D1126282

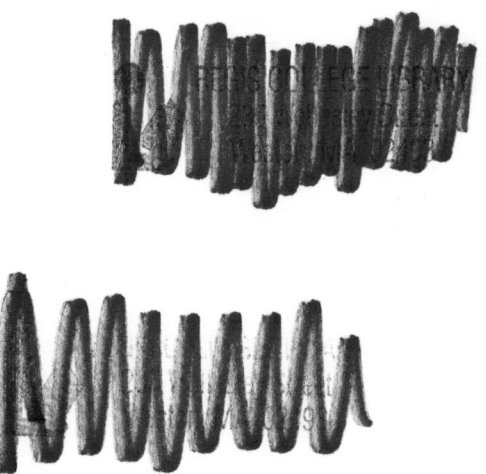

NOV   2003

GALE DIRECTORY OF PUBLICATIONS AND BROADCAST MEDIA

ISSN 1048-7972

138th Edition

Published annually since 1869

GALE DIRECTORY OF PUBLICATIONS AND BROADCAST MEDIA

(Formerly *Ayer Directory of Publications*)

An annual Guide to Publications and Broadcasting Stations
Including Newspapers, Magazines, Journals, Radio Stations,
Television Stations, and Cable Systems

Volume 3
U.S. and Canada
Broadcast Networks and
News and Feature Syndicates
Indexes and Tables

Entries 37609-38139

Alan Hedblad, Editor

GALE®

THOMSON
GALE

WITHDRAWN
FROM
LIBRARY

Detroit • New York • San Diego • San Francisco • Cleveland • New Haven, Conn. • Waterville, Maine • London • Munich

THOMSON
GALE

Gale Directory of Publications and Broadcast Media, 138th Edition

Project Editor
Alan Hedblad

Editorial
Dawn DesJardins, Kristin B. Mallegg, Jackie
Mueckenheim, Terry Peck, Jeff Sumner,
Chrystal Rozsa

Editorial Support Services
Emmanuel T. Barrido, Scott Flaugher

Data Capture
Matthew Barringer, Katrina Coach, Nikita
Greene, Cynthia Jones, Arlene Kevonian,
Elizabeth Pilette, Lindsay Trevarrow

Product Design
Cynthia Baldwin, Kate Scheible

Composition and Electronic Prepress
Evi Seoud

Manufacturing
Rhonda Williams

ISBN 0-7876-7124-X (set)
ISBN 0-7876-7125-8 (Volume 1)
ISBN 0-7876-7126-6 (Volume 2)
ISBN 0-7876-7127-4 (Volume 3)
ISBN 0-7876-7128-2 (Volume 4)
ISBN 0-7876-7129-0 (Volume 5)
ISSN 1048-7972

Printed in the United States of America
10 9 8 7 6 5 4 3 2 1

Contents

Volume 3: Indexes

Volume 4: Regional Market Index

Volume 5: International

The *Gale Directory of Publications and Broadcast Media (GDPBM)* has been the definitive media source since its inception in 1869. Formerly the *Ayer Directory of Publications,* and now in its 138th edition, *GDPBM* has grown with U.S., Canadian, and international media, and increased its scope to include the communication technologies of the twentieth century. *GDPBM* now covers over 56,000 newspapers, magazines, journals, and other periodicals, as well as radio, television, and cable stations and systems. Organized to help users find facts fast, GDPBM covers the whole media picture—ad rates, circulation statistics, local programming, names of key personnel, and other useful, accurate information. In addition, *GDPBM* offers a geographic arrangement that provides easy access to listings. Only *GDPBM* presents print and broadcast entries in one geographic sort, then alphabetically within state, province, territory, region, or country; city; and media category (Print or Broadcast).

Highlights of this Edition

In response to customer feedback, we have eliminated little-used state/province fact pages from Volumes 1 and 2, as well as the map sections from Volumes 4 and 5. The net gain in pages is being put to better use with enhanced indexing for the international entries comprising the fifth volume, which now features a Publishers Index and 12 subject indexes in addition to its Master Index.

In addition, the 138th Edition of *Gale Directory of Publications and Broadcast Media* features more than 1,400 new listings.

Scope and Preparation

The following categories of publications are ***excluded*** from the *Gale Directory of Publications and Broadcast Media*'s coverage of the U.S., Canadian, and international print and broadcast arenas: • newsletters • directories.

Information provided in *GDPBM* is obtained primarily through questionnaire responses from organizations listed. Some clarification and verification of data is obtained through telephone calls. Other published sources are used to verify some information, such as the audited circulation data in publication listings.

Organizations identified as defunct are removed from the main body of entries and listed in the Master Name and Keyword Index as "Ceased." The same basic procedure is followed for listings that cannot be located either through direct mail or subsequent attempts at telephone follow-up; these entries are listed in the Master Index as "Unable to locate." Efforts to clarify the status of such nonrespondents are ongoing.

Free Update Issued Between Editions

Approximately midway between main editions of *GDPBM,* a supplementary Update is sent free to all subscribers. It provides new listings as well as critical updates to listings of newspapers, magazines, journals, radio stations, television stations, and cable systems that are listed in the current edition of the *Directory.*

Acknowledgments

The editors are grateful to the many media professionals who generously responded to our requests for updated information, provided additional data by telephone or fax, and helped in the shaping of this edition with their comments and suggestions throughout the year. A special thanks to Hilary Weber and Lisa DeShantz-Cook for their contributions.

Available in Electronic Formats

Licensing. *Gale Directory of Publications and Broadcast Media* is available for licensing. The complete database is provided in a fielded format and is deliverable on such media as disk or CD-ROM. For more information, contact Gale's Business Development Group at 1-800-877-GALE, or visit our web site at www.gale.com/bizdev.

Online. *Gale Directory of Publications and Broadcast Media* (along with *Directories in Print* and *Newsletters in Print*) is accessible as File 469: *Gale Database of Publications and Broadcast Media* through the Dialog Corporation's DIALOG service. *GDPBM* is also accessible as PUBBRD through LexisNexis. For more information, contact The Dialog Corporation, 11000 Regency Parkway, Ste. 400, Cary, NC 27511; phone: (919) 462-8600; toll-free: 800-3-DIALOG; or

LexisNexis, P.O. Box 933, Dayton, OH 45401-0933; phone (937) 865-6800; toll-free: 800-227-4908.

The *Directory* is also available through InfoTrac as part of *Gale's Ready Reference Shelf.* For more information, call 1-800-877-GALE.

Comments and Suggestions Welcome

If you have questions, concerns, or comments about *Gale Directory of Publications and Broadcast Media* or other Gale products, please contact Alan Hedblad, Managing Editor, Business Product. Matters pertaining to specific listings in

GDPBM, as well as suggestions for new listings, should be directed to Jeff Sumner, Editor.

Please write or call:

Gale Directory of Publications and Broadcast Media
Gale Group
27500 Drake Rd.
Farmington Hills, MI 48331-3535
Phone: (248) 699-4253
Toll-free: 800-347-GALE
Fax: (248) 699-8070
Email: BusinessProducts@gale.com

Gale Directory of Publications and Broadcast Media comprises five volumes:

- Volume 1 includes U.S. entries from Alabama to New Hampshire.

- Volume 2 encompasses U.S. listings from New Jersey to Wyoming and Canadian entries.

- Volume 3 contains U.S. and Canadian broadcast & cable networks, news & feature syndicates, and 21 indexes.

- Volume 4 contains the U.S. and Canadian regional market index.

- Volume 5 includes entries from Albania to Zimbabwe and 14 indexes to International listings.

The samples and notes below offer more details on specific content and how to use the *Directory*'s listings and indexes. Please note that entry information appearing in this section has been fabricated.

Sample Entries

The samples that follow are fabricated entries in which each numbered section designates information that might appear in a listing. The numbered items are explained in the descriptive paragraphs following each sample.

Sample Publication Listing

❚1❚ 222
❚2❚ American Computer Review
❚3❚ Jane Doe Publishing Company, Inc.
❚4❚ 199 E. 49th St.
PO Box 724866
Salem, NY 10528-5555
❚5❚ Phone: (518)555-9277
❚6❚ Fax: (518)555-9288
❚7❚ Free: 800-555-5432
❚8❚ Publication E-mail: acr@jdpci.com
❚9❚ Publisher E-mail: jdpci@jdpci.com

❚10❚ Magazine for users of Super Software Plus products. **❚11❚ Subtitle:** The Programmer's Friend. **❚12❚ Founded:** June 1979. **❚13❚ Freq:** Monthly (combined issue July/Aug.). **❚14❚ Print Method:** Offset. **❚15❚ Trim Size:** 8/12 x 11. **❚16❚ Cols./Page:** 3. **❚17❚ Col. Width:** 24 nonpareils. **❚18❚ Col. Depth:** 294 agate lines. **❚19❚ Key Personnel:** Ian Smith, Editor, phone (518)555-1201, fax (518)555-1202, ismith@jdpci.com; James Newman, Publisher; Steve Jones Jr., Advertising Mgr. **❚20❚ ISSN:** 5555-6226. **❚21❚ Subscription Rates:** $25; $30 Canada; $2.50 single issue. **❚22❚ Remarks:** Color advertising not accepted. **❚23❚ Online:** Lexis-Nexis **URL:** http://www.acrmagazine.com. **❚24❚ Alternate Format(s):** Braille; CD-ROM; Microform. **❚25❚ Formerly:** Computer Software Review (Dec. 13, 1986). **❚26❚ Feature Editors:** Ann Walker, *Consumer Affairs, Editorials,* phone (518)555-2306, fax (518)555-2307, aw@jdpci.com. **❚27❚ Additional Contact Information: Advertising:** 123 Main St., New York, NY 10016, (201)555-1900, fax: (201)555-1908. **❚28❚ Ad Rates:** BW: $850, PCI: $.75 **❚29❚ Circulation:** 25,000

Description of Numbered Elements

❚1❚ Symbol/Entry Number. Each publication entry number is preceded by a symbol (a magazine or newspaper) representing the publishing industry. Entries are numbered sequentially. Entry numbers, rather than page numbers, are used in the index to refer to listings.

❚2❚ Publication Title. Publication names are listed *as they appear on the masthead or title page,* as provided by respondents.

❚3❚ Publishing Company. The name of the commercial publishing organization, association, or academic institution, as provided by respondents.

❚4❚ Address. Full mailing address information is provided wherever possible. This may include: street address; post office box; city; state or province; and ZIP or postal code. ZIP plus-four numbers are provided when known.

❚5❚ Phone. Phone numbers listed in this section are usually the respondent's switchboard number.

❚6❚ Fax. Facsimile numbers are listed when provided.

❚7❚ Free. Toll-free numbers are listed when provided.

❚8❚ Publication E-mail. Electronic mail addresses for the publication are included as provided by the listee.

❚9❚ Publisher E-mail: Electronic mail addresses for the publishing company are included as provided by the listee.

❚10❚ Description. Includes the type of publication (i.e., newspaper, magazine) as well as a brief statement of purpose, intended audience, or other relevant remarks.

❚11❚ Subtitle. Included as provided by the listee.

❚12❚ Founded. Date the periodical was first published.

❚13❚ Frequency. Indicates how often the publication is issued—daily, weekly, monthly, quarterly, etc. Explanatory remarks sometimes accompany this information (e.g., for weekly titles, the day of issuance; for collegiate titles, whether publication is limited to the academic year; whether certain issues are combined.)

|14| Print Method. Though offset is most common, other methods are listed as provided.

|15| Trim Size. Presented in inches unless otherwise noted.

|16| Number of Columns Per Page. Usually one figure, but some publications list two or more, indicating a variation in style.

|17| Column Width. Column sizes are given exactly as supplied, whether measured in inches, picas (6 picas to an inch), nonpareils (each 6 points, 72 points to an inch), or agate lines (14 to an inch).

|18| Column Depth. Column sizes are given exactly as supplied, whether measured in inches, picas (6 picas to an inch), nonpareils (each 6 points, 72 points to an inch), or agate lines (14 to an inch).

|19| Key Personnel. Presents the names and titles of contacts at each publication. May include phone, fax, and e-mail addresses if different than those for the publication and company.

|20| International Standard Serial Number (ISSN). Included when provided. Occasionally, United States Publications Serial (USPS) numbers are reported rather than ISSNs.

|21| Subscription Rates. Unless otherwise stated, prices shown in this section are the individual annual subscription rate. Other rates are listed when known, including multiyear rates, prices outside the United States, discount rates, library/institution rates, and single copy prices.

|22| Remarks. Information listed in this section further explains the Ad Rates.

|23| Online. If a publication is accessible online via computer, that information is listed here. If the publication is available online but the details of the URL (universal resource locator) or vendor are not known, the notation "Available Online" will be listed.

|24| Alternate Format(s). Lists additional mediums in which a publication may be available (other than online), including CD-ROM and microform.

|25| Variant Name(s). Lists former or variant names of the publication, including the year the change took place, when known.

|26| Feature Editors. Lists the names and beats of any feature editors employed by the publication.

|27| Additional Contact Information. Includes mailing, advertising, news, and subscription addresses and phone numbers when different from the editorial/publisher address and phone numbers.

|28| Ad Rates. Respondents may provide non-contract (open) rates in any of six categories:

    GLR = general line rate
    BW = one-time black & white page rate

    4C = one-time four-color page rate
    SAU = standard advertising unit rate
    CNU = Canadian newspaper advertising unit rate
    PCI = per column inch rate

Occasionally, explanatory information about other types of advertising appears in the Remarks section of the entry.

|29| Circulation. Figures represent various circulation numbers; the figures are accompanied by a symbol (except for sworn and estimated figures). Following are explanations of the eight circulation classifications used by *GDPBM,* the corresponding symbols, if any, are listed at the bottom of each right hand page. All circulation figures *except* publisher's reports and estimated figures appear in boldface type.

These audit bureaus are independent, nonprofit organizations (with the exception of VAC, which is for-profit) that verify circulation rates. Interested users may contact the association for more information.

- **ABC:** Audit Bureau of Circulations, 900 N. Meacham Rd., Schaumburg, IL 60173; (847)605-0909

- **CAC:** Certified Audit of Circulations, Inc., 155 Willowbrook Blvd., 4th Fl., Wayne, NJ 07470-7036; (973)785-3000

- **CCAB:** Canadian Circulations Audit Board, 90 Eglinton Ave. E, Ste. 980, Toronto, ON Canada M4P 2Y3; (416)487-2418

- **VAC:** Verified Audit Circulation, 517 Jacoby St., Ste. A, San Rafael, CA 94901; (800)775-3332

- **Post Office Statement:** These figures were verified from a U.S. Post Office form.

- **Publisher's Statement:** These figures were accompanied by the signature of the editor, publisher, or other officer.

- **Sworn Statement:** These figures, which appear in **boldface** without a symbol, were accompanied by the notarized signature of the editor, publisher, or other officer of the publication.

- **Estimated Figures:** These figures, which are shown in lightface without a symbol, are the unverified report of the listee.

The footer on every odd-numbered page contains a key to circulation and entry type symbols, as well as advertising abbreviations.

Sample Broadcast Listing

|1| 111
|2| WCAF-AM—1530
|3| 199 E. 49th St.
PO Box 724866
Salem, NY 10528-5555
|4| Phone: (518)555-9277
|5| Fax: (518)555-9288
|6| Free: 800-555-5432
|7| E-mail: wcaf@wcaf.com

|8| Format: Classical. **|9|** Simulcasts: WCAF-FM. **|10|** Network(s): Westwood One Radio; ABC. **|11|** Owner: Affici Communications, Inc., at above address. **▌12▌ Founded:** 1996. **▌13▌ Formerly:** WCAH-AM (1992). **▌14▌ Operating Hours:** Continuous; 90% local, 10% network. **▌15▌ ADI:** Elmira, NY. **▌16▌ Key Personnel:** James Smith, General Mgr., phone (518)555-1002, fax (518)555-1010, jsmith@wcaf.com; Don White, Program Dir. **▌17▌ Cities Served:** Salem, NY. **▌18▌ Postal Areas Served:** 10528; 10529. **▌19▌ Local Programs:** Who's Beethoven? Clement Goebel, Contact, (518)555-1301, fax (518)555-1320. **▌20▌ Wattage:** 5000. **▌21▌ Ad Rates:** Underwriting available. $10-15 for 30 seconds; $30-35 for 60 seconds. Combined advertising rates available with WCAF-FM. **▌22▌ Additional Contact Information:** Mailing address: PO Box 555, Elmira, NY, 10529. **▌23▌ URL:** http://www.wcaf.com.

Description of Numbered Elements

▌1▌ Entry Number. Each broadcast or cable entry is preceded by a symbol (a microphone) representing the broadcasting industry. Entries are numbered sequentially. Entry numbers (rather than page numbers) are used in the index to refer to listings.

▌2▌ Call Letters and Frequency/Channel or **Cable Company Name.**

▌3▌ Address. Location and studio addresses appear as supplied by the respondent. If provided, alternate addresses are listed in the Additional Contact Information section of the entries (see item 22 below).

▌4▌ Phone. Telephone numbers are listed as provided.

▌5▌ Fax. Facsimile numbers are listed when provided.

▌6▌ Free. Toll-free numbers are listed when provided.

▌7▌ E-mail. Electronic mail addresses are included as provided by the listee.

▌8▌ Format. For television station entries, this subheading indicates whether the station is commercial or public. Radio station entries contain industry-defined (and, in some cases, station-defined) formats as indicated by the listee.

▌9▌ Simulcasts. Lists stations that provide simulcasting.

▌10▌ Network(s). Notes national and regional networks with which a station is affiliated. The term "independent" is used if indicated by the listee.

▌11▌ Owner. Lists the name of an individual or company, supplemented by the address and telephone number, when provided by the listee. If the address is the same as that of the station or company, the notation "at above address" is used, referring to the station or cable company address.

▌12▌ Founded. In most cases, the year the station/company began operating, regardless of changes in call letters/names and ownership.

▌13▌ Variant Name(s). For radio and television stations, former call letters and the years in which there were changes are presented as provided by the listee. Former cable company names and the years in which they were changed are also noted when available.

▌14▌ Operating Hours. Lists on-air hours and often includes percentages of network and local programming.

▌15▌ ADI (Area of Dominant Influence). The Area of Dominant Influence is a standard market region defined by the Arbitron Ratings Company for U.S. television stations. Some respondents also list radio stations as having ADIs.

▌16▌ Key Personnel. Presents the names and titles of contacts at each station or cable company.

▌17▌ Cities Served. This heading is primarily found in cable system entries and provides information on channels and the number of subscribers.

▌18▌ Postal Areas Served. This heading is primarily found in cable system entries and provides information on the postal (zip) codes served by the system.

▌19▌ Local Programs. Lists names, air times, and contact personnel of locally-produced television and radio shows.

▌20▌ Wattage. Applicable to radio stations, the wattage may differ for day and night in the case of AM stations. Occasionally a station's ERP (effective radiated power) is given in addition to, or instead of, actual licensed wattage.

▌21▌ Ad Rates. Includes rates for 10, 15, 30, and 60 seconds as provided by respondents. Some stations price advertisement spots "per unit" regardless of length; these units vary.

▌22▌ Additional Contact Information. Includes mailing, advertising, news, and studio addresses and phone numbers when different from the station, owner, or company address and phone numbers.

▌23▌ Online. If a radio station or cable company is accessible online via computer, that information is listed here. If the station or company is available online but the details of the URL (universal resource locator) or vendor are not known, the notation "Available Online" will be listed.

Index Notes

Volumes 3 and 5 of the *Gale Directory of Publications and Broadcast Media* each feature a publishers index, referring to main section listings by entry number. Both volumes also include an index to subject terms, multiple subject indexes, and a master name and keyword index. These indexes refer to main section listings in Volumes 1 and 2 (U.S. and Canada) and Volume 5 (International) by entry number and geographic location. Volume 4 features a regional market index to all U.S. and Canadian listings, divided by publication or broadcast type. This index also refers back to main section listings in the first two volumes by entry number.

Publishers Index The Publishers Indexes in Volumes 3 (U.S. and Canada) and 5 (International) provide an alphabetical listing of the more than 25,000 publishers whose publications are listed in *GDPBM*. Entries in these indexes include publisher name, address, phone and fax numbers, and periodicals published. Multiple addresses for publishers are listed geographically by state, province, or country.

Index to Subject Terms The Index to Subject Terms is a consolidated alphabetical listing of the nearly 1,000 subject terms appearing in the Subject Indexes. Terms listed in this index are followed by page numbers in the appropriate subject index. Multiple page number citations indicate repeated uses of the terms. Additionally, "see" and "see also" references are provided.

Subject Indexes Seventeen indexes in Volume 3 (U.S. and Canada) and twelve indexes in Volume 5 (International) group listings by broad type or subject. These indexes have been arranged under several major categories with bleed tabs to facilitate use. Citations are presented in one of two formats:

- geographically, by states, provinces, and countries

- by subject, and within subject, geographically

Major categories are noted in the Table of Contents. Subcategories, shown as subheadings in the indexes, are listed alphabetically in the Index to Subject Terms.

Citations in the indexes refer to entry number, and for publications, provide circulation figures. (Circulation symbols are explained in footnotes on odd-numbered pages.) Additionally, the Daily Newspapers Indexes provide complete address and telephone information, and the College Publications Indexes include the names of issuing colleges and universities.

Master Name and Keyword Index The two Master Indexes provide comprehensive listings of all entries, both print and broadcast, included in Volumes 1 and 2 (U.S. and Canada) and Volume 5 (International) of *GDPBM.* Citations in these indexes are interfiled alphabetically throughout, regardless of media type.

Publication citations include the following:

- titles

- keywords within titles

- titles of cessations

- former titles

- foreign-language titles

- alternate titles

Broadcast media citations include the following:

- station call letters

- cable company names (U.S. and Canada)

- former call letters

- former cable company names (U.S. and Canada)

- radio, television, and cable company cessations

Indexing is word-by-word rather than letter-by-letter. Thus, "New York" is listed before "News." Current listings in the Index include geographic information and entry number. Former names, whether publication or broadcast, are indicated by an * and do not include a geographic designation.

Regional Market Index Volume 4 of the *Gale Directory of Publications and Broadcast Media (GDPBM)* features a regional market index, referring to main section entries in Volumes 1 and 2 (U.S. and Canada) by entry number. This index is divided into five sections:

- Newspaper Index

- Periodical Index

- Cable Index

- Radio Index

- Television Index

Each section is arranged geographically by region and then sorted by circulation, number of subscribing households, or Area of Dominant Influence (ADI). *[Note: Occasionally an ADI will appear under a region other than that listed. This is the result of an ADI designation which covers multiple neighboring states and will be represented multiple times.]* Newspaper and Periodical Index citations include publication title, entry number (given in parentheses immediately following the title), publisher name, address, phone and fax numbers, publication subject, and circulation figures. Cable Index citations include cable company name, entry number (given in parentheses immediately following the title), address, phone and fax numbers, cities served and number of subscribing households. Radio and Television Index citations include station call letters, entry number (given in parentheses immediately following the title), address, phone and fax numbers, and station format.

The regions have been defined as follows:

Great Lakes States

Illinois
Indiana
Michigan
Minnesota
Ohio
Wisconsin

Great Plains States

Iowa
Kansas
Missouri
Nebraska
North Dakota
South Dakota

Middle Atlantic States

Delaware
District of Columbia
Maryland
Virginia
West Virginia

Northeastern States

Connecticut
Maine
Massachusetts
New Hampshire
New Jersey
New York
Pennsylvania

Rhode Island
Vermont

South Central States

Arkansas
Louisiana
Oklahoma
Texas
New Mexico

Southern States

Alabama
Florida
Georgia
Kentucky
Mississippi
North Carolina
Puerto Rico
South Carolina
Tennessee

Western States

Alaska
Arizona
California
Colorado
Hawaii

Idaho
Montana
Nevada
Oregon
Utah
Washington
Wyoming

Central Canadian Provinces

Ontario
Manitoba
Saskatchewan

Eastern Canadian Provinces

Newfoundland and Labrador
Prince Edward Island
Nova Scotia
New Brunswick
Quebec

Northern Canadian Provinces

Northern Territories
Yukon Territories

Western Canadian Provinces

British Columbia
Alberta

Geographic Abbreviations

U.S. State and Territory Postal Codes

AK	Alaska
AL	Alabama
AR	Arkansas
AZ	Arizona
CA	California
CO	Colorado
CT	Connecticut
DC	District of Columbia
DE	Delaware
FL	Florida
GA	Georgia
HI	Hawaii
IA	Iowa
ID	Idaho
IL	Illinois
IN	Indiana
KS	Kansas
KY	Kentucky
LA	Louisiana
MA	Massachusetts
MD	Maryland
ME	Maine
MI	Michigan
MN	Minnesota
MO	Missouri
MS	Mississippi
NC	North Carolina
ND	North Dakota
NE	Nebraska
NH	New Hampshire
NJ	New Jersey
NM	New Mexico
NV	Nevada
MT	Montana
NC	North Carolina
ND	North Dakota
NE	Nebraska
NH	New Hampshire
NJ	New Jersey
NM	New Mexico
NV	Nevada
NY	New York
OH	Ohio
OK	Oklahoma
OR	Oregon
PA	Pennsylvania
PR	Puerto Rico
RI	Rhode Island
SC	South Carolina
SD	South Dakota
TN	Tennessee
TX	Texas
UT	Utah
VA	Virginia
VT	Vermont
WA	Washington
WI	Wisconsin
WV	West Virginia
WY	Wyoming

Canadian Province and Territory Postal Codes

AB	Alberta
BC	British Columbia
MB	Manitoba
NB	New Brunswick
NL	Newfoundland and Labrador
NS	Nova Scotia
NT	Northwest Territories
ON	Ontario
PE	Prince Edward Island
QC	Quebec
SK	Saskatchewan
YT	Yukon Territory

Australian State and Territory Codes

ACT	Australian Capitol Territory
NSW	New South Wales
NT	Northern Territory
QLD	Queensland
SA	South Australia
TAS	Tasmania
VIC	Victoria
WA	Western Australia

Chinese Province and Region Codes

AN	Anhui
FJ	Fujian
GS	Gansu
GD	Guangdong
GZ	Guangxi Zhuangzu
GH	Guizhou
HB	Hebei
HL	Heilongjiang
HN	Henan
HU	Hubeu
HA	Hunan
JS	Jiangsu
JX	Jiangxi
JI	Jilin
LI	Liaoning
NM	Nei Monggol Zizhiqu
NH	Ningxia Huizu
QI	Qinghai
SH	Shaanxi
SD	Shandong
SX	Shanxi
SI	Sichuan
XU	Xinjiang Uygur Zizhigu
XZ	Xizang
YU	Yunnan
ZH	Zhejiang

Indian State and Territory Codes

AN	Andaman and Nicobar
AP	Andhra Pradesh
AR	Arunachal Pradesh
AS	Assam
BH	Bihar
CH	Chandigarh
DN	Dadra and Nagar Haveli

DH	Delhi
GD	Goa Daman and Diu
GJ	Gujarat
HY	Haryana
HP	Himachal Pradesh
JK	Jammu and Kashmir
KA	Karnataka
KE	Kerala
LC	Laccadive Minicoy and Amindivi
MP	Madhya Pradesh
MH	Maharashtra
MN	Manipur
MG	Meghalaya
MZ	Mizoram
MY	Mysore
NG	Nagaland
OR	Orissa
PN	Pondicherry
PJ	Punjab
RJ	Rajasthan
SK	Sikkim
TN	Tamil Nadu
TR	Tripura
UP	Uttar Pradesh
WB	West Bengal (W. Bengal)

Irish County Codes

CV	Cavan
CA	Carlow
CL	Clare
CK	Cork
DO	Donegal
DU	Dublin
GL	Galway
KR	Kerry
KL	Kildare
KK	Kilkenny
LA	Laoighis
LE	Leitrim
LI	Limerick
LO	Longford
LU	Louth
MA	Mayo
ME	Meath
MO	Monaghan
OF	Offaly
RO	Roscommon
SL	Sligo
TP	Tipperary
WA	Waterford
WE	Westmeath
WX	Wexford
WI	Wicklow

Mexican State Codes

AG	Aguascalientes
BN	Baja California Norte
BS	Baja California Sur
CM	Campeche
CP	Chiapas
CH	Chihuahua
CO	Coahuila
CL	Colima
DF	Distritto Federal
DU	Durango
GJ	Guanajuato
GU	Guerrero
HD	Hidalgo
JA	Jalisco
ME	Mexico
MI	Michoacan
MO	Morelos
NY	Nayarit
NL	Nuevo Leon
OX	Oaxaca
PU	Puebla
QT	Queretaro
QR	Quintana Roo
SP	San Luis Potosi
SN	Sinaloa
SR	Sonora
TB	Tabasco
TM	Tamaulipas
TL	Tlaxcala
VC	Veracruz
YU	Yucatan
ZA	Zacatecas

Nigerian States

AN	Anambra
BA	Bauchi
BE	Bendel
BN	Benue
BR	Borno
CR	Cross River
GO	Gongola
IM	Imo
KD	Kaduna
KN	Kano
KW	Kwara
LG	Lagos
NG	Niger
OG	Ogun
ON	Ondo
OY	Oyo
PL	Plateau
RV	Rivers
SK	Sokoto

Country Abbreviations

For England, Northern Ireland, Scotland, and Wales, please see United Kingdom (GBR).

ALB	Albania
ALG	Algeria
ANG	Angola
AIA	Anguilla
ATG	Antigua-Barbuda
ARG	Argentina
AMA	Armenia
AUS	Australia
AUT	Austria
AJN	Azerbaijan
BHS	Bahamas
BHR	Bahrain
BGD	Bangladesh
BRB	Barbados
BLR	Belarus
BEL	Belgium
BLZ	Belize
BEN	Benin
BMU	Bermuda
BTN	Bhutan
BOL	Bolivia
HBO	Bosnia-Hercegovina
BWA	Botswana
BRZ	Brazil
BUL	Bulgaria
BFA	Burkina Faso
BDI	Burundi
CMB	Cambodia
CMR	Cameroon
CYM	Cayman Islands
CHL	Chile
CHN	People's Republic of China
COL	Colombia
CRI	Costa Rica
COT	Cote d'Ivoire
CTA	Croatia
CUB	Cuba
CYP	Cyprus
CZE	Czech Republic
DEN	Denmark
DMA	Dominica
DOM	Dominican Republic
ECU	Ecuador
EGY	Egypt
ELS	El Salvador
EST	Estonia
ETH	Ethiopia
FAR	Faroe Islands
FIJ	Fiji
FIN	Finland
FRA	France
GAB	Gabon
GBR	United Kingdom
GMB	Gambia
GRG	Georgia
GER	Germany
GHA	Ghana
GRC	Greece
GUM	Guam
GTM	Guatemala
GIN	Guinea
GUY	Guyana
HND	Honduras
HKG	Hong Kong

HUN	Hungary	SYC	Seychelles	APO	Army Post Office
ICE	Iceland	SLE	Sierra Leone	Apt.	Apartment
IND	India	SGP	Singapore	Assn.	Association
IDN	Indonesia	SLK	Slovakia	Assoc.	Associate
IRN	Iran	SVA	Slovenia	Asst.	Assistant
IRQ	Iraq	SLM	Solomon Islands	Ave.	Avenue
IRL	Ireland	SAF	Republic of South Africa	Bldg.	Building
ISR	Israel			Blvd.	Boulevard
ITA	Italy	SPA	Spain	boul.	boulevard
JAM	Jamaica	SRI	Sri Lanka	BPA	Business Publications Audit of Circulations
JPN	Japan	SDN	Sudan		
JOR	Jordan	SWZ	Swaziland		
KAZ	Kazakhstan	SWE	Sweden		
KEN	Kenya	SWI	Switzerland	BTA	Best Time Available
KGA	Kirgizstan	SYR	Syrian Arab Republic		
KOR	Republic of Korea			BW	One-time Black & White Page Rate
KWT	Kuwait	TWN	Taiwan		
LAT	Latvia	TDN	Tajikistan		
LBN	Lebanon	TZA	United Republic of Tanzania	C	Central
LIT	Lithuania			CAC	Certified Audit of Circulations
LUX	Luxembourg	THA	Thailand		
MEC	Macedonia	TGO	Togo	CCAB	Canadian Circulations Audit Board
MWI	Malawi	TGA	Tonga		
MYS	Malaysia	TTO	Trinidad and Tobago		
MDV	Maldives			CEO	Chief Executive Officer
MLI	Mali	TUN	Tunisia		
MAL	Malta	TUR	Turkey	Chm.	Chairman
MUS	Mauritius	UGA	Uganda	Chwm.	Chairwoman
MEX	Mexico	URE	Ukraine	CNU	Canadian Newspaper Advertising Unit Rate
MDI	Moldova	UAE	United Arab Emirates		
MCO	Monaco				
MNG	Mongolia	GBR	United Kingdom		
MON	Montenegro	URY	Uruguay	c/o	Care of
MOR	Morocco	UZN	Uzbekistan	Col.	Column
MOZ	Mozambique	VAT	Vatican City	Coll.	College
NAM	Namibia	VEN	Venezuela	Comm.	Committee
NPL	Nepal	VNM	Vietnam	Co.	Company
NLD	Netherlands	BVI	British Virgin Islands	COO	Chief Operating Officer
NAT	Netherlands Antilles				
		VIR	Virgin Islands of the United States	Coord.	Coordinator
NCL	New Caledonia			Corp.	Corporation
NZL	New Zealand			Coun.	Council
NCG	Nicaragua	YEM	Yemen	CP	case postale
NER	Niger	ZMB	Zambia	Ct.	Court
NGA	Nigeria	ZWE	Zimbabwe	Dept.	Department
NOR	Norway			Dir.	Director
OMN	Oman	**Miscellaneous Abbreviations**		Div.	Division
PAK	Pakistan	&	And	Dr.	Doctor, Drive
PAN	Panama	4C	One-Time Four Color Page Rate	E.	East
PNG	Papua New Guinea			EC	East Central
				ENE	East Northeast
PER	Peru	ABC	Audit Bureau of Circulations	ERP	Effective Radiated Power
PHL	Philippines				
POL	Poland	Acad.	Academy	ESE	East Southeast
PRT	Portugal	Act.	Acting	Eve.	Evening
ROM	Romania	Adm.	Administrative, Administration	Exec.	Executive
RUS	Russia			Expy.	Expressway
RWA	Rwanda	Admin.	Administrator	Fed.	Federation
SLC	St. Lucia	AFB	Air Force Base	Fl.	Floor
SAU	Saudi Arabia	AM	Amplitude Modulation	FM	Frequency Modulation
SEN	Senegal				
SER	Serbia	Amer.	American	FPO	Fleet Post Office

Fri.	Friday	NNE	North Northeast	Sr.	Senior
Fwy.	Freeway	NNW	North Northwest	SSE	South Southeast
Gen.	General	No.	Number	SSW	South Southwest
GLR	General Line Rate	NW	Northwest	St.	Saint, Street
Hd.	Head	Orgn.	Organization	Sta.	Station
Hwy.	Highway	PCI	Per Column Inch Rate	Ste.	Sainte, Suite
Inc.	Incorporated	Pkwy.	Parkway	Sun.	Sunday
Info.	Information	Pl.	Place	Supt.	Superintendent
Inst.	Institute	PO	Post Office	SW	Southwest
Intl.	International	Pres.	President	Terr.	Terrace
ISSN	International Standard Serial Number	Prof.	Professor	Thurs.	Thursday
		Rd.	Road	Tpke.	Turnpike
		RFD	Rural Free Delivery	Treas.	Treasurer
Jr.	Junior			Tues.	Tuesday
Libn.	Librarian	Rm.	Room	Univ.	University
Ln.	Lane	ROS	Run of Schedule	USPS	United States Publications Serial
Ltd.	Limited	RR	Rural Route		
Mgr.	Manager	Rte.	Route	VAC	Verified Audit Circulation
mi.	miles	S.	South		
Mktg.	Marketing	Sat.	Saturday	VP	Vice President
Mng.	Managing	SAU	Standard Advertising Unit Rate	W.	West
Mon.	Monday			WC	West Central
Morn.	Morning			Wed.	Wednesday
N.	North	SC	South Central	WNW	West Northwest
NAS	Naval Air Station	SE	Southeast	WSW	West Southwest
Natl.	National	Sec.	Secretary	x/month	Times per Month
NC	North Central	Soc.	Society	x/week	Times per Week
NE	Northeast	Sq.	Square	x/year	Times per Year

An alphabetical listing of newly added and recently defunct media outlets. New listings precede cessations, and International citations follow those of the United States and Canada in each instance.

New Listings

United States and Canada

American Literary Realism (Albuquerque, NM)

American Philosophical Quarterly (University Park, PA)

American Police Beat (Cambridge, MA)

Ars Combinatoria (Winnipeg, MB)

Augustinian Studies (Charlottesville, VA)

Bar & Beverage Business Magazine (Winnipeg, MB)

The Barefoot Tattler (Barefoot Bay, FL)

BB Gun Magazine (Hoboken, NJ)

Bedroom (Providence, RI)

Beethoven Forum (Chapel Hill, NC)

Big City Blues Magazine (Royal Oak, MI)

The Bulletin of Symbolic Logic (Boston, MA)

C Store Canada (Winnipeg, MB)

The Canadian Fly Fisher (Belleville, ON)

Ceramic Source (Westerville, OH)

City & Community (Chicago, IL)

Colorado Springs Independent (Colorado Springs, CO)

Combat (Circleville, WV)

Conde News (Doland, SD)

Consulting (Peterborough, NH)

Converge (Folsom, CA)

Cottage (Vancouver, BC)

County Line Advertiser (Chillicothe, OH)

Crazy for Cross Stitch (Berne, IN)

Crisis (Baltimore, MD)

Crochet! (Berne, IN)

Cultic Studies Review (Bonita Springs, FL)

DallasChild (Addison, TX)

Dayspa (Van Nuys, CA)

Dekalb Advertiser (Fort Payne, AL)

Doland Times Record (Doland, SD)

The Dolphin (Torrington, CT)

Downers Grove Sun (Naperville, IL)

EGA Needle Arts Magazine (Dillwyn, VA)

El Mundo (Wenatchee, WA)

Epoche (Villanova, PA)

Equipment Solutions (Chicago, IL)

Ethnomusicology (Champaign, IL)

Far Eastern Affairs (Minneapolis, MN)

Femme Fatales (Los Angeles, CA)

Fence (New York, NY)

FOUND (Ann Arbor, MI)

Glen Ellyn Sun (Naperville, IL)

Glennville Sentinel (Glennville, GA)

Healthy Cooking (Riverside, CA)

Hinge Music Magazine (Orlando, FL)

History of Philosophy Quarterly (Vancouver, BC)

Home Business (Huntington Beach, CA)

Hume Studies (Santa Clara, CA)

HYLE (Charlottesville, VA)

Idealistic Studies (Worcester, MA)

Information Systems Research (ISR) (Linthicum, MD)

INFORMS Journal on Computing (Linthicum, MD)

Inquiry (Bowling Green, OH)

International Journal of Applied Philosophy (Ft. Pierce, FL)

Journal of the Abraham Lincoln Association (Springfield, IL)

Journal of Musicological Research (Philadelphia, PA)

Kingwood Observer (Kingwood, TX)

Klublife (Toronto, ON)

L I T: Literature Interpretation Theory (Philadelphia, PA)

Law and History Review (Chicago, IL)

LawNow (Edmonton, AB)

Lincoln Times (Hamlin, WV)

M&SOM (Manufacturing & Service Operations Management) (Linthicum, MD)

Montreal Serai (Montreal, QC)

The Montrose Sun (Cleveland, OH)

The National Hobby News (New Philadelphia, OH)

New England Wine Gazette (Bernardsville, NJ)

N.W. Navigator (Silverdale, WA)

101 Fun Things to Do (Marble Falls, TX)

Open City (New York, NY)

OR/MS Today (Linthicum, MD)

The Owl of Minerva (Chicago, IL)

Pasta Magazine (Riverside, CA)

Perspectives on Work (Champaign, IL)

Philosophy Now (Charlottesville, VA)

The Picayune (Marble Falls, TX)

Pipeline News (Houston, TX)

Plastics Auxiliaries & Machinery (Denver, CO)

The Post (Willingboro, NJ)

Power & Gas Marketing (Houston, TX)

The Prosecutor (Alexandria, VA)

Public Affairs Quarterly (Pittsburgh, PA)

Questions (Charlottesville, VA)

Rehabilitation Technology (Houston, TX)

REITStreet Magazine (Walnut Creek, CA)

Remix (Emeryville, CA)

RINSE (Toronto, ON)

River Cities Tribune (Marble Falls, TX)

Rocky Mountain Golf Magazine (Steamboat Springs, CO)

Roctober (Chicago, IL)

Seattle's Child (Snohomish County Edition) (Seattle, WA)

Sewing Savvy (Berne, IN)

Shareholder Value (Peterborough, NH)

The Shuttle Sheet (Greensboro, NC)

Silk & Satin (Dorval, QC)

Skyscraper (New York, NY)

South County Independent (Wakefield, RI)

Southern California Brides (Riverside, CA)

Southern California Golf (Riverside, CA)

Soviet Metal Technology (New York, NY)

State Politics & Policy Quarterly (Champaign, IL)

The Sun (Cleveland, OH)

Sun Marketplace (Hanover, PA)

theIndian (Westland, MI)

Today's OEA (Portland, OR)

Tourist (Oakville, ON)

Union Hidpana (Santa Ana, CA)

Vail International Dance Festival (Steamboat Springs, CO)

Verse (Florence, MA)

Wax Poetics (Brooklyn, NY)

WDMG-FM (Douglas, GA)

West Akron Sun (Cleveland, OH)

Western Hotelier (Winnipeg, MB)

Working Money (Seattle, WA)

World Futures (Philadelphia, PA)

X-Ray News (Nashville, TN)

International

A & U (Tokyo, JPN)

Abacus (Oxford, GBR)

Abu Dhabi Economy (Abu Dhabi, UAE)

Academy of Medicine, Singapore Annals (Singapore, SGP)

Acta Anatomica Nipponica (Tokyo, JPN)

Acta Arachnologica (Osaka, JPN)

Acta Asiatica (Tokyo, JPN)

Acta Criminologiae et Medicinae Legalis Japonica (Tokyo, JPN)

Acta Dipterologica (Fukuoka, JPN)

Acta Geologica Taiwanica (Taipei, TWN)

Acta Histochemica et Cytochemica (Kyoto, JPN)

Acta Medica et Biologica (Niigata, JPN)

Acta Medica Kinki University (Osaka, JPN)

Acta Medica Nagasakiensia (Nagasaki, JPN)

Acta Medica Okayama (Okayama, JPN)

Acta Neurologica Taiwanica (Taipei, TWN)

Acta Neuropsychiatrica (Maastricht, NLD)

Acta Oceanographica Taiwanica (Taipei, TWN)

Acta Paediatrica Sinica Taiwanica (Taipei, TWN)

Acta Phytotaxonomica et Geobotanica (Kyoto, JPN)

Acta Zoologica Taiwanica (Taipei, TWN)

Actinomycetologica (Tokyo, JPN)

Action Asia (Hong Kong, CHN)

Ad-Vocate (Dubai, UAE)

Adasiaonline (Singapore, SGP)

Administrative Sciences Journal of King Saud University (Riyadh, SAU)

Advances in Neurotrauma Research (Tokyo, JPN)

African Studies (Taipei, TWN)

Afro-Asian Journal of Rural Development (New Delhi, DH, IND)

Afsaar Magazine (Dubai, UAE)

Agricultural Engineering Journal (Bangkok, THA)

Agricultural Journal of Kyushu University (Fukuoka, JPN)

Agricultural Sciences Journal of King Saud University (Riyadh, SAU)

Agro Food (Milan, ITA)

Aikido Journal (Kanagawa, JPN)

Aikuiskasvatus (Helsinki, FIN)

Akita Journal of Medicine (Akita, JPN)

AKK-Motorsport (A-lehdet, FIN)

Al Shindagah (Dubai, UAE)

Alexandria (Aldershot, GBR)

AMA - Agricultural Mechanization in Asia, Africa and Latin America (Tokyo, JPN)

Analytical Sciences (Tokyo, JPN)

Anatomical Science (Oxford, GBR)

Animal Science Journal (Oxford, GBR)

Animal Science Journal (Tokyo, JPN)

Annals of Nuclear Medicine (Tokyo, JPN)

Annals of Saudi Medicine (Riyadh, SAU)

Annals of Thoracic and Cardiovascular Surgery (Tokyo, JPN)

Anritsu Technical Review (Tokyo, JPN)

Antarctic Record (Tokyo, JPN)

Anthropological Science (Tokyo, JPN)

APLAR Journal of Rheumatology (Oxford, GBR)

APO Productivity Journal (Tokyo, JPN)

Apparel Production News (Tokyo, JPN)

Applied Entomology and Zoology (Tokyo, JPN)

Applied Human Science (Tokyo, JPN)

Apu (A-lehdet, FIN)

Arab Gulf Journal of Scientific Research (Bahrain, SAU)

Arab Journal of Library and Information Science (Riyadh, SAU)

Arab News (Jeddah, SAU)

Arabian Business (Dubai, UAE)

Arabian Computer News (Dubai, UAE)

Arabian Journal for Science and Engineering (Dhahran, SAU)

Arabian Woman (Dubai, UAE)

Architecture and Planning Journal of King Saud University (Riyadh, SAU)

Archives of Histology and Cytology (Niigata, JPN)

Archives of Pharmacal Research (Seoul, KOR)

Art Corridor (Petaling Jaya, MYS)

Artificial Life and Robotics (Tokyo, JPN)

The Arts (Singapore, SGP)

Arts of Asia (Hong Kong, CHN)

Arts Journal of King Saud University (Riyadh, SAU)

Artslink (Hong Kong, CHN)

Arttu! (Helsinki, FIN)

Asahi Evening News (Tokyo, JPN)

Asia Asset Management (Hong Kong, CHN)

Asia Electronics Industry (Tokyo, JPN)

Asia Labour Monitor (Hong Kong, CHN)

Asia Law and Practice (Hong Kong, CHN)

Asia Money (Hong Kong, CHN)

Asia-Pacific Aviation and Engineering Journal (Singapore, SGP)

Asia-Pacific Information Technology Times (Singapore, SGP)

Asia-Pacific Journal of Education (Singapore, SGP)

Asia Pacific Journal of Finance (Singapore, SGP)

Asia Pacific Journal of Management (Singapore, SGP)

Asia-Pacific Journal of Molecular Biology & Biotechnology (Serdang, MYS)

Asia-Pacific Journal of Operational Research (Singapore, SGP)

Asia-Pacific Journal of Ophthalmology (Singapore, SGP)

Asia-Pacific Journal of Pharmacology (Singapore, SGP)

Asia-Pacific Military Balance (Kuala Lumpur, MYS)

Asia Textile & Apparel Journal (Hong Kong, CHN)

The Asia Water (Singapore, SGP)

Asian Affairs (Hong Kong, CHN)

Asian Air Transport (Taipei, TWN)

Asian Airlines & Aerospace (Kuala Lumpur, MYS)

Asian-Australasian Journal of Animal Sciences (Kyunggi-do, KOR)

Asian Building & Construction (Singapore, SGP)

Asian Case Research Journal (Singapore, SGP)

Asian Cultural Studies (Tokyo, JPN)

Asian Culture (Singapore, SGP)

Asian Defence and Diplomacy (Kuala Lumpur, MYS)

Asian Defence Journal (Kuala Lumpur, MYS)

Asian Diver (Singapore, SGP)

Asian Financial Law Briefing (Hong Kong, CHN)

Asian Furniture (Singapore, SGP)

Asian Home Gourmet (Singapore, SGP)

Asian IP (Hong Kong, CHN)

Asian Journal of Control (Tokyo, JPN)

Asian Journal of Marketing (Singapore, SGP)

Asian Journal of Microbiology, Biotechnology and Environmental Sciences (Aligarh, UP, IND)

Asian Journal of Oral and Maxillofacial Surgery (Yokohama, JPN)

Asian Journal of Political Science (Singapore, SGP)

Asian Legal Business (Singapore, SGP)

Asian Oil and Gas (Tokyo, JPN)

Asian-Pacific Book Development (Tokyo, JPN)

Asian Pacific Culture Quarterly (Taipei, TWN)

Asian Pacific Journal of Allergy and Immunology (Bangkok, THA)

Asian Pacific Journal of Social Work (Singapore, SGP)

Asian and Pacific Labour (Singapore, SGP)

Asian Perspective (Seoul, KOR)

Asian Printer (Singapore, SGP)

Asian Research Trends (Tokyo, JPN)

Asian Sources Computer Products (Singapore, SGP)

Asian Sources Gifts and Home Products (Singapore, SGP)

Asian Sources Security Products (Singapore, SGP)

Asian Timber (Singapore, SGP)

The Asset (Hong Kong, CHN)

Atoms in Japan (Tokyo, JPN)

Aunt Webby (Singapore, SGP)

Australian Women's Book Review (St. Lucia, QL, AUS)

Auto China (Beijing, CHN)

Auto International (Kuala Lumpur, MYS)

Avotakka (A-lehdet, FIN)

Axis (Tokyo, JPN)

B & I Magazine (Kuala Lumpur, MYS)

BAMBI Magazine (Bangkok, THA)

Bamboo Journal (Tokyo, JPN)

Bangkok Magazine (Chiang Mai, THA)

Bangkok Post Student Weekly (Bangkok, THA)

Bank of Korea Quarterly Economic Review (Seoul, KOR)

Banker's Journal Malaysia (Kuala Lumpur, MYS)

Banter (Singapore, SGP)

BBnGG - Beautiful Brides & Gorgeous Grooms (Singapore, SGP)

bc magazine (Singapore, SGP)

Bee Sagheer (Abu Dhabi, UAE)

Beijing Review (Beijing, CHN)

Beijing This Month (Beijing, CHN)

Benthos Research (Tokyo, JPN)

BigO (Singapore, SGP)

Biological Sciences in Space (Kanagawa, JPN)

Biology of Inland Waters (Nara, JPN)

Biology Today (New Delhi, DH, IND)

Biomedical Research (Tokyo, JPN)

Biomedical Research on Trace Elements (Tokyo, JPN)

Biophysics (Tokyo, JPN)

Bioscience, Biotechnology, and Biochemistry (Tokyo, JPN)

Biotronics (Fukuoka, JPN)

Borneo Review (Kota Kinabalu, MYS)

Brain Tumor Pathology (Tokyo, JPN)

Breeding Science (Tokyo, JPN)

Buffalo Journal (Bangkok, THA)

Bug (Seoul, KOR)

Building and Estate Management Society Proceedings (Singapore, SGP)

Building Journal Hong Kong (Hong Kong, CHN)

Business Beijing (Beijing, CHN)

Business Day (Bangkok, THA)

Business and Industry: Taiwan (Taipei, TWN)

Business in Thailand Magazine (Bangkok, THA)

Business Times (Bangkok, THA)

The Business Times (Singapore, SGP)

Business Times (Kuala Lumpur, MYS)

By the Way (Tokyo, JPN)

Calorimetry and Thermal Analysis (Tokyo, JPN)

Canada Hong Kong Business (Hong Kong, CHN)

Catalysts & Catalysis (Tokyo, JPN)

The Catholic News (Singapore, SGP)

The Caving Journal (Yamaguchi, JPN)

CDA (Milan, ITA)

Cell Structure and Function (Kyoto, JPN)

Centerpoint (Taipei, TWN)

CFO Asia (Hong Kong, CHN)

Channel Middle East (Dubai, UAE)

Charged Middle East (Dubai, UAE)

Chemistry Today (New Delhi, DH, IND)

Chiangmai Mail (Chiang Mai, THA)

Chimica Oggi (Chemistry Today) (Milan, ITA)

China Aero Information (Beijing, CHN)

China and Africa (Beijing, CHN)

China Auto (Beijing, CHN)

China Books (Beijing, CHN)

China Business (Beijing, CHN)

China Chemical Week (Beijing, CHN)

China Computer Reseller World (Beijing, CHN)

China Environment News (Beijing, CHN)

China Mail (Singapore, SGP)

The China News (Taipei, TWN)

China Pictorial (Beijing, CHN)

The China Post (Taipei, TWN)

China Screen (Beijing, CHN)

China Sports (Beijing, CHN)

China & the World (Beijing, CHN)

China's Foreign Trade (Beijing, CHN)

China's Refractories (Henan, CHN)

Chinese Journal of Administration (Taipei, TWN)

Chinese Journal of Materials Science (Chutung Hsinchu, TWN)

Chinese Journal of Physics (Taipei, TWN)

Chinese Journal of Physiology (Taipei, TWN)

Chinese Journal of Psychology (Taipei, TWN)

Chinese Medical Journal (Taipei, TWN)

Chinese Medical Journal (Beijing, CHN)

Chromosome Science (Higashi-Hiroshima City, JPN)

Chubu Weekly (Aichi, JPN)

Cine News (Singapore, SGP)

City Times (Dubai, UAE)

Class NK Magazine (Chiba, JPN)

Clinical and Experimental Nephrology (Tokyo, JPN)

Clinical Pediatric Endocrinology (Sapporo, JPN)

CMPnet Asia (Singapore, SGP)

Coastal Engineering Journal (Singapore, SGP)

Cognitiva (San Sebastian de los Reyes, SPA)

Colmed (Genval, BEL)

Commentarii Mathematici Universitatis Sancti Pauli (Tokyo, JPN)

Commercial & Industrial Guide (Singapore, SGP)

Commodity Price Statistics Monthly in Taiwan Area (Taipei, TWN)

Communications Africa (Dubai, UAE)

Communications of COLIPS (Singapore, SGP)

Communications in Contemporary Mathematics (Singapore, SGP)

Communications Egypt (Dubai, UAE)

Communications Maghreb (Dubai, UAE)

Communications Middle East & Africa (Dubai, UAE)

Communications Research Laboratory Journal (Tokyo, JPN)

The Communist (Tokyo, JPN)

Computer Era (Singapore, SGP)

Computer and Information Sciences Journal of King Saud University (Riyadh, SAU)

Computer Today Monthly (Hong Kong, CHN)

Computerworld Singapore (Singapore, SGP)

Computing and Informatics (Bratislava, SLK)

Computing Japan (Tokyo, JPN)

Concrete Library International (Tokyo, JPN)

Confluence (Bangkok, THA)

Congenital Anomalies (Kyoto, JPN)

Connective Tissue (Yokosuka, JPN)

Contemporary Southeast Asia (Singapore, SGP)

Coutoure (Hong Kong, CHN)

Crusades (Aldershot, GBR)

Crustacean Research (Tokyo, JPN)

Cultura y Educacion (San Sebastian de los Reyes, SPA)

CW Magazine (Singapore, SGP)

Cytologia (Tokyo, JPN)

Daily News Nagoya (Aichi, JPN)

Daruma Magazine (Amagasaki, JPN)

Decor International Magazine (Bangkok, THA)

Demi (A-lehdet, FIN)

The Dental Mirror (Singapore, SGP)

Dentistry in Japan (Tokyo, JPN)

The Design Journal (Aldershot, GBR)

Development and Society (Seoul, KOR)

Dharma (Kuala Lumpur, MYS)

Dharma World (Tokyo, JPN)

Diamond Industria (Tokyo, JPN)

Digital Nanyang Chronicle (Singapore, SGP)

Digital Studio (Dubai, UAE)

Digital Times (Taipei, TWN)

Discovering Mathematics (Kuala Lumpur, MYS)

Dokkyo Journal of Medical Sciences (Tochigi, JPN)

Doshisha American Studies (Kyoto, JPN)

Doshisha Literature (Kyoto, JPN)

Dubai International (Dubai, UAE)

Dynasty (Taipei, TWN)

e-Health Business (London, GBR)

Earth Planets and Space (Tokyo, JPN)

Earth Science (Tokyo, JPN)

East (Singapore, SGP)

Ecological Review (Miyagi, JPN)

Economic Journal of Hokkaido University (Sapporo, JPN)

Economic Review (Tokyo, JPN)

Educational Sciences and Islamic Studies Journal of King Saud University (Riyadh, SAU)

Eeva (A-lehdet, FIN)

8 Days (Singapore, SGP)

Electronic Journal of School of Advanced Technologies (Bangkok, THA)

Elements (London, GBR)

Emirates Inflight (Dubai, UAE)

Emirates Medical Journal (Dubai, UAE)

Emirates Woman (Dubai, UAE)

Endocrine Surgery (Tokyo, JPN)

EndoSource Magazine (Singapore, SGP)

Energy Asia (Singapore, SGP)

Energy in Japan (Tokyo, JPN)

Engineering Science and Technology (Kuala Lumpur, MYS)

Engineering Sciences Journal of King Saud University (Riyadh, SAU)

The English Teacher Online (Bangkok, THA)

Enquires (Singapore, SGP)

Entomological Science (Mito, JPN)

Environmental Economics and Policy Studies (Tokyo, JPN)

Environmental Medicine (Aichi, JPN)

Environmental Mutagen Research (Tokyo, JPN)

Environmental News Digest (Penang, MYS)

Environmental Policy Monthly (Taipei, TWN)

Environmental Sciences (Tokyo, JPN)

Envision (Singapore, SGP)

Esso in Malaysia (Kuala Lumpur, MYS)

Estudios de Psicologia (San Sebastian de los Reyes, SPA)

Ethos (Petaling Jaya, MYS)

ETRI Journal (Taejon, KOR)

The European Union (Oxford, GBR)

The European Yearbook of Business History (Aldershot, GBR)

Evensongs (Taipei, TWN)

Experimental Animals (Tokyo, JPN)

Experimental and Molecular Medicine (Seoul, KOR)

Export Processing Zone Concentrates (Kaohsiung, TWN)

Extremophiles (Tokyo, JPN)

Ezyhealth Chinese (Singapore, SGP)

Ezyhealth Malaysia (Petaling Jaya, MYS)

Ezyhealth Singapore (Singapore, SGP)

Family Law Journal (London, GBR)

FDM Asia (Singapore, SGP)

Female Brides (Singapore, SGP)

Female Cookbook (Singapore, SGP)

Feminine (Petaling Jaya, MYS)

FHM Singapore (Singapore, SGP)

Financial Statistics Monthly (Taipei, TWN)

Financial Times Japan (Tokyo, JPN)

Fish Pathology (Hiroshima, JPN)

Fisheries Science Research (Kunsan, KOR)

Flow of Funds (Taipei, TWN)

Folia Ugentia (Genval, BEL)

F1 Racing (A-lehdet, FIN)

Food & Entertainment (Singapore, SGP)

Food Science and Agricultural Chemistry (Taipei, TWN)

Food Science and Technology Research (Tokyo, JPN)

Forma (Tokyo, JPN)

Formosan Journal of Surgery (Taipei, TWN)

Formosan Science (Taipei, TWN)

Four Walls (Singapore, SGP)

4x4 Magazine (Singapore) (Singapore, SGP)

Fractals (Singapore, SGP)

Fraunhofer (English) (Munich, GER)

FRI Journal of Forest Science (Suwon, KOR)

Fu Jen Studies (Taipei, TWN)

Fujitsu Ten Technical Journal (Hyogo, JPN)

Fukuoka Now (Fukuoka, JPN)

Fukushima Journal of Medical Science (Fukushima, JPN)

Funkcialaj Ekvacioj, Serio Internacia (Hyogo, JPN)

Futari (A-lehdet, FIN)

The Gaijin Gleaner (Fukuoka, JPN)

Galaxie (Petaling Jaya, MYS)

Garden Asia (Singapore, SGP)

Gastric Cancer (Tokyo, JPN)

The Gazette of Patents and Trademarks (Budapest, HUN)

Genes & Genetic Systems (Shizuoka, JPN)

Geochemical Journal (Tokyo, JPN)

Geophysics Journal of Hokkaido University (Sapporo, JPN)

Geotechnical Engineering (Bangkok, THA)

Gifu Journal of Maternal Health (Gifu, JPN)

Glass's Guide to Used Vehicle Prices (Weybridge, GBR)

Global Economic Review (Seoul, KOR)

Golf (Singapore, SGP)

Golf Malaysia (Petaling Jaya, MYS)

Gondwana Research (Kochi, JPN)

Good Morning Chiangmai News Magazine (Bangkok, THA)

Graphic Design in Japan (Tokyo, JPN)

Graphical Survey of the Economy (Taipei, TWN)

Graphs and Combinatorics (Tokyo, JPN)

Grassland Science (Tochigi, JPN)

Groom n' Bride (Singapore, SGP)

Guide to Japanese Taxes (Tokyo, JPN)

Gulf Industry Magazine (Dubai, UAE)

Gulf Marketing Review (Dubai, UAE)

Gulf News (Dubai, UAE)

The Gulf Today (Dubai, UAE)

Hand Surgery (Singapore, SGP)

Happening (Singapore, SGP)

Hardware Mag (Singapore, SGP)

Health Policy and Planning (London, GBR)

HealthToday (Singapore, SGP)

Heart and Vessels (Tokyo, JPN)

Heavyrock (Madrid, SPA)

Her World (Kuala Lumpur, MYS)

Her World (Singapore, SGP)

Her World Brides (Singapore, SGP)

Heterocycles (Tokyo, JPN)

Highway Magazine (Singapore, SGP)

Hinge (Hong Kong, CHN)

Hippo (Finland, FIN)

Hirosaki Medical Journal (Aomori, JPN)

Hiroshima Journal of Mathematics Education (Hiroshima, JPN)

Hiroshima Mathematical Journal (Hiroshima, JPN)

Hirsilehti (A-lehdet, FIN)

Historia Scientiarum (Tokyo, JPN)

Hitachi Cable Review (Tokyo, JPN)

Hitachi Zosen News (Osaka, JPN)

Hitotsubashi Journal of Arts and Sciences (Tokyo, JPN)

Hobby Electronics (Bangkok, THA)

Hokkaido Journal of Medical Science (Hokkaido, JPN)

Hokkaido Journal of Primary Care (Sapporo, JPN)

Hokkaido Mathematical Journal (Sapporo, JPN)

Home Concepts (Singapore, SGP)

Home & Decor (Singapore, SGP)

Home Journal (Hong Kong, CHN)

Hong Kong Apparel (Hong Kong, CHN)

Hong Kong for the Business Visitor (Hong Kong, CHN)

Hong Kong Dermatology and Venereology Bulletin (Hong Kong, CHN)

Hong Kong Design Services (Hong Kong, CHN)

Hong Kong Electronic Components & Parts (Hong Kong, CHN)

Hong Kong Electronics (Hong Kong, CHN)

Hong Kong Enterprise (Hong Kong, CHN)

Hong Kong Fabrics & Accessories (Hong Kong, CHN)

Hong Kong Fashion Flash (Hong Kong, CHN)

Hong Kong Footwear (Hong Kong, CHN)

Hong Kong Gifts, Premiums & Stationery (Hong Kong, CHN)

Hong Kong Household (Hong Kong, CHN)

Hong Kong Industrialist (Hong Kong, CHN)

Hong Kong Jewellery Collection (Hong Kong, CHN)

Hong Kong Jewelry Express Magazine (Hong Kong, CHN)

Hong Kong Journal of Applied Linguistics (Hong Kong, CHN)

Hong Kong Journal of Mental Health (Hong Kong, CHN)

The Hong Kong Journal of Orthopaedic Surgery (Hong Kong, CHN)

Hong Kong Journal of Paediatrics (Hong Kong, CHN)

The Hong Kong Journal of Psychiatry (Hong Kong, CHN)

The Hong Kong Journal of Social Work (Hong Kong, CHN)

The Hong Kong Journal of Sports Medicine and Sports Science (Hong Kong, CHN)

Hong Kong Law Reports & Digest (Hong Kong, CHN)

Hong Kong Lawyer (Hong Kong, CHN)

Hong Kong Leather Goods & Bags (Hong Kong, CHN)

The Hong Kong Medical Diary (Hong Kong, CHN)

Hong Kong Medical Journal (Hong Kong, CHN)

The Hong Kong Nursing Journal (Hong Kong, CHN)

Hong Kong Optical (Hong Kong, CHN)

Hong Kong Packaging (Hong Kong, CHN)

Hong Kong Physiotherapy Journal (Hong Kong, CHN)

The Hong Kong Practitioner (Hong Kong, CHN)

Hong Kong Printing (Hong Kong, CHN)

Hong Kong Productivity News (Hong Kong, CHN)

The Hong Kong Racing Journal (Hong Kong, CHN)

Hong Kong Toys (Hong Kong, CHN)

Hong Kong Trade Services (Hong Kong, CHN)

Hong Kong Watches and Clocks (Hong Kong, CHN)

Hongkong Tatler (Hong Kong, CHN)

Human Factors and Aerospace Safety (Aldershot, GBR)

Hydrocarbon Asia (Singapore, SGP)

Hydrology (Ibaraki, JPN)

Hypertension Research - Clinical and Experimental (Osaka, JPN)

Hyva Ateria (A-lehdet, FIN)

I-S Magazine (Singapore, SGP)

Iberoamericana (Tokyo, JPN)

IBS Asian Electronics News (Taipei, TWN)

IBS Electronic Component & Equipment Exhibition (Taipei, TWN)

Ichthyological Research (Tokyo, JPN)

Idea (Tokyo, JPN)

The IEA Journal of Ergonomics (Singapore, SGP)

IEICE Journal (Tokyo, JPN)

IHI Engineering Review (Tokyo, JPN)

Illustrated Flora of Hokkaido (Hokkaido, JPN)

Illustration in Japan (Tokyo, JPN)

In-House Briefing Asia Pacific (Hong Kong, CHN)

Incentives & Meetings Asia (Singapore, SGP)

Industrial Health (Kanagawa, JPN)

Industries of Japan (Tokyo, JPN)

Industry of Free China (Taipei, TWN)

Industry Weekly (Taipei, TWN)

Infancia Y Aprendizaje/Journal for the Study of Education and Development (San Sebastian de los Reyes, SPA)

Infinite Dimensional Analysis, Quantum Probability and Related Topics (Singapore, SGP)

INFOFISH International (Kuala Lumpur, MYS)

Informatization White Paper (Tokyo, JPN)

Infrared and Raman Spectroscopy (Saitama, JPN)

Innovation (Singapore, SGP)

Innovations in Materials Research (Singapore, SGP)

Inquiry into the Future (Seoul, KOR)

Intelligent Enterprise Asia (Singapore, SGP)

Intercommunication (Tokyo, JPN)

Internal Combustion Engine (Tokyo, JPN)

Internal Medicine (Tokyo, JPN)

International Game Theory Review (Singapore, SGP)

International Journal of Algebra and Computation (Singapore, SGP)

International Journal of Artificial Intelligence Tools (Singapore, SGP)

International Journal of Bifurcation and Chaos in Applied Sciences and Engineering (Singapore, SGP)

International Journal of Clinical Oncology (Tokyo, JPN)

International Journal of Computational Geometry and Applications (Singapore, SGP)

International Journal of Computer Processing of Oriental Languages (Hong Kong, CHN)

International Journal of Electrical Machining (Tokyo, JPN)

International Journal of Foundations of Computer Science (Singapore, SGP)

International Journal of Genome Research (Singapore, SGP)

International Journal of Hematology (Kyoto, JPN)

International Journal of High Speed Computing (Singapore, SGP)

International Journal of High Speed Electronics and Systems (Singapore, SGP)

International Journal of Image and Graphics (Hong Kong, CHN)

International Journal of Information and Management Sciences (Tamsui, TWN)

International Journal of Information Technology (Singapore, SGP)

International Journal of Innovation Management (Singapore, SGP)

International Journal of Japan Society for Precision Engineering (Tokyo, JPN)

International Journal of Kobe University Law Review (Hyogo, JPN)

International Journal of Manufacturing System Design (Singapore, SGP)

International Journal of Mathematical Logic (Singapore, SGP)

International Journal of Mathematics (Singapore, SGP)

International Journal of Modern Physics A (Singapore, SGP)

International Journal of Modern Physics B (Singapore, SGP)

International Journal of Modern Physics C: Physics and Computers (Singapore, SGP)

International Journal of Modern Physics D: Gravitation, Astrophysics and Cosmology (Singapore, SGP)

International Journal of Modern Physics E: Report on Nuclear Physics (Singapore, SGP)

International Journal of Neural Systems (Singapore, SGP)

International Journal of Pattern Recognition and Artificial Intelligence (Singapore, SGP)

International Journal of Peace Studies (Taipei, TWN)

International Journal of PIXE (Singapore, SGP)

International Journal of Reliability, Quality & Safety Engineering (Singapore, SGP)

International Journal of Shaping Modeling (Singapore, SGP)

International Journal of Software Engineering and Knowledge Engineering (Singapore, SGP)

International Journal of Theoretical and Applied Finance (Singapore, SGP)

International Journal of Uncertainty, Fuzziness and Knowledge-Based Systems (Singapore, SGP)

International Medical Journal (Tokyo, JPN)

International Medical News (Tokyo, JPN)

International Travel Plan (Tokyo, JPN)

Investment Now (Kempston, GBR)

Investor (Bangkok, THA)

Investors Digest Magazine (Kuala Lumpur, MYS)

Investor's Guide to Singapore (Singapore, SGP)

Ionizing Radiation (Tokyo, JPN)

Islamic World Medical Journal (Jeddah, SAU)

Island Studies in Okinawa (Okinawa, JPN)

ISO Link (Singapore, SGP)

IT Asia (Singapore, SGP)

Jacket (Balmain, NW, AUS)

Japan Architect (Tokyo, JPN)

Japan Automotive News (Tokyo, JPN)

Japan Camera Trade News (Tokyo, JPN)

Japan Graphic Arts (Tokyo, JPN)

Japan Harvest (Tokyo, JPN)

Japan Insurance News (Tokyo, JPN)

Japan International Journal (Tokyo, JPN)

Japan Journal of Industrial and Applied Mathematics (Tokyo, JPN)

Japan Law Journal (Tokyo, JPN)

Japan Marketing Data (Tokyo, JPN)

Japan Mission Journal (Tokyo, JPN)

Japan Quarterly (Tokyo, JPN)

Japan Times (Tokyo, JPN)

Japan Today (Tokyo, JPN)

Japan Update (Okinawa City, JPN)

Japanese Circulation Journal (Kyoto, JPN)

The Japanese Economic Review (Oxford, GBR)

Japanese Economy & Labor Series (Tokyo, JPN)

Japanese Heart Journal (Tokyo, JPN)

Japanese Journal of Animal Psychology (Ibaraki, JPN)

Japanese Journal of Applied Physics (Tokyo, JPN)

Japanese Journal of Bacteriology (Tokyo, JPN)

Japanese Journal of Behavior Therapy (Ibaraki, JPN)

Japanese Journal of Biofeedback Research (Tokyo, JPN)

Japanese Journal of Biometeorology (Tokyo, JPN)

Japanese Journal of Biometrics (Tokyo, JPN)

Japanese Journal of Breast Cancer (Tokyo, JPN)

Japanese Journal of Chemotherapy (Tokyo, JPN)

Japanese Journal of Clinical and Experimental Medicine (Fukuoka, JPN)

Japanese Journal of Crop Science (Sendai, JPN)

Japanese Journal of Environment, Entomology and Zoology (Osaka, JPN)

Japanese Journal of Health and Human Ecology (Tokyo, JPN)

Japanese Journal of Herpetology (Kyoto, JPN)

Japanese Journal of Hygiene (Tokyo, JPN)

Japanese Journal of Infectious Diseases (Tokyo, JPN)

Japanese Journal of Limnology (Tokyo, JPN)

Japanese Journal of Lymphology (Tokyo, JPN)

Japanese Journal of Mathematics (Tokyo, JPN)

Japanese Journal of Medical Imaging and Information Sciences (Kyoto, JPN)

Japanese Journal of Medical Mycology (Tokyo, JPN)

Japanese Journal of Nematology (Ibaraki, JPN)

Japanese Journal of Obstetrical, Gynecological and Neonatal Hematology (Shizuoka, JPN)

Japanese Journal of Optics (Tokyo, JPN)

Japanese Journal of Ornithology (Tokyo, JPN)

The Japanese Journal of Pharmacology (Kyoto, JPN)

Japanese Journal of Physical Fitness (Tokyo, JPN)

Japanese Journal of Physiology (Tokyo, JPN)

Japanese Journal of Protozoology (Gifu, JPN)

Japanese Journal of Rheumatism and Joint Surgery (Shiga, JPN)

Japanese Journal of Sanitary Zoology (Tokyo, JPN)

Japanese Journal of Toxicology (Tokyo, JPN)

Japanese Journal of Tropical Medicine and Hygiene (Nagasaki, JPN)

Japanese Journal of Veterinary Research (Sapporo, JPN)

Japanese Poultry Science (Ibaraki, JPN)

Japanese Progress in Climatology (Tokyo, JPN)

Japanese Religions (Kyoto, JPN)

Japan's Iron and Steel Industry (Tokyo, JPN)

JCA Forecast (Singapore, SGP)

JEOL News: Analytical Instrumentation (Tokyo, JPN)

JEOL News: Electron Optics Instrumentation (Tokyo, JPN)

Jikeikai Medical Journal (Tokyo, JPN)

JJAP Series (Tokyo, JPN)

Joint (Yokohama, JPN)

Journal of Acarological Society of Japan (Chiba, JPN)

Journal of the Acoustical Society of Japan (Tokyo, JPN)

Journal of Advanced Computational Intelligence (Tokyo, JPN)

Journal of African Earth Sciences (Amsterdam, NLD)

Journal of Agricultural Meteorology (Tokyo, JPN)

Journal of Agricultural Research of China (Taipei, TWN)

Journal of American and Canadian Studies (Tokyo, JPN)

Journal of Anesthesia (Tokyo, JPN)

Journal of Antibiotics (Tokyo, JPN)

Journal of Aomori Society of Obstetricians and Gynecologists (Aomori, JPN)

Journal of Applied Medicine (Kyoto, JPN)

Journal of Architecture, Planning and Environmental Engineering (Tokyo, JPN)

Journal of Artificial Organs (Tokyo, JPN)

Journal of Asian Earth Sciences (Amsterdam, NLD)

Journal of Atherosclerosis and Thrombosis (Tokyo, JPN)

Journal of Biochemistry (Tokyo, JPN)

Journal of Biological Systems (Singapore, SGP)

Journal of Bioscience and Bioengineering (Osaka, JPN)

Journal of Bone and Mineral Metabolism (Tokyo, JPN)

Journal of Brain Science (Okayama, JPN)

Journal of the Ceramic Society of Japan (Tokyo, JPN)

Journal of Chemical Engineering of Japan (Tokyo, JPN)

Journal of Chemical Software (Fukui, JPN)

Journal of the China University of Geosciences (Beijing, CHN)

Journal of Chinese Agricultural Chemical Society (Taipei, TWN)

Journal of Chinese Chemical Society (Taipei, TWN)

Journal of Chinese Institute of Chemical Engineers (Hsinchu, TWN)

Journal of Chinese Institute of Engineers (Taipei, TWN)

Journal of Circuits, Systems and Computers (Singapore, SGP)

Journal of Clinical Biochemical and Nutrition (Ibaraki, JPN)

Journal of Clinical and Experimental Medicine (Tokyo, JPN)

Journal of College of International Studies (Aichi, JPN)

Journal of Communications and Networks (Seoul, KOR)

Journal of Computational Acoustics (Singapore, SGP)

Journal of Dermatology (Tokyo, JPN)

Journal of Development Assistance (Tokyo, JPN)

Journal of Diplomatic Studies (Riyadh, SAU)

Journal of Earthquake Engineering (Singapore, SGP)

Journal of Economic Integration (Seoul, KOR)

Journal of Education (UKM Bangi, MYS)

Journal of Educational Media and Library Sciences (Tamsui, TWN)

Journal of Electrical Engineering and Information Science (Seoul, KOR)

Journal of Electronics Manufacturing (Singapore, SGP)

Journal of Enterprising Culture (Singapore, SGP)

Journal of Environmental Assessment Policy and Management (Singapore, SGP)

Journal of Environmental Chemistry (Ibaraki, JPN)

Journal of Ethnic and Migration Studies (JEMS) (Brighton, GBR)

Journal of Ethology (Tokyo, JPN)

Journal of Euro-Asian Management (Bangkok, THA)

Journal of the Experimental Forest of National Taiwan University (Nan-Tou Hsien, TWN)

Journal of Explosives and Propellants (Taoyuan, TWN)

Journal of Faculty of Applied Biological Science of Hiroshima University (Higashi-Hiroshima City, JPN)

Journal of the Faculty of Fisheries Prefectural University Mie (Mie, JPN)

Journal of Faculty of Marine Science and Technology of Tokai University (Shizuoka, JPN)

Journal of Faculty of Nutriiton of Kobe Gakuin University (Hyogo, JPN)

Journal of the Faculty of Science and Technology of Kinki University (Osaka, JPN)

Journal of Ferrocement (Bangkok, THA)

Journal of Fertilization and Implantation (Tokyo, JPN)

Journal of Food Hygienic Society of Japan (Tokyo, JPN)

Journal of the Formosan Medical Association (Taipei, TWN)

Journal of Fujita Technical Research Institute (Kanagawa, JPN)

Journal of Gastroenterology (Tokyo, JPN)

The Journal of General and Applied Microbiology (Tokyo, JPN)

Journal of Geodetic Society of Japan (Ibaraki, JPN)

Journal of Geographical Science (Taipei, TWN)

Journal of Geological Society of China (Taipei, TWN)

Journal of Geological Society of Japan (Tokyo, JPN)

Journal of Geosciences (Osaka, JPN)

Journal of Germfree Life and Gnotobiology (Kobe, JPN)

Journal of Groundwater Hydrology (Tokyo, JPN)

Journal of Health Science (Tokyo, JPN)

Journal of Hepato-Biliary-Pancreatic Surgery (Tokyo, JPN)

Journal of Himeji Red Cross Hospital (Hyogo, JPN)

Journal of Hiroshima City Medical Association (Hiroshima, JPN)

Journal of Hiroshima University Dental Society (Hiroshima, JPN)

Journal of Home Economics of Japan (Tokyo, JPN)

Journal of the Hong Kong College of Cardiology (Hong Kong, CHN)

The Journal of the Hong Kong Geriatrics Society (Hong Kong, CHN)

Journal of Human Ergology (Tokyo, JPN)

Journal of Human Genetics (Tokyo, JPN)

Journal of Humanities (Seoul, KOR)

Journal of Humanities and Natural Sciences (Tokyo, JPN)

Journal of Hydroscience and Hydraulic Engineering (Tokyo, JPN)

Journal of Hyogo University of Teacher Education Series 3 (Hyogo, JPN)

Journal of Infection and Chemotherapy (Tokyo, JPN)

Journal of Institute for the Comprehensive Study of Lotus Sutra (Tokyo, JPN)

Journal of Institute of Electrostatics (Tokyo, JPN)

Journal of Institute of International Sociology (Hyogo, JPN)

Journal of the Institution of Engineers, Federation of Malaysia (Petaling Jaya, MYS)

The Journal of International Commercial Law (Swansea, GBR)

Journal of International Studies (Tokyo, JPN)

Journal of Ion Exchange (Tokyo, JPN)

Journal of Islamic University of Imam Muhammad Ibn Saud (Riyadh, SAU)

Journal of Japan Biomagnetism and Bioelectromagnetics Society (Tokyo, JPN)

Journal of Japan Broncho-Esophagological Society (Tokyo, JPN)

Journal of Japan Glaucoma Society (Miyazaki, JPN)

Journal of Japan Institute of Navigation (Tokyo, JPN)

Journal of Japan Medical Society of Paraplegia (Tokyo, JPN)

Journal of Japan Salivary Gland Society (Kanagawa, JPN)

Journal of Japan Society of Aesthetic Surgery (Tokyo, JPN)

Journal of Japan Society of Polymer Processing (Tokyo, JPN)

Journal of Japan Spine Research Society (Tokyo, JPN)

Journal of Japan Statistical Society (Tokyo, JPN)

Journal of Japan Welding Society (Tokyo, JPN)

Journal of Japanese Association for Chest Surgery (Kyoto, JPN)

Journal of Japanese Forestry Society (Tokyo, JPN)

Journal of Japanese Paediatric Orthopaedic Association (Sendai, JPN)

Journal of Japanese Society of Autologous Blood Transfusion (Okayama, JPN)

Journal of Japanese Society for Clinical Surgery (Tokyo, JPN)

Journal of Japanese Society of Computational Statistics (Tokyo, JPN)

Journal of Japanese Society of Dialysis Therapy (Tokyo, JPN)

Journal of Japanese Society for Horticultural Science (Tokyo, JPN)

Journal of Japanese Trade and Industry (Tokyo, JPN)

Journal of Juzen Medical Society (Ishikawa, JPN)

Journal of Kagawa Nutrition College (Tokyo, JPN)

Journal of Kansai Medical University Journal (Osaka, JPN)

Journal of Kansai Society of Naval Architects (Osaka, JPN)

Journal of Knot Theory and Its Ramifications (Singapore, SGP)

Journal of Korean Astronomical Society (Seoul, KOR)

Journal of Kyoto Entomological Society (Kyoto, JPN)

Journal of Kyoto Prefectural University of Medicine (Kyoto, JPN)

Journal of Magnetics Society of Japan (Tokyo, JPN)

Journal of the Malaysian Branch of the Royal Asiatic Society (Kuala Lumpur, MYS)

Journal of Marine Science Museum of Tokai University (Shizuoka, JPN)

Journal of Marine Science and Technology (Tokyo, JPN)

Journal of Mathematical Sciences (Tokyo, JPN)

Journal of Mathematics (Tokushima, JPN)

Journal of the Medical Association of Thailand (Bangkok, THA)

Journal of Medical and Dental Sciences (Tokyo, JPN)

Journal of Medical Investigation (Tokushima, JPN)

Journal of Meteorological Society of Japan (Tokyo, JPN)

The Journal of Microbiology (Seoul, KOR)

Journal of Microbiology, Immunology and Infection (Taipei, TWN)

Journal of Microwave Surgery (Osaka, JPN)

Journal of Mineralogy, Petrology and Economic Geology (Sendai, JPN)

Journal of Modern Literature in Chinese (Hong Kong, CHN)

Journal of Musculoskeletal Research (Singapore, SGP)

Journal of National Defense Medical College (Saitama, JPN)

Journal of National Research Council of Thailand (Bangkok, THA)

Journal of Nippon Medical School (Tokyo, JPN)

Journal of Nonlinear Optical Physics and Materials (Singapore, SGP)

Journal of Northern Occupational Health (Sapporo, JPN)

Journal of Nuclear Science and Technology (Tokyo, JPN)

Journal of Nursing Research (Taipei, TWN)

Journal of Obstetrics and Gynaecology (Tokyo, JPN)

Journal of Occupational Health (Tokyo, JPN)

Journal of Oil Palm Research (Kuala Lumpur, MYS)

Journal of Operations Research Society of Japan (Tokyo, JPN)

Journal of Oral Science (Tokyo, JPN)

Journal of Orthopaedic Science (Tokyo, JPN)

Journal of Osaka Dental University (Osaka, JPN)

Journal of Pacific Society (Tokyo, JPN)

Journal of Pesticide Science (Osaka, JPN)

Journal of Pharmaceutical Science and Technology (Tokyo, JPN)

Journal of Physical Education & Recreation (Hong Kong, CHN)

Journal of Physical Society of Japan (Tokyo, JPN)

Journal of Physical Therapy Science (Tokyo, JPN)

Journal of Phytogeography and Taxonomy (Kanazawa, JPN)

Journal of Plant Biology (Seoul, KOR)

Journal of Plant Research (Tokyo, JPN)

Journal of Plasma and Fusion Research (Nagoya, JPN)

Journal of Plasma and Fusion Research (Aichi, JPN)

Journal of Population, Health and Social Welfare (Seoul, KOR)

Journal of Population and Health Studies (Seoul, KOR)

Journal of Population and Social Studies (Nakhon Pathom, THA)

Journal of Radiation Research (Chiba, JPN)

Journal of Reproduction and Development (Tokyo, JPN)

Journal of Research Methodology (Bangkok, THA)

Journal of Robotics and Mechatronics (Tokyo, JPN)

Journal of Rubber Research (Kuala Lumpur, MYS)

Journal of Science Education in Japan (Tokyo, JPN)

Journal of Science of Labour (Kanagawa, JPN)

Journal of Science Policy and Research Management (Tokyo, JPN)

Journal of the Science Society of Thailand (Bangkok, THA)

Journal of Sedimentological Society of Japan (Matsumoto, JPN)

Journal of Seismological Society of Japan (Tokyo, JPN)

Journal of Sericultural Science of Japan (Ibaraki, JPN)

Journal of Smooth Muscle Research (Tokyo, JPN)

Journal of Social Science (Tokyo, JPN)

Journal of Social Science (Taipei, TWN)

Journal of Social Sciences and Philosophy (Taipei, TWN)

Journal of Sociology (Taipei, TWN)

Journal of South American Earth Sciences (Amsterdam, NLD)

Journal of the Southeast Asian Archives (Kuala Lumpur, MYS)

Journal of Southeast Asian Education (Bangkok, THA)

Journal of Space Technology and Science (Tokyo, JPN)

Journal of Speleological Society of Japan (Yamaguchi, JPN)

Journal of Structural and Construction Engineering (Tokyo, JPN)

Journal of Structural Engineering B (Tokyo, JPN)

Journal of Taiwan Museum (Taipei, TWN)

Journal of the Taiwan Society of Anesthesiologists (Taipei, TWN)

Journal of Textile Engineering (Osaka, JPN)

Journal of Tezukayama College Food Sciences (Nara, JPN)

Journal of Thai Chamber of Commerce (Bangkok, THA)

Journal of Three Dimensional Images (Tokyo, JPN)

Journal of Toho University Medical Society (Tokyo, JPN)

Journal of Tokyo Dental College Society (Chiba, JPN)

Journal of Tokyo University of Fisheries (Tokyo, JPN)

Journal of Tokyo University of Mercantile Marine (Tokyo, JPN)

Journal of Tosoh Research (Yamaguchi, JPN)

Journal of Toxicological Sciences (Tokyo, JPN)

Journal of Traditional Medicines (Toyama, JPN)

Journal of Transportation Medicine (Tokyo, JPN)

Journal of Tropical Agriculture & Food Science (Kuala Lumpur, MYS)

Journal of Tropical Forest Products (Kuala Lumpur, MYS)

Journal of Tropical Forest Science (Kuala Lumpur, MYS)

Journal of University of Occupational and Environmental Health (Fukuoka, JPN)

Journal of Veterinary Medical Science (Tokyo, JPN)

Journal of Visualization (Tokyo, JPN)

Journal of Water and Environmental Issues (Tokyo, JPN)

Journal of Wood Science (Tokyo, JPN)

Journal of World Affairs (Tokyo, JPN)

Journal of Yamashina Institute for Ornithology (Chiba, JPN)

Journals in Art and Architectural History (Aldershot, GBR)

JSME International Journal Series A (Tokyo, JPN)

JSME International Journal Series B Fluids and Thermal Engineering (Tokyo, JPN)

JSME International Journal Series C Dynamics, Control, Robotics, Design and Manufacturing (Tokyo, JPN)

Juice (Singapore, SGP)

Jurnal Ekonomi Malaysia (UKM Bangi, MYS)

Jurnal Sains Nuklear Malaysia (Kajang, MYS)

Jurutera (Petaling Jaya, MYS)

Kansai Scene (Osaka, JPN)

Kaohsiung Journal of Medical Sciences (Kaohsiung, TWN)

Kasetsart Journal (Bangkok, THA)

Katso (A-lehdet, FIN)

Kauneus ja Terveys (A-lehdet, FIN)

Kawasaki Medical Journal (Okayama, JPN)

KDB Report (Seoul, KOR)

Keidanren Review (Tokyo, JPN)

Keio Business Review (Tokyo, JPN)

Keio Economic Studies (Tokyo, JPN)

Keio Journal of Medicine (Tokyo, JPN)

Keretapi (Kuala Lumpur, MYS)

Khaleej Times (Dubai, UAE)

King Abdul Aziz Medical Journal (Jeddah, SAU)

Kinnaree Magazine (Bangkok, THA)

Kobe Journal of Mathematics (Hyogo, JPN)

Kobe Journal of Medical Sciences (Hyogo, JPN)

Kobe University Economic Review (Hyogo, JPN)

Korea Business World (Seoul, KOR)

Korea Buyers Guide Electronics (Seoul, KOR)

Korea Development Bank: Its Functions and Activities (Seoul, KOR)

Korea Economic Weekly (Seoul, KOR)

Korea Focus on Current Topics (Seoul, KOR)

Korea Herald (Seoul, KOR)

Korea Non-Life Insurance (Seoul, KOR)

The Korea Post (Seoul, KOR)

Korea Trade (Seoul, KOR)

Korea Trade and Investment (Seoul, KOR)

Korean Business Journal (Seoul, KOR)

Korean Economic and Financial Outlook (Seoul, KOR)

Korean Financial Review (Seoul, KOR)

Korean Journal of Breeding (Suwon, KOR)

Korean Journal of Chemical Engineering (Seoul, KOR)

The Korean Journal of Defense Analysis (Seoul, KOR)

Korean Journal of International Studies (Seoul, KOR)

Korean Journal of Mycology (Seoul, KOR)

The Korean Journal of Parasitology (Seoul, KOR)

Korean Journal of Pharmacognosy (Seoul, KOR)

Korean Journal of Physiology and Pharmacology (Seoul, KOR)

Korean Journal of Public Health (Seoul, KOR)

The Korean Journal of Systematic Zoology (Jeonju, KOR)

Korean Journal of Zoology (Seoul, KOR)

Korean Physical Society Journal (Seoul, KOR)

Korean Social Science Journal (Seoul, KOR)

Korean Society of Oceanography Journal (Seoul, KOR)

KSME International Journal (Seoul, KOR)

Kultaraha (A-lehdet, FIN)

Kumamoto Journal of Mathematics (Kumamoto, JPN)

Kumamoto Medical Journal (Kumamoto, JPN)

Kurume Medical Journal (Fukuoka, JPN)

Kyodo News (Tokyo, JPN)

Kyoto Journal (Kyoto, JPN)

The Kyoto Shimbun News (Kyoto, JPN)

Kyoto University Research Activities in Civil Engineering and Related Fields (Kyoto, JPN)

Kyushu American Literature (Fukuoka, JPN)

Lamellicornia (Tokyo, JPN)

Language and Culture (Sapporo, JPN)

Language Teacher (Tokyo, JPN)

Law Gazette (Singapore, SGP)

LawLink (Singapore, SGP)

Let's Talk in English (Taipei, TWN)

Lex (London, GBR)

Library and Information Science (Tokyo, JPN)

Lien (Singapore, SGP)

Lifelong Learning in Europe (Helsinki, FIN)

Lime (Singapore, SGP)

Living in the Gulf (Dubai, UAE)

Living in Thailand (Bangkok, THA)

London Housing (London, GBR)

LookBook (Singapore, SGP)

LookEast (Bangkok, THA)

Low Temperature Medicine (Tokyo, JPN)

Madame (A-lehdet, FIN)

Maison (Seoul, KOR)

Malayan Naturalist (Batu Caves, MYS)

Malayan Nature Journal (Batu Caves, MYS)

Malaysia Tatler (Hong Kong, CHN)

Malaysiakini (Kuala Lumpur, MYS)

The Malaysian Forester (Kuala Lumpur, MYS)

Malaysian Journal of Economic Studies (Kuala Lumpur, MYS)

Malaysian Journal of Family Studies (Kuala Lumpur, MYS)

Malaysian Journal of Library and Information Science (Kuala Lumpur, MYS)

The Malaysian Journal of Pathology (Kuala Lumpur, MYS)

Malaysian Journal of Science Series A: Life Sciences (Kuala Lumpur, MYS)

Malaysian Journal of Science Series B: Physical & Earth Sciences (Kuala Lumpur, MYS)

Malaysian Journal of Tropical Geography (Kuala Lumpur, MYS)

Malaysian Panorama (Kuala Lumpur, MYS)

The Malaysian Surveyor (Petaling Jaya, MYS)

Male by Birth, Man by Choice (Singapore, SGP)

Mallal's Monthly Digest (Singapore, SGP)

Mammalian Mutagenicity Study Group Communications (Kanagawa, JPN)

Man and Society (Kuala Lumpur, MYS)

Marie Claire (Kuala Lumpur, MYS)

Marie Claire (Seoul, KOR)

Marine Science Journal of King Abdul Aziz University (Jeddah, SAU)

Marketwatch (Singapore, SGP)

Material Science Study (Kyoto, JPN)

Mathematica Japonica (Osaka, JPN)

Mathematical Education (Seoul, KOR)

Mathematical Journal of Ibaraki University (Ibaraki, JPN)

Mathematical Journal of Okayama University (Okayama, JPN)

Mathematical Models and Methods in Applied Sciences (Singapore, SGP)

Mathematics Journal of Toyama University (Toyama, JPN)

Medical Electron Microscopy (Tokyo, JPN)

Medical Imaging Technology (Tokyo, JPN)

Medical Journal of Aomori Prefectural Central Hospital (Aomori, JPN)

Medical Journal of Asahi General Hospital (Chiba, JPN)

Medical Journal of the Government Printing Bureau (Tokyo, JPN)

Medical Journal of Hiroshima Prefectural Hospital (Hiroshima, JPN)

Medical Journal of Hiroshima University (Hiroshima, JPN)

Medical Journal of Ishikawa Prefectural Central Hospital (Ishikawa, JPN)

Medical Journal of Iwate Prefectural Miyako Hospital (Iwate, JPN)

The Medical Journal of Malaysia (Kuala Lumpur, MYS)

MEED - The Middle East Business Weekly (Dubai, UAE)

Meidan Mokki (A-lehdet, FIN)

Meidan Talo (A-lehdet, FIN)

MEJ (Tokyo, JPN)

Messenger (Singapore, SGP)

Metals and Materials (Seoul, KOR)

Metro Magazine (Bangkok, THA)

Metropolis (Tokyo, JPN)

Mezzo (London, GBR)

Microbiology and Immunology (Tokyo, JPN)

Microcomputer (Bangkok, THA)

Microcomputer User Magazine (Bangkok, THA)

Mineral Resources Engineering (Singapore, SGP)

Mirror of Opinion (Singapore, SGP)

Mitsubishi Electric Advance (Tokyo, JPN)

Mitsubishi Heavy Industries Technical Review (Yokohama, JPN)

Mobile Executive (Dubai, UAE)

Mode Hong Kong (Hong Kong, CHN)

Modern Physics Letters A (Singapore, SGP)

Modern Physics Letters B (Singapore, SGP)

Money Works Magazine (Dubai, UAE)

Monthly Journal of Entomology (Tokyo, JPN)

Monumenta Nipponica (Tokyo, JPN)

Motherhood (Singapore, SGP)

Motherhood Handbook (Singapore, SGP)

Motor China (Beijing, CHN)

Motorcycle Japan (Tokyo, JPN)

Motorhome ABC (Oostende, BEL)

Motoring (Singapore, SGP)

Motoring Annual (Singapore, SGP)

Movie -TV Marketing (Tokyo, JPN)

MuangBoran Journal (Bangkok, THA)

Multi-Skills (Kenilworth, GBR)

Nagoya Mathematical Journal (Nagoya, JPN)

Nanzan Review of American Studies (Aichi, JPN)

National Junior Magazine (Bangkok, THA)

Natural Medicines (Tokyo, JPN)

Natural Product Sciences (Seoul, KOR)

Nature Aquarium World (Singapore, SGP)

Nature Watch (Singapore, SGP)

Naval Architecture and Ocean Engineering (Tokyo, JPN)

Network Middle East (Dubai, UAE)

Neuro-Ophthalmology Japan (Kanagawa, JPN)

Neurologia Medico-Chirurgica (Tokyo, JPN)

New Cicada (Fukushima, JPN)

New Diamond and Frontier Carbon Technology (Tokyo, JPN)

New Entomologist (Minamiminowa, JPN)

New Sabah Times (Sabah, MYS)

The New Straits Times (Kuala Lumpur, MYS)

New Sunday Times (Kuala Lumpur, MYS)

New Zealand Journal of Archaeology (Dunedin North, NZL)

Newman (Singapore, SGP)

News from Nisshin Steel (Tokyo, JPN)

NewsToday.co.th (Phattaya, THA)

Nihongo Journal (Tokyo, JPN)

Nihonkai Mathematical Journal (Niigata, JPN)

Nikkei Electronics Asia (Hong Kong, CHN)

Nikkei Net Interactive (Tokyo, JPN)

The Nikkei Weekly (Tokyo, JPN)

9to5Asia.com (Singapore, SGP)

Nippon Steel News (Tokyo, JPN)

Nippon Tungsten Review (Fukuoka, JPN)

Nipponia (Tokyo, JPN)

NIRA Review (Tokyo, JPN)

North Korea News (Seoul, KOR)

NUS Economic Journal (Singapore, SGP)

Ocean Research (Seoul, KOR)

Oceanographical Magazine (Tokyo, JPN)

Office Equipment and Products (Tokyo, JPN)

Okajima's Folia Anatomica Japonica (Tokyo, JPN)

On Air Magazine (Nonthaburi, THA)

Openings (Jinan, SD, CHN)

Optical Review (Tokyo, JPN)

Oral Radiology (Tokyo, JPN)

Orient Aviation (Hong Kong, CHN)

Orientations (Hong Kong, CHN)

Orthopaedic Ceramic Implants (Osaka, JPN)

Orthopaedic and Traumatic Surgery (Tokyo, JPN)

Osaka Journal of Mathematics (Osaka, JPN)

Pacific Focus (Inchon, KOR)

The Padang (Singapore, SGP)

Paper Asia (Singapore, SGP)

Papers in Meteorology and Geophysics (Ibaraki, JPN)

Parallel Processing Letters (Singapore, SGP)

Patents and Licensing (Tokyo, JPN)

PC Magazine Middle & Near East (Dubai, UAE)

PC World Hong Kong (Hong Kong, CHN)

PC World Malaysia (Kuala Lumpur, MYS)

PC World Singapore (Singapore, SGP)

Peatlands International (Jyvaskyla, FIN)

Pediatric Dental Journal (Tokyo, JPN)

Pedologist (Ibaraki, JPN)

Penang Tourist Newspaper (Penang, MYS)

People's Daily (Beijing, CHN)

Peptide Information (Osaka, JPN)

Performance Arts and Films (Seoul, KOR)

Pertanika Journal of Science and Technology (Serdang, MYS)

Pertanika Journal of Social Science and Humanities (Serdang, MYS)

Pertanika Journal of Tropical Agricultural Science (Serdang, MYS)

Petromin (Singapore, SGP)

Pharma Japan (Tokyo, JPN)

Pharmacometrics (Sendai, JPN)

Photography Middle East (Dubai, UAE)

The Phuket Gazette (Phuket, THA)

Physico-Chemical Biology (Kanagawa, JPN)

Physics For You (New Delhi, DH, IND)

Physiology and Ecology Japan (Kyoto, JPN)

Phytotaxonomy (New Delhi, DH, IND)

Pink Ink (Bangkok, THA)

Pit & Quarry (Walkerville, SAF)

Plane Talk (Manchester, GBR)

Planews (Singapore, SGP)

Plankton Biology and Ecology (Tokyo, JPN)

The Plant Pathology Journal (Seoul, KOR)

Plant Production Science (Tanashi, JPN)

Plasma Processing (Tokyo, JPN)

Plastichem (Singapore, SGP)

Plastics & Rubber Singapore Journal (Singapore, SGP)

Poetry Kanto (Yokohama, JPN)

Polar Bioscience (Tokyo, JPN)

Politeia (Singapore, SGP)

Polymer Journal (Tokyo, JPN)

Population Ecology (Tokyo, JPN)

Population Headliners (Bangkok, THA)

Port O'Call (Singapore, SGP)

Postal Service Today (Taipei, TWN)

Pregnancy & Babycare (Singapore, SGP)

Premier Golf Annual (Singapore, SGP)

Primates (Aichi, JPN)

Production Research (Tokyo, JPN)

Profile (Hong Kong, CHN)

Progress of Theoretical Physics (Kyoto, JPN)

Progress of Theoretical Physics - Supplement (Kyoto, JPN)

Psychologia (Kyoto, JPN)

ptah (Helsinki, FIN)

Publications of Amakusa Marine Biological Laboratory (Kumamoto, JPN)

Publications of Astronomical Society of Japan (Tokyo, JPN)

Publications of Seto Marine Biological Laboratory (Wakayama, JPN)

Quantitative Structure-Activity Relationships (Bonn, GER)

Quaternary Research (Tokyo, JPN)

Questions and Answers in General Topology (Osaka, JPN)

RaceWeek (Dubai, UAE)

Radio Japan News (Tokyo, JPN)

Radioisotopes (Tokyo, JPN)

Rare Earths (Osaka, JPN)

Reformation (Aberystwyth, GBR)

Regional Development Dialogue (Aichi, JPN)

Regional Development Studies (Aichi, JPN)

Regional Outlook: Southeast Asia (Singapore, SGP)

Renal Transplantation, Vascular Surgery (Tokyo, JPN)

Research Notes and Memoranda of Applied Geometry for Prevenient Natural Philosophy (Chiba, JPN)

Research and Practice in Forensic Medicine (Miyagi, JPN)

Research and Practice in Human Resource Management (Singapore, SGP)

Research Reports on Information Science and Electrical Engineering (Fukuoka, JPN)

Resource Geology (Tokyo, JPN)

Review of Economics and Business (Osaka, JPN)

Review of Industrial Property Protection and Copyright (Budapest, HUN)

Review of Laser Engineering (Osaka, JPN)

Review of Modern Literature in Chinese (Hong Kong, CHN)

Review of Pacific Basin Financial Markets and Policies (Singapore, SGP)

Reviews on Heteroatom Chemistry (Tokyo, JPN)

Reviews in Mathematical Physics (Singapore, SGP)

Revista de Psicologia Social (San Sebastian de los Reyes, SPA)

Rigaku Journal (Tokyo, JPN)

RIST Journal of R & D (Pohang, KOR)

Riyadh Daily (Riyadh, SAU)

Rocket (Petaling Jaya, MYS)

RSYC (Singapore, SGP)

RTI—Redes, Telecom and Instalacoes (Sao Paulo, SP, BRZ)

The Rubber International (Bangkok, THA)

Rural and Environmental Engineering (Tokyo, JPN)

SABRAO Journal of Breeding and Genetics (Nakhon Pathom, THA)

Sago Communication (Ibaraki, JPN)

Saitama Mathematical Journal (Saitama, JPN)

Sapporo Medical Journal (Sapporo, JPN)

Saudi Arabia Business Week (Riyadh, SAU)

Saudi Gazette (Jeddah, SAU)

Saudi Heart Journal (Jeddah, SAU)

The Saudi Journal of Disability and Rehabilitation (SJDR) (Riyadh, SAU)

The Saudi Journal of Gastroenterology (Riyadh, SAU)

Saudi Journal of Kidney Diseases and Transplantation (Riyadh, SAU)

Saudi Medical Journal (Riyadh, SAU)

Science Asia (Bangkok, THA)

Science and Engineering Review of Doshisha University (Kyoto, JPN)

Science and Industry (Osaka, JPN)

Science Journal of King Saud University (Riyadh, SAU)

Sciences (Tokyo, JPN)

Sea and Sky (Kobe, JPN)

SEAISI - Quarterly Journal (Shah Alam, MYS)

SEAMEO Regional Language Centre Guidelines (Singapore, SGP)

Seishin Studies (Tokyo, JPN)

Sensors and Materials (Tokyo, JPN)

Seoul Journal of Economics (Seoul, KOR)

Seoul Journal of Korean Studies (Seoul, KOR)

Seoul National University Journal of Agricultural Sciences (Suwon, KOR)

SET Journal (Bangkok, THA)

Setsunan University Review of Humanities and Social Sciences (Osaka, JPN)

SG News (Singapore, SGP)

Sgezine (Singapore, SGP)

Shakespeare Studies (Tokyo, JPN)

The Shakespearean International Yearbook (Aldershot, GBR)

Shanghai Today (Shanghai, CHN)

Shimane Journal of Medical Science (Shimane, JPN)

The Shinano Mainichi Shimbun (Nagano City, JPN)

Shipping Times (Singapore, SGP)

Shipping and Trade News (Tokyo, JPN)

Show Daily (Kuala Lumpur, MYS)

Showcase (Singapore, SGP)

Shukan ST (Tokyo, JPN)

Signature (Singapore, SGP)

Silver Kris (Singapore, SGP)

Singapore Accountant (Singapore, SGP)

Singapore Architect (Singapore, SGP)

Singapore Economic Review (Singapore, SGP)

The Singapore Family Physician (Singapore, SGP)

Singapore Journal of Legal Studies (Singapore, SGP)

Singapore Journal of Obstetrics & Gynaecology (Singapore, SGP)

Singapore Journal of Primary Industries (Singapore, SGP)

Singapore Journal of Tropical Geography (Singapore, SGP)

Singapore Law Review (Singapore, SGP)

Singapore Management Review (Singapore, SGP)

Singapore National Academy of Science Journal (Singapore, SGP)

Singapore Paediatric Journal (Singapore, SGP)

Singapore Source Book for Architects & Designers (Singapore, SGP)

Singapore Visitor (Singapore, SGP)

Sinorama Magazine (Taipei, TWN)

Siriraj Hospital Gazette (Bangkok, THA)

Smart Investor (Singapore, SGP)

The SMS Magazine (Singapore, SGP)

Social Science Research of University of Tokushima (Tokushima, JPN)

Soil Microorganisms (Matsudo City, JPN)

Soil Science and Plant Nutrition (Tokyo, JPN)

Soils & Foundations (Tokyo, JPN)

Sojourn (Singapore, SGP)

Solvent Extraction Research and Development, Japan (Sendai, JPN)

Sonderhefte (Hannover, GER)

Songlines (Windsor, GBR)

Soochow Journal of Economics and Business (Taipei, TWN)

Soochow Journal of Foreign Languages and Literatures (Taipei, TWN)

Soochow Journal of History (Taipei, TWN)

Soochow Journal of Political Science (Taipei, TWN)

Soochow Journal of Social Work (Taipei, TWN)

Sophia (Melbourne, VI, AUS)

The Sound Magazine (Telford, GBR)

Soundi (A-lehdet, FIN)

South Pacific Study (Kagoshima, JPN)

South Review (Kuala Lumpur, MYS)

South Seas Society Journal (Singapore, SGP)

Southeast Asian Affairs (Singapore, SGP)

Southeast Asian Journal of Social Sciences (Singapore, SGP)

Space (Singapore, SGP)

Space (Seoul, KOR)

Space in Japan (Tokyo, JPN)

Species Diversity (Tokyo, JPN)

Spinal Surgery (Osaka, JPN)

Sports (Singapore, SGP)

Square Rooms (Singapore, SGP)

The Standard (Hong Kong, CHN)

The Star (Petaling Jaya, MYS)

Stationery and Office Supplies (Taipei, TWN)

Statistica Sinica (Taipei, TWN)

Stock Market in Thailand (Bangkok, THA)

The Straits Times (Singapore, SGP)

Structural Engineering - Earthquake Engineering (Tokyo, JPN)

Structural Engineering and Mechanics (Taejon, KOR)

Studies of Broadcasting (Tokyo, JPN)

Studies in English Literature (Tokyo, JPN)

Studio Classroom (Taipei, TWN)

Study of Elementary Particles (Kyoto, JPN)

Study of Medical Supplies (Tokyo, JPN)

Suara SAM (Penang, MYS)

Sumo World (Tokyo, JPN)

Surface Review and Letters (Singapore, SGP)

Surgery Today (Tokyo, JPN)

Survival (London, GBR)

SUT Journal of Mathematics (Tokyo, JPN)

The Taiwan Economic News (Taipei, TWN)

Taiwan International Trade (Taipei, TWN)

Taiwan News (Taipei, TWN)

Taiwan Outlook (Taipei, TWN)

The Taiwanese Journal of Mathematics (Hsinchu, TWN)

Tamkang Journal of Futures Studies (Tamsui, TWN)

Tamkang Journal of International Affairs (Tamsui, TWN)

Tamkang Journal of Mathematics (Tamsui, TWN)

Tamkang Journal of Tamkang Review (Tamsui, TWN)

Teach (Singapore, SGP)

Technical Journal of Telecommunication Laboratories (Chungli, TWN)

Techno Japan (Tokyo, JPN)

Teenage (Singapore, SGP)

teens (Singapore, SGP)

Teens Annual (Singapore, SGP)

TeenzSpot.com (Sharjah, UAE)

Telcom Journal (Bangkok, THA)

Telecom Asia (Hong Kong, CHN)

Telecom Tribune (Tokyo, JPN)

Tenders Estimating Data Service (Singapore, SGP)

Tensor (Kanagawa, JPN)

TF-bladet (Stockholm, SWE)

Thai-American Business (Bangkok, THA)

Thai Economic Review (Bangkok, THA)

Thai Journal of Agricultural Science (Bangkok, THA)

Thai Journal of Anesthesiology (Bangkok, THA)

Thai Journal of Development Administration (Bangkok, THA)

Thai Junior Red Cross Magazine (Bangkok, THA)

Thailand Airline Timetable (Bangkok, THA)

Thailand Travel Magazine (Bangkok, THA)

Thailand Update (Bangkok, THA)

Third World Economics (Penang, MYS)

Third World Resurgence (Penang, MYS)

This Month in Korea (Seoul, KOR)

Time Asia (Hong Kong, CHN)

Time Out Dubai (Dubai, UAE)

TM (Tokyo, JPN)

Tobacco Asia (Bangkok, THA)

Today's Parents (Singapore, SGP)

Tohoku Geophysical Journal (Miyagi, JPN)

Tohoku Journal of Agricultural Research (Miyagi, JPN)

Tohoku Journal of Experimental Medicine (Miyagi, JPN)

Tohoku Mathematical Journal (Miyagi, JPN)

Tohoku Psychologica Folia (Miyagi, JPN)

Tokyo Journal (Tokyo, JPN)

Tokyo Journal of Mathematics (Tokyo, JPN)

Tokyo Scene (Tokyo, JPN)

Tombo (Tokyo, JPN)

Top Fashion Magazine (Bangkok, THA)

Tour Companion (Tokyo, JPN)

Toyota Technical Review (Tokyo, JPN)

Travel Agency (Kuala Lumpur, MYS)

Travel Asia (Singapore, SGP)

Travel In Taiwan (Taipei, TWN)

Travel Trade Gazette Asia (Singapore, SGP)

Travel Trade Report (Bangkok, THA)

Traveller Magazine (Bangkok, THA)

Trends in Glycoscience and Glycotechnology (Osaka, JPN)

Tropical Medicine (Nagasaki, JPN)

Trusts & Estates Tax Journal (London, GBR)

TSEA: Targeting Singapore Electronics Audience (Singapore, SGP)

Tsuda Review (Tokyo, JPN)

Tsukuba Journal of Mathematics (Ibaraki, JPN)

Tumor Research: Experimental and Clinical (Sapporo, JPN)

Tuulilasi (A-lehdet, FIN)

Twenty Four Seven (Singapore, SGP)

Unibeam (Singapore, SGP)

Union Herald (Petaling Jaya, MYS)

Union of Japanese Scientists and Engineers Reports of Statistical Application Research (Tokyo, JPN)

University of Singapore History Society Journal (Singapore, SGP)

University of Tsukuba Institute of Geoscience Science Reports Section A: Geographical Sciences (Ibaraki, JPN)

Update Magazine (Bangkok, THA)

UPDATE Magazine (Dubai, UAE)

Utusan Malaysia (Kuala Lumpur, MYS)

Vantage Point (Seoul, KOR)

Venus: Japanese Journal of Malacology (Tokyo, JPN)

Veterinary Anaesthesia and Analgesia (Midlothian, GBR)

Veterinary Dermatology (Middlesex, GBR)

Viherpiha (A-lehdet, FIN)

Vision KL (Kuala Lumpur, MYS)

Viva Origino (Osaka, JPN)

Voi Hyvin (A-lehdet, FIN)

Watan (Kuala Lumpur, MYS)

Water Report (Tokyo, JPN)

Wedding & Travel (Singapore, SGP)

The Weekend Magazine (Dubai, UAE)

Welcome to Chiangmai & Chiangrai Magazine (Chiang Mai, THA)

What's On (Dubai, UAE)

Wheat Information Service (Kanagawa, JPN)

Windows Middle East (Dubai, UAE)

Windows Southern Africa (Dubai, UAE)

Wine & Dine (Singapore, SGP)

Wolgan Mot (Seoul, KOR)

Woman's World (Singapore, SGP)

Women (Seoul, KOR)

Women's Weekly (Seoul, KOR)

World Friends (Seoul, KOR)

World Literature Written in English (Singapore, SGP)

Xene (Hokkaido, JPN)

The Yoke (Yokohama, JPN)

Yonsei Business Review (Seoul, KOR)

Yonsei Medical Journal (Seoul, KOR)

Yonsei Reports on Tropical Medicine (Seoul, KOR)

Young Buddhist (Singapore, SGP)

Young Generation (Singapore, SGP)

Young Parents (Singapore, SGP)

Young Times (Dubai, UAE)

Zaiken (Tokyo, JPN)

Zhongguo Yike Daxue Xuebao (Shenyang, LI, CHN)

Zoological Science (Tokyo, JPN)

Zoological Studies (Taipei, TWN)

Cessations

United States and Canada

ADC News & Solutions (Newton, MA)

Advancing the Consumer Interest (Ames, IA)

Advantage (Nashville, TN)

Africa Information Afrique (New York, NY)

Air Traffic Research Quarterly (Hoboken, NJ)

Allen County News (Scottsville, KY)

Alliance (Ottawa, ON)

Amelia (Bakersfield, CA)

Analytical Methods and Instrumentation (Hoboken, NJ)

Antique Gazette (Iola, WI)

Applied Geographic Studies (Hoboken, NJ)

Arrive (Bethesda, MD)

ASA News (Chicago, IL)

Asia Pacific Journal of Management (Hoboken, NJ)

Auction Times for the West (Iola, WI)

Behavioral Residential Treatment (Hoboken, NJ)

Biblion (New York, NY)

Biospectroscopy (Hoboken, NJ)

Biotechnology Software Internet Report (Larchmont, NY)

Blackjack Forum (Las Vegas, NV)

Blues Access (Boulder, CO)

Boone County Headlight (Harrison, AR)

Boswell Enterprise (Boswell, IN)

Brandywine.net Business Report (Oxford, PA)

British Car (Los Altos, CA)

British Journal of Management (Hoboken, NJ)

Budget Watch (Washington, DC)

Business Change and Re-engineering (Hoboken, NJ)

Calgary Families (Vancouver, BC)

California Grower (Carpinteria, CA)

The Canadian Forum (Halifax, NS)

Canfield Family Association (Wichita, KS)

Changes (Hoboken, NJ)

The Chemical Intelligencer (New York, NY)

Cicada (Bakersfield, CA)

Commodity Markets and the Developing Countries (Washington, DC)

Communications Standards Review (Palo Alto, CA)

Communications Standards Summary (Palo Alto, CA)

The Constantian (McMurray, PA)

Contemporary Education (Terre Haute, IN)

Corporate Executive (Dartmouth, NS)

Country Living (Wappingers Falls, NY)

Creative Classroom (New York, NY)

Credit Union Executive Journal (Madison, WI)

Cultural Diversity and Mental Health (Hoboken, NJ)

Dallas & Fort Worth Home Living (Addison, TX)

Databased Web Advisor (San Diego, CA)

Depression (Hoboken, NJ)

Edmonton Families (Vancouver, BC)

L'Eglise Canadienne (Montreal, QC)

The Einstein Quarterly (New York, NY)

Electronic Publishing (Hoboken, NJ)

Elk Valley Miner (Fernie, BC)

Embedded Systems Development (Cleveland, OH)

Environmental Manager (Hoboken, NJ)

Environmental Regulation and Permitting (Hoboken, NJ)

Environmental Toxicology and Water Quality (Hoboken, NJ)

Equity & Excellence in Education (Westport, CT)

Erickson Publishing, LLC (Madison, WI)

Farm/Ranch Exchange (Scottsbluff, NE)

Favorite Brand Name Recipes Magazine (Ames, IA)

Field Analytical Chemistry and Technology (Hoboken, NJ)

Fishing Tackle Trade News (Rockport, ME)

Focus on Renewable Natural Resources (Moscow, ID)

Freedom Review (New York, NY)

Future of Print Media (Kent, OH)

Global Commodity Markets (Washington, DC)

Gurnee Sun (Naperville, IL)

Hawkeye Booster (Elgin, IA)

Healthcare Products Today (Richmond, VA)

Heterogeneous Chemistry Reviews (Hoboken, NJ)

Home Care Provider (St. Louis, MO)

Home Report (Etobicoke, ON)

The Hospice Journal (Pittsburgh, PA)

The Hospice Professional (Alexandria, VA)

Hosta Magazine (Peabody, MA)

IEEE Computer Applications in Power (Columbus, OH)

Illinois Libraries (Springfield, IL)

Indicators of Industry and Services (Washington, DC)

Infrastructure (Hoboken, NJ)

The Inside Line (Maple Grove, MN)

Insight IS (Westminster, CO)

Interior Landscape (Chicago, IL)

International Insurance Monitor (Mount Vernon, NY)

International Journal of Applied Economics and Econometrics (Somerset, NJ)

International Journal of Human Resource Management (Greenwich, CT)

International Journal of Methods in Psychiatric Research (Hoboken, NJ)

International Journal of Microwave and Millimeter-Wave Computer-Aided Engineering (Hoboken, NJ)

International Journal of Modelling & Simulation (Calgary, AB)

International Petroleum Abstracts (Hoboken, NJ)

Internet Java & ActiveX Advisor (San Diego, CA)

Internetworking (Hoboken, NJ)

Island Business (Honolulu, HI)

Jones Intercable (Independence, MO)

Journal of Adolescent Chemical Dependency (Chester, PA)

Journal of Biochemistry, Molecular Biology and Biophysics (Honolulu, HI)

Journal of Biomolecular Screening (Larchmont, NY)

Journal of the Clinical Orthopaedic Society (Hoboken, NJ)

Journal of Environmental Permitting (Secaucus, NJ)

Journal of Geriatric Drug Therapy (Athens, GA)

Journal of Human Virology (Baltimore, MD)

Journal of Inflammation (Hoboken, NJ)

Journal of Public Administration Research and Theory (Somerset, NJ)

Journal of Quality Management (Tempe, AZ)

Journal Shopping News (Hamilton, OH)

Journal of Youth Services in Libraries (Chicago, IL)

KAIN-AM (Natchez, MS)

KAMD-AM (Camden, AR)

KAPB-AM (Marksville, LA)

KBBD-FM (Beaver, UT)

KBLE-AM (Mercer Island, WA)

KEMM-FM (Gatesville, TX)

Kentucky Review (Lexington, KY)

KIFO-AM (Honolulu, HI)

KUDY-AM (Spokane, WA)

La Barrique (Montreal, QC)

Laboratory Robotics and Automation (Hoboken, NJ)

Land Degradation & Rehabilitation (Secaucus, NJ)

Le Meunier (St. Hyacinthe, QC)

Leader Extra (Tomahawk, WI)

Leadership Montreal (Montreal, QC)

Letters of Credit Report (Secaucus, NJ)

Libertyville/Mundelein/Vernon Hills Sun (Naperville, IL)

Living Fit (Woodland Hills, CA)

Loadstar (Shreveport, LA)

Loadstar Quarterly (Shreveport, LA)

Loan Officer's Legal Alert (Secaucus, NJ)

Lookout Non-Foods (Naples, NY)

MacWeek (San Francisco, CA)

Markup Languages (Cambridge, MA)

Mathematical Modeling and Computational Experiment (Hoboken, NJ)

M.D. Computing (New York, NY)

Mental Retardation and Developmental Disabilities Research Reviews (Hoboken, NJ)

Mercator's World (Eugene, OR)

Minnesota River Valley Shopper (Faribault, MN)

Missions & Missionaries (Portland, OR)

Mixer (New York, NY)

Moffat Communications Ltd. (Winnipeg, MB)

The Mountain/Plains Business Journal (Omaha, NE)

NAMIC State Government Observer (Indianapolis, IN)

Natural Toxins (Hoboken, NJ)

The New Advocate (Norwood, MA)

The Nonprofit Counsel (Secaucus, NJ)

North Sea Monitor (Hoboken, NJ)

North-South (Somerset, NJ)

NT Update (Westminster, CO)

Nursingworld Journal (Weston, MA)

Oracle Update (Westminster, CO)

OSP Engineering & Construction (Nashua, NH)

Oswego/Montgomery Sun (Naperville, IL)

Ottawa Families (Vancouver, BC)

Periodico La Opinion Central (Humacao, PR)

Photographica (New York, NY)

PIMA's Papermaker Magazine (Glenview, IL)

Pioneer Clubs Perspective (Wheaton, IL)

Pipe Line & Gas Industry (Houston, TX)

Pipeline (Mountain Home, ID)

Plant Protection News (Gainesville, FL)

Pollution Prevention Review (Hoboken, NJ)

Primary Voices K-6 (Urbana, IL)

The Publick Enterprise (Annapolis, MD)

Quality in Manufacturing (Solon, OH)

Quebec Construction (Saint-Laurent, QC)

Quilting Today (Montrose, PA)

Real Estate Finance Today (Washington, DC)

Regina's Reviews (Fayetteville, GA)

Relief Report (Washington, DC)

The Report Newsmagazine—Alberta Edition (Edmonton, AB)

Research News (Ann Arbor, MI)

Review of Financial Markets (Hoboken, NJ)

Review of the National Literatures and World Report (Whitestone, NY)

Saint John Times Globe (St. John, NB)

Scranton Federation Reporter (Vestal, NY)

Security Advisor (San Diego, CA)

Self Reliance Journal (Orange, CA)

The Server Foodservice News (Pittsburgh, PA)

Shop Owner (Cleveland, OH)

Show Music (East Haddam, CT)

Small Town (Burton, WA)

Solar Industry Journal (Arlington, VA)

South County Chronicle (Leavenworth, KS)

Space Age Bachelor Magazine (Columbia, SC)

Speaker Builder (Peterborough, NH)

Sports Cards Magazine & Price Guide (Iola, WI)

Springer ExprESS (Orr, MN)

SPSM&H (Bakersfield, CA)

The Stratford Journal (Abbotsford, WI)

Surveys on Mathematics for Industry (New York, NY)

TECHNOCRACY DIGEST (Aldergrove, BC)

Technos Quarterly for Education and Technology (Bloomington, IN)

Telecommunications & Radio Engineering (Hoboken, NJ)

Telling It Like It Is (Rockville, MD)

Test & Measurement Europe (Newton, MA)

Time Digital (New York, NY)

Today's Collector (Iola, WI)

Tranputer Communications (Hoboken, NJ)

Tri-County Shopper (De Soto, MO)

Triangle City Facts (Raleigh, NC)

Trucking Canada (Toronto, ON)

Tucumcari Literary Review (Los Angeles, CA)

UN News (Huntsville, AL)

Urasian Soil Science (Hoboken, NJ)

Valuation (Herndon, VA)

Victoria Magazine (New York, NY)

Virginia Cavalcade (Richmond, VA)

Visualization of Engineering Research (Hoboken, NJ)

VSAM Update (Westminster, CO)

Washington County Observer (Prairie Grove, AR)

Waterford Eccentric (Livonia, MI)

Weekend Plus (Winchester, KY)

Weekender Cover Story (Lebanon, PA)

WFXW-AM (St. Charles, IL)

WHLO-AM (Independence, OH)

Williams-Sonoma TASTE (San Francisco, CA)

WKXC-FM (Atlanta, GA)

WorldViews (Cedar, MI)

WSTD-FM (Pigeon, MI)

International

Aeronautica Meridiana (Sinoville, SAF)

African Mining Monitor (Coventry, GBR)

Aftersales Management (Peterborough, GBR)

Asia-Pacific Purchasing & Materials Management (Vienna, AUT)

Asian Review of Business and Technology (London, GBR)

Asthetische Chirurgrie (Berlin, GER)

Australian Innovation Magazine (Canberra, AC, AUS)

Automotive Digest (Peterborough, GBR)

Barn och Familj (Skillingfors, SWE)

Braille Science Journal (Edinburgh, GBR)

Cabala (Caracas, VEN)

Codex (Ascot Vale, VI, AUS)

Cokemaking International (Dusseldorf, GER)

Contemporary Reviews in Obstetrics & Gynecology (Lancaster, GBR)

Corporate Citizen (London, GBR)

CRI/NCB Abstracts (Ballagarh, HY, IND)

Current Therapeutics (Frenchs Forest, NS, AUS)

Disaster Management (Gurgaon, HY, IND)

EA Magazine (London, GBR)

EMA Network (Chertsey, GBR)

Equal Voices (Glasgow, GBR)

Euro-Japanese Journal (London, GBR)

European Access (Cambridge, GBR)

European Purchasing & Materials Management (Vienna, AUT)

EXE (London, GBR)

eyepiece (Cambridge, GBR)

FDI World (Lowestoft, GBR)

Food & Drink Exporter (London, GBR)

Foreign Trade—Trends & Tidings (New Delhi, DH, IND)

Going Places (Warwick, GBR)

Homeopathy (London, GBR)

IBAF World Baseball Magazine (Lausanne, SWI)

ICSSR Research Abstracts Quarterly (New Delhi, DH, IND)

Indian Dissertation Abstracts (New Delhi, DH, IND)

Jamsides (Stockholm, SWE)

Journal of Banking and Financial Services (Melbourne, VI, AUS)

Journal of the Royal Statistical Society (London, GBR)

Kapital DATA (Oslo, NOR)

Lifeboat International (Poole, GBR)

Logistics Focus (Corby, GBR)

Modern Management (Lichfield, GBR)

NA'AMAT Magazine (Tel Aviv, ISR)

Navy News - Sea Cadet Edition (London, GBR)

New Builder (London, GBR)

News of Liturgy (Cambridge, GBR)

Newsidic (Eggenstein-Leopoldshafen, GER)

Noticias Agricocas (Caracas, VEN)

OE Report & Fibre News (High Peak, GBR)

Online Praxis (Dusseldorf, GER)

PC Magazine Norge (Oslo, NOR)

Physiotherapy Moves (St. Kilda, VI, AUS)

Prenatal & Neonatal Medicine (Lancaster, GBR)

The Regent (Newbliss, MO, IRL)

Restitution Law Review (London, GBR)

Review of Theological Literature (Poole, GBR)

Shipyards Orders Weekly Report (Redhill, GBR)

Smallwoods (Pontesbury, GBR)

Smart Users: SMUG Journal (Colchester, GBR)

Soundtrack (Mechelen, BEL)

STOA (Lueven, BEL)

Total Rugby League (Brighouse, GBR)

Waste & Environment Today (Abingdon, GBR)

BROADCAST AND CABLE NETWORKS

A selection of networks and programming providers in the U.S. and Canada. Entries are arranged alphabetically within Radio, Television, and Cable headings.

RADIO NETWORKS

37609 ABC Radio Networks
125 West End Ave.   Phone: (917)441-4368
New York, NY 10023-6298

Format comprises ABC Contemporary; ABC Direction; ABC Entertainment; ABC FM; ABC AM; ABC Information; ABC Rock; and Satellite Music. **Owner:** Capital Cities/ABC Inc. **Key Personnel:** Robert F. Callahan, Jr., President; Derek Berghuis, Programming and Affiliate Mktg. Sr. VP; Stuart Krane, VP/Group Dir.; Corinne L. Baldassano, Programming VP. **Additional Contact Info: Regional Office(s):** 2040 Avenue of the Stars, Century City, CA 90067, (310)557-7777.

37610 ABN Radio Network
1515 W. Lane Ave.   Phone: (614)486-9577
Columbus, OH 43221   Fax: (614)487-8205
                                 Free: (800)686-8299

Ohio agricultural radio format. **Key Personnel:** Ed Johnson, President; Bart Johnson, General Mgr., bjohnson@abnradio.com; David Conley, Dir. of Operations, dconley@abnradio.com. **URL:** http://www.abnradio.com.

37611 AgriAmerica Network
One Emmis Plaza   Phone: (317)637-3276
40 Monument Circle, Ste. 400   Fax: (317)684-2008
Indianapolis, IN 46204

Format comprises agricultural radio programming. **Key Personnel:** Gary Truitt, Dir. of Network Operations, phone (317)684-4168; John Emerson, Affiliate Relations, phone (361)684-4171; Jeanette Merritt, Farm Dir., phone (317)684-4173. **URL:** http://www.agriamerica.com.

37612 Agrinet Farm Radio Network
179 Lovers Ln., Ste. A   Phone: (252)491-2414
Elizabeth City, NC 27909

Format comprises news, weather, and short national and international events. **Key Personnel:** Bill Ray, Farm Dir.; Scott Fortenberry, Chief Engineer.

37613 American Ag Network
Box 1197   Phone: (605)224-9911
Pierre, SD 57501   Fax: (605)224-8984

37614 American Stock Exchange Radio AMEX
86 Trinity Pl.   Phone: (212)306-1637
New York, NY 10006

Business news/stock report format. **Key Personnel:** Yolanda Cain, Contact.

37615 American Urban Radio Networks
655 3rd Ave., 24th Fl.   Phone: (212)883-2100
New York, NY 10017   Fax: (212)297-2571
                                 Free: (800)455-4211

The only African-American owned network radio company in the United States. Comprises four programming networks and one promotion network, including SPM Urban Network. **Formed by the merger of:** National Black Networks Broadcasting Inc.; Sheridan Broadcasting Network. **Key Personnel:** Ronald R. Davenport, Co-Chairman, phone (412)456-4004, fax (412)456-4022, rdavenportsr@aol.com; Sydney L. Small, Co-Chairman, phone (212)714-1000, fax (212)714-1563, slurban@aol.com; E.J. "Jay" Williams, Jr., President, phone (212)883-2109, fax (212)557-5706, presaurn@aol.com.

37616 Associated Press, Broadcast Services
1825 K St. NW   Phone: (202)736-1100
Ste. 800   Fax: (202)736-1199
Washington, DC 20006   Free: (800)821-4747

Owner: Associated Press Broadcast Services. **Key Personnel:** Brad Kalbfeld, Deputy Dir./Mng. Editor. **URL:** http://apbroadcast.com.

37617 Associated Press Network
1825 K St. NW   Phone: (202)736-1100
Ste. 710   Fax: (202)736-1199
Washington, DC 20006   Free: (800)821-4747

Key Personnel: Louis D. Boccardi, President; Jim Williams, Vice President.

37618 Brownfield Network
505 Hobbs Rd.   Phone: (573)893-7200
Jefferson City, MO 65109-6829   Fax: (573)893-8094

Format comprises agricultural news, markets, and weather. **Owner:** Learfield Communications Inc. **Key Personnel:** Clyde G. Lear, President; Chuck Zimmerman, Farm Dir./Gen. Mgr., czimmerman@learfield.com. **URL:** http://www.brownfieldnetwork.com.

37619 California Agri-Radio Network
1700 S. 1st Ave.   Fax: (520)782-1474
Ste. 214   Free: (800)944-6077
Yuma, AZ 85364

Agricultural news format. **Owner:** Western Agri-Radio Networks. **Key Personnel:** George G. Gatley, Pres./Dir.

37620 Canadian Broadcasting Corporation CBC/ Societe Radio Canada SRC
250 Lanark Ave.   Phone: (613)724-1200
PO Box 3220
Sta. C
Ottawa, ON, Canada K1Y 1E4

News and information format. **Key Personnel:** Perrin Beatty, President; Guylaine Saucier, Chw.; Louise Tremblay, Sr. VP Resources; Michael McEwen, Sr. Advisor; Robert Hertzog, VP Internal Audit; Gerald Flaherty, VP Gen. Counsel/Corp. Sec.; George C.B. Smith, VP Human Resources; Robert O'Reilly, Acting Sr. Dir. Corp. Comm. and Public A. **Additional Contact Info: Regional Office(s):** Box 500, Sta. A, Toronto, ON, Canada M5W 1E6, (416)205-3311; Box 6000, Montreal, QC, Canada H3C 3A8, (514)597-5970.

37621 Capitol AgriBusiness
711 Hilsborough St.   Phone: (919)890-6046
Box 12800   Fax: (919)890-6024
Raleigh, NC 27605

Agricultural format. **Formerly:** Tobacco Radio Network. **Key Personnel:** Ardie Gergory, VP/GM; Barb Deniston, Sales Mgr.; Ken Tanner, Farm Ed.; Dan Wilkinson, Farm Dir.; Tracy Rich, Sales Rep.; Natalie Burgin, Sales Rep.

37622 Capitol Sports Network
711 Hilsborough   Phone: (919)890-6030
Raleigh, NC 27605   Fax: (919)890-6024

Key Personnel: Bev Holt, Operations Mgr.; Steve Richards, Racing Coord.; Melissa Lambeth, Carolina Panthers Affiliations.

37623 CBS Radio Networks
51 W. 52nd St.   Phone: (212)975-4321
New York, NY 10019   Fax: (212)975-1519

Owner: CBS Inc. **Key Personnel:** Nancy C. Widmann,

President. **Additional Contact Info: Regional Office(s):** 7800 Beverly Blvd., Los Angeles, CA 90036, (213)852-2345.

37624 Chancellor Broadcasting Network
Union Plaza Hotel   Phone: (702)798-1798
1 Main St.   Fax: (702)798-2922
Las Vegas, NV 89101

Talk radio format. **Key Personnel:** David Papandrea, CEO/Pres.; Art Bell, Affiliate Relations Mgr.

37625 CNN Radio Network
One CNN Center   Phone: (404)827-2750
Box 105366
Atlanta, GA 30348-5366
E-mail: cnnradio@cnn.com

Key Personnel: Robert Garcia, VP. **URL:** http://www.cnnradionet.com.

37626 Concert Music Network
100 Park Ave.   Phone: (212)309-9370
New York, NY 10017-5516   Fax: (212)309-9380
                                 Free: (800)722-3332

Classical music format. **Key Personnel:** Peter J. Cleary, President; Roy Lindall, Vice President, roy_lindall@intertep.com. **URL:** http://www.classicaliscool.com.

37627 Creative Radio Network
PO Box 7749   Phone: (818)991-3892
Thousand Oaks, CA 91359   Fax: (818)991-3894

Key Personnel: Darwin Lamm, President.

37628 CRN International Inc.
1 Circular Ave.   Phone: (203)288-2002
Hamden, CT 06514   Fax: (203)281-3291

News, sports, and weather format. **Key Personnel:** Barry Berman, President; S. Richard Kalt, Sr. VP; Gary E. Zenobia, Network Operations Dir.; Lucille Fortunado, Affiliate Relations Dir.

37629 Dow Jones Radio Network
200 Liberty St.   Phone: (212)416-2381
14th Fl.   Fax: (212)416-4195
New York, NY 10281

Key Personnel: Peggy Belden, Dir. Broadcast Services; Debra Adamski, Affiliate Relations Coordinator.

37630 Eastern Public Radio Network
301 N. Beauregard St.   Phone: (703)658-4851
No. 1417   Fax: (703)658-1742
Alexandria, VA 22312-2914

Public radio format. **Key Personnel:** Marion van den Bosch, Exec. Dir.

37631 ESPN Radio, Inc.
ESPN Plaza   Phone: (203)585-2000
935 Middle St.
Bristol, CT 06010

37632 Family Stations Inc.
290 Hegenberger Rd.   Phone: (510)568-6200
Oakland, CA 94621   Fax: (510)633-7983
E-mail: info@familyradio.com

Key Personnel: Harold E. Camping, Pres./Gen. Mgr. **URL:** http://www.familyradio.com.

37633 Financial News Network
2200 Fletcher Ave. Phone: (201)585-2622
Fort Lee, NJ 07024

37634 Flix
1633 Broadway Phone: (212)708-1600
37th Fl. Fax: (212)208-1212
New York, NY 10019

37635 Gear Broadcasting International, Inc. (GBI)
PO Box 28404 Phone: (401)331-6072
Providence, RI 02908-0404 Free: (800)468-8424

Cable news format. **Key Personnel:** Edward R. Robalisky, Chm./Pres.; Jack G. Thayer, Exec. VP; G.A. Rainone, Finance VP; Noel Howard, Engineering VP; James Raposa, Broadcast Development Services.

37636 Georgia Network
1819 Peachtree St. NE
Ste. 700
Atlanta, GA 30309-1849

37637 Georgia Public Radio
260 14th St., NW Phone: (404)685-2690
Atlanta, GA 30318 Fax: (404)685-2684
  Free: (800)654-3038
E-mail: gpr@gpb.org

Formerly: Peach State Public Radio Network. **Key Personnel:** Jim Lyle, Exec. Dir; Amy Fegebank, Director. **URL:** http://www.gpb.org.

37638 IDB Communications Group Inc.
10525 W. Washington Blvd. Phone: (213)870-9000
Culver City, CA 90232 Fax: (213)240-3901

Key Personnel: Jeffrey P. Sudkoff, Chmn. & CEO; Edward R. Cheramy, President; Peter F. Hartz, Sr. VP Marketing; Dave Anderson, VP Operations.

37639 Jones Satellite Networks
8250 S. Akron Fax: (303)799-0551
Ste. 205 Free: (800)784-8700
Englewood, CO 80112

Format comprises adult Hit Radio; Good Time Oldies; Soft Hits; Z Spanish; U.S. Country; CD Country; NAC; and Rock Alternative all 24 hour. **Key Personnel:** Eric Hauenstein, VP/Gen. Mgr.; Phil Barry, Programming and Operations VP.

37640 K-State Radio Network
McCain Auditorium, Rm. 20 Phone: (785)532-5851
Kansas State University Fax: (785)532-5709
Manhattan, KS 66506-4701
E-mail: kksu@oznet.ksu.edu

Format comprises news, agricultural information, education and talk. **Owner:** Kansas State University, at above address. **Formerly:** KKSU-AM (1902); KSAC-AM (1984). **Key Personnel:** Larry Jackson, Radio Coord., ljackson@oznet.ksu.edu; Richard Baker, News Dir., rbaker@oznet.ksu.edu. **URL:** http://www.oznet.ksu.edu/radio.

37641 Kansas Agriculture Network/Kansas Information Network
1210 SW Executive Dr. Phone: (785)272-3456
Topeka, KS 66615 Fax: (785)228-7282
E-mail: jweil@radionetworks.com

Format comprises adult Contemporary; Easy Listening; Goldies; Great American Country; Prime Demo. **Key Personnel:** Craig Colbach, General Mgr.; Kelly Lenz, Farm Dir., phone (785)272-2199; Craig Colboch, General Mgr., phone (785)272-2199; Ed O'Donnell, Operations Dir., phone (785)272-2199; Jason T. Weil, Sales Mgr., Ag., phone (785)272-2199; Kim Stolle, Sales Mgr. Information, phone (785)272-2199. **URL:** http://www.radionetworks.com.

37642 Linder Farm Network
1929 Cedar Ave. S Phone: (507)444-9224
Owatonna, MN 55060 Fax: (507)444-9080

Key Personnel: Lynn Ketelson, Farm Dir.; Terri Weldele, Farm Broadcaster.

37643 Lode Star
1102 N. Springbrook Phone: (503)223-6146
Newberg, OR 97132 Fax: (503)538-9382

Formerly: Northwest News Network. **Key Personnel:** Fred W. Hudson, President; Mike Beard, Managing Editor.

37644 Longhorn Radio Network
Univ. of Texas at Austin Phone: (512)471-1631
Communication Bldg. B Fax: (512)471-3700
Austin, TX 78712-1090
E-mail: john-hanson@mail.utexas.edu

Key Personnel: John L. Hanson, Jr., Exec. Producer, john-hanson@mail.utexas.edu. **URL:** http://www.kut.org.

37645 Louisiana Agri-News Network/Louisiana Network
263 3rd St. Phone: (225)383-8695
5th Fl. Fax: (225)383-5020
Baton Rouge, LA 70801

Key Personnel: Bill Rigell, President, bill_rigell@la-net.net; Michael Hudson, VP Sales and Mktg., michael@la-net.net; Rhett McMahon, VP Technology, rhett@la-net.net; Shellie Schmidt, Affiliate Mgr., shellie@la-net.net; Don Molino, Farm Dir., don@la-net.net; Carolyn Roche, Business Mgr., carolyn@la-net.net. **URL:** http://www.la-net.net.

37646 Mid-America Ag Network
1632 S. Maize Rd. Phone: (316)721-8484
Wichita, KS 67209 Fax: (316)721-8276

Key Personnel: Larry Steckline, Pres./Owner.

37647 Moody Broadcasting Network
820 N. LaSalle Blvd. Phone: (312)329-4000
Chicago, IL 60610 Fax: (312)329-4339
  Free: (800)621-7031

Key Personnel: Robert Neff, VP of Broadcasting, phone (312)329-4305. **URL:** http://www.moody.edu.

37648 MRN Motor Racing Network Radio
1801 International Speedway Phone: (904)947-6400
Blvd. Fax: (904)947-6716
Daytona Beach, FL 32114

Sports format including NASCAR stock car racing and related programming. **Key Personnel:** C. David Hyatt, Pres./General Mgr.; Cheryl Knight, Dir. of Affiliates; Steve Harrison, National Sales Mgr.; T.G. Ailstock, Operations Dir. **URL:** http://www.mrnradio.com.

37649 Mutual Broadcasting System, Inc.
8403 Colesville Rd., No. 15
Silver Spring, MD 20910-3474

Talk radio and news format. **Owner:** Westwood One Inc. **Key Personnel:** Jack B. Clements, President; George Barber, Station Relations VP; Margaret M. Solomon, Operations VP; Barton J. Tessler, News VP.

37650 National Public Radio NPR
635 Massachuetts Ave. NW Phone: (202)513-2000
Washington, DC 20001 Fax: (202)513-3329

National network of news and cultural programs for radio. **Key Personnel:** Kevin Klose, President. **URL:** http://www.npr.org.

37651 North Carolina News Network
Box 12900 Phone: (919)890-6030
Raleigh, NC 27605 Fax: (919)890-6024

News Network. **Key Personnel:** Ardie Gregory, General Mgr., phone (919)890-6101; Ellen Reinhardt, News Dir., phone (919)890-6115; Joe Formicola, Operations Dir., phone (919)890-6125; Rob Hankin, Network Mgr., phone (919)890-6128, rhankin@ncnn.com. **URL:** http://www.ncnn.com.

37652 Oklahoma Agrinet/Oklahoma News Network
Box 1000 Phone: (405)858-1400
Oklahoma City, OK 73101 Fax: (405)840-5808
  Free: (800)327-6638
E-mail: waynegriggs@clearchannel.com

State and agricultural news format. **Key Personnel:** Derrick Nance, General Mgr., fax (405)858-5313, derricknance@clearchannel.com; Ron Hays, Farm Dir., phone (405)858-1400, fax (405)858-5313, ronhays@clearchannel.com; Wayne Griggs, OPD, phone (405)858-1400, fax (405)858-5313, waynegriggs@clearchannel.com.

37653 Olympia Broadcasting Networks
7745 Carondelet Ave. Phone: (314)727-8900
St. Louis, MO 63105 Fax: (314)727-4115

Format comprises sports, comedy, and country music. **Key Personnel:** Stephen Bunyard, President; Jay Goldman, Vice President; Bill Latz, Vice President; John McElfresh, Vice President.

37654 Pacifica Network News
2390 Champlain St. NW Phone: (202)588-0988
1st Fl. Fax: (202)588-0986
Washington, DC 20009-2620

News format. **Owner:** Pacifica Foundation, (202)588-0999. **Key Personnel:** Patricia Guadalupe, News Dir.; Josephine Reed, Anchor Pacifica Network News, phone (212)209-2812, fax (212)968-0504; Amy Goodman, Anchor Democracy Now!. **URL:** http://www.pacifica.org.

37655 PIA Radio Sports
625 N. Michigan Ave., Ste. 500 Phone: (312)943-8888
Chicago, IL 60611-3193 Fax: (312)943-5464

Key Personnel: Brad Saul, CEO; Chuck Kellner, Vice President.

37656 PMP Network
24 Hollytree Rd. Phone: (781)341-8332
Stoughton, MA 02072 Fax: (781)344-7207
E-mail: pmpco@aol.com

Owner: Mark Snyder. **URL:** http://www.pmpnetwork.com.

37657 Public Radio International
100 N. 6th St. Phone: (612)338-5000
Suite 900A Fax: (612)330-9222
Minneapolis, MN 55403

Format comprises news/Information; Classical Music; Contemporary Music; and Comedy/Variety. **Formerly:** American Public Radio. **Key Personnel:** Stephen L. Salyer, Pres./CEO; Bruce Theriault, Sr. VP Network Operations; Melinda Ward, Sr. VP Programming; Timothy Engel, VP Finance & Administration; Doug Eichten, VP Development; Janet de Acevedo, Dir. National Promotion & Media Relation. **URL:** http://www.pri.org.

37658 Radio Iowa
2700 Grand Ave. Phone: (515)282-1984
Ste. 103 Fax: (515)282-1879
Des Moines, IA 50312
E-mail: radioiowa@learfield.com

News state radio format. **Owner:** Learfield Communications. **Key Personnel:** Clyde G. Lear, Owner; Steve Mays, General Mgr.; Charles Peters, Chief Engineer; O. Kay Henderson, News Dir. **URL:** http://www.radioiowa.com.

37659 Radio Pennsylvania Inc.
1982 Locust Ln. Phone: (717)232-8400
PO Box 2954 Fax: (717)232-7612
Harrisburg, PA 17105

Key Personnel: Douglas F. Easter, General Mgr.; Craig Rhodes, News Dir.; Mark O'Neill, Sports Dir.

37660 Radiomutuel Inc.
1717 boul. Rene-Levesque est Phone: (514)529-3210
Montreal, QC, Canada H2L 4E8 Fax: (514)529-3219

Key Personnel: Normand Beauchamp, CEO.

37661 Ray Sports Radio Network
PO Box 3810 Phone: (252)480-1576
Kill Devil Hills, NC 27948-3810 Fax: (252)480-4655

Key Personnel: Bill Ray, President; Gem Megers, Sports Dir. **Additional Contact Info: Regional Office(s):** 1500 S. Croatan Hwy., Ste. 104, Kill Devil Hills, NC 27948.

37662 SBS Network Inc.
26 W. 56th St. Phone: (212)541-6700
New York, NY 10019 Fax: (212)541-8535

Key Personnel: Carey Davis, VP/GM; Mickie Reyes, Sales Mgr.; David Wilkes, Local Sales Mgr.

37663 South Carolina News Network
3710 Landmark Dr., Ste. 100 Phone: (803)790-4300
Columbia, SC 29204-4034 Fax: (803)790-4309

Sports and news format. **Key Personnel:** John Winfield, Operations Mgr., phone (601)957-1700, fax (601)956-5228, jwinfield@telesouth.com; Phil Kornblut, Sports Dir., phone (803)790-4305, pkornblut@scnewsnet.com; Claudia Mauldin, Traffic Mgr., cmauldin@scnewsnet.com; William Christopher, News Dir., wchristopher@scnewsnet.com; Tom Jackson, General Mgr., tjackson@scnewsnet.com.

37664 Southern Farm Network
3012 Highwoods Blvd Phone: (919)876-0674
Raleigh, NC 27604 Fax: (919)790-8369
E-mail: bprice@southernfarmnetwork.com

Agricultural format. **Key Personnel:** Barbara Price. **URL:** http://www.southernfarmnetwork.com.

37665　Southwest Agri-Radio Network
1700 S. 1st Ave.　　　　　　　　Phone: (800)944-6077
Ste. 214　　　　　　　　　　　　Fax: (520)782-1474
Yuma, AZ 85364

Agricultural news format. **Owner:** Western Agri-Radio Networks. **Key Personnel:** George G. Gatley, Pres./Dir.

37666　Standard Broadcast News
2 St. Claire Ave. W　　　　　　　Phone: (416)323-6824
Toronto, ON, Canada M4V 1L6　　Fax: (416)323-6825

News wire format.

37667　Superadio Network
56 Central St.　　　　　　　　　Phone: (508)608-2000
Southborough, MA 01745

Open House Party Network; and Prime FM formats. **Key Personnel:** John Garabedian, President; Rich O'Brien, VP Sales; Mike Ortolano, Dir. Programming.

37668　Telemedia Radio Inc.
1411 rue Peel　　　　　　　　　Phone: (514)845-6291
Montreal, QC, Canada H3A 3L5　Fax: (514)845-6939

Format comprises talk, news, and information. **Former name:** Telemedia Communications Inc. (July 28, 1900).

37669　Tennessee Agri-Net/Tennessee Radio Network
55 Music Sq. W.　　　　　　　　Phone: (615)664-2400
Nashville, TN 37203　　　　　　Fax: (615)687-9797
E-mail: billstorey@clearchannel.com

Format comprises news, farm, sports, traffic, business, and country music. **Key Personnel:** Steve Sullivan, News Dir., stevesullivan@clearchannel.com; Gary Jackson, Farm Dir., phone (419)223-2060, garyjackson@clearchannel; Janet Patterson, General Sales Mgr., janetpatterson@clearchannel.com; Doug Combs, Affiliate Relations, dougcombs@clearchannel.com.

37670　Tribune Radio Networks
435 N. Michigan Ave.　　　　　　Phone: (312)222-3342
Chicago, IL 60611　　　　　　　Fax: (312)222-5165

Sports and agriculture formats. **Key Personnel:** Kenton Morris, General Mgr.; Allison Clark, Business Admin. Mgr.

37671　UPI Radio Network
1510 H St. NW, Ste. B2　　　　　Phone: (202)898-8111
Washington, DC 20005　　　　　Fax: (202)898-8147

Format comprises sports, newscasts, and entertainment. **Key Personnel:** Howard Dicus, General Mgr.; Ron Colbert, News Dir.; Warren Corbett, Business Mgr.; Diane Burr, Resources and Planning Mgr. **Additional Contact Info: Regional Office(s):** 6701 Center Dr. W., Los Angeles, CA 90045, (310)670-1100; 1819 Peachtree Rd. NE, Atlanta, GA 30309, (404)355-3700; 203 N. Wabash, Chicago, IL 60601, (312)781-1600; 5 Penn Plaza, 461 8th Ave., New York, NY 10001-1803, (212)560-1100.

37672　USA Radio Network
2290 Springlake Rd.　　　　　　Phone: (972)484-3900
Ste. 107　　　　　　　　　　　　Fax: (972)243-3489
Dallas, TX 75234　　　　　　　　Free: (800)829-8111

Format comprises news, sports, updates and long-form programming. **Key Personnel:** Marlin Maddoux, Pres./CEO, phone (972)692-1317; Tom Tradup, VP/GM, phone (972)692-1338, tradup@usaradio.com; Mark Maddoux, CFO/VP, phone (972)692-1357, mark@usaradio.com; Bob Morrison, News Dir., phone (972)692-1375, bobm@usaradio.com; Bob Faulkner, Affiliate Relations Dir., phone (972)692-1344, bobf@usaradio.com; Chuck Roberts, Operations, phone (972)692-1366, croberts@usaradio.com; Jeff Dorf, Sales Mgr., phone (972)692-1356, jdor@usaradio.com; Susan Henderson, Traffic Dir., phone (972)692-1353, susan@usaradio.com. **URL:** http://www.usaradio.com.

37673　VSA Radio Network
PO Box 1000
Oklahoma City, OK 73101-1000

Texas agriculture format. **Key Personnel:** Joe Jeldy, Sales & Mktg., phone (405)858-1400, fax (405)858-5313, joejeldy@clearchannel.com; Larry Rhat, Operations Dir., phone (405)858-1458; Wayne Griggs, Affiliations Dir., phone (405)858-1400, fax (405)858-5313, waynegriggs@clearchannel.com; Roddy Peeples, Sr. Farm Broadcaster.

37674　Wall Street Journal Radio Network
200 Liberty St.　　　　　　　　Phone: (212)416-2380
14th Fl.　　　　　　　　　　　　Fax: (212)416-4195
New York, NY 10281

Key Personnel: Robert Rush, Director.

37675　Wataway Radio Network
PO Box 1180　　　　　　　　　　Phone: (807)737-2760
Sioux Lookout, ON, Canada P8T　Fax: (807)737-3224
1B7

News and information format.

37676　West Virginia Metronews Radio Network
1251 Earl Core Rd.　　　　　　　Phone: (304)296-0029
Morgantown, WV 26505

Key Personnel: Dale Miller, President; Harvey Kercheval, News VP; Tony Caridi, Sports VP; Joe Parsons, Sales VP; Noel Richardson, Chief Engineer. **URL:** http://www.wvmetronews.com.

37677　Western Agri-Radio Networks, Inc. DBA: California Agri-Radio Network; Southwest Agri-Radio Network.
1700 S. 1st Ave., Ste. 214　　　Phone: (928)782-1440
Yuma, AZ 85364　　　　　　　　Fax: (928)782-1474
　　　　　　　　　　　　　　　　Free: (800)944-6077

Agricultural news format. **Owner:** George G. Gatley, at above address. **Key Personnel:** George G. Gatley, Pres./Dir., ggatley@sprynet.com; George G. Gatley. **URL:** http://www.westernagri-radio.net.

37678　Westwood One Radio Network
9540 Washington Blvd.　　　　　Phone: (310)840-4000
Culver City, CA 90232　　　　　Fax: (310)840-4052

Owner: Westwood One Inc. **Key Personnel:** Thomas A. Ferro, Exec. VP/Gen. Mgr., phone (310)840-4203, fax (310)840-4061. **Additional Contact Info: Regional Office(s):** 111 E. Wacker Dr., Ste. 1321, Chicago, IL 60601, (312)938-0222; 3250 W. Big Beaver Rd., Troy, MI 48084, (248)649-6300; 1700 Broadway, New York, NY 10019, (212)237-2500.

37679　Winners News Network
6699 N. Federal Hwy.　　　　　Phone: (561)988-5470
Boca Raton, FL 33487

Talk and business format.

37680　Zondervan Radio Network
5300 Patterson Ave. SE　　　　Phone: (616)698-6900
Grand Rapids, MI 49530　　　　Fax: (616)698-3223
　　　　　　　　　　　　　　　　Free: (800)9BO-OKIT

Talk format.

TELEVISION NETWORKS

37681　ABC
77 W. 66th St.　　　　　　　　　Phone: (212)456-7777
New York, NY 10023-6298

Format comprises news, entertainment, sports, and information. **Owner:** Capital Cities/ABC Inc. **Key Personnel:** Thomas S. Murphy, Chm./CEO. **Additional Contact Info: Regional Office(s):** 2040 Avenue of the Stars, Century City, CA 90067, (310)557-7777.

37682　ABN TV
1515 W. Lane Ave.　　　　　　Phone: (614)486-9577
Columbus, OH 43221　　　　　Fax: (614)487-8205
　　　　　　　　　　　　　　　Free: (800)686-8299

Agricultural format. **Key Personnel:** Ed Johnson, Pres./Host; Bart Johnson, General Mgr., bjohnson@abnradio.com; David Conley, Dir. of Operations, dconley@abnradio.com. **URL:** http://www.agricountry.com.

37683　American Telecommunications Group Assn.
1400 E. Touhy Ave.　　　　　　Phone: (847)390-8700
Des Plaines, IL 60018　　　　　Fax: (847)390-9435
E-mail: gerie@atgonline.org

Format comprises children's education and public broadcasting. Administrative agency for the American Center for Children and Media (ACCM), Center for Education Initiatives (CEI), Central Education Network (CEN), Continental Program Marketing (CPM), Hartford Gunn Institute, and Higher Education Telecommunications Consortium (HETC). **Key Personnel:** James A. Fellows, President, jfellows@atgonline.org; Joan C. Lence, Programming VP, jlence@atgonline.com; Helen Marie McNeilly, Finance and Admin. VP, helenmarie@atgonline.org; David Kleeman, Exec. Dir., ACCM, phone (847)390-6499, dkleeman@atgonline.org.

37684　AP-TMS Information Service AP Business Plus
1825 K St. NW　　　　　　　　Phone: (202)736-1100
Ste. 710
Washington, DC 20006

37685　ATV (Atlantic Television System)
2885 Robie St.　　　　　　　　Phone: (902)453-4000
Halifax, NS, Canada B3K 5Z4　Fax: (902)454-3270

Owner: Bell Globe Media (CTV). **URL:** http://www.atv.ca.

37686　BCTV (British Columbia Television)
7850 Enterprise St.　　　　　　Fax: (604)421-9420
Burnaby, BC, Canada V5A 1V7

News format. **Owner:** Global Communications Limited/Global Television Network Inc., at above address, Canada.

37687　California-Oregon Broadcasting Inc.
PO Box 1489　　　　　　　　　Phone: (541)779-5555
Medford, OR 97501　　　　　　Fax: (541)779-1151
E-mail: kobi@kobi5.com

Key Personnel: Patricia C. Smullin, President; Dee Domke, Vice President. **URL:** http://www.localnewscomesfirst.com.

37688　Canadian Broadcasting Corporation (CBC)/ Societe Radio Canada (SRC)
250 Lanark Ave.　　　　　　　Phone: (613)724-1200
PO Box 3220, Sta. C
Ottawa, ON, Canada K1Y 1E4

News and information format. **Key Personnel:** Perrin Beatty, Pres./CEO; Guylaine Saucier, Chw.; Louise Tremblay, Sr. VP Resources; Michael McEwen, Sr. Advisor; Robert Hertzog, VP Internal Audit; Gerald Flaherty, VP Gen. Counsel/Corp. Sec.; George C.B. Smith, VP Human Resources; Robert O'Reilly, Acting Sr. Dir., Corp. Comm./Public Aff. **Additional Contact Info:** Regional Office(s): Box 500, Sta. A, Toronto, ON, Canada M5W 1E6, (416)205-3311; Box 6000, Montreal, QC, Canada H3C 3A8, (514)597-5970.

37689　CBS
51 W. 52nd St.　　　　　　　　Phone: (212)554-0080
New York, NY 10019

Format comprises news, information, and entertainment. **Owner:** CBS Inc. **Key Personnel:** Laurence A. Tisch, Chm./Pres./CEO; Jay L. Kriegel, Sr. VP. **Additional Contact Info:** Regional Office(s): 7800 Beverly Blvd., Los Angeles, CA 90036, (213)852-2345.

37690　Central Independent Television USA, Inc.
610 5th Ave.　　　　　　　　　Phone: (212)582-6688
Ste. 401
New York, NY 10020

Key Personnel: Kevin Morrison, President.

37691　Corporation for Public Broadcasting
901 E St. NW　　　　　　　　Phone: (202)879-9600
Washington, DC 20004-2037　Fax: (202)783-1019

Format comprises public broadcasting and cultural and educational programming. **Key Personnel:** Martha Buchanan, Vice Chm.; Sheila Tate, Chm.

37692　Dakota Giant Network
4th & Broadway　　　　　　　Phone: (701)255-5757
Box 1738-58502　　　　　　　Fax: (701)255-8220
Bismarck, ND 58501

Key Personnel: Judith Ekberg Johnson, Pres./CEO; Tom Barr, General Mgr.; Penny Borg, Natl. Regional Sales Mgr.

37693　4X Network
3425 S. Broadway　　　　　　Phone: (701)852-2104
Box 1686　　　　　　　　　　Fax: (701)838-9360
Minot, ND 58702

Local news (CBS affiliate) format. **Key Personnel:** David Reiten, Pres./Gen. Mgr.

37694　Fox Broadcasting Company
10201 W. Pico Blvd.　　　　　Phone: (310)369-1000
Los Angeles, CA 90035

Entertainment format. **Owner:** Fox Inc. **Key Personnel:** Rupert Murdoch, Chm./CEO, Fox Inc.; Jamie Kellner, Pres./COO. **Additional Contact Info:** Regional Office(s): 205 N. Michigan Ave., Ste. 48, Chicago, IL 60601, (312)946-0018; 1211 Avenue of the Americas, 3rd Fl., New York, NY 10036, (212)556-2400.

37695　Global Television Network
81 Barber Green Rd.　　　　　Phone: (416)446-5311
Don Mills, ON, Canada M3C　Fax: (416)446-5543
2A2

Entertainment format. **Key Personnel:** Jim Seward, Pres./COO; Kevin Shea, Pres./COO; Doug Hoover, Natl. VP Programming and Promotion; John Burgis, VP Finance and Admin.; Ken Johnson, VP Sales and Mktg.

37696 IDB Communications Group Inc.
10525 W. Washington Blvd.   Phone: (213)870-9000
Culver City, CA 90232

Full-service satellite transmission provider. **Absorbed**: Hughes Television Network. **Key Personnel:** Jeffrey Sudikoff, Chm./CEO; Edward Cheramy, President; John Tagliaferro, Pres., IDB Broadcast Group.

37697 Inuit Broadcasting Corporation
301-331 Cooper St.   Phone: (613)235-1892
Ottawa, ON, Canada K2P 0G5   Fax: (613)230-8824

Format comprises educational, cultural, and local current events programs.

37698 Iowa Public Television
PO Box 6450   Phone: (515)242-3100
Johnston, IA 50131-6450

Format comprises educational and cultural programming. **Key Personnel:** C. David Bolender, Exec. Dir.; Daniel Miller, Program Dir.; Sid Sprecher, News and Public Affairs Dir.; Doug Brooker, Sports Dir.; Paula Adams Johnson, Dir. Educ. Telecommunications; Don Saveraid, Dir. Engineering.

37699 KBS Inc.
Box 12   Phone: (316)838-1212
Wichita, KS 67201   Fax: (316)832-1043

Key Personnel: Ron Collins, Pres./Gen. Mgr.; Gale Clevenger, News Dir.

37700 KELO-LAND TV
KELO Bldg.   Phone: (605)336-1100
501 S. Phillips Ave.   Fax: (605)334-3447
Sioux Falls, SD 57104

Commercial television station, CBS affiliate. **Key Personnel:** Mark Antonitts, General Mgr.; Mark Millage, News Dir.; Karen Floyd, Program Dir.; Jay Huizenga, Sales Mgr.; Devin Duncan, Promotion Dir.

37701 KSN Television Group
833 N. Main St.   Phone: (316)265-3333
Wichita, KS 67201   Fax: (316)292-1195

Key Personnel: Allan Buch, Gen. Mgr. KSNW, KSNC, KSNG, KSNK; Gary McNair, Gen. Mgr. KSNT.

37702 Minnesota Independent Network Inc.
1640 Como Ave.   Phone: (612)646-2300
St. Paul, MN 55101

Format comprises commercial and family programming. **Key Personnel:** Donald W. O'Conner, Pres./Gen. Mgr.; Mike Gillhan, General Sales Mgr.; Brenda Wilson, Program Dir.

37703 Minnesota Public Television Association
172 E. 4th St.   Phone: (651)222-1717
St. Paul, MN 55101

Format comprises public, educational, and cultural programming. **Key Personnel:** Dennis Falk, President; Jim Carufel, Treasurer; Barry Baker, Sec.

37704 National Educational Telecommunications Association
Box 50008   Phone: (803)799-5517
Columbia, SC 29250   Fax: (803)771-4831

Public broadcasting association and program distributor. **Formerly:** Southern Educational Communications Association. **Key Personnel:** Skip Hinton, President; Chuck McConnell, Contact. **URL:** http://www.netaonline.org.

37705 NBC (National Broadcasting Company)
30 Rockefeller Plz.   Phone: (212)664-4444
New York, NY 10112

Information and entertainment formats. **Owner:** General Electric. **Key Personnel:** Robert Wright, Pres./CEO. **Additional Contact Info: Regional Office(s):** 3000 Alameda Ave., Burbank, CA 91523, (818)840-4444; 1331 Pennsylvania Ave. NW, Ste. 930N, Washington, DC 20004, (202)885-4000.

37706 NTV Network/KHGI-TV
Box 220   Phone: (308)743-2494
Kearney, NE 68848   Fax: (308)743-2644
E-mail: news@ntv.kearney.net

Entertainment and information formats. **Key Personnel:** Steve Morris, General Mgr.; Mark Baumert, News Dir.; Jerry Fueherer, Chief Engineer.

37707 NTV (Newfoundland Television)
PO Box 2020   Phone: (709)722-5015
St. Johns, NL, Canada A1C 5S2   Fax: (709)726-5107

Format comprisese ducational, cultural, and children's programming.

37708 Odyssey
1177 Avenue of the Americas,   Phone: (212)780-1515
  15th Fl.   Fax: (212)694-5968
New York, NY 10036-2714

Religious programming format. **Owner:** National Interfaith Cable Coalition/Liberty Media Corporation. **Formerly:** Vision Interfaith Satellite Network (VISN). **Key Personnel:** Garry E. Hill, P; David Macaione, VP Business Affairs; William Bote, CFO; Jeffrey Weber, Pres. Odyssey Productions, Ltd.

37709 Ohio Educational Telecommunications Network Commission
2470 N. Star Rd.   Phone: (614)644-1714
Columbus, OH 43221   Fax: (614)644-3112

Format comprises public, educational, cultural, and children's programming. **Formerly:** Ohio Educational Broadcasting Network Commission. **Key Personnel:** Dave L. Fomshell, Exec. Dir.; Blanford W. Fuller, Asst. Dir.

37710 PBS (Public Broadcasting Service)
1320 Braddock Pl.   Phone: (703)739-5000
Alexandria, VA 22314-1698   Fax: (703)739-0775
E-mail: viewer@pbs.org

A private, nonprofit organization owned and operated by 347 public television stations nationwide. Format comprises educational and cultural programming. **Key Personnel:** Pat Mitchell, Pres./CEO. **URL:** http://www.pbs.org. **Additional Contact Info: Regional Office(s):** 1790 Broadway, New York, NY 10019-1412, (212)708-3000.

37711 Pennsylvania Public Television Network
24 Northeast Dr.   Phone: (717)533-6010
Box 397   Fax: (717)533-4236
Hershey, PA 17033

Public television format. **Key Personnel:** H. Sheldon Parker, Jr., General Mgr.

37712 The Shopping Channel
59 Ambassador Dr.   Phone: (416)785-3500
Mississauga, ON, Canada L5T   Fax: (416)785-1300
2B9

37713 SJL Broadcast Management Corp.
3203 3rd Ave. N., Ste. 300   Phone: (406)256-0705
Billings, MT 59101   Fax: (406)252-9144

Key Personnel: George D. Lilly, President; Dave McCurdy, VP/Treas.; Pamela D. Heilman, Sec. **Additional Contact Info: Regional Office(s):** 633 Picacho Ln., Montecito, CA 93108, (805)969-9278, fax: (805)969-2399.

37714 Telemundo Group, Inc.
1775 Broadway, 3rd Fl.   Phone: (212)977-1535
New York, NY 10019-1740   Fax: (212)459-9498

Spanish language format. **Key Personnel:** Saul P. Steinberg, Chm.; Joaquin F. Blaya, Pres./CEO.

37715 TQS Television Network
612 Saint-Jacques, Bureau 100   Phone: (514)390-6035
Montreal, QC, Canada H3C 5R1   Fax: (514)390-6066

Format comprises sports, movies, entertainment, and news. **Formerly:** Television Quatre Saisons. **Key Personnel:** Rene Guimond, President; Jean Durocher, VP, Sales & Marketing; Luc Doyon, VP, Operations & Programming; Hugues Beaudoin, Sales VP; Ghyslain St. Pierre, Engineering VP; Francois Laurin, Admin. VP.

37716 TV Ontario
PO Box 200, Sta. Q   Phone: (416)484-2600
Toronto, ON, Canada M4T 2T1   Fax: (416)484-4234

Educational and entertainment formats. **Key Personnel:** Peter Herrndorf, CEO; Peter Bowers, General Mgr.

37717 TVA
1600 boul. de Maisonneuve est   Phone: (514)526-0476
Montreal, QC, Canada H2L 4P2   Fax: (514)526-8399

Key Personnel: Denis Lacroix, Pres./Gen. Mgr.

37718 United Paramount Network
11800 Wilshire Blvd.   Phone: (310)575-7000
Los Angeles, CA 90025

Entertainment format. **Key Personnel:** Lucie Salhany, Pres./

CEO; Michael Sullivan, Pres. of Entertainment; Len Grossi, Sr. Exec. VP.

37719 Univision
605 3rd Ave., 12th Fl.   Phone: (212)455-5200
New York, NY 10158-0182   Fax: (212)867-6710

Spanish language format. **Key Personnel:** Luis Nogales, President; John Pero, VP/Natl. Sales Mgr. **Additional Contact Info: Regional Office(s):** 2030 Main St., Ste. 235, Irvine, CA 92614-7231, (714)474-8585, fax: (714)474-8385; 6701 Center Dr. W., 2nd Fl., Los Angeles, CA 90045, (310)338-0700, fax: (310)348-3459; 2200 Palou, San Francisco, CA 94124, (415)824-4384, fax: (415)824-1906; 9405 NW 41st St., Miami, FL 33178, (305)471-3900, fax: (305)471-4027; 401 E. Illinois St., Ste. 325, Chicago, IL 60611-4305, (312)321-8200, fax: (312)321-8223; 30700 Telegraph Rd., Ste. 3640, Bingham Farms, MI 48025, (248)540-5705, fax: (248)540-2419; 600 E. Colinas Blvd., Ste. 348, Irving, TX 75039, (214)869-0202, fax: (214)869-2635.

37720 Wall Street Journal Television Network
200 Liberty St.   Phone: (212)416-2380
New York, NY 10281

Format comprises personnel, business, and finance programming. **Key Personnel:** Robert Rush, General Mgr.; Chris Graves, News Dir.; Susan Strekel, Station Relations Mgr.; Consuelo Mack, Business Commentator/News Ed./Reporter, phone (r).

37721 Warner Brothers Studios
4000 Warner Blvd.   Phone: (818)954-6000
Burbank, CA 91522

Entertainment format. **Key Personnel:** Robert A. Daly, Co-Chairman and co-CEO; Terry Semel, Co-Chairman and co-CEO; Barry M. Meyer, COO.

37722 Wisconsin Public Television Network
3319 W. Beltline Hwy.   Phone: (608)264-9600
Madison, WI 53713-4296   Fax: (608)264-9622

Public television format. **Key Personnel:** Thomas L. Fletemeyer, Exec. Dir.

CABLE NETWORKS

37723 A&E (Arts and Entertainment Network)
235 E. 45th St.   Phone: (212)986-8046
New York, NY 10017   Fax: (212)949-7147

Format comprises comedy, drama, documentary, and performing arts. **Owner:** Hearst, Capital Cities/ABC, and NBC. **Key Personnel:** Nickolas Davatzes, Pres./CEO; Seymour Lesser, Exec. VP/CFO; Whitney Goit II, Sales/Marketing Exec. VP. **Additional Contact Info: Regional Office(s):** 1800 Century Park E., Ste. 450, Los Angeles, CA 90067, (310)933-9600; 111 E. Wacker Dr., Ste. 2206, Chicago, IL 60601, (312)819-1486.

37724 ACTS Satellite Network (American Christian Television Service)
6350 West Fwy.   Phone: (817)737-3241
Fort Worth, TX 76150   Fax: (817)737-8209

Inspirational programming. **Key Personnel:** Jack Johnson, President; Michael Wright, Affiliate Relations VP.

37725 American Movie Classics
1111 Stewart Ave.   Phone: (516)364-1160
Bethpage, NY 11714   Fax: (516)364-8929

Format includes movies; original programs on American film history and movie stars. **Owner:** Rainbow Program Enterprises. **Key Personnel:** Joshua Sapan, President; Kate McEnroe, VP/Gen. Mgr. **Additional Contact Info: Regional Office(s):** 2450 Santa Monica Blvd., Ste. 500, Los Angeles, CA 90025, (213)453-4493; 1040 Crown Point Pkwy., Ste. 1040, Atlanta, GA 30338, (404)395-9000; 1111 E. Touhy Ave., Ste. 280, Des Plaines, IL 60018, (708)296-0272.

37726 ANC/All News Channel
3415 University Ave.   Phone: (612)642-4645
Minneapolis, MN 55414-3327   Fax: (612)642-4680
E-mail: comments@allnews.com

Format comprises news programming. **Owner:** Conus Communications, at above address. **Key Personnel:** Terry O'Reilly, President, toreilly@conus.com; Michael McIntee, Sr. Mgr. of Programming & Syndication, mmcintee@allnews.com; Sara Harrell, VP of Marketing & Development, sharrell@conus.com; Robert Thomas, Sr. Managing Producer, sthomas@allnews.com; Cathy Colbeck, Chief Editor, ccolbeck@allnews.com; Glen Hinz, Production Dir., ghinz@allnews.com. **URL:** http://www.allnews.com.

37727 BET Action Pay Per View Network
1900 W Pl. NE Phone: (202)269-9436
Washington, DC 20018

Key Personnel: Curtis Symonds, Pres./COO.

37728 BET (Black Entertainment Television)
1900 W Pl. NE Phone: (202)269-9436
Washington, DC 20018 Fax: (202)608-2597

Format comprises music videos, sports, news, public affairs, and family entertainment. **Key Personnel:** Robert Johnson, CEO/Chm.; Debra Lee, Pres./COO; Curtis Symonds, Exec. VP/Affiliate Sales and Mktg. **Additional Contact Info: Regional Office(s):** 2425 Olympic Blvd., No. 4050 W., Santa Monica, CA 90404, (310)453-4500, fax: (310)998-9173; 380 Madison Ave., 20th Fl., New York, NY 10017, (212)697-5500, fax: (212)697-2050.

37729 BIZ NET/American Business Network
1615 H St. NW Phone: (202)463-5921
Washington, DC 20062 Fax: (202)463-3186

Format comprises business and finance programming. **Key Personnel:** Densil Allen, General Mgr.; Barton Eckert, Operations Mgr.

37730 Bravo
1111 Stewart Ave. Phone: (516)803-1500
Bethpage, NY 11714 Fax: (516)803-5108
E-mail: programming@bravotv.com

Format comprises American independent and international films, performing arts, music and comedy series. **Owner:** Rainbow Program Enterprises. **Key Personnel:** Joshua Sapan, President; Kathy Dore, VP/Gen. Mgr.; Jonathan Sehring, Programming VP. **URL:** http://www.bravotv.com. **Additional Contact Info: Regional Office(s):** Farmington, CT.

37731 C-SPAN/C-SPAN II (Cable Satellite Public Affairs Network)
400 N. Capital St. NW, Ste. 650 Phone: (202)737-3220
Ste. 650 Fax: (202)737-3323
Washington, DC 20001

Programming features coverage of U.S. Congress and public affairs events (C-SPAN, House of Representatives; C-SPAN II, Senate). **Key Personnel:** Brian Lamb, Pres./COO; Susan Swain, Sr. VP; Rob Kennedy, Sr. VP; Terry Murphy, Programming Dir.

37732 Cable Satellite Entertainment Network
6233 Variel Ave. Phone: (818)704-5154
Woodland Hills, CA 91367 Fax: (818)704-3934

Key Personnel: Joseph D. Preston, Chm./CEO.

37733 The California Channel
1121 L St., Ste. 110 Phone: (916)444-9792
Sacramento, CA 95814 Fax: (916)444-9812
E-mail: calchannel@aol.com

Format features coverage of California State government/legislative sessions and hearings. **Key Personnel:** John Hancock, President; James Gualtieri, Broadcast Operations Mgr. **URL:** http://www.calchannel.com.

37734 CBN/Christian Broadcasting Network
700 CBN Center Phone: (804)424-7777
Virginia Beach, VA 23463 Fax: (804)523-7959

Christian format. **Key Personnel:** Pat Robertson, General Mgr.

37735 ChicagoLand TV (CLTV)
2000 York Rd., Ste. 114 Phone: (630)368-4000
Oak Brook, IL 60523 Fax: (630)571-0489

Format comprises local and regional news, information, and entertainment. **Key Personnel:** Denise Palmer, Pres./CEO, phone (630)368-4085.

37736 Cinemax
1100 Avenue of the Americas Phone: (212)512-1000
New York, NY 10036

Format features movies, music, and comedy. **Owner:** Home Box Office. **Key Personnel:** Michael Fuchs, Chairman/CEO; Jeff Bewkes, Pres./COO; Peter Frame, Exec. VP, Affiliate Operations. **Additional Contact Info: Regional Office(s):** 2049 Century Park E., Ste. 4100, Los Angeles, CA 90067, (310)201-9200; 2 Embarcadero Center, Ste. 840, San Francisco, CA 94111, (415)765-7700; The Quadrant, 5445 DTC Pkwy., Ste. 700, Englewood, CO 80111, (303)220-2900; Lenox Bldg., 3399 Peachtree Rd. NE, Ste. 1600, Atlanta, GA 30326, (404)239-6600; 6250 River Rd., Ste. 10-300, Rosemont, IL 60018, (708)318-5100; 9401 Indian Creek Pkwy., Ste. 850, Overland Park, KS 66210, (913)451-1511; 401 City Ave., Ste. 620, Bala Cynwyd, PA 19004, (215)668-6500; 12750 Merit Dr., Ste. 1105, Dallas, TX 75251, (214)450-1000.

37737 CNBC (Consumer News & Business Channel)
2200 Fletcher Ave. Phone: (201)585-2622
Fort Lee, NJ 07024 Fax: (201)585-6393

Business, financial, and consumer news formats. **Owner:** NBC. **Key Personnel:** Albert F. Barber, President; Caroline Vanderlip, Mktg. and Affiliate Relations VP.

37738 CNN (Cable News Network)/Headline News
1 CNN Center Phone: (404)827-1503
Atlanta, GA 30348-5366

News and information format. **Owner:** Turner Broadcasting System. **Key Personnel:** Tom Johnson, President; Jon Petrovich, Exec. VP. **Additional Contact Info: Regional Office(s):** Los Angeles, CA; San Francisco, CA; Atlanta, GA; Chicago, IL; Detroit, MI; New York, NY.

37739 Comedy Central
1775 Broadway Phone: (212)767-8600
New York, NY 10019 Fax: (212)767-8582

Format comprises continuous comedy programming. **Formed by the merger of:** HA! The TV Comedy Network; The Comedy Channel. **Key Personnel:** Larry Divney, Pres./CEO; Bill Hilary, Exec. VP & General Mgr.; John Cucci, Chief Operating Officer; Hank Close, Exec. VP, Advertising Sales; Tony Fox, Exec. VP, Corporate Communications; Brad Samuels, Exec. VP, Affiliate Relations; Cathy Tankosic, Sr. VP, Marketing. **URL:** http://www.comedycentral.com. **Additional Contact Info: Regional Office(s):** 2049 Century Park E., Ste. 4170, Los Angeles, CA 90067; 541 N. Fairbanks Ct., Ste. 2050, Chicago, IL 60611; 38710 Woodward Ave., Ste. 200, Bloomfield Hills, MI 48304.

37740 Country Music Television
2806 Opryland Dr. Phone: (615)316-6170
Nashville, TN 37214 Fax: (615)871-5835

Format is country music videos. **Key Personnel:** James Guercio, Chm.; Stan Hitchcock, Sr. VP; Nan Olson, Advertising Sales VP; Rene Ray, Affiliate Relations Dir.; Robert H. Baker, General Mgr.; Tracy Storey, Program Dir.

37741 Court TV
600 3rd Ave. Phone: (212)973-2800
New York, NY 10016

Formerly: In Court Television.

37742 Courtroom Television Network
600 3rd Ave., 2nd Fl. Phone: (212)973-2800
New York, NY 10016 Fax: (212)973-2889

Format comprises live coverage of trials and legal news. **Key Personnel:** Stephen Cohen, Exec. Producer.

37743 Deep Dish TV
339 Lafayette St. Phone: (212)473-8933
New York, NY 10012 Fax: (212)420-8223

Educational programming format. **Key Personnel:** Loannis Mookas, Operations Mgr.; Kai Lumumba Barrow, Exective Dir.

37744 The Discovery Channel
7700 Wisconsin Ave. Phone: (301)986-0444
Bethesda, MD 20814 Fax: (301)986-4826

Format features documentaries on exploration, history, nature, and science. **Owner:** Cable Education Network, Inc. **Key Personnel:** John Hendricks, Chm./CEO; Ruth Otte, Pres./COO; Greg Moyer, Programming Group Sr. VP. **Additional Contact Info: Regional Office(s):** 625 N. Michigan Ave., Chicago, IL 60611, (312)751-4265; 641 Lexington, 8th Fl., New York, NY 10022, (212)751-2120.

37745 The Disney Channel
3800 W. Alameda Ave. Phone: (818)569-7500
Burbank, CA 91505 Fax: (818)566-1358

Family programming format. **Key Personnel:** John Cooke, President; Mark Handler, Sales and Affiliate Mktg. VP.

37746 E!
5670 Wilshire Blvd., 2nd Fl. Phone: (323)938-2336
Los Angeles, CA 90036 Fax: (323)954-2620

Format is entertainment/pop cuture news and information. **Formerly**: Movietime; E! (Entertainment Television). **Key Personnel:** Lee Masters, Pres./CEO; David Cassaro, Sr. VP Advertising Sales; Christopher Fager, Sr. VP Intl. Development; Mark Feldman, Gen. Counsel/Sr. VP Business/Legal Aff.; Debra Green, Sr.VP Affiliate Relations; Dale Hopkins, Sr. VP Mktg.; William Keenan, CFO/Sr. VP Finance; Fran Shea, Sr. VP Programming; Patricia Robinson, Sr. VP Human Resources. **Additional Contact Info: Regional Office(s):** Hartford Affiliate Sales, 10 Columbus Blvd., Hartford, CT 06106, (860)249-3700, fax: (860)247-8009; Chicago Ad Sales, 333 N. Michigan Ave., Ste. 2132, Chicago, IL 60601, (312)609-0360, fax: (312)609-0363; New York Ad Sales, 11 W. 42nd St., 19th Fl., New York, NY 10036-8002, (212)852-5100, fax: (212)852-5151.

37747 The ECO Channel
9171 Victoria Dr. Phone: (410)750-7291
Ellicott City, MD 21042

Key Personnel: Eric Mclamb, Founder/Chm./CEO.

37748 ESPN
935 Middle St. Phone: (860)585-2000
Bristol, CT 06010

Sports format. **Owner:** ABC, Inc., a wholly owned subsidiary of The Walt Disney Company. **Formerly**: ESPN (Entertainment and Sports Programming Network). **Key Personnel:** Steven M. Bornstein, Pres./CEO; George W. Bodenheimer, Exec. VP Sales and Mktg.; Edwin M. Durso, Exec. VP Admin.; Howard C. Katz, Exec. VP Production; Reginald R. Thomas, Exec. VP Operations Eng. and New Tech.; Michael Chico, Sr. VP Integrated Sales/Market Research; Len DeLuca, Sr. VP Programming Development; Christine F. Driessen, Sr. VP/CFO; Judy Fearing, Sr. VP Consumer Mktg.; Rosa M. Gatti, Sr. VP Communications/Employee Relations; Richard K. Glover, Sr. VP ESPN Enterprises; Jacques Kremer, Sr. VP/Gen. Mgr. Latin America Ad Sales; Jeffrey S. Mahl, Sr. VP Ad. Sales; Betsy Goff, Sr. VP, Programming & Talent Negotiation; L. Patrick Mellon, Sr. VP Affiliate Sales and Mktg.; Chuch Pagano, Sr. VP Operations and Engineering Projec; David Pahl, Sr. VP/Gen. Counsel; Jeffrey R. Ruhe, Sr. VP Event Mngt.; John A. Walsh, Sr. VP/Exec. Ed.; John Wildhack, Sr. VP Programming; David F. Zucker, Sr. VP and Mng. Dir. ESPN Intl. **Additional Contact Info: Regional Office(s):** 605 3rd Ave., New York, NY 10158, (212)916-9200; 962 N. La Cienega Blvd., Los Angeles, CA 90069, (310)358-5300; 5251 DTC Pkwy., 1 DTC, Ste. 410, Englewood, CO 80111, (303)740-8940; Blvd. Towers, 205 N. Michigan Ave., Ste. 3914, Chicago, IL 60601, (312)228-5800; Timberland Office Park, 5445 Corporate Dr., Bldg. 3, Troy, MI 48098, (248)641-1540.

37749 Eternal Word Television Network (EWTN)
5817 Old Leeds Rd. Phone: (205)271-2900
Birmingham, AL 35210 Fax: (205)271-2925
E-mail: marketing@ewtn.com

Religious cable network, offering programming for all ages. Spanish SAP available. **Key Personnel:** Bill Steltemeier, Chairman of the Board; Michael Warshaw, President. **URL:** http://www.ewtn.com.

37750 FamilyNet
6350 West Freeway Phone: (817)737-4011
Fort Worth, TX 76116-4511 Free: (800)832-6638

Based in Fort Worth, Texas, FamilyNet is a 24-hour television network airing more than 50 hours of original, values-based programs weekly. FamilyNet broadcasts to a potential 33 million TV households and is available on cable systems and broadcast stations nationwide. FamilyNet also produces five radio programs that are heard by 3.7 million listeners weekly in the U.S. and around the world. For more information please visit the FamilNet Web site at www.FamilyNet.com or call (800) 832-6638. **Key Personnel:** Dr. David W. Clark, President; David Lewis, Dir. of Programming & Traffic; Risa Hubbard, Affiliate Relations Manager; R. Martin Coleman, VP Production; Glenn McEowen, VP Engineering; Darin S. Davis, National Sales Mgr.; Denise Cook, Public Relations/Program Marketing Mgr. **URL:** http://www.FamilyNet.com.

37751 Fox Family Channel
2877 Guardian Ln. Phone: (757)459-6000
Virginia Beach, VA 23452 Fax: (757)459-6420

Format comprises family-oriented series, movies, and specials. **Owner:** International Family Entertainment, Inc. **Key Personnel:** Haim Saban, CEO; Maureen Smith, President; Mark Ittner. **Additional Contact Info: Regional Office(s):** 3350 Peachtree Rd., Ste. 1600, Atlanta, GA 30326, (404)504-0580, fax: (404)504-0581; 10960 Wilshire Blvd., 20th Fl., Los Angeles, CA 90024, (310)235-9877, fax: (310)235-9302; 444 North Michigan Ave., Ste. 1710, Chicago, IL 60611, (312)396-8920, fax: (312)396-8921; 1133 Avenue of the Americas, 36th Fl., New York, NY 10036, (212)782-1860, fax: (212)782-1865.

37752 Fox Net
10201 W. Pico Blvd., Bldg. 89, 4th Fl. Phone: (310)369-3628
Fax: (310)969-1360
Los Angeles, CA 90035

Format comprises Fox network programming, syndicated programs, movies, and series for areas of the country unable to receive an over-the-air FOX broadcast affiliate. **Key Personnel:** Mark Handwerger, Dir., National Sales, phone (212)556-2478, fax (212)299-0815; Betty Wang, Dir., Promotion & Marketing, phone (310)369-3681, fax (310)969-1361; Wendy Chambers, Dir., Affiliate Relations, phone (310)369-3490, fax (310)969-1361; Dwayne Bright, Dir., Programming, phone (310)369-3382; Keith Goldberg, Dir., Technical Operations, phone (310)369-3434; Steve Nazar, Traffic Operations Mgr., phone (310)369-3684. **URL:** http://www.fox.com. **Additional Contact Info: Regional Office(s):** 1211 Avenue of the Americas, 2nd Fl., New York, NY 10036, (212)556-2478, fax: (212)299-0815.

37753 FX
Box 900   Phone: (310)444-8123
Beverly Hills, CA 90213

General entertainment format. **Key Personnel:** Mark L. Sennenberl, Exec. VP.

37754 FXTV: Fitness and Exercise Television
Box 5767   Phone: (310)271-5400
Beverly Hills, CA 90209   Fax: (310)271-3479

Fitness and exercise format. **Key Personnel:** Alan Mruvka, Co-Chm.; Larry Namer, Co-Chm.

37755 GalaVision
6701 Center Dr. W., 6th Fl.   Phone: (310)348-3640
Los Angeles, CA 90045   Fax: (310)348-3643

Format comprises Spanish language variety programming. **Owner:** Univisa. **Key Personnel:** Jaime Davila, Group VP; G.S. Livingston III, VP Broadcast Operations.

37756 Game Show Network
10202 W. Washington Blvd.   Phone: (310)244-2222
Culver City, CA 90232   Fax: (310)280-2080

Formerly: The Game Show Channel. **Key Personnel:** Micheal Fleming, President; Russell Myerson, Network Operations Sr. VP; Dick Block, Advertising Sales VP; Elaine Parrish, Sales and Affiliate Marketing Sr. VP. **URL:** http://www.sony.com.

37757 GEMS Television
4380 NW 128th St.   Phone: (305)769-4555
Opa Locka, FL 33054   Fax: (305)681-0412

Key Personnel: Gary McBride, Pres./CEO; Alexander Berger, COO.

37758 GoodLife Television Network
650 Massachuetts Ave. NW   Phone: (202)289-6633
Washington, DC 20001   Fax: (202)289-6632

Entertainment format. **Formerly:** Nostalgia Television. **Key Personnel:** Squire Rushnell, Pres./CEO; srushnell@goodtv.com; Diane Fuller, CFO, dfuller@goodtv.com. **URL:** http://www.goodtv.com.

37759 Headline News
1 CNN Center   Phone: (404)827-2608
Box 105306   Fax: (404)827-3181
Atlanta, GA 30348-5366

Key Personnel: Tom Johnson, President.

37760 Home Box Office (HBO)
1100 Avenue of the Americas   Phone: (212)512-1000
New York, NY 10036

Format comprises movies, music, comedy, and sports. **Owner:** Time Warner, Inc. **Key Personnel:** Michael Fuchs, Chm./CEO; Jeff Bewkes, Pres./COO; Peter Frame, Exec. VP Affiliate Operations. **Additional Contact Info: Regional Office(s):** 2049 Century Park E., Ste. 4100, Los Angeles, CA 90067, (310)201-9200; 2 Embarcadero Center, Ste. 840, San Francisco, CA 94111, (415)765-7700; The Quadrant, 5445 DTC Pkwy., Ste. 700, Englewood, CO 80111, (303)220-2900; Lenox Bldg., 3399 Peachtree Rd. NE, Ste. 1600, Atlanta, GA 30326, (404)239-6600; 6250 N. River Rd., 10th Fl., Rosemont, IL 60018, (708)318-5100; 401 City Ave., Ste. 620, Bala Cynwyd, PA 19004, (215)668-6500; 12750 Merit Dr., Ste. 1105, Dallas, TX 75251, (214)450-1000.

37761 Home and Garden Channel (HGTV)
PO Box 50970   Phone: (865)694-2700
Knoxville, TN 37950

37762 Home Shopping Network
PO Box 9090   Phone: (727)872-1000
Clearwater, FL 33758-9090   Fax: (727)572-8854

Home shopping format. **Key Personnel:** Alan Garson, Executive VP; Gerald Hogan, Pres./CEO; Charles H. Bohart, Broadcast/Satellite Services Sr. VP; Scott Campbell, Cable Affiliates Sr. VP.

37763 Home Shopping Network II
PO Box 9090   Phone: (727)872-1000
Clearwater, FL 33758-9090

37764 International Channel Networks
4100 E. Dry Creek Rd., Ste.   Phone: (303)712-5400
A300   Fax: (303)712-5401
Centennial, CO 80122
E-mail: teresa.wiedel@i-channel.com

Format comprises international foreign language news, sports, drama, and comedy. **Owner:** Liberty Media Group. **Key Personnel:** Kent Rice, President/COO, phone (303)712-5404, fax (303)712-5401, kent.rice@i-channel.com; Jim Honiotes, VP Marketing & Communications, phone (303)268-5450, fax (303)268-5465, jim.honiotes@i-channel.com; Berto Guzman, Sr. VP Affiliate Relations, phone (303)414-2146, fax (303)414-2101, berto.guzman@i-channel.com; Raoul DeSota, VP Affiliate Sales, phone (303)712-5431, fax (303)712-5401, raoul.desota@i-channel.com. **URL:** http://www.internationalchannel.com. **Additional Contact Info: Regional Office(s):** 570 Lexington Ave., 36th Fl., New York, NY 10022, (212)527-9917, fax: (212)527-9915; 2700 River Rd., Ste. 108, Des Plaines, IL 60018, (847)298-9390, fax: (847)298-9491; 2250 E. Imperial Hwy., Ste. 630, El Segundo, CA 90245, (310)414-2100, fax: (310)414-2101.

37765 Jewish Television Network
8383 Wilshire Blvd., Ste. 1010   Phone: (323)852-9494
Beverly Hills, CA 90211   Fax: (323)852-9498

Format comprises news, arts, culture, entertainment and religious programming of interest to the Jewish community. **Key Personnel:** Jay Sanderson, Exec.Dir.; Harvey Lehrer, Dir. of Production; Jonathan Schreiber, Dir. of Development and Mktg.

37766 The Learning Channel
7700 Wisconsin Ave.   Phone: (301)986-1999
Bethesda, MD 20814-3522   Fax: (301)986-4826
                                      Free: (800)346-0032

Educational format. **Key Personnel:** Dr. Harold Morse, Chm./CEO; Robert Shuman, Pres./COO; Henry Schlenker, Sr. VP/CFO; Robert Sestill, Programming VP; John Ford, General Mgr.

37767 Madison Square Garden Network
2 Penn Plaza   Phone: (212)465-6727
New York, NY 10121

Key Personnel: Douglas Moss, General Mgr.; Marty Brooks, Program Dir.

37768 Mind Extension University
9697 E. Mineral Ave.   Phone: (303)784-8920
Englewood, CO 80112   Fax: (303)792-5608

Format comprises college instructional programming. **Owner:** Jones International, Ltd. **Key Personnel:** Glenn Jones, Chm./CEO; Gregory Liptak, Group Pres.; Victor Harrison, General Mgr.

37769 The Movie Channel (TMC)
1633 Broadway, 37th Fl.   Phone: (212)708-1500
New York, NY 10019

Format comprises movies. **Owner:** Showtime Networks. **Key Personnel:** Tony Cox, Chm./CEO; Matt Blank, Pres./COO; Jack Heim, Sales and Affiliate Mktg. Exec. VP. **Additional Contact Info: Regional Office(s):** 10 Universal City Plaza, 31st Fl., Universal City, CA 91608, (818)505-7700; 8101 E. Prentice Ave., Ste. 704, Englewood, CO 80111, (303)850-7380; 5 Concourse Pkwy., Ste. 2100, Atlanta, GA 30328, (404)396-1333; 401 N. Michigan, Ste. 1600, Chicago, IL 60611, (312)645-1100; 15301 N. Dallas Pkwy., Ste. 1000, Dallas, TX 75248, (214)788-5000.

37770 MTV (Music Television)
1515 Broadway   Phone: (212)965-6000
New York, NY 10036

Format comprises music videos, news, and specials. **Owner:** MTV Networks. **Key Personnel:** Tom Freston, Chm./CEO. **Additional Contact Info: Regional Office(s):** 10 Universal City Plaza, 30th Fl., Universal City, CA 91608, (818)505-7800; 3399 Peachtree Rd. NE, Ste. 990, Atlanta, GA 30326, (404)841-3099; 401 N. Michigan Ave., Ste. 1500, Chicago, IL 60611, (312)755-0310; 2301 Big Beaver Rd., Ste. 621, Troy, MI 48084, (248)649-7170; 35 Adams Ave., Hauppauge, NY 11788, (516)435-4900; 15301 N. Dallas Pkwy., Ste. 1000, Dallas, TX 75248, (214)788-5000.

37771 Nationality Broadcasting Network
11906 Madison Ave.   Phone: (216)221-0330
Lakewood, OH 44107   Fax: (216)221-3638

Format comprises international programming. **Key Person-**

nel: Miklos Kossanyi, President; John Sedivy, Operations Mgr.

37772 NECN/New England Cable News
160 Wells Ave.   Phone: (617)630-5000
Newton, MA 02459-3302   Fax: (617)630-5055

Format comprises general public interest, sports, and news programming. **Key Personnel:** Lawrence Meli, General Mgr.; Mike Adams, Sports Dir.

37773 New York One
75 9th Ave., 6th Fl.   Phone: (212)465-0111
New York, NY 10011-7006   Fax: (212)563-7632

News format. **Key Personnel:** Paul Sagan, Program Dir.; Kevin Garrity, Sports Dir.

37774 Nickelodeon/Nick at Nite
1515 Broadway   Phone: (212)258-7500
New York, NY 10036   Fax: (212)846-1724

Format comprises children's programming (6 a.m.-8 p.m.) and classic television shows (8 p.m.-6 a.m.). **Owner:** MTV Networks. **Key Personnel:** Geraldine Laybourne, President; Rich Cronin, Mktg. Sr. VP. **Additional Contact Info: Regional Office(s):** 10 Universal City Plaza, 30th Fl., Universal City, CA 91608, (818)505-7800; 3399 Peachtree Rd., Ste. 900 NE, Atlanta, GA 30326, (404)841-3099; 401 N. Michigan Ave., Ste. 1500, Chicago, IL 60611, (312)755-0310; 2301 W. Big Beaver Rd., Ste. 621, Troy, MI 48084; 15301 N. Dallas Pkwy., Ste. 1000, Dallas, TX 75240, (214)404-0793.

37775 The Outdoor Channel
43445 Business Park Dr., Ste.   Phone: (909)699-6991
103   Fax: (909)699-6313
Temecula, CA 92590   Free: (800)770-5750
E-mail: info@outdoorchannel.com

Outdoor sports format (hunting, fishing, camping). **Key Personnel:** Andy Dale, CEO, andydale@outdoorchannel.com; Wade Sherman, Business Development VP; Amy Hendrickson, Affiliate Mktg. VP. **URL:** http://www.outdoorchannel.com.

37776 PASS (Pro-Am Sports System)
550 W. Lafayette Blvd.   Phone: (313)222-7277
PO Box 3040   Fax: (313)223-2299
Detroit, MI 48231

Sports format. **Key Personnel:** Jeffrey H. Genthner, General Mgr.; Kathy Salazar, Business Mgr.

37777 PCOM West Moreland Communication, Inc.
PO Box 38307   Phone: (412)782-2921
Pittsburgh, PA 15238-8306   Fax: (412)782-4242

Formerly: Gaming and Entertainment Network. **Key Personnel:** Nelson L. Goldberg, Consultant. **Additional Contact Info: Regional Office(s):** 201 Freeport Rd.

37778 Prevue Guide
1 Technology Plz.   Phone: (918)488-4000
7140 S. Lewis Ave.   Fax: (918)663-6228
Tulsa, OK 74136

Format comprises programming promotions. **Owner:** Prevue Networks Inc. **Key Personnel:** Joe Batson, COO; Daniel J. Sweeney, Sales and Mktg. VP.

37779 Prime Network
5251 Gulston   Phone: (713)661-0078
Houston, TX 77081

Key Personnel: Dan Wilhelm, General Mgr.; Lynne Haddow, Program Dir.

37780 Prime Ticket Network
10000 Santa Monica Blvd.   Phone: (310)286-3800
Los Angeles, CA 90067-7007   Fax: (310)286-3875

Key Personnel: Roger Werner, General Mgr.; Debra Vinson, Operations Mgr.; Monique Stokes, Program Dir.

37781 QVC Network, Inc.
Goshen Corporate Park   Phone: (215)430-1000
1365 Enterprise Dr.   Fax: (215)431-6499
West Chester, PA 19380

Home shopping format. **Key Personnel:** Douglas S. Briggs, Programming Exec. VP; William F. Costello, Exec. VP/CFO.

37782 The Sci-Fi Channel
1230 Avenue of the Americas   Phone: (212)413-5000
New York, NY 10020   Fax: (212)408-8228

Format comprises science fiction movies and television shows. **Key Personnel:** Kay Koplovitz, Pres./CEO; Barry Schulman, VP Programming.

37783 Shop Television Network
1845 Empire Ave.   Phone: (818)840-1400
Burbank, CA 91504   Fax: (818)845-4702

Home shopping format. **Key Personnel:** Michael Rosen, Chm./CEO; Joseph Naughton, Exec. VP/COO; Brian Layfield, CFO.

37784 Showtime
1633 Broadway, 37th Fl.   Phone: (212)708-1600
New York, NY 10019   Fax: (212)708-1530

Movies, specials, and sports formats. **Owner:** Showtime Networks. **Key Personnel:** Tony Cox, Chairman/CEO; Matt Blank, Pres./COO; Jack Heim, Sales and Affiliate Exec. VP. **Additional Contact Info: Regional Office(s):** 10 Universal City Plaza, Universal City, CA 91608, (818)505-7700; 8101 E. Prentice Ave., Ste. 704, Englewood, CO 80111, (303)850-7380; 5 Concourse Pkwy., Ste. 2100, Atlanta, GA 30328, (404)396-1333; 401 N. Michigan Ave., Ste. 1500, Chicago, IL 60611, (312)755-0310; 1633 Broadway, New York, NY 10019, (212)708-1600; 15301 N. Dallas Pkwy., Ste. 1000, Dallas, TX 75248, (214)788-5000.

37785 Spanish Broadcasting System
26 W. 56th St.   Phone: (212)541-6700
New York, NY 10019   Fax: (212)541-6904

Format comprises ethnic programming. **Key Personnel:** Raul Alarcone, Owner/CEO; Dan Lohse, Chief Eng.

37786 Sportschannel America
150 Crossways Park Dr.   Phone: (516)921-3764
Woodbury, NY 11797   Fax: (516)364-1943

Sports format. **Owner:** Rainbow Programming Holdings, Inc., Cablevision Systems. **Key Personnel:** Jeff Ruhe, Pres./COO; Sharon Portin, Affiliate Sales and Mktg. VP.

**37787 Texas Cable & Telecommunications
    Association**
506 W 16th St.   Phone: (512)474-2082
Austin, TX 78701   Fax: (512)474-0966

Key Personnel: Amanda Batson, PhD, General Mgr. **URL:** http://www.txcable.com.

37788 TNN (The Nashville Network)
250 Harbor Plaza Dr.   Phone: (203)965-6000
Stamford, CT 06904   Fax: (203)965-6315

Country music and lifestyle format. **Owner:** Group W Satellite Communications. **Key Personnel:** Don Mitzner, President. **Additional Contact Info:** Regional Office(s): 685 3rd Ave., 20th Fl., New York, NY 10017, (212)916-1000.

37789 The Travel Channel
7700 Wisconsin Ave.   Phone: (301)986-0444
Bethesda, MD 20814-3522   Fax: (301)771-4053

Travel information and entertainment format. **Key Personnel:** Gail Gleeson, VP Programming; Karen Hanley, VP Programming. **URL:** http://travel.discovery.com.

37790 Trinity Broadcasting Network (TBN)
Box A   Phone: (714)731-1000
Santa Ana, CA 92711

Format comprises religious programming. **Key Personnel:** T. Bahnson Stanley, GM; Dana Michaelis, VP, Affiliate Sales; Lindee Youngman, Programming Dir. **Additional Contact Info: Regional Office(s):** 313 Rosedale Ave., Gadsden, AL 35901, (205)546-8860; 2528 U.S. 31 S., Greenwood, IN 46143, (317)535-5542; 9020 Yates, Westminster, CO 80030, (303)650-5515.

37791 Turner Classic Movies
1050 Techwood Dr.   Phone: (404)885-5535
Atlanta, GA 30318   Fax: (404)885-4318

Key Personnel: Scott Sassa, President.

37792 Univision
605 3rd Ave., 12th Fl.   Phone: (212)455-5200
New York, NY 10158-0180   Fax: (212)867-6710

Format comprises Spanish language programming. **Owner:** Univision Communications Inc. **Key Personnel:** Luly Estevez, Dir. Affiliate Sales. **Additional Contact Info: Regional Office(s):** 6701 Center Dr. W., 15th Fl., Los Angeles, CA 90045, (310)348-3642, fax: (310)348-3643.

37793 USA Network
1230 Avenue of the Americas   Phone: (212)413-5000
New York, NY 10020   Fax: (212)408-3600

Entertainment format. **Key Personnel:** Kay Koplovitz, Pres./CEO; Steve Brenner, Business Affairs and Operations Sr. VP. **Additional Contact Info: Regional Office(s):** 2049 Century Pkwy. E., Ste. 2550, Los Angeles, CA 90067, (310)277-0199; 401 N. Michigan Ave., Chicago, IL 60611, (312)644-1522; 2000 Town Center, Ste. 2640, Southfield, MI 48075, (248)353-1200.

37794 VH-1 (Video Hits One)
1515 Broadway   Phone: (212)258-7800
New York, NY 10036   Fax: (212)258-7955

Format comprises music videos. **Owner:** MTV Networks. **Key Personnel:** Ed Bennett, President; Julie Davidson, Programming Sr. VP; Barry Kluger, Public Relations VP. **Additional Contact Info: Regional Office(s):** 10 Universal City Plaza, 30th Fl., Universal City, CA 91608, (818)505-7800; 3399 Peachtree Rd. NE, Ste. 900, Atlanta, GA 30326, (404)841-3099; 401 N. Michigan Ave., Ste. 1500, Chicago, IL 60611, (312)755-0310; 2301 W. Big Beaver Rd., Ste. 621, Troy, MI 48084, (248)649-7170; 15301 N. Dallas Pkwy., Ste. 1020, Dallas, TX 75248, (214)458-4600.

37795 The Weather Channel
300 Interstate North Pkwy.   Phone: (770)226-0000
Atlanta, GA 30339

Format comprises international, national, and local weather. **Owner:** Landmark Communications, Inc. **Key Personnel:** Michael Eckert, CEO; Paul FitzPatrick, President; Rebecca Ruthven, Affiliate Sales and Service VP. **URL:** http://www.weather.com. **Additional Contact Info: Regional Office(s):** 1925 Century Park E., Ste. 830, Los Angeles, CA 90067, (213)785-0511; 180 N. Stetson, Ste. 5025, Chicago, IL 60601, (312)946-0892; 2690 Crooks Rd., Ste. 217, Troy, MI 48084, (248)362-2290; 780 3rd Ave., 23rd Fl., New York, NY 10017, (212)308-3055.

NEWS AND FEATURE SYNDICATES

A selection of print media services and bureaus in the U.S. and Canada. Entries are arranged alphabetically.

37796 A & A
PO Box 941293
Plano, TX 75094-1293
E-mail: aaartwork@aol.com
Phone: (972)671-1638
Fax: (972)671-1638

Cartoon strips including The Romanticats, Cow-Town, Party Gators, Golden Gourmets, Star Staples, Collegiate Crunchies, Culinary Court, and Frisky Investigators. Mary & Rufus, Pony Place. **Key Personnel:** Elaine Abramson, President; Martin Stanley, Vice President; Deborah Sue, Special Projects; Mitchell Lee, VP, Marketing/Sales. **URL:** http://www.aaartwork.com.

37797 Abrahamian Feature Syndicate
198 Robinhill Dr.
Williamsville, NY 14221
Phone: (716)688-0902

Cartoons and graphic design. **Key Personnel:** Emil V. Abrahamian, President.

37798 AccuWeather, Inc.
385 Science Park Rd.
State College, PA 16803
E-mail: info@accuwx.com
Phone: (814)237-0309
Fax: (814)235-8609

Commercial weather service and distributor of weather forecasts, broadcasts, presentations, systems, data and Internet content to more than 1,500 radio and television stations, newspapers and cable systems. **Key Personnel:** Dr. Joel N. Myers, President, fax (814)235-8509, myersj@accuwx.com; Barry Lee Myers, Exec. VP, phone (814)235-8520, fax (814)235-8529, myersb@accuwx.com; Elliot Abrams, Sr. VP, phone (814)235-8745, fax (814)238-1339, abrams@accuwx.com; Joseph Sobel, Sr. VP, phone (814)235-8760, fax (814)237-8769, sobel@accuwx.com; Evan E. Myers, Sr. VP, phone (814)235-8503, fax (814)235-8519, myerse@accuwx.com; Michael E. Steinberg, Sr. VP, phone (814)235-8535, fax (814)235-8539, steinberg@accuwx.com; Jainene Long, Exec. Dir. of Customer Service, phone (814)235-8775, fax (814)235-8779, long@accuwx.com; Jim Candor, VP, New Media Marketing, phone (814)235-8755, fax (814)235-8519, candorjim@accuwx.com. **URL:** http://www.accuweather.com. **Additional Contact Info: Regional Office(s):** AP Photo Archive Office, Two Greenwood Sq., 331 Street Rd., Ste. 440, Bensalem, PA 19020, (215)244-5316, fax: (215)244-5329.

37799 ACME Features Syndicate
147 NE Yamhill
Sheridan, OR 97378
E-mail: binky@acmefeatures.com
Phone: (503)843-4555
Fax: (503)843-4001

Distributes only the Life in Hell cartoon strip. **Key Personnel:** Sondra Gatewood, Exec. Ed., robogate@acmefeatures.com.

37800 A.D. Kahn Inc.
35336 Spring Hill Rd.
Farmington Hills, MI 48331-2044
Phone: (248)661-8585
Fax: (248)788-1022
Free: (888)844-5570
E-mail: kahn@olmarket.com

Key Personnel: A. David Kahn, Editor. **URL:** http://www.olmarket.com.

37801 Adrienne Sioux Koopersmith's World of Eventology & EAT-ventology
1437 W. Rosemont, Ste. 1W
Chicago, IL 60660-1319
E-mail: la_koop@yahoo.com
Phone: (773)743-5341
Fax: (773)743-5395

Creates, publishes, promotes, and distributes daily, weekly, and monthly original literature known as "holidates." Includes goodwill, humanitarian, altruistic, educational, recreational, spiritual, fun-time, and fun-type holidays, for a total of 1361 "holidates to celebrate" falling into 34 categories. **Owner:** Adrienne Sioux Koopersmith, at above address. **Key Person-**

nel: Adrienne Sioux Koopersmith, Founder/CEO. **URL:** http://www.eventology.com. **Also known as:** Adrienne Sioux Koopersmith's Kreative Kingdom & Kalendar: A Return to Utopia.

37802 Advertising Workshop
University of Alaska/JPC
3211 Providence Dr.
Anchorage, AK 99508
E-mail: afjra2@uaa.alaska.edu
Phone: (907)786-4187
Fax: (907)786-4190

Key Personnel: Jim Avery, Self-Syndicator.

37803 Advice Goddess
171 Pier Ave., No. 280
Santa Monica, CA 90405
E-mail: flame777@aol.com
Phone: (310)306-6160
Fax: (310)578-6970

Humorous, but practical, syndicated love advice columns entitled Ask the Advice Goddess and Ask Amy Alkon. **Key Personnel:** Amy Alkon; Lucy Furry, Assistant. **URL:** http://www.advicegoddess.com.

37804 The Advisor Group
18530 Mack Ave., No. 229
Grosse Pointe Farms, MI 48236
Phone: (313)822-7712

Distributes automotive travel car and truck features and photographs. **Key Personnel:** Bruce Hubbard, Author, brucehubbard@earthlink.net; Holly Olmsted Hubbard, Author, hollyhubbard@earthlink.net. **Additional Contact Info: Regional Office(s):** 6708 Auburn Ave. W., Bradenton, FL 34207, (941)758-5039.

37805 Agence France-Presse
1015 15th St. NW, Ste. 500
Washington, DC 20005
Phone: (202)289-0700
Fax: (202)414-0634
Free: (800)786-9380
E-mail: afp@cais.com

Distributes news photographs and text. **Key Personnel:** Georges Biannic, Exec. Dir., phone (202)414-0570, fax (202)414-0600; Gilles Tarot, Reg. Mktg. Sales Dir., N. America, phone (202)414-0637; Sue Mendives, Sales Rep., phone (202)414-0555; Jacques Rigolage, U.S. Admin.; Joseph Soares, Tech. Dir. for Americas.

37806 Agencia Efe/Efe News Service
1252 National Press Bldg.
Washington, DC 20045
Phone: (202)745-7692
Fax: (202)393-4119

Key Personnel: Fernando Pajares, Bureau Chief.

37807 The Agency
PO Box 139
Kings Park, NY 11754
Phone: (631)544-0705
Fax: (631)544-0705
Free: (800)296-5684
E-mail: cooksreviews@optonline.net

Distributes magazine articles and newspaper columns. **Key Personnel:** Joel Cook, Ed./Author; Sue Portnoy, Ed./Admin.

37808 AgeVenture Syndicated News Service
19432 Preserve Dr.
Boca Raton, FL 33498-4818
E-mail: newsdesk@demko.com
Phone: (561)482-6271

Syndicates headline news and trends on Aging America, feature columns, book reviews, profiles, and thoughts-for-the-day. **Owner:** Demko Publishing, at above address. **Key Personnel:** David J. Demko, Ed.-in-Chief Aging America News Net; Marie Mentzer, Author Health Care & Housing; Elizabeth Rupich, Author Arts & Entertainment; Dorothy Harris, Author Education. **URL:** http://www.demko.com.

37809 AIM (Accuracy in Media) Report
4455 Connecticut Ave. NW
Ste. 330
Washington, DC 20008
E-mail: ar1@aim.org; aimeditor@yahoo.com
Phone: (202)364-4401
Fax: (202)364-4098

Distributes newsletters and newspapers. **Key Personnel:** Reed Irvine, Chm.; Donald K. Irvine, Exec. Sec.; Deborah Lambert, Pub. Aff. Dir. **URL:** http://www.aim.org.

37810 A.J. Cook
6785 Slash Pine
Memphis, TN 38119
Phone: (901)754-8925

Distributes federal tax columns. **Key Personnel:** A.J. Cook, Author/Owner, phone (901)754-8925, ajcook@taxfables.com. **URL:** http://www.taxfables.com.

37811 Alan Lavine, Inc.
PO Box 14697
North Palm Beach, FL 33408-0697
Phone: (561)630-7112
Fax: (561)630-7398
E-mail: mwliblavat@aol.com

Trade and professional financial columns covering mutual funds, insurance, and family finance, as well. **Key Personnel:** Alan Lavine, Editor; Gail Liberman, Editor.

37812 Allsport Photography USA
2450 Colorado Ave., No. 500 W.
Santa Monica, CA 90404-3575
Phone: (310)998-2700

Photographic coverage from over 130 different sports worldwide. **Key Personnel:** Greg Walker, g.walker@allsport.com; Mike Powell, m.powell@allsport.com; Tony Coles, Vice President, t.coles@allsport.com; Chris Eisenberg, Picture Desk Supervisor, c.eisenberg@allsport.com.

37813 American Crossword Federation
PO Box 69
Massapequa Park, NY 11762
Phone: (516)795-8823

Daily Newsday Crossword and a Netword Puzzle via the Internet. **Key Personnel:** Stanley Newman, President/Editor-in-Chief; Joseph Vallely, VP, Sales Manager; Jonathan Delfin, VP, Senior Editor.

37814 American Press Service and Features Syndicate
PO Box 917
Van Nuys, CA 91408-0917
E-mail: iscs3assoc@aol.com
Phone: (818)997-6497

Distributes news features and entertainment columns. **Key Personnel:** Israel Bick, VP/Gen. Mgr./Sr. Ed., ISCS3ASSOC@aol.com.

37815 Ampersand Communications
2311 S. Bayshore Dr.
Miami, FL 33133
E-mail: amprsnd@aol.com
Phone: (305)285-2200

Distributes EnviroScan; HealthScan; Golden Years; Business Insights; Business Travel; also Pet Insights; Southern Book Reviews; Traveling the South; Food for Thought; Travel Adventures; House and Home; and Timeshare Topics. **Key Personnel:** Rosalie Leposky, Managing Partner; George Leposky, Editor. **URL:** http://www.ampersandcom.com.

37816 And Sew On
PO Box 71   Phone: (908)722-5676
Martinsville, NJ 08836

Distributes sewing/needlecraft column. **Key Personnel:** Alida Macor, Pres./Author.

37817 Aquino International
PO Box 15760
Stamford, CT 06901-0760
E-mail: aquinoint@aol.com

Distributes photography. **Key Personnel:** Andres Aquino, Owner. **URL:** http://www.aaquino.com.

37818 Arrigoni Travel Syndication
PO Box 1004   Phone: (415)454-0876
Fairfax, CA 94978   Fax: (415)456-2697

Distributes destinations and senior travel trips. **Key Personnel:** Patricia Arrigoni, President.

37819 Arthur's International
2613 High Range Dr.   Phone: (702)228-3731
Las Vegas, NV 89134
E-mail: arthurintl@aol.com

Key Personnel: Marvin C. Arthur, President.

37820 ArtistMarket.com
35336 Spring Hill Rd.   Phone: (248)661-8585
Farmington Hills, MI 48331-2044   Fax: (248)788-1022
   Free: (888)844-5570
E-mail: editor@artistmarket.com

Written features, editorial cartoon panels, comic strips, and caricatures. **Key Personnel:** A. David Kahn, Editor-in-Chief, editors@artistmarket.com. **URL:** http://www.artistmarket.com. **Formerly:** A.D. Kahn, Inc.

37821 Artists and Writers Syndicate
PO Box 60688   Phone: (202)882-8882
Washington, DC 20039-0688   Fax: (202)829-9283
E-mail: srcmarjorie@aol.com

Distributes "These Two Wheels" features to daily newspapers in the US and Canada. **Key Personnel:** Philip Steitz, Pres. Exec. Ed.; Marjorie Steitz, Managing Editor.

37822 Ascher Features Syndicate
214 Boston Ave.   Phone: (609)927-1842
Egg Harbor Township, NJ 08234

Key Personnel: Sidney Ascher, President; Evelyn Ascher, Sec./Treas.

37823 Ashleigh Brilliant
117 W. Valerio St.   Phone: (805)682-0531
Santa Barbara, CA 93101
E-mail: ashleigh@west.net

Distributes cartoon feature. **Key Personnel:** Ashleigh Brilliant, President; Dorothy Brilliant, Vice President. **URL:** http://www.ashleighbrilliant.com.

37824 Ask the Builder
3166 N. Farmcrest Dr.   Phone: (513)531-9229
Cincinnati, OH 45213-1112
E-mail: pr@askbuild.com

Weekly home improvement newspaper column; weekly local and national radio show; website; and weekly TV home improvement vignettes. **Owner:** Tim Carter, at above address. **Key Personnel:** Tim Carter, Author, tim@askbuild.com. **URL:** http://www.askthebuilder.com.

37825 Associated Press/AP Newsfeatures
50 Rockefeller Plaza   Phone: (212)621-1821
New York, NY 10020

Distributes news wire service. **Key Personnel:** Louis Boccardi, Pres./CEO; James Kennedy, Business Ed.; William Ahearn, VP/Exec. Ed.; Norm Goldstein, Dir./APN Spec. Proj.

37826 Associated Press/Wide World Photo
50 Rockefeller Plaza   Phone: (212)621-1930
New York, NY 10020   Fax: (212)621-1955

Key Personnel: Patricia Lantis, Director.

37827 Atlantic Feature Syndicate
PO Box 994   Phone: (781)665-4442
Melrose, MA 02176   Fax: (781)977-5073
E-mail: lreznick@offthemark.com

Key Personnel: Mark Parisi, President; Lynn Reznick, Mktg. Dir. **URL:** http://www.offthemark.com.

37828 Auto Digest Syndicate
PO Box 459   Phone: (541)416-9555
Prineville, OR 97754-0459   Fax: (541)346-9002
E-mail: adigest@iname.com

Distributes weekly automotive columns. **Key Personnel:** Bill Schaffer, President; Barbara Schaffer, Editor.

37829 Avanti NewsFeatures
29106 Palomino Dr.   Phone: (586)573-2755
Warren, MI 48093-3505   Fax: (586)573-2755
E-mail: avanti1054@aol.com

Syndicate for web sites, newspapers, and magazines. **Key Personnel:** Anne Fracassa, Editor-in-Chief; Craig Oldani, Tech. Ed.; Michael Raveane, Politics Ed.; Tracey Lee-Petri, Parenting Columnist; El Lee, Music Ed.; Anthony W. Guerrero, Motorcycle Ed.; Francesca Fracassa, Food Ed.; Paul-Michael Turkal, Medical Ed.; Karen Oldani, Arts & Crafts Ed.; Frank Zuckero, Tools Ed.; Jeff Lee, Sports Ed.; A.M. Schlosser, Lifestyle Ed. **Formerly:** Avanti & Co.

37830 The Bascome Syndicate
PO Box 638   Phone: (516)749-0111
Shelter Island, NY 11964

Distributes "Along the Food Trail.". **Key Personnel:** Rosemary Bascome, Editor.

37831 Bay City News Service
1390 Market St.   Phone: (415)552-8900
Ste. 324   Fax: (415)552-8912
San Francisco, CA 94102
E-mail: baycitynews@pacbell.net

Distributes regional wire service. **Key Personnel:** Dick Fogel, Editor; Marcia Fogel, Entertainment Ed.; Aimee Strain, Managing Editor; Wayne Futak, General Mgr.

37832 Beaver Creek Features
3508 W. 151 St.   Phone: (216)251-1389
Cleveland, OH 44111-2105
E-mail: dnorman@en.com

Distributes cartoon features about wildlife and outdoor recreation. **Owner:** Dean Norman. **URL:** http://www.wallyswoods.com.

37833 Best Buys In Wine
1406 Thomas Pl.   Phone: (817)732-4758
Fort Worth, TX 76107   Fax: (817)732-3247
E-mail: reniesteves@msn.com

Freelance articles for Fort Worth Star-Telegram. **Key Personnel:** Renie Steves, reniesteves@msn.com; Sterling Steves; Renie Steves, Contact.

37834 Better Homes & Gardens Features Syndicate
1716 Locust St.   Fax: (800)678-5994
Des Moines, IA 50309-3023   Free: (800)678-8135

Key Personnel: Jerry Ward, VP Pub. Group; Gary Fees, Business Mgr.; Dennis Christensen, Western Rep.; Robert Krisch, Northeast Rep.

37835 Bettman Archive
902 Broadway   Phone: (212)777-6200
New York, NY 10010   Fax: (212)533-4034

Key Personnel: Herbert Gstalder, President; Anne Rudden, Assoc. Dir.; Darby Harper, Res. Mgr.; Dann Peirce, Mktg. Dir.

37836 Big Red Hen Productions
Box 807   Free: (888)BIG-REDH
45 Tudor City Pl.
New York, NY 10017

Key Personnel: Frances K. Grace, Self-Syndicator.

37837 Bio File
995 Teaneck Rd., No. 3N   Phone: (201)862-1438
Teaneck, NJ 07666   Fax: (201)862-1438
E-mail: mrbiofile@aol.com

Biographical articles. **Key Personnel:** Mark Malinowski, Editor/Reporter. **URL:** http://www.thebiofile.com.

37838 Black Press Service Inc.
166 Madison Ave.   Phone: (212)686-6850
New York, NY 10016   Fax: (212)686-7308
E-mail: news@blackradionetwork.com

Distributes news wire service. **Key Personnel:** Jay R. Levy, President; Roy Thompson, Editor; Bill Baldwin, Assoc. Ed.; Peter Knight, Sales Mgr.

37839 Bloomberg Business News
499 Park Ave.   Phone: (212)318-2300
15th Fl.   Fax: (212)980-2480
New York, NY 10022   Free: (800)448-5678

Key Personnel: Matthew Winkler, Editor-in-Chief.

37840 BONAT's Diversified
255 N. El Cielo   Phone: (760)324-1503
Ste. 688
Palm Springs, CA 92262

Distributes feature articles concerning women, including beauty, health, exercise, hair and make-up, puzzles, and cartoons. **Owner:** Natalie Carlton, at above address. **Key Personnel:** Natalie Carlton, President; Teresa Carlton, VP/Sec.; Sylvia Resnick, Beauty; Sheila Cluff, Fitness; Frances Sheridan Goulard, Health and Diet.

37841 Boston Features Syndicate
42 Eugenia St.   Phone: (617)963-5073
Randolph, MA 02368

Distributes Mini-Bopper cartoon. **Key Personnel:** Harry Privette, President; Martin Hanna, Director.

37842 BPI Entertainment News Wire
100 Boylston St. Ste. 210   Phone: (617)482-9447
Boston, MA 02116   Fax: (617)482-9562

Distributes magazine, newspaper, and feature articles. **Key Personnel:** John Morgan, VP News and Photo Serv.; Don Gallagher, Managing Editor; Judy Webb, Sales Mgr.

37843 Brenafeatures
PO Box 233   Phone: (617)444-8244
Needham, MA 02492

Key Personnel: John Brennan, Pres./Ed.; Alice F. Brennan, VP/Assoc. Ed.

37844 Broadcast News Ltd.
36 King St. E   Phone: (416)364-3172
Toronto, ON, Canada M5C 2L9   Fax: (416)364-8896
E-mail: info@broadcastnews.ca

Distributes news to television and radio broadcasters. **Key Personnel:** Eric Morrison, President, phone (416)507-2135, fax (416)507-2070, emorrison@cp.org; David Ross, CFO, phone (416)507-2101, fax (416)507-2071, dross@cp.org; Wayne Waldroff, VP Broadcasting, phone (416)5072123, wwaldroff@cp.org; Michelle Poulin, Business Mgr., phone (416)507-2125, mpoulin@cp.org; Mike Omelus, General News Dir., phone (416)507-2175, momelus@cp.org; Terry Scott, Exec. Client Liaison, phone (416)507-2126, tscott@cp.org; Rina Steuerman, Satellite Serv. Mgr., phone (416)507-2127, rsteuerman@cp.org. **URL:** http://www.cp.org.

37845 Buddy Basch Feature Syndicate
720 West End Ave., No. 1216   Phone: (212)666-2300
New York, NY 10025-6299

37846 Business Features Syndicate
PO Box A   Phone: (603)922-8338
North Stratford, NH 03590   Fax: (603)922-8339
E-mail: bfs@writers-editors.com

Distributes business management, how-to, sales, marketing, home-business, and retailing features. **Key Personnel:** Dana K. Cassell, Editor. **URL:** http://www.writers-editors.com.

37847 Business Wire
44 Montgomery St.   Phone: (415)986-4422
39th Fl.   Fax: (415)788-5335
San Francisco, CA 94104   Free: (800)227-0845

Distributes press releases. **Key Personnel:** Lorry I. Lokey, Chm./CEO; Cathy Baron Tamraz, Pres./C.O.O., phone (212)252-9600, fax (212)752-9698; Pat Evans, VP Ops.; Michael Lissauer, Sr. VP Mktg. & Creative Svcs., phone (212)252-9600, fax (212)252-9698. **URL:** http://www.businesswire.com.

37848 California Features International Inc.
PO Box 58   Phone: (310)441-0565
Beverly Hills, CA 90213   Fax: (310)441-4544

Distributes celebrity, lifestyle, and travel features. **Key Personnel:** Brad Eltermann, P; Stan Findellem, Vice President.

37849 California News Service
121 N. Gate Hall   Phone: (510)642-9054
Berkeley, CA 94720   Fax: (510)643-9136

Distributes political features. **Key Personnel:** Susan Rasky, Editor.

37850 Canada Wide Feature Service Limited
Box 345   Phone: (416)947-2191
Sta. A   Fax: (416)947-2450
Toronto, ON, Canada M5W 1C2

Distributes comic strips, crosswords, and news features. **Key Personnel:** Richard Vroom, Sales Rep./Miller Feat. Syn.; Wanda Goodwin, Photo Sales; Glenn Garnett, Editor; Joe Marino, General Mgr.; Kevin Taite, Project Coord.

37851 The Canadian Press & Broadcast News
36 King St. E   Phone: (416)364-0321
Toronto, ON, Canada M5C 2L9   Fax: (416)364-0207
E-mail: cp@canpress.ca

Key Personnel: Donald Jarrett, VP Fin. & Admin.; Jim Poling, VP Editorial/Acting GM; Wayne Waldroff, VP Broadcasting; Denis Tremblay, VP French Svcs.; M. Sifton, Chm.; W. Waldroff, VP Broadcasting/GM Broadcast News. **URL:** http://www.xe.net/canpress.

37852 Cannery Row Creations
69 Pasa Hondo   Phone: (408)659-1845
Carmel Valley, CA 93924   Fax: (408)659-1399

Distributes humor column. **Key Personnel:** Yavor Bachev, Self-Syndicator/Owner.

37853 Capital Connections
1698 32nd St. NW   Phone: (202)337-2044
Washington, DC 20007   Fax: (202)338-4750
E-mail: news@karenfeld.com

Distributes political and celebrity columns for print and broadcast. **Owner:** Karen Feld, at above address. **Key Personnel:** Karen Feld, Contact. **URL:** http://www.karenfeld.com.

37854 Capitol News Service
530 Bercut Dr., Ste. E   Phone: (916)445-6336
Sacramento, CA 95814   Fax: (916)443-5871
E-mail: webmaster@capitolnews.com

Distributes information related to state legislature, senior citizen issues, and other features in California. **Key Personnel:** David Kline, Contact, phone (916)445-6331, dave@capitolnews.com. **URL:** http://www.mnc.net/capitol.htm.

37855 Cartoonews, Inc.
375 Park Ave., Ste. 1301
New York, NY 10152
E-mail: cartoonews@aol.com

Lurie's Newscartoons and Lurie's World Leaders in color and black and white. **Key Personnel:** T. R. Fletcher, President, phone (212)980-0855; R. R. Lurie, CEO/Editor, phone (212)980-0311; Carol Schachter, Administration Director, phone (212)980-0248. **Additional Contact Info:** Regional Office(s): Trump Tower, 721 5th Ave., Apts. 53-H, 59-H, 60-H, New York, NY 10022-2523.

37856 Cartoonists & Writers Syndicate
67 Riverside Dr.   Phone: (212)362-9256
Ste. 1-D   Fax: (212)595-4218
New York, NY 10024
E-mail: cws@cartoonweb.com; http://www.cartoonweb.com

Distributes political and humor cartoons. **Key Personnel:** Jerry Robinson, Pres./Edit. Dir.; Bojan Jovanovic, Assoc. Ed.

37857 The Caruba Organization
9 Brookside Rd.   Phone: (201)763-6392
Maplewood, NJ 07040-0040
E-mail: acaruba@aol.com

Distributes the National Anxiety Center, bookviews.com, and other features like "Warning Signs.". **Key Personnel:** Alan Caruba, President, acaruba@aol.com. **URL:** http://www.anxietycenter.com; http://www.bookviews.com.

37858 Catholic News Service
3211 4th St. NE   Phone: (202)541-3250
Washington, DC 20017-1100   Fax: (202)541-3255
E-mail: cns@catholicnews.com

Distributes general news concerning Catholics. **Key Personnel:** Thomas N. Lorsung, Dir./Ed.-in-Chief; James M. Lackey, Gen. News Ed.; David Gibson, Features Ed.; Julie L. Asher, Natl. Ed. **URL:** http://www.catholicnews.com; http://www.originsonline.com.

37859 Century News Service
929 W. Broad St.   Phone: (703)532-3267
Ste. 200   Fax: (703)532-3396
Falls Church, VA 22046

Distributes Eye on Washington.

37860 Changing Times-The Kiplinger Washington Editors Inc.
1729 H St. NW   Phone: (202)887-6400
Washington, DC 20006

Distributes Kiplinger Finance Magazine, Washington Letter, Tax Letter, Agriculture Letter, Florida Letter, and California Letter.

37861 Charlene Lichtenstein
PO Box 1726   Phone: (212)243-5462
Old Chelsea Sta.
New York, NY 10011
E-mail: lichtenstein@accessnewage.com; astroweek@aol.com

Humorous and entertaining weekly and monthly horoscopes syndicated worldwide. **URL:** http://www.accessnewage.com; http://www.thestarryeye.com.

37862 Chesstours
PO Box 1182   Phone: (702)786-3178
Reno, NV 89504
E-mail: chesstours@cs.com

Key Personnel: Larry Evans, Author/Owner.

37863 Chicago-Sun Times Features Inc.
401 N. Wabash Ave.   Phone: (312)321-2890
Ste. 532-A   Fax: (312)321-2336
Chicago, IL 60611
E-mail: elschiele@aol.com

Key Personnel: Elizabeth Owens-Schiele, Syndicate Mgr. **URL:** http://www.suntimes.com.

37864 Chronicle Features
901 Mission St.   Phone: (415)777-7250
San Francisco, CA 94103   Fax: (415)362-0279
E-mail: cfeatures@aol.com

Distributes cartoons, columns, and news articles. **Key Personnel:** Stuart Dodds, Ed./Gen. Mgr.; Rennie Kirby, Office Mgr.; Susan Peters, Assoc. Ed.; Harley Colbert, Prod. Mgr.; Sue Fenstermaker, Ed. Prod. Mgr.; Hilda Bloom, Perm. Ed.

37865 Cineman Syndicate, LLC
16 School St. 105
Rye, NY 10580-2952
E-mail: cineman@frontiernet.net

Distributes book, movie, and music reviews; horoscopes; trivia quiz. **Key Personnel:** Jay A. Brown, Publisher; John P. McCarthy, Editor; Robert Edelstein, Assoc. Ed. **URL:** http://www.frontiernet.net/~cineman.

37866 City News Service Inc.
1900 Avenue of the Stars   Phone: (310)201-9120
Ste. 1870   Fax: (310)201-9124
Los Angeles, CA 90067

Distributes news wire service. **Key Personnel:** Vicki Psomas, Business Mgr.; Douglas Faigin, President; Yet Lock, Vice President; Pat Teague, Editor.

37867 Commodity Quotations Inc.
600 Merinock Ave.   Phone: (914)381-7000
Harrison, NY 10528

Distributes real time financial information. **Key Personnel:** Grace Gassney, President; Russ Schiff, Vice President.

37868 Communications International/National News
1423 N. Orange Grove Ave.   Phone: (323)876-1668
PO Box 46-181   Fax: (323)876-1404
Los Angeles, CA 90046

Distributes Bonnie Churchill Reporting Leisure Time and Youth Parade, Kitchen Celebrities, and Travel Time. **Key Personnel:** Bonnie Churchill, Lead Columnist, bchurchill@earthlink.net; Stuart Allengham, Editor; Hillary Bekins, President. **URL:** http://www.bchurchill.com.

37869 Community Press Service
117 W. 2nd St.   Phone: (502)223-1736
PO Box 717   Fax: (502)223-0232
Frankfort, KY 40602

Distributes horoscopes, editorials, cartoons, and crosswords. **Key Personnel:** Judy Penn, Editor; Phyllis Corneth, Editor.

37870 ComputerUser
220 S. 6th St.   Phone: (612)339-7571
Ste. 500
Minneapolis, MN 55402-4507
E-mail: cueditor@usinternet.com

Key Personnel: Steve Deyo, Editor; Rachel Hanlein, Managing Editor.

37871 Congressional Quarterly Inc.
1414 22nd St. NW   Phone: (202)887-8500
Washington, DC 20037   Fax: (202)728-1863
                                     Free: (800)432-2250
E-mail: customerservice@cq.com

Distributes congressional features. **Owner:** St. Petersburg Times, PO Box 1121, St. Petersburg, FL 33731, Free: (800)333-7505. **Key Personnel:** Robert Merry, Pub./Pres., phone (202)887-8564, rmerry@cq.com; David Rapp, Exec. Ed./Sr. VP, phone (202)887-8535, drapp@cq.com; Rick Rockelli, Assoc. Pub./Sr. VP, phone (202)887-8571, rrockelli@cq.com; Jim Gale, Circulation Sales Dir., phone (202)822-1422, jgale@cq.com. **URL:** http://www.cq.com.

37872 Consider This . . .
PO Box 2534   Phone: (307)527-7017
Cody, WY 82414   Fax: (307)527-6971
E-mail: treetop@wavecom.net

Weekly inspirational column. **Key Personnel:** Mike Johnson, Author, treetop@wavecom.net. **URL:** http://www.mikeleejohnson.com.

37873 Continental Features/Continental News Service
501 W. Broadway   Phone: (858)492-8696
PMB 265
Plaza A
San Diego, CA 92101
E-mail: continentalnewstime@lycos.com

Distributes items of world and national news/analysis. Covers Unreported/Under- Reported News Stories. **Key Personnel:** Gary P. Salamone, Editor-in-Chief.

37874 Copley News Service
123 Camino de la Reina   Phone: (619)293-1818
Ste. E-250   Free: (800)238-6196
PO Box 120190
San Diego, CA 92112
E-mail: infofax@copleynews.com

Distributes feature stories and political cartoons. **Key Personnel:** David C. Copley, President; Patricia E. Gonzalez, VP/Bus. Mgr.; Glenda Winders, Ed. Dir.

37875 Cox Newspapers Inc.
400 N. Capitol St., Ste. 750   Phone: (202)331-0900
Washington, DC 20001   Fax: (202)331-1055

Key Personnel: Andrew Alexander, Bureau Chief; Art Dalgish, News Editor; Rick Christie, Foreign Editor; Susan Burns, Business Mgr.

37876 Creative Comic Syndicate
1608 S. Dakota Ave.   Phone: (605)336-9434
Sioux Falls, SD 57105   Fax: (605)338-3501
                                     Free: (800)423-7158

Comic strips; state coloring books; and cartoon educational books and videos. **Key Personnel:** Ken Alyine, Owner, kenalyine@aol.com. **URL:** http://www.creativecomics.net.

37877 Creators Syndicate
5777 W. Century Blvd.   Phone: (310)337-7003
Ste. 700   Fax: (310)337-7625
Los Angeles, CA 90045
E-mail: cre8ors@aol.com

International distribution of cartoons and editorials including Ann Landers, BC, and Wizard of Id. **Key Personnel:** Richard S. Newcombe, President; Lori Sheehey, Dir. of Operations; Margo Sugrue, Sales Exec. **URL:** http://www.creators.com.

37878 Cricket Communications
PO Box 527   Phone: (610)924-9158
Ardmore, PA 19003   Fax: (610)924-9159
E-mail: 76550.42@compuserve.com; relating@aol.com

Key Personnel: Edwin Marks, Pres./Pub.; Mark E. Battersby, Editor.

37879 Cromley News-Features
1912 Martha's Rd.   Phone: (703)695-5118
Alexandria, VA 22307   Fax: (703)693-7206

Key Personnel: Ray Cromley, President.

37880 Crown Syndicate Inc.
3817 W. Parkmount Pl.   Phone: (206)285-1888
PO Box 99126
Seattle, WA 98199

Key Personnel: L.M. Boyd, President; Patricia Boyd, Vice President.

37881 Cuisine Concepts
1406 Thomas Pl.   Phone: (817)732-4758
Fort Worth, TX 76107   Fax: (817)732-3247
E-mail: reniesteves@msn.com

Distributes tax and finance information. **Key Personnel:**
Renie Steves, Writer, reniesteves@msn.com; Sterling Steves,
Writer; Renie Steves, Contact.

37882 Curt Schleier Reviews
646 Jones Rd.   Phone: (201)391-7135
River Vale, NJ 07675
E-mail: writa@optonline.net

Distributes book and television reviews, author/celebrity interviews, and industry news. **Key Personnel:** Curt Schleier,
President.

37883 Dan's Cartoons & Graphic Humor
PO Box 410   Phone: (906)482-6234
Chassell, MI 49916-0410   Fax: (906)483-6234
E-mail: danscartoons@msn.com

Distributes cartoons. Danscartoons.com provides an online
catalog of cartoons and a porfolio, providing illustraton
services. **Key Personnel:** Dan Rosandich, President. **URL:**
http://www.danscartoons.com.

37884 DANY News Service
22 Lesley Dr.   Phone: (516)921-4611
Syosset, NY 11791

Distributes education, sports, and entertainment features.
Owner: David Nydick. **Key Personnel:** David Nydick, President; Robert Manhemer, Editor.

37885 Didato Associates
106 Antler Ridge   Phone: (914)923-1182
Ossining, NY 10562
E-mail: didato@frogmet.com

Psychological quizzes and behavior behind the news. **Key**
Personnel: S.V. Didato, President, didato@frognet.com; P.
Hathway, Chief Editor.

37886 Dona Z. Meilach Features
2018 Saliente Way   Phone: (760)436-4395
Carlsbad, CA 92009   Fax: (760)436-1402
E-mail: dmeilach@msn.com

Key Personnel: Dona Z. Meilach, President.

37887 Don't Laugh, You're Next
PO Box 32221   Phone: (202)337-1560
Washington, DC 20007   Fax: (202)625-1999

Distributes weekly humor column. **Key Personnel:** Russell
Warren Howe, Author. **Formerly:** Arms & the World.

37888 Dorothy Ahle Caricatures
8 Grimshaw St.   Phone: (781)321-8302
Malden, MA 02148   Fax: (781)321-8302
E-mail: dorothyahle@hotmail.com

Caricatures tri-weekly via mail. **Key Personnel:** Dorothy Ahle,
Artist, dorothyahle@hotmail.com.

37889 Dow Jones Financial News Service
200 Liberty St.   Phone: (212)416-2414
14th Fl.   Free: (800)223-2274
New York, NY 10281

Distributes international financial and corporate business
news. **Key Personnel:** Craig O. Allsopp, Vice President; Bob
Williams, Dir.-Admin.; Robert Prinsky, Managing Editor; Neal
Lipschutz, Deputy Mng. Ed.

37890 Downtown
PO Box 219
Grand Gorge, NY 12434-0219

Key Personnel: James Rosenbrick, Publisher; Mary Hyatt,
Manager.

37891 Dunkel Sports Research Service, News-Journal
Com.
PO Box 2831   Phone: (386)252-1511
Daytona Beach, FL 32120   Fax: (386)252-1515
E-mail: dindex.jduck@att.net

Distributes statistical rating systems for professional, college
and high school football; men and women professional and
college basketball; and professional hockey. **Key Personnel:**
Bob Dunkel, Author/Owner; John Duck, Exec. Producer,
dindex.jduck@att.net. **URL:** http://www.n-jcenter.com.

37892 Editorial Consultant Service
PO Box 524   Phone: (516)481-5487
West Hempstead, NY 11552   Fax: (516)481-5487
E-mail: almgo42033@aol.com

Automotive columns and feature articles. **Key Personnel:**
Arthur A. Ingoglia, Editorial Director; John Riley, Book Editor;
L. Taylor, Feature Editor.

37893 Editor's Copy Syndicate
3803 Pin Oaks St.   Phone: (941)366-2169
Sarasota, FL 34232

Distributes current editorials, features, and newspaper fillers to
newspapers throughout the United States. **Key Personnel:**
Edward H. Sims, Editor and Publisher; Bente Christensen,
Business Mgr.; Frederik Sims, Circulation Mgr.

37894 Empire Information Services
PO Box 742   Phone: (518)372-0785
Schenectady, NY 12301   Fax: (518)372-0787
                                   Free: (800)552-2194
E-mail: info@eisinc.com

Wire service. Also operates a press release delivery service,
web design and web hosting. **Key Personnel:** Peter G. Pollak,
CEO. **URL:** http://www.eisinc.com; http://www.eisnx.com;
http://www.findweb.com.

37895 Entertainment News Syndicate
PO Box 276
Murray Hill Station
New York, NY 10156

Distributes gossip, theatre, and travel reviews. **Owner:**
(212)679-9968, Fax: (212)649-9969. **Key Personnel:** Lee
Canaan, Theatre and Travel Ed., lee@entertainmentnewssyn-
dicate; Jed Canaan, Sports Ed.; Barbara Marsten, Fashion/
Beauty Ed.; Joan Young, Hospitality Ed.; Robert Michaels,
Music Film Ed.

37896 Exclusive Press Syndicate
108 E. 66th St.   Phone: (212)988-5190
Ste. 6A   Fax: (212)628-1153
New York, NY 10021

Distributes news features. **Key Personnel:** Dina Dellale,
Managing Editor.

37897 Executive Intelligence Review News Services
PO Box 17390   Phone: (703)777-9451
Washington, DC 20041   Fax: (703)771-9492
                                   Free: (888)347-3258
E-mail: eirns@larouchepub.com

37898 Exhibitor Relations Co.
15760 Venture Blvd.   Phone: (310)657-2005
Ste. 806   Fax: (310)657-7283
Encino, CA 91436-3018
E-mail: boxofficeinfo@aol.com

Key Personnel: Paul Dergarabedian, President; Randy Sanchez, Exec. VP; Allan Staker, VP of Operations. **URL:** http://
www.exhibitoRelations.com.

37899 The Extra Mile
399 Beech St.   Phone: (570)648-4225
Coal Township, PA 17866
E-mail: publisher@newsitem.com

Weekly syndicated automotive feature. **Key Personnel:** Greg
Zyla, Author, phone (570)644-6397, fax (570)648-7581, gzy-
la@ptd.net. **URL:** http://www.newsitem.com/extramile. **Addi-**
tional Contact Info: Regional Office(s): 707 Rock St.,
Shamokin, PA 17872.

37900 Extra Newspaper Features
18 1st Ave. SE   Phone: (507)285-7671
PO Box 6118   Fax: (507)285-7666
Rochester, MN 55903-6118

Key Personnel: Kelly J. Boldan, Ed./Dir.

37901 ExtremeInk.com
4477 Woodman Ave., No. 206   Phone: (818)386-9552
Sherman Oaks, CA 91423
E-mail: info@extremeink.com

Weekly tidbits puzzles and Comedian Argus Hamilton's
Humor Column six times per week. **Key Personnel:** Susan
Shelley, President, sshelley@extremeink.com. **URL:** http://
www.extremeink.com.

37902 Fairchild News Service
7 W. 34th St.   Phone: (212)630-4000
New York, NY 10001

Distributes fashion and lifestyle photographs and articles. **Key**
Personnel: Olivia Thompson, Exec. VP Publishing.

37903 Family Features Editorial Syndicate Inc.
8309 Melrose Dr.   Phone: (913)888-3800
Shawnee Mission, KS 66214   Fax: (913)888-3503
                                   Free: (800)800-5579

Key Personnel: David Hogerty, President, davidh@culi-
nary.net; Linda Wiedmaier, Dir. Media Communications. **URL:**
http://www.culinary.net.

37904 Fashion 'n Figure/World Travel Features
PO Box 1183   Phone: (330)659-6231
Bath, OH 44210-1183

Distributes fashion and travel photographs and press releases
with black and white glossies to illustrate copy. **Key Person-**
nel: Paige Palmer, President, sunbrook@raex.com.

37905 Feature Photo Service Inc.
62 W. 45th St.   Phone: (212)944-1060
New York, NY 10036   Fax: (212)944-7801
E-mail: fpsphoto@aol.com

Distributes business feature photos. **Key Personnel:** Bob
Goldberg, President; O Ren Hellner, Vice President. **URL:**
http://www.featurephoto.com.

37906 Features International of London
90 Riverside Dr., Apt. 15-B   Phone: (212)873-0772
New York, NY 10024-5322
E-mail: itpnyc@aol.com

Distributes news, features, and stories from the UK. **Key**
Personnel: Jeffrey Blyth, U.S. Ed., jblythnyc@aol.com.

37907 Feeley News Bureau
3141 Washington Ave.   Phone: (708)251-7191
Wilmette, IL 60091-2082

Distributes general news. **Key Personnel:** Jim Feeley, Bureau
Chief.

37908 Financial News Syndicate
22115 O'Connell Rd.   Phone: (815)568-8267
Marengo, IL 60152   Fax: (815)568-0487
E-mail: reliance@cin.net

Distributes consumer news and personal finance. **Key Per-**
sonnel: Edward F. Mrkvicka, Editor.

37909 The 5th Wave
16 Rowe Pt.   Phone: (978)546-2448
Rockport, MA 01966   Fax: (978)546-7747

Owner: 16 Rowe Point, Rockport, MA 01966. **Key Person-**
nel: Rich Tennant, Cartoonist, rich@the5thwave.com; Cindy
Johnson, Asst., cindy@the5thwave.com. **URL:** http://
www.the5thwave.com.

37910 FNA News
PO Box 11999   Phone: (801)355-3336
Salt Lake City, UT 84147   Fax: (801)596-8148
E-mail: rng2@utah.edu

Key Personnel: Richard Goldberger, Managing Editor; Fran-
cine Modderno, Wash. Bureau Chief; Pamela Teplick, Society
Ed., phone (801)355-3666; Connie Terry, Health Ed./Bureau
Chief, Los Angeles, fax (310)625-9780; L. Long, Legal Affs.
Ed., phone (801)322-4666; Marlon U. Stones, Tech Ed.; K.
Rossi, Energy Ed./Acting Bureau Chief, Houston; Kenneth
Lozier, Photo Bureau Chief, phone (801)205-7697. **Formerly:**
FNS Agency.

37911 Food Nutrition Health News Service
1712 Taylor St. NW   Phone: (202)723-2477
Washington, DC 20011   Fax: (202)882-9335
E-mail: goody@cpcmg.org

Distributes features and special reports. **Key Personnel:**
Goody L. Solomon, Author/Owner/Exec. Ed., goody@
cpcuq.org; German Munoz, Assoc. Ed. **URL:** http://
www.fnhnews.com.

37912 Fotopress Independent News Service
International (FPINS)
27 St. Clair E.   Phone: (705)652-8476
Box 1268, Sta. Q   Fax: (705)652-3559
Toronto, ON, Canada M4T 2P4
E-mail: operations@fotopressnews.com

Key Personnel: John M. Kubik, Ops. Dir., kubikjm@foto-
pressnews.com; Steven Brown, Accts. Admin.; Robert
O'Connor, United Kingdom Photographer; Wes Jonasson,

Europe Photographer; Y. Kenditos, Middle East Photographer; David Tam-Baryohi, Africa Photographer; Mulenga Chola, Africa Photographer; Obafimi Oredein, Africa Photographer; Pin Chek Chong, Indochina Photographer; Nohiro Kimura, Japan Photographer; Vincent Delgado, Central America Photographer; Edward Walker, North America Photographer; Frank King, North America Photographer; Eloy Yaltiera, North America Photographer; Peter Kozak, Australia Photographer. **URL:** http://www.fotopressnews.com.

37913 Four Geez Press
1911 Douglas Blvd.　　Phone: (916)781-3440
Ste. 85　　Fax: (916)781-6837
Roseville, CA 95661
E-mail: ggolomb@ns.net

Distributes health and lifestyle column.

37914 From the Ground Up
4621 Congress Dr.　　Phone: (517)631-2333
Midland, MI 48642
E-mail: echutchi@aol.com

Distributes weekly and seasonal lawn and garden features. **Key Personnel:** Edward Hutchison, Author/Owner.

37915 Future Features Syndicate
1923 N. Wickham Rd.　　Phone: (407)259-3822
Ste. 117　　Fax: (407)259-1471
Melbourne, FL 32935
E-mail: futrfeat@iu.net

Distributes cartoon panels and strips, editorial cartoon services, caricatures, illustrations, and cartoon graphics. **Key Personnel:** Ada Lewis Forney, President; Jerome L. Forney, Creative Dir. **URL:** http://www.spindata.com/futrfeat.

37916 Gambill Arts & Graphix Syndicate
12561 Palm Dr.　　Phone: (760)251-2401
Desert Hot Springs, CA 92240　　Fax: (760)251-2401
E-mail: gagstoons@aol.com; valleybreeze@aol.com

Distributes cartoon panels and The Valley Breeze monthly newspaper. **Key Personnel:** George Gambill, Creator/Owner/Artist, gagstoons@aol.com; Suzanne Gambill, Feature Ed., valleybreezesuze@aol.com. **URL:** http://arts.gs/buzzgambill.

37917 Gannett News Service
1000 Wilson Blvd.　　Phone: (703)276-5800
10th Fl.　　Fax: (703)558-3813
Arlington, VA 22229-0001

Distributes news wire service. **Key Personnel:** Robert W. Ritter, Editor; J. Ford Huffman, Man. Ed. Features, Graphics, & Photograp; Jefferey Stinson, Reg. Ed.; Ron Cohen, Natl. Ed.; Judi Austin, Reg. Ed./West; Phil Pruitt, Reg. Ed./East; Jerry Langdon, Mng. Ed./Sports; Emilie Davis, Copy Desk Chief; Craig Schwed, Bus. Ed.

37918 The Gelman Feature Syndicate
PO Box 399　　Phone: (607)498-4700
Roscoe, NY 12776

Off the Beaten Track column. **Key Personnel:** Bernard Gelman, Owner & Editor.

37919 Gemini News Service
90 Riverside Dr., Apt. 15-B　　Phone: (212)873-0772
New York, NY 10024-5322
E-mail: itpnyc@aol.com

Distributes news and features for the United Kingdom. **Key Personnel:** J. Blyth, Contact.

37920 German Press Agency
405 E. 42nd St.　　Phone: (212)355-0318
United Nations Rm. S-352　　Fax: (212)753-6168
New York, NY 10017

Key Personnel: Helmut Raether, Chief Corr.

37921 Gil Christ Features
448 Main St.　　Phone: (860)738-4026
Winsted, CT 06098　　Fax: (860)738-1380

Column titled Night Lights & Pillow Fights. **Key Personnel:** Jedd Gould, President, jgvoice@aol.com; Kedi D'Ouefrio, Syndication Mgr.

37922 Glasserfide Directory
10240 Camarillo St., Ste. 210　　Phone: (818)769-4774
Toluca Lake, CA 91602

Nonfiction articles, light verse, contests, sweepstakes, humor, puns, parodies and the columns Rime Time and Star Stanzas (horoscope). **Key Personnel:** Selma Glasser, Editor and Publisher. **Also known as:** Glasser Guide to Writing (Humor/Fillers/Contests).

37923 Global Features Syndicate
6326 Matte　　Phone: (514)322-4578
North Montreal, QC, Canada
H1G 2E8

Key Personnel: Nick Trezza, President.

37924 Global Horizons
1330 New Hampshire Ave. NW　　Phone: (202)966-8636
Ste. 609　　Fax: (202)244-1242
Washington, DC 20036

Distributes environmental column. **Key Personnel:** Edward Flattau, President; Pamela Ebert, Manager.

37925 Globe Photos Inc.
275 7th Ave.　　Phone: (212)645-9292
New York, NY 10001　　Fax: (212)627-8932
E-mail: info@globephoto.com

Distributes celebrity/personality photos, light news, general stock. **Key Personnel:** Mary Beth Whelan, President; Raymond D. Whelan, Vice President; Dick Denuet, Bureau Chief; Raymond F. Whelan, Assignment Ed. **URL:** http://www.globephotos.com. **Additional Contact Info:** Regional Office(s): 292 S. LaCierega Blvd., Beverly Hills, CA 90211, (310)657-5457, fax: (310)657-5491.

37926 Globe Syndicate
499 Richardson Rd.　　Phone: (540)635-3229
Strasburg, VA 22657-5236　　Fax: (703)519-8275
E-mail: editor@globessyndicate.com

Distributes editorial commentary columns. **Key Personnel:** Monte Bourjaily, Jr., Editor and Publisher, bourjjr@adelphia.net; Monte Bourjaily III, Ed./Assoc. Pub., bourjaily@home.com. **URL:** http://www.globessyndicate.com. **Additional Contact Info:** Regional Office(s): 218 S. Fairfax St., Alexandria, VA 22314, (703)549-2322, fax: (703)519-8275.

37927 Golf Publishing Syndicate
2743 Saxon St.　　Phone: (610)437-4982
Allentown, PA 18103　　Fax: (610)437-4982

Distributes columns concerning golf, trends, equipment, etiquette, instruction, and analysis. **Key Personnel:** Karl Gilbert, President.

37928 Graham News Syndicate
2770 W. 5th St.　　Phone: (718)372-1920
Ste. G-20
Brooklyn, NY 11224

Distributes columns on food, restaurants, travel, lifestyles, fashion, and consumer products. **Key Personnel:** Paula Royce Graham, Pres./Ed.; Lane W. Hall, Corr.; Liz Clifton, Corr.

37929 Green Grass Syndicated Features
2972 115th St.　　Phone: (419)726-1027
Toledo, OH 43611-2838

Animal articles, including Living with Horses and Living with Pets. **Key Personnel:** Marcia King, Owner. **URL:** http://www.geocities.com/greengrasssyndicated/.

37930 The Green Thumb
PO Box 579　　Phone: (585)374-5400
Naples, NY 14512

Distributes gardening questions and answers. **Key Personnel:** George Abraham, Editor; Katherine Abraham, Asst. Ed.

37931 Griffith News Feature Service Worldwide
PO Box 7294
Albany, NY 12224-0294

Distribute features stories, with or without pictures. By contract. **Key Personnel:** Bill Griffith, Reporter.

37932 Groene & Groene
206 Lake Mamie Rd.　　Phone: (386)736-0313
DeLand, FL 32724
E-mail: jgroene2@earthlink.net

Distributes columns on travel, food, automotive, and outdoors. **Key Personnel:** Janet Groene, Writer; Janet Groene, Owner. **URL:** http://www.gordonandjanetgroene.com.

37933 Gulbranson Communications Group
5317 Spy Glass Dr.　　Phone: (804)366-5224
Norfolk, VA 23518　　Fax: (804)366-0661
E-mail: karen5@ix.netcom.com

Distributes humor/lifestyle column. **Key Personnel:** Karen Gulbranson, Principal.

37934 Harmon Football Forecast
PO Box 994　　Phone: (516)432-6376
Long Beach, NY 11561

Distributes weekly college and NFL forecasts. **Key Personnel:** James M. Harmon, Editor and Publisher.

37935 Have Fun at the Movies
10717 Bushire Dr.　　Phone: (214)902-0942
Dallas, TX 75229　　Fax: (214)363-9598
　　Free: (888)229-9831
E-mail: nreagan@aol.com

Distributes film and video recommendations. **Key Personnel:** Gail Reagan, Columnist, nreagan@aol.com; Sophie Redditt, Ed./Computer Layout, phone (214)350-3063, redditt777@aol.com.

37936 Headbone Interactive
4509 Interlake Ave. N 333　　Phone: (206)378-1259
Seattle, WA 98103-6782　　Fax: (206)378-0188
E-mail: info@headbone.com

Weekly kid activity pages and an online children's website. **URL:** http://www.headbone.com.

37937 Health and Fitness News Service
Times Mirror Sq.　　Phone: (213)237-7987
Los Angeles, CA 90053

Distributes health and fitness news and features. **Key Personnel:** Karin Hsiao, Editor.

37938 Health Promotion Features
PO Box 21529
Carson City, NV 89721-1529

Key Personnel: John Yacenda, Ed./Dir., jyacenda@intercomm.com. **Formerly:** Health Promotion Features & Training Consultants.

37939 Hearst News Service
1701 Pennsylvania Ave. NW　　Phone: (202)298-6920
Washington, DC 20006　　Fax: (202)333-1184

Distributes news columns. **Key Personnel:** Charles Lewis, Wash. Bureau Chief; Kristen Collie, Office Mgr.

37940 HFM Medical Publications
3283 Casorso Rd.　　Phone: (250)868-8603
Ste. 104　　Fax: (250)868-8601
Kelowna, BC, Canada V1W 3L6
E-mail: dr.frank@cyberstore.com

Key Personnel: Dr. Frank MacInnis, Author. **URL:** http://www.drfrank.com.

37941 Hispanic Link News Service
1420 N St. NW　　Phone: (202)234-0280
Ste. 101　　Fax: (202)234-4090
Washington, DC 20005
E-mail: CarlosE@HispanicLink.org

Distributes Hispanic news. **Key Personnel:** Arlene Martinez, Editor, arlene@hispaniclink.org; Charles Ericksen, Publisher, charlie@hispaniclink.org. **URL:** http://www.HispanicLink.org.

37942 Hollywood Inside Syndicate
PO Box 49957　　Phone: (818)509-7840
Los Angeles, CA 90049-0957　　Fax: (818)754-0751
E-mail: holywood@ez2.net

Distributes Books of the Week, Celebri-Quotes, and Hollywood Inside weekly columns. **Key Personnel:** John Austin, Editor-in-Chief. **URL:** http://www.ez2.net/hollywood.

37943 Hollywood News Calendar
15030 Ventura Blvd.　　Phone: (818)990-5945
Ste. 742　　Fax: (818)789-8047
Sherman Oaks, CA 91403
E-mail: editor@newscalendar.com

Distributes entertainment news and features. **Key Personnel:** Carolyn Fox, Editor-in-Chief; Susan Fox-Davis, Editor. **URL:** http://www.newscalendar.com.

37944 Home Focus
2140 Sul Ross　　Phone: (713)630-0049
Houston, TX 77098

Distributes interior design and decoration column. **Key Personnel:** Gay Elliott McFarland, Author; Blair Pittman, Photographer.

37945 Home Improvement Time
7425 Steubenville Pike　　Phone: (412)787-2881
PO Box 247　　Fax: (412)787-3233
Oakdale, PA 15071
E-mail: hitdirect@aol.com

Distributes non-copyrighted home and property improvement editorial publicity to daily and weekly newspapers. **Key Personnel:** James A. Stewart, Jr., President; Carole C. Stewart, Vice President. **URL:** http://www.homeimprovementtime.com.

37946 HomeStyles Publishing and Marketing Inc.
213 E. 4th St.   Phone: (651)602-5000
St. Paul, MN 55101   Fax: (651)602-5001
                                  Free: (888)626-2026

Distributes blueprints for houses. **Key Personnel:** Roger Heegaard, Publisher; Jeff Heegaard, President; Craig Bryan, Mktg. Dir. **URL:** http://www.homestyles.com.

37947 Hopkins Syndicate Inc.
802 S. Washington   Phone: (812)331-7753
Bloomington, IN 47401

Distributes educational material, children's books, and psychology books. **Key Personnel:** S.L. Abram, Ed./Gen. Mgr.

37948 Hulton/Archive by Getty Images
75 Varick St., Fl. 5   Phone: (800)876-5115
New York, NY 10013-1917   Fax: (646)613-4191
E-mail: valerie.zars@gettyimages.com

Licenses historical stock footage and stock photos. **URL:** http://www.gettyimages.com; http://www.hultonarchive.com. **Formerly:** Archive Films/Archive Photos.

37949 In a Nutshell
119 Washington Ave.   Phone: (718)698-6979
Staten Island, NY 10314   Fax: (718)698-3535
E-mail: nutshell@h2net.net

Distributes humor column. **Key Personnel:** Barbara Naness, Author/Owner. **URL:** http://www.h2net.net/p/nutshell.

37950 Independence Feature Syndicate
14142 Denver W. Pkwy.   Phone: (303)279-6536
Ste. 185   Fax: (303)279-4176
Golden, CO 80401-3134
E-mail: ron@i2i.org

Distributes opinion columns. **Key Personnel:** David Kopel, Editor, david@i2i.org. **URL:** http://www.independenceinstitute.org.

37951 Inter Press Service Distributed by Global Information Network
1293 National Press Bldg.   Phone: (202)662-7160
Washington, DC 20045   Fax: (202)662-7164

Distributes Third World news wire service. **Key Personnel:** Yvette Collymore, Bureau Chief.

37952 Interior Design Teacher
74 Chestnut St.   Phone: (732)370-1441
Lakewood, NJ 08701   Fax: (732)370-1441

Manuscript on interior design including an illustration. **Key Personnel:** Michael A. Guarini Asid, Author, guariniasid@msn.com.

37953 International Business Information Services
PO Box 4082   Phone: (714)552-8494
Irvine, CA 92616

Distributes business, international business, and entrepreneurial columns. **Key Personnel:** Andrew Raymond, Mktg. and Service Mgr.

37954 International BusinessMan News Bureau
535 5th Ave.   Phone: (212)476-0802
33rd Fl.   Fax: (212)663-1663
PO Box 5595
New York, NY 10185
E-mail: 3418747@mcimail.com

Distributes media consultation information. **Key Personnel:** J.J. Edwards, Chairman/CEO/Ed.-in-Chief; Ellen M. Vahidi, President; E.J. Edwards, VP/Bureau Chief; C.P. Hennessy, VP/Food Ed. Test Kitchen.

37955 International Entertainment and Travel News
2902 29th Way   Phone: (561)582-6038
West Palm Beach, FL 33407   Fax: (561)585-5434

Distributes celebrity interviews, entertainment column, movie reviews, singles' column, fashion and travel. **Key Personnel:** Elliott S. Kravetz, Bureau Chief; Jay N. Kravetz, Editor, jkravetz1@earthlink.net. **Formerly:** International Photo News (Sept. 11, 1901).

37956 International Features Inc.
184 Kanan Dume Rd.   Phone: (818)889-6988
Malibu, CA 90265

Distributes news features. **Key Personnel:** Colin Dangaard, President; Linda Fox, Vice President; Rod Barrand, Editor.

37957 International News Agency
2445 Pine Tree Dr., Ste. 20   Phone: (305)674-9746
Miami Beach, FL 33140-4611   Fax: (305)674-1939

Distributes features on conventions, conferences, trade shows, expositions, sporting events, cruise ships, hotels, restaurants, and attractions in the southeast U.S. and the Caribbean islands. **Owner:** Charles Reader. **Key Personnel:** C.H. Garvey, Bureau Chief; R.J. Sherker, Exec.Ed.; T.M. Mosburg, Asst. Ed.; Larry Lowis, Managing Editor; Donna Shaw, Arts Dept.; Ed Dever, Bus. Dept.; Ed Hayden, Charity Dept.; Roz Sholin, Food; Pat Simpson, Sports; Judy Putnam, Travel.

37958 Interpress of London and New York
90 Riverside Dr., Apt. 15-B   Phone: (212)873-0772
New York, NY 10024-5322
E-mail: itpnyc@aol.com

Distributes news features to UK and European publications. **Key Personnel:** Jeffrey Blyth, Editor-in-Chief.

37959 Interpress Service
1293 National Press Bldg.   Phone: (202)662-7160
Washington, DC 20045   Fax: (202)662-7164

Distributes Third World economic activity, news, features. **Key Personnel:** James Lobe, Bureau Chief.

37960 Interstate News Service
237 S. Clark Ave.   Phone: (314)522-1300
St. Louis, MO 63135   Fax: (314)522-1999
                                 Free: (800)522-1301

Distributes general travel and state capital news. **Key Personnel:** Michael J. Olds, Pres./Mng. Ed.; James J. Olds, Vice President; Ellen M. Olds, Sec./Treas.; Diane Ross, Asst. Mng. Ed.

37961 ITAR-TASS News Agency
50 Rockefeller Plaza   Phone: (212)245-4250
Ste. 501   Fax: (212)245-4258
New York, NY 10020
E-mail: itar@aol.com

Distributes general news. **Key Personnel:** Alex Berezhkov, Bureau Chief. **Formerly:** Tass News Agency.

37962 J Features
PO Box 70   Phone: (781)383-9858
Cohasset, MA 02025-0070
E-mail: jfeatures@aol.com

Distributes personal finance and investment features. **Key Personnel:** Charles A. Jaffe, Columnist; Susan Biddle Jaffe, Syn. Mgr.

37963 Jack Posner Syndicate
216 Ellesmere E.   Phone: (954)427-8068
Deerfield Beach, FL 33442

37964 James Raia
706 56th St., Ste. 150   Phone: (916)451-8452
Sacramento, CA 95819   Fax: (916)452-3255
E-mail: raiaruns@aol.com

Distributes running health and fitness and cycling column. **Key Personnel:** James Raia, Self-Syndicator, raiaruns@aol.com. **URL:** http://www.byjamesraia.com.

37965 Jan & Bill Moeller
4912 Hickory St.   Phone: (402)250-2809
Omaha, NE 68106

Authors of travel, historical, and RVing columns. **Key Personnel:** Jan Moeller, Author; Bill Moeller, Author.

37966 Jandon Features
53961 222nd St.   Phone: (712)527-9517
Glenwood, IA 51534   Fax: (712)527-5063

Distributes garden columns and features to newspaper and magazines. **Key Personnel:** Don Riggenbach, Manager.

37967 The Jerusalem Post Foreign Service
270 Lafayette St., Ste. 505   Phone: (212)226-0955
New York, NY 10012
E-mail: jpedt@jpost.co.il

Key Personnel: Marilyn Henry, NY Corr.; Nina Keren-David,

Electronic Publishing; Hillel Kuttler, Wash. Corr. **URL:** http://www.jpost.co.il.

37968 Jewish Telegraphic Agency Inc.
330 7th Ave.   Phone: (212)643-1890
11th Fl.   Fax: (212)643-8498
New York, NY 10001-5010
E-mail: jtany@aol.com; info@jta.org

Distributes Jewish news articles. **Key Personnel:** Mark Joffe, Exec. Ed./Pub., fax (212)643-8499; Norman Lipoff, President, fax (212)643-8499; Lisa Hostein, Editor; Michael Arnold, Managing Editor; Caryn Rosen Adelman, Chairperson, fax (212)643-8499. **URL:** http://www.jta.org.

37969 Jiji Press America Ltd.
120 W. 45th St.   Phone: (212)575-5830
Ste. 1401   Fax: (212)764-3950
New York, NY 10036
E-mail: edit@jijiusa.com

Key Personnel: Katsuhiko Kabasawa, President; Manabu Seki, Managing Editor.

37970 Joseph Peter Simini
PO Box 31420   Phone: (415)282-1950
San Francisco, CA 94131-0420

Distributes column on business and personal finance. **Key Personnel:** Joseph Peter Simini, Self-Syndicator.

37971 Journal Press Syndicate
PO Box 931   Phone: (212)580-8559
Grand Central Sta.   Fax: (212)769-4384
New York, NY 10163-0931
E-mail: ijbnyc@aol.com

Distributes columns, comic strips, and news features. **Owner:** Irwin J. Breslauer, at above address. **Key Personnel:** Irwin J. Breslauer, Editor, ijbnyc@aol.com; John Lynker, Managing Editor; William Kresse, Art Dir.; Eugene R. Smith, Asst. Ed. **Additional Contact Info: Regional Office(s):** 545 West End Ave., New York, NY 10024.

37972 Just for Men/Male Call/Dress for Excellence
721 Shore Acres Dr.   Phone: (914)698-0721
Mamaroneck, NY 10543

Distributes men's clothing column. **Key Personnel:** Lois Fenton, Editor, lois.fenton@oceanfree.net.

37973 Karen M. Engberg M.D.
2329 Oak Park Ln.   Phone: (805)682-8844
Santa Barbara, CA 93105   Fax: (805)682-6499
E-mail: KEngbergMD@aol.com

Key Personnel: Karen M. Engberg, Bureau Chief.

37974 Keister-Williams Newspaper Services, Inc.
Special Advertising Sales, Inc. Phone: (434)293-4709
  (SASI)   Fax: (434)293-4884
PO Box 8005   Free: (800)293-4709
Charlottesville, VA 22906-8005
E-mail: kw@kwnews.com

Distributes religious and "kids page" features. **Key Personnel:** Meta L. Nay, Mktg. Dir., meta@kwnews.com; Walton C. (Ky) Lindsay, President, ky@kwnews.com; Billie P. Hogan, Business Mgr. **URL:** http://www.kwnews.com. **Also known as:** Special Advertising Sales, Inc. (SASI).

37975 Keystone Press Agency Inc.
202 E. 42nd St.   Phone: (212)924-8123
4th Fl.   Fax: (212)924-8123
New York, NY 10017
E-mail: balpert@worldnet.att.com

Key Personnel: Brian F. Alpert, Managing Editor.

37976 King Features Syndicate Inc.
888 7th Ave. Ph. 2   Free: (800)526-5464
New York, NY 10106-0003

Distributes automotive, business, and personal finance commentary; entertainment, graphic services, humor, lifestyle, advice. mental and physical fitness, and sports columns; comics, games, and puzzles. **Key Personnel:** Joseph F. D'Angelo, President; Lawrence T. Olsen, Exec. VP & Gen. Mgr.; Ted Hannah, Dir. Adv. & PR; Jay Kennedy, Comics Ed.; Paul G. Eberhart, Dir. Ops.; Maria Carmicino, Managing Editor; George Haeberlein, Dir. Sales; Mary Anne Miller, Intl. Sales Mgr.; John Killian, Asst. Sales Mgr./Midwest Sales; Dick Lafave, Southwest Sales; John Perry, Southeast Sales; Richard Heimlich, Southwest Sales; Dennis Danko, Telemarketing Sales Mgr.; Chris Monahan, Telemarketing Sales Rep.; James F. Nolan, Color Comics Mgr.; Jack Walsh, Dir. Print Sales; Richard Wilson, Weekly Serv. Natl. Sales Dir.; Diane Eckert, Weekly Serv. Mng. Ed.; Bradley Elson, Weekly Serv Sales Mgr.; Charlotte Bruckner, Admin. Asst.; Ita Golzman, Sr.

Dir.-Domestic Lic.; Irene Ackerman, Domestic Lic. Mgr.; Cathleen Titus, Dir. Intl.Lic.; Pete Gibilaro, Mgr. Prod. & Ship.; Venetta Smith, Mgr. Wire Servs.

37977 King & Kango
PO Box 7914
Vallejo, CA 94590
Phone: (707)550-3374
Fax: (707)554-9079
E-mail: tucky@2xtreme.net

URL: http://www.2xtreme.net/tucky.

37978 Knight-Ridder/Tribune Information Services
790 National Press Bldg.
Washington, DC 20045
Phone: (202)383-6095
Fax: (202)393-2460
Free: (800)435-7578

Distributes news wire service, photos, and graphics. **Key Personnel:** Mike Duggan, Managing Editor, News Service/KRT Kids, phone (202)383-6081, mduggan@krtinfo.com; Jane Scholz, Editor, phone (202)383-6085, jscholz@krtinfo.com; Harry Walker, Dir. of Photography, phone (202)383-3736, fax (202)628-6797, hwalker@krtinfo.com; Wes Albers, Dir. of Graphics, phone (202)383-6068, fax (202)347-2630, walbers@krtinfo.com; Robert Harris, Dir. of Business News; Lily Chin, Dir. Interactives, fax (202)628-6797, lchin@krtinfo.com; Walter Mahoney, Sales Dir., wmahoney@tribune.com. **URL:** http://www.online.presslink.com. **Additional Contact Info: Regional Office(s):** 435 N. Michigan Ave., Ste. 1500, Chicago, IL 60611, (312)222-4695.

37979 Krebbs Cycle Productions
3940 Hilyard St.
Eugene, OR 97405
Phone: (503)344-3416
Fax: (503)344-3057
E-mail: pysamer@aol.com

Key Personnel: Yuri Samer, Author/Owner.

37980 Kyodo News Serivce
50 Rockerfeller Plaza
Ste. 816
New York, NY 10020
Phone: (212)603-6600
Fax: (212)603-6621
E-mail: kyodony@aol.com

Distributes American news forwarded to Japanese wire service and newspapers. **Key Personnel:** Kunihiko Suzuki, NY Bureau Chief; Akihiro Onoda, Dep Bureau Chief; Masaru Imai, Dept. Bureau Chief; Shitaro Nishiyama, Office Mgr.; Toru Maruyama, Corr.; Hitoshi Kawahara, Coor.; Hiroki Sugita, Corr.; Yasuki Matsumoto, Corr.; Miho Tabuchi, Corr.; Hajime Miyagawa, Corr.; Manabu Matsuse, Corr.; Takaya Uno, Editor. **URL:** http://www.kyodo.co.jp.

37981 Landmark Designs Inc.
33127 Saginaw Rd. E
Cottage Grove, OR 97424
Phone: (541)767-0660
Fax: (541)767-0075
Free: (800)562-1041
E-mail: orders@landmarkdesigns.com

Distributes weekly home design column. **Owner:** W. Scott McAlexander, at above address. **Key Personnel:** W. Scott McAlexander, President, scottm@landmarkdesigns.com. **URL:** http://www.landmarkdesigns.com.

37982 Learning Tree Features
3922 Alsace Pl.
Indianapolis, IN 46224
Phone: (317)898-3728

Key Personnel: Charles Coffey, Editor, coffeyc@iquest.net.

37983 Lester Syndicate
PO Box 1183
Cupertino, CA 95015
Phone: (408)257-9567

Distributes information on food, wine, religion, and politics. **Key Personnel:** Mary Lester, Publisher; William Lester, Exec. Ed.

37984 Letter for Animals
PO Box 7
La Plume, PA 18440
Phone: (570)945-5312
Fax: (570)945-3471

Biweekly column covering animal advocacy issues. **Key Personnel:** Lynn Manheim, Creator, lmanheim@aol.com.

37985 Lighthouse Syndications
PO Box 779
Canyon, TX 79015
Phone: (806)655-7121

Columns on business, health, education, psychology, and lifestyle, including Minding Your Own Business, Midlife Moments, Cop and Attitude, and The Professor on Education. **Key Personnel:** Brad Tooley, President, tooley@canyonnews.com; Billy Smith, Vice President. **URL:** http://www.lighthousenews.com.

37986 Listening Inc.
8716 Pine Ave.
Gary, IN 46403
Phone: (219)938-6962
E-mail: addup@crown.net

Distributes parenting and family features including The Add Attention Deficit Disorder, Family Today, The Second Time Around, and The Divorced Family.

37987 Lona O'Connor
10887 Old Bridgeport Ln.
Boca Raton, FL 33498
Phone: (561)487-5104
E-mail: lona13@aol.com

Distributes workplace advice column. **Key Personnel:** Lona O'Connor, Author.

37988 Los Angeles Features Syndicate
650 Winnetka Mews
Ste. 110
Winnetka, IL 60093
Phone: (847)446-4082
Fax: (847)446-4804
E-mail: LAFS@aol.com

Distributes Hollywood Behind the Scenes, book reviews, film reviews, and celebrity interviews. **Key Personnel:** Alice O'Neill, Managing Editor; A.V. Licht, President.

37989 Los Angeles Times Syndicate
218 S. Spring St.
Los Angeles, CA 90012
Phone: (213)237-5485
Fax: (213)237-3698

Distributes advice, art, authoritative commentary, business, humor, lifestyle, politics, and sports columns, comic strips, puzzles, and news services. **Key Personnel:** Willard Colston, Chm.; Jesse E. Levine, Pres./CEO; Steven Christensen, VP/Gen. Mgr.; Jim Lomenzo, Sales Exec./East & Ohio; Beth Barber, Dir. Acct. Relations & Article Sales; Tom Griffiths, Sales Exec./West & South; Lupe Salazar, Reprints & Perms.; Gary Neeleman, VP/Dir.-Sales-LATSI; Grant Armendariz, Sales Exec./Midwest & South; Cathryn Irvine, Promo. Mgr.

37990 Los Angeles Times Syndicate International
2 Park Ave., Ste. 1802
New York, NY 10016
Phone: (212)447-1450
Fax: (212)447-1454

Distributes international sales of the Los Angeles Times Syndicate material. **Key Personnel:** Jesse E. Levine, Pres./CEO; Gary Neeleman, VP Dir of Sales Utah Office; Beth Barber, Dir. Acct Relations and Article Sales Ne; Charles Curmi, Sales-Europe Middle East Near East & Afr; Maryann Grau, Sales-Europe London Office. **Additional Contact Info: Regional Office(s):** 143 S. Main St., Salt Lake City, UT 84111, (801)363-4934, fax: (801)363-4941.

37991 Los Angeles Times/Washington Post News Service
1150 15th St. NW
Washington, DC 20071
Phone: (202)334-6173
Fax: (202)334-5096
E-mail: latwp@atsnewservice.com

Distributes celebrity, commentary, entertainment, food, gardening, health, hobbies, humor, media, money, news, sports, and travel columns; book reviews, and photographs. **Key Personnel:** Al Leeds, Pres./Ed. Dir.; John W. Payne, VP/Gen. Mgr.; Denise J. Bennett, Managing Editor; Bao N. Dang, Treas.; Kate Carlisle, Mng. Ed. Wash.; Robert S. Cleland, Marketing and Technology Dir. **URL:** http://www.newsservice.com.

37992 Lynch News Service
5805 Wilson Ln.
Bethesda, MD 20817-6204
Phone: (301)229-3123

Distributes news features. **Key Personnel:** David Lynch, Bureau Chief.

37993 Mark-Morgan Inc.
14 E. Washington St.
Newnan, GA 30263
Phone: (770)253-5355

Distributes political cartoons. **Key Personnel:** Robert David Boyd, President; Rosalyn M. Boyd, Sec./Treas.

37994 Market News Service
100 William St.
3rd Fl.
New York, NY 10038-3284
Phone: (212)509-4444
Fax: (212)509-5520

Distributes interational financial market news, including politics. **Key Personnel:** Tony Mace, Managing Editor, tony@atsmarketnews.com; Denis Guino, Wash. Bureau Chief; John Carter, Euro. Ed. **URL:** http://www.marketnews.com.

37995 The MarketPlace Project
566 Fairfield Rd.
East Windsor, NJ 08520
Phone: (609)443-4012
Fax: (609)443-9841
Free: (866)658-6283
E-mail: marketproject@aol.com

Key Personnel: Lawrence H. Zisman, Author; Anabel Kligerman, Author.

37996 Marks & Frederick Associates Inc.
PO Box 267
Kent, CT 06757
Phone: (860)927-3948
Fax: (860)927-3959
E-mail: teetah@aol.com

Distributes general news, international news, and financial information. **Key Personnel:** Ted Marks, President.

37997 Masterfile
175 Bloor St. E.
South Tower
2nd Fl.
Toronto, ON, Canada M4W 3R8
Fax: (416)929-2104
Free: (800)387-9010

Key Personnel: Steve Pigeon, Pres./Gen. Mgr. **URL:** http://www.masterfile.com.

37998 Mature Life Features
PO Box 9720
San Diego, CA 92169
Phone: (858)483-3412

Distributes book reviews, government affairs, health and fitness, lifestyles, personal finance, and travel columns; personality profiles of mature adults. **Key Personnel:** Igor Lobanov, Travel Ed., phone (858)270-9002; Cecil Scaglione, Editor-in-Chief; James Gaffney, Health Editor.

37999 Media General News Service Inc.
1214 National Press Bldg.
Washington, DC 20045
Phone: (202)662-7660

Distributes general news. **Key Personnel:** John Hall, Bureau Chief.

38000 The Media Maven
3793 Plume Fern Ct.
Douglasville, GA 30135-2784
Phone: (770)947-0117

Distributes column on entertainment, movies, and media. **Key Personnel:** Howard Hopwood, Self-Syndicator.

38001 Medical Insurance Claims Inc.
Kinnelon Professional Complex
170 Kinnelon Rd.
Ste. 10
Kinnelon, NJ 07405
Phone: (973)492-2828
Fax: (973)492-9068
E-mail: bdcmic@aol.com

Distributes Understanding Your Health Insurance.

38002 Medill News Service
1325 G St. NW
Ste. 730
Washington, DC 20005-3195
Phone: (202)347-8700
Fax: (202)662-1814

Distributes political/federal government news.

38003 Merrell Enterprises
2610 Garfield St. NW
Washington, DC 20008-4101
Phone: (202)265-1925
Fax: (202)265-8721
E-mail: jessemerrell@aol.com

URL: http://www.merrellenterprises.com.

38004 Metro Publishing Group/Metro Features
PO Box 104
Oradell, NJ 07649-0104
Phone: (201)385-2000
E-mail: metropub@aol.com

Publishes weekly newspaper/special interest publications. **Key Personnel:** Bob Nesoff, Contact, bobmetnews@aol.com. **Formerly:** GSM News Service.

38005 Michaels News
Rte. 5, Box 367
Black River Falls, WI 54615-9160
Phone: (715)284-5638

Distributes columns on the environment, health, safety, folk cures, travel, parenting, general advice, and teaching book reviews, as well as occasional video and magazine reviews. **Key Personnel:** Marion Michaels, Pres./Ed.; E. Spangler, Seniors Editor.

38006 Military Update
PO Box 231111
Centreville, VA 20120-1111
Phone: (703)830-6863
E-mail: milupdate@aol.com

Key Personnel: Tom Philpott, Self-Syndicator.

38007 Milligan Syndicate
981 Long Meadow Ct.
Barrington, IL 60010
Phone: (847)382-1593
Fax: (847)382-1593

Astrology and home decorating columns, including Olga Knows, The Dirt-Cheap Decorator, and Your Home Decorator. **Key Personnel:** Molly Milligan, Editor, mcmilligan@aol.com; Ann Milligan, Editor.

38008 Minority Features Syndicate
PO Box 421   Phone: (724)981-3751
Farrell, PA 16121   Fax: (724)981-3751
E-mail: bmgraphics@surf724.com

Distributes columns and cartoons. **Key Personnel:** Bill Murray, President; Merry Frable, Editor.

38009 Morris News Service
229 Peachtree St. NE   Phone: (404)589-8424
202 Cain Tower
Atlanta, GA 30303

Distributes news.

38010 Motor Matters
4635 Bailey Dr.   Phone: (302)998-1650
Wilmington, DE 19808

Distributes automotive news. **Key Personnel:** Bill McCormick, General Mgr.

38011 Motor News Media Corp.
7177 Hickman Rd., Ste. 11-D   Phone: (515)270-6782
PO Box 7543   Fax: (515)270-8752
Urbandale, IA 50322-7543
E-mail: mnmedia@qwest.net

Columns including Roadworthy, Hard Bargains, Dateline Detroit, Car Concerns first look and Wish List, Ask Dr. Gizmo. Also includes photography database of automotive images. **Key Personnel:** Kenneth Chester, Jr., President. **URL:** http://www.motornewsmedia.com. **Formerly:** ABP Writers Syndicate; AutoBuyer Plus Corporation.

38012 Motoring Road
PO Box M   Phone: (508)528-6211
Franklin, MA 02038-0389   Fax: (508)528-6211

Monthly technical columns and reviews, including Auto-How-To's and Photo How-To's. Automotive trade magazine for northeast. **Key Personnel:** J. A. Kruza, Owner; J. A. Kruza, Contact.

38013 Musick Toons
PO Box 1215   Phone: (419)562-4778
Bucyrus, OH 44820-4215   Fax: (419)562-4778

Distributes cartoons and comic strips. **Key Personnel:** Earl T. Musick, Managing Editor. **URL:** http://www.musicktoons.com.

38014 The Name Game Co. Inc.
401 SW 54th Ave.   Phone: (954)321-0032
Plantation, FL 33317   Fax: (954)321-8617
E-mail: namegameco@aol.com

Distributes circulation and ad promotions contests. **Key Personnel:** Melodye Hecht Icart, President; Mitchell J. Free, VP Sales & Dev.; Gary Zehner, Exec. Dir.

38015 National News Bureau
PO Box 43039   Phone: (215)849-9016
Philadelphia, PA 19129   Fax: (215)893-5394
E-mail: nnbfeature@aol.com

Syndicates entertainment and leisure-oriented features to more than 300 publications. **Key Personnel:** Andy Edelman, Vice President; Harry Jay Katz, Publisher. **URL:** http://www.nationalnewsbureau.com.

38016 National Press Syndicate
401 E. 74th St., Ste. 15-M   Phone: (212)744-4623
New York, NY 10021   Fax: (212)744-4623
E-mail: romresorts@aol.com

Travel news syndicate specializing in hotel and resort news. **Key Personnel:** Paulette Cooper, Publisher. **URL:** http://www.nationalpresssyndicate.com.

38017 New England News Service Inc.
66 Alexander Rd.   Phone: (617)969-4102
Newton, MA 02461

Distributes information on New England and U.S. District courts, and general news for regional and overseas interests. **Key Personnel:** Eleanor Gun, Pres./CEO; Milton J. Gun, Bureau Chief/Sports Ed.; Eleanor Margolis, Living/Leisure; Steven Richards, Computer/Tech.; Howard Neal, Business; Lee Ann Jacob, Lifestyle.

38018 New Wave Syndication
PO Box 232   Phone: (617)471-8733
North Quincy, MA 02171

Distributes comics, and weekly columns of general interest. **Key Personnel:** Tim Lynch, Editor and Publisher.

38019 New York Press Photographers Association
225 E. 36th St.   Phone: (212)889-6633
New York, NY 10016   Fax: (212)889-6634
E-mail: NYPPA@aol.com

Key Personnel: Joe DeMaria, President.

38020 New York Times News Service
229 W. 43rd St.   Phone: (212)556-1927
Rm. 943   Fax: (212)556-3535
New York, NY 10036
E-mail: robison@nytimes.com

Distributes news. **Key Personnel:** James Robison, Exec. Ed.; Lila Locksley, Assoc. Ed.; Deborah Marchand, Dir. Graphics/ Photo; Barbara Mancuso, Dir. Permissions.

38021 New York Times Syndication Sales Corporation
122 E. 42nd St.   Phone: (212)499-3300
14th Fl.   Fax: (212)499-3382
New York, NY 10168   Free: (800)972-3550

Distributes features, graphics service, magazines, news services, and photographs. **Key Personnel:** John Brewer, Pres./ Ed-in-Chief; Karl Horwitz, Pres.-Intl.; Paul Finch, VP Central & South America; Gloria Brown Anderson, VP/Exec. Ed.; Bab Farnell, Sales Exec. North America; Connie White, Sales Exec. North America; Patrick Vance, Dir. Spec. Proj.; Peter Trigg, Dir. Comm. & Tech. **URL:** http://www.yourhealthdaily.com.

38022 Newhouse News Service
1101 Connecticut Ave. NW   Phone: (202)383-7800
Washington, DC 20036   Fax: (202)296-9537

Distributes news service. **Key Personnel:** Deborah Howell, Wash. Bureau Chief/Ed., phone (202)383-7843, fax (202)872-1316, Deborah.Howell@Newhouse.com; Linda Fibich, National Ed., phone (202)383-7850, Linda.Fibich@Newhouse.com; Susan Avanzado, Office Mgr., phone (202)383-7811, Susan.Avanzado@Newhouse.com. **URL:** http://www.newhousenews.com.

38023 Newsbytes News Network
Carriage House   Phone: (612)430-1100
406 W. Olive St.   Fax: (612)430-0441
Stillwater, MN 55082

Distributes news. **Key Personnel:** Wendy Woods, Ed./Gen. Mgr.

38024 Newspaper Enterprise Association
200 Madison Ave.   Phone: (212)293-8500
4th Fl.   Fax: (212)293-8600
New York, NY 10016   Free: (800)221-4816

Distributes various features including children's commentary, consumer, business, entertainment, food, graphics, health, sports, comic strips, and editorial cartoons. **Owner:** The E.W. Scripps Co. **Key Personnel:** Douglas R. Stern, Pres./CEO; Lisa Klem Wilson, VP Sales & Mktg., phone (212)293-8612, lwilson@unitedmedia.com; John B. Matthews, Natl. Sales Dir., jmatthews@unitedmedia.com; Amy Lago, VP, Comics & Graphics, phone (212)293-8640, fax (212)293-8720, alago@unitedmedia.com; Anna Soler, Mgr. Intl. Syndications, phone (212)293-8723, fax (212)293-8720, asoler@unitedmedia.com; Liz Martinez-DeFranco, Mng. Ed. UFS & NEA, phone (212)293-8784, fax (212)293-8760, ldefranco@unitedmedia.com; Mary Anne Grimes, Exec. Dir., Public Relations, phone (212)893-8626, fax (212), magrimes@unitedmedia.com; Carmen Puello, Customer Serv. Mgr., phone (212)293-8602, cpuello@unitedmedia.com. **URL:** http://www.unitedmedia.com.

38025 Newspaper Features Inc.
14 High St.   Phone: (516)759-9709
Locust Valley, NY 11560

38026 Newsportraits Syndicate
PO Box 564   Phone: (201)342-2985
Hackensack, NJ 07602-0564

Distributes news. **Key Personnel:** Y.L. Tiajcliff, Exec. Ed.; Martin Sager, Business Mgr.

38027 NewsUSA
7777 Leesburg Pike, No. 307   Fax: (703)734-6321
South   Free: (800)355-9500
Falls Church, VA 22043

Features, columns, filler and photos for newspapers; free radio scripts for radio stations. **Key Personnel:** Diana Duvall, Exec. Editor, dduvall@newsusa.com; Zoey Rawlins, Dir. of Creative Operations, zrawlins@newsusa.com. **URL:** http://www.newsusa.com.

38028 Ohio Washington News Service
529 14th St. NW   Phone: (202)737-1888
Washington, DC 20009

38029 Olshan's Sports Features
9255 Sunset Blvd., Ste. 523   Phone: (310)274-0848
Los Angeles, CA 90069-3301   Fax: (310)273-5932
                                   Free: (800)798-GOLD
E-mail: goldshee@goldsheet.com

Articles on football and basketball handicapping. **Key Personnel:** Mort Olshan, President; Carl Giordano, Managing Editor; Gary Olshan, Chief Analyst; Chuck Sippl, Senior Analyst. **URL:** http://www.goldsheet.com.

38030 Online USA
2450 Colorado Ave., No. 5000   Phone: (310)587-0025
W.   Fax: (310)587-0027
Santa Monica, CA 90404-3575
E-mail: info@onlineusa.com

Photo/news wire service. **Key Personnel:** Brad Elterman, Photo Desk; Paul Harris, Features Desk. **URL:** http://www.onlineusa.com.

38031 Ottaway Newspapers
1025 Connecticut Ave. NW   Phone: (202)828-3390
Ste. 310
Washington, DC 20036

Distributes news service. **Key Personnel:** William Schmick III, Bureau Chief; Winston Wood, Dept. Chief; Kevin McCaney, Feature Ed.

38032 Pacific News Service
660 Market St., Rm. 210   Phone: (415)438-4755
San Francisco, CA 94104   Fax: (415)438-4935
E-mail: pacificnews@pacificnews.org

Distributes news service. **Key Personnel:** Sandy Close, Exec. Ed., sclose@pacificnews.org; Franz Schurmann, Associate Ed., fschurmann@pacificnews.org; Richard Rodriguez, Associate Ed., rrodriguez@pacificnews.org; Andrew Lam, Assoc. Editor, alam@pacificnews.org; Nicole Sawaya, Assoc. Editor, sawaya@pacificnews.org. **URL:** http://www.pacificnews.org.

38033 Parwell-Davis Features Syndicate
3741 N. 400 E., Ste. A   Phone: (260)782-2345
Lagro, IN 46941-9664
E-mail: parwell@email.com

Sons of Liberty, a weekly cartoon strip on American history. **Key Personnel:** R. J. Lynn, Editor, editor@parwell.hypermart.net. **URL:** http://parwell.hypermart.net.

38034 Pen Tip Illustrations
869 Smith Rd.   Phone: (973)515-0744
Parsippany, NJ 07054-3341
E-mail: pkolsti@optonline.net

Editorial illustrations. **Key Personnel:** Paul Kolsti, President. **URL:** http://www.pentip.com. **Formerly:** Pen Tip International Features, Inc. (Apr. 1, 1902).

38035 Photo International/Photo Associate News Service
PO Box 2163   Phone: (703)346-9595
Reston, VA 20195   Fax: (703)866-7744
E-mail: panspi@juno.com

Photo news service specializing in political photo-journalism, celebrities, and East Coast city scapes. **Key Personnel:** Peter Heimsath, Bureau Manager.

38036 Plexers Inc.
3827 Los Santos Dr.   Phone: (916)677-3632
Cameron Park, CA 95682-8601

Distributes word puzzles. **Key Personnel:** Joe Scales, President; Thomas J. Lester, V; David Hammond, Treas.

38037 The Poynor Group
444 E. 82nd St., Ste. 28C   Phone: (212)734-5909
New York, NY 10028   Fax: (212)734-5909

Distributes the Balloonatics, View from My House, and Women's Humor Columns. **Key Personnel:** Jay Poynor, President, jpoynor@webspan.net.

38038 PR Newswire
810 7th Ave.   Free: (800)832-5522
35th Fl.
New York, NY 10019

Distributes news wire service. **Key Personnel:** Ian Capps, President; John Williams, Senior VP; Ken Dowell, Ed. Dir.; Fred Ferguson, Features Coord. **URL:** http://www.prnewswire.com.

38039 Press Associates Union News Service
1000 Vermont Ave. NW   Phone: (202)898-4825
Ste. 101   Fax: (202)898-9004
Washington, DC 20005
E-mail: unionnews@hotmail.com

Distributes news concerning legislative issues, politics, unemployment, court decisions, labor cases, national health, Social Security, and Medicare; The Washington Window, a commentary column; Work & Health, a job safety column; How to Buy, a consumer column. **Key Personnel:** Mark J. Gruenberg, President/Editor; Janet Brown, Editor. **URL:** http://www.inetba.com/pressassociates.

38040 Press News Ltd.
36 King St. E.   Phone: (416)364-0321
Toronto, ON, Canada M5C 2L9 Fax: (416)594-2163

Key Personnel: Jim Poling, General Mgr.; Michael Sifton, Chm.

38041 Press News Syndicate
2073 Gerritsen Ave.   Phone: (718)339-1417
Brooklyn, NY 11229

Key Personnel: Martin Pine, Travel Columnist.

38042 Press Photo Service
79-14 Parsons Blvd.   Phone: (718)969-7444
Flushing, NY 11366

Key Personnel: Harris Sutter, Pres./Ed.; Mike Weber, Vice President; Charles Phillips, General Mgr.; Jeff Hollander, Entertainment/Sports Ed.

38043 Print Marketing Concepts
10590 Westoffice Dr.   Phone: (713)780-7055
Ste. 250   Fax: (713)780-9731
Houston, TX 77042

Key Personnel: Charles Dye, President; Robin L. Good, VP-Natl. Sales; Nancy Kissman, Controller.

38044 Punch In Travel & Entertainment News Syndicate
400 E. 59th St.   Phone: (212)755-4363
Ste. 9-F
New York, NY 10022
E-mail: punchin@usa.net

Key Personnel: J. Walman, President; Jerry Preiser, Managing Editor; Nancy Preiser, Managing Editor. **URL:** http://inx.net:80/punchin/; http://www.junchin.com.

38045 Quiz Features
4007 Connecticut Ave. NW   Phone: (202)966-0025
Washington, DC 20008   Fax: (202)966-4074
E-mail: mbds@erols.com

Distributes question and answer quizzes. **Key Personnel:** Donald Saltz, Author; Mozelle Saltz, Research Dir.

38046 Real Estate Matters Syndicate
395 Dundee Rd.   Phone: (847)835-3450
Glencoe, IL 60022   Fax: (847)835-3451
E-mail: thinkglink@aol.com

Publishes and syndicates information about residential real estate and personal finance. **Owner:** Think Glink, Inc., at above address. **Key Personnel:** Ilyce R. Glink, Publisher; Samuel J. Tamkin, Editor. **URL:** http://www.thinkglink.com.

38047 Religion News Service
1101 Connecticut Ave. NW   Phone: (202)463-8777
Ste. 350   Fax: (202)463-0033
Washington, DC 20036   Free: (800)767-6781
E-mail: info@religionnews.com

News and photo service with a focus on religion and ethics. **Key Personnel:** Christina Denny, Editorial and Publishing Coordinator; David E. Anderson, Editor. **URL:** http://www.religionnews.com. **Formerly:** Religious News Service.

38048 Retail News Bureau
Div. of Retail Reporting Corp. Phone: (212)279-7000
302 5th Ave.   Fax: (212)279-7014
New York, NY 10001

Distributes women's fashion news. **Key Personnel:** John Burr, Publisher; Bridget Biggane, Editor.

38049 Rich Markgraf
1830 Ave. del Mundo   Phone: (619)435-2514
No. 1107
Coronado, CA 92118

Distributes weekly humor columns. **Key Personnel:** Richard Markgraf, Self-Syndicator.

38050 Richard Lynn Enterprises
3741 N. 400 E   Phone: (260)782-2345
Lagro, IN 46941

Distributes educational weekly cartoon strip (Colonial Heroes). **Key Personnel:** R.J. Lynn, President, rjlynn@parwell.hypermart.net. **URL:** http://parwell.hypermart.net.

38051 RMS Syndication
14713 Pleasant Hill Rd.   Phone: (704)588-2453
Charlotte, NC 28278-7927

Key Personnel: David A. Butler, President.

38052 Roll Call Report Syndicate
Thomas Reports Inc.   Phone: (202)737-1888
1257-B National Press Bldg.
Washington, DC 20045
E-mail: roll-call-votes@atsmsu.com

Distributes congressional news. **Key Personnel:** Richard G. Thomas, Editor and Publisher; Cora Hoopes, Associate Ed.; David K. Martin, Associate Ed.; Patrick Harden, Associate Ed. **URL:** http://www.roll-call-votes.com.

38053 Ron Bernthal
PO Drawer 259   Phone: (845)292-3071
Hurleyville, NY 12747   Fax: (845)434-4806
E-mail: rbern@sullivan.suny.edu

Distributes radio commentary on travel books food and wine.

38054 Royal Features
PO Box 58174   Phone: (281)532-2145
Houston, TX 77258-8714

Key Personnel: Fay W. Henry, Exec. Dir.

38055 San Francisco Style International
PO Box 330063   Phone: (415)788-6589
San Francisco, CA 94133-4063

38056 Schlein News Bureau
308 E. Capitol St. NE   Phone: (202)544-5893
Ste. 9
Washington, DC 20003

38057 Schmidt Services Inc.
720 Creek Rd.   Phone: (716)591-3010
Attica, NY 14011

Key Personnel: Stephen P. Schmidt, President.

38058 Schwadron Cartoon & Illustration Service
PO Box 1347   Phone: (734)426-8433
Ann Arbor, MI 48106   Fax: (734)426-8433
E-mail: schwadron@schwadroncartoons.com

Distributes cartoons. **Key Personnel:** Harley Schwadron, Editor; Sally Booth, Sec. **URL:** http://www.schwadroncartoons.com.

38059 Science Communications
5318 Stirling Ct.
Newark, CA 94560

Distributes gardening column. **Key Personnel:** Pat Kite, Writer/Ed.

38060 Science Service
1719 N St. NW   Phone: (202)785-2255
Washington, DC 20036   Fax: (202)659-0365
E-mail: scinews@sciserv.org

Distributes science media news. **Key Personnel:** Don Harless, Publisher; Julie Miller, Contact. **URL:** http://www.sciserv.org.

38061 Scramble-Gram Inc.
41 Park Dr.   Phone: (419)734-2600
Port Clinton, OH 43452

Crosswords including Giant Crosswords; CowCross Crosswords; Bigfoot Crosswords; and newspaper features Scrambler, Watchword, and The Lost Word. **Key Personnel:** C.R. Elum, President; Scott M. Bowers, General Mgr.; Mary Kessler, Marketing Director.

38062 Screening Room
PO Box 2236   Phone: (413)442-1256
Pittsfield, MA 01202-2236   Fax: (413)443-2445

Key Personnel: Jonathan Levine, Self-Syndicator.

38063 Scripps-McClatchy Western Service
1090 Vermont Ave. NW   Phone: (202)408-2730
Ste. 1000
Washington, DC 20005

Distributes general news. **Key Personnel:** Dan Thomasson, Ed./Bureau Chief; Marvin West, Managing Editor; Sid Goldberg, Ed. Dev.; Irwin Breslauer, Gen. Exec. **URL:** http://www.shns.com.

38064 Senior Wire News Service
2377 Elm St.   Phone: (303)355-3882
Denver, CO 80207   Fax: (303)355-2720
E-mail: clearmountain1@msn.com

Distributes Washington Watch; national news/analysis; Joking Around; political commentary; financial advice and commentary; food column; pet column; golf column; Grandparents Corner; Attic Antiques; Health Briefs; puzzles; seasonal/holiday information columns; automotive/technical; computers/Internet; investment information; RV Travel; Home Alone; humor columns, aging issues, gaming and horse racing, nursing home column, political cartoons, travel tips, destination travel, travel with grandchildren. **Key Personnel:** Allison St. Claire, Editor and Publisher. **URL:** http://seniorwire.net.

38065 Joe Sharpnack
PO Box 3325   Phone: (319)338-9609
Iowa City, IA 52244   Fax: (319)338-9609
E-mail: joe@sharptoons.com

Self-syndicated editorial cartoonist. **URL:** http://www.sharptoons.com.

38066 Shetland Productions
4679 Goodland Park Rd.   Phone: (608)222-5522
Madison, WI 53711

Key Personnel: Eleanor Williams, Editor; Alexander Schiller, Office Mgr.; Robert Kovalic, Business Mgr.; Becky Weiner, Associate Ed. **URL:** http://www.msn.fullfeed.com/muskrat.

38067 SIPA News Service
59 E. 54th St.   Phone: (212)759-5571
New York, NY 10022   Fax: (212)593-5194

Latin America newspapers syndicate. **Key Personnel:** Henry O. Dormann, Chm./Ed.; Darrell Brown, Pres./Exec. Ed.

38068 Skin Talk
32905 W. 12 Mile Rd., No. 330 Phone: (248)553-2900
Farmington Hills, MI 48334

Question and answers about skin problems. **Owner:** Jon Blum, MD. **Key Personnel:** Jon Blum, M.D., Editor.

38069 Slightly Off
1168 Sagebrush Trail   Phone: (847)639-1232
Cary, IL 60013   Fax: (847)639-1232
E-mail: sltlyoff@mc.net

Distributes family humor columns. **Key Personnel:** Deb DiSandro, Author/Owner. **URL:** http://www.mc.net/slightlyoff.

38070 Small Talk
74 Commonwealth Ave., Apt. 11 Phone: (617)267-1396
Boston, MA 02116-3031   Fax: (509)275-4252
                            Free: (877)997-8679

Distributes comic single panel. **Key Personnel:** Alan H. Kelly, Jr., Creative Dir.; Frances Kelly, Talent.

38071 SNG Inc. (Washington Bureau)
1183 National Press Bldg.   Phone: (202)662-7240
Washington, DC 20045

Distributes SNG newspapers, Kankakee, IL; Washington Bureau.

38072 Solaman Productions
701 S. Mt. Vernon Ave.   Phone: (909)862-2985
San Bernardino, CA 92410   Fax: (909)862-2985
E-mail: sola6@earthlink.net

Q & A column dealing with the prevention and care of athletic injuries (in English and Spanish). **Key Personnel:** Mike Sola.

38073 Southam Syndicate
151 Sparks St.   Phone: (613)236-0491
Ste. 200   Fax: (613)236-1788
Ottawa, ON, Canada K1P 5E3

Distributes features and wire stories for seven of Canada's major newspapers including the Calgary Herald, Edmonton Journal, Montreal Gazette, Ottawa Citizen, Vancouver Province, and the Vancouver Sun. **Key Personnel:** Ros Guggi, Manager, rguggi@southam.ca; Dan Smythe, Ed. Coord.; Allison McLean, Business Mgr.

38074 Southern California Focus
1720 Oak St.
Phone: (213)452-3918
Santa Monica, CA 90405
E-mail: tdelias@aol.com

Distributes general news, politics, and sports columns. **Key Personnel:** Thomas Elias, Author. **Also known as:** California Focus.

38075 Speaking of Soaps Inc.
331 Boyle Ave.
Phone: (201)790-1582
Totowa, NJ 07512
Fax: (201)790-1936

Key Personnel: Mary Ann Cooper, Contact, maryann917@ aol.com. **URL:** http://www.soapoperastore.com

38076 Specialty Features Syndicate
PO Box 19268
Phone: (313)533-1846
Detroit, MI 48219-0268

Distributes literary condensations, health, and nutrition columns. **Key Personnel:** Lewis Kaye, President; Verdice Kordel, Food Ed.; L.E. Crandall, Manager.

38077 Spectrum Features
400 E. 2nd St.
Phone: (570)389-4825
BCH 106
Bloomsburg, PA 17815
E-mail: brasch@bloomu.edu

Distributes humor, political, social issues, regional features, and entertainment. **Key Personnel:** Rose Renn, Exec. Ed.; John Michaels, Associate Ed.; Jessica Snyder, Business Mgr.; MaryJayne Reibsome, Production Dir.; Matt Gerber, Sports Editor. **URL:** http://www.org5.bloomu.eduspectrum.

38078 Sports Adviser Features
1323 S. 6th St.
Phone: (630)377-6676
PO Box 891
Fax: (630)513-5438
St. Charles, IL 60174

Publishers of The Sport Psychology Adviser column. **Key Personnel:** P. Andrew Andersen, Pres./Owner.

38079 Sports Biofile & Bio-Toons
71 Dockerty Hollow Rd.
Phone: (201)728-0591
West Milford, NJ 07480
Fax: (201)728-0591

Key Personnel: Mark Malinowski, Editor; Bud Boccone, Artist. **URL:** http://espnet.sportszone.com/editors/zoned/biofiles.

38080 Sports by Voort
255 Main St.
Phone: (201)593-0563
Ste. C-2
Fax: (201)593-0099
Madison, NJ 07940
E-mail: kvoort@worldnet.att.net

Distributes sports cartoons, illustrations, and animation. **Owner:** Kenneth Vandervoort, at above address. **URL:** http://www.sportsbyvoort.com.

38081 Sportsbuff Features
PO Box 197
Phone: (978)468-2632
Hamilton, MA 01936
Fax: (978)468-7601
E-mail: sportsbuff@atti.com

Distributes weekly sports crossword puzzle. **Key Personnel:** Steve Ollove, Editor; Michael C. Smith, Assoc. Ed.

38082 Stadium Circle Features
335 Court St.
Phone: (718)797-0210
Ste. 85
Fax: (718)797-0210
Brooklyn, NY 11231-4335
E-mail: newyorkbob@prodigy.net

Distributes weekly personal computer column, and offers computer and technology features to newspapers and magazines. **Owner:** Robert S. Anthony, at above address. **Key Personnel:** Robert S. Anthony, Ed./Columnist. **URL:** http://www.paperpc.net.

38083 States News Service
NY Times Subscriber Service
Phone: (202)628-3100
1331 Pennsylvania Ave., NW,
Fax: (202)737-9818
Ste. 524 N.
Washington, DC 20004

Distributes news from Washington, DC that affects individual states. **Key Personnel:** Leland Schwartz, Editor. **URL:** http://www.statesnews.com.

38084 Steve Brock Book Reviews on the Internet
164 Bulkley Ave.
Phone: (415)332-7324
Sausalito, CA 94965-2143

Key Personnel: Steve Brock, Book Reviewer, stevo@prospero.com.

38085 The Straight Dope, Chicago Reader
11 E. Illinois St.
Phone: (312)828-0350
Chicago, IL 60611
E-mail: webmaster@straightdope.com

Key Personnel: Jane Levine, Publisher, jlevine@chicagoreader.com; Lisa Martain Hoffer, Special Projects Coordinator, lhoffer@chicagoreader.com. **URL:** http://www.straightdope.com.

38086 The Strategist
1300 3rd St. S
Phone: (239)434-5555
Ste. 203E
Fax: (239)434-5604
Naples, FL 34102
E-mail: alegatz@comcast.net

Owner: Fax: (239)434-2817. **Key Personnel:** Alan Legatz, Proprietor, alegatz@comcast.net; Janet Long, Asst., phone (989)479-3315; Ivy Peden, Asst. **URL:** http://www.thestrategist.com.

38087 Sun Features Inc.
45 Kennedy Pkwy.
Phone: (619)431-1660
PO Box 45
Fax: (619)431-1669
Cardiff, CA 92007

Key Personnel: Joyce Lain Kennedy, President, jlk@sunfeatures.com; Tim K. Horrell, Vice President.

38088 Sun Media Corporation
333 King St. E.
Phone: (416)947-2257
Toronto, ON, Canada M5A 3X5
Fax: (416)947-2043
Free: (877)624-1463
E-mail: research@sunpub.com

Key Personnel: Julie Kirsh, Director, Electronic Information, jkirsh@sunpub.com.

38089 Sunshine Press Services
325 Pennsylvania Ave. SE
Phone: (202)544-3647
Washington, DC 20003
Fax: (202)544-4887

Key Personnel: Edward Roeder, Editor.

38090 Sylvia Di Pietro
55 W. 14th St.
Phone: (212)255-4059
Ste. 4-H
Fax: (212)255-4059
New York, NY 10011
E-mail: qbly@prodigy.com

Distributes column on children, romance, career, and finance. **Key Personnel:** Sylvia Di Pietro, Self-Syndicator.

38091 Sylvia Syndicate
1440 N. Dayton
Phone: (312)943-4862
Chicago, IL 60622

Distributes Sylvia cartoon strip. **Key Personnel:** Nicole Hollander, President.

38092 Taming the Workplace
3003 14th Ave. W., Ste. 201
Phone: (206)284-9566
Seattle, WA 98119
Fax: (425)977-0218
E-mail: mrscribe@aol.com

Distributes weekly column on workplace issues. **Key Personnel:** Eric L. Zoeckler, Columnist.

38093 Ted Larsen Media
96 Columbus Ave.
Phone: (978)741-4949
Salem, MA 01970
Fax: (978)741-3916
E-mail: tlmedia@aol.com

Distributes weekly column on seasonal food, travel, and wine recipes; radio version also available. **Key Personnel:** Ted Larsen, Editor and Publisher.

38094 Tel-aire Publications Inc.
3105 E. Carpenter Fwy.
Phone: (972)438-4111
Irving, TX 75062
Fax: (972)579-7483
Free: (800)749-1841
E-mail: info@tel-aire.com

Distributes TV listings and TV feature packages. **Key Personnel:** David A. McGee, President; Richard Stein, Natl. Sales Mgr., rstein@tel-aire.com. **URL:** http://www.tel-aire.com.

38095 TheRomantic.com
PO Box 1567
Phone: (919)462-0900
Cary, NC 27512
E-mail: column@theromantic.com

The Romantic syndicated column. **Key Personnel:** Michael Webb. **URL:** http://www.theromantic.com.

38096 This Side of 60
PO Box 332
Phone: (316)283-2309
North Newton, KS 67117
E-mail: thisside60@aol.com

Distributes weekly column–This Side of 60. **Owner:** Marie Snider. **Key Personnel:** Marie Snider, Self-Syndicator. **URL:** http://www.visit-snider.com.

38097 Time Data Syndicate
PO Box 717
Phone: (603)623-7733
Manchester, NH 03105-0717
Free: (800)322-5101
E-mail: star2020@time-data.com

Distributes astrology features. **Key Personnel:** Larry White, Director, star2020@time-data.com; Marcia White, Treas. **URL:** http://www.time-data.com.

38098 Times News Service
6883 Commercial Dr.
Phone: (703)750-8125
Springfield, VA 22159-0200
Fax: (703)750-8781

Owner: Army Times Publishing Co., at above address. **Key Personnel:** Kent Miller, phone (703)750-8871, fax (703)750-8871, kmiller@atpco.com.

38099 Tiptoe Literary Service
434 6th St., No. 206
Phone: (360)942-4596
Raymond, WA 98577-1804
E-mail: anne@willapabay.org

Distributes title updates and manuscript information. **Key Personnel:** Anne Louise Grimm, Owner. **URL:** http://www.willapabay.org/~anne.

38100 Tom & Joanne O'Toole
4603 Wood St.
Phone: (440)942-5455
Willoughby, OH 44094-5821

Distributes international, domestic, and cruise travel articles and color slides, as well as wide-ranging outdoor articles to North American. **Key Personnel:** Thomas J. O'Toole, Journalist/Photographer; Joanne R. O'Toole, Journalist.

38101 Torstar Syndication Services
1 Yonge St.
Phone: (416)869-4989
Toronto, ON, Canada M5E 1E6
Fax: (416)869-4587
E-mail: syndicate@thestar.ca

Distributes general news. **Key Personnel:** Robin Graham, Sales Mgr.; Ted Cowan, Sales Rep.; Wendy Watts, Photo Sales; Joanne MacDonald, Sales Asst.

38102 Trade News Service
3701 Rte. 21 S.
Phone: (716)396-0027
Canandaigua, NY 14424-9020
E-mail: tns@fats-and-oils.com

Distributes edible and inedible fats and oils pricing and fundamental and trade data. **Key Personnel:** Dennis C. Maxfield, Senior Ed. **URL:** http://www.fats-and-oils.com.

38103 Travel & Leisure Features
66 Alexander Rd.
Phone: (617)969-4102
Newton, MA 02461

Distributes travel, leisure, and home columns. **Key Personnel:** Eleanor Margolis, Destinations Ed.; Milton Gun, Cruise News; Howard Neal, Travel Away.

38104 Tribune Media Services Inc.
435 N. Michigan Ave.
Phone: (312)222-4444
Ste. 1500
Fax: (312)222-8620
Chicago, IL 60611
Free: (800)245-6536
E-mail: tms@tribune.com

Distributes political, medical, and financial columns. **Key Personnel:** David D. Williams, Pres./CEO; Walter F. Mahoney, VP-Sales Syndicate & KRT Products; Barbara Needleman, VP-Data Base & Advertising; Michael A. Silver, VP-Editorial & Business Dev.

38105 TV Data
333 Glen St.
Phone: (518)792-9914
Glens Falls, NY 12801
Fax: (800)660-7185
Free: (800)833-9581
E-mail: features@tvdata.com

Key Personnel: Monique Skotnicki, Features Managing Editor, mskotnicki@tvdata.com; Tom Cronin, VP, Cable Sales, fax (518)792-4671, tcroning@tvdata.com. **URL:** http://www.clicktv.com. **Additional Contact Info: Regional Office(s):** 307 W. 7th St., Ste. 910, Fort Worth, TX 76101, (817)877-1400, fax: (817)336-7901, free: (800)749-1404.

38106 U-Bild Newspaper Features
PO Box 2383
Fax: (818)785-3229
Van Nuys, CA 91409
Free: (800)828-2453
E-mail: ubild@aol.com

Distributes information about woodworking and handicraft items. **Key Personnel:** Kevin Taylor, President; Gina Rosa, General Mgr.; Jeffrey Reeves, Feature Ed.

38107 United Feature Syndicate Inc.
200 Madison Ave. Phone: (212)293-8500
New York, NY 10016 Fax: (212)293-8760
  Free: (800)221-4816

Owner: The E. W. Scripps Co. **Key Personnel:** Douglas R. Stern, Pres./CEO; Sidney Goldberg, Sr. VP/Gen. Mgr.-Syndication, phone (212)293-8606, sgoldberg@unitedmedia.com; Lisa Klem Wilson, VP-Sales & Mktg., phone (212)293-8612, lwilson@unitedmedia.com; John B. Matthews, Natl. Sales Dir., jmatthews@unitedmedia.com; Amy Lago, VP, Comics & Graphics, phone (212)293-8640, fax (212)293-8720, alago@unitedmeida.com; Anna Soler, Mgr.-International Syndication, phone (212)293-8723, fax (212)293-8720, asoler@unitedmedia.com; Liz Martinez DeFranco, Mng. Ed.-UFS & NEA, (212)293-8784, ldefranco@unitedmedia.com; Mary Anne Grimes, Exec. Dir., Public Relations, phone (212)293-8626, magrimes@unitedmedia.com; Carmen Puello, Customer Service Mgr., phone (212)293-8602, cpuello@unitedmedia.com. **URL:** http://www.unitedmedia.com.

38108 United Media
200 Madison Ave. Phone: (212)293-8500
New York, NY 10016 Fax: (212)293-8600
  Free: (800)221-4816

Distributes comics, general features. **Owner:** The E.W. Scripps Co. **Key Personnel:** Douglas R. Stern, Pres./CEO; Paul Crystal, Sr., VP-Finance & Admin., phone (212)293-8670, fax (212)293-8717, pcrystal@unitedmedia.com; Sidney Goldberg, Sr., VP/Gen. Mgr.-Syndication (212)293-8606, sgoldberg@unitedmedia.com; Joshua Kislentz, Sr. VP-U.S. Licensing, phone (212)293-8522, fax (212)293-8550, jkislevitz@unitedmedia.com; Lisa Klem Wilson, VP-Sales & Mktg., phone (212)293-8612, lwilson@unitedmedia.com; John B. Matthews, Natl. Sales Dir., jmatthews@unitedmedia.com; Amy Lago, VP, Comics & Graphics, phone (212)293-8640, fax (212)293-8720, alago@unitedmedia.com; Anna Soler, Mgr.-International Syndication, phone (212)293-8723, fax (212)293-8720, asoler@unitedmedia.com; Mary Anne Grimes, Exec. Dir. Public Relations, phone (212)293-8626, magrimes@unitedmedia.com; Rita Rubin, SVP,-International Licensing, phone (212)293-8521, fax (212)293-8551, rrubin@unitedmedia.com. **URL:** http://www.unitedmedia.com.

38109 United Press International
1510 H St., NW Phone: (202)898-8000
Washington, DC 20005 Fax: (202)898-8057
E-mail: feedback@upi.com

Distributes general news, graphics, and photographs. **Key Personnel:** John R. Hayes, CEO; Peter Leach, VP-Operations; Ron MacIntyre, VP-Sales & Mktg.; Anthony Jay, Jr., CFO; Robert Martin, Mng. Ed.-International; Tobin Beck, Mng. Ed.-North America; Raphael Calis, Exec. Ed.; Kathleen Silvassy, Washington Bureau Mgr.; Helen Thomas, UPI White House Bureau Mgr.; Lin Coppedge-Martin, Dir.-HR; Larry Shuster, Science Ed.; Ian Love, Sports Ed.; Valerie Kuklenski, Entertainment Ed. **URL:** http://www.upi.com.

38110 U.S. Newswire
1230 National Press Bldg. Phone: (202)347-2770
Washington, DC 20045 Fax: (202)347-2767
E-mail: newsdesk@usnewswire.com

Distributes general news advisories and statements. **URL:** http://www.usnewswire.com.

38111 Universal Press Syndicate
4520 Main St. Phone: (816)932-6600
Kansas City, MO 64111-7701 Free: (800)255-6734

Distributes cartoons, text features, and columns such as WorkWise. **Key Personnel:** John McMeel, Pres./CEO; Kathleen Andrews, VP/Co. Chm.; Thomas Thornton, Vice President; Lee Salem, VP/Ed.; Robert Duffy, President; Kathie Kerr, Communications Dir., kkerr@uexpress.com; Dr. Mildred Culp, Columnist/Contact, WorkWise, culp@workwise.net. **URL:** http://www.uexpress.com.

38112 The Usual Suspects/Mystery Fiction Lineup
Box 3308 Merchandise Mart Phone: (708)909-5809
Chicago, IL 60654-0308
E-mail: specializedmedia@yahoo.com

Distributes author interviews and book reviews.

38113 Wagner International Photos Inc.
62 W. 45th St., 6th Fl. Phone: (212)944-7744
New York, NY 10036-4208 Fax: (212)944-9536

Key Personnel: Larry Lettera, President; Jeff Connell, Chief Photographer.

38114 Washington G2 Reports
1111 14th St. NW Phone: (202)789-1034
Ste. 711
Washington, DC 20005

Distributes information for clinical laboratories and hospitals. **Key Personnel:** Dennis Weissman, Pres./Pub.; D.J. Curren, Editor.

38115 The Washington Post Writers Group
1150 15th St. NW Phone: (202)334-6375
Washington, DC 20071-9200 Fax: (202)334-5669
  Free: (800)879-9794
E-mail: writersgrp@washpost.com

Newspaper Syndicate. **Key Personnel:** Alan Shearer, Editorial Dir./Gen. Mgr., phone (202)334-6377; James Hill, Assoc. Ed., phone (202)334-6376; Mary Fleming Svensson, Sales Mgr./International, phone (202)334-7131; Karisue Wyson, Sales Mgr./North America, phone (202)334-7209; Suzanne Whelton, Comics Ed., phone (202)334-6510; Russell James, Permissions Ed., phone (202)334-4376, fax (202)334-7862; Maria Gatti, Sales Rep., phone (202)334-4466; Karen H. Greene, Operations Mgr., phone (202)334-4511. **URL:** http://www.postwritersgroup.com.

38116 Washington Small Business News Roundup
5317 Canary Ansas Dr. Phone: (504)887-9462
Kenner, LA 70065

Business articles including Washington Small Business News Roundup and Minding Your Business. **Key Personnel:** Channing Hayden, Publisher, cfhjr@bellsouth.net.

38117 W.D. Farmer Residence Designer Inc.
2007 Montreal Rd. Phone: (770)934-7380
Tucker, GA 30084 Fax: (770)934-1700
  Free: (800)225-7526
E-mail: wdfarmer@wdfarmerplans.com

Distributes weekly feature, homes, releases. **Key Personnel:** W.D. Farmer, President; Vickie F. Starkey, Asst. Sec.-Treas./Dir. Advertising. **URL:** http://www.wdfarmerplans.com.

38118 WeatherData, Incorporated
245 N. Waco St., Ste. 310 Phone: (316)265-9127
Wichita, KS 67202 Fax: (316)265-1949
E-mail: sales@weatherdata.com

Weather packages, customized forecasts, and online data services, as well as expert and historical weather-related topics. **Key Personnel:** Mike Smith, President, phone (316)265-9127. **URL:** http://www.weatherdata.com.

38119 West Coast Syndicate
320 Vista Linda Dr. Phone: (415)388-2024
Mill Valley, CA 94941

Distributes business, food, and wine features; puzzles. **Key Personnel:** Carol Townsend, Pres./Exec. Ed.

38120 The Western Producer Newsfeature Service
2310 Millar Ave. Phone: (306)665-3591
PO Box 2500 Fax: (306)934-2401
Saskatoon, SK, Canada S7K
2C4

Key Personnel: Michael Gillgannon, Managing Editor; Sean Pratt, Reporter/Ed.

38121 What's Brewing
160 Dexter Ave. Phone: (203)235-1758
Meriden, CT 06450
E-mail: jimzebora@cox.net

Distributes information on beer and brewing. **Key Personnel:** Jim Zebora, Self-Syndicator.

38122 What's New in Medicine
1143 Chamberlain Hwy. Phone: (203)828-5016
Kensington, CT 06037

Distributes weekly medical column containing health news and commentary. **Key Personnel:** L.A. Chotkowski, MD, Author/Owner, drchot@aol.com.

38123 What's Up Information Services
1200 Ashwood Pkwy. Phone: (404)671-0200
No. 575 Fax: (404)671-0110
Atlanta, GA 30338 Free: (888)942-8787
E-mail: sales@whatsup.com

Distributes press releases. **Owner:** Commlink Interactive, LLC. **Key Personnel:** Richard Warner, President; Chad Hansen, VP Sales; Lynn Lebreton, VP Tech.; Malenka Warner, Vice President; Hannah Hite, Dir. Internet Mktg. **URL:** http://www.whatsup.com.

38124 Whitegate Features Syndicate
71 Faunce Dr. Phone: (401)274-2149
Providence, RI 02906
E-mail: 102404.574@compuserve.com

Key Personnel: Ed Issac, President; Steve Corey, VP/Gen. Mgr.; Eve Green, Talent Mgr./Special Sales; Mary Howard, Office Mgr.

38125 Wieck Photo DataBase, Inc.
dba Wieck Media Services Phone: (972)392-0888
4002 Belt Line Rd., No. 150- Fax: (972)934-8848
LB7
Addison, TX 75001-4337
E-mail: desk@wieckphoto.com

Database and web services company that distributes text, graphics and photos for news services, newspaper groups, and other sources. **Key Personnel:** James F. Wieck, Chairman; Marge Boatright, President; Linda Hughs, Exec. VP; Tim Roberts, VP/General Mgr.; Jere Cox, Managing Editor; Alex Sian, Webmaster; Christy Brown, Managing Editor. **URL:** http://www.wieck.com.

38126 William A. Alan
26 McKelvey Ave. Phone: (412)242-2332
Pittsburgh, PA 15218

Distributes business/industry economic news, especially automotive data. **Key Personnel:** William A. Alan, Columnist.

38127 Williams Syndications Inc.
8645 W. Foster Phone: (773)589-1180
Chicago, IL 60656 Fax: (773)589-1180

Columns on angels, ghosts, and word games. **Key Personnel:** James Williams, jameswilliams44@aol.com.

38128 WINGS: Women's International News Gathering Service
PO Box 33220 Phone: (512)416-9000
Austin, TX 78764
E-mail: wings@wings.org

Distributes radio news and current affairs programs by and about women around the world. **Key Personnel:** Frieda Werden, Producer. **URL:** http://www.wings.org.

38129 Wireless Flash News Service
PO Box 639111 Phone: (619)220-7191
San Diego, CA 92163-9111 Fax: (619)220-8590
E-mail: newsdesk@flashnews.com

Daily news feed focusing on offbeat, quirky, and popular culture news. **Key Personnel:** Patrick Glynn, Managing Editor, pglynn@flashnews.com; David Moye, Associate Editor, dmoye@flashnews.com; Elaine Camuso, Associate Editor, ecamuso@flashnews.com; David Louie, Sales/Marketing Manager, dslouie@flashnews.com; Gregg Fogg, Assoc. Ed., gfogg@flashnews.com; Adam Gnade, Associate Editor, agnade@flashnews.com. **URL:** http://www.flashnews.com.

38130 Women's Wear Daily
7 W. 34th St. Phone: (212)630-4000
New York, NY 10001 Fax: (212)630-3566

Distributes items on the fashion industry.

38131 World Features Syndicate
5842 Sagebrush Rd. Phone: (619)468-1099
La Jolla, CA 92037 Fax: (619)456-6264

Distributes daily and weekly columns. **Key Personnel:** Ronald A. Sataloff, President; Karl A. Van Asselt, Assoc. Ed.

38132 World News Syndicate Ltd.
PO Box 419 Phone: (213)469-2333
Hollywood, CA 90078 Fax: (213)469-2333
E-mail: worldnewssyndicate@yahoo.com

Distributes beauty, book review, entertainment, and medical columns. **Key Personnel:** William C. Lane, Managing Editor; Laurie A. Williams, Entertainment Ed.; William P. Jenkins, General Mgr.

38133 World Press
2547 Monroe St. Phone: (313)563-0360
Dearborn, MI 48124-3013 Fax: (248)669-0636
E-mail: worldpress@aol.com

Key Personnel: Stephen R. Castor, Editor.

38134 World Union Press
Rm. 373 Phone: (212)688-7557
Press Section Fax: (212)688-7557
United Nations
New York, NY 10017

Distributes political news, United Nations and world events.

Key Personnel: David Horowitz, Editor; Gregg Sitrin, Assoc. Ed.; Raymond Reuven Solomon, Staff.

38135 World Watch/Foreign Affairs Syndicate
144-21 Charter Rd.   Phone: (718)591-7246
Ste. 5C
Jamaica, NY 11435

Distributes political and foreign affairs news. **Key Personnel:** John J. Metzler, Editor.

38136 Worldwide Media
24226 Davida Ln.   Phone: (949)215-3751
Laguna Niguel, CA 92677
E-mail: wwm@wwmedia.net; pr@wwmedia.net

Syndicates features and columns on celebrities, health, fitness, family, business, pets, travel, self-help and women's issues. **Key Personnel:** Helen J. Lee, Licensing Dir., hlee@wwmedia.net; Mayra Gomez, Licensing Dir., mgomez@wwmedia.net. **Formerly:** Singer Media Corp.

38137 Yossarian News Service
PO Box 236   Phone: (415)588-5990
Millbrae, CA 94030

International distribution of parody news stories, political and social satire. **Key Personnel:** Charlie Chase, Exec. Ed.; Elio Ligi, Managing Editor; Paul Fericano, Editor; Pamela Meuser, Managing Editor; Katherine Daly, Edit. Dir.; Bruce Pryor, Assoc. Ed.

38138 Zondervan Press Syndicate
5300 Patterson Ave. SE   Phone: (616)698-6900
Grand Rapids, MI 49530   Fax: (616)698-3223
E-mail: zpub@zph.com

Distributes feature articles, short quotes, money columns, cartoons, and puzzles. **Key Personnel:** Judy Waggoner, Managing Editor. **URL:** http://www.zondervan.com.

38139 Zwita Productions
PO Box 112486   Phone: (203)973-0151
Stamford, CT 06911   Fax: (203)327-7909

Key Personnel: Angel Beck, Columnist, beckwk@aol.com.

Publishers Index

Index entries are arranged alphabetically by publishing company name. Publishers with multiple addresses are arranged alphabetically by state/province, and then by city. Citations in the index include publishing company name; street address; phone, fax, toll-free, cable, and telex numbers; publication titles published at that address; and corresponding entry numbers. Publications are arranged alphabetically under each publishing company address.

A & E Television Networks
235 E. 45th St.
New York, NY 10017
Phone: (212)210-9750
Fax: (212)210-1326

Publications: Biography (21316)

A M & M Publications
306 55th Pl.
Downers Grove, IL 60516

Publications: Metmenys (8484)

A. R. Heath Publishing Ltd.
19-11th St. N.E.
Weyburn, SK, Canada S4H 1J1
Phone: (306)842-3900
Fax: (306)842-2515

Publications: Estevan This Week (37590) • Weyburn This Week (37592)

AAA Auto Club of Missouri
12901 N 40 Dr.
St. Louis, MO 63141
Phone: (314)523-7350
Fax: (314)523-6982
Free: 800-222-7623

Publications: Midwest Traveler (17471)

AAA Auto Club South
1515 N. Westshore Blvd.
Tampa, FL 33607
Phone: (813)289-5923
Fax: (813)289-6245

Publications: AAA Going Places (6757)

AAA Auto Club of South Jersey
700 Laurel Oak Rd.
PO Box 1953
Voorhees, NJ 08043
Phone: (856)783-4222
Fax: (856)627-9100

Publications: SJ First (19703)

AAA Automobile Club of Hartford
815 Farmington Ave.
West Hartford, CT 06119-1584
Phone: (860)236-3261
Fax: (860)523-1797
Free: 800-842-4320

Publications: Journeys (5204)

AAA Automobile Club of Michigan
1 Auto Club Dr.
Dearborn, MI 48126
Phone: (313)336-1506
Fax: (313)336-1344

Publications: Michigan Living (14905)

AAA Automobile Club of Western New York
100 International Dr.
Williamsville, NY 14221-5769
Phone: (716)633-9860
Fax: (716)634-2504

Publications: The Motorist (23584)

AAA Carolinas
6600 AAA Dr.
Charlotte, NC 28212
Phone: (704)569-3600
Fax: (704)569-7815

Publications: GO Magazine (23744)

AAA Chicago Motor Club
999 E Touhy Ave.
Des Plaines, IL 60018
Phone: (847)390-9000
Fax: (847)390-9112

Publications: Home & Away (8399)

AAA Cincinnati
15 W Central Pkwy.
Cincinnati, OH 45202
Phone: (513)762-3301

Publications: Home and Away (24802)

AAA Colorado, Inc.
4100 E Arkansas Ave.
Denver, CO 80222
Phone: (303)753-8800
Fax: (303)758-8515

Publications: Rocky Mountain Motorist (4353)

AAA East Penn
1020 Hamilton St.
PO Box 1910
Allentown, PA 18105-1910
Phone: (610)434-5141
Fax: (610)778-3381

Publications: AAA Traveler (26624)

AAA Mid-Atlantic
c/o Brian Case
2040 Market St.
Philadelphia, PA 19103
Phone: (215)851-0291
Fax: (215)851-0297
Free: 888-222-4252

Publications: AAA World (27353)

AAA Midwest Magazine Network
10703 J St.
Omaha, NE 68127
Phone: (402)592-5000
Fax: (402)331-5194

Publications: AAA—Chicago Motor Club Home & Away (8037) • Home & Away (18198)

AAA Minnesota/Iowa
2900 AAA Ct.
Bettendorf, IA 52722
Phone: (563)332-7400
Fax: (563)332-1098

Publications: Home & Away (Minnesota Edition) (10621)

AAA New Jersey Automobile Club
1 Hanover Rd.
Florham Park, NJ 07932
Phone: (973)377-7200
Fax: (973)377-2979

Publications: AAA Traveler (18823)

AAA Ohio Motorists Association
5700 Brecksville Rd.
Independence, OH 44131
Phone: (216)606-6194
Fax: (216)606-6710

Publications: Ohio Motorist (25252)

AAA Southern Pennsylvania
PO Box 12005
York, PA 17402-0675
Phone: (717)845-2222
Fax: (717)845-5444

Publications: Car & Travel (28205)

AAA Southern Traveler
12901 N. 40th Dr.
St. Louis, MO 63141
Phone: (314)523-7350
Fax: (314)523-6982

Publications: AAA Southern Traveler (17402)

AAA Washington
1745-114th Ave., SW
Bellevue, WA 98004
Phone: (425)462-2222
Fax: (425)646-2193

Publications: Motorist (32667)

AAA World Publishing
c/o Brian Case
2040 Market St.
Philadelphia, PA 19103
Phone: (215)851-0291
Fax: (215)851-0297
Free: 888-AAA-4252

Publications: AAA World—Delaware (27354) • AAA World—Keystone (27355) • AAA World—Maryland (27356) • AAA World—Potomac (27357) • AAA World—Shore (27358) • AAA World—Valley (27359) • AAA World—Virginia (27360)

AACE International
209 Prairie Ave., Ste. 100
Morgantown, WV 26501
Phone: (304)296-8444
Fax: (304)291-5728
Free: 800-858-COST

Publications: Cost Engineering (33391)

AAFO, Inc.
106 S Kent St.
Winchester, VA 22601-5052
Phone: (540)662-2200
Fax: (703)665-8910
Free: 800-441-3850

Publications: The Functional Orthodontist (32629)

AANA Publishing, Inc.
222 S Prospect Ave.
Park Ridge, IL 60068
Phone: (847)692-7050
Fax: (847)692-7137

Publications: AANA Journal (9403)

Aardvark-Vanaheim Inc.
PO Box 1674, Sta. C
Kitchener, ON, Canada N2G 4R2
Phone: (519)576-0610
Fax: (519)576-0955

Publications: Cerebus (35959)

AAVC
Alumnae House
161 Raymond Ave.
Poughkeepsie, NY 12603
Phone: (845)437-5445
Fax: (845)437-7425

Publications: Vassar Quarterly (23150)

Abarta Media
516 N. Charles St., Ste. 300
Baltimore, MD 21201
Phone: (410)539-4373
Fax: (410)539-4381

Publications: WHERE Baltimore (13261)

Abarta Metro Publishing
225 S. Westmonte Dr., Ste. 1100
Altamonte Springs, FL 32714
Phone: (407)767-8338
Fax: (407)767-8348

Publications: WHERE Orlando (6510)

Abarta Metro Publishing
301 S. 19th St., Ste. 1C
Philadelphia, PA 19103
Phone: (215)893-5100
Fax: (215)893-5105

Publications: WHERE Philadelphia (27720)

Abarta Metro Publishing
Urb, Highland Garden C-8
Calle Marginal
Guaynabo, PR 00969
Phone: (787)272-3095
Fax: (787)272-3075

Publications: WHERE Puerto Rico (28246)

Abarta Metro Publishing
4809 Cole Ave., Ste. 205
Dallas, TX 75205
Phone: (214)522-0050
Fax: (214)522-0504

Publications: WHERE Dallas (30188) • WHERE Ft.
Worth (30356)

Abatech Inc.
1274 Rt. 113
PO Box 356
Blooming Glen, PA 18911
Phone: (215)258-3640
Fax: (772)679-2464

Publications: Journal of Applied Asphalt Binder
Technology (26716)

The Abbeville Herald
PO Box 609
Abbeville, AL 36310
Phone: (334)585-2331
Fax: (334)585-6835

Publications: The Abbeville Herald (1)

Abbeville Meridional
318 N Main St.
PO Box 400
Abbeville, LA 70510
Phone: (337)893-4223
Fax: (337)898-9022

Publications: Abbeville Meridional (12455)

Abbotsford Times
30887 Peardonville Rd.
Abbotsford, BC, Canada V2T 6K2
Phone: (604)854-5244
Fax: (604)854-1140

Publications: Abbotsford Times (34876)

Abbott & Hast Publications
761 Lighthouse Ave., Ste. A
Monterey, CA 93940-1033
Phone: (831)657-9403
Fax: (831)657-9137
Free: 800-453-1199

Publications: Mortuary Management (2583)

ABC Capital City
349 New Haven Ave.
PO Box 5339
Milford, CT 06460
Phone: (203)876-6800
Fax: (203)877-4772
Free: 800-238-3226

Publications: Elm City Citizen Newspaper (4954)

ABC Quincy Newspaper, Inc.
130 S 5th St.
PO Box 909
Quincy, IL 62306-0909
Phone: (217)223-5100
Fax: (217)223-9757
Free: 800-373-9444

Publications: The Quincy Herald Whig (9474)

Abenaki Publishers Inc.
160 Benmont Ave.
PO Box 4100
Bennington, VT 05201-4100
Phone: (802)447-1518
Fax: (802)447-2471

Publications: Fly Tyer (31498) • Saltwater Fly Fishing (31501)

Abernathy Weekly Review
916 Ave. D
PO Box 160
Abernathy, TX 79311-0160
Phone: (806)298-2033
Fax: (806)298-2033

Publications: Abernathy Weekly Review (29651)

Abilene Christian University
ACU Box 27892
Abilene, TX 79699-7892
Phone: (915)674-2482
Fax: (915)674-2139

Publications: Optimist (29654)

Abilene Reflector-Chronicle
303 N Broadway
Box 8
Abilene, KS 67410
Fax: (785)263-1645
Free: 800-339-1157

Publications: Northwestern Kansas Register (11783)

Abilene Reporter-News
101 Cypress St.
PO Box 30
Abilene, TX 79604
Phone: (915)673-4271
Fax: (915)670-5242
Free: 800-588-6397

Publications: Abilene Reporter-News (29652)

Ability Magazine
1001 W. 17th St.
Costa Mesa, CA 92627
Phone: (949)854-8700
Fax: (949)548-5966

Publications: Ability Magazine (1771)

Abingdon Newspaper, Inc.
143 West Main St.
PO Box 399
Abingdon, VA 24212
Phone: (540)628-7101
Fax: (540)628-9396

Publications: Washington County News (31627)

Abingdon Virginian
170 E Main St.
Abingdon, VA 24210
Phone: (540)628-2962
Fax: (540)676-6220

Publications: Abingdon Virginian (31625)

Able
PO Box 395
Old Bethpage, NY 11804
Phone: (516)939-2253
Fax: (516)939-0540

Publications: Able Newspaper (23036)

Aboriginal Multi Media Society
13245, 146 St.
Edmonton, AB, Canada T5L 4S8
Phone: (780)455-2700
Fax: (780)455-7639
Free: 800-661-5469

Publications: Alberta Sweetgrass (34700) • Windspeaker (34738)

About Face, Inc.
131 Main St.
Southwest Harbor, ME 04679-4607
Phone: (207)774-9703
Fax: (207)774-3233

Publications: Face Magazine (13058)

About.Time Magazine, Inc.
283 Genesee St.
Rochester, NY 14611
Phone: (585)235-7150
Fax: (585)235-7195

Publications: About.Time (23207)

Above Rubies
PO Box 681687
Franklin, TN 37068-1684
Phone: (931)729-9861
Fax: (931)729-1474

Publications: Above Rubies (29193)

Abrasives Engineering Society
144 Moore Rd.
Butler, PA 16001
Phone: (724)282-6210
Fax: (724)282-6210

Publications: Abrasive Users News Fax (26742)

Abraxas Press Inc.
PO Box 260113
Madison, WI 53726-0113
Phone: (608)238-0175

Publications: Abraxas (33915)

The ABWA Company Inc.
9100 Ward Pkwy.
PO Box 8728
Kansas City, MO 64114-0728
Phone: (816)361-6621
Fax: (816)361-4991
Free: 800-228-0007

Publications: Women in Business (17204)

ACA International
4040 W. 70th St.
Minneapolis, MN 55435
Phone: (952)926-6547
Fax: (952)926-1624

Publications: Collector (16068)

Academic International Press
PO Box 1111
Gulf Breeze, FL 32562-1111
Fax: (850)934-0953

Publications: Russia & Eurasia Documents Annual (6180) • Russia & Eurasia Military Review Annual (6181)

Academic Press
525 B St., Ste. 1900
San Diego, CA 92101-4495
Phone: (619)231-0926
Free: 888-677-7357

Publications: Advances in Applied Mathematics (3107) • Advances in Mathematics (14312) • Anaerobe (3112) • Analytical Biochemistry (3113) • Annals of Physics (3114) • Applied and Computational Harmonic Analysis (3115) • Archives of Biochemistry and Biophysics (3116) • Atomic Data and Nuclear Data Tables (3118) • Biochemical and Biophysical Research Communications (3120) • Biological Control (3121) • Bioorganic Chemistry (29765) • Blood Cells, Molecules, & Diseases (3122) • Brain, Behavior, and Immunity (3124) • Brain and Cognition (3125) • Brain and Language (15353) • Cell Biology International (3128) • Cellular Immunology (13323) • Clinical Immunology (2242) • Cognitive Psychology (3129) • Computer Speech & Language (3130) • Computer Vision and Image Understanding (3131) • Consciousness and Cognition (3134) • Contemporary Educational Psychology (3135) • Cryobiology (3137) • Cytokine (3138) • Developmental Biology (3140) • Developmental Review (3141) • Digital Signal Processing (3142) • Drug Delivery (3143) •

Ecotoxicology and Environmental Safety (19903) • Environmental Research (3145) • Epilepsy & Behavior (3146) • Experimental Cell Research (3147) • Experimental Eye Research (3148) • Experimental and Molecular Pathology (3149) • Experimental Neurology (3150) • Experimental Parasitology (3151) • Explorations in Economic History (3152) • Finite Fields and Their Applications (3154) • Food Microbiology (3156) • Frontiers in Neuroendocrinology (3157) • Fungal Genetics and Biology (3159) • Fungal Genetics and Biology (3158) • Games and Economic Behavior (3160) • General and Comparative Endocrinology (3161) • Genomics (3162) • Graphical Models (3163) • Gynecologic Oncology (3166) • Historia Mathematica (3167) • Hormones and Behavior (3168) • Icarus (3169) • ICES Journal of Marine Science (3170) • ImmunoMethods (3173) • Information and Computation (14070) • Journal of Algebra (3176) • Journal of Algorithms (3177) • Journal of Anthropological Archaeology (3179) • Journal of Approximation Theory (3180) • The Journal of Biomedical Informatics (22012) • Journal of Catalysis (1531) • Journal of Colloid and Interface Science (3181) • Journal of Combinatorial Theory, Series A (3182) • Journal of Combinatorial Theory, Series B (3183) • Journal of Comparative Economics (4944) • Journal of Complexity (3184) • Journal of Computational Physics (3185) • Journal of Computer and System Sciences (3186) • Journal of Differential Equations (3187) • Journal of Economic Theory (3189) • Journal of Environmental Economics and Management (3190) • Journal of Environmental Management (3191) • Journal of Environmental Psychology (3192) • Journal of Experimental Child Psychology (3193) • Journal of Experimental Social Psychology (3194) • Journal of Financial Intermediation (3195) • Journal of Food Composition and Analysis (3196) • Journal of Functional Analysis (3197) • Journal of Housing Economics (3198) • Journal of Invertebrate Pathology (3199) • Journal of the Japanese and International Economics (3200) • Journal of Magnetic Resonance (3202) • Journal of Magnetic Resonance (3203) • Journal of Magnetic Resonance (3201) • Journal of Mathematical Psychology (3204) • Journal of Memory and Language (3205) • Journal of Molecular Spectroscopy (3206) • Journal of Multivariate Analysis (3207) • Journal of Network and Computer Applications (3208) • Journal of Number Theory (3209) • Journal of Parallel and Distributed Computing (3210) • Journal of Research in Personality (3211) • Journal of Solid State Chemistry (15354) • Journal of Structural Biology (3213) • Journal of Surgical Research (3214) • Journal of Urban Economics (3215) • Journal of Visual Communication and Image Representation (3216) • Journal of Vocational Behavior (3217) • Learning and Motivation (3222) • Metabolic Engineering (3228) • Methods (3229) • Methods (3230) • Methods in Immunology and Immunochemistry (3231) • Microchemical Journal (12639) • Microvascular Research (3232) • Molecular and Cellular Neurosciences (3234) • Molecular Genetics and Metabolism (3235) • Molecular Phylogenetics and Evolution (3236) • Molecular Therapy (3237) • Neurobiology of Disease (3239) • Neurobiology of Learning and Memory (3240) • NeuroImage (3241) • Nitric Oxide (3242) • Nuclear Data Sheets (3243) • Optical Fiber Technology (3244) • Organizational Behavior and Human Decision Processes (3245) • Pesticide Biochemistry and Physiology (1817) • Plasmid (3246) • Preventive Medicine (3248) • Protein Expression and Purification (3250) • Quality Assurance (3251) • Quaternary Research (3252) • Real-Time Imaging (3253) • Regulatory Toxicology and Pharmacology (3254) • Research in Economics (3255) • Review of Economic Dynamics (3256) • Seminars in Cell and Developmental Biology (3273) • Social Science Research (3276) • Theoretical Population Biology (3278) • Toxicological Sciences (3281) • Toxicology and Applied Pharmacology (3282) • Virology (3288)

Academic Press
525 B Street, Ste. 1900
San Diego, CA 92101-4459
Phone: (619)231-6616

Publications: Graphical Models (3164)

Academic Printing and Publishing
9-3151 Lakeshore Rd., Ste. 403
Kelowna, BC, Canada V1W 3S9
Phone: (250)764-6427
Fax: (250)764-6428

Publications: Lumen (37552) • Philosophy in Review/Comptes rendus Philosophiques (34725)

Academic Publishing Co.
PO Box 145
Mount Royal, QC, Canada H3P 3B9
Phone: (514)738-5255

Publications: Economic Planning in Free Societies (37252)

Academy of Accounting Historians
c/o Kathy H. Rice
Culverhouse School of Accountancy
PO Box 870220
University of Alabama
Tuscaloosa, AL 35487
Phone: (205)348-9784
Fax: (205)348-8453

Publications: Accounting Historians Journal (480)

The Academy of American Franciscan History
The Catholic University of America Press
Leahy Hall, Rm. 240
Washington, DC 20064
Phone: (202)319-5052
Fax: (202)319-4985

Publications: The Americas (5349)

The Academy of American Poets
588 Broadway, Ste. 604
New York, NY 10012
Phone: (212)274-0343
Fax: (212)274-9427

Publications: American Poet (21205)

Academy of General Dentistry
211 E Chicago Ave., Ste. 900
Chicago, IL 60611-1999
Phone: (312)440-4300
Fax: (312)440-4261
Free: 888-AGD-DENT

Publications: AGD Impact (8247) • General Dentistry (8385)

Academy of Medicine of Cleveland/ Northern Ohio Medical Association
6000 Rockside Woods Blvd., No. 150
Cleveland, OH 44131-2352
Phone: (216)520-1000
Fax: (216)520-0999

Publications: Cleveland Physician (24873)

The Academy of Medicine of Toledo and Lucas County
4428 Secor Rd.
Toledo, OH 43623
Phone: (419)473-3200
Fax: (419)475-6744

Publications: Toledo Medicine (25571)

Academy of Political Science
475 Riverside Dr., Ste. 1274
New York, NY 10115-1274
Phone: (212)870-2500
Fax: (212)870-2202

Publications: Political Science Quarterly (22577)

Academy of Rehabilitative Audiology
PO Box 26532
Minneapolis, MN 55426
Phone: (952)920-0484
Fax: (952)920-6098

Publications: Journal of the Academy of Rehabilitative Audiology (30162)

Academy of Religion and Psychical Research
PO Box 614
Bloomfield, CT 06002-0614
Phone: (860)242-4593

Publications: Journal of Religion and Psychical Research (18737)

Academy of Television Arts and Sciences
5220 Lankershim Blvd.
North Hollywood, CA 91601-3109
Phone: (818)754-2800
Fax: (818)761-2827

Publications: Emmy (2642)

ACBJ Business Publications
137 N Main St., Ste. 400
Dayton, OH 45402
Phone: (513)222-6900
Fax: (513)222-9967

Publications: The Business News (25108)

ACC Communications Inc.
245 Fischer Ave., B-2
Costa Mesa, CA 92626
Phone: (714)751-1883
Fax: (714)751-4106

Publications: Workforce (1783)

Accent West
PO Box 1504
Amarillo, TX 79105
Phone: (806)371-8411
Fax: (806)371-7347

Publications: Accent West (29693)

Access Communications
155 N Winter
Adrian, MI 49221
Phone: (517)263-0800
Fax: (517)263-8809

Publications: Access (14707)

Accommodations, Inc., Subsidiary
200 W College Ave.
Tallahassee, FL 32301
Phone: (850)224-2888
Fax: (850)222-1752
Free: 800-476-FHMA

Publications: Florida Hotel & Motel Journal (6713)

Accountants Media Group
395 Hudson St.
New York, NY 10014
Phone: (212)337-8444
Fax: (212)337-8445
Free: 888-949-6699

Publications: Accounting Technology (21135)

ACETO Bookmen
98 St. James Ave.
Milton, NH 03851-4620

Publications: Chips from Many Trees and Growing Roots (18580)

Achill River Corp.
PO Box 2329
Asheville, NC 28802
Phone: (828)254-7334
Fax: (828)253-0677

Publications: Aquaculture Magazine (23626)

ACJ Communication Inc.
85 Broadway
Amityville, NY 11701
Phone: (631)264-0077
Fax: (631)264-5310

Publications: Amityville Record (20035) • Massapequa Post (20049)

Ackley World Journal
712 Main
Ackley, IA 50601
Phone: (641)847-2592
Fax: (641)847-3010

Publications: World Journal (10570)

Acme Newspapers, Inc.
311 E. Lancaster Ave.
Ardmore, PA 19003
Phone: (610)642-4300
Fax: (610)642-9704

Publications: Germantown Courier (26659) • Main Line Times (26662) • Mt. Airy Times Express (27575)

Acme Newspapers, Inc.
Manoa Shopping Center
Havertown, PA 19083
Phone: (610)446-8700
Fax: (610)449-0419

Publications: News of Delaware County (27030)

Acorn Whistle
907 Brewster Ave.
Beloit, WI 53511

Publications: Acorn Whistle (33573)

Acoustic Guitar
PO Box 767
San Anselmo, CA 94979
Phone: (415)485-6946
Fax: (415)485-0831
Free: 800-827-6837

Publications: Acoustic Guitar Magazine (3081)

Acre Press
3003 Ponce De Leon St.
New Orleans, LA 70119
Phone: (504)943-5198

Publications: Fell Swoop (12729)

Acres of Sky Communications, Inc.
PO Box 84
Lanark, IL 61046-0084
Phone: (815)493-2560
Fax: (815)493-2561

Publications: Prairie Advocate (9066)

Acres U.S.A.
PO Box 91299
Austin, TX 78709
Phone: (512)892-4400
Fax: (512)892-4448

Publications: Acres U.S.A. (29750)

ACT, Inc.
123 Chestnut St., Ste. 202
Philadelphia, PA 19106
Phone: (215)629-1666
Fax: (215)923-8358

Publications: Advertising/Communications Times (27364)

ACTA Press
4500 16th Ave. NW, Ste. 80
Calgary, AB, Canada T3B 0M6
Phone: (403)288-1195
Fax: (403)247-6851

Publications: International Journal of Computers and Applications (34646) • International Journal of Parallel and Distributed Systems and Networks (34647) • International Journal of Power and Energy Systems (34648)

Acting World Books
PO Box 3899
Los Angeles, CA 90078-3899
Phone: (818)905-1345
Fax: (818)905-1345
Free: 800-210-1197

Publications: The Agencies (2203)

Action
555 Broadway
New York, NY 10012
Phone: (212)343-6620
Fax: (212)682-1405

Publications: Action (21146)

Action Plus Shopper
827 S Halleck St.
Box 110
DeMotte, IN 46310
Phone: (219)987-5111
Fax: (219)987-5119
Free: 888-809-5561

Publications: Action Plus Shopper (9923)

Action Publications
17 Fond du Lac St.
Waupun, WI 53963-1598
Phone: (920)324-4717
Fax: (920)324-3773

Publications: Action Advertiser (34425) • Action Shopper (34426)

Action Shopper
307 S Front St., Ste. 101
PO Box 610
Marquette, MI 49855
Phone: (906)228-8920
Fax: (906)228-5777

Publications: Action Shopper (15337)

Action Unlimited
100-1
Domino Dr.
Concord, MA 01742
Phone: (508)371-2442

Publications: About Action Unlimited (14142)

Active Aging
125 S West St., Ste. 105
Wichita, KS 67213
Phone: (316)942-5385
Fax: (316)946-9180

Publications: Active Aging Publishing, Inc. (11880)

Actuarial Digest
PO Box 1127
Ponte Vedra Beach, FL 32004
Phone: (904)273-1245

Publications: Actuarial Digest (6593)

Ad Express
Box 610
Centerville, IA 52544
Phone: (515)856-6336

Publications: Ad Express (10687)

Ad Graphics
PO Box 398
Yorktown, TX 78164

Publications: The Yorktown News (31312)

AD Group WC, Inc.
613 S Main St.
Newark, NY 14513
Phone: (315)331-6956

Publications: Lyons Shopping Guide (22995) • Newark Pennysaver (22996) • Sodus Pennysaver (22997)

Ad-Mast Publishing, Inc.
Anthony T. Davis Bldg.
3101 Martin Luther King, Jr. Blvd.
Dallas, TX 75215
Phone: (214)428-8958
Fax: (214)428-2807

Publications: The Dallas Weekly Newspaper (30150)

AD-PAK of North Carolina
PO Box 191
Raleigh, NC 27602-9150
Phone: (919)832-9496
Fax: (919)832-7281

Publications: The AD-PAK (Raleigh Edition) (24123)

Ad Pro, Inc.
PO Box 520
Oxford, PA 19363-0520
Phone: (610)932-2462
Fax: (610)932-2246

Publications: Chester County Press (27348)

Ad Sack
PO Box 8729
Corpus Christi, TX 78468
Phone: (361)854-0137
Fax: (361)854-2439
Free: 800-659-0137

Publications: Ad Sack (30075)

Ad-Vantage Publishing Co.
PO Box 11555
Houston, TX 77293-1555
Phone: (281)449-9945
Fax: (281)987-8522

Publications: Northeast News (30511)

The AD-vertiser, Inc.
600 Charlevoix Ave.
PO Box 826
Petoskey, MI 49770
Phone: (231)347-8186
Fax: (231)347-5744
Free: 800-735-5729

Publications: The AD-vertiser (15434)

Ad-Visor
10575 Main St.
Honor, MI 49640-9761
Phone: (231)325-8600
Fax: (231)325-8602

Publications: Ad-Visor (15182)

Ada Evening News
116 N Broadway
PO Box 489
Ada, OK 74820
Phone: (580)332-4433
Fax: (580)332-8734

Publications: Ada Evening News (25723)

ADA Publishing
211 E Chicago Ave.
Chicago, IL 60611
Phone: (312)440-2810
Fax: (312)440-3538
Free: 800-621-8099

Publications: ADA News (8242) • Journal of the American Dental Association (8430)

Adair County Free Press
108 E Iowa St.
Box 148
Greenfield, IA 50849
Phone: (641)743-6121
Fax: (641)743-6378

Publications: Adair County Free Press (10930)

The Adair News
403 Audubon St.
PO Box 8
Adair, IA 50002-0008
Phone: (641)742-3241
Fax: (641)742-3489

Publications: The Adair News (10571)

Adam Fuerstenberg
90 Charlton Blvd.
Toronto, ON, Canada M2M 1B9
Phone: (416)221-2088
Fax: (416)635-1408

Publications: Parchment (36697)

Adam and Gillian's Sensual Whips and Toys Since 1987
40 Grant Ave.
Copiague, NY 11726
Phone: (516)842-1711
Fax: (516)842-7518
Free: 888-4SM-TOYS

Publications: The SandMUtopian Guardian (22704)

Adams Beverage Group
420 S. Palm Canyon Dr., 2nd Fl.
Palm Springs, CA 92262
Phone: (760)770-4370
Fax: (760)323-4370

Publications: Beverage Dynamics (2754)

Adams Business Media
420 S. Palm Canyon Dr.
Palm Springs, CA 92262-7304

Publications: Candy Business (2755) • Commodity Price Charts (2757) • Futures (2759) • GEO Europe (2760) • Investor Direct (2761) • JQ (2762) • Professional Candy Buyer (2765) • Tobacco Retailer (2768) • Truck Fleet Management (2769)

Adams Business Media
50 Washington St., 10th Fl.
Norwalk, CT 06854
Phone: (203)855-8499
Fax: (203)855-9446

Publications: Beverage & Food Dynamics (5050) • Business Geographics (5051) • Cheers (5052) • StateWays (5074)

Adams Business Media
250 S. Wacker Dr., Ste. 1150
Chicago, IL 60606
Phone: (312)977-0999
Fax: (312)980-3135

Publications: Arbor Age (8266) • AS/400 Systems Management (8276) • California Fairways (8297) • GeoWorld (8386) • Motor Service (8495) • Recreation Resources (8553) • sportsTURF (8571)

Adams Business Media
250 S. Wacker, Ste. 1150
Chicago, IL 60606
Phone: (847)427-2002
Fax: (847)427-2006

Publications: NPN International (8513)

Adams Business Media/Green Media
250 S. Wacker Dr., Ste. 1150
Chicago, IL 60606-5827
Phone: (312)977-0999

Publications: Irrigation Journal (8420) • Landscape Design (8456) • Landscape & Irrigation (8457) • Outdoor Power Equipment (8521)

Adams County Leader
PO Box R
Council, ID 83612
Phone: (208)253-6961
Fax: (208)253-6801
Free: 800-253-6961

Publications: Adams County Record (7850)

Adams State College
208 Edgemont Rd.
Alamosa, CO 81102
Phone: (719)587-7011
Fax: (719)587-7522
Free: 800-824-6494

Publications: South Coloradan (4131)

Adcraft Club of Detroit
3011 W Grand Blvd., Ste. 1715
Detroit, MI 48202
Phone: (313)872-7850
Fax: (313)872-7858

Publications: The Adcrafter (14913)

ADD, Inc.
1564 Kingsley Ave.
Orange Park, FL 32073-4594
Phone: (904)264-3200
Fax: (904)269-6958

Publications: Clay Today (6487)

Add, Inc.
100 Executive Way, Ste. 105
Ponte Vedra Beach, FL 32082
Phone: (904)285-8831

Publications: The Mirror (6333)

Add, Inc.
14 Park Pl.
PO Box 300
Lee, MA 01238-0300
Phone: (413)243-2341
Fax: (413)243-4662

Publications: The Berkshire Penny Saver (14269)

Add Inc.
195 Union St.
Newark, OH 43058
Phone: (740)522-2502
Fax: (740)522-2498

Publications: The Newark-Licking Advertiser (25425)

ADD, Inc.
109 South St.
Bennington, VT 05201
Phone: (802)447-3381
Fax: (802)447-3270
Free: 800-234-1432

Publications: Pennysaver Press (31500)

ADD, Inc.
121 N. Main St.
Jefferson, WI 53549
Phone: (414)674-2672
Fax: (414)674-6322

Publications: Jefferson County Advertiser (33868)

ADD, Inc.
416 N. Water St.
PO Box 283
New London, WI 54961
Phone: (920)982-2511
Fax: (920)982-7672

Publications: New London Buyers' Guide (34191) • New London Press-Star (34192)

ADD, Inc.
24 West Rives
Rhinelander, WI 54501
Phone: (715)369-3331
Fax: (715)369-4859

Publications: Rhinelander Our Town (34285)

ADD, Inc.
PO Box 276
Seymour, WI 54165
Phone: (920)833-2517
Fax: (920)833-2454

Publications: Seymour Buyers' Guide and Times Press (34315)

Add Inc.
PO Box 267
Waupaca, WI 54981
Phone: (715)258-3207
Fax: (715)258-8207

Publications: Rhinelander/Hodag Buyers' Guide (34284) • Stevens Point Buyers' Guide (34344) • Waupaca Buyers' Guide (34420) • Wisconsin Rapids Buyers' Guide (34464)

ADD, Inc.
600 Industrial Dr.
Waupaca, WI 54981
Phone: (715)258-8450
Fax: (715)258-8524

Publications: Wausau Buyers' Guide (34430)

Add Inc.—Ohio Group
61234 Southgate Pkwy.
Cambridge, OH 43725
Phone: (740)432-7077
Fax: (740)439-7072

Publications: The Guernsey-Noble Advertiser (24725)

Add Inc.—Ohio Group
147 W. Water St.
Chillicothe, OH 45601
Phone: (740)773-5010
Fax: (740)773-5021

Publications: County Line Advertiser (24762) • The Ross County Advertiser (24764)

Add Inc.—Ohio Group
1204 N. Court St.
Circleville, OH 43113
Phone: (740)477-3386
Fax: (740)474-9750

Publications: The Pickaway County Advertiser (24852)

Add Inc.—Ohio Group
1104 Fairy Falls Dr.
Coshocton, OH 43812
Phone: (740)622-4122
Fax: (740)623-0618

Publications: The Coshocton County Advertiser (25095)

Add Inc.—Ohio Group
300 Morton St.
Jackson, OH 45640
Phone: (740)286-7571
Fax: (740)286-4766

Publications: The Jackson County Advertiser (25256) • The Vinton County Advertiser (25258)

Add Inc.—Ohio Group
116 S. Main St.
New Lexington, OH 43764
Phone: (740)342-5483
Fax: (740)342-5305

Publications: The Buckeye Lake Advertiser (25411) • The Morgan County Advertiser (25412) • The Perry County Advertiser (25413)

Add Inc.—Ohio Group
201 E Emmitt Ave., Ste. B
Waverly, OH 45690
Phone: (740)947-7084
Fax: (740)947-7916

Publications: The Pike County Advertiser (25624)

Add Inc.—Ohio Group
760 Linden Ave., No. 2353
PO Box 2353
Zanesville, OH 43701-3355
Phone: (740)453-0615
Fax: (740)453-9504

Publications: Lancaster Fairfield Advertiser (25290) • Zanesville Muskingum Advertiser (25769)

Addison County Independent
PO Box 31
Middlebury, VT 05753
Phone: (802)388-4944

Publications: Addison County Independent (31555)

Adirondack Life
PO Box 410
Jay, NY 12941
Phone: (518)946-2191
Fax: (518)946-7461

Publications: Adirondack Life (20847)

Adirondack Mountain Club Inc.
814 Goggins Rd.
Lake George, NY 12845-4117
Phone: (518)668-4447
Fax: (518)668-3746
Free: 800-395-8080

Publications: Adirondac (20871)

Adirondack Publishing Co.
61 Broadway
PO Box 318
Saranac Lake, NY 12983
Phone: (518)891-2600
Fax: (518)891-2756

Publications: Adirondack Daily Enterprise (23297)

The Adit
1003 11th Ave.
PO Box 1244
Helena, MT 59624
Phone: (406)443-3690
Fax: (406)449-8170

Publications: The Adit (17816)

The Adler Group, Inc.
8601 Georgia Ave., Ste. 1001
Silver Spring, MD 20910-3440
Phone: (301)588-0681
Fax: (301)588-0924

Publications: Manager's Source Guide (13737)

ADMAR Associates
3140-B Tilghman St.
Box 204
Allentown, PA 18104
Phone: (610)439-1291
Fax: (610)398-5663

Publications: ARTS ALIVE! Magazine (26626)

Administrative Science Quarterly
20 Thornwood Dr., Ste. 100
Ithaca, NY 14850-1265
Phone: (607)254-8306
Fax: (607)254-7100

Publications: Administrative Science Quarterly (20787)

ADMIX Publishing
29 Barlett Ave.
Delmar, NY 12054-1105
Fax: (518)439-9004
Free: 888-439-4146

Publications: Access to Travel Magazine (20527)

The Adobe Foundation
707 Marble Ave. NW
Albuquerque, NM 87102-2066
Fax: (505)243-7801

Publications: The Adobe Journal (19762)

Adoptive Families
42 W. 38th St. Ste. 901
New York, NY 10018
Phone: (646)366-0830
Fax: (646)366-0842
Free: 800-372-3300

Publications: Adoptive Families (21150)

Adoremus: Society for the Renewal of the Sacred Liturgy
PO Box 3286
St. Louis, MO 63130
Phone: (314)863-8385
Fax: (314)863-5858

Publications: Adoremus Bulletin (17404)

Adrian Journal
130 Main St.
PO Box 378
Drexel, MO 64742
Phone: (816)657-2222
Fax: (816)657-2045

Publications: Drexel Star (17039)

The Adrian Journal Inc.
39 E Main
Box 128
Adrian, MO 64720
Phone: (816)297-2100
Fax: (816)297-2149

Publications: The Adrian Journal (16886) • The Archie News (16887) • Star Lite Shoppers Guide (16888)

ADSUM
Garrison Valcartier
C.P. 1000
Succ. Forces
Courcelette, QC, Canada G0A 4Z0
Phone: (418)844-5000
Fax: (418)844-6934

Publications: ADSUM (37083)

Adult Video News
9414 Eton Ave.
Chatsworth, CA 91311
Phone: (818)786-4286
Fax: (818)718-5799
Free: 800-521-2474

Publications: Adult Video News (1685)

Advance Magazine Publishers, Inc.
5520 Park Ave.
Trumbull, CT 06611
Phone: (203)373-7176
Fax: (203)371-2132

Publications: Golf Digest (5182) • Golf World (5183) • Golf World Business (5184)

Advance News
PO Box 30
Ligonier, IN 46767
Phone: (219)894-3102
Fax: (219)894-3104

Publications: Advance Leader (10272) • The Monday Leader (10273)

Advance Newspapers
2141 Port Sheldon Rd.
PO Box 9
Jenison, MI 49428-9301
Phone: (616)669-2700
Fax: (616)669-1162
Free: 800-439-0960

Publications: Ada/Cascade/Forest Hills Advance (14706) • East Grand Rapids Advance (15093) • Grand Rapids Advance (15094) • Grand Valley East Advance (14851) • Grand Valley West Advance (15228) • Kentwood Advance (15263) • Northfield Advance (15098) • Ottawa Advance (14891) • Rockford/Cedar Springs Advance (15469) • South Advance (15569) • Sparta/Kent City Advance (15230) • Walker/Westside Advance (15655) • Wyoming Advance (15687)

Advance Nickel & Dime News, Inc.
2048 Rte. 37
Lakehurst, NJ 08733-5645
Phone: (732)657-8936
Fax: (732)657-2970

Publications: Advance News (19157)

Advance Printing Ltd.
Box 669
Kemptville, ON, Canada K0G 1J0
Phone: (613)258-3451
Fax: (613)258-7734

Publications: The Advance (35928)

Advance Publications, Inc.
101 S. Main
PO Box 550
Holstein, IA 51025
Phone: (712)368-4368
Fax: (712)368-4369

Publications: The Advance (10951)

Advance Publications, Inc.
950 Fingerboard Rd.
Staten Island, NY 10305
Phone: (718)981-1234
Fax: (718)982-5789

Publications: Staten Island Advance (23361)

Advance Publications of Perry & Juniata Counties, Inc.
PO Box 130
New Bloomfield, PA 17068
Phone: (717)582-4305
Fax: (717)582-7933

Publications: Duncannon Record (26842) • Perry County Times (27313)

Advance Publishing Company
1101 N Cage Twin Palm Plz., Ste. C1
Pharr, TX 78577
Phone: (956)783-0036
Fax: (956)787-8824

Publications: Advance News Journal (30933)

Advance Publishing Co., Inc.
PO Box 669
Vidalia, GA 30474
Phone: (912)537-3131
Fax: (912)537-4899

Publications: The Advance Progress (7628) • The Advantage (7629)

Advance Publishing Co., Inc.
PO Box 2826
McAllen, TX 78502-2826
Phone: (210)783-0036
Fax: (210)783-0036

Publications: Pharr Advance News (30786) • The South Texas Business Journal (30787) • Sunshine (30788)

Advance-Reporter
101 W Jackson
PO Box 377
West Unity, OH 43570
Phone: (419)924-2382
Fax: (419)924-2382

Publications: Advance-Reporter (25635)

Advance Star Record
PO Drawer A
Rotan, TX 79546
Phone: (915)735-2562
Fax: (915)735-2230

Publications: Advance Star Record (30994)

Advanced Research Press, Inc.
690 Rte. 25A
Setauket, NY 11733-1200
Free: 800-645-5626

Publications: Muscular Development (23326)

Advanstar Communications
201 Sandpointe Ave., Ste. 600
Santa Ana, CA 92707
Phone: (714)513-8400
Fax: (714)513-8414
Free: 800-854-3112

Publications: America's Network (3619) • CADALYST (3621) • Comunicaciones (3623) • Dealernews (3624) • Hospitality Product News (3627) • Telecom Asia (3633) • Video Store (3635)

Advanstar Communications
440 Wheelers Farm Rd., Ste. 101
Milford, CT 06460-1847
Phone: (203)882-1300
Fax: (203)882-1800

Publications: American Salon (4952)

Advanstar Communications
100 W. Monroe, Ste. 1100
Chicago, IL 60603-1905
Phone: (312)553-8900
Fax: (312)553-8926

Publications: Chilton's Motor Age (8331)

Advanstar Communications
Raritan Plaza III
101 Fieldcrest Ave.
Edison, NJ 08837
Phone: (732)225-9500
Fax: (732)225-0211

Publications: Applied Clinical Trials (18786) • BioPharm (26314) • Frontline Solutions (24900) • GPS World (26317) • LCGC (26321) • Pharmaceutical Executive (26330) • Pharmaceutical Technology (26331) • Spectroscopy (18789)

Advanstar Communications
1 Park Ave.
New York, NY 10016-5802
Phone: (212)951-8700
Fax: (212)951-6793

Publications: Art Business News (21252) • Geriatrics (24903) • Modern Medicine (22349)

Advanstar Communications
7500 Old Oak Blvd.
Cleveland, OH 44130-3369
Phone: (440)243-8100
Fax: (440)891-2727

Publications: Aftermarket Business (24853) • Aftermarket Business AAIW Show Daily (24854) • Dermatology Times (24880) • DVM Newsmagazine (24883) • Formulary (24898) • Hotel & Motel Management (24909) • Landscape Management (24918) • LP-Gas (24922) • Managed Healthcare (24924) • Ophthalmology Times (24938) • Paperboard Packaging Worldwide (24939) • Pest Control (24940) • Pit & Quarry (24942) • R.S.I. Magazine (24951) • Urology Times (24959)

The Advantage
237 W. North St.
PO Box 488
Albemarle, NC 28002
Phone: (704)982-2121
Fax: (704)983-7999

Publications: The Advantage (23617)

Advantage Canada Inc.
466 Speers Rd. Ste. 220
Oakville, ON, Canada L6K 3W9
Phone: (905)845-8300
Fax: (905)845-9086

Publications: Business Executive (36136)

Advent Christian General Conference
14601 Albemarle Rd.
PO Box 23152
Charlotte, NC 28227
Phone: (704)545-6161
Fax: (704)573-0712

Publications: Advent Christian Witness (23734)

Adventure Media, Inc.
PO Box 3210
Incline Village, NV 89450
Phone: (775)832-3700
Fax: (775)832-3775

Publications: Adventure Travel Business (18356) • Adventure West (18357)

Adventure Publishing Group, Inc.
1501 Broadway, Ste. 500
New York, NY 10036-5501
Phone: (212)575-4510
Fax: (212)575-4521

Publications: The Licensing Book (22252) • The Toy Book (22850)

Adventures in Publishing
4721 Trousdale Dr., Ste. 120
Nashville, TN 37220
Phone: (615)333-9600
Fax: (615)333-0171

Publications: X-Ray News (29504)

Adventuresses of Sherlock Holmes
360 W 21st St.
New York, NY 10011

Publications: The Serpentine Muse (22733)

The Advertiser
920 1st. Ave.
Box 300
Beaverlodge, AB, Canada T0H 0C0
Phone: (403)354-2460
Fax: (403)354-2460

Publications: The Advertiser (34617)

The Advertiser
116 S. Magnolia
PO Box 289
Elmwood, IL 61529
Phone: (309)742-2521
Fax: (309)742-2511

Publications: The Advertiser (8842)

The Advertiser
345 S. High St.
Muncie, IN 47305
Phone: (765)213-5700
Fax: (765)213-5937

Publications: The Advertiser (10325)

The Advertiser
406 Stevens
Box 640
Iowa Falls, IA 50126
Phone: (641)648-2521
Fax: (641)648-4765
Free: 800-373-1719

Publications: The Advertiser (10999)

The Advertiser
110 W. Main
Rockford, IA 50468

Publications: Advertiser-Register (11182)

Advertiser
PO Box 309
Concordia, KS 66901-0309

Publications: Advertiser (11397)

Advertiser
PO Box 518
Maysville, KY 41056
Phone: (606)564-9091
Fax: (606)564-6893

Publications: Advertiser (12288)

Advertiser
PO Box 158
Paris, KY 40362-0158
Phone: (606)987-1870
Fax: (606)987-3729

Publications: Bourbon County Citizen (12353) •
Citizen-Advertiser (12354)

Advertiser
PO Box 628
Edgefield, SC 29824
Phone: (803)637-3540
Fax: (803)637-0602

Publications: Advertiser (28599)

Advertiser
PO Box 1900
Gillette, WY 82717-1900
Phone: (307)686-6123
Fax: (307)686-9030

Publications: The Gillette Area Advertiser (34526)

The Advertiser-Gleam
2218 Taylor St.
PO Box 190
Guntersville, AL 35976
Phone: (256)582-3232
Fax: (256)582-3231
Free: 800-239-5319

Publications: The Advertiser-Gleam (254)

Advertiser - North and South Edition
121 N. Main St.
Jefferson, WI 53549
Phone: (414)674-2672
Fax: (414)674-6322

Publications: Advertiser - North and South Edition
(33867)

Advertiser Publishing Co.
19 Church St.
PO Box 660
Calais, ME 04619-0660
Phone: (207)454-3561
Fax: (207)454-3458

Publications: The Calais Advertiser (12938)

Advertiser-Tribune
320 Nelson St.
PO Box 778
Tiffin, OH 44883-0778
Phone: (419)448-3200
Fax: (419)447-3274
Free: 800-448-3235

Publications: Advertiser-Tribune (25559)

Advertising Research Foundation
641 Lexington Ave.
New York, NY 10022
Phone: (212)751-5656
Fax: (212)319-5265

Publications: Journal of Advertising Research
(21976)

Advertising Specialty Institute
4800 St. Rd.
Trevose, PA 19053-6698
Phone: (215)942-8600
Fax: (215)953-3107

Publications: The Counselor (28056)

The Advisor
83 State St.
Box 460
North Haven, CT 06473-0071
Phone: (203)239-5404
Fax: (203)239-7097

Publications: The Advisor (5047)

Advisor Media, Inc.
4849 Viewridge Ave.
San Diego, CA 92123
Phone: (858)278-5600
Fax: (858)278-0300
Free: 800-336-6060

Publications: Access VB- SQL Advisor (3104) •
Lotus Advisor Magazine (3227) • Mobile Business
Advisor (3233)

Advisor & Source Newspapers
48075 Van Dyke Ave.
Shelby Township, MI 48317
Phone: (586)731-1000
Fax: (586)731-8172

Publications: The Advisor (15370) • The Advisor
(14998) • Macomb County Legal News (15536) •
Romeo-Washington Source (15537) • Sterling
Heights Source (15576) • The Voice News (15398) •
Warren Advisor (15665)

Advocado Press Inc.
PO Box 145
Louisville, KY 40201
Phone: (502)894-9492
Fax: (502)899-9562

Publications: The Disability Rag's Ragged Edge
Magazine (12215)

The Advocate
4917B-49th St.
Athabasca, AB, Canada T9S 1C5
Fax: (403)675-3143

Publications: The Advocate (34609)

Advocate
487 S Main
Clifton, IL 60927
Phone: (815)694-2122
Fax: (815)694-3770

Publications: Advocate (8681)

Advocate
PO Box 36
Harper, KS 67058
Phone: (620)896-7311
Fax: (620)896-2754

Publications: Harper Advocate (11478)

The Advocate
111 Mass Moca Way
North Adams, MA 01247
Phone: (413)664-6900
Fax: (413)664-7900

Publications: The Advocate (14416) • The Advocate (14417)

The Advocate
22 N. 1st St.
Newark, OH 43055-5608
Phone: (740)345-4053
Fax: (740)345-1634

Publications: The Advocate (25424)

Advocate
Box 465
Allen, OK 74825
Phone: (405)857-2687
Fax: (405)857-2573

Publications: Advocate (25729)

The Advocate-Democrat
509 Cook St.
PO Box 8
Madisonville, TN 37354
Phone: (423)442-4575
Fax: (423)442-1416

Publications: The Democrat-Observer (29340)

Advocate-Messenger Co.
330 S 4th St.
Danville, KY 40422-2033
Phone: (606)236-2551
Fax: (606)236-9566
Free: 800-428-0409

Publications: Advocate-Messenger (12036)

Advocate Printing and Publishing
George St.
PO Box 1000
Pictou, NS, Canada B0K 1H0
Phone: (902)485-1990
Fax: (902)485-6353

Publications: Pictou Advocate (35602) • Total
Health (35603)

Advocate Printing and Publishing
72 Main St.
Springhill, NS, Canada V0M 1X0
Phone: (902)597-3731
Fax: (902)667-1402

Publications: Springhill-Parrsboro Record (35606)

The Advocate-Tribune
PO Box 99
Granite Falls, MN 56241-0099
Phone: (320)564-2126
Fax: (320)564-4293

Publications: The Advocate-Tribune (15934)

Adweek LP
100 Boylston St., Ste. 210
Boston, MA 02116-4610
Phone: (617)482-0876
Fax: (617)482-2921

Publications: Adweek/New England (13846)

ADWEEK Magazines
770 Broadway, 7th Fl.
New York, NY 10003
Phone: (646)654-5174
Fax: (646)654-5351
Free: 800-468-2395

Publications: Mediaweek Magazine (22309)

Adwise
PO Box 2181
Middletown, NY 10940
Phone: (914)342-9090

Publications: Big Saver (21079)

AEA (Aircraft Electronics Association)
4217 S. Hocker Dr.
Independence, MO 64055-4723
Phone: (816)373-6565
Fax: (816)478-3100

Publications: Avionics News (17107)

Aeon: A Journal of Myth and Science
3908 Marigold Dr.
Ames, IA 50014-2918
Phone: (515)292-6565
Fax: (515)292-2603

Publications: Aeon (10588)

AERO Sun-Times
432 N Last Chance Gulch St.
Helena, MT 59601-5014
Phone: (406)443-7272
Fax: (406)442-9120

Publications: AERO Sun-Times (17817)

Aeronautica and Air Label Collectors Club
PO Box 1239
Elgin, IL 60121-1239
Phone: (847)468-0840
Fax: (847)468-0840

Publications: Aeronautica & Air Label Collectors Club (8822)

Aeronautics Education Enterprises
2900 E Weymouth
Tucson, AZ 85716-1249
Phone: (520)881-2232
Fax: (520)795-6776

Publications: Contact! (Tucson) (942)

Aerospace Medical Association
320 S. Henry St.
Alexandria, VA 22314-3579
Phone: (703)739-2240
Fax: (703)739-9652

Publications: Aviation, Space, and Environmental Medicine (31645)

Aerotech
456 East Ave. K4, Ste. 8
Lancaster, CA 93535
Phone: (661)945-5634
Fax: (661)723-7757

Publications: Aerotech News & Review (2146) • Astro News (1867) • Barstow Log (1480) • Desert Wings (1841) • The Lighthouse (2317) • Tiefort Telegraph (1925)

Aetherius Society
6202 Afton Pl.
Hollywood, CA 90028
Phone: (323)465-9652

Publications: Cosmic Voice (2051)

A.F. Keller & Assoc. Ltd.
Bag 6000
Spruce Grove, AB, Canada T7X 2Z5
Phone: (780)962-9228
Fax: (780)962-1021

Publications: Calmar Community Voice (34674) • Onoway Community Voice (34820) • Wabamun Community Voice (34853)

Affirmative Action, Inc.
8356 Olive Blvd.
St. Louis, MO 63132
Phone: (314)991-1335
Fax: (314)997-1788
Free: 800-537-0655

Publications: Affirmative Action Register (17405)

AFL-CIO
815 16th St. NW, 5th Fl.
Washington, DC 20006
Phone: (202)637-5000
Fax: (202)508-6908

Publications: America Work (5322)

Africa Resource Center
Dept. of Africana Studies
Binghamton University
Vestal Parkway
Binghamton, NY 13902-6000
Phone: (607)786-5040

Publications: African Philosophy (20151) • Ijele (20155) • Jenda (20159) • Journal on African Immigration (JAI) (20161) • West Africa Review (20220)

African Studies Association
Rutgers
The State University of New Jersey
132 George St.
New Brunswick, NJ 08901-1400
Phone: (732)932-8173
Fax: (732)932-3394

Publications: African Studies Review (19324)

African Studies Center
PO Box 951310
University of California
Los Angeles, CA 90095-1310
Phone: (310)825-1218
Fax: (310)206-2250

Publications: African Arts (2201)

African Studies Quarterly
427 Grinter Hall
PO Box 115560
Gainesville, FL 32611
Phone: (352)392-2183
Fax: (352)392-2134

Publications: African Studies Quarterly (6129)

The Afro-American Co.
2519 N Charles St.
Baltimore, MD 21218
Phone: (410)554-8200
Fax: (410)554-8213
Free: 800-AFRO-892

Publications: Baltimore Afro-American (13128)

Afro-American Historical Association of the Niagara Frontier, Inc.
PO Box 63
Buffalo, NY 14216
Phone: (716)691-4257

Publications: Afro-Americans in New York Life and History (20362)

Afro-American Historical and Genealogical Society
Box 73067
Washington, DC 20056-3067
Phone: (202)234-5350
Fax: (202)829-8970

Publications: Afro-American Historical and Genealogical Society Journal (5315)

The Afro News
PO Box 1101
Aldergrove, BC, Canada V4W 2V1
Phone: (604)856-4838
Fax: (604)856-1074

Publications: The Afro News (34879)

Afronet
PO Box 43631
Los Angeles, CA 90043

Publications: Afronet Magazine (2202)

AFSA
2101 E. St. NW
Washington, DC 20037
Phone: (202)338-4045
Fax: (202)338-6820
Free: 800-704-AFSA

Publications: Foreign Service Journal (5500)

AFSM International
1342 Colonial Blvd., Ste. 25
Fort Myers, FL 33907-1007
Phone: (941)275-7887
Fax: (941)275-0794
Free: 800-333-9786

Publications: AFSM International Professional Journal (6093)

After Five Magazine
PO Box 492905
Redding, CA 96049-2905
Phone: (530)335-5360
Fax: (530)335-5335
Free: 800-637-3540

Publications: After Five Magazine (2886)

The Afton-Fairland American
PO Box 339
Fairland, OK 74343
Phone: (918)676-3484

Publications: The Afton-Fairland American (25832)

Afton Star-Enterprise
Box 128
Afton, IA 50830
Phone: (515)347-8721

Publications: Afton Star-Enterprise (10573)

Ag Journal
122 San Juan
PO Box 500
La Junta, CO 81050-0500
Phone: (719)384-8121
Fax: (719)384-2867
Free: 800-748-1997

Publications: Ag Journal (4526)

The Ag Journal
PO Box 500
La Junta, CO 81050
Phone: (719)384-8121
Fax: (719)384-2867
Free: 800-748-1997

Publications: Cattle Guard (4137)

Ag Press, Inc.
1531 Yuma
Box 1009
Manhattan, KS 66502-0037
Phone: (785)539-7558
Fax: (785)539-2679

Publications: Grass & Grain (11620)

AG Retailer
11701 Borman Dr.
St. Louis, MO 63146
Phone: (314)569-2700
Fax: (314)569-1083

Publications: Ag Retailer Magazine (16208)

AG Service Publications
PO Box 559
LaFayette, NY 13084
Phone: (315)677-7818
Fax: (315)677-3852

Publications: Agricultural News (Lafayette) (20869)

Against the Grain
The Citadel, MSC 98
209 Richardson Ave.
Charleston, SC 29409
Phone: (843)723-3536
Fax: (843)723-3536

Publications: Against the Grain (28504)

Agency Photo Services
PO Box 273
Whitsett, NC 27377
Phone: (336)449-0809

Publications: American Modeler (24288)

Agnes Scott College
141 E College Ave.
Decatur, GA 30030-3797
Phone: (404)471-6000
Fax: (404)471-6298

Publications: Agnes Scott Alumnae Magazine (7233) • The Profile (7237)

AGNI
Boston University Creative Writing Program
236 Bay State Rd.
Boston, MA 02215
Phone: (617)353-7135
Fax: (617)353-7134

Publications: AGNI (13847)

Agra USA
2302 W. 1st St.
Cedar Falls, IA 50613-1879
Phone: (319)277-3599
Fax: (319)277-3783
Free: 800-959-3276

Publications: Implement & Tractor (10657) • Seed & Crops Digest (10662)

Agri-News Publications
420 2nd St.
La Salle, IL 61301
Phone: (815)223-2558
Fax: (815)223-5997
Free: 800-426-9438

Publications: Illinois Agri-News (9055) • Indiana Agri-News (10121)

Agricom
2474 rue Champlain
Clarence Creek, ON, Canada K0A 1N0
Phone: (613)488-2651
Fax: (613)488-2541

Publications: Agricom (35736)

Agricore United
PO Box 9800
Winnipeg, MB, Canada R3C 3K7
Phone: (204)954-1400
Fax: (204)954-1422
Free: 800-782-0794

Publications: The Manitoba Co-operator (35337)

Agricore United
2800-201 Portage Ave.
PO Box 6600
Winnipeg, MB, Canada R3C 3A7
Phone: (204)944-5511
Fax: (204)944-5454

Publications: Grainews (35330)

Agricultural Economics & Agribusiness
101 Agricultural Administration Building
Louisiana State University
Baton Rouge, LA 70803-5604
Phone: (225)578-3282
Fax: (504)388-2716

Publications: Louisiana Rural Economist (12503)

Agricultural Institute of Canada
141 Laurier Ave. W., Ste. 1112
Ottawa, ON, Canada K1P 5J3
Phone: (613)232-9459
Fax: (613)594-5190

Publications: Canadian Journal of Agricultural Economics (36200) • Canadian Journal of Animal Science (36201) • Canadian Journal of Plant Science (36212) • Canadian Journal of Soil Science (36219)

Agriculture and Agri-Food Canada
1391 Sandford St.
London, ON, Canada N5X 2M8
Phone: (519)457-1470
Fax: (519)457-3997

Publications: Canadian Plant Disease Survey (35980)

Agriculture Dept.
PO Box 371954
Pittsburgh, PA 15250-7954

Publications: Fire Management Today (27789)

AGRR (AutoGlass Repair and Replacement)
PO Box 569
Garrisonville, VA 22463
Phone: (540)720-5584
Fax: (540)720-5687

Publications: AGRR: AutoGlass Repair and Replacement (32102)

Agudath Israel of America
42 Broadway, 14th Fl.
New York, NY 10004
Phone: (212)797-9000
Fax: (646)254-1600

Publications: The Jewish Observer (21964)

Ahora Spanish News
30 Mary St., Ste. 2
PO Box 3582
Reno, NV 89509
Phone: (775)323-6811
Fax: (775)323-6995

Publications: Ahora Spanish News (18416)

Ahwautkee Foothills News
10631 S. 51st St., Ste. 1
Phoenix, AZ 85044
Phone: (480)898-7900
Fax: (480)893-1684

Publications: Ahwatukee Foothills News (772)

A.I. Root Co.
PO Box 706
Medina, OH 44258
Phone: (330)725-6677
Fax: (330)725-5624
Free: 800-289-7668

Publications: Bee Culture (25372)

AIA Wisconsin
321 S Hamilton St.
Madison, WI 53703-4000
Phone: (608)257-8477
Fax: (608)257-0242

Publications: Wisconsin Architect (33978)

AIACC
1303 J St., Ste. 200
Sacramento, CA 95814
Phone: (916)448-9082
Fax: (916)442-5346

Publications: arcCa (2977)

Aid Association for Lutherans
4321 N. Ballard Rd.
Appleton, WI 54919
Phone: (920)734-5721
Fax: (920)730-4765

Publications: Correspondent (33536)

Aigis Publications
PO Box 637
Littleton, CO 80160

Publications: Democracy and Nature (4546)

Aim Publications
PO Box 1174
Maywood, IL 60153
Phone: (708)344-4414

Publications: Aim—America's Intercultural Magazine (9163)

Air Age Publishing, Inc.
100 East Ridge
Ridgefield, CT 06877
Phone: (203)431-9000
Fax: (203)431-3000

Publications: Model Airplane News (5099) • Radio Control Boat Modeler (5100) • Radio Control Car Action (5101)

Air Cargo News Inc.
Marine Air Terminal
La Guardia Airport, NY 11371
Phone: (718)651-3591
Fax: (718)740-0761

Publications: Air Cargo News (23168)

Air Courier Conference of America
C/O Sage Communications
181 Pork St.
Montclair, NJ 07042
Phone: (201)744-5771
Fax: (201)744-6353

Publications: ACCA Express (19239)

Air Force Association
1501 Lee Hwy.
Arlington, VA 22209-1198

Publications: Air Force Magazine (31768)

Air Force News Service
203 Norton St.
San Antonio, TX 78226-1848
Phone: (210)925-7757
Fax: (210)925-7219

Publications: Airman (31024)

Air Force Reserve Command
HQ AFRC/PA
Robins AFB, GA 31098-1637
Phone: (478)327-1773
Fax: (478)327-0878

Publications: Citizen Airman (7499)

Air Force Sergeants Association
PO Box 50
Temple Hills, MD 20757-0050
Phone: (301)899-3500
Fax: (301)899-8136
Free: 800-638-0594

Publications: Sergeants (13754)

Air Line Pilots Association
535 Herndon Pkwy.
PO Box 1169
Herndon, VA 20170
Phone: (703)689-2270
Fax: (703)689-4370

Publications: Air Line Pilot (32159)

The Air Pulse
Public Affairs
55th WG
Offutt A F B, NE 68113-3206
Phone: (402)294-3663
Fax: (402)294-7172

Publications: The Air Pulse (18187)

Air Service Directory, Inc.
280 N. Bedford Rd.
Mount Kisco, NY 10549
Phone: (914)242-8700
Fax: (914)242-5422

Publications: ABD (21098)

Air and Space Power Journal
Cadre/ARJ
401 Chennault Cir.
Maxwell AFB, AL 36112-6428
Phone: (334)953-5322
Fax: (334)953-5811

Publications: Air and Space Power Journal (315)

Air Traffic Control Association (ATCA)
2300 Clarendon Blvd., Ste. 711
Arlington, VA 22201
Phone: (703)522-5717
Fax: (703)527-7251

Publications: Journal of Air Traffic Control (31800)

Air & Waste Management Association
One Gateway Ctr., 420 Ft. Duquesne Blvd.
Pittsburgh, PA 15222
Phone: (412)232-3444
Fax: (412)232-3450

Publications: EM (27783)

Airforce Productions, Ltd.
PO Box 2460, Sta. D
Ottawa, ON, Canada K1P 5W6
Phone: (613)992-5184
Fax: (613)995-2196

Publications: Airforce (36184)

AIS Communications Ltd.
145 Thames Rd. W.
Exeter, ON, Canada N0M 1S3
Phone: (519)235-2400
Fax: (519)235-0798

Publications: Canadian Rental Service (35824) • Glass Canada (35826) • Ground Water Canada (35827)

AIUM
14750 Sweitzer Ln., Ste. 100
Laurel, MD 20707-5906
Phone: (301)498-4100
Fax: (301)498-4450
Free: 800-638-5352

Publications: Journal of Ultrasound in Medicine (13920)

AJ Press
108 Hedge Nettle Crossing
Savannah, GA 31406-7220
Phone: (912)352-9300

Publications: Animation Journal (7530)

AJA Enterprises
11740 S Elizabeth
Chicago, IL 60643
Phone: (773)785-5384
Fax: (773)785-5413

Publications: The New Chicago Shoreland News (8323)

AJES, Paul Smith's College
Rte. 86 & 30
PO Box 265
Paul Smiths, NY 12970
Phone: (518)327-6377
Fax: (518)327-6369

Publications: Adirondack Journal of Environmental Studies (23083)

Ajo Copper News
10 Pajaro
PO Box 39
Ajo, AZ 85321
Phone: (520)387-7688
Fax: (520)387-7505

Publications: Ajo Copper News (655)

A.J.'s Printing
309 W Spring Ave.
Conway Springs, KS 67031
Phone: (620)456-2232

Publications: The South Haven New Era (11401)

Akademiska Dzive/Academic Life
1 Vincent Ave. S
Minneapolis, MN 55405-1953
Phone: (612)374-3009

Publications: Akademiska Dzive/Academic Life (16055)

Akron Bugle
7263 Downey Rd.
Akron, NY 14001
Phone: (716)542-9615

Publications: Akron Bugle (19977)

The Akron Legal News
60 S Summit St.
Akron, OH 44308
Phone: (330)376-0917
Fax: (330)376-7001

Publications: The Akron Legal News (24573)

The Akron News-Reporter
69 Main St.
Akron, CO 80720
Phone: (970)345-2296
Fax: (970)345-6638

Publications: The Akron News-Reporter (4130)

Akwekon Press
Cornell University
450 Caldwell Hall
Ithaca, NY 14853
Free: 800-9NA-TIVE

Publications: Native Americas (20810)

Alabama Agricultural Experiment Station
Auburn University
7 Comer Hall
Auburn, AL 36849-7425
Phone: (334)844-4877

Publications: Highlights of Agricultural Research (41)

Alabama Cattleman's Association
201 S. Bainbridge St.
PO Box 2499
Montgomery, AL 36102-2499
Phone: (205)265-1867
Fax: (334)834-5326

Publications: The Alabama Cattleman (356)

Alabama Counseling Association
217 Darryl St.
Livingston, AL 35470
Phone: (205)652-1712
Fax: (205)652-1576
Free: 888-655-5460

Publications: Alabama Counseling Association Journal (305)

Alabama Dept. of Conservation and Natural Resources
64 N Union St.
Montgomery, AL 36130-1901
Phone: (334)242-3151
Fax: (334)242-1880
Free: 800-262-3151

Publications: Outdoor Alabama (372)

Alabama Development Office
401 Adams Ave.
Montgomery, AL 36130
Phone: (334)242-0400
Fax: (334)242-2414
Free: 800-248-0033
Telex: 592471

Publications: Developing Alabama (364)

Alabama Forestry Association
555 Alabama St.
Montgomery, AL 36104-4395
Phone: (334)265-8733
Fax: (334)262-1258

Publications: Alabama Forests (357)

Alabama Heritage
University of Alabama
Box 870342
Tuscaloosa, AL 35487-0342
Phone: (205)348-7467
Fax: (205)348-7473

Publications: Alabama Heritage (483)

Alabama League of Municipalities
535 Adams Ave.
PO Box 1270
Montgomery, AL 36104
Phone: (334)262-2566
Fax: (334)263-0200

Publications: Alabama Municipal Journal (359)

Alabama Rural Electric Association of Cooperatives
340 Technacenter Dr.
Montgomery, AL 36124
Phone: (334)215-2732
Fax: (334)215-2733

Publications: Alabama Living (358)

Alabama State Council on the Arts
201 Monroe St. Ste. 110
Montgomery, AL 36130-1800
Phone: (334)242-4076
Fax: (334)240-3269

Publications: Alabama Arts (355)

The Alabamian
University of Montevallo
Station 6222
Montevallo, AL 35115
Phone: (205)665-6222
Fax: (205)665-6232

Publications: The Alabamian (354)

Alam Attijarat (The World of Business)
2700 Virginia Ave. NW, Ste. 107
Washington, DC 20037
Phone: (202)337-2413
Fax: (202)337-3383

Publications: Alam Attijarat (The World of Business) (5320)

Alameda-Contra Costa Medical Association
6230 Claremont Ave.
Oakland, CA 94618
Phone: (510)654-5383

Publications: Alameda-Contra Medical Association (2663)

Alameda County Bar Association
610 16th St., Ste. 426
Oakland, CA 94612
Phone: (510)632-7884
Fax: (510)893-3119

Publications: Alameda County Bar Association Bulletin (2664)

Alameda County Central Labor Council
7992 Capwell Dr.
Oakland, CA 94621
Phone: (510)632-4242
Fax: (510)632-3993

Publications: East Bay Labor Journal (2679)

The Alameda Publishing Corp./Oakland Post
PO Box 1350
Oakland, CA 94604-1350
Phone: (510)763-1120
Fax: (510)763-9670

Publications: Berkeley Tri City Post (1499) • El Mundo (2680) • Richmond Post (2921) • San Francisco Post (3438)

Alamosa Newspapers, Inc.
401 State Ave.
PO Box 1099
Alamosa, CO 81101
Phone: (719)589-2553
Fax: (719)589-6573

Publications: The Valley Courier (4132)

The Alan Guttmacher Institute
120 Wall St.
New York, NY 10005
Phone: (212)248-1111
Fax: (212)248-1951
Free: 800-765-7514

Publications: Guttmacher Report on Public Policy (21784) • International Family Planning Perspectives (21897) • Perspectives on Sexual and Reproductive Health (22545)

Alan Squire Enterprises
4948 St. Elmo Ave., Ste. 208
Bethesda, MD 20814
Phone: (301)986-7901
Fax: (301)986-9525
Free: 877-326-2649

Publications: SportsFan Magazine (13382)

Alarm Clock
PO Box 1551
Royal Oak, MI 48068
Phone: (248)442-8634
Fax: (248)478-7241

Publications: Alarm Clock (15476)

Alaska Business Publishing Co., Inc.
PO Box 241288
Anchorage, AK 99524-1288
Phone: (907)276-4373
Fax: (907)279-2900
Free: 800-770-4373

Publications: Alaska Business Monthly (520)

Alaska Department of Fish and Game
Box 25526
Juneau, AK 99802-5526
Phone: (907)465-4210
Fax: (907)465-2604

Publications: Alaska Fishery Research Bulletin (594)

Alaska Geographic Society
PO Box 93370
Anchorage, AK 99509
Phone: (907)562-0164
Fax: (907)562-0479
Free: 888-255-6697

Publications: Alaska Geographic (521)

Alaska Highway Publications Ltd.
PO Box 1129
Delta Junction, AK 99737
Free: 800-895-4369

Publications: Alaska Highway News (560)

Alaska Historical Society
PO Box 100299
Anchorage, AK 99510-0299
Phone: (907)276-1596
Fax: (907)276-1596

Publications: Alaska History (522)

Alaska Newspapers, Inc.
301 Calista Ct., Ste. B
Anchorage, AK 99518
Phone: (907)349-6226
Fax: (907)272-9512
Free: 800-770-9830

Publications: The Arctic Sounder (621) • The Bristol BayTimes (562) • The Dutch Harbor Fisherman (564) • First Alaskans (525) • The Seward Phoenix LOG (637)

Alaska Newspapers, Inc.
PO Box 200
Cordova, AK 99574
Phone: (907)424-7181
Fax: (907)424-5799

Publications: The Cordova Times (558)

Alaska Post
600 Richardson Dr. No. 5900
Public Affairs Office
Fort Richardson, AK 99505-5900
Phone: (907)384-1539
Fax: (907)384-2060

Publications: Alaska Post (581)

Alaska Publications
16941 N. Eagle River Loop Rd.
Eagle River, AK 99577
Phone: (907)694-2727
Fax: (907)694-1545

Publications: Alaska Star (565)

The Alaskan Viewpoint
HCR 64; Box 453
Seward, AK 99664
Phone: (907)288-3168

Publications: The Alaskan Viewpoint (636)

AlbAmerica Trade & Consulting International
8578 Gwynedd Way
Springfield, VA 22153

Publications: Albanian Times (32538)

Albany Area Advertiser
132 Pine Ave.
Albany, GA 31701
Phone: (229)888-7653
Fax: (229)438-7593
Free: 800-676-0414

Publications: Albany Area Advertiser (6902)

Albany Catholic Press Association, Inc.
40 N. Main Ave.
Albany, NY 12203
Phone: (518)453-6688
Fax: (518)453-8448

Publications: The Evangelist (19985)

The Albany Herald
126 N Washington
Albany, GA 31701
Phone: (912)888-9300
Fax: (912)888-9357

Publications: The Albany Herald (6903)

The Albany Journal
PO Box 1628
Albany, GA 31702-1628
Phone: (229)435-6222
Fax: (229)435-0557

Publications: The Albany Journal (6904)

Albany Law School
80 New Scotland Ave.
Albany, NY 12208
Phone: (518)445-2372
Fax: (518)472-5857

Publications: Albany Law Review (19980)

Albany Student Press Corporation
State University Of New York
1400 Washington Ave.
Albany, NY 12222
Phone: (518)442-5660
Fax: (518)442-5664

Publications: Albany Student Press (19981)

Alberni Valley Times
4918 Napier St.
Box 400
Port Alberni, BC, Canada V9Y 7N1
Phone: (604)723-8171
Fax: (604)723-0586

Publications: Alberni Valley Times (35048)

Albert Lea Publishing Co.
808 W Front St., No. 60
Albert Lea, MN 56007
Phone: (507)373-1411
Fax: (507)373-0333
Free: 800-657-4996

Publications: Tribune (15706)

Alberta Energy and Utilities Board
640 5th Ave., SW
Calgary, AB, Canada T2P 3G4
Phone: (403)297-8311
Fax: (403)297-7040

Publications: Alberta Drilling Progress Weekly Report (34626)

Alberta Medical Association
12230 106 Ave. NW
Edmonton, AB, Canada T5N 3Z1
Phone: (780)482-2626
Fax: (780)482-5445

Publications: The Alberta Doctors' Digest (34698)

Alberta Pork Producers Development Corp.
10319 Princess Elizabeth Ave.
Edmonton, AB, Canada T5G 0Y5
Phone: (403)474-8288
Fax: (780)479-5128

Publications: Western Hog Journal (34734)

Alberta Teachers' Association (ATA)
11010 142nd St.
Edmonton, AB, Canada T5N 2R1
Phone: (780)447-9400
Fax: (780)455-6481

Publications: The ATA Magazine (34701)

Albia Newspapers Inc.
PO Box 338
Albia, IA 52531
Phone: (641)932-7121
Fax: (641)932-2822

Publications: Monroe County News (10575) • Union Republican (10576)

Albion
ASU Box 32072
Appalachian State University
Boone, NC 28608-2072
Phone: (828)262-6004
Fax: (828)262-2592

Publications: Albion (23651)

Albion News
328 W Church
Box 431
Albion, NE 68620
Phone: (402)395-2115
Fax: (402)395-2772

Publications: Albion News (17926)

Albion Recorder
111 W. Center St.
Albion, MI 49224-1755
Phone: (517)629-3984
Fax: (517)629-5790

Publications: Albion Recorder (14715)

Albuquerque Archaeological Society
PO Box 4029
Albuquerque, NM 87196
Phone: (505)881-1675

Publications: Pottery Southwest (19941)

Albuquerque Publishing Co.
7777 Jefferson NE
Albuquerque, NM 87109
Phone: (505)823-3393
Fax: (505)823-3369
Free: 800-641-3451

Publications: Albuquerque Journal (19763)

Alcan
PO Box 1370
Jonquiere, QC, Canada G7S 4K9
Phone: (418)699-4010
Fax: (418)699-4100

Publications: Le Lingot (37012)

Alcester Union
PO Box 227
Alcester, SD 57001
Phone: (605)934-2640
Fax: (605)934-2096

Publications: Alcester Union (28801)

Alcohol Research Information Service
430 Lathrop St.
Lansing, MI 48912-2410
Phone: (517)485-9900
Fax: (517)485-1928

Publications: Monday Morning Report (15294)

Alcona County Review
111 Lake St.
PO Box 548
Harrisville, MI 48740
Phone: (517)724-6384
Fax: (517)724-6655
Free: 877-873-8439

Publications: Alcona County Review (15146)

Aldebaran
PO Box 1908
Liberty, TX 77575
Phone: (936)336-6416
Fax: (936)336-9400

Publications: The Liberty Gazette (30689) • Pony Express Mail (30691)

The Alden Advance
150 E. Main
Box 485
Alden, MN 56009
Phone: (507)874-3440
Fax: (507)874-3440

Publications: The Alden Advance (15711)

Aldergrove Star
3089-272 St.
Aldergrove, BC, Canada V4W 3R9
Phone: (604)856-8303
Fax: (604)856-5212

Publications: Aldergrove Star (34880)

Alderson-Broaddus College
PO Box 2158
Philippi, WV 26416
Phone: (304)457-1700
Fax: (304)457-1700

Publications: Battler Columns (33432)

Aldrich Chemical Company Inc.
1001 W. St. Paul Ave.
Milwaukee, WI 53233
Phone: (414)273-3850
Fax: (414)273-4979
Free: 800-558-9160

Publications: Aldrichimica Acta (34056)

Aldrich Publishing Co., Inc.
6A Main St.
PO Box 329
Ramsey, NJ 07446
Phone: (201)327-1212
Fax: (201)327-3684

Publications: The Home and Store News (19489)

ALER, Inc.
PO Box 3532
Vero Beach, FL 32964-3532

Publications: Antitrust Law and Economics Review (6834)

Alex
163 rue Collin
St.-Jean-sur-Richelieu, QC, Canada J3B 6B6
Phone: (514)932-6094
Fax: (514)932-4134

Publications: Missions des Franciscains (37187)

Alex Wilson Coldstream Ltd.
Box 3009
Dryden, ON, Canada P8N 2Y9
Phone: (807)223-2390
Fax: (807)223-2907
Free: 800-465-7230

Publications: The Dryden Observer (35790)

Alexander City Outlook Inc.
548 Cherokee Rd.
PO Box 999
Alexander City, AL 35010-0999
Phone: (205)234-4281
Fax: (205)234-6550

Publications: Alexander City Outlook (6)

Alexander Graham Bell Association for the Deaf
3417 Volta Pl. NW
Washington, DC 20007-2778
Phone: (202)337-5220
Fax: (202)337-8314

Publications: The Volta Review (5840) • Volta Voices (5841)

The Alexandria Herald
531 Main St.
PO Box 450
Alexandria, SD 57311
Phone: (605)239-4521
Fax: (605)239-4521

Publications: The Alexandria Herald (28802)

The Alexandria News Weekly
PO Box 608
Alexandria, LA 71309
Phone: (318)443-7664

Publications: The Alexandria News Weekly (12457)

ALFA/Alabama Farmers Federation
PO Box 11000
Montgomery, AL 36191-0001
Phone: (334)288-3900
Fax: (334)284-3957

Publications: Alfa News (360) • Neighbors (371)

Alfred University
Kanakadea Hall
Alfred, NY 14802
Phone: (607)871-2217
Fax: (607)871-3366

Publications: Historical Reflections/Reflexions Historiques (20024)

The Alger County Shopper
113 W Superior
PO Box 38
Munising, MI 49862
Phone: (906)387-3282
Fax: (906)387-4054

Publications: The Alger County Shopper (15385)

Algoma News Review
37 Ste. Marie St.
PO Box 528
Wawa, ON, Canada P0S 1K0
Phone: (705)856-2267
Fax: (705)856-4952
Free: 800-461-9209

Publications: Algoma News Review (36865)

Algona Publishing Co.
14 E Nebraska
PO Box 400
Algona, IA 50511
Phone: (515)295-3535
Fax: (515)295-7217
Free: 800-444-1957

Publications: The Algona Upper Des Moines (10579) • The Reminder (10580) • The Weekend Express (10581)

Algonquin College
1385 Woodroffe Ave., Rm. E121
Nepean, ON, Canada K2G 1V8
Fax: (613)727-7684

Publications: Algonquin Times (36099)

Algonquin Graphics Ltd.
PO Box 360
Haliburton, ON, Canada K0M 1S0
Phone: (705)457-1037
Fax: (705)457-3275

Publications: Haliburton County Echo & Minden Recorder (35872) • The Times (35873)

ALI-ABA Committee on Continuing Professional Education
4025 Chestnut St.
Philadelphia, PA 19104
Phone: (215)243-1604
Fax: (215)243-1664
Free: 800-253-6397

Publications: ALI-ABA Business Law Course Materials Journal (27367) • The Practical Lawyer (27641)

Alicia Patterson Foundation
1730 Pennsylvania Ave. NW, Ste. 850
Washington, DC 20006
Phone: (202)393-5995
Fax: (301)951-8512

Publications: APF Reporter (5357)

Aliso Viejo News
22481 Aspan St.
Lake Forest, CA 92630-1630
Phone: (949)768-3631

Publications: Aliso Viejo News (2142)

ALIVE Magazine
7432 Fraser Park Dr.
Burnaby, BC, Canada V5J 5B9
Phone: (604)435-1919
Fax: (604)435-4888
Free: 800-663-6580

Publications: alive (34888)

All About Kids, Inc.
1077 Celestial St. Ste. 101
Cincinnati, OH 45202
Phone: (513)684-0501
Fax: (513)684-0507

Publications: All About Kids (24768)

All American Crafts, Inc.
243 Newton-Sparta Rd.
Newton, NJ 07860
Phone: (973)383-8080
Fax: (973)383-8133

Publications: Creative Woodworks and Crafts (19370) • Paint Works (19373) • The Quilter (19374)

All Printing & Publications Inc.
407 S Orange St.
PO Box 25
Albion, IN 46701
Phone: (260)636-2727
Fax: (260)636-2042
Free: 877-636-2727

Publications: Albion New Era (9781)

Allan Kaye Publications, Inc.
10300 Watson Rd.
St. Louis, MO 63127-1106

Publications: Allan Kaye's Sports Cards News & Price Guides (17408)

Alleghany Highlander
PO Box 271
Covington, VA 24426
Phone: (540)962-2121
Fax: (540)962-5072
Free: 800-537-3006

Publications: Alleghany Highlander (31981)

Alleghany News Publishing Company Inc.
20 S Main St.
Sparta, NC 28675
Phone: (336)372-8999
Fax: (336)372-5707

Publications: The Alleghany News (24240)

Allegheny College
520 N. Main St.
Meadville, PA 16335
Phone: (814)332-3100
Fax: (814)333-8180

Publications: Film Criticism (27234)

Allegheny County Medical Society
713 Ridge Ave.
Pittsburgh, PA 15212
Phone: (412)321-5030
Fax: (412)321-5323

Publications: Bulletin of Allegheny County Medical Society (27763)

Allen Marketing and Management
PO Box 1902
Lawrence, KS 66044
Phone: 800-627-0326
Fax: (785)843-1244

Publications: American Journal of Cosmetic Surgery (11547)

Allen Press
810 E. 10th
Lawrence, KS 66044
Phone: (785)843-1234
Fax: (785)843-1244
Free: 800-627-0326

Publications: The Bryologist (8115) • Chemical Times & Trends (11549) • The Cleft Palate-Craniofacial Journal (23704) • Evolution (11550) • Invertebrate Biology (3684) • Journal of Avian Medicine and Surgery (11554) • Journal of Neuropathology & Experimental Neurology (11556) • Journal of Paleontology (11557) • Journal for Vascular Ultrasound (13606) • Lepidopterists Society Journal (2501) • Paleobiology (5713) • Weed Science (11570) • Weed Technology (11571) • Wilson Bulletin (11572)

Alliance Communications Group
810 E. Tenth
Lawrence, KS 66044
Phone: (785)843-1235
Fax: (785)843-1853
Free: 800-627-0932

Publications: Ambulatory Pediatrics (11546)

Alliance of Manufacturers & Exporters Canada
5995 Avebury Rd.
Mississauga, ON, Canada L5R 3P9
Phone: (905)568-8300
Fax: (905)528-8330

Publications: Alliance Magazine (36053)

Alliance Printers and Publishers, Inc.
5711 N. Milwaukee
Chicago, IL 60646
Phone: (773)763-3343
Fax: (773)763-3825

Publications: Polish Daily News (8536)

Alliance Publishing Co., Inc.
40 S. Linden Ave.
PO Box 2180
Alliance, OH 44601
Phone: (330)821-1200
Fax: (330)821-8258
Free: 800-778-0098

Publications: The News Leader (25392) • The News Leader (25328) • The Review (24605)

Alliance Publishing Co., Inc.
PO Box 777
Waynesburg, OH 44688
Fax: (216)821-8258

Publications: Press-News (25627)

Alliance Times-Herald
114 E 4th St.
PO Box G
Alliance, NE 69301
Phone: (308)762-3060

Publications: Alliance Times-Herald (17927)

Allied Management
PO Box 9121
Mount Prospect, IL 60056
Phone: (847)797-9051
Fax: (847)797-9075

Publications: Program (9249)

Alliston Press Ltd.
169 Dufferin St. South, Unit 22
Alliston, ON, Canada L9R 1E6
Phone: (705)435-6228
Fax: (705)435-3342

Publications: The Herald (35630)

Allstar Bass Fishing Tournaments, Inc.
PO Box 859
Mesa, AZ 85211

Publications: Arizona Hunter & Angler (743)

Allured Publishing Corp.
362 S. Schmale Rd.
Carol Stream, IL 60188-2787
Phone: (630)480-2997
Fax: (630)653-2192

Publications: Cosmetics & Toiletries (8142) • Global Cosmetic Industry (8144) • Perfumer and Flavorist (8152) • Skin Inc. (8155)

Almaguin Publishing
185 Ontario St.
PO Box 518
Burks Falls, ON, Canada P0A 1C0
Phone: (705)382-3843
Fax: (705)382-3440
Free: 800-731-6397

Publications: The Almaguin News (35712)

Alpena News Publishing Co.
130 Park Pl.
PO Box 367
Alpena, MI 49707
Phone: (989)354-3111
Fax: (989)354-2096
Free: 800-448-0254

Publications: Alpena News (14735)

Alpha Epsilon Pi Fraternity
8815 Wesleyan Rd.
Indianapolis, IN 46268-1171
Phone: (317)876-1913
Fax: (317)876-1057
Publications: The Lion of Alpha Epsilon Pi (10149)

Alpha Gamma Rho Fraternity
10101 N Ambassador Dr.
Kansas City, MO 64153
Phone: (816)891-9200
Fax: (816)891-9401
Publications: Sickle & Sheaf (17196)

Alpha General Corp.
421 W MacArthur Blvd.
Oakland, CA 94609
Phone: (510)420-1381
Fax: (510)420-1383
Publications: Lifestyle (2686)

Alpha Kappa Alpha Sorority Inc.
5656 S Stony Island Ave.
Chicago, IL 60637-1997
Phone: (773)684-1282
Fax: (773)288-8251
Publications: Ivy Leaf (8423)

Alpha Omega Alpha Honor Medical Society
525 Middlefield Rd., Ste. 130
Menlo Park, CA 94025
Phone: (415)329-0291
Fax: (415)329-1618
Publications: The Pharos (2525)

Alpha Omega Communications
37 Hillsmount Rd.
London, ON, Canada N6K 1W1
Phone: (519)472-4807
Publications: The Hellenic News (35982)

Alpha Omicron Pi Fraternity, Inc.
5390 Virginia Way
Brentwood, TN 37027-7529
Phone: (615)370-4424
Publications: To Dragma (29064)

Alpine Avalanche
Box 719
Alpine, TX 79831
Phone: (915)837-3334
Fax: (915)837-7181
Publications: Alpine Avalanche (29682)

Alpine Sun
2144 Alpine Blvd.
PO Box 1089
Alpine, CA 91901
Phone: (619)445-3288
Fax: (619)445-6776
Publications: Alpine Sun (1392)

Alta Mira Press, Inc.
1630 N. Main St., No. 367
Walnut Creek, CA 94596
Phone: (925)938-7243
Fax: (925)933-9720
Publications: Curator (4051)

Altamont Enterprise and Albany County Post
123 Maple Ave.
PO Box 654
Altamont, NY 12009
Phone: (518)861-6641
Fax: (518)861-5105
Publications: Altamont Enterprise and Albany County Post (20027)

Altamont News Banner
118 N Main St.
Altamont, IL 62411
Phone: (618)483-6176
Fax: (618)483-5177
Publications: The Altamont News (8008)

Altamont Press
67 Broadway St.
Asheville, NC 28801-2919
Phone: (828)253-0467
Fax: (828)253-7952
Publications: FIBERARTS (23629)

Alternative Cinema Inc.
PO Box 371
Glenwood, NJ 07418
Phone: (973)509-1616
Fax: (973)746-6464
Publications: Alternative Cinema (19240)

Alternative Media, Inc.
111 W. Jefferson St., Ste. 200
Orlando, FL 32801-1023
Phone: (407)377-0400
Fax: (407)377-0420
Publications: Orlando Weekly (6505)

Alternative Press Index
PO Box 33109
Baltimore, MD 21218
Phone: (410)243-2471
Fax: (410)235-5325
Publications: Alternative Press Index (13111)

Alternative Publications, Inc.
413 N. 2nd St., No. 150
Milwaukee, WI 53203-3110
Phone: (414)276-2222
Fax: (414)276-3312
Free: 800-516-2220
Publications: The Mature American (34079) • Shepherd Express (34101)

Alternatives, Inc.
University of Waterloo
c/o Faculty of Environmental Studies
Waterloo, ON, Canada N2L 3G1
Phone: (519)888-4442
Fax: (519)746-0292
Free: (866)437-2587
Publications: Alternatives Journal (36845)

Altier & Maynard Communications, Inc.
53 Oakwood Dr.
Madison, CT 06443-1823
Phone: (203)431-3454
Publications: Annals of Ophthalmology (4926) • Black Health (4927)

Altoona Herald-Mitchellville Index
809 8th St. SW, Ste. C
PO Box 427
Altoona, IA 50009
Phone: (515)967-4224
Fax: (515)967-0553
Publications: Altoona Herald-Mitchellville Index (10586)

Altus Times
218-20 W Commerce St.
PO Box 578
Altus, OK 73521
Phone: (580)482-1221
Fax: (580)482-5709
Publications: Patriot (25731)

Alumnae Association of Smith College
Smith College
Alumnae House, 33 Elm St.
Northampton, MA 01063
Fax: (413)585-2015
Free: 800-526-2023
Publications: Smith Alumnae Quarterly (14430)

Alumni Association of City College of New York
PO Box 177
New York, NY 10027
Phone: (212)234-3000
Fax: (212)368-6576
Publications: City College Alumnus (21421)

Alumni Association of the U-M
200 Fletcher St.
Ann Arbor, MI 48109-1007
Phone: (734)764-0384
Fax: (734)764-4506
Free: 800-847-4764
Publications: Michigan Alumnus (14760)

Alumni Association of the University of Missouri
407 Donald W. Reynolds Alumni and Visitor Center
Columbia, MO 65211
Phone: (573)882-7357
Fax: (573)882-7290
Publications: MIZZOU Magazine (17006)

Alumni Association of the University of Nebraska
Lincoln, NE 68588
Phone: (402)472-7211
Fax: (402)472-9289
Free: 888-353-1874
Publications: Nebraska (18097)

Alumni Society of Williams College, Hopkins Hall
75 Park St.
PO Box 38
Williamstown, MA 01267-0038
Phone: (413)597-4278
Fax: (413)597-4158
Publications: Williams Alumni Review (14660)

Alverno College
3400 S. 43rd St.
PO Box 343922
Milwaukee, WI 53234-3922
Phone: (414)382-6000
Fax: (414)382-6322
Free: 800-933-3401
Publications: Alverno Today (34057)

Always Jukin'
404 E Howell, No. 100
Seattle, WA 98122
Phone: (206)652-4005
Fax: (206)652-4007
Publications: Always Jukin' Magazine (32938)

A.M. Best Company
Ambest Rd.
Oldwick, NJ 08858
Fax: (908)439-2200
Publications: Best's Review (19395)

Am-Pol Eagle
3620 Harlem Rd.
Cheektowaga, NY 14215
Phone: (716)835-9454
Fax: (716)835-9457
Publications: Am-Pol Eagle (20455)

Amalgamated Transit Union, AFL-CIO, CLC
5025 Wisconsin Ave. NW
Washington, DC 20016-4139
Phone: (202)537-1645
Fax: (202)244-7824
Publications: In Transit (5541)

Amarillo College
PO Box 447
Amarillo, TX 79178
Phone: (806)371-5290
Fax: (806)371-5398
Publications: AC Current (29692) • The Ranger (29698)

Amarillo Globe-News
PO Box 2091
Amarillo, TX 79166
Phone: (806)376-4488
Fax: (806)376-9217
Publications: Amarillo Globe-News (29694)

Amateur Telescope Making Journal
2500 15th Ave. W
Seattle, WA 98166
Phone: (206)283-7242
Fax: (206)281-4921
Publications: The Amateur Telescope Making Journal (32939)

Amber Printers and Publishers Ltd.
125 Broadview Ave.
Toronto, ON, Canada M4M 2E9
Phone: (416)466-1514
Fax: (416)465-8168
Publications: Latvija Amerika (36649)

The Amboy News
219 E Main St.
PO Box 162
Amboy, IL 61310
Phone: (815)857-2311
Fax: (815)857-2517

Publications: The Amboy News (8012)

Ambush, Inc.
828-A Bourbon St.
New Orleans, LA 70116-3137
Phone: (504)522-8049
Fax: (504)522-0907

Publications: Ambush Magazine (12726)

aMedia, Inc.
677 5th Ave., 3rd Fl.
New York, NY 10022
Phone: (212)593-8089
Fax: (212)593-8082
Free: 800-446-6235

Publications: aMagazine (21176)

The American
25 Main St. NW
PO Box 100
Blackduck, MN 56630
Phone: (218)835-4211
Fax: (218)835-6992

Publications: The American (15753)

American Academy of Actuaries
1100 17th St., NW, 7th Fl.
Washington, DC 20036
Phone: (202)223-8196
Fax: (202)872-1948

Publications: Contingencies (5441)

American Academy of Advertising
Dept. of Comm. (E-509 HFAC)
Brigham Young Univ.
Provo, UT 84602
Phone: (801)422-6845
Fax: (801)422-0160

Publications: Journal of Advertising (10590)

American Academy of Arts & Sciences
Norton's Woods
136 Irving St.
Cambridge, MA 02138
Phone: (617)491-2600
Fax: (617)576-5088

Publications: DAEDALUS (14048)

American Academy of Clinical Neurophysiology
104 13th St.
Hudson, WI 54016
Phone: (715)381-3440

Publications: Neurology & Clinical Neurophysiology (33796)

American Academy of Family Physicians
11400 Tomahawk Creek Pkwy.
Leawood, KS 66211
Phone: (913)906-6000
Fax: (913)906-6080
Free: 800-274-2237

Publications: American Family Physician (11583) • Family Practice Management (11584)

American Academy of the History of Dentistry
100 S Vail Ave.
Arlington Heights, IL 60005-1866
Phone: (847)670-7561

Publications: Journal of the History of Dentistry (8024)

American Academy of Ophthalmology
PO Box 7424
San Francisco, CA 94120
Phone: (415)561-8500

Publications: EyeNet (3359) • Ophthalmology Journal (2352)

American Academy of Orthopaedic Surgeons
Cunningham Associates
180 Old Tappan Rd.
Old Tappan, NJ 07675
Phone: (201)767-4170
Fax: (201)767-8065

Publications: The American Academy of Orthopaedic Surgeons Bulletin (19393) • Journal of the American Academy of Orthopaedic Surgeons (19394)

American Academy of Pediatrics
141 Northwest Point Blvd.
Elk Grove Village, IL 60007-1098
Phone: (847)434-4000
Fax: (847)434-8000
Free: 800-433-9016

Publications: Pediatrics (8833)

The American Academy of Periodontology
737 N. Michigan Ave., Ste. 800
Chicago, IL 60611-2690
Phone: (312)787-5518
Fax: (312)573-3225

Publications: Journal of Periodontology (8447)

American Academy of Religion
825 Houston Mill Rd., Ste. 300
Atlanta, GA 30329-4246
Phone: (404)727-3049
Fax: (404)727-7959

Publications: Openings (7034)

American Academy of Sleep Medicine
One Westbrook Corporate Ctr., Ste. 920
Westchester, IL 60154-5767
Phone: (708)492-0930
Fax: (708)492-0943
Free: 888-41-AWAKE

Publications: Sleep (9752)

American Accounting Association
5717 Bessie Dr.
Sarasota, FL 34233
Phone: (941)921-7747
Fax: (941)923-4093

Publications: Accounting Horizons (6652) • Accounting Review (6653) • American Taxation Association Journal (29752) • Auditing (6976) • Behavioral Research in Accounting (14982) • Issues in Accounting Education (6657) • Journal of Information Systems (6658) • Journal of Management Accounting Research (36853)

American Aging Association
110 Chesley Dr.
Media, PA 19063
Phone: (610)627-2626
Fax: (610)565-9747

Publications: Age (27241)

American Air Mail Society
PO Box 110
Mineola, NY 11501

Publications: Airpost Journal (33173)

American Airlines Publishing
4255 Amon Carter Blvd.
MD 4255
Fort Worth, TX 76155
Phone: (817)967-1804
Fax: (817)931-5782

Publications: American Way (30329) • Southwest Airlines Spirit (30352)

American Alcohol and Drug Information Foundation
PO Box 10212
Lansing, MI 48901-0212
Phone: (517)484-2636
Fax: (517)484-0444

Publications: Journal of Alcohol and Drug Education (18200)

American Alliance for Health, Physical Education, Recreation & Dance
1900 Association Dr.
Reston, VA 20191
Phone: (703)476-3400
Fax: (703)476-9527
Free: 800-213-7193

Publications: AAHPERD Update (32354) • American Journal of Health Education (32360) • Journal of Health Education (32381) • Journal of Physical Education, Recreation & Dance (JOPERD) (32390) • Research Quarterly for Exercise and Sport (32413) • Strategies (32416) • Strategies (32415)

American Alliance for Theatre & Education
Theatre Department
Arizona State University
PO Box 872002
Tempe, AZ 85287-2002
Phone: (480)965-6064
Fax: (480)965-5351

Publications: Stage of the Art (915) • Youth Theatre Journal (918)

The American Alternative Foundation
3200 N St., NW (PMB 175)
Washington, DC 20007-2829
Phone: (202)659-7922
Fax: (202)659-7923

Publications: The American Spectator (5344)

American Amateur Press Association
PO Box 18117
Fountain Hills, AZ 85269

Publications: American Amateur Journalist (710)

American Angler
160 Benmont Ave.
PO Box 4100
Bennington, VT 05201-4100
Phone: (802)447-1518
Fax: (802)447-2471

Publications: American Angler (31496)

American Animal Hospital Association
PO Box 150899
Denver, CO 80215-0899
Phone: (303)986-2800
Fax: (303)986-1700
Free: 800-252-2242

Publications: Journal of the American Animal Hospital Association (4333) • TRENDS Magazine (4364)

American Anthropological Association
2200 Wilson Blvd., Ste. 600
Arlington, VA 22201
Phone: (703)528-1902
Fax: (703)528-3546

Publications: American Anthropologist (31770) • American Ethnologist (31771) • Anthropology of Consciousness (31774) • Anthropology and Education Quarterly (31775) • Anthropology and Humanism (31776) • Cultural Anthropology (31784) • Ethos (31789) • Journal of Latin American Anthropology (31802) • Journal of Linguistic Anthropology (3647) • Medical Anthropology Quarterly (31807) • Museum Anthropology (31809) • Political and Legal Anthropological Review (31818) • SACC Notes—Teaching Anthropology (31826)

American Anti-Vivisection Society
Noble Plz., Ste. 204
801 Old York Rd.
Jenkintown, PA 19046-1685
Phone: (215)887-0816
Fax: (215)887-2088
Free: 800-SAY-AAVS

Publications: The AV Magazine (27083)

American Arachnological Society
University of Maryland
College Park, MD 20742-4454
Phone: (301)405-7519
Fax: (301)314-9290

Publications: Journal of Arachnology (13424)

American Arbitration Association
335 Madison Ave.
New York, NY 10017-4605
Phone: (212)716-5800
Fax: (212)716-5906

Publications: Arbitration Times (21241) • Dispute Resolution Journal (21558) • Dispute Resolution Times (21559) • Labor Arbitration in Government (22230) • The Punch List (22614) • Summary of Labor Arbitration Awards (22806)

American Association for the Advancement of Science
1200 New York Ave., NW
Washington, DC 20005
Phone: (202)326-6400
Fax: (202)371-9849

Publications: Science (5778) • Science Books & Films (5780)

American Association of Airport Executives
601 Madison St., Ste. 400
Alexandria, VA 22314-1756
Phone: (703)824-0500
Fax: (703)820-1395

Publications: Airport Magazine (31632)

American Association for Artificial Intelligence
445 Burgess Dr.
Menlo Park, CA 94025-3496
Phone: (650)328-3123
Fax: (650)321-4457

Publications: AI Magazine (2521)

American Association of Blood Banks
8101 Glenbrook Rd.
Bethesda, MD 20814
Phone: (301)907-6977
Fax: (301)907-6895

Publications: Transfusion (16136)

American Association for Cancer Research, Inc.
615 Chestnut St., 17th Fl.
Philadelphia, PA 19106-4404
Phone: (215)440-9300
Fax: (215)440-9313

Publications: Cancer Epidemiology, Biomarkers & Prevention (27391) • Cancer Research (27392) • Clinical Cancer Research (30463) • Molecular Cancer Research (27572)

American Association of Cereal Chemists
3340 Pilot Knob Rd.
St. Paul, MN 55121-2097
Phone: (651)454-7250
Fax: (651)454-0766
Free: 800-328-7560

Publications: Cereal Chemistry (16368) • Cereal Foods World (16369)

American Association for Clinical Chemistry
2101 L St. NW, Ste. 202
Washington, DC 20037-1526
Phone: (202)857-0717
Fax: (202)887-5093
Free: 800-892-1400

Publications: Clinical Chemistry (31924) • Clinical Laboratory News (5420)

American Association of Colleges of Pharmacy
1426 Prince St.
Alexandria, VA 22314
Phone: (703)739-2330
Fax: (703)836-8982
Free: 800-510-2227

Publications: American Journal of Pharmaceutical Education (7095)

American Association of Community Colleges (AACC)
1 Dupont Cir., NW, Ste. 410
Washington, DC 20036
Phone: (202)728-0200
Fax: (202)223-9390

Publications: Community Colleges Journal (5429)

American Association for Counseling and Development
5999 Stevenson Ave.
Alexandria, VA 22304-3300
Phone: (703)823-9800
Fax: (703)823-0252
Free: 800-347-6647

Publications: Career Development Quarterly (31651) • Journal of Employment Counseling (31694)

American Association of Critical-Care Nurses
101 Columbia
Aliso Viejo, CA 92656
Phone: (949)362-2000
Fax: (949)362-2049
Free: 800-809-2273

Publications: American Journal of Critical Care (1389)

American Association of Diabetes Educators
100 W. Monroe, Ste. 400
Chicago, IL 60603
Phone: (312)424-2426
Fax: (312)424-2427
Free: 800-338-3633

Publications: The Diabetes Educator (8353)

American Association of Engineering Societies
1828 L St. NW, Ste. 906
Washington, DC 20036
Phone: (202)296-2237
Fax: (202)296-1151
Free: 888-400-AAES

Publications: Engineers (5479)

American Association of Family and Consumer Sciences
1555 King St.
Alexandria, VA 22314-2738
Phone: (703)706-4600
Fax: (703)706-4663

Publications: AAFCS Action (31629) • Journal of Family and Consumer Sciences: From Research to Practice (31695)

American Association of Health Plans
1129 20th St. NW, Ste. 600
Washington, DC 20036-3421
Phone: (202)778-3245
Fax: (202)331-7487

Publications: Healthplan (5524)

American Association of Hospital Podiatrists
3984 S. Figueroa St.
Los Angeles, CA 90037
Phone: (213)747-7272
Fax: (310)476-8003

Publications: Hospital Podiatrist (2294)

American Association of Individual Investors
625 N. Michigan Ave., Ste. 1900
Chicago, IL 60611
Phone: (312)280-0170
Fax: (312)280-1625
Free: 800-428-2244

Publications: AAII Journal (8240) • Computerized Investing (8341)

American Association of Kidney Patients
3505 E. Frontage Rd., Ste. 315
Tampa, FL 33607-1796
Phone: (813)636-8100
Fax: (813)636-8122
Free: 800-749-2257

Publications: aakpRENALIFE (6758)

American Association for Laboratory Animal Science
9190 Crestwyn Hills Dr.
Memphis, TN 38125-8538
Phone: (901)754-8620
Fax: (901)753-0046

Publications: Comparative Medicine (29363)

American Association of Law Libraries
53 W. Jackson Blvd., Ste. 940
Chicago, IL 60604
Phone: (312)939-4764
Fax: (312)431-1097

Publications: Law Library Journal (8119)

American Association for Marriage and Family Therapy
1133 15th St. NW, Ste. 300
Washington, DC 20005-2710
Phone: (202)452-0109

Publications: Family Therapy News (5491) • Journal of Marital & Family Therapy (30713)

American Association of Medical Assistants
20 N. Wacker Dr., Ste. 1575
Chicago, IL 60606
Phone: (312)899-1500
Fax: (312)899-1259

Publications: The PMA (8534)

American Association of Medical Dosimetrists (AAMD)
One Physics Ellipse
PO Box 1502
College Park, MD 20740
Phone: (301)209-3320
Fax: (301)209-3343

Publications: Medical Dosimetry (13434)

American Association on Mental Retardation
444 N. Capitol St. NW, Ste. 846
Washington, DC 20001-1512
Phone: (202)387-1968
Fax: (202)387-2193
Free: 800-424-3688

Publications: American Journal on Mental Retardation (5333) • Mental Retardation (5647)

American Association of Museums
1575 I St. NW, Ste. 400
Washington, DC 20005
Phone: (202)289-1818
Fax: (202)289-6578

Publications: Museum News (5664)

American Association of Petroleum Geologists
1444 S. Boulder
PO Box 979
Tulsa, OK 74101-0979
Phone: (918)584-2555
Free: 800-364-AAPG

Publications: AAPG Bulletin (26104) • AAPG Explorer (26105)

American Association of Physics Teachers
One Physics Ellipse
College Park, MD 20740-3845
Phone: (301)209-3350
Fax: (301)209-0845

Publications: American Journal of Physics (13789) • Announcer (13411) • The Physics Teacher (23655)

American Association of Public Health Dentistry
1224 Centre W., Ste. 400B
Springfield, IL 62704
Phone: (217)391-0218

Publications: Journal of Public Health Dentistry (23713)

American Association of Retired Persons (AARP)
601 E St. NW
Washington, DC 20049
Phone: (202)434-2277
Fax: (202)434-6451

Publications: AARP Bulletin (5307) • Modern Maturity (5657)

American Association of School Administrators
801 N. Quincy St., Ste. 700
Arlington, VA 22203-1730
Phone: (703)528-0700
Fax: (703)841-1543

Publications: The School Administrator (31827)

American Association of School Librarians
50 E Huron St.
Chicago, IL 60611
Phone: (312)944-7298
Fax: (312)664-7459
Free: 800-545-2433

Publications: School Library Media Quarterly (8561)

American Association of Spinal Cord Injury Nurses
Eastern Paralyzed Veterans Association
75-20 Astoria Blvd.
Jackson Heights, NY 11372
Phone: (718)803-3782
Fax: (718)803-0414

Publications: SCI Nursing (20828)

American Association for State & Local History
1717 Church St.
Nashville, TN 37203-2991
Phone: (615)320-3203
Fax: (615)327-9013

Publications: History News (29458)

American Association of Stratigraphic Palynologists Foundation
Anthropology Bldg. (TAMU 4352)
Texas A & M University
College Station, TX 77843-4352
Phone: (979)845-5242
Fax: (979)845-4070

Publications: Palynology (30047)

American Association of Teachers of Arabic
Department of Modern Languages and Literatures
College of William and Mary
Williamsburg, VA 23187-8795
Phone: (757)221-7412
Fax: (757)221-3637

Publications: Al-Arabiyya (32612)

American Association of Teachers of French
Mailcode 4510
Department of Foreign Languages
Southern Illinois University
Carbondale, IL 62901-4510
Phone: (618)453-5731
Fax: (618)453-5733

Publications: French Review (8117)

American Association of Teachers of German Inc.
112 Haddontowne Ct., No. 104
Cherry Hill, NJ 08034-3668
Phone: (856)795-5553
Fax: (856)795-9398

Publications: Die Unterrichtspraxis/Teaching German (18734) • German Quarterly (18735)

American Association of Teachers of Italian
Dept. of Foreign Languages
Arizona State University
Tempe, AZ 85281
Phone: (602)965-6282
Fax: (602)965-0135

Publications: Italica (25022)

American Association of Textile Chemists and Colorists
PO Box 12215
Research Triangle Park, NC 27709
Phone: (919)549-8141
Fax: (919)549-8933

Publications: AATCC Review (24182)

American Association of University Professors
1012 14th St. NW, Ste. 500
Washington, DC 20005
Phone: (202)737-5900
Fax: (202)737-5526
Free: 800-424-2973

Publications: Academe: Bulletin of the AAUP (5312)

American Association of University Women
1111 16th St. NW
Washington, DC 20036
Phone: (202)785-7700
Fax: (202)872-1425
Free: 800-326-AAUW

Publications: AAUW in Action (5308) • AAUW Outlook (5309)

American Association of Variable Star Observers
25 Birch St.
Cambridge, MA 02138
Phone: (617)354-0484
Fax: (617)354-0665

Publications: Journal of the American Association of Variable Star Observers (14073)

American Association of Woodturners
3499 Lexington Ave. N, Ste. 103
Shoreview, MN 55126
Phone: (651)484-9094
Fax: (651)484-1724

Publications: American Woodturner (16446)

American Association of Zoo Keepers Inc.
3601 SW 29th St., Ste. 133
Topeka, KS 66614-2054
Phone: (785)273-9149
Fax: (785)273-1980
Free: 800-242-4519

Publications: Animal Keepers' Forum (11814)

American Association of Zoo Veterinarians
6 N. Pennell Rd.
Media, PA 19063
Phone: (610)892-4812
Fax: (610)892-4813

Publications: Journal of Zoo and Wildlife Medicine (27242)

American Astronautical Society
6352 Rolling Mill Pl., Ste. 102
Springfield, VA 22152
Phone: (703)866-0020
Fax: (703)866-3526

Publications: The Journal of the Astronautical Sciences (10548)

American Atheist Press
PO Box 5733
Parsippany, NJ 07054
Phone: (908)259-0700
Fax: (908)259-0748

Publications: American Atheist (19410)

American Bamboo Society
7548 Ravenna Ave. NE
Seattle, WA 98115-4662

Publications: Bamboo Science & Culture (32946)

American Banker/Bond Buyer Inc.
1 State St. Plz.
New York, NY 10004
Phone: (212)803-8200
Fax: (212)843-9600
Free: 800-982-0633

Publications: American Banker (21180)

American Bankers Association
1120 Connecticut Ave., NW
Washington, DC 20036-3971
Phone: (202)663-5378
Fax: (202)828-4540
Free: 800-BAN-KERS

Publications: ABA Bank Marketing Magazine (5310) • ABA Consumer Credit Delinquency Bulletin (5311) • Journal of Agricultural Lending (5568)

American Baptist Churches, USA
PO Box 851
Valley Forge, PA 19482-0851
Phone: (610)768-2000
Fax: (610)768-2320
Free: 800-ABC-3USA

Publications: American Baptists in Mission (28090) • The Secret Place (28091)

American Baptist Historical Society
PO Box 851
Valley Forge, PA 19482-0851
Phone: (610)768-2269
Fax: (610)768-2266

Publications: American Baptist Quarterly (28089)

American Bar Association
750 N. Lake Shore Dr.
Chicago, IL 60611
Phone: (312)988-5000

Publications: ABA Journal (8241) • The Brief (8291) • Business Law Today (797) • The Business Lawyer (29447) • The Compleat Lawyer (8339) • Criminal Justice Magazine (8348) • EDT (8361) • Family Advocate (8373) • Family Law Quarterly (11817) • Jurimetrics (909) • LAMPlighter (8455) • Law Practice Management (8459) • National Security Law Report (8500) • Probate and Property (8540) • Public Contract Law Journal (8543) • Student Lawyer (8572) • The Tax Lawyer (5812) • Tort & Insurance Law Journal (8585) • The Urban Lawyer (8595)

American Beethoven Society
San Jose State University
1 Washington Sq.
San Jose, CA 95192-0171
Phone: (408)924-4590
Fax: (408)924-4715

Publications: The Beethoven Journal (3511)

The American Benedictine Review
St. Benedict's Abbey
Atchison, KS 66002

Publications: The American Benedictine Review (24533)

American Bible Society
1865 Broadway
New York, NY 10023
Phone: (212)408-8731
Fax: (212)408-1456
Free: 800-322-4253

Publications: American Bible Society Record (21181)

American Birding Association Inc.
PO Box 6599
Colorado Springs, CO 80934
Phone: (719)578-9703
Fax: (719)578-1480
Free: 800-850-2473

Publications: Birding (4236)

American Board of Family Practice
2228 Young Dr.
Lexington, KY 40505
Phone: (859)269-5626
Fax: (859)335-7501
Free: 888-995-5700

Publications: Journal of the American Board of Family Practice (32976)

American Bonanza Society
PO Box 12888
Wichita Midcontinent Airport
Wichita, KS 67277
Phone: (316)945-1700
Fax: (316)945-1710

Publications: ABS Magazine (11879)

American Bonsai Society Inc.
PO Box 1136
Puyallup, WA 98371
Phone: (253)841-8992

Publications: Bonsai Journal (17835)

American Botanical Council
6200 Manor Rd.
Austin, TX 78723
Phone: (512)926-4900
Fax: (512)926-2345
Free: 800-373-7105

Publications: HerbalGram (29778)

American Bowling Congress
5301 S. 76th St.
Greendale, WI 53129
Phone: (414)321-8310
Fax: (414)321-8356

Publications: Bowling Magazine (33757)

American Brewer
PO Box 20268
Alexandria, VA 22320-1268
Phone: (703)567-1962
Free: 800-474-7291

Publications: American Brewer (31635)

American Breweriana Association, Inc.
PO Box 11157
Pueblo, CO 81001
Phone: (719)544-9267
Fax: (719)544-4289

Publications: American Breweriana (4597)

American Bungalow Magazine
PO Box 756
Sierra Madre, CA 91025-0756

Publications: American Bungalow (3764)

American Bus Association
1100 New York Ave. NW, Ste. 1050
Washington, DC 20005
Phone: (202)842-1645
Fax: (202)842-0850
Free: 800-283-2877

Publications: Destinations (5462)

American Business
80 Central Park West, Ste. 16B
New York, NY 10023
Phone: (212)581-2000

Publications: American Business (21182) • Better
Living (21302)

American Business Law Association
Marquette University
College of Business Administration
Milwaukee, WI 53201-1881

Publications: American Business Law Journal
(34058)

American Camellia Society
Massee Ln. Gardens
100 Massee Ln.
Fort Valley, GA 31030-9100
Phone: (478)967-2358
Fax: (478)967-2083

Publications: The Camellia Journal (7285)

American Camping Association
5000 State Rd. 67 N.
Martinsville, IN 46151-7902
Phone: (765)342-8456
Fax: (765)349-6357
Free: 800-428-CAMP

Publications: Camping Magazine (10293)

American Canal & Transportation Center
333 Beach Dr.
Annapolis, MD 21403-3904
Phone: (410)263-1303

Publications: The Best from American Canals
(13089)

American Catholic Press
16565 S State St.
South Holland, IL 60473
Phone: (708)331-5485
Fax: (708)331-5484

Publications: Parish Liturgy (9616)

The American Ceramic Society
735 Ceramic Pl.
Westerville, OH 43081
Phone: (614)890-5890
Fax: (614)899-5892

Publications: American Ceramic Society Bulletin
(25636) • Ceramic Engineering and Science Proceedings (25637) • Ceramic Source (25638) • Ceramics Monthly (25639) • Journal of the American
Ceramic Society (25641) • Pottery Making Illustrated
(25644)

American Cetacean Society
PO Box 1391
San Pedro, CA 90733
Phone: (310)548-6279
Fax: (310)548-6950

Publications: Whalewatcher (3597)

American Chemical Society
1155 16th St. NW
Washington, DC 20036
Phone: (202)872-4600
Fax: (202)872-4615
Free: 800-227-5558

Publications: Biomacromolecules (5376) • Chem-
Matters (5406) • Crystal Growth & Design (5451) •
Environmental Science & Technology (5482) • Jour-

nal of Combinatorial Chemistry (5578) • Journal of
Natural Products (5604) • Modern Drug Discovery
(5656) • Organic Letters (5711) • Organic Process
Research & Development (25056)

American Chemical Society
PO Box 20453
Newark, NJ 07101
Phone: (973)482-5744

Publications: Polymer Preprints (19363)

American Chianina Association
1708 N. Prairie View Rd.
PO Box 890
Platte City, MO 64079
Phone: (816)431-2808
Fax: (816)431-5381

Publications: American Chianina Journal (17348)

American Choral Directors Association
PO Box 6310
Lawton, OK 73506-0310
Fax: (405)248-1465

Publications: Choral Journal (25885)

American City Business Journals, Inc.
120 W. Morehead St., Ste. 200
Charlotte, NC 28202
Phone: (704)973-1000
Fax: (704)973-1001

Publications: Atlanta Business Chronicle (6967) •
Baltimore Business Journal (13129) • Birmingham
Business Journal (57) • Business First (23735) •
Business First of Buffalo (20371) • The Business
Journal of Charlotte (23736) • The Business Journal
of Phoenix (795) • Business Journal - Serving Metro-
politan Kansas City (23737) • Business Journal -
Serving Phoenix and the Valley of the Sun (796) •
Capital District Business Review (20931) • The Den-
ver Business Journal (4321) • Easy Bay Business
Times (2853) • Houston Business Journal (30480) •
Kansas City Business Journal (17178) • Minneapo-
lis-St. Paul CityBusiness (23750) • Orlando Business
Journal (6502) • Pacific Business News (7713) •
Pittsburgh Business Times (27830) • Portland Busi-
ness Journal (26501) • Puget Sound Business Jour-
nal (33007) • Sacramento Business Journal
(23752) • St. Louis Business Journal (17496) • The
San Antonio Business Journal (31045) • San Francisco Business Times (3431) • San Jose Business
Journal (3535) • Silicon Valley/San Jose Business
Journal (23753) • Washington Business Journal
(5843) • Wichita Business Journal (11890)

American Coaster Enthusiasts
Box 352
Penfield, NY 14526
Phone: (716)381-1012
Fax: (716)381-1012

Publications: RollerCoaster! (23090)

**American College of Allergy, Asthma, &
Immunology**
85 W Algonquin Rd., Ste. 550
Arlington Heights, IL 60005
Phone: (847)427-1200
Fax: (847)427-1294

Publications: Annals of Allergy, Asthma, & Immunology (16306)

American College of Dentists
4403 Marlborough Ave.
San Diego, CA 92116
Phone: (619)584-8288
Fax: (619)283-2203

Publications: Journal of the American College of
Dentists (3178)

American College of Forensic Examiners
2750 E. Sunshine Rd.
Springfield, MO 65802

Publications: Forensic Examiner (17600)

American College of Forensic Psychiatry
Box 5870
Newport Beach, CA 92662
Phone: (949)673-7773
Fax: (949)673-7710

Publications: American Journal of Forensic Psychiatry (2621) • American Journal of Forensic Psychology (2622)

**American College of Health Care Admin-
istrators**
300 N Lee St., Ste. 301
Alexandria, VA 22314-2640
Phone: (703)739-7900
Fax: (703)739-7901
Free: 888-88A-CHCA

Publications: Balance (31646)

**American College of Healthcare Execu-
tives**
1 N Franklin St. Ste. 1700
Chicago, IL 60606
Phone: (312)424-2800
Fax: (312)424-0023

Publications: Healthcare Executive (8396)

American College of Musicians
PO Box 1807
Austin, TX 78767-1807
Phone: (512)478-5775
Fax: (512)478-5843

Publications: Piano Guild Notes (29797)

**American College of Physician Execu-
tives**
4890 W Kennedy Blvd., Ste. 200
Tampa, FL 33609
Phone: (813)287-2000
Fax: (813)287-8993
Free: 800-562-8088

Publications: Physician Executive (6777)

American College of Physicians
190 N Independence Mall W
Philadelphia, PA 19106-1572
Phone: (215)351-2400
Fax: (215)351-2799
Free: 800-523-1546

Publications: ACP Observer (27362) • Annals of
Internal Medicine (27379)

**American College of Veterinary Radiolo-
gy**
2520 Beechridge Rd.
Raleigh, NC 27608
Phone: (919)510-0560
Fax: (919)510-0560

Publications: Veterinary Radiology & Ultrasound
(24158)

American Concrete Institute
38800 Country Club Dr.
Farmington Hills, MI 48331
Phone: (248)848-3700
Fax: (248)848-3701

Publications: ACI Structural Journal (15015) • Concrete Abstracts (15017) • Concrete International
(15018)

**American Congress on Surveying and
Mapping**
6 Montgomery Village Ave., Ste. 403
Gaithersburg, MD 20879-3557
Phone: (240)632-9716
Fax: (240)632-1321

Publications: ACSM Bulletin (13531) • Cartography
and Geographic Information Science (13532) • Surveying and Land Information Science (13548)

American Consolidated Media
100 W. Polk
PO Box 160
Burnet, TX 78611
Phone: (512)756-6136
Fax: (512)756-8911

Publications: Burnet Bulletin (29991)

American Corporate Counsel Association
1025 Connecticut Ave. NW, Ste. 200
Washington, DC 20036-5425
Phone: (202)293-4103
Fax: (202)293-4701

Publications: ACCA Docket (5314)

American Correctional Association
4380 Forbes Blvd.
Lanham, MD 20706-4322
Phone: (301)918-1800
Fax: (301)918-1886
Free: 800-222-5646

Publications: CORRECTIONS TODAY (13599) •
Journal of Correctional Best Practices (13603)

American Council of the Blind
1155 15th St. NW, Ste. 1004
Washington, DC 20005
Phone: (202)467-5081
Fax: (202)467-5085
Free: 800-424-8666

Publications: Braille Forum (5382)

American Council on Consumer Interests
415 S Duff Ave., Ste. C
Ames, IA 50010-6600
Phone: (515)956-4666
Fax: (515)233-3101

Publications: Journal of Consumer Affairs (10591)

American Council on Education
1 Dupont Cir.
Washington, DC 20036-1193
Phone: (202)939-9380
Fax: (202)833-4760

Publications: The Presidency (5727)

American Council on Exercise
Box 910449
San Diego, CA 92191-0449
Phone: (858)279-8227
Fax: (858)279-8064
Free: 800-825-3636

Publications: ACE FitnessMatters (3105)

American Council For Polish Culture
67 Lower Orchard Dr.
Levittown, PA 19056-2722
Phone: (215)946-5723

Publications: Polish Heritage (27189)

American Council on Rural Special Education
Bluemont Hall, No. 306
Kansas State University
Manhattan, KS 66506
Phone: (785)532-5717
Fax: (785)532-7732

Publications: Rural Special Education Quarterly (33396)

American Council on the Teaching of Foreign Languages
6 Executive Plz.
Yonkers, NY 10701-6801
Phone: (914)963-8830
Fax: (914)963-1275

Publications: Foreign Language Annals (23599)

American Counseling Association
5999 Stevenson Ave.
Alexandria, VA 22304
Phone: (703)823-9800
Fax: (703)823-0252
Free: 800-347-6647

Publications: Adultspan Journal (31630) • Counseling Today (31661) • Counseling and Values (31662) • Counselor Education and Supervision (31663) • Government Relations Update (31676) • Journal of Addictions and Offender Counseling (31685) • Journal of Counseling and Development (31692) • Journal of Counseling & Development (20360) • Journal of Humanistic Counseling & Development (31698) • Journal of Multicultural Counseling and Development (31699)

American Cowboy
PO Box 6630
Sheridan, WY 82801
Phone: (307)672-7171
Fax: (307)672-7766
Free: 800-369-0196

Publications: American Cowboy (34587)

American Craft Council
72 Spring St.
New York, NY 10012-4019
Phone: (212)274-0630
Fax: (212)274-0650
Free: 888-313-5527

Publications: American Craft (21186)

American Cueist Magazine
5100 Eldorado Pkwy., Ste. 102
PMB 728
McKinney, TX 75070

Publications: American Cueist Magazine (30801)

American Culinary Federation, Inc.
10 San Bartola Dr.
St. Augustine, FL 32086
Phone: (904)824-4468
Fax: (904)825-4758
Free: 800-624-9458

Publications: The National Culinary Review (6616)

American Dairy Science Association
1111 N. Dunlap Ave.
Savoy, IL 61874
Phone: (217)356-5146
Fax: (217)398-4119

Publications: Journal of Dairy Science (31874)

American Dance Therapy Association
2000 Century Plaza, Ste. 108
10632 Little Patuxent Pkwy.
Columbia, MD 21044
Phone: (410)997-4040
Fax: (410)997-4048

Publications: American Journal of Dance Therapy (13451)

American Demographics
PO Box 2042
Marion, OH 43306-8142
Free: 800-529-7502

Publications: American Demographics (25350)

American Dental Assistants Association
35 E Wacker Dr., Ste. 1730
Chicago, IL 60601-2211
Phone: (312)541-1550
Fax: (312)541-1496

Publications: The Dental Assistant (8352)

American Dental Education Association
1625 Massachusetts Ave. NW
Washington, DC 20036-2212
Phone: (202)667-9433
Fax: (202)667-0642

Publications: Journal of Dental Education (31033)

American Dental Hygienists' Association
444 N. Michigan Ave., Ste. 3400
Chicago, IL 60611
Phone: (312)440-8900
Fax: (312)440-6780
Free: 800-243-ADHA

Publications: Journal of Dental Hygiene (8436)

American Diabetes Association
1701 N. Beauregard St.
Alexandria, VA 22311
Phone: (703)549-1500
Fax: (703)683-2890

Publications: Diabetes Care (31665) • Diabetes Forecast (31666)

American Dietetic Association
216 W. Jackson Blvd.
Chicago, IL 60606
Phone: (312)899-0040
Fax: (312)899-4899

Publications: Journal of the American Dietetic Association (8431)

American Drama Institute
University of Cincinnati
Dept. of English
Cincinnati, OH 45221-0069
Phone: (513)556-3914
Fax: (513)556-5960

Publications: America Drama (24769)

American Economic Association
2014 Broadway, Ste. 305
Nashville, TN 37203-2418
Phone: (615)322-2595
Fax: (615)343-7590

Publications: American Economic Review (19452) • Journal of Economic Literature (3796) • Journal of Economic Perspectives (16087)

American Educational Research Association
1230 17th St. NW
Washington, DC 20036-3078
Phone: (202)223-9485
Fax: (202)775-1824

Publications: American Educational Research Journal (5326) • Educational Evaluation and Policy Analysis (5473) • Educational Researcher (5474) • Journal of Educational and Behavioral Statistics (5583) • Review of Educational Research (5765)

American Educational Trust
PO Box 53062
Washington, DC 20009
Phone: (202)939-6050
Fax: (202)265-4574

Publications: Washington Report on Middle East Affairs (5852)

American Electroplaters and Surface Finishers Society
12644 Research Pkwy.
Orlando, FL 32826-3298
Phone: (407)281-6441
Fax: (407)281-6446

Publications: Plating & Surface Finishing (6507)

American Enterprise Institute
1150 17th St. NW
Washington, DC 20036-4670
Phone: (202)862-5800
Fax: (202)862-5886
Free: 888-295-9007

Publications: The American Enterprise (5328)

The American Entomological Society
The Academy of Natural Sciences
1900 Benjamin Franklin Pkwy.
Philadelphia, PA 19103-1195
Phone: (215)561-3978
Fax: (215)299-1028

Publications: Entomological News (19697) • Transactions of the American Entomological Society (27708)

American Express Publishing Corp.
1120 Avenue of the Americas
New York, NY 10036
Phone: (212)536-2025
Fax: (212)536-2020
Free: 800-295-5527

Publications: Food & Wine (21713) • SkyGuide (22743) • Travel Leisure (22858)

American Family Foundation
PO Box 2265
Bonita Springs, FL 34133
Phone: (239)514-3081

Publications: Cultic Studies Review (5947)

American Family Records Association
PO Box 15505
Kansas City, MO 64106

Publications: Family Records, TODAY (17168)

American Farm Publications, Inc.
505 Brookletts Ave.
PO Box 2026
Easton, MD 21601
Phone: (410)822-3965
Fax: (410)822-5068
Free: 800-634-5021

Publications: The Delmarva Farmer (13487) • The New Jersey Farmer (13488)

American Fastener Journal
293 Hopewell Dr.
Powell, OH 43065
Phone: (614)848-3232
Fax: (614)848-5045
Free: 800-848-0304

Publications: American Fastener Journal (25489)

American Federation of Aviculture
PO Box 7312
North Kansas City, MO 64116-0012
Phone: (816)421-BIRD
Fax: (816)421-3214

Publications: AFA Watchbird (17318)

American Federation of Musicians
1501 Broadway, Ste. 600
New York, NY 10036
Phone: (212)869-1330
Fax: (212)302-4374

Publications: International Musician (21927)

American Federation of State, County & Municipal Employees
1625 L St. NW
Washington, DC 20036-5687
Phone: (202)429-1000
Fax: (202)429-1293

Publications: The Public Employee Magazine (5749)

American Federation of Teachers
555 New Jersey Ave. NW
Washington, DC 20001-2079
Phone: (202)879-4400
Fax: (202)879-2014
Free: 800-238-1133

Publications: American Educator (5327) • American Teacher (5346)

American Fern Society, Inc.
Dept. of Biology
2801 S. University Ave.
University of Arkansas
Little Rock, AR 72204
Phone: (501)569-3270
Fax: (501)569-8020

Publications: American Fern Journal (1211)

American Field
542 S Dearborn St.
Chicago, IL 60605-1598
Phone: (312)663-9797
Fax: (312)663-5557

Publications: American Field (8256)

American Fire Journal
9072 E Artesia Blvd., Ste. 7
Bellflower, CA 90706-6299
Phone: (562)866-1664
Fax: (562)867-6434

Publications: American Fire Journal (1484)

American Fire Sprinkler Association
9696 Skillman St., Ste. 300
Dallas, TX 75243
Phone: (214)349-5965
Fax: (214)343-8898

Publications: Sprinkler Age (30182)

American Fisheries Society
5410 Grosvenor Ln., Ste. 110
Bethesda, MD 20814
Phone: (301)897-8616
Fax: (301)897-8096

Publications: Fisheries (13336) • Journal of Aquatic Animal Health (13349) • North American Journal of Aquaculture (13365) • North American Journal of Fisheries Management (13366) • Transactions of the American Fisheries Society (13385)

American Fitness
15250 Ventura Blvd., Ste. 200
Sherman Oaks, CA 91403
Phone: (818)905-0040
Fax: (818)990-5468
Free: 800-225-2322

Publications: American Fitness (3759)

American Forensic Association
PO Box 256
River Falls, WI 54022
Phone: (715)425-3198
Fax: (715)425-9533
Free: 800-228-5424

Publications: Argumentation and Advocacy (34306)

American Forest Foundation
1111 19th St., NW, Ste. 780
Washington, DC 20036
Phone: (202)463-2462
Fax: (202)463-2461
Free: 888-889-4466

Publications: Tree Farmer (5830)

American Forest and Paper Association
Forest & Paper Information Center
1111 19th St. NW, Ste. 700
Washington, DC 20036
Phone: (202)463-2422
Fax: (202)463-2785

Publications: Paper, Paperboard, and Wood Pulp Monthly Statistical Summary (5714)

American Forests
PO Box 2000
Washington, DC 20013
Phone: (202)955-4500
Fax: (202)955-4588
Free: 800-368-5748

Publications: American Forests (5329)

American Foundrymen's Society
505 State St.
Des Plaines, IL 60016-8399
Phone: (847)824-0181
Fax: (847)824-7848
Free: 800-537-4237

Publications: Modern Casting Magazine (8764)

American-French Genealogical Society
PO Box 830
Woonsocket, RI 02895-0870
Phone: (401)765-6141
Fax: (401)765-6141

Publications: Je Me Souviens (28363)

American Friends Service Committee (AFSC)
2161 Massachusetts Ave.
Cambridge, MA 02140
Phone: (617)661-6130
Fax: (617)354-2832

Publications: Peacework (14088)

American Gas Association
400 N. Capitol St., NW
Washington, DC 20001
Phone: (202)824-7000
Fax: (202)824-7115

Publications: American Gas (5330)

The American Genealogist
PO Box 398
Demorest, GA 30535-0398
Phone: (706)865-6440
Fax: (706)865-6440

Publications: The American Genealogist (7239)

American Geographical Society
120 Wall Street, Ste. 100
New York, NY 10005
Phone: (212)422-5456
Fax: (212)422-5480

Publications: Geographical Review (21753)

American Geological Institute
4220 King St.
Alexandria, VA 22302
Phone: (703)379-2480
Fax: (703)379-7563

Publications: Geotimes (31675)

American Geophysical Union
2000 Florida Ave. NW
Washington, DC 20009
Phone: (202)462-6900
Fax: (202)328-0566
Free: 800-966-2481

Publications: Computational Seismology (5430) • EOS (5483) • International Journal of Geomagnetism and Aeronomy (5553) • Journal of Geophysical Research (5594) • Radio Science (26385) • Reviews of Geophysics (5767) • Tectonics (5817) • Water Resources Research (5857)

American Guernsey Association
7614 Slate Ridge Blvd.
PO Box 666
Reynoldsburg, OH 43068
Phone: (614)864-2409
Fax: (614)864-5614

Publications: Guernsey Breeders' Journal (25494)

American Guild of Organists
475 Riverside Dr., Ste. 1260
New York, NY 10115
Phone: (212)870-2310
Fax: (212)870-2163
Free: 800-246-5115

Publications: The American Organist (21203)

The American Harp Society, Inc.
3006 Woodlawn Ave.
Falls Church, VA 22042
Phone: (703)553-9132
Fax: (703)532-8386

Publications: The American Harp Journal (32041)

American Health Care Association
1201 L St. NW
Washington, DC 20005
Phone: (202)842-4444
Fax: (202)842-3860
Free: 800-321-4444

Publications: Provider (5735)

American Health Consultants, Inc.
3525 Piedmont Rd., Bldg. 6, Ste. 400
Atlanta, GA 30305
Phone: (404)262-7436
Fax: (404)262-7837
Free: 800-688-2421

Publications: BioWorld Magazine (6978)

American Health Information Management Association
233 N. Michigan Ave., Ste. 2150
Chicago, IL 60601
Phone: (312)233-1100
Fax: (312)233-1090
Free: 800-224-4621

Publications: Journal of AHIMA (8429)

The American Health Quality Association
1140 Connecticutt Ave., N.W., Ste. 1050
Washington, DC 20036
Phone: (202)331-5790
Fax: (202)331-9334

Publications: Quality Matters (5753)

American Heart Association
7272 Greenville Ave.
Dallas, TX 75231
Phone: (214)373-6300
Fax: (214)691-6342

Publications: Arteriosclerosis, Thrombosis, and Vascular Biology (10969)

American Helicopter Society International
217 N Washington St.
Alexandria, VA 22314
Phone: (703)684-6777
Fax: (703)739-9279

Publications: Journal of the American Helicopter Society (31686) • Vertiflite (31749)

American Heritage
28 W. 23rd St.
New York, NY 10010-8882
Phone: (212)367-3100
Fax: (212)367-3151
Free: 800-777-1222

Publications: American Heritage (21188)

American Hibiscus Society
PO Box 321540
Cocoa Beach, FL 32932-1540
Phone: (321)783-2576
Fax: (321)783-2576

Publications: The Seed Pod (6634)

American Highland Cattle Association
200 Livestock Exchange Bldg.
4701 Marion St.
Denver, CO 80216
Phone: (303)292-9102
Fax: (303)292-9171

Publications: The Bagpipe (4306)

American Historical Association
400 A St. SE
Washington, DC 20003-3889
Phone: (202)544-2422
Fax: (202)544-8307

Publications: The American Historical Review (9823)

American Historical Print Collectors Society, Inc.
1920 Blue Ridge Rd.
Charlottesville, VA 22903
Phone: (434)293-4979

Publications: Imprint (31930)

American Horticultural Society
7931 East Blvd. Dr.
Alexandria, VA 22308-1300
Phone: (703)768-5700
Fax: (703)768-7533
Free: 800-777-7931

Publications: The American Gardener (31636)

American Hotel & Lodging Association
1201 New York Ave. NW, Ste. 600
Washington, DC 20005-3931
Phone: (202)289-3100
Fax: (202)289-3199

Publications: Construction & Modernization Report (5436) • Lodging Magazine (5640)

American Humanist Association
National Office
1777 T Street, NW
Washington, DC 20009-7125
Phone: (202)238-9088
Fax: (202)238-9003
Free: 800-837-3792

Publications: The Humanist (5536)

American Image Inc.
6495 Shallowford Rd.
Lewisville, NC 27023
Phone: (336)945-9867
Fax: (336)945-3711
Free: 800-654-9557

Publications: Today's Photographer Magazine (24039)

American Indian Studies Center
3220 Campbell Hall
Box 951548
Los Angeles, CA 90095-1548
Phone: (310)825-7315
Fax: (310)206-7060

Publications: American Indian Culture and Research Journal (2208)

American Indian Studies Center
Sanford Hall
Bemidji State University
1500 Birchmont Dr., NE, No. 19
Bemidji, MN 56601-2699
Phone: (218)755-3968
Fax: (218)755-4115

Publications: Oshkaabewis Native Journal (15738)

American Industrial Hygiene Association
2700 Prosperity Ave., Ste. 250
Fairfax, VA 22031
Phone: (703)849-8888
Fax: (703)207-3561

Publications: American Industrial Hygiene Association Journal (32004) • Synergist (32032)

American Institute of Aeronautics and Astronautics
1801 Alexander Bell Dr., Ste. 500
Reston, VA 20191-4344
Phone: (703)264-7500
Fax: (703)264-7551
Free: 800-639-2422

Publications: Aerospace America (32356) • Aerospace America (32355) • AIAA Journal (32357) • AIAA Student Journal (32358) • Finding Guide to AIAA Meeting Papers (32365) • International Aerospace Abstracts (32366) • Journal of Aircraft (32369) • Journal of Guidance, Control, and Dynamics (32380) • Journal of Propulsion and Power (32392) • Journal of Spacecraft and Rockets (32395) • Journal of Thermophysics and Heat Transfer (32398)

American Institute of Baking
1213 Bakers Way
PO Box 3999
Manhattan, KS 66505-3999
Phone: (785)537-4750
Fax: (785)537-1493

Publications: American Institute of Baking Technical Bulletin (11619) • Maintenance Engineering Bulletins (11628)

American Institute of Biological Sciences
1444 Eye St. NW, Ste. 200
Washington, DC 20005
Phone: (202)628-1500
Fax: (202)628-1509
Free: 800-992-2427

Publications: BioScience (5378)

The American Institute of Certified Public Accountants
1211 Ave. of the Americas
New York, NY 10036-8775
Phone: (212)596-6200
Fax: (212)596-6213
Free: 888-777-7077

Publications: Journal of Accountancy (19142)

American Institute of Chemical Engineers
3 Park Ave.
New York, NY 10016-5991
Phone: (212)591-7845
Fax: (212)591-8883
Free: 800-242-4363

Publications: AICHE Journal (21166) • Chemical Engineering Progress (21401)

American Institute for Conservation of Historic & Artistic Works
1717 K St. NW, Ste. 200
Washington, DC 20006
Phone: (202)452-9545
Fax: (202)452-9328

Publications: American Institute for Conservation of Historic and Artistic Works Journal (5331)

American Institute of CPAs
Harborside Financial Center
201 Plaza III
Jersey City, NJ 07311
Phone: (201)938-3806

Publications: CPA Client Bulletin (19135) • Tax Adviser (19145)

American Institute of Graphic Arts
164 5th Ave.
New York, NY 10010
Phone: (212)255-4004
Fax: (212)807-1799

Publications: Gain (21745) • Trace: AIGA Journal of Design (22851)

American Institute of the History of Pharmacy
University of Wisconsin
School of Pharmacy
777 Highland Ave.
Madison, WI 53705
Phone: (608)262-5378

Publications: Pharmacy in History (33968)

American Institute of Hydrology
2499 Rice St., Ste. 135
St. Paul, MN 55113-3724
Phone: (651)484-8169
Fax: (651)484-8357

Publications: Hydrological Science and Technology (16380)

American Institute of Organbuilders
Box 130982
Houston, TX 77219-0982
Phone: (713)529-2212

Publications: Journal of American Organbuilding (30495)

American Institute of Parliamentarians
PO Box 2173
Wilmington, DE 19899
Phone: (302)762-1811
Fax: (302)762-2170
Free: 888-664-0428

Publications: Parliamentary Journal (5294)

American Institute of Physics
1 Physics Ellipse
College Park, MD 20740-3843
Phone: (301)209-3000
Fax: (301)209-0842

Publications: Applied Physics Letters (13412) • The Astronomical Journal (32943) • Bulletin of the American Astronomical Society (5388) • Bulletin of the American Physical Society (13413) • CHAOS (13414) • Current Physics Index (13415) • The Industrial Physicist (13421) • JETP Letters (13422) • Journal of Applied Physics (13423) • The Journal of Chemical Physics (13425) • Journal of Experimental and Theoretical Physics (JETP) (13427) • Journal of Mathematical Physics (13428) • Journal of Optical Technology (13429) • Journal of Physical and Chemical Reference Data (13430) • Journal of Rheology (22179) • Journal of Vacuum Science and Technology A & B (24186) • Low Temperature Physics (13433) • Medical Physics (22310) • Physical Review A (23190) • Physics of Fluids (3651) • Physics of Particles and Nuclei (13435) • Physics of Plasmas (19468) • Physics Today (13436) • Publication of the Astronomical Society of the Pacific (914) • Reviews of Modern Physics (33016) • Semiconductors (13440) • Technical Physics (13441) • Technical Physics Letters (13442) • Virtual Journal of Biological Physics Research (13444) • Virtual Journal of Nanoscale Science & Technology (13445) • Virtual Journal of Quantum Information (13446)

American Institute of Steel Construction Inc.
1 E. Wacker Dr., Ste. 3100
Chicago, IL 60601-2000
Phone: (312)670-2400
Fax: (312)670-0341

Publications: Engineering Journal (8369) • Modern Steel Construction (8493)

American-International Charolais Association
PO Box 20247
Kansas City, MO 64195
Phone: (816)464-5977
Fax: (816)464-5759

Publications: Charolais Journal (17161)

American International College
University of Chicago Press
5720 S. Woodlawn Ave.
Chicago, IL 60637

Publications: American International College Journal of Business (8257)

American International College
1000 State St.
Springfield, MA 01109-3189
Phone: (413)205-3201

Publications: Yellow Jacket (14553)

American Israel Numismatic Association
12555 Biscayne Blvd. Ste. 733
North Miami, FL 33181
Phone: (305)466-2833
Fax: (305)466-2834

Publications: Shekel (6466)

American Jail Association
1135 Professional Ct.
Hagerstown, MD 21740-5853
Phone: (301)790-3930
Fax: (301)790-2941

Publications: American Jails (13562)

American Jersey Cattle Association
6486 E. Main St.
Reynoldsburg, OH 43068-2362
Phone: (614)861-3636
Fax: (614)861-8040

Publications: Jersey Journal (25495)

American Jesuits
PO Box 60790
Chicago, IL 60660-0790
Phone: (773)761-9432
Fax: (773)761-9443
Free: 800-955-5538

Publications: Company (8338)

American Jewish Archives
3101 Clifton Ave.
Cincinnati, OH 45220
Phone: (513)221-1875
Fax: (513)221-7812

Publications: American Jewish Archives (24770)

American Jewish Committee
165 E 56th St.
New York, NY 10022-2746
Phone: (212)751-4000
Fax: (212)891-1470
Free: 800-551-3253

Publications: Commentary (21454)

American Jewish Congress
15 E 84th St.
New York, NY 10028-0458
Phone: (212)879-4500

Publications: Congress Monthly (21483) • Judaism (3685)

American Jewish Historical Society
160 Herrick Rd.
Newton Centre, MA 02459-2237
Phone: (617)559-8880
Fax: (617)559-8881

Publications: American Jewish History (14414)

American Jewish World Publishing, Inc.
4509 Minnetonka Blvd.
St. Louis Park, MN 55416-4027
Phone: (952)259-5280
Fax: (952)920-6205

Publications: American Jewish World (16359)

American Journal
4 Dana St.
Westbrook, ME 04092
Phone: (207)854-2577
Fax: (207)854-0018

Publications: American Journal (13074)

American Journal of Comparative Law
School of Law (Boalt Hall)
University of California
Berkeley, CA 94720-7200
Phone: (510)643-6115
Fax: (510)643-2698

Publications: American Journal of Comparative Law (1489)

American Journal of Islamic Social Sciences
PO Box 669
Herndon, VA 20172-0669
Phone: (703)471-1133
Fax: (703)471-3922

Publications: American Journal of Islamic Social Sciences (32160)

American Journal of Nursing
1111 Bethlehem Pike
PO Box 908
Springhouse, PA 19477
Phone: (212)646-8700
Fax: (212)654-2585
Free: 800-627-0484

Publications: American Journal of Nursing (28013)

The American Journal of Pathology
9650 Rockville Pke.
Bethesda, MD 20814-3993
Phone: (301)634-7959
Fax: (301)634-7961

Publications: The American Journal of Pathology (13302)

American Journal of Science
210 Whitney Ave
PO Box 208109
New Haven, CT 06520
Phone: (203)432-3131
Fax: (203)432-5668

Publications: American Journal of Science (4982)

American Journalism Review
University of Maryland
1117 Journalism Bldg.
College Park, MD 20742-7111
Phone: (301)405-2399
Fax: (301)314-9166

Publications: American Journalism Review (13410)

American Kinesiotherapy Association
Toledo, OH 43606
Phone: (419)537-2743

Publications: Clinical Kinesiology (25565)

American Labor Conference on International Affairs
275 7th Ave.
New York, NY 10001
Phone: (212)807-8240
Fax: (212)727-2229

Publications: New Leader (22431)

American Law Institute-American Bar Association
4025 Chestnut St.
Philadelphia, PA 19104-3099
Phone: (215)243-1604
Fax: (215)243-1664
Free: 800-253-6397

Publications: ALI-ABA Estate Planning Course Materials Journal (27368) • The CLE Journal (27407) • The Practical Litigator (27642) • The Practical Real Estate Lawyer (27643) • The Practical Tax Lawyer (27644)

The American Lawyer
10 United Nations Plaza, 3rd Fl.
San Francisco, CA 94102
Fax: (415)352-0118
Free: 800-628-1160

Publications: Texas Lawyer (3451)

American Lawyer Media, L.P.
10 United Nations Plz., 3rd Fl.
San Francisco, CA 94102-4911
Phone: (415)749-5400
Fax: (415)749-5449
Free: 800-244-5399

Publications: Cal Law (3334) • The Recorder (3421)

American Lawyer Media, L.P.
1730 M St. NW, Ste. 802
Washington, DC 20036
Phone: (202)457-0686
Fax: (202)785-4539
Free: 800-933-4317

Publications: Legal Times (5635)

American Lawyer Media, L.P.
1 SE 3rd Ave., Ste. 900
Miami, FL 33131
Phone: (305)377-3721
Fax: (305)374-8474
Free: 800-777-7300

Publications: Daily Business Review (6347)

American Lawyer Media, L.P.
190 Pryor St., SW
Atlanta, GA 30303
Phone: (404)521-1227
Fax: (404)659-4739

Publications: Daily Report (6998) • Daily Report (6997)

American Lawyer Media L.P.
238 Mulberry St.
PO Box 20081
Newark, NJ 07101-6081

Publications: Corporate Counsel (19352)

American Lawyer Media, L.P.
345 Park Ave. S.
New York, NY 10010
Phone: (212)779-9200

Publications: Broward Daily Business Review (6072) • Palm Beach Daily Business Review (6847)

American Legion Auxiliary's National News
777 N Meridian, St., 3rd Fl.
Indianapolis, IN 46204-1189
Phone: (317)955-3845
Fax: (317)955-3884

Publications: American Legion Auxiliary's National News (10079)

American Legion—Dept. of Texas
3401 Ed Bluestein Blvd.
Austin, TX 78721-2902
Phone: (512)472-4138
Fax: (512)472-0603

Publications: TEXAS LEGION TIMES (29833)

The American Legion, Indiana Dept.
777 N Meridian St.
Indianapolis, IN 46204
Phone: (317)630-1300
Fax: (317)237-9891
Free: 888-723-7999

Publications: The Hoosier Legionnaire (10117)

The American Legion Mississippi Dept.
PO Box 688
Jackson, MS 39205
Phone: (601)353-3681
Fax: (601)352-7181

Publications: Mississippi Legionnaire (16704)

American Legion National Headquarters
PO Box 1055
Indianapolis, IN 46206
Phone: (317)630-1200
Fax: (317)630-1369

Publications: American Legion Magazine (10080)

The American Legion/South Dakota Department
PO Box 67
Watertown, SD 57201
Phone: (605)886-3604
Fax: (605)886-2870

Publications: South Dakota Legion News (29018)

American Letters & Commentary, Inc.
850 Park Ave., Ste. 5B
New York, NY 10021
Phone: (212)734-2233
Fax: (212)327-0706

Publications: American Letters & Commentary (21201)

American Library Association
50 E. Huron St.
Chicago, IL 60611
Phone: (312)944-7298
Fax: (312)280-4380
Free: 800-545-2433

Publications: American Libraries (8259) • Book Links: Connecting Books, Libraries and Classrooms (8286) • Booklist (8287) • Choice (4943) • Library Administration & Management (8462) • Library Resources & Technical Services (8463) • Library Technology Reports (8464) • Public Libraries (8545) • Reference and User Services Quarterly (25941)

American Littoral Society
Sandy Hook
Highlands, NJ 07732
Phone: (732)291-0055
Fax: (732)872-8041

Publications: Underwater Naturalist (18874)

American Logistics Association
1133 15th St. NW, Ste. 640
Washington, DC 20005
Phone: (202)466-2520
Fax: (202)296-4419

Publications: Interservice (5559)

American Lung Association
61 Broadway
New York, NY 10019
Phone: (212)315-8700
Fax: (212)265-5642

Publications: American Review of Respiratory Disease (21206)

American Management Association
1601 Broadway
New York, NY 10019-7420
Phone: (212)586-8100
Fax: (212)903-8083
Free: 800-313-8650

Publications: Compensation & Benefits Review (21467) • Organizational Dynamics (22502)

American Marketing Association
311 S. Wacker Dr., Ste. 5800
Chicago, IL 60606-2266
Phone: (312)542-9000
Fax: (312)542-9001
Free: 800-262-1150

Publications: Journal of Marketing (8443) • Journal of Marketing Research (8444) • Journal of Public Policy & Marketing (8449) • Marketing Health Services (8477) • Marketing Management (8478) • Marketing News (8479) • Marketing Research (8480)

American Massage Therapy Association
820 Davis St. Ste. 100
Evanston, IL 60201-4444
Phone: (847)864-0123
Fax: (847)864-1178

Publications: Massage Therapy Journal (8867)

American Mathematical Society
201 Charles St.
Providence, RI 02904-2294
Phone: (401)455-4000
Fax: (401)331-3842
Free: 800-321-4267

Publications: Abstracts of Papers Presented to the American Mathematical Society (28384) • Bulletin (New Series) of the American Mathematical Society (28392) • Current Mathematical Publications (28394) • Employment Information in the Mathematical Sciences (28396) • Journal of the American Mathematical Society (28402) • Mathematical Reviews (28404) • Mathematics of Computation (28405) • Memoirs of the American Mathematical Society (28409) • Notices of the American Mathematical Society (28410) • Proceedings of the American Mathematical Society (28413) • St. Petersburg Mathematical Journal (28423) • Sugaku Expositions (28424) • Theory of Probability & Mathematical Statistics (28425) • Transactions of the American Mathematical Society (28426) • Transactions of the Moscow Mathematical Society (28427)

American Matthay Association
2447 Hwy. 45 By-pass
Jackson, TN 38305

Publications: The Matthay News (29230)

American Medical Association
515 N. State St.
PO Box 10946
Chicago, IL 60610
Phone: (312)670-7827
Free: 800-262-2350

Publications: Archives of General Psychiatry (13838)

American Medical Association Alliance
515 N. State St.
Chicago, IL 60610
Phone: (312)464-5000
Fax: (312)464-5020

Publications: AMA Alliance Today (8251) • American Medical News (8260) • Archives of Dermatology (8267) • Archives of Family Medicine (27383) • Archives of Internal Medicine (8268) • Archives of Neurology (30123) • Archives of Ophthalmology (8269) • Archives of Otolaryngology—Head & Neck Surgery (8270) • Archives of Pathology & Laboratory Medicine (8271) • Archives of Pediatrics & Adolescent Medicine (8272) • Archives of Surgery (8274) • JAMA (8424)

American Medical Group Association
1422 Duke St.
Alexandria, VA 22314
Phone: (703)838-0033
Fax: (703)548-1890

Publications: Group Practice Journal (31677)

American Medical Technologists
710 Higgins Rd.
Park Ridge, IL 60068-5765
Phone: (847)823-5169
Fax: (847)823-0458

Publications: AMT Events (9404)

American Medical Women's Association
Eastern Virginia Medical School
825 Fairfax Ave.
Norfolk, VA 23507-1912
Phone: (757)446-7468
Fax: (757)446-7442

Publications: Journal of the American Medical Women's Association (21983)

American Meteorological Society
45 Beacon St.
Boston, MA 02108
Phone: (617)227-2425
Fax: (617)742-8718

Publications: Bulletin of the AMS (13867) • Journal of Applied Meteorology (13912) • Journal of Atmo-

spheric and Oceanic Technology (13913) • Journal of Climate (13914) • Journal of Physical Oceanography (13917) • Monthly Weather Review (13929) • Weather and Forecasting (13970)

American Midland Naturalist
University of Notre Dame, PO Box 369
Notre Dame, IN 46556
Phone: (219)631-7481
Fax: (219)631-7413

Publications: American Midland Naturalist (10366)

American Ministry Resources LLC
PO Box 681868
Franklin, TN 37068-1868
Phone: (615)599-9889
Fax: (615)599-8985

Publications: Preaching (29198)

American Monument Association
70 N. Market St.
Mount Sterling, OH 43143
Phone: (740)869-9990
Fax: (740)869-9991

Publications: Stone in America (25397)

American Morgan Horse Association
PO Box 960
Shelburne, VT 05482-0960
Phone: (802)985-4944
Fax: (802)985-8897

Publications: The Morgan Horse (31599)

American Mothers, Inc.
878 Walnut Shade Rd.
Dover, DE 19901
Phone: (302)697-6811
Fax: (302)674-1830
Free: 888-822-8486

Publications: The American Mother (5243)

American Motorcycle Association
13515 Yarmouth Dr.
Pickerington, OH 43147
Phone: (614)856-1900
Fax: (614)856-1920
Free: 800-262-5646

Publications: American Motorcyclist (25477)

American Moving & Storage Association
1611 Duke St.
Alexandria, VA 22314
Phone: (703)683-7410
Fax: (703)548-1845

Publications: Direction (31667) • Direction (31668) • The Moving World (31711)

American Museum of Natural History
79th St. & Central Park W.
New York, NY 10024-5192
Phone: (212)769-5000
Fax: (212)769-5511

Publications: American Museum Novitates (21202) • Natural History Magazine (22405)

American Music Therapy Association
8455 Colesville Rd., Ste. 1000
Silver Spring, MD 20910
Phone: (301)589-3300
Fax: (301)589-5175

Publications: Journal of Music Therapy (13731)

American Musicological Society, Inc.
201 S. 34th St.
Philadelphia, PA 19104
Phone: (215)898-8698
Fax: (215)573-3673
Free: 888-611-4267

Publications: American Musicology Society Journal (10367)

American Muslim Support Group
PO Box 5670
St. Louis, MO 63121
Phone: (314)291-3711
Fax: (314)291-3711

Publications: The American Muslim (17412)

American Name Society
17 Lexington Ave.
New York, NY 10010
Phone: (212)387-1597
Fax: (212)387-1591

Publications: Names (8739)

American Nature Study Society
Pocono Environmental Education Ctr.
RR 2, Box 1010
Dingmans Ferry, PA 18328
Phone: (717)828-9692
Fax: (717)828-9695

Publications: Nature Study (26828)

American Navion Society
PO Box 1810
Lodi, CA 95241-1810
Phone: (209)339-4213
Fax: (209)339-1701

Publications: Navioneer (4479)

American Nephrology Nurses' Association
E. Holly Ave.
Box 56
Pitman, NJ 08071-0056
Phone: (856)589-2300
Fax: (856)589-7463

Publications: Nephrology Nursing Journal (19436)

The American News
1583 W Baseline St.
San Bernardino, CA 92411-1756
Phone: (909)889-7677
Fax: (909)889-2882

Publications: The San Bernardino American News (3090)

American Nuclear Society
555 N Kensington Ave.
La Grange Park, IL 60526
Phone: (708)352-6611
Fax: (708)352-6464
Free: 800-NUC-NEWS

Publications: Fusion Technology (9705) • Nuclear News (9052) • Nuclear Science and Engineering (9053) • Nuclear Technology (9054)

American Numismatic Association
818 N. Cascade Ave.
Colorado Springs, CO 80903-3279
Phone: (719)632-2646
Fax: (719)634-4085
Free: 800-367-9723

Publications: The Numismatist (4253)

American Nurseryman Publishing Co.
223 W. Jackson Blvd., Ste. 500
Chicago, IL 60606-6904
Phone: (312)427-7339
Fax: (312)427-7346
Free: 800-621-5727

Publications: American Nurseryman (8261)

American Nurses Association
600 Maryland Ave. SW, Ste. 100 W.
Washington, DC 20024-2571
Phone: (202)651-7000
Fax: (202)651-7000
Free: 800-284-2378

Publications: The American Nurse (5337)

American Occupational Therapy Association Inc.
PO Box 31220
Bethesda, MD 20824-1220
Phone: (301)652-2682
Fax: (301)652-7711
Free: 800-877-1383

Publications: The American Journal of Occupational Therapy (13301) • OT Practice (13370)

The American Oil and Gas Reporter
PO Box 343
Derby, KS 67037
Phone: (316)788-6271
Fax: (316)788-7568
Free: 800-847-8301

Publications: The American Oil and Gas Reporter (11406)

American Opinion Publishing, Inc.
PO Box 8040
Appleton, WI 54912
Phone: (920)749-3784
Fax: (920)749-3785
Free: 800-727-TRUE

Publications: The New American (33540)

American Optometric Association
243 N. Lindbergh Blvd.
St. Louis, MO 63141-7881
Phone: (314)991-4100
Fax: (314)991-4101

Publications: AOA News (17416) • Optometry
(17479)

American Oriental Society
University of Colorado
Dept. of East Asian Language
279 UCB
Boulder, CO 80301

Publications: Journal of the American Oriental Society (4173)

The American Orthopaedic Society for Sports Medicine
6300 N River Rd.
Rosemont, IL 60018
Phone: (847)292-4900
Fax: (847)292-4905

Publications: The American Journal of Sports Medicine (31914)

American Orthopsychiatric Association
330 7th Ave., 18th Fl.
New York, NY 10001
Phone: (212)564-5930
Fax: (212)564-6180

Publications: American Journal of Orthopsychiatry (21197) • Readings (22629)

American Orthotic & Prosthetic Association
330 John Carlyle St., Ste. 200
Alexandria, VA 22314
Phone: (703)836-7116
Fax: (703)836-0838

Publications: JPO: Journal of Prosthetics & Orthotics (31704) • O & P Almanac (31717)

American Osteopathic Association
142 E. Ontario St.
Chicago, IL 60611
Phone: (312)202-8000
Fax: (312)202-8200
Free: 800-621-1773

Publications: The DO (8355) • Journal of the American Osteopathic Association (8432)

American Paint Horse Association
PO Box 961023
Fort Worth, TX 76161-0023
Phone: (817)834-2742
Fax: (817)222-8466

Publications: Paint Horse Journal (30350)

American Penstemon Society
1569 S Holland Ct.
Lakewood, CO 80232
Phone: (303)986-8096

Publications: American Penstemon Society Bulletin (4530)

American Pharmaceutical Association
2215 Constitution Ave., NW
Washington, DC 20037-2985
Phone: (202)628-4410
Fax: (202)783-2351
Free: 800-237-2742

Publications: Journal of the American Pharmaceutical Association (5570) • Journal of Pharmaceutical Sciences (5612) • Pharmacy Today (5719)

American Pheasant and Waterfowl Society
W. 2270 U.S Hwy. 10
Granton, WI 54436-8854
Phone: (715)238-7291
Fax: (715)238-4623

Publications: APWS Magazine (33736)

American Philatelic Society
100 Oakwood Ave.
PO Box 8000
State College, PA 16803-8000
Phone: (814)237-3803
Fax: (814)237-6128

Publications: The American Philatelist (28016) • Philatelic Literature Review (28020)

American Philosophical Society
104 S 5th St.
Philadelphia, PA 19106
Phone: (215)440-3425
Fax: (215)440-3450

Publications: Proceedings of the American Philosophical Society (27648)

American Physical Society
One Physics Ellipse
College Park, MD 20740-3844
Phone: (301)209-3000
Fax: (301)209-0844

Publications: Physical Review B (23191) • Physical Review C (23192) • Physical Review D (23193) • Physical Review E (23194) • Physical Review Letters (23195) • Physical Review Special Topics (23196)

American Physical Society
1 Physics Ellipse
PO Box 9000
College Park, MD 20740-3844
Phone: (301)209-3200
Fax: (301)209-0865

Publications: Physical Review Abstracts (21056)

American Physical Therapy Association
1111 N. Fairfax St.
Alexandria, VA 22314-1488
Phone: (703)706-3171
Fax: (703)706-3396
Free: 800-999-2782

Publications: Physical Therapy (31722) • PT, Magazine of Physical Therapy (31731)

The American Physiological Society
9650 Rockville Pke.
Bethesda, MD 20814-3991
Phone: (301)634-7164

Publications: Advances in Physiology Education (13294) • American Journal of Physiology: Cell Physiology (13303) • American Journal of Physiology (Consolidated) (13304) • American Journal of Physiology: Endocrinology and Metabolism (13305) • American Journal of Physiology: Gastrointestinal and Liver Physiology (13306) • American Journal of Physiology: Heart and Circulatory Physiology (13307) • American Journal of Physiology: Lung Cellular and Molecular Physiology (13308) • American Journal of Physiology: Regulatory, Integrative and Comparative Physiology (13309) • American Journal of Physiology: Renal Physiology (13310) • Journal of Applied Physiology (13348) • Journal of Neurophysiology (13353) • News in Physiological Sciences (NIPS) (13364) • Physiological Genomics (13373) • Physiological Reviews (13374)

The American Phytopathological Society
3340 Pilot Knob Rd.
St. Paul, MN 55121
Phone: (651)454-7250
Fax: (651)454-0766
Free: 800-328-7560

Publications: Molecular Plant-Microbe Interactions (MPMI) (16397) • Phytopathology (16405) • Plant Disease (16406)

American Planning Association
122 S. Michigan Ave., Ste. 1600
Chicago, IL 60603-6107
Phone: (312)431-9100
Fax: (312)431-9985

Publications: Journal of the American Planning Association (JAPA) (26483) • Planning (8532)

American Podiatric Medical Association
9312 Old Georgetown Rd.
Bethesda, MD 20814
Phone: (301)581-9200
Fax: (301)530-2752
Free: 800-ASK-APMA

Publications: APMA News (13312) • Journal of the American Podiatric Medical Association (13347)

American Police Beat
4 Brattle St., Ste. 308
Cambridge, MA 02138-3714
Fax: (617)354-6515
Free: 800-234-0056

Publications: American Police Beat (14037)

American Political Science Association
1527 New Hampshire Ave. NW
Washington, DC 20036-1206
Phone: (202)483-2512
Fax: (202)483-2657

Publications: American Political Science Review (5338) • PS (5736)

American Polygraph Association
PO Box 8037
Chattanooga, TN 37414-0037
Phone: (423)892-3992
Fax: (423)894-5435
Free: 800-APA-8037

Publications: Polygraph (29091)

American Postal Workers Union, AFL-CIO
1300 L St. NW
Washington, DC 20005
Phone: (202)842-4200
Fax: (202)842-4297

Publications: The American Postal Worker (5339)

American Power Boat Association
17640 E. 9 Mile Rd.
Eastpointe, MI 48021-0377
Phone: (586)773-9700
Fax: (586)773-6490

Publications: Propeller Magazine (14999)

American Press
125 W. Springfield St.
St. James, MO 65559-1929
Phone: (314)265-3321
Fax: (314)265-3197

Publications: Leader-Journal (17388)

American Press
Hwy. 270 E.
Box 606
Wilburton, OK 74578
Phone: (918)465-3851
Fax: (918)465-2170

Publications: Latimer County Today (26196)

American Primrose Society
PO Box 210913
Auke Bay, AK 99821
Phone: (907)789-5860

Publications: Primroses (597)

American Print Alliance
302 Larkspur Turn
Peachtree City, GA 30269-2210

Publications: Contemporary Impressions (7479)

American Psychiatric Publishing Inc.
1000 Wilson Blvd.
Arlington, VA 22209
Phone: (703)907-7300

Publications: American Journal of Addictions (31772) • American Journal of Psychiatry (31773) • Journal of Neuropsychiatry and Clinical Neurosciences (31803) • Journal of Psychiatric Research (31804) • Psychiatric News (31819) • Psychosomatics (31820)

American Psychological Association
750 1st St. NE
Washington, DC 20002-4242
Phone: (202)336-5510
Free: 800-374-2721

Publications: American Psychologist (5340) • APA Monitor (5356) • Behavioral Neuroscience (5375) • Contemporary Psychology (5440) • Developmental Psychology (5463) • Health Psychology (5522) • Journal of Abnormal Psychology (5566) • Journal of Applied Psychology (5572) • The Journal of Consulting and Clinical Psychology (5579) • Journal of Counseling Psychology (13426) • Journal of Educational Psychology (5584) • Journal of Experimental Psychology: Animal Behavior Processes (5588) • Journal of Experimental Psychology: Human Perception and Performance (5589) • Journal of Experimental Psychology: Learning, Memory and Cognition (5590) • Journal of Family Psychology (5591) • Journal of Personality and Social Psychology (5611) • Monitor on Psychology (5660) • Neuropsychology (5692) • Neuropsychology Abstracts (5693) • Professional Psychology: Research and Practice (5732) • Psychological Abstracts (5738) • Psychological Assessment (5739) • Psychological

Bulletin (5740) • Psychological Review (5741) • Psychology and Aging (5743) • PsycSCAN: Applied Psychology (5744) • PsycSCAN: Behavior Analysis & Therapy (5745) • PsycSCAN: Clinical Psychology (5746) • PsycSCAN: LD/MR (5747)

American Psychotherapy Association
2750 E. Sunshine Rd.
Springfield, MO 65804
Phone: (417)823-0173

Publications: Annals of the American Psychotherapy Association (17592)

American Public Health Association
800 I St. NW
Washington, DC 20001-3710
Phone: (202)777-2472
Fax: (202)777-2531

Publications: American Journal of Public Health (5334) • The Nation's Health (5687)

American Public Power Association
2301 M St. NW
Washington, DC 20037-1484
Phone: (202)467-2900
Fax: (202)467-2910

Publications: Public Power (5752)

American Public Welfare Association
810 First St., N.E., Ste. 500
Washington, DC 20002-4267
Phone: (202)682-0100

Publications: Policy and Practice of Public Human Services (5720)

American Publish Co.
PO Box 606
Oquawka, IL 61469
Phone: (309)867-2515
Fax: (309)867-6215

Publications: Oquawka Current (9386)

American Publishing
417 York St.
PO Box 340
Helena, AR 72342
Fax: (501)338-9184

Publications: The Daily World (1174)

American Publishing
35 S. Vine St.
Harrisburg, IL 62946-1725
Phone: (618)253-7146
Fax: (618)252-0863

Publications: The Daily Register (8972)

American Publishing
115 Main St.
Eau Claire, MI 49111
Phone: (616)461-6941
Fax: (616)461-6816

Publications: Central County (15001) • Twin City (15003)

American Publishing
818 Washington St.
PO Box 707
Chillicothe, MO 64601
Fax: (816)646-2028

Publications: Constitution-Tribune (16977)

American Publishing
806 Central Ave.
PO Box 757
Nebraska City, NE 68410
Phone: (402)873-3334
Fax: (402)873-5436

Publications: Nebraska City News-Press (18166)

American Publishing
405 E. Collin
PO Box 622
Corsicana, TX 75151-9006
Phone: (214)872-3931
Fax: (903)872-6878

Publications: Corsicana Daily Sun (30101)

American Publishing Co.
298 N. Pine St.
PO Box 31
Globe, AZ 85502
Phone: (520)425-7121
Fax: (520)425-7001

Publications: Arizona Silver Belt (717)

American Publishing Co.
PO Box 70
Malvern, AR 72104
Phone: (501)922-1900
Fax: (501)922-0958
Free: 800-833-4050

Publications: La Villa News (1262)

American Publishing Co.
PO Box 70
Blackfoot, ID 83221
Phone: (208)785-1100
Fax: (208)785-4239

Publications: The Morning News (7800)

American Publishing Co.
323-325 E. Main St.
PO Box 190
Carmi, IL 62821
Phone: (618)382-4176
Fax: (618)384-2163

Publications: Carmi Times (8131)

American Publishing Co.
606 N. Van Buren
Marion, IL 62959
Phone: (618)993-1711

Publications: Chariton Courier (9141) • Daily News (12293) • Harrison Daily Times (9142) • The Milton Daily Standard/The Lewisburg Daily Journal (27270)

American Publishing Co.
PO Box 650
Monmouth, IL 61462
Phone: (309)734-3176

Publications: The Daily American (9214) • Daily Journal (9215) • Murphysboro American (9217)

American Publishing Co.
123 S. Jefferson St.
Hartford City, IN 47348
Phone: (317)348-0110
Fax: (317)348-0112

Publications: Hartford City News Times (10060)

American Publishing Co.
PO Box 429
Winchester, IN 47394
Phone: (317)584-4501
Fax: (317)584-3066

Publications: The News Gazette (10566)

American Publishing Co.
207 N. Madison St.
Kosciusko, MS 39090-3526
Fax: (601)289-2254

Publications: The Star-Herald (16734)

American Publishing Co.
13 E. Jefferson St.
PO Box 210
Pontotoc, MS 38863
Fax: (601)489-6714

Publications: The Pontotoc Progress (16823)

American Publishing Co.
316 University Dr.
PO Drawer 1068
Starkville, MS 39759
Fax: (601)323-6586

Publications: The Starkville Daily News (16845)

American Publishing Co.
412 High St.
Boonville, MO 65233
Phone: (816)882-5335
Fax: (816)882-2256

Publications: News & Advertiser (16914)

American Publishing Co.
PO Box 471
Fredericktown, MO 63645
Fax: (314)783-6890

Publications: Democrat-News (17074)

American Publishing Co.
506 W. Potter
PO Box 828
Kirksville, MO 63501
Phone: (816)665-4663
Fax: (816)665-3048
Free: 800-830-5360

Publications: The Crier (17225)

American Publishing Co.
204 W. Bourke St.
PO Box 7
Macon, MO 63552-1503
Phone: (816)385-3121
Fax: (816)385-3082
Free: 800-475-3121

Publications: The Journal (17258) • Macon Chronicle-Herald (17259)

American Publishing Co.
4242 Lindell Blvd.
St. Louis, MO 63108-2916
Phone: (314)533-8000
Fax: (314)533-0038

Publications: St. Louis American (17493)

American Publishing Co.
PO Box 578
Waynesville, MO 65583
Phone: (314)336-3711
Fax: (314)336-4640

Publications: Daily Guide (17709)

American Publishing Co.
85 Canisteo St.
Hornell, NY 14843-1544
Phone: (607)324-1425
Fax: (607)324-1462

Publications: The Evening Tribune (20751) • Stamps (20752) • Stamps Auction News (20753)

American Publishing Co.
36 River St., No. 42
Salamanca, NY 14779
Phone: (716)945-1644
Fax: (716)945-4285

Publications: Press (23293)

The American Publishing Co.
159 N. Main St.
Wellsville, NY 14895-1149
Phone: (716)593-5300
Fax: (716)593-5303

Publications: The Allegany County Pennysaver (23532) • The Wellsville Daily Reporter (23533)

American Publishing Co.
504 W. Wilson St.
PO Box 1199
Tarboro, NC 27886
Phone: (919)823-3106
Fax: (919)823-4599

Publications: The Daily Southerner (24254)

American Publishing Co.
1219 Washington
Commerce, TX 75428
Phone: (903)886-3196
Fax: (903)886-3198

Publications: Commerce Journal (30067)

American Publishing Co.
549 4th St.
PO Box 789
Port Arthur, TX 77641
Phone: (409)985-5541
Fax: (409)982-4903

Publications: Port Arthur News (30953)

American Publishing Co.
1910 S. Interstate Hwy. 35
PO Box 1109
San Marcos, TX 78666-5901
Phone: (512)392-2458
Fax: (512)392-1514

Publications: San Marcos Daily Record (31085)

American Publishing Co. of Indiana
135 S Franklin St.
PO Box 106
Greensburg, IN 47240

Publications: Greensburg Times (10044)

American Publishing Company of Michigan
505 W Locust St.
Three Oaks, MI 49128
Phone: (616)756-2421
Fax: (616)756-7220
Publications: South County Gazette and Shopper (15591)

American Publishing of Michigan
109 Arlington St.
Sault Sainte Marie, MI 49783-1901
Phone: (906)632-2235
Fax: (906)632-1222
Publications: Evening News (15526) • Tri-County Buyers' Guide (15528)

American Publishing of Ohio
102 E Spring St.
St. Marys, OH 45885
Phone: (419)394-7414
Fax: (419)394-7202
Publications: The Evening Leader (25504)

American Quarter Horse Association
1600 Quarter Horse Dr.
PO Box 32470
Amarillo, TX 79120
Phone: (806)376-4888
Fax: (806)349-6400
Publications: The American Quarter Horse Journal (29695) • The Quarter Racing Journal (29697)

American Quilt Study Group
35th & Holdrege, E Campus Loop
PO Box 4737
Lincoln, NE 68504-0737
Phone: (402)472-5361
Fax: (402)472-5428
Publications: Uncoverings (18125)

American Quilter's Society
PO Box 3290
Paducah, KY 42002-3290
Phone: (270)898-7903
Fax: (270)898-1173
Free: 800-626-5420
Publications: American Quilter (12337)

American Radio Relay League Inc.
225 Main St.
Newington, CT 06111
Phone: (860)594-0200
Fax: (860)594-0303
Free: 888-277-5289
Publications: QST (5037)

American Real Estate and Urban Economics Association
Kelley School of Business
Indiana University
1309 E. Tenth St., Ste. 738
Bloomington, IN 47405
Phone: (812)855-7794
Fax: (812)855-8679
Publications: Real Estate Economics (9850)

American Red Brangus Association
3995 E. Highway 290
Dripping Springs, TX 78620-4205
Phone: (512)858-7285
Fax: (512)858-7084
Publications: American Red Brangus Journal (30250)

American Red Cross
PO Box 37243
Washington, DC 20013
Free: 800-HELP-NOW
Publications: The Humanitarian (5537)

American Rental Association
1900 19th St.
Moline, IL 61265
Phone: (309)764-2475
Fax: (309)764-1533
Free: 800-334-2177
Publications: Rental Management (9207)

American-Republican, Inc.
389 Meadow St.
Waterbury, CT 06722
Phone: (203)574-3636
Fax: (203)596-9277
Free: 800-992-3232
Publications: Republican-American (5193)

American Research Press
PO Box 141
Rehoboth, MN 87322
Publications: Smarandache Notions Journal (19912)

American Resort Development Association
1201 15th St. NW, Ste. 400
Washington, DC 20005
Phone: (202)371-6700
Fax: (202)289-8544
Publications: Developments (5464)

American Revenue Association
PO Box 56
Rockford, IA 50468
Phone: (515)756-3542
Publications: The American Revenuer (11183)

American Rhododendron Society
11 Pinecrest Dr.
Fortuna, CA 95540
Phone: (707)725-3043
Fax: (707)725-1217
Publications: Journal of the American Rhododendron Society (1929)

American Risk and Insurance Association
716 Providence Rd.
PO Box 3028
Malvern, PA 19355
Phone: (610)640-1997
Fax: (610)725-1007
Publications: The Journal of Risk and Insurance (27213)

American River College
4700 College Oak Dr.
Sacramento, CA 95841
Phone: (916)484-8304
Fax: (916)484-8674
Publications: The Current (2994)

American Rivers
1025 Vermont Ave., NW, Ste. 720
Washington, DC 20005
Phone: (202)347-7550
Fax: (202)347-9240
Publications: Mississippi Monitor (5653)

American Roamer Co.
1835 Thomas Rd.
Memphis, TN 38134
Phone: (901)377-8585
Fax: (901)377-8189
Publications: Roaming Guide (29379)

American Rose Society
PO Box 30000
Shreveport, LA 71130-0030
Phone: (318)938-5402
Fax: (318)938-5405
Publications: American Rose (12816)

American Safe Deposit Association
140 E. Jefferson St.
Franklin, IN 46131-2323
Phone: (317)888-1118
Fax: (317)738-5267
Publications: Access (10004)

American Salers Association
19590 E. Main St., Ste. 202
Parker, CO 80138-7371
Phone: (303)770-9292
Fax: (303)770-9302
Free: 888-972-5377
Publications: American Salers (4596)

American-Scandinavian Foundation
58 Park Ave.
New York, NY 10016
Phone: (212)879-9779
Fax: (212)249-3444
Publications: Scandinavian Review (22708)

American School Board Journal
1680 Duke St.
Alexandria, VA 22314
Phone: (703)838-6722
Publications: The American School Board Journal (31637)

American School of Classical Studies at Athens
6-8 Charlton St.
Princeton, NJ 08540-5232
Phone: (609)683-0800
Fax: (609)924-0578
Publications: Hesperia (19461)

American School Counselor Association
801 N. Fairfax St., Ste. 310
Alexandria, VA 22314
Phone: (703)683-2722
Fax: (703)683-1619
Publications: Professional School Counseling (31729)

American School Food Service Association
700 S. Washington St., Ste. 300
Alexandria, VA 22314-4287
Phone: (703)739-3900
Fax: (703)739-3915
Free: 800-877-8822
Publications: School Foodservice & Nutrition (31735)

American School Health Association
PO Box 708
Kent, OH 44240
Phone: (330)678-1601
Fax: (330)678-4526
Publications: Journal of School Health (25274)

American Sciences Press Inc.
20 Cross Rd.
Syracuse, NY 13224-2104
Phone: (315)446-1843
Publications: American Journal of Mathematical and Management Sciences (23386)

American Scientific Affiliation
PO Box 668
Ipswich, MA 01938
Phone: (978)356-5656
Fax: (978)356-4375
Publications: Perspectives on Science and Christian Faith (14257)

American Scientific Publishers
25650 N. Lewis Way
Stevenson Ranch, CA 91381-1439
Phone: (661)254-0807
Fax: (661)254-1207
Publications: Journal of Nanoscience and Nanotechnology (3804)

American Shipper
PO Box 4728
Jacksonville, FL 32201-4728
Phone: (904)355-2601
Fax: (904)791-8836
Free: 800-874-6422
Publications: American Shipper (6209)

American Shorthorn Association
8288 Hascall St.
Omaha, NE 68124
Phone: (402)393-7200
Fax: (402)393-7203
Publications: Shorthorn Country (18208)

American Showcase
584 Broadway, Rm. 303
New York, NY 10012-3229
Phone: (212)673-6600
Fax: (212)673-9795
Free: 800-894-7469
Publications: Lurzer's International Archive (22271)

American Slovenian Catholic Union
2439 Glenwood Ave.
Joliet, IL 60435
Phone: (815)730-3510
Fax: (815)741-2002

Publications: Glasilo KSKJ (Americanski Slovenec) (9033)

American Small Businesses Association
PO Box 3323
Oakton, VA 22124
Phone: (202)628-6316
Fax: (703)255-3815

Publications: ASBA Today (32316)

American Society on Aging
833 Market St., Ste. 511
San Francisco, CA 94103-1824
Phone: (415)974-9600
Fax: (415)974-0300
Free: 800-537-9728

Publications: Aging Today (3325) • Generations, Journal of the American Society on Aging (3365)

American Society of Agricultural Engineers
2950 Niles Rd.
St. Joseph, MI 49085-9659
Phone: (269)429-0300
Fax: (269)429-3852
Free: 800-371-2723

Publications: Applied Engineering in Agriculture (15511) • Resource (15513) • Transactions of the ASAE (15514)

American Society of Agronomy
677 S Segoe Rd.
Madison, WI 53711
Phone: (608)273-8080
Fax: (608)273-2021

Publications: Agronomy Journal (33916) • Journal of Environmental Quality (33951)

American Society of Andrology
1111 N. Plaza Dr., Ste. 550
Schaumburg, IL 60173
Phone: (847)619-4909
Fax: (847)517-7229
Free: 800-627-0629

Publications: Journal of Andrology (16086)

American Society of Appraisers
PO Box 101923
Denver, CO 80250
Fax: (303)758-6164

Publications: Business Valuation Review (3332)

American Society of Association Executives
1575 I St. NW
Washington, DC 20005-1103
Phone: (202)626-2723
Fax: (202)371-1673

Publications: ASAE Association Law and Policy (5363) • Association Management (5370)

American Society of Bariatric Physicians
5453 E Evans Pl.
Denver, CO 80222-5234
Phone: (303)770-2526
Fax: (303)779-4834

Publications: American Journal of Bariatric Medicine (4304)

American Society for Biochemistry and Molecular Biology, Inc
9650 Rockville Pike.
Bethesda, MD 20814-3996
Phone: (301)634-7140
Fax: (301)634-7108

Publications: The Journal of Biological Chemistry (13350)

American Society for Bone and Mineral Research
2025 M St. NW, Ste. 800
Washington, DC 20036-3309
Phone: (202)367-1161
Fax: (202)367-2161

Publications: Journal of Bone and Mineral Research (23829)

American Society of Brewing Chemists
3340 Pilot Knob Rd.
St. Paul, MN 55121
Phone: (651)454-7250
Fax: (651)454-0766
Free: 800-328-7560

Publications: Journal of the American Society of Brewing Chemists (16381)

American Society of Cataract and Refractive Surgery
4000 Legato Rd., Ste. 850
Fairfax, VA 22033
Phone: (703)591-2220
Fax: (703)591-0614
Free: 800-451-1339

Publications: Journal of Cataract and Refractive Surgery (32019)

American Society of Certified Engineering Technicians
Box 1348
Flowery Branch, GA 30542-0023
Phone: (770)967-9173
Fax: (770)967-8049

Publications: Certified Engineering Technician (7273)

American Society of Church History
PO Box 8517
Red Bank, NJ 07701
Phone: (732)345-1787
Fax: (732)345-1788

Publications: Church History (23814)

American Society of Civil Engineers
1801 Alexander Bell Dr.
Reston, VA 20191
Phone: (703)295-6300
Fax: (703)295-6222
Free: 800-548-2723

Publications: ASCE News (32361) • Civil Engineering-ASCE (32363) • Journal of Aerospace Engineering (32368) • Journal of Architectural Engineering (32370) • Journal of Bridge Engineering (32371) • Journal of Cold Regions Engineering (32372) • Journal of Composites for Construction (32373) • Journal of Computing in Civil Engineering (32374) • Journal of Construction Engineering and Management (32375) • Journal of Energy Engineering (32376) • Journal of Engineering Mechanics (32377) • Journal of Environmental Engineering (32378) • Journal of Geotechnical and Geoenvironmental Engineering (32379) • Journal of Hydraulic Engineering (32382) • Journal of Hydrologic Engineering (32383) • Journal of Infrastructure Systems (32384) • Journal of Irrigation and Drainage Engineering (32385) • Journal of Management in Engineering (32386) • Journal of Materials in Civil Engineering (32387) • Journal of Performance of Constructed Facilities (32389) • Journal of Professional Issues in Engineering Education and Practice (32391) • Journal of Structural Engineering (32396) • Journal of Surveying Engineering (32397) • Journal of Transportation Engineering (32399) • Journal of Urban Planning and Development (32400) • Journal of Water Resources Planning and Management (32401) • Journal of Waterway, Port, Coastal, and Ocean Engineering (32402) • Natural Hazards Review (32408) • Practice Periodical of Hazardous, Toxic, and Radioactive Waste Management (32410) • Practice Periodical on Structural Design and Construction (32411)

The American Society for Clinical Nutrition
9650 Rockville Pike
Bethesda, MD 20814-3998
Phone: (301)530-7110
Fax: (301)571-1863

Publications: American Journal of Clinical Nutrition (1810)

American Society of Clinical Pathologists
2100 W. Harrison St.
Chicago, IL 60612
Phone: (312)738-1336
Fax: (312)738-0101

Publications: Laboratory Medicine (8454)

American Society for Competitiveness
Box 1658
Indiana, PA 15705
Phone: (724)357-5759
Fax: (724)357-5743

Publications: Advances in Competitiveness Research (27071) • Competitveness Review (27072) • Global Competitiveness (27074)

American Society of Consultant Pharmacists
1321 Duke St., 4th Fl.
Alexandria, VA 22314
Phone: (703)739-1300
Fax: (703)739-1321
Free: 800-355-2727

Publications: The Consultant Pharmacist (31660)

American Society of Dentistry for Children
875 N Michigan Ave., Ste. 4040
Chicago, IL 60611-1901
Phone: (312)943-1244
Fax: (312)943-5341
Free: 800-637-2732

Publications: Journal of Dentistry for Children (8437)

The American Society of Dowsers
PO Box 24
Danville, VT 05828
Phone: 800-711-9530
Fax: (802)684-2565
Free: 800-711-9530

Publications: The American Dowser (31538)

American Society of Electroneurodiagnostic Technologists, Inc.
426 W. 42nd St.
Kansas City, MO 64111
Phone: (816)931-1120
Fax: (816)931-1145

Publications: American Journal of Electroneurodiagnostic Technology (33329)

American Society for Engineering Education
1818 N. St., NW, Ste. 600
Washington, DC 20036-2479
Phone: (202)331-3500
Fax: (202)265-8504

Publications: ASEE Prism (5364)

American Society for Engineering Education
1419 Knoy Hall
Purdue University
West Lafayette, IN 47907-1419
Phone: (765)494-6170
Fax: (765)494-9267

Publications: Engineering Design Graphics Journal (10546)

American Society for Ethnohistory
Dept. of Anthropology
McGraw Hall
Cornell University
Ithaca, NY 14853

Publications: Ethnohistory (33936)

American Society of Farm Managers and Rural Appraisers
950 S Cherry St., Ste. 508
Denver, CO 80246-2664
Phone: (303)758-3513
Fax: (303)758-0190

Publications: Journal of the ASFMRA (4335)

American Society of Health-System Pharmacists
7272 Wisconsin Ave.
Bethesda, MD 20814
Phone: (301)657-3000
Fax: (301)657-8857

Publications: American Journal of Health-System Pharmacy (13300) • International Pharmaceutical Abstracts (13346)

American Society for Healthcare Risk Management
One N Franklin
Chicago, IL 60606
Phone: (312)422-3980
Fax: (312)422-4580

Publications: Journal of Healthcare Risk Management (8440)

American Society of Heating, Refrigerating and Air-Conditioning Engineers Inc.
1791 Tullie Cir. NE
Atlanta, GA 30329
Phone: (404)636-8400
Fax: (404)321-5478
Free: 800-527-4723

Publications: ASHRAE Journal (6966) • International Journal of Heating, Ventilating, Air-Conditioning and Refrigeration Research (HVAC & R Research) (7018)

American Society for Horticultural Science (ASHS)
113 S West St., Ste. 200
Alexandria, VA 22314-2851
Phone: (703)836-4606
Fax: (703)836-2024

Publications: Hort Technology (31678) • HortScience (31679) • Journal of the American Society for Horticultural Science (31687)

American Society of Ichthyologists and Herpetologists
c/o Sabrina Mowry
PO Box 1897
Lawrence, KS 66044-8897
Phone: (785)843-1234
Fax: (785)843-1274

Publications: Copeia (902)

The American Society of Interior Designers
608 Massachusetts Ave., NE
Washington, DC 20002
Phone: (202)546-3480
Fax: (202)546-3240

Publications: ASID ICON (5367)

American Society of Internal Medicine
2011 Pennsylvania Ave. NW, Ste. 800
Washington, DC 20006-1834
Phone: (202)835-2746
Fax: (202)835-0441

Publications: Today's Internist (5825)

American Society of International Law
2223 Massachusetts Ave. NW
Washington, DC 20008
Phone: (202)939-6000
Fax: (202)797-7133

Publications: American Journal of International Law (5332) • International Legal Materials (5556)

American Society of Landscape Architects
636 Eye St., NW
Washington, DC 20001-3736
Phone: (202)898-2444
Fax: (202)898-1185

Publications: Landscape Architecture (5629)

American Society of Law, Medicine & Ethics, Inc.
765 Commonwealth Ave., Ste. 1634
Boston, MA 02215
Phone: (617)262-4990
Fax: (617)437-7596

Publications: American Journal of Law & Medicine (13849) • The Journal of Law, Medicine & Ethics (13916)

American Society of Mammalogists
810 E 10th St.
PO Box 1897
Lawrence, KS 66044-8897
Phone: (785)843-1235
Fax: (785)843-1274
Free: 800-627-0629

Publications: Journal of Mammalogy (23925) • Mammalian Species (14429)

American Society of Mechanical Engineers
3 Park Ave.
New York, NY 10016-5990
Phone: (973)882-1167
Free: 800-843-2763

Publications: Applied Mechanics Reviews (18811) • ASME News (21266) • Heat Transfer-Recent Contents (18813) • Journal of Applied Mechanics (21991) • Journal of Biomechanical Engineering (22011) • Journal of Dynamic Systems, Measurement, and Control (22051) • Journal of Energy Resources Technology (22060) • Journal of Engineering for Gas Turbines and Power (22061) • Journal of Engineering for Industry (22062) • Journal of Fluids Engineering (22071) • Journal of Heat Transfer (22086) • Journal of Pressure Vessel Technology (22165) • Journal of Tribology (22208) • Journal of Turbomachinery (22210) • Mechanical Engineering (22305) • Mechanical Engineering-CIME (22306)

American Society of Military Comptrollers
2034 Eisenhower Ave., Ste. 145
Alexandria, VA 22314-4650
Phone: (703)549-0360
Fax: (703)549-3181
Free: 800-462-5637

Publications: Armed Forces Comptroller (31643)

American Society of Missiology
204 N Lexington Ave.
Wilmore, KY 40390-1199
Phone: (859)858-2216
Fax: (859)858-2375

Publications: Missiology (12453)

American Society for Nondestructive Testing Inc.
1711 Arlingate Ln.
PO Box 28518
Columbus, OH 43228-0518
Phone: (614)274-6003
Fax: (614)274-6899
Free: 800-222-2768

Publications: Materials Evaluation (25030)

American Society of Ophthalmic Registered Nurses
PO Box 193030
San Francisco, CA 94119
Phone: (415)561-8513
Fax: (415)561-8531

Publications: Insight (10973)

American Society of Parasitologists
PO Box 1897
Lawrence, KS 66044-8897

Publications: The Journal of Parasitology (24320)

American Society for Parenteral and Enteral Nutrition
8630 Fenton St., Ste. 412
Silver Spring, MD 20910-3805
Phone: (301)587-6315
Fax: (301)587-3323
Free: 800-727-4567

Publications: JPEN: Journal of Parenteral and Enteral Nutrition (13734) • NCP: Nutrition in Clinical Practice (13742)

American Society for Pharmacology and Experimental Therapeutics
9650 Rockville Pke.
Bethesda, MD 20814-3995
Phone: (301)634-7060
Fax: (301)634-7061

Publications: Journal of Pharmacology & Experimental Therapeutics (13355) • Molecular Pharmacology (13362) • Pharmacological Reviews (18207)

American Society for Photobiology
1021 15th St. Ste. 9
Augusta, GA 30901

Publications: Photochemistry and Photobiology (18113)

The American Society for Productive Medicine
1209 Montgomery Hwy.
Birmingham, AL 35216
Phone: (205)978-5000
Fax: (205)978-5005

Publications: Fertility and Sterility (16308)

American Society for Psychical Research, Inc.
5 W. 73rd St.
New York, NY 10023
Phone: (212)799-5050
Fax: (212)496-2497

Publications: Journal of the American Society for Psychical Research (21985)

American Society for Public Administration
1120 G St. NW, No. 700
Washington, DC 20005
Phone: (202)393-7878
Fax: (202)638-4952

Publications: PA Times (5712) • Public Administration Review (5748)

American Society for Quality
PO Box 3005
Milwaukee, WI 53201-3005
Phone: (414)272-8575
Fax: (414)272-1734
Free: 800-248-1946

Publications: Quality Management Journal (34095)

American Society of Radiologic Technologists
15000 Central Ave. SE
Albuquerque, NM 87123-3917
Phone: (505)298-4500
Fax: (505)298-5063
Free: 800-444-2778

Publications: Radiologic Technology (19785)

American Society of Safety Engineers
1800 E Oakton St.
Des Plaines, IL 60018-2187
Phone: (847)699-2929
Fax: (847)296-3769

Publications: Professional Safety (8769)

American Society for Training & Development
1640 King St.
Box 1443
Alexandria, VA 22313-2043
Phone: (703)683-8100
Fax: (703)683-8103
Free: 800-NAT-ASTD

Publications: INFO-LINE (31683) • TD Magazine (31740)

American Society of Transportation and Logistics, Inc.
PO Box 55199
Atlanta, GA 30308-5199
Phone: (404)524-3555
Fax: (404)524-7776

Publications: Transportation Journal (7056)

American Sociological Association
1307 New York Ave. NW, Ste. 700
Washington, DC 20005-4701
Phone: (202)383-9005
Fax: (202)638-0882

Publications: American Sociological Review (33918) • Contemporary Sociology (10545) • Journal of Health & Social Behavior (31875) • Social Psychology Quarterly (3797) • Sociology of Education (5798) • Teaching Sociology (5815)

American Solar Energy Society Inc.
2400 Central Ave. G-1.
Boulder, CO 80301
Phone: (303)443-3130
Fax: (303)443-3212

Publications: Solar Today (4191)

American Songwriter Magazine
50 Music Square West, Ste. 604
Nashville, TN 37203-3227
Phone: (615)321-6096
Fax: (615)321-6097
Free: 800-739-8712

Publications: American Songwriter (29440)

American Speech-Language-Hearing Association
10801 Rockville Pike
Rockville, MD 20852
Phone: (301)897-5700
Fax: (301)897-7348
Free: 888-498-6699

Publications: Asha (13675) • Journal of Speech and Hearing Research (20649) • Journal of Speech, Language, and Hearing Research (13685) • Language, Speech, and Hearing Services in Schools (13686)

American Sports Network, Inc.
PO Box 6100
Rosemead, CA 91770
Phone: (626)292-2222
Fax: (626)292-2221

Publications: American Sports (2967)

American Squaredance
661 Middlefield Rd.
Salinas, CA 93906
Fax: (408)443-6902

Publications: American Squaredance (3066)

American Statistical Association
1429 Duke St.
Alexandria, VA 22314-3415
Phone: (703)684-1221
Fax: (703)684-2036
Free: 888-231-3473

Publications: The American Statistician (31638) • Amstat News (31640) • Journal of the American Statistical Association (31688) • Journal of Business & Economic Statistics (31689) • Journal of Computational and Graphical Statistics (31690) • Journal of Statistics Education (31703) • Technometrics (4362)

American Stroke Association
7272 Greenville Ave.
Dallas, TX 75231-5129
Phone: (214)706-1572
Fax: (214)706-5231
Free: 888-4-STROKE

Publications: Stroke Connection Magazine (30183)

American Student Dental Association
211 E. Chicago Ave., Ste. 1160
Chicago, IL 60611
Phone: (312)440-2795
Fax: (312)440-2820
Free: 800-621-8099

Publications: ASDA News (8277) • Mouth (8496)

American Studies Association, Kentucky-Tennessee Chapter
Department of English
Middle Tennessee State University
Murfreesboro, TN 37132
Phone: (615)898-2664
Fax: (615)898-5098

Publications: Border States (29429)

American Studies International
George Washington University
2108 G St. NW
Washington, DC 20052
Phone: (202)994-7368
Fax: (202)994-8651

Publications: American Studies International (5345)

American Symphony Orchestra League
33 W. 60th St., Fifth Fl.
New York, NY 10023-7905
Phone: (212)262-5161
Fax: (212)262-5198

Publications: SYMPHONY (22813)

American Tinnitus Association (ATA)
PO Box 5
Portland, OR 97207-0005
Phone: (503)248-9985
Fax: (503)248-0024
Free: 800-634-8978

Publications: Tinnitus Today (26510)

American Topical Association
PO Box 57
Arlington, TX 76004-0057
Phone: (817)274-1181
Fax: (817)274-1184

Publications: Topical Time (32583)

American Trade Magazine
500 N Dearborn St.
Chicago, IL 60610
Phone: (312)337-7700
Fax: (312)337-8654

Publications: American Laundry News (8258)

American Trade Magazines
500 N Dearborn St., Ste. 1100
Chicago, IL 60610
Phone: (312)337-7700
Fax: (312)337-8654

Publications: American Clean Car (8253) • American Coin-Op (8254) • American Drycleaner (8255)

American Truck Historical Society
PO Box 901611
Kansas City, MO 64190-1611
Phone: (816)890-9900
Fax: (816)890-9903

Publications: Wheels of Time (17203)

American Trucking Associations Inc. (ATA)
2200 Mill Rd.
Alexandria, VA 22314-4677
Phone: (703)838-1700
Fax: (703)683-2292
Free: 800-517-7370

Publications: Transport Topics (31747) • Utility Fleet Management (31748)

American University Eagle
227 Mary Graydon
4400 Massachusetts Ave., NW
Washington, DC 20016
Phone: (202)885-1400
Fax: (202)885-1428

Publications: The Eagle-News (5466)

American Urological Association
351 W. Camden St.
Baltimore, MD 21201
Phone: (410)727-1100
Fax: (410)528-4452
Free: 800-222-3790

Publications: AUA Today (31916)

American Veterinary Medical Association
1931 N. Meacham Rd, Ste. 100
Schaumburg, IL 60173-4360
Phone: (847)925-8071
Fax: (847)925-1329

Publications: American Journal of Veterinary Research (9583) • Journal of the American Veterinary Medical Association (9584)

American Visions Media, Inc.
1101 Pennsylvania Ave. NW, Ste. 820
Washington, DC 20004
Phone: (202)347-3820
Fax: (202)347-4096

Publications: American Visions (5348)

American Volkssport Association (AVA)
1001 Pat Booker Rd., Ste. 101
Universal City, TX 78148
Phone: (210)659-2112
Fax: (210)659-1212
Free: 800-830-9255

Publications: The American Wanderer (31224)

American Volleyball Coaches Association
1227 Lake Plaza Dr., Ste. B
Colorado Springs, CO 80906
Phone: (719)576-7777
Fax: (719)576-7778

Publications: Coaching Volleyball (4242)

American Water Resources Association
PO Box 1626
Middleburg, VA 20118-1626
Phone: (540)687-8390
Fax: (540)687-8395

Publications: Journal of the American Water Resources Association (32272)

American Water Works Association
6666 W. Quincy Ave.
Denver, CO 80235
Phone: (303)794-7711
Fax: (303)794-3951

Publications: Journal of the American Water Works Association (4334)

American Welding Society (AWS)
550 LeJeune Rd. NW
Miami, FL 33126
Phone: (305)443-9353
Fax: (305)443-5951
Free: 800-443-9353

Publications: Welding Journal (6391)

American Wholesale Marketers Association
1128 16th St. NW
Washington, DC 20036-4802
Phone: (202)463-2124
Fax: (202)463-6467
Free: 800-482-2962

Publications: Distribution Channels (5465)

American Window Cleaner Magazine
PO Box 70888
Richmond, CA 94807-0888
Phone: (510)233-4011
Fax: (510)223-4111

Publications: American Window Cleaner Magazine (2920)

American Wine Society
3006 Latta Rd.
Rochester, NY 14612-3298
Phone: (585)225-7613
Fax: (585)225-7613

Publications: American Wine Society Journal (23209)

American Youth Soccer Organization
12501 S. Isis Ave.
Hawthorne, CA 90250
Phone: (310)643-6455
Fax: (310)643-5310
Free: 800-USA-AYSO

Publications: Soccer Now (2040)

American Youth Work Center
1200 17th St. NW, 4th Fl.
Washington, DC 20036-3006
Phone: (202)785-0764
Fax: (202)728-0657

Publications: Youth Today (5874)

Americans United for Separation of Church & State
518 C St., NE
Washington, DC 20002
Phone: (202)466-3234
Fax: (202)466-2587

Publications: Church & State (5415)

America's Christian Newspaper
PO Box 747
Madisonville, KY 42431-0747
Phone: (270)821-2915
Fax: (270)821-2419

Publications: America's Christian Newspaper (12270)

America's Community Bankers
900 19th St. NW, Ste. 400
Washington, DC 20006
Phone: (202)857-3100
Fax: (202)296-8716
Free: 888-872-0275

Publications: Community Banker (5428)

The Americas Publishing Co.
2900 NW 39th St.
Miami, FL 33142
Phone: (305)633-3341
Fax: (305)635-4002

Publications: Diario las Americas (6348)

Amerikan Uutiset Inc.
PO Box 8147
Lantana, FL 33462
Phone: (561)588-9770
Fax: (561)588-3229
Free: 800-888-4738

Publications: Amerikan Uutiset (6298)

AMG Publishers
6815 Shallowford Rd.
Chattanooga, TN 37421
Phone: (423)894-6060
Fax: (423)510-8074
Free: 800-251-7206

Publications: Pulpit Helps (29092)

Amherst College
Box 5000
Amherst, MA 01002-5000
Phone: (413)542-2000
Fax: (413)542-2117

Publications: Amherst (13790)

Amherst College
PO Box 1912
Amherst, MA 01002-5000
Phone: (413)542-2000
Fax: (413)542-2305

Publications: Amherst Student (13792)

Amherst Press
PO Box 370
Amherst, TX 79312
Phone: (806)385-6444
Fax: (806)385-5385
Free: 800-687-6444

Publications: Amherst Press (30696)

Amherst Publishing
113 2nd St.
PO Box 90
Amherst, VA 24521
Phone: (804)946-7195
Fax: (804)946-2684

Publications: Nelson County Times (31760) • New Era-Progress (31761)

Amherst Writers & Artists Press Inc.
PO Box 1076
Amherst, MA 01004

Publications: Peregrine (13804)

Amigo Publications
1502 Ave. M
Lubbock, TX 79401
Phone: (806)763-3841
Fax: (806)741-1110

Publications: El Editor (30711)

Amite Tangi-Digest
120 NE Central
PO Box 698
Amite, LA 70422
Phone: (985)748-7156
Fax: (985)748-7104

Publications: Amite Tangi-Digest (12470)

Ammons Scientific, Ltd.
Box 9229
Missoula, MT 59807-9229
Phone: (406)728-1710

Publications: Perceptual and Motor Skills (17874) • Psychological Reports (17875)

Amnesty International USA
322 8th Ave.
New York, NY 10001
Phone: (212)807-8400
Fax: (212)627-1451
Free: 800-266-3789

Publications: Amnesty Action (21210)

Amoco Enterprises, Inc.
200 E Randolph Dr.
Chicago, IL 60601
Phone: (312)856-5316
Fax: (312)856-2379

Publications: Adventure Road (8244)

The Amory Advertiser
PO Box 519
Amory, MS 38821
Phone: (662)256-5647
Fax: (662)256-5701

Publications: The Amory Advertiser (16545)

Amos Press, Inc.
911 Vandemark Rd.
PO Box 150
Sidney, OH 45365-0150
Phone: (937)498-2111
Fax: (937)498-0812
Free: 800-673-8311

Publications: Coin World (25516) • Enon Messenger (25517) • Miamisburg Sun (25519) • The Sidney Daily News (25521)

Amsterdam News
2340 Frederick Douglass Blvd.
New York, NY 10027
Phone: (212)932-7440
Fax: (212)222-3842

Publications: Amsterdam News (21211)

AMVETS
4647 Forbes Blvd.
Lanham, MD 20706
Phone: (301)459-9600
Fax: (301)459-7924
Free: 877-726-8387

Publications: The National AMVET (13607)

Anagram
Johns Hopkins Univ.
113 Garland Hall
3400 N. Charles St.
Baltimore, MD 21218

Publications: Anagram (13122)

Anais Nin Foundation
2335 Hidalgo Ave.
Los Angeles, CA 90039

Publications: Anais (13834)

Analytic Press
101 West St.
Hillsdale, NJ 07642-1422
Phone: (201)358-9477
Fax: (201)358-4700
Free: 800-627-0629

Publications: Gestalt Review (18876) • Journal of the American Psychoanalytic Association (21984) • Psychoanalytic Dialogues (18877) • Psychoanalytic Inquiry (18878) • Studies in Gender and Sexuality (22801)

Anamosa Publications
PO Box 108
Anamosa, IA 52205
Phone: (319)462-3511
Fax: (319)462-4540

Publications: Anamosa Journal-Eureka (10601)

The Anchor
887 Highland Ave.
PO Box 7
Fall River, MA 02722
Phone: (508)675-7151
Fax: (508)675-7048

Publications: The Anchor (14180)

Anchor Associates Inc.
22 Juniper Rd.
Port Washington, NY 11050
Phone: (516)767-9331
Fax: (516)767-3710

Publications: Retail Roundup (23135)

Anchorage Daily News
1001 Northway Dr.
PO Box 149001
Anchorage, AK 99514-9001
Phone: (907)257-4200
Fax: (907)258-2157

Publications: Anchorage Daily News (523)

Andalusia Star
PO Box 430
Andalusia, AL 36420
Phone: (334)222-2402
Fax: (334)222-6597

Publications: The Butler County News (12)

The Andalusia Star News
209 Dunson St.
PO Drawer 430
Andalusia, AL 36420-0430
Phone: (334)222-2402
Fax: (334)222-6597

Publications: The Andalusia Star News (11)

Anderson Herald-Bulletin
PO Box 1090
Anderson, IN 46015
Phone: (317)622-1212
Fax: (317)649-3271

Publications: Anderson Herald-Bulletin (9783)

Anderson Independent-Mail
1000 Williamston Rd.
PO Box 2507
Anderson, SC 29622
Phone: (864)224-4321
Fax: (864)260-1276
Free: 800-859-6397

Publications: Anderson Independent-Mail (28473)

Jerry Anderson
Box 528
Cimarron, KS 67835
Fax: (316)855-2489

Publications: Jacksonian (11383)

Anderson Publishing Ltd.
1301 W Park Ave.
Ocean, NJ 07712
Phone: (732)695-0600
Fax: (732)695-9501

Publications: Applied Radiology (19387)

Anderson University
1100 E. 5th St.
Anderson, IN 46012-3495
Phone: (765)649-9071
Fax: (765)641-3851

Publications: Signatures (9784)

The Anderson Valley Advertiser
Boonville, CA 95415
Phone: (707)895-3016
Fax: (707)895-3355

Publications: The Anderson Valley Advertiser (1592)

The Andover Journal Publishing, Inc.
202 E Rhondda Ave. Ste. C
Andover, KS 67002
Phone: (316)733-2002
Fax: (316)733-4221

Publications: The Andover Journal Advocate (11338)

The Andover Townsman
33 Chestnut St.
Andover, MA 01810
Phone: (978)475-7000
Fax: (978)475-5731

Publications: The Andover Townsman (13811)

Andrew Mowbray Publishing, Inc.
Box 460
Lincoln, RI 02865
Phone: (401)726-8011
Fax: (401)726-8061
Free: 800-999-4697

Publications: Man at Arms (28362)

Andrews News
210 E Broadway
Andrews, TX 79714
Phone: (915)523-2085
Fax: (915)523-9492

Publications: Andrews County News (29723)

Andrews Publications
175 Strafford Ave., Bldg. 4, Ste. 140
Wayne, PA 19087
Phone: (610)225-0510
Fax: (610)225-0501
Free: 800-328-4880

Publications: Asbestos Property Litigation Reporter (28124) • Automotive Litigation Reporter (28125) • Bank and Lender Liability Litigation Reporter (28126) • Breast Implant Litigation Reporter (28127) • Civil RICO Litigation Reporter (28128) • Computer & Online Industry Litigation Reporter (28130) • Corporate Officers and Directors Liability Litigation Reporter (28131) • General Aviation Accident Report (19434) • Hazardous Waste Litigation Reporter (28132) • Health Law Litigation Reporter (28133) • Securities Litigation & Regulation Reporter

(28135) • Tobacco Industry Litigation Reporter (28137)

Andrews University Press
213 Info Services Bldg.
Berrien Springs, MI 49104-1700
Phone: (616)471-6915
Fax: (616)471-6224

Publications: Student Movement (14814)

Andy Anderson Corp.
501 N School St.
PO Box 187
Beaver Dam, KY 42320
Phone: (270)274-4949
Fax: (270)274-4949

Publications: Ohio County Messenger (11930)

Andy Anderson Inc.
108 Ctr. St.
PO Box 226
Hartford, KY 42347
Phone: (270)298-7100
Fax: (270)298-9572

Publications: Ohio County Times-News (12112)

ANG Newspapers
PO Box 28884
Oakland, CA 94604-8884
Phone: (510)208-6300
Fax: (510)293-2697
Free: 800-743-8742

Publications: The Argus (1938) • Argus Enterprise (2666) • The Daily Review (2041) • The Oakland Tribune (2692)

Angbase
PO Box 131041
Houston, TX 77219

Publications: Angbase (30456)

Angelina College
PO Box 1768
Lufkin, TX 75902-1768
Phone: (936)633-5288
Fax: (936)633-4299

Publications: The Pacer (30741)

Angelina Free Press, Inc.
201 N Temple
Diboll, TX 75941-1701
Phone: (936)829-1806
Fax: (936)829-1811

Publications: Free Press (30248)

Angelo State University
2601 West Ave. N
San Angelo, TX 76909
Phone: (915)942-2322
Fax: (915)942-2078

Publications: The Ram Page (31007)

Angelus Press
2918 Tracy Ave.
Kansas City, MO 64109
Phone: (816)753-3150
Fax: (816)753-3557
Free: 800-966-7337

Publications: The Angelus (17154)

Angleton Times
700 Western Ave.
Angleton, TX 77515
Phone: (979)849-8581
Fax: (979)849-0230

Publications: Angleton Times (29725)

Angolite
Louisiana State Penitentiary
Angola, LA 70712
Phone: (504)655-4411

Publications: Angolite (12472)

Angus Prodcutions, Inc.
3201 Frederick Ave.
St. Joseph, MO 64506
Phone: (816)383-5200
Fax: (816)233-6575
Free: 800-821-5478

Publications: Angus Beef Bulletin (17389) • Angus Journal (17390)

Angus Topics, Inc.
PO Box 397
Carmi, IL 62821
Phone: (618)382-8553
Fax: (618)382-3436

Publications: Angus Topics (8130)

Animal People
PO Box 960
Clinton, WA 98236-0960
Phone: (360)579-2505
Fax: (360)579-2575

Publications: Animal People (32719)

Animal Protection Institute
1122 S. St.
PO Box 22505
Sacramento, CA 95822
Phone: (916)447-3085
Fax: (916)447-3070
Free: 800-348-7387

Publications: Animal Issues (2976)

Animals Exotic and Small
1320 Mountain Ave.
Norco, CA 92860-2852
Phone: (909)371-4307
Fax: (909)371-4779

Publications: Animals Exotic and Small (2640)

Animas Publishing
1275 Main Ave.
Durango, CO 81301

Publications: Dolores Star (4401)

Animas Publishing Inc.
PO Box J
Cortez, CO 81321
Phone: (970)565-8527
Fax: (970)565-8532

Publications: Cortez Journal (4289) • The Mancos Times (4571) • Sentinel (4290)

Anita Tribune
850 Main St.
PO Box 216
Anita, IA 50020-0216
Phone: (712)762-4188
Fax: (712)762-4189

Publications: Anita Tribune (10603)

The Ann Arbor News
340 E. Huron St., PO Box 1147
Ann Arbor, MI 48104-1147
Phone: (734)994-6989

Publications: The Ann Arbor News (14742)

Ann Arbor Observer Co.
201 Catherine St.
Ann Arbor, MI 48104
Phone: (734)769-3175
Fax: (734)769-3375

Publications: Ann Arbor Observer (14743)

Annali d'Italianistica, Inc.
141 Dey Hall
CB 3170
University of North Carolina
Chapel Hill, NC 27599-3170
Phone: (919)962-1470
Fax: (919)962-5457

Publications: Annali D'Italianistica (23698)

Annals of the Association of American Geographers
1710 16th St. NW
Washington, DC 20009
Phone: (202)234-1450
Fax: (202)234-2744

Publications: Annals of the Association of American Geographers (5351)

Annals of Balloon History and Museology
15155 County Rd. 32
Mayer, MN 55360

Publications: Annals of Balloon History and Museology (16048)

Annals of Mathematics
Princeton University
Washington Rd.
309 Fine Hall
Princeton, NJ 08544
Phone: (609)258-4191
Fax: (609)258-1367

Publications: Annals of Mathematics (19453)

Annals Publishing Co.
4507 Laclede Ave.
St. Louis, MO 63108
Phone: (314)367-4987
Fax: (314)367-4988

Publications: Annals of Otology, Rhinology and Laryngology (17415)

Annandale Advocate
73 Oak Ave.
PO Box D
Annandale, MN 55302
Phone: (320)274-3052
Fax: (320)274-2301

Publications: Annandale Advocate (15717)

Anne Arundel Community College
101 College Pkwy.
Arnold, MD 21012-1857
Phone: (410)777-2803
Fax: (410)777-2201

Publications: Campus Crier (13105)

Annex Publishing & Printing
25 Townline Rd.
Box 190
Tillsonburg, ON, Canada N4G 4H6
Phone: (519)688-6397
Fax: (519)688-5323

Publications: The Daily Sentinel-Review (36907) • Delhi News-Record (36449) • Oxford Shopping News (36908)

Annex Publishing & Printing, Inc.
222 Argyle Ave.
Delhi, ON, Canada N4B 2Y2
Phone: (519)582-2513
Fax: (519)582-4040
Free: 800-265-2827

Publications: Bakers Journal (35763) • Canada Poultry Magazine/La Revue Canadienne D'Aviculture (35764) • Canadian Pizza Magazine (35765) • The Canadian Tobacco Grower (35766) • Canadian Vending Magazine (35767) • Fire Fighting in Canada (35768) • Fruit and Vegetable Magazine (35769) • Greenhouse Canada (35770)

Annex Publishing & Printing, Inc.
6200 Dixie Rd., Ste. 220
Mississauga, ON, Canada L5T 2E1
Phone: (905)795-0110
Fax: (905)795-2967
Free: 877-779-8877

Publications: Canadian Auto World (36057) • Helicopters Magazine (36070) • Wings Magazine (36092) • World of Wheels (36093)

Annex Publishing & Printing Inc.
46 Main St.
PO Box 459
Norwich, ON, Canada N0J 1P0
Phone: (519)863-2262
Fax: (519)863-3229

Publications: Norwich Gazette (36134)

The Anniston Star
PO Box 189
Anniston, AL 36202
Phone: (256)236-1551
Fax: (256)241-1991
Free: 888-649-1551

Publications: The Anniston Star (15)

Announcer-Star Herald
PO Box 837
Luverne, MN 56156-0837
Phone: (507)283-2333
Fax: (507)283-2335

Publications: Luverne Announcer (16013) • Rock County Star Herald (16014)

Annual Reviews Inc.
4139 El Camino Way
PO Box 10139
Palo Alto, CA 94303-0139
Phone: (650)493-4400
Fax: (650)424-0910
Free: 800-523-8635

Publications: Annual Review of Astronomy and Astrophysics (2788) • Annual Review of Earth and Planetary Sciences (2789) • Annual Review of Genetics (2790) • Annual Review of Medicine (2791) • Annual Review of Microbiology (2792) • Annual Review of Psychology (2793) • Annual Review of Sociology (2794)

Anoka County Shopper
4101 Coon Rapids Blvd.
Coon Rapids, MN 55433-2585
Phone: (763)421-4444
Fax: (763)421-4315

Publications: Anoka County Shopper (15814) • Anoka County Union (15815) • Blaine Spring Lake Park Life (15756) • Coon Rapids Herald (15816)

L'Anse Sentinel Inc.
202 N. Main
PO Box 7
Lanse, MI 49946
Phone: (906)524-6194
Fax: (906)524-6197

Publications: L'Anse Sentinel (15273)

Anson Record Messenger and Intelligences
PO Box 959
210 E Morgan St.
Wadesboro, NC 28170
Phone: (704)694-2161
Fax: (704)694-7060

Publications: Anson Record-Messenger & Intelligencer (24260)

Anteebo Publishers
96 Kercheval Ave.
Grosse Pointe Farms, MI 48236
Phone: (313)882-0294
Fax: (313)882-1585

Publications: The Connection (15139) • Grosse Pointe News (15140)

Antelope Valley Newspapers, Inc.
PO Box 4050
Palmdale, CA 93590-4050
Phone: (661)273-2700
Fax: (661)947-4870

Publications: Antelope Valley Press (2782) • Cover Story (2783)

Anti-Racist Action (ARA)/ People Against Racist Terror
PO Box 1055
Culver City, CA 90232
Phone: (310)495-0299

Publications: Turning the Tide (1795)

Antigo Shoppers
Civic Bldg.
813 5th Ave.
Antigo, WI 54409
Phone: (715)623-5024
Fax: (715)623-5389

Publications: Antigo Area Shoppers Guide (33530)

The Antigonish Review
St. Francis Xavier University
PO Box 5000
Antigonish, NS, Canada B2G 2W5
Phone: (902)867-3962
Fax: (902)867-5563

Publications: The Antigonish Review (35536)

The Antioch Review
Box 148
Yellow Springs, OH 45387
Phone: (937)769-1365

Publications: The Antioch Review (25690)

Antique Automobile Club of America
501 W. Governor Rd.
PO Box 417
Hershey, PA 17033-0417
Phone: (717)534-1910
Fax: (717)534-9101

Publications: Antique Automobile (27040)

Antique Bottle and Glass Collector
102 Jefferson St.
Box 180
East Greenville, PA 18041
Phone: (215)679-5849
Fax: (215)679-3068

Publications: Antique Bottle and Glass Collector (26845)

Antique and Collectible Tools, Inc.
27 Ficket Rd.
Pownal, ME 04069
Phone: (207)688-4962
Fax: (207)688-4831
Free: 800-248-8114

Publications: Fine Tool Journal (13033)

Antique Power
PO Box 838
Yellow Springs, OH 45387
Phone: (937)767-1433
Fax: (937)767-2726
Free: 800-767-5828

Publications: Vintage Truck (25691)

Antique Radio Classified
PO Box 2-V75
Carlisle, MA 01741
Phone: (978)371-0512
Fax: (978)371-7129

Publications: Antique Radio Classified (14120)

Antique Trader Publications
PO Box 1050
Dubuque, IA 52004
Phone: (563)588-2073
Fax: (563)588-0888
Free: 800-482-0148

Publications: Postcard Collector (10844)

The Antiquer
PO Box 2054
New York, NY 10159-2054
Phone: (212)725-1106
Fax: (212)725-1107
Free: 888-294-9750

Publications: The Antiquer (21223) • The Antiquer (21222)

Antiques and Collectibles, Inc.
PO Box 33
Westbury, NY 11590
Phone: (516)334-9650

Publications: Antiques & Collectibles Magazine (23551)

Antlers American
PO Box 578
Antlers, OK 74523
Phone: (580)298-3314
Fax: (580)298-3316

Publications: Antlers American (25743)

Anton Community Newspapers
132 E. 2nd St.
Mineola, NY 11501
Phone: (516)747-8282
Fax: (516)742-5867

Publications: Farmingdale Observer (20595) • Floral Park Dispatch (20604) • Garden City Life (20641) • Glen Cove Record Pilot (20660) • Great Neck Record (20688) • Hicksville Illustrated News (20738) • The Illustrated News (21110) • Levittown Tribune (20941) • Manhasset Press (21006) • Massapequan Observer (21025) • Mineola American (21086) • Oyster Bay Enterprise Pilot (23069) • Plainview Herald (23098) • Port Washington News (23133) • The Roslyn News (23278) • Syosset/Jericho Tribune (20850) • The Three Village Times (20582) • The Westbury Times (23560)

Antwerp Bee-Argus
113 N Main
PO Box 1065
Antwerp, OH 45813
Phone: (419)258-8161
Fax: (419)258-9365

Publications: Antwerp Bee-Argus (24612)

AOAC International
481 N Frederick Ave., Ste. 500
Gaithersburg, MD 20877-2417
Phone: (301)924-7077
Fax: (301)924-7089
Free: 800-379-2622

Publications: Inside Laboratory Management (13543) • Journal of AOAC International (13544)

AOCS Press
PO Box 3489
Champaign, IL 61826
Phone: (217)359-2344
Fax: (217)351-8091
Free: 800-336-AOCS

Publications: INFORM (International News on Fats, Oils and Related Materials) (8190) • Journal of the American Oil Chemists' Society (8194) • Lipids (8203)

AOPA Pilot
421 Aviation Way
Frederick, MD 21701-4756
Phone: (301)695-2000
Fax: (301)695-2375

Publications: AOPA Pilot (13505)

AORN, Inc.
2170 S. Parker Rd., Ste. 300
Denver, CO 80231-5711
Phone: (303)755-6300
Fax: (303)750-3441
Free: 800-755-AORN

Publications: AORN Journal (4305) • SSM (4358) • SSM Online (4359)

The Apache County Reporter
PO Box 867
Eagar, AZ 85925-0867
Phone: (928)333-2033
Fax: (928)333-2033
Free: 800-648-3921

Publications: The Apache County Reporter (691)

Apache News
Box 778
Apache, OK 73006
Phone: (580)588-3862
Fax: (580)588-3862

Publications: Apache News (25744)

Apartment Age Magazine
621 S Westmoreland Ave.
Los Angeles, CA 90005
Phone: (213)384-4131
Fax: (213)382-3970

Publications: Apartment Age Magazine (2211)

Apartment News Publications, Inc.
15502 Graham St.
Huntington Beach, CA 92649
Phone: (714)893-3971
Fax: (714)893-6484
Free: 800-931-6666

Publications: Apartment Management Magazine (2059)

A.P.C.H.Q.
5930, boul. Louis H. Lafontaine
Anjou, QC, Canada H1M 1S7
Phone: (514)353-9960
Fax: (514)353-4825
Free: 800-361-4572

Publications: Quebec Habitation (36938)

APCO International, Inc.
351 N Williamson Blvd.
Daytona Beach, FL 32114-1112
Phone: (904)322-2500
Fax: (904)322-2501
Free: 888-272-6911

Publications: Public Safety Communications (6039)

Aperture
20 E. 23rd St.
New York, NY 10010
Phone: (212)505-5555
Fax: (212)598-4015
Free: 800-929-2323

Publications: Aperture (21224)

Apex Publications, Inc.
185 St. Paul
Quebec, QC, Canada G1K 3W2
Phone: (418)692-2110
Fax: (418)692-3392
Free: 800-905-7468

Publications: Master Guide (37292)

Apex Publishing, Ltd.
89 Skyway Ave., Suite 200
Etobicoke, ON, Canada M9W 6R4
Phone: (416)798-9778
Fax: (416)798-9671

Publications: Dogs in Canada (35814)

APMI International
105 College Rd. E
Princeton, NJ 08540
Phone: (609)452-7700
Fax: (609)987-8523

Publications: International Journal of Powder Metallurgy (19463)

APMS
606 N Van Buren
Marion, IL 62959

Publications: Portsmouth Daily Times (25484) • Times-Tribune (12020)

The Apopka Chief
439 W Main St.
Apopka, FL 32712
Phone: (407)886-2777
Fax: (407)889-4121

Publications: The Apopka Chief (5908)

The Apostles of Infinite Love
Editions Magnificat
PO Box 4478
Mount-Tremblant, QC, Canada J8E 1A1
Phone: (819)688-5225
Fax: (819)688-6548

Publications: Magnificat (37253)

Apostleship of Prayer
661 Greenwood Ave.
Toronto, ON, Canada M4J 4B3
Phone: (416)466-1195

Publications: Canadian Messenger (36518) • Messenger of the Sacred Heart (36663)

Apostolic Lutheran Church of America
Book Concern
PO Box 2126
Battle Ground, WA 98604-2126
Phone: (360)687-6493
Fax: (360)687-6493

Publications: Christian Monthly (26621)

Appalachian Log Publishing Co.
PO Box 20297
Charleston, WV 25362-1297

Publications: The Southern Journal (33272)

Appalachian Mountain Club
5 Joy St.
Boston, MA 02108
Phone: (617)523-0636
Fax: (617)523-0722

Publications: AMC Outdoors (13848)

Appalachian State University
Belk Library
PO Box 32026
Boone, NC 28608
Phone: (828)262-4072
Fax: (828)262-2553

Publications: Appalachian Journal (23652)

Appalachian Trail Conference
799 Washington St.
Harpers Ferry, WV 25425
Phone: (304)535-6331
Fax: (304)535-2667
Free: 888-287-8673

Publications: Appalachian Trailway News (33333)

Appaloosa Horse Club
2720 W. Pullman Rd.
Moscow, ID 83843
Phone: (208)882-5578
Fax: (208)882-8150

Publications: Appaloosa Journal (7911)

Apparel News Group
110 E 9th St., Ste. A-777
Los Angeles, CA 90079-1777
Phone: (213)623-5509
Fax: (213)627-5707

Publications: Apparel News South (2212) • California Apparel News (2230) • Chicago Apparel News (8306) • Dallas Apparel News (30143) • New York Apparel News (2346)

The Apparel Strategist
PO Box 406
Fleetwood, PA 19522
Phone: (610)944-5995
Fax: (610)944-5149

Publications: The Apparel Strategist (26920)

Appeal Democrat
1530 Ellis Lake Dr.
Marysville, CA 95901
Phone: (530)741-2345
Fax: (530)741-1195
Free: 800-831-2345

Publications: CoverStory (2516)

Appeal Publishing Company
PO Box 207
Paris, MO 65275
Phone: (660)327-4192
Fax: (660)327-4847

Publications: Monroe County Appeal (17332)

Appendx
48 Quincy St. S103
Cambridge, MA 02138
Phone: (617)495-4115
Fax: (617)495-8916

Publications: Appendx (14038)

Apple Press, Inc.
PO Box 30348
Indianapolis, IN 46230
Phone: (317)255-5594

Publications: Branches Magazine (10099)

Appleton Press
241 W Snelling
Appleton, MN 56208
Phone: (320)289-1323

Publications: Appleton Press (15719)

Appliance Manufacturer
5900 Harper Rd., Ste. 105
Solon, OH 44139-1835
Phone: (440)349-3060
Fax: (440)498-9121

Publications: Appliance Manufacturer (25524)

Appliance Service News
PO Box 809
St. Charles, IL 60174

Publications: Appliance Service News (9562)

Applied Arts Inc.
18 Wynford Dr., Ste. 411
North York, ON, Canada M3C 3S2
Phone: (416)510-0909
Fax: (416)510-0913

Publications: Applied Arts Magazine (36120)

Applied Computer Research
PO Box 82266
Phoenix, AZ 85071-2266
Phone: (602)216-9100
Fax: (602)216-9200
Free: 800-234-2227

Publications: Computer Literature Index (800)

Applied Industrial Hygiene, Inc.
1330 Kemper Meadow Dr., Ste. 600
Cincinnati, OH 45240
Phone: (513)742-2020
Fax: (513)742-3355

Publications: Applied Occupational & Environmental Hygiene (24774)

Appraisal Institute of Canada
203-150 Isabella St.
Ottawa, ON, Canada K1S 1V7
Phone: (613)234-6533
Fax: (613)234-7197

Publications: The Canadian Appraiser (35319)

Aqua-Field Publishing Company, Inc.
39 Ave. of the Common
Shrewsbury, NJ 07702
Phone: (732)935-1222

Publications: Aqua-Field Turkey Hunting Guide (19546) • Blackpowder Hunter (19547) • Bowhunting (19548) • Decks & Backyard Projects (19549) • Deer Hunting North America (19550) • Fishing Smart! (19551) • Fly Fishing Made Easy (19552) • Fly Fishing Quarterly (19553) • Fly Fishing in Saltwater (19554) • Fly Fishing for Trout (19555)

The Aquaculture News
15 Foster Mound Rd.
Natchez, MS 39120
Phone: (601)443-9882
Fax: (601)443-9880

Publications: The Aquaculture News (16791)

Aquatic Therapy & Rehab Institute Inc.
3650 Center Cir., Ste. A
Fort Mill, SC 29715-8735

Publications: Aquatic Therapy Journal (28611)

L'Aquilon
PO Box 1325
Yellowknife, NT, Canada X1A 2N9
Phone: (867)873-6603
Fax: (867)873-2158

Publications: L'Aquilon (35522)

Aquinas College Publications Board
1607 Robinson Rd. SE
Grand Rapids, MI 49506-1799
Phone: (616)459-8281
Fax: (616)732-4487

Publications: Aquinas Times (15088)

Aquino International
PO Box 15760
Stamford, CT 06901-0760

Publications: Club Modele Magazine (5143) • Kids Creative Resources (5152)

A.R. Harding Publishing Co.
2878 E Main St.
Columbus, OH 43209
Phone: (614)231-9585

Publications: FUR-FISH-GAME (25018)

Arab Tribune
PO Box 310
Oneonta, AL 35121
Phone: (205)625-3231
Fax: (205)625-3239

Publications: The Blount County Shopping Guide (405)

Arabian Horse Times
1050 NE 8th St. NE
PO Box 1469
Waseca, MN 56093-9803
Phone: (507)835-3204
Fax: (507)835-5138

Publications: Arabian Horse Times (16499)

Arabian Horse World
1316 Tamson Dr., Ste. 101
Cambria, CA 93428
Phone: (805)771-2300
Fax: (805)927-6522
Free: 800-955-9423

Publications: Arabian Horse World (1648) • Horse World (1650)

Arachne, Inc.
2363 Page Rd.
Kennedy, NY 14747

Publications: Arachne (20858)

Aramco Services Company
Box 2106
Houston, TX 77252-2106
Phone: (713)432-4000

Publications: Saudi Aramco World (30527)

The Aransas Pass Progress/Ingleside Index
PO Box 2100
Aransas Pass, TX 78335
Phone: (361)758-5391
Fax: (361)758-5393
Free: 800-307-4882
Publications: Aransas Pass Progress (29727) • The Ingleside Index (29729)

Arapahoe Public Mirror
420 Nebraska Ave.
PO Box 660
Arapahoe, NE 68922-0348
Phone: (308)962-7261
Fax: (308)962-7865
Publications: Arapahoe Public Mirror (17934)

The Arbiter
1910 University Dr.
Boise, ID 83725
Phone: (208)345-8204
Fax: (208)345-3198
Publications: The Arbiter (7802)

The Arc
1010 Wayne Ave., Ste. 650
Silver Spring, MD 20910-5638
Phone: (301)565-3842
Fax: (301)565-5342
Free: 800-433-5255
Publications: The Arc's Government Report (13723)

The Arcadia News-Leader
625 Dettloff Dr.
PO Box 220
Arcadia, WI 54612
Phone: (608)323-3366
Fax: (608)323-2185
Publications: The Arcadia News-Leader (33553)

The Arcadia Progress
PO Box 29
Arcadia, LA 71001-0029
Phone: (318)263-2922
Fax: (318)268-8897
Publications: The Arcadia Progress (12475)

Arcam Publishing, Inc.
1760 Reston Pkwy.
Reston, VA 20190
Phone: (703)437-5400
Fax: (703)437-5317
Publications: Reston/Herndon Times-Mirror (32414) • Vienna Times (32585)

Archaeological Institute of America
3636 33rd St.
Long Island City, NY 11106
Phone: (212)732-5154
Publications: Archaeology (20961) • Archaeology's Dig (20962)

Archaeological Society of Delaware
Box 12483
Wilmington, DE 19850
Publications: Archaeological Society of Delaware Bulletin (5288)

Archbold Buckeye, Inc.
207 N Defiance St.
Archbold, OH 43502
Phone: (419)445-4466
Fax: (419)445-4177
Publications: Archbold Buckeye (24613)

Archie Comic Publications, Inc.
PO Box 559
Stamford, CT 06913
Phone: (914)381-4015
Publications: Archie Comics (5140)

Architectural Designs, Inc.
274 Riverside Ave.
Westport, CT 06880-4823
Phone: (203)222-1113
Fax: (203)221-9202
Publications: Architectural Designs (5211)

Architecture Minnesota
275 Market St., Ste. 54
Minneapolis, MN 55405-1621
Phone: (612)338-6763
Fax: (612)338-7981
Publications: Architecture Minnesota (16058)

The Arco Advertiser
PO Box 803
Arco, ID 83213-0803
Phone: (208)527-3038
Fax: (208)527-8210
Free: 800-927-3038
Publications: The Arco Advertiser (7799)

ARCOM, Inc.
16 W. Main
PO Box 32
Berryville, VA 22611
Phone: (703)955-1111
Fax: (703)955-1334
Publications: Clarke Times-Courier (31864)

Arcom Publishing Inc.
13873 Park Center Rd., Ste. 301
Herndon, VA 20171
Phone: (703)478-6666
Fax: (703)435-9754
Publications: Centerville Times (32161) • Eastern Loudoun Times (32184) • Fauquier Times-Democrat (32601) • Herndon Times (32163) • Rappahannock News (32165)

Arctic Institute of North America
University of Calgary
2500 University Dr. NW
Calgary, AB, Canada T2N 1N4
Phone: (403)220-7515
Fax: (403)282-4609
Publications: Arctic (34627)

Area Auto Racing News
PO Box 8547
Trenton, NJ 08650
Phone: (609)888-3618
Fax: (609)888-2538
Publications: Area Auto Racing News (19653)

Area Wide Media
PO Box 248
Salem, AR 72576
Phone: (870)895-3207
Fax: (870)895-4277
Free: 800-995-3209
Publications: The News (1335)

Areawide Media, Inc.
101 Chestnut St.
Thayer, MO 65791
Phone: (417)264-3085
Fax: (417)264-3814
Free: 800-995-3209
Publications: The South Missourian News (17648)

Arena Publishing Co.
17230 13 Mile Rd.
Roseville, MI 48066
Phone: (810)774-4311
Fax: (810)774-5450
Publications: Movie Collector's World (15475)

Arenac County Independent
203 E Cedar
PO Box 699
Standish, MI 48658
Phone: (989)846-4531
Fax: (989)846-9868
Free: 800-831-7669
Publications: Arenac County Independent (15575)

Arens Publications
PO Box 69
Covington, OH 45318
Phone: (937)473-2028
Fax: (937)473-2500
Free: 800-421-8051
Publications: Penny Saver (25099) • Stillwater Valley Advertiser (25100)

Arete Press
1420 N. Claremont Blvd., No. 204C-D
Claremont, CA 91711

Publications: Aikido Today Magazine (1722)

The Argonaut
Student Media
301 Student Union
Moscow, ID 83843
Phone: (208)885-7845
Publications: Idaho Argonaut (7915)

The Argonaut Inc.
PO Box 11209
Marina del Rey, CA 90295-7209
Phone: (310)822-1629
Fax: (310)822-2089
Publications: The Argonaut (2504)

Argosy Communications Ltd.
PO Box 956
East Greenwich, RI 02818-0960
Phone: (508)987-7717
Fax: (508)987-1662
Publications: Rhode Island Boating (28342)

The Argus
Wesleyan Sta.
PO Box 7055
Middletown, CT 06459
Phone: (860)685-3324
Fax: (860)685-3411
Publications: The Wesleyan Argus (4947)

Argus
217 N. 4th St.
Niles, MI 49120-2301
Publications: Argus (15004) • Niles Daily Star (15404)

Argus Business
6151 Powers Ferry Rd.
Atlanta, GA 30339-2941
Phone: (770)955-2500
Publications: Art Material Trade News (6964) • Business Atlanta (6982) • EMC Test & Design (7002) • Modern Paint and Coatings (7027)

Argus News
Box 37
Stickney, SD 57375-0037
Phone: (605)732-4555
Fax: (605)732-4452
Free: 800-583-9041
Publications: The Stickney Argus (28998)

The Argus-Press Co.
201 E. Exchange St.
PO Box 399
Owosso, MI 48867
Phone: (989)725-5136
Publications: The Argus-Press (15428) • The Durand Express (15429)

Ariel Communications, Inc.
PO Box 202380
Austin, TX 78720-3550
Phone: (512)250-1700
Fax: (512)219-3156
Publications: Corel (29771)

The Aristos Foundation
PO Box 1955, Radio City Sta.
New York, NY 10101
Publications: Aristos (21248)

Arizona Archaeological and Historical Society
Arizona State Museum
University of Arizona
Tucson, AZ 85721
Publications: Kiva (952)

Arizona Archaeological Society, Inc.
Box 9665
Phoenix, AZ 85068
Phone: (480)830-6055
Publications: Arizona Archaeologist (928)

Arizona Farm Bureau Federation
3401 E Elwood St.
Phoenix, AZ 85040-1625
Phone: (602)659-7000
Fax: (602)659-7073
Publications: Arizona Farm Bureau News (777)

Arizona Grocers Publishing Co., Inc.
120 E Pierce St.
Phoenix, AZ 85004
Phone: (602)252-9761
Fax: (602)252-9021

Publications: Arizona Food Industry Journal (778)

Arizona Highways
2039 W Lewis Ave.
Phoenix, AZ 85009
Phone: (602)712-2000
Fax: (602)254-4505
Free: 800-543-5432

Publications: Arizona Highways (779)

Arizona Historical Society
949 E 2nd St.
Tucson, AZ 85719
Phone: (520)628-5774
Fax: (520)628-5695

Publications: Journal of Arizona History (950)

Arizona Informant
1746 E Madison, No. 2
Phoenix, AZ 85034
Phone: (602)257-9300
Fax: (602)257-0547

Publications: Arizona Informant (780)

Arizona Medical Association, Inc.
810 W Bethany Home Rd.
Phoenix, AZ 85013
Phone: (602)347-6900
Fax: (602)242-6283
Free: 800-482-3480

Publications: AZ Med (793)

Arizona News Service Inc.
PO Box 2260
Phoenix, AZ 85002
Phone: (602)258-7026
Fax: (602)253-7636

Publications: Arizona Capitol Times (776)

Arizona Pennysaver, L.L.C.
PO Box 14110
Scottsdale, AZ 85267-4110
Phone: (602)968-5700
Fax: (602)968-8694

Publications: Arizona Pennysaver (866)

Arizona Quarterly
University of Arizona
1731 E. 2nd St.
PO Box 210014
Tucson, AZ 85721
Phone: (602)621-6396
Fax: (520)621-7397

Publications: Arizona Quarterly (933)

Arizona Senior World
7070 N. Oracle Rd., Ste. 260
Tucson, AZ 85704
Phone: (520)297-1220
Fax: (520)297-0704

Publications: Arizona Senior World (934)

Arizona State University
Tempe, AZ 85287-0405
Phone: (480)727-7204
Fax: (480)965-2659

Publications: Journal of Historical Research in Music Education (907)

Arizona State University
PO Box 871405
Tempe, AZ 85287-1405
Phone: (480)965-7572
Fax: (480)965-1000

Publications: KAET Magazine (910) • State Press (916)

Arizona Western College
PO Box 929
Yuma, AZ 85369

Publications: The Western Voice (1021)

Arizona Zoological Society
455 N Galvin Pkwy.
Phoenix, AZ 85008
Phone: (602)273-1341
Fax: (602)273-7078

Publications: Arizoo (783)

Arjuna Library Press
1025 Garner St., D, Space 18
Colorado Springs, CO 80905-1774

Publications: Journal of Regional Criticism (4250)

The Ark Publishing Co.
Box 1054
Tiburon, CA 94920
Phone: (415)435-2652
Fax: (415)435-0849

Publications: The Ark (3926)

Ark Valley News
210 W Main
PO Box 218
Valley Center, KS 67147
Phone: (316)755-0821
Fax: (316)755-0644

Publications: Ark Valley News (11857)

Arkansas Aging Foundation
706 S Pulaski St.
Little Rock, AR 72201
Phone: (501)376-6083
Fax: (501)376-6084

Publications: Aging Arkansas (1208)

Arkansas Bankers Association
The Carvill Building
1220 W. 3rd St.
Little Rock, AR 72201
Phone: (501)376-3741
Fax: (501)376-9243

Publications: Arkansas Banker (1212)

Arkansas Business Publishing Group
122 E Second St.
PO Box 3686
Little Rock, AR 72203
Phone: (501)372-1443
Fax: (501)375-7933

Publications: Arkansas Business (1213) • Little Rock Family (1233)

Arkansas Catholic
2500 N Tyler
PO Box 7417
Little Rock, AR 72217-7417
Phone: (501)664-0340
Fax: (501)661-9075

Publications: Arkansas Catholic (1214)

Arkansas Cattlemen's Association
310 Executive Ct.
Little Rock, AR 72205
Phone: (501)224-2114
Fax: (501)224-5377

Publications: Arkansas Cattle Business (1215)

Arkansas Democrat-Gazette, Inc.
Capitol Ave. & Scott St.
PO Box 2221
Little Rock, AR 72203
Phone: (501)378-3400
Fax: (501)372-3908

Publications: Arkansas Democrat-Gazette (1216)

Arkansas Education Association
1500 W. 4th St.
Little Rock, AR 72201
Phone: (501)375-4611
Fax: (501)375-4620

Publications: Arkansas Educator (1217)

Arkansas Electric Cooperative, Inc.
8000 Scott Hamilton Dr.
PO Box 510
Little Rock, AR 72203-0510
Phone: (501)570-2200
Fax: (501)570-2205

Publications: Rural Arkansas (1236)

Arkansas Farm Bureau Federation
10720 Kanis Rd.
PO Box 31
Little Rock, AR 72211-3825
Phone: (501)224-4400
Fax: (501)228-1557

Publications: Front Porch (1229)

Arkansas Game & Fish Commission
2 Natural Resources Dr.
Little Rock, AR 72205
Phone: (501)223-6300
Fax: (501)223-6447
Free: 800-364-GAME

Publications: Arkansas Wildlife (1223)

Arkansas Genealogical Society Inc.
1411 Shady Grove Rd.
PO Box 908
Hot Springs, AR 71902-0908
Phone: (501)262-4513
Fax: (501)262-4513

Publications: Arkansas Family Historian (1183)

Arkansas Historical Association
University of Arkansas
History Dept., 416 Old Main
Fayetteville, AR 72701
Phone: (479)575-5884
Fax: (479)575-2775

Publications: Arkansas Historical Quarterly (1116)

Arkansas Medical Society
PO Box 55088
Little Rock, AR 72215
Phone: (501)224-8967
Fax: (501)224-6489

Publications: The Journal of the Arkansas Medical Society (1231)

Arkansas Municipal League
PO Box 38
North Little Rock, AR 72115-0038
Phone: (501)374-3484
Fax: (501)374-0541

Publications: City & Town (1299)

Arkansas Pharmacist's Association, Inc.
417 S Victory
Little Rock, AR 72201-2923
Phone: (501)372-5250

Publications: Arkansas Pharmacist (1219)

Arkansas Review
Arkansas State University
Department of English & Philosophy
Box 1890
State University, AR 72467
Phone: (870)972-3043
Fax: (870)972-3045

Publications: Arkansas Review (1348)

Arkansas State University
Box 1930
State University, AR 72467
Phone: (870)972-3024
Fax: (870)972-3828

Publications: The Herald of Arkansas State University (1349)

Arkansas Tech University
Bryan Hall, Rm. 102
Russellville, AR 72801-2222
Phone: (479)968-0343
Fax: (479)890-8074

Publications: Arka Tech (1331)

Arkansas Tech University
Russellville, AR 72801
Phone: (479)968-0256

Publications: Nebo (1332)

Arkansas Times
PO Box 34010
Little Rock, AR 72203-4010
Phone: (501)375-2985
Fax: (501)375-3523

Publications: Arkansas Living (1218) • Arkansas Times (1221)

The Arkansas Traveler
University of Arkansas
119 Kimpel Hall
Fayetteville, AR 72701
Phone: (501)575-3406
Fax: (501)575-3306

Publications: The Arkansas Traveler (1118)

Numbers cited after listings are entry numbers rather than page numbers.

Arkansas Trucking Association
1401 W. Capitol Ave., Ste. 185
Little Rock, AR 72201
Phone: (501)372-3462
Fax: (501)376-1810

Publications: Arkansas Trucking Report (1222)

Arkansas Valley Publishing Co.
PO Box 460
Bailey, CO 80421-0460
Phone: (303)838-4423

Publications: Park County Republican and The Fairplay Flume (4152)

Arkansas Valley Publishing Co.
125 E. 2nd St.
PO Box 189
Salida, CO 81201-0189
Phone: (719)539-1455
Fax: (719)539-6630

Publications: Chaffee County Times (4618) • The Herald Democrat (4619) • The Mountain Mail (4620)

ARL
21 Dupont Cir., NW
Washington, DC 20036-1118
Phone: (202)296-2296
Fax: (202)872-0884

Publications: SPEC Kit (5800)

Arlington Enterprise
402 W Alden St.
Arlington, MN 55307

Publications: Arlington Enterprise (15721)

Arlington Herald
200 N Glebe Rd., Ste. 600
Arlington, VA 22203
Phone: (202)841-2530
Fax: (703)524-2782

Publications: Arlington Catholic Herald (31777)

Arlington Historical Society Inc.
PO Box 402
Arlington, VA 22210-0402
Phone: (703)892-4204

Publications: Arlington Historical Magazine (31778)

Arlington Times
123 N Olympic
PO Box 67
Arlington, WA 98223
Phone: (360)435-5757
Fax: (360)435-0999

Publications: Arlington Times (32654)

Armada Times
PO Box 915
Armada, MI 48005-0915
Phone: (586)784-5551
Fax: (586)784-8710

Publications: Armada Times (14782)

The Armchair Detective
549 Park Ave., Ste. 252
Scotch Plains, NJ 07076
Fax: (908)226-9702

Publications: The Armchair Detective (19533)

Armed Forces Communications & Electronics Association (AFCEA)
4400 Fair Lakes Ct.
Fairfax, VA 22033

Publications: SIGNAL (32029)

Armenian General Benevolent Union
55 E 59th St.
New York, NY 10022-1112
Phone: (212)319-6383
Fax: (212)319-6508

Publications: Ararat (21240) • Hoosharar Mioutune (21817)

Armenian Numismatic Society
8511 Beverly Park Pl.
Pico Rivera, CA 90660-1920
Phone: (562)695-0380

Publications: Armenian Numismatic Journal (2839)

Armour Chronicle
PO Box 129
Armour, SD 57313-0129
Phone: (605)724-2747
Fax: (605)946-5179

Publications: Armour Chronicle (28804)

Arms Control Association
1726 M St. NW, Ste. 201
Washington, DC 20036
Phone: (202)463-8270
Fax: (202)463-8273

Publications: Arms Control Today (5361)

Armstrong Advertiser
Okanagan St.
PO Box 610
Armstrong, BC, Canada V0E 1B0
Phone: (250)546-3121
Fax: (250)546-3636

Publications: Armstrong Advertiser (34882)

Armstrong Atlantic State University
11935 Abercorn St.
Savannah, GA 31419
Phone: (912)927-5289
Free: 800-633-2349

Publications: Southern Poetry Review (7539)

Army Aviation Publications, Inc.
755 Main St. Ste. 4D
Monroe, CT 06468-2830

Publications: Army Aviation Magazine (4962)

Army Times Publishing Co.
6883 Commercial Dr.
Springfield, VA 22159-0001
Phone: (703)750-9000
Fax: (703)750-8767

Publications: Air Force Times (32537) • Army Times (32540) • Defense News (32542) • Federal Times (32544) • Navy Times (32549)

Arnazella
3000 Landerholm Cir., SE
Bellevue, WA 98007
Phone: (425)603-4032

Publications: Arnazella (32662)

Arnold A. Auguste Associates Ltd.
658 Vaughan Rd.
Toronto, ON, Canada M6E 2Y5
Phone: (416)656-3400
Fax: (416)656-3711

Publications: Share (36739)

Arnold Arboretum
125 Arborway
Jamaica Plain, MA 02130-3500
Phone: (617)524-1718
Fax: (617)524-1418

Publications: Arnoldia (14258)

Arnold Press
PO Box 67
Tonica, IL 61370-0067
Phone: (815)442-8419
Fax: (815)339-6PCR

Publications: The Tonica News (9693)

Around the Town
1245 Colonial Dr.
Lexington, KY 40504
Phone: (606)277-5494
Fax: (606)389-7560

Publications: Around the Town (12160)

Arquidicesis de Miami
9401 Biscayne Blvd.
Miami, FL 33138-2970
Phone: (305)757-6241
Fax: (305)762-1223

Publications: La Voz Catolica (6367)

Arrow Lakes News
PO Box 189
Nakusp, BC, Canada V0G 1R0
Phone: (250)265-3823
Fax: (250)265-3841

Publications: Arrow Lakes News (35017)

Arrow Shopper
15811 Bridge St.
Ettrick, WI 54627
Phone: (608)525-5771
Fax: (608)525-2617

Publications: Arrow Shopper (33691)

Art Access
PO Box 4163
Seattle, WA 98104
Phone: (206)855-9668
Fax: (206)855-7854

Publications: Art Access (32941)

Art Calendar
PO Box 2675
Salisbury, MD 21802
Phone: (410)749-9625
Fax: (410)749-9626
Free: (866)4AR-TCAL

Publications: Art Calendar (13706)

Art City Publishing
161 S Main
Springville, UT 84663
Phone: (801)489-5651
Fax: (801)489-7021

Publications: Eureka Reporter (31476) • Springville Herald (31477)

The Art of Eating
Box 242
Peacham, VT 05862
Phone: (802)592-3144
Fax: (802)542-3400
Free: 800-495-3944

Publications: The Art of Eating (31578)

Art Institute of Chicago
Publications Department
111 S. Michigan Ave.
Chicago, IL 60603-6110
Phone: (312)443-3540
Fax: (312)443-1334

Publications: Art Institute of Chicago Museum Studies (8275)

Art Instruction Schools
3309 Broadway St. NE
Minneapolis, MN 55413
Phone: (612)362-5121
Fax: (612)362-5260

Publications: Illustrator (16085)

Art/Life Limited Editions
PO Box 23020
Ventura, CA 93002
Phone: (805)648-4331

Publications: Art/Life (4000)

Art: Mag
PO Box 70896
Las Vegas, NV 89170
Phone: (702)734-8121

Publications: Art (18360)

Art News LLC
48 W. 38th St.
New York, NY 10018-6238
Phone: (212)398-1690
Fax: (212)819-0394

Publications: ARTnews Magazine (21257)

Art Now, Inc.
97 Grayrock Rd.
PO Box 5541
Clinton, NJ 08809
Phone: (908)638-5255
Fax: (908)638-8737

Publications: Art Now Gallery Guide—Boston/New England Edition (18759) • Art Now Gallery Guide—Chicago/Midwest Edition (18760) • Art Now Gallery Guide—International Edition (18761) • Art Now Gallery Guide—New York Edition (18762) • Art Now Gallery Guide—Philadelphia Edition (18763) • Art Now Gallery Guide—Southeast Edition (18764) • Art Now Gallery Guide—Southwest Edition (18765) • Art Now Gallery Guide—West Coast Edition (18766)

Art Papers, Inc.
PO Box 5748
Atlanta, GA 31107
Phone: (404)588-1837
Fax: (404)588-1836

Publications: Art Papers Magazine (6965)

Art et architecture Quebec
405-1625 Bourg-du-lac
Sainte-Adele, QC, Canada J8B 3A2
Phone: (514)523-6832

Publications: ARQ, La revue d'architecture (37370)

Art Therapy
1202 Allanson Rd.
Mundelein, IL 60060-3808
Phone: (847)949-6064
Fax: (847)566-4580
Free: 888-290-0878

Publications: Art Therapy (9256)

ArtByte Magazine Inc.
39 E. 78th St., Ste. 501
New York, NY 10021
Phone: (212)988-5959
Fax: (212)988-6107

Publications: ArtByte (21254)

Artemis Creations Publishing
3395 Nostrand Ave., No. 2J
Brooklyn, NY 11229-4053
Phone: (718)648-8215
Fax: (718)648-8215

Publications: Matriarch's Way (20330)

Artesia Daily Press
PO Box 190
Artesia, NM 88211-0190
Phone: (505)746-3524
Fax: (505)746-8795

Publications: Artesia Daily Press (19817)

Arthur Enterprise
PO Box 165
Arthur, NE 69121-0165
Phone: (308)764-2402

Publications: Arthur Enterprise (17936)

Arthur Graphic Clarion
PO Box 19
Arthur, IL 61911
Phone: (217)543-2151
Fax: (217)543-2152

Publications: Arthur Graphic Clarion (8027)

Artichoke Publishing
901 Jervis St., No. 208
Vancouver, BC, Canada V6E 2B6
Phone: (604)683-1941
Fax: (604)683-1941

Publications: Artichoke (35122)

Artificial Language Laboratory
405 Computer Ctr.
East Lansing, MI 48824-1042
Phone: (517)353-0870
Fax: (517)353-4766

Publications: Communication Outlook (14983)

Artist-Blacksmith's Association of North America
PO Box 816
Farmington, GA 30638-0816
Phone: (706)310-1030
Fax: (706)769-7147

Publications: The Anvil's Ring (2002)

Arts & Activities
591 Camino de la Reina, Ste. 200
San Diego, CA 92108
Phone: (619)297-5350
Fax: (619)297-5353
Free: 800-537-3006

Publications: Arts & Activities (3117)

Arts Atlantic Inc.
PO Box 36007
RPO Spring Garden
Halifax, NS, Canada B3J 3S9
Phone: (902)420-5045
Fax: (902)491-8624

Publications: Arts Atlantic (35558)

Arts End Books
PO Box 703
Spencer, MA 01562
Phone: (508)885-9904

Publications: Nostoc Magazine (14549)

Arts & Media Inc.
PO Box 678
Richboro, PA 18954-0678
Phone: (215)826-1799
Fax: (215)860-1812

Publications: Glass Craftsman (27933)

Artvoice
810-812 Main St.
Buffalo, NY 14202
Phone: (716)881-6604
Fax: (716)881-6682

Publications: Artvoice (20363)

ARTWEEK
PO Box 26340
San Jose, CA 95159-6340
Phone: (408)441-7065
Fax: (408)441-9519
Free: 800-733-2916

Publications: ARTWEEK (3510)

ASA/USA Softball
2801 NE 50th St.
Oklahoma City, OK 73111
Phone: (405)424-5266
Fax: (405)424-4734

Publications: Ballard Strikes Softball Magazine (25953)

Asahi Shimbun
845 3rd Ave.
New York, NY 10022
Phone: (212)755-3900
Fax: (212)317-3025

Publications: Asahi Shimbun (21259)

ASCR International
8229 Cloverleaf Dr., Ste. 460
Millersville, MD 21108-1538
Phone: (410)729-9900
Fax: (410)729-3603
Free: 800-272-7012

Publications: Cleaning & Restoration (13630)

John M. Ashbrook Center for Public Affairs
401 College Ave.
Ashland, OH 44805
Phone: (419)289-5411
Fax: (419)289-5425
Free: 877-289-5411

Publications: Collegian (24618)

Ashburn Newspapers
109 Gordon St.
Ashburn, GA 31714
Phone: (229)567-3655
Fax: (229)567-4402

Publications: The Wiregrass Farmer (6927)

Asheville Citizen-Times Publishing Co.
14 O. Henry Ave.
Asheville, NC 28801
Phone: (828)252-5611
Fax: (828)251-2659
Free: 800-800-4204

Publications: Asheville Citizen-Times (23627) • Good News (23630)

Ashland Publishing Co.
22417th St., No. 311
Ashland, KY 41101-7606
Fax: (606)324-8434
Free: 800-955-5860

Publications: The Daily Independent (11917)

Ashland Publishing Co., LLC
255 W. Main
Loudonville, OH 44842
Phone: (419)994-4166
Fax: (419)994-4617
Free: 800-842-6859

Publications: The Loudonville Times and The Loudonville Mohican Area Shopper (25317)

Ashlee Publishing Company, Inc.
18 E. 41st St.
New York, NY 10017
Phone: (212)376-7722
Fax: (212)376-7723

Publications: Contemporary Dialysis & Nephrology (21491) • Fenestration (21686) • Glass Digest (21766) • Glass Industry (21767) • Tile & Decorative Surfaces (22836)

Ashley County Publishing Co., Inc.
PO Box 798
Crossett, AR 71635
Phone: (501)364-5186
Fax: (501)364-2116

Publications: Ashley News Observer (1092)

Ashley Publishing Co., Inc.
107 Main St.
PO Box 471
Hamburg, AR 71646
Phone: (501)853-2424
Fax: (501)853-8203
Free: (870)853-2424

Publications: Ashley County Ledger (1164)

Ashtabula Star-Beacon
4626 Park Ave.
PO Box 2100
Ashtabula, OH 44004
Phone: (440)994-3241
Fax: (440)992-9655

Publications: Ashtabula Star-Beacon (24623)

The Ashton Gazette
PO Box 287
Ashton, IL 61006
Phone: (815)453-2551
Fax: (815)453-2551

Publications: The Ashton Gazette (8029)

Asia Market Information & Development Co.
15002 225th Ave. NE
Woodinville, WA 98072-5123
Phone: (425)844-8585
Fax: (425)844-8515

Publications: China Markets for Melamine (33208) • China Paints and Coatings: Market and Opportunities (33209) • China Synthetic Rubber Markets (33210) • China Wood Preservatives (33211) • Chinese Markets for Dimethylacetamide (33212)

Asia Pacific Economic Review
1025 S. King St.
Seattle, WA 98104
Phone: (206)860-4970
Fax: (206)860-4895

Publications: Asia Pacific Economic Review (32942)

Asian-American Civic Association
200 Tremont St.
Boston, MA 02116-4705
Phone: (617)426-9492
Fax: (617)482-2316

Publications: Sampan (13958)

ASIS International
1625 Prince St.
Alexandria, VA 22314-2818
Phone: (703)519-6200
Fax: (703)519-6299

Publications: Security Management (31736)

Askov American
PO Box 275
Askov, MN 55704
Phone: (320)838-3151
Fax: (320)838-3152

Publications: Askov American (15722)

ASM International
9639 Kinsman Rd.
Materials Park, OH 44073-0002
Phone: (440)338-5151
Fax: (440)338-4634
Free: 800-336-5152

Publications: Advanced Materials & Processes (25363) • Alloy Digest (25364) • International Materials Reviews (25366) • Journal of Materials Engineering and Performance (2303) • Journal of Phase Equilibria (25367) • Journal of Thermal Spray Technology (23371)

ASM Journals
1752 N St. NW
Washington, DC 20036-2904
Phone: (202)942-9207
Fax: (202)942-9333

Publications: Antimicrobial Agents and Chemotherapy (5355) • Applied and Environmental Microbiology (5358) • ASM News (5368) • Clinical and Diagnostic Laboratory Immunology (5419) • Clinical Microbiology Reviews (5421) • Infection and Immunity (5543) • Journal of Bacteriology (5575) • Journal of Clinical Microbiology (5577) • Journal of Virology (5618) • Microbiology and Molecular Biology Reviews (5648) • Molecular and Cellular Biology (5658)

ASMC Foundation
1010 Wisconsin Ave. NW, Ste. 9
Washington, DC 20007-3603

Publications: ASMC Sales & Marketing Magazine (5369)

ASMSU Exponent
Strand Union Bldg. 330
Bozeman, MT 59717-4200
Phone: (406)994-2224
Fax: (406)994-2253

Publications: The Exponent (17752)

Asociacion de Literatura Fenemina Hispanica
University of Wisconsin
Dept of Spanish and Portuguese
Madison, WI 53706
Phone: (608)262-9663
Fax: (608)262-9671

Publications: Letras Femeninas (33958)

Asp Westward
PO Box 7
Edgewood, TX 75117
Phone: (903)896-4401
Fax: (903)962-3660

Publications: Edgewood Enterprise (30270)

ASP Westward/Douglas County Publishing
PO Box 340
Woodland Park, CO 80866
Phone: (719)687-3006
Fax: (719)687-3009

Publications: The Gold Rush (4690)

Asp Westward LP
213B Scurry
Drawer M
Daingerfield, TX 75638
Phone: (903)645-3948
Fax: (903)645-3731

Publications: The Bee (30118)

ASP Westward, L.P.
PO Box 556
Hempstead, TX 77445
Phone: (979)826-3361
Fax: (979)826-3360
Free: 800-660-1397

Publications: The Waller County News-Citizen (30439)

Aspen Law & Business
1185 Ave. of the Americas
New York, NY 10036
Phone: (212)597-0219

Publications: American Journal of Family Law (21193) • Banking & Financial Services Policy Report (21288) • The Business Torts Reporter (21360) • The Computer & Internet Lawyer (21475) • Environmental Claims Journal (21614) • Insights (21877) • IP Litigator (21948) • Journal of Insurance Coverage (22098) • Journal of Internet Law (22106) • The Licensing Journal (22253) • Of Counsel (22485) • The Trial Lawyer (22864)

Aspen Publishers
1185 Avenue of the Americas
New York, NY 10036
Phone: (212)597-0200

Publications: Asset Protection Journal (21267) • Benefits Law Journal (21295) • Compensation & Benefits Management (21466) • Corporate Business Taxation Monthly (21500) • Derivatives Quarterly (21544) • Elder's Advisor (21591) • Employee Relations Law Journal (21602) • Financial Crime Review

(21695) • Infrastructure Finance (21873) • Institutional Investor (21880) • Institutional Investor (International Edition) (21881) • The International Tax Journal (21938) • The Journal of Alternative Investments (13796) • Journal of Deferred Compensation (22047) • The Journal of Derivatives (22048) • The Journal of Fixed Income (23712) • The Journal of Investing (30947) • The Journal of Investment Compliance (22108) • Journal of Pension Benefits (22152) • Journal of Pension Planning and Compliance (22153) • The Journal of Portfolio Management (22164) • The Journal of Private Equity (10456) • Journal of Property Tax Management (22166) • The Journal of Risk Finance (22180) • Journal of State Taxation (22192) • The Journal of Structured and Project Finance (5617) • Municipal Finance Journal (22382) • Real Estate Finance (14667) • Strategic Investor Relations (5806)

Aspen Publishers
1185 Avenue of the Americas, 37th Fl.
New York, NY 10036
Phone: (212)597-0200
Fax: (212)597-0390
Free: 800-447-1717

Publications: Alzheimer's Care Quarterly (21175) • Bank Accounting & Finance (14143) • Biomedical Safety and Standards (21322) • Commercial Lending Review (14146) • Intellectual Property and Technology Law Journal (21887) • Journal of Controversial Medical Claims (22039) • Managed Care Quarterly (22277) • Medical Benefits (5019) • Special Education Report (22771) • Student Aid News (22798)

Aspen Publishers Inc.
1185 Ave. of the Americas
New York, NY 10036
Phone: (212)597-0200
Fax: (212)597-0338
Free: 800-234-1660

Publications: Advances in Nursing Science (21156) • Critical Care Nursing Quarterly (21519) • Family & Community Health (21678) • Health Care Management Review (21792) • The Health Care Manager (21794) • Holistic Nursing Practice (21807) • Infants and Young Children (13542) • Journal of Ambulatory Care Management (21981) • Journal of Cardiovascular Nursing (22018) • Journal of Head Trauma Rehabilitation (22083) • Journal of Health Care Compliance (22084) • Journal of Health Care Finance (22085) • Journal of Nursing Care Quality (22147) • Journal of Perinatal and Neonatal Nursing (22154) • Nursing Administration Quarterly (22472) • Quality Management in Health Care (13547) • Topics in Clinical Chiropractic (22844) • Topics in Clinical Nutrition (13549) • Topics in Emergency Medicine (13550) • Topics in Geriatric Rehabilitation (22845) • Topics in Health Information Management (22846) • Topics in Language Disorders (22847)

Aspen Times
310 E. Main St.
Aspen, CO 81611
Phone: (970)925-3414
Fax: (970)925-6240

Publications: Aspen Times (4142)

The Asphalt Contractor
204 W. Kansas Ave., Ste. 103
Independence, MO 64050-3700
Phone: (816)343-6462
Fax: (816)254-2128
Free: 800-254-2123

Publications: The Asphalt Contractor (17106)

ASPRSN
E. Holly Ave.
Box 56
Pitman, NJ 08071-0056
Phone: (856)256-2300
Fax: (856)256-2345

Publications: Plastic Surgery Nursing (19440)

Asset Beam Publishing Ltd.
1 Cleopatra Dr., Ste. 202
Nepean, ON, Canada K2G 3M9
Phone: (613)224-3460
Fax: (613)224-1076

Publications: The Ottawa Construction News (36101)

Asset International, Inc.
125 Greenwich Ave.
Greenwich, CT 06830
Phone: (203)629-5014
Fax: (203)629-5024

Publications: Global Custodian (4873) • Plan Sponsor (4875)

The Assiniboia Times
PO Box 910
Assiniboia, SK, Canada S0H 0B0
Phone: (306)642-5901
Fax: (306)642-4519

Publications: The Assiniboia Times (37451)

Assistive Technology News
19 Crescent Ct.
Sterling, VA 20164
Phone: (703)406-7831
Fax: (703)406-3728

Publications: Assistive Technology News (32562)

Associate Alumnae of Douglass College
80 Clifton Ave.
New Brunswick, NJ 08901-1568
Fax: (908)247-1974

Publications: Douglass Alumnae Magazine (19330)

Associated Alumni of Acadia University
Box 520
Wolfville, NS, Canada B0P 1X0
Phone: (902)542-0240
Fax: (902)542-0240

Publications: Acadia Bulletin (35622)

Associated Builders & Contractors Inc.
1300 N 17th St.
Arlington, VA 22209
Phone: (703)812-2000
Fax: (703)812-8203

Publications: ABC Today (31767)

Associated Business Publications Co., Ltd.
317 Madison Ave.
New York, NY 10017
Phone: (212)490-3999
Fax: (212)986-7864

Publications: NASA Tech Briefs (22393)

Associated Desert Newspapers, Inc.
205 N. 8th St.
El Centro, CA 92243-2301
Phone: (619)337-3400
Fax: (619)353-3003

Publications: Imperial Valley Press (1851)

Associated Desert Shoppers, Inc.
73-400 Hwy. 111
Palm Desert, CA 92260
Phone: (760)365-6361
Fax: (760)346-7350
Free: 800-678-4237

Publications: North San Bernardino Green Sheet (3088) • Ontario Green Sheet (2718) • Redlands Green Sheet (2906) • Riverside Green Sheet (2944) • Valley Shopper-The El Centro Advertiser (1852) • Victorville Green Sheet (2744) • West San Bernardino Green Sheet (3093) • White Sheet-The Blythe Advertiser (1588) • White Sheet-The Indio Advertiser (2745) • White Sheet-The Lake Havasu City Advertiser (736) • White Sheet-The Morongo Basin Advertiser (2602) • White Sheet-The Palm Desert Advertiser (2746) • White Sheet-The Palm Springs Advertiser (2770) • White Sheet-The Parker Advertiser (764) • White Sheet-The Tri-State Advertiser (2747)

Associated Equipment Distributors
615 W 22nd St.
Oak Brook, IL 60523
Phone: (630)574-0650
Fax: (630)574-0132
Free: 800-388-0650

Publications: Construction Equipment Distribution (9345)

Associated General Contractors Information
333 John Carlyle St., Ste. 200
Alexandria, VA 22314
Phone: (703)837-5355
Fax: (703)837-5402

Publications: CONSTRUCTOR (31659)

Associated Locksmiths of America
3003 Live Oak St.
Dallas, TX 75204
Phone: (214)827-1701
Fax: (214)827-1810

Publications: Keynotes (30166)

Associated Motor Carriers
PO Box 14620
Oklahoma City, OK 73113
Phone: (405)843-9488
Fax: (405)843-7310
Free: 800-368-9576

Publications: Oklahoma Motor Carrier (25982)

Associated Newspapers
800 Hingham St.
PO Box 309
Rockland, MA 02370
Phone: (781)878-1111
Fax: (781)878-3333

Publications: Abington Standard (14506) • Avon Messenger (13827) • Braintree Gazette (14003) • Bridgewater Independent (14006) • Brockton News Tribune (14011) • Canton Register (14118) • Daily Mercury (14320) • East Bridgewater Star (14008) • Easton Bulletin (14173) • Hanover Branch (14227) • Hanson Town Crier (14229) • Holbrook Times (14236) • Mansfield Reporter (14303) • Milton Townsman (14337) • Norton Courier (14437) • Randolph Herald (14495) • Raynham Journal (14497) • Rockland Standard (14507) • Sharon Sentinel (14519) • Stoughton Chronicle (14508) • West Bridgewater Times (14624) • Weymouth Dispatch (14653) • Whitman Times (14658)

Associated Plumbing Heating & Cooling
PO Box 36972
Birmingham, AL 35236-6972
Phone: (205)985-9488
Fax: (205)733-1006

Publications: Associated Plumbing Heating & Cooling (55)

Associated Publications Corp.
495 E Summerlin St.
Bartow, FL 33830
Phone: (863)533-4114
Fax: (863)534-1758

Publications: The Citrus Industry (5917)

Associated Publications, Inc.
875 N Michigan Ave., Ste. 3434
Chicago, IL 60611-1901
Phone: (312)266-8680

Publications: Complete Woman (8340)

Associated Publications, Inc.
PO Box 250
Pineville, KY 40977
Phone: (606)337-2333
Fax: (606)337-2360

Publications: The Pineville Sun (12367)

Associated Publishers
PO Box 140103
Gainesville, FL 32614-0103
Phone: (352)371-4071
Fax: (352)378-6045

Publications: Contributions on Entomology International (6134) • Oriental Insects (6152)

Associated Texas Newspapers, Inc.
1601 Ave. K
PO Box 400
Hondo, TX 78861-0400
Phone: (830)426-3346
Fax: (830)426-3348
Free: 800-725-3346

Publications: Hondo Anvil Herald (30451) • Sabinal Sampler (31002)

Associated University Presses
2010 Eastpark Blvd.
Cranbury, NJ 08512
Phone: (609)655-4770
Fax: (609)655-8366

Publications: Shakespeare Studies (18770)

Associates for Biblical Research
PO Box 356
Landisville, PA 17538
Phone: (717)892-1044
Fax: (301)892-3049
Free: 800-430-0008

Publications: Bible and Spade (27157)

Association for the Advancement of Computing in Education
PO Box 3728
Norfolk, VA 23514
Phone: (757)623-7588
Fax: (703)997-8760

Publications: Educational Technology Review (32282) • Information Technology in Childhood Education Annual (32283) • International Journal of Educational Telecommunications (32284) • Journal of Educational Multimedia and Hypermedia (32285) • Journal of Interactive Learning Research (32288) • Journal of Technology & Teacher Education (32289) • WebNet Journal (32297)

Association of American Colleges & Universities
1818 R St. NW
Washington, DC 20009
Phone: (202)387-3760
Fax: (202)265-9532
Free: 800-297-3775

Publications: Liberal Education (5636)

Association of American Geographers, Southeastern Division
Department of Geography
University of Georgia
Athens, GA 30602-2502
Phone: (706)542-2350
Fax: (706)542-2388

Publications: Southeastern Geographer (6950)

Association of American Medical Colleges
2450 N. St. NW
Washington, DC 20037
Phone: (202)828-0416
Fax: (202)828-1123

Publications: Academic Medicine (5313)

Association of American Veterinary Medical Colleges
1101 Vermont Ave., NW, Ste. 710
Washington, DC 20005
Publications: Journal of Veterinary Medical Education (31877)

Association for Asian Studies Inc.
1021 E. Huron St.
Ann Arbor, MI 48104
Phone: (734)665-2490
Fax: (734)665-3801

Publications: Early Modern Japan (14746) • The Journal of Asian Studies (31433)

Association for Assessment in Counseling
5999 Stevenson Ave.
Alexandria, VA 22304-3300
Phone: (703)823-9800
Fax: (703)823-0252
Free: 800-347-6647

Publications: Measurement and Evaluation in Counseling and Development (31708)

Association of Biomolecular Resource Facilities
2019 Galisteo St.Bldg.
Santa Fe, NM 87505
Phone: (505)983-8102
Fax: (505)989-1073

Publications: Journal of Biomolecular Techniques (29371)

Association of Black Anthropologists
4350 N. Fairfax Dr. Ste. 640
Arlington, VA 22203-1620
Phone: (703)528-1902
Fax: (703)528-3546

Publications: Transforming Anthropology (31837)

Association Blais d'Amerique
Case Postale 6700
Sillery, QC, Canada G1T 2W2
Publications: Le Journal des Blais (37400)

Association for Business Communication
Department of Communication Studies
Baruch College, Box B8-240
One Bernard Baruch Way
New York, NY 10010
Phone: (646)312-3726
Fax: (646)349-5297

Publications: Business Communication Quarterly (21353) • The Journal of Business Communication (15035)

Association of California School Administrators
1517 L St.
Sacramento, CA 95814
Phone: (916)444-3216
Fax: (916)444-3245
Free: 800-890-0325

Publications: Leadership Magazine (3005)

Association of Canadian College and University Teachers of English
Department of English
1125 Colonel By Dr.
Ottawa, ON, Canada K1S 5B6
Phone: (613)520-2600
Fax: (613)520-3544

Publications: English Studies in Canada (ESC) (36241)

Association for Canadian Jewish Studies
Dept. of Religion
Concordia University
1455 de Maisonneuve Blvd. W
Montreal, QC, Canada H3G 1M8
Phone: (514)848-2065
Fax: (514)848-4541

Publications: Canadian Jewish Studies/Etudes Juives Canadiennes (37094)

Association for Canadian Studies in the United States (ACSUS)
1317 F St., NW, Ste. 920
Washington, DC 20004-1151
Phone: (202)393-2580
Fax: (202)393-2582

Publications: American Review of Canadian Studies (5342)

Association Canado-Americaine
52 Concord St.
PO Box 989
Manchester, NH 03101-1806
Phone: (603)625-8577
Free: 800-222-8577

Publications: Le Canado-Americain (18557)

Association for Career and Technical Education
1410 King St.
Alexandria, VA 22314
Phone: (703)683-3111
Fax: (703)683-7424
Free: 800-826-9972

Publications: Techniques (31741)

Association of Caribbean Studies
PO Box 22202
Lexington, KY 40502
Phone: (606)257-6966
Fax: (606)323-1072

Publications: Journal of Caribbean Studies (12167)

Association for Childhood Education International
17904 Georgia Ave., Ste. 215
Olney, MD 20832
Phone: (301)570-2111
Fax: (301)570-2212
Free: 800-423-3563

Publications: Journal of Research in Childhood Education (13643)

Association of Christian Librarians Inc.
PO Box 4
Cedarville, OH 45314
Phone: (937)675-3799
Fax: (937)766-2337

Publications: The Christian Librarian (24745)

Association of College and Research Libraries
50 E. Huron St.
Chicago, IL 60611
Phone: (312)280-2513
Fax: (312)280-2520
Free: 800-545-2433

Publications: College and Research Libraries (6932) • College and Research Libraries News (8336)

Association of College and University Housing Officers-International (ACUHO-I)
941 Chatham Ln., Ste. 318
Columbus, OH 43221-2416
Phone: (614)292-0099
Fax: (614)292-3205

Publications: Journal of College and University Student Housing (6146)

Association for Community Based Education
1805 Florida Ave. NW
Washington, DC 20009
Phone: (202)462-6333

Publications: Journal of the Association for Communication Administration (JACA) (5574)

Association for Computing Machinery
1515 Broadway
New York, NY 10036
Phone: (212)626-0500
Fax: (212)944-1318
Free: 800-342-6626

Publications: ACM Computing Surveys (21136) • ACM Transactions on Computer Systems (21137) • ACM Transactions on Database Systems (21138) • ACM Transactions on Graphics (21139) • ACM Transactions on Information Systems (21140) • ACM Transactions on Mathematical Software (21141) • ACM Transactions on Programming Languages and Systems (21142) • ACM Transactions on Software Engineering and Methodology (21143) • Collected Algorithms (CALGO) Supplements (21437) • Communications of the ACM (21459) • Computer-Human Interaction (TOCHI) (21474) • Computing Reviews (21480) • Design Automation of Electronic Systems (TODAES) (21545) • Information and Systems Security (TISSEC) (21871) • interactions (21889) • Journal of the Association for Computing Machinery (22001) • Journal of Experimental Algorithmics (JEA) (22067) • Mobile Networks and Applications (22342) • Modeling and Computer Simulation (TOMACS) (22344) • netWorker (22419) • Networking (TON) (22420) • StandardView (22789)

Association of Departments of English
26 Broadway, 3rd Fl.
New York, NY 10004-1789
Phone: (646)576-5133
Fax: (646)458-0033

Publications: ADE Bulletin (21149)

Association des Diplomes de Polytechnique
CP 6079 SUCC Centre-Ville
Montreal, QC, Canada H3C 3A7
Phone: (514)340-4764
Fax: (514)340-4472

Publications: L'Ingenieur (37131)

Association of Drilled Shaft Contractors
PO Box 550339
Dallas, TX 75355-0339
Phone: (214)343-2091
Fax: (214)343-2384

Publications: Foundation Drilling (30158)

Association for Education in Journalism & Mass Communication
234 Outlet Pointe Blvd., Ste. A
Columbia, SC 29210-5667
Phone: (803)798-0271
Fax: (803)772-3509

Publications: Journalism and Mass Communication Educator (29279) • Journalism and Mass Communication Quarterly (28555) • Mass Communication and Society (23715)

Association for Educational Communications and Technology
1800 N. Stonelake Dr., Ste. 2
Bloomington, IN 47404
Phone: (812)335-7675
Fax: (812)335-7678
Free: 877-677-2328

Publications: TechTrends: for Leaders in Education & Training (9853)

Association for Evolutionary Economics
226 Ayres Hall
Knoxville, TN 37996-1320
Phone: (423)974-6514
Fax: (423)974-4352

Publications: J E I (29274)

Association for Financial Professionals
7315 Wisconsin Ave., Ste. 600 W.
Bethesda, MD 20814
Phone: (301)907-2862
Fax: (301)907-2864

Publications: AFP Exchange (13295)

Association For Facilities Engineering
8160 Corporate Park Dr., Ste. 125
Cincinnati, OH 45242
Phone: (513)489-2473
Fax: (513)247-7422

Publications: AFE Facilities Engineering Journal (24767)

Association des industries Forestieres du Quebec, Ltee.
Place Iberville II
1175 Ave. Lavigerie, Ste. 201
Sainte-Foy, QC, Canada G1V 4P1
Phone: (418)651-9352
Fax: (418)266-2015

Publications: Papetier (37375)

Association of Former Students of Texas A&M University
PO Box 7368
College Station, TX 77844-7368
Phone: (409)845-7514
Fax: (409)845-9263

Publications: The Texas Aggie (30053)

Association for Global Business
Box 1381
Harrisonburg, VA 22803
Phone: (540)433-7403
Fax: (540)433-7403

Publications: Journal of Global Business (32139)

Association of Governing Boards of Universities and Colleges
1 Dupont Circle, Ste. 400
Washington, DC 20036
Phone: (202)296-8400
Fax: (202)223-7053
Free: 800-356-6317

Publications: Trusteeship (5832)

Association of Government Accountants
2208 Mt. Vernon Ave.
Alexandria, VA 22301-1314
Phone: (703)684-6931
Fax: (703)548-9367
Free: 800-AGA-7211

Publications: Journal of Government Financial Management (31697)

Association for Gravestone Studies
278 Main St., Ste. 207
Greenfield, MA 01301-3230
Phone: (413)772-0836

Publications: Markers (14221)

Association of Illinois Electric Cooperatives
PO Box 3787
Springfield, IL 62708
Phone: (217)529-5561
Fax: (217)529-5810

Publications: Illinois Rural Electric News (9630)

Association for Information and Image Management International Headquarters
1100 Wayne Ave., Ste. 1100
Silver Spring, MD 20910
Phone: (301)587-8202
Fax: (301)587-2711
Free: 800-477-2446

Publications: INFORM (13727)

Association Internationale des familles Rivard
2120 ave. T.-D. Bouchard
Saint-Hyacinthe, QC, Canada J2S 7Z6

Publications: La Rivardiere (37349)

Association for Investment Management & Research
560 Ray C. Hunt Dr.
PO Box 3668
Charlottesville, VA 22903-0668
Phone: (434)951-5499
Fax: (434)951-5262
Free: 800-247-8132

Publications: CFA Digest (31922)

Association of Iron and Steel Engineers
3 Gateway Center, Ste. 1900
Pittsburgh, PA 15222-1004
Phone: (412)281-6323
Fax: (412)281-4657
Free: 800-966-6323

Publications: AISE Steel Technology (27754)

Association of Legal Administrators
175 E. Hawthorn Pkwy., Ste. 325
Vernon Hills, IL 60061-1428
Phone: (847)816-1212
Fax: (847)816-1213

Publications: ALA News (9727) • Legal Management (9728)

Association of Louisiana Electric Cooperatives, Inc.
10725 Airline Hwy.
Baton Rouge, LA 70816
Phone: (504)293-3450
Fax: (504)296-0924
Free: 800-355-3450

Publications: Louisiana Country (12497)

Association of Manitoba Municipalities
Box 397
Portage La Prairie, MB, Canada R1N 3B7
Phone: (204)857-8666
Fax: (204)856-2370

Publications: Municipal Leader (35283)

Association of Marian Helpers
Eden Hill
Stockbridge, MA 01263
Phone: (413)298-3691
Fax: (413)298-3583
Free: 800-462-7426

Publications: Marian Helper (14567)

Association of Military Surgeons of the U.S. (AMSUS)
9320 Old Georgetown Rd.
Bethesda, MD 20814
Phone: (301)897-8800
Fax: (301)530-5446
Free: 800-761-9320

Publications: Military Medicine (13361)

Association of Missouri Electric Cooperatives, Inc.
PO Box 1645
PO Box 1645
Jefferson City, MO 65102
Phone: (573)635-6857
Fax: (573)635-2314

Publications: Rural Missouri (17132)

L'Association Nationale des Camionneurs Artisans Inc.
670 Bouvier St., Ste. 235
Quebec, QC, Canada G2K 1A7
Phone: (418)623-7923
Fax: (418)623-0448

Publications: L'Ancai, La Voix du Vrac (37280)

Association of Naval Aviation, Inc.
2550 Huntington Ave, No. 201
Alexandria, VA 22303-1400
Phone: (703)960-2490
Fax: (703)960-4490

Publications: Wings of Gold (31753)

Association for Nonprofit Architectural Fieldwork
1326 11th Ave. SE
Calgary, AB, Canada T2G 0Z5
Phone: (403)266-5827

Publications: Onsite Review (34652)

Association of Ontario Land Surveyors
1043 McNicoll Ave.
Toronto, ON, Canada M1W 3W6
Phone: (416)491-9020
Fax: (416)491-2576
Free: 800-268-0718

Publications: The Ontario Land Surveyor (36683)

Association des Optometristes du Quebec
1265 Berri St., Ste. 740
Montreal, QC, Canada H2L 4X4
Phone: (514)288-6272
Fax: (514)288-7071

Publications: L'Optometriste (37198)

Association of Partners for Public Lands
2401 Blueridge Ave., Ste. 303
Wheaton, MD 20902
Phone: (301)946-9475
Fax: (301)946-9478

Publications: Psychiatric Services (13781)

Association for Politics and the Life Sciences
Political Science Dept.
Utah State University
Logan, UT 84322-0725
Phone: (435)797-8104
Fax: (435)797-3751

Publications: Politics and the Life Sciences (13437)

Association for Pre- and Perinatal Psychology and Health (APPPAH)
340 Colony Rd.
Geyserville, CA 95441
Phone: (707)857-4041
Fax: (707)857-4042

Publications: The Pre- & Perinatal Psychology Journal (7435)

Association for Preservation Technology International
4513 Lincoln Ave.
Suite 213
Lisle, IL 60532
Phone: (630)241-3100
Fax: (630)241-0142

Publications: Association for Preservation Technology (19982)

Association for the Preservation of Virginia Antiquities (APVA)
204 W. Franklin St.
Richmond, VA 23220-5012
Phone: (804)648-1889
Fax: (804)775-0802

Publications: The Journal of the Jamestown Rediscovery Center (32441)

Association of Professional Directors of YMCAs in the U.S.
Kendall & Co.
4A Damonmill Sq.
Concord, MA 01742
Phone: (978)369-6393
Fax: (978)371-7117

Publications: Perspective (14148)

Association of Professional Engineers, Geologists, and Geophysicists of Alberta
1500 Scotia One
10060 Jasper Ave.
Edmonton, AB, Canada T5J 4A2
Phone: (780)426-3990
Fax: (780)426-1877
Free: 800-661-7020

Publications: The PEGG (34724)

The Association of Professional Engineers and Geoscientists of British Columbia
200-4010 Regent St.
Burnaby, BC, Canada V5C 6N2
Phone: (604)430-8035
Fax: (604)430-8085
Free: 888-430-8035

Publications: Innovation (34902)

Association of Progressive Rental Organizations
1504 Robinhood Trail
Austin, TX 78703
Phone: (512)794-0095
Fax: (512)794-0097
Free: 800-204-APRO

Publications: Progressive Rentals (29799)

Association for Promotion of Jewish Secularism, Inc.
22 E. 17th St., Ste. 601
New York, NY 10003-1919
Phone: (212)924-5740
Fax: (212)414-2227

Publications: Jewish Currents (21962)

Association for Psychohistory
140 Riverside Dr., Ste. 14H
New York, NY 10024
Phone: (212)799-2294
Fax: (212)799-1728

Publications: The Journal of Psychohistory (22168)

Association for Quality and Participation
Executive Bldg., Ste. 200
2368 Victory Pkwy.
Cincinnati, OH 45206
Phone: (513)381-1959
Fax: (513)381-0070
Free: 800-733-3310

Publications: The Journal for Quality and Participation (24808)

Association de la construction du Quebec
7400, Boulevard les Galeries d'Anjou, Bureau 205
Anjou, QC, Canada H1M 3M2
Phone: (514)354-0609
Fax: (514)354-8292

Publications: Construire (36937)

Association Quebecoise des Loisirs Folkloriques
4545 ave. Pierre Coubertin
C.P. 1000, Sta. M
Montreal, QC, Canada H1V 3R2
Phone: (514)252-3022
Fax: (514)251-8038

Publications: Folk-Lore (37117)

Association of Record Managers and Administrators
4200 Somerset Dr, Ste. 215
Prairie Village, KS 66208
Phone: (913)341-3808
Fax: (913)341-3742
Free: 800-422-2762

Publications: Information Management Journal (29272)

The Association of School Business Officials International
11401 N. Shore Dr.
Reston, VA 20190-4200
Phone: (703)478-0405
Fax: (703)478-0205

Publications: Journal of Education Finance (8196)

Association of Schools & Colleges of Optometry
6110 Exec. Blvd., No. 510
Rockville, MD 20852
Phone: (301)231-5944
Fax: (301)770-1828

Publications: Optometric Education (13691)

The Association for Services Management International
1342 Colonial Blvd., Ste. 25
Fort Myers, FL 33907
Phone: (239)275-7887
Fax: (239)275-0794
Free: 800-333-9786

Publications: Sbusiness (6097)

Association for the Sociological Study of Jewry
7605 Old York Rd.
Melrose Park, PA 19027
Phone: (215)635-7300
Fax: (215)635-7320

Publications: Contemporary Jewry (27245)

Association for the Sociology of Religion
3520 Wiltshire Dr.
Holiday, FL 34691-1239
Phone: (727)844-5990
Fax: (727)844-7332

Publications: Sociology of Religion (35397)

Association of Students of M.S.U., Billings
1500 University Dr.
Billings, MT 59101-0298
Phone: (406)657-2194
Fax: (406)657-2191

Publications: The Retort (17733)

Association for the Study of Afro-American Life and History
7961 Eastern Ave., Ste. 301
Silver Spring, MD 20910
Phone: (301)587-5900
Fax: (301)587-5915

Publications: Journal of Negro History (13732)

Association for the Study of Humor
Department of English
St. Louis University
3800 Lindell
St. Louis, MO 63108
Phone: (314)977-3068
Fax: (314)977-1514

Publications: Thalia (17523)

Association for Symbolic Logic
Vassar College
124 Raymond Ave.
Box 742
Poughkeepsie, NY 12604
Phone: (845)437-7080
Fax: (845)437-7830

Publications: The Bulletin of Symbolic Logic (13868) • The Journal of Symbolic Logic (23147)

Association for Systems Management
1903 David Ave.
Cleveland, OH 44134-6820
Phone: (216)243-6900
Fax: (216)234-2930

Publications: Journal of Systems Management (24917)

Association of Teachers of Technical Writing
Dept. of Rhetoric
University of Minnesota
64 Classroom Office Bldg.
1994 Buford Ave.
St. Paul, MN 55108
Phone: (612)624-9729
Fax: (612)624-3617

Publications: Technical Communication Quarterly (16410)

Association of Third World Studies, Inc.
PO Box 1232
Americus, GA 31709
Phone: (229)931-2078
Fax: (229)931-2960

Publications: Journal of Third World Studies (6922)

Association Trends Publications
3327 Duluth Hwy., Ste. 201
Duluth, GA 30096-3339
Phone: (770)495-7702
Fax: (770)495-7703

Publications: Shuttle Spindle & Dyepot (7257)

Association of Trial Lawyers of America
1050 31st. St. NW
Washington, DC 20007
Phone: (202)965-3500
Fax: (202)965-0030
Free: 800-424-2725

Publications: TRIAL (5831)

Association for Tropical Lepidotera
Box 141210
Gainesville, FL 32614-1210
Phone: (352)372-3505
Fax: (352)373-3249

Publications: Holarctic Lepidoptera (6143) • Tropical Lepidoptera (6159)

Association of the U.S. Army (AUSA)
2425 Wilson Blvd.
Arlington, VA 22201
Phone: (703)841-4300

Publications: ARMY Magazine (31780)

Association of Universities and Colleges of Canada
350 Albert St., Ste. 600
Ottawa, ON, Canada K1R 1B1
Phone: (613)563-1236
Fax: (613)563-9745

Publications: University Affairs (Affaires Universitaires) (36278)

The Association for Work Process Improvement
185 Devonshire St, Ste. 770
Boston, MA 02110
Phone: (617)426-1167
Fax: (617)521-8675
Free: 800-99T-AWPI

Publications: Today Magazine (13070)

Association for Worksite Health Promotion
60 Revere Dr., No. 500
Northbrook, IL 60062
Phone: (847)480-9574
Fax: (847)480-9282

Publications: AWHP's Worksite Health (9312)

Associations Publications, Inc.
PO Box 2755
Cordova, TN 38088
Phone: (901)751-1698
Fax: (901)751-9856

Publications: Shelter (29152)

ASTED Inc.
3414, avenue du Parc Ste. 202
Montreal, QC, Canada H2X 2H5
Phone: (514)281-5012
Fax: (514)281-8219

Publications: Documentation et Bibliotheques (37110)

Astorian Budget Publishing Co.
PO Box 210
Astoria, OR 97103
Phone: (503)325-3211
Fax: (503)325-6573

Publications: The Daily Astorian (26224)

Astronomical Society of the Pacific
390 Ashton Ave.
San Francisco, CA 94112
Phone: (415)337-1100
Fax: (415)337-5205
Free: 800-335-2624

Publications: Mercury (3390)

The Astrophysical Journal
Steward Observatory
933 N. Cherry Ave.
Tucson, AZ 85721
Phone: (520)621-5145
Fax: (520)621-5153

Publications: Astrophysical Journal Supplement Series (936)

ASU Travel Guide
1525 Francisco Blvd. E
San Rafael, CA 94901
Phone: (415)459-0300
Fax: (415)459-0494

Publications: ASU Travel Guide (3598)

At the Park
PO Box 597783
Chicago, IL 60659-7783
Phone: (773)465-4880
Fax: (773)465-0084

Publications: At the Park (8278)

Atascadero News
PO Box 6068
Atascadero, CA 93423
Phone: (805)466-2585
Fax: (805)466-2714

Publications: Atascadero News (1435)

The Atchison County Mail
300 S Main St.
PO Box 40
Rock Port, MO 64482-0040
Phone: (660)744-6245
Fax: (660)744-2645

Publications: The Atchison County Mail (17377)

Atchison Daily Globe
1015-25 Main St.
PO Box 247
Atchison, KS 66002
Phone: (913)367-0583
Fax: (913)367-7531
Free: 800-748-7615

Publications: Atchison Daily Globe (11345)

Athen Review
PO Box 32
Athens, TX 75751
Phone: (903)675-5626
Fax: (903)675-9450

Publications: The Advertiser (29745)

Athens News Courier
410 W Green St.
PO Box 670
Athens, AL 35611-2518
Phone: (256)232-2720
Fax: (256)233-7753
Free: 800-844-5480

Publications: Athens News Courier (27)

Athens News Inc.
PO Box 543
Athens, OH 45701
Phone: (740)594-8219
Fax: (740)592-5695

Publications: The Athens News (24629)

Athletes in Action
651 Taylor Dr.
Xenia, OH 45385
Phone: (937)352-1000
Fax: (937)352-1091

Publications: Athletes in Action (25685)

Athletic Business Publications, Inc.
4130 Lien Rd.
Madison, WI 53704
Phone: (608)249-0186
Fax: (608)249-1153
Free: 800-722-8764

Publications: AQUA Magazine (33921) • Hardwood Floors (33945)

Athletics Magazine
1185 Eglinton Ave. E., Ste. 302
Toronto, ON, Canada M3C 3C6
Phone: (416)426-7215
Fax: (416)426-7358

Publications: Athletics Magazine (36465)

Athol Press
225 Exchange St.
Athol, MA 01331
Phone: (978)249-3535
Fax: (978)249-9630

Publications: Athol Daily News (13824)

Atikokan Printing (1994) Ltd.
109 Main Ste.
PO Box 220
Atikokan, ON, Canada P0T 1C0
Phone: (807)597-2731
Fax: (807)597-6103

Publications: The Atikokan Progress (35639)

The Atkins Chronicle
204 Ave. One N.E.
PO Box 188
Atkins, AR 72823
Phone: (479)641-7161
Fax: (479)641-1604

Publications: Chronicle (1037)

Atkinson County Citizen, Inc.
PO Box 398
Pearson, GA 31642
Phone: (912)422-3824
Fax: (912)422-6050

Publications: Atkinson County Citizen (7482)

The Atkinson Graphic
207 E State St.
PO Box 159
Atkinson, NE 68713
Phone: (402)925-5411

Publications: The Atkinson Graphic (17938)

The Atlanta Citizens Journal
PO Box 1188
Atlanta, TX 75551
Phone: (903)796-3655
Fax: (903)796-3294

Publications: Citizens Journal (29748)

Atlanta Daily World
145 Auburn Ave. NE
Atlanta, GA 30303
Phone: (404)659-1110

Publications: Atlanta Daily World (6968)

Atlanta Historical Society, Inc.
130 W Paces Ferry Rd.
Atlanta, GA 30305
Phone: (404)814-4085
Fax: (404)814-2041

Publications: Atlanta History Center (6969)

The Atlanta Inquirer
947 Martin Luther King Jr. Dr. NW
Atlanta, GA 30314
Phone: (404)523-6086
Fax: (404)523-6088

Publications: The Atlanta Inquirer (6971)

The Atlanta Journal and Constitution
72 Marietta St. NW
PO Box 4689
Atlanta, GA 30303
Phone: (404)577-5772
Fax: (404)526-5746
Free: 800-846-6672

Publications: The Atlanta Journal and Constitution (6972) • Gwinnett Extra (7461)

The Atlanta Metro
4405 Mall Blvd., No. 521
Union City, GA 30291
Phone: (770)969-7711
Fax: (770)969-7811

Publications: The Atlanta Metro (7613)

Atlanta Parent, Inc.
2346 Perimeter Park Dr., Ste. 101
Atlanta, GA 30341
Phone: (770)454-7599
Fax: (770)454-7699

Publications: Atlanta Parent (6973)

The Atlanta Pride Committee
57 Executive Park S., Ste. 380
Atlanta, GA 30329
Phone: (404)929-0071
Fax: (404)929-0056

Publications: Southern Voice (7045)

Atlanta University
223 James P. Brawley Drive SW
Atlanta, GA 30314
Phone: (404)880-8903

Publications: Clark Atlanta University Magazine (6986)

Atlanta University Center
PO Box 3191
Atlanta, GA 30302
Phone: (404)523-6136
Fax: (404)523-5467

Publications: AUC Digest (6975)

The Atlanta Voice
633 Pryor St. SW
Box 92405
Atlanta, GA 30314-0405
Phone: (404)524-6426
Fax: (404)523-7853

Publications: The Atlanta Voice (6974)

Atlantic Co-operative Publishers
123 Halifax St.
Moncton, NB, Canada E1C 8N5
Phone: (506)858-6614
Fax: (506)858-6615

Publications: The Atlantic Co-operator (35411)

Atlantic Communications of Georgia, Inc.
315 N Camellia Blvd.
PO Box 899
Fort Valley, GA 31030
Fax: (912)232-8666
Free: 800-236-0060

Publications: Fort Valley Herald (7286)

Atlantic Communications, L.L.C.
1635 W. Alabama
Houston, TX 77006-4196
Phone: (713)529-1616
Fax: (713)523-7804
Free: 800-654-1480

Publications: Offshore Engineer (30514)

Atlantic Control States Beverage Journal, Inc.
3 Twelfth St.
Wheeling, WV 26003
Phone: (304)232-7620
Fax: (304)233-1236

Publications: Atlantic Control States Beverage Journal (33500)

Atlantic County Newspaper Group
115 12th St.
PO Box 596
Hammonton, NJ 08037
Phone: (609)641-3100
Fax: (609)567-2249
Free: 800-489-4464

Publications: Egg Harbor News (18863) • Mainland Journal (18865)

Atlantic County Weekly Newspaper Group
115 12th St.
PO Box 596
Hammonton, NJ 08037
Phone: (609)641-3100
Fax: (609)646-0561
Free: 800-489-4464

Publications: Atlantic County Record (18862)

Atlantic Economic Society
4949 W Pine Blvd., 2nd Fl.
St. Louis, MO 63108-1431
Phone: (314)454-0100
Fax: (314)454-9109

Publications: Atlantic Economic Journal (17417) • International Advances in Economic Research (17446)

Atlantic Geoscience Society
Box 116
Acadia University
Wolfville, NS, Canada B0P 1X0
Phone: (902)585-1276
Fax: (902)585-1816

Publications: Atlantic Geology (35623)

Atlantic Information Services, Inc.
1100 17th St. NW, No. 300
Washington, DC 20036
Phone: (202)775-9008
Fax: (202)331-9542
Free: 800-521-4323

Publications: State Health Monitor (5804)

The Atlantic Monthly Co.
77 N. Washington St.
Boston, MA 02114
Phone: (617)854-7700
Fax: (617)854-7876

Publications: The Atlantic Monthly (13851)

Atlantic News-Telegraph
410 Walnut St.
PO Box 230
Atlantic, IA 50022
Phone: (712)243-2624
Fax: (712)243-4988

Publications: Atlantic News-Telegraph (10610)

Atlantic Progress
1660 Hollis St., Ste. 603
Halifax, NS, Canada B3J 1V7
Phone: (902)494-0999
Fax: (902)494-0997

Publications: Atlantic Progress Magazine (35559)

Atlantic Provinces Library Association (APLA)
Dalhousie University
School of Library and Information Studies
Halifax, NS, Canada B3H 4H8
Phone: (902)424-5264
Fax: (902)542-2128

Publications: APLA Bulletin (35557)

Atlantic Provinces Trucking Association
266 Dieppe Blvd
Dieppe, NB, Canada E1A 6P8
Phone: (506)855-2782
Fax: (506)853-7424

Publications: Atlantic Trucking (36466)

Atlantic Publication Group, Inc.
PO Box 30007
Charleston, SC 29417-0007
Phone: (803)747-0025
Fax: (803)744-0816

Publications: Commerce Magazine (28512)

Atlantic Salmon Federation
PO Box 5200
St. Andrews, NB, Canada E5B 3S8
Phone: (506)529-4581
Fax: (506)529-4438

Publications: Atlantic Salmon Journal (35429)

Atlantic Snowmobiler Publishing Inc.
527 Beaverbrook Ct., Ste. 510
Fredericton, NB, Canada E3B 1X6
Phone: (506)444-6489
Fax: (506)444-6453
Free: 888-661-7469

Publications: Atlantic Snowmobiler (35390)

ATQ
University of Rhode Island
English Department
Kingston, RI 02881
Phone: (401)874-2576
Fax: (401)874-2580

Publications: ATQ (28358)

Attica Independent
115 N Main
Attica, KS 67009
Phone: (620)254-7660

Publications: Attica Independent (11347)

Aubrey Daniels International
3531 Habersham at Northlake
Tucker, GA 30084-4009
Phone: (770)493-5080
Fax: (770)493-5095

Publications: Performance Management Ezine (7611)

Auburn Bulletin
PO Box 3240
Auburn, AL 36831-3240
Phone: (334)821-7150
Fax: (334)887-0037

Publications: The Auburn Bulletin (38)

Auburn Citizen
110 N 5th St.
Auburn, IL 62615
Phone: (217)438-6155
Fax: (217)438-6156

Publications: Auburn Citizen (8032)

Auburn Journal
1030 High St.
PO Box 5910
Auburn, CA 95603-4707
Phone: (530)885-5656
Fax: (530)887-1231

Publications: Auburn Journal (1436)

Auburn Newspapers
PO Box 250
Auburn, NE 68305
Phone: (402)274-3185
Fax: (402)274-3273

Publications: Auburn Press-Tribune (17939) • Nemaha County Herald (17940)

Auburn Publishers, Inc.
25 Dill St.
Auburn, NY 13021
Phone: (315)253-5311
Fax: (315)253-6031
Free: 800-878-5311

Publications: The Citizen (20105)

Auburn University
B-100 Foy Union Bldg.
Auburn, AL 36849
Phone: (334)844-4130
Fax: (334)844-9114

Publications: The Auburn Plainsman (40)

Auburn University
9088 Haley Center
Auburn, AL 36849
Phone: (334)844-9088
Fax: (334)844-9027

Publications: Southern Humanities Review (45)

Auburn University
3084 Haley Ctr.
Auburn, AL 36849-5218
Phone: (334)844-5793
Fax: (334)844-5785

Publications: Professional Educator (44)

Auburn University
6030 Haley Center
Auburn University, AL 36849

Publications: Bulletin of the Comediantes (49)

Auburn University Alumni Association
317 S. College St.
Auburn University
Auburn, AL 36849-5150
Phone: (334)844-2586
Fax: (334)844-1477

Publications: Auburn Magazine (39)

Auburn University at Montgomery
PO Box 244023
Montgomery, AL 36124-4023
Phone: (334)244-3561
Fax: (334)244-3792

Publications: Southern Business & Economic Journal (377)

Audio Amateur Corp., Inc.
PO Box 876
Peterborough, NH 03458-0876
Phone: (603)924-9464
Fax: (603)924-9467
Free: 888-924-9465

Publications: audioXpress (18617)

Audio Engineering Society
60 E 42nd St., Rm. 2520
New York, NY 10165-2520
Phone: (212)661-8528
Fax: (212)682-0477

Publications: Journal of the Audio Engineering Society (22003)

AudioFile
37 Silver St.
Box 109
Portland, ME 04112-0109
Phone: (207)774-7563
Fax: (207)775-3744
Free: 800-506-1212

Publications: AudioFile (13005)

AudioVideo International
275 Madison Ave.
New York, NY 10016
Phone: (212)682-3755
Fax: (212)682-2730

Publications: AudioVideo International (21271)

Audubon County Newspapers
301 Broadway
PO Box 247
Audubon, IA 50025-0247
Phone: (712)563-2661
Fax: (712)563-3118
Free: 800-798-2635

Publications: Audubon County Advocate Journal (10614)

Aufbau Trust
2121 Broadway
New York, NY 10023
Phone: (212)873-7400
Fax: (212)496-5736
Free: 800-215-9948

Publications: AUFBAU - The Transatlantic Jewish Paper (21273)

Augsburg Fortress, Publishers
100 S. Fifth St., Ste. 700
PO Box 1209
Minneapolis, MN 55440-1209
Phone: (612)330-3300
Fax: (612)330-3583
Free: 800-426-0115

Publications: The Lutheran (8473) • Lutheran Partners (8474) • Lutheran Woman Today (16095)

August Home Publishing
2200 Grand Ave.
Des Moines, IA 50312
Phone: (515)282-7000
Fax: (515)283-2003
Free: 800-311-3991

Publications: Cuisine (10779) • Garden Gate (10786) • ShopNotes (10808) • Woodsmith (10816) • Workbench (10817)

Augusta Area Times
PO Box 465
Augusta, WI 54722
Phone: (715)286-2655
Fax: (715)597-2705

Publications: Augusta Area Times (33559)

The Augusta Chronicle
News Bldg.
725 Broad St.
PO Box 1928
Augusta, GA 30903
Phone: (706)724-0851
Fax: (706)722-7403

Publications: The Augusta Chronicle (7096)

Augusta Daily Gazette
204 E 5th St.
PO Box 9
Augusta, KS 67010
Phone: (316)775-2218
Fax: (316)775-3220

Publications: Augusta Daily Gazette (11350)

The Augusta Focus
1143 Lenny Walker Blvd.
PO Box 10112
Augusta, GA 30903
Phone: (706)724-7855
Fax: (706)724-6969
Free: 800-531-0542

Publications: Augusta Focus (7097)

Augusta Historical Society
PO Box 686
Staunton, VA 24402
Phone: (540)248-4151

Publications: Augusta Historical Bulletin (32553)

Augustana College
639 38th St.
Rock Island, IL 61201
Phone: (309)794-7000
Fax: (309)794-7422

Publications: Augustana College Magazine (9516) • Augustana Observer (9517)

Augustana College
29th & Summit
Sioux Falls, SD 57197
Phone: (605)274-0770
Fax: (605)336-4999

Publications: Augustana Mirror (28961)

AUPELF - UREF
B.P. 400, succ. Cote-des-Neiges
Montreal, QC, Canada H3S 2S7
Phone: (514)343-7232
Fax: (514)343-2107

Publications: Universites (37232)

The Aurora
500 Vanier Ave.
Box 423
Labrador City, NL, Canada A2V 2K7
Phone: (709)944-3239
Fax: (709)944-2958

Publications: The Aurora (35469)

The Aurora Advertiser
226 West Church
PO Box 509
Aurora, MO 65605
Phone: (417)678-2115
Fax: (417)678-2117

Publications: The Aurora Advertiser (16894)

Aurora Rising
PO Box 33459
Decatur, GA 30033
Phone: (404)315-8040
Fax: (404)315-8040
Free: 800-368-9026

Publications: Aurora Rising (7234)

Aurora University
347 S. Gladstone Ave.
Aurora, IL 60506
Phone: (630)892-6431
Fax: (630)844-5463

Publications: Aurora Borealis (8039)

Austin Business Journal, Inc.
111 Congress Ave., Ste. 750
Austin, TX 78701
Phone: (512)494-2500
Fax: (512)494-2525

Publications: Austin Business Journal (29756)

Austin Chronicle
PO Box 49066
Austin, TX 78765
Phone: (512)454-5766
Fax: (512)458-6910

Publications: Austin Chronicle (29757)

Austin County Publishing Co.
PO Box 98
Bellville, TX 77418
Phone: (409)865-3131
Fax: (409)865-3132

Publications: Times (29914)

Austin Daily Herald
310 Second St. NE
PO Box 578
Austin, MN 55912-0578
Phone: (507)433-8851
Fax: (507)437-8644

Publications: Austin Daily Herald (15723)

Austin Genealogical Society
Box 1507
Austin, TX 78767-1507

Publications: Austin Genealogical Society Quarterly (29758)

Austin-Healey Club
PO Box 6197
San Jose, CA 95150
Phone: (408)541-9608
Fax: (408)541-9320

Publications: Austin-Healey Magazine (3827)

Austin Peay State University
PO Box 4634
Clarksville, TN 37044-0001
Phone: (931)221-7376
Fax: (931)221-7377

Publications: The All State (29114)

Auto Merchandising News
2370 North Ave., No. 2C
Bridgeport, CT 06604-2326
Phone: (203)335-6181
Fax: (203)335-6222

Publications: Auto Merchandising News (4710)

Auto News of America
1075 Bellevune NE, Ste. 606
Bellevue, WA 98004
Phone: (425)455-4481
Fax: (425)462-1163

Publications: Auto News of America (32663)

Auto Revista
14330 Midway Rd., Ste. 202
Dallas, TX 75244
Phone: (972)386-0040
Fax: (972)386-4255
Free: 877-386-0092

Publications: Auto Revista (30125)

Autograph Press
PO Box 803
Lorton, VA 22199
Phone: (703)339-1043

Publications: Journal of the Lincoln Assassination (32198)

Autograph Times
12213 W Bell Rd.
Suite 212
Surprise, AZ 85374
Phone: (623)544-4037
Fax: (623)214-5419
Free: 877-860-0349

Publications: Autograph Times (899)

Automatic Machining
1066 Gravel Rd., Ste. 201
Webster, NY 14580
Phone: (585)787-0820
Fax: (585)787-0868
Free: 800-610-6950

Publications: Automatic Machining (23526)

Automatism Press
PO Box 12308
San Francisco, CA 94112

Publications: Ongaku Otaku (3409)

Automedia
55 S. 11th St.
PO Box 568
Brooklyn, NY 11211-0568
Phone: (718)963-2603
Fax: (718)963-2603

Publications: Semiotext (20347)

Automobile Club of New York
1415 Kellum Pl.
Garden City, NY 11530-1690
Phone: (516)873-2249
Fax: (516)873-2355

Publications: Car & Travel Monthly (20635)

Automobile Quarterly
137 East Market St.
New Albany, IN 47150
Phone: (812)948-2886
Fax: (812)948-2816
Free: (866)838-2886
Telex: aqspec@fast.net

Publications: Automobile Quarterly (10338)

Automobile of S. California
3333 Fairview Rd., A327
Costa Mesa, CA 92626
Phone: (714)885-2376
Fax: (714)885-2335

Publications: Avenues (1772) • Westways (1781)

Automotive Aftermarket Industry Association
4600 East-West Hwy., Ste. 300
Bethesda, MD 20814-3415
Phone: (301)654-6664
Fax: (301)654-3299

Publications: Aftermarket Insider (13296)

Automotive Auction Publishing, Inc.
1713 Ardmore Blvd.
Pittsburgh, PA 15221
Phone: (412)242-3900
Fax: (412)242-7033

Publications: Automotive Market Report (27760)

Automotive Contact
PO Box 517
Terre Haute, IN 47808

Publications: Automotive Contact (10484)

Automotive Counseling & Publishing Co.
PO Box 46937
Seattle, WA 98146-0937
Phone: (206)935-3336
Fax: (206)937-9732
Free: 800-850-9288

Publications: Northwest Motor (32994)

Automotive Counseling & Publishing Co., Inc.
450 Lincoln St., Ste. 110
Denver, CO 80203-3459
Phone: (303)765-4664
Fax: (303)765-4650
Free: 800-530-8557

Publications: Parts & People (4347)

Automotive Industry Action Group (AIAG)
26200 Lahser Rd., Ste. 200
Southfield, MI 48034-7100
Phone: (248)358-3570
Fax: (248)358-3253

Publications: ActionLINE Magazine (15541)

The Automotive Messenger
PO Box 527
Hazelwood, MO 63042
Phone: (314)831-4000
Fax: (314)831-3610

Publications: The Automotive Messenger (17095)

Automotive Recyclers Association
3975 Fair Ridge Dr., Ste. 20-N.
Terrace Level North
Fairfax, VA 22033
Phone: (703)385-1001
Fax: (703)385-1494
Free: 888-385-1005

Publications: Automotive Recycling (32007)

Automotive Retailers' Publishing Co., Ltd.
8980 Fraserwood Ct., Unit 1
Burnaby, BC, Canada V5J 5H7
Phone: (604)432-7987
Fax: (604)432-1756

Publications: Collision Quarterly (34895)

Automotive Service Association
PO Box 929
Bedford, TX 76095-0929
Phone: (817)283-6205
Fax: (817)685-0225
Free: 800-272-7467

Publications: AutoInc (29913)

AutoMundo Productions, Inc.
2960 S.W. 8th St., 2nd Fl.
Miami, FL 33135-2827
Phone: (305)541-4198
Fax: (305)541-5138

Publications: Automundo Magazine (6340)

Avance Weekly
1803 Manhattan Ave.
Union City, NJ 07087
Phone: (201)865-1900

Publications: AVANCE Weekly (19689)

L'Avenir de Brome Missisquoi
322A, rue Principale Est
Farnham, QC, Canada J2N 1L7
Phone: (514)293-3138
Fax: (514)293-2093

Publications: L'Avenir de Brome Missisquoi (36994)

Avenue
823 United Nations Plz., Fl. 10
New York, NY 10017-3541
Phone: (212)983-7126
Fax: (212)758-7395

Publications: Avenue (21281)

The Avenue, Inc.
442 Eastern Blvd.
Baltimore, MD 21221
Phone: (410)687-7775
Fax: (410)687-7881

Publications: Avenue News (13127)

Avicultural Advancement Council of Canada
PO Box 1160
Chemainus, BC, Canada V8R 6N4
Phone: (250)246-4803
Fax: (250)246-4912

Publications: Avicultural Journal (34923)

Avid Media Inc.
210-340 Ferrier St.
Markham, ON, Canada L3R 2Z5
Phone: (905)475-8440
Fax: (905)475-9246

Publications: Canadian Gardening (36017) • Canadian Home and Country (36018) • Canadian Home Workshop (36020) • Snow Goer (36032)

Avotaynu Inc.
155 N Washington Ave.
Bergenfield, NJ 07621
Phone: (201)387-7200
Fax: (201)387-2855
Free: 800-286-8296

Publications: Avotaynu (18673)

Avoyelles Publishing Co.
637 Evergreen Hwy.
PO Box 179
Bunkie, LA 71322
Phone: (318)346-7253
Fax: (318)253-7223

Publications: Avoyelles Journal (12541) • The Bunkie Record (12542)

The Aylmer Express, Ltd.
PO Box 160
390 Talbot St. E
Aylmer, ON, Canada N5H 2R9
Phone: (519)773-3126
Fax: (519)773-3147

Publications: The Aylmer Express (35654)

Aynor Journal
PO Box 665
Aynor, SC 29511
Phone: (803)358-2010
Fax: (803)358-0250

Publications: Aynor Journal (28478)

Ayr News Ltd.
PO Box 1173
Ayr, ON, Canada N0B 1E0
Phone: (519)632-7432
Fax: (519)632-7743

Publications: Ayr News (35656)

A.Z. Ltd. Inc.
1415 W Genessee St.
Syracuse, NY 13204
Phone: (315)422-7011
Fax: (315)422-1721

Publications: Syracuse New Times (23428)

Azerbaijan International
PO Box 5217
Sherman Oaks, CA 91413
Phone: (818)785-0077
Fax: (818)997-7337

Publications: Azerbaijan International (3760)

Azle News
321 W. Main
Azle, TX 76020
Phone: (817)270-3340
Fax: (817)270-5300

Publications: Azle News (29886)

Azteca News
PO Box 207
Santa Ana, CA 92702-0207
Phone: (714)972-9912

Publications: Azteca News (3620)

Azure Publishing Inc.
460 Richmond St. W., Ste. 601
Toronto, ON, Canada M5V 1Y1
Phone: (416)203-9674
Fax: (416)203-9842

Publications: Azure Magazine (36469)

Azusa Pacific University
Box 9521, Unit 5504
Azusa, CA 91702-7000
Phone: (626)815-6000
Fax: (626)812-3017

Publications: Clause (1445)

B & B Publishing Co.
500 Brown Blvd.
Bourbonnais, IL 60914
Phone: (815)933-1131
Fax: (815)933-3785

Publications: The Herald/Country Market (8094)

B & L Publishing
11215 Jasper Ave., Ste. 438
Edmonton, AB, Canada T5K 0L5
Fax: (780)414-2044
Free: 888-241-5124

Publications: Sheep Canada (34730)

Charles Babbage Research Centre
PO Box 272, St. Norbert Postal Sta.
Winnipeg, MB, Canada R3V 1L6
Phone: (204)772-2612

Publications: Ars Combinatoria (35310)

Babbitt Publishing
7 Central Blvd.
Babbitt, MN 55706-1129
Phone: (218)827-2363
Fax: (218)827-2363

Publications: Babbitt Weekly News (15726)

Babcox
3550 Embassy Pkwy.
Akron, OH 44333-8318
Phone: (330)670-1234
Fax: (330)670-0874

Publications: BodyShop Business (24575) • Counterman (24578) • Engine Builder (24579) • Import Car (24581) • Tire Review (24590) • Underhood Service (24591)

Babe Ruth League, Inc.
PO Box 5000
Trenton, NJ 08638
Phone: (609)695-1434
Fax: (609)695-2505

Publications: Bullpen (19654)

Babson College
Nichols Hall
Babson Park, MA 02457
Phone: (781)239-5256
Fax: (781)239-5497

Publications: Babson Alumni Magazine (13830)

Baby Diaper Service
15417 204th Ave. SE
Renton, WA 98059
Phone: (425)235-6826
Fax: (425)228-2503

Publications: Northwest Baby & Child (32925)

babysue
PO Box 33369
Decatur, GA 30033
Phone: (404)320-1178

Publications: babysue (7235)

Back Fence Publishing, Inc.
PO Box 756
Chillicothe, OH 45601
Phone: (740)772-2165
Fax: (740)773-7626
Free: 800-718-5727

Publications: Over the Back Fence (24763)

Back of the Yards Journal, Inc.
4642 S Damen
Chicago, IL 60609
Phone: (773)927-7200
Fax: (773)927-7940

Publications: Back of the Yards Journal (8279)

Background Notes on the Countries of the World
Superintendent of Documents, G.
PO Box 371954
Pittsburgh, PA 15250-7954

Publications: Background Notes on the Countries of the World (27762)

BackOffice Magazine
10 Tara Blvd., 5th Fl.
Nashua, NH 03062-2801
Phone: (603)891-9281
Fax: (603)891-9297
Free: 800-225-0555

Publications: BackOffice Magazine (18582)

Backpacker Magazine
33 E. Minor St.
Emmaus, PA 18098
Phone: (610)967-5171
Fax: (610)967-8963

Publications: Backpacker Magazine (26873)

Backwoods Home Magazine, Inc.
PO Box 712
Gold Beach, OR 97444
Phone: (541)247-8900
Fax: (541)247-8600

Publications: Backwoods Home Magazine (26359)

Bad Attitude
PO Box 390110
Cambridge, MA 02139

Publications: Bad Attitude (14040)

The Baffler
PO Box 378293
Chicago, IL 60637
Phone: (773)493-0413

Publications: The Baffler Magazine (8280)

Baikar Association, Inc.
755 Mt. Auburn St.
Watertown, MA 02472
Phone: (617)924-4420
Fax: (617)924-3860

Publications: The Armenian Mirror-Spectator (14610)

The Bainbridge Post-Searchlight, Inc.
301 N. Crawford St.
PO Box 277
Bainbridge, GA 31717-3612
Phone: (229)246-2827
Fax: (229)246-7665
Free: 800-521-5232

Publications: The Post-Searchlight (7118) • The Post-Searchlight Extra (7119)

Bairdland Broadcasting
1747 E 3rd
Truth or Consequences, NM 87901-2042
Phone: (505)894-3088
Fax: (505)894-3998

Publications: Sierra County Sentinel (19969)

Baker College
1116 W Bristol Rd.
Flint, MI 48507
Phone: (810)766-4390
Fax: (810)766-4399
Free: 800-469-3165

Publications: Journal of Leadership and Organizational Studies (15036)

The Baker County Press
104 S 5th St.
PO Box 598
Macclenny, FL 32063-0598
Phone: (904)259-2400
Fax: (904)259-6502

Publications: The Baker County Press (6316)

Baker Newspaper Group
1901 Westcliff Dr., Ste. 11
Newport Beach, CA 92660
Phone: (949)722-1286
Fax: (949)722-6632

Publications: Newport Beach 714 (2632)

Baker Observer
5240 Groom Rd.
Baker, LA 70714
Phone: (225)775-2315
Fax: (225)774-9212

Publications: Baker Observer (12478)

The Baker Street Journal
550 Ellen St.
Hellertown, PA 18055

Publications: The Baker Street Journal (27037)

Baker & Taylor
1120 Rte. 22E.
Bridgewater, NJ 08807
Phone: (908)541-7000
Free: 800-775-1500

Publications: Books for Growing Minds (18693) • Books and More for Growing Minds (18694) • Forecast (18695) • Hot Picks (18696) • Now Hear This (18697) • Paper Clips (18698) • School Selection Guide (18699) • Spirit (18700) • TopCats! (18702) • Travel Guide (18703)

The Bakersfield Californian
PO Box BIN 440
Bakersfield, CA 93302
Phone: (661)395-7500
Fax: (661)395-7519
Free: 800-404-4949

Publications: The Bakersfield Californian (1447)

Bakersfield News Observer
1219 20th St.
Bakersfield, CA 93301
Phone: (661)324-9466
Fax: (661)324-9472
Free: 800-482-6156

Publications: Bakersfield News Observer (1448)

Bakery, Confectionery, Tobacco Workers and Grain Millers International Union (BCTGM)
10401 Connecticut Ave.
Kensington, MD 20895-3961
Phone: (301)933-8600
Fax: (301)946-8452

Publications: BCTGM News (13590)

Balance Publishing, Inc.
200 Elm St., Ste. 200
Birmingham, MI 48009
Phone: (810)642-7849
Free: 800-287-8888

Publications: Balance (14823)

Balaton Publishing
PO Box 310
Balaton, MN 56115
Phone: (507)734-5421
Fax: (507)734-2316

Publications: Balaton-Press-Tribune (15729)

Bald Knob Banner
PO Box 1480
Bald Knob, AR 72010-1480
Phone: (501)724-0398
Fax: (501)724-6362
Free: 888-515-3255

Publications: Bald Knob Banner (1038)

Balducci Publications
1248 Oak Bark Dr.
St. Louis, MO 63146
Phone: (314)993-1633
Fax: (314)993-1633

Publications: Snicker (17511)

Baldwin-Wallace College
275 Eastland Rd.
Berea, OH 44017-2012
Phone: (440)826-2356
Fax: (440)826-2388

Publications: The Exponent (24676)

Baldwyn News
102 W Main
PO Drawer 130
Baldwyn, MS 38824
Phone: (662)365-3232
Fax: (662)365-7989

Publications: The Baldwyn News (16549)

Bale Communications, Inc.
80 Park Lawn Rd., Ste. 212
Toronto, ON, Canada M8Y 3H8
Phone: (416)252-9400
Fax: (416)252-8002

Publications: Adnews (36461)

Balita Media Inc.
520 E. Wilson Blvd., Ste. 115
Glendale, CA 91206
Phone: (818)552-4503
Fax: (818)550-7635

Publications: Weekend Balita (2013)

Ball Publishing
335 N River St.
Batavia, IL 60510
Phone: (630)208-9080
Fax: (630)208-9350
Free: 888-888-0013

Publications: FloraCulture International Magazine (8052) • Green Profit Magazine (8053) • Grower Talks (8054)

Ball Publishing Co.
5312 Sebring-Warner Rd.
Greenville, OH 45331
Phone: (937)548-3330
Fax: (937)548-3376
Free: 800-548-5312

Publications: The Early Bird (25228)

Ball State University
Teachers College 1008
Muncie, IN 47306
Phone: (765)285-5453
Fax: (765)285-5455

Publications: The Teacher Educator (10329)

Ball State University Daily News
AJ 276
Muncie, IN 47306
Phone: (765)285-8580
Fax: (765)285-8248

Publications: Ball State Daily News (10326)

The Ballinger Ledger
810 Hutchins
Ballinger, TX 76821
Phone: (915)365-3501
Fax: (915)365-5389

Publications: The Ballinger Ledger (29887)

Balloon Life Magazine, Inc.
2336 47th Ave. SW
Seattle, WA 98116-2331
Phone: (206)935-3649
Fax: (206)935-3326

Publications: Balloon Life (32945)

The Baltimore Chronicle
30 W 25th St.
Baltimore, MD 21218
Phone: (410)243-4141

Publications: The Baltimore Chronicle (13130)

Baltimore Magazine
1000 Lancaster St., Ste. 400
Baltimore, MD 21202
Phone: (410)752-4200
Fax: (410)625-0280
Free: 800-935-0838

Publications: Baltimore Magazine (13134)

The Baltimore Sun
501 N. Calvert St.
Baltimore, MD 21278-0001
Phone: (410)332-6000
Fax: (410)752-6049
Free: 800-829-8000

Publications: The Baltimore Sun (13135)

Baltimore Times
2513 N. Charles St.
Baltimore, MD 21218
Phone: (410)366-3900
Fax: (410)243-1627

Publications: Annapolis Times (13124) • Baltimore Times (13136) • Prince George's Times (13239) • Shore Times (13247)

Baltimore's Child
11 Dutton Ct.
Baltimore, MD 21228
Phone: (410)367-5883
Fax: (410)719-9342

Publications: Baltimore's Child (13137)

Balzekas Museum of Lithuanian Culture
6500 S Pulaski Rd.
Chicago, IL 60629-5136
Phone: (773)582-6500
Fax: (773)582-5133

Publications: Lithuanian Museum Review (8467)

BAM Media, Inc.
1351 Apple Dr.
Concord, CA 94518-3700
Phone: (925)934-3700
Fax: (925)946-2985

Publications: BAM Magazine (1750)

Bamboo Ridge Press
PO Box 61781
Honolulu, HI 96839-1781
Phone: (808)626-1481
Fax: (808)626-1481

Publications: Bamboo Ridge (7680)

Bancraft-Whitney Co.
50 California St., 19th Fl.
San Francisco, CA 94111-4624
Fax: (415)732-8792
Free: 800-537-2707

Publications: California Official Reports (3338)

Bancroft Publishing Co.
PO Box 175
Bancroft, IA 50517-0038
Phone: (515)885-2753
Fax: (515)885-2692

Publications: The Bancroft Register (10616)

Bandera Bulletin
Box 697
Bandera, TX 78003
Phone: (830)796-3718
Fax: (830)796-4885

Publications: Bulletin (29888)

Banff Crag & Canyon
201 Bear St.
PO Box 129
Banff, AB, Canada T1L 1H2
Phone: (403)762-2453
Fax: (403)762-5274

Publications: Banff Crag & Canyon (34613)

Bangor Daily News
491 Main St.
PO Box 1329
Bangor, ME 04402-1329
Phone: (207)990-8000
Fax: (207)941-0885
Free: 800-432-7964

Publications: Bangor Daily News (12903)

Bank Administration Institute
1 N. Franklin St., Ste. 1000
Chicago, IL 60606-3421

Publications: Banking Strategies (8281)

Bank & Corporate Governance Law Reporter
1601 Connecticut Ave., NW, No. 602
Washington, DC 20009
Phone: (202)462-5755
Fax: (202)328-2430

Publications: Bank & Corporate Governance Law Reporter (5372)

Bank Marketing Association
1120 Conneticut Ave., NW, Ste. 600
Washington, DC 20036
Phone: (202)663-5268
Fax: (202)828-4540
Free: 800-433-9013

Publications: Bank Marketing (5373)

Bank News Inc.
5115 Roe Blvd., Ste. 200
PO Box 29156
Shawnee Mission, KS 66201
Phone: (913)261-7000
Fax: (913)261-7010
Free: 800-336-1120

Publications: Bank News (11803)

Bankers Digest
9550 Forest Ln., Ste. 125
Dallas, TX 75243-5928
Phone: (214)221-4544
Fax: (214)221-4546

Publications: Bankers Digest (30126)

Banner
407N. Main St.
PO Box 10
St. Elmo, IL 62458
Phone: (618)829-3246
Fax: (618)483-6176

Publications: Banner (9576)

Banner Corp.
PO Box 769
Abbeville, SC 29620
Phone: (864)459-5461
Fax: (864)459-5463

Publications: The Press and Banner (28464)

Banner-Democrat
313 Lake St.
Lake Providence, LA 71254-2688
Phone: (318)559-2750
Fax: (318)559-2750

Publications: Banner-Democrat (12652)

Banner Independent
PO Box 10
Booneville, MS 38829
Phone: (662)728-6214
Fax: (662)728-1636

Publications: Banner Independent (16571)

Banner Journal
409 E Main St.
Black River Falls, WI 54615
Phone: (715)284-4304
Fax: (715)284-4634

Publications: Banner Journal (33591)

Banner-News Publishing Co.
134 S. Washington
Box 100
Magnolia, AR 71753
Phone: (870)234-5130
Fax: (870)234-2551

Publications: Banner-News (1258)

The Banner-Press
103 Walnut St.
PO Box 109
Marble Hill, MO 63764
Phone: (573)238-2821
Fax: (573)238-0020

Publications: The Banner-Press (17262)

The Banner Press Newspaper
1217 Bowie
PO Box 490
Columbus, TX 78934
Phone: (979)732-6243
Fax: (979)732-6245

Publications: The Banner Press Newspaper (30064)

Banner Publications, Inc.
350 N 1st
PO Box 500
Cuba, IL 61427
Phone: (309)785-5058
Fax: (309)785-5050

Publications: Banner Sheep Magazine (8699)

Banner Publishing Co.
109 E Morris St.
PO Box 912
Seymour, TX 76380
Phone: (940)889-2616
Fax: (940)889-3610

Publications: The Baylor County Banner (31102)

Banner Publishing, Inc.
425 Main St.
Bennington, VT 05201
Phone: (802)447-7567
Fax: (802)442-3413

Publications: The Bennington Banner (31497)

Banner Times Publications
PO Box 71
Mason City, IL 62664
Phone: (217)482-3276
Fax: (217)482-3277

Publications: Manito Review (9156)

Baptist Convention of Maryland/Delaware
10255 Old Columbia Rd.
Columbia, MD 21046-1716
Phone: (410)290-5290
Fax: (410)290-6627
Free: 800-466-5290

Publications: BaptistLIFE (13454)

Baptist Courier, Inc.
PO Drawer 2168
Greenville, SC 29602
Phone: (864)232-8736
Fax: (803)232-8488
Free: 888-667-4693

Publications: The Baptist Courier (28621)

Baptist General Conference
2002 S Arlington Heights Rd.
Arlington Heights, IL 60005
Phone: (847)228-0200
Fax: (847)228-5376
Free: 800-323-4215

Publications: The Standard (8026)

Baptist General Convention of Oklahoma
3800 N May Ave.
Oklahoma City, OK 73112-6506
Phone: (405)942-3800
Fax: (405)942-3075

Publications: Baptist Messenger (25954)

The Baptist Message
1223 MacArthur Dr.
Alexandria, LA 71301
Phone: (318)442-7728
Fax: (318)445-8328
Free: 888-442-7760

Publications: Louisiana Baptist Message (LBM) (12459)

Baptist Missionary Association of Arkansas
10712 Interstate 30
PO Box 192208
Little Rock, AR 72219-2208
Phone: (501)565-4601
Fax: (501)565-NEWS

Publications: Baptist Trumpet (1225)

Baptist Progress
PO Box 2085
Waxahachie, TX 75168-2085
Phone: (214)923-0756
Fax: (214)923-2679

Publications: Baptist Progress (31269)

Baptist Standard Publishing Co.
PO Box 660267
Dallas, TX 75266-0267
Phone: (214)630-4571
Fax: (214)638-8535
Free: 800-749-4610

Publications: The Baptist Standard (30127)

Baptist Women's of Ontario & Quebec
414-195 The West Mall
Etobicoke, ON, Canada M9C 5K1
Phone: (416)622-8600
Fax: (416)695-0938

Publications: Link & Visitor (35817)

Pibul Baquirin
PO Box 387
San Martin, CA 95046
Phone: (408)686-1911
Fax: (408)686-1912

Publications: The Filipino Monitor (3582)

Bar Association of Lehigh County
1114 Walnut St.
Allentown, PA 18102-4734
Phone: (610)433-6204
Fax: (610)770-9826

Publications: Lehigh Law Journal (26628)

The Bar Association of Metropolitan St. Louis (BAMSL)
720 Olive St., Ste. 2900
St. Louis, MO 63101-2308
Phone: (314)421-4134
Fax: (314)421-0013

Publications: St. Louis Lawyer (17503)

Bar Association of San Francisco
465 California St., Ste. 1100
San Francisco, CA 94104-1826
Phone: (415)982-1600
Fax: (415)782-2388

Publications: San Francisco Attorney Magazine (3427)

Baraboo News Republic
219 1st St.
PO Box 9
Baraboo, WI 53913
Phone: (608)356-4808
Fax: (608)356-0344
Free: 800-773-4808

Publications: Baraboo News Republic (33562)

Barash Group
403 S. Allen St.
PO Box 77
State College, PA 16804-0077
Phone: (814)238-5051
Fax: (814)238-3415
Free: 800-326-9584

Publications: Town & Gown (28021)

Barber County Index
PO Box 349
Medicine Lodge, KS 67104
Phone: (620)886-5617

Publications: Barber County Index (11649)

Barbour Publishing Co.
113 Church St.
Philippi, WV 26416
Phone: (304)457-2222
Fax: (304)457-2703

Publications: Barbour Democrat (33431)

Bard College
PO Box 5000
Annandale-on-Hudson, NY 12504
Phone: (845)758-7200
Fax: (845)758-7625

Publications: Hudson Valley Regional Review (20060)

The Barefoot Tattler
937 Barefoot Blvd., Ste. B
PO Box 779-176
Barefoot Bay, FL 32976
Phone: (772)664-9381
Fax: (772)664-6236

Publications: The Barefoot Tattler (5915)

Bargain Browser
101 Highland Dr.
PO Box 347
White House, TN 37188
Phone: (615)672-3555
Fax: (615)672-5971

Publications: Bargain Browser (29646)

The Bargain Bulletin
306 W Washington St.
Appleton, WI 54912
Phone: (920)733-3460
Fax: (920)996-7233

Publications: The Bargain Bulletin (33535)

Bargain News L.L.C.
30 Nutmeg Dr.
Trumbull, CT 06611
Phone: (203)377-3000

Publications: The Bargain News (5180)

Bargain Sheet
107 Gerald St.
State College, PA 16801
Phone: (814)237-1900
Fax: (814)237-4036
Free: 800-526-7355

Publications: Bargain Sheet (26694)

The Bark
2810 8th St.
Berkeley, CA 94710
Phone: (510)704-0827
Fax: (510)704-0933

Publications: The Bark (1494)

David W. Barker
1320 2nd St.
PO Box 88
Napa, CA 94559
Fax: (707)226-3707

Publications: The Napa County Record (2610)

Barks Publications Inc.
400 N Michigan Ave., Ste. 900
Chicago, IL 60611-4104
Phone: (312)321-9440
Fax: (312)321-1288

Publications: Electrical Apparatus (8363)

Barnard Bulletin
105 McIntosh Student Ctr.
Barnard College
3009 Broadway
New York, NY 10027-6598
Phone: (212)854-2119
Fax: (212)749-6531

Publications: Barnard Bulletin (21290)

Barnsdall Times
Box 469
Barnsdall, OK 74002
Phone: (918)847-2916
Fax: (918)847-2115

Publications: Barnsdall Times (25753)

The Barnstable Patriot Newspaper, Inc.
4 Barnstable Rd.
PO Box 1208
Hyannis, MA 02601
Phone: (508)771-1427
Fax: (508)790-3997

Publications: The Barnstable Patriot (14249)

Barnwood Press
PO Box 146
Selma, IN 47383
Phone: (765)288-0145
Fax: (765)285-3765

Publications: Barnwood (10447)

Barre Gazette
5 Exchange St.
Barre, MA 01005
Phone: (978)355-4000
Fax: (978)355-6274

Publications: Barre Gazette (13833)

Barreau du Quebec
445 St. Lawrence Blvd.
Montreal, QC, Canada H2Y 3T8
Phone: (514)954-3400
Fax: (514)954-3477
Free: 800-361-8495

Publications: La Revue du Barreau (37152)

Barrhead Leader
PO Box 4520
Barrhead, AB, Canada T7N 1A4
Phone: (403)674-3823
Fax: (403)674-6337

Publications: Barrhead Leader (34614)

The Barrie Examiner, Inc.
16 Bayfield St.
PO Box 370
Barrie, ON, Canada L4M 4T6
Phone: (705)726-6537
Fax: (705)726-7245

Publications: The Barrie Examiner (35658) • The Barrie Examiner This Week (35659)

Barron News Shield
219 E LaSalle
PO Box 100
Barron, WI 54812
Phone: (715)537-3117
Fax: (715)537-3118

Publications: Barron News Shield (33565)

Barrows Co.
116 E 66th St.
New York, NY 10021
Phone: (212)772-1199
Fax: (212)288-7242
Free: 800-227-7697

Publications: Asia & Australasia—Basic Oil Laws & Concession Contracts (21260) • Central American & Caribbean—Basic Oil Laws & Concession Contracts (21389) • Europe—Basic Oil Laws & Concession Contracts (21634) • Middle East—Basic Oil Laws & Concession Contracts (22333) • North Africa—Basic Oil Laws & Concession Contracts (22469) • South America—Basic Oil Laws & Concession Contracts (22765) • South & Central Africa—Basic Oil Laws & Concession Contracts (22766)

Barr's Post Card News
70 S 6th St.
Lansing, IA 52151
Phone: (319)538-4500
Fax: (319)538-4038
Free: 800-397-0145

Publications: Barr's Post Card News (11030)

Barry County Advertiser
904 West St.
PO Box 488
Cassville, MO 65625
Phone: (417)847-4475
Fax: (417)847-4523

Publications: Barry County Advertiser (16964)

Barry, Inc.
PO Box 551
Wilmington, MA 01887-0551
Phone: (978)658-0441
Fax: (978)657-8691

Publications: Property Digest and Economic Development Magazine (14663)

Barry's Bay
41 Bay St.
PO Box 220
Barry's Bay, ON, Canada K0J 1B0
Phone: (613)756-2944
Fax: (613)756-2994

Publications: Barry's Bay This Week (35666)

Barter News
PO Box 3024
Mission Viejo, CA 92690
Phone: (949)831-0607
Fax: (949)831-9378

Publications: Barter News (2547)

Bartlett Newspapers, Inc.
PO Box 34967
Memphis, TN 38184-0967
Phone: (901)388-1500
Fax: (901)386-3157

Publications: The Bartlett Express (29358)

Barton College
College Sta.
Wilson, NC 27893
Phone: (919)237-6585
Fax: (919)237-4957
Free: 800-345-6305

Publications: The Collegiate (24311)

Bartow Communications
7016 Buxton Terr.
Bethesda, MD 20817-4404
Phone: (301)468-7001
Fax: (301)468-7005

Publications: New Homes Register (13363)

Baseball America, Inc.
PO Box 2089
Durham, NC 27702
Phone: (919)682-9635
Fax: (919)682-2880
Free: 800-845-2726

Publications: Baseball America (23809)

The Basement Magazine
39 Setalcott Pl.
Setauket, NY 11733

Publications: The Basement Magazine (23325)

The Basile Weekly
PO Box 578
Basile, LA 70515
Phone: (337)432-6807
Fax: (337)432-6807

Publications: The Basile Weekly (12482)

Basin Publishing Co.
PO Box O
Othello, WA 99344
Phone: (509)488-3342
Fax: (509)488-3345

Publications: The Othello Outlook (32875)

BASS/ESPN Outdoors
5845 Carmichael Rd.
Montgomery, AL 36117-2329
Phone: (334)272-9530
Fax: (334)279-7148

Publications: Bassmaster Magazine (361) • Fishing Tackle Retailer (365) • Guns&Gear (366)

Bassano Publishers
402 1st Ave.
PO Box 780
Bassano, AB, Canada T0J 0B0
Phone: (403)641-3636
Fax: (403)641-3952

Publications: The Bassano Times (34616)

BAST Music Magazine
334 Hyde St., No. 2
San Francisco, CA 94109

Publications: BAST Music Magazine (3328)

Bastrop Newspapers, Inc.
119 E. Hickory
PO Box 311
Bastrop, LA 71221
Phone: (318)281-2691
Fax: (318)283-1699

Publications: Bastrop Daily Enterprise (12483)

Batavia Newspapers Corp.
2 Apollo Dr.
Batavia, NY 14021
Phone: (716)343-8000
Fax: (716)343-2623

Publications: The Drummer Pennysaver (20120) • News (20121)

Bates College Publishing Association
Chase Hall
309 Bates College
Lewiston, ME 04240
Phone: (207)786-6255
Fax: (207)786-6035

Publications: The Bates Student (12975)

Batesville Guard-Record Co., Inc.
258 W. Main St.
Box 2036
Batesville, AR 72501
Phone: (870)793-2383
Fax: (870)793-9268

Publications: Batesville Guard (1040)

Baton Rouge Weekly Press
1283 Rosenwald Rd., Ste. 1
Baton Rouge, LA 70807-4173
Phone: (225)775-2002
Fax: (225)775-4216

Publications: Baton Rouge Weekly Press (12485)

Battelle Communications Office
505 King Ave.
Columbus, OH 43201-2693
Phone: (614)424-5336
Fax: (614)424-3889

Publications: Batelle Solutions Update (25000)

Battle Creek Enterprise
PO Box 70
Battle Creek, NE 68715
Phone: (402)675-5333
Fax: (402)371-0621

Publications: Battle Creek Enterprise (17945)

Battlefords Publishing, Ltd.
892 104 St.
PO Box 1029
North Battleford, SK, Canada S9A 3E6
Phone: (306)445-7261
Fax: (306)445-3223
Free: (866)549-9979

Publications: Mirror (37493) • News-Optimist (37508) • Regional Optimist/Advertiser-Post (37509) • The Riverbend Review (37510) • Sunday Edition News-Optimist (37511)

The Baudette Region
Drawer C
Baudette, MN 56623
Phone: (218)634-1722
Fax: (218)634-1224

Publications: The Baudette Region (15731)

Phyllis J. Bauer, Editor and Publisher
5747 Fieldstone Trl.
McHenry, IL 60050-2283
Phone: (815)385-9626

Publications: Lynn—Linn Lineage Quarterly (9165)

Bauer Publishing Co.
270 Sylvan Ave.
Box 1648
Englewood Cliffs, NJ 07632
Phone: (201)569-6699
Fax: (201)569-6264

Publications: First for Women (18800) • Soap Opera Update (18803)

Baum Publications Ltd.
201 - 2323 Boundary Rd.
Vancouver, BC, Canada V5M 4V8
Phone: (604)291-9900
Fax: (604)291-1906

Publications: Canadian Environmental Protection (35131) • Healthcare Product News (35146) • Heavy Equipment Guide (35147) • Landscaping & Groundskeeping Journal (35152) • Oil & Gas Product News (35154) • Recycling Product News (35163) • Specialty Wood Journal (35168)

The Baxley News-Banner
PO Box 410
Baxley, GA 31515
Phone: (912)367-2468
Fax: (912)367-0277

Publications: The Baxley News-Banner (7123)

The Baxter Bulletin
PO Drawer A
Mountain Home, AR 72653
Phone: (870)425-3133
Fax: (870)425-5091

Publications: The Baxter Bulletin (1285)

Baxter Publishing Co.
310 Dupont St.
Toronto, ON, Canada M5R 1V9
Phone: (416)968-7252
Fax: (416)968-2377

Publications: Canadian Defence Quarterly (Revue Canadienne de Defense) (36496) • Canadian Travel Press (36533) • Rendez-Vous Canada (36727) • Travel Courier (36772)

Bay Area Employment Listings Magazine
PO Box 60935
Sunnyvale, CA 94088
Phone: (408)730-1970

Publications: Employment Listings (3828)

Bay City Newspapers, Inc.
PO Box 2450
Bay City, TX 77404
Phone: (979)245-5555
Fax: (979)244-5908

Publications: The Daily Tribune (29891)

The Bay City Times
311 5th St.
Bay City, MI 48708
Phone: (989)895-8551
Fax: (989)895-5910
Free: 800-875-4444

Publications: The Bay City Times (14802)

Bay Publishing
216 Frankfort St.
PO Box 68
Brooksville, KY 41004
Phone: (606)735-2198
Fax: (606)735-2199

Publications: Bracken County News (11966)

Bay Saint Louis Newspapers
124 Ct. St.
PO Box 2009
Bay St. Louis, MS 39521
Phone: (228)467-5474
Fax: (228)467-0333

Publications: The Sea Coast Echo (16552)

Bay Sports Review
PO Box 4520
Berkeley, CA 94704
Phone: (510)526-3388
Fax: (925)526-3993

Publications: Bay Sports Review (1495)

Bay Windows
631 Tremont St.
Boston, MA 02118-1201
Phone: (617)266-6670
Fax: (617)266-5973

Publications: Bay Windows (13852)

Bayard Press
49 Front St. East, 2nd Fl.
Toronto, ON, Canada M5E 3B1
Phone: (416)340-2700
Fax: (416)340-9769

Publications: Chickadee (36548) • OWL (36693)

The Bayard Transcript
336 Main
PO Box 626
Bayard, NE 69334
Phone: (308)586-1313

Publications: The Bayard Transcript (17946)

Baylor College of Dentistry
3302 Gaston Ave.
Dallas, TX 75246
Phone: (214)828-8214
Fax: (214)828-8906

Publications: Baylor Dental Journal (30129)

Publishers

Baylor University
Waco, TX 76798-8006
Phone: (254)710-4290
Fax: (254)710-2271

Publications: Entrepreneurship Theory and Practice (31246)

Baylor University
PO Box 97330
Waco, TX 76798-7330
Phone: (254)710-1711
Fax: (254)710-1714

Publications: The Lariat (31251)

Bayonne Community News
13 E 21st St.
Bayonne, NJ 07002
Phone: (201)437-2460
Fax: (201)437-7127

Publications: Bayonne Community News (18666)

Bayshore Press, Inc.
PO Box 399
Middletown, NJ 07748
Phone: (732)957-0070
Fax: (732)957-0143

Publications: The Courier (19234)

Baywood Publishing Company Inc.
26 Austin Ave.
PO Box 337
Amityville, NY 11701
Phone: (631)691-1270
Fax: (631)691-1770
Free: 800-638-7819

Publications: Abstracts in Anthropology (20034) • A Current Bibliography on African Affairs (20037) • Imagination, Cognition and Personality (4990) • International Journal of Aging and Human Development (20038) • International Journal of Health Services (20039) • The International Journal of Psychiatry in Medicine (20040) • International Quarterly of Community Health Education (13795) • Journal of Applied Fire Science (20041) • Journal of Collective Negotiations in the Public Sector (20042) • Journal of Drug Education (20043) • Journal of Educational Computing Research (20044) • Journal of Educational Technology Systems (23370) • Journal of Environmental Systems (20045) • Journal of Individual Employment Rights (20046) • Journal of Recreational Mathematics (20047) • Journal of Technical Writing and Communication (20048) • New Solutions (20051) • North American Archaeologist (20052) • OMEGA-Journal of Death and Dying (20053)

BB Gun Magazine
PO Box 5074
Hoboken, NJ 07030

Publications: BB Gun Magazine (18900)

BBS Press Service Inc.
1047-B Gage Blvd.
Topeka, KS 66604
Phone: (785)271-0932
Fax: (785)271-0192

Publications: Hi-Tech Home (11822)

B.C. Bookworld
3516 West 13th Ave.
Vancouver, BC, Canada V6R 2S3
Phone: (604)736-4011
Fax: (604)736-4011

Publications: B.C. Bookworld (35123)

B.C. Decker, Inc.
20 Hughson St. S., 10th Fl.
PO Box 620, LCD 1
Hamilton, ON, Canada L8N 3K7
Phone: (905)522-7017
Fax: (905)522-7839
Free: 800-568-7281

Publications: Biological Therapies in Dentistry (35874) • Healthy Weight Journal (35880) • International Journal of Infectious Diseases (35882) • Journal of the American Academy of Audiology (35883) • Journal of Child Neurology (18201) • Journal of Continuing Education in the Health Professions (35884) • Journal of Esthetic and Restorative Dentistry (35885) • Journal of Travel Medicine (35886) • Physiotherapy Canada (36708) • Seminars in Headache Management (35889)

BC Landscape & Nursery Assn.
101-5830 176A St.
Surrey, BC, Canada V3S 4E3
Phone: (604)574-7772
Fax: (604)574-7773

Publications: Hort West (35108)

B.C. Sport Fishing Magazine
909 Jackson Crescent
New Westminster, BC, Canada V3L 4S1
Fax: (604)683-7716

Publications: B.C. Sport Fishing Magazine (35027)

The Beacher
911 Franklin St.
Michigan City, IN 46360
Phone: (219)879-0088
Fax: (219)879-8070

Publications: The Beacher (10303)

Beacon
Box 366
Cannon Falls, MN 55009
Phone: (507)263-3991

Publications: Beacon (15788) • Cannon Shopper (15789)

Beacon Communications of Rhode Island
1944 Warwick Ave.
Warwick, RI 02889-5000
Phone: (401)732-3100
Fax: (401)732-3110

Publications: Cranston Herald (28332) • East Side Monthly (28449) • Pennysaver (28451) • Warwick Beacon (28453)

The Beacon Herald of Stratford Ltd.
108 Ontario St.
PO Box 430
Stratford, ON, Canada N5A 6T6
Phone: (519)271-2220
Fax: (519)271-1026

Publications: The Beacon Herald (36409) • Marketplace (36410)

The Beacon Hill Times
25 Myrtle St.
Boston, MA 02114
Phone: (617)523-9490
Fax: (617)523-8668

Publications: The Beacon Hill Times (13853)

The Beacon-News
101 S River St.
Aurora, IL 60506
Phone: (630)844-5844
Fax: (630)844-5818
Free: 800-844-5844

Publications: The Beacon-News (8040)

Beacon News Publishing
PO Box 100
Paris, IL 61944
Phone: (217)465-6424
Fax: (217)463-1232
Free: 800-587-5955

Publications: Beacon-News (9399)

Beacon Newspapers
1181 E. John Sims Pkwy.
Niceville, FL 32578
Phone: (850)678-1080
Fax: (850)729-3225

Publications: Bay Beacon (6460) • Beacon Express (6461)

Beacon Newspapers
5 Centre St.
Hempstead, NY 11550-2422
Phone: (516)481-5400

Publications: East Meadow Beacon (20549) • Hempstead Beacon (20728) • Merrick Beacon (21072) • Syosset Tribune (23383) • Uniondale Beacon (23465) • West Hempstead Beacon (23542)

Beacon Newspapers, Inc.
220 Deer Park Ave.
PO Box 670
Babylon, NY 11702
Phone: (516)587-0198

Publications: Photo News (20111)

The Beacon-Observer
PO Box 330
Overton, NE 68863
Phone: (308)987-2451
Fax: (308)987-2452

Publications: The Beacon-Observer (18242)

The Beacon Publishing Company
597 Valley Rd.
PO Box 1887
Clifton, NJ 07015-1887
Phone: (973)279-8845
Fax: (973)279-2265

Publications: The Beacon (18751)

The Bear News Publishing, Inc.
79 Front St.
PO Box 660
Hornepayne, ON, Canada P0M 1Z0
Phone: (807)868-2701
Fax: (807)868-3337

Publications: Bear News (35916)

Beard Group, Inc.
PO Box 4250
Frederick, MD 21705
Phone: (240)629-3300
Fax: (240)629-3360

Publications: Troubled Company Prospector (13523) • Troubled Company Reporter (13524)

Beardsley Publishing Corp.
45 Main St. N.
PO Box 644
Woodbury, CT 06798
Phone: (203)263-0888
Fax: (203)266-0452

Publications: Ski Area Management (5236)

Beardstown Newspapers, Inc.
1210 Wall St.
Beardstown, IL 62618
Phone: (217)323-1010
Fax: (217)323-5402

Publications: Cass County Star-Gazette (8055) • Star Gazette Extra (8056)

Bearhouse Publishing
14781 Memorial Dr., 10
Houston, TX 77079
Phone: (281)920-1795

Publications: Lucidity (30504)

Beatrice Daily Sun
200 N 7th St.
PO Box 847
Beatrice, NE 68310-3916
Phone: (402)223-5233
Fax: (402)228-3571

Publications: Beatrice Daily Sun (17947)

The Beaufort Gazette
1556 Salem Rd.
PO Box 399
Beaufort, SC 29901
Phone: (843)524-3183
Fax: (843)524-8728

Publications: The Beaufort Gazette (28487)

Beaumont Chamber of Commerce
1110 Park St.
PO Box 3150
Beaumont, TX 77701
Phone: (409)838-6581
Fax: (409)833-6718

Publications: Metropolitan Beaumont (29899)

Beaumont Printing Co.
PO Box 2140
Nederland, TX 77627
Phone: (409)722-0479
Fax: (409)729-7626

Publications: Mid County Chronicle (30857)

Beauport Express
3333, rue du Carrefour, Ste. 212
Beauport, QC, Canada G1C 5R9
Phone: (418)663-6131
Fax: (418)663-3469

Publications: Beauport Express (36948)

Beaver County Times
400 Fair Ave.
PO Box 400
Beaver, PA 15009-0400
Phone: (412)775-3200
Fax: (412)775-7212

Publications: Beaver County Times (26684)

The Beaver Press
40 E Ctr. St.
PO Box 351
Beaver, UT 84713
Phone: (435)438-2891
Fax: (435)438-8804

Publications: The Beaver Press (31320)

Becker Associates
PO Box 507, Sta. Q
Toronto, ON, Canada M4T 2M5
Phone: (416)483-7282

Publications: Urban History Review (36783)

Beckett Publications
15850 Dallas Pkwy.
Dallas, TX 75248
Phone: (972)991-6657
Fax: (972)991-8930

Publications: Dragon Ball Z Collector (30152)

Bedford Communications, Inc.
1410 Broadway Fl. 21
New York, NY 10018-5007

Publications: Computer Buyer's Guide & Handbook (21473)

Bedford County Historical Society
250 Riverbend Rd.
Shelbyville, TN 37160-7217

Publications: Bedford Historical Quarterly (29546)

Bedford Gazette
PO Box 671
Bedford, PA 15522
Phone: (814)623-1151
Fax: (814)623-5055

Publications: Bedford Daily Gazette (26688) • Inquirer (26689)

Bedrock Communications
650 First Ave., 7th Fl.
New York, NY 10016
Phone: (212)532-4150
Fax: (212)213-6382

Publications: Facilities & Event Management (21674)

Bee Group Newspapers
5564 Main St.
PO Box 150
Williamsville, NY 14231-0150
Phone: (716)632-4700
Fax: (716)633-8601

Publications: Cheektowaga Bee (20456) • East Aurora Bee (23583)

Bee and Herald Publishing Co., Inc.
214 N Wilson Ave.
PO Box 440
Jefferson, IA 50129
Phone: (515)386-4161
Fax: (515)386-4162

Publications: The Bee (11005) • The Jefferson Herald (11006)

Bee Publications, Inc.
5564 Main St.
PO Box 150
Buffalo, NY 14231-0150
Phone: (716)632-4700
Fax: (716)633-8601

Publications: Clarence Bee (20461) • Depew Bee (20377) • East Aurora Bee (20540) • Ken-Ton Bee (20383) • Lancaster Bee/Depew Bee (20883) • Orchard Park Bee (23057) • West Seneca Bee (23547)

Bee Publishing Co., Inc.
5 Church Hill Rd.
PO Box 5503
Newtown, CT 06470
Phone: (203)426-3141
Fax: (203)426-1394

Publications: Antiques and the Arts Weekly (5039) • The Newtown Bee (5045)

Beebe News
PO Box 910
Beebe, AR 72012-0910
Phone: (501)882-5414
Fax: (501)882-3576

Publications: Beebe News (1045)

Beecher City Journal
PO Box 38
Beecher City, IL 62414
Phone: (618)487-5634

Publications: Beecher City Journal (8058)

Beef Promotion and Research Board
PO Box 3316
Englewood, CO 80155
Phone: (303)220-9890
Fax: (303)220-9280

Publications: National Cattlemen Magazine (4226)

Beeville Publishing Company
111 N. Washington St.
Beeville, TX 78102-4508
Phone: (361)358-2550
Fax: (361)358-5323

Publications: Beeville Bee—Picayune (30934)

Begell House Inc.
145 Madison Ave., No. 6
New York, NY 10016-6717
Phone: (212)725-1999
Fax: (212)213-8368

Publications: Atomization and Sprays (21270) • Critical Reviews in Therapeutic Drug Carrier Systems (21520) • Heat Exchanger Design Update (21798)

Beirut Times
PO Box 93475
Los Angeles, CA 90093
Phone: (323)978-8888
Fax: (323)978-4444
Free: 888-678-1304

Publications: Beirut Times (2218)

Belgrade Observer
PO Box 279
Belgrade, MN 56312
Phone: (320)254-8250
Fax: (320)254-3215

Publications: Belgrade Observer (15735)

The Bell Press Inc.
18289 Alberta St.
PO Box 4399
Oneida, TN 37841-4399
Phone: (423)569-8351
Fax: (423)569-4500

Publications: Scott County News (29554)

Bell Press, Inc.
PO Box 189
Ladysmith, WI 54848
Phone: (715)532-5591
Fax: (715)532-6644

Publications: Ladysmith News (33900)

Bell Publications
2403 Champa St.
Denver, CO 80205-2621
Phone: (303)296-1600
Fax: (303)295-2159

Publications: Arizona Beverage Analyst (774) • Colorado Beverage Analyst (4311) • Nebraska Beverage Analyst (18098) • New Mexico Beverage Analyst (19937)

The Belle Banner
PO Box 711
Belle, MO 65013
Phone: (573)859-3328
Fax: (573)859-6274

Publications: The Belle Banner (16899)

Belle Plaine Herald
108 S Meridian
PO Box 7
Belle Plaine, MN 56011
Phone: (952)873-2261
Fax: (952)873-2262

Publications: Belle Plaine Herald (15736)

The Belle Plaine News
431 N Merchant
PO Box 128
Belle Plaine, KS 67013
Phone: (316)488-2234

Publications: The Belle Plaine News (11354) • The Oxford Register (11355)

Bellerophon Publications, Inc.
61 W. 23rd St., 4th Fl.
New York, NY 10010
Phone: (212)627-9977
Fax: (212)627-9988
Free: 800-344-3046

Publications: Metropolis Magazine (22327)

Belles Lettres
1243 Maple View Dr.
Charlottesville, VA 22902
Phone: (804)984-2144
Fax: (804)984-5226

Publications: Belles Lettres (31918)

Belleville Recorder
619 River St.
PO Box 50
Belleville, WI 53508
Phone: (608)424-3232

Publications: Belleville Recorder (33572)

Bellevue Community College
3000 Landerholm Circle SE, C 212
Bellevue, WA 98007
Phone: (425)564-2434
Fax: (425)564-4152

Publications: The Jibsheet (32666)

Bellevue Leader
604 Fort Crook Rd. N
Bellevue, NE 68005
Phone: (402)733-7300
Fax: (402)733-9116

Publications: Bellevue Leader (17951)

Bellevue RFD News
PO Box 367
Bellevue, OH 44811-0367

Publications: Bellevue RFD News (24670)

The Bellingham Business Journal, L.L.C.
1521 King St
Bellingham, WA 98229
Phone: (360)647-8805

Publications: The Bellingham Business Journal (32675)

Bellingham Review
Western Washington University
Mail Stop 9053
Bellingham, WA 98225
Phone: (360)650-4863

Publications: Bellingham Review (32676)

Bellowing Ark Press
PO Box 55564
Seattle, WA 98155
Phone: (206)440-0791

Publications: Bellowing Ark (32949)

Belmond Independent
215 E Main St.
Box 126
Belmond, IA 50421
Phone: (641)444-3333

Publications: Belmond Independent (10620)

Belmont Banner
PO Box 589
Belmont, NC 28012
Phone: (704)827-7526
Fax: (704)827-1037

Publications: Belmont Banner (23642)

The Belmont and Tishomongo Journal, Inc.
PO Box 70
Belmont, MS 38827
Phone: (662)454-7196
Fax: (662)454-7196

Publications: Belmont-Tishomingo Journal (16557)

Belmont University
1900 Belmont Blvd.
Nashville, TN 37212
Phone: (615)460-6433
Fax: (615)460-5532

Publications: Belmont Vision (29444)

A. H. Belo
PO Box 1670
Cadiz, KY 42211
Phone: (502)522-6605
Fax: (502)522-3001

Publications: The Cadiz Record (12002) • Herald Ledger (12003)

Beloit College
700 College St.
Beloit, WI 53511
Phone: (608)363-2000

Publications: Round Table (33576)

Beloit Daily News Publishing Co.
149 State St.
Beloit, WI 53511
Phone: (608)365-8811
Fax: (608)365-1420
Free: 800-356-3411

Publications: Beloit Daily News (33574)

Beloit Newspapers
119 E Main
PO Box 366
Beloit, KS 67420
Phone: (785)738-3537
Fax: (785)738-6442

Publications: Beloit Call (11361)

The Beloit Poetry Journal Foundation, Inc.
24 Berry Cove Rd.
Lamoine, ME 04605
Phone: (207)667-5598

Publications: The Beloit Poetry Journal (12959)

The Belton Journal
210 N Penelope
PO Box 180
Belton, TX 76513
Phone: (254)939-5754
Fax: (254)939-2333

Publications: The Belton Journal (29916)

Belton Publishing Company Inc.
419 Main St.
Belton, MO 64012
Phone: (816)331-5353
Fax: (816)322-2943

Publications: The Star Herald (16901)

Belvidere Daily Republican
401 Whitney Blvd.
Belvidere, IL 61008
Phone: (815)547-0084
Fax: (815)544-6334

Publications: Belvidere Daily Republican (8062)

The Belzoni Banner
115 E. Jackson St.
PO Box 610
Belzoni, MS 39038-0610
Phone: (662)247-3373
Fax: (662)247-3372

Publications: The Belzoni Banner (16558)

Bemidji State University
Bemidji, MN 56601-2699
Phone: (218)444-6265
Fax: (218)444-5105

Publications: Germanic Notes and Reviews (15737)

Benchmark Publications, Ltd.
PO Box 26
Los Altos, CA 94023
Phone: (650)941-3823
Fax: (650)941-3845

Publications: Narrow Gauge and Short Line Gazette (2194)

Benchmark Publishing Inc.
PO Box 95769
Seattle, WA 98145-2769
Phone: (206)547-9660
Fax: (206)547-0128

Publications: The Seattle Press (33022)

Bend of the River Magazine
PO Box 859
Maumee, OH 43537
Phone: (419)893-0022
Fax: (419)893-0022

Publications: Bend of the River Magazine (25368)

Benedict College
Harden & Blanding Sts.
Columbia, SC 29204
Phone: (803)253-5297

Publications: Benedict Tiger (28543)

Benedictine Sisters of Perpetual Adoration
800 N Country Club Rd.
Tucson, AZ 85716-4583
Phone: (520)325-6401

Publications: Spirit & Life (964)

Benedictine University
5700 College Rd.
Lisle, IL 60532-0900
Phone: (630)829-6000
Fax: (630)960-1126

Publications: Voices Magazine (9112)

Benkelman Post and News-Chronicle
513 Chief St.
PO Box 800
Benkelman, NE 69021-0800
Phone: (308)423-2337
Fax: (308)423-5555

Publications: Benkelman Post and News-Chronicle (17952)

Bennett Publishing Ltd.
PO Box 130
Keremeos, BC, Canada V0X 1N0
Phone: (250)497-2653
Fax: (250)499-2645

Publications: Keremeos Review (34996) • Okanagan Falls Review (35037)

The Benning Leader
PO Box 711
Columbus, GA 31902
Phone: (706)571-8574
Fax: (706)576-6290

Publications: The Benning Leader (7280)

Benro Enterprises, Inc.
395 Ninth St.
San Francisco, CA 94103-3831
Phone: (415)861-5019
Fax: (415)891-8144

Publications: Bay Area Reporter (3329)

Benson County Farmers Press
120 B Ave. N
PO Box 98
Minnewaukan, ND 58351-0098
Phone: (701)473-5436
Fax: (701)473-5736

Publications: Benson County Farmers Press (24503)

Bent County Democrat
516 Carson
PO Box 467
Las Animas, CO 81054
Phone: (719)456-1333
Fax: (719)456-1402

Publications: Bent County Democrat (4542)

Bentley College
175 Forest St.
Waltham, MA 02452
Phone: (781)891-2241
Fax: (781)891-3165

Publications: Bentley Observer (14596)

Bentley College
310M Student Center
385 Beaver St.
Waltham, MA 02452
Phone: (781)891-2912
Fax: (781)891-2574

Publications: The Vanguard (14605)

Bentley Systems, Incorporated
685 Stockton Dr.
Exton, PA 19341-0678
Phone:

Publications: Enterprise Engineering Modeling World (26917)

Benton County Daily Record
104 SW A St.
PO Box 1049
Bentonville, AR 72712
Phone: (501)271-3700
Fax: (501)273-7777

Publications: Benton County Daily Record (1049)

Benton County Enterprise, Inc.
PO Box 128
Warsaw, MO 65355
Phone: (660)438-6312
Fax: (660)438-3464

Publications: Benton County Enterprise (17703)

Benton Evening News Co.
111 E Church
Benton, IL 62812-2238
Phone: (618)438-5611
Fax: (618)435-2413

Publications: News (8072)

Benton Publishing Co., Inc.
321 N Market St.
Benton, AR 72015
Phone: (501)315-8228
Fax: (501)315-1920

Publications: The Benton Courier (1047)

The Benton Review
102 E 5th St.
PO Box 527
Fowler, IN 47944
Phone: (765)884-1902
Fax: (765)884-8110
Free: 888-805-5821

Publications: Benton Review (9996)

Berea Citizen
PO Box 207
Berea, KY 40403
Phone: (859)986-0959
Fax: (859)986-0960

Publications: Berea Citizen (11937)

Berea College
College PO Box 2166
Berea, KY 40404
Phone: (859)985-3000
Fax: (859)985-7300

Publications: Appalachian Heritage (11936)

Berea College
CPO 2302
Berea, KY 40404
Phone: (859)985-3000
Fax: (859)985-3556
Free: 800-457-9846

Publications: Berea College Magazine (11938) • Pinnacle (11939)

Bergen Gazette
48 Harrison Ave.
Garfield, NJ 07026
Phone: (973)473-1927
Fax: (973)546-4233

Publications: The Messenger (18843)

Bergen News Publishing Co.
111 Grand Ave.
Palisades Park, NJ 07650
Phone: (201)947-5000
Fax: (201)947-6968

Publications: Bergen News (19398) • Press Journal/Valley Star (18797) • Sun Bulletin (19399)

Berghahn Books Inc.
604 W 115th St.
New York, NY 10025-7712
Phone: (212)222-6502
Fax: (212)222-5209
Free: 800-540-8663

Publications: Critical Survey (21521) • European Journal of Social Quality (21651) • European Judaism (21654) • French Politics, Culture and Society (21735) • German Politics and Society (21759) • Nomadic Peoples (22464) • Sartre Studies International (22705) • Theoria (22829)

Berkeley Democrat
PO Box 792
Athens, GA 30603

Publications: Berkeley Democrat (6931)

Berklee College of Music
1140 Boylston St.
Boston, MA 02215
Phone: (617)747-2325
Fax: (617)247-8788

Publications: Berklee Today (13854)

Berkley House Direct
809 Virginia Ave.
Martinsburg, WV 25401-2131
Phone: (304)267-2673
Fax: (304)262-0676
Free: 800-665-4237

Publications: House, Home and Garden (33379)

Berks County Bar Association
PO Box 1058
544-546 Court St.
Reading, PA 19603
Phone: (610)375-4593
Fax: (610)373-0256

Publications: Berks County Law Journal (27917)

Berks County Genealogical Society
3618 Kutztown Rd.
Laureldale, PA 19605-1842

Publications: Berks County Genealogical Society Journal (27167)

Berks-Mont Newspapers, Inc.
124 N. Chestnut St.
PO Box 565
Boyertown, PA 19512
Phone: (610)367-6041
Fax: (610)369-0233

Publications: The Boyertown Area Times (26726)

Berkshire Record
21 Elm St.
Great Barrington, MA 01230
Phone: (413)528-5380
Fax: (413)528-9449

Publications: Berkshire Record (14214)

Berlin Journal Newspapers
PO Box 10
Berlin, WI 54923-0010
Phone: (920)361-1515
Fax: (920)361-1518

Publications: Berlin Journal (33580) • The Fox Lake Representative (33582) • Green Lake County Reporter (33583) • Omro Herald (33584) • Princeton Times-Republic (33585)

Berling Communications, Inc.
1235 10th St.
Berkeley, CA 94710
Phone: (510)528-5000
Fax: (510)528-5177

Publications: Soccer America (1560)

Bernard Shaw Society, Inc.
PO Box 1159
Madison Sq. Sta.
New York, NY 10159-1159
Phone: (212)982-9885

Publications: Independent Shavian (21861)

Berne Tri-Weekly News
PO Box 324
153 S. Jefferson St.
Berne, IN 46711
Phone: (219)589-2101
Fax: (219)589-8614

Publications: Berne Tri-Weekly News (9802)

Berner Bros. Publishing Co., Inc.
612 Superior St.
Antigo, WI 54409
Phone: (715)623-4191
Fax: (715)623-4193

Publications: Antigo Daily Journal (33531) • The Journal Express (33533)

Berreth Publications
PO Box 67
Norwood, MN 55368
Phone: (612)467-2271
Fax: (612)467-2294

Publications: Norwood-Young America Times (16241)

Berrett-Koehler Communications Inc.
235 Montgomery St., Ste. 650
San Francisco, CA 94104
Phone: (415)288-0260
Fax: (415)362-2512
Free: 800-929-2929

Publications: Advances in Developing Human Resources (3324)

Berrien County Record
206 Main St.
PO Box 191
Buchanan, MI 49107
Phone: (616)695-3878
Fax: (616)695-3880

Publications: Berrien County Record (14840)

The Berrien Press
Box 455
Nashville, GA 31639
Phone: (229)686-3523
Fax: (229)686-7771

Publications: The Berrien Press (7452)

Berry College
520 Mt. Berry Sta.
Mount Berry, GA 30149-0520
Phone: (706)236-2294
Fax: (706)236-2248

Publications: Campus Carrier (7502)

Bertelsen Publishing Co.
1582 Glen Lake Rd.
Hoffman Estates, IL 60195
Phone: (847)882-2552
Fax: (847)882-7082

Publications: Danish Pioneer (8999)

The Bertrand Herald
PO Box 425
Bertrand, NE 68927
Phone: (308)472-3217
Fax: (308)472-5165

Publications: The Bertrand Herald (17953)

The Bertrand Russell Research Centre
McMaster University
Hamilton, ON, Canada L8S 4M2
Phone: (905)525-9140
Fax: (905)577-6930

Publications: Russell: The Journal of Bertrand Russell Studies (35888)

Best-Met Publishing Co., Inc.
5537 Twin Knolls Rd., Ste. 438
Columbia, MD 21045
Phone: (410)730-5013
Fax: (410)740-4680
Free: 800-860-1510

Publications: Food Trade News (26736) • Food World (13460)

Best Press
110 S Main
PO Box 155
Woodville, WI 54028
Phone: (715)698-2401
Fax: (715)698-2952

Publications: Woodville Leader (34473)

Best Publishing, Inc.
2325 W Victory Blvd.
Burbank, CA 91506
Phone: (818)566-4030
Fax: (818)566-4295

Publications: Entertainment Today (1617)

Best Read Guide
PO Box 1958
Orleans, MA 02653
Phone: (508)240-1212
Fax: (508)240-2912

Publications: Best Read Guide (14454)

Bethany College
PO Box 209
Bethany, WV 26032
Phone: (304)829-7500
Fax: (304)829-7950

Publications: The Tower (33250)

Bethany College Press
421 N 1st St.
Lindsborg, KS 67456-1897
Phone: (785)227-3311
Fax: (785)227-2289

Publications: Bethany Messenger (11610)

Bethany Printing Co.
PO Box 351
Bethany, MO 64424
Phone: (660)425-6325
Fax: (660)425-3441

Publications: Bethany Republican-Clipper (16902) • Pony Express (16903)

Bethel College
300 E. 27th St.
North Newton, KS 67117
Phone: (316)283-2500
Fax: (316)284-5286

Publications: Bethel College Context (11676)

Bethel College
3900 Bethel Dr.
St. Paul, MN 55112
Phone: (612)638-6214
Fax: (612)638-6001

Publications: The Clarion (16371)

The Bethel Oxford County Citizen
Box 109
Bethel, ME 04217
Phone: (207)824-2444
Fax: (207)824-2426
Free: 800-ABC-NEWS

Publications: The Bethel Oxford County Citizen (12921)

Bethune-Cookman College
640 Mary McLeod Bethune Blvd.
Daytona Beach, FL 32114
Phone: (386)481-2707
Fax: (386)481-2701

Publications: Voice (6040)

Beverage Journal Inc.
PO Box 8900
Elkridge, MD 21075-8900
Phone: (410)796-5455
Fax: (410)796-5511

Publications: Maryland Beverage Journal (13493) • Washington DC Beverage Journal (5844)

Beverage Media
116 John St. Fl. 21
New York, NY 10038
Phone: (212)620-0100
Fax: (212)620-0473

Publications: Beverage Media (21304)

Beverage World
770 Broadway
New York, NY 10003-9595
Phone: (646)654-4500
Fax: (646)654-7727

Publications: Beverage Aisle (21303) • Beverage World (21305) • Beverage World en Espanol (21306) • Beverage World International (21307)

The Beverly Hills Courier
8840 W Olympic Blvd.
Beverly Hills, CA 90211
Phone: (213)278-1322
Fax: (213)271-5118

Publications: The Beverly Hills Courier (1569)

Beverly Page
11407-50th St.
Edmonton, AB, Canada T5W 3B5
Phone: (403)479-3959
Fax: (403)479-3959

Publications: Beverly Page (34702)

Beverly Winters
7025 Monarch St.
Corpus Christi, TX 78413-4329
Phone: (512)808-9600
Fax: (512)808-9606

Publications: South Texas Informer & Business Journal (30079)

BFC Montreal
Garnison Saint-Jean
Richelain, QC, Canada J0J 1R0
Phone: (514)358-7099
Fax: (514)358-7423

Publications: Servir (37306)

BHG Inc.
PO Box 309
Garrison, ND 58540
Phone: (701)463-2201
Fax: (701)463-7487
Free: 800-658-3485

Publications: Beulah Beacon (24347) • Center Republican (24553) • Hazen Star (24470) • The Leader-News (24554) • McLean County Independent (24448) • McLean County Journal (24542) • Mountrail County Record (24530) • Underwood News (24543)

Bi-County Herald
115 S Church St.
PO Box 87
Hudson, MI 49247
Phone: (517)448-2201
Fax: (517)448-2201

Publications: Bi-County Herald (15200)

Bibb Publications
32 Ct.Sq. W.
PO Box 127
Centreville, AL 35042
Phone: (205)926-9769
Fax: (205)926-9760

Publications: Centreville Press (151)

The Bible Holiness Movement
PO Box 223, Sta. A
Vancouver, BC, Canada V6C 2M3
Phone: (250)492-3376

Publications: Hallelujah! (35145)

The Bible Sabbath Association
HC 60, Box 8
Fairview, OK 73737-9504
Phone: (580)227-3200
Fax: (580)227-4495
Free: 888-687-5191

Publications: The Sabbath Sentinel (25834)

Biblical Recorder, Inc.
PO Box 18808
Raleigh, NC 27619
Phone: (919)847-2127
Fax: (919)847-6939

Publications: Biblical Recorder (24126)

Biblical Theology Bulletin, Inc.
PO Box 1038
South Orange, NJ 07079
Phone: (973)761-9006
Fax: (973)275-2333

Publications: Biblical Theology Bulletin (19583)

Bibliographical Society of America
520 Butler Library
535 W. 114th St.
Columbia University
New York, NY 10027
Phone: (212)452-2710
Fax: (212)452-2710

Publications: Papers of the Bibliographical Society of America (28561)

Bicentennial Publishing Corp.
333 W 38th St.
New York, NY 10018
Phone: (212)594-2266
Fax: (212)594-2383

Publications: Polish Daily News (22571)

Bicycling
135 N. Sixth St.
Emmaus, PA 18098-0099
Phone: (610)967-5171
Fax: (610)967-8960

Publications: Bicycling (26874)

Bienville Democrat/Ringgold Record
1952 Railroad St.
PO Box 29
Arcadia, LA 71001-0029
Phone: (318)263-2922
Fax: (318)263-8897

Publications: Bienville Democrat/Ringgold Record (12476)

Biere Mag
102 Burlington
Ottawa, ON, Canada K1T 3K5
Phone: (613)737-3715
Fax: (613)737-3715

Publications: BiereMag (36187)

Big Bend Community College
7662 Chanute St.
Moses Lake, WA 98837
Phone: (509)762-5351
Fax: (509)762-6329

Publications: Tumbleweed Times (32840)

Big Buck Enterprises Corporation
243 Adilman Dr.
Saskatoon, SK, Canada S7K 7R6
Phone: (306)382-2723
Fax: (306)931-2394

Publications: Big Buck (37548)

Big City Blues Magazine
PO Box 1805
Royal Oak, MI 48068
Phone: (248)582-1544
Fax: (248)582-8242

Publications: Big City Blues Magazine (15477)

Big Grove Publications
PO Box 35
Fremont, IA 52561-0035

Publications: Batavia Beacon (10917) • Forum (10918)

Big Horn County News
204 N Ctr. Ave.
Hardin, MT 59034-1533
Phone: (406)665-1008
Fax: (406)665-1012
Free: 800-735-8736

Publications: Big Horn County News (17811)

The Big Lake Wildcat, Inc.
309 2nd St.
PO Box 946
Big Lake, TX 76932-0946
Phone: (915)884-2215
Fax: (915)884-5771

Publications: The Big Lake Wildcat (29919)

Big Muddy
MS 2650 English Dept.
Southeast Missouri State University
Cape Girardeau, MO 63701

Publications: Big Muddy (16943)

Big Pasture News
PO Box 508
Grandfield, OK 73546-0608
Phone: (580)479-5757
Fax: (580)479-5232

Publications: Big Pasture News (25845)

Big River Association
634 N. Grand Blvd., 12th Fl.
St. Louis, MO 63103
Phone: (314)533-4541
Fax: (314)533-3345

Publications: River Styx (17489)

The Big Sandy News
115 Louisa Plz., Ste. 4
PO Box 766
Louisa, KY 41230
Phone: (606)638-4581
Fax: (606)638-9949

Publications: The Big Sandy News (12208)

Big Spring Herald
710 Scurry
PO Box 1431
Big Spring, TX 79720
Phone: (915)263-7331
Fax: (915)264-7205

Publications: Big Spring Herald (29924)

Big Stone Publishers
1101 Village Rd., Ste. UL-4D
Carbondale, CO 81623-2518
Phone: (970)704-1442
Fax: (970)963-4965
Free: 877-762-5423

Publications: Rock & Ice (4217)

The Big Takeover
249 Eldridge St., No. 14
New York, NY 10002-1345
Phone: (212)533-6057

Publications: The Big Takeover (21309)

Big World
PO Box 7656
Lancaster, PA 17601
Phone: (717)569-0217

Publications: Big World (27139)

Bigfork Eagle
PO Box 406
Bigfork, MT 59911
Phone: (406)837-5131
Fax: (406)837-1132

Publications: Bigfork Eagle (17728)

Bilbey Publications, LLC
PO Box 1653
Vassar, MI 48768
Phone: (989)823-8651
Fax: (989)823-2531

Publications: Cass River Trader (15651)

Bilingual Review/Press
Hispanic Research Ctr.
Arizona State University
PO Box 872702
Tempe, AZ 85287-2702
Phone: (480)965-3867
Fax: (480)965-8309

Publications: Bilingual Review/Revista Bilingue (900)

Bill Communications, Inc.
1115 Northmeadow Pkwy.
Roswell, GA 30076
Phone: (770)569-5105
Fax: (770)569-5105
Free: 800-241-9034

Publications: Apparel Industry International (7512) • Automotive & Transportation Interiors (7514) • Retail Operations & Construction (7518) • Sporting Goods Dealer (7519) • Truck Accessory News (7520)

Bill Communications, Inc.
770 Broadway
New York, NY 10003-9595
Phone: (646)654-4500
Fax: (646)654-7212

Publications: Hospitality Design (21819) • Incentive (21859) • Meeting News (22313) • Sales & Marketing Management (22701) • Supermarket Business (22808)

Bill Communications, Inc.—A VNU Co.
1500 Hampton St., Ste. 150
Columbia, SC 29202
Phone: (803)771-7500
Fax: (803)779-1461
Free: 800-845-8820

Publications: Bobbin Magazine (28545) • La Bobina (28556)

Bill Foster Pub.
PO Box 38
Moody, TX 76557-0038
Phone: (254)754-3511
Fax: (254)754-3541

Publications: The Moody Courier (30837)

Billian/Transworld Publishing Inc.
2100 Powers Ferry Rd.
Ste. 300
Atlanta, GA 30339
Phone: (770)955-8484
Fax: (770)955-8485
Free: 800-533-8484

Publications: Art & Antiques (6963) • Textile Industries (7053) • Textiles Panamericanos (28627)

The Billings Gazette
401 N Broadway
PO Box 36300
Billings, MT 59107
Phone: (406)657-1200
Fax: (406)657-1345
Free: 800-543-2505

Publications: The Billings Gazette (17729)

The Billings Times
2919 Montana Ave.
Billings, MT 59101
Phone: (406)245-4994
Fax: (406)245-5115

Publications: The Billings Times (17731)

The Billy Graham Evangelistic Association
PO Box 779
Minneapolis, MN 55440
Phone: (612)338-0500
Fax: (612)335-1299

Publications: Decision (16072)

Bingo and Gaming News
349 Flagstone Ct.
Vacaville, CA 95687-4325
Phone: (707)451-4646
Fax: (707)281-1658

Publications: Bingo and Gaming News (3973)

Binoculus Publishing
740 Piney Acres Cir.
PO Box 3727
Dillon, CO 80435-3727
Phone: (970)262-0753
Fax: (970)262-0753

Publications: Binocular Vision & Strabismus Quarterly (4399)

Biodynamic Farming & Gardening Association
PO Box 29135
San Francisco, CA 94129-0135
Phone: (415)561-7797
Fax: (415)561-7796
Free: 888-516-7797

Publications: Biodynamics (3331)

Biola University
13800 Biola Ave.
La Mirada, CA 90639-0001
Phone: (310)903-4880
Fax: (310)903-4748

Publications: The Chimes (2125)

Biomedical Engineering Society
Dept. of Bioengineering
Rice University
PO Box 1892
Houston, TX 77251-1892

Publications: Annals of Biomedical Engineering (30457)

Biophysical Society
9650 Rockville Pke., Ste. 0512
Bethesda, MD 20814
Phone: (301)634-7114
Fax: (301)634-7133

Publications: Biophysical Journal (13321)

Bioresources Development and Conservation Programme
11303 Amherst Ave., Ste. 2
Silver Spring, MD 20902-4600
Phone: (301)962-6201
Fax: (301)962-6205

Publications: Journal of Ethnomedicine and Drug Development (13730)

Bird City Times
PO Box 220
Bird City, KS 67731-0220
Phone: (913)734-2621
Fax: (913)332-3001

Publications: Bird City Times (11362)

Bird Watcher's Digest Press
PO Box 110
Marietta, OH 45750
Phone: (740)373-5285
Fax: (740)373-8443
Free: 800-879-2473

Publications: Bird Watcher's Digest (25343)

The Birmingham News
2200 4th Ave. N.
PO Box 2553
Birmingham, AL 35202-2553
Phone: (205)325-2222
Fax: (205)325-3246
Free: 800-283-4051

Publications: The Birmingham News (58)

Birmingham Post Co.
PO Box 2553
Birmingham, AL 35202
Phone: (205)325-2214
Fax: (205)325-2410

Publications: Birmingham Post-Herald (60)

The Birmingham Times Publishing Co.
115 3rd Ave. W
PO Box 10503
Birmingham, AL 35202
Phone: (205)251-5158
Fax: (205)323-2294

Publications: Birmingham Times (61)

Birmingham World
407 15th St. N
PO Box 2285
Birmingham, AL 35203-1877
Phone: (205)251-6523
Fax: (205)328-6729

Publications: Birmingham World (62)

The Bisbee Observer
7 Bisbee Rd., Ste. L
Bisbee, AZ 85603
Phone: (520)432-7254
Fax: (520)432-4192

Publications: The Bisbee Observer (659)

Bishop Museum
1525 Bernice St.
Honolulu, HI 96817-2704
Phone: (808)848-4115
Fax: (808)847-8252

Publications: Indo-Pacific Fishes (7704)

Bittner Schatz Publishing Inc.
PO Box 668
Glen Ullin, ND 58631
Phone: (701)348-3325
Fax: (701)348-3325

Publications: Glen Ullin Times (24449)

BIV Publications Ltd.
500-1155 W. Pender St.
Vancouver, BC, Canada V6E 2P4
Phone: (604)688-2398
Fax: (604)688-1963

Publications: Business in Vancouver Media Group (35128)

Bixby Bulletin
8545 E 41st. St.
Tulsa, OK 74145
Phone: (918)663-1414

Publications: Bixby Bulletin (25763)

Black Bird Creek Printing Co.
PO Box 365
Unionville, MO 63565-0365
Phone: (816)947-2222
Fax: (816)947-2223

Publications: Unionville Republican & Putnam County Journal (17658)

The Black Chronicle
PO Box 17498
Oklahoma City, OK 73136
Phone: (405)424-4695
Fax: (405)424-6708

Publications: The Black Chronicle (25955)

Black Dress Press
PO Box 1373
New York, NY 10276
Phone: (212)504-8222
Fax: (212)504-8222

Publications: Spinning Jenny (22773)

Black Enterprise Unlimited
130 5th Ave., 10th Fl.
New York, NY 10011
Phone: (212)242-8000
Fax: (212)886-9509

Publications: Kidpreneurs News (22220) • Teenpreneur (22819)

Black Hawk College
6600 34th Ave.
Moline, IL 61265
Phone: (309)796-5000
Fax: (309)792-5976
Free: 800-334-1311

Publications: The Chieftain (9203)

Black Hills State University
PO Box 9003
1200 University
Spearfish, SD 57799
Phone: (605)642-6011
Fax: (605)642-6762

Publications: Today (28994)

Black Moon Publishing
Box 622
Logan, OH 43138-0622

Publications: Cincinnati Journal of Magic (25310)

Black Mountain News, Inc.
PO Box 9
Black Mountain, NC 28711
Phone: (828)669-8727
Fax: (828)669-8619

Publications: The Black Mountain News (23646)

Black River Publishing Co., Inc.
E. Schuyler St.
PO Box 372
Boonville, NY 13309
Phone: (315)942-4449
Fax: (315)942-4440

Publications: Boonville Herald & Adirondack Tourist (20237)

The Black Scholar
PO Box 22869
Oakland, CA 94618
Phone: (510)547-6633
Fax: (510)547-6679

Publications: The Black Scholar (2668)

Black Swan Press/Surrealist Editions
PO Box 6424
Evanston, IL 60204
Phone: (773)465-7774

Publications: Arsenal (8849)

Black Tennis Magazine
PO Box 210767
Dallas, TX 75211
Phone: (214)670-7618
Fax: (214)330-1318

Publications: Black Tennis Magazine (30133)

Black Voice News
PO Box 1581
Riverside, CA 92502
Phone: (909)682-6070
Fax: (909)276-0877

Publications: Black Voice News (2931)

BlackLightning Publishing, Inc.
Riddle Pond Rd.
West Topsham, VT 05086
Phone: (802)439-6462

Publications: Flash Magazine (31616)

Blacksburg Times
PO Box 155
Blacksburg, SC 29702
Phone: (864)839-2621
Fax: (864)839-5710

Publications: Blacksburg Times (28496)

Blackwell Journal-Tribune
113 E Blackwell Ave.
Blackwell, OK 74631
Phone: (580)363-3370
Fax: (580)363-4415

Publications: Blackwell Journal-Tribune (25765)

Blackwell Publishers
350 Main St.
Malden, MA 02148
Phone: (781)388-8200
Fax: (781)388-8210

Publications: American Journal of Agricultural Economics (14289) • Canadian Journal of Economics (Revue Canadienne d'Economique) (37097) • Choices (14290) • City & Community (8333) • Epilepsia (14291) • Journal of the American Geriatrics Society (14293) • Journal of Neurochemistry (14295) • Journal of Personality (4837) • Learning Disabilities Research and Practice (14758) • Mathematical Finance (8482) • The Russian Review (14299) • Sociological Methodology (14300) • Sociological Theory (14301)

Blackwell Publishing
350 Main St.
Malden, MA 02148
Phone: (781)388-8200
Free: 800-216-2552

Publications: Curriculum Inquiry (36565) • The Journal of Aesthetics and Art Criticism (14292) • Middle East Policy (14298) • New Perspectives Quarterly (2345) • Psychology of Women Quarterly (23936) • The Yale Review (5009)

Blackwell Publishing Ltd.
9600 Garsington Rd.
Oxford OX4 2DQ, United Kingdom
Phone: 44 1865778315
Fax: 44 1865471775

Publications: The Review of Income and Wealth (22659)

Blackwell Science Inc.
Commerce Pl.
350 Main St.
Malden, MA 02148
Phone: (781)388-8200
Fax: (781)388-8255
Free: 800-759-6120

Publications: Journal of Experimental Therapeutics and Oncology (14294) • Journal of Phycology (13001)

The Blade
801 Main St.
PO Box 400
Bridgeport, NE 69336
Phone: (308)262-0675
Fax: (308)262-0675

Publications: Bridgeport News-Blade (17964)

Blaine Banner
12570 Radisson Rd. NE
Blaine, MN 55449
Phone: (763)755-3832
Fax: (763)755-3832

Publications: Blaine Banner (15755)

Blaine County Publishing
PO Box 579
Canton, OK 73724
Phone: (580)822-4401
Fax: (580)886-3320

Publications: The Canton Times (25778)

The Blair Press
109 N Gilbert St.
Box 187
Blair, WI 54616
Phone: (608)989-2531
Fax: (608)989-9615

Publications: The Blair Press (33594)

Blalock Publishing
219 2nd Ave. SE
Cullman, AL 35055
Phone: (205)739-1351
Fax: (205)739-4422

Publications: The Cullman Tribune (161)

Blanco County News
PO Box 429
Blanco, TX 78606
Phone: (830)833-4812
Fax: (830)833-4246

Publications: Blanco County News (29927)

The Blazer News
PO Box 806
Jackson, MI 49204
Phone: (517)787-3018
Fax: (517)788-5300

Publications: Blazer News (15220)

Bleezarde Publishing, Inc.
164 Main St.
Ravena, NY 12143
Phone: (518)756-2030
Fax: (518)756-8555

Publications: News-Herald (23177)

Blegen Publishing, Inc.
Box 69
De Smet, SD 57231
Phone: (605)854-3331
Fax: (605)854-9977

Publications: The De Smet News (28841)

Blenheim News-Tribune
62 Talbot St.
Blenheim, ON, Canada N0P 1A0
Phone: (519)676-3321
Fax: (519)676-3454

Publications: Blenheim News-Tribune (35686)

Blessed Sacrament Fathers
4450 Rue St.-Hubert
Montreal, QC, Canada H2J 2W9
Phone: (514)525-6210
Fax: (514)521-8752

Publications: Pretre et Pasteur (37208)

Blethen Maine Newspapers
PO Box 1460
Portland, ME 04104
Phone: (207)791-6650
Fax: (207)791-6920
Free: 800-442-6036

Publications: Maine Sunday Telegram (13012) • Portland Press Herald (13017)

Blindskills, Inc.
PO Box 5181
Salem, OR 97304-0181
Phone: (503)581-4224
Fax: (503)581-0178
Free: 800-860-4224

Publications: Dialogue (26567)

Blitz
PO Box 48124
Los Angeles, CA 90048-0124
Phone: (818)985-8618

Publications: Blitz (2222)

BLK Publishing Company
Box 83912
Los Angeles, CA 90083-0912
Phone: (310)410-0808
Fax: (310)410-9250

Publications: Black Dates (2219) • Black Lace (2220) • Blackfire (2221) • BLK (2223) • Kuumba (2310)

Blood-Horse Publications
PO Box 4038
Lexington, KY 40544-4038
Phone: (859)278-2361
Fax: (859)276-4450
Free: 800-866-2361

Publications: The Blood-Horse (12161) • The Horse (12165)

Blood Tribe Comm. News
PO Box 410
Standoff, AB, Canada T0L 1Y0
Phone: (403)737-2121
Fax: (403)737-2336

Publications: Kainai News (34854)

Bloom Publishing Co.
112 S 4th Ave.
PO Box 148
Logan, IA 51546
Phone: (712)644-2705
Fax: (712)644-2788

Publications: Logan Herald-Observer (11040)

Bloomberg L.P.
100 Business Park Dr.
PO Box 888
Princeton, NJ 08542-0888
Phone: (609)279-3000
Fax: (609)683-7523
Free: 800-388-2749

Publications: Bloomberg Markets Magazine (19454)

Bloomberg Publishing
499 Park Ave.
New York, NY 10022
Phone: (212)893-5555

Publications: Angel Advisor (21214)

Bloomer Advance
PO Box 25
Bloomer, WI 54724
Phone: (715)568-3100
Fax: (715)568-3111

Publications: Bloomer Advance (33596)

Bloomfield College
229 Liberty St.
Bloomfield, NJ 07003
Fax: (201)743-2040

Publications: On the Green (18688)

Bloomfield Democrat
PO Box 10
Bloomfield, IA 52537

Publications: The Bloomfield Democrat (10622)

Bloomfield Monitor
110 N Broadway
PO Box 367
Bloomfield, NE 68718
Phone: (402)373-2332

Publications: Bloomfield Monitor (17961)

The Bloomfield News
29 W Main St.
Bloomfield, IN 47424-0311
Phone: (812)384-3501
Fax: (812)384-3741

Publications: The Bloomfield News (9820)

Blooming Prairie Times
411 E Main St.
PO Box 247
Blooming Prairie, MN 55917
Phone: (507)583-4431
Fax: (507)583-4445

Publications: Blooming Prairie Times (15757)

Blooming Prairie Warehouse
2340 Heinz Rd.
Iowa City, IA 52240
Phone: (319)337-6448
Fax: (319)337-4592

Publications: Prairie News (10985)

The Bloomington Independent
PO Box 1035
Westfield, IN 46074-1035
Phone: (812)331-0963
Fax: (812)337-3308

Publications: The Bloomington Independent (9824)

Bloomington Pantagraph
301 W. Washington
Bloomington, IL 61701-3827
Free: 800-747-7323

Publications: Mahomet Citizen (9138)

Bloomsburg University
The Voice
PO Box 97 KUB
Bloomsburg, PA 17815
Phone: (717)389-4457
Fax: (717)389-3905

Publications: The Voice (26719)

The Bloomsbury Review
PO Box 8928
Denver, CO 80201
Phone: (303)455-3123
Fax: (303)455-7039
Free: 800-783-3338

Publications: The Bloomsbury Review (4309)

BLSS, Inc.
Box 164509
Miami, FL 33116-4509
Phone: (305)254-7006
Fax: (305)254-9662

Publications: Journal of Security Administration (6366)

The Blue Army of Our Lady of Fatima
PO Box 976
Washington, NJ 07882-0976
Phone: (908)213-2223
Fax: (908)213-2263
Free: (866)513-1917

Publications: Hearts Aflame (19708) • Soul Magazine (19709)

Blue Diamond Growers
1802 C St.
PO Box 1768
Sacramento, CA 95814
Phone: (916)442-0771
Fax: (916)325-2880

Publications: Almond Facts (2975)

Blue & Gold Illustrated
PO Box 1007
Notre Dame, IN 46556
Phone: (574)255-9800
Fax: (574)255-9700

Publications: Blue & Gold Illustrated—Notre Dame Football (10368)

Blue Hill Leader
514 Gage St.
Box 38
Blue Hill, NE 68930
Phone: (402)756-2077
Fax: (402)756-2097

Publications: Blue Hill Leader (17962)

Blue Line Magazine
4981 Hwy. 7 E, Unit 12A, No. 254
Markham, ON, Canada L3R 1N1
Phone: (905)640-3048
Fax: (905)640-7547

Publications: Blue Line Magazine (36014)

Blue Mound Leader
PO Box 318
Blue Mound, IL 62513-0318
Phone: (217)692-2323
Fax: (217)692-2323

Publications: Blue Mound Leader (8088)

The Blue Ridge Digest Publishing Co., Inc.
PO Box 1758
Asheville, NC 28802-1758
Phone: (828)667-1607
Fax: (828)667-1607

Publications: The Digest (23628)

Blue Ridge Leader
769 E. Main St.
Purcellville, VA 20132-3129
Phone: (540)338-6200
Fax: (540)338-2647

Publications: Blue Ridge Leader (32339)

The Blue Springs Examiner
PO Box 1057
Blue Springs, MO 64013
Phone: (816)229-9161

Publications: Blue Springs Examiner (Daily Edition) (16908) • Blue Springs Examiner (Wednesday Edition) (16909)

Blue Unicorn Inc.
22 Avon Rd.
Kensington, CA 94707
Phone: (510)526-8439

Publications: Blue Unicorn (2100)

Bluebonnet Media
PO Box 897
Big Sandy, TX 75755
Phone: (903)636-4351
Fax: (903)636-5091

Publications: The Big Sandy & Hawkins Journal and Tri Area News (29920)

BlueCross BlueShield-Rochester
165 Ct. St.
Rochester, NY 14647
Phone: (716)454-1700
Fax: (716)238-4233

Publications: INQUIRY (23228)

Bluefield Automobile Club
622 Commerce St.
Bluefield, WV 24701-3107
Phone: (304)327-8187
Fax: (304)325-5137

Publications: AAA Today (33252)

Bluefield State College
219 Rock St.
Bluefield, WV 24701-2198
Phone: (304)327-4186
Fax: (304)327-4188

Publications: Bluefieldian (33253)

Bluegrass Unlimited, Inc.
9514 James Madison Hwy.
Warrenton, VA 20186
Phone: (540)349-8181
Fax: (540)341-0011
Free: 800-258-4727

Publications: Bluegrass Unlimited (32599)

Blues Revue
Rte. 1
PO Box 75
Salem, WV 26426-9604
Phone: (304)782-1971
Fax: (304)782-1993
Free: 800-258-7388

Publications: Blues Revue (33463)

Bluffton News
101 N Main St.
PO Box 49
Bluffton, OH 45817
Phone: (419)358-8010
Fax: (419)358-5027
Free: 800-358-4732

Publications: Bluffton News (24682) • Boys' Quest (24683)

Bluffton Printing & Publishing Co.
114 N Main St.
PO Box 67
North Baltimore, OH 45872
Phone: (419)257-2771
Fax: (419)257-3058

Publications: The North Baltimore News (25432)

Blytheville Courier News
PO Box 1108
Blytheville, AR 72316
Phone: (870)763-4461
Fax: (870)763-6874

Publications: Courier News (1058)

BMW Car Club of America, Inc.
640 S Main St. Ste. 201
Greenville, SC 29601-2564
Free: 800-878-9292

Publications: Roundel Magazine (28626)

B'nai B'rith
2020 K St., NW, 7th Fl.
Washington, DC 20006
Phone: (202)857-6600
Fax: (202)296-1092

Publications: B'nai B'rith (5379)

B'nai B'rith District One
823 United Nations Plz.
New York, NY 10017
Phone: (212)687-2257
Fax: (212)986-7487

Publications: The Star (22790)

B'nai B'rith Youth Organization
1640 Rhode Island Ave. NW
Washington, DC 20036
Phone: (202)857-6600
Fax: (202)857-6568

Publications: Shofar (5792)

Bo Shart Publishing
PO Box 111
Deer Lodge, MT 59722
Phone: (406)846-2424
Fax: (406)846-2453

Publications: Banner (17780) • Silver State Post (17781)

Board for Communication Services/The Lutheran Church—Missouri Synod
1333 S Kirkwood Rd.,
St. Louis, MO 63122-7295
Phone: (314)965-9000

Publications: Lutheran Witness (17468)

Board Member, Inc.
PO Box 3468
Brentwood, TN 37024
Phone: (615)309-3200
Fax: (615)371-0899
Free: 800-452-9875

Publications: Bank Director (29060)

Board of Student Publications
Kapiolani Community College
4303 Diamond Head Rd.
Honolulu, HI 96816
Phone: (808)734-9120
Fax: (808)734-9287

Publications: Kapio (7706)

Board of Trustees of the Anglican Church of Canada
600 Jarvis St.
Toronto, ON, Canada M4Y 2J6
Phone: (416)924-9192
Fax: (416)921-4452

Publications: Anglican Journal/Journal Anglican (36462)

The Board of Trustees of the S.C. United Methodist Advocate
4908 Colonial Dr., Ste. 207
Columbia, SC 29203-6070
Phone: (803)786-9486
Fax: (803)735-8168
Free: 888-678-6272

Publications: South Carolina United Methodist Advocate (28567)

Boardman News
6221 Market St.
Boardman, OH 44512
Phone: (330)758-6397
Fax: (330)758-2658

Publications: Boardman News (24684)

Boat Owners Association of The United States
880 S. Pickett St.
Alexandria, VA 22304
Phone: (703)823-9550
Fax: (703)461-2855

Publications: BoatU.S. Magazine (31648)

Bobit Publishing
21061 S Western Ave.
Torrance, CA 90501
Phone: (310)533-2400
Fax: (310)533-2500

Publications: Automotive Fleet (3927) • Contemporary Orthopaedics (3930) • Contemporary Surgery (3931) • Emergency (3933) • LCT (3934) • Metro Magazine (3937) • Mobile Electronics Magazine (3939) • Police (3940) • School Bus Fleet (3942) • Security Sales (3943)

BOCA International
4051 W Flossmoor Rd.
Country Club Hills, IL 60478
Phone: (708)799-2300
Fax: (708)799-4981

Publications: International Code Council (8689)

The Bodega Bay Navigator
1925 Bay Flat Rd.
PO Box 969
Bodega Bay, CA 94923
Phone: (707)875-3574

Publications: The Bodega Bay Navigator (1590)

Body Positive
19 Fulton St., Ste. 308B
New York, NY 10038
Phone: (212)566-7333
Fax: (212)566-4539
Free: 800-566-6599

Publications: Body Positive (21330)

Bogg Publications
422 N Cleveland St.
Arlington, VA 22201
Phone: (703)243-6019

Publications: Bogg (31782)

The Boise City News
105 W Main
PO Box 278
Boise City, OK 73933-0278
Phone: (580)544-2222
Fax: (580)544-3281

Publications: The Boise City News (25766)

Boise Family Magazine
13191 W Scotfield St.
Boise, ID 83713-0899
Phone: (208)938-2119
Fax: (208)938-2117

Publications: Boise Family Magazine (7803)

Boise Weekly
PO Box 1657
Boise, ID 83701
Phone: (208)344-2055
Fax: (208)342-4733

Publications: Boise Weekly (7804)

Boissevain Recorder
561 Stephen St.
Box 220
Boissevain, MB, Canada R0K 0E0
Phone: (204)534-6479
Fax: (204)534-2977

Publications: Boissevain Recorder (35252)

Bolchazy-Carducci Publishers Inc.
1000 Brown St., Unit 101
Wauconda, IL 60084
Phone: (847)526-4344
Fax: (847)526-2867
Free: 800-392-6453

Publications: The Classical Bulletin (9742)

Bolton Enterprise
2 Marconi Ct., Unit 13
Box 99
Bolton, ON, Canada L7E 5T1
Phone: (905)857-3433
Fax: (905)857-5002

Publications: The Enterprise (35690)

Bolton Newspapers, Inc.
126 Hines St.
PO Box 826
Monroeville, AL 36461-0826
Phone: (334)575-3282
Fax: (334)575-3284
Free: 800-239-1985

Publications: The Monroe Journal (351)

Bomar Publishing Inc.
364 Supertest Rd., 2nd Fl.
North York, ON, Canada M3J 2M2
Phone: (416)667-9945
Fax: (416)667-0609

Publications: Marketnews (36130)

The Bond Buyer
One State St. Plaza, 26th Fl.
New York, NY 10004
Phone: (212)803-8263
Fax: (212)843-9615

Publications: The Bond Buyer (21332)

Boney Publishers, Inc.
Box 431
Graham, NC 27253
Phone: (336)228-7851
Fax: (336)229-9602

Publications: Alamance News (23912)

Bongo Productions
PO Box 65856
Los Angeles, CA 90065
Phone: (323)257-2328
Fax: (323)257-2461

Publications: The Beat (Los Angeles) (2217)

The Bonham Daily Favorite
200 Beech St.
Durant, OK 74701

Publications: The Bonham Daily Favorite (25803) • The Honey Grove Signal-Citizen (25806)

Bonkers?
PO Box 189
Palm Beach, FL 33480
Phone: (561)659-0975
Fax: (561)659-2295
Free: 800-403-8850

Publications: Bonkers? (6541)

The Bonner County Daily Bee
PO Box 159
Sandpoint, ID 83864
Phone: (208)263-9534
Fax: (208)263-9091

Publications: The Bonner County Daily Bee (7977)

Bonners Ferry Herald
PO Box 539
Bonners Ferry, ID 83805
Phone: (208)267-5521
Fax: (208)267-5523

Publications: Bonners Ferry Herald (7836)

Bonnyville Nouvelle, Ltd.
5304 - 50 Ave.
Bonnyville, AB, Canada T9N 1Y4
Phone: (780)826-3876
Fax: (780)826-7062

Publications: Bonnyville Nouvelle (34621)

Book News, Inc.
5739 NE Summer
Portland, OR 97218
Phone: (503)281-9230
Fax: (503)287-4485

Publications: Reference & Research Book News (26504) • Sci Tech Book News (26507)

Bookbird
Box 807
Highland Park, IL 60035-0807
Phone: (847)432-4038
Fax: (847)432-4038

Publications: Bookbird (13138)

Booker
204 S Main
PO Box 807
Booker, TX 79005
Phone: (806)658-4732

Publications: The Booker News (29936)

Booklocker Com, Inc.
PO Box 2399
Bangor, ME 04402-2399
Fax: (207)262-5544

Publications: The Write Markets Report (12905)

Boone County Journal
PO Box 197
Ashland, MO 65010
Phone: (573)657-2334
Fax: (573)657-2002

Publications: Boone County Journal (16893)

Boone County Shopper Inc.
112 Leonard Ct.
Belvidere, IL 61008
Phone: (815)544-2166
Fax: (815)544-5558

Publications: Boone County Shopper, Inc. (8063)

Boone Newspaper
914 E Channing Ave.
PO Box 506
Fergus Falls, MN 56537
Phone: (218)736-7511
Fax: (218)736-5919
Free: 800-726-1781

Publications: Fergus Fall Daily Journal (15897)

Boone Newspapers, Inc.
PO Drawer 28
Atmore, AL 36504
Phone: (205)368-2123
Fax: (205)368-2124

Publications: Atmore Advance (33)

Boone Newspapers, Inc.
315 E. Jefferson
PO Box 860
Demopolis, AL 36732-0860
Phone: (334)289-4017
Fax: (334)289-4019

Publications: The Demopolis Times (178)

Boone Newspapers, Inc.
200 W. Marvin
PO Box 877
Waxahachie, TX 75165-3040
Phone: (214)937-3310
Fax: (214)937-1139

Publications: Waxahachie Daily Light (31271)

Boone Today
2136 Mamie Eisenhower
PO Box 375
Boone, IA 50036
Phone: (515)432-6694
Fax: (515)232-8395
Free: 888-270-0090

Publications: Boone Today (10626)

Booth Newspapers
214 S Jackson St.
Jackson, MI 49201-2282
Phone: (517)781-2300
Fax: (517)787-9711
Free: 800-878-6397

Publications: The Jackson Citizen Patriot (15221)

Booth Newspapers
401 S. Burdick St.
Kalamazoo, MI 49007
Phone: (269)345-3511

Publications: Kalamazoo Gazette (15242)

Booth Newspapers, Inc.
155 Michigan St. NW
Grand Rapids, MI 49503-2302
Phone: (616)459-1400
Fax: (616)459-1502

Publications: The Grand Rapids Press (15096)

Bootstrappin' Entrepreneur Bulletin
PO Box 881495
Los Angeles, CA 90009
Phone: (310)568-9861

Publications: Bootstrappin' Entrepreneur Bulletin (2225)

Booz Allen & Hamilton
101 Park Ave.
New York, NY 10178
Phone: (212)551-6222
Fax: (212)551-6008

Publications: strategy business (22796)

Borden Citizen
CFB Bldg. S-138
Borden, ON, Canada L0M 1C0
Phone: (705)423-2496
Fax: (705)423-3452

Publications: Borden Citizen (35691)

The Borden Star
PO Box 137
Gail, TX 79738
Phone: (806)756-4402
Fax: (806)756-4310

Publications: The Borden Star (30375)

Border Crossings Magazine
500-70 Arthur St.
Winnipeg, MB, Canada R3B 1G7
Phone: (204)942-5778
Fax: (204)949-0793
Free: (866)825-7165

Publications: Border Crossings Magazine (35317)

Borderland Sciences Research Foundation
PO Box 6250
Eureka, CA 95502
Phone: (707)445-2247
Fax: (707)445-1401

Publications: The Journal of Borderland Research (1893)

Borderlands: Texas Poetry Review
PO Box 33096
Austin, TX 78764

Publications: Borderlands: Texas Poetry Review (29766)

The Borderline
106 W Ctr. St.
PO Box 220
Roseau, MN 56751
Phone: (218)463-1521
Fax: (218)463-1530

Publications: The Borderline (16327)

Bordighera, Inc.
Department of Languages and Linguistics
Florida Atlantic University
777 Glades Rd.
Boca Raton, FL 33431
Phone: (561)297-3861
Fax: (561)297-2657

Publications: Voices in Italian Americana (10255)

Borealis Press Limited
9 Ashburn Dr.
Nepean, ON, Canada K2E 6N4
Phone: (613)224-6837
Fax: (613)829-7783

Publications: Journal of Canadian Poetry (36254)

Eli Bornstein
Box 378
RPO University
University of Saskatchewan
Saskatoon, SK, Canada S7N 4J8
Phone: (306)966-4198
Fax: (306)966-4197

Publications: The Structurist (37558)

Bort Productions
PO Box 325
Lake Orion, MI 48361-0325
Phone: (248)814-0627
Fax: (248)814-0627

Publications: Automotive Fine Art Journal (15269)

Bossier Newspapers
PO Box 6267
Bossier City, LA 71171
Phone: (318)747-7900
Fax: (318)747-5298

Publications: Bossier Banner-Progress (12536) • Bossier Press Tribune (12537)

Boston Airport Journal
256 Marginal St.
East Boston, MA 02128-2823
Phone: (617)561-4000
Fax: (617)561-2821

Publications: Boston Airport Journal (13855) • Boston Seaport Journal (13862) • Travel New England (14166)

The Boston Book Review
331 Harvard St., Ste. 17
Cambridge, MA 02139
Phone: (617)497-0344

Publications: The Boston Book Review (14041)

Boston College
McElroy Commons, No. 113
Chestnut Hill, MA 02467
Phone: (617)552-4820
Fax: (617)552-4823

Publications: The Heights (14128) • Journal of Teacher Education (10801) • Philosophy & Social Criticism (14132)

Boston College School of Law
885 Centre St.
Newton, MA 02459
Phone: (617)552-4352
Fax: (617)552-2615

Publications: Alledger (14383) • Boston College Environmental Affairs Law Review (14384)

Boston Common Press
17 Station St.
Brookline, MA 02445
Phone: (617)232-1000

Publications: Cook's Illustrated (14018)

Boston Herald
One Herald Sq.
PO Box 2096
Boston, MA 02106-2096
Phone: (617)426-3000
Fax: (617)542-1315
Free: 800-225-2040

Publications: Boston Herald (13858)

The Boston Jewish Times
15 School St.
Boston, MA 02108-4307
Phone: (617)227-7979
Fax: (617)367-9310

Publications: The Boston Jewish Times (13859)

Boston Magazine
300 Massachusetts Ave.
Boston, MA 02115
Phone: (617)262-9700
Fax: (617)262-4925

Publications: Boston Magazine (13860)

Boston & Maine Railroad Historical Society Inc.
PO Box 469
Derry, NH 03038-0469
Phone: (603)628-4053

Publications: B&M Bulletin (14532)

The Boston Parents' Paper
670 Centre St., Ste. 9, 3rd Fl.
Jamaica Plain, MA 02130
Phone: (617)522-1515
Fax: (617)522-1694
Free: 800-733-3771

Publications: The Rhode Island Parents' Paper (14261)

Boston Review
E53-407
MIT
Cambridge, MA 02139-4307
Phone: (617)258-0805
Fax: (617)252-1549

Publications: Boston Review (14042)

Boston Society of Civil Engineers Section
Engineering Ctr.
1 Walnut St.
Boston, MA 02108
Phone: (617)227-5551
Fax: (617)227-6783

Publications: Civil Engineering Practice (13878)

Boston University
236 Bay State Rd.
Boston, MA 02215
Phone: (617)353-2505

Publications: Boston University Today (13866) • Partisan Review (13947) • Studies in Romanticism (13966)

Boston University
10 Lenox St.
Brookline, MA 02446
Phone: (617)353-3180
Fax: (617)353-6488

Publications: BOSTONIA (14016)

Boston University School of Law
765 Commonwealth Ave.
Boston, MA 02215
Phone: (617)353-8368
Fax: (617)353-8369

Publications: Boston University Journal of Science & Technology Law (13865)

Botanical Society of America
Business Office
1735 Neil Ave.
Columbus, OH 43210-1293
Phone: (614)292-3519
Fax: (614)247-6444

Publications: American Journal of Botany (20789)

Bottom Line Publications, Inc.
75 Clegg Rd.
Markham, ON, Canada L6G 1A1
Phone: (905)479-2665
Fax: (905)479-3758
Free: 800-668-6481

Publications: The Bottom Line (36015)

Boucher Communications Inc.
1300 Virginia Dr., Ste. 400
Fort Washington, PA 19034-3221
Phone: (215)643-8000
Fax: (215)643-8099

Publications: Contact Lens Spectrum (26926) • Eyecare Business (26930) • Optometric Management (26932)

Boulder City News
1227 Arizona St.
PO Box 60065
Boulder City, NV 89006
Phone: (702)293-2302
Fax: (702)294-0977

Publications: Boulder City News (18325)

Boulder County Business Report
3180 Sterling Circle, Ste. 201
Boulder, CO 80301-2338
Phone: (303)440-4950
Fax: (303)440-4950

Publications: The Boulder County Business Report (4157)

Boulder Monitor, Inc.
104 W Centennial
PO Box 66
Boulder, MT 59632
Phone: (406)225-3821
Fax: (406)225-3821

Publications: Boulder Monitor (17750)

Boulder Planet
1301 Spruce St.
Boulder, CO 80302
Phone: (303)440-4950
Fax: (303)440-8954

Publications: Boulder Planet (4158)

Boulder Weekly, Inc.
690 S Lashley Ln.
Boulder, CO 80303
Phone: (303)494-5511
Fax: (303)494-2585

Publications: Boulder Weekly (4159)

Boundary Creek Times Printing & Publishing Company Ltd.
PO Box 99
Greenwood, BC, Canada V0H 1J0
Phone: (250)445-2233
Fax: (250)445-2240

Numbers cited after listings are entry numbers rather than page numbers.

Publications: Big White Mountaineer (34885) • Boundary Creek Times Mountaineer (34973)

Boundry Publishers Ltd.
PO Box 730
Estevan, SK, Canada S4A 2A6
Phone: (306)634-2654
Fax: (306)634-3934

Publications: The Estevan Mercury (37465) • Trader Express (37466)

Bow & Swing
34 E Main St.
Apopka, FL 32703
Fax: (407)886-7151

Publications: Bow & Swing (5909)

The Bowdle Pioneer
PO Box 368
Bowdle, SD 57428
Phone: (605)285-6101
Fax: (605)285-6520
Free: 800-491-6101

Publications: The Bowdle Pioneer (28808)

Bowdoin College
4104 College Station
Brunswick, ME 04011-8432
Phone: (207)725-3136
Fax: (207)725-3003

Publications: BOWDOIN Magazine (12934)

Bowdon Bulletin
PO Box 460
Carrollton, GA 30112
Phone: (770)834-6631
Fax: (770)834-9991
Free: 800-830-9425

Publications: Bowdon Bulletin (7155)

Bowers & Merena Galleries
PO Box 1224
Wolfeboro, NH 03894
Phone: (603)569-5095
Fax: (603)569-5319
Free: 800-222-5993

Publications: Rare Coin Review (18655)

Bowes Publication
PO Box 580
Port Elgin, ON, Canada N0H 2C0
Phone: (519)832-9001
Fax: (519)389-4793

Publications: Shoreline Beacon Times (36333)

Bowes Publishers
12040 149 St.
Edmonton, AB, Canada T5V 1P2
Phone: (780)453-9001
Fax: (780)447-7333

Publications: The Edmonton Examiner (34708)

Bowes Publishers, Inc.
324 S Railway
PO Box 1356
Winkler, MB, Canada R6W 4B3
Phone: (204)325-4771
Fax: (204)325-5059

Publications: The Winkler Times (35307)

Bowes Publishers Ltd.
201 Bear St.
Banff, AB, Canada T1L 1H2
Phone: (403)762-2453
Fax: (403)762-5274

Publications: Banff Crag and Canyon (34612)

Bowes Publishers Limited
4903 49 Ave.
Camrose, AB, Canada T4V 0M9
Phone: (780)672-4421
Fax: (780)672-5323

Publications: Camrose Canadian (34676)

Bowes Publishers Ltd.
PO Box 268
Cold Lake, AB, Canada T9M 1P1
Phone: (780)594-5881
Fax: (780)594-2120

Publications: Cold Lake Sun (34687)

Bowes Publishers Ltd.
8550 Franklin Ave.
Fort McMurray, AB, Canada T9H 3G1
Phone: (780)743-8186
Fax: (780)790-1006

Publications: Fort McMurray Today (34767)

Bowes Publishers Ltd.
10420 98th Ave., No. 155
Fort Saskatchewan, AB, Canada T8L 2N6
Phone: (403)998-7070
Fax: (403)998-5515

Publications: The Fort Saskatchewan Record (34771) • The Record (34772)

Bowes Publishers Ltd.
10604 100th St., Bag 3000
Grande Prairie, AB, Canada T8V 6V4
Phone: (780)532-1110
Fax: (780)532-2120

Publications: Daily Herald-Tribune (34774) • Peace Country Extra (34775)

Bowes Publishers Ltd.
104 McLeod Ave.
Hinton, AB, Canada T7V 2A9
Phone: (403)865-3115
Fax: (403)865-1252

Publications: Parklander (34785)

Bowes Publishers Ltd.
5714 44th St.
Lloydminster, AB, Canada T9V 0B6
Phone: (780)875-3362
Fax: (780)875-3423

Publications: Lloydminster Daily Times (34802)

Bowes Publishers Ltd.
Box 599
Mayerthorpe, AB, Canada T0E 1N0
Phone: (403)786-2602
Fax: (403)786-2663

Publications: Mayerthorpe Freelancer (34808)

Bowes Publishers Ltd.
10009 100 Ave.
PO Box 6870
Peace River, AB, Canada T8S 1S6
Phone: (780)624-2591
Fax: (780)624-8600

Publications: Record-Gazette (34822)

Bowes Publishers Ltd.
323 McLeod Ave.
PO Box 4206
Spruce Grove, AB, Canada T7X 3B4
Fax: (403)962-0658

Publications: The Grove Examiner (34852)

Bowes Publishers Ltd.
5006 50th St.
Stony Plain, AB, Canada T7Z 1T3
Phone: (780)963-2291
Fax: (780)963-9716

Publications: The Reporter (34857)

Bowes Publishers Ltd.
5104 53rd Ave.
PO Box 6900
Wetaskiwin, AB, Canada T9A 2G5
Phone: (780)352-2231
Fax: (780)352-4333

Publications: Wetaskiwin Times Advertiser (34873)

Bowes Publishers Ltd.
PO Box 630
Whitecourt, AB, Canada T7S 1N7
Phone: (403)778-3977
Fax: (403)778-6459

Publications: Whitecourt Star (34875)

Bowes Publishers Ltd.
13226 N. Victoria Rd.
PO Box 309
Summerland, BC, Canada V0H 1Z0
Phone: (250)494-5406
Fax: (250)494-5453

Publications: The Bulletin (35102) • Summerland Review (35103)

Bowes Publishers Ltd.
Box 700
Altona, MB, Canada R0G 0B0
Phone: (204)324-5001
Fax: (204)324-1402

Publications: The Red River Valley Echo (35247)

Bowes Publishers Ltd.
1941 Saskatchewan Ave. W.
PO Box 130
Portage La Prairie, MB, Canada R1N 3B4
Phone: (204)857-3427
Fax: (204)239-1270

Publications: The Daily Graphic (35281) • Herald Leader Press (35282)

Bowes Publishers Ltd.
238 Dalhousie St.
Amherstburg, ON, Canada N9V 1W4
Phone: (519)736-2147
Fax: (519)736-8384

Publications: The Amherstburg Echo (35632)

Bowes Publishers Ltd.
Box 39
Clinton, ON, Canada N0M 1L0
Phone: (519)482-3443
Fax: (519)482-7341

Publications: Clinton News-Record (35737)

Bowes Publishers Ltd.
33 Main St. S
PO Box 1620
Kenora, ON, Canada P9N 3X7
Phone: (807)468-5555
Fax: (807)468-4318

Publications: Daily Miner & News (35929)

Bowes Publishers Ltd.
1980 Hyde Park Rd.
London, ON, Canada N6H 5L9
Phone: (519)471-8520
Free: 877-890-9876

Publications: Airdrie Echo (34608)

Bowes Publishers Ltd.
1147 Gainsborough Rd.
PO Box 7400
London, ON, Canada N5Y 4X3
Phone: (519)471-8520
Fax: (519)471-1892
Free: 800-463-0626

Publications: The Nanton News (34817) • Ontario Dairy Farmer (35988) • Ontario Farmer (35989) • Ontario Hog Farmer (35990) • St. Thomas Times-Journal (36363) • The Shoreline News (35992)

Bowes Publishers Ltd.
1383 Confederation St.
Sarnia, ON, Canada N7S 5P1
Phone: (519)336-1100
Fax: (519)336-1833

Publications: Lambton Shopping News (36364)

Bowes Publishers Ltd.
PO Box 2014
Nipawin, SK, Canada S0E 1E0
Phone: (306)862-4618
Fax: (306)862-4566

Publications: Nipawin Journal (37506) • Nipawin N.E. Region Community Booster (37507)

Bowes Publishing
59 Grand River St. N.
Paris, ON, Canada N3L 2N9
Phone: (519)442-7866
Fax: (519)442-3100

Publications: Paris Star (36306)

Bowie County Citizens Tribune
129 East North Front
New Boston, TX 75570-0608
Phone: (903)628-2329
Fax: (903)628-8272

Publications: Bowie County Citizens Tribune (30860)

The Bowie News
218 W. Tarrant St.
Box 831
Bowie, TX 76230
Phone: (940)872-2247
Fax: (940)872-4812

Publications: The Bowie News (29939)

Bowling Green State University
Bowling Green, OH 43403
Phone: (419)372-2725
Fax: (419)372-6805

Publications: Mid-American Review (24696)

Bowling Green State University
Office of Marketing & Communications
Bowling Green, OH 43403
Phone: (419)372-2531

Publications: (Bowling Green) BGSU Magazine (24689)

Bowling Green State University
214 West Hall
Bowling Green, OH 43403
Phone: (419)372-2601
Fax: (419)372-0202

Publications: The BG News (24688)

Bowling Proprietors Association of America
615 Six Flags Dr.
Arlington, TX 76011
Phone: (817)640-5050
Fax: (817)633-2940
Free: 800-343-1329

Publications: Bowling Proprietor (29731)

Bows
PO Box 669
42 Montreal St.
Mitchell, ON, Canada E1C 8P3
Phone: (519)348-8431
Fax: (519)348-8836

Publications: The Mitchell Advocate (36094)

Box Elder News Journal
55 S. 100 W.
PO Box 370
Brigham City, UT 84302
Phone: (435)723-3471
Fax: (435)723-5247

Publications: Box Elder News Journal (31324)

Boy Scouts of America
1325 W. Walnut Hill Ln.
PO Box 152079
Irving, TX 75015-2079
Phone: (972)580-2000
Fax: (972)580-2079

Publications: Boys' Life (30604) • Scouting (30608)

Boyd Printing Co.
49 Sheridan Ave.
Albany, NY 12210
Phone: (518)436-9686
Fax: (518)436-7433
Free: 800-877-2693

Publications: Journal of Special Education Technology (18367) • Teacher Education and Special Education (24821) • Twentieth Century Literature (20007)

Jessie M. Boyett
PO Box 568
Bernice, LA 71222
Phone: (318)285-7424
Fax: (318)285-7420

Publications: Bernice Banner News (12532)

Boys & Girls Club of Greater Nashua
47 Grand Ave.
Nashua, NH 03060
Phone: (603)883-0523

Publications: The Clubhouse (18586)

Boysville Publishing
803 Church St.
Honesdale, PA 18431
Phone: (717)253-1080
Fax: (717)253-0179

Publications: Highlights for Children (27048)

BPI Communications Inc.
575 Prospect Ave.
Lakewood, NJ 08701
Phone: (732)363-5679
Fax: (732)363-0338
Free: 888-463-6110

Publications: SHOOT (19158)

BPS Communications
PO Box 340
Willow Grove, PA 19090
Phone: (215)830-8467
Fax: (215)830-8490

Publications: The National Clothesline (28193)

Brabant Newspapers
47
Ancaster, ON, Canada L9H 1B5
Phone: (905)648-4464
Fax: (905)648-7458

Publications: Ancaster News-Journal (35633)

Brabant Newspapers
333 Arvin Ave.
PO Box 9208
Stoney Creek, ON, Canada L8E 2M6
Phone: (416)561-1090
Fax: (416)664-3102

Publications: Hamilton Mountain News (36405)

Bracebridge Examiner
PO Box 1049
PO Box 1049
Bracebridge, ON, Canada P1L 1V2
Phone: (705)645-8771
Fax: (705)645-1718

Publications: Bracebridge Examiner Limited (35694)

The Bradford Bridge
PO Box 463
Bradford, NH 03221
Phone: (603)938-5029
Fax: (603)938-5702

Publications: The Bradford Bridge (18460)

The Bradford Era
43 Main St.
PO Box 365
Bradford, PA 16701
Phone: (814)368-3173
Fax: (814)362-6510

Publications: The Bradford Era (26727)

Bradford Journal
265 S Ave.
PO Box 17
Bradford, PA 16701-0017
Phone: (814)362-6563
Fax: (413)403-7272

Publications: Bradford Journal/Miner (27298)

Bradford Telegraph
135 W Call St.
PO Drawer A
Starke, FL 32091
Phone: (904)964-6305
Fax: (904)964-8628

Publications: Bradford County Telegraph (6689) • Lake Region Monitor (6690)

Bradley Communications Corp.
135 E. Plumstead Ave.
PO Box 1206
Lansdowne, PA 19050-8206
Phone: (610)259-0707
Fax: (610)284-3704
Free: 800-553-8002

Publications: Radio-TV Interview Report (27162)

The Bradley County Weekly Inc.
PO Box 4602
Cleveland, TN 37320
Phone: (423)472-2882
Fax: (423)339-2135

Publications: Bradley News Weekly (29120)

Brady Standard-Herald
PO Box 1151
Brady, TX 76825
Phone: (915)597-2959
Fax: (915)597-1434

Publications: The Brady Herald (29943)

Braille Institute Press
741 N Vermont Ave.
Los Angeles, CA 90029
Phone: (323)663-1111
Fax: (323)663-0867
Free: 800-BRA-ILLE

Publications: The Braille Mirror (2226)

The Brainerd Daily Dispatch
506 James St.
PO Box 974
Brainerd, MN 56401
Phone: (218)829-4705
Fax: (218)829-7735
Free: 800-432-5703

Publications: Dispatch (15766)

Brampton Guardian
685 Queen St. W
Brampton, ON, Canada L6V 1A1
Phone: (905)454-4344
Fax: (905)454-4385

Publications: The Brampton Guardian (35698)

Branch-Smith, Inc.
120 St. Louis Ave.
PO Box 1868
Fort Worth, TX 76101
Phone: (817)882-4120
Fax: (817)882-4121
Free: 800-433-5612

Publications: Garden Center Merchandising & Management (30339) • Garden Center Products & Supplies (30340) • Greenhouse Management and Production (30341) • Nursery Management and Production (30349)

Brandeis University
PO Box 549110 / MS 068
Waltham, MA 02454

Publications: The Justice (14601)

Brandon Sun
501 Rosser Ave.
Brandon, MB, Canada R7A 0K4
Phone: (204)727-2451
Fax: (204)727-0385
Free: 877-786-5786

Publications: Brandon Sun (35254)

Brandywine Press
Box 2594
Rancho Cucamonga, CA 91729

Publications: Skinner Kinsmen Update (2877)

Brandywyne Books
3976 Oak Hill Rd.
Oakland, CA 94605
Phone: (510)569-5675
Fax: (510)632-8868

Publications: Affaire de Coeur (2662)

Branford News, Inc.
PO Box 148
Branford, FL 32008
Phone: (386)935-1427
Fax: (904)935-3043

Publications: The Branford News (5962)

Brangus Journal
5750 Epsilon
San Antonio, TX 78249
Phone: (210)696-4343
Fax: (210)696-5031

Publications: Brangus Journal (31026)

Brannon Publishing Inc.
1306 Gaskins Rd.
Richmond, VA 23233
Phone: (804)754-2101
Fax: (804)754-1534
Free: 888-724-2101

Publications: UDC Magazine (32458)

Branson TriLakes Daily News
200 Industrial Park Dr.
Hollister, MO 65672
Phone: (417)334-3161
Fax: (417)334-4299

Publications: Branson Daily News (17100)

Brant Publications Inc.
575 Broadway
New York, NY 10012-3230
Phone: (212)941-2884
Fax: (212)941-2844

Publications: Art in America (21249) • The Magazine Antiques (22274)

The Brantley Enterprise
PO Box 454
Nahunta, GA 31553
Phone: (912)462-6776
Fax: (912)462-6776

Publications: Brantley Enterprise (7451)

Brantwood Publications, Inc.
2410 Northside Dr.
Clearwater, FL 33761
Phone: (727)786-9771
Fax: (727)791-4126

Publications: Interiorscape (5986) • Nursery Business Retailer (5989) • Southern Golf (5990)

BrassRing Diversity
170 High St.
Waltham, MA 02453-5914
Phone: (617)577-7790
Fax: (617)577-7799
Free: 800-CBA-FORU

Publications: Careers and the MBA (14597) • Careers and the Technology Undergrad (14598)

Bratstvo (Fraternity)
1 Secroft Crescent
North York, ON, Canada M3N 1R5
Phone: (416)663-3409
Fax: (416)665-3564

Publications: Bratstvo (Fraternity) (36122)

Brattleboro Town Crier
Putney Rd., Windham
PO Box 537
Brattleboro, VT 05302-0537
Phone: (802)257-7771
Fax: (802)257-2211

Publications: The Brattleboro Town Crier (31509)

Bravo Editions
1081 Trafalgar St.
Teaneck, NJ 07666-1929

Publications: Bravo (19608)

Braxton Citizen's News
PO Box 516
PO Box 516
Sutton, WV 26601
Phone: (304)765-5193
Fax: (304)765-2754

Publications: Braxton Citizens' News (33475)

Braxton Democrat-Central
205 Main
Sutton, WV 26601
Phone: (304)765-5555
Fax: (304)765-5555

Publications: Braxton Democrat-Central (33476)

The Brazil Times Publishing Corp.
100 N Meridian St.
PO Box 429
Brazil, IN 47834
Phone: (812)446-2216
Fax: (812)446-0938
Free: 800-489-5090

Publications: The Brazil Times (9869) • Times Advantage (9870)

The Brazoria County News
PO Box 488
West Columbia, TX 77486
Phone: (979)345-3127
Fax: (979)345-5308

Publications: The Brazoria County News (31283)

Brazzil
PO Box 50536
Los Angeles, CA 90050-0536
Phone: (323)255-8062
Fax: (323)257-3497

Publications: Brazzil (2227)

BRD Corp.
PO Box 183
Killington, VT 05751
Phone: (802)422-2399
Fax: (802)422-2395
Free: 800-564-6970

Publications: The Mountain Times (31547)

BREBCO, Inc.
68 Sykes St. N.
Meaford, ON, Canada N4L 1R2
Phone: (519)538-1421
Fax: (519)538-5028

Publications: The Express (36036)

BREBCO, Inc.
51 Bruce St.
PO Box 190
Thornbury, ON, Canada N0H 2P0
Fax: (519)599-3214

Publications: Courier-Herald (36434)

Breckenridge American
PO Box 871
Breckenridge, TX 76424
Phone: (254)559-5412
Fax: (254)559-3491

Publications: Breckenridge American (29946)

Breckinridge County Herald-News
US 60 E
PO Box 6
Hardinsburg, KY 40143
Phone: (270)756-2109
Fax: (270)756-1003

Publications: Breckinridge County Herald-News (12103)

Breda News
PO Box 183
Breda, IA 51436-0183
Phone: (712)673-2318
Fax: (712)673-4246

Publications: Breda News (10630)

Breese Journal
8060 Old Hwy. 50
PO Box 405
Breese, IL 62230
Phone: (618)526-7211
Fax: (618)526-2590

Publications: Breese Journal (8097)

Breeze-Courier
212 S Main St.
PO Box 440
Taylorville, IL 62568
Phone: (217)824-2233
Fax: (217)824-2026
Free: 800-200-6397

Publications: Breeze-Courier (9678)

Breeze Publishing Co.
10700 Stringfellow Rd. Ste. 60
Bokeelia, FL 33922
Phone: (239)283-2022
Fax: (239)283-0232

Publications: The Pine Island Eagle (5974)

Breeze Publishing Co.
PO Box 151306
Cape Coral, FL 33915-1306
Phone: (941)574-1110
Fax: (941)574-3403

Publications: The Cape Coral Daily Breeze (5971) • Lee County Shopper (5973)

Breeze Publishing Co.
19260 San Carlos Blvd.
Fort Myers Beach, FL 33931
Phone: (941)463-4421
Fax: (941)463-1402

Publications: Fort Myers Beach Bulletin (6117)

Breeze Publishing Co.
PO Box 56
Sanibel, FL 33957-0056

Publications: The Islander (6651)

Breeze Publishing Co.
PO Box 1180
Wewahitchka, FL 32465
Phone: (904)639-2706

Publications: The Gulf County Breeze (6862)

Brehm Comm.
1226 Ave. H
Fort Madison, IA 52627-4544
Phone: (319)372-6421
Fax: (319)372-3867
Free: 800-798-8819

Publications: Ft. Madison Daily Democrat (10916)

Brehm Communications, Inc.
180 N. Washington
Wickenburg, AZ 85390-1298
Phone: (520)684-7218
Fax: (520)684-3185

Publications: The Wickenburg Sun (1005)

Brehm Communications, Inc.
Box 2410
Lake Arrowhead, CA 92352-2410
Phone: (909)337-6145
Fax: (909)337-5275

Publications: Mountain News (2138) • Mountain Shopper (2139)

Brehm Communications, Inc.
74-617 Highway 111
Palm Desert, CA 92261
Fax: (619)773-5400

Publications: Rancho Mirage Post (2879)

Brehm Communications, Inc.
PO Box 159
Twentynine Palms, CA 92277
Phone: (760)367-3577
Fax: (760)367-1798

Publications: The Desert Trail (3964)

Brehm Communications, Inc.
c/o Daily Gate City
1016 Main St.
PO Box 430
Keokuk, IA 52632
Phone: (319)524-8300
Fax: (319)524-4363

Publications: Daily Gate City (11013)

Brehm Inc.
4253 Rocklin Rd.
Rocklin, CA 95677-2831
Phone: (916)624-9713
Fax: (916)624-7469

Publications: Placer Herald (2956)

Bremond Press
PO Box 490
Bremond, TX 76629
Phone: (254)746-7033
Fax: (254)746-7089

Publications: Bremond Press (29947)

Brepols Publishers
Begijnhof 67
B-2300 Turnhout, Belgium
Phone: 32 14448020
Fax: 32 14428919

Publications: Manuscripta (17470)

Brevard Community College
1519 Clearlake Rd.
Cocoa, FL 32922
Phone: (321)632-1111
Fax: (321)633-4565

Publications: The Capsule (5999)

The Brewers Bulletin
PO Box 677
Thiensville, WI 53092-0677
Phone: (262)242-6105
Fax: (414)351-5710

Publications: The Brewers Bulletin (34365)

Brewers Digest
PO Box 677
Thiensville, WI 53092-0677
Phone: (262)463-3400
Fax: (262)463-4962

Publications: Brewers Digest (34366)

Brewster Quad City Herald Publishing
PO Box 37
PO Box 37
Brewster, WA 98812
Phone: (509)689-2507
Fax: (509)689-2508

Publications: Brewster Quad-City Herald (32696)

Brewton Newspapers, Inc.
PO Box 887
Brewton, AL 36427
Phone: (205)867-4876
Fax: (205)867-4877

Publications: The Brewton Standard & The Plus (136)

Briarpatch, Inc.
2138 McIntyre St.
Regina, SK, Canada S4P 2R7
Phone: (306)525-2949

Publications: Briarpatch (37525)

Brick
PO Box 537, Stn. Q
Toronto, ON, Canada M4T 2M5
Phone: (416)593-9684

Publications: Brick (36477)

Bridge City Publishing, Inc.
111 W. 3rd St.
PO Box 250
Mobridge, SD 57601-0250
Phone: (605)845-3646
Fax: (605)845-7659
Free: 800-594-9418

Publications: The Mobridge Tribune (28905) • The Monday Reminder (28906)

Bridge Publications, Inc.
PO Box C
Scappoose, OR 97056
Phone: (503)543-6387
Fax: (503)543-6380

Publications: The South County Spotlight (26578)

Bridge U.S.A.
20300 S. Vermont Ave., No. 200
Torrance, CA 90502
Phone: (310)532-5921
Fax: (310)532-1184

Publications: Bridge U.S.A. (3928)

Bridgeport News
3252 S Halsted
Chicago, IL 60608-6698
Phone: (312)842-5883
Fax: (312)842-5097

Publications: Bridgeport News (8290)

Bridgeton Evening News
100 Commerce
PO Box 596
Bridgeton, NJ 08302-2602
Phone: (609)451-1000
Fax: (609)451-7214

Publications: Bridgeton Evening News (18690)

Bridgton News Corp.
42 Main St.
PO Box 244
Bridgton, ME 04009
Phone: (207)647-2851
Fax: (207)647-5001

Publications: The Bridgton News (12930)

Bridwell Publishing
PO Box 1150
Bridgeport, TX 76426
Phone: (940)683-4412
Fax: (940)683-3841

Publications: Chico Texan (30016)

Brigham Young Daily Universe
Brigham Young University
Provo, UT 84602
Phone: (801)378-4636

Publications: The Daily Universe (31402)

Brigham Young University
290 Life Science Museum
Provo, UT 84602-0200
Phone: (801)378-6688
Fax: (801)378-3733

Publications: Western North American Naturalist (31409)

Brigham Young University
207 UPB
Provo, UT 84602
Phone: (801)378-4900
Fax: (801)422-0687

Publications: BYU Magazine (31399) • BYU Studies (31400)

Bright Side
PO Box 935
Kennesaw, GA 30144
Phone: (770)423-9555

Publications: Bright Side (7353)

Brill Academic Publishers Inc.
112 Water St., Ste. 400
Boston, MA 02109
Phone: (617)263-2323
Fax: (617)263-2324
Free: 800-337-9255

Publications: Central European History (13871) • Central European History (2934)

The Brinton Group Inc.
49 Eaton Rd., Ste. 100
Framingham, MA 01701-2727

Publications: EOS/ESD Technology (14195)

Bristol Acquisition Corp.
44 Union St.
PO Box 250
Thomaston, CT 06787
Phone: (860)283-4355
Fax: (860)283-4356
Free: 800-220-6229

Publications: Thomaston Express (5174)

The Bristol Press
99 Main St.
Bristol, CT 06010-6579
Phone: (203)584-0501
Fax: (203)584-2192

Publications: The Bristol Press (4721)

Bristol Press Publishing Co.
1522 Hopmeadow St.
PO Box 477
Simsbury, CT 06070-1419
Fax: (203)658-2898

Publications: Farmington Valley Herald (4822)

Britannia.com, LLC
PO Box 136
Yorklyn, DE 19736
Phone: (610)388-6841
Fax: (610)388-1747

Publications: Britannia (5305)

British-America Business Inc.
52 Vanderbilt, 20th Fl.
New York, NY 10017
Phone: (212)661-4060
Fax: (212)661-4074

Publications: UK & USA (22880)

British America Publishing Company Ltd.
Canadian Orange Headquarters
94 Sheppard Ave. W.
Willowdale, ON, Canada M2N 1M5
Phone: (416)223-1690
Fax: (416)223-1324
Free: 800-565-6248

Publications: The Sentinel (36884)

British Columbia Genealogical Society
PO Box 88054, Lansdowne Mall
Richmond, BC, Canada V6X 3T6
Phone: (604)502-9119
Fax: (604)502-9119

Publications: British Columbia Genealogist (35074)

British Columbia Institute of Technology Student Association
3700 Willingdon Ave.
Burnaby, BC, Canada V5G 3H2
Phone: (604)432-8974
Fax: (604)431-7619

Publications: BCIT Link (34892)

British Columbia Magazine
302, 3939 Quadna St.
Victoria, BC, Canada V8X 1J5
Phone: (250)380-7611
Fax: (250)384-9926
Free: 800-663-7611

Publications: British Columbia Magazine (35210)

British Columbia Medical Association
115-1665 W. Broadway
Vancouver, BC, Canada V6J 5A4
Phone: (604)736-5551
Fax: (604)733-7317

Publications: BCMJ (The British Columbia Medical Journal) (35126)

British Columbia Ministry of Finance and Corporate Relations
PO Box 9410 Stn. Prov. Gov't
Victoria, BC, Canada V8W 9V1
Phone: (250)387-0359
Fax: (250)387-0380

Publications: British Columbia Business Indicators (35208) • British Columbia Origin Exports (35211) • British Columbia Regional Index (35212) • Economic Accounts (35215) • Labour Force Survey (35218)

British Columbia Pharmacy Association
1530-1200 West 73rd Ave.
Vancouver, BC, Canada V6P 6G5
Phone: (604)261-2092
Fax: (604)261-2097
Free: 800-663-2840

Publications: BC Pharmacy (35124)

British Columbia Vital Statistics Agency
818 Fort St.
Victoria, BC, Canada V8W 1H8
Phone: (250)952-2681
Fax: (250)952-2527

Publications: British Columbia Division of Vital Statistics Quarterly Digest (35209)

British Columbia Waterfront and Island Magazine
PO Box 1310
Port Alberni, BC, Canada V9Y 7M2

Publications: B.C. Waterfront & Island Magazine (35049)

British North America Philatelic Society Ltd.
University of Ottawa
Mathematics Dept.
Ottawa, ON, Canada K1N 6N5

Publications: BNA Topics (35761)

Britton Journal Inc.
706 7th St.
PO Box 69
Britton, SD 57430
Phone: (605)448-2281
Fax: (605)442-2282

Publications: Journal (28810)

Broad River Genealogical Society, Inc.
Box 2261
Shelby, NC 28151-2261

Publications: Eswau Huppeday (24226)

Broad Top Bulletin
PO Box 188
900 6th St.
Saxton, PA 16678-0188
Phone: (814)635-2851

Publications: Broad Top Bulletin (27944)

Broadaxe Publishers
PO Box 286
112 W. 7th Ave.
Floodwood, MN 55736
Phone: (218)476-2232
Fax: (218)476-2782

Publications: The Forum (15904)

       Numbers cited after listings are entry numbers rather than page numbers.

Broadcast Cable Financial Management Association
701 Lee St., No. 640
Des Plaines, IL 60016
Phone: (847)296-0200
Fax: (847)296-7510

Publications: Financial Manager for the Media Professional (8761)

Broadcast Education Association
1771 N St., NW
Washington, DC 20036
Phone: (202)429-5355
Fax: (202)775-2981

Publications: Feedback (26847)

Broadcast Education Association
515 N. Park Ave.
Department of Telecommunication
Indiana University
Bloomington, IN 47405

Publications: Journal of Broadcasting & Electronic Media (5576)

Broadcaster Publications, Inc.
PO Box 369
Deer Park, TX 77536
Phone: (281)479-5263
Fax: (281)479-3415

Publications: Deer Park Broadcaster/Progress (30223)

Broadside
George Mason University
4400 University Dr.
Mail Stop 2C5
Fairfax, VA 22030-4444
Phone: (703)993-2950
Fax: (703)993-2948

Publications: Broadside (32010)

Brock University
500 Glen Ridge Ave.
St. Catharines, ON, Canada L2S 3A1
Phone: (905)688-5550
Fax: (905)641-7581

Publications: The Brock Press (36350)

Broken Bow News
108 N Broadway
Broken Bow, OK 74728
Phone: (405)584-6210
Fax: (405)584-9466

Publications: Broken Bow News (25774)

Broken Pencil
PO Box 203, Sta. P
Toronto, ON, Canada M5S 2S7
Phone: (416)531-2813

Publications: Broken Pencil (36479)

Broker News
PO Box 20287
Fountain Hills, AZ 85269-0287
Phone: (602)816-1400
Fax: (602)816-1804
Free: 800-475-3565

Publications: Broker News (9620)

Bromeliad Society, Inc.
720 Millertown Rd.
Auburn, CA 95602
Phone: (530)885-0201
Fax: (530)885-0201

Publications: Bromeliad Society Journal (1437)

Bronxville Women's Club
135 Midland Ave.
Bronxville, NY 10708
Phone: (914)337-3252

Publications: The Villager (20294)

Lawrence Brook
Box 130052
Birmingham, AL 35213
Phone: (205)595-9255
Fax: (205)595-9256

Publications: Deep South Jewish Voice (67)

The Brooke County Review
319 Charles St.
PO Box 591
Wellsburg, WV 26070
Phone: (304)737-0946
Fax: (304)737-0297

Publications: The Brooke County Review (33494)

Brookfield Publishing Co.
107 N Main
PO Box 40
Brookfield, MO 64628
Fax: (816)258-7238
Free: 800-685-6012

Publications: The Daily News-Bulletin (16927)

Brookhaven College
3939 Valley View Ln.
Farmers Branch, TX 75244
Phone: (972)860-4787
Fax: (972)860-4142

Publications: The Courier (30314)

Brookings Institution Press
1775 Massachusetts Ave. NW
Washington, DC 20036
Phone: (202)797-6000
Fax: (202)797-6004
Free: 800-275-1447

Publications: Brookings Papers on Economic Activity (5384) • The Brookings Review (5385) • Capital Idea$ (5393) • Economia (5471)

Brookings Publishing Co.
312 5th St.
PO Box 177
Brookings, SD 57006-0177
Phone: (605)692-6271
Fax: (605)692-2979
Free: 800-568-5032

Publications: The Brookings Register (28812)

Brookings Register
312 5th St.
PO Box 177
Brookings, SD 57006
Phone: (605)692-6271
Fax: (605)692-2979

Publications: Prairie Profile (28815)

Brooklyn Botanic Garden
1000 Washington Ave.
Brooklyn, NY 11225
Phone: (718)623-7200
Fax: (718)622-7839

Publications: Plants & Gardens News (20338)

Brooklyn Chronicle
Box 533
Brooklyn, IA 52211
Phone: (641)522-7155
Fax: (641)522-7909

Publications: Brooklyn Chronicle (10633)

Brooklyn College
2900 Bedford Ave.
Brooklyn, NY 11210
Phone: (718)951-5335

Publications: Kingsman (20326) • Night Call (20334)

Brooklyn Journal
129 Montague St.
Brooklyn, NY 11201-3504
Phone: (718)858-2300
Fax: (718)629-2716

Publications: Brooklyn Heights Press (20301) • Brooklyn Record (20304) • Daily Bulletin (20309)

Brooklyn New York Recorder
86 Bainbridge St.
Brooklyn, NY 11233
Phone: (718)493-4616

Publications: Brooklyn New York Recorder (20302)

Brooklyn Paper Publications
26 Ct. St.
Brooklyn, NY 11242-0009
Phone: (718)834-9350
Fax: (718)834-9278

Publications: The Brooklyn Paper/Brooklyn's Weekly Newspaper (20303) • Downtown News (20315) • Park Slope Paper (20335)

Brooks Community Newspapers, Inc.
542 Westport Ave.
Norwalk, CT 06851
Phone: (203)849-1600
Fax: (203)849-4844

Publications: Fairfield Citizen-News (4787) • Inside FC (5065) • New Canaan Lifestyles (5071) • Norwalk Citizen-News (5072) • Norwalk Lifestyles (5073) • Westport News (5080) • Wilton Lifestyles (5081)

Brotherhood of Locomotive Engineers
1370 Ontario St.
Cleveland, OH 44113
Phone: (216)241-2630
Fax: (216)861-0932

Publications: Locomotive Engineers Journal (24921)

Brotherhood of Maintenance of Way Employees
26555 Evergreen Rd., Ste. 200
Southfield, MI 48076
Phone: (248)948-1010
Fax: (248)948-7150

Publications: BMWE Journal (15542)

Brotherhood of Railroad Signalmen
601 W Golf Rd.
Mount Prospect, IL 60056-4276
Phone: (847)439-3732
Fax: (847)439-3743

Publications: Signalman's Journal (9250)

Broward Community College
North Campus
1000 Coconut Creek Blvd.
Pompano Beach, FL 33066
Phone: (954)973-2237
Fax: (954)968-2448

Publications: The Observer (6034)

The Broward Informer
PO Box 130207
Sunrise, FL 33313
Phone: (954)370-6009

Publications: The Broward Informer (6699)

Browbeat Magazine
PO Box 11124
Oakland, CA 94611-1124
Phone: (510)652-2441

Publications: Browbeat Magazine (2670)

Brown & Brown Publishers
9192 W Cactus, Ste. C
Peoria, AZ 85381
Phone: (602)878-2210

Publications: Sun Life Magazine (770)

The Brown City Banner
4241 Main St.
Box 250
Brown City, MI 48416-9701
Phone: (810)346-2753
Fax: (810)346-2579

Publications: The Brown City Banner (14839)

Brown County Press
PO Box 453
Mount Orab, OH 45154
Phone: (937)444-3441
Fax: (937)444-2652

Publications: Brown County Press (25396)

Brown County Publishing Co.
138 Main St.
PO Box 610
Denmark, WI 54208
Phone: (920)863-2154
Fax: (920)863-6102

Publications: The Denmark Press (33657)

The Brown Daily Herald, Inc.
195 Angell St.
PO Box 2538
Providence, RI 02906-0538
Phone: (401)351-3260
Fax: (401)351-9297

Publications: Brown Daily Herald (28391)

Brown Publications
1455 W. Main St.
Tipp City, OH 45371
Phone: (937)667-8512
Fax: (937)667-8987

Publications: New Carlisle Sun (25408)

Brown Publishing
111 W. Cherry St.
PO Box 169
Georgetown, OH 45121-0169
Phone: (513)378-6161
Fax: (513)378-2004

Publications: The News Democrat (25216)

Brown Publishing
5412 Courseview Dr., Ste. 200
Mason, OH 45040
Phone: (513)459-2500
Fax: (513)459-2515

Publications: The Daily Advocate (25227)

Brown Publishing Co.
PO Box 498
210 N. Court St.
Circleville, OH 43113
Phone: (614)474-3131
Fax: (614)474-9525

Publications: Circleville Herald (24850)

Brown Publishing Co.
295 Broadway
PO Box 270
Jackson, OH 45640
Phone: (740)286-2187
Fax: (740)286-5854
Free: 800-933-6502

Publications: Times Journal (25257)

Brown Publishing Co.
72 E. Main St.
PO Box 758
Logan, OH 43138-0758
Fax: (614)385-4514

Publications: Logan Daily News (25312)

Brown Publishing Co.
310 Patrick Ave.
Urbana, OH 43078
Phone: (937)652-2100
Fax: (937)748-1165

Publications: The Ada Herald (24570) • Eaton Register-Herald (25174) • Press-Gazette (25243) • Star Republican (25606) • Wilmington News-Journal (25667)

Brown Publishing Co.
220 E. Court St.
PO Box 191
Urbana, OH 43078
Phone: (513)652-1331
Fax: (513)652-1336

Publications: Urbana Daily Citizen (25607)

Brown Publishing, Inc.
3085 Woodman Dr., Ste. 170
Kettering, OH 45420-1159
Phone: (937)294-7000
Fax: (937)294-2981

Publications: The Centerville-Bellbrook Times (24753) • Fairborn Daily Herald (25187) • Kettering-Oakwood Times (25284) • Skywrighter (25684) • West Carrollton Times (25632)

Brown Thompson Newspapers, Inc.
8230 W. High St.
PO Box 151
Union City, PA 16438-0151
Phone: (814)438-7666
Fax: (814)438-2898
Free: 800-352-9191

Publications: Cosmopolite Herald (26943) • The Independent-Enterprise (26862) • North East Breeze (27340) • Times-Leader (28066)

Brown University
Box 0
Providence, RI 02912
Phone: (401)863-3042
Fax: (401)863-7261

Publications: Brasil - Brazil (28389)

Brown University
PO Box 1854, 71 George St.
Providence, RI 02912-3613
Phone: (401)863-2873
Fax: (401)863-9599

Publications: Brown Alumni Magazine (28390)

Brownfield News, Inc.
409 W. Hill St.
PO Box 1272
Brownfield, TX 79316
Phone: (806)637-4535
Fax: (806)637-3795

Publications: Brownfield News (29953)

Brownwood Newspapers, Inc.
700 Carnegie St.
PO Box 1189
Brownwood, TX 76801
Phone: (915)646-2541
Fax: (915)646-6835

Publications: Brownwood Bulletin (29965)

Brule County News
Box 46
Kimball, SD 57355-0046
Phone: (605)778-6253
Fax: (605)778-6959

Publications: Brule-Buffalo County News (28879)

Brunico Communications, Inc.
366 Adelaide St. W., Ste. 500
Toronto, ON, Canada M5V 1R9
Phone: (416)408-2300
Fax: (416)408-0870
Free: 888-278-6426

Publications: Playback (36711) • Strategy (36749)

Brunswick Beacon
PO Box 2558
Shallotte, NC 28459
Phone: (910)754-6890
Fax: (910)754-5407

Publications: Brunswick Beacon (24223)

Brunswick News Inc
179 Main St.
PO Box 2756
Grand Falls, NB, Canada E3Z 2W1
Phone: (506)473-3083
Fax: (506)473-3105

Publications: The Cataract (35406)

Brunswick News Publishing Co.
3011 Altama Ave.
PO Box 1557
Brunswick, GA 31521
Phone: (912)265-8320
Fax: (912)264-4973

Publications: The Brunswick News (7139)

Brunswick Publishing Co.
PO Box 698
Industry Rd.
Brunswick, ME 04011
Phone: (207)729-8753
Fax: (207)729-5728

Publications: Church World (13008)

Brunswickan Publishing Inc.
The Brunswickan
100 Pacey Dr., UNB
Fredericton, NB, Canada E3B 5A3
Phone: (506)453-4983
Fax: (506)453-4983

Publications: The Brunswickan (35391)

The Brunswicker
118 E Broadway
PO Box 188
Brunswick, MO 65236
Phone: (660)548-3171
Fax: (660)388-6688

Publications: The Brunswicker (16928)

Brush News-Tribune
PO Box 8
Brush, CO 80723
Phone: (970)842-5516
Fax: (970)842-5519

Publications: Brush News-Tribune (4209)

BRUSHWARE
Centaur S
5515 Dundee Rd.
Huddleston, VA 24104
Phone: (540)297-1517
Fax: (540)297-1519

Publications: Brushware (32171)

Bryan-College Station Eagle
1729 Briarcrest Dr.
PO Box 3000
Bryan, TX 77802
Phone: (979)776-4444
Fax: (979)774-0496
Free: 800-299-7355

Publications: Bryan-College Station Eagle (29973)

Bryan Publications
300 4th St. SE
Cullman, AL 35055
Fax: (205)737-1020

Publications: The Leeds News (302)

Bryan Publishing Co.
127 S. Walnut St.
PO Box 471
Bryan, OH 43506
Phone: (419)636-1111
Fax: (419)636-8937

Publications: The Bryan Times (24714) • The Countyline (24715) • The Leader-Enterprise (25395)

Bryant College
1150 Douglas Pike
PO Box 7
Smithfield, RI 02917-1284
Phone: (401)232-6028
Fax: (401)232-6710

Publications: The Archway (28442)

Bryant Klippenstein
PO Box 190
Manitou, MB, Canada R0G 1G0
Phone: (204)242-2555
Fax: (204)242-3137

Publications: The Western Canadian (35272)

Bryant News, Inc.
108 Locust St.
Hickman, NE 68372-0148
Phone: (402)792-2255
Fax: (402)792-2256

Publications: The VOICE News (18048)

Robert Bryant
PO Box 2048
Port Townsend, WA 98368-0239

Publications: Recumbent Cyclist News (32895)

Andy Bryson
210 Water St.
Woodbury, TN 37190
Phone: (615)563-2512
Fax: (615)563-4502

Publications: Cannon Courier (29649)

BSC Center for International Understanding
219 Rock St.
Bluefield, WV 24701-2198
Phone: (304)327-4036
Fax: (304)327-3425

Publications: Commonwealth Novel in English (33254)

BSDA News Magazine
No. 2, 19299-94 Ave.
Surrey, BC, Canada V4N 4E6
Phone: (604)513-2205
Fax: (604)513-2206

Publications: BSDA News Magazine (35106)

BSK Communications and Associates
1356 Glenns Bay Rd., Apt. 205M
Myrtle Beach, SC 29575-4756

Publications: Today's $85,000 Freelance Writer (28704)

2306

Numbers cited after listings are entry numbers rather than page numbers.

B2B Portales
901 Ponce de Leon Blvd., Ste. 901
Coral Gables, FL 33134
Phone: (305)448-6875
Fax: (305)448-9942
Free: 800-622-6657

Publications: Artes Graficas (6004) • Tecnologia del Plastico (6013)

Buckeye Publishing Co., Inc.
308 W Maple St.
Lisbon, OH 44432
Phone: (330)424-9541
Fax: (330)424-0048
Free: 800-862-6224

Publications: Central Shopper (25307) • Morning Journal (25308)

Buckeye Review Publishing Co.
1201 Belmont Ave.
PO Box 287
Youngstown, OH 44501
Phone: (330)743-2250
Fax: (330)746-2340

Publications: The Buckeye Review (25694)

Buckeye Valley News
PO Box 217
Buckeye, AZ 85326
Phone: (602)386-4426
Fax: (602)386-4427

Publications: Buckeye Valley News (662)

Buckley Newspapers, Inc.
3362 Hwy 15
PO Box 449
Bay Springs, MS 39422
Phone: (601)764-3104
Fax: (601)764-3106

Publications: Jasper County News (16554)

Buckley Newspapers, Inc.
PO Box 4406
Laurel, MS 39441
Phone: (601)649-1129
Fax: (601)649-0424

Publications: Impact of Hattiesburg (16739) • Impact of Laurel (16740)

Buckmasters
10350 Hwy. 80 E.
Montgomery, AL 36117
Phone: (334)215-3337
Fax: (334)215-3535

Publications: Buckmasters Whitetail Magazine (362) • Young Bucks Outdoors (381)

Bucknell University
Judd House
Lewisburg, PA 17837
Phone: (570)577-3260
Fax: (570)577-3683

Publications: Bucknell World (27191)

Bucks County Bar Association
135 E. State St.
PO Box 300
Doylestown, PA 18901-0300
Phone: (215)348-9413
Fax: (215)348-3277
Free: 800-479-8585

Publications: Bucks County Law Reporter (26830)

The Bucyrus Telegraph-Forum
PO Box 471
Bucyrus, OH 44820
Phone: (419)562-3333

Publications: The Bucyrus Telegraph-Forum (24718)

The Buddhist Ray, Inc.
92 Vandam St.
New York, NY 10013
Phone: (212)645-1143
Fax: (212)645-1493

Publications: Tricycle (22866)

Buena Vista County Journal
PO Box 666
Newell, IA 50568
Phone: (712)272-4417

Publications: Buena Vista County Journal (11114)

Buena Vista University
610 W Fourth St.
Storm Lake, IA 50588-1798
Phone: (712)749-2120
Fax: (712)749-1459
Free: 800-383-2821

Publications: Buena Vista Today (11243) • The Tack (11246)

Buffalo Bulletin
PO Box 730
Buffalo, WY 82834
Phone: (307)684-2223
Fax: (307)684-7431

Publications: Buffalo Bulletin (34478)

Buffalo County Journal
PO Box 40
Cochrane, WI 54622
Phone: (608)248-2451
Fax: (608)248-2422

Publications: Buffalo County Journal (33640)

Buffalo Criterion
409 E Utica
Buffalo, NY 14206
Phone: (716)853-2973
Fax: (716)882-9570

Publications: Buffalo Criterion (20364)

Buffalo Jewish Review
15 E Mohawk
Buffalo, NY 14203
Phone: (716)854-2192
Fax: (716)854-2198

Publications: Buffalo Jewish Review (20365)

Buffalo Press
Drawer B
Buffalo, TX 75831
Phone: (903)322-4248
Fax: (903)322-4023

Publications: Buffalo Press (29986)

Buffalo Reflex
114 E Lincoln
PO Box 770
Buffalo, MO 65622
Phone: (417)345-2224
Fax: (417)345-2235
Free: 800-862-8186

Publications: Buffalo Reflex (16929)

The Buffalo Rocket
2507 Delaware Ave.
Buffalo, NY 14216
Phone: (716)873-2594
Fax: (716)873-0809

Publications: The Buffalo Rocket (20369) • West Side Times (20391)

Buffalo Spree Magazine
5678 Main St.
Williamsville, NY 14221
Phone: (716)634-0820
Fax: (716)810-0075

Publications: Buffalo Spree (23582)

BuffaloBeat
25 Boxwood Ln.
Buffalo, NY 14225
Phone: (716)656-5219
Fax: (718)668-2640

Publications: BuffaloBeat (20370)

Bugle Publications
7400 Waukekan Rd.
Niles, IL 60714
Phone: (847)588-1900
Fax: (847)588-1911

Publications: The Niles Bugle (9291)

Buhl Herald, Inc.
PO Box 312
Buhl, ID 83316
Phone: (208)543-4335
Fax: (208)543-6834

Publications: Buhl Herald (7838)

Building Industry Association of Southeastern Michigan
30375 Northwestern Hwy., Ste. 100
Farmington Hills, MI 48334
Phone: (248)737-4477
Fax: (248)862-1055

Publications: Building Business & Apartment Management (15016)

The Building Materials Retailers Association of Quebec
474, Trans-Canada
Longueuil, QC, Canada J4G 1N8
Phone: (514)646-5842
Fax: (514)646-6171
Free: 877-723-6220

Publications: Quart de Rond (37058)

Building Owners & Managers Association International
1201 New York Ave. NW, Ste. 300
Washington, DC 20005
Phone: (202)408-2662
Fax: (202)371-0181

Publications: Boma (5380)

Building Service Contractors Association Int'l.
10201 Lee Hwy., Ste. 225
Fairfax, VA 22030-2222
Phone: (703)359-7090
Fax: (703)352-0493
Free: 800-368-3414

Publications: Services (32028)

Bull & Bear Financial Newspaper
PO Box 917179
Longwood, FL 32791
Phone: (407)682-6170
Fax: (407)682-6170
Free: 800-336-BULL

Publications: Bull & Bear Financial Report (6312)

The Bulletin
PO Box 49708
PO Box 2560
Sarasota, FL 34230
Phone: (941)953-3990

Publications: The Bulletin (6655)

Bulletin
PO Box 46
Litchville, ND 58461-0046
Phone: (701)762-4267
Fax: (701)762-4267

Publications: Bulletin (24496)

The Bulletin
PO Box 2426
Angleton, TX 77516
Phone: (409)849-5407

Publications: The Bulletin (29726)

Bulletin
PO Box 76
Baldwin, WI 54002
Phone: (715)684-2484
Fax: (715)684-4937

Publications: Bulletin (33560)

Bulletin of Concerned Asian Scholars
3693 S Bay Bluffs Dr.
Cedar, MI 49621
Phone: (231)228-7116
Fax: (231)228-7116

Publications: Bulletin of Concerned Asian Scholars (14863)

Bulletin of the Council for Research in Music Education
School of Music
University of Illinois
1114 W. Nevada
Urbana, IL 61801
Phone: (217)333-1027
Fax: (217)244-4585

Publications: Bulletin of the Council for Research in Music Education (9698)

Bulletin of the Oklahoma Ornithological Society
Dept. of Biological Sciences
University of Tulsa
Tulsa, OK 74104-3189
Phone: (918)631-3943
Fax: (918)631-2762

Publications: Bulletin of the Oklahoma Ornithological Society (26107)

Bulletin Press
PO Box 477
Sioux Rapids, IA 50585
Phone: (712)283-2500
Fax: (712)283-2500

Publications: Sioux Rapids Bulletin-Press (11227)

Bulletin Times
Box 152
Bolivar, TN 38008
Phone: (731)658-3691
Fax: (731)658-7222
Free: 800-748-9232

Publications: Bulletin Times (29057)

Bunker Hill Publications
PO Box 606
Brighton, IL 62012
Phone: (618)372-8451
Fax: (618)372-8451

Publications: The Southwestern Journal (8098) • Southwestern Shoppers Guide (8099)

Bunker Hill Publications
PO Box Z
Bunker Hill, IL 62014
Phone: (618)585-4411
Fax: (618)585-3354

Publications: The Bunker Hill Gazette-News (8101)

Bunker Hill Publications
PO Box 490
Worden, IL 62097-0490
Phone: (618)459-3655
Fax: (618)459-3655

Publications: Madison County Chronicle (9773)

Bureau of Business and Economic Research
University of Montana
Gallagher Business Bldg.
Missoula, MT 59812
Phone: (406)243-5113
Fax: (406)243-2086

Publications: The Montana Business Quarterly (17870)

Bureau of Business and Economic Research
West Virginia University
PO Box 6201
Morgantown, WV 26506
Phone: (304)293-0111
Fax: (304)293-7061

Publications: Journal of Small Business Management (33395)

Bureau County Republican
316 S. Main St.
PO Box 340
Princeton, IL 61356
Phone: (815)875-4461
Fax: (815)875-1235
Free: 800-639-7237

Publications: Bureau County Republican (9467)

Bureau of National Affairs, Inc.
1231 25th St. NW
Washington, DC 20037
Phone: (202)452-4200
Fax: (202)452-4644
Free: 800-452-7773

Publications: Chemical Regulation Reporter (5404)

The Bureaucrat, Inc.
12007 Titian Way
Potomac, MD 20854
Phone: (301)279-9445
Fax: (301)251-5872

Publications: The Public Manager (13659)

Burke County Tribune
Box 40
Bowbells, ND 58721
Phone: (701)377-2626
Fax: (701)377-2717

Publications: Burke County Tribune (24379)

Burke Gazette
PO Box 359
Burke, SD 57523
Phone: (605)775-2612
Fax: (605)775-2612

Publications: Burke Gazette (28827)

Burleson Publishing Co., Inc.
205 W Buck St.
Caldwell, TX 77836-1798
Phone: (979)567-3286
Fax: (979)567-7898

Publications: Burleson County Citizen-Tribune (29994)

Burlington Free Press
191 College St.
Burlington, VT 05402-0010
Phone: (802)863-3441
Fax: (802)660-1802
Free: 800-427-3126

Publications: The Burlington Free Press (31514)

Burlington Post
2321 Fairview St.
Burlington, ON, Canada L7R 2E3
Phone: (905)632-4444
Fax: (905)632-6604

Publications: Burlington Post (35714)

Burlington Record
PO Box 459
Burlington, CO 80807
Phone: (719)346-5381
Fax: (719)346-5514

Publications: Burlington Record & Plains Dealer (4210)

Burlington Times, Inc.
4284 Rte. 130
Willingboro, NJ 08046
Phone: (609)871-8000
Fax: (609)877-2706

Publications: Airtides (19752) • Burlington County Times (19753) • The Post (19754)

Burnaby NOW
201A-3430 Brighton Ave.
Burnaby, BC, Canada V5A 3H4
Phone: (604)444-3451
Fax: (604)444-3460

Publications: Burnaby Now (34894)

Burnett County Sentinel
114 Madison Ave.
Box 397
Grantsburg, WI 54840-0397
Phone: (715)463-2341
Fax: (715)463-5138

Publications: Burnett County Sentinel (33737)

Burns Times-Herald
355 N Broadway Ave.
Burns, OR 97720-1704
Phone: (541)573-2022
Fax: (541)573-3915

Publications: Burns Times-Herald (26259)

Burping Lula
PO Box 14738
Richmond, VA 23221
Phone: (804)225-7950

Publications: Burping Lula (32431)

Burwell Tribune Newspapers
103 N 1st St.
PO Box 547
Sargent, NE 68874
Phone: (308)527-4210
Fax: (308)346-4018

Publications: Burwell Tribune (18259) • Sargent Leader (18260) • Taylor Clarion (18294) • Wheeler County Independent (18261)

Bus Conversions
7246 Garden Grove Blvd.
Westminster, CA 92683-2225
Phone: (714)799-0062
Fax: (714)799-0042

Publications: Bus Conversions (4074)

Bus History Association, Inc.
195 Lancelot Dr.
Manchester, NH 03104-1420
Phone: (603)669-7160
Fax: (603)542-0103

Publications: Bus Industry Magazine (18555)

The Bush Blade
PO Box 168
Anchor Point, AK 99556
Phone: (907)566-8406
Fax: 888-776-6789
Free: 888-776-6789

Publications: The Bush Blade (519)

Business in Broward
PO Box 460669
Fort Lauderdale, FL 33346-0699
Phone: (954)763-3338
Fax: (954)763-4481

Publications: Business in Broward (6073)

Business in Calgary magazine
215, 16 St. SE
PO Box 2400, Station M
Calgary, AB, Canada T2P 0W8
Phone: (403)569-4700
Fax: (403)569-4799

Publications: Business in Calgary (34630)

Business Communications Company Inc.
25 Van Zant St.
Norwalk, CT 06855-1781
Phone: (203)853-4266
Fax: (203)853-0348

Publications: Advanced Transportation Technology News (5049) • Nanoparticle News (5070)

Business Day, Inc.
18717 76th Ave. W, Ste. B
Lynnwood, WA 98037
Phone: (425)775-2911
Fax: (425)775-1760

Publications: RV Life (32825)

Business Ethics
2845 Harriet Ave., Ste. 207
PO Box 8439
Minneapolis, MN 55408
Phone: (612)879-0695
Fax: (612)879-0699
Free: 800-601-9010

Publications: Business Ethics (16063)

Business Examiner Newspaper Group
1517 South Fawcett St., Ste. 350
Tacoma, WA 98402-1807
Phone: (253)404-0891
Fax: (253)404-0892
Free: 800-540-8322

Publications: The Business Examiner (33144)

Business Farmer, Inc.
22 W 17th
Box 2364
Scottsbluff, NE 69361
Phone: (308)635-3110
Fax: (308)635-7435

Publications: Business Farmer (18262) • Business Farmer-Stockman (18263)

Business First
465 Main St.
Buffalo, NY 14203-1793

Publications: Buffalo Law Journal (20366)

Business First
471 E Broad St., Ste. 1500
Columbus, OH 43215
Phone: (614)461-4040
Fax: (614)365-2967

Publications: Business First-Columbus (25003)

Business Forum Software Digest
3955 Denlinger Rd.
Dayton, OH 45426
Phone: (937)837-5888
Fax: (513)837-5888

Publications: Business Forum Software Digest (25107)

Business Information Group
1450 Don Mills Rd.
East Tower, Ste. 705
Toronto, ON, Canada M3B 2X7
Phone: (416)442-2122
Fax: (416)442-2214
Free: 800-668-2374

Publications: L'Automobile (36468) • Bodyshop (36476) • Broadcaster (36478) • Cablecaster (36484) • Cabling Systems (36485) • Canadian Architect (36491) • Canadian Consulting Engineer (36495) • Canadian Industrial Equipment News (36506) • Canadian Mining Journal (36519) • Canadian Occupational Health and Safety News (COHSN) (36521) • Canadian Plastics (36525) • Canadian Transportation & Logistics (36532) • Centre (36544) • Dental Guide (Don Mills) (36568) • Dental Practice Management (36569) • Gifts & Tablewares (36604) • Hardware and Home Centre Magazine (36610) • Housewares Canada (36619) • Jobber News (36631) • Laboratory Product News (36647) • Machinery & Equipment MRO (36653) • Motor Truck (36669) • The Northern Miner (36677) • OH&S Canada (36680) • Oral Health (36690) • Service Station and Garage Management (36738) • Solid Waste & Recycling (36743) • Specialty & Performance Magazine (36745) • The Standard (35802) • Truck News (36774) • Truck West (36775)

Business Information Group
1 Holiday St., East Tower, Ste. 705
Pointe-Claire, QC, Canada H9R 5N3
Phone: (514)630-5955
Fax: (514)630-5980
Free: 800-363-1327

Publications: Les Papetieres du Quebec (37275) • Pulp & Paper Canada (37277)

The Business Journal
1315 Van Ness, Ste. 200
Fresno, CA 93721
Phone: (559)490-3400
Fax: (559)490-3532

Publications: The Business Journal (1943)

The Business Journal
1401 21st. St., Ste. 200
Sacramento, CA 95814-5221
Phone: (916)447-7661
Fax: (916)444-7779

Publications: The Business Journal (2978)

The Business Journal Serving Greater Milwaukee
600 W Virginia St. Ste. 500
Milwaukee, WI 53204
Phone: (414)278-7788
Fax: (414)278-7028

Publications: The Business Journal Serving Greater Milwaukee (34060)

Business Journals Inc.
50 Day St.
PO Box 5550
Norwalk, CT 06856
Phone: (203)853-6015
Fax: (203)852-8175
Free: 800-521-0227

Publications: Accessories (5048) • Modern Brewery Age (5068) • Modern Brewery Age Tabloid Edition (5069) • Travelware (5077) • Turbomachinery International (5078)

Business Ledger
153 E. Chestnut Hill Rd., Ste. 104
Newark, DE 19713-4054
Phone: (302)737-0923
Fax: (302)737-9019

Publications: Business Ledger (5269)

Business Magazine, Inc.
PO Box 580
Carlisle, IA 50047-0580
Phone: (515)989-2099
Fax: (515)989-2098

Publications: Business & Industry (10648)

Business Monthly
245 W. Saginaw
PO Box 26
Hemlock, MI 48626
Phone: (517)642-6397
Fax: (517)642-3600

Publications: Business Monthly (15158)

Business News Publishing
1050 IL Rte. 83, Ste. 200
Bensenville, IL 60106
Fax: (630)227-0527

Publications: Food Engineering (North American Edition) (8067)

Business News Publishing
1050 Rte. 83, No. 200
Bensenville, IL 60106
Phone: (630)616-0200
Fax: (630)227-0214

Publications: Industrial Paint and Powder (8068) • SECURITY (8071)

Business News Publishing Co.
23211 S. Pointe Dr., Ste. 101
PO Box 30700
Laguna Hills, CA 92653
Phone: (949)830-0881
Fax: (949)859-7845

Publications: Reeves Journal (2135)

Business News Publishing Co.
1050 Illinois Rte. 83, Ste. 200
Bensenville, IL 60106-1096
Phone: (847)297-3714
Fax: (847)297-8371

Publications: Prepared Foods (8069)

Business News Publishing Co.
755 W. Big Beaver Rd., Ste. 1000
Troy, MI 48084
Phone: (248)362-3700
Fax: (248)362-0317

Publications: Air Conditioning, Heating and Refrigeration News (15616) • CircuiTree (15617) • Contemporary Stone and Tile Design (19401) • Energy User News (15622) • Engineered Systems (15623) • Environmental Design and Construction (15624) • Floor Covering Installer (15626) • Modern Woodworking (15629) • National Driller (15630) • Packaging Strategies (15631) • PM Engineer (15633) • P.O.B. (Point of Beginning) (15634) • Process Cooling and Equipment (15637) • Roofing Contractor (15638) • Security Distributing & Marketing (SDM) (15639) • Service and Contracting (S & C) (8826) • Walls & Ceilings (15644) • World Trade (3464)

Business News Publishing Company
2820 Audubon Village Dr.
Norristown, PA 19403-2262

Publications: Industrial Safety and Hygiene News (27335)

Business News Publishing Co.
Manor Oak One
1910 Cochran Rd., Ste. 450
Pittsburgh, PA 15220
Phone: (412)531-3370
Fax: (412)531-3375

Publications: Industrial Heating (27799)

Business News Publishing Co. II, L.L.C.
22801 Ventura Blvd., Ste. 115
Woodland Hills, CA 91364-1222
Phone: (818)224-8035
Fax: (818)224-8042
Free: 800-835-4398

Publications: Commercial Floor Care (4101) • ICS Cleaning Specialist (4107) • National Floor Trends Magazine (4112)

Business News Publishing Co., Inc.
PO Box 400
Flossmoor, IL 60422
Phone: (708)922-0761
Fax: (708)922-0762

Publications: Adhesives & Sealants Industry (8891)

Business News Publishing Co., Inc.
755 W. Big Beaver Rd., Ste. 1000
Troy, MI 48084
Phone: (248)362-3700
Fax: (248)362-0317

Publications: Process Heating (8070)

The Business Products Industry Association
301 N. Fairfax St.
Alexandria, VA 22314
Phone: (703)549-9040
Fax: (703)683-7552
Free: 800-542-6662

Publications: Business Products Industry Report (31650)

Business & Professional Ethics Journal
PO Box 15017
Gainesville, FL 32604
Phone: (352)475-1608
Fax: (352)392-5577

Publications: Business & Professional Ethics Journal (6131)

Business and Professional Women/USA
1900 M St. NW, Ste. 310
Washington, DC 20036
Phone: (202)293-1100
Fax: (202)861-0298

Publications: BusinessWoman Magazine (5392)

Business Professionals of America
5454 Cleveland Ave.
Columbus, OH 43231
Phone: (614)895-7277
Fax: (614)895-1165

Publications: COMMUNIQUE (25011)

Business Publications Corp.
The Depot at Fourth
100 4th St.
Des Moines, IA 50309
Phone: (515)288-3336
Fax: (515)288-0309

Publications: The Business Daily (10772) • Cityview (10776) • Des Moines Business Record (10780) • Intro (10788) • Iowa Business & Technology Resource Guide (10789)

Business Publications, Inc.
150 Dow St.
Manchester, NH 03101
Phone: (603)624-1442
Fax: (603)624-1310

Publications: New Hampshire Business Review (18558)

Business Publishers Co.
PO Box 643
Blountville, TN 37617-0643
Phone: (423)323-7111
Fax: (423)323-5352

Publications: Business Journal of Tri-Cities TN/VA (29055)

Business Publishers Inc.
8737 Colesville Rd., Ste. 1100
Silver Spring, MD 20910-3928
Phone: (301)589-5103
Fax: (301)589-8493
Free: 800-274-6737

Publications: Mental Health Report (13738)

Business Service Corp.
PO Box 60762
San Diego, CA 92166
Phone: (619)263-1763
Fax: (619)263-1763
Free: 800-809-1763

Publications: Business Opportunities Journal (3126)

Business & Society Review
200 W 57th St., 15th Fl.
New York, NY 10019
Phone: (212)399-1088
Fax: (212)245-1973

Publications: Business & Society Review (21359)

Business Strategies Inc.
1240 Jefferson Rd.
Rochester, NY 14623-3104
Phone: (585)292-0171

Publications: Business Strategies Newspaper (23213)

Business Technology Association
12411 Wornall Rd.
Kansas City, MO 64145
Phone: (816)941-3100
Fax: (816)941-2829
Free: 800-366-6950

Publications: BTA Solutions (17158)

The Business Times of Western Colorado
618 Walnut Ave.
Grand Junction, CO 81501
Phone: (970)241-0177
Fax: (970)241-9730
Free: 888-382-8692

Publications: The Business Times of Western Colorado (4477)

The Business Word
11211 E. Arapahoe Rd., Ste. 101
Centennial, CO 80112-3851
Phone: (303)290-8500
Fax: (303)290-9025
Free: 800-328-3211

Publications: Healthcare Advertising Review (4224) • Twins Magazine (4228)

BUSU Communications, Inc.
270 18th St.
Brandon, MB, Canada R7A 6A9
Phone: (204)727-9667
Fax: (204)727-3498

Publications: The Quill (35255)

Busy Shopper, Inc.
1819 Cross St.
Fort Oglethorpe, GA 30742
Phone: (706)866-1020
Fax: (706)866-1128

Publications: Busy Shopper (7284)

But Viet Weekly News
9780 Walnut St., Ste. 180
Dallas, TX 75243-2396
Phone: (214)319-7740
Fax: (214)319-7313

Publications: But Viet Weekly News (30135)

The Butler Bulletin
108 E Main St.
Butler, IN 46721
Phone: (260)868-5501
Fax: (260)868-5501

Publications: The Butler Bulletin (9876)

The Butler County and Green River Republican Banner
Box 219
Morgantown, KY 42261
Phone: (270)526-4151
Fax: (270)526-3111

Publications: The Butler County and Green River Republican Banner (12310)

Butler County Publishing
208 Poplar St.
PO Box 7
Poplar Bluff, MO 63901
Phone: (573)785-1414
Fax: (573)785-2706

Publications: Daily American Republic (17357)

The Butte Gazette
Box 6
Butte, NE 68722-0006
Phone: (402)775-2431
Fax: (402)775-2431

Publications: The Butte Gazette (17968)

Butte Valley Star
111 W 3rd St.
PO Box 708
Dorris, CA 96023
Phone: (530)397-2601

Publications: Butte Valley Star (1833)

Butterick Co., Inc.
11 Penn Plaza Fl. 18
New York, NY 10001-2006

Publications: Butterick (21363) • Vogue Patterns Magazine (22904)

Buttermilk Falls Co.
PO Box 523
Leechburg, PA 15656
Phone: (412)567-5656
Fax: (412)568-3818

Publications: Apollo News-Record (27180) • Leechburg Advance (27181)

Butterworth-Heinemann
200 Wheeler Rd.
Burlington, MA 01803-5501
Phone: (781)313-4700
Fax: (781)933-6333
Free: 800-366-2665

Publications: European Journal of Purchasing and Supply Management (14027) • Journal of Air Transport Management (14028) • Journal of Retailing and Consumer Services (14029) • Journal of Vocational Rehabilitation (14030) • The Knee (14031) • Supramolecular Science (14033) • Transport Policy (14034) • Ultrasonics Sonochemistry (14035)

Button
PO Box 26
Lunenburg, MA 01462

Publications: Button (14283)

The Buy Line
109 N. Lafayette St.
PO Box 340
Greenville, MI 48838
Phone: (616)754-9301
Fax: (616)754-8559
Free: 800-968-9301

Publications: The Buy Line (15134)

Buy and Sell Press
350 Columbia St.
New Westminster, BC, Canada V3L 1A6
Phone: (604)540-4455
Fax: (604)540-6451
Free: 800-661-1199

Publications: Vancouver Buy and Sell Press (35032)

Buyer Guide
1826 E Sheridan Ave.
Cody, WY 82414
Phone: (307)587-5989
Fax: (307)587-2551

Publications: Buyer's Guide (34512)

Buyers Express
1523 Rose St.
La Crosse, WI 54603
Phone: (608)791-7171
Fax: (608)791-7107
Free: 800-326-7217

Publications: Buyers Express (33884)

Buyers Guide
2251 NW 41st St., Ste. B
Gainesville, FL 32606-6668
Phone: (904)372-5468
Fax: (904)373-9178
Free: 800-372-5468

Publications: Buyers' Guide (6132)

The Buyer's Guide
1118 W. Cloud
Salina, KS 67401-0134
Phone: (785)823-3209
Fax: (785)823-3176

Publications: The Buyer's Guide (11780) • Country Roads (11782)

Buyers' Guide Group
1212 S. Central Ave., Ste. B
Marshfield, WI 54449-4134
Phone: (715)384-4440
Fax: (715)384-4085

Publications: Marshfield Buyers' Guide (34026)

Buyers' Guide Group
321 Watson
Ripon, WI 54971
Phone: (715)258-8450
Fax: (715)258-8469

Publications: Berlin/Ripon Buyers' Guide (33581)

Buyer's Guide Shopper
317 E Jefferson
PO Box 365
Cuba, IL 61427-0365
Phone: (309)785-8500
Fax: (309)785-4541

Publications: Buyer's Guide Shopper (8700)

The Buzz
PO Box 1945
Charlottetown, PE, Canada C1A 7N5
Phone: (902)628-1958
Fax: (902)628-1953

Publications: The Buzz (36912)

The Byelorussian-American Association, Inc.
166-34 Gothic Dr.
Jamaica, NY 11432
Phone: (908)247-1822
Fax: (908)418-9838

Publications: Bielarus/The Belarusan (20831)

Byelorussian Publishing Association
Box 26
South River, NJ 08882
Phone: (732)613-7171
Fax: (732)257-3994

Publications: Bielaruskaya Dumka (19592)

Byerly Publications
1000 Armory Dr.
Franklin, VA 23851
Phone: (757)562-3187
Fax: (757)562-6795

Publications: Brunswick Times-Gazette (32178) • Independent-Messenger (32079) • The Tidewater News (32080)

ByLine
PO Box 5240
Edmond, OK 73083-5240
Phone: (405)348-5591

Publications: ByLine (25813)

Bypass Publishing
PO Box 243512
Anchorage, AK 99524-3512
Phone: (907)561-7711
Fax: (907)561-7778

Publications: Sourdough Sentinel (532)

The Byte Buyer Inc.
3655 Ruffin Rd., Ste.100
San Diego, CA 92123
Phone: (858)573-0315
Fax: (619)573-0205
Free: 800-573-3247

Publications: ComputorEdge (3132)

The Byzantine Catholic Diocese
445 Lackawanna Ave.
West Paterson, NJ 07424
Phone: (201)890-7794
Fax: (201)890-7175

Publications: Eastern Catholic Life (19728)

C. A. Publications, Inc.
1500 Massachusetts Ave. NW, No. 732
Washington, DC 20005
Phone: (202)331-9763
Fax: (202)331-9751

Publications: CovertAction Quarterly (5446)

C & D Publishing
20518 9th Ave. E
Spanaway, WA 98387-8117
Phone: (206)847-1054
Fax: (206)847-9866

Publications: On Target Computing (33091)

C. E. Publishing
30400 Van Dyke
Warren, MI 48093-2368
Phone: (586)574-9100
Fax: (248)447-7566

Publications: Chevy Outdoors (15657) • Corvette Quarterly (15658) • Vista USA (15664)

C. G. Jung Institute of Los Angeles
10349 W. Pico Blvd.
Los Angeles, CA 90064
Phone: (310)556-1193
Fax: (310)556-2290

Publications: Psychological Perspectives (2374)

C & G Publishing
13650 E. Eleven Mile Rd.
Warren, MI 48089
Phone: (586)498-8000
Fax: (586)498-9631

Publications: Warren Weekly (15666)

C & H Publishing
116 E Franklin
Sesser, IL 62884
Phone: (618)625-2711
Fax: (618)625-6221

Publications: American Cooner (9597)

C-K Publishing, Inc.
3110 Pleasant Dr.
Box 247
Wonder Lake, IL 60097
Phone: (815)728-0912

Publications: Die Casting Management (9770)

C P Publishing, Inc.
104 S Main St., 7th Fl.
PO Box 267
Fond du Lac, WI 54936-0267
Phone: (920)923-3700
Fax: (920)923-6805

Publications: Cooking for Profit (33696)

C The Visual Arts Foundation
984 Queen St. W
Toronto, ON, Canada M6J 1H1
Phone: (416)539-9495
Fax: (416)539-9903

Publications: C International Contemporary Art (36481) • C Magazine (36482)

Jolanta Cabaj
PO Box 161, Sta. P
Toronto, ON, Canada M5S 2S7
Phone: (416)259-4353
Fax: (416)259-4353

Publications: Polish Canadian Courier/Nowy Kurier (36713)

The Cabinet Press, Inc.
54 School St.
PO Box 180
Milford, NH 03055-0180
Phone: (603)673-3100
Fax: (603)673-8250
Free: 800-773-3102

Publications: Bedford Journal (18576) • The Cabinet (18577) • Hollis Brookline Journal (18578) • Merrimack Journal (18579)

Cable Printing Co.
117 S Main
PO Box 768
Lindsay, OK 73052
Phone: (405)756-4045
Fax: (405)756-2729
Free: 800-533-0116

Publications: Lindsay News (25899)

Cable World
5680 Greenwood Plz. Blvd., Ste. 100
Englewood, CO 80111-2404
Phone: (303)837-0900
Fax: (303)837-0915

Publications: Cable World (4412)

Cabool Enterprise, Inc.
525 Main St.
PO Box 40
Cabool, MO 65689
Phone: (417)962-4411
Fax: (417)962-4455

Publications: The Cabool Enterprise (16934)

The Cache Citizen
570 Research Park Way, Ste. 106
North Logan, UT 84341
Phone: (435)753-5070
Fax: (435)752-0037

Publications: The Cache Citizen (31347)

Cache Times Weekly
2101 N Sheridan
PO Box 1283
Lawton, OK 73502
Phone: (580)357-8200
Fax: (580)353-6646

Publications: Cache Times Weekly (25884)

Cactus and Succulent Society of America, Inc.
2391 E Cactus St.
Pahrump, NV 89048
Phone: (775)751-1320
Fax: (775)751-1357

Publications: Cactus and Succulent Journal (2576)

CAD Communications, Inc.
338-4195 Dundas St. W.
Toronto, ON, Canada M8X 1Y4
Phone: (416)236-5856
Fax: (416)236-5219

Publications: AutoCAD User (36467)

Caddo Citizen
Box 312
Vivian, LA 71082-0312
Phone: (318)375-3294
Fax: (318)375-4578

Publications: Caddo Citizen (12871)

Caddo Gap Press
3145 Geary Blvd., No. 275
San Francisco, CA 94118
Phone: (415)392-1911
Fax: (415)956-3702

Publications: Educational Foundations (3355) • Educational Leadership and Administration (3356) • Journal of Critical Inquiry into Curriculum and Instruction (3379) • Journal of Curriculum Theorizing (3380) • Journal of Thought (3385) • Multicultural Education (3392) • Notes and Abstracts in American and International Education (3408) • Summer Academe (3444) • Taboo (3449) • Teacher Education Quarterly (3450) • Vitae Schololasticae (3460)

Cadence Jazz and Blues Magazine
Cadence Bldg.
Redwood, NY 13679-9612
Phone: (315)287-2852
Fax: (315)287-2860

Publications: Cadence Jazz and Blues Magazine (23179)

Cadenza
Washington University
Campus Box 1039
St. Louis, MO 63130
Phone: (314)935-5941
Fax: (314)935-5938

Publications: Cadenza (17419)

Cadet Activities Fund, U.S. Military Academy
Eisenhower Hall, Bldg. 655
West Point, NY 10996
Phone: (914)938-7989

Publications: Pointer (23546)

Cadillac News
130 N. Mitchell St.
Cadillac, MI 49601-1865
Phone: (231)775-6565
Fax: (231)775-8790

Publications: Cadillac News (14842)

The Cadiz Record
214 W. Main
PO Box 370
Morganfield, KY 42437
Phone: (270)389-1833
Fax: (502)522-3001

Publications: The Union County Advocate (12307)

Cadmus Journal Services
940 Elkridge Landing Rd.
Linthicum, MD 21090-2908
Phone: (410)850-0500
Fax: (410)691-6203
Free: 800-257-5021

Publications: Emergency Medicine (13619) • Financial Services Review (7007)

Cadogan Publishing Ltd.
175 General Mansion Way
PO Box 500
Miramichi, NB, Canada E1V 3M6
Phone: (506)622-2600
Fax: (506)622-6506

Publications: Miramichi Leader (35408) • Miramichi Weekend (35409)

Cadogan Publishing, Ltd.
PO Box 40
Sussex, NB, Canada E0E 1P0
Phone: (506)433-1070
Fax: (506)432-3532

Publications: Kings County Record (35438)

Cadott Sentinel
Box 70
Cadott, WI 54727
Phone: (715)289-4978
Fax: (715)239-6200

Publications: Cadott Sentinel (33613)

Cafh Foundation
168 West Kerley Rd.
Tivoli, NY 12583
Phone: (212)724-4260
Fax: (914)962-1677

Publications: Seeds of Unfolding (22721)

Cahners Publishing
2000 Clearwater Dr.
Oak Brook, IL 60523
Phone: (630)320-7000
Free: 800-826-6270

Publications: Metal Center News (9360)

CAHPERD National Office
403-2197 Riverside Dr.
Ottawa, ON, Canada K1H 7X3
Phone: (613)523-1348
Fax: (613)523-1206
Free: 800-663-8708

Publications: Physical & Health Education Journal (36270)

Cairo Messenger Inc.
31-35 1st Ave. NE
PO Box 30
Cairo, GA 31728
Phone: (229)377-2032
Fax: (229)377-4640

Publications: Cairo Messenger (7148)

Cairo Record
Box 540
Cairo, NE 68824
Phone: (308)485-4284
Fax: (308)485-4286
Free: 800-658-3241

Publications: Cairo Record (17969)

Cake
4513 Madison St. NE
Columbia Heights, MN 55421-2363
Phone: (612)781-9141
Fax: (612)781-9181

Publications: Cake (15810)

CAL Press
PO Box 1446
Columbia, MO 65205
Phone: (573)442-4352

Publications: Anarchy (16988)

Calaveras First Newspapers
PO Box 1197
San Andreas, CA 95249
Phone: (209)754-3861
Fax: (209)754-5135
Free: 888-811-3861

Publications: The Calaveras Enterprise (3079) • Calaveras Prospect (Weekly, Citizen & Chronicle) (3080)

The Caldwell Messenger
PO Box 313
Caldwell, KS 67022
Phone: (620)845-2320
Fax: (620)845-6461

Publications: The Caldwell Messenger (11372)

Caldwell Watchman Progress
PO Box 1269
Columbia, LA 71418
Phone: (318)649-6411
Fax: (318)649-7776

Publications: Caldwell Watchman Progress (12548)

Caledonia Argus
121 W Main St.
Box 227
Caledonia, MN 55921
Phone: (507)724-3475
Fax: (507)725-8610

Publications: Caledonia Argus (15783)

Caledonia Courier
PO Box 1298
Fort St. James, BC, Canada V0J 1P0
Phone: (250)996-8482
Fax: (250)996-7973

Publications: Caledonia Courier (34958)

Caledonian-Record Publishing Co., Inc.
190 Federal St.
PO Box 8
St. Johnsbury, VT 05819
Phone: (802)748-8121
Fax: (802)748-1613
Free: 800-523-6397

Publications: Caledonian-Record (31593)

CALF News Magazine Ltd.
10720 Black Forest Dr. S
Colorado Springs, CO 80906
Phone: (719)495-0303
Fax: (719)495-9204

Publications: CALF News Magazine (4238)

The Calgary Sun
2615 12th St., NE
Calgary, AB, Canada T2E 7W9
Phone: (403)250-4200
Fax: (403)250-4258

Publications: The Calgary Mirror (Northside and Southside) (34632) • The Calgary Sun (34633)

Calhoun County Journal
PO Box 278
Bruce, MS 38915
Phone: (662)983-2570
Fax: (662)983-7667

Publications: Calhoun County Journal (16581)

Calhoun News-Herald
310 S County Rd.
PO Box 367
Hardin, IL 62047
Phone: (618)576-2345
Fax: (618)576-2245

Publications: Calhoun News-Herald (8971)

Calhoun Publishing
PO Box 400
Grantsville, WV 26147
Phone: (304)354-6917
Fax: (304)354-7142

Publications: Calhoun Chronicle (33328)

The Calhoun Times
PO Box 176
St. Matthews, SC 29135
Phone: (803)874-3137
Fax: (803)874-1588

Publications: The Calhoun Times (28752)

California Academy of Family Physicians
1520 Pacific Ave.
San Francisco, CA 94109
Phone: (415)345-8667
Fax: (415)345-8668

Publications: California Family Physician (3336)

California Advocate
1715 E St., No. 108
PO Box 11826
Fresno, CA 93706
Phone: (559)268-0941
Fax: (559)268-0943

Publications: California Advocate (1944)

California Agriculture
DANR-University of California
1111 Franklin St., 6th Fl.
Oakland, CA 94607-5200
Phone: (510)987-0044
Fax: (510)465-2659

Publications: California Agriculture (2671)

California Alumni Association
Alumni House
Berkeley, CA 94720-7520
Phone: (510)642-5781
Fax: (510)642-6252
Free: 888-CAL-ALUM

Publications: California Monthly (1504)

California Association of Realtors
14011, Ventura Blvd. Ste.406
Sherman Oaks, CA 91423
Phone: (818)501-0133
Fax: (818)905-6091

Publications: California Real Estate Magazine (3761)

California Baptist College
8432 Magnolia Ave.
Riverside, CA 92504-3297
Phone: (909)689-5771
Fax: (909)351-1808

Publications: The Banner (2930)

California Bowling News
2606 W Burbank Blvd.
Burbank, CA 91505-2303
Phone: (818)849-4664
Fax: (818)845-6321

Publications: California Bowling News (1615)

California Builder & Engineer, Inc.
7133 Magnolia Ave.
Riverside, CA 92504
Phone: (909)328-1920
Fax: (909)328-1928

Publications: California Builder & Engineer (2933)

California Cattlemen's Association
29802 Road 44
Visalia, CA 93291
Phone: (559)651-3083
Fax: (559)651-3086

Publications: California Cattleman (2979)

California Community Care News
PO Box 163270
Sacramento, CA 95816-9270
Phone: (916)455-0723
Fax: (916)455-7201

Publications: California Community Care News/Senior Citizens Today (2980)

California Community News Corp.
330 W. Bay St.
PO Box 1560
Costa Mesa, CA 92627
Phone: (949)642-4321
Fax: (949)642-7667

Publications: Newport Beach/Costa Mesa Daily Pilot (2631)

California Community News Corp.
425 W. Broadway, Ste. 300
Glendale, CA 91204
Phone: (818)241-4141

Publications: Burbank Leader (1614)

California Community News Corp.
18682 Beach Blvd., Ste. 160
Huntington Beach, CA 92648
Phone: (714)965-3030
Fax: (714)965-7174

Publications: Huntington Beach/Fountain Valley Independent (1935)

California Continuing Education of the Bar
2300 Shattuck Ave.
Berkeley, CA 94704
Fax: (510)642-3788
Free: 800-232-3444

Publications: Estate Planning and California Probate Reporter (1518)

California Courier
PO Box 5390
Glendale, CA 91221
Phone: (818)409-0949
Fax: (818)409-9207

Publications: California Courier (2007)

California Dairy Herd Improvement Association
PO Box 626
Clovis, CA 93613-0626
Phone: (559)298-6675
Fax: (559)323-6016

Publications: California Dairy (1731)

California Dental Association
1201 'K' St. Mall
PO Box 13749
Sacramento, CA 95853
Phone: (916)443-0505
Fax: (916)443-2943
Free: 800-736-7071

Publications: CDA Update (2992) • Journal of the California Dental Association (3003)

California Department of Conservation
Division of Mines & Geology
Geologic Information & Publications
801 K St., MS 14-33
Sacramento, CA 95814-3532
Phone: (916)445-4716
Fax: (916)327-1853

Publications: California Geology Magazine (2982)

California Engineer Publishing Co.
University of California, Berkeley
221 Bechtel Engineering Ctr.
Berkeley, CA 94720-0001
Phone: (510)642-8679

Publications: California Engineer (1501)

California Farm Bureau Federation
2300 River Plaza Dr.
Sacramento, CA 95833
Phone: (916)446-4647
Fax: (916)561-5695

Publications: Ag Alert (2974)

California Genealogical Society
1611 Telegraph Ave., Ste. 100
Oakland, CA 94612-2154
Phone: (510)663-1358
Fax: (510)663-1596

Publications: The Nugget and CGS News (2689)

California Hungarians
PO Box 370305
Reseda, CA 91337-0305
Phone: (818)996-7685
Fax: (818)996-5306

Publications: California Hungarians (2917)

The California Institute of Technology
Caltech 1-71
Pasadena, CA 91125
Phone: (626)395-3630
Fax: (626)577-0636

Publications: The California Tech (2813) • Engineering & Science (2815)

California Land Surveyors Association
PO Box 9098
Santa Rosa, CA 95405
Phone: (707)578-6016
Fax: (707)578-4406

Publications: The California Surveyor (3724)

California Malacozoological Society, Inc.
Santa Barbara Museum Of Natural History
2559 Puesta Del Sol Rd.
Santa Barbara, CA 93105
Phone: (805)682-4711
Fax: (805)963-9679

Publications: The Veliger (3661)

California Manufacturers Association
980 9th St., Ste. 2200
Sacramento, CA 95814
Phone: (916)441-5420
Fax: (916)441-5449
Free: 800-655-2640

Publications: California Manufacturer (2985)

California Music Education Association
3924 Cottonwood Dr.
Concord, CA 94519
Fax: (510)687-5246

Publications: CMEA News (1751)

California Newspaper Partnership DBA
2041 E. 4th St.
Ontario, CA 91761
Phone: (909)987-6397
Fax: (909)948-3197

Publications: Inland Valley Daily Bulletin (2716)

California Newspaper Publishers Association
1225 8th St., Ste. 260
Sacramento, CA 95814
Phone: (916)288-6000
Fax: (916)288-6002

Publications: California Publisher (2987)

California Newspapers, Inc.
150 Alameda Del Prado
Novato, CA 94949
Phone: (415)883-8600
Fax: (415)883-5458

Publications: Marin Independent Journal (2651)

California Nurses Association
2000 Franklin St., Ste. 300
Oakland, CA 94612-2908
Phone: (510)273-2000
Fax: (510)663-0629

Publications: California Nurse (2674)

California Pharmacists Association
1112 I St. Ste. 300
Sacramento, CA 95814
Phone: (916)444-7811
Fax: (916)444-7929
Free: 800-444-3851

Publications: California Pharmacist (2986)

California Psychoanalytic Circle
916 Ashbury St.
San Francisco, CA 94117
Phone: (415)753-2845
Fax: (415)664-9584

Publications: (a) (3323)

California School Boards Association
3100 Beacon Blvd.
PO Box 1660
West Sacramento, CA 95691
Phone: (916)371-4691
Fax: (916)372-3369
Free: 800-266-3382

Publications: California Schools (4064)

California School Employees Association
2045 Lundy Ave.
PO Box 640
San Jose, CA 95106
Phone: (408)263-8000
Fax: (408)954-0948
Free: 800-632-2128

Publications: Newslink (3529)

The California Society of Certified Public Accountants
1235 Radio Rd.
Redwood City, CA 94065
Phone: (650)802-2600
Fax: (650)802-2230

Publications: California CPA (2913)

California Society of Health-System Pharmacists
725 30th St., Ste. 208
Sacramento, CA 95816
Phone: (916)447-1033
Fax: (916)447-2396

Publications: California Journal of Health-System Pharmacy (2984)

California Southern Baptist Convention
678 E Shaw Ave.
Fresno, CA 93710-7704
Phone: (559)229-9533
Fax: (559)229-2824

Publications: The California Southern Baptist (1946)

California Staats-Zeitung
1201 N Alvarado
PO Box 26308
Los Angeles, CA 90026
Phone: (213)413-5500
Fax: (213)413-5469

Publications: California Staats-Zeitung (2232)

California State Association of Counties
1100 K St., Ste. 101
Sacramento, CA 95814
Phone: (916)327-7500
Fax: (916)441-5507

Publications: California State Association of Counties California County (2988)

California State Automobile Association
150 Van Ness Ave.
San Francisco, CA 94102
Phone: (415)565-2454
Fax: (415)552-5825
Free: 800-468-7563

Publications: VIA (3458)

California State Coastal Conservancy
1330 Broadway, Ste. 1100
Oakland, CA 94612-2530
Phone: (510)286-0934
Fax: (510)286-0470

Publications: California Coast & Ocean (2673)

California State Firefighters Association
2701 K St., Ste. 201
Sacramento, CA 95816-5113
Fax: (916)446-9889
Free: 800-451-2732

Publications: California Fire Service (2981)

California State Polytechnic University
3801 W. Temple Ave., Bldg. 1-210
Pomona, CA 91768-4007
Phone: (909)869-3530
Fax: (909)869-3863

Publications: The Poly Post (2861)

California State Polytechnic University
San Luis Obispo, CA 93407
Phone: (805)756-1111
Fax: (805)756-1143

Publications: Mustang Daily (3566)

California State University
College of Communication
Chico, CA 95929-0600
Phone: (530)898-4237
Fax: (530)898-4799

Publications: The Orion (1695)

California State University
5151 State University Dr.
Los Angeles, CA 90032
Phone: (323)343-2273
Fax: (323)343-5337

Publications: University Times (2423)

California State University, Fresno
5244 N. Jackson, KC42
Fresno, CA 93740-8023
Phone: (559)278-5735
Fax: (559)278-2679

Publications: The Collegian (1949)

California State University, Fullerton
College Park Building
2600 E. Nutwood Ave., Ste. 660
Fullerton, CA 92831-3110
Phone: (714)278-2128
Fax: (714)278-2702

Publications: Daily Titan (1989)

California State University, Los Angeles
School of Business & Economics
5151 State University Dr.
Los Angeles, CA 90032
Phone: (323)343-2273

Publications: Business Forum (2229)

California State University, Stanislaus
801 W. Monte Vista Ave.
Turlock, CA 95380
Phone: (661)259-1000
Fax: (661)284-6703

Publications: The Signal (3957)

California Teachers Association
1705 Murchison Dr.
PO Box 921
Burlingame, CA 94010
Phone: (650)697-1400
Fax: (650)552-5002

Publications: California Educator (1631)

California Territorial Quarterly
6848U Skyway
Paradise, CA 95969
Phone: (530)872-3363

Publications: California Territorial Quarterly (2805)

California Thoroughbred Breeders Association
201 Colorado Pl.
PO Box 60018
Arcadia, CA 91066-6018
Phone: (626)445-7800
Fax: (626)574-0852

Publications: California Thoroughbred (1427)

California Veterinary Medical Association
1400 River Park Dr., Ste. 100
Sacramento, CA 95815-4505
Phone: (916)344-4985
Fax: (916)344-6147

Publications: California Veterinarian (2990)

California Voice
270 Francisco St.
San Francisco, CA 94133-2012
Phone: (415)391-2030
Fax: (415)391-2527

Publications: California Voice (3339)

California Yoga Teachers Association
2054 University Ave.
Berkeley, CA 94704
Phone: (510)841-9200
Fax: (510)644-3101
Free: 800-IDO-YOGA

Publications: Yoga Journal (1566)

The Californian
28765 Single Oak Dr. Ste. 100
Temecula, CA 92590
Phone: (909)676-4315
Fax: (909)699-1467

Publications: The Californian (3841)

Calkins Inc
15 NE 1st Rd.
Homestead, FL 33030
Phone: (305)245-2311
Fax: (305)248-0596

Publications: South Dade News Leader (6205)

Calkins Newspapers, Inc.
333 N Broad St., No. 858
Doylestown, PA 18901-0858
Phone: (215)345-3000
Fax: (215)345-3150

Publications: The Intelligencer Record (26832) •
The Record (27063)

The Call
75 Main St.
PO Box A
Woonsocket, RI 02895
Phone: (401)762-3000
Fax: (401)765-2834

Publications: The Call (28460)

Call and Post
11800 Shaker Blvd
Box 6237
Cleveland, OH 44120
Phone: (216)791-7600
Fax: (216)791-6568

Publications: Call and Post (24865)

The Callaway Courier
PO Box 69
Callaway, NE 68825
Phone: (308)836-2200

Publications: The Callaway Courier (17970)

Caller-Times
820 N. Lower Broadway
PO Box 9136
Corpus Christi, TX 78469
Phone: (361)884-2011
Free: 800-827-2011

Publications: Corpus Christi Caller-Times (30076)

Callers Digest, Inc.
701 Stokes Rd.
Medford, NJ 08055
Phone: (609)953-9110
Fax: (609)953-7961

Publications: BBS Magazine (19220)

Calmar Courier
PO Box 507
Calmar, IA 52132
Phone: (563)562-3329
Fax: (563)562-3940

Publications: Calmar Courier (10647)

The Caloose Belle
PO Box 518
La Belle, FL 33935-0518
Phone: (863)675-2541
Fax: (863)675-1449

Publications: Caloosa Belle (6267) • Immokalee
Bulletin (6268)

The Calumet Press
8411 Kennedy Ave.
Highland, IN 46322-1175
Phone: (219)838-0717
Fax: (219)838-1338

Publications: The Calumet Press (10062)

The Calvert Independent
PO Box 910
Prince Frederick, MD 20678
Phone: (301)855-1000
Fax: (301)855-9070

Publications: The Calvert Independent (13667)

Calvin College
3201 Burton SE
Grand Rapids, MI 49546
Phone: (616)526-7031
Free: 800-688-0122

Publications: Chimes (15090)

Calyx Books
PO Box B
Corvallis, OR 97339
Phone: (541)753-9384
Fax: (541)753-0515
Free: 888-336-2665

Publications: CALYX (26285)

Cam-Glo Newspapers
PO Box 67
Blackwood, NJ 08012-0067
Phone: (856)228-7300
Fax: (856)232-0213

Publications: News Report (18681) • Plain Dealer
(18682) • Record Breeze (18683)

CAM Publications
PO Box 2607
Cinnaminson, NJ 08077-2607
Phone: (856)786-4719
Fax: (856)786-3208

Publications: Riverside Reporter (18743) • South
Jersey Advisor (18744) • Southern New Jersey
Swapper (18745) • Town News (18746)

The Cambrian
PO Box 67
2442 Main St
Cambria, CA 93428
Phone: (805)927-8652
Fax: (805)927-4708

Publications: The Cambrian (1649)

Cambridge Daily Reporter
26 Ainslie St. S.
PO Box 1510
Cambridge, ON, Canada N1R 3K1
Phone: (519)621-3810
Fax: (519)621-8239

Publications: Cambridge Daily Reporter (35723)

Cambridge Entomological Club
26 Oxford St.
Cambridge, MA 02138-2902
Phone: (617)496-1034
Fax: (617)495-1224

Publications: Psyche (14091)

The Cambridge News
201 W North St.
PO Box 8
Cambridge, WI 53523
Phone: (608)423-3213
Fax: (608)423-7802

Publications: The Cambridge News (33614)

The Cambridge Reporter
26 Ainslie St. S
Cambridge, ON, Canada N1R 3K1
Fax: (519)621-3810

Publications: The Cambridge Reporter (35724)

Cambridge Scientific Abstracts
7200 Wisconsin Ave., Ste. 601
Bethesda, MD 20814
Phone: (301)961-6700
Fax: (301)961-6720

Publications: Agricultural and Environmental Bio-
technology Abstracts (13297) • Algology, Mycology
& Protozoology: Microbiology Abstracts, Section C
(13299) • Alloys Index (24647) • Animal Behavior
Abstracts (13311) • ASFA 2: Ocean Technology,
Policy & Non-Living Resources (13313) • ASFA 3:
Aquatic Pollution and Environmental Quality
(13314) • ASFA Aquaculture Abstracts (13315) •
ASFA/Aquatic Sciences & Fisheries Abstracts Part 1:
Biological Sciences & Living Resources (13316) •
ASFA Marine Biotechnology Abstracts (13317) •
Bacteriology: Microbiology Abstracts, Section B
(13319) • BioEngineering Abstracts (13320) • Calci-
um and Calcified Tissue Abstracts (13322) • Chemo-
reception Abstracts (13324) • Computer and Infor-
mation Systems Abstracts Journal (13326) • Conference Papers Index (13327) • CSA Neurosciences
Abstracts (13328) • Ecology Abstracts (13329) •
EIS: Digests of Environmental Impact Statements
(13331) • Electronics & Communications Abstracts
Journal (13333) • Entomology Abstracts (13334) •
Health and Safety Science Abstracts (13342) • Immunology Abstracts (13344) • Industrial and Applied
Microbiology: Microbiology Abstracts, Section A
(13345) • Linguistics and Language Behavior Abstracts (13357) • Mechanical Engineering Abstracts
(13358) • Medical and Pharmaceutical Biotechnology Abstracts (13359) • Metalforming Technology
Digest (24652) • Metals Abstracts (24653) • Nonferrous Alert (24654) • Nucleic Acids Abstracts
(13368) • Oceanic Abstracts (13369) • Pollution
Abstracts (13376) • Polymers/Ceramics/Composites
Alert (24655) • Risk Abstracts (13377) • Sociological
Abstracts (13379) • Solid State and Superconductivity Abstracts (13380) • Steels Alert (24657) • Toxicology Abstracts (13384) • Virology and AIDS Abstracts
(13387) • World Calendar (13389)

Cambridge Times
240 Holiday Times Inn Dr.
Cambridge, ON, Canada N3C 3X4
Fax: (519)651-2358

Publications: Cambridge Times (35725)

Cambridge University Press
40 W. 20th St.
New York, NY 10011-4211
Phone: (212)924-3900
Fax: (212)691-3239
Free: 800-221-4512

Publications: Abstracts of Working Papers in Economics (AWPE) (2111) • Acta Numerica (21145) •
Ageing and Society (21164) • AI EDAM (14675) •
Ancient Mesoamerica (29442) • Anglo-Saxon England (21216) • Annals of Human Genetics
(21217) • Annual Review of Applied Linguistics
(694) • Applied Psycholinguistics (21232) • Arabic
Sciences and Philosophy (21239) • Architectural
Research Quarterly (16057) • Behavioral and Brain
Sciences (21294) • Biological Reviews of the Cambridge Philosophical Society (21318) • Bird Conservation International (21327) • The British Journal for
the History of Science (21340) • British Journal of
Music Education (21341) • British Journal of Political
Science (21342) • Bulletin of the London Mathematical Society (21351) • Cambridge Archaeological
Journal (21366) • The Cambridge Law Journal
(21367) • Cambridge Opera Journal (21368) • Cambridge Quarterly of Healthcare Ethics (1506) • Camden Fifth Series (21369) • Clinics in Developmental

Medicine (21430) • Combinatorics, Probability and
Computing (21451) • Comparative Criticism
(21463) • Comparative Studies in Society & History
(14745) • Computer Bulletin (21472) • Contemporary European History (21492) • Continuity and
Change (21496) • Current Directions in Psychological Science (21524) • Development and Psychopathology (23223) • Developmental Medicine and Child
Neurology (21548) • Early Music History (21574) •
Econometric Theory (4987) • Economics and Philosophy (21581) • Edinburgh Journal of Botany
(21584) • English Today (21606) • Epidemiology
and Infection (21624) • Ergodic Theory and Dynamical Systems (21626) • European Journal of Applied
Mathematics (21639) • European Journal of Phycology (21647) • European Journal of Sociology
(21653) • Experimental Agriculture (21663) • Experimental Physiology (21667) • Fetal and Maternal
Medicine Review (21687) • Field Mycology
(21689) • Financial History Review (21697) • Genetical Research (21752) • Geological Magazine
(21755) • The Historical Journal (21806) • International Journal of Middle East Studies (14753) •
International Journal of Technology Assessment in
Health Care (21921) • International Labor and Working-Class History (21926) • International Organization (14071) • International Review of Social History
(21936) • Japanese Journal of Political Science
(21957) • JINS (2114) • JMBA: Journal of the Marine Biological Association (21967) • The Journal of
African History (21977) • The Journal of Agricultural
Science (21979) • Journal of American Studies
(21986) • Journal of Anatomy (21988) • Journal of
Child Language (22024) • Journal of Dairy Research
(22046) • The Journal of Ecclesiastical History
(22053) • The Journal of Economic History
(22055) • Journal of Fluid Mechanics (22070) •
Journal of French Language Studies (3644) • Journal of Functional Programming (22073) • Journal of
Germanic Languages (22080) • Journal of Latin
American Studies (22110) • Journal of Linguistics
(22112) • Journal of the London Mathematical Society (22116) • Journal of the Marine Biological Association of the United Kingdom (22121) • Journal of
Modern African Studies (22135) • Journal of Navigation (22139) • Journal of Physiology (22159) • Journal of Plasma Physics (22161) • Journal of Public
Policy (22173) • Journal of the Royal Asiatic Society
(22181) • Journal of Social Policy (22187) • Journal
of Tropical Ecology (22209) • The Knowledge Engineering Review (20327) • Language in Society
(953) • Language Teaching (22233) • Language
Variation and Change (22234) • Laser and Particle
Beams (22236) • Legal Theory (3223) • LMS Journal of Computation and Mathematics (22264) •
Mathematical Proceedings of the Cambridge Philosophical Society (22297) • Mathematical Structures
in Computer Science (22298) • Meteorological Applications (22325) • Modern Asian Studies (22347) •
Mycological Research (22387) • The Mycologist
(22388) • Nations and Nationalism (22401) • Natural
Language Engineering (23608) • The New Phytologist (22433) • New Testament Studies (22435) •
New Theatre Quarterly (22436) • Parasitology
(22523) • Personal Relationships (9303) • Phonology (22550) • Plainsong and Medieval Music
(14415) • Polar and Glaciological Abstracts
(22569) • Polar Record (22570) • Popular Music
(22580) • Probability in the Engineering and Informational Sciences (1552) • Prospects (22600) • Protein
Science (10254) • Psychological Medicine (22604) •
Psychophysiology (22606) • Quarterly Review of
Biophysics (5000) • ReCall (22638) • Religious
Studies (22645) • Review of International Studies
(22661) • Risk, Decision and Policy (22670) • RNA
(22672) • Robotica (22673) • Royal Historical Society Transactions (22678) • Rural History (22681) •
Science in Context (22711) • Social Anthropology
(22753) • Social Philosophy and Policy (24702) •
Studies in American Political Development (2407) •
Studies in Second Language Acquisition (9852) •
Urban History (2425) • Visual Neuroscience
(30541) • Zygote (19724)

Camden House
Boydell & Brewer
668 Mt. Hope Ave.
Rochester, NY 14620
Phone: (585)275-0419
Fax: (585)271-8778

Publications: Fifteenth Century Studies (23226)

Camden Publications, Inc.
331 E. Bell St.
Camden, MI 49232
Phone: (517)368-0365
Fax: (517)368-5131
Free: 800-222-6336

Publications: The Farmers' Advance (14852)

Cameron Newspapers, Inc.
PO Box 498
Cameron, MO 64429
Phone: (816)632-6543
Fax: (816)632-4508

Publications: Cameron Citizen Observer (16938) •
The Cameron Shopper (16939)

Cameron Parish Pilot
PO Box 995
DeQuincy, LA 70633
Phone: (318)786-8004
Fax: (318)786-8131
Free: 800-256-7323

Publications: Cameron Parish Pilot (12544)

Cameron Publications
170 Commercial St.
Box 640
Berwick, NS, Canada B0P 1E0
Phone: (902)538-3189
Fax: (902)538-8533

Publications: The Register (35541)

Cameron University
Dept. of English, Foreign Languages, and Journalism
2800 W. Gore Blvd.
Lawton, OK 73505-6377
Phone: (580)581-2260
Fax: (580)581-2897

Publications: Collegian (25886)

The Camilla Enterprise
PO Box 365
Camilla, GA 31730-0365
Phone: (912)336-5265
Fax: (912)336-8476

Publications: The Camilla Enterprise & The Pelham Journal (7152)

Camp Chase Publishing Co., Inc.
Box 707
Marietta, OH 45750
Phone: (740)373-1865
Fax: (740)374-5710
Free: 800-449-1865

Publications: Camp Chase Gazette (25344)

The Camp Verde Journal
PO Box 2048
Camp Verde, AZ 86322
Phone: (928)567-3341
Fax: (928)567-2373

Publications: The Camp Verde Journal (668)

Campbell River/Comox Valley North Islander
1040 Cedar St.
PO Box 310
Campbell River, BC, Canada V9W 5B6
Phone: (250)287-7464
Fax: (250)287-8891

Publications: Campbell River/Comox Valley North Islander (34916)

Campbell River Courier-Islander
1040 Cedar St.
PO Box 310
Campbell River, BC, Canada V9W 5B6
Phone: (250)287-7464
Fax: (250)287-8891

Publications: Campbell River Courier-Islander (34917)

Campbell University
PO Box 567
Buies Creek, NC 27506
Phone: (910)893-1524
Fax: (910)893-1922

Publications: The Campbell Times (23668)

Campbellsport News
101 N Fond du Lac Ave.
PO Box 138
Campbellsport, WI 53010
Phone: (920)533-8338
Fax: (920)533-5579

Publications: Campbellsport News (33616)

Campus Communications, Inc.
PO Box 14257
Gainesville, FL 32605-2257
Phone: (352)376-4446
Fax: (352)376-4556

Publications: The Independent Florida Alligator (6145)

Campus Crusade for Christ
100 Lake Hart Dr.
Orlando, FL 32832-0100
Phone: (407)826-2390
Fax: (407)826-2374
Free: 800-688-4992

Publications: Worldwide Challenge (6511)

The Camrose Booster
4925 48th St.
Camrose, AB, Canada T4V 1L7
Phone: (780)672-3142
Fax: (780)672-2518

Publications: The Camrose Booster (34675)

Canada & Arab World
602 Millwood Rd.
Toronto, ON, Canada M4S 1K8
Phone: (416)362-0304
Fax: (416)816-0238

Publications: Canada & Arab World (36487)

Canada Computer Paper Inc.
425 Carrall St., Ste. 503
Vancouver, BC, Canada V6B 6E3
Phone: (604)608-2688
Fax: (604)608-2686

Publications: Canadian Computer Wholesaler (35130)

Canada Law Book Inc.
240 Edward St.
Aurora, ON, Canada L4G 3S9
Phone: (905)841-6472
Fax: (905)841-5574
Free: 800-263-3269

Publications: Canadian Business Law Journal (35641) • Criminal Law Quarterly (35646) • Estates, Trusts & Pensions Journal (35648) • Law Times (35651)

Canada Mortgage and Housing Corp.
700 Montreal Rd.
Ottawa, ON, Canada K1A 0P7
Phone: (613)748-2000
Fax: (613)748-2156

Publications: CMHC Housing Outlook, National Edition (36237)

Canada Safety Council
1020 Thomas Spratt Place
Ottawa, ON, Canada K1G 5L5
Phone: (613)739-1535
Fax: (613)739-1566

Publications: Living Safety Magazine (36260)

Canada Wide Magazines & Communications Ltd.
4180 Lougheed Hwy., 4th Fl.
Burnaby, BC, Canada V5C 6A7
Phone: (604)299-7311
Fax: (604)299-9188

Publications: Award Magazine (34889) • B. C. Business (34890)• BC Business Magazine (34891) • Going Places (34899) • Grocer Today Magazine (34900) • Hospitality Today (34901) • TV Week Magazine (34908) • Westworld (34910) • Westworld Alberta (34911) • Westworld British Columbia (34912) • Westworld Saskatchewan (34913)

Canada's National History Society
c/o A. Greenberg
478 167 Lombard Ave.
Winnipeg, MB, Canada R3B 0T6
Phone: (204)988-9300
Fax: (204)988-9309
Free: 800-816-6777

Publications: The Beaver (35314)

Canadian Academic Accounting Association
3997 Chesswood Dr.
Toronto, ON, Canada M4N 2G1
Phone: (416)486-5361
Fax: (416)486-6158

Publications: Contemporary Accounting Research (36559)

Canadian-American Center
154 College Ave.
Orono, ME 04473-1591

Publications: Canadian-American Public Policy (12999)

Canadian Anesthesiologists' Society
1 Eglinton Ave.; Ste. 208
Toronto, ON, Canada M4P 3A1
Phone: (416)480-0602
Fax: (416)480-0320

Publications: Canadian Journal of Anesthesia (Journal canadien d'anesthesie) (37095)

Canadian Art Foundation
56 The Esplanade, Ste. 310
Toronto, ON, Canada M5E 1A7
Phone: (416)368-8854
Fax: (416)368-6135

Publications: Canadian Art (36492)

Canadian Association for Distance Education
260 Dalhousie St., Ste. 204
Ottawa, ON, Canada K1N 7E4
Phone: (613)241-0018
Fax: (613)241-0019

Publications: Journal of Distance Education (34718)

Canadian Association of Geographers
805 Sherbrooke St. W.
Dept. of Geography
McGill University
Montreal, QC, Canada H3A 2K6
Phone: (514)398-4946
Fax: (514)398-7437

Publications: The Canadian Geographer (37093)

Canadian Association for Health, Physical Education, Recreation and Dance
403-2197 Riverside Dr.
Ottawa, ON, Canada K1H 7X3
Phone: (613)523-1348
Fax: (613)523-1206
Free: 800-663-8708

Publications: Avante (36185)

Canadian Association of Insurance and Financial Advisors
41 Lesmill Rd.
North York, ON, Canada M3B 2T3
Phone: (416)444-5251
Fax: (416)444-8031
Free: 800-563-5822

Publications: CAIFA Forum (36123)

Canadian Association for Japanese Language Education (CAJLE)
Centre D'Etudes De L'Asie De L'Est
University of Montreal
Montreal, QC, Canada
Phone: (450)923-9600
Fax: (450)923-9788

Publications: Journal CAJLE (37137)

Canadian Association for Latin American and Caribbean Studies
c/o CETASE
Universite de Montreal
CP6128 Succ. Centre-ville
Montreal, QC, Canada H3C 3J7
Phone: (514)343-6569
Fax: (514)343-7716

Publications: Canadian Journal of Latin American and Caribbean Studies (35978)

Canadian Association of Medical Radiation Technologists
130 Albert St., Ste. 1510
Ottawa, ON, Canada K1P 5G4
Phone: (613)234-0012
Fax: (613)234-1097
Free: 800-463-9729

Publications: Canadian Journal of Medical Radiation Technology (36207)

Canadian Association of Occupational Therapists
Carleton Technology & Training Centre, Ste. 3400
1125 Colonel By Dr.
Ottawa, ON, Canada K1S 5R1
Phone: (613)523-2268
Fax: (613)523-2552
Free: 800-434-2268
Publications: The Canadian Journal of Occupational Therapy (Revue Canadienne d'Ergotherapie) (36209) • Occupational Therapy NOW (35242)

Canadian Association for Photographic Art/L'Association canadienne d'art photographique
31858 Hopedale Ave.
Clearbrook, BC, Canada V2T 2G7
Phone: (604)855-4848
Fax: (604)859-6288
Publications: Canadian Camera (36869)

Canadian Association of Physicists
150 Louis Pasteur Ave., Ste. 112
McDonald Bldg.
Ottawa, ON, Canada K1N 6N5
Phone: (613)562-5614
Fax: (613)562-5615
Publications: Physics in Canada (36271)

Canadian Association of Provincial Court Judges
PO Box 339
Grand Bank, NL, Canada A0E 1W0
Phone: (709)832-1450
Fax: (709)832-1758
Publications: Provincial Judges Journal/Journal des Juges Provinciaux (35460)

Canadian Association for Scottish Studies
Department of History
University of Guelph
Guelph, ON, Canada N1G 2W1
Phone: (519)824-4120
Publications: Scottish Tradition (35867)

Canadian Association of University Teachers/L'Association Canadienne des Professeures et Professeurs d'Universite
2675 Queensview Dr.
Ottawa, ON, Canada K2B 8K2
Phone: (613)820-2270
Fax: (613)820-2417
Publications: CAUT (ACPPU) Bulletin (36232)

Canadian Aviation Historical Society
PO Box 224, Sta. A
Willowdale, ON, Canada M2N 5S8
Phone: (416)410-9774
Publications: C.A.H.S. Journal (36875)

The Canadian Bankers Association
Commerce Court West, 30th Fl.
PO Box 348
Toronto, ON, Canada M5L 1G2
Phone: (416)362-6093
Fax: (416)362-5658
Free: 800-263-0231
Publications: Bank Facts (36470) • Canadian Banker (36493)

The Canadian Baptist
195 The West Mall, No. 414
Etobicoke, ON, Canada M9C 5K1
Phone: (416)622-8600
Fax: (416)622-2308
Free: 800-387-7890
Publications: The Canadian Baptist (35813)

The Canadian Bar Foundation
Dow's Lake Court
865 Carling Ave., Ste. 500
Ottawa, ON, Canada K1S 5S8
Phone: (613)237-2925
Fax: (613)237-0185
Free: 800-267-8860
Publications: The Canadian Bar Review (La Revue du Barreau Canadien) (36190) • NATIONAL (36262)

Canadian Biker Publication Ltd.
735 Market St.
PO Box 4122
Victoria, BC, Canada V8T 2E2
Phone: (250)384-0333
Fax: (250)384-1832
Publications: Canadian Biker (35213)

Canadian Catholic Historical Association
History Office
10 Mary St., Ste. 508
Toronto, ON, Canada M4Y 1P9
Phone: (416)934-3400
Fax: (416)934-3444
Publications: Historical Studies (36615)

Canadian Ceramic Society
2175 Sheppard Ave. E., Ste. 310
Willowdale, ON, Canada M2J 1W8
Phone: (416)491-2886
Fax: (416)491-1670
Publications: Canadian Ceramics Quarterly (36876)

Canadian Chiropractic Association
1396 Eglinton Ave. W.
Toronto, ON, Canada M6C 2E4
Phone: (416)781-5656
Fax: (416)781-7344
Publications: Journal of the Canadian Chiropractic Association (36632)

Canadian Co-Operative Wool Growers Ltd.
c/o Ontario Stockyards Inc.
RR 1, Hwy. 89
Cookstown, ON, Canada L0L 1L0
Phone: (705)458-4800
Fax: (705)458-0186
Publications: Canadian Cooperative Wool Growers Magazine (35752)

Canadian Coast Guard
200 Kent St., 5th Fl., Sta. 13228
Ottawa, ON, Canada K1A 0E6
Phone: (613)993-0999
Fax: (613)990-1866
Publications: Radio Aids to Marine Navigation (36274)

Canadian College of Health Service Executives
350 Sparks St., Ste. 402
Ottawa, ON, Canada K1R 7S8
Phone: (613)235-7218
Fax: (613)235-5451
Free: 800-363-9056
Publications: Healthcare Management Forum (36247)

Canadian Committee on Labour History
Memorial University of Newfoundland
Arts Publication, FM 2005
St. John's, NL, Canada A1C 5S7
Phone: (709)737-2144
Fax: (709)737-4342
Publications: Labour/Le Travail (35488)

Canadian Conference of Catholic Bishops
2500 Don Reid Dr.
Ottawa, ON, Canada K1H 2J2
Phone: (613)241-9461
Fax: (613)241-5090
Free: 800-769-1147
Publications: Caravan (36231)

Canadian Conference of Mennonite Brethren Churches
3-169 Riverton Ave.
Winnipeg, MB, Canada R2L 2E5
Phone: (204)654-5760
Fax: (204)654-1865
Free: 888-669-6575
Publications: Mennonite Brethren Herald (35342) • Mennonite Review (35343)

Canadian Controlled Media Communications
5397 Eglinton Ave. W., Ste. 101
Toronto, ON, Canada M9C 5K6
Phone: (416)928-2909
Fax: (416)966-1181
Free: 800-320-6420

Publications: Campus.ca (36486) • Score (36736) • Scoregolf for Women (36737)

Canadian Council of Teachers of English Language Arts
10-730 River Rd.
Winnipeg, MB, Canada R2M 5A4
Phone: (204)255-1676
Fax: (204)253-2562
Publications: English Quarterly (35327)

Canadian Criminal Justice Association
383 Parkdale Ave., Ste. 207
Ottawa, ON, Canada K1Y 4R4
Phone: (613)725-3715
Fax: (613)725-3720
Publications: Canadian Journal of Criminology/Revue Canadienne de Criminologie (36204)

Canadian Dental Association
1815, Alta Vista Dr.
Ottawa, ON, Canada K1G 3Y6
Phone: (613)523-1770
Fax: (613)523-7736
Free: 800-267-6354
Publications: Journal of the Canadian Dental Association (Journal de l'Association Dentaire Canadienne) (36253)

Canadian Diabetes Association
15 Toronto St., Ste. 800
Toronto, ON, Canada M5C 2E3
Phone: (416)363-3373
Fax: (416)363-3393
Publications: Diabetes Dialogue (36573)

Canadian Disarmament Information Service
736 Bathurst St.
Toronto, ON, Canada M5S 2R4
Fax: (416)531-6214
Publications: Peace Magazine (36699)

Canadian Education Association
317 Adelaide St. W., Ste. 300
Toronto, ON, Canada M5V 1P9
Phone: (416)591-6300
Fax: (416)591-5345
Publications: Education Canada (36578)

Canadian Ethnic Studies Journal
c/o University of Calgary
2500 University Dr. NW
Calgary, AB, Canada T2N 1N4
Phone: (403)220-7257
Fax: (403)284-5467
Publications: Canadian Ethnic Studies Journal (34634)

Canadian Family Camping Federation, Inc.
Box 397
Rexdale, ON, Canada M9W 5L4
Publications: Canadian Camper (36341)

Canadian Federation of Students-Services
45 Charles St., E., Ste. 100
Toronto, ON, Canada M4Y 1S2
Phone: (416)966-2887
Fax: (416)966-4043
Publications: The Student Traveller (36750)

Canadian Firefighter Publications, Ltd.
480 Prince Edward Dr.
Toronto, ON, Canada M8X 2M5
Phone: (416)233-2516
Fax: (416)233-2051
Publications: The Canadian Firefighter (36498)

The Canadian Fly Fisher
389 Bridge St. W., RR2
Belleville, ON, Canada K8N 4Z2
Phone: (613)966-8017
Fax: (613)966-5002
Free: 888-805-5608
Publications: The Canadian Fly Fisher (35677)

Numbers cited after listings are entry numbers rather than page numbers.

Canadian Forces Base Cold Lake Courier
PO Box 6190
Coldlake, AB, Canada T9M 2C5
Phone: (403)594-5206
Fax: (403)594-2139

Publications: Canadian Forces Base Cold Lake Courier (34688)

Canadian Forces Base Esquimalt
PO Box 17000
STN Forces
Victoria, BC, Canada V9A 7N2
Phone: (250)363-3014
Fax: (250)363-3015

Publications: Campbell River Mirror (34918) • Cowichan News Leader (34950) • Ladysmith-Chemainus Chronicle (35001) • The Lookout (35220) • The Pictorial (34951)

Canadian Forces Base Moncton
PO Box 6100
Moncton, NB, Canada E1C 9L4
Phone: (506)851-0500
Fax: (506)851-0670

Publications: The Moncton Provider (35412)

Canadian Free Press
PO Box 771 Sta. A
Toronto, ON, Canada M5W 1G3
Phone: (904)254-4920
Free: 800-259-4919

Publications: Canadian Free Press (36499)

Canadian Gemmological Association
1767 Avenue Rd.
North York, ON, Canada M5M 3Y8
Phone: (416)785-0962
Fax: (416)785-9043
Free: 877-244-3090

Publications: Canadian Gemmologist (36197)

Canadian Geographic Enterprises
39 McArthur Ave.
Ottawa, ON, Canada K1L 8L7
Phone: (613)745-4629
Fax: (613)744-0947
Free: 800-267-0824

Publications: Canadian Geographic (36198)

Canadian Health Libraries Association/Association des bibliotheques de la sante Canada
3332 Yonge St.
PO Box 94038
Toronto, ON, Canada M4N 3R1

Publications: Bibliotheca Medica Canadiana (35315)

The Canadian Home Economics Association/L'Association canadienne d'economie familiale
151 Slater St., Ste. 307
Ottawa, ON, Canada K1P 5H3
Phone: (613)238-8817
Fax: (613)238-8972

Publications: Canadian Home Economics Journal (Revue Canadienne d'Economie Familiale) (36199)

Canadian Home Publishers, Inc.
511 King St. W., Ste. 120
Toronto, ON, Canada M5V 2Z4
Phone: (416)593-0204
Fax: (416)591-1630
Free: 800-559-8868

Publications: Canadian House & Home Magazine (36503)

Canadian Home Workshop
340 Ferrier St., Ste. 210
Markham, ON, Canada L3R 2Z5
Phone: (905)475-8440
Fax: (905)475-9246

Publications: Canadian Home Workshop (36019)

Canadian Horse Publications
PO Box 670
Aurora, ON, Canada L4G 4J9
Phone: (905)727-0107
Fax: (905)841-1530
Free: 800-505-7428

Publications: Horse-Canada.com Magazine (35649)

Canadian Horse Publications Inc.
225 Industrial Pkwy. S.
PO Box 670
Aurora, ON, Canada L4G 4J9
Phone: (905)727-0107
Fax: (905)841-1530
Free: 800-505-7428

Publications: Canadian Thoroughbred (35644)

Canadian Humanist Publications
PO Box 3769, Sta. C.
Ottawa, ON, Canada K1Y 4J8
Phone: (613)749-8929
Fax: (613)749-8929

Publications: Humanist in Canada (36250)

Canadian Industrial Publishing Inc.
919 Fraser Dr., Ste. 7
Burlington, ON, Canada L7L 4X8
Phone: (905)637-2317
Fax: (905)634-2776

Publications: Canadian Industrial Machinery (35715)

Canadian Institute of Chartered Accountants
277 Wellington St. W.
Toronto, ON, Canada M5V 3H2
Phone: (416)977-3222
Fax: (416)977-8585
Free: 800-268-3793

Publications: CA Magazine (36483)

Canadian Institute of Forestry/Institut Forestier du Canada
151 Slater St., Ste. 606
Ottawa, ON, Canada K1P 5H3
Phone: (613)234-2242
Fax: (613)234-6181

Publications: The Forestry Chronicle (36243)

Canadian Institute of Geomatics
1390 Prince of Wales Dr., Ste. 400
Ottawa, ON, Canada K2C 3N6
Phone: (613)224-9851
Fax: (613)224-9577

Publications: Geomatica (36246)

Canadian Institute of International Affairs
Glendon Hall, Glendon College
2275 BayView Ave.
Toronto, ON, Canada M4N 3M5
Phone: (416)487-6830
Fax: (416)487-6831

Publications: Behind the Headlines (36473)

Canadian Institute of International Affairs
2275 Bayview Ave.
Toronto, ON, Canada M4N 3M6
Phone: (416)487-6830
Fax: (416)487-6831
Free: 800-668-2442

Publications: International Journal (36623)

The Canadian Institute of Management
2175 Sheppard Ave. E., Ste. 310
Toronto, ON, Canada M2J 1W8
Phone: (416)493-0155
Fax: (416)491-1670
Free: 800-387-5774

Publications: The Canadian Manager (36516)

Canadian Institute of Mining, Metallurgy, and Petroleum
Xerox Tower
3400 de Maisonneuve Blvd. W., Ste. 1210
Montreal, QC, Canada H3Z 3B8
Phone: (514)939-2710
Fax: (514)939-2714

Publications: CIM Bulletin (Canadian Mining & Metallurgical Bulletin) (37103) • CIM Reporter (37104)

The Canadian Jewish News
1500 Don Mills Rd., Ste. 205
North York, ON, Canada M3B 3K4
Phone: (416)391-1836
Fax: (416)391-0829

Publications: The Canadian Jewish News (36124)

Canadian Jewish Outlook Society
6184 Ash St., Ste. 3
Vancouver, BC, Canada V5Z 3G9
Phone: (604)324-5101
Fax: (604)325-2570

Publications: Outlook (35156)

Canadian Journal of Neurological Sciences
7015 Macleod Trail SW, Ste. 709
Calgary, AB, Canada T2H 2K6
Phone: (403)229-9575
Fax: (403)229-1661

Publications: Canadian Journal of Neurological Sciences (34637)

Canadian Journal of Regional Science
Departement de Geographie
Universite de Montreal
Montreal, QC, Canada H3C 3J7
Phone: (514)343-8061
Fax: (514)343-8008

Publications: Canadian Journal of Regional Science (37098)

Canadian Journal of Women and the Law/Revue Femmes et Droit
Osgoode Hall Law School
York University
4700 Keele St.
Toronto, ON, Canada M3J 1P3
Phone: (416)736-5041
Fax: (416)736-5736

Publications: Canadian Journal of Women and the Law/Revue Femmes et Droit (36513)

Canadian Lawyer Magazine Ltd.
240 Edward St.
Aurora, ON, Canada L4G 3S9
Phone: (905)841-6480
Fax: (905)841-5078

Publications: Canadian Lawyer (35642)

Canadian Library Association
328 Frank St.
Ottawa, ON, Canada K2P 0X8
Phone: (613)232-9625
Fax: (613)563-9895

Publications: Feliciter (36242)

The Canadian Locksmith Press
137 Vaughan Rd.
Toronto, ON, Canada M6C 2L9
Phone: (416)653-2199
Fax: (416)656-3068

Publications: The Canadian Locksmith Magazine (36514)

Canadian Mathematical Society
577 King Edward, Ste. 109
PO Box 450, Sta. A
Ottawa, ON, Canada K1N 6N5
Phone: (613)562-5702
Fax: (613)565-1539

Publications: Canadian Journal of Mathematics (35132) • Crux Mathematicorum with Mathematical Mayhem (36240)

Canadian Medical Association
1867 Alta Vista Dr.
Ottawa, ON, Canada K1G 3Y6
Fax: (613)236-8864
Free: 800-457-4205

Publications: Canadian Association of Radiologists Journal (36189) • Canadian Journal of Respiratory Therapy (36217) • Canadian Journal of Rural Medicine (36218) • Canadian Journal of Surgery (36220) • CMA News (36235) • CMAJ/JAMC (Canadian Medical Association Journal)/(Journal de l'Association Medicale Canadienne) (36236) • Journal of Psychiatry and Neuroscience (36255)

Canadian MoneySaver
PO Box 370
Bath, ON, Canada K0H 1G0
Phone: (613)352-7448
Fax: (613)352-7700

Publications: Canadian MoneySaver (35667)

Canadian National Railways
Public Affairs & Advertising
PO Box 8100
Montreal, QC, Canada H3C 3N4
Phone: (514)399-5430
Fax: (514)399-5344

Publications: Movin' (37194)

Canadian Nature Federation
1 Nicholas St., Ste. 606
Ottawa, ON, Canada K1N 7B7
Phone: (613)562-3447
Fax: (613)562-3371
Free: 800-267-4088

Publications: Nature Canada (36263)

Canadian Nurses Association
50 Driveway
Ottawa, ON, Canada K2P 1E2
Phone: (613)237-2133
Fax: (613)237-3520
Free: 800-361-8404

Publications: Canadian Nurse (L'Infirmiere Canadienne) (36223)

Canadian Ophthalmological Society/Societe Canadienne d'Ophtalmologie
1525 Carling Ave., Ste. 610
Ottawa, ON, Canada K1Z 8R9
Phone: (613)729-6779
Fax: (613)729-7209
Free: 800-267-5763

Publications: Canadian Journal of Ophthalmology (Journal Canadien d'Ophtalmologie) (36210)

Canadian Owners and Pilots Association
75 Albert St., Ste. 207
Ottawa, ON, Canada K1P 5E7
Phone: (613)236-4901
Fax: (613)236-8646

Publications: Canadian Flight (36195) • Canadian Flight Annual (36196)

Canadian Parliamentary Review
151 Sparks St., Rm. 1200
Ottawa, ON, Canada K1A 0A6
Phone: (613)996-1662
Fax: (613)995-5357

Publications: Canadian Parliamentary Review (36224)

Canadian Pharmacists Association
1785 Alta Vista Dr.
Ottawa, ON, Canada K1G 3Y6
Phone: (613)523-7877
Fax: (613)523-0445
Free: 800-917-9489

Publications: Canadian Pharmaceutical Journal (36225) • Compendium of Pharmaceuticals and Specialties (36238) • Provincial Drug Benefit Programs (36273)

Canadian Political Science Association
260 Dalhousie, Ste. 204
Ottawa, ON, Canada K1N 7E4
Phone: (613)562-1202
Fax: (613)241-0019

Publications: Canadian Journal of Political Science (Revue canadienne de science politique) (36213)

Canadian Postmasters and Assistants Association
281 Queen Mary
Ottawa, ON, Canada K1K 1X1
Phone: (613)745-2095
Fax: (613)745-5559

Publications: The Canadian Postmaster (Le Maitre de Poste Canadien) (36226)

Canadian Power & Sail Squadrons
26 Golden Gate Ct.
Scarborough, ON, Canada M1P 3A5
Phone: (416)293-2438
Fax: (416)293-2445

Publications: The Port Hole (Le Hublot) (36383)

Canadian Process Equipment & Control News Ltd.
343 Eglinton Ave. E.
Toronto, ON, Canada M4P 1L7
Phone: (416)481-6483
Fax: (416)481-6436
Free: 800-483-9234

Publications: Canadian Process Equipment & Control News (36527)

Canadian Psychiatric Association
441 MacLaren St., Ste. 260
Ottawa, ON, Canada K2P 2H3
Phone: (613)234-2815
Fax: (613)234-9857

Publications: The Canadian Journal of Psychiatry (36214)

Canadian Public Health Association
1565 Carling Ave., Ste. 400
Ottawa, ON, Canada K1Z 8R1
Phone: (613)725-3769
Fax: (613)725-9826

Publications: Canadian Journal of Public Health (36215)

Canadian Railroad Historical Association
Box 22, Sta. B
Montreal, QC, Canada H3B 3J5

Publications: Canadian Rail/Rail Canadien (37099)

The Canadian Record
211 Main St.
PO Box 898
Canadian, TX 79014
Phone: (806)323-6461
Fax: (806)323-5738

Publications: The Canadian Record (29997)

Canadian Register Ltd.
1155 Yonge St., Ste. 401
Toronto, ON, Canada N4T 1W2
Phone: (416)934-3410
Fax: (416)934-3409

Publications: Catholic Register (36542)

Canadian Remote Sensing Society
1685 Russell Rd., Unit 1-R
Ottawa, ON, Canada K1G 0N1
Phone: (613)234-0191
Fax: (613)234-9039

Publications: Canadian Journal of Remote Sensing (36216)

Canadian Review of Studies in Nationalism, Inc.
c/o University of Prince Edward Island
Charlottetown, PE, Canada C1A 4P3
Phone: (902)894-4409
Fax: (902)628-4323

Publications: Canadian Review of Studies in Nationalism (36913)

Canadian Rodeo News Ltd.
223 Stockmans Centre
2116 27th Ave. NE
Calgary, AB, Canada T2E 7A6
Phone: (403)250-7292
Fax: (403)250-6926

Publications: Canadian Rodeo News (34639)

Canadian Schizophrenia Foundation
16 Florence Ave.
Toronto, ON, Canada M2N 1E9
Phone: (416)733-2117
Fax: (416)733-2352

Publications: Journal of Orthomolecular Medicine (36636)

Canadian Shareowner
121 Richmond St. W. 7th Fl.
Toronto, ON, Canada M5H 2K1
Phone: (416)595-9600
Fax: (416)595-0400

Publications: Canadian Shareowner (36530)

Canadian Slavonic Papers
200 Arts Bldg.
University of Alberta
Edmonton, AB, Canada T6G 2E6
Phone: (780)492-2566
Fax: (780)492-9106

Publications: Canadian Slavonic Papers/Revue Canadienne des Slavistes (34704)

Canadian Society of Agricultural Engineering
Box 381
RPO University
Saskatoon, SK, Canada S7N 4J8
Phone: (306)966-5319
Fax: (306)966-5334

Publications: Canadian Biosystems Engineering (37549)

Canadian Society of Hospital Pharmacists (CSHP)
1145 Hunt Club Rd., Ste. 350
Ottawa, ON, Canada K1V 0Y3
Phone: (613)736-9733
Fax: (613)736-5660

Publications: Canadian Journal of Hospital Pharmacy (36206)

Canadian Society for Medical Laboratory Science
PO Box 2830, LCD 1
Hamilton, ON, Canada L8N 3N8
Phone: (905)528-8642
Fax: (905)528-4968

Publications: Canadian Journal of Medical Laboratory Science (CJLMS) (35877)

Canadian Society for the Study of Names
c/o Prof. W. Ahrens
Dept. of Languages, Literatures, and Linguistics
York University
Toronto, ON, Canada M3J 1P3
Phone: (416)736-5016
Fax: (905)264-7517

Publications: Onomastica Canadiana (36681)

Canadian Sociology & Anthropology Association
1455 De Maisonneuve W., SB-323
Montreal, QC, Canada H3G 1M8
Phone: (514)848-8780
Fax: (514)848-8780

Publications: Canadian Review of Sociology and Anthropology (37100)

Canadian Speeches
Box 250
Woodville, ON, Canada K0M 2T0
Phone: (705)439-2580
Fax: (705)439-1208

Publications: Canadian Speeches (36910)

Canadian Sportfishing Productions Inc.
937 Centre Rd., Dept. 2020
Waterdown, ON, Canada L0R 2H0
Phone: (905)689-1112
Fax: (905)689-2065

Publications: Canadian Sportfishing (36844)

The Canadian Sportsman
25 Old Plank Rd.
PO Box 129
Straffordville, ON, Canada N0J 1Y0
Phone: (519)866-5558
Fax: (519)866-5596

Publications: The Canadian Sportsman (36408)

Canadian Tax Foundation
595 Bay St., Ste. 1200
Toronto, ON, Canada M5G 2N5
Phone: (416)599-0283
Fax: (416)599-9283
Free: 877-733-0283

Publications: Canadian Tax Journal (Revue fiscale canadienne) (36531)

Canadian Trotting Association
2150 Meadowvale Blvd.
Mississauga, ON, Canada L5N 6R6
Phone: (905)858-3060
Fax: (905)858-3111

Publications: Trot (36090)

Canadian Veterinary Medical Association
339 Booth St.
Ottawa, ON, Canada K1R 7K1
Phone: (613)236-1162
Fax: (613)236-9681
Free: 800-567-2862

Numbers cited after listings are entry numbers rather than page numbers.

Publications: Canadian Journal of Veterinary Research (36221) • Canadian Veterinary Journal (36229)

Canadian Vocational Association
PO Box 3435 Sta. D
Ottawa, ON, Canada K1P 6L4
Phone: (613)838-6012
Fax: (613)838-6012

Publications: Canadian Vocational Journal (36230)

Canadian Wireless Telecommunications Association
130 Albert St., Ste. 1110
Ottawa, ON, Canada K1P 5G4
Phone: (613)233-4888
Fax: (613)233-2032

Publications: Wireless Telecom (36280)

Canadian Wood Council
1400 Blair Pl., Ste. 210
Ottawa, ON, Canada K1J 9B8
Phone: (613)747-5544
Fax: (613)747-6264
Free: 800-463-5091

Publications: Wood Design & Building (36281)

Canandaigua Messenger, Inc.
73 Buffalo St.
Canandaigua, NY 14424
Phone: (716)394-0770
Fax: (716)394-1675
Free: 800-724-2099

Publications: The Daily Messenger (20420)

Canarsie Publications Courier, Inc.
1142 E 92 St.
Brooklyn, NY 11236
Phone: (718)257-0600
Fax: (718)272-0870

Publications: Canarsie Courier (20305)

Canisius College
2001 Main St.
Buffalo, NY 14208-1098
Phone: (716)888-5000
Fax: (716)888-2525

Publications: The Griffin (20380)

Canmore Leader
50 Lincoln Park, Ste. 100
Canmore, AB, Canada T1W 1N8
Phone: (403)678-2365
Fax: (403)678-2996

Publications: Canmore Leader (34678)

Canoe & Kayak, Inc.
10526 NE 68th St., Ste. 3
Kirkland, WA 98083
Phone: (425)827-6363

Publications: Canoe and Kayak Magazine (32797)

Canon Communications LLC
11444 W Olympic Blvd., Ste. 900
Los Angeles, CA 90064-1549
Phone: (310)445-4200
Fax: (310)445-3799

Publications: Injection Molding Magazine (4330) • Plastics Auxiliaries & Machinery (4348)

Canora Courier Ltd.
Box 746
Canora, SK, Canada S0A 0L0
Phone: (306)563-5131
Fax: (306)563-6144

Publications: Canora Courier (37455) • Kamsack Times (37478) • Norquay North Star (37456) • Preeceville Progress (37457)

Canton Jewish Community Federation
2631 Harvard Ave., NW
Canton, OH 44709
Phone: (330)453-0132
Fax: (330)452-4487

Publications: Stark Jewish News (24732)

Cantorial Council of America
500 W 185th St.
New York, NY 10033
Phone: (212)960-5353
Fax: (212)960-5359

Publications: Journal of Jewish Music and Liturgy (22109)

Canvet Publications Ltd.
359 Kent St., Ste. 407
Ottawa, ON, Canada K2P 0R6
Phone: (613)235-8741
Fax: (613)233-7159

Publications: Legion Magazine (36258)

CanWest Interactive
11 Thornhill Dr., Burnside
Dartmouth, NS, Canada B3B 1R9
Phone: (902)468-1222
Fax: (902)468-3609
Free: 800-565-2601

Publications: The Daily News (35545)

The Canyon News
1500 5th Ave.
Canyon, TX 79015
Phone: (806)655-7121
Fax: (806)655-0823

Publications: The Canyon News (30000)

Canyouth Publications Ltd.
1345 Baseline Rd.
Ottawa, ON, Canada K2C 0A7
Phone: (613)224-5131
Fax: (613)224-3571

Publications: The Canadian Leader (36222)

Capamara Communications, Inc.
5001 Forbidden Plateau Rd.
Courtenay, BC, Canada V9J 1R3
Phone: (250)338-2455
Fax: (250)338-2466
Free: 800-661-0368

Publications: Northern Aquaculture Magazine (34932)

Cape Breton Post
255 George St.
PO Box 1500
Sydney, NS, Canada B1P 6K6
Phone: (902)564-5451
Fax: (902)562-7077

Publications: Cape Breton Post (35607)

Cape Cod Times
319 Main St.
Hyannis, MA 02601
Phone: (508)775-1200
Free: 800-451-7887

Publications: Cape Cod Times (14250)

Cape Coral Daily Breeze
128 W Charlotte Ave.
Punta Gorda, FL 33950
Phone: (941)639-1136
Fax: (941)639-4832

Publications: Charlotte Shopping Guide (6607)

The Cape Courier
PO Box 6242
Cape Elizabeth, ME 04107
Phone: (207)767-5023

Publications: The Cape Courier (12945)

Cape Gazette
PO Box 213
Lewes, DE 19958
Phone: (302)645-7700
Fax: (302)645-1664

Publications: Cape Gazette (5258)

Cape Publications, Inc.
Gannett Plaza
PO Box 419000
Melbourne, FL 32941-9000
Phone: (407)242-3500
Fax: (407)242-6620
Free: 800-633-8449

Publications: Florida Today (6334)

Capers Aweigh Press
19 Cliff St.
Glace Bay, NS, Canada B1A 1B3
Phone: (902)489-0822

Publications: Capers Aweigh Annual Anthology (35554)

Capilano Courier Publishing Society
Capilano College
2055 Purcell Way
North Vancouver, BC, Canada V7J 3H5
Phone: (604)984-4949
Fax: (604)984-4985

Publications: Capilano Courier (35033)

The Capilano Review
2055 Purcell Way
North Vancouver, BC, Canada V7J 3H5
Phone: (604)984-1712
Fax: (604)990-7837

Publications: The Capilano Review (35034)

Capital Cities/ABC, Inc.
825 7th Ave., 6th Fl.
New York, NY 10019
Phone: (212)887-8400
Fax: (212)887-8484

Publications: Fort Worth Star-Telegram (30338)

Capital City Press
525 Lafayette St.
Baton Rouge, LA 70802-5410
Phone: (225)388-0216
Fax: (225)388-0348
Free: 800-960-6397

Publications: The Advocate (12484)

The Capital-Gazette Newspapers
2000 Capital Dr.
Annapolis, MD 21401
Phone: (410)268-5000
Fax: (410)268-4643
Free: 800-327-1583

Publications: The Capital (13090)

Capital Gazette Printing
306 Crane Hwy.
Glen Burnie, MD 21061
Phone: (410)766-3700
Fax: (410)766-3017

Publications: The Maryland Gazette (13555)

Capital Press
PO Box 2048
Salem, OR 97308
Phone: (503)364-4431
Fax: (503)370-4383
Free: 800-882-6789

Publications: Capital Press (26565)

Capital Publishers
226 Argyle Ave.
Ottawa, ON, Canada K2P 1B9
Phone: (613)230-0333
Fax: (613)230-4441

Publications: WHERE Ottawa (36279)

Capital Publishing Co.
PO Box 770
Bowie, MD 20715
Phone: (301)262-3700
Fax: (301)464-7027

Publications: Blade-News (13391)

Capital Publishing Co.
575 Lexington Ave.
New York, NY 10022
Phone: (212)223-3100
Fax: (212)223-1598
Free: 800-777-1851

Publications: Worth Magazine (22946)

Capital Region Weekly Newspaper Group
750 Pierce Rd.
Clifton Park, NY 12065
Phone: (518)877-7160
Fax: (518)877-7824

Publications: Ballston Journal (20119) • Ballston-Malta Pennysaver (20118) • Clifton Park North Pennysaver (20462) • Clifton Park South Pennysaver (20463) • Latham Pennysaver (20466) • Moneysaver (20467)

The Capital Times
1901 Fish Hatchery Rd.
PO Box 8060
Madison, WI 53708
Phone: (608)252-6400
Fax: (608)252-6445

Publications: The Capital Times (33925)

Capital University
2199 E. Main St.
Columbus, OH 43209
Phone: (614)236-6614
Fax: (614)236-6916

Publications: The Chimes (25006)

Capitol City Publishing Co., Inc.
Southand at Perry St.
Trenton, NJ 08602
Phone: (609)989-7800
Fax: (609)394-1358

Publications: The Trentonian (19670)

Capitol Hill Beacon
124 W Commerce
Oklahoma City, OK 73109
Phone: (405)232-4151
Fax: (405)235-0818

Publications: Capitol Hill Beacon (25957)

Capitol Outlook
602 N Adams St.
Tallahassee, FL 32301-1114
Phone: (850)681-1852
Fax: (850)681-1093

Publications: Capital Outlook (6702)

Capper's
1503 SW 42nd St.
Topeka, KS 66609-1265
Phone: (785)274-4300
Fax: (785)274-4305
Free: 800-678-5779

Publications: Capper's (11816)

Car Buyer's Market, Inc.
55 Northern Blvd.
Great Neck, NY 11023
Phone: (516)482-0292
Free: 800-288-4226

Publications: Car Buyer's Market (20687)

Car Collector Magazine, Inc.
5095 S. Washington Ave.
Titusville, FL 32780
Phone: (321)267-8011
Fax: (321)269-7004

Publications: Car Collector (6817)

Carberry News-Express
34 Main St.
Box 220
Carberry, MB, Canada R0K 0H0
Phone: (204)834-2153
Fax: (204)834-2714

Publications: Carberry News-Express (35259)

Card-Zine Communications, Inc.
8912 Ewing Ave.
Evanston, IL 60203

Publications: Patient Care and Nursing Products (8868)

Cardan, Inc.
261 Atlantic Ave.
PO Box 340
Dassel, MN 55325
Phone: (320)275-2192
Fax: (320)275-2193

Publications: Enterprise Dispatch (15824)

Carden Jennings Publishing
375 Greenbrier Dr., Ste. 100
Charlottesville, VA 22901-1618
Phone: (434)817-2000
Fax: (434)817-2020

Publications: Albemarle (31913)

Cardiff Communications Ltd.
130 Belfield Rd.
Etobicoke, ON, Canada M9W 1G1
Phone: (416)614-0955
Fax: (416)614-2781

Publications: Automotive Parts & Technology (35811)

Career Communications Group, Inc.
729 E. Pratt St., No. 504
Baltimore, MD 21202
Phone: (410)244-7101
Fax: (410)752-1837
Free: 800-932-7101

Publications: Hispanic Engineer (13168) • USBE & Information Technology (13258)

Career Recruitment Media
1800 Sherman Ave., Ste. 300
Evanston, IL 60201-3769
Phone: (847)448-1000
Fax: (847)475-8839

Publications: Graduating Engineer & Computer Careers (8860)

Cargo Network Services
Garden City Plz., Ste. 312
Garden City, NY 11530-3325
Phone: (516)747-3312
Fax: (516)747-3431

Publications: CNS Focus (20636)

Carib News
15 W 39th St.
New York, NY 10018
Phone: (212)944-1991
Fax: (212)944-2089

Publications: NY Carib News (22477)

Caribbean Review Inc.
9700 SW 67th Ave.
Miami, FL 33156
Fax: (305)284-1019

Publications: Caribbean Review (6344)

Caribbean Studies
PO Box 23361
San Juan, PR 00931-3361
Phone: (787)764-0000
Fax: (787)764-3099

Publications: Caribbean Studies (28291)

Caribbean Travel and Life, Inc.
460 N Orlando Ave., Ste. 200
Winter Park, FL 32789-2900
Phone: (407)647-2170
Fax: (407)628-7061

Publications: Caribbean Travel and Life (6878) • Latitudes (6882)

Caribe Comm.
408 S. Huntington Ave.
Boston, MA 02130
Phone: (617)522-5060
Fax: (617)524-5886

Publications: El Mundo (13888)

Cariboo Press Ltd.
128 4th St.
PO Box 190
Ashcroft, BC, Canada V0K 1A0
Phone: (250)453-2261
Fax: (250)453-9625

Publications: Ashcroft Journal (34883)

Cariboo Press Ltd.
Box 309
Burns Lake, BC, Canada V0J 1E0
Phone: (250)692-7526

Publications: Lakes District News (34915)

Cariboo Press Ltd.
1365 B Dalhousie Drive
Kamloops, BC, Canada V2C 5P6
Phone: (604)374-7467
Fax: (604)374-1033

Publications: Kamloops This Week (34978)

Cariboo Press Ltd.
PO Box 1007
Vanderhoof, BC, Canada V0J 3A0
Phone: (250)567-9258
Fax: (250)567-2070

Publications: Omineca Express (35198)

Cariboo Press (1969) Ltd.
188 N. 1st Ave.
Williams Lake, BC, Canada V2G 2A8
Phone: (250)392-2331
Fax: (250)392-1140

Publications: Eagle Valley News (35089) • Quesnel Cariboo Observer (35069) • The Tribune (35243)

Caribou County Sun
PO Box 815
Soda Springs, ID 83276
Phone: (208)547-3260
Fax: (208)547-4422

Publications: Caribou County Sun (7982)

Caribou Press Ltd.
4407 25th Ave.
Vernon, BC, Canada V1T 1P5
Phone: (250)545-3322
Fax: (250)542-1510

Publications: The Morning Star (35201)

Carieoo Press
402 W. 3rd St.
PO Box 20
Revelstoke, BC, Canada V0E 2S0
Phone: (250)837-4667
Fax: (250)837-2003

Publications: Revelstoke Times Review (35071)

Carl A. Jones Newspapers
204 W Main St.
PO Box 1717
Johnson City, TN 37601
Phone: (423)929-3111
Fax: (423)461-9558

Publications: Johnson City Press (29251)

Carl Albert State College
1507 S McKenna
Poteau, OK 74953-5208
Phone: (918)647-1200
Fax: (918)647-1266

Publications: Viking Banner (26046)

Carl Vinson Institute of Government
201 N. Milledge Ave.
Athens, GA 30602-5482
Phone: (706)542-2736
Fax: (706)542-6239

Publications: State and Local Government Review (6952)

Carleton College
1 N College St.
Northfield, MN 55057
Phone: (507)646-4000
Fax: (507)646-4146

Publications: The Carletonian (16233) • German Studies Review (16234)

Carleton University School of Journalism
1231 Colonel By Dr.
Ottawa, ON, Canada K1S 5B6
Fax: (613)788-5604

Publications: Centretown News (36233)

The Carlisle Citizen
PO Box 370
Carlisle, IA 50047
Phone: (515)989-0525

Publications: The Carlisle Citizen (10649)

Carlisle Communications, Inc.
PO Box 616
Carlisle, MA 01741
Phone: (978)369-8313
Fax: (978)369-3569

Publications: Carlisle Mosquito (14121)

Carlsbad Current-Argus
PO Box 1629
Carlsbad, NM 88220
Phone: (505)887-5501
Fax: (505)885-1066

Publications: Carlsbad Current-Argus (19822)

Carlyle Observer
Box 160
Carlyle, SK, Canada S0C 0R0
Phone: (306)453-2525
Fax: (306)453-2938

Publications: Carlyle Observer (37458)

Carmel Communications
PO Box G-1
Carmel, CA 93921
Phone: (831)620-2010
Fax: (831)624-8463

Publications: Carmel Pine Cone (1670)

The Carmelites
1540 E. Glenn St.
Tucson, AZ 85719-2632
Phone: (520)326-4967
Fax: (520)326-7366

Publications: The Carmelite Review (938)

Carmichael Times
PO Box 88
Carmichael, CA 95609
Phone: (916)483-0946
Fax: (916)483-1902

Publications: Carmichael Times (1675)

Carnegie Council on Ethics and International Affairs
170 E 64th St.
New York, NY 10021
Phone: (212)838-4120
Fax: (212)752-2432

Publications: Ethics and International Affairs (21633)

Carnegie Endowment for International Peace
1779 Massachusetts Ave. NW
Washington, DC 20036
Phone: (202)483-7600
Fax: (202)483-1840

Publications: Foreign Policy (5499)

Carnegie Herald Publishing Co.
14 W Main
PO Box 129
Carnegie, OK 73015-0129
Phone: (580)654-1443
Fax: (580)654-1608
Free: 888-235-0194

Publications: Carnegie Herald (25779)

Carnegie Mellon University
Box 17
Pittsburgh, PA 15213
Phone: (412)268-2111
Fax: (412)268-1596

Publications: The Tartan (27848)

Carnegie Museums of Pittsburgh
4400 Forbes Ave.
Pittsburgh, PA 15213
Phone: (412)622-3315
Fax: (412)688-8624

Publications: Carnegie Magazine (27764)

Caro Publishing Co.
344 N. State St.
PO Box 106
Caro, MI 48723
Phone: (989)673-7671
Fax: (989)673-5662
Free: 800-221-SOLD

Publications: Shoppers Advantage (14856) • Shopper's Guide (14857)

Carolina Bird Club, Inc.
11 West Jones St.
Raleigh, NC 27601-1029
Phone: (919)733-7450
Fax: (919)715-6439

Publications: The Chat (24132)

Carolina Christian Publications, Inc.
PO Box 1369
Yadkinville, NC 27055
Phone: (336)374-3199

Publications: Carolina Christian (24338)

Carolina Gardener, Inc.
1306 W Wendover Ave., Ste. 100
Greensboro, NC 27408
Phone: (336)574-0087
Fax: (336)574-3848
Free: 800-245-0142

Publications: Carolina Gardener (23918)

Carolina Newspapers
PO Box 38
Clover, SC 29710
Phone: (803)684-9903
Fax: (803)628-0300

Publications: Clover Herald (28542)

Carolina Newspapers
PO Box 30
York, SC 29745
Phone: (803)684-9903
Fax: (803)628-0300

Publications: Yorkville Enquirer (28790)

Carolina Parenting Inc.
1100 S Mint St., Ste. 201
Charlotte, NC 28203
Phone: (704)344-1980
Fax: (704)344-1983
Free: (866)932-6459

Publications: Charlotte Parent (23740)

Carolina Parenting, Inc.
5716 Fayetteville Rd., Ste. 201
Durham, NC 27713
Phone: (919)956-2430
Fax: (919)956-2427

Publications: Carolina Parent (23811)

Carolina Peacemaker
400 Summit Ave.
PO Box 20853
Greensboro, NC 27420-0853
Phone: (336)274-6210
Fax: (336)273-5103

Publications: Carolina Peacemaker (23919)

The Carolina Times
PO Box 3825
Durham, NC 27702
Phone: (919)682-2913
Fax: (919)682-2913

Publications: The Carolina Times (23812)

Carolina Woman Inc.
PO Box 3529
Cary, NC 27519
Phone: (919)852-5900
Fax: (919)852-5910

Publications: Carolina Woman (23685)

The Carolinian
610 Maywood Ave.
PO Box 25308
Raleigh, NC 27611
Phone: (919)834-5558
Fax: (919)832-3243

Publications: The Carolinian (24131)

The Carousel News & Trader Magazine
87 Park Ave., Ste. 206
Mansfield, OH 44902
Phone: (419)529-4999
Fax: (419)529-2321

Publications: The Carousel News & Trader Magazine (25330)

CARP
27 Queen St. E., Ste. 1304
Toronto, ON, Canada M5C 2M6
Phone: (416)363-8748
Fax: (416)363-8747

Publications: CARPNews Fifty Plus (36536)

Carroll County News
163 Court Sq.
PO Box 389
Huntingdon, TN 38344
Phone: (731)986-2253
Fax: (731)986-3585
Free: 800-706-6397

Publications: Carroll County News (29229)

Carroll County Newspapers
PO Box 232
Berryville, AR 72616-0232
Phone: (870)423-6636
Fax: (870)423-6640

Publications: Star Tribune (1054)

Carroll County Review
Box 369
Thomson, IL 61285
Phone: (815)259-2131
Fax: (815)259-3226

Publications: Carroll County Review (9683)

Carroll County Times
PO Box 346
Westminster, MD 21158
Phone: (410)848-4400

Publications: The Carroll County Times (13775)

The Carroll News
PO Box 487
Hillsville, VA 24343
Phone: (276)728-7311
Fax: (276)728-4119

Publications: The Carroll News (32167)

Carroll Papers, Inc.
14 E Main
Flora, IN 46929-0026
Phone: (219)967-4135
Fax: (219)967-3384

Publications: Carroll County Comet (9962)

Carroll Publishing
4701 Sangamore Rd., Ste. S-155
Bethesda, MD 20816
Phone: (301)263-9800
Fax: (301)263-9801
Free: 800-336-4240

Publications: Catholic Standard (13586)

Carroll Publishing Co.
145 Taylor St., NE
Washington, DC 20017
Phone: (202)281-2406
Fax: (202)281-2408

Publications: El Pregonero (5475)

Carroll Today Newspaper
102 W 6th St.
Carroll, IA 51401
Phone: (712)792-2179
Fax: (712)792-2309

Publications: Carroll Today (10651)

Carrollton Daily Democrat
Highway 65 S
PO Box 69
Carrollton, MO 64633
Phone: (660)542-0881
Fax: (660)542-0889

Publications: Carrollton Daily Democrat (16955)

Carrollton Gazette Patriot, Inc.
PO Box 231
Carrollton, IL 62016
Phone: (217)942-3626
Fax: (217)942-3699

Publications: Greene County Shopper (8160) • Jersey County Shopper (8162)

Carrollton Publishing Company Inc.
43 E Main St.
PO Box 37
Carrollton, OH 44615-9982
Phone: (330)627-5591
Fax: (330)627-3195

Publications: The Free Press-Standard (24742)

Cars & Parts Magazine
911 Vandemark Rd.
PO Box 482
Sidney, OH 45365
Phone: (937)498-0803
Fax: (937)498-0808
Free: 800-448-3611

Publications: Car & Parts Magazine (25515)

Carstens Publications Inc.
PO Box 700
Newton, NJ 07860-0700
Phone: (973)383-3355
Fax: (973)383-4064
Free: 800-474-6995

Publications: Flying Models (19371) • RailFan & Railroad (19375) • Railroad Model Craftsman (19376)

Carswell
One Corporate Plaza
2075 Kennedy Rd.
Toronto, ON, Canada M1T 3V4
Phone: (416)609-8000
Fax: (416)298-5094
Free: 800-387-5164
Publications: Banking and Finance Law Review (36471) • Canadian Family Law Quarterly (36497) • Education & Law Journal (36580) • Intellectual Property Journal (36622) • Journal of Environmental Law and Practice (36635) • National Journal of Constitutional Law (36672) • University of Toronto Faculty of Law Review (36779)

Carswell
2075 Kennedy Rd.
Toronto, ON, Canada M1T 3V4
Phone: (416)609-3800
Fax: (416)298-5082
Free: 800-387-5164
Publications: Canadian HR Reporter (36504)

Carter-Hubbard Publishing Co., Inc.
711 Main St.
Box 70
North Wilkesboro, NC 28659
Phone: (336)838-4117
Fax: (336)838-9864
Publications: Journal-Patriot (24108)

Carter Publications, Inc.
869 Dulles Ave., Ste. C
Stafford, TX 77477
Phone: (281)499-5600
Fax: (281)499-5002
Publications: Fort Bend Business Journal (31126)

Carteret Publishing Co.
Box 1679
Morehead City, NC 28557
Phone: (252)726-7081
Fax: (252)726-6016
Free: 800-849-6397
Publications: Carteret County News-Times (24070) • Tideland News (24250)

Carthage Courier
509 N Main St.
PO Box 239
Carthage, TN 37030
Phone: (615)735-1110
Fax: (615)735-0635
Publications: Carthage Courier (29081)

The Carthage Press
527 S. Main St.
PO Box 678
Carthage, MO 64836
Phone: (417)358-2191
Fax: (417)358-7428
Publications: The Carthage Press (16959)

Carthaginian
PO Box 457
Carthage, MS 39051
Phone: (601)267-4501
Fax: (601)267-5290
Publications: Carthaginian (16586)

Cartoonist and Comic Artist Magazine
2747 N Grand Ave., PMB 250
Santa Ana, CA 92705
Phone: (714)550-9933
Fax: (714)550-9696
Publications: Cartoonist and Comic Artist Magazine (3622)

Cartoonist Profiles
PO Box 325
Fairfield, CT 06430-0325
Phone: (203)227-2542
Fax: (203)227-9508
Publications: Cartoonist Profiles (4786)

Carus Publishing
315 5th St.
Peru, IL 61354
Phone: (815)224-5803
Fax: (815)224-6615
Free: 800-588-8585
Publications: Spider (9450)

Carver County News
Box 188
101 Lewis Ave. N.
Watertown, MN 55388
Phone: (952)955-1111
Fax: (952)955-2241
Publications: Carver County News (16503)

Casa Grande Valley Newspapers, Inc.
PO Box 15002
Casa Grande, AZ 85230-5002
Phone: (520)836-7461
Fax: (520)836-0343
Free: 800-821-1746
Publications: Casa Grande Dispatch (669) • Eloy Enterprise (692)

Cascade Courier
100 1st St. N
Cascade, MT 59421
Phone: (406)468-9231
Fax: (406)468-3030
Publications: Cascade Courier (17768)

Cascade Magazine
PO Box 1390
Klamath Falls, OR 97601-1390
Phone: (541)885-4460
Fax: (541)885-4447
Free: 800-275-0788
Publications: Cascade Cattleman (26382) • Cascade Horseman (26383)

Cascade Pioneer
PO Box 9
Cascade, IA 52033
Phone: (563)852-3217
Fax: (563)852-7188
Publications: Cascade Pioneer (10655)

Cascade Publishing Ltd.
207 McDougal Rd.
PO Box 990
Fort Smith, NT, Canada X0E 0P0
Phone: (867)872-2784
Fax: (867)872-2754
Free: 877-355-2734
Publications: Slave River Journal (35514)

Cascadia Times
25-6 NW 23rd Pl., No. 406
Portland, OR 97210
Publications: Cascadia Times (26472)

Casco Communication, Inc.
PO Box 933
Warrenton, VA 20188
Phone: (540)341-1951
Fax: (540)341-1953
Publications: Virginia Heritage (32602)

Case Alumni Association
The Case School of Engineering
107 Crawford Hall
10900 Euclid Ave.
Cleveland, OH 44106
Phone: (216)231-4567
Fax: (216)368-4714
Publications: Case Alumnus (24866)

Case Publishing Inc.
20 NW 20th Ave.
Battle Ground, WA 98604
Phone: (360)687-5151
Fax: (360)681-5162
Publications: The Reflector (WA) (32661)

Case Western Reserve University
11111 Euclid Ave.
Cleveland, OH 44106
Phone: (216)368-2916
Fax: (216)368-2914
Publications: The Observer (24935)

Case Western Reserve University
10900 Euclid Ave.
Cleveland, OH 44106
Phone: (216)368-5298
Fax: (216)368-4835
Publications: CWRU (24878)

Casey Publishing, Inc.
1904 3rd Ave., Ste. 1007
Seattle, WA 98101-1199
Phone: (206)448-5902
Fax: (206)448-5494
Publications: Voices of Experience (33038)

The Cash-Book Journal
210 W Main St.
PO Box 369
Jackson, MO 63755-0369
Phone: (573)243-3515
Fax: (573)243-3517
Publications: The Cash-Book Journal (17118)

The Cashton Record
713 Broadway St.
PO Box 100
Cashton, WI 54619
Phone: (608)654-7330
Fax: (608)654-7324
Publications: The Cashton Record (33618)

Casiano Communications, Inc.
1700 Fernandez Juncos Ave.
San Juan, PR 00909
Phone: (787)728-3000
Fax: (787)728-7325
Free: 800-468-8167
Publications: Buena Vida (28289) • Caribbean Business (28290) • Imagen (28295)

Casino Journal Publishing Group
Bayport One, Ste. 470
8025 Black Horse Pike
West Atlantic City, NJ 08232
Phone: (609)484-8866
Fax: (609)645-1661
Free: 800-394-2467
Publications: New Jersey Casino Journal (19716)

Casino Journal Publishing Group
8025 Black Horse Pke., Ste. 470
West Atlantic City, NJ 08232
Phone: (609)484-8866
Fax: (609)645-1661
Free: 800-486-7529
Publications: Casino Journal (19713) • Casino Player (19714) • Nevada Hospitality (19715) • The Poker Digest Magazine (19717) • Strictly Slots (19718)

The Casket Printing and Publishing Co.
88 College St.
PO Box 1300
Antigonish, NS, Canada V2G 2L7
Phone: (902)863-4370
Fax: (902)863-5808
Publications: The Casket (35537)

Casper College
125 College Dr.
Casper, WY 82601-4699
Phone: (307)268-2447
Fax: (307)268-6282
Publications: Chinook (34483)

Casper Journal
351 N Lenox
Casper, WY 82601
Phone: (307)265-3870
Fax: (307)265-4616
Free: (866)265-3870
Publications: Casper Journal (34481)

Casper Star-Tribune
170 Star Ln.
PO Box 80
Casper, WY 82602
Phone: (307)266-0500
Fax: (307)266-0501
Publications: Casper Star-Tribune (34482)

Cass City Chronicle
6550 Main St.
Cass City, MI 48726
Phone: (989)872-2010
Fax: (989)872-3810
Publications: Cass City Chronicle (14862)

Cass County Publishing Co.
301 S Lexington St.
Harrisonville, MO 64701
Phone: (816)380-3228
Fax: (816)380-7650

Publications: Cass County Shopper (17094)

Cass County Reporter
PO Box 190
Casselton, ND 58012
Phone: (701)347-4493
Fax: (701)347-4495

Publications: Cass County Reporter (24386)

Cass County-Sun
104 E Houston
PO Box 779
Linden, TX 75563
Phone: (903)756-7396
Fax: (214)796-3294

Publications: Cass County Sun (30694)

Cassens Company
419 2nd Ave
PO Box 660
Edgemont, SD 57735
Phone: (605)662-7201
Fax: (605)662-7201

Publications: Edgemont Herald-Tribune (28849)

Cassville Democrat
600 Main
PO Box 486
Cassville, MO 65625
Phone: (417)847-2610
Fax: (417)847-3092

Publications: Cassville Democrat (16965)

Castle Press Publications
PO Box 247
Washington, NJ 07882
Phone: (908)689-7512
Fax: (908)689-6320

Publications: Doll Castle News (19707)

Castro County News
PO Box 67
Dimmitt, TX 79027-0067
Phone: (806)647-3123

Publications: Castro County News (30249)

Cat Fanciers' Association Inc.
1805 Atlantic
PO Box 1005
Manasquan, NJ 08736-0805
Phone: (732)528-9797
Fax: (732)528-7391

Publications: Cat Fanciers' Almanac (19212)

Cat World International
PO Box 35635
Phoenix, AZ 85069
Phone: (602)995-1822
Fax: (602)995-1822

Publications: Cat World International (798)

Catahoula News-Booster
103 3rd St
PO Box 188
Jonesville, LA 71343
Phone: (318)339-7242
Fax: (318)339-7243

Publications: Catahoula News-Booster (12610)

Catalyst Channel Marketing
5750 Timberlake Blvd.
Mississauga, ON, Canada L4W 2S5
Phone: (905)602-5278
Fax: (905)602-6126

Publications: Patron Magazine (36084)

Catamaran Media
1212 Atlantic Ave.
PO Box 469
Wildwood, NJ 08260
Phone: (609)522-3423
Fax: (609)522-7451

Publications: Gazette Leader (19751)

Catawba Valley Publishing Co., Inc.
PO Box 2650
Hickory, NC 28603-2650
Phone: (704)328-6164
Fax: (704)322-6398

Publications: Extra (23987) • Hickory News (23988)

Cathedral Foundation, Inc.
320 Cathedral St.
PO Box 777
Baltimore, MD 21203
Phone: (410)547-5380
Fax: (410)385-0113

Publications: The Catholic Review (13144)

Cathedral Publishing Corp.
1123 S Church St.
Charlotte, NC 28203
Phone: (704)370-3333
Fax: (704)370-3382

Publications: The Catholic News & Herald (23739)

The Catholic Advance
424 N Broadway St.
Wichita, KS 67202-2310
Phone: (316)269-3965
Fax: (316)269-3936

Publications: The Catholic Advance (11881)

The Catholic Advocate
171 Clifton Ave.
PO Box 9500
Newark, NJ 07104-9500
Phone: (973)497-4000
Fax: (973)497-4192

Publications: The Catholic Advocate (19351)

Catholic Aid Association
3499 N. Lexington Ave.
St. Paul, MN 55126-8098
Phone: (651)490-0170
Fax: (651)490-0746
Free: 800-568-6670

Publications: Catholic Aid News (16365)

Catholic Biblical Association of America
Catholic University of America
Leahy Hall, Rm. 297
Washington, DC 20064
Phone: (202)319-5519
Fax: (202)319-4799

Publications: The Catholic Biblical Quarterly (5399)

Catholic Charities USA
1731 King St.
Alexandria, VA 22314
Phone: (703)549-1390
Fax: (703)549-1656

Publications: Catholic Charities USA (31652)

Catholic Church Extension Society
150 S Wacker Dr., 20th Fl.
Chicago, IL 60606-4103
Phone: (312)236-7240
Fax: (312)236-5276
Free: 888-4R-FAITH

Publications: Extension (8372)

Catholic Communications Corp.
65 Elliot St.
PO Box 1730
Springfield, MA 01101-1730
Phone: (413)732-3175
Fax: (413)747-0273

Publications: The Catholic Observer (14550)

Catholic Digest
2115 Summit Ave.
St. Paul, MN 55105-1081
Phone: (651)962-6725
Fax: (651)962-6755

Publications: Catholic Digest (16366)

Catholic Diocese of Amarillo
1800 N Spring St.
PO Box 5644
Amarillo, TX 79107-7252
Phone: (806)383-2243
Fax: (806)383-2137

Publications: West Texas Catholic (29699)

Catholic Diocese of Boston
141 Tremont St.
Boston, MA 02111-1209
Phone: (617)482-4316
Fax: (617)482-5647

Publications: The Pilot (13949)

Catholic Diocese of Jackson
237 E Amite
PO Box 2130
Jackson, MS 39201
Phone: (601)969-1880
Fax: (601)960-8455

Publications: Mississippi Today (16709)

Catholic Diocese of San Angelo
804 Ford St.
PO Box 1829
San Angelo, TX 76902-1829
Phone: (915)651-7500
Fax: (915)651-6688

Publications: West Texas Angelus (31011)

Catholic Diocese of Spokane
1023 W Riverside Ave.
Spokane, WA 99201
Phone: (509)358-7300

Publications: Inland Register (33094)

Catholic Diocese of Victoria in Texas
1505 E Mesquite Ln.
Victoria, TX 77901
Phone: (512)573-0828
Fax: (512)573-5725

Publications: The Catholic Lighthouse (31234)

Catholic East Texas
1015 E SE Loop 323
Tyler, TX 75701-9663
Phone: (903)534-1077
Fax: (903)534-1370

Publications: Catholic East Texas (31197)

Catholic Explorer
402 S Independence Blvd.
Romeoville, IL 60446
Phone: (815)838-6475
Fax: (815)834-4068

Publications: Catholic Explorer (9552)

Catholic Exponent, Inc.
PO Box 6787
Youngstown, OH 44501
Phone: (330)744-5251
Fax: (330)744-2848

Publications: Catholic Exponent (25695)

Catholic Family Life Insurance
PO Box 11563
Milwaukee, WI 53211-0563
Phone: (414)961-0500
Fax: (414)961-0103

Publications: The Family Friend (34068)

Catholic Golden Age
PO Box 249
Olyphant, PA 18447
Free: 800-836-5699

Publications: CGA World (27347)

Catholic Health Association of the United States
4455 Woodson Rd.
St. Louis, MO 63134-3797
Phone: (314)427-2500
Fax: (314)253-3540

Publications: Catholic Health World (17420) • Health Progress (17444)

Catholic Insight
31 Adelaide St., E
PO Box 625; Adelaide Stn.
Toronto, ON, Canada M5C 2J8
Phone: (416)204-9601
Fax: (416)204-1027

Publications: Catholic Insight (36539)

Catholic Knights of America
3525 Hampton Ave.
St. Louis, MO 63139
Phone: (314)351-1029

Publications: The CK of A Journal (17422)

Catholic Knights Insurance
1100 W. Wells St.
PO Box 05900
Milwaukee, WI 53233
Phone: (414)273-6266
Fax: (414)223-3201
Free: 800-927-2547

Publications: Catholic Knight Magazine (34062)

Catholic League for Religious and Civil Rights
450 7th Ave.
New York, NY 10123
Phone: (212)371-3191
Fax: (212)371-3394

Publications: Catalyst (21381)

Catholic Library Association
100 North St., Ste. 224
Pittsfield, MA 01201-5109
Phone: (413)443-2252
Fax: (413)442-2252

Publications: Catholic Library World (14470)

Catholic Light Publishing Co.
300 Wyoming Ave.
PO Box 708
Scranton, PA 18501-0708
Phone: (570)207-2229
Fax: (570)207-2271

Publications: Catholic Light (27958)

The Catholic Messenger
736 Federal St.
PO Box 460
Davenport, IA 52805-0460
Phone: (563)323-9959
Fax: (563)323-6612
Free: (866)843-9959

Publications: The Catholic Messenger (10735)

The Catholic Mirror
601 Grand Ave.
Des Moines, IA 50309
Phone: (515)243-7653
Fax: (515)244-3761
Free: 800-CA-RE002

Publications: The Catholic Mirror (10773)

Catholic Missions In Canada
201-1155 Yonge St.
Toronto, ON, Canada M4T 1W2
Phone: (416)934-3424
Fax: (416)934-3425
Free: 800-361-1128

Publications: Catholic Missions in Canada (36540)

Catholic Near East Welfare Association
1011 1st Ave.
New York, NY 10022
Phone: (212)826-1480
Fax: (212)826-8979
Free: 800-44-CNEWA

Publications: CNEWA World (21434)

Catholic New Times
80 Sackville St.
Toronto, ON, Canada M5A 3E5
Phone: (416)361-0761
Fax: (416)361-0796
Free: 800-320-4609

Publications: Catholic New Times (36541)

Catholic New York
1011 1st Ave., Ste. 1721
New York, NY 10022-4106
Phone: (212)688-2399
Fax: (212)688-2642

Publications: Catholic New York (21382)

The Catholic Outlook
2830 E 4th St.
Duluth, MN 55812
Phone: (218)724-9111
Fax: (218)724-1056

Publications: The Catholic Outlook (15834)

Catholic Pastoral Center
523 N Duluth Ave.
Sioux Falls, SD 57104-2714
Phone: (605)988-3791
Fax: (605)988-3746

Publications: The Bishop's Bulletin (28962)

Catholic Post
409 N Monroe
PO Box 1722
Peoria, IL 61603
Phone: (309)673-3603
Fax: (309)673-0334
Free: 800-340-5630

Publications: Catholic Post (9416)

Catholic Press of Wilmington, Inc.
PO Box 2208
1925 Delaware Ave.
Wilmington, DE 19899-2208
Phone: (302)573-3109
Fax: (302)573-2397

Publications: The Dialog (5293)

The Catholic Spirit
1213 Byron St.
PO Box 230
Wheeling, WV 26003
Phone: (304)233-8551
Fax: (304)233-0890
Free: 888-434-6237

Publications: The Catholic Spirit (33501)

The Catholic Spirit Publishing Co.
244 Dayton Ave.
St. Paul, MN 55102
Phone: (651)291-4444
Fax: (651)291-4460

Publications: The Catholic Spirit (16367)

Catholic Standard and Times Publishing Co.
222 N 17th St.
Philadelphia, PA 19103-1202
Phone: (215)587-3660
Fax: (215)587-3979

Publications: Catholic Standard (27395)

Catholic Star Herald
1845 Haddon Ave.
Camden, NJ 08103
Phone: (856)756-7900
Fax: (856)756-7938

Publications: Catholic Star Herald (18713)

Catholic Telegraph
100 E 8th St.
Cincinnati, OH 45202
Phone: (513)421-3131
Fax: (513)381-2242
Free: 800-686-2724

Publications: Catholic Telegraph (24780)

The Catholic Times, Inc.
197 E. Gay St.
Columbus, OH 43215
Phone: (614)224-5195

Publications: The Catholic Times (25005)

The Catholic Transcript, Inc.
467 Bloomfield Ave.
Bloomfield, CT 06002
Phone: (860)286-2828
Fax: (860)726-0000
Free: 800-726-2391

Publications: The Catholic Transcript (4701)

Catholic Universe Bulletin Publishing Co., Inc.
1027 Superior Ave.
Cleveland, OH 44114-2556
Phone: (216)696-6525
Fax: (216)696-6519
Free: 800-869-6525

Publications: Catholic Universe Bulletin (24867)

The Catholic University of America
620 Michigan Ave. NE
McMahon Hall, Rm. 311
Washington, DC 20064
Phone: (202)319-5000
Fax: (202)319-4440

Publications: C.U.A. Magazine (5452)

Catholic University Law Review
Columbus School of Law
The Catholic University of America
Cardinal Sta.
Washington, DC 20064
Phone: (202)319-5159
Fax: (202)319-4459

Publications: Catholic University Law Review (5401)

The Catholic Virginian
PO Box 26843
Richmond, VA 23261
Phone: (804)359-5654
Fax: (804)359-5689

Publications: The Catholic Virginian (32432)

Catholic Vision
PO Box 31
Tucson, AZ 85702
Phone: (520)792-3410
Fax: (520)838-2583

Publications: Catholic Vision (939)

The Catholic Voice
3014 Lakeshore Ave.
Oakland, CA 94610-3615
Phone: (510)893-5339
Fax: (510)893-4734

Publications: The Catholic Voice (2675)

The Catholic Voice Publishing Co.
PO Box 4010
Omaha, NE 68104-0010
Phone: (402)558-6611
Fax: (402)558-6614

Publications: The Catholic Voice (18192)

Catholic War Veterans, U.S.A.
National Headquarters
441 N. Lee St.
Alexandria, VA 22314-2301
Phone: (703)549-3622
Fax: (703)684-5196

Publications: The Catholic War Veteran (31653)

The Catholic Week
356 Government St.
PO Box 349
Mobile, AL 36601
Phone: (205)432-3529
Fax: (205)434-1547

Publications: The Catholic Week (316)

Catholic Worker
36 E. 1st St.
New York, NY 10003
Phone: (212)677-8627

Publications: Catholic Worker (21383)

Catholics for a Free Choice
1436 U St. NW, No. 301
Washington, DC 20009-3997
Phone: (202)986-6093
Fax: (202)332-7995

Publications: Conscience (5435)

Cato Institute
1000 Massachusetts Ave. NW
Washington, DC 20001-5403
Phone: (202)842-0200
Fax: (202)842-3490
Free: 800-767-1241

Publications: Regulation (5760)

Catolog of Homes
1390 Millburn Dr.
Conklin, NY 13748
Phone: (607)775-1226
Fax: (607)775-3839
Free: 800-422-3960

Publications: Rural Pennysaver, Inc. (20494)

Catoosa County News
7513 Nashville St.
PO Box 40
Ringgold, GA 30736
Phone: (706)935-2621
Fax: (706)965-5934

Publications: Catoosa County News (7497)

CATS
4909 SW 26th St.
Oklahoma City, OK 73128
Publications: CATJ (25958)

Catskill Mountain News
PO Box 515
Arkville, NY 12406-0515
Phone: (845)586-2601
Fax: (845)586-2366
Publications: Catskill Mountain News (20063)

Catskill Shopper
PO Box 389
Liberty, NY 12754
Phone: (845)292-0500
Fax: (845)292-0585
Publications: Catskill Shopper-Sullivan & Ulster County Editions (20943)

Cattle Today, Inc.
204 Temple Ave. S
Fayette, AL 35555
Phone: (205)932-8000
Fax: (205)932-8000
Publications: Cattle Today (213)

Cavalier Chronicle
PO Box 20
Cavalier, ND 58220
Phone: (701)265-8844
Fax: (701)265-8089
Publications: The Cavalier Chronicle (24387)

Cavanaugh Publishing
10900 Los Alamitos Blvd., Ste. 150
Los Alamitos, CA 90720
Phone: (714)527-8210
Fax: (562)493-2310
Publications: News-Enterprise (2191)

Cave County Newspapers
570 S Dixie
PO Box 340
Horse Cave, KY 42749
Phone: (502)773-3401
Fax: (502)773-8950
Publications: The Progress (KY) (12138)

C.A.W. Locals
1855 Turner Rd.
Windsor, ON, Canada N8W 3K2
Phone: (519)258-6400
Fax: (519)258-0424
Publications: The Guardian (36886)

Cawker City Ledger
PO Box 7
Cawker City, KS 67430
Phone: (785)781-4831
Fax: (785)781-4831
Publications: Cawker City Ledger (11375)

Cayo
3668 Silverado Dr.
Carson City, NV 89705-6827
Publications: Cayo (18326)

CB Media Ltd.
777 Bay St., 5th Fl.
Toronto, ON, Canada M5W 1A7
Phone: (416)596-5999
Fax: (416)596-5111
Publications: Canadian Business (36494) • Profit (36719)

CBA Service Corp., Inc.
9240 Explorer Dr.
PO Box 62000
Colorado Springs, CO 80962
Phone: (719)576-7880
Fax: (719)576-0795
Free: 800-252-1950
Publications: CBA Marketplace (4239)

CBIA
350 Church St.
Hartford, CT 06103-1126
Phone: (860)244-1900
Fax: (860)278-8562
Publications: CBIA News (4886)

CBJ Inc.
5700 Wilshire Blvd., Ste. 170
Los Angeles, CA 90036
Phone: (323)549-5225
Fax: (323)549-5255
Publications: San Fernando Valley Business Journal (2383)

CCBC Catonsville
800 S Rolling Rd.
Baltimore, MD 21228
Phone: (410)455-4485
Fax: (410)719-6556
Publications: Red & Black (13241)

CCH Incorporated (a Wolters Kluwer Company)
2700 Lake Cook Rd.
Riverwoods, IL 60015
Phone: (847)267-7000
Fax: (847)267-2945
Free: 800-449-6435
Publications: Bankruptcy Law Reports (9501) • Copyright Law Reports (6622) • Doing Business in Europe (9502) • Doing Business in Europe (9503) • Federal Audit Guides (9504) • Financial and Estate Planning (9505) • Labor Law Journal (9506) • Pension Plan Guide (9507) • Tax Treaties (9509) • Taxes—The Tax Magazine (9510)

CCI/Crosby Publishing
214 Lincoln St., Ste. 112
Boston, MA 02134-1348
Phone: (617)254-9481
Fax: (617)254-9776
Publications: Cable in the Classroom (13870)

CCIM Institute
430 N Michigan Ave., Ste. 800
Chicago, IL 60611-4092
Phone: (312)321-4460
Fax: (312)321-4530
Publications: Commercial Investment Real Estate (8337)

CCL Canadian Children's Literature
University of Guelph
Slapsie
Guelph, ON, Canada N1G 2W1
Phone: (519)824-4120
Fax: (519)837-1315
Publications: CCL Canadian Children's Literature (Litterature Canadienne pour la Jeunesse) (35860)

CCM Communications
104 Woodmont Blvd., Third Fl.
Nashville, TN 37205
Phone: (615)386-3011
Fax: (615)386-3380
Publications: Youthworker (1850)

CCN-Tex Press
PO Box 935
Franklin, TX 77856
Phone: (409)828-3221
Fax: (409)828-5536
Publications: Franklin News Weekly (30362)

C.C.S.O. Bread of Life Renewal Centre
209 MacNab St. N.
PO Box 395
Hamilton, ON, Canada L8N 3H8
Phone: (905)529-4496
Fax: (905)529-5373
Publications: The Bread of Life (35849)

Cecil Whig
601 Bridge St.
PO Box 429
Elkton, MD 21922-0429
Phone: (410)398-3311
Fax: (410)398-4044
Free: 800-220-3311
Publications: Cecil Whig (13495)

Cedar County
Box 977
Hartington, NE 68739
Phone: (402)254-3997
Fax: (402)254-3999
Publications: Cedar County News (18034)

Cedar County Republican
PO Box 1068
Stockton, MO 65785
Phone: (417)276-4211
Fax: (417)276-5760
Publications: Cedar County Republican (17639)

Cedar Hill Sentinel
PO Box 545
Cedar Hill, TX 75106-0545
Phone: (972)291-6762
Fax: (972)291-9176
Publications: Cedar Hill Sentinel (30010)

Cedar Key Beacon
PO Box 532
Cedar Key, FL 32625-0532
Phone: (352)543-5701
Fax: (352)543-5928
Publications: Cedar Key Beacon (5979)

Cedar Lake-Lowell Star
112 W Clark St.
PO Box 419
Crown Point, IN 46308-0419
Phone: (219)663-4212
Fax: (219)663-0137
Publications: Cedar Lake-Lowell Star (9914)

Cedar Rapids Press
PO Box D
Spalding, NE 68665
Phone: (308)497-2153
Fax: (308)497-2153
Publications: Cedar Rapids Press (17971)

Cegep Andre Laurendeau
1111 rue Lapierre
La Salle, QC, Canada H8N 2J4
Phone: (514)364-3320
Fax: (514)364-7130
Publications: La Protesta (37021)

Cegep d'Ahuntsic
9155 Rue St-Hubert
Montreal, QC, Canada H2M 1Y8
Phone: (514)382-2936
Fax: (514)389-5276
Publications: Le Misanthrope (37171)

Cegep de l'Abitibi-Temiscamingue
425, boul. du College
Rouyn-Noranda, QC, Canada J9X 5E5
Fax: (819)762-3815
Publications: Le Declin (37322)

Cegep de Maisonneuve
3800, rue Sherbrooke Est
Montreal, QC, Canada H1X 2A2
Phone: (514)256-6891
Fax: (514)259-2105
Publications: Le Trait d'Union (37173)

Cegep de Rosemont
6400, 16 Eme Ave.
Montreal, QC, Canada H1X 2S9
Phone: (514)725-7898
Fax: (514)376-8279
Publications: Nouveau Quartier Libre (37196)

Cegep de Saint-Hyacinthe
3000 rue Boulle
Saint-Hyacinthe, QC, Canada J2S 1H9
Publications: Assetu (37347)

Cegep de Victoriaville
475 Rue Notre-Dame Est
Victoriaville, QC, Canada G6P 4B3
Phone: (819)758-6401
Fax: (819)758-0333
Publications: La Replique (37432)

Cegep Vieux-Montreal
255 Ontario est
Box 1444, Sta. N
Montreal, QC, Canada H2X 3M8
Fax: (514)982-3448
Publications: La Republique (37151)

Ceilings and Interior Systems Construction Association
1500 Lincoln Hwy., No. 202
St. Charles, IL 60174
Phone: (630)584-1919
Fax: (630)584-2003

Publications: Interior Construction (9570)

Cell Press
1100 Massachusetts Ave.
Cambridge, MA 02138
Phone: (617)661-7057
Fax: (617)661-7061

Publications: Cell (14045) • Immunity (14069) • Neuron (14085)

Celtic Moon Publishing Inc.
PO Box 1264
Camp Hill, PA 17001
Phone: (717)730-6263
Fax: (717)730-7385
Free: 877-730-6263

Publications: Early American Life (26750)

Cembal Publications (1981) Ltd.
3 McGill St.
PO Box 250
Marmora, ON, Canada K0K 2M0
Phone: (613)472-2431
Fax: (613)472-5026

Publications: Hastings Star (35905) • Havelock Citizen (35906) • Madoc Review (36005) • Marmora Herald (36034) • Stirling News-Argus (36403)

Cenflo, Inc.
205 W Wacker Dr., Ste. 1040
Chicago, IL 60606-3508
Phone: (312)739-5000
Fax: (312)739-0739
Free: 800-732-4581

Publications: Flora Magazine (8378) • Flower News (8379) • Nursery News (8516)

Centaur Press
201 Railroad Ave.
Westminster, MD 21157
Phone: (410)875-5400
Fax: (410)857-5702

Publications: The Johns Hopkins News-Letter (13175)

Center for Advanced Judaic Studies
420 Walnut St.
Philadelphia, PA 19106-3703
Phone: (215)238-1290
Fax: (215)238-1540

Publications: The Jewish Quarterly Review (27510)

Center for Advanced Studies in Management
1574 Mallory Ct.
Bowling Green, KY 42103-1300
Phone: (270)782-2601
Fax: (270)782-2601

Publications: International Journal of Organizational Analysis (11946)

The Center for AIDS: Hope & Remembrance Project
1407 Hawthorne
Houston, TX 77266-6306
Phone: (713)527-8219
Fax: (713)521-3679
Free: 888-341-1788

Publications: Research Initiative/Treatment Action! (30524)

Center for Appalachian Studies and Services
East Tennessee State Univ.
Box 70556
Johnson City, TN 37614-1707
Phone: (423)439-5348
Fax: (423)439-6340

Publications: Now & Then (29253)

Center for Business and Economic Research
University of Alabama
Box 870221
Tuscaloosa, AL 35487-0221
Phone: (205)348-6191
Fax: (205)348-2951

Publications: Alabama Economic Outlook (482)

Center for Business and Economic Research
University of Arkansas
RCED 217 - Sam M. Walton College of Business
Fayetteville, AR 72701
Phone: (479)575-4151
Fax: (479)575-7687

Publications: Arkansas Business & Economic Review (1115)

Center for Caregiver and Patient Advocacy (CCPA)
2000 Franklin St., Ste. 400
Oakland, CA 94612
Phone: (510)273-2290
Fax: (510)663-0629

Publications: RevolutioN Magazine (2697)

Center for Changes
7012 Michigan Ave.
Detroit, MI 48210
Phone: (313)841-0161
Fax: (313)841-8884

Publications: Against the Current (14914)

Center for Critical Education, Inc.
PO Box 382616
Cambridge, MA 02238-2616
Phone: (617)876-7324

Publications: Radical Teacher (14096)

Center on Disability Studies
University of Hawaii at Manoa
1776 University Ave., No. UA4-6
Honolulu, HI 96822
Phone: (808)956-9202
Fax: (808)956-3162

Publications: Disability Studies Quarterly (8354)

Center for Economic Development and Business Research
Wichita State University
W Frank Barton School of Business
Campus Box 121
Wichita, KS 67260-0121
Phone: (316)978-3225
Fax: (316)978-3950

Publications: Kansas Economic Report (11885)

Center for Economic and Management Research
307 W. Brooks, Rm. 208
Norman, OK 73019-0450
Phone: (405)325-6311
Fax: (405)325-7688

Publications: Oklahoma Business Bulletin (25938)

Center for Great Plains Studies
University of Nebraska-Lincoln
1155 Q St., Hewit Pl.
PO Box 880214
Lincoln, NE 68588-0214
Phone: (402)472-3082
Fax: (402)472-0463

Publications: Great Plains Research (18086)

Center for Media & Democracy
520 University Ave., Ste. 310
Madison, WI 53703
Phone: (608)260-9713
Fax: (608)260-9714

Publications: PR Watch (33969)

Center for Migration Studies of New York Inc.
209 Flagg Pl.
Staten Island, NY 10304-1122
Phone: (718)351-8800
Fax: (718)667-4598

Publications: International Migration Review (23358) • Migration World Magazine (23360)

Center for Neighborhood Technology
2125 W North Ave.
Chicago, IL 60647
Phone: (312)278-4800
Fax: (312)278-3840

Publications: The Neighborhood Works (8503)

Center for Photography at Woodstock
59 Tinker St.
Woodstock, NY 12498-9984
Phone: (845)679-9957
Fax: (845)679-6337

Publications: Photography Quarterly (23595)

Center for Professional Responsibility
541 N Fairbanks Ct.
Chicago, IL 60611-3314
Phone: (312)988-5294
Fax: (312)988-5280
Free: 800-285-2221

Publications: The Professional Lawyer (8541)

Center for Psychiatric Rehabilitation
930 Commonwealth Ave., 2nd Fl.
Boston, MA 02215
Phone: (617)353-3549
Fax: (617)353-7700

Publications: Community Support Network News (13880)

Center for Scotch-Irish Studies
PO Box 71
Glenolden, PA 19036-0071

Publications: Journal of Scotch-Irish Studies (26946)

Center for the Study of the First Americans
210 Anthropology Bldg.
4352 TAMU
Texas A&M University
College Station, TX 77843-4352
Phone: (979)845-4046
Fax: (979)845-4070

Publications: Mammoth Trumpet (12923)

Center for the Study of Popular Culture
PO Box 67398
Los Angeles, CA 90067
Phone: (310)843-3699
Fax: (310)843-3692
Free: 800-752-6562

Publications: Heterodoxy (2289)

Center for the Study of the Presidency
1020 19th St. NW, Ste. 250
Washington, DC 20036
Phone: (202)872-9800
Fax: (202)872-9811

Publications: Presidential Studies Quarterly (5728)

Center for the Study of Southern Culture
University of Mississippi
301 Hill Hall
PO Box 1848
University, MS 38677
Phone: (662)915-5993
Fax: (662)915-7842
Free: 800-390-3527

Publications: Living Blues (16866)

Centers for Disease Control and Prevention
Epidemiology Program Office
1600 Clifton Rd.
Mail Stop C08
Atlanta, GA 30333
Phone: (404)639-3636
Fax: (404)639-4198

Publications: Morbidity and Mortality Weekly Report (7028)

Centerville News, Inc.
204 E Main St.
PO Box 97
Centerville, TX 75833-0097
Phone: (903)536-2015
Fax: (903)536-2329

Publications: Centerville News (30015)

Central Alberta Life
2950 Bremner Ave., Bag 5200
Red Deer, AB, Canada T4N 5G3
Phone: (403)343-2400
Fax: (403)342-4051

Publications: Central Alberta Life (34829)

Central Association of the Miraculous Medal
475 E. Chelten Ave.
Philadelphia, PA 19144-5785
Phone: (215)848-1010

Publications: The Miraculous Medal (27570)

The Central Baptist Church of Little Rock
15601 Taylor Loop Rd.
Little Rock, AR 72223-4356

Publications: The Baptist Challenge (1224)

Central Bureau of the Catholic Central Verein of America
3835 Westminster Pl.
St. Louis, MO 63108
Phone: (314)371-1653
Fax: (314)371-0883

Publications: Social Justice Review (17512)

Central CA Weeklies, Inc.
PO Box 547
Lemoore, CA 93245
Phone: (559)585-6880
Fax: (559)924-6220
Free: 800-262-3488

Publications: Coalinga Record (1735) • The Lemoore Advance (2152)

The Central California Catholic Life
1550 N Fresno St.
Fresno, CA 93703-3788
Phone: (559)488-7414
Fax: (559)488-7435

Publications: The Central California Catholic Life (1947)

Central City Times-Argus
202 W Broad st.
Central City, KY 42330-1540
Phone: (502)754-2331
Fax: (502)754-1805

Publications: Central City Times-Argus (12014)

Central Coast Publishing Co.
PO Box 10
Florence, OR 97439
Phone: (541)997-3441
Fax: (541)997-7979

Publications: The Siuslaw News (26353)

Central Idaho Publishing
1000 N 1st St.
McCall, ID 83638-3848
Phone: (208)634-2123
Fax: (208)634-4950

Publications: The Star-News (7905)

Central Iowa Publishing, Inc.
PO Box 130
Bayard, IA 50029
Phone: (712)651-2321
Fax: (712)651-2599
Free: 800-962-2485

Publications: News Gazette (10617) • Scranton Journal (10618)

Central Michigan University
8 Anspach Hall
Mount Pleasant, MI 48859
Phone: (989)774-4000
Fax: (989)774-7805

Publications: Central Michigan Life (15375)

Central Missouri News
PO Box 1086
Sedalia, MO 65302
Phone: (660)827-2425
Fax: (660)827-2427
Free: 888-827-2425

Publications: Central Missouri News (17569)

Central Missouri State University
Martin 30
Warrensburg, MO 64093
Phone: (660)543-4430
Fax: (660)543-8663

Publications: Muleskinner (17668)

Central Missouri State University
Warrensburg, MO 64093
Phone: (314)516-5498
Fax: (314)516-5816

Publications: Missouri Speech & Theatre Journal (17667)

Central New York Genealogical Society Inc.
PO Box 104, Colvin Sta.
Syracuse, NY 13205

Publications: Tree Talks (23432)

Central Newspapers, Inc.
1201 3rd St.
P.O. Box 7558
Alexandria, LA 71306
Phone: (318)487-6397
Fax: (318)487-6315
Free: 800-523-8391

Publications: Alexandria Daily Town Talk (12456)

Central Ohio Printing
30 S Oak St.
PO Box 390
London, OH 43140-1079
Phone: (740)852-1616
Fax: (740)852-1620
Free: 800-282-3838

Publications: Madison Press (25326) • Mechanicsburg Telegram (25371) • Plain City Advocate (25479) • The Tribune (25398)

Central Oklahoma Home Builders Association
625 NW Grand Blvd.
Oklahoma City, OK 73118
Phone: (405)843-1508
Fax: (405)843-6714

Publications: Central Oklahoma Home Builder (25959)

Central Oregon Community College
2600 NW College Way
Bend, OR 97701
Phone: (541)383-7700
Fax: (541)383-7508

Publications: The Broadside (26240)

Central PA Magazine
1982 Locust Ln.
PO Box 2954
Harrisburg, PA 17109
Phone: (717)221-2800
Fax: (717)221-2630
Free: 800-366-9483

Publications: Central PA (26985)

The Central Peace Signal
4720-50th St.
PO Box 250
Rycroft, AB, Canada T0H 3A0
Fax: (403)765-2188

Publications: The Central Peace Signal (34840)

Central Publications
Box 37
Sanborn, MN 56083
Phone: (507)648-3515
Fax: (507)648-3515

Publications: The Comfrey Times (15811) • Mountain Lake/Butterfield Observer/Advocate (16202)

Central Publishing Co.
205 Pennsylvania Ave. W
PO Box 188
Warren, PA 16365-2412
Phone: (814)723-8200
Fax: (814)723-6922

Publications: Warren Times Observer (28105)

Central Record
106 Richmond St.
PO Box 800
Lancaster, KY 40444-0492
Phone: (606)792-2831
Fax: (606)792-3448

Publications: Central Record (12152)

Central Record, Inc.
PO Box 1027
Medford, NJ 08055-0127
Phone: (609)654-5000
Fax: (609)654-8237

Publications: The Central Record (19222)

Central St. Croix News
815 Davis
Box 208
Hammond, WI 54015
Phone: (715)796-2356
Fax: (715)796-2355

Publications: Central St. Croix News (33773)

Central States Archaeological Societies Inc.
11552 Patty Ann Dr.
St. Louis, MO 63146-5471
Phone: (314)872-3247

Publications: Central States Archaeological Journal (16974)

Central States Communication Association
East Central University
Box A-6
Ada, OK 74820-6899

Publications: Communication Studies (25724)

Central Valley Newspapers, Inc.
10776 Argonaut Ln.
Jackson, CA 95642-9465
Phone: (209)223-1767
Fax: (209)223-4245

Publications: Calaveras Ledger Dispatch (2095)

Central Valley Publishing
350, 6th St. 1417
Hollister, CA 95023
Phone: (831)637-5566
Fax: (831)637-4104

Publications: The Free Lance (2050)

Central Valley Publishing
PO Box 305
Oakhurst, CA 93644-0305
Phone: (559)683-4464
Fax: (559)683-8102

Publications: Sierra Home Advertiser (2659)

Central Virginia Newspapers
110 Berry Hill Rd.
Orange, VA 22960
Phone: (703)672-1266
Fax: (703)899-4623

Publications: The Bullet (32084)

Central Virginia Weekly Group
110 Berry Hill Rd.
PO Box 589
Orange, VA 22960
Phone: (703)672-1266
Fax: (703)672-5831

Publications: Greene County Record (32552) • Madison County Eagle (32220) • Orange County Review (32321) • Richlands News Press (32322)

The Central Virginian
PO Box 464
Louisa, VA 23093
Phone: (540)967-0368
Fax: (540)967-0457
Free: 800-969-0368

Publications: The Central Virginian (32200)

Central Wisconsin Publications, Inc.
116 S. Wisconsin Ave.
PO Box 180
Medford, WI 54451
Phone: (715)748-2626
Fax: (715)748-2699

Publications: The Star News (34034)

Centrale de l'enseignement du Quebec
9405 Sherbrooke St. E.
Montreal, QC, Canada H1L 6P3
Phone: (514)356-8888
Fax: (514)356-9999

Publications: Nouvelles CEQ (37197)

Centralia Press, Ltd.
232 E. Broadway
PO Box 627
Centralia, IL 62801
Phone: (618)532-5604
Fax: (618)532-5919
Free: 800-371-9892
Publications: Centralia Sentinel (8174) • Morning
Sentinel (8175)

Centre for Addiction and Mental Health
33 Russell St.
Toronto, ON, Canada M5S 2S1
Phone: (416)595-6558
Fax: (416)595-6881
Free: 800-661-1111
Publications: CrossCurrents (36564)

Centre for Bioethics
Clinical Research Institute of Montreal
110 Pine Ave. W.
Montreal, QC, Canada H2W 1R7
Phone: (514)987-5617
Fax: (514)987-5695
Publications: Journal of Palliative Care (37144)

Centre College
600 W. Walnut St.
Danville, KY 40422
Phone: (606)238-5500
Fax: (606)238-5507
Free: 800-423-6236
Publications: Centrepiece (12037)

Centre County Historical Society
1001 E College Ave.
State College, PA 16801
Phone: (814)234-4779
Fax: (814)234-1694
Publications: Centre County Heritage (28017)

Centre Justice et Foi
25, Jarry Ouest
Montreal, QC, Canada H2P 1S6
Phone: (514)387-2541
Fax: (514)387-0206
Publications: Relations (37215)

Centre for Reformation and Renaissance Studies
71 Queen's Park Crescent E
Toronto, ON, Canada M5K 1K7
Phone: (416)585-4465
Fax: (416)585-4430
Publications: Renaissance and Reformation/Renaissance et Reforme (36726)

Centre for Research of Air and Space Law
3661 Peel St.
Montreal, QC, Canada H3A 1X1
Phone: (514)398-5095
Fax: (514)398-8197
Publications: Annals of Air and Space Law/Annales de Droit Aerien et Spatial (37084)

Century Publishing
990 Grove St.
Evanston, IL 60201
Phone: (847)491-6440
Fax: (847)491-0459
Publications: Wrestling Digest (8874)

Century Publishing Co.
990 Grove St.
Evanston, IL 60201-4370
Phone: (847)491-6440
Fax: (847)491-0459
Publications: Auto Racing Digest (8850) • Baseball Digest (8851) • Basketball Digest (8852) • Bowling Digest (8853) • Football Digest (8859) • Hockey Digest (8861) • Soccer Digest (8870)

The Ceres Courier
2940 4th St.
PO Box 7
Ceres, CA 95307
Phone: (209)537-5032
Fax: (209)537-0543
Publications: The Ceres Courier (1682)

Cerritos College
11110 Alondra Blvd.
Norwalk, CA 90650-6298
Phone: (562)860-2451
Fax: (562)467-5044
Publications: Talon Marks (2649)

Certified General Accountants Association of Canada
700-1188 W. Georgia St.
Vancouver, BC, Canada V6E 4A2
Phone: (604)669-3555
Fax: (604)689-5845
Publications: CGA Magazine (35135)

Cervantes Society of America
Excelsior College
7 Columbia Circle
Albany, NY 12203
Publications: Cervantes: Bulletin of the Cervantes Society of America (19983)

CFB Comox Totem Times
Lazo, BC, Canada V0R 2K0
Phone: (250)339-2541
Fax: (250)339-5209
Publications: CFB Comox Totem Times (35008)

CFO Publishing
253 Summer St.
Boston, MA 02210
Phone: (617)345-9700
Fax: (617)951-9306
Publications: CFO (13872)

C.F.W. Enterprises, Inc.
4201 Vanowen Pl.
Burbank, CA 91505-1139
Phone: (818)845-2656
Fax: (818)845-7761
Free: 800-332-3330
Publications: Action Pursuit Games (1613) • Inside Kung-Fu (1619) • Martial Arts (1620) • Martial Arts Presents (1621) • Paintball Magazine (1622)

C.F.Y.
PO Box 19271
Stanford, CA 94309
Phone: (650)714-4891
Fax: (650)324-9495
Free: 800-742-6048
Publications: Birth of Tragedy Magazine (3794)

Chadron Record
PO Box 1141
Chadron, NE 69337-1141
Phone: (308)432-5511
Fax: (308)432-2385
Publications: Chadron Record (17973)

Chadron State College
227 Kline Bldg.
1000 Main St.
Chadron, NE 69337
Phone: (308)432-6303
Fax: (308)432-6464
Free: 800-CHA-DRON
Publications: The Eagle (17974)

Chadwyck-Healey Inc.
300 N. Zeeb Rd.
Ann Arbor, MI 48103-1553
Free: 800-752-0515
Publications: European Access (14749)

Chagrin Valley Publishing Co.
525 E Wash St.
PO Box 150
Chagrin Falls, OH 44022
Phone: (440)247-5335
Fax: (440)247-5615
Publications: The Chagrin Valley Times (24756) • Currents (24757) • The Solon Times (25528)

Chalcedon, Inc.
PO Box 158
Vallecito, CA 95251
Phone: (209)736-4365
Fax: (209)736-0536
Publications: Chalcedon Report (3983)

Chalkboard Communications, LLC
PO Box 22
Keyport, NJ 07735
Phone: (732)264-0460
Fax: (732)264-0460
Free: 800-964-0763
Publications: Careers & Colleges (19155)

The Challenge Group
1195 Alantic Ave.
Brooklyn, NY 11216
Phone: (718)636-9500
Fax: (718)857-9115
Publications: Afro-American Times (20295)

Challenge Publications, Inc.
8381 Canoga Ave.
Canoga Park, CA 91304
Phone: (818)700-6868
Fax: (818)700-6282
Publications: Air Classics (1654) • Car Toy Collectibles (1655) • Kart Racer (1657) • Mountain Biking (1658) • Scale Ship Modeler (1659) • Sea Classics (1660) • Warbirds International (1661)

Challenge Publications, Ltd.
PO Box 508
Macomb, IL 61455-0508
Phone: (309)833-1902
Fax: (309)833-1902
Publications: PALAESTRA (9131)

The Challenger
1303 Fillmore Ave.
Buffalo, NY 14211
Phone: (716)897-0442
Fax: (716)897-3307
Publications: The Challenger (20372)

Challenger Newspapers
PO Box 73
Franklin, IN 46131
Phone: (317)888-3376
Fax: (317)888-3377
Publications: Franklin Challenger (10006)

Chamber Music America
305 7th Ave., 5th Fl.
New York, NY 10001
Phone: (212)242-2022
Fax: (212)242-7955
Publications: Chamber Music (21395)

Chamberlain News
120 S Main
PO Box 550
Chamberlain, SD 57325
Phone: (605)734-6360
Fax: (605)734-6418
Free: 800-371-6360
Publications: Chamberlain-Oacoma Register (28831)

Champaign County Genealogical Society
c/o Champaign County Historical Archives
201 S. Race St.
Urbana, IL 61801-3283
Phone: (217)367-4025
Fax: (217)367-4061
Publications: Champaign County Genealogical Society Quarterly (9699)

The Champion
2404 Stoney Way, Apt. H
Kissimmee, FL 34744-5907
Phone: (407)242-8491
Publications: The Champion (6260)

Champion Newspapers
13179 9th St.
Chino, CA 91710-4126
Phone: (909)628-5501
Fax: (909)591-6296
Publications: Chino Champion (1708) • Chino Hills Champion (1709)

Champlain Graphics
3464 Kingston Rd., Ste. 204
Scarborough, ON, Canada M1M 1R5
Phone: (416)261-1607
Fax: (416)261-1679
Publications: Comda Key (36375)

Champlain Planning Press
PO Box 4295
Burlington, VT 05406
Phone: (802)864-9083
Fax: (802)862-1882

Publications: Planning Commissioners Journal (31517)

Champlain Regional College Student Association
Room D-103, 900 Riverside Dr.
Saint-Lambert, QC, Canada J4P 3P2
Phone: (450)466-4436
Fax: (450)672-9299

Publications: The Champlain Edge (37358)

Champs-Elysees, Inc.
PO Box 158067
Nashville, TN 37215-8067
Phone: (615)383-8534
Fax: (615)297-3138
Free: 800-824-0829

Publications: Acquerello Italiano (29439) • Champs-Elysees (29449) • Puerta del Sol (29482) • Schau ins Land (29485)

Chandler & Brownsboro
PO Box 168
Brownsboro, TX 75756
Phone: (903)852-7641
Fax: (903)852-7631

Publications: Chandler & Brownsboro Statesman (29955)

Kevin Chanel
PO Box 225029
San Francisco, CA 94122

Publications: ChinMusic Magazine (3342)

The Channel 10/36 Friends, Inc.
Foundation Hall, 5th Fl.
700 W. State St.
Milwaukee, WI 53233-1443
Phone: (414)297-8000
Fax: (414)297-8007

Publications: Fine Tuning (34069)

Channel Town Press
PO Box 575
La Conner, WA 98257
Phone: (360)466-3315
Fax: (360)466-1195

Publications: Channel Town Press (32801)

Chanute Publishing Co.
15 N Evergreen
PO Box 559
Chanute, KS 66720
Phone: (620)431-4100
Fax: (620)431-2635

Publications: The Chanute Tribune (11377)

Chapel Hill News
505 W Franklin St.
PO Box 870
Chapel Hill, NC 27516
Phone: (919)967-7045
Fax: (919)968-4953

Publications: Chapel Hill News (23702)

The Chapman Advertiser & Enterprise Journal
1118 W Cloud St.
Salina, KS 67401-7063
Phone: (785)922-6856
Fax: (785)922-6856

Publications: The Chapman Advertiser & Enterprise Journal (11781)

Chapman University
333 N. Glassell St.
Orange, CA 92866
Phone: (714)997-6870
Fax: (714)744-7021

Publications: Panther (2725)

The Chappell Register
273 Vincent Ave.
PO Box 528
Chappell, NE 69129
Phone: (308)874-2207
Fax: (308)874-2207

Publications: The Chappell Register (17977)

Char-Jay
200 SE Clematis Ave.
Shelton, WA 98584
Phone: (206)426-7409

Publications: Char-Jay (33078)

Charhdi Kala Weekly Punjabi Newspaper
7743 128th St., Unit 6
Surrey, BC, Canada V3W 4E6
Phone: (604)590-6397
Fax: (604)591-6397

Publications: Akal Guardian (35105) • Charhdi Kala (35107)

Chariton Newspapers
817 Braden Ave.
Chariton, IA 50049
Phone: (641)774-2137
Fax: (641)774-2139

Publications: The Chariton Leader (10692) • Herald-Patriot (10693)

Charlatan Publications, Inc.
Carleton University
531 Unicentre
1125 Colonel By Drive
Ottawa, ON, Canada K1S 5B6
Phone: (613)520-6680
Fax: (613)520-4051

Publications: The Charlatan (36234)

Charles City Press
801 Riverside
PO Box 397
Charles City, IA 50616-0397
Phone: (641)228-3211
Fax: (641)228-2641

Publications: Charles City Press (10695)

Charles Mix County News
PO Box 257
Geddes, SD 57342
Phone: (605)337-2571
Fax: (605)337-2571

Publications: Charles Mix County News (28860)

Charles Simpson Ministries
PO Box 850067
Mobile, AL 36685-0067
Phone: (334)633-7900
Fax: (334)639-0489
Free: 888-811-2276

Publications: Christian Conquest Magazine (317)

The Charleston City Paper
689 King St.
Charleston, SC 29403
Phone: (843)577-5304
Fax: (843)853-6899

Publications: The Charleston City Paper (28511)

Charleston Daily Mail
1001 Virginia St. E.
Charleston, WV 25331
Phone: (304)348-5140
Fax: (304)348-4847

Publications: Charleston Daily Mail (33267)

Charleston Express
PO Box 39
Charleston, AR 72933
Phone: (479)965-7368
Fax: (479)965-7206

Publications: Charleston Express (1076)

Charleston Newspapers
1001 Virginia St. E.
Charleston, WV 25301
Phone: (304)348-5140

Publications: Sunday Gazette-Mail (33273)

Charleston Southern University
PO Box 118087
Charleston, SC 29423-8087
Phone: (843)863-8042
Fax: (843)863-7021

Publications: Buc In Print (28506)

Charleston Sun-Sentinel
PO Box 250
Charleston, MS 38921
Phone: (662)647-8462
Fax: (662)647-3830

Publications: Charleston Sun-Sentinel (16587)

Charlestown Patriot Publications Inc.
1 Thompson Sq.
Charlestown, MA 02129
Phone: (617)241-9511

Publications: Charlestown Patriot & Somerville Chronicle (14123)

Charlevoix Courier
112 Mason St.
PO Box 117
Charlevoix, MI 49720-0117
Phone: (231)547-6558
Fax: (231)547-4992

Publications: Charlevoix Courier (14864)

Charlie Maas & Associates
2300 W. Story Rd.
PO Box 167098
Irving, TX 75016
Phone: (972)660-6485
Fax: (972)660-6477

Publications: The Journal of African Human Resources and Business Issues (30605)

Charlotte Post Pub.
1531 Camden Rd.
PO Box 30144
Charlotte, NC 28230
Phone: (704)376-0496
Fax: (704)342-2160

Publications: The Charlotte Post (23741)

Charlotte Publishing
Box 214
Drakes Branch, VA 23937-0214
Phone: (434)568-3341
Fax: (434)568-3731

Publications: Charlotte Gazette (31998)

The Charlotte World
8701 Mallard Creek Rd.
Charlotte, NC 28262
Phone: (704)548-1737
Fax: (704)503-6691

Publications: The Charlotte World (23742)

Charolais Banner, Ltd.
1933 8th Ave., No. 200
Regina, SK, Canada S4R 1E9
Phone: (306)546-3940
Fax: (306)546-3942

Publications: Charolais Banner (37527) • Charolais Connection (37528)

Chart Communications
41 Britain St., Ste. 200
Toronto, ON, Canada M5A 1R7
Phone: (416)363-3101
Fax: (416)363-3109

Publications: Chart Magazine (36546)

Chartwell Communications Inc.
380 E NW Hwy., Ste. 300
Des Plaines, IL 60016
Phone: (847)390-6700
Fax: (847)795-7690

Publications: CabinetMaker (8751) • udm/Upholstery Design and Management (8772)

The Chase
1150 Industry Rd.
Lexington, KY 40505
Phone: (859)254-4262
Fax: (859)254-3145

Publications: The Chase (12162)

Chase County Leader-News
PO Box K
Cottonwood Falls, KS 66845-0436
Phone: (620)273-6391
Fax: (620)273-8674

Publications: Chase County Leader-News (11402)

Chatham College Students
Woodland Rd.
Pittsburgh, PA 15232
Phone: (412)365-1100
Fax: (412)365-1505
Free: 800-837-1290

Publications: The Communique (27767)

Chatham Daily News
45 4th St.
PO Box 2007
Chatham, ON, Canada N7M 2G4
Phone: (519)354-2000
Fax: (519)436-0949

Publications: Chatham Daily News (35729)

Chatham News Publishing Co.
PO Box 459
Pittsboro, NC 27312
Phone: (919)542-3013
Fax: (919)542-2590

Publications: Chatham Record (24118)

The Chatham News Publishing Co.
PO Box 290
Siler City, NC 27344
Phone: (919)663-3232
Fax: (919)663-4042

Publications: The Chatham News (24230)

Chattanooga Publishing Co.
400 E. 11th St.
PO Box 1447
Chattanooga, TN 37401
Phone: (423)756-1234
Fax: (423)752-3388

Publications: Chattanooga Times & Free Press (29087)

Chautauqua Institution
Box 1095
Chautauqua, NY 14722-1095
Phone: (716)357-2000
Fax: (716)357-6369

Publications: Chautauquan Daily (20453)

CHB Co., Inc.
PO Box 5627
Bellingham, WA 98227-5627
Phone: (360)676-4146
Fax: (360)647-1311

Publications: Vacation Ownership World (32691)

Cheallaigh Shamrock
PO Box 190
Dodson, LA 71422
Phone: (318)628-8671
Fax: (318)628-8673

Publications: The Piney Woods Journal (12567) •
Quote (12568)

Cheboygan Daily Tribune, Inc.
308 N Main
PO Box 290
Cheboygan, MI 49721
Phone: (231)627-7144
Fax: (231)627-5331

Publications: Daily Tribune (14872) • Shoppers Fair (14873)

Chedmount Investments Ltd.
38 Fairmount Crescent
Toronto, ON, Canada M4L 2H4
Phone: (416)466-2328
Fax: (416)466-4220

Publications: Taxi News (36753)

Cheektowaga Times, Inc.
343 Maryvale Dr.
Cheektowaga, NY 14225
Phone: (716)892-5323
Fax: (716)892-4925

Publications: Cheektowaga Times (20457)

Cheese Market News
PO Box 620244
Middleton, WI 53562-0244
Phone: (608)831-6002
Fax: (608)831-1004

Publications: Cheese Market News (34050)

The Cheese Reporter Publishing Co., Inc.
4210 E Washington Ave.
Madison, WI 53704-3742
Phone: (608)246-8430
Fax: (608)246-8431

Publications: The Cheese Reporter (33926)

Cheever Publishing Inc.
14210 W Yosemite Dr.
Sun City West, AZ 85375-5647
Free: 800-787-8444

Publications: Accent on Living (897)

Chefs Association of the Pacific Coast, Inc.
942 Market, No. 412
San Francisco, CA 94102
Phone: (415)834-9462
Fax: (415)834-9467

Publications: The Culinarian (3347)

Chelo Publishing, Inc. and Pumpkin Press, Inc.
The Empire State Bldg.
350 Fifth Ave., Ste. 3323
New York, NY 10118
Phone: (212)947-4322
Fax: (212)563-4774

Publications: Exercise For Men Only (21662)

Chelsea Associates, Inc.
PO Box 773
Cooper Sta.
New York, NY 10276-0773
Phone: (212)989-3083
Fax: (212)989-3083

Publications: Chelsea (21398)

Chelsea Reporter
245 W 6th St.
Chelsea, OK 74016
Phone: (918)789-2331
Fax: (918)789-2373

Publications: Chelsea Reporter (25782)

Chelsie Communications, Inc.
61 Alness St., Ste. 224
North York, ON, Canada M3J 2H2
Phone: (416)663-9229
Fax: (416)663-2353

Publications: Toys & Games (36132)

Chemeketa Community College
PO Box 14007
Salem, OR 97309
Phone: (503)399-5104
Fax: (503)399-2519

Publications: Chemeketa Courier (26566)

Chemical Abstracts Service
2540 Olentangy River Rd.
PO Box 3012
Columbus, OH 43210
Phone: (614)447-3600
Fax: (614)447-3713
Free: 800-753-4227

Publications: CA Selects (25004)

The Chemical Educator
Boise State University
1910 University Dr.
Boise, ID 83725
Phone: (208)426-4491
Fax: (208)426-4493

Publications: The Chemical Educator (7805)

The Chemical Institute of Canada
130 Slater St., Ste. 550
Ottawa, ON, Canada K1P 6E2
Phone: (613)232-6252
Fax: (613)232-5862

Publications: Canadian Chemical News (L'Actualite Chimique Canadienne) (36191) • Canadian Journal of Chemical Engineering (37096)

Chemical Waste Litigation Reporter
1601 Connecticut Ave., NW, No. 602
Washington, DC 20009
Phone: (202)482-5855
Fax: (202)328-2430

Publications: Chemical Waste Litigation Reporter (5405)

Chemical Week Associates
110 Williams St., 11th Fl.
New York, NY 10038
Phone: (212)621-4900
Fax: (212)621-4949

Publications: Chemical Engineering (21400) • Chemical Specialties (21404) • Lubricants World (22268) • Modern Plastics (22350) • Soap and Cosmetics (22751)

Chemung County Historical Society
415 E Water St.
Elmira, NY 14901
Phone: (607)734-4167
Fax: (607)734-1565

Publications: Chemung Historical Journal (20572)

Chenango American, Whitney Point Reporter, and Oxford Review Times
PO Box 566
Greene, NY 13778
Phone: (607)656-4511
Fax: (607)656-8544

Publications: Chenango American, Whitney Point Reporter, and Oxford Review Times (20697)

Cherokee Messenger & Republican
216 S Grand Ave.
PO Box 245
Cherokee, OK 73728
Phone: (405)596-3344
Fax: (405)596-2959

Publications: Cherokee Messenger & Republican (25783)

Cherokee Nation
1000, Connecticut Ave. NW. Ste.309
Washington, DC 20036
Phone: (202)331-2133
Fax: (202)331-4784

Publications: Cherokee Advocate (5407)

Cherry Lane Magazines
6 E. 32nd St., 6th Fl.
New York, NY 10016

Publications: Music Alive! (22384)

Chesapeake Bay Communications
1819 Bay Ridge Ave.
Annapolis, MD 21403
Phone: (410)263-2662
Fax: (410)267-6924

Publications: Chesapeake Bay Magazine (13091)

Chesapeake Publishing Corp.
214 W. Belair Ave.
Aberdeen, MD 21001
Phone: (410)398-3311
Fax: (410)398-4044

Publications: The Bargaineer (13084)

Chesapeake Publishing Corp.
535 Poplar St.
Cambridge, MD 21613-1833
Phone: (410)228-0222
Fax: (410)228-0685

Publications: The Dorchester Star (13399)

Chesapeake Publishing Corp.
114 Broadway
Centreville, MD 21617
Phone: (410)758-1400
Fax: (410)758-1701

Publications: Record Observer (13404)

Chesapeake Publishing Corp.
219 Market
Denton, MD 21629
Phone: (410)479-1800
Fax: (410)479-3174

Publications: Times/Record (13482)

Chesapeake Publishing Corp.
PO Box 600
Easton, MD 21601
Phone: (410)822-1500
Fax: (410)770-4019

Publications: The Calvert County Recorder (13486) • The Caroline Progress/Caroline Express

(31895) • Leader & State Register (5285) • The Northumberland Echo (32158) • St. Mary's Enterprise (13616) • Star-Democrat & Sunday Star (13489)

Chesapeake Publishing Corp.
PO Box 30
Upper Marlboro, MD 20773
Phone: (301)627-2833
Fax: (301)627-2835

Publications: Enquirer Gazette (13768)

Chesapeake Publishing Corp.
7 Industrial Park
Waldorf, MD 20602
Phone: (301)645-9480
Fax: (301)884-9403
Free: 800-843-3357

Publications: Maryland Independent (13772)

Chesapeake Publishing Corp.
132 Court Circle
PO Box 8
Warsaw, VA 22572
Phone: (804)333-3655
Fax: (804)333-0033

Publications: Northern Neck News (32606)

Chesnee Publishing Co.
PO Box 158
Chesnee, SC 29323
Phone: (864)476-3513
Fax: (864)476-3511

Publications: Chesnee Tribune (28530)

Chester County Bar Association
PO Box 3191
West Chester, PA 19381-3191
Phone: (610)692-1889
Fax: (610)692-9546

Publications: Chester County Law Reporter (28144)

Chester Herald
4418 S. 58th St.
Lincoln, NE 68516-1404
Phone: (402)324-5764
Fax: (402)324-5764

Publications: Chester Herald (18078)

Chesterton Tribune
193 S Calumet Rd.
PO Box 919
Chesterton, IN 46304
Phone: (219)926-1131
Fax: (219)926-6389

Publications: Chesterton Tribune (9886)

Chesterville Record
PO Box 368
Chesterville, ON, Canada K0C 1H0
Phone: (613)448-2321
Fax: (613)448-3260

Publications: Chesterville Record (35735)

Chestnut Hill Community Association
8434 Germantown Ave.
Philadelphia, PA 19118
Phone: (215)248-8800
Fax: (215)248-8814

Publications: Chestnut Hill Local (27400)

The Chetek Alert
312 Knapp St.
PO Box 5
Chetek, WI 54728
Phone: (715)924-4118
Fax: (715)924-4122

Publications: The Chetek Alert (33622)

Chetwynd Echo
5208 N. Access Rd.
Chetwynd, BC, Canada V0C 1J0
Phone: (250)788-2246
Fax: (250)788-9988

Publications: Chetwynd Echo (34924) • The Northern Horizon (34925)

Chevron Publishing Corp.
5018 Dorsey Hall Dr., Ste. 104
Ellicott City, MD 21042
Phone: (410)740-0065
Fax: (410)740-9213

Publications: International Journal of Emergency Mental Health (13498)

Chewelah Independent, Inc.
PO Box 5
Chewelah, WA 99109
Phone: (509)935-8422
Fax: (509)935-8426

Publications: The Independent (32716)

Cheyenne Star
PO Box 250
Cheyenne, OK 73628
Phone: (580)497-3324
Fax: (580)497-3516

Publications: Cheyenne Star (25784)

Chicago Business
5801 S Ellis Ave.
Chicago, IL 60637-1404

Publications: Chicago Business (8307)

Chicago Computer Guide, Inc.
954 W Washington, 5th Fl.
Chicago, IL 60607
Phone: (312)432-1662
Fax: (312)432-0022

Publications: The Chicago Computer Guide (8309)

Chicago County Press
Box 748
Lindstrom, MN 55045-0748
Phone: (651)257-5115
Fax: (651)257-5500

Publications: Chicago County Press (16002)

Chicago Dental Society
401 N Michigan Ave., Ste. 300
Chicago, IL 60611-4272
Phone: (312)836-7305
Fax: (312)836-7337

Publications: CDS Review (8302) • Chicago Dental Society News (8312)

Chicago Historical Society
Clark St. at North Ave.
Chicago, IL 60614
Phone: (312)642-4600
Fax: (312)266-2077

Publications: Chicago History (8313)

Chicago Home & Garden
825 S Waukegan Rd., No. A8-146
Lake Forest, IL 60045

Publications: Chicago Home and Garden (9061)

Chicago Independent Bulletin
2037 W 95th St.
Chicago, IL 60643-1129
Phone: (773)783-1040

Publications: Independent Bulletin (8411)

Chicago Lerner Newspapers
7331 N Lincoln Ave.
Lincolnwood, IL 60646
Phone: (847)329-2000
Fax: (847)329-2060

Publications: Lincoln-Belmont Booster (9096) • North Center-Irving Park Booster (9101) • Uptown News Star (9106)

Chicago Life
PO Box 11311
Chicago, IL 60611-0311
Phone: (773)880-1360

Publications: Chicago Life (8315)

The Chicago Maroon
Ida Noyes Hall
1212 E. 59th St.
Lower Level
Chicago, IL 60637-1604
Phone: (773)702-1403
Fax: (773)702-3032

Publications: The Chicago Maroon (8317)

Chicago Medical Society
The Medical Society of Cook County
515 N. Dearborn St.
Chicago, IL 60610
Phone: (312)670-2550
Fax: (312)670-3646

Publications: Chicago Medicine (8318)

Chicago Press Corp.
1112 N. Homan Ave.
Chicago, IL 60651
Phone: (773)276-1500

Publications: Burroughs Bulletin (12211)

Chicago Reader, Inc.
11 E. Illinois
Chicago, IL 60611
Phone: (312)828-0350
Fax: (312)828-0305

Publications: Chicago Reader (8319)

Chicago Shimpo
4670 N Manor Ave.
Chicago, IL 60625
Phone: (773)478-6170
Fax: (773)478-9360

Publications: Chicago Shimpo (8322)

Chicago South Shore Scene
7426 S Constance
Chicago, IL 60649
Phone: (773)221-1760
Fax: (773)363-0441

Publications: Chicago South Shore Scene (8324)

Chicago State University
Tempo SUB 230
95th at King Dr.
Chicago, IL 60628-1598
Phone: (773)995-2000
Fax: (773)995-3593

Publications: Tempo (8582)

Chicago Studies
1800 N Hermitage Ave.
Chicago, IL 60622-1101
Phone: (773)486-8970
Fax: (773)486-7094
Free: 800-933-4213

Publications: Chicago Studies (8325)

Chicago Sun-Times Inc.
401 N. Wabash Ave.
Chicago, IL 60611-3593
Phone: (312)321-3000
Fax: (312)321-3084

Publications: Chicago Sun-Times (8326)

Chicago Tribune
820 N. Orleans, Ste. 400
Chicago, IL 60610
Phone: (312)654-3000
Fax: (312)654-3027

Publications: Exito! (8371)

Chicago Tribune
435 N. Michigan Ave.
Chicago, IL 60611
Phone: (312)222-3232
Fax: (312)222-3162

Publications: Chicago Tribune Magazine (8328)

Chicagoland Golf Publishing Co.
PO Box 4116
Wheaton, IL 60189-4116
Phone: (630)719-1000
Fax: (630)719-1030

Publications: Chicagoland Golf (9771)

Chicago's Amateur Athlete
7840 N Lincoln Ave., Ste. 208
Skokie, IL 60077
Phone: (847)675-0200
Fax: (847)675-2903

Publications: Chicago's Amateur Athlete (9602)

Chicken Dinner News
PO Box 1267
Phenix City, AL 36868
Phone: (205)298-0679
Fax: (205)298-0690

Publications: The Phenix Citizen (424)

Chico Community Publishing, Inc.
353 E 2nd St.
Chico, CA 95928
Phone: (530)894-2300
Fax: (530)894-0143

Publications: Chico News & Review (1693)

Chicot County Spectator
105 N Ct. St.
PO Box 552
Lake Village, AR 71653
Phone: (870)265-2071
Fax: (870)265-2807

Publications: Chicot County Spectator (1205)

Chief Executive
110 Summit Ave.
Montvale, NJ 07645
Phone: (201)930-5959
Fax: (201)930-5956

Publications: Chief Executive (19244)

Chief Printing Co.
1323 2nd St.
PO Box 98
Perry, IA 50220
Phone: (515)465-4666
Fax: (515)465-3087

Publications: Chiefland Shopper (11155) • Perry Chief (11156)

Chiefland Citizen
PO Box 980
Chiefland, FL 32644
Phone: (904)493-4796
Fax: (904)493-9336

Publications: Chiefland Citizen (5981)

The Chieftain
Box 529
Iroquois, ON, Canada K0E 1K0
Phone: (613)652-4395
Fax: (613)652-2508

Publications: The Chieftain (35923)

Chieftan
PO Box 256
128 Oak
Bonner Springs, KS 66012
Phone: (913)724-1887
Fax: (913)422-4233

Publications: Chieftain (11363) • Chieftain Shopper (11364) • Sentinel (11365)

Child Evangelism Fellowship, Inc.
Box 348
Warrenton, MO 63383
Phone: (636)456-4321
Fax: (636)456-4321

Publications: Evangelizing Today's Child (17683)

Child Welfare League of America Inc.
440 1st St. NW, 3rd Fl.
Washington, DC 20001-2085
Phone: (202)638-2952
Fax: (202)638-4004
Free: 800-275-2952

Publications: Child Welfare (5408) • Children's Voice (5410)

Children of Aging Parents
1609 Woodbourne Rd., Ste. 302A
Levittown, PA 19057-1506
Phone: (215)945-6900
Fax: (215)945-8720
Free: 800-227-7294

Publications: CAPsule (27187)

Children's Apparel Manufacturers' Association
6900 Decarie Blvd., Ste. 3110
Montreal, QC, Canada H3X 2T8
Phone: (514)731-7774
Fax: (514)731-7459

Publications: KIDS CREATIONS (37147)

Children's Art Foundation, Inc.
PO Box 83
Santa Cruz, CA 95063
Phone: (831)426-5557
Fax: (831)426-1161
Free: 800-447-4569

Publications: Stone Soup (3690)

Children's Better Health Institute
1100 Waterway Blvd.
PO Box 567
Indianapolis, IN 46202-2156
Phone: (317)636-8881
Fax: (317)684-8094
Free: 800-558-2376

Publications: Child Life (10100) • Children's Digest (10101) • Children's Playmate Magazine (10102) • Humpty Dumpty's Magazine (10119) • Jack And Jill (10138) • Turtle Magazine for Preschool Kids (10177) • U.S. Kids (10179)

Children's Book and Play Review
Harold B. Lee Library
Brigham Young University
Provo, UT 84602
Phone: (801)378-6685
Free: (801)378-4636

Publications: Children's Book and Play Review (31401)

Children's House, Inc.
PO Box 111
Caldwell, NJ 07006
Phone: (201)239-3442
Fax: (201)483-1234

Publications: Children's House/Children's World (18711)

Children's Literature Association
PO Box 138
Battle Creek, MI 49016
Phone: (269)965-8180
Fax: (269)965-3568

Publications: Children's Literature Association Quarterly (14793)

Children's Software Revue
120 Main St.
Flemington, NJ 08822
Phone: (908)284-0404
Fax: (908)284-0405
Free: 800-993-9499

Publications: Children's Software Revue (CSR) (18818)

The Childress Index
224 Main St.
PO Box 1210
Childress, TX 79201-1210
Phone: (940)937-2525
Fax: (940)937-2239

Publications: The Childress Index (30017)

John A. Childs
PO Box 7188
Oxford, AL 36203

Publications: The Oxford Independent (415)

Chile Pepper Magazine
1701 River Run, No. 702
Fort Worth, TX 76107
Phone: (817)877-1048
Fax: (817)877-8870
Free: 888-774-2946

Publications: Chile Pepper Magazine (30332)

Chilkat Valley News
Main St.
Box 630
Haines, AK 99827
Phone: (907)766-2688

Publications: Chilkat Valley News (584)

Chillicothe Gazette
50 West Main St.
Chillicothe, OH 45601
Fax: (740)772-9501

Publications: Chillicothe Gazette (24761)

Chilliwack Progress Ltd.
45860 Spadina Ave.
Chilliwack, BC, Canada V2P 6H9
Phone: (604)792-1931
Fax: (604)792-4936

Publications: The Chilliwack Progress (34926) • Chilliwack Progress Weekender Edition (34927)

Chilton County News
PO Box 189
Clanton, AL 35046
Phone: (205)755-0110
Fax: (205)755-6227

Publications: Chilton County News (154)

China News Digest International, Inc.
PO Box 10111
Gaithersburg, MD 20898-0111

Publications: China News Digest—Canada (13533) • China News Digest—Global (13534) • China News Digest—US (13535) • China News—Europe/Pacific (13536) • Hua Zia Wen Zhai (13541)

China Stamp Society, Inc.
c/o Donald R. Alexander
1021 Valley View
Norman, OK 73069
Phone: (405)912-5042

Publications: China Clipper (25933)

The Chincoteague Beachcomber
PO Box 249
Onley, VA 23418-0249

Publications: The Chincoteague Beachcomber (31971)

Chinese American Daily News
673 Monterey Pass Rd.
Monterey Park, CA 91754
Phone: (626)281-2989
Fax: (626)281-0859

Publications: Chinese American Daily News (2592)

Chinese American Forum
PO Box 719
St. Charles, MO 63302-0719
Phone: (636)561-8134
Fax: (636)561-8134

Publications: Chinese American Forum (17383)

Chinese Daily News, Inc.
1588 Corporate Center Dr.
Monterey Park, CA 91754
Phone: (323)268-4982
Fax: (323)265-3476

Publications: Chinese Daily News,Inc (2593)

Chinese Historical Society of America
965 Clay St.
San Francisco, CA 94108-1527
Phone: (415)391-1188
Fax: (415)391-1150

Publications: Chinese America (3340)

Chinese L.A. Daily News
9639 Telstar Ave.
El Monte, CA 91731
Phone: (626)453-8800
Fax: (626)453-8822

Publications: Chinese L.A. Daily News (1865)

Chinese Language Teachers Association
Center for Chinese Studies
1890 East-West Rd.
Moore Hall 416
University of Hawaii
Honolulu, HI 96822
Phone: (808)956-2692
Fax: (808)956-2682

Publications: Chinese Language Teachers Association Journal (7684)

Chinese Times
849 Kearny St.
San Francisco, CA 94108-1303
Phone: (415)982-0135
Fax: (415)982-3387

Publications: Chinese Times (3341)

Chippewa Publishing Co.
321 Frenette Drive
PO Box 69
Chippewa Falls, WI 54729
Phone: (715)723-5515
Fax: (715)723-9644
Free: 800-236-5515

Publications: Chippewa Herald (33626)

Chiridion Wild Wings, Inc.
5312 Wolf Knoll
Orr, MN 55771
Phone: (218)343-6253
Fax: (218)343-6258

Publications: Spaniels in the Field (16244)

Chiron Review Press
702 N Prairie
Saint John, KS 67576-1516
Phone: (620)786-4955

Publications: Chiron Review (11777)

Chiropractic History
PO Box 1045
Richlands, VA 24641
Phone: (540)963-0395
Fax: (540)964-2225

Publications: Chiropractic History (32425)

The Chisholm Tribune-Press
327 W Lake St.
Chisholm, MN 55719-1717
Phone: (218)254-4432
Fax: (218)254-7141

Publications: The Chisholm Tribune-Press (15796)

Chitra Publications
2 Public Ave.
Montrose, PA 18801
Phone: (570)278-1984
Fax: (570)278-2223
Free: 800-628-8244

Publications: Miniature Quilts (27290) • Quiltworks Today (27291)

CHNI Media, LLC
135 S Franklin St.
PO Box 106
Greensburg, IN 47240
Phone: (812)663-3111
Fax: (812)663-2985

Publications: The Greensburg Daily News (10043)

Choctaw Advocate
PO Box 475
Butler, AL 36904
Phone: (205)459-2858
Fax: (205)459-3000

Publications: Choctaw Advocate (140)

Choctaw County Times
300 NB.
Hugo, OK 74743
Phone: (580)326-8353
Fax: (580)326-5388

Publications: Choctaw County Times (25871)

Choice Media, LLC
PO Box 580
New Haven, CT 06513-0580
Phone: (203)782-1420
Fax: (203)782-3793

Publications: Business Times (4984) • Fairfield County Business Times (4988)

Chokio Review
PO Box 96
Chokio, MN 56221
Phone: (320)324-2405
Fax: (320)324-2449

Publications: Chokio Review (15797)

Choral Research
Division of Education and Music Therapy
University of Kansas
448 Murphy Hall
1530 Naismith Dr.
Lawrence, KS 66045-7574

Publications: International Journal of Research in Choral Singing (11553)

Chosun Daily
35-11 Farrington St.
Flushing, NY 11354
Phone: (718)463-1400
Fax: (718)359-2067

Publications: Chosun Daily (20607)

Choteau Acantha
216 1st Ave. NW
PO Box 320
Choteau, MT 59422
Phone: (406)466-2403
Fax: (406)466-2403

Publications: Choteau Acantha (17771)

Christendom Press
134 Christendom Dr.
Front Royal, VA 22630
Phone: (540)636-2900
Fax: (540)636-2170
Free: 800-698-6649

Publications: Faith & Reason (32094)

Christian Appalachian Project
PO Box 459
Hagerhill, KY 41222
Phone: (606)789-9791
Fax: (606)789-4865

Publications: The Mountain Spirit (12102)

Christian Association for Psychological Studies
PO Box 310400
New Braunfels, TX 78131-0400
Phone: (830)629-2277
Fax: (830)629-2342

Publications: Journal of Psychology and Christianity (1446)

Christian Brothers University
650 E. Parkway S.
Box T12
Memphis, TN 38104-5581
Phone: (901)321-3000
Fax: (901)321-3586

Publications: The Cannon (29360)

Christian Camping International/USA
PO Box 62189
Colorado Springs, CO 80962-2189
Phone: (719)260-9400
Fax: (719)260-6398

Publications: Christian Camp & Conference Journal (4240)

The Christian Century
104 S Michigan Ave., Ste. 700
Chicago, IL 60603
Phone: (312)263-7510
Fax: (312)263-7540
Free: 800-208-4097

Publications: The Christian Century (8332)

Christian Church in the Upper Midwest
3300 University Ave.
PO Box 41217
Des Moines, IA 50311
Phone: (515)255-3168
Fax: (515)255-2625

Publications: The Christian News (10775)

Christian Civic League
PO Box 5459
Augusta, ME 04332
Phone: (207)622-7634
Fax: (207)621-0035
Free: 800-769-4132

Publications: The Christian Civic League Record (12890)

Christian Farmers' Federation of Ontario
5653 Hwy. 6 N. RR5
Guelph, ON, Canada N1H 6J2

Publications: Earthkeeping Ontario (35861)

The Christian Index
1585 S Ponce De Leon Ave. NE
Atlanta, GA 30307
Phone: (770)261-0600
Fax: (770)261-0610
Free: 877-424-6339

Publications: The Christian Index (6983)

Christian Medical & Dental Society
PO Box 7500
Bristol, TN 37621
Phone: (423)874-1000

Publications: Today's Christian Doctor (29066)

Christian New Age Quarterly
PO Box 276
Clifton, NJ 07015-0276

Publications: Christian New Age Quarterly (18752)

Christian News Northwest
PO Box 974
Newberg, OR 97132
Phone: (503)537-9220
Fax: (503)537-9220

Publications: Christian News Northwest (26443)

The Christian Observer, Inc.
9400 Fairview Ave., Ste. 200
Manassas, VA 20110
Phone: (703)335-2844
Fax: (703)368-4817

Publications: The Christian Observer (32221)

Christian Record Services
PO Box 6097
Lincoln, NE 68506
Phone: (402)488-0981
Fax: (402)488-7582

Publications: The Children's Friend (18079) • Christian Record (18080) • The Student (18122) • Young & Alive (18129)

Christian Restoration Association
7133 Central Parke Blvd.
Mason, OH 45040-7451
Phone: (513)229-8000

Publications: The Restoration Herald (25359)

Christian Schools International
3350 East Paris Ave., SE
Grand Rapids, MI 49512-3054
Phone: (616)957-1070
Fax: (616)957-5022
Free: 800-635-8288

Publications: Christian Home & School (15091)

The Christian Science Publishing Society
One Norway St.
Boston, MA 02115
Phone: (617)450-2000
Fax: (617)450-2930
Free: 800-288-7090

Publications: The Christian Science Journal (13874) • The Christian Science Monitor (13875) • Christian Science Quarterly-Weekly Bible Lessons (13876) • Christian Science Sentinel (13877) • The Herald of Christian Science (13900)

Christian Sons of Liberty
National Headquarters
PO Box 48
Langley, WA 98260
Phone: (360)579-3916

Publications: Alarming Cry News (32805)

Christian Theological Seminary
1000 W 42nd St.
Indianapolis, IN 46208
Phone: (317)931-2370
Fax: (317)923-1961

Publications: Encounter (10110)

Christianity Today International
465 Gundersen Dr.
Carol Stream, IL 60188
Phone: (630)260-6200
Fax: (630)260-9401

Publications: Books & Culture (8134) • Campus Life (8135) • Christian History Magazine (8138) • Christian Parenting Today (8139) • Christian Reader (8140) • Christianity Today (8141) • Leadership (8147) • Marriage Partnership (8148) • Men of Integrity (8149) • Today's Christian Woman (9759) • Virtue (8156) • Your Church (8158)

Christianson
University of Illinois
504 E. Pennsylvania Ave.
244 Law Bldg.
Champaign, IL 61820-6996
Phone: (217)333-6756
Fax: (217)244-1478

Publications: University of Illinois Law Review (8221)

Christopher Reeve Paralysis Foundation
500 Morris Ave.
Springfield, NJ 07081
Phone: (973)379-2690
Fax: (973)912-9433
Free: 800-225-0292

Publications: Progress in Research (19596)

Christy Publishing
Box 669
Waukomis, OK 73773
Phone: (580)758-3255
Fax: (580)758-3255

Publications: The Oklahoma Hornet (26182)

Chroma, Inc.
PO Box 8887
Chattanooga, TN 37414
Phone: (423)899-1753
Fax: (423)490-0791
Free: 800-624-4141

Publications: CRANIO (29088)

The Chronicle
PO Box 148
1 Chronicle Rd.
Willimantic, CT 06226-0148
Phone: (203)423-8466
Fax: (203)423-7641

Publications: The Chronicle (5220)

Chronicle
PO Box 132
Cambridge, IL 61238
Phone: (309)937-3303
Fax: (309)937-3303
Free: (309)944-5615

Publications: Chronicle (8108)

Chronicle
308 E. Main St.
Hoopeston, IL 60942
Phone: (217)283-5111
Fax: (217)283-5846

Publications: Extra Shopping Guide (9004)

Chronicle
PO Box 171
Clearfield, IA 50840-0155
Phone: (515)333-2810

Publications: Chronicle (10709)

Chronicle
PO Box 40
Lamoni, IA 50140-0040
Phone: (515)784-6397
Fax: (515)784-7669

Publications: Chronicle (11028)

The Chronicle
305 Main St.
Colfax, LA 71417
Phone: (318)627-3737
Fax: (318)627-3019

Publications: The Chronicle (12547)

The Chronicle
200 Hofstra University
242 Student Center
Hempstead, NY 11549
Phone: (516)463-6965
Fax: (516)463-6977

Publications: The Chronicle (20727)

The Chronicle
PO Box 428
Creswell, OR 97426
Phone: (541)895-2197
Fax: (541)895-2361
Free: 877-554-7340

Publications: Country Mile Media, Inc. (26297)

The Chronicle
PO Box 448
Humboldt, TN 38343
Phone: (731)784-2531
Fax: (731)784-2533

Publications: The Chronicle (29224)

The Chronicle
109 N. 5th St.
PO Box 60
Wills Point, TX 75169
Phone: (903)873-2525
Fax: (903)873-4321

Publications: Wills Point Chronicle (31301)

The Chronicle
PO Box 660
Barton, VT 05822
Phone: (802)525-3531
Fax: (802)525-3200

Publications: the Chronicle (31493)

The Chronicle
PO Box 580
Centralia, WA 98531
Phone: (360)736-3311
Fax: (360)736-1568
Free: 800-562-6084

Publications: The Chronicle (32704)

The Chronicle
106 E. Hogg St.
PO Box 8
Melrose, WI 54642
Phone: (608)488-3201
Fax: (608)488-7851

Publications: Melrose Chronicle (34037)

Chronicle Adviser
138 Main St.
Penn Yan, NY 14527-1219
Phone: (315)536-4422
Fax: (315)536-0682

Publications: Chronicle Ad-Viser (23091)

Chronicle Communications Corp.
1109 King St.
PO Box 20548
Charleston, SC 29413-0548
Phone: (803)723-2785
Fax: (803)577-6099

Publications: The Charleston Chronicle (28510)

Chronicle & Democrat-Voice
PO Box 840
Coleman, TX 76834
Phone: (915)625-4128
Fax: (915)625-4129

Publications: Chronicle & Democrat-Voice (30035)

Chronicle-Guide Newspapers Ltd.
116 John St.
Arnprior, ON, Canada K7S 2N6
Phone: (613)623-6571
Fax: (613)623-7518

Publications: Chronicle-Guide (35635) • Chronicle Weekender (35636) • West Carleton Review (35638)

The Chronicle of Higher Education
1255 23rd St. NW, Ste. 700
Washington, DC 20037-1125
Phone: (202)466-1000
Fax: (202)452-1033

Publications: The Chronicle of Higher Education (5413)

The Chronicle of the Horse, Inc.
PO Box 46
Middleburg, VA 20118
Phone: (540)687-6341
Fax: (540)687-3937

Publications: The Chronicle of the Horse (32271)

Chronicle-Independent
909 W DeKalb St.
Box 1137
Camden, SC 29020
Phone: (803)432-6157
Fax: (803)432-7609

Publications: Chronicle-Independent (28499)

The Chronicle-Journal
75 Cumberland St. S.
Thunder Bay, ON, Canada P7B 1A3
Phone: (807)343-6200
Fax: (807)345-5991

Publications: The Chronicle-Journal (36438)

The Chronicle of Mt. Juliet
11509 Lebanon Rd.
PO Box 647
Mount Juliet, TN 37122
Phone: (615)754-6111
Fax: (615)754-8203

Publications: The Chronicle of Mt. Juliet (29425)

Chronicle Newspapers, Inc.
1000 Randall Rd.
Geneva, IL 60134
Phone: (630)232-9222
Fax: (630)232-4976

Publications: Chronicle Extra (8917) • Kane County Chronicle (8918)

The Chronicle of Philanthropy
1255 23rd St. NW, Ste. 700
Washington, DC 20037
Phone: (202)466-1200
Fax: (202)466-2078

Publications: The Chronicle of Philanthropy (5414)

Chronicle Shopper
505 Cherokee
Leavenworth, KS 66048
Phone: (913)682-1334
Fax: (913)682-1089
Free: 800-521-1447

Publications: The Chronicle Shopper (11578) • Fort Leavenworth Lamp (11579)

Chronotype Publishing Co.
28 S. Main St.
Rice Lake, WI 54868
Phone: (715)234-2121
Fax: (715)234-5232

Publications: Early Bird (34293) • Rice Lake Chronotype (34294)

Chuck Stock's
PO Box 7127
Albuquerque, NM 87194
Phone: (505)243-9515
Fax: (505)243-9598

Publications: Arizona Cattlelog (19766)

Church of the Brethren General Board
1451 Dundee Ave.
Elgin, IL 60120
Phone: (847)742-5100
Fax: (847)742-6103
Free: 800-323-8039

Publications: Messenger (8825)

Church of God (Seventh Day)
PO Box 33677
Denver, CO 80233

Publications: Bible Advocate (4307)

Church of God World Missions
PO Box 8016
Cleveland, TN 37320-8016
Phone: (423)478-7202
Fax: (423)478-7155

Publications: Save Our World (29122)

Church of Jesus Christ of Latter-day Saints
50 E North Temple St.
Salt Lake City, UT 84150-3220
Phone: (801)240-2951
Fax: (801)240-2270

Publications: The Friend (31428) • New Era (31436)

Church Music Association of America
134 Christendom Dr.
Front Royal, VA 22630
Phone: (540)636-2900
Fax: (540)636-1655

Publications: Sacred Music (32095)

Church Point News
315 N Main
Drawer 319
Church Point, LA 70525
Phone: (337)684-5711

Publications: Church Point News (12545)

Church of Scientology International
6331 Hollywood Blvd., Ste. 1200
Los Angeles, CA 90028-6329
Phone: (323)960-3500
Fax: (323)960-3508

Publications: FREEDOM Magazine (2275)

Church Women United
475 Riverside Dr., Ste. 1626
New York, NY 10115
Phone: (212)870-2347
Fax: (212)870-2338
Free: 800-298-5551

Publications: Churchwoman (21417)

Churches of Christ in Christian Union
1426 Lancaster Pke.
PO Box 30
Circleville, OH 43113
Phone: (740)474-8856
Fax: (740)477-7766

Publications: The Evangelical Advocate (24851)

Churches of God, General Conference
700 E. Melrose Ave.
PO Box 926
Findlay, OH 45839
Phone: (419)424-1961
Fax: (419)424-3433

Publications: The Church Advocate (25193)

Churchill Centre
1150 17th St., NW, Ste. 307
Washington, DC 20036
Phone: (202)223-5511
Fax: (202)223-4944
Free: 888-WSC-1874

Publications: Journal of Winston Churchill (5619)

Churchill Livingston
15 E. 26th St., 15th Fl.
New York, NY 10010-1505

Publications: International Journal of Obstetric Anesthesia (21912)

Churm Publishing, Inc.
1451 Quail St., Ste. 201
Newport Beach, CA 92660
Phone: (949)757-1404
Fax: (949)757-1996

Publications: OC Metro (2633)

Churubusco News and Printing
123 N Main St.
PO Box 8
Churubusco, IN 46723
Phone: (219)693-3949
Fax: (219)693-6545

Publications: Churubusco News (9889)

Ciao Magazine
1081 Bas L'Assomption Nord
L'Assomption, QC, Canada J0K 1G0

Publications: Ciao Magazine (37034)

Cibola County Beacon
523 W. Santa Fe Ave.
PO Box 579
Grants, NM 87020
Phone: (505)287-4411
Fax: (505)287-7822

Publications: Beacon (19862)

Cie Imprimerie & Pub. Rive Sud Ltee.
267 St-Charles Ouest
Longueuil, QC, Canada J4H 1E3
Phone: (450)646-3333
Fax: (450)674-0205

Publications: Le Courrier du Sud (The South Shore Courier) (37053)

Cinahl Information Systems
1509 Wilson Terr.
Glendale, CA 91206
Phone: (818)409-8005
Fax: (818)546-5679
Free: 800-959-7167

Publications: Cumulative Index to Nursing & Allied Health Literature (Print Index) (2008)

Cincinnati Business Courier
101 W. 7th St.
Cincinnati, OH 45202-2306
Phone: (513)621-6665
Fax: (513)621-2462

Publications: Cincinnati Business Courier (24783)

The Cincinnati Herald
354 Hearne Ave.
Cincinnati, OH 45229
Phone: (513)961-3331
Fax: (513)961-0304
Free: 800-961-3371

Publications: The Cincinnati Herald (24786)

Cincinnati Magazine Inc.
One Centennial Plz.
705 Central Ave., Ste. 175
Cincinnati, OH 45202
Phone: (513)421-4300
Fax: (513)562-2746

Publications: Cincinnati Magazine (24787) • Cincinnati Wedding (24789)

Cincinnati Museum Center and The Filson Historical Society
1310 S. Third St.
Louisville, KY 40208
Phone: (502)635-5083
Fax: (502)635-5086

Publications: Ohio Valley History (12233)

CineAction!
40 Alexander St., Ste. 705
Toronto, ON, Canada M4Y 1B5
Phone: (416)964-3534

Publications: CineAction! (36550)

Cineaste Publishers, Inc.
Peter Stuyvesant Sta.
PO Box 2242
New York, NY 10003-1503
Phone: (212)366-5720
Fax: (212)366-5724

Publications: Cineaste (21419)

Cinefantastique
3740 Overland Ave., Ste. E
Los Angeles, CA 90034
Phone: (310)204-2029
Fax: (310)204-0825

Publications: Cinefantastique (2239) • Femme Fatales (2269)

Cinefex
PO Box 20027
Riverside, CA 92516
Phone: (909)781-1917
Fax: (909)788-1793

Publications: Cinefex (2935)

Cinema Le Clap
2360, Chemin Ste-Foy
Sainte-Foy, QC, Canada G1V 4H2
Phone: (418)653-2470
Fax: (418)653-6018
Free: 800-361-2470

Publications: Magazine Le Clap (37374)

CIO Communications
492 Old Connecticut Path
PO Box 9208
Framingham, MA 01701-9208
Phone: (508)872-8200
Fax: (508)872-0618
Free: 800-788-4605

Publications: CIO Magazine (14192) • CIO Web Business (14193)

The Circle
PO Box 6026
Minneapolis, MN 55406-0026
Phone: (612)722-3686
Fax: (612)722-3773

Publications: The Circle (16064)

Circle Media
PO Box 373
Mount Morris, IL 61054
Phone: (815)288-5600
Fax: (815)288-5157
Free: 800-421-3230

Publications: National Catholic Register (9242)

Circuit Cellar, Inc.
PO Box 5650
Hanover, NH 03755

Publications: Circuit Cellar INK (18515)

Circus Enterprises
6 W 18th St., 2nd Fl.
New York, NY 10011
Phone: (212)242-4902
Fax: (212)242-5734

Publications: Circus Magazine (21420)

Circus Historical Society
2515 Dorset Rd.
Columbus, OH 43221
Phone: (614)294-5361
Fax: (614)294-1633

Publications: Bandwagon (24999)

The Cisco Press
PO Box 470
Cisco, TX 76437-0470
Phone: (254)442-2244
Fax: (254)629-2092

Publications: The Cisco Press (30020)

Cissna Park News/Rankin Independent
PO Box 8
Cissna Park, IL 60924-0008

Publications: Cissna Park News (8678) • Rankin Independent (8680)

CITA International (USA)
3464 W. Earll Dr., Ste. E
Phoenix, AZ 85017
Phone: (602)447-0480
Fax: (602)447-0305

Publications: For Formulation Chemists Only (804)

The Citadel
171 Moultrie St.
Charleston, SC 29409
Phone: (843)953-5000
Fax: (843)953-6767

Publications: Mark Twain Circular (28515)

The Citizen
150 Brunswick St.
PO Box 5700
Prince George, BC, Canada V2L 5K9
Phone: (250)562-2441
Fax: (250)562-7453

Publications: The Prince George Citizen (35057)

The Citizen
112 S Park St.
PO Box A
Boyne City, MI 49712
Phone: (231)582-6761
Fax: (231)582-6762

Publications: The Citizen (14832)

The Citizen
11901 Joseph Campau Ave.
Hamtramck, MI 48212
Phone: (313)365-9500

Publications: The Citizen (14918)

Citizen Communications, Inc.
101 W Potomac St.
Brunswick, MD 21716
Phone: (301)834-7722

Publications: The Brunswick Citizen (13395) • The Middletown Valley Citizen (13628)

Citizen Gazette
PO Box 43
Burnet, TX 78611-0043
Phone: (512)756-6640
Fax: (512)756-6640

Publications: Citizen Gazette (29992)

The Citizen-News
PO Box 448
Edgefield, SC 29824
Phone: (803)637-5306
Fax: (803)637-5661

Publications: The Citizen-News (28600)

Citizen Newspapers
601 E 6th St.
PO Box 948
Waynesboro, GA 30830
Phone: (706)554-2111
Fax: (706)554-2437

Publications: The Signal (7283) • The True Citizen (7649)

Citizen Newspapers
412 E. 87th St.
Chicago, IL 60619
Phone: (773)783-1251
Fax: (773)487-7931

Publications: Chatham-Southeast Citizen (8304) • Chicago Weekend (8329) • Hyde Park Citizen (8402) • South End Citizen (8566) • South Suburban Citizen (8567)

Citizen Newspapers, LLC
805 Park Ave.
Beaver Dam, WI 53916
Phone: (920)887-0333
Fax: (920)887-8790

Publications: Columbus Journal-Republican (33642) • Neighbors (34427) • Shopping Reminder (33643)

Citizen Publications
107 S. Main St.
PO Box 90
Culver, IN 46511
Phone: (219)842-3229
Fax: (219)935-0083

Publications: Culver Citizen (9916)

Citizen Publishing
Box 548
Columbus, TX 78934
Fax: (409)732-8804

Publications: Colorado County Citizen (30065)

Citizen Publishing Co.
171 Fair St.
Laconia, NH 03246
Phone: (603)524-8300
Fax: (603)524-6702
Free: 800-564-3806

Publications: Citizen (18536)

Citizen Publishing Co.
805 Park Ave.
Beaver Dam, WI 53916
Phone: (920)885-7800
Fax: (920)887-8790
Free: 800-777-9470

Publications: Daily Citizen (33567) • Monday Marketeer (34024) • Tri County Citizen (33568)

Citizen-Standard
104 W. Main St.
PO Box 147
Valley View, PA 17983
Phone: (570)682-9081
Fax: (570)682-8734

Publications: Citizen-Standard (28093)

Citizen-Statesman Corp.
801 E Lake Ave.
PO Box 670
Celina, TN 38551
Phone: (931)243-2235
Fax: (931)243-2232

Publications: Citizen-Statesman (29084)

The Citizen-Times
PO Box 310
Scottsville, KY 42164
Phone: (270)237-3441
Fax: (270)237-4943
Free: 888-237-3443

Publications: The Citizen-Times (12394)

Citizen Voice, Inc.
108 Ct. St.
PO Box 660
Irvine, KY 40336
Phone: (606)723-5161
Fax: (606)723-5509

Publications: Citizen Voice & Times (12141)

Citizens Communication Group
49 Main St.
Bobcaygeon, ON, Canada K0M 1D0
Fax: (705)738-4332

Publications: Independent (35689)

Citizens Communication Group
1186 Ringwell Dr.
Dresden, ON, Canada L3Y 7V1
Phone: (905)830-1201
Fax: (905)830-1991

Publications: Voice of the Essex Farmer (35810) • Voice of the Lambton Farmer (35967) • Voice of the Middlesex Farmer (36037)

Citizens Communication Group
254 Main St.
Dresden, ON, Canada N0P 1M0

Publications: North Kent Leader (35931)

Citizens Communication Group Inc.
1183 Ringwell Dr.
Newmarket, ON, Canada L3Y 7V1
Phone: (905)830-0523
Fax: (905)830-1992

Publications: Brock Citizen (35672)

Citizens Publishing & Printing Co.
835 Lawrence Ave.
Ellwood City, PA 16117
Phone: (724)758-5573
Fax: (724)758-2410

Publications: Ellwood City Ledger (26871)

City College of San Francisco
50 Phelan Ave., V-67
San Francisco, CA 94112
Phone: (415)239-3446
Fax: (415)239-3884

Publications: The Guardsman (3368)

City-County Magazine
PO Box 517
Burlington, NC 27216
Phone: (336)226-8436
Fax: (336)226-8437

Publications: City-County Magazine (23671)

City Family, Inc.
275 7th Ave., 20th Fl.
New York, NY 10001-0577
Phone: (646)486-7100

Publications: City Family (21422) • La Familia de la Ciudad (22227)

City on a Hill Press
Student Press Ctr., University of California Santa Cruz
1156 High St.
Santa Cruz, CA 95064
Phone: (831)459-4350
Fax: (831)459-4696

Publications: City on a Hill (3682)

City Limits Community Information Service
120 Wall St., 20th Fl.
New York, NY 10005
Phone: (212)479-3344
Fax: (212)344-6457

Publications: City Limits (21425)

City News Publishing Co.
PO Box 1247
Mount Pleasant, SC 29465-1247
Phone: (843)881-8733
Fax: (843)881-4007
Free: 800-506-8733

Publications: Vital Speeches (28695) • Vital Speeches of the Day (28696)

City Newspaper Group
PO Box 1604
Colton, CA 92324
Phone: (909)370-2774
Fax: (909)370-1193

Publications: Colton City News (1740) • Grand Terrace City News (1742) • Loma Linda City News (1743)

City Pages, Inc.
401 N 3rd St., Ste. 550
Minneapolis, MN 55401
Phone: (612)375-1015
Fax: (612)372-3737

Publications: City Pages (16065)

City Parent
467 Speers Rd.
Oakville, ON, Canada L6K 3S4
Phone: (905)815-0017
Fax: (905)337-5571
Free: 800-265-3673

Publications: City Parent (36143)

City Press Publishing, Inc.
2120 Eighth Ave. S.
Nashville, TN 37204
Phone: (615)244-7989
Fax: (615)244-8578

Publications: Nashville Scene (29473)

City of Spokane
Washington City Clerk Municipal Bldg., 5th Fl.
W. 808 Spokane Falls Blvd.
Spokane, WA 99201-3342
Phone: (509)625-6070

Publications: Spokane, Washington, Official Gazette (33100)

City Sports, Inc.
444 S. Cedros Ave., No. 185
Solana Beach, CA 92075
Phone: (858)793-2711
Fax: (858)793-2710

Publications: City Sports (3767)

City Sports Publishing (Canada) Ltd.
676 B Leg in Boot Square
Vancouver, BC, Canada V5Z 4B4
Phone: (604)876-4980
Fax: (604)876-4966

Publications: Coast Magazine—Ontario Edition (36552)

City University of New York
2001 Oriental Blvd., Rm. M230
Brooklyn, NY 11235
Phone: (718)368-5603
Fax: (718)368-4833

Publications: Scepter (20345)

City University of New York
365 Fifth Ave.
New York, NY 10016-4309
Phone: (212)817-8686
Fax: (212)817-1645

Publications: Comparative Politics (21464)

City of Vancouver
PO Box 1995
Vancouver, WA 98668-9866
Phone: (360)696-8077
Fax: (360)696-8942

Publications: Senior Messenger (33179)

CityBusiness
527 Marquette Ave. Ste. 300
Ste. 300, Rand Tower
Minneapolis, MN 55402
Phone: (612)288-2100
Fax: (612)288-2121

Publications: CityBusiness (16066)

Civil Air Patrol, Inc.
105 S Hansell St.
Maxwell AFB
Montgomery, AL 36112
Phone: (334)953-5700
Fax: (334)953-4245

Publications: Civil Air Patrol News (363)

The Civil War Lady
PO Box 351
Clarinda, IA 51632-0351

Publications: The Civil War Lady (10701)

Numbers cited after listings are entry numbers rather than page numbers.

Civitan International
1 Civitan Place
PO Box 130744
Birmingham, AL 35213-0744
Phone: (205)591-8910
Fax: (205)592-6307

Publications: Civitan Magazine (64)

Clackamas County News
PO Box 549
Estacada, OR 97023
Phone: (503)630-3241
Fax: (503)630-5840

Publications: Clackamas County News (26313)

Claiborne Progress
PO Box 40
Tazewell, TN 37879
Phone: (423)626-3222
Fax: (423)626-6868

Publications: Claiborne Progress (29625)

Claiborne Publishing Co., Inc.
708 Market
PO Box 1002
Port Gibson, MS 39150-1002
Phone: (601)437-5103
Fax: (601)437-4410

Publications: The Port Gibson Reveille (16826)

Claims
23002 35th Ave. W
Brier, WA 98036
Phone: (425)774-8267

Publications: CLAIMS (32698)

Clansman Publishing Ltd.
PO Box 8805, Sta. A
Halifax, NS, Canada B3K 5M4
Phone: (902)835-6244
Fax: (902)835-0080

Publications: Celtic Heritage (35560)

Clapper Publishing Co., Inc.
2400 Devon, Ste.375
Des Plaines, IL 60018-4618
Phone: (847)635-5800
Fax: (847)635-6311
Free: 800-CRA-FTSI

Publications: Bridal Crafts (8750) • Crafts 'N Things (8756) • The Cross Stitcher (8758) • Pack-O-Fun (8766) • Painting (8767)

Clara City Herald
Box 458
Clara City, MN 56222
Phone: (320)847-3130
Fax: (320)847-2630

Publications: Clara City Herald (15798)

Clare County Review
431 N. McEwan St.
Clare, MI 48617-1402
Phone: (989)386-4414
Fax: (989)386-2412

Publications: Clare County Review (14878)

The Clare Sentinel
112 W 4th St.
Clare, MI 48617
Phone: (989)386-9937
Fax: (989)386-9311

Publications: The Clare Sentinel (14879)

The Claremont Colleges
175 E 8th St.
Claremont, CA 91711
Phone: (909)624-1887
Fax: (909)607-7825

Publications: Collage (1724)

Claremont Review Publishers
4980 Wesley Rd.
Victoria, BC, Canada V8Y 1Y9
Phone: (250)658-5221
Fax: (250)658-5387

Publications: The Claremont Review (35214)

Claremore Progress
PO Box 248
Claremore, OK 74018
Phone: (918)785-7810
Fax: (918)341-1131

Publications: Claremore Daily Progress (25788)

The Clarence Courier
106 E Maple St.
Box 10
Clarence, MO 63437-0010
Phone: (816)699-2344
Fax: (816)699-2194

Publications: The Clarence Courier (16980)

The Clarendon Enterprise
105 S Kearney St.
PO Box 1110
Clarendon, TX 79226-1110
Phone: (806)874-2259
Fax: (806)874-2423

Publications: The Clarendon Enterprise (30021)

Claretian Publications
205 W. Monroe
Chicago, IL 60606
Phone: (312)236-7782
Fax: (312)236-8207
Free: 800-328-6515

Publications: U.S. Catholic (8591)

Claridge Community Newspaper Ltd.
Box 119
Grand Valley, ON, Canada L0N 1G0
Phone: (519)941-2230
Fax: (519)941-9361

Publications: Star and Vidette (35855)

Clarington / Courtice
62-66 King St. W.
PO Box 190
Bowmanville, ON, Canada L1C 3K9
Phone: (905)623-3303
Fax: (905)623-6161

Publications: Clarington / Courtice (35692)

Clarington Museums
37 Silver St.
PO Box 188
Bowmanville, ON, Canada L1C 3K9
Phone: (905)623-2734
Fax: (905)623-5684
Free: 888-567-2598

Publications: Epoch (35693)

Clarion Herald Publishing Co., Inc.
1000 Howard Ave., Ste. 400
New Orleans, LA 70113
Phone: (504)524-1618
Fax: (504)596-3020

Publications: Clarion Herald (12727)

Clarion Publications
15717 Lakewood Blvd., Ste. C
Paramount, CA 90723
Phone: (562)633-1234
Fax: (562)630-8141
Free: 800-540-1870

Publications: The Paramount Journal (2810)

Clarion Publishing Co.
136 E Waterman St.
PO Box 220
Dumas, AR 71639
Phone: (870)382-4925
Fax: (870)382-6421

Publications: Dumas Clarion (1105)

Clarion University of Pennsylvania
Gemmell Complex
Clarion, PA 16214
Phone: (814)226-2380
Fax: (814)226-2557

Publications: The Clarion Call (26779)

Clark Community College
1800 E McLoughlin Blvd.
Vancouver, WA 98663
Phone: (360)992-2000

Publications: The Independent (33176)

Clark County Clipper
Box 457
Ashland, KS 67831
Phone: (620)635-2312
Fax: (620)635-2643

Publications: Clark County Clipper (11344)

Clark Pepper
PO Box 10
Shellbrook, SK, Canada S0J 2E0
Phone: (306)747-2442
Fax: (306)747-3000

Publications: Shellbrook Chronicle (37571) • Spiritwood Herald (37572)

Clark University
950 Main St.
Worcester, MA 01610
Phone: (508)793-7311
Fax: (508)793-8881

Publications: Economic Geography (14678)

Clark University
950 Main St., Box B-13
Worcester, MA 01610
Phone: (508)793-7508

Publications: The Scarlet (14687)

Clarke College
1550 Clarke Dr.
Dubuque, IA 52001-3198
Phone: (563)588-6351
Fax: (563)588-6789
Free: 800-383-2345

Publications: Clarke Courier (10841)

Clarke County Democrat
PO Box 39
Grove Hill, AL 36451-0039
Phone: (251)275-3375
Fax: (251)275-3060

Publications: Clarke County Democrat (247)

Clarke County Publishing Inc.
PO Box 447
Osceola, IA 50213
Phone: (641)342-2131
Fax: (641)342-2060

Publications: Osceola Sentinel-Tribune (11133)

Clarke Historical Library
Central Michigan University
Mount Pleasant, MI 48859-0001
Phone: (989)774-3352
Fax: (989)774-2160

Publications: Michigan Historical Review (15376)

Clarksburg Publishing
324 Hewes Ave.
Clarksburg, WV 26301-2744
Phone: (304)624-6411
Fax: (304)622-3629
Free: 800-982-6034

Publications: Clarksburg Exponent (33293) • Clarksburg Telegram (33294)

The Clarksville Times
106 E Main St.
PO Box 1018
Clarksville, TX 75426
Phone: (903)427-5616
Fax: (903)427-3068

Publications: The Clarksville Times (30022)

Class Actions Reports, Inc.
4900 Massachusetts Ave. NW, Ste. 230
Washington, DC 20016
Phone: (202)364-1031
Fax: (202)363-6912

Publications: Class Action Reports (5417)

Classic Boating
280 Lac La Belle Dr.
Oconomowoc, WI 53066
Phone: (262)567-4800

Publications: Classic Boating (34201)

Classical Association of the Atlantic States
Department of Humanities
University of the Sciences
600 S. 43rd St.
Philadelphia, PA 19104-4495
Phone: (215)596-8504

Publications: The Classical World (27406)

Classical Association of the Middle West & South, Inc.
Dept. of Classics
University of Virginia
Charlottesville, VA 22903
Phone: (804)924-6672
Fax: (804)982-3062

Publications: Classical Journal (31923)

Classified Flea Market
6001 Telegraph Ave.
Oakland, CA 94609
Phone: (510)420-1972
Fax: (510)420-1919
Free: 800-980-3532

Publications: The Classified Flea Market (2676)

The Classified Gazette, Inc.
716 4th St.
San Rafael, CA 94901
Phone: (415)457-4888
Fax: (415)454-9849
Free: 800-794-4888

Publications: Classified Gazette (3599)

The Classified Gazette, Inc.
532 College Ave.
Santa Rosa, CA 95404
Phone: (707)526-2434
Fax: (707)527-9251
Free: 888-526-2434

Publications: The Classified Gazette (Sonoma County Edition) (3773)

Clatskanie Chief
PO Box 8
Clatskanie, OR 97016
Phone: (503)728-3350

Publications: Clatskanie Chief (26268)

Clay County Advocate Press, Inc.
105 W. North Ave.
PO Box 519
Flora, IL 62839-1613
Phone: (618)662-2108
Fax: (618)662-2939

Publications: Daily Clay County Advocate-Press (8890)

Clay County Courier
PO Box 128, Hwy. 67 N
Corning, AR 72422
Phone: (870)857-6397
Fax: (870)857-5204

Publications: Clay County Courier (1090)

Clay County Leader
Drawer 10
Henrietta, TX 76365-0010
Phone: (817)538-4333
Fax: (817)538-4542

Publications: Clay County Leader (30442)

Clay County News
207 N Saunders
Box 405
Sutton, NE 68979-0405
Phone: (402)773-5576
Fax: (402)773-5577

Publications: Clay County News (18292)

Clay County Progress
PO Box 483
Hayesville, NC 28904
Phone: (704)389-8431
Fax: (704)389-9997

Publications: The Clay County Progress (23980)

Clay County Republican
124 S Church St.
PO Drawer B
Louisville, IL 62858
Phone: (618)665-3135
Fax: (618)665-3135

Publications: Louisville Clay County Republican (9119)

Clay Times
15481 Second St.
PO Box 365
Waterford, VA 20197

Publications: Clay Times (32609)

The Clay Times Journal
60132 Hwy. 49
PO Box 97
Lineville, AL 36266
Phone: (205)396-5760
Fax: (205)396-5760

Publications: The Clay Times Journal (304)

Clayton-Davis & Associates
8229 Maryland Ave.
St. Louis, MO 63105
Phone: (314)862-7800
Fax: (314)721-5171

Publications: Health Perspective (17443) • Managed Care/Innovations (17469)

Clayton-Fillmore Ltd.
125 Dorset Ct.
Castle Rock, CO 80104-9285
Phone: (303)663-0606
Fax: (303)663-1616

Publications: The CF Apartment Reporter (4220) • Clayton-Fillmore Report (4221)

The Clayton Record
PO Box 69
Clayton, AL 36016
Phone: (334)775-3254
Fax: (334)775-8554

Publications: The Clayton Record (158)

CLB Media Inc.
135 Spy Ct.
Markham, ON, Canada L3R 5H6
Phone: (905)477-3222
Fax: (905)477-4320

Publications: Canadian Electronics (36016) • Design Product News (36023) • Metalworking Production and Purchasing (36028) • Produits Pour L'Industrie Quebecoise (36031) • Woodworking (36033)

Cleaning Management Institute
13 Century Hill Dr.
Latham, NY 12110-2197
Phone: (518)783-1281
Fax: (518)783-1386

Publications: Cleaning and Maintenance Management Magazine (20932)

The Clear Creek Courant
1634 Miner St.
PO Box 2020
Idaho Springs, CO 80452
Phone: (303)567-4491
Fax: (303)567-4492

Publications: The Clear Creek Courant (4519)

Clear Lake Courier
Box 830
Clear Lake, SD 57226
Phone: (605)874-2499
Fax: (605)874-2642

Publications: Clear Lake Courier (28833)

Clear Lake Mirror
12 N. 4th St.
Clear Lake, IA 50428
Phone: (641)357-2131
Fax: (641)357-2133

Publications: Clear Lake Mirror Reporter (10706)

The Clearwater Progress, Inc.
417 Main St.
PO Box 428
Kamiah, ID 83536-0428
Phone: (208)935-0838
Fax: (208)935-0973

Publications: The Clearwater Progress (7885)

Clearwater Tribune
161 Main St.
PO Box 71
Orofino, ID 83544
Phone: (208)476-4571
Fax: (208)476-0765

Publications: Clearwater Tribune (7938)

Clemmons Courier
PO Drawer 765
Clemmons, NC 27012
Phone: (336)766-4126

Publications: Clemmons Courier (23787)

Clemson University
Box 340523
Clemson, SC 29634-0523
Phone: (864)656-5399
Fax: (864)656-1345

Publications: South Carolina Review (28533)

Clemson University
Clemson
PO Box 2337
Clemson, SC 29633
Phone: (864)656-3311
Fax: (864)656-4772

Publications: The Tiger (28535)

The Clergy Journal
6160 Carmen Ave. E
Inver Grove Heights, MN 55076
Phone: (612)451-9945
Fax: (612)457-4617
Free: 800-328-0200

Publications: The Clergy Journal (15971)

The Clermont Sun
465 E Main St.
PO Box 366
Batavia, OH 45103
Phone: (513)732-2511
Fax: (513)732-6344
Free: 800-404-3157

Publications: The Clermont Sun (24643)

Cleveland Athletic Club
1118 Euclid Ave.
Cleveland, OH 44115
Phone: (216)861-4170
Fax: (216)861-4263

Publications: CAC Journal (24864)

Cleveland Bar Association
113 St. Clair Ave., NE, Ste. 100
Cleveland, OH 44144-1253
Phone: (216)696-3525
Fax: (216)696-2413

Publications: Cleveland Bar Journal (24869)

Cleveland Clinic Foundation
9500 Euclid Ave., NA 32
Cleveland, OH 44195-5058
Phone: (216)444-2661
Fax: (216)444-9385

Publications: Cleveland Clinic Journal of Medicine (24870)

Cleveland Enterprise Magazine
EDI
11000 Cedar Ave., 4th Fl.
Cleveland, OH 44106
Phone: (216)229-9445
Fax: (216)229-3236

Publications: Cleveland Enterprise Magazine (24871)

Cleveland Institute of Electronics
1776 E 17th St.
Cleveland, OH 44114
Phone: (216)781-9400
Fax: (216)781-0331
Free: 800-243-6446

Publications: The Electron (24889)

Cleveland Jewish Publication Co.
23880 Commerce Pk., No. 1
Beachwood, OH 44122
Phone: (216)454-8300
Fax: (216)454-8100

Publications: Cleveland Jewish News (24651)

Cleveland Museum of Natural History
1 Wade Oval Dr.
Cleveland, OH 44106
Phone: (216)231-4600
Fax: (216)231-5919

Publications: Explorer (24894)

Cleveland Newspapers Inc.
PO Box 3600
Cleveland, TN 37320-3600
Phone: (423)472-5041
Fax: (423)476-1046
Free: 800-803-3321

Publications: The Cleveland Daily Banner (29121)

Cleveland State University
Cleveland, OH 44115
Phone: (216)687-2336
Fax: (216)687-6881

Publications: Journal of Law and Health (24915)

Cleveland State University
2121 Euclid Ave., Rm. 10
Cleveland, OH 44115
Phone: (216)687-2475
Fax: (216)687-5155

Publications: The Cauldron (24868)

Cleveland State University
Cleveland, OH 44115
Phone: (216)687-2056
Fax: (216)687-6943

Publications: Whiskey Island Magazine (24965)

Clifford/Elliot Ltd.
209-3228 S. Service Rd.
Burlington, ON, Canada L7N 3H8
Phone: (905)634-2100
Fax: (905)634-2238
Free: 800-268-7977

Publications: Canadian Occupational Safety (35716) • PEM Plant Engineering and Maintenance (35718)

The Clifton Record
PO Box 353
Clifton, TX 76634
Phone: (254)675-3336
Fax: (254)675-4090
Free: 800-241-5504

Publications: The Clifton Record (30031)

Clinch Valley News
PO Box 977
Tazewell, VA 24651
Phone: (276)988-4770
Fax: (276)963-0123

Publications: Clinch Valley News (32570)

Clinch Valley Publishing Co., Inc.
16541 Russell St.
PO Drawer 817
St. Paul, VA 24283-0817
Phone: (276)762-7671
Fax: (276)762-0929
Free: 888-533-1908

Publications: Clinch Valley Times (32520)

Clinical Cardiology Publishing Co., Inc.
PO Box 832
Mahwah, NJ 07430-0832
Phone: (201)818-1010
Fax: (201)818-0086
Free: 800-443-0263

Publications: Clinical Cardiology (19189)

Clinical Laboratory Management Association
989 Old Eagle School Rd., Ste. 815
Wayne, PA 19087
Phone: (610)995-9580
Fax: (610)995-9568

Publications: Clinical Leadership and Management Review (28129)

Clinical Psychology Publishing Co., Inc.
4 Conant Sq.
Brandon, VT 05733
Phone: (802)247-6871
Fax: (802)247-6853
Free: 800-433-8234

Publications: Journal of Clinical Psychology (25968)

Clinicians Publishing Group
2 Brighton Rd., Ste. 300
Clifton, NJ 07012
Phone: (973)916-0100

Publications: Clinician Reviews (18753)

Kirk Clinkscales Sr.
PO Box 96
Caney, KS 67333
Phone: (316)879-5460
Fax: (316)879-2264
Free: 800-942-6397

Publications: Good News (11373)

Clinton Chronicle
513 N Broad St.
PO Box 180
Clinton, SC 29325
Phone: (864)833-1900
Fax: (864)833-1902

Publications: Clinton Chronicle (28539)

Clinton Color Crafters
422 S. Main St.
Clinton, IN 47842
Phone: (765)832-2443

Publications: The Daily Clintonian (9891)

Clinton Community College
1000 Lincoln Blvd.
Clinton, IA 52732
Phone: (563)244-7046
Fax: (563)244-7107
Free: 800-637-0559

Publications: The Gallery (10711)

Clinton County Publishing Co.
129 5th St.
Renovo, PA 17764

Publications: The Record (27931)

Clinton Daily Journal
PO Box 615
Rte. 54 W.
Clinton, IL 61727
Phone: (217)935-3171
Fax: (217)935-6086

Publications: Clinton Daily Journal (8682)

Clinton Daily News Co.
522 Avant Ave.
Clinton, OK 73601-3431
Phone: (580)323-5151
Fax: (580)323-5154

Publications: The Clinton Daily News (25790)

Clinton/East Feliciana Watchman
PO Box 368
Clinton, LA 70722-0368
Fax: (504)683-8982

Publications: Clinton/East Feliciana Watchman (12546)

The Clinton Local
108 Tecumseh St.
PO Box B
Clinton, MI 49236
Phone: (517)456-4100
Fax: (517)456-6372

Publications: The Clinton Local (14883)

The Clinton Topper
242 Allen St.
Box 569
Clinton, WI 53525-0569
Phone: (608)676-4111
Fax: (608)676-4664

Publications: The Clinton Topper (33635)

Clintonville Publishing Co.
13 11th St.
Clintonville, WI 54929-1514
Phone: (715)823-3151
Fax: (715)823-7479

Publications: Clintonville Tribune-Gazette (33637)

Clintonville Shopper's Guide
17 9th St.
PO Box 330
Clintonville, WI 54929
Phone: (715)823-3107
Fax: (715)823-1364

Publications: Clintonville Shopper's Guide (33636)

Clintron Publishers
PO Box 30998
Spokane, WA 99223
Phone: (509)458-3924
Fax: (509)458-3947
Free: 800-869-7923

Publications: Ag Equipment Power (33092)

Clipper Publishing
1370 South 500 West
PO Box 267
Bountiful, UT 84010
Phone: (801)295-2251
Fax: (801)295-3044

Publications: Davis County Clipper (31322)

Clipper Publishing Co.
PO Box 640
Shelton, NE 68876
Phone: (308)647-5158

Publications: The Shelton Clipper (18277)

Cloquet Journal
813 Cloquet Ave.
Cloquet, MN 55720
Phone: (218)879-1950

Publications: Cloquet Journal (15801)

Cloquet Newspapers
813 Cloquet Ave.
Cloquet, MN 55720-1613
Phone: (218)879-6761
Fax: (218)879-6696

Publications: The Pine Knot (15802)

Close-Up Business Services Ltd.
4535 Greig Ave.
PO Box 446
Terrace, BC, Canada V8G 4B1
Fax: (604)635-7269

Publications: Terrace Review (35111)

Closeout News, Inc.
5900 Wilshire Blvd., Ste. 510
Los Angeles, CA 90036-5005
Free: 800-600-7040

Publications: Closeout News Magazine (2243)

Cloverdale Reveille
207 N Cloverdale Blvd.
PO Box 157
Cloverdale, CA 95425-3318
Phone: (707)894-3339
Fax: (707)894-3343

Publications: Cloverdale Reveille (1730)

The Clovis Independent
420 Bullard, No. 105
Clovis, CA 93612
Phone: (559)298-8081
Fax: (559)298-0459

Publications: The Clovis Independent (1733)

Clovis News Journal
PO Box 1689
Clovis, NM 88102
Phone: (505)763-3431
Fax: (505)762-3879
Free: 800-819-9925

Publications: Clovis News Journal (19830)

Clownskull Graphics
Box 02007
Detroit, MI 48202
Phone: (313)871-8419
Fax: (313)871-4840

Publications: Motorbooty (14940)

Club Publications
665 La Villa Dr.
Miami Springs, FL 33166-6029
Phone: (305)887-1701
Fax: (305)885-1923
Free: 800-887-2550

Publications: Airline, Ship & Catering ONBOARD SERVICES Magazine (6421) • City & Country Club Life (6422)

ClubCorp Publications, Inc.
3030 LBJ Fwy., Ste. 350
Dallas, TX 75234-7395
Phone: (972)888-7547
Fax: (972)888-7338
Free: 800-433-5079

Publications: Private Clubs (30178)

Clubhouse Publishing, Inc.
601 S Osprey Ave.
Sarasota, FL 34236-7526
Fax: (813)365-7272

Publications: Sarasota Magazine (6664)

The Clyde Journal
PO Box 979
Clyde, TX 79510
Phone: (915)893-4244
Fax: (915)893-2780

Publications: Journal (30034)

Clyde Republican
305 Washington
PO Box 397
Clyde, KS 66938-0397
Phone: (785)446-2201

Publications: Clyde Republican (11385)

Clydesdale Breeders of the United States
17346 Kelly Rd.
Pecatonica, IL 61063
Phone: (815)247-8780
Fax: (815)247-8337

Publications: Clydesdale News (9413)

CM Media
PO Box 29913
Columbus, OH 43229-7513
Phone: (614)888-4567
Fax: (614)848-3838

Publications: Columbus Monthly (25009)

CMD Group
30 Technology Pkwy., No. 100
Norcross, GA 30092
Phone: (770)417-4000
Fax: (770)417-4002

Publications: Construction Market Data, A/E/C Magazine (7457)

CME, Inc.
2801 McGaw Ave.
Irvine, CA 92614-5835
Phone: (949)250-1008
Free: 800-933-2632

Publications: The Psychiatric Times (2089)

CMJ Network
151 W. 25th St., 12th Fl.
New York, NY 10001
Phone: (917)606-1908
Fax: (917)606-1914

Publications: CMJ New Music Monthly (21432) • CMJ New Music Report (21433)

CMMTQ
8175 Saint-Laurent Blvd.
Montreal, QC, Canada H2P 2M1
Phone: (514)382-2668
Fax: (514)382-1566

Publications: Inter-Mecanique du Batiment (37134)

CMN Associates, Inc.
1445 Donlon St., Ste. 16
Ventura, CA 93003
Phone: (805)642-9735
Fax: (805)642-8820
Free: 800-344-BLDR

Publications: Automated Builder (4001)

CMP Game Group
600 Harrison St.
San Francisco, CA 94107
Phone: (415)947-6000
Fax: (415)947-6055

Publications: Game Developer (3364)

CMP Media LLC
600 Harrison St.
San Francisco, CA 94107
Phone: (415)538-8800

Publications: CADENCE (3333) • DV Media Group (3351) • Transform Magazine (22853)

CMP Media LLC
2800 Campus Dr.
San Mateo, CA 94403
Phone: (650)513-4300
Fax: (650)513-4618

Publications: Dr. Dobb's Journal (3585) • Windows Developer's Journal (3591)

CMP Media, LLC
600 Community Dr.
Manhasset, NY 11030
Phone: (516)562-5000

Publications: Action Sports (20990) • Call Center Magazine (20991) • Communication Systems Design (20992) • Computer Retail Week (20993) • CRN (20994) • Database Programming & Design (20995) • Diagnostic Imaging (20996) • Digital Video Magazine (20997) • EBN (20998) • Electronic Engineering Times (20999) • Embedded Systems Programming (21000) • Gavin (21001) • Home PC (21002) • Imaging Magazine (21003) • InformationWEEK (21004) • Internet Week (21005) • Network Computing (21007) • Network Magazine (21008) • PC Fab (7035) • Performance Computing (21009) • Printed Circuit Design & Manufacture (21010) • Printed Circuit Fabrication (21011) • Pulp & Paper International (21012) • Software Development (21013) • Technology & Learning (21014) • Teleconnect Magazine (21015) • VARBUSINESS (21016) • Wall Street and Technology (21017) • Windows Magazine (21018) • Wood Technology (21019)

CN Publishing
PO Box 5084
Costa Mesa, CA 92628-5084
Phone: (310)427-7433
Fax: (310)427-6685

Publications: Cycle News (1773)

CNHI
3800 Colonnade Pkwy., Ste. 450
Birmingham, AL 35243

Publications: Frederick Leader (25839)

CNHI
701 Tekulve Rd
PO Box 89
Batesville, IN 47006
Phone: (812)934-4343
Fax: (812)934-6406

Publications: The Herald-Tribune (9796)

CNHI
303 Scribner Dr.
PO Box 997
New Albany, IN 47150
Phone: (812)944-6481
Fax: (812)949-6585

Publications: The New Albany Tribune (10339)

C.N.I.
PO Box 792
Athens, GA 30603

Publications: The Weekly Observer (28659)

CNI
PO Box 1040
Cashiers, NC 28717
Phone: (704)743-5101
Fax: (704)743-4173

Publications: Crossroads Chronicle (23694)

CNI Newspapers
15770 W. Cleveland Ave.
New Berlin, WI 53151
Phone: (262)938-5000
Fax: (262)938-5001

Publications: The Bay Viewer (34166) • Brookfield News (34167) • Brown Deer Herald (34168) • Cudahy Reminder/Enterprise (34169) • Elm Grove Elm Leaves (34170) • Fox Point-Bayside-River Hills Herald (34171) • Franklin-Hales Corners Hub (34172) • Germantown Banner Press (34173) • Glendale Herald (34174) • Greendale Village Life (34175) • Greenfield Observer (34176) • Menomonee Falls News (34177) • Mequon-Thiensville Courant (34178) • Muskego Sun (34179) • New Berlin Citizen (34180) • Oak Creek Pictorial (34182) • Shorewood Herald (34185) • South Milwaukee Voice Graphic (34186) • Sussex-Lannon-Lisbon News (34187) • Wauwatosa News-Times (34188) • West Allis Star (34189) • Whitefish Bay Herald (34190)

CNNI
208 N Main
Bourbon, IN 46504
Phone: (219)342-5143
Fax: (219)342-3002
Free: 800-933-0356

Publications: Bourbon News-Mirror (9868)

CNS This Week
PO Box 341890
Columbus, OH 43234
Phone: (614)855-2774
Fax: (614)855-2857

Publications: Johnstown Independent (25271)

CNS/This Week Newspapers
670 Lakeview Plz. Blvd.
Worthington, OH 43085
Phone: (614)841-1781
Fax: (614)841-0436

Publications: Rocky Fork Enterprise (25681)

CNY Business Review, Inc.
231 Walton St.
Syracuse, NY 13202-1226
Phone: (315)472-3104
Fax: (315)472-3644
Free: 800-836-3118

Publications: Central N.Y. Business Journal (23393)

Coaching Women's Basketball
4646 Lawrenceville Hwy.
Lilburn, GA 30047-3620
Phone: (770)279-8027
Fax: (770)279-8473

Publications: Coaching Women's Basketball (7371)

Coal People Magazine
PO Box 6247
Charleston, WV 25362
Phone: (304)342-4129
Fax: (304)343-3124
Free: 800-235-5188

Publications: Coal People Magazine (33269)

Coal Valley News
PO Box 508
Madison, WV 25130
Phone: (304)369-1165
Fax: (304)369-1166

Publications: Coal Valley News (33374)

Coalgate Record-Register
115 N. Main St.
Coalgate, OK 74538-2834
Phone: (405)927-2355
Fax: (405)927-3800

Publications: Coalgate Record-Register (25793)

Coast Magazine
240 Newport Center Dr., Ste 290
Newport Beach, CA 92660
Phone: (949)644-4700
Fax: (949)644-4055

Publications: Coast Magazine (2624)

Coast Mountain News
Box 250
Hagensborg, BC, Canada V0T 1H0
Phone: (250)982-2696
Fax: (250)982-2512

Publications: Coast Mountain News (34974)

Coast Publishing Ltd.
5435 Portland Pl.
Halifax, NS, Canada B3K 6R7
Phone: (902)422-6278
Fax: (902)425-0013

Publications: The Coast (35562)

The Coast Star
13 Broad St.
Manasquan, NJ 08736
Phone: (732)223-0076
Fax: (732)223-8212

Numbers cited after listings are entry numbers rather than page numbers.

Publications: The Coast Star (19213)

Coast Weekly
668 William Ave.
Seaside, CA 93955
Phone: (831)394-5656

Publications: Coast Weekly (3750)

Coastal Carolina University
PO Box 261954
Conway, SC 29528-6054
Phone: (843)347-3161
Fax: (843)349-2317

Publications: The Chanticleer (28588)

Coastal Communications Corp.
2650 N Military Trl., Ste. 250
Boca Raton, FL 33431-6309
Phone: (561)989-0600
Fax: (561)989-9509

Publications: Corporate & Incentive Travel (5929) •
Insurance Meetings Management (5933)

The Coastal Courier
PO Box 498
Hinesville, GA 31313
Phone: (912)876-0156
Fax: (912)368-6329

Publications: The Coastal Courier (7330)

Coastal Empire Media, Inc.
5 Oglethorpe Professional Blvd., Ste. 100
Savannah, GA 31406
Phone: (912)351-9122
Fax: (912)351-9045

Publications: The Business Report & Journal (7531)

Coastal Journal
PO Box 705
Bath, ME 04530
Phone: (207)443-6241
Fax: (207)443-5605
Free: 800-649-6241

Publications: Coastal Journal (12918)

Coastal Observer
97 Commerce Dr.
PO Box 1170
Pawleys Island, SC 29585
Phone: (843)237-8438
Fax: (843)235-0084

Publications: Coastal Observer (28742)

Coastal View
4856 Carpinteria Ave.
Carpinteria, CA 93013
Phone: (805)684-4428
Fax: (805)684-4650

Publications: Coastal View (1676)

Cobblestone Publishing Co.
30 Grove St., Ste. C
Peterborough, NH 03458
Phone: (603)924-7209
Fax: (603)924-7380
Free: 800-821-0115

Publications: Appleseeds (18616) • California
Chronicles (18618) • Calliope (18619) • Cobblestone (18621) • Faces (18623) • Footsteps
(18624) • Odyssey (18626)

Cobden Sun
36 Crawford St.
PO Box 100
Cobden, ON, Canada K0J 1K0
Phone: (613)646-2380
Fax: (613)646-2700

Publications: The Cobden Sun (35740)

Cochise College
Hwy. 80 W
Douglas, AZ 85607
Phone: (602)364-0323
Fax: (602)364-0320

Publications: The Argus (685) • The Mirage (687)

The Cochran Journal Inc.
PO Box 856
Cochran, GA 31014-0856
Phone: (478)934-6303
Fax: (478)934-6800

Publications: The Cochran Journal (7178)

Cochrane Times
315-1st East
Cochrane, AB, Canada T0L 0W1
Phone: (403)932-3500
Fax: (403)932-3935

Publications: Cochrane Times (34685)

Cochran's Corner
1003 Tyler Ct.
Waldorf, MD 20602
Phone: (301)870-1664

Publications: Cochran's Corner (13771)

Coe College
1220 1st Ave. NE
Cedar Rapids, IA 52402
Phone: (319)399-8000

Publications: Coe Review (10670)

Coeur d'Alene Press
201 N. 2nd St.
Coeur d'Alene, ID 83814
Phone: (208)664-8176
Fax: (208)664-0212
Free: 800-374-5380

Publications: Coeur d'Alene Press (7844)

Coffee County News & Shopper, Inc.
213 N Peterson Ave.
Douglas, GA 31533
Phone: (912)384-9112
Fax: (912)384-4220

Publications: Coffee County News (7243) • The
Douglas Shopper (7245)

Coffeyville Community College
400 West 11th St.
Coffeyville, KS 67337
Phone: (620)251-7700
Fax: (620)251-7098

Publications: The Collegian (11387)

**Cognitive Neuroscience Institute and MIT
Press**
PO Box 274
Sharon, VT 05065-0274

Publications: Journal of Cognitive Neuroscience
(31598)

Coin Laundry Association
1315 Butterfield Rd., Ste. 212
Downers Grove, IL 60515
Phone: (630)963-5547
Fax: (630)963-5864
Free: 877-CLA-IDEA

Publications: Journal of the Coin Laundry and
Drycleaning Industry (8787)

Colby College
5500 Mayflower Hill Dr.
Waterville, ME 04901-8855
Phone: (207)872-3406
Fax: (207)872-2037

Publications: Colby (13071)

The Colby Echo
5921 Mayflower Hill
Waterville, ME 04901
Phone: (207)872-3349
Fax: (207)872-3555

Publications: Colby Echo (13072)

Colby Free Press
155 W 5th St.
Box 806
Colby, KS 67701-2312
Phone: (785)462-3963
Fax: (785)462-7749

Publications: Colby Free Press (11388)

Cold Spring Harbor Laboratory
500 Sunnyside Blvd.
Woodbury, NY 11797
Phone: (516)349-1930
Fax: (516)349-1946
Free: 800-843-4388

Publications: Genome Research (23590)

Cold Spring Harbor Laboratory Press
500 Sunnyside Blvd.
Woodbury, NY 11797-2924
Phone: (516)422-4100
Fax: (516)422-4097
Free: 800-843-4388

Publications: Learning & Memory (20484)

Cold Spring Record Inc.
PO Box 456
Cold Spring, MN 56320
Phone: (320)685-8621
Fax: (320)685-8885

Publications: Cold Spring Record (15803)

Coldwater Daily Reporter
15 W. Pearl St.
Coldwater, MI 49036-1912
Phone: (517)278-2318
Fax: (517)278-6041

Publications: Coldwater Daily Reporter (14887)

Coleopterists Society
Louisiana State University
Department of Entomology
Baton Rouge, LA 70803-1710
Phone: (225)578-1634
Fax: (225)578-1643

Publications: The Coleopterists Bulletin (12487)

Coleridge Blade
PO Box 8
Coleridge, NE 68727
Phone: (402)283-4267
Fax: (402)283-4267

Publications: Coleridge Blade (17979)

The Colfax County Press
242 Pine
PO Box 266
Clarkson, NE 68629
Phone: (402)892-3544
Fax: (402)892-3141

Publications: The Colfax County Press (17978)

Colfax Record
25 W Church
PO Box 755
Colfax, CA 95713
Phone: (916)346-2232
Fax: (916)346-2700

Publications: Colfax Record (1739)

Colgate University
13 Oak Dr.
Hamilton, NY 13346
Phone: (315)228-1000
Fax: (315)228-7798

Publications: Colgate Scene (20707)

Collectors Club Inc.
22 E 35th St.
New York, NY 10016-3806
Phone: (212)683-0559
Fax: (212)481-1269

Publications: The Collectors Club Philatelist (13672)

College of American Pathologists
325 Waukegan Rd.
Northfield, IL 60093-2750
Phone: (847)832-7000
Fax: (847)832-8150
Free: 800-323-4040

Publications: CAP Today (9325)

College Art Association
275 7th Ave.
New York, NY 10001
Phone: (212)691-1051
Fax: (212)627-2381

Publications: Art Bulletin (21251) • Art Journal
(21253)

College de Bois-de-Boulogne
10550 Boulogne
Montreal, QC, Canada H4N 1L4
Phone: (514)332-3000
Fax: (514)332-9579

Publications: L'Infomane (37128)

College of DuPage
425 Fawell Blvd.
Glen Ellyn, IL 60137
Phone: (630)942-2379
Fax: (630)942-3747

Publications: Courier (8926)

College of Eastern Utah
451 N 400 E
Price, UT 84501
Phone: (435)613-5213
Fax: (435)613-5042

Publications: The Eagle (31392)

The College of Family Physicians of Canada
2630 Skymark Ave.
Mississauga, ON, Canada L4W 5A4
Phone: (905)629-0900
Fax: (905)629-0893
Free: 800-387-6197

Publications: Canadian Family Physician (36058)

College of the Holy Cross
PO Box 32-A
Worcester, MA 01610
Phone: (508)793-2668
Fax: (508)793-3020

Publications: The Crusader (14677)

College Jean-de-Brebeuf
5625 Decelles
Montreal, QC, Canada H3T 1W4
Phone: (514)342-3663
Fax: (514)342-0693

Publications: Le Graffiti (37161)

College of Lake County
19351 W Washington St.
Grayslake, IL 60030
Phone: (847)223-3634
Fax: (847)223-9266

Publications: The Chronicle (8952)

College Language Association
Morehouse College
Atlanta, GA 30314
Phone: (404)681-2800
Fax: (404)614-3786

Publications: CLA Journal (6985)

College Marketing Bureau, Inc.
4124 Oakton St.
Skokie, IL 60076
Phone: (847)673-3703
Fax: (847)329-0358

Publications: INsider Magazine (9607)

College of New Jersey
Department of Technological Studies
103 Armstrong Hall
PO Box 7718
Ewing, NJ 08628-0718
Phone: (609)771-3332
Fax: (609)771-3330

Publications: TIES Magazine (18805)

College of Optometrists in Vision Development
243 N Lindbergh Blvd., Ste. 310
St. Louis, MO 63141
Phone: (314)991-4007
Fax: (314)991-1167
Free: 888-268-3770

Publications: Journal of Optometric Vision Development (17457)

College of the Ozarks
PO Box 17
Point Lookout, MO 65726
Phone: (417)334-6411

Publications: The Outlook (17353)

College of Physicians of Philadelphia
19 S 22nd St.
Philadelphia, PA 19103-3097
Phone: (215)563-3737
Fax: (215)569-0356

Publications: Transactions and Studies of the College of Physicians of Philadelphia (27709)

College Reading and Learning Association
University of Northern BC
3333 University Way
Prince George, BC, Canada V2N 4Z9

Publications: Journal of College Reading and Learning (35056)

College of the Redwoods
883 W Washington Blvd.
Crescent City, CA 95531
Phone: (707)465-2360
Fax: (707)464-6867

Publications: The Kerf (1787)

College Relations
Presser Hall
421 N. 1st St.
Lindsborg, KS 67456-1897
Phone: (785)227-3311
Fax: (913)227-2004

Publications: Bethany Magazine (11609)

College of Saint Benedict
37 S. College Ave.
St. Joseph, MN 56374
Phone: (320)363-5011

Publications: Studio One/HCC (16358)

College of St. Francis
500 Wilcox
Joliet, IL 60435
Phone: (815)740-3360
Fax: (815)740-4285

Publications: The Encounter (9031)

College of St. Scholastica
1200 Kenwood
Duluth, MN 55811
Phone: (218)723-6187
Fax: (218)723-6290

Publications: CSS Cable (15835)

College of Santa Fe
St. Michael's Dr.
Santa Fe, NM 87505

Publications: Countermeasures (19933)

The College Store
500 E Lorain St.
Oberlin, OH 44074-1294
Phone: (216)775-7777
Fax: (216)775-4769
Free: 800-622-7498

Publications: The College Store (25444)

College Student Affairs Journal
College of Education
Northwestern State University
Natchitoches, LA 71497
Phone: (318)357-6289
Fax: (318)357-6275

Publications: College Student Affairs Journal (12715)

College of William and Mary
Campus Center
PO Box 8795
Williamsburg, VA 23187
Phone: (757)221-3290

Publications: William and Mary Review (32624)

College of William and Mary
Williamsburg, VA 23187-8795

Publications: Chasqui (32615)

College of William and Mary
PO Box 8795
Williamsburg, VA 23187-8795
Phone: (757)221-4000

Publications: Business and Economic History (32614)

College of William and Mary School of Law
Box 8795
Williamsburg, VA 23187-8795
Phone: (757)221-4000

Publications: William & Mary Bill of Rights Journal (32621) • William and Mary Law Review (32622)

College of Wooster
Ebert Hall
Wooster, OH 44691-2363
Phone: (330)263-2000
Fax: (330)263-2594

Publications: Wooster (25673)

Collegian Reporter
Morningside College
1501 Morningside Ave.
Sioux City, IA 51106
Phone: (712)274-5801
Fax: (712)274-5664
Free: 800-831-0806

Publications: Collegian Reporter (11212)

Collegiate Baseball Newspaper, Inc.
PO Box 50566
Tucson, AZ 85703
Phone: (520)623-4530
Fax: (520)624-5501

Publications: Collegiate Baseball Newspaper (941)

Collegiate Times
363 Squires Student Ctr.
Blacksburg, VA 24060
Phone: (540)231-9860
Fax: (540)231-5057

Publications: Collegiate Times (31867)

Colleyville News and Times, Inc.
1256 Main St., Ste. 278
Southlake, TX 76092-7624

Publications: Colleyville News and Times (31122)

Collier County Publishing Co.
1075 Central Ave.
Naples, FL 34102
Phone: (239)262-3161
Fax: (239)435-3451

Publications: Naples Daily News (6445)

Lawrence J. Collins
381 Broadway
Westwood, NJ 07675
Phone: (201)358-2929
Fax: (201)358-2824

Publications: Steppin' Out Magazine (19748)

Color Printing
PO Box 5091
Columbus, MS 39704-5091

Publications: Fayette County Review (29607) • Mid-South Horse Review (16604)

Colorado Archaeological Society, Inc.
PO Box 486
Castle Rock, CO 80104
Phone: (303)814-1432
Fax: (303)753-0444

Publications: Southwestern Lore (4357)

Colorado Baptist General Convention
7393 S Alton Way
Centennial, CO 80112
Phone: (303)771-2480
Fax: (303)771-6272
Free: 888-771-2480

Publications: Rocky Mountain Baptist (4227)

Colorado Bar Association
1900 Grant St., Ste. 900
Denver, CO 80203
Phone: (303)860-1118
Fax: (303)830-3990

Publications: The Colorado Lawyer (4315)

Colorado Community Newspapers
1200 E Hwy. 24
PO Box 340
Woodland Park, CO 80863
Phone: (719)687-3006
Fax: (719)687-3009

Publications: Ute Pass Courier (4691)

Colorado Daily
2610 Pearl St.
Boulder, CO 80302
Phone: (303)443-6272
Fax: (303)443-9357

Publications: Colorado Daily (4161)

Colorado Division of Wildlife
6060 Broadway
Denver, CO 80216-1000
Phone: (303)291-7469
Fax: (303)291-7109

Publications: Colorado Outdoors (4319)

Colorado Language Arts Society
English Department
Colorado State University
Eddy Bldg.
Fort Collins, CO 80523-1773
Phone: (970)491-5264
Fax: (970)491-5601

Publications: Statement (Fort Collins) (4439)

The Colorado Leader
3480 W 1st Ave.
Denver, CO 80219
Phone: (303)922-0589
Fax: (303)922-2106

Publications: The Colorado Leader (4316)

Colorado Medical Society
7351 Lowry Blvd.
Denver, CO 80230
Phone: (720)859-1001
Free: 800-654-5653

Publications: Colorado Medicine (4317)

Colorado Municipal League
1144 Sherman St.
Denver, CO 80203-2207
Phone: (303)831-6411
Fax: (303)860-8175

Publications: Colorado Municipalities (4318)

Colorado Press Association
1336 Glenarm Pl.
Denver, CO 80204
Phone: (303)571-5117
Fax: (303)571-1803

Publications: Colorado Editor (4313)

Colorado Printing of Pueblo
447 Park Dr.
Pueblo, CO 81005
Phone: (719)561-4008
Fax: (719)561-4007

Publications: The Colorado Tribune (4598)

Colorado Record
PO Box 92
Colorado City, TX 79512
Phone: (325)728-3413
Fax: (325)728-3414

Publications: Colorado City Record (30063)

Colorado Rural Electric Association
5400 N. Washington
Denver, CO 80216
Phone: (303)455-4111
Fax: (303)455-2807

Publications: Colorado Country Life (4312)

Colorado School of Mines
Golden, CO 80401
Phone: (303)273-3690
Fax: (303)273-3199
Free: 800-245-1060

Publications: Colorado School of Mines Quarterly (4465)

Colorado School of Mines Alumni Association
PO Box 1410
Golden, CO 80401-1410
Phone: (303)273-3295
Fax: (303)273-3583
Free: 800-446-9488

Publications: Mines Magazine (4470)

Colorado School of Mines Press
Arthur Lakes Library
Golden, CO 80401
Phone: (303)273-3690
Fax: (303)273-3199
Free: 800-446-9488

Publications: Mines Oredigger (4471)

Colorado Springs Independent
121 E. Pikes Peak Ave., Ste. 455
Colorado Springs, CO 80903

Publications: Colorado Springs Independent (4243)

Colorado State University
Fort Collins, CO 80523
Phone: (970)491-5449

Publications: Colorado Review (4428)

Colorado State University
Lory Student Center Box 13
Box 13
Fort Collins, CO 80523
Phone: (970)491-1146
Fax: (970)491-1690

Publications: The Rocky Mountain Collegian (4438)

Colorado-Wyoming Academy of Science
University of Northern Colorado
Dept. of Psychology, McKee 14
Greeley, CO 80639

Publications: Journal of the Colorado-Wyoming Academy of Science (4498)

ColorsNW Magazine
1319 Dexter Ave. N. Ste. 190
Seattle, WA 98109
Phone: (206)444-9251
Fax: (206)281-7490

Publications: ColorsNW Magazine (32956)

Columbia City Publishing Co.
PO Box 128
Columbia City, IN 46725
Phone: (260)248-5112
Fax: (260)244-7598

Publications: The Post & Mail (9893)

The Columbia Club
121 Monument Cir.
Indianapolis, IN 46204
Phone: (317)767-1361
Fax: (317)638-3137
Free: 800-635-1361

Publications: The Columbian (10103)

Columbia College Center for Black Music Research
600 S Michigan Ave.
Chicago, IL 60605
Phone: (312)344-7559
Fax: (312)344-8029

Publications: Black Music Research Journal (8285) • Lenox Avenue (8460)

Columbia College Today
Columbia University
2960 Broadway
New York, NY 10027-6902
Phone: (212)854-1754

Publications: Columbia College Today (21442)

Columbia County News Times
4143 Columbia Rd., Ste. C
Martinez, GA 30907
Phone: (706)863-6165

Publications: Columbia County News Times (7426)

Columbia County Publications
195 S 15th St.
PO Box 1153
St. Helens, OR 97051
Phone: (503)397-0116
Fax: (503)397-4093

Publications: Chronicle/Sentinel-Mist (26563)

Columbia Journalism Review
2950 Broadway, Journalism Bldg.
Columbia University
New York, NY 10027
Phone: (212)854-1881
Fax: (212)854-8580

Publications: Columbia Journalism Review (21447)

Columbia Law School
435 W 116th St.
New York, NY 10027-7201
Phone: (212)854-1601
Fax: (212)854-7946

Publications: Columbia Human Rights Law Review (21444) • Columbia Law Review (21448) • Columbia Law School News (21449)

The Columbia Press
PO Box 130
Warrenton, OR 97146
Phone: (503)861-3331

Publications: The Columbia Press (26610)

Columbia Publishing
417 N 20th Ave.
Yakima, WA 98902-7008
Phone: (509)248-2452
Fax: (509)248-4056
Free: 800-900-2452

Publications: Carrot Country (33218) • Fresh Cut (33220) • Potato Country (33221) • The Tomato Magazine (33222)

The Columbia Star
PO Box 5955
Columbia, SC 29250-5955
Phone: (803)771-0219
Fax: (803)252-6397

Publications: The Columbia Star (28547)

Columbia Union Conference of Seventh-day Adventists
5427 Twin Knolls Rd.
Columbia, MD 21045
Phone: (301)596-0800
Fax: (410)997-7420

Publications: Columbia Union Visitor (13459)

Columbia University
520 Philosophy Hall
New York, NY 10027
Phone: (212)854-3208
Fax: (212)854-5863

Publications: Romanic Review (22676)

Columbia University
435 W. 116th St.
Box C-10
New York, NY 10027
Phone: (212)854-5510
Fax: (212)854-7946

Publications: Columbia Journal of Asian Law (21445)

Columbia University
Mail Code 3513
New York, NY 10027
Phone: (212)854-1606
Fax: (212)854-7946

Publications: Columbia Journal of Environmental Law (21446)

Columbia University
304 Low Library
New York, NY 10027
Phone: (212)854-3282
Fax: (212)678-4817

Publications: Columbia University Record (21450)

Columbia University School of International Public Affairs
Box 4, International Affairs Bldg.
New York, NY 10027

Publications: Journal of International Affairs (22102)

Columbia University/Spectator Publishing Co.
2875 Broadway, 3rd Fl.
New York, NY 10025
Phone: (212)854-9555
Fax: (212)854-9553

Publications: Columbia Daily Spectator (21443)

The Columbian Publishing Co.
PO Box 180
Vancouver, WA 98666
Phone: (360)694-3391
Fax: (360)699-6033

Publications: The Columbian (33175)

Columbus Alive, Inc.
1079 N High St.
Columbus, OH 43201-2439
Phone: (614)221-2449
Fax: (614)221-2456

Publications: Columbus Alive (25007)

The Columbus Gazette
209 Main St.
PO Box 267
Columbus Junction, IA 52738
Phone: (319)728-2413
Fax: (319)728-3272

Publications: The Columbus Gazette (10718)

The Columbus Medical Association
431 E. Broad St., Ste. 300
Columbus, OH 43215
Phone: (614)240-7410
Fax: (614)240-7415

Publications: Columbus Physician (25010)

Columbus Messenger Co.
3378 Sullivant Ave.
Columbus, OH 43204-1887
Phone: (614)272-5422
Fax: (614)272-0684

Publications: Eastside Messenger (25016) • Madison Messenger (25325) • Southeast Messenger (25062) • Southwest Messenger (25063) • Westside Messenger (25068)

Columbus Telegram
1254 27th Ave.
PO Box 648
Columbus, NE 68601
Phone: (402)563-7547
Fax: (402)563-7500
Free: 800-279-1123

Publications: Columbus Telegram (17981)

Columbus Times
2230 Buena Vista Rd.
PO Box 2845
Columbus, GA 31906
Phone: (706)324-0401
Fax: (706)596-0657

Publications: The Columbus Times (7183)

Combat
PO Box 3
Circleville, WV 26804

Publications: Combat (33292)

The Comer News
PO Box 7
1976 Main St.
Comer, GA 30629
Phone: (706)783-2553
Fax: (706)783-2553

Publications: The Comer News (7197)

Comic Shop News
4135 LaVista Rd., No. 610-110
Tucker, GA 30085-5003
Phone: (770)939-1364

Publications: Comic Shop News (7410)

Commandant of the Marine Corps. (PAMCN)
Headquarters - U.S. Marine Corps
Division of Public Affairs, Marine Corps News
Rm. 3134, 2 Navy Annex
Washington, DC 20380-1775
Phone: (703)614-7678
Fax: (703)614-1874

Publications: Marines Magazine (5644)

Commander Naval Reserve Force
4400 Dauphine St.
New Orleans, LA 70146-5046
Phone: (504)678-6058
Fax: (504)678-5049

Publications: Naval Reservist News (12742)

Commentator Publishing Company Ltd.
PO Box 580
Bow Island, AB, Canada T0K 0G0
Phone: (403)545-2258
Fax: (403)545-6886

Publications: The 40-Mile County Commentator (34622)

Comments from the Friends
PO Box 819
Assonet, MA 02702

Publications: Comments from the Friends (13823)

The Commercial Dispatch Publishing, Inc.
PO Box 511
Columbus, MS 39703-0511
Phone: (601)328-2424
Fax: (601)329-8937
Free: 877-328-2430

Publications: The Commercial Dispatch (16603)

Commercial Finance Association
225 W. 34th St., Ste. 1815
New York, NY 10122
Phone: (212)594-3490
Fax: (212)564-6053

Publications: The Secured Lender (22718)

The Commercial Record
280 Summer St.
Boston, MA 02210

Publications: The Commercial Record (13879)

Commercial Recorder
PO Box 11038
Fort Worth, TX 76110
Phone: (817)926-5351
Fax: (817)926-5377

Publications: Commercial Recorder (30335)

The Commercial Review
309 W Main
PO Box 1049
Portland, IN 47371
Phone: (219)726-8141
Fax: (219)726-8143

Publications: The Commercial Review (10403)

Common Ground
305 San Anselmo Ave. Ste. 313
San Anselmo, CA 94960
Phone: (415)459-4900
Fax: (415)459-4974
Free: 800-442-4922

Publications: Common Ground (3082)

Common Ground
225 Reinekers Ln., Ste. 300
Alexandria, VA 22314
Fax: (703)684-1581

Publications: Common Ground (31656)

Common Lives/Lesbian Lives
1802 7th Ave. Ct.
Iowa City, IA 52240
Phone: (319)353-6265

Publications: Common Lives/Lesbian Lives (10970)

Commonweal Foundation
475 Riverside Dr., Rm. 405
New York, NY 10115
Phone: (212)662-4200
Fax: (212)662-4183
Free: 888-495-6755

Publications: Commonweal (21458)

Commonwealth
PO Box 277
Ash Grove, MO 65604
Phone: (417)751-2322
Fax: (417)751-2322

Publications: Commonwealth (16892)

Commonwealth Business Media
400 Windsor Corporate Park
50 Millstone Rd., Ste. 200
East Windsor, NJ 08520-1415
Phone: (609)371-7700
Fax: (609)371-7885
Free: 800-221-5488

Publications: Pacific Shipper (2172)

Commonwealth Times
VCU Box 2010
Richmond, VA 23284
Phone: (804)828-1058
Fax: (804)828-9201

Publications: Commonwealth Times (32434)

Commtronics Engineering
10718 Manzanita Tr.
Dewey, AZ 86327-5304

Publications: World Scanner Report (684)

Communication Arts
110 Constitution Dr.
Menlo Park, CA 94025-1107
Phone: (650)326-6040
Fax: (650)326-1648
Free: 800-258-9111

Publications: Communication Arts (2523)

Communication Voir Inc.
355 Ste-Catherine St. W
Montreal, QC, Canada H3B 1A5
Phone: (514)848-0805
Fax: (514)848-9004

Publications: Voir (37236)

Communication Workers of America
275 Seventh Ave., 17th Fl.
New York, NY 10001
Phone: (212)633-2666
Fax: (212)633-6753

Publications: New York Generator (22444)

Communications Camping Caravaning Inc.
4545 Pierre-De Coubertin Ave.
C.P. 1000, Succursale M.
Montreal, QC, Canada H1V 3R2
Phone: (514)252-3003
Fax: (514)254-0694
Free: (866)237-3722

Publications: Camping Caravaning (37092)

Communications Engineering & Design
PO Box 266006
Highlands Ranch, CO 80163-6006
Phone: (303)470-4800
Fax: (303)470-4890

Publications: CED (Communications Engineering & Design) (4516)

Communications Famille Inc.
Family Communications Inc.
2260 des Patriotes
Laval, QC, Canada H7L 3K8
Phone: (450)622-0091
Fax: (450)622-0099

Publications: C'est Pour Quand? (37035) • Mon Bebe (37043)

Communications Ten Ltd.
197 Water St.
PO Box 2356, Sta. C
St. John's, NL, Canada A1C 6E7
Phone: (709)726-9300
Fax: (709)726-3013

Publications: Atlantic Business Magazine (35485)

Communicator
Spokane Falls Community College
3410 W. Fort George Wright Dr.
MS 3050
Spokane, WA 99224-5288
Phone: (509)533-3602
Fax: (509)533-3651

Publications: Communicator (33093)

The Communictions Office
Texas Department of Mental Health and Mental Retardation
PO Box 12668
Austin, TX 78711
Phone: (512)206-4540
Fax: (512)206-5093

Publications: Impact (Austin) (29780)

Communio-International Catholic Review
PO Box 4557
Washington, DC 20017
Phone: (202)526-0251
Fax: (202)526-1934

Publications: Communio-International Catholic Review (5427)

Community Affairs
Department of Community Affairs
318 Forum Bldg.
Harrisburg, PA 17120-0001

Publications: Community Affairs (26988)

Numbers cited after listings are entry numbers rather than page numbers.

Community College of Allegheny County
Boyce Campus
595 Beatty Rd.
Monroeville, PA 15146
Phone: (412)371-8651
Fax: (412)325-6799

Publications: The Boyce Collegian (27275)

Community Communications Corp.
38 Bellevue Ave., Ste. F
PO Box 159
Newport, RI 02840-0002
Phone: (401)847-7766
Fax: (401)846-4974
Free: 800-322-7361

Publications: Newport This Week (28372)

The Community Crier
345 Fleet St.
Plymouth, MI 48170
Phone: (313)453-6860

Publications: The Community Crier (15447)

Community Digest Multicultural Publications
1755 Robson St., Ste. 216
Vancouver, BC, Canada V6G 3B7
Phone: (604)875-8313
Fax: (604)875-0336

Publications: Community Digest, Alberta Edition (34640) • Community Digest, BC Edition (35136)

The Community Ear
300 NE Multnomah St., No. 2
Portland, OR 97232
Phone: (503)233-1353
Fax: (503)233-1460

Publications: The Community Ear (26474)

Community Gazette Inc.
597 Manhattan Ave.
Brooklyn, NY 11222
Phone: (718)389-6067
Fax: (718)349-3471

Publications: Greenpoint Gazette (20318)

Community Journal
Box 619
Wading River, NY 11792
Phone: (516)929-8882

Publications: Community Journal (23495)

Community Media Group
108 E. 5th St.
PO Box 468
Vinton, IA 52349
Phone: (319)472-2311
Fax: (319)472-4811
Free: 800-388-9335

Publications: Cedar Valley Times (11282)

Community Media LLC
487 Greenwich St., Ste. 6A
New York, NY 10013
Phone: (212)242-6162
Fax: (212)229-2790

Publications: Downtown Express (21567)

Community Media Newspapers, Inc.
112 3rd St., Box 869
Hearne, TX 77859
Phone: (409)279-3411
Fax: (409)279-5401

Publications: The Hearne Democrat (30435)

Community News
5748 Helen Ave.
St. Louis, MO 63136
Phone: (314)261-5555
Fax: (314)261-2776

Publications: Community News (17425)

Community News
22 N. Main
PO Box C
Northwood, ND 58267
Phone: (701)587-6126
Fax: (701)587-5219

Publications: Gleaner (24527)

The Community News
213 E. Oak St.
PO Box 1031
Aledo, TX 76008
Phone: (817)441-7661
Fax: (817)441-7881

Publications: The Community News (29677)

Community News Inc.
PO Box 730
Bryson City, NC 28713
Phone: (704)488-2189
Fax: (704)488-0315

Publications: Smoky Mountain Times (23666)

Community Newspaper
PO Box 1555
Cornelia, GA 30531-0190
Phone: (706)778-4215
Fax: (706)778-4114

Publications: The Northeast Georgian (7207)

Community Newspaper
923 G Rte. 6A
Yarmouth Port, MA 02675
Phone: (508)375-4945
Fax: (508)375-4903
Free: 800-660-8999

Publications: Bourne Courier (14001) • Brewster Oracle (14005) • Cape Cod News (14119) • Chatham Current (14125) • Eastham-Wellfleet Oracle (14172) • Mashpee Messenger (14311) • Orleans Oracle (14703) • The Register (14705) • Wellfleet Oracle (14622)

Community Newspaper Company
254 2nd Ave.
Needham, MA 02494
Phone: (781)433-6700
Free: 800-397-5852

Publications: Abington/Rockland Mariner (13785) • Arlington Advocate (13817) • Ashland TAB (13822) • Bedford Minuteman (13835) • Belmont Citizen-Herald (13839) • Billerica Minuteman (14349) • Boston TAB (13864) • Braintree Forum (14350) • Brookline TAB (14017) • Burlington Union (14351) • Cambridge Chronicle (14352) • Cambridge TAB (14043) • Cape Codder (14353) • Chelmsford Independent (14145) • Cohasset Mariner (14141) • Daily Transcript (14154) • Danvers Herald (14354) • Dover-Sherborn TAB (14160) • The Flyer (6354) • Framingham TAB (14196) • Hamilton-Wenham Chronicle (14225) • Hanover Mariner (14228) • Harwich Oracle (14230) • Hingham Journal (14355) • Holbrook Sun (14235) • Holliston TAB (14238) • Ipswich Chronicle (14356) • Lexington Minuteman (14147) • Lincoln Journal (14358) • Littleton Independent (14276) • Malden Observer (14323) • Marblehead Reporter (14304) • Marlborough Enterprise (14307) • Marshfield Mariner (14359) • Mass Bay Antiques (14360) • Maynard Beacon (14315) • Melrose Free Press (14328) • Metro West Daily News (14361) • Milford Daily News (14362) • Natick TAB (14348) • Needham TAB (14365) • News Tribune (14602) • Newton Graphic (14407) • Newton TAB (14367) • North Andover Citizen (14368) • North Shore Sunday (14153) • Norwell Mariner (14444) • Parkway Transcript (14369) • Pembroke Mariner (14465) • Saugus Advertiser (14324) • Scituate Mariner (14518) • Sharon Advocate (14370) • Southborough Villager (14546) • Stoughton Journal (14371) • The Sudbury Town Crier (14579) • Swampscott Reporter (14583) • Tewksbury Advertiser (14587) • Wayland Town Crier & TAB (14616) • Wellesley Townsman (14618) • The Wellesley Townsman (14372) • West Roxbury Transcript (14373) • Weston Town Crier & TAB (14652) • Weymouth News (14654) • Winchester Star (14275)

Community Newspaper Company
923G Rte. 6A
Box 400
Yarmouth Port, MA 02675
Phone: (508)375-4990
Fax: (508)375-4901

Publications: The Register (14704)

Community Newspaper Company/Northwest
150 Baker Ave., Ste. 305
PO Box 9191
Concord, MA 01742-9191
Phone: (978)371-5754
Fax: (978)371-9058

Publications: The Beacon (14144) • The Westford Eagle (14646) • Woburn Advocate (14149)

Community Newspaper Holdings
116 N. Main St.
Albion, NY 14411-1232
Fax: (716)589-4488

Publications: Albion Advertiser (20019)

Community Newspaper Holdings, Inc
3500 Colonnade Pkwy., Ste 600
Birmingham, AL 35243
Phone: (205)298-7100
Fax: (205)298-7101

Publications: The Chronicle-Express (23092) • Norris City Banner (9311) • The Ottumwa Courier (11140)

Community Newspaper Holdings, Inc.
3800 Colonade Pkwy., Ste. 450
Birmingham, AL 35243
Phone: (205)298-7100
Fax: (205)298-7101

Publications: Altus Times (25730) • Athens Daily Review (29746) • Booneville Democrat (1063) • Borger News-Herald (29937) • Cedar Creek Pilot (30009) • Chico Enterprise-Record (1692) • Clinton Herald (10710) • The Daily Herald (29136) • Daily Siftings Herald (1030) • The Daily World (32647) • Ely Daily Times (18340) • Express-Star (25785) • Gainesville Daily Register (30376) • Glasgow Daily Times (12090) • Guymon Daily Herald (25855) • Henryetta Daily Free-Lance (25863) • Kilgore News Herald (78) • Las Vegas Review-Journal (18374) • The Morning News of Northwest Arkansas (1327) • The Norman Transcript (25937) • Orchid Isle Television (84) • The Oskaloosa Herald (11134) • Pauls Valley Daily Democrat (26029) • Pawhuska Journal-Capital (26030) • Picayune Item (16819) • Pine Bluff Commercial (1314) • The Ridgway Record (27935) • Southwest Times Record (1143) • Ukiah Daily Journal (3967) • Vallejo Times-Herald (3984) • Washington Times-Herald (10540) • Weatherford Democrat (31273) • West Hawaii Today (7766)

Community Newspaper Holdings, Inc.
3500 Colonnade Pkwy., Ste. 600
Birmingham, AL 35243
Phone: (205)298-7100
Fax: (205)298-7102

Publications: Alamogordo Daily News (19758) • The Chronicle (11151) • Cleburne Times-Review (30025) • The Daily Herald (7429) • Durant Daily Democrat (25804) • The Sampson Independent (23789) • Stanly News and Press (23618) • The Union-Recorder (7436)

Community Newspaper Holdings, Inc.
120 Wilson St.
PO Box 190
Russell Springs, KY 42642
Phone: (502)866-3191
Fax: (502)866-3198

Publications: The Times Journal (12387)

Community Newspaper Holdings, Inc.
121 W 5th St.
PO Box 1028
Lumberton, NC 28359
Phone: (910)739-4322
Fax: (910)739-6553

Publications: The Robesonian (24051)

Community Newspaper Holdings, Inc.
200 W. Front Ave.
PO Box 1028
Orange, TX 77630-0128
Phone: (409)883-3571
Fax: (409)883-6342

Publications: Opportunity Valley News (30887) • The Orange Leader (30888)

Community Newspapers
1467 Marion St.
PO Box 128
Kingsburg, CA 93631
Phone: (209)897-2993
Fax: (209)897-4868

Publications: Recorder (2106)

Community Newspapers
PO Box 43-1970
Miami, FL 33143
Phone: (305)669-0419
Fax: (305)661-0954

Publications: Coral Gables News (6005) • Hialea-Opa Locka News (6359) • Kendall News (6250) • Miami Shores News (6371) • North Miami Beach News (6468) • Palmetto Bay News (6204) • Pinecrest Tribune (6375) • South Miami News (6381)

Community Newspapers
152 Sylvan St.
Danvers, MA 01923-3568
Phone: (617)233-2040
Fax: (617)231-8064

Publications: Advertiser (14152)

Community Newspapers
239 S. Cochran
Charlotte, MI 48813
Phone: (517)543-9913
Fax: (517)543-3677
Free: 800-543-9913

Publications: Charlotte Shopping Guide (14866) • The Clinton County News (15509) • Delta Waverly Community News (14867) • DeWitt Bath Review (14868) • Eaton Rapids Community News (14869) • The Grand Ledge Independent (14870)

Community Newspapers
PO Box 250
Andrews, NC 28901
Phone: (828)321-4271
Fax: (828)321-5890

Publications: The Andrews Journal (23619)

Community Newspapers
PO Box 249
Highlands, NC 28741
Phone: (828)526-4114
Fax: (828)526-3658

Publications: The Highlander (24008)

Community Newspapers
111 A Ave.
PO Box 548
Lake Oswego, OR 97034
Phone: (503)635-8811
Fax: (503)635-8817

Publications: Lake Oswego Review (26404) • West Linn Tidings (26611)

Community Newspapers
1325 SW Custer Dr.
Portland, OR 97219-2750

Publications: Beaverton Valley Times (26470) • Tigard Times (26596)

Community Newspapers
PO Box 1389
Cheraw, SC 29520
Phone: (803)537-5261
Fax: (803)537-4518

Publications: The Cheraw Chronicle (28527)

Community Newspapers
PO Box 880
Marion, SC 29571
Phone: (803)423-4002
Fax: (803)423-2542

Publications: Lake City News & Post (28688)

Community Newspapers
PO Box 40
Dyersburg, TN 38025-0040
Phone: (901)287-1555
Fax: (901)287-1551

Publications: Dyersburg News (29174)

Community Newspapers
460 W. Main St.
Wytheville, VA 24382
Phone: (276)228-6611
Fax: (276)228-7260
Free: 800-655-1406

Publications: Enterprise Buyers' Catalogue (32642) • Smyth County News & Messenger (32226)

Community Newspapers, Inc.
225 E. Hancock Ave.
Athens, GA 30601
Phone: (706)548-0010
Fax: (706)548-0808
Free: 800-226-0692

Publications: The Hartwell Sun (7321)

Community Newspapers Inc.
PO Box 225
Dawsonville, GA 30534
Phone: (706)265-2345
Fax: (706)265-7842

Publications: Dawson News & Advertiser (7232)

Community Newspapers Inc.
707 Osborne St.
Box 470
St. Marys, GA 31558
Phone: (912)882-4927
Fax: (912)882-6519

Publications: Tribune & Georgian (7524)

Community Newspapers Inc.
240 Elm St., Ste. 22
Somerville, MA 02144
Phone: (617)628-3380
Fax: (617)629-3381

Publications: Dollar Saver (14533) • Newsweekly (14537)

Community Newspapers, Inc.
PO Box 190
Murphy, NC 28906
Phone: (828)837-5122

Publications: Cherokee Scout (24088)

Community Newspapers, Inc.
105 E. Washington St.
Rockingham, NC 28379
Phone: (919)997-3111
Fax: (919)997-4321

Publications: Richmond County Daily Journal (24201)

Community Newspapers Inc.
200 Lee Ave.
PO Box 625
Hampton, SC 29924
Phone: (803)943-4645
Fax: (803)943-9365

Publications: Hampton County Guardian (28655)

Community Post
PO Box 155
Minster, OH 45865-0155
Phone: (419)628-2369
Fax: (419)628-4712

Publications: Community Post (25394)

Community Publications
520 6th St.
PO Box 285
Armstrong, IA 50514
Phone: (712)868-3460

Publications: The Armstrong Journal (10607) • Pocahontas County Advertiser (11161) • Pocahontas Record Democrat (11162) • The Ringsted Dispatch (10608)

Community Publications
216 Main St.
PO Box 485
Odebolt, IA 51458
Phone: (712)668-2253
Fax: (712)668-4364
Free: 800-397-8317

Publications: The Chronicle (11122)

Community Publications of America Inc.
55 W 14th St., No. 17D
New York, NY 10011-7400
Phone: (212)243-6800
Fax: (212)243-7457

Publications: Buying & Dining Guide (21364) • TV News (22877)

Community Publishers, Inc.
PO Box 1049
Bentonville, AR 72712
Phone: (479)271-3726
Fax: (479)273-7777

Publications: The Herald-Leader (1050) • Neighbor Shopper (1051) • Rogers Hometown News (1328) • The Weekly Vista (1046)

Community Publishers, Inc.
PO Box 7
Decatur, AR 72722
Fax: (501)524-3612

Publications: Decatur Herald (1104)

Community Publishers, Inc./Missouri
335 S Springfield
PO Box 330
Bolivar, MO 65613-0330
Phone: (417)326-7636
Fax: (417)326-8701

Publications: Bolivar Herald-Free Press (16911)

Community Publishing Co.
238 E Main St.
Gas City, IN 46933
Phone: (765)674-0070

Publications: Twin City Journal-Reporter (10020)

Community Quest
5787 South Hampton, Ste. 330-LB116
Dallas, TX 75232
Phone: (214)330-5065
Fax: (214)330-5046

Publications: Community Quest (30138)

Community Renewal Society
332 S Michigan Ave., Ste. 500
Chicago, IL 60604-9863
Phone: (312)427-4830
Fax: (312)427-6130

Publications: The Chicago Reporter (8320)

Community Service Publications
PO Box 211
Whitmire, SC 29178
Phone: (803)694-4444
Fax: (803)694-4444

Publications: The Whitmire News (28785)

Community Shoppers Guide Inc.
117 N Farmer St.
PO Box 168
Otsego, MI 49078-0168
Phone: (269)694-9431
Fax: (269)694-9145

Publications: Shoppers Guide (15426)

Community Shoppers, Inc.
120 N. Wright St.
PO Box 367
Delavan, WI 53115-0367
Phone: (262)728-3424
Fax: (262)728-5479

Publications: The Janesville Sunday Messenger (33859) • Stateline Shopping News (33577) • Walworth County Shopper Advertiser & Shopper Sunday (33654)

Community Spirit Publications
Box 4628
Carmel, CA 93921
Phone: (831)625-1557
Fax: (831)625-3424

Publications: Community Spirit Magazine (Carmel) (1671)

The Community Voice
PO Box 2038
Rohnert Park, CA 94927
Phone: (707)584-2222
Fax: (707)584-2233

Publications: The Community Voice (2961)

Community Voice
3046 Lafayette St.
Fort Myers, FL 33916-4324

Publications: Community Voice (6095)

Community Webb Inc.
PO Box 370
Arlington, SD 57212
Phone: (605)983-5491
Fax: (605)983-5715

Publications: Arlington Sun (28803)

Commuter Air International
6151 Powers Ferry Rd. NW
Atlanta, GA 30339-2941
Fax: (404)618-0343

Publications: Commuter Air International (6988)

Comox Valley Record
PO Box 3729
Courtenay, BC, Canada V9N 7P1
Phone: (250)338-5811
Fax: (250)338-5568

Publications: Comox Valley Record (34931)

Compagnie d'Edition Andre Paquette Inc.
299 est, rue Principale
C.P. 1000
Hawkesbury, ON, Canada K6A 3H1
Phone: (613)632-4155
Fax: (613)632-8601
Free: 800-267-0850

Publications: Le Carillon (35907)

Compagnie d'edition Andre-Paquette Inc.
299 Main St. E
PO Box 1000
Hawkesbury, ON, Canada K6A 3H1
Phone: (613)632-4155
Fax: (613)632-8601
Free: 800-267-0850

Publications: Le Journal de Cornwall (35753) • The Tribune/Express (35908)

Compagnie d'edition Andre Paquette, Inc.
52, rue Principale
PO Box 220
Lachute, QC, Canada J8H 3A8
Phone: (450)562-8593
Fax: (450)562-1434
Free: 800-561-5738

Publications: Tribune Express Progres Watchman (37030)

Comparative Legislative Research Center
University of Iowa
334 Schaeffer Hall
Iowa City, IA 52242
Phone: (319)335-2361
Fax: (319)335-3211

Publications: Legislative Studies Quarterly (10980)

Comparative Toxicology Laboratories
Kansas State University
1800 Denison Ave. M213 Morier Hall
Manhattan, KS 66506-5705
Phone: (785)532-4334
Fax: (785)532-4481

Publications: Veterinary and Human Toxicology (11630)

Compass Publications, Inc.
1501 Wilson Blvd., Ste. 1001
Arlington, VA 22209-2403
Phone: (703)524-3136
Fax: (703)841-0852

Publications: Sea Technology (31831)

Compass Publications, Inc., Fisheries Division
PO Box 37
Stonington, ME 04681
Phone: (207)367-2396
Fax: (207)367-2490
Free: 800-989-5253

Publications: Commercial Fisheries News (13062) • Fish Farming News (13063) • Marine Performance and Fisheries Product News (13065)

Compassion Publishing, Ltd.
3315 N. 124th St. Ste. J
Brookfield, WI 53005
Phone: (262)317-3493
Fax: (262)783-2360

Publications: Reclaiming Children and Youth (28885)

Composites Fabricators Association
1010 N. Globe Rd., Ste. 450
Arlington, VA 22201
Phone: (703)525-0511
Fax: (703)525-0743

Publications: Composites Fabrication (31783)

Compressed Air
253 E.Washington Ave.
Washington, NJ 07882-2495
Phone: (908)850-7817
Fax: (908)689-3095

Publications: Compressed Air (19706)

Compressor Tech. Two
20855 Watertown Rd.
Waukesha, WI 53186-1873
Phone: (414)784-9177
Fax: (414)784-8133

Publications: Compressor Tech Two (34400)

Comprint Military Publications
9030 Comprint Court
Gaithersburg, MD 20877
Phone: (301)921-2800

Publications: Pentagram (31816)

Computer Assisted Language Instruction
214 Centennial Hall
601 University Dr.
San Marcos, TX 78666
Phone: (512)245-1417
Fax: (512)245-9089

Publications: CALICO (31083)

Computer Bits
PO Box 2695
Clackamas, OR 97015-2695

Publications: Computer Bits (26266)

Computer Law Reporter
1601 Connecticut Ave., NW, No. 602
Washington, DC 20009
Phone: (202)462-5755
Fax: (202)328-2430

Publications: Computer Law Reporter (5431)

Computer Living/New York
PO Box 1252
Bronx, NY 10471
Phone: (718)601-1326
Fax: (718)601-4165

Publications: Computer Living/New York (20264)

Computer Output Printing, Inc.
4101 Dorectors Row
Houston, TX 77092-8703
Phone: (713)666-0911
Fax: (713)666-0957

Publications: COPI Press (30465)

Computer Publishing Group, Inc.
PMB 283
258 Harvard St.
Brookline, MA 02446-2904
Phone: (617)641-9101
Fax: (617)641-9102

Publications: Server/Workstation Expert (14025) • Server/Workstation Expert (14024) • WebServer On-Line (14026)

Computer Reporter Inc.
12424 Lamar Ave.
Overland Park, KS 66209-2703
Phone: (913)341-6881
Fax: (913)341-3890

Publications: KC Computer User (11718)

Computer Times
3206 Kings Ct.
Bardstown, KY 40004
Phone: (502)349-1664

Publications: Computer Times (11925)

ComputerTalk Associates, Inc.
492 Norristown Rd., Ste. 160
Blue Bell, PA 19422-2355
Phone: (610)825-7686
Fax: (610)825-7641

Publications: ComputerTalk for the Pharmacist (26723)

ComputerUser.com, Inc.
3020 El Cerrito Plz., No. 404
El Cerrito, CA 94530
Free: 800-365-7773

Publications: Computer Currents (1860)

ComputorEdge Magazine
PO Box 83086
San Diego, CA 92138
Phone: (858)573-0315
Fax: (858)573-0205

Publications: ComputorEdge (3133)

Comstock Publishing, Inc.
3090 Fite Cir., Ste. 101
Sacramento, CA 95827
Phone: (916)364-1000
Fax: (916)364-0280

Publications: Comstock's Business Magazine (2993)

Comtech Group
360 Hunyadi Ave.
Fairfield, CT 06430

Publications: MacII Review (4791)

Concepts Travel Media Ltd.
282 Richmond St. E., Ste. 100
Toronto, ON, Canada M5A 1P4
Phone: (416)365-1500
Fax: (416)365-1504
Free: 800-727-1429

Publications: Travelweek (36773)

Conchologists of America
1222 Holsworth Ln.
Louisville, KY 40222-6616
Phone: (502)423-0469

Publications: American Conchologist (12210)

Conciliar Press
PO Box 76
Ben Lomond, CA 95005
Phone: (831)336-5118
Fax: (831)336-8882
Free: 800-967-7377

Publications: AGAIN Magazine (1486)

Concord Feminist Health Center
38 S Main St.
Concord, NH 03301
Phone: (603)225-2739
Fax: (603)228-6255

Publications: WomenWise (18475)

Concord Monitor
1 Monitor Dr.
PO Box 1177
Concord, NH 03302-1177
Phone: (603)224-5301
Fax: (603)224-8120

Publications: Concord Monitor (18471)

Concord Publishing House, Inc.
301 Broadway
PO Box 699
Cape Girardeau, MO 63701
Phone: (573)335-6611
Fax: (573)334-7288
Free: 800-879-1210

Publications: Sioux Valley News (10723) • Southeast Missourian (16945) • Southeast Missourian Plus (16946)

Concordant Publishing Concern Inc.
15570 Knochaven Rd.
Santa Clarita, CA 91387
Phone: (661)252-2112
Fax: (661)252-2112

Publications: Unsearchable Riches (3680)

Concordia College
FPO 104, Concordia College 901 8th St. S.
Moorhead, MN 56562
Phone: (218)299-3826
Fax: (218)299-4143

Publications: The Concordian (16188)

Concordia Publishing House
3558 S. Jefferson Ave.
St. Louis, MO 63118
Phone: (314)268-1000
Fax: (314)268-1329
Free: 800-325-3381

Publications: Happy Times (17442) • Portals of Prayer (17484)

The Concordia Sentinel
PO Box 1485
Ferriday, LA 71334
Phone: (318)757-3646
Fax: (318)757-3001

Publications: The Concordia Sentinel (12579)

Concordia Theological Seminary
6600 N Clinton
Fort Wayne, IN 46825
Phone: (260)452-2172
Fax: (260)452-2270

Publications: Concordia Theological Quarterly (9966)

The Concordian, Inc.
714 S Main St.
PO Box 999
Concordia, MO 64020-0999
Phone: (660)463-7522
Fax: (660)463-7942

Publications: The Concordian (17026)

Concourse Communications
1175 Shaw Ave., Ste. 104
PMB 304
Clovis, CA 93612
Phone: (559)322-2215
Fax: (559)322-2219

Publications: California Legionnaire (1732)

Conde Nast Publications, Inc.
4 Times Sq., 17th Fl.
New York, NY 10036
Phone: (212)286-3700
Fax: (212)286-5960

Publications: Allure (21174) • Architectural Digest (2214) • Bon Appetit (2224) • Bride's Magazine (21339) • Conde Nast Traveler (21481) • Glamour (21764) • Gourmet-The Magazine of Good Living (21776) • GQ (Gentlemen's Quarterly) (21777) • Lucky (22269) • The New Yorker (22457) • SELF Magazine (22722) • Vanity Fair (22895) • Vogue (22903)

The Conference Board Inc.
845 3rd Ave.
New York, NY 10022-6679
Phone: (212)759-0900
Fax: (212)980-7014

Publications: Across the Board (21144) • HR Executive Review (21825)

Conference of Educational Administrators Serving the Deaf
800 Florida Ave. NE
Washington, DC 20002
Phone: (202)651-5488
Fax: (202)651-5489

Publications: American Annals of the Deaf (5323)

Confrontation/Change Review
3955 Denlinger Rd.
Dayton, OH 45426
Phone: (513)837-0498
Fax: (513)837-5888

Publications: Confrontation/Change Review (25112)

Cong Thuong
PO Box 1975
New York, NY 10013
Phone: (212)434-6580
Fax: (212)434-6580

Publications: Cong Thuong (21482)

Congregation of Blessed Sacrament
5384 Wilson Mills Rd.
Cleveland, OH 44143-3092
Phone: (440)449-2103
Fax: (440)449-3862

Publications: Emmanuel (24891)

Congregation of Marians
Eden Hill
Stockbridge, MA 01263
Phone: (413)298-3691
Fax: (413)298-3583
Free: 800-462-7426

Publications: Roze Maryi (14568)

Congregational Library
14 Beacon St.
Boston, MA 02108
Phone: (617)523-0470
Fax: (617)523-0491

Publications: Congregational Library Bulletin (13881)

Congressional Digest Corp.
3231 P St. NW
Washington, DC 20007-2772
Phone: (202)333-7332
Fax: (202)625-6670

Publications: Congressional Digest (5434) • Supreme Court Debates (5808)

Congressional Quarterly
1414 22nd St. NW
Washington, DC 20037
Phone: (202)887-8605
Fax: 800-380-3810
Free: 800-432-2250

Publications: Congress in Print (5432) • The CQ Researcher (5447) • CQ Weekly (5448)

Conley Publishing
805 Park Ave.
Beaver Dam, WI 53916
Phone: (920)887-8790

Publications: The Daily News (34445)

Conley Publishing Co.
7000 E. Tanque Verde
Tucson, AZ 85715
Phone: (520)721-2929
Fax: (520)721-8665

Publications: Tucson Lifestyle Magazine (968)

Conley Publishing Company
212 E Wisconsin Ave.
Oconomowoc, WI 53066
Phone: (262)567-5511
Fax: (262)567-4422

Publications: Lake Area Sunday Post (34202)

Connaught Press, Inc.
225 Long Ave, No. 15
PO Box 278
Hillside, NJ 07205

Publications: Modern Nutrition News (18879)

Conneautville Courier
4177 Perry Hwy. Rte. 19
Cochranton, PA 16314
Phone: (814)587-2033
Fax: (814)587-3720

Publications: Area Shopper (26794) • Conneautville Courier (26795)

Connecticut Ancestry Society, Inc.
Box 249
Stamford, CT 06904

Publications: Connecticut Ancestry (5144)

Connecticut Bar Associaiton
30 Bank St.
PO Box 350
New Britain, CT 06050-0350
Phone: (860)223-4400
Fax: (860)223-4488

Publications: Connecticut Bar Journal (4973) • Connecticut Lawyer (4974)

Connecticut College
270 Mohegan Ave.
PO Box 4970
New London, CT 06320
Phone: (860)439-2650
Fax: (860)439-2843

Publications: The College Voice (5016) • The Connecticut College Journal (5017)

Connecticut Department of Economic and Community Development
505 Hudson St.
Hartford, CT 06106
Phone: (860)270-8000
Fax: (860)270-8188
Free: 888-860-GOCT

Publications: Connecticut Housing Production and Permit Authorized Construction (4887)

Connecticut Jewish Ledger
740 N Main St.
West Hartford, CT 06117
Phone: (860)231-2424
Fax: (860)231-2428
Free: 800-286-6397

Publications: Connecticut Jewish Ledger (5202)

Connecticut Law Review Association
65 Elizabeth St.
Hartford, CT 06105-2290

Publications: Connecticut Law Review (4888)

Connecticut Magazine
35 Nutmeg Dr.
Trumbull, CT 06611
Phone: (203)380-6600
Fax: (203)380-6610

Publications: Connecticut Magazine (5181)

Connecticut Motor Club AAA
2276 Whitney Ave.
Hamden, CT 06518-3505
Phone: (203)765-4222

Publications: Connecticut Traveler (4880)

Connecticut Parent Magazine
420 E. Main St., Ste. 18
Branford, CT 06405

Publications: Connecticut Parent Magazine (4708)

Connecticut Pharmacists Association
35 Cold Spring Rd., Ste. 125
Rocky Hill, CT 06067-3167
Phone: (860)563-4619
Fax: (860)257-8241

Publications: Connecticut Pharmacist (5106)

Connecticut Poetry Society
PO Box 4053
Waterbury, CT 06704-0053
Phone: (203)753-7815
Fax: (203)753-1703

Publications: Connecticut River Review (5191)

Connecticut Post
410 State St.
Bridgeport, CT 06604-4501
Free: 800-423-8058

Publications: Business Woman (4712) • Connecticut Post (4713)

Connecticut State Medical Society
160 St. Ronan St.
New Haven, CT 06511
Phone: (203)865-0587
Fax: (203)865-4997

Publications: Connecticut Medicine (4986)

Connecticut's County Kids
877 Post Rd. E
Westport, CT 06880-5224
Phone: (203)226-8877
Fax: (203)221-7540

Publications: Connecticut's County Kids (5212)

The Connection
129 S 6th St.
Box 449
Seward, NE 68434
Phone: (402)643-3676
Fax: (402)643-6774

Publications: The Connection (18275)

Connection Newspapers, LLC
7913 Westpark Dr.
Mc Lean, VA 22102-4201
Phone: (703)821-5050
Fax: (703)917-0991

Publications: The Burke/Fairfax Station Connection (31908) • CentreView (31910) • The Fairfax Connection (32015) • The Great Falls Connection (32118) • The Herndon Connection (32246) • The Loudoun Connection (32248) • The Mc Lean Connection (32249) • The Reston Connection (32253) • The Springfield Connection (32551) • The Vienna/Oakton Connection (32584)

Connection Publishing, Inc.
10220 River Rd., No. 303
Potomac, MD 20854
Phone: (301)983-3350

Publications: Potomac/Bethesda Almanac (13658)

Connection Publishing, Inc.
1610 King St.
Alexandria, VA 22314
Phone: (703)549-7185
Fax: (703)549-9655

Publications: Alexandria Gazette Packet (31633) • Mt. Vernon Gazette (31710)

ConnectPress, Ltd.
2530 Camino Entrada
Santa Fe, NM 87505-4835
Phone: (505)474-5150
Fax: (505)474-5001

Publications: PRO/E (19942) • SOLID Solutions Magazine (19946)

Connell Communications Inc.
86 Elm St.
Peterborough, NH 03458-1052
Phone: (603)924-7271
Fax: (603)924-7013

Publications: CD Review (18620) • Take One (18631) • Video Event (18632)

Connersville News Examiner
406 Central Ave.
PO Box 287
Connersville, IN 47331-0287
Phone: (765)825-0585
Fax: (765)825-4599
Free: 888-906-1700

Publications: Connersville News-Examiner (9900) • Whitewater Valley Market Guide (9902)

Conolly Publishing Ltd.
1 Young St.
PO Box 1030
Brighton, ON, Canada K0K 1H0
Phone: (613)475-0255
Fax: (613)475-4546
Free: 800-267-8012

Publications: Brighton Independent (35707)

Conrad N. Hilton College
4407 Oak Trl. Ct.
Sugar Land, TX 77479
Phone: (713)743-2458
Fax: (713)743-2427

Publications: Asia Pacific Journal of Tourism Research (31136)

Conscious Choice Subscriptions
920 N. Franklin St., Ste. 202
Chicago, IL 60610
Phone: (312)440-4373
Fax: (312)751-3973

Publications: Conscious Choice (8342)

Conservation Federation of Missouri
728 W Main
Jefferson City, MO 65101
Phone: (573)634-2322
Fax: (573)634-8205
Free: 800-575-2322

Publications: Missouri Wildlife (17130)

Conservation Law Foundation
62 Summer St.
Boston, MA 02110
Phone: (617)350-0990
Fax: (617)350-4030

Publications: Conservation Matters (13883)

The Conservative News
919.5 W Washtenaw St.
PO Box 11099
Lansing, MI 48901

Publications: The Conservative News (15274)

Conservative Publishing Co.
Box 271
Tipton, IA 52772
Phone: (319)886-2131
Fax: (319)886-6466

Publications: Clarence-Lowden Sun News (11268) • The Tipton Conservative and Advertiser (11269)

Conservatory of American Letters
PO Box 298
Thomaston, ME 04861
Phone: (207)354-0998
Fax: (207)354-8953
Free: 877-594-9116

Publications: Northwoods Journal (13066)

The Conshohocken Recorder
6220 Ridge Ave.
Philadelphia, PA 19128
Phone: (215)483-7300
Fax: (215)483-2073

Publications: The Coshohocken Recorder (26803)

Consolate General of Sweden in New York
1 Dag Hammarskjold Plz., 45th Fl.
New York, NY 10017-2201
Phone: (212)583-2550
Fax: (212)755-2732

Publications: Fresh From Sweden (21736)

Consolidated Marketing Services Inc.
Drop Shipping News
PO Box 7838
New York, NY 10150
Phone: (212)688-8797

Publications: Drop Shipping News (21570)

Consolidated Publishing
926 Ross St.
PO Box 67
Heflin, AL 36264
Phone: (256)463-2872
Fax: (256)463-7127
Free: 800-408-2872

Publications: The Cleburne News (266)

Consolidated Publishing Co., Inc.
4 Sylacauga Hwy.
PO Box 977
Talladega, AL 35160
Phone: (205)362-1000
Fax: (205)249-4315

Publications: The Daily Home (465)

Consolidating Publishing
203 Pelham Rd. S
Jacksonville, AL 36265
Phone: (256)435-5021
Fax: (256)435-1028

Publications: The Jacksonville News (294)

Consort Enterprise
Box 129
Prospect Ave. & Mary St.
Consort, AB, Canada T0C 1B0
Phone: (403)577-3337
Fax: (403)577-3611

Publications: Consort Enterprise (34689)

Constitutional Commentary, Inc.
229 19th Ave. S.
Minneapolis, MN 55455

Publications: Constitutional Commentary (16070)

Construction Alberta News
10536 106 St.
Edmonton, AB, Canada T5H 2X6
Fax: (403)425-5886

Publications: Construction Alberta News (34707)

Construction Association of Michigan
43636 Woodward Ave.
PO Box 3204
Bloomfield Hills, MI 48302-3204
Phone: (248)972-1000
Fax: (248)972-1001

Publications: CAM Magazine (14828)

Construction Bulletin
9443 Science Ctr. Dr.
New Hope, MN 55428-3636
Phone: (763)537-1122
Fax: (763)537-1363
Free: 888-296-9945

Publications: Construction Bulletin Magazine (16206)

Construction Digest
5804 W 74th St.
Indianapolis, IN 46278
Phone: (317)293-6860
Fax: (317)293-7840
Free: 888-893-6860

Publications: Construction Digest (10104)

Construction Equipment Guide
470 Maryland Dr.
Fort Washington, PA 19034
Phone: (215)885-2900
Fax: (215)885-2910
Free: 800-523-2200

Publications: Construction Equipment Guide-Northeast (26925)

Construction Financial Management Association
29 Emmons Dr., Ste. F-50
Princeton, NJ 08540
Phone: (609)452-8000
Fax: (609)452-0417

Publications: C.F.M.A. Building Profits (19456)

Construction Industries of Massachusetts
1500 Providence Hwy.
PO Box 667
Norwood, MA 02062
Phone: (617)551-0182
Fax: (617)551-0916

Publications: CIM Construction Journal (14445)

Construction Labor News
2102 Almaden Rd., Ste. 204
San Jose, CA 95125-2194
Phone: (408)265-6280
Fax: (408)265-7371

Publications: Construction Labor News (3514)

Construction Market Data Canada, Inc.
280 Yorkland Blvd.
North York, ON, Canada M2J 4Z6
Phone: (416)494-4990
Fax: (416)756-2767

Publications: Daily Commercial News and Construction Record (36126)

Construction News
24 Crownpoint Rd.
Little Rock, AR 72227-2930

Publications: Construction News (1227)

Construction Publications, Inc.
829-2nd Ave. S.E.
PO Box 1689
Cedar Rapids, IA 52403
Phone: (319)366-1597
Fax: (319)362-8808

Publications: Construction Equipment Operation and Maintenance (10672)

The Construction Specifications Institute
99 Canal Center Plz., Ste. 300
Alexandria, VA 22314
Fax: (703)684-8436
Free: 800-689-2900

Publications: The Construction Specifier (31658)

Consultants CGEI, Inc.
3281 Jean-Beraud Ave.
Laval, QC, Canada H7T 2L2
Phone: (514)334-5912
Fax: (450)688-6269

Publications: Touring (37044)

Consumer Alert
1001 Connecticut Ave. NW, Ste. 1128
Washington, DC 20006
Phone: (202)467-5809
Fax: (202)467-5814

Publications: Consumer Comments (5438)

Consumer Communications Industries
1720 Dixie Hwy.
Louisville, KY 40210
Phone: (502)772-2591
Fax: (502)775-8655

Publications: Louisville Defender (12229)

Consumer & Community Publishing, Inc.
PO Box 399
Berlin, NJ 08009-0399
Phone: (856)767-1640
Fax: (856)768-4320

Publications: The Journal (18674)

Consumer Connection
30 Nick Rd.
Middlebury, CT 06762-2110

Publications: Consumer Connection (4942)

Consumer News
110 Main St.
PO Box 5548
Cortland, NY 13045
Phone: (607)756-5665
Fax: (607)756-5665

Publications: Consumer News (20511)

Consumer Publications Inc.
292 St. Joseph Blvd. W.
Montreal, QC, Canada H2V 2N7
Phone: (514)272-5555
Fax: (514)273-0797

Publications: Lemon-Aid (37174)

Consumers Digest Inc.
8001 N. Lincoln Ave.
Skokie, IL 60077-3657
Phone: (847)763-9200
Fax: (847)763-0200
Free: 800-727-4438

Publications: CONSUMERS DIGEST (9604) • Your Money (9613)

Consumers' Guide
44 Pitt St.
Cornwall, ON, Canada K6J 3P3
Phone: (613)933-3160
Fax: (613)933-7521

Publications: Smart Shoppers (35754)

Consumers' Research
800 Maryland Ave. NE
Washington, DC 20002
Phone: (202)546-1713
Fax: (202)546-1638

Publications: Consumers' Research (5439)

Consumers Union of U.S., Inc.
101 Truman Ave.
Yonkers, NY 10703-1057
Phone: (914)378-2000
Fax: (914)378-2904
Free: 800-234-2188

Publications: Consumer Reports (23598) • Zillions (23604)

Contact
PO Box 288
Perham, MN 56573
Phone: (218)346-5900
Fax: (218)346-5901

Publications: Contact (16264)

CONTACT
8 Wing/CFB Trenton
PO Box 1000
STN Forces, Ste. 40
Astra, ON, Canada K0K 3W0
Phone: (613)965-7248
Fax: (613)965-7490

Publications: CONTACT (36824)

Contact Information
200 Highpoint Dr., Ste. 215
Chalfont, PA 18914
Phone: (215)822-7935
Fax: (215)997-9582
Free: 888-447-4478

Publications: HealthQuest (26767)

Contemporary Graphics Ltd.
PO Box 760
Didsbury, AB, Canada T0M 0W0
Phone: (403)335-3301
Fax: (403)335-8143

Publications: The Didsbury Review (34694)

Contemporary Media, Inc.
460 Tennessee St.
Memphis, TN 38103
Phone: (901)521-9000
Fax: (901)521-0129

Publications: The Memphis Flyer (29375) • Memphis Magazine (29376)

Contemporary Record Society
724 Winchester Rd.
Broomall, PA 19008
Phone: (610)544-5920
Fax: (610)544-5921

Publications: Contemporary Record Society News Magazine (26735)

Continental Features/Continental News Service
501 W Broadway, Plz. A
PMB No. 265
San Diego, CA 92101
Phone: (858)492-8696

Publications: Continental Newstime (3136)

Continuing Education of the Bar
300 Frank H. Ogawa Plz., Ste. 410
Oakland, CA 94612
Phone: (510)302-2000
Fax: (510)302-2001
Free: 800-232-3444

Publications: California Business Law Reporter (2672) • Real Property Law Reporter (2696)

Continuity Publishing, Inc.
1300 N State St., Ste. 105
Bellingham, WA 98225
Phone: (360)676-0789
Fax: (360)676-0932
Free: 800-463-9243

Publications: New Age Retailer (32677)

Contra Costa College
2600 Mission Bell Dr.
San Pablo, CA 94806
Phone: (510)235-7800
Fax: (510)235-NEWS

Publications: The Advocate (3594)

Contra Costa News Register
1601 N Main St., Ste. 107
PO Box 4779
Walnut Creek, CA 94596
Phone: (510)934-2780
Fax: (510)934-2532

Publications: Contra Costa News Register (4049)

Contra Costa Newspapers, Inc.
2640 Shadelands Dr.
Walnut Creek, CA 94598-2513
Phone: (925)935-2525
Fax: (925)943-8362
Free: 800-465-0780

Publications: Contra Costa Sun (2131) • Contra Costa Times (4050) • The Ledger Dispatch (1425) • San Ramon Valley Times (1809) • Valley Times (2856)

Contractor Marketing
7600 Dayton Rd.
Fairborn, OH 45324
Phone: (937)864-5854

Publications: Contractor Marketing (25186)

Contractors Association of West Virginia
2114 Kanawha Blvd. E.
Charleston, WV 25311
Phone: (304)342-1166
Fax: (304)342-1074

Publications: West Virginia Construction News (33275)

Contractors Equipment Guide
50 Central Ave.
PO Box 324
Needham Heights, MA 02494
Phone: (781)449-1250
Fax: (781)449-7768
Free: 800-225-8448

Publications: Contractors Equipment Guide (14376)

The Convention News Co., Inc.
PO Box 277
Midland Park, NJ 07432-0277
Phone: (201)444-5075
Fax: (201)444-4647

Publications: Aviation International News (19236)

ConventionSouth Magazine
PO Box 2267
Gulf Shores, AL 36547
Phone: (334)968-5300
Fax: (334)968-4532

Publications: ConventionSouth (250)

The Conway Daily Sun
PO Box 1940
North Conway, NH 03860
Phone: (603)356-3456
Fax: (603)356-8774

Publications: The Conway Daily Sun (18614)

Conway Data Inc.
35 Technology Pkwy., Ste. 150
Norcross, GA 30092
Phone: (770)446-6996
Fax: (770)263-8825

Publications: Site Selection Magazine (7469)

Conway Springs Star
214 W Spring Ave.
PO Box 158
Conway Springs, KS 67031
Phone: (316)456-2473
Fax: (316)456-2472

Publications: Conway Springs Star and the Argonia Argosy (11400)

Cook News
PO Box 1179
Cook, MN 55723
Phone: (218)666-5944
Fax: (218)666-5609

Publications: Cook News-Herald (15813)

Cook Publishing Co.
202 W. 4th St.
Adel, GA 31620
Free: 800-861-6353

Publications: Lanier County News (7366)

Cooke Communications LLC
3420 Northside Dr.
Key West, FL 33040
Phone: (305)292-7777
Fax: (305)294-0768

Publications: Key West Citizen (6253)

Cookson Hills Publishers, Inc.
111 N. Oak St.
Sallisaw, OK 74955
Phone: (918)775-4433
Fax: (918)775-3023

Publications: Sequoyah County Times (26053)

Coon Rapids Enterprise
504 Main St.
Coon Rapids, IA 50058
Fax: (712)684-7783

Publications: Coon Rapids Enterprise (10720)

Cooper Extension Service
Oregon State University
Horticulture Department
4017 ALS Bldg.
Corvallis, OR 97331-7304
Fax: (503)737-3479

Publications: Ornamentals Northwest (26290)

Cooper Ornithological Society
Zoology Dept.
Arizona State University
Tempe, AZ 85287-1501
Phone: (602)965-9483
Fax: (602)965-3209

Publications: The Condor (901)

Cooperative Extension Association of Cayuga, Onondaga and Oswego Counties
3288 Main St.
Mexico, NY 13114

2350

Numbers cited after listings are entry numbers rather than page numbers.

Publications: AgNews of Central New York (21075)

Cooperative Extension Associations of Erie and Wyoming Counties
21 S. Grove St., Ste. 240
East Aurora, NY 14052
Phone: (716)652-5400
Fax: (716)652-5073

Publications: Farm News of Erie and Wyoming Counties (20542)

Copiah-Lincoln Community College
PO Box 649
Wesson, MS 39191
Phone: (601)643-8354
Fax: (601)643-8226

Publications: Wolf Tales (16873)

Copley Corp.
601 Pulaski St.
Lincoln, IL 62656-2825
Phone: (217)732-2101
Fax: (217)732-7039
Free: 800-397-8757

Publications: Courier (9082)

Copley Newspapers/Copley Press
PO Box 1530
La Jolla, CA 92038
Phone: (858)454-0411
Fax: (858)454-5014

Publications: The Courier News (8823) • Herald-News (9034)

Copley Newspapers, Inc.
PO Box 1530
La Jolla, CA 92038
Phone: (858)454-0411

Publications: Borrego Sun (1593)

Copley Ohio Newspapers, Inc.
50 North Ave. NW
Massillon, OH 44647
Phone: (330)833-2631
Fax: (330)833-2635

Publications: The Independent (25360)

Copper Area Publishing
PO Box 579
Kearny, AZ 85237
Phone: (520)363-5554
Fax: (520)363-9663

Publications: Copper Basin News (727)

Copper Country News
247 S. Hill St.
Globe, AZ 85501
Phone: (928)425-0355
Fax: (928)425-6535

Publications: Copper Country News (718)

Copper Pig Writers' Society
Box 4727
Edmonton, AB, Canada T6E 5G6
Phone: (780)413-0215
Fax: (780)413-1538

Publications: On Spec (34722)

Copper Queen Publishing Co., Inc.
Drawer 48
Bisbee, AZ 85603
Phone: (520)432-2244
Fax: (520)432-2247

Publications: Pay Dirt Magazine (660)

Copperopolis Herald
PO Box 220
Copperopolis, CA 95228
Phone: (209)887-3112

Publications: Copperopolis Herald (1763)

Coppersfield Publishing Inc.
60 W. 400 S.
Salt Lake City, UT 84101
Phone: (801)575-7003
Fax: (801)575-6106

Publications: Salt Lake City Weekly (31438)

Coquille Valley Sentinel
1 Barton's Alley
Coquille, OR 97423-0400
Phone: (541)396-3191
Fax: (541)396-3624

Publications: Coquille Valley Sentinel (26281)

Coracle
1516 Euclid Ave.
Berkeley, CA 94708

Publications: Coracle (1511)

The Corcoran Journal
PO Box 487
Corcoran, CA 93212
Phone: (559)992-3115
Fax: (559)992-5543

Publications: The Corcoran Journal (1765)

Cordele Dispatch
PO Box 1058
Cordele, GA 31015
Phone: (229)273-2277
Fax: (229)273-7239

Publications: Cover Story (7204)

CoreNet Global
260 Peachtree St. NW, Ste. 1500
Atlanta, GA 30303-1237
Phone: (404)589-3200
Fax: (404)589-3201
Free: 800-726-8111

Publications: Corporate Real Estate Executive (6994) • Corporate Real Estate Leader (6995)

The Corinthian Publishing Company Ltd.
225 Industrial Pkwy. S.
PO Box 670
Aurora, ON, Canada L4G 4J9
Phone: (905)727-0107
Fax: (905)841-1530
Free: 800-505-7428

Publications: The Corinthian Horse Sport (35645) • Horsepower, Magazine for Young Horse Lovers (35650)

The Coriolis Group, LLC
14455 N. Hayden Rd., Ste. 220
Scottsdale, AZ 85260
Fax: (602)483-0193
Free: 800-410-0192

Publications: Visual Developer (875)

Cornell Alumni Federation
Campus Information and Visitor Relations
Day Hall Lobby
Ithaca, NY 14853
Phone: (607)254-INFO
Free: 800-724-8458

Publications: Cornell Alumni Magazine (20791)

Cornell College
810 Commons Circle
Mount Vernon, IA 52314
Phone: (319)895-4499
Fax: (319)895-5264

Publications: The Cornellian (11096)

The Cornell Daily Sun Inc.
119 S. Cayuga St.
Ithaca, NY 14850
Phone: (607)273-3606
Fax: (607)273-0746

Publications: The Cornell Daily Sun (20792)

Cornell Political Forum
Day Hall Lobby
Cornell University
Ithaca, NY 14853
Phone: (607)254-INFO

Publications: Cornell Political Forum (20798)

Cornell University
B46 Olin Hall
Ithaca, NY 14853
Phone: (607)255-3312
Fax: (607)255-9606

Publications: Cornell Science & Technology Magazine (20799)

Cornell University
College of Human Ecology
1150 Comstock
Ithaca, NY 14853-0901
Phone: (607)255-1852
Fax: (607)255-9873

Publications: Human Ecology Forum (20802)

Cornell University
Department of Applied Economics and Management
357 Warren Hall
Ithaca, NY 14853-7801
Phone: (607)255-4534
Fax: (607)255-1589

Publications: Agricultural Finance Review (20788)

Cornell University
158 Ives Hall
Ithaca, NY 14853-3901
Phone: (607)255-3295
Fax: (607)255-8016

Publications: Industrial and Labor Relations Review (20804)

Cornell University
257 Statler Hall
Ithaca, NY 14853

Publications: Cornell International Law Journal (20795)

Cornell University Cooperative Extension Association of Saratoga County
50 W. High St.
Ballston Spa, NY 12020
Phone: (518)798-8228

Publications: Agricultural News (23171)

Cornell University Cooperative Extension of Suffolk County
246 Griffing Ave.
Riverhead, NY 11901
Phone: (516)727-7850
Fax: (516)727-7130

Publications: Suffolk County Agricultural News (23204)

Cornell University Experiment Station
1150 Comstock Hall
Ithaca, NY 14853-0901
Phone: (607)255-4326
Fax: (607)255-9873

Publications: Cornell Focus (20793)

Cornell University Law School
Myron Taylor Hall
Ithaca, NY 14853-4901
Phone: (607)255-0526
Fax: (607)255-7193

Publications: Cornell Journal of Law and Public Policy (20796)

Cornell University Law School
137 Myron Taylor Hall
Ithaca, NY 14853
Phone: (607)255-3387
Fax: (607)255-7193

Publications: Cornell Law Review (20797)

Cornell University School of Hotel Administration
Statler Hall
Ithaca, NY 14853-6902
Phone: (607)255-9393
Fax: (607)255-4179

Publications: The Cornell Hotel and Restaurant Administration Quarterly (20794)

Cornerstone Communications, Inc.
939 W Wilson Ave.
Chicago, IL 60640-5706
Phone: (773)561-2450
Fax: (773)989-2076

Publications: Cornerstone (8344)

Corning Pennysaver
57 S. Carroll St.
Horseheads, NY 14845
Phone: (607)796-6031
Fax: (607)796-5833

Publications: Corning Pennysaver (20759)

Corning Publishing
111 E. Poplar
Paragould, AR 72450
Phone: (870)239-5000
Fax: (870)239-3403

Publications: NE AR Tribune (1307)

Cornwall Publishing Company Ltd.
PO Box 2680, STN Terminal
Vancouver, BC, Canada V6B 3W8
Phone: (604)879-4991
Fax: (604)879-5110
Free: 800-263-1088

Publications: Gardens West (35142)

Coronation Review
Box 70
Coronation, AB, Canada T0C 1C0
Phone: (403)578-4111
Fax: (403)578-2088

Publications: Coronation Review (34690)

Corporate Cashflow
6151 Powers Ferry Rd. NW
Atlanta, GA 30339-2941

Publications: Corporate Cashflow (6993)

Corporate Communications
333 Pfingsten Rd.
Northbrook, IL 60062
Phone: (847)272-8800
Fax: (847)509-6235

Publications: On the Mark (9319)

Corporate Marketing & Publishing
6506 E Calle Bellatrix, Ste. 100
Tucson, AZ 85710
Phone: (520)790-4044

Publications: College & Career Guide News for College Students (940) • Working Moms & Dads Magazine (974)

The Corp.
610 Main Ave.
St. Maries, ID 83861-1838
Phone: (208)245-4538
Fax: (208)245-4991

Publications: St. Marie's Gazette-Record (7972)

Corp. of Master Electricians of Quebec
5925, Blvd. Decarie, Ste. 100
Montreal, QC, Canada H3W 3C9
Phone: (514)738-2184
Fax: (514)738-2192
Free: 800-361-9061

Publications: Electricite Quebec (37113)

Correctional News
517 Jacoby St., Ste. C
San Rafael, CA 94901
Phone: (415)460-6185
Fax: (415)460-6288

Publications: Correctional News (3600)

Correctional Service of Canada/Service correctionnel du Canada
2B-340 Laurier Ave., W.
Ottawa, ON, Canada K1A 0P9
Phone: (613)947-2915
Fax: (613)941-8477

Publications: Forum on Corrections Research (36244)

The Corrigan Times
PO Box 115-V
Corrigan, TX 75939
Phone: (936)398-2535
Fax: (936)327-7156

Publications: The Corrigan Times (30100)

Corry Journal
28 W South St.
Corry, PA 16407
Phone: (814)665-8291
Fax: (814)664-2288

Publications: Corry Journal (26809)

Corry Publishing, Inc.
2840 W. 21st St.
Erie, PA 16506-9945
Phone: (814)838-0025
Fax: (814)836-9605
Free: 800-368-9597

Publications: Builder/Dealer (26893) • Business Solutions (26894)

Corsicana Daily
PO Box 622
Corsicana, TX 75110
Phone: (903)874-7355
Fax: (903)872-6878

Publications: Navarro County Sun Extra (30102)

Cortland Group
7 Skyline Dr.
Hawthorne, NY 10532
Phone: (914)347-3800
Fax: (914)347-3801

Publications: Cortland Forum (20725)

Cortland Standard Printing Co., Inc.
PO Box 5548
Cortland, NY 13045
Phone: (607)756-5665
Fax: (607)756-5665

Publications: Cortland Standard (20512)

Corwin Press
2455 Teller Rd.
Thousand Oaks, CA 91320
Phone: (805)499-4224
Fax: (805)499-5323
Free: 800-818-7243

Publications: Education Administration Quarterly (34066) • Education and Urban Society (3863) • Educational Administration Abstracts (3864) • Educational Policy (14127) • Urban Education (3919)

Coshocton Tribune
550 Main St.
PO Box 10
Coshocton, OH 43812
Phone: (740)622-1122
Fax: (740)622-7341
Free: 800-589-8689

Publications: Coshocton Tribune (25096)

Costilla County Free Press
PO Box 306
San Luis, CO 81152
Phone: (719)672-3764
Fax: (719)672-3895
Free: 800-652-2181

Publications: Costilla County Free Press (4623)

Costume Society of America
PO Box 73
Earleville, MD 21919-0073
Phone: (410)275-1619
Fax: (410)275-8936
Free: 800-CSA-9447

Publications: Dress (13485)

Coteau Shopper, Inc.
Box 1176
Watertown, SD 57201
Phone: (605)882-1358
Fax: (605)882-1158

Publications: Coteau Shopper (29017)

Cottage Press
2318 2nd Ave., No. 366A
Seattle, WA 98121
Phone: (206)441-8123

Publications: Belltown Dispatch (32950)

Cotton Digest International
PO Box 820768
Houston, TX 77282-0768
Phone: (713)977-1644
Fax: (713)977-8193

Publications: Cotton Digest International (30467)

Cottonwood Chronicle
503 King St.
Box 157
Cottonwood, ID 83522
Phone: (208)962-3851
Fax: (208)962-7131

Publications: Cottonwood Chronicle (7849)

Cottonwood County Citizen
260 10th St.
PO Box 309
Windom, MN 56101
Phone: (507)831-3455
Fax: (507)831-3740

Publications: Cottonwood County Citizen (16523)

Cottonwood Journal Extra
PO Box 2266
Cottonwood, AZ 86326
Phone: (928)634-8551
Fax: (928)634-1080

Publications: Cottonwood Journal Extra (679)

Coulee News
153 S Leonard St.
West Salem, WI 54669
Phone: (608)786-1950
Fax: (608)786-1670

Publications: Economy Shopper (34449)

The Coulter Press
156 Church St.
Clinton, MA 01510
Phone: (978)368-0176
Fax: (978)368-1151

Publications: The Item (14139) • Item Extra (14140)

Council for Advancement and Support of Education
1307 New York Ave. NW, Ste. 1000
Washington, DC 20005-4701
Phone: (202)328-2273
Fax: (202)387-4973
Free: 800-554-8536

Publications: Currents (5455)

Council of the Alleghenies Inc.
Box 514
Frostburg, MD 21532
Phone: (301)689-8173

Publications: Journal of the Alleghenies (13527)

Council of Better Business Bureaus, Inc.
PO Box 79168
Baltimore, MD 21279-0168
Phone: (301)617-7810
Fax: (301)206-9789

Publications: NAD KARU Case Reports (13223)

Council for Exceptional Children
1110 N Glebe Rd.
Arlington, VA 22201-5704
Phone: (703)620-3660
Fax: (703)264-9494
Free: 888-232-7733

Publications: Education and Training in Developmental Disabilities (903)

Council for Exceptional Children
1110 N. Glebe Rd. Ste. 300
Arlington, VA 22201-5704
Phone: (703)620-3660
Fax: (703)264-9494
Free: 888-232-7733

Publications: Assessment for Effective Information (28505)

Council for Exceptional Children
1110 N. Glebe Rd., 300
Arlington, VA 22201
Phone: (703)264-9470
Fax: (703)620-2521
Free: 800-224-6830

Publications: Exceptional Child Education Resources (31790) • Exceptional Children (31791) • Physical Disabilities—Education & Related Services (31817) • Teaching Exceptional Children (14134)

Council on Foreign Relations, Inc.
58 E 68th St.
New York, NY 10021
Phone: (212)434-9000
Fax: (212)434-9859

Publications: Foreign Affairs (21725)

Numbers cited after listings are entry numbers rather than page numbers.

Council on Foundations
1828 L St. NW, Ste. 300
Washington, DC 20036
Phone: (202)466-6512
Fax: (202)785-3926

Publications: Foundation News & Commentary (5501)

Council Grove Republican
208 W Main
PO Box 237
Council Grove, KS 66846
Phone: (620)767-5123
Fax: (620)767-5124

Publications: Council Grove Republican (11404)

Council on Hotel, Restaurant, and Institutional Education
2613 N Parham Rd., 2nd Fl.
Richmond, VA 23294-4650
Phone: (804)747-4971
Fax: (804)747-5022

Publications: Journal of Hospitality & Tourism Research (32440)

Council for Learning Disabilities
PO Box 40303
Overland Park, KS 66204
Phone: (913)492-8755
Fax: (913)492-2546

Publications: Learning Disability Quarterly (11719)

Council of Residential Specialists
430 N Michigan Ave., Ste. 300
Chicago, IL 60611-4092
Phone: (312)321-4400
Fax: (312)329-8882
Free: 800-462-8841

Publications: The Residential Specialist (8554)

Council for Secular Humanism
PO Box 664
Amherst, NY 14226-0664
Phone: (716)636-7571
Fax: (716)636-1733
Free: 800-458-1366

Publications: Free Inquiry (20030)

Council for Social and Economic Studies Inc.
1133 13 St. NW, Ste. C-2
Washington, DC 20005
Phone: (202)371-2700
Fax: (202)371-1523

Publications: Journal of Social, Political & Economic Studies (5615)

Council on Social Work Education
1725 Duke St., Ste. 500
Alexandria, VA 22314
Phone: (703)683-8080
Fax: (703)683-8099

Publications: Journal of Social Work Education (31702)

Council of Societies for the Study of Religion
CSSR Executive Office
Valparaiso University
Valparaiso, IN 46383-6493
Phone: (219)464-5515
Fax: (219)464-6714
Free: 888-422-2777

Publications: CSSR Bulletin (10509) • Religious Studies Review (10510)

Council of State Governments
2760 Research Park Dr.
PO Box 11910
Lexington, KY 40578-1910
Phone: (859)244-8000
Fax: (859)244-8001
Free: 800-800-1910

Publications: Spectrum: Journal of State Government (12176) • State Government News (12177)

The Counselors of Real Estate
430 N Michigan Ave.
Chicago, IL 60611
Phone: (312)329-8427
Fax: (312)329-8881

Publications: Real Estate Issues (8548)

Counterterrorism & Security, Inc.
Box 10265
Arlington, VA 22210
Phone: (703)243-0993
Fax: (703)243-1197

Publications: International Counterterrorism & Security (31799)

Countian
PO Box 333
Riley, KS 66531
Phone: (913)485-2290

Publications: The Riley Countian (11769)

Country Almanac
3525 Alameda De Las Pulgas
Menlo Park, CA 94025
Phone: (650)854-2626
Fax: (650)854-0677

Publications: The Almanac (2522)

Country Charm Magazine
PO Box 696
Palmerston, ON, Canada N0G 2P0
Phone: (519)343-3059

Publications: Country Charm Magazine (36304)

Country Folks of Pennsylvania
141 Ulster Ave.
Saugerties, NY 12477
Phone: (914)246-4985
Fax: (914)246-5108

Publications: Country Folks (23306) • Mohawk Valley Pennysaver (23307) • Mountain Pennysaver (20439) • Saugerties Post Star (23308)

Country Gazette
PO Box 1231
Orting, WA 98360-1231
Phone: (360)893-5103
Fax: (360)893-2277

Publications: Country Gazette (32874)

Country Grapevine Co.
PO Box 380219
Murdock, FL 33938
Phone: (941)625-8486
Fax: (941)625-1172
Free: 800-738-9642

Publications: Country Grapevine (6437)

Country Journal Publishing Co., Inc.
3065 Pershing Ct.
Decatur, IL 62526
Phone: (217)877-9660
Fax: (217)877-6647
Free: 800-728-7511

Publications: Milling Journal (8713)

Country Media
PO Box 749
Hettinger, ND 58639
Phone: (701)567-2424
Fax: (701)567-2425

Publications: Adams County Record (24472)

Country Media
710 3rd St.
Langdon, ND 58249
Phone: (701)256-5311
Fax: (701)256-5841

Publications: Cavalier County Republican (24489)

Country Media
PO Box 129, 1022 Main St.
Sturgis, SD 57785
Phone: (605)347-2503
Fax: (605)347-2525
Free: 800-253-3656

Publications: Black Hills Press (28999) • Butte County Valley Irrigator (28910) • The Lawrence County Centennial (28881) • Meade County Times-Tribune (29000) • Tri-State Livestock News (29001)

Country Media, Inc.
Box 8700
Scottsbluff, NE 69363
Phone: (308)635-1892
Fax: (308)635-5041

Publications: The Hot Springs Star (28867)

Country Music Association, Inc.
1 Music Cir. S.
Nashville, TN 37203-4312
Phone: (615)244-2840
Fax: (615)242-4783

Publications: Close Up Magazine (29451)

Country Music Foundation Press
222 5th Ave. S
Nashville, TN 37203
Phone: (615)416-2001
Fax: (615)255-2245

Publications: Journal of Country Music (29462)

Country Music News
PO Box 7323, Vanier Terminal
Ottawa, ON, Canada K1L 8E4
Phone: (613)745-6006
Fax: (613)745-0576

Publications: Country Music News (36239)

Country Peddler
PO Box 492
Bowling Green, KY 42102
Phone: (270)842-3314
Fax: (270)842-4220

Publications: Country Peddler (11942)

Country Sampler Group
707 Kautz Rd.
St. Charles, IL 60174
Phone: (630)377-8000
Fax: (630)377-8914

Publications: Country Business (9563) • Country Sampler (9564) • Country Sampler Decorating Ideas (9565)

Country Skier L.L.C
PO Box 550
Cable, WI 54821
Phone: (612)377-0312
Fax: (612)381-9182
Free: 800-827-0607

Publications: Cross Country Skier (33612)

Country Weekly
5401 NW Broken Sound Blvd.
Boca Raton, FL 33487

Publications: Country Weekly (5930)

Countryside Publications, Ltd.
W11564 Hwy. 64
Withee, WI 54498
Phone: (715)785-7979
Fax: (715)785-7414

Publications: Dairy Goat Journal (34468) • Sheep! Magazine (34469)

County College of Morris
214 Ctr. Grove Rd.
Randolph, NJ 07869
Phone: (973)328-5471
Fax: (973)328-5425

Publications: Journal of New Jersey Poets (19495)

County Courier
PO Box 440
206-208 W. Main St.
Buffalo, MO 65622
Phone: (417)345-2323
Fax: (417)345-6800

Publications: County Courier (16930)

County Courier
PO Box 398
Enosburg, VT 05450
Phone: (802)933-4375
Fax: (802)933-4907

Publications: County Courier (31541)

The County Democrat Publishing Co.
226 N Broadway
PO Box 367
Shawnee, OK 74802
Phone: (405)273-8888
Fax: (405)275-6473

Publications: The County Democrat Publishing Co. (26061)

County Engineers Association of Ohio
37 W. Broad St., Ste. 660
Columbus, OH 43215-4132
Phone: (614)221-0707
Fax: (614)221-5761

Publications: Ohio County Engineer (25042)

The County Journal
PO Box 637
Washburn, WI 54891
Phone: (715)373-5500
Fax: (715)373-5546

Publications: The County Journal (34388)

County News
PO Box 70
Iuka, MS 38852
Phone: (662)423-2211
Fax: (662)423-2214

Publications: Tishomingo County News (16691)

County News
PO Box 407
Statesville, NC 28687
Phone: (704)873-1054
Fax: (704)873-1054

Publications: County News (24246)

County Press
1521 Imlay City Rd.
Lapeer, MI 48446
Phone: (810)664-0811
Fax: (810)664-5852
Free: 800-994-0811

Publications: County Press (15308) • The Thumb Blanket (14786)

The County Press
PO Box 9
Benson, NC 27504
Phone: (919)894-3331
Fax: (919)894-1069

Publications: The Clayton News-Star (23644) • Four Oaks-Benson News in Review (23645)

County Press
3732 West Chester Pike
PO Box 249
Newtown Square, PA 19073
Phone: (610)356-3820
Fax: (610)353-5321

Publications: County Press (27328) • Haverford Press (27329) • Upper Darby and Drexel Hill Press (27334)

County Progress
500 Chestnut St., Ste. 2000
Abilene, TX 79602
Phone: (915)673-4822
Fax: (915)677-2631

Publications: County Progress (29653)

County Publishers Corp.
24 S Main St.
Montrose, PA 18801
Phone: (570)278-6397
Fax: (570)278-4305

Publications: Susquehanna County Independent (27292)

The County Record
PO Box 366
Blountstown, FL 32424
Phone: (850)674-5041
Fax: (850)674-5008

Publications: The County Record (5925)

County Transcript
212-216 Exchange St.
Susquehanna, PA 18847
Phone: (717)853-3134
Fax: (717)853-4707
Free: 800-372-7051

Publications: County Transcript (28041)

County Wide Communications, Inc.
PO Box 497
Machias, ME 04654
Phone: (207)564-7548

Publications: County Wide Newspaper (12985) • Maine Magazine (12987)

Countywide News
101 N Broadway
PO Box 38
Tecumseh, OK 74873-0038
Phone: (405)598-3793
Fax: (405)598-3891

Publications: Countywide News (26099)

Coup de Pouce
2001 University, Ste. 900
Montreal, QC, Canada H3A 2A6
Free: 800-528-3836

Publications: Coup de Pouce (37106)

Courier
PO Box 189
Danville, AR 72833
Fax: (501)495-3501

Publications: Yell County Record (1096)

Courier
100 Ford Ln.
PO Box 349
Washington, IL 61571
Phone: (309)444-3139
Fax: (309)444-8505

Publications: Courier (9735)

Courier
PO Box O
Reinbeck, IA 50669-0177
Phone: (319)345-2031
Fax: (319)345-6767

Publications: Courier (11174)

Courier
PO Box 160
Sutherland, IA 51058
Phone: (712)446-3450
Fax: (712)446-3450

Publications: Courier (11259)

The Courier
3030 Barrow St.
PO Box 2717
Houma, LA 70361
Fax: (504)857-2233

Publications: The Courier (12601)

The Courier
PO Box 949
Winona, MN 55987-0949
Phone: (507)454-4643
Fax: (507)454-8106

Publications: The Courier (16526)

Courier
103 S. Ragsdale St.
PO Box 351
Hazlehurst, MS 39083
Phone: (601)894-3141
Fax: (601)894-3144

Publications: Copiah County Courier (16678)

The Courier
244 Whaley St.
Freeport, NY 11520
Phone: (516)378-5002

Publications: The Courier (23486)

Courier
PO Box 950
308 S. Main St
Freeman, SD 57029
Phone: (605)925-7033
Fax: (605)925-4684

Publications: Courier (28857)

Courier
PO Box 169
Sisseton, SD 57262
Phone: (605)698-7642
Fax: (605)698-3641

Publications: Courier (28991)

The Courier
803-805 Main St.
PO Box 340
Savannah, TN 38372
Fax: (901)925-6310

Publications: Courier (29584)

The Courier
114 N. Monroe St.
PO Box 6
Waterloo, WI 53594
Phone: (920)478-2188
Fax: (920)478-3618

Publications: The Courier (34391)

Courier Communications
174 N 16th St.
PO Box 268
Reedsport, OR 97467
Phone: (541)271-3633
Fax: (503)271-3138
Free: 800-222-NEWS

Publications: The Courier (26553)

Courier Enterprises, Inc.
4 Meadow St.
PO Box 294
Clinton, NY 13323-0294
Phone: (315)853-3490
Fax: (315)853-3522

Publications: The Clinton Courier (20470)

The Courier Express
341 3rd Ave. S.
PO Box 151
Glasgow, MT 59230
Phone: (406)228-9301
Fax: (406)228-2665

Publications: The Courier Express (17792)

Courier Express
500 Jeffers St.
PO Box 407
Du Bois, PA 15801
Phone: (814)371-4200
Fax: (814)371-3241

Publications: Courier Express (26837)

Courier-Gazette
613 S Main St.
Newark, NY 14513
Phone: (315)331-1000
Fax: (315)331-1053

Publications: Courier-Gazette (22994)

Courier-Gazette, Inc.
301 Park St.
PO Box 249
Rockland, ME 04841
Phone: (207)594-4401
Fax: (207)596-6981

Publications: The Courier-Publications (13044)

Courier-Index
PO Box 569
Marianna, AR 72360-0569
Phone: (870)295-2521
Fax: (870)295-9662

Publications: Courier-Index (1267)

Courier-Journal Co.
525 W. Broadway St.
Louisville, KY 40202-7431
Phone: (502)582-4011
Fax: (502)582-4075
Free: 800-765-4011

Publications: The Courier-Journal (12213)

Courier/Journal, Inc.
140 N Main
PO Box 353
Kingman, KS 67068
Phone: (316)532-3151
Fax: (316)532-3152

Publications: Kingman Journal (11539) • Kingman Leader-Courier (11540)

The Courier-Leader
32280 E Red Arrow Hwy.
Paw Paw, MI 49079-0129
Phone: (616)657-3072
Fax: (616)657-5723

Publications: The Courier-Leader (15433)

Courier Life Publications
1733 Sheepshead Bay Rd.
Brooklyn, NY 11235-3606
Phone: (718)769-4400
Fax: (718)769-5048

Publications: Bay News (20299) • Bay Ridge Courier (20300) • Canarsie Digest (20306) • Caribbean Life (20307) • Flatbush Life (20317) • Kings Courier (20325)

Courier News
1201 Rte. 22 W
Bridgewater, NJ 08807
Phone: (908)722-8800
Fax: (908)707-3205
Free: 800-675-0298

Publications: Strictly Hunterdon (18701) • Strictly Somerset (19567)

The Courier-News
233 N. Hicks St.
PO Box 270
Clinton, TN 37716
Phone: (865)457-2515
Fax: (865)457-1586

Publications: The Courier-News (29129)

Courier News Weekly
PO Box 204
Harleysville, PA 19438
Phone: (215)256-6100
Fax: (215)256-9799

Publications: Courier News Weekly (26981)

Courier Press Ltd.
955 Alexander Ave.
PO Box 1054
Winnipeg, MB, Canada R3C 2X8
Phone: (204)774-1883
Fax: (204)783-5740

Publications: KANADA KURIER (35335)

Courier Publications
PO Box 249
Rockland, ME 04841
Phone: (207)594-4401
Fax: (207)596-6981
Free: 800-559-4401

Publications: The Bar Harbor Times (12917) • The Camden Herald (12941) • Capital Weekly (12889) • Lincoln County Weekly (13045) • The Republican Journal (12920)

Courier Publishing
PO Box 129
Campton, KY 41301
Phone: (606)668-3595
Fax: (606)662-4010

Publications: Wolfe County News (12010)

Courier Publishing Co.
409 SE 7th St.
PO Box 1468
Grants Pass, OR 97526
Phone: (541)474-3700
Fax: (541)474-3814
Free: 800-228-0457

Publications: Grants Pass Daily Courier (26362)

Courier Register Corp.
246 Harrison St.
Thompson, IA 50478-0350
Phone: (641)584-2770
Fax: (641)584-2802

Publications: The Thompson Courier-Rake Register (11266)

The Courier-Sentinel
405 W Ctr. St.
Kiester, MN 56051
Phone: (507)294-3400

Publications: The Courier-Sentinel (15985)

Courier-Times
201 S 14th St.
New Castle, IN 47362-3328
Phone: (765)529-1111
Fax: (765)529-1731

Publications: Courier-Times (10342)

Courier-Times
PO Box 367
Sutherland, NE 69165
Phone: (308)386-4617
Fax: (308)386-2437

Publications: Courier-Times (18291)

Courier-Times
109 Clayton Ave.
PO Box 311
Roxboro, NC 27573
Phone: (336)599-0162
Fax: (336)597-2773

Publications: Courier-Times (24209)

Courier Tribune
512 Main
Seneca, KS 66538
Phone: (785)336-2175
Fax: (785)336-3475

Publications: Courier Tribune (11798)

Courrier Frontenac Inc.
541 Boul Smith nord
C.P. 789
Thetford Mines, QC, Canada G6G 5V3
Phone: (418)338-5181
Fax: (418)338-5482

Publications: Le Courrier Frontenac (37410)

Court & Commercial Record
41 E Washington St.,
200
Indianapolis, IN 46204
Phone: (317)636-0200
Fax: (317)263-5259

Publications: Court & Commercial Record (10105)

Courtland Journal-Empire
Box 318
Courtland, KS 66939
Phone: (785)374-4428
Fax: (785)374-4209

Publications: Courtland Journal-Empire (11405)

The Coushatta Citizen Shopper
1703 Ringgold Ave.
PO Drawer 1365
Coushatta, LA 71019-2006
Phone: (318)932-4201
Fax: (318)932-4285

Publications: The Coushatta Citizen (12551) • The Coushatta Citizen Shopper (12552)

The Cousteau Society
870 Greenbrier Cir., Ste. 402
Chesapeake, VA 23320
Phone: (757)523-9335
Fax: (757)523-2747
Free: 800-441-4395

Publications: Calypso Log (31964)

Covenant Publications
5101 N. Francisco Ave.
Chicago, IL 60625
Phone: (773)784-3000
Fax: (773)784-4366

Publications: The Covenant Companion (8345)

Coventry Broadcaster, Inc.
130 Old Town Rd
PO Box 27
Rockville, CT 06066
Phone: (860)877-3366
Fax: (860)872-4614

Publications: The Broadcaster (5105)

Cover Story
6 Louise St.
PO Box 220
Truro, NS, Canada B2N 5C3
Phone: (902)893-9405
Fax: (902)893-0518

Publications: Colchester Sunday (35615)

Covey Communications Corp.
PO Box 2267
Gulf Shores, AL 36547
Phone: (251)968-5300
Fax: (251)968-4532

Publications: Crossties (251)

The Covington Leader
2001 Hwy. 51 S
PO Box 529
Covington, TN 38019-0529
Phone: (901)476-7116
Fax: (901)476-0373

Publications: The Covington Leader (29153)

Covington Newspaper Co., Inc.
1148 Monticello St.
PO Box 1249
Covington, GA 30014
Phone: (770)787-6397
Fax: (770)786-6451

Publications: Covington News (7210) • Multi-County Star (7211)

Covington Record
Main St.
PO Drawer L
Covington, OK 73730-0535

Publications: Covington Record (25795)

Covington Virginian, Inc.
128 N. Maple Ave.
PO Box 271
Covington, VA 24426
Phone: (540)962-2121
Fax: (540)902-5072

Publications: Virginian Review (31982)

Cow Neck Peninsula Historical Society
336 Port Washington Blvd.
Port Washington, NY 11050
Phone: (516)365-9074

Publications: Cow Neck Peninsula Historical Society Journal (23123)

Cowboy Publishing Group
PO Box 9707
Fort Worth, TX 76147
Phone: (817)737-6397

Publications: The Horsetrader (30342)

Cowboys for Christ
PO Box 7557
Fort Worth, TX 76111
Phone: (817)236-0023
Fax: (817)236-0024

Publications: Christian Ranchman (30333)

The Cowichan Valley Citizen
469 Whistler St
Duncan, BC, Canada V9L 4X5
Phone: (250)748-2666
Fax: (250)748-1552

Publications: The Citizen (34949)

Cowles Enthusiast Media
6405 Flank Dr.
Harrisburg, PA 17112

Publications: Figurines & Collectibles (26990)

Cowles Magazines Inc.
6 Commercial St.
Hicksville, NY 11801
Phone: (516)433-4672

Publications: Horse & Rider (20739)

Cowles Publishing Co.
999 W Riverside Ave.
PO Box 2160
Spokane, WA 99210
Phone: (509)459-5000
Fax: (509)459-5258
Free: 800-789-0029

Publications: The Spokesman-Review (33101)

Cowley County Community College
125 S 2nd
Arkansas City, KS 67005
Phone: (316)441-5287
Fax: (816)441-5377
Free: 800-593-2222

Publications: The Press (11340)

Cox
402 SE 2nd St.
PO Box 128
Snow Hill, NC 28580
Phone: (919)747-3883
Fax: (919)747-7656

Publications: Snow Hill Standard-Laconic (24234)

Eric M. Cox
24 N Washington St.
PO Box 116
Knightstown, IN 46148
Phone: (765)345-2292
Fax: (765)345-2113

Publications: Knightstown Banner (10236)

Cox, Matthews, & Associates, Inc.
10520 Warwick Ave., Ste. B-8
Fairfax, VA 22030
Phone: (703)385-2980
Fax: (703)385-1839
Free: 800-783-3199

Publications: Black Issues Book Review (32008) • Black Issues in Higher Education (32009) • Community College Week (32012)

Cox Newspapers
1400 Lake Hearn Dr. NE
Atlanta, GA 30319
Phone: (404)843-5000

Publications: The Pflugerville Pflag (30932)

Cox Newspapers
PO Box 1089
Lufkin, TX 75902-1089
Phone: (409)632-6631
Fax: (409)632-6655

Publications: The Lufkin Daily News (30739) • Nacogdoches Daily Sentinel (30740) • Rocky Mount Telegram (24205)

Cox North Carolina Publications
209 S Highland Ave.
PO Box 369
Grifton, NC 28530
Phone: (252)524-4376
Fax: (252)524-3312

Publications: The Times-Leader (23977)

Cox North Carolina Publications
119 W Grubb St.
PO Box 277
Hertford, NC 27944
Phone: (919)426-5728
Fax: (919)426-4625

Publications: Perquimans Weekly (23986)

Cox North Carolina Publications Inc.
421 S Broad St.
PO Box 207
Edenton, NC 27932
Phone: (919)482-4418
Fax: (919)482-4410

Publications: The Chowan Herald (23856)

Cox North Carolina Publications, Inc.
PO Box 1967
Greenville, NC 27835
Phone: (252)752-6166
Fax: (252)752-8181
Free: 800-849-6166

Publications: Bertie Ledger-Advance (24316) • Campus Express (23961) • The Daily Reflector (23962)

Cox Ohio Publishing
PO Box 147
Springboro, OH 45066
Phone: (937)748-2550
Fax: (937)746-6013

Publications: The Star Press (25531)

Cox Publications (North Carolina) Inc.
PO Box 69
Kenansville, NC 28349
Phone: (910)296-0239
Fax: (910)296-9545

Publications: Duplin Times Progress (24019)

Cox Publishing Co.
120 N 12th Ave.
Durant, OK 74701-4718
Phone: (405)924-1770
Fax: (405)924-1792

Publications: Grayson County Shopper (25805) • The Shopper (Zone I) (25808) • The Shopper (Zone II) (25809)

Cox Publishing Co., Inc.
303 N. W. Murray Rd. Ste.6A,
Portland, OR 97229
Phone: (503)643-9380

Publications: Pacific Coast Nurseryman and Garden Supply Dealer (26496)

Cox Texas Publications, Inc.
Austin360
305 S. Congress Ave.
Austin, TX 78701
Phone: (512)912-2591
Fax: (512)912-2926

Publications: Austin American-Statesman (29755)

C.P.A., Inc.
PO Box 1090
Polson, MT 59860
Phone: (406)676-3800
Fax: (406)883-4349

Publications: Lake County Advertiser (17898) • Lake County Leader (17899)

CPCU Society
PO Box 3009
720 Providence Rd.
Malvern, PA 19355-0709
Phone: (610)251-2728
Fax: (610)251-2780
Free: 800-932-2728

Publications: CPCU Journal (27210)

CPO Publishing
PO Box 129
Mansfield, PA 16933
Phone: (570)549-2282
Fax: (570)549-3366
Free: 888-548-2282

Publications: Christian Motorsports Illustrated (27217) • Chrysler Power (27218)

CPS Communications, Inc.
7200 W Camino Real, Ste. 215
Boca Raton, FL 33433
Phone: (561)368-9301
Fax: (561)368-7870
Free: 800-346-2015

Publications: Medical Marketing & Media (5936)

Crafts Fair Guide
PO Box 688
Corte Madera, CA 94976-0688
Phone: (415)924-3259
Fax: (415)924-3259
Free: 800-871-2341

Publications: The Crafts Fair Guide (1770)

The Crafts Report
100 Rogers Rd.
Wilmington, DE 19801
Phone: (302)656-2209
Fax: (302)656-4894
Free: 800-777-7098

Publications: The Crafts Report (5289)

Craig Kelman and Associates Ltd.
3C-2020 Portage Ave.
Winnipeg, MB, Canada R3J 0K4
Phone: (204)985-9780
Fax: (204)985-9795

Publications: Professional Photographers of Canada (35350) • Western Canada Highway News (35358) • WRLA Yardstick (35365)

Craik Weekly News
PO Box 360
Craik, SK, Canada S0G 0V0
Phone: (306)734-2313
Fax: (306)734-2789

Publications: Craik Weekly News (37461)

Crain Communications Inc
1725 Merriman Rd.
Akron, OH 44313-5283
Phone: (330)836-9180
Fax: (330)836-2365

Publications: European Rubber Journal (24580) • Plastics News (24585) • Rubber & Plastics News (24587) • Tire Business (24589) • Urethanes Technology (24592)

Crain Communications Inc.
777 E. Speer Blvd.
Denver, CO 80203-4214
Phone: (303)733-2500
Fax: (303)733-2244

Publications: RCR Wireless News (4351)

Crain Communications, Inc.
360 N Michigan Ave.
Chicago, IL 60601
Phone: (312)649-7844
Fax: (312)280-3174
Free: 800-678-2724

Publications: Advertising Age (8245) • BtoB Magazine (8294) • Business Insurance (8296) • Crain's Chicago Business (8346) • Investment News (8419) • Modern Healthcare (8490) • Modern Physician (8492)

Crain Communications, Inc.
1155 Gratiot Ave.
Detroit, MI 48207-2997
Phone: (313)446-6000
Fax: (313)446-0347
Free: 800-678-9595

Publications: Automotive News (14915) • AutoWeek (14916) • Crain's Detroit Business (14920) • Crain's Nonprofit News (14921) • Electronic Media (14931) • Waste News (14952)

Crain Communications, Inc.
711 3rd Ave., 3rd Fl.
New York, NY 10017
Phone: (212)210-0100
Fax: (212)210-0244
Free: 800-446-1420

Publications: Crain's New York Business (21511) • Pensions & Investments (22537)

Crain Communications, Inc.
700 W. St. Clair, Ste. 310
Cleveland, OH 44113
Phone: (216)522-1383
Fax: (216)694-4264

Publications: Crain's Cleveland Business (24877)

Cranberries
PO Box 190
Rochester, MA 02770-0190
Phone: (508)763-8080

Publications: Cranberries (14505)

The Crane News
401 S Gaston
Crane, TX 79731
Phone: (915)558-3541
Fax: (915)558-2676

Publications: The Crane News (30105)

Cranston Mirror Co., Inc.
87 Myrtle Ave.
Cranston, RI 02910-5727
Phone: (401)467-7079

Publications: The Cranston Mirror (28333)

Craven County Publications, Inc.
1423 S Glenburnie Rd.
New Bern, NC 28562
Phone: (252)633-1153
Fax: (252)633-2663

Publications: The New Bern Shopper (24096)

Crawdaddy
PO Box 232517
Encinitas, CA 92023

Publications: Crawdaddy! (1883)

The Crawford Clipper/Harrison Sun
435 2nd St.
Crawford, NE 69339
Phone: (308)665-2310
Fax: (308)665-2310

Publications: The Crawford Clipper/Harrison Sun (17989)

Crawford County Avalanche
102 Michigan Ave.
PO Box 490
Grayling, MI 49738
Phone: (989)348-6811
Fax: (989)348-6806

Publications: Crawford County Avalanche (15131)

CRC Press L.L.C.
2000 Corporate Blvd. NW
Boca Raton, FL 33431
Phone: (561)994-0555
Fax: (561)998-2514

Publications: Critical Reviews in Environmental Science and Technology (25013) • International Journal of Geomechanics (5934)

CRC Publications
2850 Kalamazoo Ave. SE
Grand Rapids, MI 49560
Fax: (616)224-0834
Free: 800-333-8300

Publications: The Banner (15089)

Creation Research Society
PO Box 8263
St. Joseph, MO 64508-8263
Phone: (816)279-2312
Fax: (816)279-2312

Publications: Creation Research Society Quarterly (17391)

Creations Magazine
PO Box 970
Black Mountain, NC 28711
Phone: (828)664-0000
Fax: (828)664-0100
Free: 888-745-7337

Publications: Creations (23647)

Creative Age Publications, Inc.
7628 Densmore Ave.
Van Nuys, CA 91406-2042
Phone: (818)782-7328
Fax: (818)782-7450
Free: 800-442-5667

Publications: Dayspa (3986) • Dialysis & Transplantation (3987) • Nailpro (3994)

Creative Brilliance Associates
PO Box 32
Clam Lake, WI 54517
Phone: (715)794-2186

Publications: Brilliant Ideas for Publishers (33634)

Creative Communications for the Parish
1564 Fencorp Dr.
Fenton, MO 63026
Phone: (636)305-9777
Fax: (636)305-9333
Free: 800-325-9414

Publications: Healing Words (17060) • Living Faith (17061)

Creative Loafing
750 Willoughby Way
Atlanta, GA 30312
Phone: (404)688-5623
Fax: (404)614-3599
Free: 800-953-5623

Publications: Creative Loafing (6996)

Creative Marketing Plus
19 W 21st St., No. 403
New York, NY 10010
Phone: (212)727-1210
Fax: (212)727-1218

Publications: Outerwear Magazine (22513)

Creative Motion Publishing
2915 19th St. NE, Ste. 202
Calgary, AB, Canada T2E 7A2
Phone: (403)250-1090
Fax: (403)291-9546

Publications: Alberta Beef Magazine (34625)

Creative Nonfiction
5501 Walnut St., Ste. 202
Pittsburgh, PA 15232
Phone: (412)688-0304
Fax: (412)683-9173

Publications: Creative Nonfiction (27772)

Creative Printers, Inc.
238 Main St.
Stapleton, NE 69163
Phone: (308)636-2444
Fax: (308)636-2445

Publications: Arnold Sentinel (18285) • The Graphic (18286) • The Stapleton Enterprise (18287)

Creative Publications of Virginia, Inc.
20735 Ashburn Rd.
Ashburn, VA 20147
Phone: (703)858-5300
Fax: (703)858-7651

Publications: Loudoun Easterner (31853)

Creative Radio Network
PO Box 7749
Thousand Oaks, CA 91359
Phone: (818)991-3892
Fax: (818)991-3894

Publications: Elvis International Forum (3866)

Creative Video Consulting, Inc.
648 Broadway
New York, NY 10012-2314
Phone: (212)533-9870
Fax: (212)473-3772

Publications: CVC Report (21527)

Creative Writing Program
University of British Columbia (UBC)
Buch.
E. 462 - Main Mall
Vancouver, BC, Canada V6T 1Z1
Phone: (604)822-2514
Fax: (604)822-3616

Publications: PRISM International (35159)

Creative Writing Program
Kresge College
University of California
Santa Cruz, CA 95064

Publications: Scintilla (3689)

Credit Union Central BC
1441 Creekside Dr.
Vancouver, BC, Canada V6J 4S7
Phone: (604)734-2511
Fax: (604)730-6434

Publications: Enterprise (35140)

Credit Union National Association Inc.
PO Box 431
Madison, WI 53701-0431
Phone: (608)231-4080
Fax: (608)231-4370

Publications: Credit Union Magazine (33929)

Credit Union National Association Inc.
Publications Dept.
PO Box 431
Madison, WI 53701-0431
Phone: (608)231-4075
Fax: (608)231-4370
Free: 800-356-9655

Publications: Credit Union National Association GAC, Governmental Affairs Conference (33930) • Home & Family Finance (33948)

Cree Yadio Services
Box 9787
Fresno, CA 93794
Phone: (559)448-0700
Fax: (559)448-0761

Publications: One to One (1954) • One to One II (1955)

Creemore Echo Communications
176 Mill St.
PO Box 180
Creemore, ON, Canada L0M 1G0

Publications: Creemore Echo (35760)

Creemore Picnic
179 Mill St.
PO Box 70
Creemore, ON, Canada L1M 1G0
Phone: (705)466-2002
Fax: (705)466-3433

Publications: Elmvale Lance (35806)

CREES, MCIS, University of Toronto
1 Devonshire Place
Toronto, ON, Canada M5S 3K7
Phone: (416)946-8938
Fax: (416)946-8939

Publications: Bulletin on Current Research in Soviet and East European Law (36480)

Creighton University
California St. at 24th
Omaha, NE 68178
Phone: (402)280-1784
Fax: (402)280-2549

Publications: Creighton University Magazine (18193)

Creighton University
Dept. of Journalism & Mass Communication
2500 California St.
Omaha, NE 68178-0100
Phone: (402)280-2826

Publications: Creightonian (18194)

Cremation Association of North America
401 N Michigan Ave.
Chicago, IL 60611
Phone: (312)644-6610
Fax: (312)321-4098

Publications: The Cremationist of North America (8347)

Crescent
150 Main St.
Climax, MI 49034
Phone: (269)746-4331

Publications: Crescent (14882)

Crescent Publishing
301 S Main
PO Box 457
Hills, MN 56138
Phone: (507)962-3239
Fax: (507)962-3211

Publications: The Hills Crescent (15961)

Cresent International
300 Steelcase Rd. W, Unit 8
Markham, ON, Canada L3R 2W2
Phone: (905)474-9292
Fax: (905)474-9293

Publications: Crescent International (36022)

The Cresset
Valparaiso University
Valparaiso, IN 46383
Phone: (219)464-6809
Fax: (219)464-5511

Publications: The Cresset (10508)

Crested Butte Chronicle & Pilot
PO Box 369
Crested Butte, CO 81224
Phone: (970)349-0500
Fax: (970)349-6116

Publications: Crested Butte Chronicle & Pilot (4298)

Crestline Advocate, Inc.
312 N Seltzer
PO Box 226
Crestline, OH 44827
Phone: (419)683-3355
Fax: (419)683-0175

Publications: The Crestline Advocate (25101)

Creston Publishing Co.
503 W. Adams St.
PO Box 126
Creston, IA 50801
Phone: (641)782-2141
Fax: (641)782-2141

Publications: Creston News Advertiser (10732)

Creston Valley Advance
115 10th Ave.
PO Box 1279
Creston, BC, Canada V0B 1G0
Phone: (250)428-2266
Fax: (250)428-3320

Publications: Creston Valley Advance (34939)

The Crete News
1201 Linden
PO Box 40
Crete, NE 68333
Phone: (402)826-2147
Fax: (402)826-5072

Publications: The Crete News (17993)

The Cricket Magazine Group
315 5th St.
Peru, IL 61354
Phone: (815)224-5803
Fax: (815)224-6615
Free: 800-588-8585

Publications: Babybug (9446) • Cricket Magazine (9447) • Ladybug (9448)

Cricket Press, Inc.
PO Box 357
Manchester, MA 01944-0357
Phone: (978)526-7131
Fax: (978)526-8193

Publications: The Manchester Cricket (14302)

CRISES Press, Inc.
1716 SW Williston Rd.
Gainesville, FL 32608-4049
Phone: (352)335-2200

Publications: Counterpoise (6135) • Librarians at Liberty (6150)

Crisis
4805 Mount Hope Dr.
Baltimore, MD 21215-3206

Publications: Crisis (13153)

The Criterion
1400 N. Meridian St.
Indianapolis, IN 46206-1717
Phone: (317)236-1570
Fax: (317)236-1434
Free: 800-382-9836

Publications: The Criterion (10106)

Critical Care Nurse
101 Columbia
Aliso Viejo, CA 92656
Phone: (949)362-2000
Fax: (949)362-2049
Free: 800-899-1712

Publications: Critical Care Nurse (1391)

The Crittenden Press, Inc.
PO Box 191
Marion, KY 42064
Phone: (270)965-3191
Fax: (270)965-2516

Publications: The Crittenden Press (12281)

Crixon Communications Corp.
RR 3, Box 219B
Cobleskill, NY 12043
Phone: (518)234-8215
Fax: (518)234-8520

Publications: My Shopper (20478)

Croatian Catholic Union of U.S.A. and Canada
PO Box 602
Hobart, IN 46342-0602
Phone: (219)942-1191
Fax: (219)942-8808

Publications: Our Hope (10064)

Croatian Fraternal Union
100 Delaney Dr.
Pittsburgh, PA 15235-5416
Phone: (412)351-3909

Publications: Junior Magazine (27806) • Zajednicar (27856)

Croatian Philatelic Society
PO Box 696
Fritch, TX 79036-0696
Phone: (806)857-0129

Publications: The Trumpeter (30374)

Crompton Publishing
Box 856
Aberdeen, ID 83210
Phone: (208)397-4440
Fax: (208)226-5295

Publications: The Aberdeen Times (7797)

Crompton Publishing
PO Box 547
American Falls, ID 83211
Phone: (208)226-5294
Fax: (208)226-5295

Publications: The Power County Press (7798)

Crone Corporation
PO Box 457
Laurel, MT 59044-3048
Phone: (406)628-6243
Fax: (406)628-6243

Publications: Crone Chronicles (17845)

Crooklyn Publishers
209 E Vance
PO Box 669
Fuquay Varina, NC 27526
Phone: (919)552-4112
Fax: (919)552-7564

Publications: Fuquay Varina Independent (23903)

Crookston Times Printing Co.
124 S Broadway
PO Box 615
Crookston, MN 56716
Phone: (218)281-2730
Fax: (218)281-7234

Publications: Crookston Daily Times (15819)

Crop Science Society of America
677 S Segoe Rd.
Madison, WI 53711
Phone: (608)273-8080
Fax: (608)273-2021

Publications: Crop Science (33931)

Crosby County News & Chronicle
109 W Aspen
Crosbyton, TX 79322
Phone: (806)675-2881
Fax: (806)675-2855

Publications: Crosby County News & Chronicle (30109)

Crosby-Ironton Courier, Inc.
12 E Main St.
PO Box 67
Crosby, MN 56441
Phone: (218)546-5029
Fax: (218)546-8352

Publications: Crosby-Ironton Courier (15822)

Cross-Cultural Shamanism Network
PO Box 270
Williams, OR 97544
Phone: (541)846-1313
Fax: (541)846-1204

Publications: Shaman's Drum (26612)

Cross Currents
475 Riverside Dr., Ste. 1945
New York, NY 10115
Phone: (212)870-2544
Fax: (212)870-2539

Publications: Cross Currents (21522)

Crossville Chronicle
125 West Ave.
Crossville, TN 38555
Phone: (931)484-5145
Fax: (931)456-7683

Publications: Crossville Chronicle (29157)

Crothersville Times
510 Moore St., Ste. 100
PO Box 141
Crothersville, IN 47229
Phone: (812)793-2188
Fax: (812)793-2188

Publications: Crothersville Times (9913)

Crow Publications, Inc.
650 S. Lipan
Denver, CO 80223
Phone: (303)722-7600
Fax: (303)772-0155

Publications: Western Livestock Journal (4366)

Crowell, Inc.
PO Box 207
Chetopa, KS 67336
Fax: (316)795-2128

Publications: The Chetopa Advance (11380)

Crowley Post-Signal
602 N Parkerson Ave.
Box 1589
Crowley, LA 70526
Phone: (337)783-3450
Fax: (337)788-0949

Publications: The Crowley Post-Signal (12557)

Crowley Publishing, Inc.
PO Box 300
Crowley, TX 76036
Phone: (817)297-6707
Fax: (817)295-0486

Publications: Crowley Review (30112)

Crown Jewels of the Wire
PO Box 1003
St. Charles, IL 60174
Phone: (630)513-1544
Fax: (630)513-8278

Publications: Crown Jewels of the Wire (9566)

Crown Point Star
112 W Clark St.
PO Box 419
Crown Point, IN 46308
Phone: (219)663-4212
Fax: (219)663-0137

Publications: Crown Point Star (9915)

The Croydon Group, Ltd.,
833 Featherstone Rd.
Rockford, IL 61107-6302
Phone: (815)399-8775
Fax: (815)484-7701

Publications: The FABRICATOR (9527) • Practical Welding Today (9530) • Stamping Journal (9533) • TPJ—The Tube & Pipe Journal (9534)

Cruise & Freighter Association
PO Box 580188
Flushing, NY 11358
Phone: (718)939-2400
Fax: (718)939-2047
Free: 800-872-8584

Publications: TravLtips (20614)

Crusader Newspapers
6429 S Martin Luther King Dr.
Chicago, IL 60637
Phone: (773)752-2500
Fax: (773)752-2817

Publications: Chicago Crusader (8310)

The Crustacean Society
PO Box 1897
Lawrence, KS 66044-8897
Phone: (785)843-1221
Fax: (785)843-1274
Free: 800-627-0629

Publications: Journal of Crustacean Biology (6684)

Cryptosystems Journal
485 Middle Holland Rd.
Holland, PA 18966
Phone: (215)579-9888

Publications: Cryptosystems Journal (27046)

CSA Fraternal Life
122 W 22nd St.
Oak Brook, IL 60523
Phone: (630)472-0500
Fax: (630)472-1100
Free: 800-543-3272

Publications: CSA Journal (9347)

CSC Publishing
622 Gardenia Ct.
Golden, CO 80401
Phone: (303)277-9840
Fax: (303)278-9909

Publications: Advertising & Marketing Review (4462)

CSC Publishing, Inc.
1155 Northland Dr.
St. Paul, MN 55120-1288
Phone: (651)282-5600
Fax: (651)282-5650

Publications: Powder and Bulk Engineering (16407)

CSICOP Inc.
PO Box 703
Amherst, NY 14226
Phone: (716)636-1425
Fax: (716)636-1733
Free: 800-634-1610

Publications: The Skeptical Inquirer (19786)

CSS Publications, Inc.
16 Fite Rd.
Saugerties, NY 12477
Phone: (845)246-6944
Fax: (845)246-6944

Publications: ART TIMES (21100)

CTB International Publishing Inc.
PO Box 218
Maplewood, NJ 07040
Phone: (973)379-7749
Fax: (973)379-1158

Publications: Clinical Trials Monitor (19215)

CTI Publications Inc.
2 Oakway Rd.
Timonium, MD 21093-4247
Phone: (410)308-2080
Fax: (410)308-2079

Publications: Food Production Management (13757)

CUA Press
240 Leahy Catholic University
Washington, DC 20064
Phone: (202)319-5052
Fax: (202)319-4985

Publications: Anthropological Quarterly (5354) • The Catholic Historical Review (5400)

Cuba Free Press
110 S Buchanon
PO Box 568
Cuba, MO 65453
Phone: (573)885-7460
Fax: (573)885-3803

Publications: Cuba Free Press (17029)

The Cuero Record
119 E Main St.
Box 351
Cuero, TX 77954
Phone: (361)275-3464
Fax: (361)275-3131

Publications: The Cuero Record (30115)

Cuizine Magazine
1106 Stokes Ave.
Collingswood, NJ 08108
Fax: (609)869-5247

Publications: Cuizine Magazine (18767)

Culinaire Inc.
40 Mills St.
Morristown, NJ 07960
Phone: (973)993-5500
Fax: (973)993-8779
Free: 800-768-2789

Publications: Art Culinaire (19310)

Cullman Times
300 4th Ave. SE
Cullman, AL 35055
Phone: (256)734-2131
Fax: (256)734-7310
Free: 800-844-5369

Publications: The Cullman Times (160)

Cultural Survival Inc.
215 Prospect St.
Cambridge, MA 02139
Phone: (617)441-5400
Fax: (617)441-5417

Publications: Cultural Survival Quarterly (14047)

Culver-Stockton College
One College Hill
Canton, MO 63435-1257
Phone: (217)231-6380
Fax: (217)231-6611
Free: 800-537-1883

Publications: Megaphone (16941)

Cumberland Advocate
1375 2nd Ave.
PO Box 637
Cumberland, WI 54829
Phone: (715)822-4469
Fax: (715)822-4451

Publications: Cumberland Advocate (33648)

Cumberland County News
PO Box 307
Burkesville, KY 42717
Phone: (270)864-3891
Fax: (270)864-3497

Publications: Cumberland County News (11999)

Cumberland Presbyterian Church, Office of General Assembly
1978 Union Ave.
Memphis, TN 38104
Phone: (901)276-4581
Fax: (901)272-3913

Publications: The Cumberland Presbyterian (29365)

Cumberland Publishers, Inc.
457 E North St.
PO Box 130
Carlisle, PA 17013
Phone: (717)243-2611
Fax: (717)241-3511

Publications: Sentinel (26761)

Cumberland Publishing Ltd.
10 Lawrence St.
PO Box 280
Amherst, NS, Canada B4H 3Z2
Phone: (902)667-5102
Fax: (902)667-0419

Publications: Amherst Daily News (35532)

Cummins Publishing Co., Inc.
2563 Ashburton Ct.
Rochester, MI 48306-4926
Free: 800-552-5110

Publications: Wayland-Weston Town Crier (15671)

Cunningham Associates
180 Old Tappan Rd.
Old Tappan, NJ 07675
Phone: (201)767-4170
Fax: (201)767-8065

Publications: The Journal of Histotechnology (13392)

CurAnt Communications, Inc.
6701 Ctr. Dr. West, Ste. 450
Los Angeles, CA 90045
Phone: (310)642-4400
Fax: (310)641-4444

Publications: Respiratory Therapy Products (2379)

Current Digest of the Soviet Press
3857 N High St.
Columbus, OH 43214-3747
Phone: (614)292-4234
Fax: (614)267-6310

Publications: Current Digest of the Post-Soviet Press (25014)

Current History, Inc.
4225 Main St.
Philadelphia, PA 19127
Phone: (215)482-4464
Fax: (215)482-9923
Free: 800-726-4464

Publications: Current History (27433)

The Current Local
PO Box 100
Van Buren, MO 63965
Phone: (573)323-4515

Publications: The Current Local (17661)

The Current Newspapers, Inc.
PO Box 40400
Washington, DC 20016-0400
Phone: (202)244-7223
Fax: (202)363-9850

Publications: The Georgetown Current (5509) • The Northwest Current (5697)

Current Wave Newspaper
PO Box 728
Eminence, MO 65466-9998
Phone: (573)226-3335
Free: 800-353-9283

Publications: The Current Wave (17049)

Curry County Reporter
PO Box 766
Gold Beach, OR 97444
Phone: (503)247-6643
Fax: (503)247-6644
Free: 800-526-3059

Publications: Curry County Reporter (26360)

Curtains, Inc.
301 W 45th St., No. 5A
New York, NY 10036
Phone: (212)245-9186

Publications: Stages (22783)

Curtis Magazine Group
1000 Waterway Blvd.
Indianapolis, IN 46202
Phone: (317)633-8800
Fax: (317)633-8813

Publications: Trap & Field (10176)

Curtis Publishing Co.
8033 NW 36th St., No. S-438
Miami, FL 33166
Phone: (305)594-0508
Fax: (305)594-0518
Free: 800-334-4005

Publications: Dolphin Digest (6349)

Cushman Foundation for Foraminiferal Research
MRC-121
Dept. of Paleobiology
Smithsonian Institute
Washington, DC 20560
Phone: (202)357-1390
Fax: (202)786-2832

Publications: Journal of Foraminiferal Research (5276)

Custer County Chief
305 S 10th
PO Box 190
Broken Bow, NE 68822-0190
Phone: (308)872-2471
Fax: (308)872-2415

Publications: Custer County Chief (17965)

Custer Publishing, Inc.
PO Box 405
Challis, ID 83226
Phone: (208)879-4445
Fax: (208)879-5276

Publications: The Challis Messenger (7842)

Custom Media, Inc.
PO Box 23069
Chagrin Falls, OH 44023
Phone: (440)543-9451
Fax: (440)543-9764

Publications: Electronic Distribution Today (25491)

Custom News, Inc.
4341 Montgomery Ave.
Bethesda, MD 20814-4401
Phone: (301)951-1881
Fax: (301)656-2845
Free: 800-627-8723

Publications: U.S.A.E. (13386)

Custom Tailors and Designers Association of America, Inc.
PO Box 53052
Washington, DC 20009
Phone: (202)387-7220
Fax: (202)387-7713

Publications: The Custom Tailor (5457)

Cut Bank Pioneer Press
Box 847
517 E. Main
Cut Bank, MT 59427
Phone: (406)873-2201
Fax: (406)873-2443

Publications: Cut Bank Pioneer Press (17778)

Cutler Publishing Inc.
4500 Campus Dr. Ste. 480
Newport Beach, CA 92660-1872
Phone: (949)852-1990
Fax: (949)852-0231

Publications: Building Products Digest (2623) • The Merchant Magazine (2630)

Cuyahoga Community College
2900 Community College Ave.
Cleveland, OH 44115
Phone: (216)987-3030
Fax: (216)987-4119
Free: 800-954-8742

Publications: The High Point (24907) • The Mosaic (24929)

C.W. Post/Long Island University
199 Hillwood Commons
Greenvale, NY 11548
Phone: (516)299-2618
Fax: (516)626-1139

Publications: Pioneer (20699)

Cyberactive Media Group, Inc
64 Danbury Rd., Ste. 500
Wilton, CT 06897
Phone: (203)761-6167
Fax: (203)761-6184

Publications: IE Magazine (5228)

Cycle News Inc.
3505-M Cadillac Ave,
Costa Mesa, CA 92626
Phone: (714)751-7433
Fax: (714)751-6685

Publications: Personal Watercraft Illustrated (1780)

Cygnus Business Media
1233 Janesville Ave.
Fort Atkinson, WI 53538
Free: 800-547-7377

Publications: Aircraft Maintenance Technology (33703) • Airport Business (33704) • Automatic Merchandiser (33705) • Equipment Today (33707) • Farm Equipment (33708) • Feed & Grain (33709) • Fleet Maintenance Supervisor (33710) • Laminating Design and Technology (33712) • Law Enforcement Technology (33713) • Mass Transit (33714) • OEM Off-Highway (33715) • Pavement (33716) • Pro (33717) • Professional Tool & Equipment News (33718) • Qualified Remodeler Magazine (33719) • Rental Product News (33720) • Today's Distributor (33721) • Wood Digest (33722) • Yard and Garden (33723)

Cygnus Business Media Inc.
445 Broad Hollow Rd.
Melville, NY 11747
Phone: (631)845-2700
Fax: (631)845-2798
Free: 800-308-6397

Publications: Advanced Imaging (21039) • Army-Navy Store and Outdoor Merchandiser (21040) • The Commerical Image (21041) • Firehouse Magazine (21044) • Health Products Business (21045) • Kitchen and Bath Design Ideas (21046) • Kitchen and Bath Design News (21047) • Maintenance Supplies (21048) • Modern Jeweler (21049) • Modern Reprographics (21050) • The Pet Dealer (21053) • Photo Trade News (21054) • Photographic Video Trade News (21055) • Plastics World (21058) • Printing News (21060) • Printing News/East (21061) • PTN (Photographic Trade News) (21062) • Quick Printing (21063) • Soap/Cosmetics/Chemical Specialties (21064) • Wall & Window Trends (21065)

Cygnus Publishing Inc.
110 N Bell, Ste. 300
Shawnee, OK 74801
Phone: (405)275-3100
Fax: (405)275-3101

Publications: CPA Software News (26062)

Cynthiana Democrat
412 Webster Ave.
Cynthiana, KY 41031
Phone: (859)654-3333
Fax: (859)654-4365

Publications: The Falmouth Outlook (12355) • The Shopper's Outlook (12356)

Cypress Media, Inc.
211 State St.
PO Box 277
Clarks Summit, PA 18411
Phone: (717)587-1148
Fax: (717)586-3980

Publications: Abington Journal (26785)

Czech-American Heritage Center
2340 S 61st Ave.
Chicago, IL 60804
Phone: (708)656-1050

Publications: Hlas Naroda (Voice of the Nation) (8398)

D/FW Grocers Association
1720 S. Edmonds Ln., No. 29
Lewisville, TX 75067-5863
Phone: (972)353-5885

Publications: Food Herald (30686)

D Magazine
4311 Oak Lawn Ave., Ste. 100
Dallas, TX 75219
Phone: (214)939-3636
Fax: (214)748-4153

Publications: D Magazine (30140)

Da Capo Publishing
PO Box 1164, 255 So. Champlain St.
Burlington, VT 05402
Phone: (802)864-5684
Fax: (802)865-1015

Publications: Seven Days (31518)

Dadant & Sons Inc.
51 S. 2nd St.
Hamilton, IL 62341
Phone: (217)847-3324
Fax: (217)847-3660
Free: 800-637-7468

Publications: American Bee Journal (8968)

Daedalian Foundation
Box 249
Randolph AFB, TX 78148-0249
Phone: (210)945-2113
Fax: (210)945-2112

Publications: Daedalus Flyer (30969)

Daedalus Enterprises, Inc.
PO Box 29686
Dallas, TX 75229
Phone: (972)243-2272
Fax: (972)484-6010

Publications: AARC Times (30120)

The Dahlonega Nugget
1074 W Main St.
PO Box 36
Dahlonega, GA 30533
Phone: (706)864-3613
Fax: (706)864-4360

Publications: The Dahlonega Nugget (7219)

The Daily Advance
216 S Poindexter St.
PO Box 588
Elizabeth City, NC 27909-4835
Phone: (919)335-0841
Fax: (919)335-4415

Publications: The Daily Advance (23860)

Daily American
334 W. Main St.
PO Box 638
Somerset, PA 15501
Phone: (814)444-5900
Fax: (814)445-2935
Free: 800-452-0823

Publications: Daily American (28002) • The Sunday Shopper (28003)

The Daily Ardmoreite
PO Box 1328
Ardmore, OK 73402-1328
Phone: (580)221-6500
Fax: (580)226-2363
Free: 800-873-0211

Publications: The Daily Ardmoreite (25745)

Daily Breeze
5215 Torrance Blvd.
Torrance, CA 90503-4077
Phone: (310)540-5511
Fax: (310)540-6272

Publications: Daily Breeze (3932) • South Bay Extra (3944)

The Daily Camera
1048 Pearl St.
PO Box 591
Boulder, CO 80306

Publications: Daily Camera (4164)

The Daily Cardinal Newspaper Corp.
2142 Vilas Communication Hall
821 University Ave.
Madison, WI 53706-1497
Phone: (608)262-8000
Fax: (608)262-8100

Publications: The Daily Cardinal (33932)

Daily Challenge
1360 Fulton St.
Brooklyn, NY 11216
Phone: (718)636-9500
Fax: (718)857-9115

Publications: Daily Challenge (20310)

Daily Chronicle
PO Box 240
Reading, MA 01867
Phone: (781)944-2200
Fax: (781)942-0884

Publications: Daily Chronicle (14498)

The Daily Citizen
308 S. Thornton
Dalton, GA 30722
Phone: (706)278-1011
Fax: (706)275-6641

Publications: The Daily Citizen-News (7222)

The Daily Comet
705 W 5th Ave.
PO Box 5238
Thibodaux, LA 70302
Phone: (504)447-4055
Fax: (504)448-7606
Free: 800-256-1305

Publications: Daily Comet (12858)

Daily Commercial
PO Box 490007
Leesburg, FL 34749-0007
Phone: (352)365-8200
Fax: (352)365-1951

Publications: Daily Commercial (6301)

Daily Commercial Record
706 Main St.
Dallas, TX 75202
Phone: (214)741-6366

Publications: Daily Commercial Record (30142)

The Daily Corinthian
1607 S Harper Rd.
PO Box 1800
Corinth, MS 38834
Phone: (601)287-6111
Fax: (601)287-3525

Publications: The Daily Corinthian (16615)

The Daily Courier
147 N Cortez
Prescott, AZ 86301
Phone: (928)445-3333

Publications: The Prescott Courier (848)

The Daily Courier
550 Doyle Ave.
PO Box 40
Kelowna, BC, Canada V1Y 7V1
Phone: (604)762-4445
Fax: (604)762-3866

Publications: The Daily Courier (34988)

The Daily Courier
127 N. Apple St.
Connellsville, PA 15425-3196
Phone: (724)628-2000
Fax: (724)626-3568
Free: 800-801-9000

Publications: The Daily Courier (26801)

2360

Numbers cited after listings are entry numbers rather than page numbers.

Daily Court Review
6897 Wynnwood
PO Box 1889
Houston, TX 77251-1889
Phone: (713)869-5434
Fax: (713)869-8887

Publications: Daily Court Review (30469)

Daily Dispatch
530 11th St.
PO Drawer H
Douglas, AZ 85608
Phone: (520)364-3424
Fax: (520)364-6750

Publications: The Daily Dispatch (686)

The Daily Dunklin Democrat
203 1st St.
Kennett, MO 63857
Phone: (314)888-4505
Fax: (314)888-5114

Publications: The Daily Dunklin Democrat (17217)

Daily Freeman
79 Hurley Ave.
Kingston, NY 12401
Phone: (914)331-5000
Fax: (914)338-0672

Publications: Daily & Sunday Freeman (20860)

Daily Freeman-Journal
7 22nd St.
PO Box 490
Webster City, IA 50595
Phone: (515)832-4350
Fax: (515)832-2314

Publications: Daily Freeman-Journal (11313)

The Daily Gazette
PO Box 498
Sterling, IL 61081
Phone: (815)625-3600
Fax: (815)625-9390

Publications: The Daily Gazette (9663)

Daily Gazette Co.
2345 Maxon Rd. Ext.
PO Box 1090
Schenectady, NY 12301-1090
Phone: (518)374-4141
Fax: (518)395-3089
Free: 800-262-2211

Publications: The Daily Gazette (23314)

The Daily Gleaner
984 Prospect St. W.
PO Box 3370
Fredericton, NB, Canada E3B 2T8
Phone: (506)452-6671
Fax: (506)452-7405

Publications: The Daily Gleaner (35392)

Daily Globe
300 11th St.
PO Box 639
Worthington, MN 56187
Phone: (507)376-9711
Fax: (507)376-5202

Publications: Daily Globe (16539)

The Daily Item
200 Market St.
PO Box 607
Sunbury, PA 17801-0607
Phone: (717)286-5671
Fax: (717)286-2570

Publications: The Daily Item (28038)

Daily Jefferson County Union
28 W Milwaukee Ave.
Fort Atkinson, WI 53538
Phone: (920)563-5553
Fax: (920)563-2329
Free: 800-236-1013

Publications: Daily Jefferson County Union (33706)

Daily Journal of Commerce
2840 N.W. 35th Ave. 97210
PO Box 10127
Portland, OR 97296
Phone: (503)226-1311
Fax: (503)224-7140

Publications: Daily Journal of Commerce (26475)

Daily Journal of Commerce
83 Columbia St.
Seattle, WA 98104
Phone: (206)622-8272
Fax: (206)622-8416

Publications: Seattle Daily Journal of Commerce (33019)

Daily Journal Corp.
915 E. 1st St.
Los Angeles, CA 90012-4050
Phone: (213)229-5300
Fax: (213)680-3682
Free: (866)226-8740

Publications: California Lawyer (3337) • California Real Estate Journal (2231) • Daily Commerce (2251) • The Daily Recorder (2995) • The Inter-City Express (2682) • Los Angeles Daily Journal (2321) • San Diego Commerce (3259) • San Jose Post-Record (3537)

Daily Journal Messenger
Box 547
Seneca, SC 29679
Phone: (864)882-2375
Fax: (864)882-2381

Publications: Daily Journal Messenger (28754)

Daily Local News Co.
250 N Bradford Ave.
West Chester, PA 19382
Phone: (215)430-1134
Fax: (215)430-1180

Publications: The Homes Magazine (28147)

Daily Mail
PO Box 484
Catskill, NY 12414
Phone: (518)943-2100
Fax: (518)943-2063

Publications: Daily Mail (20438)

The Daily Mail
PO Box 128
Windham, NY 12496
Phone: (518)943-2100
Fax: (518)734-5179

Publications: The Windham Journal (23587)

The Daily Mining Gazette
PO Box 368
Houghton, MI 49931
Phone: (906)482-1500
Fax: (906)482-2726
Free: 800-682-7607

Publications: The Daily Mining Gazette (15183)

Daily Mountain Eagle
1301 Viking Dr.
PO Box 1469
Jasper, AL 35501
Phone: (205)221-2840
Fax: (205)221-2421

Publications: Jasper Mountain Eagle (296)

The Daily News
324 High St.
Palo Alto, CA 94301
Phone: (650)327-9090
Fax: (650)853-0904

Publications: Palo Alto Daily News (2800)

Daily News
PO Box 4200
Woodland Hills, CA 91365
Phone: (818)713-3000
Free: 800-346-6397

Publications: Daily News (4102)

Daily News
71 Weid Dr.
Naugatuck, CT 06770
Phone: (203)729-2228
Fax: (203)729-9099

Publications: Naugatuck News (4972)

Daily News
PO Box 130
Sullivan, IN 47882
Phone: (812)268-6356
Fax: (812)268-3110
Free: 800-264-6356

Publications: Daily Times (10474)

Daily News
813 College St.
PO Box 90012
Bowling Green, KY 42102
Phone: (270)781-1700
Fax: (502)781-0726
Free: 800-599-6397

Publications: Daily News (11943)

The Daily News
109 N. Lafayette St.
Greenville, MI 48838-9998
Phone: (616)754-9301
Fax: (616)754-8559
Free: 800-968-9301

Publications: The Daily News (15135)

The Daily News
215 E. Ludington St.
PO Box 460
Iron Mountain, MI 49801-2917
Phone: (906)774-2772
Fax: (906)774-1285
Free: 800-743-2088

Publications: The Daily News (15208)

Daily News
PO Box 760
Wahpeton, ND 58074-0760
Phone: (701)642-8585
Fax: (701)642-1501
Free: 800-666-4492

Publications: Daily News (24549)

The Daily News
PO Box 8330, Sta. A
Halifax, NS, Canada B3K 5M1
Phone: (902)461-6161
Fax: (902)468-2092

Publications: The Daily News Worldwide (35563)

The Daily News
770 11th Ave.
PO Box 189
Longview, WA 98632

Publications: The Daily News (32812)

Daily News-Journal
224 N Walnut St.
PO Box 68
Murfreesboro, TN 37133-0068
Phone: (615)893-5860
Fax: (615)896-8702

Publications: Daily News-Journal (29430)

Daily News of Los Angeles
21221 Oxnard St.
Woodland Hills, CA 91367
Phone: (818)546-1624
Fax: (818)713-3029
Free: 800-234-3348

Publications: Vecinos del Valle (4116)

The Daily News Publishing Co.
409 Walnut St.
Mc Keesport, PA 15132
Phone: (412)664-9161
Fax: (412)664-3972

Publications: The Daily News (27228)

The Daily News Publishing Co.
193 Jefferson Ave.
Memphis, TN 38103
Phone: (901)523-1561
Fax: (901)526-5813

Publications: The Daily News (29367)

Daily News Publishing, Inc.
813 College St.
PO Box 90012
Bowling Green, KY 42102
Phone: (270)781-1700
Fax: (270)781-0726
Free: 800-599-6397

Publications: Daily News Express (11944) • Daily News Shopping Guide (11945)

The Daily Nonpareil
117 Pearl St.
Council Bluffs, IA 51503
Phone: (712)328-1811
Fax: (712)328-1597

Publications: The Daily Nonpareil (10726)

The Daily Orange Corp.
744 Ostrom Ave.
Syracuse, NY 13210
Phone: (315)443-2314
Fax: (315)443-3689

Publications: The Daily Orange (23399)

Daily Packet and Times
31 Colborne St. E.
PO Box 220
Orillia, ON, Canada L3V 6J5
Phone: (705)325-1355
Fax: (705)325-7691

Publications: Daily Packet and Times (36174) • The Packet & Times This Week (36176)

The Daily Pennsylvanian, Inc.
4015 Walnut St.
Philadelphia, PA 19104
Phone: (215)898-6581
Fax: (215)898-2050

Publications: The Daily Pennsylvanian (27448)

Daily Pilot
330 W Bay St.
Costa Mesa, CA 92627
Fax: (714)631-5902

Publications: Daily Pilot (1774)

Daily Post Athenian
PO Box 340
Athens, TN 37371-0340

Publications: Daily Post-Athenian (29052)

The Daily Press
PO Box 1389
Victorville, CA 92393-1389
Phone: (760)241-7744
Fax: (760)241-7145
Free: 800-553-2006

Publications: The Daily Press (4031) • Daily Press Preview (4032)

The Daily Press
600 Ludington St.
Escanaba, MI 49829
Phone: (906)786-2021
Fax: (906)786-3752
Free: 800-743-0609

Publications: The Daily Press (15007)

The Daily Press
187 Cedar St. S.
PO Box 560
Timmins, ON, Canada P4N 7G1
Phone: (705)268-5050
Fax: (705)268-7373

Publications: The Daily Press (36453) • The Daily Press, E.M.C. (36454)

The Daily Press
245 Brussels St.
PO Box 353
St. Marys, PA 15857-0353
Phone: (814)781-1596
Fax: (814)834-7473

Publications: The Daily Press (27942)

The Daily Progress
685 W Rio Rd.
PO Box 9030
Charlottesville, VA 22906
Phone: (804)978-7200
Fax: (804)978-7223

Publications: The Daily Progress (31926)

Daily Publication Society/Le Delit Francais
3480 McTavish St. Rm. B-24
Montreal, QC, Canada H3A 1X9
Phone: (514)398-6784
Fax: (514)398-8318

Publications: The McGill Daily (37182)

Daily Racing Form
100 Broadway, 7th Fl.
New York, NY 10005
Phone: (212)366-7600
Fax: (212)366-7738
Free: 800-669-0449

Publications: Daily Racing Form (21532)

Daily Record
1209 State St.
PO Box 559
Lawrenceville, IL 62439
Phone: (618)943-2331
Fax: (618)943-3976

Publications: Daily Record (9068) • Lawrence County News (9069)

Daily Record
800 Jefferson Rd.
PO Box 217
Parsippany, NJ 07054
Phone: (973)428-6200
Fax: (973)428-6666
Free: 800-398-8990

Publications: Daily Record (19411)

The Daily Record Co.
1025 Vermont Ave., NW, Ste. 1110
Washington, DC 20005
Phone: (202)737-6860
Fax: (202)737-6848
Free: 800-878-5627

Publications: The Corridor Real Estate Journal (5443) • Real Estate Journal/Tri-State (REJ) (5759)

The Daily Record Co.
11 E. Saratoga St.
Baltimore, MD 21202
Phone: (410)752-3849
Fax: (410)752-2894
Free: 800-296-8181

Publications: The Daily Record (13154)

The Daily Record Corp.
11 Centre Park
PO Box 30006
Rochester, NY 14603-3006
Phone: (585)232-6920
Fax: (585)232-2740

Publications: The Daily Record (23220)

Daily Report Co.
190 Pryor St. SW
Atlanta, GA 30303
Phone: (404)521-1227
Fax: (404)523-5924

Publications: Fulton County Daily Report (7009)

Daily Reporter
22 W. New Rd.
PO Box 279
Greenfield, IN 46140
Phone: (317)462-5528
Fax: (317)467-6009

Publications: The Advertiser (10039) • Daily Reporter (10040)

The Daily Reporter
310 E. Milwaukee
PO Box 197
Spencer, IA 51301
Phone: (712)262-6610
Fax: (712)262-3044
Free: 800-383-0964

Publications: Cherokee Daily Times (10699) • The Daily Reporter (11230)

The Daily Reporter, Inc.
580 S. High St., S-316
Columbus, OH 43215
Phone: (614)224-4835
Fax: (614)224-8649

Publications: The Daily Reporter (25015) • Ohio Tavern News (25053)

Daily Reporter Publishing Co.
225 E. Michigan St., Ste. 540
Milwaukee, WI 53202
Phone: (414)276-0273
Fax: (414)276-8057
Free: 800-508-3800

Publications: Wisconsin Law Journal (34110)

Daily Republic
1250 Texas St.
PO Box 47
Fairfield, CA 94533-0747
Phone: (707)425-4646
Fax: (707)425-5924

Publications: Daily Republic (1909)

Daily Republican Register
115 E 4th St.
PO Box 550
Mount Carmel, IL 62863-0550
Phone: (618)262-5144
Fax: (618)263-4437

Publications: Daily Republican Register (9231)

The Daily Review
1014 Front St.
PO Box 948
Morgan City, LA 70381
Phone: (985)384-8370
Fax: (985)384-4255

Publications: The Daily Review (12707)

The Daily Sentinel
734 S. 7th St.
PO Box 668
Grand Junction, CO 81502-0668
Phone: (970)242-5050
Fax: (970)241-6860
Free: 800-332-5832

Publications: The Daily Sentinel (4478)

The Daily Sentinel
4920 Colonial Dr.
Nacogdoches, TX 75963
Phone: (936)564-8361
Fax: (936)560-4267

Publications: The Daily Sentinel (30849)

The Daily Sitka Sentinel
112 Barracks
Sitka, AK 99835
Phone: (907)747-3219
Fax: (907)747-8898

Publications: The Daily Sitka Sentinel (638)

Daily Sparks Tribune
1002 C St.
PO Box 887
Sparks, NV 89431-4929
Phone: (775)358-8061
Fax: (775)359-3837
Free: 800-669-1338

Publications: Daily Sparks Tribune (18445)

The Daily Standard
123 E Market St.
PO Box 140
Celina, OH 45822
Phone: (419)586-2371
Fax: (419)586-6271

Publications: The Daily Standard (24749)

The Daily Star-Journal
135 E Market
PO BOX 68
Warrensburg, MO 64093
Phone: (816)747-8123
Fax: (816)747-8741

Publications: The Daily Star-Journal (17666)

Daily Star Publishing Co.
PO Box 1149
Hammond, LA 70404-1149
Phone: (985)254-7827
Fax: (985)542-0242
Free: 800-844-2333

Publications: Hammond Daily Star (12590) • Star Shopping Guide (12593)

The Daily Sun
PO Box 2768
Warner Robins, GA 31098-2768
Phone: (912)923-6432
Fax: (912)328-7682

Publications: Robins Rev-Up (7637)

Daily Sun News
PO Box 878
Sunnyside, WA 98944
Phone: (509)837-4500
Fax: (509)837-6397

Publications: Daily Sun News (33142)

The Daily Targum
126 College Ave., Ste. 431
New Brunswick, NJ 08901
Phone: (732)932-7051
Fax: (732)246-7299

Publications: The Daily Targum (19329)

The Daily Telegram
133 N. Winter St.
PO Box 647
Adrian, MI 49221
Phone: (517)265-5111
Fax: (517)263-4152
Free: 800-968-5111

Publications: The Daily Telegram (14708)

The Daily Telegram
1226 Ogden Ave.
Superior, WI 54880
Phone: (715)394-4411
Fax: (715)394-9404

Publications: The Daily Telegram (34359)

Daily Telegraph
928 Bluefield Ave.
Bluefield, WV 24701-2744
Phone: (304)327-2800
Free: 800-763-2459

Publications: Daily Telegraph (33255)

The Daily Times
115 E. Carroll St.
Salisbury, MD 21802
Phone: (410)749-7171
Fax: (410)543-8736

Publications: The Daily Times (13707)

Daily Times
1 Arrow Dr.
Woburn, MA 01801
Phone: (978)658-2346
Fax: (978)658-2266

Publications: Wilmington-Tewksbury Town Crier (14588)

The Daily Times
201 N. Allen Ave.
PO Box 450
Farmington, NM 87401-6212
Phone: (505)325-4545
Fax: (505)564-4630
Free: 800-395-6397

Publications: The Daily Times (19846)

The Daily Times
307 E. Harper St.
PO Box 9740
Maryville, TN 37802
Phone: (423)981-1100
Fax: (423)681-1175

Publications: The Daily Times (29347)

The Daily Times
114 Lee Ave.
Weirton, WV 26062-4619
Phone: (304)748-0606
Fax: (304)748-2202

Publications: The Daily Times (33489)

Daily Times Leader
227 Court St.
PO Box 1176
West Point, MS 39773
Phone: (662)494-1422
Fax: (662)494-1414

Publications: Daily Times Leader (16875)

The Daily Tribune
220 1st Ave. S.
Wisconsin Rapids, WI 54495
Phone: (715)423-7200
Fax: (715)421-1545
Free: 800-632-8315

Publications: The Daily Tribune (34463)

The Daily Utah Chronicle
University of Utah
200 S. Central Campus Dr. No. 236
Salt Lake City, UT 84112
Free: (801)581-NEWS

Publications: Daily Utah Chronicle (31425)

Daily World
2781 F49 S Service Rd.
PO Box 1179
Opelousas, LA 70571-1179
Phone: (337)942-4971
Fax: (337)948-6572
Free: 800-256-4522

Publications: Daily World (12791)

Dairy Business Communications
6437 Collamer Rd.
East Syracuse, NY 13057
Phone: (315)703-7979
Fax: (315)703-7988
Free: 800-334-1904

Publications: Holstein World (20558) • The Western Dairyman (1768)

Daisy/Hi-Torque Publishing Co., Inc.
25233 Anca Dr.
Valencia, CA 91355
Phone: (805)295-1910
Fax: (805)295-1278
Free: 800-767-0345

Publications: Mountain Bike Action (3981)

Dakota County Tribune, Inc.
12190 County Rd. 11
Burnsville, MN 55337
Phone: (952)894-1111
Fax: (952)846-2010

Publications: Dakota County Tribune (15782)

Dakota Postal History Society
PO Box 600039
St. Paul, MN 55106

Publications: Dakota Collector (16373)

Da'Laine Publishing
PO Box 320
Bluffs, IL 62621-0320
Phone: (217)754-3369
Fax: (217)754-3369

Publications: Bluffs Times (8089) • Meredosia Budget (8090) • Triopia Tribune (8091)

Dalhart Publishing Co.
410 Denrock Ave.
Dalhart, TX 79022
Phone: (806)244-4511
Fax: (806)244-2395

Publications: Dalhart Daily Texan (30119)

**Dalhousie Gazette Publications Society/
Dalhousie University**
Student Union Bldg.
Halifax, NS, Canada B3H 4S2
Phone: (902)494-2507
Fax: (902)494-1280

Publications: The Dalhousie Gazette (35565)

Dalhousie University
Halifax, NS, Canada B3H 4H9
Phone: (902)494-3744
Fax: (902)494-1316

Publications: Hearsay (35567)

Dalhousie University
Macdonald Bldg., Rm. 100
Halifax, NS, Canada B3H 3J5
Phone: (902)494-2071
Fax: (902)494-1141
Free: 800-565-9969

Publications: Dalhousie Alumni Magazine (35564)

Dallas County News, Inc.
Box 190
Adel, IA 50003
Phone: (515)993-4233
Fax: (515)993-4235

Publications: The Round-up (10572)

Dallas-Fort Worth Suburban Newspapers, Inc.
1000 Ave. H East
Arlington, TX 76011
Phone: (817)695-0560
Fax: (817)695-0508

Publications: The Garland News (30384) • Metrocrest News (30004) • Richardson News (30978)

Dallas Genealogical Society
Box 12446
Dallas, TX 75225-0446
Phone: (469)948-1106

Publications: Dallas Journal (30146)

Dallas New Era
121 W Spring St.
PO Box 530
Dallas, GA 30132
Phone: (770)445-3379

Publications: Dallas New Era (7221)

The Dallas Post
PO Box 366
Dallas, PA 18612-0366
Phone: (570)675-5211

Publications: The Dallas Post (26816)

Dallas Theological Seminary
3909 Swiss Ave.
Dallas, TX 75204
Phone: (214)824-3094
Fax: (214)841-3664
Free: 800-992-0998

Publications: Bibliotheca Sacra (30132)

Dallas Tribune
508 Young St.
PO Box 655237
Dallas, TX 75265
Phone: (214)977-8222
Fax: (214)977-8638
Free: 800-431-0010

Publications: The Dallas Morning News (30147)

Dallas Tribune
2726 S. Beckley
Dallas, TX 75224
Phone: (214)946-7678
Fax: (214)946-6823

Publications: Dallas Post Tribune (30149)

The Dalton Gazette & Kidron News
PO Box 495
Dalton, OH 44618
Phone: (330)828-8401
Fax: (330)828-8401

Publications: The Dalton Gazette & Kidron News (25105)

Dan Chung News
10 Winterbranch
Irvine, CA 92604
Fax: (714)552-1791

Publications: Dan Chung News (2077)

Dan & Joan Poppers
PO Box 1040
Rancho Mirage, CA 92270
Phone: (760)836-3700
Fax: (760)836-3703

Publications: GOLF NEWS Magazine (2878)

Dan Kiedrowski Co.
P.O. Drawer A
La Honda, CA 94020
Phone: (650)747-0549
Fax: (650)747-0549

Publications: Schnauzer Shorts (2109) • Terrier Type (2110)

Dana Chase Publications, Inc.
1110 Jorie Blvd., CS 9019
Oak Brook, IL 60522-9019
Phone: (630)990-3484
Fax: (630)990-0078

Publications: Appliance (9337) • Appliance China Edition (9338) • Appliance European Edition (9339) • Appliance Latin America Edition (9340)

Dana School of Music
One University Plaza
Youngstown, OH 44555-3636
Phone: (330)742-1827
Fax: (330)742-1490

Publications: Contributions to Music Education (25696)

Danbury Reporter
PO Box 647
Walnut Cove, NC 27052
Phone: (336)591-8191
Fax: (336)591-4379

Publications: Danbury Reporter (24267)

Dance Magazine
111 Myrtle St., Ste. 203
Oakland, CA 94607
Phone: (510)839-6060
Fax: (510)839-6066

Publications: Dance Magazine (21535)

Dance Research Foundation, Inc.
37 W 12th St., No. 7/J
New York, NY 10011
Phone: (212)924-5183
Fax: (212)924-2176

Publications: Ballet Review (21285)

The Dandelion
PO Box 205
Cornucopia, WI 54827
Phone: (715)742-3940
Fax: (715)742-3940

Publications: The Dandelion (33645)

Dandick Co.
PO Box 8508
Scottsdale, AZ 85252
Phone: (480)948-1799
Fax: (602)994-9284

Publications: Arizona Trends (867)

Daniels County Leader
23 Main St.
PO Box 850
Scobey, MT 59263
Phone: (406)487-5303
Fax: (406)487-5304

Publications: Daniels County Leader (17903)

The Danish Villages Voice
PO Box 469
Elk Horn, IA 51531-0469
Phone: (712)764-4800
Fax: (712)764-4801

Publications: The Danish Villages Voice (10872)

Dan's Papers
PO Box 630
Bridgehampton, NY 11932
Phone: (631)537-0500
Fax: (631)537-3330

Publications: Dan's Paper (20243)

Dansville-Wayland Pennysaver
25 Main St.
Canisteo, NY 14823
Phone: (607)698-4771
Fax: (607)698-4388

Publications: Dansville-Wayland Pennysaver (20427)

Darby Printers
1111 E 60th St.
University of Chicago Law School
Chicago, IL 60637-2786
Fax: (312)702-0730

Publications: The University of Chicago Law Review (8592)

Darby Printing
6215 Purdue Dr. SW
Atlanta, GA 30336
Phone: (404)344-2665
Free: 800-241-5292

Publications: Florida Administrative Weekly (6705)

The Darien News
PO Box 496
Darien, GA 31305
Phone: (912)437-4251
Fax: (912)437-2299

Publications: The Darien News (7228)

The Dartmouth
6175 Robinson Hall
Hanover, NH 03755
Phone: (603)646-2600

Publications: The Dartmouth (18516)

Dartmouth College Library
Rm 115 Baker
Hanover, NH 03755-3525
Phone: (603)646-2236
Fax: (603)646-3702

Publications: Dartmouth Alumni Magazine (18517) • Dartmouth College Library Bulletin (18518)

Dartmouth Medical School
1 Medical Ctr. Dr., HB7070
Lebanon, NH 03756
Phone: (603)653-0772
Fax: (603)653-0775

Publications: Dartmouth Medicine (18542)

The Dartnell Corp.
360 Hiatt Dr.
Palm Beach Gardens, FL 33418
Phone: (561)622-6520
Fax: (561)622-2423
Free: 800-621-5463

Publications: Selling (6545)

Darvin Weaver Inc.
PO Box 6
Liberal, MO 64762
Phone: (417)843-5315
Fax: (417)843-5315

Publications: Liberal News (17247)

Data Centrum
21 W 38th St., 4th Fl.
New York, NY 10018-5506
Phone: (212)997-9800
Fax: (212)226-8847

Publications: Data Centrum (21537)

Data Enterprises, Inc.
3501 Napolean Ave.
New Orleans, LA 70125
Phone: (504)822-4433
Fax: (504)821-0320

Publications: New Orleans Data News Weekly (12744)

Data and Research Technology Corp.
1102 McNeilly Ave.
Pittsburgh, PA 15216-3402

Publications: Answers (27759)

Data Trace Publishing Co.
110 West Rd., Ste. 227
Towson, MD 21204
Phone: (410)494-4994
Fax: (410)494-0515
Free: 800-342-0454

Publications: JNMS: Journal of the Neuromusculoskeletal System (13760)

Daughters of St. Paul Provincial House
50 St. Paul's Ave.
Jamaica Plain
Boston, MA 02130
Phone: (617)522-8911
Fax: (617)524-8648

Publications: My Friend (13930)

Dauphin Herald
120 1st Ave., NE
PO Box 548
Dauphin, MB, Canada R7N 2V4
Phone: (204)638-4420
Fax: (204)638-8760

Publications: Dauphin Herald (35263)

Dauphin Island Sea Lab
101 Bienville Blvd.
Dauphin Island, AL 36528
Phone: (251)861-2141

Publications: Gulf of Mexico Science (169)

The David and Lucile Packard Foundation
300 2nd St., Ste. 200
Los Altos, CA 94022-3643
Phone: (650)948-7658
Fax: (650)941-2273

Publications: The Future of Children (2192)

Davidson College
PO Box 7171
Davidson, NC 28036
Phone: (704)894-2240
Fax: (704)894-2499

Publications: Davidson Journal (23799)

Davidson Leader
PO Box 786
205 Washington St.
Davidson, SK, Canada S0G 1A0
Phone: (306)567-2047
Fax: (306)567-2900

Publications: Davidson Leader (37463)

Davie County Enterprise-Record
PO Box 765
Clemmons, NC 27012
Phone: (704)634-2129

Publications: Davie County Enterprise-Record (23788)

Davies Communications, Inc.
135 S Christian
PO Box 720
Moundridge, KS 67107
Phone: (620)345-6353
Fax: (620)345-2170
Free: 800-378-2117

Publications: The Ledger (11659)

The Davis News
400 E Main St.
PO Box 98
Davis, OK 73030-0098
Phone: (580)369-2807
Fax: (580)369-2574

Publications: The Davis News (25799)

Davis Publications, Inc.
PO Box 187
Valley Falls, KS 66088
Phone: (785)945-3257
Fax: (785)995-3444

Publications: The Oskaloosa Independent (11687) • Valley Falls Vindicator (11858)

The Davison Index
220 N Main St.
PO Box 100
Davison, MI 48423-0100
Phone: (810)653-3511

Publications: The Davison Index (14897)

Davon Press Inc.
Box 457
West Fargo, ND 58078
Phone: (701)282-2443
Fax: (701)282-9248

Publications: The Midweek (24556) • West Fargo Pioneer (24557)

Dawn Media
PO Box 33148
San Diego, CA 92163-3148
Phone: (619)229-0500
Fax: (619)229-6907
Free: 800-331-1751

Publications: Update (3285)

The Dawson News
139 W Lee St.
PO Box 350
Dawson, GA 39842
Phone: (229)995-2175
Fax: (229)995-2176

Publications: The Dawson News (7229)

Dawson News & Advertiser
255 E. Hancock Ave.
PO Box 792
Athens, GA 30603
Phone: (706)479-3383
Fax: (706)479-1044
Free: 800-226-0692

Publications: Graham Star (24200)

Dawson Publications, Inc.
2236 Greenspring Dr.
Timonium, MD 21093
Phone: (410)560-5600
Fax: (410)560-5601

Publications: Place (14944)

Day County Printing Co.
PO Box 30
Webster, SD 57274
Phone: (605)345-3356
Fax: (605)345-4614

Publications: Reporter and Farmer (29027)

Day Publishing Co.
47 Eugene O'Neill Dr.
New London, CT 06320-1231
Phone: (860)442-2200
Fax: (860)442-5599
Free: 800-542-3354

Publications: The Day (5018)

Days Communications
1208 Juniper St.
Quakertown, PA 18951-1520
Phone: (215)538-1240
Fax: (215)538-1208

Publications: Police & Security News (27915)

The Dayspring Press
18600 W 58th St.
Golden, CO 80403-1070

Publications: Dayspring (4466) • Fiction Forum (4467) • Poet's Forum (4473)

Dayton Chronicle
358 E Main St.
PO Box 6
Dayton, WA 99328
Phone: (509)382-2221

Publications: Dayton Chronicle (32734)

Dayton Newspapers Inc.
45 S. Ludlow St.
Dayton, OH 45402
Phone: (973)225-7479

Publications: Dayton Daily News (25113)

Dayton Review
24 E Skillet
Box 6
Dayton, IA 50530
Phone: (515)547-2811
Fax: (515)547-2337

Publications: Dayton Review (10753)

The Dayton Tribune
PO Box 69
Dayton, OR 97114
Phone: (503)864-2310
Fax: (503)864-2310

Publications: The Dayton Tribune (26305)

Daytona Times, Inc.
427 S. Dr. M. L. King Jr. Blvd.
Daytona Beach, FL 32114
Phone: (386)253-0321
Fax: (386)254-7510

Publications: Daytona Times (6036)

db, The Sound Engineering Magazine
203 Commack Rd., No. 1010
Commack, NY 11725

Publications: db, The Sound Engineering Magazine (20488)

DBA bizlife Magazine
4101A Piedmont Pkwy.
Greensboro, NC 27410-8110
Phone: (336)812-8801
Fax: (336)812-8832

Publications: Business Life Magazine (23917)

DBC Communications, Inc.
655 Ste-Anne St.
Saint-Hyacinthe, QC, Canada J2S 5G4
Phone: (450)773-6028
Fax: (450)773-3115

Publications: Le Clairon Regional de St. Hyacinthe (37350)

DC & D Technologies, Inc.
8602 N 40th St.
Tampa, FL 33604
Phone: (813)989-9300
Fax: (813)980-3982
Free: 800-533-5680

Publications: Design Cost Data (6761)

De Anza College
21250 Stevens Creek Blvd.
Cupertino, CA 95014
Phone: (408)864-5626
Fax: (408)864-5533

Publications: La Voz (1798) • Red Wheelbarrow (1799)

De Baca County News
PO Box 448
502 Fort Summer
Fort Sumner, NM 88119
Phone: (505)355-2462
Fax: (505)355-7253

Publications: De Baca County News (19855)

De Camp Publishing Co.
Drawer 280
Gaffney, SC 29342-0280
Fax: (803)489-2324

Publications: Grit and Steel (28616)

Aldine de Gruyter
200 Saw Mill River Rd.
Hawthorne, NY 10532
Phone: (914)747-0110
Fax: (914)747-1326

Publications: Human Nature (19773)

De Pauw University
609 S. Locust St.
Greencastle, IN 46135
Phone: (765)658-5998
Fax: (765)658-5991

Publications: The De Pauw (10034)

De Pere Journal
126 S. Broadway
PO Box 5066
De Pere, WI 54115-5066
Phone: (920)336-4221

Publications: De Pere Journal (33651)

De Queen Bee Co.
404 De Queen Ave.
PO Box 1000
De Queen, AR 71832
Phone: (870)642-2111
Fax: (870)642-3138

Publications: De Queen Bee (1099)

De Queen Daily Citizen
404 De Queen Ave.
PO Box 1000
De Queen, AR 71832
Phone: (870)642-2111

Publications: De Queen Daily Citizen (1100)

de Sitter Publications
374 Woodsward Rd.
Willowdale, ON, Canada M2L 2T6

Publications: International Journal of Comparative Sociology (36879) • Journal of Asian and African Studies (36880)

De Witt Publishing Co.
PO Box 431
PO Box 431
De Witt, AR 72042
Phone: (870)946-3241
Fax: (870)946-1888

Publications: De Witt Era-Enterprise (1103)

De Witt Times News
PO Box 457
Wilber, NE 68465-0457
Phone: (402)683-5215
Fax: (402)821-2586

Publications: De Witt Times-News (18315)

Deaf Missions
21199 Greenview Rd.
Council Bluffs, IA 51503
Phone: (712)322-5493
Fax: (712)322-7792

Publications: Daily Devotions for the Deaf (10725)

The Deal, LLC
105 Madison Ave., 4th Fl.
New York, NY 10016
Phone: (212)313-9200
Fax: (212)481-8319
Free: 888-667-DEAL

Publications: The Deal (21541)

Dean of Education
University of Alberta
Edmonton, AB, Canada T6G 2G5
Phone: (780)492-3751
Fax: (780)492-0236

Publications: The Alberta Journal of Educational Research (34699)

DEC/CEC
1920 Association Dr.
Reston, VA 20191-1589

Publications: Journal of Early Intervention (23711)

DECA
1908 Association Dr.
Reston, VA 20191
Phone: (703)860-5000
Fax: (703)860-4013

Publications: DECA Dimensions (32364)

Decatur Publishing Co., Inc.
141 S 2nd St.
PO Box 1001
Decatur, IN 46733
Phone: (260)724-2121
Fax: (260)724-7981

Publications: Decatur Daily Democrat (9922)

Decatur Republican
Box 36
Decatur, MI 49045
Phone: (269)423-2411

Publications: Decatur Republican (14911)

Decatur Voice of the Black Community
625 E Wood St.
Decatur, IL 62523
Phone: (217)423-2231

Publications: Decatur Voice of the Black Community (8710)

December Press Inc.
PO Box 302
Highland Park, IL 60035
Phone: (847)940-4122

Publications: December (8991)

Decision Games
PO Box 21598
Bakersfield, CA 93390
Phone: (661)587-9633
Fax: (661)587-5031

Publications: Strategy & Tactics (1453)

Decker Advertising, Inc.
97 Main St., No. 5
Delhi, NY 13753-1234
Phone: (607)746-2178
Fax: (607)746-6272
Free: 888-746-3085

Publications: County Shopper—Catskill Park Edition (20523) • County Shopper—Delaware Edition (20524)

Decker Publications
3302 Gaston Ave., Rm. 610
Dallas, TX 75246
Fax: (214)828-8286

Publications: AAC (18077)

Decker Publications, Inc.
4601 Excelsior Blvd., No. 337
Minneapolis, MN 55416
Phone: (952)924-2322

Publications: Format Magazine (16038)

The Declaration & Blue Ridge Sun
PO Box 70
Independence, VA 24348
Fax: (540)773-2287

Publications: The Declaration & Blue Ridge Sun
(32172)

Decorah Newspapers
107 E Water St.
Box 350
Decorah, IA 52101
Phone: (319)382-4221
Fax: (319)382-5949

Publications: Journal (10756) • Public Opinion
(10758)

Decoy Magazine
PO Box 787
Lewes, DE 19958
Phone: (302)644-9001
Fax: (302)644-9003

Publications: Decoy Magazine (5259)

The Dedham Times
395 Washington St.
Dedham, MA 02026
Phone: (781)329-5553
Fax: (781)329-8291

Publications: The Dedham Times (14155)

Deep River Community Association
Box 310
Deep River, ON, Canada K0J 1P0
Phone: (613)584-4161
Fax: (613)584-1062

Publications: North Renfrew Times (35762)

Deer Creek Pilot
PO Box 398
Rolling Fork, MS 39159-0398
Phone: (662)873-4354
Fax: (662)873-4355

Publications: Deer Creek Pilot (16838)

Deer River Publishing
PO Box 427
Deer River, MN 56636
Phone: (218)246-8533
Fax: (218)246-8540
Free: 800-685-0800

Publications: Western Itasca Review (15826)

Deerfield Publishers
43 NE 2nd St.
Deerfield Beach, FL 33441
Phone: (954)428-9045
Fax: (954)428-9096

Publications: Observer Community Newspaper
(6051)

Defenders of Wildlife
1101 14th St. NW, Ste. 1400
Washington, DC 20005
Phone: (202)682-9400
Fax: (202)682-1331

Publications: DEFENDERS Magazine (5460)

Defense Acquisition University Press
9820 Belvoir Rd.
Fort Belvoir, VA 22060-5565
Phone: (703)805-3801
Fax: (703)805-2917

Publications: Acquisition Review Quarterly (32078)

Defense Institute of Security Assistance Management
DISAM-DRP
Bldg. 125
Wright Patterson AFB, OH 45433-7803
Phone: (937)255-5567

Publications: DISAM Journal (25683)

Defense News Media Group
6883 Commercial Dr.
Springfield, VA 22159
Phone: (703)750-9000
Fax: (703)848-0480

Publications: Armed Forces Journal International
(32539)

Defiance Publishing Co.
624 W Second St.
PO Box 249
Defiance, OH 43512
Phone: (419)784-5441
Fax: (419)784-1492
Free: 800-589-5441

Publications: Crescent-News (25157)

Deja Vu Publishing
2210 Harold Way
Berkeley, CA 94704-1425
Phone: (510)644-1600
Fax: (510)644-1686
Free: 800-433-5288

Publications: Psychic Reader (1553)

Dekalb Advertiser
PO Box 680559
Fort Payne, AL 35968-1606
Phone: (256)845-6156

Publications: Dekalb Advertiser (230)

DeKalb County Record-Herald
PO Box 98
Maysville, MO 64469
Phone: (816)449-2121
Fax: (816)449-2808

Publications: DeKalb County Record-Herald
(17280)

Del Mar College
101 Baldwin Blvd.
Corpus Christi, TX 78404
Phone: (361)698-1200
Free: 800-652-3357

Publications: The Foghorn (30077)

Del Property Management, Inc.
4800 Dufferin St.
Toronto, ON, Canada M3H 5S9

Publications: Del Condominium Life (36567)

Del Rio News-Herald
PO Box 4020
Del Rio, TX 78840
Phone: (512)775-1551
Fax: (512)774-2610

Publications: Del Rio News-Herald (30224)

The Delavan Times
314 Locust St.
PO Box 199
Delavan, IL 61734
Phone: (309)244-7111

Publications: The Delavan Times (8746)

Delaware County Journal
Box 1050
Jay, OK 74346
Phone: (918)253-4322
Fax: (918)253-4380

Publications: Delaware County Journal (25878)

Delaware County Times, Inc.
56 Main St.
Delhi, NY 13753
Phone: (607)746-2176
Fax: (607)746-3135

Publications: Delaware County Times (20525) •
Kaatskill Life (20526)

Delaware Gazette
40-44 S Vernon St.
PO Box 59
Sunbury, OH 43074-0059
Fax: (614)965-3992

Publications: News (25552)

The Delaware Gazette Co.
18 E. William St.
PO Box 100
Delaware, OH 43015
Phone: (740)363-1161
Fax: (740)363-6262

Publications: Gazette (25160)

Delaware Genealogical Society
505 Market St. Mall
Wilmington, DE 19801-3901

Publications: Delaware Genealogical Society Journal (5290)

Delaware Today
3301 Lancaster Pike, Ste. 5-C
Wilmington, DE 19805-1436
Phone: (302)656-1809
Fax: (302)656-5843
Free: 800-285-0400

Publications: Delaware Today (5292)

Delete Prefin, Inc.
38 Ctr. St. W, No. 42
Britt, IA 50423-1655
Phone: (515)843-3851

Publications: The Britt News-Tribune (10631) •
Town & County Advertiser (10632)

The Delhi Dispatch
603 Louisa
PO Box 209
Rayville, LA 71269
Phone: (318)878-2444
Fax: (318)878-3186

Publications: Richland Beacons News (12804)

Dell Magazines
475 Park Ave. S, 11th Fl.
New York, NY 10016
Phone: (212)686-7188
Fax: (212)686-7414

Publications: Alfred Hitchcock's Mystery Magazine
(21170) • Dell Horoscope Magazine (21542) • Ellery
Queen's Mystery Magazine (21597)

Delmont Record
PO Box 129
Armour, SD 57313
Phone: (605)724-2747
Fax: (605)946-5179

Publications: Delmont Record (28805)

Delphos Herald Inc.
405 N. Main
Delphos, OH 45833
Phone: (419)695-0015
Fax: (419)692-7704

Publications: Mercer County Chronicle (24997)

The Delta Atlas
212 Main St.
Delta, OH 43515-1312
Phone: (419)822-3231

Publications: The Delta Atlas (25164)

Delta Delta Delta
PO Box 5987
Arlington, TX 76005-5987
Phone: (817)633-8001
Fax: (817)652-0212

Publications: The Trident of Delta Delta Delta
(29737)

The Delta Optimist
5485 Ladner Trunk Rd.
Delta, BC, Canada V4K 1X2
Phone: (604)946-4451
Fax: (604)946-5680

Publications: The Delta Optimist (34945)

Delta Press Publishing Co.
123 2nd St.
PO Box 1119
Clarksdale, MS 38614
Phone: (662)627-2201
Fax: (662)624-5125

Publications: The Clarksdale Press Register
(16588)

Delta Productions
PO Box 2237
Vashon, WA 98070
Phone: (206)567-4373
Fax: (206)567-5711

Publications: PARA DOXA (33183)

Delta Publications, Inc.
606 Fremont St.
Kiel, WI 53042
Phone: (920)894-2828
Fax: (920)894-2161

Publications: Tempo (33881) • Tri-County News (33882)

Delta Publishing
127 W Main
PO Box 701
Malden, MO 63863
Phone: (573)276-5148
Fax: (573)276-3687

Publications: Delta News-Journal (17260)

Delta Publishing Co.
209 W. Main St.
PO Box 59
Piggott, AR 72454-0059
Phone: (870)598-2201
Fax: (870)598-5189

Publications: The Piggott Times (1313)

Delta Publishing Co.
PO Box 366
Rector, AR 72461
Phone: (870)595-3611
Fax: (870)595-3611

Publications: Clay County Democrat (1324)

Delta Publishing Co.
133 S. Walnut
PO Box 579
Dexter, MO 63841
Phone: (314)624-4545
Fax: (314)624-7449

Publications: The Daily Statesman (17032) • The North Stoddard Countian (16907)

The Delta Reporter
600 Ludington St., No. 2
Escanaba, MI 49829
Phone: (906)789-9122
Fax: (906)789-9006

Publications: The Delta Reporter (15008)

Delta Society
580 Naches Ave., SW, No. 101
Renton, WA 98055
Phone: (425)226-7357
Fax: (425)235-1076

Publications: InterActions (32924)

Democrat
PO Box 328
Marks, MS 38646
Phone: (601)326-2181
Fax: (601)326-6077

Publications: Quitman County Democrat (16759)

The Democrat
219 E. Main St.
PO Box 369
Senatobia, MS 38668
Phone: (662)562-4414
Fax: (662)562-8866

Publications: The Democrat (16841)

Democrat
319 S. High St.
PO Box 126
California, MO 65018
Phone: (314)796-2135
Fax: (314)796-4220

Publications: Democrat (16935)

Democrat
121 S. Main St.
Memphis, MO 63555
Phone: (660)465-7016
Fax: (660)465-2803

Publications: Memphis Democrat (17281)

Democrat Journal
PO Box 508
Stilwell, OK 74960
Phone: (918)696-2228
Fax: (918)696-7066

Publications: Democrat-Journal (26088)

The Democrat-Message, Inc.
110 W Main St.
PO Box 71
Mount Sterling, IL 62353
Phone: (217)773-3371
Fax: (217)773-3369

Publications: The Democrat-Message (9252)

Democrat-Missourian
301 S. Lexington
PO Box 329
Harrisonville, MO 64701
Phone: (816)380-3228
Fax: (816)380-7650

Publications: Cass County Democrat-Missourian (17093)

Democrat/Pathfinder
108 N. Court St.
PO Box 458
Glenville, WV 26351-1119
Phone: (304)462-7309
Fax: (304)462-7300

Publications: The Glenville Democrat (33322) • The Glenville Pathfinder (33323)

Democrat Publications Ltd.
3110 Boundary Rd.
Burnaby, BC, Canada V5M 4A2
Phone: (604)430-8600
Fax: (604)432-9517
Free: 800-216-3637

Publications: The Democrat (34896)

Democrat Publishing Co., Inc.
212 S. Washington
PO Box 586
Clinton, MO 64735
Phone: (816)885-2281
Fax: (816)885-2265
Free: 800-748-8473

Publications: The Clinton Daily Democrat (16983) • The Kayo (16984)

The Democrat-Reporter
PO Box 480040
Linden, AL 36748
Phone: (334)295-5224

Publications: The Democrat-Reporter (303)

Democrat-Tribune
334 High St.
Mineral Point, WI 53565
Phone: (608)987-2141
Fax: (608)935-9531

Publications: Democrat-Tribune (34145)

Democratic Socialists of America
180 Varick St., 12th Fl.
New York, NY 10014
Phone: (212)727-2207
Fax: (212)727-8616

Publications: The Activist (21148) • Democratic Left (21543) • Socialist Forum (22758)

Dempsey Management Services
2336 Wisteria Dr., Ste. 230
Snellville, GA 30078
Phone: (678)344-6283
Fax: (678)344-6299
Free: 800-822-4342

Publications: Fencepost Magazine (7557)

The Denison Bulletin/Review
1410 Broadway
Denison, IA 51442-0550
Phone: (712)263-2121
Fax: (712)263-2125

Publications: Ad-Visor (10764) • Bulletin (10765) • Review (10766)

Denison University
Box A
Granville, OH 43023
Phone: (740)587-6267
Fax: (740)587-6364

Publications: Denison Magazine (25221)

Denison University
PO Box H
Granville, OH 43023
Phone: (740)587-6276

Publications: The Denisonian (25222)

Denmark Sports
PO Box 4323
Chapel Hill, NC 27515-4323
Phone: (919)967-7789
Free: 800-447-7667

Publications: ACC Sports Journal (23697)

Dennis Publishing
1040 Ave. of the Americas, 12th Fl.
New York, NY 10018
Phone: (212)372-3801
Fax: (212)302-2635

Publications: Maxim (22300) • Stuff Magazine (22802)

Dental Learning Systems Co., Inc.
Div. of Medical World Communications, Inc.
241 Forsgate Dr.
PO Box 505
Jamesburg, NJ 08831-0505
Phone: (732)656-1143
Fax: (732)656-1148
Free: 800-926-7636

Publications: The Compendium of Continuing Education in Dentistry (19128)

Denton Publications
1 High St.
Elizabethtown, NY 12932
Phone: (518)873-6368
Fax: (518)873-6360
Free: 800-277-6567

Publications: The Adirondack Journal (23504) • North Country Free Trader (20564) • The North Countryman (23102) • Plattsburgh Free Trader (20565) • Times of Ticonderoga (20566) • Tri Lakes Free Trader (20567) • The Valley News (20568) • The Warrensburg-Lake George News (23505)

Denton Publishing Co.
314 E. Hickory
PO Box 369
Denton, TX 76201
Phone: (940)387-3811
Fax: (940)381-9666
Free: 800-275-1722

Publications: Denton Record Chronicle (30235) • The Grapevine Sun (30412) • Lewisville News (30688)

The Denver Post
1560 Broadway
Denver, CO 80202-1577
Phone: (303)820-1010
Free: 800-336-7678

Publications: The Denver Post (4324)

Denver Quarterly
University of Denver
Dept. of English
Denver, CO 80208
Phone: (303)871-2892
Fax: (303)871-2853

Publications: Denver Quarterly (4325)

Denver University College of Law
University of Denver, 2199 S. University Blvd.
Denver, CO 80208
Phone: (303)871-2000

Publications: Denver University Law Review (4326)

Depart des Industrielles
Local 3129, J.-A.-DeSeve
Universite Laval
Quebec, QC, Canada G1K 7P4
Phone: (418)656-2468
Fax: (418)656-3175

Publications: Revue Relations Industrielles/Industrial Relations (37296)

Department of Classical Studies
420 GCB/University of Missouri
Columbia, MO 65211
Phone: (573)882-3352

Publications: Classical and Modern Literature (16989)

Department of Commerce and Housing
1000 SW Jackson St.
Ste. 100
Topeka, KS 66612-1354
Phone: (785)296-3479
Fax: (785)296-6988
Free: (866)526-7624

Publications: Kansas! (11824)

Department of Conservation
PO Box 180
2901 W. Truman Blvd.
Jefferson City, MO 65109
Phone: (573)751-4115
Fax: (573)751-4467

Publications: Missouri Conservationist (17124)

Department of Education, General Conference of Seventh-Day Adventists
12501 Old Columbia Pke.
Silver Spring, MD 20904-6600
Phone: (301)680-5075
Fax: (301)622-9627

Publications: The Journal of Adventist Education (13729)

Department of Elder Affairs
4040 Esplanade Way
Tallahassee, FL 32399-7000
Phone: (904)414-2000
Fax: (904)414-2004

Publications: Elder Update (6703)

Department of Energy
PO Box 2008
Oak Ridge, TN 37831-6144
Phone: (423)574-7183
Fax: (423)574-1001

Publications: Oak Ridge National Laboratory Review (29550)

Department of Environmental Protection
PO Box 402
Trenton, NJ 08625-0402
Phone: (609)777-4182
Fax: (609)292-3198
Free: 800-645-0038

Publications: New Jersey Outdoors (19662)

Department of Geology & Mineral Industries
800 NE Oregon St., Ste. 965
Portland, OR 97232
Phone: (503)731-4100
Fax: (503)731-4066

Publications: Oregon Geology (26491)

Department of Health
Research & Statistics Office
Box 3378
Honolulu, HI 96801

Publications: Population Reports (7718)

Department of Labor
45 State House Sta.
Augusta, ME 04333-0045
Phone: (207)624-6440
Fax: (207)624-6449
Free: 877-723-3345

Publications: Fatal Occupational Injuries in Maine (12891)

Department of Language and Modern Literature
18525 Tarragon Way
Germantown, MD 20874-2026

Publications: The Journal of Afro-Latin American Studies and Literatures (13554)

Department of Military Affairs
Public Affairs Office
1301 N. Mac Arthur
Springfield, IL 62702-2399
Phone: (217)785-3569
Fax: (217)785-3527

Publications: Patriots of the Heartland (9640)

Department of Natural Resources
500 Lafayette Rd.
St. Paul, MN 55155-4046
Phone: (651)296-6157
Fax: (651)297-3618
Free: 888-646-6367

Publications: Minnesota Conservation Volunteer (16390)

Department of Natural Resources
Box 7921
Madison, WI 53707
Phone: (608)266-1510
Fax: (608)264-6293

Publications: Wisconsin Natural Resources (33988)

Department of Water Resources
PO Box 942836
Sacramento, CA 94236-0001
Phone: (916)653-1097

Publications: Management of the California State Water Project (3006)

Department of Wildlife Conservation
PO Box 53465
Oklahoma City, OK 73152
Phone: (405)521-3855
Fax: (405)521-6535
Free: 800-777-0019

Publications: Outdoor Oklahoma (25990)

DePaul University
2219 N. Kenmore Ave.
Chicago, IL 60614-3504
Phone: (773)325-7267
Fax: (773)325-7268

Publications: Philosophy Today (8529)

The DeQuincy News
203 E Harrsion
PO Box 995
DeQuincy, LA 70633
Phone: (318)786-8004
Fax: (318)786-8131
Free: 800-256-7323

Publications: The DeQuincy News (12563)

Der Yid Publication Association
84 Broadway
Brooklyn, NY 11211
Phone: (718)797-3900
Fax: (718)797-1985

Publications: Der Yid (20313)

Derksen Printers Ltd.
377 Main
PO Box 1209
Steinbach, MB, Canada R0A 2A0
Phone: (204)326-3421
Fax: (204)326-4860
Free: 800-442-0463

Publications: The Carillon (35294)

The Derrick
PO Box 928
Oil City, PA 16301
Phone: (814)676-7444
Fax: (814)677-8347

Publications: The Derrick (27346)

Derrickson Printing Corp.
122 S Main St.
PO Box 297
Licking, MO 65542
Phone: (573)674-2412
Fax: (573)624-2412

Publications: Licking News (17252)

Derry Publishing Co.
46 W Broadway
PO Box 307
Derry, NH 03038-2329
Phone: (603)437-7000
Fax: (603)432-4510

Publications: Derry News (18488)

Derus Media Service, Inc.
712 Vandustrial Dr.
Westmont, IL 60559
Phone: (630)960-4690
Fax: (630)960-4695

Publications: Editorial Pace (9754)

Des Plaines Valley News
PO Box 348
Summit, IL 60501
Phone: (708)594-9340
Fax: (708)594-9494

Publications: Des Plaines Valley News (9674)

Descant Arts and Letters Foundation
PO Box 314, Sta. P
Toronto, ON, Canada M5S 2S8
Phone: (416)593-2557
Fax: (416)593-9362

Publications: Descant (36570)

Descendants of Mexican War Veterans
Box 830482
Richardson, TX 75083-0482

Publications: Mexican War Journal (30977)

Descriptive Video Service
WGBH
125 Western Ave.
Boston, MA 02134
Phone: (617)300-3600
Fax: (617)300-1020

Publications: DVS Guide (13887)

Deseret Book Co.
40 E. South Temple
Salt Lake City, UT 84111
Phone: (801)517-3328
Fax: (801)517-3125
Free: 800-922-9681

Publications: Church News (31423)

Deseret News Publishing Co.
30 East 100 South
Salt Lake City, UT 84111

Publications: Deseret News (31426)

Desert Botanical Garden
1201 N Galvin Pkwy.
Phoenix, AZ 85008
Phone: (480)941-1225
Fax: (480)481-8124

Publications: Agave (771)

Desert Dispatch
130 Coolwater Ln.
Barstow, CA 92311-3222
Phone: (619)256-2257
Fax: (619)256-0685

Publications: Desert Dispatch (1481)

Desert Foothills Newspapers, Inc.
290 S 1st Ave., Ste. 4
Yuma, AZ 85364
Phone: (480)488-3436
Fax: (480)488-4779

Publications: Foothills Sentinel (1017)

Desert Mailer News
PO Box 4050
Palmdale, CA 93590-4050
Phone: (805)945-8671
Fax: (805)942-6418

Publications: Desert Mailer News (2784)

Desert Plants
2120 E Allen Rd.
Tucson, AZ 85719
Phone: (520)318-7046
Fax: (520)318-7272

Publications: Desert Plants (945)

Desert Post WEEKLY
68-625 Perez Rd., Ste. 6
Cathedral City, CA 92234
Phone: (760)202-3200
Fax: (760)324-2751

Publications: Desert Post WEEKLY (1679)

Desert Publication Inc.
303 N. Indian Canyon Dr.
PO Box 2724
Palm Springs, CA 92263
Phone: (760)325-2333
Fax: (760)325-7008

Publications: Palm Springs Life's Desert Guide (2764)

Desert Sun Publishing Co.
PO Box 2734
Palm Springs, CA 92263
Phone: (760)322-8889
Fax: (760)778-4513
Free: 800-834-6052

Publications: Coachella Valley Sun (2756)

Design Book Review
1418 Spring Way
Berkeley, CA 94708
Phone: (510)486-1956
Fax: (510)644-3930

Publications: Design Book Review (1513)

Design History Foundation
201B Higgins Hall
Pratt School of Architecture
200 Willoughby Ave.
Brooklyn, NY 11205
Phone: (718)399-4313

Publications: PLACES (20337)

Design Management Institute
29 Temple Pl., 2nd Fl.
Boston, MA 02111-1350
Phone: (617)338-6380
Fax: (617)338-6570

Publications: Design Management Journal (13885) • DMI Academic Review (13886)

Design Methods Institute
Box 3
San Luis Obispo, CA 93406

Publications: Design Methods (3565)

Designer/Builder
2405 Maclovia Ln.
Santa Fe, NM 87505
Phone: (505)438-2436
Fax: (505)471-4549

Publications: Designer/Builder (19934)

DeSoto County Tribune
8885 Goodman
PO Box 1486
Olive Branch, MS 38654
Phone: (662)895-6220
Fax: (662)895-4377
Free: 800-558-7025

Publications: DeSoto County Tribune (16804) • Home Market Magazine (16805)

The DeSoto Press
212 Redstone Dr.
Bristol, TN 37620-2938

Publications: American Journal of Italian Studies (29065)

The Destin Log
PO Box 957
Destin, FL 32540
Phone: (850)654-8484
Fax: (850)654-5982

Publications: The Destin Log (6059)

Destiny Productions for Print, Radio & Cable Promotions
3395 S Jones Blvd., No. 217
Las Vegas, NV 89146-6770
Phone: (702)438-1470
Fax: (702)438-2790

Publications: Cocktails Magazine (18361) • Healing Arts Quarterly (18363) • Kosher for Health (18370) • New Age Networking Magazine (18381)

Detroit Athletic Club
241 Madison Ave.
Detroit, MI 48226
Phone: (313)442-1034
Fax: (313)442-1047

Publications: D.A.C. News (14923)

Detroit Educational Television Foundation
7441 Second Ave.
Detroit, MI 48202
Phone: (313)873-7200
Fax: (313)876-8118

Publications: Signal (14946)

Detroit Institute of Arts
5200 Woodward Ave.
Detroit, MI 48202
Phone: (313)833-7900
Fax: (313)833-6409

Publications: Bulletin of the Detroit Institute of Arts (14917)

The Detroit Jewish News
29200 Northwestern Hwy. Ste.110c
Southfield, MI 48034
Phone: (248)354-6060
Fax: (248)354-6069

Publications: The Detroit Jewish News (14925)

Detroit Legal News Co.
1409 Allen Dr., Ste. B
Troy, MI 48083
Phone: (248)577-6100
Fax: (248)577-6111
Free: 800-875-5275

Publications: Detroit Legal News (15618)

Detroit Regional Chamber
1 Woodward Ave., Ste. 1900
PO Box 33840
Detroit, MI 48232
Phone: (313)596-0384
Fax: (313)964-0183

Publications: Detroiter (14929)

Detroit Society for Genealogical Research, Inc.
The Burton Historical Collection
Detroit Public Library
5201 Woodward Ave. & Kirby
Detroit, MI 48202-4093
Phone: (313)833-1480

Publications: Detroit Society for Genealogical Research Magazine (14928)

Deutsche Presse (German Press)
455 Spadina Ave., Ste. 303
Toronto, ON, Canada M5S 2G8
Phone: (416)595-9714
Fax: (416)595-9716

Publications: Deutsche Presse (German Press) (36572)

Deux Montagnes Inc.
Center Heights
50B, rue Turgeon
Ste.-Therese, QC, Canada J7E 3H4
Fax: (514)435-0588

Publications: La Voix des Mille Iles (37368)

DeVaul Publishing, Inc.
459 NE Washington Ave.
Chehalis, WA 98532
Phone: (360)748-6848
Fax: (360)748-6841

Publications: East County Journal (32836) • The Tenino Independent & Sun News (33163)

Devil's River News
228 E Main
Sonora, TX 76950
Phone: (915)387-2507
Fax: (915)387-5691

Publications: Devil's River News (31119)

Devine Media
492 Grand Ave.
Rahway, NJ 07065

Publications: The Citizen (19485)

Devine News
216 S Bright
PO Box 508
Devine, TX 78016-0508
Phone: (210)663-3685

Publications: The Devine News (30247)

Devlin Newspapers, Inc.
PO Box 100
Staples, MN 56479

Publications: Sunday Square Shooter (16461)

Devlin Publications, Inc.
Box 525
Cooperstown, ND 58425
Phone: (701)797-3331

Publications: Griggs County Sentinel-Courier (24388)

Dewitt County Genealogical Society
PO Box 632
Clinton, IL 61727
Phone: (217)935-3493

Publications: Dewitt County Genealogical Society Quarterly (8683)

The DeWitt Observer Publishing Co., Inc.
512 7th St.
PO Box 49
De Witt, IA 52742
Phone: (563)659-3121
Fax: (563)659-3778

Publications: The Observer (10755)

DFW Community Newspapers
PO Box 860248
Plano, TX 75086
Phone: (972)335-1176
Fax: (972)424-8388

Publications: The Allen American (29681) • The Colony Courier-Leader (30062) • Coppell Gazette (30072) • Flower Mound Leader (30321) • Fort Worth Business Press (30337) • The Frisco Enterprise (30371) • Lewisville Leader (30687) • The Little Elm Journal (30695) • McKinney Messenger (30778) • The Mesquite News (30808) • Plano Star Courier (30948) • The Rowlett Lakeshore Times (30998) • Southlake Times (31123)

DGM Associates
Box 10639
Marina del Rey, CA 90295-6639
Phone: (310)578-1428

Publications: HR/PC (2508)

DGR Publication
1256 Principale N. St., Ste. 203
L'Annonciation, QC, Canada J0T 1T0
Phone: (819)275-3293
Fax: (819)275-3293

Publications: Emploi Plus (36939)

Diablo Publications
2520 Camino Diablo
Walnut Creek, CA 94596-3944
Phone: (510)943-1111
Fax: (510)943-1045

Publications: Diablo (4052) • Diablo Arts (4053)

The Diagonal Progress
PO Box 77
Diagonal, IA 50845-0077

Publications: The Diagonal Progress (10839)

Dialysis, Inc.
4881 Topanga Canyon Blvd. No. 201
Woodland Hills, CA 91364
Phone: (818)704-5555
Fax: (818)704-6500
Free: 800-401-9215

Publications: For Patients Only (4106)

Diamond Headache Clinic Research & Educational Foundation
467 W Deming Pl.
Suite 500
Chicago, IL 60614-1726
Phone: (773)388-6363
Fax: (773)477-9712
Free: 800-432-3224

Publications: Headache Quarterly (8391)

Diamond Research Corp.
530 W. Ojai Ave., Ste. 108
Ojai, CA 93023-2471
Phone: (805)640-9081
Fax: (805)640-1607

Publications: Imaging News Online (2713)

Diamond Trail News
PO Box 267
Sully, IA 50251-0267
Phone: (641)594-4488
Fax: (641)594-4498

Publications: Diamond Trail News (11257)

Diarist's Journal
209 E 38th St.
Covington, KY 41015
Phone: (606)491-2369

Publications: Diarist's Journal (12026)

John DiCarlo
1241 Soto St., Ste. 213
Los Angeles, CA 90023
Phone: (323)881-6515
Fax: (323)881-6524

Publications: Novedades (2350)

The Dickey County Leader
216 Main Ave.
PO Box 9
Ellendale, ND 58436
Phone: (701)349-3222
Fax: (701)349-3229

Publications: The Dickey County Leader (24407)

Dickinson College
PO Box 4888
Carlisle, PA 17013
Phone: (717)245-1410
Fax: (717)245-1899

Publications: The Dickinsonian (26759)

The Dickinson Press
1815 W 1st St.
PO Box 1367
Dickinson, ND 58601
Phone: (701)225-8111
Fax: (701)225-4205

Publications: The Dickinson Press (24394)

Dickinson School of Law
150 S College St.
Carlisle, PA 17013
Phone: (717)240-5000
Fax: (717)241-3511

Publications: Dickinson Law Review (26758)

Dickinson State College
291 Campus Dr.
PO Box 165
Dickinson, ND 58602-0165
Phone: (701)483-2844
Fax: (701)483-2059

Publications: Western Concept (24395)

The Dickson Herald
104 Church St.
Dickson, TN 37055
Phone: (615)446-2811
Fax: (615)446-5560

Publications: The Dickson Herald (29165)

Dickson Media, Inc.
115 Main St.
Eau Claire, MI 49111
Phone: (616)461-6941
Fax: (616)461-6816

Publications: Twin City Trade Lines Shopper's Guide (14809)

Dickson Media, Inc.
18 S. Main
PO Drawer F
Bowman, ND 58623
Phone: (701)523-5623
Fax: (701)523-3441
Free: 800-732-0738

Publications: Bowman County Pioneer (24380) • The Finder - Bowman Edition (24381)

Dickson Press
119 W. Elwood Ave.
Box 550
Raeford, NC 28376
Phone: (910)875-2121
Fax: (910)875-7256

Publications: Fort Bragg Paraglide (24120) • News-Journal (24121) • Spring Lake News (23881)

Die Hausfrau, Inc.
103 E Meadow Dr.
Athens, GA 30605
Phone: (706)548-4382
Fax: (706)548-8856
Free: 800-398-7753

Publications: Das Fenster Nach Druben (6936)

Diesel & Gas Turbine Publications
20855 Watertown Rd.
Waukesha, WI 53186
Phone: (262)832-5000
Fax: (262)832-5075
Free: 800-558-4322

Publications: Diesel & Gas Turbine Worldwide (34401) • Diesel Progress International Edition (34402) • Diesel Progress North American Edition (34403)

Dietary Managers Association (DMA)
406 Surrey Woods Dr.
St. Charles, IL 60174
Phone: (630)587-6336
Fax: (630)587-6308
Free: 800-323-1908

Publications: Dietary Manager Magazine (9567)

Dietitians of Canada
480 University Ave., Ste. 604
Toronto, ON, Canada M5G 1V2
Phone: (416)596-0857
Fax: (416)596-0603

Publications: Canadian Journal of Dietetic Practice and Research (36021)

The Digby Courier
PO Box 670
Digby, NS, Canada B0V 1A0
Phone: (902)245-4715
Fax: (902)245-4715

Publications: The Digby Courier (35552)

The Digest
224 S Dixie Hwy.
Hallandale, FL 33009
Phone: (305)457-8029
Fax: (305)457-1284
Free: 800-344-3780

Publications: The Digest (6184)

Digest of Neurology and Psychiatry
200 Retreat Ave.
Hartford, CT 06106
Fax: (860)545-7068
Free: 800-673-2411

Publications: Digest of Neurology and Psychiatry (4889)

The Dighton Herald
113 E Long
PO Box 637
Dighton, KS 67839-0637
Phone: (316)397-5347
Fax: (316)397-2618

Publications: The Dighton Herald (11412)

Digital Journal, Inc.
31 Adelaide St. E.
PO Box 1046
Toronto, ON, Canada M5C 2K4
Phone: (416)410-9675

Publications: Digital Journal.com (36575)

Digital Output
5150 Palm Valley Rd., Ste. 103
Ponte Vedra Beach, FL 32082-4630
Phone: (904)285-6020
Fax: (904)285-9944

Publications: Digital Output (6594)

Dillon Tribune
22 S Montana
PO Box 911
Dillon, MT 59725-0911
Phone: (406)683-2331
Fax: (406)683-2332

Publications: Dillon Tribune (17782) • Tribune Advertiser (17783)

Dillsburg Banner
31 S. Baltimore St.
Dillsburg, PA 17019
Phone: (717)432-3456
Fax: (717)432-1518

Publications: Dillsburg Banner (26826)

Dime Novel Roundup
PO Box 226
Dundas, MN 55019-0226
Phone: (507)645-5711

Publications: Dime Novel Roundup (15860)

Dinwiddie Monitor
PO Box 66
Dinwiddie, VA 23841-0066
Phone: (804)733-8636

Publications: Dinwiddie Monitor (31997)

Diocese of Baton Rouge
1800 S Acadian Thruway
PO Box 14746
Baton Rouge, LA 70808-1663
Phone: (225)387-0983
Fax: (225)336-8789

Publications: The Catholic Commentator (12486)

Diocese of Beaumont
703 Archie
Beaumont, TX 77701
Phone: (409)838-0451
Fax: (409)838-4511

Publications: East Texas Catholic (29898)

Diocese of Bismack
520 N Washington St.
PO Box 1137
Bismarck, ND 58502
Phone: (701)222-3035
Fax: (701)223-3693

Publications: Dakota Catholic Action (24350)

Diocese of Chicago
65 E Huron St.
Chicago, IL 60611
Phone: (312)751-4207
Fax: (312)787-4534

Publications: Anglican Advance (8263)

Diocese of Colorado
1300 Washington St.
Denver, CO 80203-2008
Phone: (303)837-1173
Fax: (303)837-1311

Publications: Colorado Episcopalian (4314)

The Diocese of Gallup
PO Box 1338
Gallup, NM 87301
Phone: (505)863-4406
Fax: (505)722-9131

Publications: The Voice of the Southwest (19858)

Diocese of Jefferson City
609 Clark Ave.
PO Box 1107
Jefferson City, MO 65102
Phone: (573)635-9127
Fax: (573)635-2286

Publications: The Catholic Missourian (17120)

Diocese of Lake Charles
PO Box 3223
Lake Charles, LA 70602-3223
Phone: (337)439-7426
Fax: (337)439-7428

Publications: The Southwest Catholic (12644)

Diocese of Memphis
5825 Shelby Oaks Dr.
Memphis, TN 38134-7389
Phone: (901)373-1213
Fax: (901)373-1269

Publications: The West Tennessee Catholic (29384)

Diocese of Nashville
2400 21st Ave. S
Nashville, TN 37212
Phone: (615)383-6393
Fax: (615)783-0285
Free: 800-273-0256

Publications: The Tennessee Register (29493)

Diocese of Orange
Marywood Ctr.
2811 E. Villa Real Dr.
Orange, CA 92867-1999
Phone: (714)282-3000
Fax: (714)282-3029

Publications: Diocese of Orange Bulletin (2722)

Diocese of Springfield-Cape Girardeau
601 S Jefferson Ave.
Springfield, MO 65806-3143
Phone: (417)866-0841
Fax: (417)866-1140

Publications: The Mirror (17605)

Diocese of Steubenville
422 Washington St.
PO Box 160
Steubenville, OH 43952-2181
Phone: (740)282-3631
Fax: (740)282-3238

Publications: The Steubenville Register (25540)

Diocese of Yakima
5301-A Tieton Dr.
Yakima, WA 98908-3493
Phone: (509)965-7117
Fax: (509)966-8334

Publications: Central Washington Catholic (33219)

Directions Publishing, Inc.
21 N Henry St.
Edgerton, WI 53534-1821
Phone: (608)884-3367
Fax: (608)884-8187

Publications: Career Directions (33686)

Directories International Ltd.
2087 Castlefield Crescent
Oakville, ON, Canada L6H 5B6
Phone: (905)337-3030
Fax: (905)338-1364

Publications: Pakeeza International (36150) • The South Asian Voice (36151)

Directors and Boards
1845 Walnut St., Ste. 900
Philadelphia, PA 19103-4709
Phone: (215)567-3200
Fax: (215)405-6078
Free: 800-637-4464

Publications: Directors & Boards (27452)

Dirty Linen
POB 66600
Baltimore, MD 21239-6600
Phone: (410)583-7973
Fax: (410)337-6735

Publications: Dirty Linen (13157)

Disability Statistics Center
Institute for Health and Aging
3333 California St., Rm 340
University of California
San Francisco, CA 94118
Phone: (415)502-5210
Fax: (415)502-5208

Publications: Disability Statistics Report (3349)

Disabled American Veterans
3725 Alexandria Pike
Cold Spring, KY 41076
Free: 877-426-2838

Publications: DAV Magazine (12017)

Disabled Sports, USA
451 Hungerford Dr., Ste. 100
Rockville, MD 20850
Phone: (301)217-0960
Fax: (301)217-0968

Publications: Challenge Magazine (13676)

Disaster Recovery Journal
PO Box 510110
St. Louis, MO 63151
Phone: (314)894-0276
Fax: (314)894-7474

Publications: Disaster Recovery Journal (17434)

Disciples of Christ Historical Society
1101 19th Ave. S.
Nashville, TN 37212
Phone: (615)327-1444
Fax: (615)327-1445

Publications: Discipliana (29454)

Discover Magazine, Inc.
20533 Biscayne Blvd., Ste. 126
Aventura, FL 33180
Phone: (305)932-2400
Fax: (305)933-8876

Publications: Aventura Magazine (5912)

Discovery Publications, Inc.
400 Grand Ave., Ste. B.
Kansas City, MO 64106
Phone: (816)474-1516
Fax: (816)474-1427
Free: 800-899-9730

Publications: Discover Mid-America (17164) • eKC (17167)

Disney Publishing
244 Main St.
Northampton, MA 01060
Phone: (413)585-0444
Fax: (413)586-5724

Publications: FamilyFun (14428)

Disney Publishing Worldwide
114 Fifth Ave.
New York, NY 10011
Phone: (212)633-4400
Fax: (212)633-4817

Publications: Discover (21555)

Dispatch
Box 3009
Kenai, AK 99611
Phone: (907)283-7551
Fax: (907)283-8144

Publications: Dispatch (606)

The Dispatch
6400 Monterey Rd.
PO Box 22365
Gilroy, CA 95020
Phone: (408)842-6400
Fax: (408)842-6411

Publications: The Dispatch (2003)

The Dispatch
30 E. 1st Ave.
PO Box 908
Lexington, NC 27293
Phone: (336)249-3981

Publications: The Dispatch (24040)

The Dispatch News
434 Textile Ave.
Dracut, MA 01826
Phone: (978)957-0007
Fax: (978)957-1051

Publications: The Dispatch News (14161)

Dispatch News
314 S Pine St.
Spartanburg, SC 29302-2617
Phone: (803)359-3195
Fax: (803)359-1378

Publications: Dispatch-News (28758)

The Dispatch Printing Co.
34 S. 3rd St.
Columbus, OH 43215
Phone: (614)461-5000
Fax: (614)461-7580

Publications: The Columbus Dispatch (25008)

Distributor's Link Inc.
4297 Corporate Sq. N
Naples, FL 34104
Phone: (239)643-2713
Fax: (239)643-5220
Free: 800-356-1639

Publications: Link (6443)

The District of Columbia Bar
1250 H St. NW, 6th Fl.
Washington, DC 20005-5937
Phone: (202)737-4700
Fax: (202)626-3472

Publications: The Washington Lawyer (5847)

Dive Training Ltd.
5215 Crooked Rd.
Parkville, MO 64152-3737
Phone: (816)741-5151
Fax: (816)741-6458
Free: 800-444-9932

Publications: Dive Training (17335)

Diversified Business Communications
121 Free St.
PO Box 7437
Portland, ME 04112-7437
Phone: (207)842-5500
Fax: (207)842-5503

Publications: Seafood Business (13019)

Diversified Business Publications
121 Free St.
PO Box 7437
Portland, ME 04101
Phone: (207)842-5608
Fax: (207)842-5509

Publications: Alaska Fisherman's Journal (13004)

Diversified Publications Ltd.
264 Queen's Quay W.
Box 803
Toronto, ON, Canada M5J 1B5
Phone: (416)260-9364
Fax: (416)260-9372

Publications: Broadcast TechnologyMedia Production (34629)

Diversions Publications, Inc.
6 North East St., No. 301
Frederick, MD 21701-5601
Phone: (301)662-8171
Fax: (301)662-8399
Free: 800-272-2014

Publications: Frederick Magazine (13512)

Divibest, Inc.
PO Box 191125
Dallas, TX 75219-1125
Phone: (214)871-2913

Publications: Builder Insider (30134)

Divine Word Missionaries
PO Box 6099
Techny, IL 60082-6099
Phone: (847)272-7600
Fax: (847)272-8572

Publications: Divine Word Missionaries (9681)

A Division of Business Link LLC
2127 Paradise Rd.
Las Vegas, NV 89104-2515
Phone: (702)735-7003
Fax: (702)733-5953
Free: 800-242-0164

Publications: Nevada Business Journal (18378)

A Division of Caro Publishing
PO Box 106
Caro, MI 48723
Phone: (517)673-3181
Fax: (517)673-5662
Free: 800-821-7653

Publications: Tuscola County Advertiser (14858)

Division of Cleveland Newspapers, Inc.
PO Box 1050 821 N. Chrisman Ave.
Cleveland, MS 38732
Phone: (601)843-4241
Fax: (601)843-1830

Publications: Bolivar Commercial (16590)

Division Street News
PO Box 339
Cobleskill, NY 12043
Phone: (518)234-2515
Fax: (518)234-7898

Publications: Times-Journal (20479)

Divison of United Communications Corp.
715 58th St.
Lower Level
Kenosha, WI 53140
Fax: (414)656-1255
Free: 800-846-1101

Publications: Kenosha Bulletin (33871)

Dix Communications
40 E 2nd St.
Ashland, OH 44805
Phone: (419)281-0581
Fax: (419)281-5591

Publications: Ashland Times-Gazette (24617)

Dixie County Advocate
PO Box 5030
Cross City, FL 32628
Phone: (904)498-3312
Fax: (904)498-0420

Publications: Dixie County Advocate (6029)

Dixie News, Inc.
6603 Dixie Hwy.
Florence, KY 41042-2199
Phone: (606)371-6177
Fax: (606)371-6306

Publications: Dixie News (12059)

Dixon Telegraph Inc.
113-115 S Peoria Ave.
Dixon, IL 61021
Phone: (815)284-2222
Fax: (815)284-2870

Publications: The Telegraph (8776)

Dixon Tribune
145 E A St.
Dixon, CA 95620
Phone: (707)678-5594
Fax: (707)678-5404

Publications: The Dixon Tribune (1831)

Dixon's Independent Voice
529 N. Adams St. Ste. A
Dixon, CA 95620-2927
Phone: (707)678-8917
Fax: (707)678-4056

Publications: Dixon's Independent Voice (1832)

DJE Publications Ltd.
222 W 37th St.
New York, NY 10018
Phone: (212)967-0750
Fax: (212)967-1689

Publications: For the Bride by Demetrios (21717)

DM News
100 6th Ave.of the Americas
New York, NY 10013
Phone: (212)925-7300
Fax: (212)925-8752

Publications: DM News (21561)

DNA Publications
PO Box 2988
Radford, VA 24143-2988
Phone: (540)763-2925
Fax: (540)763-2924

Publications: Absolute Magnitude (32344)

Doane Agricultural Services
11701 Borman Dr., Ste. 300
St. Louis, MO 63146-4199
Phone: (314)569-2700
Fax: (314)569-1083
Free: 800-535-2342

Publications: Agri Marketing (17407)

Doane College
1014 Boswell Ave.
Crete, NE 68333
Phone: (402)826-6731
Fax: (402)826-8278

Publications: Doane Owl (17994)

Doctorow Communications Inc.
1011 Clifton Ave.
Clifton, NJ 07013-3518
Phone: (973)779-1600
Fax: (973)779-3242

Publications: Home Lighting & Accessories (18755)

Document Management Industries Association
433 E Monroe Ave.
Alexandria, VA 22301
Phone: (703)836-6225
Fax: (703)549-4966
Free: 800-336-4641

Publications: Print Solutions (31726)

DOD High School News Service
9420 Third Ave., Ste. 110
Norfolk, VA 23511-2029
Phone: (757)444-1442
Fax: (757)445-7782

Publications: Profile (Norfolk) (32292)

Dodge Center Star-Record
PO Box 279
Box 279
Dodge Center, MN 55927
Phone: (507)374-6531
Fax: (507)374-9327

Publications: Dodge Center Star-Record (15833)

Dodge County Independent
105 1st Ave. NW
PO Box 367
Kasson, MN 55944
Phone: (507)634-7503
Fax: (507)634-4446

Publications: Dodge County Independent (15982)

Dodge County Independent News
122 S Main
PO Box 167
Juneau, WI 53039
Phone: (920)386-2421
Fax: (920)386-2422

Publications: Dodge County Independent News (33869)

Dodge Criterion
140 Oak St.
PO Box 68
Dodge, NE 68633-0068
Phone: (402)693-2415
Fax: (402)693-2415

Publications: Dodge Criterion (17999)

Dodge Magazine
PO Box 5075
Troy, MI 48007-5075

Publications: Dodge Magazine (15620)

Dodson Publications, Inc.
546 Ct. St.
Reno, NV 89501
Phone: (775)333-1080
Fax: (775)333-1081

Publications: Architectural West (18417) • Western Roofing/Insulation/Siding (18426)

Doland Times Record
PO Box 387
Doland, SD 57436-0387
Phone: (605)897-6636
Fax: (605)897-6636

Publications: Conde News (28844) • Doland Times Record (28845)

Dollar Saver
33523 8 Mile Rd., No. C
Livonia, MI 48152-4104
Fax: (313)476-2793

Publications: Dollar Saver (15314)

Dollarsaver
340 N Jacinto St.
Hemet, CA 92543
Phone: (909)658-3117
Fax: (909)925-0394

Publications: Dollarsaver (2047)

Dominic Welch
400 Tribune Bldg.
Salt Lake City, UT 84111
Phone: (801)257-9500
Fax: (801)257-8515

Publications: The Salt Lake Tribune (31440)

Dominican Fathers, Province of St. Joseph
487 Michigan Ave. NE
Washington, DC 20017
Phone: (202)529-5300
Fax: (202)636-4460

Publications: The Thomist (5822)

Dominican University Graduate School of Library and Information Science
7900 W. Division
River Forest, IL 60305
Phone: (708)524-6845
Fax: (708)524-6657

Publications: World Libraries (9493)

Dominion Post
Greer Bldg.
1251 Earl L Core Rd.
Morgantown, WV 26505
Phone: (304)292-6301
Fax: (304)291-2326
Free: 800-654-4676

Publications: Dominion Post (33393)

Donaldsonville Chief
402 Railroad Ave.
PO Box 309
Donaldsonville, LA 70346
Phone: (225)473-3101
Fax: (225)473-4060

Publications: Donaldsonville Chief (12569)

Donalsonville News
PO Box 338
Donalsonville, GA 31745
Phone: (229)524-2343
Fax: (229)524-2343

Publications: Donalsonville News (7240)

Dongola Tri-County Record
130 NE Front St.
Box 189
Dongola, IL 62926
Phone: (618)827-4353

Publications: Dongola Tri-County Record (8778)

Donham Springs Publishing
688 Hatchell Ln.
PO Box 1529
Denham Springs, LA 70727
Phone: (504)665-5176
Fax: (504)667-0167

Publications: News (12562)

The Doniphan Herald
304 Campbell Ave
Doniphan, NE 68832
Phone: (402)845-2728
Fax: (402)845-2220

Publications: The Doniphan Herald (18000)

Donohue-Meehan Publishing Co.
2700 River Rd., Ste. 303
Des Plaines, IL 60018
Phone: (847)299-4430
Fax: (847)296-1968

Publications: Modern Baking (8763)

Donrey Media Group
700 Brookside Ave.
Redlands, CA 92373
Phone: (909)793-3221
Fax: (909)793-9588

Publications: Redland's Daily Facts (2905)

Donrey Media Group
100 Commerce Dr.
Glasgow, KY 42141
Phone: (502)678-5171
Fax: (502)678-5052

Publications: Glasgow Republican (12091)

Donrey Media Group
109 W. Pearl St.
PO Box 549
Poplarville, MS 39470
Phone: (601)795-2247
Fax: (601)795-2248

Publications: Poplarville Democrat (16824)

Donrey Media Group
1111 W. Bonzana Rd.
Las Vegas, NV 89106
Phone: (702)383-0211

Publications: Herald Democrat (31103)

Doody's Review Service
1100 W Lake St., No. 306
Oak Park, IL 60301-9918
Phone: (708)386-9500
Fax: (708)386-0860
Free: 800-219-9500

Publications: Doody's Health Sciences Book Review Journal (9374)

Dooly Newspapers, Inc.
115 E Union St.
PO Box 186
Vienna, GA 31092
Phone: (229)268-2096
Fax: (229)268-1924

Publications: The News Observer (7633)

Doon Press
209 Hubbard Ave.
Doon, IA 51235
Phone: (712)726-3313
Fax: (712)726-3334

Publications: Doon Press (10840)

Door County Publishing Co.
Box 130
Sturgeon Bay, WI 54235-0130
Phone: (920)746-9440
Fax: (920)743-5817

Publications: Door County Advocate (34350) • The Kewaunee County Star (33521) • Key to the Door. . .Illustrated (34351)

Door and Hardware Institute
14150 Newbrook Dr., Ste. 200
Chantilly, VA 20151-2223
Phone: (703)222-2010
Fax: (703)222-2410

Publications: Doors and Hardware (31911)

Door Reminder
PO Box 198
Sister Bay, WI 54234
Phone: (920)854-2662
Fax: (920)854-2788

Publications: Door Reminder (34329)

Dordt College
498 4th Ave. NE
Sioux Center, IA 51250-1697
Phone: (712)722-6000
Fax: (712)722-1185

Publications: Diamond (11205) • PRO REGE (11206)

Dorn Publications, Inc.
93 West St.
Medfield, MA 02052

Publications: Jazz Player (14316) • Saxophone Journal (14318)

Dos Mondos Bilingual Newspaper
902-A SW Blvd.
Kansas City, MO 64108
Phone: (816)221-4747
Fax: (816)221-4894

Publications: Dos Mundos Bilingual Newspaper (17165)

DOT/FAA
AFS-805
800 Independence Ave., SW
Washington, DC 20591
Phone: (202)267-8212
Fax: (202)267-9463

Publications: FAA Aviation News (5489)

The Dothan Progress
PO Box 1927
Dothan, AL 36302
Phone: (334)793-9586
Fax: (334)702-6043

Publications: The Dothan Progress (186) • The Headland Observer (187)

DoubleTake Limited Edition Prints
55 Davis Sq.
Somerville, MA 02144
Phone: (617)591-9389
Fax: (617)591-6478
Free: 800-964-8301

Publications: Double Take (14534)

Doug Penner
Box 578
Morris, MB, Canada R0G 1K0
Phone: (204)746-2823
Fax: (204)746-8867

Publications: Crow Wing Warrior (35275)

Douglas College
PO Box 2503
New Westminster, BC, Canada V3L 5B2
Phone: (604)527-5293
Fax: (604)527-5095

Publications: Event (35028)

Douglas County Historical Society
733 W Ballf St.
Roseburg, OR 97470

Publications: Umpqua Trapper (26556)

Douglas County Mail
119 S Main St.
PO Box 729
Myrtle Creek, OR 97457
Phone: (541)863-5233
Fax: (541)863-5234

Publications: Umpqua Free Press (26601)

Douglas County Publishing
PO Box 1270
Castle Rock, CO 80104
Phone: (303)688-3128
Fax: (303)660-0240

Publications: Douglas County News Press/Highlands Ranch Herald (4222)

Douglas County Publishing
PO Box 45
Corsica, SD 57328
Phone: (605)946-5489
Fax: (605)946-5197

Publications: Corsica Globe (28834)

Douglas County Tri-County News
6405 Fairbyrn Rd.
PO Box 1586
Douglasville, GA 30134-6911
Fax: (404)949-7556

Publications: Douglas County Sentinel (7249)

The Douglas Enterprise & Bonus
1823 S Peterson Ave.
PO Box 750
Douglas, GA 31533
Phone: (912)384-2323
Fax: (912)283-0218

Publications: The Douglas Enterprise & Bonus (7244)

Douglas Publications, Inc.
2807 N. Parham Rd., Ste. 200
Richmond, VA 23294
Phone: (804)762-9600
Fax: (804)217-8999

Publications: American Paint and Coatings Journal (4565) • American Painting Contractor (4235) • Compliance Magazine (32435) • FacilityCare (8023) • Flooring Magazine (4559) • Lifting & Transportation International (32443) • Robotics World (4560)

Douglass College
80 Clifton Ave.
DPO 153
New Brunswick, NJ 08901-1568

Publications: The Caellian (19327)

Douthit Communications, Inc.
525 Warren St.
Sandusky, OH 44870
Phone: (419)625-5825
Fax: (419)625-2834

Publications: The North Ridgeville Press & Light (25508) • The Press, Metro Edition (25385)

Dove Creek Press
PO Box 598
Dove Creek, CO 81324
Phone: (970)677-2214

Publications: Dove Creek Press (4400)

Dover Post Co.
609 E. Division St.
PO Box 664
Dover, DE 19903
Phone: (302)678-3616
Fax: (302)678-8291
Free: 800-942-1616

Publications: The Airlifter (5242) • Better Years (5244) • Brandywine Community News (5245) • Dover Post (5247) • Greenville Community News (5248) • Hockessin Community News (5249) • Middletown Transcript (5261) • Mill Creek Community News (5250) • Smyrna/Clayton Sun-Times (5287) • Sussex Countian (5253)

DoveTale Publishers
1 Thomas Circle NW
Washington, DC 20005-5802

Publications: Old-House Journal (5707)

Dow Jones & Co., Inc.
201 California St., Ste. 1350
San Francisco, CA 94111
Phone: (415)986-6886
Fax: (415)956-0797

Publications: Wall Street Journal (Western Edition) (3461)

Dow Jones & Co., Inc.
1 S. Wacker Dr., Ste. 2100
Chicago, IL 60606
Phone: (312)750-4000
Fax: (312)750-4153

Publications: The Wall Street Journal (Midwest Edition) (8602)

Dow Jones & Co., Inc.
PO Box 300
Princeton, NJ 08543
Phone: (609)520-4305
Fax: (609)520-7315
Free: 800-JOB-HUNT

Publications: Dowline (19459)

Dow Jones & Co., Inc.
200 Liberty St.
New York, NY 10281
Phone: (212)416-2000
Fax: (212)416-2658
Free: 800-832-1234

Publications: The Asian Wall Street Journal Weekly Edition (21265) • Barron's (21292) • Wall Street Journal (22906) • The Wall Street Journal—Classroom Edition (22907)

Dowagiac Daily News Inc.
205 Spaulding St.
Box 30
Dowagiac, MI 49047-1474
Phone: (269)782-2101
Fax: (269)782-5290

Publications: Dowagiac Daily News (14977)

Dowden Publishing Co., Inc.
110 Summit Ave.
Montvale, NJ 07645
Phone: (201)391-3365
Fax: (201)505-5890
Free: 800-707-7040

Publications: Mayo Clinic Proceedings (16309) • Podiatry Today (19272)

Dowling College
Idle Hour Blvd.
Oakdale, NY 11769
Phone: (631)244-3214

Publications: Journal of Business and Economic Studies (23029)

Down East Enterprise, Inc.
PO Box 679
Camden, ME 04843-0679
Phone: (207)594-9544
Fax: (207)594-7215
Free: 800-766-1670

Publications: Down East Magazine (12942) • Fly Rod & Reel (12943)

Downey Communications, Inc.
4800 Montgomery Ln., Ste. 710
Bethesda, MD 20814-3461
Phone: (301)718-7600
Fax: (301)718-7604

Publications: Military Grocer (13360)

Downhome Publications, Inc.
Box 16445
Jackson, MS 39236
Phone: (601)982-8418
Fax: (601)982-8418

Publications: Mississippi Magazine (16706)

Downs News and Times
717 E Railroad St.
Downs, KS 67437
Phone: (913)454-3514
Fax: (785)454-3866

Publications: Downs News and Times (11420)

Downtown Detroit Monitor, Inc.
33490 Groesbeck
Fraser, MI 48026
Phone: (586)296-6007
Fax: (586)296-6072

Publications: The Monitor (14939)

The Downtown Fun Zone
832 Hwy. 101
PO Box 49
Port Orford, OR 97465
Phone: (541)332-6565
Fax: (541)332-6565

Publications: Port Orford Today (26466)

Downtown Planet
841 Bishop St., Ste. 133
Honolulu, HI 96813
Phone: (808)524-8074
Fax: (808)538-6041

Publications: Downtown Planet (7686)

Doyle Publishing Company Inc.
15018 Mintz Ln.
Houston, TX 77014-1404
Phone: (281)440-0278
Fax: (281)440-4867
Free: 800-457-6459

Publications: UnderWater Magazine (30539)

The Draft Horse Journal
Box 670
Waverly, IA 50677
Phone: (319)352-4046
Fax: (319)352-2232

Publications: The Draft Horse Journal (11307)

The Dragon's Blood
Box 354
Sussex, NJ 07461
Fax: (201)702-7230

Publications: The Dragon's Blood (19607)

The Drain Enterprise
309 1st St.
PO Box 26
Drain, OR 97435
Phone: (541)836-2241
Fax: (541)836-2243

Publications: The Drain Enterprise (26306)

Drake University
316 Old Main
Des Moines, IA 50311
Phone: (515)271-2169
Fax: (515)271-3798

Publications: Drake Update (10783)

Drake University/Board of Student Communications
124 N. Meredith Hall
2507 University Ave.
Des Moines, IA 50311
Phone: (515)271-2020
Fax: (515)271-2798

Publications: The Times-Delphic (10812)

Drake Unviersity
Cartwright Hall
Des Moines, IA 50311
Phone: (515)271-2930
Fax: (515)271-4926

Publications: Drake Law Review (10782)

The Dramatists Guild of America, Inc.
1501 Broadway, Ste. 701
New York, NY 10036-3988
Phone: (212)398-9366
Fax: (212)944-0420

Publications: The Dramatist (21568)

Drawing Board Atlanta, Inc.
PO Box 15556
Atlanta, GA 30333-0556
Phone: (404)624-3999
Fax: (404)624-4063

Publications: Best Sellers Collection (6977)

Drayton Valley Western Review
PO Box 6960
Drayton Valley, AB, Canada T7A 1S3
Phone: (780)542-5380
Fax: (780)542-9200

Publications: Drayton Valley Western Review (34695)

Dream Magazine
PO Box 2027
Nevada City, CA 95959

Publications: Dream Magazine (2615)

Dreams and Nightmares
1300 Kicker Rd.
Tuscaloosa, AL 35404-3954
Phone: (205)553-2284

Publications: Dreams and Nightmares (486)

Dresden Transcript
17 E. 9th St.
PO Box 105
Dresden, OH 43821-0105
Phone: (614)754-1608
Fax: (614)754-1609

Publications: Dresden Transcript (25167)

Drew University
36 Madison Ave.
Madison, NJ 07940
Phone: (973)408-3000

Publications: Drew Magazine (19180)

Drexel University
3141 Chestnut St.
Philadelphia, PA 19104
Phone: (215)895-2585
Fax: (215)895-5935

Publications: The Triangle (27712)

Driftwood Enterprises
153 Balsam
PO Box 989
Ignace, ON, Canada P0T 1T0
Phone: (807)934-6482
Fax: (807)934-6667

Publications: Ignace Driftwood (35920)

Driftwood Publishing Ltd.
328 Lower Ganges Rd.
Salt Spring Island, BC, Canada V8K 2V3
Phone: (250)537-9933
Fax: (250)537-2613

Publications: Gulf Islands Driftwood (35086)

Drilling Contractor Publications, Inc.
15810 Park 10 Pl., Ste. 222
Houston, TX 77084
Phone: (281)578-7171
Fax: (281)398-7602
Free: 800-578-IADC

Publications: Drilling Contractor (30470)

DRIVE! Magazine
1300 Galaxy Way, Ste. 15
Concord, CA 94520
Phone: (925)682-9900
Fax: (925)682-9907
Free: 800-764-6278

Publications: DRIVE! (1752)

DRJES
Dawson College
c/o Jaleel Ali, Chemistry Dept., Rm. 7B.16
3040 Sherbrooke St. W.
Westmount, QC, Canada H3Z 1A4

Publications: The Dawson Research Journal of Experimental Science (DRJES) (37442)

The Drumheller Mail
368 Centre St.
PO Box 1629
Drumheller, AB, Canada T0J 0Y0
Phone: (403)823-2580
Fax: (403)823-3864

Publications: The Drumheller Mail (34696)

Drury University
900 N Benton Ave.
Springfield, MO 65802
Phone: (417)873-7318
Fax: (417)873-7533

Publications: The Drury Mirror (17595)

DSA Community Publishing
250 Miller Pl.
Hicksville, NY 11801
Phone: (516)393-9300
Fax: (516)393-9304

Publications: Results Media Shopper's Guide (20744)

DSN, Inc.
PO Box 3000
Winnemucca, NV 89446
Phone: (775)623-5011
Fax: (775)623-5243

Publications: The Humboldt Sun (18450)

DTH Publishing Corp.
PO Box 3257
Chapel Hill, NC 27515-3257

Publications: The Daily Tar Heel (23706)

Dubois Spencer Counties Publishing Co., Inc.
PO Box 38
Ferdinand, IN 47532
Phone: (812)367-2041
Fax: (812)367-2371
Free: 800-463-9720

Publications: The Ferdinand News (9955) • Spencer County Leader (9917)

The Dubuque Advertiser, Inc.
2966 J.F.K. Rd.
Dubuque, IA 52002
Phone: (319)588-0162
Fax: (319)582-0335

Publications: The Dubuque Advertiser (10842)

The Duckburg News
3010 Wilshire Blvd., Ste. 362
Los Angeles, CA 90010-1146
Phone: (213)388-2364

Publications: The Duckburg Times (2254)

Ducks Unlimited
1 Waterfowl Way
Memphis, TN 38120
Phone: (901)758-3825
Fax: (901)758-3850
Free: 800-45D-UCKS

Publications: Ducks Unlimited (29370)

Dudley Printing
931 Main St.
PO Box 40
Manson, IA 50563
Phone: (712)469-3381
Fax: (712)469-2648

Publications: Calhoun County Journal'herald (11050)

Dudley Printing
204 W. 1st St.
PO Box 279
Pomeroy, IA 50575
Phone: (712)468-2266
Fax: (712)468-2266

Publications: Journal Herald (11164)

Dudley Printing Inc.
PO Box 106
Rockwell City, IA 50579-0106
Phone: (712)297-8931
Fax: (712)297-7193

Publications: Calhoun County Reminder (11185)

2374

Numbers cited after listings are entry numbers rather than page numbers.

Duerr and Tierney Ltd.
15612 Hwy. 7, Ste. 235
Minnetonka, MN 55345
Phone: (952)935-5850
Fax: (952)935-6546
Free: 800-937-9194

Publications: Art of the West (16167)

Duke University
Box 90103
Durham, NC 27708
Phone: (919)684-6456
Fax: (919)681-4262

Publications: Greek, Roman, and Byzantine Studies (23823)

Duke University
Box 90233
Durham, NC 27708-0233
Phone: (919)684-5321
Fax: (919)684-5833

Publications: Southeastern Geology (23845)

Duke University
PO Box 90858, Duke Sta.
Durham, NC 27706
Phone: (919)684-3811
Fax: (919)684-8295

Publications: The Chronicle (23813)

Duke University Press
PO Box 90660
Durham, NC 27708-0660
Phone: (919)687-3600
Fax: (919)688-4574

Publications: American Literature (23806) • American Speech (23807) • Boundary 2 (23810) • Comparative Studies of South Asia, Africa, and the Middle East (23815) • Differences (28395) • Duke Mathematical Journal (23819) • Eighteenth-Century Life (32616) • French Historical Studies (1815) • GLQ (23822) • History of Political Economy (23825) • Hopscotch (23826) • IMRN (23827) • Journal of Health Politics, Policy and Law (4994) • Journal of Medieval and Early Modern Studies (23830) • Mediterranean Quarterly (5646) • Modern Language Quarterly (32988) • Nepantla (23835) • The Opera Quarterly (23234) • Pedagogy (15100) • Poetics Today (23840) • positions (33005) • Public Culture (8544) • Radical History Review (22621) • SAQ (23843) • Social Science History (27843) • Social Text (19339) • Socialist Review (23844) • Theater (5003) • Transition (14109)

Duke University School of Law
PO Box 90364
Durham, NC 27708-0364
Phone: (919)613-7171
Fax: (919)613-7231

Publications: Alaska Law Review (23805) • Duke Environmental Law and Policy Forum (23816) • Duke Journal of Comparative and International Law (23817) • Duke Law Journal (23818) • Law and Contemporary Problems (23833)

Dulcimer Player News
PO Box 2164
Winchester, VA 22604
Phone: (540)678-1305
Fax: (540)678-1151

Publications: Dulcimer Players News (32627)

Duluth AFL-CIO Central Labor Body
2002 London Rd., No. 110
Duluth, MN 55812
Phone: (218)728-4469
Fax: (218)724-1413

Publications: Labor World (15838)

Duluth Budgeteer News
222 W Superior St., No. 100
Duluth, MN 55802-1907
Phone: (218)723-1207
Fax: (218)727-7348

Publications: Duluth Budgeteer News (15836)

Duluth Chamber of Commerce
5 W. 1st St., Ste. 101
Duluth, MN 55802-2115
Phone: (218)722-5501
Fax: (218)722-3223

Publications: The Duluthian (15837)

The Duncan Banner
1001 Elm St.
PO Box 1268
Duncan, OK 73534-1268
Phone: (580)255-5354
Fax: (580)255-8889

Publications: The Duncan Banner (25800)

Duncan McIntosh Co., Inc.
17782 Cowan
Irvine, CA 92614
Phone: (949)660-6150
Fax: (949)660-6172

Publications: Sea Magazine (2090) • Waterfront Southern California News (2092)

The Dundee Observer
PO Box 127
Dundee, NY 14837
Phone: (607)243-7600
Fax: (607)243-5833

Publications: The Dundee Observer (20534)

Dune Buggies & Hot VWs
2950 Airway, Ste. A7
PO Box 2260
Costa Mesa, CA 92626
Phone: (714)979-2560
Fax: (714)979-3998

Publications: Dune Buggies & Hot VWs (1775)

Dunedin Times Co.
PO Box 493
Dunedin, FL 34697-0493
Phone: (727)447-8353
Fax: (727)738-1854

Publications: The Dunedin Times/The Palm Harbor Sounder (6061)

Dunklin County Press
114 Commercial St.
PO Box 356
Senath, MO 63876
Phone: (314)738-2604
Fax: (314)738-2604

Publications: Dunklin County Press (17575)

Dunlap Reporter
114 Iowa Ave.
Dunlap, IA 51529
Phone: (712)643-5380
Fax: (712)643-2173

Publications: The Dunlap Reporter (10857)

Dunn County Herald
PO Box 609
Killdeer, ND 58640
Phone: (701)764-5312
Fax: (701)764-5049

Publications: Dunn County Herald (24485)

Dunn County Reminder
PO Box 40
Menomonie, WI 54751-0040
Phone: (715)235-9011
Fax: (715)235-2946

Publications: Dunn County Reminder (34039)

The Dunnville Chronicle
131 Lock St. E
Dunnville, ON, Canada N1A 1J6
Phone: (905)774-7632
Fax: (905)774-5744

Publications: The Dunnville Chronicle (35795)

Dunnville Shoppers Guide
131 Lock St. E.
Dunnville, ON, Canada N1A 2X5
Phone: (416)774-7632
Fax: (416)774-5744

Publications: Dunnville Shoppers Guide (35796)

The Duplex Planet
Box 1230
Saratoga Springs, NY 12866
Phone: (518)692-7410
Fax: (518)692-8208

Publications: The Duplex Planet (23301)

duPont Publishing, Inc.
3051 Tech Dr.
St. Petersburg, FL 33716
Phone: (727)573-9339
Fax: (727)489-0255
Free: 800-233-1731

Publications: The duPont Registry: A Buyer's Gallery of Fine Automobiles (6623) • The duPont Registry: A Buyer's Gallery of Fine Boats (6624) • The duPont Registry: A Buyer's Gallery of Fine Homes (6625)

Duquesne School of Law
Duquesne University
900 Locust St.
Pittsburgh, PA 15282
Phone: (412)396-5017
Fax: (412)396-6314

Publications: Juris (27807)

Duquesne University
D.P.C.C., Rm. 417
1330 Stevenson St.
Pittsburgh, PA 15282
Phone: (412)396-6629
Fax: (412)396-5496

Publications: The Duquesne Duke (27782)

Duquesne University
105 Des Places
Pittsburgh, PA 15282
Phone: (412)396-6415
Fax: (412)396-4894

Publications: Critica Hispanica (27773)

Durango Herald Inc.
PO Drawer A-0950
Durango, CO 81302-0950
Phone: (970)247-3504
Fax: (970)259-5011
Free: 800-530-8318

Publications: Durango Herald (4402)

Durantech
3410 La Sierra Ave., F-391
Riverside, CA 92503
Phone: (818)413-0826

Publications: Breastcare (2932) • Women's Imaging (2949)

Durham College
2000 Simcoe St. N
Box 385
Oshawa, ON, Canada L1H 7L7
Phone: (416)576-0210
Fax: (416)436-9774

Publications: The Chronicle (36180)

Dustbooks
PO Box 100
Paradise, CA 95967
Phone: (530)887-6110
Fax: (530)877-0222
Free: 800-477-6110

Publications: Small Press Review (2808)

Duval Publications Inc.
PO Box 12955
Albuquerque, NM 87195
Phone: (505)247-9195
Fax: (505)842-5129

Publications: New Mexico Woman (19783)

Duxbury Clipper
PO Box 1656
Duxbury, MA 02331
Phone: (617)934-2811
Fax: (617)934-5917

Publications: Duxbury Clipper (14162)

DVL Publishing Inc.
PO Box 1509
Liverpool, NS, Canada B0T 1K0

Publications: Atlantic Beef Quarterly (35587) • Atlantic Forestry Review (35588) • Atlantic Horse & Pony (35589) • Rural Delivery (35590)

D.W. Moore
158 Main St.
PO Box 220
Dutton, ON, Canada N0L 1J0
Phone: (519)762-2310

Publications: Dutton Advance (35799)

Dwight King Publishing
PO Box 11688
Newport Beach, CA 92658-5038
Phone: (949)759-3553

Publications: Ex-CBI Roundup (2626)

Dynamic Chiropractic
5406 Bolsa Ave.
PO Box 4109
Huntington Beach, CA 92605-4109
Phone: (714)230-3150
Fax: (714)899-4273

Publications: Dynamic Chiropractic (2060)

The Dysart Reporter
PO Box 70
Dysart, IA 52224
Phone: (319)476-3550
Fax: (319)476-2813

Publications: The Dysart Reporter (10862)

e-Business Advisor
PO Box 429002
San Diego, CA 92142-9002
Phone: (858)278-5600
Fax: (858)278-0300
Free: 800-336-6060

Publications: e-Business Advisor (3144)

E. J. Gossett Publishing, Inc.
7145 S. Maplewood Ave.
Chicago, IL 60629-2045
Phone: (773)476-5978
Fax: (773)476-3259
Free: 800-779-JMNR

Publications: JMNR (8426)

E. Kootenay Newspapers Ltd.
822 Cranbrook St. N.
Cranbrook, BC, Canada V1C 3R9
Phone: (604)426-5201
Fax: (604)426-5003

Publications: Cranbrook Daily Townsman (34934)

E & PJ Enterprises, Inc.
PO Box 777
North Scituate, RI 02857
Phone: (401)647-9688
Fax: (401)647-3227
Free: 800-333-6236

Publications: The Northeast Square Dancer Magazine (28378)

E-Z Shopper, Inc.
57 S. Carroll St.
Horseheads, NY 14845
Phone: (607)796-2800
Fax: (607)796-0319

Publications: The Shopper (20760)

EAA Experimenter
PO Box 3086
Oshkosh, WI 54903-3086
Phone: (920)426-4800
Fax: (920)426-4828

Publications: EAA Experimenter (34221)

Eagle
227 N. Oates St.
PO Box 1968
Dothan, AL 36302
Phone: (334)792-3141
Fax: (334)712-7979

Publications: The Dothan Eagle (185)

The Eagle
14 S. Park St.
PO Box 36
Cambridge, NY 12816
Phone: (518)677-5158
Fax: (518)677-8323

Publications: The Eagle (20416)

Eagle Butte News
PO Box 210
Eagle Butte, SD 57625
Phone: (605)964-2100
Fax: (605)964-2100

Publications: Eagle Butte News (28847)

Eagle-Gazette
PO Box 848
Lancaster, OH 43130
Phone: (740)654-1321
Fax: (740)681-4505
Free: 888-420-3883

Publications: Eagle-Gazette (25289)

Eagle Group Communications, Inc.
011 Eagle Park E Dr.
PO Box 450
Eagle, CO 81631
Phone: (303)328-6656
Fax: (303)328-6393

Publications: The Eagle Valley Enterprise (4408)

Eagle Grove Eagle
314 W Broadway
PO Box 6
Eagle Grove, IA 50533-0006
Phone: (515)448-4745
Fax: (515)448-3182

Publications: Eagle Grove Eagle (10863) • Wright County Shopper's Guide (10864)

Eagle Newspapers
5910 Firestone Dr.
Syracuse, NY 13206
Phone: (315)434-8889
Fax: (315)434-8883

Publications: Baldwinsville Messenger (23388) • The Camillus Advocate (20417) • Canastota Bee-Journal (20425) • Cazenovia Republican (20441) • Chittenango-Bridgeport Times (20426) • DeWitt Times (20531) • Fayetteville Eagle Bulletin (23403) • Hamilton/Morrisville Tribune (20442) • Liverpool Review (20954) • Marcellus Observer (21021) • Marcellus Observer (23410) • The Messenger (23412) • North Syracuse Star-News (23014) • The Review (20955)

Eagle Newspapers
PO Box 108
Dallas, OR 97338
Phone: (503)623-2373
Fax: (503)623-2395

Publications: Polk County Itemizer Observer (26300)

Eagle Newspapers
419 State Ave.
PO Box 390
Hood River, OR 97031
Phone: (541)386-1234
Fax: (541)386-6796

Publications: Hood River News (26376)

Eagle Newspapers
241 SE 6th St.
Madras, OR 97741
Phone: (541)475-2275
Fax: (541)475-3710

Publications: The Madras Pioneer (26412)

Eagle Newspapers
558 N. Main St.
Prineville, OR 97754
Phone: (541)447-6205
Fax: (541)447-1754

Publications: Central Oregonian (26548) • X-TRA (26549)

Eagle Newspapers
30250 SW Parkway Ave. No. 10
Wilsonville, OR 97070
Phone: (503)682-3935

Publications: The Canby Herald (26613) • Wilsonville Spokesman (26617)

Eagle Newspapers
220 E. Jewett Blvd.
PO Box 218
White Salmon, WA 98672
Phone: (509)493-2112
Fax: (509)493-2399

Publications: The Enterprise (33206)

The Eagle Press
PO Box 1810
Fritch, TX 79036
Phone: (806)857-2123

Publications: The Eagle Press (30373)

Eagle Printing Company
120 Franklin St., No. 1B
Slippery Rock, PA 16057-1101
Phone: (412)794-6797
Fax: (412)794-5694

Publications: Slippery Rock Eagle (27998)

Eagle Printing Co.
PO Box 77
Marinette, WI 54143
Phone: (715)735-6611
Fax: (715)735-0229

Publications: Marinette Eagle-Star (34018)

Eagle Printing Co., Inc.
114 W Diamond St.
Butler, PA 16001-5747
Phone: (724)282-7209
Fax: (724)282-1780

Publications: Butler Eagle (26743) • Cranberry Eagle/The News Weekly (26815)

Eagle Pub.
PO Box 257
Augusta, IL 62311
Phone: (217)392-2715
Fax: (217)392-2619

Publications: Eagles Scribe (8036)

Eagle Publications
107 S. Main
PO Box 259
Avon, IL 61415
Phone: (309)462-5758
Fax: (309)462-3221
Free: 800-500-1961

Publications: Avon Sentinel (8047)

Eagle Publications
PO Box 581
Newbury, NH 03255
Phone: (603)763-9541
Fax: (603)763-9544

Publications: Argus-Champion (18613)

Eagle Publications, Inc.
42400 Grand River, Ste. 103
Novi, MI 48375-2572
Phone: (248)347-3486
Fax: (248)347-3079
Free: 800-783-3491

Publications: American Tool, Die & Stamping News (15407) • Filtration News (15408)

Eagle Publications, Inc.
RR 2, Box 301
Claremont, NH 03743-9308
Phone: (603)543-3100
Fax: (603)542-9705

Publications: Eagle Times (18465)

Eagle Publications of Western Illinois Inc.
125 S. Randolph St.
Macomb, IL 61455-2207
Phone: (309)837-4428
Fax: (309)837-7188
Free: 800-500-1961

Publications: Abingdon Argus (9128) • Roseville Independent (9132)

Eagle Publishing
Black Mountain Rd.
PO Box 802
Brattleboro, VT 05301-0802
Phone: (802)254-2311
Fax: (802)257-1305
Free: 800-649-2311

Publications: Brattleboro Reformer (31508)

Eagle Publishing Co.
PO Box 66
Ekalaka, MT 59324
Phone: (406)775-6245
Fax: (406)775-8750

Publications: Eagle (17786)

Eagle Publishing Inc.
One Massachusetts Ave. NW
Washington, DC 20001
Phone: (202)216-0600
Fax: (202)216-0610

Publications: Human Events (5535)

Eagle Publishing Inc.
220 E. Main
PO Box 67
Eagle Lake, TX 77434-0067
Phone: (979)234-5521

Publications: Eagle Lake Headlight (30256)

The Eagle-Record
5549 Memorial Blvd.
PO Drawer 278
St. George, SC 29477
Phone: (843)563-3121

Publications: The Eagle-Record (28750)

Eagle River Publications, Inc.
346 W Division St.
PO Box 1929
Eagle River, WI 54521
Phone: (715)479-4421
Fax: (715)479-6242

Publications: North Woods Trader (33662) • The Three Lakes News (33663) • Vacation Week (33664) • Vilas County News Review (33665)

Eagle-Scribe
Box 257
Augusta, IL 62311
Phone: (217)392-2715

Publications: Eagle-Scribe (8035)

Eagle Summit Publishing
PO Box 329
Frisco, CO 80443
Phone: (970)668-3998
Fax: (970)668-3859

Publications: Summit Daily (4456)

Eagle Times
PO Box 582
Reading, PA 19603-0582
Free: 800-633-7222

Publications: Reading Eagle (27919) • Reading Times (27920)

Eagle-Tribune
PO Box 100
Lawrence, MA 01842
Phone: (978)946-2000
Fax: (978)685-1588

Publications: The Eagle-Tribune (14266)

Eagle/Webb Press
650 N 1st St.
PO Box 96
Woodburn, OR 97071
Phone: (503)981-3441
Fax: (503)981-1253

Publications: Woodburn Independent (26619)

The Ear
Irvine Valley College
5500 Irvine Center Dr.
Irvine, CA 92620
Phone: (949)451-5341

Publications: The Ear (2078)

Earl Barron Publications, Inc.
225 E 36 St.
New York, NY 10016
Phone: (212)725-2303

Publications: MascuLines (22288)

Earl Graves Publishing Co.
130 5th Ave.
New York, NY 10011
Phone: (212)242-8000
Fax: (212)886-9600
Free: 800-727-7777

Publications: Black Enterprise (21328)

The Earlville Leader
124 W Railroad St.
Earlville, IL 60518-0606
Phone: (815)246-6911
Fax: (815)246-6911

Publications: The Earlville Leader (8802)

Early American Industries Association Inc.
167 Bakerville Rd.
South Dartmouth, MA 02748
Phone: (508)993-9578

Publications: Early American Industries Association Chronicle (28366)

The Early County News
PO Box 748
Blakely, GA 31723
Phone: (229)723-4376
Fax: (229)723-6097

Publications: Early County News (7130)

Early Music America
2366 Eastlake Ave. E.
PO Box 429
Seattle, WA 98102
Phone: (206)720-6270
Fax: (206)720-6290
Free: 888-SAC-KBUT

Publications: Early Music America (31786)

Early Typewriter Collectors Association
PO Box 641824
Los Angeles, CA 90064
Phone: (310)477-5229
Fax: (310)268-8420

Publications: ETCetera (2266)

Earnshaw Publications, Inc.
112 W 34th St. Ste 1515
New York, NY 10120
Phone: (212)563-2742
Fax: (212)629-3249

Publications: Earnshaw's Review (21576) • Small World (22747)

Earth Action Network
28 Knight St.
Norwalk, CT 06851
Phone: (203)854-5559
Fax: (203)866-0602

Publications: E (5057)

Earth Action Network
PO Box 5098
Westport, CT 06881
Phone: (203)854-5559
Fax: (203)866-0602

Publications: E (5056)

Earth Island Institute
300 Broadway, Ste. 28
San Francisco, CA 94133-3312
Phone: (415)788-3666
Fax: (415)788-7324

Publications: Earth Island Journal (3352)

The Earth Times
PO Box 3363, Grand Central Sta.
New York, NY 10163
Phone: (212)297-0488
Fax: (212)297-0566

Publications: The Earth Times (21577)

Earth Weekly News
PO Box 687
Earth, TX 79031
Fax: (806)257-2196

Publications: Earth Weekly News (30262)

EarthLight Magazine
111 Fairmount Ave.
Oakland, CA 94611
Phone: (510)451-4926
Fax: (510)451-3505

Publications: EarthLight Magazine (2678)

Earth's Daughters
Box 41, Central Park Sta.
Buffalo, NY 14215

Publications: Earth's Daughters (20378)

Easley Publications llc
PO Box 709
Easley, SC 29641
Phone: (864)855-0355
Fax: (864)855-6825

Publications: The Easley Progress (28598)

East Allen Courier
Box 77
Grabill, IN 46741-0077
Phone: (219)627-2728
Fax: (219)627-2519

Publications: East Allen Courier (10032)

East Asian Studies Center
Memorial Hall W., Ste. 207
1021, Third St.
Bloomington, IN 47405-7005
Phone: (812)855-4848
Fax: (812)855-7762

Publications: Journal of Japanese Linguistics (9842)

East Aurora Advertiser
710 Main St.
East Aurora, NY 14052-2486
Phone: (716)652-0320
Fax: (716)652-8383

Publications: East Aurora Advertiser (20539)

East Bay Newspapers
1 Bradford St.
PO Box 90
Bristol, RI 02809
Phone: (401)253-6000
Fax: (401)253-6055

Publications: Barrington Times (28324) • Bristol Phoenix (28326) • Sakonnet Times (28327) • Shopping News South (28328) • Warren Times-Gazette (28448)

East Carolina University
Greenville, NC 27858-4353
Phone: (252)328-1537
Fax: (252)328-4889

Publications: NCLR (23966)

East Carolina University
Student Publications Bldg., 2nd Fl.
Greenville, NC 27858-4353
Phone: (252)328-6366
Fax: (252)328-6558

Publications: The East Carolinian (23963)

East Carolina University
Greenville, NC 27858-4353
Phone: (252)328-1537
Fax: (252)328-4889

Publications: Tar River Poetry (23970)

East Central College
1964 Prairie Dell Rd.
Union, MO 63084-4344
Phone: (314)583-5195
Fax: (314)583-6637

Publications: Cornerstone (17657)

East Central Communications, Inc.
310 N. Sangamon
Gibson City, IL 60936
Phone: (217)784-4244
Fax: (217)784-4246
Free: 800-784-4243

Publications: Target (8919)

East Central Communications, Inc.
118 E Washington
PO Box 110
Monticello, IL 61856
Phone: (217)762-2511
Fax: (217)762-8591

Publications: Piatt County Journal-Republican (9222)

East Central Communications, Inc.
1332 Harmon Dr. E.
PO Box 5110
Rantoul, IL 61866
Phone: (217)892-9613
Fax: (217)892-9451
Free: 800-776-8555

Publications: Gibson City Courier (9487) • Rantoul Press (9488)

East Central Ohio Food Dealers Association, Inc.
1200 Rear N. Main St.
North Canton, OH 44720
Phone: (330)494-2302
Fax: (330)494-6963

Publications: ECO Communicator (25434)

East Central Oklahoma Publishers, Inc.
PO Box 840
Bristow, OK 74010-0840
Phone: (918)367-2282
Fax: (918)367-2724

Publications: The Bristow News (25767) • The Record-Citizen (25768)

East Central Press Ltd.
PO Box 576
Watson, SK, Canada S0K 4V0
Phone: (306)287-4388
Fax: (306)287-3308
Free: 888-310-4388

Publications: East Central Connection (37586) • The Naicam News (37587)

East Coast Newspapers
124 Main St.
PO Box 250
Fort Mill, SC 29716-0250
Phone: (803)547-2353
Fax: (803)547-2321

Publications: Fort Mill Times (28612)

East Coast Publications
PO Box 55
Accord, MA 02018
Phone: (617)878-4540
Fax: (617)871-1853
Free: 800-654-4993

Publications: New England Real Estate Journal (14442) • New York Real Estate Journal (14443)

East Dubuque Register
141 Sinsinawa Ave.
East Dubuque, IL 61025
Phone: (815)747-3171
Fax: (815)747-3215

Publications: Register (8803)

East European Quarterly
PO Box 10039
Bradenton, FL 34282-0039
Phone: (941)753-4782
Fax: (941)753-4782

Publications: East European Quarterly (5958)

The East Hampton Star
PO Box 5002
East Hampton, NY 11937
Phone: (516)324-0002
Fax: (516)324-7943
Free: 800-997-1968

Publications: The East Hampton Star (20545)

East Holmes Publishing Enterprises, Inc.
308 Ct. Sq.
PO Box 60
Lexington, MS 39095
Phone: (662)834-1151
Fax: (662)834-1074

Publications: Holmes County Herald (16746)

East Lauderdale News
PO Box 479
Rogersville, AL 35652
Phone: (256)247-5565
Fax: (256)247-1902

Publications: East Lauderdale News (440)

East Los Angeles College
Journalism Dept.
1301 Avenida Cesar Chavez
Monterey Park, CA 91754
Phone: (323)265-8819
Fax: (323)265-8975

Publications: Campus News (2591)

East Oregonian Publishing Co.
205 Bolstacl AVEE, Suite 2
PO Box 427
Long Beach, WA 98631
Phone: (360)642-8181
Fax: (360)642-8105
Free: 800-643-3703

Publications: Chinook Observer (32810)

East Oregonian Publishing Co., Inc.
211 S.E. Byers
PO Box 1089
Pendleton, OR 97801
Phone: (541)276-2211
Fax: (541)276-8314
Free: 800-522-0255

Publications: Blue Mountain Eagle (26378) • East Oregonian (26458)

East Penn Publishing
1633 N 26th St.
Allentown, PA 18104
Phone: (610)740-0944
Fax: (610)740-0947

Publications: East Penn Press (26627)

East Prairie Eagle News
PO Box 10
East Prairie, MO 63845
Phone: (573)649-3541
Fax: (573)683-2217

Publications: East Prairie Eagle (17040)

East St. Louis Monitor Publishing, Inc.
1501 State St.
PO Box 2137
East St. Louis, IL 62205
Phone: (618)271-0468
Fax: (618)271-0468

Publications: East St. Louis Monitor (8807)

East Side Revue
1736 East 33rd Ave.
Vancouver, BC, Canada V5N 3E2
Phone: (604)327-1665

Publications: East Side Revue (35139) • West Side Revue (35178)

East Side Suburban Newspapers
4309 E Michigan St., No. 11042
Indianapolis, IN 46201-3652
Phone: (317)356-2487
Fax: (317)356-5871

Publications: The East Side Herald (10108) • The Indianapolis Herald (10130) • The Northeast Herald (10156)

East Tennessee State University
Box 70688
Johnson City, TN 37614
Phone: (423)929-6315
Fax: (423)439-8407

Publications: East Tennessean (29250)

East Texas Historical Association
Box 6223, SFA Sta.
Nacogdoches, TX 75962
Phone: (936)468-2407
Fax: (936)468-2190

Publications: East Texas Historical Journal (30850)

East View Publications
3020 Harbor Ln. N
Minneapolis, MN 55447
Phone: (763)550-0961
Fax: (763)559-2931
Free: 800-477-1005

Publications: Far Eastern Affairs (16078) • Military Thought (16098)

East Washingtonian
742 Main St.
PO Box 70
Pomeroy, WA 99347
Phone: (509)843-1313
Fax: (509)843-3911

Publications: East Washingtonian (32887)

East West Journal
1150 S King St., Ste. 103
Honolulu, HI 96814
Phone: (808)596-0099
Fax: (808)596-2292

Publications: East West Journal (7687)

Easter Island Foundation
PO Box 6774
Los Osos, CA 93412
Phone: (805)528-8558
Fax: (805)534-9301

Publications: Rapa Nui Journal (2483)

Eastern Arizona College
3714 W. Church St.
Thatcher, AZ 85552-0769
Phone: (520)428-8321
Fax: (520)428-8462
Free: 800-678-3808

Publications: The Gila Monster (924)

Eastern Band of Cherokee Indians
PO Box 501
Cherokee, NC 28719
Phone: (828)497-3005
Fax: (828)497-4810

Publications: The Cherokee One Feather (23783)

Eastern Colorado News, Inc.
1522 Main St.
PO Box 555
Strasburg, CO 80136
Phone: (303)622-4417
Fax: (303)622-9717

Publications: Eastern Colorado News (4643)

Eastern Colorado Plainsmen
505 3rd Ave.
Box 98
Hugo, CO 80821
Phone: (719)743-2371

Publications: Eastern Colorado Plainsmen (4518)

Eastern Colorado Publishing Co.
329 Main St.
PO Box 4000
Fort Morgan, CO 80701
Phone: (970)867-5651
Fax: (970)867-7448

Publications: The Fort Morgan Times (4446)

Eastern Colorado Publishing Co.
108 Cedar
Julesburg, CO 80737
Phone: (970)474-3388
Fax: (970)474-3389

Publications: Julesburg Advocate (4523)

Eastern Colorado Publishing Co.
310 S. 5th St.
PO Box 1217
Lamar, CO 81052-1217
Phone: (719)336-2266
Fax: (719)336-2526

Publications: Lamar Daily News and Holly Chieftain (4537)

Eastern Connecticut State College
110 Student Ctr.
83 Windham St.
Willimantic, CT 06226-2308
Phone: (860)465-4445
Fax: (860)465-4685

Publications: Campus Lantern (5219)

The Eastern Door
PO Box 1170
Kahnawake, QC, Canada J0L 1B0
Phone: (450)635-3050
Fax: (450)635-8479

Publications: The Eastern Door (37017)

Eastern Economic Association
Iona College
715 North Ave.
New Rochelle, NY 10801
Phone: (914)633-2088
Fax: (914)633-2549

Publications: Eastern Economic Journal (26849)

Eastern Finance Association
Florida State University
Dept. of Finance
Tallahassee, FL 32306-1042
Phone: (904)644-4220
Fax: (904)644-4225

Publications: Financial Review (16993)

The Eastern Gazette
PO Box 306
Dexter, ME 04930
Phone: (207)924-7402
Fax: (207)924-6215
Free: 800-287-2295

Publications: The Eastern Gazette (12951)

Numbers cited after listings are entry numbers rather than page numbers.

Eastern Group Publications Inc.
2500 S. Atlantic Blvd., No. A
Los Angeles, CA 90040-2004
Phone: (213)263-5743
Fax: (213)263-9169

Publications: City Terrace Comet (2240) • Eastside Sun (2258) • E.L.A. Brooklyn-Belvedere Comet (1485) • Mexican American Sun (2332) • Montebello Comet (2580) • Monterey Park Comet (2595) • Northeast Sun Commerce Comet (2349) • Wyvern-wood Chronicle (2443)

Eastern Illinois University
600 Lincoln Ave.
Charleston, IL 61920-3099
Phone: (217)581-2812
Fax: (217)581-2923

Publications: Daily Eastern News (8234)

Eastern Itascan
310 Central Ave.
Nashwauk, MN 55769
Phone: (218)885-2100
Fax: (218)885-1222

Publications: Eastern Itascan (16203)

Eastern Michigan University
18-B Goddard
Ypsilanti, MI 48197
Phone: (734)487-0397
Fax: (734)487-1241

Publications: Eastern Echo (15690)

Eastern Middlesex Press Publications, Inc.
277 Commercial St.
Malden, MA 02148
Phone: (617)321-8000
Fax: (617)321-8008

Publications: Malden Evening News (14296)

Eastern Missouri Publishing Co.
1513 St. Joe Dr.
PO Box A
Park Hills, MO 63601
Phone: (573)431-2010
Fax: (573)431-7640

Publications: The Daily Journal (17334)

Eastern Nazarene College
25 E Elm St.
Wollaston, MA 02170
Phone: (617)745-3577

Publications: Campus Camera (14671)

Eastern Oklahoma Catholic
PO Box 690240
Tulsa, OK 74169-0240
Phone: (918)294-1904
Fax: (918)294-0920

Publications: Eastern Oklahoma Catholic (26114)

Eastern Oregon University
L Ave.
La Grande, OR 97850
Phone: (541)962-3386

Publications: The Eastern Voice (26398)

The Eastern Progress
117 Donovan Annex
Richmond, KY 40475
Phone: (859)622-1881
Fax: (859)622-2354

Publications: The Eastern Progress (12382)

Eastern Publishing Ltd.
232 Main St., Ste. 7
Fort Fairfield, ME 04742
Phone: (207)472-3111
Fax: (207)473-7977

Publications: Fort Fairfield Review (12963)

Eastern Publishing Ltd.
202 Penobscot Ave.
PO Box 330
Millinocket, ME 04462
Phone: (207)723-8118
Fax: (207)723-4434

Publications: The Katahdin Times (12990)

Eastern Sierra Publishing, Inc.
955 Kuenzli St.
Reno, NV 89502-1160
Phone: (702)883-4322
Fax: (702)883-4311

Publications: Pennysaver (18422)

Eastern Townships Research Centre
Lennoxville, QC, Canada J1M 1Z7
Phone: (819)822-9600
Fax: (819)822-9661

Publications: The Campus (37046)

Eastland County Newspaper, Inc.
PO Box 29
Eastland, TX 76448
Phone: (817)629-1707
Fax: (817)629-2092

Publications: Eastland Telegram (30264) • The Rising Star (30265)

Eastman School of Music
26 Gibbs St.
Rochester, NY 14604

Publications: Integral (23230)

Easy Reader/Redondo Beach Hometown News
832 Hermosa Ave.
PO Box 427
Hermosa Beach, CA 90254
Phone: (310)372-4611
Fax: (310)318-6292

Publications: Easy Reader/Redondo Beach Hometown News (2908)

Eating Well, Inc.
823A Ferry Rd.
PO Box 1010
Charlotte, VT 05445
Phone: (802)425-5700
Fax: (802)425-3700
Free: 800-344-3350

Publications: Eating Well Magazine (21579)

Eaton Hall Publishing
256 Columbia Tpke.
Florham Park, NJ 07932
Phone: (973)514-5900
Fax: (973)514-5977
Free: 800-746-9646

Publications: Exhibit Marketing Magazine (18824)

Eaton Publishing
PO Box 1070
Westborough, MA 01581-6070
Phone: (508)614-1414
Fax: (508)616-2930

Publications: BioTechniques (14635) • Peptide Research (14638)

Eau Claire Press Co.
PO Box 570
Eau Claire, WI 54702
Phone: (715)833-9200
Fax: (715)833-9244
Free: 800-236-8808

Publications: Leader-Telegram (33672)

Eau Claire Press Co.
701 S. Farwell St.
Eau Claire, WI 54701
Phone: (715)833-9270
Fax: (715)858-7307
Free: 800-236-4004

Publications: The Country Today (33668)

Ecclesia Publishing Corp.
9 St. Johns Ave.
Winnipeg, MB, Canada R2W 1G8
Phone: (204)586-3093
Fax: (204)582-5241

Publications: The Herald (Visnyk) (35332)

EC.COM Magazine
PO Box 6
Saratoga, CA 95071-0006
Phone: (408)867-6300
Fax: (408)867-9800

Publications: EC.COM Magazine (3744)

L'Echo de la Baie
140 Boul Perron Ouest
PO Box 129
New Richmond, QC, Canada G0C 2B0
Phone: (418)392-5083
Fax: (418)392-6605

Publications: L'Echo de la Baie (37258)

L'Echo de Frontenac
5040, boul. des Veterans
Lac Megantic, QC, Canada G6B 2G5
Phone: (819)583-1630
Fax: (819)583-1124

Publications: L'Echo de Frontenac (37028)

Echo-Pilot Newspaper
Box 159
Greencastle, PA 17225
Phone: (717)597-2164
Fax: (717)597-3754

Publications: Echo-Pilot (26949)

Echo Press
225 7th Ave. E
PO Box 549
Alexandria, MN 56308
Phone: (320)763-3133
Fax: (320)763-3258

Publications: The Echo/Press (15712) • Lakeland Shopping Guide (15713)

Echo Publishing Co.
401 Church St.
Sulphur Springs, TX 75482
Phone: (903)885-8663
Fax: (903)885-8768

Publications: Hopkins County Echo (31165)

Echo Publishing Co.
219 Back Fork St.
Webster Springs, WV 26288
Phone: (304)847-5828
Fax: (304)847-5991

Publications: Webster Echo (33485)

Echo Publishing Inc.
PO Box 900
Oakridge, OR 97463
Phone: (541)782-4241
Fax: (541)782-3323

Publications: Dead Mountain Echo (26452)

Echo Publishing & Printing, Inc.
PO Box 240
Pequot Lakes, MN 56472
Phone: (218)568-8521
Fax: (218)568-5407
Free: 800-450-8521

Publications: Echoland Shopper (16262)

Echoes-Sentinel
256 Mercer St.
Stirling, NJ 07980
Phone: (908)647-0412
Fax: (908)647-5952
Free: 800-624-3684

Publications: Echoes-Sentinel (19601)

Echos-Vedettes
801 Sherbrooke Est., Ste. 202
Montreal, QC, Canada H2L 4X9
Phone: (514)528-7111
Fax: (514)528-7115

Publications: Echos-Vedettes (37111)

Eclipse-News-Review
503 Coates St.
PO Box 340
Parkersburg, IA 50665
Phone: (319)346-1461

Publications: Eclipse-News-Review (11149)

ECM Group
234 S Main St.
PO Box 352
Cambridge, MN 55008-0352
Phone: (763)689-1981
Fax: (763)689-4372
Free: 800-473-1981

Publications: County News (15785) • Scotsman (15786)

E.C.M. Publishers, Inc.
208 N La Grande Ave.
Princeton, MN 55371-0278
Phone: (763)389-4710
Fax: (763)389-1728
Free: 800-631-1222

Publications: Princeton Union-Eagle (16284) • Town and Country Shopper (16285)

ECM Publishers, Inc. - Forest Lake
880 SW 15th St.
Forest Lake, MN 55025
Phone: (651)464-4601
Fax: (651)464-4605

Publications: Forest Lake Times (15905) • St. Croix Valley Peach (15906)

ECM Publishers, Inc. - North Branch
6354 Main St.
North Branch, MN 55056
Phone: (612)464-4601
Fax: (612)464-4605

Publications: ECM Post-Review (16221)

ECM Publishing
506 Freeport
PO Box 330
Elk River, MN 55330
Phone: (763)241-8146
Fax: (763)441-6401

Publications: Elk River Star News (15878) • Elk River Star Shopper (15879)

Ecole des Haules Etudes Commerciales
3000 Chemin Cote-Sainte-Catherine
Montreal, QC, Canada H3T 2A7
Phone: (514)340-6677
Fax: (514)340-6975

Publications: Geston (37120)

Ecological Society of America
1707 H. St. NW
Washington, DC 20006
Phone: (202)833-8773
Fax: (202)833-8775

Publications: Ecological Applications (20800)

Ecology Center
2530 San Pablo Ave.
Berkeley, CA 94702
Phone: (510)548-2220
Fax: (510)548-2240

Publications: Ecology Terrain (1516)

Ecom Publishing
PO Box 507
Wakarusa, IN 46573
Fax: (219)293-3705

Publications: Wakarusa Tribune (10533)

eCompany Now
One California St. 29th Flr.
San Francisco, CA 94111
Phone: (415)293-4800
Fax: (415)293-5900

Publications: eCompany Now (3354)

The Econometric Society
Department of Economics
Northwestern University
Evanston, IL 60208
Phone: (847)491-3615

Publications: Econometrica (14050)

Economic Affairs Bureau
740 Cambridge St.
Cambridge, MA 02141
Phone: (617)876-2434
Fax: (617)876-0008

Publications: Dollars & Sense (14049)

Economic Geology Publishing Company, Inc.
7811 Shaffer Pkwy.
Littleton, CO 80127
Phone: (720)981-7882
Fax: (720)981-7874

Publications: Economic Geology (4547)

Economics Press Inc.
12 Daniel Rd.
Fairfield, NJ 07004-2565
Phone: (973)227-1224
Fax: (973)227-9742
Free: 800-526-2554

Publications: Bits & Pieces (18812)

Economist Group
33 Washington St., Fl. 13
Newark, NJ 07102-3107
Free: 800-245-8723

Publications: Traffic World (5827)

Eden Echo
Drawer V
Eden, TX 76837
Phone: (915)869-3561

Publications: The Eden Echo (30269)

Edgecombe Publishing, Inc.
PO Box 379
Minden, NE 68959-0379
Phone: (308)832-2220
Fax: (308)832-2221

Publications: The Minden Courier (18163)

The Edgeley Mail
PO Box 278
Edgeley, ND 58433
Phone: (701)493-2261
Fax: (701)493-2261

Publications: The Edgeley Mail (24404)

Edgell Communications, Inc.
4 Middlebury Blvd.
Randolph, NJ 07869-4214
Phone: (973)252-0100
Fax: (973)252-9020

Publications: Consumer Goods Technology (19494) • Retail Info Systems News (19497) • Retail Systems Reseller (19498) • Selling Christmas Decorations (18850)

Edgerton Enterprise
831 Main St.
PO Box 397
Edgerton, MN 56128
Phone: (507)442-6161
Fax: (507)631-0061

Publications: The Edgerton Enterprise (15873)

Edgewood Reminder
Box 458
Edgewood, IA 52042
Phone: (563)928-6876

Publications: Edgewood Reminder (10867)

Edison Electric Institute
701 Pennsylvania Ave. NW
Washington, DC 20004-2696
Phone: (202)508-5714
Fax: (202)508-5759

Publications: Electric Perspectives (5476)

Editador (9012-3993 Quebec inc.)
4545 Pierre-De Coubertin Ave.
C.P. 1000, Succursale M.
Montreal, QC, Canada H1V 3R2
Phone: (514)252-3017
Fax: (514)252-3154

Publications: Virage (37235)

Editions Continuite Inc.
82, Grande Allee Ouest
Quebec, QC, Canada G1R 2G6
Phone: (418)647-4525
Fax: (418)647-6483

Publications: Continuite (37282)

Editions Cooperatives du Ven'd'Est, Ltee.
C.P. 266
Bathurst, NB, Canada E2A 3Z2
Fax: (506)545-6299

Publications: Ven'd'Est (35379)

Editions C.R. Inc.
PO Box 1010
Victoriaville, QC, Canada G6P 8Y1
Phone: (819)752-4243
Fax: (819)382-2970

Publications: 2x4 (All About Wood) (37433)

Editions E.J.S. and FDO Communications
909 blvd. Pierre Butrand, 110
Vanier, QC, Canada G1M 3R8
Phone: (418)686-1940
Fax: (418)686-1942

Publications: Pensez-Y Bien! (37428)

Editions Info Presse Inc.
4310, boul. Saint-Laurent
Montreal, QC, Canada H2W 1Z3
Phone: (514)842-5873
Fax: (514)842-2422

Publications: Info Presse Communications (37127)

Editions du Journal de l'Assurance Inc.
321, Rue de la Commune W., Ste. 100
Montreal, QC, Canada H2Y 2E1
Phone: (514)289-9595
Fax: (514)289-9527

Publications: The Insurance Journal (37133) • Journal de l'Assurance (37143) • Magazine Finance (37180)

Editions Parachute
4060, boul. St-Laurent, Bureau 501
Montreal, QC, Canada H2W 1Y9
Phone: (514)842-9805
Fax: (514)287-7146

Publications: Parachute (37204)

Editions Themis
C.P. 6128, Succ. Centre-Ville
Montreal, QC, Canada H3C 3J7
Phone: (514)343-6627
Fax: (514)343-6779

Publications: Revue Juridique Themis (37219)

Editions 2000 Neuf
606 Cathcart, Ste. 330
Montreal, QC, Canada H3B 1K9
Phone: (514)868-0383
Fax: (514)868-0608

Publications: Artere (37086)

Editions Versicolores Inc.
1320, boul. St-Joseph
Quebec, QC, Canada G2K 1G2
Phone: (418)628-8690
Fax: (418)628-0524

Publications: Espaces Verts (37283) • Fleur Design (37284) • Fleurs, Plantes et Jardins (37285) • Option Serre (37294) • Quebec Vert (37295)

Editor & Publisher Magazine
770 Broadway
New York, NY 10003-9595
Fax: (646)654-5360
Free: 800-336-4380

Publications: Editor & Publisher (21585)

Editorial Projects in Education, Inc.
6935 Arlington Rd., Ste. 100
Bethesda, MD 20814
Phone: (301)280-3100
Fax: (301)280-3250

Publications: Education Week (13330) • Teacher Magazine (13383)

Editorial Services Company
812 South 3rd St.
Louisville, KY 40203
Phone: (502)584-2720
Fax: (502)584-2722
Free: 800-888-0695

Publications: Kentucky Travel Guide (12226) • Welcome to Greater Louisville (12244)

Editorial Televisa
6355 NW 36th St.
Miami, FL 33166-7099
Phone: (305)871-6400
Fax: (305)871-4939

Publications: Buenhogar (6342) • Cosmopolitan en Espanol (6346) • Geomundo (6356) • Harper's Bazaar en Espanol (6357) • Hombre Internacional (6360) • Ideas prara Su Hogar (Ideas for Your Home) (6362) • Mecanica Popular (6385) • Tu Internacional (6385) • TV y Novelas (6386) • Vanidades Continental (6388)

Edmonton Chamber of Commerce
10123-99th St., Ste. 600
Edmonton, AB, Canada T5J 3G9
Phone: (780)426-4620
Fax: (780)424-7946

Publications: Commerce News (34706)

Edmonton and Homersham Commerce & Industry
11802 124th St., Ste. 215
Edmonton, AB, Canada T5L 0M3
Phone: (403)454-5540
Fax: (403)453-2553

Publications: Edmonton and Homersham Commerce & Industry (34709)

Edmonton Jewish Life
107-10342 107 St.
Edmonton, AB, Canada T5J 1K2
Phone: (780)488-7276
Fax: (780)487-4342
Free: 877-355-4331

Publications: Edmonton Jewish Life (34710)

Edmonton Laser Graphics
12227 107 Ave., Ste. 1
Edmonton, AB, Canada T5M 1Y9
Phone: (780)488-3693
Fax: (780)488-3859

Publications: Ukrainian News (34732)

Edmunds Enterprises Incorporated
PO Box 21
North Sutton, NH 03260
Phone: (603)927-4028
Fax: (603)927-4129

Publications: InterTown Record (18615)

Edna Herald Publishing Co., Inc.
PO Box 1099
Edna, TX 77957-1502
Phone: (512)782-3547
Fax: (512)782-6002

Publications: Jackson County Herald-Tribune (30275)

The Edon Commercial
PO Box 218
Edon, OH 43518
Phone: (419)272-2413
Fax: (419)298-2360

Publications: The Edon Commercial (25177)

Edson Leader
PO Box 6330
Edson, AB, Canada T7E 1T8
Phone: (403)723-3301
Fax: (403)723-5171

Publications: Edson Leader (34758)

Education California
1517 L St.
Sacramento, CA 95814
Phone: (916)444-3216
Fax: (916)444-1085
Free: 800-890-0325

Publications: Education California (EDCAL) (2996)

The Education Center, Inc.
3515 W. Market St. Ste. 200
Greensboro, NC 27403
Phone: (336)851-8351
Fax: (336)851-8365
Free: 800-334-0298

Publications: Learning (23926)

Education Commission of the States
700 Broadway, Ste. 1200
Denver, CO 80203-3460
Phone: (303)299-3600
Fax: (303)296-8332

Publications: State Education Leader (4360)

Education Minnesota
41 Sherburne Ave.
St. Paul, MN 55103
Phone: (651)227-9541
Fax: (651)292-4802
Free: 800-652-9073

Publications: Minnesota Educator (16391)

Education Update, Inc.
276 5th Ave., Ste. 1005
New York, NY 10001
Phone: (212)481-5519
Fax: (212)481-3919

Publications: Education Update (21588)

Educational Communication Center
1830 Walnut St.
Camp Hill, PA 17011
Phone: (717)761-6620

Publications: Journal of Educational Relations (26752)

Educational Development Center Inc.
55 Chapel St.
Newton, MA 02458-1060
Phone: (617)969-7100

Publications: Innovations in End-of-Life Care (14399)

Educational Foundation for Nuclear Science
6042 S Kimbark
Chicago, IL 60637
Phone: (773)702-2555
Fax: (773)702-0725

Publications: Bulletin of the Atomic Scientists (8295)

Educational Leadership
1703 N. Beauregard St.
Alexandria, VA 22311-1714
Fax: (703)578-5400

Publications: Educational Leadership (31669)

Educational Media, LLC
488 Main Ave.
Norwalk, CT 06851-1008
Phone: (203)847-7200
Fax: (203)846-1866

Publications: Curriculum Administrator (5054)

Educational News Service
PO Box 60478
Florence, MA 01062
Phone: (413)586-4490
Fax: (413)586-3448
Free: 800-600-4494

Publications: Perspectiva (14187)

Educational Publishing Foundation
750 1st St. NE
Washington, DC 20002-4242
Phone: (202)408-9804
Fax: (202)336-5568

Publications: Consulting Psychology Journal: Practice and Research (5437) • Psychology of Addictive Behaviors (5742)

Educational Technology Publications
700 Palisade Ave.
Englewood Cliffs, NJ 07632-0564
Phone: (201)871-4007
Fax: (201)871-4009
Free: 800-952-BOOK

Publications: Educational Technology (18799)

Educational Theatre Association
2343 Auburn Ave.
Cincinnati, OH 45219
Phone: (513)421-3900
Fax: (513)421-7077

Publications: Dramatics Magazine (24795) • Teaching Theatre (24822)

EDUCAUSE
4772 Walnut St., Ste. 206
Boulder, CO 80301-2538
Phone: (303)939-0321
Fax: (303)440-0461

Publications: EDUCAUSE Quarterly (4166)

EDventure Holdings Inc.
104 5th Ave., 20th Fl.
New York, NY 10003
Phone: (212)924-8800
Fax: (212)924-0240

Publications: Release 1.0 (22643)

Edward A. Sherman Publishing Co.
PO Box 420
101 Malbone Rd.
Newport, RI 02840
Phone: (401)849-3300
Fax: (401)849-3306

Publications: The Newport Daily News (28368) • Newport Mercury (28370) • The Newport Navalog (28371)

Edwards Publications
608 E Pershing
PO Box 1782
Riverton, WY 82501
Phone: (307)857-6114
Fax: (307)856-4356

Publications: The ADvertiser (34575)

Edwards Publishing
212 1/2 Main St.
Alta, IA 51002
Phone: (712)284-2300
Fax: (712)732-3152

Publications: Alta Advertiser (10585)

Edwards Publishing Co.
16 Waterbury Rd.
PO Box 7193
Prospect, CT 06712
Phone: (203)758-4474
Fax: (203)758-4475

Publications: Job Shop Technology (JST) (5092)

Edwardsville Publishing Co., Inc.
117 N 2nd St.
PO Box 70
Edwardsville, IL 62025-1938
Phone: (618)656-4700
Fax: (618)656-7618

Publications: Command Post (8811) • Edwardsville Intelligencer (8812)

EERC@emdUniversity of Tennessee
311 Conference Center Bldg.
Knoxville, TN 37996-4134
Phone: (865)974-5774
Fax: (865)974-8491

Publications: FORUM for Applied Research and Public Policy (29271)

Effingham Daily News
201 N Banker St.
PO Box 370
Effingham, IL 62401-2304
Phone: (217)347-7151
Fax: (217)342-9315
Free: 800-526-7205

Publications: Effingham Daily News (8816)

Effingham Herald
270 Columbia Ave.
PO Box 799
Rincon, GA 31326
Phone: (912)826-5012
Fax: (912)826-0381

Publications: Effingham Herald (7496)

Eganville Leader Publishing Ltd.
154 John St., Box 310
Eganville, ON, Canada K0J 1T0
Phone: (613)628-2332
Fax: (613)628-3291

Publications: The Eganville Leader (35800)

Eglise Unie Du Canada
1332, Victoria
Longueuil, QC, Canada J4V 1L8
Phone: (514)466-7733
Fax: (514)466-2664

Publications: Aujourd'hui Credo (37051)

EGS Press
128 Danforth Ave., No. 119
Toronto, ON, Canada M4K 1N1
Phone: (416)465-6618
Fax: (416)465-0036

Publications: Poiesis (36712)

EGW.com, Inc.
1041 Shary Cir.
Concord, CA 94518
Phone: (925)671-9852
Fax: (925)671-0692

Publications: Tole World (1755) • Veggie Life (1756) • Weekend Woodcrafts (1758) • Wood Strokes & Woodcrafts (1759)

Egypt Today
PO Box 914
Ashburn, VA 20146-0914
Phone: (703)328-0886
Fax: 800-859-9507

Publications: Business Today Egypt (31850) • Egypt Today (31851)

EH Publishing, Inc.
526 Boston Post Rd., Ste. 150
PO Box 340
Wayland, MA 01778
Phone: (508)358-3400
Fax: (508)358-5195
Free: 800-375-8015

Publications: Electronic House (14614) • Popular Home Automation (14615)

Ehlert Publishing Group, Inc.
6420 Sycamore Ln., Ste. 100
Maple Grove, MN 55369
Phone: (763)383-4400
Fax: (763)383-4499
Free: 800-848-6247

Publications: Archery Business (16036) • Bowhunting World (16037) • Powersports Business (16039) • Snow Week (16040)

EIDOS
1144 Chestnut St.
Newton, MA 02464-1309
Phone: (617)262-0096
Fax: (617)364-0096

Publications: EIDOS (14393)

18 Media inc.
618 Santa Cruz Ave.
Menlo Park, CA 94025
Phone: (650)324-1818
Fax: (650)324-1888

Publications: Gentry Magazine and Northern California Home & Design (2524)

Eintracht Inc.
9456 N Lawler Ave.
Skokie, IL 60077
Phone: (847)677-9456
Fax: (847)677-9471

Publications: Harmony (9605)

EIR News Service
PO Box 17390
Washington, DC 20041
Phone: (703)777-9451
Fax: (703)777-9492

Publications: Executive Intelligence Review (5485)

EIS International
1401 Rockville Pke., Ste. 500
Rockville, MD 20852
Phone: (301)738-6900
Fax: (301)738-1026
Free: 800-999-5009

Publications: Hazard Technology (13681)

El Bohemio News
4178 Mission St.
San Francisco, CA 94112
Phone: (415)469-9579
Fax: (415)469-9481

Publications: El Bohemio News (3357)

El Campo Newspapers, Inc.
203 E Jackson St.
PO Box 1180
El Campo, TX 77437-1180
Phone: (979)543-3363
Fax: (979)543-0097

Publications: El Campo Leader-News (30276)

EL CENTRAL Newspaper
4124 W Vernor
Detroit, MI 48209
Phone: (313)841-0100
Fax: (313)841-0155

Publications: EL CENTRAL Newspaper (14930)

El Clasificado
1125 Goodrich Blvd.
Los Angeles, CA 90022
Phone: (323)278-5310
Fax: (323)278-5315
Free: 800-242-2527

Publications: El Clasificado (2262)

El Crepusculo, Inc.
226 Albright St.
PO Box U
Taos, NM 87571
Phone: (505)758-2241
Fax: (505)758-9647
Free: 800-207-5479

Publications: The Taos News (19963)

El Dia Inc.
PO Box 9067512
San Juan, PR 00906-7512
Phone: (787)641-8000

Publications: El Nuevo Dia (28292)

El Dia Newspaper
5718 W Cermak Rd.
Cicero, IL 60804-2444
Phone: (708)652-6396
Fax: (708)652-6653

Publications: El Dia Newspaper (8673)

El Diario/La Prensa
345 Hudson St.
New York, NY 10014
Phone: (212)807-4600
Fax: (212)807-4617

Publications: El Diario/La Prensa (21590)

El Dorado Gazette/Georgetown Gazette and Town Crier
2775 Miners Flat
PO Box 49
Georgetown, CA 95634-0156
Phone: (530)333-4481
Fax: (530)333-0152

Publications: El Dorado Gazette/Georgetown Gazette and Town Crier (1863)

El Dorado News Times
111 N. Madison
PO Box 912
El Dorado, AR 71731-0912
Phone: (870)862-6611
Fax: (870)862-5226

Publications: El Dorado News-Times (1106)

El Dorado Springs Sun
PO Box 71
El Dorado Springs, MO 64744
Phone: (417)876-3841
Fax: (417)876-3848

Publications: El Dorado Springs Sun (17042)

El Editor Permian Basin
1401 Rankin Hwy.
Midland, TX 79701
Phone: (915)570-0405
Fax: (915)580-5560
Free: 800-938-4399

Publications: El Editor Permian Basin (30871)

El Especial
3510 Bergenline Ave.
Union City, NJ 07087-4751
Phone: (201)348-1959
Fax: (201)348-3385

Publications: El Especial (19690)

El Extra
PO Box 270432
Dallas, TX 75227
Phone: (214)309-0990
Fax: (214)309-0204

Publications: El Extra (30154)

El Heraldo Catolico
5890 Newman Ct.
Sacramento, CA 95819
Phone: (916)452-3344
Fax: (916)452-2945

Publications: Catholic Herald (2991) • El Heraldo Catolico (2997)

El Hispano
8605 West Chester Pke.
Upper Darby, PA 19082
Phone: (610)789-5512
Fax: (610)789-5524

Publications: El Hispano (28088)

El Manana
6140 W Deamak Rd.
Chicago, IL 60804
Phone: (708)652-5841
Fax: (708)652-6945

Publications: El Manana News (8362)

El Mensajero
PO Box 895
Amarillo, TX 79105
Phone: (806)371-7084
Fax: (806)371-7090

Publications: El Mensajero (29696)

El Mexicalo
931 Niles St.
Bakersfield, CA 93305-4535
Phone: (805)323-9334
Fax: (805)323-6951

Publications: El Mexicalo (1450)

El Mundo Communications Inc.
PO Box 2231
Wenatchee, WA 98807
Phone: (509)663-5737
Fax: (509)663-6957

Publications: El Mundo (33193)

El Norte, Acquisitions, Inc.
PO Box 140995
Arecibo, PR 00614
Phone: (787)262-0130
Fax: (787)262-0160

Publications: El Norte (28223)

El Nuevo Patria Publishing Co.
PO Box 2, Jose Marti Sta.
Miami, FL 33135-0002
Phone: (305)530-8787

Publications: El Nuevo Patria (6350)

El Observador
99 N. 1st St., Ste. 100
San Jose, CA 95113-1203
Phone: (408)938-1700
Fax: (408)938-1705

Publications: El Observador (3516)

El Paso Times
Times Plaza
El Paso, TX 79901-1470
Phone: (915)546-6104
Fax: (915)546-6496
Free: 800-351-1677

Publications: El Paso Times (30280)

El Periodico, U.S.A.
1016 Ivy Ave.
McAllen, TX 78501-4309
Phone: (210)631-5628
Fax: (210)631-0832

Publications: El Periodico, U.S.A. (30783)

El Popular
212 Goodman St.
Bakersfield, CA 93305
Phone: (661)398-1000
Fax: (661)325-1351

Publications: El Popular (1451)

El Popular
2413 Dundas St W.
Toronto, ON, Canada M6P 1X3
Phone: (416)531-2495
Fax: (416)531-7187

Publications: El Popular (36581)

El Puente
PO Box 553
Goshen, IN 46527-0553
Phone: (219)533-9082
Fax: (219)537-0552

Publications: El Puente (10022)

El Segundo Herald, Inc.
PO Box 188
El Segundo, CA 90245
Phone: (310)322-1830
Fax: (310)322-2787

Publications: El Segundo Herald (1868)

El Tiempo de New York
37-37-88 St.
Ste. 8-A
Jackson Heights, NY 11372
Phone: (718)507-0832
Fax: (718)507-2105
Free: 800-921-1148

Publications: El Tiempo de New York (20827)

The Elba Clipper
PO Drawer A
Elba, AL 36323
Phone: (334)897-2823
Fax: (334)897-3434
Free: 888-216-8050

Publications: The Elba Clipper (197)

The Elberton Star
25 N Public Sq.
PO Box 280
Elberton, GA 30635-0280
Phone: (706)283-8500
Fax: (706)283-9700

Publications: The Elberton Star & Examiner (7267)

Eldorado Courier
507 W Main St.
PO Box 160
Eldorado, OK 73537
Phone: (405)633-2376
Fax: (405)633-2375

Publications: Eldorado Courier (25818)

Eldredge Publishing Co.
1015 Lincoln Ave.
Harvey, ND 58341
Phone: (701)324-4646

Publications: The Herald-Press (24468)

Electra Star News
PO Box 1192
Electra, TX 76360
Phone: (940)495-2149
Fax: (940)495-2627

Publications: Electra Star-News (30306)

The Electric Cooperatives of South Carolina
808 Knox Abbott Dr.
Cayce, SC 29033-3311
Phone: (803)796-6060
Fax: (803)796-6064

Publications: Living in South Carolina (28503)

Electric Power Association of Mississippi, Inc.
PO Box 3300
Ridgeland, MS 39158-3300
Phone: (601)922-2341
Fax: (601)922-9869

Publications: TODAY in Mississippi (16835)

Electrical Generating Systems Association (EGSA)
1650 S. Dixie Hwy., Ste. 500
Boca Raton, FL 33432-7462
Phone: (561)750-5575
Fax: (561)395-8557

Publications: Powerline (5938)

Electrical News
PO Box 660760
Arcadia, CA 91066-0760
Phone: (626)446-8652
Fax: (626)447-6047
Free: 800-782-5493

Publications: Electrical News (1428)

The Electricity Journal
655 Ave. of Americas
New York, NY 10010-1570
Phone: (212)989-5800
Fax: (212)462-1974
Free: 888-437-4636

Publications: The Electricity Journal (21592)

Electrifying Times
63600 Deschutes Market Rd.
Bend, OR 97701
Phone: (541)388-1908
Fax: (541)388-2750

Publications: Electrifying Times (26242)

Electrochemical Society Inc.
65 S Main St.
Pennington, NJ 08534-2839
Phone: (609)737-1902
Fax: (609)737-2743

Publications: The Electrochemical Society Interface (19420)

Electronic Commerce World
2021 Coolidge St.
Hollywood, FL 33020
Phone: (954)925-5900
Fax: (954)925-7533
Free: 800-336-4889

Publications: Electronic Commerce World (6193)

The Electronic Journal of Combinatorics
Dept. of Mathematical Sciences
Clemson University
Clemson, SC 29634-1907
Phone: (864)656-3311
Fax: (864)656-5230

Publications: The Electronic Journal of Combinatorics (28532)

Element K Journals
2165 Brighton-Henrietta Townline Rd., Ste.3
Rochester, NY 14623
Fax: (585)292-4392
Free: 800-223-8720

Publications: Inside the Internet (23229)

Elevator World Inc.
356 Morgan Ave.
PO Box 6507
Mobile, AL 36660
Phone: (251)479-4514
Fax: (251)479-7043
Free: 800-730-5093

Publications: Elevator World (319)

ELF Publications, Inc.
5285 W Louisiana Ave.
Lakewood, CO 80232-5976
Phone: (303)975-0075
Free: 800-922-8513

Publications: Community Pharmacist (4531) • HealthCare Distributor (4532)

Eligible
PO Box 57466
Sherman Oaks, CA 91413
Phone: (818)760-4112

Publications: Eligible (3762)

Elitispano
928 2nd St. 300
PO Box 2856
Sacramento, CA 95812
Phone: (916)442-0267
Fax: (916)443-2818

Publications: El Hispano (2998)

Elizabethton Star
300 Sycamore St.
PO Box 1960
Elizabethton, TN 37644-1960
Phone: (423)542-4151
Fax: (423)542-2004

Publications: Elizabethton Star (29179)

Elk County Historical Society
PO Box 361
Ridgway, PA 15853

Publications: Elk Horn (27934)

Elk Island Triangle News
Box 170
St. Michael, AB, Canada T0B 4B0
Phone: (780)896-2223
Fax: (780)896-2281
Free: 888-896-1223

Publications: The Triangle (34843)

Elk Point Review
4813-50 Ave.
PO Box 309
Elk Point, AB, Canada T0A 1A0
Phone: (780)724-4087
Fax: (780)645-2346

Publications: Elk Point Review (34763)

Elk Printing Co.
PO Box 180
Clay, WV 25043
Phone: (304)587-4253
Fax: (304)587-7300

Publications: Clay County Free Press (33297)

Elk Publishing, Inc.
181 S. Union St.
Burlington, VT 05401-5275
Phone: (802)860-0003
Fax: (802)860-0005
Free: 800-499-0447

Publications: Outdoors Magazine (31516) • Vermont Business Magazine (31519)

Elkhart Tri-State News
PO Box 777
Elkhart, KS 67950
Phone: (620)697-4716

Publications: Elkhart Tri-State News (11422)

The Elkhorn Independent
11 W Walworth St.
Elkhorn, WI 53121
Phone: (414)723-2250
Fax: (414)723-7424

Publications: The Elkhorn Independent (33688)

Elko Daily Free Press
3720 Idaho St.
Elko, NV 89801
Phone: (702)738-3118
Fax: (702)738-2215

Publications: Elko Daily Free Press (18335)

The Elks Magazine
425 W. Diversey Pkwy.
Chicago, IL 60614-6196
Phone: (773)755-4900
Fax: (773)755-4792
Free: 877-ELK-SMAG

Publications: The Elks Magazine (8366)

Ellinghouse Publishing Co., Inc.
PO Box 97
Piedmont, MO 63957
Phone: (573)223-7122
Fax: (573)223-7871
Free: 800-923-7122

Publications: Reynolds County Courier (17047) • Wayne County Journal-Banner (17343)

Elliot Institute
PO Box 7348
Springfield, IL 62791-7348
Phone: (217)525-8202
Fax: (217)525-8212

Publications: The Post-Abortion Review (9641)

Elliott Publishing, Inc.
202 E. State
Camp Point, IL 62320
Phone: (217)593-6515
Fax: (217)593-7720

Publications: Camp Point Journal (8109) • Golden-Clayton New Era (8946) • Mendon Dispatch-Times (9173)

Elliott Publishing, Inc.
PO Box 198
Liberty, IL 62347
Phone: (217)645-3033
Fax: (217)645-3083
Free: 800-648-3033

Publications: Liberty Bee-Times (9076)

ellipse
471 Smythe, No. 27009
Fredericton, NB, Canada E3B 3E3
Phone: (506)451-0408
Fax: (506)455-9980

Publications: ellipse (35393)

Bob Ellis
PO Box 50733
Tucson, AZ 85703
Phone: (520)622-7176
Fax: (520)792-8382

Publications: The Weekly Observer (973)

Ellis County Capital
PO Box 236
Arnett, OK 73832-0236
Phone: (580)885-7788
Fax: (580)885-7296

Publications: Ellis County Capital (25750)

Ellis County Newspapers, Inc.
213 N Dallas St.
PO Box 100
Ennis, TX 75120
Phone: (972)875-3801
Fax: (972)875-9747
Free: (866)890-3207

Publications: Ellis County News (30308) • Ennis Daily News (30309)

Ellis County Star
708 Main St.
Hays, KS 67601
Fax: (913)625-7359

Publications: Ellis County Star (11479)

The Ellis Review
Box 227
1018 Washington
Ellis, KS 67637
Phone: (785)726-4583
Fax: (785)726-3821

Publications: The Ellis Review (11425)

Ellsworth American, Inc.
30 Water St.
PO Box 509
Ellsworth, ME 04605-0509
Phone: (207)667-2576
Fax: (207)667-7656

Publications: The Ellsworth American (12955)

The Ellsworth Reporter
202 N. Douglas Ave.
Ellsworth, KS 67439-3216
Phone: (785)472-3103
Fax: (785)472-3268

Publications: The Ellsworth Reporter (11426) • Kanhistique (11427) • Marquette Tribune (11428)

Elm City Newspapers
349 New Haven Ave.
PO Box 5339
Milford, CT 06460-6647
Phone: (203)876-6800
Fax: (203)877-4772
Free: 800-238-3226

Publications: The Bulletin (4953) • Milford Reporter (4956) • Stratford Bard (4958) • West Haven News (5207)

Elm Street
655 Bay St., Ste. 1100
Toronto, ON, Canada M5G 2K4
Phone: (416)595-9944
Fax: (416)595-7217

Publications: Elm Street (36582)

Elma Review
PO Box 118
Elma, NY 14059
Phone: (716)652-0327
Fax: (716)652-8383

Publications: Elma Review (20570)

Elmer Times Co.
PO Box 1160
Elmer, NJ 08318
Phone: (856)358-6171
Fax: (856)358-7951

Publications: Elmer Times (18793)

Elmhurst College
190 Prospect
Elmhurst, IL 60126
Phone: (630)617-3500
Fax: (630)617-3657

Publications: Prospect The Magazine of Elmhurst College (8837)

Elmont Herald
591 Bauer Ct.
Elmont, NY 11003
Phone: (516)437-1731
Fax: (516)328-1099
Free: (866)HER-ALD1

Publications: Elmont Herald (20581)

Elmwood Argus
PO Box 69
Spring Valley, WI 54767
Phone: (715)778-4395

Publications: Elmwood Argus (33690)

The Eln City Newspapers
349 New Haven Ave.
PO Box 5339
Milford, CT 06460
Phone: (203)876-6800
Fax: (203)877-4772
Free: 800-238-3226

Publications: The Advertiser (4951)

Elsberry News, Inc.
PO Box 105
Elsberry, MO 63343
Phone: (573)898-9814
Fax: (573)898-2173

Publications: Elsberry Democrat (17048)

Elsevier
100 Prospect St.
Stamford, CT 06901
Phone: (203)323-9606
Fax: (203)357-8846

Publications: The Quarterly Review of Economics and Finance (8214)

Elsevier Advanced Technology
PO Box 150
Kidlington OT1 ORD, United Kingdom
Phone: 44 1865843687
Fax: 44 1865843971

Publications: The Leadership Quarterly (30714)

Elsevier Science
The Curtis Center
625 Walnut St.
Philadelphia, PA 19106-3399
Phone: (215)238-7800
Fax: (215)238-7883
Free: 800-523-1649

Publications: Advanced in Renal Replacement Therapy (21153) • American Journal of Contact Dermatitis (30122) • The American Journal of Emergency Medicine (27371) • American Journal of Kidney Diseases (16056) • American Journal of Otolaryngology (27373) • Anesthesiology Clinics of North America (27376) • Annals of Diagnostic Pathology (27377) • Applied Nursing Research (24856) • Archives of Physical Medicine and Rehabilitation (8273) • Archives of Psychiatric Nursing (4983) • Arthroscopy (24318) • Blood (27389) • Cardiology Clinics (27393) • Cardiology Clinics: Annual of Drug Therapy (27394) • Cell Stress and Chaperones (27396) • Chest Surgery Clinics (27399) • Child and Adolescent Psychiatric Clinics (27401) • Clinical Excellence for Nurse Practitioners (14345) • Clinical Journal of Women's Health (14919) • Clinical Oncology (27408) • Clinical Pediatric Emergency Medicine (27409) • Clinical Perspectives in Gastroenterology (27410) • Clinical Techniques in Small Animal Practice (27412) • Clinical Techniques in Small Animal Practice (27411) • Clinics in Chest Medicine (27413) • Clinics in Family Practice (27414) • Clinics in Geriatric Medicine (27415) • Clinics in Laboratory Medicine (27416) • Clinics in Liver Disease (27417) • Clinics in Perinatology (27418) • Clinics in Plastic Surgery (27419) • Clinics in Podiatric Medicine and Surgery (27420) • Clinics in Sports Medicine (27421) • Complementary Medicine for the Physician (27425) • Comprehensive Psychiatry (27426) • Critical Care Clinics (27429) • Critical Care Nursing Clinics (27430) • CRNA (27431) • Dental Clinics (27449) • Dermatologic Clinics (27450) • Endocrinology and Metabolism Clinics (27459) • Facial Plastic Surgery Clinics (27466) • Foot and Ankle Clinics (27471) • Gastroenterology (27473) • Gastroenterology Clinics (27474) • Gastrointestinal Endoscopy Clinics (27475) • Growth Hormone and IGF Research (27477) • Hand Clinics (27478) • Hematology/Oncology Clinics (27480) •

Human Pathology (27487) • Immunology and Allergy Clinics (27489) • Infectious Disease Clinics (27491) • Infertility and Reproductive Medicine Clinics (27492) • The Journal of Arthroplasty (27516) • Journal of Cardiac Failure (3378) • Journal of Cardiothoracic and Vascular Anesthesia (12220) • Journal of Cardiovascular Pharmacology and Therapeutics (27519) • Journal of Critical Care (36634) • Journal of Digital Imaging (6147) • Journal of Electrocardiology (2170) • Journal of Gynecologic Techniques (27529) • Journal of Hand Surgery (17455) • Journal of Oral and Maxillofacial Surgery (12168) • Journal of Pain (27542) • Journal of Pediatric Nursing (2304) • The Journal of Pediatric Oncology Nursing (30498) • Journal of Pediatric Surgery (10141) • Journal of PeriAnesthesia Nursing (7100) • Journal of Pharmacy Practice (27546) • Journal of Professional Nursing (27548) • Journal of Prosthodontics (27549) • Journal of Renal Nutrition (18420) • Journal of Stroke and Cerebrovascular Diseases (10142) • Journal of Surgical Outcomes (27552) • Liver Transplantation (31707) • The Medical Clinics (27564) • Metabolism - Clinical and Experimental (32130) • Molecular Diagnosis (27573) • Neurologic Clinics (27576) • Neurology Network Commentary (27578) • Neurosurgery Clinics (27580) • Nurse Practitioner Forum (27588) • The Nursing Clinics of North America (27590) • Obstetrics and Gynecology Clinics (27594) • Operative Techniques in Cataract and Refractive Surgery (27600) • Operative Techniques in General Surgery (16310) • Operative Techniques in Gynecologic Surgery (27601) • Operative Techniques in Neurosurgery (27602) • Operative Techniques in Oculoplastic, Orbital and Reconstructive Surgery (27603) • Operative Techniques in Orthopaedics (27604) • Operative Techniques in Otolaryngology (27605) • Operative Techniques in Plastic and Reconstructive Surgery (27606) • Operative Techniques in Sports Medicine (27607) • Operative Techniques in Thoracic and Cardiovascular Surgery (6448) • Oral and Maxillofacial Surgery Clinics (27608) • The Orthopedic Clinics (27609) • The Otolaryngologic Clinics (27611) • Pediatric Clinics (27614) • Physical Medicine and Rehabilitation Clinics (27638) • Primary Care (27645) • Progress in Cardiovascular Diseases (20281) • Psychiatric Clinics (27650) • Radiologic Clinics of North America (27652) • Regional Anesthesia and Pain Medicine (33014) • Seizure (27657) • Seminars in Anesthesia, Perioperative Medicine and Pain (27658) • Seminars in Arthritis and Rheumatism (6379) • Seminars in Arthroplasty (27659) • Seminars in Avian and Exotic Pet Medicine (27660) • Seminars in Breast Disease (27661) • Seminars in Cardiothoracic and Vascular Anesthesia (27662) • Seminars in Clinical Neuropsychiatry (33029) • Seminars in Colon and Rectal Surgery (14032) • Seminars in Cutaneous Medicine and Surgery (27664) • Seminars in Cutaneous Medicine and Surgery (27663) • Seminars in Diagnostic Pathology (27665) • Seminars in Gastrointestinal Disease (27666) • Seminars in Hematology (5788) • Seminars in Laparoscopic Surgery (7102) • Seminars in Neonatology (27667) • Seminars in Nephrology (30717) • Seminars in Nuclear Medicine (20286) • Seminars in Oncology (17009) • Seminars in Oncology Nursing (27668) • Seminars in Ophthalmology (27841) • Seminars in Pediatric Infectious Diseases (30529) • Seminars in Pediatric Neurology (27669) • Seminars in Pediatric Surgery (10170) • Seminars in Perinatology (27670) • Seminars in Perioperative Nursing (27671) • Seminars in Radiation Oncology (23722) • Seminars in Radiologic Technology (27672) • Seminars in Respiratory Infections (10171) • Seminars in Roentgenology (27673) • Seminars in Spine Surgery (27674) • Seminars in Thoracic and Cardiovascular Surgery (6449) • Seminars in Thoracic & Cardiovascular Surgery (13959) • Seminars in Ultrasound, CT and MRI (27675) • Seminars in Urologic Oncology (27676) • Seminars in Vascular Surgery (4625) • The Surgical Clinics of North America (27697) • Techniques in Gastrointestinal Endoscopy (27698) • Techniques in Regional Anesthesia and Pain Management (20389) • Techniques in Vascular and Interventional Radiology (27700) • Transfusion Medicine Reviews (35892) • Transplantation Reviews (27710) • The Urologic Clinics (27715) • Veterinary Clinics (27717) • Veterinary Surgery (1818)

Elsevier Science BV
Sara Burgehartstraat 25
NL-1055 KV Amsterdam, Netherlands
Phone: 31 204852911
Fax: 31 204852457

Publications: North American Journal of Economics and Finance (1725)

Elsevier Science Inc.
360 Park Ave. S, No. 11
New York, NY 10010-1710
Phone: (212)633-3730
Fax: (212)633-3680
Free: 888-437-4636

Publications: ACC Current Journal Review (21133) • The Air Pollution Consultant (21168) • The American Journal of Gastroenterology (21194) • American Journal of Ophthalmology (21196) • American Journal of Preventive Medicine (21198) • Biotechnology Advances (36846) • Business Horizons (21357) • Cognitive Science (21435) • Domestic Animal Endocrinology (21566) • Environmental & Experimental Botany (21616) • Evolution and Human Behavior (21659) • Federal Practitioner (21681) • Global Finance Journal (21771) • Industrial Marketing Management (4895) • Intelligence (21888) • International Journal of Developmental Neuroscience (30381) • International Review of Economics and Finance (25121) • International Review of Financial Analysis (74) • Journal of the American College of Surgeons (21982) • Journal of Asian Economics (21999) • Journal of Cultural Heritage (22044) • Journal of International Accounting, Auditing and Taxation (15239) • Journal of Light Metals (22111) • The Journal of Socio-Economics (22188) • Journal of Substance Abuse Treatment (22196) • The Journal of Supercritical Fluids (22199) • Materials and Processing Report (22290) • Metal Finishing (22321) • NUTRITION (22476) • Race & Society (22620) • Serials Review (11948) • Survey of Ophthalmology (22812) • Technology and Disability (20390) • Thrombosis Research (22833) • Vaccine (22894)

Elsevier Science Ltd.
The Boulevard
Langford Ln.
Kidlington OX5 1GB, United Kingdom
Phone: 44 1865843000
Fax: 44 1865843010

Publications: The History of the Family (5273) • The Social Science Journal (11836)

Elsworth Reporter
PO Box 526
Wilson, KS 67490
Phone: (913)658-2235

Publications: Wilson World (11908)

ELT Press
English Dept.
University of North Carolina
PO Box 26170
Greensboro, NC 27402-6170
Phone: (336)334-5446
Fax: (336)334-3281

Publications: English Literature in Transition (23922)

Elwood Bulletin
308 Smith
PO Box 115
Elwood, NE 68937
Phone: (308)785-2251
Fax: (308)785-2251

Publications: Elwood Bulletin (18003)

Elwood Publishing Co.
317 S. Anderson St.
PO Box 85
Elwood, IN 46036-2018
Phone: (765)552-3355
Fax: (765)552-3358

Publications: Alexandria Times-Tribune (9782) • The Call-Leader (9932) • Tipton Tribune (10506)

The Elysian Enterprise
PO Box 119
Elysian, MN 56028-0028
Phone: (507)267-4323
Fax: (507)362-4458

Publications: The Elysian Enterprise (15883)

EMAP Petersen
110 5th Ave., 2nd Fl.
New York, NY 10011
Phone: (212)886-3600
Fax: (212)886-2806

Publications: Stock Car Racing (6292)

Embarcadero Publishing Co.
703 High St.
PO Box 1610
Palo Alto, CA 94302
Phone: (650)326-8210
Fax: (650)326-3928

Publications: Palo Alto Weekly (2801)

Embroiderers Guild of America, Inc.
335 W. Broadway, Ste. 100
Louisville, KY 40202
Phone: (502)589-6956
Fax: (502)584-7900

Publications: EGA Needle Arts Magazine (31996)

Emerson College
120 Boylston St
120 Boylston St.
Boston, MA 02116
Phone: (617)824-8753
Fax: (617)824-8991

Publications: Ploughshares (13950)

Emery County Progress
PO Box 589
Castle Dale, UT 84513
Phone: (435)381-2431
Fax: (435)381-5431

Publications: Emery County Progress (31333)

The Emery Enterprise
143 N 3rd St.
PO Box 244
Emery, SD 57332
Phone: (605)449-4420
Fax: (605)449-4430

Publications: The Emery Enterprise (28852)

EMIS
PO Box 794
Wheaton, IL 60189
Phone: (630)752-7158
Fax: (630)752-7155

Publications: Evangelical Missions Quarterly (EMQ) (9755)

Emmerich Enterprises, Inc.
PO Box 1171
Columbia, MS 39429
Phone: (601)736-2611
Fax: (601)736-4507

Publications: Columbian-Progress/Marion County Advertiser (16599)

Emmetsburg Publishing Co.
Box 73
Emmetsburg, IA 50536
Phone: (712)852-2323
Fax: (712)852-3184

Publications: Democrat (10876) • Reporter (10877)

Emmis Publishing Corp.
40 Monument Circle, No. 100
Indianapolis, IN 46204-3908
Phone: (317)237-9288
Fax: (317)684-8356
Free: 800-876-5133

Publications: Indianapolis Monthly (10131)

Emmons County Record
201 N Broadway
PO Box 38
Linton, ND 58552
Phone: (701)254-4537
Fax: (701)254-4909

Publications: Emmons County Record (24492)

Emory University
Drawer W.
Atlanta, GA 30322
Phone: (404)727-6178
Fax: (404)727-3613

Publications: The Emory Wheel (7005)

Emory University
1655 N. Decatur Rd.
Atlanta, GA 30322
Phone: (404)727-0162

Publications: Emory Magazine (7004)

Empire Publishing Company Ltd.
Box 250
Virden, MB, Canada R0M 2C0
Phone: (204)748-3931
Fax: (204)748-1816

Publications: Virden Empire-Advance (35306)

Empire State Report
25-35 Beechwood Ave.
PO Box 9001
Mount Vernon, NY 10552-9001
Phone: (914)699-2020
Fax: (914)699-2025

Publications: Empire State Report (21102)

Empire State Weeklies, Inc.
2010 Empire Blvd.
Webster, NY 14580
Phone: (585)671-1533
Fax: (585)671-7067

Publications: Wayne County Mail (23527) • Webster Herald (23528)

Employee Assistance Professionals
2101 Wilson Blvd., Ste. 500
Arlington, VA 22201-3062
Phone: (703)522-6272

Publications: EAP Association Exchange (31785)

Employee Benefit Research Institute
2121 K St. NW, Ste. 600
Washington, DC 20037-1896
Phone: (202)659-0670
Fax: (202)775-6312

Publications: EBRI Issue Brief (5469) • EBRI Quarterly Pension Investment Report (5470)

Employee Relocation Council (ERC)
1717 Pennsylvania Ave., NW, Ste. 800
Washington, DC 20006
Phone: (202)857-0857
Fax: (202)659-8631

Publications: Mobility (5655)

Employment Marketplace
12015 Robyn Park Dr.
St. Louis, MO 63131
Phone: (314)569-3095
Fax: (636)458-4955

Publications: Employment Marketplace (17436)

Emporia Gazette
517 Merchant St.
Emporia, KS 66801
Phone: (316)342-4800
Fax: (316)342-8108

Publications: The Emporia Gazette (11429)

Emporia State University
Division of Social Sciences
CB 4032
Emporia, KS 66801
Phone: (620)341-1200

Publications: Teaching History: A Journal of Methods (17354)

Emporia State University Printing Service
1200 Commercial
Emporia, KS 66801-5087

Publications: Kansas Biology Teacher (11430)

EMS Press Ltd.
PO Box 520
Claresholm, AB, Canada T0L 0T0
Phone: (403)625-4474
Fax: (403)625-2828

Publications: Claresholm Local Press (34683)

Emu Today and Tomorrow
PO Box 7
Nardin, OK 74646-0007
Phone: (580)628-2933
Fax: (580)628-2011

Publications: Emu Today & Tomorrow (25927)

En Foco, Inc.
32 E Kingsbridge Rd.
Bronx, NY 10468
Phone: (718)584-7718
Fax: (718)584-7718

Publications: Nueva Luz (20279)

Encore Publishing, Inc.
87 Wall St.
Seattle, WA 98121
Phone: (206)443-0445
Fax: (206)443-1246

Publications: ENCORE (32963)

Enderlin Independent
209 4th Ave.
Enderlin, ND 58027
Phone: (701)437-3131
Fax: (701)437-3131
Free: 888-993-3131

Publications: Enderlin Independent (24410)

Endocrine Society
4350 East West Highway Ste. 500
Bethesda, MD 20814-4410
Phone: (301)941-0200
Fax: (301)941-0259
Free: 800-467-6663

Publications: Endocrine Reviews (30379) • Endo-crinology (2264) • Molecular Endocrinology (24927)

Energy Information Administration, EI 30
1000 Independence Ave. SW
Washington, DC 20585
Phone: (202)586-8800
Fax: (202)586-0727

Publications: Annual Energy Review 2000 (5352) •
Natural Gas Monthly (5688)

Energy Information Administration, National Energy Information Center
Department of Energy
1000 Independence Ave. SW
Washington, DC 20585
Phone: (202)586-8800
Fax: (202)586-0727

Publications: Petroleum Supply Monthly (5718)

Energy Intelligence Group
5 E. 37th St., 5th Fl.
New York, NY 10016
Phone: (212)532-1112
Fax: (212)532-4479
Free: 888-427-7496

Publications: Natural Gas Week (22403)

Energy Times, Inc.
548 Broadhollow Rd.
Melville, NY 11747
Phone: (631)777-7773

Publications: Energy Times (21043)

Enfoque Comunal, Inc.
3565 7 St.
Philadelphia, PA 19140
Phone: (215)227-0628
Fax: (215)227-0646

Publications: Community Focus (27424)

Engel Publishing Partners
820 Bear Tavern Rd., Ste. 300
West Trenton, NJ 08628
Phone: (609)530-0044
Fax: (609)530-0207

Publications: Med Ad News (19742) • Medical
Advertising (19743)

Engineering Contractors Association
8310 Florence Ave.
Downey, CA 90240
Phone: (562)861-0929
Fax: (562)923-6179

Publications: ECA Magazine (1835)

Engineering Information Inc.
1 Castle Point Terrace
Hoboken, NJ 07030-5996
Phone: (201)216-8500
Fax: (201)216-8532
Free: 800-221-1044

Publications: Abstract Bulletin of the Institute of
Paper Science and Technology (18880)

The Engineering Society of Baltimore, Inc.
11 W Mount Vernon Pl.
Baltimore, MD 21201
Phone: (410)539-6914
Fax: (410)783-9372

Publications: Quicks Professional Journal (13240)

Engineers' Forum
Virgina Technological University
333 Norris Hall
Blacksburg, VA 24061-0000
Phone: (540)231-7738

Publications: Engineers' Forum (31870)

The England Democrat
PO Drawer 250
121 E Haywood
England, AR 72046
Phone: (501)842-3111
Fax: (501)842-3081

Publications: The England Democrat (1111)

Engle Printing and Publishing Company
1425 W. Main St.
PO Box 500
Mount Joy, PA 17552
Phone: (717)492-2536
Fax: (717)653-6165
Free: 800-800-1833

Publications: Where & When Pennsylvania's Travel
Guide (27299)

Englewood Sun Herald
200 E Venice Ave.
Venice, FL 34285
Phone: (941)484-2611
Fax: (941)485-3036

Publications: Englewood Sun Herald (6829)

English Department
99 Thomas Nelson Dr.
Hampton, VA 23666
Phone: (757)825-3663
Fax: (757)825-3842

Publications: Harrington Gay Men's Fiction Quarter-ly (32129)

English Digest Press Corps.
201 W 21st St. Ste. 10E
New York, NY 10011
Phone: (212)686-9080
Fax: (212)686-9098

Publications: English Digest (21605)

English Language Notes
University of Colorado
CB 226
Boulder, CO 80309
Phone: (303)492-7176
Fax: (303)492-3521

Publications: English Language Notes (4167)

The Engravers Journal
PO Box 318
26 Summit St.
Brighton, MI 48116
Phone: (810)229-5725
Fax: (810)229-8320

Publications: The Engravers Journal (14836)

Enlace, U.S.A.
Newspaper Div.
PO Box 720224
McAllen, TX 78504
Phone: (210)682-5519

Publications: Enlace, U.S.A. (30784)

Eno Transportation Foundation, Inc.
1634 I St., N.W.
Suite 500
Washington, DC 20006-4003
Phone: (202)879-4700
Fax: (202)879-4719

Publications: Transportation Quarterly (5829)

Enoteca Wine and Food Magazine
PO Box 37
Concord, ON, Canada L4K 1B2
Phone: (905)760-1724
Fax: (905)760-1718

Publications: Enoteca Wine and Food Magazine
(35751)

The Enquirer-Journal
500 W Jefferson St.
PO Box 5040
Monroe, NC 28111-4657
Phone: (704)289-1541
Fax: (704)289-2929

Publications: The Enquirer-Journal (24066)

THE ENSIGN Magazine
PO Box 31664
Raleigh, NC 27622
Phone: (919)821-0892
Fax: 888-304-0813
Free: 888-FOR-USPS

Publications: The Ensign (24134)

The Enterprise
PO Box 218
Claxton, GA 30417
Phone: (912)739-2132
Fax: (912)739-2140
Free: 800-794-3924

Publications: The Enterprise (7171)

Enterprise
PO Box 449
Manchester, KY 40962
Phone: (606)598-6174
Fax: (606)598-2330

Publications: Enterprise (12278)

The Enterprise
202 Adams St.
PO Box 840
Mansfield, LA 71052
Phone: (318)872-4120
Fax: (318)872-6038

Publications: Mansfield Enterprise-Progress
(12668)

The Enterprise
PO Box 218
Ponchatoula, LA 70454
Phone: (985)386-6537
Fax: (985)386-6537

Publications: The Enterprise (12796)

Enterprise
60 Main St.
PO Box 1450
Brockton, MA 02303
Phone: (508)586-6200
Fax: (508)427-4949
Free: 800-462-5569

Publications: The Enterprise (14012)

The Enterprise
106 W. Main St.
PO Box 387
Williamston, NC 27892-0387
Phone: (252)792-1181
Fax: (252)792-1921

Publications: The Enterprise (24290)

The Enterprise
231 Ambridge Dr.
PO Box 834
Iroquois Falls, ON, Canada P0K 1G0
Phone: (705)232-4081
Fax: (705)232-4235

Publications: The Enterprise (35924)

Enterprise
PO Box 546
Platte, SD 57369
Phone: (605)337-3101
Fax: (605)337-3433

Publications: Enterprise (28928)

The Enterprise-Bulletin
77 St. Marie St.
PO Box 98
Collingwood, ON, Canada L9Y 3Z4
Phone: (705)445-4611
Fax: (705)444-6477

Publications: The Enterprise-Bulletin (35748)

The Enterprise-Courier
206 S Main St.
PO Box 69
Charleston, MO 63834-0069
Phone: (573)683-3351
Fax: (573)683-2217

Publications: The Enterprise-Courier (16972)

Enterprise Inc.
PO Box 348
Stuart, VA 24171-0348
Phone: (276)694-3101
Fax: (276)694-5110

Publications: The Enterprise (32564)

Enterprise Ledger
PO Box 311130
Enterprise, AL 36331
Phone: (334)347-9533
Fax: (334)347-0825

Publications: Enterprise Ledger (201)

Enterprise Publications
400 E 59th St., No. 9-F
New York, NY 10022
Phone: (212)755-4363

Publications: Computer Survival Journal (21479)

Enterprise Publishing Co., Inc.
138 N. 16th St.
PO Box 328
Blair, NE 68008-0328
Phone: (402)426-2121
Fax: (402)426-2227

Publications: Arlington Citizen (17935) • Blair Enterprise (17954) • Clipper (17955) • Clipper Shopper (17956) • Douglas County Post-Gazette (18002) • Nebraska & Iowa Explorer (17957) • Sarpy County Extra (17958)

Enterprise Publishing Co., Inc.
213 E. Main
PO Box 577
Olney, TX 76374
Phone: (940)564-5558

Publications: The Olney Enterprise (30885)

Enterprises Publishing
400 E 59th St., Ste. 9F
New York, NY 10022
Phone: (212)755-4363

Publications: Computer Survival Guide (21478) • Punch in International Travel and Entertainment Magazine (22613)

Entertainment Law Reporter Publishing Co.
2118 Wilshire Blvd., No. 311
Santa Monica, CA 90403-5784
Phone: (310)829-9335
Fax: (310)829-9335

Publications: Entertainment Law Reporter; Movies Music Broadcasting Theater Publishing Multimedia Sports (3706)

Entertainment News & Views
4141 NE 2 Ave., No. 105A
Miami, FL 33137
Phone: (305)576-8566
Fax: (305)576-8529
Free: 800-921-7721

Publications: Entertainment News & Views (6351)

Entomological Society of America
9301 Annapolis Rd.
Lanham, MD 20706
Phone: (301)731-4535
Fax: (301)731-4538

Publications: American Entomologist (13597) • Annals of the Entomological Society of America (13598) • Environmental Entomology (13601) • Environmental Entomology (13600) • Journal of Economic Entomology (13604) • Journal of Medical Entomology (13605)

Entomological Society of Canada
393 Winston Ave.
Ottawa, ON, Canada K2A 1Y8
Phone: (613)725-2619
Fax: (613)725-9349

Publications: The Canadian Entomologist (36193)

Entomological Society of Washington
Smithsonian Institution, NMNH, MRC-168
Dept. of Systematic Biology
PO Box 37012
Washington, DC 20013-7012
Phone: (202)382-1786

Publications: Proceedings of the Entomological Society of Washington (5730)

Entrepreneur Media Inc.
2445 McCabe Way, Ste. 400
Irvine, CA 92614
Phone: (949)261-2325
Fax: (949)261-0234

Publications: Entrepreneur Magazine (2079) • Entrepreneur's Bizstartups.com (2080)

Environmental Information Ltd.
5775 Wazata Blvd., Ste. 820
St. Louis Park, MN 55416-1234
Phone: (952)831-2473
Fax: (952)831-6550

Publications: EI Digest (16360)

Environmental Law Institute
1616 P St. NW, Ste. 200
Washington, DC 20036
Phone: (202)939-3800
Fax: (202)939-3868
Free: 800-433-5120

Publications: The Environmental Forum (5481)

Environmental News Network
2020 Milvia St., Ste. 411
Berkeley, CA 94704-1156

Publications: Environmental News Network (1517)

Environmental Nutrition, Inc.
52 Riverside Dr., 15A
New York, NY 10024
Phone: (212)362-0424
Fax: (212)362-2066
Free: 800-996-7522

Publications: Environmental Nutrition (21622)

Environmental Philosophy, Inc.
Center for Environmental Philosophy
University of North Texas
Box 310980
Denton, TX 76203-0980
Phone: (940)565-2727
Fax: (940)565-4439

Publications: Environmental Ethics (30237)

Environmental Science & Engineering Publications Inc.
220 Industrial Pkwy. S., Unit 30
Aurora, ON, Canada L4G 3V6
Phone: (905)727-4666
Fax: (905)841-7271

Publications: Environmental Science & Engineering (35647)

Environmental Systems Research Institute
380 New York St.
Redlands, CA 92373-8100
Phone: (909)793-2853
Fax: (909)793-5953

Publications: Arc News (2900)

eob inc.
2938 Dundas St. W., Ste. 688
Toronto, ON, Canada M6P 4E7
Phone: (416)410-9880
Fax: (416)656-5041

Publications: KnitNet (36645)

EPA Administrative Law Reporter
1601 Connecticut Ave., NW, No. 602
Washington, DC 20009
Phone: (202)462-5755
Fax: (202)328-2430

Publications: EPA Administrative Law Reporter (5484)

The Episcopal Church Publishing Co.
PO Box 1170
Rockport, ME 04856
Phone: (207)763-2990
Fax: (207)763-2991
Free: 800-300-0702

Publications: The Witness (13047)

The Episcopal Church in the United States
815 2nd Ave.
New York, NY 10017
Phone: (212)867-8400
Fax: (212)949-8059
Free: 800-334-7626

Publications: Episcopal Life (21625)

The Episcopal Diocese of Alabama
521 N 20th St.
Birmingham, AL 35203-2682
Phone: (205)715-2060
Fax: (205)715-2066

Publications: The Apostle (54)

The Episcopal Diocese of Los Angeles
PO Box 512164
Los Angeles, CA 90051
Phone: (213)482-2040
Fax: (213)240-7670

Publications: The Episcopal News (2265)

Episcopal Diocese of Maine
143 State St.
Portland, ME 04101
Phone: (207)772-6923
Fax: (207)773-0095
Free: 800-244-6062

Publications: The Northeast (13014)

Episcopal Diocese of Massachusetts
138 Tremont St.
Boston, MA 02111
Phone: (617)482-5800
Fax: (617)482-8431

Publications: The Episcopal Times (13889)

Episcopal Diocese of Newark
31 Mulberry St.
Newark, NJ 07102
Phone: (973)622-4306
Fax: (973)622-3503

Publications: The Voice (19367)

Episcopal Diocese of Northern California
1318-27th St.
PO Box 161268
Sacramento, CA 95816-1268
Phone: (916)442-6918
Fax: (916)442-6927

Publications: Missionary (3009)

Episcopal Diocese of Oregon
11800 SW Military Ln.
Portland, OR 97219-8436
Phone: (503)636-5613
Fax: (503)636-5616
Free: 800-452-2562

Publications: The Oregon Episcopal Church News (26490)

Episcopal Diocese of Western N.Y.
1114 Delaware Ave.
Buffalo, NY 14209-1604
Phone: (716)881-0660
Fax: (716)881-1624

Publications: Church Acts of Western New York (20375)

Epitaph News
116 E Commercial St.
Viola, WI 54664
Phone: (608)627-1830
Fax: (608)627-1838

Publications: Epitaph News (33897)

EPRI
3412 Hillview Ave.
PO Box 10412
Palo Alto, CA 94303-0813
Phone: (650)855-2000
Fax: (972)556-6521
Free: 800-313-3774

Publications: EPRI Journal (2795)

Equal Access Media, Inc.
4201 Wilshire Blvd., Ste. 600
Los Angeles, CA 90010
Phone: (323)556-5720
Fax: (323)932-8250

Publications: The Beach Reporter (2500) • Los Angeles Independent (2323) • Palos Verdes Peninsula News (2804)

Equal Opportunity Publications, Inc.
445 Broad Hollow Rd., Ste. 425
Melville, NY 11747
Phone: (631)421-9421
Fax: (631)421-0359

Publications: Workforce Diversity (21066) • Workforce Diversity for Engineering and IT Professionals (21067)

Equator Publications
287 Beaverdam Rd.
Candler, NC 28715
Phone: (828)665-4466
Fax: (828)667-1717

Publications: Belize First Magazine (23682)

The Equinox
Fairleigh Dickinson University
1000 River Rd., T-SU2-03
1000 River Rd., T-SU2-03
Teaneck, NJ 07666
Phone: (201)692-2046
Fax: (201)692-2376

Publications: The Equinox (19609)

Equities Magazine Co.
PO Box 130 H
Scarsdale, NY 10583
Phone: (914)723-6702

Publications: Equities Magazine Co. (23312)

E.R. Publishing, Inc.
1911 NW 114 Ave.
Cooper City, FL 33026
Phone: (954)431-0161
Fax: (954)431-4661

Publications: Lacja's World (6003)

Eramosa Community News
180 St. Andrews E.
PO Box 189
Drayton, ON, Canada N0G 1P0
Fax: (519)638-3066

Publications: Eramosa Community News (35786)

e.Republic, Inc.
100 Blue Ravine Rd.
Folsom, CA 95630
Phone: (916)932-1300
Fax: (916)932-1470

Publications: Converge (1917)

Erickson Publishing, LLC
PO Box 45050
Madison, WI 53744-5050
Phone: (608)831-2131
Fax: (608)831-2141
Free: 800-722-6461

Publications: Dane County KIDS (33933) • Fox Valley KIDS (33942) • N.E.W. Kids (33965)

Erie Community College
6205 Main St.
Amherst, NY 14221
Phone: (716)634-0800
Fax: (716)851-1335

Publications: Northstar (20032)

The Erie Record
317 South Main
PO Box 159
Erie, KS 66733
Phone: (620)244-3371
Fax: (620)244-3371

Publications: The Erie Record (11436)

Erie Times News
205 W. 12th St.
Erie, PA 16534-0001
Phone: (814)453-4691
Fax: (814)870-1615
Free: 800-352-0043

Publications: Erie Daily Times (26896) • Erie Times-News (26897) • Morning News (26901)

Erin Advocate, Inc.
8 Thompson Cres.
8 Thompson Cres.
Erin, ON, Canada N0B 1T0
Phone: (519)833-9603
Fax: (519)833-9605

Publications: The Erin Advocate (35807)

Error Trends Coin Magazine
PO Box 158
Oceanside, NY 11572-0158
Phone: (516)764-8063

Publications: Error Trends Coin Magazine (23030)

Erskine Echo
309 1st St.
Box A
Erskine, MN 56535
Phone: (218)687-3775
Fax: (218)687-3744

Publications: Erskine Echo (15884)

Erwin Record
PO Box 700
Erwin, TN 37650
Phone: (423)743-4112
Fax: (423)743-6125

Publications: The Erwin Record (29184)

Escambia Sun-Press, Inc.
PO Box 4625
Pensacola, FL 32507
Phone: (850)456-3121
Fax: (850)456-0103

Publications: The Escambia Sun-Press (6565)

Escondido Genealogical Society
Box 2190
Escondido, CA 92033-2190

Publications: Hidden Valley Journal (1890)

ESM Association
2211 York Rd., Ste. 207
Oak Brook, IL 60523-2371
Phone: (630)368-1280
Fax: (630)368-1286

Publications: Employee Services Management (9351)

ESP Magazine
PO Box 1009
High Point, NC 27261-1009
Phone: (336)888-3648
Fax: (336)884-0008

Publications: ESP Magazine (23996)

ESP Publications
127 E Main St.
PO Box 925
Smithtown, NY 11787
Phone: (631)265-3500
Fax: (631)265-3504

Publications: Brookhaven Review (23336) • Ronkonkoma Review (23272) • Smithtown Messenger (23340)

ESPY Pub. Co.
PO Box 310
Summerville, GA 30747
Phone: (706)857-2494
Fax: (706)857-2393

Publications: The Summerville News (7575)

Esquire Sportsman
250 W 55th St.
New York, NY 10019
Phone: (212)649-4050

Publications: Esquire Sportman (21628)

Essays in International Business
University of South Carolina
College of Business Administration
Columbia, SC 29208
Phone: (803)777-6942
Fax: (803)777-3609

Publications: Essays in International Business (28548)

Essence Communications, Inc.
1500 Broadway, 6th Fl.
New York, NY 10036
Phone: (212)642-0600
Fax: (212)921-5173
Free: 800-274-9398

Publications: Essence (21629)

Essential Information, Inc.
PO Box 19405
Washington, DC 20036
Phone: (202)387-8030
Fax: (202)234-5176

Publications: Multinational Monitor (5663)

Essex Community College
7201 Rossville Blvd.
Baltimore, MD 21237-3898
Phone: (410)780-6576
Fax: (410)686-9503

Publications: The Montage (13222)

Essex County Newspaper
23 Liberty St.
Newburyport, MA 01950
Phone: (508)462-6666
Fax: (508)465-8505

Publications: Newburyport Daily News (14381)

The Essex Independent
Box 59
Essex, IA 51638-0059
Phone: (712)379-3313

Publications: The Essex Independent (10878)

Essex Reporter
1700 Hegeman Ave
PO Box 116
Colchester, VT 05446
Phone: (802)878-5282
Fax: (802)872-7611

Publications: Essex Reporter (31531)

Essex Society of Genealogists
Box 313
Lynnfield, MA 01940-0313

Publications: Essex Genealogist (14287)

Estelline Journal
PO Box 50
Castlewood, SD 57223
Phone: (605)873-2475

Publications: Estelline Journal (28829)

Estes Park Trail-Gazette
PO Box 1707
Estes Park, CO 80517
Phone: (970)586-3356
Fax: (970)586-9532

Publications: Trail-Gazette (4424)

Estonian Publishing Co.
958 Broadview Ave.
Toronto, ON, Canada M4K 2R6
Phone: (416)466-0951
Fax: (416)461-0448

Publications: Meie Elu (36661)

Estuarine Research Foundation
PO Box 510
Port Republic, MD 20676
Phone: (410)586-8707
Fax: (410)586-9226

Publications: Estuaries (16864)

The Eternal Flame
110 E 12th St.
New York, NY 10003
Phone: (212)477-2030
Fax: (212)477-2185

Publications: The Eternal Flame (21630)

Ethikos
154 E. Boston Post Rd.
Mamaroneck, NY 10543
Phone: (914)381-7475
Fax: (914)381-6947

Publications: Ethikos (20985)

The Ethiopian Mirror
PO Box 6881
Beverly Hills, CA 90212
Phone: (323)939-3059
Fax: (323)939-2636

Publications: The Ethiopian Mirror (1572)

Ethnic Newspaper
7307 3rd Ave.
Brooklyn, NY 11209-2466
Phone: (718)748-6704
Fax: (718)748-1426

Publications: Laiks (Time) (20329)

L'Etincelle
193 St-Georges
Windsor, QC, Canada J1S 1J7
Phone: (819)845-2705
Fax: (819)845-5520

Publications: L'Etincelle (37450)

Eudora Enterprise
PO Box 552
Lake Village, AR 71653
Fax: (501)265-2807

Publications: Eudora Enterprise (1112)

The Eufaula Tribune Corp.
PO Box 628
Eufaula, AL 36072-0628

Publications: The Cuthbert Times & News Record (204)

European Association for Aquatic Mammals WIU Regional Center
3561 60th St.
Moline, IL 61265
Phone: (309)762-9481
Fax: (309)762-6989

Publications: Aquatic Mammals (9202)

Evangel University
1111 N Glenstone Ave.
PO Box 728
Springfield, MO 65802-2191
Phone: (417)865-2815
Fax: (417)865-9599

Publications: The Lance (17604)

Evangelical Church Library Association
PO Box 353
Glen Ellyn, IL 60138-0353
Phone: (630)375-7865
Fax: (847)296-0754

Publications: Church Libraries (8925)

The Evangelical Free Church of America
901 E 78th St.
Minneapolis, MN 55420-1334
Phone: (952)854-1300

Publications: The Evangelical Beacon (16076)

The Evangelical Homiletics Society
Gordon-Conwell Theological Seminary
120 Essex St.
South Hamilton, MA 01982-2317
Phone: (978)646-4152
Fax: (978)468-6208

Publications: Journal of the Evangelical Homiletics Society (14544)

Evangelical Theological Society
112 Russell Woods Dr.
Lynchburg, VA 24502-3530
Phone: (804)237-5309
Fax: (804)582-2575

Publications: Journal of the Evangelical Theological Society (24261)

Evangeline Publishing Co.
PO Box 220
Ville Platte, LA 70586
Phone: (318)363-3939
Fax: (318)363-2841

Publications: Ville Platte Gazette (12865)

Evans Communications, Inc.
24 Laurel Bark Ave.
Deposit, NY 13754
Phone: (607)467-3600
Fax: (607)467-5330

Publications: Deposit Courier (20529)

Evans Printing & Publishing
135 E. main St. PO Box 89
Le Roy, MN 55951-0089
Phone: (507)324-5325
Fax: (507)324-5267

Publications: Le Roy Independent (15999)

Evansville Review
PO Box 77
Evansville, WI 53536
Phone: (608)882-5220
Fax: (608)882-5221

Publications: Evansville Review (33692)

Evening Journal Association
30 Journal Sq.
Jersey City, NJ 07306
Phone: (201)653-1000
Fax: (201)653-1414

Publications: The Hudson Dispatch (19139) • Jersey Journal (19141) • This Week in Bayonne (19146) • This Week in Jersey City (19147)

The Evening News
221 Spring St.
PO Box 867
Jeffersonville, IN 47131-0867
Phone: (812)283-6636
Fax: (812)284-7080

Publications: Clark County Journal (10224) • The Evening News (10225)

Evening Post Publishing Co.
134 Columbus St.
Charleston, SC 29403
Phone: (843)577-7111
Fax: (843)937-5579

Publications: Aiken Standard (28467) • The News (28674) • The Post and Courier (28517)

The Evening Sun
135 Baltimore St.
Hanover, PA 17331
Phone: (717)637-3736
Fax: (717)637-7730

Publications: The Community Sun (26973) • The Evening Sun (26974) • Sun Marketplace (26977)

The Evening Telegram
111 Green St.
Herkimer, NY 13350
Phone: (315)866-2220
Fax: (315)866-5913

Publications: The Evening Telegram (20732)

The Evening Telegram
150 Howard St.
PO Box 1080
Rocky Mount, NC 27802-1080
Phone: (919)446-5161
Fax: (919)446-4057

Publications: The Evening Telegram (24204)

The Evening World
31 W Main St.
PO Box 311
Bloomfield, IN 47424
Phone: (812)384-3501
Fax: (812)384-3741

Publications: The Evening World (9821)

Everest World
133 W 8th St.
Horton, KS 66439-1601
Phone: (785)486-2512
Fax: (785)486-2512

Publications: Everest World (11496)

Everett Community College
801 Wetmore
Everett, WA 98201
Phone: (425)388-9100
Fax: (425)339-9129

Publications: Clipper (32760)

Evergreen Newspapers, Inc.
27902 Meadow Dr. 200
Evergreen, CO 80439-2106

Publications: Canyon Courier (4425)

Everton Publishers Inc.
PO Box 368
Logan, UT 84323-0368
Phone: (435)752-6022
Fax: (435)752-0425
Free: 800-443-6325

Publications: Everton's Family History Magazine (31348) • Genealogical Helper (31349)

Evidence Photographers International Council
600 Main St.
Honesdale, PA 18431
Phone: (570)253-5450
Fax: (570)253-5011
Free: 800-356-3742

Publications: Journal of Evidence Photography (27050)

E.W. Scripps Co.
125 E. Court St.
Cincinnati, OH 45202
Phone: (513)352-2000
Fax: (513)621-3962

Publications: The Cincinnati Post (24788)

E.W. Scripps Co.
312 Walnut St., Ste. 2800
Cincinnati, OH 45202
Phone: (513)977-3000

Publications: The Commercial Appeal (29362) • The Sun (32695)

E.W. Williams Publications
2125 Ctr. Ave., Ste. 305
Fort Lee, NJ 07024
Phone: (201)592-7007
Fax: (201)592-7171

Publications: Auto Laundry News (18831) • LDB Interior Textiles (22241) • Private Label (18833) • Quick Frozen Foods International (18834)

EWA Publications
2446 E 65th St.
Brooklyn, NY 11234
Phone: (718)763-7034
Fax: (718)763-7035

Publications: Arts and Leisure Times (20296) • Consumer Info News (20308) • Entertainment Lifestyles (20316) • Metropolitan News (20331) • New York Entertainment Scene (20333) • Restaurant/Food Review (20342) • Travel International (20350) • Travel National (20351)

The Examiner
410 S Liberty St.
Independence, MO 64050-3805
Phone: (816)254-8600
Fax: (816)836-3805

Publications: Blue Springs & Independence Examiner Extra (Daily Edition) (17108) • Blue Springs & Independence Examiner Suburban Life (Wednesday Edition) (17109) • Independence Examiner (Daily Edition) (17113) • Independence Examiner (Wednesday Edition) (17114)

Examiner
730 The Kingsway
PO Box 3890
Peterborough, ON, Canada K9J 8L4
Phone: (705)745-4641
Fax: (705)741-3217

Publications: The Peterborough (36317)

Examiner Publications
4N781 Gerber Rd.
Bartlett, IL 60103
Phone: (630)830-4145

Publications: Bartlett Examiner (8050) • Carol Stream Examiner (8136) • Hanover Park Examiner (8970) • Streamwood Examiner (9668)

Excel Promotions Corp.
150 W. Hoffman Ave.
Lindenhurst, NY 11757
Phone: (631)226-2636

Publications: Babylon South Bay's Shopper (20946) • Deer Park South Bay's Shopper (20947) • Lindenhurst/South Bay's Shopping Newspaper (20948) • South Bay's Shopping Newspaper (20950)

Excelsior Publishing Co., Inc.
417 Thompson Ave.
PO Box 7
Excelsior Springs, MO 64024
Phone: (816)637-3147
Fax: (816)637-8411

Publications: The Daily Standard (17050) • The Excelsior (17236) • Town & Country Leader (17051)

Excerpta Medica, Inc.
655 Ave. of the Americas
New York, NY 10010
Phone: (212)989-5800

Publications: The American Journal of Cardiology (21190) • American Journal of Medicine (21195) • American Journal of Surgery (21200) • Urology (22891)

Exchange
404 S Main St.
PO Box 490
Fayetteville, TN 37334
Phone: (931)433-9737
Fax: (931)433-0053
Free: 800-247-7318

Publications: Exchange (29189) • Farmers Exchange (29190)

Exchange Publishing Corp.
PO Box 45
New Paris, IN 46553
Phone: (574)831-2138
Fax: (574)831-2131

Publications: Farmer's Exchange (10347)

Executive Business Media, Inc.
825 Old Country Rd.
PO Box 1500
Westbury, NY 11590-0812
Phone: (516)334-3030
Fax: (516)334-3059

Publications: College Store Executive (23553) • Exchange & Commissary News (23554) • Government Food Service (23555) • Government Recreation and Fitness (23556) • Military Club & Hospitality (23557) • R & R Shopper's News (23559)

Executive Sciences Institute
1005 Mississippi Ave.
Davenport, IA 52803

Publications: Operations Research/Management Science (10737) • Quality Control and Applied Statistics (10739)

Exhibit Builder, Inc.
PO Box 4144
Woodland Hills, CA 91365
Phone: (818)225-0100
Fax: (818)225-0138
Free: 800-356-4451

Publications: Exhibit Builder (4103)

Exile
PO Box 67 Sta. B
Toronto, ON, Canada M5T 1C0
Phone: (416)922-8221

Publications: Exile (36586)

Exit 13 Magazine
PO Box 423
Fanwood, NJ 07023-1162
Phone: (908)889-5298

Publications: Exit 13 Magazine (18815)

Experimental Aircraft Association, Inc. (EAA)
3000 Poberenzy Rd.
Oshkosh, WI 54902
Phone: (920)426-4800
Fax: (920)426-4828
Free: 800-843-8612

Publications: EAA Sport Aviation (34222)

EXPO Magazine, Inc.
11600 College Blvd.
Overland Park, KS 66210
Phone: (913)469-1185
Fax: (913)469-0806

Publications: Expo (11712)

Exponent
160 S. Main
Brooklyn, MI 49230
Phone: (517)592-2122
Fax: (517)592-3241

Publications: The Exponent (14838)

Exponent
PO Box 285
East Grand Forks, MN 56721-0285
Phone: (218)773-2808
Fax: (218)773-9212
Free: 800-956-2808

Publications: Exponent (15865)

Exponent
University of Wisconsin-Platteville
1 University Plaza
Platteville, WI 53818
Phone: (608)342-1471
Fax: (608)342-1671

Publications: Exponent (34240)

Exponent II, Inc.
Box 128
Arlington, MA 02476
Fax: (617)868-3464

Publications: Exponent II (13818)

Export Leads
Circulation Dept.
1741 Kekamek NW
Poulsbo, WA 98370
Phone: (360)779-1511
Fax: (360)697-4696

Publications: Export Leads (32897)

Exports of Canadian Grain and Wheat Flour
1054 Pembina Highway
Winnipeg, MB, Canada R3T 1Z8
Phone: (204)983-2790
Fax: (204)984-5131
Free: 800-853-6705

Publications: Exports of Canadian Grain and Wheat Flour (35328)

The Expositor
53 Dalhousie St.
Brantford, ON, Canada N3T 5S8
Phone: (519)756-2020
Fax: (519)756-4911

Publications: The Brantford Expositor (35703)

L'Express
17 Carlaw Rd., 2nd Fl.
Toronto, ON, Canada M4M 2R6
Phone: (416)465-2107
Fax: (416)465-3778

Publications: L'Express (36589)

The Express
9-11 W. Main St.
PO Box 208
Lock Haven, PA 17745-1217
Phone: (717)748-6791
Fax: (717)748-1544

Publications: The Express (27204)

Express News
PO Box 2171
San Antonio, TX 78297-2171
Phone: (210)250-3000

Publications: Express-News (31029)

Express Publishing, Inc.
PO Box 1013
Ketchum, ID 83340
Phone: (208)726-8060
Fax: (208)726-2329

Publications: Idaho Mountain Express (7887)

Express Shopper
1405 Broadway
PO Box 1709
Scottsbluff, NE 69363-1709
Phone: (308)632-9000
Fax: (308)632-9001
Free: 800-846-6102

Publications: Express Shopper (18264)

The Express-Times
30 N. 4th S.
PO Box 391
Easton, PA 18044
Phone: (610)258-7171
Fax: (610)258-2130

Publications: The Express-Times (26850)

Extra Equity for Homebuyers
216 Greens Farms Sta.
Greens Farms, CT 06436
Phone: (203)254-1690
Fax: (203)255-3707

Publications: Extra Equity for Homebuyers (4871)

EXTRA Publications, Inc.
3918 W North Ave.
Chicago, IL 60647
Phone: (312)252-3534
Fax: (312)252-6031

Publications: Logan Square Extra (8469) • Metro EXTRA (8486) • Northwest Extra (8510) • Pilsen/Little Village/Cicero/Berwyn EXTRA (8531) • Southwest EXTRA (8568) • West Suburban Extra (8604) • Wicker Park/West Town EXTRA (8606)

Extra Touch Florists
33031 Schoolcraft Rd.
Livonia, MI 48150

Publications: The Extra Touch Online (15315)

Exxon Corp.
5959 Las Colinas Blvd.
Irving, TX 75039-2298
Phone: (972)444-1115
Fax: (972)444-1139

Publications: Lamp (New York) (30606)

Eye Communications, Ltd.
471 Adelaide St. W.
Toronto, ON, Canada M5V 1T1
Phone: (416)504-4339
Fax: (416)504-4339

Publications: Eye (36590) • Eye Weekly (36591)

Ezra Taft Benson Agriculture and Food Institute
Brigham Young University
B-49
Provo, UT 84602
Phone: (801)378-2607
Fax: (801)378-0099

Publications: Benson Institute Review (31398)

F & B Publications, Inc.
PO Box 53461
Fayetteville, NC 28305
Phone: (910)484-6200
Fax: (910)484-9218

Publications: Up & Coming Weekly (23882)

F & W Publications
4700 E. Galbraith Rd.
Cincinnati, OH 45236
Phone: (513)531-2690
Fax: (513)531-0798
Free: 800-289-0963

Publications: Horticulture (13903)

F & W Publications, Inc.
4700 E. Galbraith Rd.
Cincinnati, OH 45236-6708
Phone: (513)531-2690
Fax: (513)531-2902
Free: 800-289-0963

Publications: The Artist's Magazine (24775) • Decorative Artist's Workbook (24792) • HOW (24804) • Writer's Digest (24829)

F.A. Communications
PO Box 508
Lac La Biche, AB, Canada T0A 2C0
Phone: (780)623-4221
Fax: (780)623-4230
Free: 888-626-4221

Publications: Lac La Biche Post (34790)

Fabricare Canada
Box 968
Oakville, ON, Canada L6J 5E8
Phone: (905)337-0516
Fax: (905)337-0525

Publications: Fabricare Canada (36144)

Facts
700 Brookside Ave.
PO Box 2240
Redlands, CA 92373
Phone: (909)793-3221
Fax: (909)793-9588

Publications: Facts (2903)

Facts & Comparisons
111 W. Port Plaza, Ste. 300
St. Louis, MO 63146
Phone: (314)216-2100
Fax: (314)878-5563
Free: 800-223-0554

Publications: Facts and Comparisons (17437) • Hospital Pharmacy (17445) • Patient Drug Facts (17482) • Pharmacy Practice Management Quarterly (17483)

Facts Newspaper
2765 E Cherry St.
PO Box 22015
Seattle, WA 98122
Phone: (206)324-0552
Fax: (206)324-1007

Publications: Facts Newspaper (32964)

Facts On File News Services
512 7th Ave., 22nd Fl.
New York, NY 10018-4721
Phone: (212)290-8090
Free: 800-363-7976

Publications: World News Digest (22943)

The Fader
71 W. 23rd St., Ste. 903
New York, NY 10010
Phone: (212)741-7100
Fax: (212)741-4747

Publications: The FADER (21675)

Fag Rag Books
PO Box 15331, Kenmore Sta.
Boston, MA 02215
Phone: (617)661-7534

Publications: Fag Rag (13891)

Fahy-Williams Publishing Inc.
171 Reed St.
PO Box 1080
Geneva, NY 14456
Phone: (315)789-0458
Fax: (315)789-4263
Free: 800-344-0559

Publications: Educational Dealer (20652)

Faimon Publications, LLC
324 Hudson
PO Box A
Burlington, KS 66839

Publications: Coffey County Republican (11370)

FAIR
112 W 27 St., 6th Fl.
New York, NY 10001
Phone: (212)633-6700
Fax: (212)727-7668
Free: 800-847-3993

Publications: EXTRA! (21670)

Fairbanks Daily News-Miner
PO Box 70710
Fairbanks, AK 99707
Phone: (907)456-6661
Fax: (907)452-5054

Publications: Fairbanks Daily News-Miner (567)

Fairbury Journal-News
516 5th St.
PO Box 415
Fairbury, NE 68352
Phone: (402)729-6141
Fax: (402)729-3892

Publications: Fairbury Journal-News (18005)

Fairchild Publications
7 W. 34th St.
New York, NY 10001
Phone: (212)630-4000
Free: 800-247-2160

Publications: Jane (21955)

Fairchild Publications, Inc.
7 W. 34th St.
New York, NY 10001
Phone: (212)630-4000

Publications: Brand Marketing (21337) • Children's Business (21410) • Daily News Record (21531) • Executive Technology (21661) • Footwear News (FN) (21716) • High Points (23999) • Home Furnishings News (HFN) (21808) • Salon News (22702) • SalonNews (22703) • Supermarket News (22809) • W (22905) • Women's Wear Daily (22936)

Fairfax Chief
153 E Elm
Fairfax, OK 74637
Phone: (918)642-3814
Fax: (918)642-1376

Publications: Fairfax Chief (25831)

The Fairfax Forum
PO Box 349
Fairfax, MO 64446
Phone: (660)686-2741

Publications: The Fairfax Forum (17053)

The Fairfax News
PO Box 353
Fairfax, VT 05454
Phone: (802)862-6045
Fax: (802)863-5229

Publications: The Fairfax News (31543)

Fairfax Standard - Gazette
102 SE 1st
Box 589
Fairfax, MN 55332
Phone: (507)426-7235
Fax: (507)426-7264

Publications: Fairfax Standard (15888)

Fairfield County Catholic
238 Jewett Ave.
Bridgeport, CT 06606
Phone: (203)372-4301
Fax: (203)374-2044

Publications: Fairfield County Catholic (4714)

The Fairfield Ledger
112 E Broadway Ave.
Box 171
Fairfield, IA 52556-3202
Phone: (641)472-4129
Fax: (641)472-1916

Publications: The Fairfield Ledger (10882)

The Fairfield Recorder
101 E Commerce
Fairfield, TX 75840
Phone: (903)389-3334
Fax: (903)389-8255

Publications: The Fairfield Recorder (30311)

Fairleigh Dickinson University
285 Madison Ave.
Madison, NJ 07940
Phone: (973)443-8564
Fax: (973)443-8364

Publications: The Literary Review (19182)

Fairmont Photo Press
112 E 1st St.
PO Box 973
Fairmont, MN 56031
Phone: (507)238-9456
Fax: (507)238-9457

Publications: Fairmont Photo Press (15889)

Fairmont Press Inc.
700 Indian Trl.
Lilburn, GA 30047
Phone: (770)925-9388
Fax: (770)381-9865

Publications: Cogeneration and Competitive Power Journal (7372) • Energy Engineering (7373) • Strategic Planning for Energy and the Environment (7374)

Fairmont State College
1201 Locust Ave.
Fairmont, WV 26554-2491
Phone: (304)367-4740
Fax: (304)367-4896

Publications: The Columns (33312)

Fairview Enterprise
PO Box 98
Fairview, KS 66425
Phone: (785)467-3461

Publications: Fairview Enterprise (11439)

The Fairview Post
10118-110 St.
PO Box 1900
Fairview, AB, Canada T0H 1L0
Phone: (780)835-4925
Fax: (780)835-4227

Publications: The Fairview Post (34764)

Fairview Republican
112 N Main St.
PO Box 497
Fairview, OK 73737
Phone: (580)227-4439
Fax: (580)227-4430

Publications: Fairview Republican (25833)

The Fairway Group
75 King St. S, Ste. 209
Waterloo, ON, Canada N2J 1P7
Phone: (519)885-4902
Fax: (519)885-5907

Publications: New Hamburg Independent (36103) • Visitor (36858)

Faith & Fellowship Press
1020 W Alcott Ave.
PO Box 655
Fergus Falls, MN 56538
Phone: (218)736-7357
Fax: (218)736-2200

Publications: Faith and Fellowship (15896)

Faith & Life Resources
718 Main St.
PO Box 347
Newton, KS 67114-0347
Phone: (316)283-5100
Fax: (316)283-0454
Free: 800-743-2484

Publications: With (11671)

Falfurrias Publishing Co., Inc.
219 E Rice St.
PO Box 619
Falfurrias, TX 78355
Phone: (512)325-2200
Fax: (512)325-2200

Publications: Falfurrias Facts (30313)

Fall Line Publishing, Inc.
PO Box 487
Louisville, GA 30434
Phone: (478)625-7722
Fax: (478)625-8816

Publications: News & Former & Wadley Herald/The Jefferson Reporter (7376)

Fallon County Times
PO Box 679
Baker, MT 59313
Phone: (406)778-3344
Fax: (406)778-3347

Publications: Fallon County Times (17722)

Falmouth Publishing Co.
50 Depot Ave.
Falmouth, MA 02540
Phone: (508)548-4700
Fax: (508)540-8407
Free: 800-286-7744

Publications: The Bourne Enterprise (14002) • Enterprise Newspapers (14182)

Falsoft Ink, Inc.
5803 Timber Ridge Dr.
Prospect, KY 40059-9317
Phone: (502)228-4492
Fax: (502)228-5121

Publications: Rainbow-Pcar Reviews On-Line (12377)

Falun Dafa Information Center
c/o The Universe Publishing
331W. 57th St. PMB 09,
New York, NY 10019

Publications: Compassion (21465)

FAMILIES Magazines, Inc.
462 Herdon Pkwy., Ste. 206
Herndon, VA 20170
Phone: (703)318-1385
Fax: (703)318-5509

Publications: North Florida FAMILIES Magazine (6216) • Washington FAMILIES Magazine (32166)

Families, Systems & Health
PO Box 20838
Rochester, NY 14602-0838
Phone: (585)482-1390
Fax: (585)482-2901

Publications: Families, Systems & Health (23225)

Family, Career and Community Leaders of America
1910 Association Dr.
Reston, VA 20191
Phone: (703)476-4900
Fax: (703)860-2713

Publications: Teen Times (32421)

The Family Circle, Inc.
375 Lexington Ave.
New York, NY 10017
Phone: (212)499-2000
Fax: (212)483-1006

Publications: Christmas Helps & Holiday Baking (21413) • Fitness Diet and Exercise Guide (21704)

Family Communications Inc.
65 The East Mall
Etobicoke, ON, Canada M8Z 5W3
Phone: (416)537-2604
Fax: (416)538-1794

Publications: Best Wishes Magazine (35812) • Expecting (35815) • Today's Bride Magazine (35820)

The Family Digest
PO Box 26126
Minneapolis, MN 55426
Phone: (952)929-6765
Free: 800-722-0985

Publications: The Family Digest (9967)

Family Helper Publishing
Box 1353
Southampton, ON, Canada N0H 2L0
Publications: Adoption Helper (36399) • Post-adoption Helper (36400)

Family Medicine
PO Box 8729
Kansas City, MO 64114
Free: 800-274-2237

Publications: Family Medicine (31030)

Family Motor Coaching Inc.
8291 Clough Pke.
Cincinnati, OH 45244
Phone: (513)474-3622
Fax: (513)388-5286
Free: 800-543-3622

Publications: Family Motor Coaching (24797)

Family Newspapers, Inc.
241 Clay St.
PO Box 809
Tecumseh, NE 68450-0809
Phone: (402)335-3394
Fax: (402)335-3496

Publications: Chieftain (18295)

Family Practice Recertification
241 Forsgate Dr.
Jamesburg, NJ 08831
Phone: (732)656-1140
Fax: (732)656-0059

Publications: Family Practice Recertification (19129)

Family Support America
20 N Wacker Dr., Ste. 1100
Chicago, IL 60606
Phone: (312)338-0900
Fax: (312)338-1522

Publications: America's Family Support Magazine (8262)

Family Times, Inc.
1080 N Delaware Ave., No. 702
Philadelphia, PA 19125-4330

Publications: Family Times (27467)

The Family Tree
PO Box 4311
Boise, ID 83711
Phone: (208)853-1624
Free: 800-297-8656

Publications: Genealogical Journal of Jefferson County, New York (7806) • Genealogical Journal of Oneida County, New York (7807)

Fancy Publications
3 Burroughs
PO Box 6050
Mission Viejo, CA 92690
Phone: (949)855-8822
Fax: (949)855-3045

Publications: Aquarium Fish Magazine (2546) • Bird Talk (2548) • Cat Fancy Magazine (2549) • Dog Fancy Magazine (2550) • Dog World (2551) • Dogs USA (2552) • Hawaii (2553) • Horse Illustrated (2554) • Pet Product News (2556) • Reptiles (2557) • WildBird Magazine (2558) • Young Rider (2559)

Fanfare
PO Box 17
Tenafly, NJ 07670
Phone: (201)567-3908
Fax: (201)816-0125

Publications: Fanfare (19613)

Fannie Mae Foundation
4000 Wisconsin Ave. NW, North Twr., Ste. 1
Washington, DC 20016-2804
Phone: (202)274-8000
Fax: (202)274-8111

Publications: Housing Policy Debate (5530) • Journal of Housing Research (5597)

Fannin County
2501 N Ctr., Ste. A
Bonham, TX 75418
Phone: (903)583-3556
Fax: (903)583-9459

Publications: Fannin County Special (29933)

Fanning Publishing Company Inc.
39 E. 78th St.
Ste. 501
New York, NY 10021
Phone: (212)988-5959
Fax: (212)988-6107
Free: 800-685-9777

Publications: Arton Paper (21258)

Fantagraphics Books
7563 Lake City Way NE
Seattle, WA 98115
Phone: (206)524-1967
Fax: (206)524-2104
Free: 800-657-1100

Publications: The Comics Journal (32958)

Faribault County Register
125 N. Main St.
PO Box 98
Blue Earth, MN 56013
Phone: (507)526-7324
Fax: (507)526-4080
Free: 888-877-0643

Publications: Faribault County Register (15762)

Farm Business Communications
Agricore United
Box 9800
Winnipeg, MB, Canada R3C 3A7
Phone: (204)954-1400
Fax: (204)942-8463

Publications: Cattlemen (35321) • Country Guide (35324) • Dairy Update-Demographic Section of Country Guide Magazine (35326)

Farm & Home Research Quarterly
Box 2231
South Dakota State University
Brookings, SD 57007
Phone: (605)688-4187
Fax: (605)688-5683

Publications: Farm & Home Research Quarterly (28813)

Farm Impact
Drawer C
Mascoutah, IL 62258
Phone: (618)566-8282
Fax: (618)566-8283

Publications: Farm Impact (9152)

Farm Journal, Inc.
1818 Market St., 31st Fl.
Philadelphia, PA 19103-3654
Phone: (215)557-8900
Fax: (215)568-4238
Free: 800-523-1538

Publications: Beef Today (11403) • Dairy Today (16184) • Farm Journal (27468) • Hogs Today (17356) • Top Producer (27705)

Farm Midwifery Center
42 The Farm
Summertown, TN 38483-9626
Phone: (931)964-2293
Fax: (931)964-3798

Publications: Birth Gazette (29622)

Farm Press
2302 W First St.
Cedar Falls, IA 50613
Phone: (319)277-1094
Fax: (319)277-3783
Free: 800-959-3276

Publications: Western Turf & Landscape Press (10664)

Farm Progress Companies
191 S Gary Ave.,
Carol Stream, IL 60188-2095
Phone: (630)462-2900
Fax: (630)462-2869

Publications: The Beef Producer (8709) • Carolina Farmer (24310) • Carolina/Virginia Farmer (8137) • Colorado Farmer-Stockman (33174) • Dakota Farmer (15922) • The Farmer (15923) • Florida Farmer (7278) • Idaho FarmekraHJJmpw- (11275) • Indiana Prairie Farmer (8712) • Kansas Farmer (11517) • Kentucky Farmer (12070) • Louisiana Farmer (12739) • Mississippi Farmer (16822) • Missouri Ruralist (17004) • Nebraska Farmer (8150) • New England Farmer (8151) • The Ohio Farmer (25291) • Oklahoma Farmer-Stockman (26036) • Oregon FarmekraHJJmpw- (1754) • Tack'n Togs Merchandising (16176) • Texas Farmer-Stockman (26038) • Wallaces Farmer (10814) • Washington FarmekraHJJmpw- (1757) • The Western Bec- Producer (1875) • Western Farmer-Stockman (8157) • Wisconsin Agriculturist (11277)

Farm Progress Companies, Inc.
191 S. Gary Ave.
Carol Stream, IL 60188
Phone: (630)690-5600
Fax: (630)462-2869
Free: 800-441-1410

Publications: The Hog Producer (8145)

Farm Pulp
PO Box 2151
Seattle, WA 98111-2151

Publications: Farm Pulp (32965)

Farm and Ranch Guide
4023 N State St.
PO Box 1977
Bismarck, ND 58503-1977
Phone: (701)255-4905
Fax: (701)255-2312

Publications: Farm and Ranch Guide (24352)

Farm & Ranch News
PO Box 160
Lithia, FL 33547-0160
Phone: (813)737-6397

Publications: Farm and Ranch News (6304)

Farm Show Publishing, Inc.
20088 Kenwood Trl.
Box 1029
Lakeville, MN 55044
Phone: (612)469-5572

Publications: Farm Show (15994)

Farm Talk Publishing
1801 S Hwy. 59
PO Box 601
Parsons, KS 67357
Phone: (316)421-9450
Fax: (316)421-9473
Free: 800-356-8255

Publications: Farm Talk (11743)

Farmers Independent
PO Box 130
Bagley, MN 56621
Phone: (218)694-6265
Fax: (218)694-6015

Publications: Farmers Independent (15727)

Farmers Insurance Group of Companies
4680 Wilshire Blvd.
Los Angeles, CA 90010

Publications: Friendly Exchange (2277)

Farmers Union of Nebraska
1305 Plum
Box 22667
Lincoln, NE 68542-2667
Phone: (402)476-8815
Fax: (402)476-8859

Publications: Nebraska Union Farmer (18106)

Farmers' Weekly Review
100 Manhattan Rd.
Joliet, IL 60433
Phone: (815)727-4811
Fax: (815)727-5570

Publications: Farmers' Weekly Review (9032)

Farmington Press
218 N Washington
Farmington, MO 6360
Phone: (573)756-8927
Fax: (573)756-9160

Publications: Farmington Press (17054)

Farmland Industries, Inc.
PO Box 20111
KC. MO 64195
Kansas City, MO 64195
Phone: (816)713-7000
Fax: (816)713-6979
Free: 800-821-8000

Publications: Farmland System News (17169)

Farmland News
104 Depot St.
PO Box 240
Archbold, OH 43502-0240
Phone: (419)445-9456
Fax: (419)445-4444

Publications: Farmland News (24614)

Farmville Enterprise
Box 247
Farmville, NC 27828
Phone: (252)753-4126
Fax: (252)753-4127

Publications: Farmville Enterprise (23877)

The Farmville Herald
114 North St.
PO Box 307
Farmville, VA 23901
Phone: (434)392-4151
Fax: (434)392-6298

Publications: The Farmville Herald (32067)

Farragut Media Group
1916 Wilson Blvd., Ste. 204
Arlington, VA 22201
Phone: (703)527-7860
Fax: (703)527-0369

Publications: El Tiempo Latino (31787)

Fast Company Magazine
77 N. Washington St.
Boston, MA 02114
Phone: (617)973-0300
Fax: (617)973-0373

Publications: Fast Company (13892)

Fastline
4900 Fox Run Rd.
PO Box 248
Buckner, KY 40010
Fax: (502)222-0615
Free: 800-626-6409

Publications: Fastline—Bluegrass Truck Edition (11968) • Fastline—Dakota Farm Edition (11969) • Fastline—Dixie Truck Edition (11970) • Fastline—Far West Farm Edition (11971) • Fastline—Florida Truck Edition (11972) • Fastline—Georgia Truck Edition (11973) • Fastline—Illinois Farm Edition (11974) • Fastline—Indiana Farm Edition (11975) • Fastline—Iowa Farm Edition (11976) • Fastline—Kansas Farm Edition (11977) • Fastline—Kentucky Farm Edition (11978) • Fastline—Mid-Atlantic Farm Edition (11979) • Fastline—Mid-South Farm Edition (11980) • Fastline—Mid-West Truck Edition (11981) • Fastline—Minnesota Farm Edition (11982) • Fastline—Missouri Farm Edition (11983) • Fastline—Nebraska Farm Edition (11984) • Fastline—Northeast Farm Edition (11985) • Fastline—Northland Truck Edition (11986) • Fastline—Northwest Farm Edition (11987) • Fastline—Ohio Farm Edition (11988) • Fastline—Oklahoma Farm Edition (11989) • Fastline—Ontario Farm Edition (11990) • Fastline—Rocky Mountain Farm Edition (11991) • Fastline—South Central Truck Edition (11992) • Fastline—Southeast Farm Edition (11993) • Fastline—Tennessee Farm Edition (11994) • Fastline—Tennessee Truck Edition (11995) • Fastline—Texas Farm Edition (11996) • Fastline—Tri-State Truck Edition (11997) • Fastline—Wisconsin Farm Edition (11998)

Fat Tuesday Productions
560 Manada Gap Rd.
Grantville, PA 17028
Phone: (717)469-7159

Publications: Fat Tuesday (26948)

FATE Magazine
PO Box 460
Lakeville, MN 55044
Phone: (952)431-2050
Fax: (952)891-6091
Free: 800-728-2730

Publications: FATE Magazine (15995)

Fatima Family Apostolate
3050 Gap Knob Rd.
New Hope, KY 40052
Phone: (502)325-3829
Fax: (502)325-3091

Publications: Fatima Family Messenger (12323)

The Fauquier Citizen
17 S. 5th St.
PO Box 3430
Warrenton, VA 20188
Phone: (540)347-5522
Fax: (540)347-7363

Publications: The Fauquier Citizen (32600)

Fawcette Technical Publications
913 Emerson St.
Palo Alto, CA 94301-2415
Phone: (650)833-7100
Fax: (650)853-0230
Free: 800-848-5523

Publications: Java Pro (2796) • Microsoft Interactive Developer (2799)

The Fayette Chronicle
PO Box 536
Fayette, MS 39069
Phone: (601)786-3661
Fax: (601)786-3661

Publications: The Fayette Chronicle (16623)

Fayette County Record
127 S Washington St.
Box 400
La Grange, TX 78945
Phone: (979)968-3155
Fax: (979)968-6767

Publications: The Fayette County Record (30656)

Fayette County Union, Inc.
Box 153
West Union, IA 52175-0153
Phone: (563)422-3888
Fax: (563)422-5557

Publications: Fayette County Union (11326)

Fayette Falcon
PO Box 39
Somerville, TN 38068
Phone: (901)465-3567
Fax: (901)465-3568

Publications: Fayette Falcon (29608)

Fayette Leader
PO Box 220
Fayette, IA 52142
Phone: (563)425-4162

Publications: Fayette Leader (10889)

Fayette Newspapers, Inc.
180 Church St.
PO Box 96
Fayetteville, GA 30214
Phone: (770)461-6317
Fax: (770)460-8172

Publications: Fayette Daily News (7271)

Fayette Tribune
417 Main St.
PO Box 139
Oak Hill, WV 25901
Phone: (304)469-3373
Fax: (304)469-4105

Publications: Fayette Tribune (33417)

Fayetteville Publishing Co.
PO Box 849
458 Whitfield St.
Fayetteville, NC 28302
Phone: (910)323-4848
Fax: (910)486-3531

Publications: The Fayetteville Observer (23879)

FCN Publishing
734 W. 79th St.
Chicago, IL 60620
Phone: (773)602-1230
Fax: (773)602-1013

Publications: The Final Call (8376)

FCW Div.
645 Stewart Ave.
Garden City, NY 11530-4709
Phone: (516)229-3600
Fax: (516)227-1342

Publications: Floor Covering Weekly (20639)

FCW Government Technology Group
3141 Fairview Park Dr., Ste. 777
Falls Church, VA 22042
Phone: (703)876-5100

Publications: Government E-Business (32047)

FD Communications Inc.
3100 Bayview Ave., Unit 4
Toronto, ON, Canada M2N 5L3
Phone: (416)224-5055
Fax: (416)224-5455

Publications: Geriatrics Today (36602) • Obesity Surgery (36679)

FDC Reports, Inc.
5550 Friendship Blvd., Ste. 1
Chevy Chase, MD 20815
Phone: (301)657-9830
Fax: (301)656-3094

Publications: The Rose Sheet (13409)

Fealty Enterprises
3050 Yonge St., Ste. 206-B
Toronto, ON, Canada M4N 2K4
Phone: (416)482-2897
Fax: (416)482-4909

Publications: Monarchy Canada (36667)

Feather Publishing
PO Box B
Quincy, CA 95971
Phone: (530)283-0800
Fax: (530)283-3952

Publications: Chester Progressive (1691) • Feather River Bulletin (2869) • Indian Valley Record (2870) • Lassen County Times (3832) • Portola Reporter (2864)

Feather River Canyon News
PO Box 4006
Yankee Hill, CA 95965
Phone: (530)534-6397

Publications: Feather River Canyon News (4118)

Feature Publishing Ltd.
2100 St. Catherine St. W., 2nd Fl.
Montreal, QC, Canada H3H 2T3
Phone: (514)939-5024
Fax: (514)939-8027
Free: (866)332-8878

Publications: Feature (37115) • Primeurs (37209)

February 11th Interactive Publishing, Ltd.
PO Box 88
Stirling, ON, Canada K0K 3E0
Phone: (613)395-3015
Fax: (613)395-2992

Publications: The Community Press (36402)

Federal Bar Association
2215 M St., NW
Washington, DC 20037
Phone: (202)785-1614
Fax: (202)785-1568

Publications: The Federal Lawyer (5493)

Federal Communications Bar Association
211 S. Indiana Ave.
Bloomington, IN 47405-7001
Phone: (812)855-5952
Fax: (812)855-0555

Publications: Federal Communications Law Journal (9826)

Federal Reserve Bank of Atlanta
1000 Peachtree St., NE
Atlanta, GA 30309-3904
Phone: (404)745-9068
Fax: (404)521-8050

Publications: Economic Review (7000) • Econ-South (7001)

Federal Reserve Bank of Boston
PO Box 2076
Boston, MA 02106-2076
Phone: (617)973-3397
Fax: (617)973-4292

Publications: Federal Reserve Bank of Boston Regional Review (13893) • New England Economic Indicators (13932) • New England Economic Review (13933)

Federal Reserve Bank of Chicago
Public Affairs Department
230 S. LaSalle
Chicago, IL 60604
Phone: (312)322-5860
Fax: (312)322-5515

Publications: Economic Perspectives (8358)

Federal Reserve Bank of Cleveland
Human Resources
1455 E. 6th
Cleveland, OH 44114
Phone: (216)579-2000
Fax: (216)579-3050

Publications: Economic Commentary (24885) • Economic Review (24886) • Economic Trends (24887)

Federal Reserve Bank of Dallas
Public Affairs Department
Sta. K
Dallas, TX 75222

Publications: Economic and Financial Policy Review (30153)

Federal Reserve Bank of Kansas City
925 Grand Blvd.
Kansas City, MO 64198-0001
Phone: (816)881-2683
Fax: (816)881-2569

Publications: Economic Review (17166)

Federal Reserve Bank of Minneapolis
90 Hennepin Ave.
PO Box 291
Minneapolis, MN 55401
Phone: (612)204-5000

Publications: Federal Reserve Bank of Minneapolis Quarterly Review (16080)

Federal Reserve Bank of New York
Public Information Department
33 Liberty St.
New York, NY 10045
Phone: (212)720-5012
Fax: (212)720-7459

Publications: Federal Reserve Bank of New York Economic Policy Review (21682)

Federal Reserve Bank of Philadelphia
100 N. 6th St.
Philadelphia, PA 19106
Phone: (215)574-6428
Fax: (215)574-4364

Publications: Business Review (27390) • Federal Reserve Bank of Philadelphia Business Review (27469)

Federal Reserve Bank of Richmond
701 E. Byrd St.
Richmond, VA 23219
Phone: (804)697-8000
Fax: (804)697-8287

Publications: Federal Reserve Bank of Richmond Economic Quarterly (32437) • Region Focus (32448)

Federated Publications, Inc.
217 N 6th St.
Lafayette, IN 47901-1448
Phone: (317)423-5511
Fax: (317)742-5633
Free: 800-456-3223

Publications: Journal and Courier (10251)

Federation of America Societies for Experimental Biology
Office of Publications
9650 Rockville Pike
Bethesda, MD 20814-3998
Phone: (301)634-7100
Fax: (301)634-1855
Free: 800-439-2732

Publications: The FASEB Journal (13335)

Federation CJA
5151 Cote St. Catherine Rd.
Montreal, QC, Canada H3W 1M6
Phone: (514)735-3541
Fax: (514)735-8972

Publications: In Montreal (37125)

Federation of General Practitioners of Quebec
1440 Ste-Catherine St. W, Ste. 1000
Montreal, QC, Canada H3G 1R8
Phone: (514)878-1911
Fax: (514)878-2659

Publications: Le Medecin du Quebec (37170)

Federation of New York State Bird Clubs, Inc.
PO Box 440
Loch Sheldrake, NY 12759
Phone: (914)277-8264

Publications: Kingbird (23343)

Federation of Ontario Naturalists
355 Lesmill Rd.
Don Mills, ON, Canada M3B 2W8
Phone: (416)444-8419
Fax: (416)444-9866
Free: 800-440-2366

Publications: Seasons (35777)

Federation of Societies for Coatings Technology
492 Norristown Rd.
Blue Bell, PA 19422-2350
Phone: (610)940-0777
Fax: (610)940-0292

Publications: Journal of Coatings Technology (26725)

Federation of State Medical Boards of the United States, Inc.
Federation Pl.
PO Box 619850
Dallas, TX 75261
Phone: (817)868-4000
Fax: (817)868-4098

Publications: Federation Bulletin (30155) • Federation Exchange (30156) • Model for the Preparation of a Guidebook on Medical Discipline (30168)

Feed-Lot Magazine
Box 850
Dighton, KS 67839-0850
Phone: (620)397-2838
Fax: (620)397-2839
Free: 800-798-9515

Publications: Feed-Lot (11413)

H. R. Felgenhauer, Part Time Publisher
Box 146486
Chicago, IL 60614
Phone: (773)772-8686

Publications: Insects are People Too (8415)

Fellom Publishing Co.
170 S Spruce Ave., Ste. 120
South San Francisco, CA 94080
Phone: (415)588-8832
Fax: (415)588-0901

Publications: Light Metal Age (3789)

Fellowship Publications
PO Box 271
Nyack, NY 10960
Phone: (845)358-4601
Fax: (845)358-4924

Publications: Fellowship (23027)

Feminist Bookstore News
PO Box 882554
San Francisco, CA 94188
Phone: (415)642-9993
Fax: (415)642-9995

Publications: Feminist Bookstore News (3360)

Feminist Press at The City University of New York
The Graduate Center
365 Fifth Ave.
New York, NY 10016
Phone: (212)817-7920
Fax: (212)817-1593

Publications: Women's Studies Quarterly (22935)

Femme-Lines
225 E 36 St., 4 N
New York, NY 10016
Phone: (212)683-6593

Publications: Femme-Lines (21684)

Fen! Press
200 E Tenth St., Ste. 603
New York, NY 10002-7702

Publications: Meshuggah (22317)

Fence Books
14 Fifth Ave., Ste. 1A
New York, NY 10011

Publications: Fence (21685)

Fennimore Times
1150 Lincoln Ave.
PO Box 177
Fennimore, WI 53809
Phone: (608)822-3912
Fax: (608)822-3916

Publications: Fennimore Times (33693)

Ferguson & Ferguson
PO Box 38
Hominy, OK 74035
Phone: (918)885-2101

Publications: News Progress (25870)

Ferndale Enterprise, Inc.
PO Box 1066
Ferndale, CA 95536
Phone: (707)786-4611
Fax: (707)786-4311

Publications: The Ferndale Enterprise (1914)

Ferndale Record, Inc.
2008 Main St.
PO Box 38
Ferndale, WA 98248-0038
Phone: (360)384-1411
Fax: (360)384-1417

Publications: Westside Record-Journal (32769)

Ferris State University
805 Campus Dr.
Rankin Center
Box 15
Big Rapids, MI 49307
Phone: (231)591-2609
Fax: (231)591-3617

Publications: Ferris State Torch (14815)

Ferrum College
PO Box 1000
Ferrum, VA 24088
Phone: (540)365-4300
Fax: (540)365-4229
Free: 800-868-9797

Publications: Ferrum Magazine (32073)

Fibonacci Association
Central Missouri State University
Dept. of Math & Comp. Science
Warrensburg, MO 64093-5045
Phone: (660)543-8851

Publications: The Fibonacci Quarterly (28806)

FIC America
3 S. Broadway
Nyack, NY 10960
Phone: (845)353-8361
Fax: (845)353-2941
Free: 888-659-8720

Publications: Cucinazte (23026)

Fichera Publications
441 S State Rd., Ste. 14
Margate, FL 33068
Phone: (954)971-4360
Fax: (954)971-4362
Free: 800-327-8999

Publications: Dealer Communicator (6324)

The Fiddlehead
Campus House
University of New Brunswick
PO Box 4400
Fredericton, NB, Canada E3B 5A3
Phone: (506)453-3501
Fax: (506)453-5069

Publications: The Fiddlehead (35394)

Fidelity Institutional Retirement Services Company (FIRSCO)
PO Box 9017
Boston, MA 02205-9017

Publications: Stages (13962)

Fidelity Publishing
Box 990593
Boston, MA 02199
Phone: (617)266-8557
Fax: (617)266-1125

Publications: The Guide (13897)

Fifth Estate
PO Box 201016
Ferndale, MI 48220-9016

Publications: Fifth Estate (15028)

Fifty Plus
PO Box 51277
Durham, NC 27717
Phone: (919)493-5900
Fax: (919)490-1925

Publications: Fifty Plus (23821)

50 Plus Lifestyles
PO Box 44327
Madison, WI 53744
Phone: (608)274-5200
Fax: (608)274-5492

Publications: 50 Plus Lifestyles (33939)

Filipinas Publishing, Inc.
1486 Huntington Ave., Ste. 300
South San Francisco, CA 94080
Phone: (650)872-8650
Fax: (650)872-8651
Free: 800-654-7777

Publications: Filipinas Magazine (3788)

The Filipino-American Headliner
1680 Civic Ctr. Dr., Ste. A
Santa Clara, CA 95050
Phone: (408)322-0043

Publications: The Filipino-American Headliner (3670)

Filling Station
PO Box 22135 Bankers Hall
Calgary, AB, Canada T2P 4J5

Publications: Filling Station (34644)

Fillmore County News
181 E Seneca
PO Box 115
Exeter, NE 68351

Publications: Fillmore County News (18004)

Film Arts Foundation
145 9th St. No. 101
San Francisco, CA 94103
Phone: (415)552-8760
Fax: (415)552-0882

Publications: Release Print (3423)

Film Bill, Inc.
250 W 54th St.
New York, NY 10019
Phone: (212)977-4140
Fax: (212)977-4404

Publications: Film Bill (21692)

Film Score Monthly
8503 Washington Blvd.
Culver City, CA 90232
Phone: (310)253-9595
Fax: (310)253-9588
Free: 888-345-6335

Publications: Film Score Monthly (1793)

Film Society of Lincoln Center
70 Lincoln Ctr. Plz.
New York, NY 10023
Phone: (212)875-5610
Fax: (212)875-5636

Publications: Film Comment (21693)

Film and TV Documentation Center
Richardson 390C SUNYA
1400 Washington Ave.
Albany, NY 12222
Phone: (518)442-5745
Fax: (518)442-5367

Publications: Film Literature Index (19986)

The Filson Historical Society
1310 S 3rd St.
Louisville, KY 40208
Phone: (502)635-5083
Fax: (502)635-5086

Publications: Filson History Quarterly (12216)

Finan Publishing
107 W. Pacific Ave.
St. Louis, MO 63119-3776
Phone: (314)961-6644
Fax: (314)961-4809

Publications: Resort Management & Operations (17486)

Finan Publishing Co., Inc.
107 W Pacific Ave.
St. Louis, MO 63119
Phone: (314)961-6644
Fax: (314)961-4809
Free: 800-333-7993

Publications: Club Management (17424) • Painting & Wallcovering Contractor (17481) • St. Louis Construction News & Review (17498)

Finance & Commerce, Inc.
730 2nd Ave., No. 100
Minneapolis, MN 55402-3400
Phone: (612)333-4244
Fax: (612)333-3243
Free: 800-397-4348

Publications: Finance and Commerce (16081)

Financial Executives Institute
200 Campus Dr.
PO Box 674
Florham Park, NJ 07932-0674
Phone: (973)898-4600
Fax: (973)538-6144

Publications: Financial Executive (18825)

Financial Management Association
School of Business
University of South Florida
Tampa, FL 33620-5500
Phone: (813)974-2084
Fax: (813)974-3318

Publications: Financial Management (6762)

Financial Planning Association
3801 E. Florida Ave., Suite 708
Denver, CO 80210
Phone: (303)759-4900
Fax: (303)759-0749
Free: 800-322-4237

Publications: Journal of Financial Planning (4337)

Financial Research Associates Inc.
203 Ave. A NW, Ste. 202
Winter Haven, FL 33881
Phone: (863)299-3969
Fax: (863)299-2131

Publications: Financial Studies of the Small Business (6866)

The Findlay Publishing Company
701 W. Sandusky St.
Findlay, OH 45840
Phone: (419)422-5151
Fax: (419)422-2937

Publications: The Courier (25194)

Findrinny Press
2800 Victory Blvd.
Staten Island, NY 10314

Publications: Outerbridge (22512)

Fine Print Publishers
PO Box 193397
San Francisco, CA 94119
Phone: (415)567-9113
Fax: (415)567-9150

Publications: Fine Print (30679)

Finger Lake Community Newspaper
PO Box 714
Trumansburg, NY 14886
Phone: (607)387-3181
Fax: (607)387-9421

Publications: Finger Lake Community Newspaper (23461) • Ovid Gazette (23462) • Random Harvest Weekly (23349) • Trumansburg Free Press (23463)

Finger Lakes Media
210 N Franklin St.
Watkins Glen, NY 14891
Phone: (607)535-2711
Fax: (607)535-2500

Publications: Watkins Review & Express (23525)

Finger Lakes Printing Co.
218 Genesee St.
PO Box 393
Geneva, NY 14456
Phone: (315)789-3376
Fax: (315)789-4077
Free: 800-388-6652

Publications: Finger Lakes Times (20653)

Fireside Guard
118 W Sneed St.
PO Box 7
Centralia, MO 65240
Phone: (573)682-2133
Fax: (573)682-3361

Publications: Fireside Guard (16969)

Fireweed
PO Box 279, Sta. B
Toronto, ON, Canada M5T 2W2
Phone: (416)504-1339

Publications: Fireweed (36595)

Firm Noncommittal
5 Vonda Ave.
North York, ON, Canada M2N 5E6
Phone: (416)222-8599

Publications: Firm Noncommittal (36127)

First Amendment Inc.
PO Box 146
New London, OH 44851-0146

Publications: Firelands Farmer (25417) • New London Record (25419)

First American Pub.
PO Box 1075
Pembroke, NC 28372
Phone: (910)521-2826
Fax: (910)521-1975

Publications: The Carolina Indian Voice (24114)

First Call Insider Research
1455 Research Blvd.
Rockville, MD 20850
Phone: (301)545-4000
Fax: (301)545-6650
Free: 800-243-2324

Publications: First Call/Thomson Financial Insiders' Chronicle (13679)

First Catholic Slovak Ladies Association
24950 Chagrin Blvd.
Beachwood, OH 44122
Phone: (216)464-8015
Fax: (216)464-9260
Free: 800-464-4642

Publications: Fraternally Yours, Zenska Jednota (28094)

First Catholic Slovak Union
1011 Rosedale Ave.
Middletown, PA 17057
Phone: (717)944-0461
Fax: (717)944-3107

Publications: Jednota (Union) (27253)

First Down Publications
4528 S Sheridan, Ste. 216
Tulsa, OK 74145
Phone: (918)622-1136

Publications: Aggies Illustrated (26106) • Sooners (26132)

First Intensity
PO Box 665
Lawrence, KS 66044
Phone: (785)749-1501

Publications: First Intensity (11551)

First-Line Publishers/L.A. Metro Group
14621 Titus St., Ste. 228
Van Nuys, CA 91402
Phone: (818)782-8695
Fax: (818)782-2924

Publications: Compton Metropolitan Gazette (1749) • Long Beach Express (2171) • Pasadena Gazette (2822) • San Fernando Gazette Express (2742)

FIS Publishing, Inc.
4209 21st Ave. W., Ste. 402
Seattle, WA 98199
Phone: (206)216-0111
Fax: (206)216-0222
Free: 877-990-0111

Publications: Pacific Fishing (33000)

Fisher Reporter
114 S 3rd St.
PO Box 400
Fisher, IL 61843
Phone: (217)897-1525
Fax: (217)897-1525

Publications: Fisher Reporter (8889)

The Fisherman Publishing Society
326-12th St., 1st Fl.
New Westminster, BC, Canada V3M 4H6
Phone: (604)519-3638
Fax: (604)524-6944

Publications: The Fisherman (35029)

Fisk News
1000 17th Ave. N
Nashville, TN 37208
Phone: (615)329-8710

Publications: Fisk News (29455)

Fitchburg Star
PO Box 26
Fitchburg, WI 53575-0026
Phone: (608)273-3576
Fax: (608)835-0130

Publications: Ftichburg Star (33694)

Fitness Publishing, Inc.
213 Danbury Rd.
Wilton, CT 06897
Phone: (203)761-1113
Fax: (203)761-9933

Publications: Running Times (5230)

Fivash Publishing Group
1500 114th Ave. SE, Ste. 101
Bellevue, WA 98004-6902
Phone: (206)441-8415
Fax: (206)441-8325
Free: 800-659-6236

Publications: Washington Magazine (32670)

Five Fingers Press
PO Box 4
San Leandro, CA 94577-0100
Phone: (510)632-5769
Fax: (510)632-5769

Publications: Five Fingers Review (3561)

588049 Saskatchewan Ltd.
Box 399
Herbert, SK, Canada S0H 2A0
Phone: (306)784-2422
Fax: (306)784-3246

Publications: The Herald (37474)

514766 NB Inc.
1 Concorde Gate, Ste. 300
Toronto, ON, Canada M3C 3N6
Phone: (416)486-4900
Fax: (416)489-2068

Publications: MetroToday (36664)

The Five Owls
PO Box 235
Marathon, TX 79842-0235
Phone: (915)386-4257
Fax: (915)386-9087

Publications: The Five Owls (30758)

Five Star Publishing
PO Box 1119
Sierra Vista, AZ 85636
Phone: (520)458-3340
Fax: (520)458-9338

Publications: The Huachuca Scout (887) • The Mountain View News (888)

5280 Publishing, Inc.
PO Box 40194
Denver, CO 80204
Phone: (303)832-5280
Fax: (303)832-0470

Publications: 5280 (4327) • Interactive (4331)

The Flagler News
321 Main Ave.
PO Box 188
Flagler, CO 80815
Phone: (719)765-4468
Fax: (719)765-4517
Free: (719)765-4468

Publications: The Flagler News & Mile Save Shopper (4426)

Flagpole Magazine
112 S Foundry St.
Athens, GA 30601
Phone: (706)549-9523
Fax: (706)548-8981

Publications: Flagpole Magazine (6937)

The Flagstaff Institute
PO Box 986
Flagstaff, AZ 86002
Phone: (928)779-0052
Fax: (928)774-8589

Publications: Journal of the Flagstaff Institute (697)

Flagstaff Printing
PO Box 567
Sedgewick, AB, Canada P0B 4C0
Phone: (780)384-2389
Fax: (780)384-2244

Publications: Community Press (34846) • The Weekly Review (34866)

Flashes, Inc.
17 W Flagler Ave.
Stuart, FL 34994
Phone: (772)287-0650
Fax: (772)283-5090

Publications: Flashes Shopping Guide (6692)

Flashes Publishers
595 Jenner Dr.
Allegan, MI 49010-1567
Phone: (269)324-1000
Fax: (269)673-4761
Free: 800-968-4415

Publications: Flashes Kalamazoo Shopper (15236) • Holland Flashes Shopping Guide (15173) • Zeeland Flashes Shopping Guide (14725)

Flashes Publishers Inc.
595 Jenner Dr.
Allegan, MI 49010
Phone: (616)673-2141
Fax: (616)673-4761
Free: 800-968-4415

Publications: Allegan Flashes (14720) • Kalamazoo Flashes (14721) • Lakeshore Flashes Shopping Guide (14722) • Senior Times (14723)

Flashes Shoppers Guide & News
115 Grand St.
PO Box 156
Eaton Rapids, MI 48827
Phone: (517)663-2361
Fax: (517)663-2381
Free: 877-212-4615

Publications: Flashes Shoppers Guide & News (15000)

The Flat Hat
The Campus Center
College of William and Mary
Williamsburg, VA 23185
Phone: (757)221-3283
Fax: (757)221-3242

Publications: The Flat Hat (32617)

Flathead Indian Reservation
PO Box 98
Pablo, MT 59855
Phone: (406)675-3000
Fax: (406)675-3001

Publications: Char-Koosta News (17889)

Flatiron Magazine
101 W. 23rd St.
New York, NY 10010
Phone: (212)627-5400
Fax: (212)214-0443

Publications: Flatiron Magazine (21706)

Fleet Reserve Association
125 N West St.
Alexandria, VA 22314-2754
Phone: (703)683-1400
Fax: (703)549-6610
Free: 800-FRA-1924

Publications: Naval Affairs (31715)

Fleisher Fine Arts Inc.
15 McMurrich St., Ste. 706
Toronto, ON, Canada M5R 3M6
Phone: (416)925-5564
Fax: (416)925-2972

Publications: ARTFOCUS (36463)

The Fleming Gazette
PO Box 32
Flemingsburg, KY 41041
Phone: (606)845-9211
Fax: (606)845-3299
Free: 877-845-9211

Publications: The Fleming Gazette (12057)

Fletcher Herald Publishing Co.
Box 469
Fletcher, OK 73541
Phone: (580)549-6045
Fax: (580)549-6107

Publications: Fletcher Herald (25835)

Fletcher School of Law & Diplomacy
160 Packard Ave.
Medford, MA 02155
Phone: (617)623-3610
Fax: (617)627-3979

Publications: The Fletcher Forum of World Affairs (14321)

Fleur de Lis Publishing, Inc.
1354 Hancock St., Ste. 300
Quincy, MA 02169
Phone: (617)328-5005
Fax: (617)328-5999

Publications: American Journal of Transportation (14488)

Flight Safety Foundation Inc.
601 Madison St., Ste. 300
Alexandria, VA 22314-1756
Phone: (703)739-6700
Fax: (703)739-6708

Publications: Aviation Mechanics Bulletin (31644) • Flight Safety Digest (31673)

Flight Training Ltd.
421 Aviation Way
Frederick, MD 21701-4756

Publications: Flight Training (13510)

The Flint Journal
200 E. 1st St.
Flint, MI 48502-1925
Free: (810)766-6100

Publications: The Clio Messenger (14885) • The Davison Flagstaff (14896) • The Flint Journal (15033) • The Flint Township News (15034) • The Flushing Observer (15050) • The Grand Blanc News (15083) • The Swartz Creek News (15584)

Flint Publishing Inc.
PO Box 511
Toppenish, WA 98948
Phone: (509)865-4055
Fax: (509)865-2655

Publications: Review Independent (33166) • Review Independent (33167) • Viva (33168)

Floating Island Publications
PO Box 276
Cedarville, CA 96104
Phone: (530)279-2766

Publications: Floating Island (1681)

Floor Focus, Inc.
28 Old Stone Hill Rd.
Pound Ridge, NY 10576
Phone: (914)764-0556
Fax: (914)764-0560

Publications: Floor Focus (23165)

Florence Citizen
200 S Pike.S Peak
Florence, CO 81226
Phone: (719)784-6383
Fax: (719)784-6384

Publications: Florence Citizen (4427)

Floresville Chronicle-Journal
1433 3rd St.
PO Box 820
Floresville, TX 78114
Phone: (830)393-2111
Fax: (830)393-9012

Publications: Floresville Chronicle-Journal (30318)

Floricanto Press
650 Castro St., Ste. 120-331
Mountain View, CA 94041-2055
Phone: (415)552-1879
Fax: (702)995-1410

Publications: La Red—The Net (2607)

Florida A&M University
309 Tucker Hall
Tallahassee, FL 32307
Phone: (904)599-3159
Fax: (904)561-2570

Publications: The Famuan (6704)

Florida Anthropological Society, Inc.
9907 High Meadow Ave.
Thonotosassa, FL 33592-2458

Publications: The Florida Anthropologist (6816)

Florida Association of Dive Operators
2320 Apalache Pkwy.
Tallahassee, FL 32301
Phone: (850)656-3483
Fax: (850)656-5732

Publications: Bluewater Scuba Electronic & Fax Update (6701)

Florida Association of PHCC
PO Box 13089
Tallahassee, FL 32317
Fax: (904)878-1291

Publications: Florida Contractor (6708)

Florida Association of Realtors
PO Box 725025
Orlando, FL 32872-5025
Phone: (407)438-1400
Fax: (407)438-1411

Publications: Florida Realtor (6492)

Florida Bankers Association
1001 Thomasville Rd., Ste 201
Tallahassee, FL 32303
Phone: (850)224-2265
Fax: (850)224-2423
Free: 800-852-6894

Publications: Florida Banking (6706)

Florida Baptist Witness
1230 Hendricks Ave.
Jacksonville, FL 32207
Phone: (904)396-2351
Fax: (904)346-0696
Free: 800-226-8584

Publications: Florida Baptist Witness (6210)

The Florida Bar
650 Apalachee Pkwy.
Tallahassee, FL 32399-2300
Phone: (850)561-5600
Fax: (850)681-3859

Publications: The Florida Bar Journal (6707)

The Florida Catholic
9401 Biscayne Blvd.
Miami, FL 33138
Phone: (305)762-1131
Fax: (305)762-1132
Free: 800-377-3438

Publications: The Florida Catholic (6352)

The Florida Catholic Newspaper
PO Box 609512
Orlando, FL 32860-9512
Phone: (407)423-3438
Fax: (407)660-2977
Free: 800-377-3438

Publications: The Florida Catholic (6490)

Florida Cattleman's Association
PO Box 421403
Kissimmee, FL 34742-1403
Phone: (407)846-6221
Fax: (407)933-8209
Free: 800-647-0026

Publications: Florida Cattleman and Livestock Journal (6261)

Florida Community College at Jacksonville
3939 Roosevelt Blvd.
Jacksonville, FL 32205
Phone: (904)381-3511

Publications: Kalliope (6215)

Florida Defense Lawyers Association
2202 North West Shore, Ste. 200
Tampa, FL 33607
Phone: (813)639-7585
Fax: (813)639-7586

Publications: Trial Advocate Quarterly (6782)

Florida Dental Association
1111 E Tennessee St.
Tallahassee, FL 32308-6914
Phone: (850)681-3629
Fax: (850)561-0504

Publications: Today's FDA (6740)

Florida Department of Agriculture and Consumer Services
1911 SW 34th St.
PO Box 147100
Gainesville, FL 32614-7100
Phone: (352)372-3505
Fax: (352)334-1719

Publications: Tri-Ology (6158)

Florida Department of Agriculture & Consumer Services
545 S Calhoun St., Ste. 234
Tallahassee, FL 32399-6555

Publications: Florida Market Bulletin (6714)

Florida Department of State
500 S Bronough St.
Tallahassee, FL 32399-0250

Publications: Orange Seed Technical Bulletin (6727)

Florida Economic Development Council
335 Beard St.
Tallahassee, FL 32303

Publications: On Track (6726)

Florida Engineering Society
125 S Gadsden St.
Tallahassee, FL 32301
Phone: (850)224-7121
Fax: (850)222-4349

Publications: Florida Engineering Society Journal (6710)

Florida Entomological Society
PO Box 1007
Lutz, FL 33548-1007
Phone: (813)903-9234

Publications: Florida Entomologist (6203)

Florida Farm Bureau Federation
PO Box 147030
Gainesville, FL 32614-7030
Phone: (352)378-1321
Fax: (352)374-1530

Publications: FloridAgriculture (6140)

Florida Funeral Directors Services, Inc.
PO Box 10727
Tallahassee, FL 32302-2727
Phone: (850)224-1969
Fax: (850)224-7965
Free: 800-226-3332

Publications: Florida Funeral Director (6712) • Thanatos (6739)

Florida Grape Growers Association
335 Beard St.
Tallahassee, FL 32303
Phone: (850)222-6000

Publications: Grape Times (6723)

Florida Grocer Publications, Inc.
PO Box 430760
South Miami, FL 33243-0760
Phone: (305)661-0792
Fax: (305)661-6720
Free: 800-440-3067

Publications: Today's Grocer (6686)

Florida Hiker Magazine
PO Box 1212
Geneva, FL 32732
Phone: (407)349-0710
Fax: (407)349-5236

Publications: Florida Hiker Magazine (6171)

Florida Institute of Certified Public Accountants, Inc.
PO Box 5437
Tallahassee, FL 32314

Publications: Florida CPA Today (6709)

Florida International University
University Park DM 300B
Miami, FL 33199
Phone: (305)348-1914
Fax: (305)348-6586

Publications: Japan Studies Review (6364)

Florida International University
3000 NE 151st St.
North Miami, FL 33181-3000

Publications: FIU Hospitality Review (6465)

Florida Keys Keynoter
3015 Overseas Hwy.
PO Box 158
Marathon, FL 33050
Phone: (305)743-5551
Fax: (305)743-6397

Publications: Florida Keys Keynoter (6321)

Florida League of Cities
301 S. Bronough St., Ste. 300
Tallahassee, FL 32302-1757
Phone: (850)222-9684
Fax: (850)222-3806

Publications: Quality Cities (6729)

Florida Marine Research Institute
100 8th Ave. SE
St. Petersburg, FL 33701-5095
Phone: (727)896-8626
Fax: (727)823-0166

Publications: Florida Marine Research Institute Technical Reports (6626) • Florida Marine Research Publications (6627) • Memoirs of the Hourglass Cruises (6631)

Florida Mariner
PO Box 1220
Venice, FL 34284
Phone: (941)488-9307
Fax: (941)488-9309
Free: 800-388-9307

Publications: Florida Mariner (6830)

Florida Media, Inc.
102 Drennen Rd. Ste. C5
Orlando, FL 32806
Phone: (407)816-9596
Fax: (407)801-9373
Free: 888-352-5484

Publications: Florida Monthly Magazine (6491)

Florida Medical Association, Inc.
PO Box 10269
Tallahassee, FL 32302
Phone: (850)224-6496
Fax: (850)222-8030
Free: 800-762-0233

Publications: Florida Medical Association (6715)

Florida Municipal Electric Association, Inc.
PO Box 2114, 417 E. College
Tallahassee, FL 32302
Phone: (850)224-3314
Fax: (850)224-2831

Publications: Relay Magazine (6730)

Florida Music Educators Association
207 Office Plaza Dr.
Tallahassee, FL 32301
Phone: (850)878-6844
Fax: (850)942-1793
Free: 800-301-3632

Publications: Florida Music Director (6716)

The Florida Newspaper
PO Box 97-1490
Miami, FL 33197
Phone: (305)254-3400
Fax: (305)254-6007
Free: 800-445-1746

Publications: The Florida Newspaper (6353)

Florida Ornithological Society
13093 Henry Beadel Dr.
Tallahassee, FL 32312

Publications: Florida Field Naturalist (6711)

Florida Pharmacy Association
610 N. Adams St.
Tallahassee, FL 32301-1114
Phone: (850)926-2405
Fax: (850)926-2411

Publications: Florida Pharmacy Today (6717)

Florida Psychological Association
408 Office Plaza Dr.
Tallahassee, FL 32301-2757
Phone: (850)656-2222
Fax: (850)942-4586

Publications: Florida Psychologist (6718)

Florida Real Estate Magazine, L.P.
PO Box 4258
Vero Beach, FL 32964

Publications: Florida Real Estate (6835)

Florida Rental Association
335 Beard St.
Tallahassee, FL 32303
Phone: (850)222-6000
Fax: (850)681-2890

Publications: Florida Rental Association News (6719)

Florida Sentinel-Bulletin
2207-21st Ave.
PO Box 3363
Tampa, FL 33601
Phone: (813)248-1921
Fax: (813)248-4507

Publications: Florida Sentinel-Bulletin (6763)

Florida Southern College
111 Lake Hollingsworth Dr.
Lakeland, FL 33801-5698
Phone: (863)680-4111
Fax: (863)680-6244

Publications: The Southern (6291)

Florida Star Times
PO Box 40629
Jacksonville, FL 32203
Phone: (904)766-8834
Fax: (904)765-1673

Publications: Florida Star Times (6211)

Florida State Firemen's Association, Inc.
PO Box 968
Avon Park, FL 33825
Phone: (863)453-4817
Fax: (863)453-7450

Publications: Florida Fireman (6590)

Florida State University
151 Dodd Hall
Tallahassee, FL 32306-1500
Phone: (850)644-0220
Fax: (850)644-3832

Publications: Social Theory and Practice (6735)

Florida State University
1211 Brandt Dr.
Tallahassee, FL 32308-5210
Phone: (850)877-2459
Fax: (850)877-2459

Publications: Psychomusicology (6728)

Florida Sun Publications
717 1st St.
Bradenton, FL 34206
Phone: (941)748-4140
Fax: (941)747-3699

Publications: The Beach Weekly (6654) • Bradenton Shopping Guide (5957) • Okeechobee Shoppers Guide (6482) • Venice Weekly (6668)

Florida Sun Publications
PO Box 422068
Kissimmee, FL 34742-2068
Phone: (407)846-7600
Fax: (407)846-8516

Publications: Osceola News-Gazette (6262) • Osceola Shopper (6263) • South Orange News (6264)

Florida Sun Publications
1010 US 27 N.
Sebring, FL 33870
Phone: (813)382-1142

Publications: Sebring Shopping Guide (6680)

Florida Sun Review
PO Box 2348
Orlando, FL 32802-2348
Phone: (407)423-1156
Fax: (407)849-1286

Publications: Florida Sun Review (6494)

Florida Trucking Association, Inc.
350 E. College Ave.
Tallahassee, FL 32301-1565
Phone: (850)222-9900

Publications: Florida Truck News (6720)

Florist's Review Enterprises, Inc.
3641 SW Plass Ave.
Topeka, KS 66611-2588
Phone: (785)266-0888
Fax: (785)266-0333
Free: 800-367-4708

Publications: Florists' Review Magazine (11819)

Floyd County Newspapers, Inc.
PO Box 391
Prestonsburg, KY 41653
Fax: (606)886-3603

Publications: The Floyd County Times (12370)

The Flyer
201 Kelsey Ln.
Tampa, FL 33619
Phone: (813)626-9430
Fax: (813)626-8923

Publications: The Flyer (6764)

Flyer Media Inc.
PO Box 39099
Lakewood, WA 98439-0099
Phone: (253)471-9888
Fax: (253)471-9911
Free: 800-426-8538

Publications: General Aviation News (32804)

Flyer Publications, Inc.
PO Box 199
Oregon, WI 53575-0199
Phone: (608)835-7063

Publications: Midwest Flyer Magazine (34217) • World Airshow News (34219)

Flying Physicians Association, Inc.
PO Box 677427
Orlando, FL 32867-7427
Phone: (407)359-1423
Fax: (407)359-1167

Publications: Flying Physician (6495)

FO Publishers.
PO Box 598
Sulphur Springs, TX 75483
Phone: (903)885-8663
Fax: (908)885-8768

Publications: News-Telegram (31166)

Foam Lake Review
324 Main St.
PO Box 550
Foam Lake, SK, Canada S0A 1A0
Phone: (306)272-3262
Fax: (306)272-4521

Publications: Foam Lake Review (37468) • Ituna News (37469)

The Foard County News
Box 489
Crowell, TX 79227-0489
Phone: (940)684-1355
Fax: (940)684-1700

Publications: The Foard County News (30111)

Focal Point Press
321 City Island Ave.
Bronx, NY 10464
Phone: (718)885-1403
Fax: (718)885-1451

Publications: Viewfinder Journal of Focal Point Gallery (20289)

Focus on the Family
8605 Explorer Dr.
Colorado Springs, CO 80920-1051
Phone: (719)531-3400
Free: 800-232-6459

Publications: Breakaway Magazine (4237) • Clubhouse Jr. (4241) • Focus on the Family Clubhouse (4246) • Focus on the Family Magazine (4247) • Physician Magazine (4254)

Focus on Farming
6 Central St.
PO Box 591
Moravia, NY 13118
Phone: (315)497-1551

Publications: Focus on Farming (21095)

Focus KAFB Newspaper
209 Palomas NE, Ste. C
Albuquerque, NM 87108
Phone: (505)892-9400
Fax: (505)255-3346

Publications: Focus KAFB Newspaper (19771)

Focus Publications, Inc.
22 S. Parsonage St.
Rhinebeck, NY 12572
Phone: (845)876-2936

Publications: FOCUS: Journal for Respiratory Care Managers and Educators (23183)

Focus Publishing Ltd.
345 Huskey Dr.
Seymour, TN 37865-4513

Publications: Fitness Plus Magazine (29597)

Focus on Security
115 N Grant St.
Moscow, ID 83843
Phone: (208)883-0817
Fax: (208)883-5353

Publications: Focus on Security (7914)

Foley Publishing
PO Box 158
Liberty Corner, NJ 07938
Phone: (908)766-6006
Fax: (908)766-6607

Publications: Bartender Magazine (19169)

The Folger Shakespeare Library
201 E Capitol St. SE
Washington, DC 20003-1094
Phone: (202)544-7077
Fax: (202)544-4623

Publications: Shakespeare Quarterly (5790)

Folio Publishing, Inc.
9456 Phillips Hwy., Ste. 11
Jacksonville, FL 32256
Phone: (904)260-9770
Fax: (904)260-9773

Publications: Folio Weekly (6213)

Fontana Herald Publishing
16981, Foothill Blvd. Ste. N
Fontana, CA 92335
Phone: (909)822-2231
Fax: (909)355-9358

Publications: Fontana Herald-News (1918)

Fontanelle Observer
PO Box 248
Fontanelle, IA 50846-0248
Phone: (641)745-3161
Fax: (641)745-1201

Publications: Fontanelle Observer (10890)

Food Chemical News
1101 Pennsylvania Ave. SE
Washington, DC 20003
Phone: (202)887-6320
Fax: (202)546-3890
Free: 800-272-7732

Publications: Food Chemical News (5497)

Food Distributors International
201 Park Washington Ct.
Falls Church, VA 22046
Phone: (703)532-9400
Fax: (703)538-4673

Publications: Food Distributor (32045)

Food Industry Alliance of NYS
130 Washington Ave.
Albany, NY 12210
Phone: (518)434-1900
Fax: (212)558-6214

Publications: Food Industry Advocate (19987)

The Food Institute
1 Broadway, 2nd Fl.
Elmwood Park, NJ 07407
Phone: (201)791-5570
Fax: (201)791-5222

Publications: Food Institute Report (18794)

Food Marketing Institute
655 15th St., NW, Ste. 700
Washington, DC 20005
Phone: (202)452-8444
Fax: (202)429-4529

Publications: Food Marketing Industry Speaks (5498)

Food & Nutrition Press Inc.
6527 Main St.
Trumbull, CT 06611-1338
Phone: (203)261-8587
Fax: (203)261-9724

Publications: Journal of Texture Studies (5185)

Foodservice Equipment Distributors Association
223 W. Jackson Blvd., Ste. 620
Chicago, IL 60606
Phone: (312)427-9605
Fax: (312)427-9607

Publications: FEDA News and Views (8375)

Football News, Inc.
8033 NW 36 St.
Miami, FL 33166
Phone: (305)594-0508
Fax: (305)594-0518
Free: 800-334-4005

Publications: Football News (6355)

Foothills Trader
PO Box 665
Torrington, CT 06790
Phone: (860)626-6047

Publications: Foothills Trader (5178)

Footprints
Wayland Baptist University, No. 437
Plainview, TX 79072
Phone: (806)291-3600
Fax: (806)291-1966

Publications: Footprints (30938)

Forbes Magazine
60 5th Ave.
New York, NY 10011
Phone: (212)620-2200
Fax: (212)206-5174

Publications: Forbes (21718) • Forbes ASAP (21719) • Forbes FYI (21720) • Forbes MediaCritic (21721)

Forbes Newspapers
44 Veterans Memorial Pkwy. E
PO Box 699
Somerville, NJ 08876
Phone: (908)722-3000
Fax: (908)526-2509

Publications: Bound Brook Chronicle (19571) • Cranford Chronicle (18771) • Franklin Focus (18835) • Highland Park Herald (18873) • Hills-Bedminster Press (18668) • Metuchen Edison Review (18787) • Middlesex Buyer's Guide (19335) • Middlesex Chronicle (19574) • The Review (19577) • Scotch Plains-Fanwood Press (19534) • Somerset County Buyer's Guide (19578)

Forced Exposure
PO Box 9102
Waltham, MA 02451
Phone: (781)562-0507
Fax: (781)562-0533

Publications: Forced Exposure (14599)

Ford County Press
115 W Main
PO Box 195
Melvin, IL 60952
Phone: (217)388-7721
Fax: (217)388-2864

Publications: Ford County Press (9171)

Fordham University
PO Box B
Bronx, NY 10458
Phone: (718)817-4398
Fax: (718)817-4319

Publications: The RAM (20282)

Fordham University
113 W. 60th St.
Rm. 408
New York, NY 10023
Phone: (212)636-6016
Fax: (212)636-7213

Publications: The Observer (22482)

Fordham University School of Law
140 W. 62nd St. Rm. 03
Lincoln Center
New York, NY 10023-7485
Phone: (212)636-6881
Fax: (212)636-6694

Publications: Fordham Law Review (21723) • Fordham Urban Law Journal (21724)

Fordyce Publishing Co.
304 Spring St.
PO Box 559
Fordyce, AR 71742
Phone: (501)352-3144
Fax: (501)352-8091

Publications: News-Advocate (1135)

The Forecaster
PO Box 66797
Falmouth, ME 04105-6797
Phone: (207)781-3661
Fax: (207)781-2060

Publications: The Forecaster—Northern Edition (12957) • The Forecaster—Southern Edition (12958)

Forefront Publishing
PMB 113, 5 River Rd.
Wilton, CT 06897-4069
Phone: (203)834-0631
Fax: (203)834-0940

Publications: Neurological Research (14941)

Foreign Language Center
Presidio
Monterey, CA 93944-5006
Phone: (831)242-5638
Fax: (831)242-5850

Publications: Applied Language Learning (2581)

Foreign Tax Law Inc.
PO Box 2189
Ormond Beach, FL 32175-2189
Phone: (386)253-5785
Fax: (386)257-3003

Publications: Foreign Tax Law Bi-Weekly Bulletin (6533)

Forest-Blade Publishing Inc.
Box 938
Swainsboro, GA 30401
Phone: (478)237-9971
Fax: (478)237-9451

Publications: The Blade (7578)

Forest City Publishing Co.
PO Box 350
Forest City, IA 50436-0350
Phone: (641)585-2112
Fax: (641)585-4442

Publications: Forest City Summit (10891)

Forest City Publishing Co., Inc.
601 Oak St.
PO Box 1149
Forest City, NC 28043-1149
Phone: (828)248-5203
Fax: (828)248-2790
Free: 888-245-6431

Publications: County News-Enterprise (23893) •
The Daily Courier (23894)

Forest History Society
701 Vickers Ave.
Durham, NC 27701-3162
Phone: (919)682-9319
Fax: (919)682-2349

Publications: Environmental History (23820)

Forest Landowners Association
PO Box 450209
Atlanta, GA 31145-0209
Phone: (404)325-2954
Fax: (404)325-2955
Free: 800-325-2954

Publications: Forest Landowner (7008)

Forest Press
PO Box 366
Tionesta, PA 16353
Phone: (814)755-4900
Fax: (814)755-4429

Publications: The Forest Press (28049)

Forest Products Society
2801 Marshall Ct.
Madison, WI 53705-2295
Phone: (608)231-1361
Fax: (608)231-2152

Publications: Forest Products Journal (33941)

Forest Standard
1 King St.
Box 220
Forest, ON, Canada N0N 1J0
Phone: (519)786-5242
Fax: (519)786-4884

Publications: The Forest Standard (35838)

Forkart Treasures
14212 El Pico St.
Winter Garden, FL 34787-9414

Publications: Folkart Treasures (6864)

The Formalist
320 Hunter Dr.
Evansville, IN 47711
Phone: (812)425-7684

Publications: The Formalist (9933)

Formula Publications
447 Speers Rd., Ste. 4
Oakville, ON, Canada L6K 3S7
Phone: (905)842-6591
Fax: (905)842-6843

Publications: Carguide Magazine (Le Magazine
Carguide) (36142)

Forney Messenger Inc.
201 W Broad St.
PO Box 936
Forney, TX 75126
Phone: (972)564-3121
Fax: (972)552-3599

Publications: Forney Messenger (30325)

Forsyth County News
121 Dahlonega St.
PO Box 210
Cumming, GA 30028
Phone: (404)887-3126
Fax: (404)887-6017

Publications: Forsyth County News (7215)

Fort Bend Publishing Group
10707 Corporate Dr., No. 170
Stafford, TX 77477
Phone: (281)240-2445
Fax: (281)240-5079

Publications: Houston Lifestyle & Homes Magazine
(31127)

Fort Dix Public Affairs Office
AFRC-FA-PA-CI
Bldg. 5407 Pennsylvania Ave.
Fort Dix, NJ 08640-5075
Phone: (609)562-5037
Fax: (609)562-3337

Publications: The Fort Dix Post (18830)

Ft. Frances Times and Rainy Lake Herald
116 1st St
PO Box 339
Fort Frances, ON, Canada P9A 3M7
Phone: (807)274-5373
Fax: (807)274-7286
Free: 800-465-8508

Publications: The Daily Bulletin (35840) • Ft.
Frances Times and Rainy Lake Herald (35841)

Fort Hays State University
Malloy Hall Rm. 106
600 Park St.
Hays, KS 67601

Publications: The University Leader (11481)

Fort Hood Sentinel
PO Box 6114
Temple, TX 76503-6114
Phone: (817)778-4444
Fax: (817)771-3516

Publications: Fort Hood Sentinel (31177)

Fort Nelson News
5004 52nd Ave., W
Box 600
Fort Nelson, BC, Canada V0C 1R0
Phone: (250)774-2357
Fax: (250)774-3612

Publications: Fort Nelson News (34956)

Fort Payne Newspapers, Inc.
PO Box 680349
Fort Payne, AL 35968-1604
Phone: (256)845-2550
Fax: (256)845-7459
Free: 800-348-4637

Publications: Times-Journal (231) • The Times-
Journal Midweek (232)

Fort Peck Assiniboine and Sioux Tribes
400 Ct. Ave.
PO Box 1027
Poplar, MT 59255
Phone: (406)768-5155
Fax: (406)768-5473

Publications: Wotanin-Wowapi (17901)

Ft. Polk Guardian
716 E Napolean
PO Box 1999
Sulphur, LA 70664-1999
Phone: (318)463-6204
Fax: (318)463-5347

Publications: Ft. Polk Guardian (12850)

Ft. Qu'Appelle Times
141 Broadway St. E.
PO Box 940
Fort Qu'Appelle, SK, Canada S0G 1S0
Phone: (306)332-5526
Fax: (306)332-5414

Publications: Ft. Qu'Appelle Times (37470)

Fort Smith Historical Society, Inc.
c/o Fort Smith Public Library
3201 Rogers Ave.
PO Box 3676
Fort Smith, AR 72913
Phone: (501)783-0229

Publications: Fort Smith Historical Society Journal
(1142)

Fort Stockton Pioneer
210 N Nelson St.
PO Box 1528
Fort Stockton, TX 79735-6724
Phone: (915)336-2281
Fax: (915)336-6432

Publications: Fort Stockton Pioneer (30326)

Fort Wayne Journal-Gazette
600 W. Main St.
Fort Wayne, IN 46802-1498
Phone: (260)461-8853
Fax: (260)461-8893
Free: 800-444-3303

Publications: Fort Wayne Journal-Gazette (9968)

Fortnightly Al-Hilal
338 Hollyberry Trail
Willowdale, ON, Canada M2H 2P6
Phone: (416)493-4374
Fax: (416)493-4374

Publications: Fortnightly Al-Hilal (36877)

Fortuna Communications Corp.
PO Box 690
Fortuna, CA 95540-0690
Phone: (707)725-6951
Fax: (707)725-4311
Free: 800-345-8876

Publications: Satellite TV Week (1930)

Forty-Niner Advertising
California State University, Long Beach
1250 Bellflower Blvd.
SSPA 010-B
Long Beach, CA 90840-4601
Phone: (562)985-8001
Fax: (562)985-1740

Publications: Daily Forty-Niner (2165)

Forum Communications Co.
PO Box 826
Detroit Lakes, MN 56502
Phone: (218)847-3151
Fax: (218)847-9409
Free: 800-422-1409

Publications: Becker County Record (15828) • Detroit Lakes Tribune (15829) • Lake Area Press
(15830)

Forum Communications Company
PO Box 639
Worthington, MN 56187
Phone: (507)376-9711
Free: 800-642-3243

Publications: Worthington Globe (16540)

Forum Communications Co.
Box 2020
101 5th St. N.
Fargo, ND 58102-4826
Phone: (701)241-5402
Fax: (701)241-5406

Publications: Advisor (28899) • The Daily Republic
(28900) • The Forum (24411)

Forum Publishing
346 S Jefferson
Box 31
Wadena, MN 56482-0031
Phone: (218)631-2561
Fax: (218)631-1621

Publications: Intercom (16489) • Pioneer Journal
(16490)

Forum Publishing Co.
383 E. Main St.
Centerport, NY 11721
Phone: (631)754-5000

Publications: Retailers Forum Magazine (20446) •
Swap Meet Magazine (20447)

Forum Publishing Group, Inc.
1701 Green Rd., Ste. B
Deerfield Beach, FL 33064
Phone: (954)698-6397
Fax: (954)429-1207
Free: 800-275-8820

Publications: Boynton Beach Times (5948)

Forum Publishing, Inc.
679 Thomas Jefferson Rd.
Wayne, PA 19087-1027
Phone: (610)385-3258
Fax: (610)337-8463

Publications: Occupational Therapy Forum (28134)

Forum for Scriptural Christianity, Inc.
308 E Main St.
PO Box 150
Wilmore, KY 40390
Phone: (859)858-4661
Fax: (859)858-4972
Free: 800-487-7784

Publications: Good News (12452)

Forward Association, Inc.
45 E. 33rd St.
New York, NY 10016
Phone: (212)889-8200
Fax: (212)684-3949
Free: 800-266-0773

Publications: Jewish Forward (21963)

Forward Movement Publications
412 Sycamore St.
Cincinnati, OH 45202-4195
Phone: (513)721-6659
Fax: (513)721-0729
Free: 800-543-1813

Publications: Dia a Dia (24793) • Forward Day by Day (24798)

Forward Times Publishing Co.
5407 Chenevert St., Ste. 203
PO Box 8346
Houston, TX 77288-8346
Phone: (713)526-4727
Fax: (713)526-3170

Publications: Houston Forward Times (30484)

Foster City Islander
1185 Chess Dr., Ste. B
Foster City, CA 94404
Phone: (650)574-5952
Fax: (650)574-1096

Publications: Foster City Islander (1932)

Foster's Democrat
333 Central Ave.
Dover, NH 03820-4127
Phone: (603)742-4455
Fax: (603)742-4455
Free: 800-660-8310

Publications: Foster's Democrat (18491)

Foto News Publications, Inc.
1905 E 14th St.
Merrill, WI 54452-3849
Phone: (715)536-7121
Fax: (715)539-3686

Publications: Foto News (34045)

FOUND Magazine
3455 Charing Cross Rd.
Ann Arbor, MI 48108-1911

Publications: FOUND (14750)

Foundation for Advanced Critical Studies, Inc.
8721 Santa Monica Blvd., PMB 6
West Hollywood, CA 90069
Phone: (323)876-4508
Fax: (323)876-5061

Publications: Art Issues (4061)

The Foundation for Cultural Review, Inc.
850 7th Ave., Ste. 400
New York, NY 10019
Phone: (212)247-6980
Fax: (212)247-3127

Publications: The New Criterion (22428)

Foundation for Economic Education Inc.
30 S Broadway
Irvington on Hudson, NY 10533-1861
Phone: (914)591-7230
Fax: (914)591-8910
Free: 800-452-3518

Publications: The Freeman (20784)

Foundation of Flexographic Technical Association
900 Marconi Ave.
Ronkonkoma, NY 11779-7212
Phone: (631)737-6020
Fax: (631)737-6813

Publications: FLEXO (23268) • FLEXO ESPANOL (23269)

Foundation for National Progress
731 Market St. Ste. 600
6TH Fl.
San Francisco, CA 94103
Phone: (415)665-6637
Fax: (415)665-6696

Publications: Mother Jones (3391)

Foundation of the New York State Psychological Association, Inc.
6 Executive Park Dr.
Albany, NY 12203
Phone: (518)437-1050
Fax: (518)437-0177
Free: 800-732-3933

Publications: NYSPA Notebook/Psychologist (20002)

Foundation for Student Communication, Inc.
305 Aaron Burr Hall
Princeton University
Princeton, NJ 08540
Phone: (609)258-1111
Fax: (609)258-1222

Publications: Business Today (Princeton) (19455)

The Founders Journal
PO Box 150931
Cape Coral, FL 33915
Phone: (239)772-1400
Fax: (239)772-1140

Publications: The Founders Journal (5972)

Four Corners Pub., Inc.
108 S Kaufman St.
Mount Vernon, TX 75457
Phone: (903)537-2228
Fax: (903)537-2227

Publications: Optic-Herald (30843)

408 Printing & Publishing
410 West St.
New York, NY 10014
Phone: (212)929-8994
Fax: (212)924-6040

Publications: The Militant (22336)

Four Stars Publishing Co., Inc.
197 Tranquility Rd.
Middlebury, CT 06762-2230

Publications: Business Digest of Greater Waterbury (4941)

The Four-Town Journal
Box 68
Langenburg, SK, Canada S0A 2A0
Phone: (306)743-2617
Fax: (306)743-2299

Publications: The Four-Town Journal (37488)

4 Ward Corp.
107 Mill Plain Rd.
Danbury, CT 06811
Phone: (203)730-4090
Fax: (203)730-4094
Free: 800-825-0900

Publications: Party & Paper Retailer (4749)

Fourteen Hills
SFSU
Dept. of Creative Writing
1600 Holloway Ave.
San Francisco, CA 94132-1722
Phone: (415)338-3083

Publications: Fourteen Hills (3362)

Fourth Publishing Co.
PO Box A
Central City, IA 52214
Phone: (319)438-1313

Publications: Linn News-Letter (10691)

Fox Valley Shopping News
PO Box 609
Yorkville, IL 60560-0609
Phone: (630)553-7431
Fax: (630)553-0310

Publications: Fox Valley Shopping News (9775)

The Foxfire Fund Inc.
PO Box 541
Mountain City, GA 30562-0541
Phone: (706)746-5828
Fax: (706)746-5829

Publications: The Foxfire Magazine (7449)

Foxxy Shopper
PO Box 526
Sparta, WI 54656
Phone: (608)269-5054
Fax: (608)269-1488

Publications: Foxxy Shopper (34330) • Triad (34333)

Framingham State College
100 State St.
Framingham, MA 01701
Phone: (508)626-4605
Fax: (508)875-1287

Publications: The Gatepost (14197)

France Press, Inc.
1 Hallidie Plz., Ste. 505
San Francisco, CA 94102
Phone: (415)981-9088
Fax: (415)981-9177
Free: 800-232-1549

Publications: France Today (3363) • Journal Francais (3381)

Francesville Tribune
PO Box 458
Francesville, IN 47946
Phone: (219)567-2221

Publications: Francesville Tribune (9998)

Franchise UPDATE Publications, Inc.
6489 Camden Ave., Ste. 205
San Jose, CA 95160
Phone: (408)997-7795
Fax: (408)997-9377

Publications: Franchise UPDATE (3517)

Franciscan Fathers-Publishers
361 Highland Blvd.
Brooklyn, NY 11207
Phone: (718)235-5962

Publications: Darbininkas (The Worker) (20311)

Franciscan Friars of California, Inc.
1500 34th Ave.
Oakland, CA 94601
Phone: (916)443-5717
Fax: (916)443-2019

Publications: The Way of St. Francis (3021)

Franciscan Institute
St. Bonaventure University
St. Bonaventure, NY 14778
Phone: (716)375-2105
Fax: (716)375-2156

Publications: The Cord (23287)

Frank Amato Publications, Inc.
PO Box 82112
Portland, OR 97282
Phone: (503)653-8108
Fax: (503)653-2766
Free: 800-541-9498

Publications: Flyfishing & Tying Journal (26478) • Salmon Trout Steelheader (26506)

Frankenmuth News
231 Hubinger
PO Box 252
Frankenmuth, MI 48734-1703
Phone: (989)652-3246
Fax: (989)652-3247

Publications: Frankenmuth News (15052)

Frankfort Area News
PO Box 156
Frankfort, KS 66427-0156
Phone: (785)292-4726
Fax: (785)292-4726

Publications: Frankfort Area News (11446)

Frankfort Publishing Co.
321 W. Main St.
Frankfort, KY 40601-1864
Phone: (502)227-4556
Fax: (502)227-2831

Publications: State Journal (12076)

Frankfort Times, Inc.
251 E Clinton St., No. 9
Frankfort, IN 46041-1906
Phone: (765)659-4622
Fax: (765)654-7031

Publications: Times (9999)

Franklin Advocate
PO Box 576
Meadville, MS 39653
Phone: (601)384-2484
Fax: (601)384-2276

Publications: Franklin Advocate (16766)

Franklin Banner-Tribune
115 Wilson St.
PO Box 566
Franklin, LA 70538-6150
Phone: (337)828-3706
Fax: (337)828-2874

Publications: Franklin Banner-Tribune (12582)

Franklin County Graphic
PO Box 160
Connell, WA 99326
Phone: (509)234-3181
Fax: (509)234-3182

Publications: Franklin County Graphic (32730)

Franklin County Newspapers, Inc.
109 S Bickett Blvd.
Box 119
Louisburg, NC 27549-0119
Phone: (919)496-6503
Fax: (919)496-1689

Publications: Franklin Times (24049)

Franklin County Newspapers, Inc.
310 S. Lane
PO Box 250
Rocky Mount, VA 24151
Phone: (540)483-5113
Fax: (540)483-8013

Publications: Franklin News-Post (32512)

Franklin County Times Inc.
PO Box 1088
Russellville, AL 35653
Phone: (256)332-1881
Fax: (256)332-1883

Publications: Franklin County Times (441)

Franklin Journal
2033 Richard Jones Rd.
Nashville, TN 37215-2803

Publications: Franklin Journal (29456)

Franklin and Marshall College
Box 3003
Lancaster, PA 17604-3003
Phone: (717)291-4095
Fax: (717)291-3886

Publications: The College Reporter (27140)

The Franklin Press
PO Box 350
Franklin, NC 28744
Phone: (704)524-2010
Fax: (704)524-8821

Publications: The Franklin Press (23898)

Franklin Publications
11050 Santa Monica Blvd.
Los Angeles, CA 90025
Phone: (310)445-7500
Fax: (310)445-7583
Free: 800-225-6473

Publications: Let's Live (2315)

Franklin Publishing Co., Inc.
99 High St.
Boston, MA 02110-2320
Phone: (781)878-3333

Publications: Suburban News (14570)

Franklin Publishing Co., Inc.
121 2nd Ave. N.
Franklin, TN 37064
Phone: (615)791-3254
Fax: (615)790-0522

Publications: Brentwood Journal (29195) • Review-Appeal (30363)

The Franklin Shopper
25 Penncraft Ave.
Chambersburg, PA 17201
Phone: (717)263-0359
Fax: (717)263-1314
Free: 800-486-3060

Publications: The Franklin Shopper (26768)

Franklin Times Publishing
208 Main
Franklin, IL 62638
Phone: (217)675-2461
Fax: (217)675-2470

Publications: The Franklin Times (8896)

The Frankston Citizen
PO Box 188
Frankston, TX 75763
Phone: (903)876-2218
Fax: (903)876-4974

Publications: The Frankston Citizen (30364)

Franmore Communications, Inc.
4999 St. Catherine St. W, Ste. 215
Westmount, QC, Canada H3Z 1T3
Phone: (514)487-9868
Fax: (514)487-9276

Publications: Aggregates & Roadbuilding Magazine (37441)

Fraser Valley Record Limited
33047 First Ave.
Mission, BC, Canada V2V 1G2
Phone: (604)826-6221
Fax: (604)826-8266

Publications: The Mission City Record (35016)

Fraternal Order of Eagles
1623 Gatewat Cir.
Grove City, OH 43123-9309

Publications: Eagle Magazine (25231)

The Frederick News-Post
200 E. Patrick St.
PO Box 578
Frederick, MD 21705-0578
Phone: (301)662-1177
Fax: (301)662-8299

Publications: The Frederick-News Post (13513)

The Frederick Press
117 N 9th
Frederick, OK 73542
Phone: (580)335-3893
Fax: (580)335-5400

Publications: The Frederick Press (25840)

Fredhartman Interprise
PO Box 585
Brenham, TX 77834
Fax: (409)830-8577

Publications: The Banner Press (29948)

Fredonia Pennysaver Inc.
25 Water St.
PO Box 493
Fredonia, NY 14063
Phone: (716)679-1509
Fax: (716)672-2626
Free: 877-679-1501

Publications: Dunkirk-Fredonia-Westfield Pennysaver (20621) • Lakeshore Pennysaver (20622)

The Free Lance-Star Publishing Co.
616 Amelia St.
Fredericksburg, VA 22401

Publications: The Free Lance-Star (32085)

Free Lunch Arts Alliance
PO Box 717
Glenview, IL 60025-0717
Phone: (847)729-3595

Publications: Free Lunch (8935)

Free Methodist Church of North America
PO Box 535002
Indianapolis, IN 46253-5002
Phone: (317)244-3660
Fax: (317)248-9055
Free: 800-342-5531

Publications: Light and Life (10147)

Free People Press
10547 State Hwy. 110 N
Tyler, TX 75704-3731
Phone: (903)592-4263

Publications: Both Sides Now (31196)

Free Press
215 4th St.
PO Box 459
100 Mile House, BC, Canada V0K 2E0
Phone: (604)395-2219
Fax: (604)395-3939

Publications: Free Press (35040)

Free Press
PO Box 469
Islamorada, FL 33036
Phone: (305)664-2266
Fax: (305)664-8411

Publications: Free Press (6208)

Free Press
198 Chambers St.
Phillipsburg, NJ 08865
Phone: (908)859-6000
Fax: (908)859-3084

Publications: Free Press (19421)

The Free Press
2103 N. Queen St.
Kinston, NC 28501
Phone: (252)527-3191
Fax: (252)527-8838

Publications: The Free Press (24027)

Free Press
16 Centre St.
Essex, ON, Canada N8M 1N9
Phone: (519)776-8511
Fax: (519)776-4014

Publications: Free Press (35809)

The Free Press
248 1st St.
PO Box 37
Midland, ON, Canada L4R 4K6
Phone: (705)526-5431
Fax: (705)526-1771

Publications: The Free Press (36041) • The Free Press This Week (36042)

The Free Press
312 W. Broad St.
Quakertown, PA 18951
Phone: (215)536-6820
Fax: (215)536-7201

Publications: The Free Press (27914)

The Free Press
3470 Jack Hays Tr.
Buda, TX 78610
Phone: (512)262-6397
Fax: (512)268-0262

Publications: The Free Press (29985)

Free Press Company
PO Box 3287
Mankato, MN 56002-3287
Phone: (507)625-4451
Fax: (507)388-4355
Free: 800-657-4662

Publications: Free Press (16026)

Free Press Co., Inc.
PO Box 3169
Mankato, MN 56001
Phone: (507)345-4523
Free: 800-657-4665

Publications: The Land (16028)

Free Press & Economist
167 Main St. W.
PO Box 100
Shelburne, ON, Canada L0N 1S0
Phone: (519)925-2832
Fax: (519)925-5500

Publications: Free Press & Economist (36389)

Free Press Inc.
112 W State
PO Box 130
Nokomis, IL 62075-0130
Phone: (217)563-2115
Fax: (217)563-7464

Publications: Free Press-Progress (9294)

The Free Press Newspapers
PO Box 327
Wilmington, IL 60481
Phone: (815)476-7966

Publications: The Braidwood Journal (8686) • The Coal City Courant (9765)

Free Press Publishing Co.
1010 Cass St.
Tampa, FL 33606
Phone: (813)254-5888
Fax: (813)251-0511

Publications: Free Press (6765)

Free Scout Press, Inc.
PO Box E
Herman, MN 56248

Publications: Grant County Herald (15950)

Free Sons of Israel
24725 Jamaica Ave.
Bellerose, NY 11426-1541

Publications: Free Sons Reporter (20145)

Free Times Inc.
6904 N. Main St.
PO Box 8295
Columbia, SC 29202
Phone: (803)765-0707
Fax: (803)765-0727

Publications: Free Times (28550)

Freebies Publishing Co.
PO Box 21957
Santa Barbara, CA 93121-1957
Phone: (805)566-1225
Fax: (805)566-0305

Publications: Freebies (3640)

The Freeburg Tribune
820 S State
Box 98
Freeburg, IL 62243
Phone: (618)539-3320

Publications: The Freeburg Tribune (8897)

Freedom Communication Inc.
1310 S Commerce
PO Box 511
Harlingen, TX 78551
Phone: (956)430-6200
Fax: (956)430-6231

Publications: Valley Morning Star (30425)

Freedom Communications Inc.
1530 Ellis Lake Dr.
PO Box 431
Marysville, CA 95901-4269
Phone: (916)741-2345
Fax: (916)741-1195
Free: 800-831-2345

Publications: Appeal Democrat (2515)

Freedom Communications Inc.
115 E. Oak
PO Box 151
Porterville, CA 93257
Phone: (209)784-5000
Fax: (209)784-1689

Publications: Porterville Recorder (2862)

Freedom Communications, Inc.
95 Avenida Del Mar
San Clemente, CA 92672

Publications: Sun Post News (3103)

Freedom Communications Inc.
1225 Airport Rd.
PO Box 957
Destin, FL 32541
Phone: (850)837-0068
Fax: (850)654-5982

Publications: The Walton Log (6060)

Freedom Communications Inc.
200 Racetrack Rd. NW
Fort Walton Beach, FL 32548
Fax: (904)862-5230
Free: 800-755-1185

Publications: Northwest Florida Daily News (6121)

Freedom Communications Inc.
501 W. 11th St.
Panama City, FL 32402
Phone: (904)763-7621
Fax: (904)763-4636

Publications: News Herald (6556)

Freedom Communications Inc.
119 N. Green St.
PO Box 512
Crawfordsville, IN 47933
Phone: (317)362-1200
Fax: (317)364-5424
Free: 800-488-4414

Publications: Journal Review (9909)

Freedom Communications Inc.
988 N. Broadway
PO Box 1618
Greenville, MS 38702
Phone: (601)335-1155
Fax: (601)335-2860
Free: 800-844-1618

Publications: Delta Democrat Times (16631)

Freedom Communications Inc.
2500 E. Franklin Blvd.
PO Box 1538
Gastonia, NC 28053
Phone: (704)864-3291
Fax: (704)867-6988

Publications: Gaston Gazette (23907)

Freedom Communications Inc.
724 Bell Fork Rd.
PO Box 196
Jacksonville, NC 28546
Phone: (910)353-1171
Fax: (910)353-7316
Free: 800-659-2873

Publications: Daily News (24011)

Freedom Communications Inc.
3200 Wellons Blvd.
PO Box 1149
New Bern, NC 28562
Phone: (919)638-8101
Fax: (919)638-4664

Publications: Sun Journal (24097)

Freedom Communications Inc.
PO Box 351
Brownsville, TX 78522-0351
Phone: (210)542-4301
Fax: (210)542-0840

Publications: Brownsville Herald (29959)

Freedom Communications Inc.
PO Box 760
McAllen, TX 78505-0760
Phone: (210)686-4343
Fax: (210)686-4370

Publications: The Monitor (30785)

The Freedom Forum Media Studies Center
1207 18th Ave. S
Nashville, TN 37212-2807

Publications: Media Studies Journal (29471)

Freedom From Religion Foundation, Inc.
PO Box 750
Madison, WI 53701
Phone: (608)256-8900
Fax: (608)256-1116

Publications: Freethought Today (33943)

Freedom Newspapers
2055 S. Arizona Ave.
Yuma, AZ 85365
Phone: (928)783-3333
Fax: (928)782-7369

Publications: The Sun Visitor (1019)

Freedom Newspapers of New Mexico
902 S 1st St.
PO Drawer 1408
Tucumcari, NM 88401
Phone: (505)461-1952
Fax: (505)461-1965

Publications: Quay County Sun (19971)

Freedom Socialist Party
5018 Rainier Ave. S
Seattle, WA 98118
Phone: (206)722-2453
Fax: (206)723-7691

Publications: Freedom Socialist (32967)

Freedom Technology Media Group
17666 Fitch
Irvine, CA 92614-6022
Phone: (212)333-7600

Publications: Knowledge Management (2082)

Freedonia Group, Inc.
767 Beta Dr.
Cleveland, OH 44143
Phone: (440)684-9600
Fax: (440)646-0484
Free: 800-927-5900

Publications: Research Studies (24949)

Freemont Current
PO Box 1800
Idaho Falls, ID 83403-1800
Phone: (208)624-4500

Publications: Freemont Current (7863)

Freemont-Mills Beacon
PO Box 299
Tabor, IA 51653
Phone: (712)629-2255
Fax: (712)629-7405

Publications: Fremont-Mills Beacon Enterprise (11261)

Freeport News
129 Division St.
Freeport, MI 49325
Phone: (616)765-8511

Publications: Freeport News (15055) • Record (15056)

The Freer Press
309 East Hahl
Box 567
Freer, TX 78357
Phone: (361)394-7402
Fax: (361)394-5386
Free: 800-460-7402

Publications: The Freer Press (30367)

Freeville Publishing Co., Inc.
9 Main St.
PO Box 210
Freeville, NY 13068
Phone: (607)844-9119
Fax: (607)844-3381

Publications: Suburban Cortland-Ithaca Shopper (20627)

Freie Zeitung Inc.
500 S 31st St.
Kenilworth, NJ 07033
Phone: (908)245-7995
Fax: (908)245-7997

Publications: Freie Zeitung (19153)

French-Canadian Genealogical Society of Connecticut, Inc.
Box 928
Tolland, CT 06084-0928
Phone: (860)872-2597

Publications: Connecticut Maple Leaf (5175)

French Forum Publishers Inc.
108 Paddock Dr.
Nicholasville, KY 40356
Phone: (859)885-1446

Publications: French Forum (12324)

Fresh Cup Publishing Company
PO Box 14827
Portland, OR 97293-0827
Phone: (503)236-2587
Fax: (503)236-3165
Free: 800-868-5866

Publications: Fresh Cup Magazine (26479)

Friendly Woman
3960 Winding Way
Cincinnati, OH 45229
Phone: (513)861-4353

Publications: Friendly Woman (24799)

Friends of Animals, Inc.
777 Post Rd., Ste. 205
Darien, CT 06820-4721
Phone: (203)656-1522
Fax: (203)656-0267

Publications: Friends of Animals Actionline (4772)

Friends of the Earth
1025 Vermont Ave. NW
Washington, DC 20005
Phone: (202)783-7400
Fax: (202)783-0444

Publications: Atmosphere (5371)

Friends for Long Island's Heritage
1864 Muttontown Rd.
Syosset, NY 11791
Phone: (516)571-7600
Fax: (516)571-7623

Publications: Long Island Forum (23591)

Friends of the National Zoo
3001, National Zoological Park
Connecticut Ave., NW
Washington, DC 20008
Phone: (202)673-4711
Fax: (202)673-4738

Publications: ZooGoer (5875)

Friends of New Mystery
101 W 23rd St.
New York, NY 10011
Phone: (212)353-3495
Fax: (212)353-3495

Publications: New Mystery (22432)

Friends of the new renaissance, Inc.
26 Heath Rd., No. 11
Arlington, MA 02474-3645
Phone: (781)646-0118

Publications: the new renaissance (13821)

Friends United Meeting
101 Quaker Hill Dr.
Richmond, IN 47374-1980
Phone: (765)962-7573
Fax: (765)966-1293

Publications: Quaker Life (10421)

Friends of the Washington Review of the Arts, Inc.
PO Box 50132
Washington, DC 20091-0132
Phone: (202)638-0515

Publications: Washington Review (5853)

Frio-Nueces Publications Ltd.
PO Box 1208
Pearsall, TX 78061
Phone: (830)334-3643
Fax: (830)334-3647
Free: 800-843-7428

Publications: Frio-Nueces Current (30920)

Friona Stan
916 Main
Friona, TX 79035
Phone: (806)250-2211
Fax: (806)250-5127

Publications: The Friona Star (30370)

Frisbie Publishing
190 S Florida Ave.
Bartow, FL 33830
Phone: (863)533-4183
Fax: (863)533-0402

Publications: The Fort Meade Leader (6092) • The Polk County Democrat (5918)

Front Page Group, Inc.
2703 S Park Ave.
Lackawanna, NY 14218
Phone: (716)823-8222
Fax: (716)821-0550

Publications: The Front Page (20867) • South Buffalo News (20868)

Front Royal Publishing Co.
PO Box 1297
Front Royal, VA 22630
Phone: (540)635-4174
Fax: (540)635-7478

Publications: Warren Sentinel (32096)

Frost, Inc.
3121 S. Calhoun St.
Fort Wayne, IN 46807
Phone: (260)745-0552

Publications: Frost Illustrated (9969)

Frostbite Publications LLC
PO Box 220168
Anchorage, AK 99522
Phone: (907)258-6898
Fax: (907)258-4354
Free: 888-477-4568

Publications: Northern Pilot Magazine (529)

Frozen Food Digest Inc.
271 Madison Ave.
New York, NY 10016
Phone: (212)557-8600
Fax: (212)986-9868

Publications: Frozen Food Digest Magazine (21738)

FRSA
4111 Metric Dr.
PO Box 4850
Winter Park, FL 32793
Phone: (407)671-3772
Fax: (407)679-0010

Publications: Florida Forum (6879)

Fruita Times
217 E Aspen Ave.
Fruita, CO 81521-2238
Phone: (970)858-3924
Fax: (970)858-7658

Publications: Fruita Times (4458)

Fry Communications, Inc.
800 W. Church St.
Mechanicsburg, PA 17055
Phone: (717)766-0211
Fax: (717)691-5796

Publications: The Guide News (26994)

FTD Association
PO Box 7051
Downers Grove, IL 60515
Free: 800-383-4383

Publications: Florist (8785)

Fulda Free Press
PO Box 439
Fulda, MN 56131
Phone: (507)425-2303
Fax: (507)425-2501

Publications: Fulda Free Press (15914)

Ray Fullenkamp
PO Box 66
West Point, IA 52656
Phone: (319)837-6722
Fax: (319)372-3867

Publications: Donnellson Star (11324) • West Point Bee (11325)

Fulton County Historical Society, Inc.
37 East 375 North
Rochester, IN 46975-8384
Phone: (574)223-4436

Publications: Fulton County Images (10430)

Fulton County News
Box 635
McConnellsburg, PA 17233
Phone: (717)485-3811
Fax: (717)485-5187

Publications: Fulton County News (27230)

Fulton Democrat
165 W Lincoln
PO Box 191
Lewistown, IL 61542
Phone: (309)547-3055
Fax: (309)543-6844

Publications: Fulton Democrat (9075)

Fulton Newspapers, Inc.
117 Oneida St.
Fulton, NY 13069
Phone: (315)598-6397

Publications: The Valley News (20631) • The Valley Shopper (20632)

The Fulton Patriot
PO Box 299
Fulton, NY 13069
Phone: (315)592-2459

Publications: The Fulton Patriot (20630)

The Fulton Press
PO Box 30
Fulton, IL 61252
Phone: (815)589-2424

Publications: Fulton Press (8902) • Whiteside Shopper (8903)

Fulton Publishing Co.
Box 1200
Fulton, KY 42041
Phone: (270)472-3439
Fax: (270)472-1129

Publications: The Fulton Leader (12084)

The Fulton Sun Gazette
115 E. 5th St.
PO Box 550
Fulton, MO 65251-0541
Phone: (573)642-7272
Fax: (573)642-0656

Publications: The Fulton Sun (17076)

Fun Publications, Inc.
225 Cattle Baron Park Dr.
Fort Worth, TX 76108
Phone: (817)448-9863
Fax: (817)448-9843

Publications: Master Collector (30347)

Fundy Group Publications Ltd.
2 2nd St.
PO Box 128
Yarmouth, NS, Canada B5A 4B1
Phone: (902)742-7111
Fax: (902)742-2311
Free: 800-717-4442

Publications: Advance (35586) • The Coast Guard (35604) • Yarmouth Vanguard (35624)

Funny Times, Inc.
PO Box 18530
Cleveland Heights, OH 44118
Phone: (216)371-8600
Fax: (216)371-8696
Free: 800-811-5267

Publications: Funny Times (24993)

Numbers cited after listings are entry numbers rather than page numbers.

Furman University
3300 Poinsett Hwy.
PO Box 28584
Greenville, SC 29613
Phone: (864)294-2077
Fax: (864)294-3339

Publications: The Paladin (28625)

Futura Publishing Company Inc.
135 Bedford Rd.
Armonk, NY 10504-0418
Phone: (914)273-1014
Fax: (914)273-1015
Free: 800-877-8761

Publications: Echocardiography (20075) • Journal of Cardiac Surgery (20084) • Journal of Cardiovascular Electrophysiology (20085) • Journal of Interventional Cardiology (20086) • Noninvasive Electrocardiology (20089) • PACE: Pacing and Clinical Electrophysiology (20090)

Future Business Leaders of America - Phi Beta Lambda, Inc.
1912 Association Dr.
Reston, VA 20191-1591
Phone: (703)860-3334
Fax: (703)758-0749

Publications: P.B.L. Business Leader (32409)

Futures Magazine
833 W. Jackson 7th Fl.
Chicago, IL 60607
Phone: (312)977-0999
Fax: (312)977-1042
Free: 800-972-9316

Publications: Futures Magazine (8383)

Futurific, Inc., Foundation for Optimisim
305 Madison Ave.
Concourse 10-B
New York, NY 10165
Phone: (212)297-0502
Fax: (212)297-0502
Free: 800-696-2836

Publications: FUTURIFIC (21744)

F.W. Gray & Associates Ltd.
Box 279
801 Canal St., No. 279
Ottawa, IL 61350-4901
Phone: (815)433-5595
Fax: (815)433-5596
Free: 800-527-4729

Publications: Thrif-T-Nickel Weekly News-Tab (9391) • Town & Country (9596)

G J USA Publishing
375 Lexington Ave.
New York, NY 10017-5514
Phone: (212)499-2000

Publications: Child (21409) • Family Circle (21677) • Fitness Magazine (21705) • McCall's (22301) • McCall's Prime Time (22302) • Parents Baby (22526) • Parents Expecting (22527) • Parents Magazine (22528) • Parents Pregnancy (22529) • Ser Padres (22732) • Target The Family (22815) • YM (22950)

G & M Communications
1050 Illinois Route 63, Ste. 200
Bensenville, IL 60106-1096
Phone: (847)588-3333
Fax: (847)647-7055

Publications: Contractors Guide (8065)

Gadsden County Times
PO Box 790
Quincy, FL 32353-0790
Phone: (850)627-7649
Fax: (850)627-7191

Publications: Gadsden County Times (6612)

The Gadsden Times, Inc.
401 Locust St.
PO Box 188
Gadsden, AL 35901-3737
Phone: (205)549-2000
Fax: (205)549-2105

Publications: Gadsden Times (234)

The Gaffney Ledger
1604 Baker Blvd.
PO Box 670
Gaffney, SC 29342
Phone: (864)489-1131
Fax: (864)487-7667

Publications: The Gaffney Ledger (28615)

The Gage Record
PO Box 236
Arnett, OK 73832
Phone: (405)885-7788

Publications: The Gage Record (25751)

Gahan Publishing Company Inc.
217 N Oakland Ave.
Oakland, NE 68045
Phone: (402)685-5624
Fax: (402)685-5625

Publications: Oakland Independent (18186)

Gaines County News
1026 Nambe St.
Hobbs, NM 88240-0971

Publications: Gaines County News (19863)

The Gainesville Iguana
PO Box 14712
Gainesville, FL 32604

Publications: The Gainesville Iguana (6141)

The Gainesville Sun
2700 SW 13th St.
Gainesville, FL 32608
Phone: (352)378-1411
Fax: (904)338-3128
Free: 800-443-9493

Publications: The Gainesville Sun (6142)

Galaxy Publishing
3413 3rd St. N.
St. Cloud, MN 56302
Phone: (320)252-4400
Fax: (320)252-1031

Publications: The Shopping News (16347)

Galena Gazette Publications, Inc.
716 S. Bench St.
Galena, IL 61036-0319
Phone: (815)777-0019
Fax: (815)777-3809
Free: 800-373-6397

Publications: Galena Gazette and Advertiser (8904)

Galena Times
511 Main St.
Galena, KS 66739
Phone: (620)783-5034
Fax: (620)783-1388

Publications: Galena Sentinel-Times (11448)

Galesburg Printing and Publishing Co.
214 Exchange St.
Galesburg, IL 61401
Phone: 800-747-7181
Fax: (309)342-5171

Publications: Galva News (8911)

Galilean Electrodynamics
141 Rhinecliff St.
Arlington, MA 02476-7331
Phone: (781)643-3155
Fax: (781)646-8114

Publications: Galilean Electrodynamics (13819)

Gallatin County News
211 3rd St.
Box 435
Warsaw, KY 41095
Phone: (859)567-5051
Fax: (859)567-6397

Publications: Gallatin County News (12432)

Gallatin News Examiner
1 Examiner Ct.
Gallatin, TN 37066
Phone: (615)452-2561
Fax: (615)452-9110

Publications: Star News (29220)

Gallatin Publishing Co.
203 N Main
PO Box 37
Gallatin, MO 64640
Phone: (660)663-2154
Fax: (660)663-2498

Publications: Moila Temple Bulletin (17393) • North Missourian (17081)

Gallaudet Research Institute
800 Florida Ave. NE
HMB S-439
Washington, DC 20002-3695
Phone: (202)651-5530
Fax: (202)651-5860

Publications: National Genealogical Society Quarterly (5671)

Gallup Independent Co.
500 N. 9th St.
PO Box 1210
Gallup, NM 87305
Phone: (505)863-6811
Fax: (505)722-5750

Publications: The Independent (19856)

Gallup Organization
901 F St., NW
Washington, DC 20004
Phone: (202)715-3030
Fax: (202)715-3042
Free: 877-242-5587

Publications: Gallup Poll Tuesday Briefing (5504)

GAMA International Journal
2901 Telestar Ct., Ste. 140
Falls Church, VA 22042-1205
Phone: (703)770-8184
Fax: (703)770-8182
Free: 800-345-2687

Publications: GAMA International Journal (32046)

Gambit Communications
Morial Convention Cenetr
New Orleans, LA 70119
Phone: (504)486-5900
Fax: (504)483-3156

Publications: Gambit Weekly (12731)

Gambling Times Inc.
3883 W. Century Blvd., Ste. 608
Inglewood, CA 90303-1003
Phone: (310)674-3365
Fax: (310)674-3205

Publications: Gambling Times (2071)

Game Revolution
740 Gilman St.
Berkeley, CA 94710

Publications: Game Revolution (1523)

Gamit Enterprises, Inc.
1917 South St.
Geneva, IL 60134
Phone: (630)845-9481
Fax: (630)845-9483
Free: 877-747-1625

Publications: Appliance Service News (9561)

Gammon, LLC
3565 Airway Dr.
Santa Rosa, CA 95403
Phone: (707)575-8282
Fax: (707)546-7368

Publications: North Bay Biz (3731)

Gannett
950 W. Basin Rd.
PO Box 15505
New Castle, DE 19720
Phone: (302)324-2898
Fax: (302)324-5518
Free: 800-235-9100

Publications: The News Journal (5267)

Gannett Co.
PO Box 357
Granville, OH 43023-0357
Phone: (740)587-3397
Fax: (740)587-3398

Publications: Community Booster (25220) • Granville Sentinel (25223)

Gannett Co., Inc.
35 Kennedy Blvd.
East Brunswick, NJ 08816
Phone: (732)246-5500
Fax: (732)937-6046
Free: 800-822-9770

Publications: Asbury Park Press (18779) • The Home News & Tribune (18781)

Gannett Co., Inc.
7950 Jones Branch Dr.
Mc Lean, VA 22107
Phone: (703)854-6000

Publications: Argus Leader (32240) • Battle Creek Enquirer (14791) • The Bellingham Herald (32242) • Chronicle-Tribune (10287) • The Cincinnati Enquirer (24785) • The Clarion Ledger (16695) • Commercial-News (8701) • Community News (20464) • The Courier-News (19572) • Courier-Post (18733) • Delaware Beachcomber (5283) • Delaware Coast Press (5284) • Democrat and Chronicle (23222) • The Des Moines Register (10781) • The Desert Sun (2758) • The Detroit News (14927) • Fort Collins Coloradoan (4431) • Great Falls Tribune (17799) • Hattiesburg American (16661) • The Herald-Dispatch (32245) • The Idaho Statesman (7811) • The Indianapolis Star (10133) • Iowa City Press Citizen (10974) • The Jackson Sun (32247) • Madison County Herald (16583) • Mount Vernon Daily Argus (21103) • The News-Examiner (29203) • The Olympian (32251) • Ossining Citizen Register (32252) • Poughkeepsie Journal (23149) • Poultry and Egg Marketing (7293) • Poultry Times (7294) • Press & Sun-Bulletin (20211) • Public Opinion (26769) • Reno Gazette-Journal (18423) • Rockford Register Star (9532) • Rockland Journal-News (32254) • Star Advocate (6821) • Tarrytown Daily News (32569) • The Tennessean (32256) • This Week (27160) • USA Today (32257) • USA Weekend (32259) • Valley Scene (32260) • Wausau Daily Herald (32261) • White Plains Reporter Dispatch (32262) • Yonkers Herald Statesman (32263)

Gannett Satellite Information Network
1700 Cedar St.
PO Box 1230
Fremont, OH 43420
Phone: (419)332-5511
Fax: (419)332-9750
Free: 800-766-6397

Publications: The News-Messenger (25202)

Gannon University
University Sq.
Box 2142
Erie, PA 16541-0001
Phone: (814)871-7294
Fax: (814)871-7208
Free: 800-GAN-NONU

Publications: The Gannon Knight (26899)

Garber-Billing News
516 Main St.
Box 9
Garber, OK 73738
Phone: (580)863-2240

Publications: Garber-Billings News (25842)

Gardena Valley News
16417 S. Western Ave.
PO Box 219
Gardena, CA 90247
Phone: (310)329-6351
Fax: (310)329-7501

Publications: Gardena Valley News (2000)

Gardening Life Publishing
511 King St. W., Ste. 120
Toronto, ON, Canada M5V 2Z4
Phone: (416)593-0204
Fax: (416)591-1630

Publications: Gardening Life (36599)

Gardenwise Magazine
4180 Lougheed Hwy., 4th Fl.
Burnaby, BC, Canada V5C 6A7
Phone: (604)299-7311
Fax: (604)299-9188
Free: 800-663-0518

Publications: Gardenwise Magazine (34898)

The Gardner News, Inc.
309 Central St.
Gardner, MA 01440
Phone: (978)632-8000
Fax: (978)630-2231

Publications: The Gardner News (14209)

Gardner Publications, Inc.
6915 Valley Ave.
Cincinnati, OH 45244-3029
Phone: (513)527-8977
Fax: (513)527-8801
Free: 800-950-8020

Publications: Automotive Design and Production (24776) • Automotive Design and Production (24777) • Automotive Finishing (24778) • Metalworking Insiders' Report (20920) • Modern Machine Shop (24810) • Plastics Technology (22564) • Products Finishing (24813)

Garfield County News
120 N Main
PO Box 127
Tropic, UT 84776
Phone: (435)679-8730
Fax: (435)679-8847

Publications: Garfield County News (31482)

Gargano Communications, Inc.
PO Box 157
Humboldt, IA 50548
Phone: (515)332-2514

Publications: Humboldt Independent (10957)

Garlinghouse Inc.
174 Oakwood Dr.
Glastonbury, CT 06033-2432
Phone: (860)659-5667
Fax: (860)659-5692
Free: 800-895-3715

Publications: Garlinghouse Home Plans Guide (4868)

Garner, Inc.
905c 5th Ave.
PO Box 466
Garner, NC 27529
Phone: (919)772-7751
Fax: (919)779-7824

Publications: Garner News (23904)

Garner Leader and Signal
365 State St.
Garner, IA 50438
Phone: (641)923-2684
Fax: (641)923-2685

Publications: Garner Leader and Signal (10919)

Garnet Valley Press
PO Box 1001
Glen Mills, PA 19342
Phone: (610)358-1516
Fax: (610)558-3406

Publications: Garnet Valley Press (26945)

Garnett Publishing, Inc.
PO Box 409
Garnett, KS 66032
Phone: (785)448-2500
Fax: (785)448-6253

Publications: Eastern Kansas Senior Star (11458) • Review (11459)

Garretson Weekly
512 Main Ave.
Box 310
Garretson, SD 57030-0310
Phone: (605)594-6315
Fax: (605)594-3442

Publications: Garretson Weekly (28858)

The Garrett Clipper
106 S Randolph St.
PO Box 59
Garrett, IN 46738
Phone: (260)357-4123
Fax: (260)357-4124

Publications: The Garrett Clipper (10014)

Garrett Publishing Co., Inc.
111 S Church St.
PO Box 929
Lockhart, TX 78644-0360
Phone: (512)398-4886
Fax: (512)398-4888

Publications: Lockhart Post-Register (30703)

Gary New Crusader
1549 Broadway
Gary, IN 46407
Phone: (219)885-4357
Fax: (219)885-4359

Publications: Gary New Crusader (10015)

Gas Industries & E.A. News Inc.
PO Box 558
Park Ridge, IL 60068
Phone: (224)693-3682
Fax: (224)696-3445

Publications: Gas Industries (30159)

Gas Technology Institute
1700 S. Mount Prospect Rd.
Des Plaines, IL 60018
Phone: (847)768-0662
Fax: (847)768-0669

Publications: gasLine (8762)

Gastar Roca Inc.
PO Box 9023831
San Juan, PR 00902-3831
Phone: (809)721-2300
Fax: (809)725-8422

Publications: El Vocero de Puerto Rico (28294)

Gaston-Lincoln Genealogical Society
Box 584
Mount Holly, NC 28120

Publications: Footprints in Time (24084)

Gateway Press
610 Beatty Rd.
PO Box 6429
Monroeville, PA 15146-1502
Phone: (412)856-7400
Fax: (412)856-7954

Publications: Advance Leader Star (27274) • Cranberry Star (27277) • The Progress Star (27284) • The Record Star (27295)

Gateway Publications
610 Beatty Rd.
Monroeville, PA 15146
Phone: (412)856-7400
Fax: (412)856-7954

Publications: Coraopolis Record Star (27276) • Moon Record Star (27278) • Murrysville Star (27279) • Norwin Star Star (27280) • Oakmont Advance Leader (27281) • Penn Hills Progress Star (27282) • Plum Advance Leader Star (27283) • Sewickley Herald Star (27285) • Signal Item Star (27286) • South Hills Record (27845) • Times-Express Star (27287) • Woodland Hills Progress (27288)

Gateway Publishing
PO Box 248
Eatonville, WA 98328
Phone: (360)832-4411
Fax: (360)832-6606

Publications: South Pierce County Dispatch (32744)

Gault Publications, Inc.
Box 10
Boody, IL 62514
Phone: (217)865-2332
Fax: (217)865-2334

Publications: Full Cry (8093)

Gauntlet
5307 Arroyo St.
Colorado Springs, CO 80922-3625

Publications: Gauntlet (4248)

Gauntlet Publications Society/University of Calgary
Calgary, AB, Canada T2N 1N4
Phone: (403)220-7750
Fax: (403)282-3218

Publications: The Gauntlet (34645)

Gavea-Brown Publications
Brown University
Dept. of Portuguese and Brazilian Studies
Box O
Providence, RI 02912
Phone: (401)863-3042
Fax: (401)863-7261

Publications: Gavea-Brown (28398)

Gay Alliance of Genesee Valley, Inc.
179 Atlantic Ave.
Rochester, NY 14607-1255
Phone: (585)244-9030
Fax: (585)244-8246

Publications: Empty Closet (23224)

Gay & Lesbian Review, Inc.
Box 180300
Boston, MA 02118
Phone: (617)421-0082

Publications: Gay and Lesbian Review Worldwide (13895)

Gayme
PO Box 15645
Kenmore Sta.
Boston, MA 02215
Phone: (617)695-8015

Publications: Gayme (13896)

The Gazette
1171 Main St.
East Hartford, CT 06108
Phone: (860)289-6468
Fax: (860)289-6469

Publications: The Gazette (4778)

Gazette
Box 7
Neola, IA 51559-0007
Phone: (712)485-2276
Fax: (712)485-2277

Publications: Gazette (11192)

Gazette
PO Box 370
Red Lake Falls, MN 56750
Phone: (218)253-2594
Fax: (218)253-4114

Publications: Gazette (16292)

The Gazette
1518 Silver St.
Box 127
Ashland, NE 68003-0127
Phone: (402)944-3397
Fax: (402)944-3398

Publications: The Ashland Gazette (17937)

The Gazette
160 Cleveland Dr.
PO Box 810
Croton On Hudson, NY 10520
Phone: (914)271-2088
Fax: (914)271-4219

Publications: The Gazette (20515)

The Gazette
PO Box 151
29 Lackawanna Ave.
Norwich, NY 13815
Phone: (607)334-3276
Fax: (607)334-8273
Free: 800-836-6780

Publications: The Gazette (23021)

Gazette Daily Inc.
1001 Virginia St. E
PO Box 2993
Charleston, WV 25301
Phone: (304)348-5100
Fax: (304)348-5133
Free: 800-982-6397

Publications: Charleston Gazette (33268)

The Gazette Newspapers
13 E. Patrick St.
Frederick, MD 21701
Phone: (301)607-1015
Fax: (301)682-4046

Publications: Aspen Hill Gazette (13506) • Burtonsville Gazette (13507) • Business Gazette (13508) •

College Park Gazette (13509) • Damascus Courier-Gazette (13481) • Frederick Gazette (13511) • The Gaithersburg Gazette (13540) • The Germantown Gazette (13553) • Kensington Gazette (13515) • Montgomery Village Gazette (13516) • New Market/Urbana Gazette (13517) • North Potomac Gazette (13518) • Poolesville Gazette (13519) • Silver Spring Gazette (13521) • Takoma Park (13522) • Walkersville/Thurmont Gazette (13525)

Gazette Newspapers
2899 Hubbard Rd.
Madison, OH 44057-2933

Publications: The Free Enterprise (25215)

Gazette Newspapers, Inc.
5225 E. Second St.
Long Beach, CA 90803
Phone: (562)433-2000
Fax: (562)434-8826

Publications: Downtown Gazette (2166) • Grunion Gazette (2168)

Gazette Newspapers, Inc.
PO Box 482
Troy, MI 48099
Phone: (248)524-4868
Fax: (248)524-9140

Publications: Troy-Somerset Gazette (15643)

Gazette North Island
7305 Market
Port Hardy, BC, Canada V0N 2P1
Phone: (250)949-6225
Fax: (250)949-7655

Publications: North Island Gazette (35051) • North Island Televiewer (35052)

Gazette-Patriot
428 N Main St.
PO Box 231
Carrollton, IL 62016-0231
Phone: (217)942-3626
Fax: (217)942-3699

Publications: Gazette-Patriot (8159)

Gazette-Post-News
PO Box 220
Carnduff, SK, Canada S0C 0S0
Phone: (306)482-3252
Fax: (306)482-3373

Publications: Gazette-Post-News (37459)

Gazette Press Ltd.
25 Chisholm Ave.
PO Box 263
St. Albert, AB, Canada T8N 1N3
Phone: (780)460-5500
Fax: (780)460-8220

Publications: The Alberta Game Warden (34841) • St. Albert Gazette (34842)

Gazette Printers
PO Box 11
Kendrick, ID 83537
Phone: (208)289-5731
Fax: (208)289-4656

Publications: Gazette News (7886)

Gazette Printing Co., Inc.
34 S Chestnut St.
Jefferson, OH 44047
Phone: (440)576-9115
Fax: (440)576-4337
Free: 800-860-2775

Publications: The Courier (Conneaut) (25261) • The Gazette (25262) • The Lake County Gazette (25263) • The New Senior Life Styles Vista (25264) • Pymatuning Area News (24611) • The Sentinel (25265) • Shores News (25500) • The Tribune (25266) • The Valley News (25267)

Gazette Publishing Co.
Box 280
Baldur, MB, Canada R0K 0B0
Phone: (204)535-2127
Fax: (204)535-2350

Publications: Gazette-News (35251)

Gazette Publishing Co.
97 N Main St.
PO Box 180
Swanton, OH 43558
Phone: (419)826-3580
Fax: (419)826-3590

Publications: The Swanton Enterprise (25553)

Gazette Publishing Co.
PO Box 38
Wellington, OH 44090
Fax: (216)607-3172

Publications: Wellington Enterprise (25628)

Gazette Publishing Co.
PO Box 671
Bedford, PA 15522
Phone: (814)623-1151
Fax: (814)623-5055
Free: 800-242-4250

Publications: The Shoppers Guide (26914)

Gazette Publishing Co., Inc.
107 N. Sandusky St.
Bellevue, OH 44811
Phone: (419)483-4190
Fax: (419)483-3737

Publications: The Bellevue Gazette (24669) • The Clyde Enterprise (24996) • News-Tribune (25446) • The Shopping News (25449)

Gazette Publishing Co., Inc.
PO Box 367
Bellevue, OH 44811
Phone: (419)483-7410
Fax: (419)483-3737

Publications: Bucyrus RFD News (24671)

Gazette Shopping Guide
PO Box 708
Tifton, GA 31793
Phone: (912)382-4321
Fax: (912)387-7322

Publications: Gazette Shopping Guide (7595)

Gazette-Times
147 W Willow
PO Box 337
Heppner, OR 97836
Phone: (541)676-9228
Fax: (541)676-9211

Publications: Gazette-Times (26367)

The Gazette Virginian
PO Box 337
Chase City, VA 23924
Fax: (804)372-3911

Publications: The News-Progress (31959)

Gazette Virginian
PO Box 524
South Boston, VA 24592
Phone: (434)572-3945
Fax: (434)572-1173

Publications: Gazette Virginian (32530)

GBSC of North Carolina
603 S Wilmington St.
Raleigh, NC 27601
Phone: (919)821-7466
Fax: (919)836-0061

Publications: Baptist Informer (24125)

GC Publishing Co., Inc.
1 University Dr., Ste. 200
Hackensack, NJ 07601
Phone: (201)488-1800
Fax: (201)488-7357

Publications: Modern Grocer (18852)

Geary Star
114 W Main
Geary, OK 73040
Phone: (405)884-2424
Fax: (405)884-2424

Publications: Star (25843)

Geist
1014 Homer St., No. 103
Vancouver, BC, Canada V6B 2W9
Phone: (604)681-9161
Fax: (604)669-8250
Free: 888-434-7834

Publications: Geist (35143)

Gem Publishers, Inc.
2414 Morris Ave.
Union, NJ 07083
Phone: (908)964-5060
Fax: (908)964-1472

Publications: New Jersey Beverage Journal (19684)

Gemini Publications
549 Ottawa Ave. NW, Ste. 201
Grand Rapids, MI 49503-1444
Phone: (616)459-4545
Fax: (616)459-4800

Publications: Grand Rapids Magazine (15095)

Gemological Institute of America
Robert Mouawad Campus
5345 Armada Dr.
Carlsbad, CA 92008
Phone: (760)603-4502
Fax: (760)603-4595
Free: 800-421-7250

Publications: Gems & Gemology (1665)

GEMS L.L.C.
3 E Main
PO Box 85
Salina, UT 84654
Phone: (801)528-3111
Fax: (801)528-7634

Publications: The Salina Sun (31336)

Genealogical Society of Hispanic America
Box 9606
Denver, CO 80209-0606
Phone: (720)564-0631
Fax: (720)390-1486

Publications: Nuestras Raices/Our Roots (4345)

General Accounting Office
Rm. 7826
441 G St. NW
Washington, DC 20548-0001
Phone: (202)512-4707
Fax: (202)512-4021

Publications: International Journal of Government Auditing (5554)

General Assembly Council, Presbyterian Church (U.S.A.)
100 Witherspoon St., Rm. 5630
Louisville, KY 40202-1396
Phone: (502)569-5770
Fax: (502)569-8632

Publications: Monday Morning (12231)

General Assembly Cumberland Presbyterian Church in America
226 Church St.
Huntsville, AL 35801
Phone: (256)536-7481
Fax: (256)536-7482

Publications: The Cumberland Flag (268)

General Board of Church and Society, The United Methodist Church
100 Maryland Ave. NE
Washington, DC 20002
Phone: (202)548-4002
Fax: (202)488-1617
Free: 800-967-0880

Publications: Christian Social Action (5412)

General Church of the New Jerusalem
PO Box 277
Bryn Athyn, PA 19009
Phone: (215)947-6225
Fax: (215)947-3078

Publications: New Church Life (26739)

General Communications, Inc.
100 Garfield St.
Denver, CO 80206
Phone: (303)322-6400
Fax: (303)322-0627

Publications: Law Enforcement Product News (4338) • Public Safety Product News (4350)

General Conference of Seventh-Day Adventists
12501 Old Columbia Pike
Silver Spring, MD 20904
Phone: (301)680-6000
Fax: (301)680-6502

Publications: Adventist Review (13722) • Ministry (13739)

General Council of the Assemblies of God
1445 N. Boonville Ave.
Springfield, MO 65802-1894
Phone: (417)862-9533
Fax: (417)862-0416

Publications: Christian Education Counselor (17593) • Club Connection (17594) • Enrichment Journal (17597) • High Adventure (17602) • Mountain Movers (17607) • Today's Pentecostal Evangel (17614) • Woman's Touch (17618)

General Federation of Women's Clubs
1734 N St. NW
Washington, DC 20036
Phone: (202)347-3168
Fax: (202)835-0246

Publications: GFWC Clubwoman Magazine (5514)

General Learning Communications
900 Skokie Blvd., Ste. 200
Northbrook, IL 60062
Phone: (847)205-3000
Fax: (847)564-8197

Publications: In Motion (9317)

General Media
11 Penn Plaza, 12th Fl.
New York, NY 10001
Phone: (212)702-6000
Fax: (212)702-6262

Publications: Forum (21729) • Penthouse Variations (22539)

General Mills
One General Mills Blvd.
Minneapolis, MN 55426
Phone: (763)764-3155
Fax: (763)764-7995

Publications: Pillsbury Classic Cookbooks (16119)

General Society of Mayflower Descendants
PO Box 3297
Plymouth, MA 02361
Phone: (508)746-5058

Publications: The Mayflower Quarterly (19217)

Genesee County Herald
PO Box 127
Mount Morris, MI 48458
Phone: (810)686-3842
Fax: (810)686-9181

Publications: Genesee County Herald (15373)

Genesee Valley Parent Magazine
1 Grove St., Ste. 204
Pittsford, NY 14534
Phone: (585)264-9955
Fax: (716)264-0647

Publications: Genesee Valley Parent Magazine (23097)

Genesee Valley Publications Inc.
1471 Rte. 15
Avon, NY 14414
Phone: (716)226-8111
Fax: (716)226-3390

Publications: Genesee Valley (20109)

Geneseeway Shopper
113 Main St.
Dansville, NY 14437
Phone: (716)335-2271
Fax: (716)335-6957

Publications: Geneseeway Shopper (20518)

Genesis Publications, Inc.
40 Violet Ave.
Poughkeepsie, NY 12601
Phone: (914)454-7420

Publications: Genesis (19403)

Genessee Country Express
113 Main St.
Dansville, NY 14437
Phone: (585)335-2121
Fax: (585)335-6957

Publications: Genessee Country Express (20519)

Genetics Society of America
9650 Rockville Pke.
Bethesda, MD 20814-3998
Phone: (301)571-1825
Fax: (301)530-7079

Publications: Genetics (27791)

Geneva College
3200 College Ave.
Beaver Falls, PA 15010
Phone: (724)846-5100
Fax: (724)847-5017
Free: 800-847-8255

Publications: Geneva Magazine (26685)

Geneva Publications Inc.
PO Box 160
Geneva, AL 36340
Phone: (334)684-2287
Fax: (334)684-3099

Publications: Geneva County Reaper (239) • Hartford News-Herald (240) • Ledger (241)

Genki Publishing, Inc.
476 Commonwealth Ave.
Boston, MA 02215-2712
Phone: (617)262-9390
Fax: (617)262-8036

Publications: J Magazine (13909)

GenLaw Resources
PO Box 9187
Gaithersburg, MD 20898-9187

Publications: Western Maryland Genealogy (13551)

Genoa Leader-Times
PO Box 429
Genoa, NE 68640
Phone: (402)993-2205

Publications: Genoa Leader-Times (18017)

Genre
University of Oklahoma
Dept. of English
760 Van Vleet Oval
Norman, OK 73019
Phone: (405)325-2908

Publications: Genre (25934)

The Gentle Revolution Press
810 Gleneagles Ct., Ste. 305
Towson, MD 21286
Phone: (410)337-5400
Fax: (410)337-3544

Publications: The IN-REPORT (13759)

Geological Society of America Inc.
PO Box 9140
Boulder, CO 80301
Phone: (303)447-2020
Fax: (303)357-1070
Free: 800-472-1988

Publications: Abstracts with Programs (4154) • Geological Society of America Bulletin (4168) • Geology (4169)

George County Times
PO Box 238
Lucedale, MS 39452
Phone: (601)947-2967
Fax: (601)947-6828

Publications: George County Times (16753)

Numbers cited after listings are entry numbers rather than page numbers.

George J. Foster Co.
PO Box D
Sanford, ME 04073
Phone: (207)324-5986
Fax: (207)490-1431

Publications: The Sanford News (13049)

George Mason Law Review
3401 N Fairfax Dr.
Arlington, VA 22201
Phone: (703)993-8161
Fax: (703)993-8148

Publications: George Mason University School of Law (31794)

George Mason University
Dept. of Economics
Fairfax, VA 22030
Phone: (703)993-1155
Fax: (703)993-1133

Publications: Journal of Labor Research (32022)

George Mason University
4400 University Dr.
Fairfax, VA 22030-4444
Phone: (703)993-1099
Fax: (703)993-1096

Publications: Women and Language (32034)

George Mason University
4400 University Dr., MSN 3A2
Fairfax, VA 22030-4444
Phone: (703)993-1246
Fax: (703)993-1251

Publications: Journal of Social History (32024) •
Phoebe (32026)

The George Meany Memorial Archives
10000 New Hampshire Ave.
Silver Spring, MD 20903
Phone: (301)431-5457
Fax: (301)431-0385

Publications: Labor's Heritage (13735)

The George P. Stewart Printing, Inc.
2901 N Tacoma Ave.
PO Box 18499
Indianapolis, IN 46218-2700
Phone: (317)924-5143
Fax: (317)924-5148

Publications: The Indianapolis Recorder (10132)

George Sand Studies
Romance Languages
Tufts University
Medford, MA 02155
Phone: (617)627-2626
Fax: (617)627-3944

Publications: George Sand Studies (14322)

The George Washington Law Review
2008 G St. NW, 2nd Fl.
Washington, DC 20052
Phone: (202)676-3868
Fax: (202)676-3876

Publications: The George Washington Law Review (5508)

George Washington University
2140 G St. NW
Washington, DC 20052
Phone: (202)994-7079
Fax: (202)994-1309

Publications: The GW Hatchet (5521)

Georgetown College
400 E College St.
Georgetown, KY 40324
Phone: (502)863-8009
Fax: (502)868-8888

Publications: The Georgetonian (12087)

Georgetown Family Center
4400 MacArthur Blvd. NW, Ste. 103
Washington, DC 20007
Phone: (202)965-4400
Fax: (202)965-1765

Publications: Family Systems (5490)

Georgetown Newspapers, Inc.
1481 Cherry Blossom Way
Georgetown, KY 40324-8953
Phone: (502)863-1111
Fax: (502)863-6296

Publications: The Georgetown-News Graphic (12088)

Georgetown Time
PO Box 2778
Georgetown, SC 29442-0546
Phone: (803)546-4148
Fax: (803)546-2395

Publications: Georgetown Time (28618)

Georgetown University
413 Leavey Center
Washington, DC 20057-1066
Phone: (202)687-6780
Fax: (202)687-6763

Publications: The Georgetown Voice (5511)

Georgetown University
421 Leavey Student Center
PO Box 571065
Washington, DC 20057-1065
Phone: (202)687-3415
Fax: (202)687-2741

Publications: The HOYA (5533)

Georgetown University
2115 Wisconsin Ave., Ste. 500
Washington, DC 20007
Phone: (202)687-4317
Fax: (202)687-2311

Publications: Georgetown Magazine (5510)

Georgetown University Law Center
Office of Journal Administration
Law & Policy in International Business
Washington, DC 20001
Phone: (202)662-9000

Publications: American Criminal Law Review (5325)

Georgetown University Law Center
600 New Jersey Ave. NW
Washington, DC 20001
Phone: (202)662-9690
Fax: (202)662-9313

Publications: Law and Policy in International Business (5633)

Georgia Academy of Science
Department of Science
Georgia Perimeter College
Lawrenceville, GA 30043
Phone: (678)407-5044

Publications: Georgia Journal of Science (7367)

Georgia Association of Future Farmers of America
Dept. of Vocational Education
Twin Towers East, Rm. 1766
Atlanta, GA 30334
Phone: (404)656-2562
Fax: (404)651-8984

Publications: Georgia Future Farmer (7012)

Georgia Botanical Society
7575 Rico Rd.
Palmetto, GA 30268
Phone: (770)463-4227

Publications: Tipularia (7478)

The Georgia Bulletin
680 W Peachtree St. NW
Atlanta, GA 30308-1984
Phone: (404)877-5500
Fax: (404)877-5505

Publications: The Georgia Bulletin (7011)

Georgia College Alumni Association, Inc.
CBX 097
Milledgeville, GA 31061
Phone: (478)445-6804
Fax: (478)445-6795
Free: 800-342-0471

Publications: Georgia College & State University Connection (7434)

Georgia Dental Hygienists' Association
1181 Burnett Rd.
Byron, GA 31008

Publications: Flossline (7147)

Georgia Dept. of Agriculture
Agriculture Bldg., Capitol Sq., Rm. 226
19 Martin Luther King Jr. Dr.
Atlanta, GA 30334-4250
Phone: (404)656-3682
Fax: (404)651-7957
Free: 800-282-5852

Publications: Farmers & Consumers Market Bulletin (7006)

Georgia Dept. of Veterans Service
Floyd Veterans Bldg., 970-E
Atlanta, GA 30334
Phone: (404)656-5933
Fax: (404)656-7006

Publications: Veterans' Bulletin (7058)

Georgia Electric Membership Corp.
PO Box 1707
Tucker, GA 30085
Phone: (770)270-6950
Fax: (770)270-6995
Free: 800-544-4362

Publications: GEORGIA Magazine (7610)

Georgia Farm Bureau Federation
1620 Bass Rd.
Macon, GA 31210
Phone: (478)474-8411

Publications: Georgia Farm Bureau News (7381)

Georgia Food Industry Association
1260 Winchester Pkwy., Ste. 216
Smyrna, GA 30080
Phone: (770)438-7744
Fax: (770)438-7761

Publications: Georgia Food Connection (7554)

Georgia Forestry Association, Inc.
500 Pinnacle Ct., Ste. 505
Norcross, GA 30071
Phone: (770)416-7621
Fax: (770)840-8961

Publications: TOPS (7470)

Georgia Historical Society
501 Whitaker St.
Savannah, GA 31401
Phone: (912)651-2125
Fax: (912)651-2831

Publications: Georgia Historical Quarterly (7532)

Georgia Institute of Technology
353 Ferst Dr., Rm. 137
Atlanta, GA 30332-0290
Phone: (404)894-2830
Fax: (404)894-1650

Publications: The Technique (7052)

Georgia Music Educators Association
145 B North Main St.
Jonesboro, GA 30236
Phone: (770)472-4632

Publications: Georgia Music News (6941)

Georgia Perimeter College
2101 Womack Rd.
Dunwoody, GA 30338-4497
Phone: (770)551-3019

Publications: The Chattahoochee Review (7258)

The Georgia Post
PO Box 860
Roberta, GA 31078
Phone: (478)836-3195
Fax: (478)836-9634

Publications: The Georgia Post (7498)

The Georgia Review
The University of Georgia
Athens, GA 30602-9009
Phone: (706)542-3481
Fax: (706)542-0047
Free: 800-542-3481

Publications: The Georgia Review (6942)

Georgia Southern University
PO Box Box 8001
Statesboro, GA 30460
Phone: (912)681-0069
Fax: (912)486-7113

Publications: The George-Anne (7560) • Southern Reflector (7563)

Georgia Southern University
PO Box 8101
Statesboro, GA 30460-8101
Phone: (912)681-0572
Fax: (912)681-5348

Publications: Politics and Policy (7561)

Georgia Southwestern State University
800 Wheatley Street
Americus, GA 31709
Phone: (912)931-2035
Fax: (912)931-2059

Publications: The Sou'Wester (6923)

Georgia State University
MSC 8R0322
33 Gilmer St., SE, Unit 8
Atlanta, GA 30303-3088
Phone: (404)651-3733
Fax: (404)651-1710

Publications: Studies in the Literary Imagination (7047)

Georgia Tech Alumni Association
190 North Ave. NW
Atlanta, GA 30313
Phone: (404)894-2391
Fax: (404)894-5113

Publications: Georgia Tech Alumni Magazine (7013) • Tech Topics (7050)

Georgian Bay Today
29 Bernard Ave.
Toronto, ON, Canada M5R 1R3
Phone: (416)944-1217
Fax: (416)944-0133

Publications: Georgian Bay Today (36600)

Georgina Advocate
461 The Queensway South
Keswick, ON, Canada L4P 2C9
Phone: (905)722-3289
Fax: (905)476-5785

Publications: Georgina Advocate (35932)

Geoscience Publications
Box 16010
Baton Rouge, LA 70893-6010
Phone: (225)388-6245
Fax: (225)388-4420

Publications: Journal of Mayan Linguistics (12490)

Gerald L. Sprouse Publishing Co.
PO Drawer 830
Ooltewah, TN 37363

Publications: The International American Sunbeam (29558)

Geraldton-Longlac Times-Star
4147 Main St.
PO Box 490
Geraldton, ON, Canada D0T 1M0
Phone: (807)854-1919
Fax: (807)854-1682

Publications: Geraldton-Longlac Times-Star (35846)

Gering Courier
1428 10th St.
PO Box 70
Gering, NE 69341
Phone: (308)436-2222
Fax: (308)436-7127

Publications: Gering Courier (18018)

Jim Gerki
106 W Main
PO Box 110
Bowling Green, MO 63334
Phone: (573)324-2222
Fax: (573)324-3991

Publications: The Bowling Green Times (16915) • Democrat (16916)

German American Chamber of Commerce of the Midwest
401 N Michigan Ave., Ste. 2525
Chicago, IL 60611-4212
Phone: (312)644-2662
Fax: (312)644-0738

Publications: Chamber Way Germany/Midwest (8303)

German Philatelic Society
Box 779
Arnold, MD 21012
Phone: (410)757-2344
Fax: (410)757-6857

Publications: The German Postal Specialist (13106)

German Shepherd Dog Club of America
1902C N Abrego Dr.
Green Valley, AZ 85614
Phone: (520)625-9528
Fax: (520)625-4789

Publications: German Shepherd Dog Review (721)

Germantown Historical Society
5501 Germantown Ave.
Philadelphia, PA 19144
Phone: (215)844-0514
Fax: (215)844-2831

Publications: Germantown Crier (27476)

The Germantown Press
PO Box 159
Germantown, OH 45327
Phone: (937)855-2300
Fax: (937)855-3860

Publications: Booster (25217) • The Germantown Press (25218)

Gernhardt Publications
3115 N Broadway St.
Chicago, IL 60657-4522
Phone: (312)327-7271
Fax: (312)327-0112

Publications: Gay Chicago Magazine (8384)

Gernsback Publications Inc.
275-G Marcus Blvd.
Hauppauge, NY 11788
Phone: (631)592-6720
Fax: (631)592-6723

Publications: Electronics Now (20717) • Poptronics (20722) • Poptronics (20721)

Gerontological Society of America
1030 15th St., NW, Ste. 250
Washington, DC 20005-1503
Phone: (202)842-1275
Fax: (202)842-1150

Publications: The Gerontologist (5513) • Journals of Gerontology (5620) • The Journals of Gerontology; Psychological Sciences & Social Sciences (5621)

Gesar
2910 San Pablo Ave.
Berkeley, CA 94704
Phone: (510)548-5407
Fax: (510)548-2230

Publications: Gesar (1524)

Gettysburg College
300 N. Washington St
Gettysburg, PA 17325
Phone: (717)337-6000
Fax: (717)337-6775

Publications: The Gettysburg Review (26938) • The Gettysburgian (26940)

Ghotek International
119 Rockland Ctr., Ste. 219
Nanuet, NY 10954
Phone: (914)371-2001
Fax: (914)371-2001

Publications: Wazobia News (21105)

Giant Robot
PO Box 642053
Los Angeles, CA 90064
Phone: (310)479-7311

Publications: Giant Robot (2278)

Gibbon Gazette
PO Box 456 Gibbone
Gibbon, MN 55335
Phone: (507)834-6966
Fax: (507)834-6966

Publications: The Gibbon Gazette (15916)

The Gibbon Reporter
PO Box 820
Gibbon, NE 68840
Phone: (308)468-5393
Fax: (308)468-5222

Publications: The Gibbon Reporter (18021)

Gibson D. Lewis Center for Business and Economic Research
Sam Houston State University
PO Box 2056
Huntsville, TX 77341
Phone: (936)294-1518
Fax: (936)294-3957

Publications: Journal of Business Strategies (30596)

Gibson Printing Co., Inc.
116 Washington St.
PO Box 360
Albany, KY 42602
Phone: (606)387-5144
Fax: (606)387-7949

Publications: Clinton County News (11914)

Gibson Publications, Inc.
820 1st St.
Benicia, CA 94510-3216
Phone: (707)745-0733
Fax: (707)557-6380

Publications: Benicia Herald (1487)

Gibson Publications, Inc.
PO Box 3067
Vallejo, CA 94590
Phone: (707)643-1706
Fax: (707)557-6380

Publications: Martinez News-Gazette (2514)

Gibson Publishing Co.
Box 7
Ipswich, SD 57451
Phone: (605)426-6471
Fax: (605)426-6202

Publications: The Ipswich Tribune (28873) • Roscoe-Hosmer Independent (28874)

Giddings Times and News
170 N Knox Ave.
PO Box 947
Giddings, TX 78942
Phone: (409)542-2222

Publications: Giddings Times and News (30395)

GIE Media, MC
4012 Bridge Ave.
Cleveland, OH 44113
Phone: (216)961-4130
Fax: (216)961-0364
Free: 800-456-0707

Publications: Lawn & Landscape Magazine (24919) • Pest Control Technology (24941) • Recycling Today (24948)

Gilchrist County Journal
207 N Main St.
Trenton, FL 32693
Phone: (352)463-7135
Fax: (352)463-7393

Publications: Gilchrist County Journal (6824)

Gillespie Area News
112-16 W Chestnut St.
PO Box 209
Gillespie, IL 62033-0209
Phone: (217)839-2130
Fax: (217)839-2139

Publications: Gillespie Area News (8920)

Gilman Research Corp.
PO Box 3390
South Pasadena, CA 91031
Phone: (626)403-6090

Publications: The Business Picture (3786)

Gilmore Publications Ltd.
5160 Skyline Way NE
Calgary, AB, Canada T2E 6V1
Phone: (403)274-1734
Fax: (403)275-4999

Publications: Canadian Hereford Digest (34635)

Giornale di Sicilia
2708 Jane St.
Downsview, ON, Canada M3L 1S4

Publications: Giornale di Sicilia (35783)

Girl Guides of Canada
50 Merton St.
Toronto, ON, Canada M4S 1A3
Phone: (416)487-5281
Fax: (416)487-5570

Publications: Canadian Guider (36501)

Girl Scouts of U.S.A.
420 5th Ave.
New York, NY 10018-2798
Phone: (212)852-8000
Fax: (212)852-6511
Free: 800-478-7248

Publications: Girl Scout Leader (21763)

G.K. Chesterton Society
c/o Rev. Ian Boyd, C.S.B
Seton Hall University
400 S. Orange Ave.
South Orange, NJ 07079-2687
Phone: (973)275-2430
Fax: (973)275-2594
Free: 800-526-7022

Publications: The Chesterton Review (19584)

Glacier Reporter
PO Box 349
Browning, MT 59417
Phone: (406)338-2090
Fax: (406)338-2410

Publications: Glacier Reporter (17760)

Glades County Democrat
PO Box 70
Moore Haven, FL 33471-0070
Phone: (941)946-0511
Fax: (941)983-7537

Publications: Glades County Democrat (6436)

Gladwin County Record and Beaverton Clarion
1100 W. Cedar Ave.
Gladwin, MI 48624
Phone: (517)426-9292

Publications: Gladwin County Record and Beaverton Clarion (15080)

Gladys Price Press
PO Box 898
McCrory, AR 72101
Phone: (870)731-2263
Fax: (870)731-5899

Publications: McCrory Monitor-Leader-Advocate (1271)

The Glasford Gazette
309E Main St.
Glasford, IL 61533
Phone: (309)389-2811

Publications: The Glasford Gazette (8923)

The Glasgow Courier
PO Box 151
Glasgow, MT 59230
Phone: (406)228-9301
Fax: (406)228-2665

Publications: The Glasgow Courier (17793)

The Glasgow Missourian
PO Box 248
Glasgow, MO 65254
Phone: (660)338-2195
Fax: (660)338-2494

Publications: The Glasgow Missourian (17083)

Glass Art Society
1305 Fourth Ave., Ste. 711
Seattle, WA 98101-2401
Phone: (206)382-1305
Fax: (206)382-2630

Publications: Glass Art Society Journal (32968)

Glass New England
PO Box 389
Franklin, MA 02038-0389
Phone: (508)528-6211
Fax: (508)528-6211

Publications: Glass New England (14205)

Glass Patterns Quarterly, Inc.
8300 Hidden Valley Rd.
Westport, KY 40077
Phone: (502)222-5631
Fax: (502)222-4527
Free: 800-719-0769

Publications: Glass Patterns Quarterly (12437)

The Glass Press, Inc.
PO Box 553
Marietta, OH 45750
Phone: (740)373-9959
Fax: (740)373-6917
Free: 800-533-3433

Publications: Glass Collector's Digest (25345)

The Glastonbury Citizen, Inc.
PO Box 373
87 Nutmeg Ln.
Glastonbury, CT 06033
Phone: (860)633-4691
Fax: (860)657-3258

Publications: The Glastonbury Citizen (4869) • Rivereast News Bulletin (4870)

Gleaner Life Insurance Society
5200 W U.S 223
Adrian, MI 49221
Phone: (517)263-2244
Fax: (517)265-7745
Free: 800-992-1894

Publications: The National Gleaner Forum (14710)

Glen Rose Inc.
PO Box 2009
Glen Rose, TX 76043-2009
Phone: (254)897-2282
Fax: (254)897-9423

Publications: Glen Rose Reporter (30398)

Glen Street Publications, Inc.
W4652 Glen St.
Appleton, WI 54913-9563
Phone: (920)749-4880
Fax: (920)749-4877

Publications: Milk & Liquid Food Transporter (33538)

The Glencoe Enterprise
831 11th St.
PO Box 97
Glencoe, MN 55336
Phone: (320)864-4715
Fax: (320)864-4715

Publications: The Glencoe Enterprise (15917)

Glendale College
1500 N Verdugo
Glendale, CA 91208
Phone: (818)240-1000
Fax: (818)549-9436

Publications: El Vaquero (2009)

Glendale Publishing Corp.
934 W Glenoaks Blvd., Ste. 1
Glendale, CA 91202-2755
Phone: (818)500-1872

Publications: Administrative Radiology Journal (2006)

Glendi Publications, Inc.
7002 W Butler Pke.
Ambler, PA 19002
Phone: (215)643-6385
Fax: (215)628-3571

Publications: Fly! (26650)

The Glengarry News Ltd.
3 Main St.
PO Box 10
Alexandria, ON, Canada K0C 1A0
Phone: (613)525-2020
Fax: (613)525-3824

Publications: The Glengarry News (35629)

Glenmary Home Missioners
PO Box 465618
Cincinnati, OH 45246
Phone: (513)874-8900
Fax: (513)874-1690
Free: 800-935-0975

Publications: Glenmary Challenge (24800)

Glennville Sentinel
PO Box 218
Glennville, GA 30427-0218
Phone: (912)654-2515
Fax: (912)654-2527

Publications: Glennville Sentinel (7305)

Glenrock Independent
207 S 4th St.
PO Box 9
Glenrock, WY 82637
Phone: (307)436-2211
Fax: (307)436-8803

Publications: Glenrock Independent (34531)

Glenville State College
200 High St.
PO Box 207
Glenville, WV 26351
Phone: (304)462-7361

Publications: Mercury (33324)

Glenwood Opinion Tribune
PO Box 191
Glenwood, IA 51534
Phone: (712)527-3191
Fax: (712)527-3193

Publications: Glenwood Opinion Tribune (10923)

Glenwood Post
2014 Grand Ave.
Glenwood Springs, CO 81601
Phone: (970)945-8515
Fax: (970)945-4487

Publications: Glenwood Post (4459)

Glidden Graphic
PO Box 607
Glidden, IA 51443
Phone: (712)659-3144
Fax: (712)659-3143

Publications: Glidden Graphic (10924)

Glider Rider, Inc.
PO Box 6009
Chattanooga, TN 37401
Phone: (423)629-5375
Fax: (423)629-5379

Publications: Ultralight Flying! (29094)

Global Business and Finance Review
413 Holiday Dr., Ste. 101G
Thibodaux, LA 70301
Phone: (985)448-4189

Publications: Global Business and Finance Review (12859)

Global Finance Media, Inc.
411 5th Ave., 7th Fl.
New York, NY 10016-2203
Phone: (212)768-1100
Fax: (212)768-2020

Publications: Global Finance (21770)

Global Information Network
146 W. 29th St., Ste. 7E
New York, NY 10001
Phone: (212)244-3123
Fax: (212)244-3522

Publications: Environment (News) (21612)

Global Options
PO Box 40601
San Francisco, CA 94140-0601
Phone: (510)550-1703
Fax: (510)620-0668

Publications: Social Justice (3443)

Global Publications, Inc.
420 Washington St., Ste. 104
Braintree, MA 02184-4755
Fax: (617)849-0228

Publications: Paper Age (18847)

Global Technology Business Publishing Inc.
1931 Old Middlefield Way, Ste. Z
Mountain View, CA 94043-2559
Phone: (650)937-1418
Fax: (650)934-2306

Publications: Global Technology Business (2606)

Globe Communications
5401 NW Broken Sound Blvd.
Boca Raton, FL 33487-3587
Phone: (561)994-7210
Fax: (561)241-5689
Free: 800-749-7733

Publications: Globe (5931) • National Examiner (5937) • Your Health (5942)

Globe Communications Corp.
Three E. 54th St., 15th Fl.
New York, NY 10022
Phone: (212)838-7733

Publications: Bridal Guide (21338)

Globe Leader
129 W Neshannock Ave.
PO Box 226
New Wilmington, PA 16142
Phone: (724)946-3501
Fax: (724)946-8098
Free: 800-995-0305

Publications: Globe (27323)

The Globe & Mail
444 Front St. W.
Toronto, ON, Canada M5V 2S9
Phone: (416)585-5406
Fax: (416)585-5641

Publications: The Globe and Mail (36606) • The Globe and Mail Report on Business Magazine (36607) • Rob Magazine (36731)

Globe Publishing Co.
118 E McLeod Ave.
Ironwood, MI 49938
Phone: (906)932-2211
Fax: (906)932-5358
Free: 800-236-2887

Publications: Ironwood Daily Globe (15213)

GLOBETECH Publishing Inc.
8 Cannon Rd.
Wilton, CT 06897
Phone: (203)762-3432
Fax: (203)762-8640

Publications: Critical Care International (5224) • Labmedica (5229)

Gloucester City News
34 S Broadway
PO Box 151
Gloucester City, NJ 08030
Phone: (856)456-1199
Fax: (856)456-1330

Publications: Gloucester City News (18849)

Gloucester County College
1400 Tanyard Rd.
College Center, Ste. 100
Sewell, NJ 08080
Phone: (856)468-5000
Fax: (856)464-9153

Publications: The Gazette (19545)

Gloucester County Sentinel
189 N Delsea Dr.
PO Box 367
Franklinville, NJ 08322-0367

Publications: Gloucester County Sentinel (18837)

Gloucester Publishers
108 E. Main St.
Gloucester, MA 01930-3846
Phone: (978)283-3200
Fax: (978)283-4629
Free: 800-356-9313

Publications: Old-House Interiors (14210)

GLS Diocesan Reports
1520 Ct. St.
PO Box 1405
Saginaw, MI 48605-1405
Phone: (989)793-7661
Fax: (989)793-7663

Publications: The Catholic Times (15049) • The Catholic Weekly (15489)

GNC Venture Group, Inc.
1479 S. E. Ave.
Vineland, NJ 08360
Phone: (609)691-8908
Fax: (609)691-2831
Free: 800-844-8631

Publications: The New Jersey Angler (19699)

Go Go Communications, Inc.
201 WestMoore, Ste.200
Terrell, TX 75160-4852
Phone: (972)563-7001
Fax: (972)563-7004

Publications: America's Barrel Racer (31182)

GOAL/QPC
2 Manor Pky.
Salem, NH 03079
Phone: (603)890-8800
Fax: (603)870-9122
Free: 800-643-4316

Publications: Journal of Innovative Management (18644)

The Goderich Signal-Star
Box 220, Industrial Park
120 Huckins St.
Goderich, ON, Canada N7A 4B6
Phone: (519)524-2614
Fax: (519)524-5145

Publications: The Goderich Signal-Star (35851) • The Teeswater News (35852)

God's Word Today
2115 Summit Ave.
St. Paul, MN 55105-1082
Phone: (651)962-6336
Fax: (651)962-6755

Publications: God's Word Today (16378)

Goering Publishing Co., Inc.
522 S Main
PO Box 849
Hugoton, KS 67951
Phone: (316)544-4321
Fax: (316)544-7321

Publications: The Hugoton Hermes (11499)

Going Places (Minot)
1601 18th Ave. NW
Minot, ND 58703-1108
Phone: (701)858-1600
Fax: (701)858-1644
Free: 800-658-3540

Publications: Going Places (Minot) (24504)

Gold Coast Marketing
PO Box 880306
Boca Raton, FL 33488-0306
Phone: (407)750-7765
Fax: (407)750-7049

Publications: Today's Boca Woman News Magazine (5940)

Gold Country Media
PO Box 755
Colfax, CA 95713
Phone: (530)346-2232
Fax: (530)346-2700

Publications: Cover Story (1920)

Gold Nugget Publications, Inc.
PO Box 440
Virden, IL 62690
Phone: (217)965-3355
Fax: (217)965-4512

Publications: The Girard Gazette (8922) • The Panhandle Press (9489)

Gold River News
11230 Gold Express Dr., No. 310-102
Gold River, CA 95670
Phone: (916)392-5843
Fax: (916)392-5843

Publications: Gold River News (3000)

Golden Bell Press
2403 Champa St.
Denver, CO 80205
Phone: (303)296-1600
Fax: (303)295-2159

Publications: Watch & Clock Review (4365)

Golden Gate Gazette
11725 Collier Blvd., No. C
Naples, FL 34116
Phone: (239)353-0444
Fax: (239)353-9040

Publications: Golden Gate Gazette (6439)

Golden Gate University School of Law
536 Mission St.
San Francisco, CA 94105
Phone: (415)442-6680
Fax: (415)442-6609

Publications: Golden Gate University Law Review (3366)

Golden Plains Publications
PO Box 528
Cimarron, KS 67835
Phone: (316)855-3902
Fax: (316)655-2489
Free: 800-658-3755

Publications: Bucklin Banner (11381) • Harper County Journal (25777) • Haskell County Monitor-Chief (11382)

Golden Prairie News
301 S Chestnut
Assumption, IL 62510
Phone: (217)226-3721
Fax: (217)226-3579

Publications: Golden Prairie News (8030)

Golden Rain Foundation
PO Box 2190
Walnut Creek, CA 94595
Fax: (510)935-8348

Publications: Rossmoor News (4056)

The Golden Star
413 A 9th Ave. N.
PO Box 149
Golden, BC, Canada V0A 1H0
Phone: (250)344-5251
Fax: (250)344-7344

Publications: The Golden Star (34966)

Golden Times
Piano Works Mall, Ste. 1025
349 W. Commerical St.
East Rochester, NY 14445
Phone: (585)586-1445
Fax: (585)586-2093

Publications: Golden Times (20552)

Golden West College
15744 Golden West St.
Huntington Beach, CA 92647
Phone: (714)895-8786
Fax: (714)895-8795

Publications: The Western Sun (2066)

Golden West Free Press, Inc.
Drawer A
109 S. Poplar St.
Kermit, TX 79745-0769
Phone: (915)586-2561
Fax: (915)586-2562

Publications: The Jal Record (19871) • The Winkler County News (30638)

Goldendale Publisher
117 W Main St.
Goldendale, WA 98620
Phone: (509)773-3777
Fax: (509)773-4737

Publications: The Goldendale Sentinel (32776)

Goldfish Press
PO Box 74
Kingston, ON, Canada K7L 4V6
Phone: (416)760-0831

Publications: Quarry Magazine (35943)

Goldstein & Associates
1150 Yale St., Ste. 12
Santa Monica, CA 90403
Phone: (310)828-1309

Publications: Neonatal Intensive Care (3713) • TradeShow & Exhibit Manager (3718)

Golf Range Magazine
PO Box 1265
New Canaan, CT 06840
Phone: (203)972-6201
Fax: (203)972-1667

Publications: Golf Range Magazine (4978)

Golf Today
204 Industrial Way
San Carlos, CA 94070
Phone: (650)802-8165
Fax: (650)802-8114
Free: 800-465-3788

Publications: Golf Today (3099)

Golfer Magazines, Inc.
10301 Northwest Fwy., No. 418
Houston, TX 77092
Phone: (713)680-1680
Fax: (713)680-0130

Publications: Texas Golfer (30534)

Golfweek
1500 Park Ctr. Dr.
Orlando, FL 32835
Phone: (407)563-7000
Fax: (407)563-7076

Publications: GOLFWEEK (6496)

Gonzales Weekly
PO Box 38
Gonzales, LA 70707-0038
Phone: (225)647-4569
Fax: (225)644-8238

Publications: Community Mirror (12586) • Gonzales Weekly (12587)

Good Day Sunshine
315 Derby Ave.
Orange, CT 06477-1345
Phone: (203)891-8131
Fax: (203)891-8433

Publications: Beatles Fan Magazine (5090)

Good Hope Enterprises Inc.
8204 Elmbrook Dr., Ste. 217
Dallas, TX 75247
Phone: (214)823-7666
Fax: (214)823-7373

Publications: African Herald (30121)

Good Morning Advertiser, Inc.
136 W Main St.
Whitewater, WI 53190
Phone: (262)473-2711
Fax: (262)753-0001
Free: 800-747-4647

Publications: Good Morning Advertiser (34456)

Good News Inc.
131 Reed
PO Box 407
Akron, IA 51001
Phone: (712)568-2551
Fax: (712)568-3171

Publications: Akron Register-Tribune (10574)

Good News Publishers Inc.
PO Box 2660
Vista, CA 92085
Phone: (760)724-3075

Publications: Good News Etc. (4045)

Good News Publishing Co.
7022 S.W. 53rd Ln.
Miami, FL 33155
Phone: (305)665-8101
Fax: (305)666-1449

Publications: Social (6380)

Good News Radio Broadcasting
3222 S. Richey Ave.
Tucson, AZ 85713
Phone: (520)790-2440
Fax: (520)790-2937

Publications: Good News Magazine (947)

Goodman Media Group, Inc.
250 W 57th St., Ste. 710
New York, NY 10107-0799
Phone: (212)246-1212

Publications: American Country Collectibles (21185) • Collectibles, Flea Market Finds (21438) • Country Accents (21504) • Fit Magazine (21703) • Log Homes Illustrated (22265)

Goodson Newspaper Group
1009 Lennox Ave.
Lawrenceville, NJ 08648
Phone: (609)895-2600
Fax: (609)895-9759

Publications: The Mercury (27899) • The Oneida Daily Dispatch (23045)

The Goose Creek Gazette
PO Box 304
Goose Creek, SC 29445
Phone: (803)572-0511
Fax: (803)572-0312

Publications: The Goose Creek Gazette (28620)

Gordon and Breach Publishers
PO Box 32160
Newark, NJ 07102-0560
Phone: (973)643-7500
Fax: (973)643-7676

Publications: Marine and Freshwater Behavior and Physiology (19359)

Gordon Journal
210 N Main
PO Box 270
Gordon, NE 69343
Phone: (308)282-0118
Fax: (308)282-1120

Publications: Gordon Journal (18022)

Goreville Gazette
Hwy. 37
PO Box 70
Goreville, IL 62939
Phone: (618)995-9445
Fax: (618)995-9445

Publications: Goreville Gazette (8948)

The Gorman Progress
106 S Kent
PO Box 68
Gorman, TX 76454-0068
Phone: (254)734-2410
Fax: (254)734-2799
Free: 800-613-0773

Publications: The Gorman Progress (30401)

Goshen College
1700 S Main St.
Goshen, IN 46526-9988
Phone: (219)535-7000
Fax: (219)535-7660
Free: 800-348-7422

Publications: Goshen College Bulletin (10023)

The Goshen News
PO Box 569
Goshen, IN 46526-0569
Phone: (219)533-2151
Fax: (219)533-0839
Free: 800-487-2151

Publications: The Goshen News (10024)

Goss Publications, Inc.
512 Green Bay Rd.
Kenilworth, IL 60043-1073
Phone: (847)256-7111
Fax: (847)256-5898
Free: 800-533-9734

Publications: Arabian Horse Express (9043)

The Gothenburg Times
Box 385
Gothenburg, NE 69138
Phone: (308)537-3636
Fax: (308)537-7554
Free: 877-537-3636

Publications: The Gothenburg Times (18024)

Goucher College
1021 Dulaney Valley Rd.
Baltimore, MD 21204
Phone: (410)337-6000

Publications: Goucher College Quarterly (13166)

Gould Publications
1333 N. U.S. Hwy. 17-92
Longwood, FL 32750-3724
Free: 800-847-6502

Publications: New York Town Law (6313)

Gouverneur Tribune-Press Inc.
74 Trinty Ave
Gouverneur, NY 13642
Phone: (315)287-2100

Publications: Gouverneur Tribune-Press (20674)

Gove County Advocate
PO Box 365
Quinter, KS 67752
Phone: (785)754-3651
Fax: (785)754-3878

Publications: Gove County Advocate (11768)

Government Finance Officers Association
203 N. LaSalle St.
Chicago, IL 60601-7401
Phone: (312)977-9700
Fax: (312)977-4806

Publications: Government Finance Review (8388)

Governors State University
Student Life Campus Center
University Pkwy.
University Park, IL 60466-3186
Phone: (708)534-5000
Fax: (708)534-8953

Publications: The GSU Innovator (9697)

Gowdy Printcraft Press, Inc.
22 N. Sierra Madre St.
Colorado Springs, CO 80903-3311
Phone: (719)634-1593
Fax: (719)867-0265
Free: 877-462-5546

Publications: Academy Spirit (4651) • Mountaineer (4252) • Space Observer (4257)

Gowrie News
Box 473
Gowrie, IA 50543
Phone: (515)352-3325
Fax: (515)352-3309

Publications: The Gowrie News (10927)

Grace McNamara Inc.
4215 White Bear Pkwy., Ste. 100
St. Paul, MN 55110
Phone: (651)293-1544
Fax: (651)653-4308
Free: 800-869-6882

Publications: American Cake Decorating (16363) • Fine Furnishings International (FFI) (16376) • Wall Fashions Magazine (16415) • Window Fashions (16417)

Grace University
1311 S. 9th St.
Omaha, NE 68108-3629
Phone: (402)449-2800
Fax: (402)341-9587

Publications: Grace Tidings (18196)

The Graceville News
PO Box 187
Graceville, FL 32440
Phone: (904)263-6015
Fax: (904)263-1042

Publications: The Graceville News (6173)

Graceway Publishing Co.
350 Northern Blvd., Ste. 203
Great Neck, NY 11021
Phone: (516)504-7576
Fax: (516)498-2029
Free: 800-440-0499

Publications: Journal of Business Forecasting Methods (20691)

**Graduate School of Library and Informa-
tion Sciences**
University of Illinois
505 E. Daniel St.
MC-493
Champaign, IL 61820
Phone: (217)244-0324
Fax: (217)333-5603

Publications: The Bulletin of the Center for Children's Books (8182)

The Graettinger Times
102 E Robbins Ave.
PO Box 118
Graettinger, IA 51342
Phone: (712)859-3780
Fax: (712)859-3039

Publications: The Graettinger Times (10928)

Graf Printing Co., Inc.
136 E Fort St.
PO Box 155
Hermann, MO 65041
Phone: (573)486-5700
Fax: (573)486-5524

Publications: Advertiser-Courier (17096)

Graham Newspapers, Inc.
PO Box 600
Graham, TX 76450
Phone: (940)549-7800
Fax: (940)549-4364

Publications: The Graham Leader (30402)

Grain Dealers Mutual Insurance Co.
1752 N. Meridian St., Box 1747
Indianapolis, IN 46206
Phone: (317)923-2453
Fax: 800-828-4124

Publications: Our Paper (10158)

Grand Forks Herald, Inc.
375 2nd Ave. N.
PO Box 6008
Grand Forks, ND 58206
Phone: (701)780-1100
Fax: (701)780-1211
Free: 800-477-6572

Publications: AGWEEK (24453)

Grand Haven Publishing Corp.
301 N 3rd St.
Grand Haven, MI 49417
Phone: (616)847-3493
Fax: (616)842-9584

Publications: Tribune (15085)

Grand Island Independent
422 W 1st St.
PO Box 1208
Grand Island, NE 68802
Phone: (308)382-1000
Fax: (308)382-8129
Free: 800-658-3160

Publications: Grand Island Independent (18025)

Grand Junction Newspapers, Inc.
1635 N. First St.
Grand Junction, CO 81501
Phone: (970)242-5555
Fax: (970)245-9250

Publications: The Nickel Want Ads (4480)

Grand Lodge AF & AM
71 W 23rd St.
New York, NY 10010
Phone: (212)741-4500
Fax: (212)633-2639
Free: 800-362-7664

Publications: Empire State Mason (20956)

Grand Lodge A.F. and A.M.
PO Box 1019
Guthrie, OK 73044
Phone: (405)282-3212
Fax: (405)282-3244

Publications: The Oklahoma Mason (25854)

**The Grand Lodge of AF & AM of North
Carolina**
126 Arbor Dr.
Washington, NC 27889

Publications: The North Carolina Mason (24272)

**Grand Lodge of Massachusetts, Order of
the Sons of Italy**
93 Concord Ave.
Belmont, MA 02478
Phone: (617)489-5235
Fax: (617)489-5371

Publications: IDB America (13840)

Grand Lodge of Montana
Box 362
Lakeside, MT 59922
Phone: (406)442-9638

Publications: The Montana Masonic News (17844)

Grand Lodge of Pennsylvania
Curtis Ctr.
601 Walnut St., No. L45
Philadelphia, PA 19106-3323
Phone: (215)592-1713
Fax: (215)592-9152
Free: 800-621-0062

Publications: Sons of Italy Times (27689)

**Grand Marais Pilot & Pictured Rocks Re-
view**
PO Box 334
Grand Marais, MI 49839
Phone: (906)494-2391
Fax: (906)494-2527

Publications: Grand Marais Pilot & Pictured Rocks
Review (15534)

Grand Rapids Community College
143 Bostwick NE
Grand Rapids, MI 49503
Phone: (616)234-4000
Fax: (616)771-4005

Publications: The Collegiate (15092)

The Grand Rapids Times
PO Box 7258
Grand Rapids, MI 49510
Phone: (616)245-8737
Fax: (616)245-1026

Publications: The Grand Rapids Times (15097)

The Grand River Sachem
3 Sutherland W.
Caledonia, ON, Canada N3W 1C1
Phone: (905)765-4441
Fax: (905)765-3651

Publications: The Grand River Sachem (35721)

Grand Street
214 Sullivan St., No. 6C
New York, NY 10012-1354
Phone: (212)533-2944
Fax: (212)533-2737

Publications: Grand Street (21778)

Grand Times Publishing
403 Village Dr.
El Cerrito, CA 94530
Phone: (510)527-4337

Publications: Grand Times (1861)

**Grande Cache Mountaineer Publishing
Co.**
PO Box 660
Grande Cache, AB, Canada T0E 0Y0
Phone: (780)827-3539
Fax: (780)827-3530

Publications: Grande Cache Mountaineer (34773)

Grandview Exponent
416 Main St.
Box 39
Grandview, MB, Canada R0L 0Y0
Phone: (204)546-2555
Fax: (204)546-3081

Publications: Grandview Exponent (35269)

Grandview Tribune
Drawer 440
Grandview, TX 76050
Phone: (817)866-3391
Fax: (817)866-3869

Publications: Grandview Tribune (30408)

Granite City Journal
1815 Delmar
Granite City, IL 62040
Phone: (618)877-7700
Fax: (618)876-4240

Publications: Sunday Home Journal (8949)

Granite Quill
PO Box 1190
Hillsboro, NH 03244-1190
Phone: (603)464-3388
Fax: (603)464-4106
Free: 800-281-2859

Publications: The Messenger (18525) • The Messenger (18524)

Grant County Herald Independent
208 W Cherry
Lancaster, WI 53813
Phone: (608)723-2151
Fax: (608)723-7272

Publications: Grant County Herald Independent
(33907)

Grant County News
151 N. Main
PO Box 308
Williamstown, KY 41097
Phone: (859)824-3343
Fax: (859)824-5888

Publications: Grant County News (12448)

Grant County News
Box 100
Elgin, ND 58533-0100
Phone: (701)584-2900

Publications: Carson Press (24405) • Grant County
News (24406)

Grant County News
PO Box 49
Medford, OK 73759-0049
Phone: (580)395-2212
Fax: (580)395-2907

Publications: Medford Patriot-Star and Grant County
Journal (25915)

Grant County Press
Box 39
Petersburg, WV 26847
Phone: (304)257-1844
Fax: (304)257-1691

Publications: Grant County Press (33429)

Grant County Review
PO Box 390
Milbank, SD 57252-0390
Phone: (605)432-4516
Fax: (605)432-5042
Free: 800-517-1420

Publications: Grant County Review (28893)

Grant MacEwan Community College
Journalism Dept.
City Center Campus
D-5-174H, 10700-104 Ave.
Edmonton, AB, Canada T5J 4S2
Phone: (780)497-5623
Fax: (780)497-5630

Publications: The MacEwan Journalist (34721)

Granville Publishing
PO Box 726
Creedmoor, NC 27522
Phone: (919)528-3909
Fax: (919)528-0288
Free: 800-736-3909

Publications: Butner-Creedmoor News (23794)

Grapeland Printing
Box 99
Grapeland, TX 75844
Phone: (936)687-2424
Fax: (936)687-2424

Publications: The Grapeland Messenger (30410)

Grapevine Independent
3338 Mather Field Rd.
Rancho Cordova, CA 95670
Phone: (916)361-1234
Fax: (916)361-0491

Publications: Grapevine Independent (2874)

Grapevine Press, Inc.
1000 RIDC Plz. Veyerka, No. 301
Pittsburgh, PA 15238
Publications: Grapevine Weekly (27793)

Graphcom Publishing, Inc.
1995 NE 150 St., Ste. 107
Miami, FL 33181
Phone: (305)945-7403
Fax: (305)947-6410
Publications: Pleasure Boatings Caribbean Sports &
Travel Magazine (6376)

Graphic Art Publishing
5325 Kendall
Boise, ID 83706
Phone: (208)375-1010
Fax: (208)376-0434
Publications: Gunfighter (7808)

**Graphic Communications International
Union**
1900 L St. NW
Washington, DC 20036
Phone: (202)462-1400
Fax: (202)721-0600
Publications: Graphic Communicator (5519)

Graphic Media, Inc.
2021 Warren Ave.
Cheyenne, WY 82001-4843
Phone: (307)634-8895
Fax: (307)634-8530
Free: 800-634-8895
Publications: Trader's Shopper's Guide (34496)

The Graphic Printing Co., Inc.
PO Box 1049
Portland, IN 47371
Phone: (219)726-8141
Fax: (219)726-8143
Publications: Dunkirk News & Sun (10404)

Graphic Publications, Inc.
7368 County Rd. 623
PO Box 358
Millersburg, OH 44654
Phone: (330)674-2300
Fax: (330)674-2461
Free: 888-674-1010
Publications: The Holmes County Bargain Hunter
(25387) • Tuscarawas Bargain Hunter (25389) •
The Wayne Journal (25390)

Graphis, Inc.
307 5th Ave., 10th Fl.
New York, NY 10016-6517
Phone: (212)532-9387
Fax: (212)213-3229
Publications: Graphis (21780)

Grass Shack Productions
720 Iwilei Rd., Ste. 415
Honolulu, HI 96817
Phone: (808)537-1868
Fax: (808)521-7936
Publications: Hawaii Bar Journal (7689)

Grasslands Review
Box 626
Berea, OH 44017
Phone: (440)826-8071
Publications: Grasslands Review (24677)

Gravel Subscriptions Ltd.
611 Main St.
PO Box 1017
Gravelbourg, SK, Canada S0H 1X0
Phone: (306)648-3479
Fax: (306)648-2520
Publications: Tribune (37471)

Gravenhurst Banner
PO Box 849
Gravenhurst, ON, Canada P1P 1X2
Phone: (705)687-6674
Fax: (705)687-7213
Publications: Gravenhurst Banner (35856)

Graves Publishing Co.
PO Box 297
Nashville, AR 71852
Phone: (870)845-2010
Fax: (870)845-5091
Publications: Montgomery County News (1283) •
Murfreesboro Diamond (1293)

Gray Areas, Inc.
PO Box 808
Broomall, PA 19008-0808
Publications: Gray Areas (26737)

Gray Communications Systems
166 Buford Dr.
Lawrenceville, GA 30045
Phone: (770)963-9205
Fax: (770)338-7353
Publications: Gwinnett Daily Post (7368)

Gray County Newspapers LLC
403 W Atchison
PO Box 2198
Pampa, TX 79066
Phone: (806)669-2525
Fax: (806)669-2520
Free: 800-687-3348
Publications: The Pampa News (30900)

The Gray News
20 Main St.
Gray, ME 04039
Phone: (207)657-2200
Fax: (207)657-2427
Publications: The Gray News (12966)

Gray Union Publishing, Inc.
PO Box 9338
Raytown, MO 64133
Phone: (816)353-5545
Publications: Raytown Post (17369)

Great Ad-ventures Publishing, Inc.
2057 Mitchell Ave.
PO Box 5006
Oroville, CA 95966
Phone: (530)533-2170
Fax: (530)533-2181
Publications: The Digger Shopper & News (2728)

Great American Publishing Co.
PO Box 128
Sparta, MI 49345
Phone: (616)887-9008
Fax: (616)887-2666
Publications: The Fruit Growers News (15568) •
The Vegetable Growers News (15570)

Great Expeditions
PO Box 18036
Raleigh, NC 27619-8036
Phone: (919)846-3600
Fax: (919)846-3600
Publications: Great Expeditions (24137)

Great Lakes Historical Society
PO Box 435
Vermilion, OH 44089-0435
Phone: (440)967-3467
Fax: (440)967-1519
Free: 800-893-1485
Publications: Inland Seas (24610)

Great Lakes Media, Inc.
7232 E. Michigan Ave.
Pigeon, MI 48755
Phone: (517)453-3100
Fax: (517)453-3877
Free: 800-733-4780
Publications: Huron County Press & Newsweekly
(15533)

Great Lakes Publishing Co.
1422 Euclid Ave., Hanna Bldg., Ste. 730
Cleveland, OH 44115
Phone: (216)771-2833
Fax: (216)781-6318
Publications: Cleveland Magazine (24872) • Inside
Business (24912)

Great Lakes Sports Publications, Inc.
3588 Plymouth Rd., No. 245
Ann Arbor, MI 48105-2603
Phone: (734)507-0241
Fax: (734)434-4765
Publications: Michigan Golfer (14763) • Michigan
Runner & Fitness Sports (14769)

Great Midwestern Publishing Co.
Box 97
Elgin, IA 52141-0097
Publications: The Elgin Echo (10871)

Great Oak Publications, Inc.
7 Bow St.
North Reading, MA 01864
Phone: (978)664-4761
Fax: (978)664-4954
Publications: The Lynnfield Villager (14288) • North
Reading Transcript (14426)

Great Valley Publishing Co.
3801 Schuylkill Rd.
Spring City, PA 19475
Phone: (610)948-9500
Fax: (610)948-7202
Free: 800-278-4400
Publications: For the Record (28008)

Greater Austin Community Newspapers
PO Box 659
Smithville, TX 78957
Phone: (512)237-4655
Fax: (512)237-5443
Publications: The Smithville Times (31113)

Greater Houston Dental Society
1 Greenway Plz., Ste. 110
Houston, TX 77046
Phone: (713)961-4337
Fax: (713)961-3617
Publications: The Journal of the Greater Houston
Dental Society (30496)

Greater Houston Partnership
1200 Smith, Ste. 700
Houston, TX 77002-4400
Phone: (713)844-3600
Fax: (713)844-0200
Publications: Houston Economic Highlights (30483)

Greater Los Angeles Zoo Association
5333 Zoo Dr.
Los Angeles, CA 90027
Phone: (323)644-6400
Fax: (323)644-4720
Publications: Zoo View (2444)

Greater Media Newspapers
2 Kennedy Blvd.
East Brunswick, NJ 08816
Phone: (732)247-6161
Fax: (732)247-0215
Publications: The News Transcript (18839) • Senti-
nel (18840) • Suburban (18841)

Greater Media Newspapers
PO Box 5001
Freehold, NJ 07728
Phone: (732)358-5200
Free: 800-660-4ADS
Publications: Bayshore Independent (18838) • Mid-
dletown Independent (19235)

**Greater Mercer County Chamber of Com-
merce**
2550 Kuser Rd.
PO Box 8307
Trenton, NJ 08650
Phone: (609)586-2056
Fax: (609)586-8052
Publications: Mercer Business Magazine (19658)

Greater North Dakota Association
PO Box 2639
Bismarck, ND 58502-2639
Phone: (701)222-0929
Fax: (701)222-1611
Free: 800-382-1405
Publications: North Dakota Horizons (24355)

Greater Northwest Printing Co.
117 Main St., Box 99
Stanley, ND 58784
Phone: (701)628-2333
Fax: (701)628-2694

Publications: Mountrail County Promoter, Inc. (24537)

Greater Northwest Publishing, Inc.
PO Box 877
Minot, ND 58702
Phone: (701)838-0227
Fax: (701)852-4908

Publications: Renville County Farmer (24520)

Greater Oklahoma City Chamber of Commerce
123 Park Ave.
Oklahoma City, OK 73102
Phone: (405)297-8900
Fax: (405)297-8916

Publications: The Point! (25993)

Greater Philadelphia Newspapers
8400 Rte. 13
Levittown, PA 19057
Phone: (215)949-4000
Fax: (215)949-4114

Publications: Bucks County Courier Times (27186)

Greater Pugent Sound
18943-120th Ave. NE, Ste. 102
Bothell, WA 98011
Free: 800-235-0080

Publications: Apartments for Rent Magazine (32690)

Greater Rochester Advertiser
201 Main St.
East Rochester, NY 14445
Fax: (716)385-3507
Free: 800-388-1514

Publications: Shopping Bag & Advertiser (20554)

GreatLander Bush Mailer
3110 Spenard Rd.
Anchorage, AK 99503
Phone: (907)274-0611
Fax: (907)272-2105
Free: 888-746-7452

Publications: GreatLander Bush Mailer (526)

Greek Orthodox Archdiocese Press
E. 79th St.
New York, NY 10021
Phone: (212)570-3500
Fax: (212)570-3569

Publications: Orthodox Observer (22505)

Greeley County Republican
507 Broadway
Box 610
Tribune, KS 67879
Phone: (620)376-4264
Fax: (620)376-2433

Publications: Greeley County Republican (11848)

Greeley Publishing Co.
501 8th Ave.
PO Box 1690
Greeley, CO 80632
Phone: (970)352-0211
Fax: (970)352-4059
Free: 800-275-0321

Publications: The Greenly Tribune (4497)

Greeley Publishing Co.
423 Main St.
Windsor, CO 80550
Phone: (970)686-5898
Fax: (970)686-5694
Free: 800-275-5646

Publications: The Fence Post (4686)

Green Anarchy
PO Box 11331
Eugene, OR 97440

Publications: Green Anarchy (26318)

Green Banner Publications, Inc.
PO Box 38
Pekin, IN 47165-0038
Phone: (812)967-3176
Fax: (812)967-3194
Free: 800-264-7336

Publications: Austin Chronicle (10392) • The Banner-Gazette (10393) • The Giveaway (10444) • The Leader (9885) • Scott County Journal (10445) • The Washington County Edition (10441)

Green Bay News-Chronicle
133 S. Monroe St.
PO Box 2467
Green Bay, WI 54306
Phone: (920)432-2941
Fax: (920)432-8581

Publications: Green Bay News-Chronicle (33740)

Green Bay Press-Gazette
PO Box 23430
Green Bay, WI 54305-3430

Publications: Green Bay Press-Gazette (33741)

Green Bay Register, Inc.
1825 Riverside Dr.
Box 23825
Green Bay, WI 54305-3825
Phone: (920)437-7531
Fax: (920)437-9356
Free: 877-500-3580

Publications: The Compass (33739)

The Green Center for Science and Society
The University of Texas at Dallas
PO Box 830688, MS JO 30
Richardson, TX 75083-0688
Phone: (214)883-6325
Fax: (214)883-6327
Free: 800-345-8112

Publications: Issues in Science and Technology (30975)

Green County Spectrum
37 S Detroit St.
PO Box 400
Xenia, OH 45385
Phone: (513)372-4444

Publications: Green County Spectrum (25686)

Larry Green
PO Box 38
Turon, KS 67583-0038
Phone: (316)497-6448
Fax: (316)497-6435

Publications: The Record (11852)

Green Leaf Publishing Inc.
198 SW 2nd St.
PO Box 219
Stevenson, WA 98648
Phone: (509)427-8444
Fax: (509)427-4229

Publications: Skamania County Pioneer (33141)

Green Line Media, Inc.
PO Box 144
Asheville, NC 28802
Phone: (828)251-1333
Fax: (828)251-1311

Publications: Mountain Xpress (23632)

Green River Community College
12401 SE 320th St.
Auburn, WA 98092
Phone: (253)833-9111
Fax: (253)939-5135

Publications: The Current (32655)

Green Tab Publishing Co.
518 7th St.
Moundsville, WV 26041
Phone: (304)845-4050
Fax: (304)845-4312

Publications: Green Tab-Northern Valley (33407) • Wetzel Green Tab (33414)

Green Teacher
95 Robert St.
Toronto, ON, Canada M5S 2K5
Phone: (416)960-1244
Fax: (416)925-3474

Publications: Green Teacher (36609)

Green Valley News & Sun
PO Box 567
Green Valley, AZ 85622
Phone: (520)625-5511
Fax: (520)625-8046

Publications: Green Valley News & Sun (722)

Green World
12 Dudley St.
Randolph, VT 05060-1202

Publications: Green World (31580)

Greenbelt Cooperative Publishing Association, Inc.
15 Crescent Rd., Ste. 100
Greenbelt, MD 20770-1887
Phone: (301)474-4131
Fax: (301)474-5880

Publications: Greenbelt News Review (13558)

Greenbrier Daily Newspapers Inc.
200 S. Court St.
Lewisburg, WV 24901
Phone: (304)645-1206
Fax: (304)645-7104

Publications: Greenbrier Valley Ranger (33364)

Greenbrier Historical Society
301 W Washington St.
Lewisburg, WV 24901
Phone: (304)645-3398
Fax: (304)645-5201

Publications: Greenbrier Historical Society Journal (33363)

Greenbrier Valley Advertiser
122 N Ct. St.
Lewisburg, WV 24901
Phone: (304)647-5724
Fax: (304)647-5767

Publications: Greenbrier Valley Trader (33365)

Greene County Herald
PO Box 220
Leakesville, MS 39451
Phone: (601)394-5070
Fax: (601)394-5070

Publications: Greene County Herald (16744)

Greene County Newspaper Co.
265 Prarie Ave.
PO Box 598
Eutaw, AL 35462
Phone: (205)372-3373
Fax: (205)372-2243

Publications: Greene County Democrat (208)

Greene Prairie Press
516 N M
PO Box 265
Carrollton, IL 62016
Phone: (217)374-2871
Fax: (217)742-3596

Publications: Greene Prairie Press (8161)

The Greene Recorder
219 N 2nd St.
Box 370
Greene, IA 50636
Phone: (515)823-4525
Fax: (515)823-4525

Publications: The Greene Recorder (10929)

Greeneville Sun
121 W Summer St.
PO Box 1630
Greeneville, TN 37743-4923
Phone: (615)638-4181
Fax: (615)638-3645

Publications: The Greeneville Sun (29212)

Greeneway Enterprises
PO Box 250
Gilmer, TX 75644-0250
Phone: (903)843-2503
Fax: (903)843-5123

Publications: The Gilmer Mirror (30396)

Greenfield Daily Times
345 Jefferson St.
PO Box 118
Greenfield, OH 45123
Phone: (513)981-2141
Fax: (513)981-2107

Publications: The Review Times (25225)

Greenhorn Valley-News
PO Box 19041
Colorado City, CO 81019
Phone: (719)676-3304
Fax: (719)676-3304

Publications: Greenhorn Valley-News (4233)

Greenpeace USA
702 H St., NW, Ste. 300
Washington, DC 20001
Phone: (202)462-1177
Fax: (202)483-8683
Free: 800-326-0959

Publications: Greenpeace Magazine (5520)

Greenprints
PO Box 1355
Fairview, NC 28730
Phone: (828)628-1902
Fax: (828)628-1902

Publications: Greenprints (23876)

Green's Educational Publications, Inc.
PO Box 3236
Regina, SK, Canada S4P 3H1

Publications: Green's Magazine (37530)

The Greensboro Watchman Inc.
1005 Market St.
PO Drawer 550
Greensboro, AL 36744
Phone: (334)624-8323
Fax: (334)624-8327

Publications: The Greensboro Watchman (243)

Greensburg Catholic Accent and Communications, Inc.
723 E Pittsburgh St.
Greensburg, PA 15601
Phone: (724)834-4010
Fax: (724)836-5650

Publications: The Catholic Accent (26953)

Greensheet Inc.
2601 Main St., 4th Fl.
Houston, TX 77002
Phone: (713)371-3500
Fax: (713)371-3980
Free: 800-793-6543

Publications: Austin Greensheet (29759) • Dallas Greensheet (30145) • Houston Greensheet (30485)

GreenTower Press
Department of English
Northwest Missouri State University
Maryville, MO 64468
Phone: (660)562-1265
Fax: (660)562-1731

Publications: The Laurel Review (Maryville) (17273)

Greenup Press
Box 127
Greenup, IL 62428
Phone: (217)923-3704
Fax: (217)923-3704

Publications: Greenup Press (8960)

The Greenville Advocate
305 S 2nd St.
PO Box 9
Greenville, IL 62246-1726
Phone: (618)664-3144
Fax: (618)664-1613

Publications: The Greenville Advocate (8961)

Greenville College
315 E College Ave.
PO Box 159
Greenville, IL 62246-1199
Phone: (618)664-2800
Fax: (618)664-1373

Publications: Papyrus (8962)

Greenville Herald Banner
2305 King St.
PO Box 1047
Greenville, TX 75403-1047
Phone: (903)455-4220
Fax: (903)455-6281

Publications: Greenville Herald Banner (30413)

Greenville News
PO Box 1688
Greenville, SC 29602
Phone: (864)298-4100
Fax: (864)298-4395
Free: 800-274-7879

Publications: Food Extra (28622) • The Greenville News (28623) • Tribune-Times (28756)

Greenville News Inc.
PO Box 340
109 N. Lafayette
Greenville, MI 48838-0340
Phone: (616)754-9301
Fax: (616)754-8559
Free: 800-968-9301

Publications: Carson City Gazette (14861)

Greenwich Time
20 E Elm St.
Greenwich, CT 06830-6529
Phone: (203)625-4400
Fax: (203)625-4419

Publications: Greenwich Time (4874)

Greenwood Commonwealth
329 Hwy. 82 W
PO Box 8050
Greenwood, MS 38930
Phone: (662)453-5312
Fax: (601)453-2908

Publications: Greenwood Commonwealth (16644)

Greenwood County Publishing Co.
106 W 2nd St.
PO Box 590
Eureka, KS 67045
Phone: (620)583-5721

Publications: Eureka Herald (11437)

Greenwood Democrat
PO Box 398
Greenwood, AR 72936-0398
Phone: (479)996-4494
Fax: (479)996-4122

Publications: Greenwood Democrat (1162)

Greenwood Lake News, Inc.
61 Windermere
Greenwood Lake, NY 10925
Phone: (845)477-2575
Fax: (845)477-2577

Publications: Greenwood Lake and West Milford News (20702)

Greenwood Publishing Group Inc.
88 Post Rd. W.
PO Box 5007
Westport, CT 06881-5007
Phone: (203)454-8814
Fax: (203)226-6009
Free: 800-225-5800

Publications: Bulletin of Bibliography (24127) • Journal of Accounting, Auditing & Finance (21973) • MultiCultural Review (5214)

The Greenwood and Southside Challenger
PO Box 708
Greenwood, IN 46142
Phone: (317)888-3376
Fax: (317)888-3377

Publications: The Greenwood and Southside Challenger (10046)

The Greer Citizen
PO Box 70
Greer, SC 29652
Phone: (864)877-2076
Fax: (864)877-3563

Publications: The Greer Citizen (28652)

The Greeter
108 N Main
Plentywood, MT 59254
Phone: (406)765-1733
Fax: (406)765-2106
Free: 800-637-2203

Publications: The Greeter (17894)

Gregory Times Advocate
623 Main St.
PO Box 378
Gregory, SD 57533
Phone: (605)835-8089
Fax: (605)835-8467

Publications: Gregory Times Advocate (28861)

Grenada Lake Herald
PO Box 907
Grenada, MS 38902-0907
Phone: (662)226-4321
Fax: (662)226-8310

Publications: Grenada Lake Herald (16653)

The Gresham Outlook
1190 NE Division St.
PO Box 747
Gresham, OR 97030
Phone: (503)665-2181
Fax: (503)665-2187

Publications: The Gresham Outlook (26365)

Gretna Guide & News
PO Box 240
Gretna, NE 68028
Phone: (402)332-3232
Fax: (402)332-4733

Publications: Gretna Guide & News (18033)

Greybull Standard
614 Greybull Ave.
Greybull, WY 82426
Phone: (307)765-4485
Fax: (307)568-2459

Publications: Greybull Standard (34534)

The Greyhound
4501 N Charles St.
Gardens Apts. B 01
Baltimore, MD 21210
Phone: (410)617-2282
Fax: (410)617-2982

Publications: The Greyhound (13167)

Greysmith Publishing
PO Box 681629
Franklin, TN 37068-1629
Phone: (615)790-7566
Fax: (615)790-6188
Free: 800-567-4335

Publications: Back Home in Kentucky (29194)

The Gridley Herald
630 Washington St.
PO Box 68
Gridley, CA 95948
Phone: (916)846-3661
Fax: (916)846-4519

Publications: The Gridley Herald (2032)

Griffin Daily News
323 E Solomon St.
PO Box M
Griffin, GA 30224
Phone: (770)227-3276
Fax: (770)412-1678

Publications: Griffin Daily News (7311)

Griffin Lovett
PO Drawer B, Ct. Sq. Sta.
Dublin, GA 31040-2449
Phone: (912)272-5522
Fax: (912)272-2189
Free: 800-833-8504

Publications: The Courier Herald (7251)

Griffis Management Services Ltd.
305 Main St.
Massena, NY 13662
Phone: (315)764-1555
Fax: (315)764-0782

Publications: County Pennysaver (21026)

Griffith Observatory
2800 E Observatory Rd.
Los Angeles, CA 90027
Phone: (323)664-1181
Fax: (323)663-4323

Publications: The Griffith Observer (2281)

Griffith Press, Inc.
PO Box 130
Elkader, IA 52043-0130
Phone: (319)245-1311
Fax: (319)245-1312

Publications: The Clayton County Register (10873)

Grimes and Associates
522 Kimbark
Longmont, CO 80501
Phone: (303)776-3103
Fax: (303)776-3798

Publications: Vows (4561)

Grimsrud Publishing, Inc.
225 Main St.
PO Box 97
Zumbrota, MN 55992
Phone: (507)732-7617
Fax: (507)732-7619
Free: 800-772-5384

Publications: The Country Shopper (15925) • News-Record (16542) • The News Record (16495)

Griot Communications Group Inc.
900 E Charleston Blvd.
Las Vegas, NV 89104
Phone: (702)380-8100
Fax: (702)380-8102

Publications: Las Vegas Sentinel-Voice (18375)

Griswold American
PO Box 430
Griswold, IA 51535
Phone: (712)778-4337
Fax: (712)778-4350

Publications: Griswold American (10934)

The Grizzly
42007, Forx Farm Rd. Ste. 3B
PO Box 1789
Big Bear Lake, CA 92315
Phone: (909)866-3456
Fax: (909)866-2302

Publications: Big Bear Life & the Grizzly (1580)

Grizzly Gazette 1990 Inc.
PO Box 1000
Swan Hills, AB, Canada T0G 2C0
Phone: (403)333-2100
Fax: (403)333-2111

Publications: Swan Hills Grizzly Gazette (34860)

GRL Communications
PO Box 11261, Sta. H
Nepean, ON, Canada K2H 7T9
Phone: (613)596-1358
Fax: (613)820-1461

Publications: Monitor (36100)

Groesbeck Journal, Inc.
PO Box 440
Groesbeck, TX 76642
Phone: (254)729-5103
Fax: (254)729-8310

Publications: Journal (30417)

Grossmont College
8800 Grossmont College Dr.
El Cajon, CA 92020
Phone: (619)644-7271
Fax: (619)644-7914

Publications: The Summit (1849)

Groton Regional Independent
16 N. Main
PO Box 588
Groton, SD 57445
Phone: (605)397-2676

Publications: Groton Regional Independent (28863)

Group C Communications, Inc.
PO Box 2060
Red Bank, NJ 07701
Phone: (732)919-1716
Fax: (732)919-7532
Free: 800-524-0337

Publications: Business Facilities (19500) • Today's Facility Manager (19501)

Group Publishing Inc.
1515 Cascade Ave.
Loveland, CO 80538
Phone: (970)669-3836
Fax: (970)292-4360
Free: 800-635-0404

Publications: Children's Ministry Magazine (4566) • Group Magazine (4567)

Group Travel (Voyage en Groupe)
590 Chemin St-Jean
Laprairie, QC, Canada J5R 2L1
Phone: (450)444-5870

Publications: Group Travel (Voyage en Groupe) (37033)

Groupe Constructo
200-1500 boul. Jules-Poitras
Saint-Laurent, QC, Canada H4N 1X7
Phone: (514)745-5720
Fax: (514)339-2267
Free: 800-363-0910

Publications: Journal Constructo (37363)

Groupe Media Business Inc.
324, boul. Labelle
Saint-Jerome, QC, Canada J7Z 5L3
Phone: (450)438-8383
Fax: (450)438-4174

Publications: Journal Le Nord (37356)

Groupe Quebecor Inc.
450, rue Bechard, Vanier
Quebec, QC, Canada G1M 2E9
Phone: (418)683-1573
Fax: (418)683-1027

Publications: Le Journal de Quebec (37288)

Grove City College
100 Campus Dr.
Grove City, PA 16127-2197
Phone: (724)458-2193
Fax: (724)458-3334

Publications: The Collegian (26964)

Grove City College
Public Relations Office
100 Campus Dr.
Grove City, PA 16127-2104
Phone: (724)458-3100
Fax: (724)458-3334

Publications: Grove City College Alumni Magazine (26965)

The Grove City Record
4048 Broadway
PO Box 339
Grove City, OH 43123-0339
Phone: (614)875-2307
Fax: (614)875-6028

Publications: Grove City Record (25233)

Grove Enterprises, Inc.
PO Box 98
Brasstown, NC 28902
Phone: (828)837-9200
Fax: (828)837-2216
Free: 800-438-8155

Publications: Monitoring Times (23663)

The Grove Sun Daily
14 W. 3rd St.
Grove, OK 74344
Phone: (918)786-2228
Fax: (918)786-2156

Publications: Grove Sun (25847) • The South Grand Laker (25849)

Growing Room Collective
Sta. D
Box 46160
Vancouver, BC, Canada V6J 5G5

Publications: Room of One's Own (35165)

GRQ Publications
1405 Villa Real Ct.
Gilroy, CA 95020-9218
Phone: (408)848-1313
Fax: (408)842-0451

Publications: The Rottweiler Quarterly (2004)

Gruner & Jahr USA
38 Commercial Wharf
Boston, MA 02110
Phone: (617)248-8000
Fax: (617)248-8090
Free: 800-842-1343

Publications: Inc. (13904) • Inc. Technology (13905)

GSA Business
7 Washington Park
Greenville, SC 29601
Phone: (864)235-5677
Fax: (864)235-4868

Publications: GSA Business (28624)

Guard Publishing Co.
3500 Chad Dr., 97408
PO Box 10188
Eugene, OR 97440-2188
Phone: (541)485-1234
Fax: (541)984-4699

Publications: The Register-Guard (26334)

The Guardian
165 Prince St.
PO Box 760
Charlottetown, PE, Canada C1A 4R7
Phone: (902)629-6000
Fax: (902)566-9808
Free: 800-267-6397

Publications: The Guardian (36915)

The Guardian-Journal
PO Box 119
Homer, LA 71040
Phone: (318)927-3541
Fax: (318)927-3542

Publications: The Guardian-Journal (12600)

Guelph Mercury
8-14 Macdonnell St.
PO Box 3604
Guelph, ON, Canada N1H 6P7
Phone: (519)822-4310
Fax: (519)767-1681

Publications: Guelph Mercury (35864)

Guelph Pennysaver
86 Dawson Rd.
Guelph, ON, Canada N1H 1A8

Publications: Guelph Pennysaver (35865)

Guidelines Press
1307 S Killian Dr.
Lake Park, FL 33403-1918
Fax: (407)842-2237

Publications: Kidstuff (6284)

Guideposts
39 Seminary Hill Rd.
Carmel, NY 10512
Phone: (845)225-3681
Fax: (845)228-2111
Free: 800-431-2344

Publications: Angels on Earth (20435) • Guideposts for Kids (9887) • Guideposts Magazine (21782)

Guild of American Luthiers
8222 S. Park Ave.
Tacoma, WA 98408
Phone: (253)432-7853
Fax: (253)472-7853

Publications: American Lutherie (33143)

Guilford Publications
72 Spring St.
New York, NY 10012
Phone: (212)431-9800
Fax: (212)431-9800
Free: 800-365-7006

Publications: Bulletin of the Menninger Clinic (11815) • The Psychoanalytic Review (22603)

Guinan Publishing Corp.
1538 Old Country Rd.
Plainview, NY 11803
Phone: (516)249-0750
Fax: (516)249-0789

Publications: Pennysaver (20596) • Plainview/Jericho Pennysaver (23099) • Syosset/Woodbury Pennysaver (23384)

Gujarat Vartman
250 Norfinch Dr.
Downsview, ON, Canada M3N 1Y4
Phone: (416)736-1640
Fax: (416)736-0848

Publications: Gujarat Vartman (35784)

Gulf/Atlantic Publishing, Inc.
2649 Pemberton Dr.
Apopka, FL 32703-9403
Phone: (407)628-5700
Fax: (407)628-0807
Free: 800-444-4980

Publications: Moneyworld (5910)

Gulf Breeze Publishing Co.
1200 Gulf Breeze Pky.
Gulf Breeze, FL 32561
Phone: (850)934-5108
Fax: (850)932-8765

Publications: The Gulf Breeze Sentinel (6177) • Mexico Business Journal (6178) • Perido Pelican (6179)

Gulf Coast Newspaper
PO Box 1128
128 Cove Ave.
Gulf Shores, AL 36547
Phone: (251)968-6414
Fax: (251)968-5233

Publications: Islander (252)

Gulf Coast Newspapers
PO Box 509
Robertsdale, AL 36567
Phone: (251)947-7712
Fax: (251)947-7652

Publications: Baldwin Times (51) • Fairhope Courier (436) • The Independent (437)

Gulf Coast Newspapers North
100 Ave. A
PO Box 609
Conroe, TX 77301
Phone: (409)756-6671
Fax: (409)756-6676

Publications: Conroe Courier (30070)

Gulf Coast Publishing Corp.
11201 Morning Ct.
San Antonio, TX 78213
Phone: (210)344-8300
Fax: (210)344-4258

Publications: The Beefmaster Cowman (31025) • Gulf Coast Cattleman (31031)

Gulf of Maine Times
PO Box 339
Annapolis Royal, NS, Canada B0S 1A0
Phone: (902)532-0200
Fax: (902)532-0250

Publications: Gulf of Maine Times (35534)

Gulf Pine Catholic
1790 Popps Ferry Rd.
PO Box 1189
Biloxi, MS 39533-1189
Phone: (228)702-2127
Fax: (228)702-2128
Free: 877-276-1041

Publications: Gulf Pine Catholic (16562)

Gulf Publishing Co.
3 Greenway Plz., 9th Fl.
Houston, TX 77252-2608
Phone: (713)529-4301
Fax: (713)520-4433
Free: 800-231-6275

Publications: Hydrocarbon Processing (30490) • World Oil (30542)

Gulfshore Media Inc.
9051 Tamiami Trl. N, Ste. 202
Naples, FL 34108-2520
Phone: (239)594-9980
Fax: (239)594-9986
Free: 800-220-4853

Publications: Gulfshore Life Magazine (6440) • Home & Condo (6441)

Gulp
21 Main St.
Binghamton, NY 13905
Phone: (607)723-4507

Publications: Gulp (20153)

Gunnison Country Times
218 N Wisconsin
PO Box 240
Gunnison, CO 81230
Phone: (303)641-1414
Fax: (303)641-6515

Publications: Gunnison Country Times (4509)

The Gurdon Times
PO Box 250
Gurdon, AR 71743-0250
Phone: (870)353-4482

Publications: The Gurdon Times (1163)

Gustavus Adolphus College
800 W. College Ave. PO Box A-6
St. Peter, MN 56082-1498
Phone: (507)933-7636
Fax: (507)933-7633

Publications: The Gustavian Weekly (16430)

Guthrie Center Times
205 State St.
Guthrie Center, IA 50115-1349
Phone: (515)747-3511

Publications: Guthrie Center Times (10937)

Guthrie County Vedette
111 E Main
PO Box 38
Panora, IA 50216
Phone: (641)755-2115
Fax: (641)755-2425

Publications: Guthrie County Vedette (11147)

Guttenberg Publishing
Box 937
Guttenberg, IA 52052
Phone: (563)252-2421
Fax: (563)252-1275

Publications: The Guttenberg Press (10938)

GVR Public Relations Agency
1120 NASA Rd. 1, Ste. 405
Houston, TX 77085
Phone: (281)333-1881
Fax: (281)333-1996

Publications: Maes National Magazine (30505)

Gwynedd Mercy College
1325 Sumney Town Pke.
Gwynedd Valley, PA 19437
Phone: (215)646-7300

Publications: The Gwynmercian (26968)

Gypsy Lore Society Inc.
5607 Greenleaf Rd.
Cheverly, MD 20785
Phone: (301)341-1261
Fax: (301)341-1261

Publications: Romani Studies (13407)

H and H Publications
PO Box 97
414 Main St.
Burden, KS 67019
Phone: (316)438-2370
Fax: (316)438-2370

Publications: The Cowley County Reporter (11368)

H & H Publications
226 E. Main
PO Box 417
Sedan, KS 67361
Phone: (316)725-3176
Fax: (316)725-3272

Publications: The Elk County Citizen-Advance News (11613) • Sedan Times-Star (11797)

H-I, Inc.
PO Box 31
Thermopolis, WY 82443
Phone: (307)864-2328
Fax: (307)864-5711

Publications: Independent Record (34595)

H & K Publications, Inc.
50 Buffalo St.
Hamburg, NY 14075-5002
Phone: (716)649-4413
Fax: (716)649-6374

Publications: Arcade Pennysaver (20062) • Blasdell Lackawanna Pennysaver (20234) • Franklinville Pennysaver (20620) • Hamburg Pennysaver (20703) • Springville Journal (23354) • Springville PennySaver (23355) • Sun & Erie County Independent (20705)

H. Lee Moffitt Cancer Center & Research Institute
12902 Magnolia Dr.
Tampa, FL 33612
Phone: (813)632-1349
Fax: (813)903-4950

Publications: Cancer Control Journal (6759)

Ha'Am
118 Kerckhoff Hall
308 Westwood Plaza
Los Angeles, CA 90024
Phone: (310)825-6280
Fax: (310)206-3165

Publications: Ha'Am (2285)

Habitat for Humanity International, Inc.
121 Habitat St.
Americus, GA 31709-3498
Phone: (229)924-6935
Fax: (229)924-6541

Publications: Habitat World (6921)

Hachette Filipacchi
PO Box 55394
Boulder, CO 80323
Phone: (303)604-7455

Publications: Premiere (4185)

Hachette Filipacchi Magazines, Inc.
1633 Broadway, 42nd Fl.
New York, NY 10019
Phone: (212)767-6000
Fax: (212)767-5612

Publications: Woman's Day Best Ideas for Christmas (22925) • Woman's Day Eating Light (22926) • Woman's Day Gardening & Outdoor Living (22927) • Woman's Day Holiday Baking (22928) • Woman's Day Home Decorating Ideas (22929) • Woman's Day Home Remodeling (22930) • Woman's Day Kitchens and Baths (22931)

Hachette Filipacchi Media U.S., Inc.
1633 Broadway
New York, NY 10019
Phone: (212)767-6000

Publications: American Photo (21204) • Boating Magazine (21329) • Car and Driver (21372) • Cycle World (2625) • Elle (21594) • Elle Canada (21595) • Elle Decor (21596) • Flying (4872) • Home Magazine (21809) • Home Magazine's Home Plans (21810) • Metropolitan Home (22328) • Mobile Entertainment (22341) • Popular Photography and Imaging (22581) • Road & Track (2635) • Sony Style (22763) • TV Crosswords (22873) • Weekend Decorating Projects (22913) • Woman's Day (22924)

Hachette Publications
5670 Wilshire Blvd., Ste. 500
Los Angeles, CA 90036
Phone: (213)954-0500
Fax: (213)954-4800

Publications: Home Magazine (2292)

Hack'd
PO Box 813
Buckhannon, WV 26201
Phone: (304)472-6146
Fax: (304)472-7027

Publications: Hack'd (33263)

Hacks 12Sports Magazine
9933 Alliance Rd.
Cincinnati, OH 45242
Phone: (513)794-4100

Publications: Hacks 12Sports Magazine (24801)

Hadassah, The Women's Zionist Organi-
zation of America
50 W 58th St.
New York, NY 10019
Phone: (212)688-2656
Fax: (212)446-9521

Publications: Hadassah Magazine (21785)

Hadassah-Wizo Organization of Canada
1310 Greene Ave., Rm. 900
Montreal, QC, Canada H3Z 2B8
Phone: (514)937-9431
Fax: (514)933-6483

Publications: Orah Magazine (37199)

Hadassah Zionist Youth Commission
PO Box 173
Merion Station, PA 19066
Phone: (215)642-8389

Publications: Young Judaean (22953)

Haden B. Brumbeloe and Associates,
Inc.
12972 Earhart Ave., Ste. 302
Auburn, CA 95602
Phone: (530)823-0706
Fax: (530)823-6937

Publications: FPC/Fire Protection Contractor (1438)

Hadoar Association, Inc.
426 West 58th St.
New York, NY 10019-1102
Phone: (212)957-6659
Fax: (212)957-5811

Publications: Hadoar (The Post) (21786)

Hadronic Press Inc.
35246 U.S. 19 N, No. 115
Palm Harbor, FL 34684
Phone: (727)934-9593
Fax: (727)934-9275

Publications: Algebras, Groups & Geometries
(6550) • Hadronic Journal (6551) • Hadronic Journal
Supplement (6552)

Hagadon, Inc.
813 W 3rd Ave.
Moses Lake, WA 98837-2008
Phone: (509)765-4561
Fax: (509)765-8659

Publications: Columbia Basin Herald (32838)

Hagadone Corp
PO Box 189
Columbia Falls, MT 59912
Phone: (406)892-2151
Fax: (406)892-5600

Publications: Hungry Horse News (17773)

Hagadone Corp.
515 Pavonia St.
Sioux City, IA 51102
Phone: (712)279-5026
Fax: (712)279-5059
Free: 800-397-3530

Publications: Sioux City Journal (11213)

Hagedorn Communications
135 Dreiser Loop
Bronx, NY 10475-2703
Phone: (718)671-1234

Publications: Co-Op City News (20263)

Hagedorn Communications
662 Main St.
New Rochelle, NY 10801
Phone: (914)636-7400
Fax: (914)636-2957

Publications: Parkchester News (21121) • Real
Estate Weekly (22635) • Town and Village (21123)

The Hagerstown Exponent
35 W. Main St.
Hagerstown, IN 47346
Phone: (765)489-4035
Fax: (765)489-5323

Publications: The Hagerstown Exponent (10048)

Hagon On
310 Church St.
PO Box 159
Sandpoint, ID 83864
Phone: (208)263-9534
Fax: (208)263-9091

Publications: The Daily Bee (7978)

Haight-Ashbury Publications
612 Clayton St.
San Francisco, CA 94117-2958
Phone: (415)565-1904
Fax: (415)864-6162

Publications: Journal of Psychoactive Drugs (3384)

The Haiku Society of America
PO Box 2461
Winchester, VA 22604-1661
Phone: (540)722-2156

Publications: Frogpond (32628)

Hairenik Association, Inc.
80 Bigelow Ave.
Watertown, MA 02472
Phone: (617)926-3974
Fax: (617)926-1750

Publications: The Armenian Weekly (14611)

Halana
PO Box 502
Ardmore, PA 19003-0502
Fax: (419)781-7542

Publications: Halana (26660)

Halco Press, LLC
PO Box 88
Turtle Lake, WI 54889
Phone: (715)986-4675

Publications: Turtle Lake Times (34376)

Halcyon Business Publications, Inc.
400 Post Ave.
Westbury, NY 11590
Phone: (516)338-0900
Fax: (516)338-0100
Free: 800-735-2732

Publications: Area Development Magazine (23552)

The Haldimand Advocate Ltd.
Box 369
Hagersville, ON, Canada N0A 1H0
Phone: (905)768-3111
Fax: (905)768-3340

Publications: Haldimand Press (35871)

Hale Communications, Inc.
1212 4th St.
Parker, AZ 85344
Phone: (602)669-6464
Fax: (602)669-6464

Publications: Arizona West (762)

Haleakala Times
PO Box 1080
Makawao, HI 96768
Phone: (808)572-9289
Fax: (808)572-0168

Publications: Haleakala Times (7786) • Kihei Times
(7787)

Half Bay Review
PO Box 68
Half Moon Bay, CA 94019
Phone: (415)726-4424
Fax: (415)726-7054

Publications: Half Moon Bay Review and Pescadero
Pebble (2036)

Halifax Gazette Publishing Co.
3201-3209 Halifax Rd
South Boston, VA 24592
Phone: (434)572-3945
Fax: (434)572-1173

Publications: Gazette/Virginia Shopper (32529)

The Halifax Herald Ltd.
1650 Argyle St.
Halifax, NS, Canada B3J 2T2
Phone: (902)426-2811
Fax: (902)426-1158
Free: 800-563-1187

Publications: The Chronicle Herald (35561) • The
Halifax Herald (35566)

Hall Center for the Humanities
1540 Sunflower Rd.
Lawrence, KS 66045
Phone: (913)864-4798
Fax: (913)864-3884

Publications: Journal of Dramatic Theory and Criticism (11555)

Chris Hall
188 Mary St.
Port Perry, ON, Canada L9L 1B7
Phone: (905)985-7383
Fax: (905)985-3708

Publications: Port Perry Star (36335)

Hall Johnson Consulting
9737 W. Ohio Ave.
Lakewood, CO 80226
Phone: (303)988-0056

Publications: Nurse Author and Editor (4534)

Hallettsville Publishing Co.
PO Box 1301
East Bernard, TX 77435-1301
Phone: (409)335-4014

Publications: East Bernard Tribune (30263)

Halloween Events, Inc.
36393 Dequindre
Troy, MI 48083
Phone: (248)524-9782
Fax: (248)524-1320

Publications: The Fear Finder (15625)

Halper Publishing Co.
830 Moseley Rd.
Highland Park, IL 60035
Phone: (847)780-2900
Fax: (847)780-2902

Publications: Made to Measure (8993)

Hamdani Communications Inc.
Bldg. 56, Ste. 282
2625 Piedmont Rd.
Atlanta, GA 30324

Publications: Black Employment and Education
Magazine (6979)

Hamilton College
College Publications
198 College Hill Rd.
Clinton, NY 13323
Phone: (315)859-4011
Fax: (315)859-4648
Free: 800-222-6381

Publications: Hamilton Alumni Review (20472) •
The Spectator (20474)

Hamilton County Herald
PO Box 21279
Chattanooga, TN 37424
Phone: (423)892-1336
Fax: (423)899-6393

Publications: Hamilton County Herald (29089)

Hamilton Diversified Services, Inc.
3611 Stockdale Hwy., Ste. H
Bakersfield, CA 93309

Publications: Bakersfield's Shopper (1449)

The Hamilton Herald-News
112 E Main
PO Box 833
Hamilton, TX 76531-0833
Phone: (254)386-3145
Fax: (254)386-3001

Publications: The Hamilton Herald-News (30420)

Hamilton News, Inc.
PO Box 326
Hamilton, IN 46742-0326
Phone: (260)488-3780
Fax: (260)488-4326

Publications: The Hamilton News (10049)

Hamlin County
Box 207
Hayti, SD 57241
Phone: (605)783-3636
Fax: (605)793-9140

Publications: Hamlin County Herald-Enterprise (28865)

Hamlin County Republican
Box 50
Castlewood, SD 57223
Phone: (605)793-2293
Fax: (605)793-9140

Publications: Hamlin County Republican (28830)

Hamline University
1536 Hewitt Ave.
PO Box 106
St. Paul, MN 55104
Phone: (651)523-2082
Fax: (651)523-2236

Publications: Journal of Law and Religion (16382) • The Oracle (16403)

Hammonton News
115 12th St.
PO Box 596
Hammonton, NJ 08037-0596
Phone: (609)561-2300
Fax: (609)567-2249
Free: 800-489-4464

Publications: Hammonton News (18864)

The Hampden-Sydney Tiger
PO Box 635
Hampden Sydney, VA 23943-0626
Phone: (804)223-6359
Fax: (804)223-6399

Publications: The Hampden-Sydney Tiger (32124)

Hampton Publishing Co.
9 2nd St. NW
PO Box 29
Hampton, IA 50441
Phone: (641)456-2585
Fax: (641)456-2587
Free: 800-558-1244

Publications: Conservative Chronicle (10939) • Hampton Chronicle (10940)

Hampton University
PO Box 6237
Hampton, VA 23668
Phone: (757)727-5385
Fax: (757)727-5085

Publications: Hampton Script (32128)

Hanceville Herald
PO Box 880
Hanceville, AL 35077
Phone: (205)352-4775

Publications: The Hanceville Herald (263)

Hanchett Publishing
334 E Campbell Ave.
Campbell, CA 95008
Phone: (408)374-9700
Fax: (408)374-0813

Publications: Campbell Express (1653)

Hancock Clarion
Main St.
Hawesville, KY 42348
Phone: (270)927-6945
Fax: (270)927-6947
Free: 800-337-0585

Publications: Hancock Clarion (12114)

Hancock County Journal Pilot
31 N Washington
PO Box 478
Carthage, IL 62321
Phone: (217)357-2149
Fax: (217)357-2177

Publications: Hancock County Journal Pilot (8165)

Hancock Courier Printing Co.
PO Box 547
New Cumberland, WV 26047
Phone: (304)564-3131
Fax: (304)564-3867

Publications: Hancock County Courier (33412)

Hancock-Henderson Quill, Inc.
PO Box 149
Stronghurst, IL 61480
Phone: (309)924-1871
Fax: (309)924-1212

Publications: Hancock County Quill (9671) • The Henderson County Quill (9672)

Hancock Herald
45 1/2 E Front St.
PO Box 519
Hancock, NY 13783
Phone: (607)637-3591
Fax: (607)637-4383

Publications: Hancock Herald (20710)

The Hancock News
263 Pennsylvania Ave.
Hancock, MD 21750
Phone: (301)678-6255
Fax: (301)678-5520

Publications: The Hancock News (13579)

Hanford Sentinel Inc.
2045 Grant St.
PO Box 100
Selma, CA 93662
Phone: (559)896-1976
Fax: (559)896-9160

Publications: The Selma Enterprise (3755)

Hanging Loose Press
231 Wyckoff St.
Brooklyn, NY 11217
Phone: (212)206-8465
Fax: (212)243-7499

Publications: Hanging Loose (20319)

Hanley & Belfus Inc.
210 S. 13th St.
Philadelphia, PA 19107
Phone: (215)546-7293
Fax: (215)790-9330
Free: 800-962-1892

Publications: Academic Emergency Medicine (27361) • Biomedical Instrumentation & Technology (27388) • Journal of Hand Therapy (27530) • Medical Decision Making (27565) • Medical Problems of Performing Artists (27567)

Hanley-Wood, LLC
4160 Wilshire Blvd.
Los Angeles, CA 90010
Phone: (323)801-4900
Fax: (323)801-4902

Publications: Aquatics International (2213)

Hanley-Wood, LLC.
1 Thomas Circle, Ste. 600
Washington, DC 20005
Phone: (202)452-0800
Fax: (202)785-1974

Publications: Builder (5386) • Building Products (5387) • Custom Home (5456) • Kitchen & Bath Showroom (5626) • ProSales (5734) • Remodeling (5761)

Hanley-Wood, LLC
426 S. Westgate St.
Addison, IL 60101-4546
Phone: (630)543-0870
Fax: (630)543-3112
Free: 800-837-0870

Publications: Concrete Cunstruction (8000) • Masonry Construction (8002)

The Hanna Herald
Hanna, AB, Canada T0J 1P0
Phone: (403)854-3366
Fax: (403)854-3256

Publications: The Hanna Herald (34779)

Hanna Publications
514 Prairie St.
PO Box 550
Winnsboro, LA 71295-0550
Phone: (318)435-4521
Fax: (318)435-9220

Publications: The Franklin Sun (12883)

Richard Hannagan
116 Main St.
PO Box 99
Adams, WI 53910
Phone: (608)339-7844
Fax: (608)339-3903

Publications: Adams County Times (33518) • Times Reporter (33519)

Hannibal Courier-Post
200 N 3rd St.
PO Box A
Hannibal, MO 63401
Phone: (573)221-2800
Fax: (573)221-1568
Free: 800-748-7025

Publications: Hannibal Courier-Post (17090)

Hanover News
201 Railroad
PO Box 278
Hanover, KS 66945
Phone: (785)337-2242

Publications: Hanover News (14681)

The Hanover Post
413 18th Ave.
Hanover, ON, Canada N4N 3S5
Phone: (519)364-2001
Fax: (519)364-6950

Publications: The Durham Chronicle (35798) • The Hanover Post (35900) • The Markdale Standard (36013)

Hansen Publishing LLC
611 Main St.
Ramona, CA 92065
Phone: (760)789-1350
Fax: (760)789-4057

Publications: Ramona Sentinel (2872)

The Hansford County Reporter-Statesman
213 Main St.
Spearman, TX 79081
Phone: (806)659-3434
Fax: (806)659-3368

Publications: The Hansford County Reporter-Statesman (31124)

The Hanska Herald
PO Box 45
Hanska, MN 56041
Phone: (507)439-6214

Publications: The Hanska Herald (15939)

Happenings Communications Group, Inc.
PO Box 61
Clarks Summit, PA 18411-0061
Phone: (570)587-3532
Fax: (570)586-7374

Publications: Happenings Magazine (26786)

Harbor City Star
2575 McCollough Rd., Ste. B1
Nanaimo, BC, Canada V9E 5W5
Phone: (250)758-4917
Fax: (250)758-4513

Publications: Harbor City Star (35019)

Harbor House Publishers Inc.
221 Water St.
Boyne City, MI 49712
Phone: (231)582-2814
Fax: (231)582-3392
Free: 800-491-1760

Publications: Outstate Business (14833) • Seaway Review (14834)

Harbor Sound
1326 Newcastle St.
PO Box 606
Brunswick, GA 31521
Phone: (912)264-4521
Fax: (912)264-4531

Publications: Harbor Sound (7140)

Harcourt Health Sciences
The Curtis Ctr.
Independence Sq. W.
Philadelphia, PA 19106-3399
Phone: (215)238-7800
Fax: (215)238-8772

Publications: Emergency Medicine Clinics of North America (27457)

Hard Hat News
PO Box 121
6113 State Hwy 5
Palatine Bridge, NY 13428
Phone: (518)673-3237
Fax: (518)673-2381

Publications: Hard Hat News (23075)

Hard Press, Inc.
PO Box 184
West Stockbridge, MA 01266-0184
Phone: (413)232-4690
Fax: (413)232-4675

Publications: Lingo Magazine (14627)

Hardi
1650 S. Dixie Hwy., 5th Fl.
Boca Raton, FL 33432
Phone: (561)338-3495
Fax: (561)395-8557

Publications: HVAC/R Distribution Today (5932)

Hardin County Independent
Box 328
Elizabethtown, IL 62931
Phone: (618)287-2361

Publications: Hardin County Independent (8830)

Hardin County Index
1513 Edgington Ave.
Eldora, IA 50627
Phone: (641)939-5051
Fax: (641)939-5541

Publications: Hardin County Index (10868)

Hardin County Publishing Co.
201 E. Columbus St.
Kenton, OH 43326
Phone: (419)673-1102
Fax: (419)673-1125
Free: 800-886-2412

Publications: KentonTimes (25281)

The Harding Publishing Co.
111 W Wyandot Ave.
PO Box 180
Upper Sandusky, OH 43351
Phone: (419)294-2332
Fax: (419)294-5608

Publications: Chief-Union (25604)

Hardware Trade, Inc.
PO Box 151
318 5th St.
Hull, IA 51239
Phone: (712)439-1962.

Publications: Hardware Trade (10955)

Hardwick Publishing Co., Inc.
Main St.
Box 367
Hardwick, VT 05843
Phone: (802)472-6521

Publications: The Hardwick Gazette (31544)

Hare Krishna World
PO Box 238
Alachua, FL 32616-0238
Phone: (386)462-5054
Fax: (386)462-5056

Publications: Hare Krishna World (5898)

Harford Business Ledger, Inc.
214 W Bel Air Ave.
Aberdeen, MD 21001-0075
Phone: (410)272-9243
Fax: (410)272-4208

Publications: Harford Business Ledger, Inc. (13085)

Harlan County Journal
Box 9
Alma, NE 68920
Phone: (308)928-2143
Fax: (308)928-9914

Publications: Harlan County Journal (17933)

The Harlan Daily Enterprise
1548 S. U.S. Hwy. 421
PO Box E
Harlan, KY 40831
Phone: (606)573-4510
Fax: (606)573-0042

Publications: The Harlan Daily Enterprise (12104)

Harle Publications
7002 W Butler Pke.
Ambler, PA 19002
Phone: (215)643-6385
Fax: (215)628-3871

Publications: Easy Crosswords (26647) • Easy Fill-Ins (26648)

Harmonie Park Press
23630 Pinewood
Warren, MI 48091
Phone: (586)755-2560
Fax: (586)755-4213
Free: 800-422-4880

Publications: The Music Index (15660)

Harnett County News
PO Box 939
Lillington, NC 27546
Phone: (910)893-5121
Fax: (910)893-6128

Publications: Harnett County News (24044)

Harold Wells Gulf Coast Fisherman, Inc.
PO Drawer 8
Port Lavaca, TX 77979
Phone: (361)552-8864
Fax: (361)552-8864

Publications: Gulf Coast Fisherman (30955)

Harrah News, Inc.
PO Box 778
Oklahoma City, OK 73101-0778
Publications: The Harrah News (25965)

Harris County Herald
PO Box 1420
713 Gardensview Dr.
Pine Mountain, GA 31822
Phone: (706)663-8886
Fax: (706)663-8864

Publications: Harris County Herald (7485)

Harris County Journal
PO Box 426
Manchester, GA 31816
Phone: (404)846-3188
Fax: (706)846-2206

Publications: Harris County Journal (7407)

Harris Enterprizes
PO Box 10
Burlington, IA 52601
Phone: (319)754-6824
Fax: (319)754-6824
Free: 800-397-1708

Publications: Hawk Eye (10638)

Harris Publications, Inc.
1115 Broadway, 8th Fl.
New York, NY 10010-2803
Phone: (212)807-7100
Fax: (212)627-4678

Publications: Guitar World (21783) • Hair Cut and Style (21787) • Small Business Opportunities (22746)

Harris Publishing, Inc.
360 B Street
Idaho Falls, ID 83402
Phone: (208)524-7000
Fax: (208)522-5241

Publications: Houseboat Magazine (7864) • Idaho Golf (7865) • The Mountain Gardener (7866) • Pontoon & Deck Boat Magazine (7867) • Potato Grower (7869) • SnoWest (7870) • The Sugar Producer (7871) • Today's Playground (7872)

Harrison News Herald
130 N. Main St.
Cadiz, OH 43907
Phone: (740)942-2118
Fax: (740)942-4667

Publications: Harrison News Herald (24722)

The Harriston Review
42 Elora St.
Harriston, ON, Canada N0G 1Z0
Fax: (519)338-3130

Publications: The Harriston Review (35902)

The Harrodsburg Herald
PO Box 68
Harrodsburg, KY 40330-0068
Phone: (606)734-2726
Fax: (606)734-0737
Free: 800-803-1184

Publications: The Harrodsburg Herald (12111)

Harrow & Colchester South This Week
72 King St. E.
PO Box 1210
Harrow, ON, Canada N0R 1G0
Phone: (519)738-2000
Fax: (519)738-3956

Publications: Harrow & Colchester South This Week (35903)

The Harrow News
563 Queen St.
PO Box 310
Harrow, ON, Canada N0R 1G0
Phone: (519)738-2542
Fax: (519)738-3874

Publications: The Harrow News (35904)

Harry Dennis Publishing
9 E 45th St.
New York, NY 10017
Phone: (212)309-6886

Publications: American Ceramics (21183)

The Hart Beat
PO Box 350
Hart, TX 79043-0350
Phone: (806)938-2640
Fax: (806)938-2275

Publications: The Hart Beat (30432)

Hart County News-Herald
570 S Dixie St.
PO Box 340
Horse Cave, KY 42749-0340
Phone: (502)786-1929
Fax: (502)786-4470

Publications: Hart County News-Herald (12137)

Hart-Hanks Communications
2830, Orbiter St.
Brea, CA 92821
Phone: (714)996-8900
Fax: (714)993-4711

Publications: Pennysaver (1600)

Hart Publications, Inc.
4545 Post Oak Place, Ste. 210
Houston, TX 77027
Phone: (713)993-9320
Fax: (713)840-8585
Free: 800-874-2544

Publications: Hart's Fuel Technology & Management (30476) • Hart's Lubricants World (30477) • Oil and Gas Investor (30515)

Hart Publishing Co.
PO Box 128
Glidden, WI 54527
Phone: (715)264-3481
Fax: (715)264-3481

Publications: Enterprise (33735)

Harte-Hanks, Inc.
1300 Specialty Dr.
Vista, CA 92083-8522

Publications: El Informador (4044)

The Hartford Courant
285 Broad St.
Hartford, CT 06115
Phone: (860)241-6200
Fax: (860)520-3176

Publications: The Hartford Courant (4892)

Hartford Seminary
77 Sherman St.
Hartford, CT 06105
Phone: (860)509-9500
Fax: (860)509-9509

Publications: The Muslim World (4899)

Hartley Sentinel, Inc.
71 1st St. SE
Hartley, IA 51346
Phone: (712)728-2223
Fax: (712)728-2223

Publications: Everly-Royal News (10881) • Hartley Sentinel (10948)

Hartman Group Publishing, Inc.
401 N Wabash, Ste. 534
Chicago, IL 60611
Phone: (312)822-0202
Fax: (312)822-0288

Publications: N'DIGO (8501)

Hartman Newspapers, Inc.
PO Box 585
Brenham, TX 77834
Phone: (409)836-7956
Fax: (409)830-8577

Publications: Bargain Hunter (29949)

Hartman Newspapers, Inc.
PO Box 1390
Rosenberg, TX 77471-1390
Phone: (281)342-4474
Fax: (281)342-3219

Publications: Anahuac Progress (29721) • The Bayshore Sun (30658) • Bayshore Sun Extra (30659) • The Herald Coaster (30992) • Herald Coaster Extra (30993) • Liberty Vindicator (30690)

Hartman Newspapers, Inc.
PO Box 1267
Sugar Land, TX 77487-1267
Phone: (713)242-9104

Publications: The Fort Bend Mirror (31137)

Hart's Oil and Gas World
110 William St.,
New York, NY 10038
Phone: (212)621-4900
Fax: (212)621-4949
Free: 800-874-2544

Publications: Hart's E&P (30475)

Hartselle Newspapers, LLC
407 W Chestnut St.
PO Box 929
Hartselle, AL 35640
Phone: (256)773-6566
Fax: (256)773-1953

Publications: Hartselle Enquirer (264) • Hartselle Shopping Guide (265)

Hartshorne Sun
PO Box 330
Hartshorne, OK 74547
Phone: (918)297-2577
Fax: (918)297-2577

Publications: Hartshorne Sun (25858)

Hartsville Messenger
207 E Carolina Ave.
Box 1865
Hartsville, SC 29551-1865
Phone: (843)332-6545
Fax: (843)332-1341

Publications: Messenger (28657)

The Hartsville Vidette
111 Marlene St.
PO Box 47
Hartsville, TN 37074
Phone: (615)374-3556
Fax: (615)374-4002

Publications: The Hartsville Vidette (29218)

Hartwick College
One Hartwick Dr.
Oneonta, NY 13820
Phone: (607)431-4000

Publications: Hilltops (23050)

Harvard Advocate
21 South St.
Cambridge, MA 02138
Phone: (617)495-0737

Publications: Harvard Advocate (14055)

Harvard Business School
Soldiers Field
Boston, MA 02163
Phone: (617)495-6179
Fax: (617)496-0594

Publications: Business History Review (13869)

Harvard Business School Publishing
Soldiers Field
Boston, MA 02163
Phone: (617)495-7500
Fax: (617)783-7555
Free: 800-988-0886

Publications: Harvard Business Review (13898)

Harvard Crimson, Inc.
14 Plympton St.
Cambridge, MA 02138
Phone: (617)576-6565
Fax: (617)576-6363
Free: 888-CRI-MSON

Publications: 15 Minutes (14053) • Harvard Crimson (14056)

Harvard Design Magazine
48 Quincy St.
Cambridge, MA 02138
Phone: (617)495-7814
Fax: (617)496-3391

Publications: Harvard Design Magazine (14057)

Harvard Divinity School
45 Francis Ave.
Cambridge, MA 02138-1994
Phone: (617)495-5786
Fax: (617)496-9402

Publications: Harvard Theological Review (14067)

Harvard Graduate School of Education
8 Story St., 5th Fl.
Cambridge, MA 02138
Phone: (617)495-3432
Fax: (617)496-3584
Free: 800-513-0763

Publications: Harvard Educational Review (14058)

Harvard Graduate School of Education
35 Longfellow Hall
Appian Way
Cambridge, MA 02138
Phone: (617)496-5875
Fax: (617)495-7629

Publications: Ed. (14051)

Harvard International Review
PO Box 380226
Cambridge, MA 02238-0226
Phone: (617)495-9607
Fax: (617)496-4472

Publications: Harvard International Review (14060)

Harvard Law Review
Gannett House
Cambridge, MA 02138
Phone: (617)495-7888

Publications: Harvard Law Review (14064)

Harvard Magazine
7 Ware St.
Cambridge, MA 02138
Phone: (617)495-5746
Fax: (617)495-0324

Publications: Harvard Magazine (14065)

Harvard School for Public Health
651 Huntington Ave., 7th Fl.
Boston, MA 02115
Phone: (617)432-4611
Fax: (617)432-4310

Publications: Health and Human Rights (13899)

Harvard Society for Law and Public Policy, Inc.
1541 Massachusetts Ave.
Cambridge, MA 02138
Phone: (617)495-3105
Fax: (617)496-0620

Publications: Harvard Journal of Law and Public Policy (14062)

Harvard University
79 John F. Kennedy St.
Cambridge, MA 02138
Phone: (617)496-8655
Fax: (617)384-9555

Publications: Asian American Policy Review (14039)

Harvard University
Box 1447
Duxbury, MA 02331
Phone: (781)585-8796
Fax: (781)585-8796

Publications: Journal of Turkish Studies/Turkluk Bilgisi Arastirmalari (14164)

Harvard University Gazette
Holyoke Center 1060
1350 Massachusetts Ave.
Cambridge, MA 02138
Phone: (617)495-1585
Fax: (617)495-0754

Publications: Harvard University Gazette (14068)

Harvard-Yenching Institute
2 Divinity Ave.
Cambridge, MA 02138
Phone: (617)495-2758
Fax: (617)495-7798

Publications: Harvard Journal of Asiatic Studies (14061)

Harvey Berish
11904 Long Beach Blvd.
Lynwood, CA 90262
Phone: (301)537-4240
Fax: (714)535-3552

Publications: World of Pageantry (2488)

Harvey Whitney Books Co.
Box 42696
Cincinnati, OH 45242
Phone: (513)793-3555
Fax: (513)793-3600
Free: 877-742-7631

Publications: The Annals of Pharmacotherapy (24773) • The Journal of Pharmacy Technology (24807)

Harwood Academic Publishers
Gordon and Breach
820 Town Center Dr.
Langhorne, PA 19047

Publications: Lasers in the Life Sciences (23832)

Hasbrouck Heights Publishing Co., Inc.
194 Blvd.
Hasbrouck Heights, NJ 07604
Phone: (201)288-0333
Fax: (201)288-1847

Publications: The Observer (18867) • The Weekly News (18868)

Haskell News
PO Box 158
Haskell, OK 74436
Phone: (918)482-5619

Publications: Haskell News (25859)

The Haskell Press
PO Box 555
Haskell, TX 79521-0555
Phone: (940)864-2686

Publications: The Haskell Free Press (30433)

The Hastings Center
21 Malcolm Gordon Rd.
Garrison, NY 10524-5555
Phone: (845)424-4040
Fax: (845)424-4931

Publications: Hastings Center Report (20647) • IRB (20648)

Hastings College
Gray Center
800 N. Turner
Hastings, NE 68901
Phone: (402)461-7399
Fax: (402)461-7442
Free: 800-LEARN-HC

Publications: The Collegian (18035)

Hastings College
Public Relations Office
7th and Turner Ave.
PO Box 269
Hastings, NE 68902-0269
Phone: (402)463-2402
Fax: (402)463-7490
Free: 800-532-7642

Publications: Hastings Today (18036)

Hastings & Sons
38 Exchange St.
PO Box 951
Lynn, MA 01903
Phone: (617)593-7700
Fax: (617)581-3178

Publications: Daily Evening Item (14284)

Hathaway Publishing
780 County St.
Somerset, MA 02726
Phone: (508)674-4656
Fax: (508)677-1210

Publications: The Advocate (14177) • The Chronicle (14541) • Middleboro Gazette (14331) • The Spectator (14527)

Hatton-Brown Publishers
PO Box 2268
Montgomery, AL 36102
Phone: (334)834-1170
Fax: (334)834-4525
Free: 800-669-5613

Publications: IronWorks (367) • Panel World (373) • Power Equipment Trade (375) • Southern Loggin' Times (378) • Southern Lumberman (29199) • Timber Harvesting (379) • Timber Processing (380)

Hatton Free Press
PO Box 157
Fordville, ND 58231-0157
Phone: (701)229-3641
Fax: (701)229-3217
Free: 800-568-6641

Publications: Hatton Free Press (24442)

Haughton Publishing of Texas, Inc.
3638 Executive Blvd.
Mesquite, TX 75149
Phone: (972)288-7511
Fax: (972)285-4881

Publications: Cotton Gin & Oil Mill Press (30807)

Havenhill Gazette
447 W Lowell Ave.
PO Box 991
Haverhill, MA 01831
Phone: (978)374-0321
Fax: (978)374-9631
Free: 800-370-0321

Publications: The Haverhill Gazette (14232)

Haverford College
370 W Lancaster Ave.
Box 132
Haverford, PA 19041
Phone: (610)649-9712

Publications: The Bryn Mawr & Haverford News (27028)

Havre Daily News
PO Box 431
Havre, MT 59501
Phone: (406)265-6795
Fax: (406)265-6798

Publications: Havre Daily News (17813)

Hawaii
PO Box 55796
Boulder, CO 80322-5796

Publications: Hawaii (4170)

Hawaii Agricultural Statistics Service
1428 South King St.
Honolulu, HI 96814
Phone: (808)973-9566
Fax: (808)973-2909

Publications: Hawaii Crop Weather (7694)

Hawaii Audubon Society
850 Richards St., Ste. 505
Honolulu, HI 96813-4709
Phone: (808)528-1432
Fax: (808)537-5294

Publications: Elepaio (7688)

Hawaii Beverage Guide
1311 Kapiolani Blvd.
Ste. 301
Honolulu, HI 96814
Phone: (808)591-0049
Fax: (808)591-0038

Publications: Hawaii Beverage Guide (7690)

Hawaii Catholic Herald
1184 Bishop St.
Honolulu, HI 96813
Phone: (808)533-1791
Fax: (808)521-8428
Free: 800-530-1790

Publications: Hawaii Catholic Herald (7692)

Hawaii Hochi
917 Kokea St.
Honolulu, HI 96817
Phone: (808)845-2255
Fax: (808)847-7215

Publications: Hawaii Hochi (7696)

Hawaii Medical Journal
1345 S Beretania St., No. 301
Honolulu, HI 96814-1821

Publications: Hawaii CPA News (7693) • Hawaii Dental Journal (7695) • Hawaii Medical Journal (7697)

Hawaii Pacific University
Faculty Support Center, LB402
1060 Bishop St.
Honolulu, HI 96813
Phone: (808)544-1108
Fax: (808)544-0862

Publications: Hawaii Pacific Review (7698)

Hawaii Publications Inc.
PO Box 10427
Lahaina, HI 96761
Phone: (808)667-7866
Fax: (808)667-2726

Publications: Lahaina News (7777)

Hawaiian Historical Society
560 Kawaiahao St.
Honolulu, HI 96813-5023
Phone: (808)537-6271

Publications: Hawaiian Journal of History (7699)

Hawgs Illustrated
17 1/2 East Center
Fayetteville, AR 72702

Publications: Hawgs Illustrated (1120)

Hawkinsville Publishing Co.
329 Commerce St.
PO Box 30
Hawkinsville, GA 31036
Phone: (478)783-9250
Fax: (478)783-1293

Publications: Hawkinsville Dispatch and News (7323)

Hawley Herald
608 Main St.
PO Box 709
Hawley, MN 56549
Phone: (218)483-3306
Fax: (218)483-4457

Publications: Hawley Herald (15943)

Haworth Clinical Practice Press
Purdue University Calumet Family Studies Center
Purdue University Calumet
Hammond, IN 46323
Phone: (219)989-2541
Fax: (219)989-2777

Publications: Journal of Clinical Activities, Assignments & Handouts in Psychotherapy (10051)

The Haworth Press Inc.
10 Alice St.
Binghamton, NY 13904-1580
Phone: (607)722-5857
Fax: (607)771-0012
Free: 800-429-6784

Publications: The Acquisitions Librarian (19979) • Activities, Adaptation & Aging (4545) • Administration in Social Work (2199) • Adoption Quarterly (20150) • Alcoholism Treatment Quarterly (30708) • American Journal of Pastoral Counseling (25846) • Art Reference Services Quarterly (6130) • Behavioral & Social Sciences Librarian (8731) • Cataloging and Classification Quarterly (28154) • Child and Family Behavior Therapy (19457) • Child and Youth Services (16370) • Clinical Gerontologist (2902) • The Clinical Supervisor (20376) • College & Undergraduate Libraries (23396) • Community & Junior College Libraries (29770) • Computers in the Schools (18419) • Gerontology & Geriatrics Education (14680) • Harrington Lesbian Fiction Quarterly (20154) • Health Marketing Quarterly (19721) • The Herb, Spice, and Medicinal Plant Digest (13794) • Home Health Care Services Quarterly (1618) • Intergenerational Programming Quarterly (20156) • International Journal of Hospitality & Tourism Administration (20157) • Internet Reference Services Quarterly (20158) • Journal of Addictive Diseases (21974) • Journal of African Business (20160) • Journal of Aggression, Maltreatment & Trauma (20162) • Journal of Aging and Social Policy (13911) • Journal of Agricultural and Food Information (30044) • Journal of Agromedicine (28514) • Journal of Applied Aquaculture (12064) • Journal of Applied School Psychology (19428) • Journal of Aquatic Food Product Technology (26225) • Journal of Archival Organization (20163) • Journal of Asia-Pacific Business (29252) • Journal of Bisexuality (20164) • Journal of Business and Finance Librarianship (25023) • Journal of Business-to-Business Marketing (22016) • Journal of Cannabis Therapeutics (20165) • Journal of Child and Adolescent Substance Abuse (6077) • Journal of Clinical Activities, Assignments & Handouts in Psychotherapy Practice (20166) • Journal of College Student Psychotherapy (28101) • Journal of College and University Foodservice (31873) • Journal of Consumer Health on the Internet (20167) • Journal of Convention & Exhibition Management (20168) • Journal of East-West Business (27254) • Journal of Elder Abuse and Neglect (20169) • Journal of Emotional Abuse (27033) • Journal of End User Computer Support (20170) • Journal of Ethnic & Cultural Diversity in Social Work (20171) • Journal of Ethnicity in Substance Abuse (20172) • Journal of Euromarketing (27255) • Journal of Family Psychotherapy (10052) • Journal of Family Social Work (20173) • Journal of Feminist Family Therapy (4435) • Journal of Food Products Marketing (27528) • Journal of Forensic Neuropsychology (20174) • Journal of Forensic Psychology Practice (20175) • Journal of Gay and Lesbian Social Services (2043) • Journal of Gerontological Social Work (22081) • Journal of Global Marketing (27256) • Journal of Health Care Chaplaincy (20176) • Journal of Health and Social Policy (32287) • Journal of Herbal Pharmacotherapy (20177) • Journal of Herbs, Spices & Medicinal Plants (20178) • Journal of HIV/AIDS Prevention and Education for Adolescents & Children (5203) • Journal of HIV/AIDS & Social Services (20179) • Journal of Homosexuality (3382) • Journal of Hospital Librarianship (20180) • Journal of Hospital Marketing (1534) • Journal of Hospitality and Leisure Marketing (14986) • Journal of Housing for the Elderly (16996) • Journal of Human Behavior in the Social Environment (20181) • Journal of Human Resources in Hospitality & Tourism (20182) • Journal of Immigrant & Refugee Services (20183) • Journal of Infectious Disease Pharmacotherapy (20184) • Journal of Interlibrary Loan, Document Delivery, and Information Supply (20882) • Journal of International Consumer Marketing (27257) • Journal of International Food and Agribusiness Marketing (27258) • Journal of Internet Cataloging (20185) • Journal of Internet Commerce (12691) • Journal of Lesbian Studies (20186) • Journal of Library Administration (25935) • Journal of Library & Information Services for Distance Learning (20187) • Journal of Maintenance in the Addictions (20274) • Journal of Managed Pharmaceutical Care

(20188) • Journal of Marketing Channels (30238) • Journal of Marketing for Higher Education (24806) • Journal of Ministry in Addiction and Recovery (16383) • Journal of Musculoskeletal Pain (31035) • Journal of Neuro-AIDS (3383) • Journal of Neurotherapy (20189) • Journal of New Seeds (20190) • Journal of Nonprofit & Public Sector Marketing (368) • Journal of Nutraceuticals, Functional & Medical Foods (27034) • Journal of Nutrition for the Elderly (20952) • Journal of Nutrition in Recipe and Menu Development (31876) • Journal of Offender Rehabilitation (26833) • Journal of Organizational Behavior-Management (14934) • Journal of Pain and Palliative Care Pharmacotherapy (31435) • Journal of Pharmaceutical Marketing & Management (20191) • Journal of Pharmacoepidemiology (16698) • Journal of Pharmacy Teaching (16865) • Journal of Police Crisis Negotiations (30343) • Journal of Potato Production and Postharvest Handling (7942) • Journal of Poverty (25027) • Journal of Prevention & Intervention in the Community (20192) • Journal of Progressive Human Services (13918) • Journal of Promotion Management (20193) • Journal of Psychology and Human Sexuality (16089) • Journal of Psychosocial Oncology (22171) • Journal of Psychotherapy in Independent Practice (6079) • Journal of Quality Assurance in Hospitality & Tourism (20194) • Journal of Relationship Marketing (1536) • Journal of Religion & Abuse (20195) • Journal of Religion, Disability & Health (19334) • Journal of Religion & Spirituality in Social Work: Social Thought (20196) • Journal of Religious Gerontology (9757) • Journal of Religious & Theological Information (17176) • Journal of Research in Pharmaceutical Economics (20197) • Journal of Restaurant and Foodservice Marketing (18366) • Journal of Social Service Research (20198) • Journal of Social Work in Long-Term Care (20199) • Journal of Social Work Practice in the Addictions (20200) • Journal of Sustainable Agriculture (4790) • Journal of Sustainable Forestry (4996) • Journal of Teaching in the Addictions (20201) • Journal of Teaching in International Business (27259) • Journal of Teaching in Social Work (22202) • Journal of Teaching in Travel & Tourism (20202) • Journal of Technology in Human Services (20203) • Journal of Technology in Human Services (29733) • Journal of Threat Assessment (20204) • Journal of Transnational Management Development (13919) • Journal of Trauma & Dissociation (20205) • Journal of Trauma Practice (20206) • Journal of Tree Fruit Production (13798) • Journal of Turf Grass Management (13799) • Journal of Vegetable Crop Production (25881) • Journal of Whiplash & Related Disorders (20207) • Journal of Women and Aging (6659) • Latin American Business Review (3221) • Legal Reference Services Quarterly (954) • Loss, Grief and Care (22267) • Marriage and Family Review (10150) • Medical Reference Services Quarterly (20208) • Music Reference Services Quarterly (8738) • Occupational Therapy in Health Care (23968) • Occupational Therapy in Mental Health (20209) • Physical & Occupational Therapy in Geriatrics (20280) • Physical and Occupational Therapy in Pediatrics (20210) • Psychoanalytic Social Work (14945) • The Psychotherapy Patient (22607) • Public Library Quarterly (20212) • Public Services Quarterly (20213) • The Reference Librarian (20003) • Residential Treatment for Children and Youth (8555) • Resource Sharing & Information Networks (20214) • Science & Technology Libraries (18119) • Services Marketing Quarterly (1558) • Slavic & East European Information Resources (3590) • Small Fruits Review (20215) • Social Policy Journal (20216) • Social Work with Groups (20217) • Social Work in Health Care (22757) • Social Work in Mental Health (20218) • Technical Services Quarterly (4500) • Women & Criminal Justice (27993) • Women and Health (22932) • Women & Therapy (20221)

The Haworth Press, Inc.
21 E. Broad St.
Hazleton, PA 18201
Phone: (717)459-5933
Fax: (717)459-5934

Publications: Women & Politics Journal (5863)

Hawthorne Press
463 Lafayette Ave.
PO Box 1
Hawthorne, NJ 07507
Phone: (973)427-3330

Publications: Hawthorne Press (18871)

The Haxtun-Fleming Herald
PO Box 128
Haxtun, CO 80731
Phone: (970)774-6118
Fax: (970)774-7690

Publications: The Haxtun-Fleming Herald (4514)

Hayfield Herald
108 E Main
PO Box 85
Hayfield, MN 55940
Phone: (507)477-2232
Fax: (507)374-9327

Publications: Hayfield Herald (15944)

Haymarket Group, Ltd.
45 W. 34th St., Ste. 600
New York, NY 10001
Phone: (212)239-0855
Fax: (212)967-4184

Publications: Chocolatier (21412) • Pastry Art & Design (22532)

The Haynesville News
PO Box 269
Haynesville, LA 71038

Publications: The Haynesville News (12598)

Haywood County Newspapers, LLC
42 S. Washington
Brownsville, TN 38012
Phone: (731)772-1172
Fax: (731)772-5451

Publications: Brownsville States-Graphic (29070)

Hazard Herald
548 Main St.
PO Box 869
Hazard, KY 41701
Phone: (606)436-5771
Fax: (606)436-3140

Publications: Hazard Herald (12115)

Hazleton Standard-Speaker Inc.
21 N. Wyoming St.
Hazleton, PA 18201
Phone: (717)455-3636
Fax: (717)455-4244
Free: 800-843-6680

Publications: Standard-Speaker (27035)

HB Communications Group
2949 Ash St.
Abbotsford, BC, Canada V2S 4G5
Phone: (604)854-5530
Fax: (604)854-3087
Free: 800-672-0103

Publications: Home Business Report (34878)

HBC Publications, Inc.
2300 Corporate Circle Dr., Ste. 150
Henderson, NV 89074
Phone: (702)435-7700
Fax: (702)434-3527

Publications: Henderson Home News (18353)

HCN Publications
999 8th St. SW, Ste. 300
Calgary, AB, Canada T2R 1N7
Phone: (403)209-3500
Fax: (403)245-8666
Free: 800-387-2446

Publications: Calgary Herald (34631)

Headlight Herald
PO Box 1188
Tracy, MN 56175
Phone: (507)629-4300
Fax: (507)629-4301

Publications: Headlight Herald (16476)

Health Administration Press
1 N. Franklin, Ste. 1700
Chicago, IL 60606-3491
Phone: (312)424-2800
Fax: (312)424-0014

Publications: Frontiers of Health Services Management (8382) • Journal of Healthcare Management (8439)

Health City Sun
900 Park Ave. SW
PO Box 1517
Albuquerque, NM 87103
Phone: (505)242-3010
Fax: (505)842-5464

Publications: Health City Sun (19772)

Health Communications Inc.
3201 SW 15th St.
Deerfield Beach, FL 33442-8190
Phone: 800-851-9100
Fax: (954)360-0034
Free: 800-851-9100

Publications: Counselor (6048)

The Health Connection
55 W. Oak Ridge Dr.
Hagerstown, MD 21740
Phone: (301)393-3000
Fax: (301)393-4055
Free: 800-548-8700

Publications: Listen (13566) • Winner (13571)

Health & Fitness Publishing, Inc.
1502 Augusta, Ste. 230
Houston, TX 77057
Phone: (713)552-9991
Fax: (713)552-9997
Free: 800-318-5044

Publications: Health & Fitness Sports Magazine (30478)

Health Forum, L.L.C.
One North Franklin
Chicago, IL 60606
Phone: (312)893-6800
Fax: (312)422-4600
Free: 800-621-6902

Publications: AHA News (8249) • Health Forum Journal (8395) • Hospitals & Health Networks (8401) • Materials Management in Health Care (8481) • Trustee (8588)

Health Ink & Vitality Communications
780 Township Line Rd.
Yardley, PA 19067-4200
Phone: (267)585-2800
Fax: (267)685-1228

Publications: HEALTH & YOU (28200)

Health Law Institute
University of Alberta
439 Law Centre
Edmonton, AB, Canada T6G 2H5
Phone: (780)492-8343
Fax: (780)492-9575

Publications: Health Law Journal (34715) • Health Law Review (34716)

Health Management Publications, Inc.
83 General Warren Blvd. Ste. 100
Malvern, PA 19355-1245

Publications: Extended Care Product News (27211) • The Journal of Invasive Cardiology (27212) • Ostomy/Wound Management (27215)

Health Media, Inc.
14453 29A Ave.
White Rock, BC, Canada V4P 1P7
Phone: (604)535-9000
Fax: (604)535-9000

Publications: Canadian Nursing Home Journal (35240) • Canadian Operating Room Nursing Journal (35241)

Health Research and Educational Trust
School of Public Health
408 Warren Hall 7360
Berkeley, CA 94720-7360

Publications: HSR (1527)

Health Sciences at Tulane
1430 Tulane Ave., TW 34
New Orleans, LA 70112
Phone: (504)988-4777
Fax: (504)587-2012

Publications: Health Sciences at Tulane (12732)

Healthcare Business Media Inc.
210 12th Ave. S
Nashville, TN 37203-4002
Phone: (615)620-1520

Publications: California Medicine (29448) • Health-care Business Month (29457)

Healthcare Review Northeast Network
Millyard Technology Park
20 Pine St. Extension
Nashua, NH 03060
Phone: (603)579-8900
Fax: (603)579-8998
Free: 800-325-6464

Publications: Healthcare Review (18590)

HealthForum
1 N. Franklin St., 28th Fl.
Chicago, IL 60606-3421
Phone: (312)893-6800
Fax: (312)422-4500
Free: 800-621-6902

Publications: Health Facilities Management (8394)

Healthy Weight Journal
2491 San Ramon Valley Blvd., Ste. 1-355
San Ramon, CA 94583

Publications: The Nooner Magazine (3607)

Hearst Business Communications, Inc.
Garden City, NY
Phone: (516)227-1300
Free: 800-544-0929

Publications: Electronic Products (20638)

Hearst Corporation
901 Mission St.
San Francisco, CA 94103
Phone: (415)777-1111
Fax: (415)896-1107

Publications: San Francisco Chronicle (3432)

Hearst Corp.
113 S. Main
Box 69
Vassar, MI 48768
Phone: (989)823-8579
Fax: (989)823-8778

Publications: Vassar Pioneer Times (15652)

The Hearst Corporation
1790 Broadway, 6th Fl.
New York, NY 10019-1412
Phone: (212)969-7500
Fax: (212)969-7557

Publications: Country Living Gardener (21507) • Diversion (21560)

Hearst Magazines
1790 Broadway
New York, NY 10019

Publications: Classic American Homes (21427) • Colonial Homes (21441) • Cosmopolitan (21503) • Country Living (21506) • Esquire (21627) • Good Housekeeping (21775) • Harper's Bazaar (21790) • House Beautiful (21821) • House Beautiful Kitchen/Baths (21822) • House Beautiful's Houses and Plans (21823) • Marie Claire (22281) • Motor Boating & Sailing (22371) • O (22481) • Popular Mechanics (22579) • Redbook Magazine (22639) • Sports Afield (22775) • Town & Country (22849) • Veranda (7057)

Hearst Publishing Co.
380 Main St.
PO Box 3071
Beaumont, TX 77704-3071
Phone: (409)833-3311
Fax: (409)838-2873

Publications: Beaumont Enterprise (29897)

Heart of America Genealogical Society
PO Box 481727
Kansas City, MO 64148-1727
Phone: (816)701-3445

Publications: Kansas City Genealogist (17179)

Heart-Centered Therapies Association
3716 274th Ave. SE
Issaquah, WA 98029
Fax: (425)391-9737
Free: 800-914-8348

Publications: Journal of Heart-Centered Therapies (32785)

The Hearthstone Town and Country
PO Box 446
Red Hill, PA 18076
Phone: (215)679-5060
Fax: (215)679-5077

Publications: The Hearthstone Town and Country (27926)

Heartland Communications Group, Inc.
1003 Central Ave.
PO Box 1052
Fort Dodge, IA 50501
Phone: (515)955-1600
Fax: (515)574-2182
Free: 800-673-4763

Publications: Aviators Hot Line (10894) • Business Air Today (10895) • Contractors Hot Line (10896) • Contractors Hot Line Monthly Equipment Guide (10897) • Farm Equipment Guide (10898) • Farmer's Digest (10899) • Farmers Hot Line (10900) • Industrial Machine Trader (10901) • Mid-America Weekly Trucking (10904) • Musicians Hotline (10905)

Heartland Publications
26861 Capp Rd.
Edinboro, PA 16412-4819
Phone: (814)734-8608
Free: 800-555-3841

Publications: Heartland (26861)

Heartland Publishing, Inc.
238 Main St.
Sweet Springs, MO 65351
Phone: (816)335-6366
Fax: (816)335-6366

Publications: Sweet Springs Herald (17644)

Heartland Retailer
6026 Maple St.
Omaha, NE 68104
Phone: (402)496-0717
Fax: (402)496-0678

Publications: Heartland Retailer (18197)

Heartland Trader
PO Box 376
Wauseon, OH 43567
Phone: (419)335-2010

Publications: Heartland Trader (25623)

Heather Publishing Co., Inc.
PO Box 201427
Arlington, TX 76006
Phone: (817)860-2375
Fax: (817)548-0004
Free: 800-860-2375

Publications: ServiceInsights (29735)

Heaven Bone Press
1310 Whispering Hills Dr.
Chester, NY 10918
Phone: (845)469-2326
Fax: (845)469-7880

Publications: Heaven Bone (20460)

The Heavener Ledger
507 E 1st St.
PO Box 38
Heavener, OK 74937
Phone: (918)653-2425

Publications: The Heavener Ledger (25861)

Hebcor, Inc., div. Editions Chaudet
12625 1E Ave. Est
Saint-Georges-de-Beauce, QC, Canada G5Y 2E4
Phone: (418)228-8858
Fax: (418)228-0268

Publications: L'Eclaireur-Progres/Beauce Nouvelle (37341)

L'Hebdo Du St. Maurice
2102 Champlain Ave.
PO Box 10
Shawinigan, QC, Canada G9N 6T8
Phone: (819)537-5111
Fax: (819)537-5471

Publications: L'Hebdo du St. Maurice (37391)

Hebdo Mag Inc.
130 De Liege East
Montreal, QC, Canada H2P 1J1
Phone: (514)384-7900
Fax: (514)384-2056

Publications: Auto Trader/Auto Hebdo (37089) • Bike, Boat & R.V. Trader/Moto, Bateau & Vehicules Recreatif Hebdo (37091) • Truck Trader/Camion Hebdo (37230)

L'Hebdo Mekinac/des Chenaux
2102 Champlain
CP 10
Shawinigan, QC, Canada G9N 6T8
Phone: (819)537-5111
Fax: (819)537-5471

Publications: L'Hebdo Mekinac/des Chenaux (37390)

Hebdos Monteregiens
184 rue Normandie
Boucherville, QC, Canada J4B 5S7
Phone: (450)655-5556
Fax: (450)655-9951

Publications: Le Saint Francois (37425) • Le Soleil du St. Laurent (37426)

Hebdos Transcontinental
1032, Laurier Ouest
Outremont, QC, Canada H2V 2K8
Phone: (514)276-9615
Fax: (514)274-5564

Publications: L'Express d'Outremont (37264)

Hebron Herald
PO Box 9
102 S. Park
Hebron, ND 58638
Phone: (701)878-4494
Fax: (701)878-4494

Publications: Hebron Herald (24471)

Hebron Journal Register
318 Lincoln Ave.
PO Box 210
Hebron, NE 68370
Phone: (402)768-6602
Fax: (402)768-7354

Publications: Hebron Journal Register (18045)

Heckler
1915 21st St.
Sacramento, CA 95814
Phone: (916)456-2300
Fax: (916)737-3920

Publications: Heckler (3001)

The Hegeler Institute
PO Box 600
La Salle, IL 61301
Phone: (815)224-6651
Fax: (815)223-4486

Publications: The Monist (9449)

Heimburger House Publishing Co.
7236 W. Madison St.
Forest Park, IL 60130
Phone: (708)366-1973
Fax: (708)366-1973

Publications: S Gaugian (8893) • Sn3 Modeler (8894)

William S. Hein & Company Inc.
1285 Main St.
Buffalo, NY 14209-1987
Phone: (716)882-2600
Fax: (716)883-8100
Free: 800-828-7571

Publications: Arkansas Law Review (1117) • Chicago Journal of International Law (20373) • Harvard Journal of Legislation (14063) • Immigration and Nationality Law Review (20381) • Journal of Legal Pluralism and Unofficial Law (20382)

Heinrich Bauer North America Inc.
270 Sylvan Ave.
PO Box 1648
Englewood Cliffs, NJ 07632
Phone: (201)569-0006
Fax: (201)569-3584

Publications: Woman's World (18804)

2426

Numbers cited after listings are entry numbers rather than page numbers.

Heinz & Associates, Inc.
PO Box 498338
Cincinnati, OH 45249-7338
Free: 800-500-1561

Publications: Content Networking Journal (24790)

Heldref Publications
1319 18th St. NW
Washington, DC 20036-1802
Phone: (202)296-6267
Fax: (202)296-5149
Free: 800-365-9753

Publications: ANQ (5353) • Archives of Environmental Health (5360) • Arts Education Policy Review (5362) • Asian Affairs (5366) • Behavioral Medicine (5374) • Change (5403) • The Clearing House (5418) • College Teaching (5425) • Critique (5450) • Current (5453) • Demokratizatsiya (5461) • Environment (5480) • The Explicator (5486) • Genetic, Social, and General Psychology Monographs (5506) • The Germanic Review (5512) • Historical Methods (5527) • History (5528) • Hospital Topics (5529) • The International Journal of Action Methods (5552) • Journal of American College Health (5569) • The Journal of Arts Management, Law, and Society (5573) • The Journal of Economic Education (5581) • Journal of Education for Business (5582) • The Journal of Educational Research (5585) • The Journal of Environmental Education (5586) • The Journal of Experimental Education (5587) • The Journal of General Psychology (5592) • The Journal of Genetic Psychology (5593) • Journal of Motor Behavior (5602) • Journal of Popular Film and Television (5613) • The Journal of Psychology (5614) • The Journal of Social Psychology (5616) • Perspectives on Political Science (5717) • Preventing School Failure (5729) • RE:view (5758) • ReVision (5768) • Rocks & Minerals (5770) • Romance Quarterly (5772) • Science Activities (5779) • The Social Studies (5795) • Symposium (5809) • Weatherwise (5858) • World Affairs (5866)

Helicopter Association International
1635 Prince St.
Alexandria, VA 22314
Phone: (703)683-4646

Publications: ROTOR (31734)

Hellanic Hamilton News
8 Morris Ave., No. 2
Hamilton, ON, Canada L8L 1X7
Phone: (416)549-9208
Fax: (416)549-7935

Publications: Hellenic Hamilton News (35881)

The Hellenic Calendar
2747 N Grand Ave., PMB 250
Santa Ana, CA 92705
Phone: (714)550-9933
Fax: (714)550-9696

Publications: The Hellenic Calendar (3626)

Hellenic College Press
50 Goddard Ave.
Brookline, MA 02445
Phone: (617)731-3500
Fax: (617)566-9075

Publications: Journal of Modern Hellenism (14021)

Helmer Printing, Inc.
N6402 790th St.
PO Box 40
Beldenville, WI 54003
Phone: (715)273-4601
Fax: (715)273-4769
Free: 800-533-1635

Publications: Shopper (33571)

Helmers Publishing Inc.
174 Concord St.
Peterborough, NH 03458
Phone: (603)924-9631
Fax: (603)924-7408

Publications: Supply Chain Systems Magazine (18630)

Hemmings Motor News
PO Box 100
Bennington, VT 05201
Fax: (802)447-9631

Publications: Hemmings Motor News (31499)

Henderson Community College
2660 S Green
Henderson, KY 42420-4699
Phone: (270)830-5295
Fax: (270)827-8635

Publications: The Hill (12123)

C.W. Henderson
PO Box 5528
Atlanta, GA 30307
Fax: (770)507-7788
Free: 800-633-4931

Publications: AIDS Weekly Plus (6961) • Blood Weekly (6980)

Henderson Daily News
1711 S Hwy. 79
PO Box 30
Henderson, TX 75653-0030
Phone: (903)657-2501
Fax: (903)657-2452

Publications: Henderson Daily News (30440)

Henderson Dispatch Co., Inc.
PO Box 908
Henderson, NC 27536-0908
Phone: (919)492-4001
Fax: (919)430-0125

Publications: Henderson Daily Dispatch (23981)

Henderson Independent
PO Box 8
Henderson, MN 56044-0008
Phone: (507)248-3223

Publications: Henderson Independent (15947)

The Henderson News
1021 N Main St.
Henderson, NE 68371
Phone: (402)723-5861
Fax: (402)723-5863

Publications: The Henderson News (18047)

Henderson Newspapers, Inc.
570 Dula St.
Alvin, TX 77511-2942
Phone: (281)331-4421
Fax: (281)331-4424

Publications: The Alvin Advertiser (29689) • The Alvin Sun (29690)

Hendersonville Newspaper Co.
PO Box 490
Hendersonville, NC 28793-0490
Phone: (704)692-0505
Fax: (704)692-2319

Publications: The Times-News (23984)

Hendricks County Republican, Inc.
6 E Main St.
PO Box 149
Danville, IN 46122
Phone: (317)745-2777
Fax: (317)745-2777

Publications: The Republican (9921)

Hendricks Pioneer
PO Box 5
Hendricks, MN 56136-0005
Phone: (507)275-3197

Publications: Hendricks Pioneer (15948)

Heneford Brand
PO Box 673
Hereford, TX 79045
Phone: (806)364-2030
Fax: (806)364-8364

Publications: The Hereford Brand (30443)

Henley Publishing
110 Carleton St.
Woodstock, NB, Canada E7M 1E4
Phone: (506)328-8863
Fax: (506)328-3208

Publications: The Bugle (35440)

The Hennessey Clipper
117 S Main
Box 338
Hennessey, OK 73742
Phone: (405)853-4888

Publications: Clipper (25862)

The Henning Advocate
400 Douglas Ave.
PO Box 35
Henning, MN 56551
Phone: (218)583-2935
Fax: (218)583-2909

Publications: The Henning Advocate (15949)

Henry George Institute
121 E 30th St.
New York, NY 10016
Phone: (212)689-0075

Publications: Georgist Journal (21757)

Henry News-Republican, Inc.
709 3rd St.
PO Box 190
Henry, IL 61537
Phone: (309)364-3250
Fax: (309)364-3858

Publications: Henry News-Republican (8981)

Herald
159 W. Pajarito St.
Nogales, AZ 85621-2712
Phone: (602)287-3622

Publications: Herald (754)

The Herald
1 Herald Square
PO Box 2050
New Britain, CT 06050
Phone: (860)225-4601
Fax: (203)225-4601

Publications: The Herald (4975)

Herald
711 Washington Ave.
PO Box 33
Cairo, IL 62914-0033
Phone: (618)734-4242
Fax: (618)734-4244

Publications: Herald (8105)

Herald
214 E. Partridge
Box 229
Metamora, IL 61548
Phone: (309)367-2335
Fax: (309)367-4277

Publications: Herald (9177)

The Herald
216 E. 4th
PO Box 31
Jasper, IN 47547
Phone: (812)482-2424
Fax: (812)482-4104

Publications: The Herald (10219)

The Herald
PO Box 556
Oakland, IA 51560

Publications: The Herald (11120)

Herald
PO Box 158
New York Mills, MN 56567
Phone: (218)385-2275
Fax: (218)385-3626

Publications: Herald (16220)

Herald
119 Maple Dr.
PO Box 68
Spring Grove, MN 55974
Phone: (507)498-3868

Publications: Herald (16455)

Herald
14 W. 4th St.
PO Box 1447
Williston, ND 58801
Phone: (701)572-2165
Fax: (701)572-1965
Free: 800-950-2165

Publications: Plains Reporter (24559)

The Herald
132 W. Main St.
PO Box 11707
Rock Hill, SC 29730
Phone: (803)329-4000
Fax: (803)329-4028

Publications: The Herald (28744)

The Herald
30 Pleasant St.
Box 309
Randolph, VT 05060-0309
Phone: (802)728-3232
Fax: (802)728-9275

Publications: The Herald of Randolph (31581)

The Herald
1213 Grand & California Sts.
PO Box 930
Everett, WA 98206
Phone: (425)339-3000
Fax: (425)339-3049

Publications: The Herald (32761)

Herald and Advance Newspapers, Inc.
39 Proton St. N.
PO Box 280
Dundalk, ON, Canada N0C 1B0
Phone: (519)923-2203
Fax: (519)923-2747

Publications: Dundalk Herald (35793) • Flesherton Advance (35832)

The Herald-Advocate Publishing Co., Inc.
115 S. 7th Ave.
PO Box 338
Wauchula, FL 33873
Phone: (863)773-3255
Fax: (863)773-0657

Publications: The Herald-Advocate (6841)

Herald Association, Inc.
27 Wales St.
PO Box 668
Rutland, VT 05702-0668
Phone: (802)747-6121
Fax: (802)775-2423
Free: 800-498-4296

Publications: Rutland Herald (31585)

The Herald Breeze
PO Box 1546
DeFuniak Springs, FL 32435
Phone: (850)892-3232
Fax: (850)892-2270

Publications: The Herald Breeze (6053)

Herald-Chronicle
906 Dinah Shore Blvd.
Winchester, TN 37398
Fax: (615)967-2299

Publications: Herald-Chronicle (29647)

Herald-Citizen
555 S Old Kentucky Rd.
PO Box 2729
Cookeville, TN 38502
Phone: (931)526-9715
Fax: (931)526-1209

Publications: Herald-Citizen Plus (29143)

The Herald Co.
Clinton Sq.
PO Box 4915
Syracuse, NY 13221
Phone: (315)470-0011
Fax: (315)470-3019

Publications: Syracuse Herald-Journal (23426)

The Herald Co.
PO Box 977
Lynnwood, WA 98046-0977
Phone: (425)775-7521
Fax: (425)774-8622

Publications: The Enterprise (32813)

Herald Company of Oklahoma, Inc.
PO Box 250
Healdton, OK 73438
Phone: (580)229-0132
Fax: (580)229-0132

Publications: The Healdton Herald (25860) • The Wilson Post-Democrat (26197)

Herald-Courier Virginia-Tennessean
320 Morrison Blvd.
Bristol, VA 24201-3812
Phone: (540)669-2181
Fax: (540)669-3696

Publications: Herald-Courier/Virginia-Tennessean (31897)

The Herald-Democrat
108 S Douglas
PO Box 490
Beaver, OK 73932
Phone: (580)625-3241
Fax: (580)625-4269

Publications: The Herald-Democrat (25757)

Herald Dispatch
4053 Marlton Ave.
PO Box 19027A
Los Angeles, CA 90008
Phone: (323)295-6323
Fax: (323)291-2123

Publications: Firestone Park News/Southeast News Press (1916) • Herald Dispatch (2288) • Watts Star Review (2431)

Herald-Enterprise
PO Box 400
Golconda, IL 62938
Phone: (618)683-3531
Fax: (618)683-3831

Publications: Herald-Enterprise (8945)

The Herald-Gazette
509 Greenwood St.
PO Box 220
Barnesville, GA 30204
Phone: (770)358-6397
Fax: (770)358-0754

Publications: The Herald-Gazette (7121)

The Herald-Gazette
111 E. 1st St.
PO Box 7
Trenton, TN 38382
Phone: (731)855-1711
Fax: (731)855-9587

Publications: The Herald-Gazette (29629)

The Herald Independent
PO Box 90
Winnsboro, SC 29180
Phone: (803)635-4016
Fax: (803)635-2948

Publications: Herald-Independent (28787)

The Herald Journal
PO Box 149
Greensboro, GA 30642
Phone: (706)453-7988
Fax: (404)453-2311

Publications: Crawfordville Advocate-Democrat (7214) • The Herald-Journal (7309)

Herald Journal
PO Box 1657
Spartanburg, SC 29304
Phone: (864)582-4511
Fax: (864)594-6350
Free: 800-922-4158

Publications: Herald-Journal (28759)

The Herald Journal
75 W. 300 N.
PO Box 487
Logan, UT 84323-0487
Phone: (435)752-2121
Fax: (435)753-6642
Free: 888-259-7631

Publications: The Herald Journal (31350)

Herald Journal Publishing
PO Box 129
Winsted, MN 55395
Phone: (320)485-2535
Fax: (320)485-2878
Free: 888-228-1428

Publications: Herald Journal Shopper (15965) • Howard Lake-Waverly Montrose Herald Journal

(15966) • Winsted-Lester Prairie Herald Journal (16537)

Herald-Leader
118 S 2nd St.
Bellevue, IA 52031
Phone: (319)872-4159
Fax: (319)872-4298

Publications: Herald-Leader (10619)

Herald-Ledger
1513 Edgington Ave.
Eldora, IA 50627
Phone: (641)939-5051
Fax: (641)939-5541

Publications: Herald-Ledger (10869)

Herald Ltd.
708 Railway St.
Whitewood, SK, Canada S0G 5C0
Phone: (306)735-2230
Fax: (306)735-2899

Publications: Whitewood Herald (37594)

The Herald-Mail Co.
PO Box 439
Hagerstown, MD 21741
Phone: (301)733-5131
Fax: (301)733-7264

Publications: The Daily-Mail (13563) • The Morning Herald (13568)

Herald News
PO Box 158
Cayuga, IN 47928
Phone: (765)492-4401

Publications: Herald News (9883)

Herald-News
116 S Main
PO Box 87
Edmonton, KY 42129
Phone: (270)432-3291
Fax: (270)432-4414

Publications: Herald-News (12043)

Herald-News
408 Main St.
Box 639
Wolf Point, MT 59201
Phone: (406)653-2222
Fax: (406)653-2221

Publications: Herald-News (17922)

Herald Newspaper Inc.
5240 S Harper
Chicago, IL 60615
Phone: (773)643-8533
Fax: (773)643-8542

Publications: Hyde Park Herald (8403)

Herald Newspapers
5739 N Main St.
Sylvania, OH 43560
Phone: (419)885-9222
Fax: (419)885-0764

Publications: Maumee Valley Herald (25569) • Sylvania Herald (25554) • Toledo Herald (25555)

The Herald-Palladium
3450 Hollywood Rd.
PO Box 128
St. Joseph, MI 49085
Phone: (269)429-2400
Fax: (616)429-7661
Free: 800-356-4262

Publications: The Herald-Palladium (15512)

Herald Press
PO Box 457
McClusky, ND 58463
Phone: (701)363-2492
Fax: (701)363-2492

Publications: McClusky Gazette (24502)

Herald Press
616 Walnut Ave.
Scottdale, PA 15683
Phone: (724)887-8500
Fax: (724)887-3111
Free: 800-245-7894

Publications: Builder Magazine, Uniform Series Edition (8854) • On the Line (27954) • Provident Book Finder (27955) • Purpose (27956) • Story Friends (27957)

Herald Press
519 N. Elm St.
PO Box 379
Palestine, TX 75802-0379
Phone: (903)729-0281
Fax: (903)729-0284

Publications: Palestine Herald-Press (30897)

The Herald Printing Co.
625 S. Kibler St.
PO Box 367
New Washington, OH 44854-0367
Phone: (419)492-2133
Fax: (419)492-2128
Free: 888-258-0008

Publications: New Washington Herald (25423)

Herald-Progress
11293 Air Park Rd.
Ashland, VA 23005-3452
Phone: (804)798-9031
Fax: (804)798-9036

Publications: Herald-Progress (31856)

Herald Publications
314 E. Church St.
PO Box C
Mascoutah, IL 62258
Phone: (618)566-8282
Fax: (618)566-8283

Publications: Fairview Heights Tribune (9151) • Herald Scott Flyer (9153) • Lebanon Herald (9154) • Mascoutah Herald (9155)

Herald Publications
PO Box 226
New Baden, IL 62265
Phone: (618)566-8282
Fax: (618)566-8283

Publications: Clinton County News (9280)

Herald Publishing
508 N. Court St.
Carroll, IA 51401
Phone: (712)792-3573
Fax: (712)792-5218
Free: 800-262-5495

Publications: The Times Herald (10652)

Herald Publishing, Co.
PO Box 577
Ava, MO 65608
Phone: (417)683-4181
Fax: (417)683-4102

Publications: Douglas County Herald (16896)

The Herald Publishing Co.
PO Box 1288
Dillon, SC 29536
Phone: (843)774-3311
Fax: (843)841-1930

Publications: The Dillon Herald (28597)

Herald Publishing Co., Inc.
109 Hwy. 70 E
PO Box 370
Hazen, AR 72064
Phone: (870)255-4538
Fax: (870)255-4539

Publications: The DeValls Bluff Times (1171) • Grand Prairie Herald (1172)

The Herald Publishing Co., Inc.
PO Box 14375
Gainesville, FL 32604
Phone: (386)454-1297
Fax: (386)454-4559

Publications: The High Springs Herald (6190)

Herald Publishing Co., Inc.
1204 N. Date St.
PO Box 752
Truth or Consequences, NM 87901
Phone: (505)894-2143
Fax: (505)894-7824

Publications: Chaparral Guide (19967) • The Herald (19968)

Herald Publishing Co. of North Carolina, Inc.
PO Box 684
Fairmont, NC 28340
Phone: (910)628-7125

Publications: The Times-Messenger (23872)

Herald Publishing House
PO Box 390
1001 W. Walnut
Independence, MO 64051-0390
Phone: (816)521-3015
Fax: (816)521-3066
Free: 800-767-8181

Publications: Herald (17112)

Herald Publishing House/Independence Press
PO Box 390
Independence, MO 64051
Phone: (816)521-3015
Fax: (816)521-3066
Free: 800-767-8181

Publications: Herald (17111)

The Herald Record
202 E Main St.
West Union, WV 26456
Phone: (304)873-1600

Publications: The Herald Record (33496)

Herald & Record Co.
120 W Front St.
PO Box 632
Traverse City, MI 49685-4968
Phone: (616)946-2000
Fax: (616)946-8273

Publications: Traverse City Record-Eagle (15602)

Herald-Register Publishing Co.
813 5th Ave.
PO Box 360
Grinnell, IA 50112-1653
Phone: (641)236-3113
Fax: (641)236-5135

Publications: Grinnell Herald-Register (10931)

Herald & Review Newspapers
601 E. William St.
Decatur, IL 62525
Phone: (217)429-5151

Publications: Herald & Review (8711)

Herald Standard
8-18 E Church St.
PO Box 848
Uniontown, PA 15401-3563
Phone: (412)439-7500
Fax: (412)439-7528

Publications: Herald-Standard (28067)

Herald-Star
PO Box 50
Edinburg, IL 62531-0050
Phone: (217)623-5523
Fax: (217)623-5523

Publications: The Herald-Star (8810)

Herald-Star
401 Herald Sq.
Steubenville, OH 43952
Phone: (740)283-4711
Fax: (740)282-4261

Publications: Herald-Star (25539)

Herald-Sun Papers
2828 Picket Rd.
Durham, NC 27705

Publications: The Herald-Sun (23824)

Herald Times
178 Main St.
PO Box 720
Meeker, CO 81641
Phone: (970)878-4017
Fax: (970)878-4016

Publications: The Meeker Herald (4573)

Herald-Times
10 Victoria St. N
Walkerton, ON, Canada N0G 2V0
Phone: (519)881-1600
Fax: (519)881-0276

Publications: Herald-Times (36842)

Herald-Times, Inc.
1900 S Walnut St.
PO Box 909
Bloomington, IN 47402
Phone: (812)332-4401
Fax: (812)331-4285
Free: 800-489-5090

Publications: Herald-Times (9827)

Herald-Times Reporter
902 Franklin St.
PO Box 790
Manitowoc, WI 54220-0790
Phone: (920)684-4433
Fax: (920)684-4416
Free: 800-783-7323

Publications: Herald-Times Reporter (34013)

Herald and Tribune
PO Box 277
Jonesborough, TN 37659
Phone: (423)753-3136
Fax: (423)753-6528

Publications: Herald and Tribune (29258)

Herburger Publications, Inc.
604 N. Lincoln Way
PO Box 307
Galt, CA 95632
Phone: (209)745-1551
Fax: (209)745-4492

Publications: Elk Grove Citizen (1993) • The Galt Herald (1994) • Laguna Citizen (1995)

Hereford Publications, Inc.
PO Box 014059
1501 Wyandotte
Kansas City, MO 64101-0059
Phone: (816)842-8878
Fax: (816)842-6931

Publications: Hereford World (17171)

The Herington Times
7 N Broadway
PO Box 310
Herington, KS 67449
Phone: (785)258-2211
Fax: (785)258-2400

Publications: The Herington Times (11488)

Heritage Information Holdings, Inc.
1101 Pennsylvania Ave., NW, Ste. 820
Washington, DC 20001

Publications: Minority Health Today (5652)

Heritage Music Service
4207 Fremont Ave. N., No. 1
Seattle, WA 98103-7247
Phone: (206)632-4389

Publications: Heritage Music Review (32970)

Heritage Newspapers, Inc.
159 Main St.
Belleville, MI 48111
Phone: (734)697-8255
Fax: (734)697-4610

Publications: The View (14807)

Heritage Newspapers, Inc.
20750 Old U.S. 12
Chelsea, MI 48118
Phone: (734)475-1371

Publications: The Chelsea Standard (14876) • The Dexter Leader (14976)

Heritage Newspapers, Inc.
15340 Michigan Ave.
Dearborn, MI 48126-2917
Phone: (313)943-4250
Fax: (313)846-5531

Publications: Dearborn Heights Press & Guide (14900) • Dearborn Press & Guide (14901) • Warrendale-West Detroit Press & Guide (14907)

Heritage Newspapers, Inc.
8545 Macomb St.
PO Box 233
Grosse Ile, MI 48138
Phone: (734)676-0515
Fax: (734)676-0638

Publications: The Ile Camera (15138)

Heritage Newspapers, Inc.
109 E. Main St.
PO Box 37
Manchester, MI 48158
Phone: (734)428-8173

Publications: Manchester Enterprise (15328)

Heritage Newspapers, Inc.
15649 S. Telegraph Rd.
Monroe, MI 48161-4066
Phone: (734)243-2100

Publications: The Monroe Guardian (15365)

Heritage Newspapers, Inc.
106 W. Michigan Ave.
Saline, MI 48176
Phone: (734)429-7380

Publications: Milan News-Leader (15517) • Mr. Mazoo (15518) • The Saline Reporter (15519)

Heritage Newspapers, Inc.
1 Heritage Dr., Ste. 100
Southgate, MI 48195-3407
Phone: (734)246-0800

Publications: The Suburban News (15567)

Heritage Newspapers, Inc.
1 Heritage Pl., Ste. 100
Southgate, MI 48195
Phone: (734)246-0810
Fax: (734)284-2028

Publications: Heritage Sunday (15565) • The News-Herald (15566)

Heritage Quest
669 W. 900 N.
North Salt Lake, UT 84054
Phone: (801)298-5358
Fax: (801)298-5468

Publications: Heritage Quest Magazine (31376)

Herman Review
Box E.
Herman, MN 56248-0304
Phone: (320)677-2229
Fax: (320)677-2229

Publications: Herman Review (15951)

Hermantown Star
4850 Miller Trunk, Ste. 4B
Hermantown, MN 55811
Phone: (218)727-0419
Fax: (218)722-5821

Publications: Hermantown Star (15952)

Hernando Today
15299 Cortez Blvd.
Brooksville, FL 34613
Phone: (352)796-1949
Fax: (352)799-5246

Publications: Hernando Today (5965)

Herndon Publishing Inc.
1043 Sterling Rd., Ste. 104
PO Box 109
Herndon, VA 20170
Phone: (703)437-5886
Fax: (703)834-3142

Publications: The Observer (32164)

Heron Dance
52 Seymour St.
Middlebury, VT 05753-1115
Phone: (802)388-4875
Fax: (802)388-6148
Free: 888-304-3766

Publications: Heron Dance (31556)

Heron Publishing
202 - 3994 Shelbourne St.
Victoria, BC, Canada V8N 3E2
Phone: (250)721-9921
Fax: (250)721-9924

Publications: Archaea (35206) • naturalSCIENCE (35223) • Tree Physiology (35227)

The Herpetologists' League
c/o Dr. Lynnette Sievert
Div. of Biological Sciences
Emporia State University
Emporia, KS 66801
Phone: (316)341-5606
Fax: (316)341-5607

Publications: Herpetologica (31872)

Herring Communications Inc.
185 Berry St., Ste. 4700
San Francisco, CA 94107-1768
Phone: (415)865-2277
Fax: (415)865-2280

Publications: The Red Herring (3422)

Hersam Acorn Newspapers, LLC
16 Bailey Ave.
PO Box 1019
Ridgefield, CT 06877
Phone: (203)438-6544

Publications: The Darien Times (5096) • The Lewisboro Ledger (4923) • The Redding Pilot (5102) • The Ridgefield Press (5103) • The Weston Forum (5210) • Wilton Bulletin (5231)

Hersam Publishing Co.
42 Vitti St.
PO Box 605
New Canaan, CT 06840
Phone: (203)966-9541
Fax: (203)966-8006

Publications: New Canaan Advertiser (4979)

Hershey Chronicle
513 W Chocolate Ave.
Hershey, PA 17033-1632
Phone: (717)533-2900
Fax: (717)531-2561
Free: 888-964-5454

Publications: Hershey Chronicle (27041)

Hesperian
111 E Missouri St.
Floydada, TX 79235
Phone: (806)983-3737
Fax: (806)983-3141

Publications: Floyd County Hesperian-Beacon (30322)

The Hesston Record
109 N Main
PO Box 340
Hesston, KS 67062-0340
Phone: (620)327-4831
Fax: (620)327-4830

Publications: The Hesston Record (11490)

Heyday Books
PO Box 9145
Berkeley, CA 94709
Phone: (510)549-3564
Fax: (510)549-1889

Publications: News from Native California (1546)

Heyworth Star Inc.
105 S Buchanan
Heyworth, IL 61745
Phone: (309)473-2414
Fax: (309)473-3610
Free: 800-288-2414

Publications: The Heyworth Star (8986)

Hi-Desert Publishing
PO Box 299
Lucerne Valley, CA 92356
Phone: (760)248-7878
Fax: (760)248-2042

Publications: The Leader (2485)

Hi Desert Publishing
56445 29 Palms Hwy.
PO Box 880
Yucca Valley, CA 92286-2861
Phone: (760)365-3315
Fax: (760)365-8686

Publications: Hi-Desert Star (4128)

Hi-Liter Graphics, Inc.
700 Blackhawk Dr.
PO Box 9
Burlington, WI 53105
Phone: (262)539-4200
Fax: (262)539-4240

Publications: Wisconsin Hi-Liter (33610)

Hi-Lites Graphics, Inc.
1212 Locust
Fremont, MI 49412
Phone: (616)924-0630
Fax: (616)924-5580
Free: 800-482-5262

Publications: Hi-Lites Shoppers Guide (15057)

Hi-Torque Publishing Co., Inc.
25233 Anza Dr.
Box 9502
Valencia, CA 91355
Phone: (661)295-1910
Fax: (661)295-1278
Free: 800-762-0345

Publications: BMX Plus! (3976) • Dirt Bike Magazine (3977) • Dirt Wheels (3978) • 4-Wheel ATV Action (3979) • Motocross Action (3980)

The Hiaring Co.
1800 Lincoln Ave.
San Rafael, CA 94901-1298
Phone: (415)453-9700
Fax: (415)453-2517

Publications: Wines & Vines (3604)

Hiawatha Daily World
607 Utah
Hiawatha, KS 66434
Phone: (785)742-2111
Fax: (785)742-2276

Publications: Hiawatha Daily World (11491)

The Hickman Courier
Box 70
Hickman, KY 42050-0070
Phone: (270)236-2726
Fax: (270)236-2726

Publications: The Hickman Courier (12126)

High Country Independent Press
220 S. Broadway
Belgrade, MT 59714
Phone: (406)388-6762
Fax: (406)388-6072

Publications: High Country Independent Press (17723)

High Country Media, Inc.
PO Box 1026
Blowing Rock, NC 28605
Phone: (828)295-7522
Fax: (828)295-7507

Publications: The Blowing Rocket (23650)

High Country Media , LLC
PO Box 1330
Newland, NC 28657
Phone: (828)733-2448
Fax: (828)733-0639

Publications: Avery Journal (24103)

High Country News
PO Box 1090
Paonia, CO 81428
Phone: (970)527-4898
Fax: (970)527-4897
Free: 800-905-1155

Publications: High Country News (4594)

High End Publishing
8895 Alton St.
Philadelphia, PA 19115

Publications: High End (27481)

High Level Echo
PO Box 571
La Crete, AB, Canada T0H 2H0

Publications: The Northern Pioneer (34807)

High Plains Publishers, Inc.
1500 E Wyatt Earp
PO Box 760
Dodge City, KS 67801
Phone: (620)227-7171
Fax: (620)227-7173
Free: 800-452-7171

Publications: High Plains Journal (11415)

High River Times
618 Center St. S.
High River, AB, Canada T1V 1E9
Phone: (403)652-2034
Fax: (403)652-3962

Publications: High River Times (34783)

High Speed Productions, Inc.
1303 Underwood
San Francisco, CA 94124
Phone: (415)822-3083
Fax: (415)822-8359

Publications: Juxtapoz (3386) • Slap (3441) •
THRASHER (3452)

High Tech Distributors
18600 W 58th Ave.
Golden, CO 80403-1070

Publications: New Catholic Review (4472)

Higher & Higher
PO Box 829
Geneva, FL 32732
Phone: (407)349-BLUE
Fax: (407)349-5236

Publications: Higher & Higher (6172)

Highland Echo
Maryville College
Maryville, TN 37801
Phone: (423)981-8176
Fax: (423)981-8010

Publications: Highland Echo (29348)

Highland Lakes Newspapers, Inc.
304 Gateway Loop
Marble Falls, TX 78654
Phone: (830)693-4367
Fax: (830)693-3650

Publications: The Highlander News (30759)

Highland News Leader
PO Box 250
Highland, IL 62249
Phone: (618)654-2366
Fax: (618)654-1181

Publications: Highland News Leader (8988)

The Highland Vidette
PO Box 369
Troy, KS 66087-0369
Phone: (913)442-3791
Fax: (913)442-3260

Publications: The Highland Vidette (11850)

The Highlander
87 Highland Ave.
Hull, MA 02045
Phone: (781)925-0600
Fax: (781)925-1439
Free: 800-607-4410

Publications: The Highlander (14248)

Highlands Star/Crosby Courier
PO Box 405
Highlands, TX 77562
Phone: (281)328-9605
Fax: (281)328-9605

Publications: Highland Star/Crosby Courier (30448)

Highlands Station, Inc.
2600 S Parker Rd., Ste. 1-211
Aurora, CO 80014
Phone: (303)338-1700
Fax: (303)338-1949
Free: 888-338-1700

Publications: Model Railroading (4147)

The Highmore Herald
PO Box 435
Highmore, SD 57345
Phone: (605)852-2927
Fax: (605)852-2927

Publications: The Highmore Herald (28866)

Highway 40 Courier
PO Box 639
Cut Knife, SK, Canada S0M 0N0
Phone: (306)398-4901
Fax: (306)398-4909

Publications: Highway 40 Courier (37462)

Highway 17 Almanack & Gazetteer
PO Box 3602
Santa Cruz, CA 95063-3602
Phone: (831)479-3675
Fax: (408)924-3229

Publications: Highway 17 Almanack & Gazetteer
(3683)

Hikane: The Capable Woman
PO Box 841
Great Barrington, MA 01230-0841

Publications: Hikane: The Capable Woman (14215)

The Hill
733 15th St. NW, No. 1140
Washington, DC 20005
Phone: (202)628-8500
Fax: (202)628-8503
Free: 800-284-3437

Publications: The Hill (5526)

The Hill City Times
110 N Pomeroy
PO Box 308
Hill City, KS 67642
Phone: (785)421-5700
Fax: (785)421-5712

Publications: The Hill City Times (11494)

Hill Country Community Press
PO Box 205
Johnson City, TX 78636
Phone: (830)868-7181
Fax: (830)868-7182

Publications: Johnson City Record Courier (30626)

Hill Country Recorder
PO Box 905
Boerne, TX 78006
Phone: (830)249-9524
Fax: (830)249-1189
Free: (866)249-9524

Publications: Hill Country Recorder (29930)

Hill Country Sun
PO Box 1482
Wimberley, TX 78676
Phone: (512)847-5162
Fax: (512)847-5162
Free: 877-477-5162

Publications: Hill Country Sun (31302)

The Hill Times
69 Sparks St.
Ottawa, ON, Canada K1P 5A5
Phone: (613)232-5952
Fax: (613)232-9055

Publications: The Hill Times (36248)

Hills & Plains Free Press, Inc.
419 Main St.
Box 29
Bottineau, ND 58318
Phone: (701)228-2605
Fax: (701)228-5864

Publications: Courant (24376)

Hills Publications, Inc.
5707 Redwood Rd.
Oakland, CA 94619
Phone: (510)339-4040
Fax: (510)339-4066

Publications: The Journal (2683)

Hillsboro Argus Inc.
150 SE 3rd St.
Hillsboro, OR 97123
Phone: (503)648-1131
Fax: (503)648-9191

Publications: Hillsboro Argus (26372)

Hillsboro Journal, Inc.
PO Box 100
Hillsboro, IL 62049
Phone: (217)532-3933
Fax: (217)532-3632

Publications: M & M Journal (8995)

Hillsboro Reporter
PO Box 569
Hillsboro, TX 76645
Phone: (254)582-3431
Fax: (254)582-3800

Publications: Reporter (30449)

Hillsborough Community College
PO Box 5096
Tampa, FL 33675-5096
Phone: (813)253-7664
Fax: (813)253-7622

Publications: HAWKEYE (6767)

Hillsdale College Press
33 E College St.
Hillsdale, MI 49242
Phone: (517)437-7341
Fax: (517)437-0654
Free: 800-437-2268

Publications: IMPRIMIS (15164)

The Himalayan Institute Press
RR 1, Box 405
Honesdale, PA 18431
Phone: (570)253-5551
Fax: (570)253-6360
Free: 800-822-4547

Publications: Himalayan Institute Quarterly
(27049) • Yoga International (27052)

The Hinckley News, Inc.
115 Main St.
PO Box 310
Hinckley, MN 55037
Phone: (320)384-6188
Fax: (320)384-7844

Publications: The Hinckley News (15962)

Hinton News
210 2nd Ave.
PO Box 1000
Hinton, WV 25951
Phone: (304)466-0005

Publications: Hinton News (33337)

Hinton Record
PO Box 959
Hinton, OK 73047
Phone: (405)542-6644
Fax: (405)542-3120

Publications: Hinton Record (25864)

Hip Mama
PO Box 12525
Portland, OR 97212-0525

Publications: Hip Mama (26480)

Hipple Publishing Co., Inc.
333 W Dakota
PO Box 669
Pierre, SD 57501-0669
Phone: (605)224-7301
Fax: (605)224-9210
Free: 800-658-3063

Publications: Dakota Outdoors (28916) • The Reminder Plus (28919) • The Times (28923)

Hiram College
PO Box 162
Hiram, OH 44234-0162
Phone: (330)569-5331
Fax: (330)569-5449

Publications: Hiram Poetry Review (25247)

Hirt Media
PO Box 312
New Lexington, OH 43764
Phone: (740)342-4121
Fax: (740)342-4131

Publications: Perry County Tribune (25414) • Tribune Shopping News (25415)

Hirt Publishing Co.
107 Main St.
Bellville, OH 44813-1020
Phone: (419)886-2291
Fax: (419)886-2704
Publications: The Bellville Star & Tri Forks Press (24673)

Hirt Publishing Co.
114 W. Main St.
PO Box 66
Cardington, OH 43315
Phone: (419)864-6046
Fax: (419)864-2369
Publications: Morrow County Independent (24739)

Hirt Publishing Co.
109 W. Sycamore St.
PO Box 127
Columbus Grove, OH 45830
Phone: (419)659-2173
Fax: (419)659-2760
Publications: Putnam County Vidette/Pandora Times (25091)

HIS Publishing, Inc.
PO Box 213
Berne, IN 46711
Fax: (219)589-2810
Publications: Proven Home Plans For Today (9816)

Hispanic Business Inc.
425 Pine Ave.
Santa Barbara, CA 93117-3709
Phone: (805)964-4554
Fax: (805)964-6139
Free: 800-957-9724
Publications: Hispanic Business (3641) • SuperOnda (3660)

Hispanic Press
PO Box 29
Avon Park, FL 33826
Phone: (863)382-7402
Fax: (863)382-7901
Publications: Prensa Hispana (Hispanic Press) (5913)

Hispanic Publishing Corp.
999 Ponce de Leon, Ste. 600
Coral Gables, FL 33134
Phone: (305)442-2462
Fax: (305)774-3578
Free: 800-989-9822
Publications: Vista Magazine (6014)

Hispanic Times Magazine
PO Box 579
Winchester, CA 92596
Phone: (909)926-2119
Publications: Diversity Magazine (4092) • Hispanic Times Magazine (4093)

Historic Brass Society, Inc.
148 W. 23rd St., No. 2A
New York, NY 10011
Phone: (212)627-3820
Fax: (212)627-3820
Publications: Historic Brass Society (21805)

Historic Deerfield Inc.
Box 321
Deerfield, MA 01342-0321
Phone: (413)774-5581
Fax: (413)775-7220
Publications: Historic Deerfield (14157)

Historic Madison, Inc. of Wisconsin
PO Box 2721
Madison, WI 53701-2721
Phone: (608)267-4489
Publications: Historic Madison (33946)

Historical Construction Equipment Association
16623 Liberty Hi Rd.
Bowling Green, OH 43402
Phone: (419)352-5616
Fax: (419)352-6086
Publications: Equipment Echoes (24691)

Historical Museum of Southern Florida
101 W. Flagler St.
Miami, FL 33130
Phone: (305)375-1492
Fax: (305)375-1609
Publications: Tequesta (6383)

Historical Publications, Inc.
234 Monarch Hill Rd.
Tunbridge, VT 05077
Phone: (802)889-3500
Fax: (802)889-5627
Free: 800-777-1862
Publications: The Artilleryman (31607) • The Civil War News (31608)

The Historical Society of Cecil County
135 E. Main St.
Elkton, MD 21921
Phone: (410)398-1790
Publications: Cecil Historical Journal (13494)

Historical Society of the Episcopal Church
PO Box 2247
Austin, TX 78768
Phone: (512)282-3234
Fax: (512)480-0437
Publications: Anglican & Episcopal History (29753)

Historical Society, Illinois Great Rivers Conference, United Methodist Church
Box 515
Bloomington, IL 61702-0515
Phone: (309)828-5092
Fax: (309)829-4820
Publications: The Historical Messenger (8078)

Historical Society of Pennsylvania
1300 Locust St.
Philadelphia, PA 19107-5699
Phone: (215)732-6200
Fax: (215)732-2680
Publications: Pennsylvania Magazine of History and Biography (27623)

Historical Society of Princeton
158 Nassau St.
Princeton, NJ 08542
Phone: (609)921-6748
Fax: (609)921-6939
Publications: Princeton History (19470)

Historical Society of Southern California
200 East Ave., 43
Los Angeles, CA 90031-1304
Phone: (323)222-0546
Publications: Southern California Quarterly (2397)

Historical Society of Washington, D.C.
1307 New Hampshire NW
Washington, DC 20036-1507
Phone: (202)785-2068
Fax: (202)887-5785
Publications: Washington History (5845)

Historical Trends Corp.
69A 7th Ave.
Brooklyn, NY 11217
Phone: (718)636-0788
Fax: (718)636-0750
Publications: Traditional Building (20349)

History of Economics Society
c/o Neil Niman, Secy.-Treas.
University of New Hampshire, Dept. of Economics
McConnell Hall
15 College Rd.
Durham, NH 03824
Phone: (603)862-3336
Publications: Journal of the History of Economic Thought (18500)

History Museum & Historical Society of Western Virginia
Box 1904
Roanoke, VA 24008
Phone: (540)342-5770
Fax: (540)224-1256
Publications: Journal (32490)

History of Science Society
University of Chicago Press Journals Division
1427 E. 60th St.
Chicago, IL 60637-2954
Phone: (773)753-3347
Fax: (773)753-0811
Publications: ISIS (20805)

Hit Parader Publications, Inc.
40 Violet Ave.
Poughkeepsie, NY 12601-1521
Phone: (914)454-7420
Fax: (914)454-7507
Publications: Hit Parader (19404)

Hitchcock Annual Corporation
English Dept.
Sacred Heart University
5151 Park Ave.
Fairfield, CT 06432-1000
Phone: (732)846-8467
Publications: Hitchcock Annual (4789)

The Hitchcock County News
PO Box 278
Trenton, NE 69044-0278
Phone: (308)334-5226
Fax: (308)334-5226
Publications: The Hitchcock County News (18299)

HJK Publications, Inc.
366 E Graves Ave., Ste. D
Orange City, FL 32763-5266
Phone: (386)774-8881
Fax: (386)774-8908
Publications: Markee (6486)

HM
6307 Cele Rd.
Pflugerville, TX 78660
Phone: (512)989-7309
Fax: (512)670-2764
Free: 877-897-0368
Publications: HM (30931)

HMR Publications Group, Inc.
PO Box 76002
Atlanta, GA 30358-1002
Phone: (770)457-6106
Publications: Healthcare Marketing Report (7015)

Hoa Thinh Don Viet Bao
8394-C2 Terminal Rd.
Lorton, VA 22079
Phone: (703)339-9852
Fax: (703)339-9857
Publications: Hoa Thinh Don Viet Bao (32197)

Hobart Democrat-Chief
407 S Main
PO Box 432
Hobart, OK 73651
Phone: (580)726-3333
Fax: (580)726-3431
Publications: Hobart Democrat-Chief (25865)

Hobart and William Smith Colleges
Box SF-92
Geneva, NY 14456-3397
Phone: (315)789-5500
Fax: (315)781-0643
Publications: The Herald (20654)

Hobart and William Smith Colleges
Geneva, NY 14456
Phone: (315)781-3392
Fax: (315)781-3348
Publications: Seneca Review (20655)

Hobbs News-Sun
PO Box 850
Hobbs, NM 88241
Phone: (505)393-2123
Fax: (505)397-0610
Free: 800-993-2123
Publications: Hobbs News-Sun (19864)

Hobby Greenhouse Association
8 Glen Terr.
Bedford, MA 01730-2048
Phone: (781)275-0377
Publications: Hobby Greenhouse (13836)

Hobby Publications Inc.
207 Commercial Ct.
PO Box 102
Morganville, NJ 07751
Phone: (732)536-5160
Fax: (732)446-5761
Free: 800-969-7176

Publications: Hobby Merchandiser (19286) • Picture Framing Magazine (19287)

Hocking Printing Co., Inc.
615 E. Main St.
PO Box 456
Ephrata, PA 17522
Phone: (717)738-1151
Fax: (717)733-3900

Publications: Shopping News of Lancaster County (26889)

Hocking Valley Advertiser
53 W. Main St.
PO Box 247
Logan, OH 43138
Phone: (740)385-1969
Fax: (740)385-8458

Publications: Hocking Valley Advertiser (25311)

Hockley County Publishing
Drawer 1628
Levelland, TX 79336
Phone: (806)894-3121
Fax: (806)894-7957

Publications: Levelland & Hockley County News Press (30682)

Hockomock Publishing
50 Washington St.
PO Box 300
North Easton, MA 02356
Phone: (508)238-7016
Fax: (508)230-2381

Publications: Speedway Scene (14422)

Ron Hoffer
PO Box 578
Lompoc, CA 93438
Phone: (805)736-2313
Fax: (805)736-5654

Publications: Space and Missile Times (2163)

Hoflin Publishing Inc.
4401 Zephyr St.
Wheat Ridge, CO 80033-3299
Phone: (303)420-2222
Fax: (303)422-7000

Publications: Akita World (4671) • The Boston Quarterly (4672) • The Dalmatian Quarterly (4674) • The German Shepherd Quarterly (4675) • The Irish Wolfhound Quarterly (4677) • The Labrador Quarterly (4679) • The Malamute Quarterly (4679) • The Rhodesian Ridgeback Quarterly (4681) • The Samoyed Quarterly (4682) • The Siberian Quarterly (4683)

Hogan Communications
150 E Olive Ave., Ste. 208
Burbank, CA 91502
Phone: (818)848-4876
Fax: (818)848-4995

Publications: Preview Theater Magazine (1623)

Hogan's Alley
PO Box 47684
Atlanta, GA 30362

Publications: Hogan's Alley (7016)

Hohner, Inc.
PO Box 15035
Richmond, VA 23227
Phone: (804)515-1900
Fax: (804)515-0840

Publications: Easy Reeding (32436)

Hoke Communications, Inc.
224 7th St.
Garden City, NY 11530
Phone: (516)746-6700
Fax: (516)294-8141
Free: 800-229-6700

Publications: Direct Marketing Magazine (20637) • Fund Raising Management Magazine (20640)

Hokubei Mainichi, Inc.
1746 Post St.
San Francisco, CA 94115
Phone: (415)567-7323
Fax: (415)567-1110

Publications: Hokubei Mainichi (3371)

Holden Arboretum
9500 Sperry Rd.
Kirtland, OH 44094-5172
Phone: (440)946-4400
Fax: (440)602-8012

Publications: Leaves Class and Events Magazine (25285)

The Holden Image-Progress
PO Box 8
117 E. 2nd
Holden, MO 64040
Phone: (816)732-5552
Fax: (816)732-4696

Publications: The Holden Image-Progress (17099)

Holdenville Daily News
1112 South Creek
PO Box 751
Holdenville, OK 74848
Phone: (405)379-5411
Fax: (405)379-5413

Publications: Holdenville Daily News (25869)

Holdrege Daily Citizen
PO Box 344
Holdrege, NE 68949
Phone: (308)995-4441
Fax: (308)995-5992

Publications: Holdrege Daily Citizen (18049)

Holistic Education Press
PO Box 328
Brandon, VT 05733-0328
Phone: (802)247-8312

Publications: Paths of Learning (31507)

The Holland Sentinel
54 W 8th St.
Holland, MI 49423
Phone: (616)392-2311
Fax: (616)392-3526
Free: 800-968-3497

Publications: The Holland Sentinel (15174)

Holland Society of New York
122 E 58th St.
New York, NY 10022-1939

Publications: de Halve Maen (21540)

Hollinger Canadian Newspapers
30 10th St. E
Saskatchewan, SK, Canada S6V 5R9
Phone: (306)764-4276
Fax: (306)763-3331
Free: 800-667-8245

Publications: Rural Roots (37518)

Hollinger Canadian Newspapers L.P.
1195 Galt E.
Sherbrooke, QC, Canada J1G 1Y7
Phone: (819)569-9525
Fax: (819)821-3179
Free: 800-463-9525

Publications: The Record (37395)

Hollinger Inc.
1827 W Fifth Ave.
Vancouver, BC, Canada V6J 1P5
Phone: (604)732-5638

Publications: The Kamloops News (34977)

Hollinger, Inc.
400 Water St.
Peterborough, ON, Canada K9J 8L4
Phone: (705)745-4641
Fax: (705)876-8439

Publications: Peterborough Examiner (36318)

Hollinger International, Inc.
440 E. Ogden Ave.
PO Box 151
Hinsdale, IL 60521
Phone: (630)887-0600
Fax: (630)887-9646

Publications: The Doings (8997)

Hollinger Newspapers Ltd.
7330 2nd St.
PO Box 700
Grand Forks, BC, Canada V0H 1H0
Phone: (250)442-2191
Fax: (250)442-3336

Publications: Boundary Bulletin (34970) • Gazette (34971)

The Hollins Critic
Box 9538
Hollins College, VA 24020-1538
Phone: (540)362-6275
Fax: (540)362-6642

Publications: The Hollins Critic (32169)

Holly Media Group
PO Box 49
Wimberley, TX 78676
Phone: (512)847-2202
Fax: (512)847-9054

Publications: The Wimberley View (31304)

The Hollywood Reporter
5055 Wilshire Blvd.
Los Angeles, CA 90036-4396
Phone: (323)525-2000
Fax: (323)525-2377

Publications: The Hollywood Reporter (2291)

Holmes Community College
PO Box 367
Goodman, MS 39079
Phone: (662)472-9062
Fax: (662)472-9156

Publications: The Growl (16630)

Holmes County Hub
25 N Clay St.
PO Box 151
Millersburg, OH 44654-0151
Phone: (330)674-1811
Fax: (330)674-3780

Publications: Holmes County Hub (25388)

Holmes Publications
PO Box 20
Villa Grove, IL 61956
Phone: (217)832-4201
Fax: (217)834-4001

Publications: Villa Grove News (9730)

Holmes Publishing Co. Ltd.
5111-50th St.
PO Box 180
Provost, AB, Canada T0B 3S0
Phone: (780)753-2564
Fax: (780)753-6117

Publications: The Provost News (34826)

Holmes Publishing Company Ltd.
5019 50th St.
PO Box 489
Vegreville, AB, Canada T9C 1R6
Phone: (780)632-2353
Fax: (780)632-3235

Publications: Vegreville Observer (34865)

Holmes Publishing Company Ltd.
414 10th St.
Wainwright, AB, Canada T9W 1P5
Phone: (780)842-4465
Fax: (780)842-2760

Publications: Wainwright Edge (34868) • Wainwright Star Chronicle (34869)

Holmes Publishing Co., Ltd.
Box 100
Macklin, SK, Canada S0L 2O0
Phone: (306)753-2424
Fax: (306)753-2424

Publications: Macklin Mirror (37492)

Holmes Publishing Co., Ltd
PO Box 420
Oyen, AB, Canada T0J 2J0
Phone: (403)664-3622
Fax: (403)664-3622

Publications: The Oyen Echo (34821)

Holstein Journal
9120 Leslie St., Unit 105
Richmond Hill, ON, Canada L4B 3J9
Phone: (905)886-4222
Fax: (905)886-0037

Publications: Holstein Journal (36342)

The Holton Recorder
109 W 4th St.
PO Box 311
Holton, KS 66436
Phone: (785)364-3141
Fax: (785)364-3422

Publications: The Holton Recorder (11495)

Holy Cross Orthodox Press
50 Goddard Ave.
Brookline, MA 02445
Phone: (617)731-3500
Fax: (617)850-1460

Publications: Greek Orthodox Theological Review (14019)

Holy Trinity Monastery
PO Box 36
Jordanville, NY 13361-0036
Phone: (315)858-0940
Fax: (315)858-0505

Publications: Orthodox Life (20854) • Pravoslavnaya Rus (20855) • Pravoslavnaya Zhizn (20856)

Holyoke Enterprise
PO Box 297
Holyoke, CO 80734
Phone: (970)854-2811
Fax: (970)854-2232

Publications: Holyoke Enterprise (4517)

Home & Away Magazine
8030 Excelsior Dr.
Madison, WI 53717
Phone: (608)828-2487
Fax: (608)828-2443

Publications: Home & Away Magazine (33947)

Home Builders Association of Maryland
1502 Woodlawn Dr.
Baltimore, MD 21207-4009
Phone: (410)265-7400
Fax: (410)265-6529

Publications: Mid-Atlantic Builder (13218)

Home Education Magazine
PO Box 1083
Tonasket, WA 98855-1083
Phone: (509)486-1351
Fax: (509)486-2753
Free: 800-236-3278

Publications: Home Education Magazine (33165)

Home Energy Magazine
2124 Kitteredge St., PMB No. 95
Berkeley, CA 94704
Phone: (510)524-5405
Fax: (510)486-4673

Publications: Home Energy (1526)

Home Furnishings Retailer
305 W. High St., No. 400
PO Box 2396
High Point, NC 27261
Phone: (336)886-6100
Fax: (336)886-6102
Free: 800-888-9590

Publications: Home Furnishings Retailer (24000)

Home Life, Inc.
1731 Smizer Mill Rd.
Fenton, MO 63026-2635
Phone: (636)343-6786
Fax: (636)225-0743
Free: 800-346-6322

Publications: Practical Homeschooling (17064)

Home Magazine
215 Maxfield
PO Box 2
Mankato, MN 56001
Phone: (507)387-7953
Fax: (507)387-4775

Publications: Home Magazine (16027)

Home News
766 Irving Pl.
PO Box 1100
Secaucus, NJ 07096
Phone: (201)867-2071
Fax: (201)865-3806

Publications: Home News (19538)

The Home News
PO Box 100
Marshville, NC 28103
Phone: (704)624-5068
Fax: (704)624-2371

Publications: The Home News (24060)

Home News Enterprises, LLC
2575 N. Morton St.
Franklin, IN 46131
Phone: (317)736-7101
Fax: (317)736-2759

Publications: Daily Journal (10005) • Herald Republican (10007) • The Republic (10008)

Home News Enterprizes
136 N Van Buren St.
PO Box 277
Nashville, IN 47448
Phone: (812)988-2221
Fax: (812)988-1570

Publications: Brown County Democrat (10337)

Home News, Inc.
120 S Walnut St.
PO Box 39
Bath, PA 18014
Phone: (610)837-0107
Fax: (610)837-0482

Publications: Home News (26683)

Home Planet Publications
PO Box 415
Stuyvesant Sta.
New York, NY 10009
Phone: (718)769-2854

Publications: Home Planet News (21812)

Home Power
PO Box 520
Ashland, OR 97520
Phone: (541)512-0220
Fax: (541)512-0343
Free: 800-707-6585

Publications: Home Power (26215)

Home Reporter, Inc.
8723 3rd Ave.
Brooklyn, NY 11209
Phone: (718)238-6606
Fax: (718)238-6630

Publications: Home Reporter & Sunset News (20320)

Home Service Publications, Inc.
2915 Commers Dr., Ste. 700
Eagan, MN 55121
Phone: (651)454-9200
Fax: (651)994-2250

Publications: American Woodworker (15861)

The Home Shop Machinist
2779 Aero Park Dr.
Traverse City, MI 49684
Phone: (231)946-3712
Fax: (231)946-9588
Free: 800-447-7367

Publications: Neil Knopf - Editor (15600)

Home Shopper
116 S Magnolia
Box 289
Elmwood, IL 61529
Phone: (309)742-2511
Fax: (309)742-2511

Publications: Home Shopper (8844)

Home Town Press, Inc.
PO Box 156
Ludlow, VT 05149
Phone: (802)228-8817
Fax: (802)228-8000

Publications: Black River Tribune (31549)

Homefinders
PO Box 40645
Bellevue, WA 98015-4645
Phone: (425)649-8912
Fax: (425)649-8913

Publications: Timber Bulletin (32668)

HomeFront Buyer's Guide
230 N Main St.
PO Box 1056
Fremont, NE 68025
Phone: (402)721-1030
Fax: (402)721-5276

Publications: HomeFront Buyer's Guide (18011)

Homeless Empowerment Project, Inc.
1151 Massachusetts Ave.
Cambridge, MA 02138
Phone: (617)497-1595
Fax: (617)868-0767

Publications: Spare Change (14103)

The Homer Index
122 E Main St.
PO Box 236
Homer, MI 49245
Phone: (517)568-4646
Fax: (517)568-4346

Publications: The Homer Index (15181)

Homer News
3482 Landings St.
Homer, AK 99603
Phone: (907)235-7767
Fax: (907)235-4199

Publications: Homer News (588)

Homes Publishing Group
178 Main St.
Unionville, ON, Canada L3R 2G9
Phone: (905)479-4663
Fax: (905)479-4482
Free: 800-363-4663

Publications: Active Adult (36827) • Condo Life (36828) • Homes Magazine (36829) • Renovation & Decor (36838)

Homestead
PO Box 29
323 Main
Napoleon, ND 58561
Phone: (701)754-2212
Fax: (701)754-2212

Publications: Homestead (24521)

Homestead Hotline
150 Morrow Ln.
Clayton, NJ 08312
Phone: (856)881-0319

Publications: Homestead Hotline (18750)

Homestead Publishing Co., Inc.
10 Hays St.
PO Box 189
Bel Air, MD 21014
Phone: (410)838-4400
Fax: (410)638-0357
Free: 888-879-1710

Publications: Aegis (13289) • The Weekender (13291)

Homesteader News, Inc.
15344 Werling Ct.
El Paso, TX 79928
Phone: (915)852-3235
Fax: (915)852-0123

Publications: West Texas County Courier (30453)

HomeStyles.com
213 E. 4th St., 4th Fl.
St. Paul, MN 55101
Phone: (651)602-5000
Fax: (651)602-5001
Free: 888-626-2026

Publications: Country Style Homes Plans and Designs (16372) • Distinguished Home Plans (16374) • HomeStyles Home Plans (16379) • New Country Homes (16400)

Hometown
314 E. Main St.
PO Box 549
Niles, MI 49120
Phone: (269)684-6802
Fax: (269)684-6115

Publications: Hometown News (15403)

Hometown Communication
Eight & Elm Sts.
PO Box 847
Coffeyville, KS 67337
Fax: (316)251-1905

Publications: Coffeyville Journal (11386)

Hometown Communication Network
PO Box 230
Howell, MI 48844-0230
Phone: (248)634-8219
Fax: (248)634-8233

Publications: The Fenton Independent (15191) •
Holly Herald (15192)

Hometown Communications, Inc.
209 John St.
Box 660
Sturgis, MI 49091-1459
Fax: (616)651-2296
Free: 800-686-5653

Publications: Sturgis Journal (15580)

HomeTown Golf Magazine
9933 Alliance Rd.
Cincinnati, OH 45242
Phone: (513)794-4100

Publications: HomeTown Golf Magazine (24803)

Hometown Herald
1520 E Sunrise Blvd.
Fort Lauderdale, FL 33304
Phone: (954)462-3000
Fax: (954)527-8955

Publications: El Nuevo Herald (6075) • Hometown
Herald (6076)

Hometown News
225 W. Colfax Ave.
South Bend, IN 46626
Phone: (219)235-6161
Fax: (219)235-1765

Publications: Hometown News (10455)

Hometown News
438 N. Main St.
PO Drawer 249
Woodruff, SC 29388
Phone: (864)476-3513
Fax: (864)476-3511

Publications: The Woodruff News (28788)

Hometown News Corp.
PO Box 789
Zebulon, GA 30295
Phone: (706)567-3446
Fax: (706)567-8814

Publications: Pike County Journal-Reporter (7658)

Hometown News Group Publications
207 E Main St.
Sun Prairie, WI 53590
Phone: (608)837-2521
Fax: (608)825-4460
Free: 888-330-6083

Publications: The Hometown Advertiser (34357) •
The Star (34358)

Hometown News, Inc.
109 Monroe NW
PO Box 146
Piedmont, OK 73078
Phone: (405)373-1616
Fax: (405)373-1636

Publications: Piedmont-Surrey Gazette (26035)

Hometown News Inc.
PO Box 280
Cowpens, SC 29330
Fax: (864)573-8710

Publications: Cowpens/Pacolet Tribune (28594)

Hometown Newspapers
323 E Grand River
PO Box 230
Howell, MI 48843
Phone: (517)548-2000

Publications: Brighton Argus (15190) • Fowlerville
Shopper (15051) • Hartland Shopper (15149) •
Home Town News (15193) • The Lakes Area Shopper (15195) • Livingston County Press and Argus
(15196) • Milford Times (15359) • Monday Green
Sheet (15198) • The Northville Record (15405) •
Novi News (15410) • The Pinckney Shopper
(15443) • The South Lyon Herald (15540)

Hometown Publications, Inc.
1000 Bridgeport Ave.
Shelton, CT 06484
Phone: (203)926-2080
Fax: (203)926-2091

Publications: The Amity Observer (5120) • Bridgeport News (4711) • Easton Courier (4779) • The
Hamden Journal (5122) • Huntington Herald
(5123) • The Milford Mirror (5126) • Monroe Courier
(5127) • Stratford Star (5173) • Trumbull Times
(5128) • The Valley Gazette (5129) • Weston Voice
(4699)

Hometown Publications, Inc.
41 N. Church St.
Carbondale, PA 18407-1904
Fax: (717)282-3950

Publications: Carbondale News (26756)

Hometown Publications, Inc.
RR 2, Wilson Dr.
Box 2186B
Moscow, PA 18444
Fax: (717)892-9841

Publications: Villager (27297)

Homiletic and Pastoral Review
50 S. Franklin Tpke.
PO Box 297
Ramsey, NJ 07446

Publications: Homiletic and Pastoral Review
(19490)

Honey Hill Publishing
37 Winwood Bldg.
PO Box 374
Bakerstown, PA 15007
Phone: (412)443-1891
Fax: (412)443-1877

Publications: Pittsburgh Parent (26668)

The Honolulu Advertiser
News Bldg.
605 Kapiolani Blvd.
PO Box 3110
Honolulu, HI 96802
Phone: (808)525-8090
Fax: (808)525-8037

Publications: The Honolulu Advertiser (7700)

**Honolulu Orchid Society/Pacific Orchid
Society**
c/o B. Brunson
86-560 W. Kolia Pl.
Waianae, HI 96792

Publications: Hawaii Orchid Journal (7794)

Honolulu Publishing Company Ltd.
707 Richards St., No. 525
Honolulu, HI 96813-4623
Phone: (808)524-7400
Fax: (808)531-2306
Free: 800-272-5245

Publications: Spirit of Aloha (7719)

Honolulu Weekly, Inc.
1200 College Walk, Ste. 214
Honolulu, HI 96817
Phone: (808)528-1475
Fax: (808)528-3144

Publications: Honolulu Weekly (7703)

The Honor Society of Phi Kappa Phi
PO Box 16000
Louisiana State University
Baton Rouge, LA 70893-6000
Phone: (225)388-4917
Fax: (225)388-4900
Free: 800-804-9880

Publications: Phi Kappa Phi Forum (50)

Hood County News
PO Box 879
Granbury, TX 76048
Phone: (817)573-7066
Fax: (817)279-8371
Free: 800-588-7066

Publications: Hood County News (30404)

Hood Today
401 Rosemont Ave.
Frederick, MD 21701
Phone: (301)696-3641
Fax: (301)696-3578

Publications: Hood Today (13514)

Hooker County Tribune
PO Box 125
Mullen, NE 69152
Phone: (308)546-2242
Fax: (308)546-2722

Publications: Hooker County Tribune (18165)

Hooper Publishing Co.
PO Box 929
Sanibel, FL 33957
Phone: (941)433-4090

Publications: Island Life Magazine (6649)

Hoosier-Times, Inc.
dba Reporter-Times
60 S. Jefferson St.
PO Box 1636
Martinsville, IN 46151
Phone: (765)342-3311
Fax: (765)342-1446

Publications: Reporter-Times (10294)

Hoosier Topics
PO Box 496
1 N. Main St.
Cloverdale, IN 46120
Phone: (765)795-4438
Fax: (765)795-3121

Publications: The Hoosier Topics (9892)

Hooters Magazine
1815 The Exchange
Atlanta, GA 30339
Phone: (770)951-2040
Fax: (770)618-7049

Publications: Hooters Magazine (7017)

Hope
PO Box 160
Brooklin, ME 04616
Phone: (207)359-4651
Fax: (207)359-8920

Publications: Hope (12931)

The Hope Star-Journal
611 Harrison St.
Hope, IN 47246
Phone: (812)546-4940
Fax: (812)546-4944

Publications: The Hope Star-Journal (10065)

The Hopkins Journal
411 Barnard St.
PO Box 170
Hopkins, MO 64461
Phone: (660)778-3205
Fax: (660)778-3205

Publications: The Hopkins Journal (17101)

Horizon California Publications, Inc.
450 E. Line St.
Bishop, CA 93514
Phone: (760)873-3535
Fax: (760)873-3591
Free: 800-293-3535

Publications: Inyo Register (1583) • Review-Herald
(1584)

Horizon House Publications, Inc.
685 Canton St.
Norwood, MA 02062
Phone: (781)769-9750
Fax: (781)769-9884
Free: 800-541-5970

Publications: Journal of Electronic Defense (14447) • Microwave Journal (14450) • Telecommunications Magazine (14451)

Horizon Publishing Co.
219 Locust St.
PO Box 70
Malvern, AR 72104-3721
Phone: (501)337-7523
Fax: (501)337-1226

Publications: Malvern Daily Record (1263)

Horizon Publishing Co.
930 6th St.
Box 545
Jesup, IA 50648-0545
Phone: (319)827-1128
Fax: (319)827-1125

Publications: Citizen Herald (11007)

Horizon Publishing Company LLC
7412 Calumet Ave.
Hammond, IN 46324-2692
Phone: (219)852-3200
Fax: (219)931-6487
Free: 800-233-5922

Publications: Dow Theory Forecasts (10050)

Horizons
1900 Carlton Rd.
Parma, OH 44134-3129
Phone: (216)741-3312
Fax: (216)741-9356

Publications: Horizons (25466)

Horizonte Acquisitions
Ave. Principal I-1 Urb. Baralt
Fajardo, PR 00738
Phone: (787)860-0446
Fax: (787)860-3451

Publications: Periodico Horizonte (28242)

The Horn Book, Inc.
56 Roland St., Ste. 200
Boston, MA 02129
Phone: (617)628-0225
Fax: (617)628-0882
Free: 800-325-1170

Publications: The Horn Book Guide (13901) • The Horn Book Magazine (13902)

The Horn Speaker
PO Box 1193
Mabank, TX 75147
Phone: (903)848-0304
Fax: (903)848-0596

Publications: The Horn Speaker (30751)

Horn and Whistle Enthusiasts Group
275 Windswept Dr.
North East, PA 16428
Phone: (814)725-8150

Publications: Horn and Whistle (27339)

Hornell-Canisteo Penn-E-Saver
PO Box 367
Canisteo, NY 14823
Phone: (607)698-4771

Publications: Hornell-Canisteo Penn-E-Saver (20428)

Horry County Historical Society
606 Main St.
Conway, SC 29526-4340
Phone: (843)488-1966

Publications: Independent Republic Quarterly (28590)

Horseless Carriage Club of America
49239 Golden Oak Loop
Oakhurst, CA 93644
Phone: (559)658-8800

Publications: Horseless Carriage Gazette (2658)

Horseman Publishing Co.
PO Box 8480
Lexington, KY 40533
Phone: (606)276-4026
Fax: (606)277-8100
Free: 800-860-8199

Publications: Horseman and Fair World (12166)

The Horsemen's Corral
211 W Main St.
PO Box 110
New London, OH 44851
Phone: (419)929-8200
Fax: (419)929-3800

Publications: The Horsemen's Corral (25418)

The Horsemen's Yankee Pedlar
88 Leicester St.
North Oxford, MA 01537
Phone: (508)987-5886
Fax: (508)987-5887

Publications: The Horsemen's Yankee Pedlar (14425)

Horses USA
21 Greenview Dr.
Carlsbad, CA 92009
Phone: (760)431-9696
Fax: (760)431-8848

Publications: Horses USA (1666)

Horton Headlight
133 W 8th St.
PO Box 269
Horton, KS 66439
Phone: (913)486-2512
Fax: (913)486-2512

Publications: Horton Headlight (11497)

Horvitz Newspapers, Inc.
1705 132nd Ave. NE
PO Box 90130
Bellevue, WA 98009
Phone: (425)455-2222

Publications: Eastside Journal (32665)

The Hosiery Association
3623 Latrobe Dr., Ste. 130
Charlotte, NC 28211
Phone: (704)365-0913
Fax: (704)362-2056

Publications: Hosiery News (23745)

Hospital for Joint Diseases
Bernard Aronson Plz.
301 E. 17th St.
New York, NY 10003
Phone: (212)598-6000

Publications: Hospital for Joint Diseases Bulletin (21818)

Hospitality News Group
PO Box 21027
Salem, OR 97307-1027
Phone: (503)390-8343
Fax: (503)390-8344
Free: 800-685-1932

Publications: Hospitality News for the Western United States (26568)

Hospitality Sales and Marketing Association International
8201 Greensboro Dr., No. 300
McLean, VA 22102
Phone: (703)610-9024
Fax: (703)610-9005

Publications: H.S.M.A.I. Marketing Review (32265)

Hospodar
PO Box 301
West, TX 76691-0301
Phone: (254)826-3838

Publications: Hospodar (31281)

Hosr Communications
904 N. Broadway
Lexington, KY 40505
Phone: (606)226-4542
Fax: (606)226-4575

Publications: Athletics Administration (24857)

Hot House
13 Mekeel Dr.
Dover, NJ 07801-2243
Phone: (973)627-5349
Fax: (973)586-0719

Publications: Hot House (18778)

Hotel Employees and Restaurant Employees International Union
1219 28th St. NW
Washington, DC 20007-3389
Phone: (202)393-4373
Fax: (202)965-2958

Publications: Catering Industry Employee (5397)

Hotel & Travel Index International Edition
500 Plz. Dr.
Secaucus, NJ 07094-3626
Phone: (201)902-2000
Fax: (201)319-1628

Publications: Hotel & Travel Index—International Edition (19539)

The Houghton Lake Resorter
4049 W. Houghton Lake Dr.
PO Box 248
Houghton Lake, MI 48629
Phone: (989)366-5341
Fax: (989)366-4472

Publications: The Houghton Lake Resorter (15188)

Hounds and Hunting
PO Box 372
Bradford, PA 16701
Phone: (814)368-6155
Fax: (814)368-3522

Publications: Hounds and Hunting (26728)

HOUR Media
117 W. 3rd St.
Royal Oak, MI 48067-3831
Phone: (248)691-1800
Fax: (248)691-4531

Publications: HOUR Detroit (15481) • Sport Detroit (15486)

The Hour Publishing Co.
346 Main Ave.
Norwalk, CT 06851
Phone: (203)846-3281
Fax: (203)846-9897

Publications: The Hour (5064) • The Wilton Villager (5232)

Housatonic Publications
65 Bank St.
New Milford, CT 06776
Fax: (860)354-2645

Publications: Bethel Beacon (5027) • Brookfield Journal (4725) • Business Digest (5028) • Fairfield Minuteman (5029) • Housatonic Weekend (5030) • Kent Good Times Dispatch (4920) • Litchfield Enquirer (4924) • Litchfield Weekend (5031) • New Milford Times (5032) • The Patent Trader (5033) • The Putnam County Courier (5034) • Putnam Courier Trader (5093) • Westport Minuteman (5035)

House of White Birches
306 E. Parr Rd.
Berne, IN 46711
Phone: (260)589-8741
Fax: (260)589-8093

Publications: Crazy for Cross Stitch (9803) • Creative Crafter (9805) • Crochet! (9806) • Crochet World (9807) • Doll World (9808) • Fast & Fun Crochet (9809) • Good Old Days (9810) • Good Old Days Specials (9811) • Home Cooking (9812) • Knitting Digest (9813) • Old-Time Crochet (9814) • Plastic Canvas Crafts (9815) • Quick & Easy Quilting (9817) • Quilt World (9818) • Sewing Savvy (9819)

Houston Chronicle
801 Texas Ave.
Houston, TX 77002
Phone: (713)220-7171
Fax: (713)220-6677
Free: 800-735-3800

Publications: Houston Chronicle (30481)

Houston Community Newspapers
17511 El Camino
Houston, TX 77058-3049
Phone: (281)488-1108
Fax: (281)286-0750

Publications: Clear Lake Citizen & Exchange News (30462)

Numbers cited after listings are entry numbers rather than page numbers.

Houston Community Newspapers
PO Box 1830
Pearland, TX 77588
Phone: (281)485-2785
Fax: (281)485-4464

Publications: Friendswood Journal (30916) • Pearland Journal (30917)

Houston County News
104 S Walnut, Ste. 2
PO Box 205
La Crescent, MN 55947
Phone: (507)895-2940
Fax: (507)895-2942

Publications: Houston County News (15987)

Houston Defender
PO Box 8005
Houston, TX 77288
Phone: (713)663-6996
Fax: (713)663-7116

Publications: Houston Defender (30482)

The Houston Home Journal
1210 Washington St.
PO Box 1910
Perry, GA 31069
Phone: (912)987-1823
Fax: (912)988-1181

Publications: The Houston Home Journal (7483)

Houston Newspapers Inc.
PO Box 170
Houston, MO 65483
Phone: (417)967-2000
Fax: (417)967-2096

Publications: Houston Herald (17102)

Houston Today
Houston Mall, Hwy. 16
PO Box 899
Houston, BC, Canada V0J 1Z0
Phone: (604)845-2890

Publications: Houston Today (34975)

Hoven Review
Box 37
Hoven, SD 57450
Phone: (605)948-2110
Fax: (605)948-2110

Publications: Hoven Review (28870)

Howard Payne University
1000 Fisk
Brownwood, TX 76801
Phone: (915)649-8514
Fax: (915)649-8902

Publications: Yellow Jacket (29966)

Howard Penn Hudson Associates Inc.
PO Box 311
Rhinebeck, NY 12572
Phone: (845)876-2081
Fax: (845)876-2561
Free: 800-572-3451

Publications: Public Relations Quarterly (23185)

Howard Publications
2110 Woodfall Dr., No. 10
Charleston, IL 61920-3058
Phone: (217)345-7085
Fax: (217)345-7090

Publications: Times-Courier (8236)

Howard Publications
20 S. 4th St.
PO Box 430
Pekin, IL 61554
Phone: (309)346-1111
Fax: (309)346-9815
Free: 800-888-6397

Publications: Pekin Daily Times (9414)

Howard Publications
601 W 45th Ave.
Munster, IN 46321
Phone: (219)933-3200
Fax: (219)933-3249

Publications: The Times (10053)

Howard Publications
501 Commercial St.
Waterloo, IA 50701
Phone: (319)291-1400

Publications: Waterloo-Cedar Falls Courier (11289)

Howard Publications Inc.
207 E. Pennsylvania Ave.
Escondido, CA 92025
Phone: (619)745-6611
Fax: (619)740-5433

Publications: The North County Times (2708)

Howard Publications, Inc.
132 3rd St. W.
Box 548
Twin Falls, ID 83303
Phone: (208)733-0931
Fax: (208)734-5538
Free: 800-658-3883

Publications: Times-News (7988)

Howard Query
300 N Washington Ave.
PO Box 271
Mason City, IA 50401-3222
Phone: (515)421-0500
Fax: (515)421-0516
Free: 800-421-0524

Publications: Globe-Gazette (11071)

Howard University
2225 Georgia Ave., NW
Washington, DC 20059
Phone: (202)238-2640
Fax: (202)986-0409

Publications: Howard (5531)

C. D. Howe Institute
125 Adelaide St. E.
Toronto, ON, Canada M5C 1L7
Phone: (416)865-1904
Fax: (416)865-1866

Publications: C.D. Howe Institute Commentary (36543)

Howe Printing Co., Inc.
132 S Beaumont
PO Box 149
Prairie du Chien, WI 53821
Phone: (608)326-2441
Fax: (608)326-2443

Publications: Courier-Press (34267) • Courier-Press (34266)

Howell International Enterprises
PO Box 370510
Denver, CO 80237
Phone: (303)663-7820
Fax: (303)663-7823
Free: 800-441-4748

Publications: The Mining Record (4339)

The Hoxie Sentinel
Box 78
Hoxie, KS 67740
Phone: (785)675-3321
Fax: (785)675-3421

Publications: The Hoxie Sentinel (11498)

Hoyt Publishing
7400 Skokie Blvd.
Skokie, IL 60077
Phone: (847)675-7400
Fax: (847)675-7494

Publications: P-O-P Design (9608) • P-O-P Times (9609)

H.P. Enterprise, Inc.
210 Church Ave.
PO Box 1009
High Point, NC 27261
Phone: (336)888-3500
Fax: (336)841-5165
Free: 800-933-5760

Publications: High Point Enterprise (23998)

HPC Inc.
3119 Campus Dr.
Norcross, GA 30071-1402

Publications: MicroTimes (7467)

HPC Publications
12001 N Central Expy., Ste. 640
Dallas, TX 75243
Phone: (972)239-2399
Fax: (972)239-7850

Publications: Dallas/Fort Worth New Homes Guide (30144)

H.S. Gere & Sons, Inc.
115 Conz St.
Northampton, MA 01060-3828
Phone: (413)584-5000

Publications: Amherst Bulletin (13791) • Daily Hampshire Gazette (14427)

HT Communications
Box 1401
Arvada, CO 80001
Phone: (303)420-4888
Fax: (303)420-4845

Publications: The Plantagenet Connection (4138)

H.T. Publishing Co.
PO Box 505
Schriever, LA 70395
Phone: (504)850-3132
Fax: (504)850-3215

Publications: The Bayou Catholic (12815)

HTC
4701 Patrick Henry Dr., No. 1901
Santa Clara, CA 95054-1847
Phone: (408)970-8800
Fax: (408)567-0242

Publications: High Technology Careers Magazine (3671)

HTC, Inc.
2142 1st Ave.
PO Box 38
Hibbing, MN 55746-1805
Phone: (218)262-1011
Fax: (218)262-4318
Free: 800-477-7093

Publications: Hibbing Daily Tribune (15954)

H2SO4
PO Box 423354
San Francisco, CA 94142
Phone: (415)431-2135
Fax: (415)431-2135

Publications: H2SO4 (3372)

Hub
PO Box 208
Gaylord, MN 55334
Phone: (507)237-2476

Publications: Hub (15915)

The Hub
105-3 Capital Dr.
Hay River, NT, Canada X0E 1G2
Phone: (867)874-6577
Fax: (867)874-2679

Publications: The Hub (35515)

Hubbard City News
102 N 2nd St.
PO Box 431
Mexia, TX 76667
Phone: (254)576-2516
Fax: (254)562-3121

Publications: Hubbard City News (30810)

Hubbard Marketing & Publishing Ltd.
270 Esna Park Dr., Unit 12
Markham, ON, Canada L3R 1H3
Phone: (905)513-0090
Fax: (905)513-1377
Free: 800-268-5503

Publications: Pool & Spa Marketing (36030)

Hubbard Publishing Co.
127 E. Chillicothe Ave.
Bellefontaine, OH 43311
Phone: (937)592-3060
Fax: (937)592-4463

Publications: The Bellefontaine Examiner (24666)

Hubbell Family Historical Society
2051 E McDaniel St.
PO Box 3813 GS
Springfield, MO 65808-3813
Publications: Hubbell Family Historical Society Annual (25286)

Hubbub
5344 SE 38th St.
Portland, OR 97202
Phone: (503)775-0370
Publications: Hubbub (26481)

Hubin Publishing Co., Inc.
Box 278
Hector, MN 55342
Phone: (320)365-3266
Fax: (320)365-4506
Free: 888-325-0196
Publications: Bird Island Union (15945)

Huckle Publishing, Inc.
135 West Pearl
Owatonna, MN 55060
Phone: (507)451-2840
Publications: Owatonna Area Shopper (16253)

Hudson Gazette
397 Main Rd.
PO Box 70
Hudson, QC, Canada J0P 1H0
Phone: (514)458-5482
Fax: (514)458-3337
Publications: Hudson Gazette (37001)

Hudson Herald
Box 210
Hudson, IA 50643-0210
Phone: (319)988-3855
Fax: (319)988-3855
Publications: Hudson Herald (10954)

Hudson Litchfield News
The Bell Twr.
43 Lowell Rd.
Hudson, NH 03051-2480
Phone: (603)880-1516
Fax: (603)879-9707
Publications: Hudson Litchfield News (18528)

Hudson Post Gazette
113 S Market St.
PO Box 70
Hudson, MI 49247
Phone: (517)448-2611
Publications: Hudson Post Gazette (15201)

Hudson Reporter Associates
PO Box 3069
Hoboken, NJ 07030-1601
Phone: (201)798-7800
Fax: (201)798-0018
Publications: The Current (18924) • The Hoboken Reporter (18964) • The Jersey City Reporter (19140) • The North Bergen/Reporter (18672) • The Secaucus Reporter (19541) • The Weehawken Reporter (19712)

The Hudson Review Inc.
684 Park Ave.
New York, NY 10021
Phone: (212)650-0020
Fax: (212)774-1911
Publications: The Hudson Review (21826)

Hudson Star-Observer
226 Locust St.
PO Box 147
Hudson, WI 54016
Phone: (715)386-9333
Fax: (715)386-9891
Publications: Hot Sheet Shopper TMC (33794) • Hudson Star-Observer (33795)

Hudson Valley Black Press
PO Box 2160
Newburgh, NY 12550
Phone: (845)562-1313
Fax: (845)562-1348
Publications: Hudson Valley Black Press (23001)

Hudson Valley Business Journal
84 E Main St.
Wappingers Falls, NY 12590
Phone: (845)298-6236
Fax: (845)298-6238
Publications: Hudson Valley Business Journal (23502)

Hudspeth Herald
290 Trl. West Park
PO Box 659
Dell City, TX 79837
Phone: (915)964-2426
Fax: (915)964-2426
Publications: Hudspeth County Herald-Dell Valley Review (30231)

Huerfano World
111 W 7th St.
PO Box 191
Walsenburg, CO 81089
Phone: (719)738-1720
Fax: (719)738-1727
Publications: Huerfano World (4656)

Hughes County Times
Box 38
120 S. Main
Wetumka, OK 74883
Phone: (405)452-3294
Fax: (405)452-3329
Free: 800-887-3294
Publications: Hughes County Times (26193)

Dennis & Janice Hughes
453 Benicia Dr.
Santa Rosa, CA 95409-3003
Publications: Share Guide (3734)

The Hugo Daily News
128 E. Jackson St.
Hugo, OK 74743
Phone: (580)326-3311
Fax: (580)326-6397
Free: 800-900-3311
Publications: The Hugo Daily News (25872)

Human Factors and Ergonomics Society
PO Box 1369
Santa Monica, CA 90406-1369
Phone: (310)394-1811
Fax: (310)394-2410
Publications: Ergonomics in Design (3707) • Human Factors (3711)

Human Kinetics Publishers Inc.
1607 N. Market St.
PO Box 5076
Champaign, IL 61825-5076
Fax: (217)351-1549
Free: 800-747-4457
Publications: Adapted Physical Activity Quarterly (8177) • Athletic Therapy Today (8181) • Canadian Journal of Applied Physiology (8183) • Exercise Immunology Review (8187) • International Journal of Sport Nutrition & Exercise Metabolism (8191) • Journal of Aging and Physical Activity (8193) • Journal of Applied Biomechanics (8195) • Journal of the Philosophy of Sport (8197) • Journal of Sport & Exercise Psychology (8198) • Journal of Sport Management (8199) • Journal of Sport Rehabilitation (8200) • Journal of Teaching in Physical Education (8201) • Motor Control (8204) • Pediatric Exercise Science (8210) • Quest (8215) • Sociology of Sport Journal (8216) • Sport History Review (8217) • The Sport Psychologist (8218) • Teaching Elementary Physical Education (8220)

Human Life Foundation
215 Lexington Ave., 4th Fl.
New York, NY 10016
Phone: (212)685-5210
Fax: (212)725-9793
Publications: Human Life Review (21830)

The Human Quest
4300 NW 23rd Ave.
PO Box 203
Gainesville, FL 32614-7050
Phone: (813)894-0097
Publications: The Human Quest (6144)

Human Resource Planning Society
317 Madison Ave., Ste. 1509
New York, NY 10017
Phone: (212)490-6387
Publications: Human Resource Planning (21833)

Human Rights Internet
8 York St., Ste. 302
Ottawa, ON, Canada K1N 5S6
Phone: (613)789-7407
Fax: (613)789-7414
Publications: Human Rights Tribune/Tribune Des Droits Humains (36249)

Humana Press Inc.
999 Riverview Dr., Ste. 208
Totowa, NJ 07512-1165
Phone: (973)256-1699
Fax: (973)256-8341
Publications: Applied Biochemistry and Biotechnology (14319) • Clinical Reviews in Allergy & Immunology (1813) • Molecular Biotechnology (19652)

Humane Society of the United States
2100 L St. NW
Washington, DC 20037
Phone: (202)452-1100
Publications: Animal Sheltering Magazine (5350) • HSUS News (5534)

Humanities Press Inc.
112 Water St., Ste. 400
Boston, MA 02109
Phone: (617)742-5277
Fax: (617)263-2324
Free: 877-999-7575
Publications: Radical Philosophy Review (13955) • Studies in Practical Philosophy (13965)

Humansville Star-Leader
PO Box 215
201 N Ohio
Humansville, MO 65674
Phone: (417)754-2228
Fax: (417)754-2228
Publications: Humansville Star-Leader (17323)

Loretta Humble
PO Box 509
Malakoff, TX 75148-0509
Phone: (903)489-0531
Fax: (903)489-2543
Publications: The Malakoff News (30755)

Humboldt Beacon
180 S Fortuna Blvd.
PO Box 310
Fortuna, CA 95540
Phone: (707)725-6166
Fax: (707)725-4981
Free: 800-632-NEWS
Publications: Humboldt Beacon & Advance (1928)

Humboldt Field Research Institute
PO Box 9
Steuben, ME 04680-0009
Phone: (207)546-2821
Fax: (207)546-3042
Publications: The Northeastern Naturalist (13060) • The Southeastern Naturalist (13061)

Humboldt Reminder, Inc.
512 Sumner Ave.
PO Box 549
Humboldt, IA 50548
Phone: (515)332-3425
Publications: Humboldt Reminder (10958)

The Humboldt Standard
PO Box 627
Humboldt, NE 68376-0627
Phone: (402)862-2200
Fax: (402)862-2209
Publications: The Humboldt Standard (18053)

Humboldt State University
Nelson Hall East 6
Arcata, CA 95521
Phone: (707)826-3259
Fax: (707)826-5921
Publications: The Lumberjack Newspaper (1429)

2438

Numbers cited after listings are entry numbers rather than page numbers.

The Humeston New Era
Box 377
Humeston, IA 50123
Phone: (641)443-2373
Fax: (515)872-1965

Publications: The Humeston New Era (10960)

Hummingbird Press, Inc.
36 Cooper Sq.
New York, NY 10003-7118

Publications: Cleveland Free Times (21428)

Hundman Publishing
13110 Beverly Park Rd.
Mukilteo, WA 98275
Phone: (425)743-2607
Fax: (425)787-9269
Free: 800-810-7660

Publications: Mainline Modeler (32850)

Hungarian Word, Inc.
130 E 16th St.
New York, NY 10003
Phone: (212)254-0397
Fax: (212)254-1584

Publications: Hungarian Word (Amerikai Magyar SZO) (21836)

Hunt County Shopper, Inc.
3617 Wesley
PO Box 609
Greenville, TX 75401
Phone: (903)455-5254
Fax: (903)455-3297

Publications: Hunt County Shopper (30414)

Hunt and Hunt Newspapers
320 Aetna St.
PO Box 70
Ruthton, MN 56170-0070
Phone: (507)658-3919
Fax: (507)247-5502

Publications: Buffalo Ridge Gazette (16339)

Hunt Institute for Botanical Documentation
5000 Forbes Ave.
Pittsburgh, PA 15213-3890
Phone: (412)268-2434
Fax: (412)268-5677

Publications: Huntia (27797)

Hunterdon County Democrat
PO Box 32
Flemington, NJ 08822-0032
Phone: (908)782-4747
Fax: (908)782-6572

Publications: Delaware Valley News (18819) • Hunterdon County Democrat (18820)

Hunter's Horn, Inc.
PO Box 777
Sesser, IL 62884
Phone: (618)625-2711
Fax: (618)625-6221

Publications: The Hunter's Horn (9598)

Huntingdon Gleaner, Inc.
66 Chateauguay St.
Huntingdon, QC, Canada J0S 1H0
Phone: (450)264-5364
Fax: (450)264-9521

Publications: Gleaner (37008)

Huntington Library Press
1151 Oxford Rd.
San Marino, CA 91108
Phone: (626)405-2172
Fax: (626)585-0794

Publications: Huntington Library Quarterly (3580)

Huntington Newspapers, Inc.
7 N. Jefferson St.
Huntington, IN 46750-2839
Phone: (260)356-6700
Fax: (260)356-9026

Publications: Herald-Press (10069)

Huntsville Forester
72 Main St., E.
PO Box 940
Huntsville, ON, Canada P1H 2C7
Phone: (705)789-5541
Fax: (705)789-9381

Publications: Huntsville Forester (35917)

The Huntsville Item
PO Box 539
Huntsville, TX 77342-0534
Fax: (409)293-3909

Publications: The Huntsville Item (30595)

Huntsville Literary Association
PO Box 919
Huntsville, AL 35804
Phone: (256)536-9038

Publications: Poem (273)

The Huntsville Times
PO Box 1487, West Sta.
Huntsville, AL 35807-0487
Phone: (205)532-4000
Fax: (205)532-4420
Free: 800-240-8463

Publications: The Huntsville Times (270)

Huron Daily Tribune
211 N. Heisterman St.
Bad Axe, MI 48413
Phone: (989)269-6461
Fax: (989)269-9893

Publications: Huron Daily Tribune (14785)

Hurricane Alice Foundation
Dept. of English
Rhode Island College
Providence, RI 02908
Phone: (401)456-8377
Fax: (401)456-8379

Publications: Hurricane Alice (28400)

Hurricane Breeze
PO Box 310
Hurricane, WV 25526
Phone: (304)562-9881
Fax: (304)562-9881

Publications: The Hurricane Breeze (33348)

Hurst Communications Group Inc.
204-15 Harwood Ave S
Ajax, ON, Canada L1S 2B9
Phone: (905)686-1040
Fax: (905)686-1078

Publications: Electricity Today (35627)

Huse Publishing Co.
525 Norfolk Ave.
Box 977
Norfolk, NE 68702-0977
Phone: (402)371-1020
Fax: (402)371-5802

Publications: Norfolk Daily News (18170)

Huskers Illustrated
PO Box 1604
Brentwood, TN 37024-1604
Free: 800-524-9527

Publications: Huskers Illustrated (29062)

Walter Hussman
PO Box 798
Camden, AR 71701
Fax: (501)837-1414

Publications: Camden News (1069)

Hutchinson Community College
1300 N Plum
Hutchinson, KS 67501
Phone: (620)665-3500
Fax: (620)665-3310

Publications: Hutchinson Collegian (11500)

Hutchinson Herald
PO Box 537
Menno, SD 57045-0537
Phone: (605)387-5158
Fax: (605)387-5148

Publications: Hutchinson Herald (28892)

Hutchinson Leader, Inc.
36 Washington Ave. W.
Hutchinson, MN 55350-2490
Phone: (320)587-5000
Fax: (320)587-6104
Free: 888-326-2476

Publications: Hutchinson Leader (15967)

Hutchinson Publishing Co.
300 W 2nd St.
PO Box 190
Hutchinson, KS 67504-0190
Phone: (620)694-5700
Fax: (620)662-4186
Free: 800-766-3311

Publications: The Hutchinson News (11501)

The H.W. Wilson Co.
950 University Ave.
Bronx, NY 10452
Phone: (718)588-8400
Fax: 800-590-1617
Free: 800-367-6770

Publications: Abridged Readers' Guide to Periodical Literature (20250) • Applied Science & Technology Index (20252) • Art Index (20253) • Biography Index (20254) • Biological & Agricultural Index (20255) • Book Review Digest (20256) • Business Periodicals Index (20262) • Current Biography (20265) • Education Index (20267) • General Science Index (20270) • Humanities Index (20271) • Index to Legal Periodicals & Books (20272) • Library Literature & Information Science (20275) • Readers' Guide to Periodical Literature (20283) • Social Sciences Index (20287) • Vertical File Index (20288)

HWH News & Printing
PO Box 454
Forrest City, AR 72336
Phone: (870)630-6450
Fax: (870)630-9072

Publications: Home with Homeland (1138)

The Hymn Society in the U.S. & Canada
Boston University School of Theology
745 Commonwealth Ave.
Boston, MA 02215-1401
Phone: (617)353-6493
Fax: (617)353-7322
Free: 800-843-4966

Publications: The Hymn (15758)

Hyora Publications, Inc.
60-C Munson Meeting Way
Chatham, MA 02633
Phone: (508)945-2220
Fax: (508)945-2579

Publications: The Cape Cod Chronicle (14124)

Hyper Media Communications, Inc.
710 Oakfield Dr., Ste. 202
Brandon, FL 33511-4954

Publications: New Media Magazine (5960)

HyperMedia Communications Inc.
710 Oakfield Dr., Ste. 202
Brandon, FL 33511-4954

Publications: NewMedia (5961)

Hypotheses
70 Sagamore Hill Dr.
Port Washington, NY 11050
Phone: (516)883-6734

Publications: Hypotheses (23128)

I-L Focus Inc.
3044 Bloor St. W., No. 270
Etobicoke, ON, Canada M8X 2Y8
Phone: (416)604-7552
Fax: (416)604-2545

Publications: Info-Link (35816)

IABC Communication World
1 Hallidie Plz., Ste. 600
San Francisco, CA 94102
Phone: (415)544-4700
Fax: (415)544-4747

Publications: IABC Communication World (3374)

IADT - The International Association for Document & Technologics
100 Daingerfield Rd.
Alexandria, VA 22314
Phone: (703)684-9606
Fax: (703)684-9675
Free: 888-999-4234

Publications: PaperTronix, Document Management Merging Paper & Electronics (31720)

iAm Magazine, Inc.
5525 Hansen Rd., Apt. 104
Edina, MN 55436-2323
Phone: (952)285-2670
Fax: (952)927-6143

Publications: iAm Magazine! (15875)

IAPA Press Institute
1801 SW 3rd Ave.
Miami, FL 33129
Phone: (305)634-2465
Fax: (305)635-2272
Free: 800-542-3732

Publications: Hora de Cierre (6361)

IAPC
Montclair State University
Upper Montclair, NJ 07043
Phone: (973)655-4277
Fax: (973)655-7834

Publications: Thinking (19694)

IAPMO
5001 E. Philadelphia St.
Ontario, CA 91761-2816
Phone: (909)472-4100
Fax: (909)472-4150
Free: 800-584-2766

Publications: Official Magazine (2717)

IAQ Publications, Inc.
7920 Norfolk Ave., No. 900
Bethesda, MD 20814-2502
Phone: (301)913-0115
Fax: (301)913-0119
Free: 800-394-0115

Publications: Lead Detection and Abatement Contractor (13356)

IBA, Inc.
19 River St.
Millbury, MA 01527
Phone: (508)865-2507
Fax: (508)865-5891

Publications: Dairy World (14334)

IBM Corp.
PO Box 218
Yorktown Heights, NY 10598-0218
Phone: (914)945-3836
Fax: (914)945-2018
Free: 800-IBM-JOUR

Publications: IBM Journal of Research and Development (23606) • IBM Systems Journal (23607)

IC Holdings Inc.
225 Main St., Ste. 300
Northport, NY 11768-1744
Phone: (516)261-8337
Fax: (516)261-8235
Free: 800-828-1429

Publications: The Inside Collector (23017)

ICD Publications
45 Research Way, Ste. 106
East Setauket, NY 11733
Phone: (631)246-9300
Fax: (631)246-9696

Publications: Hotel Business (20555)

Ice Skating Institute
17120 N Dallas Pkwy., Ste. 140
Dallas, TX 75248-1187
Phone: (972)735-8800
Fax: (972)735-8815

Publications: Recreational Ice Skating (30179)

ICMA
PO Box 727
Princeton Junction, NJ 08550
Phone: (609)799-4900
Fax: (609)799-7032

Publications: Card Manufacturing (19483)

Icon
PO Box 1035
Westfield, IN 46074-1035

Publications: Icon (10559)

The Iconoclast
1675 Amazon Rd.
Mohegan Lake, NY 10547-1804

Publications: The Iconoclast (Mohegan Lake) (21088)

ICR Publications Inc.
PO Box 408
Waukesha, WI 53189-0408
Phone: (262)896-9229
Fax: (262)896-9203

Publications: Championship Racing Magazine (34397)

Ida County Courier-Reminder Inc.
PO Box 249
Ida Grove, IA 51445
Phone: (712)364-3131
Fax: (712)364-3010

Publications: Ida County Courier-Reminder (10961)

Idaho Academy of Science
909 Lucille Ave.
Pocatello, ID 83201-2542
Phone: (208)234-7001

Publications: Journal of the Idaho Academy of Science (7946)

The Idaho Business Review
PO Box 8866
Boise, ID 83707
Phone: (208)336-3768
Fax: (208)336-5534

Publications: The Idaho Business Review (7809)

Idaho Catholic Register
303 Federal Way
Boise, ID 83705
Phone: (208)342-1311
Fax: (208)342-0224

Publications: Idaho Catholic Register (7810)

Idaho Cattle Association
2120 Airport Way
Boise, ID 83705
Phone: (208)343-1615
Fax: (208)344-6695

Publications: The Line Rider (7813)

Idaho County Free Press
PO Box 690
Grangeville, ID 83530
Phone: (208)983-1200
Fax: (208)983-1336

Publications: Idaho County Free Press (7857)

Idaho Education Association
PO Box 2638
Boise, ID 83701
Phone: (208)344-1732

Publications: IEA Reporter (7812)

Idaho Enterprise
PO Box 205
Malad City, ID 83252
Phone: (208)766-4773
Fax: (208)766-4774

Publications: Malad City Idaho Enterprise (7904)

Idaho Press Tribune
1618 N Midland Blvd.
PO Box 9399
Nampa, ID 83652
Phone: (208)467-9251
Fax: (208)467-9562

Publications: Idaho Press Tribune (7930)

Idaho State University
Box 8113
Pocatello, ID 83209-0009
Phone: (208)282-4384
Fax: (208)282-4472

Publications: Rendezvous (7947)

Idaho State University
Campus Box 8009
Pocatello, ID 83209
Phone: (208)282-4812
Fax: (208)282-4600

Publications: ISU Extra (7945)

IDC Financial Publishing, Inc.
Box 140
Hartland, WI 53029
Phone: (262)367-7231
Fax: (262)367-6497

Publications: Bank Financial Quarterly (33776) • Credit Union Financial Profiles (33777) • S & L— Savings Bank Financial Quarterly (33783)

Idea Group Publishing
701 E Chocolate Ave., Ste. 200
Hershey, PA 17033-1240
Phone: (717)533-8845
Fax: (717)533-8661
Free: 800-345-4332

Publications: Annals of Cases on Information Technology (ACIT) (27039) • Information Resources Management Journal (27042) • Journal of Database Management (18087) • Journal of End User Computing (27043) • Journal of Global Information Management (27044)

IDEA Inc.
6190 Cornerstone Ct. E., No. 204
San Diego, CA 92121-3773
Phone: (858)535-8979
Fax: (858)535-8234
Free: 800-999-4332

Publications: IDEA Health & Fitness Source (3171) • IDEA Personal Trainer (3172)

IDG
One Exeter Plz., 15th Fl.
Boston, MA 02116
Phone: (617)534-1200
Fax: (617)262-2300

Publications: Game Pro (13894)

IDS Publishing, Inc.
15709 E Valley Blvd.
City of Industry, CA 91744
Fax: (818)961-7056

Publications: Travel & Recreation Magazine (1719)

Idyllwild Town Crier
PO Box 157
Idyllwild, CA 92549
Phone: (909)659-2145
Fax: (909)659-2071
Free: 888-535-6663

Publications: Idyllwild Town Crier (2069)

IEEE Computer Society
10662 Los Vaqueros Cir.
PO Box 3014
Los Alamitos, CA 90720-1264
Phone: (714)821-8380
Fax: (714)821-4010
Free: 800-272-6657

Publications: Computer Magazine (2181) • Computing in Science & Engineering (2182) • IEEE Computer Graphics and Applications (2183) • IEEE Design and Test of Computers (2184) • IEEE Intelligent Systems (2185) • IEEE Internet Computing (2186) • IEEE Micro (2187) • IEEE Multimedia (2188) • IEEE Software Magazine (2189) • IT Professional (2190)

IEEE, Inc.
1446 Vista Claridad
La Jolla, CA 92037
Phone: (858)459-8305
Fax: (858)459-7140

Publications: IEEE Antennas & Propogation (2113)

IEEE, Inc.
445 Hoes Ln.
PO Box 1331
Piscataway, NJ 08855
Phone: (732)981-0060

Publications: IEEE Industry Applications Magazine (19425)

IEEE-USA
1828 L St., NW, Ste. 1202
Washington, DC 20036-5104
Phone: (202)785-0017
Fax: (202)785-0835

Publications: Today's Engineer (5824)

IFCA International
3520 Fairlanes
Box 810
Grandville, MI 49418-1536
Phone: (616)531-1840
Fax: (616)531-1814
Free: 800-347-1840

Publications: Voice (15130)

IHM Sisters
610 W Elm St.
Monroe, MI 48162
Phone: (734)241-3660
Fax: (734)240-9801
Free: (866)446-2002

Publications: IHM Connections (15362) • IHM Journal (15363)

IIAA/MSI, Inc.
127 S Peyton St.
Alexandria, VA 22314
Phone: (703)683-4422
Fax: (703)683-7556
Free: 800-221-7917

Publications: Independent Agent (31682)

IIE Transactions
3577 Parkway Ln., Ste. 200
Norcross, GA 30092
Free: 800-494-0460

Publications: IIE Transactions (8862) • IIE Transactions on Design & Manufacturing (7463) • IIE Transactions on Operations Engineering (7464) • IIE Transactions on Scheduling & Logistics (7465)

IIT Research Institute
201 Mill St.
Rome, NY 13440
Phone: (315)339-7075
Fax: (315)337-9932
Free: 888-RAC-USER

Publications: RAC Journal (23265)

Il Cittadino Canadese
5960 Jean-Talon E., Ste. 209
Montreal, QC, Canada H1S 1M2
Phone: (514)253-2332
Fax: (514)253-6574

Publications: Il Cittadino Canadese (37124)

Illini Media Co.
57 E. Green St.
Champaign, IL 61820
Phone: (217)333-3733
Fax: (217)244-6616

Publications: The Daily Illini (8185) • Illinois Technograph (8189)

Illinois Agricultural Association
1701 Towanda Ave.
Bloomington, IL 61701
Phone: (309)557-2329
Fax: 800-998-6090

Publications: FarmWeek (8077)

Illinois Association of Park Districts
211 E. Monroe St.
Springfield, IL 62701-1186
Phone: (217)523-4554
Fax: (217)523-4273

Publications: Illinois Parks & Recreation Magazine (9628)

Illinois Association of Plumbing-Heating-Cooling Contractors
821 S. Grand Ave. W.
Springfield, IL 62704
Phone: (217)522-7219
Fax: (217)522-4315
Free: 800-795-PHCC

Publications: Illinois Master Plumber (9626)

Illinois Association of School Boards
430 E. Vine St.
Springfield, IL 62703-2236
Phone: (217)528-9688
Fax: (217)528-2831

Publications: Illinois School Board Journal (9631)

Illinois Association of School Social Workers
Box 634
Algonquin, IL 60102
Fax: (847)831-5108

Publications: School Social Work Journal (9610)

Illinois Audubon Society
Box 2418
Danville, IL 61834-2418

Publications: Illinois Audubon (8045)

Illinois Bankers Association (IBA)
133 S. 4th St., Ste. 300
Springfield, IL 62701
Phone: (217)789-9340
Fax: (217)789-5410
Free: 800-783-2265

Publications: Illinois Banker (9621)

Illinois Beef Association
2060 West Iles Ave., Ste. B
Springfield, IL 62704
Phone: (217)787-4280
Fax: (217)793-3605

Publications: Illinois Beef (9622)

Illinois Beverage Media, Inc.
2260 Bracken Ln.
Northfield, IL 60093
Phone: (847)441-7776
Fax: (847)441-7796

Publications: Wisconsin Beverage Business (33979)

Illinois CPA Society
222 S Riverside Plz., Ste. 1600
Chicago, IL 60606
Phone: (312)993-0393
Fax: (312)993-7713

Publications: Illinois CPA Insight (8408) • Insight (Chicago) (8417)

Illinois Entertainer
124 W. Polk St. No.103
Chicago, IL 60605
Phone: (312)922-9333
Fax: (312)922-9369

Publications: Illinois Entertainer (8409)

Illinois Farm Bureau
1701 Towanda Ave.
Bloomington, IL 61701
Phone: (309)557-2238
Free: 800-640-1995

Publications: Partners (8080)

Illinois Historic Preservation Agency
500 E Madison
Springfield, IL 62701-1507
Phone: (217)785-4512
Fax: (217)785-7937

Publications: Journal of Illinois History (9636)

Illinois Landscape Contractor Association
2625 Butterfield Rd., Ste. 204-W
Oak Brook, IL 60523-1257
Phone: (630)472-2851
Fax: (630)472-3150

Publications: The Landscape Contractor (9355)

Illinois Lumber and Material Dealers Association, Inc.
932 S. Spring St.
Springfield, IL 62704
Phone: (217)544-5405
Fax: (217)544-4206

Publications: ILMDA Advantage (9633)

The Illinois Manufacturers' Association
1301 W 22nd St., Ste. 610
Oak Brook, IL 60523
Phone: (630)368-5300
Fax: (630)218-7467

Publications: The Illinois Manufacturers (9353)

Illinois Music Educators Association
72 Marchelle
Springfield, IL 62702
Phone: (217)787-6323
Fax: (217)787-3610

Publications: Illinois Music Educator (9627)

Illinois Optometric Association
304 W. Washington
Springfield, IL 62701
Phone: (217)525-8012
Fax: (217)525-8018
Free: 800-933-7289

Publications: Journal of the Illinois Optometric Association (9289)

Illinois Pharmacists Association
204 W. Cook St.
Springfield, IL 62704
Phone: (217)522-7300
Fax: (217)522-7349

Publications: Illinois Pharmacist (9629)

Illinois Society of Professional Engineers, Inc.
1304 S Lowell
Springfield, IL 62704
Phone: (217)544-7424
Fax: (217)544-3349

Publications: Illinois Engineer (9624)

Illinois Spirit Shopping Guide
PO Box 250
1492 E. Walnut
Watseka, IL 60970
Phone: (815)432-5227
Fax: (815)432-5159

Publications: Illinois Spirit Shopping Guide (9738)

Illinois State Bar Association
424 S. Second St.
Springfield, IL 62701-1779
Phone: (217)525-1760
Free: 800-252-8908

Publications: ISBA Bar News (8421)

Illinois State Dental Society
1010 S 2nd St.
PO Box 376
Springfield, IL 62705
Phone: (217)525-1406
Fax: (217)525-8872

Publications: Illinois Dental Journal (9623)

Illinois State Geological Survey
Natural Resources Bldg.
615 E. Peabody Dr.
Champaign, IL 61820
Phone: (217)333-5110
Fax: (217)333-2830

Publications: Oil and Gas (8208)

Illinois State Museum
502 S. Spring St.
Springfield, IL 62706-5000
Phone: (217)782-7386
Fax: (217)782-1254

Publications: The Living Museum (9639)

Illinois State University
Alumni Services
Campus Box 3100
Normal, IL 61790-3100
Phone: (309)438-2586
Fax: (309)438-8057

Publications: Illinois State Magazine (9298)

Illinois State University
4240 - English
Normal, IL 61790
Phone: (309)438-7176
Fax: (309)438-5414

Publications: Illinois English Bulletin (9297)

Illinois State University
University and Locust
Campus Box 0890
Normal, IL 61790-0890
Phone: (309)438-7685
Fax: (309)438-5211

Publications: Daily Vidette (9296)

Illinois Times Inc.
PO Box 5256
Springfield, IL 62704
Phone: (217)753-2226
Fax: (217)753-2281

Publications: Illinois Times (9632)

Illinois Transportation Association
2000 5th Ave.
River Grove, IL 60171
Phone: (847)952-6000
Fax: (847)452-3508

Publications: Illinois Truck News (9496)

Illinois Valley News
321 S Redwood Hwy.
PO Box 1370
Cave Junction, OR 97523
Phone: (541)592-2541

Publications: Illinois Valley News (26264)

Illinois Wildlife Federation
2218 Troy Rd.
Edwardsville, IL 62025-2588
Phone: (217)748-6365
Fax: (217)748-6304

Publications: Illinois Wildlife (8813)

Illuminating Engineering Society
120 Wall St., 17th Fl.
New York, NY 10005-4001
Phone: (212)248-5000
Fax: (212)248-5017

Publications: LDA (22240)

Illustrated Graphic Communications
2400 E Katella Ave., Ste. 1100
Anaheim, CA 92806
Phone: (714)939-2400
Fax: (714)978-6390

Publications: Turbo & Hi-Tech Performance (1419)

Imagine Media
150 N. Hill Dr.
Brisbane, CA 94005
Phone: (415)468-4684
Fax: (415)468-4686

Publications: Maximum PC (1606) • The Net (1607) • Next Generation (1608) • PC Accelerator (1609) • PC Gamer (1610) • PSM (PlayStation Magazine) (1611)

The Imaging and Geospatial Information Society
5410 Grosvenor Ln., Ste. 210
Bethesda, MD 20814
Phone: (301)493-0290
Fax: (301)493-0208

Publications: PE & RS Photogrammetric Engineering & Remote Sensing (13372)

IMAS Publishing Inc.
5827 Columbia Pike
PO Box 1214
Falls Church, VA 22041
Phone: (703)998-7600
Fax: (703)998-2966

Publications: Radio World (32056) • TV Technology (32059)

Impacto Latin News
853 Broadway, Ste. 811
New York, NY 10003
Phone: (212)505-0288
Fax: (212)598-9414

Publications: Impacto Latin News (21855)

Implosion Press
4975 Comanche Trl.
Stow, OH 44224
Phone: (330)688-5210
Fax: (330)688-5210

Publications: Impetus (25546)

L'Imprimerie Populaire
2050 De Bleury St., 9th Fl.
Montreal, QC, Canada H3A 3M9
Phone: (514)985-3399
Fax: (514)985-3390

Publications: Le Devoir (37159)

Imprint Newspapers
99 Main St.
Bristol, CT 06010
Phone: (860)236-3571
Fax: (860)233-2080

Publications: Avon News (4696) • Bloomfield Journal (4700) • Canton News (4732) • The Newington Town Crier (5036) • Rocky Hill Post (4722) • Simsbury News (5130) • West Hartford News (4723) • Wethersfield Post (4724) • Windsor Locks Journal (5234)

Imprint Publications
University of Waterloo
200 University Ave., W
Student Life Ctr., Rm. 1116
Waterloo, ON, Canada N2L 3G1
Phone: (519)888-4048
Fax: (519)884-7800

Publications: Imprint (36852)

Imprint Publications Inc.
207 E Ohio St., Ste. 377
Chicago, IL 60611
Phone: (312)337-9268
Fax: (773)288-0792

Publications: The Journal of Comparative Asian Development (8434)

Impulse Publications, Inc.
1 Bel Air S. Parkway
Bel Air, MD 21015
Phone: (410)569-1700
Fax: (410)569-1704

Publications: Impulse (13290)

IMS LLC
900 Central Ave., Ste. 1
Fort Dodge, IA 50501
Phone: (515)574-2234
Fax: (515)574-2202
Free: 888-247-2007

Publications: Packaging and Converting Hotline (10906) • Plastics Hot Line (10907)

In-Fisherman
2 In-Fisherman Dr.
Baxter, MN 56425-8098
Phone: (218)829-1648

Publications: Walleye In-Sider (15732)

The In-Home Show
4-2650 Meadowvale Blvd.
Mississauga, ON, Canada L5N 6M5
Phone: (905)567-1440
Fax: (905)567-1442
Free: 888-567-7366

Publications: Homes & Cottages (36071)

In Pittsburgh Newsweekly
1701 Walnut St., Fl. 4
Philadelphia, PA 19103-5220

Publications: In Pittsburgh Newsweekly (27490)

In The Dark Enterprises
117 E 3rd St.
Bloomington, IN 47401
Phone: (812)339-2002
Fax: (812)339-2002

Publications: The Ryder (9851)

In Tune
2851 Johnston St., No. 215
Lafayette, LA 70503
Fax: (318)232-2718

Publications: In Tune (12617)

Inanna Publications, Inc.
York University
212 Founders College
4700 Keele St.
Toronto, ON, Canada M3J 1P3
Phone: (416)736-5356
Fax: (416)736-5765

Publications: Canadian Woman Studies (Les Cahiers de la Femme) (36535)

InBusiness Media Network Inc.
1686 Woodward Dr.
Ottawa, ON, Canada K2C 3R8
Phone: (613)230-8699
Fax: (613)230-9606
Free: 800-776-1072

Publications: Ottawa Business Journal (36264)

Incarnate Word College
4301 Broadway
San Antonio, TX 78209-6397
Phone: (210)829-3811

Publications: Logos (31037)

Incursion Publishing
53 Macamo Ct.
Maple, ON, Canada L6A 1G1
Phone: (905)737-7292

Publications: Incursion Music Review (36010)

Independence Daily Reporter
320 N 6th St.
PO Box 869
Independence, KS 67301
Phone: (316)331-3550
Fax: (316)331-3550

Publications: Independence Daily Reporter (11509)

The Independence News
210 W Main
Independence, KS 67301
Phone: (316)331-4950
Fax: (316)251-1905

Publications: The Independence News (11510)

The Independent
PO Box 31
Hawarden, IA 51023
Fax: (712)552-2503

Publications: The Independent (10950)

Independent
PO Box 45
Lakin, KS 67860-0045
Phone: (620)355-6162

Publications: Independent (11544)

The Independent
PO Box 360
Hillsdale, NY 12529
Phone: (518)325-4400
Fax: (518)325-4497

Publications: The Independent (20748)

The Independent
840 Queen St.
PO Box 1240
Kincardine, ON, Canada N2Z 2Z4
Phone: (519)396-3111
Fax: (519)396-3899

Publications: The Independent (35933)

The Independent
23 N. Main St.
PO Box 27
Deerfield, WI 53531
Phone: (608)764-5515
Fax: (608)825-4460

Publications: The Independent (33652)

Independent Battery Manufacturers Association Inc.
100 Larchwood Dr.
Largo, FL 33770
Phone: (727)586-1408
Fax: (727)586-1400
Free: 800-237-6126

Publications: The Battery Man (6299)

Independent Berkeley Student Publishing Company Inc.
600 Eshleman Hall
University of California Berkeley
Berkeley, CA 94720
Phone: (510)548-8300
Fax: (510)849-2803

Publications: The Daily Californian (1512)

Independent Coast Observer, Inc.
PO Box 1200
Gualala, CA 95445
Phone: (707)884-3501
Fax: (707)884-1710

Publications: Independent Coast Observer (2034)

2442

Numbers cited after listings are entry numbers rather than page numbers.

Independent Community Bankers of America
One Thomas Circle, NW, Ste. 400
Washington, DC 20005
Phone: (202)659-8111
Fax: (202)659-1413

Publications: Independent Banker (5542)

Independent-Enterprise
124 S. Main St.
Payette, ID 83661
Phone: (208)642-3357
Fax: (208)642-3560

Publications: Independent-Enterprise (7943)

The Independent Herald
Box 100
Pineville, WV 24874-0100
Phone: (304)732-6060
Fax: (304)732-8228

Publications: The Independent Herald (33436)

The Independent-Journal
119 E High St.
PO Box 340
Potosi, MO 63664
Phone: (573)438-5141
Fax: (573)438-4472

Publications: The Independent-Journal (17364)

Independent-Journal Newspapers
1032 Broadway
Santa Monica, CA 90401-2808

Publications: The Good Life (3710)

Independent Lubricant Manufacturers Association
651 S. Washington St.
Alexandria, VA 22314-4109
Phone: (703)684-5574
Fax: (703)836-8503

Publications: Compoundings (31657)

Independent Media Group, Inc.
219 First St.
PO Box 9
Baraboo, WI 53913
Phone: (608)356-4808
Fax: (608)356-0344

Publications: News Republic Cent Saver (33563)

Independent Media Group, Inc.
321 Frenette Dr.
PO Box 69
Chippewa Falls, WI 54729-0069
Phone: (715)723-9104

Publications: Chippewa Herald Telegram (33627) • Stoplight (33629)

Independent Media Group, Inc.
PO Box 470
Portage, WI 53901
Phone: (608)742-2111
Fax: (608)742-8346

Publications: Cent Saver Buyer's Guide (34252) • Cent Saver Extra (34253) • Cent Saver Reminder (34254) • Daily Register (34255) • Elroy Wonewoc Keystone Tribune (34256) • Mauston Star Times (34258) • Portage Daily Register (34259) • West Salem Coulee News (34261)

Independent and Montgomery Transcript
350 Walnut St.
PO Box 39
Collegeville, PA 19426-3601
Fax: (215)489-8633

Publications: Independent and Montgomery Transcript (26797)

The Independent-News
20747 N Lake Dr.
Walkerton, IN 46574-9292
Phone: (219)586-3139
Fax: (219)586-3139

Publications: The Independent-News (10534)

Independent News Group
1828 El Camino Real, Ste. 508
Burlingame, CA 94010
Phone: (650)692-9406
Fax: (650)692-7587

Publications: Independent News Group (1632)

Independent News Herald
310 Main St.
PO Box 188
Clarissa, MN 56440-0188
Phone: (218)756-2131
Fax: (218)756-2126

Publications: Independent News Herald (15799)

Independent Newspaper Group
1828 El Camino Real
Burlingame, CA 94010-1205
Phone: (650)692-9406
Fax: (650)692-7587

Publications: Millbrae Sun (2543)

Independent Newspaper Group
385 Broadway, Ste. 105
Revere, MA 02151
Phone: (781)284-2400
Fax: (781)485-1403

Publications: Chelsea Record (14499) • East Boston Sun Transcript (14500) • Revere Journal (14502) • Winthrop Sun Transcript (14503)

The Independent Newspapers
385 Broadway, Ste. 105, Citizens Bank Bldg.
Revere, MA 02151
Phone: (781)485-0588
Fax: (781)485-1403

Publications: The Everett Independent (14501)

Independent Newspapers
253 E Chicago St., Ste. A
PO Box 96
Jonesville, MI 49250
Phone: (517)849-9880
Fax: (517)849-7401

Publications: Jonesville Independent (15231)

Independent Newspapers, Inc.
23043 N. 16th Ln.
Phoenix, AZ 85027
Phone: (623)445-2800
Fax: (623)445-2740

Publications: Apache Junction Independent (656) • Chandler Independent (674) • East Mesa Independent (657) • Gilbert Independent (712) • North Scottsdale Independent (872) • Paradise Valley Independent (761) • Sun Cities Independent (896)

Independent Newspapers, Inc.
PO Box 737
Dover, DE 19903
Phone: (302)674-3600
Fax: (302)741-8261
Free: 800-282-8586

Publications: Crisfield Times (13473) • Delaware State News (5246)

Independent Newspapers, Inc.
PO Box 7001
Dover, DE 19903-7001
Phone: (302)741-8270
Fax: (302)674-5910

Publications: Clewiston News (5997) • Okeechobee News (6481)

Independent Newspapers Inc.
PO Box 239
Harrington, DE 19952
Phone: (302)674-3600
Fax: (302)741-8252

Publications: Harrington Journal (5257)

Independent Newspapers Inc.
210 E. 3rd St.
Royal Oak, MI 48067-2603
Phone: (248)414-9500
Fax: (248)541-7041

Publications: The Daily Tribune (15480) • The Weekly Tribune Plus (15487)

Independent Observer
PO Box 269
Oswego, KS 67356

Publications: Oswego Independent-Observer (11688)

Independent-Observer
PO Box 966
Conrad, MT 59425
Phone: (406)271-5561
Fax: (406)271-5562

Publications: Independent-Observer (17776)

Independent Press
80 South St.
New Providence, NJ 07974-1991
Phone: (908)464-1025
Fax: (908)464-9085
Free: 800-472-0119

Publications: Independent Press (19347)

The Independent Printers Ltd.
PO Box 40
Biggar, SK, Canada S0K 0M0
Phone: (306)948-3344
Fax: (306)948-2133
Free: 800-213-8016

Publications: The Independent (37452)

Independent Publisher's Group
Box 40611
Memphis, TN 38174
Phone: (901)272-7462

Publications: Cinema Revue (29361)

Independent Publishing Co.
7762 N. Holiday Dr.
Sarasota, FL 34231-5312
Phone: (941)924-3201
Fax: (941)925-4468

Publications: Writer's Guidelines Magazine (6669) • Yesterday's Magazette (6670)

Independent Publishing, Inc.
PO Box 8275
Missoula, MT 59807
Phone: (406)543-6609
Fax: (406)543-4367

Publications: Missoula Independent (17868)

Independent Record
PO Box 4249
317 Cruse Ave.
Helena, MT 59601-5003
Phone: (406)442-7190

Publications: Independent Record (17818)

The Independent-Register, Inc.
922 Exchange St.
PO Box 255
Brodhead, WI 53520
Phone: (608)897-2193
Fax: (608)897-4137

Publications: Independent-Register (33601)

Independent-Sentinel
PO Box 128
Canton, PA 17724-0128
Phone: (570)673-5151
Fax: (570)673-5152

Publications: Independent-Sentinel (26755)

The Independent Tribune
924 Cloverleaf Plz.
Kannapolis, NC 28082
Phone: (704)782-3155
Fax: (704)786-0645

Publications: The Independent Tribune (24016)

The Independent Weekly
2810 Hillsborough Rd.
PO Box 2690
Durham, NC 27705

Publications: Independent Weekly (23828)

Independent Women's Forum
PO Box 3058
Arlington, VA 22203-0058
Phone: (703)558-4991
Fax: (703)558-4994
Free: 800-224-6000

Publications: Women's Quarterly (31842)

The Index
108 Polk St.
PO Box 127
Hermitage, MO 65668
Phone: (417)745-6404
Fax: (417)745-2222
Free: 800-828-3107

Publications: The Index (17097)

The Index
PO Box 158
1269 Center Ave.
Mitchell, NE 69357
Phone: (308)623-1322
Fax: (308)586-2312

Publications: The Index (18164)

Index
PO Box 550
Ingleside, TX 78362-0550
Phone: (361)758-5391
Fax: (361)758-5393

Publications: Index (29728)

Index-Journal
610 Phoenix
PO Box 1018
Greenwood, SC 29648
Phone: (864)223-1411
Fax: (864)223-7331

Publications: Index-Journal (28646)

Index News
PO Box 370
Mineral Wells, TX 76067
Phone: (817)325-4466
Fax: (817)325-2020

Publications: Index (30832)

India Abroad Publications, Inc.
43 W. 24th St.
New York, NY 10010
Phone: (646)432-6029
Fax: (212)691-0873

Publications: India Abroad (21862)

India Currents
PO Box 21285
San Jose, CA 95151
Phone: (408)274-6966
Fax: (408)274-2733

Publications: India Currents (3519)

India in New York, Inc.
43 W. 24th St.
New York, NY 10010
Phone: (212)741-3742
Fax: (212)627-9503

Publications: India in New York (21863)

India Tribune Publications
3302 W Peterson Ave.
Chicago, IL 60659
Phone: (773)588-5077
Fax: (773)588-7011

Publications: India Tribune (8412)

India West Publications
933 Mac Arthur Blvd.
San Leandro, CA 94577
Phone: (510)383-1140
Fax: (510)383-1155

Publications: India West (3562)

Indian Artifact Magazine, Inc.
245 Fairview Rd.
Turbotville, PA 17772-9063
Phone: (570)437-3698
Fax: (570)437-3411

Publications: Indian Artifact Magazine (28063)

Indian Country Communications, Inc.
8558N County Rd., K
Hayward, WI 54843-5800
Phone: (715)634-5226
Fax: (715)634-3243

Publications: News from Indian Country (33785)

Indian Head-Wolseley News
PO Box 70
307 Grand Ave.
Indian Head, SK, Canada S0G 2K0
Phone: (306)695-3565
Fax: (306)695-3448

Publications: Indian Head-Wolseley News (37477)

Indian Nations Communications, Inc.
PO Box 550
Westville, OK 74965
Phone: (919)723-5445
Fax: (919)723-5511

Publications: Tahlequah Daily Press (26191) • The Westville Reporter (26192)

Indiana Association of Plumbing Heating Cooling Contractors, Inc.
9595 Whitley Dr., Ste. 208
Indianapolis, IN 46240
Phone: (317)575-9292
Fax: (317)575-9378

Publications: Indiana Contractor (10125)

Indiana Audubon Society, Inc.
1005 Buffalo Run Way
Indianapolis, IN 46227
Phone: (317)883-2010

Publications: Indiana Audubon Quarterly (10122)

Indiana Bankers Association
3135 N. Meridian St.
Indianapolis, IN 46208-4717
Phone: (317)921-3135
Fax: (317)921-3131

Publications: Hoosier Banker (10115)

Indiana Beef Cattle Association
8770 Guion Rd., Ste. A
Indianapolis, IN 46268
Phone: (317)872-2333
Fax: (317)872-2364

Publications: Indiana Beef (10123)

Indiana Business Magazine
55 Monument Cir., Ste. 300
Indianapolis, IN 46204
Phone: (317)692-1200
Fax: (317)692-4250

Publications: Indiana Business Magazine (10124)

Indiana Business Research Center
Indiana University
School of Business
Bloomington, IN 47405
Phone: (812)855-5507
Fax: (812)855-7763

Publications: Indiana Business Review (9831)

Indiana Farm Bureau, Inc.
225 South East St.
PO Box 1290
Indianapolis, IN 46206
Phone: (317)692-7822
Fax: (317)692-7854
Free: 800-FARM-BUR

Publications: The Hoosier Farmer (10116)

Indiana Gazette
899 Water St.
PO Box 10
Indiana, PA 15701-1705
Phone: (724)465-5555
Fax: (724)349-4550

Publications: Gazette (27073)

Indiana Herald
2170 N Illinois St.
Indianapolis, IN 46202
Phone: (317)923-8291
Fax: (317)923-8292

Publications: Indiana Herald (10126)

Indiana Historical Society Press
450 W. Ohio St.
Indianapolis, IN 46202-3269
Phone: (317)232-1882
Fax: (317)233-0857
Free: 800-447-1830

Publications: Traces of Indiana and Midwestern History (10175)

Indiana Library Federation
941 E 86th St
Indianapolis, IN 46240
Phone: (317)257-2040
Fax: (317)257-1393

Publications: Indiana Libraries (9834)

Indiana Music Educators Association
Ball State University
School of Music
Muncie, IN 47306
Phone: (765)285-5496
Fax: (765)285-1139

Publications: Indiana Musicator (10327)

Indiana Petroleum Marketers and Convenience Store Association (IPCA)
101 W. Washington St., Ste. 1338 E
Indianapolis, IN 46204
Phone: (317)633-4662
Fax: (317)630-1827

Publications: Fueling Indiana (10113)

Indiana Pharmacists Association
729 North Penn
Indianapolis, IN 46204
Phone: (317)634-4968
Fax: (317)632-1219

Publications: Indiana Pharmacist (10129)

Indiana Review
Ballantine Hall 465
1020 E. Kirkwood Ave.
Bloomington, IN 47405-7103
Phone: (812)855-3439
Fax: (812)855-4253

Publications: Indiana Review (9836)

Indiana School Boards Association
One N. Capitol, Ste. 1215
Indianapolis, IN 46204
Phone: (317)639-0330
Fax: (317)639-3591

Publications: ISBA Journal (10136)

Indiana State Bar Association
230 E. Ohio St., 4th Fl.
Indianapolis, IN 46204-2199
Phone: (317)639-5465
Fax: (317)266-2588
Free: 800-266-2581

Publications: Res Gestaie (10167)

Indiana State Teachers Association
150 W. Market St., Ste. 900
Indianapolis, IN 46204-2875
Phone: (317)637-7481
Fax: (317)631-8715

Publications: ISTA Advocate (10137)

Indiana State University
HMSU No. 719
Terre Haute, IN 47809
Phone: (812)237-3025
Fax: (812)237-7629

Publications: The Indiana Statesman (10486)

Indiana Statewide Rural Electric Cooperative
PO Box 24517
Indianapolis, IN 46224
Phone: (317)487-2220
Fax: (317)247-5220
Free: 800-340-7362

Publications: Electric Consumer (10109)

Indiana University
Ernie Pyle Hall, Rm. 120
Bloomington, IN 47405
Phone: (812)855-0763
Fax: (812)855-8009

Publications: Indiana Daily Student (9832)

Indiana University
211 S. Indiana Ave.
Bloomington, IN 47405
Phone: (812)855-7995
Fax: (812)855-0555

Publications: Indiana Law Journal (9833)

Indiana University
1121 W. Michigan St., Rm. S411
Indianapolis, IN 46202
Phone: (317)278-4800
Fax: (317)278-4900

Publications: Operative Dentistry (10157)

Indiana University Alumni Association
1000 E. 17th St.
Bloomington, IN 47408-1521
Phone: (812)855-4822
Fax: (812)855-4228
Free: 800-824-3044

Publications: Indiana Alumni Magazine (9830)

Indiana University Mathematics Journal
Indiana University
Rawles Hall 115
Bloomington, IN 47405
Phone: (812)855-2252
Fax: (812)855-0046

Publications: Indiana University Mathematics Journal (9837)

Indiana University Northwest
3400 Broadway
Gary, IN 46408
Phone: (219)980-6795
Fax: (219)981-4233

Publications: The Northwest Phoenix (10017)

Indiana University of Pennsylvania
Indiana, PA 15705
Phone: (724)357-2261
Fax: (724)357-3056

Publications: Studies in the Humanities (27077) • Works and Days (27078)

Indiana University Press
601 N. Morton St.
Bloomington, IN 47404
Phone: (812)855-8817
Free: 800-842-6796

Publications: Africa Today (9822) • History & Memory (9828) • Hypatia (9829) • Indiana Magazine of History (9835) • Israel Studies (9838) • Jewish Social Studies (9839) • Journal of Folklore Research (9841) • Journal of Modern Literature (9843) • The Journal of Women's History (9844) • NWSA Journal (9846) • Philosophy of Music Education Review (9849) • Research in African Literatures (25058) • Victorian Studies (9854)

Indiana University - Purdue University Fort Wayne
2101 E. Coliseum Blvd.
Fort Wayne, IN 46805
Phone: (260)481-6753
Fax: (260)481-6985

Publications: CLIO (9965)

Indiana University-Purdue University at Indianapolis
425 University Blvd.
Indianapolis, IN 46202
Phone: (317)274-3455
Fax: (317)274-2953

Publications: The Sagamore (10168)

Indiana University School of Law-Indianapolis
Indiana University
530 W. New York St.
Indianapolis, IN 46202
Phone: (317)274-4440
Fax: (317)278-3326

Publications: Indiana Law Review (10128)

Indianapolis Athletic Club
350 N Meridian St.
Indianapolis, IN 46204-1709
Phone: (317)634-4331
Fax: (317)686-4155

Publications: Indac Magazine (10120)

Indianapolis Convention and Visitors Association
One RCA Dome, Ste. 100
Indianapolis, IN 46225
Phone: (317)639-4282
Fax: (317)684-2598
Free: 800-323-INDY

Publications: This is Indianapolis (10174)

Indianapolis Museum of Art
1200 W 38th St.
Indianapolis, IN 46208-4196
Phone: (317)923-1331
Fax: (317)920-2671

Publications: Previews (10162)

The Indianola News
PO Box 130
Indianola, NE 69034
Phone: (308)364-2130
Fax: (308)364-2316

Publications: The Indianola News (18056)

Indianola Publishing Co.
Box 650
Indianola, MS 38751
Phone: (662)887-2222
Fax: (662)887-2999

Publications: Enterprise-Tocsin (16687)

Indigenous Women's Network
13621 FM 2769
Austin, TX 78726
Phone: (512)258-3880
Fax: (512)258-1858

Publications: Indigenous Woman (29781)

Indira Publishing House
Box 250456
West Bloomfield, MI 48325-0456
Phone: (248)661-2529
Fax: (248)661-4066

Publications: International Journal of Acarology (15675)

Industrial Accident Prevention Association
207 Queens Quay W., Ste. 550
Toronto, ON, Canada M5B 2N4
Phone: (416)506-8888
Fax: (416)506-8880
Free: 800-669-4939

Publications: Accident Prevention (36460)

Industrial Diamond Association of America
6023 Cleveland Ave.
Columbus, OH 43231
Phone: (614)797-2265
Fax: (614)797-2264

Publications: Finer Points Magazine (25017)

Industrial Fabrics Association International
1801 County Rd. B W.
Roseville, MN 55113-4061
Phone: (651)222-2508
Fax: (651)225-6966
Free: 800-225-4324

Publications: Fabric Architecture (16331) • Geotechnical Fabrics Report (16332) • Industrial Fabric Products Review (16333)

Industrial Fire World
589 Graham Rd., Ste. A
College Station, TX 77845-9662
Phone: (409)690-7559
Fax: (409)690-7562

Publications: Industrial Fire World (30043)

Industrial Reporting, Inc.
10244 Timber Ridge Dr.
Ashland, VA 23005-8135
Phone: (804)550-0323
Fax: (804)550-2181
Free: 800-805-0263

Publications: Pallet Enterprise (31857)

Industrial Research Institute, Inc.
1550 M. St. NW, Ste. 1100
Washington, DC 20005-1712
Phone: (202)296-8811
Fax: (202)776-0756

Publications: Research-Technology Management (5763)

Industry Canada
365 Laurier Ave. W., 8th Fl.
Ottawa, ON, Canada K1A 0C8
Phone: (613)946-2160
Fax: (613)946-2168

Publications: Insolvency Bulletin (36251)

Industry Publications, Inc.
171 Mayhew Way, Ste. 202
Pleasant Hill, CA 94523
Phone: (925)932-4999
Fax: (925)932-4966

Publications: Beverage Industry News (2852)

Industry Shopper Publishing, Inc.
PO Box 160
Gardnerville, NV 89410
Phone: (775)782-0222
Fax: (775)782-0266
Free: 800-576-4624

Publications: Motorcycle Industry Magazine (18348)

Industry.net Inc.
15 Inverness Way E, B106
Englewood, CO 80112-5776
Phone: (303)397-2383
Fax: (303)705-4205

Publications: www.industry.net (4417)

Indy Suburban Newspapers
119 W North St.
PO Box 602
Greenfield, IN 46140
Phone: (317)462-7368
Fax: (317)462-7779

Publications: Ad News (10038) • Indy Suburban Newspapers (10041) • Westside Enterprise (10042)

Indy's Child, Inc.
836 E 64th St.
Indianapolis, IN 46220
Phone: (317)722-8500
Fax: (317)722-8510

Publications: Indy's Child (10135)

Info-Industriel Inc.
2370 Henri-Bourassa Blvd. E.
Montreal, QC, Canada H2B 1T6
Phone: (514)388-8801
Fax: (514)388-7871

Publications: Journal Industriel du Quebec (37141) • Le Journal Industriel du Quebec (37162)

Info Plein Air
174 Greber Blvd.
Gatineau, QC, Canada J8T 6Z5
Phone: (819)568-1234
Fax: (819)568-4464
Free: 888-568-4818

Publications: Info Plein Air (36998)

Info Printing & Publishing, Inc.
1953 Broadway
Gary, IN 46407
Phone: (219)882-5591
Fax: (219)886-1090

Publications: Info (10016)

Informant Communications Group
10519 E. Stockton Blvd., Ste. 100
Elk Grove, CA 95624-9703
Phone: (916)686-6610
Fax: (916)686-8497

Publications: Delphi Informant (1871) • Web Publisher (1874)

L'Information
135 Doucet
Mont-Joli, QC, Canada G5H 1R3
Phone: (418)775-4381
Fax: (418)775-7768

Publications: L'Information (37073)

Information Gatekeepers Inc.
320 Washington St., Ste. 302
Boston, MA 02135
Phone: (617)232-3111
Fax: (617)734-8562
Free: 800-323-1088

Publications: China Telecom (13873)

Information for Public Affairs, Inc.
2101 K St.
Sacramento, CA 95816
Phone: (916)444-2840
Fax: (916)446-5369

Publications: California Journal (2983)

Information Today, Inc.
143 Old Marlton Pike
Medford, NJ 08055-8750
Phone: (609)654-6266
Fax: (609)654-4309

Publications: Computers in Libraries (19223) • Information Science Abstracts (19224) • Information Today (19225) • Internet & Personal Computing

Abstracts (19226) • KMWorld (19227) • Link-Up (19228) • Marketing Asst. (19229) • Marketing Library Services (19230) • MultiMedia Schools (19231) • Searcher (19232)

Informer Star
417 Avenue C
Burkburnett, TX 76354-3424
Phone: (817)569-2191

Publications: Informer Star (29987)

The Informer & Texas Freeman
PO Box 3086
Houston, TX 77253
Phone: (713)218-7400
Fax: (713)218-7077

Publications: The Informer & Texas Freeman (30491)

Inforonics
30 Porter Rd.
Littleton, MA 01460-1414
Phone: (978)698-7358
Fax: (978)698-7500

Publications: Meteorological & Geoastrophysical Abstracts (14277)

InfoText Publishing, Inc.
201 Sandpointe Ave., Ste. 600
Santa Ana, CA 92707
Phone: (714)850-0585
Fax: (714)493-3018

Publications: InfoText (3628)

InfoWorld
155 Bovet Rd.
San Mateo, CA 94402
Phone: (650)572-7341
Fax: (415)312-0580
Free: 800-227-8365

Publications: InfoWorld (3587)

Ingersoil Times
19 King St. W.
Ingersoll, ON, Canada E3B 2T8
Phone: (519)485-3631
Fax: (519)485-6652

Publications: Ingersoll Times (35921)

Iniquities Publications
167 Sierra Bonita Ave.
Pasadena, CA 91106

Publications: Iniquities (2818)

Initial Publications, Inc.
3869 Darrow Rd., Ste. 109
Stow, OH 44224
Phone: (330)686-9544
Fax: (330)686-9563

Publications: Fastener Technology International (25545) • Wire & Cable Technology International (25548)

Inky Trail News
55 N Walnut, No. 226
Mount Clemens, MI 48043

Publications: Inky Trail News (15371)

Inland Empire Community Newspapers
PO Box 6247
San Bernardino, CA 92412-6247
Phone: (909)381-9898
Fax: (909)384-0406

Publications: Colton Courier (1741) • El Chicano (3086) • Rialto Record (2919)

Inland Publications, Inc.
1020 W. Riverside Ave.
Spokane, WA 99201-1100
Phone: (509)325-0634
Fax: (509)325-0638

Publications: The Pacific Northwest Inlander (33097)

Inman Times
PO Drawer 7
Inman, SC 29349
Phone: (864)472-9548
Fax: (864)476-5398

Publications: Inman Times (28667)

Inn Room Visitors Magazine
210 S Juniper, Ste. 215
Escondido, CA 92025
Phone: (760)489-5252
Fax: (760)489-6752
Free: 888-990-6901

Publications: Inn Room Visitors Magazine (1891)

Inner City Press/Community on the Move Inc.
PO Box 580188
Mount Carmel Sta.
Bronx, NY 10458
Phone: (718)716-3540
Fax: (718)716-3161

Publications: Inner City Press (20273)

Inner-View Publishing Co., Inc.
PO Box 66156
Houston, TX 77266
Fax: (713)527-0606

Publications: Inner-View (30492)

Innes Publishing Co.
28100 N Ashley
PO Box 7280
Libertyville, IL 60048-7280
Phone: (847)816-7900
Fax: (847)247-8855

Publications: High Volume Printing (9077) • In-Plant Printer & Electronic Publisher (9078) • Instant and Small Commercial Printer (9079)

Innisfail Publishing, Inc.
4932 49th St.
Innisfail, AB, Canada T4G 1N2
Phone: (403)227-3477
Fax: (403)227-3330

Publications: Innisfail Booster (34786) • Innisfail Province (34787)

InnoVision Communications, LLC
169 Saxony Rd., Ste. 104
Encinitas, CA 92024
Phone: (760)633-3910
Fax: (760)633-3918
Free: (866)828-2962

Publications: Alternative Therapies in Health and Medicine (1882)

The Inquirer and Mirror, Inc.
1 Old South Rd.
Nantucket, MA 02554
Phone: (508)228-0001
Fax: (508)325-5089

Publications: The Inquirer and Mirror (14340)

Inquirer Publishing Co., Inc.
620 N St. Paul St.
PO Box 616
Gonzales, TX 78629
Phone: (512)672-2861
Fax: (512)672-7029

Publications: The Gonzales Inquirer (30400)

Inquires Newspaper Group
PO Box 1260
Hartford, CT 06143
Phone: (860)522-1462
Fax: (860)522-3014

Publications: Hartford Inquirer (4893)

Inroads
3777 Kent Ave., Ste. A
PO Box 77042
Ottawa, ON, Canada H3S 1N4
Phone: (613)230-5835

Publications: Inroads (36102)

Inside Communications, Inc.
1830 N. 55th St.
Boulder, CO 80301
Phone: (303)440-0601
Fax: (303)444-6788

Publications: Inside Triathlon (4171) • VeloNews (4194)

Inside Film Magazine
8421 Wilshire Blvd.
Beverly Hills, CA 90211-3205
Phone: (213)852-0434

Publications: Inside Film Magazine (1575)

Inside Passage
419 6th St.
Juneau, AK 99801
Phone: (907)586-2237
Fax: (907)463-3237

Publications: Inside Passage (595)

Inside Publications
4710 N Lincoln Ave.
Chicago, IL 60625-2010
Phone: (773)878-7333
Fax: (773)878-0959

Publications: Inside (8416)

Inside Texas Running
PO Box 19909
Houston, TX 77224
Phone: (281)759-0555
Fax: (281)759-7766
Free: 800-441-9837

Publications: Inside Texas Running (30493)

Insider Business Journal
PO Box 230
Howell, MI 48844-0230

Publications: Insider Business Journal (15194)

INSIEME
4358, rue Charleroi
Montreal, QC, Canada H1H 1T3
Phone: (514)328-2062
Fax: (514)328-6562
Free: 877-689-2924

Publications: INSIEME (37132)

Insight Publications
PO Box 130
Durham, ON, Canada N0G 1R0
Fax: (519)369-5096

Publications: The Citizen (Mount Forest Citizen) (35797)

Insomniac Press
Ste. 403, 192 Spadina Ave.
Toronto, ON, Canada M5T 2C2
Phone: (416)504-6270
Fax: (416)504-9313

Publications: Word (36794)

Instant Karma Press
3075 Harness Dr.
Florissant, MO 63033

Publications: The Lowell Review (17069)

Institut d'histoire de l'Amerique francaise
261 Avenue Bloomfield
Montreal, QC, Canada H2V 3R6
Phone: (514)278-2232
Fax: (514)271-6369

Publications: Revue d'histoire de l'Amerique francaise (37218)

Institute of Chartered Accountants of B.C.
One Bentall Centre, Ste. 500
505 Burrard St.
Box 22
Vancouver, BC, Canada V7X 1M4
Phone: (604)681-3264
Fax: (604)681-1523
Free: 800-663-2677

Publications: Beyond Numbers (35127)

Institute for Criminal Justice Ethics
John Jay College
899 10th Ave.
New York, NY 10019
Phone: (212)237-8000

Publications: Criminal Justice Ethics (21517)

Institute for Democratic Development
560 Herrick Rd.
Benson, VT 05743

Publications: Central Asia Monitor (31504)

Institute of Druze Studies
San Diego State University
PO Box 22828
San Diego, CA 92192
Phone: (619)594-1880

Publications: Journal of Druze Studies (3188)

Institute of East Asian Studies
2223 Fulton St., 6th Fl.
Berkeley, CA 94720-2318
Phone: (510)643-6325
Fax: (510)643-7062

Publications: Early China (1514)

The Institute of Electrical & Electronics Engineers, Inc.
445 Hoes Ln.
Piscataway, NJ 08855
Phone: (732)981-0060
Fax: (732)981-1855

Publications: IEEE Circuits and Devices (13462) • IEEE Electrical Insulation Magazine (19423) • IEEE Engineering in Medicine and Biology Magazine (19424) • IEEE Transactions on Components, Packaging & Manufacturing Technology, Part B (19426) • IEEE Transactions on Components, Packaging & Manufacturing Technology, Part C (19427)

Institute of Electrical and Electronics Engineers, Inc.
3 Park Ave., 17th Fl.
New York, NY 10016-5997
Phone: (212)419-7900
Fax: (212)752-4929

Publications: IEEE Aerospace and Electronic Systems Magazine (21843) • IEEE Communications Magazine (21844) • IEEE Computational Science and Engineering (21845) • IEEE Network (21846) • IEEE Potentials (21847) • IEEE Signal Processing Letters (21848) • IEEE Spectrum (21849) • IEEE Transactions on Automatic Control (14020) • IEEE Transactions on Components, Packaging & Manufacturing Technology, Part A (13420) • IEEE Transactions on Industrial Electronics (21850) • Personal Communications Magazine (22543) • Proceedings of the IEEE (22597) • Robotics & Automation Magazine (24152)

Institute of Environmental Sciences and Technology
5005 Newport Dr., Ste. 506
Rolling Meadows, IL 60008-3841
Phone: (847)255-1561
Fax: (847)255-1699

Publications: Journal of The Institute of Environmental Sciences and Technology (9548)

Institute of Government
Knapp Bldg., CB 3330
Chapel Hill, NC 27599-3330
Phone: (919)966-4119
Fax: (919)962-2707

Publications: Daily Bulletin (23705) • Popular Government (23719) • School Law Bulletin (Chapel Hill) (23721)

Institute of Higher Education (IHE)
Meigs Hall
Athens, GA 30602-6772
Phone: (706)542-0579
Fax: (706)583-0281

Publications: Journal of Higher Education Outreach and Engagement (JHEOE) (6944)

Institute for Historical Review
PO Box 2739
Newport Beach, CA 92659
Phone: (949)631-1490
Fax: (949)631-0981

Publications: The Journal of Historical Review (2629)

Institute of Industrial Engineers
3577 Pky. Ln., Ste. 200
Norcross, GA 30092
Phone: (770)449-0461
Fax: (770)263-8532
Free: 800-494-0460

Publications: Engineering Economist (7459) • IIE Solutions (7462) • Industrial Management (7466)

Institute for Interdisciplinary Research
1065 Pine Bluff Dr.
Pasadena, CA 91107-1751
Phone: (626)351-0419

Publications: Journal of Interdisciplinary Studies (2819)

Institute of Internal Auditors Inc.
247 Maitland Ave.
Altamonte Springs, FL 32701-4201
Free: 877-867-4957

Publications: Internal Auditor (5900)

Institute of Liberal Arts
Oklahoma City University
Oklahoma City, OK 73106
Phone: (405)521-5281
Fax: (405)521-5447

Publications: The Personalist Forum (25992)

The Institute for Local Self-Reliance
1313 5th St. SE
Minneapolis, MN 55414
Phone: (612)379-3815
Fax: (612)379-3920

Publications: New Rules Journal (16114)

Institute of Management Accountants
10 Paragon Dr.
Montvale, NJ 07645-1760
Phone: (201)573-9000
Fax: (201)474-1603
Free: 800-638-4427

Publications: Strategic Finance (19275)

Institute of Mathematical Statistics
PO Box 22718
Beachwood, OH 44122

Publications: The Annals of Applied Probability (24648) • The Annals of Probability (24649) • The Annals of Statistics (24650) • The IMS Bulletin (5171) • Statistical Science (24656)

Institute for Memetic Research, Inc.
PO Box 15812
Panama City, FL 32406-5812

Publications: The Journal of Ideas (6555)

Institute of Mind and Behavior
PO Box 522, Village Sta.
New York, NY 10014
Phone: (212)595-4853

Publications: The Journal of Mind and Behavior (13000)

Institute of Noise Control Engineering
212 Ross Hall
Dept. of Mechanical Engineering
Auburn, AL 36849-3541
Fax: (205)844-3307

Publications: Noise Control Engineer Journal (43)

Institute of Nuclear Materials Management
60 Revere Dr., Ste. 500
Northbrook, IL 60062
Phone: (847)480-9573
Fax: (847)480-9282

Publications: Journal of Nuclear Materials Management (9318)

The Institute for Operations Research and the Management Sciences
901 Elkridge Landing Rd., Ste. 400
Linthicum, MD 21090-2909
Phone: (410)850-0300
Fax: (410)684-2963
Free: 800-446-3676

Publications: Information Systems Research (ISR) (13620) • INFORMS Journal on Computing (13621) • Interfaces (28077) • Management Science (13622) • M&SOM (Manufacturing & Service Operations Management) (13623) • Marketing Science (6151) • Mathematics of Operations Research (27812) • Operations Research (14087) • OR/MS Today (13624) • Organization Science (2087) • Transportation Science (13443)

Institute for Palestine Studies
3501 M St. NW
Washington, DC 20007
Phone: (202)342-3990
Fax: (202)342-3927
Free: 800-874-3614

Publications: Journal of Palestine Studies (5610)

Institute of Public Administration of Canada
1075 Bay St., Ste. 401
Toronto, ON, Canada M5S 2B1
Phone: (416)924-8787
Fax: (416)924-4992

Publications: Canadian Public Administration (Administration publique du Canada) (36528) • Public Sector Management/Management et Secteur Public (36720)

Institute for Public Affairs Inc.
2040 N Milwaukee Ave., 2nd Fl.
Chicago, IL 60647-4002
Phone: (773)772-0100
Fax: (773)772-4180
Free: 888-READ-ITT

Publications: In These Times (8410)

Institute for Public Service and Policy Research
University of South Carolina
Carolina Plaza
Columbia, SC 29208
Phone: (803)777-8157
Fax: (803)777-4575

Publications: E2SC (28549)

Institute of Real Estate Management
430 N. Michigan Ave.
Chicago, IL 60611-4090
Phone: (312)329-6000
Fax: (312)661-0217
Free: 800-837-0706

Publications: Journal of Property Management (8448)

Institute on Religion & Public Life
156 5th Ave., Ste. 400
New York, NY 10010

Publications: FIRST THINGS (21701)

Institute for Research on Public Policy
1470 Peel St., Ste. 200
Montreal, QC, Canada H3A 1T1
Phone: (514)985-2461
Fax: (514)985-2559

Publications: Policy Options Politiques (37207)

Institute of Scrap Recycling Industries
1325 G. St. NW, Ste. 1000
Washington, DC 20005-3104
Phone: (202)737-1770
Fax: (202)626-0900

Publications: Scrap (5784)

Institute for Southern Studies
2009 Chapel Hill Rd.
P.O.B. 531
Durham, NC 27702
Phone: (919)419-8311
Fax: (919)419-8315

Publications: Southern Exposure (23846)

Institute for the Study of Man
1133 13th St. NW, No. C-2
Washington, DC 20005
Phone: (202)371-2700
Fax: (202)371-1523

Publications: The Journal of Indo-European Studies (5598)

Institute for the Study of Traditional American Indian Arts
PO Box 66124
Portland, OR 97290
Phone: (503)233-8131

Publications: American Indian Basketry Magazine (26467)

Institute for Supply Management
2055 E. Centennial Circle
PO Box 22160
Tempe, AZ 85285-2160
Phone: (480)752-6276
Fax: (480)752-7890
Free: 800-888-6276

Publications: Inside Supply Management (905) • The Journal of Supply Chain Management (908)

Institute of Textile Technology
2551 Ivy Rd.
Charlottesville, VA 22903-4614
Phone: (434)296-5511
Fax: (434)977-5400

Publications: Textile Technology Digest (31941)

Institute of Transportation Engineers
1099 14th St. NW, Ste. 300 W
Washington, DC 20005-3438
Phone: (202)289-0222
Fax: (202)289-7722

Publications: ITE Journal (5562)

Institute for Transportation Inc.
4625 Varsity Dr. NW, No. 305, Ste. 68
Calgary, AB, Canada T3A 0Z9
Phone: (403)286-7676
Fax: (403)286-9638

Publications: Journal of Advanced Transportation
(34650)

Institute of Urban Studies
346 Portage Ave.
Winnipeg, MB, Canada R3C 0C3
Phone: (204)982-1140
Fax: (204)943-4695

Publications: Canadian Journal of Urban Research
(35320)

Institutional Distribution
770 Broadway
New York, NY 10003
Phone: (646)654-5000

Publications: Institutional Distribution (21879)

Institutional Real Estate, Inc.
1475 N. Broadway, Ste. 300
Walnut Creek, CA 94596
Phone: (925)933-4040
Fax: (925)934-4099

Publications: The Institutional Real Estate Letter
(4054) • REITStreet Magazine (4055)

Instituto Literario y Cultural Hispanico
8452 Furman Ave.
Westminster, CA 92683
Phone: (714)892-8285
Fax: (714)892-8285

Publications: Alba de America (4073)

Instrumentalist Co.
200 Northfield Rd.
Northfield, IL 60093
Phone: (847)446-5000
Fax: (847)446-6263

Publications: Clavier (9326) • The Instrumentalist
(9330)

Insurance Publications, Inc.
PO Box 1131
Overland Park, KS 66207
Phone: (913)383-9191
Fax: (913)383-1247
Free: 800-762-3387

Publications: Broker World (11700)

Integral Yoga Publications
Rte. 1, Box 1720
Buckingham, VA 23921-9980
Phone: (434)969-3121
Fax: (434)969-1463
Free: 800-262-1008

Publications: Integral Yoga Magazine (31907)

Intelligence Center and Fort Huachuca
ATZS-FDR-CB
Fort Huachuca, AZ 85613-6000
Phone: (520)538-0979
Fax: (520)538-1007

Publications: Commander (708)

The Intelligencer
45 Bridge St. E.
PO Box 5600
Belleville, ON, Canada K8N 1L5
Phone: (613)962-9171
Fax: (613)962-9652

Publications: The Intelligencer (35678)

Inter-American Development Bank
1350 New York Ave., NW
Washington, DC 20577
Phone: (202)623-3210
Fax: (202)623-3531

Publications: The IDB (5540)

Inter-County Co-op Publishing Association
303 N. Wisconsin Ave.
PO Box 490
Frederic, WI 54837
Phone: (715)327-4236
Fax: (715)327-4870

Publications: Indianhead Advertiser (33726) • Inter-
County Leader (33727) • Tri-County North Advertiser
(33728) • Tri-County South Advisor (33729) • Wild
Rivers Advertiser - North (33730) • Wild Rivers
Advertiser - South (33731)

Inter County Publishing Co.
131 E 1st Ave.
PO Box 185
Stanley, WI 54768-0185
Phone: (715)644-3319
Fax: (715)644-5452

Publications: The Stanley Republican (34342)

Inter Lake Publishing Co.
727 E Idaho
PO Box 7610
Kalispell, MT 59904
Phone: (406)755-7000
Fax: (406)752-6114

Publications: The Daily Inter Lake (17836)

Intercollegiate Broadcasting System, Inc.
367 Windsor Hwy.
New Windsor, NY 12553-7900
Phone: (845)565-0003
Fax: (845)565-7446

Publications: The Journal of College Radio (21127)

Intercontinental Media Inc.
PO Box 3410
Milford, CT 06460
Phone: (203)874-1401
Fax: (203)874-1448

Publications: National Development/Desarrollo Nacional (4957)

InterCounty Newspaper Group
PO Box 90
Newtown, PA 18940
Phone: (215)968-2244

Publications: New Hope Gazette (27320)

Intercultural Institute of Montreal
4917 St. Urbain
Montreal, QC, Canada H2T 2W1
Phone: (514)288-7229
Fax: (514)844-6800

Publications: Interculture (37135)

InterfaceMediaGroup
Old Port Technology Center
164 Middle St.
Portland, ME 04101
Phone: (207)879-2277
Fax: (207)773-4385

Publications: Interface Tech News (13010)

InterfaithFamily.com, Inc.
PO Box 9129
Newton, MA 02464
Phone: (617)965-7700
Fax: (617)965-7772

Publications: InterfaithFamily.com (IFF) (14400)

Intergalactic Culture Foundation
1569 Stonewood Ct.
San Pedro, CA 90732-1502
Phone: (310)831-4226
Fax: (310)831-4226

Publications: Sudden Enlightenment Digest (3596)

Interhemispheric Resource Center
PO Box 2178
Silver City, NM 88062
Phone: (505)388-0208
Fax: (505)388-0619

Publications: Foreign Policy in Focus (19952)

The Interior Journal
111 E Main St.
Stanford, KY 40484
Phone: (606)365-2104
Fax: (606)365-2105

Publications: The Interior Journal (12416)

The Interior News
3764 Broadway Ave.
PO Box 2560
Smithers, BC, Canada V0J 2N0
Phone: (604)847-3266
Fax: (604)847-2995

Publications: The Interior News (35090)

Interlake Publishing Co.
PO Box 70
Carman, MB, Canada R0G 0J0
Phone: (204)745-2051
Fax: (204)745-3976

Publications: Carman Valley Leader (35260)

Interlake Publishing Co.
410 Main St.
PO Box 190
Stonewall, MB, Canada R0C 2Z0
Phone: (204)467-8402
Fax: (204)467-5967
Free: 888-467-2421

Publications: The Selkirk Journal (35297) • Stonewall Argus & Teulon Times (35298)

Interlake Spectator
486 Main St.
PO Box 190
Stonewall, MB, Canada R0C 2V0
Phone: (204)467-8402
Fax: (204)467-5967

Publications: Interlake Spectator (35296)

Intermountain Jewish News
1275 Sherman St.
Denver, CO 80203-2299
Phone: (303)861-2234
Fax: (303)832-6942

Publications: Intermountain Jewish News (4332)

Intermountain News
PO Box 1030
Burney, CA 96013-1030
Phone: (530)335-4533
Fax: (530)335-5335

Publications: Intermountain News (1635)

Intermountain Publishing Co.
PO Box 999
Jackson, KY 41339-0999
Phone: (606)666-2451
Fax: (606)666-5757

Publications: Beattyville Enterprise (12143) • Jackson Times (12144)

**International Academy of Business Disci-
plines**
Eberly College of Business Information Technolo-
gy
Indiana University Of Pennsylvania
PO Box 1658
Indiana, PA 15705
Phone: (412)357-2535
Fax: (412)357-5743

Publications: International Journal of Commerce
and Management (27075)

**International and American Associations
for Dental Research**
1619 Duke St.
Alexandria, VA 22314-3406
Phone: (703)548-0066
Fax: (703)548-1883

Publications: Advances in Dental Research
(31631) • Journal of Dental Research (31693)

International Arabian Horse Association
10805 E. Bethany Dr.
Aurora, CO 80014-2605
Phone: (303)696-4500
Fax: (303)696-4599

Publications: International Arabian Horse (4146)

2448

Numbers cited after listings are entry numbers rather than page numbers.

International Arthur Schnitzler Research Association
GREAL
Bowling Green State University
Bowling Green, OH 43403

Publications: Modern Austrian Literature (24697)

International Arthurian Society-North American Branch
Southern Methodist University
Dallas, TX 75275-0432
Phone: (214)768-2959
Fax: (214)768-1234

Publications: Arthuriana (30124)

International Association of Assembly Managers
635 Fritz
Coppell, TX 75019
Phone: (972)255-8020
Fax: (972)255-9582
Free: 800-935-4226

Publications: Facility Manager (30073)

International Association of Bridge, Structural & Ornamental Iron Workers
1750 New York Ave. NW, St. 400
Washington, DC 20006
Phone: (202)737-8484
Fax: (202)638-4856

Publications: The Ironworker (5561)

International Association of Campus Law Enforcement Administrators
342 North Main St.
Hartford, CT 06117-2507
Phone: (860)586-7517
Fax: (860)586-7550

Publications: Campus Law Enforcement Journal (4885)

International Association of Cancer Victors and Friends
7740 W Manchester Ave.
Ste. 203
Playa del Rey, CA 90293
Phone: (310)822-4193
Fax: (310)822-4193

Publications: Cancer Victors Journal (2851)

International Association of Chiefs of Police
515 N. Washington St.
Alexandria, VA 22314
Phone: (703)836-6767
Fax: (703)836-4543
Free: 800-843-4227

Publications: The Police Chief (31723)

International Association of Chinese Medical Specialists and Psychologists
85-25 Kendrick Pl.
Jamaica, NY 11432
Phone: (718)523-4523
Fax: (718)523-4523

Publications: International Chinese Application Psychology Journal (20833) • International Chinese Nursing Journal (20834) • International Chinese Sexology Journal (20835)

International Association of Defense Counsels
One N. Franklin, Ste. 2400
Chicago, IL 60606
Phone: (312)368-1494

Publications: Defense Counsel Journal (8351)

International Association of Electrical Inspectors (IAEI)
901 Waterfall Way, Ste. 602
Richardson, TX 75080-7702
Phone: (972)235-1455
Fax: (972)235-3855

Publications: IAEI News (30974)

International Association for Energy Economics
28790 Chagrin Blvd., Ste. 350
Cleveland, OH 44122
Phone: (216)464-5365
Fax: (216)464-2737

Publications: Energy Journal (24893)

International Association for Environmental Hydrology
5320 Marmith Ave.
Sacramento, CA 95841
Phone: (916)348-3958
Fax: (916)348-3958

Publications: Journal of Environmental Hydrology (3004)

International Association of Fairs and Expositions
3043 E. Cairo
PO Box 985
Springfield, MO 65801
Phone: (417)862-5771
Fax: (417)862-0156
Free: 800-516-0313

Publications: Fairs and Expos (17599)

International Association of Fire Fighters
1750 New York Ave. NW
Washington, DC 20006
Phone: (202)737-8484
Fax: (202)737-8418

Publications: International Fire Fighter (5551)

International Association for Food Protection
6200 Aurora Ave., Ste. 200W
Des Moines, IA 50322
Phone: (515)276-3344
Fax: (515)276-8655
Free: 800-369-6337

Publications: Journal of Food Protection (10800)

International Association for Great Lakes Research
2205 Commonwealth Blvd.
Ann Arbor, MI 48105
Fax: (734)741-2055

Publications: Journal of Great Lakes Research (14756)

International Association of Hewlett-Packard Computer Users
1192 Borregas Ave.
Sunnyvale, CA 94089
Phone: (408)747-0227
Fax: (408)747-0947

Publications: Interact (3829)

International Association for Human Resource Information Management
401 N. Michigan Ave.
Chicago, IL 60611
Phone: (312)321-5141
Fax: (312)627-6636

Publications: IHRIM Journal (8405) • IHRIM.link (8406) • IHRIM.Wire (8407)

International Association for Identification
2535 Pilot Knob Rd., Ste. 117
Mendota Heights, MN 55120-1120
Phone: (651)681-8566
Fax: (651)681-8443

Publications: Journal of Forensic Identification (16052)

International Association for Jazz Education
PO Box 724
Manhattan, KS 66505
Phone: (785)776-8744
Fax: (785)776-6190

Publications: Jazz Education Journal (11621)

International Association of Jazz Record Collectors
41 Brentwood Dr.
Dundas, ON, Canada L9H 3N4
Phone: (905)628-6813

Publications: Journal of the International Association of Jazz Record Collectors (35794)

International Association of Laryngectomees
8900 Thornton Rd.
PO Box 99311
Stockton, CA 95209
Phone: (209)472-0516
Fax: (209)472-0516
Free: 877-425-3678

Publications: IAL News (3805)

International Association of Law Libraries
Box 5709
Washington, DC 20016
Phone: (202)707-9866
Fax: (202)707-1820

Publications: International Journal of Legal Information (5555)

International Association for Orthodontics
735 N. Water St., Ste. 617
Milwaukee, WI 53202
Phone: (414)272-2757
Fax: (414)272-2754
Free: 800-447-8770

Publications: International Journal of Orthodontics (34071)

International Association of Personnel in Employment Security
1801 Louisville Rd.
Frankfort, KY 40601
Phone: (502)223-4459
Fax: (502)223-4127
Free: 888-898-9960

Publications: Workforce Professional (12077)

International Association of Plastics Distributors
4707 College Blvd., Ste. 105
Leawood, KS 66211-1667
Phone: (913)345-1005
Fax: (913)345-1006

Publications: The IAPD Magazine (11585)

International Association of Science and Technology for Development
4500 16th Ave. NW, Ste. 80
Calgary, AB, Canada T3B 0M6
Phone: (403)288-1195
Fax: (403)247-6851

Publications: Control and Intelligent Systems (34641) • International Journal of Robotics and Automation (34649)

International Association of Structural Movers
Box 1213
Elbridge, NY 13060-1213
Phone: (315)689-9498
Fax: (315)689-9498

Publications: Structural Mover (20563)

The International Biometric Society
1444 I St., NW, Ste. 700
Washington, DC 20005-2210
Phone: (202)712-9049
Fax: (202)216-9646

Publications: Biometrics (5377) • Journal of Agricultural, Biological, and Environmental Statistics (5567)

International Bottled Water Association (IBWA)
1700 Diagonal Rd., Ste. 650
Alexandria, VA 22314
Phone: (703)683-5213
Fax: (703)683-4074
Free: 800-WAT-ER11

Publications: Bottled Water Reporter (31649)

International Brotherhood of Boilermakers, Iron Shipbuilders, Blacksmiths, Forgers, and Helpers
753 State Ave., No. 570
Kansas City, KS 66101-2511
Phone: (913)371-2640
Fax: (913)281-8104

Publications: Boilermaker Reporter (11525)

International Brotherhood of Electrical Workers
1125 15th St. NW
Washington, DC 20005
Phone: (202)833-7000

Publications: IBEW Journal (5539)

International Brotherhood of Magicians
11155C South Towne Sq.
St. Louis, MO 63123-7823
Phone: (314)845-9200
Fax: (314)845-9220

Publications: Linking Ring (23834)

International Brotherhood of Teamsters
25 Louisiana Ave. NW
Washington, DC 20001-2198
Phone: (202)624-6800
Fax: (202)624-6918

Publications: The Teamster (5816)

International Business Press Publishers, Inc.
29 W. 38th St., 15th Fl.
New York, NY 10018-5583
Phone: (212)768-8450
Fax: (212)768-8472

Publications: Sportwear International (22780)

International California Mining Journal
PO Box 2260
Aptos, CA 95001
Phone: (831)479-1500
Fax: (831)479-4385

Publications: International California Mining Journal (1426)

International Cast Polymer Association
8201 Greensboro Dr., Ste. 300
Mc Lean, VA 22102
Phone: (703)610-9034
Fax: (703)610-9005
Free: 800-414-4272

Publications: Cast Polymer Connection (32243)

International Cemetery and Funeral Association
1895 Preston White Dr., Ste. 220
Reston, VA 20191
Phone: (703)391-8400
Fax: (703)391-8416
Free: 800-645-7700

Publications: International Cemetery and Funeral Management (32367)

International Chinese Snuff Bottle Society
2601 N Charles St.
Baltimore, MD 21218
Phone: (410)467-9400
Fax: (410)243-3451

Publications: International Chinese Snuff Bottle Society Journal (13172)

International Chiropractors Association
1110 N. Glebe Rd., Ste. 1000
Arlington, VA 22201
Phone: (703)528-5000
Fax: (703)528-5023
Free: 800-423-4690

Publications: ICA Review (31796)

International Church of the Foursquare Gospel
1910 W Sunset Blvd., Ste. 200
PO Box 26902
Los Angeles, CA 90026-0176
Phone: (213)989-4234
Fax: (213)989-4544

Publications: Foursquare World Advance (2274)

International Cinematographers Guild
7715 Sunset Blvd., Ste. 300
West Hollywood, CA 90046
Phone: (323)876-0160
Fax: (323)878-1180

Publications: ICG Magazine (4063)

The International Citizen
76 University Ave. W., Ste. 200
Windsor, ON, Canada N9A 5N7
Phone: (519)977-8499
Fax: (519)977-1777

Publications: The International Citizen (36888)

International City/County Management Association
777 N. Capitol St. NE, Ste. 500
Washington, DC 20002-4201
Phone: (202)289-4262
Fax: (202)962-3500

Publications: Public Management (PM) (5751)

International Civil Aviation Organization
999 University
Attn: Document Sales Unit
Montreal, QC, Canada H3C 5H7
Phone: (514)954-8022
Fax: (514)954-6769

Publications: The ICAO Journal (37123)

International Clarinet Association
University of North Texas
College of Music
PO Box 13887
Denton, TX 76203
Phone: (940)565-4096
Fax: (940)565-2002

Publications: The Clarinet (30233)

International Concrete Repair Institute
3166 S River Rd., Ste. 132
Des Plaines, IL 60018-4260

Publications: Concrete Repair Bulletin (8753)

International Cotton Advisory Committee
1629 K St. NW, Ste. 702
Washington, DC 20006
Phone: (202)463-6660
Fax: (202)463-6950

Publications: Cotton (5444)

International Daily News
870 Monterey Pass Rd.
Monterey Park, CA 91754
Phone: (213)265-1317
Fax: (213)262-1425

Publications: International Daily News (2594)

International District Energy Association
125 Turnpike Rd., Ste. 4
Westborough, MA 01581-2841
Phone: (508)366-9339
Fax: (508)366-0019

Publications: District Energy (14637)

International Documentary Association
1201 W. 5th Street
Suite M320
Los Angeles, CA 90017
Phone: (213)534-3600
Fax: (213)534-3610

Publications: International Documentary (2297)

International Dredging Review
PO Box 1487
Fort Collins, CO 80522
Phone: (970)568-0833
Fax: (970)568-0834

Publications: International Dredging Review (4433)

The International Dyslexia Association
8600 LaSalle Rd.
Chester Bldg.
Suite 382
Baltimore, MD 21286-2044
Phone: (410)296-0232
Fax: (410)321-5069
Free: 800-222-3123

Publications: The Annals of Dyslexia (13123)

The International Economy Publications, Inc.
2099 Pennsylvania Ave., NW, Ste. 950
Washington, DC 20006-6805
Phone: (202)861-0791
Fax: (202)861-0790

Publications: The International Economy (5550)

International Education Forum
Washington State University
Journals Dept.
Pullman, WA 99164
Phone: (509)335-3518
Fax: (509)335-8568

Publications: International Education Forum (32904)

InterNational Electrical Testing Association
106 Stone St.
PO Box 687
Morrison, CO 80465
Phone: (303)697-8441
Fax: (303)697-8431
Free: 800-300-6382

Publications: NETA World (4587)

International Examiner
622 S Washington St.
Seattle, WA 98104
Phone: (206)624-3925
Fax: (206)624-3046

Publications: International Examiner (32972)

International Executive Housekeepers Association, Inc.
1001 Eastwind Dr., Ste. 301
Westerville, OH 43081-3361
Phone: (614)895-7166
Fax: (614)895-1248
Free: 800-200-6342

Publications: Executive Housekeeping Today (25640)

International Executive Reports
717 D St. NW, No. 300
Washington, DC 20004-2807
Phone: (202)628-6900
Fax: (202)628-6618

Publications: East Asian Executive Reports (5467) • Middle East Executive Reports (5649)

International Fabricare Institute
12251 Tech Rd.
Silver Spring, MD 20904
Phone: (301)622-1900
Fax: (301)236-9320
Free: 800-638-2627

Publications: Fabricare (13726)

International Facility Management Association
1 E. Greenway Plaza, Ste. 1100
Houston, TX 77046
Phone: (713)623-4362
Fax: (713)623-6124

Publications: Facility Management Journal (30472)

International Figure Skating
44 Front St., no. 280
Worcester, MA 01608
Phone: (508)756-2595
Fax: (508)792-5981

Publications: International Figure Skating (14684)

International Flag & Banner Inc.
1755 W. 4th Ave.
Vancouver, BC, Canada V6J 1M2
Phone: (604)736-8161
Fax: (604)736-6439
Free: 800-663-8681

Publications: The Flag & Banner (35141)

International Flying Farmers, Inc.
2120 Airport Rd.
PO Box 9124
Wichita, KS 67277
Phone: (316)943-4234
Fax: (316)943-4235

Publications: International Flying Farmer (11882)

International Foundation for Art Research
500 5th Ave., Ste. 1234
New York, NY 10110
Phone: (212)391-6234
Fax: (212)391-8794

Publications: I.F.A.R. Journal (21851)

Numbers cited after listings are entry numbers rather than page numbers.

International Foundation of Employee Benefit Plans
18700 W Bluemound Rd.
PO Box 69
Brookfield, WI 53008-0069
Phone: (262)786-6700
Fax: (262)786-8780
Free: 888-334-3327

Publications: Employee Benefits Journal (33605)

International Foundation for Gender Education
PO Box 540229
Waltham, MA 02454-0229
Phone: (781)899-2212
Fax: (781)899-5703

Publications: Transgender Tapestry (14604)

International Franchise Association
1350 New York Ave. NW, Ste. 900
Washington, DC 20005-4709
Phone: (202)628-8000
Fax: (202)628-0812
Free: 800-543-1038

Publications: Franchising World (5503)

International Fuzzy Mathmatics Institute
PO Box 4067
El Monte, CA 91734
Phone: (626)575-8466
Fax: (626)575-0678

Publications: Journal of Fuzzy Mathematics (1866)

International Graphoanalysis Society
111 N Canal St.
Ste. 955
Chicago, IL 60606
Phone: (312)930-9446
Fax: (312)930-5903

Publications: Journal of Graphoanalysis (8438)

International Hearing Dog, Inc.
5901 E 89th Ave.
Henderson, CO 80640-8315
Phone: (303)287-3277
Fax: (303)287-3425

Publications: Paws for Silence (4515)

International Hearing Society
16880 Middlebelt Rd., Ste. 4
Livonia, MI 48154
Phone: (734)522-7200
Fax: (734)522-0200
Free: 800-521-5247

Publications: The Hearing Professional (15316)

International History Review
EAA 2010, Simon Fraser University
Burnaby, BC, Canada V5A 1S6
Phone: (604)291-3561
Fax: (604)291-3429

Publications: International History Review (34903)

International Institute for Economic Research
1539 S Orange Ave.
Sarasota, FL 34239
Phone: (941)364-5850
Fax: (941)364-9463
Free: 800-221-7514

Publications: Intermarket Review (6656)

International Journal of Philosophical Practice
561 NW 721 Rd.
Centerview, MO 64019
Phone: (660)747-0327

Publications: International Journal of Philosophical Practice (IJPP) (16968)

International Life Sciences Institute
PO Box 830430
Birmingham, AL 35283
Phone: (205)995-1587
Fax: (205)995-1588
Free: 800-633-4931

Publications: Nutrition Reviews (83)

The International Logistics Research Institute, Inc.
PO Box 2166
Ponte Vedra Beach, FL 32004-2166
Phone: (904)880-8653
Fax: (904)880-8654

Publications: The International Journal of Logistics Management (6595)

International Longshore and Warehouse Union
1188 Franklin St., 4th Fl.
San Francisco, CA 94109
Phone: (415)775-0533
Fax: (415)775-1302

Publications: The Dispatcher (3350)

International Lutheran Laymen's League
660 Mason Ridge Ctr. Dr.
St. Louis, MO 63141-8557
Phone: (314)317-4100
Fax: (314)317-4295
Free: 800-944-3450

Publications: The Lutheran Layman (17467)

International Marriage Encounter, Inc.
955 Lake Dr.
St. Paul, MN 55120
Phone: (651)454-6434
Fax: (651)452-0466
Free: 800-627-7424

Publications: Marriage Magazine (16387)

International Medical News Group
60 Columbia Rd., Bldg. B
Morristown, NJ 07960
Phone: (973)290-8200
Fax: (973)290-8245

Publications: Clinical Psychiatry News (13677) • Family Practice News (13678) • Internal Medicine News (13684) • Ob Gyn News (13690) • Pediatric News (13692) • Skin & Allergy News (13697)

International Monetary Fund
700 19th St. NW
Washington, DC 20431
Phone: (202)623-7000
Fax: (202)623-4661

Publications: Finance & Development (5495) • International Monetary Fund Staff Papers (5557) • World Economic Outlook (5869)

International Montessori Society
912 Thayer Ave.
Silver Spring, MD 20910
Phone: (301)589-1127
Fax: (301)589-0733
Free: 800-301-3131

Publications: Montessori News (13740)

International Naval Research Organization
5905 Reinwood Dr.
Toledo, OH 43613-5605
Phone: (419)472-1331

Publications: Warship International (25573)

International New Thought Alliance
5003 E Broadway Rd.
Mesa, AZ 85206
Phone: (480)830-2461
Fax: (480)830-2561

Publications: New Thought (745)

International Parking Institute
701 Kenmore Ave.
Fredericksburg, VA 22401
Phone: (540)371-7535
Fax: (540)371-8022

Publications: The Parking Professional (32086)

International Personnel Management Association (IPMA-HR)
1617 Duke St.
Alexandria, VA 22314
Phone: (703)549-7100
Fax: (703)684-0948

Publications: Public Personnel Management (31732)

International Phenomenological Society
Box 1947
Providence, RI 02912
Phone: (401)863-3215
Fax: (401)863-2719

Publications: Philosophy and Phenomenological Research (28412)

International Planetarium Society
2800 E Observatory Rd.
Los Angeles, CA 90027
Phone: (323)664-1181
Fax: (323)663-4323

Publications: Planetarian (2368)

International Prepress Association
552 W. 167th St.
South Holland, IL 60473
Phone: (708)596-5110
Fax: (708)596-5112

Publications: IPA Bulletin (9615)

International Press of Boston Inc.
PO Box 43502
Somerville, MA 02143-0007
Phone: (617)623-3016
Fax: (617)623-3101

Publications: Advances in Theoretical and Mathematics Physics (14530) • Asian Journal of Mathematics (14531) • Journal of Differential Geometry (14535) • Mathematical Research Letters (2117) • Methods and Applications of Analysis (14536)

International Publisher Direct
709 Westchester Ave.
White Plains, NY 10604-3103

Publications: Paleoclimates (958)

International Reading Association
800 Barksdale Rd.
PO Box 8139
Newark, DE 19714-8139
Phone: (302)731-1600
Fax: (302)368-2449
Free: 800-336-7323

Publications: Journal of Adolescent & Adult Literacy (5275) • Lectura y Vida (5277) • Reading Research Quarterly (18383) • The Reading Teacher (5279) • Reading Today (5280)

International Relations Program
216 Encina Hall, West
Stanford, CA 94305
Phone: (650)723-4547
Fax: (650)723-3010

Publications: Stanford Journal of International Relations (3800)

International Research Center for Energy & Economic Development
850 Willowbrook Rd.
Boulder, CO 80302
Phone: (303)442-4014
Fax: (303)442-5042

Publications: Journal of Energy and Development (4175)

International Right of Way Association
19750 S. Vermont Ave., Ste. 220
Torrance, CA 90502-1144

Publications: Right of Way (3941)

International Scientific Communications, Inc.
30 Controls Dr.
PO Box 870
Shelton, CT 06484-0870
Phone: (203)926-9300
Fax: (203)926-9310

Publications: American Biotechnology Laboratory (5117) • American Clinical Laboratory (5118) • American Laboratory News (5119) • European Clinical Laboratory (5121) • International Biotechnology Laboratory (5124) • International Laboratory (5125)

International Sleep Products Association
501 Wythe St.
Alexandria, VA 22314-1917
Phone: (703)683-8371
Fax: (703)683-4503

Publications: BEDTimes (31647)

International Social Science Review
1001 Millington, Ste. B
Winfield, KS 67156
Phone: (620)221-3128
Fax: (620)221-7124

Publications: International Social Science Review (11909)

International Socialists
PO Box 339
Sta. E
Toronto, ON, Canada M6H 4E3
Phone: (416)972-6391
Fax: (416)972-6391

Publications: Socialist Worker (36742)

International Society of Arboriculture
PO Box 3129
Champaign, IL 61826-3129
Phone: (217)355-9411
Fax: (217)355-9516
Free: 888-ISA-TREE

Publications: Arborist News Magazine (8180)

International Society of Bassists
Don Dillon Associates
13140 Coit Rd. Ste. 320
Dallas, TX 75240-5737

Publications: Bass World (30128)

International Society of Certified Employee Benefit Specialists
18700 W Bluemound Rd.
PO Box 209
Brookfield, WI 53008-0209
Phone: (262)786-8771
Fax: (262)786-8650

Publications: Benefits Quarterly (33603)

International Society of Cryptozoology
PO Box 43070
Tucson, AZ 85733
Phone: (520)884-8369
Fax: (520)884-8369

Publications: Cryptozoology (943)

International Society of Dermatology
Mayo Clinic
847, S. Randall Rd.
Elgin, IL 60123
Phone: (847)429-9535
Fax: (847)429-9545

Publications: International Journal of Dermatology (8824)

International Society of Explosives Engineers
30325 Bainbridge Rd.
Cleveland, OH 44139-2295
Phone: (440)349-4400

Publications: Journal of Explosives Engineering (24914)

International Society for General Semantics
Box 728
Concord, CA 94522
Phone: (925)798-0311
Fax: (925)798-0312

Publications: ETC: A Review of General Semantics (1753)

International Society on Metabolic Eye Disease
1125 Park Ave.
New York, NY 10128
Phone: (212)427-1246
Fax: (212)360-7009

Publications: Metabolic Pediatric and Systems Ophthalmology (22319)

International Society of Offshore & Polar Engineers
PO Box 189
Cupertino, CA 95015-0189
Phone: (650)254-1871
Fax: (650)254-2038

Publications: International Journal of Offshore and Polar Engineering (1797)

International Society for Optical Engineering
1000 20th St.
PO Box 10
Bellingham, WA 98227
Phone: (360)676-3290
Fax: (360)647-1445

Publications: Optical Engineering (32678)

International Society of Parametric Analysts
PO Box 6402
Town & County Branch
Chesterfield, MO 63006-6402
Phone: (636)527-2955
Fax: (636)256-8358

Publications: Journal of Parametrics (16975)

International Society for Pharmaceutical Engineering, Inc.
3109 W. Dr. Martin Luther King Jr. Blvd., Ste. 250
Tampa, FL 33607-6260
Phone: (813)960-2105
Fax: (813)264-2816

Publications: Pharmaceutical Engineering (6776)

International Society for Plant Molecular Biology
Dept. of Biochemistry and Molecular Biology
University of Georgia
Athens, GA 30602
Phone: (706)542-3239
Fax: (706)542-2090

Publications: Plant Molecular Biology Reporter (6948)

International Society for Research in Healthcare Financial Management Ltd.
305 W. Chesapeake Ave.
CSBA Ste. L-096
Towson, MD 21204

Publications: Research in Healthcare Financial Management (13765)

International Society for Technology in Education
1787 Agate St.
Eugene, OR 97403-1923
Phone: (541)346-4414
Fax: (541)346-5890
Free: 800-336-5191

Publications: Journal of Research on Computing in Education (11622) • Journal of Research on Technology in Education (26319)

International Society for Vehicle Preservation
PO Box 50046
Tucson, AZ 85703
Phone: (520)622-2201

Publications: Restoration (961)

International Society of Weekly Newspaper Editors
Department of Journalism
PO Box 2235
South Dakota State University
Brookings, SD 57007
Phone: (605)688-4171
Fax: (605)688-4271

Publications: Grassroots Editor (28814)

International Specialty Shops Association
PO Box 14456
Atlanta, GA 30324
Phone: (404)237-2907
Fax: (404)237-0093

Publications: Retail Ink (7041)

International Technology Education Association
1914 Association Dr., Ste. 201
Reston, VA 20191
Phone: (703)620-4146
Fax: (703)860-0353

Publications: Technology and Children (32419) • The Technology Teacher (32420)

International Test and Evaluation Association
4400 Fair Lakes Ct.
Fairfax, VA 22033-3899
Phone: (703)631-6220
Fax: (703)631-6221

Publications: ITEA Journal of Test and Evaluation (32018)

International Times.com Company
1916 Pike Pl., Ste. 831
Seattle, WA 98101
Fax: (954)301-0384

Publications: InternationalTimes.com (32973)

International Transactional Analysis Association, Inc.
436 14th St., Ste. 1301
Oakland, CA 94612-2710
Phone: (510)625-7720
Fax: (510)625-7725

Publications: Transactional Analysis Journal (2701)

International Trotting and Pacing Association, Inc.
60 Gulf Rd.
Gouverneur, NY 13642
Phone: (315)287-2294
Fax: (315)287-2294

Publications: The Trottingbred (20675)

International Union, U.A.W.
8000 E Jefferson Ave.
Detroit, MI 48214
Phone: (313)926-5291
Fax: (313)331-1520

Publications: Solidarity (14947)

International Universities Press Inc.
59 Boston Post Rd.
Madison, CT 06443-1524
Phone: (203)245-4000
Fax: (203)245-0775
Free: 800-TEL-EIUP

Publications: Depression and Stress (4928) • Gender and Psychoanalysis (4929) • Integrative Psychiatry (4930) • Journal of Clinical Psychoanalysis (4931) • Journal of Developmental and Learning Disorders (4932) • Journal of Geriatric Psychiatry (4933) • Psychoanalysis and Contemporary Thought (4935)

International Wildlife Rehabilitation Council
829 Bancroft Way
Berkeley, CA 94710
Phone: (707)864-1761
Fax: (707)864-3106

Publications: Journal of Wildlife Rehabilitation (1538)

Internet Scientific Publications L.L.C.
23 Rippling Creek Dr.
Sugar Land, TX 77479
Phone: (832)443-1193
Fax: (281)240-1533

Publications: Internet Journal of Academic Physician Assistants (31138) • Internet Journal of Advanced Nursing Practice (31139) • The Internet Journal of Anesthesiology (31140) • Internet Journal of Asthma, Allergy and Immunology (31141) • Internet Journal of Emergency and Intensive Care Medicine (31142) • Internet Journal of Family Practice (31143) • Internet Journal of Gastroenterology (31144) • Internet Journal of Gynecology and Obstetrics (31145) • Internet Journal of Health (31146) • Internet Journal of Healthcare Administration (31147) • Internet Journal of Infectious Disease (31148) • Internet Journal of Internal Medicine (31149) • Internet Journal of Law, Healthcare and Ethics (31150) • Internet Journal of Neuromonitoring (31151) • Internet Journal of Neurosurgery (31152) • Internet Journal of Ophthalmology and Visual Science (31153) • Internet Journal of Orthopedic Surgery (31154) • Internet Journal of Pain, Symptom Control and Palliative Care (31155) • Internet Journal of Pathology (31156) • Internet Journal of Pediatrics and Neonatology (31157) • Internet Journal of Perfusionists (31158) • Internet Journal of Pulmonary Medicine (31159) • Internet Journal of Radiology (31160) • Internet Journal of Rescue and Disaster Medicine (31161) • Internet Journal of Surgery (31162) • Internet Journal of Thoracic and Cardiovascular Surgery (31163)

Interpretive Birding Bulletin
1800 11th Ave. SE
St. Cloud, MN 56304
Phone: (320)252-3909

Publications: Interpretive Birding Bulletin (16342)

Intertec Publishing
11 River Bend Dr. S
Stamford, CT 06907
Phone: (203)358-9900

Publications: Association Meetings (14571) • Corporate Meetings & Incentives (14572) • Insurance Conference Planner (14573) • Medical Meetings (14574) • Religious Conference Manager (14575) • Technology Meetings (14576)

Intertec Publishing
330 N. Wabash Ave., Ste. 2300
Chicago, IL 60611-3586
Phone: (312)595-1080
Fax: (312)595-0296
Free: 800-543-7771

Publications: Upstart (8594)

Intertec Publishing
PO Box 66010
Houston, TX 77266
Phone: (713)523-8124
Fax: (713)523-8384

Publications: Modern Bulk Transporter (30508) • Refrigerated Transporter (30522) • Telecom Business (30532) • Trailer/Body Builders (30535)

Intertec Publishing Corp.
5680 Greenwood Plaza Blvd., Ste. 100
Greenwood Village, CO 80111
Phone: (303)741-2901
Fax: (720)489-3225

Publications: Stitches Magazine (4505)

Intertec Publishing Corp.
PO Box 12901
Overland Park, KS 66212-2901
Phone: (913)967-7303
Fax: (913)967-1901
Free: 800-262-1954

Publications: Cellular & Mobile International (11704)

Intertel, Inc.
PO Box 1083
Tulsa, OK 74101
Phone: (918)582-0354

Publications: Integra (31270)

Intertribal Christian Communications
PO Box 3765, RPO Redwood Centre
Winnipeg, MB, Canada R2W 3R6
Phone: (204)661-9333
Fax: (204)661-3982
Free: 800-665-9275

Publications: Indian Life (35333)

Interval International
6262 Sunset Dr.
Miami, FL 33143
Phone: (305)666-1861
Fax: (305)668-3408
Free: 800-622-1861

Publications: Vacation Industry Review (6387)

InterVarsity Christian Fellowship
6400 Schroeder Rd.
PO Box 7895
Madison, WI 53707-7895
Phone: (608)274-9001
Fax: (608)274-7882

Publications: Student Leadership Journal (33974)

Interview
575 Broadway
New York, NY 10012
Phone: (212)941-2900
Fax: (212)941-2885
Free: 800-925-9574

Publications: Interview (21944)

The InTowner Newspaper
1730-B Corcoran St., NW
Washington, DC 20009
Phone: (202)234-1717

Publications: The InTowner Newspaper (5560)

Inuit Art Foundation
2081 Merivale Rd.
Ottawa, ON, Canada K2G 1G9
Phone: (613)224-8189
Fax: (613)224-2907

Publications: Inuit Art Quarterly (36252)

Inventors Workshop International
1029 Castillo St.
Santa Barbara, CA 93101-3736
Phone: (805)962-5722
Fax: (805)899-4927

Publications: The Lightbulb/Invent! Journal (3649)

Inverness Communications Ltd.
PO Box 100
15767 Main St.
Inverness, NS, Canada B0E 1N0
Phone: (902)258-3400
Fax: (902)258-2632

Publications: The Inverness Oran (35581)

Investment Advisor Group
3 Revmont Dr., Ste. 200
Shrewsbury, NJ 07702
Phone: (732)389-8700
Fax: (732)389-6065

Publications: Investment Advisor Magazine (19556)

Investment Executive
25 Sheppard Ave. W, Ste. 100
Toronto, ON, Canada M2N 6S7
Phone: (416)733-7600
Fax: (416)218-3624
Free: 888-366-4200

Publications: Investment Executive (36624)

Investment Media, Inc.
820 Second Ave., 4th Fl.
New York, NY 10017
Phone: (212)370-3700
Fax: (212)370-4606

Publications: Global Investment Magazine (21772)

The Investment Reporter
PO Box 8049-300
Newport Beach, CA 92658
Phone: (949)724-0444
Fax: (949)724-0408

Publications: The Investment Reporter (2628)

Investor's Business Daily
12655 Beatrice St.
Los Angeles, CA 90066
Phone: (310)448-6000

Publications: Investor's Business Daily (2298)

IO Publications, Inc.
1500 Broadway
New York, NY 10036-4015
Phone: (212)642-0600
Fax: (212)768-3769
Free: 800-289-7852

Publications: Income Opportunities (21860)

The Iola Register, Inc.
302 S Washington Ave.
PO Box 767
Iola, KS 66749
Phone: (316)365-2111
Fax: (316)365-6289
Free: 800-365-1901

Publications: The Iola Register (11513)

Iona College
715 North Ave.
New Rochelle, NY 10801
Phone: (914)633-2370
Fax: (914)633-2404

Publications: The Ionian (21117)

Iona College Graduate Department of Pastoral and Family Counseling
715 North Ave.
New Rochelle, NY 10801
Phone: (914)633-2000

Publications: Journal of Pastoral Counseling (21118)

Iowa American Legion
720 Lyon St.
Des Moines, IA 50309-5417
Phone: (515)282-5068
Fax: (515)282-7583
Free: 800-365-8387

Publications: Iowa Legionnaire (10793)

Iowa Association of Electric Cooperatives
8525 Douglas, No. 48
Urbandale, IA 50322
Phone: (515)276-5350
Fax: (515)276-7946

Publications: Iowa REC News (11276)

Iowa Association of School Boards
700 2nd Ave., Ste. 100
Des Moines, IA 50309
Phone: (515)288-1991
Fax: (515)243-4992

Publications: The Iowa School Board Dialogue (10795)

Iowa Community Publications
301 Fifth St.
PO Box 904
Ames, IA 50010
Phone: (515)233-1251
Fax: (515)233-1244
Free: 800-873-1870

Publications: The Advertiser (10587)

Iowa County Farmer
100 W Main St.
PO Box 208
Marengo, IA 52301
Phone: (319)642-5506
Fax: (319)642-5509
Free: 800-414-5506

Publications: Iowa County Farmer (11061)

Iowa Dept. of Natural Resources
Wallace State Office Bldg.
Des Moines, IA 50319
Phone: (515)281-5918
Fax: (515)281-6794

Publications: Iowa Conservationist (10790)

Iowa Farm Bureau Federation
406 Stevens
Iowa Falls, IA 50126
Phone: (641)648-2521
Fax: (641)648-4606
Free: 800-442-3276

Publications: Spokesman (11000)

Iowa Farmer Today
501 2nd Ave. SE, 3rd Fl.
PO Box 5279
Cedar Rapids, IA 52406
Phone: (319)398-8461
Fax: (319)398-8482
Free: 800-475-6655

Publications: Iowa Farmer Today (10674) • Iowa Pork Today (10675)

Iowa Genealogical Society
Box 7735
Des Moines, IA 50322-7735
Phone: (515)276-0287
Fax: (515)727-1824

Publications: Hawkeye Heritage (10787)

Iowa Grocery Industry Association
2540 106th St., Ste. 102
Des Moines, IA 50322-3771
Phone: (515)270-2628
Fax: (515)270-0316

Publications: Iowa Grocer (10791)

Iowa Hospitality Association
8525 Douglas Ave., Ste. 47
Des Moines, IA 50322
Phone: (515)276-1454
Fax: (515)276-3660

Publications: Entree (10785)

Iowa Information, Inc.
227 9th St.
PO Box 160
Sheldon, IA 51201
Phone: (712)324-5347
Fax: (712)324-2345
Free: 800-247-0186

Publications: Golden Shopper (11193) • N'West Iowa Review (11194) • Sheldon Mail-Sun (11195)

Iowa Medical Society
1001 Grand Ave.
West Des Moines, IA 50265
Phone: (515)223-1401
Fax: (515)223-8420
Free: 800-747-3070

Publications: Iowa Medicine (11320)

Iowa Motor Truck Association
717 East Court Ave
600 East Court
Des Moines, IA 50309
Phone: (515)244-5193
Fax: (515)244-2204

Publications: The Iowa Trucking Lifeliner (10797)

Iowa Parent & Family
PO Box 957
Des Moines, IA 50304
Phone: (515)284-8173
Fax: (515)286-2597

Publications: Iowa Parent & Family (10794)

Iowa Pharmacy Association
Omega Pl., Ste. 16
8515 Douglas Ave.
Des Moines, IA 50322
Phone: (515)270-0713
Fax: (515)270-2979

Publications: The Journal (10799)

Iowa Poetry Assoc.
2325 61st St.
Des Moines, IA 50322
Phone: (515)279-1106

Publications: Lyrical Iowa (10803)

Iowa Pork Producers Association
Box 71009
Clive, IA 50325
Phone: (515)225-7675
Fax: (515)225-0563
Free: 800-372-7675

Publications: Iowa Pork Producer (10716)

The Iowa State Bar Association
521 E. Locust, 3rd. Fl.
Des Moines, IA 50309
Phone: (515)243-3179
Fax: (515)243-2511

Publications: The Iowa Lawyer (10792)

Iowa State Daily Publication Board
Iowa State University
Rm. 108 Hamilton Hall
Ames, IA 50011

Publications: Iowa State Daily (10589)

Iowegian
105 N. Main St.
Centerville, IA 52544
Phone: (515)856-6336
Fax: (515)856-8118

Publications: Iowegian (10688)

IP Magazine
10 United Nations Plz., 3rd Fl.
San Francisco, CA 94102

Publications: IP Magazine (3375)

IP.com Inc.
150 Lucius Gordon Dr.
West Henrietta, NY 14586
Phone: (585)427-8180
Fax: (585)427-8183

Publications: The IP.com Journal (23543)

IR Research Publications
PO Box 1092
Kingston, ON, Canada K7L 4Y5
Phone: (613)542-5596

Publications: Worklife Report (35949)

Iranian Community Newspaper
2376 Eglinton Ave. E.
PO Box 44537
Scarborough, ON, Canada M1K 5K3
Phone: (416)265-4466
Fax: (416)265-7835

Publications: Iranian Community Newspaper (36377)

Ireton Printing
PO Box 31
Ireton, IA 51027
Phone: (712)551-1051
Fax: (712)551-1057
Free: 888-828-3024

Publications: Ireton Examiner (11004)

Irish America Magazine
432 Park Ave. S, Ste. 1503
New York, NY 10016
Phone: (212)725-2993
Fax: (212)779-1198

Publications: Irish America Magazine (21949)

Irish American Cultural Institute
1 Lackawanna Place
Morristown, NJ 07960
Phone: (973)605-1991
Fax: (973)605-8875
Free: 800-232-ERIN

Publications: Eire-Ireland (19312)

Irish American News
6441 W North Ave. Ste. 215
Oak Park, IL 60302
Phone: (708)445-0700
Fax: (708)445-2003

Publications: Irish American News (9376)

Irish Echo Newspaper Corp.
309 5th Ave.
New York, NY 10016-6548
Phone: (212)686-1266
Fax: (212)683-1756

Publications: Irish Echo (21950)

Irish Genealogical Foundation
PO Box 7575
Kansas City, MO 64116

Publications: Irish Families; Journal of (17173)

The Irish Herald
2145 19th Ave., No. 203
San Francisco, CA 94116-1866
Phone: (415)752-7977
Fax: (415)750-9670

Publications: Irish Focus News (3376)

Irish Voice Newspaper
432 Park Ave. S Ste. 1503
New York, NY 10016
Phone: (212)684-3366
Fax: (212)779-1198

Publications: Irish Voice Newspaper (21951)

Iron County Miner
216 Copper St.
Hurley, WI 54534-1339
Phone: (715)561-3405

Publications: Iron County Miner (33797)

Iron Man Industries
10 E 40th St. Ste. 9
New York, NY 10016-0201

Publications: Iron Man (21952)

Iron & Steel Society
186 Thorn Hill Rd.
Warrendale, PA 15086
Phone: (724)776-1535
Fax: (724)776-0430

Publications: Iron & Steel Maker Magazine (28112)

Irondequoit Shopper
64 Orenda Dr.
Rochester, NY 14622-2055
Phone: (716)323-1560
Fax: (716)323-1029

Publications: Irondequoit Shopper (23231)

Ironman Publishing
1701 Ives Ave.
Oxnard, CA 93033
Phone: (805)385-3500
Fax: (805)385-3515
Free: 800-447-0008

Publications: Ironman (2730)

Ironton Publications, Inc.
PO Box 647
Ironton, OH 45638
Phone: (614)532-1441
Fax: (614)532-1506
Free: (866)532-1441

Publications: Tribune (25253)

ISA Services, Inc.
67 Alexander Dr.
PO Box 12277
Research Triangle Park, NC 27709
Phone: (919)549-8411
Fax: (919)549-8288

Publications: INTECH (24185)

The Isabel and Dakolan
PO Box 207
Isabel, SD 57633
Phone: (605)466-2258
Fax: (605)466-2124

Publications: The Isabel Dakotan (28876)

iSeries Network
221 E. 29th St.
Loveland, CO 80538
Phone: (970)663-4700
Fax: (970)667-2321
Free: 800-621-1544

Publications: NEWS/400 (4569)

Ishcom Publications Ltd.
2065 Dundas St. E., Ste. 201
Mississauga, ON, Canada L4X 2W1
Phone: (905)206-0150
Fax: (905)206-9972
Free: 800-201-8596

Publications: Ontario Restaurant News (36083)

The Island-Ear, Inc.
1103 Stewart Ave.
Garden City, NY 11530
Phone: (516)889-6045
Fax: (516)889-6983

Publications: The Island-Ear (20643)

The Island Packet
10 Buck Island Rd.
Bluffton, SC 29910
Phone: (843)706-8100
Fax: (843)706-5050

Publications: The Island Packet (28661)

Island Press
PO Box 790
Montague, PE, Canada C0A 1R0
Phone: (902)838-2515
Fax: (902)838-4392
Free: 800-806-5443

Publications: The Eastern Graphic (36921)

Island Press Ltd.
PO Box 339
Alberton, PE, Canada C0B 1B0
Phone: (902)853-3320
Fax: (902)853-3071

Publications: West Prince Graphic (36911)

Island Printing
PO Box 19430
Thorne Bay, AK 99919
Phone: (907)828-3377
Fax: (907)828-3351

Publications: Island News (643)

Island Publications
1558 Ben Sawyer Blvd.
Mount Pleasant, SC 29464
Phone: (843)849-1778

Publications: The Water Log Maritime Journal (28697)

Island Publications
PO Box 2014
Mount Pleasant, SC 29465
Phone: (843)849-1778
Fax: (843)849-0214
Publications: The Catalyst (28507) • Journal (28693) • Moultrie News (28694)

Island Reporter
PO Box 809
Sanibel, FL 33957
Phone: (239)472-1587
Fax: (239)472-8398
Publications: Island Reporter (6650)

The Islander
PO Box 20539
St. Simons Island, GA 31522
Phone: (912)265-9654
Fax: (912)265-3699
Publications: The Islander (7525)

Islander
PO Box 212
South Hero, VT 05486-0212
Phone: (802)372-5000
Fax: (802)372-3025
Publications: Islander (31601)

The Islander News
104 Crandon Blvd., No. 301
Key Biscayne, FL 33149
Phone: (305)361-3333
Fax: (305)361-5051
Publications: The Islander News (6251)

Islands Publishing Co.
PO Box 4728
Santa Barbara, CA 93140-4728
Phone: (805)745-7100
Fax: (805)745-7105
Free: 800-322-1161
Publications: Islands Magazine (3643) • Resorts & Great Hotels (3653) • Spa (3658)

The Issaquah Press
45 Front Street S.
PO Box 1328
Issaquah, WA 98027
Phone: (425)392-6434
Fax: (425)391-1541
Publications: The Issaquah Press (32784)

ISTE (International Society for Technology in Education)
480 Charnelton
Eugene, OR 97401-2626
Phone: (541)302-3777
Fax: (541)302-3778
Free: 800-336-5191
Publications: Learning and Leading with Technology (26322)

Isthmus Publishing
101 King St.
Madison, WI 53703
Phone: (608)251-5627
Fax: (608)251-2165
Publications: Isthmus (33949)

IT Financial Management Association
PO Box 30188
Santa Barbara, CA 93130
Phone: (805)687-7390
Fax: (805)687-7382
Publications: Journal of IS Financial Management (3645) • Journal of IT Financial Management (3646)

IT World Canada Inc.
55 Town Centre Ct., Ste. 302
Scarborough, ON, Canada M1P 4X4
Phone: (416)290-0240
Fax: (416)290-0238
Free: 800-565-4007
Publications: CIO Canada (36374) • Computerworld Canada (36376) • Network World Canada (36378) • Northern Ontario Business (36379) • Parry Sound Beacon-Star (36381) • Parry Sound North Star (36382)

Italian American Chamber of Commerce
30 S Michigan Ave., Ste. 504
Chicago, IL 60603
Phone: (312)553-9137
Fax: (312)533-9142
Publications: Italian American Chamber of Commerce of Chicago Bulletin (8422)

Italian Chamber of Commerce of Canada
550 Sherbrooke St. W, Ste. 1150
Montreal, QC, Canada G1K 7P4
Phone: (514)844-4249
Fax: (514)844-4875
Free: 800-263-4372
Publications: Italian Commerce of Commerce of Canada (37136)

Italian Chamber of Commerce of Toronto
901 Lawrence Ave. W., Ste. 306
Toronto, ON, Canada M6A 1C3
Phone: (416)789-7169
Fax: (416)789-7160
Publications: Italy Canada Trade (36627)

Italian Tribune
427 Bloomfield Ave.
Newark, NJ 07107
Phone: (973)485-6000
Fax: (973)556-1492
Publications: Italian Tribune (19354)

Itawamba Community College
602 W Hill St.
Fulton, MS 38843
Phone: (662)862-8000
Fax: (662)862-8245
Publications: Chieftain (16627)

Itawamba County Times
106 W Main
Fulton, MS 38843
Phone: (662)862-3141
Fax: (662)862-7804
Publications: Itawamba County Times (16628)

Item
3rd & State Sts.
Hamburg, PA 19526
Phone: (610)562-7515
Fax: (610)562-4644
Publications: Item (26971)

Ithaca College
Office of Marketing Communications
Ithaca, NY 14850
Phone: (607)274-3830
Fax: (607)274-1490
Publications: Ithaca College Quarterly (20806)

The Ithaca Journal
123-125 W. State St.
PO Box 430
Ithaca, NY 14850-0430
Phone: (607)272-2321
Fax: (607)272-9290
Free: 800-328-2860
Publications: The Ithaca Journal (20807)

Ithaca Times
109 N Cayuga St.
PO Box 27
Ithaca, NY 14851
Phone: (607)277-7000
Fax: (607)277-1012
Publications: Ithaca Times (20809)

Ivanhoe Times
PO Box 100
Ivanhoe, MN 56142
Phone: (507)694-1246
Fax: (507)694-1246
Publications: Ivanhoe Times (15973)

Ivey Business Journal
179 John St., Ste. 501
Toronto, ON, Canada M5T 1X4
Phone: (416)598-7775
Fax: (416)598-0669
Free: 800-646-8531
Publications: Ivey Business Journal (36628)

iVillage Parenting Network
9 Old Kings Hwy. S.
Darien, CT 06820
Phone: (203)656-3600
Fax: (203)656-2221
Publications: Lamaze Para Padres (4774) • Lamaze Parents' Magazine (4775)

Iwanna, Inc.
991 Sweeten Creek Rd.
PO Box 15228
Asheville, NC 28813
Phone: (828)274-8888
Fax: (828)258-9781
Publications: Iwanna (23631)

Izaak Walton League
707 Conservation Ln.
Gaithersburg, MD 20878
Phone: (301)548-0150
Fax: (301)548-0146
Free: 800-IKE-LINE
Publications: Outdoor America (13546)

J-Ad Corp.
1351 N M-43 Hwy.
PO Box 188
Hastings, MI 49058-0188
Phone: (269)945-9554
Fax: (269)945-5192
Free: 800-870-7085
Publications: Battle Creek Shopper News (14792) • The Hastings Banner (15152) • Hastings Reminder (15153) • Lakewood News (15268) • Maple Valley News (15154) • Marshall Community Advisor (15351) • The Sun & News (15155)

J. B. Scott Publishing
PO Box 2685
Anniston, AL 36202
Phone: (256)835-4901
Fax: (256)835-4905
Free: 800-240-2130
Publications: Through the Gears Trucking Magazine (16)

J & B Thompson
PO Box 258
Osceola, NE 68651
Phone: (402)747-2431
Fax: (402)764-5341
Publications: The Polk County News (18239)

J-D Publishing Co.
800 Davis Ave.
PO Box 46
Corning, IA 50841
Phone: (515)322-3161
Fax: (515)322-3461
Publications: Adams County Free Press (10722)

J & D Publishing Inc.
126 Main
PO Box 279
Sharon Springs, KS 67758
Phone: (785)852-4900
Fax: (785)852-4804
Free: 888-495-5002
Publications: Western Times (11799)

J Desk International
4612 Vettelson Rd.
Hartland, WI 53029
Fax: (414)367-0196
Publications: J Desk International (33779)

J-Mart Publishing Co.
280 N Main
Spanish Fork, UT 84660
Phone: (801)798-6816
Fax: (801)798-9770
Publications: Spanish Fork Press (31474)

The J-TAC
T-0440
Stephenville, TX 76402
Phone: (254)968-9056
Fax: (254)968-9709
Publications: J-TAC (31129)

J 2 Communications
10850 Wilshire Blvd., Ste. 1000
Los Angeles, CA 90024
Phone: (310)474-5252
Fax: (310)474-1219

Publications: National Lampoon (2343)

Jacaranda Publishing, Inc.
143 Newbury St., 6th Fl.
Boston, MA 02116
Phone: (617)424-9005
Fax: (617)424-8944

Publications: Newbury Street and Back Bay Guide (13938)

Jack Mackerel Magazine
PO Box 23134
Seattle, WA 98102-0434

Publications: Jack Mackerel Magazine (32974)

Jack Rabbit Publishing Co.
PO Box 217
PO Box 217
Quincy, WA 98848
Phone: (509)787-4511
Fax: (509)787-2682

Publications: Quincy Valley Post-Register (32919)

Michael Jackman
PO Box 3663, Grand Central Sta.
New York, NY 10163-3663

Publications: Inspector 18 (21878)

Jacksboro Newspapers
212 N. Church
PO Drawer 70
Jacksboro, TX 76458
Phone: (940)567-2616
Fax: (940)567-2071

Publications: Jack County Herald (30614) • Jacksboro Gazette-News (30615)

Jackson County Advocate
502 Main St.
PO Box 620
Grandview, MO 64030
Phone: (816)761-6200
Fax: (816)761-8215

Publications: Jackson County Advocate (17086)

Jackson County, Alabama Historical Association
435 Barbee Ln.
Scottsboro, AL 35769-3745
Phone: (256)574-3556

Publications: Jackson County Chronicles (446)

The Jackson County Banner
116 E Cross St.
PO Box G
Brownstown, IN 47220
Phone: (812)358-2111
Fax: (812)358-5606

Publications: The Jackson County Banner (9875)

Jackson County Publishers, Inc.
310 2nd St.
PO Box 208
Jackson, MN 56143
Phone: (507)847-3771
Fax: (507)847-5822
Free: 800-658-2393

Publications: Jackson County Pilot (15974)

Jackson County Star
PO Box 397
Walden, CO 80480
Phone: (970)723-4404
Fax: (970)723-4474

Publications: Jackson County Star (4655)

The Jackson County Sun
PO Box 130
Mc Kee, KY 40447
Phone: (606)287-7197
Fax: (606)287-7196

Publications: The Jackson County Sun (12291)

Jackson Herald, Inc.
PO Box 908
Jefferson, GA 30549
Phone: (706)367-5233
Fax: (706)367-8056

Publications: The Commerce News (7198)

Jackson Hole Guide
PO Box 7445
Jackson, WY 83002
Phone: (307)733-2047
Fax: (307)733-2138

Publications: Jackson Hole Guide (34535)

Jackson Hole News & Guide
PO Box 7445
Jackson, WY 83002-7445
Phone: (307)733-2047
Fax: (307)733-2138

Publications: Jackson Hole News & Guide (34536)

Jackson Independent
624 Hudson Ave.
PO Box 520
Jonesboro, LA 71251
Phone: (318)259-2551
Fax: (318)259-8537

Publications: Jackson Independent (12608)

Jackson Progress-Argus
PO Box 249
Jackson, GA 30233
Phone: (770)775-3107
Fax: (770)775-3855

Publications: Jackson Progress-Argus (7339)

Jackson Star News
305 N Church St
PO Box 10
Ripley, WV 25271
Phone: (304)273-9333
Fax: (304)273-3401

Publications: Jackson Star News (33449)

Jacobs
5 Possum Hollow Rd.
Andover, MA 01810-2445
Phone: (978)688-1554
Fax: (978)687-6395

Publications: Work (13814)

JADARA
PO Box 727
Lusby, MD 20657-0727
Phone: (410)495-8440
Fax: (410)495-8442

Publications: JADARA (13625)

Jade River Publishing
PO Box 798
Wrangell, AK 99929
Phone: (907)874-2301
Fax: (907)874-2303

Publications: Wrangell Sentinel (653)

JAI Press, Inc.
100 Prospect St.
PO Box 811
Stamford, CT 06904-0811
Phone: (203)323-9606
Fax: (203)357-8446

Publications: Journal of Energy, Finance and Development (527) • Journal of Urban Affairs (12222)

Jam Rag Press
Box 20076
22757 Woodward, Ste. 240
Ferndale, MI 48220
Phone: (248)336-9243

Publications: Jam Rag (15029)

Jamac Publishing Ltd.
919 Main St.
PO Box 1150
Kindersley, SK, Canada S0L 1S0
Phone: (306)463-4611
Fax: (306)463-6505

Publications: Kerrobert Citizen-Dispatch (37480) • Kindersley Clarion (37481) • The Leader News (37482) • West-Central Crossroads (37483)

Jamaica Plain Arts News
PO Box 3
Jamaica Plain, MA 02130
Phone: (617)323-5261
Fax: (617)323-8537

Publications: Jamaica Plain Arts News (14259)

James Carter Publications, Inc.
17 Woodbridge Rd.
PO Box 7
York, ME 03909
Phone: (207)363-4343
Fax: (207)351-2849

Publications: The York Weekly (13083)

James F. Lincoln Arc Welding Foundation
PO Box 17035
Cleveland, OH 44117
Phone: (216)481-4300
Fax: (216)486-1751

Publications: Welding Innovation (24962)

James Informational Media, Inc.
2720 S River Rd., Ste. 126
Des Plaines, IL 60018
Phone: (847)298-8446
Fax: (847)391-9058
Free: 800-957-9305

Publications: Better Roads (30131) • Gas Utility and Pipeline Industries (30160)

James Joyce Quarterly
University of Tulsa
600 S. College
Tulsa, OK 74104-3189
Phone: (918)631-2501
Fax: (918)584-0623

Publications: James Joyce Quarterly (26118)

James Madison University
G1 Anthony-Seeger Hall
MSC 6805
Harrisonburg, VA 22807

Publications: The Breeze (32137)

James Michael Robbins
Box 19228
Austin, TX 78760-9228
Phone: (512)292-9456

Publications: Sulphur River Literary Review (29810)

James Newspaper, Inc.
2 Bridge St.
PO Box 269
Norway, ME 04268
Phone: (207)743-8996
Fax: (207)743-2256

Publications: Advertiser-Democrat (12993)

James Publishing, Inc.
3505 Cadillac Ave., Ste. H
Costa Mesa, CA 92626-1430
Phone: (714)755-5450
Fax: (714)751-2709
Free: 800-394-2626

Publications: Law Office Computing (1776) • Legal Assistant Today (1777)

Jamestown College
6000 College Ln.
Jamestown, ND 58405
Phone: (701)252-3467
Fax: (701)253-4318

Publications: The Collegian (24475)

The Jamestown Sun
122 2nd St. NW
Jamestown, ND 58402-1760
Phone: (701)252-3120
Fax: (701)251-2873
Free: 800-657-8067

Publications: The Jamestown Sun (24476)

Janam Publications
26 St. Raymond Blvd. Ste. 206
Hull, QC, Canada J8Y 1R4
Phone: 800-520-6281
Fax: (819)595-8553

Publications: Wood Lebois (36282)

Jane Austen Society of North America
106 Barlow's Run
Williamsburg, VA 23188
Free: 800-836-3911

Publications: Persuasions (13762) • Persuasions (Online Version) (13763)

Janesville Argus
Box 220
Janesville, MN 56048
Phone: (507)234-6651
Fax: (507)234-6390

Publications: Janesville Argus (15978)

The Janesville Gazette
PO Box 5001
Janesville, WI 53547-5001
Phone: (608)754-3311
Fax: (608)754-8179

Publications: The Janesville Gazette (33858)

Jannetti Publications, Inc.
E. Holly Ave.
Box 56
Pitman, NJ 08071-0056
Phone: (856)256-2300
Fax: (856)589-7463

Publications: Dermatology Nursing (19433) • Med-Surg Nursing (19435) • Nursing Economics (19437) • Pediatric Nursing (19439)

Japan Pacific Publications, Inc.
516 6th Ave. S., Ste. 220
Seattle, WA 98104-2878
Phone: (206)622-7443
Fax: (206)621-1786

Publications: Seattle Compass (33018)

The Japanese Daily Sun-Nikkan San
845 3rd Ave.
New York, NY 10022
Phone: (212)317-3000
Fax: (212)317-3025

Publications: The Japanese Daily Sun-Nikkan San (21956)

Jason Krusa
PO Box M
Franklin, MA 02038-0822
Phone: (508)528-6211
Fax: (508)528-6211

Publications: Collision Magazine (14204) • Wheelings -New England Mechanic (14207)

Jasonville Leader
603 W Main St.
PO Box 125
Jasonville, IN 47438
Phone: (812)665-3145
Fax: (812)665-3145

Publications: Jasonville Leader (10218)

Jasper Booster
PO Box 940
Jasper, AB, Canada T0E 1E0
Phone: (403)852-3620
Fax: (403)852-3384

Publications: Jasper Booster (34789)

Jasper County Tribune
PO Box 7
Box 7
Colfax, IA 50054
Phone: (515)674-3591
Fax: (515)674-3591
Free: 800-299-3591

Publications: Jasper County Tribune (10717)

Jasper Journal
101 NE 2nd St.
Pipestone, MN 56164
Phone: (507)825-3333
Fax: (507)825-2168

Publications: Jasper Journal (15979)

The Jasper News Boy
PO Box 1419
Jasper, TX 75951-1419
Phone: (409)384-3441
Fax: (409)384-8803

Publications: The Jasper News Boy (30619)

Java Magazine
414 S Mill Ave., Ste. 201
Tempe, AZ 85281
Phone: (480)966-6352
Fax: (480)967-0168

Publications: Java Magazine (906)

Jazz Times
8737 Colesville Rd., 5th Fl.
Silver Spring, MD 20910-3921
Phone: (301)588-4114
Fax: (301)588-5531
Free: 800-866-7664

Publications: JazzTimes (13728)

Jazziz Magazine, Inc.
2650 N. Military Trail., Ste. 140
Fountain Sq. II Bldg.
Boca Raton, FL 33431
Phone: (561)893-6868
Fax: (561)893-6867

Publications: Jazziz (5935)

J.B. Lippincott Co.
PO Box 1590
Hagerstown, MD 21741
Phone: 800-777-2295
Fax: (301)824-7390

Publications: Ambulatory Medicine Letter (13561) • Lippincott's Reviews: Radiology (13565) • Nurse Educator (13569)

Jbeen NP Publishing
30423 Conwood St., Ste. 108
Agoura Hills, CA 91301
Phone: (818)706-0266
Fax: (805)379-1864

Publications: Acorn (1385)

JCF Press Association
2050 Mackay St.
Montreal, QC, Canada H3G 2J1

Publications: Journal of Canadian Fiction (37138)

JCFT Forest Communications
90 Morgan, Unit 14
Baie D'urfe', QC, Canada H9X 3A8
Phone: (514)457-2211
Fax: (514)457-2558

Publications: Canadian Forest Industries (36944) • Canadian Wood Products (36945) • Operations Forestieres et de Scierie (36946)

JCO, Inc.
1828 Pearl St.
Boulder, CO 80302
Phone: (303)443-1720
Fax: (303)443-9356

Publications: Journal of Clinical Orthodontics (4174)

JCPDS-International Centre for Diffraction Data
Newton Square Corp., 12 Campus Blvd.
Newtown Square, PA 19073-3273
Phone: (610)325-9814
Fax: (610)325-9823

Publications: Powder Diffraction (27331)

J.D. Barreth Pub.
2365 Commerce Blvd.
PO Box 82
Mound, MN 55364
Phone: (612)472-1140
Fax: (612)472-0516

Publications: The Laker (16201)

Jeff Davis Ledger
12 Latimer St.
PO Box 460
Hazlehurst, GA 31539
Phone: (912)375-4225
Fax: (912)375-3704

Publications: Jeff Davis Ledger (7325)

Jeffco Publishing, Inc.
1000 10th St.
PO Box 987
Golden, CO 80401
Phone: (303)279-5541
Fax: (303)279-7157

Publications: Golden Transcript (4468) • The Jefferson County Transcript (4469)

Jefferson Communications
1202 W. St., Ste. 100
Annapolis, MD 21401
Phone: (410)263-1641
Fax: (410)280-0255

Publications: Chesapeake Family (13092)

Jefferson County Standard Publishing Co.
122 Andrew Johnson Hwy.
PO Box 310
Jefferson City, TN 37760
Phone: (865)475-2081
Fax: (865)475-8539

Publications: Standard Banner (29247)

Jefferson Jimplecute
PO Box 1007
Jefferson, TX 75657
Phone: (903)665-2462
Fax: (903)665-3802

Publications: Jefferson Jimplecute (30624)

The Jefferson Post
PO Box 808
West Jefferson, NC 28694
Phone: (336)246-7164
Fax: (336)246-7165

Publications: The Jefferson Post (24283)

Jefferson Publishing Co., Inc.
210 N George St.
PO Box 966
Charles Town, WV 25414-0966
Phone: (304)725-2046

Publications: Spirit of Jefferson-Advocate (33266)

Jeffersonian
14 Wells St.
Croswell, MI 48422
Phone: (810)679-4500
Fax: (810)679-4504

Publications: Jeffersonian (14892)

Jeffersonian Co.
166 E. Main
PO Box 30
Barnesville, OH 43713
Phone: (740)425-1912
Fax: (740)425-2545
Free: 800-897-2262

Publications: Barnesville Enterprise (24642)

The Jeffersonian Co., Inc.
831 Wheeling Ave.
PO Box 10
Cambridge, OH 43725
Phone: (740)439-3531
Fax: (740)432-6219
Free: 800-897-2262

Publications: The Daily Jeffersonian (24724) • The New Concord Area Leader (24726)

The Jeffersonion Co.
PO Box 30
Newcomerstown, OH 43832
Phone: (740)498-7117
Fax: (740)498-5624
Free: 800-897-2262

Publications: The Newcomerstown News (25431)

Jems Communications
525 B St., Ste. 1900
San Diego, CA 92101-4495
Phone: (760)431-9797
Fax: (760)930-9567
Free: 800-266-5367

Publications: Fire-Rescue Magazine (3155) • JEMS (3175)

Jenkins Group Inc.
400 W Front St., No. 4A
Traverse City, MI 49684-2206
Phone: (231)933-0445
Fax: (231)933-0448

Publications: Independent Publisher Online (15597) • Publishing Entrepreneur (15601)

Brenda Joyce Jerome
PO Box 325
Newburgh, IN 47629-0325
Phone: (812)853-5562

Publications: Western Kentucky Journal (10350)

Jerome Press Publications, Inc.
332 Congress St.
Boston, MA 02210
Phone: (617)423-3400
Fax: (617)423-7108

Publications: Panorama (13946)

Jersey Beat
418 Gregory Ave.
Weehawken, NJ 07087
Phone: (201)864-9054

Publications: Jersey Beat (19711)

Jersey City State College
2039 Kennedy Blvd.
Jersey City, NJ 07305
Phone: (201)200-2169
Fax: (201)200-2329

Publications: The Gothic Times (19138)

The Jersey Journal
30 Journal Sq.
Jersey City, NJ 07306
Phone: (201)217-2524
Fax: (201)653-3125

Publications: Coming Up (19134) • El Nuevo Hudson (19136) • Go Out (19137)

The Jerusalem Post, International Edition
270 Lafayette St., Ste. 505
New York, NY 10012-3327
Phone: (212)226-0955
Fax: (212)599-4743

Publications: The Jerusalem Post, International Edition (21959)

JES Publishing Corp.
6413 Congress Ave., Ste. 100
Boca Raton, FL 33487
Phone: (561)997-8683
Fax: (561)997-8909

Publications: Boca Raton Magazine (5928)

JES Publishing L.P.
240 E Morris Ave., Ste. 200
Salt Lake City, UT 84119
Phone: (801)485-5100
Fax: (801)485-5133
Free: 888-710-6195

Publications: Salt Lake Magazine (31439)

The Jessamine Journal
507 N Main St.
PO Box 8
Nicholasville, KY 40340-0008
Phone: (859)885-5381
Fax: (859)887-2966

Publications: The Jessamine Journal (12325)

The Jesuit Educational Center for Human Development
400 Washington St.
Hartford, CT 06106
Phone: (203)241-8041
Fax: (203)241-8042

Publications: Human Development (4894)

The Jesuits of the Missouri Province
4511 W Pine Blvd.
St. Louis, MO 63108-2191
Phone: (314)361-7765
Fax: (314)758-7164

Publications: Jesuit Bulletin (17449)

Jet Airtransport Exchange, Inc.
48 Wellington Rd.
Milford, CT 06460
Phone: (203)301-0255
Fax: (203)301-0250
Free: 800-9-JAXFAX

Publications: JAX FAX Travel Marketing Magazine (4955)

The Jetmore Republican
PO Box 337
Jetmore, KS 67854
Phone: (620)357-8316
Fax: (620)357-8464

Publications: The Jetmore Republican (11516)

Jevco Publishing, Inc.
2021 Union St., Ste. 1150
Montreal, QC, Canada H3A 2S9
Phone: (514)284-1732
Fax: (514)289-9257

Publications: Motocycliste (37193)

Jewett Messenger, Inc.
Hwy. 79 & Division
104 N. Main
PO Box 155
Jewett, TX 75846
Phone: (903)626-4296
Fax: (903)626-5248

Publications: The Jewett Messenger (30625)

Jewett Publishing
PO Box 586
Three Forks, MT 59752
Phone: (406)285-3414
Fax: (406)285-3413

Publications: Herald (17915)

The Jewish Advocate
15 School St.
Boston, MA 02108
Phone: (617)367-9100
Fax: (617)367-9310

Publications: The Jewish Advocate (13910)

Jewish Braille Institute of America
110 E 30th St.
New York, NY 10016
Phone: (212)889-2525
Fax: (212)689-3692
Free: 800-433-1531

Publications: Jewish Braille Review (21961)

Jewish Communal Service Association
3084 State Hwy. 27, Ste. 9
Kendall Park, NJ 08824-1657
Phone: (732)821-1871
Fax: (732)821-5335

Publications: Journal of Jewish Communal Service (19152)

Jewish Community Board of Akron
750 White Pond Dr.
Akron, OH 44320
Phone: (330)869-2424
Fax: (330)867-8498

Publications: Akron Jewish News (24572)

Jewish Community Centers Association of North America
15 E. 26th St.
New York, NY 10010-1579
Phone: (212)532-4949
Fax: (212)481-4174

Publications: JCC Circle (21958)

Jewish Community Council of Ottawa
21 Nadolny Sachs Private
Ottawa, ON, Canada K2A 1R9
Phone: (613)798-4696
Fax: (613)798-4730

Publications: Ottawa Jewish Bulletin (36266)

Jewish Exponent
2100 Arch St., 4th Fl.
Philadelphia, PA 19103
Phone: (215)832-0756
Fax: (215)832-0786

Publications: Jewish Exponent Inside (27509)

Jewish Family and Life!
PO Box 9129
Newton, MA 02464
Phone: (617)965-7700
Fax: (617)965-7772
Free: 888-ILUV-JFL

Publications: GenerationJ.com (14396) • Jewish Family & Life (14402) • JewishSports.com (14403) • JVibe.com (14404) • Sh'ma (14409) • SocialAction.com (14410)

Jewish Federation
2031 3rd Ave.
Seattle, WA 98121
Phone: (206)443-5400
Fax: (206)443-0303

Publications: The Jewish Transcript (32975)

Jewish Federation of Chicago
1 S.Franklin St.
Chicago, IL 60606-4594
Phone: (312)346-6700

Publications: JUF News (8451)

The Jewish Federation of Greater Philadelphia
226 S 16th St.
Philadelphia, PA 19102
Phone: (215)832-0500
Fax: (215)546-3957

Publications: Inside (27493)

Jewish Federation of Las Vegas
2317 Renaissance Dr.
Las Vegas, NV 89119-6191
Phone: (702)732-0556
Fax: (702)967-1082

Publications: The Jewish Reporter (18365)

Jewish Federation of Omaha
333 S 132nd St.
Omaha, NE 68154-2198
Phone: (402)334-6448
Fax: (402)334-5422

Publications: Jewish Press (18199)

Jewish Federation of South New Jersey
1301 Springdale Rd., Ste. 250
Cherry Hill, NJ 08003-2769
Phone: (609)665-6100
Fax: (609)665-0074

Publications: The Jewish Community Voice (18736)

Jewish Federation of Southern Arizona
2601 N Campbell Ave., No. 205
Tucson, AZ 85719
Phone: (520)319-1112
Fax: (520)319-1118

Publications: Arizona Jewish Post (932)

Jewish Federation of the Wyoming Valley
500 Clubhouse Rd.
Vestal, NY 13850
Phone: (607)724-2360
Fax: (607)724-2311
Free: 800-779-7896

Publications: Wyoming Valley Jewish Reporter (23489)

The Jewish Herald
1689 46th St.
Brooklyn, NY 11204
Phone: (718)972-4000

Publications: The Jewish Herald (20322)

Jewish Herald-Voice
3403 Audley St.
Houston, TX 77098-1923
Phone: (713)630-0391
Fax: (713)630-0404

Publications: Jewish Herald-Voice (30494)

Jewish Institute for National Security Affairs
1717 K St. NW, Ste. 800
Washington, DC 20006
Phone: (202)833-0020
Fax: (202)296-6452

Publications: The Journal of International Security Affairs (5600)

Jewish Ledger
2535 Brighton Henrietta Town Line Rd.
Rochester, NY 14623-2711
Phone: (585)427-2434
Fax: (585)427-8521

Publications: Jewish Ledger (23232)

The Jewish Post Ltd.
117 Hutchings St.
Winnipeg, MB, Canada R2X 2V4
Phone: (204)694-3332
Fax: (204)694-3916

Publications: The Jewish Post & News (35334)

Numbers cited after listings are entry numbers rather than page numbers.

Jewish Post of New York
262 W 38th St. Ste. 904
New York, NY 10018-9173
Phone: (212)398-1313
Fax: (212)398-3933

Publications: Jewish Post of New York (21965)

Jewish Press Group of Tampa Bay (FL), Inc.
PO Box 6970
Clearwater, FL 33758-6970
Phone: (727)535-4400
Fax: (727)530-3039

Publications: Jewish Press of Pinellas County (5987) • Jewish Press of Tampa (5988)

Jewish Press, Inc.
338 3rd Ave.
Brooklyn, NY 11215-1897
Phone: (718)330-1100
Fax: (718)935-1215
Free: 800-992-1600

Publications: Jewish Press (20323)

Jewish Russian Community Centre of Toronto
5987 Bathurst, Unit 3
Toronto, ON, Canada M2R 1V1
Phone: (416)222-7105
Fax: (416)222-7872

Publications: Exodus Magazine (36587)

The Jewish Standard
1912A Avenue Rd., Ste. E5
Toronto, ON, Canada M5M 4A1
Phone: (416)537-2696

Publications: The Jewish Standard (36630)

The Jewish Star
PO Box 130603
Birmingham, AL 35213
Phone: (205)956-3929
Fax: (205)967-1417
Free: 888-261-STAR

Publications: The Jewish Star (75)

The Jewish Veteran
1811 R St. NW
Washington, DC 20009
Phone: (202)265-6280
Fax: (202)234-5662

Publications: The Jewish Veteran (5563)

The Jewish Week
1501 Broadway
New York, NY 10036
Phone: (212)921-7822
Fax: (212)921-8420

Publications: The Jewish Week (21966)

Jewish Women International
1828 L. St. NW Ste. 250
Washington, DC 20036
Phone: (202)857-1300
Fax: (202)857-1380

Publications: Jewish Woman (5564)

The Jewish World, Inc.
3 Vatrano Rd.
Albany, NY 12205-3403
Phone: (518)459-8455
Fax: (518)459-5289

Publications: The Jewish World (19990)

The JG Press, Inc.
419 State Ave.
Emmaus, PA 18049
Phone: (610)967-4135

Publications: BioCycle (26875) • Compost Science & Utilization (26876)

Jicarilla Chieftain
PO Box 507
Dulce, NM 87528-0507
Phone: (505)759-3242
Fax: (505)759-1644

Publications: Jicarilla Chieftain (19843)

Jimmy Swaggart Ministries
PO Box 262550
Baton Rouge, LA 70826
Phone: (225)768-7000

Publications: The Evangelist (12488)

JIR Publishers
PO Box 234
Chicago Heights, IL 60411
Phone: (708)747-3717
Fax: (708)747-3657

Publications: Journal of Irreproducible Results (8667)

J.M. Dawson Institute of Church-State Studies
Baylor University
PO Box 97308
Waco, TX 76798-7308
Phone: (254)710-1510
Fax: (254)710-1571

Publications: Journal of Church and State (31249)

JM Publishing
PO Box 617000
Dallas, TX 75261-9652
Fax: (705)359-2097
Free: 888-658-BOAT

Publications: DIY Boat Owner (30151)

JMH Publishing Co.
30-31 Union Wharf
Boston, MA 02109
Phone: (617)367-4540
Fax: (617)723-6988
Free: 800-838-8808

Publications: Inventors' Digest (13908)

JMS Publishing LLC
2007 Opportunity Dr., Ste. 10
Roseville, CA 95678-3007
Phone: (916)784-3880
Fax: (916)784-3995

Publications: Before & After (2970)

J.O. Emmerich & Associates, Inc.
PO Box 2009
McComb, MS 39649
Phone: (601)684-2421
Fax: (601)684-0836
Free: 800-748-9845

Publications: Enterprise-Journal (16762) • Southwest Sun (16763)

Jo Val
PO Box 1091
Montebello, CA 90640-1091
Phone: (323)864-2036

Publications: Bayou Talk (2579)

Jobson Professional Publications Group
11 Campus Blvd., Ste. 100
Newtown Square, PA 19073
Phone: (610)492-1000
Fax: (610)492-1039

Publications: Review of Optometry (27333)

Jobson Publishing Corp.
100 Avenue of the Americas
New York, NY 10013-1678
Phone: (212)274-7000
Fax: (212)219-7835

Publications: U.S. Pharmacist (18689)

Joe Christensen, Inc.
1540 Adams St.
Lincoln, NE 68521
Phone: (402)476-7535
Fax: (402)476-3094
Free: 800-228-5030

Publications: The American University Law Review (5347) • Berkeley Women's Law Journal (1500) • California Law Review (1502) • Journal of Air Law and Commerce (30163)

Joe Tong, Inc.
44 Frid St.
PO Box 300
Hamilton, ON, Canada L8N 3G3
Phone: (905)526-3333

Publications: The Spectator (35890)

Joe Williams Communications
300 SE 4th St.
PO Box 924
Bartlesville, OK 74005
Phone: (918)336-2267
Fax: (918)336-2733
Free: 800-833-5946

Publications: Community Relations Report (25754)

Johannes Schwalm Historical Association
PO Box 416
State Line, PA 17263-0416

Publications: Johannes Schwalm Historical Association Journal (28032)

John Carroll University
20700 N. Park Blvd
University Heights, OH 44118
Phone: (216)397-4398
Fax: (216)397-1729

Publications: The Carroll News (25602)

John F. Kennedy School of Government
79 John F. Kennedy St.
Cambridge, MA 02138
Phone: (617)496-0295
Fax: (617)384-9555

Publications: Q (14092) • Q Journal (14093)

John F. Kennedy Special Warfare Center and School
Attn: AOJK-DT-DM
Fort Bragg, NC 28310
Phone: (910)432-5703
Fax: (910)432-3147

Publications: Special Warfare (23897)

John Hopkins University Press
2715 N. Charles St.
Baltimore, MD 21218
Phone: (410)516-6900
Fax: (410)516-6968
Free: 800-548-1784

Publications: Studies in English Literature, 1500-1900 (SEL) (30531)

John Jay College
555 W 57th St., Ste. 608
New York, NY 10019
Phone: (212)237-8442
Fax: (212)237-8486

Publications: Law Enforcement News (22238) • The Lex Review (22249)

The John King Network
244 Madison Ave., Ste. 393
New York, NY 10016
Phone: (212)969-8715
Fax: (212)969-8715

Publications: Casting News (21378) • Models & Talent Contacts (22346) • Models & Talent Contacts (22345) • Music Gigs & Auditions U.S.A. (22385) • Show Biz News & Model News (22737) • TV & Film Extras (22876)

John Lor Publishing
PO Box 780
Patchogue, NY 11772
Phone: (631)475-1000
Fax: (631)475-1565

Publications: Suffolk County News (23311)

John P. Kameen
636 Main St.
Forest City, PA 18421
Phone: (717)785-3800
Fax: (717)785-9840

Publications: The Forest City News (26923)

John P. Scripps Newspapers
1101 Twin View Blvd.
Redding, CA 96003
Phone: (530)243-2424
Fax: (530)225-8212

Publications: Record Searchlight (2888)

John & Suzie Galer
102 E. Main St
PO Box 300
Mount Olive, IL 62069
Phone: (217)999-3941
Fax: (217)999-5105

Publications: The Mt. Olive Herald (9246)

John W. Yopp Publications, Inc.
73 Sea Island, Ste. 21
PO Box 1147
Beaufort, SC 29902
Phone: (843)521-0239
Fax: (843)521-1398
Free: 800-849-9677

Publications: Alliance (28486) • Refrigeration (28488)

John Wiley and Sons, Inc.
111 River St.
Hoboken, NJ 07030
Phone: (201)748-8866
Fax: (201)748-8824

Publications: Advanced Functional Materials (18881) • Advances in Polymer Technology (19350) • Aggressive Behavior (18882) • Agribusiness (18883) • Air Traffic Control Quarterly (31769) • American Journal of Hematology (18884) • American Journal of Human Biology (18885) • American Journal of Industrial Medicine (18886) • American Journal of Medical Genetics (18887) • American Journal of Physical Anthropology (18888) • American Journal of Primatology (18889) • The Anatomical Record (18890) • Annals of Neurology (18891) • Applied Cognitive Psychology (18892) • Applied Organometallic Chemistry (18893) • Applied Stochastic Models in Business and Industry (18894) • Aquatic Conservation (18895) • Archaeological Prospection (18896) • Archives of Insect Biochemistry and Physiology (18897) • Arthritis Care and Research (18898) • Arthritis and Rheumatism (23808) • Banks in Insurance Report (18899) • Behavioral Interventions (18901) • Behavioral Sciences and the Law (18902) • Bioelectromagnetics (18903) • Biomedical Chromatography (18904) • Biopharmaceutics and Drug Disposition (18905) • Biopolymers (18906) • Biotechnology & Bioengineering (18907) • Catheterization and Cardiovascular Diagnosis (18908) • Cell Biochemistry and Function (18909) • Cell Motility and the Cytoskeleton (18910) • Child Abuse Review (18911) • Chirality (18912) • Circulatory Shock (18913) • Clinical Anatomy (18914) • Clinical Neuroscience (18915) • Clinical Psychology & Psychotherapy (18916) • Color Research and Application (18917) • Communications in Numerical Methods in Engineering (18918) • Communications on Pure and Applied Mathematics (18919) • Complexity (18920) • Computer Aided Surgery (17426) • Computer Applications in Engineering Education (18921) • Concepts in Magnetic Resonance (18922) • Concurrency and Computation: Practice and Experience (18923) • Cytometry (18925) • Depression and Anxiety (18926) • Developmental Dynamics (18927) • Developmental Genetics (18928) • Developmental Psychobiology (18929) • Diabetes/Metabolism Review (18930) • Diagnostic Cytopathology (18931) • Doklady Earth Sciences (69) • Drug Development Research (18932) • Dyslexia (18933) • Earth Surface Processes and Landforms (18934) • Earthquake Engineering and Structural Dynamics (18935) • Electrical Engineering in Japan (18936) • Electronics and Communications in Japan (18937) • Employment Relations Today (18938) • Engineering Design and Automation (18939) • Entomological Review (70) • Environmental and Molecular Mutagenesis (18940) • Environmental Quality Management (18941) • Environmetrics (18942) • Eurasian Soil Science (71) • European Eating Disorders Review (18943) • European Journal of Personality (18944) • European Review of Social Psychology (18945) • Evolutionary Anthropology (18946) • Federal Facilities Environmental Journal (18947) • Fire and Materials (18948) • Flavour and Fragrance Journal (18949) • Genes, Chromosomes and Cancer (18950) • Genetic Epidemiology (18951) • Geoarchaeology (18952) • Geochemistry International (72) • Geological Journal (18953) • GLIA (18954) • GPS Solutions (18955) • Head & Neck (18956) • Head & Neck Surgery (18957) • Health Care Analysis (18958) • Health Economics (18959) • Heat Transfer - Japanese Research (18960) • Hematological Oncology (18961) • Heteroatom Chemistry (18962) • Hippocampus (18963) • Human Brain Mapping (18965) • Human Factors in Ergonomics and Manufacturing (18966) • Human Mutation (18967) • Human Psychopharmacology (18968) • Human Resource Management (18969) • Hydrobiological Journal (18970) • Hydrological Processes (18971) • In Session (18972) • Infant and Child Development (18973) • Infant Mental Health Journal (12734) • International Insolvency Review (18974) • International Journal of Adaptive Control and Signal Processing (18975) • International Journal of Cancer (18976) • International Journal of Chemical Kinetics (18977) • International Journal of Circuit Theory and Applications (18978) • International Journal of Climatology (18979) • International Journal of Communication Systems (18980) • International Journal of Eating Disorders (18981) • International Journal of Energy Research (18982) • International Journal of Geriatric Psychiatry (18983) • International Journal of Health Planning and Management (18984) • International Journal of Imaging Systems and Technology (18985) • International Journal of Intelligent Systems (18986) • International Journal of Intelligent Systems in Accounting, Finance, and Management (18987) • International Journal of Network Management (18988) • International Journal for Numerical and Analytical Methods in Geomechanics (18989) • International Journal for Numerical Methods in Engineering (18990) • International Journal for Numerical Methods in Fluids (18991) • International Journal of Numerical Modelling (18992) • International Journal of Osteoarchaeology (18993) • International Journal of Population Geography (18994) • International Journal of Quantum Chemistry (18995) • International Journal of Robust and Nonlinear Control (18996) • International Journal of Satellite Communications Networking (18997) • International Journal of Short-Term Psychotherapy (18998) • International Journal of Tourism Research (18999) • International Review of Industrial and Organizational Psychology (19000) • Journal of the American Society for Information Science (19001) • Journal of Applied Econometrics (19002) • Journal of Applied Polymer Science (19003) • Journal of Applied Toxicology (19004) • Journal of Automation and Information Sciences (22005) • Journal of Behavioral Decision Making (19005) • Journal of Biochemical and Molecular Toxicology (19006) • Journal of Biomedical Materials Research (19007) • Journal of Cellular Biochemistry (19008) • Journal of Cellular Physiology (19009) • Journal of Chemical Technology and Biotechnology (19010) • Journal of Chemometrics (19011) • Journal of Clinical Apheresis (19012) • Journal of Clinical Laboratory Analysis (19013) • Journal of Clinical Ultrasound (19014) • Journal of Combinatorial Designs (19015) • Journal of Communications Technology and Electronics (19016) • Journal of Community & Applied Social Psychology (19017) • Journal of Community Psychology (27522) • The Journal of Comparative Neurology (19018) • Journal of Computational Chemistry (19019) • The Journal of Corporate Accounting and Finance (19020) • Journal of Direct and Interactive Marketing (19021) • The Journal of Experimental Zoology (19022) • Journal of Forecasting (19023) • The Journal of Futures Markets (19024) • Journal of Graph Theory (19025) • Journal of Interactive Marketing (19026) • Journal of International Development (19027) • Journal of Labelled Compounds and Radiopharmaceuticals (19028) • Journal of Mass Spectrometry (19029) • Journal of Medical Virology (19030) • Journal of Microcolumn Separations (19031) • Journal of Molecular Recognition (19032) • Journal of Morphology (19033) • Journal of Multi-Criteria Decision Analysis (19034) • Journal of Neurobiology (19035) • Journal of Neuroscience Research (19036) • Journal of Organizational Behavior (19037) • Journal of Organizational Excellence (19038) • Journal of Pathology (19039) • Journal of Peptide Science (19040) • Journal of Physical Organic Chemistry (19041) • Journal of Policy Analysis and Management (13431) • Journal of Polymer Science (19042) • Journal of Quaternary Science (19043) • Journal of Raman Spectroscopy (19044) • Journal of Research in Science Teaching (19045) • Journal of Robotic Systems (19046) • Journal of the Science of Food and Agriculture (19047) • Journal of Software Maintenance (19048) • Journal of Surgical Oncology (19049) • Journal of Thermal Analysis and Calorimetry (19050) • The Journal of Trace Elements in Experimental Medicine (19051) • Journal of Visualization and Computer Animation (19052) • Lasers in Surgery and Medicine (19053) • Luminescence (19054) • Magnetic Resonance in Chemistry (19056) • Management Report for Nonunion Organizations (19057) • Managerial and Decision Economics (19058) • Mathematical Methods in the Applied Sciences (19059) • Mechanics of Advanced Materials and Structures (27562) • Medical and Pediatric Oncology (19060) • Medicinal Research Reviews (19061) • Microscopy Research and Technique (19062) • Microsurgery (19063) • Microwave and Optical Technology Letters (19064) • Molecular Carcinogenesis (19065) • Molecular Reproduction and Development (19066) • Movement Disorders (19067) • Muscle & Nerve (19068) • Natural Gas (19069) • Naval Research Logistics (19070) • Networks (19071) • Neurology and Urodynamics (19072) • Neuroscience Research Communications (19073) • NMR in Biomedicine (19074) • Numerical Linear Algebra with Applications (19075) • Numerical Methods for Partial Differential Equations (19076) • Optimal Control Applications and Methods (19077) • Packaging Technology and Science (19078) • Paleontological Journal (85) • Pediatric Pulmonology (19079) • Permafrost and Periglacial Processes (19080) • Pest Management Science (19081) • Pharmacoepidemiology and Drug Safety (19082) • Phytochemical Analysis (19083) • Phytotherapy Research (19084) • Polymer International (19085) • Polymers for Advanced Technologies (19086) • Progress in Photovoltaics (19087) • The Prostate (19088) • Proteins: Structure, Function, and Genetics (19089) • Psycho-Oncology (19090) • Psychology and Marketing (19091) • Psychology in the Schools (20385) • Public Administration and Development (19092) • Quality and Reliability Engineering International (19093) • Radiation Oncology Investigations (19094) • Random Structures & Algorithms (19095) • Rapid Communications in Mass Spectrometry (19096) • Remediation (19097) • Research in Nursing & Health (19098) • Reviews in Medical Virology (19099) • River Research and Applications (19100) • Russian Journal of Mathematical Physics (89) • Science Education (19101) • Scientific Programming (19102) • Seminars in Surgical Oncology (19103) • Software (19104) • Software Process (19105) • Statistics in Medicine (19106) • Strategic Management Journal (19108) • Stress and Health (19109) • The Structural Design of Tall Buildings (19110) • Surface and Interface Analysis (19112) • Synapse (19113) • System Dynamics Review (19114) • Systems and Computers in Japan (19115) • Teratogenesis, Carcinogenesis and Mutagenesis (19117) • Teratology (19118) • Thunderbird International Business Review (19119) • X-Ray Spectrometry (19120) • Yeast (19121) • Zoo Biology (19122)

Johns Hopkins University
3400 N. Charles St.
Baltimore, MD 21218
Phone: (410)516-8514
Fax: (410)516-5251

Publications: The Gazette (13163) • Johns Hopkins Magazine (13174)

Johns Hopkins University Applied Physics Laboratory
11100 Johns Hopkins Rd.
Laurel, MD 20723-6099
Phone: (240)228-5625
Fax: (240)228-0343

Publications: Johns Hopkins APL Technical Digest (13613)

Johns Hopkins University Press
2715 N. Charles St.
Baltimore, MD 21218-4363
Phone: (410)516-6900
Fax: (410)516-6968

Publications: American Imago (13113) • American Journal of Mathematics (13118) • American Journal of Philology (20469) • American Quarterly (13120) • Arethusa (13126) • Bulletin of the History of Medicine (13140) • Configurations (13150) • Diacritics (13155) • Eighteenth-Century Studies (8857) • The Emily Dickinson Journal (24890) • Employee Benefit Notes (5477) • English Literary History (ELH) (13159) • Henry James Review (12217) • Human Rights Quarterly (13169) • ICSID Review (13170) • Journal of Asian American Studies (13178) • Journal of Democracy (5580) • Journal of Early Christian Studies (13187) • Journal of the History of Ideas (19333) • Journal of the History of Philosophy (13192) • Journal of Modern Greek Studies (13194) • Kennedy Institute of Ethics Journal (5623) • Late Imperial China (13207) • The Lion and the Unicorn (13209) • Literature and Medicine (13210) • Modernism/Modernity (13220) • Molecular Medicine (13221) • Philosophy and Literature (13235) • Philosophy, Psychiatry & Psychology (13236) • Portal (13237) • Postmodern Culture (13238) • Proof Texts (14603) • The Review of Higher Education (14133) • Reviews in American History (13242) • SAIS Review (13243) • Theory & Event (13253) • Wide Angle (13262) • World Politics (19478) • The Yale Journal of Criticism (13264)

Numbers cited after listings are entry numbers rather than page numbers.

Johnson C. Smith University
100 Beatties Ford Rd.
Charlotte, NC 28216
Phone: (704)378-1000
Fax: (704)378-3556

Publications: Treewell (23756)

Johnson Co.
Johnson Community College
12345 College Blvd.
Overland Park, KS 66210
Phone: (913)469-8500
Fax: (913)469-2302

Publications: Campus Ledger (11702)

Johnson County Graphic, Inc
203 E. Cherry St.
Clarksville, AR
Phone: (501)754-2005
Fax: (501)754-2098

Publications: Johnson County Graphic (1080)

Johnson Media, Inc.
PO Box 409
Granby, CO 80446
Phone: (970)726-5721
Fax: (970)726-8789

Publications: Sky-Hi News (4475) • Winter Park Manifest (4476)

Johnson Newspaper Corp.
260 Washington St.
Times Bldg.
Watertown, NY 13601
Phone: (315)782-1000
Fax: (315)782-2337
Free: 800-642-6222

Publications: Carthage Republican Tribune (20437) • Greene County News (23540) • Watertown Daily Times (23514)

Johnson Newspapers, Inc.
PO Box V-1
Felton, CA 95018
Phone: (831)335-5321
Fax: (831)335-8102

Publications: Scotts Valley Banner (3748) • The Valley Press (1913)

The Johnson Pioneer
103 N Main
PO Box 10
Johnson, KS 67855
Phone: (620)492-6244

Publications: The Johnson Pioneer (11518)

Johnson Publications, Inc.
PO Box 67
Grant, NE 69140
Phone: (308)352-4311
Fax: (308)352-4101

Publications: Grant Tribune Sentinel (18032)

Johnson Publications, Inc.
PO Box 727
Imperial, NE 69033
Phone: (308)882-4453
Fax: (308)882-5167

Publications: The Imperial Republican (18054) • Wauneta Breeze (18055)

Johnson Publishing Co., Inc.
820 S. Michigan Ave.
Chicago, IL 60605-2191
Phone: (312)322-9200
Fax: (312)322-9375

Publications: Ebony (8357) • EM: Ebony Man (8367) • Jet (8425)

The Johnsonburg Press, Inc.
517 Market St.
Johnsonburg, PA 15845
Phone: (814)965-2503
Fax: (814)965-2504

Publications: The Johnsonburg Press (27085)

Johnston Democrat
103 N Neshoba
PO Box 400
Tishomingo, OK 73460
Phone: (580)371-2356
Fax: (580)371-9648

Publications: Johnston County Capital Democrat (26100)

Johnstown Breeze
PO Box 400
Johnstown, CO 80534-0400
Phone: (970)587-4525

Publications: Johnstown Breeze (4522)

The Joint Commission Journal on Quality Improvement
1 Renaissance Blvd.
Oakbrook Terrace, IL 60181
Phone: (630)792-5453
Fax: (630)792-4453

Publications: The Joint Commission Journal on Quality Improvement (9380)

Joint Council of Teamsters, No. 37
1872 NE 162nd Ave.
Portland, OR 97230-5642
Phone: (503)251-2339
Fax: (503)251-2303

Publications: Oregon Teamster (26494)

Joliet Junior College
1215 Houbolt Ave.
Joliet, IL 60431
Phone: (815)729-9020
Fax: (815)744-5507
Free: 800-369-2200

Publications: The Blazer (9030)

Jonathan Club
545 S Figueroa St.
Los Angeles, CA 90071
Phone: (213)624-0881
Fax: (213)488-1425

Publications: Jonathan (2300)

Jonathan Scott's Cigar Smoker Magazine
PO Box 2323
Glen Ellyn, IL 60138
Phone: (630)790-3433
Fax: (630)790-3077

Publications: Chicago Cigar Smoker Magazine (8924)

Jones and Bartlett Publishers, Inc.
40 Tall Pine Dr.
Sudbury, MA 01776
Phone: (978)443-5000
Fax: (978)443-8000
Free: 800-832-0034

Publications: The Cancer Journal (14578)

The Jones County News
PO Box 1538
Gray, GA 31032
Phone: (478)986-3929
Fax: (478)986-1935

Publications: The Jones County News (7308)

Jones Group
PO Box 389
Sweetwater, TN 37874
Phone: (615)337-7101
Fax: (615)337-5932

Publications: Advocate Penny Saver (29623)

Milton W. Jones
303 N Indian Canyon
PO Box 2724
Palm Springs, CA 92262-2724
Phone: (760)325-2333
Fax: (760)325-7008

Publications: Palm Springs Life (2763)

Jones Publishing Inc.
N7450 Annstad Rd.
PO Box 5000
Iola, WI 54945
Phone: (715)445-5000
Fax: (715)445-4053
Free: 800-331-0038

Publications: The Doll Artisan (33819) • Doll Costuming (33820) • Doll Crafter (33821) • Dollmaking (33822) • DOLLS (33823) • Fired Arts & Crafts (33826) • Teddy Bear Review (33847)

The Jonesboro Sun
PO Box 1249
Jonesboro, AR 72403
Phone: (501)935-5525
Fax: (501)935-1674
Free: 800-237-5341

Publications: The Jonesboro Sun (1197)

The Joplin Globe Publishing Co.
117 E. 4th St.
Box 7
Joplin, MO 64801
Phone: (417)623-3480
Fax: (417)623-8450
Free: 800-444-8514

Publications: The Joplin Globe (17141)

Jordan Associates
PO Box 263
Colebrook, NH 03576
Phone: (603)246-8998
Fax: (603)246-9918
Free: (866)246-8998

Publications: Northern New Hampshire Magazine (18469)

Joseph F. Biddle Publishing Co.
325 Penn St.
Huntingdon, PA 16652
Phone: (814)643-4040
Fax: (814)643-0376

Publications: The Daily News (27068)

Joseph F. Biddle Publishing Co.
1067 Pennsylvania Ave
Tyrone, PA 16686
Phone: (814)684-4000
Fax: (814)684-4238
Free: 800-524-7108

Publications: The Daily Herald (28064)

The Josephites
1130 N. Calvert St.
Baltimore, MD 21202
Phone: (410)727-2233
Fax: (410)752-8571

Publications: The Josephite Harvest (13176)

Jossey-Bass Publishers
989 Market St.
San Francisco, CA 94103
Phone: (415)433-1740
Fax: (415)951-8553
Free: 888-378-2537

Publications: ASHE-ERIC Higher Education Reports (5365) • Conflict Resolution Quarterly (3344) • Human Resource Development Quarterly (3373) • National Civic Review (5669) • New Directions for Adult and Continuing Education (3396) • New Directions for Child and Adolescent Development (3397) • New Directions for Community Colleges (3398) • New Directions for Evaluation (3399) • New Directions for Higher Education (3400) • New Directions for Institutional Research (3401) • New Directions for Mental Health Services (3402) • New Directions for Student Services (10593) • Nonprofit Management and Leadership (3406) • Public Productivity & Management Review (3418)

The Jotter
303 W Ct. St.
Janesville, WI 53545-3806
Phone: (608)752-3460
Fax: (608)563-7008

Publications: The Jotter (33860)

Journal
232 N. Main St.
PO Box 696
Lake Placid, FL 33852-9624
Fax: (813)699-0331

Publications: Journal (6285)

Journal
Box 237
Forreston, IL 61030
Phone: (815)938-3320
Fax: (815)732-4238

Publications: Journal (8895)

Journal
PO Box 347
Eden Valley, MN 55329

Publications: Journal (15871)

Journal
303 N. Minnesota St.
Box 487
New Ulm, MN 56073
Phone: (507)359-2911
Fax: (507)359-7362
Free: 800-967-1760

Publications: Journal (16213)

The Journal
217 N. Main
Crosby, ND 58730
Phone: (701)965-6088

Publications: The Journal (24389)

The Journal
23 Lowellville Rd.
Struthers, OH 44471
Phone: (330)755-2155
Fax: (330)755-0320

Publications: The Journal (25551)

Journal
PO Box 970
617 Main St.
Humboldt, SK, Canada S0K 2A0
Phone: (306)682-2561
Fax: (306)682-3322

Publications: Journal (37476)

The Journal
106 W. Main St.
PO Box 369
Williamston, SC 29697
Phone: (864)847-7761
Fax: (864)847-9879

Publications: The Journal (28786)

The Journal of the Academy of Florida Trial Lawyers
218 S. Monroe St.
Tallahassee, FL 32301
Phone: (850)224-9403
Fax: (850)224-4254

Publications: The Journal of the Academy of Florida Trial Lawyers (6724)

Journal-Advocate
504 N. 3rd St.
PO Box 1272
Sterling, CO 80751
Phone: (303)522-1990
Fax: (303)522-2320

Publications: Journal-Advocate (4639)

The Journal of African Travel-Writing
PO Box 346
Chapel Hill, NC 27514
Phone: (919)929-0419

Publications: Journal of African Travel-Writing (23709)

Journal of Agricultural and Applied Economics
Conner Hall
University of Georgia
Athens, GA 30602-7509
Phone: (706)542-0747
Fax: (706)542-0739

Publications: Journal of Agricultural and Applied Economics (6943)

Journal of the Alabama Academy of Science
Ralph Brown Draughon Library
Auburn, AL 36849-5606
Phone: (205)844-9262
Fax: (205)844-4065

Publications: Journal of the Alabama Academy of Science (42)

Journal America
PO Box 459
Hewitt, NJ 07421
Phone: (973)728-8355
Fax: (973)728-7128

Publications: Journal America (18872)

Journal-Argus
48-50 Water St. S.
PO Box 1030
St. Mary's, ON, Canada N4X 1B7

Publications: Journal-Argus (36360)

Journal of Biblical Studies
Hudson College
15633 Pennsylvania
Riverview, MI 48192

Publications: Journal of Biblical Studies (15465)

The Journal of Bone and Joint Surgery
20 Pickering St.
Needham, MA 02492-3157
Phone: (781)449-9780
Fax: (781)449-9787

Publications: The Journal of Bone and Joint Surgery (14357)

Journal of Child-Care Administration
202 Cirrus Rd.
Holbrook, NY 11741-4407
Phone: (631)472-8009

Publications: Journal of Child-Care Administration (20749)

Journal of Christian Education of the African Methodist Episcopal Church
500 8th Ave. S
Nashville, TN 37203
Phone: (615)242-1420
Fax: (615)726-1866

Publications: Journal of Christian Education of the African Methodist Episcopal Church (29461)

The Journal of Commerce
33 Washington St., Fl. 13
Newark, NJ 07102-3180
Phone: (973)848-7000
Fax: (973)454-6507
Free: 800-222-0356

Publications: Journal of Commerce Import Bulletin (19356)

Journal of Commerce Limited
4285 Canada Way
Burnaby, BC, Canada V5G 1H2
Phone: (604)433-8164
Fax: (604)433-9549
Free: 888-878-2121

Publications: Journal of Commerce (34904)

Journal Communications
230 Avenida Madera
Sarasota, FL 34242
Phone: (941)349-4949
Fax: (941)346-7118
Free: 888-577-6770

Publications: Pelican Press (6662)

The Journal of Criminal Law and Criminology
Northwestern University School of Law
357 E. Chicago Ave.
Chicago, IL 60611-3008
Phone: (312)503-8547
Fax: (312)503-0132

Publications: The Journal of Criminal Law and Criminology (8435)

Journal of Dispute Resolution
University of Missouri
206 Hulston Hall
Columbia, MO 65211
Phone: (573)882-9682
Fax: (573)882-3343

Publications: Journal of Dispute Resolution (16995)

Journal of Drug Issues, Inc.
PO Box 4021
Tallahassee, FL 32303

Publications: Journal of Drug Issues (6725)

Journal of Ecumenical Studies
Temple University 022-38
Philadelphia, PA 19122

Publications: Journal of Ecumenical Studies (27525)

Journal du Emigrante
4276 boul. St. Laurent
Montreal, QC, Canada H2W 1Z3
Phone: (514)843-3863
Fax: (514)843-3863

Publications: Journal do Emigrante (37140)

The Journal-Enterprise
PO Box 190
Providence, KY 42450-0190
Phone: (270)667-2068
Fax: (270)667-9160

Publications: The Journal-Enterprise (12378)

Journal/Express Inc.
122 E Robinson
PO Box 458
Knoxville, IA 50138
Phone: (641)842-2155
Fax: (641)842-2929

Publications: Journal-Express (11019) • The Reminder (11020)

Journal of Film and Video
Dept. of Communication Studies
California State University-Los Angeles
5151 State University Dr.
Los Angeles, CA 90032-8111
Phone: (323)343-4206
Fax: (323)343-6467

Publications: Journal of Film and Video (2301)

Journal of Financial & Quantitative Analysis
University of Washington
School of Business Administration
115 Lewis Hall
PO Box 353200
Seattle, WA 98195
Phone: (206)543-4598
Fax: (206)616-1894

Publications: Journal of Financial and Quantitative Analysis (32977)

The Journal Gazette Co.
600 W Main St.
PO Box 88
Fort Wayne, IN 46801-0088
Phone: (260)461-8444
Fax: (260)461-8648

Publications: The Journal Gazette (9971)

The Journal Independent
115 N Ctr. Ave.
Piedmont, AL 36272
Phone: (205)447-2837
Fax: (205)447-2837

Publications: The Journal Independent (427)

Journal of Instructional Psychology
PO Box 8826, Spring Hill Sta.
Mobile, AL 36689-0826
Phone: (334)343-1878
Fax: (334)343-1878

Publications: Journal of Instructional Psychology (321)

Journal of International Business Studies
3240 Prospect St. NW
Washington, DC 20007
Phone: (202)944-3755
Fax: (202)944-3762

Publications: Journal of International Business Studies (5599)

Journal of the International Union of Bricklayers & Allied Craftworkers
1776 Eye St. NW
Washington, DC 20006
Phone: (202)783-3788

Publications: Journal of the International Union of Bricklayers & Allied Craftworkers (5601)

Journal of Intravenous Therapy
PO Box 67159
Los Angeles, CA 90067-0159
Phone: (310)475-5339
Fax: (310)475-5339

Publications: Journal of Intravenous Therapy (2302)

Journal La Petite-Nation
70 rue Principale
Saint-Andre-Avellin, QC, Canada J0V 1W0
Phone: (819)983-2725
Fax: (819)983-6844
Free: 800-567-6898

Publications: Journal La Petite-Nation (37325)

Journal of Law and Policy
Campus Box 1120
One Brookings Dr.
St. Louis, MO 63130-4899
Phone: (314)935-6436
Fax: (314)935-6493

Publications: Washington University Journal of Law and Policy (17529)

Journal of Law and Public Policy
PO Box 117636
Gainesville, FL 32611-7636
Phone: (352)392-4980
Fax: (352)392-3800

Publications: Journal of Law and Public Policy (6148)

Journal Le Madawaska Ltee
20, rue St-Francois
Edmundston, NB, Canada E3V 1E3
Phone: (506)735-5575
Fax: (506)735-8086

Publications: Journal Le Madawaska Ltee (35385)

Journal Le Placoteux Enr.
491, 9E Ave. D'Anjou
C.P. 490
Saint-Pascal, QC, Canada G0L 3Y0
Phone: (418)492-2706
Fax: (418)492-9706

Publications: Le Placoteux (37367)

Journal Leader
PO Box 315
Caldwell, OH 43724-0390
Phone: (740)732-2341
Fax: (740)732-7288

Publications: Journal & Noble County Leader (24723)

Journal L'Eau Vive
2604, rue Central
Regina, SK, Canada S4N 2N9
Phone: (306)347-0481
Fax: (306)565-3450
Free: 888-644-3236

Publications: Journal L'Eau Vive (37531)

Journal of Lipid Research
University of Texas
Southwestern Medical Center, Y-3206
5323 Harry Hines Blvd.
Dallas, TX 75235-9052

Publications: Journal of Lipid Research (1535)

Journal L'Itineraire
1907 Amherst St.
Montreal, QC, Canada H2L 3L7
Phone: (514)597-0238
Fax: (514)597-1544

Publications: Journal L'Itineraire (37142)

Journal L'Union Inc.
43 Notre-Dame Est, C.P. 130
Arthabaska, QC, Canada G6P 3Z4
Phone: (819)758-6211
Fax: (819)758-1632

Publications: Union (36941)

Journal Management
55 Queen St. E, Ste. 1305
Toronto, ON, Canada M5C 1R6
Phone: (416)362-7466
Fax: (416)362-8251

Publications: Canadian Independent Adjuster (36505)

Journal of the Medical Association of Georgia
1330 W. Peachtree St., No. 500
Atlanta, GA 30309
Phone: (404)881-5065
Fax: (404)881-5021
Free: 800-282-0224

Publications: Journal of the Medical Association of Georgia (7022)

Journal of Men's Studies
PO Box 32
Harriman, TN 37748-0032
Phone: (423)369-2375
Fax: (423)369-1125

Publications: Journal of Men's Studies (29216)

The Journal of Molecular Diagnostics
9650 Rockville Pike
Bethesda, MD 20814-3993
Phone: (301)634-7130
Fax: (301)634-7990

Publications: The Journal of Molecular Diagnostics (13352)

Journal de Montreal
4545, rue Frontenac
Montreal, QC, Canada H2H 2R7
Phone: (514)521-4545
Fax: (514)521-4416
Free: 800-521-4545

Publications: Le Journal de Montreal (37163)

Journal of Negro Education
Howard University
PO Box 311
Washington, DC 20059
Phone: (202)806-8120
Fax: (202)806-8434

Publications: The Journal of Negro Education (5605)

Journal of Neurosurgery
1224 W Main St., Ste. 450
Charlottesville, VA 22903
Phone: (434)924-5503
Fax: (434)924-2702

Publications: Journal of Neurosurgery (31934)

The Journal News
5120 Dixie Hwy.
Fairfield, OH 45014
Phone: (513)863-3478
Fax: (513)829-7950

Publications: Fairfield Echo (25188)

Journal-News
228 Court St. & Journal Sq.
Hamilton, OH 45011
Phone: (513)863-8200
Fax: (513)896-9489

Publications: Journal-News (25235)

The Journal-News
PO Box 8
Spencerville, OH 45887
Phone: (419)647-4981

Publications: The Journal-News (25530)

Journal News Publishing
PO Box 218
Cheney, WA 99004
Phone: (509)299-5678
Fax: (509)235-2887

Publications: Cheney Free Press (32714) • Davenport Times (32733)

The Journal Newspapers
35540 Michigan Ave.
PO Box 578
Wayne, MI 48184
Phone: (734)467-1900
Fax: (734)729-6880

Publications: The Belleville Enterprise (14806) • Canton Eagle (14853) • Eyewitness (15672) • Inkster Ledger Star (15204) • Romulus Roman (15474) • Wayne Eagle (15673) • Westland Eagle (15674)

The Journal Newspapers
6408 Edsall Rd.
Alexandria, VA 22312
Phone: (703)560-4000
Fax: (703)846-8505
Free: 800-531-1223

Publications: The Alexandria Journal (31634) • The Arlington Journal (31779) • Fairfax Journal (31671) • The Journal Friday Home Report (31696) • Prince William Journal (31724)

Journal Newspapers
4610 200th St. SW, Ste. F
Lynnwood, WA 98036-6606
Phone: (425)775-2400
Fax: (425)670-0511

Publications: The Journal—Lynnwood Edition (32823) • The Journal—North Seattle Edition (32854) • The Journal—Northgate Edition (32855)

Journal Newspapers of PA, Inc.
211 Main St.
White Haven, PA 18661
Phone: (570)443-8321

Publications: The Journal Herald (28155) • Journal of the Pocono Plateau (28156) • Journal Valley News (28157) • Mountaintop Journal (27305)

Journal of Pastoral Care Publications, Inc.
1549 Clairmont Rd., Ste. 103
Decatur, GA 30033-4611
Phone: (404)320-0195
Fax: (404)320-0849

Publications: The Journal of Pastoral Care and Counseling (23681)

Journal of Philosophy, Inc.
Columbia University
1150 Amsterdam Ave.
Mail Code 4972
New York, NY 10027
Phone: (212)666-4419
Fax: (212)932-3721

Publications: The Journal of Philosophy (22158)

Journal of the Print World, Inc.
PO Box 978
Meredith, NH 03253-0978
Phone: (603)279-6479
Fax: (603)279-1337

Publications: Journal of the Print World (18574)

Journal of Psychoeducational Assessment
505 22nd St.
Knoxville, TN 37916
Fax: (865)546-0148

Publications: Journal of Psychoeducational Assessment (32618)

Journal Publications, Inc.
PO Box 1972
Santa Rosa, CA 95402-1972
Phone: (707)568-5960
Fax: (707)568-5981

Publications: The Food & Beverage Industry (3725) • The Food & Beverage Journal (3726)

Journal Publishing
PO Box 998
Ephrata, WA 98823
Phone: (509)754-4636
Fax: (509)754-5112

Publications: Grant County Journal (32756)

The Journal Publishing Co.
211 N Sale St.
PO Box 98
Ellettsville, IN 47429
Phone: (812)876-2254
Fax: (812)876-2853

Publications: Journal (9931)

Journal Publishing Co.
PO Box 909
Tupelo, MS 38802-0909
Phone: (601)842-2611
Fax: (601)842-2233
Free: 800-264-6397

Publications: Northeast Mississippi Daily Journal (16849)

Journal Publishing Co.
Box 128
Falls City, NE 68355
Phone: (402)245-2431
Fax: (402)245-4404

Publications: Journal (18009)

Journal Publishing Co.
7 Main St.
PO Box 68
Adams, NY 13605
Phone: (315)232-4586
Fax: (315)232-4586

Publications: The Empire State Farmer (19975) •
Jefferson County Journal (19976)

Journal Publishing Co.
PO Box 26370
Oklahoma City, OK 73126-0370
Phone: (405)235-3100
Fax: (405)278-6907

Publications: The Journal Record (25969)

The Journal Publishing Co., Inc.
207 W King St.
Martinsburg, WV 25401
Phone: (304)263-8931
Fax: (304)263-8058
Free: 800-448-1895

Publications: The Journal (33380)

Journal Publishing Company Ltd.
4 Queen St.
Summerside, PE, Canada C1N 4K5
Phone: (902)436-2121
Fax: (902)436-3027
Free: 800-841-2527

Publications: Journal-Pioneer (36924)

Journal Publishing Corp.
PO Box 627
Biddeford, ME 04005
Phone: (207)282-1535
Fax: (207)282-3138
Free: 888-429-1535

Publications: Journal Tribune (12922)

Journal of Pyrotechnics Inc.
1775 Blair Rd.
Whitewater, CO 81527-9513
Phone: (970)245-0692
Fax: (970)245-0692

Publications: Journal of Pyrotechnics (4685)

Journal-Register
19 W Main St.
PO Box 10
Albion, IL 62806
Phone: (618)445-2355
Fax: (618)445-3459

Publications: Journal-Register (8003)

Journal Register Co.
111 E. Broadway
PO Box 278
Alton, IL 62002-0278
Phone: (618)462-9364
Fax: (618)463-9829
Free: 800-477-1447

Publications: The Telegraph (8009)

Journal Register Co.
50 W. State St., 12th Fl.
State St. Sq.
Trenton, NJ 08608-1298
Phone: (609)396-2200
Fax: (609)396-2292

Publications: The Daily Times (27907) • The Reporter (27159)

Journal Register Corp.
State St. Sq.
50 W. State St.
Trenton, NJ 08608-1298
Phone: (609)396-2200
Fax: (609)396-2292

Publications: Ambler Gazette (26924) • The Colonial (19655) • Glenside News (19656) • Main Line Life
(19657) • Montgomery Life (19660) • News-Herald
(28004) • North Penn Life (26931) • Souderton
Independent (28005) • The Spring-ford Reporter
(19666) • Springfield Sun (19667) • Times Chronicle
(19669) • Willow Grove Guide (19671)

Journal Register Inc.
190 Water St.
PO Box 58
Torrington, CT 06790
Phone: (860)489-3121
Fax: (860)489-6790
Free: 800-489-1450

Publications: The Dolphin (5177) • The Register
Citizen (5179)

Journal-Reporter
110 N Main St.
Leon, IA 50144
Phone: (515)446-4151
Fax: (641)446-7645

Publications: Journal-Reporter (11038)

Journal and Republican
7556 State St.
Lowville, NY 13367-0033
Phone: (315)376-3525
Fax: (315)376-4136

Publications: Journal and Republican (20968)

**Journal of Rheumatology Publishing
Company Ltd.**
920 Yonge St., Ste. 115
Toronto, ON, Canada M4W 3C7
Phone: (416)967-5155
Fax: (416)967-7556

Publications: The Journal of Rheumatology (36637)

Journal des Rivieres
55 Rue DuPont
PO Box 960
Bedford, QC, Canada J0J 1A0
Phone: (450)248-3303
Fax: (450)248-7540

Publications: Journal des Rivieres (36949)

Journal of Roman Archaeology
95 Peleg Rd.
Portsmouth, RI 02871
Phone: (401)683-1955
Fax: (401)683-1975

Publications: Journal of Roman Archaeology
(28381)

Journal St. Francois, Inc.
55, rue Jacques Cartier
Valleyfield, QC, Canada J6T 4R4
Phone: (450)371-6222
Fax: (450)371-7254

Publications: Le Journal St. Francois Inc. (37424)

Journal of Scientific Exploration
810 E. 10th St.
Lawrence, KS 66044-8897
Fax: (785)843-1274
Free: 800-627-0629

Publications: Journal of Scientific Exploration
(11558)

Journal Sentinel, Inc.
PO Box 661
Milwaukee, WI 53201
Phone: (414)224-2000
Fax: (414)224-2469

Publications: Milwaukee Journal Sentinel (34084)

Journal of Services Marketing, Inc.
108 Loma Media Rd.
Santa Barbara, CA 93103
Phone: (805)564-1313
Fax: (805)504-8800

Publications: The Journal of Services Marketing
(3648)

Journal of Sociology and Social Welfare
Western Michigan University
School of Social Work
Kalamazoo, MI 49008-5354
Phone: (616)387-3205
Fax: (616)387-3217

Publications: Journal of Sociology and Social Welfare (15241)

**Journal of the South Carolina Medical
Association**
PO Box 11188
Columbia, SC 29211
Phone: (803)798-6207
Fax: (803)772-6783
Free: 800-327-1021

Publications: Journal of the South Carolina Medical
Association (28554)

Journal of Southern History
Rice University
PO Box 1892
Houston, TX 77251-1892
Phone: (713)348-6039
Fax: (713)348-4383

Publications: Journal of Southern History (30499)

The Journal-Standard
27 S State Ave.
PO Box 330
Freeport, IL 61032
Phone: (815)232-1171
Fax: (815)232-3601
Free: 800-325-6397

Publications: Freeport Journal-Standard (8898)

Journal-Star Printing Co.
PO Box 81609
Lincoln, NE 68508-1609
Phone: (402)475-4200
Fax: (402)473-7291

Publications: Lincoln Journal (18090)

The Journal Times
212 4th St.
Racine, WI 53403-1066
Phone: (262)634-3322
Fax: (262)631-1702

Publications: The Journal Times (34273) • Pennysaver (34274)

Journal-Tribune
PO Box 690
Williamsburg, IA 52361
Phone: (319)668-1240
Fax: (319)668-9112
Free: 800-414-5506

Publications: Journal-Tribune (11062)

**Journal for Vocational Special Needs
Education**
c/o Betsy Dillon
99 Woodland Dr.
Pittsburgh, PA 15228
Phone: (412)344-7854
Fax: (412)675-9067

Publications: Journal for Vocational Special Needs
Education (27805)

Journal of the West
1531 Yuma
Manhattan, KS 66502
Phone: (785)539-1888
Fax: (785)539-2233
Free: 800-258-1232

Publications: Journal of the West (11623)

Journal-World
609 New Hampshire St.
PO Box 888
Lawrence, KS 66044
Phone: (785)843-1000
Free: 800-578-8748

Publications: Journal-World (11560)

Journeywoman
50 Prince Arthur Ave. No. 1703
Toronto, ON, Canada M5R 1B5
Phone: (416)929-7654
Fax: (416)929-1433

Publications: Journeywoman Online Magazine
(36640)

Joyce Media Inc.
PO Box 57
Acton, CA 93510-0057
Phone: (661)269-1169
Fax: (661)269-2139

Publications: Acton/Aqua Dulce News (2966)

J.R. Campbell & Associates, Inc.
5 Militia Dr.
Lexington, MA 02421
Phone: (781)862-0624
Fax: (781)863-9411

Publications: CryoGas International (14271)

J.R. O'Dwyer Company, Inc.
271 Madison Ave.
New York, NY 10016
Phone: (212)679-2471
Fax: (212)683-2750

Publications: O'Dwyer's PR Services Report (22484)

JRS Publishing
730 Wordsworth
Ferndale, MI 48220

Publications: Royal Oak Courier (15484)

J.S. Paluch Co., Inc.
3825 N. Willow Rd.
PO Box 2703
Schiller Park, IL 60176
Phone: (847)678-9300
Fax: (847)671-5715
Free: 800-621-5197

Publications: AIM Liturgy Resources (9594) • Living The Word (9595)

JSN Publishing
877 Gina Ct.
North Bellmore, NY 11710-1058
Phone: (516)292-0030
Fax: (516)481-6120
Free: 888-742-6900

Publications: Jewish Singles News/Single News & Views/Singles Style (23010)

Jstor User Services
301 E. Liberty, Ste. 310
Ann Arbor, MI 48104-2262
Phone: (734)998-9101
Fax: (734)998-9113
Free: 888-388-3574

Publications: Journal of American Folklore (14754)

Juan-Jer Corporation
PO Box 402
Butler, IN 46721-0402

Publications: The National Stock Dog (9877)

Jubilee Enterprises
PO Box 1625
Duvall, WA 98019
Phone: (206)868-4837

Publications: Jubilee (32740)

Judge Advocate General's School
TJAGSA, Attn: ADL
600 Massie Rd.
Charlottesville, VA 22903-1781
Phone: (434)972-6300

Publications: Army Lawyer (31915)

Judith Basin Press
117 Central
PO Box 507
Stanford, MT 59479
Phone: (406)566-2471
Fax: (406)566-2471

Publications: Judith Basin Press (17912)

Jukebox Collector Magazine
2545 SE 60th Ct.
Pleasant Hill, IA 50327-5099
Phone: (515)265-8324
Fax: (515)265-1980

Publications: Jukebox Collector (11160)

Julian News
PO Box 639
Julian, CA 92036-0639
Phone: (760)765-2231
Fax: (760)765-1838

Publications: Julian News (2098)

Julien's Journal
PO Box 801
Dubuque, IA 52004-0801
Phone: (563)557-1914
Fax: (563)557-9635

Publications: The Dubuque Area Magazine (10843)

Jump Cut Associates
PO Box 865
Berkeley, CA 94701
Phone: (510)658-7721
Fax: (510)658-7769

Publications: Jump Cut (1539)

The Junction Eagle
PO Box 226
Junction, TX 76849
Phone: (915)446-2610
Fax: (915)446-4025
Free: 877-547-7713

Publications: The Junction Eagle (30630)

Juniata News
2241 N 5th St.
Philadelphia, PA 19133
Phone: (215)739-8197
Fax: (215)739-9290

Publications: Juniata News (27556)

Juniata Sentinel
PO Box 127
Mifflintown, PA 17059
Phone: (717)436-8206
Fax: (717)436-5174

Publications: Juniata Sentinel (27263)

Junior Statesmen of America
60 E Third Ave., Ste. 320
San Mateo, CA 94401
Phone: (650)347-1600
Fax: (650)347-7200
Free: 800-334-5353

Publications: Junior Statement (3588)

Juno Commercial Printing
Sabanetas Industrial Park Ast 22
Mercedita, PR 00715
Phone: (787)842-5866
Fax: (787)842-5823

Publications: La Perla Del Sur (28271)

Just Minor League Hockey, LLC
8917 S. Indiana Ave.
Oklahoma City, OK 73159

Publications: Just Hockey (25970)

J.W. Eedy Publications
185 Wallace Ave. N.
PO Box 97
Listowel, ON, Canada N4W 1K8
Phone: (519)291-1660
Fax: (519)291-3771

Publications: The Listowel Banner (35975)

K Communications
6205 Redwood Ln.
Alexandria, VA 22310
Phone: (703)971-7530

Publications: INTERMISSION (5549)

K-III Family Leisure Group
4 Times Sq., 6th Fl.
New York, NY 10036
Phone: (212)462-3400
Fax: (212)367-8335

Publications: Modern Bride (22348)

K-III Magazine Corp.
1440 Broadway, Ste. 21
New York, NY 10018-2301
Phone: (212)407-9700
Fax: (212)935-4237

Publications: Seventeen (22734)

A K Peters, Ltd.
63 South Ave.
Natick, MA 01760
Phone: (508)655-9933
Fax: (508)655-5847

Publications: Experimental Mathematics (14346) • Journal of Graphics Tools (14347)

K-R Publishing
4014 56th Ave. SW
Seattle, WA 98116-3502
Phone: (206)236-2353

Publications: Grain & Feed Marketing (32969)

K State Engineer
College Of Engineering
133 Ward Hall
Manhattan, KS 66506
Phone: (785)532-6026
Fax: (785)532-6952

Publications: Kansas State Engineer (11627)

KAB Enterprises, Inc.
Box 624
Monroe, IA 50170
Phone: (641)259-2708

Publications: Monroe Legacy (11087)

Kaechele Publications, Inc.
231 Trowbridge
PO Box 189
Allegan, MI 49010
Phone: (269)673-5534
Fax: (269)673-5535

Publications: The Allegan County News (14719) • The Commercial Record (15525) • The Union Enterprise (15446)

Kaercher Publications
Box 336
Ortonville, MN 56278
Phone: (320)839-6163
Fax: (320)839-3761

Publications: The Ortonville Independent (16245)

KAL Publications, Inc.
559 S Harbor Blvd., Ste. A
Anaheim, CA 92805
Phone: (714)563-9300
Fax: (714)563-9310

Publications: The Automotive Booster of California (1401) • O & A Marketing News (1411)

Kalmbach Publishing Co.
PO Box 1612
Waukesha, WI 53187-1612
Phone: (262)796-8776
Fax: (262)796-1615
Free: 800-533-6644

Publications: Astronomy (34394) • Bead and Button (34395) • Birder's World (34396) • Classic Toy Trains Magazine (34398) • Classic Trains (34399) • Dollhouse Miniatures Magazine (34404) • FineScale Modeler (34405) • Garden Railways (34406) • Model Railroader (34407) • Model Retailer (34408) • PLAYS (34410) • Trains (34413) • The Writer Magazine (34415)

Kalmbach Publishing Co.
21027 Crossroads Cir.
PO Box 1612
Waukesha, WI 53187-1612
Phone: (262)796-8776
Fax: (262)796-0126
Free: 888-558-1544

Publications: Scale Auto Magazine (34411)

The Kalona News
419 B Ave.
PO Box 430
Kalona, IA 52247-0430
Phone: (319)656-2273
Fax: (319)656-2299
Free: 800-214-0139

Publications: The Kalona News (11010)

Kalorama Information
7200 Wisconsin Ave., Ste. 601
Bethesda, MD 20814
Phone: (301)961-6700
Fax: (301)961-6720

Publications: Genetics Abstracts (13340)

KaMai Forum
1108 Vincent Way
Glendale, CA 91205
Phone: (818)956-0551
Fax: (818)956-5322

Publications: KaMai Forum (2010)

Kampana—Campana
30-96 42nd St.
Long Island City, NY 11103-3031
Phone: (718)278-3014
Fax: (718)278-3023

Publications: Kampana—Campana (20964)

Kanabec County Times
107 Park St. S
Mora, MN 55051
Phone: (320)679-2661
Fax: (320)679-2663
Publications: Kanabec County Times (16195)

Kanadske Listy (Canadian Pages)
388 Atwater Ave.
Mississauga, ON, Canada L5G 2A3
Phone: (905)278-4116
Publications: Kanadske Listy (Canadian Pages) (36072)

The Kanawha Reporter
101 N Main St.
PO Box 190
Kanawha, IA 50447
Phone: (641)762-3994
Fax: (641)762-3994
Publications: The Kanawha Reporter (11011)

Kandiyohi Publishing
PO Box 910
Spicer, MN 56288-0910
Phone: (320)796-2945
Fax: (320)796-6375
Publications: Kandiyohi County Times (16454)

Kane Communications Inc.
10 E Athens Ave., Ste. 208
Ardmore, PA 19003
Phone: (610)734-2420
Fax: (610)734-2423
Publications: Podiatry Management Magazine (26663) • Souvenirs, Gifts, & Novelties Magazine (26664) • Tourist Attractions & Parks Magazine (26665)

Kane/DeKalb News Weeklies
322 W State St.
Sycamore, IL 60178
Phone: (847)683-2627
Fax: (815)899-4329
Publications: Hampshire Register News (8969)

Kane Republican
200 N Fraley St.
Kane, PA 16735
Phone: (814)837-6000
Fax: (814)837-2227
Publications: Kane Republican (27103)

Kaneland Publications, Inc.
123 N Main St.
Elburn, IL 60119
Phone: (630)365-6446
Fax: (630)365-2251
Publications: The Elburn Herald (8821)

Kankakee Valley Genealogical Society
Box 442
Bourbonnais, IL 60914
Publications: The-A-Ki-Ki (8095)

Kankakee Valley Publishing Co.
PO Box 298
Rensselaer, IN 47978-0298
Phone: (219)866-5111
Fax: (219)866-3775
Free: 888-809-5561
Publications: Kankakee Valley Post News (10412) • Rensselaer Republican (10414) • Shoppers News (10415)

Kansan
121-125 W 6th St.
Newton, KS 67114
Phone: (316)283-1500
Fax: (316)283-2471
Free: 888-526-7261
Publications: Prairie Advisor (11670)

Kansas Academy of Science
Kansas Geological Survey
1930 Constant Ave.
Lawrence, KS 66047
Publications: Transactions of the Kansas Academy of Science (11566)

Kansas Anthropological Association
PO Box 750962
Topeka, KS 66675-0962
Phone: (785)272-8681
Fax: (785)272-8682
Publications: The Kansas Anthropologist (11825)

Kansas Association of Insurance Agents
815 SW Topeka
Topeka, KS 66612
Phone: (785)232-0561
Fax: (785)232-6817
Publications: Kansas Insurance Agent and Broker (11829)

Kansas Bankers Association
PO Box 4407
Topeka, KS 66604-0407
Phone: (785)232-3444
Publications: The Kansas Banker (11826)

Kansas Beverage News
2416 E 37th N
Wichita, KS 67219
Phone: (316)838-6700
Fax: (316)838-6795
Publications: Kansas Beverage News (11884)

Kansas Chief
123 S Main
PO Box 369
Troy, KS 66087
Phone: (785)985-2456
Fax: (785)985-2467
Publications: Green Acres (11849) • Kansas Chief (11851)

Kansas City Artists Coalition
201 Wyandotte
Kansas City, MO 64105
Phone: (816)421-5222
Fax: (816)421-0656
Publications: Forum (17170)

Kansas City Call Inc.
PO Box 410-477
Kansas City, MO 64141
Phone: (816)842-3804
Fax: (816)842-4420
Publications: Call (17159)

Kansas City Kansan
901 N 8th St.
Kansas City, KS 66101
Phone: (913)371-4300
Fax: (913)342-8620
Publications: Kansas City Kansan (11527) • Wyandotte County Shopper (11535)

Kansas City Kansas Community College
7250 State Ave.
Kansas City, KS 66112
Phone: (913)334-1100
Fax: (913)596-9606
Publications: The Advocate (11524)

Kansas City Pitch LLC
1701 Main St.
Kansas City, MO 64108
Phone: (816)561-6061
Fax: (816)756-0502
Publications: The Pitch (17193)

Kansas City Star Co.
1729 Grand Blvd.
Kansas City, MO 64108-1413
Phone: (816)234-4141
Fax: (816)234-4267
Free: 800-726-2340
Publications: The Kansas City Star (17180)

Kansas City Wyandotte Echo
PO Box 2305
Kansas City, KS 66110
Phone: (913)573-5000
Publications: Kansas City Wyandotte Echo (11528)

Kansas Electric Cooperative, Inc.
PO Box 4267
Gage Center Sta.
Topeka, KS 66604-0267
Phone: (785)478-4554
Fax: (785)478-4852
Publications: Kansas Country Living (11827)

Kansas Farm Bureau
2627 KFB Plz.
Manhattan, KS 66502
Phone: (913)587-6000
Fax: (913)587-6914
Publications: Kansas Living (11625)

Kansas Food Dealers Association, Inc.
2809 W. 47th St.
Shawnee Mission, KS 66207
Phone: (913)384-3838
Fax: (913)384-3868
Publications: Kansas Food Dealers Bulletin (11804)

Kansas 4-H Foundation Inc.
Kansas State University
116 Umberger Hall
Manhattan, KS 66506-3417
Phone: (785)532-5881
Fax: (785)539-6963
Publications: Kansas 4-H Journal (11624)

Kansas Law Review, Inc.
University of Kansas
Green Hall, Rm. 510
Lawrence, KS 66045
Phone: (785)864-3463
Fax: (785)864-3680
Publications: University of Kansas Law Review (11568)

Kansas Livestock Association
6031 SW 37th
Topeka, KS 66614
Phone: (785)273-5115
Fax: (785)273-3399
Publications: Kansas Stockman (11831)

Kansas Motor Carriers Association
2900 S. Topeka Blvd.
PO Box 1673
Topeka, KS 66601
Phone: (785)267-1641
Fax: (785)266-6551
Publications: Mid-America Transporter (11834)

Kansas Music Educators Association
Wichita State University
School of Music
Wichita, KS 67260-0053
Phone: (316)729-7450
Fax: (316)729-6785
Publications: Kansas Music Review (11886)

Kansas Newman College
3100 McCormick St.
Wichita, KS 67213
Phone: (316)942-4291
Fax: (316)942-4483
Free: 800-736-7585
Publications: Vantage (11889)

Kansas Pharmacists Association
1020 SW Fairlawn Rd.
Topeka, KS 66604
Phone: (785)228-2327
Fax: (785)228-9147
Publications: Journal of Kansas Pharmacy (11823)

Kansas State Nurses' Association
1208 SW Tyler
Topeka, KS 66612-1735
Phone: (785)233-8638
Fax: (785)233-5222
Publications: Kansas Nurse (11830)

Kansas State University Student Publications, Inc.
Manhattan, KS 66506-7167
Publications: Kansas State Collegian (11626)

Numbers cited after listings are entry numbers rather than page numbers.

Kaplan Herald
219 N Cushing Ave.
PO Box 236
Kaplan, LA 70548
Phone: (337)643-8002
Fax: (337)643-1382

Publications: Kaplan Herald (12611)

Kapp Advertising Service, Inc.
PO Box 840
Lebanon, PA 17042
Phone: (717)273-8127
Fax: (717)273-0420
Free: 800-673-2434

Publications: Dauphin Schuylkill Area Merchandiser (27169) • Gettysburg Area Merchandiser (27170) • Greater Reading Area Merchandiser (27918) • Hanover Area Merchandiser (26975) • Hershey Area Merchandiser (27171) • Lebanon Valley Area Merchandiser (27173) • Myerstown Area Merchandiser (27174) • Northern Adams-York Area Merchandiser (27175)

Kapp Crowell Communications
Box 587
Lafayette, IN 47902
Phone: (765)471-1518
Fax: (765)471-4789

Publications: Lafayette Business Digest (10252)

Kappa Delta Pi
3707 Woodview Trace
Indianapolis, IN 46268-1158
Phone: (317)871-4900
Fax: (317)704-2323
Free: 800-284-3167

Publications: Kappa Delta Pi Record (10143)

Kappa Mu Epsilon
Div. of Mathematics and Computer Science
Emporia State University
Emporia, KS 66801-5087
Phone: (620)341-5633
Fax: (620)341-6055

Publications: The Pentagon (11431)

Kappa Publishing Group
7002 W. Butler Pl.
Ambler, PA 19002
Phone: (215)643-6385

Publications: American Astrology (26646)

Karabee Publications
107 Park St. S.
Mora, MN 55051
Phone: (320)679-2661
Fax: (320)679-2663
Free: 888-679-4860

Publications: Mora Advertisers (16196)

Karamu Association English Department
Charleston, IL 61920
Phone: (217)581-6297

Publications: Karamu (8235)

S. Karger Publishers Inc.
26 W. Avon Rd.
PO Box 529
Farmington, CT 06085
Phone: (860)675-7834
Fax: (860)675-7302
Free: 800-828-5479

Publications: Acta Haematologica (4794) • American Journal of Nephrology (4795) • Analytic Psychology (4796) • Annals of Nutrition and Metabolism (4797) • Audiology and Neuro-Otology (4798) • Biology of the Neonate (4799) • Blood Purification (4800) • Cardiology (4802) • Caries Research (4803) • Cells Tissues Organs (4804) • Cellular Physiology and Biochemistry (4805) • Cerebrovascular Diseases (4806) • Chemotherapy (4807) • Chirurgische Gastroenterologie (4808) • Community Genetics (4809) • Cytogenetics and Cell Genetics (4810) • Dementia and Geriatric Cognitive Disorders (4811) • Dermatologica Helvetica (4812) • Dermatology (4813) • Dermatology Psychosomatics (4814) • Developmental Neuroscience (4815) • Digestion (4816) • Digestive Diseases (4817) • Digestive Surgery (4818) • European Addiction Research (4819) • European Neurology (4820) • European Surgical Research (4821) • Fetal Diagnosis and Therapy (4823) • Folia Phoniatrica et Logopaedica (4824) • Folia Primatologica (4825) • Forschende Komplementarmedizin und Klassische Naturheil-kunde (4826) • Gerontology (4827) • Gynaekologisch-geburtshilfliche Rundschau (4828) • Heart-Drug (4830) • Hormone Research (4831) • Human Development (4832) • Human Heredity (4833) • International Archives of Allergy and Immunology (4834) • Intervirology (4835) • Journal of Biomedical Science (4836) • Journal of Vascular Research (4838) • Kidney and Blood Pressure Research (4839) • Medical Principles and Practice (4840) • Nephron (4841) • Neuroepidemiology (4843) • Neuroimmunomodulation (4844) • Neuropsychobiology (4845) • Neurosignals (4846) • Oncology (4847) • Onkologie (4848) • Ophthalmic Research (4849) • Ophthalmologica (4850) • ORL (4851) • Oto-Rhino-Laryngologia Nova (4852) • Pathobiology (4853) • Pediatric Neurosurgery (4854) • Pharmacology (4855) • Phonetica (4856) • Psychopathology (4857) • Psychotherapy and Psychosomatics (4858) • Respiration (4859) • Skin Pharmacology and Applied Skin Physiology (4860) • Stereotactic and Functional Neurosurgery (4861) • Tumor Biology (4862) • Urologia Internationalis (4863) • Verhaltenstherapie (4864)

Karnes Multi Media, Inc.
110 S Market
PO Box 129
Karnes City, TX 78118-0129
Phone: (830)780-3924
Fax: (830)780-3711
Free: 800-286-3924

Publications: The Countywide (30632)

Lucine Kasbarian
294 Frances St.
Teaneck, NJ 07666

Publications: TransCaucasus, A Chronology (5828)

Kauai Publishing Co.
3137 Kuhio Hwy.
PO Box 231
Lihue, HI 96766
Phone: (808)245-3681
Fax: (808)245-5286

Publications: The Garden Island (7779)

Kaufman Herald
300 N Washington
Kaufman, TX 75142
Phone: (214)932-2171
Fax: (214)932-2172

Publications: The Kaufman Herald (30633)

Kayak Magazine
7432 Alban Station Blvd., Ste. B226
Springfield, VA 22150
Phone: (703)455-3419

Publications: Kayak Magazine (32547)

KCTS Television
401 Mercer
Seattle, WA 98109
Phone: (206)728-6463
Fax: (206)443-6691

Publications: KCTS Magazine (32980)

KDC Communications, Inc.
PO Box 428
North Little Rock, AR 72115
Phone: (501)758-2571
Fax: (501)758-2597

Publications: The Times (1300)

Keach & Co., Inc.
PO Box 1192
Robstown, TX 78380-1192
Phone: (512)387-4511
Fax: (512)767-8827

Publications: Nueces County Record Star (30985)

Kearney Hub Publishing Co.
PO Box 1988
Kearney, NE 68848
Phone: (308)237-2152
Fax: (308)233-9736
Free: 800-950-6113

Publications: Kearney Hub (18059)

Keats-Shelley Association of America
Rm.226 The New York Public Library
476 Fifth Avenue
New York, NY 10018-2788

Publications: Keats-Shelley Journal (8452)

Keene Publishing Corp.
60 West St.
PO Box 546
Keene, NH 03431-0546
Phone: (603)352-1234
Fax: (603)352-0437

Publications: The Keene Sentinel (18530)

Keith County News
116 W A St.
PO Box 359
Ogallala, NE 69153
Phone: (308)284-4046
Fax: (308)284-4048
Free: 800-942-9537

Publications: Keith County News (18188)

Kelco Publishers Ltd.
1000 6th St.
Box 10
Rosthern, SK, Canada S0K 3R0
Phone: (306)232-4865
Fax: (306)232-4694

Publications: Saskatchewan Valley News (37547)

The Keller Citizen
PO Box 615
Keller, TX 76244-0615
Phone: (817)431-2231
Fax: (817)431-5534

Publications: The Keller Citizen (30635)

Keller International Publishing, LLC
150 Great Neck Rd.
Great Neck, NY 11021
Phone: (516)829-9210
Fax: (516)829-5414

Publications: Agricultura de las Americas (20684) • Asian Industrial Reporter (20686) • International Instrumentation and Controls (20690) • Petroleo Internacional (20694) • World Industrial Reporter (Reportero Industrial) (20695)

Kelly Communications
PO Box 1203
Pleasanton, CA 94566-0120
Phone: (925)846-7728
Free: 800-58K-ELLY

Publications: MotoRacing (2854) • North American Pylon (2855)

Kelowna Capital News Ltd.
2495 Enterprise Way
Kelowna, BC, Canada V1X 7K2
Phone: (250)763-3212
Fax: (250)862-5275
Free: 800-787-3308

Publications: Kelowna Capital News (34989)

Keltatim Publishing Co., Inc.
Box 130
Olathe, KS 66051
Phone: (913)764-2211
Fax: (913)764-3672

Publications: The Olathe Daily News (11683)

Kemmerer Gazette
708 J.C. Penney Dr.
PO Box 30
Kemmerer, WY 83101
Phone: (307)877-3347
Fax: (307)877-3736

Publications: Kemmerer Gazette (34541)

Kemur Publishing Company Ltd.
5220 Orbitor Dr., Unit 20
Mississauga, ON, Canada L4W 4Y8
Phone: (416)594-3772

Publications: Panthers' Plus, Canadian Grey Panthers (36695)

Ken Kenward Enterprises Ltd.
26730 56 Ave., No. 105
Langley, BC, Canada V4W 3X5
Phone: (604)607-5577
Fax: (604)607-0533
Free: 800-663-4802

Publications: Supply Post (35005)

Ken Kiser
104 W. Main
PO Box 46
Wakita, OK 73771
Phone: (580)594-2440

Publications: The Wakita Herald (26179)

Ken Robinson Publications
PO Box 399
Monroe, WA 98272

Publications: The Cascade County Billboard (32833)

Kenbridge-Victoria Dispatch
PO Box 40
Victoria, VA 23974-0040
Phone: (434)696-5550
Fax: (434)696-2958

Publications: Kenbridge-Victoria Dispatch (32576)

Kendall County Record
222 Bridge St.
PO Box J
Yorkville, IL 60560
Phone: (630)553-7034
Fax: (630)553-7085

Publications: Kendall County Record (9776)

Kendall County Record Inc.
PO Box J
PO Box 669
Yorkville, IL 60560
Phone: (630)554-8573
Fax: (630)554-7560

Publications: Ledger-Sentinel (9777)

Kendallville Publishing Co., Inc.
118 W. 9th St.
PO Box 431
Auburn, IN 46706-2225
Fax: (219)925-2625

Publications: The Evening Star (9789)

Kenilworth Media Inc.
15 Wertheim Ct., Ste. 710
Richmond Hill, ON, Canada L4B 3H7
Phone: (905)771-7333
Fax: (905)771-7336
Free: 800-409-8688

Publications: PETS Magazine (36346)

Kenly News
PO Box 39
Kenly, NC 27542
Phone: (919)284-2295
Fax: (919)284-6397

Publications: Kenly News (24020)

Kenmare News
PO Box 896
Kenmare, ND 58746
Phone: (701)385-4275
Fax: (701)385-4395

Publications: Kenmare News (24484)

Kennebec Journal
274 Western Ave.
PO Box 1052
Augusta, ME 04330-4976
Phone: (207)623-3811
Fax: (207)623-3811
Free: 800-537-5508

Publications: Kennebec Journal (12892)

Kennedy Galleries Inc.
730 Fifth Ave.
New York, NY 10019
Phone: (212)541-9600
Fax: (212)977-3833

Publications: American Art Journal (21177)

Kennedy Information, Inc.
One Pheonix Mill Ln., 5th Fl.
Peterborough, NH 03458
Phone: (603)924-1006
Fax: (603)924-4034
Free: 800-531-0007

Publications: Consulting (18622) • Shareholder Value (18629)

Kennedy Newspapers, Inc.
302-A W Main
PO Box 626
Waverly, TN 37185-0626
Phone: (931)296-7705
Fax: (931)296-5156

Publications: News-Democrat (29642) • The Shopper's Guide (29643)

Kennett Communications Inc.
116 S. Union St.
Kennett Square, PA 19348
Phone: (610)444-6590
Fax: (610)444-4931

Publications: The Kennett Paper (27106)

Kenosha News Publishing Corp.
715 58th St.
Kenosha, WI 53140
Phone: (262)657-1000
Fax: (262)657-5101
Free: 800-292-2700

Publications: Kenosha News (33872)

Kent Alumni Association
Kent State University
Williamson Alumni Center
PO Box 5190
Kent, OH 44242-0001
Fax: (216)672-4723

Publications: Kent Alumni (25275)

The Kent County Daily Times
1353 Main St.
West Warwick, RI 02893
Phone: (401)821-7400
Fax: (401)828-0810

Publications: The Kent County Daily Times (28455)

Kent County News
217 High St.
Chestertown, MD 21620
Phone: (410)778-2011
Fax: (410)778-6522

Publications: Kent County News (13405)

Kent State University
Satterfield Hall
Kent, OH 44242
Phone: (330)672-2676

Publications: Luna Negra (25276)

Kent State University Press
Lowry Hall, Rm. 307
PO Box 5190
Kent, OH 44242-0001
Phone: (330)672-7913
Fax: (330)672-3104

Publications: Civil War History (25272)

Kent State University Student Publication Policy Committee
Taylor Hall, Rm. 101
Kent, OH 44242
Phone: (330)672-2584
Fax: (330)672-4880

Publications: Daily Kent Stater (25273)

Kentucky Afield Magazine
Arnold L. Mitchell Bldg.
No.1 Game Farm Rd.
Frankfort, KY 40601
Phone: (502)564-4336
Fax: (502)564-6508
Free: 800-858-1549

Publications: Kentucky Afield (12066)

Kentucky Association of Electric Cooperatives
PO Box 32170
Louisville, KY 40232
Phone: (502)451-2430
Fax: (502)459-1611
Free: 800-595-4846

Publications: Kentucky Living (12224)

Kentucky Association of Plumbing-Heating-Cooling Contractors
1501 Durrett Ln.
Louisville, KY 40213
Phone: (502)451-5577
Fax: (502)451-5551
Free: 800-527-4229

Publications: Kentucky Plumbing-Heating-Cooling Index (12225)

Kentucky Bankers Association
Waterfront Plaza, Ste. 1000
325 W. Main St.
Louisville, KY 40202
Phone: (502)582-2453
Fax: (502)584-6390

Publications: Kentucky Banker (12223)

Kentucky Bar Association
514 W. Main St.
Frankfort, KY 40601-1883
Phone: (502)564-3795
Fax: (502)564-3225

Publications: Kentucky Bench & Bar Magazine (12068)

Kentucky Cattlemen's Association
176 Pasadena Dr.
Lexington, KY 40503
Phone: (859)278-0899
Fax: (859)260-2060

Publications: Cow Country News (12163)

Kentucky Center for Public Issues
PO Box 1664
Frankfort, KY 40602-1664
Phone: (502)227-1251
Fax: (502)227-1256

Publications: The Kentucky Journal (12071)

Kentucky Council of Teachers of English-Language Arts
Dept. of English
Bowling Green, KY 42101
Phone: (270)745-5760
Fax: (270)745-2533

Publications: Kentucky English Bulletin (11947)

Kentucky Education Association
401 Capital Ave.
Frankfort, KY 40601
Phone: (502)875-2889
Fax: (502)227-8062
Free: 800-231-4532

Publications: KEA News (12065)

The Kentucky Explorer
PO Box 227
Jackson, KY 41339
Phone: (606)666-5060
Fax: (606)666-7018

Publications: The Kentucky Explorer (12145)

Kentucky Farm Bureau Federation
9201 Bunsen Pkwy.
Louisville, KY 40250-0700
Phone: (502)495-5000
Fax: (502)495-5114

Publications: All Around Kentucky (12209)

Kentucky Historical Society
100 W Broadway
Frankfort, KY 40601-1931
Phone: (502)564-1792
Fax: (502)564-4701
Free: 877-444-7867

Publications: Kentucky Ancestors (12067) • Register of Kentucky Historical Society (12075)

Kentucky Libraries
1501 Twilight Trl.
Frankfort, KY 40601
Phone: (502)223-5322

Publications: Kentucky Libraries (12072)

Kentucky Medical Association
4965 US Hwy. 42
Louisville, KY 40222-8512
Phone: (502)426-6200
Fax: (502)426-6877

Publications: Journal of the Kentucky Medical Association (12221)

Kentucky Monthly
213 St. Clair
PO Box 559
Frankfort, KY 40602-0559
Phone: (502)227-0053
Free: 888-329-0053

Publications: The Caduceus (31920)

Kentucky Music Educators Association
1007 Granville Ln.
Russellville, KY 42276
Phone: (270)726-6427
Fax: (270)726-2291

Publications: Bluegrass Music News (12388)

Kentucky New Era
1618 E. 9th St.
PO Box 1087
Hopkinsville, KY 42240
Phone: (270)886-4444
Fax: (270)887-3222
Free: 877-463-9372

Publications: Ft. Campbell Courier (12060) • Kentucky New Era (12132)

Kentucky Pharmacists Association
1228 U.S. 127 S.
Frankfort, KY 40601
Phone: (502)227-2303
Fax: (502)227-2258

Publications: The Kentucky Pharmacist (12073)

Kentucky Press Association, Inc.
101 Consumer Ln.
Frankfort, KY 40601
Phone: (502)223-8821
Fax: (502)226-3867

Publications: The Kentucky Press (12074)

Kentucky Publishing, Inc.
701 Jefferson
Paducah, KY 42001
Phone: (502)442-7389
Fax: (502)442-5220

Publications: Carlisle County News (12338) • The Livingston Ledger (12402)

Kentucky Society of Professional Engineers
160 Democrat Dr.
Frankfort, KY 40601
Phone: (502)695-5680
Fax: (502)695-0738
Free: 800-455-5573

Publications: Kentucky Engineer (12069)

Kentville Publishing Co.
9185 Commercial St.
New Minas, NS, Canada B4N 3G1
Phone: (902)681-2121
Fax: (902)681-0830

Publications: Aurora (35556) • The Kentville Advertiser (35599) • The Mirror-Examiner (35594)

Kenyon College
104 College Dr.
Gambier, OH 43022-9623
Phone: (740)427-5208
Fax: (740)427-5417

Publications: The Kenyon Review (25212) • The Psychological Record (25213)

The Kenyon Leader
638 2nd St.
Kenyon, MN 55946
Phone: (507)789-6161
Fax: (507)789-5040

Publications: The Kenyon Leader (15983)

The Keota Eagle
Box 18
Keota, IA 52248
Phone: (641)636-2309
Fax: (641)622-2766

Publications: The Keota Eagle (11017)

Keowee Publications, Inc.
50 Short St.
PO Box 528
Walhalla, SC 29691-0538
Phone: (864)638-5856
Fax: (864)638-5857

Publications: Keowee Courier (28778)

Keowee Publications, Inc.
Main St.
PO Box 278
Westminster, SC 29693
Phone: (864)647-5404
Fax: (864)647-5405

Publications: The Westminster News (28784)

Kerala Express
18 Greenbrook Dr.
Toronto, ON, Canada M6M 2J9
Phone: (416)654-0431

Publications: Kerala Express (36641)

Kerem
3035 Porter St. NW
Washington, DC 20008
Phone: (202)364-3006

Publications: Kerem (5624)

Kerens Tribune, Inc.
PO Box 280
Kerens, TX 75144
Phone: (903)396-2261
Fax: (903)396-2728

Publications: Kerens Tribune (30637)

The Kerkhoven Banner
1003 Atlantic Ave.
PO Box 148
Kerkhoven, MN 56252
Phone: (320)264-3071
Fax: (320)264-3070

Publications: The Kerkhoven Banner (15984)

Kern County Historical Society
PO Box 141
Bakersfield, CA 93302
Phone: (661)322-4962

Publications: Historic Kern (1452)

Kernel Press, Inc.
University of Kentucky
Journalism Bldg., Rm. 026
Lexington, KY 40506-0042
Fax: (606)323-1906

Publications: Kentucky Kernel (12169)

Kerrville Daily Times
429 Jefferson St.
Kerrville, TX 78028
Phone: (830)896-7000
Fax: (830)896-1150

Publications: Kerrville Daily Times (30639)

Kerrwil Publications Ltd.
5855 Kennedy Rd.
Mississauga, ON, Canada L4Z 2G3
Phone: (905)890-1846
Fax: (905)890-3829

Publications: CAD Systems (36054) • Canadian Yachting Magazine (36060) • Electrical Business (36064) • Energy Manager (36065) • Lighting Magazine (36074) • Manufacturing Automation (36075) • Structured Cabling (36088)

Kershaw News Era
103 S Hart St.
PO Box 398
Kershaw, SC 29067
Phone: (803)475-6095
Fax: (803)475-6095

Publications: News Era (28671)

Kerwest
PO Box 336
Kerman, CA 93630
Fax: (209)846-8045

Publications: The Kerman News (2101)

KETC
3655 Olive St.
St. Louis, MO 63108
Phone: (314)512-9036
Fax: (314)512-9005
Free: 800-729-9966

Publications: KETC Guide (17465)

Kevin Hensleler
108 W. Main.
PO Box 339
Crofton, NE 68730
Phone: (402)388-4355
Fax: (402)388-4336

Publications: Crofton Journal (17995)

Kewanee Star Courier
E. Central Blvd.
Kewanee, IL 61443
Fax: (309)936-7150

Publications: Atkinson-Annawan News (9044)

Kewaskum Statesman
250 Main St.
PO Box 98
Kewaskum, WI 53040
Phone: (262)626-2626
Fax: (262)626-1382

Publications: Kewaskum Statesman (33879)

Key Communications Inc.
PO Box 569
Garrisonville, VA 22463
Phone: (540)720-5584
Fax: (540)720-5687

Publications: Architects' Guide to Glass, Metal & Glazing (32103) • Plastics Fabricating & Forming (32104) • Shelter (32105) • USGlass, Metal & Glazing (32106) • Window Film (32107)

Key Magazine, Inc.
10800 N. Norway Dr.
Mequon, WI 53092
Phone: (262)242-2077
Fax: (262)242-2745

Publications: City Guide Magazine (21423) • Frontier Country Key (26063) • Key Magazine Atlanta (7573) • Key Magazine Cincinnati (25327) • Key Magazine Colorado (4550) • Key Magazine Dallas (30165) • Key Magazine Fort Worth (30344) • Key Magazine Houston (30500) • Key Magazine Las Vegas (18369) • Key Magazine Memphis (29374) • Key Magazine Palm Springs (870) • Key Magazine Phoenix/Scottsdale (714) • Key Magazine Pittsburgh (27808) • San Diego This Week (3269) • This Week New Orleans (12757)

Key Media Ltd.
59 Front St. E.
Toronto, ON, Canada M5E 1B3
Phone: (416)364-3333
Fax: (416)861-1169

Publications: Toronto Life (36768) • Toronto Life Fashion Magazine (36769)

Key Milwaukee Magazine
10800 N. Norway Dr.
Mequon, WI 53092
Phone: (262)242-2077
Fax: (262)242-2745

Publications: Key Milwaukee Magazine (34072)

Key 3Media BCR Events, Inc.
999 Oakmont Plz. Dr.
Westmont, IL 60559
Phone: (630)986-1432
Fax: (630)323-5324
Free: 800-227-1234

Publications: Business Communications Review (9753)

Key West Inc.
PO Box 336
Kerman, CA 93630
Fax: (209)846-8045

Publications: West Side Advance (2102)

Keyboard Companion
PO Box 651
Kingston, NJ 08528-0651

Publications: Keyboard Companion (19156)

Keynoter
3636 Woodview Trace
Indianapolis, IN 46268-3196
Phone: (317)875-8755

Publications: Keynoter (10144)

KFH Publications
2511 25th Ave. E.
Seattle, WA 98112-2259
Phone: (206)547-4950
Fax: (206)545-6591
Free: 800-897-8230

Publications: Puget Sound Computer User (33008)

K.G. Saur/Reed Reference Publishing
121 Chanlon Rd.
New Providence, NJ 07974
Phone: (908)464-6800
Fax: (908)771-8784
Free: 800-521-8110

Publications: Microform Review (19348)

Khang Chien
PO Box 7826
San Jose, CA 95150
Phone: (408)363-1078
Fax: (408)363-1178

Publications: Khang Chien Magazine (3520)

Kick It Over Collective
Box 1836 Guelph
Toronto, ON, Canada N1H 7A1
Phone: (519)822-3110
Fax: (519)822-7089

Publications: Kick It Over (36642)

Kids Discover
149 Fifth Ave, 12th Fl.
New York, NY 10010
Phone: (212)677-4457

Publications: Kids Discover (22221)

Kids Monthly Publications, Inc.
1122 Rte. 22 W
Mountainside, NJ 07092
Phone: (908)232-2913
Fax: (908)317-9518

Publications: Essex County Family (19316) • Middlesex County Family (19317) • Morris County Family (19318) • Union County Family (19319)

Kilgus Publishing Co.
PO Box 929
Bamberg, SC 29003-0929
Phone: (803)245-5204
Fax: (803)245-3900

Publications: Advertizer-Herald (28479) • North Trade Journal (28480)

Killeen Daily Herald
1809 Florence Rd.
PO Box 1300
Killeen, TX 76541
Phone: (254)634-2125
Fax: (254)634-3293
Free: 800-460-1809

Publications: Killeen Daily Herald (30644)

Killian Graphics
Box 91
Chatham, NJ 07928
Phone: (973)635-5844
Fax: (973)635-5844

Publications: Animaltown News (18727)

Kilpatrick Newspapers Inc.
1210 Madrid Ave.
PO Box 637
Las Cruces, NM 88004
Phone: (505)524-8061
Fax: (505)526-4621

Publications: Las Cruces Bulletin (19872)

Kimbel Publication, Inc.
4 N. Center Pl.
Dundalk, MD 21222
Phone: (410)288-6060
Fax: (410)288-2712

Publications: Dundalk Eagle (13484)

Kincardine News
708 Queen St.
Kincardine, ON, Canada N2Z 2A3
Phone: (519)396-2963
Fax: (519)396-3790

Publications: Kincardine News (35934)

Kinder Courier-News
PO Drawer A K
Kinder, LA 70648
Phone: (337)738-5642
Fax: (337)738-5630

Publications: Kinder Courier-News (12614)

Kindred Spirits
Box 491
Kensington, PE, Canada C0B 1M0
Phone: (902)436-7329
Fax: (902)436-1787
Free: 800-665-2663

Publications: Kindred Spirit (36920)

King County Newspapers, Inc.
1627 Cole St.
PO Box 157
Enumclaw, WA 98022
Fax: (206)825-1092

Publications: Enumclaw Courier-Herald (32754)

King Publications
5697 Applebutter Hill Rd.
Coopersburg, PA 18036-9560
Phone: (610)967-3901
Fax: (610)967-2128
Free: 888-437-0259

Publications: Insights for Preachers (26806)

King Times-News
PO Box 545
King, NC 27021
Phone: (910)983-3109
Fax: (910)983-8203

Publications: Times-News (24023)

Kingfisher Times and Free Press
PO Box 209
Kingfisher, OK 73750
Phone: (405)375-3220
Fax: (405)375-3222

Publications: Kingfisher Times and Free Press (25879)

King's College
133 N Franklin St.
Box SA18
Wilkes Barre, PA 18711
Phone: (570)208-5900
Fax: (570)825-9049

Publications: The Crown (28165)

Kingsport Times News
701 Lynn Garden Dr.
PO Box 479
Kingsport, TN 37662
Phone: (423)246-8121
Fax: (423)392-1392
Free: 800-251-0328

Publications: Kingsport Times News (29260)

Kingston Publications
Box 1352
Kingston, ON, Canada K7L 5C6
Phone: (613)549-8442
Fax: (613)549-4333

Publications: Key to Kingston (35937)

Kingston This Week
677 Gardiners Rd.
Kingston, ON, Canada K7M 3Y4
Phone: (613)389-7400
Fax: (613)389-7507

Publications: Kingston This Week (35938)

The Kingston Whig Standard
6 Cataraqui St.
PO Box 2300
Kingston, ON, Canada K7L 4Z7
Phone: (613)544-5000
Fax: (613)530-4118

Publications: The Kingston Whig-Standard (35939)

Kingstree Communications, Inc.
107 E Mill St.
PO Box 574
Kingstree, SC 29556
Phone: (843)355-6397
Fax: (843)355-6530

Publications: The News (28675)

Kingsville Record
PO Box 951
Kingsville, TX 78364-0951
Phone: (361)592-6397
Fax: (361)592-1015

Publications: Kingsville Record (30647)

Kingwood Observer
1129 Kingwood Dr.
Kingwood, TX 77339-3033
Phone: (281)359-2799
Fax: (281)359-0017

Publications: Kingwood Observer (30650)

Kinmundy Express
PO Box 220
Kinmundy, IL 62854
Phone: (618)547-3111

Publications: Kinmundy Express (9049)

Kinsmen & Kinette Clubs of Canada
Box KIN
Cambridge, ON, Canada N3H 5C6
Phone: (519)653-1920
Fax: (519)650-1091
Free: 800-742-5546

Publications: Kin Mag (35726)

Kiowa County Democrat
610 E St.
PO Box 305
Snyder, OK 73566
Phone: (580)569-2684
Fax: (580)569-2640

Publications: Kiowa County Democrat (26073)

Kiowa County Press
1208 Maine St.
PO Box 248
Eads, CO 81036-0248
Phone: (719)438-5800

Publications: Kiowa County Press (4407)

Kiowa News
614 Main St.
Kiowa, KS 67070
Phone: (620)825-4229
Fax: (620)825-4229

Publications: News (11541)

Kipen Publishing Corp.
5810 W. Oklahoma Ave.
Milwaukee, WI 53219-4300
Phone: (414)543-8110
Fax: (414)543-9767

Publications: Spare Time (34103)

Kiplinger Washington Editors, Inc.
1729 H St. NW
Washington, DC 20006
Phone: (202)887-6513
Fax: (202)331-8637
Free: 800-544-0155

Publications: Kiplinger's Personal Finance Magazine (5625)

Kirkland Newspapers, Inc.
PO Box 750
Farmington, ME 04938-0750
Phone: (207)778-2075
Fax: (207)778-6970
Free: 888-778-2075

Publications: Franklin Journal and Farmington Chronicle (12960) • Livermore Falls Advertiser (12984)

Kirksville Publishing Co.
110 E McPherson
PO Box 809
Kirksville, MO 63501
Phone: (660)665-4663
Fax: (660)665-2608

Publications: Kirksville Daily Express and News (17227) • The Marketplace (17228)

Kirkwood Community College
6301 Kirkwood Blvd. SW Bldg.
PO Box 2068
Cedar Rapids, IA 52404-5260
Phone: (319)398-5444
Fax: (319)398-1021

Publications: Communique (10671)

Kitchener-Waterloo Record
225 Fairway Rd. S.
Kitchener, ON, Canada N2G 4E5
Phone: (519)894-2231

Publications: Kitchener-Waterloo Record (35961)

Kitchner-Waterloo Pennysaver
685 Wabanaki
Kitchener, ON, Canada N2C 2G3
Phone: (519)894-1400
Fax: (519)894-5401

Publications: Kitchener-Waterloo Pennysaver (35960)

The Kithara
1815 NE 102nd
Portland, OR 97220

Publications: The Kithara (26484)

Kittson County Enterprise Co.
109 S 3rd St.
Hallock, MN 56728
Phone: (218)843-2868
Fax: (218)843-2312

Publications: Kittson County Enterprise (15937)

Kiwanis International
3636 Woodview Trace
Indianapolis, IN 46268-3196
Phone: (317)875-8755
Fax: (317)879-0204
Free: 800-549-2647

Publications: Kiwanis Magazine (10145)

K.K. Printing Co.
PO Box 137
Jamesport, MO 64648
Phone: (816)684-6515
Fax: (816)684-6515

Publications: Tri-County Weekly (17119)

Klaber Publishing Corp.
1301 59th St.
Emeryville, CA 94608
Phone: (510)658-9811
Fax: (510)658-9902

Publications: The East Bay Monthly (1876)

Klamath Publishing
PO Box 788
Klamath Falls, OR 97601-0320
Phone: (541)885-4410
Fax: (541)883-4007
Free: 800-275-0788

Publications: Herald and News (26384)

Don Kleinschmidt
1453 Waterways Dr.
Ann Arbor, MI 48108
Phone: (734)439-8847
Fax: (734)769-6471

Publications: Great Lakes Pilot News (14752)

The Kline
81 Canal St.
PO Box 351
Fort Plain, NY 13339
Phone: (518)993-2321
Fax: (518)993-4919

Publications: Courier-Standard-Enterprise (20618)

Klublife Publishing Inc.
275 King St. E.
Toronto, ON, Canada M5A 1K2
Phone: (416)861-9884
Fax: (416)861-1557

Publications: Klublife (36644)

Kluwer Academic/Plenum Publishing Corp.
233 Spring St.
New York, NY 10013-1578
Phone: (212)620-8000
Fax: (212)463-0742
Free: 800-221-9369

Publications: Adsorption (21151) • Advances in Computational Mathematics (21154) • Advances in Health Sciences Education (21155) • African Archaeological Review (21163) • Agricultural and Human Values (21165) • AIDS and Behavior (21167) • Air Space and Law (21169) • Algebra and Logic (21171) • Algebras and Representation Theory

(21172) • American Journal of Community Psychology (21191) • The American Journal of Psychoanalysis (21199) • Angiogenesis (21215) • Annals of Operations Research (21218) • Annals of Software Engineering (21219) • Apoptosis (21225) • Applications of Mathematics (21227) • Applied Biochemistry and Microbiology (21228) • Applied Composite Materials (21229) • Applied Mathematics and Mechanics (21230) • Applied Psychophysiology and Biofeedback (21233) • Approximation Theory and Its Applications (21234) • Aquaculture International (21235) • Aquarium Sciences and Conservation (21236) • Aquatic Ecology (21237) • Aquatic Geochemistry (21238) • Archival Science (21244) • Archives and Museum Informatics (21246) • Archives of Sexual Behavior (21247) • Art, Antiquity and Law (21250) • Asia-Pacific Financial Markets (21261) • Asia Pacific Journal of Environmental Law (21262) • Asia-Pacific Journal on Human Rights and the Law (21263) • Asia Pacific Law Review (21264) • Astrophysics (21268) • Atomic Energy (21269) • Automation and Remote Control (21275) • Autonomous Agents and Multi-Agent Systems (21279) • Autonomous Robots (21280) • Behavior Genetics (21293) • Biochemical Genetics (29764) • Biochemistry (Moscow) (21310) • BioComplexity (21311) • BioControl (21312) • Biodiversity and Conservation (21313) • Biofeedback and Self-Regulation (21314) • Biogerontology (21315) • Biological Invasions (21317) • Biology Bulletin (21319) • Biomedical Engineering (21320) • Biomedical Microdevices (21321) • BioMetals (21323) • Biomimetics (21324) • Bioscience Reports (21325) • Biotechnology Letters (21326) • Brain and Mind (21336) • BT Technology Journal (21345) • Bulletin of Experimental Biology and Medicine (21350) • Cancer Causes and Control (21370) • Cardiac Electrophysiology Review (21374) • Catalysis Letters (21379) • Catalysis Surveys from Japan (21380) • CATTECH (21384) • Cell and Tissue Banking (21386) • Cellular and Molecular Neurobiology (21387) • Cellulose (21388) • Chemical and Petroleum Engineering (21403) • Chemistry of Heterocyclic Compounds (21405) • Chemistry of Natural Compounds (21406) • Chemistry and Technology of Fuels and Oils (21407) • Children's Literature in Education (21411) • Chromosome Research (21414) • Clinical Child and Family Psychology Review (21429) • Cluster Computing (21431) • Cognitive Therapy & Research (21436) • Colloid Journal (21440) • Combustion, Explosion, and Shock Waves (21452) • Communications in Theoretical Physics (21462) • Computational Geosciences (21469) • Computational & Mathematical Organization Theory (21470) • Computational Mathematics and Modeling (21471) • Conservation Genetics (21484) • Constraints (21486) • Continental Philosophy Review (21495) • Cosmic Research (21502) • Cybernetics (21528) • Czechoslovak Journal of Physics (21529) • Czechoslovak Mathematical Journal (21530) • Data Mining and Knowledge Discovery (21538) • Design Automation for Embedded Systems (21546) • Differential Equations (21551) • Digestive Diseases and Sciences (27780) • Doklady Biological Sciences (21563) • Doklady Chemistry (21564) • Doklady Physical Chemistry (21565) • Ecotoxicology (21583) • Education and Information Technologies (21587) • Educational Psychology Review (21589) • Empirical Software Engineering (21599) • Employee Responsibilities and Rights Journal (21603) • Entrepreneurship, Innovation and Change (21610) • Environment, Development and Sustainability (21611) • Environmental Biology of Fishes (21613) • Environmental and Ecological Statistics (21615) • Environmental Fluid Mechanics (21617) • Environmental Geochemistry and Health (21618) • Environmental Modeling & Assessment (21620) • Environmental Monitoring and Assessment (21621) • The Environmentalist (21623) • Ethical Theory and Moral Practice (21631) • Ethics and Information Technology (21632) • European Environmental Law Review (21635) • European Finance Review (21636) • European Financial Law Review (21637) • European Foreign Affairs Review (21638) • European Journal of Crime, Criminal Law and Criminal Justice (21640) • European Journal of Criminal Policy and Research (21641) • European Journal for Education Law and Policy (21642) • European Journal of Epidemiology (21643) • European Journal of Health Law (21644) • European Journal of Law and Economics (21645) • European Journal of Law Reform (21646) • European Journal of Plant Pathology (21648) • European Journal of Political Research (21649) • European Journal of Population (21650) • European Journal of Social Security (21652) • European Migration and Law (21655) • European Public Law (21656) • European Review of Private Law (21657) • Evolutionary Ecology (21660) • Experimental and Applied Acarology (21664) • Experimental Astronomy (21665) • Experi-

mental Economics (21666) • Expert Evidence (21668) • Extremes (21671) • Familial Cancer (21676) • Feminist Legal Studies (21683) • Fibre Chemistry (21688) • Fish Physiology and Biochemistry (21702) • Flow, Turbulence and Combustion (21707) • Fluid Dynamics (21708) • Formal Methods in System Design (21726) • Foundations of Chemistry (21730) • Foundations of Physics (21731) • Foundations of Physics Letters (21732) • Functional Analysis and Its Applications (21741) • Functional and Developmental Morphology (21742) • Genetic Programming and Evolvable Machines (21750) • Genetic Resources and Crop Evolution (21751) • GeoJournal (21754) • Georgian Mathematical Journal (21756) • Geotechnical and Geological Engineering (21758) • Glass and Ceramics (21765) • Glass Physics and Chemistry (21768) • Global Change & Human Health (21769) • Glycoconjugate (21773) • Group Decision and Negotiation (21781) • Health Care Management Science (21793) • Health Services and Outcomes Research Methodology (21795) • Heart Failure Reviews (21797) • High Energy Chemistry (21800) • High-Purity Substances (21801) • High Temperature (21802) • Higher-Order and Symbolic Computation (21803) • The Histochemical Journal (21804) • Human Ecology (21828) • Human Physiology (21831) • Human Relations (21832) • Human Rights Case Digest (21834) • Human Studies (21835) • Husserl Studies (21837) • Hydrotechnical Construction (21839) • Hyperfine Interactions (21840) • Indo-Iranian Journal (21864) • Industrial Laboratory (21866) • Inflammation (21868) • Information Systems Frontiers (21870) • Innovative Higher Education (21874) • Inorganic Materials (21875) • Instructional Science (21882) • Instruments and Experimental Techniques (21883) • Integrated Assessment (21885) • Integrated Pest Management (21886) • Interface Science (21890) • International Applied Mechanics (21892) • International Children's Rights Monitor (21893) • International and Comparative Corporate Law Journal (21894) • International Corporate Law Bulletin (21895) • International Environmental Agreements (21896) • International Insurance Law Journal (21898) • International Journal for the Advancement of Counseling (21899) • International Journal of Cardiovascular Imaging (21900) • The International Journal of Children's Rights (21901) • International Journal of Comparative Labour Law and Industrial Relations (21902) • International Journal of Computer Vision (21903) • International Journal of Computers for Mathematical Learning (21904) • International Journal of Fracture (21906) • International Journal of Franchising and Distribution Law (21907) • International Journal of Health Care Finance and Economics (21908) • International Journal of Infrared and Millimeter Waves (21909) • The International Journal of Marine and Coastal Law (21910) • International Journal on Minority and Group Rights (21911) • International Journal of Parallel Programming (21913) • International Journal of Primatology (21915) • International Journal of Rehabilitation and Health (21916) • International Journal for the Semiotics of Law (21917) • International Journal of Sexuality and Gender Studies (21918) • International Journal of Speech Technology (21919) • International Journal of Stress Management (21920) • International Journal of Technology and Design Education (21922) • International Journal of Theoretical Physics (21923) • International Journal of Thermophysics (21924) • International Journal of Wireless Information Networks (21925) • International Negotiation (21928) • International Peacekeeping (21929) • International Politics (21930) • International Review of Education (21935) • International Tax and Public Finance (21939) • International Urology and Nephrology (21940) • Intertax (21943) • Investigational New Drugs (21945) • Irrigation and Drainage Systems (21953) • Journal of Abnormal Child Psychology (21972) • Journal of Adult Development (21975) • Journal of Aging and Identity (21978) • Journal of Algebraic Combinatorics (21980) • Journal of Analytical Chemistry (21987) • Journal of Applied Electrochemistry (21990) • Journal of Applied Mechanics and Technical Physics (21992) • Journal of Applied Phycology (21993) • Journal of Applied Psychoanalytic Studies (21994) • Journal of Applied Spectroscopy (21995) • Journal of Aquatic Ecosystem Stress and Recovery (21996) • Journal of Archaeological Method and Theory (21997) • Journal of Archaeological Research (21998) • Journal of Assisted Reproduction and Genetics (22000) • Journal of Atmospheric Chemistry (22002) • Journal of Autism and Developmental Disorders (23710) • Journal of Automated Reasoning (22004) • Journal of Behavioral Education (22006) • Journal of Behavioral Medicine (22007) • Journal of Bioeconomics (22008) • Journal of Bioenergetics and Biomembranes (22009) • Journal of Biological Physics

Kluwer Academic/Plenum Publishing Corp.
233 Spring St., 7th Fl.
New York, NY 10013-1522
Phone: (212)620-8000
Fax: (212)463-0742
Free: 800-221-9369

Publications: International Journal of Historical Archaeology (9299)

Kluwer Academic Publishers
101 Philip Dr.
Assinippi Park
Norwell, MA 02061

Publications: Journal of Agricultural and Environmental Ethics (14441)

Kluwer Academic Publishers
233 Spring St. Fl. 7
New York, NY 10013-1522
Phone: (212)620-8000

Publications: Contemporary Family Therapy (21493) • Dreaming (21569) • International Journal of Politics, Culture, and Society (21914) • Journal of Gambling Studies (22075) • Pre- and Peri-Natal Psychology Journal (22592)

Kluwer Law International
101 Philip Dr.
Norwell, MA 02061
Fax: (617)354-8595

Publications: The EDI Law Review (14440)

KMT Communications, Inc.
PO Box 1475
Sebastopol, CA 95473-1475
Phone: (707)823-6079

Publications: KMT (3751)

KMW Publishing Company Inc.
PO Box 889
Leesburg, VA 20178
Phone: (703)777-9451
Fax: (703)771-3099
Free: 888-347-3258

Publications: The New Federalist (32186)

Knehans-Miller Publications
PO Box 1033
Warrensburg, MO 64093-1033
Phone: (660)429-1102

Publications: Probation and Parole Law Reports (17669)

Knight Publishing Corp.
8060 Melrose Ave.
Los Angeles, CA 90046
Phone: (323)653-8060
Fax: (323)655-9452

Publications: Adam Film World Guide (2197)

2472

Numbers cited after listings are entry numbers rather than page numbers.

Knight-Ridder
713 Range Ln.
PO Box 1638
Cahokia, IL 62206
Phone: (618)337-7300
Fax: (618)332-1348

Publications: The Herald (8104)

Knight-Ridder, Inc.
50 W. San Fernando St.
San Jose, CA 95113
Phone: (408)938-7700

Publications: Aberdeen American News (3508) • Akron Beacon Journal (3509) • Belleville News-Democrat (8060) • Bradenton Herald (5956) • Centre Daily Times (28018) • Charlotte Observer (3512) • Columbus Ledger-Enquirer (3513) • Detroit Free Press (14924) • Duluth News Tribune (3515) • Grand Forks Herald (3518) • Lexington Herald-Leader (3522) • The Macon Telegraph (3523) • The Miami Herald (3526) • The News-Sentinel (3528) • Philadelphia Daily News (27625) • Post-Tribune (3532) • Press-Telegram (3533) • St. Paul Pioneer Press (16409) • San Jose Mercury News (3536) • The San Luis Obispo County Telegram Tribune (3569) • Seattle Times (33023) • The State (28570) • The Sun Herald (3540) • Tallahassee Democrat (3542) • Wichita Eagle (11891)

Knights of Columbus
1 Columbus Plaza
New Haven, CT 06510-3326
Phone: (203)772-2130
Fax: (203)772-1923

Publications: Columbia (4985)

KnitMedia Inc.
74 Leonard St.
New York, NY 10013

Publications: Knotes (22225)

Knitting Guild of America
1100-H Brandywine Blvd.
PO Box 3388
Zanesville, OH 43702
Phone: (740)452-4541
Fax: (740)452-2552
Free: 800-274-6034

Publications: Cast On (25716)

Knob Noster Item
111 N Jackson
Box 188
Knob Noster, MO 65336
Phone: (660)563-3606

Publications: Knob Noster Item (17233)

Knothole Publishing
PO Box 14385
St. Paul, MN 55114-0385
Phone: (651)644-8558
Free: 888-535-9742

Publications: Elysian Fields Quarterly (16375)

Knott County Publishing Co., Inc.
PO Box 1500
Hindman, KY 41822-1500
Phone: (606)785-5134
Fax: (606)785-0107

Publications: Troublesome Creek Times (12128)

Knowledge Technology, Inc.
PO Box 30130
Phoenix, AZ 85046
Phone: (602)971-1869

Publications: PC AI (808)

The Knowles Press, Inc.
316 E Maple St.
Box 428
Hartville, OH 44632
Phone: (330)877-9345
Fax: (330)877-1364

Publications: The Hartville News (25239)

Knowles Publications, Inc.
839 Water Ave.
PO Box 469
Hillsboro, WI 54634
Phone: (608)489-2264
Fax: (608)489-2348

Publications: Hillsboro Sentry-Enterprise (33791)

Knox College
2 E. S. St.
Galesburg, IL 61401-4999
Phone: (309)341-7000

Publications: Knox Student (8905)

Knox County News
110 N Central
Drawer 9
Knox City, TX 79529-0009
Phone: (940)658-3142
Fax: (940)658-3142

Publications: Knox County News (30653)

Knox County Printing Co.
PO Box 240
Fredericktown, OH 43019
Phone: (740)694-4016
Fax: (740)694-4555

Publications: The Knox County Citizen (25201)

Knoxville News Sentinel Co.
2332 News Sentinel Dr.
Knoxville, TN 37921
Phone: (865)523-3131
Fax: (865)342-6400

Publications: The Knoxville News-Sentinel (29280)

KOCE-TV Foundation
1571, Gothard St.
Huntington Beach, CA 92647
Phone: (714)895-5623
Fax: (714)895-0852
Free: 888-246-4583

Publications: KOCE Viewers Guide (2063)

Kodaly Society of Canada
19 Grey Owl
Elmira, ON, Canada N3B 1S4

Publications: Kodaly Society of Canada, Alla Breve (35548)

Kodiak Daily Mirror
1419 Selig St.
Kodiak, AK 99615
Phone: (907)486-3227
Fax: (907)486-3088

Publications: Kodiak Daily Mirror (616)

Kokomo Perspective
209 N Main St.
Kokomo, IN 46901
Phone: (765)452-0055
Fax: (765)457-7209

Publications: Kokomo Perspective (10240)

Kokomo Tribune
300 N. Union St.
Kokomo, IN 46901
Phone: (317)459-3121
Fax: (317)456-3815
Free: 800-382-0695

Publications: Kokomo Tribune (10241)

KOLA
PO Box 44595
Barclay
Montreal, QC, Canada H3S 2W6
Phone: (514)772-0060
Fax: (514)483-7213

Publications: KOLA (37148)

Kolka and Robb
30600 Telegraph Rd., Ste. 1255
Bingham Farms, MI 48025-4531
Phone: (810)642-9580
Fax: (810)642-5290

Publications: Michigan Natural Resources Magazine (15676)

Kona Communications, Inc.
707 Lake Cook Rd., Ste. 300
Deerfield, IL 60015
Phone: (847)498-3180
Fax: (847)498-3197
Free: 800-767-5662

Publications: Successful Dealer (8729) • Truck Parts & Service (8730)

Konawa Newspapers
103 S Broadway
PO Box 157
Konawa, OK 74849-0157
Fax: (405)925-3729

Publications: Konawa Leader (25880)

Koocanusa Publications, Inc.
200, 1510 2nd St. N.
Cranbrook, BC, Canada V1C 3L2
Phone: (250)426-7253
Fax: (250)426-4125
Free: 800-663-8555

Publications: Kootenay Business Magazine (34936)

Kootenay Advertiser 1997 Ltd.
1510 2nd St. N.
Cranbrook, BC, Canada V1C 3L2
Phone: (250)489-3455
Fax: (250)489-3743
Free: 800-665-2382

Publications: The Kootenay Advertiser (34935)

E. Kootenay Newspapers Ltd.
335 Spokane St.
Kimberley, BC, Canada V1A 1Y9
Phone: (250)427-5333
Fax: (250)427-5336

Publications: The Daily Bulletin (34997)

Korea Post
9505 Berger Rd.
Columbia, MD 21046
Phone: (410)381-6633
Fax: (410)290-9335

Publications: Korea Post (13464)

The Korea Times
287 Bridgeland Ave.
Toronto, ON, Canada M6A 1Z6
Phone: (416)787-1111
Fax: (416)781-7777

Publications: The Korea Times (36646)

Korean Cultural Center
5505 Wilshire Blvd.
Los Angeles, CA 90036
Phone: (323)936-7141
Fax: (323)936-5712

Publications: Korean Culture (2308)

Korean Daily News
141 N Vermont Ave.
Los Angeles, CA 90004
Phone: (213)368-4363
Fax: (213)738-1103

Publications: Korea Times (2307)

Korean Daily Tribune, Inc.
7300 Old York Rd., No. 213
Elkins Park, PA 19027
Phone: (215)935-5000
Fax: (215)935-8888

Publications: The Dong-A Daily News (26870)

Korean Journal
5455 Buford Hwy., No. 207-A
Atlanta, GA 30340
Phone: (404)451-6946
Fax: (404)451-6956

Publications: Korean Journal (7025)

Korean Southeast News
5725 Buford Hwy., No. 211
Doraville, GA 30340
Phone: (770)454-9655
Fax: (770)454-6191

Publications: Korean Southeast News (7242)

Korean Sunday News
4950 Wilshire Blvd.
Los Angeles, CA 90010
Phone: (323)954-7500
Fax: (323)954-7503

Publications: Korean Sunday News (2309)

Korean Weekly, Inc.
5415D Backlick Rd., No. 200
Springfield, VA 22151-3915
Phone: (703)941-0899
Fax: (703)941-0966

Publications: Korean Weekly (32548)

Kosmon Publishing, Inc.
2330 Suffock Ave.
Kingman, AZ 86401-1204
Phone: (692)757-4150

Publications: Kosmon Voice 2 (730)

Kostuch Publications Ltd.
23 Lesmill Rd., Ste. 101
Don Mills, ON, Canada M3B 3P6
Phone: (416)447-0888
Fax: (416)447-5333

Publications: Foodservice and Hospitality Magazine (35773) • Hotelier (35775)

The Kourier
PO Box 37
Willow Creek, CA 95573
Phone: (916)629-2811

Publications: The Kourier (4084)

Kramer Publications
PO Box 15002
Casa Grande, AZ 85222
Phone: (520)836-7461
Fax: (520)836-0343

Publications: Coolidge Examiner (677) • Florence Reminder & Blade-Tribune (707) • Wampum Saver (670)

Krause Publications Inc.
700 E. State St.
Iola, WI 54990-0001
Phone: (715)445-2214
Fax: (715)445-4087
Free: 888-457-2873

Publications: Antique & Collectables (1843) • Antique Journal for California & Nevada (1844) • Antique Journal for the Northwest (1845) • Antique Trader Weekly (33800) • Arts & Crafts (33801) • Bank Note Reporter (33802) • Beans & Bears! (33803) • The Big Reel (33804) • Blade Magazine (33805) • Blade Trade (33806) • Card Trade (33807) • CNA (33808) • Coin Prices (33809) • Coins Magazine (33810) • Collector Magazine & Price Guide (33811) • Collector's Mart (33812) • Comics Buyer's Guide (33813) • Comics & Games Retailer (33814) • Cotton & Quail Antique Gazette (33815) • Craft Supply (33816) • Deer & Deer Hunting (33817) • Discoveries (33818) • EBay Magazine (33824) • Fantasy Sports (33825) • Frame Building News (33827) • Goldmine (33828) • Great American Crafts (33829) • Gun & Knife Show Calendar (33830) • Gun List (33831) • Memory Magic (33834) • Metal Roofing Magazine (33835) • Michael's Create! (33836) • Military Trader (33837) • Military Vehicles (33838) • Numismatic News (33839) • Old Cars Price Guide (33840) • Old Cars Weekly (33841) • Rural Builder (33842) • SCD's Price Guide Weekly (33843) • Sports Collectors Digest (33844) • Stamp Collector (33845) • Stamp Wholesaler (33846) • Toy Cars & Models (33848) • Toy Shop (33849) • Trade Fax (33850) • The Trapper & Predator Caller (33851) • Tuff Stuff (33852) • Turkey and Turkey Hunting Magazine (33853) • Whitetail Business (33855) • Wisconsin Outdoor Journal (33856) • World Coin News (33857)

Kress Chronicle
7580 Fm. 145
Kress, TX 79052
Phone: (806)684-2586
Fax: (806)684-2456

Publications: Kress Chronicle (30654)

Kriedt Enterprises, Ltd.
129 S Cortez St.
New Orleans, LA 70119
Phone: (504)482-3914
Fax: (504)482-4205

Publications: Forest Chemicals Review (12730) • Louisiana Cookin' (12738) • Sugar Journal (12754)

Jamie Krier
PO Box 23
Windsor, MO 65360
Phone: (660)647-2121
Fax: (660)647-2122

Publications: Benton County Shopper (17719)

Krsek Publishing, LP
1328 Main St.
PO Box 346
St. Helena, CA 94574
Phone: (707)963-2731
Fax: (707)963-8957

Publications: St. Helena Star (3065)

Kudzu Press
Box 1384
Forest Park, GA 30298-1384
Phone: (404)366-3177

Publications: Parnassus Literary Journal (7277)

The Kulm Messenger
Box J
Kulm, ND 58456
Phone: (701)647-2411
Fax: (701)647-2411

Publications: The Kulm Messenger (24486)

Kurdish Library
345 Park Pl.
Brooklyn, NY 11238
Phone: (718)783-7930
Fax: (718)398-4365

Publications: International Journal of Kurdish Studies (20321) • Kurdish Life (20328)

Kustom Kemps of America
26 Main St.
Cassville, MO 65625-9400
Phone: (417)847-2940
Fax: (417)847-3647

Publications: Trendsetter (16966)

Kutztown University
114 N. Student Center
Old Main Bldg.
Kutztown, PA 19530
Phone: (610)683-5630
Fax: (610)683-1377

Publications: The Keystone (27129)

KW Media Group
333 Douglas Rd. E.
Oldsmar, FL 34677
Phone: (813)433-5000
Fax: (813)433-5015
Free: 877-622-8632

Publications: Mac Design Magazine (6484)

K.W. Publishing Ltd.
211 E Georgia St., Ste. 101
Vancouver, BC, Canada V6A 1Z6
Phone: (604)688-2271
Fax: (604)688-2038

Publications: The Independent Times (35149)

Kwang Hwa Publishing Co.
6300 Wilshire Blvd., Ste. 1510A
Los Angeles, CA 90048-5217
Phone: (213)782-8770
Fax: (213)782-8761

Publications: Sinorama/Kuang Hua Hua Pao (2388)

KWIR Publications
Box 5426
Cleveland, OH 44101
Phone: (216)631-8646
Fax: (216)631-1052
Free: 800-426-5947

Publications: Gay People's Chronicle (24902)

Kylix Media Inc.
5165 Sherbrooke St. W., No. 414
Montreal, QC, Canada H4A 1T6
Phone: (514)481-5892
Fax: (514)481-9699

Publications: Wine Tidings (37238)

L & H Photojournalism
620 N Pine St.
Lancaster, PA 17603
Phone: (717)393-0943

Publications: Wine East (27146)

L & L Communications, Inc.
875 Old Roswell Rd., Ste. C-100
Roswell, GA 30076
Phone: (770)587-0501
Fax: (770)642-6501

Publications: Atlanta Tribune: The Magazine (7513)

L & L Publications, Inc.
412 S Davis St.
Box 187
Hamilton, MO 64644
Phone: (816)583-2116
Fax: (816)582-2118

Publications: Braymer Bee (16926) • Hamilton Advocate (17089)

L & M Publications, Inc.
1840 Merrick Ave.
Merrick, NY 11566-2730
Phone: (516)378-5320
Fax: (516)378-0287

Publications: Bellmore Life (21070) • The Freeport-Baldwin Leader (21071) • Merrick Life (21073) • Wantagh-Seaford Citizen (21074)

L & V Publishing Co., Inc.
411 Main
Manning, IA 51455
Phone: (712)653-3854
Fax: (712)653-9430

Publications: The Manning Monitor (11049)

The La Belle Star
PO Box 66
La Belle, MO 63447
Phone: (660)213-3848
Fax: (660)727-2475

Publications: The La Belle Star (17234)

La Canada Valley Sun
No.1061 Valley Sun Ln.
La Canada, CA 91011
Phone: (818)790-8774
Fax: (818)790-5690

Publications: La Canada Valley Sun (2107)

La Cie d'Edition Andre Paquette Inc.
52 rue Principale
Lachute, QC, Canada J8H 3A8
Phone: (450)562-2494
Fax: (450)562-1434
Free: 800-561-5738

Publications: L'Argenteuil (37029)

La Cooperative Federee de Quebec
B.P. 500 Sta. Youville
Montreal, QC, Canada H2P 2W2
Phone: (514)384-6450
Fax: (514)858-2025

Publications: Le Cooperateur Agricole (37157)

La Estrella De Puerto Rico
Paris St., No. 165
Floral Park
Hato Rey, PR 00917
Phone: (809)754-4440
Fax: (809)754-4457
Free: 800-981-4738

Publications: La Estrella De Puerto Rico (28248)

La Federation des producteurs de porcs du Quebec
555 boul. Roland-Therrien
Longueuil, QC, Canada J4H 3Y9
Phone: (450)679-0530
Fax: (450)670-4788

Publications: Porc Quebec (37057)

La Feria News
104 S Main
PO Box 999
La Feria, TX 78559
Phone: (956)797-9920
Fax: (956)797-9921

Publications: La Feria News (30655)

La Follette Press
PO Box 1261
La Follette, TN 37766
Phone: (423)562-8468
Fax: (423)566-7060

Publications: La Follette Press (29308)

L.A. Free Clinic
6043 Hollywood Blvd.
Los Angeles, CA 90028-5459
Phone: (323)462-8632
Fax: (323)462-6731

Publications: Street Scene (2406)

La Frontiere
25 Gamble W.
C.P. 490
Rouyn-Noranda, QC, Canada J9X 5C4
Phone: (819)762-4361
Fax: (819)797-2450

Publications: La Frontiere (37321)

La Gaceta Publishing Inc.
3210 E 7th Ave.
Tampa, FL 33605
Phone: (813)248-3921
Fax: (813)247-5357

Publications: La Gaceta (6773)

La Gatineau
114, de la Ferme
Maniwaki, QC, Canada J9E 3J9
Phone: (819)449-1725
Fax: (819)449-5108

Publications: La Gatineau (37065)

La Gazette Populaire
942, rue Ste-Genevieve
Trois-Rivieres, QC, Canada G9A 3X6
Phone: (819)375-4012
Fax: (819)375-9670

Publications: La Gazette Populaire (37415)

La Informacion Publishing Co., Inc.
6065 Hillcroft, Ste. 400
PO Box 740426
Houston, TX 77274
Phone: (713)272-0100
Fax: (713)272-0011

Publications: La Informacion (30501)

La Junta Democrat Publishing Co.
422 Colorado Ave.
PO Box 480
La Junta, CO 81050
Phone: (719)384-4475
Fax: (719)384-4478

Publications: La Junta Tribune-Democrat (4527)

La Leche League International Inc.
1400 N Meacham Rd.
Schaumburg, IL 60173
Phone: (847)519-7730
Fax: (847)519-0035
Free: 800-525-3243

Publications: Leaven (9585) • New Beginnings (9588)

La Ligue d'Action Nationale
425 bd de Naisonneuve O., No. 1002
Montreal, QC, Canada H3A 3G5
Phone: (514)845-8533
Fax: (514)845-8529

Publications: L'Action Nationale (37079)

La Mars Daily Sentinel
PO Box 930
Le Mars, IA 51031
Phone: (712)546-7031
Fax: (712)546-7035

Publications: The Daily Sentinel (11033)

La Moure Chronicle
Box 196
La Moure, ND 58458
Phone: (701)883-5393
Fax: (701)883-5393

Publications: La Moure Chronicle (24487)

La Noticia
6101 Idlewild Rd., Ste. 328
Charlotte, NC 28212
Phone: (704)568-6966
Fax: (704)568-8936
Free: 800-486-1204

Publications: La Noticia (23747)

La Nouvelle
43 est Notre-Dame
PO Box 130
Victoriaville, QC, Canada G6P 3Z4
Phone: (819)758-6211
Fax: (819)758-2759

Publications: La Nouvelle (37431)

La Nouvelle de Beaumont News
5021 B. 52nd Ave.
Beaumont, AB, Canada T4X 1E5
Phone: (780)929-6632
Fax: (780)929-6634

Publications: Beaumont Nouvelle (34692)

La Oferta Review
1376 N Fourth St.
San Jose, CA 95112
Phone: (408)436-7850
Fax: (408)436-7861
Free: 800-336-7850

Publications: La Oferta Review (3521)

La Pean Publications
PO Box 408
Ashland, WI 54806
Phone: (715)682-8131
Fax: (715)682-6400

Publications: Evergreen Country Shopper (33555)

La Porte Herald-Argus
701 State St.
La Porte, IN 46350
Phone: (219)362-2161
Fax: (219)362-2166

Publications: La Porte Herald-Argus (10246)

La Prensa Munoz, Inc.
1950 5th Ave., Ste. 1-3
San Diego, CA 92101-2309
Phone: (619)231-2874
Fax: (619)231-9180

Publications: La Prensa San Diego (3220)

La Prensa Publications, Inc.
616 Adams St.
Toledo, OH 43604
Phone: (419)242-7744
Fax: (419)255-7700

Publications: La Prensa Nacional (25568)

La Presse Ltee.
7, rue St-Jacques
Montreal, QC, Canada H2Y 1K9
Phone: (514)285-7272
Fax: (514)845-8129

Publications: La Presse (37150)

La Revue
231, rue Ste-Marie
C.P. 55
Terrebonne, QC, Canada J6W 3L5
Phone: (450)964-4444
Fax: (450)471-1023
Free: (514)990-7314

Publications: La Revue (37409)

La Salle University
20th St. and Olney Ave.
Campus Box 417
Philadelphia, PA 19141
Phone: (215)951-1100
Fax: (215)951-1488

Publications: The Collegian (27422) • La Salle Collegian (27558)

La Semana
2413-B E South St.
Orlando, FL 32803
Phone: (407)895-4171
Fax: (407)895-0435

Publications: La Semana (6500)

La Subasta
6120 Tarnef, Ste. 110
Houston, TX 77074
Phone: (214)951-9500

Publications: La Subasta (30502)

La Terre de chez nous
555 Blvd. Roland Therrien
Longueuil, QC, Canada J4H 3Y9
Phone: (450)679-0530
Fax: (450)679-5899

Publications: Le Producteur de Lait Quebecois (37055)

La Tribuna Hispana-USA
PO Box 186
Hempstead, NY 11550
Phone: (516)486-6457
Fax: (516)292-3972

Publications: La Tribuna Hispana-USA (20729)

La Tribune Canadienne Grecque
783S b Wiseman
Montreal, QC, Canada H3N 2N8
Phone: (514)272-6873
Fax: (514)272-3157

Publications: La Tribune Canadienne Grecque (37153)

La Tribune, Inc.
1950 Roy St.
Sherbrooke, QC, Canada J1K 2X8
Phone: (819)564-5450
Fax: (819)564-8098

Publications: La Tribune (37393)

La Vernia News
PO Box 129
La Vernia, TX 78121-0129
Phone: (830)779-3751
Fax: (830)779-3751

Publications: La Vernia News (30660)

La Vie des Arts
486, Sainte-Catherine Ouest, Ste. 400
Montreal, QC, Canada H3B 1A6
Phone: (514)282-0205
Fax: (514)282-0235

Publications: Vie Des Arts (37234)

La Voix
38-A Augusta, 2nd Fl.
Sorel, QC, Canada J3P 1A3
Phone: (514)743-8466
Fax: (514)742-8567

Publications: La Voix (37404)

La Voix Acadienne Ltee.
5 Ave Maris Stella
Summerside, PE, Canada C1N 6M9
Phone: (902)436-6005
Fax: (902)888-3976

Publications: EDT (36922) • La Voix Acadienne (36925)

La Voix du Dimanche
305, De La Gare
Matane, QC, Canada J4W 3G2
Phone: (418)562-4040
Fax: (418)562-4607

Publications: La Voix du Dimanche (37068)

La Voix Gaspesienne
305, de la Gare, Bureau 107
Matane, QC, Canada G4W 3J2
Phone: (418)562-4040
Fax: (418)562-4607

Publications: La Voix Gaspesienne (37069)

La Voix de l'Est
76 Dufferin St.
Granby, QC, Canada J2G 9L4
Phone: (450)375-4555
Fax: (450)777-7221

Publications: La Voix de l'Est (37000)

La Voz
685 W. Mission Blvd.
Pomona, CA 91766
Phone: (909)629-2292
Fax: (909)629-7644

Publications: La Voz (2860)

La Voz
948 Elizabeth Ave.
PO Box 899
Elizabeth, NJ 07201
Phone: (908)352-6654
Fax: (908)352-9735

Publications: La Voz (18790)

La Voz Hispana
159 E 116th St.
New York, NY 10029
Phone: (212)348-2100
Fax: (212)348-4469

Publications: La Voz Hispana (22228)

La Voz Publishing Corp.
6101 SW Fwy., Ste. 127
Houston, TX 77057
Phone: (713)664-4404
Fax: (713)664-4414

Publications: La Voz de Houston Newspaper (30503)

L.A. Weekly
6715 Sunset Blvd.
Los Angeles, CA 90028
Phone: (323)465-9909
Fax: (323)465-3220
Free: 800-304-4414

Publications: L.A. Weekly (2313)

The Labor Paper
400 NE Jefferson, No. 400
Peoria, IL 61603
Phone: (309)674-3148
Fax: (309)674-9714

Publications: The Labor Paper (9420)

Labor Zionist Letters Inc.
275 7th Ave., 17th Fl.
New York, NY 10001-6776
Phone: (212)675-7808

Publications: Yiddisher Kemfer (Jewish Fighter) (22949)

Laborers' International Union of North America
905 16th St. NW
Washington, DC 20006
Phone: (202)737-8320
Fax: (202)737-2754

Publications: The Laborer (5627)

Lac du Flambeau Band of Lake Superior Chippewa Indians
PO Box 67
Lac du Flambeau, WI 54538
Phone: (715)588-9272
Fax: (715)588-9408

Publications: Lac du Flambeau News (33899)

The Lacombe Globe
5022 - 50 St.
Lacombe, AB, Canada T4L 1W8
Phone: (403)782-3498
Fax: (403)782-5850

Publications: The Lacombe Globe (34791)

Ladies Auxiliary to the VFW
406 W 34 St.
Kansas City, MO 64111
Phone: (816)561-7663
Fax: (816)931-4753

Publications: VFW Auxiliary (17200)

Lafayette County Democrat
107 Spruce
PO Box 507
Lewisville, AR 71845
Phone: (501)921-5711
Fax: (501)921-5712

Publications: Lafayette County Democrat (1206)

The Lafayette Leader
514 Main St.
PO Box 908
Lafayette, IN 47902-0908
Phone: (765)429-8474
Fax: (765)742-5156

Publications: The Lafayette Leader (10253)

The Lafayette Sun
PO Box 378
Lafayette, AL 36862
Phone: (334)864-8885
Fax: (334)864-8310

Publications: Lafayette Sun (300)

Lafourche Gazette News
PO Box 1450
Larose, LA 70373
Phone: (504)693-7229
Fax: (504)693-8282
Free: 888-868-5851

Publications: The Lafourche Gazette (12656)

LaFrontera Publications, Inc.
110 N Highland Ave.
PO Drawer P
Marfa, TX 79843-0459
Phone: (915)729-4342
Fax: (915)729-4601

Publications: The Big Bend Sentinel (30764)

LaGrange Publishing Co.
State Rd. 9 S.
PO Box 148
LaGrange, IN 46761
Phone: (219)463-2166
Fax: (219)463-2734

Publications: La Grange Countian (10264) • La Grange News (10265) • La Grange Standard (10266)

Laguna Journal
Village Business Center
301 Forest Ave.
Laguna Beach, CA 92651
Phone: (949)494-7121

Publications: The Laguna Journal (2133)

Lahontan Valley News/Fallon Eagle Standard
562 N Maine St.
PO Box 1297
Fallon, NV 89406-2813
Phone: (775)423-6041
Fax: (775)423-0474
Free: 800-677-8234

Publications: Lahontan Valley News/Fallon Eagle Standard (18345)

Lake Charles American Press
PO Box 2893
Lake Charles, LA 70602
Phone: (318)433-3000
Fax: (318)494-4008

Publications: Lake Charles American Press (12637)

Lake Chelan Mirror
315 E Woodin Ave.
PO Box 249
Chelan, WA 98816
Phone: (509)682-2213

Publications: Lake Chelan Mirror (32713)

Lake City Graphic
103 N Ctr. St.
PO Box 121
Lake City, IA 51449
Phone: (712)464-3188
Fax: (712)464-3188

Publications: Lake City Graphic (11023)

Lake City Graphic
101 S. 8th St.
PO Box 469
Lake City, MN 55041
Phone: (651)345-3316
Fax: (651)345-4200

Publications: Lake City Graphic (15991) • Lake City Shopper (15992)

Lake City Reporter
126 E. Duval St.
PO Box 1709
Lake City, FL 32055-4025
Phone: (386)752-1293
Fax: (386)752-9400

Publications: Lake City Reporter (6269)

Lake Country Pennysaver
170 N Main St.
PO Box 231
Albion, NY 14411
Phone: (716)589-5641
Fax: (716)589-1239

Publications: Lake Country Pennysaver (20020)

Lake Country Publications
PO Box 200
Hartland, WI 53029
Phone: (262)367-3272
Fax: (262)367-7414

Publications: The Index (33778) • Oconomowoc Buyers Guide (33782)

Lake Country Reporter
440 Cardinal Ln.
PO Box 200
Hartland, WI 53029
Phone: (262)367-3272
Fax: (262)367-7414

Publications: Lake Country Reporter (33780)

Lake County Banner
315 Church St.
Tiptonville, TN 38079
Phone: (731)253-6666
Fax: (731)253-6667

Publications: Lake County Banner (29627)

Lake County Business Journal
PO Box 656
Willoughby, OH 44096
Phone: (440)975-9580
Fax: (440)975-9299

Publications: Lake County Business Journal (25661)

Lake County Buyer's Guide
PO Box 200
Hartland, WI 53029
Phone: (262)367-3272
Fax: (262)367-7414

Publications: Lake County Buyer's Guide (33781)

Lake County Publications
PO Box 200
Hartland, WI 53029
Phone: (262)367-3272
Fax: (262)367-7414

Publications: Sussex Sun (34364)

Lake County Publications, In.
109 Waterfront Dr.
PO Box 158
Two Harbors, MN 55616
Phone: (218)834-2141
Fax: (218)834-2144

Publications: Lake County News-Chronicle (16480)

Lake County Publishing
14913 Lake Shore Dr., Ste B
PO Box 6200
Clearlake, CA 95422
Phone: (707)994-6444
Fax: (707)994-5335

Publications: Clear Lake Observer-American (1728)

Lake County Publishing
PO Box 849
Lakeport, CA 95453
Phone: (707)263-5636
Fax: (707)263-0600

Publications: Lake County Record-Bee (2143)

Lake County Reporter
Carroll College
100 N. East Ave.
Waukesha, WI 53186
Fax: (414)524-7139

Publications: The Perspective (34409)

Lake Eusaula Pub
PO Box 689
Eufaula, OK 74432
Phone: (918)689-2191
Fax: (918)689-2377

Publications: Indian Journal (25829)

Lake Front Publications
PO Box K
Port Clinton, OH 43452
Phone: (419)734-1280

Publications: Lake Front News (25481)

Lake Geneva Printing and Publishing
315 Broad St.
PO Box 937
Lake Geneva, WI 53147
Phone: (262)248-8096
Fax: (262)248-4476

Publications: Lake Geneva Regional News (33903) • Resorter (33905)

Lake Michigan College
2755 E Napier Ave.
Benton Harbor, MI 49022-1899
Phone: (269)927-3571
Fax: (269)927-4491

Publications: Lake Michigan Journal (14808)

Lake Mills Graphic
204 N Mill St.
Box 127
Lake Mills, IA 50450
Phone: (641)592-4222
Fax: (641)592-6397

Publications: Graphic (11024)

The Lake Mills Leader
320 N Main St.
PO Box 310
Lake Mills, WI 53551
Phone: (920)648-2334
Fax: (920)648-8187

Publications: The Lake Mills Leader (33906)

The Lake News
75 South Shore Rd.
PO Box 962
Lake Cowichan, BC, Canada V0R 2G0
Phone: (250)749-3143
Fax: (250)749-3143

Publications: The Lake News (35002)

Lake Orion Review
30 N Broadway
Lake Orion, MI 48362
Phone: (248)693-8331
Fax: (248)628-5712

Publications: Lake Orion Review (15271)

Lake Region Life
115 S 3rd St.
Waterville, MN 56096
Phone: (507)362-4495
Fax: (507)362-4458

Publications: Lake Region Life (16504)

Lake Region Times
513 Main
PO Box 128
Madison Lake, MN 56063-0128
Phone: (507)243-3031
Fax: (507)243-3122

Publications: Lake Region Times (16022)

Lake Shore Community Publishing Ltd.
PO Box 1057
145 Railway St.
Nipigon, ON, Canada P0T 2J0
Phone: (807)887-3583
Fax: (807)887-3720

Publications: Nipigon-Red Rock Gazette (36115)

Lake Street Publishing Co.
330 N Summit St.
Crescent City, FL 32112
Phone: (386)698-1644
Fax: (386)698-1994

Publications: Courier Journal (6022)

The Lake Sun Leader
450 N. Highway 5
Camdenton, MO 65020
Phone: (573)346-2132
Fax: (573)346-4508
Free: 800-373-0287

Publications: The Lake Sun Leader (16937)

Lake Superior Port Cities Inc.
PO Box 16417
Duluth, MN 55816-0417
Phone: (218)722-5002
Fax: (218)722-4096
Free: 888-244-5253

Publications: Lake Superior Magazine (15839)

Lake Union Conference of Seventh-day Adventists
PO Box C
Berrien Springs, MI 49103
Phone: (269)473-8242
Fax: (269)473-8209

Publications: Lake Union Herald (14813)

Lake View Resort and Green Saver
Box 470
Lake View, IA 51450
Phone: (712)657-8588
Fax: (712)657-2495

Publications: Lake View Resort and Green Saver (11026)

Lake Wales Highlander
PO Box 1440
Winter Haven, FL 33882-1440
Phone: (863)294-1100

Publications: Lake Wales Highlander (6868) • Shopper (6871)

The Lake Wales News, Inc.
140 E. Stuart Ave.
Lake Wales, FL 33853
Phone: (863)676-3467
Fax: (863)676-3468

Publications: The Lake Wales News (6286)

Lake Worth Herald Press
130 S H St.
Lake Worth, FL 33460
Phone: (561)585-9387
Fax: (561)585-5434

Publications: Lake Worth Herald (6288)

Lakefield Standard
403 Main
PO Box 249
Lakefield, MN 56150
Phone: (507)662-5555
Fax: (507)662-6770

Publications: Lakefield Standard (15993)

Lakehead University
Bookstore
955 Oliver Rd.
Thunder Bay, ON, Canada P7B 5E1
Phone: (807)343-8110
Fax: (807)343-8023

Publications: Alices (36436)

Lakehead University Student Union
955 Oliver Rd.
Thunder Bay, ON, Canada P7B 5E6
Phone: (807)344-6911
Fax: (807)343-8803

Publications: Argus (36437)

Lakeland Center for Creative Arts
115 N. Kentucky Ave.
Lakeland, FL 33801
Phone: (941)680-2787

Publications: Onionhead Literary Quarterly (6290)

Lakeland Media, Inc.
30 S. Whitney St.
PO Box 268
Grayslake, IL 60030-0268
Phone: (847)223-8161
Fax: (847)223-8810

Publications: Antioch News (8016) • Fox Lake Press (8954) • Grayslake Times (8956) • Gurnee Press (8966) • Lake Villa Record (9064) • Libertyville News (9080) • Lindenhurst News (9107) • Mundelein News (8958) • Round Lake News (9557) • Wadsworth News (9733) • Wauconda Leader (9743)

Lakeland Times
Box 790
Minocqua, WI 54548
Phone: (715)356-5236
Fax: (715)358-2121

Publications: Lakeland Times (34146)

The Laker
PO Box 271880
Tampa, FL 33688-1880
Phone: (813)963-1918
Fax: (813)963-3910
Free: 888-320-6397

Publications: The Laker (6774)

Lakes Area Advertiser, Inc.
236 Rte. 173
Antioch, IL 60002
Phone: (847)395-7500
Fax: (847)395-2814

Publications: The Advertiser (8015) • Lakes Area Advertiser (8017)

The Lakeshore Advance
58 Ontario St. N.
PO Box 1195
Grand Bend, ON, Canada N0M 1T0
Phone: (519)238-5383
Fax: (519)238-5131

Publications: The Lakeshore Advance (35854)

Lakeshore Newspapers, Inc.
N. 19 W 6733 Commerce Ct.
PO Box 47
Cedarburg, WI 53012
Phone: (262)375-5100
Fax: (262)375-5107

Publications: News Graphic (33619) • The Sunday Post-Ozaukee County (33620)

Lakeside Leader
103 3rd Ave. NE
PO Box 849
Slave Lake, AB, Canada T0G 2A0
Phone: (780)849-4380
Fax: (780)849-3903

Publications: Lakeside Leader (34848)

The Lakeville Journal Co., LLC
PO Box 1688
Lakeville, CT 06039-1688
Phone: (860)435-9873
Fax: (860)435-0146

Publications: Lakeville Journal (4921)

Lakeway Publishers, Inc.
PO Box 625
Morristown, TN 37815-0625
Phone: (423)581-5630
Fax: (423)581-3061

Publications: Citizen Tribune (29418) • Elk Valley Times (29188) • Grundy County Herald (29628) • The Tullahoma News and Guardian (29633)

Lakota American
PO Box 507
Lakota, ND 58344
Phone: (701)247-2482
Fax: (701)247-2482

Publications: Lakota American (24488)

Lally Communications Inc.
160 Birch Hill Rd.
PO Box 468
Locust Valley, NY 11560
Phone: (516)759-2639
Fax: (516)671-7442

Publications: Leader (20959)

Lamar Daily News
310 S 5th St.
PO Box 1217
Lamar, CO 81052
Phone: (719)336-2266
Fax: (719)336-2526

Publications: The Tri State Trader (4538)

The Lamar Democrat
PO Box 587
Vernon, AL 35592
Phone: (205)695-7029
Fax: (205)695-9501

Publications: The Lamar Democrat (512)

Lamar Democrat
900 N. Gulf
PO Box 458
Lamar, MO 64759
Phone: (417)682-5529
Fax: (417)682-5595

Publications: Lamar Democrat (17235)

Lamar Leader
55071 Highway 17
PO Box 988
Sulligent, AL 35586
Phone: (205)698-8148
Fax: (205)698-8146
Free: 800-269-0234

Publications: Lamar Leader (460)

Lamar Publishing Co.
4 Willow Point, Ste. 15
Hattiesburg, MS 39402-1150
Publications: Lamar County News (16662)

Lamar University
PO Box 10055, University Sta.
Beaumont, TX 77710
Phone: (409)880-8102
Fax: (409)880-8735
Publications: University Press (29900)

Lamaze International
2025 M St., NW, Ste. 800
Washington, DC 20036-4397
Phone: (202)367-1128
Fax: (202)367-2128
Free: 800-368-4404
Publications: The Journal of Perinatal Education (32442)

Lamb County Publishing Company Inc.
PO Box 310
Littlefield, TX 79339-0310
Phone: (806)385-4481
Fax: (806)385-4640
Publications: Lamb County Leader-News (30697)

Lambda Literary Foundation
PO Box 73910
Washington, DC 20056
Phone: (202)682-0952
Fax: (202)682-0955
Publications: Lambda Book Report (5628)

Lambda Publications
Laurentian University
SCE 301 Student Centre
Sudbury, ON, Canada P3E 2C6
Fax: (705)675-4849
Publications: Lambda (36417)

Lambda Publications, Inc.
1115 W. Belmont Ave., Ste. 2-D
Chicago, IL 60657
Phone: (773)871-7610
Fax: (773)871-7609
Publications: Nightlines Weekly (8509) • Out! Resource Guide (8520) • Outlines (8522)

Lamberton News
218 E Main St.
PO Box 308
Lamberton, MN 56152
Phone: (507)752-7181
Fax: (507)752-7181
Publications: Lamberton News (15997)

Lamesa Press-Reporter
523 N 1st St.
PO Box 710
Lamesa, TX 79331-0710
Phone: (806)872-2177
Fax: (806)872-2623
Publications: Lamesa Press-Reporter (30663)

Lamont Library Level 5
Harvard University
Cambridge, MA 02138
Phone: (617)495-9775
Fax: (617)496-3692
Publications: Harvard Review (14066)

Lampasas Dispatch Record
416 S Live Oak
PO Box 631
Lampasas, TX 76550
Phone: (512)556-6262
Fax: (512)556-3278
Publications: Lampasas Dispatch Record (30665)

Lana Meiier
PO Box 910
83 Third St.
Lac du Bonnet, MB, Canada R0E 1A0
Phone: (204)345-8611
Publications: Lac du Bonnet Leader (35271)

Lancaster Bar Association
28 E. Orange St.
Lancaster, PA 17602
Phone: (717)393-0737
Fax: (717)393-0221
Publications: Lancaster Law Review (27142)

Lancaster County Weeklies, Inc.
1 E Main St.
Ephrata, PA 17522
Phone: (717)733-6397
Fax: (717)733-6058
Publications: Lititz Record-Express (27203)

Lancaster County Weeklies, Inc.
1 E. Main St.
PO Box 527
Ephrata, PA 17522
Phone: (717)733-6397
Fax: (717)733-6058
Publications: The Ephrata Review (26887)

Lancaster Management
129 Caroline Ave.
PO Box 802
Pikeville, KY 41501
Phone: (606)437-4054
Fax: (606)437-4246
Publications: Appalachian News Express (12357)

Lancaster Mennonite Historical Society
2215 Millstream Rd.
Lancaster, PA 17602-1499
Phone: (717)393-9745
Fax: (717)393-8751
Publications: Pennsylvania Mennonite Heritage (27145)

Lancaster Newspapers, Inc.
8 W. King St.
PO Box 1328
Lancaster, PA 17608-1328
Phone: (717)291-8811
Fax: (717)399-6513
Free: 800-809-4666
Publications: Intelligencer Journal (27141) • Lancaster Farming (26888) • Lancaster New Era (27143) • Lancaster Sunday News (27144)

Lancaster Publications
9650 Rockville Pke. Rd.
Bethesda, MD 20814-3990
Phone: (301)530-7050
Fax: (301)571-1892
Publications: Journal of Nutrition (13354)

Land & Sea Events
40 Aldeiney Dr., Ste. 303
Dartmouth, NS, Canada B2Y 2N5
Phone: (902)464-3757
Fax: (902)464-3755
Free: 877-311-5877
Publications: Eastern Woods and Waters (35546) • Saltscapes (35550)

Land & Water
918B 1st Ave. S.
Fort Dodge, IA 50501
Phone: (515)576-3191
Fax: (515)576-2606
Publications: Land & Water (10902)

Landlaw Specialty Publishers
675 VFW Pkwy., No. 354
Chestnut Hill, MA 02467-3656
Phone: (617)879-3133
Fax: (617)879-3182
Free: 800-637-6330
Publications: Massachusetts Civil Service Reporter (14129) • Massachusetts Discrimination Law Reporter (14130)

The Landmark
1650 Main St.
PO Box 546
Holden, MA 01520
Phone: (508)829-5981
Fax: (508)829-5984
Publications: The Landmark (14237)

The Landmark
PO Box 410
Platte City, MO 64079
Phone: (816)858-0363
Fax: (816)858-2313
Publications: The Landmark (17349)

Landmark Communications
614 Lincoln St.
PO Box 2670
Las Vegas, NM 87701
Phone: (505)425-6796
Fax: (505)425-1005
Free: 800-767-6796
Publications: Las Vegas Optic (19889)

Landmark Communications, Inc.
150 W. Brambleton Ave.
Norfolk, VA 23510-2018
Phone: (757)446-2000
Free: 800-446-2004
Publications: News & Record (23930) • The Virginian-Pilot (32296) • The Virginian Pilot (12044)

Landmark Community Newspapers, Inc.
PO Box 209
New Castle, KY 40050
Phone: (502)845-2858
Fax: (502)845-2921
Publications: Henry County Local & Shopper (12322)

Landmark Community Newspapers, Inc.
PO Box 399
Shelbyville, KY 40066
Phone: (502)633-4334
Fax: (502)732-0453
Publications: The Anderson News (12154) • Bedford Bullet (31860) • Bedford Bulletin (31861) • Carroll County Times (13776) • The Casey County News (12200) • Central Kentucky News-Journal (12006) • Chester News and Reporter (28531) • Citrus County Chronicle (6030) • Community Times (12398) • The Gazette (32099) • Henry County Local (12321) • Kentucky Standard (11926) • The Lancaster News (28680) • LaRue County Herald News (12131) • Los Alamos Monitor (19893) • The News-Democrat (12011) • The Oldham Era (12151) • Pioneer News (12400) • Sentinel-News (12399) • The Spencer County Journal-Democrat (10434) • The Springfield Sun (12415) • Sumter County Times (5969) • The Trimble Banner (11931) • Vandalia Leader Union (9725)

Landmark Community Newspapers, Inc.
PO Box 98
Shepherdsville, KY 40165
Phone: (502)543-2288
Fax: (502)955-9704
Publications: Pioneer News Extra (12401)

Landmark community newspapers Inc.
502 E 4th St.
PO Box 767
Mount Vernon, IN 47620
Phone: (812)838-4811
Fax: (812)838-3696
Publications: Mt. Vernon Democrate (10323)

Landmark Publishing, Inc.
N27 W5230 Hamilton Rd.
Cedarburg, WI 53012
Phone: (262)377-7398
Fax: (262)377-1583
Publications: Wisconsin Home Gallery Magazine (33621)

Landscape Communications, Inc.
14771 Plz. Dr. Ste. M.
Tustin, CA 92780
Phone: (714)979-5276
Fax: (714)979-3543
Publications: Landscape Architect and Specifier News (3962)

Landscape Ontario Horticultural Trades Association
7856 Fifth Line S., RR4
Milton, ON, Canada L9T 2X8
Phone: (905)875-1805
Fax: (905)875-0183
Free: 800-265-5656

Publications: Horticulture Review (36048) • Landscape Trades (36049)

Lane Communications Group
201 E Main St.
Lexington, KY 40507
Phone: (859)244-3522
Fax: (859)244-3544

Publications: The Lane Report (12172)

Lane Community College
Center Bldg., Rm. 216 Ind. Tech.
4000 E. 30th
Eugene, OR 97405-0604
Phone: (541)463-5654
Fax: (541)463-3993

Publications: The LCC Torch (26320)

Langara College
100 W. 49th Ave.
Vancouver, BC, Canada V5Y 2Z6
Phone: (604)324-5415
Fax: (604)323-5398

Publications: The Voice (35176)

Langford Bugle
Main Blvd.
PO Box 69
Britton, SD 57430
Phone: (605)493-6441
Fax: (605)448-2282

Publications: Langford Bugle (28811)

Langston Graphics, Inc.
308 N West St.
Versailles, OH 45380
Phone: (937)526-9131
Fax: (937)526-9891

Publications: The Versailles Policy (25613)

Lanigan Advisor
42 Main St
PO Box 1029
Lanigan, SK, Canada S0K 2M0
Phone: (306)365-2010
Fax: (306)365-3388

Publications: Lanigan Advisor (37490)

Lanigan Advisor
30 Downing Dr.
PO Box 1029
Lanigan, SK, Canada S0K 2M0
Phone: (306)365-2010
Fax: (306)365-3388

Publications: Lanigan Advisor (37489)

Lansing State Journal
120 E. Lenawee
Lansing, MI 48919

Publications: Lansing State Journal (15277)

The Lantzville Log Society
PO Box 268
Lantzville, BC, Canada V0R 2H0
Publications: The Log (35007)

Lapeer County Buyer's Guide
1521 Imlay City Rd., No. B
Lapeer, MI 48446-3175
Phone: (810)664-1877
Fax: (810)664-4320
Free: 800-462-9966

Publications: Lapeer Buyer's Guide (15309)

LaPorte Herald-Argus
701 State. St.
La Porte, IN 46350
Phone: (219)362-2161
Fax: (219)362-2166

Publications: LaPorte Herald-Argus (10247)

Laptop Buyer's Guide & Handbook
PO Box 5020
Brentwood, TN 37024-5020

Publications: Laptop Buyer's Guide & Handbook (29063)

Laramie Newspapers, Inc.
320 E. Grand Ave
Laramie, WY 82070
Phone: (307)742-2176
Fax: (307)721-2973

Publications: Laramie Daily Boomerang (34549)

Laredo Morning Times
111 Esperanza Dr., No. 2129
Laredo, TX 78041-2607
Phone: (210)728-2500
Fax: (210)723-1227

Publications: Laredo Morning Times (30670)

Largrange Publishing Co., Inc.
PO Box 68
Middlebury, IN 46540
Phone: (219)825-9112
Fax: (219)463-2734

Publications: Middlebury Independent (10307)

Lariat Newspaper
PO Box 229
Beaverton, OR 97075-0229
Phone: (503)644-2233
Fax: (503)644-2213

Publications: The Lariat (26237)

The Larkin Group
1 Park Ave., 2nd Fl.
New York, NY 10016-5802
Phone: (212)594-0880
Fax: (212)594-8556
Free: 800-869-7469

Publications: Accent Magazine (21134)

Larkin Publications
50 Brook Rd.
Needham, MA 02494
Phone: (781)453-9310
Fax: (781)453-9389
Free: 800-964-5150

Publications: Musical Merchandise Review (14363)

Larson Worldwide, Inc.
95 Mt. Blue St.
Norwell, MA 02061-1015
Phone: (781)659-2115
Fax: (781)659-2411
Free: 800-229-3346

Publications: DDIN International (14439)

Las Cruces Publishing Co.
219 E. Maple
PO Box 881
Deming, NM 88031
Phone: (505)546-2611
Fax: (505)546-8116

Publications: Deming Headlight (19840)

Las Cruces Sun-News
PO Box 1749
Las Cruces, NM 88004-1749
Phone: (505)541-5400
Fax: (505)541-5499

Publications: Sun-News (19876)

Las Vegas Israelite
PO Box 14096
Las Vegas, NV 89114
Phone: (702)876-1255
Fax: (702)364-1009

Publications: Las Vegas Israelite (18373)

Las Vegas Press
1385 Pama Ln., Ste., 111
Las Vegas, NV 89119-3830
Phone: (702)871-6780
Fax: (702)940-1096
Free: 800-457-3077

Publications: Las Vegas CityLife (18372)

Las Vegas Review Journal
1111 W. Bonanza Rd.
Las Vegas, NV 89106
Phone: (702)369-2000
Fax: (702)383-4666

Publications: El Tiempo Libre (18362)

Last Mountain Times Ltd.
103 1st Ave. W
Box 340
Nokomis, SK, Canada S0G 3R0
Phone: (306)528-2020
Fax: (306)528-2090

Publications: Last Mountain Times (37574) • Market Connection (37573)

Last Time Table
101 1/2 East Temple
Lenox, IA 50851
Phone: (641)333-2810

Publications: Time Table (11036)

Latah County Historical Society
327 E. Second
Moscow, ID 83843
Phone: (208)882-1004
Fax: (208)882-0759

Publications: Latah Legacy (7918)

Latimer County News Tribune
111 W Ada
PO Drawer 10
Wilburton, OK 74578
Phone: (918)465-2321
Fax: (918)465-3011

Publications: Latimer County News-Tribune (26195)

Latin American Data Base
801 Yale NE
Albuquerque, NM 87131-1016
Phone: (505)277-6839
Fax: (505)277-6837
Free: 800-472-0888

Publications: SourceMex Economic News and Analysis on Mexico (19788)

Latin American Jewish Studies Association
Dept. of Modern Languages and Literatures
Swarthmore College
500 College Ave.
Swarthmore, PA 19081
Phone: (610)328-8682
Fax: (610)328-7769

Publications: Latin American Jewish Studies (28042)

Latin American Literary Review Press
PO Box 17660
Pittsburgh, PA 15235-0860
Phone: (412)824-7903
Fax: (412)824-7909

Publications: Latin American Literary Review (27809)

Latin American News and Book, Inc.
PO Box 2109
Elizabeth, NJ 07207-2109
Phone: (908)355-8835
Fax: (908)527-9160

Publications: Mensaje (18791)

Latin American Studies Association
946, William Pitt Union
University of Pittsburgh
Pittsburgh, PA 15260
Phone: (412)648-7929
Fax: (412)624-7145

Publications: Latin American Research Review (27810)

Latin Beat Magazine
15900 Crenshaw Blvd., Ste. 1-223
Gardena, CA 90249
Phone: (310)516-6767
Fax: (310)516-9916

Publications: Latin Beat Magazine (2001)

Latin Mass Magazine
PO Box 993
Ridgefield, CT 06877
Fax: (203)438-1305

Publications: Latin Mass Magazine (5097)

Latin Publications, Inc.
7453 Woodley Ave.
Van Nuys, CA 91406
Phone: (818)882-9200
Fax: (818)882-7200

Publications: La Guia Familiar (3991) • Mundo L.A. (3992)

LATINA Style
1730 Rhode Island Ave., NW, Ste. 1207
Washington, DC 20036
Phone: (202)955-7930

Publications: LATINA Style (5631)

Latinoamericana Editores
6072 Dartmouth Hall
Dartmouth College
Hanover, NH 03755
Phone: (603)646-2822
Fax: (603)646-3695

Publications: Revista de Critica Literaria Latinoamericana (18519)

Latitude 38
15 Locust Ave.
Mill Valley, CA 94941
Phone: (415)383-8200
Fax: (415)383-5816

Publications: Latitude 38 (2540)

Latitudes & Attitudes Magazine
PO Box 668
Redondo Beach, CA 90277
Phone: (310)798-3445
Fax: (310)798-3448
Free: 888-893-7245

Publications: Latitudes & Attitudes (2909)

Latrobe Printing & Publishing
520 Philadelphia Ave
PO Box 1158
Northern Cambria, PA 15714
Phone: (814)948-6210
Fax: (814)948-7563
Free: 800-446-5161

Publications: The Star Courier (27344)

The Latrobe Printing & Publishing Co., Inc.
1211 Ligonier St.
PO Box 111
Latrobe, PA 15650-0111
Phone: (724)537-3351
Fax: (724)537-0489

Publications: The Latrobe Bulletin (27165)

Laubach Literacy
1320 Jamesville Rd.
Syracuse, NY 13210
Phone: (315)422-9121
Fax: (315)422-6369

Publications: Laubach Litscape (23407)

Lauderdale County Enterprise
145 E Jackson St.
PO Drawer 289
Ripley, TN 38063
Phone: (731)635-1771
Fax: (731)635-2111

Publications: Lauderdale County Enterprise (29575)

The Lauderdale Voice
PO Box 249
Ripley, TN 38063
Phone: (901)635-1238
Fax: (901)635-3394
Free: 800-773-1761

Publications: The Lauderdale Voice (29576)

Laurel Advocate
PO Box 688
Laurel, NE 68745
Phone: (402)256-3200
Fax: (402)256-3200

Publications: Laurel Advocate (18069)

Laurel Group Press
229 Pittsburgh St.
PO Box 222
Scottdale, PA 15683
Phone: (724)887-6101
Fax: (724)887-5115
Free: 800-640-6977

Publications: The Advisor - Youngwood (27300) • The Independent-Observer (27952) • The Times Sun (28151)

Laurel Leader Call
PO Box 728
Laurel, MS 39441-0728
Phone: (601)428-0551
Fax: (601)426-3550

Publications: Laurel Leader Call (16741)

Lauren Publications, Inc.
4275 Kellway Cir., Ste. 146
Addison, TX 75001
Phone: (972)447-9188
Fax: (972)447-0633

Publications: DallasChild (29671) • FortWorthChild (29672)

Laurens County Advertiser
218 W Laurens St.
PO Box 490
Laurens, SC 29360
Phone: (864)984-2586
Fax: (864)984-4039

Publications: Laurens County Advertiser (28682)

The Laurens Sun
119 S 3rd St.
PO Box 125
Laurens, IA 50554-0125
Phone: (712)841-4541
Fax: (712)841-4542

Publications: The Laurens Reminder (11031) • The Laurens Sun (11032)

Laurentian Business Publishing, Inc.
404 Chestnut St., No. 201
Manchester, NH 03101-1831
Phone: (603)626-6354
Fax: (603)626-6359

Publications: Business NH Magazine (18556) • Northeast Export Magazine (18561)

Laurin Publishing Company Inc.
Berkshire Common
PO Box 4949
Pittsfield, MA 01202
Phone: (413)499-0514
Fax: (413)442-3180
Free: 800-553-0051

Publications: Photonics Spectra (14471)

The Laurinburg Exchange
211 Cronly St.
PO Box 459
Laurinburg, NC 28352
Phone: (919)276-2311
Fax: (919)276-3815

Publications: The Laurinburg Exchange (24033)

Law Bulletin Publishing Co.
415 N. State St.
Chicago, IL 60610-4674
Phone: (312)644-7800
Fax: (312)644-4255

Publications: Chicago Daily Law Bulletin (8311) • Chicago Lawyer (8314) • Metro Chicago Real Estate (8485) • The Michigan Real Estate Journal (15546)

Law Enforcement Legal Publications
421 Ridgewood Ave., Ste. 100
Glen Ellyn, IL 60137-4900
Phone: (630)858-6392
Fax: (630)858-6392

Publications: Law Enforcement Legal Review (8929)

The Law Enforcement Legal Reporter Inc.
PO Box 4608
Orange, CA 92863-4608
Phone: (714)637-7237
Fax: (714)637-7130
Free: 800-733-0737

Publications: Law Enforcement Journal (2724)

Law and Order
130 Waukegan Rd., Ste. 202
Deerfield, IL 60015
Phone: (847)444-3300
Fax: (847)444-3333
Free: 800-843-9764

Publications: Law and Order (8726)

Law & Politics Media Inc.
220 S. 6th St., Ste. 500
Minneapolis, MN 55402-4502
Phone: (612)335-8808
Fax: (612)335-8809

Publications: Minnesota Law & Politics (16103)

Law Reporter Co.
209 Michigan Ave.
PO Box 270
Crystal Falls, MI 49920
Phone: (906)875-6970

Publications: Indiana Law Reporter (14894)

Law and Society Association
205 Hampshire House
University of Massachusetts
131 County Circle
Amherst, MA 01003-9257
Phone: (413)545-4617
Fax: (413)545-1640

Publications: Law & Society Review (13800)

LawNow Magazine
Legal Studies Program
Faculty of Extension
8303 - 112 St.
Edmonton, AB, Canada T6G 2T4
Phone: (780)492-1751
Fax: (780)492-6180

Publications: LawNow (34719)

The Lawrence Business Ledger
426 Alabama St.
Lawrence, KS 66044-1331
Phone: (785)749-0006
Fax: (785)749-0065

Publications: The Baldwin Ledger (11548)

The Lawrence Community Journal
7968 Pendleton Pike
Indianapolis, IN 46226
Phone: (317)542-8149
Fax: (317)542-1137

Publications: Cumberland Courier (10107) • Lawrence Community Journal (10146)

Lawrence County Advocate, Inc.
PO Box 308
Lawrenceburg, TN 38464
Fax: (615)762-7874

Publications: Lawrence County Advocate (29316)

Lawrence County Historical Society
PO Box 431
Lawrenceburg, TN 38464
Fax: (931)762-2240

Publications: Yesterday and Today in Lawrence County (29317)

Lawrence County Press
534 Broad St.
PO Box 549
Monticello, MS 39654
Phone: (601)587-2781
Fax: (601)587-2794

Publications: Lawrence County Press (16788)

Lawrence County Record, Inc.
312 S Hickory
PO Box 348
Mount Vernon, MO 65712
Phone: (417)466-2185
Fax: (417)466-7865

Publications: Lawrence County Record (17299)

Lawrence Erlbaum Associates, Inc.
10 Industrial Ave.
Mahwah, NJ 07430-2262
Phone: (201)236-9500
Fax: (201)236-0072
Free: 800-9-BOOKS-9

Publications: The American Psychoanalyst (19184) • Applied Developmental Science (19185) • Applied Measurement in Education (19186) • Applied Neuropsychology (30458) • Basic and Applied Social Psychology (19187) • Children's Health Care (6094) • Children's Services (19188) • Cognition and Instruction (29452) • Communication Booknotes Quarterly (31763) • Communication Law and Policy (31868) • Creativity Research Journal (7670) • Developmental Neuropsychology (12214) • Discourse Processes (29369) • Ecological Psychology (4890) • Educational Assessment (2261) • Educational Psychologist (34897) • Educational Studies (15691) • Emergence (6438) • Ethics & Behavior (13890) • Exceptionality (24135) • Health Communication (25120) • Human-Computer Interaction (19191) • Human Performance (28076) • Identity (35984) • Infancy (29783) • The International Journal of Aviation Psychology (25270) • International Journal of Behavioral Medicine (19192) • International Journal of Cognitive Ergonomics (19193) • International Journal of Human Computer Interaction (19194) • The International Journal for the Psychology of Religion (3642) • International Journal of Testing (35150) • Journal of Applied Animal Welfare Science (13774) • Journal of Applied Mathematics and Decision Sciences (3712) • The Journal of Behavioral Finance (19195) • Journal of Clinical Child Psychology (19196) • Journal of Cognition and Development (36633) • Journal of Community Health Nursing (19755) • Journal of Consumer Psychology (19197) • Journal of Education for Students Placed at Risk (13188) • Journal of Educational and Psychological Consultation (20609) • Journal of Family Communication (32286) • Journal of Language, Identity, and Education (31034) • Journal of Latinos and Education (3087) • The Journal of the Learning Sciences (7021) • Journal of Mass Media Ethics (6629) • The Journal of Media Economics (30239) • Journal of Media and Religion (31404) • Journal of Organizational Computing and Electronic Commerce (29789) • Journal of Personality Assessment (528) • Journal of Public Relations Research (6149) • Journal of Research on Adolescence (19199) • Language Acquisition (19200) • Mathematical Thinking and Learning (19201) • Measurement (1541) • Measurement in Physical Education and Exercise Science (14551) • Media Psychology (488) • Metaphor and Symbol (3686) • Military Psychology (5306) • Mind, Culture, and Activity (19202) • Multicultural Perspectives (4976) • Multivariate Behavioral Research (911) • Neural Computing Surveys (19203) • Nutrition and Cancer (19204) • Peabody Journal of Education (29479) • Peace and Conflict (12977) • Personality and Social Psychology Review (13588) • Psychological Inquiry (24946) • Research on Language and Social Interaction (3652) • Scientific Studies of Reading (2385) • Structural Equation Modeling (1990) • Teaching and Learning in Medicine (9643) • Teaching of Psychology (7355) • Transportation Human Factors (19206) • Understanding Statistics (19207)

The Lawrence Journal-World
PO Box 888
Lawrence, KS 66044
Phone: (785)832-1000
Free: 800-578-8748

Publications: The Lawrence Journal-World (11563)

Lawrence Technological University
21000 W. 10 Mile Rd.
Southfield, MI 48075-1058
Phone: (248)204-2200
Fax: (248)204-2207

Publications: Lawrence Technological University Magazine (15544) • Tech News (15549)

The Lawson Review
405 N Pennsylvania Ave.
Box 125
Lawson, MO 64062-0125
Phone: (816)296-3412

Publications: The Lawson Review (17237)

Lawton Publishing Co.
3rd & A Ave.
PO Box 2068
Lawton, OK 73502-0848
Phone: (580)353-0620
Fax: (580)585-5134

Publications: The Cannoneer (25837) • The Lawton Constitution (25887) • Press (25888)

Lawyers Weekly Publications
41 West St.
Boston, MA 02111
Phone: (617)451-7300
Fax: (617)451-7324
Free: 800-444-5297

Publications: Lawyers Weekly USA (13922) • Massachusetts Lawyers Weekly (13928) • Michigan Lawyers Weekly (15409) • Missouri Lawyers Weekly (17473) • North Carolina Lawyers Weekly (24146) • Virginia Lawyers Weekly (32464)

Laymen's Home Missionary Movement
1156 St. Matthews Rd.
Chester Springs, PA 19425-2700
Phone: (610)827-7665

Publications: Bible Standard and Herald of Christ's Kingdom (26777) • Present Truth and Herald of Christ's Epiphany (26778)

Laymen's Retreat League
Malvern Retreat House, St. Joseph's In The Hills
315 Warren Ave.
Malvern, PA 19355
Phone: (610)644-0400
Fax: (610)644-1526

Publications: Men of Malvern (27214)

Laymon Publishing Corp.
107 E High St.
Montpelier, IN 47359
Phone: (765)728-5322
Fax: (765)728-5322

Publications: The Montpelier Herald (10321)

Damir Lazaric
217 N Franklin St.
Watkins Glen, NY 14891
Phone: (607)535-9866
Fax: (607)535-2939

Publications: The Hi-Lites (23524)

L.C. Clark Publishing
840 U.S. Hwy. 1, Ste.330
North Palm Beach, FL 33408
Phone: (561)627-3393
Fax: (561)694-6578

Publications: Draperies and Window Coverings (6846)

L.D. Enterprises, Inc.
121 E Main
Anthony, KS 67003-0031
Phone: (620)842-5129
Fax: (620)842-5117

Publications: The Anthony Republican (11339)

LDJ Corp.
70 Edwin Ave.
PO Box 2330
Waterbury, CT 06722
Phone: (203)755-0158
Fax: (203)755-3480
Free: 800-325-6745

Publications: Servicing Management (5195)

Le Bulletin des Agriculteurs
1001 Maisonneuve Blvd. W.
Montreal, QC, Canada H3A 3E1
Phone: (514)845-5141
Fax: (514)845-6261

Publications: Le Bulletin des Agriculteurs (37156)

Le Canada Francais
84 Richelieu St.
Saint-Jean, QC, Canada J3B 6X3
Phone: (514)347-0323
Fax: (514)347-4539

Publications: Le Canada Francais (37354)

Le Chef D.S.A. Inc.
252, route 171 Sud
Saint-Etienne-de-Lauzon, QC, Canada G6J 1E8
Phone: (418)831-5317
Fax: (418)831-5172
Free: 800-363-1727

Publications: Le Chef du Service Alimentaire (37330)

Le Courrier
125 Notre Dame E.
PO Box 759
Trois-Pistoles, QC, Canada G0L 4K0
Phone: (418)851-3644
Fax: (418)851-3650

Publications: Le Courrier (37414)

Le Courrier d'Oshawa
17 Carlaw Ave.
Toronto, ON, Canada M4M 2R6
Phone: (416)465-5327
Fax: (416)465-3778

Publications: Le Courrier d'Oshawa (36650)

Le Droit
47 Clarence, Ste. 222
PO Box 8860, Sta. T
Ottawa, ON, Canada K1G 3J9
Phone: (613)562-0111
Fax: (613)562-6280

Publications: Le Droit (36257)

Le Franco-Albertain Ltee.
8527 82nd Ave., Ste. 201
Edmonton, AB, Canada T6C 3N1
Phone: (403)465-6581
Fax: (403)465-3647

Publications: Le Franco-Albertain (34720)

Le Groupe Polygone Editeurs, Inc.
11450, Albert-Hudon
Montreal, QC, Canada H1G 3J9
Phone: (514)327-4464
Fax: (514)327-0602
Free: 800-563-6738

Publications: Sentier Chasse-Peche (37224)

Le Haut St. Francois
212 Principale Est.
Cookshire, QC, Canada J0B 1M0

Publications: Journal Regional le Haut-Saint-Francois (36977) • Le Haut St-Francois (36978)

Le Journal Economique de Quebec
600, Av. Belvedere
Quebec, QC, Canada G1S 3E5
Phone: (418)681-9999
Fax: (418)681-7077

Publications: Le Journal Economique de Quebec (37287)

Le Journal La Voix Nouvelle Inc.
38, rue Augusta, 2e. etage
Sorel, QC, Canada J3P 1A3
Phone: (514)743-8466
Fax: (514)742-8567

Publications: Journal La Voix (37403)

Le Journal Les Enseignants Ltee.
1316 Domaine Du Moulin
L'Ancienne-Lorett, QC, Canada G2E 4N1
Phone: (418)872-6966
Fax: (418)872-6966

Publications: Les Enseignants (37032)

Le Journal des Pays d'En Haut
1012 rue Valiquette
PO Box 1890
Ste.-Adele, QC, Canada J0R 1L0
Phone: (514)229-6664
Fax: (514)229-6063

Publications: Le Journal des Pays d'En Haut (37324)

Le Journal de Saint-Bruno
1507, rue Roberval
Saint-Bruno, QC, Canada J3V 3P8
Phone: (450)653-3685
Fax: (450)653-6967

Publications: Le Journal de Saint-Bruno (37329)

Le Journal de Saint-Hubert
5863 blvd. Cousineau
Saint-Hubert, QC, Canada J3Y 7P5
Phone: (514)445-2812
Fax: (514)445-6347

Publications: Le Journal de Saint-Hubert (37345)

Le Magazine L'agent de voyages inc.
PO Box 38
Ville D'Anjou, QC, Canada H1K 4G5
Phone: (514)881-9637
Fax: (514)881-8292

Publications: Le Magazine L'agent de voyages (37436)

Le Magazine Voyager, Inc.
11800 5th Ave., Ste. 301
Montreal, QC, Canada H1E 7C1
Phone: (514)881-8583
Fax: (514)881-8292

Publications: Tourisme Plus (37229)

Le Mars Daily Sentinel
41 1st Ave. N.E.
Le Mars, IA 51031
Phone: (712)546-7031
Fax: (712)546-7035

Publications: Daily Sentinel (11034)

Le Messager de St. Antoine
Lac Bouchette, QC, Canada G0W 1V0
Phone: (418)348-6344
Fax: (418)348-9960
Free: 800-868-6344

Publications: Le Messager de St. Antoine (37026)

Le Nouvelliste
1920 Bellefeuille St.
CP 668
Trois-Rivieres, QC, Canada G9A 3Y2
Phone: (819)376-2501
Fax: (819)376-0946

Publications: Le Nouvelliste (37416)

Le Progres du Saguenay
1051, boul. Talbot
Chicoutimi, QC, Canada G7H 5C1
Phone: (418)545-4474
Fax: (418)690-8824

Publications: Le Quotidien du Saguenay-Lac-Saint-Jean (36965) • Progres-Dimanche (36966)

Le Regional Hull-Aylmer
215 Boul. DeLacarriere, Ste. 207
Hull, QC, Canada G8T 8G1
Phone: (819)776-1063
Fax: (819)776-1668

Publications: Le Regional Hull-Aylmer (37002)

Le Reseau Select
1110 Sherbrooke Ouest, Office 2700
Montreal, QC, Canada H3A 1G9
Phone: (514)884-3131
Fax: (514)844-9679

Publications: Guide de Montreal-Nord (37121)

Le Reseau Select
625, blvd. Rene-Levesque
Ouest Bur. 800
Montreal, QC, Canada H3B 1R2
Phone: (514)866-3131

Publications: Journal de St. Michel (37146)

Le Reseau Select
625 Rene Leuesque W. Blvd. Bur. 800
Montreal, QC, Canada H3B 1R2
Phone: (514)866-3131
Fax: (514)866-3030
Free: 800-361-7262

Publications: L'Action (37010) • L'Artisan (37087) • L'avenir De L'erable (37269) • L'Avenir de l'Est (37090) • Brossard-Eclair (36951) • Coup d'Oeil (37254) • L'Echo de Louiseville (37060) • The Equity (37392) • L'Etoile du Lac (37319) • L'Eveil (37331) • L'Express (36989) • L'Hebdo-Journal (36956) • L'Hebdo Rive-Nord (37122) • Info Dimanche (37313) • L'Infomateur (37129) • L'Information de Ste. Julie (37381) • La Concorde (37332) • La Parole (36990) • La Pensee de Bagot (36929) • La Revue de Gatineau (36999) • La Sentinelle (36964) • La Voix du Sud (37027) • Le Bulletin (36952) • Le Courrier Laval du Dimanche (37158) • Le Courrier de Malartic (37063) • Le Courrier des Moulins (37041) • Le Courrier de Portneuf (36987) • Le Courrier-Sud (37259) • Le Flambeau de l'Est (37160) • Le Havre (36960) • Le Journal de Chambly Inc. (36959) • Le Journal de Rosemont et Petite Patrie (37164) • Le Journal St-Louis & Mile End (37165) • Le Journal de St-Michel (37166) • Le Nord-Est Plus (37386) • Le Nord Info (37384) • Le Pharillon (36997) • Le Progres de Coaticook (36976) • Le Radar (36954) • Le/The Monitor (37172) • L'Oeil Regional (36950) • Progres de St. Leonard (37210) • Salut Dimanche (37061)

Le Richelieu Dimanche
84 rue Richelieu
Saint-Jean, QC, Canada J3B 6X3
Phone: (450)347-0323
Fax: (450)347-4539

Publications: Le Richelieu Dimanche (37355)

Le Saint Laurent/Portage
16 Dudomaine
Riviere-du-Loup, QC, Canada G5R 2P5
Phone: (418)867-1465
Fax: (418)862-4387

Publications: Le Saint Laurent/Portage (37314)

Le Soleil
925 Chemin St. Louis
PO Box 1547
Quebec, QC, Canada G1K 7J6
Phone: (418)686-3270
Fax: (418)686-3260

Publications: Le Soleil (37290)

Le Sueur Publishing
101 Bridge St.
Le Sueur, MN 56058
Phone: (507)665-3332

Publications: Le Sueur News-Herald (16000) • Valley (16001)

Le Touladi
PO Box 430
Cabano, QC, Canada G0L 1E0
Phone: (418)854-2766
Fax: (418)854-2830

Publications: Le Touladi (36953)

Lead Courier
PO Box 310
Elk Point, SD 57025
Phone: (605)356-2632
Fax: (605)356-3626

Publications: The Leader-Courier (28850)

Leader
6008 W. Belmont Ave.
Chicago, IL 60634-5195
Phone: (773)283-7900
Fax: (773)283-7761

Publications: Northwest Leader (8511) • Suburban Leader (8573) • Suburban Post (8574)

The Leader
115 East Ave.
PO Box 97
Ogden, IL 61859
Phone: (217)582-2373
Fax: (217)582-2237

Publications: Ogden Leader (9382)

Leader
211 Hwy. 38E
Rochelle, IL 61068
Phone: (815)562-4171
Fax: (815)562-2161

Publications: Farmer's Report (9513)

Leader
PO Box 490
Washburn, IL 61570
Phone: (309)248-7413

Publications: Leader (9734)

The Leader
4 S. Main St.
PO Box 38
Knox, IN 46534
Phone: (219)772-2101
Fax: (219)772-7041
Free: 888-772-2101

Publications: The Leader (10238)

Leader
PO Box 39
Tripoli, IA 50676
Phone: (319)882-4207
Fax: (319)882-4200

Publications: Tripoli Leader (11274)

The Leader
PO Box 487
Ellinwood, KS 67526
Phone: (316)564-3116
Fax: (316)564-2550

Publications: The Ellinwood Leader (11424)

The Leader
1137 Main St.
PO Drawer F
Franklinton, LA 70438
Phone: (985)839-9077
Fax: (985)839-9077

Publications: Franklinton Era-Leader (12583)

Leader
Box 338
Marlette, MI 48453
Phone: (517)635-2435
Fax: (517)635-3769

Publications: Leader (15336)

The Leader
34 W. Pulteney St.
Corning, NY 14830
Phone: (607)936-4651
Fax: (607)936-9939

Publications: Leader (20503)

The Leader
3500 A E. TC Jester Blvd.
Houston, TX 77018
Phone: (713)686-8494
Fax: (713)686-0970

Publications: The North Freeway Leader (30510)

The Leader
119 E. Main
Tremonton, UT 84337
Phone: (435)257-5182
Fax: (435)257-6175

Publications: Leader Garland Times (31481)

The Leader Group
PO Box 50129
Jacksonville Beach, FL 32240
Phone: (904)249-9033
Fax: (904)249-1501

Publications: Beaches Leader/Ponte Vedra Leader (6247) • Sun-Times (6248)

The Leader and the Kalkaskian
318 N Cedar St.
Kalkaska, MI 49646
Phone: (231)258-4600
Fax: (231)258-4603

Publications: The Leader and the Kalkaskian (15261)

Leader-News, Inc.
110 N East St.
PO Box 740
Uvalde, TX 78801-5312
Phone: (830)278-3335
Fax: (830)278-9191

Publications: Uvalde Leader-News (31225)

Leader Newspapers, Inc.
PO Box 30486
Charlotte, NC 28230
Phone: (704)331-4842
Fax: (704)347-0358

Publications: The Leader (23748)

Leader-Observer, Inc.
PO Box 780376
Maspeth, NY 11378-0376

Publications: Leader Observer (20837) • Realty (20626)

Leader-Post
1964 Park St.
Regina, SK, Canada S4P 3G4
Phone: (306)565-8211
Fax: (306)565-8812

Publications: Leader-Post (37532)

Leader-Press
PO Box 370
Copperas Cove, TX 76522
Phone: (254)547-4207
Fax: (254)542-3299

Publications: Copperas Cove Leader-Press (30074)

Leader Printing & Supply, Inc.
121 Main St.
Anaconda, MT 59711
Phone: (406)563-5283
Fax: (406)563-5284

Publications: The Anaconda Leader (17721)

Leader Publications
3075 Smith Rd., Ste. 204
Akron, OH 44333
Phone: (330)665-0909
Fax: (330)665-0908
Free: 888-945-9595

Publications: West Side Leader (24593)

Leader Publications Ltd.
PO Box 490
Main St.
Dresden, ON, Canada N0P 1M0
Publications: Voice of the Farmer (35789)

Leader Publishing Co., Inc.
401 Meeker St.
Delta, CO 81416-1918
Phone: (970)874-4421
Fax: (970)874-4424
Publications: Delta County Independent (4302)

Leader Publishing Co., Inc.
28 Church St.
Everett, MA 02149
Phone: (617)387-4570
Fax: (617)387-0409
Publications: Leader-Herald and News Gazette (14176)

Leader Publishing Co., Inc.
6 W. 2nd St.
PO Box 29
Coudersport, PA 16915
Phone: (814)274-8044
Fax: (814)274-8120
Publications: The Potter Leader Enterprise (26811)

Leader Publishing Co., Inc.
42 N. Main St.
Port Allegany, PA 16743-1337
Phone: (814)642-2811
Fax: (814)642-7169
Publications: Port Allegany Reporter-Argus (27897)

Leader Publishing Co., Inc.
St. 11 N. Central Ave.
PO Box 59
Staunton, VA 24402
Phone: (540)885-7281
Publications: The Daily News Leader (32555)

Leader Publishing Co. of Salem, Inc.
117-119 E Walnut St.
PO Box 509
Salem, IN 47167
Phone: (812)883-3281
Fax: (812)883-4446
Publications: The Salem Democrat (10439) • The Salem Leader (10440)

Leader-Statesman
PO Box 348
Versailles, MO 65084
Phone: (573)378-5441
Fax: (573)378-4292
Publications: Leader-Statesman (17663)

Leader Tribune
205 S Broadway
PO Box 370
Laverne, OK 73848
Phone: (580)921-3391
Fax: (580)921-3392
Publications: Leader Tribune (25883)

Leader-Tribune, Inc.
PO Box 1060
Fort Valley, GA 31030-1060
Phone: (478)825-2432
Fax: (478)825-4130
Publications: Leader-Tribune (7287)

The Leader Vindicator
435 Broad St.
PO Box 158
New Bethlehem, PA 16242-1102
Phone: (814)275-3131
Fax: (814)275-3531
Publications: The Leader-Vindicator (27312)

Leader's Magazine
98 Dennis Dr.
Lexington, KY 40503
Phone: (859)277-6221
Fax: (859)277-8059
Free: 800-356-5936
Publications: Leader's Magazine (12173)

Leaders Magazine
59 E. 54th St.
New York, NY 10022
Phone: (212)758-0740
Fax: (212)593-5194
Publications: Leaders Magazine (22242)

Leaders Publications Ltd.
Box 490
Dresden, ON, Canada N0P 1M0
Publications: Grand Bend Sun (35788)

Leading Edge Magazine
3146 JKHB
Provo, UT 84602
Phone: (801)378-4455
Publications: Leading Edge Magazine (31405)

The Leaf-Chronicle
200 Commerce St.
PO Box 829
Clarksville, TN 37041-0829
Phone: (931)552-1808
Fax: (615)648-8001
Free: 800-829-1808
Publications: The Stewart-Houston Times (29182)

Leaf-Chronicle Co., Inc.
PO Box 158
Ashland City, TN 37015-0158
Phone: (931)552-1808
Fax: (615)792-3671
Publications: Ashland City Times (29051)

League of California Cities
1400 K St., 4th floor
Sacramento, CA 95814
Phone: (916)658-8223
Fax: (916)658-8289
Free: 800-262-1801
Publications: Western City (3022)

League of Kansas Municipalities
300 SW 8th Ave.
Topeka, KS 66603
Phone: (785)354-9565
Fax: (785)354-4186
Publications: Kansas Government Journal (11828)

League of Nebraska Municipalities
1335 L St.
Lincoln, NE 68508
Phone: (402)476-2829
Fax: (402)476-7052
Publications: Nebraska Municipal Review (18103)

League of Wisconsin Municipalities
202 State St., Ste. 300
Madison, WI 53703-2215
Phone: (608)267-2380
Fax: (608)267-0645
Free: 800-991-5502
Publications: The Municipality (33964)

League of Women Voters of the United States
1730 M St. NW, Ste. 1000
Washington, DC 20036
Phone: (202)429-1965
Fax: (202)429-4343
Publications: The National Voter (5683)

League of World War I Aviation Historians
3127 Penrose Place
Cincinnati, OH 45211
Publications: Over the Front (24812)

League for Yiddish, Inc.
200 W 72nd St., Ste. 40
New York, NY 10023
Phone: (212)787-6675
Fax: (718)231-7905
Publications: Afn Shvel (21162)

Leamington Post & Shopper
27 Princess St.
Leamington, ON, Canada N8H 2X8
Phone: (519)326-4434
Fax: (519)326-2171
Publications: Leamington Shopper (35969)

Learning Resources Network
PO Box 9
River Falls, WI 54022-0009
Fax: 888-234-8633
Free: 800-678-5376
Publications: LERN Magazine (34307)

Leatherdale Publishing
6102-465T
Olds, AB, Canada T4H 1M5
Phone: (403)556-3351
Fax: (403)556-3464
Publications: Olds Gazette (34819)

The Leaven
12615 Parallel Pkwy.
Kansas City, KS 66109
Phone: (913)721-1570
Fax: (913)721-5276
Publications: The Leaven (11529)

Leavenworth Times
422 Seneca
Leavenworth, KS 66048
Phone: (913)682-0305
Fax: (913)682-1114
Publications: Leavenworth Times (11580)

Lebanon Advertiser
309 W St. Louis St.
PO Box 126
Lebanon, IL 62254
Phone: (618)537-4498
Publications: Advertiser (9073)

Lebanon Daily News
718 Poplar St.
PO Box 600
Lebanon, PA 17042
Phone: (717)272-5611
Fax: (717)274-1608
Publications: Lebanon Daily News (27172)

Lebanon High School
160 Miller Rd.
Lebanon, OH 45036-1299
Phone: (513)934-5100
Fax: (513)933-2150
Publications: The Lebanon Light (25294)

The Lebanon News
PO Box 1268
Lebanon, VA 24266
Phone: (540)889-5321
Fax: (540)889-0517
Publications: The Lebanon News (32179)

Lebanon Publishing Co.
PO Box 192
Lebanon, MO 65536
Phone: (417)532-9131
Fax: (417)532-8140
Free: 800-288-9924
Publications: The Lebanon Daily Record (17238) • News Journal (17300)

The Lebanon Reporter
117 E. Washington St.
Lebanon, IN 46052
Phone: (765)482-5400
Fax: (765)482-4652
Free: 888-482-4650
Publications: The Lebanon Reporter (10270)

The Lebanon Times
PO Box 158
Lebanon, KS 66952-0158
Phone: (785)389-6631
Fax: (785)454-3866
Publications: The Lebanon Times (11587)

Lebanon Valley College
101 N. College Ave.
Annville, PA 17003
Phone: (717)867-6100
Fax: (717)867-6035
Publications: The Valley (26657)

Lebhar-Friedman, Inc.
425 Park Ave.
New York, NY 10022-3556
Phone: (212)756-5088
Fax: (212)756-5120
Free: 800-453-2427

Publications: APPAREL Merchandising (21226) •
Chain Store Age (21393) • Discount Store News
(21554) • Drug Store News (21571) • National
Home Center News (22396) • Western Itasca Review & Deerpath Shopper (22914)

The Ledger
33815 W Lime St.
PO Box 408
Lakeland, FL 33802
Phone: (941)802-7000
Fax: (941)687-7090

Publications: The Ledger (6289)

The Ledger
Smith & Clay Streets
PO Box 247
Albany, MO 64402
Phone: (660)726-3997
Fax: (660)726-3997

Publications: The Albany Ledger Headlight (16889)

The Ledger
714 Box Butte Ave.
Hemingford, NE 69348
Phone: (308)487-3334
Fax: (308)487-3347

Publications: The Ledger (18046)

The Ledger
110 Kenosha
Broken Arrow, OK 74012
Phone: (918)258-7171
Fax: (918)258-9908

Publications: The Ledger (25771)

Ledger Publishing Co.
600 Enterprise Dr., Ste. 100
Oak Brook, IL 60523
Phone: (630)571-8911
Fax: (630)571-4053

Publications: Business Ledger (9343)

Ledger Publishing Co.
631 Main Ave.
Lafayette, MN 56054
Phone: (507)228-8985
Fax: (507)228-8779

Publications: Lafayette-Nicollet Ledger (15989)

Lee A. Romano Associates, Inc.
Rte. 30
Dorset, VT 05251
Phone: (802)362-7200

Publications: Stratton Magazine (31539)

Lee College
PO Box 818
Baytown, TX 77522-0818
Phone: (281)425-6506
Fax: (832)556-4005

Publications: The Lantern (29895)

Lee County Ledger
126 4th St.
PO Box 715
Leesburg, GA 31763
Phone: (912)759-2413
Fax: (912)759-6599

Publications: Lee County Ledger (7370)

Lee County Observer, Inc.
218 Main St.
PO Box 567
Bishopville, SC 29010
Phone: (803)484-9431
Fax: (803)484-5055

Publications: Lee County Observer (28494)

Lee Enterprises
215 Main St.
Davenport, IA 52801-1924
Phone: (563)383-2100
Free: 800-264-9091

Publications: The Ledger-Independent (10736)

Lee Enterprises
707 E. Front Ave.
Bismarck, ND 58504
Phone: (701)223-2500
Fax: (701)223-4240

Publications: The Bismarck Tribune (24349)

Lee Enterprises
600 SW Jefferson Ave.
PO Box 368
Corvallis, OR 97333
Phone: (541)753-2641
Fax: (541)758-9505

Publications: The Corvallis Gazette-Times (26286)

Lee Enterprises
90 E. Grant
PO Box 459
Lebanon, OR 97355
Phone: (541)258-3151
Fax: (541)259-3569

Publications: Lebanon Express (26408)

Lee Enterprises
710 Main St.
Menomonie, WI 54751
Phone: (715)235-3411
Fax: (715)235-0936

Publications: Dunn County News, Shopper, and
Reminder (34038)

Lee Enterprises Inc.
1904 Main St
Cedar Falls, IA 50613
Phone: (319)277-3300
Fax: (319)277-3308

Publications: Hometowner, Inc. (10656)

Lee Enterprises, Inc.
400 Putnam Bldg.
215 N. Main St.
Davenport, IA 52801-1924
Phone: (319)383-2100
Fax: (319)323-9609

Publications: The Business Journal (11070)

Lee Enterprises, Inc.
400 Putnam Bldg., 215 N. Main St.
Davenport, IA 52801-1924
Phone: (319)383-2100
Fax: (319)323-9609

Publications: La Crosse Tribune (33885) • The
Mason City Shopper (11073) • The Post (11104) •
Winona Daily News (16527)

Lee Newspapers Ltd.
PO Box 121
6113 State Highway 5
Palatine Bridge, NY 13428
Phone: (518)673-3237
Fax: (518)673-2381

Publications: Farm Chronicle (23074)

Lee Publications
PO Box 6747
Great Falls, MT 59406
Phone: (406)761-2406
Fax: (406)761-8814

Publications: Consumers Press (17798)

Lee Publications, Inc.
6113 State Hwy. 5
PO Box 121
Palatine Bridge, NY 13428
Phone: (518)673-3237
Fax: (518)673-2381
Free: 800-218-5586

Publications: Country Folks Grower (23073)

Leelanau Publishing Co., Inc.
7200 E Duck Lake Rd.
Lake Leelanau, MI 49653-9779

Publications: Leelanau Enterprise & Tribune
(15267)

Lees Summit Journal, Inc.
415 S Douglas St.
PO Box 387
Lees Summit, MO 64063
Phone: (816)524-2345
Fax: (816)524-5136

Publications: Lees Summit Journal (17243) • Lees
Summit Journal-Extra (17244)

Leesburg Today
1 East Market St.
Leesburg, VA 20176
Phone: (703)771-8800
Fax: (703)771-8833

Publications: Leesburg Today (32185)

Left Curve Publications
PO Box 472
Oakland, CA 94604
Phone: (510)763-7193

Publications: Left Curve (2685)

Left Field Press
3709 N. Kenmore
Chicago, IL 60613

Publications: Another Chicago Magazine (8264)

Lefthanders Intl.
PO Box 8249
Topeka, KS 66608
Phone: (913)234-2177
Fax: (913)232-3999

Publications: Lefthander Magazine (11832)

Legal Communications Corp.
612 N. 2nd St., 4th Fl.
PO Box 88910
St. Louis, MO 63102
Phone: (314)421-1880
Fax: (314)421-0436

Publications: St. Louis Countian (17499)

Legal News Publishing Co.
2935 Prospect Ave.
Cleveland, OH 44115
Phone: (216)696-3322
Fax: (216)696-6329
Free: 800-814-6634

Publications: Daily Legal News (24879)

Legal Record Corporation
PO Box 563
Peoria, IL 61651-0563
Phone: (309)672-1600
Fax: 888-568-7488
Free: (866)672-1600

Publications: The News Bulletin (9421)

Legislative Reference Bureau
Rm. 112, State House
Springfield, IL 62706
Phone: (217)782-6625

Publications: Legislative Synopsis and Digest
(9638)

Lehigh University
436 Brodhead Ave.
Bethlehem, PA 18015-1690
Phone: (610)758-4180
Fax: (610)758-6198

Publications: Brown and White (26699) • Lehigh
Alumni Bulletin (26702) • LehighNow (26703)

Lehman Communications Corp.
350 Terry St.
PO Box 299
Longmont, CO 80502
Phone: (303)776-2244
Fax: (303)678-8615
Free: 800-796-8201

Publications: Daily Times-Call (4558) • Loveland
Daily Reporter-Herald (4568)

Leigh Communications, Inc.
150 E Huron St.
Chicago, IL 60611
Phone: (312)951-7600
Fax: (312)951-9083

Publications: Today's Chicago Woman (8583)

Leigh World
PO Box 278
Leigh, NE 68643
Phone: (402)487-2218
Fax: (402)842-3141

Publications: Leigh World (18071)

Numbers cited after listings are entry numbers rather than page numbers.

Leisure Publications
4160 Wilshire Blvd.
Los Angeles, CA 90010
Phone: (323)964-4800
Fax: (323)964-4840

Publications: Contemporary Long Term Care (2246) • Fitness Management Magazine (2271) • Pool & Spa News (2373)

Leisure Publishing Co.
3424 Brambleton Ave.
PO Box 21535
Roanoke, VA 24018-1535
Phone: (540)989-6138
Fax: (540)989-7603
Free: 800-548-1672

Publications: Blue Ridge Country (32489) • Roanoker Magazine (32493)

Leisure Times
Box 889
Liberal, KS 67905
Phone: (620)624-2541
Fax: (620)624-0735

Publications: Leisure Times (11604)

The Leisure World Golden Rain News
PO Box 2338
Seal Beach, CA 90740
Phone: (562)430-0534
Fax: (562)598-1617

Publications: The Leisure World Golden Rain News (3749)

LeJacq Communications, Inc.
3 Parklands Dr.
Darien, CT 06820-3652
Phone: (203)656-1711
Fax: (203)656-1717

Publications: American Journal of Geriatric Cardiology (4769) • Cardiovascular Reviews & Reports (4770) • Congestive Heart Failure (4771)

The Leland Progress, LLC
PO Box 72
Leland, MS 38756
Phone: (662)686-4081
Fax: (662)686-9076

Publications: The Leland Progress (16745)

Lemmon Leader
PO Box 180
Lemmon, SD 57638
Phone: (605)374-3751

Publications: Leader (28882)

LeMoyne College
16 Loyola Hall
Syracuse, NY 13214
Phone: (315)445-4542
Fax: (315)445-4520

Publications: The Dolphin (23400)

Lenior-Rhyne College
Box 7226
Hickory, NC 28603-7229
Phone: (828)328-7315
Fax: (828)328-7338

Publications: The Lenoir Rhynean (23989)

Lennox Independent
116 S Main St.
PO Box 76
Lennox, SD 57039
Phone: (605)647-2284
Fax: (605)647-2218

Publications: Lennox Independent (28884)

Lens Publishing Co., Inc.
1624 Harmon Pl., Ste. 330
Minneapolis, MN 55403
Phone: (612)338-5040

Publications: Utne (16138)

The Leon County News
PO Box 307
Crawfordville, FL 32326-0307
Phone: (850)926-7102

Publications: The Leon County News (6020)

Leonard Graphic
PO Box 1108
Leonard, TX 75452
Phone: (903)587-3303
Fax: (903)587-9893

Publications: Leonard Graphic (30681)

The Leoti
114 S 4th St.
PO Box N
Leoti, KS 67861
Phone: (316)375-2631
Fax: (316)375-2184

Publications: Leoti Standard (11600)

Lerner Communications, Inc.
7331 N. Lincoln Ave.
Lincolnwood, IL 60712
Phone: (847)329-2000
Fax: (847)329-2060

Publications: The Booster (9090) • Elmwood Park/River Grove Times (9093) • Harlem-Foster Times (9094) • Harlem-Irving Times (8390) • Jefferson Park/Portage Park Times (9095) • Lincolnwood Life (9097) • Morton Grove-Niles Life (9098) • The Niles Life (9099) • Norridge Times (9100) • North Town News-Star (9102) • Rogers Park/Edgewater/Uptown News-Star (9103) • Schiller Park (9104) • Skokie Life (9611) • Skyline (9105)

Les Amis du Vin
O A Picone 5015 Glenoak Dr.
Louisville, OH 44641-8831

Publications: The Friends of Wine (25318)

Les Deux Rives
77, rue Georges
Sorel, QC, Canada J3P 1C2
Phone: (450)742-9408
Fax: (450)742-2493

Publications: Les Deux Rives (37405)

Les Diplomes de l'Universite de Montreal
3744, rue Jean-Brillant
bureau 410
Montreal, QC, Canada H3Y 1P1
Phone: (514)343-6230
Fax: (514)343-5798

Publications: Les Diplomes (37177)

Les Echos Abitibiens
1462 Rue de La Quebecoise, 2o Etage
Val d'Or, QC, Canada J9P 5H4
Phone: (819)825-3755
Fax: (819)825-0361

Publications: L'Echo Abitibien (36928)

Les Editions Belcor
217, Avenue Leonidas
C.P. 3217, Succ. A
Rimouski, QC, Canada G5L 9G6
Phone: (418)723-4800
Fax: (418)723-1855

Publications: L'Avant-Poste (36935) • Le Rimouskois (37307) • Progres-Echo (37308)

Les Editions Bomart Ltee.
3380, Francis-Hugues
Laval, QC, Canada H7L 5A7
Phone: (450)975-7667
Fax: (450)975-4847

Publications: L'Echo du Transport (37036) • Gestion Logistique (37038) • Guide du Transport par Camion (37039)

Les Editions Heritage, Inc.
300, rue Arran
Saint-Lambert, QC, Canada J4R 1K5
Phone: (514)875-0327
Fax: (514)672-5448

Publications: ARCHIE (37357) • Le Magazine Enfants Quebec (37359)

Les Editions Le Reveil/Group Quebecor, Inc.
3388, Boul. St-Francois
C.P. 520
Jonquiere, QC, Canada G7X 7W4
Phone: (418)695-2601
Fax: (418)695-0530
Free: 800-387-2601

Publications: Le Reveil (37013)

Les Editions Logistiques Inc.
597 Rue Beaucage
Ste.-Therese, QC, Canada J7E 2K3
Phone: (450)437-0888
Fax: (450)434-0888
Free: 877-437-0888

Publications: Logistics Magazine (37369)

Les Editions Qualite Performante Inc.
1600 Boul. St-Martin Est, Bureau 870 Tour A
Laval, QC, Canada H7G 4R8
Phone: (450)669-8373
Fax: (450)669-9078

Publications: Entreprendre (37037)

Les Editions du Reveil
1570 Boul Wall Bell
Dolbeau-Mistassini, QC, Canada G8L 1H4
Phone: (418)276-5110
Fax: (418)276-5354
Free: 800-387-2601

Publications: Le Point (36986)

Les Editions Tricycle Inc.
1251 Rachel St. E
Montreal, QC, Canada H2J 2J9
Phone: (514)521-8356
Fax: (514)521-5711
Free: 800-567-8356

Publications: Geo Plein Air (37119)

Les Editions Yvon Blais Inc.
CP 180
Cowansville, QC, Canada J2K 3H6
Phone: (450)266-1086
Fax: (450)263-9256
Free: 800-363-3047

Publications: Bulletin de Droit de L'Environnement (36980) • Bulletin de Droit de la Sante (36981) • Droit de cite (36982) • Gestion Plus Info-Employeur (36983) • Resumes de droit penal (36984)

Les Hebdos Montereqiens
243, boul. d'Anjou
Chateauguay, QC, Canada J6J 2R3
Fax: (514)691-3883

Publications: L'Information Regionale (36962)

Les Hebdos Select
625 Blvd. Rene Levesque O. Bureau 800
Montreal, QC, Canada H3B 1R2
Phone: (514)866-3131
Fax: (514)866-3030
Free: 800-361-7262

Publications: Courier Laval du Jeudi (37107)

Les Missionnaires du Sacre-Coeur
2215 Marie-Victorin
Sillery, QC, Canada G1T 1J6
Phone: (418)681-3581
Fax: (418)681-1139

Publications: RND (Revue Notre-Dame) (37401)

Les Nouvelles de l'Est
3829 rue Ontario est
Montreal, QC, Canada H1W 1S5
Phone: (514)526-2224
Fax: (514)526-0515

Publications: Les Nouvelles de l'Est (37178)

Les Presses de L'Universite de Montreal
CP 6128
Succ Centre Ville
Montreal, QC, Canada H3C 3J7
Phone: (514)343-6933
Fax: (514)343-2232

Publications: Circuit (37105) • Meta (37186)

Les Productions L'Animal, Inc.
4930 Cote des Neiges
Montreal, QC, Canada H3V 1H2

Publications: Nos Animaux (37195)

Les Publications Codex
4378 Pierre de Coubertin
Montreal, QC, Canada H1V 1A6
Phone: (514)254-0346
Fax: (514)254-5010

Publications: Quebec Pharmacie (37212)

Les Publications Vacances (Quebec), Inc.
185 Saint Paul St.
Quebec, QC, Canada G1K 3W2
Phone: (418)694-1272
Fax: (418)692-3392

Publications: VOILA QUEBEC (37297)

Les Reseaux Premire Choix
2100 Sainte-Chatherine St. W., Rm. 800
Montreal, QC, Canada H3H 2T3
Fax: (514)939-3151

Publications: Super Ecran (37227)

Lesbian and Gay Community Services Center, Youth Enrichment Program
208 W 13th St.
New York, NY 10011-7702
Phone: (212)741-2247

Publications: Outyouth (22514)

The Lesbian News
PO Box 55
Torrance, CA 90507
Phone: (310)787-8658
Fax: (310)787-1965
Free: 800-458-9888

Publications: The Lesbian News (3935)

Lessiter Publications Inc.
PO Box 624
Brookfield, WI 53008-0624
Phone: (262)782-4480
Fax: (262)782-1252
Free: 800-645-8455

Publications: American Farriers Journal (33602)

The Lethbridge Herald
504 - 7th St. S.
PO Box 670
Lethbridge, AB, Canada T1J 3Z7
Phone: (403)328-4411
Fax: (403)328-4536

Publications: The Lethbridge Herald (34795)

Let's Play, Inc.
2721 E 42nd St.
Minneapolis, MN 55406
Phone: (612)729-0023
Fax: (612)729-0259

Publications: Let's Play Hockey (16091) • Let's Play Softball (16092)

Letter Arts Review
PO Box 9986
Greensboro, NC 27429
Phone: (336)272-6139
Fax: (336)272-9015
Free: 800-369-9598

Publications: Letter Arts Review (23927)

Levy County Journal
PO Box 159
Bronson, FL 32621
Phone: (352)486-2312
Fax: (352)486-5042

Publications: Levy County Journal (5964)

Lewis & Clark College
0615 SW Palatine Hill Rd. Mailstop 121
Portland, OR 97219
Phone: (503)768-7146
Fax: (503)768-7130

Publications: The Pioneer Log (26499)

Lewis County Herald
PO Box 159
Nezperce, ID 83543
Phone: (208)937-2671
Fax: (208)962-7131

Publications: Lewis County Herald (7935)

Lewis County Herald Inc.
31 Linden St.
PO Box 69
Hohenwald, TN 38462
Phone: (615)796-3191
Fax: (615)796-2153

Publications: Lewis County Herald (29223)

Lewis County Herald Publishing Co.
206 Main St.
Vanceburg, KY 41179
Phone: (606)796-2331
Fax: (606)796-3110
Free: 800-572-2685

Publications: Lewis County Herald (12423)

Lewis County Historical Society
7552 S. State St.
Box 446
Lowville, NY 13367
Phone: (315)376-8957

Publications: Lewis County Historical Society Journal (20969)

Lewis Newspapers, Inc.
111 E Main
PO Box 249
Pilot Point, TX 76258
Phone: (940)686-2169
Fax: (940)686-2437

Publications: Post Signal (30935)

The Lewis Press, Inc.
PO Box 68
Lewis, KS 67552
Phone: (620)324-5551
Fax: (620)324-5879

Publications: The Edwards County Sentinel (11601) • Lewis Press (11602)

Lewis Publishing Co., Inc.
113 N. 6th St.
PO Box 153
Lynden, WA 98264
Phone: (360)354-4444
Fax: (360)354-4445

Publications: Lynden Tribune (32820)

Lewis Publishing, Inc.
308 SWashington
PO Box 200
Clinton, KY 42031
Phone: (502)653-3381
Fax: (502)653-3322

Publications: Hickman County Gazette (12016)

Lewistown News-Argus
521 W Main St.
PO Box 900
Lewistown, MT 59457-0900
Phone: (406)538-3401
Fax: (406)538-3405
Free: 800-879-5627

Publications: Lewistown News-Argus (17848)

Lexington Theological Seminary
631 S Limestone St.
Lexington, KY 40508
Phone: (859)252-0361
Fax: (859)281-6042

Publications: Lexington Theological Quarterly (12174)

LexisNexis Butterworths
75 Clegg Rd.
Markham, ON, Canada L6G 1A1
Phone: (905)479-2665
Fax: (905)479-2826
Free: 800-668-6481

Publications: The Lawyers Weekly (36026)

L.F.P., Inc.
8484 Wilshire Blvd., Ste. 900
Beverly Hills, CA 90211
Phone: (323)651-5400
Fax: (323)651-2741

Publications: Chic Magazine (1570) • Hustler Busty Beauties (1573) • Hustler Magazine (1574) • Tips & Tricks (1577)

LGNY
145 W 28th St., No. 8RE
New York, NY 10001-6114
Phone: (212)691-1100
Fax: (212)691-6185

Publications: LGNY (22250)

L.I. Fisherman Publishing Corp.
14 Ramsey Rd.
Shirley, NY 11967
Phone: (631)345-5200
Fax: (631)345-5304

Publications: The Fisherman (23330)

The Liberal
9350 Yonge St.
PO Box 390
Richmond Hill, ON, Canada L4C 4Y6
Phone: (905)881-3373
Fax: (905)881-9924
Free: 800-565-6357

Publications: The Liberal (36343) • Vaughan Liberal (36347)

Liberal Newspapers, Inc.
PO Box 889
Liberal, KS 67905-0889
Phone: (316)624-2541
Fax: (316)624-0735

Publications: Southwest Daily Times (11605)

Liberation Publications, Inc.
6922 Hollywood Blvd., 10th Fl.
Los Angeles, CA 90028
Phone: (323)871-1225
Fax: (323)467-0173

Publications: The Advocate (2200)

Liberty Business Development Group
731 James St.
Syracuse, NY 13203
Phone: (315)472-6911

Publications: The Business Record (23391)

Liberty County Times
PO Box 689
Chester, MT 59522
Phone: (406)759-5355
Fax: (406)759-5320

Publications: Liberty County Times (17769)

Liberty Foundation
PO Box 1181
Port Townsend, WA 98368
Phone: (360)379-0242

Publications: Liberty (32893)

Liberty Group
125 W Locust St.
Fairbury, IL 61739
Phone: (815)692-2366
Fax: (815)692-3782

Publications: Blade (8878)

Liberty Group
108 W. 1st St.
Geneseo, IL 61254-0209
Phone: (309)944-2119
Fax: (309)944-5615

Publications: Geneseo Republic (8914) • Henry County Advertizer Shopper (8915) • Orion Gazette (8916)

Liberty Group
502 W Jackson St.
PO Box 490
Marion, IL 62959
Phone: (618)993-2626
Fax: (618)993-8326

Publications: Marion Daily Republican (9143)

Liberty Group
206 Whittle Ave.
PO Box 340
Olney, IL 62450
Phone: (618)393-2931
Fax: (618)392-2953

Publications: Olney Daily Mail (9384)

Liberty Group
318 N. Main St.
PO Box 170
Pontiac, IL 61764
Phone: (815)842-1153
Fax: (815)842-4388

Publications: Daily Leader (9464)

Liberty Group
PO Box 694
El Dorado, KS 67042
Phone: (316)321-1120
Fax: (316)321-7722

Publications: El Dorado Times (11421)

Liberty Group
Box 267
Halstad, MN 56548
Phone: (218)456-2133
Fax: (218)456-2567

Publications: The Shopper Diversified (15938)

The Liberty Group
PO Box 318
Marceline, MO 64658
Phone: (660)376-3508
Fax: (660)376-2757

Publications: The Marceline Press (17264)

Liberty Group Michigan Holdings, Inc.
114 N. Depot St.
Ionia, MI 48846
Phone: (616)527-2100
Fax: (616)527-6860
Free: 800-437-3281

Publications: Sentinel-Standard (15206)

Liberty Group Pub.
53 W. Elm St.
PO Box 540
Canton, IL 61520
Phone: (309)647-5100
Fax: (309)647-4665

Publications: The Daily Ledger (8110)

Liberty Group Pub.
PO Box 216
Greenfield, MO 65661
Phone: (417)637-2712
Fax: (417)637-2232

Publications: Greenfield Vedette (17088)

Liberty Group Publishing
107 N. 4th St.
PO Box 669
Heber Springs, AR 72543
Phone: (501)362-2425
Fax: (501)362-5877

Publications: Sun Times (1173)

Liberty Group Publishing
2408 Hwy., 367 N.
Newport, AR 72112
Phone: (870)523-5855

Publications: Newport Daily Independent (1298)

Liberty Group Publishing
111 W. 6th St.
Stuttgart, AR 72160
Phone: (501)673-8533
Fax: (501)673-3671
Free: (870)673-3671

Publications: The Stuttgart Daily Leader (1352)

Liberty Group Publishing
624 State St.
PO Box 269
Chester, IL 62233
Phone: (618)826-2385
Fax: (618)826-5181

Publications: Randolph County Herald Tribune (8239)

Liberty Group Publishing
105 E. Central Blvd.
Kewanee, IL 61443-0836
Phone: (309)852-2181
Fax: (309)852-0010
Free: 800-397-7827

Publications: Star-Courier (9045)

Liberty Group Publishing
400 S. Main St.
Monmouth, IL 61462
Phone: (309)734-3176
Fax: (309)734-7649

Publications: Daily Review Atlas (9216) • Pennysaver (9218)

Liberty Group Publishing
318 N. Main St.
Pontiac, IL 61764
Phone: (815)842-1153
Fax: (815)842-4388

Publications: The Flanagan Home Times (9465)

Liberty Group Publishing
PO Box 667
Teutopolis, IL 62467
Phone: (217)857-3116
Fax: (217)857-3623

Publications: Teutopolis Press and Dieterich Special Gazette (9682)

Liberty Group Publishing
101 N. Elm
PO Box 350
Cresco, IA 52136
Phone: (319)547-3601
Fax: (319)547-4602

Publications: Times-Plain Dealer (10730)

Liberty Group Publishing
11004 Johnson Dr.
Shawnee, KS 66203-2869
Phone: (913)631-2550
Fax: (913)631-6552

Publications: Shawnee Journal Herald (11801)

Liberty Group Publishing
PO Box 1007
Little Falls, NY 13365
Phone: (315)823-3680
Fax: (315)823-4086

Publications: The Evening Times (20951)

Liberty Group Publishing
516 4th St.
PO Box 1200
Devils Lake, ND 58301
Phone: (701)662-2127
Fax: (701)662-3115

Publications: Journal (24390)

Liberty Group Publishing
201 N. Lehigh Ave.
Sayre, PA 18840
Phone: (570)888-9643
Fax: (570)888-6463

Publications: The Evening Times (27945)

Liberty Group Publishing Co.
PO Box 617
West Frankfort, IL 62896
Phone: (618)937-2146
Fax: (618)937-6006

Publications: West Frankfort Daily American (9749)

Liberty Group Publishing Co.
PO Box 190
Derby, KS 67037
Phone: (316)788-2835
Fax: (316)788-0854

Publications: The Daily Reporter (11407) • The Record/Journal (11408) • The Weekly Shopper (11409) • Wichita Journal (11410)

Liberty Group Publishing Co.
300 N. Washington St.
Mexico, MO 65265-2756
Phone: (573)735-4538
Fax: (573)735-4020
Free: 800-675-5670

Publications: Mark Twain Regional News (17283) • Monroe City News (17285)

Liberty Herald
PO Box 10
Liberty, IN 47353-0010
Phone: (765)458-5114
Fax: (765)458-5115

Publications: Liberty Herald (10271)

Liberty Lobby
300 Independence Ave. SE
Washington, DC 20003
Phone: (202)544-1794

Publications: The Spotlight (5803)

The Liberty News
PO Box 69
Liberty, NC 27298
Phone: (336)622-4781
Fax: (336)622-4944

Publications: The Liberty News (24043)

Liberty Press, Inc.
19391 N Alberta St.
Oneida, TN 37841-3359
Phone: (423)569-6343
Fax: (423)569-9566

Publications: Independent Herald (29553)

Liberty Publishing Co. of NY
435 River Rd.
North Tonawanda, NY 14120-6809
Phone: (716)693-1000
Fax: (716)693-0124

Publications: Record Advertiser (23015) • Tonawanda News (23016)

Liberty Suburban Chicago Newspapers
922 Warren Ave.
Downers Grove, IL 60515
Phone: (630)257-5300
Fax: (630)969-0228

Publications: Clarendon Hills Progress (8781) • Darien Du Page Progress (8782) • Downers Grove Reporter (8784) • Willowbrook Progress (8798)

Liberty Suburban Chicago Newspapers
709 Enterprise Dr.
Oak Brook, IL 60523
Phone: (630)368-1100
Fax: (630)368-1188

Publications: Addison Press (9336) • Bensenville/Wood Dale Press (9341) • Berwyn/Stickney/Forest View LIFE (8075) • Bloomingdale/Glendale Heights Press (9342) • Bolingbrook/Romeoville Reporter (8780) • Carol Stream Press (9344) • Cicero Life (8076) • Countryside/Indian Head Park/Willow Springs/Burr Ridge/Pleasantdale Suburban Life (9346) • Darien Metropolitan (9348) • Downers Grove Progress (8783) • Elmhurst Press (9349) • Elmhurst Suburban LIFE (9350) • The Farmside: Huntley, Marengo (9006) • Geneva Republican (9569) • Glen Ellyn News (8927) • Hillside/Broadview/Berkeley/Westchester Suburban Life (9352) • Itasca/Roselle Press: Serving Bartlett/Hanover Park/Steamwood Press (9354) • Lemont Reporter/Metropolitan (8788) • Lisle Reporter (8789) • Lombard Spectator (9358) • Lombard Suburban LIFE (9359) • Naperville Reporter (8791) • North DuPage Press (8930) • North Riverside/Riverside/Riverside Lawn Suburban Life (9361) • Rancho Santa Fe Sun (9486) • Roselle Press (9364) • St. Charles Republican (9571) • SE DuPage Suburban LIFE/Reporter (8794) • Southeast DuPage Progress (8795) • Suburban LIFE Citizen (9367) • Villa Park/Oakbrook Terrace Argus (9368) • Villa Park Suburban LIFE (9369) • Warrenville Post (9572) • West Chicago Press (9573) • West DuPage Press (9574) • Western Springs Suburban Life (9370) • Westmont Progress (8797) • Wheaton Leader (9760) • Winfield Press (9575) • Woodridge Progress (8799)

Liberty Surburban Chicago Newspapers
709 Enterprise Dr.
Oak Brook, IL 60523-8814
Phone: (708)352-9852
Fax: (708)834-0910

Publications: Ad ExPress (9335) • Glen Ellyn Press (8928)

Libido, Inc.
Box 146721
Chicago, IL 60614
Phone: (773)275-0842
Fax: (773)275-0752
Free: 800-495-1988

Publications: Libido (8461)

Libra Publishers Inc.
3089C Clairemont Dr., PMB 383
San Diego, CA 92117
Phone: (858)571-1414
Fax: (858)571-1414

Publications: Adolescence (3106) • Family Therapy (3153)

The Library of Congress
Science & Technology Division
Washington, DC 20540
Phone: (202)707-5000
Fax: (202)707-1925

Publications: Current Antarctic Literature (5454)

Library and Information Technology Association
50 E. Huron St.
Chicago, IL 60611
Phone: (312)280-4270
Fax: (312)280-3257
Free: 800-545-2433

Publications: Information Technology and Libraries (8413)

Library Outreach Reporter
148 Liberty St.
Fords, NJ 08863
Phone: (732)738-5183
Fax: (732)738-5183

Publications: The Lit Page (18827) • On the Road (18828)

LIBRE
904 SW 23rd Ave.
Miami, FL 33135
Phone: (305)643-4200
Fax: (305)649-2767

Publications: Libre (6368)

Licensing Executives Society Intl.
1800 Diagonal Rd., Ste. 280
Alexandria, VA 22314
Phone: (703)836-3106
Fax: (703)836-3107

Publications: les Nouvelles (31705)

L.I.F. Publishing Corp.
14 Ramsey Rd.
Shirley, NY 11967
Phone: (516)345-5200
Fax: (516)345-5304

Publications: The Fisherman-Long Island Edition (23331)

Life Insurance Selling
1801 Park 270 Dr., Ste. 550
St. Louis, MO 63146-4016
Phone: (314)421-5445
Fax: (314)421-1070

Publications: Life Insurance Selling (17466)

Life Office Management Association
2300 Windy Ridge Pkwy., Ste. 600
Atlanta, GA 30339-8443
Phone: (770)951-1770
Fax: (770)984-6417
Free: 800-275-5662

Publications: LOMA Resource (7026) • Resource (7040)

Lifestyle Ventures LLC
250 W 57th St., Ste. 420
New York, NY 10107
Phone: (212)265-8890
Fax: (212)265-8908

Publications: American Cheerleader (21184) • Stage Directions (22782)

Lifetime Periodicals, Inc.
2131 Hollywood Blvd.
Hollywood, FL 33020
Phone: (954)925-5242
Fax: (954)925-5244

Publications: Diet & Fitness (6192) • Fell's U.S. Coins Magazine (6194) • MoneyLines Magazine (6196) • Specialty Cooking Magazine (6198)

LifeWay Christian Resources
One Lifeway Plz.
Nashville, TN 37234-0175
Phone: (615)251-2000
Fax: (615)277-8272

Publications: Home Life (29459) • National Drama Service (29474)

Lifeway Christian Resources of the Southern Baptist Convention
One Lifeway Plz.
Nashville, TN 37234-0175
Phone: (615)251-2000
Fax: (615)251-2614
Free: 800-458-2772

Publications: Mature Living (29469) • Pedalpoint (29480) • Worship (29503)

Light
PO Box 7500
Chicago, IL 60680
Phone: (847)853-1028
Fax: (847)853-1102
Free: 800-285-4448

Publications: Light (8465)

Light Bridge Publishing
RR 3
Box 242
Spring Mills, PA 16875
Phone: (814)422-8112

Publications: Universal Light Messenger (28010)

Light & Champion Newspaper
Box 1989
Center, TX 75935
Phone: (936)598-3377
Fax: (936)598-6394

Publications: Light & Champion (30012) • The Merchandiser (30013)

The Light Inc.
42 Park Ave.
Rutherford, NJ 07070-1714
Phone: (201)460-7575
Fax: (201)460-7500

Publications: The Fountain (19526)

Light Publishing Co.
Box 87
Wyoming, IA 52362
Phone: (319)488-2281

Publications: Midland Times (11331)

Lightborne Publishing, Inc.
212 E. 14th Street
Cincinnati, OH 45210

Publications: Cincinnati CityBeat (24784)

The Lighter Than Air Society
1436 Triplett Blvd.
Akron, OH 44306-3304
Fax: (330)668-1105

Publications: Buoyant Flight (24577)

Lighthouse
5334 Torrance Blvd.
Torrance, CA 90503
Phone: (310)944-3533
Fax: (310)944-3633

Publications: Lighthouse (3936)

The Lighthouse
1874 Shadyside Rd.
Coatesville, PA 19320-4821

Publications: The Lighthouse Electronic Magazine (26793)

Lighthouse Publishing Ltd.
353 York St.
Bridgewater, NS, Canada B4V 3K2
Phone: (902)543-2457
Fax: (902)543-2228
Free: 888-543-2457

Publications: Bulletin/Progress Enterprise (35542) • Lighthouse Log (35543) • Progress Enterprise 1 Bulletin (35593)

Lightner Publishing Corp.
1006 S Michigan Ave.
Chicago, IL 60605
Phone: (312)939-4767
Fax: (312)939-0053
Free: 800-762-7576

Publications: Antiques & Collecting Magazine (8265)

Lightworks Magazine, Inc.
Box 1202
Birmingham, MI 48012-1202
Phone: (248)626-8026

Publications: Lightworks (14825)

The Ligonier Echo
229, Pittsburgh St.
Scottdale, PA 15683
Phone: (724)887-7400
Fax: (724)887-5115
Free: 800-640-6977

Publications: The Ligonier Echo (27953)

Ligonier Ministries
PO Box 547500
Orlando, FL 32854
Phone: (407)333-4244
Fax: (407)333-4233
Free: 800-435-4343

Publications: Tabletalk (6509)

Liguori Publications
1 Liguori Dr.
Liguori, MO 63057
Phone: (636)464-2500
Fax: (636)464-8449
Free: 800-464-2555

Publications: Liguorian (17253)

Lilith Publications
250 W 57th, Ste. 2432
New York, NY 10107
Phone: (212)757-0818
Fax: (212)757-5705
Free: 888-254-5484

Publications: Lilith (22257)

Lillie Suburban Newspapers
2515 E. 7th Ave.
North St. Paul, MN 55109
Phone: (651)777-8800
Fax: (651)777-8288

Publications: East Side Review (16225) • Lillie Suburban Shopping Review (16226) • Maplewood Review (16227) • New Brighton-Mounds View Bulletin (16205) • Oakdale-Lake Elmo Review (16228) • Ramsey County Review (16229) • Roseville Review (16230) • The St. Anthony Bulletin (16340) • Shoreview-Arden Hills Bulletin (16447) • South-West Review (16231) • Woodbury-South Maplewood Review (16232)

Lillooet News
979 Main St.
PO Box 709
Lillooet, BC, Canada V0K 1V0
Phone: (604)256-4219
Fax: (604)256-4210

Publications: Bridge River-Lillooet News (35010)

The Lima News
3515 Elida Rd.
PO Box 690
Lima, OH 45807-0690
Phone: (419)223-1010
Fax: (419)229-0426
Free: 800-686-9914

Publications: The Lima News (25297)

Lime Springs Herald
PO Box 187
Lime Springs, IA 52155
Phone: (563)566-2687

Publications: Lime Springs Herald (11039)

Limestone Independent News
114 Roosevelt St.
Bartonville, IL 61607
Phone: (309)697-1851
Fax: (309)697-1851

Publications: Limestone Independent News (8051)

The Limon Leader
1062 Main St.
Box 1300
Limon, CO 80828
Phone: (719)775-2064
Fax: (719)775-9082

Publications: The Limon Leader (4544)

Limousin World
PO Box 850870
1050 Andrew Dr.
Yukon, OK 73085
Phone: (405)350-0040
Fax: (405)350-0054

Publications: Limousin World (26204)

LIMRA International, Inc.
PO Box 208
Hartford, CT 06141-0208
Phone: (860)688-3358
Fax: (860)298-9555
Free: 800-235-4672

Publications: Managers Handbook (4897)

Lincoln Center
140 W 62nd St.
New York, NY 10023
Phone: (212)636-6948
Fax: (212)636-6582

Publications: Fordham Intellectual Property, Media & Entertainment Law Journal (21722)

Lincoln County News
PO Box 36
Damariscotta, ME 04543
Phone: (207)563-3171
Fax: (207)563-3127
Free: 800-339-5818

Publications: Lincoln County News (12950)

Lincoln County News
309 Central Ave.
PO Box 459
Carrizozo, NM 88301-0459
Phone: (505)648-2333
Fax: (505)648-2333

Publications: Lincoln County News (19827)

Lincoln County Publishing Co., Inc.
216 W Bradley
Star City, AR 71667
Phone: (870)628-4161
Fax: (870)628-3802

Publications: Lincoln Ledger (1347)

Lincoln County Publishing Co., Inc.
718 Manvel
Box 248
Chandler, OK 74834-0248
Phone: (405)258-1818
Fax: (405)258-1824

Publications: The Lincoln County News (25780)

Lincoln County Record
PO Box 507
Pioche, NV 89043-0507
Phone: (775)726-3333
Fax: (775)726-3331

Publications: Lincoln County Record (18415)

The Lincoln Institute for Research and Education, Inc.
1001 Connecticut Ave. NW, Ste. 1135
Washington, DC 20036
Phone: (202)223-5112

Publications: Lincoln Review (5637)

The Lincoln Journal, Inc.
328 Walnut St.
PO Box 308
Hamlin, WV 25523
Phone: (304)824-5101
Fax: (304)824-5210
Free: 800-319-4204

Publications: Hamlin Weekly News Sentinel (33330) • Lincoln Journal (33331) • Lincoln Times (33332)

Lincoln Journal Star
926 P St.
PO Box 81609
Lincoln, NE 68508
Phone: (402)475-4200

Publications: Lincoln Journal Star (18091)

Lincoln Journal Star
410 Main St.
PO Box 250
Plattsmouth, NE 68048
Phone: (402)296-2141
Fax: (402)296-3401
Free: 800-742-0061

Publications: Plattsmouth Journal (18250)

Lincoln Leader
PO Box 520
Lincoln, AR 72744
Phone: (501)824-3263
Fax: (501)824-5540

Publications: Lincoln Leader (1207)

Lincoln New Era
PO Box 280
Lincoln, MO 65338
Phone: (816)668-4418
Fax: (816)668-4418

Publications: Lincoln New Era (17254)

Lincoln News
PO Box 35
Lincoln, ME 04457
Phone: (207)794-6532
Fax: (207)794-2004

Publications: Lincoln News (12981)

Lincoln Sentinel-Republican
Box 67
Lincoln, KS 67455
Phone: (785)524-4200
Fax: (785)524-4242

Publications: Lincoln Sentinel-Republican (11608)

Lincoln Trail Publishing
PO Box 158
Casey, IL 62420
Phone: (217)932-5211
Fax: (217)932-5214

Publications: The Marketplace for Greenup & Toledo (8172) • Reporter (8173)

Lincoln University
Office of Communications
PO Box 179
Lincoln University, PA 19352
Phone: (610)932-8300
Fax: (610)932-0195

Publications: The Lincolnian (27200)

Lincolnton Journal
PO Box 399
157 N Peach St.
Lincolnton, GA 30817
Phone: (706)359-3229
Fax: (706)359-2884

Publications: Lincolnton Journal (7375)

The Linden Herald
18974 E Main St.
PO Box 929
Linden, CA 95236
Phone: (209)887-3112
Fax: (209)887-3111

Publications: The Linden Herald (1764)

Linden Lane Press
PO Box 331964
Fort Worth, TX 76163
Phone: (817)731-4657
Fax: (817)738-4435

Publications: Linden Lane Magazine (30345)

Linden Publications
19033 E Main St.
PO Box 129
Linden, CA 95236-0129
Phone: (209)887-3829
Fax: (209)887-3829

Publications: California Odd Fellow and Rebekah (2154)

Lindenwood University
209 S Kingshighway
St. Charles, MO 63301
Phone: (636)949-2000
Fax: (636)949-4910

Publications: The Linden World (17384)

The Lindsay Daily Post
15 William St. N.
Lindsay, ON, Canada K9V 3Z8
Phone: (705)324-2113
Fax: (705)324-0174

Publications: The Lindsay Daily Post (35971)

Lindsay This Week
96 Albert St. South
Lindsay, ON, Canada K9V 3Z6
Phone: (705)324-8600
Fax: (705)324-5694

Publications: Lindsay This Week (35973)

Linfield College
900 SE Baker St., Unit 4009
McMinnville, OR 97128
Phone: (503)472-7715

Publications: The Linfield Review (26414)

Lingle Guide
PO Box 278
Lingle, WY 82223
Phone: (307)837-2255
Fax: (307)837-2255

Publications: Guernsey Gazette (34559) • Lingle Guide (34560)

Linguistic Analysis
Box 2418
Vashon, WA 98070
Phone: (206)567-4373
Fax: (206)567-5711

Publications: Linguistics Analysis (33185)

Linguistic Society of America
SUNY Stony Brook
Dept. of Linguistics
Stony Brook, NY 11794-4376
Phone: (631)632-8003
Fax: (631)632-9789

Publications: Language (23372)

Link Publications Society Inc.
1455 de Maisonneuve W., Rm. H-649
Montreal, QC, Canada H3G 1M8
Phone: (514)848-7405
Fax: (514)848-4540

Publications: The Link (37179)

Links Magazine
700 Canal St.
Stamford, CT 06902

Publications: Links Magazine (5154)

Linn County News
808 Main St.
PO Box 478
Pleasanton, KS 66075
Phone: (913)352-6235
Fax: (913)352-6607
Free: 888-292-6235

Publications: Linn County News (11760)

Linn's Stamp News
911 Vandemark Rd.
Sidney, OH 45365
Phone: (937)498-0802
Fax: (937)498-0807
Free: 800-572-6885

Publications: Linn's Stamp News (25518)

Linstok Press
4020 Blackburn Ln.
Burtonsville, MD 20866
Phone: (301)421-0268
Fax: (301)421-0270
Free: 800-475-4756

Publications: Sign Language Studies (13398)

Linworth Publishing Inc.
480 E. Wilson Bridge Rd., Ste. L
Worthington, OH 43085-2372
Phone: (614)436-7107
Fax: (614)436-9490
Free: 800-786-5017

Publications: The Book Report (25678) • Library Talk (25680)

Lionheart Publishing Inc.
506 Roswell St., Ste. 220
Marietta, GA 30060
Phone: (770)431-0867
Fax: (770)432-6969

Publications: APICS-The Performance Advantage (7409) • OR/MS Today (7415)

Lions Clubs International
300 W 22nd St.
Oak Brook, IL 60523-8815
Phone: (630)571-5466
Fax: (630)571-8890

Publications: Lion En Espanol (9356) • The Lion Magazine (9357)

Lippincott Williams & Wilkins
351 W. Camden St.
Baltimore, MD 21201-2436
Phone: (410)528-4294
Fax: (410)528-4452
Free: 800-222-3790

Publications: Addictive Disorders & Their Treatment (13107) • Advances in Anatomic Pathology (13108) • Advances in Gastroenterology, Hepatology and Clinical Nutrition (13109) • A.J.N. International Nursing Index (13110) • Alzheimer Disease and Associated Disorders (13112) • American Journal of Clinical Oncology (13114) • The American Journal of Dermatopathology (13115) • The American Journal of Forensic Medicine and Pathology (13117) • The American Journal of Surgical Pathology (AJSP) (13119) • Annals of Surgical Oncology (31641) • Applied Immunohistochemistry & Molecular Morphology (13125) • CA: A Cancer Journal for Clinicians (13141) • Cardiovascular and Thoracic Anesthesia Journal (13142) • Caring for the Ages (13143) • Clinical and Applied Thrombosis/Hemostasis (13145) • The Clinical Journal of Pain (13146) • Clinical Journal of Sport Medicine (13147) • Clinical Neuropharmacology (13148) • Clinical Orthopaedics and Related Research (13149) • Convulsive Therapy (13151) • Cornea (13152) • Diagnostic Molecular Pathology (13156) • Emergency Medicine News (13158) • Eye and Contact Lens: Science and Clinical Practice (13160) • Inflammatory Bowel Diseases (13171) • International Journal of Gynecological Pathology (13173) • Journal of Acquired Immune Deficiency Syndrome (JAIDS) (13177) • Journal of the American Medical Directors Association (JAMDA) (3878) • Journal of Bronchology (13180) • Journal of Cardiovascular Pharmacology (13181) • Journal of Cerebral Blood Flow and Metabolism (13182) • Journal of Clinical Gastroenterology (13183) • Journal of Clinical Neuromuscular Disease (13184) • Journal of Clinical Neurophysiology (13185) • Journal of Computer-Assisted Tomography (13186) • Journal of Electromyography and Kinesiology (13189) • Journal of Glaucoma (13190) • Journal of Immunotherapy (13193) • Journal of Neuro-Ophthalmology (14757) • Journal of Neurosurgical Anesthesiology (13196) • Journal of Orthopaedic Trauma (13197) • Journal of Pediatric Gastroenterology & Nutrition (13198) • Journal of Pediatric Hematology/Oncology (13199) • Journal of Pediatric Orthopaedics (13200) • Journal of Spinal Disorders & Techniques (13202) • Journal of Thoracic Imaging (13203) • Journal of Voice (13205) • Menopause (13217) • Neuropsychiatry, Neuropsychology, and Behavioral Neurology (13224) • Neurosurgery Quarterly (13225) • Obstetric Anesthesia Digest (13226) • Oncology Times (13227) • Ophthalmic Plastic and Reconstructive Surgery (13228) • The Otolaryngology Journal (13229) • Otology & Neurotology (13230) • The Pain Medicine Journal (13231) • Pancreas (13232) • Pediatric Critical Care Medicine (13234) • Sports Medicine and Arthroscopy Review (13249) • Surgical Laparoscopy Endoscopy & Percutaneous Techniques (13250) • Techniques in Neurosurgery (13251) • Techniques in Orthopaedics (13252) • Therapeutic Drug Monitoring (13254) • Topics in Magnetic Resonance Imaging (TMRI) (13255) • Ultrasound Quarterly (13256)

Lippincott Williams & Wilkins
16522 Hunters Green Pkwy.
Hagerstown, MD 21740-2116
Phone: (301)223-2300
Fax: (301)223-2400
Free: 800-638-3030

Publications: Journal of Behavioral Health Services & Research (6769)

Lippincott Williams & Wilkins
530 Walnut St.
Philadelphia, PA 19106
Phone: (215)521-8300
Fax: (215)521-8920

Publications: Academic Physician & Scientist (21132) • ACSM's Health & Fitness Journal (18359) • Advances in Skin & Wound Care (27363) • AIDS (27365) • AJNR: American Journal of Neuroradiology (27366) • Alcoholism: Clinical and Experimental Research (10077) • American Journal of the Medical Sciences (27372) • American Journal of Physical Medicine and Rehabilitation (10078) • American Journal of Roentgenology (32182) • Anesthesia & Analgesia (3326) • Anesthesiology (27375) • Annals of Plastic Surgery (11027) • Annals of Surgery (33920) • ASA Refresher Courses in Anesthesiology (27384) • ASAIO Journal (27385) • AUA News (27386) • Cancer Nursing (6133) • Circulation (27403) • Circulation Research (27404) • Clinical Nuclear Medicine (28197) • Clinical Nurse Specialist (26987) • Clinical Obstetrics Gynecology (31424) • Computers in Nursing (13009) • Coronary Artery Disease (27428) • Critical Care Medicine (8757) • Current Opinion in Anesthesiology (27434) • Current Opinion in Cardiology (27435) • Current Opinion in Gastroenterology (27436) • Current Opinion in Lipidology (27437) • Current Opinion in Neurology (27438) • Current Opinion in Obstetrics & Gynecology (27439) • Current Opinion in Oncology (27440) • Current Opinion in Ophthalmology (27441) • Current Opinion in Orthopaedics (27442) • Current Opinion in Pediatrics (27443) • Current Opinion in Psychiatry (27444) • Current Opinion in Rheumatology (27445) • Current Surgery (27446) • Diseases of the Colon and Rectum (16307) • Drug Metabolism and Disposition (27454) • Ear and Hearing (27455) • The Endocrinologist (27458) • Epidemiology (27462) • European Journal of Gastroenterology & Hepatology (27465) • Foot & Ankle (27470) • Gastroenterology Nursing (29732) • Genetics in Medicine (16083) • Health Physics (28513) • Home Care Manager (27485) • Home Healthcare Nurse (12218) • Home Healthcare Nurse Manager (27486) • Hypertension (27488) • International Anesthesiology Clinics (13906) • Investigative Radiology (31178) • Journal of the American Academy of Child and Adolescent Psychiatry (27512) • Journal of the American Society of Nephrology (27514) • Journal of Cardiopulmonary Rehabilitation (27518) • Journal of Child and Family Nursing (27521) • Journal of Clinical Psychopharmacology (13915) • The Journal of Craniofacial Surgery (6770) • Journal of Developmental & Behavioral Pediatrics (27524) • Journal of ECT (19357) • Journal of Endodontics (13564) • Journal of Foot and Ankle Surgery (9405) • Journal of Hypertension (27531) • Journal of Infusion Nursing (14448) • Journal of Intravenous Nursing (27532) • Journal of Investigative Medicine (27533) • The Journal of Medical Practice Management (8446) • Journal of Nervous and Mental Disease (13195) • The Journal of Neuroscience (5606) • Journal for Nurses in Staff Development (JNSD) (27540) • Journal of Nursing Administration (JONA) (27541) • Journal of Occupational and Environmental Medicine (8025) • The Journal of Orthopaedic and Sports Physical Therapy (JOSPT) (31700) • Journal of Pediatric Orthopaedics, Part B. (27544) • Journal of Pelvic Medicine & Surgery (27545) • Journal of Trauma (13036) • Journal of Urology (13204) • Journal of Vascular and Interventional Radiology (JVIR) (27555) • Laboratory Investigation (4997) • The Lancet (North American Edition) (27559) • Lippincott's Hospital Pharmacy (22259) • MCN, The American Journal of Maternal/Child Nursing (20777) • Medical Care (10152) • Medicine (13216) • Medicine and Science in Sports and Exercise (10153) • Modern Pathology (27571) • Neurology (27577) • Neurosurgery (27579) • Nurse Educator (27587) • Nursing Case Management (27589) • Nursing 96 (27593) • Nutrition Today (13941) • Obstetrical & Gynecological Survey (29477) • Office Dealer (27596) • Outcomes Management (14942) • Pathology Case Reviews (13233) • Pediatric Emergency Care (27615) • The Pediatric Infectious Disease Journal (30177) • Pediatric Physical Therapy (27618) • Pediatric Research (27619) • Physical Therapy Case Reports (27639) • Plastic and Reconstructive Surgery (14023) • Primary Care Case Reviews (4349) • Problems in Anesthesia (27647) • Psychosomatic Medicine (27651) • The Radiologist (2695) • RETINA (26944) • Sexually Transmitted Diseases (27677) • Soil Science (19340) • Spine (27693) • Sports Chiropractic & Rehabilitation (27695) • Stroke (27696) • Survey of Anesthesiology (23483) • Techniques in Hand and Upper Extremity Surgery (27699) • Transplantation (22855)

Lippincott Williams & Wilkins
1111 Bethlehem Pike
PO Box 908
Springhouse, PA 19477
Phone: 800-346-7844
Fax: (215)646-1083
Free: 800-346-7844

Publications: The Nurse Practitioner (28014)

Lipscomb University
3901 Granny White Pike
Nashville, TN 37204-3951
Phone: (615)269-1000
Free: 800-333-4358

Publications: The Babbler (29443) • The Lipscomb News (29468)

Liquid Paper Press
PO Box 4973
Austin, TX 78765

Publications: Nerve Cowboy (29793)

Liquor Control Board of Ontario
55 Lakeshore Blvd. E
Toronto, ON, Canada M5E 1A4
Phone: (416)365-5906
Fax: (416)365-5935

Publications: Food & Drink (36598)

The Listening Eye
KSU Geauga Campus
14111 Claridon-Troy Rd.
Burton, OH 44021
Phone: (440)286-3840

Publications: The Listening Eye (24721)

Litchfield Independent-Review
PO Box 921
Litchfield, MN 55355
Phone: (320)693-3266
Fax: (320)693-9177

Publications: Litchfield Independent-Review (16004)

Litchfield News-Herald, Inc.
112 E Ryder St.
PO Box 160
Litchfield, IL 62056
Phone: (217)324-2121
Fax: (217)324-2122

Publications: Litchfield News-Herald (9113)

Literary Rocket
PO Box 672
Water Mill, NY 11976-0672

Publications: Literary Rocket (23513)

Lithuanian Alliance of America
307 W 30th St.
New York, NY 10001
Phone: (212)563-2210
Fax: (212)563-2210

Publications: Tevyne (22825)

Lithuanian Canadian R.C. Cultural Society "Ziburiai"
2185 Stavebank Rd.
Mississauga, ON, Canada L5C 1T3
Phone: (416)275-4672
Fax: (416)290-9802

Publications: Teviskes Ziburiai (The Lights of Homeland) (36089)

Lithuanian Catholic Press Society
4545 W 63rd St.
Chicago, IL 60629-5589
Phone: (773)585-9500
Fax: (773)585-8284

Publications: The Friend (8381)

Lithuanian Franciscans
361 Highland Blvd.
Brooklyn, NY 11207
Phone: (718)235-5962

Publications: Varpelis (The Little Bell) (20352)

Lithuanian National League of America, Inc.
208 W Natoma Ave.
PO Box 241
Addison, IL 60101
Phone: (630)543-8198
Fax: (630)543-8198

Publications: The League-Sandara (8001)

Litmor Publications, Inc.
81 E Barclay St.
Hicksville, NY 11801
Phone: (516)931-0012
Fax: (516)931-0027

Publications: Bethpage Newsgram (20149) • Garden City News (20642) • Jericho News Journal (20849) • Mid-Island Times (20741) • New Hyde Park Herald Courier (21111) • Syosset Advance (23382) • Williston Times (23585)

Litotype Publication
2949 W Pope John Paul II Dr.
Chicago, IL 60632
Phone: (312)523-3663
Fax: (312)523-3983

Publications: Brighton Park-McKinley Park Life (8292)

Little India
Empire State Building
350 Fifth Ave., Ste. 1826
New York, NY 10118
Phone: (212)560-0608
Fax: (212)560-0609

Publications: Little India (22263)

The Little Kanawha Publishing Co.
PO Box 309
Elizabeth, WV 26143
Phone: (304)275-8981
Fax: (304)275-8981

Publications: Wirt County Journal (33304)

The Little Magazine
1400 Washington Ave.
State University of New York at Albany
English Dept.
Albany, NY 12222
Phone: (518)442-3300

Publications: The Little Magazine (19994)

Little Nickel Classifieds
3701 148th St. SW
Lynnwood, WA 98037
Phone: (425)742-7244
Fax: (425)743-5330
Free: 800-544-0505

Publications: Little Nickel Classifieds (32824)

Little Publishing Co., Inc.
PO Box 300
Westcliffe, CO 81252
Phone: (719)783-2361
Fax: (719)783-3725

Publications: Wet Mountain Tribune (4658)

Little River News
45 E Commence
PO Box 608
Ashdown, AR 71822
Phone: (870)898-3462
Fax: (870)898-6213

Publications: Little River News (1036)

Little Sisters of the Poor
601 Maiden Choice Ln.
Baltimore, MD 21228
Phone: (410)744-9367
Fax: (410)788-5614

Publications: Serenity (13245)

Littleton Independent
2329 W Main St., Ste. 103
Littleton, CO 80120
Phone: (303)794-7877
Fax: (303)794-1909

Publications: Littleton Independent (4551)

Lituanus
47 W Polk St., Ste. 100-300
Chicago, IL 60605
Phone: (312)341-9396

Publications: Lituanus (8468)

Liturgical Conference
415 Michigan Ave. NE, No. 65
Washington, DC 20017-1518
Phone: (202)832-6520
Fax: (202)832-6523
Free: 800-394-0885

Publications: Liturgy (5638)

The Liturgical Press
St. John's Abbey
Box 7500
Collegeville, MN 56321
Phone: (320)363-2213
Fax: 800-445-5899
Free: 800-858-5450

Publications: The Bible Today (15805) • Worship (15806)

Liturgical Publications Inc.
2875 S. James Dr.
New Berlin, WI 53151
Phone: (262)785-1188
Fax: (262)785-9567
Free: 800-876-4574

Publications: Prayers for Worship (34183) • Preaching: Word & Witness (34184)

Liturgy Training Publications
1800 N Hermitage Ave.
Chicago, IL 60622-1101
Phone: (773)486-8970
Fax: (773)486-7094

Publications: Catechumenate: A Journal of Christian Initiation (8300) • RITE (8557)

Live Oak Press, Inc.
PO Box 23707
Columbia, SC 29224-3707
Phone: (803)736-2424
Fax: (803)736-3404
Free: 800-849-1004

Publications: SPORTING CLASSICS (28569)

Live Oak Publications
211 Howard St. E
PO Box 370
Live Oak, FL 32060
Phone: (386)362-1734
Fax: (386)364-5578

Publications: The Jasper News (6305) • Live Oak Suwannee Democrat (6306)

Live Oak Publishing
122 S. 3rd
Oakdale, CA 95361
Phone: (209)847-3021
Fax: (209)847-9750

Publications: Escalon Times (1888) • The Riverbank News (2929)

Live Stock News Service
120 N Rayner St.
PO Box 7655
Fort Worth, TX 76111
Phone: (817)838-0106
Fax: (817)831-3117

Publications: Weekly Livestock Reporter (30355)

Livestock Market Digest, Inc.
2231 Rio Grande Blvd. NW
PO Box 7458
Albuquerque, NM 87104
Phone: (505)243-9515
Fax: (505)243-9598

Publications: Livestock Market Digest (19775)

Livewire Printing Co.
310 2nd St.
PO Box 208
Jackson, MN 56143-0208
Phone: (507)847-3771
Fax: (507)847-5822
Free: 800-658-2393

Publications: Livewire (15975)

Living Church Foundation, Inc.
816 E Juneau Ave.
PO Box 514036
Milwaukee, WI 53203-3436
Phone: (414)276-5420
Fax: (414)276-7483

Publications: Living Church (34074)

Living City of the Focolare Movement
PO Box 837
Bronx, NY 10465
Phone: (718)828-2932
Fax: (718)892-0419

Publications: Living City (20276)

The Living Light
Department of Education
3211 4th St. NE
Washington, DC 20017
Phone: (202)541-3090
Fax: (202)541-3089

Publications: The Living Light (5639)

Living Presence Ministries
6460 Oak Hill Dr.
West Farmington, OH 44491

Publications: Presence (25633)

Livingston County Extension Service Association
Agricultural Dept.
158 S. Main St.
Mount Morris, NY 14510-1594
Phone: (585)658-3250
Fax: (585)658-4707

Publications: Livingston County Agricultural News (21101)

Livingston Enterprise
119 W. Bell St.
PO Box 61
Glendive, MT 59330
Phone: (406)365-3303
Fax: (406)365-5435

Publications: Ranger-Review (17795)

Livingston Enterprise
PO Box 2000
Livingston, MT 59047
Phone: (406)222-2000
Fax: (406)222-8580
Free: 800-345-8412

Publications: Livingston Enterprise (17856)

Llano News
813 Berry St.
PO Box 187
Llano, TX 78643-1907
Phone: (915)247-4433
Fax: (915)247-3338

Publications: Llano News (30702)

Llewellyn Worldwide
PO Box 64383
St. Paul, MN 55164-0383
Phone: (651)291-1970
Fax: (651)291-1908
Free: 800-843-6666

Publications: Llewellyn's New Worlds of Mind and Spirit (16384)

LMS Associates
17 E Henrietta St.
Baltimore, MD 21230
Phone: (410)685-8621
Fax: (410)685-0870
Free: 888-371-0152

Publications: School Library Media Activities Monthly (13244)

LMT Communications, Inc.
731 Main St., Ste. A2
Monroe, CT 06468
Phone: (203)459-2888
Fax: (203)459-2889

Publications: LMT (4963)

LNG Publishing Company Inc.
6105 Arlington Blvd., Ste. G
Falls Church, VA 22044
Phone: (703)536-0800
Fax: (703)536-0803

Publications: Lube Report (32049)

Loaded-for-Bear Publishing
1535 11th Ave. 3rd Fl.
Seattle, WA 98122
Phone: (206)323-7101
Fax: (206)323-7203

Publications: The Stranger (33033)

Loafer's Choice
1400-G NW 65th Ave.
PO Box 16928
Plantation, FL 33318
Phone: (954)791-3224
Fax: (954)581-3463

Publications: Loafer's Choice (6587)

Locke Science Publishing Co., Inc.
28th E Jackson Bldg., 10th floor, Ste. L221
Chicago, IL 60604
Publications: Journal of Architectural and Planning Research (8433)

Lockeford-Clements News
20150 Sierra
PO Box 76
Lockeford, CA 95237
Phone: (209)727-5776
Publications: A Touch of Country (2156)

Lockheed Martin Aeronantics Company
Mail Zone 1503
Box 748
Fort Worth, TX 76101-0748
Phone: (817)777-5542
Fax: (817)763-4797
Publications: Code One (30334)

Lockwood Publications, Inc.
26 Broadway, Fl. 9M
New York, NY 10004-1703
Phone: (212)269-7053
Fax: (212)827-0945
Publications: California Track and Running News (14138) • SMOKE (22749)

Lockwood Trade Journal Co.
26 Broadway, Fl. 9M
New York, NY 10004-1703
Phone: (212)391-2060
Fax: (212)827-0945
Telex: 827-925 lock uf
Publications: Tea and Coffee Trade Journal (22816) • Tobacco International (22842)

Locus Publications
PO Box 13305
Oakland, CA 94661
Phone: (510)339-9196
Fax: (510)339-8144
Publications: Locus (2687)

Lodestar Publications, Inc.
N5553 Hwy. 35
Onalaska, WI 54650
Phone: (608)781-6700
Fax: (608)781-0905
Publications: Holmen Courier (34210) • Onalaska Community Life (34211)

The Lodi Enterprise
146 S Main
PO Box 16
Lodi, WI 53555
Phone: (608)592-3261
Fax: (608)592-3866
Publications: The Lodi Enterprise (33911)

Lodi Enterprise
146 S Main St
PO Box 16
Lodi, WI 53555
Phone: (608)592-3261
Fax: (608)592-3866
Publications: Prairie/Valley Shopping News (33912)

Lodi News-Merchandiser
PO Box 1360
Lodi, CA 95241-1360
Phone: (209)369-2761
Fax: (209)369-1084
Publications: Lodi News-Merchandiser (2157)

Lodi News-Sentinel
125 N. Church St.
Lodi, CA 95240-2102
Phone: (209)369-2761
Fax: (209)369-1084
Publications: Lodi News-Sentinel (2158)

Jean Loewen
208 Aztec
PO Box 188
Montezuma, KS 67867
Phone: (316)846-2312
Fax: (316)846-2312
Publications: Montezuma Press (11658)

Log Cabin Democrat
1058 Front St.
PO Box 969
Conway, AR 72032
Phone: (501)327-6621
Fax: (501)327-6787
Free: 800-678-4523
Publications: Log Cabin Democrat (1083)

The Log Newspapers
2924 Emerson St., Ste. 200
San Diego, CA 92106
Phone: (619)226-1608
Fax: (619)226-0573
Free: 800-841-4377
Publications: The Log (Los Angeles/Ventura County Edition) (3224) • The Log (Orange County Edition) (3225)

Logan Media, Inc.
PO Box 720
Logan, WV 25601
Phone: (304)752-6950
Fax: (304)752-1239
Publications: The Logan Banner (33370)

Logan Republican
101 E Main St.
Box 97
Logan, KS 67646-0097
Phone: (785)689-4339
Fax: (785)689-7492
Publications: The Logan Republican (11612)

Loggers World Publications
4206 Jackson Hwy.
Chehalis, WA 98532
Phone: (360)262-3376
Fax: (360)262-3337
Free: 800-462-8283
Publications: Log Trucker (32710) • Loggers World (32711)

Logging & Sawmilling Journal
Box 86670
North Vancouver, BC, Canada V7L 4L2
Phone: (604)990-9970
Fax: (604)990-9971
Free: (866)405-6462
Telex: 0454339
Publications: Logging & Sawmilling Journal (35035)

Logistics Management & Distribution Report
275 Washington St.
Newton, MA 02458
Phone: (617)558-4473
Fax: (617)558-4480
Publications: Logistics Management and Distribution Report (14405)

Loma Linda University
Office of University Relations
Loma Linda, CA 92350
Phone: (909)558-4526
Fax: (909)558-4181
Publications: Scope (2160) • Today (2161)

Lombardian
116 S Main St.
Lombard, IL 60148-2628
Phone: (630)627-7010
Fax: (630)627-7027
Publications: Lombardian (9116) • Villa Park Review/Lombardian (9118)

LoMo Magazine
228 Bayberry Rd.
Birmingham, AL 35214
Phone: (205)791-1663
Publications: LoMo Magazine (79)

London Business Monthly Magazine
PO Box 7400
London, ON, Canada N5Y 4X3
Phone: (519)472-7601
Fax: (519)473-2256
Publications: London Business Monthly Magazine (35986)

The London Free Press
369 York St.
London, ON, Canada N6A 4G1
Phone: (519)679-1111
Fax: (519)667-4523
Publications: The London Free Press (35987)

Lone Star Horse Report
316 Bailey Ave., No. 105
Fort Worth, TX 76107
Phone: (817)877-3050
Fax: (817)877-3060
Publications: Lone Star Horse Report (30346)

Lone Tout Publications, Inc.
PO Box 1006
Weston, CT 06883
Phone: (203)319-0873
Fax: (203)222-9332
Publications: Troika (5209)

Lone Tree Reporter
PO Box 235
Lone Tree, IA 52755
Phone: (319)629-5207
Fax: (319)629-4203
Publications: Lone Tree Reporter (11041)

Lonergan Institute at Boston College
Bapst Library
Boston College
Chestnut Hill, MA 02467-3806
Phone: (617)552-8095
Fax: (617)552-0510
Publications: Method (14131)

Long Beach City College
4901 E Carson St.
Long Beach, CA 90808-1780
Phone: (562)938-4284
Fax: (562)938-4948
Publications: Viking (2176)

Long Island Advance
20 Medford Ave.
Patchogue, NY 11772
Phone: (631)475-1000
Fax: (631)475-1565
Publications: Long Island Advance (23076)

Long Island Association Inc.
80 Hauppauge Rd.
Commack, NY 11725-4495
Phone: (631)499-4400
Fax: (631)499-2194
Free: 800-JOIN-LIA
Publications: Long Island (20489)

Long Island Business News
2150 Smithtown Ave.
Ronkonkoma, NY 11779-7358
Phone: (631)737-1700
Fax: (631)737-1890
Free: 800-LIB-NEWS
Publications: Long Island Business News (23271)

The Long Island Catholic
200 W. Centennial Ave., Ste. 201
Roosevelt, NY 11575
Phone: (516)594-1000
Fax: (516)594-1092
Free: 800-532-8542
Publications: The Long Island Catholic (23274)

Long Island Commercial Review, Inc.
2150 Smithtown Ave.
Ronkonkoma, NY 11779
Phone: (631)737-1888
Publications: LI Business News (23270)

Long Island University
Greenvale, NY 11548
Phone: (516)299-2720
Fax: (516)299-2735
Publications: Confrontation (20698)

Long Island University Press
1 University Plz., Rm. 5219
Brooklyn, NY 11201
Phone: (718)488-1591
Fax: (718)780-4182
Publications: Seawanhaka (20346)

Numbers cited after listings are entry numbers rather than page numbers.

Long Islander Newspapers Inc.
322 Main St.
Huntington, NY 11743
Phone: (631)427-7000
Fax: (631)427-5820

Publications: The Long Islander (20774) • The Northport Journal (23018) • The Record Northport (20775) • The Suffolk Lawyer (20776)

Long Prairie Leader
PO Box 479
Long Prairie, MN 56347
Phone: (320)732-2151
Fax: (320)732-2152

Publications: Long Prairie Leader (16009)

The Long Story
18 Eaton St.
Lawrence, MA 01843-1110
Phone: (978)686-7638

Publications: The Long Story (14267)

Long View Publishing Co., Inc.
235 W. 23rd St., 4th Fl.
New York, NY 10011
Phone: (212)924-2523
Fax: (212)645-5436

Publications: People's Weekly World (22541)

The Longboat Observer, Inc.
5570 Gulf of Mexico Dr.
Longboat Key, FL 34228
Phone: (941)383-5509
Fax: (941)383-7193

Publications: Black Tie (6310)

Longhurst Golf Corp.
236 Wychwood Ave.
Toronto, ON, Canada M6C 2T3
Phone: (416)654-9171
Fax: (905)764-5462

Publications: Canada's Golf Ranking Magazine (36489)

Longueuil Extra
267 rue St. Charles W
Longueuil, QC, Canada J4H 1E3
Phone: (450)646-3333
Fax: (450)674-0205

Publications: Longueuil Extra (37056)

Longview Community College
500 Longview Rd.
Lees Summit, MO 64081
Phone: (816)672-2140
Fax: (816)672-2078

Publications: The Longview Current (17245)

Longview Newspapers, Inc.
320 Methvin St.
Longview, TX 75601
Phone: (903)757-3311
Fax: (903)757-3742
Free: 800-395-8212

Publications: Longview News-Journal (30704)

Longwood University
Box 2901
Farmville, VA 23909
Phone: (434)395-2120
Fax: (804)395-2237

Publications: The Rotunda (32068)

Loogootee Tribune
PO Box 277
104 W Maine St.
Loogootee, IN 47553
Phone: (812)295-2500
Fax: (812)295-5221

Publications: Loogootee Tribune (10278)

Looking Glass Publications
Box 3604
Quincy, IL 62305

Publications: ICUC: I See You See (9473)

Loomis News
PO Box 125
Loomis, CA 95650
Phone: (916)652-7939

Publications: Loomis News (2180)

Lorain County Printing & Publishing
225 East Ave.
PO Box 4010
Elyria, OH 44036
Phone: (216)329-7000
Fax: (216)329-7282
Free: 800-848-6397

Publications: Chronicle-Telegram (25178)

The Lorain Journal Co.
1657 Broadway
Lorain, OH 44052
Phone: (216)245-6901
Fax: (216)245-5637
Free: 800-765-6901

Publications: The Morning Journal (25315)

Loris Times
4111 Walnut St.
PO Box 796
Loris, SC 29569
Phone: (843)756-7224
Fax: (843)756-7812

Publications: Loris Times (28686)

Los Angeles Area Chamber of Commerce
404 S Bixel St.
Los Angeles, CA 90017
Phone: (213)580-7500

Publications: Southern California Business Trends (2394)

The Los Angeles Athletic Club
431 W 7th St.
Los Angeles, CA 90014
Phone: (213)625-2211
Fax: (213)689-1194

Publications: Mercury (2329)

The Los Angeles Business Journal
5700 Wilshire, No. 170
Los Angeles, CA 90036
Phone: (213)549-5225
Fax: (213)549-5255

Publications: The Los Angeles Business Journal (2320)

Los Angeles County Bar Association
261 S. Figueroa St., Ste. 300
Los Angeles, CA 90012
Phone: (213)627-2727
Fax: (213)896-6500

Publications: Los Angeles Lawyer (2324)

Los Angeles County Medical Association
523, W. 6th St. 10th Floor,
Los Angeles, CA 90014-1220
Phone: (213)683-9900
Fax: (213)630-1152

Publications: LACMA Physician (2314)

Los Angeles Downtown News
1264 W 1st St.
Los Angeles, CA 90026
Phone: (213)481-1448
Fax: (213)250-4617

Publications: Los Angeles Downtown News (2322)

Los Angeles Independent Newspaper Group
4201 Wilshire Blvd., Ste. 600
Los Angeles, CA 90010
Phone: (323)556-5720
Fax: (323)932-8250

Publications: Culver City Chronicle (1791) • Edicion Bilingue Independent (2260) • Hollywood Independent (2290) • West Hollywood Independent (2432) • The Westsider (2434) • Wilshire Independent (2437)

Los Angeles International Fern Society
Box 90943
Pasadena, CA 91109-0943

Publications: Journal of the Los Angeles International Fern Society (2820)

Los Angeles Newspaper Group
21221 Oxnard St.
Woodland Hills, CA 91367
Phone: (818)713-3000
Fax: (818)713-3009

Publications: Lompoc Record (2162) • Mission Valley Review (4109)

Los Angeles Southwest College
1600 W Imperial Hwy.
Los Angeles, CA 90047
Phone: (323)241-5235

Publications: Explorer (2267)

Los Angeles Times
202 W. 1st St.
Los Angeles, CA 90012
Phone: (213)237-7811
Fax: (213)237-7386
Free: 800-LAT-IMES

Publications: Los Angeles Times (2326) • Los Angeles Times Magazine (2327)

Los Angeles Trade Technical College
400 W Washington Blvd.
Los Angeles, CA 90015
Phone: (213)763-7000
Fax: (213)748-7334

Publications: Tradewinds (2415)

Los Angeles Valley College
Journalism Dept.
5800 Fulton Ave.
Van Nuys, CA 91401
Phone: (818)781-1200
Fax: (818)785-4672

Publications: Valley Star (3997)

Los Medanos College
2700 E Leland Rd.
Pittsburg, CA 94565
Phone: (925)439-2181
Fax: (925)427-1599

Publications: Experience (2846)

Lost River Star
PO Box 768
Merrill, OR 97633
Phone: (541)798-5668
Fax: (541)798-5668

Publications: Lost River Star (26434)

Lost Treasure Inc.
PO Box 451589
Grove, OK 74345
Phone: (918)786-2182
Fax: (918)786-2192
Free: 800-423-0029

Publications: Lost Treasure (25848)

Lott Publishing Co.
PO Box 9669
Marina del Rey, CA 90295
Phone: (310)821-5437
Fax: (310)821-5437
Free: 800-359-4554

Publications: Candy World Illustrated (2505) • Cigar / Tobacco World (2506) • Cracker/Snack World (2507) • Lott's 3—in—1 Buyer's Guide (2509) • Storyette Magazine (2510)

Lotus Ltd.
Box L
College Park, MD 20741
Phone: (301)982-4054

Publications: Lotus Remarque (13432)

Loud Magazine
PO Box 56425
Phoenix, AZ 85079
Phone: (623)872-7395

Publications: Loud (806)

Loudmouth Productions, Inc.
PMB 361
10151 University Blvd.
Orlando, FL 32817
Phone: (407)263-5504

Publications: Impact (6498)

Loudoun Times-Mirror
9 E Market St.
Leesburg, VA 20176-3013
Phone: (703)777-1111
Fax: (703)771-0036

Publications: Loudoun Times-Mirror (32199)

Louisa Publishing Co., Ltd.
301 James L. Hodges Ave. S.
PO Box 306
Wapello, IA 52653-0306
Phone: (319)523-4631
Fax: (319)523-8167

Publications: Des Moines County News (11319) •
Morning Sun News-Herald (11092) • The New London Journal (11112) • Plainsman-Clarion (11177) •
Van Buren County Register (11016) • The Wapello
Republican (11285) • Wellman Advance (11317)

Louisburg Herald
15 S Broadway
Box 99
Louisburg, KS 66053-0099
Phone: (913)837-4321
Fax: (913)837-4322

Publications: Louisburg Herald (11614)

Louisiana Association of Educators
1755 Nicholson Dr.
Baton Rouge, LA 70802
Phone: (225)343-9243
Fax: (225)343-9272
Free: 800-286-4523

Publications: LAE News (12492)

Louisiana Business, Inc.
445 N Blvd., Ste. 210
PO Box 1949
Baton Rouge, LA 70821
Phone: (225)928-1700
Fax: (225)928-5019

Publications: Greater Baton Rouge Business Report
(12489)

Louisiana Cattlemen's Association
4921 I-10 Frontage Rd. W.
Port Allen, LA 70767
Phone: (504)343-3491
Fax: (504)336-0002

Publications: The Louisiana Cattleman (12798)

Louisiana College
1140 College Dr.
Pineville, LA 71360
Phone: (318)487-7011
Fax: (318)487-7310

Publications: Wildcat (12794)

Louisiana Dept. of Agriculture
PO Box 631
Baton Rouge, LA 70821
Phone: (225)922-1284
Fax: (225)922-1253

Publications: Louisiana Market Bulletin (12500)

Louisiana Engineering Society
9643 Brookline Ave., Ste. 116
Baton Rouge, LA 70809
Phone: (225)924-2021
Fax: (225)924-2049

Publications: Louisiana Engineer & Surveyor Journal (12498)

Louisiana Forestry Association
PO Drawer 5067
Alexandria, LA 71307-5067
Phone: (318)443-2558
Fax: (318)443-1713

Publications: Forests & People (12458)

Louisiana Historical Association
PO Box 42808
Lafayette, LA 70504
Phone: (337)482-6029
Fax: (337)482-6028

Publications: Louisiana History (12618)

Louisiana Library Association
421 S 4th St.
Eunice, LA 70535-5301
Phone: (337)550-7890
Fax: (337)550-7846

Publications: Louisiana Libraries (12574)

Louisiana Life Magazine
111 Veterans Blvd., Ste. 1810
Metairie, LA 70005
Phone: (504)834-9698
Fax: (504)838-7700

Publications: Louisiana Life Magazine (12677)

Louisiana Municipal Association
PO Box 4327
Baton Rouge, LA 70821
Phone: (225)344-5001
Fax: (225)344-3057

Publications: Louisiana Municipal Review (12501)

Louisiana Oil Marketers Association
PO Box 80357
Baton Rouge, LA 70898
Phone: (504)926-8300
Fax: (504)926-7722
Free: 800-375-6984

Publications: LOMA Line (12493)

Louisiana Pharmacists Association
PO Box 14446
Baton Rouge, LA 70898
Phone: (225)926-2666
Fax: (225)926-1020

Publications: The Louisiana Pharmacist (12502)

Louisiana School Boards Association
7912 Summa Ave.
Baton Rouge, LA 70809
Phone: (225)769-3191
Fax: (225)769-6108

Publications: The Louisiana Boardmember (12495)

Louisiana State Bar Association
601 St. Charles Ave.
New Orleans, LA 70130
Phone: (504)566-1600
Fax: (504)566-0930
Free: 800-421-LSBA

Publications: The Louisiana Bar Journal (12737)

Louisiana State Newspapers
602 N. Parkerson
Crowley, LA 70526
Phone: (337)774-2527

Publications: Lake Arthur Sun-Times (12558)

Louisiana State Newspapers
202 Ave. F
Kentwood, LA 70444
Fax: (504)748-7104

Publications: The Kentwood News-Ledger (12612)

Louisiana State University
43 Allen Hall
Baton Rouge, LA 70803-5005
Phone: (225)578-5108
Fax: (225)578-5098

Publications: The Southern Review (12506)

Louisiana State University
Baton Rouge, LA 70803-5001
Phone: (225)578-4079

Publications: New Delta Review (12505)

Louisiana State University at Eunice
Box 1129
Eunice, LA 70535
Phone: (337)550-1211
Fax: (337)546-6620

Publications: Bayou Bengal (12573)

Louisiana State University Law Center
Law Center
c/o Paul M. Hebert
Baton Rouge, LA 70803
Phone: (225)578-1683
Fax: (504)578-1685

Publications: Louisiana Law Review (12499)

Louisiana State University, Shreveport
1 University Pl.
Shreveport, LA 71115-2399
Phone: (318)797-5235
Fax: (318)795-4263

Publications: Q.J.I. (12818)

Louisiana Suburban Press
5240 Groom Rd.
Baker, LA 70714
Phone: (225)775-2315
Fax: (225)774-9212

Publications: St. Francisville Democrat (12812)

Louisiana Suburban Press
5145 Main St., Ste. C
Zachary, LA 70791
Phone: (225)775-2315
Fax: (225)654-8271

Publications: Zachary Plainsman-News (12884)

Louisiana Tech University
PO Box 10258
Ruston, LA 71272-0045
Phone: (318)257-4427
Fax: (318)257-4558

Publications: The Tech Talk (12807)

Louisiana Weekly
2215 Pelopidas St.
New Orleans, LA 70122
Phone: (504)282-3705
Fax: (504)282-3773
Free: 800-504-4403

Publications: Louisiana Weekly (12740)

Louisville Eccentric Observer
600 E Main, Ste. 102
Louisville, KY 40202
Phone: (502)895-9770
Fax: (502)895-9779
Free: 800-571-6873

Publications: Louisville Eccentric Observer (LEO)
(12230)

The Louisville Herald, Inc.
PO Box 170
Louisville, OH 44641-0170
Phone: (330)875-5610
Fax: (330)875-4475

Publications: The Louisville Herald (25319)

Louisville Magazine Inc.
137 W. Muhammad Ali Blvd., Ste. 101
Louisville, KY 40202-1438
Phone: (502)625-0100
Fax: (502)625-0109

Publications: Louisville (12227)

Louisville Newspapers, Inc.
PO Box 469
Louisville, MS 39339
Fax: (601)773-6242

Publications: Winston County Journal (16750)

Lounges Publications
2613 41st St.
Highland, IN 46322
Phone: (219)972-9131
Fax: (219)972-9131

Publications: The Midwest BEAT Magazine (10063)

Love Publishing Co.
9101 E Kenyon Ave., Ste. 2200
Denver, CO 80237
Phone: (303)221-7333
Fax: (303)221-7444

Publications: Focus on Exceptional Children (4328)

Lovelock Review-Miner
230 Main St.
PO Box 620
Lovelock, NV 89419
Phone: (702)273-7245
Fax: (775)273-0500
Free: 888-799-2681

Publications: Lovelock Review-Miner (18412)

lovematters.com
1840 S. Elena Ave., Ste. 103
Redondo Beach, CA 90277
Phone: (310)373-0743
Fax: (310)375-4546

Publications: lovematters.com (2910)

The Lovington Daily Leader
14 W Ave B
PO Box 1717
Lovington, NM 88260
Phone: (505)396-2844
Fax: (505)396-5775

Publications: The Lovington Daily Leader (19897)

Numbers cited after listings are entry numbers rather than page numbers.

The Low Down to Hull & Back News
759 River Rd.
PO Box 99
Wakefield, QC, Canada J0X 3G0
Phone: (819)459-2222
Fax: (819)459-3831

Publications: The Low Down to Hull & Back News (37439)

Lowell Ledger
PO Box 128
Lowell, MI 49331
Phone: (616)897-9261
Fax: (616)897-4809

Publications: Lowell Ledger (15320)

Lowell Sun Publishing Co.
15 Kearney Sq.
Lowell, MA 01853

Publications: Lowell Sun (14278)

Lower Columbia Community Action Council
PO Box 2129
Longview, WA 98632
Phone: (360)425-3430
Fax: (360)425-6657

Publications: Cowlitz-Wahkiakum Senior News (32811)

Lower Mainland Publishing
2700 Barnet Hwy.
Coquitlam, BC, Canada V3E 1B8
Phone: (604)942-4192
Fax: (604)464-4977

Publications: Coquitlam Now (34930)

Lower Mainland Publishing Group Inc.
5731 No. 3 Rd.
Richmond, BC, Canada V6X 2C9
Phone: (604)270-8031
Fax: (604)270-2248

Publications: Richmond News (35076)

Lower Mainland Publishing Ltd.
30887 Peardonville Rd.
Abbotsford, BC, Canada V2T 6K2
Phone: (604)854-5244
Fax: (604)854-1140

Publications: Abbotsford Times (34877)

Lower Mainland Publishing Ltd.
7889 - 132 St., No. 201
Surrey, BC, Canada V3W 4N2
Phone: (604)572-0064
Fax: (604)572-6438

Publications: The Now Newspaper (35109)

Loyal Christian Benefit Association
700 Peach St.
PO Box 13005
Erie, PA 16514-1305
Phone: (814)453-4331
Fax: (814)453-3211
Free: 800-234-5222

Publications: Fraternal Leader (26898)

Loyola Marymount University
Daum Hall, One LMU Dr. MS-8470
Los Angeles, CA 90045
Phone: (310)338-2879
Fax: (310)338-1901

Publications: Los Angeles Loyolan (2325)

Loyola New Orleans University School of Law
7214 St. Charles
Campus Box 901
ATTN: Business Manager-Law Journals
New Orleans, LA 70118
Phone: (504)861-5558
Fax: (504)861-5559

Publications: Loyola Law Review (12741)

Loyola Phoenix Loyola University of Chicago
6525 N. Sheridan Rd.
Chicago, IL 60626
Phone: (773)508-7110
Fax: (773)508-7121

Publications: Loyola Phoenix (8471)

Loyola University
Box 195
New Orleans, LA 70118
Phone: (504)865-2295
Fax: (504)865-2294

Publications: New Orleans Review (12748)

Loyola University of Chicago
820 N. Michigan Ave.
Chicago, IL 60611
Phone: (312)915-6407
Fax: (312)915-6450
Free: 800-424-1513

Publications: Loyola Magazine (8470)

Loyola University of Chicago
6525 Sheridan Rd.
Chicago, IL 60626
Phone: (773)508-2217
Fax: (773)508-2153

Publications: Mid-America (Chicago) (8488)

Loyola University-Chicago/School of Law
1 E. Pearson
Chicago, IL 60611
Phone: (312)915-7183
Fax: (312)915-7201

Publications: Loyola University Chicago Law Journal (8472)

Lozano Enterprises
411 W. 5th St.
Los Angeles, CA 90013-1028
Phone: (213)622-8332
Fax: (213)896-2151

Publications: La Opinion (2312)

LRP Publications
747 Dresher Rd.
PO Box 980
Horsham, PA 19044-0980
Phone: (215)784-0912
Fax: (215)784-0870
Free: 800-341-7874

Publications: Counterpoint (27057) • Current Award Trends in Personal Injury (27058) • Early Childhood Law and Policy Reporter (27059) • Human Resource Executive (27061) • Risk & Insurance (27064)

LSU Agricultural Center
101 Efferson Hall
Baton Rouge, LA 70803
Phone: (225)388-2263
Fax: (225)578-4524

Publications: Louisiana Agriculture Magazine (12494)

LSU Alumni Association
3838 W. Lakeshore Dr.
Baton Rouge, LA 70808
Phone: (225)578-3811
Fax: (225)388-3816

Publications: LSU Magazine (12504)

Lubbock Avalanche Journal
710 Ave. J, No. 491
Lubbock, TX 79401-1808
Phone: (806)762-8844
Fax: (806)744-9603
Free: 800-692-4021

Publications: Lubbock Avalanche-Journal (30715)

Lubbock Christian University
5601 19th
Lubbock, TX 79407
Phone: (806)796-8800
Fax: (806)796-8917

Publications: The Duster (30709)

Lubbock Southwest Digest
902 E 28th St.
Lubbock, TX 79404
Phone: (806)762-3612
Fax: (806)749-6303

Publications: Lubbock Southwest Digest (30716)

Luby Publishing
122 S. Michigan Ave., Ste. 1506
Chicago, IL 60603
Phone: (312)341-1110
Fax: (312)341-1469

Publications: Billiards Digest (8283) • Bowlers Journal (8288)

Lucas Publications, Inc.
49 S Main St.
PO Box 278
Albany, TX 76430
Phone: (915)762-2201
Fax: (915)762-3201

Publications: The Albany News (29676)

Lucas Publishers
21 Main St.
Sparta, NJ 07871

Publications: Printed Circuit Network (19593)

Lucas Publishing Co.
PO Box 337
Lucas, KS 67648
Phone: (785)525-6355
Fax: (785)525-6356

Publications: Lucas-Sylvan News (11615)

The Lucerne Group
1879 E Orange Blvd.
Pasadena, CA 91104

Publications: Firsts (2816)

The Lucknow Sentinel
Box 400
Lucknow, ON, Canada N0G 2H0
Phone: (519)528-2822
Fax: (519)528-3529

Publications: The Lucknow Sentinel (36004)

Ludington Daily News
202 N. Rath St.
PO Box 340
Ludington, MI 49431-0340
Phone: (231)845-5181
Fax: (231)843-4011
Free: 800-748-0407

Publications: Ludington Daily News (15322)

Luling Publishing Co., Inc.
415 E Davis
Luling, TX 78648
Phone: (830)875-2116
Fax: (830)875-2124

Publications: The Luling Newsboy & Signal (30749)

Luna Bisonte Prods
137 Leland Ave.
Columbus, OH 43214
Phone: (614)846-4126

Publications: Lost and Found Times (25029)

Lunar Reclamation Society, Inc.
PO Box 2102
Milwaukee, WI 53201-2102
Phone: (414)342-0705

Publications: Moon Miners' Manifesto (34089)

Lungta LLC
Telluride, CO 81435

Publications: Mountainfreak (4644)

The Luso-Americano
88 Ferry St.
Newark, NJ 07105-1817
Phone: (973)589-4600
Fax: (973)589-3848

Publications: The Luso-Americano (19358)

Luther College
700 College Dr.
Decorah, IA 52101-1045
Phone: (563)387-1350
Fax: (563)387-1336
Free: 800-258-8437

Publications: Luther Alumni Magazine (10757)

Lutheran Braille Evangelism Association
1740 Eugene St.
White Bear Lake, MN 55110-3312
Phone: (651)426-0469

Publications: Christian Magnifier (16509) • Tract Messenger (16513)

Lutheran Center Association
16259 Nine Mile
Eastpointe, MI 48021
Free: 800-572-6711

Publications: Detroit Lutheran (15619)

Lutheran Education
7400 Augusta St.
River Forest, IL 60305-1499
Phone: (708)209-3073
Fax: (708)209-3176

Publications: Lutheran Education Journal (9492)

Lutheran Library for the Blind
7550 Watson Rd.
St. Louis, MO 63119
Fax: (314)965-0959
Free: 800-433-3954

Publications: Teen Time (17522)

The Lutz Community News
PO Box 271880
Tampa, FL 33688-1880
Phone: (813)963-1918
Fax: (813)963-3910

Publications: The Lutz Community News (6315)

LVP Media Inc.
27-1200 Aerowood Dr.
Mississauga, ON, Canada L4W 2S7
Phone: (905)624-8100
Fax: (905)624-1760

Publications: EP&T (Electronic Products and Technology) (36066)

Lyle Printing & Publishing Co.
185-205 E. State St.
Box 38
Salem, OH 44460
Phone: (330)337-3419
Fax: (330)337-9550
Free: 800-837-3419

Publications: Farm and Dairy (25505)

Lyman County Herald
PO Box 518
Presho, SD 57568
Phone: (605)895-6397
Fax: (605)895-6377

Publications: Lyman County Herald (28930)

Lynn County News
Box 1170
Tahoka, TX 79373
Phone: (806)998-4888
Fax: (806)998-6308

Publications: Lynn County News (31174)

Lynne Rienner Publishers
1800 30th St., No. 314
Boulder, CO 80301
Phone: (303)444-6684
Fax: (303)444-0824

Publications: Global Governance (34714)

Lyon County News
Box 68
George, IA 51237
Phone: (712)475-3351
Fax: (712)475-3353

Publications: Lyon County News (10920)

Lyon County Reporter
PO Box 420
Hull, IA 51239-0420
Phone: (712)439-1075
Fax: (712)439-1076

Publications: Sioux County Index-Reporter (10956)

Lyon County Reporter
PO Box 340
Inwood, IA 51240
Phone: (712)753-2258
Fax: (712)753-4864

Publications: West Lyon Herald (10967)

Lyon Publishing, Inc.
504 Main St.
Mapleton, IA 51034
Phone: (712)882-1101
Fax: (712)882-1330

Publications: Charter Oak-Ute Newspaper (11051) • Mapleton Press (11052) • Schleswig Leader (11053)

Lyon-Sioux Newspaper Publishing
310 1st Ave. W
Rock Rapids, IA 51246
Phone: (712)472-2525
Fax: (712)472-3414
Free: 800-621-0801

Publications: Lyon County Reporter (11179)

Lyon's Mirror-Sun
214 Main St.
Box 59
Lyons, NE 68038
Phone: (402)687-2616
Fax: (402)687-2617

Publications: Lyons Mirror Sun (18151)

Lyons Publishing Co., Inc.
210 W Commercial
PO Box 560
Lyons, KS 67554-2716
Phone: (316)257-2368
Fax: (316)259-2369

Publications: Lyons Daily News (11616)

The Lyric
65 VT. State Rte. 15
Jericho, VT 05465
Phone: (802)899-3993

Publications: The Lyric (31545)

M D Publications, Inc.
PO Box 2210
Springfield, MO 65801-2210
Phone: (417)866-3917
Fax: (417)866-2781
Free: 800-274-7890

Publications: Undercar Digest (17617)

M & G S
75 Francis St.
Brookline, MA 02445
Phone: (617)730-4750
Fax: (617)739-0052

Publications: Medicine & Global Survival (14022)

M. Shanken Communications, Inc.
387 Park Ave. S.
New York, NY 10016
Phone: (212)481-8610
Fax: (212)684-5424

Publications: Cigar Aficionado (21418)

M. Shanken Communications, Inc.
387 Park Ave. S., 8th Fl.
New York, NY 10016-8810
Phone: (212)684-4224
Fax: (212)779-3334
Free: 800-866-0775

Publications: Food Arts (21710) • Impact (21854) • Market Watch (22285) • Wine Spectator (22919)

The 'M' Voice Newspaper
PO Box 8361
Greenville, NC 27834
Phone: (919)757-0365
Fax: (919)757-1793

Publications: The 'M' Voice Newspaper (23965)

MAC America Communications, Inc.
5555 N. 7th Ave., No. B200
Phoenix, AZ 85013-1755
Phone: (602)207-3750
Fax: (602)207-3777

Publications: Phoenix Magazine (809)

Mac Media, Inc.
PO Box 774328
Steamboat Springs, CO 80477-4328
Phone: (970)879-5250
Fax: (970)879-4650
Free: 800-686-6247

Publications: Rocky Mountain Golf Magazine (4630) • Vail-Beaver Creek Magazine (4634) • Vail International Dance Festival (4635)

Mac Media LLC
PO Box 4328
Steamboat Springs, CO 80477
Phone: (970)879-5250
Fax: (970)879-4650

Publications: Steamboat Magazine (4653)

MacAddict
150 N. Hill Dr.
Brisbane, CA 94005
Phone: (415)468-4684
Fax: (415)656-2594

Publications: MacAddict (1605)

Macalester College
1600 Grand Ave.
St. Paul, MN 55105
Phone: (651)696-6684
Fax: (651)696-6685

Publications: The Mac Weekly (16385)

Macalester Park Publishing Company
7317 Cahill Rd., Ste. 201
Minneapolis, MN 55439
Phone: (952)561-1234
Fax: (952)941-3010
Free: 800-407-9078

Publications: Lutheran Journal (16094)

MacDonald Publications
123 N Main St.
PO Box 10
Ithaca, MI 48847
Phone: (517)875-4151
Fax: (517)875-3159
Free: 800-519-6418

Publications: Gratiot County Herald (15219)

Macedonia
364 Kingston Rd.
PO Box 97589
Scarborough, ON, Canada M1C 4Z2
Phone: (416)286-7673
Fax: (416)286-0712

Publications: Macedonia (36870)

Macedonian Patriotic Organization
124 W Wayne
Fort Wayne, IN 46802
Phone: (260)422-5900
Fax: (260)422-1348

Publications: Macedonian Tribune (9972)

Macfadden Communications Group LLC
333 7th Ave.
New York, NY 10001
Phone: (212)979-4800

Publications: Store Equipment & Design (22795)

Macfadden Protech
908 S. 8th St., Ste. 200
Louisville, KY 40203
Phone: (502)736-9500
Fax: (502)736-9501

Publications: Pizza Today (12234)

Machias Valley Publishing Co., Inc.
PO Box 357
Machias, ME 04654-0357
Phone: (207)255-6561
Fax: (207)255-4058
Free: 800-464-6561

Publications: Machias Valley News Observer (12986)

M.A.C.I., Inc.
2432 SW Pepperwood
Topeka, KS 66614
Phone: (785)272-5280
Fax: (785)272-3729

Publications: Mid-America Commerce and Industry (11833)

Mackenzie Report Inc.
Box 686
Manning, AB, Canada T0H 2M0
Phone: (403)836-3588
Fax: (403)836-2820

Publications: Banner Post (34806)

Maclean Hunter Healthcare Ltd.
777 Bay St., 7th Fl.
Toronto, ON, Canada M5W 1A7
Phone: (416)596-5000
Fax: (416)596-3499

Publications: Pharmacy Post (36704)

Macleod Gazette Ltd.
Box 720
Fort Macleod, AB, Canada T0L 0Z0
Phone: (403)553-3391
Fax: (403)553-2961

Publications: The Macleod Gazette (34766)

Karen MacLeod
Sunrise Villas Apartments
1622-B Swallowcrest Dr.
Edgewood, MD 21040-1751
Fax: (410)676-0164

Publications: Companion in Zeor (13492)

MacMurray College
447 E College Ave.
Box 1140
Jacksonville, IL 62650
Phone: (217)479-7000
Fax: (217)245-0405

Publications: The Daily Other (9022)

The Macomb Daily
100 Macomb Daily Dr.
PO Box 707
Mount Clemens, MI 48046
Phone: (810)469-4510
Fax: (810)469-2892

Publications: The Macomb Daily (15372)

Macomb Journal
203 N. Randolph
Macomb, IL 61455
Phone: (309)833-2114
Fax: (309)833-2346
Free: 800-237-6858

Publications: Macomb Journal (9130)

Macon Beacon
PO Box 32
Macon, MS 39341
Phone: (662)726-4747
Fax: (662)726-4742

Publications: Macon Beacon (16754)

Macon County Times
PO Box 69
200 Times Ave.
Lafayette, TN 37083
Phone: (615)666-2440
Fax: (615)666-4909

Publications: Macon County Times (29312)

Macon Magazine, Inc.
227 Orange St.
Macon, GA 31201
Phone: (912)746-7779
Fax: (912)743-4608

Publications: Macon Magazine (7382)

Macoupin County Enquirer, Inc.
PO Box 200
Carlinville, IL 62626-0200
Phone: (217)854-2534
Fax: (217)854-2535

Publications: Carlinville Democrat (8125) • The Enquirer-Democrat (8126) • The Enquirer Express (8127)

MacTech Magazine
PO Box 5200
Westlake Village, CA 91359
Phone: (805)494-9797
Fax: (805)494-9798

Publications: MacTech Magazine (4071)

Mad Dog Productions
PO Box 2263
Pasadena, CA 91102

Publications: Bovine Gazette (2811)

Maddux Publishing, L.C.
PO Box 202
St. Petersburg, FL 33731
Phone: (727)823-4394
Fax: (727)821-1645
Free: 800-226-4394

Publications: Maddux Report (6630)

Madelia Media, Inc.
112 W Main St.
Madelia, MN 56062-1440
Phone: (507)642-3636
Fax: (507)642-3535

Publications: Southern Minnesota Peach (16018) • Times-Messenger (16019)

The Madill Record
211 Plz.
PO Box 529
Madill, OK 73446-0529
Phone: (580)795-3355
Fax: (580)795-3530

Publications: The Madill Record (25902)

Madison Area Technical College
3550 Anderson St.
Madison, WI 53704
Phone: (608)246-6100
Fax: (608)246-6880
Free: 800-322-6282

Publications: Clarion (33927)

Madison County Publications
2 Executive Dr.
Collinsville, IL 62234
Phone: (618)344-0264
Fax: (618)344-3611

Publications: Madison county journals (8687)

Madison County Record
PO Box 859
Madison, AL 35758
Phone: (256)772-6677
Fax: (256)772-6655

Publications: Madison County Record (310)

Madison County Record
PO Drawer A
Huntsville, AR 72740
Phone: (501)738-2141
Fax: (501)738-1250

Publications: Madison County Record (1192)

The Madison Courier
310 Courier Sq.
Madison, IN 47250
Phone: (812)265-3641
Fax: (812)273-6903

Publications: The Madison Courier (10283) • The Weekly Herald (10284)

Madison Daily Leader
214 S. Egan Ave.
PO Box 348
Madison, SD 57042
Phone: (605)256-4555
Fax: (605)256-6190
Free: 877-635-7323

Publications: Madison Daily Leader (28886)

Madison Enterprise-Recorder
PO Box 722
Madison, FL 32341
Fax: (904)973-6491

Publications: Madison Enterprise-Recorder (6318)

The Madison Journal
300 S Chestnut St.
PO Box 791
Tallulah, LA 71284
Phone: (318)574-1404
Fax: (318)574-4219

Publications: The Madison Journal (12855)

Madison Magazine
211 S. Paterson St. 100
Madison, WI 53703
Phone: (608)255-9982
Fax: (608)255-9351

Publications: Madison Magazine (33959)

The Madison News
118 S 3rd St.
Box 217
Madison, KS 66860
Phone: (316)437-2433
Fax: (316)437-2433

Publications: The Madison News (11618)

Madison Newspapers, Inc.
1901 Fish Hatchery Rd.
PO Box 8058
Madison, WI 53713
Phone: (608)252-6100
Fax: (608)252-6119

Publications: Shopper Stopper (34260) • Wisconsin State Journal (33990)

Madisonian
PO Box 365
Ennis, MT 59729-0365
Phone: (406)682-7755
Fax: (406)682-5012

Publications: The Madisonian (17787)

Madisonville Newspapers, Inc.
PO Drawer 999
Madisonville, TX 77864
Phone: (936)348-3505
Fax: (936)348-3338

Publications: The Madisonville Meteor and Times (30752)

Magazine Adorable Inc.
132, rue St-Pierre 6e etage
Quebec, QC, Canada G1K 4A7
Phone: (418)692-5123
Fax: (418)692-0942

Publications: Adorable (37279)

Magazine of Speculative Poetry
Box 564
Beloit, WI 53512

Publications: Magazine of Speculative Poetry (33575)

Magazines/Creative, Inc.
42 W. 38th St., Rm. 601
New York, NY 10018
Phone: (212)840-0160
Fax: (212)819-0945

Publications: Creative (21512)

Magic Valley Publishing Co.
133 E Main St.
Jerome, ID 83338-2332

Publications: Lincoln County Journal (7981) • North Side News (7881)

Magic Valley Publishing Co., Inc.
144 W Main
PO Box 899
Camden, TN 38320-0899
Phone: (731)584-7200
Fax: (731)584-4943

Publications: The Camden Chronicle (29078)

Magical Blend
PO Box 600
Chico, CA 95927-0600
Phone: (530)893-9037
Fax: (530)893-9076
Free: 888-296-2442

Publications: Magical Blend Magazine (1694)

Magie Enterprises, Inc.
9035 Pine
PO Box 1058
Cabot, AR 72023
Phone: (501)843-3534
Fax: (501)843-6447

Publications: Cabot Star-Herald (1067) • Carlisle Independent (1074) • Jacksonville Patriot (1195) • Lonoke Democrat (1257)

Magma Communications Ltd.
31, Auriga Dr.
Ottawa, ON, Canada K2E 1C4

Publications: Britannia (36188)

Magna Times & West Valley News
8980 West 2700 South
Magna, UT 84044
Phone: (801)250-5656
Fax: (801)250-5685
Publications: Magna Times & West Valley News (31364)

Magnet Magazine Inc.
1218 Chestnut St., Ste. 808
Philadelphia, PA 19107
Phone: (215)413-8570
Fax: (215)413-8569
Publications: MAGNET (27560)

Magnolia Gazette
PO Box 152
Magnolia, MS 39652-0152
Phone: (601)783-2441
Fax: (601)783-2091
Publications: Magnolia Gazette (16758)

Magnolia Media Group
3451 Boston Ave.
Fort Worth, TX 76116
Phone: (817)560-6100
Fax: (817)560-6196
Publications: Petlife: Your Companion Animal Magazine (30351)

Magyar Naplo (Hungarian Newspaper)
PO Box 771, Sta. A
Toronto, ON, Canada M5W 1G3
Phone: (386)254-4920
Free: 800-259-4919
Publications: Magyar Naplo (36655)

Mahatoba Ltd.
702 Railway Ave.
PO Box 10
Glenboro, MB, Canada R0K 0X0
Phone: (204)827-2343
Fax: (204)827-2207
Publications: The Glenboro Gazette (35268)

Maher Publications, Inc.
102 N Haven Rd.
Elmhurst, IL 60126
Phone: (630)941-2030
Fax: (630)941-3210
Free: 800-535-7496
Publications: Down Beat (8834) • Music Inc. (8836) • Up Beat Daily (8838)

Mailbox News Packet
3000E Race St.
PO Box 1379
Searcy, AR 72145
Phone: (501)268-6277
Fax: (501)268-8621
Publications: Mailbox News Packet (1338)

Main Street Media Company
2114 Angus Rd., Ste. 222
Charlottesville, VA 22901-2770
Phone: (804)295-0124
Fax: (804)293-4047
Publications: The Observer (31936)

Main Street Newspapers Inc.
PO Box 419
Christiansburg, VA 24068
Phone: (540)382-6171
Fax: (540)382-3009
Publications: The News-Messenger (31972)

Maine Antique Digest
911 Main St.
PO Box 1429
Waldoboro, ME 04572-1429
Phone: (207)832-7534
Fax: (207)832-7341
Publications: Maine Antique Digest (13069)

Maine Better Transportation Association
146 State St.
Augusta, ME 04330
Phone: (207)623-2928
Fax: (207)623-2928
Publications: Maine Trails (12895)

Maine Boats & Harbors
21 Elm St.
Camden, ME 04843
Phone: (207)236-8622
Fax: (207)236-0811
Publications: Maine Boats & Harbors (12944)

Maine Dept. of Inland Fisheries and Wildlife
284 State St., 415H5
Augusta, ME 04333
Phone: (207)287-8000
Fax: (207)287-6395
Publications: Maine Fish and Wildlife (12893)

Maine Folklife Center
University of Maine
5773 S. Stevens Hall
Orono, ME 04469-5773
Phone: (207)581-1891
Fax: (207)581-1823
Publications: Northeast Folklore (13002)

Maine Genealogical Society
Box 221
Farmington, ME 04938-0221
Publications: Maine Genealogist (12961)

Maine Historical Society
489 Congress St.
Portland, ME 04101
Phone: (207)774-1822
Fax: (207)775-4301
Publications: Maine History (13011)

Maine Motor Transport News
142 Whitten Rd.
PO Box 857
Augusta, ME 04332
Phone: (207)623-4128
Fax: (207)623-4096
Publications: Maine Motor Transport News (12894)

Maine-OK Enterprises
97 Townsend Ave.
Boothbay Harbor, ME 04538
Phone: (207)633-4620
Fax: (207)633-7123
Free: 877-500-6397
Publications: Boothbay Register (12925)

Maine Organic Farmers and Gardeners Association
PO Box 170
Unity, ME 04988
Phone: (207)568-4142
Publications: Maine Organic Farmer and Gardener (12982)

Maine Publishing Corp.
11 Forest Ave.
Portland, ME 04101
Publications: Casco Bay Weekly (13007)

The Maine Sportsman
PO Box 910
Yarmouth, ME 04096
Phone: (207)846-9501
Fax: (207)846-1434
Free: 800-698-9501
Publications: The Maine Sportsman (13082)

Maine Times
PO Box 2129
Bangor, ME 04402-2129
Phone: (207)947-4410
Fax: (207)991-4450
Free: 800-439-8866
Publications: Maine Times (12904)

Maine Water Utilities Association
PO Box P
Waldoboro, ME 04572
Phone: (207)832-2263
Fax: (207)832-2265
Publications: Journal of Maine Water Utilities Association (13068)

Mainichi Newspapers
2800 28th St., Ste. 103
Santa Monica, CA 90405
Phone: (310)664-1666
Fax: (310)664-1656
Publications: Fax Mainichi U.S.A. (3708)

Mainline Newspapers
PO Box 777
Ebensburg, PA 15931-0777
Phone: (814)472-4110
Fax: (814)472-2275
Publications: The Cresson/Gallitzin Mainliner (26855) • The Ebensburg News Leader (26856) • The Nanty Glo Journal (26858) • The Portage Dispatch (27898)

Mainly Marketing
403 Main St.
PO Box 748
Port Washington, NY 11050
Phone: (516)883-3382
Fax: (516)883-2162
Free: 800-462-4659
Publications: CQ Amateur Radio (23124) • Electronic Servicing & Technology (23126) • Micro Computer Journal (23130) • Popular Communications (23132)

MainStreet Newspapers Inc.
PO Box 908
Jefferson, GA 30549-0908
Phone: (706)367-5233
Fax: (706)367-8056
Publications: Banks County News (7345) • The Jackson Herald (7346)

Maison Direct Ltee
3390 Cremazie Est
Montreal, QC, Canada H2A 1A4
Phone: (514)729-0000
Fax: (514)729-2552
Publications: Maison d'Aujourd'hui (37181)

Maison Francaise
4101 Reservoir Rd., NW
Washington, DC 20007
Phone: (202)944-6069
Fax: (202)944-6594
Publications: France Magazine (5502)

Malaspina University College
c/o Dr. Cheryl Krasnick Warsh
900 5th St.
Nanaimo, BC, Canada V9R 5S5
Phone: (250)753-3245
Fax: (250)740-6459
Publications: Canadian Bulletin of Medical History/Bulletin Canadien D'historie de la Medecine (35018)

Malcolm Publishing Inc.
11450 Albert Hudon Blvd.
Montreal-Nord, QC, Canada H1G 3J9
Phone: (514)327-4464
Fax: (514)327-0514
Free: 800-563-6738
Publications: Harrowsmith Country Life (37251)

Maledicta Press
PO Box 14123
Santa Rosa, CA 95402-6123
Phone: (707)795-8178
Publications: Maledicta (3729)

The Malheur Enterprise
PO Box 310
Vale, OR 97918
Phone: (541)473-3377
Fax: (541)473-3268
Publications: Malheur Enterprise (26602)

The Malibu Surfside News
PO Box 903
Malibu, CA 90265
Phone: (310)457-2112
Fax: (310)457-9908
Publications: The Malibu Surfside News (2491)

Numbers cited after listings are entry numbers rather than page numbers.

The Malibu Times, Inc.
PO Box 1127
3864 Las Flores Canyon Rd.
Malibu, CA 90265
Phone: (310)456-5507
Fax: (310)456-8986

Publications: The Malibu Times (2492)

Mall in Your Mailbox
PO Box 9
Camden, SC 29020
Phone: (803)432-8439
Fax: (803)432-5881
Free: (866)345-5896

Publications: Mall in Your Mailbox (28500)

Malonson Company, Inc.
6130 Wheatley St.
Houston, TX 77091-3947
Phone: (713)692-1892
Fax: (713)692-1183
Free: 877-237-6397

Publications: African-American News & Issues (30455)

The Malvern Leader
PO Box 129
Malvern, IA 51551
Phone: (712)624-8512
Fax: (712)624-9041

Publications: The Leader (11044)

Mamou Acadian Press
PO Box 360
Mamou, LA 70554
Phone: (318)363-2103
Fax: (318)363-2841

Publications: Mamou Acadian Press (12666)

Management Advisory Publications
PO Box 81151
Wellesley Hills, MA 02481-0001
Phone: (781)235-2895
Fax: (781)235-5446

Publications: Contingency Planning and Recovery Journal (CPR-J) (14621)

Management Futures
297 Kimble Dr.
Fredericton, NB, Canada E3B 6Y1
Phone: (506)454-1310
Fax: (506)454-8421

Publications: Journal of Comparative International Management (35396)

Manahawkin Newspapers, Inc.
345 E Bay Ave.
Manahawkin, NJ 08050-3320
Phone: (609)597-3211
Fax: (609)597-8169
Free: 800-660-9812

Publications: Beacon Mailbag (19209) • Lacey Beacon (18829) • Tuckerton Beacon (19681)

Manassas Journal Messenger
9009 Church St.
Manassas, VA 20110
Phone: (703)368-3101
Fax: (703)368-9017

Publications: Manassas Journal Messenger (32223)

Manchester Community College
MS 7
60 Bidwell St.
Manchester, CT 06040
Phone: (203)647-6057
Fax: (203)647-6238

Publications: Live Wire (4937)

Manchester Enterprises
Box 967
Hyden, KY 41749
Phone: (606)672-2841
Fax: (606)672-7409

Publications: The Leslie County News (12139)

Manchester Newspapers
14 E Main St.
Granville, NY 12832
Phone: (518)642-1234
Fax: (518)642-1344
Free: 800-354-4232

Publications: Sentinel (20682)

Manchester Publishing Co.
109 E Delaware St.
PO Box C
Manchester, IA 52057-0703
Phone: (563)927-2020
Fax: (563)927-4945

Publications: The Manchester Press (11045)

The Manchester Signal
414 E 7th St.
Manchester, OH 45144-1402
Phone: (937)549-2800
Fax: (937)549-3611

Publications: The Manchester Signal (25329)

Manhattan College
4513 Manhattan College Pkwy.
Bronx, NY 10471-4098
Phone: (718)862-8000
Fax: (718)862-8043

Publications: Manhattan College Quadrangle (20277)

Manhattan Institute
52 Vanderbilt Ave.
New York, NY 10017
Phone: (212)599-7000
Fax: (212)599-3494

Publications: The City Journal (21424)

The Manila Bulletin USA
362 E. Grand Ave.
South San Francisco, CA 94080
Phone: (650)876-0410
Fax: (650)873-4335
Free: 800-338-5424

Publications: The Manila Bulletin USA (3790)

Manilla Printing Co.
Box 365
Manilla, IA 51454
Phone: (712)654-2911
Fax: (712)654-2910

Publications: The Manilla Times (11047)

Manisses Communications Group, Inc.
208 Governor St.
Providence, RI 02906
Phone: (401)831-6020
Fax: (401)861-6370
Free: 800-333-7771

Publications: Psychopharmacology Update (28418)

Manitoba Genealogical Society Inc.
Unit E, 1045 St. James St.
Winnipeg, MB, Canada R3H 1B1
Phone: (204)783-9139
Fax: (204)783-0190

Publications: Generations (35329)

Manitoba Historical Society
470-167 Lombard Ave.
Winnipeg, MB, Canada R3B 0T6
Phone: (204)947-0559
Fax: (204)943-1093

Publications: Manitoba History (35338)

Manitoba Library Association
606 - 100 Arthur St.
Winnipeg, MB, Canada R3B 1H3

Publications: CM (35322)

The Manitoba Museum
190 Rupert Ave.
Winnipeg, MB, Canada R3B 0N2
Phone: (204)956-2830
Fax: (204)942-3679

Publications: The Manitoba Museum Annual Report (35340)

Manitoba Society of Seniors
Ste 202-232 Portage Ave
Winnipeg, MB, Canada R3B 2C1
Phone: (204)942-3147
Fax: (204)943-1290
Free: 800-561-6767

Publications: MSOS Journal (35346)

Manitoba Theatre Centre
174 Market Ave.
Winnipeg, MB, Canada R3B 0P8
Phone: (204)956-1340
Fax: (204)947-3741
Free: 877-446-4500

Publications: Ovation (35348)

Manitoban
University of Manitoba
105 University Centre
Winnipeg, MB, Canada R3T 2N2
Phone: (204)474-6535
Fax: (204)474-7651

Publications: Manitoban (35341)

Manitoulin Media Inc.
PO Box 235
Gore Bay, ON, Canada P0P 1H0
Phone: (705)282-2003
Fax: (705)282-2432
Free: 800-561-4696

Publications: Manitoulin Recorder (36008)

Manitoulin Publishing Company Ltd.
Box 369
Little Current, ON, Canada P0P 1K0
Phone: (705)368-2744
Fax: (705)368-3822

Publications: Manitoulin Expositor (35977)

Mann Media, Inc.
PO Box 4552
Greensboro, NC 27404
Phone: (336)286-0600
Fax: (336)286-0100
Free: 800-948-1409

Publications: Our STATE (23932)

Manney's Shopper, Inc.
626 1/2 2nd Ave.
PO Box 66
Two Harbors, MN 55616
Phone: (218)834-5551
Fax: (218)834-2555

Publications: Superior Manney Shopper (34361) • Two Harbors Manney Shopper (16481)

Mannis Communications, Inc.
4645 Cass St., Ste. 201
PO Box 9550
San Diego, CA 92169
Phone: (858)270-3103
Fax: (858)270-9325

Publications: Beach & Bay Press (3119)

MANOTICK Messenger
1165 Beaverwood Rd.
PO Box 567
Manotick, ON, Canada K4M 1A5
Phone: (613)692-6000
Fax: (613)692-3758

Publications: MANOTICK Messenger (36009)

Mansfield Mirror
300 E Commercial St.
Mansfield, MO 65704
Phone: (417)924-3226
Fax: (417)924-3227

Publications: Mirror-Republican (17261)

Mansfield News-Mirror
PO Box 337
Mansfield, TX 76063
Phone: (817)473-4451
Fax: (817)473-0730

Publications: News-Mirror (30757)

Manteca Bulletin Daily Newspaper
531 E. Yosemite Ave.
PO Box 1958
Manteca, CA 95336
Phone: (209)249-3500
Fax: (209)249-3559

Publications: Manteca Bulletin (2502)

The Manteno News
120 West North St., Box 429
Peotone, IL 60468
Phone: (708)258-3473
Fax: (708)258-6295

Publications: The Manteno News (9140)

Manticore Publishers
PO Box 711
Lewiston, NY 14092
Phone: (905)945-7221
Fax: (905)945-8486
Free: 888-263-1877

Publications: Families in Society (34067)

Manufacturers' Agents National Association
One Spectrum Pointe, No. 150
Lake Forest, CA 92630-2283
Phone: (949)859-4040
Fax: (949)855-2973
Free: 877-626-2776

Publications: Agency Sales Magazine (2141)

Manufacturers' Mart Publications
16 High St.
Westerly, RI 02891-1850
Phone: (401)348-0797
Fax: (401)348-0799
Free: 800-835-0017

Publications: Manufacturer's Mart (28457)

Manufacturing Confectioner Publishing Co.
175 Rock Rd.
Glen Rock, NJ 07452
Phone: (201)652-2655
Fax: (201)652-3419

Publications: The Manufacturing Confectioner (18846)

Manuscript Press
PO Box 336
Mountain Home, TN 37684
Phone: (423)926-7495

Publications: Comics Revue (29428)

The Manuscript Society
350 N Niagara St.
Burbank, CA 91505

Publications: Manuscripts (28557)

Many Mountains Moving
420 22nd St.
Boulder, CO 80302
Phone: (303)545-9942
Fax: (303)444-6510

Publications: Many Mountains Moving (4178)

Maple Creek
PO Box 1360
Maple Creek, SK, Canada S0N 1N0
Phone: (306)662-2133
Fax: (306)662-3092

Publications: Maple Creek News (37494)

Maple Lake Messenger
PO Box 817 218 Division St. W.
Maple Lake, MN 55358
Phone: (320)963-3813
Fax: (320)963-6114

Publications: Maple Lake Messenger (16041)

Maple Leaf
351 Main St.
PO Box 70
Port Dover, ON, Canada N0A 1N0
Phone: (519)583-0112
Fax: (519)583-3200

Publications: Port Dover Maple Leaf (36332)

Maquoketa Sentinel-Press
PO Box 1150
108 W. Quarry
Maquoketa, IA 52060-1150
Phone: (563)652-2441
Fax: (563)652-6094

Publications: Maquoketa Sentinel-Press (11055)

Mar-Len Publications
131 Lincoln St.
Worcester, MA 01605
Phone: (508)752-2512
Fax: (508)752-9057

Publications: The Fifty Plus Advocate (14679) • Jewish Chronicle (14685)

Marathan Mercury
10 Peninsula Rd.
Marathon, ON, Canada P0T 2E0
Phone: (807)229-1520
Fax: (807)229-1595

Publications: Mercury (36011)

Marathon/Big Pine Key Free Press
6363 Overseas Hwy.
Marathon, FL 33050
Phone: (305)743-8766
Fax: (305)743-9977

Publications: Marathon/Big Pine Key Free Press (6322)

Marburger Publishing Co., Inc.
PO Box 158
Hartford, AR 72938-0158
Phone: (479)639-2324

Publications: The Gamecock (1170)

Marcel Dekker, Inc.
270 Madison Ave.
New York, NY 10016
Phone: (212)696-9000
Fax: (212)685-4540
Free: 800-228-1160

Publications: The American Journal of Drug and Alcohol Abuse (21192) • Analytical Letters (21212) • Applied Spectroscopy Reviews (12635) • Artificial Cells, Blood Substitutes and Immobilization Biotechnology (21256) • Cancer Investigation (21371) • Clinical and Experimental Hypertension (30464) • Clinical Research and Regulatory Affairs (2159) • Communications in Algebra (34063) • Communications in Partial Differential Equations (3795) • Communications in Soil Science and Plant Analysis (6934) • Communications in Statistics: Simulation & Computation (21460) • Communications in Statistics: Theory & Methods (21461) • Dance Chronicle (21534) • Drug and Chemical Toxicology (5272) • Drug Development and Industrial Pharmacy (29775) • Drug Metabolism Reviews (1228) • Drying Technology (21572) • Endocrine Research (20379) • Environmental Carcinogenesis & Ecotoxicology Reviews (32543) • Food Reviews International (33940) • Fullerene Science & Technology (21740) • Hemoglobin (21799) • Immunological Investigations (21852) • Immunopharmacology and Immunotoxicology (13652) • Instrumentation Science & Technology (5950) • International Journal of Food Properties (21905) • International Journal of Public Administration (27252) • Journal of Asthma (4303) • Journal of Biopharmaceutical Statistics (14074) • Journal of Carbohydrate Chemistry (17867) • Journal of Dispersion Science & Technology (22049) • Journal of Environmental Science and Health, Part A: Toxic/Hazardous Substances & Environmental Engineering (32020) • Journal of Environmental Science and Health, Part B: Pesticides, Food Contaminants, and Agricultural Wastes (32021) • Journal of Environmental Science and Health, Part C: Environmental Carcinogenesis and Ectoxicology Reviews (32545) • Journal of Immunoassay and Immunochemistry (5951) • Journal of Liposome Research (22113) • Journal of Liquid Chromatography & Related Technologies (22114) • Journal of Macromolecular Science, Part B, Physics (9713) • Journal of Plant Nutrition (6946) • Journal of Toxicology: Clinical Toxicology (21085) • Journal of Toxicology, Cutaneous and Ocular Toxicology (13812) • Journal of Toxicology Toxin Reviews (16090) • Journal of Trace and Microprobe Techniques (22206) • Journal of Wood Chemistry and Technology (23406) • Machining Science and Technology (13545) • Materials & Manufacturing Processes (32025) • Mechanics of Structures and Machines (1816) • Nucleosides & Nucleotides & Nucleic Acids (82) • Numerical Functional Analysis and Optimization (6501) • Petroleum Science & Technology (34551) • Pharmaceutical Development and Technology (9847) • Polymer-Plastics Technology and Engineering (32446) • Polymer Reaction Engineering (22578) • Preparative Biochemistry & Biotechnology (5952) • Quality Engineering (32803) • Renal Failure (23720) • Separation Science and Technology (23458) • Sequential Analysis (22731) • Solvent Extraction and Ion Exchange (8020) • Spectroscopy Letters (5168) • Stochastic Models (22792) • Substance Use & Misuse (22803) • Synthesis and Reactivity in Inorganic and Metal-Organic Chemistry (17519) • Synthetic Communications (23087) • Transport Theory and Statistical Physics (31942)

Marcellus News
PO Box 277
Marcellus, MI 49067
Phone: (269)646-2101

Publications: Marcellus News (15335)

March Street Press
3413 Wilshire Dr.
Greensboro, NC 27408
Phone: (336)282-9754
Fax: (336)282-9754

Publications: Parting Gifts (23933)

Marco Island Eagle
1075 Central Ave.
Naples, FL 34102
Phone: (239)262-3161
Fax: (239)435-3451

Publications: Marco Island Eagle (6444)

Marcus News
PO Box 445
Marcus, IA 51035
Phone: (712)376-4712
Fax: (712)376-4712

Publications: Marcus News (11058)

Marengo Publishing Corp.
PO Box 155
Marengo, IA 52301
Phone: (319)642-5506
Fax: (319)642-5509
Free: 800-414-5506

Publications: The North English Record (11118)

Mariah Media, Inc.
400 Market St.
Santa Fe, NM 87501
Phone: (505)989-7100
Fax: (505)989-4700

Publications: Outside (19940)

Mariannhill Mission Society
PO Box 87
Dearborn, MI 48121-0087
Phone: (313)561-2330

Publications: Leaves (14904)

Marianopolis College
3880 Cote Des Neiges Rd.
Montreal, QC, Canada G6V 6R8
Phone: (514)931-8792
Fax: (514)931-8790

Publications: The Paper Cut (37203)

Marietta College
Box A20
Marietta, OH 45750-4000
Phone: (614)376-4555
Fax: (614)376-4810

Publications: The Marcolian (25346)

The Marietta Times
700 Channel Ln.
PO Box 635
Marietta, OH 45750
Phone: (614)373-2121
Fax: (614)373-6251

Publications: The Marietta Times (25347)

Marin county's news monthly-Free press
PO Box 31
Bolinas, CA 94924
Phone: (415)868-1600
Fax: (415)868-0502

Publications: Coastal Post (1591)

Marin Scope Community Newspapers, Inc.
2400 Bridgeway
Ste. 290
Sausalito, CA 94965-2651
Phone: (415)332-3778
Fax: (415)332-8714

Publications: Marinscope Community Newspaper (3747) • News Pointer (3602)

Marine Biological Laboratory
7 MBL Street
Woods Hole, MA 02543
Phone: (508)289-7149
Fax: (508)289-7922

Publications: The Biological Bulletin (14672)

Marine Business Journal, Inc.
330 N Andrews Ave., 3rd Fl.
Fort Lauderdale, FL 33301
Phone: (954)522-5515
Fax: (954)522-2260

Publications: Marine Business Journal (6080)

Marine Corps Association
Box 1775
Quantico, VA 22134
Phone: (703)640-6161
Fax: (703)640-0823
Free: 800-336-0291

Publications: Leatherneck (32341) • Marine Corps Gazette (32342)

Marine Publishing, Inc.
1710 S Norman St.
Seattle, WA 98144
Phone: (206)709-1840
Fax: (206)682-4023

Publications: MARINE DIGEST (32984)

Marine Resources Foundation
Dept. of Environmental & Natural Resource Economics
University of Rhode Island
Kingston, RI 02881-0814
Phone: (401)874-4583
Fax: (401)782-4766

Publications: Marine Resource Economics (28360)

The Mariner
PO Box 429
Elkton, MD 21921
Phone: (410)287-9430
Fax: (410)287-9442

Publications: The Mariner (13496)

Mariner
7 West St.
Walpole, MA 02081
Phone: (508)668-0243
Fax: (508)668-5174

Publications: The Walpole Times (14594)

Mariner Newspapers
165 Enterprise Dr.
Marshfield, MA 02050-2132
Phone: (781)837-3500
Fax: (781)837-4540
Free: 800-649-6661

Publications: Bridgewater Townsman (14007) • Hingham Mariner (14234) • Kingston Independent Voice (14263) • Randolph Mariner (14496) • South Look (14309) • Whitman/Hanson Mariner (14657)

Marion Advertiser
PO Box 268
Marion, WI 54950
Phone: (715)754-5444

Publications: Marion Advertiser (34023)

Marion County Newspapers, Inc.
PO Box 1199
Flippin, AR 72634-1199

Publications: Mountain Echo (1134)

Marion County Newspapers, Inc.
307 1/2 Elm. Ave.
PO Box 765
South Pittsburg, TN 37380-1337
Phone: (423)837-6312
Fax: (423)837-8715

Publications: Sequatchie Valley Purchase (29609) • South Pittsburg Hustler (29610)

Marion Military Institute
PO Box 420
Marion, AL 36756
Phone: (334)683-2347
Fax: (334)683-2380

Publications: Marion Military Institute Alumni Bulletin (311)

The Marion Record
Box 298
Marion, SD 57043
Phone: (605)648-3821
Fax: (605)648-3920

Publications: The Marion Record (28889)

The Marion Star
150 Ct. St.
Marion, OH 43302
Phone: (614)387-0400
Fax: (614)382-2210

Publications: The Marion Star (25351)

Marion Star and Mullins Enterprise
211 Railroad Ave.
PO Box 880
Marion, SC 29571
Phone: (803)423-2050
Fax: (803)423-2542

Publications: Marion Star and Mullins Enterprise (28689)

Marion Times-Standard
PO Box 418
Marion, AL 36756
Phone: (334)683-6318
Fax: (334)683-4616

Publications: Marion Times-Standard (312)

Mariposa Gazette
PO Box 38
Mariposa, CA 95338
Phone: (209)966-2500
Fax: (209)966-3384

Publications: Gazette Mountain Life (2511) • Mariposa Gazette and Miner (2512)

The Mariposa Guide
PO Box 2105
Mariposa, CA 95338
Phone: (209)966-3888
Fax: (209)742-6896

Publications: The Mariposa Guide (2513)

Marist College
290 North Rd.
Poughkeepsie, NY 12601-1387
Phone: (845)575-3000
Fax: (845)471-6213

Publications: The Circle (23145)

Maritime Activity Reports, Inc.
118 E 25th St.
New York, NY 10010
Phone: (212)477-6700
Fax: (212)254-6271

Publications: Maritime Reporter and Engineering News (22284)

Mark-Age Inc.
PO Box 10
Pioneer, TN 37847
Phone: (423)784-3269
Fax: (423)784-3269

Publications: I Am Nation News (29569)

Mark I. Publications, Inc.
62-33 Woodhaven Blvd.
Rego Park, NY 11374
Phone: (718)205-8000
Fax: (718)205-0150

Publications: Queens Chronicle (23180)

Market Guide, Inc.
2001 Marcus Ave., Ste. S. 200
Lake Success, NY 11042-1011
Phone: (516)327-2400
Fax: (516)327-2425

Publications: The Market Guide—Select Over the Counter Stock Edition (20880)

Market Independent
93 Pke. St., No. 312
Seattle, WA 98101
Phone: (206)587-0351
Fax: (206)624-6960

Publications: Pike Place Market Merchants Association & Market News (33002)

Market Journal
PO Box 410
Grayslake, IL 60030-0410
Phone: (847)223-3280
Fax: (847)223-9390

Publications: Market Journal (8957)

Market Place Publications
89 Access Rd.
Norwood, MA 02062
Phone: (781)762-6600
Fax: (781)762-1300

Publications: Clinical Laboratory MarketPlace (14446) • Meeting Planners MarketPlace (14449)

Market Power, Inc.
103 2nd St. N
Hopkins, MN 55343

Publications: Mirror News Magazine (15964)

Marketing Communications, Inc.
1086 Remsen Ave.
Brooklyn, NY 11236
Phone: (718)257-8484
Fax: (718)257-8845

Publications: Doctor's Shopper (20314)

Marketing Index International Publications
6580 SW Peyton Rd.
Portland, OR 97223-7519
Phone: (503)244-7337
Fax: (503)244-7337

Publications: Pacific Marketer (26498)

Marketing & Technology Group
1415 N. Dayton St.
Chicago, IL 60622
Phone: (312)266-3311
Fax: (312)266-3363

Publications: CarneTec (8299) • Meat Marketing & Technology (8483) • Poultry Magazine (8538)

Marketing U.S.P. Inc.
554, Ave. Grosvenor
Westmount, QC, Canada H3Y 2S4
Phone: (514)935-1171
Fax: (514)935-4504

Publications: Plaisirs de Vivre (37444) • Residences (37445)

Marketnews
364 Supertest Rd., No. 200
North York, ON, Canada M3J 2M2
Phone: (416)667-9945
Fax: (416)667-0609

Publications: Market News (36129)

Marketplace Magazine
PO Box 1897
Appleton, WI 54912-1897
Phone: (920)735-5969
Fax: (920)735-5970
Free: (866)735-5969

Publications: Marketplace Magazine (33537)

Marketplace Publications
148 Rte. 17M
Box 953
Harriman, NY 10926-9766
Phone: (914)783-1111
Fax: (914)783-8053

Publications: The Marketplace Pennysaver (20711)

Marlboro Enterprise
40 Mechanic St.
Marlborough, MA 01752-4425
Phone: (508)490-7450
Fax: (508)490-7471

Publications: Hudson Daily Sun (14306)

Marlboro Publishing Co., Inc.
100 Fayetteville Ave.
PO Box 656
Bennettsville, SC 29512
Phone: (803)479-3815
Fax: (803)479-7671

Publications: Malboro Herald-Advocate (28493)

Marlee Walker's Blues To-Do's
PO Box 22950
Seattle, WA 98122-0950
Phone: (206)328-0662

Publications: Marlee Walker's Blues To-Do's (32985)

Marlin Democrat
211 Fortune St.
PO Box 112
Marlin, TX 76661-0112
Phone: (254)883-2554
Fax: (254)883-6553

Publications: Marlin Democrat (30765)

Maro Publications
327 Huffman Dr.
Exton, PA 19341
Phone: (610)303-9920
Fax: (610)303-9921

Publications: Maro Polymer Links/Alerts (26918)

Marquee Media Inc.
1325 Burnhamthorpe Rd. E.
Mississauga, ON, Canada L4Y 3V8
Phone: (905)274-7174
Fax: (905)274-9799

Publications: Marquee Magazine (36076)

Marquette Journal
1131 W. Wisconsin Ave.
Milwaukee, WI 53233
Phone: (414)288-7057
Fax: (414)288-1739

Publications: Marquette Tribune (34077) • Marquette University Journal (34078)

Marquette Magazine
Marquette University
PO Box 1881
Milwaukee, WI 53201-1881
Phone: (414)288-7448
Fax: (414)288-7197

Publications: Marquette Magazine (34076)

Marquette University Press
PO Box 3141
Milwaukee, WI 53201-3141
Phone: (414)288-1564
Fax: (414)288-7813
Free: 800-444-2419

Publications: Philosophy & Theology (34093)

Marshall County Publishing Co.
204 S Washington St.
Lacon, IL 61540
Phone: (309)246-2865
Fax: (309)246-3214

Publications: Illinois Valley Peach (9059) • Lacon Home Journal (9060)

The Marshall Democrat-News
121 N. Lafayette
PO Box 100
Marshall, MO 65340
Phone: (660)886-2233
Fax: (660)886-8544

Publications: The Marshall Democrat-News (17265)

Marshall Independent
508 W Main
PO Box 411
Marshall, MN 56258
Phone: (507)537-1551
Fax: (507)537-1557
Free: 800-640-6148

Publications: Marshall Independent (16042) • Shoppers Review (16043)

Marshalltown Newspaper, Inc.
Marshalltown, IA 50158

Publications: Times-Republican (11066)

Marshalltown Newspaper Inc.
625 2nd St.
PO Box 156
Traer, IA 50675
Phone: (319)478-2323
Fax: (319)478-2818

Publications: Star-Clipper (11273)

The Marshfield Mail
225 N Clay
PO Box A
Marshfield, MO 65706-9613
Phone: (417)468-2013
Fax: (417)859-7930

Publications: The Marshfield Mail (17271)

Marshfield News-Herald
111 W 3rd St.
PO Box 70
Marshfield, WI 54449-2811
Phone: (715)384-3131
Fax: (715)387-4175

Publications: Marshfield News-Herald (34027)

Mart Herald
420 Texas Ave.
Box 150
Mart, TX 76664-0150
Phone: (817)876-2681

Publications: The Mart Herald (30770)

Martha Pullen Co., Inc.
149 Old Big Cove Rd.
Brownsboro, AL 35741-9683
Phone: (256)533-9586
Fax: (256)533-9630

Publications: Sew Beautiful (139)

Martha Stewart Living
20 W. 43rd St. 25th Fl.
New York, NY 10036

Publications: Martha Stewart Living (22287)

Martha's Vineyard Magazine
34 S Summer St.
PO Box 66
Edgartown, MA 02539
Phone: (508)627-4311
Fax: (508)627-7444
Free: 877-850-0409

Publications: Martha's Vineyard Magazine (14174)

Martha's Vineyard Times
PO Box 4249
Vineyard Haven, MA 02568-4249
Phone: (508)696-6688
Fax: (508)696-8989

Publications: Martha's Vineyard Times (14591)

The Martin Agency
1 Shockoe Plaza
Richmond, VA 23219-4132
Phone: (804)649-1496

Publications: What's New in Advertising and Marketing (32470)

Martin Broadcasting Corp.
620 Choctaw
Alva, OK 73717
Phone: (405)327-2200
Fax: (405)327-2454

Publications: Alva Review-Courier (25737)

The Martin Group, Inc.
24901 Northwestern Hwy., Ste. 316A
Southfield, MI 48075
Phone: (248)440-6080
Fax: (248)352-4801

Publications: Health Care Weekly Review (15543)

Martin Publications, Inc.
2120 28th St.
Sacramento, CA 95818
Phone: (916)457-3643

Publications: International Travel News (3002)

Martin Publishing, Inc.
217 W. Market St.
Havana, IL 62644
Phone: (309)543-3311
Fax: (309)543-6844

Publications: Havana Mason County Democrat (8979)

Martineau Corp.
7910 Woodmont Ave., No. 1150
Bethesda, MD 20814-3062
Phone: (301)652-8666
Fax: (301)656-8654

Publications: Association Trends (13318)

Martinelli Publications
40 Larkin Plaza
Yonkers, NY 10701
Phone: (914)965-4000
Fax: (914)965-2892

Publications: The Eastchester Record (20562) • The Harrison Independent (20712) • The Mt. Vernon Independent (21104) • The North Castle News (23011) • The Pelham Sun (23089) • Rye Chronicle (23279) • The Sound View News (23601) • The Yonkers Home News & Times (23603)

Martinsville Bulletin
204 Broad St.
Martinsville, VA 24115-3199
Phone: (276)638-8801
Fax: (276)638-4153
Free: 800-234-6575

Publications: Martinsville Bulletin (32233)

Marvel Entertainment Inc.
10 E 40th St.
New York, NY 10016
Phone: (212)576-4000
Fax: (917)472-2150

Publications: Doctor Strange, Sorcerer Supreme (21562) • Ghost Rider (21760) • The Hulk (21827) • Morbius (22365)

Mary Ann Liebert, Inc. Publishers
2 Madison Ave.
Larchmont, NY 10538
Phone: (914)834-3100
Fax: (914)834-1388
Free: 800-654-3237

Publications: AIDS PATIENT CARE and STDs (20886) • AIDS Research and Human Retroviruses (20887) • Alternative & Complementary Therapies (20888) • Antioxidants and Redox Signaling (20889) • Antisense and Nucleic Acid Drug Development (20890) • Astrobiology (20891) • Biotechnology Law Report (20892) • Cancer Biotherapy and Radiopharmaceuticals (20893) • Cloning and Stem Cells (20894) • CyberPsychology and Behavior (20895) • Disease Management (20896) • DNA and Cell Biology (20897) • Election Law Journal (20898) • Environmental Engineering Science (20899) • Gaming Law Review (20900) • Genetic Engineering News (20901) • Genetic Testing (20902) • Human Gene Therapy (9124) • Hybridoma and Hybridomics (20903) • Journal of Aerosol Medicine (20904) • Journal of Aerosol Medicine (20905) • The Journal of Alternative & Complementary Medicine (20906) • Journal of Anti-Aging Medicine (20907) • Journal of Child and Adolescent Psychopharmacology (20908) • Journal of Clinical Laser Medicine & Surgery (20909) • Journal of Computational Biology (20910) • Journal of Endourology (20911) • Journal of Gynecologic Surgery (20912) • Journal of Hematotherapy & Stem Cell Research (20913) • Journal of Interferon & Cytokine Research (20914) • Journal of Laparoendoscopic and Advanced Surgical Techniques (20915) • Journal of Men's Health (20916) • Journal of Neurotrauma (20917) • Journal of Ocular Pharmacology and Therapeutics (20918) • Journal of Women's Health (20919) • Microbial Drug Resistance (20921) • Natural Pharmacy (20922) • Omics: A Journal of Integrative Biology (20923) • Pediatric Asthma, Allergy & Immunology (20924) • Pediatric Endosurgery & Innovative Techniques (20925) • Telemedicine Journal and E-Health (20926) • Thyroid (20927) • Tissue Engineering (20928) • Vector-Borne and Zoonotic Diseases (20929) • Viral Immunology (20930)

Mary Ann Publishers, Inc.
38 N Monroe
Box 216
Williamsport, IN 47993
Phone: (765)762-3322
Fax: (765)762-6418
Free: 800-301-4300

Publications: The Review-Republican (10562)

Mary Baldwin College
12th N. Naw & Fredricks
Staunton, VA 24401
Phone: (540)887-7112
Fax: (540)887-7040

Publications: Campus Comments (32554)

Mary L. Van Meter
1623 Blake St., Ste. 250
Denver, CO 80202
Phone: (303)575-9595
Fax: (303)575-9555

Publications: Newspapers & Technology (4343)

Maryknoll Fathers
PO Box 308
Maryknoll, NY 10545-0308
Phone: (914)941-7590
Fax: (914)945-0670

Publications: Maryknoll Magazine (21023) • Revista Maryknoll (21024)

Maryland Coast Dispatch
10012 Old Ocean City Blvd
PO Box 467
Berlin, MD 21811
Phone: (410)641-4561
Fax: (410)641-0966

Publications: Maryland Coast Dispatch (13293)

Maryland Historical Society
201 W. Monument St.
Baltimore, MD 21201-4674
Phone: (410)685-3750
Fax: (410)385-2105

Publications: Maryland Historical Magazine (13211)

Maryland Horse Breeders Association
PO Box 427
Timonium, MD 21094
Phone: (410)252-2100
Fax: (410)560-0503

Publications: Mid-Atlantic Thoroughbred (13758)

Maryland Media, Inc.
3150 S. Campus Dining Hall
University of Maryland
College Park, MD 20742
Phone: (301)314-8200
Fax: (301)314-8358

Publications: Diamondback (13416)

Maryland Municipal League
1212 West St.
Annapolis, MD 21401
Phone: (410)268-5514
Fax: (410)268-7004

Publications: Municipal Maryland (13094)

Maryland Music Educators Association
c/o Thomas W. Fugate
27 Meadow Ln.
Thurmont, MD 21788-1737
Phone: (301)271-7269
Fax: (301)271-7032

Publications: Maryland Music Educator (13755)

Maryland Musician Publications
1144 York Rd.
Lutherville, MD 21093-6201
Phone: (410)494-0566
Fax: (410)494-0565
Free: 800-884-4908

Publications: Music Monthly (13626)

Maryland Pharmacists Association
650 W. Lombard St.
Baltimore, MD 21201
Phone: (410)727-0746
Fax: (410)727-2253

Publications: Maryland Pharmacist (13214)

Maryland Plumbing Heating Cooling Contractors, Inc.
10176 Balto Natl. Pke., No. 205
Ellicott City, MD 21042
Phone: (410)461-5977
Fax: (410)750-2507
Free: 800-723-4900

Publications: Maryland PHCC News & Views (13499)

Maryland State Poetry and Literary Society
Drawer H
Baltimore, MD 21228
Phone: (410)747-0594

Publications: Maryland Poetry Review (13215)

The Marysville Advocate
107 S 9th
Box 271
Marysville, KS 66508-0271
Phone: (785)562-2317
Fax: (785)562-5589

Publications: The Marysville Advocate (11639)

The Marysville Globe
8213A State Ave.
PO Box 145
Marysville, WA 98270
Phone: (360)659-1300
Fax: (360)658-0350

Publications: The Marysville Globe (32828)

Marysville Newspapers, Inc.
207 N. Main St.
Box 226
Marysville, OH 43040
Phone: (937)644-9111
Fax: (937)644-9211

Publications: Marysville Journal-Tribune (25357) • The Richwood Gazette (25496)

Maryville Daily Forum
111 E. Jenkins
PO Box 188
Maryville, MO 64468
Phone: (660)562-2424
Fax: (660)562-2823
Free: 888-660-2424

Publications: Maryville Daily Forum (17274) • Weekly Bargain Shopper (17277)

Masaryk Memorial Institute, Inc.
450 Scarborough Golf Club Rd.
Scarborough, ON, Canada M1G 1H1
Phone: (416)409-4354
Fax: (416)409-6473

Publications: Novy Domov (New Homeland) (36380)

Mason City Banner Times
126 N Tonica St.
PO Box 71
Mason City, IL 62664
Phone: (217)482-3276
Fax: (217)482-3277

Publications: Mason City Banner Times (9157)

Mason County News
110 Live Oak St.
PO Box 1729
Mason, TX 76856
Phone: (915)347-5757
Fax: (915)347-5668

Publications: Mason County News (30771)

Mason Valley News
207 W Goldfield Ave.
Yerington, NV 89447-2349
Phone: (775)463-2856

Publications: Fernley Leader/Dayton Courier (18453)

The Masonry Society
3970 Broadway, Ste. 201-D
Boulder, CO 80304-1135
Phone: (303)939-9700
Fax: (303)541-9215

Publications: Masonry Society Journal (4179)

Massachusetts Association of Older Americans
108 Arlington St.
Boston, MA 02116
Phone: (617)426-0804
Fax: (617)426-0070

Publications: The Older American (13943)

Massachusetts Bar Association
20 West St.
Boston, MA 02111-1218
Phone: (617)338-0500
Fax: (617)338-0650

Publications: Lawyer's Journal (13921) • Massachusetts Bar Association Lawyers Journal (13925)

Massachusetts Center for Renaissance Studies
PO Box 2300
Amherst, MA 01004
Phone: (413)577-3603
Fax: (413)577-3605

Publications: English Literary Renaissance (13793)

Massachusetts Institute of Technology
77 Massachusetts Ave., Rm. E60-100
77 Massachusetts Ave E60-100
Cambridge, MA 02139
Phone: (617)253-7170
Fax: (617)258-9739

Publications: Sloan Management Review (14101)

Massachusetts Institute of Technology
77 Massachusetts Ave., Rm. 36-413
Cambridge, MA 02139-4307

Publications: R.L.E. Currents (14099)

Massachusetts Municipal Association
60 Temple Pl., 2nd Fl.
Boston, MA 02111
Phone: (617)426-7272
Fax: (617)695-1314
Free: 800-882-1498

Publications: The Mass Municipal Directory (13924)

Massachusetts School of Law
Woodland Park
500 Federal St.
Andover, MA 01810
Phone: (978)681-0800
Fax: (978)681-6330

Publications: The Long Term View (13813)

Massachusetts Society of Certified Public Accountants, Inc.
105 Chauncy St., 10th Fl.
Boston, MA 02111
Phone: (617)556-4000
Fax: (617)556-4126
Free: 800-392-6145

Publications: Massachusetts CPA Review Online (13927)

Massachusetts Society for the Prevention of Cruelty to Animals and the American Human Education Society
350 S. Huntington Ave.
Boston, MA 02130
Phone: (617)541-5065
Fax: (617)522-4885

Publications: Animals Magazine (13850)

Massage Magazine
1636 W. 1st Ave., Ste. 100
Spokane, WA 99204
Phone: (509)324-8117
Fax: (509)324-8606
Free: 800-872-1282

Publications: Massage Magazine (33095)

Master Drawings Association, Inc.
29 E. 36th St.
New York, NY 10016
Phone: (212)685-0008
Fax: (212)685-4740

Publications: Master Drawings (22289)

Masthead Publications, Inc.
1035 Conklin Rd.
Conklin, NY 13748
Phone: (607)775-0472
Fax: (607)775-5863

Publications: The Country Courier (20493) • The Vestal Town Crier (20495) • The Windsor Standard (20496)

The Match!
PO Box 3012
Tucson, AZ 85702

Publications: The Match! (956)

Matchbook
242 N Broad St.
Doylestown, PA 18901
Free: 877-575-0744

Publications: Matchbook (26834)

Material Handling Network, Inc.
252 E. Washington St.
PO Box 2338
East Peoria, IL 61611

Publications: Material Handling Network (8806)

Materials Information
9639 Kinsman Rd.
Materials Park, OH 44073
Phone: (216)338-5151
Fax: (216)338-4634

Publications: Engineered Materials Abstracts (25365)

Materials Research Society
506 Keystone Dr.
Warrendale, PA 15086-7573
Phone: (724)779-3003
Fax: (724)779-8313

Publications: Journal of Materials Research (28113)

Mathematical Association of America
1529 18th St. NW
Washington, DC 20036
Phone: (202)387-5200
Fax: (301)206-9789
Free: 800-741-9415

Publications: American Mathematical Monthly (5335) • College Mathematics Journal (5424) • Journal of Online Mathematics and Its Applications (5607) • Mathematics Magazine (5645)

Mathesis Publications, Inc.
Department of Philosophy
Duquesne University
Pittsburgh, PA 15282
Phone: (412)396-6500

Publications: Ancient Philosophy (27758)

Matilda Ziegler Magazine for the Blind
80 8th Ave., Rm. 1304
New York, NY 10011
Phone: (212)242-0263
Fax: (212)633-1601

Publications: Matilda Ziegler Magazine for the Blind (22299)

The Mattawa Recorder
341 McConnell St.
Box 67
Mattawa, ON, Canada P0H 1V0
Phone: (705)744-5361
Fax: (705)744-5361

Publications: The Mattawa Recorder (36035)

The Mattingley Publishing Co., Inc.
3756 Grand Ave., Ste. 205
Oakland, CA 94610-1545
Phone: (510)839-0909
Fax: (510)839-2950

Publications: TEST Engineering & Management (2700)

Mattos Newspapers, Inc.
1021 Fresno St.
PO Box 878
Newman, CA 95360
Phone: (209)862-2222
Fax: (209)862-4133

Publications: The West Side Index (2620)

Mature Market Net
1830 Hwy. 9
Toms River, NJ 08755
Phone: (732)505-9700
Fax: (732)240-0002

Publications: Spirit Plus (19645)

Maui Publishing
100 Mahalani St.
Wailuku, HI 96793

Publications: Maui News (7795)

Maurer Publishing Co.
359 Reagon St.
PO Box 277
St. Ignace, MI 49781
Phone: (906)643-9150
Fax: (906)643-9122

Publications: The Mackinac Island Town Crier (15325) • The St. Ignace News (15508)

Robert Mauro
PO Box 0897
Levittown, NY 11756-0897
Phone: (516)579-4043

Publications: PeopleNet (20942)

Maverick Media, Inc.
123 W. 17th St.
PO Box O
Syracuse, NE 68446
Phone: (402)269-2135
Fax: (402)269-2392
Free: 800-228-3325

Publications: Mighty Nickel (18026) • Penny Press 5 (17948) • Penny Press 4 (11492) • Penny Press 2 (17276) • Syracuse Journal-Democrat (18293)

Maximilian Press
Box 64841
Virginia Beach, VA 23467-0841
Phone: (757)482-2273
Fax: (757)482-0325

Publications: Journal of Information Technology Management (32587)

Maximilian Press Publishers
PO Box 64841
Virginia Beach, VA 23467-4841
Phone: (757)482-2273
Fax: (757)482-0325

Publications: Journal of Management Systems (31965)

Mayfair Glen Publishing, Inc.
Box 815
Sandy Hook, CT 06482
Phone: (203)426-8992
Fax: (203)426-9533

Publications: Mayfair Magazine (5112) • Mayfair Specials (5113)

Mayhill Publications
27 N. Jefferson St.
PO Box 90
Knightstown, IN 46148
Fax: (765)345-3398
Free: 800-876-5133

Publications: AntiqueWeek (Eastern Edition) (10233) • AntiqueWeek (Mid-Central Edition) (10234) • Farmweek (10235)

Mayo Tree Press
PO Box 248
Mayo, FL 32066
Phone: (386)294-1210
Fax: (386)294-2666

Publications: The Mayo Free Press (6332)

Mayor's Commission on Affairs of the Elderly
One City Hall Pl., Rm. 271
Boston, MA 02201
Phone: (617)635-2712
Fax: (617)635-3213

Publications: Boston Seniority (13863)

Maysville News
Box 617
Maysville, OK 73057-0617
Phone: (405)867-4457
Fax: (405)867-5115

Publications: The Maysville News (25908)

Mayville Monitor
6071 Fulton St.
Mayville, MI 48744-0299
Phone: (989)843-6441
Fax: (989)843-0054

Publications: Mayville Monitor (15352)

Mayville Publishing
Mayville House
844 Ridge Rd.
RR 1
Picton, ON, Canada K0K 2T0
Phone: (613)476-4244
Fax: (613)476-5233

Publications: Coverings (36328)

Mazda RX-7 Club
1774 S Alvira
Los Angeles, CA 90035
Phone: (323)933-6993

Publications: Rotary Review (2382)

MBA Inc.
1301 Lancaster Ave., Ste. 102
Berwyn, PA 19312-1290
Phone: (610)722-0253
Fax: (610)722-0256
Free: 800-456-0402

Publications: The Mutual Magazine (26697)

Mc Camey News
PO Drawer E
Mc Camey, TX 79752
Phone: (915)652-3312
Fax: (915)652-8995

Publications: Mc Camey News (30774)

The Mc Gregor Mirror and Crawford Sun
311 S Main
Mc Gregor, TX 76657-0415
Phone: (254)840-2091
Fax: (254)840-2091

Publications: The Mc Gregor Mirror and Crawford Sun (30775)

McArthur Foundation
666 Broadway
New York, NY 10012
Phone: (212)614-6500
Fax: (212)228-5889
Free: 800-444-4653

Publications: Harper's Magazine (21791)

McClain County Publishing Co.
225 W Main St.
PO Box 191
Purcell, OK 73080
Phone: (405)527-2126
Fax: (405)527-3299

Publications: Purcell Register (26050)

McClatchy
212 E Chatham St.
PO Box 4949
Cary, NC 27519-4949
Phone: (919)460-2600
Fax: (919)460-6034

Publications: The Cary News (23686)

The McClatchy Company
2100 Q St.
Sacramento, CA 95816
Phone: (916)321-1855
Fax: (916)321-1869
Free: 800-877-7300

Publications: The Fresno Bee (1950) • The Modesto Bee (2561) • The News Tribune (33147) • Vida En El Valle (1959)

McCormick Media, Inc.
120 Main St.
Mc Cormick, SC 29835
Phone: (864)465-3311
Fax: (864)465-3528

Publications: McCormick Messenger (28690)

McCrone Research Institute
2820 S Michigan Ave.
Chicago, IL 60616-3292
Phone: (312)842-7100
Fax: (312)842-1078

Publications: The Microscope (8487)

McCurtain Daily Gazette
PO Box 179
Idabel, OK 74745
Phone: (580)286-3321
Fax: (580)286-2208

Publications: McCurtain Daily Gazette (25875)

McDonald Communications Corp.
260 Madison Ave., Front 3
New York, NY 10016-2401
Phone: (212)445-6100
Fax: (212)445-6197
Free: 800-234-9675

Publications: Working Woman (22939)

McDonald County Press Inc.
PO Box 266
Pineville, MO 64856
Phone: (417)223-4377
Fax: (417)223-4049

Numbers cited after listings are entry numbers rather than page numbers.

Publications: McDonald County News-Gazette (17346) • McDonald County Press (17347)

McDuffie Progress
101 Church St.
PO Box 1090
Thomson, GA 30824
Phone: (706)595-1601
Fax: (706)597-8974

Publications: Dollar Saver (7591) • McDuffie Progress (7592)

McFarland & Company Inc., Publishers
Box 611
Jefferson, NC 28640
Phone: (336)246-4460
Fax: (336)246-5018
Free: 800-253-2187

Publications: Journal of Information Ethics (16344)

McGee Publishers
217 E Alameda Ave., Ste. 301
Burbank, CA 91502-1500
Phone: (818)848-2957
Fax: (818)843-3489

Publications: California Broker (1616)

McGehee Publishing Co.
PO Box 290
McGehee, AR 71654
Phone: (870)222-3922
Fax: (870)222-3726

Publications: Times-News (1272)

The McGill Alumni Association
3605 de la Montagne
Montreal, QC, Canada H3G 2M1
Phone: (514)398-3549
Fax: (514)398-7338

Publications: McGill News (37184)

McGill Law Journal/Revue de Droit de McGill
3644 Peel St.
Montreal, QC, Canada H3A 1W9
Phone: (514)398-7397
Fax: (514)398-7360

Publications: McGill Law Journal/Revue de Droit de McGill (37183)

McGill University
Arts Building, Office 305
853 Sherbrooke St. W
Montreal, QC, Canada H3A 2T6
Phone: (514)398-6588

Publications: Scrivener (37222)

McGirgan Productions
101 Jefferson
PO Box 27
La Fayette, IL 61449
Phone: (309)995-3877
Fax: (309)995-3975

Publications: Prairie Shopper (9050)

The McGraw-Hill Companies
130 E Randolph St., Ste. 400
Chicago, IL 60601
Phone: (312)233-7470
Fax: (312)233-7430
Free: 800-257-0993

Publications: Dodge Construction News (Illinois, Indiana, Wisconsin Edition) (8356)

McGraw-Hill Companies
2 Penn Plaza, 25th Fl.
New York, NY 10021-2298

Publications: International Private Power Quarterly (21931)

The McGraw-Hill Companies, Inc.
4 International Dr., Ste. 260
Rye Brook, NY 10573
Phone: (914)939-8787
Fax: (914)939-8824
Free: 800-327-2052

Publications: A/C FLYER (23282)

McGraw-Hill Companies Inc./F.W. Dodge Louisiana Contractor
4000 S Sherwood Forest Blvd., Ste. 202
Baton Rouge, LA 70816
Phone: (225)292-8980
Fax: (225)292-5089
Free: 800-786-8980

Publications: Louisiana Contractor (12496)

McGraw-Hill Healthcare Information Group
4530 W 77th St.
Minneapolis, MN 55435
Phone: (952)835-3222
Fax: (952)835-3460

Publications: Postgraduate Medicine (16121)

McGraw-Hill, Inc.
3110 N. Central, Ste. 155
Phoenix, AZ 85012
Phone: (602)631-3068
Fax: (602)631-3080
Free: 800-580-3406

Publications: Southwest Contractor (811)

McGraw-Hill, Inc.
2000 S. Colorado Blvd., Ste. 2000
Denver, CO 80222
Phone: (303)756-9995
Fax: (303)756-4465
Free: 800-323-2362

Publications: The Daily Journal (4320)

McGraw-Hill Inc.
1221 Avenue of the Americas
New York, NY 10020
Phone: (212)512-2000

Publications: Architectural Record (21243) • Aviation Week & Space Technology (21282) • Business Week (21362) • ENR: Engineering News-Record (21607) • Metals Week (22324) • New York Construction News (22439) • Power (22587)

McGraw-Hill, Inc.
505 E. Huntland Dr., No. 310
Austin, TX 78752
Phone: (512)458-1343
Fax: (512)467-2806

Publications: Texas Construction (29815)

McGraw-Hill, Inc.
PO Box 26237
Salt Lake City, UT 84126-0237
Phone: (801)972-4400
Fax: (801)972-8975

Publications: Intermountain Contractor (31431) • Utah Building Magazine (31441)

Dave McGurgan
PO Box 26039
Wilmington, DE 19899-6039
Fax: (302)651-0206

Publications: Yakuza (5296)

McHenry County College
8900 U.S Hwy. 14
Crystal Lake, IL 60012-2761
Phone: (815)455-3700
Fax: (815)455-3999

Publications: Tartan (8696)

McIntosh County Democrat
PO Box 385
Checotah, OK 74426
Phone: (918)473-2314
Fax: (918)473-6541

Publications: McIntosh County Democrat (25781)

McKenzie County Farmers Publishing Co.
PO Box 587
Watford City, ND 58854
Phone: (701)842-2351
Fax: (701)842-2352

Publications: McKenzie County Farmer (24555)

McKenzie Report, Inc.
Box 1018
High Level, AB, Canada T0H 1Z0
Phone: (403)926-2000
Fax: (403)926-2001

Publications: The Echo (34780) • Mile Zero News (34778)

McKenzie River Reflections
59059 Old McKenzie Hwy.
McKenzie Bridge, OR 97413
Phone: (541)822-3358
Fax: (541)822-3358

Publications: McKenzie River Reflections (26413)

McKinney Newspapers, Inc.
PO Box 400
Mc Kinney, TX 75071
Phone: (972)542-2631
Fax: (972)529-1684

Publications: McKinney Courier Gazette (30776) • McKinney Courier Gazette Pennysaver (30777) • North Texas Life (30781) • North Texas Life (30780)

McKinsey & Company, Inc.
55 E. 52nd St.
New York, NY 10022

Publications: McKinsey Quarterly (22303)

McKirgan Productions
101 Jefferson
PO Box 27
La Fayette, IL 61449
Phone: (309)995-3877

Publications: Prairie Times (9051)

McKnight's Long-Term Care News
Two Northfield Plz., Ste. 300
Northfield, IL 60093-1219
Phone: (847)784-8706
Fax: (847)441-3701

Publications: McKnight's Long-Term Care News (9331) • Pharmaceutical Representative (9332)

McLean Publishing Co.
175 Main St.
PO Box 498
Brookville, PA 15825-0498
Phone: (814)849-5330
Fax: (814)849-4333

Publications: Jeffersonian Democrat (26732) • Tri-County Sunday (26733)

McLeansboro Times-Leader
355 King Ave.
PO Box 416
Bathurst, NB, Canada E2A 1P4
Phone: (506)546-4491
Fax: (506)546-1491

Publications: Cordele Dispatch (7203) • Cumberland Times News (13474) • Jacksonville Journal-Courier (35377) • The Northern Light (35378) • Princeton Times (33441) • The Progress-Index (32330) • Truro Daily News (35616)

McLeod Publishing, Inc.
PO Box 188
Glencoe, MN 55336
Phone: (320)864-5518
Fax: (320)864-5510

Publications: The Bulletin (15776) • McLeod County Chronicle (15918)

The McLoud News, Inc.
109 N Main
PO Box 517
McLoud, OK 74851
Phone: (405)964-6566
Fax: (405)946-2930

Publications: The McLoud News (25914)

The McMahon Publishing Group
545 W 45th St., 8th Fl.
New York, NY 10036
Phone: (212)957-5300
Fax: (212)957-7230

Publications: Anesthesiology News (21213) • Cardiology Special Edition (21375) • Gastroenterology and Endoscopy News (21748) • General Surgery & Laparoscopy News (21749) • Orthopedic Special Edition (22506) • Pharmacy Practice News (22547)

McMaster Centre for Gerontological Studies
1280 Main St. W.
Rm. 226, Kenneth Taylor Hall
Hamilton, ON, Canada L8S 4M4
Phone: (905)525-9140
Fax: (905)525-4198

Publications: Canadian Journal on Aging (La Revue Canadienne du vieillissement) (35876)

McMaster Students Union, Inc.
McMaster University Student Center Rm. 201
McMaster University
1280 Main St. W.
Hamilton, ON, Canada L8S 4S4
Phone: (905)525-9140
Fax: (905)529-3208

Publications: Nexus (35887) • The Silhouette (35914)

McMullen Argus Publishing
299 Market St.
Saddle Brook, NJ 07663-5312
Phone: (201)712-9300
Fax: (201)712-9899

Publications: Bracket Racing USA (6917) • High Performance Mopar (19527) • High Performance Pontiac (19528) • Muscle Mustangs & Fast Fords (19529) • MuscleCars (19530) • Vette (19531)

McMullen Argus Publishing, Inc.
2400 E Katella Ave., 11th Fl.
Anaheim, CA 92806
Phone: (714)939-2400

Publications: All Chevy (1397) • Audio/Video Interiors (1399) • Auto Sound & Security (1400) • Body-Boarding Magazine (3100) • Car Audio and Electronics (1402) • Classic Trucks (1403) • 4-Wheel Drive & Sport Utility Magazine (1405) • Hot Bike (1406) • Kit Car Illustrated (1407) • Knives Illustrated (1408) • MiniTruckin' (1409) • Mustang Illustrated (1410) • Off Road (1412) • Splash (1413) • Street Cruzin Magazine (1414) • Street Rodder (1415) • Super Chevy (1416) • Surfing Magazine (1417) • Truckin' Magazine (1418) • VW Trends (1420)

McMurry Publishing Inc.
1010 E. Missouri Ave.
Phoenix, AZ 85014
Phone: (602)395-5850
Fax: (602)395-5853
Free: 888-626-8779

Publications: Vim & Vigor Magazine (813)

McMurry University
Box 277, McMurry Sta.
Abilene, TX 79697
Phone: (915)793-3842
Fax: (915)793-4879

Publications: War Whoop (29656)

McNary County Publishing Co.
111 N 2nd St.
PO Box 220
Selmer, TN 38375-0220
Phone: (731)645-5346
Fax: (731)645-3591

Publications: Independent-Appeal (29588)

McNaughton Newspapers
315 G St.
Davis, CA 95616
Phone: (530)756-0800
Fax: (530)756-6707

Publications: Davis Enterprise (1814)

McNeese State University
PO Box 93465
Lake Charles, LA 70609-3465
Phone: (337)475-5329
Fax: (337)475-5594

Publications: Contraband (12636) • McNeese Review (12638)

MCP, Inc.
200 High St.
Boston, MA 02110
Phone: (617)330-1000
Fax: (617)330-1016

Publications: Boston Business Journal (13856)

McPherson Pub. Co.
18275 Hwy. 45 N
PO Box 6
Weston, MO 64098
Phone: (816)640-2251
Fax: (816)386-2251

Publications: Weston Chronicle (17718)

McPherson Sentinel
301 S Main
McPherson, KS 67460
Phone: (620)241-2422
Fax: (620)241-2425

Publications: McPherson Sentinel (11642)

MD Publications, Inc.
3057 E. Cairo
PO Box 2210
Springfield, MO 65801-2210
Phone: (417)866-3917
Fax: (417)866-2781
Free: 800-274-7890

Publications: Transmission Digest (17616)

MDM Publications
3151 Airway Ave Ste. C-3
Costa Mesa, CA 92626
Phone: (714)751-5813
Fax: (714)755-5500

Publications: New Homes Magazine (1778)

M.E. Sharpe, Inc.
80 Business Park Dr.
Armonk, NY 10504
Phone: (914)273-1800
Fax: (914)273-2106
Free: 800-541-6563

Publications: Annual Survey of Eastern Europe and the Former Soviet Union (20064) • Anthropology & Archeology of Eurasia (20065) • Challenge (20066) • China Briefing (20067) • The Chinese Economy (20068) • Chinese Education & Society (20069) • Chinese Law and Government (20070) • Chinese Sociology and Anthropology (20071) • Chinese Studies in History (20072) • Contemporary Chinese Thought (20073) • Eastern European Economics (20074) • Emerging Markets Finance and Trade (20076) • European Education (20077) • India Briefing (20078) • International Journal of Electronic Commerce (20079) • International Journal of Mental Health (20080) • International Journal of Political Economy (20081) • International Journal of Sociology (20082) • International Studies of Management & Organization (21937) • The Japanese Economy (20083) • Journal of Post Keynesian Economics (29278) • Journal of Russian and East European Psychology (20087) • Korea Briefing (20088) • Problems of Economic Transition (20091) • Problems of Post-Communism (20092) • Russian Education and Society (20093) • Russian Politics and Law (20094) • Russian Social Science Review (20095) • Russian Studies in History (20096) • Russian Studies in Literature (20097) • Russian Studies in Philosophy (20098) • Sociological Research (20099) • Statutes and Decisions: The Laws of the USSR and its Successor Stabey (20100) • Working USA (20101)

The Meade County Messenger
235 Main St.
PO Box 678
Brandenburg, KY 40108-0678
Phone: (270)422-2155
Fax: (270)422-2110
Free: 877-422-2155

Publications: The Meade County Messenger (11963)

Meade News
PO Box 310
Meade, KS 67864
Phone: (620)873-2118
Fax: (620)873-5456

Publications: Meade County News (11646)

Meadow Grove
PO Box 5
Meadow Grove, NE 68752
Phone: (402)634-2332

Publications: Meadow Grove News (18160)

Meadow Lake Progress
311 Centre St.
Box 879
Meadow Lake, SK, Canada S9X 1Y6
Phone: (306)236-5265
Fax: (306)236-3130
Free: 888-382-8882

Publications: Meadow Lake Progress (37495)

Meadow Publications, Inc.
100 Clearbrook Rd.
Elmsford, NY 10523-1116

Publications: Spotlight Magazine (20584)

Meadow Ridge Publications Ltd.
22328-119 Ave.
Maple Ridge, BC, Canada V2X 2Z3
Phone: (604)467-1122
Fax: (604)463-4741

Publications: The Burnaby-New Westminster News Leader (34893) • Maple Ridge-Pitt Meadows News (35012) • The Tri-City News (35013)

The Meadville Tribune
947 Federal Ct.
Meadville, PA 16335-3234
Phone: (814)724-6370
Fax: (814)724-8755
Free: 800-879-0006

Publications: The Fast Track (27233) • The Meadville Tribune (27235)

Meagher County News
13 E. Main
PO Box 349
White Sulphur Springs, MT 59645
Phone: (406)547-3831
Fax: (406)547-3832
Free: 800-398-3831

Publications: The Meagher County News (17918)

Mean Street
6747-A Greenleaf Ave.
Whittier, CA 90601
Phone: (562)789-9455
Fax: (562)789-9925

Publications: Mean Street (4078)

Measure for Measure
1460 N Page Springs Rd.
Cornville, AZ 86325-6006

Publications: Measure for Measure (678)

Meaux Walsh Publishing, Inc.
309 W. Oak
Palestine, TX 75801
Phone: (903)727-0316
Fax: (903)723-0751

Publications: The Clarion (30896)

MEC Publishing Inc.
Box 335
Howells, NE 68641
Phone: (402)986-1777

Publications: Howells Journal (18052)

Mechanical Contractor's Association of South Carolina
1504 Morninghill Dr.
PO Box 384
Columbia, SC 29202
Phone: (803)772-7834
Fax: (803)731-0390

Publications: Palmetto Piper (28559)

Mecklenburg News
329 Virginia Ave.
Box 1015
Clarksville, VA 23927
Phone: (434)374-2451
Fax: (434)374-2074

Publications: The News Progress (31975)

The Mecklenburg Times
400 Clarice Ave., Ste. 100
PO Box 36306
Charlotte, NC 28236-2820
Phone: (704)377-6221
Fax: (704)377-6214

Publications: The Mecklenburg Times (23749)

MedChi
1211 Cathedral St.
Baltimore, MD 21201
Phone: (410)539-0872
Fax: (410)547-0915
Free: 800-492-1056

Publications: Maryland Medical Journal (13212)

MEDEC Dental Communications
2 Northfield Plz. No. 300
Northfield, IL 60093
Phone: (847)441-3700
Fax: (847)441-3702
Free: 800-323-3337

Publications: Dental Lab Products (9327) • Dental Products Report (9328)

Medford Mail Tribune Co.
Fir & 6th St.
PO Box 1108
Medford, OR 97501
Phone: (503)776-4422
Fax: (503)776-4369
Free: 800-366-2527

Publications: The Mail Tribune (26418)

Media
PO Box 230
Kahoka, MO 63445
Phone: (660)727-3395
Fax: (660)727-2475

Publications: Media (17151)

Media Alliance
814 Mission St., Ste. 205
San Francisco, CA 94103
Phone: (415)546-6334
Fax: (415)546-6218

Publications: MediaFile (3389) • Propaganda Review (3417)

Media America, Inc.
PO Box 682268
Franklin, TN 37068-2268
Phone: (615)790-2400
Fax: (615)794-0179

Publications: Coping with Allergies and Asthma (29196) • Coping with Cancer (29197)

Media Foundation
1243 W. 7th Ave.
Vancouver, BC, Canada V6H 1B7
Phone: (604)736-9401
Fax: (604)737-6021
Free: 800-663-1243

Publications: Adbusters (35120)

Media General Business Communications, Inc.
PO Box 85333
Richmond, VA 23219

Publications: Virginia Business (32460)

Media General Inc.
PO Box 305
Leitchfield, KY 42755-0305
Fax: (502)259-5537

Publications: The Sentinel-Echo (12203)

Media General Inc.
PO Box 1325
Ahoskie, NC 27910-1325
Phone: (919)332-2123
Fax: (919)332-3940
Free: 888-639-7437

Publications: Commonwealth Progress (23613) • Gates County Index (23909) • Roanoke Chowen News-Herald (23614)

Media General Inc.
804 Washington St.
PO Box 308
Eden, NC 27288-6031
Phone: (919)623-2155
Fax: (919)623-2228

Publications: Eden Daily News (23855)

Media General Newspapers, Inc.
208 W Murphy St.
PO Box 508
Madison, NC 27025
Phone: (336)548-6047
Fax: (336)548-2853

Publications: The Messenger (24052)

Media General Newspapers, Inc.
Woodbridge, VA 22192
Phone: (703)878-8000
Fax: (703)878-3993

Publications: Belvoir Eagle (32636)

Media Index Publishing Inc.
PO Box 24365
Seattle, WA 98124-0365
Phone: (206)382-9220
Fax: (206)382-9437
Free: 800-332-1736

Publications: Media Inc. (32986)

Media Marketing
5380 Elvas Ave.
Sacramento, CA 95819
Phone: (916)452-2671
Fax: (916)452-2690

Publications: Sierra Sacramento Valley Medicine (3019)

Media and Methods Magazine
1429 Walnut St.
Philadelphia, PA 19102
Phone: (215)563-6005
Fax: (215)587-9706
Free: 800-555-5657

Publications: Media and Methods Magazine (27563)

Media News Group
1560 Broadway, Ste. 2100
Denver, CO 80202
Phone: (303)563-6360
Fax: (303)894-9327

Publications: The Daily Democrat (4099) • Daily News (2885) • Fort Bragg Advocate-News (1922)

Media News Group, Inc.
604 Pine Ave.
Long Beach, CA 90844
Phone: (562)499-1415
Fax: (562)499-1484

Publications: El Economico (2167)

Media Source Publishing Grp.
1315 Buena Vista Dr.
Vista, CA 92083
Phone: (760)631-1202
Fax: (760)631-1206

Publications: Miata Magazine (4046)

Media Two
22 W Pennsylvania Ave.
Ste. 305
Towson, MD 21204
Phone: (410)828-0120
Fax: (410)825-1002

Publications: Port of Baltimore (13764)

Mediapolis News
Box 548
616 Main
Mediapolis, IA 52637
Phone: (319)394-3174
Fax: (319)394-3134
Free: 800-949-3175

Publications: Mediapolis News (11082)

Medica Press, Inc.
10 Dorrance St., Ste. 500
Providence, RI 02903
Phone: (401)421-4747
Fax: (401)521-9226

Publications: Medical Law's Regan Report (28407)

Medical Group Management Association
104 Inverness Terr. E.
Englewood, CO 80112-5306
Phone: (303)799-1111
Fax: (303)643-4420
Free: 877-ASK-MGMA

Publications: MGMA Connexion (4414)

Medical Library Association
65 E. Wacker Dr., Ste. 1900
Chicago, IL 60601-7298
Phone: (312)419-9094
Fax: (312)419-8950

Publications: Journal of the Medical Library Association (8445)

Medical Publications, Inc.
2020 Ardmore Blvd., Ste. 160
Pittsburgh, PA 15221
Phone: (412)273-1775
Fax: (412)273-1776
Free: 877-395-1775

Publications: Pittsburgh Hospital News (27833)

Medical Society of Delaware
131 Continental Dr., Ste. 405
Newark, DE 19713-4308
Phone: (302)658-7596
Fax: (302)658-9669

Publications: Delaware Medical Journal (5271)

Medical Society of Metropolitan Portland
4540 SW Kelly
Portland, OR 97201
Phone: (503)222-9977
Fax: (503)223-3164

Publications: The Scribe (26508)

Medical Society of New Jersey
2 Princess Rd.
Lawrenceville, NJ 08648
Phone: (609)896-1766
Fax: (609)896-1368

Publications: New Jersey Medicine (19163)

Medical Society of the State of New York
PO Box 5404
Lake Success, NY 11042
Phone: (516)488-6100
Fax: (516)328-1982
Free: 800-523-4405

Publications: The News of New York (20881)

Medical Society of Virginia
4205 Dover Rd.
Richmond, VA 23221
Phone: (804)353-2721
Fax: (804)355-6189
Free: 800-746-6768

Publications: Virginia Medical Quarterly (32466)

Medical Society of Wisconsin
330 E Lakeside St.
PO Box 1109
Madison, WI 53701
Phone: (608)442-3800
Fax: (608)442-3802
Free: (866)442-3800

Publications: Wisconsin Medical Journal (33987)

Medical World Communications
241 Forsgate Dr.
Jamesburg, NJ 08831-0505
Phone: (732)656-1140
Fax: (732)656-0059

Publications: Cardiology Review (19127) • Internal Medicine World Report (19130)

Medical World Communications
295 Promenade St., Suite 2
Providence, RI 02908-5720
Phone: (401)455-0555
Fax: (401)455-1777

Publications: Healthcare Technology Management (28399) • Medical Imaging (28406) • 24x7 (28429)

The Medicine Hat News
3257 Dunmore Rd. S.E.
PO Box 10
Medicine Hat, AB, Canada T1A 7E6
Phone: (403)527-1101
Fax: (403)527-1244

Publications: The Medicine Hat News (34810)

The Medicine Hat Shopper
922 Allowance Ave. SE
Medicine Hat, AB, Canada T1A 3G7
Phone: (403)527-5777
Fax: (403)526-7352

Publications: The Medicine Hat Shopper (34811)

Medicopea International Inc.
3333 Cote Vertu Blvd., Ste. 300
Saint-Laurent, QC, Canada H4R 2N1
Phone: (514)331-4561
Fax: (514)336-1129

Publications: Canadian Journal of Allergy & Clinical Immunology (37362) • Practical Optometry (37366)

Medieval Academy of America
104 Mt. Auburn St., 5th Fl.
Cambridge, MA 02138
Phone: (617)491-1622
Fax: (617)492-3303

Publications: Speculum, A Journal of Medieval Studies (14104)

MediMedia USA, Inc.
780 Township Line Rd.
Yardley, PA 19067
Phone: (267)685-2788
Fax: (267)685-2966
Free: 888-724-2302

Publications: Managed Care (28201)

Medina County Gazette
885 W Liberty St.
Medina, OH 44258
Phone: (216)725-4166
Fax: (216)725-4299

Publications: Medina County Gazette (25373)

Medina Daily Journal-Register, Inc.
409-13 Main St.
Medina, NY 14103-1416
Phone: (716)798-1400
Fax: (716)798-0290

Publications: Medina Daily Journal-Register—Eastern Niagara Edition (21037) • Orleans Shopper (21038)

Medina Times
501 Madrid St., No. 1
Castroville, TX 78009-4528
Phone: (210)772-3672
Fax: (210)772-3507

Publications: Medina Valley Times (30008)

Medium II Board of Publishers
University of Toronto-Erindale Campus
3359 Mississauga Rd. N.
Mississauga, ON, Canada L5L 1C6
Phone: (416)828-5260
Fax: (416)828-5402

Publications: medium II (36078)

MEDQUEST Communications LLC
3800 Lakeside Ave. E, Ste. 201
Cleveland, OH 44114-3857
Phone: (216)522-9700
Fax: (216)391-9200

Publications: Behavioral Health Management (24863) • Ear, Nose & Throat Journal (24884) • Nursing Homes (24934)

Medrid Register
102 S Main
Madrid, IA 50156
Phone: (515)795-2730
Fax: (515)795-2012

Publications: Madrid Register-News (11043)

The Meeker News
Box 686
Meeker, OK 74855
Phone: (405)279-2363
Fax: (405)279-3850

Publications: The Meeker News (25916)

The Mega Society
4177 Garrick Ave.
Warren, MI 48091
Phone: (810)757-4177

Publications: The Megarian (15659)

Megasin Publications
7501 Morrison Rd.
New Orleans, LA 70126
Phone: (504)242-6022

Publications: SENGA (12753)

Meigher Communications, Ltd.
920 3rd Ave., No. 6
New York, NY 10022

Publications: Garden Design (21747)

Meister Publishing Co.
37733 Euclid Ave.
Willoughby, OH 44094
Phone: (440)942-2000
Fax: (440)942-0662
Free: 800-572-7740

Publications: Ag Consultant (25655) • American Fruit Grower (25656) • American Vegetable Grower (25657) • Farm Chemicals (25658) • Farm Chemicals International (25659) • Florida Grower (6880) • Greenhouse Grower (25660) • Ornamental Outlook (6884) • Productores de Hortalizas (25663) • Western Fruit Grower (25664)

Meliorist Publishing Society
University of Lethbridge
4401 University Dr., Ste. 166
Lethbridge, AB, Canada T1K 3M4
Phone: (403)329-2334
Fax: (403)329-2333

Publications: The Meliorist (34797)

Melita New Era
Box 820
Melita, MB, Canada R0M 1L0
Phone: (204)522-3491
Fax: (204)522-3648

Publications: Melita New Era (35273)

Mellette County News
Hwy. 18
PO Box 229
Mission, SD 57555
Phone: (605)259-3642
Fax: (605)856-2428

Publications: Mellette County News (28897)

Melpomene Institute
1010 University Ave. W
St. Paul, MN 55104-4706
Phone: (651)642-1951
Fax: (651)642-1871

Publications: Melpomene (16388)

Melrose Beacon
PO Box 186
Melrose, MN 56352-0186
Phone: (320)256-3240
Fax: (320)256-3363

Publications: Bargain Searchlight (16050) • Beacon (16051)

Melville Advance Printing & Publishing Co., (1986) Ltd.
218 3rd Ave., W.
Box 1420
Melville, SK, Canada S0A 2P0
Phone: (306)728-5448
Fax: (306)728-4004

Publications: Advance (37500)

Memorial Art Gallery
University of Rochester
500 University Ave.
Rochester, NY 14607
Phone: (585)473-7720
Fax: (585)473-6266

Publications: Porticus (23236)

Memorial University
FM 2005
St. John's, NL, Canada A1C 5S7
Phone: (709)737-3453
Fax: (709)737-4342

Publications: Newfoundland Studies (35492)

The Memphis Democrat
Box 190
Memphis, TX 79245
Phone: (806)259-2441
Fax: (806)259-2441

Publications: The Memphis Democrat (30802)

Memphis Offset Printing Inc.
622 S Highland
Memphis, TN 38111
Phone: (901)362-8484
Fax: (901)458-3104

Publications: Southaven Press (29381)

Mena Star Co., Inc.
501-507 Mena St.
PO Box 1307
Mena, AR 71953
Phone: (479)394-1900
Fax: (479)394-1908
Free: 800-446-5158

Publications: The Mena Star (1275)

The Menard Time
Box 711
Menard, IL 62259
Phone: (618)826-5071
Fax: (618)826-2000

Publications: The Menard Time (9172)

MENC: The National Association for Music Education
1806 Robert Fulton Dr.
Reston, VA 20191
Phone: (703)860-4000
Fax: (703)860-9404
Free: 800-336-3768

Publications: General Music Today (904) • Journal of Music Teacher Education (25026) • Journal of Research in Music Education (32394) • Journal for Research in Music Education (12491) • Music Educators Journal (32405) • Teaching Music (32418) • Update (12507) • Update: Applications of Research in Music Education (32422)

Mendocino Beacon
PO Box 225
Mendocino, CA 95460
Phone: (707)937-5874
Fax: (707)937-0825

Publications: Mendocino Beacon (2519)

Mendocino County Observer
PO Box 490
Laytonville, CA 95454-0490
Phone: (707)984-6223
Fax: (707)984-8118

Publications: Mendocino County Observer (2150)

Mendota Shopping Guide
504 9th St.
Mendota, IL 61342-1794
Phone: (815)539-7476
Fax: (815)539-7477

Publications: Mendota Shopping Guide (9175)

Menifee County News
772 W 1st St.
Morehead, KY 40351
Fax: (606)484-7337

Publications: Menifee County News (12302)

Menninger Clinic
2801 Gessner Dr.
PO Box 809045
Houston, TX 77280
Phone: (713)462-6800

Publications: Menninger Perspective (30507)

The Mennonite
1700 S Main St.
Goshen, IN 46526
Phone: (574)535-6052
Fax: (574)535-6050
Free: 800-790-2493

Publications: The Mennonite (10025)

Mennonite Central Committee
108 Main St.
Akron, PA 17501
Phone: (717)859-2210
Fax: (717)859-4910

Publications: American Patchwork and Quilting (10770)

Mennonite Historical Society
Goshen College
Goshen, IN 46526-9988
Phone: (219)535-7433
Fax: (219)535-7438

Publications: The Mennonite Quarterly Review (10026)

Mennonite Publishing Service
490 Dutton Dr., Unit C5
Waterloo, ON, Canada N2L 6H7
Phone: (519)884-3810
Fax: (519)884-3331
Free: 800-378-2524

Publications: Canadian Mennonite (36847)

Mennonite Weekly Review, Inc.
Box 568
Newton, KS 67114
Phone: (316)283-3670
Fax: (316)283-6502
Free: 800-424-0718

Publications: Mennonite Weekly Review (11668)

Men's Support Center
PO Box 30564
Oakland, CA 94604

Publications: Diseased Pariah News (2677)

MEP Publications
University of Minnesota
Physics Bldg.
116 Church St. SE
Minneapolis, MN 55455-0112
Phone: (612)922-7993
Fax: (612)922-0858

Publications: NST (Nature, Society and Thought) (16118)

The Mercer Cluster
Mercer University
Campus Box 72728
Macon, GA 31207
Phone: (478)301-2871
Fax: (478)301-5544

Publications: The Mercer Cluster (7383)

Mercer Island Reporter
PO Box 38
7845 SE 30th St.
Mercer Island, WA 98040
Phone: (206)232-1215
Fax: (206)232-1284

Publications: Mercer Island Reporter (32829)

Mercer School of Theology
3001 Mercer University Dr.
Atlanta, GA 30341-4415
Phone: (770)986-3471
Fax: (770)986-3478

Publications: Perspectives in Religious Studies (11530)

Mercer University
1400 Coleman Ave.
Macon, GA 31207
Phone: (478)301-2700
Fax: (478)752-4124
Free: 800-837-2911

Publications: The Cluster (7380) • Mercer Lawyer (7384) • Mercer University Discoveries (7385) • URSA (7387)

Mercersburg Journal/Ad Journal
11 S Main St.
PO Box 239
Mercersburg, PA 17236
Phone: (717)328-3223

Publications: Mercersburg Journal/Ad Journal (27246)

Vasant V. Merchant
1436 N Evergreen Dr.
Flagstaff, AZ 86001
Phone: (928)774-4793
Fax: (928)774-4793

Publications: International Journal of Humanities and Peace (696)

Mercor Media
204 W. Kansas, Ste. 103
Independence, MO 64050
Phone: (816)254-8735
Fax: (816)254-2128
Free: 800-254-2123

Publications: Lift Equipment (17115)

MERCOR MEDIA INC.
5900 Windward Pky., Ste. 450
Alpharetta, GA 30005
Phone: (770)664-2812
Fax: (770)664-7319

Publications: CE News (6918)

Mercor Media, Inc.
744 N. Wells
Chicago, IL 60610
Phone: (312)867-9822
Fax: (312)867-9850

Publications: Structural Engineer (6919)

Mercury Capital, Inc.
8380 Santa Monica Blvd., Ste. 200
West Hollywood, CA 90069
Phone: (323)848-2222
Fax: (323)848-2231
Free: 800-769-3877

Publications: Frontiers (4062)

Mercury Inc.
PO Box 651
Oroville, CA 95965
Phone: (916)533-3131
Fax: (916)533-3127

Publications: Oroville Shopping News (2729)

Mercury Inc.
PO Box 787
Manhattan, KS 66502
Phone: (785)776-8805
Fax: (785)776-8807

Publications: Mercury (11629)

Mercury Publications Ltd.
1839 Inkster Blvd.
Winnipeg, MB, Canada R2X 1R3
Phone: (204)954-2085
Fax: (204)954-2057
Free: 800-337-6372

Publications: Bar & Beverage Business Magazine (35313) • C Store Canada (35318) • Commerce & Industry (35323) • Western Grocer (35359) • Western Hotelier (35360) • Western Restaurant News (35361)

Mercury Tri-County Market Place
24 N Hanover St.
Pottstown, PA 19464-5480
Phone: (610)323-3000
Fax: (610)327-3308

Publications: Mercury Tri-County Market Place (27900)

Meredith Corp.
1716 Locust St.
Des Moines, IA 50309-3023
Phone: (515)284-3000
Fax: (515)284-3563
Free: 800-678-2659

Publications: Successful Farming (10811) • Traditional Home (8587) • You & Your Dog (10819)

Meredith Corp.
125 Park Ave.
New York, NY 10017-5529
Phone: (212)557-6600

Publications: Better Homes and Gardens Building Ideas (21296) • Better Homes and Gardens Do It Yourself (21297) • Better Homes and Gardens: Garden, Deck and Landscape (21298) • Better Homes and Gardens Home Plan Ideas (21299) • Better Homes and Gardens Kitchen Plans (21300) • Better Homes and Gardens S.I.P.: Garden Ideas & Outdoor Living (10771) • Better Homes and Gardens Special Interest Publications Low Calorie/Low Fat Recipes (21301) • Country Home (10777) • Country Home Country Gardens (10778) • Ladies' Home Journal (22231) • Midwest Living Magazine (22335) • more (22366) • Women & Success (22933) • WOOD (10815)

Charles Meredith IV
312 W Broad St.
Quakertown, PA 18951
Phone: (215)536-3611
Fax: (215)536-7201

Publications: Artique (27913)

Meridian Printing Ltd.
5714 44th St.
Lloydminster, AB, Canada T9V 0B6
Phone: (780)875-3362
Fax: (780)875-3423

Publications: Meridian Booster (34803)

Meridian Star, Inc.
814 22nd Ave.
Box 1591
Meridian, MS 39301
Phone: (601)693-1551
Fax: (601)485-1275

Publications: Meridian Star (16769)

Merion Publications Inc.
2900 Horizon Dr.
PO Box 61556
King of Prussia, PA 19406-0956
Phone: (610)278-1400

Publications: ADVANCE for Administrators of the Laboratory (27107) • ADVANCE for Administrators in Radiation & Radiation Oncology (27108) • ADVANCE for Directors in Rehabilitation (27109) • ADVANCE for Health Information Executives (27110) • ADVANCE for Health Information Professionals (27111) • ADVANCE for Imaging and Radiation Therapy Professionals (27112) • ADVANCE for Managers of Respiratory Care (27113) • ADVANCE for Medical Laboratory Professionals (27114) • ADVANCE for Nurse Practitioners (27115) • ADVANCE for Nurses (27116) • ADVANCE for Occupational Therapy Practitioners (27117) • ADVANCE for Physical Therapists and PT Assistants (27118) • ADVANCE for Physician Assistants (27119) • ADVANCE for Providers of Post-Acute Care (27120) • ADVANCE for Respiratory Care Practitioners (27121) • ADVANCE for Speech-Language Pathologists & Audiologists (27122)

The Merkel Mail
PO Box 428
Merkel, TX 79536
Phone: (915)928-5712
Fax: (915)928-5899

Publications: The Merkel Mail (30806)

Merlyn's Pen Publishing
4 King St.
PO Box 1058
East Greenwich, RI 02818-0964
Phone: (401)885-5175
Fax: (401)885-5222
Free: 800-247-2027

Publications: Merlyn's Pen: Stories by American Students (28341)

Merritt Herald
2090 Granite Ave.
Box 9
Merritt, BC, Canada V1K 1B8
Phone: (250)378-4241
Fax: (250)378-6818

Publications: Merritt Herald (35014)

Merton Publications Ltd.
1070 Gainsborough Rd. W.
PO Box 39
Hyde Park, ON, Canada N6H 5M8
Phone: (519)471-9109

Publications: The Herald (35983) • Scope Camping News (35919)

Mesa Legend
English-Foreign Language Bldg., Rm. EF2N
1833 W Southern Ave.
Mesa, AZ 85202
Phone: (480)461-7330
Fax: (480)461-7334

Publications: Mesa Legend (744)

The Message
PO Box 4169
Evansville, IN 47724-0169
Phone: (812)424-5536
Fax: (812)424-0972
Free: 800-637-1731

Publications: The Message (9935)

The Message
166-26 89th Ave.
Jamaica, NY 11432
Phone: (718)658-5163
Fax: (718)526-3645

Publications: The Message (20838)

Messenger
PO Box 249
Minneapolis, KS 67467
Fax: (913)392-2026

Publications: The Minneapolis Messenger (11654)

The Messenger
PO Box 48
Stephen, MN 56757
Phone: (218)478-2210
Fax: (218)478-2210

Publications: The Messenger (16463)

Messenger
PO Box 546
De Kalb, MS 39328
Phone: (601)743-5760
Fax: (601)743-4430

Publications: Kemper County Messenger (16621)

Messenger
249 Main St.
Okolona, MS 38860
Phone: (662)447-5501
Fax: (662)447-5024

Publications: Okolona Messenger (16803)

Messenger
Box 307
Miles, TX 76861
Phone: (915)468-3611

Publications: Messenger (30829)

Messenger
PO Box 517
Colfax, WI 54730
Phone: (715)962-3535
Fax: (715)962-3535

Publications: Messenger (33641)

The Messenger Enterprise
35 S Main
Manti, UT 84642
Phone: (801)835-4241
Fax: (801)835-1493

Publications: The Messenger Enterprise (31366)

Messenger Index
PO Box 577
Emmett, ID 83617
Phone: (208)365-6066
Fax: (208)365-6068

Publications: Messenger Index (7855)

The Messenger Newspaper
221 S. Main St.
Madisonville, KY 42431
Phone: (270)824-3300
Fax: (270)821-6855
Free: 800-726-6397

Publications: The Messenger (12271)

Messenger Newspaper, Inc.
322 E Old Hickory Blvd.
PO Box 626
Madison, TN 37116
Phone: (615)868-0475
Fax: (615)860-2797

Publications: The Messenger (29338)

Messenger Newspapers, Inc.
201 N 8th St.
Box 709
Mayfield, KY 42066-1825
Phone: (270)247-5223
Fax: (270)247-6336

Publications: Mayfield Messenger (12284)

Messenger-Post Newspapers
73 Buffalo St.
Canandaigua, NY 14424
Phone: (716)394-0770
Fax: (716)394-1675

Publications: Brighton Pittsford Post (20419) • Brockport Post (20244) • Gates Chili Post (20421) • The Greece Post (20696) • Henrietta Post (20731) • Irondequoit Post (20783) • The New York-Pennsylvania Collector (20422) • Penfield Post Republican (20423) • Perinton-Fairport Post (20590) • The Webster Post (23530)

Messenger Publications, Inc.
213 Minnesota Ave. N
PO Box 259
Aitkin, MN 56431-0259
Phone: (218)927-3761
Fax: (218)927-3763

Publications: Aitkin Independent Age (15700) • Bargain Hunter (15701)

The Messenger Publishing Co.
Rte. 33 N. & Johnson Rd.
PO Box 4210
Athens, OH 45701
Phone: (614)592-6612
Fax: (614)592-4647

Publications: The Athens Messenger (24628)

Messenger Publishing Co.
PO Box 799
Gatesville, TX 76528
Phone: (254)865-5212
Fax: (254)865-2361

Publications: Messenger and Star-Forum (30388)

Messenger-Wolfe Publications
73 Buffalo St.
Canandaigua, NY 14424-1001
Free: 800-424-2880

Publications: East Rochester Post Herald (20551)

The Met
200 Crescent Ct., Ste. 1375
Dallas, TX 75201-6999

Publications: The Met (30167)

Metal Mammoth Inc.
N Village Ave., Ste. 12
Rockville Centre, NY 11570
Phone: (516)594-2130
Fax: (516)594-2133

Publications: Heavy Metal (23261)

Meteor Newspaper Inc.
201 E Georgetown St.
PO Box 353
Crystal Springs, MS 39059-0353
Phone: (601)892-2581
Fax: (601)892-2249

Publications: Meteor (16620)

Methodist Board of Publication, Inc.
PO Box 508
Greensboro, NC 27402-0508
Phone: (336)272-1196
Fax: (336)271-6634

Publications: North Carolina Christian Advocate (23931)

Methodist College
5400 Ramsey St.
Fayetteville, NC 28311
Phone: (910)630-7292
Fax: (910)630-2123
Free: 800-488-7110

Publications: Monarch Messenger (23880)

Methow Valley Publishing Co LLC
101 N Glover
PO Box 97
Twisp, WA 98856
Phone: (509)997-7011
Fax: (509)997-3277

Publications: Methow Valley News (33171)

The Metro Courier
PO Box 2385
Augusta, GA 30903
Phone: (404)724-6556
Fax: (404)722-7104

Publications: The Metro Courier (7101)

Metro Group Inc.
25 Boxwood Ln.
Cheektowaga, NY 14227
Phone: (716)668-5223
Fax; (716)668-4526
Free: 800-836-7262

Publications: Metro Community News (20458)

Metro Media Publishing, Inc.
PO Box 1798
Burlington, NJ 08016-7398

Publications: Bensalem Express (18704) • Bristol Express (18705) • Burlington Mail (18706) • Croydon Express (18707) • Fairless Hills Express (18708) • Levittown Express (18709) • Mount Holly Mail (18710)

Metro Newspaper
PO Box 129
Balsam Lake, WI 54810
Phone: (715)485-3121
Fax: (715)485-3037

Publications: County Ledger-Press (33561)

Metro Parent
PO Box 13491
Wauwatosa, WI 53213
Phone: (414)259-1884
Fax: (414)259-1392

Publications: Metro Parent (34443)

Metro Parent Magazine
24567 Northwestern Hwy., Ste. 150
Southfield, MI 48075
Phone: (810)352-0990
Fax: (810)352-5066

Publications: Windsor Parent Magazine (36891)

Metro Parent Publishing Group
24567 Northwestern Hwy., No. 150
Southfield, MI 48075
Phone: (248)352-0990
Fax: (248)352-5066

Publications: Metro Parent Magazine (15545)

Metro Publishing Inc.
245 Almendra Ave.
Los Gatos, CA 95030
Phone: (408)354-3110
Fax: (408)354-3917

Publications: Saratoga News (2479)

Metro Publishing, Inc.
550 S. 1st St.
San Jose, CA 95113
Phone: (408)298-8000
Fax: (408)298-0602

Publications: Los Gatos Weekly Times (2478) • Metro (3524)

Metro Publishing Inc.
115 Cooper St.
Santa Cruz, CA 95060-4526
Fax: (831)457-9000

Publications: Metro Santa Cruz (3687)

Metro Reatiler
8 South St.
Lockport, NY 14094
Phone: (716)434-4055
Fax: (716)434-6022

Publications: Metro Retailer (20957)

Metro Reporter
270 Francisco St.
San Francisco, CA 94133-2120
Phone: (415)391-2030
Fax: (415)391-2527

Publications: San Francisco (3425)

Metro Silicon Valley
550 South 1st St.
San Jose, CA 95113
Phone: (408)298-8500

Publications: Metro (3525)

Metro Times, Inc.
733 St. Antoine
Detroit, MI 48226

Publications: Metro Times (14936)

Metro West Publishing
410 Denver Ave.
PO Box 125
Fort Lupton, CO 80621
Phone: (303)857-4440
Fax: (303)659-2901

Publications: Ft. Lupton Press (4445)

Metro West Publishing, Inc.
Box 400
204 Oak St.
Frederick, CO 80530
Fax: (303)659-2901

Publications: Farmer and Miner (4455)

Metrokids
1080 N Delaware Ave., Ste. 702
Philadelphia, PA 19125
Phone: (215)291-5560
Fax: (215)291-5563

Publications: Metrokids Magazine (27568)

Metroland
Box 130
Fergus, ON, Canada N1M 2W7
Phone: (519)843-1310
Fax: (519)843-1334
Free: 888-270-1609

Publications: Fergus-Elora News Express (35829)

Metroland
3125 Wolfedale Rd.
Mississauga, ON, Canada L5C 1S1
Phone: (905)890-4606
Fax: (905)890-3999

Publications: The Mississauga Booster (36079)

Metroland
10 Tempo Ave.
Willowdale, ON, Canada M2H 2N8
Phone: (416)493-4400
Fax: (416)493-4703

Publications: North York Mirror (36881) • The Scarborough Mirror (36883)

Metroland Community Newspaper
9 Heritage Rd.
Markham, ON, Canada L3P 1M3
Phone: (905)294-2200
Fax: (905)294-1538

Publications: Economist & Sun (36024)

Metroland News
3145 Wolfedale Rd.
Mississauga, ON, Canada L5C 3A9
Phone: (905)273-8285

Publications: Mississauga Business Times (36080)

Metroland Printing & Publishing
1625 Scugog
Port Perry, ON, Canada L9L 1K6
Phone: (905)985-2511
Fax: (905)579-2238

Publications: Oshawa-Whitby-Clarington-Port Perry This Week (36181)

Metroland Printing & Publishing
9350 Yonge St.
PO Box 390
Richmond Hill, ON, Canada L4C 4Y6
Phone: (905)881-3373
Fax: (905)881-9924
Free: 800-565-6357

Publications: The Classified News (36063) • Guardian (35700) • The Liberal Newspaper (36344) • Oakville Beaver (36147)

Metroland Printing, Publishing and Distributing
467 Speers Rd.
Oakville, ON, Canada L6K 3S4
Phone: (905)815-0017
Fax: (905)337-5571
Free: 800-265-3673

Publications: Tourist (36152)

Metroland Printing, Publishing and Distributing Ltd.
884 Division St.
Unit 212, Bldg. 2
Cobourg, ON, Canada K9A 5V6
Phone: (905)373-7355
Fax: (905)373-4719

Publications: Northumberland News (35742)

Metroland Printing, Publishing and Distributing Ltd.
15 Memorial Ave.
Elmira, ON, Canada N3B 2R1
Phone: (519)669-5155
Fax: (519)669-5928
Free: 800-645-7355

Publications: The Elmira Independent (35805) • The Farm Gate and Regional Country News (35825)

Metroland Printing, Publishing & Distributing Ltd.
206-9170 County Rd. 93
Box 77
Mountainview Mall
RR 2
Midland, ON, Canada L4R 4K4
Phone: (705)527-5500
Fax: (705)527-5467

Publications: Ajax-Pickering News Advertiser (36038) • Barrie Advance (36039) • The Collingwood Connection (36040) • The Midland Mirror (36043) • Orillia Today (36044)

Metroland Printing, Publishing & Distributing Ltd.
884 Ford St.
Peterborough, ON, Canada K9J 5V3
Phone: (705)749-3383
Fax: (705)749-0074

Publications: Peterborough This Week (36319)

Metroland Printing, Publishing and Distribution
16 Bascom St.
PO Box 459
Uxbridge, ON, Canada L9P 1M9
Phone: (905)852-9141
Fax: (905)852-9341

Publications: The Bothwell Times (35787) • Uxbridge Times-Journal (36839)

Metronetics Publications
7 Elliewood Ave.
Charlottesville, VA 22903

Publications: The Blue Penny Quarterly (31919)

Metronome Magazine
PO Box 921
Billerica, MA 01821
Phone: (978)957-0925

Publications: Metronome Magazine (13845)

MetroNorth Media
6050 Riverdale Ave.
Bronx, NY 10471
Phone: (718)543-5200
Fax: (718)543-4206

Publications: Bronx Press Blue (20258) • Bronx Press Gold (20259) • Bronx Press Red (20260) • Bronx Press-Review (20261) • Riverdale Review (20285)

MetroNorth Newspapers, Inc.
PO Box 350070
Westminster, CO 80035-0070
Phone: (303)426-6000
Fax: (303)426-4209

Publications: Westminster Window (4669)

Metropolis Planet
111 E 5th St.
Box 820
Metropolis, IL 62960-0820
Phone: (618)524-2141
Fax: (618)524-4727

Publications: Metropolis Planet (9178)

Metropolitan Archdiocese of Philadelphia
827 N Franklin St.
Philadelphia, PA 19123
Phone: (215)922-5231
Fax: (215)627-0377

Publications: The Way (27718)

Metropolitan Detroit AFL-CIO
600 W Lafayette, Ste. 200
Detroit, MI 48226
Phone: (313)961-0800

Publications: Detroit Labor News (14926)

Metropolitan Indianapolis Board of Realtors, Inc.
1912 N Meridian St.
Indianapolis, IN 46202
Phone: (317)956-1912
Fax: (317)956-5050

Publications: The Voice (10181)

Metropolitan Medical Society of Greater Kansas City
3036 Gillham Rd.
Kansas City, MO 64108
Phone: (816)531-8432
Fax: (816)531-8438

Publications: Medical Directory of Greater Kansas City (17183)

Metropolitan Museum of Art
1000 5th Ave.
New York, NY 10028-0198
Phone: (212)879-5500
Fax: (212)396-5062

Publications: The Metropolitan Museum of Art Bulletin (22329)

Metropolitan News Co.
210 S. Spring St.
Los Angeles, CA 90012
Phone: (213)628-4384
Fax: (213)687-3886

Publications: Civic Center NewSource (2241) • Escondido News-Reporter (1889) • Los Angeles Bulletin (2319) • Metropolitan News-Enterprise (2331) • Riverside Bulletin (2380) • Sacramento Bulletin (3012) • San Bernardino Bulletin (3091) • San Diego Bulletin (3257) • Ventura Bulletin (4012)

Metropolitan Newspaper Corp.
PO Box 2467
Green Bay, WI 54306
Phone: (920)432-2941
Fax: (920)432-8581

Publications: Community News E/W (33738) • Country Chronicle (33656)

Metropolitan Opera Guild, Inc.
70 Lincoln Ctr. Plz.
New York, NY 10023
Phone: (212)769-7080
Fax: (212)769-8500

Publications: Opera News (22497)

Metropolitan Radio Group, Inc.
318 East Pershing
Springfield, MO 65806
Phone: (417)862-0852
Fax: (417)862-0852
Free: 800-961-5595

Publications: East Tennessee Senior Living (17596) • 4-States Senior Living (17601) • Lake of the Ozarks Senior Living (17603) • Ozarks Senior Living (17608)

Metrovalley newspaper group
PO Box 130
Bowen Island, BC, Canada V0N 1G0
Phone: (604)947-2442
Fax: (604)947-0148

Publications: The Bowen Island Undercurrent (34886)

MetroWest Daily News
33 New York Ave.
Framingham, MA 01701

Publications: The MetroWest Daily News (14199)

Metrowest Newspapers
PO Box 646
Brighton, CO 80601
Phone: (303)659-2522
Fax: (303)659-2901

Publications: The Free Advertiser (4201) • Standard Blade (4202)

Meusey Communications
1107 Hazeltine Blvd., Ste. 539
Chaska, MN 55318-1008
Phone: (952)368-4100
Fax: (952)474-7850

Publications: Engineering Minnesota (16075) • Minnesota Insurance (15794)

Mexia News
214 N Railroad St.
PO Box 431
Mexia, TX 76667
Phone: (254)562-2868
Fax: (254)562-3121

Publications: The Mexia Daily News (30811)

Mexican American Studies & Research Center
Economics Bldg., Rm. 208
Tucson, AZ 85721-0023
Phone: (520)626-8103
Fax: (520)621-7966

Publications: Perspectives in Mexican American Studies (959)

The Mexico Ledger
300 N Washington
Mexico, MO 65265-0008
Phone: (573)581-1111
Fax: (573)581-2029

Publications: The Mexico Ledger (17284)

Meyers Publishing
6211 Van Nuys Blvd.
Van Nuys, CA 91401
Phone: (818)785-3900
Fax: (818)785-4397

Publications: Import Automotive Parts & Accessories (3990) • Specialty Automotive Magazine (3995)

MFA Inc.
201 Ray Young Dr.
Columbia, MO 65201-3599
Phone: (573)876-5205
Fax: (573)876-5505

Publications: Today's Farmer (17011)

MFG Publishing
883 Ocean Blvd.
Hampton, NH 03842-2519

Publications: Midrange Enterprise (18514)

MHR Publishing Corp.
2122 28th St.
Sacramento, CA 95818
Phone: (916)457-8990
Free: 800-366-9192

Publications: Military (3008)

The Miami Chief
PO Box 396
Miami, TX 79059-0396
Phone: (806)868-2521
Fax: (806)868-6051

Publications: The Miami Chief (30813)

Miami County Publishing Co.
121 S. Pearl St.
PO Box 389
Paola, KS 66071
Phone: (913)294-2311
Fax: (913)294-5318

Publications: Miami County Republic (11741) • Osawatomie Graphic (11742)

The Miami Herald Publishing Co.
One Herald Plaza
Miami, FL 33132
Phone: (305)350-2222
Fax: (305)376-3201
Free: 800-376-3324

Publications: Herald Values (6358) • Vida Social (6389)

The Miami Times
900 NW 54th St.
Miami, FL 33127
Phone: (305)757-1147
Fax: (305)757-5770

Publications: The Miami Times (6372)

Miami University
134G Harris Dining Hall
Oxford, OH 45056
Phone: (513)529-2210
Fax: (513)529-1893

Publications: The Miami Student (25457)

Miamisburg/West Carrollton News
230 S 2nd St.
PO Box 108
Miamisburg, OH 45342
Phone: (937)866-3331
Fax: (937)866-6011

Publications: Miamisburg/West Carrollton News (25375)

Michael Publishing Inc.
8170 Wavell Rd.
Cote St.-Luc, QC, Canada H4W 1M3
Phone: (514)484-1107
Fax: (514)484-9616

Publications: The Suburban (36979)

Michiana Business Publications, Inc.
536 W Cook Rd.
Fort Wayne, IN 46825-6702
Phone: (219)497-0433
Fax: (219)497-0822

Publications: Business People Magazine (9964)

Michiana Publications, Inc.
115 Main St.
Eau Claire, MI 49111
Phone: (616)461-4411
Fax: (616)461-6816

Publications: Central County Trade Lines Shopper's Guide (15002)

The Michigan Academy of Science, Arts, & Letters
Argus Bldg. II
400 4th St.
Ann Arbor, MI 48103-4816
Phone: (734)936-2938
Fax: (734)763-6927

Publications: Michigan Academician (14759)

Michigan Association of CPAs
5480 Corporate Dr.
PO Box 5068
Troy, MI 48007
Phone: (248)267-3700
Fax: (248)267-3737

Publications: Leaders' Edge (15628)

Michigan Association for Media in Education
1407 Rensen St., Ste. 3
Lansing, MI 48910-3657
Phone: (517)699-1717
Fax: (517)694-9303

Publications: Media Spectrum (15278)

Michigan Banker Magazine
PO Box 12236
Lansing, MI 48901-2236
Phone: (517)332-7800
Fax: (517)332-7806

Publications: Michigan Banker Magazine (15280)

Michigan Botanical Club, Inc.
Dept. of Biology
Albion College
611 E. Porter St.
Albion, MI 49224-1831

Publications: Michigan Botanist (34223)

The Michigan Catholic
305 Michigan Ave.
Detroit, MI 48226
Phone: (313)224-8000
Fax: (313)224-8009

Publications: The Michigan Catholic (14937)

Michigan Christian Advocate
316 Springbrook Ave.
Adrian, MI 49221-2099
Phone: (517)265-2075
Fax: (517)263-7422

Publications: Michigan Christian Advocate (14709)

Michigan Christmas Tree Assn.
PO Box 377
Howell, MI 48844
Phone: (577)545-9971
Fax: (577)545-4501
Free: 800-589-TREE

Publications: Michigan Christmas Tree Journal (15197)

The Michigan Daily
420 Maynard St.
420 Maynard St.
Ann Arbor, MI 48109-1327

Publications: The Michigan Daily (14761)

Michigan Dental Association
230 N. Washington Ave., Ste. 208
Lansing, MI 48933
Phone: (517)372-9070
Fax: (517)372-0008
Free: 800-589-2632

Publications: Journal of the Michigan Dental Association (15275)

Michigan Department of History, Arts & Libraries
Box 30741
Lansing, MI 48909-8241
Phone: (517)373-3703
Fax: (517)241-4909
Free: 800-366-3703

Publications: Michigan History (15285) • Michigan History for Kids (15286)

Michigan Education Association
1216 Kendale Blvd.
Box 2573
East Lansing, MI 48826-2573
Phone: (517)332-6551
Fax: (517)337-5414
Free: 800-292-1934

Publications: MEA Voice (14988)

Michigan Electric Cooperative Association
2859 W. Jolly Rd.
Okemos, MI 48864
Phone: (517)351-6322
Fax: (517)351-6396

Publications: Michigan Country Lines (15416)

Michigan Entomological Society
c/o Dept. of Entomology
Michigan State University
East Lansing, MI 48824

Publications: Great Lake Entomologist (14751)

Michigan Farm Bureau
7373 W Saginaw Hwy.
PO Box 30960
Lansing, MI 48909-8460
Phone: (517)323-7000
Fax: (517)323-6541
Free: 800-292-2680

Publications: Michigan Farm News (15282)

Michigan Floral Association
1152 Haslett Rd.
Haslett, MI 48840-9778

Publications: Michigan Florist (15150)

Michigan Grocers Association
221 N. Walnut
Lansing, MI 48933
Phone: (517)372-6800
Fax: (517)372-3002
Free: 800-947-6237

Publications: Michigan Food News (15283)

Michigan Hospital Association
6215 W. St. Joseph Hwy.
Lansing, MI 48917-4846
Phone: (517)323-3443
Fax: (517)323-0946

Publications: Michigan Health and Hospitals (15284)

Michigan Journal of Gender & Law
625 S. State St.
Ann Arbor, MI 48109-1215
Phone: (734)763-7378
Fax: (734)764-6043

Publications: Michigan Journal of Gender & Law (14764)

Michigan Law Review Association
Hutchins Hall
625 S. State St.
Ann Arbor, MI 48109-1215
Phone: (734)764-1358

Publications: Michigan Law Review (14765)

Michigan Municipal League
PO Box 1487
Ann Arbor, MI 48106-1487
Phone: (734)662-3246
Fax: (734)662-8083
Free: 800-653-2483

Publications: Michigan Municipal Review (14767)

Michigan Oil and Gas News
600 W. Pickard
PO Box 250
Mount Pleasant, MI 48804-0250
Phone: (989)772-5181
Fax: (989)773-2970

Publications: Michigan Oil and Gas News (15377)

Michigan Optometric Association
530 W. Ionia St., Ste. A
Lansing, MI 48933-1062
Phone: (517)482-0616
Fax: (517)482-1611

Publications: The Michigan Optometrist (15288)

Michigan Osteopathic Association
2445 Woodlake Circle
Okemos, MI 48864-5941
Phone: (517)347-1555
Fax: (517)347-1566
Free: 800-657-1556

Publications: Triad (15417)

Michigan Pharmacists Association
815 N. Washington Ave.
Lansing, MI 48906-5198
Phone: (517)484-1466
Fax: (517)484-4893

Publications: Michigan Pharmacist (15290)

Michigan Plumbing and Mechanical Contractors Association (MPMCA)
400 N. Walnut St.
Lansing, MI 48933
Phone: (517)484-5500
Fax: (517)484-5225
Free: 800-292-1044

Publications: Michigan Master Plumber and Mechanical Contractor (15287)

The Michigan Post
PO Box 37646
Oak Park, MI 48237-0646

Publications: The Michigan Post (15413)

Michigan Roads and Construction
535 N Clippert, Ste. B
PO Box 25007
Lansing, MI 48909-5007
Phone: (517)484-7600
Fax: (517)332-7336

Publications: Michigan Roads and Construction (15291)

Michigan Snowmobiler
01615 Advance-East Jordan Rd.
PO Box 417
East Jordan, MI 49727
Phone: (231)536-2371
Fax: (231)536-7691

Publications: Michigan Snowmobiler (14980)

Michigan State AFL-CIO
419 Washington Sq. S, Ste. 200
Lansing, MI 48933
Phone: (517)487-5966
Fax: (517)487-5213

Publications: Michigan AFL-CIO News (15279)

Michigan State Grange
1730 Chamberlain
Haslett, MI 48840
Phone: (517)339-2171
Fax: (517)339-3636
Free: 800-337-1502

Publications: Michigan News (15151)

Michigan State Medical Society
PO Box 950
East Lansing, MI 48826-0950
Phone: (517)337-1351
Fax: (517)337-2490

Publications: Michigan Medicine (14989)

Michigan State University
560 Baker Hall
East Lansing, MI 48824-1118
Phone: (517)355-2197
Fax: (517)432-1787

Publications: International Journal of Comparative and Applied Criminal Justice (14985)

Michigan State University
201 Morrill Hall
East Lansing, MI 48824
Phone: (517)355-9571
Fax: (517)353-3755

Publications: Journal of South Asian Literature (14987)

Michigan State University
202 Ag Hall
East Lansing, MI 48824-1039
Phone: (517)355-4563
Fax: (517)432-1800

Publications: Agricultural Economics Report (14981)

Michigan State University Alumni Association
MSU Union
East Lansing, MI 48824-1029
Phone: (517)355-8314
Fax: (517)355-5265

Publications: MSU Alumni Magazine (14990)

Michigan State University Press
1405 S. Harrison Rd., Ste. 25
East Lansing, MI 48823-5202
Phone: (517)355-9543
Fax: 800-678-2120

Publications: The Historian (14984) • Northeast African Studies (14991)

Michigan Technological University
106 Memorial Union Bldg.
Houghton, MI 49931
Phone: (906)487-2404

Publications: Michigan Tech Lode (15184)

Michigan Traveler Publishing Company
2500 Leon Ave.
Lansing, MI 48906-3646
Phone: (517)886-0568
Free: 800-676-7997

Publications: Michigan Traveler (15293)

Michigan United Conservation Clubs
2101 Wood St.
PO Box 30235
Lansing, MI 48909
Phone: (517)371-1041
Fax: (517)371-1505
Free: 800-777-6720

Publications: Michigan Out-of-Doors (15289) • TRACKS MAGAZINE (15295)

Mickens, Inc.
PO Box 6
Liberty Center, OH 43532
Phone: (419)533-2401

Publications: The Liberty Press (25296)

Mico Graphics & Advertising, Inc.
PO Box 5132
Flint, MI 48505
Phone: (810)767-7769
Fax: (810)785-3806

Publications: The FORUM Magazine (14932)

Microdac
PO Box 68234
Virginia Beach, VA 23471-8234
Phone: (757)495-1408
Fax: (757)495-1408
Free: 800-642-7632

Publications: The Shilling (32589)

Micropaleontology Press
American Museum of Natural History
79th St. & Central Park W.
New York, NY 10024
Phone: (212)769-5656
Fax: (212)769-5653

Publications: Micropaleontology (22332)

Mid-America Folklore Society
c/o Lyon College
Batesville, AR 72501

Publications: Mid-America Folklore (1041)

Mid-America Theatre Association
Central College
Pella, IA 50219
Phone: (515)263-0110

Publications: Theatre History Studies (11152)

Mid Atlantic Gay
PO Box 22575
Baltimore, MD 21203
Phone: (410)837-7748
Fax: (410)837-8889

Publications: Baltimore Gay Paper (13132)

Mid Atlantic Media/Hanahan Publications
PO Box 60580
Charleston, SC 29419-0580
Phone: (803)747-5773
Fax: (803)744-5505

Publications: The Hanahan News (28656)

Mid-Atlantic Tech Publications Inc.
PO Box 957
Valley Forge, PA 19482-0957
Phone: (610)783-6100
Fax: (610)783-0317

Publications: U.S. Tech (28092)

Mid-Atlantic Trade Exhibition
2117 Smith Ave.
Chesapeake, VA 23320
Phone: (804)420-2434
Fax: (804)420-8021

Publications: Virginia Builder (32276)

Mid-Florida Publications, Inc.
4645 N. Hwy. 19-A
PO Box 318
Mount Dora, FL 32757
Phone: (352)735-0777
Fax: (352)357-3202

Publications: Sumter Shopper (6128)

Mid-Illinois Newspapers, Inc.
100 Broadway
Mattoon, IL 61938
Phone: (217)235-5656
Fax: (217)235-1925

Publications: Journal-Gazette (9159)

Mid-Iowa Publishing Co.
130 W Main
PO Box 634
State Center, IA 50247
Phone: (641)483-2120
Fax: (641)483-2938

Publications: Mid Iowa Enterprise (11242)

Mid Island News
PO Box 21
Centereach, NY 11720
Phone: (631)265-2100
Fax: (631)265-6237

Publications: Mid Island News (23337)

Mid-North Monitor
15-417 2nd Ave.
Espanola, ON, Canada P5E 1L1
Phone: (705)869-0588
Fax: (705)869-0587
Free: 877-869-0588

Publications: Mid-North Monitor (35808)

Mid-South Hunting & Fishing News
PO Box 198
Brownsville, TN 38012
Phone: (731)772-9962

Publications: Mid-South Hunting & Fishing News (29071)

Mid-South Newspapers, Inc.
PO Drawer 1477
Hamilton, AL 35570-1477
Phone: (205)921-3104
Fax: (205)921-3105

Publications: The Journal-Record (261)

Mid-States Newspapers, Inc.
256 W Las Cruces Ave.
Las Cruces, NM 88004
Phone: (505)541-5400
Fax: (505)541-5498

Publications: The Las Cruces Sun-News (19873)

Mid-Valley Newspaper, Inc.
401 S Iowa
Weslaco, TX 78596
Phone: (210)969-2543
Fax: (210)968-0855

Publications: Mid-Valley Town Crier (31278)

Mid Valley Publication
740 N St.
Sanger, CA 93657
Phone: (559)875-2511
Fax: (559)875-2521

Publications: The Fowler Ensign (3615)

Mid-Valley Publications
6950 Gerard St.
Winton, CA 95388
Phone: (209)358-5311
Fax: (209)358-7108

Publications: Atwater's New Times (4095) • Denair Dispatch (1824) • Hilmar Times (4096) • Hughson Chronicle (2058) • Merced County Times (4097) • The Waterford News (4057) • Winton Times (4098)

Mid-Valley Publishers, Inc.
PO Box 657
PO Box 657
Mercedes, TX 78570
Phone: (956)565-4111
Fax: (956)565-2570

Publications: The Mercedes Enterprise (30805)

Middle Atlantic Council of Latin American Studies
University of Delaware
Foreign Language & Literature
Newark, DE 19716
Phone: (302)831-2597

Publications: MACLAS Latin American Essays (5278)

Middle East Forum
1500 Walnut St., Ste. 1050
Philadelphia, PA 19102
Phone: (215)546-5406
Fax: (215)546-5409

Publications: Middle East Quarterly (27569)

Middle East Institute
1761 N St. NW
Washington, DC 20036
Phone: (202)785-1141
Fax: (202)452-8876

Publications: The Middle East Journal (5650)

Middle East Research & Information Project
1500 Massachusetts Ave. NW, Ste. 119
Washington, DC 20005
Phone: (202)223-3677
Fax: (202)223-3604

Publications: Middle East Research & Information Project (5651)

Middle Georgia College
1100 Second St. SE
Cochran, GA 31014
Phone: (478)934-6221
Fax: (478)934-3199

Publications: Kernel (7179)

Middle Park Times
Box 476
Kremmling, CO 80459
Phone: (970)724-3350
Fax: (970)724-0879

Publications: Middle Park Times (4525)

Middle Tennessee Shopper
PO Box 1424
Columbia, TN 38402
Phone: (931)381-4990
Fax: (931)381-1017

Publications: Middle Tennessee Shopper (29137)

Middle Tennessee State University
English Dept.
Murfreesboro, TN 37132
Phone: (615)898-2712

Publications: Poems and Plays (29431)

Middle Tennessee State University
1301 E. Main St.
Murfreesboro, TN 37132-0001
Phone: (615)898-2300
Fax: (615)904-8487

Publications: Sidelines (29432)

Middle Tennessee State University
PO Box 102
Murfreesboro, TN 37132
Phone: (615)898-2610
Fax: (615)898-5045

Publications: Tennessee's Business (29435)

Middlebury College Publications
Middlebury College
Middlebury, VT 05753
Phone: (802)443-5075
Fax: (802)443-2088
Free: 800-450-9571

Publications: Middlebury College Magazine (31557) • New England Review (31558)

Middletown Journal
52 S. Broad St.
PO Box 490
Middletown, OH 45044
Phone: (513)422-3611
Fax: (513)422-8698

Publications: Middletown Journal (25378)

Middletown News
106 N Fifth
Middletown, IN 47356
Phone: (765)354-2221
Fax: (765)354-2221

Publications: Middletown News (10308)

Middletown Times
21168 Calistoga St.
PO Box 608
Middletown, CA 95461
Phone: (707)987-3602
Fax: (707)987-3901

Publications: Middletown Times Star (2538)

Midland Daily News
PO Box 432
Midland, MI 48640-5161
Phone: (517)835-7171
Fax: (517)835-6991

Publications: Midland Daily News (15355)

Midland Lutheran College
Journalism Dept.
900 N. Clarkson
Fremont, NE 68025
Phone: (402)721-5480
Fax: (402)721-0250

Publications: The Midland (18012)

Midland Reporter-Telegram
201 E. Illinois St.
PO Box 1650
Midland, TX 79701-4852
Phone: (915)682-5311
Fax: (915)682-6173
Free: 800-542-3952

Publications: Midland Reporter-Telegram (30814)

Midlands Business Journal Publications
1279 S. 120th St.
Omaha, NE 68144
Phone: (402)330-1760

Publications: The Lincoln Business Journal (18202) • The Midlands Business Journal (18203) • The Omaha Business Journal (18205)

The Midlothian Mirror
110 N 8th St.
PO Box 70
Midlothian, TX 76065
Phone: (972)775-3322
Fax: (972)723-0167

Publications: The Midlothian Mirror (30826)

Midnight Publishing Corp.
55-51 69th St.
PO Box 780376
Maspeth, NY 11378
Phone: (718)639-7000
Fax: (718)429-1234

Publications: Glendale Register (20667) • Queens Ledger (23169)

Midrex Direct Reduction Corp.
2725 Water Ridge Pkwy., Ste. 100
Charlotte, NC 28217
Phone: (704)373-1600

Publications: Direct From Midrex (23743)

Midstate
PO Box 685
Lawrenceburg, TN 38464
Phone: (931)762-2222
Fax: (931)762-4191
Free: 888-471-8712

Publications: Democrat-Union (29315)

Midway Publishing Corp.
2807 N Parham Rd., Ste. 200
Richmond, VA 23294-4410

Publications: Infection Control & Sterilization Technology (32438)

The Midweek Inc.
650 Peace Rd.
PO Box 546
DeKalb, IL 60115
Phone: (815)758-0696
Fax: (815)758-1418

Publications: The MidWeek (8737)

The Midweek, Inc.
PO Box 651
Fergus Falls, MN 56538
Phone: (218)739-3308

Publications: The Heartland Shopping News (15898) • The Midweek (15899)

Midweek Printing Co.
500 Ala Moana Blvd., 7-500
Honolulu, HI 96813
Phone: (808)529-4700
Fax: (808)529-4750

Publications: Honolulu Star-Bulletin (7702)

Midwest Contractor
4005 Genessee St.
Kansas City, MO 64111-4106
Phone: (816)561-3300
Fax: (816)561-3334
Free: 800-233-2412

Publications: Midwest Contractor (17184)

Midwest History of Education Society
c/o Joseph Watras, Editor
University of Dayton
Dayton, OH 45469-0525
Phone: (937)229-3328
Fax: (937)229-2500

Publications: American Educational History Journal (25106)

Midwest Magazine Network
PO Box 88505
Indianapolis, IN 46208
Phone: (317)923-1500
Fax: (317)924-4669

Publications: Home & Away (Hoosier Edition) (10114)

Midwest Modern Language Association
302 English-Philosophy Bldg.
University of Iowa
Iowa City, IA 52242-1408
Phone: (319)335-0331
Fax: (319)335-3123

Publications: Midwest Modern Language Association Journal (10982)

MidWest Outdoors, Ltd.
111 Shore Dr.
Burr Ridge, IL 60527
Phone: (630)887-7722

Publications: Fishing Facts Magazine (8102)

The Midwest Quarterly
Pittsburg State University
Pittsburg, KS 66762
Phone: (620)235-4369
Fax: (620)235-4080

Publications: The Midwest Quarterly (11753)

Midwest Racing News
6646 W Fairview Ave.
Milwaukee, WI 53213
Phone: (414)778-4700
Fax: (414)778-4688
Free: 800-432-4212

Publications: Midwest Racing News (34081)

Midwest Retailer
8528 Columbus Ave. S
Bloomington, MN 55420-2460
Phone: (952)854-7610
Fax: (952)854-6460

Publications: Midwest Retailer (15759)

Midwest Sociological Society
Dept. of Sociology
505 Seashore Hall West
The University of Iowa
Iowa City, IA 52242-1401
Phone: (319)335-3982
Fax: (319)335-2509

Publications: The Sociological Quarterly (10987)

Midwest Suburban Publishing
6901 W 159th St.
Tinley Park, IL 60477-1604
Phone: (708)633-6880
Fax: (708)633-6999

Publications: Daily Southtown (9685)

Midwestern State University
3410 Taft Blvd.
Box 14
Wichita Falls, TX 76308-2099
Phone: (940)397-4704
Fax: (940)397-4909

Publications: The Wichitan (31294)

Midwestern States Salvage Guide
3700 Decker
Moore, OK 73160
Phone: (405)787-0795
Fax: (405)787-6388

Publications: Midwestern States Salvage Guide (25920)

Midwifery Today
Box 2672
Eugene, OR 97402
Phone: (541)344-7438
Fax: (541)344-1422
Free: 800-743-0974

Publications: Midwifery Today (26323)

Mifflinburg Telegraph
358 Walnut St.
Mifflinburg, PA 17844-0189
Phone: (570)966-2255
Fax: (570)966-0062
Free: 800-996-2879

Publications: Mifflinburg Telegraph (27262)

Mikeska Inc.
PO Box 5500
San Angelo, TX 76902
Phone: (915)658-8367
Fax: (915)653-9643
Free: 877-655-4161

Publications: San Angelo Bridal Guide Magazine (31009)

Milam County Newpaper LLC
108 E 1st St.
PO Drawer 1230
Cameron, TX 76520
Phone: (254)697-6672
Fax: (254)697-4902

Publications: The Cameron Herald (29995)

Milan Mirror-Exchange
Box 549
Milan, TN 38358
Phone: (901)686-1632
Fax: (901)686-9005

Publications: Milan Mirror-Exchange (29414)

The Milan Standard
105 S Market
Milan, MO 63556
Phone: (816)265-4244
Fax: (816)265-3180

Publications: The Milan Standard (17289)

Milan Standard-Watson Journal
Box 190
Milan, MN 56262
Phone: (320)734-4458
Fax: (320)289-2702

Publications: Milan Standard-Watson Journal (16054)

Mildmay Town & Country Crier
100 Elora St.
PO Box 190
Mildmay, ON, Canada N0G 2J0
Phone: (519)367-2681
Fax: (519)367-5417

Publications: Mildmay Town & Country Crier (36046)

Miles Media Group, Inc.
6751 Professional Pkwy. W.
Sarasota, FL 34240-8448
Phone: (941)922-3575
Fax: (941)923-6309
Free: 800-683-0010

Publications: SEE Emerald Coast (6665) • SEE Florida Keys (6666) • SEE Sarasota, Bradenton, Venice & Gulf Coast Islands Magazine (6667)

Miles Messenger
PO Box 307
Miles, TX 76861
Phone: (915)468-3611

Publications: The Concho Herald (30828) • Rowena Press (30997)

Miles Publishing Company Inc.
PO Box 360
Oneill, NE 68763
Phone: (402)336-1220
Fax: (402)336-1222

Publications: Frontier and Holt County Independent (18232)

Milestones
51 Pleasant St., Ste. 5
Malden, MA 02148

Publications: The Malden Milestone (14297)

Milestones, Inc.
2 E Sheridan
Ely, MN 55731
Phone: (218)365-3141
Fax: (218)365-3142
Free: 800-492-3555

Publications: Ely Echo (15880) • North Country Angler (15881) • North Country Saver (15882)

Milford Herald-News
18 S Axtel Ave.
PO Box 200
Milford, IL 60953-0200
Phone: (815)889-4321
Fax: (815)889-4321

Publications: Milford Herald-News (9196)

The Milford Times
PO Box 723
Milford, NE 68405-0723
Phone: (402)761-2911
Fax: (402)761-2914

Publications: The Milford Times (18162)

Military Forces Features, Inc.
51 Atlantic Ave., Ste. 200
Floral Park, NY 11001
Phone: (516)616-1930
Fax: (516)616-1936

Publications: Salute (20606)

Military Newspapers of Virginia
2509 Walmer Ave.
Norfolk, VA 23513
Phone: (757)857-1212
Fax: (804)853-1634

Publications: Casemate (32126) • Soundings (32294) • The Wheel (32280)

Military Order of the World Wars
435 N Lee St.
Alexandria, VA 22314
Phone: (703)683-4911
Fax: (703)683-4501
Free: 877-320-3744

Publications: Officer Review (31718)

Military Vehicle Preservation Association
Box 520378
Independence, MO 64052-0378
Phone: (816)833-6872
Fax: (816)832-5115

Publications: Army Motors (17105)

The Mill
PO Box 378
Bradford, VT 05033
Phone: (802)222-5281
Fax: (802)222-5438

Publications: Journal Opinion (31506)

Mill Publishing Inc.
237 Commerce St., Ste. 202
PO Box 953
Williston, VT 05495-0953
Phone: (802)862-4109
Fax: (802)862-9322

Publications: Business People Vermont (31618)

Millard County Chronicle Progress
Box 249
40 North 300 West
Delta, UT 84624
Phone: (435)864-2400
Fax: (435)864-2214

Publications: Millard County Chronicle Progress (31331)

Millard County Gazette Inc.
PO Box 609
Delta, UT 84624
Phone: (435)846-2904
Fax: (435)846-2904

Publications: Millard County Gazette (31332)

Millbrook Publishing Company
PO Box 867
Wallingford, CT 06492-0867
Phone: (203)498-5120

Publications: CT LIFE (5188)

Millbrook Times
28 King St. E.
PO Box 230
Millbrook, ON, Canada L0A 1G0
Phone: (705)932-3001
Fax: (705)932-3377

Publications: Millbrook Times (36047)

Mille Lacs County Time
225 SW 2nd St.
PO Box 9
Milaca, MN 56353
Phone: (320)983-6111
Fax: (320)983-6112

Publications: Mille Lacs County Times (16053)

Mille Lacs Messenger
280, W. Main St. PO Box 26
Isle, MN 56342
Phone: (320)676-3123
Fax: (320)676-8450

Publications: Mille Lacs Messenger (15972)

The Millen News
PO Box 909
Millen, GA 30442
Phone: (478)982-5460
Fax: (478)982-1785

Publications: Millen News (7441)

Millenium Publishing Inc.
2117 Buffalo Rd., Ste. 290
Rochester, NY 14624-1507
Phone: (585)594-9283
Fax: (585)594-9287

Publications: Computer Link Magazine (23218)

Miller County Liberal
157 E Main St.
PO Box 37
Colquitt, GA 39837-0037
Phone: (229)758-5549
Fax: (229)758-5540

Publications: Miller County Liberal (7182)

Miller Freeman, Inc.
1601 W. 23rd St., Ste. 200
Lawrence, KS 66046
Phone: (785)841-1631
Fax: (785)841-2624

Publications: Sys Admin (11565)

Miller Magazines, Inc.
4880 Market St.
Ventura, CA 93003
Phone: (805)644-3824
Fax: (805)644-3875

Publications: COINage (4002) • Rock & Gem (4009)

The Miller Press
PO Box 216
Greenfield, MO 65661-0216
Phone: (417)452-3792
Fax: (417)637-2232

Publications: The Miller Press (17290)

Miller Publishing Co.
12400 Whitewater Dr., Ste. 160
Minnetonka, MN 55343
Phone: (952)930-1832
Fax: (952)938-4390

Publications: Feedstuffs (16169)

Miller Publishing Co.
114 W. 3rd St.
PO Box 196
Miller, SD 57362
Phone: (605)853-3575
Fax: (605)853-2478
Free: 800-953-8491

Publications: The Miller Press (28896)

Miller Publishing Group
810 7th Ave., 4th Fl.
New York, NY 10019
Phone: (212)636-2700
Fax: (212)636-2710

Publications: Mountain Sports & Living (22374)

Miller Publishing Group LLC
3679 Motor Ave., Ste. 300
Los Angeles, CA 90034
Phone: (310)280-2880
Fax: (310)893-5454

Publications: WHERE Alaska & The Yukon (35181) • WHERE Atlanta (7061) • WHERE Boston (13971) • WHERE Chicago (8605) • WHERE Denver (4367) • WHERE Indianapolis (16140) • WHERE Las Vegas (18386) • WHERE Los Angeles (2435) • WHERE Miami (6392) • WHERE New Orleans (12761) • WHERE New York (22917) • WHERE Orange County (1782) • WHERE Phoenix/Scottsdale (876) • WHERE St. Louis (17532) • WHERE San Francisco (3462) • WHERE Seattle (33044) • WHERE Toronto (36791) • WHERE Twin Cities (16141) • WHERE Washington (5860)

Miller Sports Group, L.L.C.
79 Madison Ave.
New York, NY 10016-7802
Phone: (212)636-2700
Free: 800-634-1953

Publications: Cruising World Magazine (28365) • Sailing World (28373) • Tennis (22823) • Tennis Buyer's Guide (22824)

Millin Publishing Group, Inc.
1150 Connecticut Ave., NW, Ste. 900
Washington, DC 20036
Phone: (202)862-4375
Fax: (202)659-3493

Publications: EDP Weekly's IT Monitor (5472)

The Millington Star
PO Box 305
Millington, TN 38083
Phone: (901)872-2286
Fax: (901)872-2965

Publications: The Millington Star (29416) • South Tipton Star (29417)

Million Dollar Round Table
325 W Touhy Ave.
Park Ridge, IL 60068-4265
Phone: (847)692-6378
Fax: (847)518-8921

Publications: Round the Table (9408)

Milpitas Post
59 Marylinn Dr.
Milpitas, CA 95035
Phone: (408)262-2454
Fax: (408)763-9710

Publications: Milpitas Post (2545)

The Milton Courier
513 Vernal Ave.
Box 69
Milton, WI 53563
Phone: (608)868-2442
Fax: (608)868-4664

Publications: The Milton Courier (34054)

Milton-Freewater Valley Times
205 N. Main
PO Box 170
Milton-Freewater, OR 97862
Phone: (541)938-0702
Fax: (541)938-0691

Publications: Milton-Freewater Valley Times (26435)

Milton Independent
PO Box 163
Milton, VT 05468
Phone: (802)893-2028
Fax: (802)893-7407

Publications: Milton Independent (31563)

Milton Quarterly
Ohio University
PO Box 378, Ellis Hall
Athens, OH 45701
Phone: (614)593-2829
Fax: (614)593-2818

Publications: Milton Quarterly (24630)

Milton Shopping News
1158 S. Service Rd. W.
Oakville, ON, Canada L6L 5T7
Phone: (416)827-2244
Fax: (416)827-2308

Publications: Milton Shopping News (36146)

John Milton Society for the Blind
370 Lexington Ave., Rm. 1007
New York, NY 10017-6503
Phone: (212)870-3335
Fax: (212)870-3226

Publications: Adult Lessons Quarterly (21152) • Discovery Magazine (21556) • John Milton Magazine (21970)

Milwaukee Catholic Press Apostolate, Inc.
3501 S Lake Dr.
PO Box 070913
Milwaukee, WI 53207-0913
Phone: (414)769-3500
Fax: (414)769-3468

Publications: Catholic Herald (34061)

Milwaukee Community Journal, Inc.
3612 N Martin Luther King Dr.
Milwaukee, WI 53212
Phone: (414)265-5300
Fax: (414)265-1536

Publications: Milwaukee Community Journal (34082)

Milwaukee County Labor Council AFL-CIO
633 S Hawley Rd.
Milwaukee, WI 53214
Phone: (414)771-7070
Fax: (414)771-0509

Publications: Milwaukee Labor Press, AFL-CIO (34085)

Milwaukee Courier
2431 W Hopkins St.
PO Box 06279
Milwaukee, WI 53206-1298
Phone: (414)449-4860
Fax: (414)449-4872

Publications: Milwaukee Courier (34083)

Milwaukee Express News
10001 W Lisbon Ave.
Milwaukee, WI 53222
Phone: (414)466-3933
Fax: (414)466-2040

Publications: Ads Express (34055)

Milwaukee Magazine
417 E Chicago St.
Milwaukee, WI 53202-5828
Phone: (414)273-1101
Fax: (414)273-0016
Free: 800-662-4818

Publications: Milwaukee Magazine (34086)

Milwaukee Star
3815 N Teutonia Ave.
Milwaukee, WI 53206
Phone: (414)449-4870
Fax: (414)449-4872

Publications: Milwaukee Star (34087)

Milwaukee Times
1938 MLK Jr. Dr.
Milwaukee, WI 53212
Phone: (414)263-5088
Fax: (414)263-4445

Publications: Milwaukee Times (34088)

Mind Over Media Publications
535 Hazard Ave.
Enfield, CT 06082
Phone: (860)763-5632
Fax: (860)763-5639
Free: (866)763-5632

Publications: Dirt Late Model (4780) • Late Model Racer (4781) • Trackside (4782)

Minden City Herald
1524 Main St.
Minden City, MI 48456
Phone: (989)864-3630
Fax: (989)864-5363

Publications: Minden City Herald (15361)

Minden Press-Herald
203 Gleason St.
PO Box 1339
Minden, LA 71055
Phone: (318)377-1866
Fax: (318)377-1895

Publications: Minden Press-Herald (12687)

Mine Action Information Center
James Madison University
MCS 8504
Harrisonburg, VA 22807
Phone: (540)568-2756
Fax: (540)568-2718

Publications: Demining Technology Information Forum Journal (34809) • Journal of Mine Action (32140)

Mine & Quarry Trader
7355 Woodland Dr.
Indianapolis, IN 46278-1769
Phone: (317)297-5500
Fax: (317)298-7113
Free: 800-827-7468

Publications: Mine & Quarry Trader (10154)

Miner County Pioneer
PO Box 220
Howard, SD 57349
Phone: (605)772-5644

Publications: Miner County Pioneer (28871)

Miner Journal
606 2nd Ave.
Box 1000
Esterhazy, SK, Canada S0A 0X0
Phone: (306)745-6669
Fax: (306)745-2699

Publications: Potashville-Miner Journal (37464)

Mineral County Independent-News
PO Box 1270
Hawthorne, NV 89415
Phone: (775)945-2414
Fax: (775)945-1270

Publications: Mineral County Independent-News (18352)

Mineral Daily News-Tribune
24 Armstrong St.
PO Box 879
Keyser, WV 26726
Phone: (304)788-3333
Fax: (304)788-3398

Publications: Mineral Daily News-Tribune (33352) • Today's Shopper (33354)

Mineral King Publishing
120 N E St.
PO Box 7
Exeter, CA 93221
Phone: (559)592-3171
Fax: (559)592-4308

Publications: The Exeter Sun (1907)

Mineralogical Society of America
1015 18th St., NW, Ste. 601
Washington, DC 20036-5212
Phone: (202)775-4344
Fax: (202)775-0018

Publications: American Mineralogist (5336)

Miner's News
PO Box 5694
2504 Kootenai St.
Boise, ID 83705
Phone: (208)345-7488
Fax: (208)345-7905
Free: 800-624-7212

Publications: Miner's News (7814)

The Minerva Center
20 Granada Rd.
Pasadena, MD 21122-2708
Phone: (410)437-5379
Fax: (914)693-2834

Publications: Minerva (13644)

Mini-Storage Messenger
2531 W. Dunlap Ave.
Phoenix, AZ 85021
Phone: (602)678-3579
Fax: (602)678-3511
Free: 800-528-1056

Publications: The Mini-Storage Messenger (807)

The Mining Journal
PO Box 430
Marquette, MI 49855
Phone: (906)228-2500
Fax: (906)228-5556

Publications: The Mining Journal (15338)

Ministere de l'Education
300, boul. Jean-Lesage
Quebec City, QC, Canada G1K 8K6

Publications: Recueil des Sentences de l'Education (37305)

Ministry of Agriculture, Food & Rural Affairs
1 Stone Rd. W.
Guelph, ON, Canada N1G 4Y2
Phone: (519)826-4191
Fax: (519)826-4211

Publications: Agri-Food Research in Ontario/Recherche Agro-alimentaire en Ontario (35858)

Ministry of Employment and Investment
Mineral Resources Division, 5th Fl.
1810 Blanshard St.
Victoria, BC, Canada V8V 1X4
Phone: (250)751-7380
Fax: (250)751-7393

Publications: BC Mine Rescue Manual (35207)

Ministry of Energy and Mines
1810 Blanshard St., 7th Fl.
Victoria, BC, Canada V8N 9N3

Publications: PIMS (Petroleum Information Management System) (35224)

The Minnedosa Tribune
Box 930
Minnedosa, MB, Canada R0J 1E0
Phone: (204)867-3816
Fax: (204)867-5171

Publications: The Minnedosa Tribune (35274)

The Minneola Record
Box 456
Minneola, KS 67865
Phone: (316)885-4584
Fax: (316)635-2643

Publications: The Minneola Record (11655)

Minneota Mascot
201 N Jefferson
PO Box 8
Minneota, MN 56264
Phone: (507)872-6492
Fax: (507)872-6492

Publications: Minneota Mascot (16165)

Minnesota American Legion Publishing Co.
20 W. Twelfth St.
St. Paul, MN 55155-2069
Phone: (651)291-1800
Fax: (651)291-1057

Publications: Minnesota Legionnaire (16394)

Minnesota Dental Association
2236 Marshall Ave.
St. Paul, MN 55104
Phone: (651)647-6673
Fax: (651)646-8246

Publications: Northwest Dentistry (16402)

Minnesota Farm Bureau Federation
3080 Eagandale Pl.
PO Box 64370
St. Paul, MN 55164
Phone: (651)905-2100
Fax: (651)905-2159

Publications: The Voice of Agriculture (16414)

Minnesota Flyer Magazine
PO Box 750
Sandstone, MN 55072-0750
Phone: (320)295-2111
Fax: (320)295-2438

Publications: Minnesota Flyer Magazine (16434)

Minnesota Grocers Association
533 St. Clair Ave.
St. Paul, MN 55102
Phone: (651)228-0973
Fax: (651)228-1949
Free: 800-966-8352

Publications: Minnesota Grocer (16392)

Minnesota Historical Society
345 W. Kellogg Blvd.
St. Paul, MN 55102-1906
Phone: (651)296-6126
Fax: (651)297-1345
Free: 800-647-7827

Publications: Minnesota History (16393)

Minnesota Medical Association
3433 Broadway St., NE, Ste. 300
Minneapolis, MN 55413-1761
Phone: (612)378-1875
Fax: (612)378-3875
Free: 800-DIAL-MMA

Publications: Minnesota Medicine (16105)

Minnesota Monthly Publications, Inc.
730 2nd Ave. S., Ste. 600
Minneapolis, MN 55402-2420
Phone: (612)371-5800
Fax: (612)371-5801
Free: 800-933-4398

Publications: Midwest Home & Garden (16097) • Minnesota Monthly (16106)

Minnesota Neighbors
PO Box 69
Chippewa Falls, WI 54729

Publications: Rural Minnesota News (33628)

Minnesota Ornithologists' Union
James Ford Bell Museum of Natural History
University of Minnesota
10 Church St. SE
Minneapolis, MN 55455-0104
Phone: (612)825-3074
Fax: (612)825-3074

Publications: The Loon (16093)

Minnesota Spokesman-Recorder
3744 4th Ave. S.
Minneapolis, MN 55409
Phone: (612)827-4021
Fax: (612)827-0577

Publications: Minnesota Spokesman (16107)

Minnesota State Bar Association
600 Nicollet Mall, Ste. 380
Minneapolis, MN 55402
Phone: (612)333-1183
Fax: (612)333-4927
Free: 800-882-6722

Publications: Bench & Bar of Minnesota (16060)

Minnesota State Horticultural Society
1755 Prior Ave. N
Falcon Heights, MN 55113
Phone: (651)643-3601
Fax: (651)643-3638
Free: 800-676-6747

Publications: Northern Gardener (15893)

Minnesota State University, Mankato
293 CSU
Mankato, MN 56001
Phone: (507)389-1776
Fax: (507)389-5812

Publications: Reporter (16029)

Minnesota State University Student Association
108 Como Ave.
St. Paul, MN 55103
Phone: (651)224-1518
Fax: (651)224-9753

Publications: The Monitor (16398)

Minnesota Sun Publications
10917 Valley View Rd.
Eden Prairie, MN 55344
Phone: (952)829-0797

Publications: Apple Valley/Rosemount Sun Current (15718) • Bloomington Sun Current (15866) • Brooklyn Center Sun-Post (15774) • Brooklyn Park Sun-Post (15867) • Burnsville/Savage Sun Current (15781) • Crystal Robbinsdale Sun Post (15823) • Eagan Sun Current (15862) • Eden Prairie Sun Current (15869) • Edina Sun Current (15874) • Excelsior/Shorewood/Chanhassen Sun-Sailor (15887) • Hopkins/East Minnetonka Sailor-Sun (15963) • New Hope/Golden Valley Sun-Post (16207) • Richfield Sun Current (16304) • St. Louis Park Sun-Sailor (16361) • South St. Paul/Inver Grove Heights Sun Current (16453) • Wayzata/Orono/Long Lake Sun-Sailor (16280) • Wayzata Sun-Sailor (16178) • West Minnetonka/Deephaven Sun-Sailor (16179) • West Saint Paul/Mendota Heights Sun Current (16506)

Minnesota Technology magazine
111 third Ave. S. Ste. 400
5 Lind Hall
Minneapolis, MN 55401
Phone: (612)373-2900
Fax: (612)373-2901

Publications: Minnesota Technology (16109)

Minnesota Turkey Growers Association, Inc.
108 Marty Dr.
Buffalo, MN 55313-9338
Phone: (763)682-2171
Fax: (763)682-5546

Publications: Gobbles (15778)

Minnesota Valley News Publishing, LLC
PO Box 68
Le Center, MN 56057-1502
Phone: (320)357-2233
Fax: (320)357-6656

Publications: Le Center Leader (15998)

Minnesota Women's Press, Inc.
771 Raymond Ave.
St. Paul, MN 55114-1522
Phone: (651)646-3968
Fax: (651)646-2186

Publications: Minnesota Women's Press (16396)

Minority Business Entrepreneur
3528 Torrance Blvd., Ste. 101
Torrance, CA 90503
Phone: (310)540-9398
Fax: (310)792-8263

Publications: Minority Business Entrepreneur (3938)

Minot Daily News
301 4th St. SE
Minot, ND 58701
Phone: (701)857-1900
Fax: (701)857-1907
Free: 800-735-3119

Publications: The Minot Daily News (24505) • The Trading Post (24506)

MIR Communications Inc.
345 Danforth Ave.
Toronto, ON, Canada M4K 1N7
Phone: (416)466-4956
Fax: (416)466-5002

Publications: Kidsworld (36643)

Miramar Communications Inc.
23805 Stuart Ranch Rd., Ste. 235
PO Box 8987
Malibu, CA 90265-8987
Phone: (310)317-4522
Fax: (310)317-0264
Free: 800-543-4116

Publications: HomeCare Magazine (2490) • Rental Equipment Register (2494) • Special Events (2496)

Mirror-Democrat Publishing Co.
308 N Main St.
PO Box 191
Mount Carroll, IL 61053
Phone: (815)244-2411
Fax: (815)244-2965

Publications: Carroll County Mirror-Democrat (9235)

Mirror Newspapers
1523 N. Main
PO Box 430
Royal Oak, MI 48067-0430
Phone: (248)546-4900
Fax: (248)398-2353

Publications: Clawson Mirror (15478) • Huntington Woods/Berkley Mirror (15482) • Pleasant Ridge/Ferndale Mirror (15483) • Royal Oak Mirror (15485)

MIS Research Center
University of Minnesota
Carlson School of Management
321 19th Ave. S.
Minneapolis, MN 55455
Phone: (612)624-7803
Fax: (612)624-2056

Publications: MIS Quarterly (16110)

The Mishawaka Enterprise
PO Box 584
Mishawaka, IN 46546-0584
Phone: (574)255-4789
Fax: (574)255-4789

Publications: The Mishawaka Enterprise (10313)

Missing Spoke Press
PO Box 9569
Seattle, WA 98109
Phone: (206)443-4693
Fax: (206)728-1202

Publications: American Jones Building & Maintenance (32940)

Mission
33047 1st Ave.
Mission, BC, Canada V2V 1G2
Phone: (604)826-6221
Fax: (604)826-8266

Publications: Fraser Valley Record (35015)

Mission Helpers of the Sacred Heart
1001 W Joppa Rd.
Baltimore, MD 21204-3787
Phone: (410)823-8585
Fax: (410)825-6355

Publications: The Mission Helper (13219)

Mission of Our Lady of Mercy Inc.
1140 W Jackson
Chicago, IL 60607
Phone: (312)738-7560
Fax: (312)738-9250

Publications: Waifs' Messenger (8601)

Mission Publishing Co., Inc.
PO Box 353
Mission, TX 78572-0353
Fax: (512)585-2304

Publications: Progress-Times (30833)

Missionary Oblates of Mary Immaculate
486 Chandler St.
PO Box 680
Tewksbury, MA 01876
Phone: (978)858-0434
Fax: (978)858-3661

Publications: The Oblate World and Voice of Hope (14586)

Missionhurst C.I.C.M.
4651 N. 25th St.
Arlington, VA 22207
Phone: (703)528-3804
Fax: (703)522-7864

Publications: Missionhurst (31808)

Missions des Peres de Sainte-Croix
4901, rue Piedmont
Montreal, QC, Canada H3V 1E3
Phone: (514)731-6231
Fax: (514)731-7820

Publications: Orient (37202)

The Mississauga News
3145 Wolfedale Rd.
Mississauga, ON, Canada L5C 3A9
Phone: (905)273-8111
Fax: (905)273-9119

Publications: The Mississauga News (36081)

Mississippi Agricultural and Forestry Experiment Station
Box 9625
Mississippi State, MS 39762-9625
Phone: (601)325-1716
Fax: (601)325-1710

Publications: MAFES Research Highlights (16782)

Mississippi Association of Educators
775 N State St.
Jackson, MS 39202
Phone: (601)354-4463
Fax: (601)352-7054
Free: 800-530-7998

Publications: The Mississippi Educator (16701)

Mississippi Bankers Association
640 N. State St.
PO Box 37
Jackson, MS 39205
Phone: (601)948-6366
Fax: (601)355-6461

Publications: The Mississippi Banker (16699)

Mississippi Baptist Convention
PO Box 530
Jackson, MS 39205
Phone: (601)968-3800

Publications: The Baptist Record (16694)

Mississippi Business Journal
5120 Galaxie Dr.
Jackson, MS 39206
Phone: (601)364-1000
Fax: (601)364-1007

Publications: Mississippi Business Journal (16700)

Mississippi Conference of the United Methodist Church
321 Mississippi St.
PO Box 1093
Jackson, MS 39201-1002
Phone: (601)354-0515
Fax: (601)948-5982

Publications: Mississippi United Methodist Advocate (16710)

Mississippi Department of Environmental Quality
Office of Geology, Box 20307
Jackson, MS 39289
Phone: (601)961-5500
Fax: (601)961-5521

Publications: Mississippi Geology (16703)

Mississippi Farm Bureau Federation
6310 Interstate 55 N
PO Box 1972
Jackson, MS 39215
Phone: (601)957-3200

Publications: Mississippi Farm Bureau News (16702)

Mississippi Historical Society
Dept. of Archives and History
Box 571
Jackson, MS 39205
Phone: (601)359-6850
Fax: (601)359-6975

Publications: The Journal of Mississippi History (16697)

Mississippi Law Journal
Box 849
University, MS 38677-0849
Phone: (662)915-6870
Fax: (662)915-7948

Publications: Mississippi Law Journal (16867)

Mississippi Library Association
PO Box 20448
Jackson, MS 39289
Phone: (601)352-3917
Fax: (601)352-4240

Publications: Mississippi Libraries Association (16705)

Mississippi Municipal League
600 East Amite St., Ste. 104
Jackson, MS 39201
Phone: (601)353-5854
Fax: (601)353-0435

Publications: Mississippi Municipalities (16707)

Mississippi Pharmacists Association
341 Edgewood Terrace Dr.
Jackson, MS 39206-6299
Phone: (601)981-0416
Fax: (601)981-0451
Free: 800-898-0416

Publications: Mississippi Pharmacist (16708)

The Mississippi Rag, Inc.
9448 Lyndale Ave. S, No. 120
Minneapolis, MN 55420
Phone: (952)885-9918
Fax: (952)885-9943

Publications: The Mississippi Rag (16111)

Mississippi State Alumni Association
PO Box 5325
Mississippi State, MS 39762-5325
Phone: (662)325-3442
Fax: (662)325-7455

Publications: Mississippi State Alumnus (16784)

Mississippi State Medical Association
PO Box 2548
Ridgeland, MS 39158-2548
Phone: (601)853-6733
Fax: (601)853-6746
Free: 800-898-0251

Publications: Journal of the Mississippi State Medical Association (16834)

Mississippi State University
Box 5272
Mississippi State, MS 39762
Phone: (662)325-3069
Fax: (662)325-3299

Publications: The Mississippi Quarterly (16783)

Mississippi State University
PO Drawer 5407
Mississippi State, MS 39762
Phone: (662)325-2374
Fax: (662)325-8985

Publications: The Reflector (16785)

Mississippi Valley Publishing Corp.
282 Commerce Park Dr.
Ridgeland, MS 39157
Phone: (601)853-1861
Fax: (601)853-8087
Free: 800-748-9808

Publications: The Stockman Grass Farmer (16770)

Missoulian
PO Box 8029
Missoula, MT 59807
Phone: (406)523-5200
Fax: (406)523-5221
Free: 800-366-7102

Publications: Missoulian (17869)

Missouri Archaeological Society
101A Museum Support Center
Rock Quarry Rd. at Hinkson Creek
Columbia, MO 65211-3170
Phone: (573)882-3544
Fax: (573)882-9410
Free: 800-472-3223

Publications: Missouri Archaeologist (16998)

Missouri Association of Realtors
2601 Bernadette Pl.
PO Box 1327
Columbia, MO 65205
Phone: (573)445-8400
Fax: (573)445-7865

Publications: The Missouri Realtor (17002)

Missouri Athletic Club
405 Washington Ave.
St. Louis, MO 63102
Phone: (314)231-7220
Fax: (314)231-2327

Publications: Cherry Diamond (17421)

The Missouri Bar
326 Monroe St.
PO Box 119
Jefferson City, MO 65101-3158
Phone: (573)635-4128
Fax: (573)635-2811

Publications: Journal of the Missouri Bar (17123)

Missouri Beef Cattleman, Inc.
PO Box 025727
Kansas City, MO 64102
Phone: (816)471-0200
Fax: (816)471-0220

Publications: Missouri Beef Cattleman (17186)

Missouri Botanical Garden
PO Box 299
St. Louis, MO 63166
Phone: (314)577-9534
Fax: (314)577-9591

Publications: Missouri Botanical Garden Annals
(17472) • Novon (17477)

Missouri Color Web, Inc.
225 N Clay
PO Box A
Marshfield, MO 65706
Phone: (417)468-2013
Fax: (417)859-7930

Publications: The Country Mailbox (17270)

Missouri Dakota Publishing Inc.
PO Box 158
Dupree, SD 57623
Phone: (605)365-5145
Fax: (605)365-5145

Publications: West River Progress (28846)

Missouri Dental Association
PO Box 104900
3340 American Ave.
Jefferson City, MO 65110-4900
Phone: (573)634-3436
Fax: (573)635-0764

Publications: Focus MDA (17121)

Missouri Farm Bureau Federation
Box 658
Jefferson City, MO 65102
Phone: (573)893-1400
Fax: (573)893-1470
Free: 800-922-4MFB

Publications: Show Me Missouri Farm Bureau News
(17133)

Missouri Farm Publishing, Inc.
3903 W Ridge Trl. Rd.
Clark, MO 65243-9525
Phone: (573)687-3525
Fax: (573)687-3148
Free: 800-633-2535

Publications: Small Farm Today (16981)

Missouri Grocers' Association
315 N. Ken Ave.
Springfield, MO 65802
Phone: (417)831-6667
Fax: (417)831-3907
Free: 800-260-4642

Publications: Missouri Grocer (17606)

Missouri Historical Society
PO Box 11940
St. Louis, MO 63112-0040
Phone: (314)746-4599
Fax: (314)746-4548

Publications: Gateway Heritage (17441)

Missouri Municipal League
1727 Southridge Dr.
Jefferson City, MO 65109
Phone: (573)635-9134
Fax: (573)635-9009

Publications: Missouri Municipal Review (17127)

Missouri NEA
1810 E Elm
Jefferson City, MO 65101-4174
Phone: (573)634-3202
Fax: (573)634-5645
Free: 800-392-0236

Publications: Something Better (17134)

Missouri Nurses Association
1904 Bubba Ln.
PO Box 105228
Jefferson City, MO 65110
Phone: (573)636-4623
Fax: (573)636-9576
Free: 888-662-6662

Publications: The Missouri Nurse (17128)

Missouri Pharmacy Association
211 E. Capital Ave.
Jefferson City, MO 65101
Phone: (573)636-7522
Fax: (573)636-7485

Publications: Missouri Pharmacist (17129)

Missouri Press Association
802 Locust ST.
Columbia, MO 65201
Phone: (573)449-4167
Fax: (573)874-5894

Publications: Missouri Press News (17001)

Missouri School for the Deaf
505 E 5th St.
Fulton, MO 65251-1799
Phone: (573)592-4000
Fax: (573)592-2570

Publications: Missouri Record (17077)

Missouri Society of Professional Engineers
200 E McCarty St., Ste. 200
Jefferson City, MO 65101
Phone: (573)636-4861

Publications: The Missouri Engineer (17125)

Missouri State Genealogical Association
PO Box 833
Columbia, MO 65205
Phone: (573)442-2387

Publications: Missouri State Genealogical Association Journal (17005)

Missouri State Medical Association
113 Madison St.
PO Box 1028
Jefferson City, MO 65101-3015
Phone: (573)636-5151
Fax: (573)636-8552

Publications: Missouri Medicine (17126)

Missouri State Teachers Association
PO Box 458
Columbia, MO 65205-0458
Phone: (573)442-3127
Fax: (573)443-5079
Free: 800-392-0532

Publications: School and Community (17008)

Missouri Valley Merchandiser/Missouri Valley Times-News
501 E Erie
PO Box 159
Missouri Valley, IA 51555
Phone: (712)642-2791
Fax: (712)642-2595

Publications: Missouri Valley Merchandiser (11084)

Missouri Valley Observer
204 Walnut
PO Box 858
Yankton, SD 57078
Phone: (605)665-0484

Publications: Missouri Valley Observer (29036)

Missouri Valley Shopper
329 Broadway St.
PO Box 773
Yankton, SD 57078
Phone: (605)665-5884
Fax: (605)665-5882

Publications: Missouri Valley Shopper (29037)

Missouri Valley Times News
501 E Erie St.
PO Box 159
Missouri Valley, IA 51555
Phone: (712)642-2791
Fax: (712)642-2595

Publications: Missouri Valley Times News (11085)

Missouri Western State College
4525 Downs Dr. SS/C 204
St. Joseph, MO 64507
Phone: (816)271-4200
Fax: (816)271-4543

Publications: The Griffon News (17392)

Missourian News
PO Box 456
Portageville, MO 63873
Phone: (573)379-5355
Fax: (573)379-5488
Free: 800-459-9558

Publications: Missourian News (17363)

Missourian Publishing Association, Inc.
221 S. 8th St.
PO Box SM7
Columbia, MO 65205
Phone: (573)882-5700
Fax: (573)882-5702

Publications: Columbia Missourian (16991)

Missourian Publishing Co.
PO Box 336
Washington, MO 63090
Phone: (636)239-7701
Fax: (636)239-0915
Free: 888-314-7701

Publications: The Marthasville Record (17272) •
Washington Missourian (17705)

The MIT Press
5 Cambridge Ctr.
Cambridge, MA 02142-1493
Phone: (617)253-5646
Fax: (617)258-6779

Publications: AJOB (14036) • Computer Music Journal (14046) • The Harvard International Journal of Press/Politics (14059) • International Security (14072) • Journal of Cold War Studies (14075) • Journal of Economics and Management Strategy (8864) • Journal of Industrial Ecology (14076) • The Journal of Interdisciplinary History (14077) • Journal of Machine Learning Research (14078) • Leonardo Music Journal (14080) • Linguistic Inquiry (14081) • Neural Computation (14084) • PAJ: A Journal of Performing (22519) • Presence (14090) • The Quarterly Journal of Economics (14094) • Reflections (14097) • Review of Economics and Statistics (14098) • Studies in Nonlinear Dynamics and Econometrics (19341) • TDR: The Drama Review (14105) • The Washington Quarterly (14111)

Mitchell College
437 Pequot Ave.
New London, CT 06320-4498
Phone: (860)701-5000
Fax: (860)701-5090
Free: 800-443-2811

Publications: The Seal (5020)

Mitchell County Press-News
PO Box 60
112 N. 6th St.
Osage, IA 50461
Phone: (641)732-3721
Fax: (641)732-5689

Publications: Mitchell County Press-News (11131)

Mitchell News Journal
261 Locust Ave.
PO Box 339
Spruce Pine, NC 28777
Phone: (828)765-2071
Fax: (828)765-1616

Publications: Mitchell News Journal (24245)

Mitchell Publications
543 Avenida Adobe
San Clemente, CA 92672-2414
Fax: (818)443-9124

Publications: Industrial West (3101)

The Mitchell Tribune
Box 378
Mitchell, IN 47446
Phone: (812)849-2075
Fax: (812)849-2911

Publications: The Mitchell Tribune (10319)

Mitzel Outdoor Publications, Inc.
PO Box 2714
Bismarck, ND 58502
Phone: (701)255-3031
Fax: (701)255-5038
Free: 800-767-5082

Publications: Dakota Country (24351)

MLPGA, Inc.
4100 Country Club Dr.
Jefferson City, MO 65109-0302
Fax: (314)893-2623

Publications: MLPGA News (17131)

MMB Publishers
990 Motor Pky.
Central Islip, NY 11722-1001
Phone: (631)435-8890
Fax: (631)435-8925

Publications: New York Sportscene (20449)

MMG, Inc.
462 Broadway, Ste. 4000
New York, NY 10013
Phone: (212)966-8400
Fax: (212)966-9366
Free: 888-664-7827

Publications: Honcho Magazine (21815) • Mandate Magazine (22279) • Playguy Magazine (22566)

M.N.R. Promotions, Inc.
640 Palisade Ave.
Englewood Cliffs, NJ 07632
Phone: (201)871-2221
Fax: (201)871-2223

Publications: Hi Class Living (18801)

Moberly Monitor-Index & Evening Democrat
218 N. Williams St.
Moberly, MO 65270
Phone: (660)263-4123

Publications: Moberly Monitor-Index & Evening Democrat (81)

Mobile Beacon
2311 Costarides St.
PO Box 1407
Mobile, AL 36633
Phone: (251)479-0629

Publications: Mobile Beacon (323)

Mobile Beat Magazine
PO Box 309
East Rochester, NY 14445
Phone: (585)385-9920
Fax: (585)385-3637

Publications: Mobile Beat (20553)

The Mobile Press
304 Government St.
PO Box 2488
Mobile, AL 36630
Phone: (334)433-1551
Fax: (334)434-8662
Free: 800-239-1659

Publications: The Mobile Press (324)

The Mobile Register
304 Government St.
PO Box 2488
Mobile, AL 36602
Phone: (334)433-1551
Fax: (334)434-8662
Free: 800-239-1659

Publications: The Mobile Register (325)

Mobilia Corporation
461 Ave. D
Williston, VT 05495
Phone: (802)658-0164
Fax: (802)658-4761

Publications: Mobilia Magazine (31619)

MOCAL News Corp.
8046 California City Blvd.
California City, CA 93505
Phone: (760)373-4812
Fax: (760)373-2941
Free: 800-541-4460

Publications: The Mojave Desert News (1639)

Mode Magazine
17666 Fitch
Irvine, CA 92614-6022

Publications: Mode (2084)

Mode Weekly
1120 N. Third St.
Harrisburg, PA 17102
Phone: (717)234-6633
Fax: (717)703-5010

Publications: Mode Weekly (26999)

Model Aeronautics Association of Canada
5100 S. Service Rd., Unit 9
Burlington, ON, Canada L7L 6A5
Phone: (905)632-9808
Fax: (905)632-3304

Publications: Model Aviation Canada (35717)

Model T Ford Club of America
Box 126
Centerville, IN 47330-0126
Phone: (765)855-5248
Fax: (765)588-3428

Publications: Vintage Ford (9884)

Modern Communications, Inc.
2905 Seymour Rd.
Eau Claire, WI 54703
Phone: (715)835-3800
Fax: (715)835-3958

Publications: Wisconsin West Magazine (33674)

Modern Day Periodicals, Inc.
1115 Broadway
New York, NY 10010

Publications: Super Easy-To-Do (22807)

Modern Drummer Publications, Inc.
12 Old Bridge Rd.
Cedar Grove, NJ 07009
Phone: (973)239-4140
Fax: (973)239-7139

Publications: Drum Business (18720) • Modern Drummer Magazine (18721)

Modern Ferret
PO Box 1007
Smithtown, NY 11787
Phone: (631)981-3710

Publications: Modern Ferret (23338)

Modern Haiku
PO Box 68
Lincoln, IL 62656-0068

Publications: Modern Haiku (9083)

Modern Language Association
Shannon Hall 119
Saint Louis University
220 N. Grand Blvd.
St. Louis, MO 63103-2007
Phone: (314)977-3703
Fax: (314)977-3649

Publications: African American Review (17406)

Modern Language Association of America
26 Broadway, 3rd Fl.
New York, NY 10004-1789
Phone: (646)576-5000
Fax: (646)458-0030

Publications: PMLA (22567)

Modern Logic Publishing
PO Box 204
Webster City, IA 50595-0204
Free: 800-361-8012

Publications: Modern Logic: International Journal for the History of Mathematical Logic, Set Theory, and Foundation of Mathematics (11314)

The Modern News
PO Box 400
Harrisburg, AR 72432
Phone: (501)578-2121
Fax: (501)578-9415

Publications: The Modern News (1166)

The Modern Poetry Association
60 W. Walton St.
Chicago, IL 60610
Phone: (312)255-3703
Fax: (312)255-3702

Publications: Poetry (8535)

Modern Trade Communications, Inc.
7450 N Skokie Blvd.
Skokie, IL 60077
Phone: (847)674-2200
Fax: (847)674-3676

Publications: Metal Architecture (25671)

Modern Woodmen of America
1701 1st Ave.
PO Box 2005
Rock Island, IL 61204-2005
Phone: (309)786-6481
Fax: (309)793-5603

Publications: The Modern Woodmen Magazine (9518)

Modoc County Record
Box 531
Alturas, CA 96101
Phone: (530)233-2632
Fax: (530)233-5113

Publications: Modoc County Record (1394)

Moffitt Newspapers
125 Wyoming St.
PO Box 569
Welch, WV 24801
Phone: (304)436-3144
Fax: (304)436-3146

Publications: The Welch Daily News (33492)

Mohave Valley Daily News
2435 Miracle Mile
PO Box 21209
Bullhead City, AZ 86442
Phone: (928)763-2505
Fax: (928)763-7820
Free: 800-571-3835

Publications: Mohave Valley Daily News (666)

Mohawk Nation
PO Box 196
Rooseveltown, NY 13683-0196
Phone: (518)358-9531

Publications: Akwesasne Notes (23275)

Moksha Press
PO Box 2360
Lenox, MA 01240
Phone: (413)637-6000
Fax: (413)637-6015
Free: 800-376-3210

Publications: What Is Enlightenment? (14270)

Molalla Pioneer
217 Main St.
PO Box 168
Molalla, OR 97038
Phone: (503)829-2301
Fax: (503)829-2317

Publications: Molalla Pioneer (26439)

Moline Dispatch Publishing Co.
1720 5th Ave.
Moline, IL 61265
Phone: (309)764-4344
Fax: (309)797-0311

Publications: The Dispatch and the Rock Island Argus (9204) • The Gold Book (9205) • Rock Island Argus (9519)

John Moloy Zimmerman
PO Box 99
Overton, TX 75684
Phone: (903)834-6178

Publications: The Overton Press (30890)

Mom Guess What Newspaper
1103 T St.
Sacramento, CA 95814
Phone: (916)441-6397
Fax: (916)441-6422

Publications: Mom Guess What Newspaper (MGW) (3010)

Momence Progress-Reporter
110 W. River St.
Momence, IL 60954
Phone: (815)472-2000
Fax: (815)472-3877

Publications: Momence Progress-Reporter (9211)

Momentum Media
2488 N. Triphammer Rd.
Ithaca, NY 14850
Phone: (607)257-6970
Fax: (607)257-7328

Publications: Coaching Management (20790) • Training and Conditioning (20815)

Momentum Media Management
4040 Creditview Rd., Unit 11
PO Box 1800
Mississauga, ON, Canada L5C 3Y8
Phone: (905)813-7100
Fax: (905)813-7117

Publications: Charitable Business Magazine (36061) • Church Business (36062) • Government Business (36068) • School Business Magazine (36086)

The Monadnock Ledger
20 Grove St.
PO Box 36
Peterborough, NH 03458
Phone: (603)924-7172
Fax: (603)924-3681

Publications: The Monadnock Ledger (18625)

Monahans News
Box 767
Monahans, TX 79756
Phone: (915)943-4313
Fax: (915)943-4314
Free: 800-658-2752

Publications: The Monahans News (30835)

Monarch Services, Inc.
4517 Hartford Rd.
Baltimore, MD 21214
Phone: (410)254-9200
Fax: (410)254-0991

Publications: The General (13164) • Girls' Life (GL) (13165)

Moncton Publishing
939 Main St.
PO Box 1001
Moncton, NB, Canada E1C 8P3
Phone: (506)859-4900
Fax: (506)859-4899

Publications: The Times-Transcript (35413)

Monday Morning Newspapers, Inc.
31201 Chicago Rd., Ste. A-101
Warren, MI 48093
Phone: (586)939-6800
Fax: (586)939-5850

Publications: Renaissance Times—New Center News (15661) • Tech Center News (15662) • U.S. Auto Scene (15663)

Mondovi Herald-News
123 W Main
PO Box 67
Mondovi, WI 54755
Phone: (715)926-4970
Fax: (715)926-4928

Publications: Mondovi Herald-News (34149)

Monetary Research Institute
PO Box 3174
Houston, TX 77253-3174
Phone: (713)827-1796
Fax: (713)827-8665

Publications: MRI Banker's Guide to Foreign Currency (30509)

Monett Newspapers, Inc.
505 E Broadway St.
Monett, MO 65708
Phone: (417)235-3135
Fax: (417)235-8852

Publications: Monett Times (17293)

Money Digest
1 Dundas St., W, Ste. 2500
Toronto, ON, Canada M5G 1Z3
Phone: (416)340-1722

Publications: Money Digest (36668)

Money Maker's Monthly
6827 W. 171st St.
Tinley Park, IL 60477
Phone: (708)633-8888
Fax: (708)633-8889

Publications: Money Maker's Monthly (9686)

Moneysaver
355 Union St.
PO Box 1
Randolph, MA 02368-0001
Phone: (781)963-8267

Publications: Moneysaver (14494)

Moneysaver Advertising, Inc.
218 N Main St.
PO Box I
Bolivar, NY 14715-0009
Phone: (716)928-2470
Fax: (716)928-2191

Publications: Moneysaver Shopping Guide (20235) • Moneysaver Shopping News (20236)

Mongolia Society Inc.
322 Goodbody Hall, 1011 E 3rd St.
Indiana University
Bloomington, IN 47405-7005
Phone: (812)855-4078
Fax: (812)855-7500

Publications: Mongolian Studies (9845)

Monitor
PO Box 279
140 Court House Square
Danielsville, GA 30633
Phone: (706)795-3102
Fax: (706)783-2553

Publications: Monitor (7227)

The Monitor
PO Box 5147
Trenton, NJ 08638-0147
Phone: (609)406-7404
Fax: (609)406-7423

Publications: The Monitor (19659)

Monitor
PO Box 330
Marietta, OK 73448-0330
Phone: (405)276-3255
Fax: (405)276-2118

Publications: Monitor (25904)

The Monitor
PO Box 39
Naples, TX 75568-0039
Phone: (903)897-2281
Fax: (903)897-2095

Publications: The Monitor (30855)

The Monitor
PB Box 123
Amelia Court House, VA 23002
Phone: (804)561-3655
Fax: (804)561-2065

Publications: Amelia Bulletin Monitor (31759)

The Monitor-Herald
PO Box 69
Calhoun City, MS 38916-0069
Phone: (662)628-5241
Fax: (662)628-4651

Publications: The Monitor-Herald (16582)

The Monitor Review
PO Box 276
Stacyville, IA 50476
Phone: (641)710-2119
Fax: (641)737-2119

Publications: The Monitor Review (11241)

Monkeyshines Publications
PO Box 10245
Greensboro, NC 27404
Phone: (336)292-6999

Publications: Monkeyshines on America (23928) • Monkeyshines on Health and Science (23929)

Monmouth College
700 E Broadway
Monmouth, IL 61462
Phone: (309)457-3456
Fax: (309)457-2363

Publications: The Courier (9213)

Monmouth University
400 Cedar Ave.
West Long Branch, NJ 07764-1898
Phone: (732)571-3481
Fax: (732)263-5151

Publications: The Outlook (19722)

Monroe County Advocate/Democrat
PO Box 389
Sweetwater, TN 37874
Phone: (423)337-7101
Fax: (423)337-3932

Publications: Monroe County Advocate/Democrat (29624)

Monroe County Beacon
103 E Ct. St.
PO Box 70
Woodsfield, OH 43793-0070
Phone: (740)472-0734
Fax: (740)472-0735
Free: 800-320-0177

Publications: Monroe County Beacon (25670)

Monroe County Citizen
301 N Main
Tompkinsville, KY 42167
Phone: (270)487-8666
Fax: (270)487-8666

Publications: Monroe County Citizen (12421)

Monroe County Press, Inc.
105 N Main St.
Tompkinsville, KY 42167-1599
Phone: (502)487-5576
Fax: (502)487-8839

Publications: Tompkinsville News (12422)

Monroe County Publishers, Inc.
1302 River Rd.
PO Box 252
Sparta, WI 54656
Phone: (608)269-3186
Fax: (608)269-6876

Publications: Monroe County Democrat (34331) •
The Sparta Herald (34332)

Monroe County Reporter
PO Box 795
Forsyth, GA 31029
Phone: (478)994-2358
Fax: (478)994-2359

Publications: Monroe County Reporter (7279)

Monroe County Sun
PO Box 711
Brinkley, AR 72021
Phone: (501)734-1056
Fax: (501)734-1494

Publications: Monroe County Sun (1079)

Monroe Monitor
113 W Main St.
PO Box 399
Monroe, WA 98272
Phone: (360)794-7116
Fax: (360)794-6202

Publications: Monroe Monitor/Valley News (32834)

Monroe Publishing Co.
20 W. 1st St.
Monroe, MI 48161
Phone: (734)242-1100

Publications: The Monroe Evening News/The Monroe Sunday News (15364)

Monroe Publishing, LLC
1065 4th Ave. W
PO Box 230
Monroe, WI 53566
Phone: (608)328-4202
Fax: (608)328-4217
Free: 800-236-2240

Publications: The Monroe Times (34151)

The Monroe Watchman
PO Box 179
Union, WV 24983
Phone: (304)772-3016
Fax: (304)772-4052

Publications: The Monroe Watchman (33479)

Monsters in Motion
181 W. Orangethorpe Ave., Ste. E
Placentia, CA 92870
Phone: (714)577-8863
Fax: (714)577-8865

Publications: Kit Builders Magazine (2847)

Montage Media Corp.
1000 Wyckoff Ave.
Mahwah, NJ 07430
Phone: (201)891-3200
Fax: (201)891-2626

Publications: The Journal of Practical Hygiene
(19198) • Practical Procedures & Aesthetic Dentistry
(19205)

Montague County Shopper
1300 E. Wise St.
Bowie, TX 76230-4521
Fax: (940)872-3559
Free: 800-972-7730

Publications: Ratite Marketplace (29941)

Montana Farm Bureau Federation
502 S 19th Ave., No. 104
Bozeman, MT 59718
Phone: (406)587-3153
Fax: (406)587-0319

Publications: Montana Farm Bureau Spokesman
(17753)

Montana Food Distributors Association
25 Neill Ave., Ste. 101
PO Box 5775
Helena, MT 59604
Phone: (406)449-6394
Fax: (406)449-0647

Publications: The Montana Food Distributor (17821)

Montana Historical Society
225 N. Roberts
PO Box 201201
Helena, MT 59620-1201
Phone: (406)444-2694
Fax: (406)444-2696
Free: 800-243-9900

Publications: Montana (17819)

Montana Land Magazine, Inc.
PO Box 1897
Billings, MT 59103
Phone: (406)259-3534
Fax: (406)259-1676

Publications: Montana Land Magazine (17732)

Montana Living Magazine
2700 Radio Way
Missoula, MT 59808
Phone: (406)541-4975
Fax: (406)541-4953

Publications: Montana Living (17837)

Montana Magazine
PO Box 5630
Helena, MT 59604
Phone: (406)443-2842
Fax: (406)443-5480
Free: 800-654-1105

Publications: Montana Magazine (17822)

Montana Standard
PO Box 627
Butte, MT 59703
Phone: (406)496-5500
Fax: (406)496-5551
Free: 800-877-1074

Publications: Montana Standard (17761)

Montana Tech of University of Montana
1300 W Park St.
Butte, MT 59701
Phone: (406)496-4241
Fax: (406)496-4702

Publications: Technocrat (17762)

Montana Trial Lawyers Associations
32 S. Ewing Ste. 312
PO Box 838
Helena, MT 59624
Phone: (406)443-3124
Fax: (406)449-6943

Publications: Trial Trends (17823)

The Montanian
PO Box 946
Libby, MT 59923
Phone: (406)293-8202

Publications: The Montanian (17851)

Montcalm Publishing Corp.
401 Park Ave. S., 3rd Fl.
New York, NY 10016-8802
Phone: (212)779-8900
Fax: (212)725-7215

Publications: Gallery Magazine (21746)

Montclair State University
Student Center Annex, Rm. 113
Upper Montclair, NJ 07043
Phone: (973)655-5169
Fax: (973)655-7804

Publications: The Montclarion (19693)

Monterey Peninsula Herald Co.
PO Box 271
Monterey, CA 93942
Phone: (831)372-3311
Fax: (831)646-4394
Free: 800-688-1808

Publications: The Monterey County Herald (2582)

The Montesano Vidette
PO Box 671
Montesano, WA 98563
Phone: (360)249-3311

Publications: The Montesano Vidette (32835)

Montevideo Publishing Co.
Box 736
223 1st St.
Montevideo, MN 56265
Phone: (320)269-2156
Fax: (320)269-2159

Publications: American News (16180)

Montezuma Republican
406 E Main St.
PO Box 100
Montezuma, IA 50171
Phone: (641)623-5116
Fax: (641)623-5580
Free: 800-936-5611

Publications: Montezuma Republican (11088)

Montfort Publications
26 S. Saxon Ave.
Bay Shore, NY 11706-8993
Phone: (631)665-0726
Fax: (631)665-4349

Publications: Queen of All Hearts (20137)

Montgomery Advertiser Corp.
PO Box 1000
Montgomery, AL 36101-1000
Phone: (334)365-6739
Fax: (334)365-1400

Publications: The Prattville Progress (376)

Montgomery Bar Association
100 W. Airy St.
PO Box 268
Norristown, PA 19404-0268
Phone: (610)279-9660
Fax: (610)279-4846

Publications: Montgomery County Law Reporter
(27336)

Montgomery College
Takoma Park Campus
7600 Takoma Ave.
Takoma Park, MD 20912
Phone: (301)650-1592
Fax: (301)650-1486

Publications: Excalibur (13725)

Montgomery Communications, Inc.
222 W. 6th St.
Junction City, KS 66441
Phone: (785)762-5000
Fax: (785)762-4584
Free: 800-657-6096

Publications: Daily Union (11519) • Daily Union
Extra (11520) • Fort Riley Post (11442) • Gypsum
Advocate (11476) • Lindsborg News-Record
(11611) • The Smoke Signal (11861)

Montgomery County Chronicle
202 W 4th St.
PO Box 186
Caney, KS 67333
Phone: (620)879-2156
Fax: (620)879-2855

Publications: Montgomery County Chronicle
(11374)

Montgomery County Community College
340 DeKalb Pke.
Blue Bell, PA 19422
Phone: (215)619-7306
Fax: (215)619-7191

Publications: The Advantage (26722)

Montgomery County Medical Society
40 S Perry St., Ste. 100
Dayton, OH 45402
Fax: (513)223-6363

Publications: Dayton Medicine (25114)

Montgomery County News
PO Box 250
Hillsboro, IL 62049
Phone: (217)532-3929
Fax: (217)532-3522
Free: 800-529-6397

Publications: Montgomery County News (8996)

Montgomery County News, Inc.
3063 Ft. Campbell Blvd.
Clarksville, TN 37042-3063
Phone: (931)431-3574
Fax: (931)431-5153

Publications: Montgomery County News (29115)

Montgomery County Sentinel Newspa-pers
PO Box 1272
Rockville, MD 20849-1272
Phone: (301)838-0788
Fax: (301)417-1210

Publications: Montgomery County Sentinel (13687)

The Montgomery Herald
406 Lee St.
PO Box 240
Montgomery, WV 25136
Phone: (304)442-4156
Fax: (304)442-8753

Publications: The Montgomery Herald (33386)

The Montgomery Journal Newspaper
5706 Frederick Ave.
Rockville, MD 20852-1818
Phone: (301)670-1400
Fax: (301)670-1421

Publications: The Montgomery Journal (13688)

Montgomery Newspapers
290 Commerce Dr.
Fort Washington, PA 19034
Phone: (215)542-0200
Fax: (215)548-3640

Publications: Parents Express (26933) • South Jersey Parents Express (26934)

Montgomery Newspapers
123 Chestnut St., 3rd Fl.
Philadelphia, PA 19106
Phone: (215)735-8444
Fax: (215)735-8535

Publications: City Paper (27405)

Montgomery Printing
524-526 S 16th St.
Philadelphia, PA 19146-1565
Phone: (215)546-1006
Fax: (215)735-3612

Publications: The Philadelphia Tribune (27633)

Montgomery Publishing
110 Ardmore Ave.
Ardmore, PA 19003
Phone: (610)896-9555
Fax: (610)896-9560

Publications: Main Line Life (26661)

Montgomery Publishing Inc.
PO Box 151
Winona, MS 38967
Phone: (662)283-1131
Fax: (662)283-5374
Free: 800-898-0694

Publications: Conservative (16879) • The Winona Times (16880)

Montgomery Standard
115 W. 2nd St.
Montgomery City, MO 63361-1812

Publications: Montgomery Standard (17296)

Monthly Review Press
122 W. 27th St.
New York, NY 10001
Phone: (212)691-2555
Fax: (212)727-3676
Free: 800-670-9499

Publications: Monthly Review (22364)

The Monticello Express
111 E Grand
PO Box 191
Monticello, IA 52310-0191
Phone: (319)465-3555
Fax: (319)465-4611
Free: 800-841-7172

Publications: The Monticello Express (11089)

Monticello Herald Journal
114 S Main St.
PO Box 409
Monticello, IN 47960-2328
Phone: (574)583-5121
Fax: (574)583-4241

Publications: Monticello Herald Journal (10320)

Monticello News
100 W Dogwood St.
PO Box 428
Monticello, FL 32344
Phone: (904)997-3568
Fax: (904)997-3774

Publications: Monticello News (6435)

The Monticello News
237 Washington St.
PO Box 30
Monticello, GA 31064-0030
Phone: (706)468-6511
Fax: (706)468-6576

Publications: The Monticello News (7445)

Monticello Times, Inc.
116 E. River St.
PO Box 420
Monticello, MN 55362
Phone: (763)295-3131
Fax: (763)295-3080

Publications: Monticello Shopper (16185) • Times (16186)

Montmorency County Tribune
PO Box 186
Atlanta, MI 49709
Phone: (517)785-4214
Fax: (517)785-3118

Publications: Montmorency County Tribune (14783)

Montpress, Inc.
PO Box 106
Forsyth, MT 59327
Phone: (406)356-2149

Publications: The Independent Enterprise (17790)

Montreal Policemen's Brotherhood Inc.—Fraternite des Policiers et Policieres de Montreal Inc
480 Gilford St.
Montreal, QC, Canada H2J 1N3
Phone: (514)527-4161
Fax: (514)527-7830

Publications: La Flute (37149)

Montreal Serai
PO Box 72
Succursale NDG
Montreal, QC, Canada H4A 3P4

Publications: Montreal Serai (37191)

Montrose Daily Press
535 S. 1st
PO Box 850
Montrose, CO 81402
Phone: (303)249-3444
Fax: (303)249-3331

Publications: Montrose Daily Press (4580)

Moody Bible Institute
820 N. LaSalle Blvd.
Chicago, IL 60610
Phone: (312)329-2164
Fax: (312)329-2149

Publications: Moody Magazine (8494)

Moody Co.
PO Box 796
Welsh, LA 70591
Phone: (318)734-2891
Fax: (318)734-4457

Publications: Welsh Citizen (12873)

Moody Lafayette Communications
PO Box AD
Kentwood, LA 70444
Fax: (504)229-8698

Publications: Louisiana News (12613)

Moore County News
30 Hiles St.
PO Box 500
Lynchburg, TN 37352
Phone: (931)759-7302

Publications: The Moore County News (29337)

Moore County Publishing, Co. L.L.C.
PO Box 757
Dumas, TX 79029
Phone: (806)935-4111
Fax: (806)935-2348

Publications: Moore County News-Press (30251)

Moore Marketing
719 Broad St.
Durham, NC 27705-4833
Phone: (919)477-4588
Fax: (919)477-6368

Publications: North Carolina Architecture (23837)

The Moore School of Business
University of South Carolina
Columbia, SC 29208
Phone: (803)777-2510
Fax: (803)777-9344

Publications: Business & Economic Review (28546)

The Moorefield Examiner
132 S Main St.
PO Box 380
Moorefield, WV 26836-0380
Phone: (304)538-2342
Fax: (304)538-7294

Publications: The Moorefield Examiner (33389)

Mooresville Tribune
147 E. Center Ave.
PO Box 300
Mooresville, NC 28115
Phone: (704)664-5554
Fax: (704)664-3614

Publications: Mooresville Tribune (24068)

Moorhead State University
Box 306
Moorhead, MN 56563-0001
Phone: (218)236-2204
Fax: (218)287-5086

Publications: Alumnews (16187) • Moorhead State University Advocate (16189)

Moorshead Magazines Ltd.
505 Consumers Rd., No. 500
Toronto, ON, Canada M2J 4V8
Phone: (416)491-3699
Fax: (416)491-3966
Free: 877-738-7624

Publications: Family Chronicle (36593) • Government Purchasing Guide (36608)

Moose International
155 S. International Dr.
Mooseheart, IL 60539-1174
Phone: (630)859-2000
Fax: (630)859-6620

Publications: Moose Magazine (9224)

Moose Jaw This Week
44 Fairford St. W.
Moose Jaw, SK, Canada S6H 1V1
Phone: (306)692-6441
Fax: (306)692-2101
Free: 800-665-4798

Publications: Moose Jaw This Week (37501)

The Moose Jaw Times-Herald
44 Fairford St. W.
Moose Jaw, SK, Canada S6H 1V1
Phone: (306)692-6441
Fax: (306)692-2101
Free: 800-655-4768

Publications: The Moose Jaw Times-Herald (37502)

Moose River Publishing
PO Box 449
St. Johnsbury, VT 05819
Phone: (802)748-8908
Fax: (802)748-1866
Free: 800-422-7147

Publications: TURF (31594)

Moosonee Freighter
550 Lamminen
Timmins, ON, Canada P4N 4R3
Phone: (705)268-4282
Fax: (705)268-4282

Publications: Moosonee Freighter (36455)

Moravia Union
PO Box 468
Moravia, IA 52571
Phone: (641)724-3224

Publications: Moravia Union (11090) • Moulton Tribune (11091)

Moravian Church in America
Interprovincial Board of Communication
PO Box 1245
Bethlehem, PA 18016
Phone: (610)867-0593
Fax: (610)866-9223
Free: 800-732-0591

Publications: Moravian (26704)

Moravian College
1200 Main St.
Box 13
Bethlehem, PA 18018-6650
Phone: (610)866-1682

Publications: The Comenian (26700)

The Morehead News
722 W 1st St.
Morehead, KY 40351
Phone: (606)784-4116
Fax: (606)784-7337

Publications: The Morehead News (12303)

Morehead State University Board of Student Publications
115-A Breckenridge Hall
Morehead, KY 40351
Phone: (606)783-2697
Fax: (606)783-9113

Publications: The Trail Blazer (12304)

The Morenci Observer
120 North St.
Morenci, MI 49256
Phone: (517)458-6811
Fax: (517)458-6811

Publications: The Morenci Observer (15369)

Morgan County Herald
89 W Main St.
Box 268
McConnelsville, OH 43756
Phone: (614)962-3377
Fax: (614)962-6861

Publications: Morgan County Herald (25369)

The Morgan County News
243 E. 125 N.
PO Box 190
Morgan, UT 84050
Phone: (801)829-3451
Fax: (801)829-4073

Publications: Morgan County News (31371)

The Morgan Messenger
PO Box 567
Berkeley Springs, WV 25411
Phone: (304)258-1800
Fax: (304)258-8441

Publications: The Morgan Messenger (33247)

Morgan Printing
402 Hill Ave.
Box 471
Grafton, ND 58237
Phone: (701)352-0640
Fax: (701)352-1502

Publications: The Record (24450)

Morgan Publishing Group
PO Box 1613
Bowie, TX 76230
Fax: (940)872-3559
Free: 800-972-7730

Publications: Exotic Market Review (29940)

Morinville Mirror
10123-100th Ave.
PO Box 1649
Morinville, AB, Canada T0G 1P0
Phone: (403)939-2133
Fax: (403)939-2425

Publications: Morinville Mirror (34816)

Morinville Mirror Publications
PO Box 1180
Redwater, AB, Canada T0A 2W0
Fax: (403)939-2425

Publications: Redwater Tribune (34838)

Moritz Publishing Co.
117 1st Ave., E
PO Box 189
Clark, SD 57225
Phone: (605)532-5343

Publications: Clark County Courier (28832)

Moritz Publishing, Inc.
PO Box 68
Faulkton, SD 57438
Phone: (605)598-6525
Fax: (605)598-4355

Publications: Faulk County Record (28854)

Morley Publishing Group, Inc.
1814 1/2 N St., NW
Washington, DC 20036
Phone: (202)861-7790
Fax: (202)861-7788

Publications: Crisis Magazine (5449)

Mormon Historical Studies
433 E 300 S
Hyrum, UT 84319
Phone: (435)245-3507
Fax: (435)245-3507

Publications: Mormon Historical Studies (31340)

The Morning Call
101 N. 6th St., No. 1260
Allentown, PA 18101-1403
Phone: (610)820-6500
Fax: (610)820-6617

Publications: The Morning Call (26629)

Morning Star Publishing Co.
311 E. Superior
PO Box 425
Alma, MI 48801
Phone: (989)463-6071
Fax: (989)463-3338
Free: 800-499-2976

Publications: Alma Reminder (14728) • Carson City Reminder (14729) • Clare County Buyers Guide (14730) • The Edmore Advertiser (14731) • Gladwin Buyers Guide (15079) • Hemlock Shoppers Guide (14732) • Midland Buyer's Guide (15378) • The Morning Sun (15379)

Morningside House Inc.
260 Oak St.
Dayton, OH 45410-1334
Phone: (937)461-6736
Fax: (937)461-4260
Free: 800-648-9710

Publications: The Gettysburg Magazine (25117)

Morningstar Inc.
225 W. Wacker Dr., Ste. 400
Chicago, IL 60606
Phone: (312)696-6000
Fax: (312)696-6001
Free: 800-735-0700

Publications: Mutual Funds (8498)

Morocco Courier
PO Box 298
Rensselaer, IN 47978
Phone: (219)866-5111
Fax: (219)866-3775

Publications: Morocco Courier (10413)

Morris Communication Corp.
PO Box 1440
Winter Haven, FL 33882-1440
Fax: (941)294-2008

Publications: Newschief (6869)

Morris Communications
410 S Liberty St.
PO Box 459
Independence, MO 64051
Phone: (816)254-8600
Fax: (816)836-3805

Publications: The Examiner (17110)

Morris Communications
PO Box 486
Bluffton, SC 29910
Fax: (803)837-5266

Publications: Hilton Head News (28497)

Morris Communications Corp.
PO Box 936
Augusta, GA 30903
Phone: (706)724-0851
Fax: (706)823-3440

Publications: Athens Banner Herald (6928) • Athens Magazine (6929) • Athens Star (6930) • Brainerd Daily Dispatch (7098) • The Florida Times-Union (6212) • Hillsdale Daily News (15163) • Juneau Empire (596) • The St. Augustine Record (6617)

Morris Communications Corp.
121 W. 6th St.
PO Box 268
Newton, KS 67114
Phone: (316)283-1500
Fax: (316)283-2471

Publications: Newton Kansan (11669)

Morris Communications Corp.
319 Walnut St.
PO Box 56
Yankton, SD 57078
Phone: (605)665-7811
Fax: (605)665-1721
Free: 800-743-2968

Publications: Yankton Daily Press & Dakotan (29040)

Morris Magazines
735 Broad St.
Augusta, GA 30901
Phone: (706)722-5833
Fax: (706)823-3641

Publications: Gray's Sporting Journal (7099) • SPUR MAGAZINE (7103)

Morris Newspapers, Inc.
PO Box 801870
Santa Clarita, CA 91380-1870
Phone: (661)259-1000
Fax: (661)284-6703

Publications: The Signal (3679)

Morris/Stauffer Communications, Inc.
1367 33rd Ave.
PO Box 1397
Columbus, NE 68602-1397
Phone: (402)564-1025
Fax: (402)564-1403
Free: 800-639-9932

Publications: Columbus Area Choice (17980)

The Morrisburg Leader Ltd.
PO Box 891
Morrisburg, ON, Canada K0C 1X0
Phone: (613)543-2987
Fax: (613)543-3643

Publications: The Leader (36096)

Morrison County Record
216 SE 1st St.
Little Falls, MN 56345
Phone: (320)632-2345
Fax: (320)632-2348
Free: 888-637-2345

Publications: Morrison County Record (16006)

Morrisons Cove Herald
113 N Market St.
Martinsburg, PA 16662-0165
Phone: (814)793-2144
Fax: (814)793-4882

Publications: Morrisons Cove Herald (27222)

Morrisonville Times
511 Carlin St.
PO Box 16
Morrisonville, IL 62546
Phone: (217)526-3323
Fax: (217)526-3323
Free: 888-880-6397

Publications: Morrisonville Times (9228)

Mortgage Bankers Association of America
1919 Pennsylvania Ave., NW
Washington, DC 20006-3438
Phone: (202)557-2700
Fax: (202)721-0245
Free: 800-793-MBAA

Publications: Mortgage Banking Magazine (5662)

Morton Tribune
PO Box 1016
Morton, TX 79346
Phone: (806)266-5576
Fax: (806)266-8841

Publications: Morton Tribune (30839)

Mortuary Times
77 Sussex Rd.
Clifton, NJ 07012
Phone: (201)779-7959

Publications: Mortuary Times (18756)

Mosaic
208 Tier Bldg.
The University of Manitoba
Winnipeg, MB, Canada R3T 2N2
Phone: (204)474-9763
Fax: (204)474-7584

Publications: Mosaic (35345)

Mosby
360 Park Ave. S
New York, NY 10010
Fax: (212)633-3913

Publications: Aesthetic Surgery Journal (21161) • JMPT: Journal of Manipulative and Physiological Therapeutics (21968) • Journal of AAPOS (American Association for Pediatric Ophthalmology and Strabismus) (21971) • The Journal of Thoracic and Cardiovascular Surgery (22205) • Journal of Vascular Surgery (22212) • Otolaryngology—Head and Neck Surgery (22508) • Surgery (22810)

Mosby
The Curtis Center, 3rd Fl.
Independence Sq. W
Philadelphia, PA 19106-3399
Phone: (215)235-7800
Fax: (215)238-7883
Free: 800-523-1649

Publications: American Heart Journal (27370) • Journal of the American Society of Echocardiography (27513) • Journal of Emergency Nursing (27527) • Journal of Nuclear Cardiology (27539)

Mosby
625 Walnut St.
Philadelphia, PA 19106
Phone: (215)238-7872

Publications: Heart and Lung (27479) • Journal of Pediatric Health Care (27543)

Mosby Inc.
10801 Executive Center Dr., Ste. 509
Little Rock, AR 72211
Phone: (501)223-5165
Fax: (501)223-0519

Publications: Air Medical Journal (1209) • AJIC (American Journal of Infection Control) (1210) • Geriatric Nursing (1230) • Nursing Outlook (1234)

Mosby Inc.
11830 Westline Industrial Dr.
St. Louis, MO 63146
Phone: (314)872-8370
Fax: (314)432-1380
Free: 800-325-4177

Publications: American Journal of Obstetrics and Gynecology (17410) • American Journal of Orthodontics and Dentofacial Orthopedics (17411) • Annals of Emergency Medicine (17414) • Breast Diseases (17418) • The Case Manager (1226) • Clini-

cal Pharmacology and Therapeutics (17423) • Current Problems in Cardiology (17427) • Current Problems in Dermatology (17428) • Current Problems in Obstetrics, Gynecology and Fertility (17429) • Current Problems in Pediatric and Adolescent Health Care (17430) • Disease-A-Month (17435) • Gastrointestinal Endoscopy (17440) • International Journal of Trauma Nursing (17447) • The Journal of Allergy and Clinical Immunology (17451) • Journal of the American Academy of Dermatology (17452) • Journal of the American Psychiatric Nurses Association (17453) • The Journal of Evidence-Based Dental Practice (17454) • The Journal of Laboratory and Clinical Medicine (17456) • The Journal of Pediatrics (17458) • The Journal of Prosthetic Dentistry (17460) • Journal of Shoulder and Elbow Surgery (17462) • Journal of Vascular Nursing (17463) • Journal of WOCN (Wound, Ostomy, and Continence Nursing) (17464) • Oral Surgery, Oral Medicine, Oral Pathology, Oral Radiology, and Endodontics (17480)

Moscow-Pullman Daily News
409 S. Jackson St.
Moscow, ID 83843
Phone: (208)882-5561
Fax: (208)883-8205

Publications: Daily News (7912)

The Mosinee Times
407 3rd St.
Mosinee, WI 54455-1495
Phone: (715)693-2300
Fax: (715)693-1574

Publications: The Mosinee Times (34155)

Mother Road Publications
PO Box 22068
Albuquerque, NM 87154

Publications: Atom Mind (19767)

Mother Wit Publishing Co.
PO Box 534
Ottumwa, IA 52501
Phone: (515)933-4241
Fax: (515)933-4341

Publications: New Sharon Star (11113)

Mothering Magazine Inc.
PO Box 1690
Santa Fe, NM 87504
Phone: (505)984-8116
Fax: (505)986-8335

Publications: Mothering Magazine (19936)

Motion Corporation
PO Box 21730
Carson City, NV 89721-1730
Phone: (775)246-9292
Fax: (775)246-9222

Publications: MOTION (18327)

Motley County Tribune
724 Dundee
PO Box 490
Matador, TX 79244
Phone: (806)347-2400
Fax: (806)347-2774

Publications: Motley County Tribune (30772)

Motor Information Systems
8009 Lea Rd.
Bloomington, MN 55438
Phone: (952)941-4623
Free: 800-417-MOTOR

Publications: Motor Magazine (15760)

Motor Transport Association of Connecticut, Inc.
60 Forest St.
Hartford, CT 06105
Phone: (860)520-4455
Fax: (860)520-4567

Publications: Motor Transport Association Bullitin (4898)

Motorcycle Events Association, Inc.
State Publishing Company
303 E. Sioux Ave.
PO Box 100
Pierre, SD 57501
Phone: (605)224-9999
Fax: (605)224-2063
Free: 800-675-4656

Publications: Motorcycle Events Magazine (28917)

The Motorcyclist's Post
11 Haven Ln.
Huntington, CT 06484
Phone: (203)929-9409
Fax: (203)926-9347

Publications: The Motorcyclist's Post (4918)

Motoring Road Magazine
PO Box M
Franklin, MA 02038-2960
Phone: (508)528-6211
Fax: (508)528-6211

Publications: Motoring Road Magazine (14206)

MotoVenture, Inc.
PO Box 90374
Austin, TX 78709-1931
Phone: (512)858-2313
Free: 877-858-2313

Publications: Ride Texas Magazine (29802)

Mott Community College
1401 E Ct. St.
Flint, MI 48503-2089
Phone: (810)762-0315
Fax: (810)762-0257

Publications: MCC Post (15037)

Moultrie Observer
PO Box 889
Moultrie, GA 31776-0889
Phone: (229)985-4545
Fax: (229)985-3569

Publications: Moultrie Observer (7446)

Mound City News
511 State St.
PO Box 175
Mound City, MO 64470
Phone: (660)442-5423
Fax: (660)442-5423

Publications: Mound City News (17298)

Moundsville Daily Echo
713 Lafayette Ave.
PO Box 369
Moundsville, WV 26041
Phone: (304)845-2660
Fax: (304)845-2661

Publications: Moundsville Daily Echo (33408)

Mount Airy Newspapers, Inc.
319 N Renfro St.
PO Box 808
Mount Airy, NC 27030-0808
Phone: (336)786-4141
Fax: (336)789-2816
Free: 800-826-NEWS

Publications: Mount Airy News (24079) • Simple Pleasures (24080) • Surry Scene (24081)

Mount Allison University
82 York St.
Sackville, NB, Canada E4L 1G2
Phone: (506)364-2345
Fax: (506)364-2262

Publications: Mount Allison Record (35426)

Mount Desert Island Biological Laboratory
PO Box 35
Old Bar Harbor Rd.
Salsbury Cove, ME 04672
Phone: (207)288-3605
Fax: (207)288-2130

Publications: MDIBL Bulletin (13048)

The Mount Forest Confederate
277 Main St. S
PO Box 130
Mount Forest, ON, Canada N0G 2L0
Phone: (519)323-1550
Fax: (519)323-4548

Publications: The Mount Forest Confederate (36097)

The Mount Hope Clearrn
101 S Ohio
PO Box 337
Mount Hope, KS 67108
Phone: (316)667-2697
Fax: (316)667-2406
Free: 800-794-3606

Publications: The Mount Hope Clarion (11661)

Mount Marty College
1105 W 8th St.
PO Box 564
Yankton, SD 57078
Phone: (605)668-1011

Publications: Moderator (29038)

Mount Olive College Press
634 Henderson St.
Administration Bldg.
Mount Olive, NC 28365
Phone: (919)658-2502
Fax: (919)658-7180

Publications: Mount Olive Review (24085)

Mount Olive Tribune
Hwy. 55 W
PO Box 1039
Mount Olive, NC 28365
Phone: (919)658-9456
Fax: (919)658-9559

Publications: Mount Olive Tribune (24086)

Mt. Pleasant Buyers Guide
711 W Pickard St.
PO Box 447
Mount Pleasant, MI 48804-0447
Phone: (517)779-6000
Fax: (517)779-6012
Free: 800-616-6397

Publications: Buyers Guide (15374)

Mount Pleasant News
215 W Monroe St.
PO Box 240
Mount Pleasant, IA 52641-0240
Phone: (319)385-3131

Publications: Mt. Pleasant News (11094)

Mount Pleasant Publishing Corp.
229 Pittsburgh St.
PO Box 222
Scottdale, PA 15683
Phone: (724)887-7400
Fax: (724)887-5115
Free: 800-640-6877

Publications: The Mount Pleasant Journal (27301)

Mt. Pulaski Weekly News
311 S Washington St.
PO Box 114
Mount Pulaski, IL 62548
Phone: (217)792-5557
Fax: (217)792-5482

Publications: Mt. Pulaski Weekly News (9251)

Mount Rose Publishing Co.
PO Box 2973
Truckee, CA 96160
Fax: (916)587-3763

Publications: The Sierra Sun (3950)

Mt. St. Vincent University
Rosario Centre 403
166 Bedford Hwy.
Halifax, NS, Canada B3M 2J6
Fax: (902)457-0444

Publications: The Picaro (35570)

Mt. San Antonio College
1100 N Grand Ave.
Walnut, CA 91789
Phone: (909)594-5611
Fax: (909)594-7661

Publications: The Mountaineer (4047)

Mt. Sinai School of Medicine
1 E 100th St.
Box 1094
New York, NY 10029-6574
Phone: (212)241-6108
Fax: (212)722-6386

Publications: The Mount Sinai Journal of Medicine (22373)

Mt. Sterling Advocate
40 S Bank St.
PO Box 406
Mount Sterling, KY 40353
Phone: (859)498-2222
Fax: (859)498-2228

Publications: Mt. Sterling Advocate (12311) • Mt. Sterling Advocate-Advertiser (12312)

Mt. Union College
1972 Clark Ave.
PO Box 1283
Alliance, OH 44601
Phone: (330)823-7183
Fax: (330)821-0425

Publications: The Dynamo (24604)

Mt. Vernon Signal
PO Box 185
Mount Vernon, KY 40456
Phone: (606)256-2244
Fax: (606)256-9526

Publications: Mt. Vernon Signal (12314)

The Mount Washington Valley Mountain Ear
PO Box 530
Conway, NH 03818
Phone: (603)447-6336
Fax: (603)447-5474

Publications: The Mount Washington Valley Mountain Ear (18483)

Mountain Bike Magazine
33 E. Minor St.
Emmaus, PA 18098
Phone: (610)967-5171
Fax: (610)967-7522

Publications: Mountain Bike Magazine (26878)

Mountain Democrat
1360 Broadway
PO Box 1088
Placerville, CA 95667
Phone: (530)622-1255
Fax: (530)622-7894

Publications: Mountain Democrat (2848)

The Mountain Eagle
357B Hazard Rd., Pky. Plz.
PO Box 808
Whitesburg, KY 41858-0808
Phone: (606)633-2252
Fax: (606)633-2843

Publications: The Mountain Eagle (12438)

The Mountain Eagle
140 Van Wagenen Ln.
Kingston, NY 12401-7839
Phone: (518)589-7007
Fax: (518)589-7028

Publications: The Mountain Eagle (20861)

Mountain Echo, Inc.
PO Box 224
Fall River Mills, CA 96028
Phone: (530)336-6262
Free: 800-327-6471

Publications: Mountain Echo (1911)

Mountain Echo/X-Tra
110 N Main St.
PO Box 25
Ironton, MO 63650-0025
Phone: (573)546-3917
Fax: (573)546-3919

Publications: Mountain Echo/X-Tra (17117)

The Mountain Enterprise
PO Box 610
Frazier Park, CA 93225-0610
Phone: (805)245-3794
Fax: (805)245-5620

Publications: The Mountain Enterprise (1936)

Mountain Meadows Publications
PO Box 1513
Asheville, NC 28802
Phone: (828)253-9299
Fax: (828)253-9299

Publications: This Week of Western North Carolina (23634)

Mountain Messenger
Drawer A
Downieville, CA 95936-0395
Phone: (916)289-3262
Fax: (916)289-3262

Publications: The Mountain Messenger (1837)

Mountain Messenger Newspaper
122 N Ct. St.
Lewisburg, WV 24901
Phone: (304)647-5724
Fax: (304)647-5767

Publications: Mountain Messenger Newspaper (33366)

Mountain News
PO Box 2410
Lake Arrowhead, CA 92352
Phone: (909)337-6145
Fax: (909)338-4449

Publications: Crestline Courier-News (2137)

Mountain Press Inc.
119 Riverbend Dr.
Sevierville, TN 37876
Phone: (865)428-0746
Fax: (865)453-4913

Publications: Mountain Press (29589)

Mountain Statesman
914 W Main St.
PO Box 218
Grafton, WV 26354
Phone: (304)265-3333
Fax: (304)265-3342

Publications: Mountain Statesman (33325)

The Mountain Sun
301 McFarland Rd.
Kerrville, TX 78028-4429
Phone: (512)257-3300
Fax: (512)257-3329

Publications: Kerrville Mountain Sun (30640)

Mountain Wave
103 E Main
PO Box 220
Marshall, AR 72650
Phone: (870)448-3321
Fax: (870)448-5659

Publications: Mountain Wave (1269)

The Mountaineer-Herald
113 S Ctr. St.
PO Box 359
Ebensburg, PA 15931-0359
Phone: (814)472-4110
Fax: (814)472-8600

Publications: The Mountaineer-Herald (26857)

Mountaineer Newspapers
PO Box
Buckhannon, WV 26201
Phone: (304)472-2800
Fax: (304)265-3342

Publications: The Senator (33305)

Mountaineer Progress
PO Box 290130
Phelan, CA 92329
Phone: (760)868-3245
Fax: (760)868-2700

Publications: Mountaineer Progress (2837)

The Mountaineer Publishing Co.
4814 49th St.
Rocky Mountain House, AB, Canada T4T 1S8
Phone: (403)845-3334
Fax: (403)845-5570

Publications: The Mountaineer (34839)

Mountaineer Publishing Co.
105 Main St.
Drawer 2040
Grundy, VA 24614
Phone: (276)935-2123
Fax: (276)935-2125

Publications: The Virginia Mountaineer (32121)

Numbers cited after listings are entry numbers rather than page numbers.

The Mountaineer Publishing Co., Inc.
PO Box 129
Waynesville, NC 28786
Phone: (828)452-0661
Fax: (828)452-0665

Publications: The Enterprise (24278) • Mid-Week Messenger (24279) • The Mountaineer (24280)

Mountaintop Eagle
85 S Main Rd.
PO Box 10
Mountain Top, PA 18707
Phone: (570)474-6397
Fax: (570)474-9272

Publications: Mountaintop Eagle (27304)

Mountaintop Publishing, Inc.
PO Box 27467
Denver, CO 80227-0467
Phone: (303)985-3034
Fax: (303)986-5664

Publications: Rocky Mountain Oyster & National Oyster Newspaper (4355)

Mouse River Journal
PO Box 268
Towner, ND 58788-0328
Phone: (701)537-5610
Fax: (701)537-5493

Publications: Mouse River Journal (24541)

MOUTH: Voice of the Disability Nation
4201 SW 30th St.
Topeka, KS 66614
Phone: (785)272-2578
Fax: (785)272-7348

Publications: MOUTH (11835)

Movieline, Inc.
10537 Santa Monica Blvd., Ste. 250
Los Angeles, CA 90025-4952
Phone: (310)234-9501
Fax: (310)234-0332

Publications: Movieline (2338)

Moville Record
PO Box AE
Moville, IA 51039
Phone: (712)873-3141
Fax: (712)873-3142

Publications: Moville Record (11101)

Moving To Magazines Ltd.
178 Main St.
Unionville, ON, Canada L3R 2G9
Phone: (905)479-0641
Fax: (905)479-1286
Free: (866)902-6683

Publications: Moving to Alberta (36830) • Moving to Montreal (36831) • Moving to Ottawa/Outaouais (36832) • Moving to Saskatchewan (36833) • Moving to Southwestern Ontario (36834) • Moving to Toronto (36835) • Moving to Vancouver & British Columbia (36836) • Moving to Winnipeg & Manitoba (36837)

Moxie Publishing
1307 Greenfield Ave.
Nashville, TN 37216
Phone: (615)227-9125
Fax: (615)227-1630

Publications: The Bird Online (29445)

MPC Publishing Co.
100 W Main St.
Marengo, IA 52301-1412
Phone: (319)444-2520
Fax: (319)642-5509

Publications: The Belle Plaine Union (11059) • South Benton Star-Press (11064)

MPG Newspapers
9 Long Pond Rd.
PO Box 959
Plymouth, MA 02362-0959
Phone: (508)746-5555
Fax: (508)747-6616

Publications: Carver Reporter (14122) • Duxbury Reporter (14163) • Halifax/Plympton Reporter (14224) • Kingston Reporter (14264) • Marshfield Reporter (14308) • Old Colony Memorial (14479) • Pembroke Reporter (14466) • The Sentinel (14481) • Wareham Courier (14482)

MPI Medical Publishing, Inc.
14 Ronan Ave.
Toronto, ON, Canada M4N 2X9
Phone: (416)481-6384
Fax: (416)483-9689

Publications: Geriatric Medicine Quarterly (36601)

MPL Communications Inc.
133 Richmond St., Ste. 700
Toronto, ON, Canada M5H 3M8
Phone: (416)869-1177
Fax: (416)869-0616

Publications: Investor's Digest of Canada (36625)

MPLS Central Labor Union Council
312 Central Ave., Ste. 526
Minneapolis, MN 55414-1077
Phone: (612)379-4725
Fax: (612)379-1307

Publications: Minneapolis Labor Review (16099)

MSA Publishing, Inc.
Box 3326
Leduc, AB, Canada T9E 6M1
Phone: (780)986-1787
Fax: (780)980-5303
Free: (866)986-1787

Publications: Prairie Hog Country (34793)

MSDN Magazine
PO Box 56621
Boulder, CO 80322-6621
Phone: (303)678-8475
Fax: (641)842-6101
Free: 800-666-1084

Publications: MSDN Magazine (4180)

MSM Productions, Ltd.
1095 Meigs St.
Rochester, NY 14620-2405
Phone: (585)442-6372
Fax: (716)442-6371

Publications: Deaf Life (23221)

MSP Airport News, Inc.
1698 Sims Ave.
St. Paul, MN 55106-3622
Phone: (612)726-5557
Fax: (612)726-5979

Publications: MSP Airport News (16399)

MSP Communications
220 S. 6th St., Ste. 500
Minneapolis, MN 55402-4507
Phone: (612)339-7571
Fax: (612)339-5806
Free: 800-788-0204

Publications: Computer User (16069) • MPLS.ST.PAUL (16112) • U.S. ART (16137)

MSP International, Inc.
405 Main St.
Port Washington, NY 11050
Phone: (516)944-7340
Fax: (516)944-8663

Publications: International Journal of Fertility and Women's Medicine (23129)

MT Publishing Co.
Box 99
Eston, SK, Canada S0L 1A0
Phone: (306)962-3221
Fax: (306)962-4445

Publications: The Eston Press Review (37467)

M2 Communications Inc.
108-93 Lombard Ave.
Winnipeg, MB, Canada R3B 3B1
Phone: (204)985-8160
Fax: (204)943-8991

Publications: What! A Magazine (35362)

Muenster Enterprise
PO Box 190
Muenster, TX 76252-0190
Phone: (940)759-4311
Fax: (940)759-4110

Publications: Muenster Enterprise (30844)

Mukluk News
PO Box 90
Tok, AK 99780
Phone: (907)883-2571

Publications: Mukluk News (644)

Mukwonago Publications
PO Box 204
Mukwonago, WI 53149
Phone: (262)363-4045
Fax: (262)363-8573

Publications: KMA Chief II (34157) • The Mukwonago Chief (34158) • Times-Record/Bulletin (34159)

Mules and More, Inc.
PO Box 460
Bland, MO 65014-0460
Phone: (573)646-3934
Fax: (573)646-3407

Publications: Mules and More (16906)

Muleshoe Journal
304 W 2nd St.
PO Box 449
Muleshoe, TX 79347
Phone: (806)272-4536
Fax: (806)272-3567

Publications: Bailey County Journal (30845) • Muleshoe and Baily County Journal (30846)

Mullac Publishing
1364 Walker Ave.
Baltimore, MD 21239
Phone: (410)323-3883

Publications: Flower of the Forest Black Genealogical Journal (13161)

Mullen Publications, Inc.
PO Box 241028
Charlotte, NC 28224
Phone: (704)527-5111
Fax: (704)527-5114
Free: 800-738-5111

Publications: Southern Textile News (23754)

The Mullens Advocate
217 Moran Ave.
Mullens, WV 25882
Phone: (304)294-4144

Publications: The Mullens Advocate (33410)

Multi-Vision Publishing, Inc.
655 Bay St., Ste. 1100
Toronto, ON, Canada M5G 2K4
Phone: (416)595-9944
Fax: (416)595-7217

Publications: Chirp (36549) • Health Watch Canada (36612) • Images (36621) • Owl Canadian Family (36694)

Multilingual Computing, Inc.
319 N First Ave.
Sandpoint, ID 83864
Phone: (208)263-8178
Fax: (208)263-6310
Free: 800-748-9824

Publications: MultiLingual Computing & Technology (7979)

Multimed Inc.
66 Martin St.
Milton, ON, Canada L9T 2R2
Phone: (905)875-2456
Fax: (905)875-2864
Free: 888-834-1001

Publications: Peritoneal Dialysis International (36050) • The Renal Family (36051)

MultiMedia HealthCare/Freedom, LLC
Office Ctr. at Princetown Meadows, Ste. 440
Plainsboro, NJ 08536
Phone: (609)275-3800
Fax: (609)275-6076

Publications: Home Healthcare Consultant (19441) • The Journal of Gender-Specific Medicine (19442)

MultiMedia Inc.
200 Washington Ave.
PO Box 1000
Montgomery, AL 36101-1000
Phone: (334)262-1611
Fax: (334)261-1591

Publications: The Montgomery Advertiser (369)

Multimedia Nova Corporation
101 Wingold Ave.
Toronto, ON, Canada M6B 1P8
Phone: (416)785-4300
Fax: (416)488-4918
Free: 877-503-5077

Publications: Corriere Canadese/Canadian Courier (36560)

The Multiracial Activist
PO Box 8208
Alexandria, VA 22306-8208
Phone: (760)875-8547
Fax: (760)875-8547

Publications: The Multiracial Activist (31712)

Mulvane News
204 W Main St.
PO Box 157
Mulvane, KS 67110
Phone: (316)777-4233

Publications: Bandwagon (11663) • The Mulvane News (11664)

Muncie Newspapers
PO Box 2408
Muncie, IN 47307-0408
Phone: (765)213-5700
Fax: (765)213-5937

Publications: The Star Press (10328)

The Munday Courier
111 E B St.
PO Box 130
Munday, TX 76371
Phone: (940)422-4314
Fax: (940)422-4333

Publications: The Munday Courier (30848)

Mundo Hispanico
PO Box 13808
Atlanta, GA 30324-0808
Phone: (404)881-0441
Fax: (404)881-6085

Publications: Mundo Hispanico (7029)

Mundo Hispano
2350 S Cicero Ave.
Cicero, IL 60804-2469
Phone: (708)780-8808
Fax: (708)780-8818

Publications: Mundo Hispano (8675)

Mundo Medico USA, Inc
158 Danbury Rd., Ste. 8
Ridgefield, CT 06877-3200
Phone: (203)438-1056
Fax: (203)438-1057

Publications: Medicina Y Cultura (5098)

Municipal World Inc.
PO Box 399
Station Main
St. Thomas, ON, Canada N5P 3V3
Phone: (519)633-0031
Fax: (519)633-1001
Free: 888-368-6125

Publications: Municipal World (36362)

Munro Enterprises
151 Main St.
PO Box 38
Berlin, NH 03570-0038
Phone: (603)752-1200

Publications: Berlin Reporter (18455)

Murphy McGinnis Media, Inc.
PO Box 757
Grand Marais, MN 55604
Phone: (218)387-1025
Fax: (218)387-2539
Free: 800-781-1025

Publications: Cook County News-Herald (15926)

Murphy McGinnis Media, Inc.
301 1st Ave. NW
PO Box 220
Grand Rapids, MN 55744
Phone: (218)326-6623
Fax: (218)326-6627
Free: 888-515-6623

Publications: Herald-Review (15928) • Itasca Shopper (15929)

Murphy McGinnis Media, Inc.
704 7th Ave. S.
Virginia, MN 55792
Phone: (218)741-5544
Fax: (218)741-1005

Publications: Mesabi Daily News (16485)

Murphy McGinnis Media, Inc.
122 3rd St. W.
Ashland, WI 54806-1620
Phone: (715)682-2313
Fax: (715)682-4699

Publications: The Daily Press (33554)

Murphy McGinnis Media, Inc.
156173 Hwy. 63 N
PO Box 191
Hayward, WI 54843
Phone: (715)634-4881
Fax: (715)634-4191

Publications: Four Seasons Shopper (33784) • Sawyer County Record (33786)

Murphy McGinnis Media, Inc.
259 2nd Ave. N.
Park Falls, WI 54552-1217
Phone: (715)762-4940
Fax: (715)762-2757

Publications: The Park Falls Herald (34233)

Murphy McGinnis Media Inc.
115 N. Lake Ave.
Phillips, WI 54555
Phone: (715)339-3036
Fax: (715)339-4300

Publications: The Bee (34237) • The Extra Shopper (34238)

Murphy McGinnis Media, Inc.
509 Front St.
PO Box 338
Spooner, WI 54801
Phone: (715)635-2181
Fax: (715)635-2186

Publications: The Evergreen Shopping Guide (34336) • Spooner Advocate (34337)

The Murray Hill News Corp.
237 Madison Ave.
New York, NY 10016
Phone: (212)684-6728

Publications: Murray Hill News (22383)

Murray Ledger and Times
1001 Whitnell Ave.
Box 1040
Murray, KY 42071
Phone: (270)753-1916
Fax: (270)753-1927

Publications: Murray Ledger and Times (12316)

Murray Printing Co.
PO Box 57068
Salt Lake City, UT 84157-0068
Phone: (801)262-8091

Publications: West Valley Eagle (31486)

Murray State University
Murray, KY 42071
Phone: (270)762-4284
Fax: (270)762-5478

Publications: Journal of Business and Public Affairs (12315)

Murray State University
PO Box 9
Murray, KY 42071
Phone: (502)762-2998
Fax: (502)762-3175
Free: 800-272-4MSU

Publications: The Murray State News (12317)

Murrayville Gazette
208 Main
Franklin, IL 62638
Phone: (217)675-2461

Publications: Murrayville Gazette (9023)

Muscatine Journal
301 E 3rd St.
Muscatine, IA 52761
Phone: (319)263-2331
Fax: (319)262-8042
Free: 800-383-3198

Publications: Classic Images (11102) • Muscatine Journal (11103)

Muscular Dystrophy Association, Inc.
3300 E. Sunrise Dr.
Tucson, AZ 85718
Phone: (520)529-2000
Fax: (520)529-5300
Free: 800-572-1717

Publications: Quest (960)

Museum of American Financial History
26 Broadway
Room 947
New York, NY 10004
Phone: (212)908-4695
Fax: (212)908-4601
Free: 877-98-FINANCE

Publications: Financial History (21696)

Museum of Early Southern Decorative Arts
PO Box 10310
Winston-Salem, NC 27108-0310
Phone: (336)721-7360
Fax: (336)721-7367

Publications: Journal of Early Southern Decorative Arts (24319)

Museum of Modern Art
11 W. 53rd St.
New York, NY 10019
Phone: (212)557-0230
Fax: (212)333-6575

Publications: MoMA Magazine (22359)

Mushroom the Journal
1511 E. 54th St.
Chicago, IL 60615
Phone: (773)288-2873

Publications: Mushroom the Journal (8497)

Music Association of San Diego County
1717 Morena Blvd.
San Diego, CA 92110
Phone: (619)276-4324
Fax: (619)276-4876

Publications: American Federation of Musicians (3110)

Music Connection Inc.
4215 Coldwater Canyon
Studio City, CA 91604
Phone: (818)755-0101
Fax: (818)755-0102

Publications: Music Connection Magazine (3822)

Music Library Association
8551 Research Way, Ste. 180
Middleton, WI 53562
Phone: (608)836-5825
Fax: (608)831-8200

Publications: Notes (34052)

Music Maker Publications, Inc.
5412 Idylwild Trl., Ste. 100
Boulder, CO 80301
Phone: (303)516-9118
Fax: (303)516-9119

Publications: Recording (4186)

The Music Paper
PO Box 5167
Bay Shore, NY 11706
Fax: (516)666-7445

Publications: The Music Paper (20136)

The Music Player Group
2800 Campus Dr.
San Mateo, CA 94403
Phone: (650)513-4300
Fax: (650)513-4642

Publications: Bass Player (3583)

Music Teachers National Association
The Carew Tower
441 Vine St., Ste. 505
Cincinnati, OH 45202-2811
Phone: (513)421-1420
Fax: (513)421-2503
Free: 888-512-5278

Publications: American Music Teacher (24771)

Music Trades Corp.
80 West St.
Englewood, NJ 07631
Phone: (201)871-1965
Fax: (201)871-0455
Free: 800-423-6530

Publications: Music Trades (18796)

Musicians Union Local 6
116 Ninth St.
San Francisco, CA 94103
Phone: (415)575-0777
Fax: (415)863-6173

Publications: Musical News (3393)

Musicworks
179 Richmond St. W.
Toronto, ON, Canada M5V 1V3
Phone: (416)977-3546
Fax: (416)204-1084

Publications: Musicworks Magazine (36671)

The Muskegon Chronicle & The Sunday Chronicle
981 3rd St.
PO Box 59
Muskegon, MI 49443
Phone: (616)722-3161
Fax: (616)728-3330
Free: 800-783-3161

Publications: The Muskegon Chronicle & The Sunday Chronicle (15388)

Muskingum College
163 Stormont St.
New Concord, OH 43762
Phone: (740)826-8296
Fax: (740)826-8404

Publications: Black and Magenta (25409)

The Muskoka Sun Ltd.
PO Box 1600
Bracebridge, ON, Canada P1L 1V6
Phone: (705)645-4463
Fax: (705)645-3928

Publications: Muskoka Advance (35695)

The Muskokan
16 Manitoba St.
PO Box 1049
Bracebridge, ON, Canada P1L 1V2
Phone: (705)645-8771
Fax: (705)645-1718

Publications: The Muskokan (35696)

Musky Hunter Magazine
7978 Hwy., 70 E.
PO Box 340
St. Germain, WI 54558
Phone: (715)477-2178
Fax: (715)477-8858
Free: 800-236-8758

Publications: Musky Hunter (34312)

Muslim Journal Enterprises, Inc.
929 W 171st. St.
Hazel Crest, IL 60429-1901
Phone: (708)647-9600
Fax: (708)647-0754
Free: 800-837-8402

Publications: Muslim Journal (8980)

Muttmatchers Messenger
PO Box 1165
Enumclaw, WA 98022
Phone: (360)825-0741

Publications: Muttmatchers Messenger (32755)

Mycological Society of America
PO Box 1897
Lawrence, KS 66044-8897

Publications: Mycologia (11564)

MyFamily.com, Inc.
360 W. 4800 North
Provo, UT 84604
Phone: (801)705-7000
Fax: (801)705-7001
Free: 800-262-3787

Publications: Genealogical Computing (31403)

Myron J. Biggar Group, Inc.
PO Box 239
65 S. Broad St.
Nazareth, PA 18064-0239
Phone: (610)759-0406
Fax: (610)759-0223

Publications: O Guage Railroading (27311)

Myrtle Point Herald
408 Spruce
PO Box 606
Myrtle Point, OR 97458-0128
Phone: (541)572-2717
Fax: (541)572-2828

Publications: Myrtle Point Herald (26442)

Mystery Readers International
Box 8116
Berkeley, CA 94707-8116
Phone: (510)845-3600
Fax: (510)845-1975

Publications: Mystery Readers Journal (1544)

The Mystery Review
PO Box 233
Colborne, ON, Canada K0K 1S0
Phone: (613)475-4440
Fax: (613)475-3400

Publications: The Mystery Review (35747)

Mystic Seaport Museum Inc.
75 Greenmanville Ave.
PO Box 6000
Mystic, CT 06355-0990
Phone: (860)572-0711
Fax: (860)572-5348

Publications: Log of Mystic Seaport (4968)

Mythos Institute
PO Box 130
Frontenac, MN 55026-0130
Phone: (612)345-5488

Publications: Mythos Journal (15913)

The N C Catholic
715 Nazareth St.
Raleigh, NC 27606
Phone: (919)821-9700
Fax: (919)821-9705

Publications: The N C Catholic (24139)

NA'AMAT USA
350 5th Ave., Ste. 4700
New York, NY 10118-4700
Phone: (212)563-5222
Fax: (212)563-5710

Publications: NA'AMAT WOMAN (22390)

NAC International
655 Engineering Dr., Ste. 200
Norcross, GA 30092-2843
Phone: (770)447-1144
Fax: (770)447-1797

Publications: NAC Focus (7468)

NACE International
1440 S. Creek Dr.
Houston, TX 77084
Phone: (281)228-6200
Fax: (281)228-6300

Publications: Corrosion (30466) • Materials Performance (30506)

NACLA Report on the Americas
38 Greene St., 4th Fl.
New York, NY 10013
Phone: (646)613-1440
Fax: (646)613-1443

Publications: NACLA Report on the Americas (22391)

NADIG Newspapers, Inc.
4937 N Milwaukee Ave.
Chicago, IL 60630
Phone: (773)286-6100

Publications: Chicago's Northwest Side Press (8330) • Edgebrook Reporter (8359) • Journal (8427)

Nanaimo Daily News
2575 McCullough Rd., Ste. B1
Nanaimo, BC, Canada V9S 5W5
Phone: (250)729-4200
Fax: (250)729-4256

Publications: Nanaimo Daily News (35020)

Nance County Journal
416 4th
PO Box 10
Fullerton, NE 68638
Phone: (308)536-3100
Fax: (308)536-3100

Publications: Nance County Journal (18015)

Nantucket Journal, Inc.
2 Greglen Ave., Ste. 408
Nantucket, MA 02554
Phone: (508)228-8700
Fax: (508)228-9063

Publications: Nantucket Magazine (14341)

The Napa Valley Register
1615 2nd St.
PO Box 150
Napa, CA 94559
Phone: (707)226-3711
Fax: (707)224-3963

Publications: The Napa Valley Register (2611)

Napanee Beaver Publishers
72 Dundas St. E.
Napanee, ON, Canada K7R 1H9
Phone: (613)354-6641
Fax: (613)354-2622

Publications: Napanee Beaver (36098) • Picton Gazette (36329)

Naples Guide
947 4th Ave. S
Naples, FL 34102
Phone: (239)262-6524
Fax: (239)262-3468

Publications: Naples Guide (6446)

NAPM-Carolinas-Virginia
2300 W Meadowvies Rd. Ste. 117
Greensboro, NC 27407
Phone: (336)292-9228
Fax: (336)292-8415

Publications: Southern Purchaser (23940)

Napoleon, Inc.
595 E. Riverview
PO Box 567
Napoleon, OH 43545
Phone: (419)592-5055
Fax: (419)592-9778

Publications: Northwest Signal (25402) • Spotlite (25403)

Napoleon St. Cyr
PO Box 664
Stratford, CT 06615
Phone: (203)378-4066

Publications: Small Pond Magazine of Literature (5172)

Narayana Gurukula
8311 Quail Hill Rd.
Bainbridge Island, WA 98110

Publications: Gurukulam (32658)

NARSA
PO Box 97
East Greenville, PA 18041
Phone: (215)541-4500
Fax: (215)679-4977
Free: 800-551-3232

Publications: Automotive Cooling Journal (26846)

NASA Aviation Safety Reporting System
PO Box 189
Moffett Field, CA 94035-0189
Phone: (650)604-5000

Publications: ASRS Directline (2573) • Callback (2574)

Nashoba Publications, Inc.
69 Fitchburg Rd.
Ayer, MA 01432-0362
Phone: (978)772-0777
Fax: (978)772-4012
Free: 800-445-5635

Publications: Fort Devens Dispatch (13828) • The Public Spirit (13829) • Times-Free Press (14467)

Nashua Reporter and Weekly Post
216 Main St.
PO Box 67
Nashua, IA 50658
Phone: (641)435-4151

Publications: Nashua Reporter and Weekly Post (11107)

The Nashvile News
PO Box 297
Nashville, AR 71852
Phone: (870)845-2010

Publications: The Nashville News (1294)

Nashville Business Journal
344 Fourth Ave. N, Ste. 610
Nashville, TN 37219
Phone: (615)248-2222
Fax: (615)248-6246

Publications: Nashville Business Journal (29472)

The Nashville Graphic
203 W Washington St.
PO Box 1008
Nashville, NC 27856
Phone: (252)459-7101
Fax: (252)459-3052

Publications: The Nashville Graphic (24094)

Nasinec
206 E Davilla St.
Box 636
Granger, TX 76530
Phone: (512)859-2238

Publications: Nasinec (30409)

NaSPA
7044 S. 13th St.
Oak Creek, WI 53154-1429
Phone: (414)768-8000
Fax: (414)768-8001

Publications: Technical Support (34199)

Nassau Border Papers, Inc.
PO Box 227
Floral Park, NY 11002
Phone: (516)775-7700

Publications: The Floral Park Bulletin (20603) • The Gateway (20605)

Nassau Border Papers, Inc.
PO Box 155
Franklin Square, NY 11010
Phone: (516)775-7700

Publications: The Franklin Square Bulletin (20619)

Nassau Community College, State University of New York
1 Education Dr.
Garden City, NY 11530
Phone: (516)572-7792

Publications: Nassau Review (20644)

Nassau Community Newspaper Group
42 Broadway, Ste. 202
Lynbrook, NY 11563
Phone: (516)599-5400
Fax: (516)599-3535

Publications: East Rockaway/Lynbrook Observer (20973) • Long Beach Independent Voice (20974) • Lynbrook USA (20975) • The MAILeader (20976) • Malverne Times (20983) • Rockville Centre News and Owl (23262)

Nassau County Record
PO Box 609
Callahan, FL 32011
Phone: (904)879-2727
Fax: (904)879-5155

Publications: Nassau County Record (5970)

Nassau Inc.
Princeton University
Armory Bldg., Washington Rd.
Princeton, NJ 08544
Phone: (609)258-1899
Fax: (609)258-7883

Publications: Nassau Weekly (19465)

Nassau & Queens Publications
26 Jericho Tpke.
Jericho, NY 11753
Phone: (516)333-7400
Fax: (516)334-4055

Publications: Merrick/Bellmore South Shopper's Guide (20740) • Oceanside/Island Park Shopper's Guide (20743) • Rockville Centre Shopper's Guide (20745)

Natchez Democrate Inc.
300 N Fanisha
PO Box 3708
Jackson, MS 39207
Phone: (601)948-4122
Fax: (601)948-4125

Publications: Jackson Advocate (16696)

Natchez Newspapers, Inc.
PO Box 1447
Natchez, MS 39121
Phone: (601)442-9101
Fax: (601)442-7315

Publications: Miss-Lou Guide (16792) • The Natchez Democrat (16793)

Natchitoches Times Publications
PO Box 448
Natchitoches, LA 71458
Phone: (318)352-3618
Fax: (318)352-7842

Publications: The Interstate Progress (12667) • The Natchitoches Times (12718)

NatCom Inc.
15115 S 76th East Ave.
Bixby, OK 74008-4114

Publications: Bassin' (25762) • Crappie (25764)

The Nation
33 Irving Pl., 8th Fl.
New York, NY 10003
Phone: (212)209-5400
Fax: (212)982-9000
Free: 800-333-8536

Publications: The Nation (22395)

National Academy of Engineering
2101 Constitution Ave. NW
Washington, DC 20418
Phone: (202)334-1628
Fax: (202)334-1563

Publications: The Bridge (5383)

National Academy of Sciences
2101 Constitution Ave. NW, NAS 340
NAS 340
Washington, DC 20418
Phone: (202)334-2679
Fax: (202)334-2739

Publications: Proceedings of the National Academy of Sciences of the United States of America (5731)

National Ad Search, Inc.
PO Box 2083
Milwaukee, WI 53201
Phone: (414)351-1398
Fax: (414)351-0836
Free: 800-992-2832

Publications: National Ad Search (34090)

National Affairs, Inc.
1112 16th St. NW, Ste. 140
Washington, DC 20036
Phone: (202)785-8555

Publications: The Public Interest (5750)

National Agricultural Aviation Association
1005 E St. SE
Washington, DC 20003
Phone: (202)546-5722
Fax: (202)546-5726

Publications: Agricultural Aviation (5316)

National Alliance of Postal and Federal Employees
1628 11th St. NW
Washington, DC 20001
Phone: (202)939-6325
Fax: (202)939-6389

Publications: National Alliance (5668)

National Apostolate for Inclusion Ministry
PO Box 218
Riverdale, MD 20738-0218
Phone: (301)699-9500
Fax: (240)220-8374
Free: 800-736-1280

Publications: National Apostolate for Inclusion Ministry Quarterly (13673)

The National Archives & Records Admin.
8601 Adelphi Rd.
National Archives & Records Admin.
College Park, MD 20740-6001
Phone: (301)837-0482
Free: (866)272-6272

Publications: Federal Register Index (13417)

National Archives and Records Administration
8601 Adelphi Rd.
College Park, MD 20740-6001
Phone: (301)837-1850
Fax: (301)837-0319
Free: (866)272-6272

Publications: Prologue (13438)

National Art Education Association
1916 Association Dr.
Reston, VA 20190
Phone: (703)860-8000
Fax: (703)860-2960
Free: 800-299-8321

Publications: Art Education (28070) • Studies in Art Education (6736)

National Association of Attorneys General
750 1st St. NE, Ste. 1100
Washington, DC 20002
Phone: (202)326-6018
Fax: (202)408-6998

Publications: National Environmental Enforcement Journal (5670)

National Association of Biology Teachers
12030 Sunrise Valley Dr., Ste. 110
Reston, VA 20191
Phone: (703)264-9696
Fax: (703)264-7778
Free: 800-406-0775

Publications: The American Biology Teacher (32359)

National Association of Black Accountants, Inc.
7249-A Hanover Pkwy.
Greenbelt, MD 20770
Phone: (301)474-6222
Fax: (301)474-3114

Publications: Spectrum (Greenbelt) (13560)

National Association of Black Journalists
8701A Adelphi Rd.
Adelphi, MD 20783-1716
Phone: (301)445-7100
Fax: (301)445-7101

Publications: NABJ Journal (13088)

National Association for Business Economics
1233 20th St., Ste. 505
Washington, DC 20036
Phone: (202)463-6223
Fax: (202)463-6239

Publications: Business Economics (5390) • Nabe News (5666) • Nabe Quarterly Surveys (5667) • Salary Survey (5775)

National Association of Business Travel Agents
3699 Wilshire Blvd., Ste. 700
Los Angeles, CA 90010-2726
Phone: (213)382-3335

Publications: First Class Executive Travel (2270)

National Association for Campus Activities
13 Harbison Way
Columbia, SC 29212
Phone: (803)732-6222
Fax: (803)749-1047

Publications: Programming Magazine (28563)

National Association of Chiefs of Police
3801 Biscayne Blvd.
Miami, FL 33137
Phone: (321)264-0911
Fax: (321)264-0033
Free: 800-527-1517

Publications: The Chief of Police (6345)

National Association of College Auxiliary Services
PO Box 5546
Charlottesville, VA 22905
Phone: (434)245-8425
Fax: (434)245-8453

Publications: College Services (31925)

National Association of College & University Attorneys (NACUA)
One Dupont Circle NW, Ste. 620
Washington, DC 20036

Publications: Journal of College and University Law (10369)

National Association of Colleges and Employers
62 Highland Ave.
Bethlehem, PA 18017
Phone: (610)868-1421
Fax: (610)868-0208
Free: 800-544-5272

Publications: Journal of Career Planning & Employment (26701)

National Association of Congregational Christian Churches
8473 S. Howell Ave.
Oak Creek, WI 53154
Phone: (414)764-1620
Fax: (414)764-0319
Free: 800-262-1620

Publications: The Congregationalist (25331)

National Association of Counties
440 1st St., NW
Washington, DC 20001-2082
Phone: (202)393-6226
Fax: (202)393-2630

Publications: County News (5445)

National Association of Credit Management
8840 Columbia 100 Pkwy.
Columbia, MD 21045
Phone: (410)740-5560
Fax: (410)740-5574
Free: 800-955-8815

Publications: Business Credit (13455)

National Association of the Deaf
814 Thayer Ave.
Silver Spring, MD 20910-4500
Phone: (301)587-1788
Fax: (301)587-1791

Publications: NADmag (13741)

National Association of Disability Examiners
1117 Sunshine Dr.
Aurora, MO 65605
Phone: (417)888-4152
Fax: (417)888-4069
Free: 800-584-4305

Publications: The NADE Advocate (16895)

National Association for the Education of Young Children
1509 16th St. NW
Washington, DC 20036-1426
Phone: (202)232-8777
Fax: (202)328-1846
Free: 800-424-2460

Publications: Young Children (5873)

National Association of Educational Buyers, Inc. (NAEB)
450 Wireless Blvd.
Hauppauge, NY 11788
Phone: (631)273-2600
Fax: (631)952-3660

Publications: NAEB Journal (20719)

National Association of Electrical Distributors, Inc.
1100 Corporate Square Dr., Ste. 100
St. Louis, MO 63132
Phone: (314)991-9000
Fax: (314)991-3090
Free: 888-791-2512

Publications: TED The Electrical Distributor Magazine (17521)

National Association of Elementary School Principals
1615 Duke St.
Alexandria, VA 22314-3483
Phone: (703)684-3345
Fax: (703)548-6021
Free: 800-386-2377

Publications: Principal (31725)

National Association of Enrolled Agents
200 Orchard Ridge Dr., No. 302
Gaithersburg, MD 20878-1978
Phone: (301)212-9608
Fax: (301)990-1611

Publications: EA Journal (13537)

National Association of Federal Credit Unions (NAFCU)
PO Box 3769
Washington, DC 20007
Phone: (703)522-4770
Fax: (703)524-1082
Free: 800-336-4644

Publications: The Federal Credit Union (31793)

National Association of Fire Equipment Distributors
104 S Michigan Ave., Ste. 300
Chicago, IL 60603
Phone: (312)263-8100
Fax: (312)263-8111

Publications: Firewatch! (8377)

National Association of Fleet Administrators Inc.
100 Wood Ave. S., Ste. 310
Iselin, NJ 08830-2716
Phone: (732)494-8100
Fax: (732)494-6789

Publications: NAFA Fleet Executive (19126)

National Association of Forensic Economists
PO Box 30067
Kansas City, MO 64112
Phone: (816)235-2833

Publications: Journal of Forensic Economics (17174)

National Association for Gifted Children
1707 L St. NW, No. 550
Washington, DC 20036
Phone: (202)785-4268
Fax: (202)785-4248

Publications: Gifted Child Quarterly (5515) • Parenting for High Potential (5715)

National Association for Healthcare Quality
4700 W Lake Ave.
Glenview, IL 60025
Fax: 877-218-7939
Free: 800-966-9392

Publications: Journal for Healthcare Quality (8938)

National Association of Home Builders
1201 15th St., NW
Washington, DC 20005-2800
Fax: (202)866-8195
Free: 800-368-5242

Publications: Sales & Marketing Ideas (5776) • Seniors' Housing News (5789)

National Association for Home Care
228 Seventh St., SE
Washington, DC 20003
Phone: (202)547-7424
Fax: (202)547-3540

Publications: Caring (5394) • Caring People (5395)

National Association of Housing and Redevelopment Officials
630 I St. NW
Washington, DC 20001-3736
Phone: (202)289-3500
Fax: (202)289-8181
Free: 877-866-2476

Publications: Journal of Housing and Community Development (5596)

National Association of Human Rights Workers
115 S. Andrews Ave., No. A-640
Fort Lauderdale, FL 33301
Phone: (954)357-6046
Fax: (954)357-5746

Publications: Journal of Intergroup Relations (29463)

National Association for Humane and Environmental Education
PO Box 362
East Haddam, CT 06423
Phone: (860)434-8666
Fax: (860)434-9579

Publications: KIND News (4777)

National Association of Insurance Commissioners
2301 McGee St., Ste. 800
Kansas City, MO 64108-2662
Phone: (816)842-3600
Fax: (816)783-8175

Publications: Journal of Insurance Regulation (33953)

National Association of Insurance and Financial Advisors
2901 Telestar Ct.
Falls Church, VA 22042
Phone: (703)770-8100
Fax: (703)770-8212
Free: 800-247-4074

Publications: Advisor Today (32039)

National Association of Insurance Women (International)
1847 E. 15th St.
Tulsa, OK 74104-4610
Phone: (918)744-5195
Fax: (918)743-1968
Free: 800-766-NAIW

Publications: Today's Insurance Woman (26134)

National Association of Investors Corp.
711 W. 13 Mile Rd.
Madison Heights, MI 48071
Phone: (248)583-6242
Fax: (248)583-4880
Free: 877-275-6242

Publications: Better Investing (15326)

National Association of Letter Carriers
100 Indiana Ave. NW
Washington, DC 20001-2144
Phone: (202)393-4695

Publications: Postal Record (5724)

National Association of Mutual Insurance Companies
3601 Vincennes Rd.
Indianapolis, IN 46268
Phone: (317)875-5250
Fax: (317)879-8408

Publications: NAMIC National Affairs Insider (10155) • Property/Casualty Insurance (10163) • Property/Casualty Insurance Magazine (10164)

National Association of Orthopaedic Nurses
E. Holly Ave. Box 56
Pitman, NJ 08071-0056
Phone: (609)256-2310
Fax: (609)589-7463

Publications: Orthopaedic Nursing (19438)

National Association of Pastoral Musicians
962 Wayne Ave., Ste. 210
Silver Spring, MD 20910-4461
Phone: (240)247-3000
Fax: (240)247-3001

Publications: Pastoral Music (13743)

National Association of Postmasters
8 Herbert St.
Alexandria, VA 22305-2600
Phone: (703)683-9027
Fax: (703)683-6820

Publications: Postmasters Gazette (32027)

National Association of Power Engineers
One Springfield St.
Chicopee, MA 01013-2624
Phone: (413)592-6273
Fax: (413)592-1998

Publications: National Engineer (14136)

National Association for Practical Nurse Education and Service, Inc.
1400 Spring St., Ste. 330
Silver Spring, MD 20910-2735
Phone: (301)588-2491
Fax: (301)588-2839

Publications: Journal of Practical Nursing (13733)

National Association for Printing Leadership
75 W. Century Rd.
Paramus, NJ 07652
Phone: (201)634-9600
Fax: (201)634-0324
Free: 800-642-6275

Publications: Printing Manager (19406)

National Association of Professional Insurance Agents
400 N. Washington St.
Alexandria, VA 22314
Phone: (703)836-9340
Fax: (703)836-4933

Publications: Professional Agent (31727)

National Association of Realtors
430 N. Michigan Ave.
Chicago, IL 60611-4087
Phone: (312)329-8200
Fax: (312)329-8390
Free: 800-874-6500

Publications: Real Estate Today (8549) • REALTOR Magazine (8550) • REALTORS Land Institute (8551) • Today's Realtor (8584)

National Association of Rocketry
1311 Edgewood Dr.
PO Box 177
Altoona, WI 54720
Phone: (715)832-1946
Fax: (715)832-6432
Free: 800-262-4872

Publications: Sport Rocketry (19894)

National Association of School Psychologists
4340 East-West Hwy., Ste 402
Bethesda, MD 20814
Phone: (301)657-0270
Fax: (301)657-0275

Publications: Communique (13325) • School Psychology Review (13378)

National Association of Secondary School Principals (NASSP)
1904 Association Dr.
Reston, VA 20191-1537
Phone: (703)860-0200
Fax: (703)476-5432
Free: 800-253-7746

Publications: NASSP Bulletin (32406)

National Association for the Self-Employed
2121 Precinct Line Rd.
Hurst, TX 76054
Phone: (817)428-4243
Fax: (817)428-4210

Publications: Self-Employed America (30602)

National Association of Social Workers
750 1st St. NE, Ste. 700
Washington, DC 20002-4241
Phone: (202)408-8600
Fax: (202)336-8312

Publications: Children & Schools (5409) • Health & Social Work (5523) • Social Work (5796) • Social Work Research (5797)

National Association of Tax Professionals
720 Association Dr.
Appleton, WI 54914-1483
Phone: (920)749-1040
Fax: 800-839-0001
Free: 800-558-3402

Publications: TAXPRO Quarterly Journal (33545)

National Association of Temple Administrators (NATA)
c/o Brock & Associates
6114 La Salle Ave.
Box 731
Oakland, CA 94611

Publications: NATA Journal (2688)

National Association of Underwater Instructors
9942 Currie Davis Dr., Ste. H
Tampa, FL 33619-2667
Phone: (813)628-6284
Fax: (813)628-8253
Free: 800-553-6284

Publications: Sources (29806)

National Association of Watch and Clock Collectors, Inc.
514 Poplar St.
Columbia, PA 17512-2130
Phone: (717)684-8261
Fax: (717)684-0878

Publications: Bulletin of the National Association of Watch and Clock Collectors (26798)

National Athletic Trainers' Association
2952 Stemmons Fwy.
Dallas, TX 75247-6196
Phone: (214)637-6282
Fax: (214)637-2206

Publications: Journal of Athletic Training (31933)

National Auctioneers Association
8880 Ballentine
Overland Park, KS 66214
Phone: (913)541-8084
Fax: (913)894-5281

Publications: The Auctioneer (11697)

National Audubon Society, Inc.
700 Broadway
New York, NY 10003
Phone: (212)979-3000
Fax: (212)979-3188

Publications: Audubon (21272) • Field Notes (21690)

National Automobile Club
1151 E Hillsdale Blvd.
Foster City, CA 94404
Phone: (650)294-7000
Fax: (650)294-7040

Publications: National Motorist (1933)

National Automobile Dealers Association
8400 Westpark Dr.
Mc Lean, VA 22102
Phone: (703)821-7150
Fax: (703)821-7234
Free: 800-252-NADA

Publications: NADA's AutoExec Magazine (32250)

National Bar Association
1225 11th St., NW
Washington, DC 20001
Phone: (202)842-3900
Fax: (202)289-6170

Publications: NBA Magazine (5691)

National Bison Association
4701 Marion, Ste. 100
Denver, CO 80216
Phone: (303)292-2833
Fax: (303)292-2564

Publications: Bison World (4308)

National Braille Press Inc.
88 St. Stephen St.
Boston, MA 02115-4302
Phone: (617)266-6160
Fax: (617)437-0456
Free: 800-548-7323

Publications: Our Special (13945) • Syndicated Columnists Weekly (13967)

National Bureau of Economic Research Inc.
1050 Massachusetts Ave.
Cambridge, MA 02138
Phone: (617)441-3895
Fax: (617)868-2472

Publications: NBER Reporter (14083)

National Bus Trader, Inc.
9698 W Judson Rd.
Polo, IL 61064
Phone: (815)946-2341
Fax: (815)946-2347

Publications: National Bus Trader (9462) • National Bus Trader (9461)

National Business Education Association
1914 Association Dr.
Reston, VA 20191-1596
Phone: (703)860-8300
Fax: (703)620-4483

Publications: Business Education Forum (32362)

National Business Media, Inc.
PO Box 1416
Broomfield, CO 80038
Phone: (303)469-0424
Fax: (303)469-5730
Free: 800-669-0424

Publications: Digital Graphics (4204) • Printwear (4206) • Restyling Magazine (4207) • Sign Business (4208)

National Cancer Registrars Association
PO Box 15945-295
Lenexa, KS 66286
Phone: (913)438-6272
Fax: (913)541-0156

Publications: Journal of Registry Management (1232)

National Catholic Cemetery Conference
710 N River Rd.
Des Plaines, IL 60016
Phone: (847)824-8131
Fax: (847)824-9608

Publications: Catholic Cemetery (8752)

National Catholic Educational Association
1077 30th St. NW, Ste. 100
Washington, DC 20007
Phone: (202)337-6232
Fax: (202)333-6706

Publications: Momentum (5659)

National Catholic Office for the Deaf
7202 Buchanan St.
Landover Hills, MD 20784-2236
Phone: (301)577-1684
Fax: (301)577-1690

Publications: Vision (13596)

National Catholic Reporter Publishing Co., Inc.
115 E Armour Blvd.
Kansas City, MO 64111-1203
Phone: (816)531-0538
Fax: (816)968-2268
Free: 800-444-8910

Publications: Celebration (17160) • The National Catholic Reporter (17187) • Praying (17194)

National Center for Developmental Education
Reich College of Education
Boone, NC 28608
Phone: (828)262-3057
Fax: (828)262-2128

Publications: Journal of Developmental Education (23653)

National Center for Employee Ownership
1736 Franklin St., 8th Fl.
Oakland, CA 94612-3423
Phone: (510)208-1300
Fax: (510)272-9510

Publications: Journal of Employee Ownership Law and Finance (2684)

National Center for Health Statistics
6525 Belcrest Rd., No. 1064
Hyattsville, MD 20782-2003
Phone: (301)458-4636

Publications: National Vital Statistics Report (13587)

The National Center for Public Policy Research
777 N. Capitol St. NE, Ste. 803
Washington, DC 20002
Phone: (202)371-1400
Fax: (202)408-7773

Publications: Legal Briefs (5634) • Political Money Monitor (5721) • Scoop (5782)

National Children's Literacy Project, Inc.
24 Union St.
Hamburg, NY 14075-5002
Phone: (716)649-7491
Fax: (716)649-2379

Publications: Kids Courier (20704)

National Christmas Tree Association
1000 Executive Parkway Dr., No. 220
St. Louis, MO 63141-6372
Phone: (314)205-0944
Fax: (314)576-7989

Publications: American Christmas Tree Journal (17409)

National Chrysanthemum Society, Inc.
10107 Homar Pond Dr.
Fairfax Station, VA 22039-1650
Phone: (703)978-7981

Publications: Chrysanthemum (32037)

National Clearinghouse for Alcohol and Drug Information
PO Box 2345
Rockville, MD 20847-2345
Phone: (301)294-3319
Fax: (301)468-6433

Publications: Prevention Pipeline (13696)

National Club Association
1 Lafayette Centre
1120 20th St. NW, No. 725
Washington, DC 20036
Phone: (202)822-9822
Fax: (202)822-9808
Free: 800-625-6221

Publications: Club Director (5422)

National Committee for National Pilgrim Virgin of Canada
PO Box 602
Fort Erie, ON, Canada L2A 5X3
Phone: (905)871-7607
Fax: (905)871-3646
Free: 800-263-8160

Publications: The Fatima Crusader (35839)

National Communication Association
1765 N St., NW
Washington, DC 20036-2801
Phone: (202)464-4622
Fax: (202)464-4600

Publications: Journal of Applied Communication Research (5571) • Quarterly Journal of Speech (5754) • Text and Performance Quarterly (5820)

National Community Pharmacists Association
205 Daingerfield Rd.
Alexandria, VA 22314-2885
Phone: (703)683-8200
Fax: (703)683-3619
Free: 800-544-7447

Publications: America's Pharmacist (31639)

National Concrete Masonry Association
13750 Sunrise Valley Dr.
Herndon, VA 20171
Phone: (703)713-1900
Fax: (703)713-1910

Publications: CM News (32162)

National Conference of Bar Examiners
402 W Wilson St.
Madison, WI 53703-3614
Phone: (608)280-8550
Fax: (608)280-8552

Publications: The Bar Examiner (33923)

National Conference of State Legislatures
7700 E First Pl.
Denver, CO 80230-7143
Phone: (303)364-7700
Fax: (303)364-7800

Publications: State Legislatures (4361)

National Conservation Tillage Digest
PO Box 468
Perryville, MO 63775
Phone: (573)547-7212
Fax: (573)547-5663
Free: 877-489-6997

Publications: National Conservation Tillage Digest (17338)

National Contract Management Association
8260 Greensboro Dr., Ste. 200
McLean, VA 22102
Phone: (571)382-0082
Fax: (703)448-0939
Free: 800-344-8096

Publications: Contract Management (32264) • National Contract Management Journal (32266)

National Cooperative Business Association (NCBA)
1401 New York Ave. NW, Ste. 1100
Washington, DC 20005
Phone: (202)638-6222
Fax: (202)638-1374

Publications: Cooperative Business Journal (5442)

National Council on the Aging
409 3rd St. SW, 2nd Fl.
Washington, DC 20024
Phone: (202)479-1200
Fax: (202)479-0735

Publications: Innovations (5545)

National Council of Catholic Women
1275 K St. NW, Ste. 975
Washington, DC 20005
Phone: (202)682-0334
Fax: (202)682-0338
Free: 800-506-9407

Publications: Catholic Woman (5402)

National Council on Family Relations
3989 Central Ave. NE, Ste. 550
Minneapolis, MN 55421
Phone: (763)781-9331
Fax: (763)781-9348
Free: 888-781-9331

Publications: Family Relations (16077) • Journal of Marriage and Family (16088)

National Council for Geocosmic Research, Inc.
c/o Terry Lamb
712 Concepcion Ave.
Spring Valley, CA 91977
Phone: (619)303-9236

Publications: Geocosmic Magazine (3792) • NCGR Journal (14364)

National Council for Geographic Education
206-A Martin Hall
Jacksonville State University
Jacksonville, AL 36265-1602
Phone: (256)782-5293
Fax: (256)782-5336
Free: 800-346-5444

Publications: Journal of Geography (16343)

National Council of Jewish Women Inc.
53 W 23rd St.
New York, NY 10010
Phone: (212)645-4048
Fax: (212)645-7466

Publications: NCJW Journal (5215)

National Council of Juvenile and Family Court Judges
PO Box 8970
Reno, NV 89507
Phone: (775)784-6012
Fax: (775)784-1084

Publications: Juvenile and Family Court Journal (18421)

National Council for Research on Women
11 Hanover Sq., 20th Fl.
New York, NY 10005
Phone: (212)785-7335
Fax: (212)785-7350

Publications: Issues Quarterly (21954)

National Council for the Social Studies
8555 Sixteenth St., Ste. 500
Silver Spring, MD 20910
Phone: (301)588-1800
Fax: (301)588-2049
Free: 800-296-7840

Publications: Social Education (13746) • Social Studies and the Young Learner (29805) • Theory and Research in Social Education (20219)

National Council of State Garden Clubs, Inc.
4401 Magnolia
St. Louis, MO 63110
Phone: (314)776-7574
Fax: (314)776-5108

Publications: The National Gardener (17475)

National Council of the Steuben Society of America
67-05 Fresh Pond Rd.
Ridgewood, NY 11385
Phone: (718)381-0900
Fax: (718)628-4874

Publications: The Steuben News (23197)

National Council of Teachers of English
1111 W Kenyon Rd.
Urbana, IL 61801-1096
Phone: (217)328-3870
Fax: (217)278-3761
Free: 800-369-6283

Publications: College Composition and Communication (9700) • College English (9701) • The Council Chronicle (9703) • English Education (9704) • English Journal (4429) • Language Arts (9714) • Research in the Teaching of English (9717) • Teaching English in the Two-Year College (9720)

National Council of Teachers of Mathematics
1906 Association Dr.
Reston, VA 20191-1502
Phone: (703)620-9840
Fax: (703)476-2970
Free: 800-235-7566

Publications: Journal for Research in Mathematics Education (32393) • The Mathematics Teacher (32403) • Mathematics-Teaching in the Middle

School (32404) • Teaching Children Mathematics (32417)

National Council of Young Israel
3 W 16th St.
New York, NY 10011
Phone: (212)929-1525
Fax: (212)727-9526
Free: 800-617-NCYI

Publications: Young Israel Viewpoint (22952)

National Cowboy & Western Heritage Museum
1700 NE 63rd St.
Oklahoma City, OK 73111
Phone: (405)478-6404
Fax: (405)478-4714

Publications: Persimmon Hill (25991)

National Croquet Calendar
718 E Jackson St.
PO Box 208
Monmouth, OR 97361-0208
Phone: (503)838-5697

Publications: National Croquet Calendar (26440)

National Cutting Horse Association
260 Bailey Ave.
Fort Worth, TX 76107-1862
Phone: (817)244-6188
Fax: (817)244-2015

Publications: Cutting Horse Chatter (30336)

National Deaf Education Center
800 Florida Ave. NE
Washington, DC 20002
Phone: (202)651-5530
Fax: (202)651-5489
Free: 800-621-2736

Publications: World Around You (5867)

National Defense Magazine
2111 Wilson Blvd., Ste. 400
Arlington, VA 22201-3061
Phone: (703)522-1820
Fax: (703)522-1885

Publications: National Defense (31810)

National Defense Transportation Association
50 South Pickett St., Ste. 220
Alexandria, VA 22304-7296
Phone: (703)751-5011
Fax: (703)823-8761

Publications: Defense Transportation Journal (31664)

National Defense University
300 Fifth Ave.
Bldg. 62, Rm. 212
Washington, DC 20319-5066

Publications: Joint Force Quarterly (5565)

The National Dipper
1841 Hicks Rd., Ste. C
Rolling Meadows, IL 60008
Phone: (847)202-4770
Fax: (847)202-4791

Publications: The National Dipper (9549)

National District Attorneys Association
99 Canal Center Plaza, Ste. 510
Alexandria, VA 22314
Phone: (703)549-9222
Fax: (703)836-3195

Publications: The Prosecutor (31730)

National Education Association
PO Box 2035
Annapolis Junction, MD 20701
Phone: (202)822-7202
Fax: (202)822-7206
Free: 800-229-4200

Publications: NEA Today (13104)

National Education Association of the United States
1201 16th St. NW
Washington, DC 20036
Phone: (202)822-7207
Fax: (202)822-7206

Publications: Thought & Action (5823)

National Electrical Contractors Association
3 Bethesda Metro Center, Ste. 1100
Bethesda, MD 20814-5372
Phone: (301)215-4502
Fax: (301)215-4501

Publications: Electrical Contractor (13332)

National Electrical Manufacturers Association (NEMA)
1300 N. 17th St., Ste. 1847
Rosslyn, VA 22209
Phone: (703)841-3200
Fax: (703)841-3300

Publications: Electrical Standards and Product Guide (32514) • ElectroIndustry (ei) (32515)

National Enquirer
5401 NW Broken Sound Blvd.
Boca Raton, FL 33487
Phone: (561)586-1111
Fax: (561)540-1009

Publications: National Enquirer (6548)

National Environmental Health Association
720 S. Colorado Blvd., Ste. 970, South Tower
Denver, CO 80246-1925
Phone: (303)756-9090
Fax: (303)691-9490

Publications: Journal of Environmental Health (4336)

The National Exchange Club
3050 Central Ave.
Toledo, OH 43606
Phone: (419)535-3232
Fax: (419)535-1989
Free: 800-924-2643

Publications: Exchange Today (25567)

National Families Network
280 Nelson St., Ste. 224
Vancouver, BC, Canada V6B 2E2
Phone: (604)689-1331
Fax: (604)689-7011

Publications: WestCoast Families (35179)

National Farmers Union
2717 Wentz Ave.
Saskatoon, SK, Canada S7K 4B6
Phone: (306)652-9465
Fax: (306)664-6226

Publications: Union Farmer (37559)

National Federation of the Blind
1800 Johnson St.
Baltimore, MD 21230
Phone: (410)659-9314
Fax: (410)685-5653

Publications: Braille Monitor (13139) • Future Reflections (13162)

National Federation of the Blind
Diabetes Action Network
1412 I-70 Dr., SW Ste. C
Columbia, MO 65203
Phone: (573)875-8911
Fax: (573)875-8902

Publications: Voice of the Diabetic (17012)

National Federation of Modern Language Teachers Associations
618 Van Hise Hall
1220 Linden Dr.
Madison, WI 53706-1558
Phone: (608)262-5010
Fax: (608)265-4672

Publications: The Modern Language Journal (33962)

National Federation of Republican Women
310 First St. SE
Washington, DC 20003

Publications: The Republican Woman (5762)

National Federation of State High School Associations
PO Box 690
Indianapolis, IN 46206
Phone: (317)972-6900
Fax: (317)822-5700
Free: 800-776-3462

Publications: Forensic Quarterly (10112)

The National FFA Organization
6060 FFA Dr.
PO Box 68960
Indianapolis, IN 46268-0960
Phone: (317)802-6060
Fax: (317)802-6061

Publications: FFA Advisors Making a Difference (10111) • FFA New Horizons (8143)

National Fire Protection Association
1 Batterymarch Park
PO Box 9101
Quincy, MA 02269-9101
Phone: (617)745-2200
Fax: (617)770-0700
Free: 800-344-3555

Publications: Fire Technology (14489) • NFPA Journal (14490)

National Fire and Rescue
5808 Faringdon Pl., No. 200
Raleigh, NC 27609-3930
Phone: (919)872-5040
Fax: (919)876-6531

Publications: National Fire & Rescue (24140)

National Fisherman
PO Box 7438
Portland, ME 04112
Phone: (207)842-5608
Fax: (207)842-5609

Publications: National Fisherman (13013)

National Forum Journals
PO Box 7400
Lake Charles, LA 70605-7400
Phone: (337)439-1516
Fax: (337)475-5402

Publications: National Forum of Applied Educational Research Journal (12640) • National Forum of Education Administration and Supervision Journal (12641) • National Forum of Special Education Journal (12642) • National Forum of Teacher Education Journal (12643)

National Funeral Directors Association
13625 Bishop's Dr.
Brookfield, WI 53005
Phone: (262)789-1880
Fax: (262)789-6977

Publications: The Director (33604)

National Gardening Association
1100 Dorset St.
South Burlington, VT 05403
Phone: (802)863-5251
Fax: (802)863-6889
Free: 800-538-7476

Publications: National Gardening (31600)

National Geographic Society
1145 17th St. NW
Washington, DC 20036-4688
Phone: (202)857-7000
Fax: (202)459-5727
Free: 800-638-6400
Telex: 89-2398

Publications: National Geographic (5672) • National Geographic Adventure (5673) • National Geographic Traveler (5674) • National Geographic WORLD (5675)

National Glass Association
8200 Greensboro Dr., No. 302
Mc Lean, VA 22102
Phone: (703)442-4890
Fax: (703)442-0630
Free: (866)342-5642

Publications: AutoGlass (32241) • Glass Magazine (32244)

Numbers cited after listings are entry numbers rather than page numbers.

National Greyhound Association
PO Box 543
Abilene, KS 67410-0543
Phone: (785)263-4660
Fax: (785)263-4689

Publications: The Greyhound Review (11334)

National Ground Water Association
601 Dempsey Rd.
Westerville, OH 43081-8978
Phone: (614)882-8179
Fax: (614)898-7786
Free: 800-332-2104

Publications: Ground Water (33944) • Ground Water Monitoring and Remediation (15237) • Water Well Journal (25645)

National Guard Magazine
1 Massachusetts Ave. NW
Washington, DC 20001
Phone: (202)789-0031
Fax: (202)682-9358
Free: 888-226-4287

Publications: National Guard Magazine (5676)

National Guild of Community Schools of the Arts
40 N Van Brunt St., Ste. 32
PO Box 8018
Englewood, NJ 07631
Phone: (201)871-3337
Fax: (201)871-7639

Publications: Employment Opportunities (Englewood) (18795)

National Head Start Association
1651 Prince St.
Alexandria, VA 22314
Phone: (703)739-0875
Fax: (703)739-0878

Publications: Children and Families (31654)

National Health Association
PO Box 30630
Tampa, FL 33630
Phone: (813)855-6607
Fax: (813)855-8052

Publications: Health Science (6768)

National Health Federation
PO Box 688
Monrovia, CA 91017-0688
Phone: (626)357-2181
Fax: (626)303-0642

Publications: Health Freedom News (2577)

The National Horseman
16101 N 82nd St., Ste. 10
Scottsdale, AZ 85260
Phone: (480)922-5202
Fax: (480)922-5212
Free: 800-437-5202

Publications: National Horseman (871)

National Hot Rod Association
2035 Financial Way
Glendora, CA 91741
Phone: (626)914-4761
Fax: (626)335-6651

Publications: National Dragster (2024)

National Housing Institute
460 Bloomfield Ave., Ste. 211
Montclair, NJ 07042-3552
Phone: (973)509-2888
Fax: (973)509-8005

Publications: Shelterforce (19241)

National Humanities Institute
214 Massachusetts Ave., NE, Ste. 303
Washington, DC 20002

Publications: Humanitas (5538)

National Independent Automobile Dealers Association
2521 Brown Blvd.
Arlington, TX 76006
Phone: (817)640-3838
Fax: (817)649-2377
Free: 800-756-4232

Publications: Used Car Dealer (29738)

National Information Center for Children and Youth With Disabilities (NICHCY)
PO Box 1492
Washington, DC 20013-1492
Phone: (202)884-8200
Fax: (202)884-8441
Free: 800-695-0285

Publications: NICHCY News Digest (5696)

National Inner City Enterprises, Inc.
1318 Polaris Dr.
PO Box 1545
Mobile, AL 36633-1545
Phone: (334)602-0210

Publications: National Inner City (326)

National Institute on Alcohol Abuse and Alcoholism (NIAAA)
Willco Bldg.
6000 Exec. Blvd.
Bethesda, MD 20892-7003
Phone: (301)443-3860

Publications: Alcohol Research & Health (13298)

National Insulation Association
99 Canal Center Plaza, Ste. 222
Alexandria, VA 22314
Phone: (703)683-6480
Fax: (703)549-4838

Publications: Insulation Outlook (31684)

National Interest, Inc.
1615 L St., NW, Ste. 1230
Washington, DC 20036-5651
Phone: (202)467-4884
Fax: (202)467-0006

Publications: The National Interest (5677)

The National Jewish Post and Opinion
238 S Meridian, Ste. 502
Indianapolis, IN 46225
Phone: (317)972-7800
Fax: (317)972-7807

Publications: The Indiana Jewish Post and Opinion (10127)

National Journal Group Inc.
1501 M St. NW, Ste. 300
Washington, DC 20005
Phone: (202)739-8400
Fax: (202)739-8500
Free: 800-356-4838

Publications: CongressDaily/A.M. (5433) • Government Executive (5518) • National Journal (5678)

National Junior College Athletic Association
PO Box 7305
Colorado Springs, CO 80933-7305
Phone: (719)590-9788
Fax: (719)590-7324

Publications: Juco Review (4251)

The National Jurist crittenden magazines
2035 N. Lincoln St. No. 205
Arlington, VA 22207
Phone: (703)294-5500
Fax: (703)294-5512

Publications: The National Jurist (31811)

National Knife Collectors Association
PO Box 21070
Chattanooga, TN 37421
Phone: (423)892-5007
Fax: (423)899-9456
Free: 800-548-3907

Publications: National Knife Magazine (29090)

National Law Center
2008 G St. NW
Washington, DC 20052

Publications: George Washington Journal of International Law and Economics (5507)

National Lawyers Guild
Box 46205
Los Angeles, CA 90046
Phone: (213)653-4510

Publications: The Guild Practitioner (2282)

National League of Cities
1301 Pennsylvania Ave. NW, Ste 550
Washington, DC 20004-1763
Phone: (202)626-3000
Fax: (202)626-3043

Publications: Nation's Cities Weekly (5686)

National League for Nursing
61 Broadway
New York, NY 10006-2701
Phone: (212)363-5555
Free: 800-669-1656

Publications: Nursing Education Perspectives (22473)

National Legal Center for the Medically Dependent & Disabled, Inc.
3 South 6th St.
Terre Haute, IN 47807-3510
Phone: (812)232-0103
Fax: (812)232-0103

Publications: Issues in Law & Medicine (10487)

National Library Service for the Blind and Physically Handicapped
1291 Taylor St., NW
Washington, DC 20542
Phone: (202)707-5100
Fax: (202)707-0712
Free: 800-424-8567

Publications: Braille Book Review (5381) • Musical Mainstream (5665) • Talking Book Topics (5810) • Update (Library of Congress) (5837)

National Lubricating Grease Institute
4635 Wyandotte St.
Kansas City, MO 64112
Phone: (816)931-9480
Fax: (816)753-5026

Publications: NLGI Spokesman (17189)

National Lumbermens Publishing Corp.
1405 Lilac Dr. N, No. 131
Minneapolis, MN 55422
Phone: (763)544-1597
Fax: (763)582-3024

Publications: Building Material Dealer (16062)

National Management Association
2210 Arbor Blvd.
Dayton, OH 45439
Phone: (937)294-0421
Fax: (937)294-2374

Publications: Manage (25122)

National Marine Educators Association
PO Box 1470
Ocean Springs, MS 39566-1470
Phone: (601)374-7557
Fax: (601)374-5559

Publications: Current (16801)

National Masters News
PO Box 50098
Eugene, OR 97405
Phone: (503)343-7716
Fax: (503)345-2436

Publications: National Masters News (26324)

National Medical Association
1012 10th St. NW
Washington, DC 20001
Phone: (202)347-1895
Fax: (202)207-1555

Publications: Journal of the National Medical Association (5603)

National Middle School Association
4151 Executive Pkwy., Ste. 300
Westerville, OH 43081-3871
Phone: (614)895-4730
Fax: (614)895-4750
Free: 800-528-NMSA

Publications: Middle School Journal (25642)

National Ministries Division PCUSA
100 Witherspoon St.
Louisville, KY 40202-1396
Phone: (502)569-5810
Fax: (502)569-8116
Free: 888-728-7228

Publications: Church & Society (12212)

National Motorcoach Network
P.O. Box 7430
Fairfax Station, VA 22039
Phone: (703)503-3613
Fax: (703)503-5922
Free: 800-469-0062

Publications: BYWAYS (32011)

National Multiple Sclerosis Society
733 3rd Ave.
New York, NY 10017
Phone: (212)986-3240
Fax: (212)986-7981
Free: 800-FIGHT-MS

Publications: Inside MS (21876)

The National Museum of Women in the Arts
1250 New York Ave. NW
Washington, DC 20005
Phone: (202)783-5000
Fax: (202)393-3235
Free: 800-222-7270

Publications: Women in the Arts (5862)

National Muzzle Loading Rifle Association
PO Box 67
Friendship, IN 47021
Phone: (812)667-5131
Fax: (812)667-5137
Free: 800-745-1493

Publications: Muzzle Blasts (10013)

National Notary Association
PO Box 2402
Chatsworth, CA 91313-2402
Phone: (818)739-4000
Fax: (818)700-0920
Free: 800-876-6827

Publications: The National Notary (1689)

National Office
113 University Pl., 6th Fl.
New York, NY 10003
Phone: (212)254-0279
Fax: (212)254-0673

Publications: American Writer (21209)

National Office of The Delta Theta Phi Law Fraternity, International
38640 Butternut Ridge Rd.
Elyria, OH 44035
Phone: (440)458-4381
Fax: (440)458-4380
Free: 800-783-2600

Publications: The Paper Book (25179)

National Organization for Rivers
212 W Cheyenne Mtn. Blvd.
Colorado Springs, CO 80906
Phone: (719)579-8759
Fax: (719)576-6238

Publications: Currents (4244)

National Ornamental and Miscellaneous Metals Association
532 Forest Pkwy., Ste. A
Forest Park, GA 30297
Phone: (404)363-4009
Fax: (404)366-1852

Publications: Ornamental Miscellaneous Metal Fabricator (7276)

National Parking Association
1112 16th St. NW, Ste. 300
Washington, DC 20036
Phone: (202)296-4336
Fax: (202)331-8523
Free: 800-647-PARK

Publications: Parking Magazine (5716)

National Parks & Conservation Association
1776 Massachusetts Ave. NW, Ste. 200
Washington, DC 20036
Phone: (202)223-6722
Fax: (202)659-8178
Free: 800-628-7275

Publications: National Parks (5679)

National Pastoral Life Center
18 Bleecker St.
New York, NY 10012-2404
Phone: (212)431-7825
Fax: (212)274-9786

Publications: Church (21416)

National Poetry Association Inc.
SOMAR
934 Brannan St., 2nd Fl.
San Francisco, CA 94103
Phone: (415)552-9261
Fax: (415)552-9271

Publications: Poetry USA (3415)

National Police Athletic League
618 U.S Hwy. 1, Ste. 201
North Palm Beach, FL 33408
Phone: (561)844-1823
Fax: (561)863-6120

Publications: National PAL CopsnKids Chronicles (6470)

National Police Officers Association
7811 Old Tree Run
Louisville, KY 40222-4694
Phone: (502)425-9215
Fax: (502)326-3705

Publications: National Police Review (12232)

National Pre-Vue Network Inc.
7825 Fay Ave.
La Jolla, CA 92037
Phone: (858)456-5577
Fax: (858)542-0114

Publications: Pre-Vue Entertainment Magazine (2119)

National Precast Concrete Association
10333 N. Meridian St., Ste. 272
Indianapolis, IN 46290-1081
Phone: (317)571-9500
Fax: (317)571-0041
Free: 800-366-7731

Publications: MC Magazine (10151)

National Press Photographers Association
3200 Croasdaile Dr., No. 306
Durham, NC 27705
Phone: (919)383-7246
Fax: (919)383-7261

Publications: News Photographer (23836)

National Productions
5600 Monterey Rd., Ste. G
Morgan Hill, CA 95037
Phone: (408)778-5200
Fax: (408)779-1374
Free: 800-800-5600

Publications: Computer Fair Show Program (2601)

National Publishing Co., Inc.
1533 Burgundy Pkwy.
Streamwood, IL 60107
Phone: (630)837-2044
Fax: (630)837-1210

Publications: National Locksmith (9667)

National Recreation and Park Association
22377 Belmont Ridge Rd.
Ashburn, VA 20148
Phone: (703)858-0784
Fax: (703)858-0794
Free: 800-626-6772

Publications: Journal of Leisure Research (31852) • Parks & Recreation Magazine (31854) • Therapeutic Recreation Journal (31855)

National Rehabilitation Association
633 S. Washington St.
Alexandria, VA 22314
Phone: (703)836-0850
Fax: (703)836-0848
Free: 888-258-4295

Publications: Journal of Rehabilitation (31701)

National Rehabilitation Counseling Association
8807 Sudley Rd., Ste. 102
Manassas, VA 20110-4719
Phone: (703)361-2077
Fax: (703)361-2489

Publications: Journal of Applied Rehabilitation Counseling (32222)

National Religious Broadcasters
9510 Technology Dr.
Manassas, VA 20110
Phone: (703)330-7000
Fax: (703)330-7100

Publications: NRB (32224)

National Religious Vocation Conference
5420 S Cornell Ave., No. 105
Chicago, IL 60615-5604
Phone: (773)363-5454
Fax: (773)363-5530

Publications: Horizon (8400)

National Research Bureau
320 Valley
Burlington, IA 52601
Phone: (319)752-5415

Publications: Ad Trends (10636) • American Salesman (10637) • Radio Campaigns (10639) • Supervision (10640)

National Research Council Canada, NRC Research Press
1200 Montreal Rd.
Bldg. M-58
Ottawa, ON, Canada K1A 0R6
Phone: (613)993-9101
Fax: (613)952-9907
Free: 877-672-2672

Publications: Biochemistry and Cell Biology (Biochimie et Biologie Cellulaire) (35316) • Canadian Geotechnical Journal (Revue Canadienne de Geotechnique) (36059) • Canadian Journal of Chemistry (Revue Canadienne de Chimie) (36202) • Canadian Journal of Civil Engineering (Revue Canadienne de Genie Civil) (36203) • Canadian Journal of Earth Sciences (Revue Canadienne des Sciences de la Terre) (34703) • Canadian Journal of Fisheries & Aquatic Science (36205) • Canadian Journal of Microbiology (Revue Canadienne de Microbiologie) (36208) • Canadian Journal of Physiology and Pharmacology (Revue Canadienne de Physiologie et Pharmacologie) (36211) • Canadian Journal of Zoology (Revue Canadienne de Zoologie) (36125) • Environmental Reviews (Dossiers Environnement) (36314) • Genome (36128)

National Review
215 Lexington Ave.
New York, NY 10016
Phone: (212)679-7330
Fax: (212)849-2835

Publications: National Review (22400)

National Rifle Association of America
11250 Waples Mill Rd.
Fairfax, VA 22030-9400
Phone: (703)267-1300
Fax: (703)267-3800

Publications: American Hunter (32003) • American Rifleman (32005) • America's 1st Freedom (32006) • InSights (32016)

National Right to Life Committee, Inc.
419 7th St. NW, Ste. 500
Washington, DC 20004
Phone: (202)347-3089
Fax: (202)393-2610

Publications: National Right to Life News (5680)

National Roofing Contractors Association
10255 W. Higgins Rd., Ste. 600
Rosemont, IL 60018-5607
Phone: (847)299-9070
Fax: (847)299-1183
Free: 800-323-9545

Publications: Professional Roofing (9556)

National Rural Education Association
820 Van Vleet Oval
Room 227
University of Oklahoma
Norman, OK 73019
Phone: (405)325-7959

2536

Numbers cited after listings are entry numbers rather than page numbers.

Publications: The Rural Educator Journal (25942)

National Rural Electric Cooperative Association
4301 Wilson Blvd.
Arlington, VA 22203-1861
Phone: (703)907-5500
Fax: (703)907-5521

Publications: Management Quarterly (31806) • R.E. Magazine (31823) • Rural Electrification Magazine (31824)

National Rural Health Association
1 W. Armour Blvd., Ste. 203
Kansas City, MO 64111
Phone: (816)756-3140
Fax: (816)756-3144

Publications: Journal of Rural Health (17177)

National Rural Letter Carriers' Association
1630 Duke St., 4th Fl.
Alexandria, VA 22314-3465
Phone: (703)684-5545
Fax: (703)548-8735

Publications: The National Rural Letter Carrier (31714)

National Safety Council
1121 Spring Lake Dr.
Itasca, IL 60143-3201
Phone: (630)285-1121
Fax: (630)285-1315
Free: 800-621-7615

Publications: SafetyHealth (9018)

National Science Teachers Association
1840 Wilson Blvd.
Arlington, VA 22201-3000
Phone: (703)243-7100
Fax: (703)243-7177
Free: 800-722-6782

Publications: Journal of College Science Teaching (31801) • NSTA Reports! (31815) • Quantum (31822) • Science Scope (31828) • The Science Teacher (31829)

National Sculpture Society
237 Park Ave.
New York, NY 10017
Fax: (212)764-5651

Publications: Sculpture Review (22715)

National Shellfisheries Association
Natural Science Division
Southampton College LIU
Southampton, NY 11968
Phone: (631)287-8407
Fax: (631)287-8419

Publications: Journal of Shellfish Research (23344)

National Sheriffs' Association
1450 Duke St.
Alexandria, VA 22314-3490
Phone: (703)836-7827
Fax: (703)683-6541
Free: 800-424-7827

Publications: Sheriff (31737)

National Skeet Shooting Association
5931 Roft Rd.
San Antonio, TX 78253
Phone: (210)688-3371
Fax: (210)688-3014

Publications: Skeet Shooting Review (31048)

National Society of Accountants
1010 N Fairfax St.
Alexandria, VA 22314-1504
Phone: (703)549-6400
Fax: (703)549-2984
Free: 800-966-6679

Publications: National Public Accountant (31713)

National Society of Accountants for Co-operatives
6320 Augusta Dr., Ste. 800
Springfield, VA 22150
Phone: (703)569-3088
Fax: (703)569-0235

Publications: The Cooperative Accountant (32541)

National Society Daughters of the American Revolution
1776 D St. NW
Washington, DC 20006-5392
Phone: (202)628-1776
Fax: (202)879-3283

Publications: Daughters of the American Revolution Magazine (5459)

National Society of Fund Raising Executives
1101 King St., Ste. 700
Alexandria, VA 22314
Phone: (703)684-0410
Fax: (703)684-0540
Free: 800-666-FUND

Publications: Advancing Philanthropy (8243)

National Society of Professional Engineers
1420 King St.
Alexandria, VA 22314
Phone: (703)684-2875
Fax: (703)836-4875

Publications: Engineering Times (31670)

National Society Sons of the American Revolution
1000 S 4th St.
Louisville, KY 40203
Phone: (502)589-1776
Fax: (502)589-1671

Publications: The SAR Magazine (34100)

National Sojourners, Inc.
8301 East Blvd. Dr.
Alexandria, VA 22308
Phone: (703)765-5000
Fax: (703)765-8390

Publications: The Sojourner (31738)

National Speakers Association
1500 S. Priest Dr.
Tempe, AZ 85281
Phone: (480)968-2552
Fax: (480)968-0911

Publications: Professional Speaker (913)

National Speed Sport News
6509 Hudspeth Rd.
PO Box 1210
Harrisburg, NC 28075
Phone: (704)455-2531
Fax: (704)455-2605

Publications: National Speed Sport News (23978)

National Spiritual Assembly of the Baha'is of the United States
415 Linden Ave.
Wilmette, IL 60091
Phone: (847)251-1854
Fax: (847)251-3652

Publications: World Order (9764)

National Sporting Goods Association
1601 Feehanville Dr., Ste. 300
Mount Prospect, IL 60056-6035
Phone: (847)296-6742
Fax: (847)391-9827

Publications: NSGA Retail Focus (9248)

National Spotted Swine Record, Inc.
PO Box 9758
Peoria, IL 61612
Phone: (309)691-0151
Fax: (309)691-0168

Publications: Spotted News (9426)

National Stone, Sand & Gravel Association
1605 King St.
Alexandria, VA 22314
Phone: (703)525-8788
Fax: (703)525-7782
Free: 800-342-1415

Publications: Stone, Sand & Gravel Review (31739)

National Storytelling Network
101 Courthouse Sq.
Jonesborough, TN 37659
Phone: (423)913-8201
Fax: (423)753-9331
Free: 800-525-4514

Publications: Storytelling Magazine (29259)

National Strength & Conditioning Association (NSCA)
PO Box 9908
Colorado Springs, CO 80932-0908
Phone: (719)632-6722
Fax: (719)632-6367
Free: 800-815-6826

Publications: Strength and Conditioning Journal (4258)

National Student Nurses' Association, Inc.
555 W. 57th St.
New York, NY 10019
Phone: (212)581-2211
Fax: (212)581-2368

Publications: Imprint (21856)

National Sunflower Association
4023 State St.
Bismarck, ND 58503
Phone: (701)328-5138
Fax: (701)328-5101
Free: 888-718-7033

Publications: The Sunflower (24360)

National Swine Registry
1769 US Hwy. 52 W
PO Box 2417
West Lafayette, IN 47996-2417
Phone: (765)463-3594
Fax: (765)497-2959

Publications: Seedstock Edge (10552)

National Tax Association
725 15th St., NW, No. 600
Washington, DC 20005-2109
Phone: (202)737-3325

Publications: National Tax Journal (5681)

National Technical Communications Co., Inc.
PO Box 2027
Winter Park, FL 32790-2027
Phone: (407)671-7777
Fax: (407)671-7757
Free: 800-881-6822

Publications: Florida Specifier (6881)

National Telecommunications Cooperative Association
4121 Wilson Blvd., 10th Fl.
Arlington, VA 22201
Phone: (703)351-2000
Fax: (703)298-2320

Publications: Rural Telecommunications (31825)

National Telemedia Council
1922 University Ave.
Madison, WI 53726
Phone: (608)218-1182
Fax: (608)218-1183

Publications: Telemedium (33976)

National Trade Publications, Inc.
13 Century Hill Dr.
Latham, NY 12110-2124
Phone: (518)783-1281
Fax: (518)783-1386

Publications: Professional Carwashing & Detailing (20933) • Water Technology (20934)

National Traditional Country Music Association
PO Box 492
Anita, IA 50020
Phone: (712)762-4363
Fax: (712)762-4363

Publications: Tradition Magazine (10604)

National Trappers Association
PO Box 632018
Nacogdoches, TX 75963
Phone: (936)569-6444
Fax: (936)569-9805

Publications: American Trapper (34576)

National Truck Equipment Association
PO Box 522020
Longwood, FL 32752-2020
Phone: (407)327-4817
Fax: (407)327-2603

Publications: Tow Times (6314)

National Truck Equipment Association
37400 Hills Tech Dr.
Farmington Hills, MI 48331-3414
Phone: (248)489-7090
Fax: (248)489-8590
Free: 800-441-NTEA

Publications: NTEA Technical Report (15019)

National Trust for Historic Preservation
1785 Massachusetts Ave. NW
Washington, DC 20036-2117
Phone: (202)588-6296
Fax: (202)588-6223
Free: 800-944-6847

Publications: National Trust Forum (5682) • Preservation (5726)

National Ultreya Publications
PO Box 210226
Dallas, TX 75211
Phone: (214)339-6321
Fax: (214)339-6322

Publications: Ultreya Magazine (30186)

National Underwriter Co.
5081 Olympic Blvd.
Erlanger, KY 41018
Phone: (859)692-2100
Fax: 800-874-1916
Free: 800-543-0874

Publications: National Underwriter Life and Health-Financial Services Edition (12053) • National Underwriter Property and Casualty/Risk and Benefits Management (12054) • Who Writes What in Life and Health Insurance (12055)

National United Women's Societies for the Adoration of the Most Blessed Sacrament
538 Eynon St.
Scranton, PA 18504-3561

Publications: Polka—Polish Woman (27961)

National Urban League
120 Wall St., 7th Fl.
New York, NY 10005-3902
Phone: (212)558-5300
Fax: (212)344-5332

Publications: The Urban League Review (22890)

National Utility Contractors Association
4301 N. Fairfax Dr., Ste. 360
Arlington, VA 22203
Phone: (703)358-9300
Fax: (703)358-9307

Publications: The National Utility Contractor (31812)

National Vanguard Books
PO Box 330
Hillsboro, WV 24946
Fax: (304)653-4690

Publications: Free Speech (33335) • National Vanguard (33336)

National Vehicle Leasing Association
1900 Arch St.
Philadelphia, PA 19103-1498
Phone: (215)564-3484
Fax: (215)963-9785

Publications: Vehicle Leasing Today (27716)

National Water Research Institute
867 Lakeshore Rd.
Burlington, ON, Canada L7R 4L7
Phone: (905)336-4513
Fax: (905)336-6444

Publications: Water Quality Research Journal of Canada (35719)

National Wildlife Federation
11100 Wildlife Center Dr.
Reston, VA 20190-5362
Phone: (703)438-6000
Fax: (703)438-3570
Free: 800-822-9919

Publications: National Wildlife (32407) • Ranger Rick (32412) • Your Big Backyard (32424)

National Woman's Christian Temperance Union
c/o Leonard Pohl
PO Box 69
Hutchinson, KS 67504-0069
Phone: (316)665-4035
Fax: (316)665-3756

Publications: Union Signal (11502)

National Women's Political Caucus
1634 Eye St. NW, Ste.310
Washington, DC 20006
Phone: (202)785-1100
Fax: (202)785-3605

Publications: Women's Political Times (5864)

National Wood Carvers Association
7424 Miami Ave.
PO Box 43218
Cincinnati, OH 45243
Phone: (513)561-0627

Publications: Chip Chats (24781)

The National Writers Association
3140 S. Peoria St., No. 295
Aurora, CO 80014-3155
Phone: (303)841-0246
Fax: (303)841-2607

Publications: Authorship (4145)

Nations Building News
1201 15th St. NW
Washington, DC 20005
Phone: (202)822-0525
Fax: (202)861-2131

Publications: Nation's Building News (5684)

Nation's Center News
PO Box 107
Buffalo, SD 57720
Phone: (605)375-3228
Fax: (605)375-3615

Publications: Nation's Center News (28826)

Nation's Restaurant News
425 Park Ave., 6th Fl.
New York, NY 10022
Phone: (212)756-5000
Fax: (212)756-5215

Publications: Nation's Restaurant News (22402)

Nationwide Promotion Ltd.
12 Dawn Dr.
Dartmouth, NS, Canada B3B 1H9
Phone: (902)468-5141
Fax: (902)468-4843
Free: 888-468-5141

Publications: The Torch (35551)

Natoma Publishing Co.
PO Box 126
Natoma, KS 67651-0160
Phone: (785)885-4582
Fax: (785)885-4582

Publications: Natoma-Luray Independent (11665)

Natural Areas Association
PO Box 1504
Bend, OR 97709
Phone: (541)317-0199
Fax: (541)317-0140

Publications: Natural Areas Journal (26243)

Natural Business Communications
360 Interlocken Blvd.
PO Box 7370
Broomfield, CO 80021
Phone: (303)442-8983
Fax: (303)440-7741

Publications: Natural Business (4205)

Natural History Society of Maryland
2643 N Charles St.
Baltimore, MD 21218
Phone: (410)235-6116

Publications: Maryland Naturalist (13213)

Natural Life
PO Box 112
Niagara Falls, NY 14304
Free: 800-215-9574

Publications: Natural Life (23004)

Natural Resources Defense Council
40 W 20 St.
New York, NY 10011
Phone: (212)727-2700
Fax: (212)727-1773

Publications: On Earth (22488) • OnEarth (22490)

The Nature Conservancy
4245 N Fairfax Dr., Ste. 100
Arlington, VA 22203
Phone: (703)841-5300
Fax: (703)841-9692
Free: 800-628-6860

Publications: Nature Conservancy (31813)

Nature Genetics
345 Park Ave. S.
New York, NY 10010-1707
Phone: (212)545-8341
Fax: (212)726-9314

Publications: Nature Genetics (22411)

Nature Publishing Group
345 Park Ave. S.
New York, NY 10010-1707
Phone: (212)726-9200
Fax: (212)696-0052

Publications: Human & Experimental Toxicology (21829) • Lab Animal (22229) • Nature (22409) • Nature Biotechnology (22410) • Nature International Weekly Journal of Science (5689)

Naturist Life International, Inc.
PO Box 300-H
Troy, VT 05868-0300
Phone: (802)744-6565
Free: 800-NLI-7020

Publications: Naturist Life International (31606)

The Naturist Society
PO Box 132
Oshkosh, WI 54903
Phone: (920)426-5009
Fax: (920)426-5184
Free: 800-886-7230

Publications: Nude & Natural (34225)

Nautical Research Guild, Inc.
12021 Kerwood Rd.
Silver Spring, MD 20904
Phone: (301)622-2635

Publications: Nautical Research Journal (14380)

Navajo County Publisher
PO Box 670
Holbrook, AZ 86025-0670
Phone: (520)524-6203
Fax: (520)524-3541

Publications: Holbrook Tribune-News (724)

The Navajo Times
PO Box 310
Window Rock, AZ 86515-0310
Phone: (520)871-6641
Fax: (520)871-6409

Publications: The Navajo Times (1011)

Naval Facilities Engineering Command
Washington Navy Yard
1322 Patterson Ave., SE, Ste. 1000
Washington, DC 20374-5065
Phone: (202)685-9008
Fax: (202)685-1484

Publications: Navy Civil Engineer (5690)

Navasota Examiner
115 Railroad St.
PO Box 751
Navasota, TX 77868
Phone: (936)825-6484
Fax: (936)825-2230

Publications: Navasota Examiner (30856)

Navigator Publishing LLC
58 Fore St.
Portland, ME 04101
Phone: (207)772-2466
Fax: (207)772-2879

Publications: Ocean Navigator (13015) • Professional Mariner (13018)

NavPress
3820 N. 30th St.
Colorado Springs, CO 80904-5001
Phone: (719)548-9222
Fax: (719)598-7128

Publications: Discipleship Journal (4245)

Naylor Communications Ltd.
100 Sutherland Ave.
Winnipeg, MB, Canada R2W 3C7
Phone: (204)947-0222
Fax: (204)947-2047

Publications: Association (36464) • The Oil Can (35347)

N.B. Publishing Company Ltd.
210 Crown St.
PO Box 2350
St. John, NB, Canada E2L 3V8
Phone: (506)632-8888
Fax: (506)648-2652

Publications: The Telegraph Journal (35431)

N.C. Cattlemen's Association
2228 N. Main St.
Fuquay Varina, NC 27526
Phone: (919)552-9111
Fax: (919)552-9216

Publications: Carolina Cattle Connection (23902)

N.C. League of Municipalities
PO Box 3069
Raleigh, NC 27602
Phone: (919)715-4000
Fax: (919)733-9519

Publications: Southern City (24154)

N.C. Wildlife Resources Commission
512 N Salisbury St.
Raleigh, NC 27604-1188
Phone: (919)733-7123
Fax: (919)715-2381

Publications: Wildlife in North Carolina (24159)

NE Ohio Coalition for the Homeless
2012 W 25th St., No. 717
Cleveland, OH 44113
Phone: (216)241-1104
Fax: (216)241-1047

Publications: Homeless Grapevine (24908)

NE Publishing
PO Box 510
Presque Isle, ME 04769
Phone: (207)769-5061
Fax: (207)764-4499
Free: 800-924-9041

Publications: Maine Potato News (13034)

Near North News, Inc.
10 E Ontario St., No. 2505
Chicago, IL 60611-4769
Phone: (312)787-2677
Fax: (312)787-2680

Publications: Near North News (8502)

Nebraska Academy of Sciences
302 Morrill Hall
University of Nebraska
Lincoln, NE 68588-0339
Phone: (402)472-2644

Publications: Transactions of the Nebraska Academy of Sciences (18123)

The Nebraska Cattlemen, Inc.
134 S. 13th St., Ste. 900
Lincoln, NE 68508
Phone: (402)475-2333
Fax: (402)475-0822

Publications: Nebraska Cattleman (18099)

Nebraska City News Press, Inc.
806 Central
PO Box 757
Nebraska City, NE 68410
Phone: (402)873-3334
Fax: (402)873-5436
Free: 877-269-3358

Publications: Penny Press 1 (18167)

Nebraska Farm Bureau Federation
PO Box 80299
Lincoln, NE 68501-0299
Phone: (402)421-4446
Fax: (402)421-4432

Publications: Nebraska Farm Bureau News (18100)

Nebraska Game and Parks Commission
2200 N 33rd St.
PO Box 30370
Lincoln, NE 68503
Phone: (402)471-0641
Fax: (402)471-5528

Publications: NEBRASKAland (18107)

Nebraska Grocery Industry Association
5533 S. 27th St., Ste. 104
Lincoln, NE 68512
Phone: (402)423-5533
Fax: (402)423-8686

Publications: The Voice (18127)

Nebraska Journal Leader
110 East St.
PO Box 545
Ponca, NE 68770
Phone: (402)755-2203
Fax: (402)755-2205

Publications: Nebraska Journal-Leader (18252)

Nebraska Music Educators Association
128 N. 13th St., Apt. 910
Lincoln, NE 68508-1501
Phone: (402)435-6913
Fax: (402)474-3250
Free: 888-870-NMEA

Publications: Nebraska Music Educator (18104)

Nebraska Petroleum Marketers & Convenience Store Association
1320 Lincoln Mall
Lincoln, NE 68508
Phone: (402)474-6691
Fax: (402)474-2510

Publications: Marketer (18095)

Nebraska Rural Electric Association
PO Box 82048
Lincoln, NE 68501
Phone: (402)475-4988
Fax: (402)475-0835

Publications: Rural Electric Nebraskan (18117)

The Nebraska Signal
131 N 9th
PO Box 233
Geneva, NE 68361-0233
Phone: (402)759-3117
Fax: (402)759-4214

Publications: The Nebraska Signal (18016)

Nebraska State Bar Association
635 S. 14th St., No. 2
PO Box 81809
Lincoln, NE 68508-2712

Publications: The Nebraska Lawyer (18102)

Nebraska State Education Association
605 S. 14th St.
Lincoln, NE 68508
Phone: (402)475-7611
Fax: (402)475-2630

Publications: NSEA Voice (18110)

Nebraska State Historical Society
1500 R St.
PO Box 82554
Lincoln, NE 68501-2554
Phone: (402)471-3270
Fax: (402)471-3100
Free: 800-833-6747

Publications: Nebraska History (18101)

The Needlecraft Shop, LLC.
23 Old Pecan Rd.
Big Sandy, TX 75755
Phone: (903)636-4011
Fax: (903)636-4088
Free: 800-259-4000

Publications: Crazy for Cross Stitch (9804) • Hooked on Crochet (29921) • Plastic Canvas Home & Holiday (29922) • Quick & Easy Plastic Canvas (29923)

Neenah/Menasha Buyers' Guide
PO Box 1897
Appleton, WI 54912-1897
Phone: (715)258-8450
Fax: (715)258-8524

Publications: Neenah/Menasha Buyers' Guide (33539)

Negative Capability Press
62 Ridgelawn Dr. E
Mobile, AL 36608-6116
Phone: (334)343-6163
Fax: (334)344-8478

Publications: Negative Capability (327)

Neighbor Newspapers, Inc.
580 Fairground St.
PO Box 449
Marietta, GA 30060
Phone: (770)795-3000
Fax: (770)428-7945

Publications: Acworth Neighbor (6896) • Alpharetta Neighbor (6916) • Austell Neighbor (7115) • Chamblee De Kalb Neighbor (7167) • Cherokee Plus (7169) • The Clayton Neighbor (7275) • Decatur De Kalb Neighbor (7236) • Doraville De Kalb Neighbor (7241) • The Douglas Neighbor (7411) • Dunwoody De Kalb Neighbor (7259) • The East Cobb Neighbor (7177) • The Fayette Neighbor (7310) • The Henry Neighbor (7328) • Kennesaw Neighbor (7354) • Mableton Neighbor (7414) • Northside Neighbor/Sandy Springs Neighbor (7033) • Powder Springs Neighbor (7486) • Rockdale Neighbor (7500) • Roswell Neighbor (7416) • Sandy Springs Neighbor (7417) • The Smyrna Neighbor (7555) • The South De Kalb Neighbor (7418) • The South Fulton Neighbor (7419) • The Stone Mountain De Kalb Neighbor (7571) • Tucker De Kalb Neighbor (7422) • Vinings Neighbor (7423)

Neighbor Newspapers, Inc.
8545 E. 41st. St.
Tulsa, OK 74145-3390
Phone: (918)663-1414
Fax: (918)664-8161

Publications: Owasso Reporter (26028)

Neighborhood House
Jesse Epstein Bldg.
905 Spruce St.
Seattle, WA 98104
Phone: (206)461-8430
Fax: (206)461-3857

Publications: The Voice Newspaper (33037)

Neighborhood Publications Inc.
PO Box 4285
Pittsburgh, PA 15203-0285
Phone: (412)481-0266
Fax: (412)488-8011

Publications: South Pittsburgh Reporter (27846)

Neighbors
3425 N. First, Ste. 201
Fresno, CA 93726-6819
Phone: (559)441-6750

Publications: Neighbors (1952)

Neighbors
159 S. Main St.
Milford, MA 01757
Phone: (508)473-1111
Fax: (508)478-8769

Publications: Neighbors (14332)

Neighbors
51 E. John St.
PO Box 397
Markesan, WI 53946
Phone: (920)398-2334
Fax: (920)398-3835

Publications: Neighbors (34025)

Neighbors Publishing
3628 Madison Ave., No. 3
North Highlands, CA 95660-5070
Phone: (916)348-2700
Fax: (916)348-2706

Publications: Elk Grove-Laguna Neighbors (1872)

Neil Sperry's Gardens Magazine
PO Box 864
Mc Kinney, TX 75070
Phone: (972)562-5050
Fax: (214)544-1278
Free: 800-752-4769

Publications: Neil Sperry's Gardens Magazine (30779)

Nelson Daily News
266 Baker St.
Nelson, BC, Canada V1L 4H3
Phone: (250)352-3552
Fax: (250)352-2418

Publications: Nelson Daily News (35024) • West Kootenay Weekender (35025)

Nelson Gazette
63 E 4th St.
PO Box 285
Nelson, NE 68961
Phone: (402)225-2301

Publications: Nelson Gazette (18169)

Nelson Publishing, Inc.
2500 Tamiami Tr. N.
Nokomis, FL 34275-3482
Phone: (941)966-9521
Fax: (941)966-2590
Free: 800-226-6113

Publications: Communications News (6462) • Designfax (25525) • EE Evaluation Engineering (6463) • Healthcare Purchasing News (8992) • Medical Equipment Designer (25526) • Modern Applications News (MAN) (6464) • Tooling & Production (25529)

Neodesha Derrick
502 Main
PO Box 356
Neodesha, KS 66757
Phone: (620)325-3000
Fax: (620)352-2880

Publications: Neodesha Derrick (11666)

Neonatal Network
1410 Neotomas Ave., Ste. 107
Santa Rosa, CA 95405
Phone: (707)569-1415
Fax: (707)569-0786

Publications: Neonatal Network (3730)

Neosho Daily News
1006 W Harmony
PO Box 848
Neosho, MO 64850
Phone: (417)451-1520
Fax: (417)451-6408

Publications: Neosho Daily News (17304)

John A. Nesbitt
701 Oaknoll Dr.
Iowa City, IA 52246-5168
Phone: (319)466-3192

Publications: Special Recreation Digest (10988)

Nesbitt Publishing Co.
Box 1450
Brooks, AB, Canada T1R 1C3
Phone: (403)362-5571
Fax: (403)362-5080

Publications: Brooks Bulletin (34623)

Nesbitt Publishing Ltd.
353 Station Rd.
Box 160
Shoal Lake, MB, Canada R0J 1Z0
Phone: (204)759-2644
Fax: (204)759-2521

Publications: Crossroads This Week (35292)

Ness County News
PO Box C
Ness City, KS 67560
Phone: (785)798-2213
Fax: (785)798-2214

Publications: Ness County News (11667)

Ness Press, Inc.
PO Box 157, Main St.
Fordville, ND 58231
Phone: (701)229-3641
Fax: (701)229-3217

Publications: Adams Standard (24438) • Aneta Star (24439) • Edmore Herald (24440) • The Express (24441) • Larimore Leader (24443) • McVille Messenger (24444) • Nelson County Arena (24445) • Tri-County Sun (24446)

Netmar Inc.
930 Richmond St.
Chatham, ON, Canada G1K 7P4
Phone: (519)351-7331
Fax: (519)351-7774

Publications: Chatham This Week (35730)

Netmar, Inc.
369 York St.
PO Box 5020
London, ON, Canada N6A 4L6
Phone: (519)336-1100
Fax: (519)336-1833

Publications: The Courier Press (36843) • Elgin County Market (36361) • Sarnia This Week (36366)

Network World Inc./IDG
PO Box 9108
Southborough, MA 01772-9108
Phone: (508)875-6400
Fax: (508)820-3467
Free: 800-622-1108

Publications: IntraNet Magazine (14545)

Networking Alternatives for Publishers, Retailers, & Artists, Inc.
109 North Beach Rd.
PO Box 9
Eastsound, WA 98245-0009
Phone: (360)376-2702
Fax: (360)376-2704
Free: 800-367-1907

Publications: NAPRA Review (32742)

NeuroScience Publishers
6555 Carrollton Ave.
Indianapolis, IN 46220
Phone: (317)257-9672
Fax: (317)257-9674

Publications: The Journal of Cognitive Rehabilitation (10139)

Neurosurgical Focus
1224 W Main St., Ste. 450B
Charlottesville, VA 22903
Phone: (434)924-8727
Fax: (434)982-1396

Publications: Neurosurgical Focus (31935)

Nevada
401 N. Carson St.,Ste.100
Carson City, NV 89701
Phone: (775)687-5416
Fax: (775)687-6159
Free: 800-495-3281

Publications: Nevada (18328)

Nevada Appeal
PO Box 2288
Carson City, NV 89702
Phone: (775)882-2111
Free: 800-221-8013

Publications: Nevada Appeal (18329)

Nevada County
PO Box 60
Prescott, AR 71857
Phone: (501)887-2002
Fax: (501)887-2949

Publications: Nevada County Picayune (1323)

Nevada Journal
1210 6th St.
PO Box 89
Nevada, IA 50201
Phone: (515)382-2161
Fax: (515)382-4299

Publications: Money Saver (11108) • Nevada Journal (11109)

Nevada Magazine
401 N. Carson, Ste. 100
Carson City, NV 89701
Phone: (775)687-5416
Fax: (775)687-6159
Free: 800-495-3281

Publications: Nevada Events and Shows (18330)

The Nevada Rancher
PO Box 620
Lovelock, NV 89419-0620
Phone: (702)358-2681
Fax: (702)358-2686

Publications: The Nevada Rancher (18413)

Nevada Senior World
1516 E. Tropicana Ave., Ste. 105
Las Vegas, NV 89119-6526
Phone: (702)367-6709
Fax: (702)367-6883

Publications: Nevada Senior World (18380)

New Age Citizen
PO Box 419
Dearborn Heights, MI 48127
Phone: (313)563-3192
Fax: (313)563-3192

Publications: The New Age Citizen (14909)

The New Age-Examiner
PO Box 59
Tunkhannock, PA 18657
Phone: (570)836-2123
Fax: (570)836-3378

Publications: The New Age-Examiner (28062)

New Age Publishing
42 Pleasant St.
Watertown, MA 02472
Phone: (617)926-0200
Fax: (617)926-5021
Free: 800-782-7006

Publications: Body & Soul Magazine (14612)

New Albany Gazette
713 Carter Ave.
PO Box 300
New Albany, MS 38652
Phone: (662)534-6321
Fax: (662)534-6355

Publications: New Albany Gazette (16798)

New Art Examiner
314 W. Institute Pl.
Chicago, IL 60610
Phone: (312)649-9900
Fax: (312)649-9935

Publications: New Art Examiner (8504)

New Arts Publications
594 Broadway, Ste. 905
New York, NY 10012
Phone: (212)431-3943
Fax: (212)431-5880

Publications: Bomb (21331)

New Beverage Publications, Inc.
55 Clarendon St.
Boston, MA 02116-6067
Phone: (617)598-1900
Fax: (617)598-1941

Publications: Massachusetts Beverage Business (13926)

New Buffalo Times
PO Box 369
New Buffalo, MI 49117
Phone: (616)469-1100
Fax: (616)469-4812

Publications: New Buffalo Times (15399)

New Capital & Democrat
500 Second St.
PO Box 987
McAlester, OK 74502
Phone: (918)423-1700
Fax: (918)426-3081
Free: 877-307-4237

Publications: The McAlester NEWS-CAPITAL & Democrat (25909)

New Castle News
2735 N. Mercer St.
PO Box 60
New Castle, PA 16105-1728
Phone: (412)654-6651
Fax: (412)654-9393

Publications: New Castle News (27314)

New Castle Weekly
203 Delaware St.
New Castle, DE 19720
Phone: (302)328-6005

Publications: New Castle Weekly (5266)

New Catholic Miscellany
PO Box 818
Charleston, SC 29402
Phone: (843)724-8375
Fax: (843)724-8368

Publications: The Cathholic Miscellany (28508)

New Century Publishing
2005 Palo Verde Ave., Ste. 158
Long Beach, CA 90815

Publications: The Jazz Review and Collectors Discography (2169)

New City Communications Inc.
770 N. Halsted Ste. 306
Chicago, IL 60622
Phone: (312)243-8786
Fax: (312)243-8802

Publications: New City (8505)

New College of California
50 Fell St.
San Francisco, CA 94102
Phone: (415)241-1300
Fax: (415)626-5171
Free: 888-437-3460

Publications: New College of California Journal of Public Interest Law (3395)

New Communications Group Inc.
130 Belfield Rd.
Etobicoke, ON, Canada M9W 1G1
Phone: (416)614-2200
Fax: (416)614-8861

Publications: Today's Trucking (35821) • Transport Routier (35822)

New Day Publishing Enterprises
211 Glendale, Ste. 216
Highland Park, MI 48203
Phone: (313)869-0033
Fax: (313)869-0430

Publications: Michigan Citizen (15161)

The New Earth
244 Dayton Ave.
St. Paul, MN 55102
Phone: (612)291-4453
Fax: (612)291-4460

Publications: The New Earth (24412)

New England Appraisers Association
5 Gill Terrace
Ludlow, VT 05149
Phone: (802)228-7444
Fax: (802)228-7444

Publications: The Appraisers Standard (31548)

The New England Board of Higher Education
45 Temple Pl.
Boston, MA 02111
Phone: (617)357-9620
Fax: (617)338-1577

Publications: Connection (13882)

New England Botanical Club, Inc.
Harvard University Herbaria
22 Divinity Ave.
Cambridge, MA 02138
Phone: (617)627-3544
Fax: (617)627-3805

Publications: Rhodora (18501)

New England Bride Inc.
215 Newbury St., Ste. 207B
Peabody, MA 01960
Phone: (978)535-4186
Fax: (978)535-3090
Free: 800-241-5458

Publications: New England Bride (14463)

New England College
24 Bridge St.
Henniker, NH 03242
Phone: (603)428-2211
Fax: (603)428-7230

Publications: The New Englander (18522)

New England Fuel Institute
20 Summer St.
Watertown, MA 02472
Phone: (617)924-1000
Fax: (617)924-5962

Publications: Oil and Energy (13841)

New England Golfer Magazine, Inc.
148 Old Westminster Rd.
Hubbardston, MA 01452
Phone: (978)928-5300
Fax: (978)840-3209

Publications: New England Golf (14244)

New England Historic Genealogical Society
101 Newbury St.
Boston, MA 02116-3007
Phone: (617)536-5740
Fax: (617)536-7307
Free: 800-296-3447

Publications: New England Ancestors (13931) • New England Historical and Genealogical Register (13934)

The New England Journal of Medicine
860 Winter St.
Waltham Woods Corporate Center
Waltham, MA 02451-1441
Phone: (781)893-4610

Publications: The New England Journal of Medicine (13935)

New England Newspapers, Inc.
Clocktower Business Park
75 S. Church St.
Pittsfield, MA 01201
Phone: (413)496-6355
Fax: (413)499-3419

Publications: The Berkshire Eagle (14468)

New England Newspapers, Inc.
PO Box 569
Manchester Center, VT 05255
Phone: (802)362-2222
Fax: (802)362-5327

Publications: The Manchester Journal (31553)

New England School of Law
154 Stuart St.
Boston, MA 02116
Phone: (617)451-0010

Publications: New England Law Review (13936)

New England Water Works Association
125 Hopping Brook Rd.
Holliston, MA 01746
Phone: (508)893-7979
Fax: (508)893-9898

Publications: Journal of the New England Water Works Association (14239)

The New Era
PO Box 700
Davenport, OK 74026
Phone: (918)377-2259
Fax: (918)377-2213

Publications: The New Era (25797)

New Era
PO Box 39
Sweet Home, OR 97386
Phone: (541)367-2135
Fax: (541)367-2137

Publications: New Era (26593)

The New Era
350 N. Main St.
PO Box 579
Parker, SD 57053
Phone: (605)297-4419
Fax: (605)297-4015
Free: 800-469-2237

Publications: The New Era (28912)

New Era Magazine
22152 Jonesport Ln.
Huntington Beach, CA 92646
Phone: (714)962-1351
Fax: (714)962-1354
Free: 888-565-8236

Publications: New Era Magazine (2064)

New century Foundation
PO Box 527
Oakton, VA 22124
Phone: (703)716-0900
Fax: (703)716-0932

Publications: American Rennaissance (32315)

New Freeman Ltd.
1 Bayard Dr.
St. John, NB, Canada E2L 3L5
Phone: (506)653-6806
Fax: (506)653-6818

Publications: The New Freeman (35430)

New Gloucester News
PO Box 102
New Gloucester, ME 04260
Phone: (207)926-4036
Fax: (207)926-4034

Publications: New Gloucester News (12991)

New Guide
1342 Main St.
PO Box 764
Eagle Pass, TX 78852
Phone: (830)773-2309
Fax: (830)773-3398

Publications: News-Guide (30257) • Sunday News (30258)

New Hampshire Bar Association
112 Pleasant St.
Concord, NH 03301
Phone: (603)224-6942
Fax: (603)224-2910

Publications: New Hampshire Bar Journal (18473)

New Hampshire Good Roads Association
261 Sheep Davis Rd., Ste. 5
Concord, NH 03301-5750
Phone: (603)224-1823

Publications: New Hampshire Highways (18474)

New Hampshire Grocers Association
110 Stark St.
Manchester, NH 03101-1934
Phone: (603)669-9333
Fax: (603)623-1137

Publications: News & Food Report (18560)

New Hampshire Magazine
150 Dow St.
Manchester, NH 03101
Phone: (603)624-1442
Fax: (603)624-1310

Publications: New Hampshire Magazine (18559)

New Hampshire Plant Growers Association
845 Loudon Ridge Rd.
Loudon, NH 03307
Phone: (603)267-8492

Publications: The Plantsman (18554)

New Hampshire Review
PO Box 1036
Romney, WV 26757
Phone: (304)822-3871
Fax: (304)822-4487

Publications: Hampshire Review (33452)

New Hampton Publishing Co.
10 N Chestnut Ave.
PO Box 380
New Hampton, IA 50659
Phone: (641)394-2111
Fax: (641)394-2113
Free: 800-642-4169

Publications: Impact Advertiser Shopper (11110) • New Hampton Tribune (11111)

New Haven Advocate
900 Chapel St., Ste. 1100
New Haven, CT 06510
Phone: (203)789-0010
Fax: (203)787-1418

Publications: New Haven Advocate (4998)

New Haven Register
Long Wharf, 40 Sargent Dr.
New Haven, CT 06511
Phone: (203)789-5200
Fax: (203)865-7894

Publications: New Haven Register (4999)

The New Hope Gazette
6220 Ridge Ave.
Philadelphia, PA 19178
Phone: (215)862-9435
Free: 800-968-4237

Publications: The Advance of Bucks County (27327) • The New Egypt Press (19346) • The Review (27653) • Yardley News (28202)

New Hope Natural Media
1401 Pearl St.
Boulder, CO 80302
Phone: (303)939-8440
Fax: (303)998-9020
Free: 800-933-8440

Publications: Delicious Living! (4165) • Natural Foods Merchandiser (4181)

New Horizon Publishers, Inc.
PO Box 1791
San Benito, TX 78586
Phone: (956)399-2436
Fax: (956)399-2430

Publications: Port Isabel/South Padre Press (30954) • San Benito News (31081)

New Indicator
9500 Gilman Dr., 323 Student Co-Op Ctr.
La Jolla, CA 92093-5003

Publications: New Indicator (2118)

New Internationalist Publications
PO Box 1062
Niagara Falls, NY 14304
Phone: (905)946-0407
Fax: (905)946-0410

Publications: New Internationalist (23005)

New Jersey Association of Realtors
295 Pierson Ave.
PO Box 2098
Edison, NJ 08818-3118
Phone: (732)494-4705
Fax: (732)494-4723

Publications: New Jersey Realtors Magazine (18788)

New Jersey Audubon Society
Box 693
Bernardsville, NJ 07924
Phone: (908)766-5787
Fax: (908)766-7775

Publications: Records of New Jersey Birds (18680)

New Jersey Business & Industry Association
310 Passaic Ave.
Fairfield, NJ 07004-2519
Phone: (973)882-5004
Fax: (973)882-4648

Publications: New Jersey Business (18814)

New Jersey Conservation Foundation
Bamboo Brook
170 Longview Rd.
Far Hills, NJ 07931
Phone: (908)234-1225
Fax: (908)234-1189

Publications: New Jersey Conservation (18817)

New Jersey Countryside Magazine
134 S Finley Ave.
Basking Ridge, NJ 07920-1422
Phone: (908)221-1171
Fax: (908)221-1656
Free: (866)888-8174

Publications: New Jersey Countryside Magazine (18664)

New Jersey Dental Association
1 Dental Plaza
PO Box 6020
North Brunswick, NJ 08902-6020
Phone: (732)821-9400
Fax: (732)821-1082

Publications: Journal of the New Jersey Dental Association (19381)

New Jersey Education Association
180 W. State St.
PO Box 1211
Trenton, NJ 08607
Phone: (609)599-4561
Fax: (609)392-6321

Publications: NJEA Review (19665)

New Jersey Herald
2 Spring St.
PO Box 10
Newton, NJ 07860-0010
Phone: (973)383-1500
Fax: (973)383-8477

Publications: New Jersey Herald (19372) • A Shopper's Guide (19377)

The New Jersey Historical Society
52 Park Pl.
Newark, NJ 07102
Phone: (973)596-8500
Fax: (973)596-6957

Publications: Jersey Journeys (19355) • New Jersey History (19360)

New Jersey Jewish News
901 Rte. 10
Whippany, NJ 07981-1157
Phone: (973)887-8500
Fax: (973)887-5999

Publications: New Jersey Jewish News—Central Edition (19749) • New Jersey Jewish News—Metrowest Edition (19750)

New Jersey Law Journal
238 Mulberry St.
PO Box 20081
Newark, NJ 07101-6081
Phone: (973)642-0075
Fax: (973)642-0920

Publications: New Jersey Law Journal (19361)

New Jersey League of Municipalities
407 W. State St.
Trenton, NJ 08618
Phone: (609)695-3481
Fax: (609)695-0151

Publications: New Jersey Municipalities (19661)

New Jersey Motor Truck Association
160 Tices Ln.
East Brunswick, NJ 08816
Phone: (732)254-5000
Fax: (732)613-1745

Publications: Bulletin of the New Jersey Motor Truck Association (18780)

New Jersey Pharmacists Association
760 Alexander Rd.
CN 1
Princeton, NJ 08543-0001
Phone: (609)275-4246
Fax: (609)275-4066

Publications: New Jersey Journal of Pharmacy (19466)

New Jersey Principals & Supervisors Association
12 Centre Drive
Monroe, NJ 08831
Phone: (609)860-1200
Fax: (609)860-6677

Publications: Educational Viewpoints (19238)

New Jersey School Boards Association
PO Box 909
413 W. State St
Trenton, NJ 08605
Phone: (609)695-7600
Fax: (609)695-0413

Publications: New Jersey School Boards Association School Leader (19664)

New Jersey Sportsmen's Guides
PO Box 100
Somerdale, NJ 08083
Phone: (856)783-1271
Fax: (856)783-1271

Publications: Discovering and Exploring New Jersey's Fishing Streams and the Delaware River (19557) • New Jersey Lake Survey Fishing Maps Guide (19558)

New Jersey State Bar Association
New Jersey Law Center
1 Constitution Sq.
New Brunswick, NJ 08901-1500
Phone: (732)249-5000
Fax: (732)828-0034

Publications: New Jersey Lawyer (19336)

New Jersey State Safety Council
6 Commerce Dr.
Cranford, NJ 07016
Phone: (908)272-7712
Fax: (908)276-6622
Free: 800-228-3384

Publications: Safety Briefs (18772)

New Journal & Guide
PO Box 209
Norfolk, VA 23501
Phone: (757)543-6531
Fax: (757)543-7620

Publications: New Journal & Guide (32291)

The New Korea
141 S New Hampshire Ave.
Los Angeles, CA 90004
Phone: (213)382-9345
Fax: (213)382-1678

Publications: The New Korea (2344)

New Leader
PO Box 591
Richwood, WV 26261
Phone: (304)846-2666
Fax: (304)846-4972

Publications: Nicholas County News Leader (33447)

New Living
PO Box 1519
Stony Brook, NY 11790
Phone: (631)751-8819
Fax: (631)751-8910

Publications: New Living (23373)

New Mass. Media, Inc.
1 Dock St.
Stamford, CT 06902
Phone: (203)406-2406
Fax: (203)906-1099

Publications: Fairfield County Weekly (5149) • Hartford Advocate (4891) • New Haven Advocate (5156) • Valley Advocate (5161) • Westchester County Weekly (5164)

New Mexican, Inc.
202 E Marcy St.
Santa Fe, NM 87501
Phone: (505)986-3075
Fax: (505)984-1785
Free: 800-873-3362

Publications: Buzz'n (19932)

New Mexico Academy of Science
New Mexico Museum of Natural History & Science
1801 Mountain Rd., NW
Albuquerque, NM 87104
Phone: (505)841-2802

Publications: New Mexico Journal of Science (19780)

New Mexico Bureau of Geology and Mineral Resources
801 Leroy Pl.
Socorro, NM 87801-4796
Phone: (505)835-5420
Fax: (505)835-6333

Publications: New Mexico Geology (19959)

New Mexico Farm & Livestock Bureau
PO Box 20004
Las Cruces, NM 88004
Phone: (505)532-4706
Fax: (505)532-4710

Publications: New Mexico Farm and Ranch (19874)

New Mexico Jewish Link
5520 Wyoming Blvd. NE
Albuquerque, NM 87109
Phone: (505)821-3214
Fax: (505)821-3351

Publications: New Mexico Jewish Link (19779)

New Mexico Magazine
PO Box 12002
Santa Fe, NM 87504
Phone: (505)827-7447
Fax: (505)827-6496

Publications: New Mexico Magazine (19938)

New Mexico Rural Electric Cooperatives
614 Don Gaspar Ave.
Santa Fe, NM 87501
Phone: (505)982-4671
Fax: (505)982-0153

Publications: Enchantment (19935)

New Mexico State University
PO Box 30004
Dept. CC
Las Cruces, NM 88003
Phone: (505)646-NEWS
Fax: (505)646-7905

Publications: Round Up (19875)

New Mexico Stockman
PO Box 7127
Albuquerque, NM 87194
Phone: (505)243-9515
Fax: (505)243-9598

Publications: New Mexico Stockman (19782)

New Moon Publishing
34 E Superior St., Ste. 200
Duluth, MN 55802-3003
Phone: (218)728-5507
Fax: (218)728-0314
Free: 800-381-4743

Publications: New Moon (15840)

New Moon Publishing, Inc.
PO Box 1027
Corvallis, OR 97339
Phone: (541)745-7773

Publications: The Growing Edge (26288)

New Moon Rising
12345 SE Fuller Rd., Ste. 119
Milwaukie, OR 97222
Phone: (360)242-8186
Fax: (360)242-8186

Publications: New Moon Rising (26438)

New North Ventures
PO Box 750
The Pas, MB, Canada R9Q 1K8
Phone: (204)623-3435
Fax: (204)623-5601
Free: 877-232-4777

Publications: Opasquia Times (35278)

New On the Charts
70 Laurel Pl.
New Rochelle, NY 10801
Phone: (914)632-3349
Fax: (914)633-7690

Publications: New on the Charts (21119)

The New Optimist, Inc.
Box 490
Redvers, SK, Canada S0C 2H0
Phone: (306)452-3363
Fax: (306)452-6408

Publications: Optimist (37524)

New Orleans, Big Bend & Pacific Co., Publishers
PO Box 51831
New Orleans, LA 70151
Phone: (504)524-0348

Publications: New Orleans Menu (12746)

New Orleans CityBusiness
3445 N. Causeway Blvd., Ste. 400
Metairie, LA 70002
Phone: (504)309-1004
Fax: (504)309-1630

Publications: New Orleans CityBusiness (12678)

New Orleans Jazz Club
828 Royal St., Ste. 265
New Orleans, LA 70116
Phone: (504)455-6847

Publications: The Second Line (12752)

New Orleans Jazz Club of Southern California
PO Box 12267
Orange, CA 92859-8267
Phone: (949)830-0521
Fax: (949)830-0521

Publications: The Jazzologist (2723)

New Orleans Publishing Group
PO Box 52031
New Orleans, LA 70152
Phone: (504)368-8900
Fax: (504)368-8999

Publications: Daily Journal of Commerce (12728)

New Orleans Publishing Group, Inc.
111 Veterans Blvd., Ste. 1440
Metairie, LA 70005
Phone: (504)831-3731
Fax: (504)837-2258

Publications: New Orleans Magazine (12745)

New Oxford Review, Inc.
1069 Kains Ave.
Berkeley, CA 94706
Phone: (510)526-5374
Fax: (510)526-3492

Publications: New Oxford Review (1545)

New Palestine Press
PO Box 407
New Palestine, IN 46163-0407
Phone: (317)861-4242
Fax: (317)861-4201

Publications: New Palestine Press (10346)

The New Pathway Publishers Ltd.
295 College St.
Toronto, ON, Canada M5T 1S2
Phone: (416)960-3424
Fax: (416)960-1442

Publications: The New Pathway (36673)

New Pittsburgh Courier
315 E Carson St.
Pittsburgh, PA 15219
Phone: (412)481-8302
Fax: (412)481-1360
Free: 800-237-3200

Publications: New Pittsburgh Courier (27821)

New Politics Associates, Inc.
328 Clinton St.
Brooklyn, NY 11231
Phone: (718)287-2048
Fax: (718)246-9648

Publications: New Politics (20332)

New Prague Times
200 E Main St.
PO Box 25
New Prague, MN 56071
Phone: (952)758-4435
Fax: (952)758-4135

Publications: New Prague Times (16209)

New Product News
213 W Institute Pl., Ste. 704
Chicago, IL 60610
Phone: (312)932-0600
Fax: (312)932-0474

Publications: New Product News (8506)

New Prospect, Inc.
PO Box 601
Mount Morris, IL 61054-0601

Publications: The American Prospect (9236)

New Publishing Co.
816 Main St.
PO Box 55
Creighton, NE 68729
Phone: (402)358-5220
Fax: (402)358-5132

Publications: The Creighton News (17991)

New Readers Press
1320 Jamesville Ave.
Syracuse, NY 13210
Phone: (315)422-9121
Fax: (315)422-6369
Free: 800-448-8878

Publications: News for You (23414)

New Regime Press, Inc.
PO Box 96
Maunaloa, HI 96770
Phone: (808)552-2781
Fax: (808)552-2334

Publications: The Dispatch (7788)

The New Republic
PO Box 239
145 Center St.
Meyersdale, PA 15552
Phone: (814)634-8321
Fax: (814)634-5556
Free: 888-445-5660

Publications: The New Republic (27248)

The New Republic, LLC
1331 H St. NW, Ste. 700
Washington, DC 20005
Phone: (202)508-4444
Fax: (202)331-0275

Publications: The New Republic (5694)

The New Review
2175 S. Jasmine, Ste. A
Denver, CO 80222
Phone: (303)639-9000
Fax: (303)639-5125

Publications: The New Review (4342)

New Review, Inc.
611 Broadway, Ste. 842
New York, NY 10012-2608
Phone: (212)353-1478
Fax: (212)353-1478

Publications: Novyj Zhurnal (The New Review) (22470)

New Richland Star
PO Box 248
New Richland, MN 56072-0248
Phone: (507)465-8112

Publications: New Richland Star (16212)

New River Record
PO Box F
Greenbush, MN 56726
Phone: (218)782-2275
Fax: (218)782-2277

Publications: New River Record (15935)

New Salem Journal
PO Box 416
New Salem, ND 58563
Phone: (701)843-7567
Fax: (701)843-7623

Publications: New Salem Journal (24525)

New School University
55 W 13th St.
New York, NY 10011
Phone: (212)229-5776
Fax: (212)229-5476

Publications: Social Research (22756)

New South Publishing Inc.
1303 Hightower Trl., Ste. 101
Atlanta, GA 30350
Phone: (770)650-1102
Fax: (770)650-2848
Free: 800-536-5669

Publications: KNOW Atlanta Magazine (7024) • Net
News (7031)

New Texas
1512 1/2 S Congress Ave., No. 4
Austin, TX 78704-2437

Publications: New Texas (29794)

New Times
1201 E. Jefferson
PO Box 2510
Phoenix, AZ 85002
Phone: (602)271-0040
Fax: (602)340-8806

Publications: Phoenix New Times (810)

New Times
505 Higuera St.
San Luis Obispo, CA 93401
Phone: (805)546-8208
Fax: (805)546-8641
Free: 800-215-0300

Publications: New Times (3567)

New Times
2800 Biscayne Blvd., Ste. 100
PO Box 011591
Miami, FL 33137
Phone: (305)576-8000
Fax: (305)571-7677

Publications: Miami New Times (6370) • The New
Times (6374)

New Times Broward-Palm Beach
PO Box 14128
Fort Lauderdale, FL 33302-4128
Phone: (954)233-1600
Fax: (954)233-1521

Publications: New Times Broward-Palm Beach
(6081)

New Times, Inc.
1201 E. Jefferson
Phoenix, AZ 85034
Phone: (602)271-0040
Fax: (602)258-2953

Publications: Dallas Observer (30148) • Houston
Press (30488) • Scene (24952)

New Times of Mobile
PO Box 40536
Mobile, AL 36640-0536
Fax: (205)432-8320

Publications: The New Times (328)

New Times Publishing, Inc.
Sierra Center Mall 2nd Fl.
452 Old Mammoth Rd.
Mammoth Lakes, CA 93546
Phone: (760)934-3929
Fax: (760)934-3951

Publications: Mammoth Times (2498)

New Town Inc.
59 N Main St.
PO Box 730
New Town, ND 58763
Phone: (701)873-4381
Fax: (701)627-4021

Publications: New Town News (24526)

New Ulm Enterprise
PO Box 128
New Ulm, TX 78950
Phone: (979)992-3351

Publications: Enterprise (30866)

New Union Party
1821 University Ave. W, No. S-116
St. Paul, MN 55104
Phone: (651)646-5546

Publications: New Unionist (16401)

New Utah!
59 W Main
PO Box 7
American Fork, UT 84003-0007
Phone: (801)756-7669
Fax: (801)756-5274
Free: 888-201-5470

Publications: Citizen (31316) • Lehi Free Press
(31345) • New Utah! Lindon Edition (31317) • New
Utah! Lone Peak Edition (31318) • New Utah! Shopper (31319) • Pleasant Grove Review (31390)

The New Waterfront Press
PO Box 507
Lumsden, SK, Canada S0G 3C0
Phone: (306)731-3143
Fax: (306)731-2277

Publications: The New Waterfront Press (37491)

New Wave Communications Inc.
Box 1029
Inez, KY 41224
Phone: (606)298-7570
Fax: (606)298-3711

Publications: The Mountain Citizen (12140)

The New Wolcott Enterprise
125 W Market St.
PO Box 78
Wolcott, IN 47995
Phone: (219)279-2167
Fax: (219)279-2167

Publications: The New Wolcott Enterprise (10567)

New World Publications
721 N LaSalle St.
Chicago, IL 60610
Phone: (312)655-7777
Fax: (312)642-7350

Publications: The Catholic New World (8301)

New Writer's Magazine
PO Box 5976
Sarasota, FL 34277
Phone: (941)953-7903
Free: 800-249-0658

Publications: New Writer's Magazine (6660)

New York Academy of Medicine
1216 Fifth Ave., Rm. 601
New York, NY 10029
Phone: (212)822-7200
Fax: (212)996-7826

Publications: Bulletin of the New York Academy of
Medicine (21352)

New York Athletic Club
180 Central Park S, No. 1223
New York, NY 10019
Phone: (212)767-7000
Fax: (212)767-7063

Publications: The Winged Foot (22921)

New York Blade News
333 7th Ave., 14th Fl.
New York, NY 10011
Phone: (212)268-2701
Fax: (212)268-2069

Publications: New York Blade News (22438)

New York Botanical Garden Press
200th St. and Southern Blvd.
Bronx, NY 10458-5126
Phone: (718)817-8705
Fax: (718)817-8842

Publications: Advances in Economic Botany
(20251) • The Botanical Review (20257) • Economic
Botany (20266) • Flora Neotropica (20269) • North
American Flora (20278)

**New York City Association of Insurance
& Financial Advisors**
500 Fifth Ave., Ste. 330
New York, NY 10110
Phone: (212)221-3500

Publications: The Bulletin (21348)

New York City Housing Authority
250 Broadway, Rm. 917
New York, NY 10007
Phone: (212)776-5000
Fax: (212)306-6482

Publications: The Housing Authority Journal (21824)

**The New York Civil Service Employees
Publishing Co., Inc.**
277 Broadway, Ste. 1506
New York, NY 10007-2008
Phone: (212)962-2690
Fax: (212)962-2556

Publications: The Chief Civil Service Leader
(21408)

New York Credit Group
253 W. 35th St., Fl. 6
New York, NY 10001-1907

Publications: Credit Memo (21514)

The New York Evening Express
204 W 118th St.1b
PO Box 1B
New York, NY 10026-1739
Phone: (212)673-5628

Publications: The New York Evening Express
(22442)

New York Family Publications, Inc.
141 Halstead Ave., Ste. 3D
Mamaroneck, NY 10543-2652
Phone: (914)381-7474
Fax: (914)381-7672

Publications: Connecticut Family (20984) • New
York Family (20987) • Westchester Family (20988)

New York Folklore Society
PO Box 764
Schenectady, NY 12301
Phone: (518)346-7008
Fax: (518)346-6617

Publications: Voices (27244)

**New York Genealogical and Biographical
Society**
122 E 58th St.
New York, NY 10022-1939
Phone: (212)755-8532
Fax: (212)754-4218

Publications: The New York Genealogical and Biographical Record (22443)

New York Holstein Association
957 Mitchell St.
Ithaca, NY 14850-4936
Phone: (607)273-7591
Fax: (607)273-7612

Publications: New York Holstein News (20811)

New York Journal of Mathematics
Department of Mathematics and Statistics
University at Albany
Albany, NY 12222

Publications: New York Journal of Mathematics
(19995)

The New York Law Journal
345 Park Ave. S
New York, NY 10010
Phone: (212)779-9200
Fax: (212)481-8110
Free: 800-888-8300

Publications: The National Law Journal (22398) •
The New York Law Journal (22445)

Numbers cited after listings are entry numbers rather than page numbers.

New York Law School
57 Worth St.
New York, NY 10013
Phone: (212)431-2100
Fax: (212)966-1522

Publications: The L (22226)

New York Legal Publishing Corp.
136 Railroad Ave.
Albany, NY 12205
Phone: (518)459-1100
Fax: (518)459-9718
Free: 800-541-2681

Publications: City of New York Council Digest (21426)

New York Mercantile Exchange
1 N. End Ave.
World Financial Center
New York, NY 10282
Phone: (212)299-2000
Fax: (212)301-4700

Publications: Energy in the News (21604)

New York Metro Area Postal Union, Union Mail
350 W 31st St., 3rd Fl.
New York, NY 10001
Phone: (212)563-7553
Fax: (212)714-1399

Publications: New York Metro Area Postal Union, Union Mail (22447)

New York News, Inc.
450 W 33rd St.
New York, NY 10001
Phone: (212)210-2100
Fax: (212)210-2049

Publications: New York Daily News (22440)

New York Open Center
83 Spring St.
New York, NY 10012
Phone: (212)334-0210
Fax: (212)219-1347

Publications: Lapis (22235)

New York Opera Newsletter
PO Box 95490
South Jordan, UT 84095-0490
Phone: (801)254-1025
Fax: (801)254-3139

Publications: Classical Singer Magazine (31472)

New York Post Corp.
1211 6th Ave.
New York, NY 10036
Phone: (212)930-8000

Publications: New York Post (22448)

New York Press, Inc.
333 7th Ave., 14th Fl.
New York, NY 10001
Phone: (212)244-2282
Fax: (212)941-7824

Publications: Manhattan Spirit (22280) • New York Press (22449)

New York Quarterly Foundation
Box 693, Old Chelsea Sta.
New York, NY 10113
Phone: (212)255-8531

Publications: New York Quarterly (22450)

The New York Review of Books
1755 Broadway, 5th Fl.
New York, NY 10019-3780
Phone: (212)757-8070
Fax: (212)333-5374

Publications: The New York Review of Books (22451)

New York Road Runners
9 E 89th St.
New York, NY 10128
Phone: (212)860-4455
Fax: (212)423-0879

Publications: New York Runner (22452)

New York State Assembly
Legislative Office Bldg., Rm. 841
Albany, NY 12248

Publications: New York State Assembly Standing Committee on Veterans' Affairs Annual Report (19996)

New York State Bar Association
1 Elk St.
Albany, NY 12207
Phone: (518)463-3200
Fax: (518)463-8844
Free: 800-582-2452

Publications: Journal (19991) • State Bar News (20004)

New York State Dental Association
121 State St., 4th Fl.
Albany, NY 12207
Phone: (518)465-0044
Fax: (518)427-0461
Free: 800-255-2100

Publications: New York State Dental Journal (19998)

New York State Dept. of Environmental Conservation
625 Broadway, 2nd Fl.
Albany, NY 12233-4501
Phone: (518)402-8047
Fax: (518)402-8050
Free: 800-678-6399

Publications: New York State Conservationist (19997)

New York State Dept. of Labor
State Campus
Bldg. 12, Rm. 403
Albany, NY 12240
Phone: (518)457-1130
Fax: (518)457-3652

Publications: Employment Review (19984)

New York State Department of State
41 State St.
Albany, NY 12231
Phone: (518)474-6957
Fax: (518)473-9055

Publications: New York State Register (20000)

New York State Economics Association
Division of Economics and Business
SUNY-Oneonta
Oneonta, NY 13820
Phone: (607)436-3458
Fax: (607)436-2543

Publications: New York Economic Review (23051)

New York State Historical Association
PO Box 800
Cooperstown, NY 13326
Phone: (607)547-1404
Fax: (607)547-1400

Publications: Heritage (20499) • New York History (20500)

The New York State Society of Anesthesiologists, Inc.
360 Lexington Ave., Ste. 1800
New York, NY 10017
Phone: (212)867-7140
Fax: (212)867-7153

Publications: NYSSA Sphere (22480)

New York State Society of CPAs
530 Fifth Ave.
New York, NY 10036-5101
Phone: (212)719-8300
Fax: (212)719-3364

Publications: The CPA Journal (21509)

New York State Trial Lawyers Association
132 Nassau St., Ste. 200
New York, NY 10038
Phone: (212)349-5890
Fax: (212)608-2310

Publications: Trial Lawyers Quarterly (22865)

New York State United Teachers
159 Wolf Rd., Box 15-008
Albany, NY 12212-5008
Phone: (518)459-5400
Fax: (518)459-6736

Publications: The New York Teacher (20001)

The New York Times Co.
229 W. 43rd St.
New York, NY 10036-3913
Phone: (212)556-1234
Fax: (212)556-3535
Free: 888-346-9867

Publications: American Homestyle and Gardening (21189) • Lenoir News-Topic (24035) • The New York Times (22453) • The New York Times Book Review (22454) • The New York Times Large Type Weekly (22455) • Real Beauty (22630) • Sarasota Herald-Tribune (6663)

New York Times Co./Globe Newspaper Co.
135 Morrissey Blvd.
PO Box 2378
Boston, MA 02107-3310
Phone: (617)929-2935
Fax: (617)929-3192

Publications: The Boston Globe (13857)

New York Times Magazine Group
5 John Clarke Rd.
Newport, RI 02840

Publications: Tennis USTA (5186)

New York University
7 E. 12th St., Ste. 800
New York, NY 10003
Phone: (212)998-4300
Fax: (212)995-3790

Publications: The Washington Square News (22909)

New York University Law Review
110 W. Third St.
New York, NY 10012-1074
Phone: (212)998-6350
Fax: (212)998-4032

Publications: New York University Law Review (22456)

New York University Libraries
70 Washington Square S.
New York, NY 10012
Phone: (212)998-2519

Publications: Information Technology and Disabilities (21872)

The New York Voice/Harlem U.S.A.
175-61 Hillside Ave.
Ste. 201
Jamaica, NY 11432
Phone: (718)206-9866
Fax: (718)206-9803

Publications: The New York Voice/Harlem U.S.A. (20839)

New York Water Environment Association, Inc.
126 N. Salina St., Ste. 200
Syracuse, NY 13202
Phone: (315)422-7811
Fax: (315)422-3851

Publications: Clearwaters (23395)

New Yorker Staats Zeitung
PMB 703
3412 Clark Rd.
Sarasota, FL 34231-8406

Publications: New Yorker Staats Zeitung (6661)

Newark Morning Ledger Co.
1 Star-Ledger Plaza
Newark, NJ 07102-1200
Phone: (973)877-4040
Fax: (973)877-5845

Publications: Star-Ledger (19366)

The Newberg Graphic
109 N School St.
PO Box 700
Newberg, OR 97132
Phone: (503)538-2181
Fax: (503)538-1632

Publications: The Newberg Graphic (26444)

Newberry News Inc.
PO Box 46
Newberry, MI 49868
Phone: (906)293-8401
Fax: (906)293-8815

Publications: Newberry News (15400)

The Newbury Street Group, Inc.
355 Cambridge St.
Cambridge, MA 02141-1208
Phone: (617)354-9080
Fax: (617)354-2394
Free: 800-852-5212

Publications: Foodservice East (14054)

Newcastle Pacer, Inc.
PO Box 429
Newcastle, OK 73065
Phone: (405)387-5277
Fax: (405)387-9863

Publications: Early Bird Express (25928) • The
Newcastle Pacer (25929)

Newhouse Newspapers
405 Delmas Ave.
PO Box 849
Pascagoula, MS 39567
Phone: (601)762-1111
Fax: (601)934-1454
Free: 800-655-6597

Publications: Mississippi Press (16811)

Newhouse Services
1801 Superior Ave.
Cleveland, OH 44114
Phone: (216)999-6000
Fax: (216)344-4620
Free: 800-362-0727

Publications: Plain Dealer (24943)

Newkirk Herald-Journal
121 N Main St.
PO Box 131
Newkirk, OK 74647-0131
Phone: (580)362-2140
Fax: (580)362-2348

Publications: Newkirk Herald-Journal (25930)

Newman Independent
120 S Broadway
PO Box 417
Newman, IL 61942
Phone: (217)837-2414
Fax: (217)837-2071

Publications: Newman Independent (9283)

The Newnan Times-Herald
16 Jefferson St.
PO Box 1052
Newnan, GA 30264

Publications: The Newnan Times-Herald (7453)

Newport Communications
PO Box W
Newport Beach, CA 92658-8910
Phone: (714)261-1636
Fax: (714)261-2904
Free: 800-233-1911

Publications: Heavy Duty Trucking (2627) • Truck
Sales & Leasing (2636)

Newport Communications East
38 Executive Park, Ste. 300
Irvine, CA 92614
Phone: (949)261-1636

Publications: Truck Sales & Leasing Magazine
(2091)

The Newport Daily Express
PO Box 347
Newport, VT 05855
Phone: (802)334-6568
Fax: (802)334-6891
Free: 800-464-6568

Publications: The Newport Daily Express (31572)

Newport Historical Society
82 Touro St.
Newport, RI 02840
Phone: (401)846-0813
Fax: (401)846-1853

Publications: Newport History (28369)

The Newport Miner & Gem State Miner
PO Box 349
Newport, WA 99156-0349
Phone: (509)447-2433
Fax: (509)447-9222

Publications: The Newport Miner & Gem State
Miner (32851)

Newport Plain Talk
PO Box 279
Newport, TN 37821
Phone: (423)623-6171
Fax: (423)625-1995

Publications: Newport Plain Talk (29544)

News
617 N. Adams St.
PO Box 218
Sturgis, KY 42459
Phone: (502)333-5545
Fax: (502)333-9943

Publications: The Sturgis News (12420)

News
PO Box 249
Faribault, MN 55021
Phone: (507)334-1853
Fax: (507)334-8569

Publications: News (15894)

News
Box 447
Tower, MN 55790
Phone: (218)753-3170

Publications: Tower News (16475)

The News
PO Box 338
New Richmond, WI 54017-0338
Phone: (715)246-6881
Fax: (715)246-7117

Publications: The News (34193)

The News & Advance
101 Wyndale Dr.
PO Box 10129
Lynchburg, VA 24506-0129
Phone: (804)385-5450
Fax: (804)385-5472

Publications: The News & Daily Advance (32207)

News Advertiser
508 N 1st St.
Lake City, FL 32055
Phone: (904)752-8280
Fax: (904)758-5869

Publications: News Advertiser (6270)

News-Argus
310 N Berkeley Blvd.
Goldsboro, NC 27534
Phone: (919)778-2211
Fax: (919)778-9891

Publications: Goldsboro News-Argus (23910)

News Baja, Inc.
296 H St., 2nd Fl.
Nes Plaza Bldg.
Chula Vista, CA 91910
Phone: (619)425-2132

Publications: California Weekly (1713)

The News Banner
P.O. Drawer 90
Covington, LA 70433
Phone: (985)892-7980
Fax: (985)867-8572

Publications: The News Banner (12554)

The News & Banner, Inc.
210 W Court Squire
PO Box 97
Franklin, GA 30217
Phone: (706)675-3374
Fax: (706)675-3374

Publications: The News & Banner (7292)

News Banner Publications, Inc.
125 N. Johnson St.
PO Box 436
Bluffton, IN 46714
Phone: (260)824-0224
Fax: (260)824-0700

Publications: Bluffton News-Banner (9863) • The
Echo (9864) • The Ossian Journal (10385) • The
Sunriser News (10386)

News Chief Publishing Group
650 Sixth St. SW
Winter Haven, FL 33882
Phone: (863)294-1100
Fax: (863)294-2008

Publications: La Prensa Newspaper (6867) • Winter
Haven Shopper (6874)

The News-Chronicle
PO Box 606
Belton, SC 29627
Phone: (864)338-6124
Fax: (864)338-1109

Publications: The News Chronicle (28492)

News-Chronicle Co.
1011 Ritner Hwy.
Shippensburg, PA 17257
Phone: (717)532-4101
Fax: (717)532-3020

Publications: The News-Chronicle (27989) • Valley
Times-Star (27991)

News Chronicle Printing Co., Inc.
PO Box 218
Scott City, KS 67871
Fax: (316)872-3572

Publications: News Chronicle (11794)

The News Circle Publishing House
PO Box 3684
Glendale, CA 91201-0684
Phone: (818)507-0333
Fax: (818)246-1936

Publications: News Circle (2011)

News & Citizen
PO Box 369
Morrisville, VT 05661
Phone: (802)888-2212
Fax: (802)888-2173
Free: 800-734-2114

Publications: News and Citizen (31569)

The News-Commercial
104 1st St. S
PO Box 1299
Collins, MS 39428
Phone: (601)765-8275
Fax: (601)765-6952

Publications: The News-Commercial (16598)

News Communications
63 W 38th St. Ste. 206
New York, NY 10018-3818
Phone: (212)268-8600

Publications: Chelsea Clinton News (21399) • Our
Town (22509) • The Westsider (22915)

News Daily
138 Church St.
Jonesboro, GA 30236

Publications: Clayton News/Daily (7351)

News-Democrat & Leader
120 Public Sq.
PO Box 270
Russellville, KY 42276
Phone: (270)726-8394
Fax: (270)726-8398

Publications: News-Democrat & Leader (12389)

News and Eagle
227 W Broadway
PO Box 1192
Enid, OK 73702
Phone: (405)233-6600
Fax: (405)233-7645
Free: 800-299-6397

Publications: News and Eagle (25822)

Numbers cited after listings are entry numbers rather than page numbers.

News Eagle Inc.
PO Box E
Hawley, PA 18428-0176
Phone: (570)226-4547
Fax: (570)226-4548

Publications: The News Eagle (27032)

News-Enterprise
410 W. Dixie
Elizabethtown, KY 42701
Phone: (270)769-2312
Fax: (270)765-7318

Publications: Inside the Turret (12062)

News-Gazette
PO Box 86
Windsor, IL 61957
Phone: (217)459-2121
Fax: (217)459-2150

Publications: Shelby County News-Gazette (9767)

The News Gazette
Box 429
Winchester, IN 47394
Phone: (765)584-4501
Fax: (765)584-3066

Publications: News & Advertiser (10565)

News-Gazette Corp.
PO Box 1153
Lexington, VA 24450-1153
Phone: (540)463-3113
Fax: (540)464-6397

Publications: The News-Gazette (32190) • The Weekender (32193)

News-Gazette, Inc.
15 Main St.
PO Box 677
Champaign, IL 61820
Phone: (217)351-5252
Fax: (217)351-5291

Publications: County Star (9692) • The News-Gazette (8205)

News Gleaner Publications
9999 Gantry Rd.
Philadelphia, PA 19115
Phone: (215)969-5100
Fax: (215)969-5400

Publications: News Gleaner (Bustleton-Somerton Edition) (27581) • News Gleaner (Far Northeast Edition) (27582) • News Gleaner (Frankford Juniata Edition) (27583) • News Gleaner (Mayfair-Northeast Edition) (27584) • News Gleaner (Six Editions) (27585) • Northeast Breeze Edition (27586) • Olney Times (27597)

The News-Herald
PO Box 219
Owenton, KY 40359
Phone: (502)484-3431
Fax: (502)484-3221

Publications: The News-Herald (12334)

The News Herald
301 Collett St.
PO Box 280
Morganton, NC 28655-3322
Phone: (828)328-8725
Fax: (828)437-5372

Publications: The News Herald (24073)

News Herald
115 W. 2nd St.
PO Box 550
Port Clinton, OH 43452
Phone: (419)734-3141
Fax: (419)734-4662

Publications: News Herald (25482)

The News Herald
7085 Mentor Ave.
Willoughby, OH 44094
Phone: (440)951-0000
Fax: (440)975-2293
Free: 800-947-2737

Publications: The News-Herald (25662)

News-Herald
508 E. Broadway
Box 310
Lenoir City, TN 37771
Phone: (423)986-6581
Fax: (423)988-3261

Publications: News-Herald (29323)

The News Herald
PO Box 140628
Nashville, TN 37214
Phone: (615)889-1860

Publications: The News Beacon (29475) • The News Herald (29476)

The News-Herald, Inc.
164 Main St.
Ravena, NY 12143
Phone: (518)756-2030
Fax: (518)756-8555

Publications: Greenville Local (20700)

News of the Highlands, Inc.
PO Box B
Cornwall, NY 12518
Phone: (914)534-7771

Publications: Cornwall Local (20510) • News of the Highlands (20747)

News/Independent
PO Box 8
Cissna Park, IL 60924-0008
Phone: (815)457-2245
Fax: (815)437-3245

Publications: News/Independent (8679)

News India Times Group
43 W. 24th St.
New York, NY 10010
Phone: (212)675-7515
Fax: (212)675-7624

Publications: News India Times (22458)

The News-Item
707 N. Rock St.
PO Box 587
Shamokin, PA 17872
Phone: (570)644-6397
Fax: (570)644-0892

Publications: News-Item (27984)

News Journal
PO Box 911
Columbia, LA 71418-0911
Phone: (318)649-7136

Publications: News Journal (12549)

News Journal
70 W. 4th St.
PO Box 25
Mansfield, OH 44903
Phone: (419)522-3311
Fax: (419)522-2672

Publications: News Journal (25332)

The News Journal
146 W. Evans St.
Florence, SC 29501
Phone: (843)667-9656

Publications: The News Journal (28603)

News-Journal Corporation
901 6th St.
Daytona Beach, FL 32117-8099
Phone: (386)252-1511
Fax: (386)258-8465
Free: 800-252-1511

Publications: Flagler/Palm Coast News-Tribune (5967) • The New Volusian (6055) • The News-Journal (6037)

News-Leader
PO Box 766
511 Ash St.
Fernandina Beach, FL 32034
Phone: (904)261-3696
Fax: (904)261-3698

Publications: News-Leader (6069)

The News Leader
138 Church St.
Jonesboro, GA 30236
Phone: (770)478-5753

Publications: The News Leader (7521)

News-Leader
211 Hwy. 38 E.
PO Box 46
Rochelle, IL 61068
Phone: (815)562-4171
Fax: (815)562-2161

Publications: News-Leader (9514)

The News Leader
PO Box 9
Landrum, SC 29356-0009
Phone: (864)457-3337
Fax: (864)472-6900

Publications: The News Leader (28681)

The News-Leader
11 N. Central Ave.
PO Box 59
Staunton, VA 24402

Publications: The News-Leader (32556)

News Leader, Inc.
206 E. Texas
PO Box 619
Leesville, LA 71446
Phone: (337)239-3444
Fax: (337)238-1152

Publications: Leesville Daily Leader (12658)

News Leader, Inc.
716 E. Napoleon
PO Box 1999
Sulphur, LA 70664-1999
Phone: (318)527-7075
Fax: (318)528-3044

Publications: Beauregard Daily News (12564) • Builder News Extra (12878) • Guardian (12565) • The Iowa News (12851) • Southwest Daily News (12852) • The Vinton News (12869) • Westlake/Moss Bluff News (12879)

News-Ledger
816 W Acres Rd.
PO Box 463
West Sacramento, CA 95691-3222
Phone: (916)371-8030

Publications: News-Ledger (4065)

News Letter Journal
14 W Main
PO Box 40
Newcastle, WY 82701
Phone: (307)746-2777
Fax: (307)746-2660

Publications: News Letter Journal (34564)

News & Letters
36 S. Wabash
Rm. 1440
Chicago, IL 60603
Phone: (312)236-0799

Publications: News & Letters (8508)

News Media
Box 46
Rochelle, IL 61068
Phone: (815)562-4171

Publications: Bridger Valley Pioneer (34563)

News Media Corp.
703 Illinois Ave.
PO Box 300
Mendota, IL 61342
Phone: (815)539-9396
Fax: (815)539-7862

Publications: Mendota Reporter (9174)

News Media Corp.
107 2nd Ave W
PO Box 71
Flandreau, SD 57028
Phone: (605)997-3725
Fax: (605)997-3194

Publications: Moody County Enterprise (28855)

News Media Corp.
PO Box 210
Evanston, WY 82931
Phone: (307)789-6560
Fax: (307)789-2700

Publications: Uinta County Herald (34521)

News and Messenger
200 Mission St.
PO Box 248
Menard, TX 76859
Phone: (915)396-2243
Fax: (915)396-2739

Publications: News and Messenger (30804)

News Mirror
PO Box 278
Hector, MN 55342
Phone: (320)848-2248
Fax: (320)848-2249
Free: 888-325-0196

Publications: News Mirror (15946)

News Montana, Inc.
PO Box 659
Columbus, MT 59019
Phone: (406)322-5212
Fax: (406)322-5391
Free: 800-823-7426

Publications: Carbon County News (17774) • Stillwater County News (17775)

The News Observer
PO Box 989
Blue Ridge, GA 30513
Phone: (706)632-2019
Fax: (706)632-2577

Publications: The News Observer (7133)

News/Observer
PO Box 870
Chapel Hill, NC 27514
Phone: (919)967-7045
Fax: (919)968-4953

Publications: Chapel News (23703)

The News & Observer Publishing Co.
215 S. McDowell St.
PO Box 191
Raleigh, NC 27602
Phone: (919)829-4700

Publications: Eastern Wake News (24341) • The News and Observer (24141)

News Press
PO Box 23
Pembina, ND 58271
Phone: (701)825-6937
Fax: (701)229-3217
Free: 800-852-0057

Publications: New Era (24531)

News and Press
117 S Main St.
Box 513
Darlington, SC 29532
Phone: (803)393-3811
Fax: (803)393-6811

Publications: News and Press (28596)

News-Press & Gazette Co.
825 Edmond
PO Box 29
St. Joseph, MO 64501
Phone: (816)271-8500
Fax: (816)271-8692
Free: 800-779-6397

Publications: St. Joseph News-Press (17394)

News-Press Publications Inc.
2442 Dr. Martin Luther King Blvd.
Fort Myers, FL 33901
Phone: (239)335-0200
Fax: (239)369-1396

Publications: Lehigh Acres News Star (6096)

News Press Publishing Co.
311 S State St.
PO Box 663
Oscoda, MI 48750
Phone: (989)739-2054
Fax: (989)739-3201

Publications: Oscoda Press (15425)

News-Press Publishing Co., Inc.
110 W. State St.
Box 72
East Tawas, MI 48730-0072
Phone: (517)362-3456
Fax: (517)362-6601

Publications: Iosco County News Herald (14997)

News Printing Co.
101 Emerson Ave.
Aspinwall, PA 15215
Phone: (412)782-2121
Fax: (412)782-1195

Publications: The Herald (26666)

News Progress
100 W Monroe St.
PO Box 290
Sullivan, IL 61951-0290
Phone: (217)728-7381
Fax: (217)728-2020

Publications: News Progress (9673)

News Progress
Box 1015
Clarksville, VA 23927
Phone: (434)374-2451
Fax: (434)374-2074

Publications: Super Shopper (31976)

News Publishing
614 Hewett St.
PO Box 149
Neillsville, WI 54456
Phone: (715)743-2600
Fax: (715)743-5460

Publications: Black River County Shopper (34162) • The Clark County Press (34163)

News Publishing Black Earth
801 Water St.
PO Box 606
Sauk City, WI 53583
Phone: (608)643-3444
Fax: (608)643-4988

Publications: Sauk-Prairie Star (34313)

News Publishing Co.
PO Box 1633
Rome, GA 30162-1633
Phone: (706)291-6397
Fax: (706)232-9632

Publications: The Calhoun Times (7149) • The Cedartown Standard (7165) • Chattooga Press (7574) • Cherokee County Herald (148) • Rome News-Tribune (7503) • Walker County Messenger (7360)

News Publishing Co.
PO Box 309
Tell City, IN 47586
Phone: (812)547-3424
Fax: (812)547-2847

Publications: Lincolnland Shopping Guide (10481) • The Perry County News (10482)

News Publishing Co.
507 Main St.
Hays, KS 67601
Phone: (785)628-1081
Fax: (785)628-8186

Publications: The Hays Daily News (11480)

News Publishing Co.
PO Box 46
Neligh, NE 68756
Phone: (402)887-4840
Fax: (402)887-4711

Publications: Neligh News and Leader (18168)

News Publishing Company Inc.
1126 Mills St.
PO Box 286
Black Earth, WI 53515
Phone: (608)767-3655
Fax: (608)767-2222
Free: 800-762-3655

Publications: Allamakee Journal (33587) • Marquette County Tribune (34154) • Mt. Horeb Mail (34156) • North Iowa Times (33589) • Waukon Standard (11303)

News Publishing Co. of Mississippi
713 Lomax
PO Box 509
Waynesboro, MS 39367
Phone: (601)735-4341
Fax: (601)735-1111

Publications: The Wayne County News (16872)

News Publishing Inc.
PO Box 100
Postville, IA 52162
Fax: (319)864-3400

Publications: The Postville Herald-Leader (11165)

News Publishing, Inc.
7507 Hubbard Ave.
PO Box 62006
Middleton, WI 53562
Phone: (608)836-1601
Fax: (608)836-3759

Publications: Middleton Times-Tribune (34051)

The News-Record
221 E S
PO Box 49
Cerro Gordo, IL 61818-0049
Fax: (217)578-2833

Publications: The News-Record (8176)

The News Record
1201 W. 2nd St.
PO Box 3006
Gillette, WY 82716
Phone: (307)682-9306
Fax: (307)686-9306
Free: 800-447-4539

Publications: The News Record (34527)

The News Record, Inc.
PO Box 369
Marshall, NC 28753
Phone: (828)649-1075
Fax: (828)649-3722

Publications: The News Record (24059)

News-Register Publishing Co.
611 NE 3rd St.
PO Box 727
McMinnville, OR 97128

Publications: News-Register (26416)

News-Reporter
116 W Robert Toombs Ave.
PO Box 340
Washington, GA 30673
Phone: (706)678-2636
Fax: (706)678-3857

Publications: News-Reporter (7640)

News Reporter
PO Box 707
Whiteville, NC 28472
Phone: (910)642-4104
Fax: (910)642-1856

Publications: The News Reporter (24285) • News-Times (23695)

News-Review
109 N. Sanders
Ridgecrest, CA 93555
Phone: (760)371-4301
Fax: (760)371-4304

Publications: News-Review (2923)

News & Review
1015 20th St.
Sacramento, CA 95814
Phone: (916)498-1234
Fax: (916)498-7910

Publications: Sacramento News & Review (3017)

News-Review
201 N Main St.
PO Box 995
Continental, OH 45831
Phone: (419)596-3897

Publications: News-Review (25094)

News-Review Publishing Co.
345 NE Winchester
PO Box 1248
Roseburg, OR 97470
Phone: (541)672-3321
Fax: (541)673-5994

Publications: The News-Review (26555)

News-Review Publishing Co.
104 E. Central
PO Box 430
Sutherlin, OR 97479
Phone: (541)672-3321
Fax: (541)459-1542

Publications: The Sun-Tribune (26591) • The Umpqua Shopper (26592)

The News and Sentinel
1 Bridge St.
Box 39
Colebrook, NH 03576
Phone: (603)237-5501
Fax: (603)237-5060
Free: 800-521-5501

Publications: The News and Sentinel (18468)

News-Sentinel
204 S Broadway
PO Box 549
Stigler, OK 74462
Phone: (918)967-4655
Fax: (918)967-4289

Publications: News-Sentinel (26075)

News Shopper, Inc.
8608 Main St.
Woodstock, GA 30188
Phone: (770)926-4467
Fax: (770)591-8478

Publications: News Shopper (7656)

News-Standard
405 W Main
PO Box 488
Coulee City, WA 99115-0488
Phone: (509)632-5402
Fax: (509)632-5732

Publications: News-Standard (32731)

The News-Star
411 N. 4th St., No. 1502
Monroe, LA 71201
Phone: (318)322-5161
Fax: (318)362-0225
Free: 800-259-7788

Publications: The News-Star (12692)

The News-Sun
2227 U.S. 27 S.
Sebring, FL 33870
Phone: (863)385-6155
Fax: (863)385-1954

Publications: The News-Sun (6679)

News-Sun
PO Box 25
Fairmount, IN 46928-0025
Phone: (317)948-4164

Publications: News-Sun (9954)

News-Sun
102 N. Main St.
PO Box 39
Kendallville, IN 46755
Phone: (219)347-0400
Fax: (219)347-2693

Publications: News-Sun (10228)

News-Sun, Inc.
10102 Santa Fe Dr.
PO Box 1779
Sun City, AZ 85372
Phone: (602)977-8351
Fax: (602)876-3698

Publications: Daily News-Sun (895)

News-Times
PO Box 408
Forest Grove, OR 97116
Phone: (503)357-3181
Fax: (503)359-8456

Publications: News-Times (26355)

News-Times
831 NE Avery St.
PO Box 965
Newport, OR 97365
Phone: (541)265-8571
Fax: (541)265-3862

Publications: News-Times (26445)

News Tribune Co.
210 Monroe
Jefferson City, MO 65101
Phone: (573)636-3131

Publications: Jefferson City News Tribune (17122)

News-Tribune Publication
426 2nd St.
La Salle, IL 61301
Phone: (815)223-3200
Fax: (815)223-2543
Free: 800-892-6452

Publications: News-Tribune (9056)

News West Publishing Co.
PO Box 21209
Bullhead City, AZ 86439
Phone: (928)763-2505

Publications: Booster Advertiser (663) • Colorado River Weekender (664) • Laughlin Nevada Entertainer (665)

News World Communications
3600 New York Ave., NE
Washington, DC 20002
Phone: (202)636-3000
Fax: (202)529-2471
Free: 800-356-3588

Publications: Insight on the News (5547) • The Washington Times (5855)

Newsbytes News Network
1515 N. Courthouse Rd., 11th Fl.
Arlington, VA 22201

Publications: Washington Techway (31840)

Newsday
235 Pinelawn Rd.
Melville, NY 11747-4250
Phone: (516)843-2700
Fax: (516)843-2953

Publications: Newsday (21051)

Newspaper
619 Industrial Pkwy.
Heath, OH 43056
Phone: (740)522-8566

Publications: Ace News (25240)

Newspaper Association of America
1921 Gallows Rd., Ste. 600
Vienna, VA 22182-3900
Phone: (703)902-1600
Fax: (703)917-0636

Publications: Presstime (32579)

Newspaper Association of America Foundation
1921 Gallows Rd., Ste. 600
Vienna, VA 22182-3900
Phone: (703)902-1600

Publications: Foundation Update (32577)

Newspaper Division United Methodist Communications Council
PO Box 660275
Dallas, TX 75266-0275
Phone: (214)630-6495
Fax: (214)630-0079
Free: 800-947-0207

Publications: United Methodist Reporter (30187)

Newspaper Guild of New York
1501 Broadway, 7th Fl., Ste. 708
New York, NY 10036
Phone: (212)575-1580

Publications: Frontpage (21737)

Newspaper Ltd.
1163 Cedar Ave.
Trail, BC, Canada V1R 4B8
Phone: (250)368-8551
Fax: (250)368-8550

Publications: Trail Daily Times (35115)

Newspaper Research Journal
Department of Journalism
University of Memphis
Memphis, TN 38152
Phone: (901)678-4238
Fax: (901)678-4287

Publications: Newspaper Research Journal (29377)

Newspaper Service Co., Inc.
238 Market St.
PO Box 910
Jennings, LA 70546
Fax: (318)824-3019

Publications: Jennings Daily News (12606)

Newspapers
PO Box 100
Riesel, TX 76682
Fax: (817)753-3871

Publications: The Riesel Rustler (30982)

NewsPort
San Francisco State University
Humanities Bldg.
1600 Holloway Ave.
1600 Holloway Ave.
San Francisco, CA 94132
Phone: (415)338-2086

Publications: NewsPort (3403)

Newsreel, Inc.
8 E Long St., Ste. 420
Columbus, OH 43215-2914
Phone: (614)469-0700
Fax: (614)469-7077

Publications: Newsreel (25036)

NewsRX
PO Box 5528
Atlanta, GA 30307
Phone: (770)507-7777
Free: 800-726-4550

Publications: Stem Cell Week (7046) • Women's Health Weekly (7062)

Newsweek Budget Travel, Inc.
251 W. 57th St.
New York, NY 10019
Phone: (212)564-2630
Fax: (212)564-2670

Publications: Arthur Frommer's Budget Travel (21255)

Newsweek, Inc.
251 W. 57th St.
New York, NY 10019
Phone: (212)445-4000
Fax: (212)445-5068
Free: 800-634-6850

Publications: Newsweek (22459) • Newsweek International (22460) • Newsweek International - Latin America Edition (22461)

Newsweekly
PO Box 405
Moorestown, NJ 08057
Phone: (856)231-7600
Fax: (856)231-4333

Publications: Newsweekly (19521)

Newton Co. News
PO Box 65
706 Glover St.
Newton, TX 75966
Phone: (409)379-2416
Fax: (409)379-2416

Publications: Newton County News (30867)

Newton County News
PO Box 50
Granby, MO 64844
Phone: (417)472-3100
Fax: (417)472-6533

Publications: Newton County News (17085)

Newton County Times
Box 453
Jasper, AR 72641
Phone: (870)446-2645
Fax: (870)446-6286

Publications: Newton County Times (1196)

Newton Press-Mentor
700 W. Washington
PO Box 151
Newton, IL 62448
Phone: (618)783-2324
Fax: (618)783-2325

Publications: Newton Press-Mentor (9284)

Newton Printing Co.
200 1st Ave. E
Newton, IA 50208
Phone: (641)792-3121
Fax: (641)792-5505

Publications: The Newton Daily News (11115)

The Newton Record
120 S Main St.
PO Box 60
Newton, MS 39345
Phone: (601)683-2001
Fax: (601)683-2360

Publications: The Newton Record (16800)

Next Generation Publications, Inc.
PO Box 588
Groton, SD 57445
Phone: (605)397-2676
Fax: (605)397-8671

Publications: Brown County Independent (28862)

The Next Step Magazine
86 West Main St.
PO Box 405
Victor, NY 14564
Phone: (716)742-1260
Fax: (716)742-1263

Publications: The Next Step Magazine (23494)

NEXUS Magazine
2940 E Colfax, No. 131
Denver, CO 80206
Phone: (303)321-5006
Fax: (720)941-9352
Free: 888-909-7474

Publications: NEXUS Magazine (4344)

The NFIB Research Foundation
1201 F St., NW Ste. 200
Washington, DC 20004
Phone: (202)554-9000
Fax: (202)554-5572
Free: 800-552-6342

Publications: The NFIB Foundation Small Business Economic Trends (5695)

NFR Communications, Inc.
4948 Washburn Ave.S.
Minneapolis, MN 55410
Phone: (612)929-8110
Fax: (612)929-8146

Publications: Northwestern Financial Review (16117)

NHN Publishing
PO Box 612
New Philadelphia, OH 44663-0612
Phone: (330)339-6338

Publications: The National Hobby News (25420)

The Niagara Advance
PO Box 430
Virgil, ON, Canada L0S 1T0
Phone: (905)468-3283
Fax: (905)468-8137

Publications: The Niagara Advance (36841)

Niagara Farmers' Monthly
PO Box 52
Smithville, ON, Canada L0R 2A0
Phone: (416)957-3751
Fax: (416)957-0088

Publications: Niagara Farmers' Monthly (36397)

Niagara Frontier Publications
1859 Whitehaven Rd.
PO Box 130
Grand Island, NY 14072-0130
Phone: (716)773-7676
Fax: (716)773-7190

Publications: Grand Island PennySaver (20677) • Island Dispatch (20678) • Lewiston-Porter Sentinel (20679) • Niagara-Wheatfield Tribune (20680)

Niagara Gazette
310 Niagara St.
PO Box 549
Niagara Falls, NY 14302-0549
Phone: (716)282-2311
Fax: (716)286-3895

Publications: Niagara Gazette (23006)

The Niagara Journal
PO Box 217
Niagara, WI 54151
Phone: (715)696-6111
Fax: (715)696-3400

Publications: The Niagara Journal (34196)

Niagara Shopping News
4949 Victoria Ave.
Niagara Falls, ON, Canada L2E 4C7
Phone: (905)357-2440
Fax: (905)357-1620

Publications: Niagara Shopping News (36109)

Niagara University
PO Box 1919
Lower Level Gallagher Center
Niagara University, NY 14109
Phone: (716)285-1212
Fax: (716)286-8542

Publications: The Niagara Index (23009)

Nibbe, Hernandez & Associates, Inc.
4110 Rio Bravo Dr., Ste. 108
El Paso, TX 79902
Phone: (915)532-1567
Fax: (915)544-7556

Publications: Twin Plant News (30283)

Nichi Bei Times
2211 Bush St.
San Francisco, CA 94115
Phone: (415)921-6820
Fax: (415)921-0770

Publications: Nichi Bei Times (3404)

Nicholas Communications, Inc.
26012 Marguerite Pkwy., Ste. 344
Mission Viejo, CA 92692
Phone: (949)580-0230
Fax: (949)580-0231

Publications: Medical Industry Information Report (2555)

Nicholas County Publishing Co., Inc.
603 Church St.
PO Box 503
Summersville, WV 26651
Phone: (304)872-2251
Fax: (304)872-2254
Free: 800-640-5807

Publications: The Nicholas Chronicle (33473)

Nicholls State University
PO Box 2010
Thibodaux, LA 70310
Phone: (985)448-4259
Fax: (985)448-4267

Publications: The Nicholls Worth (12860)

Nichols Hills Publishing Co., Inc.
Box 20340
10801 N. Quail Plaza Dr.
Oklahoma City, OK 73156
Phone: (405)755-3311
Fax: (405)753-3315

Publications: Friday (25931)

Hugh Nicholson
884 Ford St.
Peterborough, ON, Canada K9J 5V3
Phone: (705)749-3383
Fax: (705)749-0074

Publications: The Hockey Talk (36315)

Nickel Development Institute
214 King St. W., Ste. 510
Toronto, ON, Canada M5H 3S6
Phone: (416)591-7999
Fax: (416)591-7987

Publications: Communique (36555) • Nickel (36674)

The Nickel-Kelso
1510 Grade St.
Kelso, WA 98626
Phone: (360)423-3141

Publications: The Nickel-Kelso (32786)

Nickel Saver
715 W. Third Ave.
PO Box 699
Moses Lake, WA 98837
Phone: (509)765-5681
Fax: (509)766-9977
Free: 800-962-0311

Publications: Nickel Saver (32839)

Nickel's Worth
107 N. 5th St.
PO Box 2048
Coeur d'Alene, ID 83816
Phone: (208)667-0651
Fax: (208)765-6969

Publications: Nickel's Worth (7846)

Nielson Publishing
PO Box 308
Avoca, IA 51521
Phone: (712)343-2154
Fax: (712)343-2262

Publications: Avoca Journal-Herald (10615)

Nieman Foundation
1 Francis Ave.
Cambridge, MA 02138
Phone: (617)496-2968
Fax: (617)495-8976

Publications: Nieman Reports (14086)

Nifty Nickel
909 W Bonanza Rd.
Las Vegas, NV 89106-3528
Phone: (702)224-5555
Fax: (702)382-0549

Publications: Nifty Nickel (18382)

Night Roses
PO Box 393
Prospect Heights, IL 60070
Phone: (847)392-2435

Publications: Night Roses (9471)

Nightshade Publications
PO Box 8068
Cranston, RI 02920
Phone: (401)781-9438
Fax: (401)943-0980

Publications: Haunts (28334)

Nihon Keizai Shimbun
1325 Ave. of the Americas, Ste. 2500
New York, NY 10019
Phone: (212)261-6200
Fax: (212)261-6208

Publications: The Nikkei Weekly (22463)

996963 Ontario Inc.
41 High St.
PO Box 160
Vankleek Hill, ON, Canada K0B 1R0
Phone: (613)678-3327
Fax: (613)678-2700
Free: 877-678-3327

Publications: The Review (36840)

99 North Promotions
PO Box 2289
Squamish, BC, Canada V0N 3G0
Phone: (604)892-9679
Fax: (604)892-9609

Publications: 99 North Magazine (35094)

The Ninety-Nines, Inc.
International Women Pilots Assn.
4300 Amelia Earhart Rd.
Oklahoma City, OK 73159
Phone: (405)685-7969
Fax: (405)685-7985

Publications: International Women Pilots/99 News (11883)

Ninnau Publications
11 Post Ter.
Basking Ridge, NJ 07920
Phone: (908)776-4151
Fax: (908)221-0744

Publications: Ninnau (18665)

Ninthwave Records and Publishing
PO Box 1734
Wheaton, MD 20915
Phone: (301)588-2369
Fax: (301)991-6640

Publications: Lexicon (13780)

Nisqually Valley News
PO Box 597
Yelm, WA 98597
Phone: (360)458-2681
Fax: (360)458-5741

Publications: Nisqually Valley News (33239) •
Nisqually Valley Shopper (33240)

Nite-Owl Press
137 Pointview Rd., Ste. 300
Pittsburgh, PA 15227
Phone: (412)885-3798

Publications: Nite-Writer's International Literary Arts
Journal (27822)

NIVA Inc.
300-30 Murray St.
Ottawa, ON, Canada K1N 5M4
Phone: (613)737-6000
Fax: (613)737-5868

Publications: Writer's Block (36283)

Nixon Newspapers, Inc.
26 W 3rd St.
PO Box 87
Peru, IN 46970-2155
Phone: (317)473-6641
Fax: (317)472-4438

Publications: The Good Times (10395) • The
News-Dispatch (10304) • Peru Daily Tribune (10396)

Nixon Publishing
123 W Canal St.
Box 379
Wabash, IN 46992
Phone: (219)563-2131
Fax: (219)563-0816
Free: 800-659-6321

Publications: Plain Dealer (10529)

NJN Publishing
8 Minneakoning Rd.
PO Box 32
Flemington, NJ 08822-0032
Phone: (908)575-6660
Fax: (908)575-6682

Publications: The Journal (Greenbrook-North Plainfield Edition) (19573) • Piscataway Review
(19430) • Somerset Messenger Gazette (19565) •
South Plainfield Reporter (19590) • Value Shopper
(19580)

NJN Publishing
106 E Moore St.
Hackettstown, NJ 07840
Phone: (908)852-1212
Fax: (908)852-9320

Publications: Community Forum (18856) • Suburban News (18858)

NJN Publishing
PO Box 500
Hackettstown, NJ 07840
Phone: (908)852-1212
Fax: (908)852-9320

Publications: Star Gazette (18857)

NJN Publishing
PO Box 425
Hackettstown, NJ 07840-0425
Phone: (908)362-6161
Fax: (908)852-9320

Publications: The Blairstown Press (18855)

NJW Magazine (New Jersey Woman)
177 Main St., Ste. 232
Fort Lee, NJ 07024-6936
Phone: (201)886-2185

Publications: NJW Magazine (New Jersey Woman)
(18832)

N.L. Publishing, Inc.
PO Box 69
Old Forge, NY 13420
Phone: (315)369-3078
Fax: (315)369-3736

Publications: Northern Logger and Timber Processor (23037)

Nob Hill Gazette
The Hearst Bldg., Ste. 222
5 3rd St.
San Francisco, CA 94103
Phone: (415)227-0190
Fax: (415)974-5103

Publications: Nob Hill Gazette (3405)

Noble Publishing Corp.
630 Pinnacle Ct.
Norcross, GA 30071
Phone: (770)449-6774
Fax: (770)448-2839

Publications: Applied Microwave & Wireless (7455)

Nobles County Review
PO Box 160
Adrian, MN 56110
Phone: (507)483-2213
Fax: (507)483-2219

Publications: Nobles County Review (15699)

Noblesville Times
PO Box 100
Noblesville, IN 46060
Phone: (317)773-3971
Fax: (317)773-3970

Publications: Noblesville Times (10355)

Nocona News
PO Box 539
Nocona, TX 76255
Phone: (940)825-3201

Publications: News (30868)

Nocturnal Lyric
Box 542
Astoria, OR 97103
Phone: (503)325-2340

Publications: Nocturnal Lyric (26226)

Nogales International
PO Box 579
Nogales, AZ 85628
Phone: (602)281-9706
Fax: (602)761-3115

Publications: Nogales International (755)

The Noise
74 Jamaica St.
Boston, MA 02130
Phone: (617)524-4735

Publications: The Noise (13939)

Nomis Publications Inc.
PO Box 5122
Youngstown, OH 44514
Phone: (330)965-2380
Fax: 800-321-9040
Free: 800-321-7479

Publications: YB News (25700)

Norborne Democrat-Leader
106 S Pine St.
Box 195
Norborne, MO 64668
Phone: (660)593-3712

Publications: Norborne Democrat-Leader (17317)

The Nordic Press, Inc.
243 E. 34th St.
New York, NY 10016
Phone: (212)686-3356
Fax: (212)689-2939

Publications: Vaba Eesti Sona (Free Estonian
Word) (22893)

Nordstjernan (Swedish News)
PO Box 4587
New York, NY 10163-4587
Phone: (212)490-3900
Fax: (212)490-5979
Free: 800-827-9333

Publications: Nordstjernan (Swedish News) (22468)

Norm Winick
251 E Main St.
PO Box 1
Galesburg, IL 61402
Phone: (309)342-2010
Fax: (309)342-2728
Free: 800-248-3750

Publications: The Zephyr (8907)

Normalite
102 Parkinson St.
Normal, IL 61761
Phone: (309)454-5476
Fax: (309)454-5476

Publications: Normal Normalite (9301)

Norman County Index
307 W Main St.
PO Box 148
Ada, MN 56510-0148
Phone: (218)784-2541
Fax: (218)784-2551

Publications: Norman County Index (15696)

The Normangee Star
PO Box 249
Normangee, TX 77871
Phone: (409)396-3391
Fax: (409)396-6651

Publications: The Normangee Star (30869)

Norris Publishers
PO Box 2593
Amherst, MA 01004-2593
Phone: (413)519-7288
Fax: (413)253-9525

Publications: Journal of Computing in Higher Education (13797)

Norris-Whitney Communications
23 Hannover Dr., No. 7
St. Catharines, ON, Canada L2W 1A3
Phone: (905)641-3471
Fax: (905)641-1648
Free: 800-265-8481

Publications: Canadian Music Trade (36352) • Canadian Musician (36353)

North Adams Publishing Co.
Box 473
North Adams, MA 01247
Phone: (413)663-3741
Fax: (413)662-2792

Publications: Transcript (14418)

**North American Association for the
Study of Obesity**
8630 Fenton St. Ste. 412
Silver Spring, MD 20910
Phone: (301)563-6526
Fax: (301)563-6595

Publications: Obesity Research (13942)

North American Bookdealers Exchange
PO Box 606
Cottage Grove, OR 97424

Publications: Book Dealers World (26294)

North American Deer Farmer
1720 W Wisconsin Ave.
Appleton, WI 54914-3254
Phone: (920)734-0934
Fax: (920)734-0955

Publications: The North American Deer Farmer
(33541)

North American Die Casting Association
9701 W. Higgins Rd., Ste. 880
Rosemont, IL 60018-4721
Phone: (847)292-3600
Fax: (847)292-3620

Publications: Die Casting Engineer (9555)

North American Equipment Dealers Association
1195 Smizer Mill Rd.
Fenton, MO 63026-3480
Phone: (636)349-5000
Fax: (636)349-5443

Publications: NAEDA Equipment Dealer (17062)

North American Lily Society Inc.
PO Box 272
Owatonna, MN 55060
Phone: (507)451-2170
Fax: (507)455-0087

Publications: North American Lily Society Quarterly (16252)

North American Media Group, Inc.
12301 Whitewater Dr.
Minnetonka, MN 55343
Phone: (952)988-7117
Fax: (952)936-9169
Free: 800-688-7611

Publications: Cooking Pleasures (16168) • Gardening How-To (16170) • Handy (16171) • North American Fisherman (16172) • North American Hunter (16173) • PGA Tour Partners (16174) • Today's Health & Wellness (16177)

North American Post Publishing, Inc.
PO Box 3173
Seattle, WA 98114-3173
Phone: (206)623-0100
Fax: (206)625-1424

Publications: North American Post (32991)

North American Publications
164-11 89th Ave., Ste. 190
Jamaica, NY 11432
Phone: (718)591-7777

Publications: Jamaica Shopping & Entertainment Guide (20836)

North American Publishing Co.
Pierce Financial Corp.
837 Villa Ridge Rd.
Falls Church, VA 22046-3665
Free: 800-627-2689

Publications: Catalog Success Magazine (32042) • Dealerscope: The Business of CE Retailing (32043) • Inside Direct Mail (32048) • Package Printing (32051) • Print Media (32052) • Printing Impressions (32053) • PrintMedia Magazine (32054) • Promotional Marketing (32055) • Target Marketing (32057)

North American Retail Dealers Association
10 E 22nd St., Ste. 310
Lombard, IL 60148
Phone: (630)953-8950
Fax: (630)953-8957

Publications: NARDA Independent Retailer (9117)

North American Riding for the Handicapped Association, Inc. (NARHA)
PO Box 33150
Denver, CO 80233
Phone: (303)452-1212
Fax: (303)252-4610
Free: 800-369-7433

Publications: NARHA Strides (4341)

North American Rock Garden Society
Box 67
Millwood, NY 10546
Phone: (914)762-2948

Publications: Rock Garden Quarterly (4352)

North American Shortwave Association (NASWA)
45 Wildflower Rd.
Levittown, PA 19057

Publications: North American Shortwave Association (NASWA)—The Journal (27188)

North American Vegetarian Society
PO Box 72
Dolgeville, NY 13329
Phone: (518)568-7970
Fax: (518)568-7979

Publications: Vegetarian Voice (20533)

North Bartow News
321B N Main St.
PO Box 374
Adairsville, GA 30103
Phone: (770)773-3754
Fax: (770)773-3754

Publications: North Bartow News (6898)

North Beach Now
350 Bay, Ste. 100-106
San Francisco, CA 94133
Phone: (415)391-1043
Fax: (415)398-2258

Publications: North Beach Now (3407)

North Bend Eagle
PO Box 100
North Bend, NE 68649
Phone: (402)652-8312

Publications: North Bend Eagle (18175)

North Carolina Agricultural & Technical University
1601 E. Market St.
Box E25
Greensboro, NC 27411
Phone: (336)334-7700
Fax: (336)334-3699

Publications: A & T Register (23915)

North Carolina Association of Electric Corp.
3400 Sumner Blvd. 27616
PO Box 27306
Raleigh, NC 27611
Phone: (919)872-0800
Fax: (919)878-3970
Free: 800-662-8835

Publications: Carolina Country (24130)

North Carolina Association of Pharmacists
109 Church St.
Chapel Hill, NC 27516
Phone: (919)967-2237
Fax: (919)968-9430

Publications: North Carolina Pharmacist (23718)

North Carolina Association of Plumbing, Heating and Cooling Contractors, Inc.
70 E. Business Park
145 US Hwy. 70 West
Garner, NC 27529
Phone: (919)661-8222
Fax: (919)661-8003

Publications: North Carolina Plumbing-Heating-Cooling Forum (23905)

North Carolina Bankers Association
3601 Haworth Dr.
PO Box 19999
Raleigh, NC 27619-1999
Phone: (919)781-7979
Fax: (919)881-9909
Free: 800-662-7044

Publications: Carolina Banker (24129)

North Carolina Center for Public Policy Research
PO Box 430
Raleigh, NC 27602
Phone: (919)832-2839
Fax: (919)832-2847

Publications: North Carolina Insight (24145)

North Carolina Citizens for Business and Industry
PO Box 2508
Raleigh, NC 27602
Phone: (919)836-1400
Fax: (919)836-1425

Publications: North Carolina (24143)

North Carolina Dept. of Agriculture
PO Box 27647
Raleigh, NC 27611
Phone: (919)733-4216
Fax: (919)733-5047

Publications: Agricultural Review (North Carolina) (24124)

North Carolina Genealogical Society
PO Box 22
Greenville, NC 27835-0022

Publications: North Carolina Genealogical Society Journal (23967)

North Carolina Law Review Association
University of North Carolina
School of Law
Van Hecke-Wettach Hall
Chapel Hill, NC 27599-3380
Phone: (919)962-3926
Fax: (919)962-1527

Publications: North Carolina Law Review (23717)

North Carolina Medical Journal
Woodcroft Professional Center
5501 Fortunes Ridge Dr., Ste E
Durham, NC 27713
Phone: (919)401-6599
Fax: (919)401-6899

Publications: North Carolina Medical Journal (23838)

North Carolina Museum of History
4650 Mail Service Ctr.
Raleigh, NC 27699-4650
Phone: (919)715-0200
Fax: (919)733-8655

Publications: Tar Heel Junior Historian (24155)

North Carolina Office of Archives and History
4622 Mail Service Ctr.
Raleigh, NC 27699-4622
Phone: (919)733-7442
Fax: (919)733-1439

Publications: North Carolina Historical Review (24144)

North Carolina Propane Gas Association
5112 Bur Oak Circle
Raleigh, NC 27612
Phone: (919)787-8485
Fax: (919)781-7481

Publications: NGA News (24142)

North Carolina State University
Dept. of Adult & Community College Education
310 Poe Hall
Box 7801
Raleigh, NC 27695-7801
Phone: (919)515-6248
Fax: (919)515-4039

Publications: Community College Review (24133)

North Carolina State University
PO Box 8608
Raleigh, NC 27695-8608
Phone: (919)515-2411
Fax: (919)515-5133

Publications: Technician (24156)

North Central Regional Educational Laboratory
1120 E. Diehl Rd., Ste. 200
Naperville, IL 60563-1460
Phone: (630)649-6500
Fax: (630)649-6730
Free: 800-356-2735

Publications: Learning Point (9267) • Pathways to School Improvement (9271)

North Coast Journal, Inc.
145 G St., Ste. A
Arcata, CA 95521
Phone: (707)826-2000
Fax: (707)826-2060

Publications: North Coast Journal (1430)

North Country Publishing Co.
79 Main St.
Box 28
Lancaster, NH 03584
Phone: (603)788-4939
Fax: (603)788-3022
Free: 800-643-4939

Publications: Coos County Democrat (18541)

2552

Numbers cited after listings are entry numbers rather than page numbers.

North Country Publishing Corp.
211 E 3rd St.
Harbor Springs, MI 49740
Phone: (231)526-2191
Fax: (231)526-7634

Publications: Harbor Springs Harbor Light (15144)

North Country Sun, Inc.
PO Box 425
Ironwood, MI 49938
Phone: (906)932-3530
Fax: (906)932-3074

Publications: North Country Sun (15214)

North Country This Week
PO Box 975
Potsdam, NY 13676
Phone: (315)265-1000
Fax: (315)268-8701

Publications: North Country This Week (23138) •
Northern New York Business Journal (23139)

North County Publications
1080 S Amphlett Blvd.
PO Box 5400
San Mateo, CA 94402-1860
Phone: (650)348-4321
Fax: (650)348-4446

Publications: Coastside Chronicle (3584) • Daly
City Record (1802) • Enterprise-Journal (3586) •
San Bruno Herald (3097)

North County Times
207 E. Pennsylvania Ave.
Escondido, CA 92025
Phone: (619)745-6611
Fax: (619)745-8809

Publications: North County Times (1892)

North County Times
PO Box 2800
Fallbrook, CA 92088
Phone: (619)723-1171
Fax: (619)723-4967

Publications: Enterprise (1912)

**North Dakota Association of Rural Elec-
tric Cooperatives**
3201 Nygren Dr. NW
PO Box 727
Mandan, ND 58554
Phone: (701)663-6501
Fax: (701)663-3745
Free: 800-234-0518

Publications: North Dakota REC Magazine (24498)

North Dakota Education Association
PO Box 5005
Bismarck, ND 58502
Phone: (701)223-0450
Fax: (701)224-8535

Publications: North Dakota Education News (24353)

North Dakota Game and Fish Dept.
100 N Bismarck Expy.
Bismarck, ND 58501-5095
Phone: (701)328-6300
Fax: (701)328-6352

Publications: North Dakota Outdoors (24356)

**North Dakota Motor Carriers Association,
Inc.**
PO Box 874
Bismarck, ND 58502
Phone: (701)223-2700
Fax: (701)223-4324

Publications: Rolling Along (24359)

North Dakota Printing Publishing
303 NE 1st St.
PO Box 908
Mandan, ND 58554
Phone: (701)663-6823
Fax: (701)663-2442

Publications: The Finder (Mandan) (24497)

North Dakota State College of Science
800 N 6th St.
Wahpeton, ND 58076
Phone: (701)671-2240
Fax: (701)671-2260

Publications: American Technical Education Association Journal (24547)

North Dakota State College of Science
Marketing and Communications
Wahpeton, ND 58076
Phone: (701)671-2483
Fax: (701)671-2145
Free: 800-342-4325

Publications: College Review (24548)

North Dakota State University
356 Memorial Union
Fargo, ND 58105
Phone: (701)231-8929
Fax: (701)231-9402

Publications: The Spectrum (24413)

North Dakota Stockmen's Association
407 S. 2nd St.
Bismarck, ND 58504
Phone: (701)223-2522
Fax: (701)223-2587
Free: 800-224-3031

Publications: North Dakota Stockman (24357)

North Delta Sentinel
10680 84th Ave.
Delta, BC, Canada V4C 2L2
Phone: (604)589-2233
Fax: (604)581-1519

Publications: North Delta Sentinel (34947)

North Eagle Corp. of New York
15 Arbutus Ln.
Stony Brook, NY 11790-1408

Publications: North Atlantic Review (23374)

North East Publishing, Inc.
4475 S. Clinton Ave., Ste. 201
South Plainfield, NJ 07080
Phone: (908)561-6010
Fax: (908)755-7864

Publications: Contemporary Bride Magazine
(19588)

North Georgia News
PO Box 2029
Blairsville, GA 30514
Phone: (706)745-6343
Fax: (706)745-1830

Publications: North Georgia News (7129)

North Idaho College
1000 W Garden
Coeur d'Alene, ID 83814
Phone: (208)769-3228
Fax: (208)769-3431

Publications: NIC Sentinel (7845)

North Iowa Area Community College
500 College Dr.
Mason City, IA 50401-7213
Phone: (641)423-1264
Fax: (641)422-4430
Free: 800-GO-NIACC

Publications: Logos (11072)

North Island Publishing
1606 Sedlescomb Dr., Unit 8
Mississauga, ON, Canada L4X 1M6
Phone: (905)625-7070
Fax: (905)625-4856
Free: 800-331-7408

Publications: The Graphic Monthly (36069)

North Island Publishing Ltd.
1606 Sedlescomb Dr., Unit 8
Mississauga, ON, Canada L4X 1M6
Phone: (905)625-7070
Fax: (905)625-4856
Free: 800-331-7408

Publications: Masthead (36077)

North Jackson Progress
PO Drawer 625
Stevenson, AL 35772
Phone: (256)437-2395
Fax: (256)437-2592

Publications: North Jackson Progress (290)

North Jersey Community Newspapers
12-38 River Rd.
Fair Lawn, NJ 07410-1897
Phone: (201)791-8400
Fax: (201)794-3259

Publications: Fair Lawn-Elmwood Park-Saddle
Brook Shopper (18806) • Garfield-Wallington-South
Hackensack Shopper (18842) • Hawthorne-Glen
Rock-Haledon-North Haledon-Prospect Park Shop-
per (18870) • Lodi-Hasbrouck Heights-Woodridge-
Maywood-Rochelle Park Shopper (19179) • The
News Beacon (18808) • The Week Ahead (18810)

North Jersey Community Newspapers
The Weekly Division of North Jersey Media
Group
1 Garret Mountain Plz.
PO Box 471
West Paterson, NJ 07424-0471
Phone: (973)569-7000

Publications: Belleville Times (19726) • Bloomfield
Life (19727) • Dateline Journal (18754) • Glen Ridge
Voice (19729) • The Item of Millburn- and Sho- Hills
(19730) • Lakeland Today (19731) • The Montclair
Times (19732) • Neighbor News (19522) • Northern
Valley Suburbanite (19733) • Nutley Sun (19734) •
Pascack Valley Community Life (19735) • Passaic
Valley Today (19736) • The Ridgewood News
(19737) • The Shopper News (18809) • South -
Bergenite (19738) • Suburban Life (19523) • Subur-
ban Trends (19739) • Today Newspapers (19740) •
The Town Journal (19504) • Town News (19505) •
Twin-Boro News (18774) • Verona-Cedar Grove
Times (18722) • Wayne Today (19741) • The Wyck-
off Suburban News (19506)

North Jersey Media Group
150 River St.
Hackensack, NJ 07601-7172
Phone: (201)646-4000
Fax: (201)646-4310

Publications: The Record (18854)

North Jersey Media Group
41 Oak St.
Ridgewood, NJ 07450
Phone: (201)599-6090
Fax: (201)847-1144

Publications: Berger County Newspapers, Inc.
(19502)

North Jersey Newspapers
301 Central Ave.
Clark, NJ 07066
Phone: (732)396-4404
Fax: (732)396-4770
Free: 800-472-0102

Publications: Elizabeth City News (18748)

North Jersey Newspapers
PO Box 455
Ledgewood, NJ 07852
Phone: (973)584-7176
Fax: (973)362-9223

Publications: West Morris Star Journal (19168)

North Jersey Newspapers
PO Box 52
Stanhope, NJ 07874
Phone: (973)691-9530

Publications: The Chronicle (19597) • The Journal
(19598) • The Sussex County Chronicle (19599)

North Jersey Newspapers Co.
231 Herbert Ave., Bldg. 2
Closter, NJ 07624
Phone: (201)784-0903
Fax: (201)784-2592

Publications: Teaneck Suburbanite (19610)

North Jersey Newspapers Co.
44 Veterans Memorial Pkwy. E
Somerville, NJ 08876
Phone: (908)722-3000
Fax: (908)722-8475

Publications: Record-Press (19576)

North Jersey Prospector, Inc.
85 Crooks Ave.
Clifton, NJ 07011
Phone: (973)773-8300

Publications: North Jersey Prospector (18757)

North Lake Tahoe Bonanza
917 Tahoe Blvd., Ste. 205
PO Drawer 7820
Incline Village, NV 89452
Phone: (775)831-4666
Fax: (702)831-4222

Publications: North Lake Tahoe Bonanza (18358)

North Light Book Club
4700 E Galbraith Rd.
Cincinnati, OH 45236
Phone: (513)531-2222
Fax: (513)531-4744

Publications: North Light (24811)

North Louisiana Good News
203 Gleason St.
Minden, LA 71055
Phone: (318)377-1866
Fax: (318)377-1895

Publications: North Louisiana Good News (12688)

North Louisiana Historical Association
Box 6701
Shreveport, LA 71136
Phone: (318)424-4533
Fax: (318)797-5122

Publications: North Louisiana History (12817)

North Louisiana Publishing, Inc.
Box 1007
Oak Grove, LA 71263
Phone: (318)428-3207
Fax: (318)428-2747

Publications: West Carroll Gazette (12788)

North Manchester News-Journal, Inc.
118 N Walnut St.
North Manchester, IN 46962-1844

Publications: The News Journal (10360)

North Mississippi Community Newspaper
209 Commerce St.
PO Box 279
Aberdeen, MS 39730
Phone: (601)369-4507
Fax: (601)369-4508

Publications: Aberdeen Examiner (16543)

North Mississippi Newspapers
219 E Main St.
PO Box 369
Senatobia, MS 38668
Phone: (662)562-4414
Fax: (662)562-8866

Publications: The Democrat (16842)

North Myrtle Beach Times
203 N Kings Hwy.
PO Box 725
North Myrtle Beach, SC 29597
Phone: (843)249-3525
Fax: (843)249-7012

Publications: North Myrtle Beach Times (28730)

North Newspapers Inc.
304 Davis St.
PO Box 70
Independence, VA 24348-0070
Phone: (540)773-2222
Fax: (540)773-2287

Publications: The Declaration Dynamo (32173)

North Pacific Union Conference of Seventh-Day Adventists
PO Box 871150
Vancouver, OR 98687-1150

Publications: Gleaner (26603)

The North Platte Telegraph
621 N. Chestnut
North Platte, NE 69103-0370
Phone: (308)532-6000
Fax: (308)535-9268
Free: 800-753-7092

Publications: Telegraph Happenings (18177)

The North Scott Press
214 N. Second St.
PO Box 200
Eldridge, IA 52748
Phone: (563)285-8111
Fax: (563)285-8114

Publications: The North Scott Press (10870)

North Scott Press, Inc.
101 W 4th St.
PO Box 415
Wilton, IA 52778
Fax: (319)732-3144

Publications: Wilton-Durant Advocate News (10858)

North Shore Free Press Ltd.
1139 Lonsdale Ave.
North Vancouver, BC, Canada V7M 2H4
Phone: (604)985-2131

Publications: North Shore News (35036)

North Shore Jewish Press
201 Washington St.
Ste. 14
Salem, MA 01970
Phone: (508)745-4111
Fax: (508)745-5333

Publications: The Jewish Journal/North of Boston (14513)

The North Shore Sentinel
PO Box 640
155 Main St.
Thessalon, ON, Canada P0R 1L0
Phone: (705)842-2504
Fax: (705)842-2679

Publications: The North Shore Sentinel (36433)

North-South Center Press at the University of Miami
1500 Monza Ave.
Coral Gables, FL 33146
Phone: (305)284-8914
Fax: (305)284-5089

Publications: Public Budgeting and Finance (6011)

North Star Media
PO Box 512
Cambridge, MN 55008
Phone: (763)689-1181
Fax: (763)689-1185

Publications: Cambridge Star (15784)

North Star News
PO Box 158
204, S. Main St.
Karlstad, MN 56732
Phone: (218)436-2157
Fax: (218)436-3271

Publications: North Star News (15981)

North Star Publishing Co.
1602 Hwy. 71
International Falls, MN 56649-2161
Phone: (218)285-7411
Fax: (218)285-7206

Publications: The Daily Journal (15968)

North Superior Publishing, Inc.
1145 Barton St.
Thunder Bay, ON, Canada P7B 5N3
Phone: (807)623-2348
Fax: (807)623-7515

Publications: Thunder Bay Business (36439) •
Thunder Bay Life (36442)

North Tahoe/Truckee Week
PO Box 49
Tahoe Vista, CA 96148
Phone: (530)546-5995
Fax: (530)546-8113

Publications: North Tahoe/Truckee Week (3949)

North Texas Catholic
800 W Loop 820 S
Fort Worth, TX 76108
Phone: (817)560-3300
Fax: (817)244-8839

Publications: North Texas Catholic (30348)

North Valley Newspapers, Inc.
2680 Gateway Dr.
PO Box 1148
Anderson, CA 96007
Fax: (916)365-2829

Publications: The Valley Post (1423)

North Vernon Plain Dealer & Sun
528 E O&M Ave.
PO Box 988
North Vernon, IN 47265
Phone: (812)346-3973
Fax: (812)346-8368

Publications: North Vernon Plain Dealer (10362) •
North Vernon Sun (10363)

North Virginia Community College
3001 N Beauregard
Alexandria, VA 22311
Phone: (703)845-6200

Publications: The Collective (31655)

North Warren Town and Country News
PO Box 325
Norwalk, IA 50211
Phone: (515)981-0406

Publications: North Warren Town and County News (11119)

North Weld Herald
208 First St.
PO Box 235
Eaton, CO 80615-0235
Phone: (970)454-3466

Publications: North Weld Herald (4409)

The North Woods Call
00509 Turkey Run Rd.
Charlevoix, MI 49720
Phone: (231)547-9797

Publications: The North Woods Call (14865)

Northeast Detroiter Harper Woods Herald
2648 Dorchester
Birmingham, MI 48009
Phone: (248)649-0749

Publications: Northeast Detroiter Harper Woods Herald (14826)

Northeast Louisiana University
700 University Ave.
Monroe, LA 71209
Phone: (318)342-1000
Fax: (318)342-5452

Publications: The Pow Wow (12693)

Northeast Mississippi Historical and Genealogical Society
Box 434
Tupelo, MS 38802-0434

Publications: Northeast Mississippi Historical and Genealogical Society Quarterly (16850)

Northeast Nebraska News Co.
PO Box 428
Osmond, NE 68765
Phone: (402)748-3666
Fax: (402)748-3354

Publications: Osmond Republican (18241)

Northeast Publishing Co.
PO Box 30
Dover Foxcroft, ME 04426
Phone: (207)564-8355
Fax: (207)564-7056

Publications: The Piscataquis Observer (12952)

Northeast Publishing Co.
23 Court
PO Box 456
Houlton, ME 04730
Phone: (207)532-2281
Fax: (207)532-2403

Publications: Houlton Pioneer Times (12968)

Northeast Publishing Co.
40B North St.
PO Box 510
Presque Isle, ME 04769
Phone: (207)764-4471
Fax: (207)764-7585

Publications: Star-Herald (13035)

Northeast Publishing Co.
PO Box 510
Presque Isle, ME 04769
Phone: (207)764-4471
Fax: (207)764-4499
Publications: Aroostook Republican & News (12946)

Northeast Publishing, Inc.
207 Pocasset St.
Box 2410
Fall River, MA 02722
Phone: (508)676-8211
Fax: (508)676-2566
Publications: Herald News (14181)

Northeaster
2304 Central Ave., NE
Minneapolis, MN 55418
Phone: (612)788-9003
Fax: (612)788-3299
Publications: Northeaster & Northnews (16115)

Northeastern Retail Lumber Association
585 N. Greenbush Rd.
Rensselaer, NY 12144
Phone: (518)286-1010
Fax: (518)286-1755
Free: 800-292-6752
Publications: The Lumber Co-Operator (23181)

Northeastern Science Foundation, Inc.
15 Third St.
PO Box 746
Troy, NY 12181-0746
Phone: (518)273-3247
Fax: (518)273-3249
Publications: Carbonates and Evaporites (23452) • Northeastern Geology and Environmental Sciences (23454)

The Northeastern Shopper
129 E North St.
Box 447
Tawas City, MI 48764-0447
Phone: (989)362-6111
Fax: (989)362-7080
Publications: The Northeastern Shopper (15585)

Northeastern State University
Tahlequah, OK 74464-2399
Phone: (918)683-0040
Publications: The Northeastern (26094)

Northeastern University
406 Holmes Hall
Boston, MA 02115
Phone: (617)373-2000
Publications: Studies in American Fiction (13964)

Northeastern University
Meserve Hall, 2nd Fl.
360 Huntington Ave.
Boston, MA 02115
Phone: (617)373-2734
Fax: (617)373-2661
Publications: The New England Quarterly (13937)

Northeastern University
100 City Hall Plaza
Level 2
Boston, MA 02108
Phone: (617)248-9880
Fax: (617)248-8747
Publications: The Northeastern News (13940)

Northern Arizona Newspapers, Inc.
208 W 1st St.
Box AW
Winslow, AZ 86047
Phone: (928)289-2467
Fax: (928)289-4151
Publications: The Winslow Mail (1014)

Northern Breezes, Inc.
3949 Winnetka Ave. N.
Minneapolis, MN 55427
Phone: (763)542-9707
Fax: (763)542-8998
Publications: Northern Breezes Sailing Magazine (16116)

Northern California Angler Publications
PO Box 994
Elk Grove, CA 95759-0994
Phone: (916)685-2245
Fax: (916)685-1498
Free: 800-748-6599
Publications: The Fish Sniffer (1873)

The Northern Colorado Business Report
141 S. College Ave.
Fort Collins, CO 80524-2810
Phone: (970)221-5400
Fax: (970)221-5432
Publications: The Northern Colorado Business Report (4436)

The Northern Daily News
8 Duncan Ave.
PO Box 1030
Kirkland Lake, ON, Canada P2N 3L4
Phone: (705)567-5321
Fax: (705)567-6162
Publications: The Northern Daily News (35957)

Northern Illinois University
Campus Life Bldg., Ste. 130
DeKalb, IL 60115
Phone: (815)753-0101
Fax: (815)753-0708
Publications: The Northern Star (8740)

Northern Illinois University
DeKalb, IL 60115
Phone: (815)753-1857
Fax: (815)753-2003
Publications: George Eliot—George Henry Lewes Studies (8735)

Northern Kittitas County Tribune
PO Box 308
Cle Elum, WA 98922
Phone: (509)674-2511
Fax: (509)674-5571
Publications: Northern Kittitas County Tribune (32718)

Northern Light
PO Box 2230
Conway, NH 03818
Phone: (603)447-3824
Fax: (603)447-3825
Publications: Northern Light (18484)

Northern Michigan News
130 N Mitchell St.
PO Box 640
Cadillac, MI 49601-1856
Phone: (231)775-6565
Fax: (231)775-8790
Publications: Northern Michigan News (14843)

Northern News Services Ltd.
5108-50th St.
Box 2820
Yellowknife, NT, Canada X1A 2R1
Phone: (867)873-4031
Fax: (867)873-8507
Publications: Deh Cho Drum (35523) • Inuvik Drum (35524) • News/North (35525) • Yellowknifer (35528)

Northern Ohio LIVE
11320 Juniper Rd.
Cleveland, OH 44106
Phone: (216)721-1800
Fax: (216)721-2525
Publications: Northern Ohio LIVE (24933)

Northern Oklahoma College
1220 E Grand
PO Box 310
Tonkawa, OK 74653
Phone: (580)628-6200
Fax: (580)628-6209
Publications: The Maverick (26101)

Northern Pen
PO Box 520
10-12 North St.
St. Anthony, NL, Canada A0K 4S0
Phone: (709)454-2191
Fax: (709)454-3718

Publications: Northern Pen (35482)

Northern Reporter
PO Box 310, Sta. B
Happy Valley, NL, Canada A0P 1E0
Phone: (709)896-2595
Fax: (709)896-2812
Publications: Northern Reporter (35466)

Northern Sentinel Press
626 Enterprise Ave.
Kitimat, BC, Canada V8C 2E4
Phone: (250)632-6144
Fax: (250)639-9373
Publications: Northern Sentinel (34998) • Weekend Advertiser (34999)

Northern Star
Box 368
Clinton, MN 56225
Phone: (320)325-5152
Fax: (320)325-5280
Publications: Northern Star (15800)

Northern Star Communications Ltd.
900-6 Ave. SW, 5th Fl.
Calgary, AB, Canada T2P 3K2
Phone: (403)263-6881
Fax: (403)263-6886
Free: 800-526-4177
Publications: Energy Processing/Canada (34643) • Propane/Canada (34655)

Northern Sun Print
423 2nd St.
PO Box 340
Gladbrook, IA 50635-0340
Phone: (641)473-2102
Fax: (641)473-1004
Publications: Northern Sun Print (10922)

Northern Tier Publishing Corp.
1520 Front St.
Yorktown Heights, NY 10598
Phone: (914)962-4748
Fax: (914)962-6763
Publications: North County News (23609)

Northern Times
51 Riverside Dr.
Kapuskasing, ON, Canada P5N 1A7
Phone: (705)335-2283
Fax: (705)337-1222
Publications: Northern Times (35926)

Northern Virginia Daily
152 N Holliday St.
PO Box 69
Strasburg, VA 22657-0069
Phone: (540)465-5137
Fax: (540)465-9388
Free: 800-296-5137
Publications: Northern Virginia Daily (32563)

Northern Woodlands Magazine
PO Box 471, 1776 Center Rd.
Corinth, VT 05039
Phone: (802)439-6292
Fax: (802)439-6296
Publications: Northern Woodlands (31537)

Northern Wyoming Daily News
201 N. 8th
Worland, WY 82401
Phone: (307)347-3241
Fax: (307)347-4267
Publications: Northern Wyoming Daily News (34604)

Northerner Shopping News
Vinal St.
PO Box 261
Wittenberg, WI 54499
Phone: (715)253-2291
Fax: (715)253-3555
Publications: Shopping News Northerner (34470)

Northfield News
115 W 5th St.
PO Box 58
Northfield, MN 55057
Phone: (507)645-5615
Fax: (507)645-6005

Publications: Northfield News (16236) • Northfield Shopper (16237)

Northfield News and Printery
21 East St.
Northfield, VT 05663
Phone: (802)485-3681
Fax: (802)485-7909

Publications: Northfield News (31574)

Northland Community and Technical College
1101 Hwy. One E
Thief River Falls, MN 56701
Phone: (218)681-0819
Fax: (218)683-7052
Free: 800-959-6282

Publications: Northern Light (16466)

Northland Publishers, Inc.
801 W Adams
PO Box 311
Iron River, MI 49935
Phone: (906)265-9927
Fax: (906)265-5755

Publications: Iron River Reporter (15211)

Northside People
6116 N Central Expy., Ste. 230
Dallas, TX 75206
Phone: (214)739-2244
Fax: (214)363-6948

Publications: Northside People (30170)

Northstar Travel Media
500 Plaza Dr.
Secaucus, NJ 07094-3626
Phone: (201)902-2000
Fax: (201)902-2053

Publications: Business Travel Planner - European Edition (19535) • Business Travel Planner - North American Edition (19536) • Business Travel Planner - Pacific/Asia Edition (19537) • Meetings & Conventions (19540) • Travel Weekly (19542) • TravelAge West (3453)

Northumberland Publishers
PO Box 400
Cobourg, ON, Canada K9A 4L1
Phone: (905)372-0131
Fax: (905)372-4966
Free: 800-363-5835

Publications: Colborne Chronicle (35746)

Northumberland Publishers Ltd.
99 King St. W.
PO Box 400
Cobourg, ON, Canada K9A 4L1

Publications: Cobourg Daily Star (35741)

NorthUmberland Publishing
95 Walton St.
PO Box 296
Port Hope, ON, Canada L1A 3W4
Phone: (905)885-2471
Fax: (905)885-7442

Publications: Port Hope Evening Guide (36334)

Northwest Alabamian
PO Box 430
Haleyville, AL 35565
Phone: (205)486-9461
Fax: (205)486-4849

Publications: Northwest Alabamian (257) • The Times-Record (258)

Northwest Alliance for Alternative Media & Education
2807 SE Stark
Portland, OR 97214
Phone: (503)239-4991
Fax: (503)232-3764

Publications: Portland Alliance (26500)

Northwest Anthropological Research Notes
625 N Garfield
Moscow, ID 83843-3624
Phone: (208)882-0413
Fax: (208)882-3393

Publications: Northwest Anthropological Research Notes (7920)

Northwest Arkansas Genealogical Society
Box 796
Rogers, AR 72757-0796
Phone: (479)273-3890

Publications: Backtracker (1326)

Northwest Arkansas Times
212 N East Ave.
Fayetteville, AR 72701
Phone: (479)442-1700
Fax: (479)442-5477
Free: 800-498-1991

Publications: Northwest Arkansas Times (1121)

Northwest Arkansas Times
212 N. East Ave.
PO Box 1607
Fayetteville, AR 72702
Phone: (479)442-1700
Fax: (479)442-5477

Publications: Northwest Arkansas Times (1122)

Northwest Asian Weekly
412 Maynard Ave. S
Seattle, WA 98104-2917
Phone: (206)223-0623

Publications: Northwest Asian Weekly (32993)

Northwest Atlantic Fisheries Organization
2 Morris Dr., Ste. 1000
Dartmouth, NS, Canada B2Y 3Y9
Phone: (902)468-5590
Fax: (902)468-5538

Publications: Journal of Northwest Atlantic Fishery Science (35547) • NAFO Scientific Council Studies (35549)

The Northwest-Blade
PO Box 797
Eureka, SD 57437
Phone: (605)284-2631
Fax: (605)284-2632
Free: 800-616-2631

Publications: The Northwest-Blade (28853)

Northwest Christian Journal
17806 154th Ave. SE
Renton, WA 98058
Phone: (206)255-3552
Fax: (206)228-8749

Publications: Northwest Christian Journal (32926)

Northwest Comic News
PO Box 11825
Eugene, OR 97440
Phone: (541)344-1922
Fax: (541)344-5793
Free: 888-668-1800

Publications: Northwest Comic News (26325)

Northwest Dispatch
PO Box 5637
Tacoma, WA 98415
Phone: (253)272-7587
Fax: (253)272-4418

Publications: The Northwest Dispatch (33148)

Northwest Fun & Games
27013 Pacific Hwy. South, No. 333
Des Moines, WA 98198
Phone: (253)874-5600
Fax: (253)874-5434

Publications: Northwest Fun & Games (32737)

Northwest Indiana Catholic
9292 Broadway
Merrillville, IN 46410
Phone: (219)769-9292
Fax: (219)738-9034

Publications: Northwest Indiana Catholic (10298)

Northwest Media
PO Box 90130
Bellevue, WA 98009
Phone: (425)486-1231
Fax: (425)452-3022

Publications: Bothell-Kenmore Reporter (32664)

Northwest Media
305 W. 1st St.
Port Angeles, WA 98362
Phone: (360)452-2345
Fax: (360)417-3521
Free: 800-826-7714

Publications: Peninsula Daily News (32888)

Northwest Missouri State University
800 University Dr.
Maryville, MO 64468
Phone: (660)562-1224
Fax: (660)562-1521

Publications: Northwest Missourian (17275)

Northwest Nazarene University
623 Holly St.
Nampa, ID 83686-5897
Phone: (208)467-8011
Fax: (208)467-8645

Publications: Crusader (7929)

Northwest NEWS
13342 NE 175th St.
PO Box 587
Woodinville, WA 98072
Phone: (425)483-0606
Fax: (425)486-7593

Publications: The Northlake News (33214) • Valley View (33216) • Woodinville WEEKLY (33217)

Northwest Newspapers
PO Box 250
Crystal Lake, IL 60039
Phone: (815)356-1270
Fax: (815)477-4960
Free: 800-589-8910

Publications: Northwest Herald (8695)

Northwest Oklahoman
PO Box 460
Shattuck, OK 73858
Phone: (580)938-2533
Fax: (580)938-5240

Publications: Northwest Oklahoman and Ellis County News (26060)

Northwest Parent Publishing
123 NW 36th St., Ste. 215
Seattle, WA 98107-4959
Phone: (206)441-0191
Fax: (206)441-4919

Publications: Eastside Parent (32961) • Portland Parent (33004) • Puget Sound Parent (33009) • Seattle's Child (33027) • Seattle's Child (Snohomish County Edition) (33028)

Northwest Public Power Association (NWPPA)
9817 N.E. 54th St.
Vancouver, WA 98662
Phone: (360)254-0109
Fax: (360)254-5731

Publications: Northwest Public Power Association Bulletin (33177)

Northwest Publishing
600 Lyon St. SW
PO Box 130
Albany, OR 97321-0041
Phone: (541)926-2211
Fax: (541)926-5298

Publications: Albany Democrat-Herald (26206)

Northwest Publishing
133 SW 153rd St.
Burien, WA 98166
Phone: (206)444-4873

Publications: Des Moines News (32699)

Northwest Regional Magazines
4969 Hwy. 101, No. 2
Florence, OR 97439-8896
Phone: (541)997-8401
Fax: (541)902-0400
Free: 800-348-8401

Publications: Northwest Travel (26351) • Oregon Coast (26352)

Northwest Review
369 Prince Lucien Campbell Hall
Eugene, OR 97403
Phone: (541)346-3957
Fax: (541)346-1509

Publications: Northwest Review (26326)

Northwest Runner
4831 NE 44th St.
Seattle, WA 98105
Phone: (206)527-5301
Fax: (206)527-1223

Publications: Northwest Runner (32995)

Northwest Territory Genealogical Society
502 N 7th St.
Vincennes, IN 47591
Phone: (812)886-4380

Publications: Northwest Trail Tracer (10521)

Northwest Yachting
7342 15th Ave. NW
Seattle, WA 98117-5401
Phone: (206)789-8116
Fax: (206)781-1554
Free: 888-224-7407

Publications: Northwest Yachting (32996)

Northwestern College
3003 N Snelling Ave.
St. Paul, MN 55113
Phone: (651)631-5100

Publications: The Cadence (16364)

Northwestern Food Merchants, Inc.
30300 SW Pkwy., Ave.
Wilsonville, OR 97070
Phone: (503)685-6293
Fax: (503)685-6295

Publications: Oregon Grocery Line (26615)

Northwestern Illinois Farmer
Box 536
Lena, IL 61048-0536
Phone: (815)369-2811
Fax: (815)369-2816

Publications: Northwestern Illinois Farmer (9074)

Northwestern Oklahoma State University
Jesse Dunn Annex, Rm. 232
709 Oklahoma Blvd.
Alva, OK 73717
Phone: (580)327-8479
Fax: (580)327-8660

Publications: Northwestern News (25738)

Northwestern Pacific Railroad Historical Society
PO Box 667
Santa Rosa, CA 95402-0667
Phone: (707)526-2467

Publications: Northwesterner (3732)

Northwestern School of Law
10015 SW Terwilliger Blvd.
Portland, OR 97219
Phone: (503)768-6700
Fax: (503)768-6671

Publications: Environmental Law (Portland) (26476)

Northwestern State University
Box 5306
Natchitoches, LA 71497
Phone: (318)357-4439
Fax: (318)357-6564

Publications: Current Sauce (12716)

Northwestern State University
Kyser Hall 316M
Natchitoches, LA 71497
Phone: (318)357-6272
Fax: (318)357-5942

Publications: Louisiana English Journal (12717)

Northwestern University Press
2020 Ridge Ave.
Evanston, IL 60208-4302
Phone: (847)491-4000
Fax: (847)467-2096
Free: 800-832-3615

Publications: TriQuarterly (8873)

Northwestern University School of Law
357 E. Chicago Ave.
Chicago, IL 60611
Phone: (312)503-8742
Fax: (312)503-0132

Publications: Northwestern Journal of International Law & Business (8512)

Northwestern University Students Publishing Co.
1999 S Campus Dr., Norris Center
Evanston, IL 60208
Phone: (847)491-7206
Fax: (847)491-9905

Publications: The Daily Northwestern (8856)

Northwoods Press
PO Box 28
Nevis, MN 56467
Phone: (218)652-3475

Publications: Northwoods Press (16204)

Norton Daily Telegram
215 S. Kansas Ave.
Norton, KS 67654-0320
Phone: (785)877-3361

Publications: Norton Daily Telegram (11678)

The Norton Press, Inc.
725 Park Ave.
PO Box 380
Norton, VA 24273
Phone: (276)679-1101
Fax: (276)679-5922

Publications: The Coalfield Progress (32310)

Norton Records
Box 646, Cooper Sta.
New York, NY 10276-0646
Phone: (718)789-4438
Fax: (718)789-9215

Publications: Kicks (22218)

Norwegian-American Historical Association
St. Olaf College Library
1510 St. Olaf Ave.
Northfield, MN 55057
Phone: (507)646-3221
Fax: (507)646-3734

Publications: Norwegian-American Studies (16238)

NorWest Newspapers
1205 Main St.
Goodland, KS 67735-2946
Phone: (785)899-2338
Fax: (785)899-6186

Publications: Country Advocate (11463) • The Goodland Daily News (11464)

Nor'West Newspapers
170 S Penn Ave.
Oberlin, KS 67749
Phone: (785)475-2206
Fax: (785)475-2800

Publications: The Oberlin Herald (11681)

Nor'westing Publications, Inc.
PO Box 17002
Seattle, WA 98107-0702

Publications: Nor'westing (32997)

Norwich Bulletin
66 Franklin St.
Norwich, CT 06360
Phone: (860)887-9211
Fax: (860)887-9666
Free: 800-404-9211

Publications: Norwich Bulletin (5084)

The Norwich and Sidney Pennysavers, Inc.
18-20 Mechanic St.
Norwich, NY 13815
Phone: (607)334-4714
Fax: (607)336-7318

Publications: Norwich Pennysaver (23022) • Sidney Pennysaver (23023)

Norwich University
158 Harmon Drive
65 S. Main St.
Northfield, VT 05663
Phone: (802)485-2000
Fax: (802)485-2580

Publications: The Norwich Guidon (31575)

Notional Collegiate Honors Council
Iowa State University
2130 Jisdike Honors Bldg.
Ames, IA 50011-1150
Phone: (515)294-9188
Fax: (515)294-2970

Publications: Journal of the National Collegiate Honors Council (JNCHC) (76) • National Honors Report (32345)

Notre Dame Law School
University of Notre Dame
PO Box 988
Notre Dame, IN 46556
Phone: (219)631-7097
Fax: (219)631-6379

Publications: Notre Dame Law Review (10372)

Notre Dame Technical Review
University of Notre Dame
College Of Engineering
Notre Dame, IN 46556
Phone: (219)283-1122
Fax: (219)239-8007

Publications: Notre Dame Technical Review (10374)

Nottoway Publishing Co., Inc.
111 W Maple St.
PO Box 460
Blackstone, VA 23824
Phone: (434)292-3019
Fax: (434)292-5966

Publications: Courier-Record (31892)

Nouveau Magazine
5933 Stoney Hill Rd.
New Hope, PA 18938
Phone: (215)794-5996
Fax: (215)794-8305

Publications: The Nouveau Magazine (27321)

Nouvelles Saint Laurent News
685 Decarie, Ste. 101
Saint-Laurent, QC, Canada H4L 5G4
Phone: (514)855-1292
Fax: (514)855-1855
Telex: 514-855-9916

Publications: Nouvelles Saint-Laurent News (37365)

Nova Express
PO Box 27231
Austin, TX 78755

Publications: Nova Express (29795)

Nova Media Inc.
1724 N State St.
Big Rapids, MI 49307-9073
Phone: (231)796-4637
Fax: (231)796-4637

Publications: Nova Review (14817)

Nova Science Publishers Inc.
400 Oser Ave.
Hauppauge, NY 11788-3619
Phone: (631)424-6682
Fax: (631)424-4666

Publications: International Journal of Space Research (20718) • Nova Journal of Theoretical Physics (20720) • White House Studies (20723)

Nova Scotia Department of Labour
PO Box 697
Halifax, NS, Canada B3J 2T8
Phone: (902)424-8474
Fax: (902)424-3239

Publications: Labor Legislation in Nova Scotia (35569)

Novalis
49 Front St. E., 2nd Fl.
Toronto, ON, Canada M5E 1B3
Phone: (416)363-3303
Fax: (416)363-9409
Free: 800-387-7164

Publications: Living with Christ (36259)

Novato Institute for Somatic Research and Training
1516 Grant Ave., Ste. 212
Novato, CA 94945
Phone: (415)892-0617
Fax: (415)892-4388

Publications: Somatics (2653)

Novicom, Inc.
6701 Center Dr. W., Ste. 450
Los Angeles, CA 90045
Phone: (310)642-4400
Fax: (310)641-4444

Publications: Chiropractic Products (2238) • Physical Therapy Products (2367) • Plastic Surgery Products (2369) • Podiatric Products (2371)

Now Magazine
189 Church St.
Toronto, ON, Canada M5B 1Y7
Phone: (416)364-1300
Fax: (416)364-1166

Publications: Now (36678)

Now Times Group, Inc.
102-45951 Tretheway Ave.
Chilliwack, BC, Canada V2P 1K4
Phone: (604)792-9117
Fax: (604)792-9300

Publications: Chilliwack Times (34928)

NPT Publishing Group, Inc.
120 Littleton Rd., Ste. 120
Parsippany, NJ 07054-1803
Phone: (973)394-1800
Fax: (973)734-1771

Publications: Non-profit Times (19412) • The Non-profit Times (19413)

NPTA Alliance
500 Bi County Blvd. Ste. 200
Farmingdale, NY 11735
Phone: (631)777-2223
Fax: (631)777-2224
Free: 800-355-6782

Publications: Distribution Sales and Management (20594)

NRF Enterprises, Inc.
Liberty Pl.
325 7th St. NW, Ste. 1100
Washington, DC 20004
Phone: (202)626-8101

Publications: Stores (5805)

N's M Publications
PO Box 82108
Columbus, OH 43202
Phone: (614)491-5660
Fax: (614)491-5660

Publications: Nancy's Magazine (25032)

NSBE Publications
1454 Duke St.
Alexandria, VA 22314
Phone: (703)549-2207
Fax: (703)683-5312

Publications: NSBE Magazine (31716)

NSC Press
1121 Spring Lake Dr.
Itasca, IL 60143-3201
Phone: (630)285-1121
Fax: (630)285-1315
Free: 800-621-7615

Publications: Family Safety & Health (9013) • Safe Driver (9017) • Safeworker (9019) • Today's Supervisor (9020) • Traffic Safety (9021)

NTM Publications
1000 E 1st St.
Sanford, FL 32771-1487
Phone: (407)323-3430
Fax: (407)330-0376

Publications: Brown Gold Magazine (6646)

Nuclear Age Peace Foundation
PMB 121
1187 Coast Village Rd., Ste. 1
Santa Barbara, CA 93108-2794
Phone: (805)965-3443
Fax: (805)568-0466

Publications: The Sunflower (3659)

Nuclear Plant Journal
799 Roosevelt Rd., Bldg. 6, Ste. 208
Glen Ellyn, IL 60137
Phone: (630)858-6161
Fax: (630)858-8787

Publications: Nuclear Plant Journal (8931)

Nueva Vista
201 E Illinois Ae.
Midland, TX 79701
Phone: (915)683-4201
Fax: (915)682-3793

Publications: Nueva Vista (30815)

Nuit Blanche
1026 rue Saint-Jean, No. 403
Quebec, QC, Canada G1R 1R7
Phone: (418)692-1354
Fax: (418)692-1355

Publications: Nuit Blanche (37293)

Nunatext Publishing Corp.
PO Box 8
Iqaluit, NT, Canada X0A 0H0
Phone: (867)979-5357
Fax: (867)979-4763

Publications: Nunatsiaq News (35519)

Nun's Island Journal
574 Victoria Ave.
Saint-Lambert, QC, Canada J4P 2J5
Phone: (514)671-0014

Publications: St. Lambert Journal (37360)

Nuovo Mondo Publishing
10342 - 107 St.
Edmonton, AB, Canada T5J 1K2
Fax: (403)478-5493

Publications: Italian Link (34717)

Nursecom, Inc.
1211 Locust St.
Philadelphia, PA 19107-5409
Phone: (215)545-7222
Fax: (215)545-8107
Free: 800-242-6757

Publications: Journal of Child and Adolescent Psychiatric Nursing (27520) • Journal of the Society of Pediatric Nurses (27550) • Journal of Trauma Nursing (27554) • Nursing Forum (27591) • ONS Nursing Scan in Oncology (27599)

Nurses Christian Fellowship of InterVarsity Christian Fellowship
PO Box 7895
Madison, WI 53707-7895
Phone: (608)274-4823
Fax: (608)274-7882

Publications: Journal of Christian Nursing (33950)

Nurseweek Publishing
1156-C Aster Ave.
Sunnyvale, CA 94086
Fax: (408)249-3756
Free: 800-859-2091

Publications: Nurseweek (3830)

Nursing Spectrum, Inc.
2353 Hassell Rd., Ste. 110
Hoffman Estates, IL 60195
Phone: (847)490-6650

Publications: Nursing Spectrum—Florida Edition (6082) • Nursing Spectrum—Greater Chicago/Tri-State Edition (9001) • Nursing Spectrum—New England Edition (14273) • Nursing Spectrum—New York & New Jersey Edition (23558) • Nursing Spectrum—Philadelphia/Tri-State Edition (27126) • Nursing Spectrum—Washington D.C. & Baltimore Edition (32050)

Nusand Publishing Inc.
12 Tamerlane Ct.
Toronto, ON, Canada M9B 6G4
Phone: (416)233-2487
Fax: (416)233-1746

Publications: Optical Prism (36689)

Nutrition Health Review
Box No. 406
Haverford, PA 19041
Phone: (610)896-1853
Fax: (610)896-1857

Publications: Nutrition Health Review (27029)

N.V. Business Publishers Corp.
43 Main St.
PO Box 188
Avon by the Sea, NJ 07717
Phone: (732)502-0500
Fax: (732)502-9606
Free: 800-962-3001

Publications: Board Converting News (18662)

NVST.Inc.
1100 Dexter Ave. N
Seattle, WA 98109
Phone: (425)702-9733
Fax: (425)702-9753
Free: 800-843-9559

Publications: The Comedy Magazine (32957)

NW Iowa Printing Co.
310 E Milwaukee
PO Box 197
Spencer, IA 51301
Phone: (712)262-6610
Fax: (712)262-3044

Publications: The Beacon (11236) • Northwest Iowa Shopper (11231)

NYC Poetry Calendar
39 W 14th St. No. 206
New York, NY 10011
Phone: (212)260-7097

Publications: NYC Poetry Calendar (22479)

Nytek Publishing Inc.
130 Belfield Rd.
Etobicoke, ON, Canada M9W 1G1
Phone: (416)242-8088
Fax: (416)242-8085

Publications: Plumbing & HVAC Product News (35819)

OAG Worldwide
3025 Highland Pkwy. Ste. 200
Downers Grove, IL 60515
Phone: (630)515-5300
Fax: (630)515-2071
Free: 800-342-5624

Publications: OAG Air Cargo Guide (8792) • OAG Pocket Flight Guide - Pacific Asia Edition (8793)

Oak Cliff Tribune, Ltd.
PO Box 4650
Dallas, TX 75208
Phone: (214)943-7755
Fax: (214)943-7775

Publications: Oak Cliff Tribune (30173)

Oak Grove Publications, Inc.
1220 Broadway St.
PO Box 838
Oak Grove, MO 64075
Phone: (816)690-4126
Fax: (816)690-6026

Publications: Town & Country News (16910)

Oak Hill Times, Inc.
PO Box 640
Swayzee, IN 46986
Phone: (765)674-3496
Fax: (317)674-0071

Publications: Oak Hill Times (10478)

Oak Ridge National Laboratory
Bldg. 9201-3, MS No. 8065
PO Box 2008
Oak Ridge, TN 37831-8065
Phone: (615)574-0386
Fax: (615)574-0382

Publications: Nuclear Safety (29549)

The Oak Ridger
785 Oak Ridge Turnpike
Box 3446
Oak Ridge, TN 37831-3446
Phone: (423)482-1021
Fax: (865)220-5539

Publications: The Oak Ridger (29551)

Oakdale Advertiser
PO Box 278
Oakdale, CA 95361
Phone: (209)847-3021
Fax: (209)847-9750

Publications: Oakdale Advertiser (2655)

Oakdale Journal
PO Box 668
Oakdale, LA 71463-0668
Phone: (318)335-0635
Fax: (318)335-0431

Publications: Oakdale Journal (12790)

Oakdale Leader
122 S 3rd Ave.
PO Box 278
Oakdale, CA 95361
Phone: (209)847-3021
Fax: (209)847-9750

Publications: Oakdale Leader (2656)

Oakland Community College
27055 Orchard Lake Rd.
Farmington Hills, MI 48334
Phone: (734)996-5732

Publications: Witness (15021)

Oakland Football Marketing Association (OFMA)
7901 Oakport St., Ste. 4300
Oakland, CA 94621
Phone: (510)615-1888
Fax: (510)615-1878

Publications: The Blitz (2669)

Oakland Post
PO Box 1350
Oakland, CA 94604

Publications: Oakland Post (2691)

Oakland Press Co.
48 W. Huron St., No. 436009
PO Box 9
Pontiac, MI 48342-2101
Phone: (248)332-8181
Fax: (248)332-8284

Publications: Oakland Press (15450)

The Oakley Graphic
118 Ctr.
Oakley, KS 67748-0545
Phone: (785)672-3228
Fax: (785)672-3229

Publications: The Oakley Graphic (11680)

Oakton Community College
1600 E Golf Rd.
Des Plaines, IL 60016
Phone: (847)635-1600
Fax: (847)635-2610

Publications: OCCurrence (8765)

Oakville Shopping News
1158 S. Service Rd. W.
Oakville, ON, Canada L6L 5T7
Phone: (416)827-2244
Fax: (416)827-2308

Publications: Oakville Shopping News (36148)

Oakville Today
871 Equestrian Ct. U-7
Oakville, ON, Canada L6L 6L7
Phone: (905)825-2229
Fax: (905)825-3202

Publications: Oakville Today (36149)

Oakwood Register
435 Patterson Rd.
PO Box 572
Dayton, OH 45419
Phone: (937)294-2662
Fax: (937)294-8375

Publications: Oakwood Register (25123)

Oasis
Box 626
Largo, FL 33779-0626
Phone: (727)345-8505

Publications: Oasis (6300)

O'Bannon Publishing Co.
301 N Capitol Ave.
Corydon, IN 47112
Phone: (812)738-2211
Fax: (812)738-1909

Publications: The Clarion (9904)

O'Bannon Publishing Co., Inc.
PO Box 220
Corydon, IN 47112
Phone: (812)738-2211
Fax: (812)738-1909

Publications: The Corydon Democrat (9905)

Oberdorf Publishing
246 N Derr Dr., PO Box 392
Lewisburg, PA 17837-1451
Phone: (570)524-9850
Fax: (570)524-4048

Publications: The Valley Trader (27193)

Oberlin College
Oberlin, OH 44074
Phone: (440)775-8665
Fax: (440)775-6841

Publications: Allen Memorial Art Museum Bulletin (25443)

Oberlin College
145 W. Lorain St.
Oberlin, OH 44074-1023
Phone: (440)775-8182
Fax: (440)775-6575

Publications: Oberlin Alumni Magazine (25447)

Oberlin College
Wilder Box 90
Oberlin, OH 44074
Phone: (440)775-8123
Fax: (440)775-6733

Publications: The Oberlin Review (25448)

Oberlin College Press
Oberlin College
10 N. Professor St.
Oberlin, OH 44074
Phone: (440)775-8408
Fax: (440)775-8124

Publications: Field: Contemporary Poetry and Poetics (25445)

Oblates of Mary Immaculate
8844 Notre-Dame, Est
Montreal, QC, Canada H1L 3M4
Phone: (514)351-9310
Fax: (514)351-1314

Publications: Apostolat International (37085)

Oblong Gem
PO Box 25
Oblong, IL 62449-0025
Phone: (618)592-3094
Fax: (618)592-3095

Publications: Oblong Gem (9381)

O'Bren County Bell
Box 478
Primghar, IA 51245
Phone: (712)757-4055
Fax: (712)757-4055

Publications: O'Brien County Bell (11168)

L'Observateur
PO Box 1010
LaPlace, LA 70069
Phone: (985)652-9545
Fax: (985)652-3885

Publications: L'Observateur (12655)

The Observer
580 Fremont St.
PO Box 2079
Monterey, CA 93942
Phone: (831)373-2919
Fax: (831)373-4510

Publications: The Observer (2584)

The Observer
823 S. Dixie Fwy.
PO Box 10
New Smyrna Beach, FL 32170
Phone: (386)427-1000
Fax: (386)428-1265

Publications: The Observer (6458)

The Observer
PO Box 7044
Rockford, IL 61125-7044
Phone: (815)963-3471
Fax: (815)968-2808
Free: 800-252-1775

Publications: The Observer (9528)

The Observer
Box 307
Kewanna, IN 46939
Phone: (219)653-2101
Fax: (574)653-3418

Publications: The Observer (10232)

The Observer
531 Kearny Ave.
Kearny, NJ 07032
Phone: (201)991-1600
Fax: (201)991-8049

Publications: The Observer (19151)

The Observer
10 E. 2nd St.
Dunkirk, NY 14048
Phone: (716)366-3000
Fax: (716)366-3005
Free: 800-836-0931

Publications: Observer (20537)

The Observer Community Publications
PO Box 188
Vail, IA 51465
Phone: (712)677-2438
Fax: (712)677-2402

Publications: The Observer (11280)

Observer-Dispatch
221 Oriskany Plz.
Utica, NY 13501
Phone: (315)792-5000
Fax: (315)792-5033

Publications: Observer-Dispatch (23466)

Observer & Eccentric Newspapers
36251 Schoolcraft Rd.
Livonia, MI 48150-1216
Phone: (734)591-2300
Fax: (734)953-2232

Publications: Birmingham Eccentric (14824) • Canton Observer (14854) • Clarkston Eccentric (14880) • Farmington Observer (15014) • Garden City Observer (15064) • Lake Orion Eccentric (15270) • Livonia Observer (15317) • Oxford Eccentric (15431) • Plymouth Observer (15448) • Redford Observer (15462) • Rochester Eccentric (15466) • Southfield Eccentric (15548) • Troy Eccentric (15642) • West Bloomfield Eccentric (15677) • Westland Observer (15682)

Observer/Enterprise
PO Box 1329
Robert Lee, TX 76945
Phone: (915)453-2433
Fax: (915)453-4643

Publications: Observer/Enterprise (30984)

The Observer Group
5570 Gulf Of Mexico Dr.
Longboat Key, FL 34228
Phone: (941)383-5509
Fax: (941)383-7193

Publications: The Longboat Observer (6311)

Observer News Enterprise
309 N. College Ave.
PO Box 48
Newton, NC 28658-0048
Phone: (828)464-0221
Fax: (828)464-1267

Publications: Observer-News-Enterprise (24106)

Observer Newspapers
PO Box 27521
Oakland, CA 94602-0521

Publications: Alameda County Observer (1387) • Hayward & Castro Valley Observer (2042) • Oakland Bay Area Observer (2690) • Piedmont & Berkeley Observer (2842) • Sacramento Observer (3018) • San Leandro Observer (2699)

The Observer Newspapers
PO Box 407
Bellmore, NY 11710-0407
Phone: (516)679-9888
Fax: (516)731-0338

Publications: Bellmore/Merrick Observer (20146) • Seaford/Wantagh Observer (20147)

Observer Press, Inc.
Bard College
Annandale On Hudson, NY 12504
Phone: (914)752-4183

Publications: Bard Observer (20059)

Observer Publications, Inc.
478 Huron St.
Toronto, ON, Canada M5R 2R3
Phone: (416)960-8500
Fax: (416)960-8477

Publications: The United Church Observer (36777)

Observer Publications, Inc.
1 Whipple Ln.
Box 950
Greenville, RI 02828
Phone: (401)949-2700
Fax: (401)333-4600

Publications: Johnston Sunrise (28354) • North Providence North Star (28355) • The Observer (28356)

Observer Publishing Co.
122 S. Main St.
Washington, PA 15301
Phone: (724)222-2200
Fax: (724)229-2754
Free: 800-825-8326

Publications: The Almanac (27231) • Observer-Reporter (28115)

Observer Publishing Company Ltd.
PO Box 205
Queen Charlotte, BC, Canada V0T 1S0
Phone: (250)559-4680
Fax: (250)559-8433

Publications: Queen Charlotte Islands Observer (35068)

O.C. Weekly Media, Inc.
PO Box 10788
Costa Mesa, CA 92627
Phone: (714)708-8420
Fax: (714)708-8410

Publications: O.C. Weekly (1779)

OCB Tracker
657 E. Arrow Hwy., No. M
Glendora, CA 91740
Phone: (626)914-0306
Fax: (626)914-1837

Publications: OCB Tracker (2025)

Occidental College
1600 Campus Rd.
Box M-40
Los Angeles, CA 90041
Phone: (323)259-2896
Fax: (323)341-4982

Publications: The Occidental Weekly (2351)

Ocean City Sentinel
112 E. 8th St.
PO Box 238
Ocean City, NJ 08226-0238
Phone: (609)399-5411
Fax: (609)399-0416
Free: 800-356-3791

Publications: Ocean City Sentinel (19388)

Ocean County College
College Dr.
PO Box 2001
Toms River, NJ 08754-2001
Phone: (732)255-0481
Fax: (732)255-0444

Publications: Viking News (19646)

Ocean County Journal
PO Box 250
Waretown, NJ 08758
Phone: (609)660-1900
Fax: (609)668-7209

Publications: Ocean County Journal (19705)

Ocean County Newspapers, Inc.
8 Robbins St.
Toms River, NJ 08753
Phone: (732)349-3000
Fax: (732)557-5610

Publications: Ocean County Observer (19642) • Ocean County Reporter (19643) • Senior Scoop (19644) • Weekend Reporter (19647)

Ocean Side Publications
95 Pitman St.
Providence, RI 02906
Phone: (401)331-2510
Fax: (401)331-5138

Publications: American Journal of Rhinology (28386)

Ocean Side Publications Inc.
95 Pitman St.
Providence, RI 02906-4311
Phone: (401)331-2510
Fax: (401)331-5138

Publications: Allergy and Asthma Proceedings (28385)

Ocean State Golf
375 Atwood Ave., Ste. 4
Cranston, RI 02920-8400
Phone: (401)464-8445
Fax: (401)464-8477

Publications: Ocean State Golf (28336)

Oceana Magazine
PO Box 2070
Ocean City, MD 21843-2070
Phone: (410)250-5700

Publications: Oceana Magazine (13639)

Oceana's Herald
123 State St.
Hart, MI 49420-0190
Phone: (231)861-2126
Fax: (231)873-4775

Publications: Oceana's Herald-Journal (15147)

Oceanic Navigation Research Society
3907 Vineland Ave.
Studio City, CA 91604-3915
Phone: (818)985-1345

Publications: Ship to Shore (3823)

The Ochsner Journal
1514 Jefferson Hwy.
New Orleans, LA 70121
Phone: (504)842-6096
Fax: (504)842-2013

Publications: The Ochsner Journal (12749)

Oconee Enterprise
PO Box 535
Watkinsville, GA 30677
Phone: (706)769-5175
Fax: (706)769-8532

Publications: Oconee Enterprise (7643)

Oconee Publishing
PO Box 547
Seneca, SC 29679
Phone: (864)882-2375
Fax: (864)882-2381

Publications: Golden Corner Shopper (28755)

Oconomowoc Enterprise
212 E Wisconsin Ave.
PO Box B
Oconomowoc, WI 53066-3036
Phone: (262)567-5511
Fax: (262)567-4422

Publications: Oconomowoc Enterprise (34203)

Oconto County Reporter
PO Box 200
Oconto, WI 54153
Phone: (414)834-4242
Fax: (414)834-4878

Publications: Oconto County Reporter (34204)

OCS News
5 E 44th St.
New York, NY 10017
Fax: (212)599-4528

Publications: OCS News (22483)

The Octopus
2603 W. Bradley Ave.
Champaign, IL 61821-1829
Phone: (217)398-3049
Fax: (217)398-0946

Publications: The Octopus (8207)

Odessa American
222 E. 4th
PO Box 2952
Odessa, TX 79760
Phone: (915)337-6262
Fax: (915)334-8641
Free: 800-375-4661

Publications: Odessa American (30872)

The Odessa Record
Box 458
Odessa, WA 99159
Phone: (509)982-2632
Fax: (509)982-2651

Publications: The Odessa Record (32858)

The Odessan
PO Box 80
204 W. Mason
Odessa, MO 64076
Phone: (816)230-5311
Fax: (816)230-5313

Publications: The Odessan (17319)

Odgen Newspaper
PO Box 659
Fort Dodge, IA 50501
Phone: (515)573-2141
Fax: (515)573-2148
Free: 800-622-6613

Publications: The Messenger (10903)

Odon Journal
102 1/2 W Main St.
Odon, IN 47562
Phone: (812)636-7350
Fax: (812)636-7359

Publications: Journal (10383)

O'Donnell Index-Press
PO Box 457
Odonnell, TX 79351
Phone: (806)428-3591
Fax: (806)428-3360

Publications: O'Donnell Index-Press (30884)

Odyssey Publications, Inc.
510-A S Corona Mall
Corona, CA 92879-1420
Phone: (909)371-7137
Fax: (909)371-7139
Free: 800-996-3977

Publications: Autograph Collector (1766) • Pop Culture Collecting (1767)

Oelwein Publishing Co.
PO Box 511
25 1st St. SE
Oelwein, IA 50662-2306
Phone: (319)283-2144
Fax: (319)283-3268
Free: 800-283-6371

Publications: Register (11123)

O'Fallon Progress
PO Box 970
612 E. State St.
O Fallon, IL 62269-0970
Phone: (618)632-3643
Fax: (618)632-6438
Free: 888-234-3365

Publications: The Legal Reporter (9333) • O'Fallon Progress (9334)

Off Our Backs
2337 18th St. NW
Washington, DC 20009
Phone: (202)234-8072
Fax: (202)234-8092

Publications: Off Our Backs (5704)

OffBeat Publications
421 Frenchman St., Ste. 200
New Orleans, LA 70116-2506
Phone: (504)944-4300
Fax: (504)944-4306

Publications: OffBeat Magazine (12750)

Office for the Advancement of Scholarship and Teaching
Miami University
Oxford, OH 45056
Phone: (513)529-7224
Fax: (513)529-3762

Publications: Journal on Excellence in College Teaching (25456)

Office of the City Historian
115 South Ave.
Rochester, NY 14604-1896
Phone: (716)428-8095
Fax: (716)428-8098

Publications: Rochester History (23240)

Office of General Counsel
United States Conference of Catholic Bishops
3211 Fourth St. NE
Washington, DC 20017
Phone: (202)541-3300
Fax: (202)541-3337

Publications: Law Briefs (5632)

Office of the Secretary of State
Rm 256, State Capitol
Little Rock, AR 72201-1094
Phone: (501)682-1010
Fax: (501)682-3548

Publications: Arkansas Register (1220)

Office of the State Archaeologist
700 Clinton St. Bldg.
Iowa City, IA 52242-1030

Publications: Midcontinental Journal of Archeology (10981)

Office Systems
PO Box 908
Spring House, PA 19477
Phone: (215)628-7716
Fax: (215)540-8041

Publications: Office Systems 96 (28009)

Office of University Advancement
PO Box 2537
Huntsville, TX 77341-2537
Phone: (936)294-3625
Fax: (936)294-1993

Publications: Heritage (30593)

OFFICE@Home
PO Box D-79
Bowen Island, BC, Canada V0N 1G0
Phone: (604)947-2275
Fax: (604)947-0633

Publications: OFFICE@Home (34887)

Official Michigan, Inc.
432 S Sandusky
Sandusky, MI 48471
Phone: (517)635-3000
Fax: (517)635-3000

Publications: Official Michigan (15520)

Official Publications
7002 W Butler Pke., Ste. 100
Ambler, PA 19002
Phone: (215)643-6385
Fax: (215)628-3571

Publications: All Number-Finds (26645) • Official's Cryptograms (26652) • Superb Crosswords (26654)

Official Publications, Inc.
18201 Weston Place
Tustin, CA 92780

Publications: 9-1-1 Magazine (3963)

Official Star Wars Fan Club
Box 111000
Aurora, CO 80042
Phone: (303)574-0907
Fax: (303)574-9442

Publications: Star Wars Insider (4150)

Offshore Data Services Inc.
PO Box 19909
Houston, TX 77224-1909
Phone: (713)781-2713
Fax: (713)781-9594

Publications: Gulf of Mexico Drilling Report (30473) • Gulf of Mexico Field Development Report (30474)

The Ogden
PO Box R
Ogden, IA 50212
Phone: (515)275-4101
Fax: (515)275-2844

Publications: Ogden Reporter (11125)

Ogden Newspapers, Inc.
412 S. Main St.
Lake Placid, NY 12946
Phone: (518)523-4401
Fax: (518)891-2756

Publications: The Lake Placid News (20875)

Ogden Newspapers, Inc.
PO Box 38
Westfield, NY 14787
Phone: (716)326-3163
Fax: (716)326-3165

Publications: Chautauqua News (23561) • Mayville Sentinel (23562) • Westfield/Corry Quality Guide (23563) • Westfield Quality Guide (23564) • Westfield Republican (23565)

Ogden Newspapers Inc.
1500 Main St.
Wheeling, WV 26003
Phone: (304)233-0100
Fax: (304)233-9397
Free: 800-852-5475

Publications: Intelligencer (33502) • News-Register (33503)

Ogden Newspapers of Iowa, Inc.
2221 E Ovid
Des Moines, IA 50313
Phone: (515)262-1190
Fax: (515)262-2267

Publications: Ankeny Press Citizen (11163) • Central Shopper (10774) • Leetown Shopper (10802) • Northcentral Shopper (10805) • Northeast Shopper (10806) • Southside Shopper (10810) • Valley Shopper (10813)

Ogden Newspapers of North Dakota, Inc.
PO Box 1150
Minot, ND
Phone: (701)857-1912
Fax: (701)857-1907
Free: 800-735-3119

Publications: Pierce County Tribune (24535)

Ogden Publications
1503 SW 42nd St.
Topeka, KS 66609
Phone: (785)274-4300
Fax: (785)274-4305
Free: 800-678-4883

Publications: Farm Collector (11818) • Gas Engine Magazine (11820) • Grit (11821) • Steam Traction (11837)

Ogden Publishing Corp.
332 Standard Way
PO Box 12790
Ogden, UT 84412-2790
Phone: (801)625-4200
Fax: (801)625-4508
Free: 800-234-5505

Publications: Standard-Examiner (31378)

Ogeman County Herald
215 W Houghton Ave.
PO Box 247
West Branch, MI 48661-1219
Phone: (989)345-0044
Fax: (989)345-0342

Publications: Ogemaw County Herald (15680)

Ogle County Life
311 W. Washington
PO Box 378
Oregon, IL 61061
Phone: (815)732-2156
Fax: (815)732-6154

Publications: Ogle County Life (9387)

Ogle County Newspapers
121A S 4th St.
PO Box 8
Oregon, IL 61061
Phone: (815)732-6166
Fax: (815)946-2501

Publications: Mt. Morris Times (9241)

Oglethorpe Echo
PO Box 268
Lexington, GA 30648
Phone: (706)743-3111

Publications: Oglethorpe Echo (7477)

O'Gorman King Co.
20 W Caledonia
Box 39
Hillsboro, ND 58045
Phone: (701)436-4241
Fax: (701)436-4245

Publications: Hillsboro Banner (24474)

Ohio Academy of Science
1500 W. 3rd Ave., Ste. 223
Columbus, OH 43212-2817
Phone: (614)488-2228
Fax: (614)488-2228

Publications: The Ohio Journal of Science (25277)

Ohio Antique Review, Inc.
7891 Pontius Rd.
Groveport, OH 43125-9309
Phone: (614)885-9757
Fax: (614)885-9762
Free: 800-992-9757

Publications: Antique Review (25234)

Ohio Auto Club
90 E Wilson Bridge Rd.
Worthington, OH 43085
Phone: (614)431-7919
Fax: (614)410-0756

Publications: Home & Away (Ohio Edition) (25679)

Ohio Bankers League
37 W. Broad St., Ste. 1001
Columbus, OH 43215
Phone: (614)221-5121
Fax: (614)221-3421

Publications: Ohio Record (25048)

Ohio Beverage Journal
3 12th St.
Wheeling, WV 26003
Phone: (304)232-7620
Fax: (304)233-1236

Publications: Ohio Beverage Journal (33504)

Ohio Biological Survey
1315 Kinnear Rd.
Columbus, OH 43212
Phone: (614)292-9645
Fax: (614)688-4322

Publications: Ohio Biological Survey Miscellaneous Contributions (25040)

Ohio Cattlemen's Association/Ohio Beef Council
10600 US Hwy. 42
Marysville, OH 43040
Phone: (614)873-6736
Fax: (614)873-6835

Publications: Ohio Cattleman (25358)

Ohio Department of Aging
50 W Broad St., 9th Fl.
Columbus, OH 43266
Phone: (614)466-5500
Fax: (614)466-5741
Free: 800-422-1976

Publications: Ohio's Heritage (25055)

Ohio Department of Natural Resources
1840 Belcher Dr.
Columbus, OH 43224
Phone: (614)265-6300
Free: 800-945-3543

Publications: Wild Ohio Magazine (25069)

Ohio Education Association
225 E. Broad St.
Box 2550
Columbus, OH 43216
Phone: (614)227-3014
Fax: (614)224-5659
Free: 800-282-1500

Publications: Ohio Schools (25049)

Ohio Farm Bureau Federation
PO Box 182383
Columbus, OH 43218-2383
Phone: (614)246-8229
Fax: (614)249-2200

Publications: Buckeye Farm News (25002)

Ohio Florists' Association
2130 Stella Ct., Ste. 200
Columbus, OH 43215-1033
Phone: (614)487-1117
Fax: (614)487-1216

Publications: Ohio Florists Association Bulletin (25044)

Ohio Genealogical Society
713 S. Main St.
Mansfield, OH 44907-1644
Phone: (419)756-7294
Fax: (419)756-8681

Publications: Ohio Records & Pioneer Families (25333)

Ohio Historical Society
1982 Velma Ave.
Columbus, OH 43211-2497
Phone: (614)297-2360
Fax: (614)297-2367

Publications: Ohio History (25046) • Timeline (25065)

Ohio Magazine
1422 Euclid Ave., No. 730
Cleveland, OH 44115
Phone: (216)771-2833
Free: 800-210-7293

Publications: Ohio Magazine (24937)

Ohio Northern University
Box 153
Ada, OH 45810
Phone: (419)772-2248
Fax: (419)772-2714

Publications: Ohio Northern University Law Review (24571)

Ohio Nurses Association
4000 E. Main St.
Columbus, OH 43213-2983
Phone: (614)899-1195
Fax: (614)237-6074

Publications: Ohio Nurses Review (25047)

Ohio Psychology Publications Inc.
6100 Channingway Blvd., Ste. 303
Columbus, OH 43232
Phone: (614)861-1999
Fax: (614)861-1996

Publications: The National Psychologist (25034)

Ohio Runner
1001 Eastwind Dr., No. 304
Westerville, OH 43081
Fax: (614)882-2111

Publications: Ohio Runner (25643)

Ohio Rural Electric Cooperatives, Inc.
6677 Busch Blvd.
PO Box 26036
Columbus, OH 43226-0036
Phone: (614)846-5757
Fax: (614)846-7108

Publications: Country Living (Ohio) (25012)

Ohio Society of CPAs
535 Metro Pl. S
PO Box 1810
Dublin, OH 43017
Phone: (614)764-2727
Fax: (614)764-5880
Free: 800-686-2727

Publications: The Ohio CPA Journal (25169)

Ohio Society of Professional Engineers
4795 Evanswood Dr., Ste. 201
Columbus, OH 43229
Phone: (614)228-8605
Fax: (614)228-8611

Publications: Ohio Engineer (25043)

Ohio State Grange
1031 E Broad St.
Columbus, OH 43205
Phone: (614)258-9569
Fax: (614)258-3232

Publications: Ohio Granger (25045)

Ohio State University
Western
537 East Ohio St.
Indianapolis, IN 46204
Phone: 800-807-8833
Fax: (317)636-4180

Publications: Ohio State Journal on Dispute Resolution (25051)

Ohio State University
The College of Education
341 Ramseyer Hall
29 W Woodruff Ave.
Columbus, OH 43210
Phone: (614)292-3407
Fax: (614)292-7020

Publications: Theory into Practice (25064)

Ohio State University
Engineering Communications
142 Hitchcock Hall
2070 Neil Ave.
Columbus, OH 43210-1275
Phone: (614)292-4064

Publications: The News in Engineering (25035)

Ohio State University
School of Journalism
242 W. 18th Ave.
Columbus, OH 43210
Phone: (614)292-2031
Fax: (614)292-3722

Publications: Ohio State Lantern (25052)

The Ohio State University Alumni Association, Inc.
2400 Olentangy River Rd.
Columbus, OH 43210-1061
Phone: (614)292-2970
Fax: (614)292-7697

Publications: Ohio State Alumni Magazine (25050)

The Ohio State University Press
1070 Carmack Rd.
Columbus, OH 43210-1002
Phone: (614)292-6930
Fax: (614)292-2065

Publications: Geographical Analysis (25019) • The Journal of Higher Education (25024) • Journal of Money, Credit, and Banking (25025) • Journal for the Psychoanalysis of Culture and Society (25028) • Narrative (25033)

Ohio University
20 E. Union St.
Athens, OH 45701
Phone: (740)593-4000
Fax: (740)593-0561

Publications: The Post (24631)

Ohio Valley Publishing
825 3rd Ave.
Gallipolis, OH 45631
Phone: (740)446-2342
Fax: (740)446-3008

Publications: The Daily Sentinel (25208) • Gallipolis Daily Tribune (25209) • Times-Sentinel (25210)

Ohio Wesleyan University
61st Sandusky St.
Delaware, OH 43015
Phone: (614)369-4431
Fax: (614)363-0795

Publications: Ohio Wesleyan Magazine (25161)

Ohioana Library Association
274 East First Ave
Columbus, OH 43201
Phone: (614)466-3831
Fax: (614)728-6974

Publications: Ohioana Quarterly (25054)

Oil Mill Gazetteer Publishing
PO Box 590483
Houston, TX 77259-0483
Phone: (281)480-7889
Fax: (281)338-2345

Publications: Oil Mill Gazetteer (30518)

Oildom Publishing Company of Texas Inc.
PO Box 941669
Houston, TX 77079
Phone: (281)558-6930
Fax: (281)558-7029

Publications: Pipeline News (30520) • Power & Gas Marketing (30521) • Rehabilitation Technology (30523) • Underground Construction (30538)

Ojai Valley Newspapers, LLC
PO Box 277
Ojai, CA 93024-0277
Phone: (805)646-1476
Fax: (805)646-4281

Publications: Ojai Valley News (2714) • Ojai Valley Shopper (2715)

Okaloosa Publishing Co.
301 N. Main St.
PO Box 447
Crestview, FL 32536
Phone: (850)682-6524
Fax: (850)682-2246

Publications: Crestview News Bulletin (6023) • News Extra (6024)

Okang Communications Corp.
104 Magnolia St.
PO Box 60739
Rochester, NY 14606

Publications: Communicade (23217)

Okarche Chieftain
PO Box 468
Okarche, OK 73762
Phone: (405)373-1616
Fax: (405)373-1636

Publications: Okarche Chieftain (25950)

Okawville Times
109 E Walnut
PO Box 68
Okawville, IL 62271
Phone: (618)243-5563
Fax: (618)243-5563

Publications: Times (9383)

The Okeene Record
211 N Main St.
PO Box 664
Okeene, OK 73763
Phone: (580)822-4401
Fax: (580)822-3051

Publications: The Okeene Record (25951)

Okemah News Leader
602 W Broadway
PO Box 191
Okemah, OK 74859
Phone: (918)623-0123
Fax: (918)623-0124

Publications: Okemah News Leader (25952)

Oklahoma Bankers Association
643 NE 41st St.
PO Box 18246
Oklahoma City, OK 73154-0246
Phone: (405)424-5252
Fax: (405)424-4518

Publications: Oklahoma Banker (25973)

Oklahoma Baptist University
Journalism Dept., Box 61704
500 W. University Blvd.
Shawnee, OK 74804
Phone: (405)878-2128
Fax: (405)878-2113

Publications: The OBU Bison (26064)

Oklahoma Bar Association
PO Box 53036
Oklahoma City, OK 73152
Phone: (405)416-7000
Fax: (405)416-7001

Publications: The Oklahoma Bar Journal (25974)

Oklahoma Beverage News
2416 E 37th N
Wichita, KS 67219
Phone: (316)838-6700
Fax: (316)838-6795

Publications: Oklahoma Beverage News (25975)

Oklahoma Cattlemen's Association
2500 Exchange Ave.
Oklahoma City, OK 73108
Phone: (405)235-4391
Fax: (405)235-3608

Publications: Oklahoma COWMAN (25977)

Oklahoma Christian University
PO Box 11000
Oklahoma City, OK 73136-1100
Phone: (405)425-5070
Fax: (405)425-5076

Publications: The Christian Chronicle (25961) •
Vision (25997)

Oklahoma City University
2501 N. Blackwelder Ave.
Oklahoma City, OK 73106-1402
Phone: (405)557-6068
Fax: (405)557-6069

Publications: The Campus (25956)

The Oklahoma Eagle
PO Box 3267
Tulsa, OK 74101-3267
Phone: (918)582-7124
Fax: (918)582-8905

Publications: The Oklahoma Eagle (26122)

Oklahoma Education Association
323 E. Madison
PO Box 18485
Oklahoma City, OK 73154
Phone: (405)528-7785
Fax: (405)524-0350
Free: 800-522-8091

Publications: Focus on Members (25964)

Oklahoma Farm Bureau, Inc.
2501 N Stiles
Oklahoma City, OK 73105
Phone: (405)523-2300
Fax: (405)523-2362
Free: 800-299-2412

Publications: Oklahoma Country (25976)

Oklahoma Farmers Union
6200 NW 2nd
PO Box 24000
Oklahoma City, OK 73127
Phone: (405)789-5666
Fax: (405)491-1599

Publications: Farm News & Views (25963)

Oklahoma Gazette
3701 N. Shartel
Oklahoma City, OK 73118
Phone: (405)528-6000
Fax: (405)528-4600

Publications: Oklahoma Gazette (25979)

Oklahoma Geological Survey
Energy Center
100 E. Boyd St.
Norman, OK 73019
Phone: (405)325-3031
Fax: (405)325-7069
Free: 800-330-3996

Publications: Oklahoma Geology Notes (25940)

Oklahoma Grocers Association
PO Box 18716
Oklahoma City, OK 73154
Phone: (405)525-9419
Fax: (405)525-0962

Publications: Oklahoma Grocers Journal (25980)

Oklahoma Historical Society
2100 N Lincoln Blvd.
Oklahoma City, OK 73105-4997
Phone: (405)522-5243
Fax: (405)521-2492

Publications: The Chronicles of Oklahoma (25962)

Oklahoma Living Magazine
PO Box 54309
Oklahoma City, OK 73154
Phone: (405)478-1455
Fax: (405)478-0246

Publications: Oklahoma Living Magazine (25981)

Oklahoma LP-Gas Association
4200 N. Lindsay
Oklahoma City, OK 73105
Phone: (405)424-1775
Fax: (405)424-1781

Publications: Propaneorist (25994)

The Oklahoma Observer
Box 53371
Oklahoma City, OK 73152
Phone: (405)525-5582
Fax: (405)525-3403

Publications: The Oklahoma Observer (25983)

Oklahoma Petroleum Marketers Association
5115 N. Western
Oklahoma City, OK 73118
Phone: (405)842-6625
Fax: (405)842-9564

Publications: The Marketer (25971)

Oklahoma Pharmaceutical Association
45 NE 52 St.
PO Box 18731
Oklahoma City, OK 73154-0731
Phone: (405)528-3338
Fax: (405)528-1417

Publications: Oklahoma Pharmacist (25984)

Oklahoma Press Association
3601 N. Lincoln Blvd.
Oklahoma City, OK 73105-5499
Phone: (405)524-4421
Fax: (405)524-2201
Free: 888-815-2672

Publications: Oklahoma Publisher (25986)

Oklahoma Press Publishing Co.
PO Box 1968
Muskogee, OK 74402
Phone: (918)684-2900
Fax: (918)684-2878

Publications: Phoenix & Times-Democrat (25923)

Oklahoma Publishing Co.
9000 N. Broadway
PO Box 25125
Oklahoma City, OK 73114
Phone: (405)475-3311
Fax: (405)475-3970
Free: 800-375-6397

Publications: Oklahoman (25989)

Oklahoma Restaurant Association
3800 N. Portland
Oklahoma City, OK 73112-2948
Phone: (405)942-8181
Fax: (405)942-0541

Publications: Midsouthwest Restaurant (25972)

Oklahoma Retailer Publishing Co., Inc.
4500 N Sewell, Rm. 12
Oklahoma City, OK 73118
Phone: (405)528-0903
Fax: (405)528-0903

Publications: Oklahoma Retailer (25987)

Oklahoma Society of Professional Engineers
201 NE 27th St., Rm. 125
Oklahoma City, OK 73105
Phone: (405)528-1435
Fax: (405)557-1820

Publications: Oklahoma Professional Engineer (25985)

Oklahoma State Medical Association
601 NW Grand Blvd.
Oklahoma City, OK 73118
Phone: (405)843-9571
Fax: (405)842-1834
Free: 800-522-9452

Publications: Journal (25967)

Oklahoma State University
College of Business Administration
Stillwater, OK 74078-4011
Phone: (405)744-7645
Fax: (405)774-5180

Publications: Southern Economic Journal (26081)

Oklahoma State University
121 Cordell North
Stillwater, OK 74078-2000
Phone: (405)744-6260
Fax: (405)744-8445

Publications: Oklahoma State University Magazine (26080)

Oklahoma State University
School of Journalism & Broadcasting
106 Paul Miller J/B Bldg.
Stillwater, OK 74078
Phone: (405)744-8372
Fax: (405)744-7936

Publications: The Daily O'Collegian (26077)

Oklahoma State University
205 Morrill Hall
Stillwater, OK 74078-4069
Phone: (405)744-9476
Fax: (405)744-6326

Publications: Cimarron Review (26076)

Oklahoma Today Magazine
PO Box 53384
Oklahoma City, OK 73152
Phone: (405)521-2496
Fax: (405)522-4588
Free: 800-777-1793

Publications: Oklahoma Today Magazine (25988)

The Oklee Herald
PO Box 9
Oklee, MN 56742
Phone: (218)796-5181
Fax: (218)487-5251

Publications: The Oklee Herald (16242)

The Old Berthoud Recorder
534 3rd Ave.
PO Box J
Berthoud, CO 80513
Phone: (970)532-3715
Fax: (970)532-3918

Publications: The Old Berthoud Recorder (4153)

Old Buncombe County Geological Society
PO Box 2122
Asheville, NC 28802-2122
Phone: (828)293-1894

Publications: A Lot of Bunkum (24010)

Old Dominion University
Arts and Letters Bldg.
Norfolk, VA 23529
Phone: (757)683-3949
Fax: (757)683-5844

Publications: Scotia (32293)

Old Dominion University
2101 Webb University Center
Hampton Blvd.
Norfolk, VA 23529

Publications: The Mace and Crown (32290)

Old Huntsville Magazine
716 East Clinton Ave.
Huntsville, AL 35801
Publications: Old Huntsville (271)

The Old Lyons Recorder
430 Main St.
PO Box 1729
Lyons, CO 80540
Phone: (303)823-6625
Fax: (303)823-6633
Publications: The Old Lyons Recorder (4570)

Old Mill News
5667 Leisure South Dr. SE
Kentwood, MI 49548-5814
Phone: (616)455-0609
Publications: Old Mill News (15264)

Old Sturbridge Inc.
1 Old Sturbridge Village Rd.
Sturbridge, MA 01566-1198
Phone: (508)347-3362
Fax: (508)347-0377
Free: 800-SEE-1830
Publications: Old Sturbridge Visitor (14577)

Old-Time Music Group, Inc.
1812 House Ave.
Durham, NC 27707
Phone: (919)402-8495
Fax: (919)402-8495
Publications: The Old-Time Herald (23839)

Older Persons Action Group, Inc.
325 E 3rd Ave., Ste. 300
Anchorage, AK 99501
Phone: (907)276-1059
Fax: (907)278-6724
Free: 800-478-1059
Publications: Senior Voice (531)

Ole Brook Broadcasting, Inc.
Hwy. 550 & 51
PO Box 532
Brookhaven, MS 39601
Phone: (601)833-7149
Fax: (601)833-9683
Publications: Buyers Guide (16577)

Olean Independent Press
36 River St.
Salamanca, NY 14779-1474
Phone: (716)945-1644
Publications: The Independent Olean Press (23292)

Olean Times-Herald
639 Norton Dr.
Olean, NY 14760
Phone: (716)372-3121
Fax: (716)372-0740
Publications: Houghton Star (23039) • Olean Times-Herald (23040)

Oligochaetology Laboratory
18 Broadview Ct.
Kitchener, ON, Canada N2A 2X8
Phone: (519)896-4728
Publications: Megadrilogica (35963)

Olive Hill Times
Post Office Bldg.
Olive Hill, KY 41164
Phone: (606)286-4201
Publications: Olive Hill Times (12326)

Olivet College
320 S. Main St.
Olivet, MI 49076
Phone: (269)749-7000
Publications: Shipherd's Record (15418)

Olson Communications, Inc.
PO Box 28
Nevis, MN 56467
Phone: (218)652-3475
Publications: Cass Lake Times (15790)

Olson Press
2900 E. Broadway
PO Box 1697
Bismarck, ND 58506-1697
Phone: (701)258-4970
Publications: Billings County Pioneer (24343) • Golden Valley News (24344) • Oakes Times (24358)

Olson Publications, Inc.
5137 Hwy. 92
Acworth, GA 30102
Phone: (770)974-1077
Fax: (770)974-1911
Free: 800-647-3724
Publications: Food People (6897)

The Olton Enterprise
716 Main St.
PO Drawer E
Olton, TX 79064-0437
Phone: (806)285-2631
Fax: (806)285-2632
Publications: The Olton Enterprise (30886)

Olympia Genealogical Society
Box 1313
Olympia, WA 98507-1313
Publications: Olympia Genealogical Society Quarterly (32859)

Olympic Publishing Company, Inc.
822 E. Main ST.
Puyallup, WA 98371
Phone: (253)841-2481
Fax: (206)840-8249
Publications: Puyallup Herald (32918)

Olympic View Publishing, Inc.
147 1/2 W Washington St.
PO Box 1750
Sequim, WA 98382
Phone: (360)683-3205
Fax: (360)683-6670
Free: 800-829-5810
Publications: Peninsula Business Journal (33076) • The Sequim Gazette (33077)

Omaha World-Herald Co.
1334 Dodge St.
Omaha, NE 68102-1122
Phone: (402)444-1000
Fax: (402)345-0183
Free: 800-284-6397
Publications: Omaha World-Herald (18206)

Omak Chronicle, Inc.
618 Okoma Dr., Box 553
Omak, WA 98841
Phone: (509)826-1110
Fax: (509)826-5819
Free: 800-572-3446
Publications: The Omak-Okanogan County Chronicle (32872)

Omega Group
5735 E Avapahoe, Ste. 5
Boulder, CO 80303
Phone: (303)449-3750
Fax: (303)444-5617
Free: 800-800-7630
Publications: Soldier of Fortune (4192)

Omohundro Institute of Early American History & Culture
PO Box 8781
Williamsburg, VA 23187-8781
Phone: (757)221-1120
Fax: (757)221-1047
Publications: William and Mary Quarterly (32623)

On the Town
PO Box 499
Jenison, MI 49429-0499
Phone: (616)669-1366
Fax: (616)662-4060
Publications: On the Town (15229)

Onaga Herald
PO Box 309
Onaga, KS 66521
Phone: (785)889-4681
Fax: (785)889-4610

Publications: Onaga Herald (11685)

Oncology Nursing Society
125 Enterprise Dr.
Pittsburgh, PA 15275-1214
Phone: (412)859-6100
Fax: (412)859-6163
Free: (866)257-4667
Publications: Clinical Journal of Oncology Nursing (27765) • Oncology Nursing Forum (27824)

101 Communications
9121 Oakdale Ave.
Chatsworth, CA 91311
Phone: (818)734-1520
Fax: (818)734-1522
Publications: Computerworld (14194) • Federal Computer Week (32044) • The Industry Standard (1687) • InfoWorld Direct (1688) • Macworld (3388) • PC WORLD (3413)

101communications, LLC
9121 Oakdale Ave., Ste. 101
Chatsworth, CA 91311
Phone: (818)734-1520
Publications: Enterprise Systems Journal (1686)

101communications, LLC
600 Worchester Rd., Ste. 301
Framingham, MA 01702
Phone: (508)875-6644
Fax: (508)875-6622
Publications: Application Development Trends (14191)

101communications, LLC
1300 Virginia Dr., Ste. 401
Fort Washington, PA 19034-3221
Phone: (215)643-8000
Fax: (215)643-3901
Publications: ENT (26927) • Enterprise Linux (26928) • Enterprise Systems (26929)

1059434 Ontario Inc.
7B Pleasant Blvd., Unit 966
Toronto, ON, Canada M4T 1K2
Phone: (416)535-9735
Fax: (416)535-0566
Publications: Exclaim! (36585)

1199603 Ontario Ltd.
487 Book Rd. W
Ancaster, ON, Canada L9G 3L1
Phone: (905)648-2035
Fax: (905)648-6977
Publications: Rider (35634)

1812
Box 1812
Amherst, NY 14226-7812
Phone: (716)834-1067
Publications: 1812 (20033)

1590 Broadcaster
502 W Hollis St.
PO Box 548
Nashua, NH 03061-0548
Phone: (603)882-1590
Fax: (603)886-9356
Publications: 1590 Broadcaster (18598)

1000 Islands Publishers, LTD
79 King St. E.
Gananoque, ON, Canada K7G 1E8
Phone: (613)382-2156
Fax: (613)382-3010
Publications: PIC Press (35843) • The Reporter (35844)

Oneida-Chittenango Pennysaver, Inc.
208 Lenox Ave.
PO Box 297
Oneida, NY 13421
Phone: (315)697-2969
Fax: (315)363-3119
Publications: Pennysaver (Chittenango Edition) (23046)

Oneida-Madison Pennysaver, Inc.
28 Robinson Rd.
PO Box 203
Clinton, NY 13323
Phone: (315)853-5559
Fax: (315)853-4024
Free: 800-765-2112

Publications: Farm and Home Pennysaver (20471) • Herkimer Pennysaver (20733) • Mid-York Weekly (20708) • North Country Pennysaver (20238) • Pennysaver (Oneida Edition) (20473) • Rome Pennysaver (23266) • Suburban Pennysaver (23577) • Utica Pennysaver (23468)

Oneworld Magazine, Inc.
648 Broadway, Ste. 201
New York, NY 10012
Phone: (212)941-0774
Fax: (212)941-0339

Publications: Oneworld (22491)

The Onida Watchman
116 S Main
PO Box 245
Onida, SD 57564
Phone: (605)258-2604
Fax: (605)258-2572

Publications: The Onida Watchman (28911)

Onion, Inc.
544 E. Ogden Ave., Ste. 700-388
Milwaukee, WI 53202
Phone: (414)272-1372
Fax: (414)272-3555
Free: 800-695-4376

Publications: The Onion (34091)

Online, A Division of Information Today, Inc.
213 Danbury Rd.
Wilton, CT 06897
Phone: (203)761-1466
Fax: (203)761-1444
Free: 800-248-8466

Publications: EContent (5225) • EMedia (5226) • EMedia Magazine (5227) • Online (28474) • online user (28475)

OnPoint Publishing
2 South St., Ste. 204
Auburn, NY 13021
Phone: (315)253-4601
Fax: (315)258-8148
Free: 800-529-5652

Publications: The Finger Lakes Business Almanac (20106)

Ontario Archaeological Society
11099 Bathurst St.
Richmond Hill, ON, Canada L4C 0N2
Phone: (905)787-9851
Fax: (905)787-9852
Free: 888-733-0042

Publications: Ontario Archaeology (36345)

Ontario Association of Certified Engineering Technicians and Technologists
10 Four Seasons Pl., Ste. 404
Etobicoke, ON, Canada M9B 6H7
Phone: (416)621-9621
Fax: (416)621-8694

Publications: The Ontario Technologist (35818)

Ontario Association for Mathematics Education
70 Chestnut Ct.
London, ON, Canada N6K 4J5
Phone: (519)471-6234
Fax: (519)471-6324

Publications: Ontario Mathematics Gazette (35991)

Ontario College of Pharmacists
483 Huron St.
Toronto, ON, Canada M5R 2R4
Phone: (416)962-4861
Fax: (416)847-8200

Publications: Pharmacy Connection (36703)

Ontario College of Teachers
121 Bloor St. E., 6th Fl.
Toronto, ON, Canada M4W 3M5
Phone: (416)961-8800
Fax: (416)961-8822

Publications: Professionally Speaking/Pour Parler Profession (36717)

The Ontario Dental Association
4 New St.
Toronto, ON, Canada M5R 1P6
Phone: (416)922-3900
Fax: (416)922-9005

Publications: Ontario Dentist (36682)

Ontario DX Association
PO Box 161, Sta. A
Toronto, ON, Canada M2N 5S8

Publications: Listening In (36651)

Ontario Fruit & Vegetable Growers' Association
355 Elmira Rd., N 105
Guelph, ON, Canada N1K 1S5
Phone: (519)763-8728
Fax: (519)763-6604

Publications: The Grower (35863)

Ontario Genealogical Society
40 Orchard View Blvd., Ste. 102
Toronto, ON, Canada M4R 1B9

Publications: Families (36592)

Ontario Herbalists Association
RR 1
Port Burwell, ON, Canada N0J 1T0
Phone: (416)536-1509
Free: 877-OHA-HERB

Publications: The Canadian Journal of Herbalism (36331)

The Ontario Historical Society
34 Parkview Ave.
Willowdale, ON, Canada M2N 3Y2
Phone: (416)226-9011
Fax: (416)226-2740

Publications: Ontario History (36882)

Ontario Institute for Studies in Education/UT
252 Bloor St. W.
Toronto, ON, Canada M5S 1V6
Phone: (416)923-6641
Fax: (416)926-4725

Publications: Resources for Feminist Research (Documentation sur la Recherche Feministe) (36728)

Ontario Library Association
100 Lombard St., Ste. 303
Toronto, ON, Canada M5C 1M3
Phone: (416)363-3388
Fax: (416)941-9581

Publications: Teaching Librarian (36755)

Ontario Long Term Care Association
345 Renfrew Dr., No. 202
Markham, ON, Canada L3R 9S9
Phone: (905)470-8995
Fax: (905)470-9595

Publications: Long Term Care (35637)

Ontario Medical Association
525 University Ave., Ste. 300
Toronto, ON, Canada M5G 2K7
Phone: (416)599-2580
Fax: (416)340-2232
Free: 800-268-7215

Publications: Ontario Medical Review (36684)

Ontario Milk Marketing Board
6780 Campobello Rd.
Mississauga, ON, Canada L5N 2L8
Phone: (905)821-8970
Fax: (905)821-3160

Publications: Ontario Milk Producer (36082)

Ontario Ministry of Agriculture, Food and Rural Affairs
1 Stone Rd. W.
Guelph, ON, Canada N1G 4Y2
Phone: (519)826-4191
Fax: (519)826-4211
Free: 888-466-2372

Publications: Monthly Crop and Livestock Report (35866)

Ontario Principals' Council
180 Dundaf St. W, 25th Fl.
Toronto, ON, Canada M5G 1Z8
Phone: (416)322-6600
Fax: (416)322-6618
Free: 800-701-2362

Publications: The Register (36724)

Ontario Public Service Employees Union
100 Lesmill Rd.
North York, ON, Canada M3B 3P8
Phone: (416)443-8888
Fax: (416)443-1762
Free: 800-268-7376

Publications: Our Ontario (36131)

Ontario Secondary School Teachers' Federation
60 Mobile Dr.
Toronto, ON, Canada M4A 2P3
Phone: (416)751-8300
Fax: (416)751-3875
Free: 800-267-7867

Publications: Education Forum (36579)

Ontario Snowmobiler Publishing Ltd.
78 Main St. S.
Newmarket, ON, Canada L3Y 3Y6
Phone: (905)898-8585
Fax: (905)848-8071
Free: 888-661-7469

Publications: Ontario Snowmobiler (36107)

Ontario Teachers' Federation
1300 Yonge St., Ste. 200
Toronto, ON, Canada M4T 1X3
Phone: (416)966-3424
Fax: (416)966-5450

Publications: OTF (FEO) Interaction (36692)

Ontario Tennis Association
1185 Eglinton Ave. E.
Toronto, ON, Canada M3C 3C6
Phone: (416)426-7135
Fax: (416)426-7370
Free: 800-387-5066

Publications: Ontario Tennis Association (36687)

Onti Publications
Box 20657
Cranston, RI 02920
Phone: (401)865-2690
Fax: (401)865-1264

Publications: Inti (28335)

The Ontonagon Herald
326 River St.
Ontonagon, MI 49953
Phone: (906)884-2826
Fax: (906)884-2939

Publications: The Ontonagon Herald (15422)

Oologah Lake Leader
109 S Maple
PO Box 460
Oologah, OK 74053-0460
Phone: (918)443-2428

Publications: Oologah Lake Leader (26027)

OP Publishing Ltd.
1080 Howe St., Ste. 900
Vancouver, BC, Canada V6Z 2T1
Phone: (604)606-4644
Fax: (604)687-1925

Publications: Cottage (35137) • The Outdoor Edge (35155) • Pacific Yachting (35158) • Western Sportsman (35180)

OP Travel & Tourism Marketing, Inc.
104-1260 Hornby St.
Vancouver, BC, Canada V6Z 1W2
Phone: (604)699-9990
Fax: (604)699-9993

Publications: Canadian Traveller (35134)

Opelika-Auburn News
3505 Pepperell Pkwy.
PO Box 2208
Opelika, AL 36801
Phone: (205)749-6271
Fax: (205)749-1228

Publications: Opelika-Auburn News (409)

Open City, Inc.
225 Lafayette St., Ste. 1114
New York, NY 10012
Phone: (212)625-9048
Fax: (212)625-2030
Publications: Open City (22493)

Open Communication
429 Timber Ln.
Devon, PA 19333
Phone: (610)687-2824
Fax: (610)225-2405
Publications: O2 (26825)

An Open Door to the Inner Light, Inc.
70 Valley Falls Rd.
Vernon, CT 06066
Phone: (860)875-4101
Fax: (860)875-4101
Publications: The Door Opener (5187)

Openings
202-204 W. University Ave.
Champaign, IL 61824-0526
Phone: (217)356-8391
Fax: (217)356-5733
Publications: Bulletin of the American Society of Papyrologists (19692) • Journal of Cuneiform Studies (14755) • Semeia (37556)

Opera Canada
366 Adelaide St. E, Ste. 244
Toronto, ON, Canada M5A 3X9
Phone: (416)363-0395
Fax: (416)363-0396
Free: 800-331-6014
Publications: Opera Canada (36688)

The Opp News
PO Box 870
Opp, AL 36467
Phone: (334)493-3595
Fax: (334)493-4901
Publications: The Opp News (410)

Opti Press
234 St Geoge
PO Box 189
Annapolis Royal, NS, Canada B0S 1A0
Phone: (902)532-2219
Fax: (902)532-2246
Publications: The Spectator (35535)

Optical Society of America
2010 Massachusetts Ave. NW
Washington, DC 20036-1023
Phone: (202)223-8130
Fax: (202)223-1939
Free: 800-766-405A
Publications: Applied Optics (5359) • Journal of the Optical Society of America A: Optics, Image Science,and Vision (5608) • Journal of the Optical Society of America B: Optical Physics (5609) • Optics Letters (5709) • Optics & Photonics News (5710)

Optimist International
4494 Lindell Blvd.
St. Louis, MO 63108
Phone: (314)371-6000
Fax: (314)371-6006
Free: 800-678-8389
Publications: The Optimist Magazine (17478)

Optipress Ltd.
Box 550
73 Gerrish St.
Windsor, NS, Canada B0N 2T0
Phone: (902)798-8371
Fax: (902)798-5451
Free: 800-567-7377
Publications: The Hants Journal (35619)

OR Manager, Inc.
PO Box 5303
Santa Fe, NM 87502-5303
Phone: (505)982-1600
Fax: (505)983-0790
Free: 800-442-9918
Publications: OR Manager (19939)

Oracle Corp.
500 Oracle Pkwy., M/S 10BP1
Redwood City, CA 94065
Phone: (650)506-7000
Fax: (650)633-2424
Publications: Oracle Magazine (2914) • Profit (2915)

Oral Roberts University
Student Publications LRC 230
7777 S. Lewis St.
Tulsa, OK 74171
Phone: (918)495-6346
Fax: (918)495-6345
Publications: The Oracle (26123)

Orange Coast
3701 Birch St., Ste. 100
Newport Beach, CA 92660
Phone: (949)862-1133
Fax: (949)862-0133
Publications: Orange Coast (2634)

Orange County Business Journal
2600 Michelson Dr., No. 170
Irvine, CA 92612
Publications: Orange County Business Journal (2086)

Orange County Community College
115 South St.
Middletown, NY 10940-6404
Phone: (845)344-6222
Fax: (845)343-1228
Publications: The Citadel (21080)

Orange County Multi-Housing Service Corp.
12822 Garden Grove Blvd., Ste. D
Garden Grove, CA 92843
Phone: (714)638-5550
Fax: (714)741-9457
Publications: Apartment News (1997)

Orange County News
7441 Garden Grove Blvd., Ste. G
Garden Grove, CA 92841-4209
Phone: (714)894-2575
Fax: (714)894-0809
Publications: Orange County News (1998)

Orange County Post
15 Goshen Ave.
Washingtonville, NY 10992
Phone: (845)496-3611
Fax: (845)496-1715
Publications: Orange County Post (23512)

Orange County Publishing Co.
450 W Bolivar
PO Box 1236
Vidor, TX 77670-1236
Phone: (409)769-5428
Fax: (409)769-2600
Publications: Vidorian (31243) • Vidorian Shopper (31244)

Orange County Publishing Company Inc.
PO Box 190
Paoli, IN 47454
Phone: (812)723-2572
Fax: (812)723-2592
Publications: News (10387) • Orange Countian (10388) • Republican (10389)

The Orange County Register
625 N. Grand Ave.
Santa Ana, CA 92701
Phone: (714)796-7000
Publications: Aliso Viejo News (3618) • Capistrano Valley News (3559) • Dana Point News (1805) • Laguna Niguel News (2136) • Leisure World News (2134) • Orange County Register (3630)

The Orange County Register
625 N. Grand Ave.
PO Box 11626
Santa Ana, CA 92701
Phone: (714)796-7000
Fax: (714)542-5037
Publications: Anaheim Hills News (1398)

The Orange County Register
625 N. Grand Ave.
Santa Ana, CA 92701
Phone: (714)796-7000
Publications: Rancho Santa Margarita News (2881) • Saddleback Valley News (3632) • San Clemente Sun-Post News (3102)

Orange Offset Inc.
132 W Main St.
Postal Drawer A
Goshen, NY 10924
Phone: (845)566-4539
Fax: (845)294-0532
Publications: Independent Republican (20673)

Orange Review
PO Box 3428
Charlottesville, VA 22903
Phone: (804)979-0373
Fax: (804)971-5821
Publications: Tribune (31943)

Orange Source
126 Schine Student Ctr.
Syracuse, NY 13210
Phone: (315)443-4863
Fax: (315)443-5458
Publications: Orange Source (23417)

Orangeburg Black Voice
PO Box 11128
Columbia, SC 29211
Phone: (803)799-5252
Fax: (803)799-7709
Publications: Orangeburg Black Voice (28731)

The Orangeville Banner
37 Mill St.
Orangeville, ON, Canada L9W 2M4
Phone: (519)941-1350
Fax: (519)941-9600
Publications: The Orangeville Banner (36172)

Orangeville Citizen
10 First St.
Orangeville, ON, Canada L9W 2C4
Phone: (519)941-2230
Fax: (519)941-9361
Publications: Orangeville Citizen (36173)

Oratoire St. Joseph Du-Mont-Royal
3800, Chemin Queen Mary
Montreal, QC, Canada H3V 1H6
Phone: (514)733-8211
Fax: (514)733-9735
Publications: L'Oratoire (37200) • The Oratory (37201)

Orban Communications, Inc.
25 Washington St., 4th Fl.
Morristown, NJ 07960
Phone: (973)605-2442
Fax: (973)605-2722
Publications: Cruise and Vacation Views (19311)

Orchard News
235 Windom St.
PO Box 130
Orchard, NE 68764
Phone: (402)893-2535
Fax: (402)893-2535
Publications: Orchard News (18235)

Order of Buddhist Contemplatives
Shasta Abbey
3724 Summit Dr.
Mount Shasta, CA 96067-9102
Fax: (916)926-0428
Publications: The Journal of the Order of Buddhist Contemplatives (2604)

Order of St. Benedict
100 College Dr.
Box 190
Muenster, SK, Canada S0K 2Y0
Phone: (306)682-1772
Fax: (306)682-5285
Publications: Prairie Messenger (37505)

2566

Numbers cited after listings are entry numbers rather than page numbers.

The Order of United Commercial Travelers of America
632 N Park St.
PO Box 159019
Columbus, OH 43215-8619
Phone: (614)228-3276
Fax: (614)228-1898
Free: 800-848-0123

Publications: The Sample Case (25060)

Ordre des Dentistes du Quebec
625, blvd. Western Rene-Levesque, 15th stage
Montreal, QC, Canada H3B 1R2
Phone: (514)875-8511
Fax: (514)393-9248
Free: 800-361-4887

Publications: Journal Dentaire du Quebec (JDQ) (37139)

Ordre des Ingenieurs du Quebec
2020 University St., 18th Fl.
Montreal, QC, Canada H3A 2A5
Phone: (514)845-6141
Fax: (514)845-1833

Publications: Plan (37206)

Ordre des Medecins Veterinaires du Quebec
800, ave. Sainte-Anne, bureau 200
Saint-Hyacinthe, QC, Canada J2S 5G7
Phone: (450)774-1427
Fax: (450)774-7635
Free: 800-267-1427

Publications: Le Medecin Veterinaire du Quebec (37351)

Ordre Professionel des Dietetistes du Quebec
1425 bd. Rene-Levesque O., Bur. 703
Montreal, QC, Canada H3G 1T7
Phone: (514)393-3733
Fax: (514)393-3582
Free: 888-393-8528

Publications: Dietetique en Action (37108)

Ordre des infirmieres et infirmiers du Quebec
4200, boul. Dorchester Ouest
Montreal, QC, Canada H3Z 1V4
Phone: (514)935-2501
Fax: (514)935-2055
Free: 800-363-6048

Publications: L'infirmiere du Quebec (37126)

Oregon Association of Nurserymen
29751 SW Town Center Loop W
Wilsonville, OR 97070
Phone: (503)682-5089
Fax: (503)682-5727
Free: 800-342-6401

Publications: Digger (26614)

Oregon Beef Producer
3415 Commercial St., Ste. 217
Salem, OR 97302-4668
Phone: (503)361-8941
Fax: (503)361-8947

Publications: Oregon Beef Producer (26569)

Oregon Catholic Press
5536 N.E. Hassalo
Portland, OR 97213
Phone: (503)281-1191
Fax: (503)282-3486
Free: 800-548-8749

Publications: Catholic Sentinel (26473) • Today's Liturgy (26511)

Oregon Coast Newspapers
PO Box 444
Tillamook, OR 97141
Phone: (503)842-7535
Fax: (503)842-8842

Publications: Headlight-Herald (26597)

Oregon Daily Emerald Publishing Co.
PO Box 3159
300 EMU
Eugene, OR 97403
Phone: (541)346-5511
Fax: (541)346-5578

Publications: Oregon Daily Emerald (26328)

Oregon Education Association
6900 SW Atlanta St.
Portland, OR 97223-2513
Phone: (503)684-3300
Fax: (503)684-8063

Publications: Today's OEA (26512)

Oregon Historical Society
1200 SW Park Ave.
Portland, OR 97205
Phone: (503)222-1741
Fax: (503)221-2035

Publications: Oregon Historical Quarterly (26492)

Oregon Institute of Technology
3201 Campus Dr.
Klamath Falls, OR 97601-8801
Phone: (541)885-1772
Fax: (541)885-1777

Publications: Shaw Historical Library Journal (26386)

Oregon Labor Press Publishing Co.
1827 NE 44th Ave., Ste. 200
PO Box 13150
Portland, OR 97213
Phone: (503)288-3311
Fax: (503)288-3320

Publications: Northwest Labor Press (26487)

Oregon Law Review
School of Law
1221 University of Oregon
Eugene, OR 97403-1221
Phone: (541)346-3844
Fax: (541)346-1564

Publications: Office Manager (26327)

Oregon Lithoprint
PO Box 727
McMinnville, OR 97128
Phone: (503)472-5114
Fax: (503)472-9151
Free: 800-472-1198

Publications: News-Register (26415)

Oregon Newspaper Publishers Association
7150 SW Hampton, Ste. 111
Portland, OR 97223
Phone: (503)624-6397
Fax: (503)639-9009

Publications: Oregon Publisher (26493)

Oregon PeaceWorks
104 Commercial St. NE
Salem, OR 97301-3401
Phone: (503)371-8002
Fax: (503)588-0088

Publications: Oregon Peaceworker (26570)

Oregon Secretary of State
800 Summer St. NE
Salem, OR 97310
Phone: (503)373-0701
Fax: (503)378-4118

Publications: Oregon Secretary of State Administration Rule Compilation (26571)

Oregon State Bar
5200 SW Meadows Rd.
Lake Oswego, OR 97035
Phone: (503)620-0222
Fax: (503)684-1366

Publications: Oregon State Bar Bulletin (26405)

Oregon State Pharmacists Association
29702-B SW Town Center Loop W
Wilsonville, OR 97070-6481
Phone: (503)582-9055

Publications: Oregon Pharmacist (26616)

Oregon State University
118 Memorial Union East
Corvallis, OR 97331-1614
Phone: (541)737-3374
Fax: (541)737-4999

Publications: The Daily Barometer (26287)

Oregon Wheat Growers League
115 SE 8th St.
Pendleton, OR 97801-2319
Phone: (541)276-7330
Fax: (541)276-1723

Publications: Oregon Wheat (26459)

Oregonian Publishing Co.
1320 SW Broadway
Portland, OR 97201-3469
Phone: (503)221-8327
Fax: (503)227-5306
Free: 800-452-1420

Publications: The Oregonian (26495)

Orfordville Journal and Footville News
124 E Spring St.
PO Box 248
Orfordville, WI 53576
Phone: (608)879-2211
Fax: (608)879-2211

Publications: Orfordville Journal and Footville News (34220)

Organ Historical Society
Box 26811
Richmond, VA 23261
Phone: (804)353-9226
Fax: (804)353-9266

Publications: The Tracker (32457)

Organic Preparations and Procedures, Inc.
PO Box 610009
Newton Highlands, MA 02461

Publications: Organic Preparations and Procedures International (13944)

Organization of American Historians
112 N Bryan Ave.
Bloomington, IN 47408-4199
Phone: (812)855-7312
Fax: (812)855-0696

Publications: The Journal of American History (9840)

Organization of American States
1889 F St. NW
Washington, DC 20006
Phone: (202)458-3510
Fax: (202)458-3526

Publications: Inter-American Review of Bibliography (5548)

Organization Development Institute
11234 Walnut Ridge Rd.
Chesterland, OH 44026-1299
Phone: (440)729-7419
Fax: (440)729-9319

Publications: Organization Development Journal (24760)

Organization for Economic Cooperation and Development
2001 L St. NW, Ste. 650
Washington, DC 20036-4922
Phone: (202)785-6323
Fax: (202)785-0350
Free: 800-456-6323

Publications: The DAC Journal (5458) • Energy Prices and Taxes (5478) • Financial Market Trends (5496) • Higher Education Management (5525) • International Trade by Commodities, Series C (5558) • Main Economic Indicators (5641) • Main Science & Technology Indicators (5642) • Monthly Statistics of International Trade (5661) • OECD Economic Studies (5699) • OECD Economic Surveys (5700) • OECD Journal on Budgeting (5701) • OECD Journal of Competition Law & Policy (5702) • OECD Observer (5703) • Oil, Gas, Coal and Electricity Quarterly Statistics (5706) • Quarterly Labour Force Statistics (5755) • Quarterly National Accounts (5756)

Organization for Promotion and Advancement of Small Telecommunications Companies (OPASTCO)
21 Dupont Cir. NW, Ste. 700
Washington, DC 20036
Phone: (202)659-5990
Fax: (202)659-4619

Publications: OPASTCO Roundtable (5708)

Organization for Research on Women and Communication
University of Geogia
Dept. of Speech Communication
Athens, GA 30602-1725

Publications: Women's Studies in Communication (6953)

Organize Training Center
PO Box 1297
Pacifica, CA 94044-1919
Phone: (650)557-9720
Fax: (650)557-9720

Publications: Social Policy (2739)

Orgone Biophysical Research Laboratory
Box 1148
Ashland, OR 97520
Phone: (541)552-0118

Publications: Pulse of the Planet (26216)

The Original Entertainer
PO Box 19809
Oklahoma City, OK 73144
Phone: (405)681-8073
Fax: (405)681-2454

Publications: Oklahoma Entertainment News (25978)

Original Internist, Inc.
720 Oak Knoll
Rolla, MO 65401
Phone: (573)341-8448
Fax: (573)341-8494

Publications: Original Internist (17378)

Orion
187 Main St.
Great Barrington, MA 01230
Phone: (413)528-4422
Fax: (413)528-0676
Free: 888-909-6568

Publications: Orion (14216)

Orlando Sentinel Communications
633 N Orange Ave.
Orlando, FL 32801-1300
Phone: (407)420-5000
Fax: (407)420-5661
Free: 800-347-6868

Publications: Central Florida Family Magazine (6488) • The Orlando Sentinel (6503)

The Orlando Times
4403 Vineland Rd., Ste. B-5
PO Box 555339
Orlando, FL 32855
Phone: (407)841-3052
Fax: (407)849-0434

Publications: The Orlando Times (6504)

Orlo
PO Box 10342
Portland, OR 97296
Phone: (503)242-1047

Publications: The Bear Deluxe Magazine (26469)

Ornel, Inc.
13 Lamplighter Ln.
South Easton, MD 02375

Publications: Case Digests, Human Resources Law Index (13750)

The Oromocto Post-Gazette
291 Restigouche Rd.
Oromocto, NB, Canada E2V 2H5
Phone: (506)357-9813
Fax: (506)357-5222

Publications: The Oromocto Post-Gazette (35424)

Orono Weekly Times
5310 Main St.
PO Box 209
Orono, ON, Canada L0B 1M0
Phone: (905)983-5301
Fax: (905)983-5301

Publications: Orono Weekly Times (36179)

Oroville Gazette Publishing, Ltd.
PO Box 250
Oroville, WA 98844
Phone: (509)476-3602
Fax: (509)476-3054
Free: 888-874-9820

Publications: Okanogan Valley Gazette-Tribune (32873)

The Orthodox Catholic Church of North & South America
PO Box 1213
Akron, OH 44309
Phone: (330)753-1155
Fax: (330)753-7717

Publications: The Orthodox Catholic Voice (24584)

Orthodox Christian Journal
10 Downs Dr.
Wilkes Barre, PA 18705-3802
Phone: (570)825-3158
Fax: (570)825-0136

Publications: Orthodox Christian Journal (27001)

Oryx Press
1434 E. San Miguel Ave.
Phoenix, AZ 85014-2422
Free: 800-225-5800

Publications: Current Index to Journals in Education (801)

Osage County Chronicle
107 E Santa Fe
Burlingame, KS 66413
Phone: (785)654-3621
Fax: (785)654-3438

Publications: Osage County Chronicle (11369)

Osage Valley Publishing
PO Box 23
Windsor, MO 65360
Phone: (660)647-2121
Fax: (660)647-2122

Publications: Cole Camp Courier (17720)

Osborne Publishing Co., Inc.
PO Box 130
Osborne, KS 67473
Phone: (785)346-5424
Fax: (785)346-5400

Publications: Osborne County Farmer (11686)

Oser Communications Group Inc.
1350 N. Kolb Rd., Ste. 220
Tucson, AZ 85715
Phone: (520)721-1300
Fax: (520)721-6300

Publications: Arizona Gourmet (931) • Tucson Gourmet (967)

Osgoode Hall Law Journal
4700 Keele St., Rm. 312
Toronto, ON, Canada M3J 1P3
Phone: (416)736-5354
Fax: (416)736-5869

Publications: Osgoode Hall Law Journal (36691)

O'Shillal Enterprises, Inc.
144 E Broadway
PO Box 637
Paullina, IA 51046
Phone: (712)448-3622
Fax: (712)448-2622

Publications: The Paullina Times (11150)

Oshkosh
204 Main St.
Box 290
Oshkosh, NE 69154-0290
Phone: (308)772-3555
Fax: (308)772-4475
Free: 800-774-4656

Publications: Garden County News (18240)

Oshkosh Buyer's Guide
314 N Koeller St.
Oshkosh, WI 54901-4110
Phone: (414)235-1790
Fax: (414)235-1833

Publications: Oshkosh Buyers' Guide (34227)

Oshkosh Northwestern Co.
224 State St.
PO Box 2926
Oshkosh, WI 54901-4839
Phone: (920)235-7700
Fax: (920)235-1316
Free: 800-924-6168

Publications: Northwestern (34224)

Oskaloosa Shopper
1901 A Ave. W
Box 530
Oskaloosa, IA 52577-0530
Phone: (641)672-2581
Fax: (641)672-2294

Publications: Oskaloosa Shopper (11135)

Osmon Publications
4805 Alta Canyada Rd.
La Canada, CA 91011
Phone: (818)790-0651
Fax: (818)790-2807

Publications: Not Born Yesterday (2108)

Osoyoos Times
8712 Main St.
Box 359
Osoyoos, BC, Canada V0H 1V0
Phone: (250)495-7225
Fax: (250)495-6616

Publications: Osoyoos Times (35042)

Ospery Media Group
PO Box 250
Chesley, ON, Canada N0G 1L0
Phone: (519)363-2414
Fax: (519)363-2726

Publications: The Chesley Enterprise (35734)

Osprey Media
186 Alexander St.
PO Box 190
Pembroke, ON, Canada K8A 4L9
Phone: (613)732-3691
Fax: (613)732-2645
Free: 800-265-0246

Publications: Observer (36308)

Osprey Media Group
PO Box 40
Petrolia, ON, Canada N0N 1R0
Phone: (519)882-1770
Fax: (519)882-3212

Publications: Mainly for Seniors Lambton-Kent (36326)

Osprey Media Group Inc.
Suite 110 100 Renfrew Dr.
Markham, ON, Canada L3R 9R6
Phone: (905)752-1132

Publications: Flamborough Review (36025)

Osprey Media Group Inc.
145 Old Garden River Rd.
PO Box 460
Sault Sainte Marie, ON, Canada P6A 5M5
Phone: (705)759-3030
Fax: (705)942-8690

Publications: The Sault Star (36370)

Ossain Bee
107 W Main
PO Box 96
Ossian, IA 52161-0096
Phone: (319)532-9113
Fax: (319)532-9081

Publications: The Ossian Bee (11139)

Ostdiek Publishing, Inc.
PO Box 188
Lawrence, NE 68957
Phone: (402)756-7284
Fax: (402)756-7285

Publications: Locomotive (18070)

Osteen Publishing Co., Inc.
20 N. Magnolia
PO Box 1677
Sumter, SC 29150
Phone: (803)775-6331
Fax: (803)775-1024

Publications: The Item (28768)

Osterhus Publishing House, Inc.
4500 W Broadway
Minneapolis, MN 55422
Phone: (763)537-9311
Fax: (763)537-9585

Publications: The Bible Friend (16061)

OSU Alumni Association
Oregon State University
204 CH2M-HILL Alumni Center
Corvallis, OR 97331-6303
Phone: (541)737-7851
Free: 877-305-3759

Publications: Oregon Stater (26289)

Oswego County Weeklies
N. Jefferson 80
PO Box 129
Mexico, NY 13114
Phone: (315)963-7813
Fax: (315)963-4087

Publications: Central Square Citizen Outlet (20451) • Independent Mirror (21076) • Phoenix Register (23096) • Salmon River News (21077)

Other Publications Society
Room 1020-700 Royal Ave.
Douglas College
New Westminster, BC, Canada V3L 5B2
Phone: (604)525-3542
Fax: (604)525-3505

Publications: Other Press (35030)

The Other Side
300 W. Apsley
Philadelphia, PA 19144
Phone: (215)849-2178
Fax: (215)849-3755
Free: 800-700-9280

Publications: The Other Side (27610)

Otsego County Herald Times, Inc.
PO Box 598
Gaylord, MI 49734
Phone: (989)732-1111
Fax: (989)732-3490
Free: 877-819-6170

Publications: Gaylord Herald Times (15068) • Northern Lights (15069)

Ottawa Citizen Group Inc.
1101 Baxter Rd.
PO Box 5020
Ottawa, ON, Canada K2C 3M4
Phone: (613)829-9100
Free: 800-267-6100

Publications: The Ottawa Citizen (36265)

The Ottawa County Exponent
121 W. Water St.
PO Box 70
Oak Harbor, OH 43449-0070
Phone: (419)898-5361
Fax: (419)898-0501

Publications: The Ottawa County Exponent (25442)

Ottawa Field-Naturalists Club
Box 35069, Westgate P.O.
Ottawa, ON, Canada K1Z 1A2
Phone: (613)722-3050

Publications: Canadian Field-Naturalist (36194) • Trail and Landscape (36277)

Ottawa Herald
104 S Cedar
Ottawa, KS 66067
Phone: (785)242-4700
Fax: (785)242-9420
Free: 800-467-8383

Publications: Ottawa Herald (11689)

Ottawa Publishing Co.
110 W. Jefferson
Ottawa, IL 61350
Phone: (815)433-2000
Fax: (815)433-1626

Publications: The Daily Times (9390)

The Ottawa Times
401 S Main St., Ste. 1
PO Box 246
Ottawa, KS 66067
Phone: (785)242-9200
Fax: (785)242-9595

Publications: Ottawa Times Shopper (11691)

Ottawa University
1001 S. Cedar
Box 16
Ottawa, KS 66067-3399
Phone: (785)242-5200
Fax: (785)229-1022
Free: 800-755-5200

Publications: Ottawa Spirit (11690)

The Ottawa X Press
396 Cooper, Ste. 204
Ottawa, ON, Canada K2P 2H7
Phone: (613)237-8226
Fax: (613)237-8220

Publications: The Ottawa X Press (36269)

Ottaway News Service
40 Mulberry St.
Middletown, NY 10940
Phone: (914)343-2181
Fax: (914)343-2170

Publications: Times Herald-Record (21081)

Ottaway Newspaper
PO Box 250
Oneonta, NY 13820
Phone: (607)432-1000
Fax: (607)432-5847
Free: 800-721-1000

Publications: The CoopersTown Crier (20497) • The Daily Star (23049)

Ottaway Newspaper
170 Margaret St., PO Box 459
Plattsburgh, NY 12901
Phone: (518)561-2300

Publications: Press-Republican (23103)

Ottaway Newspaper
84-88 Fowler St.
Port Jervis, NY 12771
Phone: (914)856-5383
Fax: (914)858-8484

Publications: Gazette (23119)

The Ottaway Newspapers
Whittemore St.
Gloucester, MA 01930
Phone: (508)283-7000
Fax: (508)281-5748

Publications: Times (14211)

Ottaway Newspapers, Inc.
333 Main St.
Danbury, CT 06810
Phone: (203)744-5100
Fax: (203)792-8730

Publications: News-Times (4747)

Ottaway Newspapers, Inc.
PO Box 401
Campbell Hall, NY 10916
Phone: (845)294-8181

Publications: Allied News (26963) • The Herald (27986) • Pocono Record (28035)

Ottumwa Courier
PO Box 228
Walnut St.
Eddyville, IA 52553
Phone: (515)969-4846
Fax: (515)933-4341

Publications: Eddyville Tribune (10865)

The Ouachita Citizen
PO Box 758
West Monroe, LA 71294
Phone: (318)322-3161
Fax: (318)325-2285

Publications: The Ouachita Citizen (12874)

Oughtred Society
2160 Middlefield Rd.
Palo Alto, CA 94301
Phone: (415)324-1821

Publications: Journal of Oughtred Society (2797)

Our Home Town
540 E Main St.
PO Box 101
Vanderbilt, MI 49795
Phone: (517)983-2233
Fax: (517)983-2233

Publications: Our Home Town (15650)

Our Northland Diocese
1200 Memorial Dr.
PO Box 610
Crookston, MN 56716
Fax: (218)281-5991

Publications: Our Northland Diocese (15820)

Our Sunday Visitor Publishing
200 Noll Plaza
Huntington, IN 46750
Phone: (260)356-8400
Fax: (260)356-8472
Free: 800-348-2440

Publications: The Catholic Answer (10067) • Catholic Parent (10068) • My Daily Visitor (10070) • New Covenant (10071) • Our Sunday Visitor (10072) • The Pope Speaks (10073) • The Priest (10074)

Our Town
58 W Pleasant Ave.
Maywood, NJ 07607
Phone: (201)843-5700

Publications: Our Town (19219)

Our World Publishing Corp.
1104 N Nova Rd., Ste. 251
Daytona Beach, FL 32117
Phone: (386)441-5367
Fax: (386)441-5604

Publications: Our World (6038)

Out Front Colorado
723 Sherman St.
Denver, CO 80203-3545
Phone: (303)778-7900
Fax: (303)778-7978

Publications: Out Front Colorado (4346)

Out Magazine
80 8th Ave., No. 315
New York, NY 10011-5126
Free: 800-792-2760

Publications: Out Magazine (22510)

Out Your Backdoor
4686 Meridian Rd.
Williamston, MI 48895
Phone: (517)347-1689
Fax: (517)349-5912

Publications: Out Your Backdoor (15685)

Outburn
PO Box 3187
Thousand Oaks, CA 91359
Phone: (805)493-5861

Publications: Outburn (3905)

Outcrop Ltd.
PO Box 1350
Yellowknife, NT, Canada X1A 2N9
Phone: (867)920-4343
Fax: (867)873-2844
Free: 800-661-0861

Publications: Up Here (35527)

Outdoor Canada Publishing Ltd.
340 Ferrier St., Ste. 210
Markham, ON, Canada L3R 2Z5
Phone: (905)475-8440
Fax: (905)475-9246

Publications: Outdoor Canada (36029)

Outdoor Empire Publishing Inc.
PO Box 19000
Seattle, WA 98109
Phone: (206)624-3845
Fax: (206)695-8512
Free: 800-645-5489

Publications: Fishing and Hunting News (32966)

The Outdoor Press
8716 N Forest Blvd.
Spokane, WA 99208
Phone: (509)328-9392
Fax: (509)327-9861

Publications: The Outdoor Press (33096)

Outlook Printers (1960) Ltd.
PO Box 399
Outlook, SK, Canada S0L 2N0
Phone: (306)867-8262
Fax: (306)867-9556

Publications: The Outlook (37514)

Outlook Publishing, Inc.
415 E. Main
PO Box 278
Laurel, MT 59044
Phone: (406)628-4412
Fax: (406)628-8260

Publications: Laurel Outlook (17846)

Outpost Exchange
204 E Capitol Dr.
Milwaukee, WI 53212
Phone: (414)964-7789
Fax: (414)964-0317

Publications: Outpost Exchange (34092)

Outspoken Enterprises, Inc.
1 Haight St., Ste. B
San Francisco, CA 94102
Phone: (415)863-6538
Fax: (415)863-1609

Publications: Curve (3348)

Overdrive Magazine, Inc.
PO Box 3187
Tuscaloosa, AL 35403
Phone: (205)349-2990
Fax: (205)349-6359
Free: 800-633-5953

Publications: Overdrive (490)

Overland Courier
704 E Main St.
PO Box 286
Princeton, MO 64673
Phone: (816)748-3266
Fax: (816)748-3267

Publications: Post-Telegraph (17366)

Overseas Ministries Study Center
490 Prospect St.
New Haven, CT 06511-2196
Phone: (203)624-6672
Fax: (203)865-2857

Publications: International Bulletin of Missionary Research (4992)

Overton County News
415 W Main St.
PO Box 479
Livingston, TN 38570
Phone: (931)823-6485
Fax: (931)823-6486

Publications: Overton County News (29333)

Owatonna People's Press
Box 346
135 W. Pearl St.
Owatonna, MN 55060-0346
Phone: (507)451-2840
Fax: (507)444-3282

Publications: Owatonna People's Press (16254)

Owego Pennysaver
181-183 Front St.
Owego, NY 13827
Phone: (607)687-2434

Publications: Owego Pennysaver (23067)

Owen County Historical and Genealogical Society
1819 Concord Rd.
Spencer, IN 47460
Phone: (812)829-4466

Publications: Owen County History & Genealogy (10031)

Owensboro Messenger-Inquirer
1401 Frederica St.
PO Box 1480
Owensboro, KY 42301
Phone: (270)926-0123
Fax: (270)685-3446
Free: 800-633-2008

Publications: Messenger-Inquirer (12327)

Owl and the Pussycat Publications
St. Thomas University
Fredericton, NB, Canada E3B 5G3
Phone: (506)460-0300
Fax: (506)460-0306

Publications: Aquinian (35389)

Owner-Operator Independent Drivers Association Inc.
1 NW OOIDA Dr.
PO Box 1000
Grain Valley, MO 64029
Phone: (816)229-5791
Fax: (816)229-0518
Free: 800-444-5791

Publications: Land Line (17084)

Oxbow Herald
PO Box 420
Oxbow, SK, Canada S0C 2B0
Phone: (306)483-2323
Fax: (306)483-5258

Publications: Oxbow Herald (37515)

Oxendine Publishing, Inc.
PO Box 14081
Gainesville, FL 32604-2081
Phone: (352)373-6907
Fax: (352)373-8120
Free: 888-547-6310

Publications: Florida Leader for High School Students (6138) • Florida Leader Magazine (6139)

The Oxford American
303 President Clinton Ave.
Little Rock, AR 72201
Phone: (501)907-6418
Fax: (501)907-6419
Free: 888-250-5692

Publications: The Oxford American (1235)

The Oxford Eagle
PO Box 866
Oxford, MS 38655
Phone: (662)234-4331
Fax: (662)234-4351

Publications: The Oxford Eagle (16807)

Oxford Journal Ltd.
PO Box 10
Oxford, NS, Canada B0M 1P0
Phone: (902)447-2051
Fax: (902)447-2055

Publications: The Oxford Journal (35600)

The Oxford Press
15 S. Beech St.
Oxford, OH 45056
Phone: (513)523-4139
Fax: (513)523-1935

Publications: The Oxford Press (25458)

Oxford Public Ledger
PO Box 643
Oxford, NC 27565
Phone: (919)693-2646
Fax: (919)693-3704

Publications: Oxford Public Ledger (24111)

Oxford Publishing, Inc.
307 W. Jackson Ave.
Oxford, MS 38655
Phone: (601)236-5510
Fax: (601)236-5541
Free: 800-247-3881

Publications: Nightclub & Bar Magazine (16806)

Oxford Standard
Box 125
Oxford, NE 68967
Phone: (308)824-3582
Fax: (308)824-3582

Publications: Oxford Standard (18243)

Oxford University Press
111 Market Pl. Ste. 840
Baltimore, MD 21202-6709
Phone: (410)223-1600
Fax: (410)223-1620

Publications: American Journal of Epidemiology (13116)

Oxford University Press
2001 Evans Rd.
Cary, NC 27513
Phone: (919)677-0977
Fax: (919)677-1714
Free: 800-451-7556

Publications: Cerebral Cortex (23687) • History Workshop (23688) • Journal of the American Academy of Religion (4077) • Journal of Communication (23689) • The Journal of Deaf Studies and Deaf Education (23690) • Journal of the History of Medicine and Allied Sciences (23691) • Journal of Law, Economics, and Organization (23692) • Psychotherapy Research (25459) • Public Health Reports (13954) • The Review of Financial Studies (23693)

Oyster Bay Guardian
32 E Main
PO Box 28
Oyster Bay, NY 11771
Phone: (516)922-4215
Fax: (516)922-4227

Publications: Oyster Bay-Syosset Guardian (23070)

Ozark County Times
PO Box 188
Gainesville, MO 65655
Phone: (417)679-4641
Fax: (417)679-3423

Publications: Ozark County Times (17080)

The Ozark Journal
PO Box 598
Imboden, AR 72434
Phone: (870)869-2220

Publications: The Ozark Journal (1194)

Ozark Publications Inc.
PO Box 490
Ozark, MO 65721
Phone: (417)581-3541
Fax: (417)581-3577

Publications: Christian County Headliners News (17330)

Ozark Spectator Corp.
207 W Main
Ozark, AR 72949
Phone: (501)667-2136
Fax: (501)667-4365

Publications: Ozark Spectator (1305)

The Ozarks & Mountaineer Corp.
PO Box 20
Kirbyville, MO 65679
Phone: (417)336-2665
Fax: (417)336-2679

Publications: The Ozarks Mountaineer (17224)

The Ozona Stockman
1000 Ave. E
PO Box 370
Ozona, TX 76943-2551
Phone: (915)392-2551
Fax: (915)392-2439

Publications: The Ozona Stockman (30891)

P. B & H Publishing Inc.
Main St.
PO Box 520
Tyndall, SD 57066
Phone: (605)589-3242

Publications: Tyndall Tribune & Register (29004)

P-EN Publications, Inc.
215 Allen Ave.
Glendale, CA 91201
Phone: (818)954-9495
Fax: (818)954-0452

Publications: Print-Equip News (2012)

P. H. Publishing
295 Losher St. PO Box 100
Hernando, MS 38632
Phone: (601)393-6397
Fax: (601)393-6463

Publications: DeSoto Times Today (16679)

Pace Communications, Inc.
1301 Carolina St.
Greensboro, NC 27401-1001
Phone: (336)378-6065
Fax: (336)378-8261

Publications: Attacheair Magazine (23916) • Elegant Bride (23921) • IGA Grocergram (8404) • The Shuttle Sheet (23937) • SKY Magazine—(Delta Air Lines) (23938) • United Hemispheres (23942)

PACE International Union
3340 Perimeter Hill Dr.
PO Box 1475
Nashville, TN 37202
Phone: (615)834-8590
Fax: (615)831-6791

Publications: The PACEsetter (29478)

Pace Publishing Ltd.
5160 Explorer Dr., Unit 6
Mississauga, ON, Canada L4W 4T7
Phone: (905)629-7500
Fax: (905)629-7988
Free: 800-667-8541

Publications: Equipment Journal (36067)

Pace University
Westchester Campus
861 Bedford Rd.
Pleasantville, NY 10570
Phone: (914)773-3401
Fax: (914)773-3402
Free: 800-874-PACE

Publications: The New Morning (23111)

Pace University
Wilcox Hall
861 Bedford Rd.
Pleasantville, NY 10570

Publications: New Morning (23110)

Pacific Ancient and Modern Language Association
Department of Humanities
Pepperdine University
Malibu, CA 90263-4225
Phone: (310)506-4225

Publications: Pacific Coast Philology (2493)

Pacific Basin Communications
1000 Bishop St., Ste. 405
Honolulu, HI 96813
Phone: (808)537-9500
Fax: (808)537-6455

Publications: Honolulu Magazine (7701)

Pacific Builder & Engineer
10504 NE 37th Cir., No. 7
Kirkland, WA 98033-7920
Phone: (425)486-8553
Fax: (425)488-0946
Free: 888-452-9038

Publications: Pacific Builder & Engineer (32799)

Pacific Coast Entomological Society
c/o: California Academy of Sciences
Golden Gate Park
San Francisco, CA 94118-4599
Phone: (415)750-7227
Fax: (415)750-7228

Publications: The Pan-Pacific Entomologist (3530)

Pacific Coast Newspapers
930 SE Hwy. 101
PO Box 848
Lincoln City, OR 97367
Phone: (503)994-2178
Fax: (503)994-7613

Publications: The News Guard (26411)

Pacific/Guest Life Inc.
PO Box 7540
Carmel, CA 93921-7540
Phone: (831)626-5740
Fax: (831)626-5744

Publications: Guest Life Monterey Bay (1672)

Pacific Island Publishers
818 Broughton St.
Victoria, BC, Canada V8W 1E4
Phone: (250)383-3633
Fax: (250)480-3233

Publications: WHERE Victoria (35230)

Pacific Lutheran University
1010, 122nd St. S.
Tacoma, WA 98447
Phone: (253)535-7494
Fax: (253)536-5076

Publications: The Mooring Mast (33146)

Pacific Media Group
2314 3rd Ave.
Seattle, WA 98121
Phone: (206)461-1300
Fax: (206)461-1340

Publications: Redmond Sammamish Valley News (33013)

Pacific News Service
275 9th St., 3rd Fl.
San Francisco, CA 94103-3025
Phone: (415)503-4170

Publications: JINN Magazine (3377) • New California Media (NCM) (3394) • YO! (3466)

Pacific Newspaper Group, Inc.
1-200 Granville St.
Vancouver, BC, Canada V6C 3N3
Phone: (604)605-2111
Fax: (604)605-2323

Publications: The Province (35160) • The Vancouver Sun (35175)

Pacific Press
PO Box 1452
Melville, NY 11747
Phone: (631)694-2929
Fax: (631)390-0053
Free: 877-390-7730

Publications: Physiological Chemistry and Physics and Medical NMR (21057)

Pacific Press Publishing Association
PO Box 5353
Nampa, ID 83653-5353
Phone: (208)465-2500
Fax: (208)465-2531
Free: 800-447-7377

Publications: Signs of the Times (7931)

Pacific Publishing Co.
4000 Aurora Ave. N, Ste. 100
Seattle, WA 98103-7853
Phone: (206)461-3333

Publications: The Beacon Hill News (32948) • Capitol Hill Times (32953) • Kirkland Courier (32798) • Madison Park Times (32983) • North Seattle Herald-Outlook (32992) • Queen Anne/Magnolia News (33010)

Pacific Rim Publishing, Inc.
40748 Encyclopedia Cr.
Fremont, CA 94538
Phone: (510)656-5100
Fax: (510)656-8844
Free: 800-824-2433

Publications: Kung Fu/Qigong (1939)

Pacific Sierra Publishing Co., Inc.
150 Chambers St. 9
El Cajon, CA 92020-3366

Publications: Amador Ledger-Dispatch (1842) • The Catalina Islander (1443) • The Chowchilla News (1711) • La Jolla Light (2115) • Los Banos Enterprise (1846) • Madera Tribune (1847) • Turlock Journal (3958)

Pacific Sun Publishing Co., Inc.
21 Corte Madera Ave.
Mill Valley, CA 94941
Phone: (415)383-4500
Fax: (415)383-4159

Publications: Pacific Sun (2541)

Pacific Telecommunications Council
2454 S Beretania St., 3rd Fl.
Honolulu, HI 96826-1596
Phone: (808)941-3789
Fax: (808)944-4874

Publications: Pacific Telecommunications Review (7716)

Pacific Union Conference of Seventh-day Adventists
PO Box 5005
Westlake Village, CA 91359
Phone: (805)497-9457
Fax: (805)495-2644

Publications: Pacific Union Recorder (4072)

Pacific University
2043 College Way
U.C PO Box 586
Forest Grove, OR 97116
Phone: (503)352-2855
Fax: (503)352-3130

Publications: Pacific Index (26356)

Pacifica Publishing, Inc.
P.O. Box 10860
Portland, OR 97296-0860
Phone: (503)224-6039
Fax: (503)222-5312
Free: 800-398-7842

Publications: Northwest Palate Magazine (26488)

Pacifica Tribune
59 Aura Vista
PO Box 1189
Pacifica, CA 94044
Phone: (650)359-6666
Fax: (650)359-3821

Publications: Pacifica Tribune (2738) • The Wave, The Buyer's Guide for the Coastside (2740)

PacificBasin Communications
PO Box 913
Honolulu, HI 96808
Phone: (808)537-9500
Fax: (808)537-6455

Publications: Hawaii Business (7691)

PacificBasin Communications, Inc.
1000 Bishop St., Ste. 405
Honolulu, HI 96813
Phone: (808)537-9500

Publications: Pacific Magazine with Islands Business (7714)

Packard Automobile Classics
420 S Ludlow St.
Dayton, OH 45402

Publications: Packard Cormorant (1603)

Paddock Publications
PO Box 280
Arlington Heights, IL 60006
Phone: (847)427-4300
Fax: (847)427-1550

Publications: Daily Herald (8022)

Paducah Community College
Alben Barkley Dr.
PO Box 7380
Paducah, KY 42002-7380
Fax: (502)554-6218

Publications: (The Smoke) Signal (12340)

The Paducah Post
PO Box E
Paducah, TX 79248
Phone: (806)492-3585

Publications: The Paducah Post (30893)

The Paducah Sun
PO Box 2300
Paducah, KY 42002-2300
Phone: (502)443-1771
Fax: (502)442-7859
Free: 800-959-1771

Publications: The Paducah Sun (12339)

Page One Corp.
PO Box 278
Imlay City, MI 48444
Phone: (810)724-0254
Fax: (810)724-8552

Publications: Tri-City Times (15202)

Page-Shenandoah Newspaper Corp.
PO Box 707
Luray, VA 22835
Phone: (703)743-5123

Publications: Page News and Courier (32203) •
The Shenandoah Valley-Herald (32640)

Pageantry, Talent & Entertainment Services, Inc.
PO Box 160307
Altamonte Springs, FL 32716-0307
Phone: (407)260-2262
Fax: (407)260-5131

Publications: Pageantry (5902)

The Pagosa Springs Sun
Box 9
Pagosa Springs, CO 81147
Phone: (970)264-2101

Publications: The Pagosa Springs Sun (4590)

Pahrump Valley Times
2160 E. Calvada Blvd.
Pahrump, NV 89048
Phone: (775)727-5102
Fax: (775)752-5309
Free: 800-473-2737

Publications: Pahrump Valley Times (18414)

Paint & Coatings Industry
755 W. Big Beaver Rd., Ste. 1000
Troy, MI 48084
Phone: (248)362-3700
Fax: (248)244-6439

Publications: Paint & Coatings Industry (15632)

Paint and Decorating Retailers Association
403 Axminster Dr.
Fenton, MO 63026
Phone: (636)326-2636
Fax: (636)326-1823
Free: 800-737-0107

Publications: Paint & Decorating Retailer (17063)

The Paintsville Herald
PO Box 1547
Paintsville, KY 41240
Phone: (606)789-5315
Fax: (606)789-9717
Free: 888-788-5315

Publications: The Paintsville Herald (12349)

Paisano Publications, LLC
PO Box 3000
Agoura, CA 91376
Phone: (818)889-8740
Free: 800-247-6246

Publications: American Rodder (1376) • Biker
(1377) • Easyriders (1378) • In the Wind (1386) •
Savage (1379) • Tailgate (1380) • Tattoo (1381) •
Tattoo Industry (1382) • V-Twin (1383) • V-Twin
News (1384)

Pakistan Today
13913 Seville Ave.
Fontana, CA 92335
Phone: (909)350-0348
Fax: (909)350-0359

Publications: Pakistan (1919)

Palate and Spirit
2443 Filmore St., Ste. 347
San Francisco, CA 94115-1925

Publications: Palate and Spirit (3412)

Palatka Daily News
1825 St. Johns Ave.
PO Box 777
Palatka, FL 32178

Publications: Palatka Daily News (6537)

The Palisade Tribune and Valley Report
124 W 3rd
PO Box 8
Palisade, CO 81526
Phone: (970)464-5614

Publications: The Palisade Tribune and Valley Report (4593)

Palisades Institute for Research Services
411 Lafayette St., Fl. 2
New York, NY 10003
Phone: (212)460-9700
Fax: (212)620-3379

Publications: Information Display (21869)

Palisadian-Post
839 Via De La Paz
Pacific Palisades, CA 90272
Phone: (310)454-1321
Fax: (310)454-1078

Publications: Palisadian-Post (2736)

Palladium Publishing
1175 N A St.
PO Box 308
Richmond, IN 47374-3226
Phone: (765)962-1575
Fax: (765)973-4570
Free: 800-686-1330

Publications: Palladium-Item (10420)

The Palladium-Times
140 W 1st St.
Oswego, NY 13126
Phone: (315)343-3800
Fax: (315)343-0273

Publications: The Palladium-Times (23062)

Palm Beach County Genealogical Society, Inc.
Box 1746
West Palm Beach, FL 33402-1746
Phone: (561)832-3279

Publications: Ancestry (6845)

Palm Beach Media Group
PO Box 3344
Palm Beach, FL 33480
Phone: (561)659-0210
Fax: (561)659-1736

Publications: Palm Beach Illustrated (6543)

Palm Beach Newspapers, Inc.
265 Royal Poinciana Way
Palm Beach, FL 33480-4007
Phone: (561)820-3800
Fax: (561)655-4594

Publications: Palm Beach Daily News (6542)

The Palm Beach Post
2751 S Dixie Hwy.
West Palm Beach, FL 33405
Phone: (561)820-4401
Fax: (561)820-4407
Free: 800-432-7595

Publications: The Palm Beach Post (6848)

Palm Beach Society Magazine
Box 3229
240 Worth Ave.
Palm Beach, FL 33480
Phone: (561)659-5555
Fax: (561)655-6209
Free: 800-452-7066

Publications: Palm Beach Society Magazine (6544)

Palm Beach Times
222 Lakeview Ave., Ste. 160-262
West Palm Beach, FL 33401
Phone: (561)833-5129
Fax: (561)659-2893
Free: 888-444-7188

Publications: Palm Beach and The Naples Times (6849)

Palmer Video Corp.
41B Sandra Cir., Apt. B3
Westfield, NJ 07090-1126
Phone: (908)686-3030
Fax: (908)686-2151

Publications: Palmer Video Magazine (19744) •
Palmer Video News (19745)

Palmerston Observer
171 Williams St.
PO Box 757
Palmerston, ON, Canada N0G 2P0
Phone: (519)343-2440
Fax: (519)343-2267

Publications: Palmerston Observer (36305)

Palmetto Pharmacist
1350 Browning Rd.
Columbia, SC 29210-6903
Phone: (803)354-9977
Fax: (803)354-9207
Free: 800-532-4033

Publications: Palmetto Pharmacist (28558)

Palmyra Spectator
304 S Main St.
PO Box 391
Palmyra, MO 63461
Phone: (573)769-3111
Fax: (573)769-3554

Publications: Palmyra Spectator (17331)

Palo Verde Valley Times
231 N Spring St.
PO Box 1159
Blythe, CA 92226
Phone: (760)922-3181
Fax: (760)922-3184

Publications: Palo Verde Valley Times (1587)

Palomar Community Newspapers
29277 Valley Ctr. Rd.
Valley Center, CA 92082
Phone: (760)749-1112
Fax: (760)749-1688

Publications: Valley Roadrunner (3985)

Palomino Horse Breeders of America
15253 E Skelly Dr.
Tulsa, OK 74116-2637
Phone: (918)438-1234
Fax: (918)438-1232

Publications: Palomino Horses (26124)

Pan American Health Organization
Publications Program, PAHO
525 23rd St. NW
Hanover, PA 17331
Phone: (717)632-3535
Fax: (717)633-8920

Publications: Revista Panamericana de Salud Publica (26976)

Pan Asia Venture Capital Corp.
809 Sacramento St.
San Francisco, CA 94108
Phone: (415)397-0220
Fax: (415)397-7258

Publications: AsianWeek (3327)

Pan-Japan Journal
Anthropology 4640
338 Schroeder Hall
Illinois State University
Normal, IL 61790
Phone: (309)438-7690
Fax: (309)438-7177

Publications: Pan-Japan (9302)

Panagraphics, Inc.
PO Box 328
Boston, NY 14025-0328
Phone: (716)312-8088
Free: 800-422-1275

Publications: Polish-American Journal (20239)

Pandata Corp.
7108 S Alton Way, Bldg. H
Englewood, CO 80112-2129
Phone: (303)792-2390
Fax: (303)792-2391
Free: 800-548-5536

Publications: RadioResource International (4415)

Panhandle Buyers Guide Publications, Inc.
415 Wilson St.
PO Box 2118
Martinsburg, WV 25401
Phone: (304)267-9983
Fax: (304)263-7106

Publications: Buyers Guide (33378) • Jefferson Buyers Guide (33271)

Panhandle Herald
Box 429
Panhandle, TX 79068-0429
Phone: (806)537-3634
Fax: (806)537-3634
Publications: Panhandle Herald (30903)

Pannell Kerr Forster
420 Lexington Ave.
New York, NY 10170
Phone: (212)867-8000
Publications: Trends in the Hotel Industry (22863)

Panola Watchman
109 W Panola
PO Box 518
Carthage, TX 75633
Phone: (903)693-7888
Fax: (903)693-5857
Publications: Panola Watchman (30904)

Panolian, Inc.
363 Hwy. 51 N
Batesville, MS 38606-0393
Phone: (662)563-4591
Fax: (662)563-5610
Free: 800-310-4591
Publications: The Panolian (16550)

The Pantagraph
301 W. Washington St.
PO Box 2907
Bloomington, IL 61702-2907
Phone: (309)829-9000
Fax: (309)829-8497
Free: 800-747-7323
Publications: The Pantagraph (8079)

PAO MCCDC
Public Affairs Office
14010 Smoketown Rd.
Woodbridge, VA 22192-4707
Publications: Quantico Sentry (32638)

P.A.P. Communication Inc.
1627, boul. St-Joseph
Quebec, QC, Canada G2K 1H1
Phone: (418)623-3383
Fax: (418)623-5033
Free: 800-387-3383
Publications: Magazine Circuit Industriel (37291)

The Paper
725 Bainbridge St.
Barry, IL 62312
Phone: (217)335-2112
Fax: (217)335-2112
Publications: The Paper (8049)

The Paper
Highways 24 & 13 N
PO Box 603
Wabash, IN 46992
Phone: (219)563-8326
Fax: (219)563-2863
Free: 800-766-6333
Publications: The Paper (10528)

Paper Industry
PO Box 5675
Montgomery, AL 36103-5675
Free: 888-224-6611
Publications: Paper Industry (374)

Paper Publishing Co.
365 Broadway
New York, NY 10013
Phone: (212)226-4405
Fax: (212)226-0062
Publications: Paper Magazine (22520)

PaperClip Communications
125 Paterson Ave.
Little Falls, NJ 07424
Phone: (973)256-1333
Fax: (973)256-8088
Publications: Curriculum Review (19177)

Paperplates
19 Kenwood Ave.
Toronto, ON, Canada M6C 2R8
Phone: (416)651-2551
Fax: (416)651-2910
Publications: Paperplates (36696)

The Papers, Inc.
206 S. Main St.
PO Box 188
Milford, IN 46542-0188
Phone: (574)658-4111
Fax: (574)658-4701
Free: 800-733-4111
Publications: The Mail-Journal (10309) • The Paper (Elkhart County Edition) (10027) • The Paper (Goshen Edition) (10028) • The Paper (Kosciusko Edition) (10536) • Senior Life (Allen County Edition) (10310) • Senior Life (El-Ko Edition) (10311) • Senior Life (Northwest Edition) (10312)

Papers on Language & Literature
Southern Illinois University Edwardsville
Edwardsville, IL 62026-1434
Phone: (618)650-2119
Fax: (618)650-3509
Publications: Papers on Language & Literature (8814)

Pappin Communications
The Victoria Centre
84 Isabella St.
Pembroke, ON, Canada K8A 5S5
Phone: (613)735-0952
Fax: (613)735-7983
Publications: Body Cast (36121) • Canadian Oncology Nursing Journal (36522) • Dynamics (34642)

Parade Publications
711 3rd Ave.
New York, NY 10017
Phone: (212)450-7000
Fax: (212)450-7087
Publications: Parade (22522)

Paradigm Communications Group
2701 1st Ave., Ste. 250
Seattle, WA 98121
Phone: (206)441-5871
Fax: (206)448-6939
Publications: Alaska Airlines Magazines (32937) • Horizon Air Magazine (32971) • Midwest Airlines Magazine (32987)

Paradigm Communications, Inc.
PO Box 27709
Richmond, VA 23261
Phone: (804)644-0496
Fax: (804)643-7519
Publications: Richmond Free Press (32450)

Paradise Genealogical Society, Inc.
PO Box 460
Paradise, CA 95967-0460
Phone: (530)877-2330
Publications: Genealogical Goldmine (2806)

The Paradise Post
PO Drawer 70
Paradise, CA 95967
Phone: (530)877-4413
Fax: (530)877-5213
Publications: The Paradise Post (2807)

Paragon Publications, Inc.
122 W Madison
PO Box 346
Mount Ayr, IA 50854
Phone: (641)464-2440
Fax: (641)464-2229
Publications: Mt. Ayr Record-News (11093)

Paragon Publishing, Inc.
Box 200
Sandy Hook, CT 06482
Phone: (203)426-6533
Fax: (203)426-9533
Publications: Club Confidential (5108) • Club International Magazine (5109) • Club Magazine (5110) • Club Specials Magazine (5111)

Paragould Daily Press
1401 W. Hunt St.
Paragould, AR 72450
Phone: (870)239-8562
Fax: (870)239-8565
Publications: Paragould Daily Press (1308)

Paranoia Publishing
PO Box 1041
Providence, RI 02901
Publications: Paranoia (28411)

Parapsychology Press
2741 Campus Walk Ave., Ste. 500
Durham, NC 27705
Phone: (919)688-8241
Fax: (919)683-4338
Publications: Journal of Parapsychology (23831)

Parent & Child
7048 Wilson Ln.
Bethesda, MD 20817
Phone: (301)365-5929
Publications: Parent & Child (13371)

Parent Paper, Inc.
150 River St.
Hackensack, NJ 07601
Phone: (201)646-4377
Publications: The Parent Paper (18853)

The Parenting Group
530 5th Ave., 4th Fl.
New York, NY 10036
Phone: (212)522-8989
Fax: (212)522-8699
Publications: Baby Talk (21283) • Family Life (21679) • Healthy Pregnancy (21796) • Parenting Magazine (22524)

Parents Express
PO Box 1598
San Antonio, TX 78296-1598
Phone: (512)222-1721
Publications: San Antonio Register (31047)

Parents' Press
1454 6th St.
Berkeley, CA 94710
Phone: (510)524-1602
Fax: (510)524-0912
Publications: Parents' Press (1550)

Paris Culley
20258 Fraser Hwy.
PO Box 3097
Langley, BC, Canada V3A 4R3
Phone: (604)533-4157
Fax: (604)533-0219
Publications: The Langley Times (35003)

Paris Express
PO Box 551
Paris, AR 72855
Phone: (479)963-2901
Fax: (479)963-3062
Publications: Paris Express (1311)

The Paris News
PO Box 1078
Paris, TX 75461
Phone: (903)785-8744
Fax: (903)785-1263
Free: 800-683-1929
Publications: The Paris News (30905)

Paris Publishing Co., Inc.
208 E Wood St.
PO Box 310
Paris, TN 38242-0310
Phone: (731)642-1162
Fax: (731)642-1165
Publications: The Paris Post-Intelligencer (29559)

The Paris Review
541 E 72nd St.
New York, NY 10021
Phone: (212)861-0016
Fax: (212)861-4504
Publications: The Paris Review (22530)

Park Avenue Publishing, Inc.
52 Park Ave., Ste. A4
Park Ridge, NJ 07656-1277
Phone: (201)505-9500
Fax: (201)505-9505

Publications: Kids Magazine (19409)

Park Cities People
6116 N Central Expy., Ste. 230
Dallas, TX 75206
Phone: (214)739-2244
Fax: (214)363-6948

Publications: Park Cities People (30176)

Park College
8700 NW River Park Dr.
Parkville, MO 64152
Phone: (816)741-2346
Fax: (816)741-4911

Publications: The Park Stylus (17336)

Park Communications
PO Box 355
Chatham, NY 12037
Phone: (518)392-4141
Fax: (518)392-7322

Publications: The Chatham Courier-Rough Notes (20452)

Park Communications
544 W. Main St.
PO Box 1027
Waynesboro, VA 22980
Phone: (540)949-8213

Publications: The News-Virginian (32610)

Park Communications, Inc.
110-112 E. Mount Vernon St.
PO Box 859
Somerset, KY 42502
Phone: (606)678-8191
Fax: (606)679-9225

Publications: Commonwealth-Journal (12403) • Lake Cumberland Shopper (12404)

Park Genealogical Books
PO Box 130968
Roseville, MN 55113-0968
Phone: (651)488-4416
Fax: (651)488-2653

Publications: Minnesota Genealogical Journal (16334)

Park Labrea News and Beverly Press
PO Box 36036
Los Angeles, CA 90036
Phone: (323)933-5518

Publications: Park Labrea News and Beverly Press (2358)

Park Newspaper
PO Box 409
Ogdensburg, NY 13669
Phone: (315)393-1002
Fax: (315)393-5108

Publications: Advance-News (23032) • Journal (23033)

Park Newspapers
PO Box 67
Elizabethtown, NC 28337
Phone: (919)862-4163
Fax: (919)862-6602

Publications: Bladen Journal (23864)

Park Newspapers
26 N. Logan St.
PO Box 610
Marion, NC 28752-3944
Phone: (704)652-3313

Publications: The Express (24055) • McDowell News (24056)

Park Newspapers of the Cumberlands
PO Box 9
Whitley City, KY 42653
Phone: (606)376-5356
Fax: (606)376-9565

Publications: McCreary County Record (12442)

Park Newspapers of Kentucky, Inc.
PO Box 305
Leitchfield, KY 42755
Phone: (502)259-9622
Fax: (502)259-5537

Publications: Grayson County News-Gazette (12157)

Park Newspapers of Medina, Inc.
409 Main St., No. 13
Medina, NY 14103-1416
Phone: (716)798-1400
Fax: (716)798-0290

Publications: The Journal-Register (21036)

Park Newspapers of Morehead, Inc.
722 W 1st St.
Morehead, KY 40351
Phone: (606)784-4116
Fax: (606)484-7337

Publications: Grayson Journal-Enquirer (12093) • The Greenup News (12098)

Park Newspapers of Statesville, Inc.
222 E Broad St.
PO Box 1071
Statesville, NC 28677-5325
Phone: (704)873-1451
Fax: (704)872-3150

Publications: Statesville Record and Landmark (24247)

Park Rapids Enterprise
PO Box 111
Park Rapids, MN 56470
Phone: (218)732-3364
Fax: (218)732-8757

Publications: Park Rapids Enterprise (16256)

Park Record Newspaper
PO Box 3688
Park City, UT 84060
Phone: (435)649-9014
Fax: (435)649-4942

Publications: Park Record Newspaper (31387)

Parker Publications, Inc.
PO Box 7
Denville, NJ 07834-0007
Phone: (973)627-0400
Fax: (973)627-0403

Publications: The Citizen of Morris County (18777)

Parker Publishing, Inc.
155 Main St.
Madison, NJ 07940
Phone: (908)766-3900
Fax: (908)766-6365

Publications: Hanover Eagle & Weekly Regional News (19181)

Parkers Prairie Independent
117 N Otter Ave.
Parkers Prairie, MN 56361
Phone: (218)338-2741
Fax: (218)338-2741

Publications: The Independent (16259)

The Parkersburg News
PO Box 1787
Parkersburg, WV 26102-1787
Phone: (304)485-1891
Fax: (304)485-1891
Free: 800-642-1997

Publications: The Parkersburg News (33420)

The Parkersburg Sentinel
519 Juliana St.
PO Box 1788
Parkersburg, WV 26102
Phone: (304)485-1891
Fax: (304)485-1891
Free: 800-642-1997

Publications: The Parkersburg Sentinel (33421)

The Parkhill Gazette Inc.
165 King St.
Box 400
Parkhill, ON, Canada N0M 2K0
Phone: (519)294-6264
Fax: (519)294-6391

Publications: The Parkhill Gazette (36307)

Parkhurst Publishing Ltd.
400 McGill, 3rd Fl.
Montreal, QC, Canada H2Y 2G1
Phone: (514)397-8833
Fax: (514)397-0228
Free: 800-663-7403

Publications: Doctor's Review (37109) • Parkhurst Exchange (37205)

Parkston Advance
205 W. Main St.
PO Box J
Parkston, SD 57366
Phone: (605)928-3111
Fax: (605)928-3111

Publications: The Tripp Star-Ledger (28913)

Parksville-Qualicum News
PO Box 1180
Parksville, BC, Canada V9P 2H2
Phone: (250)248-4341
Fax: (250)248-4655

Publications: Parksville-Qualicum Beach News (35043)

Parsippany News
PO Box 6123
West Caldwell, NJ 07007-6123
Phone: (973)227-4433

Publications: Parsippany News (19719)

The Parson Advocate
212 Main St.
PO Box 403
Parsons, WV 26287
Phone: (304)478-3533
Fax: (304)478-4658

Publications: The Parsons Advocate (33427)

Parsons Publishing Co.
220 S. 18th
PO Box 836
Parsons, KS 67357-0836
Phone: (620)421-2000
Fax: (620)421-2217
Free: 800-530-5723

Publications: Parsons Sun (11744)

Parthenon Publishing
28 White Bridge Rd., Ste. 209
Nashville, TN 37205

Publications: Road King (29483)

PartiLife Publications
65 Sussex St.
Hackensack, NJ 07601
Phone: (201)441-4224
Fax: (201)342-8118

Publications: Balloons & Parties Magazine (18851)

Partnership Press, Inc.
2136 Mamie Eisenhower
Boone, IA 50036
Phone: (515)432-6153
Fax: (515)432-6706

Publications: Boone County Shopping News (10624)

Pasadena Community College
1570 E Colorado Blvd.
Rm. C220
Pasadena, CA 91106
Phone: (818)585-7130
Fax: (818)585-7912

Publications: The Courier (2814)

Pasadena Weekly
50 S. DeLacey Ave. Ste. 200
Pasadena, CA 91105
Phone: (626)584-1500
Fax: (626)795-0149

Publications: Pasadena Weekly (2824)

Paseo del Rio Association
110 Broadway, Ste. 60
San Antonio, TX 78205
Phone: (210)227-4262
Fax: (210)212-7602

Publications: RIO (31044)

Paso Robles Communications Group
1636 Spring St.
PO Box 427
Paso Robles, CA 93447-0427
Phone: (805)237-6060
Fax: (805)237-6066

Publications: Paso Robles Press (2831)

Paso Robles Newspapers, Inc.
1040 Park St.
PO Box 757
Paso Robles, CA 93447-0757
Phone: (805)239-7420
Fax: (805)238-7166

Publications: Central Coast Times (2830)

Pasquia Publishing
Box 1660
1004-102 Ave.
Tisdale, SK, Canada S0E 1T0
Phone: (306)873-4515
Fax: (306)873-4712

Publications: The Parkland Review (37579)

Pasquia Publishing, Ltd.
Box 1660
1004-102 Ave.
Tisdale, SK, Canada S0E 1T0
Phone: (306)873-4515
Fax: (306)873-4712

Publications: Tisdale Recorder (37580)

The Pass Herald Ltd.
Box 960
Blairmore, AB, Canada T0K 0E0
Phone: (403)562-2248
Fax: (403)562-8379

Publications: The Pass Herald (34619)

Passaic County Community College
One College Blvd.
Paterson, NJ 07505-1179
Phone: (973)684-6555
Fax: (973)523-5843

Publications: The Paterson Literary Review (19417)

Passim, Inc.
511 W 25th St., No. 502
New York, NY 10001-5501
Phone: (646)486-0252
Fax: (646)486-0241

Publications: Trans (22852)

Passionist Missionaries of Union City
526 Monastery Pl.
Union City, NJ 07087-3306
Phone: (201)867-6400
Fax: (201)864-1337

Publications: The Passionist' Compassion (19691)

Pataskala Standard
350 S Main St.
PO Box 7
Pataskala, OH 43062-0007
Phone: (740)927-2991
Fax: (740)927-2930
Free: 800-665-2991

Publications: Pataskala Standard (25470)

P.A.T.I., Inc.
PO Box 879, JFK Sta.
Jamaica, NY 11430-0879
Phone: (718)244-6788
Fax: (718)995-3432
Free: 800-982-5832

Publications: Airport Press (20830)

Patience & Persistence in Marketing, Inc.
44 Country Rd.
North Springfield, VT 05150
Phone: (802)886-3333
Fax: (802)886-3333

Publications: Vermont Green Mountain Guide (31573)

Patrioit Publications
PO Box 38
Bronson, MI 49028
Phone: (517)369-5085
Fax: (517)369-2225

Publications: The Bronson Journal (14837)

The Patriot
208 W Main St.
Kutztown, PA 19530-1636
Phone: (610)683-7343
Fax: (610)683-5136

Publications: The Patriot (27130)

The Patriot Ledger
PO Box 699159
Quincy, MA 02269-9159
Phone: (617)786-7000
Fax: (617)786-7298
Free: 800-972-5070

Publications: The Patriot Ledger (14491)

The Patriot News
812 Market St.
Harrisburg, PA 17105
Phone: (717)255-8100
Fax: (717)255-8456
Free: 800-692-7207

Publications: The Patriot-News (27002)

Patriot Newspapers
34 Water St.
Cuba, NY 14727-1490
Phone: (585)968-2580
Fax: (585)968-2622
Free: 800-924-1123

Publications: Patriot & Free Press (20517)

Patterson Irrigator
26 N 3rd
Patterson, CA 95363
Phone: (209)892-6187
Fax: (209)892-3761

Publications: Patterson Irrigator (2832)

Patterson Publishing
PO Box 37812
Cincinnati, OH 45222
Phone: (513)475-0100
Fax: (513)475-6014
Free: 800-543-0486

Publications: Criminal Politics Magazine (24791)

Patuxent Publishing Co.
10750 Little Patuxent Pkwy.
Columbia, MD 21044
Phone: (410)730-3990
Fax: (410)997-4564

Publications: Arbutus Times (13452) • The Baltimore Messenger (13453) • Catonsville Times (13456) • Columbia Flier (13457) • Columbia Magazine (13458) • Howard County Times (13461) • Jeffersonian (13463) • Laurel Leader (13465) • North County News (13466) • Northeast Booster (13467) • Northeast Reporter (13468) • Northeast Times Booster (13469) • The Official Guide to Howard County (13470) • Owings Mills Times (13471) • Soundoff (13504) • Towson Times (13472)

Paulding Progress
111 East Fourth St.
PO Box 180
Delphos, OH 45833
Phone: (419)695-0015

Publications: Paulding Progress (25471)

Paulist National Catholic Evangelization Association
3031 4th St. NE
Washington, DC 20017
Phone: (202)832-5022
Fax: (202)269-0209
Free: 800-237-5515

Publications: Share the Word (5791)

Paul's Record Magazine
713 Gardens Dr., Apt. 203
Pompano Beach, FL 33069-0951

Publications: Paul's Record Magazine (6591)

The Pawnee Chief
PO Drawer 370
558 Illinois St.
Pawnee, OK 74058
Phone: (918)762-2552
Fax: (918)762-2564

Publications: The Pawnee Chief (Division of American-Chief Co.) (26031)

The Pawnee Republican
PO Box 111
Pawnee City, NE 68420
Phone: (402)852-2575
Fax: (402)852-2565

Publications: The Pawnee Republican (18244)

Paws & Claws
1508 E 86th St., Ste. 135
Indianapolis, IN 46240
Fax: (317)574-0181

Publications: Paws & Claws (10159)

Pax Christi-USA
532 W 8th St.
Erie, PA 16502
Phone: (814)453-4955
Fax: (814)452-4784

Publications: The Catholic Peace Voice (26895)

Paxton Media Group
PO Box 685
Bremen, GA 30110
Phone: (770)537-2434
Fax: (770)537-0826

Publications: The Haralson Gateway Beacon (7137)

Paxton Media Group
PO Box 2300
Paducah, KY 42002
Phone: (270)575-8630

Publications: The Daily Citizen (1337) • The Other Side of the Lake (8518)

Paxton Printing, Inc.
218 N. Market
PO Box 73
Paxton, IL 60957
Phone: (217)379-2356
Fax: (217)379-3104

Publications: Loda Times (9410) • Paxton Daily Record (9411)

Pazdur Publishing Inc.
2171 Campus Dr., Ste. 330
Irvine, CA 92612
Phone: (949)752-6474
Fax: (949)752-0398

Publications: Executive Golfer (2081)

Pazifische Rundschau (Pacific Review)
PO Box 88047
Richmond, BC, Canada V6X 3T6
Fax: (604)273-9365

Publications: Pazifische Rundschau (Pacific Review) (35075)

PBI Media, LLC
1201 Seven Locks Rd., Ste. 300
Potomac, MD 20854
Phone: (301)354-2000

Publications: Aviation Maintenance (13646) • Avionics Magazine (13647) • Card News (13648) • Communications (13649) • Communications Today (13650) • Diesel Fuel News (13651) • In-Motion (13653) • ISP Business News (13654) • Mobile Products Europe (13655) • Oil and Gas Interests (13656) • Petroleum Finance Week (13657) • Rotor & Wing (13660) • Telecommunications Regulatory Monitor (13661) • Via Satellite (13662) • Wireless Business & Technology (13663) • Wireless Data News (13664) • Wireless Networks (13665)

PBI Media, L.L.C.
701 Westchester Ave.
White Plains, NY 10604
Phone: (914)328-9157
Fax: (914)328-9093
Free: 800-800-5474

Publications: AV Video & Multimedia Producer (23568) • Tape/Disc Business (23575)

PC Publishing
PO Box 186
Culloden, WV 25510-0186
Phone: (304)562-6214
Fax: (304)562-6214

Publications: The Putnam - Cabell Post (33298)

P.C. Publishing Co.
2085 U. S. Route 60
Culloden, WV 25510
Phone: (304)743-6731
Fax: (304)562-6214

Publications: Putnam Democrat (33299)

PC Specialists Inc.
7810 Trade St.
San Diego, CA 92121
Phone: (619)566-8200

Publications: San Diego Computer Journal (3260)

PDA
3 Bethesda Metro Center, Ste. 1500
Bethesda, MD 20814
Phone: (301)656-5900
Fax: (301)986-0296

Publications: The PDA Journal of Pharmaceutical
Science & Technology (10983)

Peabody Essex Museum
East India Sq.
Salem, MA 01970
Phone: (978)745-9500
Fax: (978)741-9012
Free: 800-745-4054

Publications: The American Neptune (14512)

Peabody Gazette-Bulletin
118 N Walnut
PO Box 129
Peabody, KS 66866
Phone: (316)983-2185
Fax: (316)983-2700

Publications: Peabody Gazette-Bulletin (11747)

Peak Publications Society
Simon Fraser University
Burnaby, BC, Canada V5A 1S6
Phone: (604)291-3597
Fax: (604)291-3786

Publications: The Peak (34905)

Peak Publishing Ltd.
4400 Marine Ave.
Powell River, BC, Canada V8A 2K1
Phone: (604)485-5313
Fax: (604)485-5007

Publications: The Powell River Peak (35054)

Peale Center for Christian Living
66 E Main St.
Pawling, NY 12564
Phone: (845)855-5000
Fax: (845)855-1462
Free: 800-938-3322

Publications: Positive Thinking (23086)

Pearl Editions
3030 E Second St.
Long Beach, CA 90803
Phone: (562)434-4523
Fax: (562)434-4523

Publications: Pearl (2173)

Pearl Publishing Inc.
99 Kimbark Blvd.
Toronto, ON, Canada M5N 2Y3
Phone: (416)787-3322
Fax: (416)787-9299

Publications: Toronto Events Calender (36767)

PEC Inc.
Box 430
Rye, NH 03870
Phone: (603)427-1377
Fax: (603)427-1388

Publications: Personal Engineering & Instrumentation News (18643)

Peck Papers
234 E Main
Box 787
Lovell, WY 82431
Phone: (307)548-2217
Fax: (307)548-2218

Publications: The Lovell Chronicle (34561)

Pecos Enterprise
324 S Cedar St.
PO Box 2057
Pecos, TX 79772
Phone: (915)445-5475
Fax: (915)445-4321

Publications: Pecos Enterprise (30923)

Pecos Free Press
324 S. Cedar
Pecos, TX 79772
Phone: (915)445-5475
Fax: (915)445-4321

Publications: Pecos Free Press (30924)

Pedal Magazine
317 Adelaide St. W., Ste. 703
Toronto, ON, Canada M5V 1P9
Phone: (416)977-2100
Fax: (416)977-9200
Free: (866)977-3325

Publications: Pedal Magazine (36700)

Peddler
1860 Wilma Rudolph Blvd., Ste. 101
Clarksville, TN 37040
Phone: (931)552-1160
Fax: (931)552-1777

Publications: The Peddler (29116)

The Peddler of Tennessee
PO Box 701
Cookeville, TN 38503-0701
Phone: (931)526-5910
Fax: (931)528-9735
Free: 800-262-7355

Publications: The Peddler (29145)

**The Pediatric Pharmacy Advocacy Group
Inc.**
9866 W. Victoria Dr.
Littleton, CO 80128
Phone: (720)981-7356
Fax: (720)981-7357

Publications: The Journal of Pediatric Pharmacology and Therapeutics (4549)

Peep Magazine
67 Olive St.
Brooklyn, NY 11211

Publications: Peep (20336)

Pegasus Press
PO Box 2265
Fairview, NC 28730
Phone: (828)232-5146

Publications: Exemplaria (23875)

Pelican Rapids Press
29 W Mill
Box 632
Pelican Rapids, MN 56572-0632
Phone: (218)863-1421
Fax: (218)863-1423

Publications: Pelican Rapids Press (16261)

Pella Publishing Co.
337 W 36th St.
New York, NY 10018
Phone: (212)279-9586
Fax: (212)594-3602

Publications: Charioteer (21397) • Journal of the
Hellenic Diaspora (22087)

Pembroke Magazine
UNCP, Box 1510
Pembroke, NC 28372-1510
Phone: (910)521-6358
Fax: (910)521-6446
Free: 800-521-UNCP

Publications: Pembroke Magazine (24115)

Pemiscot Publishing
111 E 5th St.
PO Box 1059
Caruthersville, MO 63830
Phone: (573)333-4336
Fax: (573)333-2307

Publications: The Democrat-Argus (16963)

Pender Chronicle
PO Box 699
Wallace, NC 28466
Phone: (910)259-2351
Fax: (910)259-6277

Publications: Pender Chronicle (24264)

The Pender Times
313 Main St.
PO Box 280
Pender, NE 68047
Phone: (402)385-3013
Fax: (402)385-3013

Publications: The Pender Times (18245)

Pendle Hill Publications
338 Plush Mill Rd.
Wallingford, PA 19086
Phone: (610)566-4507
Fax: (610)366-3679
Free: 800-742-3150

Publications: Pendle Hill Pamphlets (28102)

The Pendleton Record
809 SE Ct.
PO Box 69
Pendleton, OR 97801
Phone: (541)276-2853
Fax: (541)278-2916

Publications: The Pendleton Record (26460)

Pendleton Times
PO Box 906
Franklin, WV 26807
Phone: (304)358-2304
Fax: (304)358-2304

Publications: Pendleton Times (33320)

Penfield Communications, Inc.
50 Fitch St.
New Haven, CT 06515
Phone: (203)387-0354
Fax: (203)387-2684

Publications: The Inner City Newspaper (4991)

Peninsula Gateway
3555 Erickson St.
PO Box 407
Gig Harbor, WA 98335

Publications: Peninsula Gateway (32774)

Penn Media Group, LLC
150 James Way
Southampton, PA 18966-3857
Phone: (215)322-6920
Fax: (215)322-7087

Publications: Carrier Pigeon (28006) • Philly Health
& Fitness (28007)

Penn News
PO Box 73
Murrysville, PA 15668
Phone: (412)327-3471
Fax: (412)325-4591

Publications: Penn Franklin News (27307)

Penn-Ohio Graphics, Inc.
PO Box 245
Jefferson, OH 44047
Phone: (216)576-9115
Fax: (216)576-2735
Free: 800-860-2775

Publications: Albion News (26623)

Penn State Alumni Association
Hintz Family Alumni Center
University Park, PA 16802
Phone: (814)865-6516
Fax: (814)865-3325
Free: 800-546-5466

Publications: The Penn Stater (28081)

Penn State McKeesport
4000 University Dr.
Mc Keesport, PA 15132-7698
Phone: (412)675-9466
Fax: (412)675-9278

Publications: Latin America Indian Literatures Journal (27229)

Penn State University
Penn State Harrisburg
777 W. Harrisburg Pike
Olmsted Bldg. W-341
Middletown, PA 17057
Phone: (717)948-6070
Fax: (717)948-6724

Publications: Capital Times (27251)

Penn State University
123 S. Burrowes St.
James Bldg.
University Park, PA 16802
Phone: (814)865-4700
Fax: (814)865-3848

Publications: The Daily Collegian (28074) • The Weekly Collegian (28086)

Penn State University Press
820 N. University Dr.
University Park, PA 16802-1003
Phone: (814)865-1327
Fax: (814)863-1408

Publications: The Chaucer Review (28072) • Comparative Literature Studies (28073) • Journal of General Education (28078)

The Penn State University Press
820 N University Dr.
USB 1, Ste. C
University Park, PA 16802
Phone: (814)865-1327
Fax: 877-PSU-BOOK
Free: 800-326-9180

Publications: Journal of Policy History (17459)

Penn State University Press
USB-1, Ste. C
University Park, PA 16802
Phone: (814)863-5992
Fax: (814)863-1408

Publications: Book History (28071) • The Journal of Speculative Philosophy (28079) • Philosophy and Rhetoric (28082)

Penner Publishing
9 Debbie Ln.
East Windsor, NJ 08520
Phone: (609)443-0038
Fax: (609)443-4471

Publications: Cycling Science (18785)

Pennington County Courant
Box 435
Wall, SD 57790
Phone: (605)279-2565
Fax: (605)279-2965

Publications: Pennington County Courant (29016)

The Pennsylvania Bar Association
100 South St.
PO Box 186
Harrisburg, PA 17108-0186
Phone: (717)238-6715
Fax: (717)238-2342
Free: 800-932-0311

Publications: The PBA Quarterly (27003) • Pennsylvania Bar News (27005) • The Pennsylvania Lawyer (27009)

Pennsylvania Dental Association
Box 3341
Harrisburg, PA 17105
Phone: (717)234-5941
Fax: (717)234-2186

Publications: Pennsylvania Dental Journal (27006)

Pennsylvania Farm Bureau
PO Box 8736
Camp Hill, PA 17001-8736
Phone: (717)761-2740
Fax: (717)731-3506

Publications: Country Focus (26749)

Pennsylvania Food Merchants Association
1029 Mumma Rd.
PO Box 870
Camp Hill, PA 17001-0870
Phone: (717)731-0600
Fax: (717)703-3140
Free: 800-522-9983

Publications: The Food Industry Advisor (26751)

Pennsylvania Forestry Association
56 E. Main St.
Mechanicsburg, PA 17055-3851
Phone: (717)766-5371

Publications: Pennsylvania Forests (27240)

Pennsylvania Game Commission
2001 Elmerton Ave.
Harrisburg, PA 17110-9797
Phone: (717)787-3745
Fax: (717)772-0542
Free: 888-888-1019

Publications: Pennsylvania Game News (27007)

Pennsylvania Geographical Society
Department of Geography
University of Pittsburgh at Johnstown
Johnstown, PA 15904
Phone: (814)269-2994
Fax: (814)269-7255

Publications: The Pennsylvania Geographer (27088)

Pennsylvania Historical Association
108 Weaver Bldg.
Penn State University, PA 16802
Phone: (814)238-4053
Fax: (814)863-7840

Publications: Pennsylvania History (28019)

Pennsylvania Historical and Museum Commission
Bureau of Archives and History
Division of Publications
Commonwealth Keystone Bldg., Plaza Level
300 North St.
Harrisburg, PA 17120-0024
Phone: (717)787-2407
Fax: (717)787-8312
Free: 800-747-7790

Publications: Pennsylvania Heritage (27008)

Pennsylvania Institute of Certified Public Accountants
1650 Arch St., 17th Fl.
Philadelphia, PA 19103
Phone: (215)496-9272
Fax: (215)496-9212
Free: 888-CPA-2001

Publications: Pennsylvania CPA Journal (27621)

Pennsylvania Magazine
PO Box 755
Camp Hill, PA 17011-0755
Phone: (717)697-4660
Free: 800-537-2624

Publications: Pennsylvania Magazine (26753)

Pennsylvania Medical Society
777 E Park Dr.
PO Box 8820
Harrisburg, PA 17105-8820
Phone: (717)558-7750
Fax: (717)558-7840
Free: 800-228-7823

Publications: Pennsylvania Medicine (27010)

Pennsylvania Motor Truck Association
910 Linda Ln.
Camp Hill, PA 17011-6401
Phone: (717)761-7122
Fax: (717)761-8434
Free: 800-382-1373

Publications: Penntrux (26754)

Pennsylvania Newspaper Association (PNA)
3899 N. Front St.
Harrisburg, PA 17110-1221
Phone: (717)703-3000
Fax: (717)703-3001

Publications: Press (27012)

Pennsylvania Osteopathic Medical Association
1330 Eisenhower Blvd.
Harrisburg, PA 17111-2395
Phone: (717)939-9318
Fax: (717)939-7255

Publications: Journal of the Pennsylvania Osteopathic Medical Association (26996)

Pennsylvania Pharmacists Association
508 N. 3rd St.
Harrisburg, PA 17101-1199
Phone: (717)234-6151
Fax: (717)236-1618

Publications: Pennsylvania Pharmacist (27011)

The Pennsylvania Police Criminal Law Bulletin
712 Ivy St.
Pittsburgh, PA 15232-2408
Phone: (412)687-7063
Fax: (412)687-4527

Publications: The Pennsylvania Police Criminal Law Bulletin (27826)

Pennsylvania Rural Electric Association
PO Box 1266
212 Locust St.
Harrisburg, PA 17108
Phone: (717)233-5704
Fax: (717)234-1309

Publications: Penn Lines (27004)

Pennsylvania School Boards Association
774 Limekiln Rd.
New Cumberland, PA 17070-2398
Phone: (717)774-2331
Fax: (717)774-0718

Publications: PSBA Bulletin (27319)

Pennsylvania State Association of Boroughs
2941 N. Front St.
Harrisburg, PA 17110
Phone: (717)236-9526
Fax: (717)236-8164

Publications: The Borough News Magazine (26983)

Pennsylvania State Association of Township Supervisors
4885, Woodland Dr.
Enola, PA 17025
Phone: (717)763-0930
Fax: (717)763-9732

Publications: Pennsylvania Township News (26886)

Pennsylvania State Education Association
400 N. 3rd St.
PO Box 1724
Harrisburg, PA 17105
Phone: (717)255-7134
Fax: (717)255-7124

Publications: The VOICE for Education (27014)

Pennsylvania State University
116 Deike Bldg.
University Park, PA 16802
Phone: (814)863-6546
Fax: (814)863-7708

Publications: Earth and Mineral Sciences (28075)

Pennsylvania State University
212 Earth & Engineering Sciences Bldg.
University Park, PA 16802
Phone: (814)863-4210
Fax: (814)865-3052

Publications: Journal of Wave-Material Interaction (28080)

Pennsylvania State University Press
820 N. University Dr.
University Park, PA 16802
Phone: (814)863-5992
Fax: (814)863-1408
Free: 800-326-9180

Publications: Resources for Literary Study (28084) • Shaw Annual (2767)

PennWell Corporation
100 S Atkinson Rd., Ste. 382
Grayslake, IL 60030-7817
Phone: (847)876-5602
Fax: (847)634-4240

Publications: Connector Specifier (8953) • SMT (8959)

PennWell Corp.
98 Spit Brook Rd.
Nashua, NH 03062-5737
Phone: (603)891-0123

Publications: Advanced Packaging (18581) • Cabling Installation & Maintenance (18583) • CleanRooms (18584) • CleanRooms International (18585) • Computer Design (18587) • Computer Graphics World (18588) • Electronic Publishing (18589) • Industrial Laser Solutions (18591) • InfoStor (18592) • Integrated Communications Design (18593) • Laser Focus World (18594) • Lightwave (18595) • Military & Aerospace Electronics (18597) • Portable Design (18599) • Solid State Technology (18600) • Vision Systems Design (18602) • Wireless Integration (18605)

PennWell Corporation
21-00 Route 208 S.
Fair Lawn, NJ 07410-2602
Phone: (973)251-5040
Fax: (973)251-5065
Free: 800-962-6484

Publications: Fire Engineering (18807)

PennWell Corp.
1421 S. Sheridan Rd.
Tulsa, OK 74112
Phone: (918)835-3161
Fax: (918)832-9201
Free: 800-331-4463

Publications: Control Solutions (26111) • Dental Economics (26112) • Dental Equipment & Materials (26113) • Electric Light & Power (26115) • Microlithography World (18596) • Oil, Gas & Petrochem Equipment (26121) • Potencia (26126) • Power Engineering (26127) • Power Engineering International (26128) • Prevencion de la Contaminacion (26129) • Proofs (26130) • Utility Automation (26141) • Utility Automation International (26142) • Water & Wastewater International (18603) • WaterWorld (26143) • Worldwide Waste Management (26144)

PennWell Publishing Co.
PO Box 1260
Tulsa, OK 74101-1260
Phone: (918)831-9742
Fax: (918)831-9804
Free: 800-633-1681

Publications: RDH (26131)

PennWell Publishing Co.
1700 West Loop S, Ste. 1000
Houston, TX 77027
Phone: (713)621-9720
Fax: (713)963-6296
Free: 800-736-6935

Publications: Offshore (30513) • Oil & Gas Journal (30516) • Oil & Gas Journal Latinoamerica (30517)

Penny Power Ltd.
202-212 S 3rd St.
PO Box 250
Coopersburg, PA 18036
Phone: (610)282-4808
Fax: (610)282-1932
Free: 800-573-6697

Publications: Penny Power (26807)

Penny Press, Inc.
6 Prowitt St.
Norwalk, CT 06855
Phone: (203)866-6688
Fax: (203)854-5962

Publications: Easy & Fun Word Seek Puzzles (5058) • Family Word Seek Puzzles (5059) • Favorite Variety Puzzles and Games (5060) • Favorite Word Seek Puzzles (5061) • Good Time Fill-in Puzzles (5062) • Good Time Word Seek Puzzles (5063)

Penny-Saver, Inc.
PO Box 37
Mansfield, PA 16933
Fax: (717)662-7676

Publications: Penny-Saver (27219)

Penny Saver Publications, Inc.
6901 W. 159th St.
Tinley Park, IL 60477
Phone: (708)633-6890
Fax: (708)633-4919

Publications: The Penny Saver (9688)

Pennypower Shopping News, Inc.
PO Box 4748
Springfield, MO 65808-4748
Phone: (417)887-9000
Fax: (417)887-9006

Publications: Pennypower Shopping News (17609)

The Pennysaver
2830 Orbiter St.
Brea, CA 92821-6224
Phone: (714)577-4296
Fax: (714)577-4286

Publications: The Original Pennysaver (1599) • PennySaver (1601)

Pennysaver
1400-G NW 65th Ave.
PO Box 16928
Plantation, FL 33318
Phone: (954)792-1151
Fax: (954)581-3463

Publications: Pennysaver (6588)

Pennysaver
507 E. Anson
Box 246
Marshalltown, IA 50158
Phone: (641)752-6630
Fax: (641)752-7073

Publications: Pennysaver (11065)

Pennysaver
1342 Charwood Rd.
Hanover, MD 21076
Phone: (410)684-2600
Fax: (410)684-6188
Free: 800-736-6972

Publications: Pennysaver (13580)

Pennysaver
56 Bramsteele Rd., Unit 1
Brampton, ON, Canada L6W 3M7
Phone: (905)454-0854
Fax: (905)450-5792

Publications: Brampton Pennysaver (35699) • Malton Pennysaver (36007) • Mississauga Pennysaver (35701) • Rexdale Pennysaver (35702)

Pennysaver
61 Dalkeith Dr., Unit 6
Brantford, ON, Canada N3P 1M1
Phone: (519)756-0076
Fax: (519)756-9034

Publications: Brantford Pennysaver (35704)

Pennysaver Group, Inc.
101 Executive Blvd.
Elmsford, NY 10523
Phone: (914)592-5222
Fax: (914)592-4570
Free: 800-800-5220

Publications: The Pennysaver (20583)

The Pennysaver, Inc.
607 Tenney Mtn. Hwy.
Village Sq., Ste. 137
Plymouth, NH 03264
Phone: (603)536-3160
Fax: (603)536-8150

Publications: The Penny Saver (18633)

Pennysaver/News
217 Maple St.
PO Box 130
Corinth, NY 12822
Phone: (518)654-9331
Fax: (518)654-2935

Publications: Pennysaver/News (20502)

PennySaver/San Diego South
2830 Orbiter St.
Brea, CA 92821
Phone: (714)996-8900
Fax: (714)993-4711
Free: 888-736-6972

Publications: PennySaver/San Diego South (1602)

Penobscot Bay Press
PO Box 205
Castine, ME 04421
Phone: (207)326-9300
Fax: (207)326-4383

Publications: Castine Patriot (12949)

Penobscot Bay Press, Inc.
PO Box 646
Blue Hill, ME 04614
Phone: (207)374-2341
Fax: (207)374-2343

Publications: The Weekly Packet (12924)

Penobscot Bay Press, Inc.
PO Box 36
Stonington, ME 04681
Phone: (207)367-2200
Fax: (207)367-6397

Publications: Island Ad-Vantages (13064)

Penobscot Times, Inc.
Box 568
Old Town, ME 04468
Phone: (207)827-4451
Fax: (207)827-2280

Publications: Penobscot Times, Inc. (12997)

Pensacola Historical Society
117 E Government St.
Pensacola, FL 32501
Phone: (850)434-5455
Fax: (850)433-1559

Publications: Pensacola History Illustrated (6567)

Pensacola Junior College
1000 College Blvd.
Pensacola, FL 32504
Phone: (850)484-1641

Publications: Half Tones to Jubilee (6566)

Pensacola News Journal
1 News-Journal Plaza
Pensacola, FL 32501-5670
Phone: (904)435-8500
Fax: (904)435-8633

Publications: Pensacola News Journal (6568)

Pensacola Voice
213 E Yonge St.
Pensacola, FL 32503-3766
Phone: (850)434-6963
Fax: (850)469-8745

Publications: Pensacola Voice (6569)

Pentecostal Assemblies of Canada
2450 Milltower Ct.
Mississauga, ON, Canada L5N 5Z6
Phone: (905)542-7400
Fax: (905)542-7313

Publications: Pentecostal Testimony (36085)

Pentecostal Church of God
4901 Pennsylvania
PO Box 850
Joplin, MO 64802-0850
Phone: (417)624-7050
Fax: (417)624-7102
Free: 800-444-4674

Publications: The Pentecostal Messenger (17142)

Penthouse International Ltd.
11 Penn Plaza, 12th Fl.
New York, NY 10001-2006
Phone: (212)702-6000
Fax: (212)702-6262

Publications: Penthouse (22538)

Penticton Herald
186 Nanaimo Ave. W.
Penticton, BC, Canada V2A 1N4
Phone: (604)492-4002
Fax: (604)492-2403

Publications: Penticton Herald (35044)

Penticton Western News
2250 Camrose St.
Penticton, BC, Canada V2A 8R1
Phone: (250)492-0444
Fax: (250)492-9843

Publications: Penticton Western News (35045)

Penton Media, Inc.
PO Box 385
Golden, CO 80402-0385
Phone: (303)235-9510
Fax: (303)235-9502

Publications: Boardwatch Magazine (4463) • CLEC Magazine (4464)

Penton Media, Inc.
16 Thorndal Circle
Darien, CT 06820-5421
Phone: (203)662-5889
Fax: (203)559-2840

Publications: Internet Shopper (4773)

Penton Media Inc.
2700 S. River Rd., Ste. 109
Des Plaines, IL 60018
Phone: (847)299-3101
Fax: (847)299-3018

Publications: Contractor Magazine (8755)

Penton Media, Inc.
1300 E. 9th St.
Cleveland, OH 44114-1503
Phone: (216)696-7000
Fax: (216)931-9799

Publications: Air Transport World (5318) • Airport Equipment & Technology (5319) • American Machinist (24855) • Baking Management (24859) • Contracting Business (24875) • Convenience Store Decisions (24876) • DesignMart (24881) • EE Product News (24888) • Energy & Environmental Management (24892) • Expansion Management (11761) • FLOW Manufacturing Report (24895) • Food Management (24896) • Forging (24897) • Foundry Management & Technology (24899) • Gases & Welding Distributor (24901) • Government PROcurement Magazine (24904) • Government Product News (24905) • Heating/Piping/Air Conditioning Engineering (HPAC) (24906) • Hydraulics & Pneumatics (24910) • IndustryWeek (24911) • LH (Lodging Hospitality) (24920) • Machine Design (24923) • Material Handling Management (24925) • Mechanical Solutions (24926) • Motion Systems Consultant (24930) • The Motion Systems Distributor (24931) • New Equipment Digest (24932) • Nutrition Science News (4182) • Occupational Hazards (24936) • PT Design (24947) • Restaurant Hospitality (24950) • Supply Chain Technology News (24955) • 33 Metal Producing (24956) • Transportation & Distribution (24958) • Welding Design & Fabrication (24961)

Penton Technology and Lifestyle Media
45 Eisenhower Dr., 5th Fl.
Paramus, NJ 07652
Phone: (201)845-6511
Fax: (201)845-2493
Free: 800-829-9028

Publications: Electronic Design (19402) • Microwaves & RF Magazine (19405) • Wireless Systems Design (19408)

Penumbra Press
PO Box 736
Pine Island, MN 55963
Phone: (507)367-4430

Publications: Kumquat Meringue (16271)

People of God
4000 St. Joseph Pl. NW
Albuquerque, NM 87120
Phone: (505)831-8188
Fax: (505)831-8225

Publications: People of God (19784)

People Sentinel
PO Box 1255
Barnwell, SC 29812
Phone: (803)259-3501
Fax: (803)259-2703

Publications: People-Sentinel (28482)

People's Publishing Co.
PO Box 219
San Anselmo, CA 94979
Phone: (415)454-3936
Fax: (415)454-4262

Publications: Western & Eastern Treasures (3085)

People's Translation Service
PO Box 14431
Berkeley, CA 94701-5431
Phone: (510)549-3505

Publications: Connexions (1509)

People's Tribune
League of Revolutionaries for a New America
PO Box 477113
Chicago, IL 60647
Phone: (773)486-0028
Fax: (773)486-1728
Free: 800-691-6888

Publications: People's Tribune (8528)

The Peoria Journal Star, Inc.
1 News Plaza
Peoria, IL 61643
Phone: (309)686-3000
Fax: (309)686-3296
Free: 800-225-5757

Publications: Journal Star (9419)

Pep Publishing
PO Box 4358
Boulder, CO 80306
Phone: (303)543-7540
Free: 800-424-9561

Publications: Loving More (4177)

Pepperdine University
24255 Pacific Coast Hwy.
Malibu, CA 90263-4138
Phone: (310)506-4138
Fax: (310)506-4998

Publications: The Graphic Weekly (2489)

Pequot Publishing, Inc.
PO Box 447
Southport, CT 06490-0447
Phone: (203)259-1812

Publications: Gas Turbine World (5136) • Private Power Executive (5137)

Performance Printing Ltd.
65 Lorne St.
PO Box 158
Smiths Falls, ON, Canada K7A 4T1
Phone: (613)283-3182
Fax: (613)283-7480
Free: 800-267-7936

Publications: The Record News (36395)

Performance Resource Press Inc.
1270 Rankin Dr., Ste. F
Troy, MI 48083-2843
Phone: (248)588-7733
Fax: (248)588-6633
Free: 800-453-7733

Publications: EAP Digest (15621) • Student Assistance Journal (15641)

The Performing Artist
5005 City St., No. 1326
Orlando, FL 32839
Phone: (407)852-7078

Publications: Hinge Music Magazine (6497)

Performing Arts in Canada
104 Glenrose Ave.
Toronto, ON, Canada M4T 1K8
Phone: (416)484-4534
Fax: (416)484-6214

Publications: Performing Arts in Canada (36701) • Performing Arts and Entertainment in Canada (36702)

Performing Arts Network
10350 Santa Monica Blvd., No. 350
Los Angeles, CA 90025
Phone: (310)551-1115
Fax: (310)551-2079

Publications: Performing Arts (2360)

Perham Enterprise Bulletin
222 2nd Ave SE
PO Box 288
Perham, MN 56573
Phone: (218)346-5900
Fax: (218)346-5901

Publications: Perham Enterprise Bulletin (16265)

Periodico El Oriental, Inc.
Ave. Cruz Ortiz Stella 36
Humacao, PR 00791
Phone: (787)852-1496
Fax: (787)852-3405

Publications: Periodico El Oriental (28249) • Periodico El Regional de Guayama (28250) • Periodico La Opinion Del Sur (28251)

Perkasie News-Herald
PO Box 127
Perkasie, PA 18944-0127

Publications: Perkasie News-Herald (27352)

Perkins Communications, LLC
1951 Rohwling Rd., Ste. B
Rolling Meadows, IL 60008-1300
Phone: (847)870-1576
Fax: (847)870-1594
Free: 800-607-9276

Publications: Greenhouse Business (9547)

Perks Publications Inc.
92 Church St. S., Unit 107
Ajax, ON, Canada L1S 6B4
Phone: (905)427-0080
Fax: (905)427-0087
Free: 877-880-4877

Publications: The LBMAO Reporter (36073)

The Perris Progress
240 W 4th St.
PO Box 128
Perris, CA 92572-0128
Phone: (909)657-2181
Fax: (909)657-2182

Publications: The Perris Progress (2835)

Perry Co.
59 S. Division
59 S. Division
Plainfield, IL 60544
Phone: (815)436-2431
Fax: (815)436-2592
Free: 800-997-9922

Publications: The Enterprise (9458)

Perry Herald
12 Borden Ave.
PO Box 219
Perry, NY 14530
Phone: (585)237-2212
Fax: (585)237-2211

Publications: Perry Herald (23094)

Perry Journal Co.
714 Delaware St.
PO Box 311
Perry, OK 73077-0311
Phone: (405)336-2222
Fax: (405)336-3222

Publications: The Perry Daily Journal (26032)

Perry Newspapers, Inc.
PO Box 888
Perry, FL 32347
Phone: (850)584-5513
Fax: (850)838-1566

Publications: Perry News-Herald (6581) • Perry Taco Times (6582)

Perry & Perry & Associates
Tennessee Tribune Bldg.
1501 Jefferson St.
Nashville, TN 37208
Phone: (615)321-3268
Fax: (615)321-0409

Publications: The Tennessee Tribune (29495)

Perry Publishing Co.
217 Indiana
PO Box 279
Chinook, MT 59523
Phone: (406)357-2680
Fax: (406)357-3736

Publications: The Chinook Opinion (17770)

Perry Shopper
12 Borden Ave.
PO Box 219
Perry, NY 14530-0219
Phone: (585)237-2212
Fax: (585)237-2211

Publications: Perry Shopper (23095)

The Perryton Herald
401 S Amherst
Box 989
Perryton, TX 79070
Phone: (806)435-3631
Fax: (806)435-2420

Publications: The Perryton Herald (30927)

Perryville Newspapers, Inc.
10 W. Ste. Maries St.
PO Drawer 367
Perryville, MO 63775
Phone: (573)547-4567
Fax: (573)547-1643

Publications: The Perry County Republic-Monitor (17339) • The Republic-Monitor Shopping Guide (17341)

Perryville Sun Times
PO Box 428
Ste. Genevieve, MO 63670
Phone: (573)883-2980
Fax: (573)883-2866

Publications: Perryville Sun Times (17340)

Personal Selling Power
PO Box 5467
Fredericksburg, VA 22403
Phone: (540)752-7000
Fax: (540)752-7001
Free: 800-752-7355

Publications: Selling Power (32087)

Personnel Management Abstracts
704 Island Lake Rd.
Chelsea, MI 48118
Phone: (313)475-1979

Publications: Personnel Management Abstracts (14877)

Personnel Psychology, Inc.
520 Ordway Ave.
Bowling Green, OH 43402-2756
Phone: (419)352-1562
Fax: (419)352-2645

Publications: Personnel Psychology (24698)

Perspectiva Mundial
408 Printing & Publishing Corp.
152 W. 36th St., No.401
New York, NY 10018
Phone: (212)594-1014
Fax: (212)594-1018

Publications: Perspectiva Mundial (22544)

Perspective
PO Box 2439
Cambridge, MA 02238
Phone: (617)495-4290
Fax: (617)495-4688

Publications: Perspective (14089)

The Perth Courier
PO Box 156
39 Gore St. E.
Perth, ON, Canada K7H 3E3
Phone: (613)367-1100
Fax: (613)267-3986

Publications: The Perth Courier (36312)

The Peshtigo Times
PO Box 187
Peshtigo, WI 54157
Phone: (715)582-4541
Fax: (715)582-4662

Publications: The Peshtigo Times (34236)

PESI HealthCare, LLC
PO Box 1000, 200 Spring St.
PO Box 1000
Eau Claire, WI 54703
Phone: (715)833-5431
Fax: (715)833-5493
Free: 800-843-7763

Publications: Journal of Nursing Law (33671)

The Pet Companion
3871 Piedmont Ave., PMB. 305
Oakland, CA 94611-5351
Phone: (510)533-7777
Fax: (510)533-7571

Publications: The Pet Companion (2694)

Petal Pusher Press
PO Box 280
Silvana, WA 98287
Phone: (360)652-4367
Fax: (360)719-8727

Publications: The Saponifier (33082)

Peter Katz Productions, Inc.
PO Box 831
White Plains, NY 10602-0831
Phone: (914)949-7443

Publications: Aviation Monthly (23569) • NTSB Reporter (23572)

Peter Li, Inc.
2621 Dryden Rd.
Dayton, OH 45439
Phone: (937)298-8965
Fax: (937)293-1310
Free: 800-523-4625

Publications: Catechist (25109) • College Planning and Management (25111) • Good News for Children (25118) • Promise (25124) • School Planning and Management (25125) • Seeds (25126) • Today's Catholic Teacher (25127) • Venture (25129) • Visions (25130)

Peter Piper Publishing, Inc.
3968 Long Gun Place
Victoria, BC, Canada V8N 3A9
Phone: (250)477-5543
Fax: (250)477-5390

Publications: YES Mag (35231)

The Peterborough Transcript
PO Box 419
Peterborough, NH 03458-0419
Phone: (603)924-3333
Fax: (603)924-7944
Free: 800-559-3370

Publications: The Peterborough Transcript (18627)

Peters Printing Ltd.
1462 Conrad Ave.
PO Box 628
Gull Lake, SK, Canada S0N 1A0
Phone: (306)672-3373
Fax: (306)672-3573

Publications: Gull Lake Advance (37473)

Petersburg Observer
235 E. Sangamon Ave.
Petersburg, IL 62675-1245
Phone: (217)632-2236
Fax: (217)632-2237

Publications: Ashland Sentinel (8028) • The Petersburg Observer (9454)

Petersburg Post
1412 Ave. G
PO Box 248
Petersburg, TX 79250
Phone: (806)667-3841
Fax: (806)667-3347

Publications: Petersburg Post (30930)

Petersburg Press
PO Box 177
Petersburg, NE 68652
Phone: (402)386-5384
Fax: (402)386-5384

Publications: Petersburg Press (18246)

Peterson Patriot
PO Box 126
Peterson, IA 51047
Phone: (712)295-7711
Fax: (712)295-7711

Publications: Peterson Patriot (11159)

Peterson Publishing, Inc.
PO Box 38
Munising, MI 49862
Phone: (906)387-3282
Fax: (906)387-4054

Publications: The Munising News (15386)

Petoskey News-Review, Super Shopper, and Graphic
319 State St.
PO Box 528
Petoskey, MI 49770-0528
Phone: (231)347-2544
Fax: (231)347-6833

Publications: The Graphic (15435) • Petoskey News-Review (15436) • Super Shopper (15437)

Petroleum Abstracts
600 S. College Ave.
Harwell 101
Tulsa, OK 74104-3189
Phone: (918)631-2297
Fax: (918)599-9361
Free: 800-247-8678

Publications: Petroleum Abstracts (26125)

Petroleum Newspapers of Alaska LLC
PO Box 231651
Anchorage, AK 99523-1651
Phone: (907)245-5553
Fax: (907)522-9583

Publications: Business News Alaska (524) • Petroleum News Alaska (530)

Petrolia Topic
4182 Petrolia Line
PO Box 40
Petrolia, ON, Canada M0N 1R0
Phone: (519)882-1770
Fax: (519)882-3212

Publications: Petrolia Topic (36327)

Peuple Cote Sud
80 Blvd. Tacheast
C.P. 430
Montmagny, QC, Canada G5V 3S7
Phone: (418)248-0415
Fax: (418)248-2377

Publications: Le Peuple de la Cote du Sud (37077)

Pfanstiel Publishers and Printers, Inc.
PO Box 4278
Long Beach, CA 90804
Phone: (562)438-5641
Fax: (562)438-7086

Publications: Reporter (2174)

Pfeiffer College
Hwy. 52
Misenheimer, NC 28109
Phone: (704)833-2060
Free: 800-833-2060

Publications: Falcon's Eye (24064)

Pfingsten Publishing Company, L.L.C.
1801 Park 270 Dr., Ste. 550
St. Louis, MO 63146-4016
Phone: (314)421-5445
Fax: (314)421-1070

Publications: DECOR (17432)

Pfingsten Publishing, LLC
3990 Old Town Ave., Ste. A203
San Diego, CA 92110
Phone: (619)223-9989
Fax: (619)223-9943
Free: 800-995-2090

Publications: Mortgage Originator Magazine (3238)

PFW Publications
Box 430
Kaslo, BC, Canada V0G 1M0
Phone: (250)353-2602
Fax: (250)353-7444
Free: 800-663-4619

Publications: Cast Logan/Slocan Valley Pennywise (34984) • Kaslo Pennywise (34985) • Nelson Pennywise (34986) • Trail/Beaver Valley/Salmo Pennywise (34987)

PGN
505 S. 4th St.
Philadelphia, PA 19147-1506
Phone: (215)625-8501
Fax: (215)925-6437

Publications: Philadelphia Gay News (27626)

Numbers cited after listings are entry numbers rather than page numbers.

Phan Media, Inc.
Box 216
Ocean Grove, NJ 07756
Phone: (732)988-6264
Fax: (732)988-9180

Publications: The Phantom of the Movies' Videoscope (19390)

Phare/Beacon
B.F.C. Bagotville
CP 369
Alouette, QC, Canada G0V 1A0
Phone: (418)677-4000
Fax: (418)677-4465

Publications: Phare/Beacon (36931)

Pharmaceutical Media Inc.
30 E 33rd St., 4th Fl.
New York, NY 10016
Phone: (212)684-5540
Fax: (212)685-6126

Publications: AACN's Clinical Issues in Critical Care Nursing (21129)

Pharmacists Society of the State of New York
210 Washington Ave., Ext. Ste. 101
Albany, NY 12203
Phone: (518)869-6595
Fax: (518)464-0618
Free: 800-632-8822

Publications: New York State Pharmacist (19999)

Pharmacotherapy Publications, Inc.
750 Washington Ave.
NEMC Box 806
Boston, MA 02111
Phone: (617)636-5390
Fax: (617)636-5318

Publications: Pharmacotherapy (13948)

Pharmacy Society of Wisconsin
701 Hartland Trail
Madison, WI 53717
Phone: (608)827-9200
Fax: (608)827-9292

Publications: Journal of the Pharmacy Society of Wisconsin (33954)

Pheasant Meadow Farm
1338 Hughes Shop Rd.
Westminster, MD 21158
Phone: (410)875-0118
Fax: (410)857-9145

Publications: Miniature Donkey Talk (13777)

Pheasants Forever, Inc.
1783 Buerkle Cir.
St. Paul, MN 55110
Phone: (651)773-2000
Fax: (651)773-5500
Free: 877-773-2070

Publications: Pheasants Forever (16404)

Phelps County Genealogical Society
Box 571
Rolla, MO 65402-0571

Publications: Phelps County Genealogical Society Quarterly (17379)

phenomeNEWS
18444 W. 10 Mile, Ste. 105
Southfield, MI 48075
Phone: (248)569-3888
Fax: (248)569-4512

Publications: phenomeNEWS (15547)

Phi Beta Kappa Society
1785 Massachusetts Ave., NW, 4th Fl.
Washington, DC 20036
Phone: (202)265-3808
Fax: (202)265-0083

Publications: The American Scholar (5343)

Phi Delta Kappa International
408 N Union
PO Box 789
Bloomington, IN 47402-0789
Phone: (812)339-1156
Fax: (812)339-0018
Free: 800-766-1156

Publications: Phi Delta Kappan (9848)

Phi Delta Theta Fraternity
2 S Campus
Oxford, OH 45056
Phone: (513)523-6345

Publications: Scroll of Phi Delta Theta (25460)

Phi Epsilon Kappa Fraternity
901 W. New York St.
Indianapolis, IN 46202
Phone: (317)637-8431

Publications: Physical Educator (10160)

Phi Gamma Delta Fraternity
PO Box 4599
Lexington, KY 40544-4599
Phone: (859)255-1848
Fax: (859)253-0779

Publications: The Phi Gamma Delta (12175)

Phi Rho Sigma Medical Society
PO Box 90264
Indianapolis, IN 46290
Phone: (317)255-4379
Fax: (317)253-5067

Publications: Phi Rho Sigma Journal (15356)

Philadelphia Business Journal
400 Market St., Ste. 300
Philadelphia, PA 19106
Phone: (215)238-1450
Fax: (215)238-1466

Publications: Philadelphia Business Journal (27624)

Philadelphia College of Osteopathic Medicine
Marketing and Communications
4170 City Ave.
Philadelphia, PA 19131
Phone: (215)871-6100
Fax: (215)871-6307

Publications: Digest (27451)

Philadelphia County Medical Society
2100 Spring Garden St.
Philadelphia, PA 19130
Phone: (215)563-5343
Fax: (215)563-3627

Publications: Philadelphia Medicine (27628)

Philadelphia Museum of Art
Publications Dept.
2525 Pennsylvania Ave.
Philadelphia, PA 19130
Phone: (215)763-8100
Fax: (215)235-8715

Publications: Philadelphia Museum of Art Bulletin (27629)

Philadelphia New Observer
1930 Chestnut St., Ste. 900
PO Box 30092
Philadelphia, PA 19103
Phone: (215)545-7500
Fax: (215)665-8914

Publications: Philadelphia New Observer (27630)

Philadelphia Newspapers, Inc.
400 N. Broad St.
Philadelphia, PA 19130
Phone: (215)854-2000
Fax: (215)854-4794

Publications: Philadelphia Inquirer (27627)

The Philadelphia Spotlite
3401 N I St., 5th Fl.
Philadelphia, PA 19134
Phone: (215)427-8484
Fax: (215)425-1155

Publications: The Philadelphia Spotlite (27631) • Playbill (27640)

The Philadelphia Sunday Sun
6661 Germantown Ave., No. 63
Philadelphia, PA 19119-2251
Phone: (215)848-7864
Fax: (215)848-7893

Publications: The Philadelphia Sunday Sun (27632)

Philadelphia Tribune Co.
522 S. 16th St.
Philadelphia, PA 19146
Phone: (215)893-4097
Fax: (215)735-3612

Publications: The Philadelphia Tribune Metro Edition (27634)

Philaprint, Ltd.
10 Summerhill Avenue
Toronto, ON, Canada M4T 1A8
Phone: (416)921-2073
Fax: (416)921-1282

Publications: Canadian Philatelist (36524)

Philatelic Communications Corp.
175 R Proctor Hill Rd.
Hollis, NH 03049
Phone: (603)465-9377
Fax: (603)465-9377
Free: 800-635-3351

Publications: Mekeel's Weekly Stamp News (18527)

The Philipsburg Mail
Box 160
Philipsburg, MT 59858
Phone: (406)859-3223
Fax: (406)859-3690

Publications: The Philipsburg Mail (17890)

Phillip Sanchez, Publisher
38-42 9th St., 3rd Fl.
Long Island City, NY 11101
Phone: (718)786-4343
Fax: (718)609-2676
Free: 800-432-4451

Publications: Noticias del Mundo (20965)

Phillips County Historical Review
623 Pecan St.
Helena, AR 72342
Phone: (870)338-3537

Publications: Phillips County Historical Review (1175)

Phillips County News
Box 850
Malta, MT 59538-0850
Phone: (406)654-2020
Fax: (406)654-1410

Publications: The Phillips County News (17858)

Phillips County Review
Box 446
Phillipsburg, KS 67661
Phone: (785)543-5242
Fax: (785)543-5243

Publications: Phillips County Review (11748)

Phillips Publishers Ltd.
Box 1300
Melfort, SK, Canada S0E 1A0
Phone: (306)752-5737
Fax: (306)752-5358
Free: 800-752-9559

Publications: Kinistino—Birch Hills Post—Gazette (37497) • The Melfort Journal (37498)

Phillips Publishing, Inc.
141 S Broadway
PO Box 112
Spring Valley, MN 55975
Phone: (507)346-7365
Fax: (507)346-7366

Publications: News-Record (16017) • River Valley Shopper (16457) • Spring Valley Tribune (16458)

The Philosopher's Information Center
1616 E Wooster St.
Bowling Green, OH 43402
Phone: (419)353-8830
Fax: (419)353-8920
Free: 800-476-8757

Publications: The Philosopher's Index (24699)

Philosophical Research Society Inc.
3910 Los Feliz Blvd.
Los Angeles, CA 90027
Phone: (323)663-2167
Fax: (323)663-9443
Free: 800-548-4062

Publications: Ancient Wisdom for Modern Living (2210)

Philosophy Documentation Center
PO Box 7147
Charlottesville, VA 22906-7147
Phone: (434)220-3300
Fax: (434)220-3301
Free: 800-444-2419

Publications: American Catholic Philosophical Quarterly (30603) • Augustinian Studies (31917) • Business Ethics Quarterly (5391) • Epoche (28096) • Hume Studies (3672) • HYLE (31929) • Idealistic Studies (14683) • Inquiry (24692) • International Journal of Applied Philosophy (6118) • International Philosophical Quarterly (31931) • Journal of Philosophical Research (30045) • New Vico Studies (7032) • The Owl of Minerva (8523) • Philosophy Now (31937) • Questions (31939) • Teaching Philosophy (25461)

Philosophy Education Society
The Catholic University of America
Washington, DC 20064
Phone: (202)635-8778
Fax: (202)319-4484
Free: 800-255-5924

Publications: Review of Metaphysics (5766)

Phoenix
Trinity College
Toronto, ON, Canada M5S 1H8
Phone: (416)978-3037
Fax: (416)978-4949

Publications: Phoenix (36706)

The Phoenix
Swarthmore College
500 College Ave.
Swarthmore, PA 19081-1390

Publications: The Phoenix (28043)

Phoenix Home & Garden
8501 E Princess Dr., Ste. 190
Scottsdale, AZ 85255
Phone: (480)664-3960
Fax: (480)664-3963
Free: 800-228-6540

Publications: Phoenix Home & Garden (873)

Phoenix Jewish News, Inc.
1625 E Northern Ave. Ste. 106
Phoenix, AZ 85020
Phone: (602)870-9470
Fax: (602)870-0426

Publications: Jewish News of Greater Phoenix (805)

The Phoenix Media/Communications Group
108 Grove St., Ste. 18
Worcester, MA 01605-2651
Phone: (508)767-9777
Fax: (508)795-0439

Publications: The Worcester Phoenix (13972)

Phoenix Media Group
126 Brookline Ave.
Boston, MA 02215
Phone: (617)536-5390
Fax: (617)536-1463

Publications: The Boston Phoenix (13861)

Phoenix Media Group, Inc.
1637 Lesperance Rd.
Tecumseh, ON, Canada N8N 1Y1
Phone: (519)735-2080
Fax: (519)735-2082

Publications: Lakeshore News (35675)

Phoenix Media Network Inc.
1580 NW Boca Raton Blvd.
Boca Raton, FL 33432
Phone: (561)447-0810
Fax: (561)368-9125

Publications: Produce Business (5939)

Phoenix Newspapers, Inc.
200 E. Van Buren St.
Phoenix, AZ 85004-2238
Phone: (602)444-8000
Fax: (602)444-7363

Publications: Arizona Business Gazette (775) • The Arizona Republic (782)

Phoenix Technologies Ltd.
411 E. Plumeria Dr.
San Jose, CA 95134
Phone: (408)570-1000
Fax: (408)570-1001
Free: 800-677-7305

Publications: The Phoenix (3531)

Phoenix Ventures
34 E. State St.
Salamanca, NY 14779-1232
Phone: (716)945-6489
Fax: (716)945-6494
Free: 888-271-0777

Publications: Electronic Retailer (23291) • Security Professional (23294)

The Phoenix, WMC
2 College Hill
Westminster, MD 21157-4390
Phone: (410)751-8600

Publications: The Phoenix (13778)

Photo Imaging Entrepreneur
2627 Grimsley St.
Greensboro, NC 27403
Phone: (336)854-8088
Fax: (336)854-8566
Free: 800-854-4119

Publications: Photo Imaging Entrepreneur (23934)

Photo Journal Press
525 Warren
Sandusky, OH 44870
Phone: (419)836-2221
Fax: (419)836-1319

Publications: The Press, Suburban Edition (25386)

Photo Marketing Association International
3000 Picture Pl.
Jackson, MI 49201
Phone: (517)788-8100
Fax: (517)788-8371

Publications: Photo Marketing (15223)

Photo Printing
210 S 1st St.
Carlisle, IA 50047
Phone: (515)989-3251
Fax: (515)989-0743

Publications: Marion County News (10650)

Photo Puzzlers
201 No. 8 Rd.
New Wilmington, PA 16142
Phone: (412)946-8935

Publications: 11 (27322)

The Photo Review
140 E. Richardson Ave., Ste. 301
Langhorne, PA 19047
Phone: (215)891-0214
Fax: (215)891-9358

Publications: The Photo Review (27158)

Photo Star
307 State St.
Box B
Willshire, OH 45898
Phone: (419)495-2696
Fax: (419)495-2143

Publications: Photo Star (25666)

Photographic Society of America
3000 United Founders Blvd., No. 103
Oklahoma City, OK 73112-3940
Phone: (405)843-1437
Fax: (405)843-1438

Publications: PSA Journal (25995)

Photography in New York International
64 W 89 St.
New York, NY 10024
Phone: (212)787-0401
Fax: (212)799-3054

Publications: Photography in New York (22551)

Phreno Cosmian
1200 W University Ave.
Dakota Wesleyan University Box 318
Mitchell, SD 57301
Phone: (605)995-2814
Fax: (605)995-2814

Publications: Phreno Cosmian (28901)

Phun Inc.
PO Box 1905
Boulder, CO 80306

Publications: Iron Feather Journal (4172)

The Phylaxis Society
PO Box 3151
Fort Leavenworth, KS 66027
Phone: (913)651-4584

Publications: Phylaxis Magazine (11441)

Physical Education Digest
11 Cerilli Cres.
Sudbury, ON, Canada P3E 5R3
Fax: (705)523-3331
Free: 800-455-8782

Publications: Physical Education Digest (36418)

Physicians Committee for Responsible Medicine (PCRM)
5100 Wisconsin Ave., NW, Ste. 400
Washington, DC 20016
Phone: (202)686-2210

Publications: Good Medicine Magazine (5516)

Physicians News Digest, Inc.
230 Windsor Ave.
Narberth, PA 19072
Phone: (610)668-1040
Fax: (610)668-9177
Free: 800-220-6109

Publications: Physicians News Digest (27310)

Physicians Postgraduate Press, Inc.
PO Box 752870
Memphis, TN 38175
Fax: (901)751-3444
Free: 800-489-1001

Publications: Journal of Clinical Psychiatry (29372)

Physics Essays Publication
2012 Woodglen Cres.
Ottawa, ON, Canada K1J 6G4
Phone: (819)457-1020

Publications: Physics Essays (36272)

Pi Kappa Alpha Fraternity
8347 W. Range Cove
Memphis, TN 38125
Phone: (901)748-1868
Fax: (901)748-3100

Publications: Shield & Diamond (29380)

Pi Kappa Delta
PO Box 5075
University Sta.
Fargo, ND 58105-5075
Phone: (701)231-7783
Fax: (701)231-7784

Publications: Forensic (33145)

Pi Kappa Phi Fraternity
PO Box 240526
Charlotte, NC 28224
Phone: (704)504-0888
Fax: (704)504-0880
Free: 800-929-1904

Publications: Star & Lamp (23755)

Pi Lambda Theta
4101 E 3rd St.
PO Box 6626
Bloomington, IN 47407-6626
Phone: (812)339-3411
Fax: (812)339-3462
Free: 800-487-3411

Publications: Educational Horizons (9825)

Pi Sigma Epsilon
6560 S 27th St.
Oak Creek, WI 53154
Phone: (414)328-1952
Fax: (414)761-9351
Free: 800-761-9350

Publications: The Journal of Personal Selling and Sales Management (30240)

PIA Management Services Inc.
25 Chamberlain St.
PO Box 997
Glenmont, NY 12077-0997
Phone: (518)434-3111
Fax: 888-225-6935
Free: 800-424-4244

Publications: Professional Insurance Agents (20668)

Piano Technicians Guild, Inc.
3930 Washington
Kansas City, MO 64111
Phone: (816)753-7747
Fax: (816)531-0070

Publications: Piano Technicians Journal (17192)

Piano Today
333 Adams St.
Bedford Hills, NY 10507
Phone: (914)244-8500
Fax: (914)244-8560

Publications: Piano Today (20143) • Sheet Music Magazine (20144)

Pickens County Herald
PO Box 390
Carrollton, AL 35447-0390
Phone: (205)367-2217
Fax: (205)367-2217

Publications: Pickens County Herald (146)

Pickens County Progress
PO Box 67
Jasper, GA 30143
Phone: (706)253-2457
Fax: (706)253-9738

Publications: Pickens County Progress (7341)

The Pickens Sentinel
PO Box 95
Pickens, SC 29671
Phone: (803)878-2453
Fax: (803)878-2454

Publications: The Pickens Sentinel (28743)

Pickett County Press
23 Ct.house Sq.
PO Box 268
Byrdstown, TN 38549-0268
Phone: (931)864-3675
Fax: (931)864-3695

Publications: Pickett County Press (29076)

PICT
26933 Westwood Rd., Ste, 200,
PO Box 76
Westlake, OH 44145
Phone: (419)625-5797
Fax: (419)623-3824

Publications: West Life (25649)

Pied Piper Publishing Co.
350 South Central
Hamlin, TX 79520
Phone: (915)576-3606
Fax: (915)576-3607

Publications: Hamlin Herald (30422)

The Piedmont Herald
34 Railroad St.
Piedmont, WV 26750
Phone: (304)355-2381
Fax: (304)355-2383

Publications: The Piedmont Herald (33435)

Piedmont Publishing Co.
PO Box 3159
Winston-Salem, NC 27102-3159
Phone: (336)727-7211
Fax: (336)727-7315

Publications: Winston-Salem Journal (24324)

Pierce-Arrow Society
135 Edgerton St.
Rochester, NY 14607-2945
Phone: (585)244-1664

Publications: The Arrow (23210)

Pierce County Leader
109 E Main St.
Pierce, NE 68767-1343
Phone: (402)329-4665
Fax: (402)329-6337

Publications: Pierce County Leader (18248)

Pierre Capital Journal
333 W Dakota
PO Box 878
Pierre, SD 57501
Phone: (605)224-7301

Publications: Pierre Capital Journal (28918)

Pig Iron Press
PO Box 237
Youngstown, OH 44501
Phone: (330)747-6932
Fax: (330)747-0599

Publications: Pig Iron (25698)

Pike County Publishing Co.
115 W Jefferson
Box 70
Pittsfield, IL 62363
Phone: (217)285-2345
Fax: (217)285-5222

Publications: Pike Press (9455)

Pikeville College
Humanities Dept.
Pikeville, KY 41501
Phone: (606)218-5002
Fax: (606)218-5225

Publications: Pikeville Review (12358)

Pilcher Publishing Company Inc.
116-18 Clark St.
PO Box 248
Lowell, IN 46356
Phone: (219)696-7711
Fax: (219)696-7713

Publications: Cedar Lake Journal (10279) • Lowell Tribune (10280) • The Northern Star (10281) • South Lake Advertiser (10282)

Pillar Publishing
PO Box 57744
Salt Lake City, UT 84157-0744
Phone: (801)265-0066
Fax: (801)261-2923

Publications: The Pillar (31437)

Pillsbury Co.
200 6th St., M.S. 28M7
Minneapolis, MN 55402
Phone: (612)330-8665
Fax: (612)330-4875

Publications: Classic Cookbooks (16067) • Pillsbury Fast & Healthy Magazine (16120)

Pilot
302 Locust
PO Box Drawer V
Dixon, MO 65459
Phone: (573)759-2127

Publications: Pilot (17035)

The Pilot
145 W Pennsylvania Ave.
Southern Pines, NC 28387
Phone: (910)692-7271
Fax: (910)692-9382

Publications: The Pilot (24235)

The Pilot Co.
126 E Plymouth St.
Bremen, IN 46506-0185
Phone: (219)546-2941
Fax: (219)546-3599

Publications: Bremen Enquirer (9872)

The Pilot Co., Inc.
158 W Market St.
PO Box 230
Nappanee, IN 46550
Phone: (219)773-3127
Fax: (219)936-3844

Publications: Farm and Home News (10335) • Nappanee Advance-News (10336)

The Pilot-Independent
PO Box 190
Walker, MN 56484
Phone: (218)547-1000
Fax: (218)547-3000

Publications: The Co-Pilot (16493) • The Pilot-Independent (16494)

Pilot International
244 College St.
PO Box 4844
Macon, GA 31208-4844
Phone: (478)743-7403
Fax: (478)743-2173

Publications: The Pilot Log (7386)

Pilot Publishing Inc.
PO Box 930
Petersburg, AK 99833
Phone: (907)722-9393
Fax: (907)772-4871

Publications: Petersburg Pilot (631)

Pilot-Tribune
111 W 7th
Storm Lake, IA 50588-1824
Phone: (712)732-3130
Fax: (712)732-3152
Free: 800-798-6397

Publications: The Pilot-Tribune (11244)

Piloven Publishing
2600 S Jackson St.
Seattle, WA 98144
Phone: (206)323-3070
Fax: (206)322-6518

Publications: Seattle Medium (33020) • Tacoma True Citizen (33152)

Pilsudski Institute of America
180 Second Ave.
New York, NY 10003-5778
Phone: (212)505-9077
Fax: (212)505-9052

Publications: Niepodleglosc/Independence (22462)

Pima County Community College
2202 W Anklam Rd.
Tucson, AZ 85709-0001
Phone: (520)260-6800
Fax: (520)206-6834

Publications: Aztec Press (937)

PIME Missionaries
17330 Quincy St.
Detroit, MI 48221-2765
Phone: (313)342-4066
Fax: (313)342-6816

Publications: PIME World (14943)

Pincher Creek Echo
714 Main St.
PO Box 1000
Pincher Creek, AB, Canada T0K 1W0
Phone: (403)627-3252
Fax: (403)627-3949

Publications: Pincher Creek Echo (34824)

Pinconning Journal
110 3rd St.
PO Box 626
Pinconning, MI 48650
Phone: (989)879-3811
Fax: (989)879-5529

Publications: Pinconning Journal (15444)

Pine Bluffs Post
201 E 2nd
PO Box 68
Pine Bluffs, WY 82082
Phone: (307)245-3763

Publications: Pine Bluffs Post (34566)

Pine City Pioneer
405 SE 2nd Ave.
Pine City, MN 55063
Phone: (320)629-6771
Fax: (320)629-6772

Publications: Pine City Pioneer (16268)

Pine Cone Press-Citizen
PO Box 401
Longville, MN 56655-0401
Phone: (218)363-2002
Fax: (218)363-3043

Publications: Pine Cone Press-Citizen (16012)

Pine County Courier
PO Box 230
Sandstone, MN 55072
Phone: (320)245-2368
Fax: (320)245-2438

Publications: Pine County Courier (16435)

Pine River Journal
215 Norway Ave.
Box 370
Pine River, MN 56474
Phone: (218)587-2360
Fax: (218)587-2331
Free: 800-450-8521

Publications: Pine River Journal (16274)

Pineland Publishing Co.
PO Box 750
Winnfield, LA 71483
Phone: (318)628-2712
Fax: (318)628-6196

Publications: Winn Parish Enterprise (12880)

Pinewood Country Creations
86 6th Ave.
PO Box 10
Cochrane, ON, Canada P0L 1C0
Phone: (705)272-4363
Fax: (705)272-2935

Publications: Pinewood Country Creations (35744)

Pinnacle Peak Publishing Ltd.
8711 E Pinnacle Peak Rd., No. 249
Scottsdale, AZ 85255
Phone: (480)502-2285

Publications: Document Management (868)

Pinnacle Publishing Group
2736 Sawbury Blvd.
Columbus, OH 43235
Phone: (614)336-0710
Fax: (614)336-0713

Publications: Midwest Foodservice News (25031)

Pioneer
Box 219
Mahnomen, MN 56557
Phone: (218)935-5296

Publications: Pioneer (16023)

The Pioneer/Advertiser
Box 455
Bemidji, MN 56619
Phone: (218)751-3740
Fax: (218)751-2193

Publications: The Pioneer (15739)

Pioneer Communications
218 6th Ave., Ste. 610
Des Moines, IA 50309-4009

Publications: The Iowan (10798)

Pioneer Communications, Inc.
PO Box 306
PO Box 306
Grundy Center, IA 50638

Publications: Collectors News (10935)

The Pioneer Group
502 N. State St.
Big Rapids, MI 49307
Phone: (231)796-4831
Fax: (231)796-1152
Free: 888-796-4831

Publications: Benzie County Record-Patriot (15053) • Evart Review (15013) • Freeway Shoppers Guide (15463) • The Herald-News (15464) • Lake County Star (14790) • Lakeview Enterprise (15272) • Manistee County Pioneer Press (14816) • Manistee News Advocate (15329) • The Pioneer (14818) • River Valley News Shopper (15189) • Tri-County Shoppers Guide (14819) • West Shore Shoppers Guide (15330)

Pioneer Newspaper and Commercial Printing
PO Box 830
105 W 2nd Ave.
Big Timber, MT 59011
Phone: (406)932-5298
Fax: (406)932-4931
Free: 800-253-4602

Publications: The Big Timber Pioneer (17727)

Pioneer Newspapers
401 North Main
Ellensburg, WA 98926
Phone: (509)925-1414
Fax: (509)925-5696

Publications: Daily Record (32748)

Pioneer Press
PO Box 400
Fort Jones, CA 96032
Phone: (530)468-5355
Fax: (530)468-5356

Publications: Pioneer Press (1926)

Pioneer Press Newspapers
3701 W. Lake Ave.
Glenview, IL 60025
Phone: (847)486-0600
Fax: (847)486-7416

Publications: Algonquin Countryside (8007) • Arlington Heights Post (8021) • Barrington Courier-Review (8048) • Buffalo Grove Countryside (8100) • Cary-Grove Countryside (8167) • Deerfield Review (8723) • Des Plaines Times (8759) • Edgebrook Times Review (8809) • Edison-Norwood Times Review (8360) • Elk Grove Times (8831) • Evanston Review (8858) • Glencoe News (8936) • Glenview Announcements (8937) • Grayslake Review (8955) • Gurnee Review (8967) • Highland Park News (8989) • Hoffman Estates Review (9000) • Lake Forester (9062) • Lake Zurich Courier (9065) • Libertyville Review (9081) • Maywood Herald (9164) • Melrose Park Herald (9170) • Morton Grove Champion Review (9230) • Mount Prospect Times (9247) • Mundelein Review (9258) • Niles Herald-Spectator (9292) • Norridge-Harwood Heights News (8978) • North Shore Magazine (8939) • Northbrook Star (8940) • Palatine Countryside (9395) • Park Ridge Herald-Advocate (9407) • The Review of Lake Villa/Lindenhurst (9108) • Rolling Meadows Review (9550) • Schaumburg Review (9591) • Skokie Review (9612) • Vernon Hills Review (9744) • West Proviso Herald (9472) • Wheeling Countryside (9762) • Wilmette Life (8942) • Winnetka Talk (9768)

Pioneer Printing Co., Inc.
501 Dock St.
PO Box 7900
Ketchikan, AK 99901
Phone: (907)225-3157
Fax: (907)225-1096

Publications: Ketchikan Daily News (611)

Pioneer Publications
PO Box 3838
Idaho Falls, ID 83403
Phone: (208)523-7777

Publications: Cable Scene (7862)

Pioneer Publications
PO Box P
Shelley, ID 83274
Phone: (208)357-7661

Publications: The Shelley Pioneer (7980)

Pioneer Publishing
Box 37
Rigby, ID 83442
Phone: (208)745-8701
Fax: (208)745-8703

Publications: Jefferson Star (7967)

Pioneer Publishing Co.
PO Box 1190
Bozeman, MT 59771-1190
Phone: (406)587-4491
Fax: (406)587-7995

Publications: Bozeman Daily Chronicle (17751)

Pioneer Republican
PO Box 208
Marengo, IA 52301
Phone: (319)642-5506
Fax: (319)642-5509
Free: 800-414-5506

Publications: The 4-County Market (11060) • Pioneer Republican (11063)

Pioneer-Tribune
212 Walnut St.
Manistique, MI 49854
Phone: (906)341-5200

Publications: Pioneer-Tribune (15333)

Pipestone Publishing Co.
101 2nd St. NE
Box 277
Pipestone, MN 56164-0277
Phone: (507)825-3333
Fax: (507)825-2168

Publications: Pipestone County Star (16275)

Pittsburg Publishing
701 N Locust
Pittsburg, KS 66762-0570
Phone: (620)231-8110
Fax: (620)231-0645
Free: 800-794-6536

Publications: Morning Sun (11754)

Pittsburg State University
Dept. of Economics, Finance & Banking
Pittsburg, KS 66762
Phone: (620)235-4547
Fax: (620)235-4572

Publications: Journal of Managerial Issues (11752)

Pittsburg State University
1701 S. Broadway
Pittsburg, KS 66762
Phone: (620)235-4809
Fax: (620)235-4817

Publications: Collegio (11751)

Pittsburgh Catholic Publishing Associates, Inc.
135 1st Ave., No. 200
Pittsburgh, PA 15222-1506
Phone: (412)471-1252
Fax: (412)471-4228
Free: 800-392-4670

Publications: Pittsburgh Catholic (27831)

The Pittsfield Gazette, Inc.
PO Box 2236
Pittsfield, MA 01202
Phone: (413)443-2010
Fax: (413)443-2445

Publications: Berkshire Summer (14469) • Pittsfield Gazette (14472)

Pixel Vision
154 W 57th St., No. 826
New York, NY 10019
Phone: (212)581-3000
Fax: (212)757-8283

Publications: Pixel Vision (22556)

Placer Community Newspapers Inc.
188 Cirby Way
Roseville, CA 95678
Phone: (916)786-8746
Fax: (916)786-6501

Publications: Press-Tribune (2971)

Placer Management Corp.
17951-C Skypark Circle
Irvine, CA 92614
Phone: (949)553-0836
Fax: (949)863-9261

Publications: World Dredging, Mining & Construction (2093)

Plain Truth Ministries
Pasadena, CA 91129
Phone: (626)304-6077
Fax: (626)795-5106
Free: 800-309-4466

Publications: The Plain Truth (2825)

2584

Numbers cited after listings are entry numbers rather than page numbers.

Plaindealer Publishing Co.
Box 239
Tekamah, NE 68061
Phone: (402)374-2225
Fax: (402)374-2739

Publications: Burt County Plaindealer (18296) •
Midwest Messenger (18297)

The Plaindealer Publishing Co., Inc.
PO Box 910
Ackerman, MS 39735-0910
Phone: (662)285-6248
Fax: (662)285-6695

Publications: Choctaw Plaindealer (16544)

Plainview Daily Herald
820 Broadway
Plainview, TX 79072
Phone: (806)296-1300
Fax: (806)296-1315

Publications: Plainview Daily Herald (30939)

Plainview News
Box 9
Plainview, NE 68769-0009
Phone: (402)582-4921
Fax: (402)582-4922

Publications: Plainview News (18249)

Plainville Times
400 W Mill St.
Plainville, KS 67663
Phone: (785)434-4525

Publications: Plainville Times (11759)

Planet Communications
670 5th St.
San Francisco, CA 94107-1517
Phone: (415)543-6100
Fax: (415)546-7556

Publications: Film/Tape World (3361)

Planet Underground Business Media
20550 Calumet Ave.
Lowell, IN 46356
Phone: (219)696-4015
Fax: (219)696-7989

Publications: Underground Focus (34338)

The Planter Newspaper
PO Box 880
Apopka, FL 32704-0880
Phone: (407)886-2777
Fax: (407)889-4121

Publications: The Planter Newspaper (5911)

Plaquemine Publishing, Inc.
58650 Belleview Dr.
PO Box 589
Plaquemine, LA 70764
Phone: (225)687-3288
Fax: (225)687-1814

Publications: Plaquemine Post-South (12795)

Plaquemines Newspaper Publishing, Inc.
7952 Hwy. 23
PO Box 700
Belle Chasse, LA 70037
Phone: (504)392-1619
Fax: (504)393-9327

Publications: The Plaquemines Gazette (12528) •
The Plaquemines Watchman (12529)

Plast-Ukrainian Youth Organization
2199 Bloor St. W.
Toronto, ON, Canada M6S 1N2
Phone: (416)769-7855
Fax: (416)763-0185

Publications: Yunak (36796)

The Plastic Tower
Box 702
Bowie, MD 20718

Publications: The Plastic Tower (13393)

The Plastics Distributor & Fabricator Magazine
One Riverside Rd., Ste.3D
Riverside, IL 60546
Phone: (708)447-0001
Fax: (708)447-0005

Publications: The Plastics Distributor & Fabricator
Magazine (9498)

Platte County Citizen
PO Box 888
Platte City, MO 64079
Phone: (816)858-5154
Fax: (816)858-2154

Publications: Platte County Citizen (17350)

Platte County Record Times
1007 8th St.
Wheatland, WY 82201-2602
Phone: (307)322-2627
Fax: (307)322-9612

Publications: Platte County Record Times (34601)

Platteville Journal
1190 W Hwy. 151
Platteville, WI 53818-0266
Phone: (608)348-3006
Fax: (608)348-7979

Publications: Platteville Journal (34242)

Playboy
680 N Lake Shore Dr.
Chicago, IL 60611
Phone: (312)751-8000
Fax: (312)751-2818

Publications: Playboy (8533)

Players International Publications
8060 Melrose Ave.
Los Angeles, CA 90046
Phone: (323)653-8060
Fax: (323)682-2932

Publications: Adam Magazine (2198) • Players
(2370)

Playful Productions, Inc.
PO Box 10804
Wilmington, DE 19850
Phone: (302)894-1950
Fax: (302)894-1957

Publications: Worddance (5295)

Playgirl, Inc.
801 2nd Ave.
New York, NY 10017
Phone: (212)661-7878
Fax: (212)697-6343
Free: 800-877-6139

Publications: Playgirl (22565)

Plaza Metro Ltd.
1253 McGill College, bureau 232
Montreal, QC, Canada H3B 2Y5
Phone: (514)933-3333
Fax: (514)931-9581

Publications: Montreal Scope (37190)

P.L.C. Publishing Co.
PO Box 6192
Pasadena, TX 77506
Phone: (713)477-0221
Fax: (713)477-9090

Publications: Pasadena Broadcaster (30913) •
Pasadena Citizen (30914)

Pleasant Co.
8400 Fairway Pl.
Middleton, WI 53562
Phone: (608)836-4848
Fax: (608)831-7089
Free: 800-233-0264

Publications: American Girl (34049)

Pleasant Hill Times, Inc.
126 1st St.
Box 8
Pleasant Hill, MO 64080
Phone: (816)540-3500
Fax: (816)987-5699

Publications: Pleasant Hill Times (17352)

Pleasanton Express
PO Box 880
114 Goodwin St.
Pleasanton, TX 78064-0880
Phone: (830)569-4967
Fax: (830)569-6100

Publications: Express (30952)

Pleiades Magazine
PO Box 140213
Edgewater, CO 80214-9998
Phone: (303)237-1019

Publications: Pleiades Magazine (4410)

Plexus Publishing Inc.
143 Old Marlton Pike
Medford, NJ 08055
Phone: (609)654-6500
Fax: (609)654-4309

Publications: Biology Digest (19221)

PLM Publishing Inc.
1312 Lincoln Blvd.
PO Box 1700
Santa Monica, CA 90401-1706
Phone: (310)451-1344
Fax: (310)395-9058

Publications: Focus on Imaging (3709)

Pluim Publishing, Inc.
113 Central Ave. SE
Orange City, IA 51041-1738
Phone: (712)737-4266
Fax: (712)737-3896
Free: 800-747-5846

Publications: Ad-Visor (11128) • Farmer's Cattle-
log (11129) • Sioux County Capital-Democrat
(11130)

Plumbers - Steamfitters, UA Local 38
1621 Market St.
San Francisco, CA 94103
Phone: (415)626-2000

Publications: Pipelines (3414)

Plus Magazine
823 Via Esteban, Ste. A
San Luis Obispo, CA 93401-7164
Phone: (805)544-8711
Fax: (805)544-4450

Publications: Plus Magazine (3568)

Plymouth County Development Council
32 Ct. St., 2nd Fl.
Plymouth, MA 02360
Phone: (508)747-0100
Fax: (508)747-3118

Publications: Plymouth County Business Review
(14480)

The Plymouth Review
PO Box 317, 113 E. Mill St.
Plymouth, WI 53073
Phone: (920)893-6411
Fax: (920)893-5505

Publications: The Review (34249)

PMT Publishing Co., Inc.
529 Beacon Pkwy. W, Ste. 110
Birmingham, AL 35209
Phone: (205)941-1425
Fax: (205)479-8822

Publications: Business Alabama Monthly (63)

Pocahontas Times
810 2nd Ave.
Marlinton, WV 24954
Phone: (304)799-4973
Fax: (304)799-6466

Publications: The Pocahontas Times (33376)

Poe Foundation, Inc.
1914-16 E Main St.
Richmond, VA 23223
Phone: (804)648-5523
Fax: (804)648-8729
Free: 888-21E-APOE

Publications: The Poe Messenger (32445)

Poetics, Inc.
Box 120128, Acklen Sta.
Nashville, TN 37212
Phone: (615)373-8948

Publications: Cumberland Poetry Review (29453)

Poetry Flash Inc.
1450 4th St., Ste. 4
Berkeley, CA 94710
Phone: (510)525-5476
Fax: (510)525-6752

Publications: Poetry Flash (1551)

Poetry Harbor
PO Box 103
Duluth, MN 55801
Phone: (218)279-3865

Publications: North Coast Review (15841)

Poetry in Review Foundation
205 W 89th St., No. 8F
New York, NY 10024
Phone: (212)362-3492
Fax: (212)875-0148

Publications: Parnassus (22531)

Poetry on Wings
PO Box 1000
Pearblossom, CA 93553-1000
Phone: (661)264-3726

Publications: Silver Wings Mayflower Pulpit (2833)

Poets on the Line
PO Box 020292
Brooklyn, NY 11202-0007

Publications: Poets on the Line (20339)

Poet's Roundtable
826 Ctr. St.
Terre Haute, IN 47807

Publications: Poet's Roundtable (10488)

Poets at Work
PO Box 232
Lyndora, PA 16045

Publications: Poets at Work (27208)

Poets & Writers Inc.
72 Spring St., Ste. 301
New York, NY 10012
Phone: (212)226-3586
Fax: (212)226-3963

Publications: Poets & Writers Magazine (22568)

PoetsWest
1011 Boren Ave.
PMB 155
Seattle, WA 98104
Phone: (206)682-1268

Publications: PoetsWest Online (33003)

Pohly & Partners, Inc.
27 Melcher St., 2nd Fl.
Boston, MA 02210
Phone: (617)451-1700
Fax: (617)338-7767

Publications: Continental Magazine (13884) • Living Healthy Magazine (13923) • Professional Collector Magazine (13952) • Tomorrow Magazine (13968)

Point
18 Bluff Rd.
PO Box 8325
Columbia, SC 29202
Phone: (803)808-3384
Fax: (803)808-3781
Free: 800-849-1803

Publications: Point (28562)

Point Foundation
1408 Mission Ave.
San Rafael, CA 94901
Phone: (415)256-2800
Fax: (415)256-2808
Free: 888-732-6739

Publications: Whole Earth (3603)

Point Park College
201 Wood St.
Box 627
Pittsburgh, PA 15222
Phone: (412)392-3970
Fax: (412)391-1980

Publications: The Globe (27792) • The Pioneer (27827)

Point Pleasant Register
200 Main St., No. 237
Point Pleasant, WV 25550-1030
Phone: (304)675-1333
Fax: (304)675-5234

Publications: Point Pleasant Register (33439)

Point Reyes Light
PO Box 210
Point Reyes Station, CA 94956
Phone: (415)663-8404
Fax: (415)663-8458

Publications: Point Reyes Light (2859)

The Point Weekly
3900 Lomaland Dr.
San Diego, CA 92106
Phone: (619)849-2499
Fax: (619)849-7009

Publications: The Point (3247)

Pointe Coupee Printing & Publishing Inc.
123 St. Mary St.
PO Box 400
New Roads, LA 70760
Phone: (225)638-7155
Fax: (225)638-8442

Publications: The Pointe Coupee Banner (12787)

Polebridge Press
PO Box 6144
Santa Rosa, CA 95406
Phone: (707)523-1323
Fax: (707)523-1350

Publications: Forum (3727) • The Fourth R (3728)

Policy Studies Organization
701 Devonshire Dr., Ste. C31
Champaign, IL 61820-7358
Phone: (217)352-5094
Fax: (217)352-3037

Publications: Peace, Prosperity & Democracy (8209) • Policy Studies Journal (8212)

Policy Studies Review
Policy Studies Organizaion
711 S. Ashton Lane
Champaign, IL 61820
Phone: (217)359-8541
Fax: (217)352-3037

Publications: Policy Studies Review (8213)

Polish Alliance Press Ltd.
22 Roundsvall Ave
Toronto, ON, Canada M6P 4A8
Phone: (416)531-2491
Fax: (416)531-5153

Publications: Zwiazkowiec (Alliancer) (36798)

Polish American World
3100 Grand Blvd.
Baldwin, NY 11510
Phone: (516)223-6514
Fax: (516)868-6618

Publications: Polish American World (20114)

Polish Army Veterans Association of America
17 Irving Pl.
New York, NY 10003
Phone: (212)473-0580

Publications: Weteran/Veteran (22916)

Polish Daily News, Inc.
11903 Joseph Campau St.
Hamtramck, MI 48212
Phone: (313)365-1990
Fax: (313)365-0850

Publications: The Polish Weekly (15141)

Polish Falcons of America
615 Iron City Dr.
Pittsburgh, PA 15205-4397
Phone: (412)922-2244
Fax: (412)922-5029
Free: 800-535-2071

Publications: Sokol Polski (Polish Falcon) (27844)

Polish Institute of Arts & Sciences of America
208 E 30th St.
New York, NY 10016
Phone: (212)686-4164
Fax: (212)545-1130

Publications: The Polish Review (22572)

Polish Institute of Houston, Inc.
Box 79119
Houston, TX 77279
Phone: (713)467-5836
Fax: (713)467-6348

Publications: Sarmatian Review (30526)

Polish Music Center
University of Southern California
Thornton School of Music
840 W. 34th St.
Los Angeles, CA 90089-0851
Phone: (213)740-9369
Fax: (213)740-3217

Publications: Polish Music Journal (2372)

Polish National Catholic Church
1004 Pittston Ave.
Scranton, PA 18505
Phone: (570)346-9131
Fax: (570)346-2188

Publications: Rola Boza (God's Field) (27962)

Polish Press, Ltd.
1150 Main St.
Winnipeg, MB, Canada R2W 3S6
Phone: (204)582-4392
Fax: (204)582-4392

Publications: Czas (Times) (35325)

Polish Roman Catholic Union of America
984 N Milwaukee Ave.
Chicago, IL 60622-4101
Phone: (773)782-2600
Fax: (773)278-4595
Free: 800-772-8632

Publications: Narod Polish (8499)

Political Affairs Publishers, Inc.
235 W 23rd St., 7th Fl.
New York, NY 10011-2313
Phone: (212)989-4994
Fax: (212)229-1713

Publications: Political Affairs (22574) • Political Affairs (22573)

Political Research Inc.
Tegoland at Bent Tree
16850 Dallas Pkwy.
Dallas, TX 75248
Phone: (972)931-8827
Fax: (972)248-7159
Free: 800-782-9002

Publications: Clements' International Report (30137) • World of Politics (30190)

The Polk County News
Box 365
Stromsburg, NE 68666
Phone: (402)764-5341
Fax: (402)764-5341

Publications: The Polk County News (18288)

Polk County Publishing
PO Box 551
Crockett, TX 75835
Phone: (936)544-2238
Fax: (936)544-4088

Publications: Houston County Courier (30106)

Polk County Publishing
PO Box 730
Groveton, TX 75845
Phone: (409)642-1726
Fax: (409)642-1195

Publications: Groveton News (30418)

Polk County Publishing Co., Inc.
PO Box 129
Benton, TN 37307
Phone: (615)338-2818

Publications: Polk County News-Citizen Advance (29054)

Polk County Publishing Co., Inc.
PO Box 1276
Livingston, TX 77351
Phone: (936)327-4357
Fax: (936)327-7156

Publications: Lake Livingston Progress (30699) • Polk County Enterprise (30700) • San Jacinto News Times (31082) • The Trinity Standard (31194)

Pollock Advertising, Inc.
118 1/2 Franklin St.
PO Box 97
Slippery Rock, PA 16057
Phone: (724)794-6857
Fax: (724)794-1314

Publications: Movin' Out (27996) • Tri-County News (27999)

Pollstar
4697 W. Jacquelyn Ave.
Fresno, CA 93722-6413
Phone: (559)271-7900
Fax: (559)271-7979

Publications: Pollstar (1956)

Polytechnic University
6 Metro Tech Ctr.
Brooklyn, NY 11201
Phone: (718)260-3165
Fax: (718)260-3084

Publications: The Polytechnic Reporter (20340)

Pomerado Publishing
13247 Poway Rd.
Poway, CA 92064
Phone: (858)748-2311

Publications: Corridor News (2866) • Poway News Chieftain (2867) • Rancho Bernardo News Journal (2873)

The Pompano Ledger Publishing Co.
2500 SE 5th Ct.
Pompano Beach, FL 33062
Phone: (954)532-2000

Publications: The Pompano Ledger (6592)

Ponca City Publishing Co., Inc.
300 N. 3rd St.
PO Box 191
Ponca City, OK 74602
Phone: (580)765-3311
Fax: (580)762-6397

Publications: The Ponca City News (26037)

The Ponchatoula Times
PO Box 743
Ponchatoula, LA 70454
Phone: (985)386-2877
Fax: (985)386-0458

Publications: The Ponchatoula Times (12797)

Ponoka News
PO Box 4217
Ponoka, AB, Canada T4J 1R6
Phone: (403)783-3311
Fax: (403)783-6300

Publications: Ponoka News & Advertiser (34825)

Pontchartrain Newspapers
525 Ave. V
PO Box 820
Bogalusa, LA 70427-4413
Phone: (985)732-2565
Fax: (985)732-4006

Publications: The Bogalusa Daily News (12533) • St. Tammany News-Banner (12556)

Pontchartrain Newspapers
3648 Pontchartrain Dr.
PO Box 910
Slidell, LA 70459
Phone: (504)643-4918
Fax: (504)643-4966

Publications: Slidell Sentry-News (12843)

Pony of Americas Club, Inc.
5240 Elmwood Ave.
Indianapolis, IN 46203
Phone: (317)788-0107
Fax: (317)788-8974

Publications: POA (10161)

Poodle Review
2003 E Illini Airport Rd.
Urbana, IL 61801
Phone: (217)328-7375

Publications: Poodle Review (9715)

Pool Dust
PO Box 419
Tempe, AZ 85280-0419

Publications: Pool Dust (912)

Poole Publications, Inc.
20700 Belshaw Ave.
PO Box 5427
Carson, CA 90749-5427
Phone: (310)537-6322
Fax: (310)537-8735

Publications: Trailer Boats Magazine (1677)

Pope County Tribune
14 1st Ave., SE
Glenwood, MN 56334
Phone: (320)634-4571
Fax: (320)634-5522

Publications: Pope County Tribune (15920)

Poplar Publishing
PO Box 5393
Takoma Park, MD 20913

Publications: Endangered Species & Wetlands Report (13751)

POPsmear Magazine
232 N Almont Dr.
Beverly Hills, CA 90211
Fax: (310)247-9588

Publications: POPsmear (1576)

Popular Culture Center
RR 3, Box 80
Cleveland, OK 74020
Phone: (918)243-7637
Fax: (918)243-5995

Publications: Film & History (25789)

Popular Press
Bowling Green State University
Popular Culture Center
Bowling Green, OH 43403
Phone: (419)372-7867
Fax: (419)372-8095

Publications: Journal of American Culture (24693) • Journal of Popular Culture (24695)

Popular Press
Bowling Green, OH 43403
Phone: (419)372-7866
Fax: (419)372-8095

Publications: Clues: A Journal of Detection (24690) • Journal of Cultural Geography (24694) • Popular Music and Society (24700)

Population Association of America
8630 Fenton St., Ste. 722
Silver Spring, MD 20910-3812
Phone: (301)565-6710
Fax: (301)565-7850

Publications: Demography (13724)

Population Connection
1400 16th St. NW, Ste. 320
Washington, DC 20036-2290
Phone: (202)332-2200
Fax: (202)332-2302
Free: 800-767-1956

Publications: Population Connection (5723)

Population Council
1 Dag Hammarskjold Plaza
New York, NY 10017
Phone: (212)339-0500
Fax: (212)755-6052

Publications: Population and Development Review (22583) • Studies in Family Planning (22800)

Population Reference Bureau
1875 Connecticut Ave. NW, Ste. 520
Washington, DC 20009
Phone: (202)483-1100
Fax: (202)328-3937
Free: 800-877-9881

Publications: Population Bulletin (5722)

Pork Publications, Inc.
PO Box 9114
Des Moines, IA 50306
Phone: (515)223-2600
Fax: (515)223-2646

Publications: National Pork Report (10804)

Porsche Club of America
912 Lullwater Rd.
Atlanta, GA 30307
Phone: (404)378-9823
Fax: (404)377-7041

Publications: Porsche Panorama (7038)

Port Byron Shopping Press, Inc.
101 Main St.
Port Byron, NY 13140
Phone: (315)776-5512

Publications: Port Byron Shopping Guide (23114)

The Port Orford News
PO Box 5
Port Orford, OR 97465-0005
Phone: (541)332-2361
Fax: (503)332-8101

Publications: Port Orford News (26465)

Port Townsend Publishing Co.
226 Adams St.
PO Box 552
Port Townsend, WA 98368
Phone: (360)385-2900
Fax: (360)385-3422

Publications: Port Townsend/Jefferson County Leader (32894)

Portfolio Publishing Inc.
1300 Diamond Springs Rd., Ste. 102
Virginia Beach, VA 23455
Phone: (757)222-3100
Fax: (757)363-1767

Publications: Tidewater Parent (32590)

Porthole Cruise Magazine
Wingate Commons
4517 NW 31st Ave.
Fort Lauderdale, FL 33309-3403
Phone: (954)377-7777
Fax: (954)377-7000

Publications: Porthole (6083)

Portland
578 Congress St.
Portland, ME 04101
Phone: (207)775-4339
Fax: (207)775-2334

Publications: Portland (13016)

Portland Community College
12000 SW 49th Ave.
PO Box 19000
Portland, OR 97280
Phone: (503)977-4184
Fax: (503)977-4956

Publications: The Bridge (26471)

Portsmouth Herald
111 Maplewood Ave.
Portsmouth, NH 03801
Phone: (603)436-1800
Fax: (603)427-0550

Publications: Portsmouth Herald (18637)

Portuguese Journal
5404 Valley View Rd.
El Sobrante, CA 94803-3447
Phone: (510)237-0888
Fax: (510)237-3790
Free: 800-309-0233

Publications: Portuguese Journal (1869)

Posey County News
PO Box 250
Poseyville, IN 47633
Phone: (812)874-2813
Fax: (812)874-6397

Publications: Posey County News (10407)

Positive Futures Networks
284 Madrona Way NE Ste. 116
Bainbridge Island, WA 98110-0818
Phone: (206)842-0216
Fax: (206)842-5208
Free: 800-937-4451

Publications: Yes! A Journal of Positive Futures (32659)

The Post
PO Box 250
Big Stone Gap, VA 24219
Phone: (276)523-1141
Fax: (276)523-1175

Publications: The Post (31865)

Post-Bulletin
18 1st Ave. SE
PO Box 6118
Rochester, MN 55903-6118
Phone: (507)285-7600
Fax: (507)281-7436
Free: 800-533-1727

Publications: Agri News (16305) • Post-Bulletin (16311)

Post City Magazines
30 Lesmill Rd.
Toronto, ON, Canada M3B 2T6
Phone: (416)250-7979
Fax: (416)250-1737

Publications: Bayview Post (36472) • North Toronto Post (36676) • Richmond Hill Post (36729) • Thornhill Post (36759) • Village Post (36787)

The Post-Crescent
PO Box 59
Appleton, WI 54912
Phone: (920)733-4411
Fax: (414)733-1945

Publications: The Post-Crescent (33542)

The Post Dispatch
123 E Main
PO Box 490
Post, TX 79356
Phone: (806)495-2816
Fax: (806)495-2059

Publications: The Post Dispatch (30961)

Post Falls Press
PO Box 39
Post Falls, ID 83877
Phone: (208)773-7502
Fax: (208)773-7002

Publications: Post Falls Press (7958)

Post Falls Tribune
PO Box 39
Post Falls, ID 83877
Phone: (208)773-7502
Fax: (208)773-7002

Publications: Post Falls Tribune (7959)

Post-Gazette
5 Prince St.
PO Box 135
Boston, MA 02113
Phone: (617)227-8929

Publications: Post-Gazette (13951)

Post Gazette
34 Blvd. of the Allies
Pittsburgh, PA 15222
Phone: (412)263-1100
Fax: (412)391-8452

Publications: Post-Gazette (27837)

The Post-Journal
15 W. 2nd St.
Jamestown, NY 14701
Phone: (716)487-1111
Fax: (716)664-3119

Publications: The Post-Journal (20842)

Post Newspaper Group, Inc.
1688 Meridian Ave. No. 702
PO Box 19-1870
Miami Beach, FL 33139
Phone: (305)538-9700

Publications: The Sun Post (6417)

Post Newspapers, Inc.
PO Box 955
Burgaw, NC 28425-0955
Phone: (910)259-9111
Fax: (910)259-9112

Publications: Pender Post (23670)

Post-Newsweek Business Information
10 G St. NE, Ste. 500
Washington, DC 20002-4228

Publications: Washington Technology (5854)

Post Pro Publishing, Inc.
25 Willowdale Ave.
Port Washington, NY 11050
Phone: (516)767-2500
Fax: (516)767-9335

Publications: Post (23134)

Post Publications
425 NE. 4th Ave.
Camas, WA 98607
Phone: (360)834-2141
Fax: (360)834-3423
Free: 800-765-1343

Publications: At Your Leisure (32700) • Camas-Washougal Post-Record (32701)

Post Publishing Co.
131 W. Innes St.
PO Box 4639
Salisbury, NC 28145-4639
Phone: (704)633-8950
Fax: (704)639-0003
Free: 800-633-8957

Publications: The Salisbury Post (24215)

Post Publishing Co., Inc.
800 Van Houten Ave.
PO Box 2127
Clifton, NJ 07015
Phone: (973)473-5414
Fax: (973)473-3211

Publications: Post Eagle (18758)

The Post-Register
333 Northgate Mile
PO BOX 1800
Idaho Falls, ID 83401
Phone: (208)522-1800

Publications: The Post-Register (7868)

Post-Review 1990 Ltd.
20 Railway Ave.
PO Box 10
Hudson Bay, SK, Canada S0E 0Y0
Phone: (306)865-2771
Fax: (306)865-2340

Publications: Hudson Bay Post-Review (37475)

Post Shopper
839 Via De La Paz
PO Box 725
Pacific Palisades, CA 90272-0725
Phone: (310)454-1321
Fax: (310)454-1078

Publications: Post Shopper (2737)

The Post-Star
Lawrence & Cooper St.
Glens Falls, NY 12801
Phone: (518)792-3131
Fax: (518)761-1255
Free: 800-724-2543

Publications: The Post-Star (20669)

Post and Star Publishing Co.
1000 A Waterman Ave.
East Providence, RI 02914
Phone: (401)434-7210
Fax: (401)434-9469

Publications: East Providence Post (28344)

Post-Tribune Publishing
1433 E. 83rd Ave.
Merrillville, IN 46410-6307
Phone: (219)648-3000
Free: 800-753-5533

Publications: Post-Tribune (10299)

Potash Phosphate Institute
655 Engineering Dr., Ste. 110
Norcross, GA 30092-2837
Phone: (770)447-0335
Fax: (770)448-0439

Publications: Better Crops with Plant Food (7456)

Potato Association of America
University of Maine
5715 Coburn Hall, Rm. 6
Orono, ME 04469-5715
Phone: (207)581-3042
Fax: (207)581-3015

Publications: American Journal of Potato Research (12998)

Poteau Daily News & Sun
804 N. Broadway St.
PO Box 1237
Poteau, OK 74953-3535
Phone: (918)647-3188
Fax: (918)647-8198
Free: 800-495-6397

Publications: Poteau Daily News & Sun (26045)

Pothole Publications, Inc.
PO Box 22439
Eagan, MN 55122-0439
Phone: (952)736-1020
Fax: (952)736-1030
Free: 800-221-6547

Publications: Wildlife Art (15864)

Potomac Children
3908 Underwood St.
Chevy Chase, MD 20815
Phone: (301)656-2133
Fax: (301)656-7830

Publications: Potomac Children (13408)

Potomac News
14010 Smoketown Rd.
PO Box 2470
Woodbridge, VA 22192
Phone: (703)878-8000
Fax: (703)878-3993

Publications: Potomac News (32637)

Potomac State College
308 Academy Hall
Keyser, WV 26726
Phone: (304)788-3011

Publications: Pasquino (33353)

Potsdam College
Potsdam, NY 13676
Phone: (315)267-2043
Fax: (315)267-3256

Publications: Blueline (Potsdam) (23137)

Potter Media Inc.
533 4th St. N
St. Petersburg, FL 33701
Phone: (727)894-2411
Fax: (727)894-2522

Publications: Pinellas News (6632)

Pottersfield Portfolio
PO Box 40, Sta. A
Sydney, NS, Canada B1P 6C9
Phone: (902)567-6609
Fax: (902)567-6609

Publications: Pottersfield Portfolio (35609)

Pottsville Republican
111 Mahantongo St.
Pottsville, PA 17901-3008
Phone: (717)622-3456
Fax: (717)628-6092

Publications: Pottsville Republican (27903)

Poultry Press
PO Box 542
Connersville, IN 47331
Phone: (765)827-0932
Fax: (765)827-4186

Publications: Poultry Press (9901)

POWDER
PO Box 1028
Dana Point, CA 92629
Phone: (714)496-5922
Fax: (714)496-7849
Free: 800-289-8983

Publications: POWDER (1806)

Powder River Examiner
PO Box 328
Broadus, MT 59317
Phone: (406)436-2244
Fax: (406)436-2244

Publications: Powder River Examiner (17759)

The Powell Tribune
PO Box 70
Powell, WY 82435
Phone: (307)754-2221
Fax: (307)754-4873

Publications: The Powell Tribune (34569)

Powell Valley Printing Co.
Box 459
Pennington Gap, VA 24277-0459
Phone: (276)546-1210
Fax: (276)546-5468

Publications: Powell Valley News (32326)

Power of Poetry
c/o Dominican School of Philosophy & Theology
2401 Ridge Rd.
Berkeley, CA 94709
Phone: (510)849-2030
Fax: (510)849-1372

Publications: Ruah (2698)

Power Trade Media, LLC
1550 E. Missouri Ste. 202
Phoenix, AZ 85014-2456
Phone: (602)265-7600
Fax: (602)227-7588
Free: 800-541-2670

Publications: Bus Ride (794)

Powerboat Magazine
1691 Spinnaker Dr., Ste. 206
Ventura, CA 93001-4378
Phone: (805)639-2222
Fax: (805)639-2220

Publications: Powerboat Magazine (4008)

Powerlifting USA
PO Box 467
Camarillo, CA 93011-0467
Phone: (805)482-2378
Fax: (805)987-4275
Free: 800-448-7693

Publications: Powerlifting USA Magazine (1642)

PowerOne Media, Inc.
400 Jordan Rd.
Troy, NY 12180
Free: 800-6PO-WER6

Publications: Lafayette News (23453) • Tri-County Times (23459)

Powershift Communications Inc.
245 Fairview Mall Dr., Ste. 501
Toronto, ON, Canada M2J 4T1
Phone: (416)494-1066
Fax: (416)494-2536

Publications: Benefits and Pensions Monitor (36475) • Home Improvement Retailing (36616)

Poynette Press
125 N Main
Poynette, WI 53955-0037
Phone: (608)635-2565
Fax: (608)846-5757

Publications: Poynette Press (34264)

PPA Publications & Events, Inc.
229 Peachtree St. NE, Ste. 2200
International Tower
Atlanta, GA 30303
Phone: (404)522-8600
Fax: (404)614-6406
Free: 800-339-5451

Publications: PEI Magazine (7036)

Practical Communications, Inc.
PO Box 183
Cary, IL 60013-9986
Phone: (847)639-2200
Fax: (847)639-9542

Publications: Outside Plant Magazine (8169) • Utility & Telephone Fleets (8171)

The Prague Times-Herald
1123 Broadway
PO Box U
Prague, OK 74864
Phone: (405)567-3933
Fax: (405)567-3934

Publications: The Prague Times-Herald (26048)

Prairie Catholic
1400 6th St. N
New Ulm, MN 56073-2099
Phone: (507)359-2966
Fax: (507)354-3667

Publications: Prairie Catholic (16214)

Prairie City News, Inc.
108 E Jefferson
Box 249
Prairie City, IA 50228
Phone: (515)994-2349
Fax: (515)994-3169

Publications: Prairie City News (11166)

Prairie Fire Press, Inc.
423-100 Arthur St.
Winnipeg, MB, Canada R3B 1H3
Phone: (204)943-9066
Fax: (204)942-1555

Publications: Prairie Fire (35349)

Prairie Grove Enterprise
PO Box 650
Prairie Grove, AR 72753
Phone: (501)846-2191
Fax: (479)824-2192

Publications: Prairie Grove Enterprise (1322)

Prairie Journal Trust
PO Box 61203
Calgary, AB, Canada T2L 2K6

Publications: The Prairie Journal of Canadian Literature (34654)

Prairie Media Inc.
201 Cottage Ave.
Box N
Cashmere, WA 98815
Phone: (509)782-3781
Fax: (509)548-4789

Publications: Cashmere Valley Record (32702)

Prairie Media, Inc.
215 14th St.
Leavenworth, WA 98826

Publications: The Leavenworth Echo (32809)

Prairie Pioneer
PO Box 218
Pollock, SD 57648
Phone: (605)889-2320
Fax: (605)889-2361

Publications: Prairie Pioneer (28929)

Prairie Post
PO Box 326
White City, KS 66872-0326
Phone: (785)349-5516
Fax: (785)349-5516
Free: 800-593-5516

Publications: Prairie Post (11878)

The Prairie Post
PO Box 1760
Jamestown, ND 58402-1760
Phone: (701)252-2796
Fax: (701)252-5751

Publications: The Prairie Post (24477)

Prairie Publications
1300 E Rushmore
PO Box 257
Brandon, SD 57005
Phone: (605)582-6025
Fax: (605)582-7184

Publications: Brandon Valley Challenger (28809)

Prairie State College
202 S Halsted St.
Chicago Heights, IL 60411
Phone: (708)709-3500
Fax: (708)755-2587

Publications: Prairie State College Student Review (8668)

Prakken Publications Inc.
3970 Varsity Dr.
PO Box 8623
Ann Arbor, MI 48107-8623
Phone: (734)975-2800
Fax: (734)975-2787
Free: 800-530-WORD

Publications: The Education Digest (14747) • Tech Directions (14770)

The Prarie Flyer II
PO Box 240
Bushell Park, SK, Canada S0H 0N0
Phone: (306)694-2256
Fax: (306)694-2851

Publications: The Prarie Flyer II (37454)

Pratfall
PO Box 8341
Universal City, CA 91608
Phone: (818)845-4048

Publications: Pratfall (3972)

The Pratt Tribune
320 S Main
Pratt, KS 67124
Phone: (620)672-5511
Fax: (620)672-5514

Publications: The Pratt Tribune (11764) • St. John News (11778)

Precambrian Press Publishers
141 Commercial Pl.
PO Box 887
Thompson, MB, Canada R8N 1N8
Phone: (204)677-4534
Fax: (204)677-3681

Publications: The Citizen (35300) • Thompson Nickel Belt News (35301)

Precast/Prestressed Concrete Institute
209 W Jackson Blvd., Ste. 500
Chicago, IL 60606-6938
Phone: (312)786-0300
Fax: (312)786-0353

Publications: PCI Journal (8527)

Precinct Reporter
1677 W Baseline St.
San Bernardino, CA 92411
Phone: (909)889-0597
Fax: (909)889-1706

Publications: Precinct Reporter (3089)

Precision Metalforming Association
6363 Oak Tree Blvd.
Independence, OH 44131-2500
Phone: (216)901-8800
Fax: (216)901-9190

Publications: Metalforming (25251)

Precision Shooting, Inc.
222 Mckee St.
Manchester, CT 06040
Phone: (860)645-8776
Fax: (860)643-8215

Publications: Precision Shooting (4938)

Prefin, Inc.
12 N 4th St.
Clear Lake, IA 50428
Phone: (515)357-2131
Fax: (515)357-2133

Publications: Clear Lake Reporter (10707) • The Clear Lake Reporter/Advertiser (10708)

Prehospital and Disaster Medicine
PO Box 55158
Madison, WI 53705-8958
Phone: (608)263-2063
Fax: (608)265-3037

Publications: Prehospital and Disaster Medicine (33970)

Premier Publishers Inc.
PO Box 330309
Fort Worth, TX 76163-0309
Fax: (817)293-3410

Publications: Book News & Book Business Mart (30330)

Premiere Publications
14531 Jefferson St.
Midway City, CA 92655
Phone: (714)893-0053
Fax: (714)893-5085

Publications: The Royal Spaniels (2539)

Prentiss Publishers, Inc.
PO Box 1257
Prentiss, MS 39474
Phone: (601)792-4221
Fax: (601)792-4222

Publications: The Prentiss Headlight (16827)

Presbyterian Church (U.S.A.)
100 Witherspoon St.
Louisville, KY 40202-1396
Phone: (502)569-5000
Fax: (502)569-5018
Free: 800-524-2612

Publications: Presbyterians Today (12235)

Presbyterian College
503 S. Broad St.
Clinton, SC 29325
Phone: (864)833-8281
Fax: (864)833-2820

Publications: Presbyterian College Magazine (28540)

Presbyterian Historical Society
425 Lombard St.
Philadelphia, PA 19147
Phone: (215)627-1852
Fax: (215)627-0509

Publications: The Journal of Presbyterian History (27547)

The Presbyterian Lay Committee
PO Box 2210, 136 Tremont Park Dr.
Lenoir, NC 28645
Phone: (828)758-8716
Fax: (828)758-0920

Publications: The Presbyterian Layman (24036)

The Presbyterian Outlook Foundation, Inc.
Box 85623
Richmond, VA 23285-5623
Phone: (804)359-8442
Fax: (804)353-6369
Free: 800-446-6008

Publications: The Presbyterian Outlook (32447)

Presbyterian Record Inc.
50 Wynford Dr.
Toronto, ON, Canada M3C 1J7
Phone: (416)441-1111
Fax: (416)441-2825
Free: 800-619-7301

Publications: Presbyterian Record (36714)

Presbyterian Synod of the Sun
1925 E Belt Line Rd., Ste. 220
Carrollton, TX 75006-5826
Phone: (817)382-9656
Fax: (817)383-8253
Free: 877-748-6777

Publications: The Presbyterian (30005)

Presbyterian Women in the Presbyterian Church (U.S.A.)
100 Witherspoon St.
Louisville, KY 40202-1396
Phone: (502)569-5379
Fax: (502)569-8085
Free: 888-728-7228

Publications: Horizons (12219)

Prescribing Reference, Inc.
114 W 26th St. Fl. 3
New York, NY 10001-6812
Phone: (646)638-6000
Fax: (646)638-6119

Publications: Monthly Prescribing Reference (22363)

Preservation Resource Center
923 Tchoupitoulas St.
New Orleans, LA 70130
Phone: (504)581-7032
Fax: (504)522-9275

Publications: New Orleans Preservation in Print (12747)

President & Prime Ministers
799 Roosevelt Rd., Bldg. 6, Ste. 208
Glen Ellyn, IL 60137
Phone: (630)858-6161
Fax: (630)858-8787

Publications: Presidents & Prime Ministers (8932)

Presque Newspaper
PO Box 176
Onaway, MI 49765-0176
Phone: (517)734-2105

Publications: The Onaway Outlook (15420) • Presque Isle County Advance (15421)

The Press
PO Box 300
Avon Lake, OH 44012
Phone: (440)933-5100
Fax: (440)933-7904

Publications: The Press (24640)

Press
Box 155
Floyd, VA 24091-0155
Phone: (540)745-2127
Fax: (540)745-2126

Publications: Press (32076)

The Press of Bryan-College Station
1729 Briarcrest Dr.
Bryan, TX 77802
Phone: (979)823-0088
Fax: (979)774-0053
Free: 800-299-7355

Publications: The Press of Bryan-College Station (29975)

Press Community Newspapers
5552 Cheviot Rd.
Cincinnati, OH 45247
Phone: (513)923-3111
Fax: (513)923-1806

Publications: The Bethel Journal (25321)

Press Community Newspapers
394 Wards Corner Rd.
Loveland, OH 45140
Phone: (513)248-8600
Fax: (513)248-1712

Publications: Clermont Community Journal (25322) • Community Journal (North) (25323) • Community Press of Mason (25324) • Forest Hills Journal-Press (25199) • Milford Advertiser-Press (25384)

The Press Democrat
427 Mendocino Ave.
PO Box 569
Santa Rosa, CA 95402
Phone: (707)546-2020
Fax: (707)546-2437
Free: 800-675-5056

Publications: The Press Democrat (3733)

The Press-Dispatch
PO Box 68
Petersburg, IN 47567
Phone: (812)354-8500
Fax: (812)354-2014

Publications: The Press-Dispatch (10400)

The Press-Enterprise Company
3512 Fourteenth St.
Riverside, CA 92501
Phone: (909)684-1200
Fax: (909)368-9020

Publications: Corona-Norco Independent (2641) • Lake Elsinore Valley Sun-Tribune (2940) • The Press-Enterprise (2943) • Rancho News (3842) • Sun City News (3824) • Valley Times (2600)

Press Enterprise Inc.
3185 Lackawanna Ave.
Bloomsburg, PA 17815-3398
Phone: (717)784-2121
Fax: (717)784-9226
Free: 800-228-3483

Publications: Press Enterprise (26718)

Press Gazette
531 SW Elva St.
Milton, FL 32570
Phone: (850)623-2120
Fax: (850)623-2007

Publications: Santa Rosa Free Press (6424) • Santa Rosa Press Gazette (6425)

Press Herald Publications Ltd.
304 Main St.
Box 309
Unity, SK, Canada S0K 4L0
Phone: (306)228-2267
Fax: (306)228-2767

Publications: Northwest Herald (37581) • The Wilkie Press (37595)

The Press, Inc.
PO Box 456
Ocheyedan, IA 51354
Phone: (712)758-3140
Fax: (712)758-3186

Publications: Ocheyedan Press and Melvin News (11121)

The Press Independent
PO Box 1919
Yellowknife, NT, Canada X1A 2P4

Publications: The Press Independent (35526)

Press Journal
PO Box 1268
Vero Beach, FL 32961
Phone: (561)562-2315
Fax: (561)978-2365

Publications: Press-Journal (6836)

Press Journal
PO Box 70
Strawberry Point, IA 52076
Phone: (563)933-4370
Fax: (563)933-4370

Publications: Press Journal (11253)

Press Journal Printing Corp.
3406 W Georgia
Louisiana, MO 63353-0466
Phone: (573)754-5566
Fax: (573)754-4749

Publications: The Louisiana Press-Journal (17256)

Press & Journal Publication
PO Box 310
20 S. Union St.
Middletown, PA 17057
Phone: (717)944-4628
Fax: (717)944-2083

Publications: Press & Journal (27260)

Press Media Group, L.L.C.
PO Box 519
Rustburg, VA 24588
Phone: (434)332-5728

Publications: The Lynchburg Ledger (32519)

Press-News Journal
130 N 4th St.
PO Box 227
Canton, MO 63435
Phone: (573)288-5668
Fax: (573)288-0000

Publications: Press-News Journal (16942)

Press Newspapers
204 Ballymore Rd.
PO Box 291
Springfield, PA 19064
Phone: (610)544-6660
Fax: (610)544-4530

Publications: Springfield Press (28012)

Numbers cited after listings are entry numbers rather than page numbers.

Press One Publishing
PO Box 563
Barnegat, NJ 08005
Phone: (609)660-0682
Fax: (609)660-1412
Free: 888-775-4410

Publications: DebtSmart (18663)

Press Publications
Box 10151, Grand Lake Sta.
Oakland, CA 94610
Phone: (510)428-2000

Publications: Piedmont Press (2843)

Press Publications
4779 Bloom Ave.
White Bear Lake, MN 55110
Phone: (651)407-1200
Fax: (651)429-1242

Publications: Quad Community Press (16510) • St. Croix Valley Press (16511) • Shoreview Press (16512) • Vadnais Heights Press (16514) • White Bear Press (16515)

Press Publications
PO Box 455
Ledgewood, NJ 07852-0455
Phone: (973)584-7176
Fax: (973)584-7176

Publications: Star Journal (19167)

Press Publications
26 Main St.
PO Box 637
Netcong, NJ 07857-1111
Fax: (908)362-9223

Publications: News-Leader (19323)

Press Publications, Inc.
PO Box 265
Belvidere, NJ 07823

Publications: News (18671)

Press Publishing Co.
3245 Garrett Rd.
Drexel Hill, PA 19026
Phone: (610)259-4141

Publications: Marcus Hook Press (26835) • Ridley Press (26921) • Upper Darby Press (26836) • Yeadon Times (28204)

Press Review
PO Box 368, Sta. A
Toronto, ON, Canada M5W 1C2
Phone: (416)368-0512
Fax: (416)366-0104

Publications: Press Review (36715)

The Press-Sentinel
PO Box 607
Jesup, GA 31545
Phone: (912)427-3757
Fax: (912)427-4092
Free: (866)427-3757

Publications: The Press-Sentinel (7347)

The Press & Standard
113 Washington St.
PO Box 1248
Walterboro, SC 29488
Phone: (843)549-2586
Fax: (843)549-2446

Publications: The Press and Standard (28781)

Presse-Ouest Ltee.
Box 190
St. Boniface, MB, Canada R2H 3B4
Phone: (204)237-4823
Fax: (204)231-1998
Free: 800-523-3355

Publications: La Liberte (35289)

Preston Citizen
77 S. State St.
PO Box 472
Preston, ID 83263-0472
Phone: (208)852-0155
Fax: (208)852-0158

Publications: Preston Citizen (7960)

Preston County Journal
110 W Main St.
PO Box 587
Kingwood, WV 26537
Phone: (304)329-0090
Fax: (304)329-2450
Free: 800-244-6872

Publications: Preston County Journal (33359)

Preston Publications
6600 W. Touhy Ave.
PO Box 48312
Niles, IL 60714
Phone: (847)647-2900
Fax: (847)647-1155

Publications: Boat and Motor Dealer (9286) • Journal of Analytical Toxicology (9287) • Journal of Chromatographic Science (9288) • Marina/Dock Age (9290) • Photo Techniques (9293)

Pretty Panda Publishing
PO Box 1345
Hunt Valley, MD 21030
Fax: (410)252-7232
Free: 800-417-7670

Publications: The Vintage and Classic Baseball Collector (13583)

Price County Publications
115 N. Lake Ave.
PO Box 170
Phillips, WI 54555
Phone: (715)339-3036
Fax: (715)339-4300

Publications: Phillips Bee (34239)

The Priest River Times
PO Box 10
Priest River, ID 83856
Phone: (208)448-2431
Fax: (208)448-2938

Publications: The Priest River Times (7962)

Priests of the Sacred Heart
6889 S Lovers Ln.
Hales Corners, WI 53130
Phone: (414)425-3383
Fax: (414)425-5719

Publications: Reign of the Sacred Heart (33769)

Primary Sources
PO Box 472, Cooper Sta.
New York, NY 10276-0472
Phone: (212)254-8748

Publications: Soviet Journal of Non-Ferrous Metals (22767) • Soviet Metal Technology (22768)

Prime
7116 Helen C. White Hall
Madison, WI 53706
Phone: (608)262-3262

Publications: Prime (33971)

Prime National Publishing Corp.
470 Boston Post Rd.
Weston, MA 02493
Phone: (781)899-2702
Fax: (781)899-4900

Publications: American Journal of Alzheimers Disease (14648) • American Journal of Hospice and Palliative Care (14649) • Healing Ministry (14650) • Journal of Healthcare Safety, Compliance & Infection Control (14651)

Prime Publishers, Inc.
PO Box 383
Southbury, CT 06488
Phone: (203)263-2116
Fax: (203)266-0199

Publications: Southbury Voices (5133) • Town Times (5201) • Voices (5237) • VOICES Sunday-Weekly Star (5238)

Prime Time Incorporated Newspapers
17400 Judson Rd.
San Antonio, TX 78247
Phone: (210)453-3300
Fax: (210)453-3300

Publications: Bulverde Community News (31027) • The Daily Commercial Recorder (31028) • Medical Gazette (31038) • Medical Gazette (31039) • Que Pasa San Antonio (31043)

Prime Time Publishing Co.
17400 Judson Rd.
San Antonio, TX 78247
Phone: (210)658-7424
Fax: (210)658-0390

Publications: Herald (31032)

Prime Times
185 Rte. 25A
Setauket, NY 11733-2858
Phone: (516)751-0356
Fax: (516)689-3077

Publications: Prime Times (23328)

Primedia
0326 Hwy. 133, Ste. 190
Carbondale, CO 81623
Phone: (970)963-9449
Fax: (970)963-9442
Free: 800-493-4569

Publications: Climbing Magazine (4216)

Primedia
5211 S. Washington Ave.
Titusville, FL 32780-7315
Phone: (321)269-3212
Fax: (321)267-1894

Publications: PhotoPro (6818) • Shutterbug (6819) • Shutterbug's Outdoor & Nature Photography (6820)

Primedia
260 Madison Ave., 8th Fl.
New York, NY 10016
Phone: (212)448-4500
Fax: (917)256-2282

Publications: Power and Motoryacht (22588)

Primedia
6405 Flank Dr.
Harrisburg, PA 17112
Phone: (717)540-6700
Fax: (717)657-9552

Publications: British Heritage (26984) • Country Journal (26989) • Fly Fisherman (26991)

PRIMEDIA Anaheim
2100 E Howell Ave., Ste. 209
Anaheim, CA 92806

Publications: Custom Classic Trucks (1404)

Primedia Business
6400 Hollis St., Ste. 12
Emeryville, CA 94608
Phone: (510)653-3307
Fax: (510)653-5142
Free: 800-541-7706

Publications: Electronic Musician (1877) • Mix (1879) • Mix—Edicion en Espanol (1880) • Remix (1881)

Primedia Business
5680 Greenwood Plaza Blvd., Ste. 100
Greenwood Village, CO 80111
Phone: (303)741-2901
Fax: (720)489-3101

Publications: Cable Avails (4504) • THE PRESS Magazine (4506)

Primedia Business
11 River Bend Dr. S.
PO Box 4949
Stamford, CT 06907-4949
Phone: (203)358-9900
Fax: (203)358-5834
Free: 800-776-1246

Publications: Catalog Age (5141) • Circulation Management (5142) • Customer Support Management (5147) • Direct (5148) • Fleet Owner (5150) • Folio (5151) • Operations and Fulfillment (5157) • PROMO (5158)

Primedia Business
6151 Powers Ferry Rd.
Atlanta, GA 30339
Phone: (770)955-2500
Fax: (770)618-0348

Publications: Access Control & Security Systems Integration (6959) • American City and County (6962) • Club Industry (6987) • Defense & Security Electronics (6999) • Health Management Technology (7014) • National Real Estate Investor (7030) • PENSION Management (7037) • Shopping Center

World (7042) • Swimming Pool/Spa Age (7048) • Textile World (7054) • Textile World Latina (7055) • Waste Age (7059) • Waste Age Product News (7060)

Primedia Business
29 N. Wacker Dr.
Chicago, IL 60606
Phone: (312)726-2802
Fax: (312)726-2574
Free: 800-621-9907

Publications: Paper, Film & Foil Converter (8526)

Primedia Business
PO Box 603
Indianapolis, IN 46206
Phone: (317)297-5500
Fax: (317)299-1356

Publications: American Trucker—Badger Edition (10081) • American Trucker—Buckeye Edition (10082) • American Trucker—California Edition (10083) • American Trucker—Cascade Edition (10084) • American Trucker—Central States Edition (10085) • American Trucker—Florida Edition (10086) • American Trucker—Illinois Edition (10087) • American Trucker—Indiana Edition (10088) • American Trucker—Kentucky/Tennessee Edition (10089) • American Trucker—Metro East Edition (10090) • American Trucker—Michigan Edition (10091) • American Trucker—Mid-Atlantic Edition (10092) • American Trucker—Minn/Dakota Truck Edition (10093) • American Trucker—Mountain America Edition (10094) • American Trucker—New England Edition (10095) • American Trucker—New York/Pennsylvania Edition (10096) • American Trucker—South Central Edition (10097) • American Trucker—Southern Edition (10098)

Primedia Business
9800 Metcalf Ave.
Overland Park, KS 66212
Phone: (918)341-1300
Fax: (918)967-1898

Publications: Adhesives Age (6960) • American Printer (11695) • Boxboard Containers (8289) • Broadcast Engineering (11699) • California-Arizona Farm Press (11701) • CEE News (11703) • Coal Age (11705) • Concrete Products (11707) • Electrical Construction and Maintenance (EC&M) (11708) • Electrical Wholesaling (11709) • Energy Manager (11710) • Engineering and Mining Journal (16074) • Entertainment Design (11711) • Entertainment Design Magazine (21608) • Grounds Maintenance (11713) • International Construction (11715) • Lighting Dimensions Magazine (22256) • Millimeter Magazine (11721) • Mobile Radio Technology (11722) • Retail Store Image (11728) • RF Design (11729) • Rock Products (8558) • Seguridad Latina (11730) • Sound & Video Contractor (11731) • Telephony (8581) • Transmission and Distribution World (11732) • Utility Business (11733) • Video Systems (11734) • Wearables Business (11735) • Wireless Review (11736) • World Broadcast Engineering (11737) • World Broadcast News (11738)

Primedia Business
PO Box 12901
Overland Park, KS 66212
Phone: (913)967-7453
Fax: (913)967-1901
Free: 800-654-6776

Publications: Automobile Red Book (11698)

Primedia Business
7900 International Dr., 3rd Fl.
Minneapolis, MN 55425-1510
Phone: (952)851-9329
Fax: (952)851-4601
Free: 800-722-5334

Publications: BEEF (16059) • Delta Farm Press (16073) • Farm Industry News (16079) • Hay & Forage Grower (16084) • National Hog Farmer (16113) • Southeast Farm Press (16129) • Southwest Farm Press (16130) • Soybean Digest (16132) • Western Farm Press (16139)

Primedia Business
249 W 17th St., 3rd Fl.
New York, NY 10011-5300
Phone: (212)462-3586
Fax: (212)206-3622

Publications: Registered Rep. (22642) • Trusts and Estates (22872)

Primedia Business Magazines & Media
9800 Metcalf Ave.
Overland Park, KS 66212
Phone: (913)341-1300
Fax: (913)967-1901
Free: (866)505-7173

Publications: American School & University (11696) • Home Care Magazine (11714) • PCIM Power Electronic Systems (11725) • Power Quality Assurance (11726) • Radio Magazine (11727)

Primedia Consumer Magazine Group
741 Corporate Circle, Ste. A
Golden, CO 80401
Phone: (303)278-1010
Fax: (303)277-0370

Publications: Sew News (4474)

PRIMEDIA Consumer Magazines
500 N. Dearborn, Ste. 1200
Chicago, IL 60610
Phone: (312)222-8999

Publications: Chicago Magazine (8316)

Primedia Enthusiast Group
2250 Newmarket Pkwy., Ste. 110
PO Box 721
Marietta, GA 30061-0741
Phone: (770)953-9222
Fax: (770)933-9510

Publications: Game & Fish Magazine (7412) • Georgia Sportsman (7413) • Michigan Sportsman (15292)

PRIMEDIA Enthusiast Group
260 Madison Ave., 8th Fl.
New York, NY 10016
Phone: (212)726-4300
Fax: (212)726-4310

Publications: CATS (23122) • In-Fisherman (15767)

Primedia Enthusiast Publications
6405 Flank Dr.
Harrisburg, PA 17112-2753
Phone: (717)540-6648
Fax: (717)657-9552

Publications: American History (26982) • Civil War Times Illustrated (26986)

PRIMEDIA Enthusiast Publications, Inc.
8745 Aero Dr., Ste. 105
San Diego, CA 92123
Phone: (858)694-0235
Fax: (858)694-8195

Publications: KITPLANES (3218)

Primedia Equine Group
656 Quince Orchard Rd., Ste. 600
Gaithersburg, MD 20878
Phone: (301)977-3900
Fax: (301)990-9015

Publications: Equus (13538)

Primedia History Group
6405 Flank Dr.
Harrisburg, PA 17112

Publications: MHQ (26998)

Primedia History Group
741 Miller Dr., Ste. D-2
Leesburg, VA 20175
Phone: (703)771-9400
Fax: (703)779-8345

Publications: Aviation History (32183) • Vietnam (32187)

Primedia Inc.
745 5th Ave.
New York, NY 10151
Phone: (212)745-0100
Fax: (212)745-0121

Publications: Snowboarder (22750)

Primedia Inc.
200 Madison Ave., 8th Fl.
New York, NY 10016
Phone: (212)726-4300

Publications: Automobile Magazine (14744) • New York Magazine (22446)

PRIMEDIA Los Angeles
6420 Wilshire Blvd.
Los Angeles, CA 90048
Phone: (323)782-2000

Publications: All About You (2205) • Car Craft (2233) • Chevrolet High Performance (2235) • Chevy Truck (2236) • Corvette Fever (2247) • Dirt Rider (2253) • Four Wheeler Magazine (2273) • Gun Dog (2283) • Guns & Ammo (2284) • Handguns (2286) • Home Theater (2293) • Hot Rod Magazine (2295) • JP (2305) • Kit Car (2306) • Mopar Muscle (2333) • Motor Trend (2334) • Motorcyclist (2336) • Muscle Car Review (2339) • Mustang & Fords (2340) • Mustang Monthly (2341) • Petersen's Bowhunting (2361) • Petersen's Circle Track (2362) • Petersen's 4 Wheel & Off Road (2363) • Petersen's Hunting (2364) • Petersen's Photographic Magazine (2365) • Shooting Times (9423) • Shotgun News (9425) • Skin Diver (2390) • Sport Truck (2405) • Super Ford (2408) • TEEN (2410) • Truck Trend (2416) • Wildfowl (2436) • Wing & Shot (2438)

Primedia Publishing
249 W. 17th St., 3rd Fl.
New York, NY 10011
Phone: (212)462-3300
Fax: (212)367-8332

Publications: American Baby (21179)

Primedia Special Interest Publication
260 Madison Ave., 8th Fl.
New York, NY 10016
Phone: (212)726-4300

Publications: Crafts Magazine (21510) • HandGunning (21788) • McCall's Needlework (80)

Primedia Special Interest Publications
260 Madison Ave., 8th Fl.
New York, NY 10016
Phone: (212)726-4300
Fax: (212)726-4310

Publications: Colored Stone (26823) • Lapidary Journal (26824)

PRIMEDIA Special Interest Publications, Inc.
98 N. WA St.
Boston, MA 02114
Phone: (617)720-8600
Fax: (617)723-0911

Publications: SAIL (13956)

Primedia Youth Entertainment Group
470 Park Ave. S.
New York, NY 10016
Phone: (212)684-9340
Fax: (212)532-3148

Publications: Tiger Beat Magazine (22835)

PrimeTime Newspaper
PO Box 205
Coos Bay, OR 97420-0022
Phone: (541)267-6587
Fax: (541)267-6587

Publications: Prime Time (26271)

Prince Albert Daily Herald
30 10th St. E.
PO Box 550
Prince Albert, SK, Canada S6V 5R9
Phone: (306)764-4276
Fax: (306)763-3331
Free: 800-667-8245

Publications: Prince Albert Daily Herald (37517)

Princeton Alumni Weekly
194 Nassau St., Ste.38
Princeton, NJ 08542
Phone: (609)258-4885
Fax: (609)258-2247

Publications: Princeton Alumni Weekly (19469)

Princeton Packet Inc.
Royal Plaza Center, Rte. 130 S.
Hightstown, NJ 08520
Phone: (609)448-2100
Fax: (609)448-8044

Publications: The Messenger-Press (18875)

The Princeton Packet, Inc.
300 Witherspoon St.
PO Box 350
Princeton, NJ 08542-3477
Phone: (609)924-3244
Fax: (609)924-3842

Publications: Central Post (18776) • Central Post Tempo (19380) • Cranbury Press (19458) • Franklin News Record (19460) • Hopewell Valley News (19124) • The Lawrence Ledger (19162) • The Princeton Packet (19471) • Tempo-Mercer (18861)

The Princeton Packet, Inc.
307 Omni Dr.
Somerville, NJ 08876
Phone: (908)359-0850
Fax: (908)359-3930

Publications: The Manville News (19464)

Princeton Publishing Inc.
100 N Gibson
PO Box 30
Princeton, IN 47670
Phone: (812)385-2525
Fax: (812)386-6199
Free: 800-467-5130

Publications: Gibson County Today (10408) • Oakland City Journal (10381) • Oakland City Journal Dollar Saver (10382) • Princeton Daily Clarion (10409)

Princeton Scientific Publishing Company Inc.
1108 Kingston Rd.
Princeton, NJ 08540-4132
Phone: (609)252-0814

Publications: International Journal of Occupational Medicine, Immunology and Toxicology (19462)

Princeton Theological Seminary
PO Box 821
Princeton, NJ 08542
Phone: (609)497-7714
Fax: (609)497-7870

Publications: Theology Today (19474)

Princeton University
22 Chambers St., Ste. 201
Princeton, NJ 08544
Phone: (609)258-3601
Fax: (609)258-1301

Publications: Princeton Weekly Bulletin (19472)

Princeton University Press
41 William St.
Princeton, NJ 08540
Phone: (609)258-4900
Fax: (609)258-6305

Publications: Philosophy & Public Affairs (19467)

Print Shack
499 Federal Rd.
Brookfield, CT 06804
Phone: (203)775-4515
Fax: (203)775-0180

Publications: ROTA.GENE (4729)

Printers Inc.
PO Box 187
Wagner, SD 57380
Phone: (605)384-5616
Fax: (605)384-5955

Publications: The Wagner Post and Announcer (29014)

Printers and Publishers
200 E Clay St.
PO Box 327
Whitewater, WI 53190
Phone: (262)473-3363
Fax: (262)473-5635

Publications: Palmyra Enterprise (34232) • Whitewater Register (34458)

Printing & Publishing, Inc.
109 W. Washington St.
Millstadt, IL 62260
Phone: (618)233-0145
Fax: (618)476-1616

Publications: Kansas City Commerce (9197) • Meat Business Magazine (9198)

Printing & Publishing Ltd.
PO Box 400
PO Box 310
Beansville, ON, Canada L3M 4G5
Phone: (905)945-9264
Fax: (905)945-0540

Publications: The Grimsby Independent (35671)

Priority News, Inc.
103 W 7th Ave.
Havana, FL 32333
Fax: (904)539-0454

Publications: Havana Herald (6185)

Prism Publications, Inc.
148 E Front St.
Traverse City, MI 49684
Phone: (231)941-8174
Fax: (231)941-8391
Free: 800-678-3416

Publications: Traverse, Northern Michigan's Magazine (15603)

Prison Legal News
2400 NW 80th St., No. 148
Seattle, WA 98117-4449
Phone: (206)246-1022
Fax: (206)505-9449

Publications: Prison Legal News (33006)

Pritchartt Publishing Co.
PO Box 427
Collierville, TN 38027-0427
Phone: (901)853-2241
Fax: (901)853-8507

Publications: The Collierville Herald (29133)

PRO-ED Inc.
8700 Shoal Creek Blvd.
Austin, TX 78757
Phone: (512)451-3246
Fax: (512)302-9129
Free: 800-897-3202

Publications: Communication Disorders Quarterly (29769) • Focus on Autism and Other Developmental Disabilities (11526) • Intervention in School and Clinic (32017) • Journal of Disability Policy Studies (29786) • Journal of Emotional and Behavioral Disorders (8736) • Journal of Learning Disabilities (6945) • Journal of Positive Behavior Interventions (29790) • The Journal of Special Education (29465) • Remedial and Special Education (RASE) (32209) • Topics in Early Childhood Special Education (11534)

Pro Football Weekly
302 Saunders Rd., No. 100
Riverwoods, IL 60015-3897
Phone: (847)940-1100
Fax: (847)940-1108
Free: 800-331-7529

Publications: Pro Football Weekly (9508)

Pro Group
PO Box 6585
Englewood, CO 80155

Publications: Farm Supply Retailing (4413)

Pro-Life Action League
6160 N Cicero Ave.
Chicago, IL 60646
Phone: (773)777-2900
Fax: (773)777-3061

Publications: Pro-Life Action News (8539)

Pro Quest Information and Learning
PO Box 1346
Ann Arbor, MI 48106-1346
Phone: (734)761-4700
Fax: (734)761-3940
Free: 800-521-0600

Publications: UMI's Banking Information Index (12241)

Pro Tooner
PO Box 2270
Daly City, CA 94017-2270
Phone: (650)755-4827
Fax: (650)755-4827

Publications: Pro Tooner (1804)

Processed World
1095 Market St., No. 210
San Francisco, CA 94103

Publications: Processed World (3416)

Proctor Journal
215 5th St.
Proctor, MN 55810
Phone: (218)624-3344
Fax: (218)624-7037

Publications: Proctor Journal (16289)

Producers Masterguide
60 E 8th St., 34th Fl.
New York, NY 10003-6514
Phone: (212)777-4002
Fax: (212)777-4101

Publications: Producers Masterguide (22598)

Production Update Magazine
7021 Hayvenhurst Ave., 205
Van Nuys, CA 91406
Phone: (818)785-6362
Fax: (818)785-8092

Publications: Update Magazine (3996)

Productions Tel-Art
7383 rue de la Roche
Montreal, QC, Canada H2R 2T4
Phone: (514)274-6124
Fax: (514)272-5939

Publications: Le Magazine Jeunesse (37168)

Profane Existence
PO Box 8722
Minneapolis, MN 55408
Phone: (612)558-4359

Publications: Profane Existence (16124)

Professional Convention Management Association
2301 S. Lake Shore Dr., Ste. 1001
Chicago, IL 60616-1419
Phone: (312)423-7262
Fax: (312)423-7222
Free: 877-827-7262

Publications: Convene (8343)

Professional Engineers of North Carolina
111 N Boylan Ave.
Raleigh, NC 27603-1422
Phone: (919)832-7333
Fax: (919)832-7311

Publications: The Professional Engineer (24150)

Professional Engineers Ontario
25 Sheppard Ave. W., Ste. 1000
Toronto, ON, Canada M2N 6S9
Phone: (416)224-1100
Fax: (416)224-8168
Free: 800-339-3716

Publications: Engineering Dimensions (36583)

Professional Ethics
PO Box 15017
Gainesville, FL 32604
Phone: (352)475-1608

Publications: Professional Ethics (6153)

Professional Independent Insurance Agents of Illinois
4360 Wabash Ave.
Springfield, IL 62707
Phone: (217)793-6660
Fax: (217)793-6744
Free: 800-628-6436

Publications: Insurance Insight (9634)

Professional Media Group LLC
36 Clipper Ct., Ste. B
Mystic, CT 06355-2138

Publications: Matrix: The Magazine for Leaders in Higher Education (4969)

Professional Media Group, LLC
488 Main Ave.
Norwalk, CT 06851
Phone: (203)663-0100
Fax: (203)663-0149

Publications: University Business (5079)

Professional Musicians, Local 47
817 N Vine St.
Los Angeles, CA 90038
Phone: (323)462-2161
Fax: (323)466-1289

Publications: Overture (2355)

Professional Opticians of Florida
1947 Greenwood Dr.
Tallahassee, FL 32303-4825
Phone: (850)201-2622
Fax: (850)201-2625

Publications: Focal Point (6721)

Professional Photographers of America, Inc.
229 Peachtree St. NE, Ste. 2200
Atlanta, GA 30303
Phone: (404)522-8600
Fax: (404)614-6405
Free: 800-786-6277

Publications: Professional Photographer Storytellers (7039)

Professional Resource Publishing, Inc.
PO Box 126
Girard, KS 66743
Phone: (316)724-4426
Fax: (316)724-4493

Publications: The Girard Press (11460)

Professional Rodeo Cowboys Association, Inc.
101 Prorodeo Dr.
Colorado Springs, CO 80919
Phone: (719)593-8840

Publications: Prorodeo Sports News (4255)

Professional Staff Congress
City University of New York
25 W. 43rd St.
New York, NY 10036
Phone: (212)302-1653

Publications: P S C Clarion (22516)

Professional Surveyors Publishing Co., Inc.
100 Tuscanny Dr., Ste. B1
Frederick, MD 21702
Phone: (301)682-6101
Fax: (301)682-6105

Publications: Professional Surveyor (13520)

Professional and Technical Consultants Association
PO Box 78008
San Francisco, CA 94107-8008
Phone: (408)971-5902
Fax: (408)999-0344
Free: 800-747-2822

Publications: Consulting Rates and Business Practices Annual Survey (3345)

Professional Tennis Registry
PO Box 4739
Hilton Head Island, SC 29938
Phone: (843)785-7244
Fax: (843)686-2033
Free: 800-421-6289

Publications: TennisPro (28662)

Program for Appropriate Technology in Health
1455 NW Leary Way
Seattle, WA 98107-5136
Phone: (206)285-3500
Fax: (206)285-6619

Publications: Outlook (32999)

The Progress
PO Box A
Christopher, IL 62822
Phone: (618)724-9423
Fax: (618)724-9510

Publications: The Progress (8672)

Progress
206 E. Locust St.
PO Box 291
Clearfield, PA 16830
Phone: (814)765-5581
Fax: (814)765-5165

Publications: The Progress (26788)

The Progress
Box 100
Anahuac, TX 77514
Phone: (409)267-6131
Fax: (409)267-4157

Publications: The Progress (29722)

The Progress
Box 848
Three Rivers, TX 78071
Phone: (361)786-3022
Fax: (361)786-3671

Publications: The Progress (31191)

Progress-Examiner
233 S 2nd St.
PO Box 225
Orleans, IN 47452
Phone: (812)865-3242
Fax: (812)865-3242

Publications: Progress-Examiner (10384)

The Progress-Index Extra
15 Franklin St
Petersburg, VA 23803
Phone: (804)732-3456
Fax: (804)861-9452

Publications: The Progress-Index Extra (32331)

Progress Newspapers, Inc.
1102 Churchill Rd.
Glenside, PA 19038
Phone: (215)836-5398

Publications: Far Northeast Citizen Sentinel (27060)

Progress Newspapers, Inc.
390 Easton Rd.
Horsham, PA 19044-2532
Phone: (215)368-8600
Fax: (215)836-5398

Publications: Bucks County Telegraph (26831) • Bucks County Tribune (26919) • Hatboro Progress (27027) • Progress of Montgomery County (27062)

Progress in Paper Recycling
18 Woodbury Ct.
Appleton, WI 54913-7111
Phone: (920)832-9101
Fax: (920)832-0870

Publications: Progress in Paper Recycling (33543)

Progress Publishing Co., Inc.
131 S Main St.
PO Box 460
Dawson Springs, KY 42408
Phone: (502)797-3271
Fax: (502)797-3271

Publications: The Dawson Springs Progress (12042)

Progress Publishing Co., Ltd.
Suite 200-1865 Marine Dr.
West Vancouver, BC, Canada V7V 1J7
Phone: (604)922-6717
Fax: (604)922-1739

Publications: Harbour & Shipping (35238)

Progress Review
313 Main St.
La Porte City, IA 50651
Phone: (319)342-2429
Fax: (319)342-2433

Publications: Progress Review (11022)

The Progressive
409 E Main St.
Madison, WI 53703
Phone: (608)257-4626
Fax: (608)257-3373

Publications: The Progressive (33972)

Progressive Communication Corp.
18 E. Vine
Mount Vernon, OH 43050
Phone: (614)397-5333
Fax: (614)397-1321
Free: 800-772-5333

Publications: Fairfield Leader (25189) • Mt. Vernon News (25399)

Progressive Engineer
2049 Crossroads Dr.
Lewisburg, PA 17837-9001
Phone: (570)568-8444

Publications: Progressive Engineer (27192)

Progressive Era
PO Box 100
Camden, AL 36726
Phone: (334)682-4422
Fax: (334)682-5163

Publications: Wilcox Progressive Era (143)

Progressive Labor Party
105 W. 28th St., Rm. 301
New York, NY 10001-6103

Publications: Challenge New York (21394)

The Progressive Populist
PO Box 487
Storm Lake, IA 50588
Phone: (712)732-4991
Free: 800-732-4992

Publications: The Progressive Populist (29798)

Progressive Publishers
PO Box 218
Pageland, SC 29728
Phone: (843)672-2358
Fax: (843)672-5593

Publications: The Pageland Progressive-Journal (28739)

The Progressor-Times
1198 E Findlay St.
PO Box 37
Carey, OH 43316
Phone: (419)396-7567
Fax: (419)396-7527

Publications: The Progressor-Times (24741)

Project HOPE
7500 Old Georgetown Rd., Ste. 600
Bethesda, MD 20814-6133
Phone: (301)656-7401
Fax: (301)654-2845

Publications: Health Affairs (13341)

Project Innovation
1362 Santa Cruz Ct.
Chula Vista, CA 91910-7114
Phone: (619)421-9377

Publications: Education (1714)

Project Innovation of Mobile
Spring Hill Sta.
PO Box 8508
Mobile, AL 36689-0508
Phone: (251)343-1878
Fax: (251)343-1878

Publications: College Student Journal (318) • Reading Improvement (329)

Project on Linguistic Analysis
2222 Piedmont Ave.
Berkeley, CA 94720
Phone: (510)642-5937
Fax: (510)841-7205

Publications: Journal of Chinese Linguistics (1532)

Project Management Institute
4 Campus Blvd.
Newtown Square, PA 19073-3299
Phone: (610)356-4600
Fax: (610)356-4647

Publications: PM Network (27330) • Project Management Journal (27332)

Project Ploughshares
57 Erb St. W
Waterloo, ON, Canada N2L 6C2
Phone: (519)888-6541
Fax: (519)888-0018

Publications: Ploughshares Monitor (36857)

Proleptic, Inc.
1101 Broad St.
Oriental, NC 28571
Phone: (252)249-3414
Fax: (252)249-3409

Publications: Shop Talk! (24110)

Numbers cited after listings are entry numbers rather than page numbers.

Promociones Tyson, S.A. de C.V.
7770 Regents Rd., No. 113-387
San Diego, CA 92122
Phone: (858)569-0172
Fax: (858)755-3569

Publications: Los Cabos Magazine (3226)

Promotional Products Association of Canada Inc.
4920 Ouest de Maisonneuve W., Ste. 305
Westmount, QC, Canada H3Z 1N1
Phone: (514)489-5359
Fax: (514)489-7760
Free: 800-489-8741

Publications: The Image News (37443)

Promotional Products Association International
3125 Skyway Circle N.
Irving, TX 75038
Phone: (972)258-3104
Fax: (972)258-3012

Publications: Promotional Products Business (30607)

Properties Magazine
PO Box 112127
Cleveland, OH 44111
Phone: (216)251-0035
Fax: (216)251-0064
Free: 888-641-4241

Publications: Properties Magazine (24945)

Prophetstown Echo
342 Washington St.
PO Box 7
Prophetstown, IL 61277
Phone: (815)537-5107
Fax: (815)537-2658

Publications: The Prophetstown Echo (9470)

Prospect-News
Box 367
Doniphan, MO 63935
Phone: (573)996-2103
Fax: (573)996-2217

Publications: Prospect-News (17036)

Protec Publishing
PO Box 404
Spencer, IN 47460
Phone: (812)829-1640
Fax: (812)829-1489
Free: 800-783-1639

Publications: Indiana Builder Magazine (10470)

Providence Association of Ukrainian Catholics in America
817 N. Franklin St.
Philadelphia, PA 19123
Phone: (215)627-4984
Fax: (215)238-1933

Publications: America (27369)

Providence Business News
300 Richmond St. Ste. 202
Providence, RI 02903
Phone: (401)273-2201
Fax: (401)274-0270

Publications: Providence Business News (28414)

Providence College
549 River Ave.
Providence, RI 02918-0001
Phone: (401)865-1000
Fax: (401)865-2822

Publications: The Cowl (28393)

The Providence Journal Co.
75 Fountain St.
Providence, RI 02902-0050
Phone: (401)277-7000
Fax: (401)277-7889

Publications: The Providence Journal (28415)

The Providence Visitor
184 Broad St.
Providence, RI 02903
Phone: (401)272-1010
Fax: (401)421-8418

Publications: The Providence Visitor (28417)

The Provincetown Advocate
PO Box 977
Provincetown, MA 02657-0977
Phone: (617)487-1170
Fax: (508)487-3878

Publications: The Provincetown Advocate (14485)

Provincetown Arts Inc.
650 Commercial St.
Provincetown, MA 02657
Phone: (508)487-3167
Fax: (508)487-4791

Publications: Provincetown Arts (14486)

ProvPhoenix
150 Chestnut St.
Providence, RI 02903
Phone: (401)273-6397
Fax: (401)273-0920

Publications: Providence Phoenix (28416)

PRR, Inc.
48 South Service Rd.
Melville, NY 11747-2335
Phone: (631)777-3800
Fax: (631)777-8700

Publications: Oncology (21052) • Primary Care & Cancer (21059)

Prufrock Press
100 N 6th St.
Waco, TX 76701
Phone: (254)756-3337
Fax: (254)756-3339
Free: 800-998-2208

Publications: Creative Kids (31245) • Gifted Child Today Magazine (31247) • Journal for the Education of the Gifted (29275) • Journal of Secondary Gifted Education (8865)

Pryor Publications, Inc.
Drawer 40
Fitzgerald, GA 31750
Phone: (912)423-9331
Fax: (912)423-6533

Publications: The Herald-Leader (7272)

Pryor Publishing Co.
PO Box 308
Pryor, OK 74362
Phone: (918)825-3292
Fax: (918)825-1965

Publications: Times (26049)

PSExtreme
1175 Chess Dr., E
Foster City, CA 94404
Phone: (415)372-0942
Fax: (415)372-0753

Publications: PSExtreme (1934)

PSP Communications
705 W. White St.
Champaign, IL 61820
Phone: (217)359-2633
Fax: (217)359-2744
Free: 888-777-2321

Publications: Austin Lawyer (29761) • IHRIM.LINK (8188)

PSP Sports
355 Lexington Ave.
New York, NY 10017
Phone: (212)697-1460
Fax: (212)286-8154

Publications: College Hoops Illustrated (21439) • NBA Hoop (22412) • NBA Inside Stuff (22413) • Touchdown Illustrated (22848)

Psy-Ed Corporation
65 E. Rte. 4
River Edge, NJ 07661
Phone: (201)489-4111
Fax: (201)489-0074
Free: 800-E-PARENT

Publications: Exceptional Parent (19507)

Psychiatric Rehabilitation Journal
940 Commonwealth Ave.
Boston, MA 02215
Phone: (617)353-3549
Fax: (617)353-9209

Publications: Psychiatric Rehabilitation Journal (13953)

Psychoanalytic Books, Inc.
211 E 70th St.
New York, NY 10021
Phone: (212)628-8792
Fax: (212)628-8453

Publications: Psychoanalytic Books (22602)

The Psychoanalytic Quarterly
670 Berry Ave.
Los Altos, CA 94024
Phone: (650)941-5420
Fax: (650)941-5420

Publications: The Psychoanalytic Quarterly (2195)

Psychology and Education
PO Box 7487, SCSU
Orangeburg, SC 29117
Phone: (803)836-7133
Fax: (803)536-8492

Publications: Psychology and Education (28732)

Psychonomic Society, Inc.
1710 Fortview Rd.
Austin, TX 78704
Phone: (512)462-2442
Fax: (512)462-1101

Publications: Animal Learning and Behavior (29754) • Behavior Research Methods, Instruments, & Computers (29763) • Cognitive, Affective, & Behavioral Neuroscience (29768) • Memory & Cognition (29792) • Perception & Psychophysics (29796) • Psychonomic Bulletin & Review (29800)

Psychosocial Press
59 Boston Post Rd.
PO Box 1524
Madison, CT 06443-1524
Phone: (203)245-4000
Fax: (203)245-0775
Free: 800-835-2487

Publications: Journal of Imago Relationship Therapy (4934)

Public Communications, Inc.
PO Box 4233
Ithaca, NY 14852-4233
Phone: (801)991-7656

Publications: 14850 Magazine (20812)

Public Policy Center of New Jersey
36 W Lafayette St.
Trenton, NJ 08608-2011
Phone: (609)392-2003
Fax: (609)392-1770

Publications: New Jersey Reporter (19663)

The Public Record
PO Box 2724
Palm Springs, CA 92263-2724
Phone: (760)416-9709
Fax: (760)416-9690

Publications: The Public Record (2766)

Public Relations Society of America (PRSA)
33 Irving Pl.
New York, NY 10003-2376
Phone: (212)995-2230
Fax: (212)995-0757

Publications: Public Relations Tactics (22609)

Public Relations Strategist
33 Irving Pl.
New York, NY 10003
Phone: (212)995-2230
Fax: (212)995-0757

Publications: Public Relations Strategist (22608)

Public Risk Management Association (PRIMA)
1815 Ft. Myer Dr., Ste. 1020
Arlington, VA 22209-1805
Phone: (703)528-7701
Fax: (703)528-7966

Publications: Public Risk (31821)

Public Service Research Foundation
320 D Maple Ave. E
Vienna, VA 22180
Phone: (703)242-3575
Fax: (703)242-3579

Publications: Government Union Review (32578)

Public Utilities Reports Inc.
8229 Boone Blvd., Ste. 401
Vienna, VA 22182
Phone: (703)847-7720
Fax: (703)917-0964
Free: 800-368-5001

Publications: Public Utilities Fortnightly (32580) •
Public Utilities Fortnightly (32581)

Public Works Journal Corp.
PO Box 688
200 S. Broad St.
Ridgewood, NJ 07451
Phone: (201)445-5800
Fax: (201)445-5170
Free: 800-524-2364

Publications: Public Works (19503)

Publication Management Inc.
4350 DiPaolo Ctr.
Glenview, IL 60025
Phone: (847)699-1706
Fax: (847)699-1703

Publications: Finishers' Management (8934)

Publications BLD
4388 rue Saint-Denis, Bureau 304
Montreal, QC, Canada H2J 2L1
Phone: (514)844-4388
Fax: (514)844-8407

Publications: Les Debrouillards (37176)

Publications and Communications, Inc.
11675 Jollyville Rd., Ste. 201
Austin, TX 78759
Phone: (512)250-9023
Fax: (512)331-3900
Free: 800-678-9724

Publications: Austin Home and Living (29760) •
Cisco World (29767) • The HP Chronicle (31248) •
Severworld (29804) • UNISYS World (31255)

Publications Dumont Inc.
262 Boul L' Industrie
Joliette, QC, Canada J6E 8Z1
Fax: (514)759-9828

Publications: Le Regional de Lanaudiere-Jolliette
Journal (37011)

Publications, Inc.
500 3rd Ave. SE
Cedar Rapids, IA 52401
Phone: (319)399-5900
Fax: (319)399-5918

Publications: Penny Saver (10676)

Publications, Inc.
1801 2nd St., Ste. 100
Coralville, IA 52241
Phone: (319)339-3100
Fax: (319)339-3112

Publications: The Community News Advertisers
(10971)

Publications for Industry
21 Russell Woods Rd.
Great Neck, NY 11021
Phone: (516)487-0990
Fax: (516)487-0809

Publications: American Industry (20685) • Industrial
Purchasing Agent (20689)

Publications International Ltd.
7373 N. Cicero Ave.
Lincolnwood, IL 60712-1613
Phone: (847)676-3470
Fax: (847)676-3671
Free: 800-745-9299

Publications: Collectible Automobile (9091) • Consumer Guide (9092)

Publications Le Peuple, Inc.
45 Rue. Desjardins
Levis, QC, Canada G6V 5V3
Phone: (418)833-9398
Fax: (418)833-8177

Publications: Le Peuple Tribune (37049)

Publications Le Peuple, Inc.
1000, rue St-Joseph
C.P. 130, Laurier Sta.
Quebec, QC, Canada G0S 1N0
Phone: (418)728-2131
Fax: (418)728-4819

Publications: Le Peuple de Lotbiniere (37289)

Publications Rousseau & Associe
2938, Terrasse Abenaquis
Longueuil, QC, Canada J4M 2B3
Phone: (450)448-2220
Fax: (450)448-1041

Publications: Le Garagiste (37054)

Publications Voyageur, Inc.
20 Ste-Anne Rd.
Sudbury, ON, Canada P3C 5N4
Phone: (705)673-3377
Fax: (705)673-5854
Free: (866)688-7027

Publications: Journal Le Voyageur (36416)

Publicom, Inc.
2800 E. Fort Lowell Rd.
Tucson, AZ 85716
Phone: (520)323-6144
Fax: (520)323-7412

Publications: Water Conditioning & Purification
(972)

Publicom Inc.
CP 365 Pl. D'Armes
Montreal, QC, Canada H2Y 3H1
Phone: (514)274-0004
Fax: (514)274-5884

Publications: Meetings Monthly (37185) • Spa Destinations (37225) • Spa Management (37226)

Publik Enema
25686 Nugget
El Toro, CA 92630

Publications: Public Enema (1870)

PubliPresse Inc.
11 Notre-Dame de Lourdes
C.P. 219
Ville-Marie, QC, Canada J0Z 3W0
Phone: (819)629-2618
Fax: (819)629-2661

Publications: Le Temiscamien (37437)

Publishers Development Corp.
591 Camino de la Reina, Ste. 200
San Diego, CA 92108
Phone: (619)297-5350
Fax: (619)297-5353
Free: 800-537-3006

Publications: American Handgunner (3111) • Guns
Magazine (3165) • Shooting Industry (3274)

Publishers Weekly
360 Park Avenue S.
New York, NY 10010
Phone: (646)746-6758
Fax: (646)746-6631
Free: (866)436-0727

Publications: Publishers Weekly (22610)

Publishing Board
Box 1120
Steinbach, MB, Canada R0A 2A0
Phone: (204)326-6790
Fax: (204)326-6302

Publications: Die Mennonitische Post (35295)

Publishing and Business Consultants
4427 W Slauson Ave.
Los Angeles, CA 90043-2717

Publications: The American Senior (2209) • Busi-
ness Concepts (2228) • Credit & Finance (2248) •
Current Employment (2249) • The Economic Home
Owner (2259) • Government Programs (2280) •
Health Diet & Nutrition (2287) • Innovation and Ideas
(2296) • Motor World (2335) • National Auctions and
Sales (2342) • PBC Federal Tax Guide (2359) •
Situations Digest (2389) • Soldiers Today (2391) •
U.S. Immigration (2421) • The World & Science
(2441)

Publishing Concepts Corp.
3243 Hwy. 61 E
Luttrell, TN 37779
Phone: (865)992-3892
Fax: (865)992-5259

Publications: Marine Fish Monthly (29336)

**The Publishing House Div of Colorado
  Word Works, Inc.**
7380 Lowell Blvd.
PO Box 215
Westminster, CO 80036
Phone: (303)428-9529
Fax: (303)430-1676

Publications: Denver Arts Center Programs (4662)

Publius: The Journal of Federalism
002 Kirby Hall Of Civil Rights
Lafayette College
Easton, PA 18042-1785
Phone: (610)330-5598
Fax: (610)330-5648

Publications: Publius: The Journal of Federalism
(26851)

Puckerbrush Press
76 Main St.
Orono, ME 04473
Phone: (207)866-4868

Publications: Puckerbrush Review (13003)

Pudding House Publications
81, Shadymere Lane
Columbus, OH 43213
Phone: (614)986-1881

Publications: Pudding Magazine (25057)

The Pueblo Chieftain
PO Box 4040
Pueblo, CO 81003
Phone: (719)544-3520
Fax: (719)546-3235

Publications: The Pueblo Chieftain (4599)

Pueblo Publishers, Inc.
7122 N. 59th Ave.
Glendale, AZ 85301
Phone: (623)842-6000
Fax: (623)842-6017

Publications: The Glendale Star (713) • Peoria
Times (769) • Thunderbolt (716)

Puerto Rican Catholic Conference
Apartado 41305 Est Minillas Stn.
San Juan, PR 00940-1305
Phone: (787)728-3710
Fax: (787)286-1748

Publications: El Visitante de Puerto Rico (28293)

Pulaski Citizen
308 W College St.
PO Box 905
Pulaski, TN 38478
Phone: (615)363-3544
Fax: (615)363-4319

Publications: Pulaski Citizen (29572)

Pulaski County Journal
PO Box 19
Winamac, IN 46996
Phone: (574)946-6628
Fax: (574)946-7471

Publications: Pulaski County Journal (10564)

Pulaski Publishing
PO Box 905
Pulaski, TN 38478
Phone: (615)363-4548
Fax: (615)363-4319

Publications: Giles Free Press (29571)

Pulitzer
1586 Barber Green Rd.
PO Box 587
DeKalb, IL 60115
Phone: (815)756-4841
Fax: (815)756-2079
Free: 877-688-4841

Publications: The Daily Chronicle (8734)

Pulitzer Community Newspapers
830 Petaluma Blvd. N
PO Box 1091
Petaluma, CA 94953
Phone: (707)762-4541
Fax: (707)765-1707

Publications: Petaluma Argus-Courier (2836)

Pulitzer Inc.
900 N. Tucker Blvd.
PO Box 717
St. Louis, MO 63101
Phone: (314)340-8000
Fax: (314)340-3125

Publications: The Daily Herald (17431)

Pullano Publications Inc.
PO Box 98
Berrien Springs, MI 49103-0098
Phone: (616)473-5421
Fax: (616)471-1362

Publications: The Journal Era (14812)

Pulp & Paper
55 Hawthorne, Ste. 600
San Francisco, CA 94105
Phone: (866)271-8525

Publications: Pulp and Paper (3419)

Pulp and Paper Technical Association of Canada
740 Notre Dame W., Ste. 810
Montreal, QC, Canada H3C 3X6
Phone: (514)392-6963
Fax: (514)392-0369

Publications: Journal of Pulp & Paper Science (37145)

Pulsus Group, Inc.
2902 S. Sheridan Way
Oakville, ON, Canada L6J 7L6
Phone: (905)829-4770
Fax: (905)829-4799

Publications: The Canadian Journal of Cardiology (Journal Canadien de Cardiologie) (36137) • Canadian Journal of Clinical Pharmacology (36138) • The Canadian Journal of Gastroenterology (36139) • The Canadian Journal of Plastic Surgery (36140) • Canadian Respiratory Journal (36141)

Punch In Syndicate
400 E 59th St., Ste. 9F
New York, NY 10022

Publications: Travel, Food & Wine (22857)

Puncture Publications
PO Box 14806
Portland, OR 97293
Phone: (503)777-4611

Publications: Puncture (26503)

Purdue Alumni Association, Inc.
Union Bldg.
West Lafayette, IN 47906-6212
Phone: (765)494-5182
Fax: (765)494-9179
Free: 800-414-1541

Publications: Purdue Alumnus (10551)

Purdue University
500 Oval Dr.
West Lafayette, IN 47907-2038
Phone: (765)494-3783
Fax: (765)494-3780

Publications: Modern Fiction Studies (10550) • Sycamore Review (10554)

Purdue University Press
509 Harrison St.
West Lafayette, IN 47907
Phone: (765)494-2038
Fax: (765)496-2442
Free: 800-247-6553

Publications: Anthrozoos (10544)

Putman Media
555 W. Pierce Rd., Ste. 301
Itasca, IL 60143
Phone: (630)467-0052
Fax: (630)467-1109

Publications: Chemical Processing (9009) • Control (9010) • Control Ad-Lits (9011) • Control Isa Show Reporter (9012) • Food Processing (9014) • Plant Services (9015) • Processing (9016)

Putnam County News & Recorder
86 Main St.
PO Box 185
Cold Spring, NY 10516
Phone: (845)265-2468
Fax: (845)265-2144

Publications: Putnam County News & Recorder (20483)

Putnam County Press
PO Box 608
Mahopac, NY 10541
Phone: (845)628-8400
Fax: (845)628-8400

Publications: Beacon Light (20139) • Brewster Times (20242) • Carmel Times (20436) • East Fishkill Record (20544) • Fishkill Standard (20601) • La Grange Independent (20866) • Mahopac Press (20980)

Putnam County Sentinel
PO Box 149
Ottawa, OH 45875
Phone: (419)523-5709
Fax: (419)523-3512

Publications: Putnam County Sentinel (25452)

Putnam Printing Co., Inc.
PO Box 4027
Eatonton, GA 31024
Phone: (706)485-3501
Fax: (706)485-4166
Free: 888-485-3501

Publications: The Eatonton Messenger (7264) • Messenger Plus (7265)

Puxico Weekly Press
PO Box 277
Puxico, MO 63960
Phone: (573)222-3243
Fax: (573)222-6327

Publications: Puxico Weekly Press (17367)

Pyramid Design, Inc.
PO Box 382
Salisbury, MD 21803-0382
Phone: (410)546-6388
Fax: (410)546-6387

Publications: The Metropolitan Magazine (13710)

Pyramid Publishing
49 W Main
Mount Pleasant, UT 84647
Phone: (435)462-2134
Fax: (435)462-2459
Free: 888-821-1672

Publications: The Pyramid (31372) • The Pyramid Shopper (31373)

Pyx Press
PO Box 922648
Sylmar, CA 91392-2648

Publications: Avatar (3835) • Magic Realism (3836) • Strike Through The Mask (3837) • A Theater of Blood (3838)

Q-Notes
4037 E Independence Blvd., Ste. 611
Charlotte, NC 28205
Phone: (704)531-9988
Fax: (704)531-1361

Publications: Q-Notes (23751)

QRW Publishing
24 Garfield Ave.
Winchester, MA 01890
Phone: (781)729-7132
Fax: (781)721-0572

Publications: The Quarterly Review of Wines (14666)

QST Publications, Inc.
905 Rucker Blvd.
PO Box 1536
Enterprise, AL 36331
Phone: (334)393-2969
Fax: (334)393-2987

Publications: Daleville Sun Courier (200) • The Southeast Sun (202)

Quad-City Times
500 E. 3rd St.
PO Box 3828
Davenport, IA 52801

Publications: Quad-City Times (10738)

QUAD County Printing
615 E Lyons
Marissa, IL 62257
Phone: (618)295-2812
Fax: (618)295-3422

Publications: Journal-Messenger (9149)

Quad River News
12634 Noble Rd.
Sheridan, MO 64486
Phone: (660)799-3735

Publications: Quad River News (17580)

Quadrant Healthcom
26 Main St.
Chatham, NJ 07928
Phone: (973)701-2719
Fax: (973)701-8894

Publications: CUTIS (18728)

Quadrant HealthCom Inc.
26 Main St.
Chatham, NJ 07928-2402
Phone: (973)701-8900
Fax: (973)701-8894

Publications: The American Journal of Anesthesiology (18725) • The American Journal of Orthopedics (18726) • The Female Patient (18729) • Hospital Therapy (18730) • P & T (18731) • Physicians' Travel & Meeting Guide (18732)

Quail Unlimited, Inc.
PO Box 610
Edgefield, SC 29824
Phone: (803)637-5731
Fax: (803)637-0037

Publications: Quail Unlimited (28601)

Quality Publishing
523 N. Sam Houston Pkwy. E., Ste. 300
Houston, TX 77060

Publications: OfficeSolutions (30512)

Quanah Tribune-Chief
310 Mercer St.
Quanah, TX 79252
Phone: (940)663-5333
Fax: (940)663-5073

Publications: Quanah Tribune-Chief (30963)

Quantum Graphics CFB Edmonton
PO Box 10500
Edmonton, AB, Canada T0A 2H0
Phone: (403)457-8481
Fax: (403)457-8406

Publications: Sealandair (34728)

Quarry Press
PO Box 1061
Kingston, ON, Canada K7L 4Y5
Phone: (613)548-8429
Fax: (613)548-1556

Publications: Poetry Canada (35941)

Quarter Century Wireless Association, Inc. (QCWA)
159 E. 16th St.
Eugene, OR 97401
Phone: (541)683-0987
Fax: (541)683-4181

Publications: QCWA News (26332)

The Quarterly
50 Baldwin St., Ste. 100
Toronto, ON, Canada M5T 1L4
Phone: (416)977-7187
Fax: (416)861-8804

Publications: The Quarterly (22617)

Quarto Communications
54 S. Patrick St.
Toronto, ON, Canada M5T 1V1
Phone: (416)599-2000
Fax: (416)599-0800
Free: 800-465-6183

Publications: Cottage Life (36563) • explore (36588)

Quartz Hill Journal of Theology
43543 51st St. W.
Quartz Hill, CA 93536
Phone: (661)722-0891
Fax: (661)943-3484

Publications: Quartz Hill Journal of Theology (2868)

Quatrone
410 1/2 Morris Ave.
Spring Lake, NJ 07762-1320

Publications: Passaic Review (19594)

Quebec Chronicle-Telegraph
3484 chemin Sainte Foy
Ste.-Foy, QC, Canada G1X 1S8
Phone: (418)650-1764
Fax: (418)650-5172

Publications: Quebec Chronicle Telegraph (37338)

Quebec Dans Le Monde
Case postale 8503
Ste.-Foy, QC, Canada G1V 4N5
Phone: (418)659-5540
Fax: (418)659-4143

Publications: Agenda (37334) • Quebec Info (37339)

Quebec Farmers' Advocate
PO Box 80
Ste.-Anne-de-Bellevue, QC, Canada H9X 3L4
Phone: (514)457-2010
Fax: (514)398-7972
Free: 800-363-7869

Publications: Quebecs Farmers Advocate (37328)

Quebec Federation of Home and School Associations
3285 Cavendish Blvd., Ste. 560
Montreal, QC, Canada H4B 2L9
Phone: (514)481-5619
Fax: (514)481-5610
Free: 888-808-5619

Publications: Quebec Home & School News (37211)

Quebec Science Inc.
4388 Saint-Denis St. 300
Montreal, QC, Canada H2J 2L1
Phone: (514)843-6888
Fax: (514)843-4897
Free: 800-667-4444

Publications: Quebec Science (37213)

Quebecor Inc.
100 Water St.
PO Box 637
Campbellton, NB, Canada E3N 3H1
Phone: (506)753-7637
Fax: (506)759-7738

Publications: L'Aviron (35382)

Quebecor Inc.
500, De La Madone
Mont-Laurier, QC, Canada J9L 1S5
Phone: (819)623-5250
Fax: (819)623-7148

Publications: L'Echo de la Lievre (37074)

Quebecor Media
465 Mcgill St.
Montreal, QC, Canada H2Y 2G1
Phone: (514)393-1010
Fax: (514)393-3173

Publications: Montreal Mirror (37189)

Quedecor
1107, rue de Saint-Jouite
Mont-Tremblant, QC, Canada J8E 3J9
Phone: (819)425-8658
Fax: (819)425-7713

Publications: L'Information du Nord L'Annonciation (37075) • L'Information de Ste. Agathe (37076)

Queens County Bar Association
65-32 183 St.
Flushing, NY 11365
Phone: (718)291-4500
Fax: (718)657-1789

Publications: Queens Bar Bulletin (20610)

Queens Gazette
4216 34th Ave.
Astoria, NY 11101-1110
Phone: (718)361-6161
Fax: (718)784-7552

Publications: Queens Gazette (20102)

Queens Herald Corp.
137-05 Cross Bay Blvd.
Ozone Park, NY 11417
Phone: (718)845-3221
Fax: (718)738-7645

Publications: Forum of Queens (23072)

Queen's Journal
272 Earl St.
Kingston, ON, Canada K7L 2H8
Phone: (613)533-2800
Fax: (613)533-6728

Publications: Queen's Journal (35945)

Queens Publishing Corp.
41-02 Bell Blvd., 2nd Fl.
Bayside, NY 11361
Phone: (718)229-0300
Fax: (718)225-7117

Publications: The Bayside Times (20138) • The Flushing Times (20608) • The Forest Hills Ledger (20616) • The Fresh Meadows Times (20628) • The Glen Oaks Ledger (20666) • The Laurelton Times (20939) • The Little Neck Ledger (20953) • The Queens Village Times (23170) • The Richmond Hill Times (23188) • The Whitestone Times (23581)

Queen's Quarterly
Queen's University
Kingston, ON, Canada K7L 3N6
Phone: (613)533-2667
Fax: (613)533-6822

Publications: Queen's Quarterly (35946)

Queen's University
Dept. of Alumni Affairs
Summerhill Bldg.
Kingston, ON, Canada K7L 3N6
Phone: (613)533-2060
Fax: (613)533-6828
Free: 800-267-7837

Publications: Queen's Alumni Review (35944)

Queen's University
Kingston, ON, Canada K7L 3N6
Phone: (613)533-2083
Fax: (613)533-6522

Publications: Revue Frontenac/Frontenac Review (35947)

Queen's University Engineering Society
Queen's University
Kingston, ON, Canada K7L 3N6
Phone: (613)533-3051
Fax: (613)533-6678

Publications: Golden Words (35936)

Queensmith Communications Corp.
3014 Colvin St.
Alexandria, VA 22314
Phone: (703)370-0606
Fax: (703)370-7082
Free: 800-222-3212

Publications: Professional Pilot (31728)

Queue Inc.
1450 Barnum Ave.
Bridgeport, CT 06610
Free: 800-232-2224

Publications: Renaissance Magazine (14342)

Quill & Quire
70 The Esplanade, Ste. 210
Toronto, ON, Canada M5E 1R2
Phone: (416)360-0044
Fax: (416)955-0794
Free: 800-757-6177

Publications: Quill & Quire (36721)

Quill and Scroll Society
University of Iowa
School of Journalism & Mass Communication
W312 Seashore Hall
Iowa City, IA 52242-1528
Phone: (319)335-5795
Fax: (319)335-5210

Publications: Quill & Scroll (10986)

Robin L. Quillon
122 W Spencer St.
PO Box 111
Culpeper, VA 22701
Phone: (540)825-0771
Fax: (540)825-0778

Publications: Culpeper Star-Exponent (31987)

The Quincy Sun Publishing Co., Inc.
1372 Hancock St.
Quincy, MA 02169
Phone: (617)471-3100
Fax: (617)472-3963

Publications: Sun (14492)

Quinn Publishing
PO Box 750
Fort Washington, PA 19034
Phone: (215)643-6385
Fax: (215)628-6571

Publications: Find the Word (26649)

Quintessence Publishing Company Inc.
551 Kimberly Dr.
Carol Stream, IL 60188-1881
Phone: (630)682-3223
Fax: (630)682-3288
Free: 800-621-0387

Publications: Journal of Orofacial Pain (8146) • QDT (8153) • Quintessence International (8154)

Quirk Enterprises, Inc.
PO Box 23536
Minneapolis, MN 55423-0536
Phone: (952)854-5101
Fax: (952)854-8191

Publications: Quirk's Marketing Research Review (16125)

Quitman
PO Box 312
Adel, GA 31620
Phone: (912)896-2233
Fax: (912)896-7237

Publications: Adel News-Tribune (6899) • Quitman Free Press (6900)

Quiz Graphic Arts, Inc.
305 S 16th St.
Ord, NE 68862
Phone: (308)728-3262
Fax: (308)728-5715

Publications: The Ord Quiz (18236)

The Quoddy Tides
123 Water St.
PO Box 213
Eastport, ME 04631
Phone: (207)853-4806
Fax: (207)853-4095

Publications: The Quoddy Tides (12954)

Quota International
1420 21st St. NW
Washington, DC 20036
Phone: (202)331-9694
Fax: (202)331-4395

Publications: Quotarian (5757)

R & B Publishing Co.
526 S Conkling St.
Baltimore, MD 21224
Phone: (410)732-6600
Fax: (410)732-6336

Publications: The Baltimore Guide (13133)

R/C Modeler Corp.
144 W Sierra Madre Blvd.
PO Box 487
Sierra Madre, CA 91024-2435
Phone: (626)355-1476
Fax: (626)355-6415

Publications: Freshwater & Marine Aquarium Magazine (3765) • R/C Modeler (3766)

R & W Publishing, Inc.
PO Box 3275
Evansville, IN 47731
Phone: (812)425-2210
Fax: (812)422-4984

2598

Numbers cited after listings are entry numbers rather than page numbers.

Publications: Indiana Journal of Commerce & Industry (9934)

R.A. Rapaport Publishing, Inc.
150 W 22nd St.
New York, NY 10011
Phone: (212)989-0200
Fax: (212)989-4786

Publications: Diabetes Self-Management (21549) • Practical Diabetology (22590)

RAAA National Office
4201 N. Interstate 35
Denton, TX 76207
Phone: (940)387-3502
Fax: (940)383-4036

Publications: American Red Angus (30232)

The Rabbinical Assembly
3080 Broadway
New York, NY 10027
Phone: (212)280-6065
Fax: (212)749-9166

Publications: Conservative Judaism (21485)

Rabbit Creek Journal
PO Box 309
Clipper Mills, CA 95930
Phone: (530)675-2270
Fax: (530)675-0415

Publications: Rabbit Creek Journal (1729)

Racher Press, Inc.
220 5th Ave.
New York, NY 10001-7798
Phone: (212)213-6000
Fax: (212)725-4594

Publications: Chain Drug Review (21391) • MMR (22340)

Racing Wheels
3617 NE 51st St., Apt. 4
Vancouver, WA 98661-2355
Phone: (360)892-5590
Fax: (360)892-8021
Free: 888-892-2574

Publications: Racing WHEELS Newspaper (33178)

Radcliffe Institute for Advanced Study
10 Garden St.
Cambridge, MA 02138
Phone: (617)495-8601
Fax: (617)495-8422

Publications: Radcliffe Quarterly (14095)

Raddle Moon Press
518-350 E. Second Ave.
Vancouver, BC, Canada V5T 4R8

Publications: Raddle Moon (35161)

Radford University
PO Box 6985
Radford, VA 24142-5905
Phone: (540)831-6724
Fax: (540)831-6725

Publications: The Tartan (32347)

Radiance
4788 Heyer Ave., Apt. B
Castro Valley, CA 94546
Phone: (510)885-1505

Publications: Radiance (1678)

Radiant City Publications, LLC
800 S Valley View
Las Vegas, NV 89107
Phone: (702)990-2419
Fax: (702)990-2424

Publications: Las Vegas Weekly (18376)

Radical Pedagogy
Department of Sociology
University of Southern Colorado
2200, Bonforte Blvd.
Pueblo, CO 81001
Phone: (719)549-2416
Fax: (719)549-2705

Publications: Radical Pedagogy (4600)

Radio and Records, Inc.
10100 Santa Monica Blvd., 3rd Fl.
Los Angeles, CA 90067-4004
Phone: (310)553-4330
Fax: (310)203-8727

Publications: Radio & Records (2375)

Radio-Television News Directors Association
1600 K St. NW, No. 700
Washington, DC 20006
Phone: (202)659-6510
Fax: (202)223-4007
Free: 800-807-8632

Publications: Communicator (5426)

Radiological Society of North America
820 Jorie Blvd.
Oak Brook, IL 60523-2251
Phone: (630)571-2670
Fax: (630)571-7837

Publications: RadioGraphics (9363)

RadTech International North America
60 Revere Dr., Ste. 500
Northbrook, IL 60062
Phone: (847)480-9576
Fax: (847)480-9282

Publications: RadTech Report (9321)

The Radville Star
129 Main St.
PO Box 370
Radville, SK, Canada S0C 2G0
Phone: (306)869-2202
Fax: (306)869-2533

Publications: The Radville Star (37523)

The Rafu Shimpo
259 S. Los Angeles St.
Los Angeles, CA 90012
Phone: (213)629-2231
Fax: (213)687-0737

Publications: The Rafu Shimpo (2376)

David Rago
333 N. Main St.
Lambertville, NJ 08530
Phone: (609)397-4104
Fax: (609)397-9377
Free: 888-847-6464

Publications: Modernism Magazine (19159)

Railway & Locomotive Historical Society
PO Box 517
Urbana, IL 61803-0517
Phone: (217)333-0568

Publications: Railroad History (9716)

Rain Crow Publishing
PO Box 11013
Chicago, IL 60611-0013
Phone: (773)562-5786

Publications: Rain Crow (8547)

Rain, Inc.
PO Box 30097
Eugene, OR 97403
Fax: (541)465-9192

Publications: Rain Magazine (26333)

Rainbow Publications, Inc.
24715 Rockefeller
PO Box 918
Santa Clarita, CA 91355
Phone: (805)257-4066
Fax: (805)257-3028
Free: 800-423-2874

Publications: Black Belt Magazine (3678)

Rains County Leader
PO Box 127
Emory, TX 75440
Phone: (903)473-2653
Fax: (903)473-0050

Publications: Rains County Leader (30307)

Rainy River Record
312 3rd St.
Box 280
Rainy River, ON, Canada P0W 1L0
Phone: (807)852-3366
Fax: (807)852-4434

Publications: Rainy River Record (36338)

Raivaaja Publishing Co.
PO Box 600
Fitchburg, MA 01420-0054
Phone: (978)343-3822
Fax: (978)343-8147

Publications: Pioneer (14183)

Ralls County Herald Enterprise
PO Box 426
New London, MO 63459
Phone: (573)985-5531
Fax: (573)985-5531

Publications: Ralls County Herald-Enterprise (17314)

Ralph
PO Box 93627
Vancouver, BC, Canada V6E 4L7
Phone: (604)654-2929
Fax: (604)654-1993

Publications: Ralph (35162)

Ram Press
PO Box 2060
Key Largo, FL 33037
Phone: (305)451-3287
Fax: (305)453-0255

Publications: Catamaran Sailor (6252)

RAM Publications, Inc.
1810 W. Fifth St.
Montgomery, AL 36106-1516
Phone: (334)265-7323
Fax: (334)265-7320

Publications: Montgomery Independent (370)

RAM Publishing Group
610 Colonial Park Dr.
Roswell, GA 30075-3746
Phone: (770)587-0311
Fax: (770)642-8874
Free: 800-878-0311

Publications: Over the Road (7515)

Ramp Publishing Group
610 Colonial Park Dr.
Roswell, GA 30075-3746
Phone: (770)587-0311
Fax: (770)642-8874

Publications: Pro Trucker (7517)

Ramsey News-Journal
217 S Superior St.
PO Box 218
Ramsey, IL 62080-0218
Phone: (618)423-2411
Fax: (618)423-2514

Publications: Ramsey News-Journal (9484)

Ranch Publishing
PO Box 2678
San Angelo, TX 76902
Phone: (915)655-4434
Fax: (915)658-8250

Publications: Meat Goat Monthly News (31006)

Ranch & Rural Living Magazine
PO Box 2678
San Angelo, TX 76902
Phone: (915)655-4434
Fax: (915)658-8250

Publications: Ranch & Rural Living Magazine (31008)

Ranchland News
115 Sioux Ave.
PO Box 307
Simla, CO 80835-0307
Phone: (719)541-2288
Fax: (719)541-2289

Publications: Ranchland News (4627)

Rancho Santa Ana Botanic Garden
1500 N. College Ave.
Claremont, CA 91711
Phone: (909)625-8767
Fax: (909)626-7670

Publications: Aliso (1723)

RAND
1700 Main St.
PO Box 2138
Santa Monica, CA 90407-2138
Phone: (310)393-0411
Fax: (310)451-7069

Publications: RAND Journal of Economics (3714) • RAND Review (3715)

Randall Publishing Co.
3200 Rice Mine Rd. N.E.
Tuscaloosa, AL 35406
Phone: (205)349-2990
Fax: (205)349-4174
Free: 800-633-5953

Publications: Equipment World Magazine (487) • NATSO Truckers News (489) • Trucking Co. (491)

Randall Publishing Inc.
1425 Lunt Ave.
Elk Grove Village, IL 60007
Phone: (847)437-6604
Fax: (847)437-6618

Publications: Gear Technology (8832)

The Randolph Guide
431 S. Fayetteville St.
PO Box 1044
Asheboro, NC 27204-1044
Phone: (336)625-5576
Fax: (336)625-1228

Publications: The Randolph Guide (23622)

Randolph-Macon Woman's College
2500 Rivermont Ave.
Lynchburg, VA 24503
Phone: (434)947-8000
Fax: (434)947-8323

Publications: Randolph-Macon Woman's College Alumnae Bulletin (32208) • The Sundial (32210)

The Randolph Register
220 Main St.
PO Box 98
Randolph, NY 14772
Phone: (716)358-2921
Fax: (716)358-5695

Publications: The Randolph Register (23176)

Random Lengths, Inc.
PO Box 731
San Pedro, CA 90733-0731
Phone: (310)519-1442
Fax: (310)832-1000
Free: 800-643-7746

Publications: Random Lengths/Harbor Independent News (3595)

Randy DeCur & Assoc.
PO Box 383
Marksville, LA 71351
Phone: (318)253-5413
Fax: (318)253-7223

Publications: Louisiana Roots (12674)

The Range-Ledger
PO Box 684
Cheyenne Wells, CO 80810
Phone: (719)767-5615
Fax: (719)767-5113

Publications: The Range-Ledger & Cheyenne Records (4232)

Range Magazine
PO Box 639
Carson City, NV 89702-0639
Phone: (775)884-2200
Fax: (775)884-2213
Free: 800-RANGE-4U

Publications: Range Magazine (18331)

Range Times
PO Box 169
Biwabik, MN 55708
Phone: (218)865-6265
Fax: (218)865-7007

Publications: Biwabik Times (15752)

The RangeFinder Publishing Co., Inc.
1312 Lincoln Blvd.
PO Box 1703
Santa Monica, CA 90406
Phone: (310)451-8506
Fax: (310)395-9058

Publications: The RangeFinder (3716)

Rangely Times
713 E Main
PO Box 460
Rangely, CO 81648
Phone: (970)675-5033
Fax: (970)675-8709

Publications: Rangely Times (4613)

The Ranger Publishing Co., Inc.
Box 98801
Tacoma, WA 98498
Phone: (253)581-4218
Fax: (253)581-5962

Publications: The Ranger (33149)

Rankin County News
PO Box 107
Brandon, MS 39043
Phone: (601)825-8333
Fax: (601)825-8334

Publications: Rankin County News (16575)

Rankin Publishing
118 E Main St.
PO Box 130
Arcola, IL 61910
Phone: (217)268-4959

Publications: Arcola Record Herald (8018) • Broom Brush and Mop (8019)

Rannie Printing and Publishing
PO Box 3044
St. Catharines, ON, Canada L2R 7E3
Phone: (905)948-3144
Fax: (905)957-0055

Publications: West Lincoln Review (36398)

Rannie Publications, Ltd.
91 Geneva St.
St. Catharines, ON, Canada L0R 1B0

Publications: Lincoln Post Express (35670)

Ransom County Gazette
PO Box 473
Lisbon, ND 58054-0473
Phone: (701)683-4128
Fax: (701)683-4129

Publications: Ransom County Gazette (24493)

Rapid City Journal
507 Main St.
PO Box 450
Rapid City, SD 57701
Phone: (605)394-8383
Fax: (605)394-8463
Free: 800-843-2300

Publications: Rapid City Journal (28931)

Rapid Intellect Group Inc.
PO Box 131
Stuyvesant Falls, NY 12174
Phone: (518)372-1347

Publications: Academic Exchange Quarterly (23379)

Rapid Publishing
349 W Compton
PO Box 4248
Compton, CA 90224
Phone: (310)635-6776

Publications: Carson Bulletin (1746) • Compton Bulletin (1747) • Inglewood Tribune (2073) • Lynwood Journal (2486) • Wilmington Beacon (4090)

Rappahannock Press, Inc.
PO Box 549
Urbanna, VA 23175
Phone: (804)758-2328
Fax: (804)758-5896
Free: 800-758-2329

Publications: Southside Sentinel (32572)

Rapport Publishing Co., Inc.
8128 Gould Ave.
Los Angeles, CA 90046-1960
Phone: (213)660-0433
Fax: (213)664-0434
Free: 800-397-1266

Publications: Rapport (2377)

Rare Breeds Journal
PO Box 66
Crawford, NE 69339
Phone: (308)665-1431
Fax: (308)665-1931

Publications: Rare Breeds Journal (17990)

Rare Reminders
222 Dividend St.
Rocky Hill, CT 06067-0289
Phone: (860)563-9386
Fax: (860)563-4688

Publications: The Trinity Tripod (5107)

Raritan
31 Mine St.
New Brunswick, NJ 08903
Phone: (732)932-7887
Fax: (732)932-7855

Publications: Raritan (19337)

The Raton Range
208 S 3rd St.
PO Box 1068
Raton, NM 87740
Phone: (505)445-2721
Fax: (505)445-2723
Free: 800-748-2722

Publications: The Raton Range (19910)

Ravalli Republic
232 Main St.
Hamilton, MT 59840
Phone: (406)363-3300
Fax: (406)363-3569

Publications: Post Script (17807) • Ravalli Republic (17808)

Ravellette Publications, Inc.
PO Box 309
Kadoka, SD 57543
Phone: (605)837-2259

Publications: Kadoka Press (28877)

Ravellette Publishing
Box 465
Murdo, SD 57559
Phone: (605)669-2271
Free: 800-705-1165

Publications: The Murdo Coyote (28909)

Ravellette Publishing, Inc.
Box 788
Philip, SD 57567-0788
Phone: (605)859-2516
Fax: (605)859-2410

Publications: Pioneer Review (28914)

Raven Chronicles
Richard Hugo House
1634 11th Ave.
Seattle, WA 98122-2419

Publications: Raven Chronicles (33011)

The Ravenna News
322 Grand Ave.
PO BOX 110
Ravenna, NE 68869
Phone: (308)452-3411
Fax: (308)452-3511

Publications: The Ravenna News (18254)

The Rawlins County Square Deal
114 S. Fourth St.
PO Box 371
Atwood, KS 67730
Phone: (785)626-3600
Fax: (785)626-9299

Publications: The Rawlins County Square Deal (11348)

2600

Numbers cited after listings are entry numbers rather than page numbers.

Rawlins Newspapers, Inc.
6th & Buffalo
PO Box 370
Rawlins, WY 82301
Phone: (307)324-3411
Fax: (307)324-2797
Free: 800-541-3411

Publications: Daily Times (34572)

Ray Publishing, Inc.
4891 Independence St., Ste. 270
Wheat Ridge, CO 80033
Phone: (303)467-1776
Fax: (303)467-1777

Publications: Composites Technology (4673) •
High-Performance Composites (4676)

The Raymond News
PO Box 200
Raymond, IL 62560
Phone: (217)229-3421
Fax: (217)532-3632

Publications: The Raymond News (9490)

The Raymond-Prinsburg News
204 Spicer Ave.
PO Box 157
Raymond, MN 56282
Phone: (320)967-4244
Fax: (320)967-4244

Publications: The Raymond-Prinsburg News
(16291)

**Raymondville Chronicle and Willacy
County News**
PO Box 369
Raymondville, TX 78580
Phone: (512)689-2421
Fax: (210)689-6575

Publications: Raymondville Chronicle and Willacy
County News (30970)

Rayne Acadian Tribune
108 N Adams Ave.
PO Box 260
Rayne, LA 70578
Phone: (337)334-3186
Fax: (337)334-8474

Publications: Tribune Plus (12802)

The Rayne Independent Newspaper
201 East South 1st St.
PO Box 428
Rayne, LA 70578
Phone: (318)334-2128
Fax: (318)334-2120

Publications: The Rayne Independent (12801)

RB Publishing Co.
2901 International Ln., Ste. 200
Madison, WI 53704-3177
Phone: (608)241-8777
Fax: (608)241-8666

Publications: MAST (Mailing Systems Technology)
(33961)

RBC Ministries
PO Box 2222
Grand Rapids, MI 49501-2222
Phone: (616)942-6770
Fax: (616)957-5741

Publications: Our Daily Bread (15099)

R.C. Publications, Inc.
PO Box 150278
Altamonte Springs, FL 32715-0278
Phone: (407)265-2947
Fax: (407)265-2948

Publications: Florida Plumbing Prospective (5899) •
Ohio Perspective (5901) • Wisconsin Perspective
(5903)

RCM Enterprises Inc.
PO Box 14268
St. Paul, MN 55114-0268
Phone: (651)523-0666
Fax: (651)523-0665
Free: 800-451-9278

Publications: Marine Textiles (16386) • Midwest
Players (16389) • Upholstery Journal (16412)

RCP Publications Inc.
PO Box 3486
Chicago, IL 60654
Phone: (773)227-4066

Publications: The Revolutionary Worker (8556)

Reach Out Magazine
3090 Sheridan St., Ste. 207
Hollywood, FL 33021
Phone: (954)985-0319
Fax: (954)985-0483

Publications: Reach Out Magazine (6197)

Reader's Digest
1100 Rene-Levesque Blvd. W
Montreal, QC, Canada H3B 5H5
Phone: (514)940-0751
Fax: (514)940-7338
Free: 888-459-3333

Publications: Reader's Digest Magazine (37214) •
Selection du Reader's Digest (Canadian-French Edition) (37223)

Reader's Digest Association Inc.
Reader's Digest Rd.
Pleasantville, NY 10570-7000
Phone: (914)238-1000
Fax: (914)238-4559
Free: 800-431-1726

Publications: Reader's Digest (23112)

**Reader's Guide to the Underground
Press**
537 Jones St., PMB 2386
San Francisco, CA 94102

Publications: Reader's Guide to the Underground
Press (3420)

Real American Newspaper Corp.
PO Box 840
Leakey, TX 78873
Phone: (830)232-5204
Fax: (830)232-5630

Publications: Real American (30680)

Real Change
2129 2nd Ave.
Seattle, WA 98121
Phone: (206)441-3247
Fax: (206)441-8847

Publications: Real Change (33012)

Real Data Corp.
103 Bay St.
Manchester, NH 03104-3007
Phone: (603)669-3822
Fax: (603)645-0072
Telex: real-data.com

Publications: The Registry Review (18563)

Real Detroit Weekly, L.L.C.
359 Livernois, 2nd Fl.
Ferndale, MI 48220
Phone: (248)591-7325
Fax: (248)544-9893

Publications: Real Detroit Weekly (15030)

Real Estate Center
2115 TAMU
College Station, TX 77843-2115
Phone: (979)845-2031
Fax: (979)845-0460
Free: 800-244-2144

Publications: Tierra Grande (30055)

Real Estate Media Inc.
520 Eighth Ave., 17th Fl.
New York, NY 10018
Phone: (212)929-6900
Fax: (212)929-7124

Publications: Real Estate Forum (22632) • Real
Estate New York (22633)

Real Estate News
15 Kern Rd.
Toronto, ON, Canada M3B 1S9
Phone: (416)443-8113
Fax: (416)443-9185

Publications: Real Estate News (36722)

Real Estate News Corp.
3525 W Peterson, Ste. 103
Chicago, IL 60659
Phone: (773)866-9900
Fax: (773)866-9906

Publications: Inland Architect (8414)

Real Estate Northwest
PO Box 402
Edmonds, WA 98020-0402
Phone: (360)638-0196
Fax: (360)638-0196

Publications: Real Estate Northwest (32745)

The Real Girls Papers
2519 Galbreth Rd.
Pasadena, CA 91109-3436
Phone: (510)433-2830

Publications: The REAL Girls Papers (2826)

Realty and Building Inc.
111 N Wabash, Ste. 1120
Chicago, IL 60602-2012
Phone: (312)467-1888
Fax: (312)467-0225

Publications: Realty and Building (8552)

Realty Publications Inc.
1485 Spruce, Ste. H
PO Box 20069
Riverside, CA 92516
Phone: (909)781-7300
Fax: (909)781-4721

Publications: First Tuesday (2936)

The Rearview Mirror
PO Box 130
Westport, ON, Canada K0G 1X0
Phone: (613)273-8000
Fax: (613)273-8001
Free: 800-387-0796

Publications: The Review Mirror (36871)

Reason Foundation
3415 S Sepulveda Blvd. Ste. 400
Los Angeles, CA 90034
Phone: (310)391-2245

Publications: REASON (2378)

Recharger Magazine
2800 W. Sahara Ave., Ste. 5C
Las Vegas, NV 89102-4384
Phone: (702)438-5557
Fax: (702)438-4025

Publications: Recharger Magazine (18384)

The Record
Box 279
Gold River, BC, Canada V0P 1G0
Phone: (250)283-2324

Publications: The Record (34964)

The Record
201 A 3430 Brighton Ave
New Westminster, BC, Canada V5A 3H4
Phone: (604)525-6306
Fax: (604)525-7360

Publications: The Record (35031)

The Record
530 E. Market St.
PO Box 900
Stockton, CA 95201-0900
Phone: (209)948-1702
Fax: (209)547-8181
Free: 800-606-9742

Publications: The Record (3807) • Record Weekly
(3808)

The Record
PO Box 190
Conrad, IA 50621
Phone: (641)366-2020
Fax: (641)366-2020
Free: 888-851-2020

Publications: The Record (10719)

Record
12 Spruce
Miltonvale, KS 67466-0414
Phone: (785)427-2680
Fax: (785)427-2680

Publications: Record (11652)

The Record
PO Box 1061
North Wilkesboro, NC 28659
Phone: (336)667-0134
Fax: (336)667-6694

Publications: The Record (24109)

Record-Argus
10 Penn Ave.
PO Box 711
Greenville, PA 16125-0711
Phone: (724)588-5000
Fax: (724)588-4691

Publications: Record-Argus (26958)

The Record-Courier
1503 Hwy. 395 N., Ste. G
Gardnerville, NV 89410
Phone: (775)782-5121
Fax: (775)782-6152

Publications: The Record-Courier (18349)

Record-Courier
126 N. Chestnut St.
PO Box 1201
Ravenna, OH 44266
Phone: (330)296-9657
Fax: (330)296-2698

Publications: Record-Courier (25493)

The Record-Courier
1718 Main St.
PO Box 70
Baker City, OR 97814-0070
Phone: (541)523-5353
Fax: (541)523-5353

Publications: The Record-Courier (26233)

The Record Farmer and Ranch-Statewide
PO Box 806
620 N. Main St.
Gainesville, FL 32602
Phone: (352)377-2444
Fax: (352)338-1986

Publications: The Record-Local (6155)

Record Guide Productions
4412 Braddock St.
Cincinnati, OH 45204
Phone: (513)941-1116
Free: 888-658-1907

Publications: American Record Guide (24772)

Record-Herald
1801 W. 2nd Ave., Ste. 2
PO Box 259
Indianola, IA 50125-0259
Phone: (515)961-2511
Fax: (515)961-4833

Publications: EXTRA (10964) • Record-Herald and Indianola Tribune (10965)

Record-Herald
PO Box 130
Greensburg, KY 42743
Phone: (270)932-4381
Fax: (270)932-4441

Publications: Record-Herald (12097)

Record-Herald
138 S. Fayette St.
Washington Court House, OH 43160
Phone: (740)335-3611
Fax: (740)335-5728
Free: 800-780-3079

Publications: Record-Herald (25619)

Record Herald
PO Box 271
Waynesboro, PA 17268-2156
Phone: (717)762-2151
Fax: (717)762-3824

Publications: Record Herald (28138)

Record, Inc.
218 N Murray St.
PO Box 727
Banning, CA 92220-0005
Phone: (909)849-4586
Fax: (909)849-2437

Publications: The Record-Gazette (1478) • The Record-Gazette TMC (1479)

The Record-Journal Publishing Co.
11 Crown St.
PO Box 915
Meriden, CT 06450
Phone: (203)235-1661
Fax: (203)639-0210
Free: 800-228-6915

Publications: Record-Journal (4940)

Record Newspaper Inc.
302 S McCoy
PO Box 48
Granville, IL 61326
Phone: (815)339-2321
Fax: (815)339-6727

Publications: Putnam County Record (8951)

Record Newspapers, Inc.
250 N Bradford Ave.
West Chester, PA 19382-1912
Phone: (610)696-1775
Fax: (610)430-1194
Free: 800-456-6397

Publications: The Village News (28149)

Record Press, Inc.
6980 S. Rt.1
St. Anne, IL 60964
Phone: (815)427-6734
Fax: (815)427-6751

Publications: Record (9560)

Record Printing & Publishing Co.
364 Warren St.
Hudson, NY 12534
Phone: (518)828-1616
Fax: (518)828-9437
Free: 800-400-8846

Publications: Register-Star (20767)

The Record Publications
3414 Strong Ave.
Kansas City, KS 66106
Phone: (913)362-1988
Fax: (913)362-1989

Publications: The Record (11532)

The Record Publishing Co.
PO Box 116
Hollywood, CA 90028
Phone: (213)461-4196
Fax: (213)461-1738

Publications: The National Record (2052)

Record Publishing Co.
1619 Commerce Dr.
Stow, OH 44224
Phone: (330)688-0088
Fax: (330)688-1588
Free: 800-966-6565

Publications: Aurora Advocate (24639) • Bedford Times-Register (24661) • Cuyahoga Falls News-Press (25103) • Hudson Hub-Times (25250) • Record-News (25341) • Stow Sentry (25547) • Tallmadge Express (25557) • Twinsburg Bulletin (24662)

Record Publishing Co., Inc.
99 W. Broad St.
PO Box 1448
Dunn, NC 28335

Publications: The Daily Record (23803)

Record Stockman, Inc.
4800 Wadsworth Blvd., Ste. 200
Wheat Ridge, CO 80033-3315
Phone: (303)425-5777
Fax: (303)431-8911

Publications: Record Stockman (4680)

The Recorder
14 Hope St.
PO Box 1367
Greenfield, MA 01302-1367
Phone: (413)772-0261
Fax: (413)774-5511

Publications: The Recorder (14222)

The Recorder
PO Box 309
Amsterdam, NY 12010
Phone: (518)843-1100
Fax: (518)843-1338

Publications: The Recorder (20056)

Recorder
Box 9
Wakaw, SK, Canada S0K 4P0
Phone: (306)233-4325
Fax: (306)233-4386

Publications: Recorder (37584)

The Recorder-Herald
519 Van Dreff St.
PO Box 310
Salmon, ID 83467
Phone: (208)756-2221
Fax: (208)756-2222

Publications: The Recorder-Herald (7974)

Recorder Publishing Company Inc.
17-19 Morristown Rd.
PO Box 687
Bernardsville, NJ 07924
Phone: (908)766-3900
Fax: (908)766-6365

Publications: The Bernards Township Community News (18675) • The Hills Community News (18677) • New England Wine Gazette (18678) • The Progress (18679)

Recorder Publishing Co., Inc.
254 Mercer St.
Stirling, NJ 07980
Phone: (908)647-1180

Publications: The Bernardsville News (18676) • Chatham Courier (19600) • Florham Park Eagle (18826) • Hunterdon Review (19602) • The Madison Eagle (19603) • Morris News Bee (19604) • Mount Olive Chronicle (18741) • Observer-Tribune (18742) • Randolph Reporter (19496) • Roxbury Register (19525)

Recorder Publishing of Virginia Inc.
PO Box 10
Monterey, VA 24465
Phone: (540)468-2148
Fax: (540)468-2048

Publications: The Recorder (32274)

The Recorder and Times Ltd.
23 King St. W.
PO Box 10
Brockville, ON, Canada K6V 5T8
Phone: (613)342-4441
Fax: (613)342-4456
Free: 800-267-4434

Publications: The Brockville Recorder and Times (35708)

Recreation News
7339-D Hanover Pkwy.
Greenbelt, MD 20770
Phone: (301)474-4600
Fax: (301)474-6283

Publications: Recreation News (13559)

Recreation Press Inc.
3091 Mayfield Rd. Ste. 315
Cleveland Heights, OH 44118-1732
Phone: (216)371-5751
Fax: (216)371-5440
Free: 800-321-5750

Publications: Mid-America Boating (24994)

Recreation Publications, Inc.
4090 S McCarran Blvd., Ste. E
Reno, NV 89502-7529
Phone: (775)353-5100
Fax: (775)353-5111
Free: 800-878-7886

Publications: Bay and Delta Yachtsman (18418)

Recreation Vehicle Indiana Council (RVIC)
3210 Rand Rd.
Indianapolis, IN 46241
Phone: (317)247-6258
Fax: (317)243-9174

Publications: Hoosier Outdoors (10118)

The Red Bay News
120 4th Ave., SE
PO Box 1339
Red Bay, AL 35582-1339
Phone: (256)356-2148
Fax: (256)356-2787

Publications: The Red Bay News (431)

The Red and Black Publishing Co.
123 N. Jackson St.
Athens, GA 30601
Phone: (706)543-1791
Fax: (706)548-7251

Publications: The Red and Black (6949)

Red Brick Review
315 Canal St.
Manchester, NH 03101

Publications: Red Brick Review (18562)

Red Cedar Press
17C Morrill Hall
Dept. of English
East Lansing, MI 48824
Phone: (517)355-9656

Publications: Red Cedar Review (14992)

Red Cloud Chief
322 N Webster
Box 466
Red Cloud, NE 68970
Phone: (402)746-3700

Publications: Red Cloud Chief (18255)

Red Deer Advocate Ltd.
2950 Bremner Ave.
PO Bag 5200
Red Deer, AB, Canada T4N 5G3
Phone: (403)343-2400
Fax: (403)342-4051

Publications: Red Deer Advocate (34830) • Red Deer Life (34832)

Red Deer College
PO Box 5005
Red Deer, AB, Canada T4N 5H5
Phone: (403)343-1877
Fax: (403)347-8510

Publications: Bricklayer (34827)

Red Deer Publishing
No. 121, 5301 43 St.
Red Deer, AB, Canada T4N 1C8
Phone: (403)346-3356
Fax: (403)347-6620

Publications: Central Alberta Adviser (34828) • The Red Deer Express (34831)

The Red Oak Express
2012 Commerce Dr.
Red Oak, IA 51566-1010
Phone: (712)623-2566
Fax: (712)623-2568

Publications: The Red Oak Express (11170)

Red Owl
35 Hampshire Rd.
Portsmouth, NH 03801-4815
Phone: (603)431-2691

Publications: Red Owl (18638)

Red River Valley Historical Journal
Southeastern Oklahoma State University
Durant, OK 74701
Phone: (580)745-2342

Publications: Red River Valley Historical Journal (25807)

Red River Valley Potato Growers Association
PO Box 301
East Grand Forks, MN 56721
Phone: (218)773-8405
Fax: (218)773-6227

Publications: Valley Potato Grower (24415)

Red Rocks Community College
13300 W 6th Ave., Box 7
Lakewood, CO 80228-1255
Phone: (303)914-6371
Fax: (303)914-8154

Publications: Rock On (4535)

The Red Springs Citizen
131 S Main St.
Red Springs, NC 28377
Phone: (910)843-4631
Fax: (910)843-8171

Publications: The Red Springs Citizen (24177)

Reddy Corporation International
4501 Indian School Rd. NE, Ste. 200
Albuquerque, NM 87110-3979
Phone: (505)884-7500
Fax: (505)344-3844

Publications: SourceBook (19787)

Redemptorist Fathers
PO Box 1000
Ste.-Anne-de-Beaupre, QC, Canada G0A 3C0
Phone: (418)827-4538
Fax: (418)827-4530
Free: 800-363-3585

Publications: The Annals of Saint Anne de Beaupre (37326) • Le Revue Sainte Anne de Beaupre (37327)

Redfield Press, Inc.
16 E 7th Ave.
PO Box 440
Redfield, SD 57469
Phone: (605)472-0822
Fax: (605)472-3634

Publications: The Redfield Press (28953)

Redhead Publishing
511 Beaver Ave.
PO Box 275
Wishek, ND 58495
Phone: (701)452-2331
Fax: (701)452-2340

Publications: The Wishek Star (24568)

Redlands Daily Facts
PO Box 2240
Redlands, CA 92373-0740
Phone: (909)793-3221
Fax: (909)793-9588

Publications: Globetrotter (2904)

The Redmond Spokesman
PO Box 788
Redmond, OR 97756
Phone: (541)548-2184
Fax: (541)548-3203

Publications: The Redmond Spokesman (26552)

The Redwood Crozier
24451 Sherwood. Rd.
Willits, CA 95490
Phone: (707)459-5710
Fax: (707)459-9070

Publications: The Red Wood Crozier (4082)

Redwood Custom Communications Inc.
65 Front St. E., 2nd Fl.
Toronto, ON, Canada M5E 1B5
Phone: (416)360-7339
Fax: (416)360-7339

Publications: Noise (36675) • Real You (36723) • What's Cooking Magazine (35779)

Redwood Gazette, Inc.
219 South Washington
PO Box 299
Redwood Falls, MN 56283
Phone: (507)637-2929
Fax: (507)637-3175

Publications: Redwood Gazette (16295)

Redwood Investments Corp.
2259 Bloor St. W.
Toronto, ON, Canada M6S 4W1
Phone: (416)767-3644
Fax: (416)767-4880

Publications: The Villager (36788)

Reed Business Information
5700 Wilshire Blvd., Ste. 120
Los Angeles, CA 90036
Phone: (323)857-6600
Fax: (323)965-2475

Publications: Daily Variety (21533) • Variety (2427) • Variety's on Production (2428)

Reed Business Information
1050 IL Route 83, Ste. 200
Bensenville, IL 60106-1096
Phone: (630)694-4353
Fax: (630)320-7145

Publications: Assembly (8064)

Reed Business Information
275 Washington St.
Newton, MA 02458
Phone: (617)558-4900
Fax: (617)630-3830
Free: 800-357-4745

Publications: CPI Purchasing (14385) • Datamation (14386) • Design News (14387) • Digital News & Review (14388) • EDN China (14389) • EDN Europe (14390) • EDN Magazine Edition (14391) • EDN Products and Careers (14392) • Electronic Business (14394) • Electronic - Business Asia (14395) • Global Design News (14397) • Industrial Distribution (14398) • Interior Design (14401) • Modern Materials Handling (14406) • Purchasing Magazine (14408) • Supply Chain Management Review (14411) • Test & Measurement World (14412)

Reed Business Information
301 Gibraltar Dr.
Morris Plains, NJ 07950
Phone: (973)292-5100
Fax: (973)539-3476

Publications: Biomedical Products (19288) • Chemical Equipment (19289) • Fiberoptic Product News (19290) • Food Manufacturing (19291) • Food Products and Equipment (19292) • Industrial Maintenance and Plant Operation (19293) • Industrial Product Bulletin (19294) • Laboratory Equipment (19295) • Lasers & Optronics (19296) • Material Handling Product News (19297) • Medical Design Technology (19298) • Patient Management (19299) • Pharmaceutical Laboratory (19300) • Pharmaceutical Processing (19301) • Powder/Bulk Solids (19302) • Product Design and Development (19303) • Production Technology News (19304) • R & D Magazine (19305) • Scientific -Computing & -Automation (19306) • Surgical Products (19307) • Vertical Application Reseller (19308) • Wireless Design and Development (19309)

Reed Business Information
360 Park Ave. S.
New York, NY 10014
Phone: (646)746-7764

Publications: Automotive Body Repair News (21276) • Automotive Industries (21277) • Automotive Marketing (21278) • Broadcasting & Cable (21343) • Building Design & Construction (21346) • Building Supply Home Centers (21347) • CED (21385) • Chain Leader (21392) • Commercial Carrier Journal (21456) • Construction Equipment (21487) • Construction Products (21488) • Consulting-Specifying Engineer (21490) • Converting Magazine (21499) • Dairy Foods (8066) • ECN (Electronic Component News) (21580) • Electronic Packaging & Production (21593) • Food Engineering (International Edition) (21711) • Foodservice Equipment and Supplies (21715) • Gifts & Decorative Accessories (21761) • Graphic Arts Monthly (21779) • Hardware Age's Home Improvement Market (21789) • Home Systems (21813) • Home Textiles Today (21814) • HOTELS (21820) • Jewelers' Circular-Keystone (21960) • Library Journal (22251) • Logistics Management and Distribution Report (22266) • MSI (22375) • MSI Europe (22376) • Mundo Mercantil (22381) • New York Diamonds (22441) • Owner Operator (22515) • Packaging Digest (22517) • Plant Engineering (22559) • Pollution Engineering (15635) • Professional Builder (8768) • Professional Remodeler (9362) • Restaurants & Institutions (22652) • School Library Journal (22710) • SDM Dealer/Installer Marketplace (22716) • Semiconductor International (9365) • Television Europe (22820) • TWICE (22878) • Warehousing Management (22908)

Reed Business Information
7025 Albert Pick Rd., Ste. 200
Greensboro, NC 27409
Phone: (336)605-1055
Fax: (336)605-1149
Free: 800-561-5681

Publications: Furniture Today (23997) • Plants Sites & Parks (23935)

Reed Business Information
PO Box 2754
High Point, NC 27261-2754
Phone: (336)605-0121
Fax: (336)605-3801
Free: 800-999-6311

Publications: Casual Living (23995)

Reed Business Information
Valley Forge Park Place
1018 W. 9th Ave., 3rd Fl.
King of Prussia, PA 19406-1225
Phone: (610)205-1000
Fax: (610)205-1139

Publications: Commercial Carrier Journal (CCJ)
(27123) • JCK's High-Volume Jeweler (27124)

Reed construction Data
30 Technology Pkwy. S., Ste. 100
Norcross, GA 30092
Phone: (770)417-4122
Fax: 800-930-3003
Free: 800-263-6063

Publications: Construction Market Data Inc. (7458)

Reed Print Inc.
5409 Aldrin Court
Bakersfield, CA 93313
Phone: (661)834-0496
Fax: (661)746-5571

Publications: Wasco Tribune (1454)

Reed Print, Inc.
107 E. Lerdo Hwy.
Shafter, CA 93263-2701
Phone: (661)746-4942
Fax: (661)746-5571

Publications: Arvin Tiller (3756)

Reed Print, Inc. Community Newspapers
1231 Jefferson St.
Delano, CA 93215
Phone: (805)725-0600
Fax: (805)725-4373

Publications: Delano Record (1821) • Market Shopper (1822)

Reed Print Publication
Box 548
Lamont, CA 93241
Phone: (805)845-3704
Fax: (805)845-5907

Publications: Lamont Reporter (2145)

Reed Publish Supply
South Brindlee Mountain Pkwy.
Box 605
Arab, AL 35016
Phone: (205)586-3188
Fax: (205)586-3190

Publications: The Arab Tribune (23)

Reedley Exponent, Inc.
Box 432
Reedley, CA 93654-0432
Phone: (559)638-2244
Fax: (559)638-5021

Publications: Reedley Exponent (2916)

Beverly C. Reeves
PO Box 518
Healdsburg, CA 95448
Phone: (707)433-4451
Fax: (707)431-2623

Publications: The Healdsburg Tribune (2046)

Referee Enterprises, Inc.
PO Box 161
Franksville, WI 53126
Phone: (262)632-8855
Fax: (262)632-5460
Free: 800-733-6100

Publications: Referee Magazine (34276)

Reflector Chronicle Publishing Corp.
303 N Broadway
PO Box 8
Abilene, KS 67410
Phone: (785)263-1000
Fax: (785)263-1645

Publications: Abilene Reflector Chronicle (11332) •
Central Marketplace (11333)

Reflector-Herald, Inc.
61 E. Monroe St.
Norwalk, OH 44857
Phone: (419)668-3771
Fax: (419)668-2424

Publications: Norwalk Reflector (25441)

Reflector Publications Society
4825 Richard Rd. SW
Calgary, AB, Canada T3E 6K6
Phone: (403)240-6268
Fax: (403)240-6762

Publications: The Reflector (34656)

Reflector Publishing
209 Cotanche St.
PO Box 1967
Greenville, NC 27834
Phone: (919)931-4205
Fax: (919)752-9583
Free: 800-849-6166

Publications: Homes Magazine (23964)

Reformed Faith Witness
4-261 Martindale Rd.
St. Catharines, ON, Canada L2W 1A1
Phone: (905)682-8311
Fax: (905)682-8313
Free: 800-969-4838

Publications: Christian Courier (36355)

Refugio County Press
PO Drawer 200
Refugio, TX 78377
Phone: (361)526-2397
Fax: (361)526-2398

Publications: Refugio County Press (30973)

Refundle Bundle
Box 140, Centuck Sta.
Yonkers, NY 10710
Phone: (914)472-2227
Fax: (914)725-1597

Publications: Refundle Bundle (23600)

Regal Communications Corp.
321 New Albany Rd.
Moorestown, NJ 08057-1120
Phone: (609)778-8900

Publications: Lottery Player's Magazine (19216)

Regal Publishing Co.
15300 SW 116th Ave., Ste.11
King City, OR 97224-2693
Phone: (503)639-5414
Fax: (503)968-7397
Free: 877-639-8951

Publications: The Regal Courier (26381)

Regent Park Focus Community Coalition
600 Dundas St. E., Rear Basement
Toronto, ON, Canada M5A 2B9
Phone: (416)863-1074
Fax: (416)863-9440

Publications: Catch da Flava (36538)

Regent University
252 B Robertson Hall
Virginia Beach, VA 23464-9800
Phone: (757)226-4333
Fax: (757)226-4595

Publications: Regent University Law Review (32588)

Regentin Publishing
3520 Main
PO Box 519
Deckerville, MI 48427
Phone: (810)376-3805
Fax: (810)376-4058

Publications: The Deckerville Recorder (14912)

Region News
433 Hwy. 121
Box 79
Mount Zion, IL 62549
Phone: (217)864-4212
Fax: (217)864-4711

Publications: Region News (9254)

Regional Cooperative Extension Dairy Program
56 Main St.
Owego, NY 13827
Phone: (607)687-4020
Fax: (607)687-6162

Publications: Dairy and Field Crops Digest (23066)

Regional News
PO Box 828
Westville, IN 46391-0828
Phone: (219)785-2234
Fax: (219)785-2442

Publications: Regional News (10560)

Regional Parks Botanic Garden
Tilden Regional Park
Berkeley, CA 94708-2396
Phone: (510)841-8732
Fax: (510)848-6025

Publications: The Four Seasons (1522)

Regional Press
315 Broad St.
PO Box 937
Lake Geneva, WI 53147
Fax: (414)248-4476

Publications: Peach & Leisure (33904)

Regional Publishing Corp.
12247 S. Harlem Ave.
Palos Heights, IL 60463-0932
Phone: (708)448-6161
Fax: (708)448-4012

Publications: Regional News (9397) • The Reporter (9398)

Regis University
3333 Regis Blvd.
Denver, CO 80221-1099
Phone: (303)964-5391
Fax: (303)964-5530

Publications: Highlander (4329)

Register-Herald
PO Box 2398
Beckley, WV 25802
Phone: (304)255-4400
Fax: (304)255-4427
Free: 800-950-0250

Publications: Register-Herald (33241)

The Register-Mail
140 S Prairie St.
PO Box 310
Galesburg, IL 61402-0310
Phone: (309)343-7181
Fax: (309)342-5171
Free: 800-747-7181

Publications: The Register-Mail (8906)

Register-News
118 N 9th St.
PO Box 489
Mount Vernon, IL 62864
Phone: (618)242-0113
Fax: (618)242-8286

Publications: Register-News (9253)

Register Printing Co.
601 G Ave.
Grundy Center, IA 50638-1549
Phone: (319)824-6958
Fax: (319)824-6288

Publications: The Grundy Register (10936)

Register Publications
126 W. High St.
PO Box 328
Lawrenceburg, IN 47025
Phone: (812)537-0063
Fax: (812)537-5576

Publications: Dearborn County Register (10268) •
Harrison Press (25238) • The Journal Press (10269)

Register Publishing Co., Inc.
700 Monument St.
Danville, VA 24541
Phone: (434)793-2311
Fax: (434)793-2299

Publications: Danville Register & Bee (31991)

Numbers cited after listings are entry numbers rather than page numbers.

Register-Tribune
314 N Broadway
PO Box 8
Union City, MI 49094
Phone: (517)741-8451
Fax: (517)369-2225

Publications: Register-Tribune (15646)

Registered Nurses Association of British Columbia
2855 Arbutus St.
Vancouver, BC, Canada V6J 3Y8
Phone: (604)736-7331
Fax: (604)738-2272

Publications: Nursing BC (35153)

Registered Nurses Association of Ontario
438 University Ave., Ste. 1600
Toronto, ON, Canada M5G 2K8
Phone: (416)599-1925
Fax: (416)599-1926
Free: 800-268-7199

Publications: The Registered Nurse Journal (36725)

Rehabilitation Education
Elliot & Fitzpatrick
PO Box 1945
Athens, GA 30603
Phone: (706)548-8161
Fax: (706)546-8417
Free: 800-843-4977

Publications: Rehabilitation Education (1124)

Rehabilitation Foundation, Inc.
PO Box 675
Wheaton, IL 60189
Fax: (630)221-1201
Free: 800-462-5655

Publications: Journal of Outcome Measurement (9756)

Rehabilitation International
25 E 21st St.
New York, NY 10010
Phone: (212)420-1500
Fax: (212)505-0871

Publications: International Rehabilitation Review (21934)

Rehabilitation Nursing
4700 West Lake Ave.
Glenview, IL 60025
Phone: (847)375-4710
Fax: 877-734-9384
Free: 800-229-7530

Publications: Rehabilitation Nursing (8941)

Rehabilitation Services Administration
US Department of Education
400 Maryland Ave., SW
Washington, DC 20202
Phone: (202)205-8296
Fax: (202)401-0689
Free: 800-437-0833

Publications: American Rehabilitation (5341)

Reid Newspapers, Inc.
25 Ctr. Sq.
Elizabethtown, PA 17022
Phone: (717)367-7152
Fax: (717)367-3655

Publications: Elizabethtown Chronicle (26865)

Reilly Communications Group
16 E Schaumburg Rd.
Schaumburg, IL 60194
Phone: (847)882-6336
Fax: (847)519-0166

Publications: MEEN Diagnostic and Invasive Technology (9586) • MEEN Imaging Technology News (9587) • Outpatient Care Technology (9590)

J. Patrick and T. Michael Reilly
106 W Merrimac St.
Dodgeville, WI 53533

Publications: The Dodgeville Chronicle (33658) • Pecatonica Valley Leader (33595)

Reiman Media Group
5400 S. 60th St.
Greendale, WI 53129-1404
Phone: (414)423-0100
Fax: (414)423-8463

Publications: Country (33758) • Country Extra (33759) • Country Woman (33760) • Crafting Traditions (33761) • Farm & Ranch Living (33762) • Reminisce (33763) • Taste of Home (33764)

John Reiniger
235 Main St.
PO Box 128
Rising Sun, IN 47040-0128
Phone: (812)438-2011
Fax: (812)438-3228

Publications: Ohio County News (10428) • Rising Sun Recorder (10429)

Religious Herald Publishing Association, Inc.
PO Box 8377
Richmond, VA 23226-0377
Phone: (804)672-1973
Fax: (804)672-8323

Publications: The Religious Herald (32449)

Relix Magazine
PO Box 94
Brooklyn, NY 11229
Phone: (718)258-0009

Publications: Relix Magazine (20341)

The Reminder
10 North Ave.
Flin Flon, MB, Canada R8A 0T2
Phone: (204)687-3454
Fax: (204)687-4473

Publications: The Reminder (35266)

Reminder Publications, Inc.
280 N Main St.
East Longmeadow, MA 01028-1865
Phone: (413)525-6661
Fax: (413)525-5882

Publications: The Reminder (14167) • Today's Family (14168)

Remma Inc.
328 Ct. St.
PO Box 31
Rockwell City, IA 50579-9998
Phone: (712)297-7544
Fax: (712)297-7544

Publications: Calhoun County Advocate (11184)

Remsen Bell-Enterprise
Box 209
257 Washington St.
Remsen, IA 51050
Phone: (712)786-1196
Fax: (712)786-5566

Publications: Remsen Bell-Enterprise (11175)

Remvue
304 Francis
Box 1090
Jackson, MI 49204
Phone: (517)782-0825
Fax: (517)782-4996

Publications: Jackson County Legal News (15222)

Renaissance Publications
1516 5th Ave.
Pittsburgh, PA 15219-5198
Phone: (412)391-8208
Fax: (412)391-8006

Publications: Pittsburgh Renaissance News (27835)

Renaissance Society of America
365 5th Ave., Rm. 5400
New York, NY 10016-4309
Phone: (212)817-2130
Fax: (212)817-1544

Publications: Renaissance Quarterly (22646)

Renascence
Marquette University
Helfaer Bldg., Rm. 105
PO Box 1881
Milwaukee, WI 53201-1881
Phone: (414)288-6725
Fax: (414)288-5433

Publications: Renascence (34096)

Renco Publishing, Inc.
816 E Lincoln
Olivia, MN 56277
Phone: (320)523-2032
Fax: (320)523-2033

Publications: Olivia Times-Journal (16243)

Renco Publishing Inc.
110 NW Dupont
PO Box 468
Renville, MN 56284-0468
Phone: (320)329-3324
Fax: (320)329-3432

Publications: Renville County Star Farmer News (16303)

Renegade Publishing, Inc.
710 S Kenosha
Tulsa, OK 74150
Phone: (918)592-5550
Fax: (918)592-5970

Publications: Urban Tulsa (26140)

Renfrew Newspapers
35 Opeongo Rd., Box 400
Renfrew, ON, Canada K7V 4A8
Phone: (613)432-3655
Fax: (613)432-6689

Publications: Mercury (36339)

Renninger's ANTIQUE GUIDE
PO Box 495
Lafayette Hill, PA 19444
Phone: (610)828-4614
Fax: (610)834-1599

Publications: Renninger's ANTIQUE GUIDE (27132)

The Renovator's Supply
Renovator's Old Mill
Millers Falls, MA 01349
Phone: (413)659-0211
Fax: (413)659-3796

Publications: Old Mill Marketing (14335)

Rensselaer Polytechnic Institute
Rensselaer Union
Box 35
Troy, NY 12180-3590
Phone: (518)276-6770
Fax: (518)276-8728

Publications: The Polytechnic (23455)

The Rensselaerville Institute
Rensselaerville, NY 12147
Phone: (518)797-3783
Fax: (518)797-5270

Publications: Innovating Magazine (23182)

Rental Guide Magazine
4021 Ardara Dr.
Tallahassee, FL 32309
Phone: (850)894-3278
Fax: (850)894-3271

Publications: Rental Guide (6731)

RePlay Magazine
PO Box 7004
Tarzana, CA 91357
Phone: (818)776-2880
Fax: (818)776-2888

Publications: RePlay Magazine (3839)

The Reponsive Community
2020 Pennsylvania Ave. NW, Ste. 282
Washington, DC 20006
Phone: (202)994-7997
Fax: (202)994-1606
Free: 800-245-7460

Publications: The Responsive Community (5764)

The Reporter
916 Cotting Ln.
Vacaville, CA 95688
Phone: (707)448-6401
Fax: (707)447-8411

Publications: The Weekly Star (3974)

The Reporter
PO Box 2042
Akron, OH 44309
Phone: (330)253-0007
Fax: (330)535-7333

Publications: The Akron Reporter (24574)

The Reporter
PO Box 630
Fond du Lac, WI 54936-0630

Publications: The Reporter (Fond du Lac) (33697)

The Reporter Co.
181 Delaware St.
Walton, NY 13856
Phone: (607)865-4132
Fax: (607)865-8983
Free: 800-865-4131

Publications: The Walton Reporter (23497)

The Reporter Co., Inc.
21 N. Henry St.
Edgerton, WI 53534
Phone: (608)884-3367
Fax: (608)884-8187

Publications: Advertiser (33685) • The Edgerton Reporter (33687)

Reporter Magazine
37 Lomb Memorial Dr.
Rochester, NY 14623
Phone: (716)475-2212

Publications: Reporter Magazine (23237)

Reporter Publications
1791 Vancroft Ave.
San Francisco, CA 94124
Phone: (415)931-5778
Fax: (415)931-0214

Publications: Pennisula Reporter (2544) • Sun-Reporter (3445)

Reporter Publishing Co.
Box 52193
New Orleans, LA 70152-2193
Phone: (504)366-8797
Fax: (504)366-1966

Publications: Surplus Line Reporter & Insurance News (12755) • Texas Surplus Line Reporter (12756)

Reporter-Times, Inc.
PO Box 187
Beech Grove, IN 46107
Phone: (317)787-3291
Fax: (317)787-3325
Free: 800-873-7060

Publications: The Southside Times (9801)

Reporter-Times, Inc.
23 E. Main St.
Mooresville, IN 46158
Phone: (317)831-0280
Fax: (317)831-7068

Publications: The Times (10322)

Reporters Committee for Freedom of the Press
1815 N Fort Myer Dr., Ste. 900
Arlington, VA 22209
Phone: (703)807-2100
Fax: (703)807-2109

Publications: The News Media & the Law (31814)

The Repository
500 Market Ave. S
Canton, OH 44702-2112
Phone: (216)454-5611
Fax: (216)454-5610

Publications: The Repository (24731)

Reppert Publications
PO Box 529
Anna, IL 62906
Phone: (618)833-2158
Fax: (618)833-5813
Free: (618)833-2699

Publications: Gazette-Democrat (8013) • Monday's Pub (8014)

The Republic
333 2nd St.
Columbus, IN 47201-6795
Phone: (812)372-7811
Fax: (812)379-5608

Publications: The Republic (9895)

Republic Newspaper
PO Box 769
Kings Mountain, NC 28086
Phone: (704)739-7496
Fax: (704)739-0611

Publications: Kings Mountain Herald (24025)

Republic Newspaper Inc.
107 1/2 E Main St.
PO Box 699
Cherryville, NC 28021
Phone: (704)435-6752
Fax: (704)435-8293

Publications: Cherryville Eagle (23784)

Republic Newspapers, Inc.
732 W. Montrose St.
Clermont, FL 34711
Phone: (352)394-2183
Fax: (352)394-8001

Publications: South Lake Press (5995) • Zephyrhills Shopper (5996)

Republic Times LLC
222 S Main
PO Box 147
Waterloo, IL 62298
Phone: (618)939-3814
Fax: (618)939-3815

Publications: Republic Times (9736) • The Shopper (9737)

Republican
PO Box 695
Galesville, WI 54630-0695
Phone: (608)582-2330

Publications: Galesville Republican (33732)

Republican Eagle
2760 No. Service Dr.
Box 82
Red Wing, MN 55066
Phone: (651)388-8235
Fax: (651)388-8912
Free: 800-535-1660

Publications: Republican-Eagle (16293)

Republican Journal
316 S Main St.
PO Box 20
Darlington, WI 53530
Phone: (608)776-4425
Fax: (608)776-4301

Publications: Republican Journal (33649)

Republican Liberty
611 Pennsylvania Ave. SE No. 370
Washington, DC 20003
Phone: (202)546-8749
Fax: (202)543-1603

Publications: Republican Liberty (6157)

Republican Nonpareil
PO Box 26
Central City, NE 68826
Phone: (308)946-3081
Fax: (308)946-3082
Free: 800-323-3929

Publications: Republican Nonpareil (17972)

Republican Register
6 Central St.
PO Box 591
Moravia, NY 13118
Phone: (315)497-1551

Publications: Republican-Register (21096)

Republican-Reporter
121A South 4th
PO Box 8
Oregon, IL 61061
Phone: (815)732-6166
Fax: (815)732-4238

Publications: Republican-Reporter (9388)

Republican-Rustler
409 West C
Box 640
Basin, WY 82410
Phone: (307)568-2458
Fax: (307)568-2459

Publications: Republican-Rustler (34477)

Request Magazine
10400 Yellow Cir. Dr.
Minnetonka, MN 55343
Phone: (952)931-8740
Fax: (952)931-8490
Free: 800-325-0075

Publications: REQUEST (16175)

Research Center for Religion and Human Rights in Closed Societies, Ltd.
475 Riverside Dr., Ste. 448
New York, NY 10115
Phone: (212)870-2481
Fax: (212)663-6771

Publications: RCDA (22626)

Research Magazine, Inc.
585 Howard St., 2nd Fl.
San Francisco, CA 94105-3032
Phone: (415)621-0220
Fax: (415)621-0735

Publications: Research (3424)

Research Publications
320 Kern Bldg.
University Park, PA 16802-3303
Phone: (814)865-3477
Fax: (814)863-5368

Publications: Research/Penn State (28083)

The Reserve Officers Association
1 Constitution Ave. NE
Washington, DC 20002
Phone: (202)479-2200
Fax: (202)479-0416

Publications: The Officer (5705)

Resident Publications
120 5th Ave., No. 77
New York, NY 10011-5600

Publications: The Upper East Side Resident (22888) • The Upper West Side Resident (22889)

RESNA
1700 N. Moore St., Ste. 1540
Arlington, VA 22209-1903
Phone: (703)524-6686
Fax: (703)524-6630

Publications: Assistive Technology (31781)

Resort Condominiums International, Inc.
9998 N. Michigan Rd.
Carmel, IN 46032-9640
Phone: (317)805-9800
Fax: (317)805-8229

Publications: Endless Vacation (9879) • Timeshare Business (9880)

Resource Development Press Ltd.
2235 Durand Dr.
PO Box 399
Downers Grove, IL 60515
Phone: (630)963-0398
Fax: (630)963-2625

Publications: Illinois Standardbred & Mid-America Harness News (8786)

Resource Links
PO Box 9
Pouch Cove, NL, Canada A0A 3L0
Phone: (709)335-2394
Fax: (709)335-2978

Publications: Resource Links (35481)

Resource Publications Inc.
160 E. Virginia St., No. 290
San Jose, CA 95112-5876
Phone: (408)286-8505
Fax: (408)287-8748

Publications: Ministry & Liturgy (3527)

Resource Recycling
PO Box 42270
Portland, OR 97242-0270
Phone: (503)233-1305
Fax: (503)233-1356

Publications: Resource Recycling (26505)

Resources for Feminist Research/Documentation Sur La Recherche Feministe
Ontario Institute for Studies in Education
University of Toronto
252 Bloor St. W.
Toronto, ON, Canada M5S 1V6
Phone: (416)923-6641
Fax: (416)926-4725

Publications: Confronting Violence in Women's Lives (36558)

Response TV
201 E Sandpointe Ave., Ste. 600
Santa Ana, CA 92707-5761
Phone: (714)513-8400
Fax: (714)513-8482
Free: 800-854-3112

Publications: Response TV (3631)

Rest Communicatoion
W 1st & E Sts.
PO Box 1268
McCook, NE 69001
Phone: (308)345-4500
Fax: (308)345-7881

Publications: McCook Daily Gazette (18153)

The Reston Recorder
Box 10
Reston, MB, Canada R0M 1X0
Phone: (204)877-3321
Fax: (204)877-3115

Publications: The Reston Recorder (35285)

Restoration
2888 Dafoe Rd.
Combermere, ON, Canada K0J 1L0
Phone: (613)756-3713
Fax: (613)756-0211

Publications: Restoration (35750)

Results Media
205-101 Worthington St. E
North Bay
Ontario, ON, Canada P1B 1G5
Phone: (705)495-1581
Fax: (705)495-8585
Free: 877-495-1581

Publications: Baldwin Shopper's Guide (36157) • Bayside-North Pennysaver (36158) • Bayside South/Oakland Gardens Pennysaver (35668) • Bayside West Pennysaver (35669) • Bellmore/Merrick North Shopper's Guide (36159) • Cedarhurst/Lawrence Shopper's Guide (36160) • Douglaston/Little Neck Shopper's Guide (36161) • East Flushing Pennysaver (35835) • East Meadow Shopper's Guide (36162) • Elmont Shopper's Guide (36163) • Floral Park Bellerose North Pennysaver (35833) • Floral Park Bellerose South Pennysaver (35834) • Flushing Pennysaver (35836) • Franklin Square Shopper's Guide (20736) • Freeport Shopper's Guide (20737) • Garden City Pennysaver (35845) • Hempstead Shopper's Guide (36164) • Herricks-Searingtown Pennysaver (35913) • Hewlett/Woodmere Shopper's Guide (36165) • Long Beach Shopper's Guide (36166) • Lynbrook/East Rockaway/Malverne Shopper's Guide (36167) • Mineola Pennysaver (36052) • New Hyde Park Pennysaver (36104) • North Flushing Pennysaver (35837) • Queens Village Shopper's Guide (36168) • Uniondale/Roosevelt Shopper's Guide (36169) • Valley Stream Shopper's Guide (20746) • West Hempstead Shopper's Guide (36170) • Westbury Shopper's Guide (36171) • Whitestone Pennysaver (36873)

Resumen Newspaper
6908 Roosevelt Ave.
Flushing, NY 11372
Phone: (718)899-8603
Fax: (718)899-7616

Publications: Resumen Newspaper (20612)

Retail Information Group, Inc.
226 Esna Park Dr., Ste. 23
Markham, ON, Canada L3R 1H3
Phone: (905)944-8851
Fax: (905)944-9858

Publications: Luggage, Leathergoods & Accessories (36027)

Retail News
4707 Hayes Ave.
Sandusky, OH 44870
Phone: (419)626-1442
Fax: (419)626-1436

Publications: Retail News (25509)

Retail, Wholesale and Dept. Store Union-AFL-CIO
30 E 29th St.
New York, NY 10016
Phone: (212)684-5300
Fax: (212)779-2809

Publications: RWDSU Record (22698)

Retailer and Marketing News
PO Box 191105
Dallas, TX 75219-1105
Phone: (214)871-2930

Publications: Retailer and Marketing News (30180)

Retherford Publications, Inc.
8545 E. 41st St.
Tulsa, OK 74145-3305
Phone: (918)663-1414

Publications: Catoosa Times (26108) • Tulsa County News (26135) • Tulsa Daily Commerce & Legal News (26136)

Rethinking Schools
1001 E Keefe Ave.
Milwaukee, WI 53212
Phone: (414)964-9646
Fax: (414)964-7220
Free: 800-669-4192

Publications: Rethinking Schools (34097)

The Retired Officers Association
201 N. Washington St.
Alexandria, VA 22314

Publications: The Retired Officer Magazine (31733)

The Retrospect
732 Haddon Ave.
Box 296
Collingswood, NJ 08108
Phone: (609)854-1400

Publications: The Retrospect (18768)

Reub Williams and Sons, Inc.
PO Box 1448
Warsaw, IN 46581-1448
Phone: (219)267-3111
Fax: (219)267-7784

Publications: Times-Union (10537)

Reunions Magazine
PO Box 11727
Milwaukee, WI 53211-0727
Phone: (414)263-4567
Fax: (414)263-6331
Free: 800-373-7933

Publications: Reunions Magazine (34098)

Reveille Publishing Co., Inc.
PO Box 557
Seneca Falls, NY 13148
Phone: (607)869-5344
Fax: (607)869-9208

Publications: Reveille/Between the Lakes (23324)

The Review
210 E. 4th St.
East Liverpool, OH 43920
Phone: (330)385-4545
Fax: (330)385-7114

Publications: The Review (25171)

The Review
PO Box 6
Shidler, OK 74652
Phone: (918)793-3841
Fax: (918)793-3842

Publications: The Review (26071)

Review
PO Box 851400
Yukon, OK 73085
Phone: (405)354-5264
Fax: (405)350-3044

Publications: Review (26205)

The Review
4801 Valley Way
Niagara Falls, ON, Canada L2E 1W4
Phone: (905)358-5711
Fax: (905)356-0785

Publications: The Review (36110)

Review
PO Box 519
Somerville, TN 38068
Phone: (901)465-4042
Fax: (901)465-5493

Publications: East Shelby Review (29606)

Review
116 E. 8th St.
PO Box 519
Cross Plains, TX 76443
Fax: (817)725-7225

Publications: Review (30110)

Review of Contemporary Fiction
Illinois State University
Campus Box 4241
Normal, IL 61790-4241

Publications: Review of Contemporary Fiction (9304)

Review Enterprises, Inc.
114 Lake Ave.
PO Box 99
Battle Lake, MN 56515
Phone: (218)864-5952
Fax: (218)864-5212
Free: 800-340-0426

Publications: Battle Lake Review (15730)

Review & Expositor
PO Box 6681
Louisville, KY 40206-0681
Phone: (502)327-8347
Fax: (502)327-8347

Publications: Review and Expositor (12236) • Southern Seminary Magazine (12237)

Review and Herald Publishing Association
55 W. Oak Ridge Dr.
Hagerstown, MD 21740
Phone: (301)393-3000
Fax: (301)393-4055

Publications: Liberty (13736) • Message (13567) • Vibrant Life (13570)

Review Magazine
318 S Hamilton
Saginaw, MI 48602
Phone: (517)799-6078
Fax: (517)799-6162

Publications: Review Magazine (15490)

Review-Messenger
112 Minnesota Ave. W
PO Box 309
Sebeka, MN 56477-0309
Phone: (218)837-5558
Fax: (218)837-5560

Publications: Review-Messenger (16442) • Total Shopper (16443)

Review of Politics
PO Box B
Notre Dame, IN 46556-0762
Phone: (574)631-6623
Fax: (574)631-3103

Publications: Review of Politics (10378)

Review Printing Co., Inc.
PO Box 153
Marlow, OK 73055
Fax: (405)658-6659

Publications: Marlow Review (25905)

Review of Psychology and Psychiatry
PO Box 15680
Seattle, WA 98115
Phone: (206)367-5764
Fax: (206)365-3036

Publications: Review of Existential Psychology and Psychiatry (33015)

Review Publishing Ltd.
1500 Sansom St., 3rd Fl.
Philadelphia, PA 19102
Phone: (215)563-7400
Fax: (215)563-6799

Publications: Philadelphia Weekly (27635)

Review for Religious
3601 Lindell Blvd., Rm. 428
St. Louis, MO 63108
Phone: (314)977-7363
Fax: (314)977-7362

Publications: Review for Religious (17487)

Reviews Unlimited
6060 Arthur Ave.
St. Louis, MO 63139
Phone: (314)645-3410

Publications: Reviews Unlimited (17488)

Revue Notre-Dame du Cap
626 Notre-Dame
Cap-de-la-Madeleine, QC, Canada G8T 4G9
Phone: (819)374-2441
Fax: (819)374-2441

Publications: Revue Notre-Dame du Cap (36957)

Revue Sante Mentale au Quebec, C.P.
548, Succ. Place d'Armes
Montreal, QC, Canada H2Y 3H3
Phone: (514)523-0607
Fax: (514)523-0797

Publications: Sante Mentale au Quebec (37221)

Rexburg Standard Journal
Box 10
Rexburg, ID 83440
Phone: (208)356-5441
Fax: (208)356-8312

Publications: Rexburg Standard Journal (7963)

RFD
PO Box 68
Liberty, TN 37095-0068
Phone: (615)536-5176

Publications: RFD (29332)

RFD News Group, Inc.
207 Kasan Ave.
PO Box 18
Volga, SD 57071
Phone: (605)627-9471
Fax: (605)627-9310

Publications: The Elkton Record (28851) • Tri-City Star (29030) • Volga Tribune (29012)

RFD Publications, Inc.
45-525 Luluku Rd.
Kaneohe, HI 96744-1945
Phone: (808)235-5881
Fax: (808)247-7246

Publications: Central Sun-Press (7768) • Hawaii Army Weekly (7769) • Hawaii Kai/East Oahu Sun Press (7770) • Hawaii Marine (7771) • Hawaii Navy News (7772) • Hawaiian Falcon (7773) • Midweek Magazine (7774) • Windward Sun-Press (7776)

RG
C.P. 915 Succursale C
Montreal, QC, Canada H2L 4V2
Phone: (514)523-9463
Fax: (514)523-2214

Publications: RG (37220)

Rhea County Publishing Co.
PO Box 286
Dayton, TN 37321
Phone: (423)775-6111
Fax: (423)775-8218

Publications: The Herald-News (29163) • Herald-News Sunrise Edition (29164)

Rheinwald Printing Co., Inc.
15 Main St.
PO Box 378
Brockport, NY 14420
Phone: (716)637-5100
Fax: (716)637-0111

Publications: Tri-County Advertiser (20247)

Rhetoric Society of America
c/o English Department
Brigham Young University
3146 JKHB
Box 26280
Provo, UT 84602-6280

Publications: Rhetoric Society Quarterly (31407)

Rhizome.org
180 Vaeick St., Ste. 1126
New York, NY 10014
Phone: (646)552-2313
Fax: (212)989-2335

Publications: Rhizome Digest (22666)

Rhode Island Beverage Journal, Inc.
PO Box 185159
Hamden, CT 06518-0157
Phone: (203)288-3375
Fax: (203)288-2693

Publications: Rhode Island Beverage Journal (28421)

Rhode Island Builders Association
450 Veterans Memorial Pkwy., No. 301
East Providence, RI 02914-5380
Phone: (401)431-0880
Fax: (401)438-7446

Publications: The Rhode Island Builder Report (28345)

Rhode Island College
Dept. of English
Rhode Island College
Providence, RI 02908
Phone: (401)456-8000
Fax: (401)456-8379

Publications: Literature and Psychology (28403)

Rhode Island College
Student Union, Rm. 308
600 Mt. Pleasant Ave.
Providence, RI 02908
Phone: (401)456-8000
Fax: (401)456-8792

Publications: The Anchor (28387)

Rhode Island Herald
PO Box 6063
Providence, RI 02940
Phone: (401)724-0200
Fax: (401)726-5820

Publications: Rhode Island Herald (28422)

Rhode Island Medical Society
106 Francis St.
Providence, RI 02903
Phone: (401)331-3207
Fax: (401)751-8050

Publications: Medicine and Health Rhode Island (28408)

Rhode Island Pharmacist
2484 Warwick Ave. Ste. 113
Warwick, RI 02889-4263

Publications: Rhode Island Pharmacist (28452)

Rhode Island Postal History Society
c/o Thomas Greene
Box 113822
North Providence, RI 02911
Phone: (401)353-1161

Publications: Rhode Island Postal History Journal (28377)

Rhode Island Senior Times
89 Neptune St.
Jamestown, RI 02835
Phone: (401)423-3900
Fax: (401)423-3805

Publications: Rhode Island Senior Times (28357)

Rhose Island Bar Association
115 Cedar St.
Providence, RI 02903
Phone: (401)421-5740
Fax: (401)421-5740

Publications: The Rhode Island Bar Journal (28420)

RIA Group
395 Hudson St., 4th Fl.
New York, NY 10014
Phone: (212)352-2746
Fax: (212)367-6314
Free: 800-431-9025

Publications: Business Entities (21355) • Journal of Compensation and Benefits (22033) • Journal of Cost Management (22040) • The Journal of Taxation (22201) • Practical Tax Strategies (22591)

Riccon, Inc.
211 W St. Louis St.
PO Box 47
Nashville, IL 62263-0047
Phone: (618)327-3411
Fax: (618)327-3299

Publications: The Nashville News (9277)

Rice Thresher
Rice University
6100 Main St.
Houston, TX 77005
Phone: (713)348-4801
Fax: (713)348-5238

Publications: Rice Thresher (30525)

Ricepaper Magazine
12-21, Main St.
Vancouver, BC, Canada V5T 3E3
Phone: (604)322-6616
Fax: (604)322-6616

Publications: RicePaper (35164)

Riceville Recorder
Lock Box A
Riceville, IA 50466
Phone: (641)985-2142
Fax: (641)985-4185

Publications: Riceville Recorder (11176)

Rich Hill Mining Review
PO Box 29
Rich Hill, MO 64779
Phone: (417)395-4131
Fax: (417)395-2171

Publications: Rich Hill Mining Review (17372)

Richard Bland College
11301 Johnson
Petersburg, VA 23805
Phone: (804)862-6226
Fax: (804)862-6455

Publications: Bon Homme Richard (32329)

Richard Ivey School of Business
1151 Richmond St. N.
London, ON, Canada N6A 3K7
Phone: (519)661-3309
Fax: (519)661-3838

Publications: Ivey Business Quarterly (36629)

Richards Publishing Co., Inc.
PO Box 159
Gonvick, MN 56644
Phone: (218)487-5225
Fax: (218)487-5251
Free: 800-835-8496

Publications: The Grygla Eagle (15936) • Leader-Record (15924)

Richardson Publishing Co. Luc.
70 4th St. NW
PO Box 831
Barberton, OH 44203
Phone: (330)753-1068
Fax: (330)753-1021

Publications: Barberton Herald (24641)

The Richfield Reaper
PO Box 730
Richfield, UT 84701-0730
Phone: (435)896-5476
Fax: (435)896-8123

Publications: The Richfield Reaper (31414)

The Richfield Reaper
65 W. Center
PO Box 730
Richfield, UT 84701
Phone: (801)896-5476
Fax: (801)896-8123

Publications: Reaper Extra (31413)

Richland Beacon News
PO Box 209
Rayville, LA 71269
Phone: (318)728-2250
Fax: (318)728-5991

Publications: Richland Beacon News (12803)

The Richland Mirror
Box 757
Richland, MO 65556
Phone: (573)765-3391
Fax: (573)765-3235

Publications: The Richland Mirror (17373)

Richland Observer
172 E Ct. St.
Box 31
Richland Center, WI 53581-0031
Phone: (608)647-6141
Fax: (608)647-6143

Publications: Richland Observer (34298)

Richmond News, Inc.
204 W North Main St., No. 100
PO Box 100
Richmond, MO 64085-1743
Phone: (816)776-5454

Publications: The Advantage (17374) • The Daily News (17375)

Richmond Newspapers, Inc.
300 E. Franklin St.
PO Box 85333
Richmond, VA 23293

Publications: Richmond Times-Dispatch (32452)

The Richmond Review
140-5671 No. 3 Rd.
Richmond, BC, Canada V6X 2C7
Phone: (604)247-3700
Fax: (604)606-8752

Publications: The Richmond Review (35077)

Richmond Suburban Newspapers
7235 Stonewall Pkwy.
Mechanicsville, VA 23111
Phone: (804)746-1235
Fax: (804)730-0476

Publications: Goochland Gazette (32267) • The Mechanicsville Local (32268)

Richner Communications
379 Central Ave.
Lawrence, NY 11559-1616
Phone: (516)569-4000
Fax: (516)569-4942

Publications: Baldwin Herald (20113) • Long Beach Herald (20960) • Long Island Graphic (20625) • Meadowbrook Times (20550) • Nassau Herald (21108) • Oceanside-Island Park Herald (23031) • Prime Time (20940) • Rockaway Journal (20591) • Rockville Centre Herald (23260) • Valley Stream Herald (23488) • Village Herald (20978)

The Richton Dispatch
PO Drawer X
Richton, MS 39476-1521
Phone: (601)788-6031
Fax: (601)788-6031

Publications: The Richton Dispatch (16833)

Rickard Publishing Co.
PO Box 710
Minier, IL 61759
Phone: (309)392-2414
Fax: (309)392-2169

Publications: Olympia Review (9199)

RICO Law Reporter
1601 Connecticut Ave., NW, No. 602
Washington, DC 20009
Phone: (202)462-5755
Fax: (202)328-2430

Publications: RICO Law Reporter (5769)

Rider University
2083 Lawrenceville Rd.
Lawrenceville, NJ 08648
Phone: (609)896-5000
Fax: (609)895-5440

Publications: The Rider News (19164) • Rider University (19165)

Ridge Publications
720 E Durant Ave. Ste. E8
Ste. E8
Aspen, CO 81611
Phone: (970)920-4040
Fax: (970)920-4044

Publications: Aspen Magazine (4141)

The Ridgway Sun
PO Box 529
Ridgway, CO 81432
Phone: (970)626-5100
Fax: (970)626-5100

Publications: Ouray County Plaindealer (4614) • The Ridgway Sun (4615)

Ridick Publishing
123 Main
PO Box 529
Big Sandy, MT 59520
Phone: (406)378-2176
Fax: (406)378-2176

Publications: Big Sandy Mountaineer (17726)

The Right to Die Society of Canada
PO Box 39018
Victoria, BC, Canada V8V 4X8
Phone: (604)380-1112
Fax: (604)386-3800

Publications: Last Rights (35219)

Riley Publications, Inc.
PO Box 1107.
Chautauqua Institution
Chautauqua, NY 14722
Phone: (716)357-2479
Fax: (716)357-2479

Publications: Journal of Multicultural Nursing and Health (JMCNH) (20454)

RILM Abstracts
365 5th Ave.
New York, NY 10016
Phone: (212)817-1990
Fax: (212)817-1569

Publications: RILM Abstracts of Music Literature (22668)

Rimbach Publishing, Inc.
8650 Babcock Blvd.
Pittsburgh, PA 15237
Phone: (412)364-5366
Fax: (412)369-9720
Free: 800-245-3182

Publications: Industrial Hygiene News (27800) • Pollution Equipment News (27836)

The Ring Magazine, Inc.
7002 W Butler Pke.
PO Box 910
Ambler, PA 19002
Phone: (215)643-6385
Fax: (215)628-3571

Publications: KO Magazine Superfight Color Special No. 1 (26651) • The Ring (26653)

The Ringgold Progress
Mill St.
PO Box 708
Ringgold, LA 71068-0708
Phone: (318)894-6397
Fax: (318)263-8897

Publications: The Ringgold Progress (12477)

The Ringling Eagle
103 E Main
PO Box 626
Ringling, OK 73456-0626
Phone: (405)662-2221

Publications: The Ringling Eagle (26051)

RINSE Magazine
599B Yonge St., No. 346
Toronto, ON, Canada M4Y 1Z4

Publications: RINSE (36730)

Rio Grande Sun
PO Box 790
Espanola, NM 87532
Phone: (505)753-2126
Fax: (505)753-2140

Publications: Rio Grande Sun (19844)

The Ripley Bee
Box 97
Ripley, OH 45167
Phone: (937)392-4321
Fax: (937)392-0317

Publications: The Ripley Bee (25498)

Ripley Newspaper, Inc.
PO Box 31
Ripley, WV 25271
Phone: (304)372-2421
Fax: (304)372-8240

Publications: The Jackson Herald (33448) • Star Herald (33450)

The Ripley Publishing Co.
115 S Washington St.
PO Box 158
Versailles, IN 47042
Phone: (812)689-6364
Fax: (812)689-6508

Publications: Osgood Journal (10516) • Spotlight - Advertiser (10517) • The Versailles Republican (10518)

Ripon College
300 Seward St.
PO Box 248
Ripon, WI 54971-0248
Phone: (920)748-8115
Fax: (920)748-9262

Publications: Ripon Magazine (34303)

Ripon Community Printer
PO Box 344
Ripon, WI 54971
Phone: (920)748-3017
Fax: (920)748-3028

Publications: The Ripon Commonwealth Express (34302)

The Ripon Record
130 W Main St.
Ripon, CA 95366
Phone: (209)599-2194
Fax: (209)599-2195

Publications: The Ripon Record (2928)

Riseau Envirnement
911 Jean Talon E, Office 220
Montreal, QC, Canada H2R 1V5
Phone: (514)270-7110
Fax: (514)270-7154

Publications: Vecteur Environnement (37233)

Rising Tide Studios
307 W. 36th St., 10th Fl.
New York, NY 10018
Phone: (646)473-2234
Fax: (646)473-2223

Publications: Digital Coast Reporter (21552) • Silicon Alley Reporter (22741)

Risk and Insurance Management Society, Inc.
655 Third Ave., 2nd Fl.
New York, NY 10017-5617
Phone: (212)286-9292
Fax: (212)986-9716
Free: 800-713-7467

Publications: Risk Management (22671)

Ritchie Gazette and The Cairo Standard
200 E Main St.
PO Box 215
Harrisville, WV 26362-0215
Phone: (304)643-2221
Fax: (304)643-2156

Publications: Ritchie Gazette and The Cairo Standard (33334)

Ritzville Adams County Journal Publishing
216 W Railroad Ave.
PO Box 288
Ritzville, WA 99169
Phone: (509)659-1020
Fax: (509)659-0842

Publications: The Ritzville Adams County Journal (32932)

River City Newspapers
2225 W Acoma Blvd.
Lake Havasu City, AZ 86403
Phone: (928)855-2197
Fax: (928)855-2637
Free: 800-894-2109

Publications: River Extra (734) • Today's News - Herald (735)

The River Falls Journal
PO Box 25
River Falls, WI 54022
Phone: (715)425-1561
Fax: (715)425-5666

Publications: River Falls Journal (34309)

River News Herald Co.
PO Box 786
Rio Vista, CA 94571
Phone: (707)374-6431
Fax: (707)374-6322

Publications: River News Herald & Isleton Journal (2927)

The River Press
PO Box 69
Fort Benton, MT 59442-0069
Phone: (406)622-3311
Fax: (406)622-5446

Publications: The River Press (17791)

River Publishers
115 W Burleson
PO Box 111
Wharton, TX 77488
Phone: (409)532-8840
Fax: (409)532-8845

Publications: Wharton Journal-Spectator (31284)

River Raisin Publications, Inc.
121 Newspaper St.
Blissfield, MI 49228
Phone: (517)486-2400
Fax: (517)486-4675

Publications: The Advance (14827)

The River Reporter
PO Box 150
Narrowsburg, NY 12764
Phone: (845)252-7414
Fax: (845)252-3298

Publications: The River Reporter (21107)

River Turmain Tournal
332 Main
PO Box 10
Lander, WY 82520
Phone: (307)332-2323
Fax: (307)332-9332

Publications: The Lander Wyoming State Journal (34543)

The Riverdale Press
6155 Broadway
Bronx, NY 10471
Phone: (718)543-6065
Fax: (718)548-4038

Publications: The Riverdale Press (20284)

Riverfront Times, LLC
6358 Delmar Blvd., Ste. 200
St. Louis, MO 63130-4719
Phone: (314)615-6666
Fax: (314)615-6655

Publications: The Riverfront Times (17490)

Rivers Banner
Box 70
Rivers, MB, Canada R0K 1X0
Phone: (204)328-7494
Fax: (204)328-5212

Publications: Rivers Banner (35286)

Riverside County Farm Bureau
21160 Box Springs Rd., Ste. 102
Moreno Valley, CA 92557
Phone: (909)684-6732
Fax: (909)782-0621
Free: 888-383-5684

Publications: Riverside County Agriculture (2599)

Riverside Current
31 E 1st St.
PO Box H
MF 8-5 CST
Riverside, IA 52327
Phone: (319)648-2542
Fax: (319)648-5923

Publications: Riverside Current (11178)

Riverside Publishing
2 Riverside Dr.
Kingston, MA 02364
Phone: (781)585-7472

Publications: South Shore Baby Journal (14265)

Riverton Ranger
421 E. Main St.
PO Box 993
Riverton, WY 82501
Phone: (307)856-2244
Fax: (307)856-0189
Free: 800-428-7229

Publications: The Dubois Frontier (34520) • The Riverton Ranger (34577)

Riverton Register Publishing
100 N 6th St.
Box 200
Riverton, IL 62561
Phone: (217)629-9247

Publications: Buffalo Tri City Register (9499) • Williamsville Sun (9500)

Rivertown Newspaper Group
126 S. Chestnut St.
Ellsworth, WI 54011-4117
Phone: (715)273-4334
Fax: (715)273-4335

Publications: Pierce County Herald (33689)

Rivertown Ranger
310 W 6th St.
PO Box 420
Shoshoni, WY 82649
Phone: (307)856-2244
Fax: (307)876-2627

Publications: Shoshoni Pioneer (34593)

Riverview Publishing, Inc.
PO Box 91
Kingston, ON, Canada K7L 4V6
Phone: (613)546-6723
Fax: (613)546-0707

Publications: Profile Kingston (35942)

Rizzo Management Corporation
3500 Fairlane Farms Rd., No. 9
Wellington, FL 33414-8749
Phone: (561)793-9524
Fax: (561)793-9576

Publications: Polo Players Edition (6844)

The R.J. Garbosky Co.
29 Bennitt Ave.
San Anselmo, CA 94960
Phone: (415)647-7091
Fax: (415)456-7260

Publications: FAD Magazine (3083)

RLD Communications, Inc.
155 S El Molino Ave., Ste. 100
Pasadena, CA 91101
Phone: (626)396-0250
Fax: (626)396-0248

Publications: BOXOFFICE Magazine (2812)

RLD Group, Inc.
203 N Wabash, Ste. 800
Chicago, IL 60601
Phone: (312)236-3528
Fax: (312)236-4024

Publications: Manufactured Home Merchandiser (8476)

RMA—The Risk Management Association
1 Liberty Place
1650 Market St., Ste. 2300
Philadelphia, PA 19103-7398
Phone: (215)446-4000
Fax: (215)446-4101
Free: 800-677-7621

Publications: The RMA Journal (27654)

RMV Publications Ltd.
One Palliser Sq., Ste. 250
125 Ninth Ave. SE
Calgary, AB, Canada T2G 0P6
Phone: (403)299-1885
Fax: (403)299-1899

Publications: WHERE Canadian Rockies (34660)

RO-EL Productions, Inc.
550 W. Old Country Rd. Ste. 204
Hicksville, NY 11801
Phone: (516)932-7860
Fax: (516)932-7639

Publications: Floor Covering News (20735)

Roadracing World & Motorcycle Technology
581 Birch St., Unit C
Lake Elsinore, CA 92530
Phone: (909)245-6411
Fax: (909)245-6417
Free: 800-464-8336

Publications: Roadracing World & Motorcycle Technology (2140)

Roane County News
204 Franklin St.
PO Box 610
Kingston, TN 37763
Phone: (423)376-3481
Fax: (423)376-1945

Publications: Roane County News (29269)

The Roane County News-Record
112 Pierce St.,
Rockwood, TN 37854
Phone: (865)376-3481
Fax: (865)376-1945

Publications: The Roane County News/Record (29578)

Roane Newspapers
PO Box 346
Wartburg, TN 37887
Phone: (423)346-6225
Fax: (423)346-5788

Publications: Morgan County News (29639)

Roanoke
PO Box 726
Plymouth, NC 27962
Phone: (252)793-2123
Fax: (252)793-5365

Publications: Roanoke Beacon (24119)

The Roanoke Times
201 W. Campbell Ave.
PO Box 2491
Roanoke, VA 24010-2491
Free: 800-346-1234

Publications: The Roanoke Times (32491)

Roanoke Tribune Inc.
PO Box 6021
Roanoke, VA 24017
Phone: (540)343-0326
Fax: (540)343-0326

Publications: Roanoke Tribune (32492)

Robar Industries, Inc.
3 Union Hill Rd.
West Conshohocken, PA 19428-2788
Phone: (610)834-0400
Fax: (610)834-7337

Publications: Item-Interference Technology Engineers Master (28150)

Roberts Publishing
3600 College Ave.
PO Box 949
Snyder, TX 79549
Phone: (915)573-5486
Fax: (915)573-0044

Publications: Snyder Daily News (31114)

Robertson County Times
PO Box 637
505 W. Court Sq.
Springfield, TN 37172
Phone: (615)384-3567
Fax: (615)384-1221

Publications: Robertson County Times (29618)

The Robins Review
RR 4
Box 275
Cochran, GA 31014-9252
Phone: (478)922-5758
Fax: (478)922-4559

Publications: The Robins Review (7180)

Robinson Blackmore Printing and Publishing
PO Box 39, Sta. B
Happy Valley, NL, Canada A0P 1E0
Phone: (709)896-3341
Fax: (709)896-8781

Publications: Labradorian (35465)

Robinson Blackmore Printing and Publishing
PO Box 428
Harbour Breton, NL, Canada A0H 1P0
Phone: (709)489-2162
Fax: (709)489-4817

Publications: The Coaster (35468)

Robinson Blackmore Printing and Publishing
PO Box 1210 Main St.
Lewisporte, NL, Canada A0G 3A0
Phone: (709)535-6910
Fax: (709)535-8640

Publications: The Pilot (35470)

Robinson Blackmore Printing and Publishing
PO Box 1090 Grand Bay Rd.
Port-aux-Basques, NL, Canada A0M 1C0
Phone: (709)695-3671
Fax: (709)695-7901

Publications: The Gulf News (35477)

Robinson Blackmore Printing and Publishing
36 Austin St.
PO Box 8660, Sta. A
St. John's, NL, Canada A1B 3T7
Phone: (709)579-1312
Fax: (709)722-2228

Publications: Advertiser (35484) • The Express (35487) • Express (35486) • Humber Log (35446) • Nor'Wester (35507) • Packet (35493) • The Southern Gazette (35472)

Robinson Blackmore Printing and Publishing
PO Box 283
Stephenville, NL, Canada A2N 2Z4
Phone: (709)643-4531
Fax: (709)643-5041

Publications: The Georgian (35508)

Robinson Blackmore Printing and Publishing
129 Grand Falls
Windsor, NL, Canada A2A 2J4
Phone: (709)256-4371
Fax: (709)256-3826

Publications: The Beacon (35455)

Robinson Communications
2208 NW Market St., Rm. 202
Seattle, WA 98107
Phone: (206)783-1244
Fax: (206)783-2455

Publications: Ballard News Tribune (32944)

Robinson Community Newspaper
118 E Lee Ave.
PO Box 508
Vinton, VA 24179
Phone: (540)343-0720
Fax: (540)343-2648

Publications: The Vinton Messenger (32586)

Robinson Daily News
302 S Cross St.
PO Box 639
Robinson, IL 62454
Phone: (618)544-2101
Fax: (618)544-9533

Publications: Robinson Daily News (9512)

Roblin Review
119 1st Ave. NW
Box 938
Roblin, MB, Canada R0L 1P0
Phone: (204)937-8377
Fax: (204)937-8212

Publications: Roblin Review (35287)

Rochester Business Journal
55 St. Paul St.
Rochester, NY 14604
Phone: (585)546-8303
Fax: (585)546-3398

Publications: Rochester Business Journal (23238)

Rochester Catholic Press Association
PO Box 24379
Rochester, NY 14624-0379
Phone: (585)529-9530
Free: 800-600-3628

Publications: Catholic Courier (23215)

Rochester Golf Week Newspaper
2535 Brighton Henrietta Town Line Rd.
Rochester, NY 14623-2711
Phone: (585)427-2160

Publications: Rochester Golf Week Newspaper (23239)

Rochester Museum and Science Center
657 East Ave.
Rochester, NY 14607
Phone: (716)271-4552
Fax: (716)271-2119

Publications: The Bulletin (23212)

The Rochester Sentinel
118 E 8th St.
PO Box 260
Rochester, IN 46975
Phone: (574)223-2111
Fax: (219)223-5782
Free: 800-686-2112

Publications: The Rochester Sentinel (10431)

Rock County Leader
PO Box 488
Bassett, NE 68714
Phone: (402)684-3771
Fax: (402)684-2857

Publications: Rock County Leader (17943)

The Rock River Times
128 N Church St.
Rockford, IL 61101
Phone: (815)964-9767
Fax: (815)964-9825

Publications: The Rock River Times (9531)

Rock Springs Newspapers, Inc.
PO Box 98
Rock Springs, WY 82902-0098
Phone: (307)362-3736
Fax: (307)382-2763

Publications: Daily Rocket-Miner (34581)

The Rock Valley Bee
PO Box 157
Rock Valley, IA 51247
Phone: (712)476-2795
Fax: (712)476-2796

Publications: The Rock Valley Bee (11181)

Rock Valley Publishing
11512 N. 2nd St.
Machesney Park, IL 61115
Phone: (815)877-4044
Fax: (815)654-4857

Publications: The Herald (9546) • Journal (9125) • News Gazette (9126) • Northern Ogle Tempo (9127) • The Post-Journal and Metro Rockford Journal (9529)

Rockdale Citizen
969 Main St.
PO Box 136
Conyers, GA 30012
Phone: (770)483-7108
Fax: (770)483-2955

Publications: East Metro Plus (7200) • Rockdale Citizen (7201)

The Rockdale Reporter & Messenger
221-225 E Cameron Ave.
PO Box 552
Rockdale, TX 76567
Phone: (512)446-5838
Fax: (512)446-5317

Publications: The Rockdale Reporter & Messenger (30987)

Rockefeller University Press
1114 1st Ave., 3rd Fl.
New York, NY 10021
Phone: (212)327-8572
Fax: (212)327-7944

Publications: The Journal of Cell Biology (22019) • The Journal of Experimental Medicine (22068)

Rocket Acquisition
PO Box 55
Fairbury, IL 61739-0055

Publications: The Rocket (8879)

The Rocket Courier
PO Box 187
Wyalusing, PA 18853
Phone: (570)746-1217
Fax: (570)746-7737

Publications: The Rocket-Courier (28196)

Rocket Fuel
c/o Courtney Miller
509 S. 15th St.
Philadelphia, PA 19146

Publications: Rocket Fuel Online (27655)

The Rockford Institute
928 N Main St.
Rockford, IL 61103
Phone: (815)964-5053
Fax: (815)964-9403

Publications: Chronicles (9526)

Rockford Writers' Guild
7721 Venus St.
Loves Park, IL 61111

Publications: Rockford Review (9120)

Rockhurst University
1100 Rockhurst Rd.
Kansas City, MO 64110-2561
Phone: (816)501-4051
Fax: (816)501-4290

Publications: The Rockhurst Sentinel (17195)

Rockingham Newspapers, Inc.
225 Turner Dr.
PO Box 2157
Reidsville, NC 27320-5736
Fax: (919)342-2513

Publications: The Reidsville Review (24180)

Rockingham Publishing Co., Inc.
PO Box 126
Elkton, VA 22827
Phone: (540)298-9444
Fax: (540)298-2560

Publications: The Valley Banner (32001)

Rockingham Publishing Co., Inc.
231 S. Liberty St.
PO Box 193
Harrisonburg, VA 22803
Phone: (540)574-6200
Fax: (540)433-9112
Free: 800-296-NEWS

Publications: Daily News-Record (32138)

Rockler Woodworking and Hardware
4365 Willow Dr.
Medina, MN 55340
Phone: (763)478-8306
Fax: (763)478-8396

Publications: Woodworker's Journal (16049)

The Rockport Pilot
PO Box 730
Rockport, TX 78381
Phone: (361)729-9900
Fax: (361)729-8903

Publications: The Rockport Pilot (30988)

Rockwell Publishing Co.
109 N. VanBibber
PO Box 608
Pocahontas, AR 72455
Phone: (870)892-4451
Fax: (870)892-4453

Publications: Pocahontas Star Herald (1316) • Randco Trading Post (1317)

Rocky Ford Daily Gazette
912 Elm Ave.
PO Box 430
Rocky Ford, CO 81067-0430
Phone: (719)254-3351
Fax: (719)254-3354

Publications: Rocky Ford Daily Gazette (4616)

Rocky Ford Publishing Co.
223 Main St.
Ordway, CO 81063
Phone: (719)267-3576
Fax: (719)267-4661

Publications: The Ordway New Era (4589)

Rocky Mountain Association of Geologists
820 16th St., No. 505
Denver, CO 80202-3218
Phone: (303)573-8621
Fax: (303)628-0546

Publications: Mountain Geologist (4340)

Rocky Mountain Elk Foundation
2291 W Broadway
Missoula, MT 59808
Phone: (406)523-4500
Fax: (406)523-4550
Free: 800-225-5355

Publications: Bugle (17865)

Rocky Mountain Farmers Union
10800 E Bethany Dr., 4th Fl.
Aurora, CO 80014-2632
Phone: (303)752-5800
Fax: (303)752-5810
Free: 800-373-7638

Publications: Rocky Mountain Union Farmer (4148)

Rocky Mountain Medieval and Renaissance Association
Dept. of English
University of Wyoming
Laramie, WY 82071
Phone: (307)766-6490
Fax: (307)766-3189

Publications: Quidditas (34552)

Rocky Mountain Modern Language Association
PO Box 642610
Pullman, WA 99164-2610
Phone: (509)335-4198
Fax: (509)335-3708

Publications: Rocky Mountain Review of Language and Literature (32907)

Rocky View Times
Bay 8, 206, 5th Ave. W.
Cochrane, AB, Canada T4C 1X3
Phone: (403)932-3500
Fax: (403)932-3935

Publications: Rocky View Times (34686)

Roctober Magazine
1507 E. 53rd St., No. 617
Chicago, IL 60615

Publications: Roctober (8559)

Rod & Custom
6420 Wilshire Blvd.
Los Angeles, CA 90048
Phone: (323)782-2712
Fax: (323)782-2223

Publications: Rod & Custom Magazine (2381)

Rodale Inc.
33 E. Minor St.
Emmaus, PA 18098-0099
Phone: (610)967-5171
Fax: (610)967-8181

Publications: Men's Health (26877) • Organic Gardening (26879) • Prevention (26880) • Rodale's Fitness Swimmer (26881) • Rodale's SCUBA Diving (7533) • Runner's World (26882)

Rodman Publishing Co.
70 Hilltop Rd.
Box 555
Ramsey, NJ 07446
Phone: (201)825-2552
Fax: (201)825-0553

Publications: Carpet and Rug Industry (19487) • Happi Household & Personal Products Industry (19488) • Ink World (19491) • Nonwovens Industry (19492)

Roeper School
PO Box 329
Bloomfield Hills, MI 48303
Phone: (248)203-7321
Fax: (248)203-7310

Publications: Roeper Review (14829)

Rogers Media
1001 boul. De Maisonneure Ouest
Bureau 1100
Montreal, QC, Canada H3A 3E1
Phone: (514)845-5141
Fax: (514)845-3879

Publications: L'actualite (37080) • L'Actualite Medicale (37081) • L'Actualite Pharmaceutique (37082) • Chatelaine (37102) • L'Actualite Medicale (37154)

Rogers Media Publishing
One Mount Pleasant Rd., 7th Fl.
Toronto, ON, Canada M4Y 2Y5
Phone: (416)764-2000
Fax: (416)764-1740
Free: 800-382-4957

Publications: Coatings Magazine (36553) • Heating, Plumbing, Air Conditioning Buyers' Guide (36613) • HPAC (Heating-Plumbing-Air Conditioning Magazine) (36620) • Marketing Magazine (36657) • Materials Management & Distribution (36658) • Plastics in Canada (36710)

Rogers Media Publishing
One Mount Pleasant Rd., 12th Fl.
Toronto, ON, Canada M4Y 2Y5
Phone: (416)764-2000
Free: 800-268-9119

Publications: Benefits Canada (36474) • Canadian Advertising Rates & Data (36490) • Canadian Grocer (36500) • Canadian Machinery and Metalworking (36515) • Canadian Packaging (36523) • Channel Business (36545) • Chatelaine (36547) • Civic Public Works (36551) • Cosmetics (36561) • Cosmetics (36562) • Design Engineering (36571) • L'Epicier (36584) • FLARE (36596) • Food in Canada (36597) • Hardware Merchandising (36611) • Heavy Construction News (36614) • IT Magazine (36626) • Maclean's (36654) • The Medical Post (36659) • Meetings & Incentive Travel (36660) • Modern Purchasing (36666) • Ontario Medicine (36685) • Ontario Out of Doors (36686) • Pharmacy Practice (36705) • Physician's Management Manuals (36707) • Plant (36709)

Rogers Media Publishing
777 Bay St., 6th Fl.
Toronto, ON, Canada M5W 1A7
Phone: (416)596-5898
Fax: (416)596-5965

Publications: Canadian Printer Magazine (36526)

Rogersville Review
316 E Main St.
PO Box 100
Rogersville, TN 37857-0100
Phone: (423)272-7422
Fax: (423)272-7889

Publications: Rogersville Review (29580)

Rogue Valley Genealogical Society, Inc.
95 Houston Rd.
PO Box 1468
Phoenix, OR 97535-1468
Phone: (541)512-2340

Publications: Rogue Digger (26464)

Rolin Press Group
PO Box 250
Richland, GA 31825
Phone: (912)887-3674
Fax: (912)887-2800

Publications: The Hogansville Herald (7337). • Manchester Star-Mercury (7493) • Meriwether-Vindicator (7494) • Patriot-Citizen (7495) • Stewart-Webster Journal (7569)

Roll Call, Inc.
50 F St. NW, Ste. 700
Washington, DC 20001
Phone: (202)824-6800
Fax: (202)824-0902

Publications: Roll Call (5771)

Rolla Daily News
101 W 7th St.
PO Box 808
Rolla, MO 65401-0808
Phone: (573)364-2468
Fax: (573)341-5847
Free: 888-882-2468

Publications: Rolla Daily News (17380)

Rollins College
1000 Holt Ave., 2749
Winter Park, FL 32789-4499
Phone: (407)646-2696
Fax: (407)646-1530

Publications: The Sandspur (6885)

Romaine Pierson Publishers Inc.
241 Forsgate Dr.
Jamesburg, NJ 08831
Phone: (732)656-0200
Fax: (732)656-1142

Publications: Pharmacy Times (19131) • Resident & Staff Physician (19132) • Surgical Rounds (19133)

Roman Catholic Diocese of Burlington
PO Box 489
Burlington, VT 05402
Phone: (802)658-6110
Fax: (802)863-3866

Publications: The Vermont Catholic Tribune (31520)

Roman Catholic Diocese of Helena
515 N. Ewing
PO Box 1729
Helena, MT 59624-1729
Phone: (406)442-5820
Fax: (406)442-5191

Publications: The Montana Catholic (17820)

Roman Catholic Diocese of Phoenix
400 E Monroe St.
Phoenix, AZ 85004-2336
Phone: (602)257-5565
Fax: (602)258-6404

Publications: The Catholic Sun (799)

Roman Catholic Diocese of Salt Lake City
27 C St.
Salt Lake City, UT 84103-2302
Phone: (801)328-8641
Fax: (801)537-1667

Publications: Intermountain Catholic (31430)

Roman Catholic Diocese of San Jose
900 Lafayette St., Ste. 301
Santa Clara, CA 95050-4966
Phone: (408)983-0260
Fax: (408)983-0268

Publications: The Valley Catholic Newspaper (3676)

The Roman Catholic Diocese of Worcester
51 Elm St.
Worcester, MA 01609
Phone: (508)757-6387
Fax: (508)756-8315

Publications: The Catholic Free Press (14676)

Romantic Lifelines
1224 NW 9th Ave.
Gainesville, FL 32601-4942

Publications: Relationships Today (6156)

Numbers cited after listings are entry numbers rather than page numbers.

Romantic Times Publishing Group
55 Bergen St.
Brooklyn, NY 11201
Phone: (718)237-1097
Fax: (718)624-4231
Free: 800-989-8816

Publications: Romantic Times (20343)

Rome Sentinel Co.
333 W. Dominick St.
PO Box 471
Rome, NY 13442-0471

Publications: Daily Sentinel (23264)

The Romeo Observer
124 W St. Clair
Box 96
Romeo, MI 48065-0096
Phone: (810)752-3524
Fax: (810)752-0548

Publications: The Countryman (15472) • The Romeo Observer (15473)

Rondout Valley Publishing Co., Inc.
1087 Ulster Heights Rd.
Ellenville, NY 12428-5745
Phone: (914)647-7222
Fax: (914)647-7443
Free: 800-864-0263

Publications: The Ellenville Press (20569)

Rood Printing
Box 237
Slater, IA 50244-0237
Fax: (515)685-3668

Publications: Tri County Times (11228)

Roofing, Metal and Heating Engineers, Inc.
PO Box 21187
Philadelphia, PA 19114-0387
Phone: (215)927-5262
Fax: (215)224-2690
Free: 800-237-0024

Publications: The Trade News (27707)

Room Communications and Design
PO Box 7183
Windsor, ON, Canada N9C 3Z1
Phone: (519)252-5344
Fax: (519)252-9506

Publications: Room (36889)

Roper Center for Public Opinion Research
341 Mansfield Rd.
University of Connecticut U-1164
Storrs, CT 06269-1164
Phone: (860)486-4440
Fax: (860)486-6308

Publications: Public Perspective (5167)

The Rose Hill Reporter
110 N Rose Hill Rd.
PO Box 16
Rose Hill, KS 67133
Phone: (316)776-0097

Publications: The Rose Hill Reporter (11771)

Rose-Hulman Institute of Technology
5500 Wabash Ave.
Terre Haute, IN 47803
Phone: (812)877-8258
Fax: (812)877-8362

Publications: Echoes (10485) • The Rose Thorn (10489)

Roseau Times-Region
106 W. Center St.
Roseau, MN 56751
Phone: (218)463-1521
Fax: (218)463-1530

Publications: Roseau Times-Region (16328)

Rosebud
PO Box 459
Cambridge, WI 53523
Phone: (608)423-9609
Fax: (608)423-9690
Free: 800-786-5669

Publications: Rosebud (33615)

The Rosebud News
PO Box 516
Rosebud, TX 76570
Phone: (254)583-7811
Fax: (254)583-4000
Free: 800-458-3927

Publications: The Rosebud News (30991)

Rosemead School of Psychology and Theology
Biola University
13800 Biola Ave.
La Mirada, CA 90639-0001
Phone: (562)944-0351
Fax: (562)906-4547

Publications: Journal of Psychology and Theology (2126)

Rosemont College
1400 Montgomery Ave.
Rosemont, PA 19010
Phone: (610)366-1963

Publications: Rambler (27941)

The Rosen Group, Inc.
3000 Chestnut Ave., Ste. 304
Baltimore, MD 21211
Phone: (410)889-3093
Fax: (410)243-7089

Publications: AmericanStyle Magazine (13121)

Rosenstiel School of Marine and Atmospheric Science
4600 Rickenbacker Causeway
Miami, FL 33149-1098

Publications: The Bulletin of Marine Science (6343)

Rosetown Publishing Company Ltd.
Box 130
Rosetown, SK, Canada S0L 2V0
Phone: (306)882-4202
Fax: (306)882-4204

Publications: Rosetown Eagle (37545)

The Rosholt Review
PO Box 136
Rosholt, SD 57260
Phone: (605)537-4276
Fax: (605)537-4276

Publications: The Rosholt Review (28958)

Rosicrucian Fellowship
PO Box 713
Oceanside, CA 92049-0713
Phone: (760)757-6600
Fax: (760)721-3806

Publications: Rays from the Rose Cross (2709)

Rosicrucian Order, AMORC
Rosicrucian Park
1342 Naglee Ave.
San Jose, CA 95191
Phone: (408)947-3600
Fax: (408)947-3677

Publications: Rosicrucian Digest (3534)

Ross Periodicals
42 Digital Dr., No. 5
Novato, CA 94949-5704
Phone: (415)382-0580
Fax: (415)382-0587

Publications: Sports Car International (2973) • Woodwork (2654)

Rossi Publications, Inc.
6001 N. Clark St.
Chicago, IL 60660
Phone: (773)273-2900
Fax: (773)273-2006

Publications: La Raza (8453)

Roswell Daily Record
2301 N. Main St.
PO Box 1897
Roswell, NM 88201-6452
Phone: (505)622-7710
Fax: (505)625-0421

Publications: Roswell Daily Record (19913)

Rotary International
One Rotary Center
1560 Sherman Ave.
Evanston, IL 60201
Phone: (847)866-3000
Fax: (847)866-9732

Publications: The ROTARIAN (8869)

The Round Top Register
PO Box 225
Round Top, TX 78954
Phone: (409)249-5550
Fax: (409)249-5021

Publications: The Round Top Register (30996)

Roundup Record Tribune, Inc.
PO Box 350
Roundup, MT 59072
Phone: (406)323-1105
Fax: (406)323-1761

Publications: Roundup Record-Tribune and Winnett Times (17902)

Route 66 Magazine
326 W Rte. 66
Williams, AZ 86046
Phone: (928)635-4322
Fax: (928)635-4470

Publications: Route 66 Magazine (1009)

Route 3 Press
19948 Shooting Star Rd.
Anamosa, IA 52205
Phone: (319)462-4623

Publications: Wapsipinicon Almanac (10602)

Routledge Inc.
29 W. 35th St.
New York, NY 10001-2291
Phone: (212)216-7800
Fax: (212)564-7854
Free: 800-634-7064

Publications: Journal of Strategic Marketing (22194)

Routledge Journals
325 Chestnut St., 8th Fl.
Philadelphia, PA 19106
Fax: (215)625-8914
Free: 800-354-1420

Publications: Communication Education (6933) • Communication Monographs (27423) • Critical Studies in Media Communication (6935)

Rowland Publishing, Inc.
PO Box 1837
Tallahassee, FL 32302
Phone: (904)878-0554
Fax: (904)656-1871

Publications: Tallahassee Magazine (6738)

Royal Astronomical Society of Canada
136 Dupont St.
Toronto, ON, Canada M5R 1V2
Phone: (416)924-7973
Fax: (416)924-2911

Publications: Journal of the Royal Astronomical Society of Canada (R.A.S.C.) (36638)

Royal Canadian Mounted Police Veterans' Association
Attn: The Quarterly
1200 Vanier Pkwy.
Ottawa, ON, Canada K1A 0R2
Phone: (613)993-3738
Fax: (613)993-4353

Publications: RCMP Veterans' Association Quarterly/Association des anciens de la GRC Trimestrialle (36275)

Royal Center Record
PO Box 638
Royal Center, IN 46978
Phone: (574)643-3165
Fax: (574)643-9440

Publications: Royal Center Record (10436)

Royal Gorge Publishing Corp.
701 S 9th St.
Canon City, CO 81212
Phone: (719)275-7565
Fax: (719)275-1353

Publications: Daily Record (4213)

Royal Neighbors of America
230 16th St.
Rock Island, IL 61201
Phone: (309)788-4561
Fax: (309)788-1439
Free: 800-627-4762

Publications: The Royal Neighbor (9520)

Royal Ontario Museum
100 Queen's Park
Toronto, ON, Canada M5S 2C6
Phone: (416)586-5758
Fax: (416)586-5649

Publications: Rotunda (36732)

Royal Publications Co., Inc.
112 Market St.
Sun Prairie, WI 53590
Phone: (608)837-5161
Fax: (608)825-3053

Publications: Bear Report (9257)

Royal Publishing, Inc.
PO Box 398
Glendora, CA 91740
Phone: (626)335-8069
Fax: (626)335-6127

Publications: Sharing Ideas News Magazine (2026)

Royal Winnipeg Ballet
380 Graham Ave.
Winnipeg, MB, Canada R3C 4K2
Phone: (204)956-0183
Fax: (204)943-1994
Free: 800-667-4792

Publications: Ballet-Hoo (35312)

Royalty Printing Inc.
1558 Hill St.
Radcliff, KY 40160
Phone: (270)351-4407
Fax: (270)351-4407

Publications: The Sentinel (12379)

Royann Tatro
213 E Main
PO Box 457
Glasco, KS 67445-0457
Phone: (913)568-2565

Publications: The Delphos Republican (11461) •
The Glasco Sun (11462)

Royle Publishing Co., Inc.
112 Market St.
Sun Prairie, WI 53590
Phone: (608)837-2200
Fax: (608)825-3053
Free: 800-728-6315

Publications: Live Sound! International (17181)

RPB Publications
34 E Franklin St.
Bellbrook, OH 45305-2098
Phone: (937)848-4972
Fax: (937)848-3012
Free: 888-772-2776

Publications: Racing Pigeon Bulletin (24665)

RR International Magazine, Inc.
21300 NE 24 Ct.
Miami, FL 33180
Phone: (305)933-1178
Fax: (305)933-9918

Publications: Reggae Report (6377)

RSA Publications
19 Pendelton Dr.
Box 19
Hebron, CT 06248
Phone: (860)228-0487
Fax: (860)228-4402

Publications: Radiation Protection Management
(4916) • RSO Magazine (4917)

RTP Publications
301 Friendship St.
Providence, RI 02903-4507
Phone: (401)351-0787
Fax: (401)351-0788

Publications: Bedroom (28388) • Futon Life (28397)

Rubber Division, American Chemical Society
PO Box 499
Akron, OH 44309-0499
Phone: (330)972-7814
Fax: (330)972-5269

Publications: Rubber Chemistry and Technology
(24586)

Rubber World
1867 W. Market St.
PO Box 5451
Akron, OH 44313
Phone: (216)864-2122
Fax: (216)864-5298

Publications: Rubber World (24588)

Ruben P. Bunag
12 Avalon Dr.
Daly City, CA 94015
Phone: (650)992-5474
Fax: (650)997-0673

Publications: Manila Mail (1803)

Ruffed Grouse Society
451 McCormick Rd.
Coraopolis, PA 15108
Phone: (412)262-4044
Fax: (412)262-9207
Free: 888-564-6747

Publications: RGS Magazine (26808)

Rug Hooking Magazine
1300 Market St., Ste. 202
Lemoyne, PA 17043-1420
Phone: (717)234-5091
Fax: (717)234-1359
Free: 800-233-9055

Publications: Rug Hooking Magazine (27185)

Rug News Magazine
26 Broadway, Ste. 776
New York, NY 10004
Phone: (212)269-2016
Fax: (212)269-2740

Publications: Rug News (23620)

The Rugby Press
2350 Broadway
New York, NY 10024
Phone: (212)787-1160
Fax: (212)595-0934
Free: 888-987-1010

Publications: Rugby (22679)

Ruhr Publishing, Inc.
Hwy. 20
PO Box 9
Vacherie, LA 70090
Phone: (504)265-2120
Fax: (504)265-2120

Publications: The Enterprise (12664)

Ruhr Valley Publishing, Inc.
2290 Texas St.
PO Drawer 460
Lutcher, LA 70071
Phone: (504)869-5784
Fax: (504)869-4386

Publications: News Examiner (12665)

Ruland Communications, Inc.
12 Lawton Blvd.
Toronto, ON, Canada M4V 1Z4
Phone: (416)927-9129
Fax: (416)927-9118

Publications: Canada Journal (36488) • German
American Trade (36603)

Ruminator Review
1648 Grand Ave.
St. Paul, MN 55105
Phone: (651)699-2610
Fax: (651)699-7190

Publications: Ruminator Review (16408)

Runge Newspapers
Box 430
Carleton Place, ON, Canada K7C 3P5
Phone: (613)257-1303
Fax: (613)257-7373

Publications: Carleton Place Canadian (35728)

Runge Newspapers Inc.
86 Mill St.
PO Box 130
Almonte, ON, Canada K0A 1A0
Phone: (613)256-1311
Fax: (613)256-5168

Publications: Gazette (35631)

Runge Newspapers Inc.
1120 March Drive, Unit C
Kanata, ON, Canada K2K 1X7
Phone: (613)591-3060
Fax: (613)591-8503

Publications: Kanata Kourier-Standard (35925)

Runge Newspapers Inc.
186 Alexander St.
PO Box 190
Pembroke, ON, Canada K8A 6X3
Phone: (613)735-3141
Fax: (613)732-7214

Publications: Pembroke Daily News (36309)

Runge Publishing Inc.
35 Opeongo Rd.
PO Box 400
Renfrew, ON, Canada K7V 4A8
Phone: (613)432-3655
Fax: (613)432-6689

Publications: The Renfrew Weekend News (36340)

Rungh Cultural Society
Box 66019, Sta. F
Vancouver, BC, Canada V5N 5L4
Phone: (604)873-5593
Fax: (604)837-5276

Publications: Rungh (35166)

Running Deer Press
647 N Santa Cruz Ave., Annex
Los Gatos, CA 95030
Phone: (408)354-8604

Publications: Writing For Our Lives (2480)

Running Wild
494 North Ave.
Weston, MA 02493-1806
Phone: (617)899-9896

Publications: Running Wild (14526)

Rural Heritage
281 Dean Ridge Ln.
Gainesboro, TN 38562
Phone: (931)268-0655

Publications: Rural Heritage (29201)

Rural Rambler
140 W Ormsby
Oxford, WI 53952-0105
Phone: (608)586-5461
Fax: (608)586-5744

Publications: Rural Rambler (34231)

Rural-Urban Record
24487 Squires Rd.
Box 966
Columbia Station, OH 44028
Phone: (440)236-8982
Fax: (440)236-9198

Publications: Rural-Urban Record (24998)

Rural Virginian
PO Box 9030
Charlottesville, VA 22906-9030
Phone: (434)978-7216
Fax: (434)978-7204

Publications: Rural Virginian (31940)

The Rural Voice
PO Box 429
Blyth, ON, Canada N0M 1H0
Phone: (519)523-4311
Fax: (519)523-9140

Publications: The Rural Voice (35688)

Ruralite Services, Inc.
2040 A St.
PO Box 558
Forest Grove, OR 97116
Phone: (503)357-2105
Fax: (503)357-8615

Publications: Ruralite (26357)

Numbers cited after listings are entry numbers rather than page numbers.

The Rush County News
112 W 8th
Box 60
La Crosse, KS 67548
Phone: (785)222-2555
Fax: (785)222-2557

Publications: The Rush County News (11542)

Rushville Newspapers, Inc.
PO Box 189
Rushville, IN 46173-0189
Phone: (765)932-2222
Fax: (765)932-4358

Publications: Rushville Republican (10437)

RUSPAM Communications, Inc.
205 Madison Ave.
Cresskill, NJ 07626-1301
Phone: (201)871-9200
Fax: (201)871-9639

Publications: Sugar y Azucar (18773)

Russell Banner
PO Box 100
310 Maine St.
Russell, MB, Canada R0J 1W0
Phone: (204)773-2069
Fax: (204)773-2645

Publications: Banner (35288)

Russell Daily News
802 N Maple St.
PO Box 513
Russell, KS 67665-1937
Phone: (785)483-2116
Fax: (785)483-4012
Free: 800-737-3023

Publications: Russell Daily News (11772)

Russell Publications
PO Box 429
Peotone, IL 60468
Phone: (708)258-3473
Fax: (708)258-6295

Publications: Beecher Herald (8057) • Crete Record (8693) • Grant Park Gazette (8950) • Manhattan American (9443) • Monee Monitor (9212) • New Lenox Community Reporter (9282) • Peotone Vedette (9444)

The Russell Record
802 N Maple St., No. 393
Russell, KS 67665-1937
Phone: (785)483-2111
Fax: (785)483-4012

Publications: The Russell Record (11773)

Russell Sage College
45 Ferry St.
Troy, NY 12180
Phone: (518)274-2175

Publications: The Quill (23456)

Russells Guides Inc.
PO Box 278
Cedar Rapids, IA 52406
Phone: (319)364-6138
Fax: (319)364-4853

Publications: Russell's Official National Motor Coach Guide (10677)

Russellville Newspapers
107 Harrison St.
PO Box 270
Dardanelle, AR 72834-0270
Phone: (501)229-2250
Fax: (501)229-1159

Publications: The Courier (1097) • Post Dispatch (1098)

Rust Communications
112 N Poplar
Osceola, AR 72370-2665
Phone: (501)563-2615
Fax: (501)563-2616

Publications: Osceola Times (1304)

Rust Publishing
195 S 3rd E
PO Box 1330
Mountain Home, ID 83647
Phone: (208)587-3331
Fax: (208)587-9205

Publications: Mountain Home News (7926)

Rust Publishing, MOKS, LLC
131 S Cedar
PO Box 247
Nevada, MO 64772
Phone: (417)667-3344
Fax: (417)667-8121

Publications: Nevada Daily Mail/Herald (17308)

Rustler Sentinel
PO Box 24
Hooper, NE 68031
Phone: (402)654-2218
Fax: (402)654-2130

Publications: Rustler Sentinel (18274)

Ruston Daily Leader
212 W Park Ave.,
PO Box 520
Ruston, LA 71270-4314
Phone: (318)255-4353
Fax: (318)255-4006
Free: 800-287-4176

Publications: Ruston Daily Leader (12806)

Rutgers Magazine
101 Somerset Street
New Brunswick, NJ 08901
Phone: (732)932-7084
Fax: (732)932-6950

Publications: Rutgers Magazine (19338)

Rutgers University
CMS 42 Camden Campus Center
326 Penn St.
Camden, NJ 08102
Phone: (609)225-6354
Fax: (609)225-6579

Publications: The Gleaner (18714)

Rutgers University
New Brunswick, NJ 08901-1248

Publications: Comparative Economic Studies (19328)

Rutgers University
84 College Ave.
New Brunswick, NJ 08901-8542
Phone: (732)932-7536
Fax: (732)932-1686

Publications: Italian Quarterly (19332)

Rutgers University
131 George St.
New Brunswick, NJ 08901
Phone: (732)932-4029
Fax: (732)932-9246

Publications: American Journal of Ancient History (19325)

Rutgers University
Student Activities Center
Box 50
George St.
New Brunswick, NJ 08901
Phone: (732)246-8448
Fax: (908)463-1702

Publications: Black Voice/Carta Latina (19326)

Rutgers University
15 Washington St.
Newark, NJ 07102

Publications: Rutgers Computer and Technology Law Journal (19364)

Rutgers University
123 Washington St.
Newark, NJ 07102
Phone: (973)353-5391
Fax: (973)353-1497

Publications: Rutgers Law Review (19365)

Rutgers University
350 Dr. Martin Luther King Jr. Blvd.
Newark, NJ 07102
Phone: (973)353-5023
Fax: (973)353-1333

Publications: The Observer (19362)

Rutgers University
Bldg. 100 Joyce Kilmer Ave.
Piscataway, NJ 08855-1179
Phone: (732)445-7762
Fax: (732)445-7039

Publications: Journal of Sedimentary Research (14079)

Rutgers University
607 Allison Rd.
Piscataway, NJ 08854-8001
Phone: (732)445-3510
Fax: (732)445-5944

Publications: Journal of Studies on Alcohol (19429) • Rutgers Center of Alcohol Studies (19431)

R.W. Mansfield Company
2973 Kennedy Blvd.
Jersey City, NJ 07306-3884
Phone: (201)795-0629
Fax: (201)795-5476
Free: 877-626-7353

Publications: Mansfield Stock Chart Service (19143)

R.W. Nielsen Co.
350 E Center St.
Ste. 201
Provo, UT 84606
Phone: (801)373-0013
Fax: (801)373-0015
Free: 800-748-7690

Publications: Permanent Buildings & Foundations (31406)

RW Publications
3770 Transit Rd.
Orchard Park, NY 14127
Phone: (716)662-4200
Fax: (716)662-0740

Publications: Akron-Corfu Pennysaver (19978) • Attica Pennysaver (20104) • East Aurora/Elma Pennysaver (20541) • Orchard Park Pennysaver (23058) • West Seneca Pennysaver (23548)

Rx Remedy, Inc.
PO Box 29
Westport, CT 06881-0029

Publications: Remedy (5216)

Ryan Leader
606 Washington
PO Box 220
Ryan, OK 73565
Phone: (580)757-2281

Publications: The Ryan Leader (26052)

Ryerson University
80 Gould St.
Toronto, ON, Canada M5B 2M7
Phone: (416)979-5323
Fax: (416)979-5342

Publications: The Ryersoniam (36733)

S. Carolina Black Media Group
1310 Harden
PO Box 11128
Columbia, SC 29211
Phone: (803)799-5252
Fax: (803)799-7709

Publications: Charleston Black Times (28509)

S. & G. Publications
109 Carney
Box 617
Leslie, MI 49251-0617
Phone: (517)589-8228
Fax: (517)589-8526

Publications: Leslie Local Independent (15313)

S/K Publishing Group, Inc.
257 N Main St.
PO Box 489
Wadley, GA 30477-0489
Phone: (478)252-5237
Fax: (478)252-1140
Free: 800-634-1261

Publications: Logger and Lumberman (7635)

S. Karger Publishers, Inc.
26 W. Avon Rd.
PO Box 529
Farmington, CT 06085
Phone: (860)675-7834
Fax: (860)675-7302

Publications: Brain, Behavior and Evolution (4801) • Gynecologic and Obstetric Investigation (4829) • Neuroendocrinology (4842)

Saanich News
1824 Store St.
Victoria, BC, Canada V8T 4R4
Phone: (604)920-2090
Fax: (604)920-7352

Publications: Saanich News (35225)

The Sabetha Herald
1024 Main
PO Box 208
Sabetha, KS 66534-0208
Phone: (785)284-3300
Fax: (785)284-2320

Publications: The Sabetha Herald (11776)

Sabine County Reporter
Box 700
Hemphill, TX 75948
Phone: (409)787-2172
Fax: (409)787-4300

Publications: Sabine County Reporter and the Rambler (30437)

Sabine Index
Box 850
Many, LA 71449
Phone: (318)256-3495
Fax: (318)256-9151

Publications: Sabine Index (12669)

Sabot Publishing Inc.
301 Concourse Blvd., Ste. 350
Glen Allen, VA 23059-5643
Phone: (804)346-0990
Fax: (804)346-1223

Publications: Better Nutrition Magazine (32111) • Southwest Art (30530) • Vegetarian Times (5162)

SAC Newsmonthly
PO Box 159
Bogalusa, LA 70429
Phone: (985)732-5616
Fax: (985)732-3744
Free: 800-825-3722

Publications: SAC Newsmonthly (12534)

SAC-Osghee
PO Box 580
Osceola, MO 64776
Phone: (417)646-2211
Fax: (417)646-8015

Publications: St. Clair County Buyer's Guide (17324) • St. Clair County Courier (17325)

Sac Sun
406 William St.
PO Box 426
Sac City, IA 50583-0426
Phone: (712)662-7161
Fax: (712)662-4198

Publications: Sac City Reminder (11186) • Sac Sun (11187)

The Sackville Tribune-Post
80 Main St.
Sackville, NB, Canada E4L 4A7
Phone: (506)536-2500
Fax: (506)536-4024

Publications: The Sackville Tribune-Post (35427)

The Sacramento Bee
2100 Q St.
PO Box 15779
Sacramento, CA 95852
Phone: (916)321-1000
Fax: (916)321-1524
Free: 800-876-8700

Publications: The Sacramento Bee (3011)

Sacramento City College Store
3835 Freeport Blvd.
Sacramento, CA 95822
Phone: (916)558-2561
Fax: (916)558-2282

Publications: Sacramento City College Express (3013)

Sacramento County Bar Association
901 H St., Ste. 101
Sacramento, CA 95814
Phone: (916)448-1087
Fax: (916)447-2788

Publications: Sacramento Lawyer (3015)

The Sacramento Gazette
555 University Ave., Ste. 126
Sacramento, CA 95825-6584
Phone: (916)567-9654

Publications: The Sacramento Gazette (3014)

Sacramento Magazines Corp.
706 56th St.
Sacramento, CA 95819
Phone: (916)452-6200
Fax: (916)414-6060

Publications: Sacramento Magazine (3016)

Sacred Dance Guild
201 Hewitt
Carbondale, IL 62901
Phone: (618)457-8603

Publications: Sacred Dance Guild Journal (8120)

Sacred Heart University
5151 Park Ave.
Fairfield, CT 06432
Phone: (203)371-7810

Publications: George Herbert Journal (4788)

Saddle & Bridle, Inc.
375 Jackson Ave.
St. Louis, MO 63130
Phone: (314)725-9115
Fax: (314)725-6440

Publications: Saddle & Bridle Magazine (17491)

Saddle Horse Report
PO Box 1007
Shelbyville, TN 37162-1007
Phone: (615)684-8123
Fax: (615)684-8196

Publications: Saddle Horse Report (29599) • Walking Horse Report (29601)

The Sae Gae Times
38-42 9th St.
Long Island City, NY 11101
Phone: (718)361-2600
Fax: (718)361-2368

Publications: The Sae Gae Times (20966)

SAE International
400 Commonwealth Dr.
Warrendale, PA 15096-0001
Phone: (724)776-4841
Fax: (724)776-4026

Publications: Automotive Engineering International (28111) • SAE Off-Highway Engineering (28114)

Safari Club Intl.
4800 W Gates Pass Rd.
Tucson, AZ 85745
Phone: (520)620-1220
Fax: (520)622-1205

Publications: Safari Magazine (962)

SAFE Association
PO Box 130
Creswell, OR 97426-0130
Phone: (541)895-3012
Fax: (541)895-3014

Publications: SAFE Journal (26298) • SAFE Symposium Proceedings (26299)

Safe Schools Coalition, Inc.
PO Box 1338
Holmes Beach, FL 34218-1338
Phone: (941)778-6652
Fax: (941)778-6818
Free: 800-537-4903

Publications: School Intervention Report (6202)

The Sag Harbor Express
PO Box 1620
Sag Harbor, NY 11963

Publications: The Sag Harbor Express (23283)

Sage Publications
2455 Teller Rd.
Thousand Oaks, CA 91320
Phone: (805)499-0721
Fax: (805)499-0871

Publications: Journal of the Association of Nurses in AIDS Care (3880)

Sage Publications Inc.
2455 Teller Rd.
Thousand Oaks, CA 91320
Phone: (805)499-0721
Fax: (805)499-0871
Free: 800-818-SAGE

Publications: Abstracts in Social Gerontology (3845) • Administration & Society (3846) • AFFILIA: Journal of Women and Social Work (3847) • American Behavioral Scientist (3848) • American Politics Research (3849) • American Review of Public Administration (16987) • The Annals of the American Academy of Political and Social Science (3850) • AWHONN Lifelines (3851) • Behavior Modification (3852) • Business & Society (19768) • China Report (3853) • Clinical Nursing Research (3854) • Communication Abstracts (3855) • Communication Research (3856) • Comparative Political Studies (3857) • The Counseling Psychologist (16992) • Crime & Delinquency (3858) • Criminal Justice Abstracts (3859) • Criminal Justice and Behavior (3860) • Cross-Cultural Research (3861) • Economic Development Quarterly (3862) • Educational and Psychological Measurement (3865) • Environment and Behavior (946) • Evaluation & the Health Professions (3867) • Evaluation Review (3868) • Family and Consumer Sciences Research Journal (3869) • Family Court Review (3870) • Gender & Society (19988) • Group & Organization Management (19989) • Hispanic Journal of Behavioral Sciences (3871) • Home Health Care Management and Practice (3872) • Human Resources Abstracts (3873) • Indian Economic and Social History Review (3874) • International Studies (3875) • Journal of the Academy of Marketing Science (6009) • Journal of Adolescent Research (3876) • Journal of Aging and Health (3877) • Journal of Applied Behavioral Science (3879) • Journal of Biological Rhythms (8863) • Journal of Black Psychology (3881) • Journal of Black Studies (3882) • Journal of Business and Technical Communications (3883) • Journal of Communication Inquiry (3884) • Journal of Conflict Resolution (4993) • Journal of Contemporary Ethnography (3885) • Journal of Cross-Cultural Psychology (3886) • The Journal of Diagnostic Medical Sonography (JDMS) (3887) • Journal of Early Adolescence (3888) • Journal of Family Issues (3889) • Journal of Family Nursing (3890) • Journal of Health Care for the Poor and Underserved (3891) • Journal of Holistic Nursing (29788) • Journal of Humanistic Psychology (3892) • Journal of Intensive Care Medicine (14524) • Journal of Interpersonal Violence (3893) • Journal of Language and Social Psychology (3894) • Journal of Management Education (9300) • Journal of Neuroimaging (3895) • Journal of Obstetric, Gynecologic and Neonatal Nursing (JOGNN) (3896) • Journal of Planning Literature (3898) • Journal of Research in Crime and Delinquency (3899) • Journal of Service Research (29464) • The Journal for Specialists in Group Work (3900) • Journal of Sport & Social Issues (3901) • Journal of Urban History (23746) • Latin American Perspectives (2941) • Management Communication Quarterly (3902) • Modern China (3903) • Neurohabilitation and Neural Repair (3904) • Nonprofit and Voluntary Sector Quarterly (32990) • Peace Research Abstracts Journal (3906) • Philosophy of the Social Sciences (3907) • Political Theory (31938) • Politics & Society (3908) • The Prison Journal (27646) • Public Finance Review (3909) • Public Works Management & Policy (3910) • Qualitative Health Research (34726) • Research on Aging (23842) • Research on Social Work Practice (3911) • Review of Public Personnel Administration (6733) • Sage Family Studies Abstracts (3912) • Sage Public Administration Abstracts (3913) • Sage Urban Studies Abstracts (3914) • Science Communication (13439) • Science, Technology & Human Values (3915) • Simulation & Gaming (3916) • SMR/Sociological Methods and Research (3917) • Social Science Computer Review (24153) • Urban Affairs Review (3918) • Violence Against Women (3920) • Western Journal of Nursing Research (34735) • Work and Occupations (3921) •

Numbers cited after listings are entry numbers rather than page numbers.

Written Communication (3922) • Youth & Society (3923)

Sage Publishing
Box 488
Whitefish, MT 59937
Fax: (406)862-3636

Publications: Whitefish Pilot (17919)

Sage Publishing
Drawer 109
Douglas, WY 82633
Phone: (307)358-2965
Fax: (307)358-2926

Publications: Douglas Budget (34519)

Sage Publishing Co.
PO Box 1090
Cody, WY 82414
Phone: (307)587-2231
Fax: (307)587-5208

Publications: Cody Enterprise (34513)

Sage School of Philosophy
Cornell University
327 Goldwin Smith Hall
Ithaca, NY 14853-3201
Phone: (607)255-6817
Fax: (607)255-8177

Publications: Philosophical Review (20813)

Sagebrush
1262-A N Sierra St.
Reno, NV 89503
Phone: (702)784-4033
Fax: (702)784-1955

Publications: Sagebrush (18424)

Sagebrush Publishing Co., Inc.
PO Box 220
Eddy, TX 76524-0220
Phone: (254)859-5507
Fax: (254)859-5451

Publications: The Brahman Journal (30268)

SageWoman
PO Box 641
Point Arena, CA 95468
Phone: (707)882-2052
Fax: (707)882-2793
Free: 888-724-3966

Publications: SageWoman Magazine (2858)

The Saginaw News
203 S. Washington Ave.
Saginaw, MI 48607

Publications: The Saginaw News (15491)

The Saginaw Press
410 Hancock St.
PO Box 1836
Saginaw, MI 48605-1836
Phone: (989)793-8070

Publications: The Saginaw Press (15492)

Saguache Crescent
316 4th St.
PO Box 195
Saguache, CO 81149
Phone: (719)655-2620
Fax: (719)655-2620

Publications: Saguache Crescent (4617)

Saigon Times
9129 E Valley Blvd.
Rosemead, CA 91770
Phone: (626)288-2696
Fax: (626)286-3293

Publications: Saigon Times (2969)

St. Anthony Messenger
28 W. Liberty St.
Cincinnati, OH 45202-6498
Phone: (513)241-5615
Fax: (513)241-0399
Free: 800-488-0488

Publications: St. Anthony Messenger (24814)

St. Anthony's Guild
158 W 27th St., 6th Fl.
New York, NY 10001
Phone: (212)924-1451
Fax: (212)924-1994

Publications: The Anthonian (21221)

Saint Bernard Club of America
1734 Rocky Ford Rd.
Kittrell, NC 27544
Phone: (252)431-1609

Publications: Saint Fancier (24032)

Saint Bernard Voice
PO Box 88
Arabi, LA 70032
Phone: (504)279-7488
Fax: (504)277-2231

Publications: Saint Bernard Voice (12474)

St. Bonaventure University
Drawer X
St. Bonaventure, NY 14778
Phone: (716)375-2128
Fax: (716)375-2252

Publications: The Bona Venture (23286)

The St. Catharines Standard Ltd.
17 Queen St.
St. Catharines, ON, Canada L2R 5G5
Phone: (905)684-7251
Fax: (905)684-6032

Publications: The Standard (36357)

St. Charles Herald-Guide
PO Box 1199
Boutte, LA 70039
Phone: (504)758-2795
Fax: (504)758-7000

Publications: St. Charles Herald-Guide (12540)

St. Charles Press
PO Box 617
St. Charles, MN 55972
Phone: (507)932-3663
Fax: (507)932-5537

Publications: Press (16341)

St. Clair News-Aegis
PO Box 750
Pell City, AL 35125
Phone: (205)884-2310
Fax: (205)884-2312

Publications: St. Clair News-Aegis (443)

St. Cloud Newspapers, Inc.
3000 N 7th St.
St. Cloud, MN 56301
Phone: (320)255-8700
Fax: (320)255-8773
Free: 800-955-9998

Publications: St. Cloud Times (16345)

St. Cloud State University
13 Stewart Hall
720 4th Ave. S.
St. Cloud, MN 56301-4498
Phone: (612)255-4086
Fax: (612)255-2164

Publications: University Chronicle (16348)

St. Cloud Visitor
305 7th Ave. N
PO Box 1068
St. Cloud, MN 56302
Phone: (320)251-3022
Fax: (320)251-0424

Publications: St. Cloud Visitor (16346)

St. Croix Printing and Publishing Co.
47 Milltown Blvd.
PO Box 250
St. Stephen, NB, Canada E3L 2X2
Phone: (506)466-3220
Fax: (506)466-9950

Publications: Courier Weekend (35436) • Saint Croix Courier (35437)

The St. Edward Advance
PO Box 287
St. Edward, NE 68660
Phone: (402)678-2771
Fax: (402)678-2556

Publications: The St. Edward Advance (18257)

St. Edward's University
3001 S. Congress
PO Box 1029
Austin, TX 78704
Phone: (512)448-8400
Fax: (512)448-8492

Publications: Hilltop Views (29779)

St. Francis Xavier University
Student Union
PO Box 271
Antigonish, NS, Canada B2G 1C0
Phone: (902)867-2430
Fax: (902)867-5138

Publications: Xavierian Weekly (35538)

Ste. Genevieve Newspapers, Inc.
PO Box 447
Ste. Genevieve, MO 63670
Phone: (573)883-2222
Fax: (573)883-2833

Publications: Ste. Genevieve Herald (17387)

St. Helena Echo
PO Box 190
Greensburg, LA 70441
Phone: (225)222-4541
Fax: (225)708-7104

Publications: St. Helena Echo (12589)

St. Herman of Alaska Brotherhood
Box 70
Platina, CA 96076
Phone: (530)352-4430
Fax: (530)352-4432

Publications: The Orthodox Word (2850)

St. James Publishing Co., Inc.
604 1st Ave. S
PO Box 67
St. James, MN 56081
Phone: (507)375-3161
Fax: (507)375-3221

Publications: Plaindealer (16355) • Town and Country Shopper (16356)

St. Jerome's University
200 University Ave. W.
Waterloo, ON, Canada N2L 3G3
Phone: (519)884-8110
Fax: (519)884-5759

Publications: The New Quarterly (36856)

The Saint Jo Tribune
Drawer 160
St. Jo, TX 76265
Phone: (940)995-2586
Fax: (940)995-2586

Publications: The Saint Jo Tribune (31003)

St. John Fisher College
3690 East Ave.
Rochester, NY 14618
Phone: (585)385-8000
Fax: (585)385-8129

Publications: Pioneer (23235)

St. John Valley Times
160 Main St.
PO Box 419
Madawaska, ME 04756
Phone: (207)728-3336
Fax: (207)728-3825
Free: 800-339-9502

Publications: St. John Valley Times (12989)

St. John's College, Office of Public Relations
Box 2800
Annapolis, MD 21404

Publications: The College (13093)

St. John's, Newfoundland Publications
1414, The Pastoral Centre
Bonaventure Ave.
St. John's, NL, Canada A1C 5M3
Phone: (709)739-6553
Fax: (709)739-6458

Publications: The Monitor (35489)

St. Johns Reminder
109 W Higham St.
PO Box 473
St. Johns, MI 48879-0473
Phone: (989)224-8356
Fax: (989)224-9458

Publications: St. Johns Reminder (15510)

St. John's University
8000 Utopia Pkwy.
Jamaica, NY 11439
Phone: (718)990-6756
Fax: (718)990-5849

Publications: The Torch (20841)

St. Johns University
300 Howard Ave.
Staten Island, NY 10301
Phone: (718)390-4463
Fax: (718)390-4590

Publications: The Arrow (23357)

St. John's University College of Business Administration
8000 Utopia Pkwy.
Jamaica, NY 11439

Publications: Review of Business (20840)

St. Joseph Media Ltd.
Ste. 250
125 9th Ave. SE
Calgary, AB, Canada T2G 0P6
Phone: (403)299-1888
Fax: (403)299-1899

Publications: WHERE Calgary (34659)

The St. Joseph Telegraph
PO Box 1087
St. Joseph, MO 64502-1087
Phone: (816)364-1323
Fax: (816)364-3083

Publications: The St. Joseph Telegraph (17395)

St. Laurent
7575, Transcanadienne, 401
Saint-Laurent, QC, Canada H4T 1V6
Phone: (514)956-1361
Fax: (514)956-1461

Publications: Le Monde de L'Auto (37364)

St. Lawrence College
King & W. Portsmouth Ave.
PO Box 6000
Kingston, ON, Canada K7L 5A6
Phone: (613)544-5400
Fax: (613)544-1763

Publications: Nomad (35940)

St. Lawrence County Historical Association
PO Box 8
Canton, NY 13617
Phone: (315)386-8133
Fax: (315)386-8134

Publications: The Quarterly (20430)

St. Lawrence County Newspapers
PO Box 300
Massena, NY 13662
Phone: (315)393-1002
Fax: (315)764-0337

Publications: The Daily Courier Observer (21027)

St. Lawrence Printing Co.
PO Box 549
Prescott, ON, Canada K0E 1T0
Phone: (613)925-4265
Fax: (613)925-3472

Publications: Journal (36337)

St. Lawrence University
Publications Office, Vilas Hall
Canton, NY 13617
Phone: (315)379-5560
Fax: (315)379-5502

Publications: St. Lawrence (20431)

St. Lawrence University
23 Romoda Dr.
Canton, NY 13617
Phone: (315)229-5011
Fax: (315)379-5944

Publications: The Hill News (20429)

St. Louis Argus
4595 Martin Luther King Dr.
St. Louis, MO 63113
Phone: (314)531-1323

Publications: St. Louis Argus (17494)

Saint Louis Art Museum
Publications
1 Fine Arts Dr.
Forest Park
St. Louis, MO 63110
Phone: (314)721-0072
Fax: (314)721-6172

Publications: Saint Louis Art Museum Bulletin (17495)

St. Louis Commerce
1 Metropolitain Sq., Ste. 1300
St. Louis, MO 63102
Phone: (314)340-8000
Fax: (314)340-3050
Free: 800-365-0820

Publications: St. Louis Post-Dispatch (17506)

St. Louis County Printing & Pub. Co.
200 S Bemiston, Ste. 212
St. Louis, MO 63105-1915
Phone: (314)725-1515
Fax: (314)725-1716

Publications: Franklin County Watchman (17439) • Saint Charles Watchman (17492) • St. Louis Watchman Advocate (17509)

St. Louis Crusader
715 Vandeventer Ave.
St. Louis, MO 63108-3527

Publications: St. Louis Crusader (17500)

St. Louis Jewish Light
12 Millstone Campus Dr.
St. Louis, MO 63146-5776
Phone: (314)432-3353
Fax: (314)432-0515

Publications: St. Louis Jewish Light (17501)

St. Louis Journalism Review
470 E Lockwood
WH 414
St. Louis, MO 63119
Phone: (314)968-5905
Fax: (314)963-6104

Publications: The St. Louis Journalism Review (17502)

St. Louis Metropolitan Medical Society
3839 Lindell Blvd.
St. Louis, MO 63108
Phone: (314)371-5225
Fax: (314)533-8601

Publications: St. Louis Metropolitan Medicine (17505)

St. Louis Regional Chamber & Growth Association (RCGA)
One Metropolitan Sq., Ste. 1300
St. Louis, MO 63102
Phone: (314)231-5555
Fax: (314)206-3244
Free: 877-785-7242

Publications: St. Louis Commerce (17497)

St. Louis Review
20 Archbishop May Dr.
St. Louis, MO 63119-5738
Phone: (314)531-9700
Fax: (314)531-2269

Publications: St. Louis Review (17507)

St. Louis/Southern Illinois Tribune
505 S Ewing Ave.
St. Louis, MO 63103
Phone: (314)535-9660
Fax: (314)535-2700

Publications: St. Louis/Southern Illinois Labor Tribune (17508)

St. Louis University
Dept. of Philosophy
3800 Lindell Blvd.
St. Louis, MO 63156-0907
Phone: (314)977-3155

Publications: The Modern Schoolman (17474)

St. Louis University
3674 Lindell Blvd.
St. Louis, MO 63108
Phone: (314)977-3814
Fax: (314)977-3897

Publications: Forum for Social Economics (17438)

St. Mary Journal
1014 Front St.
PO Box 31
Morgan City, LA 70381
Phone: (504)384-1350
Fax: (504)384-4255

Publications: St. Mary Journal (12708)

St. Mary's College
PO Box 4407
Moraga, CA 94575
Phone: (925)631-4279
Fax: (925)631-4675

Publications: St. Mary's Collegian (2597)

St. Marys Star
517 W Bertrand
PO Box 190
St. Marys, KS 66536-0190
Phone: (785)437-2935
Fax: (785)437-2095
Free: 800-334-9912

Publications: St. Marys Star (11779)

St. Mary's University
700 Terrace Hgts. No. 36
Winona, MN 55987
Phone: (507)457-1496
Fax: (507)457-6967
Free: 800-635-5987

Publications: The Cardinal (16525)

St. Mary's University
Student Ctr., Ste. 517
Halifax, NS, Canada B3H 3C3
Phone: (902)496-8200
Fax: (902)496-8209

Publications: The Journal (35568)

St. Nicholas Diocesan Press
2208 W Chicago Ave.
Chicago, IL 60622
Phone: (773)227-3970

Publications: The New Star (8507)

St. Olaf College
1520 St. Olaf Ave.
Northfield, MN 55057-1098
Phone: (507)646-3275
Fax: (507)663-3549

Publications: Manitou Messenger (16235)

St. Patrick Hospital
500 W Broadway
PO Box 4587
Missoula, MT 59806
Phone: (406)543-7271
Fax: (406)329-5875

Publications: St. Patrick Hospital Health Update (17876)

St. Paul Journal
4813 50th Ave.
St. Paul, AB, Canada T0A 3A0
Phone: (780)645-3342
Fax: (780)645-2346

Publications: St. Paul Journal (34844)

Numbers cited after listings are entry numbers rather than page numbers.

St. Paul Phonograph-Herald
PO Box 27
St. Paul, NE 68873
Phone: (308)754-4401
Fax: (308)754-4498

Publications: St. Paul Phonograph-Herald (18258)

The St. Pauls Review
PO Box 265
St. Pauls, NC 28384
Phone: (910)865-4179
Fax: (910)865-4995

Publications: The St. Pauls Review (24213)

St. Petersburg Junior College
PO Box 13489
St. Petersburg, FL 33733
Phone: (727)341-4459

Publications: The Wooden Horse (6636)

St. Raphael's Better Health
1450 Chapel St.
New Haven, CT 06511
Phone: (203)789-3972
Fax: (203)789-4053

Publications: Saint Raphael's Better Health (5001)

St. Rita School for the Deaf
1720 Glendale-Milford Rd.
Cincinnati, OH 45215
Phone: (513)771-7600
Fax: (513)326-8264

Publications: Silent Advocate (24819)

St. Tammany Farmer, Inc.
PO Box 269
321 N. New Hampshire St.
Covington, LA 70434
Phone: (504)892-2323
Fax: (504)892-2325

Publications: St. Tammany Farmer (12555)

St. Thomas More Institute for Legal Research
St. John's University, School of Law
8000 Utopia Pkwy.
Jamaica, NY 11439
Phone: (718)990-6655
Fax: (718)990-6649

Publications: The Catholic Lawyer (20832)

St. Thomas University School of Law
16400 NW 32nd Ave.
Miami, FL 33054
Phone: (305)623-2380
Fax: (305)474-2410

Publications: St. Thomas Law Review (6378)

SAITSA Publications/Southern Alberta Institute of Technology
1301 16th Ave. NW
V219 Campus Centre
Calgary, AB, Canada T2M 0L4
Phone: (403)284-8077
Fax: (403)284-8037

Publications: The Weal (34658)

The Sale Line, Inc.
6851 Jericho Tpke.
Syosset, NY 11791
Phone: (516)496-4300
Fax: (516)496-9898

Publications: North Shore Today (23380) • North Shore Today's Elite (23381)

Salem College
352 Lafayette
Salem, MA 01970
Phone: (508)741-6448

Publications: The Salem State Log (14515)

Salem Evening News
32 Dunham Rd.
Beverly, MA 01915
Phone: (978)922-1234
Fax: (978)922-4330

Publications: Salem Evening News (13842)

The Salem News
500 N Washington
PO Box 798
Salem, MO 65560
Phone: (573)729-4126
Fax: (573)729-4920

Publications: The Salem News (17563)

Salem News
161 N. Lincoln Ave.
Salem, OH 44460
Phone: (330)332-4601
Fax: (330)332-3084

Publications: Salem News (25506)

Salem News Publishing Co.
155 Washington St.
Salem, MA 01970
Phone: (508)744-0600
Fax: (508)744-1010

Publications: Salem News (14514)

Salem Newspapers, Inc.
93 5th St.
Salem, NJ 08079
Phone: (609)935-1500
Fax: (609)845-3139

Publications: Today's Sunbeam (19532)

Salem Observer
88 Stiles Rd., No. 103
PO Box 720
Salem, NH 03079
Phone: (603)893-4356
Fax: (603)893-0721

Publications: Salem Observer (18645)

Salem Publishing
PO Box 127
Fincastle, VA 24090
Phone: (540)473-2741
Fax: (540)473-2741

Publications: The Fincastle Herald and Botetourt County News (32075)

Salem Publishing Co.
PO Box 1125
Salem, VA 24153
Phone: (540)389-9355
Fax: (540)389-2930

Publications: The New Castle Record (32278) • Salem Times-Register (32521)

Salem Times Commoner
109 N. Walnut St.
PO Box 245
Farina, IL 62838
Phone: (618)245-6216
Fax: (618)245-6216

Publications: Farina News (8884)

Salem Times-Commoner
120 S. Broadway
PO Box 548
Salem, IL 62881
Phone: (618)548-3330
Fax: (618)548-3593

Publications: Salem Times-Commoner (9577)

Salesian Missions
2 Lefevre Ln.
PO Box 30
New Rochelle, NY 10802
Phone: (914)633-8344
Fax: (914)633-7404

Publications: Salesian (21122)

Salesmen Publications
125 E Cass St.
PO Box 5
Albion, MI 49224
Phone: (517)629-2127
Fax: (517)629-8831
Free: 800-589-2127

Publications: Morning Star: The Shopping Guide (14716)

The Salina Journal
333 S. 4th St.
PO Box 740
Salina, KS 67402-0740
Phone: (785)823-6363
Fax: (785)823-3207
Free: 800-827-6363

Publications: The Salina Journal (11784)

Salinas Newspapers, Inc.
123 W Alisal
Salinas, CA 93901
Phone: (831)424-2221
Fax: (831)754-4293
Free: 800-300-6397

Publications: The Californian (3067)

Salisbury Press-Spectator
111 S Broadway
PO Box 313
Salisbury, MO 65281
Phone: (660)388-6131
Fax: (660)388-6688

Publications: Salisbury Press-Spectator (17565)

Salisbury State University
Box 3183
Salisbury, MD 21801-6860
Phone: (410)543-6000
Fax: (410)548-2800

Publications: The Flyer (13708)

Salisbury University
1101 Camden Ave.
Salisbury, MD 21801-6860
Phone: (410)677-5357
Fax: (410)543-6068

Publications: Literature Film Quarterly (13709)

Salmon Arm Observer
51 Hudson St.
PO Box 550
Salmon Arm, BC, Canada V1E 4N7
Phone: (250)832-2131
Fax: (250)832-5140

Publications: Salmon Arm Observer (35081)

Salmon Press
PO Box 38
Center Ossipee, NH 03814
Phone: (603)539-4111
Fax: (603)539-5564

Publications: Carroll County Independent and Pioneer (18463)

Salmon Press
365 Union St.
PO Box 230
Littleton, NH 03561
Phone: (603)444-3927
Fax: (603)444-3920

Publications: The Courier (18548) • The Record Enterprise (18634)

Salmon Press
5 Water St.
Meredith, NH 03253
Phone: (603)279-4516
Fax: (603)279-3331

Publications: Granite State News (18654) • The Meredith News (18575) • Summer Week/Winter Week (18635)

Salon Communications Inc.
411 Richmond St. E., Ste. 300
Toronto, ON, Canada M5A 3S5
Phone: (416)869-3131
Fax: (416)869-3008

Publications: Salon Magazine (36734)

Salt Lake Community College
4600 S Redwood Rd.
Salt Lake City, UT 84130
Phone: (801)957-4045
Fax: (801)957-4018

Publications: Horizon (31429)

Salt Water Sportsman
263 Summer St.
Boston, MA 02210
Phone: (617)303-3660
Fax: (617)303-3661

Publications: Salt Water Sportsman (13957)

Salud Publications Intl. Inc.
2724 Erie Ave., Ste. B
Cincinnati, OH 45208-2125
Phone: (513)533-5470
Fax: (513)533-5474

Publications: El Hospital (24796)

Saluda Standard
PO Box 668
Saluda, SC 29138
Phone: (864)445-2527
Fax: (864)445-8679

Publications: Saluda Standard Sentinel (28753)

Saludos Hispanos
73121 Fred Waring Dr., No. 100
Palm Desert, CA 92260
Phone: (619)776-1206
Fax: (619)776-1214
Free: 800-371-4456

Publications: Saludos Hispanos (2743)

The Salvation Army
615 Slaters Ln.
PO Box 269
Alexandria, VA 22313

Publications: The War Cry (31750)

Salyersville Independent
7 E Maple St.
PO Box 29
Salyersville, KY 41465-9466
Phone: (606)349-2915
Fax: (606)349-2907

Publications: Salyersville Independent (12390)

Sam Houston State University
PO Box 2146
Huntsville, TX 77341-2146
Phone: (936)294-1992
Fax: (936)294-3070

Publications: The Texas Review (30597)

Sam Houston State University
PO Box 2178
Huntsville, TX 77341
Phone: (936)294-1503
Fax: (936)294-1503

Publications: The Houstonian (30594)

Samford University
S.U. Box 2269
Birmingham, AL 35229
Phone: (205)726-2011

Publications: The Samford Crimson (90)

Samson Ledger
105 Main St.
PO Box 66
Samson, AL 36477
Phone: (334)684-2280

Publications: Samson Ledger (444)

San Angelo Standard Inc.
34 W. Harris Ave.
San Angelo, TX 76903
Phone: (915)653-1221
Fax: (915)658-6192
Free: 800-588-1884

Publications: Goodfellow Monitor (31004) • San Angelo Standard-Times (31010)

San Antonio Homes & Gardens
2703 Stone Edge
San Antonio, TX 78232

Publications: San Antonio Homes & Gardens (31046)

San Augustine Tribune
315 W Columbia St.
PO Box 539
San Augustine, TX 75972
Phone: (936)275-2181
Fax: (936)275-0572

Publications: San Augustine Tribune (31080)

San Bernardino County Museum Association
2024 Orange Tree Ln.
Redlands, CA 92373
Phone: (909)307-2669

Publications: San Bernardino County Museum Association Quarterly (2907)

The San Bernardino County Sun
399 N. D St.
San Bernardino, CA 92401-1518
Phone: (909)889-9666
Fax: (909)381-3976

Publications: The San Bernardino County Sun (3092)

San Cayetano Mountain Investment Corporation
PO Box 727
Fillmore, CA 93016
Phone: (805)524-0153
Fax: (805)524-0154

Publications: The Fillmore Herald (1915)

San Diego Business Journal
4909 Murphy Canyon Rd., No. 200
San Diego, CA 92123
Phone: (858)277-6359
Fax: (858)571-3628

Publications: San Diego Business Journal (3258)

San Diego Community Newspaper Group
PO Box 9550
San Diego, CA 92169
Phone: (858)270-3103
Fax: (858)270-9325
Free: 800-669-3103

Publications: La Jolla Village News (3219)

San Diego County Medical Society
3702 Ruffin Rd., Ste. 206
San Diego, CA 92123-1842
Phone: (858)565-8888

Publications: San Diego County Physician (3261)

San Diego Daily Transcript
2131 3rd Ave.
Box 85469
San Diego, CA 92101
Phone: (619)232-4381
Fax: (619)231-4866
Free: 800-697-6397

Publications: San Diego Daily Transcript (3262)

San Diego Family Magazine
PO Box 23960
San Diego, CA 92193
Phone: (619)685-6970

Publications: San Diego Family Magazine (3263)

San Diego Floral Association
1650 El Prado, Rm. 105
San Diego, CA 92101-1622
Phone: (619)232-5762
Fax: (619)232-5762

Publications: California Garden (3127)

San Diego Historical Society
PO Box 81825
San Diego, CA 92138

Publications: Journal of San Diego History (3212)

San Diego Law Review Association
5998 University of San Diego, School of Law
5998 Alcala Park
San Diego, CA 92110
Phone: (619)260-4531
Fax: (619)260-7497

Publications: San Diego Law Review (3264)

San Diego Magazine Publishing Co.
PO Box 85409
San Diego, CA 92186
Phone: (619)230-9292
Fax: (619)230-0490
Free: 800-600-2489

Publications: San Diego Magazine (3265)

San Diego Parent Magazine
3160 Camino Del Rio S., Ste. 313
San Diego, CA 92108
Phone: (619)624-2770
Fax: (619)624-2777

Publications: San Diego Parent (3267)

San Diego Reader
PO Box 85803
San Diego, CA 92186-5803
Phone: (619)235-3000
Fax: (619)231-0489

Publications: San Diego Reader (3268)

San Diego State University
San Diego, CA 92182-7700
Phone: (619)594-4199
Fax: (619)594-7277

Publications: The Daily Aztec (3139) • The Professional Geographer (3249)

San Diego Teachers Association
10393 San Diego Mission Rd., No. 100
San Diego, CA 92108
Phone: (619)283-4411
Fax: (619)282-7659

Publications: S.D.T.A. Teacher Advocate (3272)

San Diego Union-Tribune
PO Box 120191
San Diego, CA 92112
Phone: (619)299-3131
Fax: (619)293-2436
Free: 800-244-6397

Publications: Books (3123)

The San Diego Voice and Viewpoint
PO Box 120095
San Diego, CA 92112-0095
Phone: (619)266-2233
Fax: (619)266-0533

Publications: The San Diego Voice and Viewpoint (3271)

The San Fernando Valley Sun Newspaper
601 S. Brand Blvd., Ste. 202
San Fernando, CA 91340
Phone: (818)365-3111
Fax: (818)898-7135

Publications: The San Fernando Sun Newspaper and Valley View (3322)

San Francisco AIDS Foundation
PO Box 426182
San Francisco, CA 94142-6182
Phone: (415)487-8060
Fax: (415)487-8069

Publications: BETA (Bulletin of Experimental Treatments for AIDS) (3330)

San Francisco Art Institute
800 Chestnut St.
San Francisco, CA 94133
Phone: (415)771-7020

Publications: San Francisco Art Institute Magazine (3426)

The San Francisco Bay Guardian
135 Mississippi St.
San Francisco, CA 94107-2536
Phone: (415)255-3100
Fax: (415)255-8955

Publications: East Bay Guardian (3353) • The San Francisco Bay Guardian (3429)

San Francisco Bay View
4908 Third St.
San Francisco, CA 94124
Phone: (415)671-0449
Fax: (415)822-8971

Publications: San Francisco Bay View (3430)

San Francisco Cinematheque
145 Ninth St., Ste. 240
San Francisco, CA 94103
Phone: (415)552-1990
Fax: (415)552-2067

Publications: Cinematograph (3343)

San Francisco Examiner
901 Mission St.
San Francisco, CA 94103
Phone: (415)777-1111

Publications: San Francisco Examiner (3433)

San Francisco Guide, Inc.
444 Lakeview ave.
San Francisco, CA 94112
Phone: (415)333-1834
Fax: (415)333-2534

Publications: The San Francisco and Bay Area
Guide (3428)

San Francisco Independent
1213 Evans Ave.
San Francisco, CA 94124
Phone: (415)826-1100
Fax: (415)826-5371

Publications: San Francisco Independent (3434)

San Francisco Latino Newspapers
3824 23rd St.
San Francisco, CA 94110
Phone: (415)648-1670
Fax: (415)648-3385

Publications: El Latino (3358)

San Francisco Magazine
243 Vallejo St.
San Francisco, CA 94111
Phone: (415)398-2800
Fax: (415)398-6777

Publications: San Francisco Magazine (3435)

San Francisco Medical Society
1409 Satter St.
San Francisco, CA 94109
Phone: (415)561-0850
Fax: (415)561-0833

Publications: San Francisco Medicine (3436)

San Francisco Observer
PO Box 15102
San Francisco, CA 94115
Phone: (415)863-6397
Fax: (415)431-2021

Publications: San Francisco Observer (3437)

San Francisco S.P.C.A.
2500 16th St.
San Francisco, CA 94103
Phone: (415)554-3009

Publications: Our Animals (3410)

San Francisco State University
Dept. of Journalism
1600 Holloway Ave.
San Francisco, CA 94132-1722
Phone: (415)338-3123
Fax: (415)338-3111

Publications: Golden Gate Xpress (3367)

San Gabriel Newspaper Group
7612 Greenleaf Ave.
Whittier, CA 90602
Phone: (818)962-8811
Fax: (818)962-8849
Free: 800-788-1200

Publications: Pasadena Star-News (2823) • San
Gabriel Valley Tribune (4060) • Whittier Daily News
(4080)

San Joaquin Farm Bureau Federation
PO Box 8444
Stockton, CA 95208
Phone: (209)931-4931
Fax: (209)931-1433

Publications: San Joaquin Farm Bureau News
(3507)

San Jose State University
Art Bldg. 116
San Jose, CA 95192
Phone: (408)924-4320
Fax: (408)924-4326

Publications: Switch (3541)

San Jose State University
1 Washington Sq.
San Jose, CA 95192-0149
Phone: (408)924-1000
Fax: (408)924-3282

Publications: Spartan Daily (3539)

The San Juan Record
Box 879
Monticello, UT 84535-0879
Phone: (801)587-2277
Fax: (801)587-2277

Publications: The San Juan Record (31370)

San Manuel Miner
PO Box 60
San Manuel, AZ 85631
Phone: (520)385-2266
Fax: (520)385-4666

Publications: San Manuel Miner (865)

San Marino Tribune
2260 Huntington Dr.
San Marino, CA 91108
Phone: (626)282-5707
Fax: (626)457-6436

Publications: San Marino Tribune (3581)

San Mateo Times
1080 S Amphlett Blvd.
San Mateo, CA 94402
Phone: (415)348-4321
Fax: (415)348-4446

Publications: San Mateo Times (3589)

San Miguel Basin Forum
PO Box 9
Nucla, CO 81424
Phone: (970)864-7425
Fax: (970)864-7856

Publications: San Miguel Basin Forum (4588)

San Patricio Publishing Co., Inc.
P.O. Drawer B
Sinton, TX 78387
Phone: (361)364-4243
Fax: (361)364-3833

Publications: The Mathis News (30773) • The
Odem-Edroy Times (30870) • Portland News
(31110) • San Patricio County News (31111)

San Patricio Publishing Co., Inc.
325 Green Ave.
Taft, TX 78390
Phone: (361)364-1270
Fax: (361)364-3833

Publications: The Taft Tribune (31173)

San Saba News & Star
PO Box 815
San Saba, TX 76877
Phone: (915)372-5115
Fax: (915)372-3972

Publications: San Saba News and Star (31089)

San Ysidro Publishing & Advertising Co.
601 E San Ysidro Blvd., Ste. 180
San Diego, CA 92173
Phone: (619)428-1537
Fax: (619)428-0871

Publications: Ahora Now (3109)

Sanborn Publishing Co.
Box 280
Sanborn, IA 51248
Phone: (712)729-3201

Publications: Sanborn Pioneer (11188)

Sand Mountain Reporter
1603 Progress Dr.
PO Box 1729
Albertville, AL 35950
Phone: (256)840-3000
Fax: (256)840-2987

Publications: The Sand Mountain Reporter (3)

Sand Springs Leader
303 N McKinley
Sand Springs, OK 74063
Phone: (918)245-6634
Fax: (918)241-3610

Publications: Sand Springs Leader (26054)

Sanders County Ledger
Box 219
Thompson Falls, MT 59873
Phone: (406)827-3421
Fax: (406)827-4375

Publications: Sanders County Ledger (17914)

The Sanderson Times
124 W Oak St.
Sanderson, TX 79848
Phone: (915)345-2442
Fax: (915)345-2244

Publications: The Sanderson Times (31092)

The Sandersville Georgian, Inc.
PO Box 431
Sandersville, GA 31082
Phone: (478)552-3161
Fax: (478)552-5777

Publications: Sandersville Progress (7526) • The
Wrightsville Headlight (7527)

Sandhills Publishing
120 W. Harvest Dr.
PO Box 85310
Lincoln, NE 68501-5310
Phone: (402)479-2141
Fax: (402)479-2120
Free: 800-247-4880

Publications: Controller (18082) • Machinery Trader
(Central Edition) (18092) • Machinery Trader (Eastern Edition) (18093) • Machinery Trader (Western
Edition) (18094) • PC Novice (18111) • PC Today
(18112) • Processor (18115) • Smart Computing
(18120) • Truck Paper (18124)

Sandlapper Society Inc.
PO Box 1108
Lexington, SC 29071-1108
Phone: (803)359-9954
Fax: (803)359-0629

Publications: Sandlapper (28685)

SandPaper Inc.
1816 Long Beach Blvd.
Surf City, NJ 08008
Phone: (609)494-5900
Fax: (609)494-1437

Publications: The Sandpaper (19606)

Sandusky Newspapers
116 S. Church St.
PO Box 90
Mountain City, TN 37683
Phone: (423)727-6121
Fax: (423)727-4833

Publications: The Tomahawk (29426)

Sandusky Newspapers, Inc.
314 W. Market St.
Sandusky, OH 44870-2410
Phone: (419)625-5500

Publications: Sandusky Register (25510)

Sandy Corp.
1500 W. Big Beaver Rd.
Troy, MI 48084
Phone: (248)649-0800
Fax: (248)816-2305
Free: 800-733-4739

Publications: GMC Directions (15627) • Pontiac
Excitement (15636)

Sanford Herald
1429 N Federal Hwy.
Fort Lauderdale, FL 33304
Phone: (407)778-0751
Fax: (407)323-9408

Publications: Sanford Herald (6647)

The Sanford Herald
PO Box 100
Sanford, NC 27330-0100
Phone: (919)708-9000
Fax: (919)774-9636

Publications: The Sanford Herald (24219)

Sanger Herald, Inc.
740 N St.
Sanger, CA 93657
Phone: (559)875-2511
Fax: (559)875-2521

Publications: Herald Advertiser (3616) • Sanger Herald (3617)

Sangre de Cristo Chronicle
Centro Plz.
PO Drawer I
Angel Fire, NM 87710
Phone: (505)377-2358

Publications: Sangre de Cristo Chronicle (19816)

Sanilac County Buyer's Guide
356 E Sanilac Ave.
PO Box 72
Sandusky, MI 48471
Phone: (810)648-9900
Fax: (810)648-4526
Free: 800-462-9966

Publications: Sanilac County Buyer's Guide (15521)

Sanilac County News
432 S Sandusky Rd.
Sandusky, MI 48471
Phone: (810)648-4000
Fax: (810)648-4002

Publications: Sanilac County News (15522)

Santa Barbara County Genealogical Society
Box 1303
Goleta, CA 93116
Phone: (805)884-9909

Publications: Ancestors West (2027)

Santa Barbara Independent
122 W. Figueroa St.
Santa Barbara, CA 93101-3106
Phone: (805)965-5205
Fax: (805)965-5518

Publications: Santa Barbara Independent (3654)

Santa Barbara News-Press
715 Anacapa St.
Santa Barbara, CA 93102-1359
Phone: (805)564-5200
Fax: (805)966-6258

Publications: Santa Barbara News-Press (3655)

Santa Clara University
Box 3190
Santa Clara, CA 95053
Phone: (408)554-4445
Fax: (408)554-4673

Publications: The Santa Clara (3673)

Santa Clara University School of Law
Santa Clara, CA 95053
Phone: (408)554-4000

Publications: Santa Clara Computer and High Technology Law Journal (3674) • Santa Clara Law Review (3675)

Santa Cruz Sentinel Publishers Co.
PO Box 638
Santa Cruz, CA 95061
Phone: (408)423-4242
Fax: (408)423-1154

Publications: Santa Cruz County Sentinel (3688)

The Santa Fe New Mexican
202 E. Marcy St.
Santa Fe, NM 87501-2021
Phone: (505)986-3075
Fax: (505)984-1785
Free: 800-873-3362

Publications: The Santa Fe New Mexican (19943)

Santa Fe Reporter
132 E. Marcy St.
Santa Fe, NM 87504
Phone: (505)988-5541
Fax: (505)988-5348

Publications: Santa Fe Reporter (19944)

The Santa Fean, L.L.C.
444 Galisteo
Santa Fe, NM 87501
Phone: (505)983-1444
Fax: (505)983-1555

Publications: The Santa Fean Magazine (19945)

Santa Maria Times
3200 Skyway Dr.
PO Box 400
Santa Maria, CA 93455-1896
Phone: (805)925-2691
Fax: (805)928-5657

Publications: Central Coast This Week (3695) • Santa Maria Times (3696)

Santa Monica Corsair
1900 Pico Blvd.
Santa Monica, CA 90405
Phone: (310)434-4340
Fax: (310)434-3697

Publications: Santa Monica College Corsair (3717)

Santa Rosa News
PO Box 505
Santa Rosa, NM 88435
Phone: (505)472-5454
Fax: (505)472-5453

Publications: Santa Rosa News (19951)

Santa Susana Press
University Library
18111 Nordhoff St.
Northridge, CA 91330-8326
Phone: (818)667-2638
Fax: (818)677-2676

Publications: The Daily Sundial (2646)

Sante Fe Publishing Co., Inc.
PO Box 806
Gainesville, FL 32602
Phone: (352)377-2444
Fax: (352)338-1986

Publications: The Record Farm & Ranch (6154)

The Santee Striper
369 McGee St.
PO Box 929
Bamberg, SC 29003
Phone: (803)245-5204
Fax: (803)245-3900

Publications: The Santee Striper (28481)

Santelices Communications, Inc.
3116 S Austin Blvd., No. 1
Cicero, IL 60804-3724
Phone: (708)484-1188
Fax: (708)484-0202

Publications: El Imparcial (8674)

Sapulpa Daily Herald
PO Box 1370
Sapulpa, OK 74067-1370
Phone: (918)224-5185
Fax: (918)224-5196

Publications: Sapulpa Daily Herald (26056) • Sapulpa Herald Extra (26057)

Saratoga Sun
116 E Bridge St.
Box 489
Saratoga, WY 82331
Phone: (307)326-8311
Fax: (307)326-5108

Publications: Saratoga Sun (34586)

The Saratogian, LLC
20 Lake Ave.
Saratoga Springs, NY 12866-2314
Phone: (518)584-4242
Fax: (518)587-7750

Publications: The Saratogian (23303)

Sarcoxie Publishing Co.
101 N 6th
Box 400
Sarcoxie, MO 64862
Phone: (417)548-3311
Fax: (417)548-3312

Publications: Pierce City Leader-Journal (17566) • The Sarcoxie Record (17567)

The Sarnia Observer
140 Front St. S.
PO Box 3009
Sarnia, ON, Canada N7T 7M8
Phone: (519)344-3641
Fax: (519)332-2951
Free: 800-668-0564

Publications: The Sarnia Observer (36365)

Saskatchewan Archaeological Society
1-1730 Quebec Ave.
Saskatoon, SK, Canada S7K 1V9
Phone: (306)664-4124
Fax: (306)665-1928

Publications: Saskatchewan Archaeology (37553)

Saskatchewan Archives Board
3 Campus Dr.
Murray Bldg.
University of Saskatchewan
Saskatoon, SK, Canada S7N 5A4
Phone: (306)933-5832
Fax: (306)933-7305

Publications: Saskatchewan History (37554)

Saskatchewan Genealogical Society
PO Box 1894
Regina, SK, Canada S4P 3E1
Phone: (306)780-9207
Fax: (306)781-6021

Publications: Saskatchewan Genealogical Society (37533)

Saskatchewan Ltd.
Box 100
309 Main St.
Watrous, SK, Canada S0K 4T0
Phone: (306)946-3343
Fax: (306)946-2026

Publications: The Watrous Manitou (37585)

Saskatchewan School Trustees Association
400-2222 13th Ave.
Regina, SK, Canada S4P 3M7
Phone: (306)569-0750
Fax: (306)352-9633

Publications: School Trustee (37534)

Saskatoon Heritage Society
PO Box 7051
Saskatoon, SK, Canada S7K 4J1
Phone: (306)652-9801

Publications: Saskatoon History Review (37555)

Satellite 1-416
PO Box 176, Sta. E
Toronto, ON, Canada M6H 4E2
Phone: (416)530-4232
Fax: (416)530-0069

Publications: Satellite 1-416 (36735)

The Saturday Evening Post Society
1100 Waterway Blvd.
Indianapolis, IN 46202
Phone: (317)636-8881
Fax: (317)637-0126

Publications: The Saturday Evening Post (10169)

The Satyr
211 Windsor Ln.
West Hempstead, NY 11552
Phone: (917)613-8678
Fax: (516)483-6047

Publications: The Satyr (23541)

Sauk Centre Publishers Inc.
522 Sinclair Lewis Ave.
Sauk Centre, MN 56378
Phone: (320)352-6577
Fax: (612)352-5647
Free: 877-396-6577

Publications: Herald (16436) • Sauk Rapids Herald (16437)

Sault Ste. Marie Evening News
109 Arlington St.
Sault Sainte Marie, MI 49783
Phone: (906)632-2235
Fax: (906)632-1222

Publications: Sault Ste. Marie Evening News (15527)

Sault Ste. Marie This Week
2 Towers St.
PO Box 188
Sault Sainte Marie, ON, Canada P6A 5L6
Phone: (705)949-6111
Fax: (705)942-8596

2622

Numbers cited after listings are entry numbers rather than page numbers.

Publications: Sault Ste. Marie This Week (36369)

W. B. Saunders Co.
The Public Ledger Bldg., Ste. 1250
150 S. Independence Mall W.
Philadelphia, PA 19106-3412
Phone: (215)238-7800

Publications: Journal of the American Society for Surgery (27515) • Pain Management Nursing (3411)

Saunders County Publishing Inc.
564 N Broadway
Wahoo, NE 68066
Phone: (402)443-4162
Fax: (402)443-4459

Publications: Wahoo Newspaper (18302)

Savannah
115 S 4th St.
PO Box 299
Savannah, MO 64485
Phone: (816)324-3149
Fax: (816)324-3632

Publications: Savannah Reporter and Andrew County Democrat (17568)

The Savannah Herald
1803 Barnard St.
PO Box 486
Savannah, GA 31401
Phone: (912)232-4505
Fax: (912)231-0018

Publications: The Savannah Herald (7534)

Savannah Jewish Federation
PO Box 23527
Savannah, GA 31403-3527
Phone: (912)355-8111
Fax: (912)355-8116

Publications: Savannah Jewish News (7535)

Savannah Morning News
PO Box 1088
Savannah, GA 31402-1088
Phone: (912)236-0271
Fax: (912)234-6522

Publications: Savannah Morning News (7536)

Savannah Tribune, Inc.
916 Montgomery St.
PO Box 2066
Savannah, GA 31402
Phone: (912)233-6128
Fax: (912)233-6140

Publications: The Savannah Tribune (7538)

Sawyer County Gazette
PO Box 99
Winter, WI 54896
Phone: (715)266-2511
Fax: (715)266-2511

Publications: Sawyer County Gazette (34461)

Sawyer Press
PO Box 85
North Creek, NY 12853
Phone: (518)251-3012
Fax: (518)251-4147

Publications: The North Creek News-Enterprise (23012)

Scaffold Industry Association
20335 Ventura Blvd., No. 310
Woodland Hills, CA 91364
Phone: (818)610-0320
Fax: (818)610-0323

Publications: Scaffold Industry Association Magazine (4113)

Scandia Journal
1710 M St.
Belleville, KS 66935
Phone: (785)527-5182
Fax: (785)527-2159

Publications: Scandia Journal (11358)

Scandinavian Collectors Club
102 S Main St.
Madrid, IA 50156

Publications: The Posthorn (4184)

Scanning Microscopy International
PO Box 66507
AMF OHare, IL 60666
Phone: (847)524-6677
Fax: (847)985-6698

Publications: Scanning Microscopy (8560)

Scarboro Foreign Mission Society
2685 Kingston Rd.
Scarborough, ON, Canada M1M 1M4
Phone: (416)261-7135
Fax: (416)261-0820
Free: 800-260-4815

Publications: Scarboro Missions (36384)

Scarborough College Student Press
University of Toronto
1265 Military Trail, Rm. S-364
Scarborough, ON, Canada M1C 1A4
Phone: (416)287-7054
Fax: (416)287-7055

Publications: The Underground (36386)

Scarecrow Education
4720 Boston Way, Ste. A
Lanham, MD 20706
Phone: (301)459-3366
Fax: (301)429-5747
Free: 800-462-6420

Publications: International Journal of Educational Reform (13602)

Scarecrow Press Inc.
4501 Forbes Blvd., Ste. 200
Lanham, MD 20706
Phone: (301)459-3366
Fax: (301)429-5743
Free: 888-486-9297

Publications: Voice of Youth Advocates (13609)

Scarlet Street, Inc.
PO Box 604
Glen Rock, NJ 07452
Phone: (201)445-0034
Fax: (201)445-1496

Publications: Scarlet Street (18848)

Scars Publications & Design
829 Brian Ct.
Gurnee, IL 60031-3155

Publications: Children, Churches & Daddies (8965)

SCCC Publications
Seattle Central Community College
1701 Broadway
Seattle, WA 98122
Phone: (206)587-3800

Publications: The City Collegian (32954)

Scene, Inc.
930 5th Ave.
New York, NY 10021-2651
Phone: (212)737-8100
Fax: (212)737-8884

Publications: Scene at the Movies (22709)

Scene Publications
300 N Appleton St., Ste. 2
Appleton, WI 54911
Phone: (920)733-5743
Fax: (920)733-5783

Publications: The Scene (33544)

Schaffner Publications, Inc.
205 SE Catawba Rd., Ste. G
Port Clinton, OH 43452
Phone: (419)732-2154
Fax: (419)734-5382

Publications: The Beacon (25480) • Ohio Sportsman (25483)

Schaller Herald
203 S Main
PO Box 129
Schaller, IA 51053
Phone: (712)275-4229

Publications: Schaller Herald (11189)

Schaub Publishing Inc.
Box 100
Boone, IA 50036
Phone: (515)432-1234
Fax: (515)432-7811

Publications: Boone News-Republican (10625)

Schneider Publishing Co.
11835 W Olympic Blvd., 12th Fl.
Los Angeles, CA 90064
Phone: (310)577-3700
Fax: (310)577-3715
Free: 877-577-3700

Publications: Association News (2215)

Schnell Publishing Co., Inc.
2 Rector St., 26th Fl.
New York, NY 10006-1819
Phone: (212)791-4200
Fax: (212)791-4313

Publications: Chemical Market Reporter (21402)

Scholastic Library Publishing
90 Sherman Tpke.
Danbury, CT 06816
Fax: (203)797-3657
Free: 800-621-1115

Publications: Art & Man (4735) • Choices (4736) • Coach and Athletic Director (4737) • Computing Software Review (4738) • Electronic Learning (4739) • Family Computin- (4740) • Home-Office Computing (4741) • Instructor (4742) • Junior Scholastic (4743) • Let's Find Out (4744) • Literary Cavalcade (4745) • The New York Times Upfront (4746) • Parent & Chg- (4748) • Peanut Butter (4750) • Scholastic Action (4751) • Scholastic Ars- (4752) • Scholastic Coach & Athletic Director (4753) • Scholastic DynaMath (4754) • Scholastic MATH Magazine (4755) • Scholastic News Citizen Edition (4756) • Scholastic News Explorer Edition (4757) • Scholastic News Newstime Edition (4758) • Scholastic News Pilot Edition (4759) • Scholastic News Ranger Edition (4760) • Scholastic News Trails Edition (4761) • Scholastic Scope (4762) • Science World (4763) • Storyworks (4764)

Scholl & Associates
516 Dudley Dr.
Roseville, CA 95678-3926

Publications: Single Again Magazine (2972)

School of Architecture
815 Sherbrooke St. W.
Montreal, QC, Canada H3A 2K6
Phone: (514)398-6700
Fax: (514)398-7372

Publications: Fifth Column (37116)

School Arts Magazine
50 Portland St.
Worcester, MA 01608
Phone: (508)754-7201
Fax: (508)753-3834
Free: 800-533-2847

Publications: School Arts Magazine (27131)

School of International Studies
1800 30th St., Ste. 314
Boulder, CO 80301
Phone: (303)444-6684
Fax: (303)444-0824

Publications: Latin American Politics and Society (4176)

School of Law
MSC11 6070
University of New Mexico
Albuquerque, NM 87131
Phone: (505)277-4910
Fax: (505)277-8342

Publications: New Mexico Law Review (19781)

School Science and Mathematics Association
c/o Arthur L. White
238 Arps Hall
1945 N. High St.
Ohio State University
Columbus, OH 43210-1172
Phone: (614)292-8061
Fax: (614)292-7695

Publications: School Science and Mathematics (25061)

Schroeder Publications
202 W Cottage Grove Rd., No. D
Cottage Grove, WI 53527-9632
Phone: (608)221-1544
Fax: (608)221-0463

Publications: Monona Community Herald (33646)

Schroeder Publications
120 W. Verona Ave.
Verona, WI 53593
Phone: (608)845-9559
Fax: (608)845-9550

Publications: The Verona Press (34380)

Schulenburg Sticker, Inc.
405 N Main
Schulenburg, TX 78956-0160
Phone: (979)743-3450
Fax: (979)743-4609

Publications: The Schulenburg Sticker (31093)

Jeff Schumacher
PO Box 517
New England, ND 58647
Phone: (701)579-4530
Fax: (701)579-4180

Publications: The Herald (24522)

Schurz Communications Inc./South Bend Tribune
225 W Colfax Ave.
South Bend, IN 46626
Phone: (574)235-6161
Fax: (574)236-1765

Publications: Morresville/Decatur Times (10457) • Tribune Business Weekly (10460)

Johannes Schwalm Historical Association Inc.
PO Box 416
State Line, PA 17263-0416

Publications: Journal of the Johannes Schwalm Historical Association (28033)

Schwarz Publishing Inc.
4731 Palm Ave.
La Mesa, CA 91941
Phone: (619)463-5515
Fax: (619)403-1309

Publications: San Diego Jewish Times (2123)

Science & Engineering Network News
49 Midgley Ln.
Worcester, MA 01604-3564
Phone: (508)755-5242
Fax: (508)795-1636

Publications: Science & Engineering Network News (14688)

Science Fiction Chronicle
PO Box 2988
Radford, VA 24143-2988
Phone: (540)763-2925
Fax: (540)763-2924

Publications: Science Fiction Chronicle (32346)

Science Fiction Eye
PO Box 18539
Asheville, NC 28814
Fax: (704)285-9400

Publications: Science Fiction Eye (23633)

Science Illustrated, L.P.
8428 Holly Leaf Dr.
Mc Lean, VA 22102
Phone: (703)356-1688
Fax: (703)356-1688

Publications: Science Illustrated (32255)

Science Printers and Publishers, Inc.
PO Drawer 12425
8342 Olive Blvd.
St. Louis, MO 63132-2814
Phone: (314)991-4440
Fax: (314)991-4654

Publications: ACTA Cytologica (17403) • Analytical and Quantitative Cytology and Histology (17413) • The Journal of Reproductive Medicine (17461)

Science Service, Inc.
1719 N St. NW
Washington, DC 20036
Phone: (202)785-2255
Fax: (202)785-1243

Publications: Science News (5781)

Science Weekly, Inc.
2141 Industrial Pkwy., Ste. 202
Silver Spring, MD 20904
Phone: (301)680-8804

Publications: Science Weekly (13745)

Scientific American Magazine
415 Madison Ave.
New York, NY 10017
Phone: (212)754-0550
Fax: (212)355-6245

Publications: Scientific American (22714)

The Scientist, Inc.
3535 Market St., Ste. 200
Philadelphia, PA 19104-2645
Phone: (215)386-9601
Fax: (215)386-7542
Free: 800-258-6008

Publications: The Scientist (27656)

Scioto Voice
8019 Hayport Rd.
PO Box 400
Wheelersburg, OH 45694
Phone: (614)574-8494
Fax: (614)574-2329
Free: 800-297-8494

Publications: The Scioto Voice (25650)

S.C.M. Publications, Inc.
PO Box 859
Mahwah, NJ 07430
Phone: (201)684-9222
Fax: (201)684-9228

Publications: Fashion Accessories (19190)

Scotland Journal
PO Box 388
Scotland, SD 57059
Phone: (605)583-4419

Publications: Scotland Journal (28959)

Scotsman Community Publications
PO Box 4970
Syracuse, NY 13221
Phone: (315)472-7825
Fax: (315)478-1434
Free: (866)SCOTSMAN

Publications: Auburn Pennysaver (23387) • Baldwinsville Pennysaver (23389) • Bellevue-Geddes Pennysaver (23390) • City Edition Pennysaver (23394) • Cortland Sunday/Democrat (23397) • Court-Butternut Pennysaver (23398) • East Syracuse/Minoa/Kirkville/Bridgeport Pennysaver (23401) • Eastwood Pennysaver (23402) • Fulton Pennysaver (23404) • Geneva Pennysaver (23405) • Jamesville/Dewitt/Fayetteville/Manlius Pennysaver (21020) • Liverpool-Phoenix Pennysaver (23408) • Lyncourt Pennysaver (23410) • Mattydale-North Syracuse Pennysaver (23411) • Moravia Pennysaver (23413) • North Area Pennysaver (23415) • Onondaga Valley News (23416) • Pennywise/Villager (23418) • Seneca Falls Pennysaver (23421) • Skaneateles-Marcellus Pennysaver (23422) • Solvay-Camillus Pennysaver (23423) • Strathmore-Onondaga Hill Pennysaver (23424) • Syracuse East Pennysaver (23425) • Town & Country Pennysaver (23431)

Scott County Herald Virginian Inc.
PO Box 218
Gate City, VA 24251
Phone: (276)386-7027
Fax: (276)386-2354

Publications: Scott County Virginia Star (32108)

Scott County Publishing Company
1720 5th Ave.
Moline, IL 61265
Phone: (309)386-3670
Fax: (309)386-3731

Publications: The Leader (9206)

Scott County Signal
113 S Main St.
PO Box 97
Chaffee, MO 63740
Phone: (573)887-3636
Fax: (573)887-3637

Publications: Scott County Signal (16971)

The Scott County Times Newspaper
PO Box 138
Winchester, IL 62694
Phone: (217)742-3313
Fax: (217)742-3596

Publications: Campbell Publication (9766)

Scott Publications, Inc.
801 W Norton Ave., Ste. 200
Muskegon, MI 49441
Phone: (231)733-9382
Fax: (231)733-7635
Free: 800-458-8237

Publications: Contemporary Doll Collector (15387) • Soft Dolls & Animals (15389) • Stamping Arts & Crafts (15390)

Scott Publishing Co
PO Box 828
911 Vandermark Rd.
Sidney, OH 45365-0828
Phone: (937)498-6885
Fax: (937)498-0807
Free: 800-572-6885

Publications: Scott Stamp Monthly (25520)

Scott Publishing, Inc.
PO Box 89
Forest, MS 39074
Phone: (601)469-2561
Fax: (601)469-2004

Publications: Scott County Times (16625)

Scott-Townsend Publishers
PO Box 34070
Washington, DC 20043
Phone: (202)371-2700
Fax: (202)371-1523

Publications: The Mankind Quarterly (5643)

The Scottish Banner
249 Main St.
Dunedin, FL 34698-5731
Phone: (727)738-9590
Fax: (727)738-9592

Publications: The Scottish Banner (6062)

Scottsboro Newspapers, Inc.
701 Veterans Dr.
Scottsboro, AL 35768-2132
Phone: (205)259-1020
Fax: (205)259-2709

Publications: The Daily Sentinel (445)

The Scout
Bldg. 1160, Rm. 111
Camp Pendleton, CA 92055-5001

Publications: The Scout (1652)

SCP Journal
PO Box 4308
Berkeley, CA 94704
Phone: (510)540-0300
Fax: (510)540-1107

Publications: SCP Journal (1557)

Scranton Gillette Communications Inc.
380 E NW Hwy., Ste. 200
Des Plaines, IL 60016-2282
Phone: (847)298-6622
Fax: (847)390-0408

Publications: The DIAPASON (8760) • Roads & Bridges Magazine (8770) • Seed World (8771) • Water Engineering & Management (8773) • Water & Wastes Digest (8774)

Scranton Times
812 Park Ave.
Baltimore, MD 21201-4847
Phone: (410)889-6600
Fax: (410)523-2222

Publications: Baltimore City Paper (13131)

Numbers cited after listings are entry numbers rather than page numbers.

The Scranton Times
149 Penn Ave.
PO Box 3311
Scranton, PA 18505-3311
Phone: (570)348-9154
Fax: (570)348-9135

Publications: Northeast Pennsylvania Business Journal (26717) • The Scranton Times (27963)

Screen Enterprises, Inc.
222 W Ontario St., Ste. 500
Chicago, IL 60610
Phone: (312)640-0800
Fax: (312)640-1928

Publications: Screen Magazine (8562)

Scribblefest Literary Group
542 Mitchell Dr.
Los Osos, CA 93402
Phone: 800-528-8146

Publications: Lynx Eye (2482)

Scripps Community Newspapers
405 SH 121 Bypass, Ste. 110
Lewisville, TX 75067
Phone: (972)436-3566

Publications: The Colony Leader (30685)

Scripps Howard
100 Gene Amole Way
Denver, CO 80204

Publications: Rocky Mountain News (4354)

Scripps Howard Company
545 Fifth St.
Bremerton, WA 98337-0053
Phone: (360)377-3711
Fax: (360)377-9237

Publications: North Kitsap Neighbors (32693) • South Kitsap Neighbors (32694)

Scripps Howard Group
PO Box 9009
Stuart, FL 34995-9009

Publications: Fort Pierce News (6694)

Scripps Howard, Inc.
312 Walnut, 28th Fl.
Cincinnati, OH 45202
Phone: (513)977-3000
Free: 800-888-3000

Publications: The Albuquerque Tribune (19764) • Bonita Banner (5946) • Daily Camera (4163) • The Jupiter Courier (6249) • The Kentucky Post (12027)

Scripps Marin Publishing Co.
1068 Machin Ave.
Novato, CA 94945-2458
Phone: (415)892-1516
Fax: (415)897-0940

Publications: Novato Advance (2652)

Scuba Retailers Association
335 Beard St.
Tallahassee, FL 32303

Publications: Scuba Retailer (6734)

SDB Tract and Communication Council
3120 Kennedy Rd.
PO Box 1678
Janesville, WI 53547-1678
Phone: (608)752-5055
Fax: (608)752-7711

Publications: The Sabbath Recorder (33861)

Sea-Coast Publications Inc.
128 Gerard D. Levesque Boul.
PO Box 99
New Carlisle, QC, Canada G0C 1Z0
Phone: (418)752-5400
Fax: (418)752-6932

Publications: Gaspe Spec (37255)

Sea Fog Press
447 20th Ave.
San Francisco, CA 94121
Phone: (415)221-8527

Publications: Harmony (3369)

Sea Grant Program
2700 Earl Rudder Fwy. S, Ste. 1800
College Station, TX 77845
Phone: (979)845-3854
Fax: (979)845-7525

Publications: Texas Shore Magazine (30054)

Sea Kayaker Inc.
PO Box 17029
Seattle, WA 98107-0729
Phone: (206)789-9536
Fax: (206)781-1141

Publications: Sea Kayaker Magazine (33017)

Sea Power Magazine
2300 Wilson Blvd.
Arlington, VA 22201-3308
Phone: (703)528-1775
Fax: (703)528-2333
Free: 800-356-5760

Publications: Sea Power (31830)

Seacoast Newspapers, Inc.
PO Box 250
Exeter, NH 03833-0250
Phone: (603)772-6000
Fax: (603)772-3830
Free: 800-734-7022

Publications: The Exeter News-Letter (18505) • The Hampton Union (18506) • The Rockingham News (18507)

Seacoast Publishing
850 Park Ave.
Monterey, CA 93940

Publications: Your World of Birds (2585)

Seafarers Intl. Union
5201 Auth Way
Camp Springs, MD 20746-4275
Phone: (301)899-0675
Fax: (301)899-7355

Publications: Seafarers LOG (13402)

Seago Publishing Co.
PO Box 130
Seagoville, TX 75159
Phone: (972)287-7720
Fax: (972)287-3278

Publications: Seagoville Suburbia News (31094)

Seagraphic Publications Ltd.
PO Box 1312 STN A
Delta, BC, Canada V4M 3Y8
Phone: (604)948-9937
Fax: (604)948-9985
Free: 877-974-4333

Publications: Diver Magazine (34946)

The Sealy News
Drawer 480
Sealy, TX 77474
Phone: (979)885-3562
Fax: (979)885-3564
Free: 800-236-2916

Publications: The Sealy News (31095)

Sean Waters
PO Box 185
Storden, MN 56174

Publications: Village Insight (16464)

Search Reports, Inc.
345 Blvd.
Hasbrouck Heights, NJ 07604
Phone: (201)288-4445
Fax: (201)288-8055

Publications: National Missing Persons Report (18866)

Search Shopper
PO Box 748
Lindstrom, MN 55045-0748
Phone: (651)257-5115
Fax: (651)257-5500

Publications: Search Shopper (16003)

The Searchlight
PO Box 496
Culbertson, MT 59218
Phone: (406)787-5821
Fax: (406)787-5271

Publications: The Searchlight (17777)

Seaside Press Co., Inc.
1003 Settlers Lane Ste. F
Carolina Beach, NC 28428
Phone: (910)458-8156
Fax: (910)458-0267

Publications: Island Gazette (23684)

Seaside Signal Publishing
730 Broadway
PO Box 848
Seaside, OR 97138
Phone: (503)738-5561
Fax: (503)738-5672

Publications: North Coast Tidings (26579) • Seaside Signal (26580)

Seaton Publications
908 W 2nd St.
Box 788
Hastings, NE 68902-0788
Phone: (402)462-2131
Fax: (402)461-4657

Publications: The Hastings Tribune (18037)

Seaton Publishing Co.
315 Seaton Cir.
PO Box 7
Spearfish, SD 57783
Phone: (605)642-2761
Fax: (605)642-9060
Free: 800-676-2761

Publications: Black Hills Pioneer (28993)

Seattle Post Intelligencer
101 Elliott Ave. W.
Seattle, WA 98119
Phone: (206)448-8000
Fax: (206)448-8166

Publications: Seattle Post-Intelligencer (33021)

Seattle Publishing
68 S Washington St.
Seattle, WA 98104
Phone: (206)903-1333
Fax: (206)903-8565
Free: 888-836-5720

Publications: The Bicycle Paper (32951)

Seattle University
900 Broadway
Seattle, WA 98122-4340
Phone: (206)398-4270
Fax: (206)398-4272

Publications: Seattle University Law Review (33024) • Seattle University Spectator (33025)

Seattle Weekly Media Inc.
1008 Western Ave., Ste. 300
Seattle, WA 98104-1006
Phone: (206)623-0500
Fax: (206)467-4338

Publications: Seattle Weekly (33026)

Seaways Publishing, Inc.
2271 Constitution Dr.
San Jose, CA 95124-1204
Phone: (408)978-5657
Fax: (408)978-5657

Publications: Seaways' Ships in Scale (31478)

The Sebree Banner
Box 36
Sebree, KY 42455
Phone: (270)835-7521
Fax: (270)835-9521

Publications: The Sebree Banner (12397)

Second Amendment Foundation
PO Box 488
Buffalo, NY 14209-0488
Phone: (716)885-6408
Fax: (716)884-4471

Publications: The New Gun Week (20384) • Women and Guns (20393)

Seconds Magazine
245th Ave. Apt. 405
New York, NY 10011
Phone: (212)260-0481
Fax: (212)260-0440

Publications: Seconds (22717)

Securities Data Publishing
195 Broadway, 10th Fl.
New York, NY 10007
Free: 800-455-5844

Publications: Financial Planning (21698) • Investment Dealers' Digest (21946) • Mergers & Acquisitions (22316) • Nest Egg (22417)

Securities Data Publishing Inc.
195 Broadway St., 4th Fl.
New York, NY 10007
Phone: (646)822-2000
Free: 800-455-5844

Publications: Employee Benefit News (21600)

Securities Industry Association
120 Broadway, 35th Fl.
New York, NY 10271
Phone: (212)608-1500
Fax: (212)968-0703

Publications: Operation Update (22498)

Securities Reform Act Litigation Reporter
1601 Connecticut Ave., NW, No. 602
Washington, DC 20009
Phone: (202)462-5755
Fax: (202)328-2430

Publications: Securities Reform Act Litigation Reporter (5787)

Security Media Inc.
240 Edward St.
Aurora, ON, Canada L4G 3S9
Phone: (905)713-0816
Fax: (905)841-5078

Publications: CANADIAN SECURITY (35643)

The Sedalia Democrat
7th & Massachusetts Ave.
PO Box 848
Sedalia, MO 65302
Phone: (660)826-1000
Fax: (660)826-2413

Publications: The Sedalia Democrat (17570)

Sedona Excentric
PO Box 843
Sedona, AZ 86339
Phone: (928)639-4224
Fax: (928)639-4224

Publications: Sedona Excentric (877)

Sedona Red Rock News
PO Box 619
Sedona, AZ 86339
Phone: (928)282-7795
Fax: (928)282-6011

Publications: Sedona Red Rock News (878)

The Seeley Swan Pathfinder
PO Box 702
Seeley Lake, MT 59868
Phone: (406)677-2022
Fax: (406)677-2741

Publications: The Seeley Swan Pathfinder (17905)

Seismological Society of America
201 Plaza Professional Bldg.
El Cerrito, CA 94530-4003
Phone: (510)525-5474
Fax: (510)525-7204

Publications: Bulletin (1859) • Seismological Research Letters (1862)

Selby Record
4411 Main St.
PO Box 421
Selby, SD 57472
Phone: (605)649-7866
Fax: (605)649-7054

Publications: Selby Record (28960)

Select Press
PO Box 37
Corte Madera, CA 94976-0037
Phone: (415)209-9838
Fax: (415)209-6719

Publications: Journal of Social Behavior and Personality (2650)

Self Help for Hard of Hearing People
7910 Woodmont Ave., Ste. 1200
Bethesda, MD 20814
Phone: (301)657-2248
Fax: (301)913-9413

Publications: Hearing Loss (13343)

Self-Realization Fellowship, Publishers
3208 Humboldt St.
Los Angeles, CA 90031
Phone: (323)661-8006
Fax: (323)276-6003
Free: 888-773-8680

Publications: Self-Realization (2386)

Selma Newspapers, Inc.
1018 Water Ave.
PO Box 611
Selma, AL 36701
Phone: (334)875-2110
Fax: (205)875-5896

Publications: The Selma Times-Journal (452)

Selma Times Journal
PO Box 1379
Clanton, AL 35045
Phone: (205)755-5747
Fax: (205)755-5857

Publications: The Clanton Advertiser (155)

SEMI
PO Box 3417
Northbrook, IL 60065-3417
Phone: (408)943-7047
Fax: (408)943-7965

Publications: Semiconductor Magazine (9322)

Seminar on Jesuit Spirituality
3601 Lindell Blvd.
St. Louis, MO 63108
Phone: (314)977-7257
Fax: (314)977-7263

Publications: Studies in the Spirituality of Jesuits (17518)

The Seminole Producer
121 N Main
PO Box 431
Seminole, OK 74868
Phone: (405)382-1100
Fax: (405)382-1104

Publications: The Seminole Producer (26058)

The Seminole Sentinel
406 S Main St.
Drawer 1200
Seminole, TX 79360
Phone: (915)758-3667
Fax: (915)758-2136

Publications: The Seminole Sentinel (31098)

Semiotic Society of America
Speech Communication Dept.
Southern Illinois University
Carbondale, IL 62901-6605
Phone: (618)453-1894
Fax: (618)453-2812

Publications: American Journal of Semiotics (8114)

Seneca College Student Federation
1750 Finch Ave. E.
Willowdale, ON, Canada M2J 2X5
Phone: (416)491-5050
Fax: (416)756-2765

Publications: The Impact (36878)

Seneca News-Dispatch
1103 Cherokee St.
PO Box 1110
Seneca, MO 64865
Phone: (417)776-2236
Fax: (417)776-2204

Publications: Seneca News-Dispatch (17576)

Seneca Publishing, Inc.
26 N Main St.
PO Box 516
Attica, OH 44807
Phone: (419)426-3491
Fax: (419)426-2003

Publications: Attica Hub (24638) • Bloomville Gazette (24681)

Sengstacke Newspaper Corp.
479 Ledyard St.
Detroit, MI 48201
Phone: (313)963-5522
Fax: (313)963-8788
Free: 800-203-0220

Publications: Michigan Chronicle (14938)

Senior Media Services
Lutheran Community Services NW
223 N. Yakima
Tacoma, WA 98403
Phone: (253)272-2278
Fax: (253)597-6456

Publications: Senior Scene (33150)

Senior Multimedia Inc.
6022 W. Pico Blvd., Ste. 7
Los Angeles, CA 90035
Phone: (323)933-9228
Fax: (323)933-9261
Free: 888-767-5433

Publications: Northwest Senior Life (26489) • Southern California Senior Life (1848) • Southern California Senior Life (Inland Empire Edition) (2398) • Southern California Senior Life (Los Angeles County Edition) (2399) • Southern California Senior Life (Orange County Edition) (2400) • Southern California Senior Life (Southern California Edition) (2401) • Southern California Senior Life (Southland Edition) (2402)

Senior Times, Inc.
523 N. Pines Rd., Ste. B
PO Box 142020
Spokane, WA 99214-2020
Phone: (509)924-2440
Fax: (509)927-1154

Publications: Senior Times (33099)

Sensations Magazine
PO Box 6
Ocean Grove, NJ 07756

Publications: Sensations Magazine (19391)

Sensible Sound, Inc.
403 Darwin Dr.
Snyder, NY 14226
Phone: (716)833-0930
Fax: (716)833-0929
Free: 800-695-8439

Publications: Sensible Sound (23342)

Sentinel
PO Box 9148
Auburn, CA 95604
Phone: (530)823-2463
Fax: (530)823-1309

Publications: Sentinel (1439)

The Sentinel
385 West Church St.
PO Box 277
Trenton, GA 30752
Phone: (706)657-6182
Fax: (706)657-4970

Publications: The Dade County Sentinel (7608)

Sentinel
PO Box 208
Onawa, IA 51040-0208
Phone: (712)423-2021
Fax: (712)423-3038
Free: 800-603-2021

Publications: Sentinel (11127)

Sentinel
PO Box 1015
Dawson, MN 56232

Publications: Sentinel (15825)

Sentinel
64 Downtown Plaza
PO Box 681
Fairmont, MN 56031
Phone: (507)235-3303
Fax: (507)235-3718

Publications: Sentinel (15890)

Numbers cited after listings are entry numbers rather than page numbers.

Sentinel
PO Box 270
Edina, MO 63537
Phone: (660)397-2226
Fax: (660)397-2227

Publications: Sentinel (17041)

Sentinel
Box 69
Sentinel, OK 73664
Phone: (580)393-4348
Fax: (580)393-4349

Publications: Sentinel Leader (26059)

Sentinel Communications Corp.
PO Box 1839
Tahlequah, OK 74465
Phone: (918)458-0816

Publications: The Tahlequah Times Journal (26095)

The Sentinel Co.
300 E. Poe Rd.
PO Box 88
Bowling Green, OH 43402
Phone: (419)352-4611
Fax: (419)354-0314

Publications: Sentinel-Tribune (24701)

The Sentinel Courier
13 Railway
PO Box 179
Pilot Mound, MB, Canada R0G 1P0
Phone: (204)825-2772
Fax: (204)825-2772

Publications: The Sentinel Courier (35280)

Sentinel & Enterprise
808 Main St.
Fitchburg, MA 01420
Phone: (978)343-6911
Fax: (978)342-1158

Publications: Sentinel & Enterprise (14184)

Sentinel Plus
300 W 6th St.
PO Box 9
Hanford, CA 93230
Phone: (559)582-0471
Fax: (559)587-1876

Publications: The Hanford Sentinel (2037) • Sentinel Plus (2038)

Sentinel Printing and Publishing
145 South L St.
Dinuba, CA 93618-2324
Phone: (559)591-4634
Fax: (559)591-1322

Publications: Dinuba Sentinel (1828) • The Sentinel-Advertiser (1829)

The Sentinel-Record
300 Spring St.
Hot Springs, AR 71901
Phone: (501)623-7711
Fax: (501)623-2984

Publications: The Sentinel-Record (1184)

Sentry Books, Inc.
4426 Deseret Dr.
Woodland Hills, CA 91364-4842

Publications: Airpower (4100)

Sentry Technology Group
One Research Dr.
Suite 400-B
Westborough, MA 01581-3907
Phone: (508)366-2031
Fax: (508)836-4732
Free: 800-225-9218

Publications: Client/Server Computing (14636)

Serb National Federation
1 5th Ave.
Pittsburgh, PA 15222
Phone: (412)642-7372
Fax: (412)642-1372
Free: 800-538-7372

Publications: American Srbobran (27757)

Serb World U.S.A., Inc.
415 E Mabel St.
Tucson, AZ 85705
Phone: (602)624-4887

Publications: Serb World U.S.A. (963)

Serbian League of Canada
335 Britannia Ave.
Hamilton, ON, Canada L8H 1Y4
Phone: (905)549-4079
Fax: (905)549-8552

Publications: Canadian Serbian (35878)

Serbin Communications, Inc.
511 Olive St.
Santa Barbara, CA 93101
Phone: (805)564-7636
Fax: (805)965-0496

Publications: Photographer's Forum (3650)

Serif
Dept. W-1
2038 N. Clark St.
PO Box 377
Chicago, IL 60614

Publications: Serif (8563)

Serif Publishing Company
PO Box 340
Junction City, OR 97448
Phone: (541)998-3877
Fax: (541)998-3878

Publications: Tri-County News (26379)

SERPRO COMM Inc.
8403 Rue Oscar-Roland
Montreal, QC, Canada H2M 2T4
Phone: (514)383-7700
Fax: (514)383-7691
Free: 888-383-7700

Publications: Electronique Industrielle et Commerciale (EIC) (37114)

Service Communications
1122 Saskatchewan Dr.
Regina, SK, Canada S4P 0C4
Phone: (306)525-8321
Fax: (306)569-1363

Publications: The Commonwealth (37529)

Service Publications
14 FTW/PA
PO Box 511
Columbus, MS 39710-1009
Phone: (662)742-7066
Fax: (662)434-7009

Publications: Silver Wings (16605)

SETAC
1010 N 12th Ave.
Pensacola, FL 32501-3367
Phone: (850)469-1500
Fax: (850)469-9778
Free: 800-899-2088

Publications: Environmental Toxicology and Chemistry (30471)

Setcom, Inc.
389 Johnnie Dodds Blvd. Ste. 200
Mount Pleasant, SC 29464
Phone: (843)849-3100
Fax: (843)849-3122

Publications: Charleston Regional Business Journal (28692)

Seton Hall University
Division of Business Research
c/o Mary L. Williams
South Orange, NJ 07079-2692
Phone: (973)761-9000
Fax: (973)761-9217

Publications: Mid-Atlantic Journal of Business (19585)

Seton Hill College
PO Box 343
Greensburg, PA 15601
Phone: (724)838-4280
Fax: (724)838-4203

Publications: Setonian (26954)

The Setonian
Seton Hall University
400 S. Orange Ave.
South Orange, NJ 07079
Phone: (973)761-9083
Fax: (973)761-7943

Publications: The Setonian (19586)

Seven Hills Foundation
81 Hope Avenue
PO Box 6341
Worcester, MA 01603
Phone: (508)755-2340

Publications: Home Automation (14682)

795651 Ontario Inc.
813 rue Georges
C.P. 2320
Hearst, ON, Canada P0L 1N0
Phone: (705)372-1233
Fax: (705)362-5954

Publications: Le Nord (35911)

Seventeenth-Century News
Dept. of English, 4227 TAMU
Texas A&M University
College Station, TX 77843-4227
Phone: (979)845-8340
Fax: (979)862-2292

Publications: Seventeenth-Century News (30049)

Seventh-Day Adventist Church Reform Movement
Religious Liberty Publishing Assn.
2877 E. Florence Ave.
Huntington Park, CA 90255-5751
Phone: (562)862-5252
Fax: (562)862-7166

Publications: The Sabbath Watchman (1836)

73 Magazine
70 Hancock Rd.
Peterborough, NH 03458
Phone: (603)924-4117
Fax: (603)924-9327

Publications: 73 Amateur Radio Today (18628)

Seward County Community College
Box 1137
Liberal, KS 67905-1137
Phone: (620)629-2669
Fax: (620)629-2725

Publications: The Crusader (11603)

Seward County Independent
129 S 6th St.
Box 449
Seward, NE 68434-0449
Phone: (402)643-3676
Fax: (402)643-6774

Publications: Seward County Independent (18276)

Sewing Dealers Trade Association
2724 2nd Ave.
Des Moines, IA 50313
Phone: (515)282-9101
Fax: (515)282-4483
Free: 800-367-5651

Publications: Embroidery Professional & Sewing Professional/Round Bobbin (10784)

Sexuality Information and Education Council of the United States
130 W 42nd St., Ste. 350
New York, NY 10036-7802
Phone: (212)819-9770
Fax: (212)819-9776

Publications: SIECUS Report (22740)

The Seymour Herald
116 N 4th St.
PO Box 125
Seymour, IA 52590
Phone: (641)898-7554
Fax: (641)898-7554

Publications: The Seymour Herald (11191)

SF-TH, Inc., EC L-06
DePauw University
Greencastle, IN 46135-0037
Phone: (765)658-4758
Fax: (765)658-4764

Publications: Science Fiction Studies (10035)

SF Weekly
185 Berry, Lobby 4, Ste. 3800
San Francisco, CA 94107
Phone: (415)541-0700
Fax: (415)777-1839

Publications: SF Weekly (3439)

SFR, Inc.
20 Oneil Cir.
Monroe, NY 10950
Phone: (914)774-4449
Fax: (914)774-1317
Free: 888-497-6484

Publications: Smith University Funding Report (21090)

SGM Communications
4026 Woodland Park Ave. N Ste. B
Seattle, WA 98103-7918
Phone: (206)441-3407
Fax: (206)728-1868

Publications: neo (32989)

Shadow Press
PO Box 20298
New York, NY 10009

Publications: The Shadow (22735)

Shafter Press
107 E Lerdo Hwy.
Shafter, CA 93263
Phone: (661)746-4942
Fax: (661)746-5571

Publications: Shafter Press (3757)

Shafter Shopper
PO Box 1600
Shafter, CA 93263
Phone: (661)746-4942
Fax: (661)746-5571

Publications: Shafter Shopper (3758)

Shakour Publishers
445 West St.
PO Box 487
Keene, NH 03431-0487
Phone: (603)352-5250
Fax: (603)357-9351

Publications: The Monadnock Shopper News (18531)

Shalom Foundation, Inc.
13241 Port Republic Rd.
Grottoes, VA 24441
Phone: (540)433-5351
Fax: (540)434-0247
Free: 888-833-3353

Publications: Living (32141) • Together (32142)

Share International
PO Box 971
North Hollywood, CA 91603
Phone: (818)785-6300
Fax: (818)904-9132

Publications: Share International (2644)

Sharpe Newspapers, Inc.
PO Box 100
Littleton, NC 27850-0100
Phone: (919)586-6397

Publications: The Littleton Observer (24048)

Shasta Community College
11555 N Old Oregon Trl.
PO Box 496006
Redding, CA 96049-6006
Phone: (530)225-4723
Fax: (530)225-4668

Publications: The Lance (2887)

Shattered Wig Review
425 E 31st St.
Baltimore, MD 21218-3409
Phone: (410)243-6888

Publications: Shattered Wig Review (13246)

Shaunavon Standard
346 Centre
PO Box 729
Shaunavon, SK, Canada S0N 2M0
Phone: (306)297-4144
Fax: (306)297-3357

Publications: Shaunavon Standard (37569)

Shaw Newspapers
1804 N Division St.
Morris, IL 60450
Phone: (815)942-3221
Fax: (815)942-0988

Publications: Morris Daily Herald (9225)

Shaw Publications
1111 N Green St., No. 200
McHenry, IL 60050
Phone: (815)385-0170
Fax: (815)385-0916

Publications: Northwest Herald (9166)

Shawano Leader
1464 E. Green Bay St.
Shawano, WI 54166
Phone: (715)526-2121
Fax: (715)524-3941
Free: 800-236-2105

Publications: Shawano Leader (34317)

The Shawano Shopper
109 1/2 S Main St.
Shawano, WI 54166
Phone: (715)526-6188
Fax: (715)526-6420

Publications: The Shawano Shopper (34318)

Sheaf
127 W Johnson Ave.
PO Box 45
Warren, MN 56762
Phone: (218)745-5174
Fax: (218)745-5175

Publications: Sheaf (16496)

Sheaf Publishing Society
Rm. 108 Memorial Union Bldg.
93 Campus Dr.
Saskatoon, SK, Canada S7N 5B2
Phone: (306)966-8688
Fax: (306)966-8699

Publications: The Sheaf (37557)

Shearlaw Publishing
PO Box 158
Three Hills, AB, Canada T0M 2A0
Phone: (403)443-5133
Fax: (403)443-7331

Publications: Capital (34861)

The Shearman Group
200 Church St.
PO Box 763
Trinidad, CO 81082-0763
Phone: (719)846-3311
Fax: (719)846-3612

Publications: Chronicle-News (4648)

Sheboygan Falls News
PO Box 317
Plymouth, WI 53073
Phone: (414)467-6591
Fax: (414)893-5505

Publications: Sheboygan Falls News (34250)

The Sheboygan Press
632 Center Ave.
Sheboygan, WI 53081
Phone: (920)457-7711
Fax: (920)457-0178
Free: 800-686-3900

Publications: The Sheboygan Press (34321)

Sheep & Farm Life, Inc.
5696 Johnston Rd.
New Washington, OH 44854
Phone: (419)492-2364
Fax: (419)492-2128

Publications: The Shepherd (24740)

Shelbina Democrat
115 S Center St.
PO Box 138
Shelbina, MO 63468
Phone: (573)588-2133
Fax: (573)588-2134

Publications: Shelbina Democrat (17578)

Shelby County Herald
106 E Main
PO Box 225
Shelbyville, MO 63469-0225
Phone: (573)633-2261
Fax: (573)633-2133

Publications: Shelby County Herald (17579)

Shelby County Newspapers Inc.
PO Box 947
Columbiana, AL 35051
Phone: (205)669-3131
Fax: (205)669-4217

Publications: Shelby County Reporter (159)

Shelby Daily Globe, Inc.
37 W Main St.
PO Box 647
Shelby, OH 44875
Phone: (419)342-4276
Fax: (419)342-4246

Publications: Shelby Daily Globe (25514)

The Shelby Promoter
187 Main
Box 610
Shelby, MT 59474
Phone: (406)434-5171
Fax: (406)434-5955

Publications: The Shelby Promoter (17906)

Shelby Publishing Co., Inc.
517 Green St.
Gainesville, GA 30501
Phone: (770)534-8380
Fax: (770)535-0110

Publications: Shelby Report of the Southeast (7295) • Shelby Report of the Southwest (7296) • Sunbelt Foodservice (7297)

The Shelby Star
315 E Graham St.
PO Box 48
Shelby, NC 28150
Phone: (704)484-7000
Fax: (704)484-0805

Publications: The Shelby Star (24227)

Shelby Sun Times
7508 Captial Dr.
Germantown, TN 38138-0801
Phone: (901)755-7386
Fax: (901)755-0827

Publications: Shelby Sun Times (29206)

Shelbyville Newspapers, Inc.
123 E. Washington St.
PO Box 750
Shelbyville, IN 46176
Phone: (317)398-6631
Fax: (317)398-0194
Free: 800-362-0114

Publications: The Shelbyville News (10452)

Shelbyville Times-Gazette
323 E. Depot St.
PO Box 380
Shelbyville, TN 37162
Phone: (931)684-1200
Fax: (931)684-3228

Publications: Shelbyville Times-Gazette (29600)

Shelbyville Union Bay Inc.
100 W Main St.
PO Box 347
Shelbyville, IL 62565
Phone: (217)774-2161
Fax: (217)774-5732

Publications: Union (9599)

Shellman Publishing, Inc.
107 S Main St.
PO Box 128
Oconto Falls, WI 54154-0128
Phone: (920)848-3427
Fax: (920)848-3430

Publications: The Bonus Paper (34207) • Oconto County Times-Herald (34208)

Shelter Island Reporter
PO Box 2067
Southampton, NY 11969-2067
Phone: (516)749-1000
Fax: (516)749-0144

Publications: Shelter Island Reporter (23345)

Sheltie Pacesetter
69 Beth Pl.
Jackson, TN 38305-8761
Phone: (731)424-9400
Fax: (731)424-9400

Publications: Sheltie Pacesetter (29231)

Shelton-Mason County Journal
3rd & Cota Sts.
PO Box 430
Shelton, WA 98584
Phone: (360)426-4412

Publications: Shelton-Mason County Journal (33079)

Shepherd Argus
PO Box 459
Shepherd, MI 48883
Phone: (989)828-6360
Fax: (989)828-5361

Publications: Shepherd Argus (15538)

The Shepherd College Picket
Shepherd College
Administration Box 68
Shepherdstown, WV 25443
Phone: (304)876-2511
Fax: (304)876-3262

Publications: The Shepherd College Picket (33464)

The Shepherd Media Group
PO Box 226789
Los Angeles, CA 90022-0489
Phone: (562)463-4000
Fax: (562)692-5608

Publications: Earth (2256)

The Sheptytsky Institute
St. Paul University
223 Main St.
Ottawa, ON, Canada K1S 1C4
Phone: (613)236-1393
Fax: (613)782-3026

Publications: Logos (36261)

Sherburne News
17 E State St.
Sherburne, NY 13460
Phone: (607)674-6071
Fax: (607)674-6071

Publications: Sherburne News (23329)

Sheridan Headlights
PO Box 539
Sheridan, AR 72150
Phone: (501)942-2142
Fax: (501)942-8823

Publications: Sheridan Headlight (1343)

Sheridan Newspapers, Inc.
144 Grinnell St.
PO Box 2006
Sheridan, WY 82801
Phone: (307)672-2431
Fax: (307)672-7950
Free: 800-672-2431

Publications: The Sheridan Press (34588)

Sherman County Times
Box 430
Loup City, NE 68853-0430
Phone: (308)745-1260
Fax: (308)745-0541

Publications: Sherman County Times (18150)

Sherman Publications, Inc.
PO Box 108
Oxford, MI 48371
Phone: (248)628-4801
Fax: (248)628-9750

Publications: The Clarkston News (14881) • The Oxford Leader (15432)

Sherwood Park News
168 Kaska Rd.
Sherwood Park, AB, Canada T8A 4G7
Phone: (780)464-0033
Fax: (780)464-8512

Publications: Sherwood Park News (34847)

Sheshunoff Information Services, Inc.
1 Texas Center
505 Barton Springs Rd., Ste. 1100
Austin, TX 78704
Phone: (512)472-2244
Fax: (512)305-6575

Publications: The Bank Quarterly (29762) • The S & L Quarterly (29803)

Shift Multimedia
316 W. 79th St., No. 4E
New York, NY 10024-6127
Phone: (212)633-0233

Publications: Shift (22736)

Shiner Gazette, Inc.
713 N Ave. D.
PO Box 727
Shiner, TX 77984
Phone: (361)594-3346
Fax: (361)594-2655

Publications: The Shiner Gazette (31105)

Shingwah News
795 Gerrard St. E.
Toronto, ON, Canada M4M 1Y5
Phone: (416)778-1854

Publications: Shing Wah News (36740)

The Shinnston News/The Harrison County Journal
223 Pike. St.
PO Box 187
Shinnston, WV 26431
Phone: (304)592-1030
Fax: (304)592-0603

Publications: The Shinnston News/The Harrison County Journal (33466)

Shippensburg University
Office of University Publications
1871 Old Main Dr.
Shippensburg, PA 17257-2299
Phone: (717)477-1201
Fax: (717)477-1253

Publications: The Slate (27990) • Vista (27992)

Shoe Trades Publishing Co.
PO Box 1530
Arlington, MA 02474-0023

Publications: American Shoemaking (13816) • The Leather Manufacturer (13820)

Shoemaker Publications
PO Box 305
Dushore, PA 18614-0305
Phone: (570)928-8403
Fax: (570)928-8006
Free: 800-582-1774

Publications: Sullivan Review (26844)

Shop Right
PO Box T
Ridgway, PA 15853
Phone: (814)776-2121
Fax: (814)776-1086

Publications: Shop-Right 1 (27936) • Shop-Right 1 & 2 (27937)

The Shopper
PO Box 16069
Seattle, WA 98116
Phone: (206)932-0300
Fax: (206)937-1223

Publications: The Shopper (33030)

Shopper-News Network
PO Box 4826
Des Moines, IA 50306
Phone: (515)262-2165
Fax: (515)262-2267

Publications: Northwest Shopper (10807) • Shopper-News Network (10809)

Shopper News Note
318 S Main St.
Lindsay, OK 73052-0008
Phone: (405)756-3169
Fax: (405)756-8609

Publications: Shopper News Note (25900)

Shopper Observer News
210 Woodland Estates Dr.
Ruskin, FL 33570
Phone: (813)645-3111
Fax: (813)645-4118

Publications: The Observer News (6615)

Shopper Press, Inc.
PO Box 400
120 E. Ohio
Fountain, CO 80817
Phone: (719)382-5611
Fax: (719)382-5614

Publications: El Paso County Advertiser & News (4451) • Fountain Valley News (4452)

Shopper's Edge
PO Box 3511
Enid, OK 73702
Phone: (580)233-1722
Fax: (580)233-3764
Free: 800-299-1722

Publications: Shopper's Edge (25823)

Shoppers Guide
PO Box 443
Red Hill, PA 18076
Phone: (215)679-4133
Fax: (215)679-5490

Publications: Upper Perk Shoppers Guide (27927)

Shopper's Guide, Inc.
250 W. 1st St.
Tempe, AZ 85281
Phone: (602)968-5700
Fax: (602)968-8694

Publications: Tucson Shopper (969)

Shopper's Helper
17 Main St.
PO Box 7
Greenwich, OH 44837
Phone: (419)752-3854
Fax: (419)933-2031

Publications: The Shopper's Helper (25230)

Shopper's Market
365 N. Front St.
PO Box 446
Belleville, ON, Canada K8N 5A5
Phone: (613)962-3422
Fax: (613)962-0543

Publications: Shopper's Market (35679)

The Shopper's Weekly
611 W. Cota St.
Shelton, WA 98584
Phone: (360)426-4677
Fax: (360)427-1005
Free: 800-451-7902

Publications: The Shopper's Weekly (33080)

Shopping Guide News
PO Box 229
Rochester, IN 46975
Phone: (219)223-5417
Fax: (219)223-8330

Publications: Shopping Guide News (10432)

Shopping News
2495 Brickyard Rd.
Canandaigua, NY 14424-7679
Phone: (716)394-4510
Fax: (716)394-0399

Publications: Shopping News (20424)

Shore Line Newspapers
PO Box 349
Guilford, CT 06437
Phone: (203)453-2711
Fax: (203)453-4152
Free: 800-922-7065

Publications: Clinton Recorder (4734)

Shore Line Newspapers
Sargent Dr.
New Haven, CT 06511
Phone: (203)453-2711

Publications: Branford Review (4707) • Shore Line Times (5002)

Shore Line Newspapers
PO Box 813
Old Saybrook, CT 06475
Phone: (860)388-3441
Fax: (860)388-5613

Publications: Pictorial-Gazette (5088)

Shore Publishing
724 Boston Post Rd., Ste. 202
PO Box 1010
Madison, CT 06443
Phone: (203)245-1877
Fax: (203)245-9773

Publications: The Sound (4936)

Shoreline Chronicle
PO Box 358
Sheboygan, WI 53082-0358
Phone: (414)459-8820
Fax: (414)459-7449

Publications: Shoreline Chronicle (34322)

Shoreline Community College
16101 Greenwood Ave. N
Seattle, WA 98133
Phone: (206)546-4101
Fax: (206)546-4599

Publications: Observer (32998).

Shoreline Creations, Ltd.
2465 112th Ave.
Holland, MI 49424
Phone: (616)393-2077
Fax: (616)393-0085
Free: 800-767-3489

Publications: Group Tour Magazine Great Lakes Region (15168) • Group Tour Magazine Mid-Atlantic Region (15169) • Group Tour Magazine New England Region (15170) • Group Tour Magazine Southeastern Region (15171) • Group Tour Magazine Western Region (15172)

Short Fuse
PO Box 90436
Santa Barbara, CA 93190

Publications: Short Fuse (3656)

The Short Line
1318 S Johanson Rd.
Peoria, IL 61607-1130
Phone: (309)697-1400
Fax: (309)697-5388

Publications: The Short Line (9424)

Shotgun Sports, Inc.
PO Box 6810
Auburn, CA 95604
Phone: (530)889-2220
Fax: (530)889-9106
Free: 800-676-8920

Publications: Shotgun Sports (1440)

Shots
PO Box 27755
Minneapolis, MN 55427-0775

Publications: Shots (16126)

Show Biz News & Model News
244 Madison Ave., Ste. 393
New York, NY 10016
Phone: (212)969-8715
Fax: (212)969-8715

Publications: Show Biz News & Model News (22738)

Show Me Publishing, Inc.
306 E. 12th St., Ste. 1014
Kansas City, MO 64106

Publications: Ingram's (17172)

ShowBiz Weekly
2290 Corporate Cir. Dr., Ste. 250
Henderson, NV 89074
Phone: (702)383-7185
Fax: (702)383-1089

Publications: ShowBiz Weekly (18354)

Showcase Publishing Inc.
5301 W 75th
Prairie Village, KS 66208
Phone: (913)648-5757
Fax: (913)648-5783

Publications: Kansas City Homes & Gardens (11762)

The Shreveport Sun, Inc.
PO Box 38357
Shreveport, LA 71133
Phone: (318)631-6222
Fax: (318)635-2822

Publications: The Shreveport Sun (12819)

Shuswap Market News
Box 550
Salmon Arm, BC, Canada V1E 4N7
Phone: (604)679-3554
Fax: (604)679-7677

Publications: Shuswap Market News (35082)

S.I. Communications, Inc.
PO Box 418
Scarsdale, NY 10583
Phone: (914)725-2500
Fax: (914)725-1552

Publications: The Scarsdale Inquirer (23313)

Si Magazine Limited Partners
6464 Odin St.
Los Angeles, CA 90068
Phone: (213)975-9313
Fax: (213)957-1114

Publications: Si Magazine (2387)

Sibley Printing and Publishing Co.
201 9th St.
Sibley, IA 51249
Phone: (712)754-3656
Fax: (712)754-2552

Publications: Osceola County Gazette-Tribune (11202)

Sidell Reporter
116 E Market St.
PO Box 475
Sidell, IL 61876
Phone: (217)288-9365

Publications: Sidell Reporter (9601)

The Sidney Argus-Herald
PO Box 190
Sidney, IA 51652
Phone: (712)374-2251

Publications: The Sidney Argus-Herald (11203)

SIECCAN - The Sex Information and Education Council of Canada
850 Coxwell Ave.
Toronto, ON, Canada M4C 5R1
Phone: (416)466-5304
Fax: (416)778-0785

Publications: Canadian Journal of Human Sexuality (36509)

Siena College
515 Loudon Rd.
Loudonville, NY 12211
Phone: (518)783-2300
Fax: (518)783-2493

Publications: The Promethean (20967)

Sierra Booster
PO Box 8
Loyalton, CA 96118
Phone: (916)993-4379
Fax: (916)993-4379

Publications: Sierra Booster (2484)

Sierra Club
85 Second St., 2nd Fl.
San Francisco, CA 94105-3441
Phone: (415)977-5656
Fax: (415)977-5794

Publications: Sierra (3440)

Sierra Vista Herald
102 Fab Ave.
Sierra Vista, AZ 85635
Phone: (520)458-9440
Fax: (520)459-0120

Publications: Bisbee Daily Review (885) • Sierra Vista Herald (889)

Sights and Sounds, Inc.
1410 Northport Dr., Lower Level
PO Box 8052
Madison, WI 53708-8052
Phone: (608)241-2292
Fax: (608)241-4974
Free: 800-554-9630

Publications: Drum Corps World (33934)

Sigma Chi Fraternity
1714 Hinman Ave.
PO Box 469
Evanston, IL 60204-0469
Phone: (847)869-3655
Fax: (847)869-4906

Publications: The Magazine of Sigma Chi (8866)

Sigma Phi Epsilon Fraternity, Inc.
Box 1901
Richmond, VA 23218
Phone: (804)353-1901
Fax: (804)359-8160

Publications: Sigma Phi Epsilon Journal (32454)

Sigma Theta Tau International Honor Society of Nursing
550 W North St.
Indianapolis, IN 46202
Phone: (317)634-8171
Fax: (317)634-8188
Free: 888-634-7575

Publications: Journal of Nursing Scholarship (10140) • Online Journal of Knowledge Synthesis for Nursing (27598)

Sigma Xi, The Scientific Research Society
PO Box 13975
Research Triangle Park, NC 27709-3975
Phone: (919)549-0097
Fax: (919)549-0090
Free: 800-282-0444

Publications: American Scientist (24183)

Sign Builder Illustrated
323 Clifton St., Ste. 7
Greenville, NC 27858-5053
Free: 800-638-0776

Publications: Sign Builder Illustrated (23969)

The Signal
3033 N. G St.
Merced, CA 95340
Phone: (209)358-6431
Fax: (209)357-2968

Publications: The Signal (2528)

Signal
PO Box 250
Manly, IA 50456
Phone: (641)454-2216
Fax: (641)454-2216

Publications: Signal (11048)

Signal
104 Maple St.
Box 157
Springport, MI 49284

Publications: Signal (15574)

Signal American Printers, Inc.
18 E Idaho
PO Box 709
Weiser, ID 83672
Phone: (208)549-1717
Fax: (208)549-1718

Publications: Weiser Signal American (7998)

The Signal-Enterprise
PO Box 158
Alma, KS 66401-0158
Phone: (785)765-3327
Fax: (785)765-3384

Publications: The Signal-Enterprise (11337)

Signal Star Publishing
Box 220
Goderich, ON, Canada N7A 4B6

Publications: Focus Newsmagazine (35850)

Signal Star Publishing
Box 69
Seaforth, ON, Canada N0K 1W0
Phone: (519)527-0240
Fax: (519)527-2858

Publications: Huron Expositor (36388)

Signals
University of Rio Grande
PO Box 995
Rio Grande, OH 45674-9999
Fax: (614)245-7239

Publications: Signals (25497)

The Signature Group
200 N Martingale Rd.
Schaumburg, IL 60173
Phone: (847)605-5522
Fax: (847)605-4595

Publications: VANTAGE (9592)

Signature Publishing Inc.
512 Brickhaven Dr.
Raleigh, NC 27606-1492
Phone: (919)878-6151
Fax: (919)850-0873

Publications: Piedmont Triad Newcomer (24149) • Piedmont Triad Newcomer (24148) • Triangle Newcomer (24157)

Signcraft Publishing Company Inc.
PO Box 60031
Fort Myers, FL 33906
Phone: (239)939-4644
Fax: (239)939-0607
Free: 800-204-0204

Publications: SignCraft (6098)

Signpost
15 Bridge St.
Dorchester, ON, Canada N0L 1G2
Phone: (519)268-7337
Fax: (519)268-3260

Publications: Signpost (35782)

Sigourney News-Review
114 E Washington St.
PO Box 285
Sigourney, IA 52591-0285
Phone: (515)622-3110
Fax: (515)622-2766
Free: 800-550-4237

Publications: Sigourney News-Review (11204)

SIGS Publications & Conferences
1250 Broadyway, 19th Fl.
New York, NY 10001-3701
Phone: (212)242-7447
Fax: (212)242-7545

Publications: Java Report (14198)

SIL International
7500 W. Camp Wisdom Rd.
Dallas, TX 75236-5699
Phone: (972)708-7404
Fax: (972)708-7363

Publications: Journal of Translation and Textlinguistics (30164) • Notes on Linguistics (30171) • Notes on Literacy (30172)

Silhouetee Publications
PO Box 20012
LaSalle, ON, Canada N9J 3E5
Phone: (519)250-0816
Fax: (519)250-0189

Publications: LaSalle Silhouette (35968)

Silk & Satin
1604, Boul. St-Regis
Dorval, QC, Canada H9P 1H6
Free: 888-500-4747

Publications: Silk & Satin (36988)

The Silsbee Bee
Drawer 547
Silsbee, TX 77656
Phone: (409)385-5278
Fax: (409)385-5270

Publications: The Silsbee Bee (31106)

Silver City Daily Press and Independent Publishing Co., Inc.
300 W Market St.
PO Box 740
Silver City, NM 88062
Phone: (505)388-1576
Fax: (505)388-1196

Publications: Silver City Daily Press (19953)

Silver Eagle Publishers
49 Richmondville Ave., No. 112
Westport, CT 06880-2053
Phone: (203)221-4950
Fax: (203)221-4948

Publications: Country Music (5213)

Silver Lake Leader
PO Box 343
Silver Lake, MN 55381
Phone: (612)327-2216
Fax: (612)327-2530

Publications: Silver Lake Leader (16448)

Silver Magazine
PO Box 9690
Rancho Santa Fe, CA 92067-4690
Phone: (858)756-1054
Fax: (858)756-9928
Free: 800-756-1054

Publications: Silver Magazine (2882)

Silver Publishing Co.
PO Box 100
Lake City, CO 81235
Phone: (970)944-2515

Publications: Silver World (4529)

Silver Square Tech, Inc.
12204 Covington Rd.
Fort Wayne, IN 46814
Phone: (260)625-4030
Fax: (260)625-3480

Publications: Hunter & Sport Horse (9970)

Silverton Appeal Tribune
399 S. Water
PO Box 35
Silverton, OR 97381
Phone: (503)873-8385
Fax: (503)873-8064
Free: 800-700-8385

Publications: Appeal Tribune/Mt. Angel News (26584)

The Silverton Standard and The Miner
1139 Greene St.
Silverton, CO 81433-0008
Phone: (970)387-5477
Fax: (970)387-5291

Publications: The Silverton Standard and The Miner (4626)

SIM Canada
10 Huntingdale Blvd.
Scarborough, ON, Canada M1W 2S5
Phone: (416)497-2424
Fax: (416)497-2444

Publications: SIMNOW (36385)

Simcoe and Nanticoke Times
105 Doney Dr., S.
PO Box 370
Simcoe, ON, Canada N3R 4L2
Phone: (519)426-5710
Fax: (519)426-9255

Publications: Simcoe and Nanticoke Times (36390)

The Simcoe Reformer
105 Donly Dr. S.
Simcoe, ON, Canada N3Y 4L2
Phone: (519)426-5710
Fax: (519)426-9255

Publications: The Simcoe Reformer (36391)

Simcoe-York Printing and Publishing Ltd.
PO Box 310
34 Main St. W.
Beeton, ON, Canada L0G 1A0
Phone: (905)729-2287
Fax: (905)729-2541

Publications: The Beeton Record Sentinel (35673) • Innisfil Scope (35922) • The Tottenham Times (36823)

SIMCOM International Holdings, Inc.
6111 Peachtree-Dunwoody Rd., Bldg. E
Atlanta, GA 30328-4577
Phone: (404)730-9980
Fax: (404)730-9976

Publications: The Complete European Trade Digest Electrical Edition (6989) • The Complete European Trade Digest Machinery Edition (6990) • The Complete European Trade Digest Medical Edition (6991) • The Complete European Trade Digest Semiconductor Equipment & Materials Edition (6992)

Simmental Country (1997) Ltd.
4101 19th St. NE, Ste. 13
Calgary, AB, Canada T2E 7C4
Phone: (403)250-5255
Fax: (403)250-5121

Publications: Simmental Country (34657)

Simmons-Boardman Publishing Corp.
345 Hudson St.
New York, NY 10014
Phone: (212)620-7200
Fax: (212)633-1165

Publications: ABA Banking Journal (21130) • International Railway Journal (21933) • Marine Log (22283) • Railway Age (22624) • Railway Track & Structures (8546)

Simmons College
300 The Fenway
Boston, MA 02115
Phone: (617)521-2000
Fax: (617)521-3190

Publications: Simmons Review (13960)

Simon Fraser University
515 W. Hastings St.
Vancouver, BC, Canada V6B 5K3
Phone: (604)291-5240
Fax: (604)291-5239

Publications: Canadian Journal of Communication (34636) • SR (Studies in Religion)/(Sciences Religieuses) (34731)

Simply Seafood, Inc.
1111 NW 45th St., Ste. B
Seattle, WA 98107-4627

Publications: Simply Seafood (33031)

Simpson College
701 N C St.
Indianola, IA 50125-1264
Phone: (515)961-1738
Fax: (515)961-1498

Publications: The Simpsonian (10966)

Simpson County News
120 Ct. Ave.
PO Box 97
Mendenhall, MS 39114
Phone: (601)847-2525
Fax: (601)847-2571

Publications: Simpson County News (16756)

Simpson Publishing Co.
PO Box 338
Magee, MS 39111-0338
Phone: (601)849-3434
Fax: (601)849-6828

Publications: The Magee Courier (16755) • The Simpson Shopper (16757)

Sims Publications, Inc.
17 Chestnut St.
Kingsville, ON, Canada N9Y 1J9
Phone: (519)733-2211
Fax: (519)733-6464

Publications: The Kingsville Reporter (35956)

Sincell Publishing Co., Inc.
PO Box 326
Oakland, MD 21550
Phone: (301)334-3963
Fax: (301)334-5904

Publications: The Republican (13635)

Sinclair Community College
444 W 3rd St.
Dayton, OH 45402-1460
Phone: (937)512-2744
Fax: (937)512-4586

Publications: Clarion (25110)

The Sing Out Corp.
512 E 4th St.
PO Box 5460
Bethlehem, PA 18015-0460
Phone: (610)865-5366
Fax: (610)865-5129
Free: 888-SING-OUT

Publications: Sing Out! (26705)

Sing Tao Newspapers
215 Littlefield Ave.
South San Francisco, CA 94080
Phone: (650)872-1177
Fax: (650)872-0234
Free: 888-SIN-GTAO

Publications: Sing Tao Daily (3791)

Singing News Inc.
330 University Hall Dr.
PO Box 2810
Boone, NC 28607-2810
Phone: (828)264-3700
Fax: (828)264-4621

Publications: The Singing News Magazine (23656)

Singular Publishing Group Inc.
5 Maxwell Dr.
Clifton Park, NY 12065-2919
Free: 800-521-8545

Publications: Infant—Toddler Intervention (20465)

Sinister Wisdom, Inc.
PO Box 3252
Berkeley, CA 94703-0252

Publications: Sinister Wisdom (1559)

Sino-Japanese Studies
History Department
University of California
Santa Barbara, CA 93106
Phone: (805)893-4065
Fax: (805)893-8795

Publications: Sino-Japanese Studies (3657)

The Sioux Center News
PO Box 198
Sioux Center, IA 51250
Phone: (712)722-0741
Fax: (712)722-0744

Publications: The Sioux Center News (11207)

Sioux Center Shopper
67 3rd St. NE
Sioux Center, IA 51250
Phone: (712)722-0511
Fax: (712)722-0507
Free: 800-683-5269

Publications: Sioux Center Shopper (11208)

Sioux Falls Shopping News, Inc.
4005 S. Western Ave.
PO Box 5184
Sioux Falls, SD 57117-5184
Phone: (605)339-3633
Fax: (605)335-6873
Free: 800-843-6805

Publications: Sioux Falls Shopping News (28965) • Sioux Falls Shopping News Informer (28966)

Siouxland Press
PO Box 278
Hospers, IA 51238
Phone: (712)752-8401
Fax: (712)752-8405

Publications: Siouxland Press (10952)

The Sir James Whitney School
350 Dundas St. W.
Belleville, ON, Canada K8T 1B2
Phone: (613)967-2823
Fax: (613)967-2857

Publications: The Canadian (35676)

Siskiyou Daily News
PO Box 129
Yreka, CA 96097-0129
Phone: (530)842-5777
Free: 800-540-5905

Publications: Siskiyou Daily News (4121)

Siskiyou Field Institute
The Siskiyou Project
9335 Takilma Rd.
Cave Junction, OR 97523
Phone: (541)592-4459

Publications: Mountains & Rivers (26265)

Siskiyou Newspaper
924-B Mt. Shasta Blvd.
PO Box 127
Mount Shasta, CA 96067-0127
Fax: (916)926-4166

Publications: Mount Shasta Herald, Weed Press, Dunsmuir News (2605)

Sister Cities International
1301 Pennsylvania Ave, NW, Ste. 850
Washington, DC 20004
Phone: (202)347-8630
Fax: (202)393-6524

Publications: Sister City News (5793)

Sister Miriam Teresa League of Prayer Bulletin
League Headquarters
Box 476
Convent Station, NJ 07961-0476
Phone: (973)290-4084
Fax: (973)290-5335

Publications: Sister Miriam Teresa League of Prayer Bulletin (18769)

Sister 2 Sister Inc.
6930 Carroll Ave.
Takoma Park, MD 20912
Phone: (301)270-5999
Fax: (301)270-0085

Publications: Sister 2 Sister (13752)

Sisters of the Blessed Sacrament
1663 Bristol Pke.
Bensalem, PA 19020-5796
Phone: (215)244-9900
Fax: (215)639-1154

Publications: Mission (26695)

Sisters of Providence
Gamelin St.
Holyoke, MA 01040-4083
Phone: (413)536-7511
Fax: (413)536-7917

Publications: Tracings (14241)

Sisters of St. Dominic
555 Albany Ave.
Amityville, NY 11701
Phone: (631)842-6000
Fax: (631)842-0639

Publications: Our Preaching (20054)

Siwol Media Group
17525 Ventura Blvd., Ste. 312
Encino, CA 91316-5144
Phone: (818)501-2299
Fax: (818)501-8833

Publications: Los Angeles Family Magazine (1884) • South Bay Family Magazine (1885) • Ventura Family Magazine (1886)

S.J. Rundt & Associates, Inc.
130 E 63rd St.
New York, NY 10021
Phone: (973)783-5206
Fax: (973)744-3073

Publications: Rundt's World Business Intelligence (22680)

SJS Publishing Co., Inc.
19 N Main
Perryville, MO 63775
Phone: (573)547-2244
Fax: (573)547-5663

Publications: MidAmerica Farmer Grower (17337)

SK Publications
175 May Ave.
Monrovia, CA 91016
Phone: (626)358-6255

Publications: Skinned Knuckles (2578)

Skagit Valley Publishing Co.
1000 E. College Way
PO Box 578
Mount Vernon, WA 98273-0578
Phone: (360)424-3251
Fax: (360)424-5300

Publications: Skagit Valley Herald (32845) • Skagit Weekly (32846)

The Skagway News
264 Broadway
PO Box 498
Skagway, AK 99840-0498
Phone: (907)983-2354
Fax: (907)983-2356

Publications: The Skagway News (641)

Skanner Group Inc.
415 N. Killingsworth St.
Portland, OR 97217
Phone: (503)285-5555
Fax: (503)285-2900
Free: 800-488-6397

Publications: The Portland Skanner (26502)

Skeptic Magazine
PO Box 338
Altadena, CA 91001
Phone: (626)794-3119
Fax: (626)794-1301

Publications: Skeptic (1393)

Ski Racing
1830 N. 55th St.
Boulder, CO 80301-2700
Phone: (303)440-0601

Publications: Ski Racing (4188)

Skiatook Journal
501 W Rogers Blvd.
Skiatook, OK 74070
Phone: (918)396-1616

Publications: Skiatook Journal (26072)

Skidmore College
815 N Broadway
Saratoga Springs, NY 12866
Phone: (518)580-5186
Fax: (518)580-5188

Publications: Salmagundi (23302) • The Skidmore News (23304)

Skier International Inc.
C.P. 143
Beloeil, QC, Canada J3G 4T1
Phone: (514)464-3121
Fax: (514)464-9210

Publications: Ski Presse (37072)

Skillings Mining Review
11 E Superior St. Ste. 514
Duluth, MN 55802-2007
Phone: (218)722-2310
Fax: (218)722-0134

Publications: Skillings Mining Review (15842)

Sky Publishing Corp.
49 Bay State Rd.
Cambridge, MA 02138
Phone: (617)864-7360
Fax: (617)864-6117
Free: 800-253-0245
Publications: Sky & Telescope (14100)

Skybird Publishing Co., Inc.
PO Box 24170
New Orleans, LA 70184
Phone: (504)488-7003
Fax: (504)488-7083
Publications: Play Meter Magazine (12751)

Skydiving
1725 N Lexington Ave.
DeLand, FL 32724
Phone: (386)736-4793
Fax: (386)736-9786
Publications: Skydiving (6056)

Skyscraper Magazine
PO Box 1595
New York, NY 10276
Publications: Skyscraper (22744)

Skysong Press
RR 1
Washago, ON, Canada L0K 2B0
Publications: Dreams and Visions (36175)

Skyway Publications, Inc.
3225 Lyndale Ave. S.
Minneapolis, MN 55408
Phone: (612)825-9205
Fax: (612)825-0929
Publications: Minnesota Sports (16108) • Skyway News (16127)

Skyword Marketing Inc.
4636 E Elwood St.
Suite 5
Phoenix, AZ 85040-1963
Phone: (602)997-7200
Fax: (602)997-9875
Publications: America West Airlines Magazine (773)

SL, Inc.
PO Box 4356
Los Angeles, CA 90078-4356
Phone: (323)468-1919
Fax: (323)957-9219
Publications: Freshmen (2276) • MEN (2328)

SLACK Inc.
6900 Grove Rd.
Thorofare, NJ 08086-9447
Phone: (856)848-1000
Fax: (856)853-5991
Publications: AAOHN Journal (19615) • Hem/Onc Today (19616) • Infection Control and Hospital Epidemiology (19617) • Infectious Disease News (19618) • Infectious Diseases in Children (19619) • The Journal of Continuing Education in Nursing (19620) • Journal of Gerontological Nursing (19621) • The Journal of Knee Surgery (19622) • Journal of Nursing Education (19623) • Journal of Pediatric Ophthalmology & Strabismus (19624) • Journal of Psychosocial Nursing and Mental Health Services (19625) • Journal of Refractive Surgery (19626) • Journal of Spirochetal and Tick-borne Diseases (19627) • O&P Business News (19628) • O&P World (19629) • Occupational Therapy Journal of Research (19630) • Ocular Surgery News (19631) • Ocular Surgery News Europe/Asia-Pacific Edition (19632) • Ocular Surgery News Latin America Edition (19633) • Ophthalmic Surgery Lasers and Imaging (19634) • Orthopaedics Today International (19635) • Orthopedics (19636) • Orthopedics Today (19637) • Pediatric Annals (19638) • Primary Care Optometry News (19639) • Psychiatric Annals (19640) • Today in Cardiology (19641)

Slant 6 Club of America
PO Box 4414
Salem, OR 97302
Phone: (503)581-2230
Publications: Slant 6 News (26572)

Slater Main Street News
222 N. Main St.
Slater, MO 65349
Phone: (660)529-2249
Fax: (660)529-2474
Publications: Slater Main Street News (17590)

Slaton Newspapers, Inc.
PO Box 517
Moulton, AL 35650
Phone: (205)974-1114
Fax: (205)974-3097
Publications: The Moulton Advertiser (396)

Slaton Publishing Co.
139 S 9th St.
Box 667
Slaton, TX 79364
Phone: (806)828-6201
Fax: (806)828-6202
Publications: The Slatonite (31112)

Slechta Communications, Inc.
PO Box 96
West Liberty, IA 52776-0096
Phone: (319)627-2814
Fax: (319)627-2110
Free: 800-817-8729
Publications: West Liberty Index (11323)

Sleepy Eye Herald-Dispatch
115 2nd Ave. NE
Sleepy Eye, MN 56085
Phone: (507)794-3511
Fax: (507)794-5031
Publications: Sleepy Eye Herald-Dispatch (16451)

Sliger/Livingston Publications, Inc.
323 E. Grand River
Howell, MI 48843
Phone: (517)548-2000
Fax: (517)548-3005
Publications: Highland Shopping Guide (15159)

Slippery Rock University
220 Eisenberg Classroom Bldg.
Slippery Rock, PA 16057
Phone: (724)738-2643
Fax: (724)738-4896
Publications: The Rocket (27997)

Slipstream
PO Box 2071, New Market Sta.
Niagara Falls, NY 14301
Phone: (716)282-2616
Publications: Slipstream (23007)

Sloan Management Review
77 Massachusetts Ave., Ste. E60-100
Cambridge, MA 02139-4307
Phone: (617)253-7170
Publications: MIT Sloan Management Review (14082)

Slovak Catholic Sokol
205 Madison St.
PO Box 899
Passaic, NJ 07055
Phone: (973)777-2605
Fax: (973)779-8245
Publications: Slovak Catholic Falcon (19416)

Slovene National Benefit Society
247 W Allegheny Rd.
Imperial, PA 15126-9774
Phone: (724)695-1100
Fax: (724)695-1555
Free: 800-843-7675
Publications: Prosveta (8542) • Voice of Youth (27070)

Slovenian Women's Union of America/ Slovenska Zenska Zveza Ameriki
431 N Chicago St.
Joliet, IL 60432
Phone: (773)268-4899
Fax: (312)268-7744
Publications: Dawn (8349)

Smackover Journal
PO Box 147
Smackover, AR 71762
Phone: (870)725-3131
Fax: (870)725-3131
Publications: Smackover Journal (1346)

Small Business Association of Michigan
222 N. Washington Sq., Ste. 100
PO Box 16158
Lansing, MI 48933
Phone: (517)482-8788
Fax: (517)482-4205
Free: 800-362-5461
Publications: Journal of Small Business (15276)

Small Business News, Inc.
14725 Detroit Ave. No. 300
Cleveland, OH 44107
Phone: (216)228-6397
Fax: (216)529-8924
Free: 800-988-4726
Publications: Cleveland Small Business News (24874)

Small Business Times
1123 N. Water St.
Milwaukee, WI 53202
Phone: (414)277-8181
Fax: (414)277-8191
Publications: Small Business Times (34102)

Small Farmer's Journal
PO Box 1627
Sisters, OR 97759
Phone: (541)549-2064
Fax: (541)549-4403
Free: 800-876-2893
Publications: Small Farmer's Journal (26585)

A Small Garlic Press
5445 Sheridan Rd., No. 3003
Chicago, IL 60640-7477
Phone: (773)784-3844
Publications: Agnieszka's Dowry (8248)

Small Newspaper Group
8 Dearborn Sq.
Kankakee, IL 60901
Phone: (815)937-3300
Fax: (815)937-3301
Free: 800-892-1861
Publications: The Daily Journal (9039)

The Small Press Book Review
PO Box 176
Southport, CT 06490
Phone: (203)332-7629
Fax: (203)332-7629
Publications: The Small Press Book Review (5138)

Small Publisher
PO Box 1620
Pineville, WV 24874
Phone: (304)732-8195
Fax: (304)732-8195
Publications: Small Publisher (33437)

The Smallholder Publishing Collective
Argenta, BC, Canada V0G 1B0
Phone: (250)366-4283
Publications: The Smallholder (34881)

Smart Business Publishing Inc.
20140 Valley Forge Cir.
King of Prussia, PA 19406
Phone: (610)783-5060
Fax: (610)783-1662
Publications: Smart Business Now Magazine (27127)

SmartMoney
1755 Broadway, 2nd Fl.
New York, NY 10019
Phone: (212)830-9200
Fax: (212)830-9292
Free: 800-444-4204
Publications: offspring (22486) • SmartMoney (22748)

Smith College
Capen Annex
Northampton, MA 01063
Phone: (413)585-2700
Fax: (413)585-2075

Publications: The Sophian (14431)

Smith County News
PO Box 72
Tyler, TX 75710
Phone: (903)597-6533
Fax: (903)597-4997

Publications: Smith County News (31198)

Smith County Pioneer
PO Box 266
Smith Center, KS 66967
Phone: (785)282-3371
Fax: (785)282-6383

Publications: Smith County Pioneer (11806)

Smith County Reformer
PO Box 187
Raleigh, MS 39153
Phone: (601)782-4358
Fax: (601)782-9020

Publications: Smith County Reformer (16832)

Smith Haj Group Inc.
12 E. 33 St., 6th Fl.
New York, NY 10016
Phone: (212)213-8585
Fax: (212)213-6291

Publications: The New York Beacon (22437)

Smith-Kettlewell Eye Research Institute
2318 Fillmore St.
San Francisco, CA 94115
Phone: (415)345-2124
Fax: (415)345-8455

Publications: Smith-Kettlewell Technical File (3442)

Smith News Inc.
113 Washington St.
Walterboro, SC 29488-1248
Phone: (803)549-2586
Fax: (803)549-2446

Publications: Colleton Shopper (28780)

Smith Newspapers
34 W Bockman Way
PO Box 179
Sparta, TN 38583
Phone: (615)836-3284

Publications: Expositor (29612)

Smith Publications
105 Raider Blvd.
Belle Mead, NJ 08502
Phone: (908)874-8550
Fax: (908)874-0700

Publications: Physician Assistant (18669)

The Smithfield Herald
PO Box 1417
Smithfield, NC 27577-1417
Phone: (919)934-2176
Fax: (919)989-7093

Publications: The Smithfield Herald (24232)

Smithsonian Magazine
750 9th St. NW, Ste. 7100
Washington, DC 20560
Phone: (202)786-2900

Publications: Smithsonian Magazine (5794)

The Smithtown News, Inc.
1 Brooksite Dr.
Smithtown, NY 11787-3454
Phone: (631)265-2100
Fax: (631)265-6237

Publications: Commack News (20487) • Islip News (20786) • Observer (23339) • The Smithtown News (23341)

The Smithville Lake Herald
110 N Bridge
PO Box 269
Smithville, MO 64089-0269
Phone: (816)532-4217
Fax: (816)532-4918

Publications: The Smithville Lake Herald (17591)

Smithville Review
106 S 1st Ave.
PO Box 247
Smithville, TN 37166
Phone: (615)597-5485
Fax: (615)597-5489

Publications: Smithville Review (29604)

Smoke Bend Publishing
828 Lesseps St.
New Orleans, LA 70117
Phone: (504)947-6001

Publications: New Laurel Review (12743)

Smoke-Eater Publications
109 E Main St.
Pierce, NE 68767-0129
Phone: (402)329-4665
Fax: (402)329-6337

Publications: Iowa Smoke-Eater (10796) • Minnesota Smoke-Eater (16395) • Nebraska Smoke-Eater (18247)

Smoky Lake
4924-50th St.
PO Box 328
Smoky Lake, AB, Canada T0A 3C0
Fax: (403)656-4361

Publications: Smoky Lake Signal (34851)

Smoky Mountain Historical Society
Box 5078
Sevierville, TN 37864

Publications: Smoky Mountain Historical Society Journal (29590)

SMS Students Publishing Association
St. Michael's College
PO Box 275
Colchester, VT 05439
Phone: (802)654-2442

Publications: The Defender (31530)

Snake Nation Press
574 N. Patterson St.,
Valdosta, GA 31601

Publications: Snake Nation Review (7614)

Snell Publications, Inc.
15 S Rountree
Metter, GA 30439
Phone: (912)685-6566
Fax: (912)685-4901

Publications: The Metter Advertiser (7431)

SNEWS
12119 Lupine Ln.
Klamath Falls, OR 97603-9637
Phone: (541)882-5196
Free: 800-474-5196

Publications: SNEWS (26387)

Snips Magazine
755 W. Big Beaver., Ste.1000
Troy, MI 48084-4903
Phone: (248)362-3700
Fax: (248)362-0317

Publications: Snips Magazine (15640)

Snohomish County Seniors
127 Ave. C
PO Box 499
Snohomish, WA 98291-0499
Phone: (360)568-4121
Fax: (360)568-1484

Publications: Snohomish County Seniors (33088)

Snoqualmie Valley Record
PO Box 300
Snoqualmie, WA 98065
Phone: (425)888-2311
Fax: (425)888-2427

Publications: Snoqualmie Valley Record (33090)

Snowscope
112 S Park St.
PO Box A
Boyne City, MI 49712
Phone: (616)582-6761

Publications: Snowscope (14835)

Snyder Communications Corp.
18-20 Mechanic St.
PO Box 111
Norwich, NY 13815-2038
Phone: (607)334-4714
Fax: (607)336-7318

Publications: The Evening Sun (23020) • Hall of Fame Pennysaver (20498) • Turnpike Pennysaver (23187)

Snyder County Times & Union County Times
405 E Main St.
PO Box 356
Middleburg, PA 17842-0356
Phone: (570)837-6065
Fax: (570)837-0776

Publications: Snyder County Times (27249) • Union County Times (27250)

So to Speak
George Mason Univ.
4400 University Dr., MS 2D6
Fairfax, VA 22030-4444
Phone: (703)993-3625

Publications: So to Speak (32031)

Soaring Society of America Inc.
PO Box 2100
Hobbs, NM 88241
Phone: (505)392-1177
Fax: (505)392-8154

Publications: Soaring (19865)

Sober Times
PO Box 13013
Mill Creek, WA 98082-1013

Publications: Sober Times (32832)

Sobran's
PO Box 1383
Vienna, VA 22183-1383

Publications: Sobran's (32582)

Social Anarchism
2743 Maryland Ave.
Baltimore, MD 21218
Phone: (410)243-6987

Publications: Social Anarchism (13248)

Social Register Association
381 Park Ave. S.
New York, NY 10016
Phone: (212)685-2634
Fax: (212)679-1449

Publications: Social Register Observer (22755)

Socialist Labor Party of America
PO Box 218
Mountain View, CA 94042-0218
Phone: (408)280-7266
Fax: (408)280-6964

Publications: The People (2608)

Societe Americaine de Philosophie de Langue Francaise
C/O Northern Illinois University
635 Joanne Ln.
DeKalb, IL 60115
Phone: (815)756-4639
Fax: (815)753-6302

Publications: Bulletin de la Societe Americaine de Philosophie de Langue Francaise (8732)

Societe Historique du Saguenay
930 rue Jacques-Cartier Est
Chicoutimi, QC, Canada G7H 7K9
Phone: (418)549-2805
Fax: (418)549-3701

Publications: Saguenayensia (36968)

Societe Historique de Stanstead-Stanstead Historical Society
535 Dufferin Rd.
Stanstead, QC, Canada J0B 3E0
Phone: (819)876-7322
Fax: (819)876-7936

Publications: Stanstead Historical Society Journal (37407)

Societe des Missions-Etrangeres
160 Place Juge Desnoyers
Laval, QC, Canada H7G 1A5
Phone: (450)667-4190
Fax: (450)667-3006

Publications: Missions Etrangeres (37042)

Society for Accessible Travel and Hospitality
347 5th Ave., No. 610
New York, NY 10016-5010
Phone: (212)447-7284
Fax: (212)725-8253

Publications: Open World for Disability and Mature Travel (22496)

Society of Actuaries
475 N. Martingale Rd., Ste. 800
Schaumburg, IL 60173-2226
Phone: (847)706-3500
Fax: (847)706-3599

Publications: North American Actuarial Journal (9589)

Society for Advancement of Management
Texas A&M University - Corpus Christi
College of Business
6300 Ocean Dr., FC 111
Corpus Christi, TX 78412
Phone: (361)825-6045
Fax: (361)825-2725
Free: 888-827-6077

Publications: SAM Advanced Management Journal (30078)

Society for the Advancement of Material & Process Engineering
1161 Parkview Dr.
Covina, CA 91724-3748
Phone: (626)331-0616
Fax: (626)332-8929
Free: 800-562-7360

Publications: SAMPE Journal (1786)

Society for the Advancement of Scandinavian Study
Brigham Young University
3003 JKHB
Provo, UT 84602-6118
Phone: (801)422-5598
Fax: (801)422-0307

Publications: Scandinavian Studies (31408)

Society of Allied Weight Engineers, Inc.
204 Hubbard St.
Glastonbury, CT 06033-3063
Phone: (860)633-0850
Fax: (860)633-8971

Publications: Weight Engineering (8779)

Society of the Alumni
PO Box 2100
Williamsburg, VA 23187-2100
Phone: (804)221-1167
Fax: (804)221-1186

Publications: Alumni Gazette (32613)

Society for American Archaeology
900 2nd St. NE, No. 12
Washington, DC 20002-3557
Phone: (202)789-8200
Fax: (202)789-0284

Publications: American Antiquity (5324) • Latin American Antiquity (5630) • The SAA Archaeological Record (5774)

Society of American Archivists
527 S Wells St., 5th Fl.
Chicago, IL 60607-3922
Phone: (312)922-0140
Fax: (312)347-1452

Publications: The American Archivist (8252)

Society for American Baseball Research
812 Huron Rd. E, No. 719
Cleveland, OH 44115
Phone: (216)575-0500
Fax: (216)575-0502
Free: 800-969-7227

Publications: Baseball Research Journal (24862)

Society of American Florists
1601 Duke St.
Alexandria, VA 22314-3406
Phone: (703)836-8700
Fax: (703)836-8705
Free: 800-336-4743

Publications: Floral Management (31674)

Society of American Foresters
5400 Grosvenor Ln.
Bethesda, MD 20814-2198
Phone: (301)897-8720
Fax: (301)897-3690

Publications: Forest Science (13337) • Journal of Forestry (13351) • Northern Journal of Applied Forestry (13367) • Southern Journal of Applied Forestry (13381) • Western Journal of Applied Forestry (13388)

The Society of American Military Engineers (SAME)
607 Prince St.
Alexandria, VA 22314-3117
Phone: (703)549-3800
Fax: (703)684-0231

Publications: The Military Engineer (31709)

Society for Applied Anthropology
PO Box 2436
Oklahoma City, OK 73101-2436
Phone: (405)843-5113
Fax: (405)843-8553

Publications: Human Organization (25966)

Society of Architectural Historians
1365 N. Astor St.
Chicago, IL 60610-2144
Phone: (312)573-1365
Fax: (312)573-1141

Publications: Journal of the Society of Architectural Historians (JSAH) (8450)

Society of Automotive Engineers - Detroit Section
28535 Orchard Lake Rd., Ste.200
Farmington Hills, MI 48334
Phone: (248)324-4445
Fax: (248)324-4449

Publications: Supercharger (15020)

Society of Automotive Engineers Inc.
400 Commonwealth Dr.
Warrendale, PA 15096-0001
Phone: (724)776-4841
Fax: (724)776-4026

Publications: Aerospace Engineering (28110)

Society of Bead Researchers
1600 Liverpool Court
Ottawa, ON, Canada K1A 0M5
Phone: (613)990-4814
Fax: (613)952-1756

Publications: Beads (36186)

Society of Behavioral Medicine
7611 Elmwood Ave., Ste. 201
Middleton, WI 53562
Phone: (608)827-7267
Fax: (608)831-5122

Publications: Annals of Behavioral Medicine (2112)

Society of Biblical Literature
825 Houston Mill Rd., Ste. 350
Atlanta, GA 30329
Phone: (404)727-3100
Fax: (404)727-3101

Publications: Journal of Biblical Literature (7020)

Society of Christian Philosophers
Department of Philosophy
Asbury College
Wilmore, KY 40390-1198
Phone: (606)858-3511
Fax: (606)858-3921

Publications: Faith and Philosophy (12451)

Society for Computer Simulation
4838 Ronson Ct., Ste. L
San Diego, CA 92111
Phone: (858)277-3888
Fax: (858)277-3930

Publications: Simulation (3275) • Transactions of the Society for Computer Simulation International (3283)

Society of Cost Estimating and Analysis
101 S Whiting St., Ste. 201
Alexandria, VA 22304
Phone: (703)751-8069
Fax: (703)461-7328

Publications: Journal of Cost Analysis and Management (31691)

Society for the Experimental Analysis of Behavior
JEAB Psychology Dept.
Indiana Univ.
Bloomington, IN 47405-1301
Phone: (812)339-4718
Fax: (812)855-4691

Publications: Journal of the Experimental Analysis of Behavior (33394)

Society for Experimental Mechanics
7 School St.
Bethel, CT 06801
Phone: (203)790-6373
Fax: (203)790-4472

Publications: Experimental Mechanics (4697) • Experimental Techniques (4698)

Society of Exploration Geophysicists
8801 S. Yale
Tulsa, OK 74137
Phone: (918)497-5500
Fax: (918)497-5557

Publications: Geophysics (26116) • The Leading Edge (26120)

Society of Financial Service Professionals
270 S. Bryn Mawr Ave.
Bryn Mawr, PA 19010-2195
Phone: (215)526-2500
Fax: (610)527-1499
Free: 800-392-6900

Publications: Journal of Financial Service Professionals (26741)

Society of Folk Dance Historians
2100 Rio Grande St.
Austin, TX 78705-5578
Phone: (512)478-9676

Publications: Folk Dance Problem Solver (29776)

Society for Historians of the Early American Republic
1358 University Hall
Department of History
Purdue University
West Lafayette, IN 47907-1358
Phone: (765)494-4135
Fax: (765)496-1755

Publications: Journal of the Early Republic (10549)

Society for the History of Technology
216B Ames Hall
John Hopkins University
3400 N. Charles St.
Baltimore, MD 21218
Phone: (410)516-8349
Fax: (410)516-7502

Publications: Technology and Culture (14906)

The Society for Human Performance in Extreme Environments (HPEE)
2652 Corbyton Court
Orlando, FL 32828
Phone: (407)381-7762
Fax: (407)381-7762

Publications: The Journal of Human Performance in Extreme Environments (6499)

Society for Human Resource Management
1800 Duke St.
Alexandria, VA 22314
Phone: (703)548-3440
Fax: (703)535-6490

Publications: HR News (31680) • HRMagazine (31681)

The Society for Imaging Science and Technology
7003 Kilworth Ln.
Springfield, VA 22151-4008
Phone: (703)642-9090
Fax: (703)642-9094

Publications: Journal of Imaging Science and Technology (32546)

Society for In Vitro Biology
9315 Largo Dr. W, Ste. 255
Largo, MD 20774
Phone: (301)324-5054
Fax: (301)324-5057
Free: 800-741-7476

Publications: InVitro Cellular & Developmental Biology - PLANT (13612)

Society for Industrial & Applied Mathematics
3600 University City Science Center
Philadelphia, PA 19104-2688
Phone: (215)382-9800
Fax: (215)386-7999

Publications: SIAM Journal on Applied Mathematics (27678) • SIAM Journal on Computing (27679) • SIAM Journal on Control and Optimization (27680) • SIAM Journal on Discrete Mathematics (27681) • SIAM Journal on Mathematical Analysis (27682) • SIAM Journal on Matrix Analysis and Applications (27683) • SIAM Journal on Numerical Analysis (27684) • SIAM Journal on Optimization (27685) • SIAM Journal on Scientific Computing (27686) • SIAM News (27687) • SIAM Review (27688) • Theory of Probability and Its Applications (27704)

Society of Industrial and Office Realtors
700 11th St. NW, Ste. 510
Washington, DC 20001-4507
Phone: (202)737-1150
Fax: (202)737-8796
Free: 888-891-7467

Publications: Professional Report (5733)

Society of Manufacturing Engineers
1 SME Dr.
PO Box 930
Dearborn, MI 48121-0930
Phone: (313)271-1500
Fax: (313)425-3417
Free: 800-733-4SME

Publications: Forming & Fabricating (14902) • Journal of Manufacturing Systems (14903)

Society for Military History
George C. Marshall Library
Virginia Military Institute
Lexington, VA 24450
Phone: (540)464-7468
Fax: (540)464-7330

Publications: The Journal of Military History (32189)

Society for Mining, Metallurgy, and Exploration Inc.
8307 Shaffer Pkwy.
Littleton, CO 80127
Phone: (303)973-9550
Fax: (303)948-4265
Free: 800-763-3132

Publications: Minerals and Metallurgical Processing (4552) • Mining Engineering (4553)

Society of Motion Picture and Television Engineers
595 W. Hartsdale Ave.
White Plains, NY 10607
Phone: (914)761-1100
Fax: (914)761-3115

Publications: SMPTE Journal (23573)

Society of Municipal Arborists
PO Box 641
Watkinsville, GA 30677
Phone: (706)769-7412
Fax: (706)769-7307

Publications: City Trees (14461)

Society for Music Theory
Journals Division
University of California Press
2120 Berkeley Way
Berkeley, CA 94720-5812
Phone: (510)642-5536

Publications: Music Theory Spectrum (23233)

Society of Nematologists
5988 Highway 99, Ste. 4900
Milton, FL 32583

Publications: Journal of Nematology (29277)

The Society of North American Goldsmiths
5009 Londonderry Dr.
Tampa, FL 33647
Phone: (813)977-5326
Fax: (813)977-8462

Publications: Metalsmith (34080)

Society of Nuclear Medicine Inc.
1850 Samuel Morse Dr.
Reston, VA 20190-5316
Phone: (703)708-9000
Fax: (703)708-9018

Publications: Journal of Nuclear Medicine Technology (32388)

Society for Pacific Coast Native Iris
C/O Terri Hudson, Sec.-Treasurer
33450 Little Valley Rd.
Fort Bragg, CA 95437
Phone: (707)964-3907
Fax: (707)964-3907

Publications: Almanac (2665)

Society of Paper Money Collectors
Box 793941
Dallas, TX 75379-3941

Publications: Paper Money (30175)

Society of Plastics Engineers
14 Fairfield Dr.
PO Box 0403
Brookfield, CT 06804-0403
Phone: (203)775-0471
Fax: (203)775-8490

Publications: Journal of Vinyl and Additive Technology (4726) • Plastics Engineering (4727) • Polymer Engineering and Science (4728)

Society of Police and Criminal Psychology
Hines Academy Ctr., Rm. 120
Southwest Texas State University
San Marcos, TX 78666
Phone: (512)245-2174
Fax: (512)245-8063

Publications: Journal of Police and Criminal Psychology (31084)

Society for Popular Democracy
10920 Wilshire Blvd., Ste. 150
Los Angeles, CA 90024
Phone: (310)908-9898

Publications: Amass (2206)

Society of Professional Journalists
3909 N Meridian
Indianapolis, IN 46208
Phone: (317)920-4789
Fax: (317)927-8000

Publications: Quill (10165)

Society for the Propagation of the Faith
366 5th Ave., 12th Fl.
New York, NY 10001
Phone: (212)563-8700
Fax: (212)563-8725
Free: 800-431-2222

Publications: Mission Magazine (22338)

Society for the Protection of New Hampshire Forests
54 Portsmouth St.
Concord, NH 03301-5400
Phone: (603)224-9945
Fax: (603)228-0423

Publications: Forest Notes (18472)

Society for Range Management
440 Union Blvd., Ste. 230
Lakewood, CO 80228-1259
Phone: (303)986-3309
Fax: (303)986-3892

Publications: Journal of Range Management (4533)

Society of Research Administrators
1901 N. Moore St., Ste. 1004
Arlington, VA 22209
Phone: (703)741-0140
Fax: (703)741-0142

Publications: Journal of Research Administration (31805)

Society of St. Columban
St. Columbans, NE 68056
Phone: (402)291-1920
Fax: (402)291-4984

Publications: Columban Mission (18256)

Society of St. Paul
Box 595
Canfield, OH 44406-0595
Phone: (330)533-5503
Fax: (330)533-1076

Publications: Pastoral Life (24730)

Society for the Scientific Study of Sexuality
Box 416
Allentown, PA 18105
Phone: (610)530-2483
Fax: (610)530-2485

Publications: The Journal of Sex Research (33955)

Society for the Study of Amphibians and Reptiles
PO Box 253
Marceline, MO 64658-0253
Phone: (314)977-3916
Fax: (314)977-3658

Publications: Journal of Herpetology (12591)

Society for the Study of Myth & Tradition
656 Broadway
New York, NY 10012
Phone: (212)505-6200
Fax: (212)979-7325
Free: 800-560-MYTH

Publications: Parabola (22521)

Society for the Study of Reproduction
1619 Monroe St.
Madison, WI 53711-2063
Phone: (608)256-2777
Fax: (608)256-4610

Publications: Biology of Reproduction (33924)

Society for Technical Communication
901 N Stuart St., Ste. 904
Arlington, VA 22203-1854
Phone: (703)522-4114
Fax: (703)522-2075

Publications: Intercom (31798)

Society of Toxicologic Pathologists
c/o Dr. Gordon C. Hard
American Health Foundation
1 Dana Rd.
Valhalla, NY 10595
Phone: (914)592-2600
Fax: (914)592-6317

Publications: Toxicology Pathology (23484)

Society of Tribologists and Lubrication Engineers
840 Busse Hwy.
Park Ridge, IL 60068-2376
Phone: (847)825-5536
Fax: (847)825-1456

Publications: Lubrication Engineering (9406)

Society for Utopian Studies
c/o Ken Roemer
University of Texas at Arlington
English Dept. - Box 19035
Arlington, TX 76013-1908

Publications: Utopian Studies (29739)

Society of Wetland Scientists
1313, Dolley Madison Blvd.Ste.402
McLean, VA 22101
Phone: (703)790-1745
Fax: (703)790-2672
Free: 800-627-0629

Publications: Wetlands (14772)

Society of Women Engineers
230 E. Ohio St., No. 400
2135 Lamberton Rd.
Chicago, IL 60611-3265
Phone: (312)596-5223
Fax: (312)596-5252

Publications: SWE (8579)

Society of Wood Science and Technology
1 Gifford Pinchot Dr.
Madison, WI 53726-2398
Phone: (608)231-9347
Fax: (608)231-9592

Publications: Wood & Fiber Science (31880)

Soil Science Society of America
677 S Segoe Rd.
Madison, WI 53711-1086
Phone: (608)273-8080
Fax: (608)273-2021

Publications: Soil Science Society of America Journal (33973)

Soil and Water Conservation Society
7515 NE Ankeny Rd.
Ankeny, IA 50021
Phone: (515)289-2331
Fax: (515)289-1227
Free: 800-843-7645

Publications: Conservation Voices (10605) • Journal of Soil and Water Conservation (10606)

Sojourner Feminist Institute, Inc.
42 Seaverns Ave.
Jamaica Plain, MA 02130-2865
Phone: (617)524-0415
Fax: (617)524-9397

Publications: Sojourner (14262)

Sojourners
2401 15th St. NW
Washington, DC 20009
Phone: (202)328-8842
Fax: (202)328-8757
Free: 800-714-7474

Publications: Sojourners (5799)

Sokol U.S.A.
276 Prospect St.
POBOX 189
East Orange, NJ 07019
Phone: (201)676-0280
Fax: (201)676-3348

Publications: Sokol Times (18783)

Sol de Hialeah Publishing Co.
436 Palm Ave.
Hialeah, FL 33010
Phone: (305)887-8324
Fax: (305)887-8324

Publications: El Sol de Hialeah (6187)

Soledad Bee
635 Front St.
PO Box 95
Soledad, CA 93960
Phone: (831)678-2660
Fax: (831)385-4799

Publications: Soledad Bee (3770)

Solon Economist
Box 249
Solon, IA 52333
Phone: (319)624-2233
Fax: (319)644-1356

Publications: Solon Economist (11229)

Solstice Publishing Inc.
47 Soho Sq.
Toronto, ON, Canada M5T 2Z2
Phone: (416)595-1252
Fax: (416)595-7255
Free: 800-263-5295

Publications: Ski Canada (36741)

Somerset Community College
808 Monticello St.
Somerset, KY 42501-2999
Fax: (606)679-5139

Publications: The Mirror (12405)

Somerset Pulaski News Journal
PO Box 1565
Somerset, KY 42502
Phone: (606)678-0161
Fax: (606)678-9032

Publications: Somerset Pulaski News Journal (12406)

Somerset Spectator
PO Box 41
Kingston, NJ 08528-0041
Phone: (908)359-2828
Fax: (908)359-1765

Publications: Somerset Spectator (19566)

The Somerville News
7 Davis Sq.
Somerville, MA 02144-2917
Phone: (617)666-4010
Fax: (617)666-2974

Publications: The Somerville News (14538)

The Sondheim Review
PO Box 11213
Chicago, IL 60611-0213
Phone: (773)275-4254
Fax: (773)275-4254
Free: 800-584-1020

Publications: The Sondheim Review (8565)

Sondreal Enterprises
215 S Keller Ave.
Amery, WI 54001
Phone: (715)268-8101
Fax: (715)268-5300
Free: 800-784-6993

Publications: Amery Free Press (33527)

Song Sao Cho Manh Inc.
PO Box 21245
San Jose, CA 95151-1245
Phone: (408)605-0605
Fax: (408)729-5595

Publications: Song Manh Magazine (3538)

Sonoma County Medical Association
3033 Cleveland Ave.
Santa Rosa, CA 95403
Phone: (707)525-4325
Fax: (707)525-4289

Publications: Sonoma Medicine (3735)

The Sonoma Index-Tribune
PO Box C
Sonoma, CA 95476
Phone: (707)938-2111
Fax: (707)938-1600

Publications: Shopping News/Penny Pincher (3776) • Sonoma Valley News (3778)

The Sonoma Index-Tribune Inc.
PO Box C
Sonoma, CA 95476
Phone: (707)938-2111
Fax: (707)938-1600

Publications: Headliner (3774) • Rohnert Park Community Voice (3775) • The Sonoma Index-Tribune (3777)

Sonoma Valley Publishing
PO Box C
Sonoma, CA 95476
Phone: (707)938-0637
Fax: (707)938-1600

Publications: Valley of the Moon Visitor's News (3779)

Sonoma West Publishers, Inc.
PO Box 521
Sebastopol, CA 95473-0521
Free: 800-465-0780

Publications: Sonoma West Exchange (3753) • Sonoma West Times & News (3754)

Sonora Landing Enterprises Inc.
PO Box 415
Nauvoo, IL 62354
Phone: (217)453-6771
Fax: (217)452-6771

Publications: The New Independent (9279)

Sonoran News
6812 E Cave Creek Rd.
Cave Creek, AZ 85331
Phone: (480)488-2021
Fax: (480)488-6216

Publications: Sonoran News (672)

Sons of Norway
1455 W. Lake St.
Minneapolis, MN 55408
Phone: (612)827-3611
Fax: (612)827-0658

Publications: The Sons of Norway Viking (16128)

Sooke Mirror
6595 Sooke Rd.
PO Box 339
Sooke, BC, Canada V0S 1N0
Phone: (604)642-5752
Fax: (604)642-4767

Publications: Sooke Mirror (35093)

The Sooner Catholic
7501 NW Expwy.
PO Box 32180
Oklahoma City, OK 73123
Phone: (405)721-1810
Fax: (405)721-5210

Publications: The Sooner Catholic (25996)

Soperton News Building
PO Box 527
2nd Main St.
Soperton, GA 30457
Phone: (912)529-6624
Fax: (912)529-5399

Publications: The Montgomery Monitor (7558) • The Soperton News (7559)

Soroptimist International of the Americas
2 Penn Ctr., Ste. 1000
Philadelphia, PA 19102
Phone: (215)557-9300
Fax: (215)568-5200

Publications: The Soroptimist of the Americas Magazine (27690)

Sosland Publishing Co.
4800 Main St., Ste. 100
Kansas City, MO 64112-2513
Phone: (816)756-1000
Fax: (816)756-0494
Free: 800-338-6201

Publications: Baking Buyer (17155) • Baking & Snack (17156) • Blade-Empire (17157) • Meat & Poultry (17182) • Milling & Baking News (17185) • World Grain (17205)

Sound Publishing
PO Box 758
Eastsound, WA 98245
Phone: (360)376-4500
Fax: (360)376-4501

Publications: The San Juans Beckon (32743)

Sound Publishing, Inc.
7689 NE Day Rd.
Bainbridge Island, WA 98110
Phone: (206)842-8305
Fax: (206)780-9562

Publications: The Bainbridge Island Review (32657) • Bremerton Patriot (32692) • Central Kitsap Reporter (33083) • Federal Way Mirror (32764) • The Islands' Sounder (32741) • The Journal of the San Juan Islands (32772) • Lakewood Journal (33182) • North Kitsap Herald (32899) • The Port Orchard Independent (32891) • South Whidbey Record (32807) • The Vashon Beachcomber (33184) • Whidbey News-Times (32857)

Sound Publishing Inc.
PO Box 387
Langley, WA 98260
Phone: (360)221-5300
Fax: (360)221-6474

Publications: South Whidbey Record (32806) • Southend Neighborhood Classifieds (32808)

Sound Publishing, Inc.
3098 300 Ave. West
Oak Harbor, WA 98277

Publications: Crosswind (32856)

Sound Publishing, Inc.
19062 Hwy. 305, No. 203
Poulsbo, WA 98370
Phone: (360)779-4464
Fax: (206)682-1107

Publications: North Kitsap Herald (32898)

Sound Publishing Inc.
9989 Silverdate Way, Ste. 109
Silverdale, WA 98383
Phone: (360)308-9161
Fax: (360)308-9363

Publications: N.W. Navigator (33084)

The Sound Shore Review
3 Gannett Dr.
White Plains, NY 10604
Phone: (914)694-3600
Fax: (914)694-3699

Publications: The Sound Shore Review (23574)

Sound and Vibration
PO Box 40416
Bay Village, OH 44140
Phone: (440)835-0101
Fax: (440)835-9303

Publications: Sound and Vibration (24646)

Soundings: An Interdisciplinary Journal
306 Aconda Ct.
University of Tennessee
Knoxville, TN 37996-0630
Phone: (865)974-8252
Fax: (865)974-8544

Publications: Soundings (29281)

Soundings Publications, L.L.C.
10 Bokum Rd.
Essex, CT 06426
Phone: (860)767-3200
Fax: (860)767-1048

Publications: Soundings Trade Only (4784)

Source Publications
c/o Floral Finance
4715 E. 91st St., No. 200
Tulsa, OK 74137-2804
Phone: (918)491-9933
Fax: (918)491-9080
Free: 800-477-6698

Publications: Collectors' Showcase (26109)

Source Publications, Inc.
215 Park Ave. S,
New York, NY 10003
Phone: (212)253-3700
Fax: (212)253-9344

Publications: The Source (22764)

The Souris Plaindealer
PO Box 488
Souris, MB, Canada R0K 2C0
Phone: (204)483-2070
Fax: (204)483-3866

Publications: The Souris Plaindealer (35293)

The South Alabamian
PO Box 68
Jackson, AL 36545
Phone: (251)246-4494
Fax: (334)246-7486

Publications: The South Alabamian (291)

South American Explorers
126 Indian Creek Rd.
Ithaca, NY 14850
Phone: (607)277-0488
Fax: (607)277-6122

Publications: South American Explorer (20814)

South Arkansas Accent
PO Box 766
Hampton, AR 71744
Fax: (501)798-2005

Publications: South Arkansas Accent (1165)

South Atlantic Modern Language Association
Georgia State University, MSC 8L0387
33 Gilmer St., SE Unit 8
Atlanta, GA 30303-3088
Phone: (404)651-2693
Fax: (404)651-2858

Publications: South Atlantic Review (7043)

South Bend Tribune
225 W. Colfax Ave.
South Bend, IN 46626
Phone: (574)235-6161
Fax: (574)236-1765

Publications: South Bend Tribune (10458)

South Boston Tribune
PO Box 6
South Boston, MA 02127
Phone: (617)268-3440
Fax: (617)268-6420

Publications: Dorchester Argus-Citizen (14159) •
South Boston Tribune (14540)

South Carolina Association of Young Farmers and FFA
222 McAdams Hall
Clemson University
Clemson, SC 29634

Publications: South Carolina YR and FFA (28534)

South Carolina Bar
950 Taylor St.
Columbia, SC 29202
Phone: (803)799-6653
Fax: (803)799-4118

Publications: South Carolina Lawyer (28566)

South Carolina Black Media Group
1310 Harden
PO Box 11128
Columbia, SC 29204
Phone: (803)799-5252
Fax: (803)799-7709

Publications: The Black News (28544)

South Carolina Department of Natural Resources
1000 Assembly St.
PO Box 167
Columbia, SC 29202-0167
Phone: (803)734-3944
Fax: (803)734-3968

Publications: South Carolina Wildlife (28568)

South Carolina Historical Society
Fireproof Bldg.
100 Meeting St.
Charleston, SC 29401
Phone: (843)723-3225
Fax: (843)723-8584

Publications: South Carolina Historical Magazine
(28518)

South Carolina Poultry Federation
1921-A Pickens St.
Columbia, SC 29201
Phone: (803)779-4700
Fax: (803)779-5002

Publications: Palmetto Poultry Life (28560)

South Carolina State Ports Authority
176 Concord St.
PO Box 22287
Charleston, SC 29413-2287
Phone: (843)723-8651
Fax: (843)577-8127

Publications: Port News (28516)

South Carolina Trucking Association
2425 Devine St.
PO Box 50166
Columbia, SC 29250
Phone: (803)256-4290
Fax: (803)254-7148

Publications: SCTA Hi-Lights (28564)

South Central Modern Language Association
Dept. of English
Texas A&M University
College Station, TX 77843-4227
Phone: (979)845-7041
Fax: (979)862-2292

Publications: South Central Review (30050)

South Central Ohio Shopper's Guide
138 S Fayette St.
Washington Court House, OH 43160
Phone: (614)335-3611
Fax: (614)335-5728

Publications: South Central Ohio Shopper's Guide
(25620)

South Central Wisconsin Newspapers
309 Dewitt St.
PO Box 470
Portage, WI 53901
Phone: (608)462-8224
Fax: (608)462-5678

Publications: Keystone Reporter (34257)

South Central Wisconsin Newspapers, Inc.
PO Box 269
Reedsburg, WI 53959-0269
Phone: (608)524-4336
Fax: (608)524-4337
Free: 800-638-6137

Publications: Reedsburg Times-Press (34281)

South Coast Shopper
PO Box 1440
Coos Bay, OR 97420
Phone: (541)756-5010
Fax: (541)756-8109
Free: 800-883-4455

Publications: South Coast Shopper (26272)

South Country Newspapers
635 Front St.
Soledad, CA 93960
Phone: (831)385-4880
Fax: (831)385-4799

Publications: Gonzales Tribune (3768) • King City
Rustler (3769)

South County Communications
PO Box 154
Vicksburg, MI 49097-0154
Phone: (616)649-2333
Fax: (616)649-2335

Publications: Commercial-Express (15654)

South County Journal
PO Box 130
Kent, WA 98035
Phone: (253)872-6600
Fax: (206)854-1006

Publications: South County Journal (32796)

South County Newspapers, Inc.
202 Church St.
Wakefield, RI 02879-2912
Phone: (401)789-6000
Fax: (401)792-9176

Publications: North-East Independent (28446) •
South County Independent (28447)

South County Publications
110 N 5th St.
Auburn, IL 62615
Phone: (217)438-6155
Fax: (217)438-6155

Publications: Chatham Clarion (8033) • Divernon
News (8775) • Pawnee Post (8034)

South County Publishing Co., Inc.
PO Box 460
Arroyo Grande, CA 93421
Phone: (805)489-4206
Fax: (805)473-0571

Publications: Five Cities Times Press Recorder
(1433)

South Dakota Magazine
410 E. 3rd St.
PO Box 175
Yankton, SD 57078
Phone: (605)665-6655
Fax: (605)665-6659

Publications: South Dakota Magazine (29039)

South Dakota Ornithologist's Union
1200 S Jay St.
Aberdeen, SD 57401-7198
Phone: (605)626-2456
Fax: (605)626-2635

Publications: South Dakota Bird Notes (28791)

South Dakota Pharmacists Association
215 West Sioux Avenue
PO Box 518
Pierre, SD 57501
Phone: (605)945-0409
Fax: (605)224-1280

Publications: South Dakota Pharmacist (28922)

South Dakota Rural Electric Association
222 W. Pleasant Dr.
PO Box 1138
Pierre, SD 57501
Phone: (605)224-8823
Fax: (605)224-4430

Publications: South Dakota Electric Cooperative Connections (28920)

South Dakota School of Mines & Technology
501 E. St. Joseph
PO Box 136 Surbeck Ctr.
Rapid City, SD 57701
Phone: (605)394-2511

Publications: The Tech (28933)

South Dakota State Historical Society
900 Governors Dr.
Pierre, SD 57501-2217
Phone: (605)773-3458
Fax: (605)773-6041

Publications: South Dakota History (28921)

South Dakota State Medical Association
1323 S. Minnesota Ave.
Sioux Falls, SD 57105-0624
Phone: (605)336-1965
Fax: (605)336-0270

Publications: South Dakota Journal of Medicine (28967)

South Dakota State University
Administration 200
PO Box 2201
Brookings, SD 57007
Phone: (605)688-6164
Fax: (605)688-6165

Publications: The SDSU Collegian (28816)

South Dakota Stock Growers Association
426 St. Joseph St.
Rapid City, SD 57701-2715
Phone: (605)342-0429
Fax: (605)342-0463

Publications: South Dakota Stock Grower (28932)

South Dakota Trucking Association
3801 S. Kiwanis Ave.
Sioux Falls, SD 57105
Phone: (605)334-8871
Fax: (605)334-1938

Publications: South Dakota Trucking News (28968)

South East Press Ltd.
521 Main St.
PO Box 329
Kipling, SK, Canada S0G 2S0
Phone: (306)736-2535
Fax: (306)736-8445

Publications: The Citizen (37485)

The South End News
631 Tremont St.
Boston, MA 02118
Phone: (617)266-6670
Fax: (617)266-5973

Publications: The South End News (13961)

South Fire News
PO Box 428
Alma, GA 31510-0428
Phone: (912)632-7201
Fax: (912)632-4156

Publications: Alma Times (6914)

South Florida Newspaper Network
601 Fairway Dr.
Deerfield Beach, FL 33441
Phone: (305)698-6397
Fax: (305)429-0556
Free: 800-575-8820

Publications: Eastsider (6049) • Greenacres/Lantana/Lake Worth Forum (6843) • Jewish Journal Dade (6050)

South Florida Parenting, Inc.
5555 Nob Hill Rd.
Sunrise, FL 33351
Phone: (954)747-3050
Fax: (954)747-3055
Free: 800-244-8447

Publications: South Florida Parenting (6700)

South Georgia Business Journal, Inc.
PO Box 2036
Thomasville, GA 31799
Phone: (912)228-1299
Fax: (912)228-7033

Publications: South Georgia Business Journal (7586)

South Georgia Media Group
PO Box 1247
Americus, GA 31709
Phone: (229)924-2751
Fax: (229)928-6344

Publications: Americus Times-Recorder (6920)

South Georgia News
302 W 16th Ave., Ste. D
Cordele, GA 31015
Phone: (229)273-6714
Fax: (229)273-6714

Publications: Southeastern News (7205)

South Gibson Star-Times
PO Box 70
Fort Branch, IN 47648
Phone: (812)753-3553
Fax: (812)753-4251

Publications: South Gibson Star-Times (9963)

South Hamilton Record News
PO Box 130
Jewell, IA 50130
Phone: (515)827-5931
Fax: (515)827-5760

Publications: South Hamilton Record News (11008)

South Hardin Signal-Review
Box 457
Hubbard, IA 50122
Phone: (641)864-2288

Publications: South Hardin Signal-Review (10953)

South Idaho Press
230 E Main St.
Burley, ID 83318
Phone: (208)678-2201
Fax: (208)678-0412

Publications: South Idaho Press (7839)

South Jersey Newspaper
309 S Broad St.
Woodbury, NJ 08096
Phone: (609)845-3300
Fax: (609)845-5480

Publications: Gloucester County Times (19756)

South Jersey Publishing Co.
1000 W Washington Ave.
Pleasantville, NJ 08232-3806
Phone: (609)272-7000
Fax: (609)272-7910
Free: 800-651-8279

Publications: At the Shore (19443) • The Press of Atlantic City (18658) • Shoreast Magazine (19444)

South Jersey Shoppers Guide
8 Ranoldo Ter.
Cherry Hill, NJ 08034-2132
Phone: (856)616-4900
Fax: (856)616-0299
Free: 800-229-8775

Publications: South Jersey Shoppers Guide (18738)

South Lincoln County News
PO Box 1419
Waldport, OR 97394
Phone: (541)563-5100
Fax: (541)563-5116

Publications: South Lincoln County News (26606)

South Louisiana Publishing
217 Garfield St.
Lafayette, LA 70501-7029
Phone: (337)237-3560
Fax: (337)261-2630

Publications: The Times of Acadiana (12620)

South Metro Publications
PO Box 6739
Moore, OK 73153
Phone: (405)794-5555
Fax: (405)799-8046

Publications: Moore American (25921) • South OKC Leader (25922)

South Orange County News
22481 Aspan St.
Lake Forest, CA 92630-1630

Publications: Flight Jacket (1651) • Laguna Beach News (2132)

South Peace News
Box 1000
High Prairie, AB, Canada T0G 1E0
Phone: (780)523-4484
Fax: (780)523-3039

Publications: Smoky River Express (34765) • South Peace News (34781)

South Philadelphia American
2414 S 21st
Philadelphia, PA 19147
Phone: (215)467-2713
Fax: (215)925-2339

Publications: South Philadelphia American (27691)

South Plains Catholic
4620 Fourth St.
PO Box 98700
Lubbock, TX 79499-8700
Phone: (806)792-3943
Fax: (806)792-8109

Publications: South Plains Catholic (30718)

The South Reporter
PO Box 278
Holly Springs, MS 38635
Phone: (662)252-4261
Fax: (662)252-3388
Free: 800-468-3820

Publications: Pigeon Roost News (16680) • The South Reporter (16681)

South Schuylkill Printing and Publishing
181 S. Tulpehocken St.
PO Box 7
Pine Grove, PA 17963
Phone: (570)385-3120
Fax: (570)345-8467

Publications: The Press Herald (27752)

South Schuylkill Printing & Publishing
PO Box 178
Schuylkill Haven, PA 17972
Phone: (570)385-3120
Fax: (570)385-0725

Publications: The Call (27951) • West Schuylkill Herald (28054)

South Seattle Community College
6000 16th Ave. SW
Seattle, WA 98106
Phone: (206)764-5300
Fax: (206)764-7936

Publications: The South Seattle Sentinel (33032)

South Shore Gazette
PO Box 96
South Shore, SD 57263
Phone: (605)756-4200
Publications: South Shore Gazette (28992)

South Shore Record
42 Broadway
Lynbrook, NY 11563-2519
Phone: (516)374-9200
Fax: (516)374-9209
Publications: South Shore Record (20977)

South Suburban College
15800 S State St., Rm. 3234
South Holland, IL 60473
Phone: (708)596-2000
Fax: (708)210-5776
Publications: Courier (9614)

The South Texan
PO Box 123
Kingsville, TX 78363
Fax: (512)563-3780
Publications: The South Texan (30648)

The South Texas Reporter
101 E LaFragua St.
Roma, TX 78584
Phone: (210)849-1757
Fax: (210)849-1757
Publications: The South Texas Reporter (30990)

South Washington County Bulletin
7584 80th St., S.
Cottage Grove, MN 55016
Phone: (651)459-3434
Fax: (651)459-9491
Publications: South Washington County Bulletin (15817)

Southam Inc.
352 E. River Rd.
New Glasgow, NS, Canada B2H 5E2
Phone: (902)928-3526
Fax: (902)752-1945
Publications: The Evening News (35596)

Southam Inc.
1450 Don Mills Rd.
Don Mills, ON, Canada M3B 2X7
Phone: (416)445-6641
Fax: (416)442-2213
Free: 800-387-0273
Publications: Canadian Underwriter (35772) • National Post (35776)

Southam, Inc.
4949 Victoria Ave.
Niagara Falls, ON, Canada L2E 4C7
Phone: (905)871-3100
Publications: The Times (36111)

Southam, Inc.
250 St-Antoine St. W.
Montreal, QC, Canada H2Y 3R7
Phone: (514)987-2350
Fax: (514)987-2323
Free: 800-363-6765
Publications: The Gazette (37118) • The Montreal Gazette (37188)

Southam News, Inc.
PO Box 570
North Bay, ON, Canada P1B 8J6
Phone: (705)472-3200
Fax: (705)472-5128
Publications: The North Bay Nugget (36116)

Southam Publications
10006-101 St.
Edmonton, AB, Canada T5J 0S1
Phone: (780)429-5100
Fax: (780)429-5500
Publications: The Edmonton Journal (34711)

Southam (The Fairway Group)
75 King S, Ste. 201
Waterloo, ON, Canada N2J 1P2
Phone: (519)886-2830
Fax: (519)886-9383
Publications: Waterloo Chronicle (36859)

Southampton Press-Western Edition
12 Mitchell Rd.
PO Box 1071
Westhampton Beach, NY 11978
Phone: (516)288-1100
Fax: (516)288-4965
Publications: Southampton Press-Western Edition (23567)

Southeast Asia Program Publications
369 Pine Tree Rd.
Ithaca, NY 14850
Phone: (607)255-8038
Fax: (607)255-7534
Free: 877-865-2432
Publications: Indonesia (20803)

Southeast Asia Publications
Center for Southeast Asian Studies, Adams 412
Northern Illinois University
DeKalb, IL 60115-2854
Phone: (815)753-1981
Fax: (815)753-1776
Free: 888-731-9599
Publications: Crossroads (8733)

Southeast Missouri State University
828 N. St.
Cape Girardeau, MO 63701
Phone: (573)651-2540
Fax: (573)651-2825
Publications: The Capaha Arrow (16944)

Southeast Publishing Co., Inc.
PO Box 47719
Atlanta, GA 30362
Phone: (770)452-1807
Fax: (770)457-3829
Publications: Southeast Food Service News (7044)

Southeastern College Art Conference Review
Box 508
Chapel Hill, NC 27516-0508
Phone: (919)933-1777
Fax: (919)933-0547
Publications: Southeastern College Art Conference Review (4601)

Southeastern Council on Latin American Studies
PO Box 8106
Georgia Southern University
Statesboro, GA 30460-8106
Phone: (912)681-5668
Fax: (912)681-0824
Publications: SECOLAS Annals (7562)

Southeastern Louisiana University
SLU 10877
Hammond, LA 70402
Phone: (985)549-3731
Fax: (985)549-3842
Publications: The Lion's Roar (12592)

Southeastern Newspapers, Inc.
PO Box 3009
Kenai, AK 99611
Phone: (907)283-7551
Fax: (907)283-3299
Publications: Peninsula Clarion (607)

Southeastern Peanut Farmer
PO Box 706
Tifton, GA 31793
Publications: Southeastern Peanut Farmer (7597)

Southern Advocate
PO Box 157
Ashland, MS 38603
Phone: (662)224-6681
Fax: (662)224-6681
Publications: Southern Advocate (16548)

Southern Alberta Newspaper Group
234 12B St. N.
Lethbridge, AB, Canada T1H 2K7
Phone: (403)329-8225
Fax: (403)329-8211
Publications: The Lethbridge Shopper (34796)

Southern Appalachian Botanical Society
University of North Carolina at Charlotte
Dept. of Biology
Charlotte, NC 28223
Phone: (704)687-4065
Publications: CASTANEA (23738)

Southern Baptist Convention Executive Committee
901 Commerce
Nashville, TN 37203
Phone: (615)244-2355
Fax: (615)782-8684
Publications: SBC Life (29484)

Southern Berkshire Shopper's Guide
35 Bridge St.
PO Box 89
Great Barrington, MA 01230
Phone: (413)528-0095
Fax: (413)528-4805
Publications: Southern Berkshire Shopper's Guide (14217)

Southern Beverage Journal
14337 SW 119 Ave.
Miami, FL 33186
Phone: (305)233-7230
Fax: (305)252-2580
Publications: Southern Beverage Journal (6382)

Southern Building Code Congress International Inc.
900 Montclair Rd.
Birmingham, AL 35213-1206
Phone: (205)591-1853
Fax: (205)599-9891
Free: 888-44-SBCCI
Publications: Southern Building (92)

Southern California Golf Association
PO Box 8386
North Hollywood, CA 91618-8386
Phone: (818)980-3630
Fax: (818)980-1808
Free: 800-554-7242
Publications: Fore Magazine (2643)

Southern California Guide
3461 Butler Ave.
Los Angeles, CA 90066
Phone: (310)391-8255
Fax: (310)391-8255
Publications: Southern California Guide (2395)

Southern California Magazine
3769 Tibbetts St., Ste. A
Riverside, CA 92506
Phone: (909)682-3026
Fax: (909)682-0246
Publications: Southern California Magazine (2947)

Southern California Veterinary Medical Association
8338 Rosemead Blvd.
Pico Rivera, CA 90660-5197
Phone: (562)948-4979
Fax: (562)942-2977
Publications: Pulse (2841)

Southern Comparative Literature Association
4400 University Dr.
Fairfax, VA 22030-4444
Phone: (703)993-1160
Publications: The Comparatist (32013)

Southern Connecticut Newspapers, Inc.
75 Tresser Blvd.
PO Box 9307
Stamford, CT 06901-3304
Phone: (203)964-3709
Fax: (203)964-2345
Publications: The Advocate (5139)

Southern Connection
125 N Main St.
Dawson, GA 31742-1417
Publications: Southern Connection (7230)

Southern County News
PO Box 96
Thornton, IA 50479-0096
Phone: (641)998-2712
Fax: (641)998-2712

Publications: Southern County News (11267)

The Southern Cross
PO Box 81869
San Diego, CA 92138
Phone: (858)490-8266
Fax: (858)490-8355

Publications: The Southern Cross (3277)

The Southern Democrat, Inc.
PO Box 310
Oneonta, AL 35121
Phone: (205)625-3231
Fax: (205)625-3239

Publications: The Blount Countian (404)

Southern Festivals
107 S Main St.
Blakely, GA 31723
Phone: (912)723-2778
Fax: (912)723-2779
Free: 800-558-3378

Publications: Southern Festivals (7131)

Southern Finance Association
The Darla Moore School of Business
University of South Carolina
Columbia, SC 29208

Publications: Journal of Financial Research (28552)

Southern Genealogist's Exchange Society Inc.
PO Box 2801
Jacksonville, FL 32203-2801
Phone: (904)778-1000

Publications: Southern Genealogists Exchange Quarterly (6217)

Southern Growth Policies Board
PO Box 12293
Research Triangle Park, NC 27709

Publications: Southern Growth Magazine (24187)

Southern Herald
PO Box 674
Liberty, MS 39645
Phone: (601)657-4818
Fax: (601)657-4818

Publications: The Southern Herald (16748)

Southern Hills Publishing, Inc.
PO Box 551
Custer, SD 57730
Phone: (605)673-2217
Fax: (605)574-4409

Publications: Custer County Chronicle (28836) • Hill City Prevailer-News (28837) • Western Trader (28838)

Southern Illinois University at Carbondale
Communications Bldg.
PO Box 6887
Carbondale, IL 62901
Phone: (618)536-3311
Fax: (618)453-3248

Publications: Alumnus (8113) • Daily Egyptian (8116)

Southern Illinoisan
710 N Illinois
Carbondale, IL 62901
Phone: (618)529-5454
Fax: (618)457-2935
Free: 800-228-0429

Publications: Southern Illinoisan (8121)

Southern Lakes Newspapers
140 Commerce St.
PO Box 437
Burlington, WI 53105-0437
Phone: (262)763-3511
Fax: (262)763-2238
Free: (262)642-7451

Publications: Burlington Standard Press (33608) • The East Troy News (33609) • The Sharon Reporter (34316) • Westosha Report (34377)

Southern Manitoba Review
PO Box 249
Cartwright, MB, Canada R0K 0L0
Phone: (204)529-2342
Fax: (204)529-2029

Publications: Southern Manitoba Review (35261)

Southern Media Properties, Inc.
151 N. Main St.
Collierville, TN 38017-2670
Phone: (901)853-7060
Fax: (901)854-0727

Publications: Independent (29135)

Southern Medical Association
35 Lakeshore Dr.
PO Box 190088
Birmingham, AL 35219-0088
Phone: (205)945-1840
Fax: (205)945-1830
Free: 800-423-4992

Publications: Southern Medical Journal (97)

Southern MotoRacing
1049 NW Blvd.
PO Box 500
Winston-Salem, NC 27102
Phone: (336)723-5227
Fax: (336)722-3757

Publications: Southern MotoRacing (24322)

Southern Nazarene University
6729 NW 39th Expy.
Bethany, OK 73008
Phone: (405)789-6400
Fax: (405)491-6381

Publications: The Echo (25758) • Southern Lights (25760)

Southern Nebraska Register
PO Box 80329
Lincoln, NE 68501
Phone: (402)488-0090
Fax: (402)488-3569

Publications: Southern Nebraska Register (18121)

Southern Newspaper Inc.
8522 Teichman Rd.
PO Box 628
Galveston, TX 77553
Phone: (409)683-5200
Fax: (409)744-6268

Publications: The Galveston County Daily News (30380)

Southern Newspapers
1301 Memorial Dr.
PO Box 90
Baytown, TX 77520
Phone: (281)422-8302
Fax: (281)427-5252

Publications: The Baytown Sun (29894)

Southern Newspapers Inc.
PO Box 549
720 S. Main
PO Box 549
Clute, TX 77531
Phone: (409)265-7411
Fax: (409)265-9052
Free: 800-864-8340

Publications: Brazosport Facts (30033)

Southern Newspapers, Inc.
1012 Schriewer
Seguin, TX 78155
Phone: (830)379-5402
Fax: (830)379-8328

Publications: The Seguin Gazette-Enterprise (31096)

Southern Oregon University
Stevenson Union Bldg., Rm. 103
1250 Siskiyou Blvd.
Ashland, OR 97520
Phone: (541)552-6307
Fax: (541)552-6440

Publications: The Siskiyou (26217)

Southern Polytechnic State University
110 S Marietta Pkwy.
Marietta, GA 30060

Publications: The Sting (7420)

Southern Progress
2100 Lakeshore Dr.
Birmingham, AL 35209-6721
Phone: (205)445-6000
Fax: (205)445-6860
Free: 800-366-4712

Publications: Coastal Living (65) • COOKING LIGHT (66) • Progressive Farmer (87) • Southern Accents (91) • Southern Living (93) • Southern Living Garden Guide (94) • Southern Living Home for the Holidays (95) • Southern Living Vacations (96)

Southern Public Administration Education Foundation, Inc.
2103 Fairway Ln.
Harrisburg, PA 17112

Publications: German Policy Studies (26992) • Global Virtue Ethics Review (26993) • Journal of Power and Ethics (26997)

Southern Publishing, Inc.
3818 Shelbyville Rd.
Louisville, KY 40207-3186
Phone: (502)897-8900
Fax: (502)897-8915

Publications: The Voice-Tribune (12243)

Southern Rhode Island Newspapers
187 Main St.
PO Box 232
Wakefield, RI 02880
Phone: (401)789-9744
Fax: (401)783-1550

Publications: The Chariho Times (28463) • The Coventry Courier (28444) • The East Greenwich Pendulum Times (28340) • The Narragansett Times (28445)

Southern Standard
105 College St.
PO Box 150
Mc Minnville, TN 37110
Phone: (931)473-2191
Fax: (931)473-6823

Publications: Southern Standard (29353)

The Southern Star
PO Box 1729
Ozark, AL 36361
Phone: (334)774-2715
Fax: (334)774-9619

Publications: The Southern Star (419)

Southern States Communication Association
University of Memphis
3750 Norriswood
Memphis, TN 38152-0001

Publications: Southern Communication Journal (14949)

Southern States Cooperative, Inc.
PO Box 26234
Richmond, VA 23260
Phone: (804)282-0350
Fax: (804)281-1119

Publications: The Southern States Cooperative Magazine (32455)

Southern Trade Publications, Inc.
Box 7344
Greensboro, NC 27417
Phone: (336)454-3516
Fax: (336)454-3649

Publications: Southern PHC Magazine (23939)

Southern Utah Publishing
26 N Main
Kanab, UT 84741
Phone: (435)644-2900
Fax: (435)644-2926
Free: 888-468-2900

Publications: Color Country Shopper (31341) • Southern Utah News (31342)

Southfork Publishing Co.
PO Box 129
Booneville, KY 41314
Phone: (606)593-6627
Fax: (606)598-2330

Publications: Booneville Sentinel (11940)

Southside Shopper
2339 Timber Dr.
PO Box 449
Garner, NC 27529
Phone: (919)772-9002
Fax: (919)772-4172

Publications: Southside Shopper, Inc. (23906)

Southwest Baptist University
1600 University Ave.
Bolivar, MO 65613
Phone: (417)328-1833
Fax: (417)328-1579

Publications: Omnibus (16912)

The Southwest Booster
30 4th Ave. NW
PO Box 1330
Swift Current, SK, Canada S9H 3X4
Phone: (306)773-9321
Fax: (306)773-9136

Publications: The Southwest Booster (37575)

Southwest Computer Monthly
5208 W Calavar Rd.
Glendale, AZ 85306
Phone: (602)978-4842
Fax: (602)978-4842
Free: 800-TCCM-WEB

Publications: Southwest Computer Monthly (715)

Southwest Education Council for Journalism and Mass Communication
Arkansas University
PO Box 1930
State University, AR 72467
Phone: (870)972-3075
Fax: (870)972-3856

Publications: Southwestern Mass Communication Journal (1350)

Southwest Globe Times, Inc.
2821 Island Ave.
Philadelphia, PA 19153-2314
Phone: (215)727-7777
Fax: (215)727-5116

Publications: Southwest Globe Times (27692)

Southwest Iowa Newsgroup
205 E Main
PO Box 278
Clarinda, IA 51632
Phone: (712)542-2181
Fax: (712)542-5424

Publications: The Herald-Journal (10702)

Southwest Journal
3225 Lyndale Ave. S.
Minneapolis, MN 55408
Phone: (612)825-9205
Fax: (612)825-0929

Publications: Southwest Journal (16131)

Southwest Kansas Publications, Inc.
Box 706
Ulysses, KS 67880
Fax: (316)356-4610

Publications: The Ulysses News (11854)

Southwest Kansas Senior Beacon
PO Box 1842
Syracuse, KS 67878
Phone: (316)384-7657
Fax: (316)384-6375

Publications: Southwest Kansas Senior Beacon (11811)

Southwest Messenger Press, Inc.
3840 W 147th St.
PO Box 548
Midlothian, IL 60445
Phone: (708)388-2425
Fax: (708)385-7811

Publications: Beverly News (9183) • Bridgeview Independent (9184) • Burbank Stickney Independent (9185) • Chicago Ridge Citizen (9186) • Evergreen Park Courier (9187) • Hickory Hills Citizen (9188) • Midlothian-Bremen Messenger (9189) • Mount Greenwood Express (9190) • Oak Lawn Independent (9191) • Orland Township Messenger (9192) • Palos Citizen (9193) • Scottsdale Ashburn Independent (9194) • Worth Citizen (9195)

Southwest Missouri State University
901 S. National
Springfield, MO 65804
Phone: (417)836-6784
Fax: (417)836-6738

Publications: Explorations in Renaissance Culture (17598) • The Standard (17613)

Southwest Oklahoma Genealogical Society
Box 148
Lawton, OK 73502-1048
Phone: (580)581-3450
Fax: (580)248-0243

Publications: Tree Tracers (25889)

Southwest Publisher LLC
PO Box 188
Gays Mills, WI 54631
Phone: (608)375-4458
Fax: (608)375-2369

Publications: Crawford County Independent Scout (33733)

Southwest Publishers, Inc.
128 N. Railroad Ave.
PO Box 551
Brookhaven, MS 39601
Phone: (601)833-6961
Fax: (601)833-6714

Publications: Daily Leader (16578)

Southwest Publishers, Inc.
PO Box 3306
San Angelo, TX 76902
Phone: (915)949-4611
Fax: (915)949-4614
Free: 800-284-5268

Publications: Livestock Weekly (31005)

Southwest Publishers LLC
901 Wisconisn Ave.
Boscobel, WI 53805-1531
Phone: (608)375-4458
Fax: (608)375-2369

Publications: The Boscobel Dial (33598)

Southwest Quarter Horse Track Magazine
PO Box 222
Morgan Mill, TX 76465-0222
Phone: (817)870-1990
Fax: (817)870-2087

Publications: Southwest Quarter Horse Track Magazine (30838)

Southwest Review
307 Fondren Library W
PO Box 750374
Dallas, TX 75275-0374
Phone: (214)768-1036
Fax: (214)768-1408

Publications: Southwest Review (30181)

Southwest Society on Aging
CHES Rm. 139
Oklahoma State University
Stillwater, OK 74078
Phone: (405)744-7511
Fax: (405)744-7512

Publications: Southwest Journal on Aging (26082)

Southwest Stockman
PO Box 32390
Amarillo, TX 79120
Phone: (806)373-7643

Publications: Southwest Stockman (4684)

Southwest Suburban Publishing
327 S. Marschall Rd.
PO Box 8
Shakopee, MN 55379
Phone: (952)445-3335
Fax: (952)445-3335

Publications: The Chanhassen Villager (15792) • Chaska Herald (15793) • Eden Prairie News (15868) • Jordan Independent (15980) • Prior Lake American (16288) • Savage Pacer (16441) • Shakopee Valley News (16445)

Southwest Texas State University
601 University Dr.
102 Old Main
San Marcos, TX 78666
Phone: (512)245-3487
Fax: (512)245-3708

Publications: The University Star (31086)

Southwest Virginia Enterprise
460 W Main St.
Wytheville, VA 24382
Phone: (276)228-6611
Fax: (276)228-7260
Free: 800-655-1406

Publications: Southwest Virginia Enterprise (32643)

Southwestern Entomological Society
17360 Coit Rd.
Dallas, TX 75252
Phone: (972)952-9222

Publications: Southwestern Entomologist (30051)

Southwestern Oklahoma State University
100 Campus Dr.
Journalism Dept.
Weatherford, OK 73096
Phone: (580)772-6611
Fax: (580)774-7111

Publications: The Southwestern (26185)

Southwestern Oregon Publishing Co.
350 Commercial
PO Box 1840
Coos Bay, OR 97420-0147
Phone: (503)269-1222
Fax: (503)267-0294
Free: 800-437-6397

Publications: The World (26274)

Southwestern Philosophical Society
Box 4540
Department of Philosophy
Illinois State University
Normal, IL 61790-4540
Phone: (309)438-7666
Fax: (309)438-8028

Publications: Southwest Philosophy Review (9305)

Southwestern Union Conference of Seventh-Day Adventists
PO Box 4000
Burleson, TX 76097
Phone: (817)295-0476
Fax: (817)447-2443

Publications: Southwestern Union Record (29989)

Southwestern University
675 S. Westmoreland
Los Angeles, CA 90005
Phone: (213)738-6700
Fax: (213)383-1688

Publications: The Commentator (2245)

Southwestern University
1001 E. University Ave. PO Box 770
Georgetown, TX 78626

Publications: Inside Southwestern (30390)

C.W. Soward
3155 Lynde St.
Oakland, CA 94601
Phone: (510)532-5513
Fax: (510)436-6236

Publications: Pacific Bakers News (2693)

Sow's Ear Poetry Review
19535 Pleasant View Dr.
Abingdon, VA 24211-6827
Phone: (276)628-2651

Publications: Sow's Ear Poetry Review (31626)

SPA
645 5th Ave., Ste. 703
New York, NY 10022
Phone: (212)753-6849
Fax: (212)753-6948

Publications: ICR: The International Cookbook Revue (21841)

2642

Numbers cited after listings are entry numbers rather than page numbers.

Space Publications, Inc.
1341 G St, NW
Washington, DC 20005
Phone: (202)638-0500

Publications: Arlington Sun Gazette (31642)

Space and Time
138 W 70th St., Apt. 4-B
New York, NY 10023-4468
Phone: (212)595-0894

Publications: Space and Time Magazine (22770)

Spalding Enterprise
140 S Cedar
PO Box D
Spalding, NE 68665
Phone: (308)497-2153
Fax: (308)497-2153

Publications: Spalding Enterprise (18281)

Spanish Colonial Research Center
MSC05 3020
1 University of New Mexico
Albuquerque, NM 87131-0001
Phone: (505)277-1370
Fax: (505)277-4603

Publications: Colonial Latin America Historical Review (19769)

Spanish Publications, Inc.
6601 Tarnef
Houston, TX 77074
Phone: (713)774-7640
Fax: (713)774-4666
Free: 800-248-3984

Publications: Hola Magazine (30479) • Semana (30528)

The Spanish Speaking Community of Maryland, Inc.
8519 Piney Branch Rd.
Silver Spring, MD 20901
Fax: (301)589-1397

Publications: Prensa Hispana (13744)

Sparta Newspapers Inc.
Box 179
Sparta, TN 38583

Publications: The Expositor (29613)

Spartacist Publishing Co.
PO Box 1377
New York, NY 10116
Phone: (212)732-7861
Fax: (212)406-2210

Publications: Workers Vanguard (22937)

Speakin' Out News
115 Wholesale Ave.
Huntsville, AL 35811
Phone: (205)551-1020
Fax: (205)551-0607

Publications: Speakin' Out News (274)

Spearville News
400 Main St.
PO Box 127
Spearville, KS 67876
Phone: (620)385-2200
Fax: (620)385-2610

Publications: The Spearville News (11807)

SPEBSQSA Inc.
6315 3rd Ave.
Kenosha, WI 53143-5199
Phone: (262)653-8440
Fax: (262)654-4048

Publications: The Harmonizer (33870)

Special Care Dentistry
211 E Chicago Ave., Ste. 740
Chicago, IL 60611-6994
Phone: (312)440-2660
Fax: (312)440-2824

Publications: Special Care in Dentistry (8570)

Special Interest Autos
PO Box 100
Bennington, VT 05201
Fax: (802)447-9631

Publications: Special Interest Autos (31303)

Special Libraries Association
1700 18th St. NW
Washington, DC 20009-2514
Phone: (202)234-4700
Fax: (202)234-2442

Publications: Information Outlook (5544) • SpeciaList (5801)

Special Libraries Association, Geography & Map Division
Anita T. Sprankle
406 E. Smith St.
Topton, PA 19562
Phone: (215)683-4166
Fax: (215)683-4483

Publications: Special Libraries Association, Geography & Map Division (28052)

Special Library Association
Concordia University
1455 de Maisonneuve St., Rm. 583-1
Montreal, QC, Canada H3G 1M8
Phone: (514)848-2543
Fax: (514)848-4520

Publications: Education Libraries (37112)

Specialized Agricultural Publications, Inc.
5808 Faringdon Pl., Ste. 200
Raleigh, NC 27609-3930
Phone: (919)872-5040
Fax: (919)876-6531

Publications: The Burley Tobacco Farmer (24128) • The Flue Cured Tobacco Farmer (24136) • The Peanut Farmer (24147) • Rice Journal (24151)

Specialized Systems Consultants Inc.
PO Box 55549
Seattle, WA 98155-0549
Phone: (206)782-7733
Fax: (206)782-7191

Publications: Be Magazine (32947) • Embedded Linux Journal (32962)

Specialty Digest Publications, Inc.
PO Box 24439
Edina, MN 55424-0439
Phone: (612)823-4220

Publications: Specialty Law Digest (15877)

Spectator Publications, Inc.
1310 E 9th Ave.
Tampa, FL 33605-3616
Free: 800-942-8644

Publications: Spectator Magazine (6778)

Spectrum Press
1370 South 500 West
Bountiful, UT 84010
Phone: (801)292-1088
Fax: (801)261-5623

Publications: Eagle Newspaper (31323)

Spectrum Publishing Inc.
4824 George Washington Hwy.
PO Box 978
Yorktown, VA 23692
Phone: (757)898-7225
Fax: (757)890-0119

Publications: The Flyer (32127) • The News Advance (32206) • The Poquoson Post (32645) • York Town Crier (32646)

Spectrum Student Periodical, Inc.
State University of New York at Buffalo
Student Union, Ste. 132
Buffalo, NY 14260
Phone: (716)645-2468
Fax: (716)645-2766

Publications: The Spectrum (20388)

Spectrum Unlimited
3201 General DeGaulle Dr., Ste. 107
New Orleans, LA 70114-4002
Phone: (504)365-7088
Fax: (504)365-0465

Publications: Journal for Minority Medical Students (12735) • The Keepsake (12736)

Speculations
PO Box 400
1111 W. El Camino Real, No. 109-400
Sunnyvale, CA 94087-1057

Publications: Speculations (3831)

Speech Communication Association of Ohio
University of Akron
Akron, OH 44325-1003
Phone: (330)972-7600
Fax: (330)972-8045

Publications: Ohio Speech Journal (24583)

Speedhorse Inc.
PO Box 1000
Norman, OK 73070-1000
Phone: (405)573-1050
Fax: (405)573-1059

Publications: Speedhorse Racing Report (25943)

Speedway-Northwest Press, Inc.
1564 Main St.
Indianapolis, IN 46224-6527
Phone: (317)241-4345
Fax: (317)241-4386

Publications: Speedway Town Press (10172) • West Side Messenger (10183)

The Speedy Bee
PO Box 1317
Jesup, GA 31598
Phone: (912)427-4018
Fax: (912)427-8447

Publications: The Speedy Bee (7348)

Speirs Publishing
PO Box 6830
Calgary, AB, Canada T2P 2E7

Publications: Opuntia (34653)

The Spencer Advocate
100 S Thayer
Box 187
Spencer, NE 68777
Phone: (402)589-1010
Fax: (402)589-1010

Publications: The Spencer Advocate (18282)

Charles D. Spencer & Associates Inc.
250 S Wacker Dr., Ste. 600
Chicago, IL 60606-5834
Phone: (312)993-7900
Fax: (312)993-7910
Free: 800-555-5490

Publications: Employee Benefit Plan Review (8368)

Spencer Evening World
717 Main St.
Clay City, IN 47841
Phone: (812)939-2163
Fax: (812)939-2286

Publications: The News (9890)

Spencer Evening World
114 E. Franklin St.
Spencer, IN 47460
Phone: (812)829-2255
Fax: (812)829-4666

Publications: World (10472)

Spencer Newspapers, Inc.
210 E. Main St.
Spencer, WV 25276
Phone: (304)927-2360
Fax: (304)927-2361

Publications: Roane County Reporter (33470) • Times Record (33471)

Spencer Owen Leader
114 E Franklin St.
PO Box 22
Spencer, IN 47460
Phone: (812)829-3936
Fax: (812)829-4666

Publications: Spencer Owen Leader (10471)

SPIE - The International Society for Optical Engineering
1000 20th St.
Bellingham, WA 98225
Phone: (360)676-3290
Fax: (360)647-1445

Publications: Biomedical Optics (2076) • Electronic Imaging (30040) • oemagazine (18454)

Spill Magazine
3055 Harold Sheard Dr.
Mississauga, ON, Canada L4T 1V4
Phone: (905)677-8337
Fax: (905)677-9705

Publications: The Spill Magazine (36087)

Spilogale, Inc.
PO Box 3447
Hoboken, NJ 07030-1605
Phone: (201)876-2551
Fax: (201)876-2551

Publications: The Magazine of Fantasy & Science Fiction (19055)

Spinal Column Publications
7196 Cooley Lake Rd.
PO Box 14
Union Lake, MI 48387-0014
Phone: (248)360-7355
Fax: (248)360-4711

Publications: Commerce Spinal Column Newsweekly (14890) • Highland Spinal Column Newsweekly (15160) • Milford Spinal Column Newsweekly (15538) • Novi Spinal Column Newsweekly (15411) • Waterford Spinal Column Newsweekly (15668) • West Bloomfield Spinal Column Newsweekly (15678) • White Lake Spinal Column Newsweekly (15683)

Spindle Publishing Co.
4136 Library Rd., Ste. 200
Pittsburgh, PA 15234
Phone: (412)531-9742
Fax: (412)531-2004

Publications: Baby Shop (27761)

Spirit of Change Magazine
PO Box 410
Grafton, MA 01519
Phone: (508)839-2228
Fax: (508)839-1173

Publications: Spirit of Change Magazine (14213)

Spirit Lake Publishing Co.
PO Box AE
Spirit Lake, IA 51360
Phone: (712)336-2667
Fax: (712)336-1219

Publications: Milford Mail and Terril Record (11237) • News (11238)

Spirit Newspapers of Missouri, Inc.
403 Charles Cook Plz.
PO Box 168
New Haven, MO 63068
Phone: (573)237-3222
Fax: (573)237-7222

Publications: New Haven Leader (17313)

The Spirit of Philadelphia
Pier 3 Deleware & Market St.
Philadelphia, PA 19106
Phone: (215)923-4993
Fax: (215)923-8556

Publications: The Spirit of Philadelphia (27694)

Spirit Publishing Co.
510 Pine St.
PO Box 444
Punxsutawney, PA 15767-0444
Phone: (814)938-8740
Fax: (814)938-3794

Publications: County Neighbors (27908) • The Spirit (27909) • The Spirit Extra (27910)

The Spirit That Moves Us Press
PO Box 720820-GA
Jackson Heights, NY 11372-0820
Phone: (718)426-8788

Publications: Editor's Choice (20826) • The Spirit That Moves Us (20829)

Spiritans, The Congregation of the Holy Ghost
121 Victoria Park Ave.
Toronto, ON, Canada M4E 3S2
Phone: (416)698-2003
Fax: (416)698-1884

Publications: Spiritan Missionary News (36746)

Spiritual Life Institute of America
PO Box 219
Crestone, CO 81131
Phone: (719)256-4778
Fax: (719)256-4719

Publications: Desert Call (4300)

Spiritual Massage Healing Ministry
6907 Sherman St.
Philadelphia, PA 19119
Phone: (215)842-0265
Fax: (215)842-2388

Publications: Journal of Spiritual Bodywork (27551)

Spiro Graphic
PO Box 190
212 S. Main St.
Spiro, OK 74959
Phone: (918)962-2075
Fax: (918)962-3531

Publications: Spiro Graphic (26074)

Splash Magazine
5826 New Territory Blvd., Ste. 209
Sugar Land, TX 77479-5948
Phone: (281)565-1920
Fax: (281)565-1921

Publications: Splash Magazine (31164)

Spokane Community College
1810 N Greene St.
Spokane, WA 99207
Phone: (509)536-7171
Fax: (509)533-8141

Publications: The Reporter (33098)

The Spokesman
216 N. Park Ave.
PO Box 128
Herrin, IL 62948
Phone: (618)942-5000
Fax: (618)942-4630

Publications: The Spokesman (8983)

Spondylitis Association of America
PO Box 5872
Sherman Oaks, CA 91413
Phone: (818)981-1616
Fax: (818)981-9826
Free: 800-777-8189

Publications: Spondylitis Plus (3763)

Spoon River Poetry Review
c/o Dr. Lucia Getsi
Illinois State University
4240 English
Normal, IL 61790-4240
Phone: (309)438-7906
Fax: (309)438-5414

Publications: Spoon River Poetry Review (9306)

Spoon River Press
358 E. Main St.
PO Box 269
Bushnell, IL 61422
Phone: (309)772-2129
Fax: (309)772-3994

Publications: The McDonough Democrates (8103)

Sport Prince Edward Island, Inc.
PO Box 302
Charlottetown, PE, Canada C1A 7K7
Phone: (902)368-4110
Fax: (902)368-4548

Publications: Island Sport Scene (36916)

The Sporting News Publishing Co.
10176 Corporate Square Dr., Ste. 200
St. Louis, MO 63132
Phone: (314)997-7111
Fax: (314)993-7726
Free: 800-325-4081

Publications: The Sporting News (17515)

Sportomatic Ltd.
PO Box 392
White Plains, NY 10602

Publications: Beau (23570)

Sports, Inc.
27142 Burbank
Foothill Ranch, CA 92610-2503
Phone: (949)598-5860
Fax: (949)598-5872

Publications: Jet Sports (1921)

Sports Tech Partnership
121 W 72nd St., Ste. 16D
New York, NY 10023

Publications: Sports Tech (22779)

Sportsman Pilot
PO Box 400
Asheboro, NC 27204-0400
Phone: (336)633-3954
Fax: (336)633-0165

Publications: Sportsman Pilot (23623)

The Spotlight
282 Bridge St.
PO Box 340
Princeton, BC, Canada V0X 1W0
Phone: (250)295-3535
Fax: (250)295-7322

Publications: Princeton-Similkameen Spotlight (35066)

The Spotlight
4217 S Meridian St.
Indianapolis, IN 46217-3313
Phone: (317)788-4554
Fax: (317)788-4570

Publications: The Spotlight (10173)

Spotlight Hawaii Publishing
532 Cummins St.
Honolulu, HI 96814
Phone: (808)593-9404
Fax: (808)593-9494

Publications: Spotlight Big Island (7720) • Spotlight Kauai (7721) • Spotlight Oahu (7722)

Spotlight Newspapers
125 Adams St.
PO Box 100
Delmar, NY 12054-0100
Phone: (518)439-4949
Fax: (518)439-0609

Publications: Colonie Spotlight (20485) • The Spotlight (20528)

Spout
PO Box 581067
Minneapolis, MN 55458-1067

Publications: Spout (16133)

SPPGroup LLC.
157 Primrose Way
Palo Alto, CA 94303

Publications: Meanderings (2798)

The Sprague Advocate
718 W 1st St.
Sprague, WA 99032-9638
Phone: (509)257-2227
Fax: (509)257-2227

Publications: The Sprague Advocate (33139)

Sprague Publishing
1050 Main St., Unit 32
East Greenwich, RI 02818-3164
Phone: (401)884-3003
Fax: (401)884-3223

Publications: The Rhode Island Gourmet Guide (28343)

Spring
33-54 164th St.
Flushing, NY 11358-1442
Phone: (718)353-3631
Fax: (718)353-4778

Publications: Spring (20613)

Spring Arbor University
106 E. Main
Spring Arbor, MI 49283
Phone: (517)750-6359
Fax: (517)750-6604
Free: 800-968-9103

Publications: Spring Arbor University Journal (15571)

Spring Creek Sun
1540 Van Siclen Ave.
Brooklyn, NY 11239
Phone: (718)642-2718
Fax: (718)240-4599

Publications: Spring Creek Sun (20348)

Spring Hill College
4000 Dauphin St.
Mobile, AL 36608
Phone: (334)380-3850
Fax: (334)460-2185

Publications: The Springhillian (330)

Spring Hope Enterprise/Bailey News
Box 399
Spring Hope, NC 27882
Phone: (252)478-3651
Fax: (252)478-3075

Publications: Spring Hope Enterprise/Bailey News (24244)

Spring House
434 W Downer Pl.
Aurora, IL 60506
Phone: (630)844-6911
Free: 800-950-0879

Publications: Advances in Wound Care (8038) • Nursing Management (8041)

Spring Journal
PO Box 583
Putnam, CT 06260
Phone: (860)974-3195
Fax: (860)974-3195

Publications: Spring Journal (5094)

Spring Manufacturers Institute
2001 Midwest Rd., No. 106
Oak Brook, IL 60523
Phone: (630)495-8588
Fax: (630)495-8595

Publications: Springs (9366)

Spring Valley Sun
PO Box 69
Spring Valley, WI 54767
Phone: (715)778-4395
Fax: (715)698-2952

Publications: Spring Valley Sun (34340)

Springer Publishing Co.
536 Broadway
New York, NY 10012
Phone: (212)431-4370
Fax: (212)941-7842

Publications: Care Management Journals (21377) • Complementary Health Practice Review (21468) • Contemporary Gerontology (21494) • Ethics, Law and Aging Review (25115) • International Psychogeriatrics (21932) • Journal of Aging and Ethnicity (14933) • Journal of Applied Social Studies (24913) • Journal of Brief Therapy (22014) • Journal of Cognitive Psychotherapy (22029) • Journal of Mental Health and Aging (6771) • Journal of Nursing Measurement (7023) • Journal of Nutrition, Health & Aging (25283) • Nursing History Review (27592) • Nursing Leadership Forum (22474) • Research and Theory for Nursing Practice (22649) • Violence and Victims (33036)

Springer-Verlag New York Inc.
175 5th Ave.
New York, NY 10010
Phone: (212)460-1500
Fax: (212)473-6272
Free: 800-777-4643

Publications: Abdominal Imaging (21131) • Aesthetic Plastic Surgery (21160) • Algorithmica (21173) • Annals of Vascular Surgery (21220) • Applied Mathematics and Optimization (21231) • Archives of Environmental Contamination and Toxicology (21245) • Bulletin of Environmental Contamination and Toxicology (21349) • Calcified Tissue International (21365) • CardioVascular and Interventional Radiology (21376) • Chance (21396) • Constructive Approximation (21489) • Current Microbiology (21525) • Discrete and Computational Geometry (21557) • Dysphagia (21573) • Environmental Management (21619) • Journal of Cryptology (22042) • Journal of Cutaneous Medicine (22045) • Journal of Membrane Biology (22132) • Journal of Molecular Evolution (22136) • Journal of Nonlinear Science (22145) • Journal of Plant Growth Regulation

(22160) • Kidney (22219) • Lung (22270) • Mammalian Genome (22276) • The Mathematical Intelligencer (22294) • Microbial Ecology (22330) • Osteoporosis International (22507) • Pain Digest (22518) • Pediatric Cardiology (22536) • Semigroup Forum (22723) • Surgical Endoscopy (22811) • Theory of Computing Systems (22830) • World Journal of Surgery (22941)

Springfield Advance-Press
13 S Marshall Ave.
PO Box 78
Springfield, MN 56087
Phone: (507)723-4225
Fax: (507)723-4400

Publications: Springfield Advance-Press (16459)

Springfield Business Journal
313 Park Central West
Springfield, MO 65806
Phone: (417)831-3238
Fax: (417)831-5478

Publications: Springfield Business Journal (17610)

Springfield Communications Inc.
PO Box 4749
Springfield, MO 65808
Phone: (417)831-1600

Publications: Springfield! Magazine (17611)

The Springfield News
PO Box 139
Springfield, OR 97477
Phone: (541)746-1671
Fax: (541)746-0633

Publications: The Springfield News (26586)

Springfield Newspapers, Inc.
202 N. Limestone St.
Springfield, OH 45501
Phone: (937)328-0300
Fax: (937)328-0227
Free: 800-441-6397

Publications: Springfield News-Sun (25532)

Springfield Parent & Family
313 Park Central W
Springfield, MO 65806
Phone: (417)869-9800
Fax: (417)831-5478

Publications: Springfield Parent, Inc. (17612)

Springfield Reporter
151 Summer St.
Springfield, VT 05156-3503
Phone: (802)885-2246
Fax: (802)885-9821

Publications: Springfield Reporter (31603)

Springfield Times
810 8th St.
PO Box 465
Springfield, SD 57062
Phone: (605)369-2441

Publications: Times (28997)

Springhill Press & News Journal
PO Box 669
Springhill, LA 71075
Phone: (318)539-3511
Fax: (318)539-3512

Publications: The Advertiser (12846) • Springhill Press & News Journal (12847)

Springs Valley Herald
PO Box 311
French Lick, IN 47432
Phone: (812)936-9630
Fax: (812)936-9559

Publications: Springs Valley Herald (10011)

Springview Herald
Box 369
Springview, NE 68778
Phone: (402)497-3651
Fax: (402)497-2651

Publications: Springview Herald (18283)

SQAD
303 S. Broadway
Tarrytown, NY 10591
Phone: (914)524-7600
Fax: (914)524-7650

Publications: Media Market Guide (18549)

SRDS
1700 E. Higgins Rd., 5th Fl.
Des Plaines, IL 60018-5605
Phone: (847)375-5000
Fax: (847)375-5001
Free: 800-851-7737

Publications: Consumer Magazine Advertising Source (8754)

SRI Newspapers, Inc.
187 Main St.
PO Box 232
Wakefield, RI 02880
Phone: (401)789-9744
Fax: (401)294-9736

Publications: The Standard Times (28376)

SSB of the Southern Baptist Convention
1 Lifeway Plaza
Nashville, TN 37234
Phone: (615)251-2000
Fax: (615)251-5091

Publications: Sunday School Leadership (29486)

SSC
PO Box 55549
Seattle, WA 98155-0549
Phone: (206)782-7733
Fax: (206)782-7191
Free: 888-66L-INUX

Publications: Linux Gazette (32981) • Linux Journal (32982)

SSM Health Care System
477 N Lindbergh Blvd.
St. Louis, MO 63141-7813
Phone: (314)994-7800
Fax: (314)994-7900
Free: (314)994-7800

Publications: Issues (17448)

ST Communicator
Box 111000
Aurora, CO 80011
Phone: (303)574-0907
Fax: (303)547-9442

Publications: Star Trek Communicator (4149)

ST Media Group International
407 Gilbert Ave.
Cincinnati, OH 45202
Phone: (513)421-2050
Fax: (513)421-5144
Free: 800-925-1110

Publications: The Big Picture (24779) • Screen Printing (24815)

ST Media Group International, Inc.
407 Gilbert Ave.
Cincinnati, OH 45202
Phone: (513)421-2050
Fax: (513)421-5144
Free: 800-925-1110

Publications: Signs of the Times (24817) • Signs of the Times & Screen Printing en Espanol (24818) • Visual Merchandising and Store Design (24827)

STA Communications Inc.
955 St. Jean Blvd., Ste. 306
Pointe-Claire, QC, Canada H9R 5K3
Phone: (514)695-7623
Fax: (514)695-8554

Publications: The Canadian Journal of CME (Continuing Medical Education) (37272) • The Canadian Journal of Diagnosis (37273) • Le Clinicien (37274) • Perspectives in Cardiology (37276)

Staab Typographic
Box A
408 Main St.
Emlenton, PA 16373
Phone: (724)867-2435
Fax: (724)867-5933

Publications: The Progress News (26872)

Staffer Communications
200 E 5th Ave.
Box 988
Arkansas City, KS 67005-2606
Fax: (316)442-7483

Publications: Traveler (11341)

The Stafford Courier
114 E Bdwy
PO Box 276
Stafford, KS 67578
Phone: (316)234-5241

Publications: The Stafford Courier (11808)

Stagewrite Publishing Inc.
6225 Harrison Dr., Ste. 4
Las Vegas, NV 89120
Phone: (702)798-0099
Fax: (702)798-0220

Publications: Juggle (18368) • Magic (18377)

Stagnito Communications
210 S 5th St.
St. Charles, IL 60174
Phone: (630)377-0100
Fax: (630)377-1678
Free: 800-346-6229

Publications: Food & Drug Packaging (9568)

Stagnito Communications Inc.
155 Pfingsten Rd., Ste. 205
Deerfield, IL 60015-4961
Phone: (847)205-5660
Fax: (847)205-5680

Publications: Candy Industry (8722) • Industria Alimenticia (8725) • Refrigerated and Frozen Foods (8727) • Snack Food and Wholesale Bakery (8728)

Stained Glass Association of America
10009 E. 62nd St.
Raytown, MO 64133
Phone: (816)737-2090
Fax: (816)737-2801
Free: 800-438-9581

Publications: Stained Glass Magazine (17370)

Stamats Communications, Inc.
615 5th St. SE
PO Box 1888
Cedar Rapids, IA 52401

Publications: Buildings (10669)

Stamford American
125 W McHarg St., Ste. A
Stamford, TX 79553-4603
Phone: (915)773-3621
Fax: (915)773-3622

Publications: Stamford American (31128)

Stan Hubsher, Inc.
8211 Horseshoe Bay Rd.
Boynton Beach, FL 33437
Phone: (561)733-8799

Publications: Eastern Aftermarket Journal (5949)

The Standard
14 Hillside Dr. S.
Elliot Lake, ON, Canada P5A 1M6
Phone: (705)848-7195
Fax: (705)848-0249
Free: 800-463-6408

Publications: The Marketplace (35801)

Standard Corp.
2072 Layton Hills Mall
Layton, UT 84041-2106
Phone: (801)776-4951
Fax: (801)773-7284

Publications: Lakeside Review (31343)

The Standard Democrat
205 S New Madrid St.
Sikeston, MO 63801
Phone: (314)471-1137
Fax: (314)471-6277

Publications: The Standard Democrat (17581)

Standard-Examiner
332 Standard Way
Ogden, UT 84404
Phone: (801)625-4340
Fax: (801)625-4508

Publications: Hilltop Times (31377)

Standard-Freeholder
44 Pitt St.
Cornwall, ON, Canada K6J 3P3
Phone: (613)933-3160
Fax: (613)933-7521
Free: 800-267-9832

Publications: Standard-Freeholder (35755)

Standard-Herald, Inc.
PO Box 76
Alma, MO 64001
Phone: (660)674-2250
Fax: (660)674-2250

Publications: The Santa Fe Times (16890)

Standard Herald Inc.
132 W Pine St.
PO Box 7
Warrensburg, MO 64093
Phone: (816)747-3135
Fax: (816)747-7800

Publications: Warrensburg Gazette (17670)

Standard Journal Newspapers
44 N Bridge St.
PO Box 568
St. Anthony, ID 83445-0568
Phone: (208)624-4455
Fax: (208)356-8312

Publications: Fremont County Herald-Chronicle (7971)

Standard News
PO Box 79
Mountain View, MO 65548-0052
Phone: (417)934-2025
Fax: (417)934-6481

Publications: Standard News (17303)

Standard Newspapers
615 S. Halsted
Chicago Heights, IL 60411
Phone: (708)755-5021
Fax: (708)755-5020

Publications: Chicago Standard News (8666) • South Suburban Standard (8669)

Standard & Poor's
1177 Ave. of the Americas, 18th Fl.
New York, NY 10036
Phone: (646)471-8960
Fax: (646)471-2609

Publications: Bond Guide (21333) • CreditWeek (21516) • Earnings Guide (21575) • The Review of Securities & Commodities Regulation (22662) • S & P's Insurance Digest/Life Insurance Edition (22699) • S & P's Insurance Digest/Property-Casualty & Reinsurance Edition (22700) • Standard & Poor's A.S.E. Stock Reports (22784) • Standard & Poor's Corporation Records, Current News Edition (22785) • Standard & Poor's Dividend Record (22786) • Standard & Poor's Nasdaq and Regional Exchange Stock Reports (22787) • Standard & Poor's N.Y.S.E. Stock Reports (22788) • Stock Guide (22793) • Trendline Current Market Perspectives (22861) • Trendline Daily Action Stock Charts (22862)

Standard Press
PO Box 267
Westhope, ND 58793
Phone: (701)245-6461
Fax: (701)245-6461

Publications: Standard (24558)

Standard Publishing
8121 Hamilton Ave.
Cincinnati, OH 45231-2323
Phone: (513)931-4050
Fax: (513)931-0950
Free: 800-543-1301

Publications: Christian Standard (24782) • The Lookout (24809) • Seek (24816) • Weekly Bible Reader (24828)

Standard Publishing Corp.
155 Federal St., 13th Fl.
Boston, MA 02110
Phone: (617)457-0600
Fax: (617)482-7820
Free: 800-682-5759

Publications: The Standard (13963)

Standard-Radio Post
PO Box 1639
Fredericksburg, TX 78624
Phone: (830)997-2155
Fax: (830)990-0036

Publications: Standard-Radio Post (30365)

Standard-Times Publishing Co.
25 Elm St.
New Bedford, MA 02740
Phone: (508)997-7411

Publications: The Standard-Times (14377)

Stanford Alumni Association
326 Galvez St.
Stanford, CA 94305-6105
Phone: (650)723-6105

Publications: Stanford Magazine (3803)

The Stanford Daily Publishing Corp.
Storke Publication Bldg., Ste. 101
Stanford, CA 94305-2240

Publications: The Stanford Daily (3799)

Stanford French & Italian Studies
Dept. of French and Italian
PO Box 876
Saratoga, CA 95071
Phone: (408)741-1522

Publications: Stanford French & Italian Studies (3746)

Stanford Graduate School of Business
News & Publications Office
Stanford, CA 94305-5015
Phone: (650)723-3157
Fax: (650)725-6750

Publications: Stanford Business (3798)

Stanford Law School
Stanford University
Crown Quadrangle
559 Nathan Abbott Way
Stanford, CA 94305-8610
Phone: (650)725-9301
Fax: (650)725-9786

Publications: Stanford Law Review (3801) • Stanford Lawyer (3802)

Stanford Lipsey Publishers
1 News Plz.
Buffalo, NY 14203-2994
Phone: (716)849-3434
Fax: (716)849-3409
Free: 800-777-8680

Publications: The Buffalo News (20368)

The Stanstead Journal
515 A Dufferin St.
PO Box 30
Stanstead, QC, Canada J0B 3E0
Phone: (819)876-7514
Fax: (819)876-7515
Free: 800-567-1259

Publications: The Stanstead Journal (37408)

Stanton Printing Co.
907 Ivy St.
PO Box 719
Stanton, NE 68779
Phone: (402)439-2173
Fax: (402)439-2273

Publications: The Register (18284)

Stanwood Camano News and Advertiser
PO Box 999
Stanwood, WA 98292
Phone: (360)629-2155
Fax: (360)629-4211

Publications: Stanwood/Camano News (33140)

Staplcotn
PO Box 547
Greenwood, MS 38935-0547
Phone: (662)254-6344
Fax: (662)453-6274

Publications: Staplreview (16645)

                       Numbers cited after listings are entry numbers rather than page numbers.

Staples World
224 4th St. NE
PO Box 100
Staples, MN 56479
Phone: (218)894-1112
Fax: (218)894-3570
Free: 888-894-1112

Publications: Staples World (16460)

The Star
PO Box 1800
Cardston, AB, Canada T0K 0K0
Phone: (403)653-4664
Fax: (403)653-4667

Publications: The Star (34680)

The Star
1235 Pierce St.
Lakewood, CO 80214
Phone: (303)235-0116
Fax: (303)237-6080
Free: 800-929-0892

Publications: The Star (4536)

The Star
Box 308
Port St. Joe, FL 32457
Phone: (850)227-1278
Fax: (850)227-7212

Publications: The Star (6601)

Star
102 E. 4th St.
PO Box 25
Ocilla, GA 31774
Phone: (229)468-5433
Fax: (229)468-5045

Publications: Star (7476)

Star
PO Box 7
Gilman, IL 60938
Phone: (815)265-7332
Fax: (815)265-7880

Publications: Star (8921)

Star
14 Mulberry St.
Brookville, OH 45309
Phone: (937)833-2545

Publications: Star (24712)

The Star
815 Taylor Creek Dr.
Orleans, ON, Canada K1C 1T1
Phone: (613)830-7827
Fax: (613)830-1116

Publications: The Star (36178)

The Star
106 E Buena Vista Ave.
North Augusta, SC 29841-3821
Phone: (803)279-2793
Fax: (803)278-4070

Publications: The Star (28719)

Star Banner
2121 SW 19th Ave.
PO Box 490
Ocala, FL 34478
Phone: (352)867-4010
Fax: (352)867-4018
Free: 800-541-2171

Publications: Ocala Star-Banner (6472)

The Star Co.
PO Box 8
Allison, IA 50602
Phone: (319)267-2731
Fax: (319)267-2731

Publications: Butler County Tribune Journal (10584) • Clarksville Star (10705)

Star-Courier
PO Box 1158
Northern Cambria, PA 15714-3158
Phone: (814)674-3666
Fax: (814)674-3628

Publications: Star Courier (27345)

Star-Gazette
308 Elm St.
Box 449
Moose Lake, MN 55767
Phone: (218)485-4406
Fax: (218)485-0237
Free: 800-247-0882

Publications: Star-Gazette (16194)

Star-Gazette
PO Box 285
Elmira, NY 14902
Phone: (607)734-5151
Fax: (607)734-4408
Free: 800-836-8970

Publications: Star-Gazette (20573)

The Star Group
PO Drawer 909
Burleson, TX 76097-0909
Phone: (817)295-0486
Fax: (817)295-5278

Publications: Burleson Star (29988) • Joshua Tribune (30629) • Star Review (29990)

Star-Herald
1405 Broadway
PO Box 1709
Scottsbluff, NE 69363-1709
Phone: (308)632-9000
Fax: (308)635-9001
Free: 800-846-6102

Publications: Star-Herald (18265)

Star-Journal
PO Box 145
Ainsworth, NE 69210
Phone: (402)387-2844
Fax: (402)387-1234

Publications: Star-Journal (17923)

Star-Mail
PO Box 487
Madison, NE 68748-0487
Phone: (402)454-3818
Fax: (402)454-3520

Publications: Star-Mail (18152)

Star News
321 E St.
Chula Vista, CA 91910-2012
Phone: (619)427-3000
Fax: (619)426-6346

Publications: Star-News (1715)

Star Newspapers
204 E Chippewa St.
PO Box 159
Dwight, IL 60420-0159
Phone: (815)584-3007
Fax: (815)584-1841

Publications: Dwight Star & Herald (8801) • Gardner Chronicle (8913) • Herscher Press (8985) • Reddick-Essex Courier/Herscher Press (9491)

Star Newspapers
6901 W. 159th St.
Tinley Park, IL 60477
Phone: (708)802-8800
Fax: (708)802-8899

Publications: Aslip/Crestwood/Blue Island Star (8087) • Burnham/Calumet City Star (8107) • Chicago Heights Star (9684) • Country Club Hills/Hazel Crest Star (8688) • Crete/University Park Star (9696) • Frankfort/Mokena Star (9201) • Harvey/Markham Star (8976) • Homer Township Star (9002) • Homewood/Flossmoor Star (9003) • Lansing/Lynwood Star (9067) • Matteson/Richton Star (9158) • Oak Forest/Midlothian Star (9371) • Oak Lawn Star (9372) • Orland Park Star (9389) • Palos Area Star (9687) • Park Forest Star (9402) • South Holland/Dolton Star (9617) • Tinley Park Star (9689) • Worth/Chicago Ridge Star (9690)

Star Printing Co.
811 Main St.
PO Box 47
Delta, PA 17314
Phone: (717)456-5692
Fax: (717)456-5692

Publications: Star (26822)

Star Printing & Publishing
2520 Dakota Ave.
PO Box 157
South Sioux City, NE 68776
Phone: (402)494-4264
Fax: (402)494-2414

Publications: South Sioux City Star (18280)

Star Printing & Supply Co.
818 Main St.
PO Box 1216
Miles City, MT 59301
Phone: (406)232-0450
Fax: (406)232-6687
Free: 800-323-6565

Publications: Miles City Star (17861)

Star Publications
PO Box 620
Gaylord, MI 49734
Phone: (517)732-5125
Fax: (517)732-9323
Free: 800-782-7237

Publications: Alpena Star (15066) • Charlevoix Co. Star (15067) • Northern Star (15070) • Petoskey Star Advertiser (15071) • Presque Isle Star (15072) • Star Advertiser (15073) • Star Buyer's Guide (15074) • Straits Area Star (15075)

Star Publishing
PO Box 580
Green River, WY 82935
Phone: (307)875-3103
Fax: (307)875-8778

Publications: Green River Star (34532)

Star Publishing Co.
4850 S. Park Ave.
Tucson, AZ 85726-6807
Phone: (520)573-4400

Publications: The Arizona Daily Star (929)

Star Publishing Co., Inc.
PO Box 648
Hope, AR 71802
Phone: (501)777-8841
Fax: (501)777-3311
Free: 888-840-8842

Publications: Hope Star (1178)

Star Publishing, Inc.
PO Box 150
Grand Coulee, WA 99133-0150
Phone: (509)633-1350
Fax: (509)633-3828
Free: 888-633-1350

Publications: The Star (32779) • Star Buyer's Guide (32780)

Star Tech Journal, Inc.
PO Box 35
Medford, NJ 08055
Phone: (609)654-5544
Fax: (609)654-1441

Publications: STAR TECH Journal (19233)

Star & Times
Box 670
Swan River, MB, Canada R0L 1Z0
Phone: (204)734-3858
Fax: (204)734-4935

Publications: Star & Times (35299)

Star-Times Publishing Co., Inc.
108 W Main St.
PO Box 180
Staunton, IL 62088
Phone: (618)635-2000
Fax: (618)635-5281

Publications: Staunton Star-Times (9661)

Star Tribune
425 Portland Ave.
Minneapolis, MN 55488
Phone: (612)673-4000
Fax: (612)673-7138

Publications: Star Tribune (16134)

Star Valley Independent
360 Washington
PO Box 129
Afton, WY 83110
Phone: (307)885-5727
Fax: (307)886-5742

Publications: Star Valley Independent (34474)

Star Watch
132 W Main St.
PO Box 11707
Rock Hill, SC 29730
Phone: (803)329-4000
Fax: (803)329-4028

Publications: Star Watch (28745)

Star and Wave
600 Park Blvd., Ste. 5
Cape May, NJ 08204-1265
Phone: (609)884-3465
Fax: (609)884-2893

Publications: Star and Wave (18719)

Starbucks Coffee Company
1271 Avenue of the Americas, Ste. 2872B
New York, NY 10020

Publications: Joe Magazine (21969)

StarDate & Universo Productions
2609 University Ave. 3-118
University of Texas
McDonald Observatory
Austin, TX 78712
Phone: (512)471-5285
Fax: (512)471-5060
Free: 800-782-7328

Publications: StarDate (29809)

Starlog Group Inc.
475 Park Ave. S., 8th Fl.
New York, NY 10016
Phone: (212)689-2830
Fax: (212)889-7933

Publications: Comics Scene 2000 (21453) • Starlog (22791)

Stat Publishing
PMB 803, 250 H St.
Blaine, WA 98230

Publications: Grey Book (32688)

Statabase, Inc.
15850 Dallas Pky.
Dallas, TX 75248
Phone: (972)991-6657
Fax: (972)991-8930

Publications: Beckett Sports Collectibles and Autographs (30130)

The State Bar of California
180 Howard St.
San Francisco, CA 94105
Phone: (415)538-2000

Publications: California Bar Journal (3335)

State Bar of Georgia
104 Marietta St., Ste. 100
50 Hurt Plaza
Atlanta, GA 30303
Phone: (404)527-8736

Publications: Georgia Bar Journal (7010)

State Bar of Michigan
306 Townsend St.
Lansing, MI 48933
Phone: (517)372-9030
Fax: (517)482-6248

Publications: Michigan Bar Journal (15281)

State Bar of Nevada
600 E Charleston Blvd.
Las Vegas, NV 89104
Phone: (702)382-2200
Fax: (702)385-2878
Free: 800-254-2797

Publications: Nevada Lawyer (18379)

State Bar of Texas
1414 Colorado
Austin, TX 78701
Phone: (512)463-1463
Fax: (512)463-3802
Free: 800-204-2222

Publications: Texas Bar Journal (29812)

State Bar of Wisconsin
5302 Eastpark Blvd.
PO Box 7158
Madison, WI 53707-7158
Phone: (608)257-3838
Fax: (608)257-5502
Free: 800-444-9404

Publications: Wisconsin Lawyer (33985)

State Convention of Baptists in Ohio
1680 E. Broad St.
Columbus, OH 43203-2095
Phone: (614)258-8491
Fax: (614)827-1860

Publications: Ohio Baptist Messenger (25039)

State Gazette
PO Box 808
Hwy. 51 By-Pass
Dyersburg, TN 38025
Phone: (901)285-4091
Fax: (901)285-9747

Publications: State Gazette (29175)

State Historical Society of Iowa
402 Iowa Ave.
Iowa City, IA 52240
Phone: (319)335-3916
Fax: (319)335-3935

Publications: Annals of Iowa (10968) • Iowa Heritage Illustrated (10975)

State Historical Society of Missouri
1020 Lowry St.
Columbia, MO 65201-7298
Phone: (573)882-7083
Fax: (573)884-4950

Publications: Missouri Historical Review (16999)

State Historical Society of North Dakota
North Dakota Heritage Ctr.
612 E. Boulevard Ave.
Bismarck, ND 58505
Phone: (701)328-2666
Fax: (701)328-3710

Publications: North Dakota History (24354)

The State Hornet
California State University, Sacramento
6000 J St., University Union
Sacramento, CA 95819-6102
Fax: (916)278-5578

Publications: The State Hornet (3020)

State Journal Register
1 Copley Plz.
PO Box 219
Springfield, IL 62701-1927
Phone: (217)788-1300
Fax: (217)788-1372
Free: 800-397-8757

Publications: State Journal-Register (9642)

State Line Tribune
Box 255
Farwell, TX 79325
Phone: (806)481-3681

Publications: State Line Tribune (30315)

State News, Inc.
343 Student Service Bldg.
East Lansing, MI 48824
Phone: (517)355-3447
Fax: (517)353-2599

Publications: The State News (14993)

The State Port Pilot
114 E. Moore St.
PO Box 10548
Southport, NC 28461
Phone: (919)457-4568
Fax: (919)457-9427

Publications: The State Port Pilot (24239)

State Prison of Southern Michigan
4000 Cooper St.
Jackson, MI 49201
Phone: (517)780-6000
Fax: (517)780-6021

Publications: The Spectator (15224)

State Service Systems, Inc.
10405-B E. 55th Pl.
Tulsa, OK 74146
Phone: (918)627-8000
Fax: (918)627-8660

Publications: State of the Art (26133)

State University College
Sub. 417
New Paltz, NY 12561
Fax: (914)259-3031

Publications: The Oracle (21114)

State University College at Buffalo
109 Cassety Hall
1300 Elmwood Ave.
Buffalo, NY 14222
Phone: (716)878-4000
Fax: (716)878-4539

Publications: Record (20386)

State University of New York
PO Box 7023
Albany, NY 12225
Phone: (518)473-9739
Fax: (518)486-6609

Publications: Legislative Gazette (19993)

State University of New York at Buffalo
SUNY at Buffalo
341 Student Union
Amherst, NY 14260
Phone: (716)645-6131
Fax: (716)646-2674

Publications: Generation (20031)

State University of New York at Buffalo-Amherst Campus
605 John Lord O'Brian Hall
Buffalo, NY 14260
Phone: (716)645-2000

Publications: Buffalo Law Review (20367)

State University of New York at Buffalo - School of Law
605 John Lord O'Brian Hall
Buffalo, NY 14260
Phone: (716)645-2000

Publications: Child Study Journal (20374)

State University of New York at Cobleskill
107 Knapp Hall
Cobleskill, NY 12043
Phone: (518)255-5841

Publications: The Courier (20477)

State University of New York College at Brockport
350 New Campus Dr.
Brockport, NY 14420-2914
Fax: (716)395-2723

Publications: Kaleidoscope (20245)

State University of New York College at Cortland
111 Corey Union
Cortland, NY 13045
Phone: (607)753-2526
Fax: (607)753-2807

Publications: The Dragon Chronicle (20513)

State University of New York College at Oneonta
Oneonta, NY 13820
Phone: (607)436-3500
Fax: (607)436-2415

Publications: State Times (23052)

State University of New York at Farmingdale
Knapp Hall 15
Farmingdale, NY 11735
Phone: (631)420-2047

Publications: Aitia/Humanities Magazine (20593)

State University of New York at Oswego
15B Hewitt Union
Oswego, NY 13126-3500
Phone: (315)341-2272
Fax: (315)341-3542

Publications: The Oswegonian (23061)

State University of New York at Potsdam Student Government Association
119 Barrington Union
Potsdam, NY 13676
Phone: (315)267-3287
Fax: (315)267-2798

Publications: The Racquette (23140)

State University of New York at Stony Brook
Stony Brook, NY 11794-3358
Phone: (631)632-7444
Fax: (631)632-7421

Publications: Forum Italicum (23369)

State University of New York at Stony Brook
Nicholls Rd., Student Union Rm. 258
Stony Brook, NY 11794-0001
Fax: (516)632-9128

Publications: Statesman (23376)

State University of West Georgia
Carrollton, GA 30118-2200
Phone: (770)836-6512
Fax: (770)830-2334

Publications: Christianity and Literature (7156)

Staten Island Register
2100 Clove Rd.
Staten Island, NY 10305
Phone: (718)447-4700
Fax: (718)816-7719

Publications: Staten Island Pennysaver (23362) • Staten Island Register (23363)

Statesboro Publishing Company Inc.
1 Herald Sq.
PO Box 888
Statesboro, GA 30458
Phone: (912)764-9031
Fax: (912)489-8181
Free: 888-764-9031

Publications: Statesboro Herald (7564)

Statesman-Examiner & The Sun
220 S Main
PO Box 271
Colville, WA 99114
Phone: (509)684-4567
Fax: (509)684-3849
Free: 800-488-5676

Publications: Statesman-Examiner & The Sun (32726)

Statesman Journal
280, Church St. NE
PO Box 13009
Salem, OR 97301
Phone: (503)399-6611
Fax: (503)399-6808
Free: 800-556-3975

Publications: Statesman Journal (26573)

Statistics Canada
18-K R.H. Coats Bldg.
Ottawa, ON, Canada K1A 0T6
Phone: (613)951-3634
Fax: (613)951-5403

Publications: Canadian Economic Observer (36192)

Statistics Canada
R.H. Coats Building, Lobby
Holland Ave.
Tunney's Pasture
Ottawa, ON, Canada K1A 0T6

Publications: Canadian Social Trends (36228)

Stauffer Communications
650 6th St. SW
PO Box 1440
Winter Haven, FL 33880-3325

Publications: Bartow Shopper (5916) • North Lakeland Shopper (6870) • South Lakeland Shopper (6872) • Winter Haven News Chief (6873)

Stauffer Communications, Inc.
705 2nd
Dodge City, KS 67801
Fax: (316)225-4154
Free: 800-279-8795

Publications: Dodge City Daily Globe (11414)

Stauffer Communications, Inc.
PO Box 1688
Shawnee, OK 74801
Phone: (405)273-4200
Fax: (405)273-4207

Publications: The Shawnee News-Star (26065)

Stauffer Media, Inc.
PO Box 200
Danville, PA 17821
Phone: (717)275-3235
Fax: (717)275-7624

Publications: The Danville News (26817)

Stavrolex Publications
7002 W Butler Pke.
Ambler, PA 19002
Phone: (215)643-6385

Publications: All Crosswords Special (26644) • Superior Fill-Ins (26655)

Stayner Sun
250 Main St. E
PO Box 80
Stayner, ON, Canada L0M 1S0
Phone: (705)428-2638
Fax: (705)428-6909

Publications: Stayner Sun (36401)

The Stayton Mail
400 N. 3rd
PO Box 400
Stayton, OR 97383
Phone: (503)769-6338
Fax: (503)769-6207
Free: 800-452-2511

Publications: Stayton Mail (26589)

Stealth Technologies, Inc.
539 First St.
Brooklyn, NY 11215-2305
Phone: (212)674-0952
Fax: (212)598-1856

Publications: Deolog (20312) • Satya (20344)

Steam Automobile Club of America, Inc.
1680 Dartmouth Ln.
Deerfield, IL 60015
Phone: (847)945-3911

Publications: The Steam Automobile Bulletin (9396)

Steamboat Pilot
1041 Lincoln Ave.
PO Box 4488
Steamboat Springs, CO 80477
Phone: (970)879-1502
Fax: (970)879-2888

Publications: Steamboat Pilot (4631) • The Steamboat Whistle (4633)

Steamshovel Press
PO Box 210553
St. Louis, MO 63121
Phone: (314)382-5160

Publications: Steamshovel Press (17516)

Stearn-Morrison
PO Box 310
Albany, MN 56307
Phone: (320)845-2700
Fax: (320)845-4805

Publications: Stearns-Morrison Enterprise (15704)

Steel City Media
650 Smithfield St., Ste. 2200
Pittsburgh, PA 15222
Phone: (412)316-3342
Fax: (412)316-3388

Publications: Pittsburgh City Paper (27832)

Steele County Press, Inc.
215 4th St. W
PO Box 475
Finley, ND 58230
Phone: (701)524-1640

Publications: Steele County Press (24437)

Steele Ozone-Press, Inc.
PO Box 350
Steele, ND 58482-0350
Phone: (701)475-2513

Publications: Ozone-Press (24538)

Steelville Star/Crawford Mirror
106 S 1st St.
PO Box BG
Steelville, MO 65565
Phone: (573)775-5454
Fax: (573)775-2668

Publications: Steelville Star/Crawford Mirror (17030)

The Step Saver, Inc.
213 Spring St.
Southington, CT 06489
Phone: (860)628-9645
Fax: (860)621-1841

Publications: The Observer (5134) • The Step Saver (5135)

Step by Step Graphics
6000 N Forest Park
Peoria, IL 61614
Phone: (309)688-2300
Fax: (309)688-8515
Free: 800-255-8800

Publications: Step-By-Step Graphics (9427)

Stephen F. Austin State University
PO Box 13007, SFA Sta.
Nacogdoches, TX 75962
Phone: (936)468-2059
Fax: (936)468-2190

Publications: RE:AL (30852)

Stephen F. Austin State University
13049 SFA Sta.
Nacogdoches, TX 75962
Phone: (936)468-4703
Fax: (936)468-1016

Publications: The Pine Log (30851)

Stephens College
PO Box 2014
Columbia, MO 65215
Phone: (573)876-7254
Fax: (573)876-2318

Publications: Stephens Life (17010)

Stephens Media Group
500 Sunset Ave.
PO Box 340
Asheboro, NC 27204-0340
Phone: (336)625-2101
Fax: (336)626-6120

Publications: The Courier-Tribune (23621)

Stephenville Empire-Tribune
590 South Loop
PO Box 958
Stephenville, TX 76401-4224
Phone: (254)965-3124
Fax: (254)965-4269

Publications: Stephenville Empire-Tribune (31130)

Stepping Stone Publications
654 Highland Ave., Ste. 27
Fort Thomas, KY 41075-1762
Phone: (606)283-0404
Fax: (606)283-2536

Publications: Campbell County Recorder (12063)

Stereo & Video Guide
238 Davenport Rd., No. 252
Toronto, ON, Canada M5R 1J6

Publications: Stereo Video Guide (36748)

Sterling Ag, LLC
PO Box 1626
Pendleton, OR 97801-0189
Phone: (541)276-6202

Publications: Agri-Times Northwest (26457)

Sterling Bulletin
PO Box 97
Sterling, KS 67579
Phone: (620)278-2114
Fax: (620)278-2330
Publications: Sterling Bulletin (11809)

Sterling City News & Record
305 Elm
PO Box 608
Sterling City, TX 76951
Phone: (915)378-3251
Fax: (915)378-3251
Publications: Sterling City News-Record (31134)

Sterling/Macfadden Partnership
333 Seventh Ave., Fl. 11
New York, NY 10001-5004
Phone: (212)780-3500
Fax: (212)780-3571
Publications: Daytime TV (21539) • Metal Edge (TV Picture Life) (22320) • Modern Romances Presents True Life Stories (22351) • Modern Screen's Country Music (22352) • Right On! (22667) • True Confessions (22867) • True Experience (22868) • True Love (22869) • True Romance (22870) • True Story (22871)

Sterling Newspapers
15 William St. N.
Lindsay, ON, Canada K9V 3Z8
Phone: (705)314-2114
Fax: (705)324-0174
Publications: Lindsay Performer (35972)

Sterling Newspapers Ltd.
901 100 Ave.
Dawson Creek, BC, Canada V1G 1W2
Phone: (250)782-4888
Fax: (250)782-6770
Publications: Peace River Block News (34941)

Sterling Newspapers Ltd.
342 2nd Ave.
Bag 5000
Fernie, BC, Canada V0B 1M0
Phone: (250)423-4666
Fax: (250)423-3110
Publications: The Free Press (34953)

Sterling Publishing Company Ltd.
801 2nd Ave. W.
Prince Rupert, BC, Canada V8J 1A6
Phone: (250)624-6781
Fax: (250)624-2851
Publications: The Daily News (35064)

Sterling Rose Press, Inc.
PO Box 14341
Berkeley, CA
Publications: American Spirit Newspaper (1490)

Stern Stewart Management Services, Inc.
135 Lexington Ave.
New York, NY 10022
Phone: (212)261-0600
Fax: (212)581-6420
Publications: Journal of Applied Corporate Finance (21989)

Stettler Independent Management Ltd.
Box 310
Stettler, AB, Canada T0C 2L0
Phone: (403)742-2395
Fax: (403)742-8050
Publications: The Bashaw Star (34615) • Castor Advance (34682) • The Stettler Independent (34855)

Steuben Courier-Advocate
10 W Stueben St.
Bath, NY 14810
Phone: (607)776-2121
Fax: (607)776-3967
Free: 800-776-0484
Publications: Steuben Courier-Advocate (20125)

Steve Postal Productions
108 Carraway St.
Palatka, FL 32177-1150
Phone: (386)325-9356
Publications: Cinevue Worldwide Talent Directory and Festival Program Book (6536)

Steve Simmons Photography
PO Box 2328
Corrales, NM 87048-2328
Publications: View Camera (19839)

Stevens Alumni Association
Castle Point
Hoboken, NJ 07030
Phone: (201)216-5161
Fax: (201)216-5374
Publications: The Stevens Indicator (19107)

Stevens Institute of Technology
Castle Point on Hudson
Hoboken, NJ 07030
Phone: (201)216-3404
Fax: (201)216-3479
Publications: The Stute (19111)

Stevens Publishing Corp.
5151 Belt Line Road, 10th Fl.
Dallas, TX 75254
Phone: (972)687-6700
Fax: (972)687-6799
Publications: Home Health Products (30161) • Occupational Health & Safety (30174)

Stevens Publishing Inc.
1049 Main St.
PO Box 33
Coventry, RI 02816
Phone: (401)821-2216
Fax: (401)821-0397
Publications: The Reminder (28330)

Stillwater Publishing Co.
PO Box 2288
Stillwater, OK 74076
Phone: (405)372-5000
Fax: (405)372-3112
Publications: The News Press (26079)

Stipes Publishing Co.
202-204 W University
Champaign, IL 61820
Phone: (217)356-8391
Fax: (217)356-5753
Publications: Illinois Classical Studies (9708)

Stitches Publishing Inc.
16787 Warden Ave., RR 3
Newmarket, ON, Canada L3Y 4W1
Phone: (905)853-1884
Fax: (905)853-6565
Free: 800-668-7418
Publications: Stitches (36108)

The Stittsville News
Box 610
Stittsville, ON, Canada K2S 1A7
Phone: (613)836-1357
Fax: (613)836-5621
Publications: The Stittsville News (36404)

STN Media Co., Inc.
PO Box 789
Redondo Beach, CA 90277
Phone: (310)792-2226
Fax: (310)792-2231
Publications: School Transportation News (2911)

Stockbridge Town Crier
PO Box 548
Stockbridge, MI 49285-0548
Phone: (517)851-7833
Fax: (517)851-4641
Publications: Stockbridge Town Crier (15579)

Stone County Enterprise
143 1st St.
Wiggins, MS 39577
Phone: (601)928-4802
Fax: (601)928-2191
Publications: Stone County Enterprise (16877)

Stone County Publishing Co.
PO Box 509
Mountain View, AR 72560-0509
Phone: (870)269-3841
Fax: (870)269-2171
Publications: Stone County Leader (1291)

Stone County Publishing Co., Inc.
PO Box 237
Crane, MO 65633-0401
Phone: (417)723-5248
Fax: (417)723-8490
Publications: The Crane Chronicle/Stone County Republican (17027)

Stone & Cox Ltd.
111 Peter St., Ste. 500
Toronto, ON, Canada M5V 2H1
Phone: (416)599-0772
Fax: (416)599-0867
Publications: Canadian Insurance X Canadian Insurance Magazine (36507)

Stone Lantern Publishing Co.
PO Box 324
Watertown, MA 02471
Phone: (617)926-1212
Fax: (617)926-7200
Publications: Bonsai Today (14613)

Stone Publications
PO Box 189
Grenfell, SK, Canada S0G 2B0
Phone: (306)697-2722
Fax: (306)697-2689
Publications: Broadview Express (37453) • Grenfell Sun (37472)

Stonebridge Press
110 Church St.
Whitinsville, MA 01588
Phone: (508)234-2107
Fax: (508)234-7506
Free: 800-367-9898
Publications: Blackstone Valley Tribune (14656)

Stonebridge Press Inc.
25 Elm St.
Southbridge, MA 01550
Phone: (508)764-6102
Fax: (508)764-8015
Free: 800-367-9898
Publications: The New Leader (14548) • The Southbridge Evening News (14547) • The Winchendon Courier (14664)

Stonehill College
320 Washington St. No. 1974
North Easton, MA 02357
Phone: (508)230-7830
Fax: (508)230-8268
Publications: The Summit (14423)

Stoney Creek News
333 Arvin Ave.
Stoney Creek, ON, Canada L8E 2M6
Phone: (905)523-5800
Fax: (905)664-3102
Publications: Stoney Creek News (36406)

Stonington Historical Society
PO Box 103
Stonington, CT 06378
Phone: (860)535-1131
Publications: Historical Footnotes (5165)

Storm Lake Times
PO Box 487
Storm Lake, IA 50588-0487
Phone: (712)732-4991
Fax: (712)732-4331
Publications: Storm Lake Times (11245)

The Story City Herald
423 Broad St.
Story City, IA 50248
Phone: (515)733-4318
Fax: (515)733-4319
Publications: The Story City Herald (11251) • The Story City Reminder (11252)

Stouffville Sun
6306 Main St. W.
PO Box 154
Stouffville, ON, Canada L4A 7Z5
Phone: (905)640-2612
Fax: (905)640-8778
Publications: Stouffville Sun (36407)

2650

Numbers cited after listings are entry numbers rather than page numbers.

The Stowe Reporter
School St.
PO Box 489
Stowe, VT 05672-0489
Phone: (802)253-2101
Fax: (802)253-8332

Publications: The Stowe Reporter (31604)

Straitsland Resorter
3691 Club Rd.
PO Box 579
Indian River, MI 49749
Phone: (616)238-7362
Fax: (616)238-1290

Publications: Straitsland Resorter (15203)

Strand Media Group, Inc.
1357-21st Ave. N, Ste. 102
Myrtle Beach, SC 29577
Phone: (843)626-8911
Fax: (843)626-6452

Publications: Strand Magazine (28703)

Strang Communications
600 Rineheart Rd.
Lake Mary, FL 32746-4968
Phone: (407)333-0600
Fax: (407)333-7100

Publications: Charisma (6274) • Charisma & Christian Life (6275) • Christian Retailing (6276) • Inspirational Giftware (6277) • Ministries Today (6278) • New Man (6279) • SpiritLed Woman (6280) • Vida Cristiana (6281)

Strange Magazine
11772 Parklawn Dr.
Rockville, MD 20852

Publications: Strange Magazine (13698)

Strasburg Weekly News
140 W Main St.
Box 249
Strasburg, PA 17579
Phone: (717)687-7721
Fax: (717)392-1341

Publications: Strasburg Weekly News (28034)

Strategic Account Management Association (SAMA)
150 N. Wacker Dr., Ste. 2222
Chicago, IL 60606
Phone: (312)251-3131
Fax: (312)251-3132

Publications: Velocity (8597)

Stratford Star
PO Box 8
Stratford, TX 79084
Phone: (806)366-5885

Publications: Stratford Star (31135)

Strathroy Age Dispatch Ltd.
8 Front St. E.
Strathroy, ON, Canada N7G 1Y4
Phone: (519)245-2370
Fax: (519)245-1647

Publications: The Age Dispatch (36412)

Strato Publishing Co., Inc.
405 E 56th St., Ste. 4E
New York, NY 10022
Phone: (212)223-2707
Fax: (212)371-1224

Publications: REVISTA AEREA (22665)

Stratton Publishing and Marketing, Inc.
5501 Backlick Rd., Ste. 240
Springfield, VA 22151
Phone: (703)914-9200
Fax: (703)914-6777

Publications: Defense Communities (32831) • OfficePRO (32550)

Straus Newspapers
45 Gilbert St.
Monroe, NY 10950
Phone: (914)782-4000
Fax: (914)782-1711

Publications: The Chronicle (21089) • Monroe Woodbury Photo News (23592) • The Warwick Advertiser (21091)

STRINGS
PO Box 767
San Anselmo, CA 94979
Phone: (415)485-6946
Fax: (415)485-0831
Free: 800-827-6837

Publications: STRINGS (3084)

Stroud American Inc.
PO Box 400
Stroud, OK 74079
Phone: (918)968-2581
Fax: (918)968-3864

Publications: Stroud American (26089)

Struth Publishing Co.
320 Park St E.
Killarney, MB, Canada R0K 1G0
Phone: (204)523-4611
Fax: (204)523-4445

Publications: Guide (35270)

Struve Enterprises Inc.
PO Box 647
Deshler, NE 68340
Phone: (402)365-7575
Fax: (402)265-4439
Free: 800-762-3681

Publications: The Deshler Rustler (17998)

The Stuart Herald
Box 608
Stuart, IA 50250
Phone: (515)523-1010
Fax: (515)523-2825
Free: 800-622-1010

Publications: The 5 x 80 Bulletin (11254) • The Stuart Herald (11255)

The Stuart News
PO Box 9009
Stuart, FL 34995-9009
Phone: (561)287-1550
Fax: (561)221-4250

Publications: The Stuart News (6695)

Studebaker Drivers Club, Inc.
PO Box 1040
Oswego, IL 60543
Phone: (630)554-2889

Publications: The SDC Magazine (1823)

Student Association of Southern College Seventh-day Adventists
Southern College
PO Box 370
Collegedale, TN 37315-0370

Publications: Southern Accent (29131)

Student Conservation Association
PO Box 550
Charlestown, NH 03603
Phone: (603)543-1700
Fax: (603)543-1828

Publications: Earth Work (18464)

Student Cooperative Association, Inc.
319 Pratt Dr.
Indiana, PA 15701
Fax: (724)463-9597

Publications: The Penn (27076)

Student Federation of the University of Ottawa
631 King Edward Ave 2nd. Fl.
Ottawa, ON, Canada K1N 6N5
Phone: (613)562-5260
Fax: (613)562-5259

Publications: The Fulcrum (36245)

Student Media Co.
Southern Methodist University
3140 Dyer St.
314 Hughes-Trigg Center
Dallas, TX 75275-0456
Phone: (214)768-4555
Fax: (214)768-4573

Publications: The Daily Campus (30141)

Student Media Corporation
823 16th St.
Greeley, CO 80631
Phone: (970)392-9270
Fax: (970)392-9025

Publications: The Mirror (4499)

Student Press Law Center
1815 N Fort Myer Dr., Ste. 900
Arlington, VA 22209-1817
Phone: (703)807-1904
Fax: (703)807-2109

Publications: SPLC Report (31832)

Student Publications, Inc.
201 N. Communications Center
Iowa City, IA 52242
Phone: (319)335-6063
Fax: (319)335-6184

Publications: The Daily Iowan (10972)

Student Union
13 Oak Dr.
Hamilton, NY 13346
Phone: (315)228-7744
Fax: (315)228-7745

Publications: The Colgate Maroon-News (20706)

Studia Mystica
Texas A & M University
Dept. of English
6000 J St.
College Station, TX 77843-0001

Publications: Studia Mystica (30052)

Studies in Short Fiction
Newberry College
Newberry, SC 29108
Phone: (803)321-5195
Fax: (803)321-5629

Publications: Studies in Short Fiction (28717)

Studiolot Publishing
5632 Van Nuys Blvd., Ste. 320
Van Nuys, CA 91401-4600
Phone: (818)776-2800
Free: 800-335-4335

Publications: Entertainment Employment Journal (3989)

Stumbo Publishing Company Inc.
347 Allen Dr.
PO Box 127
Ontario, OH 44862
Phone: (419)529-2847
Fax: (419)529-2847

Publications: Tribune-Courier (25451)

Stump Publishing Co.
409 W. Broadway, No. 457
Plainview, MN 55964
Phone: (507)534-3121
Fax: (507)534-3920

Publications: Plainview News (16278)

Style Communications
555 Richmond St. W, Ste. 701
Toronto, ON, Canada M5V 3B1
Phone: (416)203-6737
Fax: (416)203-1057

Publications: Canadian Jeweller (36508) • Style (36751)

Style 1900
333 N Main St.
Lambertville, NJ 08530
Phone: (609)397-4104
Fax: (609)397-9377
Free: 888-847-6464

Publications: Style 1900 (19160)

Style Weekly
1707 Summit Ave. Ste. 201
Richmond, VA 23230
Phone: (804)358-0825
Fax: (804)358-9089

Publications: Style Weekly (32456)

The Stylus
State University of New York College at Brock-
port
B30 Seymour Union
Brockport, NY 14420
Phone: (585)395-5623
Fax: (585)395-2609

Publications: The Stylus (20246)

sub-TERRAIN Magazine
175 E. Broadway, No. 204-A
PO Box 3008
Vancouver, BC, Canada V6B 3X5
Phone: (604)876-8710
Fax: (604)879-2667

Publications: sub-TERRAIN Magazine (35169)

Sublette County Newspapers, Inc.
PO Box 100
Pinedale, WY 82941
Phone: (307)367-2123
Fax: (307)367-6623

Publications: Pinedale Roundup (34568)

Subourbon Press
PO Box 9101
Warwick, RI 02889
Phone: (401)453-6457

Publications: The Hunted News (28450)

Suburban Circle Publications, Inc.
2808 Dewey Ave.
Rochester, NY 14616
Phone: (585)323-1560
Fax: (585)663-0146

Publications: Courier Journal (23219) • Greece
Pennysaver (23227) • Timesaver (23241)

Suburban Gazette
421 Locust St.
Mc Kees Rocks, PA 15136
Phone: (412)331-2645

Publications: Suburban Gazette (27227)

Suburban Journal
5050 Old Collinsville Rd.
Swansea, IL 62226-2009
Phone: (618)277-7000
Fax: (618)277-7018

Publications: Fairview Heights/O'Fallon Journal
(9677)

**Suburban Journals of Greater St. Louis,
LLC**
220 E Main
Warrenton, MO 63383
Phone: (636)456-3481
Fax: (636)456-3020

Publications: Belleville Journal (8059) • Cahokia-
Dupo Journal (17674) • Central West End Journal
(17675) • Chesterfield Journal (17676) • Citizen
Journal (17677) • Collinsville Herald-Journal
(17678) • County Journal (17679) • County Star
Journal West (17680) • Courier Journal (17065) •
East St. Louis Journal (17681) • Edwardsville Jour-
nal (17682) • Granite City Journal (17684) • Jeffer-
son County Journal (17685) • Meramec Journal
(17686) • Mid County Journal (17687) • Monroe
County Clarion Journal (17688) • Neighborhood
Journal (17476) • News Democrat Journal (17689) •
North County Journal East (17690) • North Side
Journal (17691) • Press Journal (17692) • St.
Charles Journal (17693) • St. Peters Journal
(17694) • South City Journal (17695) • South Coun-
ty Journal (17696) • South Side Journal (17697) •
Southwest City Journal (17698) • Southwest County
Journal (17699) • Warrenton Journal (17700) • West
County Journal (17701)

The Suburban News
733 Roosevelt Trl.
Windham, ME 04062
Phone: (207)892-1166
Fax: (207)892-1171

Publications: The Suburban News (13076)

Suburban News
PO Box 822
Pineville, NC 28134
Phone: (704)535-2737

Publications: Suburban News (24116)

Suburban News Publications
5257 Sinclair Rd.
PO Box 29912
Columbus, OH 43229
Phone: (614)785-1212
Fax: (614)785-1881

Publications: Bexley News (24680) • Booster
(25001) • Dublin News (25168) • Gahanna News
(25206) • German Village Gazette (25020) • Grove
City News (25232) • Hilliard Northwest News
(25242) • Northland News (25037) • Northwest Columbus News (25038) • Olentangy Valley News
(25492) • The Times (25066) • Tri-Village News
(25067) • Upper Arlington News (25603) • Westerville News & Public Opinion (25646) • Whitehall
News (25652) • Worthington News (25682)

Suburban Newspapers
1455 W. Main St.
Tipp City, OH 45371
Phone: (937)667-8512
Fax: (937)667-8987

Publications: Huber Heights Courier (25249) • Troy
Advocate (25562) • Vandalia Drummer News
(25611)

Suburban Newspapers of Dayton
1455 W Main St.
Tipp City, OH 45371-2803

Publications: West Milton Record (25563)

Suburban Newspapers, Inc.
7820 Wyatt Dr.
Fort Worth, TX 76108-2595
Phone: (817)246-2473
Fax: (817)246-2474

Publications: Benbrook News (29918) • River Oaks
News (30983) • White Settlement Bomber News
(31290)

Suburban Publications, Inc.
134 N Wayne Ave.
Wayne, PA 19087
Phone: (610)688-3000
Fax: (610)254-8522

Publications: King of Prussia Courier (27125) • The
Suburban (28136) • Suburban Advertiser (27350)

Suburban Publishing Corp.
PO Box 6039
Peabody, MA 01961-6039
Phone: (978)532-5880
Fax: (978)532-4250
Free: 800-221-2078

Publications: Lynnfield-Peabody Edition (14462) •
Peabody-Lynnfield Edition (14464)

Suburban Publishing, Inc.
22 IBM Rd., Ste. 108
Poughkeepsie, NY 12601-5461
Phone: (845)463-0542
Fax: (845)463-1544
Free: 800-274-7844

Publications: Hudson Valley Magazine (23146)

Suburban World, Inc.
992 Great Plain Ave.
PO Box 358
Needham, MA 02492
Phone: (508)653-4460
Fax: (781)444-1795
Free: 800-847-NEWS

Publications: Dover-Sherborn Suburban Press
(14523) • Medfield Suburban Press (14317) • Needham Times (14366)

Success Publishing International
11071 Ventura Blvd.
Studio City, CA 91604-3548
Phone: (818)765-2344
Fax: (818)980-7829

Publications: Money Making Opportunities (3821)

Successful Meetings
770 Broadway
New York, NY 10003
Phone: (646)654-5000

Publications: Successful Meetings (22805)

Sudbury Northern Life
158 Elgin St.
Sudbury, ON, Canada P3E 3N5
Phone: (705)673-5667
Fax: (705)673-4652

Publications: Sudbury Northern Life (36419)

The Sudbury Star
33 McKenzie St.
Sudbury, ON, Canada P3C 4Y1
Phone: (705)674-5271
Fax: (705)674-0624
Free: 800-461-1155

Publications: The Sudbury Star (36420)

Suel Printing Co., Inc.
310 1st St. S.
PO Box 49
Montgomery, MN 56069
Phone: (507)364-8601
Fax: (507)364-8602

Publications: Montgomery Messenger (16183)

Suffolk Life Newspapers
PO Box 167
Riverhead, NY 11901
Phone: (631)369-0800
Fax: (631)369-5190

Publications: Amityville Suffolk Life (20036) • Bay
Shore Suffolk Life (20135) • Bellport/East Patchogue
Suffolk Life (20148) • Brentwood Suffolk Life
(20240) • Centereach/Lake Grove Suffolk Life
(20445) • Central Islip/Hauppauge Suffolk Life
(20448) • Commack/Kings Park Suffolk Life
(20486) • Coram/Middle Island Suffolk Life
(20501) • Deer Park Suffolk Life (23199) • Dix Hills/
Melville Suffolk Life (21042) • East Islip Suffolk Life
(20548) • Hampton East Suffolk Life (20546) •
Hampton West Suffolk Life (23566) • Holbrook/
Bohemia Suffolk Life (21033) • Huntington Station
Suffolk Life (20778) • Huntington Suffolk Life
(20772) • Lindenhurst Suffolk Life (20949) • Mastic/
Shirley Suffolk Life (21030) • Medford/Holtsville Suffolk Life (21034) • Mid-Hampton Suffolk Life
(23200) • Moriches Suffolk Life (21097) • North Fork
Suffolk Life (23201) • Northport Suffolk Life
(23019) • Patchogue Suffolk Life (23077) • Port
Jefferson Suffolk Life (23116) • Riverhead Suffolk
Life (23202) • Rocky Point Suffolk Life (23263) •
Ronkonkoma Suffolk Life (23273) • St. James/Nes-
conset Suffolk Life (23290) • Sayville/Oakdale Suf-
folk Life (23310) • Selden/Farmingville Suffolk Life
(23323) • Smithtown Suffolk Life (23203) • Stony
Brook/Setauket Suffolk Life (23377) • Suffolk County
Life (23205) • West Babylon Suffolk Life (20112) •
West Islip Suffolk Life (23544)

Suffolk News-Herald
PO Box 1220
Suffolk, VA 23434
Phone: (757)539-3437

Publications: Suffolk News-Herald (32566)

The Suffolk Times
PO Box 1500
Mattituck, NY 11952-0901
Phone: (631)298-3200
Fax: (631)298-3287

Publications: The Suffolk Times (21032)

Sufi Psychology Association
Journal Subscription, Printing, and Publication
Dept.
10590 Magnolia Ave., Ste. G
Riverside, CA 92505
Fax: (909)687-4486
Free: 800-830-0320

Publications: Sufism (2948)

Sugar Mountain Press
36 W Main St.
Warner, NH 03278-9202

Publications: Color Wheel (18647)

Sugar Publications
503 Broadway
Fargo, ND 58102
Phone: (701)476-2111
Fax: (701)476-2182

Publications: The Sugarbeet Grower (24414)

Sul Ross State University
Box C-71
Alpine, TX 79832
Phone: (915)837-8179
Fax: (915)837-8381

Publications: Journal of Big Bend Studies (29683)

Sul Ross State University
Student Publications Office
PO Box C-112
Alpine, TX 79832
Phone: (915)837-8061
Fax: (915)837-8664

Publications: The Skyline (29684)

Sullivan County Democrat
5 Lower Main St.
PO Box 308
Callicoon, NY 12723
Phone: (914)887-5200
Fax: (914)887-5386

Publications: Sullivan County Democrat (20415)

Sullivan Independent News
Box 268
Sullivan, MO 63080
Phone: (573)732-3230
Fax: (573)468-4046

Publications: The Sullivan Independent News (17641)

Sulphur Institute
1140 Connecticut Ave., NW, Ste. 612
Washington, DC 20036
Phone: (202)331-9660
Fax: (202)293-2940

Publications: Sulphur in Agriculture (5807)

Summer Communications, Inc.
7626 Densmore Ave.
Van Nuys, CA 91406-2042
Phone: (818)786-4367
Fax: (818)786-9246
Free: 800-224-4367

Publications: Emergency Medical Services (3988)

Summers Road
PO Box 536
Bristol, FL 32321
Phone: (850)643-3333
Fax: (850)643-3334

Publications: The Calhoun-Liberty Journal (5963)

Summerville Journal, Inc.
PO Drawer 715
Summerville, SC 29484
Phone: (843)873-9424
Fax: (843)873-9432

Publications: Journal-Scene (28765)

Summit Herald
80 South St.
New Providence, NJ 07974
Phone: (908)464-1025
Fax: (908)464-9085

Publications: Summit Herald (19349)

Summit Publishing Co.
One IBM Plaza., Ste. 2401
330 N. Wabash Ave.
Chicago, IL 60611
Phone: (312)222-1010
Fax: (312)222-1310

Publications: Packaging World (8524)

Sumner Gazette
106 E 1st St.
Box 208
Sumner, IA 50674
Phone: (563)578-3351
Fax: (563)578-3352

Publications: Sumner Gazette (11258)

Sumner Media Group
215 S Kansas Ave.
PO Box 231
Columbus, KS 66725
Phone: (316)429-2773
Fax: (316)429-3223

Publications: Columbus Daily Advocate (11395) •
The Modern Light (11396)

The Sumner Press, Inc.
216 S Christy
PO Box 126
Sumner, IL 62466
Phone: (618)936-2212
Fax: (618)936-2858

Publications: The Sumner Press (9676)

Sumner Publishing
417 E Hwy. 60
Republic, MO 65738
Phone: (417)732-2525
Fax: (417)732-2980

Publications: Republic Monitor (17371)

Sumter County Record-Journal
210 S. Washington St.
Livingston, AL 35470
Phone: (205)652-6100
Fax: (205)652-4466

Publications: Sumter County Record-Journal (306)

The Sun
136 E. Main
PO Box 68
Sheridan, OR 97378
Phone: (503)843-2312
Fax: (503)843-3830

Publications: The Sun (26582)

The Sun
115-117 S. Water St.
PO Box C
Hummelstown, PA 17036
Phone: (717)566-3251
Fax: (717)566-6196

Publications: The Sun (27066)

The Sun
PO Box 271
Colville, WA 99114
Phone: (509)684-4567
Fax: (509)684-3849
Free: 800-488-5676

Publications: The Sun (32727)

Sun Advocate
645 E. Main St.
Price, UT 84501-2708
Phone: (435)637-0732
Fax: (435)637-2716
Free: 888-637-0732

Publications: Sun Advocate (31393)

The Sun Chronicle
34 S Main St.
Attleboro, MA 02703
Phone: (508)222-7000
Fax: (508)236-0462

Publications: The Sun Chronicle (13825)

The Sun Chronicle
36 Mechanic St.
PO Box 289
Foxboro, MA 02035
Phone: (508)543-4851
Fax: (508)543-4888

Publications: The Foxboro Reporter (14189)

Sun Coast Media
200 E Venice Ave.
Venice, FL 34285
Phone: (941)484-2611
Fax: (941)484-8450

Publications: The Advertiser (6828) • The Venice Gondolier (6831)

Sun Coast Media Group
13644 S Tamiami Tr.
North Port, FL 34287
Phone: (941)426-9544
Fax: (941)423-2318
Free: (866)562-2604

Publications: North Port Sun Herald (6471)

Sun Coast Media Group, Inc.
23170 Harborview Rd.
Port Charlotte, FL 33980

Publications: The Charlotte Sun Herald (6596)

Sun Diamond Growers of California
1050 Diamond St.
Stockton, CA 95205
Phone: (209)467-6000
Fax: (209)467-6714

Publications: Sun Diamond Grower (3809)

Sun-Gazette
252 W. 4th St.
Williamsport, PA 17701
Phone: (717)326-1551
Fax: (717)323-0948

Publications: Williamsport Sun-Gazette (28182)

Sun-Gazette Co.
Box 432
Muncy, PA 17756
Phone: (570)546-8555
Fax: (570)546-8974

Publications: The Luminary (27306)

Sun-Gazette Newspapers
PO Box 266
Hughesville, PA 17737
Phone: (570)584-2134
Fax: (570)584-5399
Free: 877-878-3076

Publications: East Lycoming Shopper and News (27065)

Sun-Journal
PO Box 4400
Lewiston, ME 04243-4400
Phone: (207)784-5611
Fax: (207)777-3436
Free: 800-482-0753

Publications: Lewiston Sun-Journal (12976)

Sun Media Corp.
380 Hunt Club Rd.
PO Box 9729, Stn. T
Ottawa, ON, Canada K1G 5H7
Phone: (613)739-7000
Fax: (613)739-9383

Publications: Ottawa Sun (36268)

Sun Media Corp.
333 King St. E
Toronto, ON, Canada M5A 3X5
Phone: (416)947-2222
Fax: (416)947-2441
Free: 877-624-1463

Publications: The Edmonton Sun (34712) • The Financial Post (36594)

Sun Media Corp.
179 rue St-Georges
Saint-Jerome, QC, Canada J7Z 4Z8
Phone: (450)436-3303
Fax: (450)431-7778

Publications: Le Riverain (37372)

Sun-News
P.O. Box 370
Lowden, IA 52255-0370
Phone: (563)886-2131
Fax: (563)886-6644

Publications: Sun-News (11042)

Sun News
12 N Main
Liberty, MO 64068
Phone: (816)781-1044
Fax: (816)781-1755

Publications: Platte County Sun Gazette (17249)

Sun News
PO Box 1749
Las Cruces, NM 88005
Phone: (505)541-5458
Fax: (505)541-5498

Publications: White Sands Missile Ranger (19974)

Sun News Idaho, Inc.
847 Washington
PO Box 278
Montpelier, ID 83254
Phone: (208)847-0552
Fax: (208)847-0553

Publications: The Bear Laker (7908) • The News-Examiner (7909)

The Sun Newspapers
216 Main St.
PO Box 755
Seal Beach, CA 90740-6318
Phone: (562)430-7555
Fax: (562)430-3469

Publications: The Sun Journal (2065)

Sun Newspapers
400A UCW, Catholic University
Washington, DC 20064
Phone: (202)319-5778
Fax: (202)319-5529

Publications: The Tower (5826)

Sun Newspapers
45-525 Luluku Rd.
Kaneohe, HI 96744
Phone: (808)235-5881
Fax: (808)247-7246

Publications: Military Sun Press (7775)

Sun Newspapers
5510 Cloverleaf Pkwy.
Cleveland, OH 44125-4887
Phone: (216)986-2600
Fax: (216)986-2380
Free: 800-362-8008

Publications: Bedford Sun Banner (24660) • Brooklyn Sun Journal (24711) • Brunswick Sun Times (24713) • Chagrin Herald Sun (24755) • Euclid Sun Journal (25184) • Garfield-Maple Sun (25342) • Lakewood Sun Post (25287) • The Medina Sun (25374) • The Montrose Sun (24928) • The News Sun (24678) • Nordonia Hills Sun (25440) • Parma Sun Post (25467) • Solon Herald Sun (25527) • The Sun (24954) • Sun Banner Pride (25614) • The Sun Courier (24706) • The Sun Herald (25438) • The Sun Messenger (24658) • The Sun Press (24659) • Sun Scoop Journal (25185) • The Sun Star (25550) • The Twinsburg Sun (25599) • West Akron Sun (24963) • West Geauga Sun (24964) • West Side Sun News (25439)

Sun Newspapers
275 Market St.
PO Box 879
Lake Dallas, TX 75065
Phone: (940)321-7378

Publications: The Argyle Sun (29730) • Denton County Express (30661) • The Lake Cities Sun (30662)

Sun Newspapers
6408 Edsall Rd.
Alexandria, VA 22312-6410
Phone: (703)204-2800
Fax: (703)204-3455

Publications: Northern Virginia Sun (32269) • Sun Gazette (32270)

Sun Newspapers, Inc.
PO Box 6192
Pasadena, TX 77506-0192

Publications: Bay Area Sun (30460) • Fort Bend/Southwest Sun (30910) • The Lake Houston Sun (30911) • The North Channel Sun (30912) • The 1960 Sun (30519)

Sun Press and News Publications
33 2nd St. NE
Box 280
Osseo, MN 55369
Phone: (763)425-3323
Fax: (763)425-2945

Publications: Champlin Dayton Press (15791) • Delano Eagle (15827) • North Crow River News (16248) • Osseo-Maple Grove Press (16249) • Rockford Area News Leader (16250) • South Crow River News (16251)

Sun Publications
1500 W. Ogden Ave.
PO Box 269
Naperville, IL 60566-0269
Phone: (630)355-0063
Fax: (630)416-5163

Publications: Batavia Sun (9260) • The Bolingbrook Sun (9261) • Downers Grove Sun (9262) • The Fox Valley Villages/60504 Sun (9263) • Geneva Sun (9264) • Glen Ellyn Sun (9265) • Homer/Lockport/Lemont Sun (9266) • The Joliet Herald News (9035) • Lincoln-Way Sun (9268) • The Lisle Sun (9269) • The Naperville Sun (9270) • Plainfield Sun

(9272) • The Romeoville Sun (9553) • St. Charles Sun (9273) • Sun Publications (9274) • Wheaton Sun (9275)

Sun Publications, Inc.
7373 W 107th St.
Overland Park, KS 66212
Phone: (913)381-1010
Fax: (913)381-9889

Publications: College Boulevard News (11706) • Gladstone News (17082) • Johnson County Sun (11716) • Kansas City Jewish Chronicle (11717) • Leawood Sun (11586) • Leawood Sun, Blue Valley Edition (11543) • Lenexa Sun (11720) • Mission Sun (11656) • Northeast Johnson County Sun (11651) • Northland News (17190) • Olathe Sun (11684) • Overland Park Sun (11723) • Overland Park Sun, Blue Valley Edition (11724) • Prairie Village Sun (11763) • Roeland Park Sun (11770) • Shawnee-Merriam Sun (11802) • Sun Newspaper (11810)

Sun Publishing Company Inc.
107 N Roberson St.
Chapel Hill, NC 27516
Phone: (919)942-5282
Fax: (919)932-3101

Publications: The Sun (23727)

Sun Publishing Co., Inc.
PO Box 997
Clarksville, VA 23927
Phone: (434)374-8152
Fax: (434)374-8153
Free: 888-786-6659

Publications: The Mecklenberg Sun (31974)

Sun Sentinel
200 E. Las Olas Blvd., 1250
Fort Lauderdale, FL 33301

Publications: City Link (6074)

Sun-Sentinel Co.
200 E Las Olas Blvd.
Fort Lauderdale, FL 33301-2293
Phone: (954)356-4000
Fax: (954)356-4093

Publications: Sun-Sentinel (6084)

The Sun Times
290 9th St. E
Owen Sound, ON, Canada N4K 5P2
Phone: (519)376-2250
Fax: (519)376-7190

Publications: The Sun Times (36299)

Sun Trenton Publishing
PO Box 118
Trenton, IL 62293
Phone: (618)224-9422
Fax: (618)224-9422

Publications: Sun (9694)

Sunbelt Newspapers, Inc.
1401 Oakfield Dr.
Brandon, FL 33511-2800
Phone: (813)689-7764
Fax: (813)689-9545

Publications: Carrollwood News (5976) • The Courier (6585) • East Bay Breeze (5907) • Plant City Shopper (6586) • The Sun (6698) • Town'n Country News (6781)

Suncoast News
6214 U.S Hwy. 19
New Port Richey, FL 34652
Phone: (727)815-1000
Fax: (727)815-1025

Publications: Suncoast News (6455) • West Pasco Press (6456)

Sundance Publications Ltd.
423 Mountain Ave.
PO Box 939
Neepawa, MB, Canada R0J 1H0
Phone: (204)476-2309
Fax: (204)476-5802

Publications: The Gladstone Enterprise (35276) • Heartland Shopper (35277)

The Sundance Times
PO Box 400
Sundance, WY 82729
Phone: (307)283-3411
Fax: (307)283-3332

Publications: The Sundance Times (34594)

Sunday Dispatch
109 New St.
Pittston, PA 18640
Phone: (717)655-1418
Fax: (717)883-1266

Publications: Sunday Dispatch (27885)

Sunday Herald, Ltd.
458 Logy Bay Rd.
PO Box 2015
St. John's, NL, Canada A1C 5R7
Phone: (709)726-7060
Fax: (709)726-6971

Publications: The Newfoundland Herald (35491)

The Sunday Post (Washington County)
PO Box 478
West Bend, WI 53095-0478
Phone: (414)334-5655
Fax: (414)334-6252
Free: 800-498-5655

Publications: The Sunday Post (Washington County) (34446)

Sundown Times
PO Box 112
PO Box 1815
Boone, NC 28607
Phone: (828)264-6397
Fax: (828)264-8536

Publications: The Mountain Times (23654)

Sundre Round Up
Box 599
Sundre, AB, Canada T0M 1X0
Phone: (403)638-3577
Fax: (403)638-3077

Publications: Round-Up (34859)

Sunfield Sentinel Publishing
PO Box 8
Sunfield, MI 48890
Phone: (517)566-8500
Fax: (517)566-8873

Publications: The Sunfield Sentinel (15583)

Sunland Publishing Co.
PO Box 16709
246 Briarwood Dr.
Jackson, MS 39236
Phone: (601)957-1122
Fax: (601)957-1533

Publications: Northside Sun (16711)

Sunny South News
PO Box 30
Coaldale, AB, Canada T1M 1M2
Phone: (403)345-3081
Fax: (403)345-5408

Publications: Sunny South News (34684)

Sunpress Publications, Inc.
13032 U.S Hwy. 301
PO Box 187
Dade City, FL 33525
Phone: (352)567-5639
Fax: (352)567-5640

Publications: Pasco News (6031) • Pasco Shopper (6032)

Sunrise Publications, Inc.
724 N. First St., 4 Fl.
Minneapolis, MN 55401-2885
Phone: (612)946-8883
Fax: (612)946-8155
Free: (866)844-GAME

Publications: Game Informer Magazine (16082)

Sunset Open House
80 Willow Rd.
Menlo Park, CA 94025
Phone: (415)321-3600
Fax: (415)321-0551
Free: 800-227-7346

Publications: Sunset Magazine (2527)

Sunshine Artist Magazine
3210 Dade Ave.
Orlando, FL 32804
Phone: (407)228-9772
Fax: (407)228-9862
Free: 800-597-2573

Publications: Sunshine Artist (6508)

Sunshine Group Worldwide Ltd.
770 Broadway
Fl. 5
New York, NY 10003-9522
Phone: (212)246-6460
Fax: (212)265-6428

Publications: Film Journal International (21694)

Sunshine Printing
3109 State Rte. 8
Lake Placid, FL 33852
Phone: (941)465-4213
Fax: (941)465-4046

Publications: Frostproof News (6127)

Suntex Communications, Inc.
PO Box 9005
Waco, TX 76714
Phone: (254)848-9393
Fax: (254)848-9779

Publications: Texas Gardener (31253)

Sunwest Publishing
3769 Tibbetts St., Ste. A
Riverside, CA 92506-2606
Phone: (909)682-3026
Fax: (909)682-0246

Publications: Healthy Cooking (2937) • Inland Empire (2939) • Pasta Magazine (2942) • Southern California Brides (2945) • Southern California Golf (2946)

SUNY Geneseo Journal of Science and Mathematics
Biology Dept.
Bailey 4
SUNY Geneseo
Geneseo, NY 14454
Phone: (716)245-5448
Fax: (716)245-5007

Publications: SUNY Geneseo Journal of Science and Mathematics (20650)

Super Markets Productions Ltd.
PO Box 6124
San Rafael, CA 94903
Phone: (415)479-0211
Fax: (415)479-0211

Publications: Grocers Report (3601)

Superintendent of Documents
PO Box 371954
MS4004-MIB
Pittsburgh, PA 15250-7954
Phone: (202)512-1800

Publications: Abridged Index Medicus (27753) • Alcohol, Health and Research World (27755) • All Hands (27756) • Code of Federal Regulations (27766) • Construction Reports: Housing Starts (C20) (27769) • Construction Reports: Housing Units Authorized by Building Permits & Contracts (C40) (27770) • Current Business Reports (27774) • Current Housing Reports (27776) • Current Population Reports (27777) • Customs Bulletin and Decisions (27778) • Diplomatic List (27781) • Employment and Earnings (27784) • Environmental Health Perspectives (27785) • FDA Consumer (27787) • Fishery Bulletin (27790) • Health Care Financing Review (27795) • Index Medicus (27798) • Internal Revenue Bulletin (27801) • Journal of Research of the National Institute of Standards and Technology (27804) • Military Law Review (27813) • The Mobility Forum (27815) • Monthly Catalog of U.S. Government Publications (27816) • Monthly Energy Review (27817) • Monthly Labor Review (27818) • Naval Aviation News (27819) • Navy Medicine (27820) • Official Summary of Security Transactions and Holdings (27823) • Patents-Official Gazette (27825) • Postal Bulletin (27838) • Resources in Education (27840) • Treasury Bulletin (27849) • Treaties and Other International Acts Series (27850) • United States Tax Court Reports (27853) • Weekly Compilation of Presidential Documents (27855)

Superintendent's Profile Product-Service Directory
525, ave. du Pont
Box 520
Alma, QC, Canada G8B 5W1
Phone: (418)668-4545
Fax: (418)668-8522

Publications: Superintendent's Profile Product-Service Directory (36930)

The Superior Express
PO Box 408
Superior, NE 68978
Phone: (402)879-3291
Fax: (402)879-3463
Free: 800-359-2120

Publications: The Superior Express (18289)

Superior Printing and Publishing
PO Box 217, Rte. 805
Cromona, KY 41810
Phone: (606)855-4541
Fax: (606)855-9290

Publications: Letcher County Community News-Press (12149)

Superior Publishing Co.
148 E 3rd St.
Box 408
Superior, NE 68978
Phone: (402)879-3291
Fax: (402)879-3463
Free: 800-359-2120

Publications: Jewell County News (11637)

Superior Publishing Co., Inc.
111 E Main
PO Box 305
Mankato, KS 66956
Phone: (785)378-3191
Fax: (785)378-5437
Free: 800-359-2120

Publications: Jewell County Record (11638)

Superior Sun
467 Main St.
Superior, AZ 85273
Phone: (520)689-2436
Fax: (520)363-9663

Publications: Superior Sun (898)

SuperMagazine
3065 boul. Levesque Ouest
Laval, QC, Canada H7V 1C5
Phone: (514)681-6361
Fax: (514)681-1638
Free: 800-361-7244

Publications: Horoscope Quotidien (37040)

The Supermarket Gourmet
102 E. 5th St.
PO Box 527
Fowler, IN 47944
Phone: (765)884-1902
Fax: (765)884-8110
Free: 888-805-5821

Publications: The Supermarket Gourmet (9997)

Supersonic Media, Inc.
PO Box 491034
Los Angeles, CA 90049
Phone: (310)449-0120
Fax: (310)449-1153

Publications: Option (2353)

Supertrax LLC
Dupont Ctr., Ste. 250
9801 Dupont Ave. S.
Bloomington, MN 55431-3197
Phone: (952)885-6884
Fax: (952)884-9836
Free: 800-905-8729

Publications: Supertrax International Magazine (15761)

Support Coalition
PO Box 11284
Eugene, OR 97440-3484
Phone: (541)345-9106
Fax: (541)345-3737
Free: 877-MADPRIDE

Publications: Dendron News (26315)

Supreme Council, Scottish Rite, NMJ, USA
PO Box 519
Lexington, MA 02420
Phone: (781)862-4410
Fax: (781)863-1833

Publications: The Northern Light (14272)

Supreme Council of the 33rd Degree
1733 16th St. NW
Washington, DC 20009-3103
Phone: (202)232-3579
Fax: (202)387-1843
Free: 800-776-2766

Publications: The Scottish Rite Journal (Southern Jurisdiction, USA) (5783)

*Surface
7 Isadora Duncan
San Francisco, CA 94102
Phone: (415)929-5100
Fax: (415)929-5103

Publications: *Surface (3446)

Surface Design Association
PO Box 360
Sebastopol, CA 95473-0360
Phone: (707)829-3110
Fax: (707)829-3285

Publications: Surface Design Journal (18798)

Surfer Publications, Inc.
Box 1028
Dana Point, CA 92629
Phone: (714)496-5922
Fax: (714)496-7849

Publications: SURFER Magazine (1807)

Surfing Girl Magazine
PO Box 54974
Boulder, CO 80322-4974
Phone: 800-876-3487

Publications: Surfing Girl (4193)

Surplus Record, Inc.
20 N Wacker Dr.
Chicago, IL 60606
Phone: (312)372-9077
Fax: (312)372-6537
Free: 800-622-5449

Publications: The Surplus Record (8578)

Survival News
95 Standard St.
Mattapan, MA 02126
Phone: (617)298-7311
Fax: (617)296-4276

Publications: Survival News (14313)

The Suspension Press
PO Box 2064
Covington, KY 41012

Publications: The Suspension Press (12028)

Susquehanna Times & Magazine, Inc.
400 Stackstown Rd.
Marietta, PA 17547-9300
Phone: (717)426-2212

Publications: Old News (27221)

Susquehanna University
514 University Ave.
Selinsgrove, PA 17870-1025
Phone: (570)371-4119
Fax: (717)374-6080

Publications: Susquehanna Today (27975)

Sussex Publishers, Inc.
49 21st St., 11th Fl.
New York, NY 10010-6213
Phone: (212)260-7210
Fax: (212)260-7566

Publications: Mother Earth News (22369) • Psychology Today (22605)

Sutphen Services
PO Box 38
Malibu, CA 90265
Phone: (818)706-0963
Fax: (818)706-3606
Free: 800-421-6603

Publications: Soaring Spirit (2495)

Suzuki Association of Americas
PO Box 17310
Boulder, CO 80308-7310
Phone: (303)444-0948
Fax: (303)444-0984
Free: 888-378-9854

Publications: American Suzuki Journal (4156)

Swan Erickson Publishing Inc.
1011 Upper Middle Rd. E, Ste. 1235
Oakville, ON, Canada L6H 5Z9
Phone: (905)475-4231
Fax: (905)475-3512

Publications: Industrial Process Products and Technology (36145)

Swank Publications
210 Rte. 4E, Ste. 211
Paramus, NJ 07652
Phone: (201)843-4004
Fax: (201)843-8636

Publications: Swank (19407)

The Swap Shop
PO Box 907
Picayune, MS 39466
Phone: (601)798-4835
Fax: (601)798-9755
Free: 800-284-5036

Publications: The Swap Shop (16820)

Swarthmore College
500 College Ave.
Swarthmore, PA 19081
Phone: (610)328-8000

Publications: Swarthmore College Bulletin (28044) • Swarthmore Phoenix (28045)

Swarthmorean
107 Rutgers
Box 59
Swarthmore, PA 19081
Phone: (610)543-0900

Publications: The Swarthmorean (28046)

Swartz-Morris Media, Inc.
189 W Athens St.
PO Drawer C
Winder, GA 30680
Phone: (770)867-7557
Fax: (770)867-1034

Publications: The Barrow County News (7652) • The Barrow County News (7653) • The Barrow County Shopper (7654)

Swea City Herald Press
PO Box 428
Swea City, IA 50590
Phone: (515)272-4660

Publications: Swea City Herald-Press (11260)

SWEAT Marketing
5743 E. Thomas Rd., No. 2
Scottsdale, AZ 85251
Phone: (480)947-3900
Fax: (480)947-1215

Publications: SWEAT Magazine (917)

Swedenborg Scientific Association
PO Box 757
Bryn Athyn, PA 19009-0757
Phone: (215)947-2977
Fax: (215)914-2986

Publications: The New Philosophy (26740)

Swedish-American Historical Society
5125 N Spaulding Ave.
Chicago, IL 60625-4816
Phone: (773)583-5722

Publications: Swedish-American Historical Quarterly (16431)

Swedish News
PO Box 1710
New Canaan, CT 06840
Free: 800-827-9333

Publications: NordicReach (4980)

Swedish Press Inc.
1294 W. 7th Ave.
Vancouver, BC, Canada V6H 1B6
Phone: (604)731-6381
Fax: (604)731-2292
Free: (866)882-0088

Publications: Scandinavian Press (35167) • Swedish Press (35170)

Sweetwater Reporter
112 W Third St.
PO Box 750
Sweetwater, TX 79556
Phone: (915)236-6677
Fax: (915)235-4967

Publications: Nolan County Shopper (31169) • Sweetwater Reporter (31170)

Swenson Swedish Immigration Research Center,
639 38th St.
Rock Island, IL 61201-2296
Phone: (309)794-7204
Fax: (309)794-7443

Publications: Swedish American Genealogist (32814)

Swettman Publications
Box 50
Pleasant Plains, IL 62677
Phone: (217)626-1711

Publications: New Berlin Bee (9281) • The Pleasant Press (9460)

Swift County Monitor-News
101 12th St. S
PO Box 227
Benson, MN 56215
Phone: (320)843-4111
Fax: (320)843-3246

Publications: Swift County Monitor-News (15747)

Swiss American Historical Society
6440 N Bosworth
Chicago, IL 60626
Phone: (773)262-9336
Fax: (773)465-5292

Publications: Swiss-American Historical Society (8580)

Swiss Journal Co.
548 Columbus Ave.
PO Box 330082
San Francisco, CA 94133-2802
Fax: (415)362-3159

Publications: Swiss Journal (3447)

Sword of the Lord Publishers
224 Bridge Ave.
PO Box 1099
Murfreesboro, TN 37133
Phone: (615)893-6700
Fax: (615)895-7447
Free: 800-247-9673

Publications: The Sword of the Lord (29433)

S.W.W. Publications, L.L.C.
114 S Michigan St.
Edgerton, OH 43517
Phone: (419)298-2369
Fax: (419)298-2360

Publications: The Edgerton Earth (25176)

Sybase Inc.
1 Sybase Dr.
Dublin, CA 94568
Phone: (925)236-5000
Fax: (925)236-6157
Free: 800-879-2273

Publications: Sybase Magazine (1839)

Syllabus Press
9121 Oakdale Ave., Ste. 101
Chatsworth, CA 91311-6526
Fax: (408)261-7280
Free: 800-773-0670

Publications: Syllabus Magazine (1690)

The Sylva Herald Publishing Co., Inc.
539 W. Main St.
PO Box 307
Sylva, NC 28779-0307
Phone: (828)586-2611
Fax: (828)586-2637

Publications: The Sylva Herald & Ruralite (24251)

Sylvania Telephone
208 N Main St.
PO Box 10
Sylvania, GA 30467-0010
Phone: (912)564-2045
Fax: (912)564-7055

Publications: Sylvania Telephone (7581)

The Sylvester Local News
103 E Kelly
PO Box 387
Sylvester, GA 31791
Phone: (229)776-7713

Publications: The Sylvester Local News (7582)

Symphony Orchestra Institute
P.O. Box 1040
Deerfield, IL 60015
Phone: (847)945-3050
Fax: (847)945-1897

Publications: Harmony (8724)

Synergy Publishing, Ltd.
407 Vine St., Dept. 189
Cincinnati, OH 45202
Phone: (513)736-4751

Publications: The Small Business Journal (24820)

Synergy Resource Group, Inc.
3131 Fernbrook Ln. N., Ste. 111
Plymouth, MN 55447-5336
Phone: (763)566-5696
Fax: (763)566-5780

Publications: Precision Manufacturing (16279)

Synod of Lincoln Trails
1100 W 42nd St.
Indianapolis, IN 46208
Phone: (317)923-3681

Publications: The Link (10148)

Syracuse Catholic Press Association Inc.
421 S. Warren St.
Syracuse, NY 13202
Phone: (315)422-8153
Fax: (315)422-7549
Free: 800-333-0571

Publications: The Catholic Sun (23392)

The Syracuse Jewish Federation, Inc.
5655 Thompson Rd.
DeWitt, NY 13214
Phone: (315)445-2040
Fax: (315)445-1559

Publications: Jewish Observer (20532)

Syracuse Journal
203 N Main
PO Box 1137
Syracuse, KS 67878
Phone: (620)384-5640
Fax: (620)384-5228

Publications: Syracuse Journal (11812)

The Syracuse Newspapers, Inc.
Clinton Sq.
PO Box 4818
Syracuse, NY 13221
Phone: (315)470-0011
Fax: (315)470-3081
Free: 800-765-4335

Publications: The Post-Standard (23419)

Syracuse University
820 Comstock Ave., Rm. 014
Syracuse, NY 13244-5040
Phone: (315)443-3784
Fax: (315)443-3786

Publications: The Syracuse Record (23429)

Syracuse University
Syracuse, NY 13244
Phone: (315)443-1315
Fax: (315)443-3660

Publications: Salt Hill (23420) • Syracuse Law Review (23427)

Syracuse University Library Associates
600 Bird Library
Syracuse, NY 13244-2010
Phone: (315)443-5533
Fax: (315)443-2060

Publications: Syracuse University Library Associates Courier (23430)

SYS-CON Media
135 Chestnut Ridge Rd.
Montvale, NJ 07645
Phone: (201)802-3000
Fax: (201)782-9601
Free: 888-303-5282

Publications: ColdFusion Developer's Journal (CFDJ) (19247) • Java Developer's Journal (19258) • Linux Business Week (19261) • Power-Builder Developer's Journal (19273) • Web Services Journal (19279) • WebLogic Developers Journal (19280) • WebSphere Developer's Journal (19281) • Wireless Business & Technology (19282) • XML Journal (19284) • XML-Journal (19283)

T P Printing Co.
103 W. Spruce St.
PO Box 667
Abbotsford, WI 54405
Phone: (715)223-2342
Fax: (715)223-3505

Publications: Tribune-Phonograph (33517)

Tabor-Loris Tribune
U.S 701 N
PO Box 67
Tabor City, NC 28463
Phone: (910)653-3153
Fax: (910)653-9440
Free: 800-672-1022

Publications: Tabor-Loris Tribune (24253)

Taconic Press
PO Box 316
Millbrook, NY 12545-0316
Phone: (845)677-8241
Fax: (845)677-6337

Publications: Gazette-Advertiser (23184) • Harlem Valley Times (20029) • Hyde Park Townsman (20779) • Millbrook Round Table (21083) • Pawling News Chronicle (23085) • Pine Plains Register Herald (21084) • Voice Ledger (23109)

Tahoe Daily Tribune
3079 Harrison Ave.
South Lake Tahoe, CA 96150
Phone: (530)541-3880
Fax: (530)541-0373

Publications: Lake Tahoe Action Magazine (3783) • Tahoe Daily Tribune (3784)

Tahoe World
500 Double Eagle Ct.
Reno, NV 89511
Phone: (775)850-7686
Fax: (775)850-7677

Publications: Tahoe World (18425)

Talbotton New Era
3051 Roosevelt Hwy
PO Box 426
Manchester, GA 31816
Phone: (706)846-3188
Fax: (706)846-2206

Publications: Talbotton New Era (7583)

Talcott Communications Corp.
2B W Kinzie, 12th Fl.
Chicago, IL 60610
Phone: (312)849-2220
Fax: (312)849-2174
Free: 800-229-1967
Telex: 3710743 TALCOTT CGO

Publications: Chef (8305) • Equipment Solutions (8370) • Fancy Food & Culinary Products (8374) • Giftware News (8387)

Talent Publishing, LLC
PO Box 657
Rison, AR 71665
Phone: (870)325-6412
Gax: (870)325-6127

Publications: Cleveland County Herald (1325)

Talisman House Publishers
PO Box 3157
Jersey City, NJ 07303-3157
Phone: (201)938-0695
Fax: (201)938-1693

Publications: Talisman (19144)

talk
250 W. 55th St.
New York, NY 10019

Publications: talk (22814)

Talk of the Town Publications
521 S. Jackson St.
Moscow, ID 83843-2232
Phone: (208)877-1550

Publications: Talk of the Town (7921)

Tall-Taylor Publishing
2nd Ave. & 2nd St.
PO Box 40
Irricana, AB, Canada T0M 1B0
Phone: (403)935-4688
Fax: (403)935-4981
Free: 888-999-4178

Publications: Carstairs Courier (34681) • Crossfield/Irricana Rocky View/Five Village Weekly (34788)

The Tallahassee Advertiser
PO Box 3696
Tallahassee, FL 32315-3696
Phone: (850)574-0520
Fax: (850)574-0459

Publications: The Tallahassee Advertiser (6737)

Tallapoosa Publishers
PO Box 999
Alexander City, AL 35010-0999
Phone: (205)234-4281
Fax: (205)234-6550

Publications: The Dadeville Record (7)

The Tallassee Tribune
301 Gilmer
PO Drawer 780730
Tallassee, AL 36078-0730
Phone: (334)283-6568
Fax: (334)283-6569

Publications: The Tallassee Tribune (467)

TAM Communications, Inc.
1010 Summer St., 3rd Fl.
Stamford, CT 06905
Phone: (203)425-8777
Fax: (203)425-8775

Publications: Motorcycle Tour & Cruiser (5155)

Tama County Publishing, Inc.
220 W 3rd St.
PO Box 118
Tama, IA 52339
Phone: (641)484-2841
Fax: (641)484-5705

Publications: Tama County Shopper-Advisor (11262) • The Tama News-Herald (11263) • Toledo Chronicle (11272)

Tamara: Journal of Critical Postmodern Organization Science
Dept. of Management MSC 3DJ
New Mexico State University
PO Box 30001
Las Cruces, NM 88003-8001
Phone: (505)646-2391
Fax: (505)646-1372

Publications: Tamara (19877)

The Tampa Bay Online
202 S. Parker St.
Tampa, FL 33606
Phone: (813)259-8010
Free: 800-527-2773

Publications: The Tampa Tribune (6780)

Tampa Bay Publications, Inc.
2531 Landmark Dr., Ste. 101
Clearwater, FL 33761
Phone: (727)791-4800

Publications: Tampa Bay Magazine (5991)

Tanner Publishing Ltd.
9343 50th St., No. 4
Edmonton, AB, Canada T6B 2L5
Phone: (780)465-3362
Fax: (780)448-0424

Publications: WHERE Edmonton (34737)

TAP Publishing Co.
174 Fourth St.
PO Box 3079
Crossville, TN 38557
Phone: (931)484-5137
Fax: (931)484-2532
Free: 800-251-6776

Publications: International Tradequip (29158) • Rock and Dirt (29159)

Taproot Press Publishing Co.
Box 204
Ambridge, PA 15003
Phone: (724)266-8476

Publications: Taproot Literary Review (26656)

Taproot Reviews
Box 585
Lakewood, OH 44107

Publications: Taproot Reviews (25288)

Target Communications Corp.
7626 W Donges Bay Rd.
Mequon, WI 53097
Phone: (262)242-3990
Fax: (262)242-7391
Free: 800-324-3337

Publications: Deer and Turkey Show Previews (34043)

Target Communications, Inc.
2201 W. Broad St. Ste. 105
Richmond, VA 23220-2022
Phone: (804)355-0111
Fax: (804)355-5442

Publications: Richmond Magazine (32451)

Target Marketing Magazine Group
167 Hwy. 72 E
PO Box 640
Collierville, TN 38017
Phone: (901)853-7720
Fax: (901)853-6437

Publications: Cutting Tool Business (29134)

Target Publishing Co., Inc.
2470 E Main St.
Columbus, OH 43209
Phone: (614)235-1022
Fax: (614)235-3584

Publications: Rinksider (25059)

Targeted Media Communications, Inc.
1241 E. Washington St., Ste. 206
Phoenix, AZ 85034
Phone: (602)230-8161
Fax: (602)230-8162

Publications: Arizona Jazz Magazine (781)

The Tarkio Avalanche
521 Main
PO Box 278
Tarkio, MO 64491
Phone: (660)736-4111
Fax: (660)736-5700

Publications: The Tarkio Avalanche (17646)

TASH
29 W Susquehanna Ave., Ste. 210
Baltimore, MD 21204
Phone: (410)828-8274
Fax: (410)828-6706
Free: 800-482-TASH

Publications: The Journal of the Association for Persons with Severe Handicaps (13179)

The Tattnall Journal
114 B North Main St., Ste. B
PO Box 278
Reidsville, GA 30453
Phone: (912)557-6761
Fax: (912)557-4132

Publications: The Tattnall Journal (7488)

Tau Beta Pi Association
PO Box 2697
Knoxville, TN 37901-2697
Phone: (865)546-4578
Fax: (865)546-4579

Publications: The Bent of Tau Beta Pi (29270)

Taunton Daily Gazette
5 Cohannet St.
Taunton, MA 02780-3903
Phone: (508)880-9000
Fax: (508)824-3487

Publications: Taunton Daily Gazette (14584)

Taunton Press
63 S. Main St., Box 5506
Newtown, CT 06470-5506
Phone: (203)426-8171
Fax: (203)426-3434
Free: 800-926-8776

Publications: Fine Cooking Magazine (5040) • Fine Gardening (5041) • Fine Homebuilding (5042) • Fine Woodworking (5043) • Kitchen Gardener (5044) • Threads (5046)

Tavern League of Wisconsin
2817 Fish Hatchery Rd.
Madison, WI 53713
Phone: (608)270-8591
Fax: (608)270-8595
Free: 800-445-9221

Publications: On Premise (33966)

Tavistock Gazette
119 Woodstock St. S.
PO Box 70
Tavistock, ON, Canada E1C 8P3
Phone: (519)655-2341
Fax: (519)655-3070

Publications: Tavistock Gazette (36430)

The Tawakoni News
PO Box 3100
Quinlan, TX 75474
Phone: (903)356-2311
Fax: (903)356-3770

Publications: The Tawakoni News (30966)

Tax Analysts
6830 N. Fairfax Dr.
Arlington, VA 22213
Phone: (703)533-4400
Fax: (703)533-4660
Free: 800-955-3444

Publications: The Exempt Organization Tax Review (31792) • Highlights and Documents (31795) • The Insurance Tax Review (31797) • State Tax Notes (31833) • Tax Notes (31835) • Tax Notes International (31836)

Tax Executives Institute, Inc.
1200 G. St. NW, Ste. 300
Washington, DC 20005-3814
Phone: (202)638-5601
Fax: (202)638-5607

Publications: The Tax Executive (5811)

Tax Management Inc.
1250 23rd St. NW
Washington, DC 20037
Phone: (202)452-4200
Fax: (202)833-7297
Free: 800-372-1033
Telex: 285656 BNAI WSH

Publications: The Tax Management International Forum (5813) • Tax Practice Adviser (5814)

Taxicab, Limousine & Paratransit Association
3849 Farragut Ave.
Kensington, MD 20895
Phone: (301)946-5701
Fax: (301)946-4641

Publications: Transportation Leader (13591)

Joanna Taylor Books
2461 El Pavo Way
Rancho Cordova, CA 95670
Phone: (916)362-6963

Publications: Journal of Applied Sport Psychology (2875) • Journal of Loss & Trauma (2876)

Taylor Communications, Inc.
128 E 6th St.
Cincinnati, OH 45202
Phone: (513)241-9906
Fax: (513)241-7235

Publications: Downtowner Newspaper (24794)

Taylor County Historical Society
Box 14
Campbellsville, KY 42719
Phone: (502)465-7033

Publications: Central Kentucky Researcher (12007)

Taylor and Francis
29 W 35th St.
New York, NY 10001
Phone: (212)216-7800
Fax: (212)564-7854

Publications: Capitalism, Nature, Socialism (3681) • Journal of the American Academy of Psychoanalysis (4702) • Journal of Personality Disorders (6365) • Journal of Social and Clinical Psychology (32023) • Journal of Systemic Therapies (35985) • Psychiatry (5737) • Pulmonary Pharmacology (22612) • Rethinking Marxism (10377) • School Psychology Quarterly (18118) • Science & Society (22713) • Social Cognition (10553) • Suicide and Life-Threatening Behavior (8575)

Taylor & Francis
325 Chestnut St., Ste. 800
Philadelphia, PA 19106
Phone: (215)625-8900
Fax: (215)625-2940
Free: 800-354-1420

Publications: Advances in Physics (14126) • Annals of Human Biology (27378) • Annals of Science (27380) • Aphasiology (12159) • Applied Artificial Intelligence (27382) • Archives of Andrology, an International Journal (28673) • Arid Land Research and Management (31346) • Behavior & Information Technology (27387) • Brain Injury (32430) • The Chemical Engineer (27397) • Chemical Engineering Research and Design (27398) • Chinese Medical Sciences Journal (27402) • Clinical Linguistics and Phonetics (12615) • Coastal Management (32955) • Community/Junior College Journal of Research and Practice (30234) • Comparative Strategy (32014) • Contemporary Physics (27427) • Cybernetics and Systems (27447) • Death Studies (29368) • Deviant Behavior: An Interdisciplinary Journal (12616) • Disability and Rehabilitation (27453) • Educational Gerontology (30236) • Electric Machines Components and Systems (27456) • Electromagnetics (8364) • Energy Sources (34548) • Energy Systems and Policy (27460) • Entrepreneurship and Regional Development (27461) • Ergonomics (27463) • Ergonomics Abstracts (27464) • Experimental Aging Research (13539) • Experimental Heat Transfer (1520) • Experimental Lung Research (24184) • Fiber and Integrated Optics (1664) • Food Additives and Contaminants (30041) • Geomicrobiology Journal (20801) • Health Care for Women International (24295) • Heat Transfer Engineering: An International Quarterly (26078) • History of Education (27482) • History and Philosophy of the Life Sciences (27483) • History and Philosophy of Logic (27484) • The Howard Journal of Communications (5532) • Human Dimensions of Wildlife (4432) • The Information Society (10076) • Inhalation Toxicology (24138) • International Journal of Computer Integrated Manufacturing (27495) • International Journal of Control (27496) • International Journal of Electronics (27497) • International Journal of Geographical Information Science (27498) • International Journal of Hyperthermia (27499) • International Journal of Lifelong Education (27500) • International Journal of Mathematical Education in Science and Technology (27501) • International Journal of Optoelectronics (27502) • International Journal of Personal Construct Psychology (27503) • International Journal of Pest Management (27504) • International Journal of Production Research (27505) • International Journal of Qualitative Studies in Education (29785) • International Journal of Radiation Biology (27506) • International Journal of Remote Sensing (27507) • International Journal of Science Education (27508) • International Reviews in Physical Chemistry (10547) • The International Trade Journal (30669) • Issues in Comprehensive Pediatric Nursing (19524) • Issues in Mental Health Nursing (29273) • Journal of Ambulatory Monitoring (27511) • Journal of Automatic Chemistry (27517) • Journal of Constructivist Psychology (29373) • Journal of Curriculum Studies (27523) • Journal of Education Policy (27526) • Journal of Health Communication (5595) • Journal of Investigative Surgery (15240) • The Journal of Legal

Medicine (9637) • Journal of Loss & Trauma (10979) • Journal of Medical Engineering & Technology (27534) • Journal of Microencapsulation (27535) • Journal of Modern Optics (27536) • Journal of Musicological Research (27537) • Journal of Natural History (27538) • Journal of Popular Music Studies (13831) • Journal of Sex & Marital Therapy (24916) • Journal of Thermal Stresses (6442) • Journal of Toxicology and Environmental Health (27553) • L I T: Literature Interpretation Theory (27557) • Leisure Sciences (23714) • Marine Geodesy (7710) • Marine Georesources and Geotechnology (7711) • Maritime Policy & Management (27561) • Medical Informatics & The Internet in Medicine (27566) • Molecular Membrane Biology (27574) • Molecular Physics (6947) • Numerical Heat Transfer (8514) • Numerical Heat Transfer, Part A: Applications (8515) • Ocean Development and International Law (27595) • Particulate Science and Technology (27612) • Pediatric Hematology and Oncology (27616) • Pediatric Pathology & Molecular Medicine (27617) • Philosophical Magazine (27636) • Philosophical Magazine Letters (27637) • Political Communication (23841) • Progress in Natural Science (27649) • Reading Psychology (30048) • Reading and Writing Quarterly: Overcoming Learning Difficulties (20611) • Social Epistemology (27842) • Society & Natural Resources (31351) • Sociological Spectrum (12619) • Studies in Conflict and Terrorism (31834) • Toxicology & Ecotoxicology News/Reviews (27706) • Transport Reviews (27711) • Ultrastructural Pathology (8590) • Women's Studies (1726) • Word & Image (27721) • Work & Stress (27722) • World Futures (27723) • Xenobiotica (27724)

Taylor & Francis Group
29 W. 35th St.
New York, NY 10001
Phone: (212)216-7800
Fax: (212)564-7854

Publications: Comments on Nuclear and Particles Physics (21455) • Comments on Toxicology (18081) • The Communication Review (9702) • Current Topics in Chinese Science Section B: Chemistry (21526) • International Journal of Environmental Studies: Sections A & B (20859) • Journal of Neurogenetics (14600) • Neutron News (22427)

Taylor & Francis, Ltd.
11 New Fetter Ln.
London EC4P 4EE, United Kingdom
Phone: 44 2075839855
Fax: 44 2078422298

Publications: Somatosensory and Motor Research (17513)

Taylor News
PO Box 550
Butler, GA 31006
Phone: (478)862-5101
Fax: (478)862-9668

Publications: Taylor County News (7146)

Taylor Publications, Inc.
PO Box 12006
1430 McCarthy Blvd.
New Bern, NC 28561
Phone: (252)633-5106
Fax: (252)633-2836
Free: 800-672-5837

Publications: Carolina Business (24095)

Taylor Publishing Group
1020 Brevik Pl., Ste. 5
Mississauga, ON, Canada L4W 4N7
Phone: (905)624-8218
Fax: (905)624-6764

Publications: Camping Canada Dealer News (36055) • Camping Canada's RV Lifestyle Magazine (36056)

The Taylorsville Times
PO Box 279
Taylorsville, NC 28681
Phone: (828)632-2532
Fax: (828)632-8233

Publications: The Taylorsville Times (24255)

Tazewell County Free Press
1249 Front St.
PO Box 1205
Richlands, VA 24641-1049
Phone: (276)963-0127
Fax: (276)963-0127

Publications: Tazewell County Free Press (32426)

T.B. Butler Publishing Co.
410 W. Erwin St.
PO Box 2030
Tyler, TX 75710
Phone: (903)597-8111
Fax: (903)595-0335

Publications: Tyler Courier-Times-Telegraph (31201) • Tyler Morning Telegraph (31203)

T.Bay Post Inc.
87 Hill St. N
Thunder Bay, ON, Canada P7A 5V6
Phone: (807)622-8588
Fax: (807)622-2779

Publications: Thunder Bay Guest Magazine (36440)

TDM Inc.
PO Box 1441
Orem, UT 84059
Phone: (801)224-7390
Fax: (801)224-5723
Free: 800-891-1736

Publications: The Doors Collectors Magazine (31384)

TDN Publishing Co.
224 S Market St.
Troy, OH 45373-3300
Phone: (937)335-5634
Fax: (937)335-3552

Publications: Miami County Advocate (25592) • Miami Valley Fifty Plus (25593) • Miami Valley Home Finder (25594) • Miami Valley Parents (25595) • Miami Valley Sunday News (25596) • Troy Daily News (25597) • T.V. Week (25598)

T.E. Smith Inc.
PO Box 14-2096
Coral Gables, FL 33114
Phone: (305)740-7170
Fax: (305)740-7153
Free: (866)946-3639

Publications: The Wine News (6015)

TEACH Magazine
258 Wallace Ave. Ste. 206
Toronto, ON, Canada M6P 3M9
Phone: (416)537-2103
Fax: (416)537-3491

Publications: TEACH Magazine (36754)

Teacher Librarian
Box 34069, Dept. 343
Seattle, WA 98124
Phone: (604)925-0266
Fax: (604)925-0566

Publications: Teacher Librarian (33034)

Teachers College Record Columbia University
525 W. 120th St.
PO Box 103
New York, NY 10027
Fax: (212)678-3790

Publications: Teachers College Record (22817)

Teachers of English to Speakers of Other Languages Inc.
700 S Washington St., Ste. 200
Alexandria, VA 22314-4287
Phone: (703)836-0774
Fax: (703)836-7864

Publications: TESOL Journal (31742) • TESOL Quarterly (31743)

Teaching/K-8
40 Richards Ave.
Norwalk, CT 06854-2509
Phone: (203)855-2650
Fax: (203)855-2656
Free: 800-249-9363

Publications: Teaching/K-8 (5075)

The Teague Chronicle
319 Main
Box 631
Teague, TX 75860
Phone: (254)739-2141
Fax: (254)739-2144

Publications: The Teague Chronicle (31176)

Cheryl Tears
70 Stevens St.
Clifton Springs, NY 14432
Phone: (315)462-6411
Fax: (315)462-7627

Publications: The Merchandiser (20468)

The Tech
PO Box 397029
Cambridge, MA 02139-7029
Phone: (617)253-1541
Fax: (617)258-8226

Publications: The Tech (14106)

Teche News
214 N Main
PO Box 69
St. Martinville, LA 70582
Phone: (337)394-6232
Fax: (337)394-7511

Publications: Teche News (12814)

TechLinks Media Inc.
3630 Stonewall Dr.
Atlanta, GA 30339
Phone: (770)436-6789

Publications: TechLINKS (7051)

Technical Analysis Inc.
4757 California Ave. SW
Seattle, WA 98116-4499
Phone: (206)938-0570
Fax: (206)938-1307
Free: 800-832-4642

Publications: Technical Analysis of Stocks & Commodities (33035) • Working Money (33045)

Technical Association of Pulp and Paper Industry (TAPPI)
Technology Park/Atlanta
PO Box 105113
Atlanta, GA 30348-5113
Phone: (770)446-1400
Fax: (770)446-6947
Free: 800-332-8686

Publications: TAPPI JOURNAL (7049)

Technical Enterprises, Inc.
7044 S 13th St.
Oak Creek, WI 53154
Phone: (414)768-8000
Fax: (414)768-8001

Publications: Engineering Professional (34198)

Technocracy, Inc.
2475 Harksell Rd.
Ferndale, WA 98248
Phone: (360)366-1012
Fax: (360)366-1409

Publications: The North American Technocrat (32768)

Technology Marketing Corp.
1 Technology Plaza
Norwalk, CT 06854
Phone: (203)852-6800
Fax: (203)853-2845
Free: 800-243-6002

Publications: CTI (5053) • Customer Interaction Solutions (5055) • Journal of Radiation Curing (5066) • Journal of Water Borne Coatings (5067) • Telemarketing & Call Center Solutions (5076)

The Technology Organization, Inc.
76 Highland Ave.
Somerville, MA 02143
Phone: (617)623-2253

Publications: Technology & Conservation of Art, Architecture & Antiquities (14539)

Technology Publishing Co.
2100 Wharton St., Ste. 310.
Pittsburgh, PA 15203
Phone: (412)431-8300
Fax: (412)431-5428
Free: 800-837-8303

Publications: Journal of Protective Coatings & Linings (27803)

Technology Review
201 Vassar St.
Cambridge, MA 02139
Phone: (617)253-8250
Fax: (617)258-5850

Publications: Technology Review (14107)

Technomic Publishing Company Inc.
2455 Teller Rd.
Thousand Oaks, CA 91320-2218

Publications: Journal of Pharmacy Practice (3897)

The Tecumseh Herald
PO Box 218
110 E. Logan
Tecumseh, MI 49286
Phone: (517)423-2174
Fax: (517)423-6258
Free: 800-832-6443

Publications: The Tecumseh Herald (15590)

Teen Generation, Inc.
202 Cleveland St.
Toronto, ON, Canada M4S 2W6
Phone: (416)487-3204
Fax: (416)481-8226

Publications: TG Magazine (36757)

TeeVee Moneysaver, Inc., Publications
52 West Main St.
PO Box 954
Somerville, NJ 08876
Phone: (908)722-6270
Fax: (908)722-7303

Publications: The Moneybook (19575) • TeeVee Moneysaver (Edition 1) (19579)

Tefft Publishers, Inc.
35 Salem St.
PO Box 185
Greenwich, NY 12834-0185
Phone: (518)692-2266

Publications: The Journal-Press (20701)

Tehachapi News Publications
411 N Mill St.
PO Box 1840
Tehachapi, CA 93561
Phone: (661)822-6828
Fax: (661)822-4053

Publications: Tehachapi News (3840)

Tekawennake
PO Box 130
Ohsweken, ON, Canada N0A 1M0
Phone: (519)753-0077
Fax: (519)753-0011

Publications: Tekawennake (36155)

Tekeyan Armenian Cultural Association
825, rue Manoogian
Saint-Laurent, QC, Canada H4N 1Z5
Phone: (514)747-6680
Fax: (514)747-6162

Publications: Abaka (37361)

Tele Guia Publications
3116 S Austin Blvd.
Cicero, IL 60804
Phone: (708)656-6666
Fax: (708)656-6679

Publications: Tele Guia de Chicago (8676)

Telecentral Electronics
Box 354
Wyoming, PA 18644-0354
Phone: (570)655-2880
Fax: (570)602-0826

Publications: Checkmate Incorporating Dungeonmaster (28198)

Teleflora
11444 W. Olympic Blvd.
Los Angeles, CA 90064
Phone: (310)231-9199
Fax: (310)966-3610
Free: 800-321-2665

Publications: Flowers (2272)

The Telegram
Columbus Dr.
PO Box 5970
St. John's, NL, Canada A1C 5X7
Publications: The Telegram (35494)

Telegram Publishing Co.
PO Box 958
Garden City, KS 67846
Phone: (316)275-8500
Fax: (316)275-5165
Free: 800-475-8600
Publications: The Garden City Telegram (11449)

The Telegram Publishing Co., Inc.
12 S Ohio Ave.
PO Box 111
Wellston, OH 45692
Phone: (614)384-6102
Publications: The Telegram (25630)

The Telegraph
17 Executive Dr.
Hudson, NH 03051
Phone: (603)882-2741
Fax: (603)882-5138
Publications: The Telegraph (18529)

The Telegraph
PO Box 1008
Nashua, NH 03061
Phone: (603)882-2741
Fax: (603)882-2681
Publications: The Telegraph (18601)

Telephone Pioneers of America
PO Box 13888
Denver, CO 80201-3888
Phone: (303)571-9274
Fax: (303)572-0520
Free: 800-872-5995
Publications: The Telephone Pioneer (4363)

Telescope Pub. Co.
1817 E U.S 81, Frontage Rd.
Belleville, KS 66935
Phone: (913)527-2224
Fax: (913)527-2225
Publications: Belleville Telescope (11356) • Farmer Stockman of the Midwest (11357)

Telfair Enterprise
237 W Oak St.
PO Box 269
Mc Rae, GA 31055
Phone: (229)868-6015
Fax: (229)868-5486
Free: 888-825-3441
Publications: Telfair Enterprise (7427)

Telluride Daily Planet
PO Box 2315
Telluride, CO 81435
Phone: (970)728-9788
Fax: (970)728-9793
Publications: Telluride Daily Planet (4645)

Telos Press Ltd.
431 E 12th St.
New York, NY 10009
Phone: (212)228-6479
Fax: (212)228-6379
Publications: American Foreign Policy Interests (21187) • New German Critique (22430) • Telos (22821)

TELOS/Springer-Verlag
1150 65th St.
Emeryville, CA 94608-1109
Phone: (510)595-7036
Fax: (510)595-7040
Free: 800-338-7638
Publications: Mathematics in Education and Research (1878)

Temas Corporation Inc.
300 W. 55th St, 14P
New York, NY 10019
Phone: (212)582-4750
Fax: (212)541-7910
Publications: Temas (22822)

Temiskaming Printing Company Ltd.
18 Wellington St.
Box 580
New Liskeard, ON, Canada P0J 1P0
Phone: (705)647-6791
Fax: (705)647-9669
Free: 800-461-8751
Publications: Temiskaming Speaker (36105)

Temple Daily Telegram
10 S 3rd St.
Temple, TX 76501
Phone: (254)778-4444
Fax: (254)771-3516
Publications: Temple Daily Telegram (31179)

The Temple Terrace Beacon
PO Box 271880
Tampa, FL 33688-1880
Phone: (813)963-1918
Fax: (813)963-3910
Publications: The Temple Terrace Beacon (6815)

Temple University
Philadelphia, PA 19122
Phone: (215)204-7331
Fax: (215)204-1185
Publications: Temple Law Review (27701)

Temple University
302 University Services Bldg.
1601 N. Broad St., Temple Zip: No. 083-43
Philadelphia, PA 19122-6099
Phone: (215)204-8963
Fax: (215)204-3753
Publications: Temple Times (27703)

Temple University
University Services Bldg., Rm. 601
Philadelphia, PA 19122
Phone: (215)204-6445
Fax: (215)204-4704
Publications: Temple Review (27702)

Ten Lakes Publishing
520 Dewey Ave
PO Box 307
Eureka, MT 59917
Phone: (406)296-2514
Fax: (406)296-2515
Publications: Tobacco Valley News (17788)

Tennessee Academy of Science
2001 Craven Ln.
Hixson, TN 37343
Phone: (615)842-6808
Publications: Tennessee Academy of Science Journal (29222)

Tennessee Bankers Association
201 Venture Circle
Nashville, TN 37228-1603
Phone: (615)244-4871
Fax: (615)244-0995
Publications: The Tennessee Banker (29488)

Tennessee Baptist Convention, Executive Board
PO Box 728
Brentwood, TN 37024
Phone: (615)371-2003
Fax: (615)371-2080
Free: 800-558-2090
Publications: Baptist and Reflector (29061)

Tennessee Dental Association
2104 Sunset Pl.
Box 120188
Nashville, TN 37212
Phone: (615)383-8962
Fax: (615)383-0214
Publications: Tennessee Dental Association Journal (29490)

Tennessee Department of Environment & Conservation
401 Church St.
L & C Annex, 8th Fl.
Nashville, TN 37243-0440
Phone: (615)532-0060
Fax: (615)532-8007
Publications: Tennessee Conservationist (29489)

Tennessee Electric Cooperative Association
710 Spence Ln.
PO Box 100912
Nashville, TN 37224
Phone: (615)367-9284
Fax: (615)367-2495
Publications: Tennessee Magazine (29492)

Tennessee Farm Bureau Federation
147 Bear Creek Pke.
PO Box 313
Columbia, TN 38402
Phone: (931)388-7872
Fax: (931)388-5818
Publications: Tennessee Farm Bureau News (29138)

Tennessee Folklore Society
Middle Tennessee State University
PO Box 529
Murfreesboro, TN 37132
Phone: (615)898-2663
Fax: (615)898-5098
Publications: Tennessee Folklore Society Bulletin (29434)

Tennessee Genealogical Society
PO Box 12124
Memphis, TN 38182
Phone: (901)327-3273
Publications: Ansearchin' News (29357)

Tennessee Historical Society
War Memorial Bldg.
Nashville, TN 37243
Phone: (615)741-8934
Fax: (615)741-8937
Publications: Tennessee Historical Quarterly (29491)

Tennessee Law Review
1505 W Cumberland
Knoxville, TN 37996-1810
Phone: (865)974-4464
Fax: (865)974-2576
Publications: Tennessee Law Review (29283)

Tennessee Municipal League
226 Capitol Blvd., Ste. 710
Nashville, TN 37219
Phone: (615)255-6416
Fax: (615)255-4752
Publications: Tennessee Town & City (29494)

Tennessee Technological University
Box 5072
Cookeville, TN 38505
Phone: (931)372-3060
Fax: (931)372-6225
Publications: The Oracle (29144)

Tennessee Trucking Association
4531 Trousdale Dr.
Nashville, TN 37204-4513
Phone: (615)777-2882
Fax: (615)777-2024
Publications: Tennessee Trucking News (29496)

Tennessee Valley Historical Society
Box 149
Sheffield, AL 35660
Phone: (256)381-2298
Publications: Journal of Muscle Shoals History (220)

Tennessee Valley Printing
201 1st Ave. SE
Decatur, AL 35601
Phone: (256)353-4612
Fax: (256)340-2366
Free: 888-353-4612
Publications: Decatur Daily (170)

Tennessee Walking Horse Breeders and Exhibitors Association
250 N. Ellington Pkwy.
Box 286
Lewisburg, TN 37091
Phone: (931)359-1567
Fax: (931)270-8743
Free: 800-467-0232

Publications: Voice of the Tennessee Walking Horse (29326)

Tennis Week
15 Elm Pl.
Rye, NY 10580
Phone: (914)967-4890
Fax: (914)967-8178
Free: 800-800-TENN

Publications: Tennis Week (23280)

Tennyson Publishing
PO Box 13
Blytheville, AR 72315
Phone: (501)763-4461
Fax: (501)763-6874

Publications: Village News (1059)

Tennyson Publishing
225 W. Main
Box 60
Steele, MO 63877
Phone: (573)695-3415
Fax: (573)695-2114

Publications: The Steele Enterprise (17638)

Tensa Gazette
PO Box 25
St. Joseph, LA 71366
Phone: (318)766-3258
Fax: (318)766-4273

Publications: The Tensas Gazette (12813)

Terminal Railroad Association Historical and Technical Society
PO Box 1688
St. Louis, MO 63188-1688
Phone: (314)535-3101

Publications: Railroads of St. Louis Magazine (17485)

Territorial Newspapers
3280 E. Hemisphere Lp., Ste. 174
PO Box 27087
Tucson, AZ 85726-7087
Phone: (520)294-1200
Fax: (520)294-4040

Publications: The Daily Territorial (944) • Inside Tucson Business (949)

Territorial Publishing Co.
PO Box 879
Guthrie, OK 73044
Phone: (405)282-2222
Fax: (405)282-7378

Publications: Guthrie News Leader (25853)

Testa Communications
25 Willowdale Ave.
Port Washington, NY 11050
Phone: (516)767-2500
Fax: (516)767-9335

Publications: DJ Times (23125) • The Music & Sound Retailer (23131) • Sound & Communications Magazine (23136)

Teton Media, Inc.
20917 Higgins Ct.
Torrance, CA 90501
Free: 800-777-4320

Publications: Cable Yellow Pages (3929)

Teton Valley News
80 E Little Ave.
Driggs, ID 83422-5138
Phone: (208)354-8101
Fax: (208)354-8621

Publications: Teton Valley News (7853)

The Texan Express
302 S Commercial
PO Box 1
Goliad, TX 77963
Phone: (361)645-2330
Fax: (361)645-2812

Publications: The Texan Express (30399)

Texan & Veteran News
PO Box 7440
Fort Worth, TX 76111-0440
Phone: (817)831-3263
Fax: (817)831-3265

Publications: Texan Veteran News (30353)

Texas A & M University
Anthropology Building (TAMU 4352)
College Station, TX 77843-4352
Phone: (979)845-5242
Fax: (979)845-4070

Publications: American Association of Stratigraphic Palynologists Contributions Series (30036)

Texas A & M University
Dept. of Psychology
College Station, TX 77843
Phone: (409)845-2576
Fax: (409)845-4727

Publications: Bulletin: Committee on South Asian Women (30038)

Texas A & M University
015 Reed McDonald Bldg.
College Station, TX 77843-1111
Phone: (979)845-2611
Fax: (979)845-2678

Publications: The Battalion (30037)

Texas A & M University-Commerce
PO Box 4104, ET Sta.
Commerce, TX 75429
Phone: (903)450-4351
Fax: (903)886-5230

Publications: The East Texan (30068)

Texas Accountants and Lawyers for the Arts
1540 Sul Ross
Houston, TX 77006
Phone: (713)526-4876
Fax: (713)526-1299
Free: 800-526-8252

Publications: Art Law & Accounting Reporter (30459)

Texas Association of Counties
1204 San Antonio St.
PO Box 2131
Austin, TX 78768
Phone: (512)478-8753
Fax: (512)477-0519

Publications: COUNTY Magazine (29772)

Texas Association of Realtors
1115 San Jacinto, 2nd Fl.
PO Box 2246
Austin, TX 78768-2246
Phone: (512)480-8200
Fax: (512)370-2390
Free: 800-873-9155

Publications: Texas Realtor (29845)

Texas Association of School Boards
PO Box 400
Austin, TX 78767
Phone: (512)467-0222
Fax: (512)483-7159
Free: 800-580-8272

Publications: Texas Lone Star (29834)

Texas Automobile Dealers Association
PO Box 1028
Austin, TX 78767-1028
Phone: (512)476-2686
Fax: (512)322-0561

Publications: Dealers' Choice (29774)

Texas Bankers Association
PO Box 29156
Shawnee Mission, KS 66201-9156
Phone: (913)261-7000
Fax: (913)261-7010
Free: 800-336-1120

Publications: Texas Banking (11805)

The Texas Catholic
3725 Blackburn
PO Box 190347
Dallas, TX 75219
Phone: (214)528-8792
Fax: (214)528-3411

Publications: The Texas Catholic (30184)

The Texas Catholic Herald
1700 San Jacinto St.
Houston, TX 77002
Phone: (713)659-5461
Fax: (713)659-3444

Publications: The Texas Catholic Herald (30533)

Texas Chiropractic Association
815 Brazos St., Ste. 802
Austin, TX 78701-2509
Phone: (512)477-9292
Fax: (512)477-9296

Publications: Texas Journal of Chiropractic (29828)

Texas City Sun
2404 S Park
Pearland, TX 77581
Phone: (409)945-3441
Fax: (409)935-0428
Free: 800-270-9175

Publications: Friendswood Reporter News & Pearland Reporter News (30369) • Pearland Reporter News (30918) • Texas City Sun (30919)

The Texas Democracy Foundation
307 W 7th St.
Austin, TX 78701
Phone: (512)477-0746
Fax: (512)474-1175

Publications: Texas Observer (29837)

Texas Dental Association
1946 S. IH35, Ste. 400
Austin, TX 78704
Phone: (512)443-3675
Fax: (512)443-3031

Publications: Texas Dental Journal (29816)

Texas Electric Cooperatives, Inc.
2550 S. IH-35
Austin, TX 78704
Phone: (512)454-0311
Fax: (512)486-6254

Publications: Texas Co-op Power (29813)

Texas Farm Bureau
PO Box 2689
Waco, TX 76702
Phone: (254)772-3030
Fax: (254)772-1766

Publications: Texas Agriculture (31252)

Texas FFA Association
6210 E. Hwy. 290, No. 410
Austin, TX 78723-1082
Phone: (512)480-8045
Fax: (512)480-0555

Publications: Texas FFA News (29819)

Texas Food Industry Association
7333 Hwy. 290 E.
Austin, TX 78723
Phone: (512)926-9285
Fax: (512)926-0917
Free: 800-856-8342

Publications: Texas Food Merchant (29820)

Texas Funeral Directors Association
PO Box 14667
Austin, TX 78761
Phone: (512)454-5262
Fax: (512)451-9556

Publications: Texas Director (29817)

Texas Hereford Association
4609 Airport Fwy.
Fort Worth, TX 76117
Phone: (817)831-3161
Fax: (817)831-3162

Publications: Texas Hereford (30354)

Texas High School Coaches Association
1011 53 1/2 St.
PO Box 14627
Austin, TX 78761
Phone: (512)454-6709
Fax: (512)454-3950

Publications: Texas Coach (29814)

Texas Highways Magazine
PO Box 149233
Austin, TX 78714
Phone: (512)486-5823
Fax: (512)486-5879

Publications: Texas Highways (29822)

Texas Longhorn Journal, Inc.
PMB 210-110
40 W Littleton Blvd.
Littleton, CO 80120-2478

Publications: Texas Longhorn Journal (4555)

Texas Medical Association
401 W. 15th St.
Austin, TX 78701
Phone: (512)370-1300
Fax: (512)370-1632
Free: 800-880-1300

Publications: Texas Medicine (29835)

The Texas Mohair Weekly
PO Box 287
Rocksprings, TX 78880
Phone: (830)683-3130

Publications: The Texas Mohair Weekly (30989)

Texas Monthly
PO Box 1569
Austin, TX 78767
Phone: (512)320-6900
Fax: (512)476-9007

Publications: Texas Monthly (29836)

Texas Municipal League
1821 Rutherford Ln., Ste. 400
Austin, TX 78754-5128
Phone: (512)231-7400
Fax: (512)231-7490

Publications: Texas Town & City (29849)

Texas Music Educators Association
PO Box 140465
Austin, TX 78714
Phone: (512)452-0710
Fax: (512)451-9213
Free: 888-318-TMEA

Publications: The Southwestern Musician (29808)

Texas Parks and Wildlife
4200 Smith School Rd.
Austin, TX 78744
Phone: (512)389-4800
Free: 800-792-1112

Publications: Texas Parks & Wildlife (29838)

Texas Pecan Growers Association
4348 Carter Creek, Ste. 101
Bryan, TX 77802
Phone: (979)846-3285
Fax: (979)846-1752

Publications: Pecan South (29974)

Texas Petroleum Marketers and Convenience Store Association (TPCA)
701 W. 15th St.
Austin, TX 78701
Phone: (512)476-9547
Fax: (512)477-4239
Free: 800-460-8662

Publications: Texas Petroleum and C-Store Journal (29839)

Texas Pharmacy Association
PO Box 14709
Austin, TX 78761
Phone: (512)836-8350
Fax: (512)836-0308
Free: 800-505-5463

Publications: Texas Pharmacy (29840)

Texas Press Association
718 W. 5th St.
Austin, TX 78701-2799
Phone: (512)477-6755
Fax: (512)477-6759

Publications: Texas Press Messenger (29841)

Texas Propane Gas Association
8408 N. Interegional Hwy.
Austin, TX 78753
Phone: (512)836-8620
Fax: (512)834-0758
Free: 800-325-7427

Publications: Texas Propane (29843)

Texas Public Employees Association
512 E. 11th St., Ste. 100
Austin, TX 78701
Phone: (512)476-2691
Fax: (512)476-1338
Free: 888-367-8732

Publications: Texas Public Employee (29844)

Texas Restaurant Association
1400 Lavaca St.
PO Box 1429
Austin, TX 78767
Phone: (512)457-4100
Fax: (512)472-2777
Free: 800-395-2872

Publications: Food & Service News (29777)

Texas Society of Architects
816 Congress Ave., Ste. 970
Austin, TX 78701-2443
Phone: (512)478-7386
Fax: (512)478-0528
Free: 877-286-4144

Publications: Texas Architect (29811)

Texas Society of Professional Engineers
3501 Manor Rd.
PO Box 2145
Austin, TX 78768
Phone: (512)472-9286
Fax: (512)472-2934
Free: 800-580-8973

Publications: Texas Professional Engineer (29842)

Texas Society of Professional Surveyors
2525 Wallingwood Dr., Ste. 300
Austin, TX 78746
Phone: (512)327-7871
Fax: (512)327-7872

Publications: The Texas Surveyor (29848)

Texas Southern University
3100 Cleburne Ave.
Houston, TX 77004-4583
Phone: (713)313-7011
Fax: (713)313-7188

Publications: The TSU Herald (30536)

Texas and Southwestern Cattle Raisers Association, Inc.
1301 W. 7th St.
Fort Worth, TX 76102
Phone: (817)332-7064
Fax: (817)332-5446
Free: 800-242-7820

Publications: The Cattleman (30331)

The Texas Spur
PO Box 430
Spur, TX 79370
Phone: (806)271-3381
Fax: (806)271-3966

Publications: The Texas Spur (31125)

Texas State Historical Association
2/306 Sid Richardson Hall
University of Texas
Austin, TX 78712
Phone: (512)471-1525
Fax: (512)471-1551

Publications: Southwestern Historical Quarterly (29807) • Texas Historian (29824)

Texas State Teachers Association
316 W. 12th St.
Austin, TX 78701
Phone: (512)476-5355
Fax: (512)469-0766

Publications: TSTA Advocate (29852)

Texas Tech University
PO Box 43081
Lubbock, TX 79409
Phone: (806)742-3603
Fax: (806)742-2434

Publications: The University Daily (30720)

Texas Tech University Press
Box 41037
Lubbock, TX 79409-1037
Phone: (806)742-2982
Fax: (806)742-2979
Free: 800-832-4042

Publications: Conradiana (16197) • Eighteenth Century (30710) • Helios (Lubbock) (30042) • Intertexts (30712)

Texas Tribune
PO Box 446
Tyler, TX 75710
Phone: (903)597-1124
Fax: (903)593-3146

Publications: Texas Tribune (31199)

Texas Veterinary Medical Association
6633 Hwy. 290 E., Ste. 201
Austin, TX 78723-1134
Phone: (512)452-4224
Fax: (512)452-6633

Publications: Texas Veterinarian (29850)

Texas Water Utilities Association
1106 Clayton Ln., Ste. 101E
Austin, TX 78723
Phone: (512)459-3124
Fax: (512)459-7124

Publications: Texas Water Utilities Journal (29851)

Texas Woman's University
PO Box 425828
Denton, TX 76204-5828
Phone: (940)898-2185
Fax: (940)898-2188

Publications: The Lasso (30241)

Texas Women in Business, Inc.
395 Sawdust, Ste. 2139
The Woodlands, TX 77380
Phone: (281)419-8961
Fax: (281)367-9343

Publications: Texas Women in Business (31308)

Texoma Enterprise
805 N Hughes
Box 488
Howe, TX 75459-0488
Phone: (903)532-6012
Fax: (903)532-6012

Publications: Texoma Enterprise (30591)

The Textile Museum
2320 S St. NW
Washington, DC 20008-4088
Phone: (202)667-0441
Fax: (202)483-0994

Publications: The Textile Museum Journal (5821)

Textile Rental Services Association of America
1800 Diagonal Rd.,Ste. 200
Alexandria, VA 22314
Phone: (954)457-7555
Fax: (954)457-3890
Free: 800-868-8772

Publications: Textile Rental Magazine (31744)

Textile Research Institute
601 Prospect Ave.
PO Box 625
Princeton, NJ 08542
Phone: (609)924-3150
Fax: (609)683-7836

Publications: Textile Research Journal (19473)

Textile Technology Centre
3000 Boulle St.
Saint-Hyacinthe, QC, Canada J2S 1H9
Phone: (514)778-1870
Fax: (514)778-9016
Free: 800-288-8378

Publications: Canadian Textile Journal (La Revue Canadienne du Textile) (37348)

T.F.H. Publications Inc.
1 T.F.H. Plaza
3rd & Union Aves.
Neptune, NJ 07753-6497
Phone: (732)988-8400
Fax: (732)988-5466
Free: 800-631-2188

Publications: Tropical Fish Hobbyist (19320)

Thaddeus Computing, Inc.
110 N. Court
PO Box 910
Fairfield, IA 52556

Publications: Pocket PC (10883)

Thamesville Herald
PO Box 580
Thamesville, ON, Canada N0P 2K0
Fax: (519)692-9515

Publications: Thamesville Herald (36432)

Theatre Communications Group
520 Eighth Ave., 24th Fl.
New York, NY 10018-4156
Phone: (212)609-5900
Fax: (212)609-5901

Publications: American Theatre (21207)

Theatre Historical Society of America
York Theatre Bldg., 2nd Fl.
152 N. York St.
Elmhurst, IL 60126-2806
Phone: (630)782-1800
Fax: (630)782-1802

Publications: Marquee (8835)

theINDIAN Group
PO Box 858030
Westland, MI 48185
Phone: (734)447-0028

Publications: theIndian (15681)

Thema
Box 8747
Metairie, LA 70011-8747
Phone: (504)887-1263

Publications: Thema (12679)

Then and There Media, LLC
PO Box 970
Wantagh, NY 11793
Phone: (212)628-1594

Publications: Films in Review (23500)

Theodor Herzl Foundation, Inc.
633 3rd Ave., 21st Fl.
New York, NY 10017-6706
Phone: (212)339-6040
Fax: (212)318-6176

Publications: Midstream (22334)

Theodore Roosevelt Association
PO Box 719
Oyster Bay, NY 11771
Phone: (516)921-6319
Fax: (516)921-6481

Publications: Theodore Roosevelt Association Journal (23071)

Theology Digest
St. Louis University
3800 Lindell Blvd.
PO Box 56907
St. Louis, MO 63108
Phone: (314)977-3410
Fax: (314)977-3704

Publications: Theology Digest (17524)

Theosophical Book Association for the Blind Inc.
516 N. Lucas Dr.
Santa Maria, CA 93454-3828
Phone: (805)646-2121
Fax: (805)646-2121

Publications: The Braille Star Theosophist (3694)

Theosophical History
20733 Via Sonrisa
Yorba Linda, CA 92886
Phone: (714)278-3727
Fax: (714)693-0142

Publications: Theosophical History (4119)

Theosophical Society in America
PO Box 270
Wheaton, IL 60189-0270
Phone: (630)668-1571
Fax: (630)668-4976

Publications: The Quest (9758)

Theosophical Society in Canada
RR No. 3
Burks Falls, ON, Canada P0A 1C0
Phone: (705)382-6012

Publications: Canadian Theosophist (35713)

Theosophical University Press
PO Box C
Pasadena, CA 91109-7107
Phone: (626)798-3378
Fax: (626)798-4749

Publications: Sunrise (2827)

The Theosophy Co.
245 W 33rd St.
Los Angeles, CA 90007
Phone: (213)748-7244
Fax: (213)748-0634

Publications: Theosophy (2412)

Thesaurus Publishing
141 NE 3rd Ave., No 604
Miami, FL 33132-2221

Publications: International Journal of Mathematical and Statistical Sciences (6363)

Thief River Falls Times, Inc.
324 Main Ave. North
PO Box 100
Thief River Falls, MN 56701
Phone: (218)681-4450
Fax: (218)681-4455

Publications: Northern Watch (16467) • Thief River Falls Times (16468)

Thiel College
Box 1654
Greenville, PA 16125
Phone: (724)589-2000

Publications: Thielensian (26959)

Thieme Medical Publishers, Inc.
333 7th Ave., 5th Fl.
New York, NY 10001
Phone: (212)760-0888
Fax: (212)947-1112
Free: 800-782-3488

Publications: Facial Plastic Surgery (21672) • Journal of Reconstructive Microsurgery (22177) • Seminars in Hearing (4356) • Seminars in Neurology (22724) • Seminars in Reproductive Endocrinology (26509) • Seminars in Respiratory and Critical Care Medicine (22725) • Seminars in Speech and Language (22726) • Seminars in Thrombosis and Hemostasis (22727) • Skull Base (22742)

Think Tank Communications Inc.
PO Box 2226
St. James, NY 11780

Publications: Professional Check Casher (23289)

Third Coast
Western Michigan Univ.
Dept. of English
Kalamazoo, MI 49008-5331
Phone: (616)387-2675
Fax: (616)387-2562

Publications: Third Coast (15245)

Third World Press
PO Box 19730
Chicago, IL 60619
Phone: (773)651-0700
Fax: (773)651-7286

Publications: Black Books Bulletin: Words Work (8284)

The Thirteen Towns of Fosston, Inc.
118 N Johnson
Fosston, MN 56542
Phone: (218)435-1313
Fax: (218)435-1309

Publications: The Thirteen Towns (15908)

13th Moon, Inc.
Dept. of English
SUNY at Albany
1400 Washington Ave.
Albany, NY 12222
Phone: (518)442-5593

Publications: 13th Moon (20005)

This Week
PO Box 130
Albany, OR 97321-0041
Fax: (503)926-5298

Publications: This Week (26207)

This Week in Cleveland Magazine
20575 Ctr. Ridge Rd., Ste. 460
Cleveland, OH 44116-3422
Phone: (440)331-8012
Fax: (440)331-1481

Publications: This Week in Cleveland Magazine (24957)

This Week Life & Times
20780 Holyoke Ave. W
PO Box 549
Lakeville, MN 55044
Phone: (612)469-2181
Fax: (612)469-2184

Publications: This Week Life & Times (15996)

This Week Publications
274 Puuhale Rd., Ste. 200
Honolulu, HI 96819-2234
Phone: (808)843-6000
Fax: (808)843-6090

Publications: Bellmore South This Week/Pennysaver (7659) • Cedarhurst Pennysaver (7661) • Elmont Pennysaver (7663) • Far Rockaway Pennysaver (7664) • Franklin Square Pennysaver (7665) • Hewlett/Woodmere Pennysaver (7669) • Long Beach Pennysaver (7784) • Lynbrook Pennysaver (7785) • Oceanside Pennysaver (7790) • Rockville Centre Pennysaver (7792) • This Week (7723) • This Week Big Island (7724) • This Week Kauai (7725) • This Week Oahu (7726) • Valley Stream Pennysaver (7793)

This Week Publications
2325 Park Lawn Dr., Ste. R.
Waukesha, WI 53186
Phone: (262)798-1234
Fax: (262)798-1222

Publications: Franklin/Hales Corners Enterprise (33768) • Greenfield/Greendale Enterprise (33765) • New Berlin Enterprise (34181) • This Week Publications (34412)

Thoi Bao
447 E Santa Clara St.
San Jose, CA 95113
Phone: (408)292-2276
Fax: (408)292-0346

Publications: Thoi Bao (3543)

Thomas Gilcrease Museum Association
1400 N. Gilcrease Museum Rd.
Tulsa, OK 74127-2100
Phone: (918)596-2700
Fax: (918)596-2759
Free: 888-655-2278

Publications: Gilcrease Journal (26117)

Thomas Jefferson Law Review
2121 San Diego Ave.
San Diego, CA 92110
Phone: (619)298-3111
Fax: (619)692-8149

Publications: Thomas Jefferson Law Review (3279)

Thomas Land Publishers Inc.
255 Jefferson Rd.
St. Louis, MO 63119-3627
Phone: (314)963-7445
Fax: (314)963-9345

Publications: Topics in Stroke Rehabilitation (17525)

Thomas Publication Co., Inc.
PO Box 5088
St. Louis, MO 63115
Phone: (314)535-4033
Fax: (314)535-4280

Publications: The St. Louis Metro Evening Whirl (17504)

Thomas Publishing Co.
5 Penn Plaza
New York, NY 10001
Phone: (212)695-0500
Fax: (212)290-7362

Publications: Inbound Logistics (21858) • Industrial Equipment News (21865) • Managing Automation (22278) • The Thomas Tribune (22832)

Thomaston Publishing Co.
PO Box 430
Thomaston, GA 30286
Phone: (706)647-7144
Fax: (706)647-2833

Publications: Thomaston Times (7585)

The Thomasville Times
21 Wilson Ave.
Thomasville, AL 36784
Phone: (334)636-2214
Fax: (334)636-9822

Publications: The Thomasville Times (470)

Thompson Newspaper
34 S. 4th St.
Zanesville, OH 43701
Phone: (740)452-4561
Fax: (740)453-9417

Publications: Times-Recorder Midweek (25718)

Thompson Publishing Group Inc.
1725 K St. NW, Ste. 700
Washington, DC 20006
Phone: (202)739-9540
Free: 800-444-8741

Publications: Section 504 Compliance Handbook (5786)

Thompson Publishing, Inc.
204 S First St.
PO Box 398
Folkston, GA 31537
Phone: (912)496-3585
Fax: (912)496-4585

Publications: Charlton County Herald (7274)

Thomsom Newspaper
PO Box 2100
Ashtabula, OH 44005-2100
Phone: (216)593-1166
Fax: (216)593-6589

Publications: The Star Beacon (24624)

Thomson-Chesapeake Publications
115 East Carroll St.
Salisbury, MD 21801
Phone: (410)749-7171

Publications: Maryland Times-Press (13638) • Somerset Herald (13669)

Thomson Financial
195 Broadway
New York, NY 10007
Phone: (646)822-2000

Publications: Bank Investment Marketing (21286) • Bank Technology News (21287) • Broker Magazine (21344) • Card Marketing (21373) • Card Technology (8298) • Corporate Taxation (21501) • Credit Card Management (21513) • Credit Union Journal (21515) • Financial Services Marketing (21699) • Future Banker (21743) • Health Data Management (8393) • Health Data Management (8392) • Insurance Networking (21884) • Internet Health Care (21941) • Investment Management Weekly (21947) • The Journal of California Taxation (22017) • The Journal of New York Taxation (22143) • Medicine and Health (22311) • Mortgage Servicing News (22367) • Mortgage Technology (22368) • National Mortgage News (22399) • On Wall Street (22489) • Origination News (22503) • The Practical Accountant (22589) • Private Equity Week (22594) • Securities Industry News (22719) • Small Business Banker (22745) • U.S. Banker (22886) • Web Finance (22912)

Thomson Financial Media
300 S. Wacker Dr. Ste. 1800
Chicago, IL 60606
Phone: (312)913-1334
Fax: (312)913-1369

Publications: Collections & Credit Risk (8335)

Thomson Healthcare
1 Mt. Pleasant Rd
Toronto, ON, Canada M5W 1A7
Phone: (416)596-5000

Publications: Patient Care (36698)

Thomson Indiana, Inc.
8109 Kingston Rd., Ste. 500
Avon, IN 46123-8211
Phone: (317)839-5129
Fax: (317)839-6546

Publications: Hendrick County Flyer/Weekend Edition (9793) • The Hendricks County Flyer (9794) • Westside Flyer (9795)

Thomson Medical Economics
5 Paragon Dr.
Montvale, NJ 07645-1742
Phone: (201)358-7200
Fax: (201)722-2680

Publications: Business & Health (19243) • Clinical Cardiology Alert (19245) • Clinical Laboratory Reference (CLR) (19246) • Contemporary OB/GYN (19248) • Contemporary Pediatrics (19249) • Contemporary Urology (19250) • Contraceptive Technology Update (19251) • Drug Topics (19252) • ED Nursing (19253) • FirstLine (19254) • Hospital Pharmacist Report (19255) • Infectious Disease Alert (19256) • Internal Medicine Alert (19257) • JobWatch (19259) • Journal of the American Academy of Physician Assistants (JAAPA) (19260) • Medical Economics (19262) • Medical Economics—Obstetrics/Gynecology Edition (19263) • Medical Economics—Orthopedic Surgery Edition (19264) • Medical Economics for Surgeons (19265) • Medical Laboratory Observer (MLO) (19266) • Nursing Opportunities (19267) • OB/GYN Clinical Alert (19268) • Office Nurse (19269) • Patient Care (19270) • Patient Care for the Nurse Practitioner (19271) • RN (19274) • Strategic Medicine (19276) • Trauma Reports (19277) • Veterinary Medicine (19278)

Thomson Newspaper
PO Box 730
Marshall, TX 75671-0730
Phone: (903)935-7914
Fax: (903)935-6242

Publications: Marshall News Messenger (30766)

Thomson Newspapers
120 W. 1st Ave.
Mesa, AZ 85210
Phone: (602)898-6500
Fax: (602)898-6463

Publications: The Tribune (746)

Thomson Newspapers
7525 E. Camelback Rd.
PO Box 1150
Scottsdale, AZ 85252-1150
Phone: (480)898-5680
Fax: (480)970-2360

Publications: Scottsdale Progress Tribune (874)

Thomson Newspapers
4403 Constitution Ln.
Marianna, FL 32446
Phone: (904)526-3614
Fax: (904)482-4478

Publications: Marianna Jackson County Floridan (6326)

Thomson Newspapers
PO Box 968
Valdosta, GA 31603-0968
Phone: (912)244-1880
Fax: (912)244-2560

Publications: The Valdosta Daily Times (7616)

Thomson Newspapers
517 E. Broadway
PO Box 210
Logansport, IN 46947
Phone: (219)722-5000
Fax: (219)732-5070
Free: 800-676-4125

Publications: Pharos-Tribune (10275)

Thomson Newspapers
34 S. 4th St.
Zanesville, OH 43701
Phone: (614)452-4561
Fax: (614)452-0750

Publications: The Times Recorder (25717)

Thomson Newspapers
65 Queen St. W.
Toronto, ON, Canada M5H 2M8
Phone: (416)864-1710
Fax: (416)864-0109

Publications: The Spectrum (31417)

Thomson Newspapers
PO Box 2008
Altoona, PA 16603
Phone: (814)946-7411
Fax: (814)946-7547
Free: 800-339-4482

Publications: Altoona Mirror (26635)

Thomson Newspapers
PO Box 100528
Florence, SC 29501-0528
Phone: (803)317-6397
Fax: (803)661-6558
Free: 888-317-NEWS

Publications: Florence Morning News (28602)

Thomson Publications
PO Box 9335
Fresno, CA 93791
Phone: (559)266-2964
Fax: (559)266-0189

Publications: Agricultural Spray Adjuvants (1942)

Thomson Publishing Inc.
PO Box 288
Tasley, VA 23441

Publications: The Eastern Shore News (32318)

Thomson-Shore, Inc.
7300 W. Joy Rd.
Dexter, MI 48130-9701
Phone: (734)426-3939
Fax: (734)426-6219

Publications: The Allegheny Review (27232)

Thorne Research Inc.
25820 Hwy. 2 W.
PO Box 25
Dover, ID 83825
Phone: (208)263-1337
Fax: (208)365-2488

Publications: Alternative Medicine Review (7852)

Thorny Locust
PO Box 32631
Kansas City, MO 64171-5631
Phone: (816)756-5096

Publications: Thorny Locust (17198)

Thorold News
13 Front St. N.
PO Box 86
Thorold, ON, Canada L2V 3Y7
Phone: (416)227-1141
Fax: (416)227-0222

Publications: Thorold News (36435)

Thoroughbred Times Company Inc.
PO Box 8237
Lexington, KY 40533
Phone: (859)260-9800
Fax: (859)260-9812

Publications: Thoroughbred Times (12178)

Thorp Courier
Box 487
Thorp, WI 54771
Phone: (715)669-5525
Fax: (715)669-5596

Publications: Thorp Courier (34367)

Thousand Islands Printing Co., Inc.
PO Box 277
Alexandria Bay, NY 13607-0277
Phone: (315)482-2581
Fax: (315)482-6315

Publications: Thousand Islands Sun (20022)

Thousand Trails, Inc.
3801 Parkwood Blvd., Ste. 100
PO Box 2529
Frisco, TX 75034
Phone: (214)618-7200
Fax: (214)618-7208
Free: 800-328-6226

Publications: Trailblazer (30372)

Three Fifty Six, Inc.
30 W. Olentangy St.
PO Box 937
Powell, OH 43065-0937
Phone: (614)848-5038
Fax: (614)436-4760
Free: 800-2CTO-MAG

Publications: Check the Oil! (25490)

Three Rivers Commerical News
124 N Main St.
Three Rivers, MI 49093
Phone: (269)279-7488
Fax: (269)279-6007

Publications: Three Rivers Commercial-News (15592)

Three Rivers Community News
130 W Michigan Ave.
Three Rivers, MI 49093
Phone: (616)279-7448
Fax: (616)279-7440

Publications: Your Community News (15593)

Three Village Herald
PO Box 703
East Setauket, NY 11733-0903
Fax: (516)751-8592

Publications: Three Village Herald (20556)

3Com Corp.
5400 Bayfront Plaza
Santa Clara, CA 95052-8145
Phone: (408)764-5000
Fax: (408)764-5001
Free: 800-NET-3CON

Publications: CONNECT (3669)

The Threepenny Review
PO Box 9131
Berkeley, CA 94709
Phone: (510)849-4545
Fax: (510)849-4551

Publications: The Threepenny Review (1564)

Thresholds in Education Foundation
EPF Dept.
225 Graham Hall
Northern Illinois University
DeKalb, IL 60115
Phone: (815)753-9359
Fax: (815)753-8750

Publications: Thresholds in Education (8741)

Thrifty Nickel
PO Box 7423
Falls Church, VA 22040
Phone: (703)536-5700
Fax: (703)536-2907

Publications: Thrifty Nickel (32058)

Thrifty Nickel Want Ads
1301 E Morgan Ave.
Evansville, IN 47711
Phone: (812)428-8484
Fax: (812)428-8491
Free: 800-467-8480

Publications: Thrifty Nickel Want Ads (9936)

Thrifty Nickel Want Ads
PO Box 6637
Lubbock, TX 79493-6637
Phone: (806)793-9990
Fax: (806)793-9922
Free: 800-822-0882

Publications: Thrifty Nickel Want Ads (30719)

Throckmorton Tribune
Box 847
Throckmorton, TX 76483
Phone: (940)849-3166
Fax: (940)849-3166

Publications: Tribune (31192)

Thunder Bay Historical Museum Society
425 Donald St. E
Thunder Bay, ON, Canada P7E 5V1
Phone: (807)623-0801
Fax: (807)622-6880

Publications: Thunder Bay Historical Museum Society, Papers and Records (36441)

Thunder Bay Post
87 Hill St. N
Thunder Bay, ON, Canada P7A 5V6
Phone: (807)346-2600
Fax: (807)622-2779

Publications: Thunder Bay Post (36443)

Thunder Prairie Publishing
161 Main
PO Box 98
Deport, TX 75435
Phone: (903)652-4205
Fax: (903)652-6041

Publications: Deport Times (30245) • Talco Times (31175)

Thunder Prairie Publishing Co.
PO Box 98
Deport, TX 75435
Phone: (903)652-4205
Fax: (903)652-6041

Publications: Blossom Times (29929) • Bogata News (29932)

The Thunderbolt, Inc.
PO Box 1211
Marietta, GA 30061

Publications: The Truth at Last (7421)

Thurman Marketing Services, Inc.
92 Argonaut, No. 275
Aliso Viejo, CA 92656
Phone: (949)581-3993
Fax: (949)581-3399

Publications: Computing News & Reviews (1390)

Thurston County Council on Aging
112 E 4th Ave.
Olympia, WA 98501
Phone: (360)586-3590
Fax: (360)586-3551

Publications: The Thurston-Mason Senior News (32860)

T.I. Publications
44 W Main
PO Box 7
Fremont, MI 49412-0007
Phone: (616)924-4400
Fax: (616)924-4066

Publications: Times-Indicator (15058)

The Ticker
Baruch College, CUNY
One Bernard Baruch Way, Ste. 3-290
New York, NY 10010
Phone: (646)312-4710
Fax: (646)312-4711

Publications: The Ticker (22834)

Tidewater Newspaper Inc.
Box J
Gloucester, VA 23061
Phone: (804)693-3101
Fax: (804)693-7844

Publications: Gloucester-Mathews Gazette-Journal (32115)

Tidewater Virginia Families
316 Littletown Quarter
Williamsburg, VA 23185-5519
Phone: (757)220-4888
Fax: (757)220-0975

Publications: Tidewater Virginia Families (32619)

The Tidings
PO Box 7
Ashland, OR 97520
Phone: (503)482-3456
Fax: (503)482-3688

Publications: The Tidings (26218)

The Tidings Corp.
3424 Wilshire Blvd., 6th Fl.
Los Angeles, CA 90010
Phone: (213)637-7360
Fax: (213)637-6360

Publications: The Tidings (2413) • Vida Nueva (2430)

TIE - The International Educator
PO Box 513
Cummaquid, MA 02637
Phone: (508)362-1414
Fax: (508)362-1411
Free: 877-375-6668

Publications: TIE (The International Educator) (14151)

TIEMPO
1917 Austin Ave., Ste. 8
Waco, TX 76701
Phone: (254)752-7528
Fax: (254)752-6715

Publications: TIEMPO (31254)

Tiftarea Shopper
147 Love Ave.
Tifton, GA 31793
Phone: (229)386-0472
Fax: (229)386-0478

Publications: Tiftarea Shopper (7598)

The Tifton Gazette
211 N. Tift Ave.
PO Box 708
Tifton, GA 31794
Phone: (229)382-4321
Fax: (229)387-7322

Publications: The Tifton Gazette (7599)

Tikkun Magazine
2342 Shattuck Ave., No. 1200
Berkeley, CA 94704-1517
Phone: (415)575-1200
Fax: (415)575-1434

Publications: Tikkun Magazine (1565)

Tilden Citizen
PO Box 280
Tilden, NE 68781
Phone: (402)368-5315
Fax: (402)368-5315

Publications: Tilden Citizen (18298)

Tile and Stone, Inc.
18 E. 41st St.,
New York, NY 10017
Phone: (212)376-7722
Fax: (212)376-7723

Publications: Stone Magazine (22794)

The Tillsonburg News
25 Townline Rd.
PO Box 190
Tillsonburg, ON, Canada N4G 4H6
Phone: (519)688-6397
Fax: (519)842-3511
Free: 800-363-2245

Publications: The Tillsonburg News (36450)

Tim Hall
Box 13261
Detroit, MI 48213-0261
Phone: (313)273-9039

Publications: Struggle (14950)

Timber Framers Guild of North America
Box 60
Becket, MA 01223
Free: 888-453-0879

Publications: Timber Framing (31571)

Timber Lake
PO Box 10
Timber Lake, SD 57656-0010
Phone: (605)865-3546
Fax: (605)865-3787

Publications: Timber Lake Topic (29003)

The Timber Producer
PO Box 1278
Rhinelander, WI 54501
Phone: (715)282-5828
Fax: (715)282-4941

Publications: The Timber Producer (34286)

Timber West Publications
PO Box 610
Edmonds, WA 98020-0610
Phone: (425)778-3388
Fax: (425)771-3623
Free: (866)221-1017

Publications: Timber West (32746)

Timberline Publishing
Box 1350
La Ronge, SK, Canada S0J 1L0
Phone: (306)425-3344
Fax: (306)425-2827

Publications: The La Ronge Northerner (37486)

Timbertimes
Box 219
Hillsboro, OR 97123
Phone: (503)293-6658
Fax: (503)615-8557
Free: 800-821-8652

Publications: Timbertimes (26373)

Time Canada Ltd.
175 Bloor St. E., Ste. 602
North Tower
Toronto, ON, Canada M4W 3R8
Phone: (416)929-1115
Fax: (416)929-0019
Free: 800-668-9934

Publications: Time (Canada) (36760)

Time Health Media, Inc.
2100 Lakeshohre Dr.
Birmingham, AL 35209-6721

Publications: Health (73)

Time Inc.
Time-Life Bldg., Rockefeller Center
1271 Avenue of the Americas
New York, NY 10020
Phone: (212)522-1212
Fax: (212)467-1396

Publications: Entertainment Weekly (21609) • Fortune (21727) • Fortune International (21728) • FSB (21739) • In Style (21857) • Life Magazine (22254) • Martha Stewart at Home (22286) • Money (22360) • On (22487) • People Weekly (22540) • Real Simple (22636) • Sports Illustrated (22776) • Sports Illustrated for Kids (22777) • Sports Illustrated for Women (22778) • Teen People (22818) • This Old House (22831) • Time (22837) • Time (Asia) (22838) • Time International (22839) • Time for Kids (22840)

Time Inc. Ventures
1325 Avenue of the Americas, 27th Fl.
New York, NY 10019
Phone: (212)522-8989
Fax: (212)522-3611

Publications: Parenting's Healthy Pregnancy (22525)

The Time Journal & Spotlight
PO Drawer 4189
Eastman, GA 31023
Phone: (478)374-5562
Fax: (478)374-3464

Publications: Times Journal Spotlight (7261)

Time Out New York
627 Broadway, 7th Fl.
New York, NY 10012
Phone: (212)539-4495
Fax: (212)673-8382

Publications: Time Out New York (22841)

Time Ventures
PO Box 59580
Boulder, CO 80322
Phone: (303)678-8475
Fax: (303)661-1181
Free: 800-477-3974

Publications: Vibe Magazine (4195)

Time4 Media, Inc.
2 Park Ave., 10th Fl.
New York, NY 10016
Phone: (212)779-5493
Fax: (212)779-5118

Publications: Field & Stream (21691) • Golf Magazine (21774) • Home Mechanix (21811) • Outdoor Life (22511) • Popular Science (22582) • Ski (4187) • Skiing (4189) • Skiing Trade News (4190) • Yachting Magazine (5082)

The Times
PO Box 308
Melbourne, AR 72556
Phone: (870)368-4421
Fax: (870)368-4721

Publications: The Times (1274)

The Times
540 MacKenzie Blvd.
PO Box 609
Mackenzie, BC, Canada V0J 2C0
Phone: (250)997-6675
Fax: (250)997-4747

Publications: The Times (35011)

Times
113 South Central Ave
PO Box 410
Blackshear, GA 31516
Phone: (912)449-6693
Fax: (912)449-1719

Publications: Times (7128)

The Times
PO Box 838
Gainesville, GA 30503
Phone: (770)532-1234
Fax: (770)532-7085

Publications: The Times (7298)

Times
PO Box 226
110 East Lafayette
Rushville, IL 62681
Phone: (217)322-3321
Fax: (217)322-2770

Publications: Times (9558)

The Times
PO Box 1603
Lafayette, IN 47902-1603
Phone: (765)742-2050
Fax: (765)742-7513

Publications: The Catholic Moment (10250)

The Times
222 Lake St.
Shreveport, LA 71101
Phone: (318)459-3200
Fax: (318)459-3301
Free: 800-551-8892

Publications: The Times (12820)

The Times
Broadway St.
PO Box 50
Treherne, MB, Canada R0G 2V0
Phone: (204)723-2542
Fax: (204)723-2754

Publications: The Times (35305)

Times
123 N. 1st St.
Harbor Beach, MI 48441-1102

Publications: Times (15143)

The Times
PO Box 122
Comfrey, MN 56019-0218
Phone: (507)877-2281
Fax: (507)877-2251

Publications: The Times (15812)

Times
PO Box 457
508 Main St.
Starbuck, MN 56381
Phone: (320)239-2244
Fax: (320)239-2254

Publications: Starbuck Times (16462)

The Times
512 Turner St.
PO Box 549
Thomasville, NC 27360
Phone: (910)472-9500
Fax: (910)476-7272
Free: 800-233-2943

Publications: The Times (24256)

The Times
PO Box 1431
Warren, OH 44482
Phone: (330)652-5841
Fax: (330)652-3948

Publications: The Times (25616)

Times
PO Box 278
109 Spalding Ave.
Brownsville, OR 97327
Phone: (541)466-5311
Fax: (541)466-5312

Publications: Times (26258)

Times
142 Chemawa Rd. N.
PO Box 20025
Keizer, OR 97303-0025
Phone: (503)390-1051

Publications: Keizertimes (26380)

TIMES: standard inc
8125 Jonestown Rd.
Harrisburg, PA 17112
Phone: (717)469-2000
Fax: (717)469-2005
Free: 888-US-TIMES

Publications: TIMES: in harness (27013)

The Times
23 Exchange St.
PO Box 307
Pawtucket, RI 02862
Phone: (401)722-4000
Fax: (401)727-9252
Free: 800-292-6838

Publications: The Times (28379)

Times
PO Box 368
Lake Preston, SD 57249
Phone: (605)847-4421
Fax: (605)847-4421

Publications: Times (28880)

The Times
PO Box 97
Waitsburg, WA 99361-0097
Phone: (509)337-6631
Fax: (509)337-6045

Publications: The Times (33186)

The Times
105 1st St.
Westby, WI 54667-1301
Phone: (608)634-4317
Fax: (608)634-6499

Publications: The Times (34450)

Times Advocate
PO Box 427
West Salem, IL 62476-0427
Phone: (618)456-8808
Fax: (618)456-8809

Publications: Times Advocate (9751)

Times-Advocate
PO Box 850
Exeter, ON, Canada E3B 2T8
Phone: (519)235-1331
Fax: (519)235-0766

Publications: Times-Advocate (35828)

The Times-Argus
540 N. Main St.
PO Box 707
Barre, VT 05641
Phone: (802)479-0191
Fax: (802)479-4032

Publications: The Times-Argus (31488)

The Times Beacon Publishing
345 E Bay Ave.
Manahawkin, NJ 08050
Phone: (609)597-3211
Fax: (609)597-8169

Publications: Manahawkin Newspaper (19210)

Times Beacon Record Newspapers
Box 707
Setauket, NY 11733
Phone: (631)751-7744
Fax: (631)751-4165

Publications: North Shore Homes (23327) • Port Times Record (23118) • The Village Beacon Record (23117) • The Village Times (20557)

Times Bonanza and Goldfield News
PO Box 193
Tonopah, NV 89049
Phone: (702)482-3365
Fax: (702)482-5042

Publications: Eureka Sentinel (18446) • Times Bonanza and Goldfield News (18447)

Times-Citizen Co.
406 Stevens
PO Box 640
Iowa Falls, IA 50126-0640
Phone: (641)648-2521
Fax: (641)648-4765

Publications: Times-Citizen (11001)

Times-Clarion
111 S Central
PO Box 307
Harlowton, MT 59036-0307
Phone: (406)632-5633
Fax: (406)632-5644

Publications: Times-Clarion (17812)

Times Colonist
2621 Douglas St.
PO Box 300
Victoria, BC, Canada V8T 4M2
Phone: (250)380-5211
Fax: (250)380-5353

Publications: Times Colonist (35226)

Times-Courier Pub.
PO Box 1076
Ellijay, GA 30540
Phone: (706)635-4313
Fax: (706)635-7006

Publications: Times-Courier (7270)

Times-Democrat
115 W Muskogee
Box 131
Sulphur, OK 73086
Phone: (580)622-2102
Fax: (580)622-2937

Publications: Times-Democrat (26090)

Times & Democrat
1010 Broughton
PO Drawer 1766
Orangeburg, SC 29115
Phone: (803)534-3352
Fax: (803)533-5526
Free: 877-536-4607

Publications: The Times & Democrat (28733)

The Times Dispatch
225 W Main St.
Box 389
Walnut Ridge, AR 72476-0389
Phone: (870)886-2464
Fax: (870)886-9369

Publications: The Times Dispatch (1363)

Times-Enterprise
PO Box 650
Thomasville, GA 31792
Phone: (912)226-2400
Fax: (912)228-5863

Publications: Times-Enterprise (7587)

The Times-Georgian
PO Box 460
Carrollton, GA 30117-0460
Phone: (404)834-6631
Fax: (404)834-9991

Publications: The Times-Georgian (7157)

Times Graphics, Inc.
891 E Oak Rd.
Vineland, NJ 08360
Phone: (609)691-5000
Fax: (609)691-2031

Publications: The Daily Journal (19698)

Times Guardian/Chronicle
PO Box 1940
Canyon Lake, TX 78133
Phone: (830)907-3882
Fax: (830)964-2771

Publications: Canyon Lake Times Guardian (30002)

Times Herald
222 N Izard St.
PO Box 1699
Forrest City, AR 72336
Phone: (870)633-3130
Fax: (870)633-0599

Publications: Times Herald (1139)

Times-Herald
PO Box 338
Kingsville, MD 21087
Phone: (410)817-9910
Fax: (410)817-9902

Publications: Times-Herald (13593)

Times-Herald
13730 Michigan Ave.
Dearborn, MI 48126
Phone: (313)584-4000
Fax: (313)584-1357

Publications: Times-Herald (14910)

The Times Herald Co.
911 Military St.
Port Huron, MI 48060
Phone: (810)985-7171
Fax: (810)989-6294
Free: 800-462-4057

Publications: Times Herald (15451)

Times Herald Publishing Co., Inc./Journal Register Co.
410 Markley St.
PO Box 591
Norristown, PA 19404
Phone: (610)272-2500
Fax: (610)272-4003
Free: 800-887-2501

Publications: The Times Herald (27337)

The Times Independent Printing Inc.
35 E Ctr.
PO Box 129
Moab, UT 84532
Phone: (435)259-7525
Fax: (435)259-7741

Publications: The Times Independent (31369)

The Times at the Jersey Shore
PO Box 5
Ocean Grove, NJ 07756
Phone: (732)775-0007
Fax: (732)774-4480

Publications: The Times At The Jersey Shore (19392)

Times-Journal
PO Box 218
Savanna, IL 61074
Phone: (815)273-2277
Fax: (815)273-2715

Publications: Northwestern Illinois Dispatch (9580) • Times-Journal (9581)

Times Journal
PO Drawer 280
Burnsville, NC 28714
Phone: (704)682-2120
Fax: (704)682-3701

Publications: The Yancey Journal (23678)

The Times-Journal
319 S. Main St.
Box 746
Condon, OR 97823
Phone: (541)384-2431
Fax: (541)384-2411

Publications: The Times-Journal (26270)

Times Leader
PO Box 439
Princeton, KY 42445
Phone: (270)365-5588
Fax: (270)365-7299

Publications: Times Leader (12374)

The Times Leader
200 S. 4th St.
Martins Ferry, OH 43935
Phone: (740)633-1131
Fax: (740)633-1122

Publications: The Times Leader (25356)

The Times Leader
15 N. Main St.
Wilkes Barre, PA 18711
Phone: (570)829-7100
Fax: (570)829-2002
Free: 800-427-8649

Publications: The Expressline (28166) • The Times Leader (28167)

The Times Mirror Co.
93 S. Chestnut St.
Ventura, CA 93001
Phone: (805)653-7566
Fax: (805)653-7576

Publications: Los Angeles Times—Ventura County Edition (4005)

Times Mirror Magazines, Inc.
Two Park Ave.
New York, NY 10016
Phone: (212)779-5000

Publications: Motorboating (22372)

The Times News
813 16th St.
PO Box 849
Bedford, IN 47421
Phone: (812)275-3355
Fax: 800-782-4405

Publications: The Times-Mail (9798)

Times-News
707 S Main St.
PO Box 481
Burlington, NC 27216
Phone: (336)227-0131
Fax: (336)229-2463
Free: 800-488-0085

Publications: Times-News (23672)

The Times News, Inc.
PO Box 239
Lehighton, PA 18235-0239
Phone: (610)826-2554
Fax: (610)377-5800

Publications: The Times News (27183)

Times & News Publishing Company
PO Box 3669
1570 Fairfield Rd.
Gettysburg, PA 17325
Phone: (717)334-1131
Fax: (717)334-4243

Publications: Gettysburg Times (26939)

The Times News Publishing Co.
96 S Main St.
PO Box 77
Nephi, UT 84648
Phone: (435)623-0525
Fax: (435)623-4735

Publications: Nephi Times-News (31375)

Times Newspaper Group
PO Box 40216
Bay Village, OH 44140

Publications: Lorain County Times (24645) • Westlaker Times (25502)

Times Newspapers
1616 W. Pioneer Pkwy.
Peoria, IL 61615
Phone: (309)692-6600
Fax: (309)692-3399

Publications: Chillicothe Times-Bulletin (8670) • El Paso Times-Journal (9418) • Morton Times News

(9229) • Peoria Times Observer (9422) • Washington Times-Reporter (9428)

Times Newspapers, Inc.
PO Box 9426
Peoria, IL 61612
Phone: (309)692-6600
Fax: (309)692-6447
Free: 800-42-TIMES

Publications: East Peoria Times-Courier (9417)

Times Newspapers, Inc.
2512 Metropolitan Dr.
Trevose, PA 19053
Phone: (215)355-9009
Fax: (215)355-4812

Publications: Bucks County Midweek (28055) • Northeast Times (28057)

Times Newsweekly
PO Box 299
Ridgewood, NY 11386
Phone: (718)821-7500
Fax: (718)456-0120

Publications: Times Newsweekly (23198)

The Times of Northeast Benton County
PO Box 25
Pea Ridge, AR 72751
Phone: (501)451-1196
Fax: (501)451-9456

Publications: The Times of Northeast Benton County (1312)

Times Observer
119 W. Nodaway
PO Box 317
Oregon, MO 64473
Phone: (660)446-3331
Fax: (660)446-3409

Publications: Times Observer (17320)

Times-Picayune Publishing Corp.
3800 Howard Ave.
New Orleans, LA 70125-1429
Phone: (504)826-3729
Fax: (504)826-3007
Free: 800-925-0000

Publications: The Times-Picayune (12758)

The Times Post
219 N Jackson St.
PO Box 629
Houston, MS 38851
Phone: (662)456-3771
Fax: (662)456-3772

Publications: The Times Post (16685)

Times-Press
115 Oak St.
Streator, IL 61364-2805
Phone: (815)673-3771
Fax: (815)672-9332

Publications: Times-Press (9669)

Times Press Recorder
PO Box 460
Arroyo Grande, CA 93421
Phone: (805)489-4206
Fax: (805)473-0571

Publications: Times Press Recorder (1434)

Times Printing Co., Inc.
501 Budleigh St.
Box 400
Manteo, NC 27954
Phone: (919)473-2105
Fax: (919)473-1515

Publications: Coastland Times (24053)

Times Printing Co., Inc.
405 2nd St.
PO Box 346
Random Lake, WI 53075-0346
Phone: (920)994-9244
Fax: (920)994-4817

Publications: The Sounder (34280)

Times Publishing
7631 Main St., Ste. 2
Ralston, NE 68127
Phone: (402)331-6300
Fax: (402)331-8050

Publications: The Ralston Recorder (18253)

Times Publishing Co.
490 1st Ave. S.
PO Box 1121
St. Petersburg, FL 33701
Phone: (727)893-8111
Fax: (727)893-8675
Free: 800-333-7505

Publications: Governing Magazine (5517) • St. Petersburg Times (6633)

Times Publishing Co.
PO Box 478
Twin Valley, MN 56584
Phone: (218)584-5195
Fax: (218)584-5196

Publications: Twin Valley Times/Gary Graphic (16479)

Times Publishing Co.
4 S. Brooks St.
PO Box 576
Manning, SC 29102
Phone: (803)435-8422
Fax: (803)435-4189

Publications: The Manning Times (28687)

Times Publishing Co.
PO Box 366
Smithfield, VA 23431

Publications: The Smithfield Times (32526)

Times Publishing LLC
PO Box 578
Fairfield, MT 59436
Phone: (406)467-2334
Fax: (406)467-3354

Publications: Fairfield Sun Times (17789)

The Times-Record
219 S College Rd.
Aledo, IL 61231
Phone: (309)582-5112
Fax: (309)582-5319

Publications: The Times-Record (8005)

Times Record
6 Industry Rd.
PO Box 10
Brunswick, ME 04011
Phone: (207)729-3311
Fax: (207)729-5728

Publications: Brunswick Times Record (12935)

Times Record News
PO Box 120
Wichita Falls, TX 76307
Phone: (940)767-8341
Fax: (940)767-1741
Free: 800-627-1646

Publications: Times Record News (31293)

Times-Reporter
629 Wabash Ave. NW
PO Box 667
New Philadelphia, OH 44663
Phone: (330)364-5577
Fax: (330)364-8449
Free: 800-686-5577

Publications: Times-Reporter (25421)

Times-Republican
PO Box 258
Corydon, IA 50060
Phone: (641)872-1234
Fax: (641)872-1965

Publications: Times-Republican (10724)

Times-Republican
Box 7
Hayes Center, NE 69032
Phone: (308)286-3325

Publications: Times-Republican (18043)

Times Review Newspapers
PO Box 1500
Mattituck, NY 11952

Publications: The News-Review (21031)

Times-Shamrock
75 N. Washington St.
Wilkes Barre, PA 18711
Phone: (570)821-2000
Fax: (717)821-2247

Publications: Citizens' Voice (28164)

Times-Shamrock Weekly Group
183 Front St.
Owego, NY 13827
Phone: (607)687-2434
Fax: (607)687-2931

Publications: Broome Pennysaver (23065)

Times-Standard
PO Box 3580
Eureka, CA 95502
Phone: (707)441-0500
Fax: (707)441-0565
Free: 800-564-5630

Publications: Times-Standard (1894)

Times Star
PO Box 417
Sedan, KS 67361
Phone: (316)725-3176
Fax: (316)725-3272

Publications: Sedan (11796)

Times & Star
Box 407
Deloraine, MB, Canada R0M 0M0
Phone: (204)747-2249
Fax: (204)747-3999

Publications: Times & Star (35265)

Times of Trenton Publishing Corp.
500 Perry St.
Trenton, NJ 08605
Phone: (609)989-5454
Fax: (609)396-3633
Free: 800-753-3088

Publications: The Times (19668)

Times-Tribune
Box 258
Beaver City, NE 68926
Phone: (308)268-2205
Fax: (308)268-4000

Publications: Times-Tribune (17950)

Times-Tribune
PO Box 585
De Forest, WI 53532
Phone: (608)846-5576
Fax: (608)846-5757

Publications: De Forest Times-Tribune (33650)

The Times Union
Box 15000, News Plz.
Albany, NY 12212
Phone: (518)454-5694
Fax: (518)454-5514

Publications: The Times Union (20006)

Times-Virginian
PO Box 2097
Appomattox, VA 24522-2097
Phone: (434)352-8215
Fax: (434)352-2216

Publications: Times-Virginian (31764)

Times-West Virginian
PO Box 2530
Fairmont, WV 26555-2530
Phone: (304)363-5000
Fax: (304)366-9620

Publications: Times-West Virginian (33313)

TimesDaily
219 W. Tennessee St.
Florence, AL 35630
Phone: (205)766-3434
Fax: (205)740-4717

Publications: TimesDaily (6071)

The J.I. Timmer Publishing Company Ltd.
201-20408 Douglas Cr.
Langley, BC, Canada V3A 4B4
Phone: (604)530-9446
Fax: (604)530-9766

2668

Numbers cited after listings are entry numbers rather than page numbers.

Publications: De Hollandse Krant (32687)

The Timmins Times
815 Pine St. S.
Timmins, ON, Canada P4N 8S3
Phone: (705)268-6252
Fax: (705)268-2255

Publications: The Timmins Times (36456)

Tin Publishing Co.
102 E Maple
Plattsburg, MO 64477
Phone: (816)539-2112
Fax: (816)539-3530

Publications: The Leader (17351)

Tioga Tribune
PO Box 700
Tioga, ND 58852
Phone: (701)664-2222
Fax: (701)664-3333

Publications: Tioga Tribune (24539)

Tipsico Coin LLC
PO Box 2067
Corvallis, OR 97339
Phone: (541)343-3132

Publications: Tipsico Bulletin (26291)

Tire Industry Association
PO Box 37203
Louisville, KY 40233-7203
Phone: (502)968-8900
Fax: (502)964-7859
Free: 800-426-8835

Publications: Tire Retreading/Repair Journal (12239)

Titan Publishers, Inc.
25 Chesterfield Rd.
Cheraw, SC 29520
Phone: (803)537-2791
Fax: (803)537-1912

Publications: Chesterfield County Shopper (28528)

Titanic Historical Society, Inc.
PO Box 51053
Indian Orchard, MA 01151-0053
Phone: (413)543-4770

Publications: Titanic Commutator (14256)

Titonka Topic
Box 329
Titonka, IA 50480
Phone: (515)928-2723
Fax: (515)928-2506

Publications: Titonka Topic (11270)

Titusville Herald
209 W Spring St.
PO Box 328
Titusville, PA 16354
Phone: (814)827-3634
Fax: (814)827-2512

Publications: The Titusville Herald (28050)

TL Enterprises, Inc.
2575 Vista Del Mar
Ventura, CA 93001
Phone: (805)667-4100
Fax: (805)667-4454

Publications: Highways (4004) • MotorHome (4006) • RV Business (4010) • Trailer Life (4011)

TMB Publishing Inc.
1838 Techny Ct.
Northbrook, IL 60062
Phone: (847)564-1127
Fax: (847)564-1264

Publications: Plumbing Engineer (9320)

TMR Publications
PO Box 381822
Cambridge, MA 02238-1822
Phone: (617)489-9120
Fax: (617)489-3437
Free: 877-532-1838

Publications: Training Media Review (14108)

Toastmasters International Inc.
23182 Arroyo Vista
Rancho Santa Margarita, CA 92688
Phone: (949)858-8255
Fax: (949)858-1207
Free: 800-993-7732

Publications: The Toastmaster (2883)

The Toccoa Record Co.
151 W Doyle St.
PO Drawer 1069
Toccoa, GA 30577
Phone: (706)886-9476
Fax: (706)886-2161

Publications: The Toccoa Record (7605)

Today Enterprises, Inc.
PO Box 1368
Miami, FL 33101
Phone: (305)358-2663

Publications: Miami Today (6373)

Today Newspapers, Inc.
1701 N. Hampton, Ste. A
DeSoto, TX 75115
Phone: (972)298-4211
Fax: (972)298-6369

Publications: Cedar Hill Today (30011) • DeSoto Today (30246) • Duncanville Today (30254) • Lancaster Today (30668) • Midlothian Today (30827)

Today in San Diego
3600 Mission Blvd.
San Diego, CA 92109
Phone: (858)488-0357
Fax: (858)488-0357

Publications: Today in San Diego (3280)

Today's Advantage
325 Belle St.
PO Box 8003
Alton, IL 62002
Phone: (618)463-0612
Fax: (618)463-0733

Publications: Today's Advantage (8010)

Today's Catholic
PO Box 11169
150 E. Doan Dr.
Fort Wayne, IN 46806
Phone: (260)456-2824
Fax: (219)744-1473

Publications: Today's Catholic (9973)

Today's Catholic
2718 W. Woodlawn
San Antonio, TX 78228-0410
Phone: (210)734-2620
Fax: (210)734-2939

Publications: Today's Catholic (31049)

Today's Parent Group
269 Richmond St. W.
Toronto, ON, Canada M5V 1X1
Phone: (416)596-8680
Fax: (416)596-1991

Publications: Mere Nouvelle (36662) • Today's Parent (36762) • Today's Parent Newborn (36763) • Today's Parent Pregnancy & Birth (36764) • Zellers Family (36797)

Today's Woman
119 S. Hurstbourne Pkwy., Ste. 202
Louisville, KY 40222
Phone: (502)327-8855
Fax: (502)327-8861

Publications: Today's Woman Magazine (12240)

Todd County Standard
PO Box 308
Public Sq.
Elkton, KY 42220
Phone: (502)265-2439

Publications: Todd County Standard (12051)

Todd County Tribune
PO Box 229
Mission, SD 57555
Phone: (605)856-4469
Fax: (605)856-2428

Publications: Todd County Tribune (28898)

Todd Publications, Inc.
105 S. Blair St.
Round Rock, TX 78664
Phone: (512)255-5827
Fax: (512)255-3733

Publications: The Round Rock Leader (30995)

Tofield Mercury
PO Box 150
Tofield, AB, Canada T0B 4J0
Phone: (403)662-4046
Fax: (403)662-3735
Free: 888-705-1585

Publications: Tofield Mercury (34862)

Token and Medal Society, Inc.
PO Box 366
Bryantown, MD 20617-0366
Phone: (301)274-3441

Publications: TAMS Journal (13397)

The Toledo Blade Co.
541 N. Superior St.
Toledo, OH 43660-1000
Phone: (419)724-6000
Fax: (419)724-6439

Publications: The Blade (25564)

Toledo Democrat
116 Ct.house Sq.
PO Box 7
Toledo, IL 62468
Phone: (217)849-2000
Fax: (217)849-3237

Publications: Toledo Democrat (9691)

The Toledo Journal
3021 Douglas Rd.
PO Box 2536
Toledo, OH 43606
Phone: (419)472-4521
Fax: (419)472-1602

Publications: The Toledo Journal (25570)

Tom White
314 N Main St.
PO Box 486
Monticello, AR 71655
Phone: (501)367-5325
Fax: (501)367-6612

Publications: Advance-Monticellonian (1278) • Drew County Shopper's Guide (1279)

Tomah Journal Newspapers
1108 Superior Ave.
PO Box 190
Tomah, WI 54660-0190
Phone: (608)372-4123
Fax: (608)372-2791
Free: 800-272-0105

Publications: Journal and Monitor-Herald (34369)

Tomahawk Leader
PO Box 345
Tomahawk, WI 54487
Phone: (715)453-2151
Fax: (715)453-1865

Publications: Tomahawk Leader (34373)

Tombstone Epitaph Corp.
Box 1880
Tombstone, AZ 85638
Phone: (602)457-2211

Publications: The National Tombstone Epitaph (925)

Tomlinson Enterprise
55 Park Pl.
PO Box 920
Morristown, NJ 07963-0920
Phone: (973)539-8230
Fax: (973)538-2953

Publications: New Jersey Monthly (19313)

Tommy Greene Publishing Co., Inc.
PO Drawer 772
Madison, FL 32341
Phone: (850)973-4141
Fax: (850)973-4121

Publications: Madison County Carrier (6317)

Toney Publishing
PO Box 488
West Columbia, TX 77486
Phone: (979)345-3127
Fax: (979)345-5308

Publications: Gulf Coast Tribune (30859) • Palacios Beacon (30894)

Tonkawa News
108 N 7th St.
Box 250
Tonkawa, OK 74653
Phone: (405)628-2532
Fax: (405)628-4044

Publications: Tonkawa News (26102)

Tony Rome Enterprises, Inc.
660 Livernois St.
Ferndale, MI 48220-2304
Phone: (248)545-9040
Fax: (248)545-1073

Publications: Cruise Entertainment Magazine (15479)

The Topeka Capital-Journal
616 SE Jefferson St.
Topeka, KS 66607
Phone: (785)295-1111
Fax: (913)295-1230
Free: 800-777-7171

Publications: The Topeka Capital-Journal (11838)

Topeka Genealogical Society Inc.
PO Box 4048
Topeka, KS 66604-0048
Phone: (785)233-5762

Publications: Topeka Genealogical Society Quarterly (11839)

TOPICATOR, Inc.
PO Box 757 CRR
Terrebonne, OR 97760
Phone: (541)923-7334

Publications: Topicator (26595)

Topics Newspapers, Inc.
13095 Publisher's Dr.
Fishers, IN 46038
Phone: (317)598-6300
Fax: (317)598-6340

Publications: Carmel News Tribune (10353) • Center Grove Gazette (9956) • The Daily Ledger (9957) • Fishers Sun-Herald (9958) • Geist Gazette (10021) • Lawrence Times (10354) • Lawrence Topics (9959) • Northside Topics (10356) • Pike Topics (10357) • Westfield Enterprise (9960) • White River Gazette (9961)

TOPS Club Inc.
PO Box 070360
Milwaukee, WI 53207-0360
Phone: (414)482-4620

Publications: TOPS News (34104)

The Torch
PO Box 647
Mancelona, MI 49659-0647

Publications: The Torch (15327)

Torch Newspapers
PO Box 187
Rockville, IN 47872
Phone: (317)569-2033
Fax: (317)569-1424

Publications: Parke County Sentinel (10435)

TORO
Box 427
Bronx, NY 10458

Publications: Farming Uncle (20268)

Toronto Business Journal
8 King W. E., Ste. 710
Toronto, ON, Canada M5C 1B5
Phone: (416)368-1886
Fax: (416)368-1889
Free: (866)410-6660

Publications: Toronto Business Journal (36765)

Toronto Committee for Links Between Southern Africa and Canada
603 1/2 Parliament St.
Toronto, ON, Canada M5X 1P9
Fax: (416)921-0071

Publications: Southern Africa Report (36744)

Toronto East End Express
80 Nashdene
Toronto, ON, Canada M1V 5E4

Publications: Toronto East End Express (36766)

Toronto Jewish Press
PO Box 142
Downsview, ON, Canada M3M 3A3
Phone: (416)633-0202

Publications: Toronto Jewish Press (35785)

Toronto Star Newspapers Ltd.
1 Yonge St., 5th Fl.
Toronto, ON, Canada M5E 1E6
Phone: (416)367-2000
Fax: (416)869-4834

Publications: Starweek Magazine (36747) • The Toronto Star (36770)

Torrey Botanical Club
Attn: Chris Cudebec
PO Box 1897
Lawrence, KS 66044
Free: 800-627-0629

Publications: Journal of the Torrey Botanical Society (11559)

Total Health Holdings LCC
165 No. 100 E, Ste. 2
St. George, UT 84770
Phone: (435)673-1789
Fax: (435)634-9336
Free: 888-316-6051

Publications: Total Health (31418)

Totem Times
Box 1000 Stn. Main
Lazo, BC, Canada V0R 2K0
Phone: (250)339-2541
Fax: (250)339-5209

Publications: Totem Times (35009)

Tourisme Jeunesse
4545 Pierre de Coubertin Ave.
Montreal, QC, Canada H1V 3R2
Phone: (514)252-3117
Fax: (514)252-3119

Publications: Tourisme Jeunesse (37228)

Towanda Printing Co.
116 Main St.
Towanda, PA 18848
Phone: (570)265-2151
Fax: (570)265-0613

Publications: The Daily Review (28053)

Tower Records, Inc.
2500 Del Monte St.
West Sacramento, CA 95691
Phone: (916)373-2500
Fax: (916)373-2480

Publications: Pulse! (4066)

Town & Country Shopper
PO Box 466
Brookings, SD 57006
Phone: (605)692-9311
Fax: (605)692-6750

Publications: Town and Country Shopper (28817)

The Town Crier
PO Box 1326
Manila, AR 72442-1326
Phone: (870)561-4634
Fax: (870)561-3602

Publications: The Town Crier (1266)

The Town Crier
121 W. Michigan Blvd.
Michigan City, IN 46360-3274
Phone: (219)362-8519
Fax: (219)325-0677
Free: 877-472-9082

Publications: The Town Crier (10305)

The Town Crier Community Newspapers
PO Box 1435
Greenfield, MA 01302
Phone: (413)774-7226
Fax: (413)774-6809
Free: 800-448-9595

Publications: The Athol/Orange Town Crier (14219) • The Greenfield Town Crier (14220)

The Town Crier Co., Inc.
138 Main St.
Los Altos, CA 94022
Phone: (650)948-9000

Publications: Los Altos Town Crier (2193)

Town Crier, Inc.
101 Wingold Ave.
Toronto, ON, Canada M6B 1P8
Phone: (416)488-4918
Fax: (416)488-3671

Publications: The Town Crier (36771)

Town Crier Publishing Co.
925 Main St.
PO Box 279
Lexington, MO 64067-0279
Fax: (816)259-4870

Publications: The Lexington News (17246)

Town Krier Publications
PO Box 422
Higginsville, MO 64037
Phone: (816)584-3611
Fax: (816)584-7966

Publications: Higginsville Advance (17098)

Town Publishing
875 Main St. W
Hamilton, ON, Canada L8S 4P9
Phone: (905)522-6117
Fax: (905)529-2242

Publications: B12-Hamilton/Halton Business Report (35875) • Hamilton Magazine (35879)

Town Talk
24 W Baltimore Pke.
Media, PA 19063
Phone: (610)566-6755
Fax: (610)566-1261

Publications: Town Talk (27243)

Town Topics
4 Mercer St.
PO Box 664
Princeton, NJ 08540
Phone: (609)924-2200

Publications: Town Topics (19475)

Towner County Record Herald
423 Main
PO Box 519
Cando, ND 58324
Phone: (701)968-3223
Fax: (701)968-3345

Publications: Towner County Record Herald (24383)

Towns County Herald
Box 365
Hiawassee, GA 30546
Phone: (706)896-4454
Fax: (706)745-1830

Publications: Towns County Herald (7329)

Townsend Communications, Inc.
7007 NE Parvin Rd.
Kansas City, MO 64117
Phone: (816)454-9660
Fax: (816)452-5889

Publications: Clay & Platte Dispatch-Tribune (17162) • Liberty Tribune (17248) • Raytown Dispatch-Tribune (17368) • The Wednesday Magazine (17202)

Townsend Letter for Doctors & Patients
911 Tyler St.
Port Townsend, WA 98368-6541
Phone: (360)385-6021
Fax: (360)385-0699

Publications: Townsend Letter for Doctors & Patients (32896)

Townsend Outlook Publishing Co.
20 E Gregory BLVD.
Kansas City, MO 64114
Phone: (816)361-0616
Fax: (816)361-6164
Free: 800-274-8867

Publications: College Outlook (17163)

The Townsend Star
PO Box 1011
Townsend, MT 59644
Phone: (406)266-3333
Fax: (406)266-5440

Publications: The Townsend Star (17916)

Townsfolk
919 N Michigan Ave.
Chicago, IL 60611
Phone: (312)787-6579

Publications: Townsfolk (8586)

Township Officials of Illinois
408 S. 5th St.
Springfield, IL 62701
Phone: (217)744-2212
Fax: (217)744-7419
Free: (866)897-4688

Publications: Township Perspective (9644)

The Townships Sun
7 Conley
C.P. 28
Lennoxville, QC, Canada J1M 1Z3
Phone: (819)566-7424
Fax: (819)566-7424

Publications: The Townships Sun (37047)

Towse Publishing Co.
1333A North Ave.
New Rochelle, NY 10804
Phone: (914)235-3095
Fax: (914)235-3278

Publications: Furniture World Magazine (21116)

Towson University
University Union 313
Towson, MD 21252
Phone: (410)704-5133
Fax: (410)704-3862

Publications: Journal of Colonialism & Colonial History (13761) • The Towerlight (13766)

Toy Tips
9663 Santa Monica Blvd.
Beverly Hills, CA 90210
Phone: (310)553-8834
Fax: (310)553-8848

Publications: Toy Tips (1578)

TP Printing Co.
103 W. Spruce St.
Abbotsford, WI 54405
Phone: (715)223-2342
Fax: (715)223-3505

Publications: Record-Review (33516)

TPG Sports Inc.
1710 N. Douglas Dr., Ste. 201
Minneapolis, MN 55422
Phone: (763)595-0808
Fax: (763)595-0016

Publications: American Hockey Magazine (4234) • Minnesota Golfer (15876) • Surprises (16135)

TR Communications, Inc.
10546 S Western Ave.
Chicago, IL 60643
Phone: (773)238-3366
Fax: (773)238-1492

Publications: The Beverly Review (8282)

Track & Field News
2570 El Camino Real, Ste. 606
Mountain View, CA 94040
Phone: (650)948-8188
Fax: (650)948-9445
Free: 800-GET-TRAK

Publications: Track & Field News (2609)

Tracy Press
145 W. 10th St.
PO Box 419
Tracy, CA 95376-3903
Phone: (209)835-3030
Fax: (209)835-0655

Publications: Tracy Press (3946)

Trade Communications, Inc.
733 15th St. NW, Ste. 1100
Washington, DC 20005
Phone: (202)737-1060
Fax: (202)783-5966

Publications: Export Today's Global Business Magazine (5488)

Trade Data Reports, Inc.
5 Hanover Sq., 21st Fl.
New York, NY 10004
Phone: (212)269-2016
Fax: (212)269-2740

Publications: The Exporter (21669)

Trade Press Publishing Corp.
2100 W. Florist Ave.
Milwaukee, WI 53209
Phone: (414)228-7701
Fax: (414)228-1134
Free: 800-727-7995

Publications: Building Operating Management (34059) • Contracting Profits (34064) • Maintenance Solutions (34075) • Progressive Railroading (34094) • Sanitary Maintenance (34099)

Trade Publishing Co.
287 Mokauea St.
Honolulu, HI 96819
Phone: (808)848-0711
Fax: (808)841-3053

Publications: Building Management Hawaii (7682)

Trade & Transactions, Inc.
1st St. & Lincoln Ave.
York, NE 68467
Phone: (402)362-5561
Fax: (402)362-3697

Publications: Trade & Transactions (18320)

Trade Winds
PO Box 277
Hastings, MN 55033
Phone: (651)437-6153
Fax: (651)437-5911

Publications: Hastings Star Gazette (15941)

Tradeline, Inc.
115 Orinda Way
PO Box 1568
Orinda, CA 94563
Phone: (925)254-1744
Fax: (925)254-1093

Publications: Tradeline's Exclusive Reports Online (2727)

Trader Media Corp.
17 Apex Rd.
Toronto, ON, Canada M6A 2V6
Phone: (416)781-5516
Fax: (416)781-5499

Publications: Hospital News Canada (36618)

Trader Publishing Co.
20200 Detroit Rd.
PO Box 161005
Rocky River, OH 44116
Phone: (216)356-4810
Fax: (216)356-2950
Free: 800-258-7355

Publications: Tradin' Times (25501)

Trader Publishing Company
8400 Blanco Rd., Ste. 201
San Antonio, TX 78216
Phone: (210)349-6667
Fax: (210)349-0421

Publications: Our Kids Magazine (31040)

Trader Publishing Co.
100 W. Plume St.
Norfolk, VA 23510
Phone: (757)640-4000

Publications: Soundings (4783) • Towing and Recovery Footnotes (32295) • Woodshop News (4785)

Traders Guide Inc.
118 Ebony Rd., Ste. 102
PO Box 30
Ebensburg, PA 15931-0030
Phone: (814)472-8600
Fax: (814)472-9292
Free: 800-482-1203

Publications: Pennysaver (26859) • Traders Guide (26860)

Traders World
2508 W. Grayrock St.
Springfield, MO 65810
Phone: (417)882-9697
Fax: (417)885-5180
Free: 800-288-4266

Publications: Traders World (17615)

Tradeshow Week, Inc.
5700 Wilshire Blvd., Ste. 120
Los Angeles, CA 90036-5804
Phone: (323)965-5300
Fax: (323)965-5304

Publications: Tradeshow Week (2414)

Traditional Fine Arts Online, Inc.
PMB 392
8502 E. Chapman
Orange, CA 92869-2461
Phone: (714)997-8500

Publications: Resource Library Magazine (2726)

Trail Blazer Horseback Trail Riding
4241 Covina Cir.
Prescott Valley, AZ 86314
Phone: (928)772-9233
Fax: (928)772-9558

Publications: Trail Blazer Horseback Trail Riding (856)

The Trailrider
14 Hillside Dr., S.
Elliot Lake, ON, Canada P5A 1M6
Phone: (705)848-7195
Fax: (705)848-0249

Publications: The Trailrider (35803)

Trails Media Group Inc.
PO Box 317
Black Earth, WI 53515-0317
Phone: (608)767-8000
Fax: (608)767-5444
Free: 800-236-8088

Publications: Corporate Report Wisconsin (33588) • Wisconsin Trails (33590)

Trajan Publishing Corp.
103 Lakeshore Rd., Ste. 202
St. Catharines, ON, Canada L2N 2T6
Phone: (905)646-7744
Fax: (905)646-0995

Publications: Antique Showcase (36349) • Canadian Coin News (36351) • The Canadian Stamp News (36354) • Collectibles Canada (36356)

Trans World Publishing, Inc.
2100 Powers Ferry Rd.
Atlanta, GA 30339
Phone: (770)955-5656
Fax: (770)952-0669
Free: 800-827-0818

Publications: Boating World (6981)

Transaction Publishers
390 Campus Dr.
Somerset, NJ 08873
Fax: (732)748-9801
Free: 888-999-6778

Publications: Academic Questions (19451) • Ageing International (35205) • The American Sociologist (19560) • Armed Forces & Society (19561) • Community Review (20963) • Current Psychology (19422) • East Asia (19331) • Gender Issues (5505) • Human Rights Review (12733) • Integrative Physiological and Behavioral Science (19562) • International Journal of the Classical Tradition (13907) • Journal of African American Men (25455) • Journal of American Ethnic History (7019) • Journal of Income Distribution (19563) • Knowledge, Technology & Policy (8118) • Publishing

Research Quarterly (22611) • Quarterly Journal of Austrian Economics (22618) • The Review of Black Political Economy (19564) • Sexuality & Culture (2175) • Society (14617) • Studies in Comparative International Development (1563) • Trends in Organized Crime (19568) • Urban Forum (19569) • Women Studies Abstracts (19570)

Transcontinental Media
1100 Rene-Levesque Blvd. W, 24th Fl.
Montreal, QC, Canada H3B 4X9
Phone: (514)392-9000
Fax: (514)392-4726
Free: 800-361-5479
Publications: Le Bel Age (37155) • Le Magazine Affaires Plus (37167) • Le Magazine PME (37169) • LES AFFAIRES (37175) • Revue Commerce (37217)

Transcontinental Publications, Inc.
25 Sheppard Ave. W, Ste. 100
Toronto, ON, Canada M2N 6S7
Phone: (416)733-7600
Fax: (416)218-3632
Publications: Homemaker's Magazine (Madame au Foyer) (36617) • Style at Home (36752) • TV Guide Canada (36776)

Transcontinental Publishing
2608 Granville St., Ste. 500
Vancouver, BC, Canada V6H 3V3
Phone: (604)877-7732
Fax: (604)877-4848
Publications: Vancouver Magazine (35174) • Western Living (34736)

Transcontinental Weeklies
1465 St. James St.
Winnipeg, MB, Canada R3H 0W9
Phone: (204)949-6100
Fax: (204)949-6122
Publications: Backspin (35311) • The Herald (35331) • The Lance (35336) • The Metro (35344) • The Times (35352)

Transcontinential IT Business Group
25 Sheppard Ave. W., Ste. 100
Toronto, ON, Canada M2N 6S7
Phone: (416)733-7600
Fax: (416)227-8324
Free: 800-387-5012
Publications: Computer Dealer News (36556) • Computing Canada (36557) • Direction Informatique (36576) • EDGE (36577) • Technology in Government (36756)

The Transcript
Ohio Wesleyan University
Phillips Hall 106
Delaware, OH 43015
Phone: (740)368-2911
Fax: (740)368-3649
Publications: The Transcript (25162)

The Transcript
Brooklyn St.
PO Box 369
Morrisville, VT 05661
Phone: (802)888-2212
Fax: (802)888-2173
Free: 800-734-2114
Publications: The Transcript (31570)

Transcript-Bulletin Publishing Co., Inc.
58 N Main St.
PO Box 390
Tooele, UT 84074
Phone: (435)882-0050
Fax: (435)882-6123
Publications: Shopper's Guide (UT) (31479) • Tooele Transcript-Bulletin (31480)

Transcript & Free Press Ltd.
243 Main St.
PO Box 400
Glencoe, ON, Canada N0L 1M0
Phone: (519)287-2615
Fax: (519)287-2408
Publications: Transcript & Free Press (35848)

Transcript Publishing
632 1st Ave. N
PO Box 752
New Rockford, ND 58356
Phone: (701)947-2417
Fax: (701)947-2418
Publications: Transcript (24524)

Transitions Abroad Publishing
PO Box 745
Bennington, VT 05201
Phone: (802)442-4827
Fax: (802)442-4827
Publications: Transitions Abroad (31495)

Transport Workers Union of America
80 West End Ave.
New York, NY 10023
Phone: (212)873-6000
Fax: (212)721-1431
Publications: TWU Express (22879)

Transportation Communications
2615 Three Oaks Rd.
Cary, IL 60013
Phone: (847)359-6100
Fax: (847)639-9542
Publications: Fleet Equipment (8168) • Transport Technology Today (8170)

Transportation Communications International Union
3 Research Pl.
Rockville, MD 20850
Phone: (301)948-4911
Fax: (301)330-7661
Publications: Interchange (Rockville) (13683) • The Winning Edge (13700)

TransWorld Media
353 Airport Rd.
Oceanside, CA 92054
Phone: (760)722-7777
Fax: (760)722-0653
Publications: FREEZE (2707) • Snowboard Life (2710) • TransWorld Skateboarding Magazine (2711) • TransWorld Snowboarding Magazine (2712)

The Transylvania Times
PO Box 32
Brevard, NC 28712-0032
Phone: (704)883-8156
Fax: (704)883-8158
Publications: The Transylvania Times (23664)

Tranter Publishing Co.
113 S State St.
South Whitley, IN 46787
Phone: (260)723-5085
Fax: (260)723-4771
Publications: Tribune News (10469)

Travel Goods Association
5 Vaughn Dr., Ste. 105
Princeton, NJ 08540-6515
Phone: (609)720-1200
Fax: (609)720-0620
Publications: Travel Goods Showcase (19476)

Travel Industry Network, Inc.
50 Washington St.
South Norwalk, CT 06854
Phone: (203)853-4955
Fax: (203)866-1153
Publications: Travel World News Magazine (5132)

Travel Tips
4901 Forest Ave.
Downers Grove, IL 60515
Phone: (630)964-1431
Fax: (630)852-0414
Publications: TRAVELtips (8796)

Travel Trade
15 W 44th St.
New York, NY 10036
Phone: (212)730-6600
Fax: (212)730-7137
Publications: Travel Trade (22859)

The Traveler-Watchman
Traveler St.
PO Box 725
Southold, NY 11971
Phone: (631)765-3425
Fax: (631)765-1756
Publications: The Traveler-Watchman (23347)

Travelhost, Inc.
10701 Stemmons Fwy.
Dallas, TX 75220-2419
Phone: (214)691-1163
Fax: (214)869-1552
Free: 800-527-1782
Publications: TRAVELHOST (30185)

Traveling Times, Inc.
25061 Ave. Stanford, Ste. 10
Valencia, CA 91355-4551
Phone: (661)295-1250
Fax: (661)295-8558
Publications: Traveling Times (3982)

Treasure Chest
22 Parsonage St.
Providence, RI 02903-4732
Publications: Treasure Chest (28428)

Treasury Management Association of Canada
8 King St. E., Ste. 1010
Toronto, ON, Canada M5C 1B5
Phone: (416)367-8501
Fax: (416)367-3240
Free: 800-449-8622
Publications: Canadian Treasurer (36534)

Treasury & Risk Management
52 Vanderbilt Ave., Ste. 514
New York, NY 10017-3808
Phone: (212)557-7480
Fax: (212)557-7653
Publications: Business Eastern Europe (21354) • Business Europe (21356) • Business Latin America (21358) • The Economist (21582) • Financing Operations (21700) • Treasury and Risk Management Magazine (22860)

Tree Care Industry Association, Inc.
3 Perimeter Rd., Unit 1
Manchester, NH 03103-3341
Phone: (603)314-5380
Fax: (603)314-5386
Free: 800-733-2622
Publications: Tree Care Industry (18564)

Tree Publishers, Inc.
PO Box 107
Lecompton, KS 66050-0107
Phone: (785)887-6324
Fax: (785)887-6734
Publications: Christmas Trees (11588)

Trend Magazine
PO Box 36160
Charlotte, NC 28236-6160
Phone: (704)566-0104
Publications: Trend Magazine (23757)

Trend Magazines Inc.
490 First Ave. S.
St. Petersburg, FL 33731
Phone: (727)822-5000
Publications: Florida Trend (6628)

Trend Publications LLC
5880 Live Oak Pkwy., Ste. 280
Norcross, GA 30093
Phone: (770)931-9505
Fax: (770)931-9410
Publications: Georgia Trend (7460)

Trend Publishing
One East Erie, Ste. 401
Chicago, IL 60611
Phone: (312)654-2300
Fax: (312)654-2323
Free: 800-278-7363
Publications: Grocery Headquarters (8389) • Modern Metals (8491)

The Trends Journal
PO Box 660
Rhinebeck, NY 12572-0660
Phone: (845)876-6700
Fax: (845)758-5252
Free: 888-ON-TREND

Publications: The Trends Journal (23186)

Trent University
1600 W. Bank Dr.
Peterborough, ON, Canada K9J 7B8
Phone: (705)748-1279
Fax: (705)748-1110

Publications: Arthur (36313) • Journal of Canadian Studies (Revue d'Etudes Canadiennes) (36316)

Trey Foerster Ink, Inc.
PO Box 235
Iola, WI 54945
Phone: (715)445-6397
Fax: (715)445-3988

Publications: Amherst Tomorrow River Times (33799) • Iola Herald (33832) • The Manawa Advocate (33833) • Waupaca County News (33854)

Tri-Cities Publishing Co.
300 N Connecticut
King City, MO 64463
Phone: (816)535-4313
Fax: (660)535-6133
Free: 800-421-1765

Publications: Tri-County News (17223)

Tri-City Herald
PO Box 2608
Pasco, WA 99302-2608
Phone: (509)582-1500
Fax: (509)582-1453
Free: 800-874-0445

Publications: Tri-City Herald (32877)

Tri-City Ledger
PO Drawer F
Flomaton, AL 36441
Phone: (334)296-3491
Fax: (334)296-0010

Publications: Tri-City Ledger (216)

Tri-City News
PO Box 490
Cumberland, KY 40823
Phone: (606)589-2588
Fax: (606)589-2589

Publications: Tri-City News (12031)

Tri-City Record
Box 7
Watervliet, MI 49098
Phone: (616)463-6397
Fax: (616)463-8329

Publications: Tri-City Record (15669)

Tri-City Reporter
101 N Main
PO Box 266
Dyer, TN 38330
Phone: (731)692-3506
Fax: (731)692-4844

Publications: Tri-City Reporter (29173)

Tri-City Review Publishing Co.
311 21st St.
Rock Island, IL 61201
Phone: (309)786-6439
Fax: (309)786-6439

Publications: Tri-City Labor Review (9521)

Tri-City Trib
617 CMR
Drawer A, Box A
Cozad, NE 69130-0006
Phone: (308)229-3644
Fax: (308)229-3647

Publications: Tri-City Trib (17986)

Tri-City Tribune
PO Box 490
Marked Tree, AR 72365
Phone: (870)358-2993
Fax: (870)358-4538

Publications: Tri-City Tribune (1268)

Tri-County Investments
122 E Columbia
Springfield, OH 45502
Phone: (513)325-7041

Publications: Tri-County Shoppers News (25533)

Tri-County Journal
7115 W North Ave., No. 308
Oak Park, IL 60302-1002
Phone: (708)524-5184
Fax: (708)606-0860

Publications: Tri-City Journal (9377)

Tri-County News
PO Box 6666
South Bend, IN 46660-6666
Phone: (574)287-0285
Fax: (574)282-1716

Publications: Tri-County News (10459)

Tri-County News
74 W. Main
PO Box 76
Cottonwood, MN 56229
Phone: (507)423-6239
Fax: (507)423-6230

Publications: Tri-County News (15818)

Tri County News
PO Box 227
Heron Lake, MN 56137
Phone: (507)793-2327
Fax: (507)793-2327

Publications: Tri County News (15953)

Tri-County News
Box 220
Kimball, MN 55353
Phone: (320)398-5000
Fax: (320)398-5000

Publications: Tri-County News (15986)

The Tri-County News
PO Box 6
Irene, SD 57037
Phone: (605)263-3339
Fax: (605)263-2425

Publications: The Tri-County News (28875)

Tri-County News
9010 Chapman Hwy.
Knoxville, TN 37920
Phone: (865)577-5935
Fax: (865)525-5756

Publications: Tri-County News (29598)

Tri-County News Edition
116 S Magnolia
PO Box 289
Elmwood, IL 61529
Phone: (309)742-2521
Fax: (309)742-2511

Publications: Elmwood Gazette (8843) • Farmington Bugle (8888) • Williamsfield Times (9763) • Yates City Banner (9774)

Tri-County Newspapers
PO Box 303
Gardner, KS 66030
Phone: (913)856-7615
Fax: (913)856-6707

Publications: Gardner News (11455) • La Latina Presencia (11456) • The Spring Hill New Era (11457)

Tri-County Newspapers
PO Box 202
Vienna, MO 65582
Phone: (573)422-3441
Fax: (573)859-6274

Publications: Maries County Gazette (17665)

Tri-County Newspapers, Inc.
101 Airport Rd.
Willows, CA 95988
Phone: (530)934-6800
Fax: (530)934-6815

Publications: Colusa Sun-Herald (4085) • Corning Observer (4086) • Orland Press-Register (4087) • The Willows Journal (4088)

Tri-County Newspapers, LLC
PO Box 711
Belle, MO 65013
Phone: (573)859-3328
Fax: (573)859-6274

Publications: Bland Courier (16900)

Tri-County Penny Saver
PO Box 498
Hinesville, GA 31313
Phone: (912)876-0156
Fax: (912)368-6329

Publications: Tri-County Penny Saver (7331)

Tri-County Press
PO Box 97
Polo, IL 61064
Phone: (815)946-2364
Fax: (815)732-4238

Publications: Tri-County Press (9463)

Tri-County Press Inc.
301 S Main St.
PO Box 869
Cuba City, WI 53807-0869
Phone: (608)744-2107
Fax: (608)744-2108

Publications: Tri-County Press (33647)

Tri-County Publications
PO Box 223859
Carmel, CA 93922
Phone: (831)624-3411
Fax: (831)625-0767

Publications: KEY Magazine, Carmel and Monterey Peninsula (1673)

Tri-County Publications
PO Box 37
Talihina, OK 74571
Phone: (918)567-2390
Fax: (918)567-2390

Publications: Talihina American (26098)

Tri-County Publishing
602 3rd St.
PO Box 68
Algoma, WI 54201
Phone: (920)487-2222
Fax: (920)487-3194

Publications: Algoma Record-Herald (33520) • Kewaunee County Sunday Chronicle (33522) • Kewaunee Enterprise (33880) • Luxemburg News (33914)

Tri-County Publishing Co., Inc.
113 Wilson St.
PO Box 139
Dresden, TN 38225-0139
Phone: (731)364-2234
Fax: (731)364-5774

Publications: Dresden Enterprise (29170)

Tri County Publishing Co., Inc.
3 Banner Row
PO Box 100
Mc Kenzie, TN 38201-0100
Phone: (901)352-3323
Fax: (901)352-3322
Free: 800-748-9686

Publications: McKenzie Banner (29352)

Tri-County Publishing, Inc.
PO Box 429
Rushford, MN 55971
Phone: (507)864-7700
Fax: (507)864-2356

Publications: Tri-County Record (16337) • Tri-County Record Special Edition (16338)

Tri-County Special
PO Box E
Auburn, IA 51433
Phone: (712)688-2216
Fax: (712)688-2216

Publications: Tri-County Special (10613)

Tri County Today
C/O Fox Alley Shopping News
PO Box 609
Yorkville, IL 60560
Phone: (815)786-2125
Fax: (815)553-0310

Publications: Tri County Today (9778)

Tri-County Tribune
PO Box 220
Deer Trail, CO 80105
Phone: (303)769-4646
Fax: (303)769-4650

Publications: Tri-County Tribune (4301)

Tri-Son, Inc.
PO Box 40328
Nashville, TN 37204-0328
Phone: (615)371-9596
Fax: (615)371-9597

Publications: International Fan Club Organization (29460)

Tri-State Defender
124 E Calhoun Ave.
PO Box 2065
Memphis, TN 38103
Phone: (901)523-1818
Fax: (901)523-1820

Publications: Tri-State Defender (29383)

Tri State Food News
1 Pky. Ctr., Ste. 202
Pittsburgh, PA 15220-3505
Phone: (412)937-1000
Fax: (412)920-6699

Publications: Griffin's Tri-State Food News (27794)

Tri-State Neighbor
309 W 43rd St.
Sioux Falls, SD 57105
Phone: (605)335-7300
Fax: (605)335-8141
Free: 800-925-6397

Publications: Tri-State Neighbor (28969)

Tri-State Tribune
120 N Connell
PO Box 307
Picher, OK 74360-0307
Fax: (918)673-1140

Publications: Tri-State Tribune (26034)

Tri-Town News, Inc.
PO Box 570
Sidney, NY 13838-0570
Phone: (607)563-3526
Fax: (607)563-7118

Publications: Tri-Town News (23332)

Tri-Valley Herald
4770 Willow Rd., No. 697
Pleasanton, CA 94588-2762
Phone: (925)416-4822
Fax: (925)416-4850

Publications: Tri-Valley Herald (2155)

Tri-Village Pennysaver, Inc.
Geneva St.
PO Box 416
Interlaken, NY 14847
Phone: (607)532-4320
Fax: (607)273-6248

Publications: Ithaca Pennysaver (20808) • Tri-Village Pennysaver (20782)

Tri-Village Publications
107 N Main St.
PO Box 589
Atwood, IL 61913
Phone: (217)578-3213
Fax: (217)578-2833

Publications: Atwood Herald (8031)

TRIAD
6525 Busch Blvd.
Columbus, OH 43229
Phone: (614)846-8761
Fax: (614)846-8763
Free: 800-288-7423

Publications: HIGHWAY BUILDER (26995) • Ohio Contractor (25041)

Triad Business News
5601 Roanne Way, Ste. 113
Greensboro, NC 27409
Phone: (336)854-3001
Fax: (336)854-3013
Free: 800-287-1094

Publications: Triad Business News (23941)

Triad News Publishing, Inc.
626 Thain Rd.
PO Box 682
Lewiston, ID 83501
Fax: (208)746-8507
Free: 800-473-4158

Publications: Idaho Moneysaver (7917) • Moneysaver (Lewiston) (7892) • Moscow Moneysaver (7919)

Triangle News
Box 689
Coronach, SK, Canada S0H 0Z0
Phone: (306)267-3381
Fax: (306)267-3381

Publications: Triangle News (37460)

Triangle Pointer, Inc.
PO Box 2777
Chapel Hill, NC 27515
Phone: (919)968-4801
Fax: (919)918-2005
Free: 800-400-1901

Publications: Triangle Pointer (23728)

Triathlete Group
2037 San Elijo Ave.
Cardiff, CA 92007
Phone: (760)634-4100
Fax: (760)634-4110

Publications: Triathlete (1663)

Trib Publications
1709 3rd Ave. N
PO Box 1900
Bessemer, AL 35020
Phone: (205)424-7827
Fax: (205)424-8118

Publications: The Western Star (52)

Tribal College Journal of American Indian Higher Education
PO Box 270
Mancos, CO 81328
Phone: (970)533-9170
Fax: (970)533-9145
Free: 888-899-6693

Publications: Tribal College Journal of American Indian Higher Education (TCJ) (4572)

Tribarts Inc.
2261 Market St., PMBSte. 644
San Francisco, CA 94114
Phone: (415)970-0220
Fax: (415)431-8321
Free: (866)882-0220

Publications: Tribal: The Magazine of Tribal Art (3454)

Tribco Inc.
174-15 Horace Harding Expy.
Fresh Meadows, NY 11365
Phone: (718)357-7400
Fax: (718)357-9417

Publications: Queens Tribune (20629)

Triboro Banner Newspaper
149 Penn Ave.
Scranton, PA 18503
Phone: (570)207-9001
Fax: (570)207-3448

Publications: Triboro Banner (27964)

Tribune
112 E. Cranston
Fowler, CO 81039
Phone: (719)263-5311
Fax: (719)263-5100

Publications: Fowler Tribune (4454)

The Tribune
PO Box 488
Monument, CO 80132
Phone: (719)481-3423
Fax: (719)481-4172

Publications: The Tribune (4584)

The Tribune
100 St. Louis Ave.
PO Box 447
Seymour, IN 47274
Phone: (812)522-4871
Fax: (812)522-7691
Free: 800-800-8212

Publications: Seymour Daily Tribune (10448)

The Tribune
317 5th St.
Ames, IA 50010
Phone: (515)232-2160
Fax: (515)232-2364

Publications: The Tribune (10594)

Tribune
124 N. Main St.
Box 367
Buffalo Center, IA 50424
Phone: (515)562-2606
Fax: (515)562-2636

Publications: Tribune (10635)

Tribune
2012 Forest Ave.
Box 228
Great Bend, KS 67530
Phone: (316)792-1211
Fax: (316)792-3441

Publications: Great Bend Tribune (11468)

Tribune
104 Ellen St.
PO Box 8
Union City, MI 49094
Phone: (517)741-8451
Fax: (517)741-8181

Publications: Tribune (15647)

Tribune
PO Box 308
Minnesota Lake, MN 56068
Phone: (507)462-3575

Publications: Tribune (16166)

Tribune
108 E. 6th St.
PO Box 470
Morris, MN 56267
Phone: (612)589-2525
Free: 888-589-2525

Publications: Sun-Tribune (16198)

The Tribune
214 E. Main St.
PO Drawer 1009
Elkin, NC 28621
Phone: (336)835-1513
Fax: (336)835-8742

Publications: The Tribune (23867)

The Tribune
3813 N. College
PO Box 40
Bethany, OK 73008
Phone: (405)789-1962
Fax: (405)789-4253

Publications: Northwest Metro Times (25759) • The Tribune (25761)

Tribune
162 King St.
Sturgeon Falls, ON, Canada P0H 2G0
Phone: (705)753-2930
Fax: (705)753-5231

Publications: Northern Agri-Source (36413) • Tribune (36414)

The Tribune
228 E. Main St.
PO Box 278
Welland, ON, Canada L3B 5P5
Phone: (905)732-2411
Fax: (905)732-3660

Publications: The Tribune (36867)

The Tribune
425 Locust St.
Johnstown, PA 15907
Phone: (814)532-5199
Fax: (814)539-1409

Publications: Tribune-Democrat (27089)

Tribune
1705 Industrial
PO Box 1177
Mount Pleasant, TX 75456-1177
Phone: (903)572-1705
Fax: (903)572-6026

Publications: Mount Pleasant Daily Tribune (30840)

Tribune
Box 43
Trenton, TX 75490
Phone: (903)989-2325

Publications: Tribune (31193)

Tribune Chronicle
240 Franklin St. SE
PO Box 1431
Warren, OH 44482
Phone: (216)841-1600
Fax: (216)841-1721

Publications: Tribune Chronicle (25617)

Tribune Company
435 N. Michigan Ave.
Chicago, IL 60611
Phone: (312)222-9100
Free: 800-874-2863

Publications: Boca Raton Community News (8092) • Broward Jewish Journal (8293) • Coral Springs/Parkland Forum (6017) • Deerfield Beach Times (8350) • Delray Beach Community News (8747) • Hi-Riser (8397) • Margate/Coconut Creek Forum (6325) • Palm Beach Jewish Journal North (8525) • Palm Beach Jewish Journal South (9750) • Pompano Times (8537) • Tamarac/North Lauderdale Forum (6018) • West Boca Community News (8603)

Tribune, Co.
7505 Warwick Blvd.
Newport News, VA 23607

Publications: Daily Press (32279)

The Tribune Corp.
201 N. Rock Island
PO Box 9
El Reno, OK 73036
Phone: (405)262-9000
Fax: (405)262-3541

Publications: The El Reno Daily Tribune (25816)

Tribune Courier
308 East 12th St.
PO Box 410
Benton, KY 42025
Phone: (270)527-3162
Fax: (270)527-4567

Publications: Leisure Scene (11932) • Tribune Courier (11933)

The Tribune/Georgian
PO Box 470
St. Marys, GA 31558-0470
Phone: (912)729-5231
Fax: (912)729-1589

Publications: The Southeast Georgian (7523)

Tribune, Inc.
104 N Main
PO Box 400
Deer Park, WA 99006
Phone: (509)276-5043
Fax: (509)276-2041

Publications: Deer Park Tribune (32735)

Tribune/Marketplace Newspapers, Inc.
127 Ave. C
PO Box 499
Snohomish, WA 98291-0499
Phone: (360)568-4121
Fax: (360)568-1484

Publications: The Monroe Tribune (33086)

Tribune-Monitor, Co.
6 E Wall St.
PO Box 150
Fort Scott, KS 66701
Phone: (620)223-1460
Fax: (620)223-1469

Publications: The Fort Scott Tribune (11443)

Tribune Newspaper
127 Ave. C
PO Box 499
Snohomish, WA 98291-0499
Phone: (360)568-4121
Fax: (360)568-1484

Publications: The Snohomish County Tribune (33089)

Tribune Newspaper Co.
120 N Main St.
PO Box 368
Greensburg, KS 67054
Phone: (316)723-2115

Publications: Kiowa County Signal (11475)

Tribune Newspapers
127 Ave. C
PO Box 499
Snohomish, WA 98291-0499
Phone: (360)568-4121
Fax: (360)568-1484

Publications: Everett News Tribune (33085) • Mukilteo Tribune (33087)

Tribune Newspapers, Inc.
1114 7th St.
PO Box 721
Harlan, IA 51537-0721
Phone: (712)755-3111
Fax: (712)755-3324
Free: 800-909-6397

Publications: News-Advertiser (10942) • Penny-Saver (10943) • Rocket Common Supplement Shopper (10944) • Tribune (10945)

Tribune Press
105 Misty Ct.
Box 38
Glenwood City, WI 54013
Phone: (715)265-4646
Fax: (715)265-7496

Publications: Tribune Press Reporter (33734)

Tribune Printing, Inc.
147 E High St.
Hicksville, OH 43526
Phone: (419)542-7764
Fax: (419)542-7370
Free: 877-777-7166

Publications: The News Tribune (25241)

Tribune Progress News
108 W Clark
PO Box 50
Bartlett, TX 76511
Phone: (254)527-4333
Fax: (254)527-4333

Publications: Tribune-Progress (29889)

The Tribune Publishers Ltd.
6 Shannon St.
PO Box 486
Campbellton, NB, Canada E3N 3G9
Phone: (506)753-4413
Fax: (506)759-9595

Publications: The Tribune (35383)

Tribune Publishing
PO Box 957
Lewiston, ID 83501
Phone: (208)743-9411
Fax: (208)746-7341

Publications: Lewiston Morning Tribune (7891)

Tribune Publishing
435 N. Michigan Ave.
Chicago, IL 60611-4041
Phone: (312)222-4150
Fax: (312)222-3935

Publications: Chicago Tribune (8327)

Tribune Publishing
373 1/2 W 19th St.
Houston, TX 77008
Phone: (713)862-9603

Publications: Houston Tribune (30489)

Tribune Publishing Co.
514 E. Barbour St.
PO Box 628
Eufaula, AL 36072
Phone: (205)687-3507
Fax: (205)687-3229

Publications: The Eufaula Tribune (205)

Tribune Publishing Co.
570 Holt Ave., No. 1
Holtville, CA 92250-1216
Phone: (619)356-2995
Fax: (619)356-4915

Publications: Calexico Chronicle (2055) • Holtville Tribune (2056) • Imperial Valley Weekly (2070)

Tribune Publishing Co.
1261 Hyde Park Ave.
Hyde Park, MA 02136
Phone: (617)361-6500
Fax: (617)361-8909

Publications: Hyde Park Mattapan Tribune (14255) • Jamaica Plain/Roxbury Citizen (14260) • Milton Record Transcript (14336)

Tribune Publishing Co.
101 N. Fourth St.
PO Box 798
Columbia, MO 65205-0798
Phone: (573)815-1500
Fax: (573)815-1701
Free: 800-333-6799

Publications: Columbia Daily Tribune (16990)

Tribune-Record-Gleaner
PO Box 187
Loyal, WI 54446-0187
Phone: (715)255-8531
Fax: (715)255-8357

Publications: Tribune-Record-Gleaner (33913)

Tribune Review Publishing Co.
622 Cabin Hill Dr.
Greensburg, PA 15601
Phone: (724)834-1151
Fax: (724)838-5171
Free: 800-433-3046

Publications: Dispatch (26714) • Standard-Observer (26955) • Tribune-Review (26956) • Valley News Dispatch (28048)

Tribune-Star
222 S. 7th St.
PO Box 149
Terre Haute, IN 47808
Phone: (812)231-4200

Publications: Tribune-Star (10490)

The Tribune Weekender
188 N. 1st Ave.
Williams Lake, BC, Canada V2G 1Y8
Fax: (604)392-7253

Publications: The Tribune Weekender (35244)

Tribute Publishing Inc.
71 Barber Greene Rd.
Don Mills, ON, Canada M3C 2A2
Phone: (416)445-0544
Fax: (416)445-2894

Publications: Teen Tribune (35778)

TriDelta, Inc.
PO Box 986
Delta Junction, AK 99737
Phone: (907)895-5115
Fax: (907)895-5116

Publications: Delta Wind (561)

Trident Military Newspaper
2740 Barrington St., CFB,
PO Box 99000
Halifax, NS, Canada B3K 5X5

Publications: TRIDENT (35571)

Trident Press Ltd.
842 Main St.
Winnipeg, MB, Canada R2W 3N8
Phone: (204)589-5871
Fax: (204)586-3618

Publications: Ukrainian Voice (35354)

TS-REN Ventures Ltd.
15 Kern Rd.
Toronto, ON, Canada M3B 1S9
Publications: KW Real Estate News (35962)

TSR Publications Inc.
PO Box 157
Sardis, MS 38666-0157
Phone: (601)487-1551
Fax: (601)487-1552
Publications: The Southern Reporter (16840)

T.T. Publications
Box 130
Grant City, MO 64456
Phone: (816)564-3603
Publications: The Grant City Times-Tribune (17087)

TT Publishing
2200 Mill Rd.
Alexandria, VA 22314
Phone: (703)838-1746
Fax: (703)838-6259
Publications: Light & Medium Truck (31706)

T.T.W. Associates Inc.
11 Middleneck Rd., Ste. 208
Great Neck, NY 11021
Phone: (516)466-0028
Fax: (516)466-0062
Publications: New York Trend (20693)

Tuba Frenzy
PO Box 576
Chapel Hill, NC 27514
Publications: Tuba Frenzy (23729)

The Tube Council
26 Park St., Ste. 2031
Montclair, NY 07042
Phone: (973)744-4551
Fax: (973)744-5568
Publications: The Tube Council News (21092)

Tucker Publications Inc.
PO Box 580
Lisle, IL 60532-0580
Phone: (630)969-3809
Fax: (630)969-3895
Publications: ABNF Journal (9109) • Journal of
Cultural Diversity (9110) • Journal of Theory Construction Testing (9111)

Tucker Publishing
149 Rte. 31 S
Flemington, NJ 08822
Phone: (908)788-3850
Fax: (908)788-3877
Publications: Today in Hunterdon (18821)

Tucson Citizen
4850 S. Park Ave.
Tucson, AZ 85714
Phone: (520)573-4561
Fax: (520)573-4569
Free: 800-695-4492
Publications: Tucson Citizen (966)

The Tucson Weekly Inc.
PO Box 27087
Tucson, AZ 85701-7087
Phone: (520)792-3630
Fax: (520)792-2096
Publications: Tucson Weekly (970)

Tuff Publications, Inc.
11725 Collier Blvd.
Naples, FL 34116-6524
Phone: (239)353-0444
Fax: (239)353-9040
Publications: Everglades Echo (6068) • Naples
Times (6447)

Tulane Journal of Technology and Intellectual Property
Tulane Law School
John Giffen Wienmann Hall
Tulane University
New Orleans, LA 70118-5670
Fax: (504)865-5830
Publications: Tulane Journal of Technology and
Intellectual Property (12759)

Tulane Publications
3439 Prytania St., Ste. 400
New Orleans, LA 70115
Phone: (504)865-5714
Fax: (504)865-5621
Publications: Tulanian (12760)

The Tule Times
PO Box 692
Springville, CA 93265
Phone: (559)539-3166
Fax: (559)539-2942
Publications: The Tule Times (3793)

The Tulia Herald
115 S Austin
PO Drawer 87
Tulia, TX 79088-0087
Phone: (806)995-3535
Fax: (806)995-3536
Publications: The Tulia Herald (31195)

Tulsa County Medical Society
5315 S. Lews Ave.
Tulsa, OK 74105-6539
Phone: (918)743-6184
Publications: Tulsa Medicine (26137)

Tulsa Studies in Women's Literature, The University of Tulsa
600 S. College Ave.
Tulsa, OK 74104-3189
Phone: (918)631-2503
Fax: (918)584-0623
Publications: Tulsa Studies in Women's Literature
(26138)

Tundra
22230 NE 28th Pl.
Sammamish, WA 98074-6408
Phone: (425)836-8875
Publications: Tundra (32935)

Tundra Drums
PO Box 868
Bethel, AK 99559
Phone: (907)543-3500
Fax: (907)543-3312
Publications: Tundra Drums (554)

Tunica Publishing Co.
991 Magnolia
PO Box 308
Tunica, MS 38676
Phone: (662)363-1511
Fax: (662)363-9969
Free: 800-775-5826
Publications: The Tunica Times (16848)

Turbopress Inc.
411 Richmond St. E, Ste. 301
Toronto, ON, Canada M5A 3S5
Phone: (416)362-7966
Fax: (416)362-3950
Publications: Cycle Canada (36566) • Moto Journal
(37192) • Motorsport Dealer & Trade (36670)

Turf and Recreation Publishing Inc.
275 James St.
Delhi, ON, Canada N4B 2B2
Phone: (519)582-8873
Fax: (519)582-8877
Publications: Turf & Recreation (35771)

Turfgrass Producers International
1855A Hicks Rd.
Rolling Meadows, IL 60008-1215
Phone: (847)705-9898
Fax: (847)705-8347
Free: 800-405-8873
Publications: Turf News (9551)

Turley Publications
24 Water St.
Palmer, MA 01069-1840
Phone: (413)283-8393
Fax: (413)289-1977
Free: 800-824-6648
Publications: The Harvard Salient (14455) • Journal
Register (14456) • The New England Antiques Journal (14609) • Ware River News (14457)

Turn For The Judges
15326 Ensenada Dr.
Houston, TX 77083-5031
Phone: (281)933-6127
Fax: (281)933-5354
Publications: Turn For The Judges (TFTJ) (30537)

Turtle Mountain Star
PO Box 849
Rolla, ND 58367-0849
Phone: (701)477-6495
Fax: (701)477-3182
Publications: Turtle Mountain Star (24534)

Turtle Mountain Times
PO Box 1270
Bia House, No. 177
Belcourt, ND 58316
Phone: (701)477-6670
Fax: (701)477-6875
Publications: Turtle Mountain Times (24345)

Turtle Press
Box 241
Nordland, WA 98358
Phone: (360)385-3626
Publications: Pangolin Papers (32853)

The Tuscaloosa News
6th St. & 20th Ave.
PO Box 20587
Tuscaloosa, AL 35401
Phone: (205)345-0505
Fax: (205)349-0845
Free: 800-866-6086
Publications: The Tuscaloosa News (492)

Tuscarora Inc.
Box 1125
Maywood, NJ 07607
Phone: (201)368-9100
Fax: (201)368-9101
Free: 800-351-ALES
Publications: Ale Street News (19218)

Tuscola Review, Inc.
PO Box 350
Tuscola, IL 61953
Phone: (217)253-2358
Fax: (217)253-3265
Publications: Review (9695)

Tuskegee Newspapers, Inc.
120 Eastside St.
PO Box 830060
Tuskegee, AL 36083
Phone: (334)727-3020
Fax: (334)727-7700
Publications: The Tuskegee News (508)

Tuskegee University
Tuskegee, AL 36083
Phone: (334)727-8710
Publications: Campus Digest (507)

TV Trade Media, Inc.
216 E 75th St., No. PW
New York, NY 10021
Phone: (212)288-3933
Fax: (212)734-9033
Publications: The TV Executive (22874) • TV Executive Daily (22875) • Video Age Daily (22897) •
Video Age International (22898)

TVA Publications Inc.
7 Chemin Bates
Outremont, QC, Canada H2V 4V7
Phone: (514)270-1100
Fax: (514)270-9618
Publications: Decoration Chez-Soi (37263) • Filles
d'Aujourd'hui (37265) • Le Lundi (37266) • Les
Idees de Ma Maison (37267) • Renovation Bricolage
(37268)

TVH, Inc.
100 Matsonford Rd., Bldg. 4
Radnor, PA 19088-0001
Phone: (717)657-1700
Fax: (717)657-2921
Free: 800-922-4678
Publications: TV Host Monthly (27916)

TVI Report
PO Box 1055
Beverly Hills, CA 90213-1055
Publications: TVI Report (1579)

TVPPA
PO Box 6189
Chattanooga, TN 37401-6189
Phone: (423)756-6511
Fax: (423)267-2280
Publications: TVPPA News (29093)

TWC Publishers
General Delivery
Del Rio, TX 78840-9999
Free: 888-490-8206
Publications: Volando (30225)

Tweed News
242 Victoria St.
PO Box 550
Tweed, ON, Canada K0K 3J0
Phone: (613)478-2017
Fax: (613)478-2749
Publications: Tweed News (36826)

20 de Mayo
1824 Sunset Blvd., Ste. 202
Los Angeles, CA 90026
Phone: (213)483-8511
Fax: (213)483-6474
Publications: 20 de Mayo (2417)

21st Century Adventures
256 Red Maple Dr.
Hampton, GA 30228
Phone: (770)234-5861
Fax: (770)234-5861
Publications: 21st Century Adventures (7320)

21st Century Science Associates, Inc.
PO Box 16285
Washington, DC 20041-6285
Phone: (703)777-7473
Fax: (703)777-8853
Publications: 21st Century Science & Technology (5833)

Twenty-Third Publications, Bayard
185 Willow St.
PO Box 180
Mystic, CT 06355
Phone: (860)536-2611
Fax: 800-572-0788
Free: 800-321-0411
Publications: Religion Teacher's Journal (4970) • Today's Parish (4971)

22 Wing
CFB North Bay
Hornel Heights, ON, Canada P0H 1P0
Phone: (705)494-6011
Publications: The Shield (35915)

The Twiggs County
PO Box 232
Cochran, GA 31014-0232
Phone: (912)945-3566
Fax: (912)986-1935
Publications: Twiggs County New Era (7181)

The Twin City Community News
202 N Ctr. St.
PO Box 1625
Bloomington, IL 61702
Phone: (309)827-8555
Fax: (309)829-6926
Publications: The Twin City Community News (8081)

The Twin-City News
PO Box 2529
Batesburg-Leesville, SC 29070
Phone: (803)532-6203
Fax: (803)532-6204
Publications: The Twin-City News (28485)

Twin City News, Inc.
PO Box 505
Chattahoochee, FL 32324
Phone: (850)663-2255
Publications: Twin City News (5980)

Twin Creek Publishing
PO Box 811
Alfred, NY 14802-0811
Phone: (607)587-8110
Fax: (607)587-8113
Publications: The Alfred Sun (20023)

Twin States Publishing
1492 E. Walnut St.
PO Box 250
Watseka, IL 60970
Phone: (815)432-5227
Fax: (815)432-5159
Publications: Iroquois County's Times-Republic (9739)

Twin States Publishing
113 S Perry St.
Attica, IN 47918-1349
Phone: (765)762-2411
Fax: (765)762-2163
Publications: The Messenger (9787) • The Neighbor (9788)

Twin States Publishing
PO Box 107
Kentland, IN 47951
Phone: (219)474-5531
Fax: (219)474-5354
Publications: Indiana Spirit Shopping Guide (10230) • Newton County Enterprise (10231)

Twin Valley Publications, Inc.
PO Box 24
West Alexandria, OH 45381
Phone: (937)839-4733
Fax: (937)839-5351
Publications: Twin Valley News & Advisor (25631)

Two-Lane Roads
PO Box 23518
Fort Lauderdale, FL 33307-3518
Phone: (954)563-9794
Free: 888-896-5263
Publications: Two-Lane Roads (6085)

Two Queens, Inc.
230 W. 17th St., 8th Fl.
New York, NY 10011
Phone: (212)352-3535
Publications: HX Magazine (21838)

2600 The Hacker Quarterly
PO Box 752
Middle Island, NY 11953-0752
Phone: (631)751-2600
Fax: (631)474-2677
Publications: The Hacker Quarterly (21078)

2D Publishing
22026 Gault St.
Canoga Park, CA 91303
Phone: (818)710-1234
Fax: (818)710-1877
Free: 888-487-2448
Publications: Junior Baseball Magazine (1656)

2wice Arts Foundation, Inc.
PO Box 980
East Hampton, NY 11937
Fax: (866)FX2-WICE
Free: (866)882-WICE
Publications: 2wice (20547)

2wo Mor Publications, Inc.
545 St. Lawrence St.
PO Box 399
Winchester, ON, Canada K0C 2K0
Phone: (613)774-2524
Fax: (613)774-3967
Publications: The Winchester Press (36885)

Tydeman Publishing
36083 97th St.
PO Box 880
Oliver, BC, Canada V0H 1T0
Phone: (250)498-4416
Fax: (250)498-3966
Publications: Oliver Chronicle (35038)

Tyler Cableguide
PO Box 34
Tyler, TX 75710
Phone: (903)597-4997
Fax: (903)597-6533
Publications: Tyler Cableguide (31200)

Tyler Junior College, Journalism Dept.
PO Box 9020
Tyler, TX 75711
Phone: (903)510-2335
Fax: (903)510-2877
Publications: Tyler Junior College News (31202)

Tyler Star-News
727 Wells St.
PO Box 191
Sistersville, WV 26175
Phone: (304)652-4141
Fax: (304)652-1454
Publications: Tyler Star-News (33467)

The Tyler Tribute
151 N Tyler St.
Box Q
Tyler, MN 56178-0466
Phone: (507)247-5502
Fax: (507)247-5502
Publications: The Tyler Tribute (16482)

The Tylertown Times
727 Beulah Ave.
PO Box 72
Tylertown, MS 39667
Phone: (601)876-5111
Fax: (601)876-5280
Publications: The Tylertown Times (16862)

Typogal, Ltee.
4117 A Boul St-Laurent
Montreal, QC, Canada H2W 1Y7
Phone: (514)844-0388
Fax: (514)844-6283
Publications: A Voz de Portugal (37237)

UAB (University of Alabama at Birmingham)
1530 3rd Ave. S.
HB205
Birmingham, AL 35294
Phone: (205)934-4250
Fax: (205)975-8125
Publications: Birmingham Poetry Review (59)

UAS Explorations
c/o Art Petersen, Editor
University of Alaska Southeast
11120 Glacier Hwy.
Juneau, AK 99801-8671
Fax: (907)465-6406
Publications: UAS Explorations (598)

UAW Local 12
2300 Ashland Ave.
Toledo, OH 43620
Phone: (419)241-9126
Publications: Toledo Union Journal (25572)

Ubyssey Publications Society
6138 Sub Blvd., Rm. 23
UBC
Vancouver, BC, Canada V6T 1Z1
Phone: (604)822-6681
Fax: (604)822-1658
Publications: The Ubyssey (35172)

U.C.L.A.
118 Kerckhoff Hall
308 Westwood Plaza
University of California, Los Angeles
Los Angeles, CA 90024
Phone: (310)825-4321
Fax: (310)206-3165
Publications: Al Talib (2204) • Pacific Ties (2357)

UCLA Applied Linguistics/TESL
3300 Rolfe Hall
PO Box 951531
Los Angeles, CA 90095-1531
Phone: (310)206-1327
Fax: (310)206-4118

2678

Numbers cited after listings are entry numbers rather than page numbers.

Publications: Issues in Applied Linguistics (IAL) (2299)

UCLA Asian American Studies Center Publications
3230 Campbell Hall
Box 951546
Los Angeles, CA 90095-1546
Phone: (310)825-2974
Fax: (310)206-9844

Publications: Amerasia Journal (2207)

UCLA Chicano Studies Research Center Press
193 Haines Hall
Los Angeles, CA 90095-1544
Phone: (310)825-2642
Fax: (310)206-1784

Publications: Aztlan (2216)

UCLA Graduate School of Education & Information Studies
204 GSE&IS Bldg.
CB 951520, 300 Charles E. Young Dr. N.
Los Angeles, CA 90095-1520
Phone: (310)206-9366
Fax: (310)267-0333

Publications: The Library Quarterly (2316)

UHF Magazine
Box 65085, Place Longueuil
Longueuil, QC, Canada J4K 5J4

Publications: UHF Magazine (37059)

Uinta County Herald
PO Box 210
Evanston, WY 82931
Phone: (307)789-6560
Fax: (307)789-2700

Publications: Uinta County Herald Shoppers Guide (34522)

Uintah Basin Standard
268 South 200 East
Roosevelt, UT 84066
Phone: (801)722-5131
Fax: (801)722-4140

Publications: Uintah Basin Standard (31415)

The Ukrainian Catholic Diocese of Stamford
14 Peveril Rd.
Stamford, CT 06902-3019
Phone: (203)358-9905
Fax: (203)967-9948

Publications: The Sower (5160)

Ukrainian Fraternal Association
1327 Wyoming Ave.
Scranton, PA 18509
Phone: (570)342-0937
Fax: (570)347-5649

Publications: Forum—A Ukrainian Review (27959) • Narodna Volya Ukrainian (27960)

Ukrainian National Association, Inc.
2200 Route 10
PO Box 280
Parsippany, NJ 07054
Phone: (973)292-9800
Fax: (973)292-0900

Publications: SVOBODA (19414) • The Ukrainian Weekly (19415)

Ukrainian National Women's League of America, Inc.
203 2nd Ave.
New York, NY 10003
Phone: (212)674-5508
Fax: (212)254-2672

Publications: Nashe Zhyttia (Our Life) (22394)

Ukrainian Orthodox Church of the U.S.A.
PO Box 495
South Bound Brook, NJ 08880-1412
Phone: (732)356-0090
Fax: (732)356-5556

Publications: Ukrainian Orthodox Word (19582)

Ukrainian Philatelic and Numismatic Society
PO Box 11184
Chicago, IL 60611-0184
Phone: (773)276-0355
Fax: (914)782-3048

Publications: Ukrainian Philatelist (8589)

Ukrainian Women's Association of Canada
202-450 Main St.
Winnipeg, MB, Canada L8L 3B4
Phone: (905)572-9626
Fax: (905)524-5362

Publications: Promin (35351)

The Ulen Union
Box 248
Ulen, MN 56585
Phone: (218)596-8813
Fax: (218)861-6708
Free: 877-674-2688

Publications: The Ulen Union (16483)

Ulster County Townsman
PO Box 308
Woodstock, NY 12498
Phone: (845)679-2145
Fax: (845)679-4304

Publications: Ulster County Townsman (23596)

Ulster Pub Co.
Box 537
New Paltz, NY 12561
Phone: (914)255-7000
Fax: (914)255-7005

Publications: The Herald (21112) • Huguenot Herald (21113)

Ulster Publishing
322 Wall St.
Kingston, NY 12402
Phone: (914)334-8200
Fax: (914)334-8202

Publications: Woodstock Times (20862)

Ultramontane Associates, Inc.
206 Marquette Ave.
South Bend, IN 46617
Fax: (219)289-1461

Publications: Culture Wars (10454)

UN Chronicle
United Nations, Rm. DC1-0530
New York, NY 10017

Publications: UN Chronicle (22882)

UNCW Magazine
The University of North Carolina at Wilmington
601 S. College Rd.
Wilmington, NC 28403-5993
Phone: (910)962-3000
Free: 800-596-2880

Publications: UNCW Magazine (24296)

Under the Sun
Tennessee Tech University
Dept. of English
Box 5053
Cookeville, TN 38505
Phone: (931)372-3768
Fax: (931)372-3484

Publications: Under the Sun (29146)

Undersea and Hyperbaric Medical Society
10531 Metropolitan Ave.
Kensington, MD 20895
Phone: (301)942-2980
Fax: (301)942-7804

Publications: Undersea & Hyperbaric Medicine (13592)

Unified Newspaper Group
845 Market St.
Box 26
Oregon, WI 53575
Phone: (608)270-7022
Fax: (608)835-0130

Publications: Oregon Observer (34218)

Uniformed Services Almanac, Inc.
PO Box 4144
Falls Church, VA 22044
Phone: (703)532-1631
Fax: (703)532-1635

Publications: American Guidance for Seniors (32040)

The Union
464 Sutton Way
Grass Valley, CA 95945
Phone: (530)273-9561
Fax: (530)273-1607

Publications: The Union (2029)

Union Advocate
411 Main St.
Room 202
St. Paul, MN 55102-1044
Phone: (651)227-0106
Fax: (651)293-1989

Publications: Union Advocate (16411)

Union of American Hebrew Congregations
633 3rd Ave.
New York, NY 10017-6778
Phone: (212)650-4240
Fax: (212)650-4249

Publications: Reform Judaism (22640)

Union Banner
671 10th St.
PO Box 220
Carlyle, IL 62231
Phone: (618)594-3131
Fax: (618)594-3115

Publications: Union Banner (8129)

Union City Daily Messenger
613 E. Jackson St.
Box 430
Union City, TN 38261
Phone: (731)885-0744
Fax: (731)885-0782

Publications: Union City Daily Messenger (29635)

Union of Concerned Scientists
2 Brattle Sq.
Cambridge, MA 02138
Phone: (617)547-5552
Fax: (617)864-9405
Free: 800-666-8276

Publications: Catalyst (14044)

Union Cooperative Publishing Co.
3030 39th Ave., Ste. 110
Kenosha, WI 53144-4210
Phone: (262)657-6116
Fax: (262)657-6153

Publications: The Labor Paper (33873)

Union County Leader
15 N 1st
PO Box 486
Clayton, NM 88415
Phone: (505)374-2587
Fax: (505)374-8117

Publications: Union County Leader (19828)

The Union County News Leader, Inc.
PO Box 866
Maynardville, TN 37807
Phone: (865)992-3392
Fax: (865)992-6861
Free: 800-546-7996

Publications: The News Leader (29351)

Union County Times
150 Main St.
Lake Butler, FL 32054
Phone: (386)496-2261
Fax: (386)964-8628

Publications: Union County Times (6691)

Union Democrat Inc.
84 S. Washington St.
Sonora, CA 95370
Phone: (209)532-7151
Fax: (209)532-5139

Publications: Union-Democrat (3780)

Union Hispana
611 W. Civic Center Dr.
Santa Ana, CA 92701
Phone: (714)541-6007
Fax: (714)541-1603

Publications: Union Hidpana (3634)

Union Jack Publishing
PO Box 1823
La Mesa, CA 91944
Phone: (619)466-3129
Free: 800-262-7305

Publications: Union Jack (2124)

Union Labor Publishing Co., Inc.
1840 Sycamore Ave.
Racine, WI 53406-4826
Phone: (262)634-7186
Fax: (262)634-7187

Publications: The Racine Labor (34275)

Union Leader Corp.
100 William Loeb Dr.
PO Box 9555
Manchester, NH 03109-5309
Phone: (603)668-4321
Fax: (603)668-0382

Publications: The Union Leader (18565)

Union of Needletrades, Industrial & Textile Employees
1710 Broadway
New York, NY 10019
Phone: (212)265-7000
Fax: (212)582-3175

Publications: Unite! Magazine (22884)

Union News & Sunday Republican
1860 Main St.
Springfield, MA 01101
Phone: (413)788-1000
Fax: (413)788-1301

Publications: Union-News & Sunday Republican (14552)

Union des Producteurs Agricoles
555, Blvd. Roland Therrien
Longueuil, QC, Canada J4H 3Y9
Phone: (450)679-8483
Fax: (450)670-4788

Publications: La Terre de Chez Nous (37052)

Union-PSCE
3401 Brook Rd.
Richmond, VA 23227
Phone: (804)355-0671
Fax: (804)278-4208
Free: 877-522-7799

Publications: Interpretation (32439) • Union Seminary Quarterly Review (32459)

Union Publishing Co.
102 Washington
PO Box 722
Farmerville, LA 71241
Phone: (318)368-9732
Fax: (318)368-7331

Publications: The Gazette (12578)

Union Springs Herald
PO Box 600
Union Springs, AL 36089
Phone: (334)738-2360
Fax: (334)738-2342

Publications: Union Springs Herald (510)

Union St-Jean-Baptiste
68 Cumberland St.
Box F
Woonsocket, RI 02895
Phone: (401)769-0520
Fax: (401)766-3014
Free: 800-225-8752

Publications: L'Union (28461)

Union Times Co., Inc.
PO Box 749
100 Times Blvd.
Union, SC 29379-0749
Phone: (864)427-1234
Fax: (864)427-1237

Publications: Union Daily Times (28776)

Union-Tribune Publishing Co.
7364 El Cajon Blvd.
San Diego, CA 92112-4106
Phone: (619)460-3667
Fax: (619)293-2064
Free: 800-244-6397

Publications: The San Diego Union-Tribune (3270)

Unique Homes Magazine, Inc.
2020 Santa Monica Blvd. Ste. 460
Santa Monica, CA 90404
Phone: (310)453-0500
Fax: (310)453-0511
Free: 800-732-4092

Publications: Unique Homes (3719)

Unisys Corp.
Unisys Way
Blue Bell, PA 19424
Phone: (215)986-6873
Fax: (215)986-2812

Publications: EXEC (26724)

The Unit for Contemporary Literature
Illinois State Univ.
Campus Box 4241
Normal, IL 61790-4241
Phone: (309)438-2127
Fax: (309)438-3523

Publications: The American Book Review (9295)

Unitarian Universalist Association
25 Beacon St.
Boston, MA 02108
Phone: (617)742-2100
Fax: (617)367-3237

Publications: UU World (13969)

United Advertising Publications
987 University Ave., Ste. 4
Los Gatos, CA 95032-7640

Publications: Bay Area Parent—East Bay Edition (2477)

United Advertising Publications
1750 Yankee Doodle Rd., No. 108
Eagan, MN 55121
Phone: (651)454-5145
Fax: (651)454-6577

Publications: Minnesota Parent (15863)

United Association of Journeymen & Apprentices of the Plumbing & Pipefitting Industry of the U.S. & Canada
901 Massachusetts Ave.
Washington, DC 20001
Phone: (202)628-5823
Fax: (202)628-5024

Publications: U.A. Journal (5834)

United Brotherhood of Carpenters and Joiners of America, AFL-CIO
101 Constitution Ave. NW
Washington, DC 20001
Phone: (202)546-6206
Fax: (202)547-8979

Publications: The Carpenter (5396)

United Caprine News
PO Box 328
Crowley, TX 76036-0328
Phone: (817)579-5211
Fax: (817)579-2606

Publications: United Caprine News (30113)

United Church of Religious Science
3251 W 6th St.
Los Angeles, CA 90020-5096
Phone: (213)388-2181
Fax: (213)388-1926

Publications: Science of Mind (2384)

United Communications Group
11300 Rockville Pike, Ste. 1100
Rockville, MD 20852
Phone: (301)816-8950
Fax: (301)816-8945
Free: 800-929-4824

Publications: 411 (13680)

United Disability Services
701 E Main St.
Akron, OH 44311
Phone: (330)762-9755
Fax: (330)762-0912

Publications: Kaleidoscope (24582)

United Electrical Radio and Machine Workers of America
1 Gateway Ctr., No. 1400
Pittsburgh, PA 15222-1416
Phone: (412)471-8919
Fax: (412)471-8999

Publications: U.E. News (27851)

United Empire Loyalists' Association of Canada
50 Baldwin St., Ste. 202
Toronto, ON, Canada M5T 1L4
Phone: (416)591-1783
Fax: (416)591-7506

Publications: Loyalist Gazette (36652)

United Entertainment Media
460 Park Ave. S., 9th Fl.
New York, NY 10016
Phone: (212)378-0400
Fax: (212)378-2160

Publications: AES Daily (21159) • DigitalTV (21553) • EQ (23127) • Government Video (11800) • Pro Sound News (22595) • Videography (22899)

United Food and Commercial Workers International Union
1775 K St. NW
Washington, DC 20006
Phone: (202)223-3111
Fax: (202)466-1562

Publications: Working America (5865)

United Jewish Council of Greater Toledo
6505 Sylvania Ave.
Sylvania, OH 43560
Phone: (419)885-4461
Fax: (419)724-0423

Publications: Toledo Jewish News (25556)

United Kennel Club, Inc.
100 E Kilgore Rd.
Kalamazoo, MI 49002-5584
Phone: (269)343-9020
Fax: (269)343-7037

Publications: Bloodlines (15232) • Coonhound Bloodlines (15235) • Hunting Retriever (15238)

United Marketing and Research Company, Inc.
8855 Atlanta Ave., Ste. 368
Huntington Beach, CA 92646
Phone: (714)968-0331
Fax: (714)962-7722

Publications: Home Business (2062)

United Methodist Board of Global Ministers
475 Riverside Dr., Rm. 1323
New York, NY 10115-0122
Phone: (212)749-3553

Publications: Response (22650)

United Methodist Communications
10330 Staples Mill Rd.
PO Box 1719
Glen Allen, VA 23060
Phone: (804)521-1100
Fax: (804)521-1173
Free: 800-768-6040

Publications: Virginia United Methodist Advocate (32114)

United Methodist Communications Council, Inc.
2400 Lone Star Dr.
Dallas, TX 75212
Phone: (214)630-6495
Fax: (214)630-0079
Free: 800-947-0207

Publications: The Florida United Methodist (30157) • National Christian Reporter (30169)

The United Methodist Publishing House
201 8th Ave. S
Nashville, TN 37203-3957
Phone: (615)749-6000
Free: (866)388-8442

Publications: Circuit Rider (29450) • Leader in Christian Education Ministries (29467) • Mature Years (29470)

United Mine Workers of America
8315 Lee Hwy.
Fairfax, VA 22031
Phone: (703)208-7200
Fax: (703)208-7227

Publications: United Mine Workers Journal (32033)

United Nations Div. for Economic and Social Information
Grand Central Sta.
PO Box 5850
New York, NY 10163
Phone: (212)963-1516
Fax: (212)963-1381

Publications: Development Business (21547)

United Nations Publications
Two UN Plz. DC2-853
New York, NY 10017
Phone: (212)832-1075
Fax: (212)963-3489
Free: 800-253-9646

Publications: Cepal Review (21390) • Commodity Trade Statistics (21457) • Current Bibliographical Information (21523) • Industry and Environment (21867) • Monthly Bibliography, Part II (22361) • Monthly Bulletin of Statistics (22362) • Permanent Missions to the United Nations (22542) • Transnational Corporations (22854) • UNDOC (22883) • United Nations Treaty Series (22885)

United Ostomy Association, Inc.
19772 MacArthur Blvd., Ste. 200
Irvine, CA 92612-2405
Phone: (714)660-8624
Fax: (714)660-9262
Free: 800-826-0826

Publications: Ostomy Quarterly (2088)

United Publications, Inc.
106 Lafayette St.
Yarmouth, ME 04096
Phone: (207)846-0600
Fax: (207)846-0657

Publications: Golf Course News (13077) • Gourmet News (13078) • HME News (13079) • IT Support News (13080) • Kitchenware News (13081)

United Schutzhund Clubs of America
3810 Paule Ave.
St. Louis, MO 63125-1718
Phone: (314)638-9686
Fax: (314)638-0609

Publications: Schutzhund USA (17510)

U.S. Air Force Academy Department of Law
CPD-JAL
Maxwell AFB, AL 36112-5712

Publications: Air Force Law Review (314)

U.S. Air Force Logistics Management Agency
Gunter Annex
Maxwell AFB, AL 36114-3236

Publications: Air Force Journal of Logistics (313)

U.S. Amateur Confederation of Roller Skating
PO Box 6579
Lincoln, NE 68506
Phone: (402)983-7551
Fax: (402)483-1465

Publications: U.S. Roller Skating (18126)

U.S. Army Armor Center
Bldg. 1109A 6th Ave., Rm. 371
Fort Knox, KY 40121-5210
Phone: (502)624-2249

Publications: Armor (12061)

United States Army Corps of Engineers
3909 Halls Ferry Rd.
Vicksburg, MS 39180-6133

Publications: Dredging Research (16870)

U.S. Army Field Artillery
PO Box 33311
Fort Sill, OK 73503-0311
Phone: (580)442-5121
Fax: (580)442-7773

Publications: Field Artillery (25838)

U.S. Army Infantry School
PO Box 52005
Fort Benning, GA 31995
Phone: (706)545-2350
Fax: (706)545-4531

Publications: Infantry (7281)

U.S. Army Intelligence Center and School
Sttn: ATZS-FOT-M
Fort Huachuca, AZ 85613-6000
Phone: (520)538-1009
Fax: (520)538-1007

Publications: Military Intelligence Professional Bulletin (709)

U.S. Army Maneuver Support Center
U.S. Army Engineer School
Attn: ATSE T PD ED
Fort Leonard Wood, MO 65473-6650

Publications: America's Insider (17070) • CML Army Chemical Review (17071) • Cuba News (17072) • Engineer: The Professional Bulletin for Army Engineers (17073)

U.S. Army Signal Regiment
USASC & FG, Bldg. 29808A (Signal Towers), Rm. 713
Fort Gordon, GA 30905
Phone: (706)791-7204
Fax: (706)791-3917

Publications: Army Communicator (7282)

U.S. Army War College
122 Forbes Ave.
Carlisle, PA 17013-5238
Phone: (717)245-4943

Publications: Parameters (26760)

U.S. Bureau of Labor Statistics
2 Massachusetts Ave. NE, Rm. 2135
Washington, DC 20212
Phone: (202)606-7828
Fax: (202)691-7890

Publications: PPI Detailed Report (5725)

U.S. Catholic Historical Society
c/o Our Sunday Visitor
200 Noll Pl.
Huntington, IN 46750
Phone: (219)356-8400
Fax: (219)359-9117
Free: 800-348-2440

Publications: U.S. Catholic Historian (10075)

U.S. Center for World Mission
1605 Elizabeth St.
Pasadena, CA 91104
Phone: (626)398-2241
Fax: (626)398-2263

Publications: Global Prayer Digest (2817) • Mission Frontiers (2821)

U.S. Chamber of Commerce
1615 H St. NW
Washington, DC 20062-2000
Phone: (202)659-6000
Fax: (202)463-3114

Publications: The Business Advocate (5389) • Nation's Business (5685)

U.S. Chess Federation
3054 NYS Rt., 9W
New Windsor, NY 12553
Phone: (914)562-8350
Fax: (914)561-2437
Free: 800-388-KING

Publications: Chess Life (21126) • SchoolMates (21128)

U.S. China Business Council
1818 N. St. NW, Ste. 200
Washington, DC 20036
Phone: (202)429-0340
Fax: (202)833-9027

Publications: The China Business Review (5411)

U.S. Commission on Civil Rights
624 Ninth St., NW
Washington, DC 20425

Publications: Civil Rights Journal (5416)

U.S. Department of Agriculture
Economic Research Service
1800 M St., NW, Rm. N4141
Washington, DC 20036

Publications: Amber Waves (5321)

U.S. Department of Agriculture
3101 Park Center Dr.
Rm. 1034
Alexandria, VA 22302-1594
Phone: (703)305-7600
Fax: (703)305-3300

Publications: Family Economics and Nutrition Review (31672)

U.S. Department of Agriculture, Rural Business - Cooperative Service
Stop 0705
1400 Independence Ave., SW
Washington, DC 20250-0705
Phone: (202)720-6483
Fax: (202)690-4083

Publications: Rural Cooperatives (5773)

U.S. Department of the Air Force
c/o Major Danielle Coleman, Editor
Langley AFB, VA 23665-2786

Publications: Combat Edge (32176)

U.S. Department of Energy
PO Box 62
Oak Ridge, TN 37831
Phone: (865)576-1035
Fax: (865)241-3826

Publications: Concentrating Solar Power (29547) • Geothermal Energy Technology (29548)

U.S. Department of Health and Human Services
National Center for Health Statistics
Division of Data Services
Hyattsville, MD 20782
Phone: (301)458-4636

Publications: Advance Data (13585)

United States Department of Veterans Affairs
103 S Gay St.
Baltimore, MD 21202-4051
Phone: (410)962-1800
Fax: (410)962-9670

Publications: Journal of Rehabilitation Research and Development (13201)

U.S. Farmers Association
1407 2nd Ave. S.
Denison, IA 51442-2017
Phone: (712)263-2679

Publications: U.S. Farm News (10767)

U.S. Federal Bureau of Investigation
FBI Academy, Madison Bldg., Rm. 209
Quantico, VA 22135
Phone: (703)632-1952
Fax: (703)632-1968

Publications: FBI Law Enforcement Bulletin (32340)

U.S. Federal Mine Safety and Health Review Commission
1730 K St. NW, 6th Fl.
Washington, DC 20006
Phone: (202)653-5633

Publications: Federal Mine Safety and Health Review (5494)

U.S. Fish and Wildlife Service
4401 N Fairfax Dr.
Rm. 670
Arlington, VA 22203
Phone: (703)358-2029
Fax: (703)358-1826

Publications: Endangered Species Bulletin (31788)

U.S. Forest Service
2150 Centre Ave. Bldg. A
Fort Collins, CO 80526
Phone: (970)498-1100
Fax: (970)498-1010

Publications: RMRScience (4437)

U.S. Frontline News
330 Madison Ave., 2nd Fl.
New York, NY 10017
Phone: (212)922-9090
Fax: (212)922-9119

Publications: U.S. Frontline News (22887)

U.S. Golf Association
Golf House
PO Box 708
Far Hills, NJ 07931-0708
Phone: (908)234-2300
Fax: (908)234-9687

Publications: Golf Journal (18816)

U.S. Gospel News
603 W Matthews
Jonesboro, AR 72401
Phone: (870)802-0414
Fax: (870)932-6397

Publications: U.S. Gospel News (1198)

U.S. Government Printing Office
PO Box 371954
Pittsburgh, PA 15250-7954
Phone: (202)512-1800
Fax: (202)512-2250

Publications: Congressional Record (27768) • Construction Reports: Value of New Construction Put in Place (C30) (27771) • Current Business Reports: Monthly Wholesale Trade, Sales, and Inventories (27775) • Decisions of the Department of the Interior (27779) • Federal Register (27788) • Occupational Outlook Quarterly (5698) • United States Army Aviation Digest (27852)

U.S. Government Printing Office
Superintendent of Documents
130 Andrews St, Suite 301
Langley AFB, VA 23665-2786
Phone: (757)873-2800

Publications: Statistics of Income - SOI Bulletin (32177)

U.S. Handball Association
2333 N. Tucson Blvd.
Tucson, AZ 85716
Phone: (520)795-0434
Fax: (520)795-0465
Free: 800-345-2048

Publications: Handball (948)

U.S. Hospitality Corp.
1940 Elm Hill Pike
Nashville, TN 37210
Phone: (615)259-4500
Fax: (615)777-5500
Free: 800-467-1218

Publications: Key Magazine Nashville (29466)

U.S. Institute for Theatre Technology
6443 Ridings Rd., Ste. 134
Syracuse, NY 13206-1111
Phone: (315)463-6463
Fax: (315)463-6525
Free: 800-93U-SITT

Publications: Theatre Design & Technology (12238)

U.S. International Trade Administration
14th St. & Constitution Ave., NW
Rm. 3414
Washington, DC 20230
Phone: (202)482-5487
Fax: (202)482-5819

Publications: Export America (5487)

United States International University
10455 Pomerado Rd,. M-2
San Diego, CA 92131
Phone: (858)635-4540
Fax: (858)635-4843

Publications: USIU Envoy (3286)

U.S. Japan Business News
312 East 1st St., Ste. 300
Los Angeles, CA 90012
Phone: (213)626-5001
Fax: (213)613-1187

Publications: U.S. Japan Business News (2422)

U.S. - Japan Women's Center
926 Bautista Ct.
Palo Alto, CA 94303-4046
Fax: (415)494-8160

Publications: U.S. - Japan Women's Journal (2802)

The U.S. Junior Chamber of Commerce
PO Box 7
Tulsa, OK 74102
Phone: (918)584-2481
Fax: (918)584-4422

Publications: Jaycees Magazine (26119)

U.S. Lighthouse Society
244 Kearny St., 5th Fl.
San Francisco, CA 94108
Phone: (415)362-7255

Publications: The Keeper's Log (3387)

U.S. Media, Inc.
3033 N G St.
PO Box 739
Merced, CA 95340
Phone: (209)722-1511
Fax: (209)384-2226

Publications: The Gustine Standard (2619)

U.S. Medicine Inc.
2021 L St. NW, Ste. 400
Washington, DC 20036-3362
Phone: (202)463-6000
Fax: (202)223-2849

Publications: U.S. Medicine (5835)

U.S. Military Traffic Management Command
200 Stovall St.
Alexandria, VA 22332-5000
Phone: (703)545-6700

Publications: Translog: Journal of Military Transportation Management (31746)

U.S. National Center for Infectious Diseases
Centers for Disease Control and Prevention
1600 Clifton Rd., Mailstop D-61
Atlanta, GA 30333
Phone: (404)371-5329
Fax: (404)371-5449

Publications: Emerging Infectious Diseases (7003)

U.S. Naval Academy Alumni Association
247 King George St.
Annapolis, MD 21402
Phone: (410)263-4448
Fax: (410)269-0151

Publications: Shipmate (13097)

U.S. Naval Institute
Preble Hall
291 Wood Rd.
Annapolis, MD 21402-5035
Phone: (410)268-6110
Fax: (410)269-7940

Publications: Naval History (13095) • Proceedings (13096)

U.S. Naval War College
686 Cushing Rd., Code 32
Newport, RI 02841-1207
Phone: (401)841-2236
Fax: (401)841-1071

Publications: Naval War College Review (28367)

U.S. News & World Report, Inc.
1050 Thomas Jefferson St., NW
Washington, DC 20007
Phone: (202)955-2000
Fax: (202)955-2685

Publications: U.S. News & World Report (5836)

U.S. 1 Publishing Co.
12 Roszel Rd.
Princeton, NJ 08540
Phone: (609)452-0038
Fax: (609)452-0033

Publications: U.S. 1 Newspaper (19477)

U.S. Pacific Command
Box 64013
Camp H M Smith, HI 96861-4013
Phone: (808)477-2813
Fax: (808)477-1471

Publications: Asia-Pacific Defense Forum (7660)

U.S. Pan Asian American Chamber of Commerce
1329-18th St. NW
Washington, DC 20036
Phone: (202)296-5221
Fax: (202)296-5225

Publications: East West Report (5468)

U.S. Parachute Association
1440 Duke St.
Alexandria, VA 22314
Phone: (703)836-3495
Fax: (703)836-2843

Publications: Parachutist (31721)

U.S. Patent and Trademark Office
Crystal Plaza 3, Rm. 2C02
PO Box 1450
Alexandria, VA 22313-1450

Publications: Trademarks (31745)

U.S. Pharmacopeial Convention Inc.
12601 Twinbrook Pkwy.
Rockville, MD 20852
Phone: (301)881-0666
Fax: (301)816-8236
Free: 800-822-8772

Publications: Pharmacopeial Forum (13693)

U.S. Pipe and Foundry Co.
PO Box 10406
Birmingham, AL 35202-0406
Phone: (205)254-7163
Fax: (205)254-7165
Free: (866)347-7473

Publications: U.S. Piper (98)

United States Professional Tennis Association Inc.
3535 Briarpark Dr., Ste. 1
Houston, TX 77042
Phone: (713)978-7782
Fax: (713)978-7780
Free: 800-877-8248

Publications: ADDvantage (30454)

United States Racquetball Association
1685 West Uintah
Colorado Springs, CO 80904-2906
Phone: (719)635-5396
Fax: (719)635-0685

Publications: RACQUETBALL Magazine (4256)

The U.S. Rowing Association
201 S. Capitol Ave., Ste. 400
Indianapolis, IN 46225
Phone: (317)237-5700
Fax: (317)237-5646
Free: 800-314-4769

Publications: USRowing (10180)

U.S. Securities and Exchange Commission
450 Fifth St. NW
Washington, DC 20549

Publications: SEC Docket (5785)

2682

Numbers cited after listings are entry numbers rather than page numbers.

United States Telecom Association (USTA)
1401 H St. NW, Ste. 600
Washington, DC 20005-2164
Phone: (202)326-7300
Fax: (202)326-7333

Publications: TeleTimes (5818)

U.S. Toy Collector Magazine
PO Box 172
Helena, MT 59624-0172

Publications: U.S. Toy Collector Magazine (17824)

U.S. Trotting Association
750 Michigan Ave.
Columbus, OH 43215
Phone: (614)224-2291
Fax: (614)222-2791

Publications: Hoof Beats (25021)

U.S. Water News, Inc.
230 Main St.
Halstead, KS 67056-9983
Phone: (316)835-2222
Fax: (316)835-2223
Free: 800-251-0046

Publications: U.S. Water News (11477)

United Steelworkers of America
5 Gateway Ctr.
Pittsburgh, PA 15222
Phone: (412)562-2442
Fax: (412)562-2445

Publications: Steelabor (27847)

United Transportation Union
14600 Detroit Ave.
Cleveland, OH 44107
Phone: (216)228-9400
Fax: (216)228-5755

Publications: UTU News (24960)

United Union of Roofers
1660 L St. NW, Ste. 800
Washington, DC 20036
Phone: (202)463-7663
Fax: (202)463-6906

Publications: Journeyman Roofer and Waterproofer (5622)

United Western Communications Ltd.
17327 106A Ave.
Edmonton, AB, Canada T5S 1M7
Phone: (780)486-2277
Fax: (780)489-3280
Free: 800-663-3500

Publications: Citizens Centre Report (34705)

Unity of the Brethren
6703 FM 2502
Brenham, TX 77833

Publications: The Brethren Journal (29950)

Unity School of Christianity
1901 NW Blue Pkwy.
Unity Village, MO 64065-0001
Phone: (816)524-3550
Fax: (816)251-3557

Publications: Daily Word (17660)

Univelt Inc.
PO Box 28130
San Diego, CA 92198-0130
Phone: (760)746-4005
Fax: (760)746-3139

Publications: Advances in Astronautical Sciences (3108)

Universal Media, Inc.
801 2nd Ave.
New York, NY 10017
Phone: (212)986-5100
Fax: (212)338-9445

Publications: Travel Agent (22856)

Universite Laval
Quebec, QC, Canada G1K 7P4
Phone: (418)656-2131
Fax: (418)656-7267

Publications: Laval Theologique et Philosophique (37286)

Universite Laval
3577 Alphonse Desjardins
Quebec, QC, Canada G1K 7P4
Phone: (418)656-2772
Fax: (418)658-2809

Publications: Au Fil des Evenements (37281)

Universite Laval
Ste.-Foy, QC, Canada G1K 7P4
Phone: (418)656-3700
Fax: (418)656-3284

Publications: Anthropologie et Societes (37335)

Universite Laval
1244, Pavillon Pollack
Ste.-Foy, QC, Canada G1K 7P4
Phone: (418)656-5079
Fax: (418)656-2398

Publications: IMPACT CAMPUS (37337)

Universite Laval
Pavillon Alexandre-Vachon
Ste.-Foy, QC, Canada G1K 7P4
Phone: (418)656-3188
Fax: (418)656-2346

Publications: Ecoscience (37336)

Universite de Montreal
C.P/ 6128, succ. Centre-ville
Montreal, QC, Canada H3C 3J7
Phone: (514)343-5970
Fax: (514)343-7716

Publications: Centre D'Etudes de L'Asie de L'Est/ Cahiers (37101)

Universite de Montreal
750 bd. Gouin est.
Montreal, QC, Canada H2C 1A6

Publications: Revue Canadienne de Psycho-Education (37216)

Universite du Quebec a Chicoutimi
555 bd. de L'Universite
Chicoutimi, QC, Canada G7H 2B1
Phone: (418)545-5011
Fax: (418)545-5012

Publications: Protee (36967)

Universite du Quebec a Hull
Public Relations Dept.
C.P. 1250 Succ. B
Hull, QC, Canada J8X 3X7
Phone: (819)595-3960
Fax: (819)595-3924
Free: 800-567-1283

Publications: L'Uniscope (37003)

Universite du Quebec a Hull
283 Alexandre-Tache
Hull, QC, Canada J8X 3X7
Phone: (819)595-3900
Fax: (819)595-2385

Publications: L'Uquoi (37004)

Universite de Sherbrooke
Services aux Etudiants, Local 107
2500 boul. l'Universite
Sherbrooke, QC, Canada J1K 2R1
Phone: (819)821-7641
Fax: (819)562-2324

Publications: Le Collectif (37394)

University of Akron
302 Buchtel Ave.
Akron, OH 44325
Phone: (330)972-7111
Fax: (330)972-7810

Publications: The Buchtelite (24576)

University of Alabama
College of Communication & Information Sciences
Box 870172
Tuscaloosa, AL 35487-0172
Phone: (205)348-0132
Fax: (205)348-2401

Publications: American Journalism (484)

University of Alabama
PO Box 861928
Tuscaloosa, AL 35486-0017
Phone: (205)348-5963
Fax: (205)348-5958

Publications: Alabama Alumni Magazine (481)

University of Alabama
PO Box 862936
Tuscaloosa, AL 35486
Phone: (205)348-4518
Fax: (205)348-8036

Publications: Black Warrior Review (485)

University of Alabama - Birmingham
HUC 135
1530 3rd Ave. S.
Birmingham, AL 35294-1150
Phone: (205)934-3216
Fax: (205)934-8050

Publications: Aura Literary/Arts Review (56)

University of Alabama at Birmingham
University Ctr.
Box 76
Birmingham, AL 35294-1150
Phone: (205)934-3354
Fax: (205)934-8050

Publications: Kaleidoscope (77) • Phoenix Magazine (86)

The University of Alabama in Huntsville
118 Alumni House
Huntsville, AL 35899

Publications: The Exponent (269) • UAH (The University of Alabama in Huntsville) Magazine (275)

University of Alaska
Wood Center
Publications Board
Fairbanks, AK 99775
Phone: (907)474-7540
Fax: (907)474-5508

Publications: Sun Star (568)

University of Alaska Fairbanks
PO Box 757140
Fairbanks, AK 99775
Phone: (907)474-5042
Fax: (907)474-6184

Publications: Agroborealis (566)

University of Albany
School of Criminal Justice
Draper Hall No. 209
135 Western Ave.
Albany, NY 12222
Phone: (518)442-5609
Fax: (518)442-5716

Publications: The Journal of Criminal Justice & Popular Culture (19992)

University of Alberta
c/o History Dept.
2-28 Tory Bldg.
Edmonton, AB, Canada T6G 2H4
Phone: (780)492-4568
Fax: (780)492-4568

Publications: Past Imperfect (34723)

University of Alberta
Students Union Bldg., Ste. 3-04
Edmonton, AB, Canada T6G 2J7
Phone: (780)492-5168
Fax: (780)492-6665

Publications: Gateway (34713)

The University of Arizona
McClelland Hall 103
Tucson, AZ 85721-0108
Phone: (520)621-2155
Fax: (520)621-2150

Publications: Arizona's Economy (935)

University of Arizona
Modern Languages Bldg., Rm. 345
PO Box 210067
Tucson, AZ 85721-0067
Phone: (520)621-9294
Fax: (520)621-5594

Publications: Studies in Latin American Popular Culture (965)

University of Arizona
1052 N. Highland Ave.
Tucson, AZ 85721
Phone: (520)621-2484
Fax: (520)621-9922

Publications: Journal of the Southwest (951)

University of Arizona
1230 N. Park Ave., No. 201
Tucson, AZ 85721
Phone: (520)621-1714
Fax: (520)621-3094

Publications: Arizona Daily Wildcat (930)

University of Arkansas Press
201 Ozark Ave.
Fayetteville, AR 72701
Phone: (501)575-3246
Fax: (501)575-6044
Free: 800-626-0090

Publications: Philosophical Topics (1123)

University of Baltimore
1420 N. Charles St.
Baltimore, MD 21202

Publications: The Law Forum (13208)

University of British Columbia
Buchanan E158
1866 Main Mall
Vancouver, BC, Canada V6T 1Z1
Phone: (604)822-2780
Fax: (604)822-5504

Publications: Canadian Literature (35133)

The University of British Columbia
1866 Main Wall
Buchanan E, Rm. 162
Vancouver, BC, Canada V6T 1Z1
Phone: (604)822-3727
Fax: (604)822-0606

Publications: BC Studies (35125)

The University of British Columbia
Pacific Affairs
No. 164-1855 West Mall
Vancouver, BC, Canada V6T 1Z2
Phone: (604)822-6508
Fax: (604)822-9452

Publications: Pacific Affairs (35157)

**University of British Columbia Alumni
Association**
6251 Cecil Green Park Rd.
Vancouver, BC, Canada V6T 1Z1
Phone: (604)822-3313
Fax: (604)822-8928
Free: 800-882-3088

Publications: Trek Magazine (35171)

University of Calgary
Calgary, AB, Canada T2N 1N4
Phone: (403)220-7317
Fax: (403)282-9298

Publications: Journal of Comparative Family Studies
(34651)

University of Calgary
SS 1152
2500 University Dr. NW
Calgary, AB, Canada T2N 1N4
Phone: (403)220-4657
Fax: (403)289-1123

Publications: ARIEL (34628)

University of Calgary Press
2500 University Dr. NW
Calgary, AB, Canada T2N 1N4
Phone: (403)220-7579
Fax: (403)282-0085

Publications: Canadian Journal of Philosophy
(34794) • Canadian Journal of Program Evaluation/
Revue Canadienne D'evaluation de Programme
(36415) • Mouseion (35490)

University of California
322 Wheeler Hall
Berkeley, CA 94720

Publications: Bad Subjects (1493)

University of California
6701 San Pablo, Rm. 408
Oakland, CA 94608
Phone: (510)642-0978
Fax: (510)643-9930

Publications: Asian Survey (2667)

University of California-Berkeley
Boalt Hall School of Law
589 Simon Tower
Berkeley, CA 94720-1900
Phone: (510)643-9643
Fax: (510)643-9643

Publications: Asian Law Journal (1491) • Asian Law
Journal (1492)

University of California, Berkeley
F501 Haas School of Business, No. 1900
Berkeley, CA 94720-1900
Phone: (510)642-7159
Fax: (510)642-1318

Publications: California Management Review (CMR)
(1503)

University of California, Berkeley
588 Simon Hall
Berkeley, CA 94704-7200
Phone: (510)643-6600
Fax: (510)643-6816

Publications: Berkeley Technology Law Journal
(1498)

University of California at Berkeley
1203 Dwinelle Hall No. 2652
Berkeley, CA 94720-2652

Publications: Linguistics of the Tibeto-Burma Area
(1540)

University of California at Berkeley
Berkeley, CA 94720
Phone: (510)642-1821
Fax: (510)642-1822

Publications: PaleoBios (1549)

University of California, Davis
25 Lower Freeborn Hall
Davis, CA 95616
Phone: (530)752-0208
Fax: (530)752-0355

Publications: The California Aggie (1811)

**University of California, Hastings College
of the Law**
200 McAllister St.
San Francisco, CA 94102-4978
Phone: (415)581-8970
Fax: (415)551-4177

Publications: Hastings Communications and Entertainment Law Journal (COMM/ENT) (3370)

University of California, Irvine
3100 Gateway Commons Bldg.
Irvine, CA 92697-4250
Phone: (949)824-4285
Fax: (949)824-4287

Publications: New University (2085)

University of California, Los Angeles
118 Kerkhoff Hall
308 Westwood Plaza
Los Angeles, CA 90024
Phone: (310)824-7010
Fax: (310)206-0906

Publications: Daily Bruin (2250) • La Gente
(2311) • NOMMO (2348)

University of California at Los Angeles
Los Angeles, CA 90095-1555
Phone: (310)825-1148
Fax: (310)206-6673

Publications: Pacific Journal of Mathematics (2356)

University of California, Los Angeles
School of Law
Rm. 2246
405 Hilgard Ave.
Los Angeles, CA 90024-1476
Phone: (310)824-7010
Fax: (310)206-6489

Publications: Chicano-Latin Law Review (2237) •
UCLA Journal of Environmental Law and Policy
(2418)

University of California, Los Angeles
10920 Wilshire Blvd., Ste. 1500
Los Angeles, CA 90024-6517
Phone: (310)794-6880
Fax: (310)794-6968

Publications: UCLA Magazine (2419)

University of California at Los Angeles
10244 Bunche Hall
Box 951310
Los Angeles, CA 90095-1310
Phone: (310)825-6059

Publications: Ufahamu (2420)

University of California, Los Angeles
308 Westwood Plaza
118 Kerckhoff Hall
Los Angeles, CA 90024
Phone: (310)824-7010
Fax: (310)206-3165

Publications: Fem (2268) • TenPercent (2411)

University of California at Los Angeles
302 Royce Hall
Los Angeles, CA 90095-1485
Phone: (310)825-1537
Fax: (310)825-0655
Cable: sullivan@humnet.u

Publications: Comitatus (2244)

University of California Press
2120 Berkeley Way
Berkeley, CA 94720
Phone: (510)642-4247
Fax: (510)643-7127

Publications: China Economic Review (1507) •
Evaluation Practice (1519) • Government Information Quarterly (6722) • The International Journal of
Accounting (1529) • International Journal of Expert
Systems (9711) • Issues in Education (1530) • The
Journal of Academic Librarianship (24805) • Journal
of Aging Studies (16994) • Journal of Entrepreneurial
and Small Firm Finance (31250) • Journal of High
Technology Management Research (1533) • Journal
of Management (28553) • Journal of Retailing
(13832) • Journal of Social and Evolutionary Systems (1537) • Journal of World Business (18088) •
Learning and Individual Differences (4543) • Public
Relations Review (13449) • Sociological Perspectives (1562)

University of California Press/Journals
2120 Berkeley Way
Berkeley, CA 94720
Phone: (510)642-4247
Fax: (510)643-7127

Publications: Agricultural History (1488) • Berkeley
Journal of Employment and Labor Law (1496) •
Berkeley Journal of International Law (1497) • California Public Employee Relations (1505) • Classical
Antiquity (1508) • Contexts (1510) • East European
Politics & Societies (21578) • Ecology Law Quarterly
(1515) • Federal Sentencing Reporter (4989) • Film
Quarterly (1521) • Gastronomica (14659) • Histori-
cal Studies in the Physical and Biological Sciences
(1525) • Index to Foreign Legal Periodicals (1528) •
Mexican Studies-Estudios Mexicanos (1542) • Mexican Studies/Estudios Mexicanos (2083) • Music Perception (1543) • Nineteenth-Century Literature
(1547) • 19th-Century Music (1548) • Oral History
Review (272) • Pacific Historical Review (26497) •
The Public Historian (1554) • Religion and American
Culture (10166) • Representations (1555) • Rhetorica (1556) • Social Problems (1561)

University of California, Riverside
Associated Students of the University of California
245 Costo Hall
Riverside, CA 92521
Phone: (909)784-3686
Fax: (909)787-5638

Publications: Highlander (2938)

University of California at San Diego
C-0108
La Jolla, CA 92093
Phone: (858)534-3652

Publications: Linguistic Notes from La Jolla (2116)

University of California at San Diego
Mail Code 0316 UCSD
9500 Gilman Dr.
La Jolla, CA 92093-0316
Phone: (619)534-3466
Fax: (619)534-7691

Publications: UCSD Guardian (2120)

University of California at San Diego
0077, UCSD
La Jolla, CA 92093
Phone: (858)534-3652

Publications: Voz Fronteriza (2121)

University of California, San Francisco
500 Parnassus Ave.
Box 0376
San Francisco, CA 94143
Phone: (415)476-2211
Fax: (415)502-4537

Publications: Synapse (3448)

University of Central Florida
PO Box 161346
Orlando, FL 32816-1346
Phone: (407)823-5152
Fax: (407)823-6582

Publications: Faulkner Journal (6489) • Florida Review (6493)

University of Chicago
5801 S. Ellis Ave., Rm. 200
Chicago, IL 60637-1473
Phone: (773)702-8360
Fax: (773)702-8324

Publications: Chicago Chronicle (8308)

University of Chicago
5801 S. Kenwood Ave.
Chicago, IL 60637
Phone: (773)702-0887
Fax: (773)702-0887

Publications: Chicago Review (8321)

University of Chicago Graduate School of Business
1101 E. 58th St.
Chicago, IL 60637
Phone: (773)702-7743
Fax: (773)834-4585

Publications: Journal of Accounting Research (8428)

University of Chicago Magazine
5801 S.Ellis Ave.
Chicago, IL 60637
Phone: (773)702-2163
Fax: (773)702-0495

Publications: University of Chicago Magazine (8593)

University of Chicago Press
1427 E. 60th St.
Chicago, IL 60637
Phone: (773)702-7600
Fax: (773)702-0694
Free: 877-705-1878

Publications: The Journal of Law and Economics (8441) • The Journal of Legal Studies (8442) • Osiris (8517) • Physiological and Biochemical Zoology (8530) • The Quarterly Review of Biology (23375) • Signs (8564) • Supreme Court Economic Review (8576) • Supreme Court Review (8577) • Winterthur Portfolio (5304)

University of Chicago Press, Journals Division
PO Box 37005
Chicago, IL 60637
Phone: (773)753-4240
Fax: (773)753-0811

Publications: Philosophy of Science (17191)

University of Cincinnati
PO Box 210136
Mail Location 0136
Cincinnati, OH 45221-0136

Publications: University of Cincinnati News Record (24824)

University of Cincinnati
Rm. 300
Cincinnati, OH 45221-0040
Phone: (513)556-6000
Fax: (513)556-6265

Publications: University of Cincinnati Law Review (24823)

University College of Cape Breton
PO Box 5300
Sydney, NS, Canada B1P 6L2
Phone: (902)563-1473
Fax: (902)562-2886

Publications: Caper Times (35608)

University of Colorado
Box 261
Boulder, CO 80309-0261
Phone: (303)492-8181
Fax: (303)492-7722

Publications: On-Stage Studies (4183)

University of Colorado
Campus Box 422
Boulder, CO 80309-0422
Phone: (303)492-8635
Fax: (303)492-2199

Publications: Colorado Engineer (4162)

University of Colorado at Boulder
School of Journalism
Campus Box 478
Boulder, CO 80309
Phone: (303)492-4557

Publications: Campus Press (4160)

University of Colorado at Boulder
301 UCB
Boulder, CO 80309
Phone: (303)492-7540
Fax: (303)492-5619

Publications: American Music Research Center Journal (4155)

University of Connecticut
11 Dog Ln.
Storrs, CT 06268
Phone: (860)486-3407
Fax: (860)486-4388

Publications: The Daily Campus (5166)

University of Connecticut
1266 Storrs Rd.
Storrs, CT 06269-5144
Phone: (860)486-3530
Fax: (860)486-4064

Publications: UConn Traditions (5169)

University of Dallas
1845 E. Northgate Dr.
U.D. Box 732
Irving, TX 75062
Phone: (972)721-5089
Fax: (972)721-4136

Publications: University News (30609)

University of Dayton
300 College Park
Dayton, OH 45469-1659
Phone: (937)229-3241
Fax: (937)229-3063

Publications: Flyer News (25116) • University of Dayton Quarterly (25128)

University of Delaware
150 S. College
Newark, DE 19716
Phone: (302)831-1422
Fax: (302)831-1445

Publications: International Journal of Conflict Management (5274)

University of Delaware
250 Perkins Student Center
Newark, DE 19716
Phone: (302)831-2771
Fax: (302)831-1396

Publications: The Review (5281)

University of Denver
Denver Research Institute
Gas Requirements Agency
Denver, CO 80220

Publications: Denver Journal of International Law and Policy (4323)

University of Denver
Student Media Board
Driscoll University Center
2055 East Evans
Denver, CO 80208
Phone: (303)871-3131
Fax: (303)871-2568

Publications: The Clarion (4310)

University of Detroit-Mercy
4001 W. McNichols
Detroit, MI 48221
Phone: (313)993-1090
Fax: (313)993-1120

Publications: Varsity News (14951)

University of Florida
141 Bruton Geer
Gainesville, FL 32611-7635
Phone: (352)392-4980
Fax: (352)392-3800

Publications: Florida Journal of International Law (6137)

University of Florida
2346 NPB 118440
Gainesville, FL 32611
Phone: (352)377-1560
Fax: (352)392-0524

Publications: Delos (6136)

University of Florida Alumni Association
2012 W. University Ave.
Gainesville, FL 32603
Phone: (352)392-1905
Fax: (352)392-8736
Free: 888-352-5866

Publications: University of Florida Today Magazine (6160)

University of Georgia
Athens, GA 30602
Phone: (706)542-5191

Publications: Georgia Law Review (6939)

University of Georgia
Selig Center Economic Growth, Terry College of Business
Athens, GA 30602
Phone: (706)542-4085
Fax: (706)542-3858

Publications: Georgia Business and Economic Conditions (6938)

University of Georgia
250 River Rd.
Athens, GA 30602
Phone: (706)542-3737
Fax: (706)542-2773

Publications: Southeastern Journal of Music Education (6951)

University of Georgia
University Communications
Alumni House
Athens, GA 30602
Phone: (706)542-5830
Fax: (706)542-9492

Publications: Georgia Magazine (6940)

University of Guelph
Guelph, ON, Canada N1G 2W1
Phone: (519)824-4120
Fax: (519)766-0844

Publications: Essays in Theatre/Etudes Theatrales (35862)

University of Hawaii
1859 East-West Rd., No. 106
Honolulu, HI 96822
Phone: (808)956-2467
Fax: (808)956-5983

Publications: Language Learning and Technology (7708)

University of Hawaii at Manoa
The Ka Leo Building
1755 Pope Rd. 31-D
Honolulu, HI 96822
Phone: (808)956-7043
Fax: (808)956-9962

Publications: The Voice of Hawai'i (7727)

University of Hawaii Press
Journals Dept.
2840 Kolowalu St.
Honolulu, HI 96822-1888
Phone: (808)956-8255
Fax: (808)988-6052
Free: 800-650-7811

Publications: Asian Perspectives (7679) • Asian Theater Journal (20297) • Biography (7681) • Buddhist-Christian Studies (12450) • China Review International (7683) • The Contemporary Pacific (7685) • Journal of World History (7705) • Korean Studies (7707) • Manoa (7709) • Oceanic Linguistics (7712) • Pacific Science (7715) • Philosophy East & West (7717)

University of Houston
651 Philip G. Hoffman Hall
Houston, TX 77204-3476
Phone: (713)743-3467
Fax: (713)743-3505

Publications: Houston Journal of Mathematics (30487)

University of Houston
Student Publications Dept.
Communications Bldg.
Houston, TX 77204-4015
Phone: (713)743-5350
Fax: (713)743-5384

Publications: The Daily Cougar (30468)

University of Idaho
Administration Bldg. Rm. 140
PO Box 870
Moscow, ID 83844-3155
Phone: (208)885-6721
Fax: (208)885-5878

Publications: Women in Natural Resources (7922)

University of Idaho
Moscow, ID 83843
Phone: (208)885-7241
Fax: (208)885-5177

Publications: Idaho Law Review (7916)

University of Idaho Library
Moscow, ID 83844-2360
Phone: (208)885-6631
Fax: (208)885-6817

Publications: Electronic Green Journal (EGJ) (7913)

University of Idaho Press
c/o Susan F. Beegel
180 Polpis Rd.
Nantucket, MA 02554
Phone: (508)325-7157
Fax: (508)325-7157
Free: 800-UI-PRESS

Publications: The Hemingway Review (14339)

University of Illinois
116 Law Bldg.
504 E Pennsylvania Ave.
Champaign, IL 61820
Phone: (217)333-9852
Fax: (217)244-1478

Publications: Comparative Labor Law & Policy Journal (8184)

University of Illinois
Springfield, IL 62794-9243
Phone: (217)206-6084
Fax: (217)206-7257

Publications: Illinois Issues (9625)

University of Illinois
Urbana, IL 61801

Publications: Illinois Archaeology (9707)

University of Illinois
109 Davenport Hall
607 S Matthews St.
Urbana, IL 61801
Phone: (217)244-0183
Fax: (217)244-3490

Publications: Steward Anthropological Society Journal (9718)

University of Illinois
273 Altgeld Hall, MC-382
1409 W. Green St.
Urbana, IL 61801
Phone: (217)333-3350
Fax: (217)265-9576

Publications: Illinois Journal of Mathematics (9709)

University of Illinois Alumni Association
227 Illini Union
1401 W Green St.
Urbana, IL 61801
Phone: (217)333-1471
Fax: (217)333-7803

Publications: Illinois Alumni (9706)

University of Illinois at Chicago
Box 8198
Chicago, IL 60680-8198
Phone: (312)996-2730
Fax: (312)413-0424

Publications: AIDS Book Review Journal (8250)

University of Illinois at Chicago
College of Dentistry
801 S. Paulina St.
M/C 621
Chicago, IL 60612-7211
Phone: (312)996-8495
Fax: (312)413-2927

Publications: Vision Magazine (8600)

University of Illinois at Chicago
601 S. Morgan St.
Chicago, IL 60607-7120
Phone: (312)413-2209
Fax: (312)413-1005

Publications: Other Voices (8519)

University of Illinois College of Agriculture
1401 W. Green St.
227 Illini Union
Urbana, IL 61801
Phone: (217)333-1000
Fax: (217)333-7803

Publications: Illinois Research (9710)

University of Illinois Graduate School of Library & Information Science
501 E. Daniel St.
Champaign, IL 61820
Phone: (217)333-1359
Fax: (217)244-7329

Publications: Library Trends (8202)

University of Illinois Press
1325 S. Oak St.
Champaign, IL 61820-6903
Phone: (217)333-0950
Fax: (217)244-8082
Free: 800-537-5487

Publications: American Journal of Psychology (8178) • American Literary Realism (19765) • American Music (8179) • American Philosophical Quarterly (28069) • Beethoven Forum (23699) • Ethnomusicology (8186) • History of Philosophy Quarterly (35148) • Journal of the Abraham Lincoln Association (9635) • The Journal of Aesthetic Education (8192) • Journal of English and Germanic Philology (9712) • Law and History Review (8458) • Northwestern University Law Review (8206) • Perspectives on Work (8211) • Public Affairs Quarterly (27839) • State Politics & Policy Quarterly (8219)

University of Illinois at Urbana-Champaign
121 Art and Design Bldg.
408 E. Peabody Dr.
Champaign, IL 61820
Phone: (217)333-4841
Fax: (217)244-7688

Publications: Visual Arts Research (8222)

University of Illinois at Urbana-Champaign
707 S. Mathews, 4088 Foreign Language Bldg.
Urbana, IL 61801
Phone: (217)333-3563
Fax: (217)333-3466

Publications: Studies in the Linguistic Sciences (9719)

University of Iowa
College of Law
Boyd Law Bldg., No. 190
Iowa City, IA 52242-1113
Phone: (319)335-9132
Fax: (319)335-9019

Publications: Iowa Law Review (10976)

University of Iowa
308 EPB
Iowa City, IA 52242
Phone: (319)335-0462

Publications: The Iowa Review (10977) • Walt Whitman Quarterly Review (10990)

University of Iowa
311 English/Philosophy Bldg.
Iowa City, IA 52242
Phone: (319)356-2318

Publications: Philological Quarterly (10984)

University of Iowa
202 Schaeffer Hall
Iowa City, IA 52242
Phone: (319)335-2323
Fax: (319)335-2326

Publications: Syllecta Classica (10989)

University of Iowa, College of Law
188 Boyd Law Bldg.
Iowa City, IA 52242-1113
Phone: (319)335-9061
Fax: (319)335-9019

Publications: Journal of Corporation Law (10978)

University of Kansas
119 Stauffer-Flint Hall
Lawrence, KS 66045
Phone: (785)864-4358
Fax: (785)864-5261

Publications: The University Daily Kansan (11567)

University of Kansas
1440 Jayhawk Blvd., Ste. 320
Lawrence, KS 66045
Phone: (785)864-4213
Fax: (785)864-3800

Publications: Latin American Theatre Review (11562)

University of Kansas Alumni Association
1266 Oread Ave.
Lawrence, KS 66044
Phone: (785)864-4412
Fax: (785)864-5397

Publications: Kansas Alumni (11561)

Univ. of Ky College of Law
Publications
Lexington, KY 40506-0001
Phone: (859)257-4747
Fax: (859)323-1061
Free: 800-241-5292

Publications: Kentucky Law Journal (12170)

University of La Verne
1950 3rd St.
La Verne, CA 91750
Phone: (909)392-2712
Fax: (909)392-2706

Publications: Campus Times (2127) • La Verne Magazine (2128)

University of Louisville
Old Student Center, Ste. 305
Louisville, KY 40292-0001
Phone: (502)852-0365
Fax: (502)588-0700

Publications: The Louisville Cardinal (12228)

University of Maine-Fort Kent
25 Pleasent
Fort Kent, ME 04743-1222
Phone: (207)834-7500

Publications: The Bengal Review (12964)

University of Manitoba
180 Dafoe Rd.
Winnipeg, MB, Canada R3T 2N2
Phone: (204)474-9946
Fax: (204)474-7531

Publications: Alumni Journal (35309)

University of Manitoba
104 Robson Hall
Winnipeg, MB, Canada R3T 2N2
Phone: (204)474-6159
Fax: (204)474-7580

Publications: Manitoba Law Journal (35339)

University of Mary Hardin Baylor
Box 8012, UMH-B Sta.
Belton, TX 76513
Phone: (254)295-4689
Fax: (254)295-4943
Publications: The Bells (29915)

University of Maryland
0103 Taliaferro
College Park, MD 20742
Phone: (301)405-7415
Fax: (301)405-8395
Publications: Feminist Studies (13418)

University of Maryland - Baltimore County
1000 Hilltop Cir.
Baltimore, MD 21250
Phone: (410)455-1000
Publications: UMBC Review (13257)

University of Maryland, College Park Campus
2115 Francis Scott Key Hall
College Park, MD 20742-7315
Phone: (301)405-7941
Publications: The Hispanic American Historical Review (13419)

University of Maryland School of Law
515 W. Lombard St.
Baltimore, MD 21201-1786
Publications: Journal of Health Care Law and Policy (13191)

University of Massachusetts
Dept. of Theatre, FAE 112
Amherst, MA 01003
Phone: (413)584-6812
Fax: (413)577-0025
Publications: Theatre Topics (13806)

University of Massachusetts
Amherst, MA 01003
Phone: (413)577-5000
Fax: (413)545-4490
Publications: Main Group Chemistry News (13801)

University of Massachusetts
No.103, Munson Hall
Amherst, MA 01003
Phone: (413)545-2991
Fax: (413)545-3824
Publications: UMASS Magazine (13807)

University of Massachusetts
113 Campus Center
Amherst, MA 01003
Phone: (413)577-5000
Fax: (413)545-1592
Publications: Massachusetts Daily Collegian (13802)

University of Massachusetts
South College
Amherst, MA 01003
Phone: (413)545-2689
Fax: (413)577-0740
Publications: The Massachusetts Review (13803)

University of Massachusetts at Amhearst
426 Thompson Hall
200 Hicks Way
Amherst, MA 01003-9277
Phone: (413)545-1354
Fax: (413)545-4902
Publications: POLITY: The Journal of the Northeastern Political Science Association (13805)

University of Massachusetts at Lowell
McGauvran, Ste. 6
71 Wilder St.
Lowell, MA 01854
Phone: (978)934-5009
Fax: (978)934-3031
Publications: UMASS Lowell Connector (14279)

University of Medicine and Dentistry of New Jersey
30 Bergen St.
Newark, NJ 07107-3000
Phone: (973)972-5521
Fax: (973)972-7261
Publications: Healthstate (19353)

University of Memphis
113 Meeman Journalism Bldg.
Memphis, TN 38152-3290
Phone: (901)678-2191
Fax: (901)678-4792
Publications: The Daily Helmsman (29366)

University of Memphis
Memphis, TN 38152
Phone: (901)678-4591
Fax: (901)678-2226
Publications: River City (29378)

University of Memphis
330 Deloach St., Ste. 221
Memphis, TN 38152-3130
Phone: (901)678-2281
Fax: (901)678-4086
Publications: Business Perspectives (29359)

University of Memphis
329 Clement Hall
3704 Walker Ave.
Memphis, TN 38152
Phone: (901)678-2669
Fax: (901)678-4365
Publications: The Southern Journal of Philosophy (29382)

University of Miami
Box 248145
Coral Gables, FL 33124
Phone: (305)284-3973
Fax: (305)284-5635
Publications: James Joyce Literary Supplement (6008)

University of Miami
PO Box 248132
Coral Gables, FL 33124
Phone: (305)284-4401
Fax: (305)284-4404
Publications: The Miami Hurricane (6010)

University of Miami School of Law
PO Box 248087
Coral Gables, FL 33124
Phone: (305)284-4456
Fax: (305)284-2861
Publications: Entertainment & Sports Law Review (6006) • Res Ipsa Loquitur (6012)

University of Michigan
525 E. University
Ann Arbor, MI 48109-1109
Phone: (734)647-4462
Fax: (734)763-0938
Publications: Michigan Mathematical Journal (14766)

University of Michigan
430 E. University, Dana Bldg.
Ann Arbor, MI 48109-1115
Phone: (734)763-3243
Fax: (734)936-2195
Publications: Endangered Species Update (14748)

University of Michigan
1122 Lane Hall
204 S. State Street
Ann Arbor, MI 48109-1290
Phone: (734)615-6610
Fax: (734)647-4943
Publications: Michigan Feminist Studies (14762)

University of Michigan
3574 Rackham Bldg.
Ann Arbor, MI 48109-1070
Phone: (734)764-9265
Publications: Michigan Quarterly Review (14768)

University of Michigan Museum of Art
434 S. State St.
Ann Arbor, MI 48109-1390
Phone: (734)647-3307
Fax: (734)763-8976
Publications: University of Michigan Museums of Art and Archaeology Bulletin (14771)

University of Minnesota
118 Kirby Student Center
Duluth, MN 55812
Phone: (218)726-8154
Fax: (218)726-8246
Publications: UMD Statesman (15843)

University of Minnesota
10 Murphy Hall
206 Church St. SE
Minneapolis, MN 55414-3070
Phone: (612)627-4080
Fax: (612)627-4159
Publications: The Minnesota Daily (16102)

University of Minnesota
229 19th Ave. S.
Minneapolis, MN 55455-0444
Phone: (612)625-9330
Fax: (612)625-3478
Publications: Minnesota Law Review (16104)

University of Minnesota Alumni Association
200 Oak St. SE, Ste. 200
Minneapolis, MN 55455-2040
Phone: (612)624-2323
Fax: (612)626-8167
Free: 800-UM-ALUMS
Publications: Minnesota (16100)

University of Minnesota Press
111 3rd Ave. S., Ste. 290
Minneapolis, MN 55401-2520
Phone: (612)627-1970
Fax: (612)627-1980
Free: 800-621-2736
Publications: Cultural Critique (16071)

University of Mississippi Alumni Association
Alumni House Rm. 172
University, MS 38677
Phone: (662)915-7375
Fax: (662)915-7756
Publications: Ole Miss Alumni Review (16868)

University of Mississippi Student Media Center
233 Farley Hall
University, MS 38677
Phone: (601)232-5503
Fax: (601)232-5703
Publications: The Daily Mississippian (16863)

University of Missouri
110 Tate Hall
Columbia, MO 65211
Phone: (573)882-3059
Fax: (573)882-5785
Publications: Minnesota Review (16997)

University of Missouri at Columbia
1 Pickard Hall
Columbia, MO 65211
Phone: (573)882-3591
Fax: (573)884-4039
Publications: Muse (17007)

University of Missouri at Columbia
1507 Hillcrest Hall
Columbia, MO 65211
Phone: (573)882-4474
Fax: (573)884-4671
Free: 800-949-2505
Publications: The Missouri Review (17003)

University of Missouri at Columbia
School of Law
15 Hulston Hall
Columbia, MO 65211
Phone: (573)882-7055
Fax: (573)882-4984
Publications: Missouri Law Review (17000)

University of Missouri at Kansas City
5101 Rockhill Rd.
Kansas City, MO 64110-2499
Phone: (816)235-1168
Fax: (816)235-2611

Publications: New Letters (17188)

University of Missouri-Kansas City
5327 Holmes St.
Kansas City, MO 64110
Phone: (816)235-6397
Fax: (816)235-6514

Publications: University News (17199)

University of Montana
Missoula, MT 59812
Phone: (406)243-6156
Fax: (406)243-4076

Publications: CutBank (17866)

University of Montana
Journalism Bldg., Rm. 206
Missoula, MT 59812
Phone: (406)243-6541
Fax: (406)243-5475

Publications: Montana Kaimin (17872)

The University of Montana
Missoula, MT 59812
Phone: (406)243-4001

Publications: Montana Journalism Review (17871)

The University of Montana
University Relations
Missoula, MT 59812
Phone: (406)243-2523
Fax: (406)243-4520

Publications: Montanan (17873)

University of Nebraska
CBA Bldg.
PO Box 880407
Lincoln, NE 68588-0407
Phone: (402)472-7931
Fax: (402)472-5180

Publications: Quarterly Journal of Business & Economics (18116)

University of Nebraska
201 Andrews Hall
Lincoln, NE 68588-0334
Phone: (402)472-0911
Fax: (402)472-9771
Free: 800-715-2387

Publications: Prairie Schooner (18114)

University of Nebraska at Kearney
905 W. 25th St.
Kearney, NE 68849
Phone: (308)865-8441
Fax: (308)865-8806

Publications: Platte Valley Review (18060)

University of Nebraska at Kearney
103 Thomas Hall
Kearney, NE 68849
Phone: (308)865-8488
Fax: (308)865-8157

Publications: Antelope Newspaper (18058)

University of Nebraska at Lincoln
Hewit Pl.
1155 Q St.
PO Box 880214
Lincoln, NE 68588-0214
Phone: (402)472-6058
Fax: (402)472-0463

Publications: Great Plains Quarterly (18085)

University of Nebraska at Lincoln
1400 R St.
Nebraska Union, Rm. 20
Lincoln, NE 68588-0448
Phone: (402)472-2588
Fax: (402)472-1761

Publications: Daily Nebraskan (18083)

University of Nebraska at Omaha
Fine Arts Bldg., No. 212
Omaha, NE 68182-0324
Phone: (402)554-3159

Publications: The Nebraska Review (18204)

University of Nebraska at Omaha
6001 Dodge St.
Omaha, NE 68182
Phone: (402)554-2800
Fax: (402)554-2735

Publications: The Gateway (18195)

University of Nebraska Press
312 N. 14th St.
Lincoln, NE 68588-0484
Phone: (402)472-5937
Fax: (402)472-6214
Free: 800-755-1105

Publications: Nineteenth Century French Studies (18109)

University of Nebraska Press
233 N. 8th St.
Lincoln, NE 68588-0255
Phone: (402)472-3581
Fax: (402)472-6214
Free: 800-755-1105

Publications: American Indian Quarterly (693) • Frontiers (18084) • Legacy: A Journal of American Women Writers (18089) • National Pastime (18096) • Nine (18108) • Studies in American Jewish Literature (28085) • Symploke (31235) • Women and Music (18128)

University of Nevada
Las Vegas, NV 89154-5034
Phone: (702)895-3458

Publications: Interim (18364)

University of New Brunswick
Department of History
Fredericton, NB, Canada E3B 5A3
Phone: (506)453-4978
Fax: (506)453-5068

Publications: Acadiensis (35388)

University of New Brunswick
PO Box 4400
Fredericton, NB, Canada E3B 5A3
Phone: (506)453-4636
Fax: (506)447-3166

Publications: International Fiction Review (35395)

University of New Mexico
Dept. of Anthropology
Albuquerque, NM 87131-1561
Phone: (505)277-4544
Fax: (505)277-0874

Publications: Journal of Anthropological Research (19774)

University of New Mexico
Marron Hall, Rm. 131
University of New Mexico
Albuquerque, NM 87131
Phone: (505)277-5656
Fax: (505)277-7531

Publications: Conceptions Helpless (19770)

University of New Mexico
Marrow Hall, Rm.131
Albuquerque, NM 87131-2061
Phone: (505)277-5656
Fax: (505)277-6228

Publications: New Mexico Daily Lobo (19777)

University of New Mexico
1013 Mesa Vista Hall
Albuquerque, NM 87131-1186
Phone: (505)277-5839
Fax: (505)277-0992

Publications: New Mexico Historical Review (19778)

University of New Mexico School of Law
1117 Stanford Dr. NE
Albuquerque, NM 87131
Phone: (505)277-4910
Fax: (505)277-8342

Publications: Natural Resources Journal (19776)

University News
20 N. Grand, Ste. 301
St. Louis, MO 63103
Phone: (314)977-2812
Fax: (314)977-1588

Publications: University News (17526)

University of North Alabama
PO Box 5077
Florence, AL 35632-0001
Phone: (256)765-4144
Fax: (256)765-4170

Publications: Journal of Legal Economics (219)

University of North Alabama
UNA Box 5300
Florence, AL 35632-0001

Publications: The Flor-Ala (218)

University of North Carolina
CB 3520
Chapel Hill, NC 27599
Phone: (919)962-8482
Fax: (919)962-3520

Publications: a/b (23696)

University of North Carolina at Chapel Hill
Greenlaw Hall, CB 3520
Chapel Hill, NC 27599-3520
Phone: (919)962-0244
Fax: (919)962-3520

Publications: The Carolina Quarterly (23701)

University of North Carolina at Chapel Hill
CB 3380
Chapel Hill, NC 27599-3380
Phone: (919)962-4402
Fax: (919)962-4713

Publications: North Carolina Journal of International Law and Commercial Regulation (23716)

University of North Carolina at Charlotte
9201 University City Blvd.
Charlotte, NC 28223-0001
Phone: (704)547-2324
Fax: (704)547-2663

Publications: The University Times (23758)

University of North Carolina General Alumni Association
PO Box 660
Chapel Hill, NC 27514
Phone: (919)962-1208
Fax: (919)962-0010

Publications: Carolina Alumni Review (23700)

University of North Carolina at Greensboro
Elliott University Center
Box 10
Greensboro, NC 27412
Phone: (336)334-3088
Fax: (336)334-3008

Publications: The Carolinian (23920)

University of North Carolina at Greensboro
134 McIver, UNCG
PO Box 26170
Greensboro, NC 27402-6170
Phone: (336)334-5459
Fax: (336)334-3281

Publications: The Greensboro Review (23923)

University of North Carolina at Greensboro
390 Bryan Building
Greensboro, NC 27402
Phone: (336)334-5836

Publications: Integers (23924)

University of North Carolina Press
Dept. of Sociology
Hamilton Hall
Chapel Hill, NC 27599-3210
Phone: (919)962-0513
Fax: (919)962-4777

Publications: Social Forces (23723)

University of North Carolina Press
116 S. Boundary St.
PO Box 2288
Chapel Hill, NC 27515-2288
Phone: (919)966-3561
Fax: (919)966-3829
Free: 800-848-6224

Publishers

Publications: Early American Literature (23707) • The High School Journal (23708) • Southern Cultures (23724) • Southern Literary Journal (23725) • Studies in Philology (23726)

University of North Dakota
Box 9003
Grand Forks, ND 58202-9003
Phone: (701)777-2941
Fax: (701)777-2217

Publications: North Dakota Law Review (24455)

University of North Dakota
PO Box 7189
Grand Forks, ND 58202-7189
Phone: (701)777-4421
Fax: (701)777-4365

Publications: Teaching & Learning (24457)

University of North Dakota
PO Box 7209
Grand Forks, ND 58202-7209
Phone: (701)777-2514
Fax: (701)777-2373

Publications: Dakota Student (24454) • North Dakota Quarterly (24456)

University of North Dakota Alumni Association & the UND Foundation
PO Box 8157
Grand Forks, ND 58202-8157
Phone: (701)777-2611
Fax: (701)777-4054
Free: 800-543-8764

Publications: University of North Dakota Alumni Review (24458)

University of North Texas
Box 310650
Denton, TX 76203-0650
Phone: (940)565-2288
Fax: (940)369-8838

Publications: Military History of the West (30242)

University of Northern Iowa
Cedar Falls, IA 50614-0406
Phone: (319)273-7343
Fax: (319)273-7103

Publications: Journal of Social Studies Research (10658) • The North American Review (10659)

University of Northern Iowa
112 Maucker Union
Cedar Falls, IA 50614

Publications: Northern Iowan (10661)

University of Northern Iowa
University of Marketing and Public Relations
127 Gilchrist Hall
Cedar Falls, IA 50614-0017
Phone: (319)273-2761
Fax: (319)273-2888

Publications: Northern Iowa Today (10660)

University of Notre Dame
538 Grace Hall
Notre Dame, IN 46556

Publications: Notre Dame Magazine (10373)

University of Notre Dame
Notre Dame, IN 46556-0780
Phone: (574)631-5918
Fax: (574)631-6371

Publications: Journal of Legislation (10370) • Notre Dame Journal of Law, Ethics & Public Policy (10371)

University of Notre Dame
1146 Flanner Hall
Notre Dame, IN 46556
Phone: (574)631-5725
Fax: (574)631-8609

Publications: Religion and Literature (10376)

University of Notre Dame
PO Box Q
Notre Dame, IN 46556
Phone: (219)631-7471
Fax: (219)239-6927

Publications: The Observer (10375)

University of Notre Dame - Ave Maria Press
Notre Dame, IN 46556

Publications: Scholastic Magazine (10379)

University of Oklahoma
860 Van Vleet Oval, 149A
Copend Hall
Norman, OK 73019-0270
Phone: (405)325-2521
Fax: (405)325-7517

Publications: The Oklahoma Daily (25939)

University of Oklahoma
Norman, OK 73019
Phone: (405)325-3967
Fax: (405)325-7383

Publications: Journal of Music Theory Pedagogy (25936)

University of Oklahoma College of Law
300 Timberdell Rd.
Norman, OK 73019
Phone: (405)325-2840
Fax: (405)325-6282

Publications: American Indian Law Review (25932)

University of Oregon
5228 University of Oregon
Eugene, OR 97403-5228
Phone: (541)346-5047
Fax: (541)346-5571

Publications: Oregon Quarterly (26329)

University of Ottawa
Alumni and Development Office
178 Laurier E.
Ottawa, ON, Canada K1N 6N5
Phone: (613)562-5857
Fax: (613)562-5113
Free: 800-465-1888

Publications: Tabaret (36276)

University of Ottawa
57 rue Louis Pasteur
Ottawa, ON, Canada K1N 6N5
Phone: (613)562-5800
Fax: (613)562-5124

Publications: Ottawa Law Review (36267)

University of Ottawa Students' Federation
85 University Priv., Rm. 07
Ottawa, ON, Canada K1N 6N5
Phone: (613)562-5264
Fax: (613)562-5265

Publications: La Rotonde (36256)

University of the Pacific
3200 Fifth Ave.
Sacramento, CA 95817

Publications: McGeorge Law Review (3007)

University of the Pacific
3601 Pacific Ave.
Hand Hall, 3rd Fl.
Stockton, CA 95211
Phone: (209)946-2115
Fax: (209)946-2195

Publications: The Pacifican (3806)

University of the Pacific School of Dentistry
2155 Webster St.
San Francisco, CA 94115
Phone: (415)929-6550
Fax: (415)929-6654

Publications: Contact Point (3346)

University of Pennsylvania
4001 Spruce St.
Philadelphia, PA 19104
Phone: (215)898-8951
Fax: (215)898-5243

Publications: Penn Dental Journal (27620)

University of Pennsylvania
3400 Chestnut St.
Philadelphia, PA 19104-6204

Publications: University of Pennsylvania Journal of International Economic Law (27713)

University of Pennsylvania
3718 Locust Walk
University of Pennsylvania
Philadelphia, PA 19104-6297
Phone: (215)898-5841
Fax: (215)573-2072

Publications: International Economic Review (27494)

University of Pennsylvania, Kelly Writer's House
3805 Locust Walk
Philadelphia, PA 19104
Phone: (215)573-9748

Publications: CrossConnect (27432)

University of Pennsylvania Law Review
3400 Chestnut St.
Philadelphia, PA 19104-6204
Phone: (215)898-7060
Fax: (215)573-2005

Publications: University of Pennsylvania Law Review (27714)

University of Pennsylvania Press
4015 Walnut St.
3533 Locust Walk
Philadelphia, PA 19104
Phone: (215)898-5555
Fax: (215)573-4812

Publications: Pennsylvania Gazette (27622)

University of Pennsylvania Wharton School
370 Jon M. Huntsman Hall
3730 Walnut St.
Philadelphia, PA 19104
Phone: (215)898-3200
Fax: (215)898-1200

Publications: The Wharton Journal (27719)

University of Pittsburgh
Dept. of Anthropology
Pittsburgh, PA 15260
Phone: (412)648-7503
Fax: (412)648-7535

Publications: Ethnology (27786)

University of Pittsburgh
400 Craig Hall
Pittsburgh, PA 15260
Phone: (412)624-4147
Fax: (412)624-1021

Publications: Pitt Magazine (27828)

University of Pittsburgh
434 William Pitt Union
Pittsburgh, PA 15260
Phone: (412)648-7980
Fax: (412)648-7978

Publications: The Pitt News (27829)

University of Pittsburgh
3900 Forbes Ave.
Pittsburgh, PA 15260
Phone: (412)648-1361
Fax: (412)648-2649

Publications: Journal of Law & Commerce (27802)

University of Pittsburgh Press
3400 Forbes Ave.
Pittsburgh, PA 15260
Fax: (412)383-2466

Publications: Milton Studies (27814)

University of Portland
5000 N. Willamette Blvd.
Portland, OR 97203
Phone: (503)943-8000
Fax: (503)283-7399

Publications: The Beacon (26468)

University Press Inc.
c/o the American Mathematical Society
201 Charles St.
Providence, RI 02904-2294
Phone: (401)455-4000
Fax: (401)331-3842
Free: 800-321-4AMS

Publications: Journal of Algebraic Geometry (28401)

University Press of Kentucky
663 S. Limestone St.
Lexington, KY 40508
Phone: (859)257-2951
Fax: (859)323-1873
Free: 800-839-6835

Publications: Southern Folklore (11949)

University of Prince Edward Island
550 University Ave.
Charlottetown, PE, Canada C1A 4P3
Phone: (902)566-0330
Fax: (902)566-0416

Publications: Exceptionality Education Canada (EEC) (36914)

University of Prince Edward Island Student Union, Inc.
550 University Ave.
Charlottetown, PE, Canada C1A 4P3
Phone: (902)566-0629
Fax: (902)566-0979

Publications: Panther Prints (36917)

University of Puerto Rico Journal of Agriculture
University of Puerto Rico, Mayaguez Campus
Agricultural Experiment Sta.
Box 21360
Rio Piedras, PR 00928
Phone: (787)767-9705
Fax: (787)777-8090

Publications: University of Puerto Rico Journal of Agriculture (28286)

University of Puget Sound
1095 Wheelock Student Center
Tacoma, WA 98416-1095
Phone: (253)879-3197
Fax: (253)879-3661

Publications: The Trail (33153)

University of Redlands
1200 E. Colton Ave.
PO Box 3080
Redlands, CA 92373-0999
Phone: (909)335-5137
Fax: (909)335-4091

Publications: Bulldog Weekly (2901)

University of Regina
3737 Wascana Pkwy.
Regina, SK, Canada S4S 0A2
Phone: (306)585-4302
Fax: (306)585-4827

Publications: Wascana Review of Contemporary Poetry and Short Fiction (37535)

University of Regina Students' Union
University Centre
Regina, SK, Canada S4S 0A2
Phone: (306)586-8867
Fax: (306)586-7422

Publications: The Carillon (37526)

University Relations
11300 NE 2nd Ave.
Miami Shores, FL 33161-6695
Phone: (305)899-3188
Fax: (305)899-3186

Publications: Barry Magazine (6420)

University of Rhode Island
Memorial Union, Rm. 125
Kingston, RI 02881
Phone: (401)874-2914
Fax: (401)874-5607

Publications: The Good Five Cent Cigar (28359)

University of Richmond
Tyler Haynes Commons, Rm. 327
Richmond, VA 23173

Publications: The Collegian (32433)

University of Rochester
Dept. of English
Morey Hall 410
Rochester, NY 14627
Phone: (585)275-3820
Fax: (585)442-5769

Publications: Blake/An Illustrated Quarterly (23211)

University of Rochester Students Association
Wilson Commons 102
CPU 277086
Rochester, NY 14627-7086
Phone: (585)275-5942
Fax: (585)273-5303

Publications: Campus Times (23214)

University of St. Thomas
3800 Montrose Blvd.
Houston, TX 77006
Phone: (713)522-7911
Fax: (713)522-9920

Publications: The Cauldron (30461)

University of San Francisco
2130 Fulton St.
San Francisco, CA 94117
Phone: (415)422-2698
Fax: (415)422-2696

Publications: University of San Francisco Magazine (3455)

University of Saskatchewan
707 Arts Bldg.
9 Campus Dr.
Saskatoon, SK, Canada S7N 5A5
Phone: (306)966-5794
Fax: (306)966-5852

Publications: Canadian Journal of History/Annales canadiennes d'histoire (37550)

University of Saskatchewan Alumni Association
223-117 Science Place
UNV of Saskatchewan
Saskatoon, SK, Canada S7N 5C8
Phone: (306)966-5186
Fax: (306)966-5571
Free: 800-699-1907

Publications: The Green and White (37551)

University of the South
735 University Ave.
Office of Communications
Sewanee, TN 37383
Phone: (931)598-1000
Fax: (931)598-1667
Free: 800-289-4919

Publications: Sewanee (29593)

University of the South
735 University Ave.
Sewanee, TN 37383-1000
Phone: (931)598-1246

Publications: The Sewanee Review (29595)

University of the South
University S.T.O.
Sewanee, TN 37375
Phone: (615)598-1000
Fax: (615)598-1145

Publications: The Sewanee Purple (29594)

University of South Alabama
Dept. Psychology
Mobile, AL 36688
Phone: (251)460-0321

Publications: Journal of Sport Behavior (322)

University of South Alabama
Humanities 344
Mobile, AL 36688
Phone: (251)460-6210
Fax: (251)460-7650

Publications: Gulf South Historical Review (320)

University of South Alabama
The Vanguard
PO Drawer U-25100
Mobile, AL 36688
Phone: (251)460-6442
Fax: (251)414-8293

Publications: The Vanguard (331)

University of South Carolina
471 University Pkwy.
Aiken, SC 29801
Phone: (803)648-6851
Fax: (803)641-3461

Publications: Pacer Times (28468)

University of South Carolina
Columbia, SC 29208
Phone: (803)777-5874
Fax: (803)777-2368

Publications: South Carolina Law Review (28565)

University of South Carolina at Spartanburg
800 University Way
Spartanburg, SC 29303
Phone: (864)503-5000
Fax: (864)503-5100

Publications: The Carolinian (28757)

University of South Dakota
English Dept.
Vermillion, SD 57069
Phone: (605)677-5966
Fax: (605)677-5184

Publications: South Dakota Review (29006)

University of South Dakota
Student Publications Board
414 E. Clark St.
Vermillion, SD 57069
Phone: (605)677-5494
Fax: (605)677-5105

Publications: Volante (29007)

University of South Florida
CPR 472
Tampa, FL 33620-5600
Phone: (813)974-6242
Fax: (813)974-4887

Publications: Oracle (6775)

University of Southern California
Office of University Public Relations
University Park (KAP 248)
Los Angeles, CA 90089-2538
Phone: (213)740-2684
Fax: (213)821-1100

Publications: USC Trojan Family Magazine (2426)

University of Southern California
Student Union 404
Los Angeles, CA 90089-0895
Phone: (213)740-2707
Fax: (213)740-5701

Publications: Daily Trojan (2252)

University of Southern California
University Park
Los Angeles, CA 90089-0071
Phone: (213)740-8475
Fax: (213)740-5502

Publications: Southern California Law Review (2396)

University of Southern California
WPH 404
Los Angeles, CA 90089-4034
Phone: (213)740-3252
Fax: (213)740-5775

Publications: Southern California Anthology (2393)

University of Southern California School of Cinema-TV
Critical Studies
Lucas 405
Los Angeles, CA 90089-2211
Phone: (213)740-3334
Fax: (213)740-9471

Publications: Spectator (Los Angeles) (2404)

University of Southern Colorado
Dept. of Mass Communications
2200 Bonforte Blvd.
Pueblo, CO 81001-4901
Phone: (719)549-2100
Fax: (719)549-2120

Publications: USC Today (4602)

University of Southern Mississippi
Box 5144, Southern Sta.
Hattiesburg, MS 39406-5144
Phone: (601)266-4321
Fax: (601)266-5757

Publications: Mississippi Review (16663)

University of Southern Mississippi
PO Box 5078, Southern Sta.
Hattiesburg, MS 39406-5078
Phone: (601)266-4370
Fax: (601)266-5757

Publications: Southern Quarterly (16664)

The University of Southern Mississippi Alumni Association
Box 5013
Hattiesburg, MS 39406-5013
Phone: (601)266-5013
Fax: (601)266-4214

Publications: The Talon (16665)

University of Southwestern Louisiana
PO Box 4-4813
Lafayette, LA 70504
Phone: (337)482-6960
Fax: (337)482-6959

Publications: The Vermilion (12621)

University of Tampa Press
401 W. Kennedy Blvd.
Box 19F
Tampa, FL 33606-1490
Phone: (813)253-6266
Fax: (813)258-7593

Publications: Tampa Review (6779)

University of Tennessee
5 Communications Bldg.
Knoxville, TN 37996-0314
Phone: (865)974-3231

Publications: Journal of Industrial Teacher Education (29276) • UT Daily Beacon (29284)

University of Tennessee Alumni Association
91 Communications Bldg.
University of Tennessee
Knoxville, TN 37996-0315
Phone: (865)974-2225
Fax: (865)974-6435

Publications: Tennessee Alumnus (29282)

University of Tennessee at Chattanooga
615 McCallie
Chattanooga, TN 37403
Phone: (423)425-4111
Fax: (423)755-5357

Publications: The University Echo (29095)

University of Tennessee at Martin
111 Business Administration Bldg.
Martin, TN 38238-5015
Phone: (731)587-7226
Fax: (731)587-7241

Publications: Journal of Business and Economic Perspectives (29342)

University of Tennessee at Martin
314 Gooch Hall
Martin, TN 38238
Phone: (731)587-7780
Fax: (731)587-7791

Publications: Pacer (29343)

University of Texas
Dept. of Mathematics
Box 19408
Arlington, TX 76019
Phone: (817)261-1179
Fax: (817)272-5802

Publications: Libertas Mathematica (29734)

University of Texas at Arlington
Box 19038
UTA Student Publications
Arlington, TX 76019
Phone: (817)272-3188
Fax: (817)272-5009

Publications: The Shorthorn (29736)

University of Texas at Brownsville & Texas Southmost College
80 Fort Brown
Brownsville, TX 78520
Phone: (956)544-8984
Fax: (956)983-7064

Publications: Extrapolation (29960)

University of Texas at El Paso
University Communications
El Paso, TX 79968-0522
Phone: (915)747-5526
Fax: (915)747-5969

Publications: NOVA Quarterly (30281)

University of Texas at El Paso Student Publications
University of Texas El Paso
500 University Ave. W.
El Paso, TX 79968-0622
Phone: (915)747-5161
Fax: (915)747-8031

Publications: Prospector (30282)

University of Texas at Houston
7000 Fannin, Ste. 1111
Houston, TX 77225
Phone: (713)500-4151

Publications: Houston Journal of International Law (30486)

University of Texas Medical Branch
301 University Blvd.
Galveston, TX 77555
Phone: (409)772-3215
Fax: (409)772-5640

Publications: Medical Humanities Review (30382)

The University of Texas—Pan American
Student Publications CAS170
Edinburg, TX 78539
Phone: (956)381-2541
Fax: (956)316-7122

Publications: The Pan American (30271)

University of Texas Press
PO Box 7819
Austin, TX 78713
Phone: (512)232-7621
Fax: (512)232-7178
Free: 800-252-3206

Publications: Cinema Journal (30136) • Journal of the History of Sexuality (29787) • Latin American Music Review (29791)

University of Texas at San Antonio
Division of Life Sciences
San Antonio, TX 78285

Publications: Pharmacology Biochemistry and Behavior (31041) • Physiology & Behavior (31042)

University of Texas School of Law Publications
727 E. Dean Keeton St., Ste. 4
Austin, TX 78705
Phone: (512)232-1149
Fax: (512)471-6988

Publications: Texas Law Review Manual on Usage and Style (29831) • Texas Law Review Texas Rules of Form (29832)

The University of Texas School of Law Publications Inc.
727 E Dean Keeton St.
Austin, TX 78705
Phone: (512)477-6397
Fax: (512)471-6988

Publications: The American Journal of Criminal Law (29751) • The Review of Litigation (29801) • Texas Environmental Law Journal (29818) • Texas Forum on Civil Liberties and Civil Rights (29821) • Texas Hispanic Journal of Law and Policy (29823) • Texas Intellectual Property Law Journal (29825) • Texas International Law Journal (29826) • Texas Journal of Business Law (29827) • Texas Journal of Women and the Law (29829) • Texas Law Review (29830) • The Texas Review of Entertainment and Sports Law (29846) • Texas Review of Law and Politics (29847)

University of Texas Student Publications
2500 Whitis
Austin, TX 78713
Phone: (512)471-4591
Fax: (512)471-2952

Publications: The Daily Texan (29773)

University of Toledo
2801 W. Baneroft St.
Toledo, OH 43606
Phone: (419)530-2721
Fax: (419)537-2108

Publications: The Collegian (25566)

University of Toronto
21 King's College Circle
Toronto, ON, Canada M5S 3J3
Phone: (416)946-7575
Fax: (416)978-3958
Free: 800-463-6048

Publications: University of Toronto Bulletin (36778) • University of Toronto Magazine (36781)

University of Toronto
214 College St., 3rd Fl.
Toronto, ON, Canada M5T 2Z9
Phone: (416)978-7984
Fax: (416)971-1378

Publications: Theatre Research in Canada/Recherches Theatrales Au Canada (36758)

University of Toronto Press
10 St. Mary St., Ste. 700
Toronto, ON, Canada M4Y 2W8
Phone: (416)978-2239
Fax: (416)978-4738
Free: 800-565-9523

Publications: Canadian Review of American Studies (36227)

University of Toronto Press - Journals Division
5201 Dufferin St.
Toronto, ON, Canada M3H 5T8
Phone: (416)667-7810
Fax: (416)667-7881
Free: 800-221-9985

Publications: Canadian Historical Review (36502) • The Canadian Journal of Linguistics/Revue canadienne de linguistique (36511) • Canadian Journal of Sociology/Cahiers canadiens de sociologie (36512) • Canadian Mathematical Bulletin (36517) • The Canadian Modern Language Review/La Revue canadienne des langues vivantes (36520) • Canadian Public Policy—Analyse de Politiques (34638) • Canadian Review of Comparative Literature (36529) • Canadian Theatre Review (35859) • Cartographica (36537) • Diaspora (36574) • Infor (37130) • Journal of Scholarly Publishing (36639) • Journal of Scholarly Publishing (4945) • Modern Drama (36665) • Seminar (34729) • The Tocqueville Review/La Revue Tocqueville (36761) • Ultimate Reality and Meaning (35355) • University of Toronto Law Journal (36780) • University of Toronto Quarterly (36782) • Victorian Periodicals Review (36786)

University of Tulsa
600 S. College
Tulsa, OK 74104
Phone: (918)631-3084
Fax: (918)631-2885

Publications: Collegian Newspaper (26110)

University of Utah
255 S. Central Campus Dr., Rm. 3500
Salt Lake City, UT 84112-0494
Phone: (801)581-6070
Fax: (801)585-5167

Publications: Western Humanities Review (31443)

University of Utah College of Law
332 S 1400 E Front
Salt Lake City, UT 84112
Phone: (801)581-3583
Fax: (801)581-6897

Publications: Journal of Land Resouces and Environmental Law (31434)

University of Vermont
Dept. of Microbiology
Stafford Bldg., Rm. B009
Burlington, VT 05405
Phone: (802)656-3131
Fax: (802)656-8749

Publications: Methods in Cell Science (31515)

University of Victoria
Box 1700, MS 7902
Victoria, BC, Canada V8W 2Y2
Phone: (250)721-7902
Fax: (250)721-6597

Publications: Fermata (35216)

University of Victoria
PO Box 1700
STN CSC
Victoria, BC, Canada V8W 2Y2
Phone: (250)721-8524
Fax: (250)472-5051

Publications: The Malahat Review (35221)

University of Victoria
Student Union Bldg.
PO Box 3035
Victoria, BC, Canada V8W 3P3
Phone: (250)721-8359
Fax: (250)472-4556

Publications: The Martlet (35222)

University of Virginia
115 Wilson Hall
PO Box 400777
Charlottesville, VA 22904-4777
Phone: (804)924-7159
Fax: (804)924-7160

Publications: Dieciocho (31928)

University of Virginia
PO Box 418 Newcomb Hall Sta.
Charlottesville, VA 22904

Publications: The Declaration (31927)

University of Virginia
PO Box 400703
Charlottesville, VA 22904-4703
Phone: (434)924-1086
Fax: (434)924-7290

Publications: The Cavalier Daily (31921)

University of Virginia
Women's Center
PO Box 800588
Charlottesville, VA 22908
Phone: (434)924-4500
Fax: (434)982-2901

Publications: IRIS (31932)

University of Virginia Alumni Association
Box 3446
Charlottesville, VA 22903
Phone: (434)971-9721
Fax: (434)296-4577

Publications: Virginia (31944)

University of Washington
Box 353587
Seattle, WA 98195-3587
Phone: (206)543-2992

Publications: Pacific Northwest Quarterly (33001)

University of Washington
Box 353650
Seattle, WA 98195-3650
Phone: (206)543-9302
Fax: (206)685-0668

Publications: Journal of Japanese Studies (32978)

University of Washington
144 Communications Bldg.
PO Box 353720
Seattle, WA 98195

Publications: The Daily (32959)

University of Waterloo
Dept. of Chemistry
Waterloo, ON, Canada N2L 3G1
Phone: (519)888-4567
Fax: (519)888-9168

Publications: Chem 13 News (36848)

University of Waterloo
Waterloo, ON, Canada N2L 3G1
Phone: (519)888-4567
Fax: (519)746-2031

Publications: Environments (36850) • Germano-Slavica (36851) • Kinema (36854)

University of West Florida
11000 University Pkwy.
Pensacola, FL 32514-5751
Phone: (850)474-2191
Fax: (850)474-2109

Publications: Voyager (6570)

University of Western Ontario
London, ON, Canada N6A 3K7
Phone: (519)661-2111
Fax: (519)661-3790

Publications: Canadian Journal of Law & Jurisprudence (35979)

University of Western Ontario
Middlesex College
London, ON, Canada N6A 5B7
Phone: (519)661-3542
Fax: (519)661-3506

Publications: Canadian Journal of Information and Library Science (36510)

University of Western Ontario
Rm. 340, U.C.C. Bldg.
London, ON, Canada N6A 3K7
Phone: (519)661-3580
Fax: (519)661-3825

Publications: The Gazette (35981) • University of Western Ontario, Gazette (35994)

University of Western Ontario
London, ON, Canada N6A 3K7
Phone: (519)661-2043
Fax: (519)661-3531

Publications: Studies in Music (35993)

University of Windsor
Windsor, ON, Canada N9B 3P4
Phone: (519)253-3000
Fax: (519)971-3610

Publications: Informal Logic (36887) • View (36890)

University of Windsor's Dept. of English
Windsor, ON, Canada N9B 3P4
Phone: (519)253-3000
Fax: (519)971-3676

Publications: Windsor Review (36892)

University of Winnipeg
515 Portage Ave.
Winnipeg, MB, Canada R3D 2E9
Phone: (204)786-7811
Fax: (204)783-7080

Publications: Uniter (35356)

University of Wisconsin
Mechanical Engineering Bldg.
1513 University Ave.
Madison, WI 53706
Phone: (608)262-3494
Fax: (608)265-4734

Publications: Wisconsin Engineer (33982)

University of Wisconsin
618 Vanhise Hall
Madison, WI 53706

Publications: L'Anello Che Non Tiene (33919)

University of Wisconsin
1800 Grand Ave.
Superior, WI 54880
Phone: (715)394-8335
Fax: (715)394-8454

Publications: Promethean (34360)

University of Wisconsin
518 S. 7th Ave.
Wausau, WI 54401-5362
Phone: (715)261-6100
Fax: (715)261-6333

Publications: The Forum (34429)

University of Wisconsin-Eau Claire
405 Hibbard Hall
Eau Claire, WI 54702-4004
Phone: (715)836-2637
Fax: (715)836-5996

Publications: Computer Science Education (33667) • Feminist Teacher (33669) • International Journal of Computer Simulation (33670)

University of Wisconsin-Eau Claire
Hibbard Humanities Hall, 108
Eau Claire, WI 54701
Phone: (715)836-2637
Fax: (715)836-5958

Publications: Spectator (33673)

University of Wisconsin-La Crosse
1725 State St.
La Crosse, WI 54601
Phone: (608)785-8381
Fax: (608)785-8856

Publications: The Racquet (33886)

University of Wisconsin at Madison
Helen C. White Hall
600 N. Park St.
Madison, WI 53706
Phone: (608)263-0566
Fax: (608)563-3709

Publications: Madison Review (33960)

University of Wisconsin-Milwaukee
PO Box 413
Milwaukee, WI 53201
Phone: (414)229-4707
Fax: (414)229-6699
Free: 888-349-3432

Publications: Digest of Middle East Studies (DOMES) (34065)

University of Wisconsin-Milwaukee
PO Box 413, Union Box 88
Milwaukee, WI 53201-0413
Phone: (414)229-4578
Fax: (414)229-4579

Publications: UWM Post (34105)

University of Wisconsin-Oshkosh
800 Algoma Blvd.
Oshkosh, WI 54901

Publications: Wisconsin Review (34228)

University of Wisconsin-Oshkosh
19 Reeve Memorial Union
Oshkosh, WI 54901
Phone: (414)424-3048
Fax: (414)424-0866

Publications: Oshkosh Advance-Titan (34226)

University of Wisconsin Press
1930 Monroe St., 3rd Fl.
Madison, WI 53711
Phone: (608)263-0668
Fax: (608)263-1173

Publications: American Orthoptic Journal (33917) • Arctic Anthropology (33922) • Contemporary Literature (33928) • Ecological Restoration (33935) • Journal of Human Resources (33952) • Land Economics (33956) • Landscape Journal (33957) • Monatshefte (33963) • Substance (33975)

University of Wisconsin Press
PO Box 7819
Madison, WI 53707
Phone: (608)265-4782
Fax: (608)262-7560

Publications: Individual Psychology (29782)

University of Wisconsin—River Falls
English Dept.
410 S. 3rd St.
River Falls, WI 54022
Phone: (715)425-3173
Fax: (715)425-0657

Publications: Literary Magazine Review (34308)

University of Wisconsin-Stevens Point
2100 Main St.
Stevens Point, WI 54481-3897
Phone: (715)346-0123

Publications: The Pointer (34343)

University of Wisconsin-Stout
302 10th Ave.
Menomonie, WI 54751
Phone: (715)232-2272
Fax: (715)232-1773

Publications: The Stoutonia (34040)

University of Wyoming
Box 3035
Laramie, WY 82071-3035
Phone: (307)766-2329
Fax: (307)766-6417

Publications: Wyoming Law Review (34553)

University of Wyoming
PO Box 3625
Laramie, WY 82071
Phone: (307)766-6190
Fax: (307)766-4027

Publications: Branding Iron (34547) • Owen Wister Review (34550)

Universty of New Mexico
200 College Rd.
Gallup, NM 87301
Phone: (505)863-7647
Fax: (505)863-7532

Publications: Paradoxism (19857)

Uno Mas Magazine
PO Box 1832
Silver Spring, MD 20915

Publications: Uno Mas Magazine (13747)

UNRESTRAINED!
3150 Spring Creek Cres.
Mississauga, ON, Canada L5N 4S2

Publications: UNRESTRAINED! (36091)

Unterrified Democrat
PO Box 109
Linn, MO 65051-0109
Phone: (573)897-3150
Fax: (573)897-0076

Publications: Unterrified Democrat (17255)

UO Inc.
455 S. 4th Ave., Ste. 1236
Louisville, KY 40202
Phone: (502)589-8250
Fax: (502)587-0848
Free: 800-888-2047

Publications: Unique Opportunities (12242)

The UP Catholic
347 Rock St.
PO Box 548
Marquette, MI 49855
Phone: (906)227-9131
Fax: (906)226-6941

Publications: The UP Catholic (15339)

UP Media Group, Inc.
2018 Powers Ferry Rd., Ste. 600
Atlanta, GA 30339
Phone: (678)589-8800
Fax: (678)589-8850

Publications: Circuits Assembly (6984)

Up North Publications, Inc.
206 N. Bridge St.
PO Box 337
Bellaire, MI 49615
Phone: (231)533-8523

Publications: Antrim County News (14805)

Up North Publications, Inc.
PO Box 335
Elk Rapids, MI 49629
Phone: (616)264-9711

Publications: The Town Meeting (15005)

Up North Publishing, Inc.
PO Box 79
Florence, WI 54121
Phone: (715)696-3400
Fax: (715)528-5976

Publications: The Florence Mining News (33695)

Upper Country News-Reporter
155 N Superior
PO Box 9
Cambridge, ID 83610
Phone: (208)257-3515

Publications: Upper Country News-Reporter (7841)

Upper Dauphin Sentinel
510 Union St.
Millersburg, PA 17061
Phone: (717)692-4737
Fax: (717)692-2420
Free: 800-959-2715

Publications: Upper Dauphin Sentinel (27265)

Upper Iowa University
PO Box 1857
Fayette, IA 52142
Phone: (319)425-5273
Fax: (319)425-5271

Publications: Collegian (10888)

Upper Rogue Independent
PO Box 900
Eagle Point, OR 97524
Phone: (541)826-7700
Fax: (541)826-1340

Publications: Upper Rogue Independent (26307)

The Upper Room
1908 Grand Ave.
PO Box 340004
Nashville, TN 37203-0004
Phone: (615)340-7200
Fax: (615)340-7552
Free: 800-972-0433

Publications: Pockets Magazine (29481) • The Upper Room Daily Devotional Guide/ (29497) • WEAVINGS (29501)

Upper Snake River Valley Historical Society
PO Box 244
Rexburg, ID 83440
Phone: (208)356-7030

Publications: Snake River Echoes (7964)

Upstate Newspapers, Inc.
PO Box 576
Columbus, NC 28722
Fax: (704)472-6900

Publications: Polk County News Journal (23792)

Ural and Associates, Inc.
Box 340525
Coral Gables, FL 33134
Phone: (305)446-9462
Fax: (305)461-0921

Publications: International Journal for Housing Science and Its Applications (6007)

URB
2410 Hyperion Ave.
Los Angeles, CA 90027
Phone: (323)993-0291
Fax: (323)466-1207
Free: 800-872-6249

Publications: URB (2424)

Urban Ecology, Inc.
414 13th St., Ste. 500
Oakland, CA 94612-2706
Phone: (510)251-6330
Fax: (510)251-2117

Publications: Urban Ecology (2702)

Urban Land Institute
1025 Thomas Jefferson, NW, Ste. 500 W.
Washington, DC 20007
Phone: (202)624-7000
Fax: (202)624-7140
Free: 800-321-5011

Publications: Urban Land Magazine (5838)

The Urban Latino West News
3288 21st St. No. 9
San Francisco, CA 94110
Phone: (415)821-4452
Fax: (415)821-4452

Publications: The Urban Latino News (3457) • The Urban Latino News (3456)

Urner Barry Publications, Inc.
PO Box 389
Toms River, NJ 08754
Phone: (732)240-5330
Fax: (732)341-0891
Free: 800-932-0617

Publications: Weekly Insiders Turkey Letter (19648)

Ursbry
41 Quinte St.
PO Box 130
Trenton, ON, Canada K8V 5R3
Phone: (613)392-6501
Fax: (613)392-0505

Publications: Trentonian and Tri-County News (36825)

Ursinus College
PO Box 1000
Collegeville, PA 19426
Phone: (610)409-3586

Publications: The Grizzly (26796)

US Lacrosse, Inc.
113 W University Pkwy.
Baltimore, MD 21210
Phone: (410)235-7392
Fax: (410)366-6735

Publications: Lacrosse (13206)

USA Cycling Inc.
1 Olympic Plaza
Colorado Springs, CO 80909-5746
Phone: (719)578-4581
Fax: (719)578-4596

Publications: USA Cycling Magazine (4259)

USA Deaf Sports Federation
102 N Krohn Pl.
Sioux Falls, SD 57103-1800
Phone: (605)367-5761
Fax: (605)367-5958

Publications: Deaf Sports Review (28963)

USA Equestrian
4047 Iron Works Pkwy.
Lexington, KY 40511-8483
Phone: (859)258-2472
Fax: (859)231-6662

Publications: Equestrian (12164)

USA Gymnastics
201 S Capitol, Ste. 300
Indianapolis, IN 46225
Phone: (317)237-5050
Fax: (317)237-5069

Publications: U.S.A. Gymnastics (10178)

USA Table Tennis
One Olympic Plz.
Colorado Springs, CO 80909
Phone: (719)866-4583
Fax: (719)632-6071

Publications: USA Table Tennis Magazine (4260)

U.S.A. Today
99 W Hawthorne Ave.
Valley Stream, NY 11580
Phone: (516)568-9191

Publications: U.S.A. Today (23487)

USA TODAY
7950 Jones Branch Dr.
Mc Lean, VA 22108
Phone: (703)854-6319
Free: 800-872-1415

Publications: USA TODAY Sports Weekly (32258)

USA Water Ski
1251 Holy Cow Rd.
Polk City, FL 33868-8200
Phone: (863)324-4341
Fax: (863)325-8259
Free: 800-533-2972

Publications: The Water Skier (6589)

USACGSC
290 Grant Ave., Bldg. 77
Fort Leavenworth, KS 66027-1254
Phone: (913)684-9327
Fax: (913)684-9328

Publications: Military Review (11440)

USA.NET, Inc.
1155 Kelly Johnson Blvd.
Colorado Springs, CO 80903
Phone: (719)265-2930
Fax: (719)265-2922

Publications: The Gazette (4249)

USFR Media Group
6688 N. Central Expy., No. 650
Dallas, TX 75206-3914
Phone: (214)750-8222
Fax: (214)750-4522
Free: 800-982-5370

Publications: Cowboys & Indians (30139)

USG Corp.
125 S Franklin St.
Chicago, IL 60606-4678
Phone: (312)606-4041
Fax: (312)606-5566
Free: 800-USG-4YOU

Publications: Form & Function (8380)

Utah Education Association
875 E. 5180 S.
Murray, UT 84107
Phone: (801)266-4461
Fax: (801)265-2249
Free: 800-594-8996

Publications: UEA Action (31374)

Utah Food Industry Association
1578 West 1700 South, Ste. 100
Salt Lake City, UT 84104
Phone: (801)973-9517
Fax: (801)972-8712

Publications: The Intermountain Retailer (31432)

Utah Genealogical Association
PO Box 1144
Salt Lake City, UT 84110-1144

Publications: Utah Genealogical Association (31442)

Utah Science
UAES (Agriculture Experimental Sta. Information Office)
Utah State University
Logan, UT 84322-4845
Phone: (435)797-2189
Fax: (435)797-3321

Publications: Utah Science (31352)

Utah State University
1420 Old Main Hill
Logan, UT 84322-1420
Phone: (435)797-1353
Fax: (435)797-1364

Publications: Utah State Magazine (31353)

Utah Valley Publishing
546 S State St.
PO Box 65
Orem, UT 84058
Phone: (801)225-1340
Fax: (801)225-1341

Publications: Orem-Geneva Times (31385)

Ute City Tea Party Ltd.
517 E. Hopkins
Aspen, CO 81611-1982
Phone: (970)925-2220
Fax: (970)920-2118

Publications: Aspen Daily News (4140)

Utica College of Syracuse University
Burrstone Rd.
Utica, NY 13502
Phone: (315)792-3111
Fax: (315)792-3073

Publications: Tangerine (23467)

The Utica Herald
120 S. Main St.
PO Box 515
Utica, OH 43080-0515
Phone: (614)892-2771

Publications: The Utica Herald (25608)

Utillaje, Inc.
20 N Wacker Dr.
Chicago, IL 60606
Phone: (312)372-9077
Fax: (312)372-6537

Publications: Utillaje (8596)

UTPress
PO Box 7819
Journals Div.
Austin, TX 78713-7819
Fax: (512)262-7560

Publications: Journal of Politics (30046)

The Utter Co.
PO Box 520
Westerly, RI 02891-0520
Phone: (401)596-7791
Fax: (401)348-5080
Free: 800-937-8759

Publications: The Westerly Sun (28458)

UVic Communications
Sedgewick C Wing
Rm. C149
Victoria, BC, Canada V8W 2Y2
Phone: (250)721-7636

Publications: UVic Ring (35228) • UVic Torch (35229)

UW - Whitewater
62 E University Ctr.
Whitewater, WI 53190
Phone: (262)472-1426
Fax: (262)472-5101

Publications: Royal Purple (34457)

V & P Publishing Co., Inc.
PO Box 134
Eureka, CA 95502
Phone: (707)443-5672
Fax: (707)443-5022

Publications: Tri-City Weekly (1895) • Tri-City Weekly (Southern Edition) (1896)

Vacation Publications, Inc.
1502 Augusta, Ste. 415
Houston, TX 77057
Phone: (713)974-6903
Fax: (713)974-0445

Publications: VACATIONS (30540)

Vagelos Alumnae Center
Barnard College
3009 Broadway
New York, NY 10027-6598
Phone: (212)854-6157
Fax: (212)854-0044

Publications: Barnard Magazine (21291)

Vail Daily
PO Box 81
Vail, CO 81658
Phone: (970)949-0555
Fax: (970)949-7096

Publications: Vail Daily (4654)

Vajra Printing & Publishing of Y.A.A.
154 Merrick Rd.
Amityville, NY 11701-3439
Phone: (516)691-8475
Fax: (516)691-8475

Publications: Moksha Journal (20050)

Val D'Or
1465 de la Quebecoise
Quebec, QC, Canada G9P 4P2
Phone: (819)825-3755
Fax: (819)825-0361

Publications: L'Echo d'Amos (36932) • L'Echo d'Abitibi Quest (37022) • L'Echo de Malartic (37064)

VAL Publications Ltd.
95 Leeward Glenway, No. 121
Don Mills, ON, Canada M3C 2Z6
Phone: (416)424-1393
Fax: (416)467-8262

Publications: Hi-Rise (35774)

The Valders Journal
204 N Liberty St.
PO Box 400
Valders, WI 54245-0400
Phone: (920)775-4431

Publications: The Valders Journal (34379)

Valdese News
PO Box 280
Morganton, NC 28680
Phone: (704)437-2161
Fax: (704)437-5372

Publications: Valdese News (24074)

Valdosta State University
PO Box 7052
Valdosta, GA 31698
Phone: (229)333-5686
Fax: (229)249-2618

Publications: Spectator (7615)

Valencia Community College
1800 S Kirkman Rd.
PO Box 3028
Orlando, FL 32802
Phone: (407)299-5000
Fax: (407)299-5000

Publications: The Paper (6506)

The Valierian
PO Box 308
Valier, MT 59486
Phone: (406)279-3719
Fax: (406)279-3686

Publications: The Valierian (17917)

Valley Breeze
2180 Mendon Rd.
Cumberland, RI 02864-3805
Phone: (401)334-9555
Fax: (401)334-9994
Free: 877-800-1559

Publications: Valley Breeze (28339)

Valley City Times-Record
146 3rd St. NE
PO Box 697
Valley City, ND 58072
Phone: (701)845-0463
Fax: (701)845-0175
Free: 800-254-0674

Publications: Valley City Times-Record (24544)

Valley Courier
218 W. Benson St.
Cincinnati, OH 45215-3206
Phone: (513)821-4575
Fax: (513)761-3304

Publications: Valley Courier (24825)

Valley Del Publications, Inc.
842 E St. Rd.
PO Box 31
Westtown, PA 19395
Phone: (610)399-1720
Fax: (610)399-9738

Publications: County Lines (28153)

The Valley Echo
Box 70
Invermere, BC, Canada V0A 1K0
Phone: (250)342-9216
Fax: (250)342-3930

Publications: The Valley Echo (34976)

Valley Farmer
905 S Henry
Bay City, MI 48706
Phone: (517)893-6507

Publications: Valley Farmer (14803)

The Valley Independent
Eastgate 19
Monessen, PA 15062
Phone: (724)684-5200
Fax: (724)684-2602

Publications: The Valley Independent (27273)

Valley Journal
115 S. Center St.
Lake Benton, MN 56149
Phone: (507)368-4275
Fax: (507)368-4276

Publications: Lake Benton Valley Journal (15990)

Valley Media, Inc.
PO Box 9
Jenison, MI 49429-0009
Phone: (616)454-9456
Fax: (616)454-4666

Publications: Cadence (15227)

Valley Media, Inc.
PO Box 4195
Brownsville, TX 78520
Phone: (210)546-5113
Fax: (210)546-0903
Free: 800-556-9876

Publications: Bargain Book (Central) (29956) • Bargain Book (North) (29957) • Bargain Book (South) (29958) • Valley Town Crier (30789)

Valley Media, Inc.
1811 N. 23rd St.
McAllen, TX 78501
Phone: (956)682-2423
Fax: (956)630-6371

Publications: Winter Texan (30790)

Valley News
423 2nd St.
PO Box 647
Solvang, CA 93464
Phone: (805)688-5522
Fax: (805)688-7685

Publications: Santa Ynez Valley News (3771)

Valley News
201 Maple
PO Box 327
Pretty Prairie, KS 67570
Phone: (620)459-6322
Fax: (620)459-6729

Publications: Ninnescah Valley News (11767)

Valley News
PO Box 339
Beardsley, MN 56211
Phone: (320)265-3491

Publications: Valley News (15734)

Valley News
7 Interchange Dr.
West Lebanon, NH 03784
Phone: (603)298-8711
Fax: (603)298-0212
Free: 800-874-2226

Publications: Valley News (18650)

The Valley News Herald
523 N Pines Rd., Ste. B
PO Box 142020
Spokane, WA 99214-2020
Phone: (509)924-2440
Fax: (509)927-1154

Publications: The Valley News Herald (33102)

Valley News Pub.
101 Emerson Ave.
Pittsburgh, PA 15215
Phone: (412)782-2121
Fax: (412)782-1195

Publications: The Herald (27796)

Valley News & Views
PO Box 309
Drayton, ND 58225
Phone: (701)454-6333
Fax: (701)454-6333

Publications: Valley News & Views (24403)

Valley Newspapers, Inc.
220 N 12th St.
PO Box 850
Lanett, AL 36863

Publications: The Valley Times-News (301)

Valley Press
478 NE 56th St.
Miami, FL 33137-2621
Phone: (305)756-8800

Publications: Thoughts for All Seasons (6384)

Valley Press
PO Box 667
Plains, MT 59859
Phone: (406)826-3402
Fax: (406)826-5577
Free: 800-440-3402

Publications: Valley Press (17893)

Valley Publication
200 Industrial Ct.
PO Box 109
Wabasha, MN 55981
Phone: (651)565-3368
Fax: (651)565-4736

Publications: Wabasha County Herald (16486)

Valley Publications
PO Box 369
Shenandoah, IA 51601
Phone: (712)246-3097
Fax: (712)246-3099

Publications: Valley News Today (11199)

Valley Publications
103 W Main
Durand, WI 54736
Phone: (715)672-4252

Publications: The Courier-Wedge (33661)

Valley Publishing
PO Box 607
Monte Vista, CO 81144-0607
Phone: (719)852-3531
Fax: (719)852-3387

Publications: Center Post-Dispatch (4229) • The Del Norte Prospector (4574) • The Monte Vista Journal (4575) • SLV Midweek (4576) • SLV Saturday Want Ads (4577) • South Fork Times (4628)

Valley Publishing Co.
7 Francis St.
Derby, CT 06418
Phone: (203)735-6696
Fax: (203)735-0334

Publications: Shopping News (4776)

Valley Publishing Co., Inc.
PO Box 370
Pikeville, TN 37367
Phone: (423)447-2996
Fax: (423)447-2997

Publications: The Bledsonian Banner (29567) • The Dunlap Tribune (29171) • The Sequatchie Valley Shopper (29568)

Valley Publishing Co., Inc.
107 Division St.
Grandview, WA 98930
Phone: (509)882-3712
Fax: (509)882-2833

Publications: Grandview Herald (32783)

Valley Publishing Co., Inc.
PO Box 750
Prosser, WA 99350
Phone: (509)786-1711
Fax: (509)786-1779

Publications: Prosser Record-Bulletin (32900)

The Valley Reporter, Inc.
Mad River Green Rte. 100
PO Box 119
Waitsfield, VT 05673
Phone: (802)496-3607
Fax: (802)496-4703

Publications: The Valley Reporter (31610)

Valley Sentinel
1012 Commerical Dr.
PO Box 688
Valemount, BC, Canada V0E 2Z0
Phone: (250)566-4425
Fax: (250)566-4528

Publications: The Valley Sentinel (35118)

The Valley Times
PO Box 9700
Moreno Valley, CA 92552
Phone: (909)247-1920
Fax: (909)247-1920

Publications: The Beacon (2503)

Valley Times LLC
67 E. State St.
PO Box 1790
Eagle, ID 83616
Phone: (208)938-6217
Fax: (208)939-6738

Publications: Valley Times (7854)

Valley Tribune
PO Box 478
Quitaque, TX 79255
Phone: (806)455-1101
Fax: (806)455-1101
Free: 877-655-1101

Publications: Valley Tribune (30967)

Valley Value Shopper
PO Box 69
Spring Valley, WI 54767

Publications: Valley Values Shopper (34341)

The Valley Vantage
23009 Ventura Blvd.
Woodland Hills, CA 91364-1107
Phone: (818)223-9545
Fax: (818)223-9552

Publications: The Valley Vantage (4115)

Valley Views Publishing Ltd.
4713-50 St.
PO Box 787
Valleyview, AB, Canada T0H 3N0
Phone: (780)524-3490
Fax: (780)524-4545

Publications: Valleyview Valley Views (34863)

Valley Wide Newspaper
16925 Main St.
PO Box 400937
Hesperia, CA 92340-0937
Phone: (760)244-3920
Fax: (760)244-6609

Publications: Hesperia Resorter (2048)

The Value News
PO Box 1060
Brentwood, CA 94513
Phone: (925)634-6393

Publications: The Value News (1604)

Value Retail News
29399 US Hwy. 19 N, Ste. 370
Clearwater, FL 33761-2137
Phone: (727)781-7557
Fax: (727)781-9717
Free: 800-669-1020

Publications: Value Retail News (5992)

Valve Manufacturers Association of America (VMA)
1050 17th St. NW, Ste. 280
Washington, DC 20036
Phone: (202)331-8105
Fax: (202)296-0378

Publications: Valve Magazine (5839)

Van Allen Publishing Co.
PO Box 354
Hicksville, NY 11802-0354

Publications: New York Auto Repair News (20742)

Van Alstyne Leader
PO Box 578
Van Alstyne, TX 75495
Phone: (903)482-5253
Fax: (903)482-5656

Publications: Van Alstyne Leader (31229)

Van Buren County Democrat
114 South Ct. St.
PO Box 119
Clinton, AR 72031-0119
Phone: (501)745-5175
Fax: (501)745-8865

Publications: Van Buren County Democrat (1082)

Van Buren County Leader-Record
102 Elm St.
PO Box 155
Farmington, IA 52626
Phone: (319)878-4111
Fax: (319)878-4111

Publications: Van Buren County Leader-Record (10887)

The Van Horn Advocate
701B W Broadway
PO Box 8
Van Horn, TX 79855
Phone: (915)283-2003
Fax: (915)283-7334

Publications: The Van Horn Advocate (31230)

Van Nostrand Reinhold Company Inc.
605 3rd Ave.
New York, NY 10158-0180
Phone: (212)254-3232
Fax: (212)254-9499
Free: 800-842-3636

Publications: Dangerous Properties of Industrial Materials Report (21536)

Van Raper Productions Co.
101 Meadow Ridge Ct.
Dingmans Ferry, PA 18328
Phone: (570)828-9800
Fax: (570)828-7959

Publications: Country Road Chronicles (26827)

Robert D. Van Vleet, Sr.
1136 Illinois
PO Box 193
Sidney, NE 69162
Phone: (308)254-2818
Fax: (308)254-3925
Free: 888-254-2818

Publications: Sidney Sun Telegraph (18278)

Van Wert Times-Bulletin
PO Box 271
700 Fox Rd.
Van Wert, OH 45891-0271
Phone: (419)238-2285
Fax: (419)238-0447
Free: 800-727-2036

Publications: Van Wert Times-Bulletin (25609)

Van Zandt Newpapers, L.L.C.
PO Box 60
Wills Point, TX 75169
Phone: (903)873-2525
Fax: (903)873-4321

Publications: Van Zandt News (31300)

Van Zandt Newspapers
103 E. Tyler
Canton, TX 75103
Phone: (903)567-4000
Fax: (903)567-6076

Publications: Canton Herald (29998)

Vance Publishing
PO Box 83, 128 1st St., Ste. 223
Tifton, GA 31793
Fax: (912)386-9772

Publications: The Peanut Grower (7596)

Vance Publishing Corp.
16057 Tampa Palms Blvd. W, No. 416
Tampa, FL 33647
Phone: (813)975-8377
Fax: (813)975-1772
Free: 800-362-1571

Publications: Citrus and Vegetable Magazine (6760)

Vance Publishing Corp.
400 Knightsbridge Pkwy.
Lincolnshire, IL 60069
Phone: (847)634-2600
Fax: (847)634-4343
Free: 800-621-2845

Publications: Accessory Merchandising (9084) • CWB: Custom Woodworking Business (9085) • Modern Salon (9086) • Residential Lighting (9087) • Salon Today Magazine (9088) • Wood & Wood Products (9089)

Vance Publishing Corp.
10901 W. 84th Terrace
Lenexa, KS 66214
Phone: (913)438-0695
Fax: (913)438-0697
Free: 800-255-5113

Publications: Dealer and Applicator Magazine (11589) • Drovers (11590) • Floral Retailing Magazine (11591) • Fresh Trends (11592) • The Grower (11593) • The Packer (11594) • Pork (11595) •

Produce Merchandising (11596) • Swine Practitioner (11597)

Vance Publishing Corp.
5050 Poplar Ave.
Memphis, TN 38157
Phone: (901)767-4020
Fax: (901)767-4026
Free: 800-888-9784

Publications: Cotton Farming (29364) • Rice Farming (2562)

Vancouver Ballet Society
Scotiabank Dance Cenre
677 Davie St., Level 6
Vancouver, BC, Canada V6G 2B6
Phone: (604)681-1525
Fax: (604)681-7732

Publications: Dance International (35138)

Vancouver Bar Association
300-1275 W. 6th Ave.
Vancouver, BC, Canada V6H 1A6
Phone: (604)732-6566
Fax: (604)732-6590

Publications: The Advocate (35121)

Vancouver Business Journal
2525 E. 4TH Plain Blvd.
Vancouver, WA 98661
Phone: (360)695-2442
Fax: (360)695-3056

Publications: Vancouver Business Journal (33180)

Vancouver Courier
1574 W. 6th Ave.
Vancouver, BC, Canada V6J 1R2
Phone: (604)738-1411
Fax: (604)731-1474

Publications: The Vancouver Courier (35173)

Vancouver Free Press
1770 Burrard St., 2nd Fl.
Vancouver, BC, Canada V6J 3G7
Phone: (604)730-7000
Fax: (604)730-7010

Publications: The Calgary Straight (35129) • Georgia Straight (35144)

Vandalia Leader-Press
108 W State
Box 239
Vandalia, MO 63382
Phone: (573)594-3322
Fax: (573)594-6741

Publications: Vandalia Leader-Press (17662)

Vanderbilt Student Communications
Vanderbilt University
Box 1669 - Sta. B
Nashville, TN 37235
Phone: (615)322-2424
Fax: (615)322-3762

Publications: Vanderbilt Hustler (29498)

Vanderbilt University
Box 6325, Sta. B
Nashville, TN 37235
Phone: (615)343-0372

Publications: Bulletin Baudelairien (29446)

Vanderbilt University
PO Box 7703, VU Sta. B. 357703
Vanderbilt Pl.
Nashville, TN 37235
Phone: (615)322-2601
Fax: (615)343-8547

Publications: Vanderbilt Magazine (29500)

Vanderbilt University School of Law
131 21st Ave., S., Rm. 047
Nashville, TN 37203
Phone: (615)322-2284
Fax: (615)322-2354

Publications: Vanderbilt Journal of Transnational Law (29499)

Vanderbilt University TV News Archive
110 21st Ave. S, Ste. 704
Nashville, TN 37203-2416
Phone: (615)322-2927
Fax: (615)343-8250

Publications: Television News Index and Abstracts (29487)

Vandergrift News
143 Washington Ave.
Vandergrift, PA 15690
Fax: (412)568-3818

Publications: The Vandergrift News (28095)

VanDerHeide Publishing Company Ltd.
PO Box 3006, Sta. LCD1
Langley, BC, Canada V3A 4R3
Phone: (604)532-1733
Fax: (604)532-1734

Publications: The Windmill Herald (35006)

Vanguard Publications, Inc.
4440 Hagadorn Rd.
Okemos, MI 48864
Phone: (517)376-1700
Fax: (517)336-1705
Free: 800-757-0667

Publications: The Corporate Board (15415)

Vanguarde Media Inc.
315 Park Ave. S., 11th Fl.
New York, NY 10010
Phone: (646)654-4200

Publications: Honey (21816) • Impact! (21853) • Savoy (22707)

Vapaa Sana Press Ltd.
50 Weybright Ct., A22
Toronto, ON, Canada M1S 5A8
Phone: (416)321-0808
Fax: (416)321-0811

Publications: Vapaa Sana (36784)

Varsity Publications
University of Toronto
21 Sussex Ave. 2nd Fl.
Toronto, ON, Canada M5S 1J6
Phone: (416)946-7600
Fax: (416)946-7606

Publications: The Varsity (36785)

Vassar College
124 Raymond Ave.
PO Box 149
Poughkeepsie, NY 12604

Publications: The Miscellany News (23148)

VBC—Vietnamese Broadcasting Corporation
PO Box 218, Sta. U
Toronto, ON, Canada M8Z 5P1
Phone: (905)607-8010
Fax: (905)607-8011

Publications: Lang Van (36648)

Vedanta West Communications
PO Box 731285
Elmhurst, NY 11373
Phone: (212)877-4730
Fax: (212)769-4280

Publications: American Vedantist (20571)

The Vega Enterprise
116 S. Main St
PO Box 130
Vega, TX 79092
Phone: (806)267-2230
Fax: (806)267-2889

Publications: The Vega Enterprise (31231)

The Vegetarian Resource Group
PO Box 1463
Baltimore, MD 21203
Phone: (410)366-8343
Fax: (410)366-8804

Publications: Vegetarian Journal (13259)

The Vegreville News Advertiser
Box 810
Vegreville, AB, Canada T9C 1R9
Phone: (780)632-2861
Fax: (780)632-7981
Free: 800-522-4127

Publications: The Vegreville News Advertiser (34864)

Velazquez Publishing, Inc.
1742 S. Main St.
Santa Ana, CA 92707
Phone: (714)547-0701
Fax: (714)547-2404

Publications: Farandula USA (3625) • Miniondas (3629)

The Velikovskian IVY Press Books
65-35 108th St., Ste. D-15
Forest Hills, NY 11375
Phone: (718)897-2403

Publications: The Velikovskian (20617)

Ventura County News
130 Palm Dr.
Oxnard, CA 93030
Phone: (805)483-1008
Fax: (805)483-6233

Publications: Ventura County Vida Newspaper (2731)

Ventura County Reporter
1567 Spinnaker Dr., Ste. 202
Ventura, CA 93001
Phone: (805)658-2244
Fax: (805)658-7803

Publications: Ventura County Reporter (4013)

Ventura County Star
5250 Ralston St.
Ventura, CA 93003
Fax: (805)482-8631
Free: 800-221-STAR

Publications: Conejo Star (4003) • Ventura County Star (4014) • Ventura County Star (Camarillo Edition) (4015)

Venture Publishing, Inc.
PO Box 7364
Menlo Park, CA 94026

Publications: SCO World Magazine (2526)

Vercauteren Publishing
19 E. Main St.
Chilton, WI 53014
Phone: (920)849-4551
Fax: (920)849-4651

Publications: The Badger Sportsman (33623) • Calumet County Shopper (33624) • Times-Journal (33625)

Verdigre Eagle
202 Main
PO Box 309
Verdigre, NE 68783
Phone: (402)668-2242
Fax: (402)668-2242

Publications: Verdigre Eagle (18301)

Verelk
1327 Pleasant Ave.
Los Angeles, CA 90033
Fax: (213)261-0522

Publications: Verelk (2429)

Vermilion County Museum Society
116 N Gilbert St.
Danville, IL 61832
Phone: (217)442-2922
Fax: (217)442-2001

Publications: Heritage of Vermilion County (8702)

Vermilion Photo Journal
630 N Main St.
PO Box 23
Vermilion, OH 44089
Phone: (440)967-5268
Fax: (440)967-2535

Publications: Vermilion Photo Journal (25612)

Vermont Bar Association
35-37 Court St.
PO Box 100
Montpelier, VT 05601-0100
Phone: (802)223-2020
Fax: (802)223-1573

Publications: The Vermont Bar Journal (31564)

Vermont Historical Society Inc.
Vermont History Center
60 Washington St.
Barre, VT 05641-4209
Phone: (802)479-8500
Fax: (802)479-8510

Publications: Vermont History (31489)

Vermont Law School
Chelsea St.
PO Box 96
South Royalton, VT 05068

Publications: The FORUM (31602)

Vermont Life Magazine
6 Baldwin St.
Montpelier, VT 05602-2109
Phone: (802)828-3241
Fax: (802)828-3366
Free: 800-455-3399

Publications: Vermont Life (31565)

Vermont Magazine
PO Box 800
Middlebury, VT 05753-0800
Phone: (802)388-8480
Fax: (802)388-8485

Publications: Vermont Magazine (31559)

Vermont Media Publishing Co.
PO Box 310
West Dover, VT 05356
Phone: (802)464-3388
Fax: (802)464-7255
Free: 800-339-3388

Publications: Deerfield Valley News (31615)

Vermont National Education Association
10 Wheelock St.
Montpelier, VT 05602
Phone: (802)223-6375
Fax: (802)223-1253
Free: 800-649-6375

Publications: Vermont-NEA Today (31566)

Vermont News Guide
PO Box 1265, Rte. 7A Main St.
Manchester Center, VT 05255
Phone: (802)362-3535
Fax: (802)362-5368

Publications: Vermont News Guide (31554)

Vermont Publishing, Inc.
281 N. Main St.
PO Box 1250
St. Albans, VT 05478
Phone: (802)524-9771
Fax: (802)527-1948

Publications: The St. Albans Messenger (31590)

The Vermont Standard
PO Box 88
Woodstock, VT 05091
Phone: (802)457-1313
Fax: (802)457-3639

Publications: The Vermont Standard (31624)

Vernal Express Publishing Co.
54 N Vernal Ave.
PO Box 1000
Vernal, UT 84078
Phone: (435)789-3511
Fax: (435)789-8690

Publications: Vernal Express (31483)

The Verndale Sun
21 1st Ave. SW
PO Box E
Verndale, MN 56481
Phone: (218)445-5779
Fax: (218)445-5779

Publications: The Verndale Sun (16484)

Vernon County Broadcaster
PO Box 472
Viroqua, WI 54665
Phone: (608)637-3137
Fax: (608)637-8557

Publications: Vernon County Broadcaster (34383)

Vernon Publications L.L.C.
12437 NE 173rd Pl.
Woodinville, WA 98072-7925
Phone: (425)488-3211
Fax: (425)488-0946

Publications: Greater Seattle InfoGuide (33213) • RV West Magazine (33215)

Vernon Publishing, Inc.
409-15 S. Maple
Eldon, MO 65026
Phone: (573)392-5658
Fax: (573)392-7755

Publications: The Eldon Advertiser (17045) • Miller County Autogram-Sentinel (17046)

Vernon Publishing, Inc.
PO Box 130
Stover, MO 65078
Phone: (573)377-4616
Fax: (573)377-4512

Publications: Morgan County Press (17640)

Vernon Publishing, Inc.
PO Box U
Tipton, MO 65081
Phone: (660)433-5721
Fax: (660)433-2222

Publications: The Tipton Times (17651)

Vernon Sun Publications Ltd.
3309 31st Ave.
Vernon, BC, Canada V1T 3H4
Fax: (250)549-4446

Publications: Sun Review (35202)

Verse Press
221 Pine St., Studio 2A3
Florence, MA 01062

Publications: Verse (14188)

Vertex Inc.
1041 Old Cassatt Rd.
Berwyn, PA 19312
Phone: (610)640-4200
Fax: (610)640-1207

Publications: Vertex National SalesTax Manuals (26698)

Verticalnet Inc.
5 Walnut Grove Dr., No. 300
Horsham, PA 19044-2201

Publications: CareerMagazine (27056)

Vesta Publications Ltd.
PO Box 1641
Cornwall, ON, Canada K6K 1E5
Phone: (613)932-2135
Fax: (613)932-7735

Publications: Writer's Lifeline (35756)

Vestkusten
237 Ricardo Rd.
Mill Valley, CA 94941
Phone: (415)381-5149
Fax: (415)381-9664

Publications: Vestkusten (2542)

VESTNIK
6100 Park Heights Ave.
Baltimore, MD 21215-3624
Phone: (410)358-0900

Publications: Vestnik (13260)

Veterans of Foreign Wars of the U.S.
1510 J St., Ste. 110
Sacramento, CA 95814-2097
Phone: (916)424-1684
Fax: (916)424-9049

Publications: The California Veteran (2989)

Veterinary Healthcare Communications
8033 Flint St.
Lenexa, KS 66214
Phone: (913)492-4300
Fax: (913)492-4157
Free: 800-255-6864

Publications: Veterinary Economics (11598)

Veterinary Learning Systems
780 Township Line Rd.
Yardley, PA 19067
Phone: (267)685-2400
Fax: (267)685-1221
Free: 800-426-9119
Publications: Compendium on Continuing Education for the Practicing Veterinarian (28199)

Vevay Newspapers, Inc.
111 W Market St.
PO Box 157
Vevay, IN 47043
Phone: (812)427-2311
Fax: (812)427-2793
Publications: The Switzerland Democrat (10519) • Vevay Reveille-Enterprise (10520)

VFW Magazine
406 W. 34th St.
Kansas City, MO 64111
Phone: (816)756-3390
Fax: (816)968-1149
Publications: VFW Magazine (17201)

VIA Magazine
150 Van Ness Ave.
San Francisco, CA 94102
Free: 800-922-8228
Publications: VIA (3459)

Via Media Publishing Co.
821 W 24th St.
Erie, PA 16502
Phone: (814)455-9517
Fax: (814)455-2726
Free: 800-455-9517
Publications: The Journal of Asian Martial Arts (26900)

Via Times Newsmagazine
PO Box 138155
Chicago, IL 60613
Phone: (312)866-0811
Fax: (312)866-9207
Publications: Via Times Newsmagazine (8598)

VIBE/SPIN Ventures, L.L.C.
215 Lexington Ave., 6th Fl.
New York, NY 10016
Phone: (212)448-7300
Fax: (212)448-7400
Publications: SPIN (22772)

Vice Postulation for the Cause of Canonization of Blessed Kateri Tekakwitha
PO Box 70
Kahnawake, QC, Canada J0L 1B0
Phone: (450)638-1546
Fax: (450)632-6031
Publications: Kateri (37018)

The Vice President for Research
Florida State University
109 Westcott Bldg.
Tallahassee, FL 32306-1330
Phone: (850)644-9694
Fax: (850)645-0108
Publications: Research in Review (6732)

Vice Publishing
75 N. 4th St., 3rd Fl.
Brooklyn, NY 11211-3105
Publications: Vice (20353)

Vickers Stock Research Corp.
226 New York Ave.
Huntington, NY 11743
Phone: (631)423-7710
Fax: (631)423-7715
Free: 800-645-5043
Publications: Institutional Holding of Oil Stocks (20773)

Vicksburg Printing & Publishing Co., Inc.
PO Box 821668
Vicksburg, MS 39182-1668
Publications: Vicksburg Evening Post (16871)

Vicksburg Publications, Inc.
PO Box 154
Vicksburg, MI 49097-0154
Phone: (616)649-2333
Fax: (616)649-2335
Publications: The Broadcast (15653)

Victimology Inc.
2333 N Vernon St.
Arlington, VA 22207
Phone: (703)536-1750
Publications: Victimology (31839)

Victor T. Craig
PO Box 234
Waldorf, MD 20604-0234
Phone: (301)843-1371
Fax: (301)843-1371
Publications: Accident Investigation Quarterly (13769) • Accident Reconstruction Journal (13770)

The Victoria Advocate
311 E. Constitution
PO Box 1518
Victoria, TX 77901
Phone: (361)575-1451
Fax: (361)574-1225
Publications: The Victoria Advocate (31236)

Victorian Studies Association of Western Canada
Department of History
University of Lethbridge
Lethbridge, AB, Canada T1K 3M4
Phone: (403)329-2543
Fax: (403)329-5108
Publications: Victorian Review (34798)

Victory Music
PO Box 2254
Tacoma, WA 98401-2254
Phone: (253)428-0823
Fax: (253)660-3263
Publications: Victory Music Review (33154)

Victory Publishing
PO Box 10
Marble Falls, TX 78654
Phone: (830)693-7152
Fax: (830)693-3085
Publications: 101 Fun Things to Do (30760) • The Picayune (30761) • River Cities Tribune (30762)

Video Librarian
8705 Honeycomb Ct. NW
Seabeck, WA 98380
Phone: (360)830-9345
Fax: (360)830-9346
Free: 800-692-2270
Publications: Video Librarian (32936)

VIDEO WATCHDOG
PO Box 5283
Cincinnati, OH 45205-0283
Phone: (513)471-8989
Free: 800-275-8395
Publications: VIDEO WATCHDOG (24826)

The Vienna Times
PO Box 457
Vienna, IL 62995
Phone: (618)658-4321
Fax: (618)658-4322
Publications: The Vienna Times (9729)

Viet Bao Kinh Te
9393 Bolsa Ave., Ste. E
Westminster, CA 92683-5975
Phone: (714)418-5099
Fax: (714)418-0705
Publications: Viet Bao Kinh Te (4075)

Viet Nam Generation Inc.
PO Box 13746
Tucson, AZ 85732
Phone: (520)733-3755
Publications: Vietnam War Generation Journal (971)

Vietnam Daily News
2350 S 10th St.
San Jose, CA 95112
Phone: (408)292-3422
Fax: (408)293-5153
Publications: Vietnam Daily News (3544)

Vietnam Hai Ngoal
PO Box 33627
San Diego, CA 92103-0580
Publications: Viet Nam Hai Ngoai (3287)

Vietnam Weekly News
3250 W Walnut St.
Garland, TX 75042
Phone: (972)272-4898
Fax: (972)272-4657
Free: 800-626-8438
Publications: Vietnam Weekly News (30385)

VietNow
PO Box 736
Pine Island, MN 55963
Publications: VietNow (16272)

The View From Here Publications
2nd Ave. North
PO Box 307
Rose Valley, SK, Canada S0E 1M0
Phone: (306)322-2051
Fax: (306)327-4911
Publications: The View From Here (37479)

Villa Narcissa
100 Vanderlip Dr.
Rancho Palos Verdes, CA 90275
Phone: (310)377-4444
Fax: (310)377-4584
Publications: Friends of French Art (2880)

Villa Rican
PO Box 757
Villa Rica, GA 30180
Fax: (404)459-4804
Publications: Villa Rican (7634)

The Village Chronicle
56 Freeway Dr.
Cranston, RI 02920
Phone: (401)467-9343
Fax: (401)467-9359
Free: 800-212-4356
Publications: The Village Chronicle (28337)

Village News, Inc.
PO Box 1108
Blytheville, AR 72316-1108
Phone: (870)763-4461
Fax: (870)763-6874
Publications: Blytheville Courier News (1057)

Village Press Publications
PO Box 1810
Traverse City, MI 49685-1810
Phone: (231)946-3712
Fax: (231)946-9588
Free: 800-447-7367
Publications: Live Steam (15598) • Machinist's Workshop (15599)

The Village Publishing Corp.
505 W. Franklin St.
Chapel Hill, NC 27516
Phone: (919)932-2000
Fax: (919)932-2027
Publications: Village Advocate (23730)

Village West Publishing
PO Box 1288
Laconia, NH 03247
Phone: (603)528-4285
Fax: (603)524-0643
Free: 800-258-3772
Publications: Hearth & Home Magazine (18537)

The Villager
8933 E. Union Ave., Ste. 230
Greenwood Village, CO 80111
Phone: (303)773-8313
Fax: (303)773-8456
Publications: The Villager (4507) • The Villager Office Park News (4508)

The Villager
487 Greenwich St., Ste. 6A
New York, NY 10013
Phone: (212)229-1890
Fax: (212)229-2365

Publications: The Villager (22901)

The Villager
1223-A Rosewood Ave.
Austin, TX 78702
Phone: (512)476-0082
Fax: (512)476-0179

Publications: The Villager (29853)

Villager Communications, Inc.
757 Snelling Ave. S
St. Paul, MN 55116-2296
Phone: (651)699-1462
Fax: (651)699-6501

Publications: Villager (16413)

Villager Journal
PO Box 480
Cherokee Village, AR 72525
Phone: (870)257-2417
Fax: (870)257-5487
Free: 800-897-2417

Publications: Villager Journal (1077)

The Villager Publication Gr.
314 Federal Blvd.
Denver, CO 80219
Phone: (303)936-7778
Fax: (303)936-0994

Publications: Denver Herald-Dispatch (4322)

The Villages Daily Sun
1100 Main St.
The Villages, FL 32159
Phone: (352)753-1119
Fax: (352)753-2380

Publications: The Villages Daily Sun (6840)

Villanova University
800 Lancaster Ave.
Villanova, PA 19085
Phone: (610)519-4499
Fax: (610)519-4496

Publications: Journal of Peace & Justice Studies (28097)

Villanova University
201 Dougherty Hall
Villanova, PA 19085
Phone: (610)519-7207
Fax: (610)519-5666

Publications: The Villanovan (28099)

Villanova University
229 N. Spring Mill Rd.
Villanova, PA 19085
Phone: (610)519-4500
Fax: (610)519-6906

Publications: Villanova Law Review (28098)

Viltis
1110 N Old World 3rd St., Ste. 420
Suite 420
Milwaukee, WI 53203
Phone: (414)225-6220
Fax: (414)225-6235

Publications: Viltis (34106)

Vincennes Sun-Commercial
PO Box 396
Vincennes, IN 47591
Phone: (812)886-9955
Fax: (812)885-2002
Free: 800-876-9955

Publications: Vincennes Sun-Commercial (10522)

Vincent Owners Club
23 Bramble Way
Common Rd.
Wincanton BA9 9HA, United Kingdom
Phone: 44 1963824416
Fax: 44 1963824417

Publications: MPH (35004)

The Vindicator Printing Co.
Vindicator Sq. No. 107
PO Box 780
Youngstown, OH 44501
Phone: (330)747-1471
Fax: (330)747-6712
Free: 800-686-5003

Publications: The Vindicator (25699)

Vineyard Gazette, Inc.
34 S. Summer St.
PO Box 66
Edgartown, MA 02539
Phone: (508)627-4311
Fax: (508)627-7444
Free: 877-850-0409

Publications: Vineyard Gazette (14175)

Vinita Printing Co., Inc.
138 S Wilson
PO Box 328
Vinita, OK 74301-0328
Phone: (918)256-6422
Fax: (918)256-7100

Publications: Nowata Star (25949) • The Vinita Daily Journal (26176)

Vintage Guitar, Inc.
PO Box 7301
Bismarck, ND 58507
Phone: (701)255-1197
Fax: (701)255-0250
Free: 800-844-1197

Publications: Vintage Guitar (24361)

Vintage Publications, Inc.
PO Box 61
Millers Falls, MA 01349
Phone: (413)659-3785
Fax: (413)659-3113

Publications: Victorian Homes (20354)

Vinton Livewire
110 E 5th St.
PO Box 468
Vinton, IA 52349
Phone: (319)472-3303
Fax: (319)472-5478

Publications: Vinton Livewire (11283)

Virginia Cattleman's Association
PO Box 9
Daleville, VA 24083-0009
Phone: (540)992-1009
Fax: (540)992-4632

Publications: Virginia Cattleman (31990)

Virginia Commonwealth University Alumni Activities
924 W. Franklin St.
PO Box 843044
Richmond, VA 23284-3044
Phone: (804)828-2586
Fax: (804)828-8197

Publications: Shafer Court Connections (32453)

Virginia Dept. of Game and Inland Fisheries
4010 W Broad St.
PO Box 11104
Richmond, VA 23230-1104
Phone: (804)367-1000
Fax: (804)367-0488

Publications: Virginia Wildlife (32468)

Virginia Education Association
116 S. 3rd St.
Richmond, VA 23219-3704
Phone: (804)648-5801
Fax: (804)775-8379
Free: 800-552-9554

Publications: Virginia Journal of Education (32463)

The Virginia Engineer
PO Box 2354
Glen Allen, VA 23058-2354
Phone: (804)779-3527
Fax: (804)779-3032

Publications: The Virginia Engineer (32113)

Virginia Farm Bureau Federation
12580 W Creek Pky.
PO Box 27552
Richmond, VA 23261-7552

Publications: Virginia Farm Bureau News (32461)

Virginia Forestry Association
8810 B Patterson Ave.
Richmond, VA 23229
Phone: (804)741-0836
Fax: (804)741-0838

Publications: Virginia Forests (32462)

Virginia Gazette Companies LLC
216 Ironbound Rd.
Williamsburg, VA 23188
Phone: (757)220-1736
Fax: (757)220-1665

Publications: Somerset/Crisfield Express (13668) • Sussex-Surry Dispatch (32598) • The Virginia Gazette (32620) • Westmoreland News (32275) • Worcester County Messenger (13645)

Virginia Genealogical Society
5001 W Broad St., Ste. 115
Richmond, VA 23230
Phone: (804)285-8954
Fax: (804)285-0394

Publications: Magazine of Virginia Genealogy (32444)

The Virginia Genealogist
Box 5860
Falmouth, VA 22405-5860
Phone: (703)371-9115
Fax: (703)374-9264

Publications: The Virginia Genealogist (32066)

Virginia Historical Society
PO Box 7311
Richmond, VA 23221-0311
Phone: (804)358-4901

Publications: Virginia Magazine of History and Biography (32465)

Virginia Journal of International Law Association
University of Virginia School of Law
580 Massie Rd.
Charlottesville, VA 22901
Phone: (804)924-3415
Fax: (804)924-3237

Publications: Virginia Journal of International Law (31945)

Virginia Law Review Association
University of Virginia School of Law
580 Massie Rd.
Charlottesville, VA 22903-1789
Phone: (434)924-3079
Fax: (434)982-2818

Publications: Virginia Law Review (31946)

Virginia, Maryland, and Delaware Association of Electric Cooperatives
4201 Dominion Blvd., Ste. 101
Glen Allen, VA 23060
Phone: (804)346-3344
Fax: (804)346-3448
Free: (866)266-7584

Publications: Rural Living (32112)

Virginia Municipal League
PO Box 12164
Richmond, VA 23241
Phone: (804)649-8471
Fax: (804)343-3758

Publications: Virginia Town & City (32467)

Virginia Museum of Natural History
1001 Douglas Ave.
Martinsville, VA 24112
Phone: (276)666-8656
Fax: (276)632-6487

Publications: Virginia Explorer (32234)

Virginia Parent News
11734 Bowman Green
Reston, VA 20190-3501
Phone: (703)834-1075
Fax: (703)834-1077

Publications: Virginia Parent News (32423)

Virginia Polytechnic Institute and State University
Blacksburg, VA 24061-0112
Phone: (540)231-8650
Fax: (540)231-5692

Publications: Stephen Crane Studies (31878)

Virginia Polytechnic Institute and State University
333 Norris Hall
Blacksburg, VA 24061
Phone: (540)231-6641
Fax: (540)231-3031

Publications: Engineering Now (31869)

Virginia Polytechnic Institute and State University
202 Media Bldg.
Blacksburg, VA 24061
Phone: (540)231-6975
Fax: (540)231-4943

Publications: 4-H for Life (31871) • Virginia Extension (31879)

Virginia Publishing Co.
625 N Euclid, Ste. 330
PO Box 4538
St. Louis, MO 63108
Phone: (314)367-6612
Fax: (314)367-0727

Publications: West End-Clayton Word (17531)

Virginia Quarterly Review
University of Virginia
1 W. Range
PO Box 400223
Charlottesville, VA 22904-4223
Phone: (434)924-3124
Fax: (434)924-1397

Publications: Virginia Quarterly Review (31947)

Virginia Union University
Attn: A.H. Benson
1500 N. Lombardy St.
Richmond, VA 23220
Phone: (804)257-5678
Fax: (804)257-5625

Publications: The V.U.U. Informer (32469)

Virginian-Leader
Drawer C
Pearisburg, VA 24134-0702
Phone: (540)921-3434
Fax: (540)921-2563

Publications: Virginian-Leader (32325)

Virginian Pilot
157 N Main St., Ste. B
Suffolk, VA 23434-4507
Phone: (757)222-5550
Fax: (757)222-5515

Publications: Sun (32567)

Virgo Publishing, Inc.
3300 N. Central Ave., Ste. 2500
Phoenix, AZ 85012
Phone: (480)990-1101
Fax: (480)990-0819

Publications: Assisted Living Success (792) • Embroidery Business News (802) • Exhibitor Times (803) • Swim Fashion Quarterly (812)

Visalia Daily
330 N West St.
Visalia, CA 93291-6010
Phone: (559)735-3200
Fax: (559)733-0826

Publications: Visalia Times-Delta (4040) • Weekly Visalia Times-Daily (4041)

Visalia Newspapers Inc.
388 E. Cross Ave.
PO Box 30
Tulare, CA 93275-0030
Phone: (209)688-0521
Fax: (209)688-7503

Publications: Advance-Register & Times (3952)

Visible Language
Rhode Island School of Design
Graphic Design Dept.
2 College St.
Providence, RI 02903
Phone: (401)454-6171
Fax: (401)454-6117

Publications: Visible Language (8599)

Vision, Inc.
Calle Post 178 Sur
Mayaguez, PR 00681
Phone: (787)834-6829
Fax: (787)833-0722

Publications: Vision (28258)

Visionaire Publishing
11 Mercer St.
New York, NY 10013
Phone: (212)274-8959
Fax: (212)343-2595

Publications: Visionaire (22902)

Visions International
1007 Ficklen Rd.
Fredericksburg, VA 22405
Phone: (540)310-0730
Fax: (540)899-6021

Publications: Visions International (32088)

Visitor Publications
818 Broughton St.
Victoria, BC, Canada V8W 1E4
Phone: (250)388-3676
Fax: (250)386-2624

Publications: Island Visitor (35217)

The Vista Advertising
Dept.100 N. University Dr.
Edmond, OK 73034
Phone: (405)341-2980
Fax: (405)330-3839

Publications: The Vista (25814)

Visual Studies Workshop Press
31 Prince St.
Rochester, NY 14607
Phone: (585)442-8676

Publications: AFTERIMAGE (23208)

Vitality Magazine
356 Dupont St.
Toronto, ON, Canada M5R 1V9
Phone: (416)964-0528

Publications: Vitality Magazine (36789)

Vivre
PO Box 1120
Cochrane, ON, Canada P0L 1C0
Phone: (705)272-2954

Publications: Vivre (35745)

VNU Business Media
50 S. 9th St.
Minneapolis, MN 55402
Phone: (612)333-0471
Fax: (612)333-6526
Free: 800-328-4329

Publications: Potentials (16122) • Presentations Magazine (16123)

VNU Business Media
770 Broadway
New York, NY 10003-9595
Phone: (646)654-5000

Publications: Facilities Design & Management (21673) • Kitchen and Bath Business (22224) • Multi-Housing News (22397) • National Jeweler (22397) • Sporting Goods Business (22774) • STACKS (22781)

VNU Business Media USA
770 Broadway
New York, NY 10003
Phone: (646)654-5000

Publications: Action Sports Retailer (21147) • Adweek (21157) • Adweek Western Edition (21158) • American Artist (21178) • American Time (21208) • Architectural Lighting (21242) • Auto Interiors (21274) • Back Stage West (21284) • Bicycle Retailer and Industry News (21308) • Bookseller (21335) • Business Travel News (21361) • Contract (21498) •

Country Airplay Monitor (21505) • Couture International Jeweler (21508) • Diamond Intelligence Briefs (21550) • Embroidery Monogram Business (21598) • Eurotec (21658) • Fly Fishing Retailer (21709) • Food Logistics (21712) • ID: The Information Source for Managers and DSRs (21842) • INTERIORS (21891) • Music and Media (22386) • Online Learning (22492) • PIX (22555) • R&B Airplay Monitor (22625) • Retail Merchandiser (22653) • Retail Tech (22654) • Rock Airplay Monitor (22674) • Ross Reports Television and Film (22677) • Satellite Broadband (22706) • Top 40 Airplay Monitor (22843) • Variety and General Merchandise TradeNews (22896) • Watercolor (22911)

VNU Business Publications
770 Broadway
New York, NY 10003
Phone: (646)654-5000
Fax: (646)654-4977

Publications: Amusement Business (29441) • FoodService Director (21714) • Giftware Business (21762) • Kirkus Reviews (22223) • Restaurant Business (22651)

VNU Business Publications, Inc
200 W. Jackson Blvd.
Chicago, IL 60606-6910
Phone: (312)464-8500
Fax: (312)464-8540

Publications: Adweek/Midwest (8246)

VNU Business Publications USA
1115 Northmeadow Pkwy.
Roswell, GA 30076
Phone: (770)569-1540
Fax: (770)569-5105
Free: 800-933-8202

Publications: Point Of Purchase (7516)

VNU eMedia, Inc.
770 Broadway, 6th Fl.
New York, NY 10003
Phone: (646)654-4500
Fax: (646)654-7370

Publications: Contract (21497)

Vogel Communications Inc
701 5th Ave. 36th Fl.
Seattle, WA 98104
Phone: (206)262-8183
Fax: (206)262-8187

Publications: DirectGuide (32960)

Vogel Satellite T.V. Publishing Inc.
1109 Toronto Dominion Tower, Edmonton Centre
10088 - 102 Ave.
Edmonton, AB, Canada T5J 2Z1
Phone: (780)424-6222
Fax: (780)425-8392

Publications: Satellite Entertainment Guide (34727) • VU Magazine (34733)

The Voice
898 Arkadelphia Rd.
Birmingham, AL 35204
Phone: (205)226-7972
Fax: (205)226-7941
Free: 888-448-6423

Publications: The Voice (99)

The Voice
326 1st St.
PO Box 130
Kersey, CO 80644
Phone: (970)356-7176
Fax: (970)356-7176

Publications: The Voice (4524)

The Voice of Florida
PO Box 030397
Fort Lauderdale, FL 33303-0397
Phone: (954)463-5556
Fax: (954)463-2674

Publications: The Voice Newspaper (6086)

Voice of South Marion
PO Box 700
Belleview, FL 34421
Phone: (352)245-3161
Fax: (352)245-3161

Publications: Voice of South Marion (5923)

2700

Numbers cited after listings are entry numbers rather than page numbers.

Voices of Central Pennsylvania
103 E Beaver Ave., Ste. 11
State College, PA 16801
Phone: (814)234-1699

Publications: Voices of Central Pennsylvania (28022)

Volunteer State Community College
1480 Nashville Pke.
Gallatin, TN 37066
Phone: (615)452-8600
Fax: (615)230-3228

Publications: Firefly Magazine (29202)

Volusia Pennysaver, Inc.
2A McCormick Dr.
Bunnell, FL 32110
Phone: (386)437-5971

Publications: Flagler Pennysaver (5968)

Volusia Pennysaver, Inc.
245 S Woodland Blvd.
DeLand, FL 32720
Phone: (386)736-2880
Fax: (386)736-3587
Free: 800-218-2186

Publications: West Volusia Pennysaver (6047)

Volusia Pennysaver, Inc.
237 Canal St.
Box 767
New Smyrna Beach, FL 32170
Phone: (904)423-2300
Fax: (904)426-2807

Publications: New Smyrna Pennysaver (6457)

Volusia Pennysaver, Inc.
454 S. Young St.
PO Box 67
Ormond Beach, FL 32174
Phone: (904)677-4262
Fax: (904)672-7453

Publications: Daytona Pennysaver (6532)

Volusia Pennysaver, Inc.
PO Box 220
Palatka, FL 32178
Phone: (386)328-4649
Fax: (386)325-4617

Publications: Putnam Pennysaver (6538)

Volusia Pennysaver, Inc.
1740 A1A South
PO Box 500
St. Augustine, FL 32085
Phone: (904)471-8488
Fax: (904)471-4519

Publications: St. John's Pennysaver (6618)

Von Meyer Publishing, Inc.
PO Box 324
St. Joseph, MN 56374
Phone: (320)363-7741
Fax: (320)363-4195
Free: 800-386-2261

Publications: Music and Dance News (16357)

Vondrac Publishing
6225 S. Kedzie Ave.
Chicago, IL 60629-3397
Phone: (312)476-4800
Fax: (312)475-7811
Free: (773)476-4800

Publications: Clear-Ridge Reporter (8334) • Southwest News-Herald (8569)

VooDoo Magazine
MIT
77 Massachusetts Ave., Rm. 50-309
Cambridge, MA 02139
Phone: (617)253-4575

Publications: VooDoo Magazine (14110)

Voodoo Souls Quarterly
PO Box 4117
Lawrence, KS 66046

Publications: Voodoo Souls Quarterly (11569)

Voxair
17 Wing
Winnipeg, MB, Canada R3J 3I5
Phone: (204)833-2500
Fax: (204)833-2809

Publications: Voxair (35357)

Voyageur Magazine
PO Box 8085
Green Bay, WI 54308-8085
Phone: (920)465-2446
Fax: (920)465-2890

Publications: Voyageur (33742)

Voz de Portugal
370 A St.
Hayward, CA 94541
Phone: (510)537-9503

Publications: Voz de Portugal (2044)

V.P. Culpeper Communications Corp.
605 S Main St.
Culpeper, VA 22701-3209
Phone: (540)825-3232
Fax: (540)825-5670

Publications: Culpeper News (31986)

VS Enterprises
PO Box 871
Clark, NJ 07066-0871
Phone: (908)486-3221
Fax: (732)396-4215

Publications: Wire Rope News & Sling Technology (18749)

The Vulcan Advocate
Box 389
Vulcan, AB, Canada T0L 2B0
Phone: (403)485-2036
Fax: (403)485-6938

Publications: The Vulcan Advocate (34867)

VV Publishing Co.
36 Cooper Sq.
New York, NY 10003-7149
Phone: (212)475-3300
Fax: (212)475-8944
Free: 800-825-0061

Publications: The Village Voice (22900)

W. A. Cleaton & Sons
PO Box 1025
Tappahannock, VA 22560
Phone: (804)443-2200
Fax: (804)443-9684
Free: 800-296-2204

Publications: Rappahannock Times (32568)

Wabash Plain-Dealer
123 W Canal St.
PO Box 379
Wabash, IN 46992
Phone: (219)563-2131
Fax: (219)563-0816

Publications: The $hopper (10530)

Wabasso Standard
PO Box 70
Wabasso, MN 56293
Phone: (507)342-5143
Fax: (507)342-5144

Publications: Wabasso Standard (16487)

Waccamaw Publishing Co.
2510 Main St.
Conway, SC 29528
Phone: (843)248-6671
Fax: (843)248-6024

Publications: The Horry Independent (28589) • The Loris Scene (28591)

Waco Citizen Newspaper
1020 N 25th St.
Waco, TX 76707-2840
Phone: (254)754-3511
Fax: (254)754-3541

Publications: Waco Citizen Newspaper (31256)

Waco Tribune-Herald
900 Franklin Ave.
Waco, TX 76701-1906
Phone: (254)757-5757
Fax: (254)757-0302
Free: 800-678-8742

Publications: Waco Tribune-Herald (31257)

Waconia Patriot
8 Elmwood S
PO Box 5
Waconia, MN 55387
Phone: (952)442-4414
Fax: (952)442-4428

Publications: Waconia Patriot (16488)

The Wadena News
102 1st St. NE
PO Box 100
Wadena, SK, Canada S0A 4J0
Phone: (306)338-2231

Publications: Kelvington Radio (37582) • The Wadena News (37583)

Wagner Announcer
209 S Main
PO Box 187
Wagner, SD 57380
Phone: (605)384-5616
Fax: (605)384-5955

Publications: Wagner Announcer (29013)

Wagner College
631 Howard Ave.
Staten Island, NY 10301
Phone: (718)390-3100
Fax: (718)390-3467

Publications: The Wagnerian (23364)

Wagoner Tribune
221 E Cherokee
Wagoner, OK 74467
Phone: (918)485-5505
Fax: (918)485-8442

Publications: Wagoner Tribune (26178)

The Wahkiakum County Eagle
77 Main St.
PO Box 368
Cathlamet, WA 98612-0368
Phone: (360)795-3391
Fax: (360)795-3983

Publications: The Wahkiakum County Eagle (32703)

Wake Forest University
Reynolda Sta., Box 7569
Winston-Salem, NC 27109
Phone: (336)758-5279
Fax: (336)758-4561

Publications: Old Gold and Black (24321)

Wake Weekly
229 E. Owen Ave.
PO Box 1919
Wake Forest, NC 27588
Phone: (919)556-3182
Fax: (919)556-2233

Publications: Wake Weekly (24262)

Wakefield Item Co.
26 Albion St.
Wakefield, MA 01880
Phone: (781)245-0080
Fax: (781)246-0061

Publications: East Boston Times (14165) • Item (14593)

Wakefield Publishing Co.
3236 Estado St.
Pasadena, CA 91107-2916
Phone: (626)793-2911
Fax: (626)793-5540
Free: 800-793-2911

Publications: Western Cleaner and Launderer (2828)

The Wakefield Republican
PO Box 110
Wakefield, NE 68784-0110
Phone: (402)287-2323

Publications: The Wakefield Republican (18303)

Wakulla Publishing Co.
PO Box 307
Crawfordville, FL 32326
Phone: (850)926-7102
Fax: (904)926-3815

Publications: The Wakulla News (6021)

Waldron News
PO Box 745
Waldron, AR 72958
Phone: (479)637-4161
Fax: (479)637-4162
Free: 800-647-4161

Publications: Waldron News (1361) • The Waldron News - Bulletin (1362)

Walhalla Mountaineer
PO Box 497
Walhalla, ND 58282
Phone: (701)549-2580

Publications: Walhalla Mountaineer (24552)

Walker
PO Box 1046, Hwy. 56
Allen, KS 66833
Phone: (316)528-3556

Publications: American Beef Cattleman (11336)

Wall Street Publications Institute Inc.
16 School St.
Yonkers, NY 10701
Phone: (914)423-4566
Fax: (914)476-1052

Publications: The Stock Market Magazine (23602)

Walla Walla Community College
500 Tausick Way
Walla Walla, WA 99362
Phone: (509)522-2500
Fax: (509)527-4480

Publications: Fourth Estate (33187)

Walla Walla Union-Bulletin
112 S. 1st Ave.
Walla Walla, WA 99362
Phone: (509)525-3300
Fax: (509)525-1232

Publications: Walla Walla Union-Bulletin (33188)

Wallace Enterprise
PO Box 699
Wallace, NC 28466-0699
Phone: (910)285-2178
Fax: (910)285-3179

Publications: Wallace Enterprise (24265)

Wallace Stevens Society, Inc.
PO Box 5750
Clarkson University
Potsdam, NY 13699-5750
Phone: (315)268-3987
Fax: (315)268-3983

Publications: Wallace Stevens Journal (23141)

The Wallis-News Review
PO Box 668
Wallis, TX 77485
Phone: (979)478-6412
Fax: (979)478-2198

Publications: Wallis News-Review (31268)

Wallkill Valley Times
23 E Main St.
PO Box 446
Walden, NY 12586
Phone: (845)778-2181
Fax: (845)778-1196

Publications: Wallkill Valley Times (23496)

Wallowa County Chieftain, Inc.
106 NW. First St.
PO Box 338
Enterprise, OR 97828
Phone: (541)426-4567
Fax: (541)426-3921

Publications: Wallowa County Chieftain (26310)

Walls Newspapers
224 N 3rd Ave.
PO Box 130
Chatsworth, GA 30705
Phone: (706)695-4646
Fax: (706)695-7181

Publications: Chatsworth Times (7168)

The Walnut Leader
110 Jackson St.
PO Box 280
Walnut, IL 61376
Phone: (815)379-9290
Fax: (815)379-2659

Publications: The Walnut Leader (9732)

Walsh County Press
PO Box 49
Park River, ND 58270
Phone: (701)284-6333
Fax: (701)284-6091

Publications: Walsh County Press (24529)

Walters Herald
112 E Colorado St.
PO Box 247
Walters, OK 73572
Phone: (580)875-3326
Fax: (580)875-3150

Publications: Walters Herald (26180)

Walton Tribune/Advertiser
PO Box 808
Monroe, GA 30655-0808
Phone: (770)267-8371
Fax: (770)267-7780

Publications: Walton Tribune/Advertiser (7442)

Walworth County Publishers
1436 Mound Rd.
PO Box 366
Delavan, WI 53115-0366
Phone: (262)728-5505
Fax: (262)728-5706
Free: 800-515-6397

Publications: The Delavan Enterprise (33653) • The Week (33655)

Walworth Newspapers, Inc.
PO Box 129
Walworth, WI 53184
Fax: (414)275-5259

Publications: Times (34386)

WAM Publishing Co.
PO Box 2247
Hendersonville, TN 37077
Phone: (615)824-6920
Fax: (615)824-7092

Publications: Weighing & Measurement (29221)

Wamego Times
PO Box 247
Wamego, KS 66547
Phone: (785)456-7838
Fax: (785)456-9668

Publications: Wamego Times (11862)

Wanderer Comm., Inc.
55 Couty Rd., Rte. 6
PO Box 102
Mattapoisett, MA 02739
Phone: (508)758-9055

Publications: The Wanderer (14314)

Wanderer Press
201 Ohio St.
St. Paul, MN 55107
Phone: (612)224-5733
Fax: (612)224-9666

Publications: The Wanderer (16416)

WANT AD Publications, Inc.
128 Boston Post Rd.
Sudbury, MA 01776-3330
Phone: (978)443-4100
Fax: (978)443-5033

Publications: The WANT ADvertiser (14580) • Wheels, Etc. (14581)

Wapakoneta Daily News
8 Willipie St.
PO Box 389
Wapakoneta, OH 45895
Phone: (419)738-2120
Fax: (419)738-5352

Publications: Wapakoneta Daily News (25615)

Wappingers Falls Shopper, Inc.
84 E. Main St.
Wappingers Falls, NY 12590
Phone: (845)297-3723
Fax: (845)297-6810

Publications: Beacon Free Press (23501) • Southern Dutchess News (23503)

War Resisters League
339 Lafayette St.
New York, NY 10012
Phone: (212)228-0450
Fax: (212)228-6193

Publications: The Nonviolent Activist (22467)

Warden Publishing Co.
106 E Washington
PO Box 540
Owensville, MO 65066-0540
Phone: (314)437-2323
Fax: (314)437-3033

Publications: East Central Ad Mart (17328) • Gasconade County Republican (17329)

Ward's Communications
3000 Town Center, Ste. 2750
Southfield, MI 48075-1212
Phone: (248)357-0800
Fax: (248)357-0810
Telex: 877-825-1815

Publications: Ward's Auto World (15550) • Ward's Automotive International (15551) • Ward's Automotive International Focus on China (15552) • Ward's Automotive Reports (15553) • Ward's Automotive Yearbook (15554) • Ward's Engine and Vehicle Technology Update (15555)

The Warner Robins Buyers' Guide
PO Box 6129
Warner Robins, GA 31095-6129

Publications: The Warner Robins Buyers Guide (7638)

Warner's New Paper
PO Box 92
Warner, NH 03278
Phone: (603)456-1423
Fax: (603)456-3087

Publications: Warner's New Paper (18648)

Warren Communications News
2115 Ward Ct. NW
Washington, DC 20037
Phone: (202)872-9200
Fax: (202)296-4397
Free: 800-771-9202

Publications: Mobile Communications Report (5654) • Satellite Week (5777) • Television & Cable Factbook (5819)

Warren County Historical Society
210 Fourth Ave.
PO Box 427
Warren, PA 16365
Phone: (814)723-1795
Fax: (814)723-1795

Publications: Stepping Stones (28104)

Warren Eagle Democrat
200 W Cypress St.
Warren, AR 71671
Phone: (870)226-5831
Fax: (870)226-6601

Publications: Shoppers Guide Weekly (1364) • Warren Eagle Democrat (1365)

Warren, Gorham & Lamont R.I.A. Group
395 Hudson St., 4th Fl.
New York, NY 10014-3669
Phone: (212)367-6300
Fax: (212)367-6305
Free: 800-742-3348

Publications: Banking Law Journal (21289) • Employee Benefits Report (21601) • Journal of Business Strategy (22015) • Journal of Construction

Accounting and Taxation (22038) • Journal of International Taxation (22104) • The Real Estate Finance Journal (22631) • Real Estate Review (22634) • Securities Regulation Law Journal (22720)

The Warrenton Clipper
407 Norwood St.
PO Box 306
Warrenton, GA 30828-0306
Phone: (706)465-3395
Fax: (706)465-3396

Publications: The Warrenton Clipper (7639)

Warrick Publishing Co.
204 W Locust St.
PO Box 71
Boonville, IN 47601
Phone: (812)897-2330
Fax: (812)897-3703

Publications: Boonville Standard (9866) • Newburgh Chandler Register (10349)

Warroad Pioneer
109 E. Lake St. PO Box E
Warroad, MN 56763
Phone: (218)386-1594
Fax: (218)386-1072
Free: 800-273-1594

Publications: The Warroad Pioneer (16497)

Warsaw-Faison News
PO Box 427
Warsaw, NC 28398
Phone: (910)293-4534

Publications: Warsaw-Faison News (24271)

Warsaw Penny Saver
72 N. Main St.
Warsaw, NY 14569
Phone: (585)786-8161
Fax: (585)786-5159

Publications: Warsaw Penny Saver (23506)

Wartburg College
C/O McElroy Communication Arts Ctr.
Waverly, IA 50677
Phone: (319)352-8200
Fax: (319)352-8610
Free: 800-772-2085

Publications: Wartburg Trumpet (11308)

Warwick Publishing Inc.
162 John St.
Toronto, ON, Canada M5V 2E5
Phone: (416)596-1555
Fax: (416)596-1520

Publications: Coda Magazine (36554)

Warwick Valley Dispatch
PO Box 594
Warwick, NY 10990-0594
Phone: (914)986-2216
Fax: (914)987-1180

Publications: Warwick Valley Dispatch (23508)

Wary Canary Press
PO Box 2204
Fort Collins, CO 80522
Phone: (303)224-0083

Publications: Environ (4430)

Wasatch Wave
PO Box 128
Heber City, UT 84032
Fax: (801)654-5085

Publications: Wasatch Wave (31337)

Waseca County News
PO Box 465
Waseca, MN 56093
Phone: (507)835-3380
Fax: (507)835-3435

Publications: Waseca County News (16500)

Washburn County Register
PO Box 455
Shell Lake, WI 54871
Phone: (715)468-2314
Fax: (715)468-2314

Publications: Washburn County Register (34326)

Washington Association of Wheat Growers
109 E. 1st Ave.
Ritzville, WA 99169
Phone: (509)659-0610
Fax: (509)659-4302

Publications: Wheat Life (32933)

The Washington Blade
1408 U St. NW, 2nd Fl.
Washington, DC 20009
Phone: (202)797-7000
Fax: (202)797-7040

Publications: The Washington Blade (5842)

Washington CEO, Inc.
1500 114th Ave. SE, Ste. 101
Bellevue, WA 98004-6902
Phone: (206)441-8415
Fax: (206)441-8325
Free: 800-488-4984

Publications: Washington CEO (32669)

Washington County Bar Association
30 E. Beau, No. 523
Washington, PA 15301
Phone: (724)225-6710
Fax: (724)225-8345

Publications: Washington County Reports (28119)

Washington County Historical Society Inc.
118 E Dickson St.
Fayetteville, AR 72701-5612
Phone: (479)521-2970

Publications: Flashback (1119)

Washington County News
PO Box 627
Chipley, FL 32428
Phone: (850)638-0212
Fax: (850)638-4601

Publications: Washington County News (5984)

Washington County News
Box 316
Washington, KS 66968
Phone: (785)325-2219
Fax: (785)325-3255

Publications: Washington County News (11863)

Washington County Publications, Inc.
305 Jordan St.
PO Box 510
Chatom, AL 36518
Phone: (334)847-2599
Fax: (334)847-3847

Publications: Washington County News (152)

The Washington Diplomat, Inc.
PO Box 1345
Wheaton, MD 20915-1345
Phone: (301)933-3552
Fax: (301)949-0065

Publications: The Washington Diplomat (13782)

The Washington Evening Journal
111 North Marion Ave.
Washington, IA 52353

Publications: The Washington Evening Journal (11286)

Washington Information Source
6506 Old Stage Rd., Ste. 100
Rockville, MD 20852-4326
Fax: (301)468-0475

Publications: Inspection Monitor (13682)

The Washington Informer
3117 Martin Luther King Jr. Ave. SE
Washington, DC 20032-1537
Phone: (202)561-4100
Fax: (202)574-3785

Publications: The Washington Informer (5846)

Washington and Jefferson College
60 S Lincoln St.
Washington, PA 15301
Phone: (724)222-4400
Fax: (724)223-5271
Free: 888-926-3529

Publications: Red and Black (28116) • Topic (Washington) (28117) • W & J Magazine (28118)

Washington Jewish Week
1500 E. Jefferson St.
Rockville, MD 20852
Phone: (301)230-2222
Fax: (301)881-1994

Publications: Washington Jewish Week (13699)

Washington & Lee University
Publications Office
Mattingly House
Lexington, VA 24450-0303
Phone: (540)463-8957
Fax: (540)463-8024

Publications: W & L (32192)

Washington Library Association
4016 1st Ave. NE
Seattle, WA 98105-6502
Phone: (206)545-1529
Free: 800-704-1529

Publications: ALKI (32759)

Washington Magazine, Inc.
1828 L St. NW, Ste. 200
Washington, DC 20036
Phone: (202)296-1246

Publications: Washingtonian Magazine (5856)

The Washington Monthly
733 15th St. NW, Ste. 520
Washington, DC 20005
Phone: (202)393-5155
Fax: (202)393-2444

Publications: The Washington Monthly (5848)

Washington Music Educator's Association
PO Box 1117
Edmonds, WA 98020-1117
Phone: (425)771-7859
Fax: (425)776-1795
Free: 800-324-WMEA

Publications: Voice of Washington Music Educators (32747)

Washington National Cathedral
3101 Wisconsin Ave. NW
Washington, DC 20016-5098
Phone: (202)537-5681
Fax: (202)364-6600

Publications: Cathedral Age (5398)

Washington News Publishing Co.
217 N Market St.
PO Box 1788
Washington, NC 27889
Phone: (252)946-2144
Fax: (252)946-9797
Free: 800-326-0762

Publications: Washington Daily News (24273)

Washington Newspaper Publishers Association
3838 Stone Way N.
Seattle, WA 98103
Phone: (206)634-3838
Fax: (206)634-3842

Publications: The Washington Newspaper (33039)

The Washington Opera
2600 Virgina Ave., Ste. 104
Washington, DC 20037
Phone: (202)295-2420
Fax: (202)295-2479

Publications: The Washington Opera Magazine (5849)

The Washington Post
1150 15th St. NW
Washington, DC 20071-2400
Phone: (202)334-6000
Fax: (202)334-5693
Free: 800-627-1150

Publications: Fast Forward (5492) • The Washington Post (5850) • The Washington Post Magazine (5851)

Washington Province of Discalced Carmelite Friars, Inc.
2131 Lincoln Rd. NE
Washington, DC 20002-1199
Fax: (202)832-8967
Free: 888-616-1713

Publications: Spiritual Life (5802)

Washington State Grange
PO Box 1186
Olympia, WA 98507-1186
Phone: (360)943-9911
Fax: (360)357-3548
Free: 800-854-1635

Publications: Washington State Grange News (32862)

Washington State Nurses Association
575 Andover Park W., No. 101
Seattle, WA 98188-3348
Phone: (206)575-7979
Fax: (206)575-1908

Publications: The Washington Nurse (33040)

Washington State Pharmacists Association
1501 Taylor Ave. SW
Renton, WA 98055-3139
Phone: (425)228-7171
Fax: (425)277-3897
Free: 800-222-WSPA

Publications: Washington Pharmacist (32927)

Washington State University
Pullman, WA 99164-5020
Phone: (509)335-3023
Fax: (509)335-2582
Free: 800-392-4059

Publications: ESQ (32903)

Washington State University
PO Box 2008
Pullman, WA 99164-0000
Phone: (509)335-4573
Fax: (509)335-7401

Publications: The Daily Evergreen (32902)

Washington State University
Pullman, WA 99164-5020
Phone: (509)335-3023
Fax: (509)335-2582
Free: 800-392-4059

Publications: Poe Studies/Dark Romanticism (32906) • Washington State University Hilltopics (32908)

Washington State University Press
PO Box 645910
Pullman, WA 99164-5910
Phone: (509)335-3518
Fax: (509)335-8568
Free: 800-354-7360

Publications: Northwest Science (32905) • The Western Journal of Black Studies (32909)

The Washington Times Corp.
3600 New York Ave. NE
Washington, DC 20002-1947
Phone: (202)636-3000
Fax: (202)636-3000
Free: 800-822-2822

Publications: Insight (5546) • The World & I (5870)

Washington Trails Association
1305 4th Ave., No. 512
Seattle, WA 98101-2401
Phone: (206)625-1367
Fax: (206)625-9249

Publications: Washington Trails (33041)

Washington University
Attn.: Student Life
PO Box 1039
St. Louis, MO 63130
Phone: (314)935-6713
Fax: (314)935-5938

Publications: Student Life (17517)

Washington University School of Law
Anheuser-Busch Hall
1 Brookings Dr. PO Box 1120
St. Louis, MO 63130-4899
Phone: (314)935-6498

Publications: The Washington University Global Studies Law Review (17528)

Washington University School of Medicine
660 S. Euclid Ave.
PO Box 8127
St. Louis, MO 63110
Phone: (314)454-8702

Publications: Diabetes (17433)

Washita County Enterprise
PO Box 68
Corn, OK 73024
Phone: (580)343-2513
Fax: (580)343-2513

Publications: Washita County Enterprise (25794)

Watauga Newspapers, Inc.
474 Industrial Park Dr.
Boone, NC 28607
Phone: (828)264-3612

Publications: Watauga Democrat (23657)

Watchtower Bible and Tract Society of New York Inc.
25 Columbia Heights
Brooklyn, NY 11201
Phone: (718)560-5000
Fax: (718)560-8850

Publications: Awake! (20298) • The Watchtower (20355)

Water Environment Federation
601 Wythe St.
Alexandria, VA 22314-1994
Phone: (703)684-2400
Fax: (703)684-2492
Free: 800-666-0206

Publications: Operations Forum (31719) • Water Environment Research (31751) • Water Environment & Technology (31752)

Water Resources Center
Rubidoux Hall 094
4501 Glenwood Dr.
Riverside, CA 92521-0436
Phone: (530)752-8050
Fax: (530)752-8345

Publications: California Water Resources Center Contribution (1812)

Waterbird Society
Pacific Cooperative Studies Unit
Department of Botany
University of Hawaii Manoa
3190 Maile Way
Honolulu, HI 96822
Phone: (808)956-8369
Fax: (808)973-2936

Publications: Waterbirds (7728)

The Waterford Post
224A N Milwaukee St.
PO Box 297
Waterford, WI 53185
Phone: (414)534-4668
Fax: (414)534-3616

Publications: The Waterford Post (34390)

Watershed Sentinel
708-207, W. Hastings St.
Vancouver, BC, Canada V6B 1H7
Phone: (604)879-2992
Fax: (604)879-2272

Publications: Watershed Sentinel (35177)

Watertown Daily Times
115 W Main St.
PO Box 140
Watertown, WI 53094-0140
Phone: (920)261-4949
Fax: (920)261-5102

Publications: Watertown Daily Times (34392)

Watertown Public Opinion
120 3rd Ave. NW
Box 10
Watertown, SD 57201
Phone: (605)886-6901
Fax: (605)886-4280
Free: 800-658-5401

Publications: Watertown Public Opinion (29019)

The Waterville Times
128 Main St.
Box C
Waterville, NY 13480
Phone: (315)841-4105
Fax: (315)841-4104

Publications: The Waterville Times (23523)

Waterways Journal, Inc.
319 N 4th St., Ste. 650
St. Louis, MO 63102
Phone: (314)241-7354
Fax: (314)241-4207

Publications: The Waterways Journal (17530)

The Waterways Project
393 St. Pauls Ave.
Staten Island, NY 10304-2127
Phone: (718)442-7429
Fax: (718)442-4978

Publications: Waterways: Poetry in the Mainstream (23365)

Waterworks Publishing
5473 Hwy. 23N
Eureka Springs, AR 72631

Publications: Aqua Terra, Meta-Ecology and Culture (1113)

Watford Guide-Advocate
5292 Nauvoo Rd.
PO Box 99
Watford, ON, Canada N0M 2S0
Phone: (519)876-2809
Fax: (519)876-2322

Publications: Watford Guide-Advocate (36864)

The Wathena Times
Box 368
Wathena, KS 66090-0368
Phone: (913)989-4415

Publications: The Wathena Times (11865)

Watkins Patriot
PO Box 347
Eden Valley, MN 55329-0347
Phone: (612)764-5375

Publications: Watkins Patriot (15872)

The Watson Witness
PO Box 129
Watson, SK, Canada S0K 4V0
Phone: (306)287-3245
Fax: (306)287-4333
Free: 888-999-6397

Publications: The Watson Witness (37588)

Watsonville Newspapers, Inc.
1000 Main St.
PO Box 50055
Watsonville, CA 95077-3732
Phone: (408)761-0611
Fax: (408)722-8386

Publications: Register-Pajaronian (4058)

Watt Publishing Co.
122 S. Wesley Ave.
Mount Morris, IL 61054-1497
Phone: (815)734-4171
Fax: (815)734-5649

Publications: Feed International (9237) • Feed Management (9238) • Industria Avicola (9239) • Meat Processing (9240) • Petfood Industry (9243) • Pig International (9244) • Poultry International (9245) • WATT Poultry USA (162)

Waukesha County Freeman
PO Box 7
Waukesha, WI 53187
Phone: (414)542-2501
Fax: (414)542-6082

Publications: Waukesha County Freeman (34414)

Waunakee Tribune
PO Box 128
Waunakee, WI 53597
Phone: (608)849-5227
Fax: (608)849-4225

Publications: Waunakee Tribune (34418)

Waupaca County Publishing Co.
PO Box 152
717 10th St.
Waupaca, WI 54981-1934
Phone: (715)258-5546
Fax: (715)258-8162
Free: 800-236-3313

Publications: The Chronicle (34451) • Silent Sports (34419) • Waupaca County Post (34421) • Wisconsin State Farmer (34422)

Waurika News-Democrat
117 W Broadway
Waurika, OK 73573
Phone: (580)228-2316
Fax: (580)228-3647

Publications: Waurika News-Democrat (26183)

The Wausa Gazette
603 East Broadway
Wausa, NE 68786-0318
Phone: (402)586-2661
Fax: (402)586-2661

Publications: The Wausa Gazette (18304)

The Wautoma Newspaper, Inc.
PO Box 838
Wautoma, WI 54982
Phone: (414)787-3334
Fax: (414)787-2883

Publications: Waushara Argus (34442)

The Wave
115 E. Carroll St.
Salisbury, MD 21801
Phone: (410)749-7171

Publications: The Wave (13711)

The Wave
107 E. Austin
PO Box 88
Port Lavaca, TX 77979
Phone: (361)552-9788
Fax: (361)552-3108
Free: 800-928-3639

Publications: The Port Lavaca Wave & Calhoun County WAVE EXTRA (30956)

The Wave
PO Box 95
Whitehall, WI 54773-0095
Phone: (715)985-3815
Fax: (715)985-9330

Publications: News-Wave (34452)

Wave Community Newspapers
2621 W. 54th St.
Los Angeles, CA 90043
Phone: (323)291-0242
Fax: (323)293-2136
Free: 800-404-WAVE

Publications: Alhambra Post Advocate (1388) • Bell Gardens Review (1483) • Bell/Maywood/Cudahy Industrial Post (1482) • Central Star/Journal Wave (2234) • Compton/Carson Wave (1748) • Culver City Star (1792) • Downey Herald American (1834) • Eagle Rock Sentinel (2255) • East Los Angeles Commerce Tribune (1840) • Eastside Journal (2257) • El Sereno Star (2263) • Huntington Park Bulletin (2068) • Inglewood/Hawthorne Wave (2072) • Lincoln Heights Bulletin-News (2318) • Lynwood Press (2487) • Mesa Tribune Wave (2330) • Monterey Park Progress (2596) • Mount Washington Star-Review (2337) • News-Herald and Journal (2347) • Norwalk Herald American (2648) • Paramount/Bellflower Herald American (2809) • Pico Rivera/Santa Fe Springs News (2840) • Rosemead/South San Gabriel Progress (2968) • South Gate Press (2392) • Southwest News Wave (2403) • Westchester Star (2433) • Whittier Independent (4070)

Wave Publishing
PO Box 7
Coalville, UT 84017
Phone: (435)654-1471
Fax: (435)654-5085

Publications: Summit County Bee (31330)

Wave Publishing Co.
8808 Rockaway Beach Blvd.
PO Box 97
Rockaway Beach, NY 11693
Phone: (718)634-4000
Fax: (718)945-0913

Publications: The Wave (20592)

WaveLength Magazine
2735 North Rd.
Gabriola Island, BC, Canada V0R 1X7
Phone: (250)247-8858
Fax: (250)247-9789
Free: 800-799-5607

Publications: WaveLength Magazine (34962)

Waverly Journal
130 S Pearl
PO Box 78
Waverly, IL 62692
Phone: (217)435-9221
Fax: (217)435-4511

Publications: Waverly Journal (9748)

Waverly News
PO Box 100
Waverly, NE 68462
Phone: (402)786-2344
Fax: (402)786-2344

Publications: Waverly News (18305)

Waverly Newspapers
311 W Bremer
PO Box 858
Waverly, IA 50677
Phone: (319)352-3334
Fax: (319)352-5135
Free: 800-369-2226

Publications: Bremer County Independent (11306) • Waverly Democrat (11309)

Wawatay Native Communications Society
16 5th Ave.
PO Box 1180
Sioux Lookout, ON, Canada P8T 1B7
Phone: (807)737-2951
Fax: (807)737-3224
Free: 800-243-9059

Publications: Wawatay News (36393)

Wax Poetics, LLC
655 Fulton St., No. 181
Brooklyn, NY 11217-1112
Phone: (718)826-0616

Publications: Wax Poetics (20356)

way station magazine
1319 S Logan St.
Lansing, MI 48910
Phone: (517)374-4702

Publications: way station magazine (15296)

Waycross Journal Herald
400 Isabella St.
PO Box 219
Waycross, GA 31502
Phone: (912)283-2244
Fax: (912)283-2815

Publications: Waycross Journal Herald (7644)

Wayfarer Publications
PO Box 39938
Los Angeles, CA 90039
Phone: (323)665-7773
Fax: (323)665-1627

Publications: T'ai Chi (2409)

Wayland Baptist University
1900 W. 7th
PO Box 759
Plainview, TX 79072
Phone: (806)296-5051
Fax: (806)296-4718

Publications: Trail Blazer (30940)

Wayland Printing, Inc.
133 E. Superior
Wayland, MI 49348
Phone: (269)792-2271
Fax: (269)792-2030
Free: 800-554-8800

Publications: Penasee Globe (15670)

The Wayne County News, Inc.
PO Box 156
Waynesboro, TN 38485
Phone: (615)722-5429
Fax: (615)722-5429

Publications: The Wayne County News (29644)

Wayne County Newspaper Inc.
PO Box 432
Monticello, KY 42633
Phone: (606)348-3338
Fax: (606)348-8848

Publications: Wayne County Outlook (12298)

Wayne County Press
213 E. Main St.
PO Box F
Fairfield, IL 62837
Phone: (618)842-2662
Fax: (618)842-7912

Publications: Wayne County Press (8880)

Wayne County Publications Inc.
310 Central Ave.
Wayne, WV 25570
Phone: (304)272-3433
Fax: (304)552-3910

Publications: Wayne County Publication Inc (33484)

Wayne County Star
PO Box 199
Red Creek, NY 13143
Phone: (315)754-6229
Fax: (315)754-6431
Free: 800-246-6229

Publications: Wayne County Star (20979)

The Wayne Herald
114 Main St.
Box 70
Wayne, NE 68787
Phone: (402)375-2600
Fax: (402)375-1888
Free: 800-672-3418

Publications: The Wayne Herald (18306)

The Wayne Independent
220 8th St., No. 122
Honesdale, PA 18431-1854
Phone: (570)253-3055
Fax: (570)253-5387

Publications: The Wayne Independent (27051)

Wayne State College
200 E 10th St.
Wayne, NE 68787
Phone: (402)375-2200
Fax: (402)375-7204

Publications: Wayne Stater (18307)

Wayne State University
441 Ferry Mall
Detroit, MI 48202-3619
Phone: (313)577-6046
Fax: (313)577-9337
Free: 877-WSU-ALUM

Publications: Wayne State Magazine (14953)

Wayne State University Press
Leonard N. Simons Bldg.
4809 Woodward Ave.
Detroit, MI 48201-1309
Phone: (313)577-4606
Fax: (313)577-6131
Free: 800-978-7323

Publications: Criticism (14922) • Human Biology (11552) • Merrill-Palmer Quarterly (14935)

Wayne State University Student Newspapers Publishing Board
5425 Woodward Ave. Ste. 100
Detroit, MI 48202
Phone: (313)577-7878
Fax: (313)993-8108

Publications: The South End (14948)

Waynedale News
2700 Lower Huntington Rd.
Fort Wayne, IN 46809
Phone: (260)747-4535
Fax: (260)747-3282

Publications: Waynedale News (9974)

Waynoka Publishing Co.
109 N Main St.
Waynoka, OK 73860
Phone: (405)824-2171
Fax: (405)824-2172

Publications: Woods County Enterprise (26184)

Wayuga Community Newspapers, Inc.
PO Box 199
Red Creek, NY 13143
Phone: (315)754-6229
Fax: (315)754-6431

Publications: Post Herald (23178)

W.B. Rogers Printing Co., Inc.
122 E 8th St.
PO Box 548
Trenton, MO 64683-0548
Phone: (816)359-2212
Fax: (816)359-4414

Publications: Republican-Times (17652)

W.D. Hoard & Sons Co.
28 West Milwaukee Ave.
Fort Atkinson, WI 53538
Phone: (920)563-5551
Fax: (920)563-7298

Publications: Hoard's Dairyman (33711)

WD Press
PO Box 24115
St. Louis, MO 63130
Phone: (314)727-8554
Fax: (314)727-8554

Publications: Synthesis/Regeneration (17520)

W.E. Upjohn Institute for Employment Research
300 S. Westnedge Ave.
Kalamazoo, MI 49007-4686
Phone: (616)343-5541
Fax: (616)343-7310

Publications: Business Outlook for West Michigan (15233)

WEA Board of Directors
33434 8th Ave. S.
Federal Way, WA 98003-6397
Phone: (253)765-7039
Fax: (253)946-7612
Free: 800-622-3393

Publications: WEA Action (32765)

Weatherford Advertising, Inc.
315 N York Ave.
Weatherford, TX 76086
Phone: (817)599-5785
Fax: (817)599-0412

Publications: Parker County Shopper (31272)

Weatherford Daily News
118, S.Broadway
Weatherford, OK 73096-0919
Phone: (580)772-3301
Fax: (580)772-7329

Publications: Weatherford Daily News (26186)

Web Craft, LTD
345 Argyle St. S
Caledonia, ON, Canada N3W 1L8
Phone: (905)765-4210
Fax: (905)765-3563

Publications: Regional News This Week (35722)

Web Press (Thunder Bay) Ltd.
866 Tungsten St.
Thunder Bay, ON, Canada P7B 6J3
Phone: (807)623-3668

Publications: Thunder Bay Real Estate News (36444)

Webb City Sentinel, Inc.
8 S Main
PO Box 150
Webb City, MO 64870
Phone: (417)673-2421

Publications: Webb City Sentinel (17712) • Wise Buyer (17713)

Webb Printing
4 N Stevens
PO Box 9
Preston, IA 52069

Publications: Preston Times (11167)

Webco Co.
PO Box 479
Devon, AB, Canada T0C 1E0
Phone: (403)987-2522
Fax: (403)987-4744

Publications: Devon Dispatch (34693)

Webco Publishers
4504-61 Ave.
Leduc, AB, Canada T9E 3Z1
Phone: (780)986-2271
Fax: (780)986-6397

Publications: Leduc Representative (34792)

Webcom Communications Corp.
7355 E Orchard Rd., Ste. 100
Englewood, CO 80111
Phone: (720)528-3770
Fax: (720)528-3771
Free: 800-803-9488

Publications: Webcom Communication Corp (4416)

Weber State University
1214 University Cir.
Ogden, UT 84408-1214
Phone: (801)626-6616

Publications: Weber Studies (31379)

Webster County Citizen
PO Box 190
Seymour, MO 65746-0190
Phone: (417)935-2257
Fax: (417)935-2487

Publications: Webster County Citizen (17577)

Webster-Kirkwood Times, Inc.
122 W Lockwood Ave., 2nd Fl.
St. Louis, MO 63119-2916
Phone: (314)968-2699
Fax: (314)968-2961

Publications: South County Times (17514) • Webster-Kirkwood Times (17714)

Webster-Ontario-Walworth Pennysaver
164 E Main St.
Webster, NY 14580
Phone: (585)265-3620
Fax: (585)265-3882

Publications: Webster-Ontario-Walworth Pennysaver (23529)

Webster Printing Co.
108 N Sparta
Steeleville, IL 62288
Phone: (618)965-3417
Fax: (618)965-3548

Publications: Steeleville Ledger (9662)

Webster Progress
PO Drawer D
Eupora, MS 39744
Phone: (662)258-7532
Fax: (662)258-6474

Publications: Webster Progress-Times (16622)

Webster Publishing Co.
219 Back Fork St
Webster Springs, WV 26288
Phone: (304)847-5828
Fax: (304)847-5991

Publications: Webster Republican (33486)

Webster University
470 E. Lockwood
St. Louis, MO 63119
Phone: (314)961-2660
Fax: (314)968-7059

Publications: The Journal (17450)

Wedding Bells
50 Wellington St. E., Ste., 200
Toronto, ON, Canada M5E 1C8
Phone: (416)862-8479
Free: 800-387-9877

Publications: Mariage Qalec (36656)

WeddingBells Inc.
34 King St. E., Ste. 800
Toronto, ON, Canada M5E 2X8
Free: 800-267-5450

Publications: WeddingBells Magazine (36790)

Wedel Anderson Publishing
PO Box 128
Canistota, SD 57012-0128

Publications: The Canova Herald (28828)

Wedel Publishing, LLC
113 1st St. W
PO Box 129
Mount Vernon, IA 52314-0129
Phone: (319)895-6216
Fax: (319)895-6217

Publications: The Hillsboro Star-Journal (11097) • The Sun (11098) • The SUNlight (11099)

Wednesday Journal, Inc.
141 S. Oak Park Ave.
Oak Park, IL 60302
Phone: (708)524-8300
Fax: (708)524-0447

Publications: Chicago Parent Magazine (9373) • Forest Park Review (9375) • Wednesday Journal of Oak Park & River Forest (9378)

WEED Foundation
517 College St., Ste. 233
Toronto, ON, Canada M6G 4A2
Phone: (416)928-0880
Fax: (416)928-9640

Publications: Women & Environments (36793)

Weekend Adventures Magazine
PO Box 1895
Cumberland, MD 21501-1895
Phone: (301)722-3533
Fax: (301)722-8020
Free: 888-805-5235

Publications: Weekend Adventures Magazine (13475)

Weekender
15 N. Main St.
Wilkes Barre, PA 18711
Phone: (570)829-7101

Publications: The Weekender (28168)

The Weekender Mountain Echo-News Tribune
PO Box 879
Keyser, WV 26726
Phone: (304)788-3333
Fax: (304)788-3398

Publications: The Weekender Mountain Echo-News Tribune (33355)

The Weekly
PO Box 921141
Norcross, GA 30010-1141
Phone: (770)446-2364
Fax: (770)263-8636

Publications: The Weekly (7472)

Weekly Alibi
2118 Central Ave. SE, Ste. 151
Albuquerque, NM 87106-4004
Phone: (505)346-0660
Fax: (505)256-9651

Publications: Weekly Alibi (19789)

Weekly Bargain Bulletin
R.R. 5
Box 662
New Castle, PA 16105
Phone: (724)654-5529

Publications: Weekly Bargain Bulletin (27315)

The Weekly Calistogan
PO Box 385
Calistoga, CA 94515
Phone: (707)942-6242
Fax: (707)942-4617

Publications: The Weekly Calistogan (1641)

The Weekly Challenger
2500 9th St. S
St. Petersburg, FL 33705
Phone: (727)896-2922
Fax: (727)823-2568

Publications: The Weekly Challenger (6635)

The Weekly Herald
106 W Main St.
Williamston, NC 27892
Phone: (252)792-1181
Fax: (252)792-1921

Publications: The Weekly Herald (24291)

The Weekly Home News
PO Box 39
Spring Green, WI 53588
Phone: (608)588-2508
Fax: (608)588-2509

Publications: The Weekly Home News (34339)

The Weekly Leader
Town Sq.
207 E. Government St.
Brandon, MS 39042
Phone: (601)825-8333
Fax: (601)825-8334

Publications: The Weekly Leader (16815)

The Weekly News, Inc.
901 NE 79th St.
Miami, FL 33138
Phone: (305)757-6333
Fax: (305)756-6488

Publications: The Weekly News (6390)

The Weekly Post
PO Box 849
Rainsville, AL 35986
Phone: (256)638-4027
Fax: (256)638-2329

Publications: The Weekly Post (429)

Weekly Reader Corp.
200 First Stamford Pl.
PO Box 120023
Stamford, CT 06912-0023
Phone: (203)705-3500
Fax: (203)705-1661

Publications: Career World (9313) • Current Events (5145) • Current Health 1 (9314) • Current Health 2 (9315) • Current Science (5146) • Know Your World Extra (5153) • Read (5159) • Weekly Reader (Pre-K edition) (5163) • Writing! (9323)

The Weekly Record
218 Main St.
New Madrid, MO 63869-1997
Phone: (573)748-2120
Fax: (573)748-5435

Publications: The Weekly Record (17315)

Weekly Recorder
256 Main St.
PO Drawer F
Claysville, PA 15323-0506
Phone: (724)663-7742

Publications: Weekly Recorder (26787)

Weekly Register-Call
220 Spring St.
PO Box 609
Central City, CO 80427-0609
Phone: (303)582-5333
Fax: (303)582-3932

Publications: Weekly Register-Call (4231)

The Weekly Reminder
PO Box 180
Paulding, OH 45879-0180
Phone: (419)399-4015
Fax: (419)399-4030

Publications: The Weekly Reminder (25472)

The Weekly Standard
1150 17th St. NW, No. 505
Washington, DC 20036
Phone: (202)293-4900
Fax: (202)293-4901

Publications: The Weekly Standard (5859)

The Weekly Star
PO Box 898
Pigeon Forge, TN 37868
Phone: (865)453-0626

Publications: The Weekly Star (29566)

Weekly World News
5401 NW Broken Sound Blvd.
Boca Raton, FL 33487

Publications: Weekly World News (5941)

Weeks Publishing Co.
3400 Dundee Rd., Ste. 100
Northbrook, IL 60062
Phone: (847)559-0385
Fax: (847)559-0389

Publications: Food Product Design (9316)

WEHCO Media Group
315 Pine St.
PO Box 621
Texarkana, TX 75504
Phone: (903)794-3311
Fax: (903)794-3315

Publications: Texarkana Gazette (31184)

Weider Publications
21100 Erwin St.
Woodland Hills, CA 91367-3712
Phone: (818)884-6800
Fax: (818)595-0463
Free: 800-423-5590

Publications: Fit Pregnancy (4104) • Flex Magazines (4105) • Men's Fitness (4108) • Muscle & Fitness (4110) • Muscle & Fitness/Hers (4111) • Shape (4114)

Weil Communications and Marketing, Inc.
PO Box 535
Olney, MD 20830
Phone: (301)924-5490
Fax: (301)924-0265

Publications: EH & S Solutions (Environmental Health & Safety Solutions) (13641) • Housing Operations Manager (13642)

Weimar Merway
200 W Main
Weimar, TX 78962
Phone: (979)725-8444
Fax: (979)725-9051

Publications: Weimar Mercury (31276)

Weinberg Inc.
252 W. 37th St., 9th Fl.
New York, NY 10018
Phone: (212)387-0299
Fax: (646)218-6950

Publications: New Russian Word (22434)

Weisbeck Publishing & Printing, Inc.
13200 Broadway
Alden, NY 14004
Phone: (716)937-9226

Publications: Alden Advertiser (20021)

Weiss Communications
6081 E. 82nd St., Ste. 401
Indianapolis, IN 46250
Phone: (317)585-5858

Publications: Indianapolis Woman (10134)

Welch Daily News, Inc.
100 Ctr. St.
PO Box 180
Iaeger, WV 24844
Phone: (304)938-2142
Fax: (304)436-3146

Publications: The Industrial News (33351)

Welch Publishing Co.
117 E. 2nd St.
PO Box 267
Perrysburg, OH 43552
Phone: (419)874-4491
Fax: (419)874-7311

Publications: The American Legion Press (25474) • Perrysburg Messenger Journal (25475) • Point and Shoreland Journal (25476) • Rossford Record Journal (25503)

Welcome Publishing Co., Inc.
1751 NE 162nd St.
Box 630-518
North Miami Beach, FL 33162-4757
Phone: (305)944-9444
Fax: (305)949-0544

Publications: Bienvenidos a Miami (6341) • Welcome to Miami and the Beaches (6469)

The Weleetkan
Box 427
Weleetka, OK 74880
Phone: (405)786-2224
Fax: (405)452-3329

Publications: The Weleetkan (26190)

Welfare Warriors
2711 W Michigan Ave.
Milwaukee, WI 53208
Phone: (414)342-6662
Fax: (414)342-6667

Publications: Welfare Warriors (34107)

Well Nations, Inc.
520 Kansas City St., Ste. 308
Rapid City, SD 57701
Phone: (605)348-9283
Fax: (605)348-9284

Publications: Well Nations Magazine (28934)

Wellesley College
Center for Research on Women
106 Central St.
Wellesley, MA 02481
Fax: (781)283-3645
Free: 888-283-8044

Publications: The Women's Review of Books (14619)

Wellington Daily News
113 W Harvey Ave.
PO Box 368
Wellington, KS 67152-3840
Phone: (620)326-3326
Fax: (316)326-3290

Publications: Wellington Daily News (11866)

Wellington Leader
913 West Ave.
Box 992
Wellington, TX 79095
Phone: (806)447-2559
Fax: (806)447-2463

Publications: Wellington Leader (31277)

The Wells Mirror
40 W Franklin
Wells, MN 56097
Phone: (507)553-3131
Fax: (507)553-3132

Publications: The Wells Mirror (16505)

Wells Publishing, Inc.
3570 Camino del Rio N, Ste. 200
San Diego, CA 92108
Phone: (619)584-1100
Fax: (619)584-1200

Publications: The Insurance Journal of Texas (29784) • The Insurance Journal of the West (3174)

Wellsville Optic-News
PO Box 73
Wellsville, MO 63384
Phone: (573)684-2929

Publications: Wellsville Optic-News (17715)

The Wenatchee Business Journal Inc.
304 S Mission St.
Wenatchee, WA 98801
Phone: (509)663-6730
Fax: (509)663-4399

Publications: Everett Business Journal (33194) • Wenatchee Business Journal (33195)

Wendell Clarion
PO Box 400
Wendell, NC 27591
Phone: (919)365-6262
Fax: (919)269-8383

Publications: Wendell Clarion (24282)

Wenner Media
1290 Avenue of the Americas
New York, NY 10104
Phone: (212)484-1616
Fax: (212)767-8209

Publications: Men's Journal (22315) • Rolling Stone (22675) • Us (22892)

Wenona Index
PO Box 190
Henry, IL 61537
Phone: (309)364-3250
Fax: (309)364-3858

Publications: Wenona Index (8982)

Don Wentworth
282 Main St.
Pittsburgh, PA 15201

Publications: Lilliput Review (27811)

Werner Publishing Corp.
12121 Wilshire Blvd., Ste. 1220
Los Angeles, CA 90025
Phone: (310)820-1500
Fax: (310)826-5008

Publications: Golf Tips (2279) • Outdoor Photographer (2354)

Wesleyan Christian Advocate, Inc.
PO Box 427
Stone Mountain, GA 30086-0427
Phone: (404)659-8809
Fax: (404)659-1727

Publications: Wesleyan Christian Advocate (7572)

Wesleyan Publishing House
7990 Castleway Dr.
Indianapolis, IN 46250
Phone: (317)570-5300
Fax: (317)570-5730
Free: 800-493-7539

Publications: The Wesleyan Advocate (10182)

Wesleyan University
Middletown, CT 06459
Phone: (860)685-3699
Fax: (860)685-3601

Publications: Wesleyan (4946)

Wessington Springs True Dakotan
113 E Main St.
PO Box T
Wessington Springs, SD 57382
Phone: (605)539-1281
Fax: (605)539-9315

Publications: Wessington Springs True Dakotan (29029)

Wessington Times Enterprise
PO Box 107
Wessington, SD 57381
Phone: (605)458-2253
Fax: (605)853-3575

Publications: Wessington Times Enterprise (29028)

West Art
PO Box 6868
Auburn, CA 95604
Phone: (530)885-0969

Publications: West Art (1441)

West Branch Times
PO Box 368
West Branch, IA 52358
Phone: (319)643-2131

Publications: West Branch Times (11318)

West Central Publishing, Inc.
PO Box 27
St. Marys, WV 26170
Phone: (304)684-2424
Fax: (304)684-2426

Publications: The Pennsboro News (33428) • Pleasants County Leader (33460) • The St. Marys Oracle (33461)

West Central Tribune
PO Box 839
Willmar, MN 56201
Phone: (320)235-1150
Fax: (320)235-6769

Publications: The Sunday Reminder (16517) • West Central Tribune (16518)

West Chester Publishing Co.
250 N Bradford Ave.
West Chester, PA 19382-2800
Phone: (610)696-1776
Fax: (610)430-1180
Free: 800-568-7355

Publications: Daily Local News (28146)

West Chester State University
253 Sykes Union Bldg.
West Chester, PA 19383-0001
Phone: (610)436-2793
Fax: (215)436-2287

Publications: The Quad (28148)

West Chester University
210 E. Rosedale Ave.
West Chester, PA 19383
Phone: (610)436-2901
Fax: (610)436-2275

Publications: College Literature (28145)

West Coast Paradise Publishing
PO Box 2093 Sardis Sta. Main
Sardis, BC, Canada V2R 1A5
Phone: (604)824-9528
Fax: (604)824-9541

Publications: Teak Roundup (35087)

West Coast Publishing Inc.
161 Worcester Rd., Ste. 201
Framingham, MA 01701
Phone: (508)879-9792
Fax: (508)879-2755

Publications: SC Magazine (14200)

West Coast Review Publishing Society
2027 E. Academic Annex
Simon Fraser University
Burnaby, BC, Canada V5A 1S6
Phone: (604)291-4287
Fax: (604)291-4622

Publications: West Coast Line (34909)

West County News
45 Conway St.
PO Box 218
Shelburne Falls, MA 01370
Phone: (413)625-4660
Fax: (413)625-4661

Publications: Shelburne Falls and West County News (14521)

West Egg Communications LLC
252 W. 37th St., 5th Fl.
New York, NY 10018
Phone: (212)736-4111

Publications: Book (21334)

West Essex Tribune, Inc.
495 S Livingston Ave.
PO Box 65
Livingston, NJ 07039-0065
Phone: (973)992-1771
Fax: (972)992-7015

Publications: West Essex Tribune (19178)

West Group
375 Hudson St.
New York, NY 10014
Phone: (212)929-7500
Fax: (212)807-6209
Free: 800-851-1133

Publications: Criminal Law Bulletin (21518)

West Group
6111 Oak Tree Blvd.
Cleveland, OH 44131
Phone: (216)520-5600
Fax: (216)520-5658
Free: 800-362-4500

Publications: Babbit's Ohio Municipal Service (24858) • Baldwin's Ohio Legislative Service, Annotated (24860) • Baldwin's Ohio Monthly Record (24861) • Domestic Relations Journal of Ohio (24882) • Probate Law Journal of Ohio (24944) • SERB Official Reporter (24953) • Worker's Compensation Journal of Ohio (24966)

West-Lane News
PO Box 188
Veneta, OR 97487
Phone: (541)935-1882
Fax: (541)935-4082

Publications: Tri-County Shopper (26604) • West-Lane News (26605)

West Liberty State College
PO Box 295
West Liberty, WV 26074-0295
Phone: (304)336-8360
Fax: (304)336-8323
Free: 800-732-6204

Publications: The Trumpet (33495)

West Michigan Senior Times
595 Jenner Dr.
Allegan, MI 49010
Phone: (616)673-2141
Fax: (616)673-4761
Free: 800-968-4415

Publications: West Michigan Senior Times (14724)

West Nebraska Register
804 W Division
PO Box 608
Grand Island, NE 68802
Phone: (308)382-4660
Fax: (308)382-4746

Publications: West Nebraska Register (18027)

The West News
214 W Oak
PO Box 38
West, TX 76691
Phone: (817)826-3718

Publications: The West News (31282)

West Orange Times
705 S. Dillard St.
Winter Garden, FL 34787-3908
Phone: (407)656-2121
Fax: (407)656-6075

Publications: West Orange Times (6865)

West Plains Daily Quill
125 N Jefferson St.
PO Box 110
West Plains, MO 65775-0110
Phone: (417)256-9191
Fax: (417)256-9196

Publications: West Plains Daily Quill (17716)

West Point News
PO Box 40
West Point, NE 68788
Phone: (402)372-2461
Fax: (402)372-3530

Publications: Elkhorn Valley Shopper (18311) • West Point News (18312)

West River Catholic
606 Cathedral Dr.
PO Box 678
Rapid City, SD 57709
Phone: (605)343-3541
Fax: (605)348-7985

Publications: West River Catholic (28935)

West Seattle Hearld/White Center News
3500 SW Alaska St.
Seattle, WA 98126
Phone: (206)932-6456
Fax: (206)937-1223

Publications: West Seattle Herald/White Center News (33042)

West Sherburne Tribune
29 S Lake St.
PO Box 276
Big Lake, MN 55309
Phone: (612)263-3602
Fax: (612)263-8458

Publications: Clearwater Tribune (15750) • West Sherburne Tribune (15751)

West Side Journal
PO Box 260
Port Allen, LA 70767
Phone: (225)343-2540
Fax: (225)344-0923

Publications: West Side Journal (12799)

West Side Publishing Co.
PO Box 5027
Salem, OR 97304
Publications: West Side (26574)

West Springfield Record, Inc.
516 Main St.
PO Box 357
West Springfield, MA 01090
Phone: (413)736-1587
Fax: (413)739-2477
Publications: West Springfield Record (14625)

West Texas Want Ads, Inc.
2903 N 3rd
Abilene, TX 79603
Phone: (915)673-4521
Fax: (915)673-4525
Publications: Thrifty Nickel Want Ads (29655)

West Valley College
14000 Fruitvale
Saratoga, CA 95070-5697
Phone: (408)867-2200
Fax: (408)867-5033
Publications: Norseman (3745)

West Valley Courier
PO Box 588
Hillsboro, OR 97123
Phone: (503)648-1131
Fax: (503)648-9191
Publications: West Valley Courier (26374)

West Valley View
200 W. Wigwam Blvd.
Litchfield Park, AZ 85340-4636
Phone: (623)535-VIEW
Fax: (623)935-2103
Publications: West Valley View (742)

West View Publications
Site 15 C 5 RR 6
Vernon, BC, Canada V1T 6Y5
Fax: (604)549-7099
Publications: Equinews (35200)

West Virginia Coal Association
PO Box 3923
Charleston, WV 25339
Phone: (304)342-4153
Fax: (304)342-7651
Publications: West Virginia Coal Facts (33274)

West Virginia Daily News
PO Box 471
Lewisburg, WV 24901
Phone: (304)645-1206
Fax: (304)645-7104
Publications: West Virginia Daily News (33367)

West Virginia Dental Association
2003 Quarrier St.
Charleston, WV 25311-2212
Phone: (304)344-5246
Fax: (304)344-5316
Publications: West Virginia Dental Journal (33276)

West Virginia Division of Culture and History
1900 Kanawha Blvd. E
Charleston, WV 25305-0300
Phone: (304)558-0220
Fax: (304)558-2779
Publications: Goldenseal (33270)

West Virginia Division of Natural Resources
State Capitol Complex
1900 Kanawha Blvd. E.
Bldg. 3, Rm. 662
Charleston, WV 25305-0312
Phone: (304)558-3315
Fax: (304)558-2768
Free: 800-225-5982
Publications: Wonderful West Virginia (33281)

West Virginia Hillbilly
407 Jackson St.
Minerva, OH 44657-1319

Publications: West Virginia Hillbilly (25393)

West Virginia Nurses Association
PO Box 1946
Charleston, WV 25327
Phone: (304)342-1169
Fax: (304)342-6973
Publications: West Virginia Nurse (33279)

West Virginia Pharmacists Association
2003 Quarrier St.
Charleston, WV 25311
Phone: (304)344-5302
Fax: (304)344-5316
Publications: West Virginia Pharmacists Association (33280)

The West Virginia State Bar
2006 Kanawha Blvd., E.
Charleston, WV 25311-2204
Phone: (304)558-2456
Fax: (304)558-2467
Publications: The West Virginia Lawyer (33277)

West Virginia State Medical Association
PO Box 4106
Charleston, WV 25364
Phone: (304)925-0342
Fax: (304)925-0345
Free: 800-257-4747
Publications: West Virginia Medical Journal (33278)

West Virginia University
Department of English
PO Box 6296
Morgantown, WV 26506
Phone: (304)293-3107
Fax: (304)293-5380
Free: (304)293-3107
Publications: Victorian Poetry (33397)

West Virginia University
PO Box 6690
Morgantown, WV 26506-6690
Phone: (304)293-6368
Fax: (304)293-4762
Publications: West Virginia University Alumni Magazine (33398)

West Virginia University
P.O. Box 6298
Morgantown, WV 26506
Phone: (304)293-5121
Fax: (304)293-7655
Publications: West Virginia University Philological Papers (33399)

West Virginia University
284 Prospect St.
Morgantown, WV 26506
Phone: (304)293-4141
Fax: (304)293-6857
Publications: The Daily Athenaeum (33392)

West Virginia University Institute of Technology
PO Box 1 Old Main
Montgomery, WV 25136
Phone: (304)442-3180
Fax: (304)442-3464
Publications: Tech Collegian (33387)

West Virginia University Press
44 Stansbury Hall
PO Box 6295
Morgantown, WV 26506
Phone: (304)293-8400
Fax: (304)293-5380
Publications: Labor Studies Journal (12171)

West Virginia Wesleyan College
59 College Ave.
Buckhannon, WV 26201-2997
Phone: (304)473-8234
Publications: Communication Quarterly (5270)

West Winfield Star
PO Box 6
West Winfield, NY 13491
Phone: (315)822-3001
Publications: Star (23550)

West World Productions
420 N Camden Dr.
Beverly Hills, CA 90210
Phone: (310)276-9500
Fax: (310)246-1405
Publications: Computer Technology Review (1571)

The Westborough News
10 E Main St.
Westborough, MA 01581
Phone: (508)366-1511
Fax: (508)366-5265
Publications: The Westborough News (14639)

Westbrook Sentinel & Tribune
621 1st Ave.
PO Box 98
Westbrook, MN 56183
Phone: (507)274-6136
Fax: (507)274-6137
Publications: Westbrook Sentinel & Tribune (16507)

Westchester Country Club
99 Biltmore Ave.
Rye, NY 10580
Phone: (914)967-6000
Fax: (914)967-3429
Publications: Westchester Country Club News (23281)

Westchester County Historical Society
2199 Saw Mill River Rd.
Elmsford, NY 10523
Phone: (914)592-4323
Fax: (914)231-1515
Publications: Westchester Historian (20585)

Westchester-Rockland Newspapers
1 Gannett Dr.
White Plains, NY 10604-3406
Phone: (914)694-9300
Fax: (914)694-5150
Publications: The Item (23571) • Mamaroneck Daily Times (20986) • New Rochelle Standard-Star (21120) • Patent Trader (21099) • Review Press (20293) • The Star (23088)

Westchester Spotlight
100 Clearbrook Rd.
Elmsford, NY 10523-1116
Phone: (914)381-4740
Fax: (914)381-4641
Publications: Westchester Spotlight (20586)

Westerly News
1701 Peninsula Rd.
Box 317
Ucluelet, BC, Canada V0R 3A0
Phone: (604)726-7029
Fax: (604)726-4282
Publications: The Westerly News (35117)

Western Academic Press
PO Box 620760
Littleton, CO 80162
Phone: (303)904-4750
Fax: (303)978-0413
Publications: International Business & Economics Research Journal (4548) • Review of Business Information Systems (4554)

Western Agricultural Economics Association
Dept. of Agriculture & Resource Economics
Colorado State University
Fort Collins, CO 80523-1172
Phone: (970)491-7220
Fax: (970)491-2067
Publications: Journal of Agricultural & Resource Economics (4434)

Western Agricultural Publishing Co., Inc.
4969 E Clinton Way, No. 104
Fresno, CA 93727-1549
Phone: (559)252-7000
Fax: (559)252-7387
Free: 888-382-9772
Publications: Agribusiness Fieldman (1941) • California-Arizona Texas Cotton (1945) • Citrograph (1948) • Grape Grower Magazine (1951) • Nut Grower (1953) • Tree Fruit (1957) • Vegetable (1958)

Western Breeze
3 E Main St.
Cut Bank, MT 59427-2917
Phone: (406)873-4128
Fax: (406)873-4129

Publications: Western Breeze (17779)

Western Builder
400 S Executive Dr., Ste. 201
Brookfield, WI 53005
Phone: (262)797-2522
Fax: (262)782-5477

Publications: Western Builder (33606)

Western Carolina Publishing Co., Inc.
119 W. Water St.
PO Box 40
Lincolnton, NC 28093
Phone: (704)735-3031
Fax: (704)735-3037

Publications: Lincoln Times-News (24045)

Western Carolina University
PO Box 66
Cullowhee, NC 28723-0066
Phone: (704)227-7267

Publications: The Western Carolinian (23795)

Western Communications
Box 46
Hermiston, OR 97838
Phone: (503)567-6457
Fax: (503)567-4125

Publications: The Hermiston Herald (26369)

Western Communications, Inc.
1777 SW Chandler Ave.
PO Box 6020
Bend, OR 97708
Phone: (541)382-1181
Fax: (541)385-5802

Publications: Baker City Herald (26232) • The Bulletin (26241) • Curry Coastal Pilot (26255) • The Observer (26399)

Western Council of Industrial Workers, AFL-CIO
12788 SE Stark St.
Portland, OR 97233-1539
Phone: (503)251-1980
Fax: (503)228-0245

Publications: The Union Register (26513)

Western Economic Association Intl.
7400 Center Ave., Ste. 109
Huntington Beach, CA 92647-3039
Phone: (714)898-3222
Fax: (714)891-6715

Publications: Contemporary Economic Policy (30039) • Economic Inquiry (2061)

Western Fairs Association
1776 Tribute, No. 210
Sacramento, CA 95815-4410
Phone: (916)927-3100
Fax: (916)927-6397

Publications: Fair Dealer (2999)

Western Field Ornithologists
1359 Solano Dr.
Pacifica, CA 94044-4258
Phone: (650)359-2068
Fax: (209)797-9388

Publications: Western Birds (2741)

Western Fraternal Life Association (WFLA)
1900 1st Ave. NE
Cedar Rapids, IA 52402
Phone: (319)363-2653
Fax: (319)363-8806

Publications: Fraternal Herald (10673)

Western Guard
PO Box 183
Madison, MN 56256-0183
Phone: (320)598-7521

Publications: Western Guard (16020)

Western History Association
Utah State University
0740 Old Main Hill
Logan, UT 84322-0740
Phone: (435)797-1301
Fax: (435)797-3899

Publications: Western Historical Quarterly (31355)

Western Horseman
PO Box 7980
Colorado Springs, CO 80933
Phone: (719)633-5524
Fax: (719)633-1392
Free: 800-874-6774

Publications: Western Horseman (4261)

Western Illinois University
Board of Trustees
1 University Circle
Macomb, IL 61455-1390

Publications: Journal of Elementary Science Education (9129)

Western Illinois University
1 University Circle
PO Box 6009
Macomb, IL 61455-1330
Phone: (309)298-1876
Fax: (309)298-2309

Publications: Western Courier (9133)

Western Kansas World
PO Box 218
205 Main St.
Wa Keeney, KS 67672
Phone: (785)743-2155
Fax: (785)743-5340

Publications: Western Kansas World (11859)

Western Kentucky University
122 Garrett Center
Bowling Green, KY 42101
Phone: (270)745-2653
Fax: (270)745-2697

Publications: College Heights Herald (11941)

Western Literature Association
3200 Old Main Hill
Utah State University
Logan, UT 84322-3200
Phone: (435)797-1603
Fax: (435)797-4099

Publications: Western American Literature (31354)

Western Livestock Reporter
18th & Minnesota
PO Box 30758
Billings, MT 59107
Phone: (406)259-5406
Fax: (406)259-6888

Publications: Western Livestock Reporter (17734)

Western Michigan University
1903 W. Michigan Ave.
Kalamazoo, MI 49008-5331
Phone: (269)387-2567
Fax: (269)387-2562

Publications: Comparative Drama (15234) • Medieval Prosopography at Medieval Institute Publications (15243) • Western Herald (15246)

Western Michigan University
1903 West Michigan Ave.
Kalamazoo, MI 49008-5200
Phone: (269)387-8400
Fax: (269)387-8422

Publications: WMU, The Magazine (15247)

Western Michigan University
Kalamazoo, MI 49008
Phone: (269)387-3470
Fax: (269)387-6272

Publications: Reading Horizons (15244)

Western Nebraska Observer
118 E 2nd St.
Kimball, NE 69145-0700
Phone: (308)235-3631
Fax: (308)235-3632

Publications: Western Nebraska Observer (18068)

Western New York Catholic
795 Main St.
Buffalo, NY 14203
Phone: (716)847-8719
Fax: (716)847-8722

Publications: Western New York Catholic (20392)

Western News
311 California Ave.
PO Box 1377
Libby, MT 59923
Phone: (406)293-4124
Fax: (406)293-7187

Publications: Western News (17852)

Western Newspapers, Inc.
116 S. Main St.
Cottonwood, AZ 86326
Phone: (520)634-2241
Fax: (520)634-2312
Free: 800-647-9565

Publications: Verde Independent (680)

Western Newspapers, Inc.
417 W. Santa Fe Ave.
Flagstaff, AZ 86001
Phone: (928)226-9696
Fax: (928)226-1115
Free: 877-627-3787

Publications: Canyon Shopper (695) • Navajo-Hopi Observer (698)

Western Newspapers, Inc.
3015 Stockton Hill Rd.
Kingman, AZ 86401
Phone: (928)753-6397
Fax: (928)753-5661

Publications: Kingman Daily Miner (729) • The Prospector (731)

Western Newspapers, Inc.
PO Box 312
Prescott, AZ 86302
Phone: (602)445-6020
Fax: (602)445-4756

Publications: Chino Valley Review (846) • Prescott Valley Tribune (849)

Western Outdoors Publications
3197-E Airport Loop Dr.
Costa Mesa, CA 92626
Phone: (714)546-4370
Fax: (714)662-3486

Publications: Western Outdoors (2637)

Western Pennsylvania Newspaper Co.
645 Main St.
PO Box 647
Clarion, PA 16214-1137
Phone: (814)226-7000
Fax: (814)226-7518

Publications: Clarion News (26780)

The Western Producer
2310 Millar Ave.
PO Box 2500
Saskatoon, SK, Canada S7K 2C4
Phone: (306)665-3500
Fax: (306)665-4961

Publications: The Western Producer (37560)

Western Publishing Co.
PO Box 599
Lexington, NE 68850
Phone: (308)324-5511
Fax: (308)324-5240
Free: 800-639-7039

Publications: Clipper-Herald (18072) • North Platte Telegraph (18176)

Western Recorder, Inc.
PO Box 43969
Louisville, KY 40253
Phone: (502)244-6470
Fax: (502)244-6474

Publications: Western Recorder (12297)

Western Retail Implement and Hardware Association
PO Box 419264
Kansas City, MO 64141
Phone: (816)561-5323
Fax: (816)561-1249
Free: 800-762-5616

Publications: Southwestern Retailer (17197)

Western Sky Communications Ltd.
301-68 E. 2nd Ave.
Vancouver, BC, Canada V5T 1B1
Phone: (604)689-1520
Fax: (604)689-1525

Publications: The Jewish Western Bulletin (35151)

Western Slope Publishing Group
POB 1150
Carbondale, CO 81623-1150

Publications: The Valley Journal (4218)

Western Society of Engineers
28 E Jackson Blvd.
Chicago, IL 60604
Phone: (312)913-1730
Fax: (312)913-1731

Publications: Midwest Engineer (8489)

The Western Star
113 S Central
PO Box 518
Coldwater, KS 67029
Phone: (316)582-2101

Publications: The Western Star (11394)

The Western Star
106 West St.
PO Box 460
Corner Brook, NL, Canada A2H 6E7
Phone: (709)634-4348
Fax: (709)634-9824
Free: 800-454-4348

Publications: The Western Star (35447)

Western Star
200 Harmon Ave.
PO Box 29
Lebanon, OH 45036
Phone: (513)932-3010
Fax: (513)932-6056

Publications: Western Star (25295)

Western States Communication Association
California State University
Fresno, CA 93740-8027
Fax: (209)278-6616

Publications: Western Journal of Communication (1960)

Western States Jewish History Association
22711 Cass Ave.
Woodland Hills, CA 91364
Phone: (818)225-9631
Fax: (818)225-8354

Publications: Western States Jewish History (4117)

Western States Publishers, Inc.
PO Box 17869
Fountain Hills, AZ 85269-7869
Phone: (480)837-1925
Fax: (480)837-1951

Publications: The Fountain Hills Times (711)

Western States Weeklies, Inc.
6312 Riverdale St.
San Diego, CA 92160-0600
Phone: (619)280-2985

Publications: San Diego Navy Dispatch (3266)

Western Texas College
6200 S College Ave.
Snyder, TX 79549
Phone: (915)573-8511
Fax: (915)573-9321

Publications: The Western Texan (31115)

Western Viking, Inc.
PO Box 70408
Seattle, WA 98107
Phone: (206)784-4617
Fax: (206)784-4856

Publications: Western Viking (33043)

Western Washington University
Viking Union 211
516 High St
Bellingham, WA 98225
Phone: (360)650-3000
Fax: (360)650-7775

Publications: The Western Front (32679)

Western Wheel Publishing
9 McRae St.
Bag 9
Okotoks, AB, Canada T0L 1T0
Phone: (403)938-6397
Fax: (403)938-2518

Publications: Okotoks Western Wheel (34818)

Western Wood Products Association
522 S.W. 5th Ave., Ste. 500
Portland, OR 97204-2122
Phone: (503)224-3930
Fax: (503)224-3934

Publications: Export Report (26477) • Injury and Illness Incidence (26482) • Monthly F.O.B. Price Summary, Past Sales (Coast Mills) (26485) • Monthly F.O.B. Price Summary, Past Sales (Inland Mills) (26486) • Western Lumber Facts (26514)

Western World Enterprises
PO Box 248
Bandon, OR 97411-0248
Phone: (541)347-2423
Fax: (541)347-2424

Publications: Western World (26236)

Westerns and Serials Fan Club
527 S Front St.
Mankato, MN 56001-3718
Phone: (507)549-3677
Fax: (507)549-3788

Publications: Favorite Westerns & Serial World (16025)

Westfield Leader
50 Elm St.
Westfield, NJ 07090
Phone: (908)232-4407
Fax: (908)232-0473

Publications: The Times of Scotch Plains-Fanwood (19746) • The Westfield Leader (19747)

Westfield News Advertiser, Inc.
62 School St., No. 64
Westfield, MA 01085-2835
Phone: (413)568-4921
Fax: (413)562-4185

Publications: The Longmeadow News (14641) • The Wallace Pennysaver (14642) • The Westfield Evening News (14643)

Westfield State College
PO Box 1630
Westfield, MA 01086
Phone: (413)572-5344
Fax: (413)562-3613

Publications: Historical Journal of Massachusetts (14640)

Westlock News
PO Box 40
Westlock, AB, Canada T0G 2L0
Phone: (403)349-3033
Fax: (403)349-3677

Publications: Westlock News (34871)

Westminister
PO Box 428
Westminster, CA 92684
Phone: (714)893-4501
Fax: (714)893-4502

Publications: Westminister Herald (4076)

Westminster College
319 S. Market St.
New Wilmington, PA 16142

Publications: Westminster College Magazine (27324)

Westminster College
1840 South 1300 East
Salt Lake City, UT 84105
Phone: (801)832-2319
Fax: (801)466-6916

Publications: The Forum (31427)

Westminster Publications, Inc.
708 Glen Cove Ave.
Glen Head, NY 11545
Phone: (516)759-0025
Fax: (516)759-5524

Publications: Angiology (20661) • Clinical Pediatrics (20662) • International Journal of Surgical Pathology (20663) • Trends in Amplification (20664) • Vascular and Endovscular Surgery (20665)

The Westmont Examiner
210 Victoria Ave.
Westmount, QC, Canada H3Z 2M4
Phone: (514)484-5610
Fax: (514)484-6028

Publications: The Westmount Examiner (37446)

Westmore News
38 Broad St.
Port Chester, NY 10573-4197
Phone: (914)939-6864
Fax: (914)939-6877

Publications: Westmore News (23115)

Westmoreland Recorder
Box 128
Westmoreland, KS 66549-0128
Phone: (785)457-3411
Fax: (785)457-3411

Publications: Westmoreland Recorder (11870)

Westmount Press
13343 20th Ave.
PO Box 1019
Blairmore, AB, Canada T0K 0E0
Phone: (403)562-8884
Fax: (403)562-2242

Publications: The Crowsnest Pass Promoter (34618)

Westmount Press, Ltd.
PO Box 2250
Strathmore, AB, Canada T1P 1K2
Phone: (403)934-3021
Fax: (403)934-5011

Publications: The Strathmore Standard (34858)

Weston County Gazette
PO Box 526
722 2nd St
Upton, WY 82730
Phone: (307)468-2642
Fax: (307)468-2642
Free: 888-648-7513

Publications: Weston County Gazette (34600)

The Weston Democrat
Box 968
Weston, WV 26452
Phone: (304)269-1600
Fax: (304)269-4035

Publications: The Weston Democrat (33497)

Westside Gazette
PO Box 5304
Fort Lauderdale, FL 33310
Phone: (954)523-5115
Fax: (954)522-2553
Free: 800-371-6310

Publications: Westside Gazette (6088)

Westside News
1835 N. Union St.
PO Box 106
Spencerport, NY 14559
Phone: (585)352-3411
Fax: (585)352-4811

Publications: Hamlin Clarkson Herald (23350) • Suburban News (North Edition) (23351) • Suburban News (South Edition) (23352) • Suburban News West (23353)

WESTVIEW
8120 Sawyer Brown Rd., ste.107
PO Box 210183
Nashville, TN 37221
Phone: (615)646-6131
Fax: (615)662-0946

Publications: WESTVIEW (29502)

Westville Indicator
Box 828
Westville, IN 46391
Phone: (219)785-2234
Fax: (219)785-2242

Publications: Westville Indicator (10561)

Westward Communications
PO Box 1628
Cleveland, TX 77327
Phone: (713)592-2626
Fax: (713)592-2629

Publications: Cleveland Advocate (30028) • Eastex News-Shopper (30029) • Spring Observer (30030)

Westward Communications
907 B Main St.
Humble, TX 77347
Phone: (281)448-5929

Publications: The Lindale News (30693)

Westward Communications
112 Quitman St.
Pittsburg, TX 75686
Phone: (903)856-6629
Fax: (903)856-0510
Free: 800-256-1679

Publications: The Pittsburg Gazette (30936)

Westward Communications LLC
305 S. Congress Ave.
Austin, TX 78704
Phone: (512)445-3500

Publications: The Bastrop Advertiser (29890) • Westlake Picayune (29854)

Westward Communications, L.L.C.
1129 Kingwood Dr.
Kingwood, TX 77339
Phone: (281)359-2799
Fax: (281)359-0017

Publications: Observer Newspapers (30651)

Westward Publications
PO Box 210
Mineola, TX 75773
Phone: (903)569-2047
Fax: (903)569-9201

Publications: Mineola Monitor (30830)

Westwind Publishing
PO Box J
Eldorado Springs, CO 80025-0028
Phone: (303)499-3228
Fax: (303)499-3494

Publications: Rocky Mountain Gardener (4411)

Westwood Press, Inc.
118 Five Mile River Rd.
Darien, CT 06820
Phone: (203)656-8680

Publications: International Journal of Instructional Media (IJIM) (5176)

Westwood Publishing
PO Box 308
Quitman, TX 75783
Phone: (903)763-4522
Fax: (903)763-2313

Publications: Wood County Democrat (30968)

WETA Publishing
2775 S. Quincy St.
Arlington, VA 22206-2236

Publications: WETA Magazine (31841)

The Wetumpka Herald, Inc.
300 Green St.
PO Box 99
Wetumpka, AL 36092-0099
Phone: (334)567-7811
Fax: (334)567-3284

Publications: The Wetumpka Herald (515)

Wetzel Tyler Newspapers
PO Box 289
New Martinsville, WV 26155
Phone: (304)455-3300
Fax: (304)455-1275

Publications: Wetzel Chronicle (33413)

Wewoka Daily Times
210 S Wewoka
PO Box 61
Wewoka, OK 74884
Phone: (405)257-3341
Fax: (405)257-3342

Publications: Wewoka Daily Times (26194)

Weyburn Review
Box 400
904 East Ave.
Weyburn, SK, Canada S4H 2K4
Phone: (306)842-7487
Fax: (306)842-0282

Publications: Booster (37589) • Weyburn Review (37591)

WFC, Inc.
3000 Hadley Rd.
South Plainfield, NJ 07080-1117
Phone: (908)769-1160
Fax: (908)769-1171

Publications: Imprinting Business (19589) • Whole Foods (19591)

WFM, Inc.
4215 White Bear Pkwy., Ste. 100
St. Paul, MN 55110
Phone: (651)762-2046
Fax: (651)762-2035

Publications: Gaming Products and Services (16377)

W.H. White Publications
Box 278
Hastings on Hudson, NY 10706
Phone: (914)478-2787
Fax: (914)478-2863

Publications: The Enterprise (20716)

W.H.A. Publications Ltd.
180 St. Andrews St. E.
PO Box 252
Fergus, ON, Canada N1M 2W8
Phone: (519)843-5410
Fax: (519)843-7607

Publications: The Wellington Advertiser (35830)

What Cheer
PO Box 414
What Cheer, IA 50268
Phone: (641)634-2092
Fax: (641)634-2122

Publications: What Cheer Paper (11327)

Whatcom County Farm Review
PO Box 153
Lynden, WA 98264
Phone: (360)354-4444
Fax: (360)354-4445

Publications: Lynden Tribune (32821)

What's Happening, Inc.
1251 Lincoln
Eugene, OR 97401
Phone: (541)484-0519
Fax: (541)484-4044

Publications: Eugene Weekly (26316)

What's On, The Las Vegas Guide
4425 Industrial Rd.
Las Vegas, NV 89103
Phone: (702)891-8811
Fax: (702)891-8804
Free: 800-494-2876

Publications: What's On, The Las Vegas Guide (18385)

Wheatley Journal
14 Talbot St. W.
PO Box 10
Wheatley, ON, Canada N0P 2P0
Phone: (519)825-4541
Fax: (519)825-4546

Publications: Wheatley Journal (36872)

Wheaton College
Norton, MA 02766
Phone: (508)285-7722
Fax: (508)286-3821

Publications: Wheaton Wire (14438)

Wheaton Gazette
1114 Broadway
Wheaton, MN 56296
Phone: (320)563-8146
Fax: (320)563-8147

Publications: Wheaton Gazette (16508)

The Wheaton Journal
PO Box 486
Cassville, MO 65625-0486

Publications: Wheaton Journal (16967)

Wheel Beers
PO Box 263
2734 Broadway
Slayton, MN 56172
Phone: (507)836-8726
Fax: (507)836-8942

Publications: Murray County Wheel/Herald (16449)

The Wheeler County Eagle
PO Box 409
Alamo, GA 30411-0409
Phone: (912)529-6624
Fax: (912)529-5399

Publications: The Wheeler County Eagle (6901)

Wheeler Times
PO Box 1080
Wheeler, TX 79096
Phone: (806)826-3123
Fax: (806)826-3123

Publications: Times (31287)

Wheelers Publishing Co.
2015 Yellowknife Rd.
Yucca Valley, CA 92284
Phone: (619)364-4317

Publications: Wheelers (4129)

WHERE Halifax
5475 Spring Garden Rd., Ste. 305
Box 14
Halifax, NS, Canada B3J 3T2
Phone: (902)420-9943
Fax: (902)429-9058

Publications: WHERE Halifax (35572)

Where Vancouver, Inc.
The Sixth Estate
2208 Spruce St.
Vancouver, BC, Canada V6H 2P3
Phone: (604)736-5586
Fax: (604)736-3465

Publications: WHERE Vancouver (35182)

Whig - Standard
306 King St. E.
PO Box 2300
Kingston, ON, Canada K7L 4Z7
Phone: (613)544-5000
Fax: (613)544-6944

Publications: Whig-Standard (35948)

Whipple Printing Company Ltd.
102 N Jefferson
PO Box 140
Kearney, MO 64060-0140
Phone: (816)628-6010
Fax: (816)628-4422

Publications: The Kearney Courier (17216)

The Whit
201 Mullica Hill Rd.
Glassboro, NJ 08028
Phone: (609)256-4530
Fax: (609)256-4929

Publications: The Whit (18844)

White County Historical Society
PO Box 537
Searcy, AR 72145

Publications: White County Heritage (1339)

The White Deer News
206 S Main St.
PO Box 728
White Deer, TX 79097
Phone: (806)883-4881
Fax: (806)883-4881

Publications: White Deer News (31289)

White Hat Communications
PO Box 5390
Harrisburg, PA 17110-0390
Phone: (717)238-3787
Fax: (717)238-2090

Publications: The New Social Worker (27000)

White Lake Beacon
PO Box 98
Whitehall, MI 49461
Phone: (616)894-5356
Fax: (616)894-2174

Publications: White Lake Beacon (15684)

White Mountain Publishing Co.
3191 S. White Mountain Rd., Ste. 4
PO Box 1570
Show Low, AZ 85902-1570
Phone: (928)537-5721
Fax: (928)537-1780

Publications: White Mountain Independent (881)

White Publishing Co.
534 Lancaster St.
Jacksonville, FL 32204-4113
Phone: (904)396-8666
Fax: (904)396-0926

Publications: Jacksonville Magazine (6214)

White Rocker
10809 Garland Rd.
PO Box 180698
Dallas, TX 75218
Phone: (214)327-9335
Fax: (214)327-9374

Publications: The White Rocker (30189)

The White Tops
70 Dublin Ave.
Nashua, NH 03063
Phone: (603)883-9405
Fax: (603)883-0604

Publications: The White Tops (18604)

White Urp Publishing
5360 Fallriver Row Ct.
Columbia, MD 21044
Phone: (410)730-4272

Publications: Abbey (13450)

White Wing Publishing House
WingNet Internet Services
PO Box 2605
Cleveland, TN 37320-2605

Publications: White Wing Messenger (29123)

Whitehall Times
PO Box 330
Granville, NY 12832-0333
Phone: (518)642-1234
Fax: (518)642-1344

Publications: Whitehall Times (20683)

Whitehall Times Inc.
36435 Main St.
Whitehall, WI 54773
Phone: (715)538-4765
Fax: (715)538-4540

Publications: Tri-County Tab (34453) • Whitehall Times (34454)

Whitehead Enterprises, Inc.
618 N Main
PO Box 475
Rusk, TX 75785
Phone: (903)683-2257
Fax: (903)683-5104

Publications: Cherokeean/Herald (30999)

Whitehorse Star (1977) Ltd.
2149 2nd Ave.
Whitehorse, YT, Canada Y1A 1C5
Fax: (867)668-7130

Publications: The Whitehorse Star (37605)

Whitesboro News-Record
130 E Main
PO Box 68
Whitesboro, TX 76273
Phone: (903)564-3565
Fax: (903)564-9655

Publications: Whitesboro News-Record (31291)

Whitewater Publications Inc.
PO Box 38
Brookville, IN 47012
Phone: (317)647-4221
Fax: (317)647-4811
Free: 888-227-6451

Publications: American (9873) • Democrat (9874)

The Whitewright Sun, Inc.
PO Box 218
Whitewright, TX 75491-0218
Phone: (903)364-2276
Fax: (903)364-2276

Publications: The Whitewright Sun (31292)

Whitley Whiz
105 S. 2nd
Williamsburg, KY 40769-1201
Phone: (606)549-9767
Fax: (859)745-0638

Publications: The Whitley Republican News Journal (12445)

Whitman College
Office of Communications
Walla Walla, WA 99362
Phone: (509)527-5768
Fax: (509)527-4963

Publications: Whitman Academic Journal (33189)

Whitman County Gazette
211 N. Main
PO Box 770
Colfax, WA 99111
Phone: (509)397-4333
Fax: (509)397-4527

Publications: Whitman County Gazette (32720)

Whitney Publishing Co., Inc.
Box 1380
Taos, NM 87571
Phone: (505)758-5404
Fax: (505)758-5404

Publications: Taos Magazine (19962)

Whittier College
Box 8613
Whittier, CA 90608
Phone: (562)907-4254
Fax: (562)945-5301

Publications: Quaker Campus (4079)

Whitworth College
ASWC
Spokane, WA 99251-4302
Phone: (509)777-3248
Fax: (509)777-3710

Publications: Whitworthian (33103)

Whole Notes Press
PO Box 1374
Las Cruces, NM 88004
Phone: (505)541-5744

Publications: Whole Notes (19878)

The Whole Shebang!
PO Box 1407
Coos Bay, OR 97420
Phone: (541)269-9571
Fax: (541)269-9571

Publications: The Whole Shebang! (26273)

Whoot Newspaper
PO Box 1293
Pleasantville, NJ 08232
Phone: (609)646-4848
Fax: (609)646-7338

Publications: Whoot Newspaper (19445)

WHYY, Inc.
150 N. Sixth St.
Philadelphia, PA 19106
Phone: (215)351-1200
Fax: (215)351-0398

Publications: Applause (27381)

The Wiarton Echo
Box 220
573 Berford St.
Wiarton, ON, Canada N0H 2T0
Phone: (519)534-1560
Fax: (519)534-4616

Publications: The Wiarton Echo (36874)

The Wibaux Pioneer-Gazette
120 S Wibaux St.
Wibaux, MT 59353
Phone: (406)796-2218
Fax: (406)796-2218

Publications: The Wibaux Pioneer-Gazette (17921)

Wicazo Sa Review
111 3rd Ave. S. Ste. 290
Minneapolis, MN 55401
Phone: (612)627-1970
Fax: (612)627-1980

Publications: Wicazo Sa Review (16290)

Wichita Pennypower News Inc.
650 N. Carraige Pkwy., No. 60
Wichita, KS 67208
Phone: (316)688-6051
Fax: (316)688-6034

Publications: Wichita Pennypower News (11892)

Wichita State University
1845 Fairmount
Wichita, KS 67260-0034
Phone: (316)978-3170
Fax: (316)978-3086

Publications: Multivariate Experimental Clinical Research (11887)

Wichita State University
1845 N. Fairmount
Campus Box 134
Wichita, KS 67208
Phone: (316)978-3644
Fax: (316)978-3778

Publications: The Sunflower (11888)

Wick Communications
333 West Wilcox Dr., Ste. 302
Sierra Vista, AZ 85635
Phone: (520)458-9440
Fax: (520)459-0120

Publications: The Copper Era (886)

Wick Communications
PO Box 9290
New Iberia, LA 70562-9290
Phone: (337)365-6773
Fax: (337)367-9640

Publications: Daily Iberian (12722)

Wick Communications
PO Box 27409
Las Vegas, NV 89126-1409
Phone: (702)871-6780
Fax: (702)871-3298

Publications: Las Vegas Business Press (18371)

Wick Communications
916 Roanoke Ave.
Roanoke Rapids, NC 27870
Phone: (919)537-2505
Fax: (919)537-2314

Publications: Daily Herald (24195)

Wick Communications
107 Main St.
Hankinson, ND 58041
Phone: (701)242-7696
Fax: (701)242-7406

Publications: Richland County News-Monitor (24467)

Wick Communications
1160 SW 4th St.
Ontario, OR 97914
Phone: (541)889-5387
Fax: (541)889-3347

Publications: Argus Observer (26453) • Treasure Valley Reminder (26454)

Wick Communications Co.
333 Wilcox Dr., Ste. 302
Sierra Vista, AZ 85635
Phone: (520)458-0200
Fax: (520)892-5719

Publications: Arizona Range News (1008) • Parker Pioneer (763) • San Pedro Valley News-Sun (658) • The Sidney Herald-Leader (17910)

Wick Communications, Inc.
5751 E Mayflower Ct.
Wasilla, AK 99654-8334
Phone: (907)376-5225
Fax: (907)352-2277

Publications: Frontiersman (649) • Valley Sun (650)

Wick Publishing
301 E Hwy. 70
PO Box N
Safford, AZ 85548
Phone: (520)428-2560
Fax: (520)428-5396

Publications: Eastern Arizona Courier (860)

Wicks
PO Box 327
Jeanerette, LA 70544-0327
Phone: (318)276-5171
Fax: (318)369-9640

Publications: Enterprise (12605)

Wickstrom Publishers
2700 S Kanner Hwy.
Stuart, FL 34994-4815
Phone: (561)219-7400
Fax: (561)219-6900

Publications: Florida Sportsman (6693)

Widener University
Box 7286
Wilmington, DE 19803
Phone: (302)477-2145
Fax: (302)477-2042

Publications: Delaware Journal of Corporate Law (5291)

Widener University
1 University Pl.
Chester, PA 19013-5792
Phone: (610)499-4042
Fax: (610)499-4059

Publications: Journal of Solid Waste Technology and Management (26775)

Widener University
1 University Pl.
PO Box 1175
Chester, PA 19013
Phone: (610)499-4000
Fax: (610)499-4531

Publications: The Dome (26774)

Widescreen Review
27645 Commerce Ctr. Dr.
Temecula, CA 92590-2521
Phone: (909)676-4914
Fax: (909)693-2960
Free: 888-WSR-SUBS

Publications: Widescreen Review (3843)

Wiesenberger
1455 Research Blvd.
Rockville, MD 20850
Phone: (301)545-4000
Fax: (301)545-6400
Free: 800-232-2285

Publications: Mutual Funds Update (13689)

Wiesner Inc.
1100 Johnson Ferry Rd. NE, Ste. 595
Atlanta, GA 30342
Phone: (404)252-6670
Fax: (404)252-6673
Free: 800-264-2456

Publications: Atlanta Homes and Lifestyles (6970)

Wiesner Publishing, LLC
7009 S Potomac St., Ste. 200
Centennial, CO 80112
Phone: (303)397-7600
Fax: (303)397-7619
Free: 888-577-7702

Publications: ColoradoBiz (4223) • Mountain Living (4225) • Trucking Times & Sport Utility News (10663)

The Wilber Republican
206 W 3rd
PO Box 457
Wilber, NE 68465
Phone: (402)821-2586
Fax: (402)821-2586

Publications: The Wilber Republican (18316)

Wilbur Register, Inc.
110 SE Main
PO Box 186
Wilbur, WA 99185
Phone: (509)647-5551
Fax: (509)647-5552

Publications: The Wilbur Register (33207)

Wild Dog
1327 Whispering Ln.
Venice, FL 34292-1449

Publications: Wild Dog (6832)

Wild Duck Review
PO Box 388
Nevada City, CA 95959
Phone: (530)478-0134
Fax: (530)265-2304

Publications: Wild Duck Review (2616)

Wild Raspberry Inc.
207 North Broadway
Billings, MT 59101
Phone: (406)247-5020
Fax: (406)247-5021

Publications: The Billings Outpost (17730)

Wildlife Conservation
2300 Southern Blvd.
Bronx, NY 10460
Phone: (718)220-5121
Fax: (718)584-2625

Publications: Wildlife Conservation (20290)

Wildlife Harvest Publications
PO Box 96
Goose Lake, IA 52750
Phone: (563)259-4000
Fax: (563)259-4483

Publications: Wildlife Harvest (10926)

Wilen Media Corp.
5 Wellwood Ave.
Farmingdale, NY 11735-1213
Phone: (631)439-5000
Fax: (631)439-4536

Publications: TV Blueprint (20597)

John Wiley & Sons Inc.
111 River St.
Hoboken, NJ 07030-5773
Phone: (201)748-6000
Free: 800-255-5945

Publications: Systems Research and Behavioral Science (19116)

Wilfrid Laurier University Press
Waterloo, ON, Canada N2L 3C5
Phone: (519)884-0710
Fax: (519)725-1399

Publications: Leisure/Loisir (36855)

Wilfrid Laurier University Student Publications
Fred Nichols Campus Centre, 3rd Fl.
75 University Ave. W.
Waterloo, ON, Canada N2L 3C5
Phone: (519)884-0710
Fax: (519)883-0873

Publications: The Cord (36849)

Wilhelm Reich Infant Trust, Orgonon
PO Box 687
Rangeley, ME 04970
Phone: (207)864-3443
Fax: (207)864-5156

Publications: Orgonomic Functionalism (13043)

Wilk-Amite Record
111 Main St.
Meadville, MS 39653
Phone: (601)384-2484
Fax: (601)384-2276

Publications: Wilk-Amite Record (16767)

Wilkes University
PO Box 111
Wilkes Barre, PA 18766
Phone: (570)408-4000
Fax: (570)831-5902
Free: 800-945-5378

Publications: Beacon (28163)

Wilkinson County News
Box 205
Irwinton, GA 31042
Phone: (478)946-2218
Fax: (478)946-2218

Publications: Wilkinson County News (7307)

Willamette Week
822 SW 10th
Portland, OR 97205
Phone: (503)243-2122
Fax: (503)243-1115

Publications: Willamette Week (26515)

The Willapa Harbor Herald
PO Box 706
Raymond, WA 98577
Phone: (360)942-3466
Fax: (360)942-3487

Publications: The Willapa Harbor Herald (32922)

Willard Times Junction
211 Myrtle Ave.
PO Box 368
Willard, OH 44890
Phone: (419)935-0184
Fax: (419)933-2031

Publications: Willard Times Junction (25654)

William B. Collins Co.
8-10 E Fulton St.
Gloversville, NY 12078-3283
Phone: (518)725-8616
Fax: (518)725-8616

Publications: The Leader-Herald (20671)

William Carlos Williams Society
PAR 108
Dept. of English
University of Texas at Austin
Austin, TX 78712-1164
Phone: (512)471-7842
Fax: (512)471-4909

Publications: William Carlos Williams Review (29855)

William J. Kline and Son, Inc.
1 Venner Rd.
Amsterdam, NY 12010
Phone: (518)548-6898
Fax: (518)548-5305
Free: 800-453-6397

Publications: Hamilton County News (20055)

William Rainey Harper College
1200 W Algonquin Rd.
Palatine, IL 60067

Publications: Harbinger (9394)

William Woods University
One University Ave.
Fulton, MO 65251
Phone: (573)592-4391
Fax: (573)592-1623

Publications: Echoes from the Woods (17075)

Williams College
SU Box 1018
Williamstown, MA 01267
Phone: (413)597-2289
Fax: (413)597-2450

Publications: The Williams Record (14661)

Numbers cited after listings are entry numbers rather than page numbers.

Williams and Crue
4 Queen St.
Box 2480
Summerside, PE, Canada C1N 4K5
Phone: (902)436-2121

Publications: The First Informer (36923)

Williams-Grand Canyon News
118 S 3rd St.
PO Box 667
Williams, AZ 86046-0667
Phone: (928)635-4426
Fax: (520)635-4887
Free: 800-408-4726

Publications: Williams-Grand Canyon News (1010)

Williamson County Sun, Inc.
Box 39
Georgetown, TX 78627-0039
Phone: (512)930-4824

Publications: Sun Advertiser (30391) • Sunday Sun (30392) • Williamson County Sun (30393)

Williamson Daily News
PO Box 1660
Williamson, WV 25661
Phone: (304)235-4242
Fax: (304)235-0730

Publications: News (33512) • Williamson Sun and Sentinel (33513)

Willis Publishing Co.
PO Box 369
Percy, IL 62272
Phone: (618)497-8272
Fax: (618)497-2607

Publications: The County Journal (9445)

Williston Daily Herald
PO Box 1447
Williston, ND 58801
Phone: (701)572-2165
Fax: (701)572-1965
Free: 800-950-2165

Publications: Williston Daily Herald (24560)

Williston Sun-Suwannee Valley News
PO Box Q
Williston, FL 32696
Phone: (352)528-6397

Publications: Williston Sun-Suwannee Valley News (6863)

The Willits News
77 W Commercial
PO Box 628
Willits, CA 95490
Phone: (707)459-4643
Fax: (707)459-1664

Publications: The Willits News (4083)

Bill Willroth
201 W Cherry St.
PO Box 256
Vermillion, SD 57069-1109
Phone: (605)624-2695
Fax: (605)624-2696

Publications: Plain Talk (29005) • Wakonda Times (29015)

Carol Willsey Bell
10460 N. Palmyra Rd.
North Jackson, OH 44451-9793
Phone: (330)538-2046

Publications: Bushong Bulletin (25436)

The Wilmington Journal
412 S 7th St.
PO Box 1020
Wilmington, NC 28401-1020
Phone: (910)762-5502
Fax: (910)343-1334

Publications: The Wilmington Journal (24297)

Wilmington Media Co.
25 N. Kerr Ave.
Wilmington, NC 28405
Phone: (910)791-0688
Fax: (910)791-9534
Free: 800-571-7304

Publications: The AD-PAK (Wilmington Edition) (24294) • The Rutherford Courier (29605) • Savannah Pennysaver (7537)

Wilmington Star-News
PO Box 840
Wilmington, NC 28402
Phone: (910)343-2000
Fax: (910)343-2227
Free: 800-272-1277

Publications: Wilmington Morning Star (24298)

The Wilmot Enterprise
PO Box 6
Wilmot, SD 57279
Phone: (605)938-4651
Fax: (605)938-4683

Publications: The Wilmot Enterprise (29031)

Wilson County Citizen
Box 330
Fredonia, KS 66736
Phone: (620)378-4415
Fax: (620)378-4688

Publications: Wilson County Citizen (11447)

Wilson County News
1012 C St.
Floresville, TX 78114
Phone: (830)216-4519
Fax: (830)393-3219

Publications: Wilson County News (30319)

Wilson Daily Times, Inc.
2001 Downing St.
PO Box 2447
Wilson, NC 27894
Phone: (252)243-5151
Fax: (252)243-2999

Publications: Wilson Daily Times (24312)

Wilson Internet Services
PO Box 308
Rocklin, CA 95677-0308

Publications: Web Commerce Today (2957) • Web Marketing Today (2958)

Wilson Publications
PO Box 300
Illiopolis, IL 62539
Phone: (217)486-6496

Publications: County Line Observer (9007) • Illiopolis Sentinel (9008)

The Wilson World
113 E Main St.
PO Box 857
Lebanon, TN 37088
Phone: (615)444-6008
Fax: (615)444-6018

Publications: The Wilson World (29321)

Winchester Star
2 N. Kent St.
Winchester, VA 22601
Phone: (540)667-3200
Fax: (540)667-1649
Free: 800-296-8639

Publications: The Winchester Star (32630)

The Winchester Sun
PO Box 4300
Winchester, KY 40392
Phone: (859)744-3123
Fax: (606)745-0638

Publications: The Winchester Sun (12454)

Windham Independent
233 Range Rd.
Windham, NH 03087
Phone: (603)898-7874

Publications: Windham Independent (18653)

Windigo Harbor Media
PO Box 182397
Shelby Township, MI 48318-2397
Phone: (586)612-0279

Publications: The Basenji (15535)

Windows Fashions Magazine
4215 White Bear Pkwy., Ste. 100
St. Paul, MN 55110-7635
Phone: (651)293-1544
Fax: (651)653-4308

Publications: Window Fashions (16418)

Windplayer
PO Box 2750
Malibu, CA 90265
Phone: (310)306-4500
Fax: (310)306-8200
Free: 800-946-3305

Publications: Windplayer (2497)

Windsor Beacon
425 Main St.
Windsor, CO 80550
Phone: (970)686-9646

Publications: Windsor Beacon (4687)

Windsor Press, Inc.
6 N. 3rd St.
PO Box 465
Hamburg, PA 19526
Phone: (610)562-2267
Fax: (610)562-2770
Free: 800-562-5521

Publications: East Penn Valley Merchandiser (26970) • Northern Berks Merchandiser (26972)

The Windsor Star
167 Ferry St.
Windsor, ON, Canada N9A 4M5
Phone: (519)255-5711
Fax: (519)255-5778

Publications: The Windsor Star (36893)

Windsport Publishing
2255 B. Queen, Ste. 3266 E
Toronto, ON, Canada M4E 1G3
Phone: (416)827-5462
Fax: (416)827-0728

Publications: Windsport Magazine (36792)

Windy City Publishing, Inc.
1450 W. Randolph
Chicago, IL 60607
Phone: (312)421-1551
Fax: (312)421-1454

Publications: Windy City Sports Magazine (8607)

Windy City Times
1115 W Belmont 2D
Chicago, IL 60657
Phone: (773)871-7610
Fax: (773)871-7609

Publications: Windy City Times (8608)

Wine Enthusiast Co.
103 Fairview Park Dr.
Elmsford, NY 10523
Phone: (914)345-8463
Fax: (914)592-0105
Free: 800-356-8466

Publications: Wine Enthusiast Magazine (20587)

Wine & Spirits Magazine Inc.
2 W. 32nd St., Ste. 601
New York, NY 10001
Phone: (212)695-4660
Fax: (212)695-2920
Free: 888-695-4660

Publications: Wine & Spirits Magazine (22920)

Wine X Magazine
880 Second St.
Santa Rosa, CA 95404-8557
Phone: (707)545-0992
Free: (866)545-0992

Publications: Wine X Magazine (3736)

Wineberg Publications
7842 N Lincoln Ave.
Skokie, IL 60077
Phone: (847)676-1900
Fax: (847)676-0063
Free: 800-323-1818

Publications: Computer Listing Service's Machinery & Equipment Guide (9603) • Industrial Market Place (9606)

Winfield Beacon & Wayland News
107 E Elm
Box F
Winfield, IA 52659
Phone: (319)257-6813
Fax: (319)257-6902

Publications: Winfield Beacon & Wayland News (11328)

Winfield Daily Courier
201 E. 9th Ave.
Winfield, KS 67156
Phone: (620)221-1050
Fax: (620)221-1101

Publications: Winfield Daily Courier (11910)

The Wingham Advance-Times
5 Diagonal Rd.
PO Box 390
Wingham, ON, Canada N0G 2W0
Phone: (519)357-2320
Fax: (519)357-2900

Publications: The Wingham Advance-Times (36902)

Wingspan
Laramie County Community College
1400 E. College Dr.
Cheyenne, WY 82007
Phone: (307)778-1304
Fax: (307)778-1177

Publications: Wingspan (34497)

Winmill Publishing
PO Box 459
Bellows Falls, VT 05101
Phone: (802)463-9591
Fax: (802)463-9818

Publications: The Bellows Falls Town Crier (31494)

Winner Advocate
PO Box 71
Winner, SD 57580
Phone: (605)842-1481
Fax: (605)842-1979

Publications: Winner Advocate (29032)

The Winnipeg Free Press
1355 Mountain Ave.
Winnipeg, MB, Canada R2X 3B6
Phone: (204)697-7001
Fax: (204)697-7465

Publications: The Winnipeg Free Press (35363)

The Winnipeg Sun
1700 Church Ave.
Winnipeg, MB, Canada R2X 3A2
Phone: (204)632-2768
Fax: (204)697-0759

Publications: Trade and Commerce (35353) • The Winnipeg Sun (35364)

Winnsboro News
PO Box 87
Winnsboro, TX 75494
Phone: (903)342-5247

Publications: The Winnsboro News (31305)

Winona Post
64 E. 2nd St.
PO Box 27
Winona, MN 55987
Phone: (507)452-1262
Fax: (507)454-6409
Free: 800-353-2126

Publications: Winona Post (16528)

Winona State University
Kryzsko Commons
PO Box 5838
Winona, MN 55987
Phone: (507)457-5677
Fax: (507)457-5317

Publications: Winonan (16529)

Winslow Communications LLC
5150 Russell Ave. NW
Seattle, WA 98107
Phone: (206)682-7813
Fax: (206)782-7778

Publications: Bulletin of the King County Medical Society (32952) • The Journal of the Seattle-King County Dental Society (32979)

Winston-Salem Chronicle
617 N. Liberty St.
PO Box 1636
Winston-Salem, NC 27101-2912
Phone: (336)722-8624
Fax: (336)723-9173

Publications: Winston-Salem Chronicle (24323)

Winter Park Publishing Co., Inc.
PO Box 2426
Winter Park, FL 32790-2426
Phone: (407)628-8500

Publications: Winter Park/Maitland Observer (6891)

Winter Publishing Inc.
PO Box 80667
South Dartmouth, MA 02748
Phone: (508)999-0078
Fax: (508)984-4040

Publications: Hair to Stay (14542)

Winters Express
312 Railroad Ave.
Winters, CA 95694-0608
Phone: (530)795-4551

Publications: Winters Express (4094)

The Winthrop News
Box A
Winthrop, IA 50682
Phone: (319)935-3027
Fax: (319)935-3082

Publications: The Winthrop News (11329)

Wire Association International Inc.
1570 Boston Post Rd.
Guilford, CT 06437
Phone: (203)453-2777
Fax: (203)453-8384

Publications: Wire Journal International (4879)

Wired USA
520 3rd St., 4th Fl.
San Francisco, CA 94107-1815
Phone: (415)276-5000
Fax: (415)276-5100
Free: 800-769-4733

Publications: Wired (3463)

Wireless Week
PO Box 266008
Littleton, CO 80163-6008
Phone: (303)393-7449
Fax: (303)399-2034

Publications: Wireless Week (4556)

Wisconsin AIDS/HIV Program
PO Box 2659
Madison, WI 53701
Phone: (608)267-5287
Fax: (608)266-2906

Publications: Wisconsin AIDS Update (33977)

Wisconsin Alumni Association
650 N. Lake St.
Madison, WI 53706
Phone: (608)262-2551
Fax: (608)262-3332
Free: 888-947-2586

Publications: ON WISCONSIN (33967)

Wisconsin Archeological Society
PO Box 1292
Milwaukee, WI 53201
Phone: (414)229-4273
Fax: (414)229-4219

Publications: Wisconsin Archeologist (34108)

Wisconsin Counties Association
22 E. Mifflin St., Ste. 900
Madison, WI 53703-4257
Phone: (608)224-5330
Fax: (608)224-5325
Free: 800-922-1993

Publications: Wisconsin Counties (33980)

Wisconsin Dells Events
PO Box 116
Wisconsin Dells, WI 53965
Phone: (608)254-8327
Fax: (608)254-8328

Publications: Wisconsin Dells Events (34462)

Wisconsin Evangelical Lutheran Synod
2929 N Mayfair Rd.
Milwaukee, WI 53222-4398
Phone: (414)256-3888
Fax: (414)256-3899

Publications: Forward in Christ (34070)

Wisconsin Farm Bureau Federation
PO Box 5550
Madison, WI 53705
Phone: (608)836-5575
Fax: (608)828-5769
Free: 800-261-3276

Publications: Farm Bureau's Rural Route (33937)

Wisconsin Federation of Co-ops
131 W Wilson St., No. 400
Madison, WI 53703-3269
Phone: (608)258-4400
Fax: (608)258-4407

Publications: Wisconsin Energy Cooperative News (33981)

Wisconsin Free Press
PO Box 164
Horicon, WI 53032
Phone: (920)485-2016
Fax: (920)485-4820

Publications: The Horicon Reporter (33793)

Wisconsin Free Press
PO Box 271
Mayville, WI 53050-0271
Phone: (920)387-2211
Fax: (920)387-5515
Free: 800-261-NEWS

Publications: The Mayville News (34032)

Wisconsin Grocers Association
1 S Pinckney Ste 504
Madison, WI 53703
Phone: (608)244-7150
Fax: (608)244-9030

Publications: Wisconsin Grocer (33983)

Wisconsin Historical Society Press
816 State St.
Madison, WI 53706-1488
Phone: (608)264-6461
Fax: (608)264-6486
Free: 800-621-2736

Publications: Wisconsin Magazine of History (33986)

Wisconsin Jewish Chronicle
1360 N Prospect Ave.
Milwaukee, WI 53202
Phone: (414)390-5888
Fax: (414)271-0487

Publications: The Wisconsin Jewish Chronicle (34109)

Wisconsin Law Review
University of Wisconsin Law School
975 Bascom Mall
Madison, WI 53706-1399
Phone: (608)262-5815
Fax: (608)262-5485

Publications: Wisconsin Law Review (33984)

Wisconsin in Motion
9231 W Bonniwell Rd.
Mequon, WI 53097-1901
Fax: (414)255-7939

Publications: Wisconsin in Motion (34044)

Wisconsin Potato and Vegetable Growers Association, Inc.
700 5th Ave.
PO Box 327
Antigo, WI 54409
Phone: (715)623-7683
Fax: (715)623-3176

Publications: The Badger Common'Tater (33532)

Wisconsin Restaurant Association
2801 Fish Hatchery Rd.
Madison, WI 53713-3120
Phone: (608)270-9950
Fax: (608)251-3666
Free: 800-589-3211

Publications: Wisconsin Restaurateur (33989)

Wisconsin Right to Life Inc.
10625 W. North Ave., Ste. LL
Milwaukee, WI 53226-2331
Phone: (414)778-5780
Fax: (414)778-5785
Free: 877-855-5007

Publications: Life Without Limits (34073)

Wisconsin Taxpayers Alliance
335 W Wilson St.
Madison, WI 53703-3694
Phone: (608)255-4581
Fax: (608)255-0642

Publications: The Wisconsin Taxpayer (33991)

Wise County Messenger
115 S Trinty
PO Box 149
Decatur, TX 76234
Phone: (940)627-5987
Fax: (940)627-1004
Free: 888-627-5987

Publications: Wise County Messenger (30221)

The Wise Woman
2441 Cordova St.
Oakland, CA 94602
Phone: (510)536-3174

Publications: The Wise Woman (2703)

Wisner News-Chronicle
1014 Ave. E
PO Box 460
Wisner, NE 68791
Phone: (402)529-3228
Fax: (402)529-3279
Free: 888-221-4338

Publications: Wisner News-Chronicle (18317)

Witness Publishing Co.
1229 Mt. Loretta Ave.
PO Box 917
Dubuque, IA 52004
Phone: (563)588-0556
Fax: (563)556-5464

Publications: The Witness (10846)

Wittenberg Press, Inc.
PO Box 190
Wittenberg, WI 54499-0190
Phone: (715)253-2737
Fax: (715)253-2700

Publications: Wittenberg Enterprise and Birnamwood News (34471)

Wittenberg Torch
PO Box 720
Springfield, OH 45501-0720
Phone: (937)327-6151
Fax: (937)327-6340

Publications: Wittenberg Torch (25534)

Wizard Entertainment
151 Wells Ave.
Congers, NY 10920
Phone: (845)268-2000
Fax: (845)268-6357

Publications: Inquest, The Gaming Magazine (20490) • Toyfare, The Toy Magazine (20491) • Wizard (20492)

Wizards of the Coast, Inc.
PO Box 707
Renton, WA 98057
Phone: (425)204-8000

Publications: Dragon Magazine (32923)

WMDA Service Station & Auto Repair Association
9420 Annapolis Rd., Ste. 307
Lanham, MD 20706-3021
Phone: (301)577-4956
Fax: (301)306-0523
Free: 800-492-0329

Publications: Nozzle & Wrench (13608)

W.M.T. Publications, Inc.
250 N Goodman St.
Rochester, NY 14607-1199
Phone: (585)244-3329
Fax: (585)244-1126

Publications: City Newspaper (23216)

WNS Publications
100 E Main St.
PO Box 31
Morrison, IL 61270
Phone: (815)772-7244
Fax: (815)772-4105
Free: 800-245-4927

Publications: The Review (8846) • Whiteside News Sentinel (9227)

WNYC
1 Centre St., 24th Fl.
New York, NY 10007
Phone: (212)669-7800
Fax: (212)669-3312

Publications: WNYC Program Guide (22923)

Woburn Daily Times, Inc.
1 Arrow Dr.
Woburn, MA 01801-3514
Phone: (781)933-3700
Fax: (781)932-3321

Publications: Daily Times Chronicle (14669) • Middlesex East Update (14670) • The Stoneham Independent (14569)

Wolfe City Mirror
PO Drawer F
Wolfe City, TX 75496-0600
Phone: (903)496-7297
Fax: (903)496-2421

Publications: The Wolfe City Mirror (31307)

Wolfe Publishing Co.
2625 Stearman Rd., Ste. A
Prescott, AZ 86301-6155
Phone: (928)445-7810
Fax: (928)778-5124
Free: 800-899-7810

Publications: Handloader (847) • Rifle (850)

Womack Publishing
14245 Moneta Rd.
PO Box 231
Moneta, VA 24121-0231
Phone: (540)297-1222
Fax: (540)297-1944

Publications: Smith Mountain Eagle (32273)

Womack Publishing Co.
PO Box 111
Chatham, VA 24531
Phone: (434)432-1654
Fax: (434)432-1005

Publications: The Altavista Journal (31756) • The Caswell Messenger (24340) • Jamestown News (24015) • Mebane Enterprise (24063) • Outer Banks Sentinel (24092) • Star-Tribune (31962) • The Union Star (31905)

Womack Publishing Co., Inc.
139 Bruton St.
PO Box 466
Troy, NC 27371
Phone: (910)576-6051
Fax: (910)576-1050

Publications: Montgomery Herald (24257)

Womack Publishing Co. Inc.
PO Box 60
South Hill, VA 23970-0060
Phone: (804)447-3178
Fax: (804)447-5931

Publications: The South Hill Enterprise (32534)

Woman Activist Fund Inc.
2310 Barbour Rd.
Falls Church, VA 22043
Phone: (703)573-8716
Fax: (703)573-8716

Publications: The Woman Activist (32060)

Woman's Art Journal
1711 Harris Rd.
Laverock, PA 19038
Phone: (215)233-0639
Fax: (215)233-0639

Publications: Woman's Art Journal (27168)

Woman's Life Insurance Society
1338 Military St.
PO Box 5020
Port Huron, MI 48061-5020
Phone: (810)985-5191
Fax: (810)985-6970
Free: 800-521-9292

Publications: Woman's Life (15452)

Woman's Missionary Union
PO Box 830010
100 Missionary Ridge
Birmingham, AL 35283-0010
Phone: (205)991-8100
Fax: (205)991-4990
Free: 800-968-7301

Publications: Dimension (68)

Women Band Directors International
345 Overlook Dr.
West Lafayette, IN 47906-1249
Phone: (765)463-1738
Fax: (765)463-1738

Publications: The Woman Conductor (10555)

Women of Diversity Productions
5790 N Park St.
Las Vegas, NV 89149-2304
Phone: (702)341-9807
Fax: (702)341-9828
Free: 800-399-7166

Publications: Women in Sport and Physical Activity Journal (18387)

Women for Faith & Family
PO Box 8326
St. Louis, MO 63132
Phone: (314)863-8385
Fax: (314)863-5858

Publications: Voices (17527)

Women Nationally Active for Christ of the National Association of Free Will Baptists
5233 Mt. View Rd.
PO Box 5002
Antioch, TN 37011-5002
Phone: (615)731-6812

Publications: Co-Laborer (29049)

Women's American ORT
250 Park Ave. S, Ste. 600
New York, NY 10003
Phone: (212)505-7700
Fax: (212)674-3057
Free: 800-51W-AORT

Publications: The Reporter (22647)

Women's Center
PO Box 354
Binghamton, NY 13902
Phone: (607)724-3462
Fax: (607)785-3915

Publications: Celebrating Voices (20152)

Women's International League for Peace & Freedom, U.S. Section
1213 Race St.
Philadelphia, PA 19107
Phone: (215)563-7110
Fax: (215)563-5527

Publications: Peace and Freedom (27613)

Women's International Network
187 Grant St.
Lexington, MA 02420-2126
Phone: (781)862-9431
Fax: (781)862-1734

Publications: WIN News (14274)

Women's League for Conservative Judaism
475 Riverside Dr.
New York, NY 10115
Phone: (212)870-1260
Fax: (212)870-1261
Free: 800-628-5083

Publications: Women's League Outlook (22934)

Women's Literary Guild
Box 7415, JFA Sta.
New York, NY 10116-4630
Phone: (212)967-8006

Publications: Free Focus (21734)

Women's Missionary Society
50 Wynford Dr.
Toronto, ON, Canada M3C 1J7
Phone: (416)441-1111
Fax: (416)441-2825
Free: 800-619-7301

Publications: Glad Tidings (36605)

Women's News
33 Halstead Ave.
Harrison, NY 10528-0829
Phone: (914)835-5400
Fax: (914)835-5718

Publications: Women's News (20713)

Women's Studies Librarian
430 Memorial Library
728 State St.
Madison, WI 53706
Phone: (608)263-5754
Fax: (608)265-2754

Publications: Feminist Periodicals (33938)

Women's Studio Workshop
PO Box 489
Rosendale, NY 12472
Phone: (845)658-9133
Fax: (845)658-9031

Publications: Binnewater Tides (23277)

Women's Voices
PO Box 1924
Sebastopol, CA 95473-1924
Phone: (707)575-5654

Publications: Sonoma County Women's Voices (3752)

Wonder and Son Publishing
720 Iowa Ave.
PO Box 418
Onawa, IA 51040-0418
Phone: (712)423-2411
Fax: (712)423-2411

Publications: Onawa Democrat (11126)

Wonewoc News
PO Box 220
Mauston, WI 53948
Phone: (608)462-8224
Fax: (608)847-6224

Publications: Wonewoc Reporter (34472)

Wood College
PO Box 289
Mathiston, MS 39752
Phone: (662)263-5352
Fax: (662)263-4172

Publications: The Breeze (16760) • Chips-O-Wood (16761)

Wood Creek Media
202 E Morrison
PO Box 32
Fayette, MO 65248-0032
Phone: (660)248-2235
Fax: (660)248-1200

Publications: The Democrat-Leader (17058) • The Fayette Advertiser (17059)

Wood Publications, Inc.
400 Fuller-Wiser, Ste. 125
Euless, TX 76039
Phone: (817)540-4666
Fax: (817)685-7562

Publications: DFW People (30310)

Wood Publishing
Old Salt Rd.
PO Box 89
Skaneateles, NY 13152-0089
Phone: (315)685-3300

Publications: Empire State Food Service News (23335)

Wood River Journal
11 E. Bullion
Hailey, ID 83333
Phone: (208)788-3444
Fax: (208)788-0083

Publications: Wood River Journal (7860)

The Wood River Sunbeam
PO Box 356
Wood River, NE 68883-0356
Phone: (308)583-2241
Fax: (308)583-2543

Publications: The Wood River Sunbeam (18318)

Woodall Publications Corp.
2575 Vista Del Mar Dr.
Ventura, CA 93001
Phone: (805)667-4100
Fax: (805)667-4468
Free: 800-323-9076

Publications: WOODALL's California RV Traveler (4016) • WOODALL's Camp-orama (4017) • WOODALL'S Camperways (4018) • WOODALL's Campground Management (10479) • WOODALL's Carolina RV Traveler (4019) • WOODALL's Midwest RV Traveler (4020) • WOODALL's Northeast Outdoors (4021) • WOODALL's Northeast Summers (4022) • WOODALL'S Southern RV (4023) • WOODALL'S Sunny Destinations (4024) • WOODALL's Texas RV (4025)

Woodall Publishing Corp.
2575 Vista Del Mar Dr.
Ventura, CA 93001
Free: 877-680-6155

Publications: Northeast Outdoors (4007)

Woodbridge Advertiser
PO Box 379
Beeton, ON, Canada L0G 1A0
Phone: (905)729-4501
Fax: (905)729-3961
Free: 888-285-4501

Publications: Woodbridge Advertiser (35674)

Woodbury Bulletin
8420 City Centre Dr.
Woodbury, MN 55125
Phone: (651)730-4007

Publications: Woodbury Bulletin (16538)

WoodenBoat Publications Inc.
Naskeag Rd.
PO Box 78
Brooklin, ME 04616
Phone: (207)359-4651
Fax: (207)359-8920
Free: 800-273-SHIP

Publications: Professional BoatBuilder (12932) • WoodenBoat (12933)

Woodford County Journal
1926 S Main St.
PO Box 36
Eureka, IL 61530
Phone: (309)467-3314
Fax: (309)467-4563

Publications: Farmer City Journal (8885) • The Le Roy Journal (9072) • Woodford County Journal-Eureka Edition (8847) • Woodford County Journal-Minonk Edition (9200) • Woodford County Journal-Roanoke Edition (9511) • Woodford Star (8848)

Woodford Sun
PO Box 29
Versailles, KY 40383-0029
Phone: (859)873-4131
Fax: (859)873-0300

Publications: Woodford Sun (12429)

Woodham Family Publications
421 S 5th St.
Florala, AL 36442-1221
Phone: (334)858-3342
Fax: (334)858-3786

Publications: DeFuniak Herald (6052) • Holmes County Advertiser (5945)

Woodland Publishing Co.
3910 Main St.
Munhall, PA 15120
Phone: (412)462-0626
Fax: (412)462-1847

Publications: The Valley Mirror (27854)

Woodmen of the World/Omaha Woodmen Life Insurance Society
1700 Farnam St.
Omaha, NE 68102
Phone: (402)342-1890
Fax: (402)271-7269
Free: 800-225-3108

Publications: WOODMEN Magazine (18209)

Woodrow Wilson Center Press
One Woodrow Wilson Plz.
1300 Pennsylvania Ave. NW
Washington, DC 20004-3027
Phone: (202)691-4000
Fax: (202)691-4001

Publications: The Wilson Quarterly (5861)

The Woodrow Wilson International Center for Scholars
Ronald Reagan Building and International Trade Center
One Woodrow Wilson Plz.
1300 Pennsylvania Ave. NW
Washington, DC 20004-3027
Phone: (202)691-4000
Fax: (202)691-4001

Publications: Cold War International History Project (5423)

Woods Hole Oceanographic Institution
86 Water St.
Woods Hole, MA 02543
Phone: (508)289-2865
Fax: (508)457-2195

Publications: Oceanus Magazine (14673)

Woodsman Publishing Co., Inc.
PO Box 339
Woodville, TX 75979
Phone: (409)283-2516
Fax: (409)283-2560

Publications: The Booster (31309)

The Woodstock Independent
671 E. Calhoun St.
Woodstock, IL 60098
Phone: (815)388-8040
Fax: (815)338-8177

Publications: The Woodstock Independent (9772)

The Woodville Republican, Inc.
425 Depot St.
PO Box 696
Woodville, MS 39669
Phone: (601)888-4293
Fax: (601)888-6156

Publications: The Woodville Republican (16882)

Woodward Communications
Box 688
Dubuque, IA 52004-0668
Phone: (563)588-5687
Fax: (563)588-5739

Publications: Dyersville Commercial (10859) • Eastern Iowa Shopping News (10860) • Freeport Shopping News (8899) • Grant, Iowa, Lafayette Shopping News (34241) • Great Dane Shopping News (34216) • Monroe Area Shopping News (34150) • Richland Center Shopping News (34297) • Stoughton Courier Hub (34349) • Telegraph Herald (10845) • Wisconsin-Iowa Shopping News (34268)

Woodward Publishing, Inc.
904 Oklahoma Ave.
PO Box 928
Woodward, OK 73801
Phone: (580)256-2200
Fax: (580)254-2159

Publications: Woodward News (26198)

Woodworkers west
PO Box 452058
Los Angeles, CA 90045
Phone: (310)216-9265
Fax: (310)216-9274

Publications: Woodworkers West (2439)

Woonsocket News
PO Box 218
Woonsocket, SD 57385-0218
Phone: (605)796-4221
Fax: (605)796-4221

Publications: Woonsocket News (29035)

Wooster Republican Printing Co.
212 E. Liberty St.
PO Box 918
Wooster, OH 44691-4348
Phone: (216)264-1125
Fax: (216)264-3756
Free: 800-686-2958

Publications: The Daily Record (25672)

Worcester Business Journal
172 Shrewsbury St.
Worcester, MA 01604-4636
Phone: (508)755-8004
Fax: (508)755-4734
Free: 800-925-8004

Publications: Worcester Business Journal (14692) • Worcester Magazine (14693)

Worcester Polytechnic Institute
100 Institute Rd.
Worcester, MA 01609-2280
Phone: (508)831-5000
Fax: (508)831-5820

Publications: Tech News (14689) • Transformations (14691)

Worcester Polytechnic Institute
Worcester, MA 01609-2280

Publications: Pi Mu Epsilon Journal (14686)

Worchester Telegram & Gazette Corp.
20 Franklin St.
PO Box 15012
Worcester, MA 01615
Phone: (508)793-9100

Publications: Telegram & Gazette (14690)

The Word Among Us Press
9639 Dr. Perry Rd., No. 126
Ijamsville, MD 21754
Phone: (301)831-1262
Fax: (301)831-1188
Free: 800-775-WORD

Publications: The Word Among Us (13589)

Word Publications
110 East Washington St., Ste. 14-B
Indianapolis, IN 46204
Phone: (317)725-8840
Fax: (317)687-8840

Publications: The Word (10184)

Word and Way
3236 Emerald Ln., Ste. 400
Jefferson City, MO 65109
Phone: (573)635-5939
Fax: (573)635-1774

Publications: Word and Way (17135)

WORD WAYS
Spring Valley Rd.
Morristown, NJ 07960
Phone: (973)538-4584

Publications: WORD WAYS (19314)

Word Weavers
PO Box 8742
Minneapolis, MN 55408-0742

Publications: Maize, A Lesbian Country Magazine (16096)

Wordright Enterprises
4718 E Cactus Rd.
Phoenix, AZ 85032-7706
Phone: (602)953-0178
Fax: (602)951-4197

Publications: Asian Sources Computer Products (784) • Asian Sources Electronic Components (785) • Asian Sources Electronics (786) • Asian Sources Fashion Accessories & Supplies (787) • Asian Sources Gifts & Home Products (788) • Asian Sources Hardwares (789) • Asian Sources Telecom Sources (790) • Asian Sources Timepieces (791)

WordSci, Inc.
61 E 8th St., Ste. 240
New York, NY 10003
Phone: (212)260-5532
Fax: (212)260-5532

Publications: Literal Latte (22260)

WordsPlus, Inc.
PO Box 15738
Tampa, FL 33684-5738
Phone: (813)689-7566
Fax: (813)654-6995

Publications: The Gazette (6766)

WordsWorth Communications, Inc.
PO Box 70
Hendersonville, NC 28793
Phone: (828)696-3838
Fax: (828)696-0700

Publications: Back Home (23983)

Workplace News
240 Edward St.
Aurora, ON, Canada L4G 3S9
Phone: (905)841-6481
Fax: (905)841-5078
Free: 800-263-2037

Publications: Workplace News (35652)

Works in Progress
PO Box 295
Olympia, WA 98507
Phone: (360)705-2726
Fax: (360)705-2726

Publications: Works in Progress (32863)

Workstyles, Inc.
5 Rose Ave.
Great Neck, NY 11021
Phone: (516)829-8829

Publications: Making It! Careers Newsmagazine (20692)

The World
403 US Rte. 302 Berlin
Barre, VT 05641
Phone: (802)479-2582
Free: 800-639-9753

Publications: The World (Vermont) (31490)

World Air Data
Box 42724
Washington, DC 20015
Phone: (301)990-6800
Fax: (301)990-8484

Publications: Air Jobs Digest (5317)

World Almanac Education Group
512 Seventh Ave.
New York, NY 10018
Phone: (646)312-6880

Publications: Editorials On File (21586)

The World Bank
PO Box 7247-7956
Philadelphia, PA 19170-7956

Publications: The World Bank Economic Review (5868)

World Banking Intelligence
c/o American Banker
1 State St. Plaza
New York, NY 10004

Publications: World Banking Abstracts (22940)

World Climate Report
PO Box 455
Ivy, VA 22945
Phone: (804)295-7462
Fax: (804)295-7549

Publications: World Climate Report (32174)

World of Fandom
PO Box 9421
Tampa, FL 33604

Publications: World of Fandom (6783)

World Federation for Mental Health
1021 Prince St.
Alexandria, VA 22314-2971
Phone: (703)838-7543
Fax: (703)519-7648

Publications: World Federation for Mental Health Annual Report (13263)

World Future Society
7910 Woodmont Ave., Ste. 450
Bethesda, MD 20814
Phone: (301)656-8274
Fax: (301)951-0394
Free: 800-989-8274

Publications: Future Survey (20870) • Futures Research Quarterly (13338) • The Futurist (13339)

The World Institute on Disability
510 16th St., Ste. 100
Oakland, CA 94612
Phone: (510)763-4100
Fax: (510)763-4109

Publications: Impact! (2681)

The World at Large, Inc.
1689-46th St.
Brooklyn, NY 11204
Phone: (718)972-4000
Fax: (718)972-9400
Free: 800-285-2743

Publications: The World at Large (20357)

World Literature Today
630 Parrington Oval. Ste. 110
University of Oklahoma
Norman, OK 73019-4033
Phone: (405)325-4531
Fax: (405)325-7495

Publications: World Literature Today (25944)

World Mining Equipment
1250 Broadway, 26th Fl.
New York, NY 10001
Phone: (212)213-6202
Fax: (212)213-1870
Free: 800-MET-AL25

Publications: World Mining Equipment (22942)

World Newspaper Publishing Inc.
7317 Cahill Rd., Ste. 201
Minneapolis, MN 55439
Phone: (952)562-1234
Fax: (952)941-3010

Publications: Minnesota Christian Chronicle (16101)

World Organization of China Painters
2641 NW 10th St.
Oklahoma City, OK 73107-5407
Phone: (405)521-1234
Fax: (405)521-1265

Publications: The China Painter (25960)

World Pioneer
PO Box 157
Williams, MN 56686-0157
Phone: (218)783-6875
Fax: (218)386-1072

Publications: The Northern Light (16516)

World Poetry, Inc.
117 S 17th St., Ste. 910
Philadelphia, PA 19103
Phone: (215)496-0439
Fax: (215)569-0808

Publications: The American Poetry Review (27374)

World Policy Institute
66 5th Ave., 9th Fl.
New York, NY 10011
Phone: (212)229-5808
Fax: (212)229-5579

Publications: World Policy Journal (22944)

World Press Review
700 Broadway
New York, NY 10003
Phone: (212)982-8880
Fax: (212)982-6968

Publications: World Press Review (22945)

World Publications, Inc.
460 N. Orlando Ave., Ste. 200
Winter Park, FL 32789
Phone: (407)628-4802
Fax: (407)628-7061

Publications: Boating Life (6877) • Marlin (6883) • Sport Diver (6886) • Sport Fishing (6887) • Wake Boarding (6888) • Waterski Magazine (6889) • Windsurfing (6890)

World Publications Service
1 Maple St., Unit 8A
East Rutherford, NJ 07073
Phone: (201)531-0760
Fax: (201)531-0827
Free: 800-507-4383

Publications: Latin Finance (18784)

World Publishing Co.
990 Grove St.
Evanston, IL 60201-4370
Phone: (847)491-6440
Fax: (847)491-0459

Publications: Cruise Travel Magazine (8855) • Travel America (8871) • TravelAmerica (8872)

World Publishing Co.
315 S. Boulder Ave.
PO Box 1770
Tulsa, OK 74103
Phone: (918)581-8300
Fax: (918)581-8353
Free: 800-999-6297

Publications: Tulsa World (26139)

World Publishing Co.
PO Box 1511
Wenatchee, WA 98807
Phone: (509)663-5161
Fax: (509)662-5413
Free: 800-572-4433

Publications: The Wenatchee World (33196)

World Publishing Co., Inc.
PO Box 99
Garden Valley, ID 83622
Phone: (208)462-3487
Fax: (208)462-3325

Publications: The Idaho World (7856)

World Reporter
4515 Eagle Rook Bldg.
Los Angeles, CA 90041
Phone: (323)344-3530
Fax: (323)344-3501

Publications: World Reporter (2440)

World Scientific Publishing
1060 Main St., Ste. 1B
River Edge, NJ 07661
Phone: (201)487-9655
Fax: (201)487-9656
Free: 800-227-7562

Publications: Journal of Modern Physics B (19518)

World Scientific Publishing
1060 Main St., Ste. 202
River Edge, NJ 07661
Phone: (201)487-9655
Fax: (201)487-9656
Free: 800-227-7562

Publications: International Journal on Artificial Intelligence Tools (19508) • International Journal of High Speed Electronics (19509) • International Journal of Intelligent and Cooperative Information Systems (19510) • International Journal of Nonlinear Optical Physics (IJNOP) (19511) • International Journal of PIXE (19512) • International Journal of Software Engineering and Knowledge Engineeg (19513) • International Journal of Uncertainty, Fuzziness, and Knowledge-Based Systems (19514) • Journal of Computational Geometry and Applications (19515) • Journal of Knot Theory and Its Ramifications (JKTR) (19516) • Journal of Modern Physics A (19517) • Nightlife (19519) • Parallel Processing Letters (19520)

World Scientific Publishing Company Inc.
1060 Main St., No. 1B
River Edge, NJ 07661-2013
Phone: (201)487-9655
Fax: (201)487-9656
Free: 800-227-7562

Publications: American Journal of Chinese Medicine (20634)

World Service Office of Narcotics Anonymous Inc.
PO Box 9999
Van Nuys, CA 91409
Phone: (818)773-9999
Fax: (818)700-0700

Publications: The N.A. Way Magazine (3993)

World Spectator
PO Box 250
624 Main St.
Moosomin, SK, Canada S0G 3N0
Phone: (306)435-2445
Fax: (306)435-3969

Publications: World Spectator (37504)

World Times, Inc.
225 Franklin St., 26th Flr.
Boston, MA 02110
Phone: (617)439-5400
Fax: (617)439-5415

Publications: The WorldPaper (13973)

World Tribune Press
606 Wilshir Bvld
Santa Monica, CA 90401
Phone: (310)260-8900
Fax: (310)260-8910

Publications: World Tribune (3720)

World Vision United States
PO Box 9716
Federal Way, WA 98063-9716
Phone: (253)815-1000
Fax: (253)815-3445
Free: 800-777-5777

Publications: World Vision Today (32766)

World War 1 Aeroplanes, Inc.
15 Crescent Rd.
Poughkeepsie, NY 12601
Phone: (845)473-3679

Publications: Skyways (32030) • WW1 Aero (23151)

World Wide Gun Report, Inc.
110 S College
PO Box 38
Aledo, IL 61231
Phone: (309)582-5311
Fax: (309)582-5555

Publications: The Gun Report (8004)

World Wide Shipping Guide, Inc.
16302 Byrnwyck Ln.
Odessa, FL 33556-2807
Phone: (813)920-4788
Fax: (813)920-8268

Publications: WWS/World Wide Shipping (6480)

World of Yesterday
104 Chestnut Wood Dr.
Waynesville, NC 28786-6514
Phone: (828)646-6864

Publications: Cliffhanger (24277) • Under Western Skies (24281)

Worldprofit, Inc.
PO Box 38-2007
Cambridge, MA 02238
Phone: (617)547-6372
Fax: (617)547-0061

Publications: Worldprofit Online Magazine (14112)

Worldradio, Inc.
2120 28th St.
Sacramento, CA 95818
Phone: (916)457-3655
Fax: (916)457-7339
Free: 800-446-3623

Publications: Worldradio (3023)

Worldwatch Institute
1776 Massachusetts Ave. NW
Washington, DC 20036
Phone: (202)452-1999
Fax: (202)296-7365
Free: 888-544-2303

Publications: World Watch (5871) • Worldwatch Paper Series (5872)

WorldWest, LLC
609 New Hampshire
Lawrence, KS 66044
Phone: (785)838-7909

Publications: The Baldwin City Signal (11351) • Craig Daily Press (4295) • EL Defensor Chieftain (19958) • Hayden Valley Press (4629) • Payson Roundup and Advisor (767) • The Ruidoso News (19928) • Steamboat Today (4632) • Tonganoxie Mirror (11813) • Valencia County News-Bulletin (19820)

Worldwide Marriage Encounter
3943 W End Rd.
Downers Grove, IL 60515

Publications: Matrimony (8790)

Worldwide Publications No. 1, Inc.
2117 Hollywood Blvd.
Hollywood, FL 33020-6706
Phone: (305)923-4510
Fax: (305)923-4533

Publications: Le Soleil de la Floride (6195)

Worm Digest
PO Box 544
Eugene, OR 97440-0544
Phone: (541)485-0456
Fax: (541)485-0456

Publications: Worm Digest (26335)

Worral Publishing, Inc.
215 Military Rd.
Buffalo, NY 14207-2631
Phone: (716)877-8400
Fax: (716)877-8742

Publications: Riverside Review (20387)

Worrall Community Newspapers
266 Liberty St.
Bloomfield, NJ 07003
Phone: (973)743-4040
Fax: (973)680-8848

Publications: Belleville Post (18685) • The Glen Ridge Paper (18686) • The Independent Press (18687)

Worrall Community Newspapers
463 Valley St.
Maplewood, NJ 07040
Phone: (973)763-0700
Fax: (973)763-2557

Publications: Vailsburg Leader (19696)

Worrall Community Newspapers
170 Scotland Rd.
Orange, NJ 07051
Phone: (973)674-8000
Fax: (973)674-2038

Publications: East Orange Record (18782) • Irvington Herald (19125) • Nutley Journal (19385) • Orange Transcript (19396) • West Orange Chronicle (19397)

Worrall Community Newspapers
1291 Stuyvesant Ave.
PO Box 3109
Union, NJ 07083
Phone: (908)686-7700
Fax: (908)686-4169

Publications: The Clark/Cranford Eagle (18747) • Echo Leader (19595) • The Leader (19683) • The Leader (19154) • News-Record (19685) • News-Record of Maplewood and South Orange (19686) • Rahway Progress (19486) • Spectator Leader (19171) • Summit Observer (19687) • Union Leader (19688)

Worth International Communications Corp.
5979 NW, 151 St., Ste. 120
Miami Lakes, FL 33014
Phone: (305)828-0123
Fax: (305)826-6950
Free: 800-447-0123

Publications: Recommend (6419)

Worthington Times
12 S. Lessie St.
Worthington, IN 47471-1513
Phone: (812)875-1504

Publications: Worthington Times (10568)

WOW
PO Box 92
Califon, NJ 07830
Free: 800-815-6973

Publications: Women's Outdoor World (WOW) (18712)

WQED Pittsburgh
4802 5th Ave.
Pittsburgh, PA 15213
Phone: (412)622-1360
Fax: (412)622-1488
Free: 800-495-7323

Publications: Pittsburgh Magazine (27834)

The Wray Gazette
411 Main St.
PO Box 7
Wray, CO 80758-0007
Phone: (970)332-4846
Fax: (970)332-4065

Publications: The Wray Gazette (4692)

Wright County Journal Press
108 Central Ave.
PO Box 159
Buffalo, MN 55313
Phone: (612)682-1221
Fax: (612)682-5458

Publications: The Drummer (15777)

Wright County Monitor
PO Box 153
Clarion, IA 50525
Phone: (515)532-2871

Publications: Wright County Monitor (10704)

Wright Foundation
Taliesin W
Cactus Rd. & 114th St.
Scottsdale, AZ 85261-4430
Phone: (602)860-2700
Fax: (602)451-8989

Publications: Frank Lloyd Wright Quarterly (869)

Wright State University
W016C Student Union
Dayton, OH 45435
Phone: (937)775-5537
Fax: (937)775-5535

Publications: The Guardian (25119)

Wright State University, Lake Campus
1280 Main St. W Togo Salmon Hall 308
Hamilton, ON, Canada L8S 4M2
Phone: (905)525-9140
Fax: (905)577-6930

Publications: Text Technology (35891)

The Writer's Center
4508 Walsh St.
Bethesda, MD 20815
Phone: (301)654-8664
Fax: (301)654-8667

Publications: Poet Lore (13375) • Writer's Carousel (13390)

Writers Guild America, West
7000 W 3rd St.
Los Angeles, CA 90048-4329
Phone: (323)782-4502
Fax: (323)782-4802

Publications: Written By Magazine (2442)

Writers' Monthly
1450 Front Street
San Diego, CA 92101
Phone: (619)230-9292
Fax: (619)230-0490

Publications: Writers' Monthly (3289)

Written Heritage
PO Box 1390
Folsom, LA 70437-1390
Phone: (985)796-5433
Fax: (985)796-9236
Free: 800-301-8009

Publications: Whispering Wind (12581)

WTTW/Chicago
5400 N St. Louis Ave.
Chicago, IL 60625-4698
Phone: (773)583-5000
Fax: (773)509-5305

Publications: Eleven (8365)

WW Publishers Inc.
55 W. 17th St., 5th Fl.
New York, NY 10011
Phone: (212)255-0352

Publications: Workers World (22938)

Wyandotte West Communications, Inc.
7735 Washington Ave.
PO Box 12003
Kansas City, KS 66112-0003
Phone: (913)788-5565
Fax: (913)788-9812

Publications: The Piper Press (11531) • The Suburban Advertiser (11533) • The Wyandotte West (11536)

The Wylie News
110 N Ballard
PO Box 369
Wylie, TX 75098
Phone: (214)442-5515
Fax: (214)442-4313

Publications: The Wylie News (31310)

Wymore Arbor State
PO Box 327
Wymore, NE 68466
Phone: (402)645-3344
Fax: (402)645-3345

Publications: Wymore Arbor State (18319)

Wynne Progress, Inc.
702 N Falls Blvd.
PO Box 308
Wynne, AR 72396
Phone: (870)238-2375
Fax: (870)238-4655

Publications: East Arkansas News Leader (1371) • Wynne Progress (1372)

Wynnewood Gazette
PO Box 309
Wynnewood, OK 73098
Phone: (405)665-4333
Fax: (405)665-4334

Publications: Wynnewood Gazette (26202)

Wynyard Advance, Ltd.
117 Ave. B East
PO Box 10
Wynyard, SK, Canada S0A 4T0
Phone: (306)554-2224
Fax: (306)554-3226

Publications: Wynyard Advance/Gazette (37597)

Wyoming Archeological Society, Inc.
1617 Westridge Terr.
Casper, WY 82604-3305
Phone: (307)268-2212
Fax: (307)268-2224

Publications: Wyoming Archeologist (34485)

Wyoming Catholic Register
PO Box 1468
Cheyenne, WY 82003
Phone: (307)638-1530
Fax: (307)637-7936
Free: 800-788-4606

Publications: Wyoming Catholic Register (34498)

Wyoming Game and Fish Dept.
5400 Bishop Blvd.
Cheyenne, WY 82006
Phone: (307)777-4544
Fax: (307)777-4610
Free: 800-548-9453

Publications: Wyoming Wildlife (34501)

Wyoming Newspapers, Inc.
PO Box 30
Lusk, WY 82225
Phone: (307)334-2867
Fax: (307)334-2514

Publications: The Lusk Herald (34562)

Wyoming Newspapers, Inc.
PO Box 1058
Torrington, WY 82240
Phone: (307)532-2184
Fax: (307)532-2283

Publications: Torrington Telegram (34597)

Wyoming Rural Electric Association
340 W B St., Ste. 101
Casper, WY 82601
Phone: (307)234-6152
Fax: (307)234-4115

Publications: The WREN Magazine (34484)

Wyoming State Bar
PO Box 109
Cheyenne, WY 82003-0109
Phone: (307)632-9061
Fax: (307)632-3737

Publications: The Wyoming Lawyer (34499)

Wyoming Stock Growers Association
113 E. 20th St.
PO Box 206
Cheyenne, WY 82003
Phone: (307)638-3942
Fax: (307)634-1210

Publications: Cow Country (34495)

Wyoming Trucking Association
555 N Poplar
Casper, WY 82601
Phone: (307)234-1579
Fax: (307)234-7082

Publications: Wyoming Trucker (34486)

Xavier University
Marketing & Public Relations
Schott Hall, Rm. 711
3800 Victory Pkwy.
Cincinnati, OH 45207-5141
Phone: (513)745-3000
Fax: (513)745-2807
Free: 800-344-4698

Publications: Xavier Magazine (24830)

Xavier University of Louisiana
Box 110C
New Orleans, LA 70125-1098
Phone: (504)483-7303
Fax: (504)485-7917

Publications: Xavier Review (12762)

Xcp: Cross Cultural Poetics
College of St. Catherine-Minneapolis
601 25th Ave. S
Minneapolis, MN 55454
Phone: (651)690-7747
Fax: (651)690-7849

Publications: Xcp: Cross Cultural Poetics (16142)

The Xenia Daily Gazette
30 S. Detroit St
PO Box 400
Xenia, OH 45385-3580
Phone: (937)372-4444
Fax: (937)372-3385

Publications: The Xenia Daily Gazette (25687)

Xephon
PO Box 350100
Westminster, CO 80035-0100
Phone: (303)410-9344
Fax: (303)438-0290

Publications: AIX Update (4659) • CICS Update (4660) • DB2 Update (4661) • Mainframe Market Monitor (4663) • MQ Update (4664) • MVS Update (4665) • News IS (4666) • RACF Update (4667) • TCP/SNA Update (4668)

Xerces Society
4828 SE Hawthorne Blvd.
Portland, OR 97215-3252
Phone: (503)232-6639
Fax: (503)233-6794

Publications: Wings (26516)

Xerolage
Rt 1, Box 131
RR 1, Box 131
La Farge, WI 54639
Phone: (608)625-4619

Publications: Xerolage (33898)

XLR8R
1388 Haight St. No. 105
San Francisco, CA 94117

Publications: XLR8R (3465)

XRX, Inc.
PO Box 1525
Sioux Falls, SD 57101-1525
Phone: (605)338-2450
Fax: (605)338-2994
Free: 800-232-KNIT

Publications: Knitter's (28964)

XTR Corp.
32 Broad St.
San Luis Obispo, CA 93405-3710
Phone: (805)546-9596
Fax: (805)546-0570
Free: 800-488-2249

Publications: Command Magazine (3564)

XXX Publishing Enterprises Ltd.
436 Frontage Rd., Ste. 100
Northfield, IL 60093
Phone: (847)784-9797
Fax: (847)784-9898

Publications: Floral & Nursery Times (9329)

Y Drych (The Mirror)
Box 8337
Utica, NY 13505-8337

Publications: Y Drych (The Mirror) (23469)

Y-Visionary Publishing, LP
265 S Anita Dr., Ste. 120
Orange, CA 92868-3310
Phone: (714)939-9991
Fax: (714)939-9901

Publications: Bow and Arrow Hunting (2721)

Yadkin Ripple, Inc.
PO Box 7
Yadkinville, NC 27055
Phone: (336)679-2341
Fax: (336)679-2340

Publications: Yadkin Ripple (24339)

The Yadkin Valley Advertiser
PO Box 1009
Elkin, NC 28621-1009
Phone: (336)835-1513
Fax: (336)835-8742

Publications: The Yadkin Valley Advertiser (23868)

Yakima Herald-Republic
114 N 4th St.
PO Box 9668
Yakima, WA 98909
Phone: (509)248-1251
Fax: (509)577-7767

Publications: Yakima Herald-Republic (33223)

Yale Daily News Publishing Co., Inc.
202 York St.
New Haven, CT 06511-4808
Phone: (203)432-2424
Fax: (203)432-7425

Publications: Yale Daily News (5004)

Yale Expositor
21 S Main St.
PO Box 158
Yale, MI 48097
Phone: (313)387-2300
Fax: (810)387-2300

Publications: Yale Expositor (15689)

The Yale Journal of Biology and Medicine, Inc.
333 Ceder St.
PO Box 208000
New Haven, CT 06520-8000
Phone: (203)785-4251
Fax: (203)785-4251

Publications: The Yale Journal of Biology & Medicine (5005)

Yale Journal of Law and Feminism
PO Box 208215
New Haven, CT 06520-8215
Phone: (203)432-4056
Fax: (203)432-2592

Publications: Yale Journal of Law and Feminism (5006)

Yale Law Journal Co.
PO Box 208215
New Haven, CT 06520-8215
Phone: (203)432-1666
Fax: (203)432-7482

Publications: The Yale Law Journal (5007)

The Yale Literary Magazine
PO Box 209087, Yale Stn.
New Haven, CT 06520-7394
Phone: (203)432-4771

Publications: The Yale Literary Magazine (5008)

Yale News
103 N Main St.
Box 307
Yale, OK 74085
Phone: (918)387-2125
Fax: (918)387-2866

Publications: News (26203)

Yale Scientific Magazine
Yale Sta.
PO Box 209117
New Haven, CT 06520

Publications: Yale Scientific Magazine (5010)

Yale University
PO Box 208109
New Haven, CT 06520-8109
Phone: (203)432-3154
Fax: (203)432-3134

Publications: Journal of Marine Research (4995)

Yankee Permaculture
PO Box 52
Sparr, FL 32192-0052

Publications: The International Permaculture Solutions Journal (6687) • Permaculture Review, Overview and Digest (6688)

Yankee Publishing Inc.
PO Box 520
Dublin, NH 03444-0520
Phone: (603)563-8111
Fax: (603)563-8252

Publications: The Old Farmer's Almanac Gardener's Companion (18499)

Yarn Tree Design, Inc.
117 Alexander Ave.
Ames, IA 50010
Phone: (515)232-3121
Fax: (515)232-0789

Publications: Needlework Retailer (10592)

Yasodhara Ashram Society
PO Box 9
Kootenay Bay, BC, Canada V0B 1X0
Phone: (250)227-9224
Fax: (250)227-9494
Free: 800-661-8711

Publications: Ascent Magazine (37088)

The Yates Center News
PO Box 285
Yates Center, KS 66783
Phone: (620)625-2181
Fax: (620)625-2081

Publications: The Yates Center News (11913)

Yazoo Newspaper Inc.
1035 Grand Ave.
PO Box 720
Yazoo City, MS 39194
Phone: (662)746-4911
Fax: (662)746-4915

Publications: The Yazoo Herald (16883)

Yellow Pages Publishers Association
820 Kirts Blvd., Ste. 100
Troy, MI 48084
Phone: (248)244-6200
Fax: (248)244-6230

Publications: Link (8466)

Yellow Springs News
253 1/2 Xenia Ave.
PO Box 187
Yellow Springs, OH 45387
Phone: (937)767-7373
Free: 888-823-3608

Publications: Yellow Springs News (25692)

Yellowback Press
PO Box 36172
Des Moines, IA 50315
Phone: (515)287-0404

Publications: Yellowback Library (10818)

Yellowhead Communication Services
PO Box 1020
Barriere, BC, Canada V0E 1E0
Phone: (604)672-5611
Fax: (604)672-9900

Publications: North Thompson Star/Journal (34884)

Yellowstone County Publishing
748 Railroad Hwy.
Huntley, MT 59037
Phone: (406)348-2649
Fax: (406)348-2650

Publications: Yellowstone County News, Inc. (17834)

Yellowstone Newspapers
204 Logan Ave.
Box 127
Terry, MT 59349
Phone: (406)635-5513
Fax: (406)635-2149

Publications: Terry Tribune (17913)

Yenor, Inc.
Box 5171
Culver City, CA 90231
Phone: (310)645-4998
Fax: (310)910-1386

Publications: Library Mosaics (1794)

Yes Books
589 Congress St.
Portland, ME 04101
Phone: (207)775-3233

Publications: The Cafe Review (13006)

Yes Canada - BC Publishing Division
5172 Kingsway, Ste. 310
Burnaby, BC, Canada V5H 2E8
Phone: (604)412-4141
Fax: (604)412-4144

Publications: REALM Magazine (34906) • Sphere Magazine (34907)

Yeshiva Birkas Reuven
PO Box 204
Brooklyn, NY 11204
Phone: (718)336-8544

Publications: Kashrus Magazine (20324)

Yeshiva University
500 W 185th St.
New York, NY 10033
Phone: (212)960-5235
Fax: (212)960-5482

Publications: Sephardic Scholar (22729)

Yeshiva University Press
500 W. 185th St.
New York, NY 10033-3201
Phone: (212)960-5400
Fax: (212)960-0043

Publications: Chronos (21415)

Yesterday's Island Inc.
1 Skyline Dr.
Nantucket, MA 02554
Phone: (508)228-9165
Fax: (508)228-1348

Publications: Yesterday's Island (14343)

Yoakum Herald-Times
PO Box 798
Yoakum, TX 77995
Phone: (361)293-5266
Fax: (361)293-5267

Publications: Yoakum Herald-Times (31311)

YodaMedia, Inc.
PO Box 1743
Tacoma, WA 98401-1743
Phone: (253)274-9320
Fax: (253)272-8824

Publications: Tacoma Reporter (33151)

Yomiuri America
666 5th Ave., 5th Fl.
New York, NY 10103
Phone: (212)765-1111
Fax: (212)765-1618

Publications: Yomiuri America (22951)

York County Bar Association
137 E. Market St.
York, PA 17401-1221
Phone: (717)854-8755
Fax: (717)843-8766

Publications: York Legal Record (28209)

York County Coast Star, Inc.
PO Box 979
Kennebunk, ME 04043-0979
Phone: (207)985-2961
Fax: (207)985-9050

Publications: York County Coast Star (12973)

York Daily Record
122 S George St.
PO Box 15122
York, PA 17405-7122
Phone: (717)771-2000
Fax: (717)771-2009
Free: 800-682-1334

Publications: York Daily Record (28207)

The York Dispatch
1517 E Philadelphia, Ste. 2807
York, PA 17403-1234
Phone: (717)854-1575
Fax: (717)843-2958

Publications: The York Dispatch (28208)

York News-Times
327 Platte Ave.
PO Box 279
York, NE 68467-3547
Phone: (402)362-4478
Fax: (402)362-6748

Publications: York News-Times (18321)

York Newspaper Co.
1891 Loucks
PO Box 14401
York, PA 17404
Phone: (717)767-6397
Fax: (717)764-6130

Publications: Weekly Record (28206) • York Sunday News (28210)

York Pioneer and Historical Society
2482 Yonge St.
PO Box 45026
Toronto, ON, Canada M4P 2H5
Fax: (416)231-1829

Publications: York Pioneer (36795)

York Publishing
PO Box 4591
Chico, CA 95927
Phone: (530)891-8410
Fax: (530)891-8443

Publications: Smart TV & Sound Magazine (1696) • Videomaker Magazine (1697)

York University
280 York Lanes
York University
4700 Keele St.
North York, ON, Canada M3J 1P3
Phone: (416)736-2100
Fax: (416)736-5681

Publications: York Gazette (36133)

York University
4700 Keele St.,
York Lanes
Toronto, ON, Canada M3J 1P3
Phone: (416)736-2100
Fax: (416)650-2979

Publications: Profiles (36718)

Yorkton This Week Ltd.
20 3rd Ave. N.
PO Box 1300
Yorkton, SK, Canada S3N 2X3
Phone: (306)782-2465
Fax: (306)786-1898

Publications: This Week Marketplace (37598) • TV This Week (37599) • Yorkton This Week & Enterprise (37600)

Yorktown News-View
PO Box 398
Yorktown, TX 78164
Phone: (361)564-2242

Publications: Yorktown News-View (31313)

Yorktown Pennysaver Corp.
1520 Front St.
Yorktown Heights, NY 10598
Phone: (914)962-3871
Fax: (914)962-5123

Publications: Yorktown Pennysaver Corp. (23610)

Larry Yoshida
593 Waikala St.
Kahului, HI 96732-1736
Phone: (808)877-5198

Publications: Shemp! (7759)

Young Entomologists' Society, Inc.
Minibeast Zooseum & Educational Ctr.
6907 W. Grand River Ave.
Lansing, MI 48906-9131
Phone: (517)886-0630
Fax: (517)886-0630

Publications: YES Quarterly (15297)

Young Horizons Indigo
PO Box 371595
Decatur, GA 30037-1595
Phone: (404)241-5003

Publications: Young Horizons Indigo (7238)

Young Voices
PO Box 2321
Olympia, WA 98507
Phone: (360)357-4683
Fax: (360)705-9669

Publications: Young Voices Magazine (32864)

Youngblood Publishing Ltd.
4580 Dufferin St., Ste. 404
Toronto, ON, Canada M3H 5Y2
Phone: (416)665-7333
Fax: (416)665-7226
Free: 800-363-3261

Publications: PrintAction (36716)

Youngstown State University
One University Plaza
Youngstown, OH 44555
Phone: (330)941-3095
Fax: (330)941-2322

Publications: The Jambar (25697)

Your Family Shopper
410 Bay St.
PO Box 366
Chippewa Falls, WI 54729-0366
Phone: (715)723-2839
Fax: (715)723-6668

Publications: Your Family Shopper (33630)

Your Life Matters
2877 Paridise Rd., Apt. 801
Las Vegas, NV 89109-5244
Phone: (702)222-1998
Fax: (702)222-1940

Publications: Your Life Matters (18388)

Youth Communication
224 W. 29th St., 2nd Fl.
New York, NY 10001
Phone: (212)279-0708
Fax: (212)242-7057

Publications: NYC/New Youth Connections (22478)

Youth Runner Magazine
PO Box 1156
Lake Oswego, OR 97035
Phone: (503)236-2524
Fax: (503)620-3800

Publications: Youth Runner Magazine (26406)

Youth for Yiddish, Inc.
200 W 72nd St., Ste. 40
New York, NY 10023-2824
Phone: (212)787-6675
Fax: (212)231-7905

Publications: Yugntruf (22954)

Yukon News
211 Wood St.
Whitehorse, YT, Canada Y1A 2E4
Phone: (867)667-6285
Fax: (867)668-3755

Publications: Yukon News (37606)

The Yuma Daily Sun
2055 S Arizona Ave.
PO Box 271
Yuma, AZ 85364
Phone: (928)783-3333
Fax: (928)343-1009

Publications: Bajo El Sol (1016) • The Prospector (1018) • Super Shopper (1020) • The Yuma Daily Sun (1022)

Yuma Pioneer
207 S Main St.
PO Box 326
Yuma, CO 80759
Phone: (970)848-2174
Fax: (970)848-2895

Publications: Yuma Pioneer (4694)

Z-Law Software, Inc
PO Box 40602
Providence, RI 02940
Phone: (401)273-5588
Fax: (401)421-5334
Free: 800-526-5588

Publications: Real Estate Software Guide (28419)

Zackin Publications, Inc.
70 Edwin Ave.
PO Box 2180
Waterbury, CT 06722
Phone: (203)755-0158
Fax: (203)755-3480
Free: 800-325-6745

Publications: Alternative Energy Retailer (5190) • Drycleaners News (5192) • Secondary Marketing Executive (5194)

Zacks Investment Research
155 N Wacker Dr.
Chicago, IL 60606
Phone: (312)630-1951
Fax: (312)630-9898
Free: 800-399-6659

Publications: Zacks Analyst Watch (8609) • Zacks Earnings Forecaster (8610) • Zacks Profit Guide (8611)

Zander Press, Inc.
425 W. Ryan St.
Brillion, WI 54110
Phone: (920)756-2131
Fax: (920)756-2701

Publications: The Brillion News (33599) • Lake to Lake Shopper (33600)

Zapata County News
PO Box 216
Zapata, TX 78076
Phone: (956)765-6931
Fax: (956)765-9058

Publications: Zapata County News (31314)

Zavala County Sentinel
PO Drawer G
Crystal City, TX 78839
Phone: (830)374-3465
Fax: (830)374-5771

Publications: Zavala County Sentinel (30114)

ZDNet
One Athenaeum St.
Cambridge, MA 02142
Phone: (617)225-3450

Publications: eWeek (14052) • Sm@rt Partner (14102)

The Zeeland Record Co.
1622 S Elm St.
Zeeland, MI 49464
Phone: (616)772-2131

Publications: Zeeland Record (15694)

Zeitgeist Publishing, Inc.
1068 National Hwy.
LaVale, MD 21502
Phone: (301)729-6190
Fax: (301)729-1720
Free: 800-875-2997

Publications: German Life (13615)

Ziegler Publishing Co., Inc.
1515 SW 1 Ave.
Fort Lauderdale, FL 33315
Phone: (954)524-9450
Fax: (954)524-9464
Free: 800-226-9464

Publications: Waterfront News (6087)

Ziff-Davis Inc.
28 E. 28th St.
New York, NY 10016-7930
Phone: (212)503-3500

Publications: Computer Life (21476) • Computer Shopper (21477) • Family PC (21680) • Internet User (21942) • PC Computing (22533) • PC Magazine (22534) • Window Sources (22918) • Wireless & Mobility (22922) • Yahoo! Internet Life (22947) • Year/2000 Journal (22948) • ZD Internet Magazine (22955) • Ziff Davis Smart Business for the New Economy (22956)

Ziff-Davis Publishing Co.
28 E. 28th St.
New York, NY 10016-7930
Phone: (212)503-3500

Publications: PC Week (22535)

Zim-mer Trade Publications, Inc.
482 Hudson Ter.
Englewood Cliffs, NJ 07632
Phone: (201)592-9100
Fax: (201)592-0809

Publications: The Produce News (18802)

Zion-Benton News
2719 Elisha Ave.
Zion, IL 60099
Phone: (847)746-9000
Fax: (847)746-9150

Publications: The Bargaineer (9779) • Zion Benton News (9780)

Zionsville Times Sentinel
250 S Elm St.
Zionsville, IN 46077-1601
Phone: (317)873-6397
Fax: (317)873-6259

Publications: Zionsville Times Sentinel (10569)

ZIP Publishing, Inc.
8298 Main St.
Ellicott City, MD 21043
Phone: (410)480-0816
Fax: (410)480-0834

Publications: The View from Ellicott City (13500)

Zonta International
557 W Randolph St.
Chicago, IL 60661
Phone: (312)930-5848
Fax: (312)930-0951

Publications: The Zontian (8612)

Zoological Society of San Diego, Inc.
2920 Zoo Dr.
PO Box 120551
San Diego, CA 92101
Phone: (619)231-1515
Fax: (619)744-3310
Free: 800-934-2267

Publications: ZOONOOZ (3290)

Zuzu's Petals Quarterly Online
PO Box 4853
Ithaca, NY 14852
Phone: (607)539-1141
Fax: (607)539-1141

Publications: Zuzu's Petals Quarterly Online (20816)

The Zygon Center for Religion and Science
1100 East 55th St.
Chicago, IL 60615-5199
Phone: (773)256-0670
Fax: (773)256-0682

Publications: Insights (8418)

ZYZZYVA
PO Box 590069
San Francisco, CA 94159-0069
Phone: (415)752-4393
Fax: (415)752-4391

Publications: ZYZZYVA (3467)

Index to Subject Terms

This is a consolidated alphabetical listing of subject terms appearing in the following six subject indexes: Agricultural Publications (by Subject); Ethnic Publications; Fraternal Publications; Magazines of General Circulation; Trade, Technical, and Professional Publications; and the Radio Station Formats index. Citations are followed by page numbers referring to indexes where the subject terms appear. In addition to actual subject headings being used, the Index to Subject Terms provides "see" and "see also" references to guide users to appropriate headings.

Agricultural Publications (by State)

Index entries are arranged geographically, first by states/provinces and then by cities. Within cities in this index, citations appear alphabetically by publication title. Citations include publication title, entry number (given in parentheses immediately following the title), and circulation figures.

Circ.

ALABAMA
Auburn
Highlights of Agricultural Research **(41)**

Birmingham
Progressive Farmer **(87)** ....(Paid) 244,000
(Non-paid) 358,000

Cullman
WATT Poultry USA **(162)** ....(Combined) 20,126

Fayette
Cattle Today **(213)** ....‡15,000

Montgomery
The Alabama Cattleman **(356)** 17,000
Alabama Living **(358)** ....(Paid) ★360,936
Alfa News **(360)** ....‡280,000
Neighbors **(371)** ....(Paid) 101,159

ALASKA
Fairbanks
Agroborealis **(566)** ....(Non-paid) 2,500

ARIZONA
Buckeye
Buckeye Valley News **(662)** 2,600

Phoenix
Arizona Farm Bureau News **(777)** ....‡3,300

Scottsdale
National Horseman **(871)** ....(Paid) 3,800
(Non-paid) 1,000

ARKANSAS
Hartford
The Gamecock **(1170)** 14,300

Little Rock
Arkansas Cattle Business **(1215)** ....(Paid) 10,000
(Controlled) 1,000
Front Porch **(1229)** ....‡231,000

CALIFORNIA
Arcadia
California Thoroughbred **(1427)** 5,500

Berkeley
Agricultural History **(1488)** ....‡1,050

Cambria
Arabian Horse World **(1648)** 10,000

Clovis
California Dairy **(1731)**

Concord
Oregon FarmekraHJJmpw- **(1754)**
Washington FarmekraHJJmpw- **(1757)**

Corona
The Western Dairyman **(1768)** ....‡17,500

Elk Grove
The Western Bec- Producer **(1875)**

Fortuna
Journal of the American Rhododendron
Society **(1929)** ....(Controlled) 6,000

Circ.

Fresno
Agribusiness Fieldman **(1941)** .....(Controlled) ‡8,058
Agricultural Spray Adjuvants **(1942)**
California-Arizona Texas Cotton **(1945)** ....‡15,000
Grape Grower
Magazine **(1951)** ....(Non-paid) 11,276
Nut Grower **(1953)** 11,993
Tree Fruit **(1957)** ....(Controlled) ‡11,008
Vegetable **(1958)** ....(Controlled) ‡8,371

Modesto
Rice Farming **(2562)** ....‡8,753

Moreno Valley
Riverside County Agriculture **(2599)** ....‡3,200

Norco
Animals Exotic and Small **(2640)** 3,500

Oakland
Almanac **(2665)** ....(Paid) 450
California Agriculture **(2671)** ....(Paid) 850
(Controlled) 19,000

Pasadena
Journal of the Los Angeles International Fern
Society **(2820)** ....(Combined) 400

Paso Robles
Paso Robles Press **(2831)** ....(Wed.) ‡12,500
(Fri.) ‡5,000

Sacramento
Ag Alert **(2974)** 44,000
Almond Facts **(2975)** ....(Controlled) 8,000
California Cattleman **(2979)** ....(Paid) ‡3,585
(Non-paid) ‡910

San Diego
California Garden **(3127)** 2,100

San Francisco
Biodynamics **(3331)** ....‡1,500

San Joaquin
San Joaquin Farm Bureau
News **(3507)** ....(Paid) ‡5,000

Stockton
Sun Diamond Grower **(3809)** ....(Controlled) ‡10,000

COLORADO
Arvada
Cattle Guard **(4137)** ....‡15,000

Aurora
International Arabian Horse **(4146)** ....‡30,000
Rocky Mountain Union
Farmer **(4148)** ....(Paid) ‡5,000
(Controlled) ‡500

Centennial
National Cattlemen
Magazine **(4226)** ....(Paid) 35,000

Colorado Springs
CALF News Magazine **(4238)** 6,000

Denver
The Bagpipe **(4306)**
Bison World **(4308)** ....‡2,000
Colorado Country Life **(4312)** 160,000
Journal of the ASFMRA **(4335)** ....(Combined) 3,000
Rock Garden Quarterly **(4352)** ....(Paid) 5,000

Circ.

Western Livestock Journal **(4366)** ......(Paid) 18,335

Englewood
Farm Supply Retailing **(4413)** .....(Controlled) 20,000

Fort Collins
Journal of Agricultural & Resource Economics **(4434)**

Frederick
Farmer and Miner **(4455)** ....‡1,300

Lakewood
Journal of Range Management **(4533)** 3,400

Littleton
Texas Longhorn Journal **(4555)** ....‡3,000

Parker
American Salers **(4596)** ....(Paid) ‡1,720

Wheat Ridge
Record Stockman **(4680)** 12,000
Southwest Stockman **(4684)** 13,250

Windsor
The Fence Post **(4686)** ....(Paid) ‡9,700
(Non-paid) ‡400

CONNECTICUT
Fairfield
Journal of Sustainable
Agriculture **(4790)** ....(Paid) ‡775

DISTRICT OF COLUMBIA
Washington
Agricultural Aviation **(5316)** ....(Controlled) 6,000
Amber Waves **(5321)**
Journal of Agricultural Lending **(5568)** .....(Paid) 580
Rural Cooperatives **(5773)** ....(Paid) 8,000
Sulphur in Agriculture **(5807)**

FLORIDA
Bartow
The Citrus Industry **(5917)** ....‡10,000

Gainesville
FloridAgriculture **(6140)** ....(Paid) ‡127,000
(Free) ‡800
The Record Farm & Ranch **(6154)** ....‡5,000
Tri-Ology **(6158)**

Havana
Havana Herald **(6185)** ....(Paid) ⊕2,600
(Free) ⊕25

Kissimmee
Florida Cattleman and Livestock
Journal **(6261)** ....(Paid) 4,383
(Non-paid) 205

Lithia
Farm and Ranch News **(6304)** ....(Paid) 6,000
(Controlled) 13,000

St. Petersburg
The Seed Pod **(6634)** ....(Controlled) 1,200

Tallahassee
Florida Market
Bulletin **(6714)** ....(Controlled) ‡15,000

Circulation: ★ = ABC; △ = BPA; ♦ = CAC; ● = CCAB; ▢ = VAC; ⊕ = PO Statement; ‡ = Publisher's Report; Boldface figures = sworn; Light figures = estimated.

Circ.　　　　　Circ.　　　　　Circ.

FLORIDA (continued)
Tampa
Citrus and Vegetable
　Magazine **(6760)** ....(Controlled) △12,000

Winter Park
Florida Grower **(6880)** ....(Controlled) 13,396
Ornamental Outlook **(6884)** 13,175

GEORGIA
Athens
Communications in Soil Science and Plant
　Analysis **(6934)** ....‡800
Journal of Agricultural and Applied
　Economics **(6943)** ....(Paid) 750

Atlanta
Farmers & Consumers Market
　Bulletin **(7006)** ....(Free) 205,428
Georgia Future Farmer **(7012)**

Augusta
SPUR MAGAZINE **(7103)** 25,000

Forsyth
Florida Farmer **(7278)**

Fort Valley
The Camellia Journal **(7285)** ....‡5,000

Gainesville
Poultry and Egg
　Marketing **(7293)** ....(Controlled) ‡11,600
Poultry Times **(7294)** ....(Paid) 10,661

Jesup
The Speedy Bee **(7348)** ....‡3,000

Macon
Georgia Farm Bureau News **(7381)** ....‡66,312

Norcross
Better Crops with Plant Food **(7456)** ......(Paid) ‡50
　　　　　　　　　　　　　　　(Non-paid) ‡16,000

Tifton
The Peanut Grower **(7596)** ....(Controlled) 22,500
Southeastern Peanut Farmer **(7597)** ....‡8,500

Tucker
GEORGIA Magazine **(7610)** ....‡448,000

HAWAII
Honolulu
Hawaii Crop Weather **(7694)**

Waianae
Hawaii Orchid Journal **(7794)** ....‡750

IDAHO
Boise
The Line Rider **(7813)** ....‡1,500

Idaho Falls
Potato Grower **(7869)** ....(Combined) 16,000
The Sugar Producer **(7871)** .....(Controlled) ‡16,000

Moscow
Appaloosa Journal **(7911)** 30,000

Parma
Journal of Potato Production and Postharvest
　Handling **(7942)**

ILLINOIS
Batavia
Grower Talks **(8054)** ....(Paid) 9,230

Bloomington
FarmWeek **(8077)** ....(Paid) 80,608
Partners **(8080)** ....(Paid) 287,683
　　　　　　　　　　　　　　　(Non-paid) 609

Carmi
Angus Topics **(8130)** ....‡8,300

Carol Stream
Carolina/Virginia Farmer **(8137)** ....‡15,177
FFA New Horizons **(8143)** .....(Controlled) ‡512,644
The Hog Producer **(8145)**
Nebraska Farmer **(8150)** ....(Paid) 16,436
　　　　　　　　　　　　　　　(Non-paid) 23,281
New England Farmer **(8151)** ....(Paid) ‡5,402
　　　　　　　　　　　　　　　(Controlled) ‡10,783
Western Farmer-Stockman **(8157)**

Champaign
Arborist News
　Magazine **(8180)** ....(Controlled) 17,000

Chicago
American Nurseryman **(8261)** ....(Paid) 14,961
CarneTec **(8299)** ....(Non-paid) 6,200
Meat Marketing &
　Technology **(8483)** ....(Combined) 20,058
Poultry Magazine **(8538)** ....(Controlled) ‡10,000

Cuba
Banner Sheep Magazine **(8699)** ....‡3,500

Decatur
The Beef Producer **(8709)**
Indiana Prairie Farmer **(8712)** ....‡35,000

Downers Grove
Illinois Standardbred & Mid-America Harness
　News **(8786)** 1,540

Hamilton
American Bee Journal **(8968)** ....(Paid) ‡12,000

Joliet
Farmers' Weekly Review **(9032)** 11,500

La Salle
Illinois Agri-News **(9055)** ....(Paid) ‡34,000

Lena
Northwestern Illinois Farmer **(9074)** ....‡6,000

Mascoutah
Farm Impact **(9152)** ....(Non-paid) 40,000

Mount Morris
Feed International **(9237)** ....(Paid) 478
　　　　　　　　　　　　　　　(Non-paid) 16,025
Feed Management **(9238)** ....(Paid) 204
　　　　　　　　　　　　　　　(Non-paid) 17,676
Industria Avicola **(9239)** 15,160
Pig International **(9244)** ....(Controlled) 17,638
Poultry International **(9245)** ......(Combined) 23,620

Pecatonica
Clydesdale News **(9413)**

Peoria
Spotted News **(9426)** ....(Paid) ‡4,000
　　　　　　　　　　　　　　　(Non-paid) ‡3,000

Rochelle
Farmer's Report **(9513)**

Rolling Meadows
Greenhouse Business **(9547)** ......(Non-paid) 18,000
Turf News **(9551)** ....‡1,700

Springfield
Illinois Beef **(9622)** ....(Controlled) ‡5,200
Illinois Rural Electric News **(9630)** ....‡142,000

Urbana
Illinois Research **(9710)** ....(Controlled) ‡7,000

INDIANA
Berne
Berne Tri-Weekly News **(9802)** ....‡2,500

Connersville
Poultry Press **(9901)** ....‡5,800

Indianapolis
Electric Consumer **(10109)** ....(Paid) 250,000
　　　　　　　　　　　　　　　(Non-paid) 172
FFA Advisors Making a
　Difference **(10111)** ....(Combined) 13,200
The Hoosier Farmer **(10116)** ....‡271,000
Indiana Agri-News **(10121)** ....(Paid) ‡8,000
　　　　　　　　　　　　　　　(Controlled) ‡21,000
Indiana Beef **(10123)** ....‡8,300
Our Paper **(10158)**
POA **(10161)** ....‡1,600

Knightstown
Farmweek **(10235)** ....(Paid) 35,141

New Paris
Farmer's Exchange **(10347)** ....(Paid) ‡13,800
　　　　　　　　　　　　　　　(Free) ‡800

West Lafayette
Seedstock Edge **(10552)** ....(Paid) 4,900
　　　　　　　　　　　　　　　(Non-paid) 250

IOWA
Cedar Falls
Implement & Tractor **(10657)** ....(Paid) ‡3,000
　　　　　　　　　　　　　　　(Non-paid) ‡4,000

Cedar Rapids
Iowa Farmer Today **(10674)** .....(Controlled) ‡71,228
Iowa Pork Today **(10675)** ......(Non-paid) ‡30,313

Clive
Iowa Pork Producer **(10716)** ......(Non-paid) ‡16,173

Cresco
Times-Plain Dealer **(10730)** ....(Paid) ‡3,450
　　　　　　　　　　　　　　　(Free) ‡7,650

Dayton
Dayton Review **(10753)** ....‡845

Des Moines
National Pork
　Report **(10804)** ....(Non-paid) ‡109,350
Successful Farming **(10811)** ....(Paid) ‡442,000
Wallaces Farmer **(10814)** ....(Paid) 12,289
　　　　　　　　　　　　　　　(Non-paid) 55,513

Elgin
The Elgin Echo **(10871)** 1,700

Fort Dodge
Farm Equipment Guide **(10898)** ....(Paid) ‡11,500
　　　　　　　　　　　　　　　(Non-paid) ‡7,500
Farmer's Digest **(10899)** 10,000
Farmers Hot Line **(10900)** ......(Non-paid) ‡47,540
　　　　　　　　　　　　　　　(Paid) ‡1,660

Gowrie
The Gowrie News **(10927)** ....‡1,400

Iowa Falls
Spokesman **(11000)** ....(Paid) 105,294

Jewell
South Hamilton Record News **(11008)** 950

Marengo
Iowa County Farmer **(11061)** ....(Paid) ‡10,140

Orange City
Farmer's Cattle-log **(11129)** ....(Free) 4,800

Peterson
Peterson Patriot **(11159)** ....‡580

Tipton
The Tipton Conservative and
　Advertiser **(11269)** ....‡4,700

Urbandale
Idaho FarmekraHJJmpw- **(11275)**
Iowa REC News **(11276)** ....(Combined) ‡93,000
Wisconsin Agriculturist **(11277)** ....(Paid) 3,205
　　　　　　　　　　　　　　　(Non-paid) 27,505

Waverly
The Draft Horse Journal **(11307)** ....(Paid) 22,000
　　　　　　　　　　　　　　　(Non-paid) 125

KANSAS
Allen
American Beef Cattleman **(11336)** ....‡20,000

Belleville
Farmer Stockman of the
　Midwest **(11357)** ....‡15,057

Council Grove
Beef Today **(11403)** ....(Controlled) 187,656

Dighton
Feed-Lot **(11413)** ....(Controlled) ‡10,777

Dodge City
High Plains Journal **(11415)** ....(Paid) 51,411

Jewell
Kansas Farmer **(11517)** ....(Paid) 12,656
　　　　　　　　　　　　　　　(Non-paid) 21,141

Lawrence
Weed Science **(11570)**
Weed Technology **(11571)**

Lecompton
Christmas Trees **(11588)** ....(Paid) ‡4,391
　　　　　　　　　　　　　　　(Controlled) ‡41

Lenexa
Dealer and Applicator
　Magazine **(11589)** ....(Controlled) ‡22,000
Drovers **(11590)** ....(Paid) 297
　　　　　　　　　　　　　　　(Controlled) 98,000
The Grower **(11593)** ....(Controlled) ‡22,000
Pork **(11595)** ....(Controlled) ‡26,299
Swine Practitioner **(11597)** ....△3,340

Manhattan
Grass & Grain **(11620)** ....‡16,500
Kansas 4-H Journal **(11624)** ....‡13,500
Kansas Living **(11625)** ....(Controlled) ‡140,000

Numbers cited after listings are entry numbers rather than page numbers.

Overland Park
California-Arizona Farm Press **(11701)**

Parsons
Farm Talk **(11743)** ....‡9,985

Scott City
News Chronicle **(11794)** ....(Paid) 2,850
(Free) 25

Topeka
Kansas Country Living **(11827)** ....‡80,957
Kansas Stockman **(11831)** ....(Paid) ‡7,025
(Non-paid) ‡410

Troy
Green Acres **(11849)** ....(Paid) 2,800
(Free) 43,500

Wichita
International Flying
Farmer **(11882)** ....(Controlled) ‡1,900

KENTUCKY
Buckner
Fastline—Dakota Farm
Edition **(11969)** ....(Combined) 22,000
Fastline—Far West Farm
Edition **(11971)** ....(Combined) 22,000
Fastline—Illinois Farm
Edition **(11974)** ....(Combined) 22,000
Fastline—Indiana Farm
Edition **(11975)** ....(Combined) 22,000
Fastline—Iowa Farm
Edition **(11976)** ....(Combined) 22,000
Fastline—Kansas Farm
Edition **(11977)** ....(Combined) 22,000
Fastline—Kentucky Farm
Edition **(11978)** ....(Combined) 22,000
Fastline—Mid-Atlantic Farm
Edition **(11979)** ....(Combined) 22,000
Fastline—Mid-South Farm
Edition **(11980)** ....(Combined) 22,000
Fastline—Minnesota Farm
Edition **(11982)** ....(Combined) 22,000
Fastline—Missouri Farm
Edition **(11983)** ....(Combined) 22,000
Fastline—Nebraska Farm
Edition **(11984)** ....(Combined) 22,000
Fastline—Northeast Farm
Edition **(11985)** ....(Combined) 22,000
Fastline—Northwest Farm
Edition **(11987)** ....(Combined) 22,000
Fastline—Ohio Farm
Edition **(11988)** ....(Combined) 22,000
Fastline—Oklahoma Farm
Edition **(11989)** ....(Combined) 22,000
Fastline—Ontario Farm
Edition **(11990)** ....(Combined) 22,000
Fastline—Rocky Mountain Farm
Edition **(11991)** ....(Combined) 22,000
Fastline—Southeast Farm
Edition **(11993)** ....(Combined) 22,000
Fastline—Tennessee Farm
Edition **(11994)** ....(Combined) 22,000
Fastline—Texas Farm
Edition **(11996)** ....(Combined) 22,000
Fastline—Wisconsin Farm
Edition **(11998)** ....(Combined) 22,000

Frankfort
Journal of Applied
Aquaculture **(12064)** ....(Paid) 301
Kentucky Farmer **(12070)** ....‡9,535

Lexington
Cow Country News **(12163)** 10,000

Louisville
All Around Kentucky **(12209)** ....(Paid) ‡387,925
(Controlled) ‡935

LOUISIANA
Baton Rouge
Louisiana Agriculture
Magazine **(12494)** ....(Controlled) ‡5,900
Louisiana Country **(12497)** ....‡130,000
Louisiana Market Bulletin **(12500)** ....‡16,800
Louisiana Rural
Economist **(12503)** ....(Controlled) ‡1,265

Lake Providence
Banner-Democrat **(12652)** ....‡2,200

New Orleans
Louisiana Farmer **(12739)**
Sugar Journal **(12754)** ....(Paid) 654
(Non-paid) 3,319

Port Allen
The Louisiana Cattleman **(12798)** ......(Paid) ‡3,900
(Non-paid) ‡800

Shreveport
American Rose **(12816)** ....(Paid) ‡22,109
(Controlled) ‡150

MAINE
Lincolnville
Maine Organic Farmer and
Gardener **(12982)** ....(Paid) ‡5,000
(Non-paid) ‡100

Orono
American Journal of Potato
Research **(12998)** ....‡1,000

Presque Isle
Maine Potato News **(13034)** ....(Free) ‡6,250

MARYLAND
Bethesda
North American Journal of
Aquaculture **(13365)** ....‡2,200

Easton
The Delmarva Farmer **(13487)** ....(Paid) ‡8,000
(Free) ‡3,702
The New Jersey Farmer **(13488)** ....(Paid) ‡2,247
(Controlled) ‡2,543

Lanham
Journal of Economic Entomology **(13604)** 1,800

MASSACHUSETTS
Amherst
Journal of Tree Fruit
Production **(13798)** ....(Paid) 96

Bedford
Hobby Greenhouse **(13836)** ....(Combined) 1,600

Boston
Horticulture **(13903)** ....(Paid) 210,000

Jamaica Plain
Arnoldia **(14258)** 4,450

Malden
American Journal of Agricultural
Economics **(14289)** 4,300
Choices **(14290)** ....(Combined) 6,100

Millbury
Dairy World **(14334)** ....(Non-paid) ‡40,999

Norwell
Journal of Agricultural and Environmental
Ethics **(14441)** ....(Paid) 211
(Non-paid) 27

Rochester
Cranberries **(14505)** ....‡1,000

MICHIGAN
Bay City
Valley Farmer **(14803)** ....‡1,450

Camden
The Farmers' Advance **(14852)** ......(Paid) ‡19,315
(Free) ‡2,512

East Lansing
Agricultural Economics
Report **(14981)** ....(Non-paid) 15

Haslett
Michigan News **(15151)** ....‡1,300

Lansing
Michigan Farm News **(15282)** ....(Paid) 48,586

Okemos
Michigan Country Lines **(15416)** 240,000

Paw Paw
The Courier-Leader **(15433)** ....(Paid) ⊕4,069
(Free) 45

St. Joseph
Applied Engineering in
Agriculture **(15511)** ....(Paid) ‡700
Resource **(15513)** ....‡9,000
Transactions of the ASAE **(15514)** ....‡1,200

Sparta
The Fruit Growers News **(15568)** .....(Paid) ‡14,235
The Vegetable Growers
News **(15570)** ....(Combined) ‡14,415

MINNESOTA
Buffalo
Gobbles **(15778)** ....‡800

Glyndon
Dakota Farmer **(15922)** ....‡37,530
The Farmer **(15923)**

Lakeville
Farm Show **(15994)** ....‡150,000

Mankato
The Land **(16028)** ....(Non-paid) ‡39,500

Minneapolis
BEEF **(16059)** ....(Controlled) ‡101,661
Delta Farm Press **(16073)** ....(Paid) 23,224
(Non-paid) 7,977
Farm Industry News **(16079)** ....(Non-paid) ‡250,000
Hay & Forage
Grower **(16084)** ....(Non-paid) ‡90,000
National Hog
Farmer **(16113)** ....(Controlled) ‡35,000
Southeast Farm
Press **(16129)** ....(Combined) 53,000
Southwest Farm Press **(16130)** ....(Paid) 25,009
(Non-paid) 21,666
Soybean Digest **(16132)** ....(Controlled) ‡214,000
Western Farm Press **(16139)** .....(Combined) 24,000

Minnetonka
Feedstuffs **(16169)** ....(Paid) 11,312
(Non-paid) 4,727

Monticello
Dairy Today **(16184)** ....(Non-paid) 70,000

New Prague
Ag Retailer Magazine **(16208)** ....(Non-paid) 21,598

Owatonna
North American Lily Society
Quarterly **(16252)** ....(Paid) 1,500

Rochester
Agri News **(16305)** ....(Paid) ‡21,500

St. Paul
Molecular Plant-Microbe Interactions
(MPMI) **(16397)** ....(Paid) 1,500
(Non-paid) 7
Plant Disease **(16406)** ....(Paid) ‡4,000
(Non-paid) ‡31
The Voice of
Agriculture **(16414)** ....(Combined) 35,000

MISSISSIPPI
Greenwood
Staplreview **(16645)** ....‡4,500

Jackson
Mississippi Farm Bureau News **(16702)** .....‡180,000

Meridian
The Stockman Grass
Farmer **(16770)** ....(Paid) 10,961

Mississippi State
MAFES Research
Highlights **(16782)** ....(Non-paid) 10,300

Pontotoc
Mississippi Farmer **(16822)**

Ridgeland
TODAY in Mississippi **(16835)** ....(Paid) ‡386,691
(Non-paid) ‡176

MISSOURI
Clark
Small Farm Today **(16981)** 12,000

Columbia
Missouri Ruralist **(17004)** ....(Paid) 17,087
(Non-paid) 17,161
Today's Farmer **(17011)** ....‡46,000

Fenton
NAEDA Equipment Dealer **(17062)** .....(Paid) △8,298
(Non-paid) △2,245

Jefferson City
Rural Missouri **(17132)** ....‡388,000
Show Me Missouri Farm Bureau
News **(17133)** ....(Controlled) ‡91,000

Kansas City
Charolais Journal **(17161)** ....‡6,000
Farmland System News **(17169)** ....‡168,000
Hereford World **(17171)** ....‡10,000

Agricultural Publications

Circulation: ★ = ABC; △ = BPA; ♦ = CAC; • = CCAB; ◻ = VAC; ⊕ = PO Statement; ‡ = Publisher's Report; Boldface figures = sworn; Light figures = estimated.

2733

Circ.　　　　　Circ.　　　　　Circ.

MISSOURI (continued)
Missouri Beef
　Cattleman **(17186)** ....(Controlled) ‡5,200
Southwestern Retailer **(17197)** ....(Paid) ‡1,100
　　　　　　　　　　　　(Controlled) ‡420
World Grain **(17205)** ....(Combined) ‡9,017

Perryville
MidAmerica Farmer
　Grower **(17337)** ....(Paid) ‡14,379
　　　　　　　　　　　(Non-paid) ‡10,451
National Conservation Tillage Digest **(17338)**

Platte City
American Chianina Journal **(17348)** ....‡1,500

Polo
Hogs Today **(17356)** ....(Non-paid) 84,547

St. Joseph
Angus Beef Bulletin **(17389)** ......(Non-paid) ‡70,000
Angus Journal **(17390)** ....‡23,000

St. Louis
Agri Marketing **(17407)** ....(Paid) 212
　　　　　　　　　　　(Controlled) 8,325
The National Gardener **(17475)** ....‡30,000

MONTANA
Billings
Western Livestock Reporter **(17734)** ....‡12,000

Bozeman
Montana Farm Bureau
　Spokesman **(17753)** ....‡9,000

Helena
AERO Sun-Times **(17817)** ....(Paid) 630
　　　　　　　　　　　(Controlled) 50

Huson
Bonsai Journal **(17835)** ....(Paid) 1,450

NEBRASKA
Lincoln
Nebraska Cattleman **(18099)** ....(Paid) ‡5,067
　　　　　　　　　　　(Controlled) ‡4,530
Nebraska Farm Bureau
　News **(18100)** ....(Paid) ‡45,000
　　　　　　　　　　　(Non-paid) ‡500
Nebraska Union Farmer **(18106)** 3,000
Rural Electric Nebraskan **(18117)** ....‡66,000

Omaha
Shorthorn Country **(18208)** ....(Paid) ‡3,500
　　　　　　　　　　　(Non-paid) ‡200

Scottsbluff
Business Farmer **(18262)** ....(Paid) 2,750
Business Farmer-Stockman **(18263)** 2,700

Tekamah
Midwest Messenger **(18297)** ....(Free) ‡154,380

NEVADA
Lovelock
The Nevada Rancher **(18413)** ....(Paid) ‡3,500
　　　　　　　　　　　(Free) ‡200

NEW HAMPSHIRE
Loudon
The Plantsman **(18554)**

Manchester
Tree Care Industry **(18564)** ......(Controlled) ‡28,000

NEW JERSEY
Hoboken
Agribusiness **(18883)** 11,900

New Brunswick
Soil Science **(19340)** ....(Paid) ‡1,113
　　　　　　　　　　　(Non-paid) ‡235

Toms River
Weekly Insiders Turkey Letter **(19648)** ....(Paid) 230

NEW MEXICO
Albuquerque
Arizona Cattlelog **(19766)** ....‡1,800
Livestock Market Digest **(19775)**
New Mexico Stockman **(19782)** ....‡10,750

Las Cruces
New Mexico Farm and
　Ranch **(19874)** ....(Paid) ‡12,500
　　　　　　　　　　　(Controlled) ‡175

Santa Fe
Enchantment **(19935)** ....‡125,000

NEW YORK
Adams
The Empire State Farmer **(19975)** .....(Free) ‡6,000

Binghamton
Journal of New Seeds **(20190)**
Small Fruits Review **(20215)** 225

Bronx
Biological & Agricultural Index **(20255)**
Farming Uncle **(20268)** ....(Paid) 400
　　　　　　　　　　　(Non-paid) 700

Brooklyn
Plants & Gardens News **(20338)** ....‡18,000

East Aurora
Farm News of Erie and Wyoming
　Counties **(20542)** ....(Paid) ‡1,600
　　　　　　　　　　　(Non-paid) ‡100

East Syracuse
Holstein World **(20558)** ....‡13,255

Gouverneur
The Trottingbred **(20675)** ....‡500

Great Neck
Agricultura de las
　Americas **(20684)** ....(Non-paid) 37,318

Ithaca
Agricultural Finance Review **(20788)** ....(Paid) 600
Cornell Focus **(20793)** ....(Non-paid) ‡4,600
New York Holstein
　News **(20811)** ....(Controlled) ‡4,300

LaFayette
Agricultural News
　(Lafayette) **(20869)** ....(Non-paid) 3,000

Mexico
AgNews of Central New York **(21075)** ....‡2,700

Moravia
Focus on Farming **(21095)** ....‡15,500

Mount Morris
Livingston County Agricultural
　News **(21101)** ....(Paid) ‡220
　　　　　　　　　　　(Controlled) ‡25

New York
Agricultural and Human Values **(21165)**
European Journal of Plant Pathology **(21648)**
Experimental Agriculture **(21663)** 550
Genetic Resources and Crop Evolution **(21751)**
Integrated Pest Management **(21886)**
Irrigation and Drainage Systems **(21953)**
The Journal of Agricultural Science **(21979)** 750
Journal of Dairy Research **(22046)** 750
New Forests **(22429)**
Plant and Soil **(22561)**

Owego
Dairy and Field Crops Digest **(23066)**

Palatine Bridge
Country Folks Grower **(23073)** ....(Combined) 25,000
Farm Chronicle **(23074)** ....(Paid) 22,000

Queensbury
Agricultural News **(23171)** ....‡4,000

Riverhead
Suffolk County Agricultural News **(23204)** ......‡800

Saugerties
Country Folks **(23306)** ....(Combined) 9,000

NORTH CAROLINA
Fuquay Varina
Carolina Cattle Connection **(23902)** ....‡7,000

Raleigh
Agricultural Review (North
　Carolina) **(24124)** ....(Controlled) ‡60,000
The Burley Tobacco
　Farmer **(24128)** ....(Controlled) 17,318
The Flue Cured Tobacco
　Farmer **(24136)** ....(Paid) 85
　　　　　　　　　　　(Controlled) 14,461
The Peanut Farmer **(24147)** ....(Paid) 48
　　　　　　　　　　　(Controlled) 17,410
Rice Journal **(24151)** ....(Paid) ‡177
　　　　　　　　　　　(Controlled) ‡10,876

Wilson
Carolina Farmer **(24310)** ....‡30,000

NORTH DAKOTA
Bismarck
Farm and Ranch Guide **(24352)** ....(Paid) 1,450
　　　　　　　　　　　40,484
North Dakota Stockman **(24357)** ....‡3,400
The Sunflower **(24360)** 16,667

Enderlin
Enderlin Independent **(24410)** ....‡1,000

Grand Forks
AGWEEK **(24453)** ....(Paid) 26,831
　　　　　　　　　　　(Controlled) 517

Mandan
North Dakota REC Magazine **(24498)** ....‡71,199

Minnewaukan
Benson County Farmers Press **(24503)** ....‡2,714

Watford City
McKenzie County Farmer **(24555)** ....‡2,300

OHIO
Archbold
Farmland News **(24614)** 7,107

Bellbrook
Racing Pigeon Bulletin **(24665)** ....‡5,000

Bellevue
Bellevue RFD News **(24670)** ....(Paid) 400
　　　　　　　　　　　(Non-paid) 9,500
Bucyrus RFD News **(24671)** ....(Paid) 300
　　　　　　　　　　　(Non-paid) 9,700

Cardington
The Shepherd **(24740)** ....‡7,500

Columbus
Buckeye Farm News **(25002)** ....(Paid) ‡215,000
　　　　　　　　　　　(Non-paid) ‡1,106
Country Living (Ohio) **(25012)** ....(Paid) 282,050
Ohio Granger **(25045)** ....‡10,000

Lancaster
The Ohio Farmer **(25291)** ....(Paid) 15,730
　　　　　　　　　　　(Non-paid) 18,862

Marysville
Ohio Cattleman **(25358)** ....‡3,000

Medina
Bee Culture **(25372)** ....(Paid) ‡15,000
　　　　　　　　　　　(Non-paid) ‡500

New London
Firelands Farmer **(25417)** ....‡5,870

Reynoldsburg
Guernsey Breeders'
　Journal **(25494)** ....(Paid) ‡1,900
　　　　　　　　　　　(Controlled) ‡190
Jersey Journal **(25495)** ....(Paid) 3,142
　　　　　　　　　　　(Non-paid) 1,649

Salem
Farm and Dairy **(25505)** ....(Paid) ‡34,800
　　　　　　　　　　　(Non-paid) ‡1,668

Willoughby
Ag Consultant **(25655)** ....(Non-paid) 17,623
American Fruit Grower **(25656)** ....(Paid) ‡58,423
American Vegetable Grower **(25657)** ....(Paid) 9,778
　　　　　　　　　　　(Non-paid) 19,711
Farm Chemicals **(25658)** ....(Paid) △550
　　　　　　　　　　　(Non-paid) △29,136
Farm Chemicals International **(25659)** 9,400
Greenhouse Grower **(25660)** ....(Controlled) 22,060
Productores de
　Hortalizas **(25663)** ....(Controlled) 10,000
Western Fruit Grower **(25664)** ....(Paid) ‡3,142
　　　　　　　　　　　22,377

OKLAHOMA
Boise City
The Boise City News **(25766)** ....(Paid) 1,800
　　　　　　　　　　　(Free) 60

Checotah
McIntosh County Democrat **(25781)** ....(Paid) ‡2,995
　　　　　　　　　　　(Free) ‡205

Lane
Journal of Vegetable Crop Production **(25881)**

Nardin
Emu Today & Tomorrow **(25927)** ......(Paid) ⊕1,000
　　　　　　　　　　　(Non-paid) ⊕100

Norman
Speedhorse Racing Report **(25943)** ....‡8,000

Oklahoma City
Farm News & Views **(25963)** 109,000
Oklahoma Country **(25976)** ....(Paid) ‡127,247
(Controlled) ‡834
Oklahoma COWMAN **(25977)** **4,784**

Ponca City
Oklahoma Farmer-Stockman **(26036)** ....(Paid) 8,948
(Non-paid) 8,825
Texas Farmer-Stockman **(26038)** ....(Paid) 15,458
(Non-paid) 25,451

Yukon
Limousin World **(26204)** ....(Paid) ‡4,800
(Non-paid) ‡5,200

OREGON
Corvallis
The Growing Edge **(26288)** ....(Paid) 20,000
(Non-paid) 1,000
Ornamentals Northwest **(26290)** ....‡4,750

Eugene
Worm Digest **(26335)** ....(Paid) ‡6,200
(Non-paid) ‡800

Forest Grove
Ruralite **(26357)** ....‡281,400

Klamath Falls
Cascade Cattleman **(26382)** 5,500
Cascade Horseman **(26383)** 10,000

Pendleton
Agri-Times Northwest **(26457)** ......(Combined) 3,700
Oregon Wheat **(26459)** ....‡5,800

Portland
Pacific Coast Nurseryman and Garden Supply
Dealer **(26496)** ....(Paid) ‡6,840
(Non-paid) ‡3,624

Salem
Capital Press **(26565)** ....(Paid) 38,966
Oregon Beef Producer **(26569)** 2,500

Sisters
Small Farmer's Journal **(26585)** 25,000

PENNSYLVANIA
Camp Hill
Country Focus **(26749)** ....(Controlled) 26,000

Emmaus
Organic Gardening **(26879)** ....(Paid) 605,980

Ephrata
Lancaster Farming **(26888)** ....(Paid) ⊕51,000
(Free) ⊕1,000

Harrisburg
Penn Lines **(27004)** ....(Paid) 143,134

Philadelphia
Farm Journal **(27468)** ....(Paid) 133,655
(Non-paid) 449,384

PUERTO RICO
Rio Piedras
University of Puerto Rico Journal of
Agriculture **(28286)**

SOUTH CAROLINA
Cayce
Living in South Carolina **(28503)** ....‡503,000

Charleston
Journal of Agromedicine **(28514)** ....(Paid) 218

Clemson
South Carolina YR and FFA **(28534)** ....‡8,000

Columbia
Palmetto Poultry Life **(28560)** ......(Controlled) 1,350

Gaffney
Grit and Steel **(28616)** ....‡6,000

SOUTH DAKOTA
Brookings
Farm & Home Research
Quarterly **(28813)** ....(Non-paid) ‡5,000

Sioux Falls
Tri-State Neighbor **(28969)** ....(Controlled) 29,500

Sturgis
Tri-State Livestock News **(29001)** .....(Paid) ‡14,000
(Free) ‡500

TENNESSEE
Columbia
Tennessee Farm Bureau News **(29138)** ....‡117,000

Dresden
Dresden Enterprise **(29170)** ....‡5,200

Fayetteville
Farmers Exchange **(29190)** ....(Free) 21,000

Gainesboro
Rural Heritage **(29201)** ....‡6,000

Lewisburg
Voice of the Tennessee Walking
Horse **(29326)** ....(Paid) ‡19,500
(Non-paid) ‡176

Memphis
Cotton Farming **(29364)** ....(Non-paid) 51,151

Nashville
Tennessee Magazine **(29492)** ....(Paid) 472,677

TEXAS
Amarillo
The American Quarter Horse
Journal **(29695)** ....(Paid) 70,052
The Quarter Racing Journal **(29697)** ....(Paid) 8,908

Austin
Acres U.S.A. **(29750)** 10,000
Texas FFA News **(29819)** ....(Controlled) 68,000

Bogata
Bogata News **(29932)** ....‡2,184

Bowie
Ratite Marketplace **(29941)** ....(Paid) 4,000

Bryan
Pecan South **(29974)** ....(Paid) ‡4,300
(Non-paid) ‡500

College Station
Journal of Agricultural and Food
Information **(30044)** ....(Paid) 200

Crowley
United Caprine News **(30113)** ....‡6,000

Denton
American Red Angus **(30232)** ....‡9,000

Dripping Springs
American Red Brangus Journal **(30250)** ....‡5,000

Eddy
The Brahman Journal **(30268)** ....(Paid) ‡2183
(Non-paid) ‡1586

Fort Worth
The Cattleman **(30331)** ....(Paid) 15,415
(Non-paid) 1,590
Christian Ranchman **(30333)** ....(Free) 39,470
Cutting Horse Chatter **(30336)** ....‡13,000
The Horsetrader **(30342)** ....‡20,452
Lone Star Horse Report **(30346)** ......(Paid) 1,000
(Controlled) 10,000
Paint Horse Journal **(30350)** ....(Paid) ‡35,038
Texas Hereford **(30354)** ....‡3,200
Weekly Livestock
Reporter **(30355)** ....(Paid) ‡11,903
(Free) ‡662

Grandview
Grandview Tribune **(30408)** ....‡1,200

Odonnell
O'Donnell Index-Press **(30884)** ....(Combined) 495

San Angelo
Livestock Weekly **(31005)** ....(Paid) ⊕18,211
Meat Goat Monthly News **(31006)** 2,500
Ranch & Rural Living
Magazine **(31008)** ....(Paid) 6,318
(Non-paid) 700

San Antonio
The Beefmaster Cowman **(31025)** ......(Paid) ‡4,835
(Non-paid) ‡211
Brangus Journal **(31026)** ....‡2,800
Gulf Coast
Cattleman **(31031)** ....(Controlled) ‡15,755

Waco
Texas Agriculture **(31252)** ....(Paid) 125,065
(Free) 1,009

UTAH
Logan
Utah Science **(31352)** ....(Non-paid) 6,000

Provo
Benson Institute Review **(31398)**

VERMONT
Randolph
Green World **(31580)** 200

Shelburne
The Morgan Horse **(31599)** ....‡8,000

VIRGINIA
Alexandria
The American Gardener **(31636)** 28,000
Hort Technology **(31678)** ....(Paid) 2,600
HortScience **(31679)** ....(Paid) 3,600
Journal of the American Society for Horticultural
Science **(31687)** ....(Paid) 2,500

Arlington
Rural Electrification
Magazine **(31824)** ....(Paid) 33,119

Blacksburg
Journal of Dairy Science **(31874)** ....‡5,062
Virginia Extension **(31879)**

Daleville
Virginia Cattleman **(31990)** ....‡10,000

Fairfax Station
Chrysanthemum **(32037)** ....(Controlled) 1,200

Glen Allen
Rural Living **(32112)** ....(Paid) 325,000

Richmond
The Southern States Cooperative
Magazine **(32455)** ....(Paid) ‡3,611
(Non-paid) ‡198,997
Virginia Farm Bureau News **(32461)** ....‡136,000

WASHINGTON
Blaine
Grey Book **(32688)**

Lynden
Lynden Tribune **(32821)** ....‡7,000

Olympia
Washington State Grange News **(32862)** .....‡38,993

Ritzville
Wheat Life **(32933)** 14,065

Seattle
Bamboo Science & Culture **(32946)**
Grain & Feed
Marketing **(32969)** ....(Controlled) ‡15,415

Spokane
Ag Equipment Power **(33092)** ...(Non-paid) ‡10,800
10,600

Vancouver
Colorado Farmer-Stockman **(33174)** .....(Paid) 3,421
(Non-paid) 6,690

Yakima
Potato Country **(33221)** ....(Controlled) ‡7,544
The Tomato
Magazine **(33222)** ....(Controlled) ‡6,742

WISCONSIN
Antigo
The Badger Common'Tater **(33532)** ......(Paid) ‡487
(Non-paid) ‡3,357

Appleton
The North American Deer
Farmer **(33541)** ....(Combined) 1,200

Brookfield
American Farriers Journal **(33602)** .....(Paid) ‡7,000
(Non-paid) ‡200

Chippewa Falls
Rural Minnesota News **(33628)** ....(Paid) 35,000

Denmark
Country Chronicle **(33656)** ....(Paid) 381
(Free) 14,631

Eau Claire
The Country Today **(33668)** ....(Paid) ‡25,000
(Free) ‡2,903

Circulation: ★ = ABC; △ = BPA; ♦ = CAC; • = CCAB; ▢ = VAC; ⊕ = PO Statement; ‡ = Publisher's Report; Boldface figures = sworn; Light figures = estimated.

2735

Agricultural Publications

Circ.   Circ.   Circ.

WISCONSIN (continued)

Fort Atkinson
Farm Equipment **(33708)** ....(Controlled) 10,000
Feed & Grain **(33709)** ....(Controlled) ‡16,505
Hoard's Dairyman **(33711)** ....(Paid) 69,672
     (Non-paid) 15,892
OEM Off-Highway **(33715)** ....(Controlled) ‡17,500

Greendale
Country Woman **(33760)**
Farm & Ranch Living **(33762)** 400,000

Madison
Agronomy Journal **(33916)** 9,500
The Cheese Reporter **(33926)** ....(Paid) 1,665
     (Free) 170
Crop Science **(33931)** ....‡4,500
Farm Bureau's Rural Route **(33937)** ....‡48,000
Food Reviews International **(33940)** 350
Soil Science Society of America
   Journal **(33973)** ....‡4,500
Wisconsin Energy Cooperative
   News **(33981)** 153,000

Waupaca
Wisconsin State Farmer **(34422)** ......(Paid) ‡23,000
     (Non-paid) ‡4,000

Withee
Dairy Goat Journal **(34468)** ....(Paid) 6,500
Sheep! Magazine **(34469)** ....(Paid) 4,000

WYOMING
Casper
The WREN Magazine **(34484)** ....(Combined) 34,141

Cheyenne
Cow Country **(34495)** ....(Paid) ‡1,335
     (Non-paid) ‡207

ALBERTA, CANADA
Calgary
Alberta Beef Magazine **(34625)** ....(Paid) 2,700
     (Controlled) 10,200
Canadian Hereford Digest **(34635)** 3,000
Canadian Rodeo News **(34639)** ....‡3,058
     (Non-paid) ‡942
Simmental Country **(34657)** ....(Paid) ‡4,500
     (Non-paid) ‡350

Edmonton
Sheep Canada **(34730)** 1,500
Western Hog Journal **(34734)** ....(Non-paid) 5,101

Leduc
Prairie Hog Country **(34793)** ......(Controlled) ‡4,775

Red Deer
Central Alberta Life **(34829)** ....(Non-paid) 37,663

BRITISH COLUMBIA, CANADA
Argenta
The Smallholder **(34881)** ....(Paid) 750

Chetwynd
The Northern Horizon **(34925)** ....(Paid) ‡2,648
     (Non-paid) ‡29,040

Vernon
Equinews **(35200)** ....(Paid) ‡17,492
     (Non-paid) ‡800

MANITOBA, CANADA
Boissevain
Boissevain Recorder **(35252)** ....‡1,650

Carberry
Carberry News-Express **(35259)** ....‡1,277

Winnipeg
Cattlemen **(35321)** ....(Paid) 25,759
Country Guide **(35324)** ....(Paid) 31,910
     16,980
Dairy Update-Demographic Section of Country Guide
   Magazine **(35326)** ....‡18,653
Exports of Canadian Grain and Wheat
   Flour **(35328)** ....(Paid) 150
Grainews **(35330)** ....(Paid) 36,977
     (Non-paid) 8,276
The Manitoba Co-operator **(35337)** .....(Paid) 13,025

NOVA SCOTIA, CANADA
Liverpool
Atlantic Beef Quarterly **(35587)** ....(Paid) 2000
     (Non-paid) 2000
Rural Delivery **(35590)** ....(Paid) 8,500
     (Non-paid) 500

ONTARIO, CANADA
Aurora
Canadian Thoroughbred **(35644)** ....‡4,500

Blyth
The Rural Voice **(35688)** ....(Paid) ‡9,831
     (Non-paid) ‡3,669

Clarence Creek
Agricom **(35736)** ....‡4,500

Cookstown
Canadian Cooperative Wool Growers
   Magazine **(35752)** ....(Non-paid) 17,000
     ⊕12,000
     5,000

Delhi
Canada Poultry Magazine/La Revue Canadienne
   D'Aviculture **(35764)** 9,000
The Canadian Tobacco
   Grower **(35766)** ....(Paid) ‡2,000
Fruit and Vegetable
   Magazine **(35769)** ....(Paid) ‡3,000
Greenhouse Canada **(35770)** ....(Paid) ‡4,200

Dresden
Voice of the Farmer **(35789)**

Essex
Voice of the Essex Farmer **(35810)** ....(Free) ‡4,360

Exeter
The Farm Gate and Regional Country
   News **(35825)** 25,800

Guelph
Agri-Food Research in Ontario/Recherche Agro-
   alimentaire en
   Ontario **(35858)** ....(Combined) 7,500
Earthkeeping Ontario **(35861)** ....(Paid) 6,500
     (Non-paid) 6,500
The Grower **(35863)** ....(Combined) ‡8939
Monthly Crop and Livestock
   Report **(35866)** ....(Non-paid) 2,600

Lambton
Voice of the Lambton
   Farmer **(35967)** ....(Free) ‡7,070

London
Ontario Dairy Farmer **(35988)** 14,411
Ontario Farmer **(35989)** ....(Paid) 34,673
     (Non-paid) 1,156
Ontario Hog Farmer **(35990)** ....(Paid) 26
     (Non-paid) 8,614

Middlesex
Voice of the Middlesex
   Farmer **(36037)** ....(Free) ‡6,350

Milton
Horticulture Review **(36048)** ....(Paid) 2,400

Mississauga
Ontario Milk Producer **(36082)** ....(Paid) ‡10,000
     (Non-paid) ‡1,200

Ottawa
Canadian Journal of Animal
   Science **(36201)** ....(Paid) 1,000
Canadian Journal of Plant
   Science **(36212)** ....‡1,100
Canadian Journal of Soil
   Science **(36219)** ....(Paid) 1,250

Richmond Hill
Holstein Journal **(36342)** ....(Paid) 4,877
     (Non-paid) 77

Smithville
Niagara Farmers'
   Monthly **(36397)** ....(Non-paid) ‡17,800

Sturgeon Falls
Northern Agri-Source **(36413)** ....(Paid) 3,066

QUEBEC, CANADA
Longueuil
La Terre de Chez Nous **(37052)** ....(Paid) 40,400
Le Producteur de Lait
   Quebecois **(37055)** ....(Combined) •10,278
Porc Quebec **(37057)** ....(Combined) 2,905

Montreal
Le Bulletin des Agriculteurs **(37156)** ....(Paid) 21,291
Le Cooperateur
   Agricole **(37157)** ....(Combined) •17,946

Mount Royal
Economic Planning in Free Societies **(37252)**

Ste.-Anne-de-Bellevue
Quebecs Farmers Advocate **(37328)** .....(Paid) 3,448

SASKATCHEWAN, CANADA
Prince Albert
Rural Roots **(37518)** ....(Controlled) 31,992

Regina
Charolais Banner **(37527)** ....‡2,100
Charolais Connection **(37528)** ....(Paid) ‡18,000
     (Non-paid) ‡300

Saskatoon
Canadian Biosystems
   Engineering **(37549)** ....(Controlled) 250
Union Farmer **(37559)** ....‡5,500
The Western Producer **(37560)** ....(Paid) 81,247
     (Non-paid) 275

Agricultural Publications (by Subject)

Index entries are arranged by subject (please refer to the Index to Subject Terms). Within the subject groupings, entries appear geographically by states/provinces and alphabetically within cities. Citations in this index include publication title, entry number (given in parentheses), and circulation figures.

Circ.

BEEKEEPING

GEORGIA
Jesup
The Speedy Bee **(7348)** ....‡3,000

ILLINOIS
Hamilton
American Bee Journal **(8968)** ....(Paid) ‡12,000

OHIO
Medina
Bee Culture **(25372)** ....(Paid) ‡15,000
(Non-paid) ‡500

DAIRYING

CALIFORNIA
Clovis
California Dairy **(1731)**

Corona
The Western Dairyman **(1768)** ....‡17,500

MASSACHUSETTS
Millbury
Dairy World **(14334)** ....(Non-paid) ‡40,999

MINNESOTA
Monticello
Dairy Today **(16184)** ....(Non-paid) 70,000

NEW YORK
New York
Journal of Dairy Research **(22046)** 750

Owego
Dairy and Field Crops Digest **(23066)**

OHIO
Reynoldsburg
Guernsey Breeders'
Journal **(25494)** ....(Paid) ‡1,900
(Controlled) ‡190
Jersey Journal **(25495)** ....(Paid) 3,142
(Non-paid) 1,649

Salem
Farm and Dairy **(25505)** ....(Paid) ‡34,800
(Non-paid) ‡1,668

TEXAS
Crowley
United Caprine News **(30113)** ....‡6,000

VIRGINIA
Blacksburg
Journal of Dairy Science **(31874)** ....‡5,062

WISCONSIN
Fort Atkinson
Hoard's Dairyman **(33711)** ....(Paid) 69,672
(Non-paid) 15,892

Madison
The Cheese Reporter **(33926)** ....(Paid) 1,665
(Free) 170

Circ.

MANITOBA, CANADA
Winnipeg
Dairy Update-Demographic Section of Country Guide
Magazine **(35326)** ....‡18,653

ONTARIO, CANADA
London
Ontario Dairy Farmer **(35988)** 14,411

Mississauga
Ontario Milk Producer **(36082)** ....(Paid) ‡10,000
(Non-paid) ‡1,200

Richmond Hill
Holstein Journal **(36342)** ....(Paid) 4,877
(Non-paid) 77

QUEBEC, CANADA
Longueuil
Le Producteur de Lait
Quebecois **(37055)** ....(Combined) •10,278

FARM BUREAU, GRANGE, AND COOPERATIVE ASSOCIATIONS

ALABAMA
Montgomery
Alfa News **(360)** ....‡280,000

ARIZONA
Phoenix
Arizona Farm Bureau News **(777)** ....‡3,300

ARKANSAS
Little Rock
Front Porch **(1229)** ....‡231,000

CALIFORNIA
Moreno Valley
Riverside County Agriculture **(2599)** ....‡3,200

Sacramento
Ag Alert **(2974)** 44,000

San Joaquin
San Joaquin Farm Bureau
News **(3507)** ....(Paid) ‡5,000

COLORADO
Aurora
Rocky Mountain Union
Farmer **(4148)** ....(Paid) ‡5,000
(Controlled) ‡500

FLORIDA
Gainesville
FloridAgriculture **(6140)** ....(Paid) ‡127,000
(Free) ‡800

GEORGIA
Macon
Georgia Farm Bureau News **(7381)** ....‡66,312

INDIANA
Indianapolis
The Hoosier Farmer **(10116)** ....‡271,000

Circ.

IOWA
Iowa Falls
Spokesman **(11000)** ....(Paid) 105,294

Urbandale
Iowa REC News **(11276)** ....(Combined) ‡93,000

KANSAS
Manhattan
Kansas Living **(11625)** ....(Controlled) ‡140,000

Topeka
Kansas Country Living **(11827)** ....‡80,957

KENTUCKY
Louisville
All Around Kentucky **(12209)** ....(Paid) ‡387,925
(Controlled) ‡935

MINNESOTA
St. Paul
The Voice of
Agriculture **(16414)** ....(Combined) 35,000

MISSISSIPPI
Greenwood
Staplreview **(16645)** ....‡4,500

Jackson
Mississippi Farm Bureau News **(16702)** .....‡180,000

MISSOURI
Jefferson City
Show Me Missouri Farm Bureau
News **(17133)** ....(Controlled) ‡91,000

NEBRASKA
Lincoln
Nebraska Farm Bureau
News **(18100)** ....(Paid) ‡45,000
(Non-paid) ‡500
Nebraska Union Farmer **(18106)** 3,000

NEW YORK
LaFayette
Agricultural News
(Lafayette) **(20869)** ....(Non-paid) 3,000

Mexico
AgNews of Central New York **(21075)** ....‡2,700

Mount Morris
Livingston County Agricultural
News **(21101)** ....(Paid) ‡220
(Controlled) ‡25

Owego
Dairy and Field Crops Digest **(23066)**

OHIO
Columbus
Ohio Granger **(25045)** ....‡10,000

OKLAHOMA
Oklahoma City
Farm News & Views **(25963)** 109,000
Oklahoma Country **(25976)** ....(Paid) ‡127,247
(Controlled) ‡834

Circ.   Circ.   Circ.

FARM BUREAU, GRANGE, AND COOPERATIVE ASSOCIATIONS (continued)

TENNESSEE
Columbia
Tennessee Farm Bureau News **(29138)** ....‡117,000

UTAH
Provo
Benson Institute Review **(31398)**

VIRGINIA
Blacksburg
Virginia Extension **(31879)**

Richmond
The Southern States Cooperative
Magazine **(32455)** ....(Paid) ‡3,611
(Non-paid) ‡198,997
Virginia Farm Bureau News **(32461)** ....‡136,000

WASHINGTON
Olympia
Washington State Grange News **(32862)** .....‡38,993

WISCONSIN
Madison
Farm Bureau's Rural Route **(33937)** ....‡48,000

QUEBEC, CANADA
Montreal
Le Cooperateur
Agricole **(37157)** ....(Combined) •17,946

SASKATCHEWAN, CANADA
Saskatoon
Union Farmer **(37559)** ....‡5,500

FARM IMPLEMENTS AND SUPPLIES

COLORADO
Englewood
Farm Supply Retailing **(4413)** .....(Controlled) 20,000

IOWA
Cedar Falls
Implement & Tractor **(10657)** ....(Paid) ‡3,000
(Non-paid) ‡4,000

Fort Dodge
Farm Equipment Guide **(10898)** ....(Paid) ‡11,500
(Non-paid) ‡7,500
Farmers Hot Line **(10900)** ....(Non-paid) ‡47,540
(Paid) ‡1,660

KENTUCKY
Buckner
Fastline—Dakota Farm
Edition **(11969)** ....(Combined) 22,000
Fastline—Far West Farm
Edition **(11971)** ....(Combined) 22,000
Fastline—Illinois Farm
Edition **(11974)** ....(Combined) 22,000
Fastline—Indiana Farm
Edition **(11975)** ....(Combined) 22,000
Fastline—Iowa Farm
Edition **(11976)** ....(Combined) 22,000
Fastline—Kansas Farm
Edition **(11977)** ....(Combined) 22,000
Fastline—Kentucky Farm
Edition **(11978)** ....(Combined) 22,000
Fastline—Mid-Atlantic Farm
Edition **(11979)** ....(Combined) 22,000
Fastline—Mid-South Farm
Edition **(11980)** ....(Combined) 22,000
Fastline—Minnesota Farm
Edition **(11982)** ....(Combined) 22,000
Fastline—Missouri Farm
Edition **(11983)** ....(Combined) 22,000
Fastline—Nebraska Farm
Edition **(11984)** ....(Combined) 22,000
Fastline—Northeast Farm
Edition **(11985)** ....(Combined) 22,000
Fastline—Northwest Farm
Edition **(11987)** ....(Combined) 22,000
Fastline—Ohio Farm
Edition **(11988)** ....(Combined) 22,000
Fastline—Oklahoma Farm
Edition **(11989)** ....(Combined) 22,000
Fastline—Ontario Farm
Edition **(11990)** ....(Combined) 22,000
Fastline—Rocky Mountain Farm
Edition **(11991)** ....(Combined) 22,000

Fastline—Southeast Farm
Edition **(11993)** ....(Combined) 22,000
Fastline—Tennessee Farm
Edition **(11994)** ....(Combined) 22,000
Fastline—Texas Farm
Edition **(11996)** ....(Combined) 22,000
Fastline—Wisconsin Farm
Edition **(11998)** ....(Combined) 22,000

MISSOURI
Fenton
NAEDA Equipment Dealer **(17062)** .....(Paid) △8,298
(Non-paid) △2,245

Kansas City
Southwestern Retailer **(17197)** ....(Paid) ‡1,100
(Controlled) ‡420

WASHINGTON
Spokane
Ag Equipment Power **(33092)** ....(Non-paid) ‡10,800
10,600

WISCONSIN
Fort Atkinson
Farm Equipment **(33708)** ....(Controlled) 10,000
OEM Off-Highway **(33715)** ....(Controlled) ‡17,500

FARM NEWSPAPERS

ARIZONA
Buckeye
Buckeye Valley News **(662)** 2,600

CALIFORNIA
Paso Robles
Paso Robles Press **(2831)** ....(Wed.) ‡12,500
(Fri.) ‡5,000

COLORADO
Frederick
Farmer and Miner **(4455)** ....‡1,300
Wheat Ridge
Record Stockman **(4680)** 12,000
Southwest Stockman **(4684)** 13,250

FLORIDA
Gainesville
The Record Farm & Ranch **(6154)** ....‡5,000
Havana
Havana Herald **(6185)** ....(Paid) ⊕2,600
(Free) ⊕25

GEORGIA
Atlanta
Farmers & Consumers Market
Bulletin **(7006)** ....(Free) 205,428

ILLINOIS
Bloomington
FarmWeek **(8077)** ....(Paid) 80,608

Carol Stream
Carolina/Virginia Farmer **(8137)** ....‡15,177
New England Farmer **(8151)** ....(Paid) ‡5,402
(Controlled) ‡10,783

Joliet
Farmers' Weekly Review **(9032)** 11,500

Lena
Northwestern Illinois Farmer **(9074)** ....‡6,000

Rochelle
Farmer's Report **(9513)**

INDIANA
Berne
Berne Tri-Weekly News **(9802)** ....‡2,500

Indianapolis
Indiana Agri-News **(10121)** ....(Paid) ‡8,000
(Controlled) ‡21,000

Knightstown
Farmweek **(10235)** ....(Paid) 35,141

New Paris
Farmer's Exchange **(10347)** ....(Paid) ‡13,800
(Free) ‡800

IOWA
Cedar Rapids
Iowa Farmer Today **(10674)** .....(Controlled) ‡71,228

Cresco
Times-Plain Dealer **(10730)** ....(Paid) ‡3,450
(Free) ‡7,650

Dayton
Dayton Review **(10753)** ....‡845

Elgin
The Elgin Echo **(10871)** 1,700

Gowrie
The Gowrie News **(10927)** ....‡1,400

Iowa Falls
Spokesman **(11000)** ....(Paid) 105,294

Jewell
South Hamilton Record News **(11008)** 950

Marengo
Iowa County Farmer **(11061)** ....(Paid) ‡10,140

Orange City
Farmer's Cattle-log **(11129)** ....(Free) 4,800

Peterson
Peterson Patriot **(11159)** ....‡580

Tipton
The Tipton Conservative and
Advertiser **(11269)** ....‡4,700

KANSAS
Dodge City
High Plains Journal **(11415)** ....(Paid) 51,411

Manhattan
Grass & Grain **(11620)** ....‡16,500

Overland Park
California-Arizona Farm Press **(11701)**

Parsons
Farm Talk **(11743)** ....‡9,985

Scott City
News Chronicle **(11794)** ....(Paid) 2,850
(Free) 25

Troy
Green Acres **(11849)** ....(Paid) 2,800
(Free) 43,500

LOUISIANA
Baton Rouge
Louisiana Market Bulletin **(12500)** ....‡16,800

Lake Providence
Banner-Democrat **(12652)** ....‡2,200

MAINE
Lincolnville
Maine Organic Farmer and
Gardener **(12982)** ....(Paid) ‡5,000
(Non-paid) ‡100

MARYLAND
Easton
The Delmarva Farmer **(13487)** ....(Paid) ‡8,000
(Free) ‡3,702

MICHIGAN
Bay City
Valley Farmer **(14803)** ....‡1,450

Camden
The Farmers' Advance **(14852)** ....(Paid) ‡19,315
(Free) ‡2,512

Lansing
Michigan Farm News **(15282)** ....(Paid) 48,586

Paw Paw
The Courier-Leader **(15433)** ....(Paid) ⊕4,069
(Free) 45

Sparta
The Fruit Growers News **(15568)** .....(Paid) ‡14,235
The Vegetable Growers
News **(15570)** ....(Combined) ‡14,415

MINNESOTA
Minneapolis
Delta Farm Press **(16073)** ....(Paid) 23,224
(Non-paid) 7,977
Southwest Farm Press **(16130)** ....(Paid) 25,009
(Non-paid) 21,666

Rochester
Agri News **(16305)** ....(Paid) ‡21,500

St. Paul
The Voice of
Agriculture **(16414)** ....(Combined) 35,000

MONTANA
Billings
Western Livestock Reporter **(17734)** ....‡12,000

NEBRASKA
Scottsbluff
Business Farmer-Stockman **(18263)** 2,700

NEVADA
Lovelock
The Nevada Rancher **(18413)** ....(Paid) ‡3,500
(Free) ‡200

NEW YORK
Adams
The Empire State Farmer **(19975)** .....(Free) ‡6,000

Moravia
Focus on Farming **(21095)** ....‡15,500

Palatine Bridge
Country Folks Grower **(23073)** ....(Combined) 25,000
Farm Chronicle **(23074)** ....(Paid) 22,000

Saugerties
Country Folks **(23306)** ....(Combined) 9,000

NORTH CAROLINA
Wilson
Carolina Farmer **(24310)** ....‡30,000

NORTH DAKOTA
Bismarck
Farm and Ranch Guide **(24352)** ....(Paid) 1,450
40,484

Enderlin
Enderlin Independent **(24410)** ....‡1,000

Grand Forks
AGWEEK **(24453)** ....(Paid) 26,831
(Controlled) 517

Minnewaukan
Benson County Farmers Press **(24503)** ....‡2,714

Watford City
McKenzie County Farmer **(24555)** ....‡2,300

OHIO
Archbold
Farmland News **(24614)** 7,107

Bellevue
Bellevue RFD News **(24670)** ....(Paid) 400
(Non-paid) 9,500

New London
Firelands Farmer **(25417)** ....‡5,870

Salem
Farm and Dairy **(25505)** ....(Paid) ‡34,800
(Non-paid) ‡1,668

OKLAHOMA
Boise City
The Boise City News **(25766)** ....(Paid) 1,800
(Free) 60

Checotah
McIntosh County Democrat **(25781)** ....(Paid) ‡2,995
(Free) ‡205

Oklahoma City
Farm News & Views **(25963)** 109,000

OREGON
Pendleton
Agri-Times Northwest **(26457)** ......(Combined) 3,700

Salem
Capital Press **(26565)** ....(Paid) 38,966

PENNSYLVANIA
Camp Hill
Country Focus **(26749)** ....(Controlled) 26,000

Ephrata
Lancaster Farming **(26888)** ....(Paid) ⊕51,000
(Free) ⊕1,000

SOUTH DAKOTA
Sioux Falls
Tri-State Neighbor **(28969)** ......(Controlled) 29,500

Sturgis
Tri-State Livestock News **(29001)** .....(Paid) ‡14,000
(Free) ‡500

TENNESSEE
Columbia
Tennessee Farm Bureau News **(29138)** ....‡117,000

Dresden
Dresden Enterprise **(29170)** ....‡5,200

TEXAS
Bogata
Bogata News **(29932)** ....‡2,184

Grandview
Grandview Tribune **(30408)** ....‡1,200

Odonnell
O'Donnell Index-Press **(30884)** ....(Combined) 495

Waco
Texas Agriculture **(31252)** ....(Paid) 125,065
(Free) 1,009

WASHINGTON
Lynden
Lynden Tribune **(32821)** ....‡7,000

WISCONSIN
Denmark
Country Chronicle **(33656)** ....(Paid) 381
(Free) 14,631

Eau Claire
The Country Today **(33668)** ....(Paid) ‡25,000
(Free) ‡2,903

Greendale
Country Woman **(33760)**

ALBERTA, CANADA
Red Deer
Central Alberta Life **(34829)** ....(Non-paid) 37,663

BRITISH COLUMBIA, CANADA
Chetwynd
The Northern Horizon **(34925)** ....(Paid) ‡2,648
(Non-paid) ‡29,040

MANITOBA, CANADA
Boissevain
Boissevain Recorder **(35252)** ....‡1,650

Carberry
Carberry News-Express **(35259)** ....‡1,277

Winnipeg
Grainews **(35330)** ....(Paid) 36,977
(Non-paid) 8,276
The Manitoba Co-operator **(35337)** .....(Paid) 13,025

NOVA SCOTIA, CANADA
Liverpool
Rural Delivery **(35590)** ....(Paid) 8,500
(Non-paid) 500

ONTARIO, CANADA
Clarence Creek
Agricom **(35736)** ....‡4,500

Dresden
Voice of the Farmer **(35789)**

Essex
Voice of the Essex Farmer **(35810)** ....(Free) ‡4,360

Exeter
The Farm Gate and Regional Country
News **(35825)** 25,800

Lambton
Voice of the Lambton
Farmer **(35967)** ....(Free) ‡7,070

London
Ontario Farmer **(35989)** ....(Paid) 34,673
(Non-paid) 1,156

Middlesex
Voice of the Middlesex
Farmer **(36037)** ....(Free) ‡6,350

Sturgeon Falls
Northern Agri-Source **(36413)** ....(Paid) 3,066

QUEBEC, CANADA
Longueuil
La Terre de Chez Nous **(37052)** ....(Paid) 40,400

SASKATCHEWAN, CANADA
Prince Albert
Rural Roots **(37518)** ....(Controlled) 31,992

Saskatoon
The Western Producer **(37560)** ....(Paid) 81,247
(Non-paid) 275

FEED AND GRAIN

ILLINOIS
Mount Morris
Feed International **(9237)** ....(Paid) 478
(Non-paid) 16,025
Feed Management **(9238)** ....(Paid) 204
(Non-paid) 17,676

INDIANA
Indianapolis
Our Paper **(10158)**

KANSAS
Dighton
Feed-Lot **(11413)** ....(Controlled) ‡10,777

MINNESOTA
Minneapolis
Hay & Forage
Grower **(16084)** ....(Non-paid) ‡90,000

Minnetonka
Feedstuffs **(16169)** ....(Paid) 11,312
(Non-paid) 4,727

MISSOURI
Kansas City
World Grain **(17205)** ....(Combined) ‡9,017

NORTH CAROLINA
Raleigh
Rice Journal **(24151)** ....(Paid) ‡177
(Controlled) ‡10,876

WASHINGTON
Blaine
Grey Book **(32688)**

Seattle
Grain & Feed
Marketing **(32969)** ....(Controlled) ‡15,415

WISCONSIN
Fort Atkinson
Feed & Grain **(33709)** ....(Controlled) ‡16,505

MANITOBA, CANADA
Winnipeg
Exports of Canadian Grain and Wheat
Flour **(35328)** ....(Paid) 150

FERTILIZER

MINNESOTA
New Prague
Ag Retailer Magazine **(16208)** .....(Non-paid) 21,598

NEW JERSEY
New Brunswick
Soil Science **(19340)** ....(Paid) ‡1,113
(Non-paid) ‡235

OHIO
Willoughby
Farm Chemicals **(25658)** ....(Paid) △550
(Non-paid) △29,136
Farm Chemicals International **(25659)** 9,400

OREGON
Eugene
Worm Digest **(26335)** ....(Paid) ‡6,200
(Non-paid) ‡800

GENERAL AGRICULTURE
See also Farm Newspapers

ALABAMA
Birmingham
Progressive Farmer **(87)** ....(Paid) 244,000
(Non-paid) 358,000

Circulation: ★ = ABC; △ = BPA; ◆ = CAC; ● = CCAB; ❑ = VAC; ⊕ = PO Statement; ‡ = Publisher's Report; Boldface figures = sworn; Light figures = estimated.

2739

Agricultural Publications

Circ.   Circ.   Circ.

GENERAL AGRICULTURE (continued)
Montgomery
Alfa News (360) ....‡280,000
Neighbors (371) ....(Paid) 101,159

ALASKA
Fairbanks
Agroborealis (566) ....(Non-paid) 2,500

CALIFORNIA
Berkeley
Agricultural History (1488) ....‡1,050

Concord
Oregon FarmekraHJJmpw- (1754)
Washington FarmekraHJJmpw- (1757)

Elk Grove
The Western Bec- Producer (1875)

Fresno
Agribusiness Fieldman (1941) ....(Controlled) ‡8,058
Grape Grower
  Magazine (1951) ....(Non-paid) 11,276
Nut Grower (1953) 11,993
Tree Fruit (1957) ....(Controlled) ‡11,008
Vegetable (1958) ....(Controlled) ‡8,371

Modesto
Rice Farming (2562) ....‡8,753

Oakland
California Agriculture (2671) ....(Paid) 850
    (Controlled) 19,000

COLORADO
Denver
Journal of the ASFMRA (4335) ....(Combined) 3,000

Fort Collins
Journal of Agricultural & Resource Economics (4434)

Windsor
The Fence Post (4686) ....(Paid) ‡9,700
    (Non-paid) ‡400

DISTRICT OF COLUMBIA
Washington
Agricultural Aviation (5316) ....(Controlled) 6,000
Amber Waves (5321)
Journal of Agricultural Lending (5568) .....(Paid) 580
Rural Cooperatives (5773) ....(Paid) 8,000
Sulphur in Agriculture (5807)

FLORIDA
Lithia
Farm and Ranch News (6304) ....(Paid) 6,000
    (Controlled) 13,000

Tallahassee
Florida Market
  Bulletin (6714) ....(Controlled) ‡15,000

Winter Park
Florida Grower (6880) ....(Controlled) 13,396

GEORGIA
Athens
Journal of Agricultural and Applied
  Economics (6943) ....(Paid) 750

Atlanta
Farmers & Consumers Market
  Bulletin (7006) ....(Free) 205,428
Georgia Future Farmer (7012)

Forsyth
Florida Farmer (7278)

Norcross
Better Crops with Plant Food (7456) ......(Paid) ‡50
    (Non-paid) ‡16,000

Tifton
The Peanut Grower (7596) ....(Controlled) 22,500

HAWAII
Honolulu
Hawaii Crop Weather (7694)

ILLINOIS
Bloomington
Partners (8080) ....(Paid) 287,683
    (Non-paid) 609

Carol Stream
FFA New Horizons (8143) .....(Controlled) ‡512,644
Nebraska Farmer (8150) ....(Paid) 16,436
    (Non-paid) 23,281

Western Farmer-Stockman (8157)

Decatur
The Beef Producer (8709)
Indiana Prairie Farmer (8712) ....‡35,000

La Salle
Illinois Agri-News (9055) ....(Paid) ‡34,000

Mascoutah
Farm Impact (9152) ....(Non-paid) 40,000

Rolling Meadows
Turf News (9551) ....‡1,700

Urbana
Illinois Research (9710) ....(Controlled) ‡7,000

INDIANA
Indianapolis
FFA Advisors Making a
  Difference (10111) ....(Combined) 13,200
Indiana Agri-News (10121) ....(Paid) ‡8,000
    (Controlled) ‡21,000

IOWA
Des Moines
Successful Farming (10811) ....(Paid) ‡442,000
Wallaces Farmer (10814) ....(Paid) 12,289
    (Non-paid) 55,513

Fort Dodge
Farmer's Digest (10899) 10,000

Urbandale
Idaho FarmekraHJJmpw- (11275)
Wisconsin Agriculturist (11277) ....(Paid) 3,205
    (Non-paid) 27,505

KANSAS
Belleville
Farmer Stockman of the
  Midwest (11357) ....‡15,057

Jewell
Kansas Farmer (11517) ....(Paid) 12,656
    (Non-paid) 21,141

Lawrence
Weed Technology (11571)

Lenexa
The Grower (11593) ....(Controlled) ‡22,000

Manhattan
Kansas 4-H Journal (11624) ....‡13,500

Wichita
International Flying
  Farmer (11882) ....(Controlled) ‡1,900

KENTUCKY
Buckner
Fastline—Dakota Farm
  Edition (11969) ....(Combined) 22,000
Fastline—Far West Farm
  Edition (11971) ....(Combined) 22,000
Fastline—Illinois Farm
  Edition (11974) ....(Combined) 22,000
Fastline—Indiana Farm
  Edition (11975) ....(Combined) 22,000
Fastline—Iowa Farm
  Edition (11976) ....(Combined) 22,000
Fastline—Kansas Farm
  Edition (11977) ....(Combined) 22,000
Fastline—Kentucky Farm
  Edition (11978) ....(Combined) 22,000
Fastline—Mid-Atlantic Farm
  Edition (11979) ....(Combined) 22,000
Fastline—Mid-South Farm
  Edition (11980) ....(Combined) 22,000
Fastline—Minnesota Farm
  Edition (11982) ....(Combined) 22,000
Fastline—Missouri Farm
  Edition (11983) ....(Combined) 22,000
Fastline—Nebraska Farm
  Edition (11984) ....(Combined) 22,000
Fastline—Northeast Farm
  Edition (11985) ....(Combined) 22,000
Fastline—Northwest Farm
  Edition (11987) ....(Combined) 22,000
Fastline—Ohio Farm
  Edition (11988) ....(Combined) 22,000
Fastline—Oklahoma Farm
  Edition (11989) ....(Combined) 22,000
Fastline—Ontario Farm
  Edition (11990) ....(Combined) 22,000
Fastline—Rocky Mountain Farm
  Edition (11991) ....(Combined) 22,000

Fastline—Southeast Farm
  Edition (11993) ....(Combined) 22,000
Fastline—Tennessee Farm
  Edition (11994) ....(Combined) 22,000
Fastline—Texas Farm
  Edition (11996) ....(Combined) 22,000
Fastline—Wisconsin Farm
  Edition (11998) ....(Combined) 22,000

Frankfort
Kentucky Farmer (12070) ....‡9,535

LOUISIANA
Baton Rouge
Louisiana Country (12497) ....‡130,000
Louisiana Rural
  Economist (12503) ....(Controlled) ‡1,265

New Orleans
Louisiana Farmer (12739)

MARYLAND
Bethesda
North American Journal of
  Aquaculture (13365) ....‡2,200

Easton
The New Jersey Farmer (13488) ......(Paid) ‡2,247
    (Controlled) ‡2,543

Lanham
Journal of Economic Entomology (13604) 1,800

MASSACHUSETTS
Malden
Choices (14290) ....(Combined) 6,100

Norwell
Journal of Agricultural and Environmental
  Ethics (14441) ....(Paid) 211
    (Non-paid) 27

Rochester
Cranberries (14505) ....‡1,000

MICHIGAN
Haslett
Michigan News (15151) ....‡1,300

Okemos
Michigan Country Lines (15416) 240,000

St. Joseph
Transactions of the ASAE (15514) ....‡1,200

Sparta
The Fruit Growers News (15568) .....(Paid) ‡14,235
The Vegetable Growers
  News (15570) ....(Combined) ‡14,415

MINNESOTA
Glyndon
Dakota Farmer (15922) ....‡37,530
The Farmer (15923)

Lakeville
Farm Show (15994) ....‡150,000

Mankato
The Land (16028) ....(Non-paid) ‡39,500

Minneapolis
Farm Industry News (16079) ....(Non-paid) ‡250,000
Southeast Farm
  Press (16129) ....(Combined) 53,000
Western Farm Press (16139) .....(Combined) 24,000

MISSISSIPPI
Jackson
Mississippi Farm Bureau News (16702) .....‡180,000

Meridian
The Stockman Grass
  Farmer (16770) ....(Paid) 10,961

Pontotoc
Mississippi Farmer (16822)

MISSOURI
Clark
Small Farm Today (16981) 12,000

Columbia
Missouri Ruralist (17004) ....(Paid) 17,087
    (Non-paid) 17,161
Today's Farmer (17011) ....‡46,000

Kansas City
Farmland System News (17169) .....‡168,000

Perryville
MidAmerica Farmer
Grower **(17337)** ....(Paid) ‡14,379
(Non-paid) ‡10,451
National Conservation Tillage Digest **(17338)**

St. Louis
Agri Marketing **(17407)** ....(Paid) 212
(Controlled) 8,325

MONTANA
Bozeman
Montana Farm Bureau
Spokesman **(17753)** ....‡9,000

Helena
AERO Sun-Times **(17817)** ....(Paid) 630
(Controlled) 50

NEBRASKA
Lincoln
Rural Electric Nebraskan **(18117)** ....‡66,000

Scottsbluff
Business Farmer **(18262)** ....(Paid) 2,750

Tekamah
Midwest Messenger **(18297)** ....(Free) ‡154,380

NEW MEXICO
Las Cruces
New Mexico Farm and
Ranch **(19874)** ....(Paid) ‡12,500
(Controlled) ‡175

NEW YORK
Bronx
Biological & Agricultural Index **(20255)**
Farming Uncle **(20268)** ....(Paid) 400
(Non-paid) 700

East Aurora
Farm News of Erie and Wyoming
Counties **(20542)** ....(Paid) ‡1,600
(Non-paid) ‡100

Great Neck
Agricultura de las
Americas **(20684)** ....(Non-paid) 37,318

Ithaca
Agricultural Finance Review **(20788)** ....(Paid) 600

LaFayette
Agricultural News
(Lafayette) **(20869)** ....(Non-paid) 3,000

Mexico
AgNews of Central New York **(21075)** ....‡2,700

New York
Irrigation and Drainage Systems **(21953)**

Queensbury
Agricultural News **(23171)** ....‡4,000

Riverhead
Suffolk County Agricultural News **(23204)** ....‡800

NORTH CAROLINA
Raleigh
Agricultural Review (North
Carolina) **(24124)** ....(Controlled) ‡60,000
The Burley Tobacco
Farmer **(24128)** ....(Controlled) 17,318

NORTH DAKOTA
Bismarck
The Sunflower **(24360)** 16,667

OHIO
Bellevue
Bellevue RFD News **(24670)** ....(Paid) 400
(Non-paid) 9,500
Bucyrus RFD News **(24671)** ....(Paid) 300
(Non-paid) 9,700

Columbus
Buckeye Farm News **(25002)** ....(Paid) ‡215,000
(Non-paid) ‡1,106

Lancaster
The Ohio Farmer **(25291)** ....(Paid) 15,730
(Non-paid) 18,862

Salem
Farm and Dairy **(25505)** ....(Paid) ‡34,800
(Non-paid) ‡1,668

Willoughby
Ag Consultant **(25655)** ....(Non-paid) 17,623

American Vegetable Grower **(25657)** ....(Paid) 9,778
(Non-paid) 19,711
Productores de
Hortalizas **(25663)** ....(Controlled) 10,000

OKLAHOMA
Ponca City
Oklahoma Farmer-Stockman **(26036)** ....(Paid) 8,948
(Non-paid) 8,825
Texas Farmer-Stockman **(26038)** ......(Paid) 15,458
(Non-paid) 25,451

OREGON
Corvallis
The Growing Edge **(26288)** ....(Paid) 20,000
(Non-paid) 1,000

Salem
Capital Press **(26565)** ....(Paid) 38,966

Sisters
Small Farmer's Journal **(26585)** 25,000

PENNSYLVANIA
Philadelphia
Farm Journal **(27468)** ....(Paid) 133,655
(Non-paid) 449,384

SOUTH CAROLINA
Charleston
Journal of Agromedicine **(28514)** ....(Paid) 218

Clemson
South Carolina YR and FFA **(28534)** ....‡8,000

TENNESSEE
Fayetteville
Farmers Exchange **(29190)** ....(Free) 21,000

Gainesboro
Rural Heritage **(29201)** ....‡6,000

TEXAS
Austin
Acres U.S.A. **(29750)** 10,000
Texas FFA News **(29819)** ....(Controlled) 68,000

Bowie
Ratite Marketplace **(29941)** ....(Paid) 4,000

Odonnell
O'Donnell Index-Press **(30884)** ....(Combined) 495

UTAH
Provo
Benson Institute Review **(31398)**

WASHINGTON
Vancouver
Colorado Farmer-Stockman **(33174)** .....(Paid) 3,421
(Non-paid) 6,690

WISCONSIN
Antigo
The Badger Common'Tater **(33532)** ......(Paid) ‡487
(Non-paid) ‡3,357

Appleton
The North American Deer
Farmer **(33541)** ....(Combined) 1,200

Greendale
Farm & Ranch Living **(33762)** 400,000

Waupaca
Wisconsin State Farmer **(34422)** ......(Paid) ‡23,000
(Non-paid) ‡4,000

BRITISH COLUMBIA, CANADA
Argenta
The Smallholder **(34881)** ....(Paid) 750

MANITOBA, CANADA
Winnipeg
Country Guide **(35324)** ....(Paid) 31,910
(Non-paid) 16,980
Grainews **(35330)** ....(Paid) 36,977
(Non-paid) 8,276

ONTARIO, CANADA
Blyth
The Rural Voice **(35688)** ....(Paid) ‡9,831
(Non-paid) ‡3,669

Clarence Creek
Agricom **(35736)** ....‡4,500

Guelph
Agri-Food Research in Ontario/Recherche Agro-
alimentaire en
Ontario **(35858)** ....(Combined) 7,500
Earthkeeping Ontario **(35861)** ....(Paid) 6,500
(Non-paid) 6,500
Monthly Crop and Livestock
Report **(35866)** ....(Non-paid) 2,600

London
Ontario Dairy Farmer **(35988)** 14,411

Smithville
Niagara Farmers'
Monthly **(36397)** ....(Non-paid) ‡17,800

QUEBEC, CANADA
Longueuil
Porc Quebec **(37057)** ....(Combined) 2,905

Montreal
Le Bulletin des Agriculteurs **(37156)** ....(Paid) 21,291

Mount Royal
Economic Planning in Free Societies **(37252)**

Ste.-Anne-de-Bellevue
Quebecs Farmers Advocate **(37328)** .....(Paid) 3,448

HORTICULTURE

CALIFORNIA
Fortuna
Journal of the American Rhododendron
Society **(1929)** ....(Controlled) 6,000

Oakland
Almanac **(2665)** ....(Paid) 450

Pasadena
Journal of the Los Angeles International Fern
Society **(2820)** ....(Combined) 400

San Diego
California Garden **(3127)** 2,100

COLORADO
Denver
Rock Garden Quarterly **(4352)** ....(Paid) 5,000

FLORIDA
Bartow
The Citrus Industry **(5917)** ....‡10,000

St. Petersburg
The Seed Pod **(6634)** ....(Controlled) 1,200

Tampa
Citrus and Vegetable
Magazine **(6760)** ....(Controlled) △12,000

Winter Park
Ornamental Outlook **(6884)** 13,175

GEORGIA
Fort Valley
The Camellia Journal **(7285)** ....‡5,000

HAWAII
Waianae
Hawaii Orchid Journal **(7794)** ....‡750

ILLINOIS
Batavia
Grower Talks **(8054)** ....(Paid) 9,230

Champaign
Arborist News
Magazine **(8180)** ....(Controlled) 17,000

Chicago
American Nurseryman **(8261)** ....(Paid) 14,961

Rolling Meadows
Greenhouse Business **(9547)** ......(Non-paid) 18,000

LOUISIANA
Shreveport
American Rose **(12816)** ....(Paid) ‡22,109
(Controlled) ‡150

MASSACHUSETTS
Bedford
Hobby Greenhouse **(13836)** ....(Combined) 1,600

Boston
Horticulture **(13903)** ....(Paid) 210,000

Agricultural Publications

Circ.   Circ.   Circ.

HORTICULTURE (continued)
Jamaica Plain
Arnoldia (14258) 4,450

MINNESOTA
Owatonna
North American Lily Society
  Quarterly (16252) ....(Paid) 1,500

St. Paul
Plant Disease (16406) ....(Paid) ‡4,000
                                    (Non-paid) ‡31

MISSOURI
St. Louis
The National Gardener (17475) ....‡30,000

MONTANA
Huson
Bonsai Journal (17835) ....(Paid) 1,450

NEW HAMPSHIRE
Loudon
The Plantsman (18554)

Manchester
Tree Care Industry (18564) ......(Controlled) ‡28,000

NEW YORK
Brooklyn
Plants & Gardens News (20338) ....‡18,000

OHIO
Willoughby
Ag Consultant (25655) ....(Non-paid) 17,623
American Fruit Grower (25656) ......(Paid) ‡58,423
American Vegetable Grower (25657) ....(Paid) 9,778
                                    (Non-paid) 19,711
Greenhouse Grower (25660) ......(Controlled) 22,060
Western Fruit Grower (25664) ......(Paid) ‡3,142
                                              22,377

OREGON
Corvallis
The Growing Edge (26288) ....(Paid) 20,000
                                    (Non-paid) 1,000
Ornamentals Northwest (26290) ....‡4,750

Portland
Pacific Coast Nurseryman and Garden Supply
  Dealer (26496) ....(Paid) ‡6,840
                                    (Non-paid) ‡3,624

PENNSYLVANIA
Emmaus
Organic Gardening (26879) ....(Paid) 605,980

VERMONT
Randolph
Green World (31580) 200

VIRGINIA
Alexandria
The American Gardener (31636) 28,000
Hort Technology (31678) ....(Paid) 2,600
HortScience (31679) ....(Paid) 3,600
Journal of the American Society for Horticultural
  Science (31687) ....(Paid) 2,500

Fairfax Station
Chrysanthemum (32037) ....(Controlled) 1,200

ONTARIO, CANADA
Delhi
Greenhouse Canada (35770) ....(Paid) ‡4,200

Milton
Horticulture Review (36048) ....(Paid) 2,400

LIVESTOCK
See also Dairying

ALABAMA
Fayette
Cattle Today (213) ....‡15,000

Montgomery
The Alabama Cattleman (356) 17,000

ARIZONA
Scottsdale
National Horseman (871) ....(Paid) 3,800
                                    (Non-paid) 1,000

ARKANSAS
Little Rock
Arkansas Cattle Business (1215) ....(Paid) 10,000
                                    (Controlled) 1,000

CALIFORNIA
Arcadia
California Thoroughbred (1427) 5,500

Cambria
Arabian Horse World (1648) 10,000

Concord
Oregon FarmekraHJJmpw- (1754)
Washington FarmekraHJJmpw- (1757)

Elk Grove
The Western Bec- Producer (1875)

Norco
Animals Exotic and Small (2640) 3,500

Sacramento
California Cattleman (2979) ....(Paid) ‡3,585
                                    (Non-paid) ‡910

COLORADO
Arvada
Cattle Guard (4137) ....‡15,000

Aurora
International Arabian Horse (4146) ....‡30,000

Centennial
National Cattlemen
  Magazine (4226) ....(Paid) 35,000

Colorado Springs
CALF News Magazine (4238) 6,000

Denver
The Bagpipe (4306)
Bison World (4308) ....‡2,000
Western Livestock Journal (4366) ......(Paid) 18,335

Littleton
Texas Longhorn Journal (4555) ....‡3,000

Parker
American Salers (4596) ....(Paid) ‡1,720

Wheat Ridge
Record Stockman (4680) 12,000

FLORIDA
Kissimmee
Florida Cattleman and Livestock
  Journal (6261) ....(Paid) 4,383
                                    (Non-paid) 205

GEORGIA
Augusta
SPUR MAGAZINE (7103) 25,000

Forsyth
Florida Farmer (7278)

IDAHO
Boise
The Line Rider (7813) ....‡1,500

Moscow
Appaloosa Journal (7911) 30,000

ILLINOIS
Carmi
Angus Topics (8130) ....‡8,300

Carol Stream
The Hog Producer (8145)
Western Farmer-Stockman (8157)

Chicago
CarneTec (8299) ....(Non-paid) 6,200
Meat Marketing &
  Technology (8483) ....(Combined) 20,058

Cuba
Banner Sheep Magazine (8699) ....‡3,500

Decatur
The Beef Producer (8709)

Downers Grove
Illinois Standardbred & Mid-America Harness
  News (8786) 1,540

Mount Morris
Pig International (9244) ....(Controlled) 17,638

Pecatonica
Clydesdale News (9413)

Peoria
Spotted News (9426) ....(Paid) ‡4,000
                                    (Non-paid) ‡3,000

Springfield
Illinois Beef (9622) ....(Controlled) ‡5,200

INDIANA
Indianapolis
Indiana Beef (10123) ....‡8,300
POA (10161) ....‡1,600

West Lafayette
Seedstock Edge (10552) ....(Paid) 4,900
                                    (Non-paid) 250

IOWA
Cedar Rapids
Iowa Pork Today (10675) ....(Non-paid) ‡30,313

Clive
Iowa Pork Producer (10716) ......(Non-paid) ‡16,173

Des Moines
National Pork
  Report (10804) ....(Non-paid) ‡109,350

Urbandale
Idaho FarmekraHJJmpw- (11275)

Waverly
The Draft Horse Journal (11307) ....(Paid) 22,000
                                    (Non-paid) 125

KANSAS
Allen
American Beef Cattleman (11336) ....‡20,000

Belleville
Farmer Stockman of the
  Midwest (11357) ....‡15,057

Council Grove
Beef Today (11403) ....(Controlled) 187,656

Dighton
Feed-Lot (11413) ....(Controlled) ‡10,777

Lenexa
Drovers (11590) ....(Paid) 297
                                    (Controlled) 98,000
Pork (11595) ....(Controlled) ‡26,299
Swine Practitioner (11597) ....△3,340

Topeka
Kansas Stockman (11831) ....(Paid) ‡7,025
                                    (Non-paid) ‡410

KENTUCKY
Lexington
Cow Country News (12163) 10,000

LOUISIANA
New Orleans
Louisiana Farmer (12739)

Port Allen
The Louisiana Cattleman (12798) ......(Paid) ‡3,900
                                    (Non-paid) ‡800

MINNESOTA
Glyndon
The Farmer (15923)

Minneapolis
BEEF (16059) ....(Controlled) ‡101,661
National Hog
  Farmer (16113) ....(Controlled) ‡35,000

MISSISSIPPI
Meridian
The Stockman Grass
  Farmer (16770) ....(Paid) 10,961

Pontotoc
Mississippi Farmer (16822)

MISSOURI
Clark
Small Farm Today (16981) 12,000

Kansas City
Charolais Journal (17161) ....‡6,000
Hereford World (17171) ....‡10,000
Missouri Beef
  Cattleman (17186) ....(Controlled) ‡5,200

Platte City
American Chianina Journal (17348) ....‡1,500

2742

Numbers cited after listings are entry numbers rather than page numbers.

Polo
Hogs Today (17356) ....(Non-paid) 84,547

St. Joseph
Angus Beef Bulletin (17389) ......(Non-paid) ‡70,000
Angus Journal (17390) ....‡23,000

MONTANA
Billings
Western Livestock Reporter (17734) ....‡12,000

NEBRASKA
Lincoln
Nebraska Cattleman (18099) ....(Paid) ‡5,067
(Controlled) ‡4,530

Omaha
Shorthorn Country (18208) ....(Paid) ‡3,500
(Non-paid) ‡200

NEVADA
Lovelock
The Nevada Rancher (18413) ....(Paid) ‡3,500
(Free) ‡200

NEW MEXICO
Albuquerque
Arizona Cattlelog (19766) ....‡1,800
Livestock Market Digest (19775)
New Mexico Stockman (19782) ....‡10,750

NEW YORK
East Syracuse
Holstein World (20558) ....‡13,255

Gouverneur
The Trottingbred (20675) ....‡500

Ithaca
New York Holstein
News (20811) ....(Controlled) ‡4,300

NORTH CAROLINA
Fuquay Varina
Carolina Cattle Connection (23902) ....‡7,000

NORTH DAKOTA
Bismarck
North Dakota Stockman (24357) ....‡3,400

OHIO
Cardington
The Shepherd (24740) ....‡7,500

Marysville
Ohio Cattleman (25358) ....‡3,000

Reynoldsburg
Guernsey Breeders'
Journal (25494) ....(Paid) ‡1,900
(Controlled) ‡190

OKLAHOMA
Nardin
Emu Today & Tomorrow (25927) ......(Paid) ⊕1,000
(Non-paid) ⊕100

Norman
Speedhorse Racing Report (25943) ....‡8,000

Oklahoma City
Oklahoma COWMAN (25977) 4,784

Yukon
Limousin World (26204) ....(Paid) ‡4,800
(Non-paid) ‡5,200

OREGON
Klamath Falls
Cascade Cattleman (26382) 5,500
Cascade Horseman (26383) 10,000

Salem
Oregon Beef Producer (26569) 2,500

Sisters
Small Farmer's Journal (26585) 25,000

SOUTH DAKOTA
Sturgis
Tri-State Livestock News (29001) .....(Paid) ‡14,000
(Free) ‡500

TENNESSEE
Lewisburg
Voice of the Tennessee Walking
Horse (29326) ....(Paid) ‡19,500
(Non-paid) ‡176

TEXAS
Amarillo
The American Quarter Horse
Journal (29695) ....(Paid) 70,052
The Quarter Racing Journal (29697) ....(Paid) 8,908

Bowie
Ratite Marketplace (29941) ....(Paid) 4,000

Crowley
United Caprine News (30113) ....‡6,000

Denton
American Red Angus (30232) ....‡9,000

Dripping Springs
American Red Brangus Journal (30250) ....‡5,000

Eddy
The Brahman Journal (30268) ....(Paid) ‡2183
(Non-paid) ‡1586

Fort Worth
The Cattleman (30331) ....(Paid) 15,415
(Non-paid) 1,590
Christian Ranchman (30333) ....(Free) 39,470
Cutting Horse Chatter (30336) ....‡13,000
The Horsetrader (30342) ....‡20,452
Lone Star Horse Report (30346) ....(Paid) 1,000
(Controlled) 10,000
Paint Horse Journal (30350) ....(Paid) ‡35,038
Texas Hereford (30354) ....‡3,200
Weekly Livestock
Reporter (30355) ....(Paid) ‡11,903
(Free) ‡662

San Angelo
Livestock Weekly (31005) ....(Paid) ⊕18,211
Meat Goat Monthly News (31006) 2,500
Ranch & Rural Living
Magazine (31008) ....(Paid) 6,318
(Non-paid) 700

San Antonio
The Beefmaster Cowman (31025) ......(Paid) ‡4,835
(Non-paid) ‡211
Brangus Journal (31026) ....‡2,800
Gulf Coast
Cattleman (31031) ....(Controlled) ‡15,755

VERMONT
Shelburne
The Morgan Horse (31599) ....‡8,000

VIRGINIA
Daleville
Virginia Cattleman (31990) ....‡10,000

WISCONSIN
Appleton
The North American Deer
Farmer (33541) ....(Combined) 1,200

Brookfield
American Farriers Journal (33602) .....(Paid) ‡7,000
(Non-paid) ‡200

Withee
Dairy Goat Journal (34468) ....(Paid) 6,500
Sheep! Magazine (34469) ....(Paid) 4,000

WYOMING
Cheyenne
Cow Country (34495) ....(Paid) ‡1,335
(Non-paid) ‡207

ALBERTA, CANADA
Calgary
Alberta Beef Magazine (34625) ....(Paid) 2,700
(Controlled) 10,200
Canadian Hereford Digest (34635) 3,000
Canadian Rodeo News (34639) ....‡3,058
(Non-paid) ‡942
Simmental Country (34657) ....(Paid) ‡4,500
(Non-paid) ‡350

Edmonton
Sheep Canada (34730) 1,500
Western Hog Journal (34734) ....(Non-paid) 5,101

Leduc
Prairie Hog Country (34793) ......(Controlled) ‡4,775

BRITISH COLUMBIA, CANADA
Vernon
Equinews (35200) ....(Paid) ‡17,492
(Non-paid) ‡800

MANITOBA, CANADA
Winnipeg
Cattlemen (35321) ....(Paid) 25,759

NOVA SCOTIA, CANADA
Liverpool
Atlantic Beef Quarterly (35587) ....(Paid) 2000
(Non-paid) 2000

ONTARIO, CANADA
Aurora
Canadian Thoroughbred (35644) ....‡4,500

Cookstown
Canadian Cooperative Wool Growers
Magazine (35752) ....(Non-paid) 17,000
⊕12,000
5,000

Guelph
Monthly Crop and Livestock
Report (35866) ....(Non-paid) 2,600

London
Ontario Hog Farmer (35990) ....(Paid) 26
(Non-paid) 8,614

Ottawa
Canadian Journal of Animal
Science (36201) ....(Paid) 1,000

Richmond Hill
Holstein Journal (36342) ....(Paid) 4,877
(Non-paid) 77

SASKATCHEWAN, CANADA
Regina
Charolais Banner (37527) ....‡2,100
Charolais Connection (37528) ....(Paid) ‡18,000
(Non-paid) ‡300

POULTRY AND PIGEONS

ALABAMA
Cullman
WATT Poultry USA (162) ......(Combined) 20,126

ARKANSAS
Hartford
The Gamecock (1170) 14,300

GEORGIA
Gainesville
Poultry and Egg
Marketing (7293) ....(Controlled) ‡11,600
Poultry Times (7294) ....(Paid) 10,661

ILLINOIS
Chicago
CarneTec (8299) ....(Non-paid) 6,200
Meat Marketing &
Technology (8483) ....(Combined) 20,058
Poultry Magazine (8538) ....(Controlled) ‡10,000

Mount Morris
Industria Avicola (9239) 15,160
Poultry International (9245) ....(Combined) 23,620

INDIANA
Connersville
Poultry Press (9901) ....‡5,800

MINNESOTA
Buffalo
Gobbles (15778) ....‡800

NEW JERSEY
Toms River
Weekly Insiders Turkey Letter (19648) ....(Paid) 230

OHIO
Bellbrook
Racing Pigeon Bulletin (24665) ....‡5,000

SOUTH CAROLINA
Columbia
Palmetto Poultry Life (28560) ......(Controlled) 1,350

Gaffney
Grit and Steel (28616) ....‡6,000

ONTARIO, CANADA
Delhi
Canada Poultry Magazine/La Revue Canadienne
D'Aviculture (35764) 9,000

Circulation: ★ = ABC; △ = BPA; ◆ = CAC; ● = CCAB; ❑ = VAC; ⊕ = PO Statement; ‡ = Publisher's Report; Boldface figures = sworn; Light figures = estimated.

2743

Circ.

Circ.

Circ.

RURAL ELECTRIFICATION
See also Power and Power Plants;
Electrical Engineering

ALABAMA
Montgomery
Alabama Living (358) ....(Paid) ★360,936

COLORADO
Denver
Colorado Country Life (4312) 160,000

GEORGIA
Tucker
GEORGIA Magazine (7610) ....‡448,000

ILLINOIS
Springfield
Illinois Rural Electric News (9630) ....‡142,000

INDIANA
Indianapolis
Electric Consumer (10109) ....(Paid) 250,000
(Non-paid) 172

IOWA
Urbandale
Iowa REC News (11276) ....(Combined) ‡93,000

KANSAS
Topeka
Kansas Country Living (11827) ....‡80,957

LOUISIANA
Baton Rouge
Louisiana Country (12497) ....‡130,000

MISSISSIPPI
Ridgeland
TODAY in Mississippi (16835) ....(Paid) ‡386,691
(Non-paid) ‡176

MISSOURI
Jefferson City
Rural Missouri (17132) ....‡388,000

NEW MEXICO
Santa Fe
Enchantment (19935) ....‡125,000

NORTH DAKOTA
Mandan
North Dakota REC Magazine (24498) ....‡71,199

OHIO
Columbus
Country Living (Ohio) (25012) ....(Paid) 282,050

OREGON
Forest Grove
Ruralite (26357) ....‡281,400

PENNSYLVANIA
Harrisburg
Penn Lines (27004) ....(Paid) 143,134

SOUTH CAROLINA
Cayce
Living in South Carolina (28503) ....‡503,000

TENNESSEE
Nashville
Tennessee Magazine (29492) ....(Paid) 472,677

VIRGINIA
Arlington
Rural Electrification
Magazine (31824) ....(Paid) 33,119
Glen Allen
Rural Living (32112) ....(Paid) 325,000

WISCONSIN
Chippewa Falls
Rural Minnesota News (33628) ....(Paid) 35,000
Madison
Wisconsin Energy Cooperative
News (33981) 153,000

WYOMING
Casper
The WREN Magazine (34484) ....(Combined) 34,141

SCIENTIFIC AGRICULTURAL PUBLICATIONS

ALABAMA
Auburn
Highlights of Agricultural Research (41)

ALASKA
Fairbanks
Agroborealis (566) ....(Non-paid) 2,500

CALIFORNIA
Fresno
Agricultural Spray Adjuvants (1942)
Oakland
California Agriculture (2671) ....(Paid) 850
(Controlled) 19,000
San Francisco
Biodynamics (3331) ....‡1,500

COLORADO
Lakewood
Journal of Range Management (4533) 3,400

CONNECTICUT
Fairfield
Journal of Sustainable
Agriculture (4790) ....(Paid) ‡775

FLORIDA
Gainesville
Tri-Ology (6158)

GEORGIA
Athens
Communications in Soil Science and Plant
Analysis (6934) ....‡800

IDAHO
Parma
Journal of Potato Production and Postharvest
Handling (7942)

ILLINOIS
Urbana
Illinois Research (9710) ....(Controlled) ‡7,000

KANSAS
Lawrence
Weed Science (11570)
Weed Technology (11571)
Lenexa
Dealer and Applicator
Magazine (11589) ....(Controlled) ‡22,000

LOUISIANA
Baton Rouge
Louisiana Agriculture
Magazine (12494) ....(Controlled) ‡5,900

MAINE
Orono
American Journal of Potato
Research (12998) ....‡1,000

MASSACHUSETTS
Malden
American Journal of Agricultural
Economics (14289) 4,300

MICHIGAN
East Lansing
Agricultural Economics
Report (14981) ....(Non-paid) 15
St. Joseph
Applied Engineering in
Agriculture (15511) ....(Paid) ‡700
Resource (15513) ....‡9,000

MINNESOTA
St. Paul
Molecular Plant-Microbe Interactions
(MPMI) (16397) ....(Paid) 1,500
(Non-paid) 7

MISSISSIPPI
Mississippi State
MAFES Research
Highlights (16782) ....(Non-paid) 10,300

NEW JERSEY
Hoboken
Agribusiness (18883) 11,900
New Brunswick
Soil Science (19340) ....(Paid) ‡1,113
(Non-paid) ‡235

NEW YORK
Binghamton
Journal of New Seeds (20190)
Small Fruits Review (20215) 225
Ithaca
Cornell Focus (20793) ....(Non-paid) ‡4,600
New York
Agricultural and Human Values (21165)
European Journal of Plant Pathology (21648)
Experimental Agriculture (21663) 550
Genetic Resources and Crop Evolution (21751)
Integrated Pest Management (21886)
Irrigation and Drainage Systems (21953)
The Journal of Agricultural Science (21979) 750
New Forests (22429)
Plant and Soil (22561)

OKLAHOMA
Lane
Journal of Vegetable Crop Production (25881)

PUERTO RICO
Rio Piedras
University of Puerto Rico Journal of
Agriculture (28286)

SOUTH DAKOTA
Brookings
Farm & Home Research
Quarterly (28813) ....(Non-paid) ‡5,000

TEXAS
College Station
Journal of Agricultural and Food
Information (30044) ....(Paid) 200

UTAH
Logan
Utah Science (31352) ....(Non-paid) 6,000

WASHINGTON
Seattle
Bamboo Science & Culture (32946)

WISCONSIN
Madison
Agronomy Journal (33916) 9,500
Crop Science (33931) ....‡4,500
Food Reviews International (33940) 350
Soil Science Society of America
Journal (33973) ....‡4,500

ONTARIO, CANADA
Guelph
Agri-Food Research in Ontario/Recherche Agro-
alimentaire en
Ontario (35858) ....(Combined) 7,500
Ottawa
Canadian Journal of Plant
Science (36212) ....‡1,100
Canadian Journal of Soil
Science (36219) ....(Paid) 1,250

SASKATCHEWAN, CANADA
Saskatoon
Canadian Biosystems
Engineering (37549) ....(Controlled) 250

SOCIALIZED FARMING

CALIFORNIA
Fresno
California-Arizona Texas Cotton (1945) ....‡15,000
Sacramento
Almond Facts (2975) ....(Controlled) 8,000
Stockton
Sun Diamond Grower (3809) ....(Controlled) ‡10,000

FLORIDA
Tampa
Citrus and Vegetable
Magazine (6760) ....(Controlled) △12,000

GEORGIA
Tifton
Southeastern Peanut Farmer **(7597)** ....‡8,500

HAWAII
Waianae
Hawaii Orchid Journal **(7794)** ....‡750

IDAHO
Idaho Falls
Potato Grower **(7869)** ....(Combined) 16,000
The Sugar Producer **(7871)** .....(Controlled) ‡16,000

ILLINOIS
Rolling Meadows
Turf News **(9551)** ....‡1,700

KANSAS
Lecompton
Christmas Trees **(11588)** ....(Paid) ‡4,391
                                    (Controlled) ‡41

KENTUCKY
Frankfort
Journal of Applied
   Aquaculture **(12064)** ....(Paid) 301

LOUISIANA
New Orleans
Sugar Journal **(12754)** ....(Paid) 654
                              (Non-paid) 3,319

MAINE
Presque Isle
Maine Potato News **(13034)** ....(Free) ‡6,250

MASSACHUSETTS
Amherst
Journal of Tree Fruit
   Production **(13798)** ....(Paid) 96

MINNESOTA
Minneapolis
Soybean Digest **(16132)** ....(Controlled) ‡214,000

MISSISSIPPI
Greenwood
Staplreview **(16645)** ....‡4,500

NORTH CAROLINA
Raleigh
The Flue Cured Tobacco
   Farmer **(24136)** ....(Paid) 85
                              (Controlled) 14,461
The Peanut Farmer **(24147)** ....(Paid) 48
                              (Controlled) 17,410
Rice Journal **(24151)** ....(Paid) ‡177
                              (Controlled) ‡10,876

OREGON
Pendleton
Oregon Wheat **(26459)** ....‡5,800

TENNESSEE
Memphis
Cotton Farming **(29364)** ....(Non-paid) 51,151

TEXAS
Bryan
Pecan South **(29974)** ....(Paid) ‡4,300
                                (Non-paid) ‡500

WASHINGTON
Ritzville
Wheat Life **(32933)** 14,065

Yakima
Potato Country **(33221)** ....(Controlled) ‡7,544
The Tomato
   Magazine **(33222)** ....(Controlled) ‡6,742

ONTARIO, CANADA
Delhi
The Canadian Tobacco
   Grower **(35766)** ....(Paid) ‡2,000
Fruit and Vegetable
   Magazine **(35769)** ....(Paid) ‡3,000

Guelph
The Grower **(35863)** ....(Combined) ‡8939

Circulation: ★ = ABC; △ = BPA; ♦ = CAC; ● = CCAB; ❑ = VAC; ⊕ = PO Statement; ‡ = Publisher's Report; Boldface figures = sworn; Light figures = estimated.

2745

Black Publications

Index entries are arranged geographically, first by states/provinces and then by cities. Within cities in this index, citations appear alphabetically by publication title. Citations include publication title, entry number (given in parentheses immediately following the title), and circulation figures.

Circ.

ALABAMA
Birmingham
Birmingham Times **(61)** ....(Paid) ‡10,000
(Free) ‡350

Birmingham World **(62)** ....(Paid) ‡12,600
Pure Heart Magazine **(88)**

Eutaw
Greene County Democrat **(208)** ....‡3,500

Huntsville
Speakin' Out News **(274)** ....‡24,000

Mobile
Mobile Beacon **(323)** ....‡4,952
National Inner City **(326)** ....‡8,000
The New Times **(328)** ....(Paid) ‡5,000
(Free) ‡150

Tuskegee
Campus Digest **(507)** ....(Non-paid) 2,000

ARIZONA
Phoenix
Arizona Informant **(780)** ....‡1,800

CALIFORNIA
Bakersfield
Bakersfield News Observer **(1448)**

Berkeley
Berkeley Tri City Post **(1499)** ....(Free) ‡20,000

Beverly Hills
The Ethiopian Mirror **(1572)** ....(Paid) 11,000
(Non-paid) 15,000

Compton
Carson Bulletin **(1746)** ....(Paid) 8,000
(Free) 9,000
Compton Bulletin **(1747)** ....(Paid) 12,000
(Free) 10,000
Compton/Carson Wave **(1748)** .....(Non-paid) 40,365
Compton Metropolitan
Gazette **(1749)** ....(Free) 60,000

Culver City
Culver City Star **(1792)** ....(Non-paid) 29,109

Firestone Park
Firestone Park News/Southeast News
Press **(1916)** ....(Paid) ‡18,000
(Free) ‡6,000

Fresno
California Advocate **(1944)** 22,500

Inglewood
Inglewood/Hawthorne
Wave **(2072)** ....(Non-paid) 45,453
Inglewood Tribune **(2073)** ....(Paid) 1,000
(Free) 9,000

Long Beach
Long Beach Express **(2171)** ....(Free) 60,000

Los Angeles
Afronet Magazine **(2202)**
Black Dates **(2219)**
Blackfire **(2221)**
BLK **(2223)**
Central Star/Journal
Wave **(2234)** ....(Combined) 37,210

Herald Dispatch **(2288)** ....‡35,000
Kuumba **(2310)**
Mesa Tribune Wave **(2330)** 31,609
NOMMO **(2348)** ....(Non-paid) 10,000
Players **(2370)** 50,000
Southwest News Wave **(2403)** 38,932
Watts Star Review **(2431)** ....‡30,000
Westchester Star **(2433)** ....(Non-paid) 9,956

Lynwood
Lynwood Journal **(2486)**
Lynwood Press **(2487)** 12,500

Oakland
The Black Scholar **(2668)** ....(Paid) 10,000
(Non-paid) 60,000
Oakland Post **(2691)** ....(Free) ‡62,496

Pacoima
San Fernando Gazette
Express **(2742)** ....(Free) 60,000

Palo Alto
Meanderings **(2798)**

Pasadena
Pasadena Gazette **(2822)** ....(Free) 60,000

Richmond
Richmond Post **(2921)** ....(Free) ‡21,900

Riverside
Black Voice News **(2931)** ....‡7,500

Sacramento
Sacramento Observer **(3018)** ....‡49,090

San Bernardino
Precinct Reporter **(3089)** ....‡55,000
The San Bernardino American
News **(3090)** 5,000

San Diego
The San Diego Voice and
Viewpoint **(3271)** 13,000

San Francisco
California Voice **(3339)** ....(Free) 37,325
San Francisco **(3425)** ....(Combined) ‡108,895
San Francisco Bay View **(3430)** ....(Paid) ‡500
(Non-paid) ‡19,500
San Francisco Post **(3438)** ....(Free) ‡18,289
Sun-Reporter **(3445)** ....‡11,249

Thousand Oaks
Journal of Black Psychology **(3881)** .....(Paid) 1,200
Journal of Black Studies **(3882)** ....(Paid) ‡1,000

Torrance
Minority Business Entrepreneur **(3938)** 40,000

Wilmington
Wilmington Beacon **(4090)**

CONNECTICUT
Hartford
Hartford Inquirer **(4893)** 125,000

Madison
Black Health **(4927)** ....(Paid) ‡2,340
(Free) ‡25,000

New Haven
The Inner City Newspaper **(4991)** .....(Free) ‡35,000

DISTRICT OF COLUMBIA
Washington
Afro-American Historical and Genealogical Society
Journal **(5315)** ....(Paid) 910
American Visions **(5348)** ....(Paid) 125,000
(Controlled) 5,000
Howard **(5531)** ....(Combined) 50,000
Journal of the National Medical
Association **(5603)** ....(Paid) 6,000
(Controlled) 31,000
The Journal of Negro
Education **(5605)** ....(Paid) ‡2,300
(Controlled) ‡100
Lincoln Review **(5637)** ....(Non-paid) ‡7,000
The Washington Informer **(5846)** ....‡27,000

FLORIDA
Daytona Beach
Daytona Times **(6036)** ....‡20,150
Voice **(6040)** ....‡3,000

Fort Lauderdale
Westside Gazette **(6088)** ....(Paid) ‡7,000
(Free) ‡14,500

Jacksonville
Florida Star Times **(6211)** ....(Thurs.) 1,399

Miami
The Miami Times **(6372)** ....(Wed.) 22,050

Orlando
Florida Sun Review **(6494)**
The Orlando Times **(6504)** 11,000

Pensacola
Pensacola Voice **(6569)** ....‡35,896

St. Petersburg
The Weekly Challenger **(6635)** 45,000

Sarasota
The Bulletin **(6655)** ....(Paid) 16,500

Tallahassee
Capital Outlook **(6702)** 11,333
The Famuan **(6704)** ....(Free) ‡3,400

Tampa
Florida Sentinel-Bulletin **(6763)** ....‡23,345

GEORGIA
Atlanta
Atlanta Daily World **(6968)** ....‡10,000
The Atlanta Inquirer **(6971)** ....(Paid) 61,082
The Atlanta Voice **(6974)** 50,000
AUC Digest **(6975)** ....(Paid) ‡100
(Non-paid) ‡20,000
Black Employment and Education
Magazine **(6979)** ....(Paid) ‡25,000
(Controlled) ‡150,000

Augusta
The Metro Courier **(7101)** ....‡28,760

Columbus
The Columbus Times **(7183)** ....‡20,000

Cordele
Southeastern News **(7205)**

Fort Valley
Fort Valley Herald **(7286)** ....‡6,000

Circulation: ★ = ABC; △ = BPA; ♦ = CAC; • = CCAB; ❏ = VAC; ⊕ = PO Statement; ‡ = Publisher's Report; Boldface figures = sworn; Light figures = estimated.

2747

Circ.   Circ.   Circ.

GEORGIA (continued)
Roswell
Atlanta Tribune: The
  Magazine **(7513)** ....(Paid) ‡22,000
                                     (Non-paid) ‡10,000

Savannah
The Savannah Herald **(7534)** ....(Paid) 8,500
The Savannah Tribune **(7538)** ....(Paid) ‡8,000
                                     (Free) ‡8,000

ILLINOIS
Chicago
Black Books Bulletin: Words Work **(8284)**
Chatham-Southeast Citizen **(8304)** ....(Paid) ‡20,597
                                     (Free) ‡9,365
Chicago Crusader **(8310)** ....(Paid) ‡57,000
The New #Chicago Shoreland
  News **(8323)** 38,000
                                     (Paid) 9,880
Chicago South Shore Scene **(8324)** ...(Paid) ‡1,000
                                     (Free) ‡19,000
Chicago Weekend **(8329)** ....(Paid) ‡22,583
                                     (Free) ‡2,053
Ebony **(8357)** ....(Paid) 1,728,986
EM: Ebony Man **(8367)** ....(Paid) 171,391
The Final Call **(8376)** 400,000
                                     (Free) 2,000
Hyde Park Citizen **(8402)** ....‡17,000
Ivy Leaf **(8423)** 40,000
Jet **(8425)** ....(Paid) 944,073
N'DIGO **(8501)** ....(Combined) 125,000
South End Citizen **(8566)** ....(Free) ‡19,586
                                     (Paid) ‡9,121
South Suburban Citizen **(8567)** ....(Free) ‡12,750
                                     (Paid) 8,750

Chicago Heights
Chicago Standard News **(8666)** 16,000
South Suburban Standard **(8669)** 15,000

Decatur
Decatur Voice of the Black
  Community **(8710)** ....(Paid) ‡16,000
                                     (Non-paid) ‡3,000

East St. Louis
East St. Louis Monitor **(8807)** ....‡22,500

Hazel Crest
Muslim Journal **(8980)** ....‡16,000

Oak Park
Tri-City Journal **(9377)** 50,000

INDIANA
Fort Wayne
Frost Illustrated **(9969)** ....(Paid) ‡1,342
                                     (Free) ‡32

Gary
Gary New Crusader **(10015)** ....‡27,000
Info **(10016)** ....(Paid) ‡18,640
                                     (Free) ‡2,415

Indianapolis
The Indianapolis Recorder **(10132)** 13,300

KENTUCKY
Covington
The Suspension Press **(12028)** ....(Paid) ‡38,000
                                     (Free) ‡3,200

Louisville
Louisville Defender **(12229)** ....(Non-paid) ♦536
                                     (Paid) ♦2,689

LOUISIANA
Alexandria
The Alexandria News Weekly **(12457)** ....‡13,750

Baton Rouge
Baton Rouge Weekly Press **(12485)** .....(Paid) 7,500

New Orleans
Louisiana Weekly **(12740)** 20,000
New Orleans Data News
  Weekly **(12744)** ....(Paid) ‡380
                                     (Free) ‡20,000
SENGA **(12753)**

Shreveport
The Shreveport Sun **(12819)** ....(Paid) 4,968
                                     (Free) 102

MARYLAND
Baltimore
Alternative Press Index **(13111)** ....(Paid) ‡550
                                     (Controlled) ‡200
Baltimore Afro-American **(13128)** ....(Sat.) 9,947
Crisis **(13153)**
USBE & Information
  Technology **(13258)** ....(Non-paid) 35,000

Hagerstown
Message **(13567)** ....(Paid) ‡78,273
                                     (Non-paid) ‡56

Silver Spring
Journal of Negro History **(13732)** ....(Paid) ‡3,700
                                     (Non-paid) ‡300

Takoma Park
Sister 2 Sister **(13752)** ....(Paid) ★150,000

MICHIGAN
Detroit
Michigan Chronicle **(14938)** ....‡47,428

Grand Rapids
The Grand Rapids Times **(15097)**

Highland Park
Michigan Citizen **(15161)** ....(Paid) 51,442
                                     (Free) 918

Jackson
Blazer News **(15220)** ....‡2,000

MINNESOTA
Minneapolis
Minnesota Spokesman **(16107)** ....(Paid) ‡3,790
                                     (Free) ‡517

MISSISSIPPI
Jackson
Jackson Advocate **(16696)** ....(Paid) ‡20,000
                                     (Free) ‡3,000

University
Living Blues **(16866)** ....‡25,000

MISSOURI
Kansas City
Call **(17159)** ....(Fri.) 17,310

St. Louis
African American Review **(17406)** ....(Paid) 4,200
                                     (Non-paid) 167
St. Louis American **(17493)** ....(Paid) 393
                                     (Non-paid) 62,880
St. Louis Argus **(17494)** 33,000
St. Louis Crusader **(17500)** ....(Paid) ‡9,000
                                     (Controlled) ‡150
The St. Louis Metro Evening
  Whirl **(17504)** ....‡49,500

NEVADA
Las Vegas
Las Vegas Sentinel-Voice **(18375)** 5,000

NEW HAMPSHIRE
Peterborough
Footsteps **(18624)** 6,000

NEW JERSEY
New Brunswick
Black Voice/Carta Latina **(19326)** ....(Free) ‡4,000

Somerset
The Review of Black Political
  Economy **(19564)** ....(Paid) ‡1,000

NEW YORK
Brooklyn
Afro-American Times **(20295)** 55,000
Brooklyn New York Recorder **(20302)**
Daily Challenge **(20310)** 79,000

Buffalo
Afro-Americans in New York Life and
  History **(20362)** ....(Paid) 600
Buffalo Criterion **(20364)**
The Challenger **(20372)** ....‡10,000

Jamaica
Jamaica Shopping & Entertainment
  Guide **(20836)** ....(Free) ‡30,000
The New York Voice/Harlem
  U.S.A. **(20839)** ....(Paid) ‡70,000

New York
Amsterdam News **(21211)** ....(Wed.) 51,133
Black Enterprise **(21328)** ....(Paid) 421,169
Essence **(21629)** ....(Paid) 1,004,452
Honey **(21816)** ....(Combined) 200,000
The New York Beacon **(22437)** 71,750
The New York Evening
  Express **(22442)** ....(Paid) 1,200
NY Carib News **(22477)** ....(Paid) ‡67,000
                                     (Free) ‡4,500
Right On! **(22667)** ....(Paid) 77,247
Savoy **(22707)** ....(Combined) 200,000

Newburgh
Hudson Valley Black Press **(23001)** ....‡42,500

Rochester
About...Time **(23207)** ....(Paid) ‡56,000
Communicade **(23217)** ....(Paid) 2,800
                                     (Free) 200

NORTH CAROLINA
Charlotte
The Charlotte Post **(23741)** ....‡11,500

Durham
The Carolina Times **(23812)** ....‡5,800

Greensboro
A & T Register **(23915)** 3,000
Carolina Peacemaker **(23919)** ....‡6,400

Greenville
The 'M' Voice Newspaper **(23965)** ....(Paid) ‡16,000
                                     (Non-paid) ‡12,000

Raleigh
The Carolinian **(24131)** ....(Paid) ‡12,000
                                     (Free) ‡225

Statesville
County News **(24246)** ....(Paid) ‡2,500
                                     (Free) ‡2,500

Wilmington
The Wilmington Journal **(24297)** 9,000

Winston-Salem
Winston-Salem Chronicle **(24323)** ....(Paid) 5,292
                                     (Non-paid) 497

OHIO
Akron
The Akron Reporter **(24574)** 17,000

Cincinnati
The Cincinnati Herald **(24786)** ....‡24,500

Cleveland
Call and Post **(24865)** ....‡43,283

Toledo
The Toledo Journal **(25570)** 19,000

Youngstown
The Buckeye Review **(25694)** ....(Paid) ‡5,000
                                     (Free) ‡100

OKLAHOMA
Oklahoma City
The Black Chronicle **(25955)** ....(Paid) ‡28,927

Tulsa
The Oklahoma Eagle **(26122)** ....‡12,800

OREGON
Portland
The Portland Skanner **(26502)** ....(Paid) ‡20,000

PENNSYLVANIA
Chalfont
HealthQuest **(26767)** ....(Paid) 1,000

Lincoln University
The Lincolnian **(27200)** ....(Free) 1,500

Philadelphia
Philadelphia New
  Observer **(27630)** ....(Paid) ‡10,303
                                     (Free) ‡70,697
The Philadelphia Tribune **(27633)** .....(Tues.) 13,196
                                     (Fri.) 9,269
The Philadelphia Tribune Metro
  Edition **(27634)** ....(Sun.) ♦47,408
                                     (Tues.) ♦20,250
                                     (Wed.) ♦34,000
                                     (Thurs.) ♦64,000
                                     (Fri.) ♦10,643

Pittsburgh
New Pittsburgh Courier **(27821)** ....‡30,000

SOUTH CAROLINA
Charleston
Charleston Black Times **(28509)** 6,883
The Charleston Chronicle **(28510)** ....(Paid) 3,000
(Free) 3,000

Columbia
The Black News **(28544)**

Orangeburg
Orangeburg Black Voice **(28731)** 5,365

TENNESSEE
Memphis
Tri-State Defender **(29383)** ....‡15,000

Nashville
Fisk News **(29455)** ....(Free) 1,000
The Tennessee Tribune **(29495)** ......(Paid) ‡25,000

TEXAS
Austin
The Villager **(29853)** ....(Free) ‡6,000

Dallas
African Herald **(30121)** ....(Paid) 12,500
Black Tennis Magazine **(30133)** ....‡5,000
Dallas Post Tribune **(30149)** ....‡20,000
The Dallas Weekly Newspaper **(30150)** ....(Paid) 78
(Free) 15,258

Houston
African-American News &
Issues **(30455)** ....(Combined) 350,000
Houston Defender **(30482)** ....(Paid) ‡23,000
(Free) ‡4,000
Houston Forward Times **(30484)** ....‡64,580
The Informer & Texas Freeman **(30491)** 30,000

Lubbock
Lubbock Southwest Digest **(30716)** .....(Paid) ‡3,137
(Free) ‡1,243

San Antonio
San Antonio Register **(31047)** ....(Paid) ‡7,800
(Non-paid) ‡200

VIRGINIA
Alexandria
NSBE Magazine **(31716)** ....(Paid) ‡8,000
(Non-paid) ‡14,934

Fairfax
Black Issues Book
Review **(32008)** ....(Combined) ★54,853
Black Issues in Higher Education **(32009)**

Norfolk
New Journal & Guide **(32291)** ....(Combined) 25,000

Roanoke
Roanoke Tribune **(32492)** ....‡5,200

WASHINGTON
Pullman
The Western Journal of Black
Studies **(32909)** ....(Paid) ‡400
(Non-paid) ‡30

Seattle
Facts Newspaper **(32964)** ....(Paid) 13,000
(Free) 29,650
Seattle Medium **(33020)** 37,000

Tacoma
The Northwest Dispatch **(33148)** .....:...(Paid) ‡7,700
(Free) ‡3,900
Tacoma True Citizen **(33152)** 13,500

WISCONSIN
Madison
Prime **(33971)**

Milwaukee
Milwaukee Community
Journal **(34082)** ....(Paid) 4,960
(Free) 35,000
Milwaukee Courier **(34083)** 40,000
Milwaukee Star **(34087)** ....(Free) 20,000
Milwaukee Times **(34088)** ....(Non-paid) ‡7,500

BRITISH COLUMBIA, CANADA
Aldergrove
The Afro News **(34879)**

ONTARIO, CANADA
Toronto
Share **(36739)** ....(Combined) 153,000

QUEBEC, CANADA
Montreal
KOLA **(37148)** ....(Combined) 325

Circulation: ★ = ABC; △ = BPA; ♦ = CAC; ♦ = CCAB; ❑ = VAC; ⊕ = PO Statement; ‡ = Publisher's Report; Boldface figures = sworn; Light figures = estimated.

2749

Foreign Language Publications

This index lists newspapers and other periodicals that are published entirely or partly in a language other than English. Index entries are arranged by languages (please refer to the Index to Subject Terms). Within these groupings, entries are arranged geographically by states/provinces and alphabetically within cities. Citations include the publication title, entry number (given in parentheses), and circulation figures.

ALBANIAN

NEW YORK
Brooklyn
The Watchtower **(20355)** ....‡23,042,000

VIRGINIA
Springfield
Albanian Times **(32538)**

ARABIC

CALIFORNIA
Glendale
News Circle **(2011)** ....(Paid) ‡3,000

Los Angeles
Beirut Times **(2218)** ....(Non-paid) 15,000

DISTRICT OF COLUMBIA
Washington
Alam Attijarat (The World of
  Business) **(5320)** ....(Non-paid) ‡20,954
Finance &
  Development **(5495)** ....(Controlled) 95,000
International Journal of Government Auditing **(5554)**

NEW YORK
Brooklyn
The Watchtower **(20355)** ....‡23,042,000

Great Neck
World Industrial Reporter (Reportero
  Industrial) **(20695)** ....(Non-paid) ‡71,101

New York
Action **(21146)** ....(Paid) 5,000
                                              (Free) 2,000

VIRGINIA
Williamsburg
Al-Arabiyya **(32612)**

ONTARIO, CANADA
Scarborough
Iranian Community Newspaper **(36377)**

Toronto
Canada & Arab World **(36487)** ....(Paid) ‡7,900
                                              (Non-paid) ‡5,300

ARMENIAN

CALIFORNIA
Los Angeles
Verelk **(2429)**

MASSACHUSETTS
Watertown
The Armenian Mirror-Spectator **(14610)** 2,800

NEW YORK
Brooklyn
The Watchtower **(20355)** ....‡23,042,000

New York
Ararat **(21240)** ....‡1,800

The Eternal Flame **(21630)** ....(Non-paid) 3,300
Hoosharar Mioutune **(21817)** ....‡7,500

QUEBEC, CANADA
Saint-Laurent
Abaka **(37361)** ....(Paid) ‡875
                                              (Free) ‡75

BULGARIAN

INDIANA
Fort Wayne
Macedonian Tribune **(9972)** ....‡1,600

NEW YORK
Brooklyn
The Watchtower **(20355)** ....‡23,042,000

BYELORUSSIAN

NEW YORK
Jamaica
Bielarus/The Belarusan **(20831)** ....‡2,000

CHINESE

CALIFORNIA
City of Industry
Travel & Recreation
  Magazine **(1719)** ....(Combined) 20,000

El Monte
Chinese L.A. Daily
  News **(1865)** ....(Combined) 103,000

Monterey Park
Chinese American Daily
  News **(2592)** ....(Combined) 30,000
Chinese Daily News,Inc **(2593)** ....‡85,000
International Daily News **(2594)** ....(Paid) 23,000
                                              (Non-paid) 1,000

San Francisco
Chinese Times **(3341)** ....‡11,000

South San Francisco
Sing Tao Daily **(3791)**

DISTRICT OF COLUMBIA
Washington
The China Business Review **(5411)** ....(Paid) ‡5,600
                                              (Non-paid) ‡100
Finance &
  Development **(5495)** ....(Controlled) 95,000

HAWAII
Honolulu
China Review International **(7683)** ....(Paid) 600
                                              (Controlled) 45

MARYLAND
Gaithersburg
Hua Zia Wen Zhai **(13541)**

MISSOURI
St. Charles
Chinese American Forum **(17383)** ....(Paid) ‡500
                                              (Non-paid) ‡750

NEW YORK
Brooklyn
The Watchtower **(20355)** ....‡23,042,000

WASHINGTON
Seattle
Northwest Asian Weekly **(32993)** ....(Paid) ‡9,000
                                              (Free) ‡6,000
Outlook **(32999)** ....(Non-paid) 20,000

ONTARIO, CANADA
Toronto
Shing Wah News **(36740)** ....(Paid) 1,000
                                              (Free) 9,000

CROATIAN

See also Serbian

INDIANA
Hobart
Our Hope **(10064)** ....(Paid) ‡50
                                              (Free) ‡3,500

NEW YORK
Brooklyn
The Watchtower **(20355)** ....‡23,042,000

PENNSYLVANIA
Pittsburgh
Junior Magazine **(27806)** ....(Non-paid) 15,000
Zajednicar **(27856)** ....(Non-paid) 40,000

TEXAS
Fritch
The Trumpeter **(30374)** ....(Paid) ‡600
                                              (Controlled) ‡700

CZECH

ILLINOIS
Chicago
Hlas Naroda (Voice of the Nation) **(8398)**

Oak Brook
CSA Journal **(9347)**

NEW YORK
Brooklyn
The Watchtower **(20355)** ....‡23,042,000

New York
Applications of Mathematics **(21227)**
Czechoslovak Mathematical Journal **(21530)**

TEXAS
Granger
Nasinec **(30409)** ....(Paid) ⊕300

West
Hospodar **(31281)** ....(Paid) ‡400

Circ. Circ. Circ.

CZECH (continued)

ONTARIO, CANADA
Mississauga
Kanadske Listy (Canadian Pages) **(36072)** .... ‡2,800

Scarborough
Novy Domov (New Homeland) **(36380)** .... ‡2,700

Toronto
Satellite 1-416 **(36735)** .... (Combined) 1,500

DANISH

ILLINOIS
Hoffman Estates
Danish Pioneer **(8999)** .... (Paid) ‡3,000
(Non-paid) ‡250

MASSACHUSETTS
Boston
Christian Science Quarterly-Weekly Bible
Lessons **(13876)**
The Herald of Christian Science **(13900)**

NEW YORK
Brooklyn
The Watchtower **(20355)** .:.............. ‡23,042,000

PENNSYLVANIA
Chester Springs
Present Truth and Herald of Christ's
Epiphany **(26778)** .... (Paid) ‡1,100

DUTCH

MASSACHUSETTS
Boston
Christian Science Quarterly-Weekly Bible
Lessons **(13876)**
The Herald of Christian Science **(13900)**

NEW YORK
Brooklyn
The Watchtower **(20355)** .... ‡23,042,000

WASHINGTON
Blaine
De Hollandse Krant **(32687)** .... (Paid) •7,364

BRITISH COLUMBIA, CANADA
Langley
The Windmill Herald **(35006)** .... ‡11,500

ONTARIO, CANADA
St. Catharines
Christian Courier **(36355)** .... (Paid) ‡4,400
(Non-paid) ‡100

ESKIMO DIALECTS

NORTHWEST TERRITORIES, CANADA
Iqaluit
Nunatsiaq News **(35519)** .... (Combined) ‡9,800

ESTONIAN

NEW YORK
Brooklyn
The Watchtower **(20355)** .... ‡23,042,000

New York
Vaba Eesti Sona (Free Estonian
Word) **(22893)** .... ‡2,750

ONTARIO, CANADA
Toronto
Meie Elu **(36661)** .... ‡2,500

FILIPINO

ILLINOIS
Chicago
Via Times
Newsmagazine **(8598)** .... (Combined) 60,000

FINNISH

FLORIDA
Lantana
Amerikan Uutiset **(6298)** 5,000

MASSACHUSETTS
Fitchburg
Pioneer **(14183)** .... ‡2,000

NEW YORK
Brooklyn
The Watchtower **(20355)** .... ‡23,042,000

ONTARIO, CANADA
Toronto
Vapaa Sana **(36784)** .... (Paid) 1,707
(Non-paid) 107

FRENCH

CALIFORNIA
San Francisco
Journal Francais **(3381)** .... ‡20,000

Santa Barbara
Journal of French Language Studies **(3644)** 600

CONNECTICUT
Farmington
Annals of Nutrition and Metabolism **(4797)** 1,250
Audiology and Neuro-Otology **(4798)** 1,650
Cells Tissues Organs **(4804)** 1,200
Cytogenetics and Cell Genetics **(4810)** 1,800
Dermatologica Helvetica **(4812)** ...... (Combined) 500
Folia Phoniatrica et Logopaedica **(4824)** 1,100
Folia Primatologica **(4825)** 850
Gynaekologisch-geburtshilfliche
Rundschau **(4828)** 1,750
Ophthalmologica **(4850)** 1,250
Oto-Rhino-Laryngologia Nova **(4852)** .... ‡1,000
Phonetica **(4856)** 1,150
Respiration **(4859)** 1,200

New Haven
Columbia **(4985)** .... ‡1,600,000

Wilton
Critical Care
International **(5224)** .... (Controlled) ‡26,000

DISTRICT OF COLUMBIA
Washington
Finance &
Development **(5495)** .... (Controlled) 95,000
Inter-American Review of
Bibliography **(5548)** .... (Paid) ‡400
(Non-paid) ‡400
International Journal of Government Auditing **(5554)**

FLORIDA
Hollywood
Le Soleil de la Floride **(6195)** .... (Paid) 40,000
(Controlled) 10,000

ILLINOIS
DeKalb
Bulletin de la Societe Americaine de Philosophie de
Langue Francaise **(8732)**

MARYLAND
Baltimore
Journal of the History of
Philosophy **(13192)** 1,600

MASSACHUSETTS
Boston
Christian Science Quarterly-Weekly Bible
Lessons **(13876)**
The Herald of Christian Science **(13900)**

NEW HAMPSHIRE
Manchester
Le Canado-Americain **(18557)** .... (Paid) ‡36,000
(Controlled) ‡1,333

NEW JERSEY
Fort Lee
Quick Frozen Foods
International **(18834)** .... (Paid) ‡6,011
(Controlled) ‡5,528

NEW YORK
Brooklyn
The Watchtower **(20355)** .... ‡23,042,000

New York
Applications of Mathematics **(21227)**
Current Bibliographical Information **(21523)**
Czechoslovak Mathematical Journal **(21530)**
Editorials On File **(21586)** .... (Paid) ‡800
(Non-paid) ‡1,000
European Journal of Population **(21650)**
France-Amerique **(21733)** .... ‡20,000
International Family Planning
Perspectives **(21897)** .... (Paid) ‡30,000
(Non-paid) ‡1,000
International Journal for the Semiotics of
Law **(21917)**
International Railway
Journal **(21933)** .... (Combined) 10,314
International Review of Education **(21935)**
Journal of the History of International Law **(22090)**
The Legal History Review **(22244)**
Monthly Bibliography, Part II **(22361)**
Monthly Bulletin of Statistics **(22362)**
Scientific American **(22714)** .... (Paid) 687,437
Monthly Bulletin of Statistics **(22882)** ... (Paid) ‡9,000
(Controlled) ‡22,000
UN Chronicle **(22882)** .... (Paid) ‡9,000
(Controlled) ‡22,000

PENNSYLVANIA
Chester Springs
Bible Standard and Herald of Christ's
Kingdom **(26777)** .... (Paid) ‡3,500
Present Truth and Herald of Christ's
Epiphany **(26778)** .... (Paid) ‡1,100

RHODE ISLAND
Woonsocket
L'Union **(28461)** .... (Non-paid) ‡25,000

TENNESSEE
Bristol
American Journal of Italian Studies **(29065)** 300

Cleveland
White Wing Messenger **(29123)** .... ‡9,000

Nashville
Champs-Elysees **(29449)**

WASHINGTON
Seattle
Outlook **(32999)** .... (Non-paid) 20,000

ALBERTA, CANADA
Calgary
Canadian Public Policy–Analyse de
Politiques **(34638)** .... (Paid) ‡1,100
(Non-paid) ‡32

Edmonton
Canadian Journal of Earth Sciences (Revue
Canadienne des Sciences de la
Terre) **(34703)** .... ‡2,200
Le Franco-Albertain **(34720)** .... (Paid) 4,300
(Free) 50
SR (Studies in Religion)/(Sciences
Religieuses) **(34731)** .... ‡1,450

Lethbridge
Canadian Journal of Philosophy **(34794)** 950

BRITISH COLUMBIA, CANADA
Burnaby
Sphere Magazine **(34907)** .... (Combined) 185,000

Vancouver
Canadian Journal of Mathematics **(35132)** 1,226
Canadian Literature **(35133)** .... (Paid) ‡1,500
(Non-paid) ‡150
Hallelujah! **(35145)** .... (Combined) ‡5,000

MANITOBA, CANADA
St. Boniface
La Liberte **(35289)** 6,000

Winnipeg
Biochemistry and Cell Biology (Biochimie et Biologie
Cellulaire) **(35316)** .... ‡1,225

NEW BRUNSWICK, CANADA
Campbellton
L'Aviron **(35382)** .... ‡8,000

Edmundston
Journal Le Madawaska
Ltee **(35385)** .... (Wed.) ‡7,724

Fredericton
ellipse (35393) ....(Combined) 560

Grand Falls
The Cataract (35406) ....‡4,875

ONTARIO, CANADA
Cambridge
Kin Mag (35726) ....(Paid) ISSN 002311436

Cochrane
Pinewood Country Creations (35744) ....(Paid) 1,978
Vivre (35745) ....(Paid) ‡3,100
(Free) ‡600

Cornwall
Le Journal de Cornwall (35753) ....(Paid) ‡1,023
(Free) ‡1,077

Etobicoke
Transport Routier (35822) ....(Combined) •12,022

Guelph
CCL Canadian Children's Literature (Litterature
Canadienne pour la Jeunesse) (35860) .....‡1,000

Hamilton
Canadian Journal of Medical Laboratory Science
(CJLMS) (35877) ....(Paid) 14,326
(Controlled) 451

Hawkesbury
Le Carillon (35907) ....(Free) ‡16,000
(Paid) ‡450
The Tribune/Express (35908) ....(Free) 23,200

Hearst
Le Nord (35911) ....(Paid) 3,455
(Free) 45

Kingston
Revue Frontenac/Frontenac Review (35947)

Markham
Produits Pour L'Industrie
Quebecoise (36031) ....(Combined) 15,074

Mississauga
Canadian Family
Physician (36058) ....(Combined) 33,908
Canadian Geotechnical Journal (Revue Canadienne
de Geotechnique) (36059) ....‡2,700
Trot (36090) ....(Paid) $20,000
(Non-paid) ‡2,000

North York
CAIFA Forum (36123) ....(Paid) ‡1,500
(Controlled) ‡18,000
Canadian Journal of Zoology (Revue Canadienne de
Zoologie) (36125) ....‡1,300
Genome (36128) ....‡1,400

Ottawa
The Canadian Bar Review (La Revue du Barreau
Canadien) (36190) ....(Paid) ‡38,128
(Non-paid) ‡2
Canadian Chemical News (L'Actualite Chimique
Canadienne) (36191) ....(Paid) 4,171
(Non-paid) 814
Canadian Journal of Chemistry (Revue Canadienne
de Chimie) (36202) ....‡1,700
Canadian Journal of Civil Engineering (Revue
Canadienne de Genie Civil) (36203) ....‡2,885
Canadian Journal of Hospital
Pharmacy (36206) ....(Paid) 2,513
(Controlled) 741
Canadian Journal of Medical Radiation
Technology (36207) ....(Paid) ‡9,798
(Non-paid) ‡89
Canadian Journal of Microbiology (Revue Canadienne
de Microbiologie) (36208) ....‡1,725
Canadian Journal of Physiology and Pharmacology
(Revue Canadienne de Physiologie et
Pharmacologie) (36211) ....‡1,000
Canadian Journal of Political Science (Revue
canadienne de science politique) (36213) 3,000
Canadian Nurse (L'Infirmiere
Canadienne) (36223) ....(Combined) 111,563
Canadian Parliamentary Review (36224) 2,000
500
The Canadian Postmaster (Le Maitre de Poste
Canadien) (36226) ....‡9,500
Crux Mathematicorum with Mathematical
Mayhem (36240) 800
Journal of the Canadian Dental Association (Journal
de l'Association Dentaire
Canadienne) (36253) ....(Combined) •19,897
La Rotonde (36256) ....‡8,000
Le Droit (36257) ....(Mon.-Fri.) ★34,968
(Sat.) ★39,843
Living Safety Magazine (36260) ....‡100,000

Physical & Health Education Journal (36270)
Tabaret (36276) ....(Non-paid) ‡88,000
University Affairs (Affaires
Universitaires) (36278) ....(Combined) 22,480

Peterborough
Journal of Canadian Studies (Revue d'Etudes
Canadiennes) (36316) ....‡1,350

Scarborough
The Port Hole (Le
Hublot) (36383) ....(Controlled) ‡35,000

Sudbury
Journal Le Voyageur (36416) 10,000

Toronto
L'Automobile (36468) ....(Combined) •12,087
CA Magazine (36483) ....(Paid) 71,448
(Non-paid) 3,386
Canadian Historical Review (36502) 2,100
The Canadian Journal of Linguistics/Revue
canadienne de
linguistique (36511) ....(Combined) 800
The Canadian Modern Language Review/La Revue
canadienne des langues
vivantes (36520) ....(Combined) 1,200
Canadian Public Administration (Administration
publique du Canada) (36528) 3,400
Canadian Woman Studies (Les Cahiers de la
Femme) (36535) ....(Paid) ‡3,000
(Non-paid) ‡120
Direction Informatique (36576) ....(Combined) 20,585
L'Epicier (36584) ....(Controlled) 12,806
L'Express (36589) ....(Paid) 20,000
(Non-paid) 5,000
Homemaker's Magazine (Madame au
Foyer) (36617) ....(Paid) 550,000
(Non-paid) 270,349
OTF (FEO)
Interaction (36692) ....(Non-paid) ‡130,000
Pharmacy Post (36704) ....(Combined) 18,529
Resources for Feminist Research (Documentation sur
la Recherche Feministe) (36728) ....‡2,000
The Tocqueville Review/La Revue
Tocqueville (36761) ....(Combined) 500

Unionville
Moving to Ottawa/Outaouais (36832)

PRINCE EDWARD ISLAND, CANADA
Summerside
EDT (36922) ....‡1,000
La Voix Acadienne (36925) ....(Controlled) 1,050

QUEBEC, CANADA
Abitibiens
L'Echo Abitibien (36928) ....(Wed.) 15,000

Acton Vale
La Pensee de
Bagot (36929) ....(Controlled) ‡13,333

Alma
Superintendent's Profile Product-Service
Directory (36930) ....(Free) 19,957

Alouette
Phare/Beacon (36931) ....(Controlled) 2,500

Amos
L'Echo d'Amos (36932) ....‡3,921

Amqui
L'Avant-Poste (36935) ....(Controlled) 8,542

Anjou
Construire (36937) ....(Combined) 27,400

L'Annonciation
Emploi Plus (36939) ....(Combined) 500

Arthabaska
Union (36941) ....‡25,000

Baie D'urfe'
Operations Forestieres et de
Scierie (36946) ....(Non-paid) •5,615

Bedford
Journal des Rivieres (36949) ....(Free) 6,650

Beloeil
L'Oeil Regional (36950) ....(Controlled) 29,350

Brossard
Brossard-Eclair (36951) ....(Controlled) ‡24,635

Buckingham
Le Bulletin (36952) ....(Controlled) 10,892

Cabano
Le Touladi (36953) ....(Free) ‡9,600

Cap-aux-Meules
Le Radar (36954) ....(Fri.) 2,300

Cap-de-la-Madeleine
L'Hebdo-Journal (36956) ....(Controlled) 44,691
Revue Notre-Dame du Cap (36957) ....‡65,000

Chambly
Le Journal de Chambly
Inc. (36959) ....(Controlled) ‡20,700

Chandler
Le Havre (36960) ....(Controlled) ‡7,493

Chateauguay
L'Information Regionale (36962) ....(Free) ‡27,105

Chibougamau
La Sentinelle (36964) ....(Tues.) 2,394

Chicoutimi
Le Quotidien du
Saguenay-Lac-Saint-Jean (36965).(Mon.-Sat.)28,914
Progres-Dimanche (36966) ....(Sun.) 41,231
Saguenayensia (36968)

Coaticook
Le Progres de
Coaticook (36976) ....(Controlled) 7,578

Cookshire
Le Haut St-Francois (36978) ....(Free) ‡8,300

Cowansville
Bulletin de Droit de L'Environnement (36980)

Dolbeau-Mistassini
Le Point (36986) 11,466

Drummondville
L'Express (36989) ....(Controlled) 43,876
La Parole (36990) ....(Controlled) ‡35,435

Farnham
L'Avenir de Brome Missisquoi (36994) ....‡8,733

Gaspe
Le Pharillion (36997) ....(Controlled) 9,188

Gatineau
Info Plein Air (36998) ....(Non-paid) 75,000
La Revue de
Gatineau (36999) ....(Controlled) ‡37,180

Granby
La Voix de l'Est (37000) ....(Mon.-Fri.) 15,281
(Sat.) 18,668

Hull
L'Uquoi (37004) ....(Free) 2,000

Huntingdon
Gleaner (37008) ....(Wed.) 3,534

Joliette
L'Action (37010) ....(Controlled) 45,140
Le Regional de Lanaudire-Jolliette
Journal (37011) ....(Free) ‡40,500

Jonquiere
Le Lingot (37012) ....‡16,000
Le Reveil (37013) ....(Free) ‡69,376

Kahnawake
Kateri (37018) 10,000

La Salle
La Protesta (37021)

La Sarre
L'Echo d'Abitibi Quest (37022) ....‡3,212

Lac Bouchette
Le Messager de St. Antoine (37026) ....⊕51,000

Lac Etchemin
La Voix du Sud (37027) ....(Controlled) ‡19,144

Lac Megantic
L'Echo de Frontenac (37028) ....(Paid) 4,580
(Free) 3,992
(Non-paid) 4,089

Lachute
L'Argenteuil (37029) ....(Combined) ‡13,500

L'Ancienne-Lorett
Les Enseignants (37032) ....‡5,000

Ethnic Publications

Circulation: ★ = ABC; △ = BPA; ♦ = CAC; • = CCAB; ❑ = VAC; ⊕ = PO Statement; ‡ = Publisher's Report; Boldface figures = sworn; Light figures = estimated.

2753

Circ.

FRENCH (continued)

Laprairie
Group Travel (Voyage en
  Groupe) **(37033)** ....(Paid) 415
                                   (Controlled) 11,750

Laval
L'Echo du Transport **(37036)** .....(Controlled) 18,625
Entreprendre **(37037)** ....(Combined) ‡60,000
Gestion Logistique **(37038)** 10,104
Horoscope Quotidien **(37040)** ....(Paid) ‡13,000
                                     (Non-paid) ‡12,000
Le Courrier des
  Moulins **(37041)** ....(Controlled) ‡38,792
Missions Etrangeres **(37042)** ....‡25,000

Levis
Le Peuple Tribune **(37049)** ....(Free) ‡26,033

Longueuil
La Terre de Chez Nous **(37052)** ....(Paid) 40,400
Le Courrier du Sud (The South Shore
  Courier) **(37053)** ....(Free) 120,000
Le Garagiste **(37054)** ....(Combined) 16,363
Le Producteur de Lait
  Quebecois **(37055)** ....(Combined) •10,278
Longueuil Extra **(37056)** ....(Controlled) 54,200
Quart de Rond **(37058)** ....(Combined) 3,000

Louiseville
L'Echo de Louiseville **(37060)** ....(Wed.) 5,387
Salut Dimanche **(37061)** ....(Combined) 17,377

Malartic
Le Courrier de Malartic **(37063)** .....(Controlled) 891
L'Echo de Malartic **(37064)** ....‡914

Maniwaki
La Gatineau **(37065)** ....(Free) ‡9,000

Matane
La Voix Gaspesienne **(37069)** ....(Wed.) 4,979

Mont-Joli
L'Information **(37073)** ....(Free) ‡11,920

Mont-Laurier
L'Echo de la Lievre **(37074)** ....(Free) ‡11,600

Mont-Tremblant
L'Information du Nord
  L'Annonciation **(37075)** ....(Paid) ‡7,500
L'Information de Ste.
  Agathe **(37076)** ....(Free) ‡14,700

Montmagny
Le Peuple de la Cote du
  Sud **(37077)** ....(Free) ‡16,250

Montreal
L'Action Nationale **(37079)** ....(Paid) ‡3,000
L'actualite **(37080)** ....(Paid) 190,745
ADSUM **(37083)** ....(Free) ‡5,000
Apostolat International **(37085)** ....‡17,000
L'Artisan **(37087)** ....(Controlled) ‡47,722
L'Avenir de l'Est **(37090)** ....(Controlled) ‡44,070
Camping Caravaning **(37092)** ....(Paid) 4,046
                                   (Non-paid) 23,176
Canadian Jewish Studies/Etudes Juives
  Canadiennes **(37094)** ....(Paid) 354
Canadian Journal of Economics (Revue Canadienne
  d'Economique) **(37097)**
Centre D'Etudes de L'Asie de
  L'Est/Cahiers **(37101)** ....(Controlled) 300
Chatelaine **(37102)** ....(Paid) 182,099
Circuit **(37105)** ....(Combined) 1,500
Coup de Pouce **(37106)** ....(Paid) 172,413
Courier Laval du Jeudi **(37107)** ....(Free) 106,877
Dietetique en Action **(37108)**
Documentation et Bibliotheques **(37110)** 800,000
Echos-Vedettes **(37111)** ....(Sat.) 76,119
Electricite Quebec **(37113)** ....(Controlled) 9,670
Electronique Industrielle et Commerciale
  (EIC) **(37114)** ....(Controlled) 9,202
Geston **(37120)** ....(Paid) 5,500
Guide de
  Montreal-Nord **(37121)** ......(Controlled) 32,869
L'Hebdo Rive-Nord **(37122)** ....(Controlled) 45,118
The ICAO Journal **(37123)** 58,482
L'Infomeo **(37128)** 1,500
L'Infomateur **(37129)** ....(Controlled) 17,448
Infor **(37130)** 1,125
L'Ingenieur **(37131)** ....‡17,500
Inter-Mecanique du
  Batiment **(37134)** ....(Combined) •6,350
Italian Commerce of Commerce of
  Canada **(37136)** ....(Non-paid) ‡8,000
Journal CAJLE **(37137)**
Journal of Canadian Fiction **(37138)** 1,500

Circ.

Journal Dentaire du Quebec
  (JDQ) **(37139)** ....‡5,300
Journal Industriel du
  Quebec **(37141)** ....(Combined) 20,431
Journal de
  l'Assurance **(37143)** ....(Controlled) 26,000
Journal de St. Michel **(37146)** ....(Free) ‡22,500
KIDS CREATIONS **(37147)** ....(Paid) 7,571
La Presse **(37150)** ....(Mon.-Fri.) 170,362
                                       (Sat.) 268,420
                                       (Sun.) 180,426
La Republique **(37151)** ....(Free) 3,500
La Revue du Barreau **(37152)** ....‡9,662
La Tribune Canadienne
  Grecque **(37153)** ....(Paid) 200
                                     (Free) 13,500
L'Actualite Medicale **(37154)** .....(Non-paid) 16,511
                                     (Paid) 730
Le Bel Age **(37155)** ....(Paid) 149,754
Le Bulletin des Agriculteurs **(37156)** ....(Paid) 21,291
Le Cooperateur
  Agricole **(37157)** ....(Combined) •17,946
Le Courrier Laval du
  Dimanche **(37158)** ....(Controlled) 106,877
Le Devoir **(37159)** ....(Mon.-Fri.) 25,080
                                       (Sat.) 38,236
Le Flambeau de l'Est **(37160)** ....(Controlled) 50,671
Le Graffiti **(37161)** ....(Free) 1,500
Le Journal Industriel du
  Quebec **(37162)** ....(Combined) 19,652
Le Journal de
  Montreal **(37163)** ....(Mon.-Fri.) ★259,594
                                    (Sat.) ★312,153
                                    (Sun.) ★266,656
Le Journal de Rosemont et Petite
  Patrie **(37164)** ....(Controlled) 58,741
Le Journal St-Louis & Mile
  End **(37165)** ....(Combined) 20,000
Le Journal de
  St-Michel **(37166)** ....(Controlled) 22,500
Le Magazine Affaires Plus **(37167)** .....(Paid) 92,887
Le Magazine PME **(37169)** ......(Combined) •39,764
Le Medecin du
  Quebec **(37170)** ....(Combined) 18,200
Le Misanthrope **(37171)** ....(Free) 3,000
Le/The Monitor **(37172)** ....(Combined) 29,500
Le Trait d'Union **(37173)** ....(Non-paid) 2,800
Lemon-Aid **(37174)** 20,000
LES AFFAIRES **(37175)**
Les Debrouillards **(37176)** ....(Controlled) 37,500
Les Nouvelles de
  l'Est **(37178)** ....(Controlled) 27,338
Maison d'Aujourd'hui **(37181)** .....(Combined) 14,860
The McGill Daily **(37182)** ....(Free) 11,000
Meta **(37186)** ....‡1,800
Missions des Franciscains **(37187)** .....(Paid) ‡6,000
                                     (Non-paid) ‡1,000
Moto Journal **(37192)** ....(Paid) 8,000
                                     (Non-paid) 1,000
Motocycliste **(37193)** ....(Paid) 1,229
                                     (Non-paid) 28,103
Nos Animaux **(37195)** ....(Paid) 14,000
                                     (Non-paid) 11,000
Nouveau Quartier Libre **(37196)**
L'Optometriste **(37198)** ....(Controlled) ‡4,400
L'Oratoire **(37200)** ....(Paid) ‡40,000
                                     (Non-paid) ‡2,000
Orient **(37202)** ....(Paid) ‡4,800
                                     (Non-paid) ‡50
Parachute **(37204)** ....(Paid) ‡2500
                                     (Non-paid) ‡350
Plan **(37206)** ....(Combined) 48,000
Policy Options Politiques **(37207)** .....(Paid) 3,100
                                     (Non-paid) 3,100
Pretre et Pasteur **(37208)** ....(Paid) ‡2,800
                                     (Controlled) ‡300
Primeurs **(37209)** ....(Combined) 450,000
Progres de St.
  Leonard **(37210)** ....(Controlled) 30,054
Quebec Pharmacie **(37212)** ....(Controlled) 7,422
Quebec Science **(37213)** ....(Paid) 22,601
Reader's Digest
  Magazine **(37214)** ....(Paid) 1,025,256
Relations **(37215)** ....‡4,000
Revue Commerce **(37217)** ....(Paid) 43,111
Selection du Reader's Digest (Canadian-French
  Edition) **(37223)** 225,000
Sentier Chasse-Peche **(37224)** ....(Paid) ★45,091
                                     (Non-paid) ★1,260
Tourisme Jeunesse **(37228)** ....(Controlled) 75,000
Tourisme Plus **(37229)** ....(Combined) 9,341
TV Hebdo **(37231)** ....(Paid) 190,123
Universites **(37232)**
Vecteur Environnement **(37233)** ....(Combined) 4,000
Vie Des Arts **(37234)** ....(Paid) •4,072
                                     (Non-paid) •1,728

Circ.

Mount-Tremblant
Magnificat **(37253)** 15,000

Napierville
Coup d'Oeil **(37254)** ....(Controlled) ‡13,350

New Richmond
L'Echo de la Baie **(37258)** ....(Paid) ‡1,152
                                     (Free) ‡16,842

Nicolet
Le Courrier-Sud **(37259)** ....(Controlled) ‡20,047

Outremont
Decoration Chez-Soi **(37263)** ....(Paid) 65,386
L'Express
  d'Outremont **(37264)** ....(Controlled) 16,000
Filles d'Aujourd'hui **(37265)** ....(Paid) 56,532
Le Lundi **(37266)** ....(Paid) 52,507
Les Idees de Ma Maison **(37267)** ......(Paid) 53,529
Renovation Bricolage **(37268)** ....(Paid) 35,576

Plessisville
L'avenir De L'erable **(37269)** ....(Tues.) 11,093

Pointe-Claire
Les Papetieres du
  Quebec **(37275)** ....(Combined) ‡4,348

Quebec
Au Fil des Evenements **(37281)** ....(Free) 15,000
Continuite **(37282)** ....⊕5,000
                                       ⊕3,920
Espaces Verts **(37283)** ....‡2,250
Fleur Design **(37284)** ....‡1,850
Laval Theologique et Philosophique **(37286)**
Le Journal Economique de
  Quebec **(37287)** ....(Combined) 11,234
Le Journal de
  Quebec **(37288)** ....(Mon.-Fri.) ★96,646
                                    (Sat.) ★120,743
                                    (Sun.) ★99,094
Le Peuple de Lotbiniere **(37289)** ......(Free) ‡11,900
Le Soleil **(37290)** ....(Mon.-Fri.) ★81,045
                                    (Sat.) ★112,951
                                    (Sun.) ★90,304
Magazine Circuit
  Industriel **(37291)** ....(Controlled) 17,652
Nuit Blanche **(37293)** ....(Controlled) 3,400
Option Serre **(37294)** ....‡1,580
Quebec Vert **(37295)** ....‡3,760
Revue Relations Industrielles/Industrial
  Relations **(37296)** ....(Paid) 1,500
                                     (Non-paid) 150
VOILA QUEBEC **(37297)** ....(Controlled) 88,766

Quebec City
Recueil des Sentences de l'Education **(37305)**

Richelain
Servir **(37306)** 3,300

Rimouski
Le Rimouskois **(37307)** ....(Free) 23,463

Riviere-du-Loup
Info Dimanche **(37313)** ....(Controlled) 29,118

Roberval
L'Etoile du Lac **(37319)** ....(Controlled) 12,800

Rouyn-Noranda
La Frontiere **(37321)** ....(Wed.) 5,614
Le Declin **(37322)** ....(Controlled) ‡900

Ste.-Adele
Le Journal des Pays d'En Haut **(37324)** 17,000

Saint-Andre-Avellin
Journal La Petite-Nation **(37325)** ....(Free) ‡8,002

Ste.-Anne-de-Beaupre
Le Revue Sainte Anne de Beaupre **(37327)**

Saint-Bruno
Le Journal de Saint-Bruno **(37329)** 17,573

Saint-Etienne-de-Lauzon
Le Chef du Service
  Alimentaire **(37330)** ....(Controlled) •20,629

Saint-Eustache
L'Eveil **(37331)** ....(Controlled) 37,925
La Concorde **(37332)** ....(Controlled) ‡28,650

Ste.-Foy
Agenda **(37334)** 2,000
IMPACT CAMPUS **(37337)** ....(Free) 15,000
Quebec Info **(37339)** 2,000

Saint-Georges-de-Beauce
L'Eclaireur-Progres/Beauce
Nouvelle **(37341)** ....(Paid) 1,000
(Free) 25,000

Saint-Hubert
Le Journal de Saint-Hubert **(37345)** ....‡28,800

Saint-Hyacinthe
Assetu **(37347)** ....(Free) 2,000
La Rivardiere **(37349)**
Le Clairon Regional de St.
Hyacinthe **(37350)** 33,926
Le Medecin Veterinaire du
Quebec **(37351)** ....(Non-paid) ‡2,700

Saint-Jean
Le Canada Francais **(37354)** ....(Wed.) 14,431
Le Richelieu
Dimanche **(37355)** ....(Controlled) 35,500
(Paid) 9

Saint-Lambert
ARCHIE **(37357)** ....(Combined) ‡165,000

Saint-Laurent
Abaka **(37361)** ....(Paid) ‡875
(Free) ‡75
Journal Constructo **(37363)** ......(Combined) 3,345
Nouvelles Saint-Laurent
News **(37365)** ....(Free) 26,300

Saint-Pascal
Le Placoteux **(37367)** ....(Paid) ‡60
(Non-paid) ‡17,142

Ste.-Therese
La Voix des Mille Iles **(37368)** ....(Free) ‡42,650

Sainte-Adele
ARQ, La revue
d'architecture **(37370)** ....(Controlled) 3,485

Sainte-Foy
Magazine Le Clap **(37374)** ....(Combined) 98,900

Sainte-Julie
L'Information de Ste.
Julie **(37381)** ....(Controlled) 21,082

Sainte-Therese
Le Nord Info **(37384)** ....(Controlled) 48,775

Sept-Iles
Le Nord-Est Plus **(37386)** ....(Controlled) 14,022

Shawinigan
L'Hebdo Mekinac/des
Chenaux **(37390)** ....(Free) 12,716

Shawville
The Equity **(37392)** ....(Wed.) 4,300

Sherbrooke
La Tribune **(37393)** ....(Mon.-Fri.) 30,731
(Sat.) 38,741
Le Collectif **(37394)** ....(Free) ‡5,000

Sillery
Le Journal des Blais **(37400)**
RND (Revue Notre-Dame) **(37401)** ....‡100,000

Sorel
Journal La Voix **(37403)** ....(Free) ‡28,185
Les Deux Rives **(37405)** ....(Free) ‡28,000

Terrebonne
La Revue **(37409)** ....(Free) ‡45,100

Thetford Mines
Le Courrier Frontenac **(37410)** ....(Free) 20,572

Trois-Rivieres
Le Nouvelliste **(37416)** ....(Mon.-Fri.) 44,094
(Sat.) 48,256

Valleyfield
Le Soleil du St.
Laurent **(37426)** ....(Controlled) 26,275

Victoriaville
La Nouvelle **(37431)** 40,000
La Replique **(37432)** ....(Non-paid) 500

Ville D'Anjou
Le Magazine L'agent de
voyages **(37436)** ....(Combined) 8,456

Ville-Marie
Le Temiscamien **(37437)** ....(Controlled) ‡8,380

Westmount
Plaisirs de Vivre **(37444)** ....(Non-paid) 65,691
(Paid) 2,092

Windsor
L'Etincelle **(37450)** ....(Free) ‡8,700

SASKATCHEWAN, CANADA
Regina
Journal L'Eau Vive **(37531)** ....(Paid) ‡1,400
(Free) ‡100

GERMAN

CALIFORNIA
Los Angeles
California Staats-Zeitung **(2232)** 18,700

CONNECTICUT
Farmington
Analytic Psychology **(4796)** 1,700
Annals of Nutrition and Metabolism **(4797)** 1,250
Cells Tissues Organs **(4804)** 1,200
Chirurgische
Gastroenterologie **(4808)** ....(Combined) 4,000
Cytogenetics and Cell Genetics **(4810)** 1,800
Dermatologica Helvetica **(4812)** ......(Combined) 500
Dermatology Psychosomatics **(4814)**
Folia Phoniatrica et Logopaedica **(4824)** 1,100
Folia Primatologica **(4825)** 850
Forschende Komplementarmedizin und Klassische
Naturheilkunde **(4826)** ....(Combined) 4,000
Gynaekologisch-geburtshilfliche
Rundschau **(4828)** 1,750
Onkologie **(4848)** 800
Ophthalmologica **(4850)** 1,250
Oto-Rhino-Laryngologia Nova **(4852)** ....‡1,000
Phonetica **(4856)** 1,150
Respiration **(4859)** 1,200
Verhaltenstherapie **(4864)** ....‡4,000

Wilton
Critical Care
International **(5224)** ....(Controlled) ‡26,000

FLORIDA
Sarasota
New Yorker Staats Zeitung **(6661)** 14,450

GEORGIA
Athens
Das Fenster Nach Druben **(6936)** .....(Paid) ‡15,000
(Free) ‡100

ILLINOIS
Skokie
Harmony **(9605)** ....‡25,000

MARYLAND
Baltimore
Journal of the History of
Philosophy **(13192)** 1,600

MASSACHUSETTS
Boston
Christian Science Quarterly-Weekly Bible
Lessons **(13876)**
The Herald of Christian Science **(13900)**

MISSOURI
St. Louis
Portals of Prayer **(17484)** 950,000

NEW JERSEY
Fort Lee
Quick Frozen Foods
International **(18834)** ....(Paid) ‡6,011
(Controlled) ‡5,528

Kenilworth
Freie Zeitung **(19153)** ....‡3,000

NEW YORK
Brooklyn
The Watchtower **(20355)** ....‡23,042,000

New York
Applications of Mathematics **(21227)**
AUFBAU - The Transatlantic Jewish
Paper **(21273)** ....‡13,000
Czechoslovak Mathematical Journal **(21530)**
International Railway
Journal **(21933)** ....(Combined) 10,314
International Review of Education **(21935)**
Scientific American **(22714)** ....(Paid) 687,437

PENNSYLVANIA
Chester Springs
Bible Standard and Herald of Christ's
Kingdom **(26777)** ....(Paid) ‡3,500
Present Truth and Herald of Christ's
Epiphany **(26778)** ....(Paid) ‡1,100

TENNESSEE
Nashville
Schau ins Land **(29485)**

TEXAS
Fritch
The Trumpeter **(30374)** ....(Paid) ‡600
(Controlled) ‡700

WISCONSIN
Madison
Monatshefte **(33963)** ....‡1,000

BRITISH COLUMBIA, CANADA
Richmond
Pazifische Rundschau (Pacific
Review) **(35075)** ....(Combined) ‡12,390
(Free) ‡110

MANITOBA, CANADA
Steinbach
Die Mennonitische Post **(35295)** ....‡5,200

Winnipeg
KANADA KURIER **(35335)** ......(Combined) ‡25,000
Mennonite Review **(35343)** ....(Paid) ¥900
(Non-paid) ‡1,000

ONTARIO, CANADA
Toronto
Canada Journal **(36488)** ....(Combined) 24,000
Deutsche Presse (German
Press) **(36572)** ....‡30,000

GREEK

MASSACHUSETTS
Boston
Christian Science Quarterly-Weekly Bible
Lessons **(13876)**
The Herald of Christian Science **(13900)**

NEW YORK
Brooklyn
The Watchtower **(20355)** ....‡23,042,000

Long Island City
Kampana–Campana **(20964)** ....‡8,800

New York
Orthodox Observer **(22505)** 140,000

ONTARIO, CANADA
Hamilton
Hellenic Hamilton News **(35881)** ....(Paid) ‡500
(Non-paid) ‡1,500

London
The Hellenic News **(35982)** ....(Paid) ‡850
(Non-paid) ‡4,150

QUEBEC, CANADA
Montreal
La Tribune Canadienne
Grecque **(37153)** ....(Paid) 200
(Free) 13,500

HEBREW

See also Yiddish

NEW YORK
Brooklyn
The Watchtower **(20355)** ....‡23,042,000

New York
Hadoar (The Post) **(21786)** ....(Paid) ‡3,500
(Free) ‡870

HINDI

NEW YORK
Brooklyn
The Watchtower **(20355)** ....‡23,042,000

Circulation: ★ = ABC; △ = BPA; ♦ = CAC; ● = CCAB; ❑ = VAC; ⊕ = PO Statement; ‡ = Publisher's Report; Boldface figures = sworn; Light figures = estimated.

2755

Circ.

HUNGARIAN

CALIFORNIA
Reseda
California Hungarians **(2917)** ....‡2,000

NEW YORK
Brooklyn
The Watchtower **(20355)** ....‡23,042,000

New York
Hungarian Word (Amerikai Magyar
SZO) **(21836)** ....(Paid) ‡1,000
(Free) ‡150

ONTARIO, CANADA
Toronto
Magyar Naplo **(36655)** ....(Paid) ‡5,000
(Free) ‡4,000

ICELANDIC

NEW YORK
Brooklyn
The Watchtower **(20355)** ....‡23,042,000

INDONESIAN

MASSACHUSETTS
Boston
Christian Science Quarterly-Weekly Bible
Lessons **(13876)**
The Herald of Christian Science **(13900)**

NEW YORK
Brooklyn
The Watchtower **(20355)** ....‡23,042,000

ITALIAN

CONNECTICUT
Wilton
Critical Care
International **(5224)** ....(Controlled) ‡26,000

FLORIDA
Tampa
La Gaceta **(6773)** ....‡18,079

MASSACHUSETTS
Boston
Christian Science Quarterly-Weekly Bible
Lessons **(13876)**
The Herald of Christian Science **(13900)**

NEW YORK
Brooklyn
The Watchtower **(20355)** ....‡23,042,000

New York
Scientific American **(22714)** ....(Paid) 687,437

OHIO
Columbus
Italica **(25022)** ....‡1,600

PENNSYLVANIA
Philadelphia
Sons of Italy Times **(27689)** ....‡15,500

TENNESSEE
Bristol
American Journal of Italian Studies **(29065)** 300

Nashville
Acquerello Italiano **(29439)**

WISCONSIN
Madison
L'Anello Che Non Tiene **(33919)**

ALBERTA, CANADA
Edmonton
Italian Link **(34717)** ....‡5,000

ONTARIO, CANADA
Downsview
Giornale di Sicilia **(35783)**

Circ.

Toronto
Corriere Canadese/Canadian
Courier **(36560)** ....(Controlled) ‡32,630

QUEBEC, CANADA
L'Assomption
Ciao Magazine **(37034)** ....(Paid) ‡30,000
(Non-paid) ‡10,000

Montreal
INSIEME **(37132)** ....(Paid) ‡18,000
(Free) ‡20,000

Italian Commerce of Commerce of
Canada **(37136)** ....(Non-paid) ‡8,000

JAPANESE

CALIFORNIA
Glendale
KaMai Forum **(2010)** ....‡12,000

Los Angeles
The Rafu Shimpo **(2376)** ....(Paid) 15,500
Southern California Guide **(2395)**
U.S. Japan Business
News **(2422)** ....(Combined) 40,000

San Francisco
Hokubei Mainichi **(3371)** 10,000
Nichi Bei Times **(3404)** ....(Combined) 8,000

Santa Monica
Fax Mainichi U.S.A. **(3708)** ....(Combined) 1,500

Torrance
Bridge U.S.A. **(3928)** ....(Combined) 35,000
Lighthouse **(3936)** ....(Combined) 31,200

HAWAII
Honolulu
East West Journal **(7687)** ....(Combined) 5,000
Hawaii Hochi **(7696)** ....(Combined) 8,000

ILLINOIS
Chicago
Chicago Shimpo **(8322)** ....(Combined) 5,000

MASSACHUSETTS
Boston
Christian Science Quarterly-Weekly Bible
Lessons **(13876)**
The Herald of Christian Science **(13900)**
J Magazine **(13909)** ....(Combined) 15,000

NEW YORK
Brooklyn
The Watchtower **(20355)** ....‡23,042,000

New York
Asahi Shimbun **(21259)** ....(Combined) 12,000
The Japanese Daily Sun-Nikkan San **(21956)**
OCS News **(22483)** ....(Combined) 19,000
Scientific American **(22714)** ....(Paid) 687,437
U.S. Frontline News **(22887)** ......(Combined) 29,000
Yomiuri America **(22951)** ....(Combined) 19,600

WASHINGTON
Seattle
North American Post **(32991)** ....(Fri.) 5,000
(Combined) 8,000
Seattle Compass **(33018)** ....(Non-paid) 20,000

WISCONSIN
Hartland
J Desk International **(33779)** ......(Combined) 1,000

QUEBEC, CANADA
Montreal
Journal CAJLE **(37137)**

KOREAN

CALIFORNIA
Los Angeles
Korea Times **(2307)**
Korean Culture **(2308)** ....(Paid) 1,500
(Non-paid) 200
Korean Sunday News **(2309)** .....(Combined) 22,000
The New Korea **(2344)** ....(Paid) ‡3,000
(Non-paid) ‡100

GEORGIA
Atlanta
Korean Journal **(7025)** ....(Paid) 2,389
(Non-paid) 97,811

Circ.

Doraville
Korean Southeast
News **(7242)** ....(Combined) 20,000

HAWAII
Honolulu
Korean Studies **(7707)** ....(Paid) 160
(Controlled) 60

MARYLAND
Columbia
Korea Post **(13464)** ....(Combined) 13,000

NEW YORK
Brooklyn
The Watchtower **(20355)** ....‡23,042,000

Flushing
Chosun Daily **(20607)**

Long Island City
The Sae Gae Times **(20966)** ....(Combined) 40,000

PENNSYLVANIA
Elkins Park
The Dong-A Daily
News **(26870)** ....(Combined) 23,000

VIRGINIA
Springfield
Korean Weekly **(32548)** ....(Combined) 12,000

BRITISH COLUMBIA, CANADA
Vancouver
Hallelujah! **(35145)** ....(Combined) ‡5,000

ONTARIO, CANADA
Toronto
The Korea Times **(36646)** ....(Paid) ‡8,200
(Free) ‡1,500

LATIN

KANSAS
Lawrence
Mycologia **(11564)** ....‡2,100

LATVIAN

NEW YORK
Brooklyn
Laiks (Time) **(20329)** 10,500
The Watchtower **(20355)** ....‡23,042,000

ONTARIO, CANADA
Toronto
Latvija Amerika **(36649)** ....(Paid) ‡3,000

LITHUANIAN

ILLINOIS
Addison
The League-Sandara **(8001)** ....(Paid) ‡1,000

Chicago
The Friend **(8381)** ....‡6,200

NEW YORK
Brooklyn
Varpelis (The Little Bell) **(20352)** ......(Paid) ‡1,500
The Watchtower **(20355)** ....‡23,042,000

New York
Tevyne **(22825)** ....‡3,500

ONTARIO, CANADA
Mississauga
Teviskes Ziburiai (The Lights of
Homeland) **(36089)** ....(Paid) ‡3,286
(Free) ‡142

MACEDONIAN

NEW YORK
Brooklyn
The Watchtower **(20355)** ....‡23,042,000

ONTARIO, CANADA
West Hill
Macedonia **(36870)** ....(Paid) 1,800
(Free) 50

Numbers cited after listings are entry numbers rather than page numbers.

MALAY

PENNSYLVANIA
Chester Springs
Bible Standard and Herald of Christ's
   Kingdom **(26777)** ....(Paid) ‡3,500

NORWEGIAN

MASSACHUSETTS
Boston
Christian Science Quarterly-Weekly Bible
   Lessons **(13876)**
The Herald of Christian Science **(13900)**

MINNESOTA
Minneapolis
The Sons of Norway
   Viking **(16128)** ....(Combined) ‡56,000

NEW YORK
Brooklyn
The Watchtower **(20355)** ....‡23,042,000

PENNSYLVANIA
Chester Springs
Present Truth and Herald of Christ's
   Epiphany **(26778)** ....(Paid) ‡1,100

WASHINGTON
Seattle
Western Viking **(33043)** ....‡3,000

POLISH

ILLINOIS
Chicago
Narod Polish **(8499)** ....(Non-paid) ‡25,000
Polish Daily News **(8536)** ....(Paid) ‡10,847
                                          (Free) ‡203

Mount Prospect
Program **(9249)** ....(Combined) 28,000

MASSACHUSETTS
Boston
Christian Science Quarterly-Weekly Bible
   Lessons **(13876)**

Stockbridge
Roze Maryi **(14568)** ....(Paid) ‡6,000
                                          (Controlled) ‡1,500

MICHIGAN
Hamtramck
The Polish Weekly **(15141)** ....‡2,000

NEW YORK
Boston
Polish-American Journal **(20239)** ....‡14,500

Brooklyn
The Watchtower **(20355)** ....‡23,042,000

New York
Polish Daily News **(22571)** ....(Paid) 39,000
                                          (Free) 450

Weteran/Veteran **(22916)**

PENNSYLVANIA
Chester Springs
Bible Standard and Herald of Christ's
   Kingdom **(26777)** ....(Paid) ‡3,500
Present Truth and Herald of Christ's
   Epiphany **(26778)** ....(Paid) ‡1,100

Pittsburgh
Sokol Polski (Polish
   Falcon) **(27844)** ....(Free) ‡15,000

Scranton
Rola Boza (God's Field) **(27962)** ....‡7,700

MANITOBA, CANADA
Winnipeg
Czas (Times) **(35325)** ....(Paid) 3,000
                                          (Free) 1,000

ONTARIO, CANADA
Toronto
Zwiazkowiec (Alliancer) **(36798)** ....(Fri.) 11,000

PORTUGUESE

CALIFORNIA
El Sobrante
Portuguese Journal **(1869)** ....‡9,000

Hayward
Voz de Portugal **(2044)** ....‡3,200

DISTRICT OF COLUMBIA
Washington
Inter-American Review of
   Bibliography **(5548)** ....(Paid) ‡400
                                          (Non-paid) ‡400

KANSAS
Fort Leavenworth
Military Review **(11440)** ....(Paid) ‡5,000
                                          (Controlled) ‡20,000

MASSACHUSETTS
Boston
Christian Science Quarterly-Weekly Bible
   Lessons **(13876)**
The Herald of Christian Science **(13900)**

NEW HAMPSHIRE
Hanover
Revista de Critica Literaria Latinoamericana **(18519)**

NEW JERSEY
Newark
The Luso-Americano **(19358)**

NEW YORK
Brooklyn
The Watchtower **(20355)** ....‡23,042,000

New York
Popular Mechanics **(22579)** ....(Paid) 1,224,960
REVISTA AEREA **(22665)** ....(Controlled) 11,200

RHODE ISLAND
Providence
Gavea-Brown **(28398)**

WASHINGTON
Seattle
Outlook **(32999)** ....(Non-paid) 20,000

QUEBEC, CANADA
Montreal
Journal do Emigrante **(37140)** ....(Free) 10,000
A Voz de Portugal **(37237)** ....(Paid) ‡3,755
                                          (Free) ‡6,245

ROMANIAN

NEW YORK
Brooklyn
The Watchtower **(20355)** ....‡23,042,000

RUSSIAN

MARYLAND
Baltimore
Vestnik **(13260)** ....(Combined) 10,000

NEW YORK
Brooklyn
The Watchtower **(20355)** ....‡23,042,000

Jordanville
Pravoslavnaya Rus **(20855)** ....‡1,850
Pravoslavnaya Zhizn **(20856)** ....‡1,900

New York
New Russian Word **(22434)**
Novyj Zhurnal (The New Review) **(22470)** 500

PENNSYLVANIA
Horsham
Far Northeast Citizen Sentinel **(27060)** ....(Paid) 250
                                          (Free) 14,250

WASHINGTON
Seattle
Outlook **(32999)** ....(Non-paid) 20,000

BRITISH COLUMBIA, CANADA
Vancouver
Hallelujah! **(35145)** ....(Combined) ‡5,000

ONTARIO, CANADA
Toronto
Exodus Magazine **(36587)** ....(Paid) 15,000
                                          (Non-paid) 3,000

QUEBEC, CANADA
Montreal
The ICAO Journal **(37123)** 58,482

SERBIAN

See also Croatian

NEW YORK
Brooklyn
The Watchtower **(20355)** ....‡23,042,000

PENNSYLVANIA
Pittsburgh
American Srbobran **(27757)** ....‡12,000

TEXAS
Fritch
The Trumpeter **(30374)** ....(Paid) ‡600
                                          (Controlled) ‡700

ONTARIO, CANADA
Hamilton
Canadian Serbian **(35878)** 1,000

North York
Bratstvo (Fraternity) **(36122)** ....(Paid) 1,500
                                          (Controlled) 700

SLOVAK

NEW YORK
Brooklyn
The Watchtower **(20355)** ....‡23,042,000

PENNSYLVANIA
Middletown
Jednota (Union) **(27253)** ....(Paid) ‡535
                                          (Free) ‡35,105

Vandergrift
Fraternally Yours, Zenska
   Jednota **(28094)** ....(Controlled) ‡30,800

SLOVENE

ILLINOIS
Chicago
Dawn **(8349)** ....(Paid) ‡4,800
                                          (Controlled) ‡25
Prosveta **(8542)** ....‡21,000

Joliet
Glasilo KSKJ (Americanski Slovenec) **(9033)**

NEW YORK
Brooklyn
The Watchtower **(20355)** ....‡23,042,000

PENNSYLVANIA
Imperial
Voice of Youth **(27070)** ....‡4,000

SPANISH

ARIZONA
Tempe
Bilingual Review/Revista Bilingue **(900)**

Yuma
Bajo El Sol **(1016)** ....(Non-paid) ♦20,369

CALIFORNIA
Bakersfield
El Mexicalo **(1450)** ....(Paid) ‡9,676
                                          (Free) ‡5,563
El Popular **(1451)** 25,000

Belvedere
E.L.A. Brooklyn-Belvedere
   Comet **(1485)** ....(Paid) ♦26
                                          (Free) ♦5,300

Emeryville
Mix—Edicion en
   Espanol **(1880)** ....(Combined) 20,000

Circulation: ★ = ABC; △ = BPA; ♦ = CAC; ● = CCAB; ▢ = VAC; ⊕ = PO Statement; ‡ = Publisher's Report; Boldface figures = sworn; Light figures = estimated.

2757

Circ.   Circ.   Circ.

SPANISH (continued)

Fresno
Vida En El Valle **(1959)** ....(Free) 29,190
(Paid) 46

Irvine
Mexican Studies/Estudios Mexicanos **(2083)**

Los Angeles
City Terrace Comet **(2240)** ....(Paid) ◆211
(Free) ◆4,528
Eastside Sun **(2258)** ....(Paid) ◆24,000
(Free) ‡22,500
El Clasificado **(2262)** ....(Non-paid) 130,000
La Opinion **(2312)** ....(Mon.-Fri.) ★126,189
(Sat.) ★102,473
(Sun.) ★72,601
Mexican American Sun **(2332)** ....(Paid) ◆104,000
(Free) ◆13,770
Novedades **(2350)** ....(Combined) 50,000
20 de Mayo **(2417)** 25,000
Wyvernwood Chronicle **(2443)** ....(Paid) ◆2
(Free) ◆1,948

Montebello
Montebello Comet **(2580)** ....(Paid) ◆10
(Free) ◆15,657

Monterey Park
Monterey Park Comet **(2595)** ....(Paid) 23
(Free) 104,000

Oakland
El Mundo **(2680)** ....(Free) ‡31,864

Oxnard
Ventura County Vida Newspaper **(2731)** 35,000

Palm Desert
Saludos Hispanos **(2743)** 300,000

Pomona
La Voz **(2860)** ....(Paid) 200
(Free) 19,800

Sacramento
El Heraldo Catolico **(2997)** ....‡20,000
El Hispano **(2998)** ....(Paid) ‡3,250
(Free) ‡17,000

San Bernardino
El Chicano **(3086)** ....(Free) ‡16,000

San Diego
Ahora Now **(3109)** ....(Paid) 100
(Free) 20,000
La Prensa San Diego **(3220)** ....‡30,000

San Francisco
El Bohemio News **(3357)** ....(Free) 60,000
The Urban Latino News **(3457)** 20,000-25,000

San Jose
El Observador **(3516)** ....(Paid) 451
(Free) 75,549
La Oferta Review **(3521)** 54,915

Santa Ana
Azteca News **(3620)** ....(Free) ‡33,000

Van Nuys
La Guia Familiar **(3991)** ....(Free) ‡242,375

Vista
El Informador **(4044)** ....(Combined) 28,229

Westminster
Alba de America **(4073)** ....(Paid) 500

Winchester
Hispanic Times Magazine **(4093)** ....(Paid) ‡628
(Controlled) ‡60,000

CONNECTICUT
Darien
Lamaze Para Padres **(4774)** ....(Non-paid) △750,000

New Haven
Columbia **(4985)** ....‡1,600,000

Wilton
Critical Care
International **(5224)** ....(Controlled) ‡26,000

DISTRICT OF COLUMBIA
Washington
El Pregonero **(5475)** ....(Non-paid) 27,154
Finance &
Development **(5495)** ....(Controlled) 95,000
Inter-American Review of
Bibliography **(5548)** ....(Paid) ‡400
(Non-paid) ‡400

International Journal of Government Auditing **(5554)**

FLORIDA
Avon Park
Prensa Hispana (Hispanic
Press) **(5913)** ....(Free) 30,000

Cooper City
Lacja's World **(6003)** ....(Controlled) 20,000

Coral Gables
Artes Graficas **(6004)** 24,112

Fort Lauderdale
El Nuevo Herald **(6075)** ....(Mon.-Sat.) 90,543
(Sun.) 97,705

Hialeah
El Sol de Hialeah **(6187)** ....(Non-paid) ‡24,000

Homestead
Florida Entomologist **(6203)** ....‡1,000

Lake Mary
Vida Cristiana **(6281)**

Miami
Automundo Magazine **(6340)** ....(Paid) 25,000
(Non-paid) 25,000
Bienvenidos a Miami **(6341)** ......(Non-paid) ‡16,000
Buenhogar **(6342)** ....‡18,449
Cosmopolitan en Espanol **(6346)** ....(Paid) 49,568
Diario las Americas **(6348)** ......(Mon.-Fri.) ‡65,670
(Sun.) ‡69,580
El Nuevo Patria **(6350)** ....(Paid) ‡12,910
(Free) ‡17,090
The Florida Catholic **(6352)** ....(Paid) 144,250
The Flyer **(6354)** ....(Non-paid) ‡1,018,449
Geomundo **(6356)**
Harper's Bazaar en Espanol **(6357)** ....‡13,108
Hombre Internacional **(6360)** ....‡12,749
Hora de Cierre **(6361)** ....(Controlled) 10,000
Ideas para Su Hogar (Ideas for Your
Home) **(6362)** ....‡10,848
La Voz Catolica **(6367)** ....(Free) ❑58,025
Libre **(6368)** ....(Paid) 2,000
(Free) 8,000
Mecanica Popular **(6369)** ....‡14,977
Tu Internacional **(6385)** ....‡11,452
TV y Novelas **(6386)** ....(Paid) 136,708
Vanidades Continental **(6388)** ......(Paid) 92,777
Vida Social **(6389)** ....(Combined) 277,385

Orlando
La Semana **(6500)** ....(Non-paid) 66,390
(Paid) 10

South Miami
Today's Grocer **(6686)** ....(Controlled) ‡19,500

Tampa
La Gaceta **(6773)** ....‡18,079

Winter Haven
La Prensa Newspaper **(6867)** ....(Free) ‡19,828

Winter Park
Latitudes **(6882)** ....(Controlled) 105,000

GEORGIA
Atlanta
Mundo Hispanico **(7029)** ....(Combined) 57,500

Roswell
Apparel Industry
International **(7512)** ....(Controlled) ‡13,750

ILLINOIS
Chicago
Back of the Yards
Journal **(8279)** ....(Combined) 44,000
El Manana News **(8362)** ....(Combined) ‡140
La Raza **(8453)** ....(Paid) ◆12,159
(Non-paid) ◆130,686
Logan Square Extra **(8469)** ....(Free) ‡16,000
Northwest Extra **(8510)** ....(Free) 10,000
The Revolutionary Worker **(8556)**
Utillaje **(8596)** ....(Paid) 500
(Controlled) 30,250

Cicero
El Dia Newspaper **(8673)** ....(Paid) 3,000
(Free) 27,000
El Imparcial **(8674)** ....(Free) 30,000

Deerfield
Industria Alimenticia **(8725)** ....△18,000

Mount Morris
Industria Avicola **(9239)** 15,160

Oak Brook
Lion En Espanol **(9356)**

INDIANA
Goshen
El Puente **(10022)** ....(Combined) 6,050

KANSAS
Fort Leavenworth
Military Review **(11440)** ....(Paid) ‡5,000
(Controlled) ‡20,000

Gardner
La Latina Presencia **(11456)** ....(Non-paid) 5,000

Overland Park
Seguridad Latina **(11730)** ....(Combined) 16,000

MAINE
Orono
American Journal of Potato
Research **(12998)** ....‡1,000

MARYLAND
Silver Spring
Prensa Hispana **(13744)**

MASSACHUSETTS
Boston
Christian Science Quarterly-Weekly Bible
Lessons **(13876)**
El Mundo **(13888)** 27,000
The Herald of Christian Science **(13900)**

Florence
Perspectiva **(14187)** 15,000

MICHIGAN
Detroit
EL CENTRAL
Newspaper **(14930)** ....(Combined) 14,000

MISSOURI
Kansas City
Dos Mundos Bilingual Newspaper **(17165)** 20,000

Unity Village
Daily Word **(17660)** ....‡1,500,000

NEVADA
Reno
Ahora Spanish News **(18416)** ....(Paid) 620
(Free) 11,380

NEW HAMPSHIRE
Hanover
Revista de Critica Literaria Latinoamericana **(18519)**

NEW JERSEY
Cresskill
Sugar y Azucar **(18773)** ....(Paid) 506
(Controlled) 4,707

Elizabeth
La Voz **(18790)** ....⊕38,000
Mensaje **(18791)** ....(Paid) 52,000

Union City
El Especial **(19690)** ....(Paid) 71,250
(Free) 1,400

NEW MEXICO
Santa Rosa
Santa Rosa News **(19951)** ....‡2,200

NEW YORK
Flushing
Resumen Newspaper **(20612)** ....‡27,500

Great Neck
Agricultura de las
Americas **(20684)** ....(Non-paid) 37,318
Petroleo Internacional **(20694)** ....(Non-paid) 9,313
World Industrial Reporter (Reportero
Industrial) **(20695)** ....(Non-paid) ‡71,101

Jackson Heights
El Tiempo de New York **(20827)** ......(Paid) ‡48,000
(Free) ‡500

Long Island City
Noticias del Mundo **(20965)** ....(Paid) 37,000

New York
Beverage World en
Espanol **(21306)** ....(Combined) ‡11,100
City Family **(21422)**

El Diario/La Prensa (21590) ......(Mon.-Fri.) 53,843
(Sat.) 46,090
(Sun.) 36,152
Impacto Latin News (21855) 128,000
International Family Planning
Perspectives (21897) ....(Paid) ‡30,000
(Non-paid) ‡1,000
International Railway
Journal (21933) ....(Combined) 10,314
La Familia de la Ciudad (22227)
La Voz Hispana (22228) 60,082
Mundo Mercantil (22381) ....(Combined) 10,000
Perspectiva Mundial (22544) ....‡4,300
Popular Mechanics (22579) ....(Paid) 1,224,960
REVISTA AEREA (22665) ....(Controlled) 11,200
Scientific American (22714) ....(Paid) 687,437
Temas (22822) ....(Paid) 107,000
(Non-paid) 6,200

Ronkonkoma
FLEXO ESPANOL (23269) ....(Paid) ‡2,500
(Non-paid) ‡5,500

NORTH CAROLINA
Charlotte
La Noticia (23747) ....⊕26,000

OHIO
Cincinnati
Dia a Dia (24793) ....(Paid) 12,000
El Hospital (24796) ....(Controlled) ‡15,500
Signs of the Times & Screen Printing en
Espanol (24818) ....(Paid) 540
(Non-paid) 15,950

OKLAHOMA
Tulsa
Potencia (26126)
Prevencion de la Contaminacion (26129)

PENNSYLVANIA
Philadelphia
Community Focus (27424) ....(Free) ‡16,000
25,000

PUERTO RICO
Humacao
Periodico El Regional de
Guayama (28250) ....(Non-paid) 39,800

San Juan
Caribbean Studies (28291)
El Nuevo Dia (28292) ....(Mon.-Sat.) 200,484
(Sun.) 239,494
El Visitante de Puerto Rico (28293) ....(Paid) 65,000
(Free) 400
El Vocero de Puerto
Rico (28294) ....(Mon.-Fri.) 181,168
(Sat.) 156,051

RHODE ISLAND
Cranston
Inti (28335) ....(Controlled) 1,000

SOUTH CAROLINA
Columbia
La Bobina (28556) ....(Controlled) ‡13,600

Greenville
Textiles
Panamericanos (28627) ....(Controlled) 13,000

TENNESSEE
Cleveland
White Wing Messenger (29123) ....‡9,000

Nashville
Puerta del Sol (29482)

TEXAS
Dallas
El Extra (30154) ....(Free) ❑27,298

Fort Worth
Linden Lane Magazine (30345) ....(Paid) 2000

Houston
Key Magazine
Houston (30500) ....(Combined) ‡41,505
La Informacion (30501) 84,000
La Voz de Houston
Newspaper (30503) ....(Non-paid) 96,780
Oil & Gas Journal Latinoamerica (30517)

Waco
TIEMPO (31254)

WASHINGTON
Seattle
Outlook (32999) ....(Non-paid) 20,000

Wenatchee
El Mundo (33193) ....(Paid) ❑235
(Non-paid) ❑14,643

BRITISH COLUMBIA, CANADA
Vancouver
Hallelujah! (35145) ....(Combined) ‡5,000

ONTARIO, CANADA
Toronto
El Popular (36581) ....‡10,500

QUEBEC, CANADA
Montreal
The ICAO Journal (37123) 58,482

SWAHILI

NEW YORK
Brooklyn
The Watchtower (20355) ....‡23,042,000

SWEDISH

CALIFORNIA
Mill Valley
Vestkusten (2542) ....(Paid) ‡1,800
(Free) ‡400

MASSACHUSETTS
Boston
Christian Science Quarterly-Weekly Bible
Lessons (13876)
The Herald of Christian Science (13900)

NEW YORK
Brooklyn
The Watchtower (20355) ....‡23,042,000

New York
Nordstjernan (Swedish
News) (22468) ....(Paid) ‡5,000
(Free) ‡100

BRITISH COLUMBIA, CANADA
Vancouver
Swedish Press (35170) ....(Paid) 4,000
(Non-paid) 1,000

TAMIL

NEW YORK
Brooklyn
The Watchtower (20355) ....‡23,042,000

PENNSYLVANIA
Chester Springs
Bible Standard and Herald of Christ's
Kingdom (26777) ....(Paid) ‡3,500

TURKISH

NEW YORK
Brooklyn
The Watchtower (20355) ....‡23,042,000

UKRAINIAN

CONNECTICUT
Stamford
The Sower (5160) ....(Paid) ‡8,220
(Non-paid) ‡140

ILLINOIS
Chicago
The New Star (8507) ....(Paid) 36,129
(Controlled) 2,035

NEW JERSEY
Parsippany
SVOBODA (19414) ....(Paid) ‡12,500
(Free) ‡300

South Bound Brook
Ukrainian Orthodox Word (19582) 8,200

NEW YORK
Brooklyn
The Watchtower (20355) ....‡23,042,000

New York
Nashe Zhyttia (Our Life) (22394) ....(Paid) ‡3,000
(Non-paid) ‡50

PENNSYLVANIA
Philadelphia
America (27369)
The Way (27718) ....(Paid) 7,000

Scranton
Narodna Volya Ukrainian (27960) ......(Paid) ‡3,000
(Free) ‡200

ALBERTA, CANADA
Edmonton
Ukrainian News (34732) ....(Paid) 4,487
(Non-paid) 2,000

MANITOBA, CANADA
Winnipeg
The Herald (Visnyk) (35332) ......(Paid) ‡7,500
(Non-paid) 250
Promin (35351) ....‡1,637
Ukrainian Voice (35354) ....(Paid) 1,880
(Free) 50

ONTARIO, CANADA
Toronto
The New Pathway (36673) ....(Paid) ‡4,500
(Free) ‡110
Yunak (36796)

URDU

ONTARIO, CANADA
Oakville
Pakeeza International (36150) ....(Paid) ‡35
(Non-paid) ‡8,000
The South Asian Voice (36151) ....(Paid) 35
(Non-paid) 8,000

Willowdale
Fortnightly Al-Hilal (36877) ....(Paid) ‡4,000
(Free) ‡1,500

VIETNAMESE

CALIFORNIA
Irvine
Dan Chung News (2077) ....(Combined) 10,000

Rosemead
Saigon Times (2969) ....(Combined) 20,000

San Diego
Viet Nam Hai Ngoai (3287) ....(Paid) ‡5,000
(Non-paid) ‡2,500

San Jose
Khang Chien Magazine (3520) ....(Paid) 7,000
(Non-paid) 2,000
Song Manh Magazine (3538) 10,000
Thoi Bao (3543) ....(Combined) 12,000
Vietnam Daily News (3544) 13,000

Westminster
Viet Bao Kinh Te (4075)

NEW YORK
Brooklyn
The Watchtower (20355) ....‡23,042,000

TEXAS
Dallas
But Viet Weekly
News (30135) ....(Combined) 27,500

Garland
Vietnam Weekly
News (30385) ....(Combined) 12,000

VIRGINIA
Lorton
Hoa Thinh Don Viet
Bao (32197) ....(Combined) 6,000

ONTARIO, CANADA
Toronto
Lang Van (36648) ....(Controlled) 1,800

Circulation: ★ = ABC; △ = BPA; ♦ = CAC; • = CCAB; ❑ = VAC; ⊕ = PO Statement; ‡ = Publisher's Report; Boldface figures = sworn; Light figures = estimated.

2759

Circ.

Circ.

Circ.

WELSH

NEW JERSEY
Basking Ridge
Ninnau **(18665)** ....(Paid) ‡2,500
(Non-paid) ‡500

NEW YORK
Utica
Y Drych (The Mirror) **(23469)** ....(Paid) ‡2,500
(Non-paid) ‡500

YIDDISH

See also Hebrew

NEW YORK
Brooklyn
Der Yid **(20313)** ....(Paid) ‡41,000
(Free) ‡2,500

New York
Afn Shvel **(21162)** ....(Paid) ‡1,100
(Non-paid) 100
Jewish Forward **(21963)** 25,000
Yiddisher Kemfer (Jewish Fighter) **(22949)**

Hispanic Publications

Index entries are arranged geographically, first by states/provinces and then by cities. Within cities in this index, citations appear alphabetically by publication title. Citations include publication title, entry number (given in parentheses immediately following the title), and circulation figures.

Circ.

CALIFORNIA
Bakersfield
El Mexicalo **(1450)** ....(Paid) ‡9,676
(Free) ‡5,563
El Popular **(1451)** 25,000

Belvedere
E.L.A. Brooklyn-Belvedere
Comet **(1485)** ....(Paid) ♦26
(Free) ♦5,300

Irvine
Mexican Studies/Estudios Mexicanos **(2083)**

La Jolla
Voz Fronteriza **(2121)** 8,000

Los Angeles
City Terrace Comet **(2240)** ....(Paid) ♦211
(Free) ♦4,528
Eastside Sun **(2258)** ....(Paid) ♦24,000
(Free) ‡22,500
La Gente **(2311)** ....(Non-paid) 20,000
La Opinion **(2312)** ....(Mon.-Fri.) ★126,189
(Sat.) ★102,473
(Sun.) ★72,601
Mexican American Sun **(2332)** ....(Paid) ♦104,000
(Free) ♦13,770
20 de Mayo **(2417)** 25,000
Wyvernwood Chronicle **(2443)** ....(Paid) ♦2
(Free) ♦1,948

Montebello
Montebello Comet **(2580)** ....(Paid) ♦10
(Free) ♦15,657

Monterey Park
Monterey Park Comet **(2595)** ....(Paid) 23
(Free) 104,000

Oakland
El Mundo **(2680)** ....(Free) ‡31,864

Oxnard
Ventura County Vida Newspaper **(2731)** 35,000

Palm Desert
Saludos Hispanos **(2743)** 300,000

Pomona
La Voz **(2860)** ....(Paid) 200
(Free) 19,800

Riverside
Latin American Perspectives **(2941)** ....(Paid) ‡1,550
(Non-paid) ‡83

Sacramento
El Heraldo Catolico **(2997)** ....‡20,000
El Hispano **(2998)** ....(Paid) ‡3,250
(Free) ‡17,000

San Bernardino
El Chicano **(3086)** ....(Free) ‡16,000

San Diego
Ahora Now **(3109)** ....(Paid) 100
(Free) 20,000
La Prensa San Diego **(3220)** ....‡30,000
The San Diego Voice and
Viewpoint **(3271)** 13,000

San Francisco
El Bohemio News **(3357)** ....(Free) 60,000
The Urban Latino News **(3456)** ....(Non-paid) 20,000

The Urban Latino News **(3457)** 20,000-25,000
San Jose
El Observador **(3516)** ....(Paid) 451
(Free) 75,549
La Oferta Review **(3521)** 54,915

Santa Ana
Azteca News **(3620)** ....(Free) ‡33,000
Union Hidpana **(3634)** ....(Non-paid) 35,000

Santa Barbara
Hispanic Business **(3641)** ....(Paid) 65,000
(Controlled) 165,000
SuperOnda **(3660)** ....(Combined) 102,016

Thousand Oaks
Hispanic Journal of Behavioral
Sciences **(3871)** ....(Paid) 500

Torrance
Minority Business Entrepreneur **(3938)** 40,000

Van Nuys
La Guia Familiar **(3991)** ....(Free) ‡242,375

Winchester
Hispanic Times Magazine **(4093)** ....(Paid) ‡628
(Controlled) ‡60,000

Woodland Hills
Vecinos del Valle **(4116)** ....(Free) 48,371

COLORADO
Denver
Nuestras Raices/Our
Roots **(4345)** ....(Controlled) 550

CONNECTICUT
New Haven
The Inner City Newspaper **(4991)** .....(Free) ‡35,000

DELAWARE
Newark
Lectura y Vida **(5277)** ....(Paid) 1,900
(Controlled) 30

DISTRICT OF COLUMBIA
Washington
El Pregonero **(5475)** ....(Non-paid) 27,154
Inter-American Review of
Bibliography **(5548)** ....(Paid) ‡400
(Noh-paid) ‡400
Latin American Antiquity **(5630)** ....‡1,500
LATINA Style **(5631)** ....(Paid) 150,000

FLORIDA
Coral Gables
Artes Graficas **(6004)** 24,112
Vista Magazine **(6014)** ....(Non-paid) 960,716

Fort Lauderdale
El Nuevo Herald **(6075)** ....(Mon.-Sat.) 90,543
(Sun.) 97,705

Gulf Breeze
Mexico Business Journal **(6178)**

Hialeah
El Sol de Hialeah **(6187)** ....(Non-paid) ‡24,000

Miami
Automundo Magazine **(6340)** ....(Paid) 25,000
(Non-paid) 25,000
Bienvenidos a Miami **(6341)** ......(Non-paid) ‡16,000
Buenhogar **(6342)** ....‡18,449
Cosmopolitan en Espanol **(6346)** ....(Paid) 49,568
Diario las Americas **(6348)** ....(Mon.-Fri.) ‡65,670
(Sun.) ‡69,580
El Nuevo Patria **(6350)** ....(Paid) ‡12,910
(Free) ‡17,090
The Florida Catholic **(6352)** ....(Paid) 144,250
The Flyer **(6354)** ....(Non-paid) ‡1,018,449
Geomundo **(6356)**
Harper's Bazaar en Espanol **(6357)** ....‡13,108
Hombre Internacional **(6360)** ....‡12,749
Ideas para Su Hogar (Ideas for Your
Home) **(6362)** ....‡10,848
La Voz Catolica **(6367)** ....(Free) ❑58,025
Libre **(6368)** ....(Paid) 2,000
(Free) 8,000
Mecanica Popular **(6369)** ....‡14,977
Tu Internacional **(6385)** ....‡11,452
TV y Novelas **(6386)** ....(Paid) 136,708
Vanidades Continental **(6388)** ....(Paid) 92,777

Orlando
La Semana **(6500)** ....(Non-paid) 66,390
(Paid) 10

Tampa
La Gaceta **(6773)** ....‡18,079

Winter Haven
La Prensa Newspaper **(6867)** ....(Free) ‡19,828

GEORGIA
Atlanta
Mundo Hispanico **(7029)** ....(Combined) 57,500

ILLINOIS
Chicago
El Manana News **(8362)** ....(Combined) ‡140
La Raza **(8453)** ....(Paid) ♦12,159
(Non-paid) ♦130,686
Logan Square Extra **(8469)** ....(Free) ‡16,000
Northwest Extra **(8510)** ....(Free) 10,000
The Revolutionary Worker **(8556)**
Wicker Park/West Town EXTRA **(8606)**

Cicero
El Dia Newspaper **(8673)** ....(Paid) 3,000
(Free) 27,000
El Imparcial **(8674)** ....(Free) 30,000
Mundo Hispano **(8675)** ....(Controlled) 20,000
Tele Guia de Chicago **(8676)** ....(Paid) 9,516
(Non-paid) 11,121

Deerfield
Industria Alimenticia **(8725)** ....△18,000

Mount Morris
Industria Avicola **(9239)** 15,160

Oak Brook
Lion En Espanol **(9356)**

IOWA
Columbus Junction
The Columbus Gazette **(10718)** ....‡1,600

Circulation: ★ = ABC; △ = BPA; ♦ = CAC; ● = CCAB; ❑ = VAC; ⊕ = PO Statement; ‡ = Publisher's Report; Boldface figures = sworn; Light figures = estimated.

Circ.

Circ.

Circ.

MARYLAND
Baltimore
Alternative Press Index **(13111)** ....(Paid) ‡550
(Controlled) ‡200
Hispanic Engineer **(13168)** ....‡15,000

College Park
The Hispanic American Historical
Review **(13419)** ....‡2,200

Silver Spring
Prensa Hispana **(13744)**

MASSACHUSETTS
Boston
El Mundo **(13888)** 27,000

MISSOURI
Kansas City
Dos Mundos Bilingual Newspaper **(17165)** 20,000

Unity Village
Daily Word **(17660)** ....‡1,500,000

NEVADA
Reno
Ahora Spanish News **(18416)** ....(Paid) 620
(Free) 11,380

NEW JERSEY
East Rutherford
Latin Finance **(18784)**

Elizabeth
La Voz **(18790)** ....⊕38,000
Mensaje **(18791)** ....(Paid) 52,000

Jersey City
El Nuevo Hudson **(19136)** ....(Non-paid) ♦55,525

New Brunswick
Black Voice/Carta Latina **(19326)** ....(Free) ‡4,000

Union City
AVANCE Weekly **(19689)** 25,000
El Especial **(19690)** ....(Paid) 71,250
(Free) 1,400

NEW YORK
Flushing
Resumen Newspaper **(20612)** ....‡27,500

Great Neck
Agricultura de las
Americas **(20684)** ....(Non-paid) 37,318
Petroleo Internacional **(20694)** ....(Non-paid) 9,313

Jackson Heights
El Tiempo de New York **(20827)** .....(Paid) ‡48,000
(Free) ‡500

Long Island City
Noticias del Mundo **(20965)** ....(Paid) 37,000

New York
El Diario/La Prensa **(21590)** ......(Mon.-Fri.) 53,843
(Sat.) 46,090
(Sun.) 36,152
Impacto Latin News **(21855)** 128,000
La Voz Hispana **(22228)** 60,082
Perspectiva Mundial **(22544)** ....‡4,300
REVISTA AEREA **(22665)** ....(Controlled) 11,200
Sephardic Scholar **(22729)** ....(Paid) 5,000
Ser Padres **(22732)** ....(Controlled) 500,000
Temas **(22822)** ....(Paid) 107,000
(Non-paid) 6,200

OHIO
Cincinnati
El Hospital **(24796)** ....(Controlled) ‡15,500

Toledo
La Prensa Nacional **(25568)** ....(Paid) 6,000

Willoughby
Productores de
Hortalizas **(25663)** ....(Controlled) 10,000

PENNSYLVANIA
Philadelphia
Community Focus **(27424)** ....(Free) ‡16,000
25,000

Pittsburgh
Critica Hispanica **(27773)**
Latin American Literary
Review **(27809)** ....(Combined) 1,250

PUERTO RICO
San Juan
El Nuevo Dia **(28292)** ....(Mon.-Sat.) 200,484
(Sun.) 239,494
El Visitante de Puerto Rico **(28293)** ....(Paid) 65,000
(Free) 400
El Vocero de Puerto
Rico **(28294)** ....(Mon.-Fri.) 181,168
(Sat.) 156,051
Imagen **(28295)** ....‡70,000

SOUTH CAROLINA
Columbia
La Bobina **(28556)** ....(Controlled) ‡13,600

Greenville
Textiles
Panamericanos **(28627)** ....(Controlled) 13,000

TEXAS
Amarillo
El Mensajero **(29696)** ....(Paid) 500
(Non-paid) 14,500

Austin
Latin American Music Review **(29791)** ....(Paid) 600
Texas Hispanic Journal of Law and
Policy **(29823)** ....(Combined) 300

Dallas
Auto Revista **(30125)** ....(Free) 41,000
El Extra **(30154)** ....(Free) ❑27,298

Houston
Hola Magazine **(30479)** ....(Free) 65,000
La Informacion **(30501)** 84,000
La Subasta **(30502)** ....(Free) 101,168

Lubbock
El Editor **(30711)** ....(Controlled) ‡15,000

Midland
Nueva Vista **(30815)**

VIRGINIA
Williamsburg
Chasqui **(32615)** ....(Combined) 385

WASHINGTON
Toppenish
Viva **(33168)** ....(Non-paid) 15,000

Wenatchee
El Mundo **(33193)** ....(Paid) ❑235
(Non-paid) ❑14,643

WISCONSIN
Madison
Letras Femeninas **(33958)** ....(Paid) 500
(Non-paid) 40

ONTARIO, CANADA
Toronto
El Popular **(36581)** ....‡10,500

Jewish Publications

Index entries are arranged geographically, first by states/provinces and then by cities. Within cities in this index, citations appear alphabetically by publication title. Citations include publication title, entry number (given in parentheses immediately following the title), and circulation figures.

Circ.

ALABAMA
Birmingham
Deep South Jewish Voice **(67)** ....(Combined) 3,200
The Jewish Star **(75)** ....‡8,000

ARIZONA
Phoenix
Jewish News of Greater Phoenix **(805)** ....‡6,500

Tucson
Arizona Jewish Post **(932)** 6,800

CALIFORNIA
Berkeley
Tikkun Magazine **(1565)** ....(Combined) 20,000

Oakland
NATA Journal **(2688)**

Santa Cruz
Judaism **(3685)** ....‡5,500

COLORADO
Denver
Intermountain Jewish News **(4332)** .....(Paid) ‡9,750
(Free) ‡165

CONNECTICUT
West Hartford
Connecticut Jewish Ledger **(5202)** ....‡30,000

Westport
NCJW Journal **(5215)** ....(Paid) 100,000

DISTRICT OF COLUMBIA
Washington
B'nai B'rith **(5379)** ....(Paid) ‡169,434
(Non-paid) ‡2,042
The Jewish Veteran **(5563)** ....(Paid) 40,000
(Non-paid) 5,000
Jewish Woman **(5564)** ....(Combined) ‡75,000
Shofar **(5792)** ....‡30,000

FLORIDA
Clearwater
Jewish Press of Pinellas
County **(5987)** ....(Controlled) 4,967
Jewish Press of Tampa **(5988)** ....(Controlled) 6,984

GEORGIA
Douglas
Coffee County News **(7243)** ....(Paid) ‡7,800

Savannah
Savannah Jewish News **(7535)** ....‡1,700

ILLINOIS
Chicago
Broward Jewish Journal **(8293)** ....(Free) 72,000
JUF News **(8451)** 50,000
Palm Beach Jewish Journal
North **(8525)** ....(Combined) 21,575

West Palm Beach
Palm Beach Jewish Journal
South **(9750)** ....(Combined) 26,500

INDIANA
Bloomington
Jewish Social Studies **(9839)** 600

Indianapolis
The Indiana Jewish Post and Opinion **(10127)**

KANSAS
Overland Park
Kansas City Jewish Chronicle **(11717)**

MARYLAND
Rockville
Washington Jewish Week **(13699)** ....‡13,000

MASSACHUSETTS
Boston
The Boston Jewish Times **(13859)** ....‡11,000
The Jewish Advocate **(13910)** 22,000

Newton
GenerationJ.com **(14396)**
InterfaithFamily.com (IFF) **(14400)** 11,000
Jewish Family & Life **(14402)**
JewishSports.com **(14403)**
JVibe.com **(14404)**
Sh'ma **(14409)** ....(Paid) ‡6,287
(Non-paid) ‡377
SocialAction.com **(14410)**

Newton Centre
American Jewish History **(14414)** ....‡3,550

Salem
The Jewish Journal/North of
Boston **(14513)** 13,500

Worcester
Jewish Chronicle **(14685)** ....‡4000

MICHIGAN
Detroit
The Detroit Jewish News **(14925)** ......(Paid) 20,555
(Free) 300

MINNESOTA
St. Louis Park
American Jewish World **(16359)** ....‡7,000

MISSOURI
St. Louis
St. Louis Jewish Light **(17501)** ....‡14,800

NEBRASKA
Omaha
Jewish Press **(18199)** 3,800

NEVADA
Las Vegas
The Jewish Reporter **(18365)** .....(Controlled) 13,000
Las Vegas Israelite **(18373)** ....(Paid) ‡10,000
(Free) ‡33,000

NEW JERSEY
Bergenfield
Avotaynu **(18673)** ....(Combined) 3,400

Cherry Hill
The Jewish Community
Voice **(18736)** ....(Paid) ‡8,400
(Free) ‡2,100

Kendall Park
Journal of Jewish Communal
Service **(19152)** ....‡4,000

Whippany
New Jersey Jewish News—Central
Edition **(19749)** ....(Paid) 7,000
New Jersey Jewish News—Metrowest
Edition **(19750)** ....(Paid) 28,186

NEW MEXICO
Albuquerque
New Mexico Jewish
Link **(19779)** ....(Combined) 20,000

NEW YORK
Albany
The Jewish World **(19990)** ....(Paid) ‡3,311

Bellerose
Free Sons Reporter **(20145)** ....(Controlled) 4,600

Brooklyn
Der Yid **(20313)** ....(Paid) ‡41,000
(Free) ‡2,500
The Jewish Herald **(20322)** ....‡312,000
Jewish Press **(20323)** ....(Paid) ⊕105,203
(Free) ⊕1,930
Kashrus Magazine **(20324)** ....‡10,000

Buffalo
Buffalo Jewish Review **(20365)** ....‡4,100

DeWitt
Jewish Observer **(20532)** 4,500

New York
Afn Shvel **(21162)** ....(Paid) ‡1,100
(Non-paid) 100
AUFBAU - The Transatlantic Jewish
Paper **(21273)** ....‡13,000
Chronos **(21415)**
Commentary **(21454)** ....(Paid) 26,000
(Non-paid) 600
Congress Monthly **(21483)** ....‡30,000
Conservative Judaism **(21485)** ....‡2,600
Hadassah Magazine **(21785)** ....(Paid) 272,131
Hadoar (The Post) **(21786)** ....(Paid) ‡3,500
(Free) ‡870
JCC Circle **(21958)** ....‡35,000
The Jerusalem Post, International
Edition **(21959)** 4,200
Jewish Braille Review **(21961)** .....(Non-paid) ‡2,000
Jewish Currents **(21962)** 2,100
Jewish Forward **(21963)** 25,000
The Jewish Observer **(21964)** ....‡15,000
Jewish Post of New
York **(21965)** ....(Controlled) 18,000
The Jewish Week **(21966)** ....(Paid) ★72,421
Lilith **(22257)** ....‡10,000
Midstream **(22334)** ....‡8,000
NA'AMAT WOMAN **(22390)** ....‡20,000
Reform Judaism **(22640)** ....‡305,000
The Reporter **(22647)** ....(Paid) ‡50,000
Sephardic Scholar **(22729)** ....(Paid) 5,000
The Star **(22790)** ....‡60,000

Circulation: ★ = ABC; △ = BPA; ♦ = CAC; • = CCAB; ❑ = VAC; ⊕ = PO Statement; ‡ = Publisher's Report; Boldface figures = sworn; Light figures = estimated.

2763

Circ.

Circ.

Circ.

NEW YORK (continued)

Women's League
  Outlook **(22934)** ....(Controlled) ‡95,000
Yiddisher Kemfer (Jewish Fighter) **(22949)**
Young Israel Viewpoint **(22952)** ....‡35,000
Young Judaean **(22953)** ....(Paid) ‡5,000
                                    (Non-paid) ‡3,864
Yugntruf **(22954)** ....(Paid) 1000

North Bellmore
Jewish Singles News/Single News & Views/Singles
  Style **(23010)**

Rochester
Jewish Ledger **(23232)** ....(Paid) ‡7,000
                                      (Free) ‡1,000

Vestal
Wyoming Valley Jewish
  Reporter **(23489)** ....(Paid) ⊕2,000

OHIO
Akron
Akron Jewish News **(24572)** ....(Non-paid) 3,200

Beachwood
Cleveland Jewish News **(24651)** ....(Paid) 16,000

Canton
Stark Jewish News **(24732)** ....(Controlled) 2,000

Cincinnati
American Jewish Archives **(24770)**

Sylvania
Toledo Jewish News **(25556)** ......(Controlled) 3,000

PENNSYLVANIA
Melrose Park
Contemporary Jewry **(27245)** ....(Paid) 500

Philadelphia
Inside **(27493)** ....(Paid) 200
                                    (Non-paid) 58,000
Jewish Exponent Inside **(27509)** ......(Paid) ♦38,007
                                 (Non-paid) ♦3,206
The Jewish Quarterly Review **(27510)** 800

Swarthmore
Latin American Jewish Studies **(28042)**

University Park
Studies in American Jewish
  Literature **(28085)** ....(Combined) 450

RHODE ISLAND
Providence
Rhode Island Herald **(28422)** ....(Paid) ‡5,600
                                    (Non-paid) ‡20,000

TEXAS
Houston
Jewish Herald-Voice **(30494)** ....(Paid) ‡7,000
                                         (Free) ‡53

WASHINGTON
Seattle
The Jewish Transcript **(32975)** ....‡4,500

WISCONSIN
Milwaukee
The Wisconsin Jewish
  Chronicle **(34109)** ....(Paid) ⊕2,525
                                    (Non-paid) ⊕130

ALBERTA, CANADA
Edmonton
Edmonton Jewish Life **(34710)** ....(Paid) ⊕1,415

BRITISH COLUMBIA, CANADA
Vancouver
The Jewish Western
  Bulletin **(35151)** ....(Combined) 2,587
Outlook **(35156)** 2,000

MANITOBA, CANADA
Winnipeg
The Jewish Post & News **(35334)** ......(Paid) •2,306
                                    (Non-paid) •755

ONTARIO, CANADA
Downsview
Toronto Jewish Press **(35785)**

North York
The Canadian Jewish
  News **(36124)** ....(Paid) 44,152
                                       (Free) 2,995

Ottawa
Ottawa Jewish Bulletin **(36266)** ....(Controlled) 9,200

Toronto
Exodus Magazine **(36587)** ....(Paid) 15,000
                                    (Non-paid) 3,000

The Jewish Standard **(36630)**

QUEBEC, CANADA
Montreal
Canadian Jewish Studies/Etudes Juives
  Canadiennes **(37094)** ....(Paid) 354
In Montreal **(37125)** ....(Paid) 30,000
Orah Magazine **(37199)** 12,582

College Publications

Index entries are arranged geographically, first by states/provinces and then by cities. Within cities in this index, citations appear alphabetically by publication title. Citations include publication title, name of college or university, entry number (given in parentheses immediately following the title), and circulation figures.

Circ.

ALABAMA
Auburn
Auburn Magazine—Auburn University Alumni
Association **(39)** ....‡53,000
The Auburn Plainsman—Auburn
University **(40)** 19,500

Birmingham
Kaleidoscope—University of Alabama at
Birmingham **(77)** ....(Paid) 300
(Free) 8,000
Phoenix Magazine—University of Alabama at
Birmingham **(86)** ....(Non-paid) ‡2,500
The Samford Crimson—Samford
University **(90)** ....(Non-paid) ‡3,500

Florence
The Flor-Ala—University of North
Alabama **(218)** ....(Paid) 300
(Non-paid) 4,700

Huntsville
The Exponent—The University of Alabama in
Huntsville **(269)** ....(Non-paid) 3,500
UAH (The University of Alabama in Huntsville)
Magazine—The University of Alabama in
Huntsville **(275)** ....‡19,000

Marion
Marion Military Institute Alumni Bulletin—Marion
Military Institute **(311)** ....(Controlled) ‡10,000

Mobile
The Springhillian—Spring Hill
College **(330)** ....(Free) ‡2,000
The Vanguard—University of South
Alabama **(331)** ....(Combined) ‡8,000

Montevallo
The Alabamian—The Alabamian **(354)** ......(Paid) 40
(Non-paid) 2,500

Troy
Tropolitan—Troy State
University **(474)** ....(Free) 4,000

Tuscaloosa
Alabama Alumni Magazine—University of
Alabama **(481)** ....(Non-paid) 34,000

Tuskegee
Campus Digest—Tuskegee
University **(507)** ....(Non-paid) 2,000

ALASKA
Fairbanks
Sun Star—University of
Alaska **(568)** ....(Free) ‡4,000

ARIZONA
Douglas
The Argus—Cochise
College **(685)** ....(Controlled) 3,000

Mesa
Mesa Legend—Mesa
Legend **(744)** ....(Free) ‡15,000

Tempe
State Press—Arizona State
University **(916)** ....(Free) ‡18,000

Thatcher
The Gila Monster—Eastern Arizona
College **(924)** ....(Free) 1,000

Tucson
Arizona Daily Wildcat—University of
Arizona **(930)** ....(Free) ‡20,000
Aztec Press—Pima County Community
College **(937)** ....(Free) ‡6,000

Yuma
The Western Voice—Arizona Western
College **(1021)** ....(Free) 1,000

ARKANSAS
Fayetteville
Hawgs Illustrated—Hawgs
Illustrated **(1120)** ....(Paid) 7,000
(Non-paid) 1,000

Russellville
Arka Tech—Arkansas Tech
University **(1331)** ....(Free) ‡2,500
Nebo—Arkansas Tech University **(1332)**

State University
The Herald of Arkansas State University—Arkansas
State University **(1349)** ....‡8,000

CALIFORNIA
Arcata
The Lumberjack Newspaper—Humboldt State
University **(1429)** ....(Free) ‡6,500

Azusa
Clause—Azusa Pacific
University **(1445)** ....(Non-paid) 2,600

Berkeley
Asian Law Journal—University of
California-Berkeley **(1492)** ....(Paid) 200
California Engineer—California Engineer Publishing
Co. **(1501)** ....(Controlled) ‡10,000
California Monthly—California Alumni
Association **(1504)** ....(Paid) ‡81,800
(Non-paid) ‡3,400
The Daily Californian—Independent Berkeley Student
Publishing Company Inc. **(1512)** ....(Paid) 200
(Free) 23,000

Chico
The Orion—California State
University **(1695)** ....‡10,000

Claremont
Collage—The Claremont
Colleges **(1724)** ....(Controlled) 8,500

Cupertino
La Voz—De Anza College **(1798)** ......(Free) ‡3,000

Davis
The California Aggie—University of California,
Davis **(1811)** ....(Free) ‡13,000

El Cajon
The Summit—Grossmont
College **(1849)** ....(Free) ‡2,000

Fresno
The Collegian—California State University,
Fresno **(1949)** ....(Free) 5,000

Fullerton
Daily Titan—California State University,
Fullerton **(1989)** ....(Free) ‡6,000

Glendale
El Vaquero—Glendale
College **(2009)** ....(Free) ‡3,500

Huntington Beach
The Western Sun—Golden West
College **(2066)** ....(Free) ‡4,500

Irvine
New University—University of California,
Irvine **(2085)** ....(Free) ‡10,000

La Jolla
New Indicator—New Indicator **(2118)** .....(Paid) ‡100
(Free) ‡7,900
UCSD Guardian—University of California at San
Diego **(2120)** ....(Combined) 12,000
Voz Fronteriza—University of California at San
Diego **(2121)** 8,000

La Mirada
The Chimes—Biola University **(2125)** ....(Free) 2,000

La Verne
Campus Times—University of La
Verne **(2127)** ....(Free) 2,200

Loma Linda
Scope—Loma Linda
University **(2160)** ....(Free) ‡36,000
Today—Loma Linda
University **(2161)** ....(Non-paid) 4,000

Long Beach
Daily Forty-Niner—Forty-Niner
Advertising **(2165)** ....(Free) ‡10,000
Viking—Long Beach City
College **(2176)** ....(Free) 6,500

Los Angeles
Al Talib—U.C.L.A. **(2204)** ....(Controlled) 20,000
The Commentator—Southwestern
University **(2245)** ....(Non-paid) 2,000
Daily Bruin—University of California, Los
Angeles **(2250)** ....(Free) 22,000
Daily Trojan—University of Southern
California **(2252)** ....‡10,000
Explorer—Los Angeles Southwest College **(2267)**
Ha'Am—Ha'Am **(2285)**
La Gente—University of California, Los
Angeles **(2311)** ....(Non-paid) 20,000
Los Angeles Loyolan—Loyola Marymount
University **(2325)** ....(Free) ‡5,000
The Occidental Weekly—Occidental
College **(2351)** ....(Paid) ‡250
(Free) ‡1,800
Pacific Ties—U.C.L.A. **(2357)** .....(Controlled) ‡5,000
Tradewinds—Los Angeles Trade Technical
College **(2415)** ....(Free) 2,000
UCLA Magazine—University of California, Los
Angeles **(2419)** 110,000
University Times—California State
University **(2423)** ....(Free) ‡9,000
USC Trojan Family Magazine—University of Southern
California **(2426)** ....(Controlled) ‡195,000

Malibu
The Graphic Weekly—Pepperdine
University **(2489)** ....(Free) ‡3,750

Circulation: ★ = ABC; △ = BPA; ♦ = CAC; • = CCAB; ❑ = VAC; ⊕ = PO Statement; ‡ = Publisher's Report; Boldface figures = sworn; Light figures = estimated.

2765

Circ.

Circ.

Circ.

CALIFORNIA (continued)
Monterey Park
Campus News—East Los Angeles
College **(2591)** ....(Free) ‡500

Moraga
St. Mary's Collegian—St. Mary's
College **(2597)** 4,500

Northridge
The Daily Sundial—Santa Susana Press **(2646)**

Norwalk
Talon Marks—Cerritos
College **(2649)** ....(Free) 4,000

Orange
Panther—Chapman
University **(2725)** ....(Non-paid) ‡3,500

Pasadena
The California Tech—The California Institute of
Technology **(2813)** ....(Paid) ‡3,400
(Free) ‡100
The Courier—Pasadena Community
College **(2814)** ....‡5,000
Engineering & Science—The California Institute of
Technology **(2815)** ....(Paid) 200
(Non-paid) 15,500

Pittsburg
Experience—Los Medanos
College **(2846)** ....(Free) 2,000

Pomona
The Poly Post—California State Polytechnic
University **(2861)** ....(Free) ‡6,500

Redding
The Lance—Shasta Community
College **(2887)** ....(Non-paid) ‡5,000

Redlands
Bulldog Weekly—University of
Redlands **(2901)** ....(Free) 2,000

Riverside
The Banner—California Baptist
College **(2930)** ....(Free) ‡1,000
Highlander—University of California,
Riverside **(2938)** ....(Free) ‡10,000

Sacramento
The Current—American River
College **(2994)** 5,000
Sacramento City College Express—Sacramento City
College Store **(3013)** ....(Free) 3,000
The State Hornet—The State Hornet **(3020)**

San Diego
The Daily Aztec—San Diego State
University **(3139)** ....(Free) 13,000
The Point—The Point Weekly **(3247)** ....‡1,500

San Francisco
Contact Point—University of the Pacific School of
Dentistry **(3346)** ....(Non-paid) ‡6,500
Golden Gate Xpress—San Francisco State
University **(3367)** ....‡10,000
The Guardsman—City College of San
Francisco **(3368)** ....‡10,000
NewsPort—NewsPort **(3403)**
Synapse—University of California, San
Francisco **(3448)** 4,500
University of San Francisco Magazine—University of
San Francisco **(3455)** ....(Controlled) 75,000

San Jose
Spartan Daily—San Jose State
University **(3539)** ....(Paid) 100
(Free) 7,400

San Luis Obispo
Mustang Daily—California State Polytechnic
University **(3566)** ....(Free) 7,000

San Pablo
The Advocate—Contra Costa
College **(3594)** ....(Free) ‡2,500

Santa Clara
The Santa Clara—Santa Clara
University **(3673)** ....(Free) ‡3,500

Santa Cruz
City on a Hill—City on a Hill
Press **(3682)** ....(Free) ‡7,000
Scintilla—Creative Writing Program **(3689)**

Santa Monica
Santa Monica College Corsair—Santa Monica
Corsair **(3717)** ....(Free) 5,000

Saratoga
Norseman—West Valley
College **(3745)** ....(Free) 4,000

Stanford
Stanford Business—Stanford Graduate School of
Business **(3798)** ....(Paid) 24,000
(Controlled) 4,000
The Stanford Daily—The Stanford Daily Publishing
Corp. **(3799)** ....(Free) ‡13,500
Stanford Lawyer—Stanford Law
School **(3802)** ....(Controlled) 15,000
Stanford Magazine—Stanford Alumni
Association **(3803)** ....(Controlled) 127,000

Stockton
The Pacifican—University of the
Pacific **(3806)** ....(Free) 5,000

Turlock
The Signal—California State University,
Stanislaus **(3957)** ....(Free) ‡2,200

Van Nuys
Valley Star—Los Angeles Valley
College **(3997)** ....(Free) ‡7,000

Walnut
The Mountaineer—Mt. San Antonio
College **(4047)** ....(Free) ‡4,000

Whittier
Quaker Campus—Whittier
College **(4079)** ....(Free) 1,800

COLORADO
Alamosa
South Coloradan—Adams State
College **(4131)** ....(Free) ‡2,000

Denver
The Clarion—University of
Denver **(4310)** ....(Free) 4,000
Highlander—Regis University **(4329)** 1,000

Fort Collins
The Rocky Mountain Collegian—Colorado State
University **(4438)** ....(Free) ‡11,000

Golden
Mines Oredigger—Colorado School of Mines
Press **(4471)** ....(Paid) ‡500
(Free) ‡3,000

Greeley
The Mirror—Student Media
Corporation **(4499)** ....(Free) 7,000

Lakewood
Rock On—Red Rocks Community
College **(4535)** ....(Free) ‡2,000

Pueblo
USC Today—University of Southern
Colorado **(4602)** ....(Mon.-Thurs.) 1,591,629
(Fri.) 2,008,940

CONNECTICUT
Manchester
Live Wire—Manchester Community
College **(4937)** ....(Free) ‡3,000

Middletown
Wesleyan—Wesleyan
University **(4946)** ....(Controlled) 30,000
The Wesleyan Argus—The Argus **(4947)** 3,200

New Haven
Yale Daily News—Yale Daily News Publishing Co.,
Inc. **(5004)** ....(Paid) ‡200
(Free) ‡7,500

New London
The College Voice—Connecticut
College **(5016)** ....(Paid) 300
(Free) 2,400
The Connecticut College Journal—Connecticut
College **(5017)**

Rocky Hill
The Trinity Tripod—Rare
Reminders **(5107)** ....(Paid) 500
(Free) 3,000

Storrs
The Daily Campus—University of
Connecticut **(5166)** ....(Combined) ‡10,000
UConn Traditions—University of
Connecticut **(5169)** ....(Controlled) 160,000

Willimantic
Campus Lantern—Eastern Connecticut State
College **(5219)** ....(Controlled) 2,900

DELAWARE
Newark
The Review—University of
Delaware **(5281)** ....(Paid) ‡15,000

DISTRICT OF COLUMBIA
Washington
The Eagle-News—American University
Eagle **(5466)** ....(Paid) 150
(Free) 8,000
Georgetown Magazine—Georgetown
University **(5510)** ....(Free) ‡140,000
The Georgetown Voice—Georgetown
University **(5511)** ....(Free) ‡8,400
The GW Hatchet—George Washington
University **(5521)** ....(Paid) ‡150
(Free) ‡12,000
Howard—Howard
University **(5531)** ....(Combined) 50,000
The HOYA—Georgetown
University **(5533)** ....(Paid) ‡500
(Free) ‡8,400
The Tower—Sun Newspapers **(5826)** ....(Free) 5,000

FLORIDA
Cocoa
The Capsule—Brevard Community
College **(5999)** ....‡4,000

Coral Gables
The Miami Hurricane—University of
Miami **(6010)** ....(Free) ‡10,000
Res Ipsa Loquitur—University of Miami School of
Law **(6012)** ....(Free) 2,000

Davie
The Observer—Broward Community
College **(6034)** ....(Free) 10,000

Daytona Beach
Voice—Bethune-Cookman College **(6040)** .....‡3,000

Gainesville
Florida Leader Magazine—Oxendine Publishing,
Inc. **(6139)** ....(Controlled) ‡25,000
The Independent Florida Alligator—Campus
Communications, Inc. **(6145)** ....(Paid) ‡93
(Free) ‡31,907
University of Florida Today Magazine—University of
Florida Alumni
Association **(6160)** ....(Controlled) ‡50,000

Lakeland
The Southern—Florida Southern
College **(6291)** ....(Free) ‡2,500

Miami Shores
Barry Magazine—University
Relations **(6420)** ....(Non-paid) 40,000

Orlando
The Paper—Valencia Community
College **(6506)** ....(Free) ‡6,000

Pensacola
Voyager—University of West
Florida **(6570)** ....(Free) ‡12,000

St. Petersburg
The Wooden Horse—St. Petersburg Junior
College **(6636)** ....(Free) 6,000

Tallahassee
The Famuan—Florida A&M
University **(6704)** ....(Free) ‡3,400
Research in Review—The Vice President for
Research **(6732)**

Tampa
HAWKEYE—Hillsborough Community
College **(6767)** ....(Free) ‡5,000
Oracle—University of South
Florida **(6775)** ....(Paid) ‡150
(Free) ‡16,850

Winter Park
The Sandspur—Rollins College **(6885)** 1,500

GEORGIA
Americus
The Sou'Wester—Georgia Southwestern State
University **(6923)** ....(Free) ‡1,500

Athens
Georgia Magazine—University of
Georgia **(6940)** ....‡30,000
The Red and Black—The Red and Black Publishing
Co. **(6949)** ....(Free) 16,000

Atlanta
AUC Digest—Atlanta University
Center **(6975)** ....(Paid) ‡100
(Non-paid) ‡20,000
Clark Atlanta University Magazine—Atlanta
University **(6986)** ....(Controlled) 18,000
Emory Magazine—Emory
University **(7004)** ....(Non-paid) ‡78,000
The Emory Wheel—Emory
University **(7005)** ....(Combined) 7,500
Georgia Tech Alumni Magazine—Georgia Tech
Alumni Association **(7013)** ....(Paid) 33,000
Tech Topics—Georgia Tech Alumni
Association **(7050)** ....(Controlled) **100,000**
The Technique—Georgia Institute of
Technology **(7052)** ....(Paid) ‡300
(Non-paid) ‡10,700

Cochran
Kernel—Middle Georgia
College **(7179)** ....(Free) ‡1,000

Decatur
Agnes Scott Alumnae Magazine—Agnes Scott
College **(7233)** ....(Non-paid) 15,000
The Profile—Agnes Scott
College **(7237)** ....(Paid) ‡75
(Free) ‡925

Macon
The Cluster—Mercer
University **(7380)** ....(Paid) ‡30,000
The Mercer Cluster—The Mercer
Cluster **(7383)** ....(Free) ‡2,000
URSA—Mercer University **(7387)**

Marietta
The Sting—Southern Polytechnic State
University **(7420)** ....(Free) ‡2,500

Milledgeville
Georgia College & State University Connection—
Georgia College +Alumni Association,
Inc. **(7434)** ....(Free) ‡23,000

Rome
Campus Carrier—Berry College **(7502)** ....(Paid) 100
(Free) 1,900

Statesboro
The George-Anne—Georgia Southern
University **(7560)** ....(Free) ‡7,000
Southern Reflector—Georgia Southern
University **(7563)** ....(Paid) 100
(Controlled) 4,500

Valdosta
Spectator—Valdosta State
University **(7615)** ....(Combined) 5,000

HAWAII
Honolulu
Kapio—Board of Student
Publications **(7706)** 3,000
The Voice of Hawai'i—University of Hawaii at
Manoa **(7727)** ....(Mon.-Fri.) ‡18,000

IDAHO
Boise
The Arbiter—The Arbiter **(7802)** ....(Free) ‡6,000

Coeur d'Alene
NIC Sentinel—North Idaho
College **(7845)** ....(Non-paid) 4,000

Moscow
Idaho Argonaut—The Argonaut **(7915)** ....(Paid) 250
(Free) 6,000

Nampa
Crusader—Northwest Nazarene
University **(7929)** ....(Paid) 100
(Non-paid) 1,400

Pocatello
ISU Extra—Idaho State
University **(7945)** ....(Free) ‡5,000

ILLINOIS
Aurora
Aurora Borealis—Aurora
University **(8039)** ....(Free) ‡2,000

Carbondale
Alumnus—Southern Illinois University at
Carbondale **(8113)** 105,000
Daily Egyptian—Southern Illinois University at
Carbondale **(8116)** ....(Free) ‡22,500

Champaign
The Daily Illini—Illini Media Co. **(8185)** ......‡20,000

Charleston
Daily Eastern News—Eastern Illinois
University **(8234)** ....‡9,000

Chicago
Chicago Business—Chicago
Business **(8307)** ....(Paid) ‡300
(Non-paid) ‡2,500
Chicago Chronicle—University of
Chicago **(8308)** ....(Paid) 500
(Free) 13,500
The Chicago Maroon—The Chicago
Maroon **(8317)** ....‡13,000
Loyola Magazine—Loyola University of
Chicago **(8470)** ....(Non-paid) 120,000
Loyola Phoenix—Loyola Phoenix Loyola University of
Chicago **(8471)** ....(Free) 7,000
Loyola University Chicago Law Journal—Loyola
University-Chicago/School of
Law **(8472)** ....(Controlled) ‡650
Tempo—Chicago State
University **(8582)** ....(Free) 6,000
University of Chicago Magazine—University of
Chicago Magazine **(8593)** ....(Non-paid) ‡110,000
Vision Magazine—University of Illinois at
Chicago **(8600)** ....(Non-paid) 5,500

Chicago Heights
Prairie State College Student Review—Prairie State
College **(8668)**

Crystal Lake
Tartan—McHenry County
College **(8696)** ....(Free) ‡2,000

DeKalb
The Northern Star—Northern Illinois
University **(8740)** ....(Free) ‡16,000
(Fri.) 12,000

Des Plaines
OCCurrence—Oakton Community
College **(8765)** ....(Free) ‡3,750

Elmhurst
Prospect The Magazine of Elmhurst College—
Elmhurst College **(8837)** ....(Controlled) ‡35,000

Evanston
The Daily Northwestern—Northwestern University
Students Publishing Co. **(8856)** ....(Paid) ‡300
(Free) ‡7,000

Galesburg
Knox Student—Knox College **(8905)** ....‡1,800

Glen Ellyn
Courier—College of DuPage **(8926)** ....(Free) ‡5,000

Grayslake
The Chronicle—College of Lake
County **(8952)** ....(Free) 4,000

Greenville
Papyrus—Greenville College **(8962)** 1,000

Jacksonville
The Daily Other—MacMurray
College **(9022)** ....(Non-paid) ‡700

Joliet
The Blazer—Joliet Junior
College **(9030)** ....(Free) ‡3,000
The Encounter—College of St.
Francis **(9031)** ....(Free) ‡1,200

Lisle
Voices Magazine—Benedictine
University **(9112)** ....(Non-paid) ‡25,000

Macomb
Western Courier—Western Illinois
University **(9133)** ....(Free) ‡6,500

Moline
The Chieftain—Black Hawk
College **(9203)** ....(Free) ‡2,000

Monmouth
The Courier—Monmouth
College **(9213)** ....(Free) 1,000

Normal
Daily Vidette—Illinois State
University **(9296)** ....(Paid) ‡300
(Free) ‡15,700
Illinois State Magazine—Illinois State
University **(9298)** ....(Non-paid) ‡124,000

Palatine
Harbinger—William Rainey Harper
College **(9394)** ....(Free) ‡5,000

River Grove
Fifth Avenue Journal—Triton
College **(9495)** ....(Free) ‡5,000

Rock Island
Augustana College Magazine—Augustana
College **(9516)** ....(Controlled) ‡26,500
Augustana Observer—Augustana
College **(9517)** ....(Paid) 300
(Free) 2,600

Skokie
INsider Magazine—College Marketing Bureau,
Inc. **(9607)** ....(Paid) 1,000,000

South Holland
Courier—South Suburban College **(9614)** ......‡3,500

University Park
The GSU Innovator—Governors State
University **(9697)** ....(Free) ‡3,000

Urbana
Illinois Alumni—University of Illinois Alumni
Association **(9706)** ....(Paid) ‡90,000

INDIANA
Anderson
Signatures—Anderson
University **(9784)** ....(Free) ‡24,000

Bloomington
Indiana Alumni Magazine—Indiana University Alumni
Association **(9830)** ....‡75,000
Indiana Daily Student—Indiana
University **(9832)** ....‡17,000

Gary
The Northwest Phoenix—Indiana University
Northwest **(10017)** ....(Free) ‡2,500

Goshen
Goshen College Bulletin—Goshen
College **(10023)** ....‡23,000

Greencastle
The De Pauw—De Pauw
University **(10034)** ....(Paid) 400
(Free) 3,000

Indianapolis
The Sagamore—Indiana University-Purdue University
at Indianapolis **(10168)** ....(Free) ‡13,000

Muncie
Ball State Daily News—Ball State University Daily
News **(10326)** 14,000

Notre Dame
Blue & Gold Illustrated—Notre Dame Football—Blue
& Gold Illustrated **(10368)** ....(Paid) 55,000
Notre Dame Magazine—University of Notre
Dame **(10373)** ....(Controlled) ‡140,000
The Observer—University of Notre
Dame **(10375)** 12,500
Scholastic Magazine—University of Notre Dame - Ave
Maria Press **(10379)** 8,000

Terre Haute
Echoes—Rose-Hulman Institute of
Technology **(10485)** ....(Free) 22,000
The Indiana Statesman—Indiana State
University **(10486)** ....(Free) ‡7,000
The Rose Thorn—Rose-Hulman Institute of
Technology **(10489)** ....(Free) ‡1,500

West Lafayette
Purdue Alumnus—Purdue Alumni Association,
Inc. **(10551)** 55,000

IOWA
Ames
Iowa State Daily—Iowa State Daily Publication
Board **(10589)** 14,000

Cedar Falls
Northern Iowa Today—University of Northern
Iowa **(10660)** ....‡77,000
Northern Iowan—University of Northern
Iowa **(10661)** ....‡9,000

Fraternal Publications

Circulation: ★ = ABC; △ = BPA; ◆ = CAC; ● = CCAB; ❑ = VAC; ⊕ = PO Statement; ‡ = Publisher's Report; Boldface figures = sworn; Light figures = estimated.

2767

	Circ.

IOWA (continued)
Cedar Rapids
Communique—Kirkwood Community
College (10671) ....(Free) ‡4,000

Clinton
The Gallery—Clinton Community
College (10711) ....(Paid) ‡1,000
(Controlled) ‡1,000

Des Moines
Drake Update—Drake
University (10783) ....(Controlled) 52,000
The Times-Delphic—Drake University/Board of
Student Communications (10812) .....(Free) 2,700

Dubuque
Clarke Courier—Clarke
College (10841) ....(Free) 1,000

Fayette
Collegian—Upper Iowa University (10888) 750

Indianola
The Simpsonian—Simpson
College (10966) ....‡1,400

Mason City
Logos—North Iowa Area Community
College (11072) ....(Non-paid) 3,000

Mount Vernon
The Cornellian—Cornell
College (11096) ....(Paid) 200
(Free) 1,100

Sioux Center
Diamond—Dordt College (11205) ....‡1,100
PRO REGE—Dordt
College (11206) ....(Non-paid) ‡3,100

Sioux City
Collegian Reporter—Collegian
Reporter (11212) ....(Free) 1,000

Storm Lake
Buena Vista Today—Buena Vista
University (11243) ....(Controlled) ‡18,000
The Tack—Buena Vista
University (11246) ....(Non-paid) 1,200

Waverly
Wartburg Trumpet—Wartburg
College (11308) ....(Paid) 1,850
(Free) 350

KANSAS
Arkansas City
The Press—Cowley County Community
College (11340) ....(Free) 1,200
(Free) ‡1,200

Coffeyville
The Collegian—Coffeyville Community
College (11387) ....‡1,000

Hays
The University Leader—Fort Hays State
University (11481) ....(Free) ‡3,700

Hutchinson
Hutchinson Collegian—Hutchinson Community
College (11500) ....(Free) ‡1,200

Kansas City
The Advocate—Kansas City Kansas Community
College (11524) ....(Free) ‡2,000

Lawrence
Kansas Alumni—University of Kansas Alumni
Association (11561) ....(Paid) ‡30,000
(Non-paid) ‡1,500
The University Daily Kansan—University of
Kansas (11567) ....(Free) 200
(Paid) 11,300

Liberal
The Crusader—Seward County Community
College (11603) ....(Free) ‡2,000

Lindsborg
Bethany Magazine—College
Relations (11609) ....(Controlled) ‡10,500
Bethany Messenger—Bethany College
Press (11610) 700

Manhattan
Kansas State Collegian—Kansas State University
Student Publications, Inc. (11626) .....(Paid) ‡312
(Free) ‡14,260

Kansas State Engineer—K State
Engineer (11627) ....(Paid) ‡100
(Non-paid) ‡3,000

North Newton
Bethel College Context—Bethel
College (11676) ....(Free) ‡13,000

Ottawa
Ottawa Spirit—Ottawa
University (11690) ....(Controlled) ‡14,500

Overland Park
Campus Ledger—Johnson
Co. (11702) ....(Free) 5,600

Pittsburg
Collegio—Pittsburg State
University (11751) ....(Free) ‡5,000

Wichita
The Sunflower—Wichita State
University (11888) ....(Mon.) 8,000
(Wed.) 8,000
(Fri.) 8,000

Vantage—Kansas Newman
College (11889) ....(Free) ‡1,500
(Paid) 20

KENTUCKY
Berea
Berea College Magazine—Berea
College (11938) ....‡45,000
Pinnacle—Berea College (11939) ......(Paid) ‡1,800
(Free) ‡50

Bowling Green
College Heights Herald—Western Kentucky
University (11941) ....(Free) 10,000

Danville
Centrepiece—Centre College (12037) ....‡18,000

Georgetown
The Georgetonian—Georgetown
College (12087) ....(Free) ‡2,000

Henderson
The Hill—Henderson Community
College (12123) ....(Non-paid) ‡1,200

Lexington
Kentucky Kernel—Kernel Press,
Inc. (12169) 17,000

Louisville
The Louisville Cardinal—University of
Louisville (12228) ....(Free) 17,000
Southern Seminary Magazine—Review &
Expositor (12237) ....(Controlled) 33,000

Morehead
The Trail Blazer—Morehead State University Board of
Student Publications (12304) ....(Paid) 523
(Free) 7,200

Murray
The Murray State News—Murray State
University (12317) ....(Paid) ‡250
(Free) ‡7,000

Paducah
(The Smoke) Signal—Paducah Community
College (12340)

Richmond
The Eastern Progress—The Eastern
Progress (12382) ....(Free) ‡10,000

Somerset
The Mirror—Somerset Community
College (12405) ....(Non-paid) ‡1,000

LOUISIANA
Baton Rouge
LSU Magazine—LSU Alumni
Association (12504) ....‡24,000

Eunice
Bayou Bengal—Louisiana State University at
Eunice (12573) ....(Non-paid) 1,000

Hammond
The Lion's Roar—Southeastern Louisiana
University (12592) ....(Free) ‡5,500

Lafayette
The Vermilion—University of Southwestern
Louisiana (12621) ....(Free) ‡10,000

Lake Charles
Contraband—McNeese State
University (12636) ....‡4,500

Monroe
The Pow Wow—Northeast Louisiana
University (12693) ....‡7,000

Natchitoches
College Student Affairs Journal—College Student
Affairs Journal (12715) ....(Paid) 1,200
Current Sauce—Northwestern State
University (12716) ....‡3,500

New Orleans
Health Sciences at Tulane—Health Sciences at
Tulane (12732) ....(Non-paid) 21,000
Tulanian—Tulane
Publications (12760) ....(Controlled) 83,000

Pineville
Wildcat—Louisiana College (12794) .....(Free) 1,000

Ruston
The Tech Talk—Louisiana Tech
University (12807) ....(Paid) ‡8,000

Thibodaux
The Nicholls Worth—Nicholls State
University (12860) ....‡5,500

MAINE
Brunswick
BOWDOIN Magazine—Bowdoin
College (12934) ....(Non-paid) ‡21,000

Fort Kent
The Bengal Review—University of Maine-Fort
Kent (12964) ....(Free) ‡1,300

Lewiston
The Bates Student—Bates College Publishing
Association (12975)

Waterville
Colby—Colby College (13071) ....(Non-paid) ‡26,000
Colby Echo—The Colby Echo (13072) 4,000

MARYLAND
Annapolis
The College—St. John's College, Office of Public
Relations (13093) ....(Non-paid) 20,000
Shipmate—U.S. Naval Academy Alumni
Association (13097) ....‡42,500

Arnold
Campus Crier—Anne Arundel Community
College (13105) ....‡3,000

Baltimore
The Gazette—Johns Hopkins
University (13163) ....(Free) ‡16,000
Goucher College Quarterly—Goucher
College (13166) 15,000
The Greyhound—The
Greyhound (13167) ....(Free) 3,000
Johns Hopkins Magazine—Johns Hopkins
University (13174) ....(Controlled) ‡121,000
The Johns Hopkins News-Letter—Centaur
Press (13175) ....(Free) 7,000
The Law Forum—University of
Baltimore (13208) ....(Controlled) 8,000
The Montage—Essex Community
College (13222) ....‡1,000
Red & Black—CCBC
Catonsville (13241) ....(Non-paid) 4,000
UMBC Review—University of Maryland - Baltimore
County (13257)

College Park
Diamondback—Maryland Media,
Inc. (13416) ....‡19,000

Frederick
Hood Today—Hood Today (13514) ....(Free) ‡1,250

Salisbury
The Flyer—Salisbury State
University (13708) ....(Free) ‡2,500

Silver Spring
Excalibur—Montgomery
College (13725) ....(Free) ‡2,200
(Free) 500

Towson
The Towerlight—Towson
University (13766) ....‡10,000

Westminster
The Phoenix—The Phoenix, WMC (13778) ....‡1,500

MASSACHUSETTS
Amherst
Amherst—Amherst College **(13790)**
Amherst Student—Amherst
　College **(13792)** ....(Controlled) 2,500
Massachusetts Daily Collegian—University of
　Massachusetts **(13802)** ....(Free) ‡17,000
UMASS Magazine—University of
　Massachusetts **(13807)** ....(Free) ‡155,000

Andover
The Long Term View—Massachusetts School of
　Law **(13813)** ....(Non-paid) 5,000

Babson Park
Babson Alumni Magazine—Babson
　College **(13830)** ....(Controlled) 32,000

Boston
Boston University Today—Boston
　University **(13866)** ....(Paid) ‡500
　　　　　　　　　　　　　　(Free) ‡16,000
The Northeastern News—Northeastern
　University **(13940)** ....(Free) ‡10,000
Simmons Review—Simmons
　College **(13960)** ....(Non-paid) 35,000

Brookline
BOSTONIA—Boston
　University **(14016)** ....(Paid) 2,000
　　　　　　　　　　　　(Non-paid) 200,000

Cambridge
Ed.—Harvard Graduate School of Education **(14051)**
Harvard Crimson—Harvard Crimson,
　Inc. **(14056)** ....‡10,000
Harvard Magazine—Harvard
　Magazine **(14065)** ....(Paid) ‡19,560
　　　　　　　　　　　　(Non-paid) ‡200,150
Radcliffe Quarterly—Radcliffe Institute for Advanced
　Study **(14095)** ....(Free) ‡33,500
The Tech—The Tech **(14106)** ....(Paid) ‡500
　　　　　　　　　　　　　　(Free) ‡8,500
Technology Review—Technology
　Review **(14107)** ....(Paid) 221,784
VooDoo Magazine—VooDoo
　Magazine **(14110)** ....(Non-paid) 8,000

Chestnut Hill
The Heights—Boston
　College **(14128)** ....(Free) 10,000

Framingham
The Gatepost—Framingham State
　College **(14197)** ....(Free) ‡2,000

Lowell
UMASS Lowell Connector—University of
　Massachusetts at Lowell **(14279)** ....(Free) ‡3,500

North Easton
The Summit—Stonehill
　College **(14423)** ....(Free) 1,700

Northampton
Smith Alumnae Quarterly—Alumnae Association of
　Smith College **(14430)** ....‡40,000
The Sophian—Smith College **(14431)** ....‡3,500

Norton
Wheaton Wire—Wheaton College **(14438)**

Palmer
The Harvard Salient—Turley
　Publications **(14455)** 4,500

Salem
The Salem State Log—Salem
　College **(14515)** ....(Free) ‡4,000

Springfield
Yellow Jacket—American International
　College **(14553)** 800

Waltham
Bentley Observer—Bentley
　College **(14596)** ....(Controlled) 52,000
The Justice—Brandeis
　University **(14601)** ....(Paid) 300
　　　　　　　　　　　　　　(Free) 4,200
The Vanguard—Bentley
　College **(14605)** ....(Free) ‡4,000

Williamstown
Williams Alumni Review—Alumni Society of Williams
　College, Hopkins Hall **(14660)** ......(Free) ‡30,417
The Williams Record—Williams
　College **(14661)** ....(Paid) ‡500
　　　　　　　　　　　　　　(Free) ‡3,000

Wollaston
Campus Camera—Eastern Nazarene
　College **(14671)**

Worcester
The Crusader—College of the Holy
　Cross **(14677)** ....‡4,000
The Scarlet—Clark
　University **(14687)** ....(Free) 2,000
Tech News—Worcester Polytechnic
　Institute **(14689)** ....(Paid) ‡100
　　　　　　　　　　　　　　(Free) ‡2,650
Transformations—Worcester Polytechnic
　Institute **(14691)** ....(Non-paid) ‡28,000

MICHIGAN
Ann Arbor
Michigan Alumnus—Alumni Association of the
　U-M **(14760)** 100,000
The Michigan Daily—The Michigan
　Daily **(14761)** ....(Free) ‡18,000
Michigan Feminist Studies—University of
　Michigan **(14762)** ....(Controlled) 250

Benton Harbor
Lake Michigan Journal—Lake Michigan
　College **(14808)**

Berrien Springs
Student Movement—Andrews University
　Press **(14814)** ....(Free) 2,500

Big Rapids
Ferris State Torch—Ferris State
　University **(14815)** ....(Free) ‡6,000

Detroit
The South End—Wayne State University Student
　Newspapers Publishing
　Board **(14948)** ....(Free) ‡10,000
Varsity News—University of
　Detroit-Mercy **(14951)** ....(Free) ‡5,000

East Lansing
MSU Alumni Magazine—Michigan State University
　Alumni Association **(14990)** 37,000
The State News—State News,
　Inc. **(14993)** ....‡33,000

Flint
MCC Post—Mott Community
　College **(15037)** ....(Non-paid) ‡4,200

Grand Rapids
Aquinas Times—Aquinas College Publications
　Board **(15088)** ....(Non-paid) ‡1,500
Chimes—Calvin College **(15090)** ....(Paid) ‡90
　　　　　　　　　　　　　　(Free) ‡3,500
The Collegiate—Grand Rapids Community
　College **(15092)** ....(Free) ‡3,500

Houghton
Michigan Tech Lode—Michigan Technological
　University **(15184)** ....(Free) 5,000

Kalamazoo
Western Herald—Western Michigan
　University **(15246)** ....(Combined) 12,500
WMU, The Magazine—Western Michigan
　University **(15247)** ....(Free) 80,000

Mount Pleasant
Central Michigan Life—Central Michigan
　University **(15375)** ....(Paid) ‡700
　　　　　　　　　　　　　　(Free) ‡14,900

Olivet
Shipherd's Record—Olivet
　College **(15418)** ....(Non-paid) 12,000

Southfield
Tech News—Lawrence Technological
　University **(15549)** ....(Non-paid) ‡3,000

Spring Arbor
Spring Arbor University Journal—Spring Arbor
　University **(15571)** ....(Controlled) 17,000

Ypsilanti
Eastern Echo—Eastern Michigan
　University **(15690)** ....(Free) ‡10,000

MINNESOTA
Duluth
CSS Cable—College of St.
　Scholastica **(15835)** ....(Controlled) ‡1,000
UMD Statesman—University of
　Minnesota **(15843)** 6,000

Mankato
Reporter—Minnesota State University,
　Mankato **(16029)** ....(Free) 7,500

Minneapolis
Minnesota—University of Minnesota Alumni
　Association **(16100)** 43,000
The Minnesota Daily—University of
　Minnesota **(16102)** ....(Free) ‡27,000
Minnesota Technology—Minnesota Technology
　magazine **(16109)** ....(Non-paid) ‡3,000

Moorhead
Alumnews—Moorhead State
　University **(16187)** ....(Non-paid) ‡35,000
The Concordian—Concordia
　College **(16188)** ....‡4000
Moorhead State University Advocate—Moorhead State
　University **(16189)** ....(Free) ‡5,500

Northfield
The Carletonian—Carleton
　College **(16233)** ....(Paid) 500
　　　　　　　　　　　　(Non-paid) 2,500
Manitou Messenger—St. Olaf
　College **(16235)** ....(Free) ‡3,800

St. Cloud
University Chronicle—St. Cloud State
　University **(16348)** ....(Free) ‡7,000

St. Paul
The Cadence—Northwestern
　College **(16364)** ....(Non-paid) 3,000
The Clarion—Bethel
　College **(16371)** ....(Controlled) ‡2,500
The Mac Weekly—Macalester
　College **(16385)** ....‡1,600
The Monitor—Minnesota State University Student
　Association **(16398)** ....(Non-paid) ‡19,000
The Oracle—Hamline University **(16403)** ......‡1,600

St. Peter
The Gustavian Weekly—Gustavus Adolphus
　College **(16430)** ....(Free) ‡2,500

Thief River Falls
Northern Light—Northland Community and Technical
　College **(16466)** ....(Non-paid) ‡1,500

Winona
The Cardinal—St. Mary's
　University **(16525)** ....(Paid) 50
　　　　　　　　　　　　(Non-paid) 1,500
Winonan—Winona State
　University **(16529)** ....(Free) ‡5,000

MISSISSIPPI
Fulton
Chieftain—Itawamba Community
　College **(16627)** ....(Free) ‡2,000

Goodman
The Growl—Holmes Community
　College **(16630)** ....(Paid) 3,750
　　　　　　　　　　　　　(Free) 5,100

Hattiesburg
The Talon—The University of Southern Mississippi
　Alumni Association **(16665)** ....‡14,500

Mathiston
The Breeze—Wood
　College **(16760)** ....(Free) ‡1,200
Chips-O-Wood—Wood
　College **(16761)** ....(Free) ‡6,500

Mississippi State
Mississippi State Alumnus—Mississippi State Alumni
　Association **(16784)** ....(Non-paid) ‡28,500
The Reflector—Mississippi State
　University **(16785)** ....(Free) ‡12,000

University
The Daily Mississippian—University of Mississippi
　Student Media Center **(16863)** ....‡11,500
Ole Miss Alumni Review—University of Mississippi
　Alumni Association **(16868)** ....(Paid) 20,000
　　　　　　　　　　　　(Controlled) 50,000

Wesson
Wolf Tales—Copiah-Lincoln Community
　College **(16873)** ....(Free) ‡2,000

MISSOURI
Bolivar
Omnibus—Southwest Baptist
　University **(16912)** ....(Free) ‡1,400

Circulation: ★ = ABC; △ = BPA; ◆ = CAC; ● = CCAB; ❑ = VAC; ⊕ = PO Statement; ‡ = Publisher's Report; Boldface figures = sworn; Light figures = estimated.

2769

Circ.   Circ.   Circ.

MISSOURI (continued)
Canton
Megaphone—Culver-Stockton
  College **(16941)** ....(Free) ‡1,000

Cape Girardeau
The Capaha Arrow—Southeast Missouri State
  University **(16944)** ....‡6,000

Columbia
MIZZOU Magazine—Alumni Association of the
  University of
  Missouri **(17006)** ....(Non-paid) ‡157,500
Stephens Life—Stephens
  College **(17010)** ....(Paid) 150
                                    (Non-paid) 1,850

Fulton
Echoes from the Woods—William Woods
  University **(17075)** ....(Controlled) 1,000

Kansas City
The Rockhurst Sentinel—Rockhurst
  University **(17195)** ....(Free) 1,900
University News—University of Missouri-Kansas
  City **(17199)** ....(Controlled) 8,000

Kirksville
Index - Chappell—Truman
  University **(17226)** ....(Free) 6,000

Lees Summit
The Longview Current—Longview Community
  College **(17245)** ....‡2,000

Maryville
Northwest Missourian—Northwest Missouri State
  University **(17275)** 8,000

Parkville
The Park Stylus—Park
  College **(17336)** ....(Paid) ‡2,200
                                    (Free) ‡200

Point Lookout
The Outlook—College of the Ozarks **(17353)**

St. Charles
The Linden World—Lindenwood
  University **(17384)** ....(Non-paid) 1500

St. Joseph
The Griffon News—Missouri Western State
  College **(17392)** ....(Free) ‡3,500

St. Louis
The Journal—Webster
  University **(17450)** ....(Free) ‡3,000
Student Life—Washington
  University **(17517)** ....(Paid) ‡500
                                    (Free) ‡6,500
University News—University
  News **(17526)** ....(Paid) 250

Springfield
The Drury Mirror—Drury
  University **(17595)** ....(Paid) 4,177
                                    (Controlled) 6,000
The Lance—Evangel
  University **(17604)** ....(Free) ‡1,400
The Standard—Southwest Missouri State
  University **(17613)** ....(Free) ‡7,000

Union
Cornerstone—East Central
  College **(17657)** ....(Free) 1,000

Warrensburg
Muleskinner—Central Missouri State
  University **(17668)** 6,000

MONTANA
Billings
The Retort—Association of Students of M.S.U.,
  Billings **(17733)** ....(Free) 2,000

Bozeman
The Exponent—ASMSU
  Exponent **(17752)** ....(Free) ‡7,000

Butte
Technocrat—Montana Tech of University of
  Montana **(17762)** ....(Free) ‡1,150

Missoula
Montana Kaimin—University of
  Montana **(17872)** ....(Free) 6,000
Montanan—The University of
  Montana **(17873)** ....(Controlled) 60,000

NEBRASKA
Chadron
The Eagle—Chadron State
  College **(17974)** ....(Free) 2,500

Crete
Doane Owl—Doane College **(17994)** ....(Paid) 1,100

Fremont
The Midland—Midland Lutheran
  College **(18012)** ....(Free) ‡1,500

Hastings
The Collegian—Hastings
  College **(18035)** ....(Paid) ‡1,050
                                    (Free) ‡98
Hastings Today—Hastings
  College **(18036)** ....(Non-paid) ‡28,000

Kearney
Antelope Newspaper—University of Nebraska at
  Kearney **(18058)** ....‡4,600

Lincoln
Daily Nebraskan—University of Nebraska at
  Lincoln **(18083)** 14,000
Nebraska—Alumni Association of the University of
  Nebraska **(18097)** ....‡24,000

Omaha
Creighton University Magazine—Creighton
  University **(18193)**
Creightonian—Creighton
  University **(18194)** ....(Paid) ‡4,600
                                    (Free) ‡200
The Gateway—University of Nebraska at
  Omaha **(18195)** ....(Free) 6,000
Grace Tidings—Grace
  University **(18196)** ....(Non-paid) 24,000

Wayne
Wayne Stater—Wayne State
  College **(18307)** ....(Paid) 800
                                    (Non-paid) 4,000

NEVADA
Reno
Sagebrush—Sagebrush **(18424)** ....(Free) ‡6,000

NEW HAMPSHIRE
Hanover
The Dartmouth—The Dartmouth **(18516)** ......‡3,000
Dartmouth Alumni Magazine—Dartmouth College
  Library **(18517)** ....(Paid) ‡41,251
                                    (Non-paid) ‡2,727

Henniker
The New Englander—New England
  College **(18522)** ....(Free) ‡1,500

NEW JERSEY
Camden
The Gleaner—Rutgers
  University **(18714)** ....(Free) 6,000

Glassboro
The Whit—The Whit **(18844)** ....(Non-paid) 4,000

Hoboken
The Stevens Indicator—Stevens Alumni
  Association **(19107)** ....(Non-paid) 21,000
The Stute—Stevens Institute of
  Technology **(19111)** ....(Free) 2,500

Jersey City
The Gothic Times—Jersey City State
  College **(19138)** ....(Free) ‡2500

Lawrenceville
The Rider News—Rider University **(19164)** ....‡3,200
Rider University—Rider
  University **(19165)** ....(Non-paid) ‡37,000

Madison
Drew Magazine—Drew
  University **(19180)** ....(Controlled) ‡19,500

New Brunswick
Black Voice/Carta Latina—Rutgers
  University **(19326)** ....(Free) ‡4,000
The Caellian—Douglass
  College **(19327)** ....(Free) ‡4,000
The Daily Targum—The Daily
  Targum **(19329)** ....‡17,000
Douglass Alumnae Magazine—Associate Alumnae of
  Douglass College **(19330)** ....‡11,000
Rutgers Magazine—Rutgers
  Magazine **(19338)** ....‡70,000

Newark
The Observer—Rutgers
  University **(19362)** ....(Non-paid) 10,000

Princeton
Business Today (Princeton)—Foundation for Student
  Communication,
  Inc. **(19455)** ....(Controlled) 200,000
Nassau Weekly—Nassau
  Inc. **(19465)** ....(Non-paid) ‡6,000
Princeton Alumni Weekly—Princeton Alumni
  Weekly **(19469)** 60,000
Princeton Weekly Bulletin—Princeton
  University **(19472)** ....(Paid) 4,403
                                    (Non-paid) 9,800

Sewell
The Gazette—Gloucester County
  College **(19545)** ....(Free) 4,500

South Orange
The Setonian—The
  Setonian **(19586)** ....(Non-paid) 4,000

Teaneck
The Equinox—The Equinox **(19609)** .....(Free) 2,000

Toms River
Viking News—Ocean County
  College **(19646)** ....(Free) ‡5,000

Upper Montclair
The Montclarion—Montclair State
  University **(19693)** 5,000

West Long Branch
The Outlook—Monmouth
  University **(19722)** ....(Paid) ‡25
                                    (Free) ‡3,575

NEW MEXICO
Albuquerque
New Mexico Daily Lobo—University of New
  Mexico **(19777)** ....‡14,500

Las Cruces
Round Up—New Mexico State
  University **(19875)** ....(Paid) 15
                                    (Free) 13,000

NEW YORK
Albany
Albany Student Press—Albany Student Press
  Corporation **(19981)** ....(Free) ‡8,000

Amherst
Generation—State University of New York at
  Buffalo **(20031)** ....(Non-paid) ‡10,000
Northstar—Erie Community
  College **(20032)** ....(Free) ‡4,000

Annandale On Hudson
Bard Observer—Observer Press, Inc. **(20059)**

Brockport
Kaleidoscope—State University of New York College
  at Brockport **(20245)** ....(Combined) 58,000
The Stylus—The Stylus **(20246)** ....(Free) ‡5,000

Bronx
Manhattan College Quadrangle—Manhattan
  College **(20277)** 2,500
The RAM—Fordham
  University **(20282)** ....(Free) ‡7,000

Brooklyn
Kingsman—Brooklyn College **(20326)** 10,000
Night Call—Brooklyn
  College **(20334)** ....(Free) ‡10,000
The Polytechnic Reporter—Polytechnic
  University **(20340)** ....(Free) ‡3,000
Scepter—City University of New York **(20345)**
Seawanhaka—Long Island University
  Press **(20346)** ....(Free) ‡3,500

Buffalo
The Griffin—Canisius
  College **(20380)** ....(Free) ‡2,000
Record—State University College at
  Buffalo **(20386)** ....(Free) ‡15,000
The Spectrum—Spectrum Student Periodical,
  Inc. **(20388)** ....(Free) ‡10,000

Canton
The Hill News—St. Lawrence
  University **(20429)** ....(Free) ‡3,500

Clinton
Hamilton Alumni Review—Hamilton
  College **(20472)** ....(Non-paid) ‡19,500

The Spectator—Hamilton
College **(20474)** ....(Combined) ‡3,200

Cobleskill
The Courier—State University of New York at
Cobleskill **(20477)**

Cortland
The Dragon Chronicle—State University of New York
College at Cortland **(20513)** ....(Free) ‡5,500

Geneva
The Herald—Hobart and William Smith
Colleges **(20654)** ....(Free) 2,200

Greenvale
Pioneer—C.W. Post/Long Island
University **(20699)** ....(Free) ‡7,000

Hamilton
The Colgate Maroon-News—Student
Union **(20706)** ....(Free) ‡4,500
Colgate Scene—Colgate
University **(20707)** ....(Free) ‡39,000

Hempstead
The Chronicle—The
Chronicle **(20727)** ....(Free) ‡6,500

Ithaca
Cornell Alumni Magazine—Cornell Alumni
Federation **(20791)** ....‡28,250
The Cornell Daily Sun—The Cornell Daily Sun
Inc. **(20792)** ....‡4,000
Cornell Political Forum—Cornell Political
Forum **(20798)** ....(Non-paid) 8,000
Ithaca College Quarterly—Ithaca
College **(20806)** ....(Free) ‡47,000
Ithaca Times—Ithaca
Times **(20809)** ....(Free) ‡20,159
(Paid) ‡274

Jamaica
The Torch—St. John's
University **(20841)** ....(Free) ‡6,500

Loudonville
The Promethean—Siena
College **(20967)** ....(Free) ‡1,500

Middletown
The Citadel—Orange County Community
College **(21080)** ....(Non-paid) 1,500

New Paltz
The Oracle—State University
College **(21114)** ....(Free) 8,000

New Rochelle
The Ionian—Iona College **(21117)** ....(Free) 6,000

New York
Barnard Bulletin—Barnard
Bulletin **(21290)** ....(Combined) 2,500
Barnard Magazine—Vagelos +Alumnae
Center **(21291)** ....(Controlled) ‡23,500
City College Alumnus—Alumni Association of City
College of New
York **(21421)** ....(Non-paid) 24,000
Columbia College Today—Columbia College
Today **(21442)** ....(Controlled) 47,000
Columbia Daily Spectator—Columbia University/
Spectator Publishing Co. **(21443)** ......(Paid) ‡250
(Free) ‡9,750
Columbia Law School News—Columbia Law
School **(21449)** ....(Controlled) 1,200
Columbia University Record—Columbia
University **(21450)** ....(Controlled) ⊕18,500
The L—New York Law School **(22226)** ....‡5,000
The Lex Review—John Jay College **(22249)**
The Observer—Fordham
University **(22482)** ....(Free) ‡3,000
P S C Clarion—Professional Staff Congress **(22516)**
The Ticker—The Ticker **(22834)** ....(Free) ‡5,000
The Washington Square News—New York
University **(22909)** ....(Free) ‡10,000

Niagara University
The Niagara Index—Niagara
University **(23009)** ....(Free) ‡1,500

Olean
Houghton Star—Olean
Times-Herald **(23039)** ....‡1,000

Oneonta
Hilltops—Hartwick College **(23050)** .....(Free) ‡1,750
State Times—State University of New York College
at Oneonta **(23052)** ....(Free) ‡5,000

Oswego
The Oswegonian—State University of New York at
Oswego **(23061)** ....(Free) 6,000

Pleasantville
New Morning—Pace
University **(23110)** ....(Free) ‡3,500
The New Morning—Pace University **(23111)**

Potsdam
The Racquette—State University of New York at
Potsdam Student Government
Association **(23140)** ....(Free) 3,500

Poughkeepsie
The Circle—Marist
College **(23145)** ....(Non-paid) 3,100
The Miscellany News—Vassar
College **(23148)** ....(Paid) 100
(Free) 2,900
Vassar
Quarterly—AAVC **(23150)** ......(Non-paid) ‡30,000

Rochester
Campus Times—University of Rochester Students
Association **(23214)** ....(Controlled) 5,000
Pioneer—St. John Fisher
College **(23235)** ....(Free) ‡3,000
Reporter Magazine—Reporter
Magazine **(23237)** ....(Controlled) ‡10,000

St. Bonaventure
The Bona Venture—St. Bonaventure
University **(23286)** ....‡3,500

Saratoga Springs
The Skidmore News—Skidmore
College **(23304)** 2,000

Staten Island
The Arrow—St. Johns
University **(23357)** ....(Free) 2,500
The Wagnerian—Wagner
College **(23364)** ....(Free) ‡2,000

Stony Brook
Statesman—State University of New York at Stony
Brook **(23376)** ....‡24,000

Syracuse
The Daily Orange—The Daily Orange
Corp. **(23399)** ....(Free) 9,000
The Dolphin—LeMoyne College **(23400)** 2,500
Orange Source—Orange Source **(23417)**
The Syracuse Record—Syracuse
University **(23429)** ....(Free) 13,500

Troy
The Polytechnic—Rensselaer Polytechnic
Institute **(23455)** ....(Paid) 50
(Free) 8,000
The Quill—Russell Sage
College **(23456)** ....(Free) ‡2,500

Utica
Tangerine—Utica College of Syracuse
University **(23467)** ....(Free) ‡2,500

West Hempstead
The Satyr—The Satyr **(23541)** ....(Free) ‡6,000

West Point
Pointer—Cadet Activities Fund, U.S. Military
Academy **(23546)** ....(Non-paid) ‡4,300

NORTH CAROLINA
Buies Creek
The Campbell Times—Campbell
University **(23668)** ....(Free) 2,000

Chapel Hill
Carolina Alumni Review—University of North Carolina
General Alumni Association **(23700)** ....‡55,000
The Daily Tar Heel—DTH Publishing
Corp. **(23706)** ....(Free) ‡20,000

Charlotte
Treewell—Johnson C. Smith
University **(23756)** ....(Paid) 150
The University Times—University of North Carolina at
Charlotte **(23758)** ....(Paid) ‡193
(Free) ‡10,000

Cullowhee
The Western Carolinian—Western Carolina
University **(23795)** ....(Free) 7,000

Davidson
Davidson Journal—Davidson
College **(23799)** ....(Controlled) 22,500

Durham
The Chronicle—Duke University **(23813)** .....‡15,000

Fayetteville
Monarch Messenger—Methodist
College **(23880)** ....(Free) ‡1,200

Greensboro
A & T Register—North Carolina Agricultural &
Technical University **(23915)** 3,000
The Carolinian—University of North Carolina at
Greensboro **(23920)** ....(Free) 6,000

Greenville
Campus Express—Cox North Carolina Publications,
Inc. **(23961)** ....(Free) ‡18,500
The East Carolinian—East Carolina
University **(23963)** ....(Free) ‡9,000

Hickory
The Lenoir Rhynean—Lenior-Rhyne
College **(23989)** ....(Paid) 100
(Non-paid) 2,000

Misenheimer
Falcon's Eye—Pfeiffer College **(24064)** 500

Raleigh
Technician—North Carolina State
University **(24156)** ....(Free) 18,000

Wilmington
UNCW Magazine—UNCW
Magazine **(24296)** ....(Non-paid) 37,000

Wilson
The Collegiate—Barton
College **(24311)** ....(Free) ‡1,000

Winston-Salem
Old Gold and Black—Wake Forest
University **(24321)** ....(Paid) ‡1,000
(Free) ‡4,500

NORTH DAKOTA
Dickinson
Western Concept—Dickinson State
College **(24395)** ....‡1,500

Fargo
The Spectrum—North Dakota State
University **(24413)** ....‡7,000

Grand Forks
Dakota Student—University of North
Dakota **(24454)** ....‡6,500
University of North Dakota Alumni Review—University
of North Dakota Alumni Association & the UND
Foundation **(24458)** ....(Free) ‡80,000

Jamestown
The Collegian—Jamestown **(24475)** ....(Non-paid) ‡1,000

Wahpeton
College Review—North Dakota State College of
Science **(24548)** ....(Controlled) ‡29,000

OHIO
Ada
Ohio Northern University Law Review—Ohio Northern
University **(24571)** ....(Paid) 850

Akron
The Buchtelite—University of
Akron **(24576)** ....(Free) ‡15,000

Alliance
The Dynamo—Mt. Union College **(24604)** 1,200

Ashland
Collegian—John M. #Ashbrook Center for Public
Affairs **(24618)** ....(Free) ‡2,600

Athens
The Post—Ohio University **(24631)** ....(Paid) 76
(Free) 14,000

Berea
The Exponent—Baldwin-Wallace
College **(24676)** 3,000

Bowling Green
The BG News—Bowling Green State
University **(24688)** ....(Free) ‡9,500
(Bowling Green) BGSU Magazine—Bowling Green
State University **(24689)** ....(Controlled) ‡94,000

Cincinnati
University of Cincinnati News Record—University of
Cincinnati **(24824)** ....(Free) ‡10,000

Fraternal Publications

Circ.

OHIO (continued)

Xavier Magazine—Xavier
University **(24830)** ....(Non-paid) ‡38,000

Cleveland
Case Alumnus—Case Alumni
Association **(24866)** ....(Non-paid) ‡16,000
The Cauldron—Cleveland State
University **(24868)** ....‡‡5,000
CWRU—Case Western Reserve
University **(24878)** ....(Controlled) 98,000
The High Point—Cuyahoga Community
College **(24907)** ....(Free) 2,000
The Mosaic—Cuyahoga Community
College **(24929)** ....(Free) ‡3,000
The Observer—Case Western Reserve
University **(24935)** 6000

Columbus
The Chimes—Capital
University **(25006)** ....(Free) 2,000
The News in Engineering—Ohio State
University **(25035)** ....(Combined) 30,000
Ohio State Alumni Magazine—The Ohio State
University Alumni Association,
Inc. **(25050)** ....‡121,200
Ohio State Lantern—Ohio State
University **(25052)** ....(Free) ‡28,000

Dayton
Clarion—Sinclair Community
College **(25110)** ....(Free) ‡5,000
Flyer News—University of
Dayton **(25116)** ....(Paid) ‡20
(Free) ‡5,000
The Guardian—Wright State
University **(25119)** ....(Free) 5,000
University of Dayton Quarterly—University of
Dayton **(25128)** ....(Non-paid) ‡90,000

Delaware
Ohio Wesleyan Magazine—Ohio Wesleyan
University **(25161)** ....(Non-paid) ‡27,000
The Transcript—The
Transcript **(25162)** ....(Paid) ‡175
(Free) ‡1,825

Granville
Denison Magazine—Denison
University **(25221)** ....(Controlled) ‡30,000
The Denisonian—Denison
University **(25222)** ....‡2,200

Kent
Daily Kent Stater—Kent State University Student
Publication Policy
Committee **(25273)** ....(Free) ‡12,000
Kent Alumni—Kent Alumni
Association **(25275)** ....(Controlled) ‡15,000
Luna Negra—Kent State University **(25276)**

Marietta
The Marcolian—Marietta
College **(25346)** ....(Paid) ‡250
(Free) ‡3,750

New Concord
Black and Magenta—Muskingum
College **(25409)** ....(Paid) 1,500
(Free) 1,900

Oberlin
Oberlin Alumni Magazine—Oberlin
College **(25447)** ....(Non-paid) 33,000
The Oberlin Review—Oberlin
College **(25448)** ....(Free) 3,500

Oxford
The Miami Student—Miami
University **(25457)** ....(Free) 10,000

Rio Grande
Signals—Signals **(25497)** ....(Free) ‡2,000

Springfield
Wittenberg Torch—Wittenberg
Torch **(25534)** ....(Controlled) ‡2,300

Toledo
The Collegian—University of
Toledo **(25566)** ....(Free) 10,000

University Heights
The Carroll News—John Carroll
University **(25602)** ....(Free) ‡5,000

Wooster
Wooster—College of
Wooster **(25673)** ....(Controlled) 26,000

Youngstown
The Jambar—Youngstown State University **(25697)**

OKLAHOMA

Alva
Northwestern News—Northwestern Oklahoma State
University **(25738)** 2,000

Bethany
The Echo—Southern Nazarene
University **(25758)** 1,200
Southern Lights—Southern Nazarene
University **(25760)** ....(Non-paid) ‡20,000

Edmond
The Vista—The Vista Advertising **(25814)** .....‡5,000

Lawton
Collegian—Cameron University **(25886)** ....‡3,000

Norman
The Oklahoma Daily—University of
Oklahoma **(25939)** 12,500

Oklahoma City
The Campus—Oklahoma City
University **(25956)** ....(Non-paid) 1,200
Vision—Oklahoma Christian University **(25997)**

Poteau
Viking Banner—Carl Albert State
College **(26046)** ....‡2,000

Shawnee
The OBU Bison—Oklahoma Baptist
University **(26064)** ....(Free) ‡2,000

Stillwater
The Daily O'Collegian—Oklahoma State
University **(26077)** ....(Paid) ‡11,400
Oklahoma State University Magazine—Oklahoma
State University **(26080)** ....(Paid) ‡21,000
(Controlled) ‡500

Tahlequah
The Northeastern—Northeastern State
University **(26094)**

Tonkawa
The Maverick—Northern Oklahoma
College **(26101)** ....(Free) 1,500

Tulsa
Aggies Illustrated—First Down
Publications **(26106)** ....(Paid) 5,000
Collegian Newspaper—University of
Tulsa **(26110)** ....‡4,000
The Oracle—Oral Roberts
University **(26123)** ....‡2,500
Sooners—First Down Publications **(26132)** 16,000

Weatherford
The Southwestern—Southwestern Oklahoma State
University **(26185)** ....‡5,000

OREGON

Ashland
The Siskiyou—Southern Oregon
University **(26217)** ....(Free) ‡3,000

Bend
The Broadside—Central Oregon Community
College **(26240)** ....(Non-paid) ‡2,500

Corvallis
The Daily Barometer—Oregon State
University **(26287)** ....(Non-paid) 10,000
Oregon Stater—OSU Alumni Association **(26289)**

Eugene
The LCC Torch—Lane Community
College **(26320)** ....‡4,000
Oregon Daily Emerald—Oregon Daily Emerald
Publishing Co. **(26328)** ....(Free) 10,000
Oregon Quarterly—University of
Oregon **(26329)** ....(Controlled) ‡100,000

Forest Grove
Pacific Index—Pacific
University **(26356)** ....(Free) ‡2,000

La Grande
The Eastern Voice—Eastern Oregon
University **(26398)** ....(Free) ‡1,500

McMinnville
The Linfield Review—Linfield
College **(26414)** ....(Combined) 1,500

Circ.

Portland
The Beacon—University of
Portland **(26468)** ....(Free) ‡3,000
The Bridge—Portland Community
College **(26471)** ....(Free) ‡5,000
The Pioneer Log—Lewis & Clark
College **(26499)** ....(Free) 3,000

Salem
Chemeketa Courier—Chemeketa Community
College **(26566)** ....(Free) ‡1,500

PENNSYLVANIA

Annville
The Valley—Lebanon Valley
College **(26657)** ....(Non-paid) ‡16,000

Beaver Falls
Geneva Magazine—Geneva
College **(26685)** ....(Controlled) ‡21,000

Bethlehem
Brown and White—Lehigh
University **(26699)** 7,000
The Comenian—Moravian
College **(26700)** ....(Free) 1200
Lehigh Alumni Bulletin—Lehigh
University **(26702)** ....(Controlled) ‡60,000
LehighNow—Lehigh
University **(26703)** ....(Free) ‡4,000

Bloomsburg
The Voice—Bloomsburg
University **(26719)** ....(Free) ‡5,000

Blue Bell
The Advantage—Montgomery County Community
College **(26722)** ....(Free) 6,000

Carlisle
Dickinson Law Review—Dickinson School of
Law **(26758)** ....‡2,000
The Dickinsonian—Dickinson
College **(26759)** ....(Paid) 250
(Non-paid) 2200

Chester
The Dome—Widener
University **(26774)** ....(Paid) ‡25
(Free) ‡2,475

Clarion
The Clarion Call—Clarion University of
Pennsylvania **(26779)** ....(Paid) ‡100
(Free) ‡5,900

Collegeville
The Grizzly—Ursinus
College **(26796)** ....(Free) ‡2,000

Erie
The Gannon Knight—Gannon
University **(26899)** ....(Free) 3,000

Gettysburg
The Gettysburgian—Gettysburg
College **(26940)** ....(Paid) ‡800
(Free) ‡2,600

Greensburg
Setonian—Seton Hill College **(26954)** .....(Free) 800

Greenville
Thielensian—Thiel College **(26959)** ....(Free) 800

Grove City
The Collegian—Grove City College **(26964)** ......‡15
(Free) ‡2,150
Grove City College Alumni Magazine—Grove City
College **(26965)** ....(Free) ‡22,000

Gwynedd Valley
The Gwynmercian—Gwynedd Mercy
College **(26968)** ....(Free) ‡1,000

Haverford
The Bryn Mawr & Haverford News—Haverford
College **(27028)** ....(Free) ‡2,000

Indiana
The Penn—Student Cooperative Association,
Inc. **(27076)** ....(Free) ‡11,000

Kutztown
The Keystone—Kutztown
University **(27129)** ....(Free) ‡4,000

Lancaster
The College Reporter—Franklin and Marshall
College **(27140)** ....(Free) 3,000

2772

Numbers cited after listings are entry numbers rather than page numbers.

Lewisburg
Bucknell World—Bucknell
University **(27191)** ....(Non-paid) ‡44,500
The Valley Trader—Oberdorf
Publishing **(27193)** ....(Controlled) ‡3,029

Lincoln University
The Lincolnian—Lincoln
University **(27200)** ....(Free) 1,500

Meadville
The Allegheny Review—Thomson-Shore,
Inc. **(27232)** ....(Paid) 1,000

Middletown
Capital Times—Penn State
University **(27251)** ....(Non-paid) 1,000

Monroeville
The Boyce Collegian—Community College of
Allegheny County **(27275)** ....(Free) ‡1,700

New Wilmington
Westminster College Magazine—Westminster
College **(27324)** ....(Controlled) ‡22,500

Philadelphia
The Collegian—La Salle
University **(27422)** ....(Free) ‡3,000
The Daily Pennsylvanian—The Daily Pennsylvanian,
Inc. **(27448)** ....(Free) ‡14,000
Digest—Philadelphia College of Osteopathic
Medicine **(27451)** ....(Controlled) ‡10,600
La Salle Collegian—La Salle
University **(27558)** ....(Non-paid) 38,000
Pennsylvania Gazette—University of Pennsylvania
Press **(27622)**
Temple Review—Temple
University **(27702)** ....(Non-paid) ‡180,000
Temple Times—Temple
University **(27703)** ....(Free) ‡15,000
The Triangle—Drexel
University **(27712)** ....(Free) ‡7,000
The Wharton Journal—University of Pennsylvania
Wharton School **(27719)** 5,000

Pittsburgh
The Communique—Chatham College
Students **(27767)** ....(Non-paid) 900
The Duquesne Duke—Duquesne
University **(27782)** ....(Paid) ‡300
(Free) ‡4000
The Globe—Point Park
College **(27792)** ....(Free) 2,600
The Pioneer—Point Park
College **(27827)** ....(Non-paid) 1,500
Pitt Magazine—University of
Pittsburgh **(27828)** ....(Non-paid) ‡205,000
The Pitt News—University of
Pittsburgh **(27829)** ....(Free) ‡14,000
The Tartan—Carnegie Mellon
University **(27848)** ....(Non-paid) ‡7,000

Rosemont
Rambler—Rosemont College **(27941)**

Selinsgrove
Susquehanna Today—Susquehanna
University **(27975)** ....(Non-paid) ‡17,000

Shippensburg
The Slate—Shippensburg
University **(27990)** ....(Non-paid) 4,000
Vista—Shippensburg University **(27992)** 47,500

Slippery Rock
The Rocket—Slippery Rock
University **(27997)** ....(Free) 7,000

Swarthmore
The Phoenix—The
Phoenix **(28043)** ....(Combined) 2,000
Swarthmore College Bulletin—Swarthmore
College **(28044)** ....(Non-paid) ‡22,500
Swarthmore Phoenix—Swarthmore
College **(28045)** ....(Free) ‡2,500

University Park
The Daily Collegian—Penn State
University **(28074)** ....(Free) ‡20,300
The Penn Stater—Penn State Alumni
Association **(28081)** 124,000
The Weekly Collegian—Penn State
University **(28086)** ....(Paid) 5,250
(Free) 13

Villanova
Villanova Law Review—Villanova
University **(28098)** ....‡890
The Villanovan—Villanova
University **(28099)** ....‡8,000

Washington
Red and Black—Washington and Jefferson
College **(28116)** ....(Non-paid) 1,000
W & J Magazine—Washington and Jefferson
College **(28118)** ....(Free) ‡12,500

West Chester
The Quad—West Chester State
University **(28148)** ....(Combined) ‡77,500

Wilkes Barre
Beacon—Wilkes University **(28163)** ....(Paid) 100
(Non-paid) 1,500
The Crown—King's College **(28165)** ....(Free) ‡2,000

RHODE ISLAND
Kingston
The Good Five Cent Cigar—University of Rhode
Island **(28359)**

Providence
The Anchor—Rhode Island
College **(28387)** ....‡5,000
Brown Alumni Magazine—Brown
University **(28390)** ....(Non-paid) 78,000
Brown Daily Herald—The Brown Daily Herald,
Inc. **(28391)** ....‡5,500
The Cowl—Providence College **(28393)** 4,000

Smithfield
The Archway—Bryant
College **(28442)** ....(Free) ‡3,000

SOUTH CAROLINA
Aiken
Pacer Times—University of South
Carolina **(28468)** ....(Free) 2,000

Charleston
Buc In Print—Charleston Southern
University **(28506)** ....(Free) ‡2,000
The Catalyst—Island
Publications **(28507)** ....(Free) ‡7,000

Clemson
The Tiger—Clemson
University **(28535)** ....(Free) 12,000

Clinton
Presbyterian College Magazine—Presbyterian
College **(28540)** ....(Non-paid) 14,000

Columbia
Benedict Tiger—Benedict
College **(28543)** ....(Non-paid) 2,500

Conway
The Chanticleer—Coastal Carolina
University **(28588)** ....(Free) ‡2,500

Greenville
The Paladin—Furman
University **(28625)** ....(Combined) ‡3,000

Spartanburg
The Carolinian—University of South Carolina at
Spartanburg **(28757)** ....(Free) ‡2,500

SOUTH DAKOTA
Brookings
The SDSU Collegian—South Dakota State
University **(28816)** ....(Free) ‡4,500

Mitchell
Phreno Cosmian—Phreno Cosmian **(28901)** 800

Rapid City
The Tech—South Dakota School of Mines &
Technology **(28933)** ....(Free) ‡1,000

Sioux Falls
Augustana Mirror—Augustana
College **(28961)** 1700

Spearfish
Today—Black Hills State
University **(28994)** ....‡1,500

Vermillion
Volante—University of South
Dakota **(29007)** ....(Paid) ‡200
(Free) ‡6,500

Yankton
Moderator—Mount Marty
College **(29038)** ....(Free) ‡1,000

TENNESSEE
Brentwood
Huskers Illustrated—Huskers
Illustrated **(29062)** 14,000
To Dragma—Alpha Omicron Pi Fraternity,
Inc. **(29064)**

Chattanooga
The University Echo—University of Tennessee at
Chattanooga **(29095)** ....‡4,000

Clarksville
The All State—Austin Peay State
University **(29114)** ....‡3,000

Collegedale
Southern Accent—Student Association of Southern
College Seventh-day
Adventists **(29131)** ....(Paid) ‡150
(Free) ‡1,850

Cookeville
The Oracle—Tennessee Technological
University **(29144)** ....(Non-paid) 5,000

Johnson City
East Tennessean—East Tennessee State
University **(29250)** ....(Free) ‡4,000

Knoxville
Tennessee Alumnus—University of Tennessee Alumni
Association **(29282)** ....‡58,000
UT Daily Beacon—University of
Tennessee **(29284)** ....(Free) ‡16,000

Martin
Pacer—University of Tennessee at
Martin **(29343)** ....(Free) 3,000

Maryville
Highland Echo—Highland
Echo **(29348)** ....(Free) 1,250

Memphis
The Cannon—Christian Brothers
University **(29360)** ....(Free) ‡1,100
The Daily Helmsman—University of
Memphis **(29366)** ....(Free) ‡9,500
River City—University of
Memphis **(29378)** ....(Controlled) 1,500
Shield & Diamond—Pi Kappa Alpha
Fraternity **(29380)** ....‡90,000

Murfreesboro
Sidelines—Middle Tennessee State
University **(29432)** ....(Free) ‡8,000

Nashville
The Babbler—Lipscomb
University **(29443)** ....(Free) ‡2,000
Belmont Vision—Belmont
University **(29444)** ....(Free) ‡2,500
Fisk News—Fisk News **(29455)** ....(Free) 1,000
The Lipscomb News—Lipscomb
University **(29468)** ....(Free) ‡57,000
Vanderbilt Hustler—Vanderbilt Student
Communications **(29498)** 7,000
Vanderbilt Magazine—Vanderbilt
University **(29500)** ....(Paid) 32,000
(Non-paid) 3,000

Sewanee
Sewanee—University of the
South **(29593)** ....(Free) ‡33,500
The Sewanee Purple—University of the
South **(29594)** ....(Paid) 800
(Free) 1,300

TEXAS
Abilene
Optimist—Abilene Christian
University **(29654)** ....(Free) ‡3,800
War Whoop—McMurry
University **(29656)** ....(Non-paid) 1,000

Alpine
The Skyline—Sul Ross State
University **(29684)** ....(Paid) ‡2,000

Amarillo
AC Current—Amarillo
College **(29692)** ....(Non-paid) 2,500
The Ranger—Amarillo
College **(29698)** ....(Free) ‡2,500

Arlington
The Shorthorn—University of Texas at
Arlington **(29736)** ....‡11,000

Circulation: ★ = ABC; △ = BPA; ♦ = CAC; ● = CCAB; ❑ = VAC; ⊕ = PO Statement; ‡ = Publisher's Report; Boldface figures = sworn; Light figures = estimated.

2773

Circ. Circ. Circ.

TEXAS (continued)

Austin
The Daily Texan—University of Texas Student
 Publications (29773) ....‡30,000
Hilltop Views—St. Edward's
 University (29779)....................(Free) 3,000

Baytown
The Lantern—Lee College (29895) .....(Free) ‡1,250

Beaumont
University Press—Lamar
 University (29900) ....(Free) 7,000

Belton
The Bells—University of Mary Hardin Baylor (29915)

Brownwood
Yellow Jacket—Howard Payne
 University (29966) ....(Free) ‡1,500

College Station
The Battalion—Texas A & M
 University (30037) ....(Paid) ‡22,000
The Texas Aggie—Association of Former Students of
 Texas A&M University (30053) 60,000

Commerce
The East Texan—Texas A & M
 University-Commerce (30068) 4,500

Corpus Christi
The Foghorn—Del Mar
 College (30077) ....(Free) ‡5,000

Dallas
Baylor Dental Journal—Baylor College of
 Dentistry (30129) ....(Controlled) 7,500
The Daily Campus—Student Media
 Co. (30141) ....(Free) 5,000

Denton
The Lasso—Texas Woman's
 University (30241) 3,000

Edinburg
The Pan American—The University of Texas—Pan
 American (30271) 8,000

El Paso
NOVA Quarterly—University of Texas at El
 Paso (30281) ....(Controlled) ‡40,000
Prospector—University of Texas at El Paso Student
 Publications (30282) ....‡7,000

Farmers Branch
The Courier—Brookhaven
 College (30314) ....(Free) 2,500

Georgetown
Inside Southwestern—Southwestern
 University (30390)

Houston
The Cauldron—University of St.
 Thomas (30461) ....(Free) ‡2,300
The Daily Cougar—University of
 Houston (30468) ....(Free) ‡13,000
Rice Thresher—Rice
 Thresher (30525) ....(Free) ‡6,000
The TSU Herald—Texas Southern
 University (30536) ....(Non-paid) 10,000

Huntsville
Heritage—Office of University Advancement (30593)
The Houstonian—Sam Houston State
 University (30594) ....(Free) ‡5,500

Irving
University News—University of
 Dallas (30609) ....(Free) ‡2,000

Kingsville
The South Texan—The South
 Texan (30648) ....(Free) ‡5,000

Lubbock
The Duster—Lubbock Christian
 University (30709) 1,000
The University Daily—Texas Tech
 University (30720) ....‡17,000

Lufkin
The Pacer—Angelina
 College (30741) ....(Free) ‡2,500

Nacogdoches
The Pine Log—Stephen F. Austin State
 University (30851) ....(Free) ‡6,500

Plainview
Footprints—Footprints (30938) ....(Free) ‡16,000

Trail Blazer—Wayland Baptist
 University (30940) 900

San Angelo
The Ram Page—Angelo State
 University (31007) ....(Free) ‡4,500

San Antonio
Logos—Incarnate Word College (31037) .....‡3,000

San Marcos
The University Star—Southwest Texas State
 University (31086) ....(Free) 20,000

Snyder
The Western Texan—Western Texas
 College (31115) ....(Free) 1,200

Stephenville
J-TAC—The J-TAC (31129) ....‡4,000

Tyler
Tyler Junior College News—Tyler Junior College,
 Journalism Dept. (31202) ....(Free) 2,500

Waco
The Lariat—Baylor University (31251) .....(Paid) 500
 (Non-paid) 7,000

Wichita Falls
The Wichitan—Midwestern State
 University (31294) ....(Paid) ‡50
 (Free) ‡2,500

UTAH
Logan
Utah State Magazine—Utah State
 University (31353) ....(Controlled) 96,000

Price
The Eagle—College of Eastern
 Utah (31392) ....(Free) 3,000

Provo
BYU Magazine—Brigham Young
 University (31399) ....(Non-paid) 186,000
The Daily Universe—Brigham Young Daily
 Universe (31402) 18,500

Salt Lake City
Daily Utah Chronicle—The Daily Utah
 Chronicle (31425) ....‡15,000
The Forum—Westminster
 College (31427) ....(Free) 1,000
Horizon—Salt Lake Community
 College (31429) ....(Free) ‡10
 (Free) ‡6,000

VERMONT
Colchester
The Defender—SMS Students Publishing
 Association (31530) ....(Paid) 75
 (Free) 3,000

Middlebury
Middlebury College Magazine—Middlebury College
 Publications (31557) 35,000

Northfield
The Norwich Guidon—Norwich
 University (31575) ....(Free) ‡2,000

VIRGINIA
Alexandria
The Collective—North Virginia Community
 College (31655) 4,000

Blacksburg
Collegiate Times—Collegiate
 Times (31867) ....(Free) ‡14,000

Charlottesville
The Cavalier Daily—University of
 Virginia (31921) ....(Free) ‡10,000
The Declaration—University of
 Virginia (31927) ....(Free) ‡5,000
Virginia—University of Virginia Alumni
 Association (31944) ....(Paid) 51,500

Fairfax
Community College Week—Cox, Matthews, &
 Associates, Inc. (32012)

Farmville
The Rotunda—Longwood
 University (32068) ....(Free) ‡3,000

Ferrum
Ferrum Magazine—Ferrum
 College (32073) ....(Controlled) ‡14,000

Fredericksburg
The Bullet—Central Virginia
 Newspapers (32084) ....(Free) 3,500

Hampden Sydney
The Hampden-Sydney Tiger—The Hampden-Sydney
 Tiger (32124) ....(Paid) ‡105
 (Free) ‡1,300

Hampton
Hampton Script—Hampton
 University (32128) ....(Combined) 5,000

Harrisonburg
The Breeze—James Madison
 University (32137) ....(Free) ‡17,000

Lexington
W & L—Washington & Lee
 University (32192) ....(Controlled) ‡25,000

Lynchburg
Randolph-Macon Woman's College Alumnae
 Bulletin—Randolph-Macon Woman's
 College (32208) ....(Controlled) ‡15,000
The Sundial—Randolph-Macon Woman's
 College (32210) 1,200

Norfolk
The Mace and Crown—Old Dominion
 University (32290) ....(Free) ‡17,000

Petersburg
Bon Homme Richard—Richard Bland
 College (32329) ....(Free) 600

Radford
The Tartan—Radford
 University (32347) ....(Free) ‡5,000

Reston
P.B.L. Business Leader—Future Business Leaders of
 America - Phi Beta Lambda, Inc. (32409)

Richmond
The Collegian—University of
 Richmond (32433) ....(Free) ‡3,500
Commonwealth Times—Commonwealth
 Times (32434) 3,000
Shafer Court Connections—Virginia Commonwealth
 University Alumni
 Activities (32453) ....(Controlled) 25,000
Sigma Phi Epsilon Journal—Sigma Phi Epsilon
 Fraternity, Inc. (32454) ....(Controlled) 150,500
Union Seminary Quarterly
 Review—Union-PSCE (32459) ....(Paid) ‡1,100
 (Non-paid) ‡100
The V.U.U. Informer—Virginia Union
 University (32469) ....(Free) ‡2,000

Staunton
Campus Comments—Mary Baldwin
 College (32554) ....(Non-paid) 1,000

Williamsburg
Alumni Gazette—Society of the
 Alumni (32613) ....‡60,000
The Flat Hat—The Flat Hat (32617) .....(Paid) ‡400
 (Free) ‡7,000

WASHINGTON
Bellevue
The Jibsheet—Bellevue Community
 College (32666) ....(Free) 3,000

Bellingham
The Western Front—Western Washington
 University (32679)

Everett
Clipper—Everett Community
 College (32760) ....(Controlled) 2,000

Moses Lake
Tumbleweed Times—Big Bend Community
 College (32840) ....(Free) 2,000

Pullman
The Daily Evergreen—Washington State
 University (32902) ....(Non-paid) 12,000
Washington State University Hilltopics—Washington
 State University (32908) ....‡110,000

Seattle
The City Collegian—SCCC
 Publications (32954) ....(Free) 25,000
The Daily—University of
 Washington (32959) 17,000
Observer—Shoreline Community
 College (32998) ....(Non-paid) 2,200

Numbers cited after listings are entry numbers rather than page numbers.

Seattle University Spectator—Seattle
  University (33025) 4,200
The South Seattle Sentinel—South Seattle Community
  College (33032) ....(Free) 1,200

Spokane
Communicator—Communicator (33093).(Free)‡3,000
The Reporter—Spokane Community
  College (33098) ....(Free) ‡2,500
Whitworthian—Whitworth College (33103) 2,200

Tacoma
The Mooring Mast—Pacific Lutheran
  University (33146) ....(Free) ‡3,000
The Trail—University of Puget
  Sound (33153) ....(Free) ‡1,800

Vancouver
The Independent—Clark Community
  College (33176) ....(Free) ‡3,000

Walla Walla
Fourth Estate—Walla Walla Community
  College (33187) ....(Controlled) ‡1,000
Whitman Academic Journal—Whitman
  College (33189)

WEST VIRGINIA
Bethany
The Tower—Bethany
  College (33250) ....(Paid) 1,000

Bluefield
Bluefieldian—Bluefield State
  College (33253) 1,000

Elkins
The Senator—Mountaineer
  Newspapers (33305) 1,000

Fairmont
The Columns—Fairmont State
  College (33312) ....(Free) 3,000

Glenville
Mercury—Glenville State
  College (33324) ....(Paid) 200
                        (Free) 2,000

Keyser
Pasquino—Potomac State
  College (33353) ....(Free) ‡2,200

Montgomery
Tech Collegian—West Virginia University Institute of
  Technology (33387) ....(Free) ‡2,500

Morgantown
The Daily Athenaeum—West Virginia
  University (33392) ....(Free) ‡15,000
West Virginia University Alumni Magazine—West
  Virginia University (33398) ....(Controlled) 104,000

Philippi
Battler Columns—Alderson-Broaddus
  College (33432) ....(Non-paid) ‡1,200

Shepherdstown
The Shepherd College Picket—The Shepherd College
  Picket (33464) ....(Free) 4,000

West Liberty
The Trumpet—West Liberty State
  College (33495) ....(Free) ‡1,500

WISCONSIN
Beloit
Round Table—Beloit
  College (33576) ....(Free) 2,000

Eau Claire
Spectator—University of Wisconsin-Eau
  Claire (33673) ....(Mon.-Fri.) 107,137
                        (Sat.) 127,707

La Crosse
The Racquet—University of Wisconsin-La
  Crosse (33886) ....(Free) ‡5,000

Madison
Clarion—Madison Area Technical
  College (33927) ....(Non-paid) 4,000
The Daily Cardinal—The Daily Cardinal Newspaper
  Corp. (33932) ....(Free) ‡10,000
ON WISCONSIN—Wisconsin Alumni
  Association (33967) ....‡260,000
Student Leadership Journal—InterVarsity Christian
  Fellowship (33974) ....‡10,000

Menomonie
The Stoutonia—University of
  Wisconsin-Stout (34040) ....‡5,500

Milwaukee
Alverno Today—Alverno
  College (34057) ....(Free) 20,000
Marquette Tribune—Marquette
  Journal (34077) ....‡7,500
Marquette University Journal—Marquette
  Journal (34078) ....(Non-paid) ‡3,000
UWM Post—University of
  Wisconsin-Milwaukee (34105) ....(Free) 12,500

Oshkosh
Oshkosh Advance-Titan—University of
  Wisconsin-Oshkosh (34226) ....(Free) ‡9,000

Platteville
Exponent—Exponent (34240) ....‡3,500

Ripon
Ripon Magazine—Ripon
  College (34303) ....(Controlled) ‡13,000

Stevens Point
The Pointer—University of Wisconsin-Stevens
  Point (34343) 4,000

Superior
Promethean—University of
  Wisconsin (34360) ....(Paid) ‡1,500
                    (Non-paid) ‡1,500

Waukesha
The Perspective—Lake County
  Reporter (34409) ....(Free) 1,200

Wausau
The Forum—University of
  Wisconsin (34429) ....(Non-paid) 800

Whitewater
Royal Purple—UW - Whitewater (34457) ......‡7,000

WYOMING
Casper
Chinook—Casper College (34483) ....(Paid) 300
                      (Free) 2,500

Cheyenne
Wingspan—Wingspan (34497) .....(Non-paid) ‡1,000

Laramie
Branding Iron—University of
  Wyoming (34547) ....(Free) 7,000

ALBERTA, CANADA
Calgary
The Gauntlet—Gauntlet Publications Society/University
  of Calgary (34645) ....(Free) 12,000
The Reflector—Reflector Publications
  Society (34656) ....(Non-paid) ‡10,000
The Weal—SAITSA Publications/Southern Alberta
  Institute of Technology (34658) ......(Free) ‡4,000

Edmonton
Gateway—University of Alberta (34713) 10,000
The MacEwan Journalist—Grant MacEwan Community
  College (34721) ....(Controlled) ‡4,000

Lethbridge
The Meliorist—Meliorist Publishing
  Society (34797) ....(Free) ‡3,000

Red Deer
Bricklayer—Red Deer College (34827) ....‡2000

BRITISH COLUMBIA, CANADA
Burnaby
BCIT Link—British Columbia Institute of Technology
  Student Association (34892) ....(Free) ‡3,500
The Peak—Peak Publications
  Society (34905) ....(Paid) ‡150
                    (Free) ‡9,850

North Vancouver
Capilano Courier—Capilano Courier Publishing
  Society (35033) ....(Free) 3,000

Vancouver
Trek Magazine—University of British Columbia Alumni
  Association (35171) ....(Combined) ‡130,000
The Ubyssey—Ubyssey Publications
  Society (35172) ....(Free) ‡12,000
The Voice—Langara College (35176) ....‡2,000

Victoria
The Martlet—University of
  Victoria (35222) ....(Free) 10,000

UVic Ring—UVic
  Communications (35228) ....(Combined) 7,000
UVic Torch—UVic Communications (35229)

MANITOBA, CANADA
Brandon
The Quill—BUSU Communications,
  Inc. (35255) ....(Free) ‡2,000

Winnipeg
Alumni Journal—University of
  Manitoba (35309) ....‡118,000
Manitoban—Manitoban (35341) ....‡13,000
Uniter—University of
  Winnipeg (35356) ....(Free) 4,000

NEW BRUNSWICK, CANADA
Fredericton
Aquinian—Owl and the Pussycat
  Publications (35389)
The Brunswickan—Brunswickan Publishing
  Inc. (35391) ....‡11,000

Sackville
Mount Allison Record—Mount Allison
  University (35426) ....(Controlled) 18,500

NOVA SCOTIA, CANADA
Antigonish
Xavierian Weekly—St. Francis Xavier
  University (35538) ....(Free) 2,000

Halifax
The Dalhousie Gazette—Dalhousie Gazette
  Publications Society/Dalhousie
  University (35565) 10,000
Hearsay—Dalhousie University (35567) 5,000
The Journal—St. Mary's
  University (35568) ....(Free) 10,000
The Picaro—Mt. St. Vincent
  University (35570) 4,000

Sydney
Caper Times—University College of Cape
  Breton (35608) ....(Free) 2,000

Wolfville
Acadia Bulletin—Associated Alumni of Acadia
  University (35622) ....(Non-paid) 22,000

ONTARIO, CANADA
Hmilton
The Silhouette—McMaster Students Union,
  Inc. (35914) 10,500

Kingston
Golden Words—Queen's University Engineering
  Society (35936) ....(Paid) ‡20
                    (Free) ‡9,000
Nomad—St. Lawrence
  College (35940) ....(Free) 2,000
Queen's Alumni Review—Queen's
  University (35944) ....(Paid) ‡100
               (Controlled) ‡89,000
Queen's Journal—Queen's
  Journal (35945) ....‡10,000

London
The Gazette—University of Western
  Ontario (35981) ....(Free) ‡16,000

Mississauga
medium II—Medium II Board of
  Publishers (36078) ....(Free) ‡5,000

Nepean
Algonquin Times—Algonquin
  College (36099) ....(Free) 5,000

North York
York Gazette—York University (36133)

Oshawa
The Chronicle—Durham
  College (36180) ....(Free) ‡3,000

Ottawa
The Charlatan—Charlatan Publications,
  Inc. (36234) ....(Free) ‡10,000
The Fulcrum—Student Federation of the University of
  Ottawa (36245) 10,000
La Rotonde—University of Ottawa Students'
  Federation (36256) ....‡8,000

Peterborough
Arthur—Trent University (36313) ....(Free) ‡3,000

Circulation: ★ = ABC; △ = BPA; ◆ = CAC; ● = CCAB; ❑ = VAC; ⊕ = PO Statement; ‡ = Publisher's Report; Boldface figures = sworn; Light figures = estimated.

2775

Circ.

Circ.

Circ.

ONTARIO, CANADA (continued)
St. Catharines
The Brock Press—Brock
University **(36350)** ....(Free) 5,000

Scarborough
The Underground—Scarborough College Student
Press **(36386)** ....(Free) 8,000

Sudbury
Lambda—Lambda
Publications **(36417)** ....(Free) 3,300

Thunder Bay
Argus—Lakehead University Student
Union **(36437)** 4,000

Toronto
Profiles—York
University **(36718)** ....(Non-paid) **123,850**
The Ryersoniam—Ryerson
University **(36733)** 4,000
The Varsity—Varsity
Publications **(36785)** ....(Free) ‡25,000

Waterloo
The Cord—Wilfrid Laurier University Student
Publications **(36849)** ....(Free) ‡6,000
Imprint—Imprint
Publications **(36852)** ....(Free) 11,000
(Paid) 50

Willowdale
The Impact—Seneca College Student
Federation **(36878)** ....(Free) 5,000

Windsor
View—University of Windsor **(36890)** ....⊕**60,000**

PRINCE EDWARD ISLAND, CANADA
Charlottetown
Panther Prints—University of Prince Edward Island
Student Union, Inc. **(36917)** ....(Free) 2,500

QUEBEC, CANADA
Hull
L'Uniscope—Universite du Quebec a
Hull **(37003)** ....(Non-paid) ‡600
L'Uquoi—Universite du Quebec a
Hull **(37004)** ....(Free) 2,000

La Salle
La Protesta—Cegep Andre Laurendeau **(37021)**

Lennoxville
The Campus—Eastern Townships Research
Centre **(37046)** 2,250

Montreal
La Republique—Cegep
Vieux-Montreal **(37151)** ....(Free) 3,500
Le Graffiti—College
Jean-de-Brebeuf **(37161)** ....(Free) 1,500
Le Misanthrope—Cegep
d'Ahuntsic **(37171)** ....(Free) 3,000
Le Trait d'Union—Cegep de
Maisonneuve **(37173)** ....(Non-paid) 2,800
Les Diplomes—Les Diplomes de l'Universite de
Montreal **(37177)** ....(Controlled) 160,000
The Link—Link Publications Society
Inc. **(37179)** ....(Free) 10,000
The McGill Daily—Daily Publication Society/Le Delit
Francais **(37182)** ....(Free) 11,000
McGill News—The McGill Alumni
Association **(37184)** ....(Controlled) ‡65,000
Nouveau Quartier Libre—Cegep de
Rosemont **(37196)**
The Paper Cut—Marianopolis
College **(37203)** ....(Free) 1,000

Quebec
Au Fil des Evenements—Universite
Laval **(37281)** ....(Free) 15,000
Laval Theologique et Philosophique—Universite
Laval **(37286)**

Rouyn-Noranda
Le Declin—Cegep de
l'Abitibi-Temiscamingue **(37322)**.(Controlled)‡900

Ste.-Foy
Anthropologie et Societes—Universite Laval **(37335)**
IMPACT CAMPUS—Universite
Laval **(37337)** ....(Free) 15,000

Saint-Hyacinthe
Assetu—Cegep de
Saint-Hyacinthe **(37347)** ....(Free) 2,000

Saint-Lambert
The Champlain Edge—Champlain Regional College
Student Association **(37358)** ....(Free) 2,500

Sherbrooke
Le Collectif—Universite de
Sherbrooke **(37394)** ....(Free) ‡5,000

Victoriaville
La Replique—Cegep de
Victoriaville **(37432)** ....(Non-paid) 500

Westmount
The Dawson Research Journal of Experimental
Science (DRJES)—DRJES **(37442)**

SASKATCHEWAN, CANADA
Regina
The Carillon—University of Regina Students'
Union **(37526)** ....(Free) ‡5,000

Saskatoon
The Green and White—University of Saskatchewan
Alumni Association **(37551)** .....(Controlled) 80,000
The Sheaf—Sheaf Publishing
Society **(37557)** ....(Free) ‡10,000

Fraternal Publications

Index entries are grouped beneath subheadings for fraternal organizations (please refer to the Index to Subject Terms). Within this broad subject arrangement, entries appear geographically by states/provinces and alphabetically within cities. Citations in this index include the publication title, entry number (given in parentheses), and circulation figures.

Circ.

Circ.

Circ.

EAGLES

OHIO
Grove City
Eagle Magazine **(25231)** ....(Paid) 68,100

ELKS, BENEVOLENT AND PROTECTIVE ORDER OF

ILLINOIS
Chicago
The Elks Magazine **(8366)** ....(Paid) 1,126,090

KNIGHTS OF COLUMBUS

CONNECTICUT
New Haven
Columbia **(4985)** ....‡1,600,000

MASONS

DISTRICT OF COLUMBIA
Washington
The Scottish Rite Journal (Southern Jurisdiction,
    USA) **(5783)** ....(Non-paid) ‡400,000

KANSAS
Fort Leavenworth
Phylaxis Magazine **(11441)** 3,000

MASSACHUSETTS
Lexington
The Northern Light **(14272)** ....(Paid) ‡720
                                    (Non-paid) ‡278,000

MISSOURI
St. Joseph
Moila Temple Bulletin **(17393)** ....‡4,500

MONTANA
Lakeside
The Montana Masonic News **(17844)**

NEW YORK
Lockport
Empire State Mason **(20956)** ....(Paid) ‡94,000
                                    (Non-paid) ‡3,394

NORTH CAROLINA
Washington
The North Carolina
    Mason **(24272)** ....(Free) ‡67,023

OKLAHOMA
Guthrie
The Oklahoma Mason **(25854)** ....‡39,000

VIRGINIA
Alexandria
The Sojourner **(31738)** ....(Paid) ‡9,500
                                    (Non-paid) ‡200

MODERN WOODMEN OF AMERICA

ILLINOIS
Rock Island
The Modern Woodmen
    Magazine **(9518)** ....‡400,000

MOOSE INTERNATIONAL

ILLINOIS
Mooseheart
Moose Magazine **(9224)** ....(Controlled) ‡950,000

ODD FELLOWS, INDEPENDENT ORDER OF

CALIFORNIA
Linden
California Odd Fellow and
    Rebekah **(2154)** ....‡8,125

ROTARIANS, INTERNATIONAL FELLOWSHIP OF

CONNECTICUT
Brookfield
ROTA.GENE **(4729)** ....(Paid) ‡300
                                    (Non-paid) ·‡150

ROYAL NEIGHBORS OF AMERICA

ILLINOIS
Rock Island
The Royal Neighbor **(9520)** ....‡190,000

UNCLASSIFIED FRATERNAL

DISTRICT OF COLUMBIA
Washington
Daughters of the American Revolution
    Magazine **(5459)** ....‡40,000

FLORIDA
Dunedin
The Scottish Banner **(6062)** ....‡62,708

GEORGIA
Macon
The Pilot Log **(7386)** ....(Controlled) ‡15,000

ILLINOIS
Addison
The League-Sandara **(8001)** ....(Paid) ‡1,000

Chicago
Prosveta **(8542)** ....‡21,000

Evanston
The Magazine of Sigma Chi **(8866)** ....‡55,000

Oak Brook
CSA Journal **(9347)**
Lion En Espanol **(9356)**
The Lion Magazine **(9357)** ....(Paid) 503,016

INDIANA
Indianapolis
Kiwanis Magazine **(10145)** ....(Paid) 258,674
The Lion of Alpha Epsilon Pi **(10149)** 30,000

IOWA
Cedar Rapids
Fraternal Herald **(10673)** ....(Non-paid) ‡24,400

KENTUCKY
Lexington
The Phi Gamma Delta **(12175)** ....‡90,000

MICHIGAN
Midland
Phi Rho Sigma
    Journal **(15356)** ....(Non-paid) 12,500

Port Huron
Woman's Life **(15452)** ....(Non-paid) 32,000

MINNESOTA
Minneapolis
The Sons of Norway
    Viking **(16128)** ....(Combined) ‡56,000

MISSOURI
Kansas City
Sickle & Sheaf **(17196)** ....‡40,000

NEW HAMPSHIRE
Manchester
Le Canado-Americain **(18557)** ....(Paid) ‡36,000
                                    (Controlled) ‡1,333

NEW JERSEY
East Orange
Sokol Times **(18783)** 5,000

Passaic
Slovak Catholic Falcon **(19416)** ....(Paid) ‡10,494
                                    (Non-paid) ‡200

NEW YORK
New York
Ararat **(21240)** ....‡1,800
Hadassah Magazine **(21785)** ....(Paid) 272,131
Hoosharar Mioutune **(21817)** ....‡7,500
Nashe Zhyttia (Our Life) **(22394)** ......(Paid) ‡3,000
                                    (Non-paid) ‡50

NORTH CAROLINA
Charlotte
Star & Lamp **(23755)** ....‡60,000

OHIO
Columbus
The Sample Case **(25060)** ....(Paid) 145,000

Elyria
The Paper Book **(25179)** ....(Combined) 12,500

Oxford
Scroll of Phi Delta Theta **(25460)**

Circulation: ★ = ABC; △ = BPA; ♦ = CAC; • = CCAB; ❑ = VAC; ⊕ = PO Statement; ‡ = Publisher's Report; Boldface figures = sworn; Light figures = estimated.

2777

Circ.

Circ.

Circ.

UNCLASSIFIED FRATERNAL (continued)

Toledo
Exchange Today **(25567)** ....(Paid) ‡30,000
(Controlled) ‡750

PENNSYLVANIA
Berwyn
The Mutual Magazine **(26697)** ....‡8,500

Erie
Fraternal Leader **(26898)** ....(Non-paid) 23,000

Imperial
Voice of Youth **(27070)** ....‡4,000

Middletown
Jednota (Union) **(27253)** ....(Paid) ‡535
(Free) ‡35,105

Philadelphia
Sons of Italy Times **(27689)** ....‡15,500

Pittsburgh
American Srbobran **(27757)** ....‡12,000
Junior Magazine **(27806)** ....(Non-paid) 15,000
Sokol Polski (Polish
Falcon) **(27844)** ....(Free) ‡15,000
Zajednicar **(27856)** ....(Non-paid) 40,000

RHODE ISLAND
Woonsocket
L'Union **(28461)** ....(Non-paid) ‡25,000

TENNESSEE
Brentwood
To Dragma **(29064)**

Memphis
Shield & Diamond **(29380)** ....‡90,000

TEXAS
Arlington
The Trident of Delta Delta
Delta **(29737)** ....‡129,000

VIRGINIA
Charlottesville
The Caduceus **(31920)** 122,000

Richmond
Sigma Phi Epsilon
Journal **(32454)** ....(Controlled) 150,500

WISCONSIN
Milwaukee
Catholic Knight
Magazine **(34062)** ....(Controlled) ‡60,000
The Family Friend **(34068)** ....(Non-paid) 33,000
The SAR Magazine **(34100)** ....‡26,000

NOVA SCOTIA, CANADA
Dartmouth
The Torch **(35551)** ....(Non-paid) 30,000

ONTARIO, CANADA
Toronto
Zwiazkowiec (Alliancer) **(36798)** ....(Fri.) **11,000**

Willowdale
The Sentinel **(36884)** ....(Paid) ‡2,229

WOODMEN OF THE WORLD

NEBRASKA
Omaha
WOODMEN Magazine **(18209)** ....‡485,000

Religious Publications

Index entries are arranged geographically, first by states/provinces and then by cities. Within cities in this index, citations appear alphabetically by publication title. Citations include publication title, entry number (given in parentheses immediately following the title), and circulation figures.

Circ.

ALABAMA
Birmingham
The Apostle (54) ....(Non-paid) ‡13,000
Dimension (68) ....(Paid) 25,000
Pure Heart Magazine (88)
The Voice (99) ....(Paid) 4,000

Huntsville
The Cumberland Flag (268) ....(Paid) ‡600
(Non-paid) ‡25

Mobile
The Catholic Week (316) ....(Paid) 16,797
(Non-paid) 400

Christian Conquest
Magazine (317) ....(Non-paid) ‡10,000

ALASKA
Juneau
Inside Passage (595) ....(Paid) 2,267

ARIZONA
Mesa
New Thought (745) ....‡3,000

Phoenix
The Catholic Sun (799) ....(Paid) 108,579

Tucson
The Carmelite Review (938) ....(Paid) ‡3,700
(Controlled) ‡25
Catholic Vision (939)
Good News Magazine (947) ......(Controlled) 29,500
Spirit & Life (964) ....‡10,000

ARKANSAS
Jonesboro
U.S. Gospel News (1198) ....(Paid) 60,000
(Non-paid) 25,000

Little Rock
Arkansas Catholic (1214) ....‡7,000
The Baptist Challenge (1224) ....(Free) ‡6,000
Baptist Trumpet (1225) ....‡12,700

CALIFORNIA
Azusa
Journal of Psychology and
Christianity (1446) ....(Paid) ‡2,300
(Non-paid) ‡200

Ben Lomond
AGAIN Magazine (1486) ....(Paid) 5,000
(Free) 50

Berkeley
Gesar (1524) ....‡3,000
New Oxford Review (1545) ....‡14,635

Downey
The Sabbath Watchman (1836) ....‡750

El Cajon
Youthworker (1850)

Fresno
The California Southern Baptist (1946) ....‡10,000
The Central California Catholic
Life (1947) ....(Non-paid) 20,000

La Mirada
Journal of Psychology and
Theology (2126) ....‡1,350

Los Angeles
Ancient Wisdom for Modern
Living (2210) ....(Free) 20,000
The Episcopal News (2265) ....‡30,000
Foursquare World
Advance (2274) ....(Controlled) ‡95,000
Science of Mind (2384) ....(Paid) ‡45,000
(Controlled) ‡32,495
Self-Realization (2386) 25,000
The Tidings (2413) ....‡40,547
Verelk (2429)

Monterey
The Observer (2584) ....‡16,500

Mount Shasta
The Journal of the Order of Buddhist
Contemplatives (2604) ....(Paid) 375
(Non-paid) 175

Oakland
The Catholic Voice (2675) ....(Paid) 82,500
(Free) 500
NATA Journal (2688)
Ruah (2698) ....(Combined) 300

Oceanside
Rays from the Rose
Cross (2709) ....(Combined) ‡650

Orange
Diocese of Orange Bulletin (2722) .....(Free) 47,100

Pasadena
Global Prayer Digest (2817)
Mission Frontiers (2821) ....‡80,000
The Plain Truth (2825) ....(Paid) 75,000

Pearblossom
Silver Wings Mayflower Pulpit (2833) ......(Paid) 250

Platina
The Orthodox Word (2850) ....(Paid) ‡2,790
(Controlled) ‡400

Point Arena
SageWoman Magazine (2858) ....(Paid) ‡20,000
(Non-paid) ‡100

Quartz Hill
Quartz Hill Journal of Theology (2868) 200

Sacramento
Catholic Herald (2991) ....(Paid) 23,500
El Heraldo Catolico (2997) ....(Paid) ‡20,000
Missionary (3009)
The Way of St. Francis (3021) ....(Controlled) 5,000

San Anselmo
Common Ground (3082) ....(Paid) ‡2,000
(Non-paid) ‡103,000

San Diego
Journal of Druze Studies (3188)
The Southern Cross (3277) ....‡36,000

San Jose
Ministry & Liturgy (3527) ....(Paid) 20,000
(Non-paid) 10,000

Santa Clara
The Valley Catholic
Newspaper (3676) ....(Paid) 27,500
(Free) 840

Santa Clarita
Unsearchable Riches (3680) ....‡2,000

Santa Monica
World Tribune (3720) ....(Paid) 29,000

Santa Rosa
Forum (3727) ....(Paid) 805.
The Fourth R (3728) ....(Paid) 1,500

Vallecito
Chalcedon Report (3983) ....(Non-paid) ‡6,000

Westlake Village
Pacific Union Recorder (4072) ....(Non-paid) ‡59,000

Whittier
Journal of the American Academy of
Religion (4077) 10,500

Willits
The Red Wood Crozier (4082) ....(Paid) 12,000
(Free) 11,000

COLORADO
Centennial
Rocky Mountain Baptist (4227) ....‡6,000

Colorado Springs
Breakaway Magazine (4237) ....(Paid) 90,000
CBA Marketplace (4239) ....(Paid) ‡8,514
(Non-paid) ‡567

Christian Camp & Conference
Journal (4240) ....‡8,500
Clubhouse Jr. (4241) ....(Controlled) 88,000
Discipleship Journal (4245) ....(Paid) ‡126,820
(Non-paid) ‡4,959

Focus on the Family
Clubhouse (4246) ....(Paid) 115,000
Focus on the Family
Magazine (4247) ....(Free) 2,200,000
Physician Magazine (4254) ....‡71,000

Crestone
Desert Call (4300) ....(Paid) 3,000
(Non-paid) 200

Denver
Bible Advocate (4307) ....(Controlled) ‡12,200
Colorado Episcopalian (4314) .....(Non-paid) ‡15,500

Golden
New Catholic Review (4472) ....(Paid) ‡620
(Non-paid) ‡72

Loveland
Children's Ministry Magazine (4566) ....(Paid) 55,000
(Non-paid) 5,000
Group Magazine (4567) ....‡55,000

CONNECTICUT
Bloomfield
The Catholic Transcript (4701) ....(Paid) ⊕67,000
(Non-paid) ⊕456

Bridgeport
Fairfield County Catholic (4714) ....‡90,000

Circulation: ★ = ABC; △ = BPA; ♦ = CAC; ● = CCAB; ❑ = VAC; ⊕ = PO Statement; ‡ = Publisher's Report; Boldface figures = sworn; Light figures = estimated.

2779

Circ.

Circ.

Circ.

CONNECTICUT (continued)
Hartford
Human Development **(4894)** ....(Paid) ‡10,000
(Non-paid) ‡300
The Muslim World **(4899)** ....‡1,000

Mystic
Religion Teacher's Journal **(4970)** ......(Paid) 36,000
Today's Parish **(4971)** ....‡12,000

New Haven
International Bulletin of Missionary
Research **(4992)** ....(Paid) 6,000
(Non-paid) 300

Ridgefield
Latin Mass Magazine **(5097)** ....(Paid) 13,000
(Non-paid) 1,500

Stamford
The Sower **(5160)** ....(Paid) ‡8,220
(Non-paid) ‡140

DELAWARE
Wilmington
The Dialog **(5293)** ....‡52,300

DISTRICT OF COLUMBIA
Washington
The Catholic Biblical
Quarterly **(5399)** ....(Paid) ‡4,200
(Non-paid) ‡56
The Catholic Historical
Review **(5400)** ....(Paid) ‡1,926
(Non-paid) ‡166
Catholic Woman **(5402)** 10,500
Christian Social Action **(5412)** ....(Paid) ‡2,000
(Non-paid) ‡1,000
Church & State **(5415)** ....(Paid) ‡33,000
(Controlled) ‡2,600
Communio-International Catholic
Review **(5427)** ....(Paid) ‡2,500
(Non-paid) ‡150
Conscience **(5435)** ....(Combined) 10,000
Crisis Magazine **(5449)** ....(Paid) 20,000
(Non-paid) 3,000
El Pregonero **(5475)** ....(Non-paid) 27,154
Kerem **(5624)**
Liturgy **(5638)** 1,800
The Living Light **(5639)** ....(Paid) 1,200
Momentum **(5659)** ....(Paid) ‡24,500
ReVision **(5768)** ....(Paid) ‡900
Share the Word **(5791)** ....(Paid) ‡17,500
Sojourners **(5799)** ....(Paid) ‡24,000
(Non-paid) 3,000
Spiritual Life **(5802)** 12,000
The Thomist **(5822)** ....(Paid) 1000
(Controlled) 50

FLORIDA
Alachua
Hare Krishna World **(5898)** ....(Paid) ⊕8,000

Cape Coral
The Founders Journal **(5972)** ....(Paid) 1,000

Gainesville
The Human Quest **(6144)** ....‡2,200

Jacksonville
Florida Baptist Witness **(6210)** ....(Paid) ‡42,000
(Free) ‡1,500

Kissimmee
The Champion **(6260)** ....(Paid) ‡3,000
(Free) ‡2,000

Lake Mary
Charisma **(6274)** ....(Paid) 220,000
(Non-paid) 2,000
Charisma & Christian Life **(6275)**
Christian Retailing **(6276)** ....(Controlled) ‡10,500
Inspirational Giftware **(6277)**
Ministries Today **(6278)**
New Man **(6279)**
SpiritLed Woman **(6280)**
Vida Cristiana **(6281)**

Miami
The Florida Catholic **(6352)** ....(Paid) 144,250

Orlando
The Florida Catholic **(6490)** ....⊕142,000
Tabletalk **(6509)** ....(Paid) ⊕50,000
(Non-paid) ⊕10,000
Worldwide Challenge **(6511)** 95,000

Sanford
Brown Gold Magazine **(6646)** ....(Paid) 38,582
(Controlled) 12,344

GEORGIA
Americus
Habitat World **(6921)** ....(Free) 1,050,000

Atlanta
The Christian Index **(6983)** ....(Paid) 62,000
(Non-paid) 2,000
The Georgia Bulletin **(7011)** 77,000
Journal of Biblical Literature **(7020)**

Carrollton
Christianity and Literature **(7156)** ....(Paid) 1,100

Stone Mountain
Wesleyan Christian Advocate **(7572)** ....‡21,000

HAWAII
Honolulu
Hawaii Catholic Herald **(7692)** ....(Paid) ‡7,000
(Non-paid) ‡500

IDAHO
Boise
Idaho Catholic Register **(7810)** ....‡16,000

Nampa
Signs of the Times **(7931)** ....‡200,000

ILLINOIS
Arlington Heights
The Standard **(8026)** ....(Paid) 8,000
(Non-paid) 1,000

Bloomington
The Historical Messenger **(8078)** ....(Paid) ‡290
(Non-paid) ‡140

Carbondale
Sacred Dance Guild Journal **(8120)**

Carol Stream
Books & Culture **(8134)** ....(Paid) 14,743
(Non-paid) 6,009
Campus Life **(8135)** ....(Combined) 96,657
Christian History Magazine **(8138)** ....‡50,000
Christian Parenting Today **(8139)** .....(Paid) ‡87,194
(Non-paid) ‡23,889
Christian Reader **(8140)** ....(Paid) 171,990
(Non-paid) 3,659
Christianity Today **(8141)** ....(Paid) ‡149,125
(Non-paid) 1,572
(Non-paid) 2,502
Leadership **(8147)** ....(Combined) 73,000
Marriage Partnership **(8148)** ....(Paid) 59,000
(Non-paid) 27,000
Men of Integrity **(8149)** ....(Paid) 86,979
Virtue **(8156)** ....(Paid) ‡100,000
(Non-paid) ‡10,000
Your Church **(8158)** ....(Controlled) 150,000

Chicago
Anglican Advance **(8263)** 17,500
Catechumenate: A Journal of Christian
Initiation **(8300)** ....(Paid) 4,100
(Non-paid) 175
The Catholic New World **(8301)** ....‡75,000
Chicago Studies **(8325)** ....(Paid) 3,000
The Christian Century **(8332)** ....‡30,000
Company **(8338)** ....(Controlled) ‡100,000
Cornerstone **(8344)** ....(Controlled) ‡35,000
The Covenant Companion **(8345)** ......(Paid) 17,000
(Non-paid) 500
Extension **(8372)** ....(Controlled) ‡95,000
The Friend **(8381)** ....‡6,200
Hlas Naroda (Voice of the Nation) **(8398)**
Horizon **(8400)** ....(Paid) 2,200
(Controlled) 72
The Lutheran **(8473)** ....‡640,000
Lutheran Partners **(8474)** ....(Paid) 70
(Controlled) 20,000
Moody Magazine **(8494)** ....‡98,000
Narod Polish **(8499)** ....(Non-paid) ‡25,000
The New Star **(8507)** ....(Paid) 36,129
(Controlled) 2,035
RITE **(8557)** ....(Paid) ‡4,800
(Non-paid) ‡2,000
U.S. Catholic **(8591)** 40,000
Waifs' Messenger **(8601)** 190,000

Downers Grove
Matrimony **(8790)**

Elgin
Messenger **(8825)** ....‡19,500

Evanston
Builder Magazine, Uniform Series
Edition **(8854)** 6,500

Hazel Crest
Muslim Journal **(8980)** ....‡16,000

Joliet
Glasilo KSKJ (Americanski Slovenec) **(9033)**

Mount Morris
National Catholic Register **(9242)** ....(Paid) 15,000
(Free) 453

Peoria
Catholic Post **(9416)** 28,900

River Forest
Lutheran Education Journal **(9492)** ....‡4,200

Rockford
The Observer **(9528)** ....(Paid) ‡38,000
(Non-paid) ‡309

Romeoville
Catholic Explorer **(9552)** ....‡22,500

Schiller Park
AIM Liturgy Resources **(9594)** .....(Paid) 20,000
Living The Word **(9595)** ....‡22,000

South Holland
Parish Liturgy **(9616)** ....(Paid) 1,600
(Non-paid) 200

Techny
Divine Word Missionaries **(9681)** ......(Free) 210,000

Wheaton
Evangelical Missions Quarterly
(EMQ) **(9755)** ....‡6,500
Journal of Religious Gerontology **(9757)** 691
Today's Christian Woman **(9759)** ......(Paid) ‡256,000
(Non-paid) ‡6,892

Wilmette
World Order **(9764)** ....‡1,500

INDIANA
Chesterton
Guideposts for Kids **(9887)**

Evansville
The Message **(9935)** ....(Controlled) ‡7,200

Fort Wayne
Concordia Theological
Quarterly **(9966)** ....(Paid) 400
(Non-paid) 9,000
The Family Digest **(9967)** ....(Non-paid) ‡150,000
Today's Catholic **(9973)** ....‡16,500

Goshen
The Mennonite **(10025)** ....‡15,000
The Mennonite Quarterly
Review **(10026)** ....(Paid) ‡820
(Controlled) ‡180

Hobart
Our Hope **(10064)** ....(Paid) ‡50
(Free) ‡3,500

Huntington
The Catholic Answer **(10067)** ....(Paid) 43,863
(Non-paid) 923
Catholic Parent **(10068)** ....(Paid) 20,000
My Daily Visitor **(10070)** ....‡29,277
New Covenant **(10071)** ....‡25,000
Our Sunday Visitor **(10072)** 85,000
The Pope Speaks **(10073)** ....(Combined) 4,500
The Priest **(10074)** 7,200
U.S. Catholic Historian **(10075)**

Indianapolis
The Criterion **(10106)** ....(Combined) 72,500
Encounter **(10110)** ....(Paid) ‡568
(Non-paid) ‡58
Light and Life **(10147)** ....(Paid) ‡20,000
(Controlled) ‡200
The Link **(10148)** ....(Non-paid) 10,000
The Wesleyan Advocate **(10182)** ......(Paid) ‡18,000
(Controlled) ‡500

Lafayette
The Catholic Moment **(10250)** ....‡28,309

Merrillville
Northwest Indiana
Catholic **(10298)** ....(Paid) ‡19,750

Richmond
Quaker Life **(10421)** 7,000

South Bend
Culture Wars **(10454)** ....(Paid) ‡10,000

Valparaiso
The Cresset **(10508)** ....‡4,700
CSSR Bulletin **(10509)** ....‡6,500
Religious Studies Review **(10510)** ....‡3,500

IOWA
Council Bluffs
Daily Devotions for the
   Deaf **(10725)** ....(Non-paid) 20,000

Davenport
The Catholic Messenger **(10735)** ....(Paid) 19,962
(Free) 33

Des Moines
The Catholic Mirror **(10773)** ....‡31,000
The Christian News **(10775)** ....‡18,000

Dubuque
The Witness **(10846)** ....(Paid) ‡18,880
(Free) 100

Sioux Center
PRO REGE **(11206)** ....(Non-paid) ‡3,100

KANSAS
Kansas City
The Leaven **(11529)** ....(Paid) ‡47,453
(Non-paid) ‡384
Perspectives in Religious Studies **(11530)** ....‡550

Newton
Mennonite Weekly Review **(11668)** ....(Paid) ‡10,200
(Free) ‡840
With **(11671)** 6,000

Salina
Northwestern Kansas
   Register **(11783)** ....(Paid) 7,800
(Non-paid) 50

Wichita
The Catholic Advance **(11881)** ....‡27,882

KENTUCKY
Hagerhill
The Mountain Spirit **(12102)** ....(Paid) 24,000

Lexington
Lexington Theological
   Quarterly **(12174)** ....(Non-paid) 2,300

Louisville
Church & Society **(12212)** ....(Paid) 5,000
Horizons **(12219)** ....(Paid) 28,000
(Non-paid) 1,000
Monday Morning **(12231)** 10,500
Presbyterians Today **(12235)** ....‡80,000
Review and Expositor **(12236)** ....(Paid) ‡2,400
Southern Seminary
   Magazine **(12237)** ....(Controlled) 33,000

Madisonville
America's Christian Newspaper **(12270)**

Middletown
Western Recorder **(12297)** ....(Paid) 48,500
(Free) 1,120

New Hope
Fatima Family Messenger **(12323)**

Wilmore
Buddhist-Christian Studies **(12450)** ....(Paid) 700
(Controlled) 60
Faith and Philosophy **(12451)** ....(Paid) 1,800
Good News **(12452)** 40,000
Missiology **(12453)** ....‡2,000

LOUISIANA
Alexandria
Louisiana Baptist Message
   (LBM) **(12459)** ....(Paid) 45,000

Baton Rouge
The Catholic Commentator **(12486)** ....‡50,000
The Evangelist **(12488)**

Lake Charles
The Southwest Catholic **(12644)** ....(Paid) 3,000
(Non-paid) 1,000

Minden
North Louisiana Good News **(12688)**

New Orleans
Clarion Herald **(12727)** ....(Paid) ‡75,000

Schriever
The Bayou Catholic **(12815)** ....(Paid) ‡33,000
(Free) ‡0

MAINE
Augusta
The Christian Civic League
   Record **(12890)** ....(Paid) ‡2,500
(Non-paid) ‡500

Portland
Church World **(13008)** ....‡6,271
The Northeast **(13014)** ....‡10,000

Rockport
The Witness **(13047)** ....(Paid) ‡3,000
(Non-paid) ‡500

MARYLAND
Baltimore
The Catholic Review **(13144)** ....‡68,000
The Josephite Harvest **(13176)** ....(Paid) 15,000
(Free) 70,000
The Mission Helper **(13219)** ....(Controlled) 9,500
Serenity **(13245)** ....(Free) 67,000

Columbia
BaptistLIFE **(13454)** 21,000
Columbia Union
   Visitor **(13459)** ....(Controlled) ‡40,000

Hagerstown
Message **(13567)** ....(Paid) ‡78,273
(Non-paid) ‡56
Vibrant Life **(13570)** ....‡35,000

Hyattsville
Catholic Standard **(13586)** ....‡51,000

Ijamsville
The Word Among Us **(13589)** ....(Paid) 200,000

Landover Hills
Vision **(13596)** 1,000

Riverdale
National Apostolate for Inclusion Ministry
   Quarterly **(13673)** ....(Paid) 500

Silver Spring
Adventist Review **(13722)** ....‡47,000
The Journal of Adventist
   Education **(13729)** ....(Paid) ‡7,500
(Non-paid) ‡250
Liberty **(13736)**
Ministry **(13739)** ....(Paid) ‡20,000
(Controlled) ‡50,000

MASSACHUSETTS
Arlington
Exponent II **(13818)** 4,000

Assonet
Comments from the Friends **(13823)**

Boston
The Christian Science Journal **(13874)**
Christian Science Quarterly-Weekly Bible
   Lessons **(13876)**
Christian Science
   Sentinel **(13877)** ....(Paid) ⊕50,000
Congregational Library Bulletin **(13881)** ....(Paid) 925
The Episcopal Times **(13889)** ....(Free) ‡40,000
The Herald of Christian Science **(13900)**
My Friend **(13930)** ....‡11,500
The Pilot **(13949)** 31,000
UU World **(13969)** ....(Controlled) ‡120,000
(Paid) ‡1,000

Brookline
Greek Orthodox Theological Review **(14019)** ....‡800

Cambridge
Harvard Theological Review **(14067)** 1,500

Fall River
The Anchor **(14180)** ....‡29,890

Holyoke
Tracings **(14241)** ....(Free) ‡3,250

Ipswich
Perspectives on Science and Christian
   Faith **(14257)** ....‡2,500

Lenox
What Is Enlightenment? **(14270)** ....(Paid) 40,000

Pittsfield
Catholic Library World **(14470)** ....‡1,200

South Hamilton
Journal of the Evangelical Homiletics
   Society **(14544)** ....(Paid) 800

Springfield
The Catholic Observer **(14550)** 12,000

Stockbridge
Marian Helper **(14567)** ....(Controlled) 650,000
Roze Maryi **(14568)** ....(Paid) ‡6,000
(Controlled) ‡1,500

Stow
Religious Conference Manager **(14575)**

Tewksbury
The Oblate World and Voice of Hope **(14586)**

Weston
Healing Ministry **(14650)** 1,100

Worcester
The Catholic Free Press **(14676)** ....‡24,500

MICHIGAN
Adrian
Michigan Christian Advocate **(14709)** ....‡8,500

Berrien Springs
Lake Union Herald **(14813)** ....(Paid) 29,000

Dearborn
Leaves **(14904)** ....(Free) 75,000

Detroit
The Michigan Catholic **(14937)** ....‡35,000
PIME World **(14943)** 12,000

Flushing
The Catholic Times **(15049)** ....(Paid) 6,125
(Non-paid) 157

Grand Rapids
The Banner **(15089)** ....(Paid) ‡30,000
(Controlled) ‡255
Christian Home & School **(15091)** ......(Paid) ‡1,000
(Controlled) ‡69,000
Our Daily Bread **(15099)** ......(Non-paid) ⊕1,600,000

Grandville
Voice **(15130)** ....(Paid) ‡7,000
(Non-paid) ‡3,000

Marquette
The UP Catholic **(15339)** ....(Paid) 25,000

Monroe
IHM Connections **(15362)** ....(Paid) 1,250

Riverview
Journal of Biblical Studies **(15465)**

Saginaw
The Catholic Weekly **(15489)** ....(Paid) ⊕11,464
(Free) ⊕583

Troy
Detroit Lutheran **(15619)** ....(Paid) ‡8,600
(Free) ‡45

MINNESOTA
Bloomington
The Hymn **(15758)** ....(Paid) ⊕2,847

Collegeville
The Bible Today **(15805)** ....(Paid) 6,900
(Non-paid) 155
Worship **(15806)** 5,000

Crookston
Our Northland Diocese **(15820)** ....‡14,950

Duluth
The Catholic Outlook **(15834)** 31,484

Fergus Falls
Faith and Fellowship **(15896)** ....(Paid) ‡8,500
(Controlled) ‡100

Inver Grove Heights
The Clergy Journal **(15971)** ....(Paid) ‡6,000

Minneapolis
The Bible Friend **(16061)** ....(Paid) 8,000
(Non-paid) 3,000
Decision **(16072)** ....(Paid) 350,000
(Non-paid) 1,300,000
The Evangelical Beacon **(16076)** 37,500
Lutheran Journal **(16094)** ....‡550
(Non-paid) ‡120,000
Lutheran Woman Today **(16095)** ......(Paid) 150,000

Fraternal Publications

Circ.   Circ.   Circ.

MINNESOTA (continued)

Minnesota Christian
  Chronicle **(16101)** ....(Paid) 23,000

New Ulm
Prairie Catholic **(16214)** ....(Combined) ⊕**26,500**

St. Cloud
St. Cloud Visitor **(16346)** ....(Paid) 46,000
                          (Non-paid) 185

St. Paul
Catholic Aid News **(16365)** 40,000
Catholic Digest **(16366)** ....(Paid) 400,000
The Catholic Spirit **(16367)** ....(Paid) 87,000
God's Word Today **(16378)** ....‡55,000
The Wanderer **(16416)** ....‡35,000

White Bear Lake
Christian Magnifier **(16509)** ......(Controlled) 2,200
Tract Messenger **(16513)** ....(Controlled) 475

Winona
The Courier **(16526)** ....‡39,700

MISSISSIPPI
Biloxi
Gulf Pine Catholic **(16562)** ....‡5,100

Jackson
The Baptist Record **(16694)** ....(Paid) ‡108,000
                     (Controlled) ‡500
Mississippi Today **(16709)** 13,500
Mississippi United Methodist
  Advocate **(16710)** 13,000

MISSOURI
Fenton
Healing Words **(17060)** ....‡20,000
Living Faith **(17061)** ....(Paid) 725,000

Independence
Herald **(17111)**
Herald **(17112)** ....‡25,000

Jefferson City
The Catholic Missourian **(17120)** ......(Paid) ‡20,211
Word and Way **(17135)** ....‡23,000

Joplin
The Pentecostal Messenger **(17142)** ....‡6,000

Kansas City
The Angelus **(17154)**
Celebration **(17160)** ....‡11,000
The National Catholic
  Reporter **(17187)** ....(Paid) ‡50,000
                     120,000
Praying **(17194)** ....‡15,000

Liguori
Liguorian **(17253)** 230,000

St. Louis
Adoremus Bulletin **(17404)** ....(Non-paid) 25,000
The American Muslim **(17412)** 2,000
Catholic Health World **(17420)** ....(Paid) ‡300
                   (Non-paid) ‡10,500
The CK of A Journal **(17422)** ....‡8,500
Happy Times **(17442)** ....‡35,000
Jesuit Bulletin **(17449)** ....(Non-paid) 20,000
The Lutheran Layman **(17467)** ....‡135,000
Lutheran Witness **(17468)** ....‡275,000
Portals of Prayer **(17484)** 950,000
Review for Religious **(17487)** ....(Paid) ‡7,000
                    (Non-paid) ‡242
St. Louis Review **(17507)** ....‡90,000
Studies in the Spirituality of
  Jesuits **(17518)** 5,300
Teen Time **(17522)**
Theology Digest **(17524)** ....‡2,300

Springfield
Christian Education Counselor **(17593)** ....‡20,000
Club Connection **(17594)** ....‡12,000
Enrichment Journal **(17597)** ....‡32,000
High Adventure **(17602)** ....‡88,000
The Mirror **(17605)** ....‡17,500
Mountain Movers **(17607)** ....(Non-paid) ‡220,000
Today's Pentecostal
  Evangel **(17614)** ....(Paid) ‡258,000
Woman's Touch **(17618)** ....‡10,000

Unity Village
Daily Word **(17660)** ....‡1,500,000

Warrenton
Evangelizing Today's Child **(17683)** ....‡14,000

MONTANA
Helena
The Montana Catholic **(17820)** ....‡9,200

NEBRASKA
Grand Island
West Nebraska Register **(18027)**

Lincoln
Southern Nebraska Register **(18121)** ....‡21,500

Omaha
The Catholic Voice **(18192)** ....‡69,326
Grace Tidings **(18196)** ....(Non-paid) 24,000

St. Columbans
Columban Mission **(18256)** .....(Controlled) ‡120,000

NEW JERSEY
Camden
Catholic Star Herald **(18713)** ....‡35,000

Clifton
The Beacon **(18751)** ....(Paid) ‡32,761
Christian New Age Quarterly **(18752)**

Convent Station
Sister Miriam Teresa League of Prayer
  Bulletin **(18769)** ....(Paid) ‡3,000

New Brunswick
Journal of Religion, Disability &
  Health **(19334)** ....(Paid) 335

Newark
The Catholic Advocate **(19351)** ......(Paid) ‡122,300
                     (Free) ‡4,800
The Voice **(19367)** ....‡15,200

Passaic
Slovak Catholic Falcon **(19416)** ....(Paid) ‡10,494
                    (Non-paid) ‡200

Princeton
Theology Today **(19474)** ....‡14,000

Ramsey
Homiletic and Pastoral Review **(19490)** ......‡14,500

South Bound Brook
Ukrainian Orthodox Word **(19582)** 8,200

South Orange
Biblical Theology Bulletin **(19583)** 1,600

Trenton
The Monitor **(19659)** ....‡20,000

Union City
The Passionist'
  Compassion **(19691)** ....(Controlled) 7,200

Washington
Hearts Aflame **(19708)** ....‡5,000
Soul Magazine **(19709)** 47,000

West Paterson
Eastern Catholic Life **(19728)** ....(Paid) ‡11,400
                  (Controlled) ‡718

NEW MEXICO
Albuquerque
People of God **(19784)** ....(Non-paid) ‡39,000

Gallup
The Voice of the Southwest **(19858)** ....‡2,500

NEW YORK
Albany
The Evangelist **(19985)** 57,300

Amityville
Moksha Journal **(20050)** ....(Controlled) 200
Our Preaching **(20054)** 5,500

Bay Shore
Queen of All Hearts **(20137)** ....‡2,500

Binghamton
Journal of Religion & Spirituality in Social Work:
  Social Thought **(20196)** ....‡1,000

Bronx
Living City **(20276)** ....(Paid) 7,200

Brooklyn
Awake! **(20298)** ....‡20,682,000
Darbininkas (The Worker) **(20311)** ....‡14,000
Deolog **(20312)**
Der Yid **(20313)** ....(Paid) ‡41,000
                    (Free) ‡2,500

Varpelis (The Little Bell) **(20352)** ....(Paid) ‡1,500
The Watchtower **(20355)** ....‡23,042,000

Buffalo
Church Acts of Western New
  York **(20375)** ....(Free) ‡8,750
Western New York
  Catholic **(20392)** ....(Paid) 70,000

Carmel
Angels on Earth **(20435)** ....(Paid) 647,478

DeWitt
Jewish Observer **(20532)** 4,500

Elmhurst
American Vedantist **(20571)** ....(Paid) 125
                   (Non-paid) 125

Jamaica
The Catholic Lawyer **(20832)** 1,000
The Message **(20838)**

Jordanville
Orthodox Life **(20854)** ....‡1,500
Pravoslavnaya Rus **(20855)** ....‡1,850
Pravoslavnaya Zhizn **(20856)** ....‡1,900

Maryknoll
Maryknoll Magazine **(21023)** ....(Paid) 600,000
Revista Maryknoll **(21024)** 90,000

New Rochelle
Journal of Pastoral Counseling **(21118)**
Salesian **(21122)** 1,500,000

New York
Adult Lessons Quarterly **(21152)** ....(Non-paid) 2,350
American Bible Society
  Record **(21181)** ....(Controlled) ‡250,000
The Anthonian **(21221)** ....(Controlled) 110,000
Catalyst **(21381)** 80,000
Catholic New York **(21382)** ......(Paid) ★**135,415**
Catholic Worker **(21383)** 85,000
Church **(21416)** 8,600
Churchwoman **(21417)** ....(Paid) 3,831
                   (Non-paid) 1,978
CNEWA World **(21434)** ....(Paid) ‡90,000
Commonweal **(21458)** ....‡19,000
Compassion **(21465)**
Cross Currents **(21522)** ....(Paid) ‡4,000
                   (Controlled) ‡400
Discovery Magazine **(21556)** .....(Non-paid) 1,200
Episcopal Life **(21625)** ....(Paid) ‡280,000
The Eternal Flame **(21630)** ....(Non-paid) 3,300
FIRST THINGS **(21701)** ....‡32,000
Guideposts Magazine **(21782)** ......(Paid) 2,590,323
                 (Non-paid) 101,785
John Milton Magazine **(21970)** ......(Non-paid) 3,591
Mission Magazine **(22338)** ......(Non-paid) 1,000,000
New Testament Studies **(22435)** 2400
Orthodox Observer **(22505)** 140,000
RCDA **(22626)** ....(Paid) ‡2,000
                   (Non-paid) ‡500
Religious Studies **(22645)** 1,200
Response **(22650)** 83,500
Seeds of Unfolding **(22721)**
Tricycle **(22866)** ....(Paid) 55,000

Nyack
Fellowship **(23027)** ....(Paid) ‡8,700

Pawling
Positive Thinking **(23086)** ....(Paid) ‡600,000
                 (Non-paid) ‡600,000

Rochester
Catholic Courier **(23215)** ....(Paid) ⊕**44,299**

Roosevelt
The Long Island
  Catholic **(23274)** ....(Paid) ★**111,908**

St. Bonaventure
The Cord **(23287)** ....(Paid) 1,200
                   (Non-paid) 56

Syracuse
The Catholic Sun **(23392)** ....‡32,000

NORTH CAROLINA
Calabash
The Journal of Pastoral Care and
  Counseling **(23681)** ....(Paid) ‡9,000

Charlotte
Advent Christian Witness **(23734)** 5,000
The Catholic News &
  Herald **(23739)** ....(Paid) ⊕**49,000**
The Charlotte World **(23742)** ....(Paid) ‡1,800
                   (Non-paid) ‡8,200

Numbers cited after listings are entry numbers rather than page numbers.

Durham
Church History **(23814)** ....‡3,123

Greensboro
North Carolina Christian
  Advocate **(23931)** ....‡15,577

Lenoir
The Presbyterian
  Layman **(24036)** ....(Free) ‡580,000

Raleigh
Baptist Informer **(24125)** ....(Paid) ‡6,500
                                  (Non-paid) ‡2,000
Biblical Recorder **(24126)** ....‡55,000
The N C Catholic **(24139)** ....(Paid) ‡55,000

Wake Forest
Journal of the Evangelical Theological
  Society **(24261)** 3,000

Yadkinville
Carolina Christian **(24338)** ....‡1,200

NORTH DAKOTA
Bismarck
Dakota Catholic Action **(24350)** ....(Non-paid) 16,800

Fargo
The New Earth **(24412)** 32,000

Richardton
The American Benedictine Review **(24533)** 950

OHIO
Akron
The Orthodox Catholic Voice **(24584)** ....(Paid) ‡323
                                  (Non-paid) ‡52

Canfield
Pastoral Life **(24730)** ....‡1,400

Cedarville
The Christian Librarian **(24745)** ....(Paid) 700
                                  (Non-paid) 100

Cincinnati
Catholic Telegraph **(24780)** ....(Paid) ‡24,100
                                  (Free) ‡400
Christian Standard **(24782)** ....‡53,080
Dia a Dia **(24793)** ....(Paid) 12,000
Forward Day by Day **(24798)** 400,000
Friendly Woman **(24799)** ....(Paid) ‡800
Glenmary Challenge **(24800)** .....(Non-paid) 140,000
The Lookout **(24809)** 100,000
St. Anthony Messenger **(24814)** ....‡330,000
Seek **(24816)** ....‡45,000
Weekly Bible Reader **(24828)** ....‡104,000

Circleville
The Evangelical Advocate **(24851)** .....(Paid) ‡2,000
                                (Non-paid) ‡1,550

Cleveland
Catholic Universe Bulletin **(24867)** ....‡32,485
Emmanuel **(24891)** 4,500

Columbus
The Catholic Times **(25005)**
Ohio Baptist Messenger **(25039)** ....‡30,000

Dayton
Catechist **(25109)** ....(Paid) ‡48,000
                                (Non-paid) ‡536
Good News for Children **(25118)**
Promise **(25124)**
Seeds **(25126)**
Today's Catholic Teacher **(25127)** .....(Paid) ‡48,000
                                (Non-paid) ‡2,000
Venture **(25129)**
Visions **(25130)**

Findlay
The Church Advocate **(25193)** ....‡16,000

Mansfield
The Congregationalist **(25331)** ....(Controlled) 8,000

Mason
The Restoration Herald **(25359)** ....‡6,500

Parma
Horizons **(25466)** ....(Paid) 5,779
                                (Non-paid) 295

Steubenville
The Steubenville Register **(25540)** ....(Paid) ⊕18,490
                                (Free) ⊕120

West Farmington
Presence **(25633)**

Xenia
Athletes in Action **(25685)** ....(Paid) 13,700
                                (Free) 300

Youngstown
Catholic Exponent **(25695)** 38,000

OKLAHOMA
Fairview
The Sabbath Sentinel **(25834)** ....(Paid) ‡650
                                (Non-paid) ‡200

Grove
American Journal of Pastoral
  Counseling **(25846)** 1,000

Oklahoma City
Baptist Messenger **(25954)** ....(Paid) ‡92,000
                                (Non-paid) ‡1,500
The Christian Chronicle **(25961)** 100,000
The Sooner Catholic **(25996)** ....(Paid) 8,108
                                (Free) 23,987

Tulsa
Eastern Oklahoma
  Catholic **(26114)** ....(Combined) 19,000
The Oracle **(26123)** ....‡2,500

OREGON
Newberg
Christian News
  Northwest **(26443)** ....(Non-paid) 30,000

Portland
Catholic Sentinel **(26473)** ....‡16,176
The Oregon Episcopal Church
  News **(26490)** ....(Combined) 10,350
Today's Liturgy **(26511)** ....‡22,500

Vancouver
Gleaner **(26603)** ....‡40,000

Yamhill
Christian Monthly **(26621)** ....‡1,100
                                (Non-paid) ‡500

PENNSYLVANIA
Allentown
The A.D. Times **(26625)** 59,350

Bensalem
Mission **(26695)** ....(Paid) 3,300
                                (Controlled) 1,000

Bethlehem
Moravian **(26704)** ....‡25,000

Bryn Athyn
New Church Life **(26739)** ....(Paid) ‡1,480
                                (Non-paid) ‡130

Chester Springs
Bible Standard and Herald of Christ's
  Kingdom **(26777)** ....(Paid) ‡3,500
Present Truth and Herald of Christ's
  Epiphany **(26778)** ....(Paid) ‡1,100

Coatesville
The Lighthouse Electronic
  Magazine **(26793)** ....(Free) 30,000

Coopersburg
Insights for Preachers **(26806)** ....(Paid) ‡500
                                (Controlled) ‡50

Erie
The Catholic Peace Voice **(26895)** .....(Paid) 15,000
                                (Non-paid) 10,000

Greensburg
The Catholic Accent **(26953)** ....‡54,000

Harrisburg
Orthodox Christian Journal **(27001)** ....‡3,800

Lancaster
Pennsylvania Mennonite
  Heritage **(27145)** ....(Combined) 3,000

Malvern
Men of Malvern **(27214)** ....(Non-paid) 25,000

Mansfield
Christian Motorsports
  Illustrated **(27217)** ....(Paid) 20,000

Middletown
Jednota (Union) **(27253)** ....(Paid) ‡535
                                (Free) ‡35,105

Olyphant
CGA World **(27347)** ....‡200,000

Philadelphia
America **(27369)**
Catholic Standard **(27395)** ....‡62,500
Friends Journal **(27472)** ....‡8,100
Jewish Exponent Inside **(27509)** ......(Paid) ♦38,007
                              (Non-paid) ♦3,206
Journal of Ecumenical Studies **(27525)**
The Journal of Presbyterian History **(27547)** ....‡800
The Miraculous Medal **(27570)** ....(Paid) 215,000
                            (Controlled) 2,000
The Other Side **(27610)** ....‡12,000
The Way **(27718)** ....(Paid) 7,000
World Futures **(27723)**

Pittsburgh
Pittsburgh Catholic **(27831)** ....‡110,470

Scottdale
On the Line **(27954)** ....(Combined) 5,500
Provident Book Finder **(27955)** .....(Controlled) 8,000
Purpose **(27956)** 10,000
Story Friends **(27957)** ....‡6,500

Scranton
Catholic Light **(27958)** ....‡48,000
Polka—Polish Woman **(27961)** ....‡1,352
Rola Boza (God's Field) **(27962)** ....‡7,700

Valley Forge
American Baptist Quarterly **(28089)** ....(Paid) ‡1,030
                                (Non-paid) ‡56
American Baptists in Mission **(28090)** 39,000
The Secret Place **(28091)** ....‡150,000

Vandergrift
Fraternally Yours, Zenska
  Jednota **(28094)** ....(Controlled) ‡30,800

Wallingford
Pendle Hill Pamphlets **(28102)** ....(Paid) ‡1,500
                                (Free) ‡100

PUERTO RICO
San Juan
El Visitante de Puerto Rico **(28293)** ....(Paid) 65,000
                                (Free) 400

RHODE ISLAND
Providence
The Providence Visitor **(28417)** 36,674

Warwick
The Hunted News **(28450)**

Woonsocket
L'Union **(28461)** ....(Non-paid) ‡25,000

SOUTH CAROLINA
Charleston
The Cathholic Miscellany **(28508)** ....‡27,000

Columbia
South Carolina United Methodist
  Advocate **(28567)** ....‡10,000

Greenville
The Baptist Courier **(28621)** ....(Paid) ‡125,000
                              (Non-paid) ‡1,000

SOUTH DAKOTA
Rapid City
West River Catholic **(28935)** ....(Paid) 13,004

Sioux Falls
The Bishop's Bulletin **(28962)** ....‡40,000

TENNESSEE
Antioch
Co-Laborer **(29049)** ....(Paid) ‡8,000
                              (Controlled) ‡1,000

Brentwood
Baptist and Reflector **(29061)** ....‡52,000

Chattanooga
Pulpit Helps **(29092)** ....(Paid) ‡16,000
                              (Free) ‡60,000

Cleveland
Save Our World **(29122)** ....(Free) ‡75,000
White Wing Messenger **(29123)** ....‡9,000

Franklin
Preaching **(29198)** ....‡8,000

Circulation: ★ = ABC; △ = BPA; ♦ = CAC; ● = CCAB; ❑ = VAC; ⊕ = PO Statement; ‡ = Publisher's Report; Boldface figures = sworn; Light figures = estimated.

Circ.   Circ.   Circ.

TENNESSEE (continued)

Memphis
The Cumberland Presbyterian **(29365)** ....‡7,300
The West Tennessee
Catholic **(29384)** ....(Paid) 17,000

Murfreesboro
The Sword of the Lord **(29433)**

Nashville
Circuit Rider **(29450)** ....(Paid) ‡500
      (Non-paid) ‡42,000
Discipliana **(29454)** ....(Paid) ‡5,400
      (Controlled) ‡50
Home Life **(29459)** ....(Paid) ‡500,000
      (Controlled) ‡500
Journal of Christian Education of the African
  Methodist Episcopal
  Church **(29461)** ....(Paid) ‡3,526
      (Free) ‡50
Leader in Christian Education
  Ministries **(29467)** ....(Paid) 3,000
      (Controlled) 1,000
Mature Living **(29469)** ....‡330,000
Mature Years **(29470)** ....‡55,000
National Drama Service **(29474)** ....(Paid) 6,000
Pockets Magazine **(29481)** ....‡96,000
      (Controlled) ‡3,000
SBC Life **(29484)** ....‡70,000
Sunday School Leadership **(29486)**
The Tennessee Register **(29493)** .....(Paid) ‡17,000
      (Free) ‡330
The Upper Room Daily Devotional
  Guide/ **(29497)** 2,750,000
WEAVINGS **(29501)** ....(Paid) 35,000
      (Non-paid) 200

TEXAS
Amarillo
West Texas Catholic **(29699)**

Austin
Anglican & Episcopal History **(29753)** ....‡1,500

Beaumont
East Texas Catholic **(29898)** ....(Paid) 15,000

Brenham
The Brethren Journal **(29950)** ....‡1,500

Burleson
Southwestern Union
  Record **(29989)** ....(Paid) ‡23,000
      (Controlled) ‡400

Carrollton
The Presbyterian **(30005)** ....(Non-paid) ‡118,089

Dallas
The Baptist Standard **(30127)** ....‡120,000
Bibliotheca Sacra **(30132)** ....‡11,500
The Florida United
  Methodist **(30157)** ....(Paid) 1,084
      (Non-paid) 9,100
National Christian Reporter **(30169)** 17,000
The Texas Catholic **(30184)** ....(Paid) ⊕51,000
      (Free) ⊕900
Ultreya Magazine **(30186)** 4,000
United Methodist
  Reporter **(30187)** ....(Paid) ⊕130,000

Fort Worth
Christian Ranchman **(30333)** ....(Free) 39,470
North Texas Catholic **(30348)** ....(Paid) 26,500
      (Non-paid) 700

Houston
The Texas Catholic
  Herald **(30533)** ....(Paid) ‡158,500
      (Controlled) ‡192,500

Irving
American Catholic Philosophical
  Quarterly **(30603)** ....‡1,800

Lubbock
South Plains Catholic **(30718)** ....(Paid) ‡8,500

Pflugerville
HM **(30931)** ....(Combined) ⊕15,000

San Angelo
West Texas Angelus **(31011)** ....(Paid) ‡18,950
      (Non-paid) ‡1,050

San Antonio
Today's Catholic **(31049)** ....‡24,000

Tyler
Catholic East Texas **(31197)** 12,979

Victoria
The Catholic
  Lighthouse **(31234)** ....(Non-paid) 22,000

Waxahachie
Baptist Progress **(31269)** ....(Paid) ‡12,000
      (Non-paid) ‡300

UTAH
Hyrum
Mormon Historical Studies **(31340)** ....(Paid) ‡500
      (Non-paid) ‡15

Salt Lake City
Church News **(31423)** ....(Paid) ‡232,000
The Friend **(31428)** 275,000
Intermountain Catholic **(31430)** ....‡14,000
New Era **(31436)** ....(Combined) ‡230,000

VERMONT
Burlington
The Vermont Catholic
  Tribune **(31520)** ....(Paid) 21,000

VIRGINIA
Alexandria
The Catholic War Veteran **(31653)** ....(Paid) ‡24,000
      (Free) ‡1,000
Counseling and Values **(31662)** ....(Paid) 3,200
The War Cry **(31750)** 25,000

Arlington
Arlington Catholic Herald **(31777)** ......(Paid) 53,000
      (Non-paid) 369
Missionhurst **(31808)** ....(Controlled) 48,000

Front Royal
Faith & Reason **(32094)** ....‡500
Sacred Music **(32095)** ....‡1,000

Glen Allen
Virginia United Methodist
  Advocate **(32114)** 12,000

Harrisonburg
Living **(32141)** ....(Non-paid) 125,000
Together **(32142)** ....(Free) ‡200,000

Herndon
American Journal of Islamic Social
  Sciences **(32160)** 1,700

Manassas
The Christian Observer **(32221)** ....(Paid) ‡2,000
      (Non-paid) ‡20

Richmond
The Catholic Virginian **(32432)**
Interpretation **(32439)** ....‡7,000
The Presbyterian Outlook **(32447)** ......(Paid) 11,020
The Religious Herald **(32449)** 25,040
Union Seminary Quarterly
  Review **(32459)** ....(Paid) ‡1,100
      (Non-paid) ‡100

WASHINGTON
Federal Way
World Vision Today **(32766)** .....(Controlled) 490,000

Langley
Alarming Cry News **(32805)** ....(Combined) 1,500

Renton
Northwest Christian
  Journal **(32926)** ....(Controlled) ‡27,000

Spokane
Inland Register **(33094)** ....‡11,000

Yakima
Central Washington
  Catholic **(33219)** ....(Non-paid) 22,000

WEST VIRGINIA
Wheeling
The Catholic Spirit **(33501)** ....(Paid) ‡3,200

WISCONSIN
Appleton
Correspondent **(33536)** ....(Controlled) 930,000

Green Bay
The Compass **(33739)** ....‡25,060

Hales Corners
Reign of the Sacred Heart **(33769)**

Janesville
The Sabbath Recorder **(33861)** ....(Non-paid) ‡2,400

Madison
Journal of Christian
  Nursing **(33950)** ....(Paid) ‡10,000
      (Controlled) ‡150
Student Leadership Journal **(33974)** ....‡10,000

Milwaukee
Catholic Herald **(34061)** ....(Paid) ‡68,247
      (Free) ‡3,336
The Family Friend **(34068)** .....(Non-paid) 33,000
Forward in Christ **(34070)** ....(Paid) ‡55,000
      (Controlled) ‡3,000
Living Church **(34074)** ....(Paid) ‡8,738
      (Non-paid) ‡294
Renascence **(34096)** ....(Paid) ‡650
      (Non-paid) ‡25

New Berlin
Prayers for Worship **(34183)** .....(Combined) ⊕1,200
Preaching: Word &
  Witness **(34184)** ....(Combined) 1,400

WYOMING
Cheyenne
Wyoming Catholic Register **(34498)** ....(Paid) 18,500

ALBERTA, CANADA
Edmonton
SR (Studies in Religion)/(Sciences
  Religieuses) **(34731)** ....‡1,450

BRITISH COLUMBIA, CANADA
Vancouver
Hallelujah! **(35145)** ....(Combined) ‡5,000

MANITOBA, CANADA
Steinbach
Die Mennonitische Post **(35295)** ....‡5,200

Winnipeg
The Herald (Visnyk) **(35332)** ....(Paid) ‡7,500
      (Non-paid) 250
Indian Life **(35333)** ....(Paid) ‡16,530
      (Non-paid) ‡3,175
Mennonite Brethren Herald **(35342)** ....‡17,000
Mennonite Review **(35343)** ....(Paid) ‡900
      (Non-paid) ‡1,000

NEW BRUNSWICK, CANADA
St. John
The New Freeman **(35430)** ....(Paid) ‡7,300
      (Non-paid) ‡173

NEWFOUNDLAND AND LABRADOR, CANADA
St. John's
The Monitor **(35489)** 5,800

ONTARIO, CANADA
Burks Falls
Canadian Theosophist **(35713)**

Combermere
Restoration **(35750)** ....(Paid) 8,000

Etobicoke
The Canadian Baptist **(35813)** ....‡12,000
Link & Visitor **(35817)** ....(Combined) 4,400

Fort Erie
The Fatima
  Crusader **(35839)** ....(Non-paid) ‡500,000

Gloucester
The Bread of Life **(35849)** 4,000

Guelph
Earthkeeping Ontario **(35861)** ....(Paid) 6,500
      (Non-paid) 6,500

Markham
Crescent International **(36022)** ....(Paid) ‡15,000
      (Controlled) ‡6,000

Mississauga
Church Business **(36062)** ....(Controlled) ‡12,487
Pentecostal Testimony **(36085)** ....‡19,000

North York
The Canadian Jewish
  News **(36124)** ....(Paid) 44,152
      (Free) 2,995

Numbers cited after listings are entry numbers rather than page numbers.

Orillia
Dreams and Visions **(36175)** ....(Paid) 200

Ottawa
Caravan **(36231)** ....(Paid) ‡1,000
                     (Non-paid) ‡100
Living with Christ **(36259)** ....(Paid) 125,000

St. Catharines
Christian Courier **(36355)** ....(Paid) ‡4,400
                     (Non-paid) ‡100

Scarborough
Scarboro Missions **(36384)** ....(Paid) 8,000
                     (Non-paid) 5,000
SIMNOW **(36385)** ....(Controlled) ‡132,000

Toronto
Anglican Journal/Journal
  Anglican **(36462)** ....(Paid) ‡263,000
Canadian Messenger **(36518)** ....‡13,000
Catholic Insight **(36539)** ....(Paid) 3,300
                     (Non-paid) 400
Catholic Missions in Canada **(36540)**
Catholic New Times **(36541)** ....‡7,000
Catholic Register **(36542)** ....‡23,000
Glad Tidings **(36605)** ....(Paid) ‡5,000
                     (Non-paid) ‡200
Messenger of the Sacred
  Heart **(36663)** ....(Paid) 13,000
                     (Controlled) 70
Presbyterian Record **(36714)** ....‡47,500
Spiritan Missionary
  News **(36746)** ....(Controlled) 9,000
The United Church Observer **(36777)** ....‡95,000

Waterloo
Canadian Mennonite **(36847)** ....‡17,500

QUEBEC, CANADA
Cap-de-la-Madeleine
Revue Notre-Dame du Cap **(36957)** ....‡65,000

Kahnawake
Kateri **(37018)** 10,000

Lac Bouchette
Le Messager de St. Antoine **(37026)** ....⊕**51,000**

Laval
Missions Etrangeres **(37042)** ....‡25,000

Longueuil
Aujourd'hui Credo **(37051)** 900

Montreal
Apostolat International **(37085)** ....‡17,000
Missions des Franciscains **(37187)** .....(Paid) ‡6,000
                     (Non-paid) ‡1,000
L'Oratoire **(37200)** ....(Paid) ‡40,000
                     (Non-paid) ‡2,000
The Oratory **(37201)** ....(Paid) 7,500
Orient **(37202)** ....(Paid) ‡4,800
                     (Non-paid) ‡50
Pretre et Pasteur **(37208)** ....(Paid) ‡2,800
                     (Controlled) ‡300

Mount-Tremblant
Magnificat **(37253)** 15,000

Ste.-Anne-de-Beaupre
The Annals of Saint Anne de
  Beaupre **(37326)** ....(Paid) 35,000
Le Revue Sainte Anne de Beaupre **(37327)**

Sillery
RND (Revue Notre-Dame) **(37401)** ....‡100,000

SASKATCHEWAN, CANADA
Muenster
Prairie Messenger **(37505)** ....(Paid) ‡7,300

Saskatoon
Semeia **(37556)** 1,500

Circulation: ★ = ABC; △ = BPA; ◆ = CAC; ● = CCAB; ❏ = VAC; ⊕ = PO Statement; ‡ = Publisher's Report; Boldface figures = sworn; Light figures = estimated.

2785

Women's Publications

Index entries are arranged geographically, first by states/provinces and then by cities. Within cities in this index, citations appear alphabetically by publication title. Citations include publication title, entry number (given in parentheses immediately following the title), and circulation figures.

Circ.

ALABAMA
Birmingham
Dimension **(68)** ....(Paid) 25,000

CALIFORNIA
Berkeley
Berkeley Women's Law Journal **(1500)**
Connexions **(1509)** ....(Paid) ‡1,000
         (Non-paid) ‡150
Sinister Wisdom **(1559)** ....(Paid) ‡3,000
         (Non-paid) ‡500

Castro Valley
Radiance **(1678)**

Claremont
Women's Studies **(1726)** ....(Paid) 500

Irvine
Mode **(2084)** ....(Paid) 615,436

Los Angeles
Black Lace **(2220)** ....(Paid) 9,000
         (Non-paid) 200
Fem **(2268)** ....(Non-paid) ‡10,000

Los Gatos
Writing For Our Lives **(2480)** ....(Paid) 500

Oakland
The Wise Woman **(2703)**

Palo Alto
U.S. - Japan Women's Journal **(2802)**

Point Arena
SageWoman Magazine **(2858)** ....(Paid) ‡20,000
         (Non-paid) ‡100

Riverside
Breastcare **(2932)**
Southern California Brides **(2945)**

San Francisco
Curve **(3348)** ....(Paid) 68,800
         (Non-paid) 305
Feminist Bookstore News **(3360)** ....(Paid) ‡800
         (Non-paid) ‡50

Sebastopol
Sonoma County Women's
  Voices **(3752)** ....(Paid) 300
         (Non-paid) 5,700

Sherman Oaks
Eligible **(3762)** ....(Paid) 80,000
         (Non-paid) 5,000

Thousand Oaks
AFFILIA: Journal of Women and Social
  Work **(3847)** ....(Paid) ‡700
Violence Against Women **(3920)**

Torrance
The Lesbian News **(3935)** ....‡110,000
Minority Business Entrepreneur **(3938)** 40,000

Woodland Hills
Fit Pregnancy **(4104)**
Shape **(4114)** ....(Paid) 1,538,192

COLORADO
Fort Collins
Journal of Feminist Family Therapy **(4435)**

CONNECTICUT
Bridgeport
Business Woman **(4712)** ....(Combined) 15,000

Darien
Lamaze Parents'
  Magazine **(4775)** ....(Non-paid) 2,700,000

New Haven
Yale Journal of Law and
  Feminism **(5006)** ....(Paid) 1,100

Westport
NCJW Journal **(5215)** ....(Paid) 100,000

DELAWARE
Dover
The American Mother **(5243)** ....(Non-paid) 4,000

Harrington
Harrington Journal **(5257)** ....‡2,300

DISTRICT OF COLUMBIA
Washington
AAUW in Action **(5308)** ....(Non-paid) 150,000
AAUW Outlook **(5309)** ....(Controlled) ‡150,000
BusinessWoman
  Magazine **(5392)** ....(Controlled) ‡70,000
Catholic Woman **(5402)** 10,500
Conscience **(5435)** ....(Combined) 10,000
Gender Issues **(5505)** ....(Paid) ‡700
GFWC Clubwoman Magazine **(5514)** ....‡18,000
Jewish Woman **(5564)** ....(Combined) ‡75,000
Lambda Book Report **(5628)** ....(Paid) 8,000
         (Non-paid) 150
LATINA Style **(5631)** ....(Paid) 150,000
Off Our Backs **(5704)** ....(Paid) 2,500
         (Non-paid) 18,000
The Republican
  Woman **(5762)** ....(Controlled) 100,000
Women in the Arts **(5862)**
Women's Political Times **(5864)**

FLORIDA
Altamonte Springs
Pageantry **(5902)** ....(Combined) 68,000

Boca Raton
Today's Boca Woman News
  Magazine **(5940)** ....(Paid) ‡590
         (Non-paid) ‡25,000

Gainesville
The Gainesville Iguana **(6141)** ....(Paid) 700
         (Non-paid) 3,000

Jacksonville
Kalliope **(6215)** ....(Paid) 1,500
         (Non-paid) 100

Lake Mary
SpiritLed Woman **(6280)**

Miami
Buenhogar **(6342)** ....‡18,449
Cosmopolitan en Espanol **(6346)** ....(Paid) 49,568
Harper's Bazaar en Espanol **(6357)** ....‡13,108

Ideas para Su Hogar (Ideas for Your
  Home) **(6362)** ....‡10,848
The New Times **(6374)** ....(Paid) ‡1,500
         (Free) ‡21,500
Tu Internacional **(6385)** ....‡11,452
Vanidades Continental **(6388)** ....(Paid) 92,777

Sarasota
Journal of Women and Aging **(6659)** 467

GEORGIA
Athens
Women's Studies in Communication **(6953)**

Atlanta
Women's Health Weekly **(7062)**

Lilburn
Coaching Women's
  Basketball **(7371)** ....(Paid) 5,000
         (Non-paid) 200

IDAHO
Moscow
Women in Natural Resources **(7922)**

ILLINOIS
Carol Stream
Virtue **(8156)** ....(Paid) ‡100,000
         (Non-paid) ‡10,000

Chicago
Complete Woman **(8340)** ....(Paid) 350,000
         (Non-paid) 5,000
Ivy Leaf **(8423)** 40,000
Signs **(8564)** ....‡3,149
SWE **(8579)** ....‡15,000
Today's Chicago
  Woman **(8583)** ....(Non-paid) 70,000
The Zontian **(8612)** ....‡36,000

Gurnee
Children, Churches & Daddies **(8965)**

Schaumburg
Leaven **(9585)** ....(Paid) ⊕6,849
         (Controlled) ⊕225
New Beginnings **(9588)** ....(Paid) ⊕29,463
         (Controlled) ⊕300

Wheaton
Today's Christian Woman **(9759)** ....(Paid) ‡256,000
         (Non-paid) ‡6,892

INDIANA
Berne
Crazy for Cross Stitch **(9803)** ....(Combined) 60,000
Creative Crafter **(9805)** ....‡179,650
Crochet! **(9806)** ....(Combined) 56,000
Sewing Savvy **(9819)** ....(Paid) 57,000

Bloomington
Hypatia **(9829)** 1,600
The Journal of Women's
  History **(9844)** ....(Paid) ‡1,500
         (Non-paid) ‡50
NWSA Journal **(9846)** ....‡1,300

Indianapolis
Indianapolis Woman **(10134)** ....(Non-paid) 58,227

Circulation: ★ = ABC; △ = BPA; ♦ = CAC; • = CCAB; ▢ = VAC; ⊕ = PO Statement; ‡ = Publisher's Report; Boldface figures = sworn; Light figures = estimated.

2787

Circ.   Circ.   Circ.

IOWA
Clarinda
The Civil War Lady **(10701)**

Iowa City
Common Lives/Lesbian Lives **(10970)**

KANSAS
Wichita
International Women Pilots/99
  News **(11883)** ....‡7,000

KENTUCKY
Louisville
Horizons **(12219)** ....(Paid) 28,000
  (Non-paid) 1,000

Today's Woman
  Magazine **(12240)** ....(Non-paid) ‡46,000

MARYLAND
Baltimore
Alternative Press Index **(13111)** ....(Paid) ‡550
  (Controlled) ‡200
Menopause **(13217)** 2,639

College Park
Feminist Studies **(13418)** 6,000

Pasadena
Minerva **(13644)** ....(Paid) ‡500
  (Non-paid) ‡20

Takoma Park
Sister 2 Sister **(13752)** ....(Paid) ★150,000

MASSACHUSETTS
Arlington
Exponent II **(13818)** 4,000

Boston
Our Special **(13945)** ....‡2,000

Cambridge
Bad Attitude **(14040)** ....(Paid) ‡5,000
Q Journal **(14093)**
Radical Teacher **(14096)** 2,000

Great Barrington
Hikane: The Capable Woman **(14215)**

Jamaica Plain
Sojourner **(14262)** 30,000

Lexington
WIN News **(14274)** ....‡1,100

Wellesley
The Women's Review of
  Books **(14619)** ....(Paid) ‡12,000
  (Non-paid) ‡500

MICHIGAN
Ann Arbor
Michigan Feminist
  Studies **(14762)** ....(Controlled) 250
Michigan Journal of Gender &
  Law **(14764)** ....(Paid) 230

Mount Clemens
Inky Trail News **(15371)** 500

Port Huron
Woman's Life **(15452)** ....(Non-paid) 32,000

MINNESOTA
Edina
iAm Magazine! **(15875)** 50,000

Minneapolis
Lutheran Woman Today **(16095)** ......(Paid) 150,000
Maize, A Lesbian Country Magazine **(16096)**

St. Paul
Melpomene **(16388)** ....(Paid) 1,700
  (Non-paid) 173
Minnesota Women's Press **(16396)** ....(Paid) 500
  (Free) 40,000

MISSOURI
Kansas City
Women in Business **(17204)** ....(Paid) 50,000

St. Louis
Voices **(17527)** ....(Non-paid) 10,000

Springfield
Woman's Touch **(17618)** ....‡10,000

MONTANA
Laurel
Crone Chronicles **(17845)** ....(Combined) 5,540

NEBRASKA
Lincoln
Frontiers **(18084)**
Legacy: A Journal of American Women
  Writers **(18089)**
Women and Music **(18128)**

NEVADA
Las Vegas
Women in Sport and Physical Activity
  Journal **(18387)** ....(Paid) 250

NEW HAMPSHIRE
Concord
WomenWise **(18475)** ....(Paid) 600
  (Non-paid) 1,400

NEW JERSEY
Califon
Women's Outdoor World
  (WOW) **(18712)** ....(Paid) 30,000

Englewood Cliffs
First for Women **(18800)** ....(Paid) 1,542,566
Woman's World **(18804)** ....(Paid) 1,604,003

Fort Lee
NJW Magazine (New Jersey
  Woman) **(18832)** ....(Paid) 15,000
  (Non-paid) 30,000

Somerset
Women Studies Abstracts **(19570)** .....(Paid) ‡1,000

NEW MEXICO
Albuquerque
New Mexico Woman **(19783)** ....(Paid) ‡2,000
  (Non-paid) ‡10,000

Santa Fe
Mothering Magazine **(19936)** ....(Paid) ‡90,000
  (Non-paid) ‡500

NEW YORK
Albany
Gender & Society **(19988)** ....(Paid) ‡2,650
  (Non-paid) ‡153

13th Moon **(20005)**

Binghamton
Celebrating Voices **(20152)** 775
Jenda **(20159)**
Women & Therapy **(20221)** ....(Paid) 823

Bronxville
The Villager **(20294)** ....(Paid) 450
  (Non-paid) 40

Brooklyn
Matriarch's Way **(20330)**

Buffalo
Earth's Daughters **(20378)** ....(Paid) 1,000
Women and Guns **(20393)** ....‡18,000

Harrison
Women's News **(20713)** ....‡250,000

Larchmont
Journal of Women's Health **(20919)**

New York
Allure **(21174)** ....(Paid) 876,584
Churchwoman **(21417)** ....(Paid) 3,831
  (Non-paid) 1,978
Cosmopolitan **(21503)** ....(Paid) 2,592,887
Elle **(21594)** ....(Paid) 1,000,638
Elle Canada **(21595)**
Essence **(21629)** ....(Paid) 1,004,452
Family Circle **(21677)** ....(Paid) 5,002,042
Feminist Legal Studies **(21683)**
Fit Magazine **(21703)** ....(Paid) 149,162
Free Focus **(21734)** 600
Glamour **(21764)** ....(Paid) 2,147,263
Good Housekeeping **(21775)** ....(Paid) 4,558,524
Hadassah Magazine **(21785)** ....(Paid) 272,131
Hair Cut and Style **(21787)**
Healthy Pregnancy **(21796)**
Honey **(21816)** ....(Combined) 200,000
Human Life Review **(21830)** ....(Paid) 6,000
Issues Quarterly **(21954)**
Journal of the American Medical Women's
  Association **(21983)** ....‡10,000

Ladies' Home Journal **(22231)** ......(Paid) 4,101,550
Lilith **(22257)** ....‡10,000
Lucky **(22269)**
Martha Stewart at Home **(22286)**
McCall's **(22301)** ....(Paid) 4,005,961
more **(22366)** ....(Paid) 850,000
NA'AMAT WOMAN **(22390)** ....‡20,000
O **(22481)**
Playgirl **(22565)** 350,000
Real Beauty **(22630)**
Real Simple **(22636)** ....(Paid) ‡1,200,000
Redbook Magazine **(22639)** ....(Paid) 2,338,941
The Reporter **(22647)** ....(Paid) ‡50,000
SELF Magazine **(22722)** ....(Paid) 1,190,707
Sports Illustrated for Women **(22778)**
Town & Country **(22849)** ....(Paid) 430,367
True Story **(22871)** ....(Paid) 234,717
W **(22905)** ....(Paid) 451,883
Woman's Day **(22924)** ....(Paid) 4,167,933
Women and Health **(22932)** ......(Controlled) ‡1,010
Women & Success **(22933)**
Women's League
  Outlook **(22934)** ....(Controlled) ‡95,000
Women's Studies Quarterly **(22935)** ....‡1,500
Women's Wear Daily **(22936)** ....(Mon.-Fri.) 44,015
Working Woman **(22939)** ....(Paid) 630,343
YM **(22950)** ....(Paid) 2,202,979

Port Washington
International Journal of Fertility and Women's
  Medicine **(23129)**

Rosendale
Binnewater Tides **(23277)** ....(Paid) ‡1,000
  (Non-paid) ‡6,000

NORTH CAROLINA
Cary
Carolina Woman **(23685)** ....‡40,000
History Workshop **(23688)** ....(Paid) 2,100

Greensboro
Psychology of Women
  Quarterly **(23936)** ....(Paid) 4437
  (Non-paid) 75

Wilmington
Health Care for Women
  International **(24295)** ....‡696

OHIO
Cincinnati
Friendly Woman **(24799)** ....(Paid) ‡800

OKLAHOMA
Tulsa
Today's Insurance Woman **(26134)** ....‡15,000
Tulsa Studies in Women's
  Literature **(26138)** 1,000

OREGON
Corvallis
CALYX **(26285)** ....(Paid) 4,500
  (Non-paid) 500

Portland
Hip Mama **(26480)** ....(Paid) 5,000

PENNSYLVANIA
Laverock
Woman's Art Journal **(27168)** .....(Combined) ‡1,800

Philadelphia
Peace and Freedom **(27613)**
The Soroptimist of the Americas
  Magazine **(27690)** ....(Paid) 50,000

Scranton
Polka—Polish Woman **(27961)** ....‡1,352

Shippensburg
Women & Criminal
  Justice **(27993)** ....(Controlled) ‡382

PUERTO RICO
San Juan
Imagen **(28295)** ....‡70,000

RHODE ISLAND
Providence
Differences **(28395)** 800
Hurricane Alice **(28400)** ....(Paid) ‡500
  (Non-paid) ‡300

TENNESSEE
Summertown
Birth Gazette **(29622)** 2,500

TEXAS
Austin
Indigenous Woman **(29781)** 4,000
(Non-paid) 1,000
Texas Journal of Women and the
Law **(29829)** ....(Combined) 450

College Station
Bulletin: Committee on South Asian Women **(30038)**

Denton
The Lasso **(30241)** 3,000

The Woodlands
Texas Women in Business **(31308)**

VIRGINIA
Arlington
Women's Quarterly **(31842)**

Charlottesville
Belles Lettres **(31918)** ....(Paid) ‡6,000
(Controlled) ‡2,000
IRIS **(31932)** ....(Paid) 3,500

Fairfax
So to Speak **(32031)**
Women and Language **(32034)** ......(Combined) 400

Falls Church
The Woman Activist **(32060)** 200

WASHINGTON
Seattle
Freedom Socialist **(32967)** 10,000
Outlook **(32999)** ....(Non-paid) 20,000

WISCONSIN
Eau Claire
Feminist Teacher **(33669)** ....(Paid) 900

Greendale
Country Woman **(33760)**

Madison
Feminist Periodicals **(33938)** 1,000
Letras Femeninas **(33958)** ....(Paid) 500
(Non-paid) 40

Milwaukee
Welfare Warriors **(34107)** ....(Paid) 250
(Non-paid) 16,000

BRITISH COLUMBIA, CANADA
Vancouver
Room of One's Own **(35165)** ....(Paid) ‡1,000
(Non-paid) ‡200

ONTARIO, CANADA
Etobicoke
Link & Visitor **(35817)** ....(Combined) 4,400

Toronto
Canadian Journal of Women and the Law/Revue
Femmes et Droit **(36513)** ......(Controlled) 15,000
Canadian Woman Studies (Les Cahiers de la
Femme) **(36535)** ....(Paid) ‡3,000
(Non-paid) ‡120
Chatelaine **(36547)** ....(Paid) 716,727
Confronting Violence in Women's Lives **(36558)**
Elm Street **(36582)** ....(Paid) 44,842
(Non-paid) 597,736
Fireweed **(36595)** 1,500
FLARE **(36596)** ....(Paid) 160,220
Homemaker's Magazine (Madame au
Foyer) **(36617)** ....(Paid) 550,000
(Non-paid) 270,349
Images **(36621)** ....(Non-paid) ‡490,000
Journeywoman Online Magazine **(36640)**
Kick It Over **(36642)** ....(Paid) ‡1,500
(Non-paid) ‡500
Real You **(36723)**
Resources for Feminist Research (Documentation sur
la Recherche Feministe) **(36728)** ....‡2,000
Scoregolf for Women **(36737)** ....(Paid) 1,000
(Non-paid) 59,000
Women & Environments **(36793)** 2,000

QUEBEC, CANADA
Dorval
Silk & Satin **(36988)**

Montreal
Chatelaine **(37102)** ....(Paid) 182,099
Coup de Pouce **(37106)** ....(Paid) 172,413

Outremont
Filles d'Aujourd'hui **(37265)** ....(Paid) 56,532

Circulation: ★ = ABC; △ = BPA; ♦ = CAC; ● = CCAB; ❑ = VAC; ⊕ = PO Statement; ‡ = Publisher's Report; Boldface figures = sworn; Light figures = estimated.

2789

Fraternal Publications

Daily Periodicals

Index entries are arranged geographically, first by states/provinces and then by cities. Within cities in this index, citations appear alphabetically by publication title. Citations include publication title, entry number (given in parentheses immediately following the title), and circulation figures.

Circ.

ARIZONA
Tucson
The Daily Territorial **(944)** ....(Paid) 892
(Free) 100

CALIFORNIA
Los Angeles
The Hollywood Reporter **(2291)** ....(Mon.-Fri.) 24,608
(Tues.) 32,799

San Francisco
The Recorder **(3421)** ....‡6,600

COLORADO
Denver
The Daily Journal **(4320)** ....(Paid) ‡1,206
(Controlled) ‡3,859

FLORIDA
Miami
Daily Business Review **(6347)** ....(Paid) 10,184
(Controlled) 286

GEORGIA
Atlanta
Fulton County Daily Report **(7009)** ......(Paid) 5,270
(Non-paid) 552

Norcross
Construction Market Data
Inc. **(7458)** ....(Combined) ‡3,000

ILLINOIS
Chicago
Chicago Daily Law Bulletin **(8311)** ....‡6,633
Dodge Construction News (Illinois, Indiana, Wisconsin
Edition) **(8356)** ....(Paid) ‡650

Peoria
The News Bulletin **(9421)** ....(Paid) 2,000
(Free) 3,800

LOUISIANA
New Orleans
Daily Journal of Commerce **(12728)**

MARYLAND
Baltimore
The Daily Record **(13154)** ....(Paid) ‡7,597
(Free) ‡1,747

MICHIGAN
Troy
Detroit Legal News **(15618)** ....⊕**1,850**

MINNESOTA
Minneapolis
Finance and Commerce **(16081)** ....‡1,500

MISSOURI
St. Louis
St. Louis Countian **(17499)** 1,300
St. Louis Watchman
Advocate **(17509)** ....(Combined) ‡40,000

Circ.

NEW YORK
Brooklyn
Daily Bulletin **(20309)** ....‡5,200

Chautauqua
Chautauquan Daily **(20453)** ....‡2,500

New York
Daily News Record **(21531)** ....(Paid) 17,069
Daily Racing Form **(21532)** ....(Mon.) 18,467
(Tues.) 10,481
(Fri.) 40,319
(Sat.) 63,430
(Sun.) 46,672
Standard & Poor's Corporation Records, Current
News Edition **(22785)** ....‡5,600
Standard & Poor's Dividend Record **(22786)**
Standard & Poor's N.Y.S.E. Stock
Reports **(22788)** ....‡5,368

OHIO
Cleveland
Daily Legal News **(24879)** ....‡1,300

Columbus
The Daily Reporter **(25015)** ....(Paid) 5,300
(Free) 64

OKLAHOMA
Oklahoma City
The Journal Record **(25969)** ....(Mon.-Fri.) ★**3,214**

Tulsa
Tulsa Daily Commerce & Legal
News **(26136)** ....‡450

OREGON
Portland
Daily Journal of Commerce **(26475)** .....(Paid) 3,341
(Controlled) 809

PENNSYLVANIA
Pittsburgh
Congressional Record **(27768)**
Federal Register **(27788)**

TEXAS
Dallas
Daily Commercial Record **(30142)**

Fort Worth
Commercial Recorder **(30335)** ....‡600

Houston
Daily Court Review **(30469)** 2,120

WASHINGTON
Seattle
Seattle Daily Journal of
Commerce **(33019)** ....‡5,500

ONTARIO, CANADA
North York
Daily Commercial News and Construction
Record **(36126)** 3,500

Circ.

Circulation: ★ = ABC; △ = BPA; ♦ = CAC; ● = CCAB; ❏ = VAC; ⊕ = PO Statement; ‡ = Publisher's Report; Boldface figures = sworn; Light figures = estimated.

2791

Magazines of General Circulation

Index entries are arranged by subject (please refer to the Index to Subject Terms). Within the subject groupings, entries appear geographically by states/provinces and alphabetically within cities. Citations in this index include publication title, entry number (given in parentheses), and circulation figures.

Circ.

ABORTION

DISTRICT OF COLUMBIA
Washington
Conscience **(5435)** ....(Combined) 10,000

ILLINOIS
Springfield
The Post-Abortion
  Review **(9641)** ....(Controlled) 1050

WISCONSIN
Milwaukee
Life Without Limits **(34073)** ....(Non-paid) ⊕**35,000**

AGNOSTIC AND FREE THOUGHT

CALIFORNIA
San Diego
Truth Seeker **(3284)** ....(Non-paid) 20,000

ILLINOIS
Chicago
News & Letters **(8508)** ....‡7,000

ALTERNATIVE AND UNDERGROUND

ARIZONA
Mesa
New Thought **(745)** ....‡3,000

Tempe
Java Magazine **(906)** ....(Controlled) 27,000

Tucson
The Match! **(956)** 1,750

CALIFORNIA
Agoura
Savage **(1379)**

Berkeley
American Spirit Newspaper **(1490)**
SCP Journal **(1557)** ....(Paid) 15,000

Beverly Hills
POPsmear **(1576)**

Chico
Magical Blend Magazine **(1694)** ....(Paid) 85,000
  (Non-paid) 15,000

El Toro
Public Enema **(1870)** ....(Non-paid) 250

Emeryville
Remix **(1881)**

Hollywood
Cosmic Voice **(2051)**

Los Angeles
Street Scene **(2406)** ....(Non-paid) 1,000

Malibu
Soaring Spirit **(2495)** ....(Controlled) 65,000

Oakland
Browbeat Magazine **(2670)** ....(Paid) 2,000

Circ.

EarthLight Magazine **(2678)** ....(Paid) 6,500
  (Non-paid) 500
Left Curve **(2685)** ....(Paid) 1850
  2000

San Francisco
BAST Music Magazine **(3328)**
H2SO4 **(3372)** ....(Combined) ‡1000
Propaganda Review **(3417)**
Reader's Guide to the Underground
  Press **(3420)** ....(Paid) 1,250

Santa Cruz
Highway 17 Almanack &
  Gazetteer **(3683)** ....(Paid) 3,500
  (Non-paid) 1,500

Santa Rosa
Maledicta **(3729)** ....(Paid) 2,000

Stanford
Birth of Tragedy
  Magazine **(3794)** ....(Combined) 6,000

Thousand Oaks
Outburn **(3905)** 15,000

COLORADO
Boulder
Iron Feather Journal **(4172)** ....(Combined) 3,500

Littleton
Democracy and Nature **(4546)** ....(Paid) 950
  (Controlled) 50

CONNECTICUT
Hartford
Hartford Advocate **(4891)** ....(Paid) 55,000

DELAWARE
Wilmington
Yakuza **(5296)**

FLORIDA
Fort Lauderdale
City Link **(6074)** ....(Non-paid) 51,798

Gainesville
Counterpoise **(6135)**

Orlando
Impact **(6498)** ....(Non-paid) 12,000

GEORGIA
Athens
Flagpole Magazine **(6937)** ....(Combined) 13,803

Decatur
babysue **(7235)** ....(Controlled) 5,000

Marietta
The Truth at Last **(7421)** ....(Paid) ‡30,000
  (Free) ‡12,000

ILLINOIS
Champaign
The Octopus **(8207)** ....(Combined) 22,000

Circ.

Chicago
The Baffler Magazine **(8280)** ....(Paid) 30,000
Chicago Reader **(8319)** ....(Non-paid) 133,158
  (Paid) 291
News & Letters **(8508)** ....‡7,000

INDIANA
Indianapolis
Branches Magazine **(10099)** ....(Combined) 25,000

MARYLAND
Baltimore
Shattered Wig Review **(13246)**
Social Anarchism **(13248)**

Rockville
Strange Magazine **(13698)** ....(Combined) 15,500

Wheaton
Lexicon **(13780)**

MASSACHUSETTS
Cambridge
Spare Change **(14103)** ....(Paid) 25,000
VooDoo Magazine **(14110)** ....(Non-paid) 8,000

Waltham
Transgender Tapestry **(14604)** .....(Combined) 8,000

Watertown
Body & Soul Magazine **(14612)** ....(Paid) 261,000
  (Non-paid) 14,000

MICHIGAN
Ann Arbor
FOUND **(14750)**

Detroit
Motorbooty **(14940)** ....(Paid) 25,000

MINNESOTA
Lakeville
FATE Magazine **(15995)** ....(Paid) 20,000
  (Free) 200

Minneapolis
City Pages **(16065)** ....(Free) 116,697
Profane Existence **(16124)** ....(Combined) 20,000
Utne **(16138)** ....(Paid) 232,629

St. Paul
Llewellyn's New Worlds of Mind and
  Spirit **(16384)** ....(Combined) ‡80,000

MISSOURI
Columbia
Anarchy **(16988)** ....(Paid) 5,200

St. Louis
Steamshovel Press **(17516)** ....(Paid) 5,000

MONTANA
Belgrade
Trout Wrapper **(17724)**

Missoula
Missoula Independent **(17868)** ....(Combined) 25,000

Circulation: ★ = ABC; △ = BPA; ◆ = CAC; ● = CCAB; ❑ = VAC; ⊕ = PO Statement; ‡ = Publisher's Report; **Boldface figures = sworn**; Light figures = estimated.

2793

Circ.   Circ.   Circ.

ALTERNATIVE AND UNDERGROUND (continued)

NEVADA
Las Vegas
Art **(18360)** 100

NEW JERSEY
Hoboken
BB Gun Magazine **(18900)**

Weehawken
Jersey Beat **(19711)** ....(Combined) 2,500

NEW MEXICO
Albuquerque
Atom Mind **(19767)** ....(Paid) 800
(Non-paid) 350

Santa Fe
Mothering Magazine **(19936)** ....(Paid) ‡90,000
(Non-paid) ‡500

NEW YORK
Amityville
Moksha Journal **(20050)** ....(Controlled) 200

Bronx
Farming Uncle **(20268)** ....(Paid) 400
(Non-paid) 700

Brooklyn
Peep **(20336)** ....(Paid) 4,000
Vice **(20353)** ....(Non-paid) ‡75,000

Buffalo
BuffaloBeat **(20370)** ....(Combined) 50,000

New York
The Nonviolent Activist **(22467)** ....(Paid) 8,000
(Non-paid) 1,500
The Shadow **(22735)**
The Source **(22764)** ....(Paid) 454,726

Niagara Falls
Natural Life **(23004)** ....(Combined) 35,000

OHIO
Columbus
Nancy's Magazine **(25032)** ....(Combined) 2,000

Logan
Cincinnati Journal of Magic **(25310)**

OREGON
Astoria
Nocturnal Lyric **(26226)** ....(Paid) 400

Eugene
Green Anarchy **(26318)**

Milwaukie
New Moon Rising **(26438)** 4,000

Portland
Portland Alliance **(26500)** ....(Combined) 7,000

PENNSYLVANIA
Philadelphia
MAGNET **(27560)** 35,000
Philadelphia Weekly **(27635)** ....(Free) 111,613
Rocket Fuel Online **(27655)**

Wilkes Barre
The Weekender **(28168)** ....(Non-paid) ‡42,000

RHODE ISLAND
Providence
Paranoia **(28411)** ....(Paid) 5,000

TENNESSEE
Ooltewah
The International American
Sunbeam **(29558)** ....‡75,000

TEXAS
Tyler
Both Sides Now **(31196)** ....‡200

VERMONT
Troy
Naturist Life
International **(31606)** ....(Controlled) 1,700

VIRGINIA
Richmond
Burping Lula **(32431)** ....(Controlled) 5,000

Vienna
Sobran's **(32582)** ....(Combined) ‡3,000

WEST VIRGINIA
Hillsboro
Free Speech **(33335)** ....(Paid) 3,800
National Vanguard **(33336)** ....‡9,100

WISCONSIN
Oshkosh
Nude & Natural **(34225)** ....(Paid) 18,650
(Non-paid) 6,350

ONTARIO, CANADA
Mississauga
UNRESTRAINED! **(36091)**

Toronto
Broken Pencil **(36479)** ....(Combined) 3,000
Now **(36678)** ....(Paid) 55
(Free) 106,103
RINSE **(36730)**
Socialist Worker **(36742)** ....‡2,000

PRINCE EDWARD ISLAND, CANADA
Kensington
Kindred Spirit **(36920)** ....(Paid) 1,800

ANTIQUES

CALIFORNIA
El Cajon
Antique & Collectables **(1843)** ....(Combined) 25,000
Antique Journal for California &
Nevada **(1844)** ....(Combined) 40,000
Antique Journal for the
Northwest **(1845)** ....(Combined) 28,000

Sierra Madre
American Bungalow **(3764)**

ILLINOIS
Chicago
Antiques & Collecting
Magazine **(8265)** ....(Paid) ‡10,000
(Non-paid) ‡6,000

INDIANA
Knightstown
AntiqueWeek (Eastern Edition) **(10233)** 64,959
AntiqueWeek (Mid-Central Edition) **(10234)** 64,959

IOWA
Grundy Center
Collectors News **(10935)** ....‡10,000

MAINE
Waldoboro
Maine Antique Digest **(13069)** ....(Paid) ‡33,000
(Non-paid) ‡1,500

MASSACHUSETTS
Carlisle
Antique Radio
Classified **(14120)** ....(Combined) 7,000

Ware
The New England Antiques
Journal **(14609)** ....(Paid) 5,000
(Controlled) 20,000

MISSOURI
Kansas City
Discover Mid-America **(17164)** .....(Non-paid) 30,000

MONTANA
Helena
U.S. Toy Collector Magazine **(17824)** 2,800

NEW YORK
Canandaigua
The New York-Pennsylvania
Collector **(20422)** ....(Paid) 5,000
(Non-paid) 2,500

New York
The Antiquer **(21223)** ....(Controlled) 35,000
Collectibles, Flea Market
Finds **(21438)** ....(Paid) 150,000

Westbury
Antiques & Collectibles
Magazine **(23551)** ....(Non-paid) 6,000

OHIO
Marietta
Glass Collector's Digest **(25345)** ....‡6,500

New Philadelphia
The National Hobby News **(25420)**

PENNSYLVANIA
Camp Hill
Early American Life **(26750)** ....(Paid) 100,000

Lafayette Hill
Renninger's ANTIQUE
GUIDE **(27132)** ....(Paid) ‡5,000
(Non-paid) ‡45,000

Quakertown
Artique **(27913)** ....(Paid) 213
(Non-paid) 16,000

RHODE ISLAND
Providence
Treasure Chest **(28428)** ....(Non-paid) ‡50,000
(Paid) ‡250

WISCONSIN
Iola
Cotton & Quail Antique
Gazette **(33815)** ....(Combined) 30,000

ONTARIO, CANADA
St. Catharines
Antique Showcase **(36349)** ....(Paid) 9,400

ART

ALASKA
Seward
The Alaskan Viewpoint **(636)**

ARIZONA
Douglas
The Mirage **(687)** ....(Non-paid) 2,000

Tempe
Java Magazine **(906)** ....(Controlled) 27,000

CALIFORNIA
Auburn
West Art **(1441)** ....‡4,000

Cedarville
Floating Island **(1681)**

Nevada City
Dream Magazine **(2615)**

Oakland
Left Curve **(2685)** ....(Paid) 1850
2000

Orange
Resource Library
Magazine **(2726)** ....(Non-paid) 8,000

Palo Alto
Meanderings **(2798)**

San Francisco
Juxtapoz **(3386)** ....‡54,000
SF Weekly **(3439)** ....(Non-paid) 123,462
*Surface **(3446)** ....(Paid) 112,000

San Jose
ARTWEEK **(3510)** ....(Paid) ‡12,000
(Non-paid) ‡3,000

CONNECTICUT
Newtown
Antiques and the Arts
Weekly **(5039)** ....(Paid) ‡24,255
(Non-paid) ‡231

Magazines *(side margin)*

DISTRICT OF COLUMBIA
Washington
Cathedral Age **(5398)** ....‡36,000
The World & I **(5870)** ....(Paid) 20,056
(Non-paid) 2,781

FLORIDA
Jacksonville
Kalliope **(6215)** ....(Paid) 1,500
(Non-paid) 100

Longboat Key
Black Tie **(6310)**

Naples
Naples Guide **(6446)** ....(Controlled) ‡270,000

GEORGIA
Atlanta
Art & Antiques **(6963)** ....(Paid) 195,805
Art Material Trade News **(6964)** ....(Paid) 168
(Non-paid) 8,100

Peachtree City
Contemporary Impressions **(7479)**

ILLINOIS
Chicago
New Art Examiner **(8504)** ....(Paid) ‡4,000
‡10,000

Des Plaines
Pack-O-Fun **(8766)** ....(Paid) ⊕105,000

Gurnee
Children, Churches & Daddies **(8965)**

Springfield
The Living Museum **(9639)** ....(Non-paid) ‡18,000

INDIANA
Indianapolis
Previews **(10162)** ....(Controlled) ‡12,000

IOWA
Grundy Center
Collectors News **(10935)** ....‡10,000

KANSAS
Ellsworth
Kanhistique **(11427)** ....‡5,215

LOUISIANA
Lafayette
In Tune **(12617)** ....(Paid) ‡100
(Non-paid) ‡20

New Orleans
New Orleans Preservation in Print **(12747)**

MAINE
Waldoboro
Maine Antique Digest **(13069)** ....(Paid) ‡33,000
(Non-paid) ‡1,500

MARYLAND
Baltimore
AmericanStyle Magazine **(13121)**
The Yale Journal of Criticism **(13264)** 606

MASSACHUSETTS
Arlington
the new renaissance **(13821)** ....(Combined) 910

Deerfield
Historic Deerfield **(14157)**

Edgartown
Martha's Vineyard
Magazine **(14174)** ....(Paid) ‡7,600
(Non-paid) ‡4,400

Jamaica Plain
Jamaica Plain Arts News **(14259)**

Needham
Mass Bay Antiques **(14360)** ....‡22,000

Ware
The New England Antiques
Journal **(14609)** ....(Paid) 5,000
(Controlled) 20,000

Watertown
Bonsai Today **(14613)** ....‡8,012

MICHIGAN
Big Rapids
Nova Review **(14817)** ....(Non-paid) 12,000

Birmingham
Lightworks **(14825)** ....(Combined) 2,000

Jenison
On the Town **(15229)** ....(Controlled) 36,500

Lansing
The Conservative News **(15274)** 13,000

MINNESOTA
Eagan
Wildlife Art **(15864)** ....‡65,000

Minneapolis
U.S. ART **(16137)** ....(Controlled) 55,000

Minnetonka
Art of the West **(16167)** ....(Paid) ‡25,000
(Non-paid) ‡5,000

NEVADA
Las Vegas
Art **(18360)** 100

NEW HAMPSHIRE
Meredith
Journal of the Print World **(18574)** 10,000

Portsmouth
Red Owl **(18638)** ....(Paid) 50
(Non-paid) 50

NEW JERSEY
Clinton
Art Now Gallery Guide–Boston/New England
Edition **(18759)** ....(Non-paid) 15,000
Art Now Gallery Guide–Chicago/Midwest
Edition **(18760)** ....(Non-paid) 12,000
Art Now Gallery Guide–International
Edition **(18761)** 4,072
Art Now Gallery Guide–New York
Edition **(18762)** ....(Non-paid) 40,000
Art Now Gallery Guide–Philadelphia
Edition **(18763)** ....(Non-paid) 8,000
Art Now Gallery Guide–Southeast
Edition **(18764)** ....(Paid) 18,000
Art Now Gallery Guide–Southwest
Edition **(18765)** ....(Non-paid) ‡13,169
Art Now Gallery Guide–West Coast
Edition **(18766)** ....(Non-paid) 30,000

Newton
Paint Works **(19373)**

River Edge
Nightlife **(19519)** ....(Paid) 50
(Controlled) 16,000

Sussex
The Dragon's Blood **(19607)** ....(Paid) 2,000

NEW YORK
Brooklyn
Peep **(20336)** ....(Paid) 4,000

Chautauqua
Chautauquan Daily **(20453)** ....‡2,500

Mount Marion
ART TIMES **(21100)** ....(Paid) ‡1,000
(Non-paid) ‡25,000

New York
American Artist **(21178)** ....(Paid) 180,471
Art in America **(21249)** ....(Paid) 69,583
ARTnews Magazine **(21257)** ....(Paid) 82,911
Bomb **(21331)** ....(Paid) ‡12,000
(Non-paid) ‡3,000
Chelsea **(21398)** ....(Paid) 2,200
(Non-paid) 300
Elle Decor **(21596)** ....(Paid) 467,367
Home Planet News **(21812)** ....(Paid) 700
(Non-paid) 200
The Magazine Antiques **(22274)** ....(Paid) 70,605
The New Criterion **(22428)** 7,000
(Non-paid) 1,000
Seconds **(22717)** ....(Paid) 30,000
(Non-paid) 8,000
Visionaire **(22902)** 5,000

Rockville Centre
Heavy Metal **(23261)** ....(Paid) 100,000
(Non-paid) 1,000

OHIO
Chagrin Falls
Currents **(24757)** 65,000

Cincinnati
The Artist's Magazine **(24775)** ....(Paid) 225,000
Decorative Artist's Workbook **(24792)** ....‡86,779
North Light **(24811)** ....(Non-paid) 68,635

Columbus
Timeline **(25065)** ....‡20,000

Groveport
Antique Review **(25234)** ....(Paid) ‡8,000
(Controlled) ‡2,500

OKLAHOMA
Oklahoma City
Persimmon Hill **(25991)** ....‡15,000

PENNSYLVANIA
Allentown
ARTS ALIVE!
Magazine **(26626)** ....(Controlled) ‡18,000

Camp Hill
Early American Life **(26750)** ....(Paid) 100,000

Hershey
Antique Automobile **(27040)** ....‡40,000

Laverock
Woman's Art Journal **(27168)** .....(Combined) ‡1,800

New Hope
The Nouveau
Magazine **(27321)** ....(Non-paid) 10,000

Philadelphia
Philadelphia Museum of Art
Bulletin **(27629)** ....(Paid) ‡4,000
(Non-paid) ‡4,000

TEXAS
Austin
Indigenous Woman **(29781)** 4,000
(Non-paid) 1,000

Houston
Southwest Art **(30530)** ....(Paid) 65,052

VERMONT
Burlington
Seven Days **(31518)** ....(Free) ⊔23,732
(Paid) ⊔48

Middlebury
Heron Dance **(31556)**

VIRGINIA
Fredericksburg
Visions International **(32088)** ....(Paid) 750
(Non-paid) 80

WASHINGTON
Olympia
Young Voices Magazine **(32864)** 3,000

Seattle
Art Access **(32941)** ....(Combined) 6,500

Shelton
Char-Jay **(33078)**

WISCONSIN
Iola
Antique Trader Weekly **(33800)** ....(Paid) ‡42,045
Collector's Mart **(33812)** ....(Paid) 88,129

BRITISH COLUMBIA, CANADA
Vancouver
Artichoke **(35122)** ....(Paid) 1,500

MANITOBA, CANADA
Winnipeg
Border Crossings Magazine **(35317)** 6,500

Circulation: ★ = ABC; △ = BPA; ◆ = CAC; ● = CCAB; ⊔ = VAC; ⊕ = PO Statement; ‡ = Publisher's Report; Boldface figures = sworn; Light figures = estimated.

2795

Circ.

Circ.

Circ.

ART (continued)

ONTARIO, CANADA
St. Catharines
Antique Showcase (36349) ....(Paid) 9,400
Collectibles Canada (36356) ....(Paid) 20,200

Toronto
ARTFOCUS (36463) 9,000
C International Contemporary Art (36481) 7,000
Canadian Art (36492) ....(Paid) ‡15,828
(Non-paid) ‡4,864
Rotunda (36732) 25,000

QUEBEC, CANADA
Montreal
Montreal Serai (37191)
Parachute (37204) ....(Paid) ‡2500
(Non-paid) ‡350
Vie Des Arts (37234) ....(Paid) •4,072
(Non-paid) •1,728

ASTROLOGY

NEW YORK
New York
Dell Horoscope Magazine (21542) ....‡132,000

PENNSYLVANIA
Ambler
American Astrology (26646) 100,000

QUEBEC, CANADA
Laval
Horoscope Quotidien (37040) ....(Paid) ‡13,000
(Non-paid) ‡12,000

ATHEISM

NEW JERSEY
Parsippany
American Atheist (19410) ....(Paid) ‡25,000
(Non-paid) ‡5,000

WISCONSIN
Madison
Freethought Today (33943) ....(Paid) ‡5,300
(Non-paid) ‡300

AUTOMOTIVE (CONSUMER)

See also (Auto Racing)

ARIZONA
Tucson
Restoration (961) ....(Paid) ‡1,500
(Controlled) ‡3,500

CALIFORNIA
Agoura
American Rodder (1376) ....(Paid) 46,517
Tailgate (1380) ....(Paid) ‡41,250

Anaheim
All Chevy (1397) ....‡100,000
Auto Sound & Security (1400) ....(Paid) 27,330
Car Audio and Electronics (1402) ......(Paid) 72,809
Classic Trucks (1403) ....(Paid) 57,035
Custom Classic Trucks (1404) ....(Paid) 99,594
4-Wheel Drive & Sport Utility
Magazine (1405) ....(Paid) 53,774
Kit Car Illustrated (1407) 85,000
MiniTruckin' (1409) ....‡325,000
Mustang Illustrated (1410) ....‡100,000
Off Road (1412)
Street Cruzin Magazine (1414)
Street Rodder (1415) ....(Paid) 132,567
Super Chevy (1416) ....(Paid) 190,480
Truckin' Magazine (1418) ....(Paid) 2,02,255
VW Trends (1420) ....(Paid) 74,164

Concord
DRIVE! (1752) ....(Non-paid) ‡135,000

Costa Mesa
Avenues (1772) ....(Paid) 2,738,634
Dune Buggies & Hot VWs (1775) ....‡68,324

Delhi
The SDC Magazine (1823) ....(Paid) ‡12,800
(Non-paid) ‡50

Lake Elsinore
Roadracing World & Motorcycle
Technology (2140) ....(Paid) ‡20,000

Los Angeles
Car Craft (2233) ....(Paid) 375,186
Chevrolet High
Performance (2235) ....(Paid) 219,621
Chevy Truck (2236) ....(Combined) 100,000
Corvette Fever (2247)
Four Wheeler Magazine (2273) ....(Paid) 325,441
Hot Rod Magazine (2295) ....(Paid) 805,035
JP (2305) ....(Combined) 80,000
Mopar Muscle (2333) ....(Paid) 69,621
Motor Trend (2334) ....(Paid) 1,285,178
Motor World (2335) ....(Paid) 120,000
Muscle Car Review (2339)
Mustang & Fords (2340) ....(Paid) 95,538
Mustang Monthly (2341)
Petersen's Circle Track (2362) ....(Paid) 130,212
Rod & Custom Magazine (2381) ......(Paid) 164,221
Rotary Review (2382) 1300
Sport Truck (2405) ....(Paid) 202,635
Super Ford (2408) ....(Paid) 46,656
Truck Trend (2416)

Monrovia
Skinned Knuckles (2578) ....(Paid) 7,500

Newport Beach
Road & Track (2635) ....(Paid) 771,024

Ross
Sports Car International (2973) ....(Paid) ‡50,000
(Non-paid) ‡1,200

San Francisco
VIA (3458) ....(Paid) 4,000,000
VIA (3459)

Sunnyvale
Austin-Healey Magazine (3827) ....(Paid) ‡1,550
(Non-paid) ‡100

Vista
Miata Magazine (4046) ....(Paid) 28,000
(Non-paid) 10,000

Westminster
Bus Conversions (4074) ....(Paid) 10,000

COLORADO
Denver
Rocky Mountain
Motorist (4353) ....(Controlled) ‡265,000

Lakewood
The Star (4536) ....(Paid) ‡30,000
(Non-paid) ‡2,000

CONNECTICUT
Trumbull
The Bargain News (5180) ....(Paid) 42,000

West Hartford
Journeys (5204) 245,000

FLORIDA
Fort Lauderdale
Two-Lane Roads (6085)

Miami
Automundo Magazine (6340) ....(Paid) 25,000
(Non-paid) 25,000

St. Petersburg
The duPont Registry: A Buyer's Gallery of Fine
Automobiles (6623) ....(Paid) 105,037

Titusville
Car Collector (6817)

GEORGIA
Atlanta
Porsche Panorama (7038) ....(Paid) ‡51,500
(Non-paid) ‡2,000

ILLINOIS
Chicago
Home & Away (8399) 370,000

Lincolnwood
Collectible Automobile (9091) ....‡55,000

Palatine
The Steam Automobile Bulletin (9396) ....(Paid) 600

INDIANA
Indianapolis
American Trucker—Florida
Edition (10086) ....(Combined) 44,297
American Trucker—Kentucky/Tennessee
Edition (10089) ....(Combined) 56,559
American Trucker—Southern
Edition (10098) ....(Combined) 49,599
Home & Away (Hoosier
Edition) (10114) ....‡221,977

New Albany
Automobile Quarterly (10338)

IOWA
Bettendorf
Home & Away (Minnesota
Edition) (10621) ....(Paid) 225,000
(Controlled) 400

MARYLAND
College Park
Lotus Remarque (13432) ....(Paid) ‡1,250
(Non-paid) ‡45

MASSACHUSETTS
Sudbury
Wheels, Etc. (14581) ....‡17,000

MICHIGAN
Ann Arbor
Automobile Magazine (14744) ....(Paid) 653,574

Detroit
AutoWeek (14916) ....(Paid) 360,000

Lake Orion
Automotive Fine Art Journal (15269) 5,000

Oak Park
The Michigan Post (15413) ....(Paid) 10,000

Troy
Dodge Magazine (15620)
GMC Directions (15627) ....(Non-paid) 850,000
Pontiac Excitement (15636) ......(Non-paid) 850,000

Warren
Chevy Outdoors (15657) ....(Paid) 80
(Non-paid) 999,950
Corvette Quarterly (15658) ......(Non-paid) ‡230,000
U.S. Auto Scene (15663) 8,000

MISSOURI
Cassville
Trendsetter (16966)

St. Louis
AAA Southern Traveler (17402) ......(Paid) ‡172,971
(Non-paid) ‡939

MONTANA
Helena
U.S. Toy Collector Magazine (17824) 2,800

NEBRASKA
Omaha
Home & Away (18198) ....(Paid) 3,355,000

NEW JERSEY
Florham Park
AAA Traveler (18823) ....(Free) 220,000

Saddle Brook
High Performance Mopar (19527) ....‡55,000
High Performance Pontiac (19528) ....‡47,000
MuscleCars (19530) ....‡45,000
Vette (19531) ....(Paid) 60,000

NEW YORK
New York
Car and Driver (21372) ....(Paid) 1,402,657
Mobile Entertainment (22341) ....(Paid) 102,992

Rochester
The Arrow (23210) ....‡1,100
(Non-paid) ‡50

OHIO
Cincinnati
Family Motor Coaching (24797) .....(Paid) ⊕125,000
Home and Away (24802) ....‡200,000

Numbers cited after listings are entry numbers rather than page numbers.

Independence
Ohio Motorist **(25252)** ....‡430,000

Sidney
Car & Parts Magazine **(25515)** 86,381

Worthington
Home & Away (Ohio
　Edition) **(25679)** ....(Controlled) 590,000

Yellow Springs
Vintage Truck **(25691)** ....(Paid) 28,000

OREGON
Bend
Electrifying Times **(26242)** 10,000

Salem
Slant 6 News **(26572)** ....(Paid) ‡1,950
　　　　　　　　　　　　　　(Controlled) ‡50

PENNSYLVANIA
Allentown
AAA Traveler **(26624)** ....(Controlled) ‡150,000

Hershey
Antique Automobile **(27040)** ....‡40,000

Mansfield
Christian Motorsports
　Illustrated **(27217)** ....(Paid) 20,000
Chrysler Power **(27218)** ....(Paid) 25,000

Philadelphia
AAA World **(27353)**
AAA World—Delaware **(27354)** 2,300,000
AAA World—Keystone **(27355)** 2,300,000
AAA World—Maryland **(27356)** 2,300,000
AAA World—Shore **(27358)** 2,300,000

York
Car & Travel **(28205)** ....(Non-paid) ‡151,936

SOUTH CAROLINA
Greenville
Roundel Magazine **(28626)** ....(Paid) 48,000

TEXAS
Wimberley
Special Interest Autos **(31303)** ....(Paid) ‡34,434
　　　　　　　　　　　　　　(Non-paid) ‡410

VERMONT
Bennington
Hemmings Motor News **(31499)** ....(Paid) 245,287

Williston
Mobilia Magazine **(31619)** ....(Paid) 29,000

WASHINGTON
Bellevue
Auto News of America **(32663)** 100,000
Motorist **(32667)** ....‡330,000

WEST VIRGINIA
Bluefield
AAA Today **(33252)** ....‡14,695

WISCONSIN
Iola
Military Vehicles **(33838)** ....(Paid) ‡18,000
Old Cars Price Guide **(33840)** ....(Paid) 41,116
Old Cars Weekly **(33841)** ....(Paid) ‡60,514

Madison
Home & Away Magazine **(33947)** ....‡292,822

BRITISH COLUMBIA, CANADA
Burnaby
Going Places **(34899)** ....(Paid) 106,654
Westworld **(34910)** ....(Paid) ‡853,237
　　　　　　　　　　　　　　(Controlled) ‡2,387
Westworld Alberta **(34911)** ....(Paid) 378,022
Westworld Saskatchewan **(34913)** .....(Paid) 108,880

ONTARIO, CANADA
Mississauga
World of Wheels **(36093)** ....(Paid) 32,761

Oakville
Carguide Magazine (Le Magazine
　Carguide) **(36142)** ....(Combined) 333,043

QUEBEC, CANADA
Montreal
Auto Trader/Auto Hebdo **(37089)**
Lemon-Aid **(37174)** 20,000

Saint-Laurent
Le Monde de L'Auto **(37364)** .....(Controlled) 30,000

AVIATION
ALASKA
Anchorage
Northern Pilot Magazine **(529)** ....(Paid) 15,000

CALIFORNIA
Canoga Park
Air Classics **(1654)**
Warbirds International **(1661)**

San Diego
KITPLANES **(3218)** ....(Paid) 75,984

CONNECTICUT
Greenwich
Flying **(4872)** ....(Paid) 313,246

KANSAS
Wichita
International Women Pilots/99
　News **(11883)** ....‡7,000

MARYLAND
Frederick
AOPA Pilot **(13505)** ....(Paid) 341,339

MINNESOTA
St. Paul
MSP Airport News **(16399)** ....(Free) ‡23,000

Sandstone
Minnesota Flyer Magazine **(16434)** ......(Paid) 3,702
　　　　　　　　　　　　　　(Non-paid) 500

NEW MEXICO
Hobbs
Soaring **(19865)** 15,911

NORTH CAROLINA
Asheboro
Sportsman Pilot **(23623)** ....‡3,000

OHIO
Cincinnati
Over the Front **(24812)** ....(Paid) 1,400

TENNESSEE
Chattanooga
Ultralight Flying! **(29094)** ....‡17,704

VIRGINIA
Leesburg
Aviation History **(32183)** ....(Controlled) 76,102

WISCONSIN
Oregon
Midwest Flyer Magazine **(34217)** ....(Paid) ‡1,000
　　　　　　　　　　　　　　(Non-paid) ‡25,000
World Airshow News **(34219)** ....(Paid) ‡2,000
　　　　　　　　　　　　　　(Non-paid) ‡1,500

Oshkosh
EAA Experimenter **(34221)** 18,000
EAA Sport Aviation **(34222)** ....(Paid) 167,000

ONTARIO, CANADA
Ottawa
Canadian Flight **(36195)** ....‡18,000

BABIES
See also Parenting

COLORADO
Centennial
Twins Magazine **(4228)** ....(Paid) ★25,624
　　　　　　　　　　　　　　(Non-paid) ★22,080

CONNECTICUT
Darien
Lamaze Para Padres **(4774)** ....(Non-paid) △750,000
Lamaze Parents'
　Magazine **(4775)** ....(Non-paid) 2,700,000

ILLINOIS
Schaumburg
Leaven **(9585)** ....(Paid) ⊕6,849
　　　　　　　　　　　　　　(Controlled) ⊕225
New Beginnings **(9588)** ....(Paid) ⊕29,463
　　　　　　　　　　　　　　(Controlled) ⊕300

KENTUCKY
Louisville
Developmental Neuropsychology **(12214)**

MARYLAND
Gaithersburg
Infants and Young Children **(13542)** .....(Paid) 2,600

MASSACHUSETTS
Kingston
South Shore Baby
　Journal **(14265)** ....(Combined) 16,000

NEW YORK
New York
American Baby **(21179)** ....(Paid) 193,063
　　　　　　　　　　　　　　(Non-paid) 963,020
Baby Talk **(21283)** ....(Paid) 976
　　　　　　　　　　　　　　(Controlled) 1,801,016
Child **(21409)** ....(Paid) 921,332
　　　　　　　　　　　　　　(Non-paid) 100,185
Healthy Pregnancy **(21796)**
Parenting's Healthy
　Pregnancy **(22525)** ....(Paid) △67,166
　　　　　　　　　　　　　　(Non-paid) △2,255,258
Parents Baby **(22526)** ....(Controlled) ‡3,700,000
Parents Expecting **(22527)** .....(Non-paid) ‡1,300,000
Parents
　Pregnancy **(22529)** ....(Controlled) ‡2,000,000

OREGON
Eugene
Midwifery Today **(26323)** ....(Combined) ‡2,400

TENNESSEE
Summertown
Birth Gazette **(29622)** 2,500

VIRGINIA
Richmond
The Journal of Perinatal
　Education **(32442)** ....(Paid) ‡5,224
　　　　　　　　　　　　　　(Non-paid) ‡408

WASHINGTON
Renton
Northwest Baby & Child **(32925)** ......(Free) ‡27,000

WISCONSIN
Milwaukee
Life Without Limits **(34073)** ....(Non-paid) ⊕35,000

ONTARIO, CANADA
Etobicoke
Expecting **(35815)** ....(Non-paid) 143,041

Southampton
Adoption Helper **(36399)** ....(Paid) 700

Toronto
Today's Parent Pregnancy &
　Birth **(36764)** ....(Non-paid) 199,575

BLIND AND VISUALLY CHALLENGED
CALIFORNIA
Los Angeles
The Braille Mirror **(2226)** ....(Controlled) 3,000

San Francisco
Smith-Kettlewell Technical File **(3442)** .....(Paid) 250

Santa Maria
The Braille Star
　Theosophist **(3694)** ....(Non-paid) 5,000

Circulation: ★ = ABC; △ = BPA; ◆ = CAC; • = CCAB; ❑ = VAC; ⊕ = PO Statement; ‡ = Publisher's Report; Boldface figures = sworn; Light figures = estimated.

Circ.　　　　　　　　　　　　　Circ.　　　　　　　　　　　　　Circ.

BLIND AND VISUALLY CHALLENGED (continued)

DISTRICT OF COLUMBIA
Washington
Braille Book Review (5381) ....(Non-paid) ‡15,000
Musical Mainstream (5665) ....(Non-paid) ‡3,600
RE:view (5758) ....(Combined) ‡4,850
Talking Book Topics (5810) ....(Free) ‡286,000

ILLINOIS
Quincy
ICUC: I See You See (9473) ....(Paid) 300

MARYLAND
Baltimore
Braille Monitor (13139) ....(Non-paid) 40,000
Future Reflections (13162) ....(Combined) ‡13,000

MASSACHUSETTS
Boston
Christian Science Quarterly-Weekly Bible Lessons (13876)
DVS Guide (13887) ....(Combined) 24,688
The Herald of Christian Science (13900)
Our Special (13945) ....‡2,000

MINNESOTA
White Bear Lake
Tract Messenger (16513) ....(Controlled) 475

NEBRASKA
Lincoln
The Children's Friend (18079) .....(Non-paid) ‡1,300
Christian Record (18080) ....(Non-paid) ‡2,900
The Student (18122) ....(Non-paid) ‡4,180
Young & Alive (18129) ....(Non-paid) ‡26,200

NEW YORK
New York
Jewish Braille Review (21961) .....(Non-paid) ‡2,000
Matilda Ziegler Magazine for the Blind (22299) ....(Non-paid) ‡20,000
The New York Times Large Type Weekly (22455) ....(Paid) 15,000

OHIO
Columbus
Newsreel (25036) ....(Combined) 1000

OREGON
Salem
Dialogue (26567) ....(Paid) ‡1,500

BRIDES

CALIFORNIA
Riverside
Southern California Brides (2945)

ILLINOIS
Des Plaines
Bridal Crafts (8750) ....(Paid) 52,066

MASSACHUSETTS
Peabody
New England Bride (14463) ......(Non-paid) ‡15,075

NEW JERSEY
South Plainfield
Contemporary Bride Magazine (19588) ....(Non-paid) ‡110,000

NEW YORK
New York
Bridal Guide (21338) ....(Paid) 205,858
Bride's Magazine (21339) ....(Paid) 388,180
For the Bride by Demetrios (21717) ....(Paid) 135,143
Modern Bride (22348) ....(Paid) 371,160

NORTH CAROLINA
Greensboro
Elegant Bride (23921) ....(Paid) ‡134,177

OHIO
Cincinnati
Cincinnati Wedding (24789) ....(Combined) 15,000

TEXAS
San Angelo
San Angelo Bridal Guide Magazine (31009) ....(Non-paid) ⊕6,000

ONTARIO, CANADA
Etobicoke
Today's Bride Magazine (35820) ....(Paid) 27,395
(Non-paid) 72,890

Toronto
Mariage Quebec (36656) ....(Combined) 22,413
WeddingBells Magazine (36790) ....(Paid) 26,369
(Non-paid) 80,114

BUSINESS

ALASKA
Anchorage
Alaska Business Monthly (520) ....(Paid) ‡3,000
(Non-paid) ‡7,000

ARIZONA
Phoenix
The Business Journal of Phoenix (795) ....(Paid) 13,677

Tucson
Inside Tucson Business (949) ....(Paid) 2,000
(Non-paid) 6,000

CALIFORNIA
Huntington Beach
Home Business (2062)

Irvine
Entrepreneur Magazine (2079) ....(Paid) 563,492

Los Angeles
Bootstrappin' Entrepreneur Bulletin (2225)
Business Concepts (2228) ....(Paid) 120,000
Credit & Finance (2248) ....(Paid) 120,000
First Class Executive Travel (2270) 21,000
U.S. Japan Business News (2422) ....(Combined) 40,000

Newport Beach
OC Metro (2633) ....(Combined) 90,000

Palm Springs
Investor Direct (2761)

San Francisco
PC WORLD (3413) ....(Paid) 1,268,016

San Ramon
The Nooner Magazine (3607) ....(Paid) 11
(Non-paid) 16,000

Studio City
Money Making Opportunities (3821) ....(Controlled) ⊕220,000

Sunnyvale
Employment Listings (3828)

Walnut Creek
REITStreet Magazine (4055) ....(Non-paid) 4,000

COLORADO
Fort Collins
The Northern Colorado Business Report (4436) ....(Combined) 12,000

CONNECTICUT
Greens Farms
Extra Equity for Homebuyers (4871) ....(Controlled) 234,000

FLORIDA
Fort Lauderdale
Broward Daily Business Review (6072) ....(Paid) 2,736
(Non-paid) 154

Hollywood
MoneyLines Magazine (6196)

West Palm Beach
Palm Beach Daily Business Review (6847) ....(Paid) 1,852
(Non-paid) 16

ILLINOIS
Champaign
IHRIM.LINK (8188) ....(Non-paid) 6,000
(Paid) 5,000

INDIANA
Fort Wayne
Business People Magazine (9964) ....(Controlled) 8,000

LOUISIANA
Metairie
New Orleans CityBusiness (12678) ....(Combined) 12,800

MARYLAND
Frederick
Business Gazette (13508) ....(Non-paid) 28,191

MASSACHUSETTS
Boston
Stages (13962)

Waltham
Careers and the MBA (14597) ....(Paid) 4,000
(Non-paid) 18,500

MICHIGAN
Traverse City
Publishing Entrepreneur (15601)

NEW HAMPSHIRE
Manchester
New Hampshire Magazine (18559) ....(Combined) 26,000

NEW JERSEY
Barnegat
DebtSmart (18663)

Jersey City
CPA Client Bulletin (19135)

NEW YORK
New York
American Business (21182) ....‡110,000
Business Week (21362) ....(Paid) 949,860
Digital Coast Reporter (21552)
The Economist (21582) ....(Paid) 342,677
Forbes ASAP (21719)
Incentive (21859) ....(Non-paid) 40,050
Income Opportunities (21860) ....(Paid) 140,728
Leaders Magazine (22242) ....(Non-paid) ‡35,120
Nest Egg (22417) 2,200,000
Silicon Alley Reporter (22741)
SmartMoney (22748) ....(Paid) 822,436
U.S. Frontline News (22887) ......(Combined) 29,000
Working Woman (22939) ....(Paid) 630,343
Worth Magazine (22946) ....(Paid) 501,071
Ziff Davis Smart Business for the New Economy (22956)

Rochester
Rochester Business Journal (23238) ....(Combined) 70,000

NORTH CAROLINA
Charlotte
Business First (23735) ....(Paid) 10,734

OHIO
Cleveland
Inside Business (24912) ....(Non-paid) 30,000

Columbus
Rinksider (25059) ....(Paid) ‡750
(Non-paid) ‡1,750

Dayton
Business Forum Software Digest (25107) ....(Paid) ‡2,000
(Non-paid) ‡2,000

PENNSYLVANIA
Bloomsburg
Northeast Pennsylvania Business Journal **(26717)**

TENNESSEE
Blountville
Business Journal of Tri-Cities
　TN/VA **(29055)** ....(Paid) 3,400
　　　　　　　　　　　　　　(Controlled) 5,000

TEXAS
Corpus Christi
South Texas Informer & Business
　Journal **(30079)** ....(Non-paid) 60,000

The Woodlands
Texas Women in Business **(31308)**

VIRGINIA
Richmond
Region Focus **(32448)**

WASHINGTON
Seattle
Midwest Airlines
　Magazine **(32987)** ....(Non-paid) 33,000
Working Money **(33045)** ....(Paid) 165,000

WEST VIRGINIA
Pineville
Small Publisher **(33437)** ....(Paid) ‡1,000
　　　　　　　　　　　　　　(Free) ‡4,900

WISCONSIN
Madison
Home & Family Finance **(33948)** ....‡350,000

ALBERTA, CANADA
Calgary
Business in Calgary **(34630)** ......(Combined) 30,368

BRITISH COLUMBIA, CANADA
Abbotsford
Home Business Report **(34878)** ....(Paid) 1,881
　　　　　　　　　　　　　　(Non-paid) 43,346

Bowen Island
OFFICE@Home **(34887)**

Burnaby
BC Business Magazine **(34891)** ....(Paid) •9,150
　　　　　　　　　　　　　　(Non-paid) •11,866

NOVA SCOTIA, CANADA
Halifax
Atlantic Progress
　Magazine **(35559)** ....(Controlled) •24,447
　　　　　　　　　　　　　　(Paid) •335

ONTARIO, CANADA
Bath
Canadian MoneySaver **(35667)** ....‡19,100

Ottawa
Ottawa Business
　Journal **(36264)** ....(Combined) •20,000

Toronto
The Globe and Mail Report on Business
　Magazine **(36607)** ....(Controlled) ‡320,000
Money Digest **(36668)**
Toronto Business Journal **(36765)**

QUEBEC, CANADA
Anjou
Quebec Habitation **(36938)** ....(Combined) 30,000

Montreal
Le Magazine Affaires Plus **(37167)** .....(Paid) 92,887

CAREER DEVELOPMENT AND EMPLOYMENT

ARIZONA
Tucson
College & Career Guide News for College
　Students **(940)** ....(Non-paid) 10,000

CALIFORNIA
Sunnyvale
Employment Listings **(3828)**

FLORIDA
Fort Lauderdale
Nursing Spectrum—Florida Edition **(6082)**

Gainesville
Florida Leader
　Magazine **(6139)** ....(Controlled) ‡25,000

ILLINOIS
Hoffman Estates
Nursing Spectrum—Greater Chicago/Tri-State
　Edition **(9001)**

MASSACHUSETTS
Lexington
Nursing Spectrum—New England Edition **(14273)**

Waltham
Careers and the MBA **(14597)** ....(Paid) 4,000
　　　　　　　　　　　　　　(Non-paid) 18,500

NEW YORK
Victor
The Next Step
　Magazine **(23494)** ....(Non-paid) 440,000

Westbury
Nursing Spectrum—New York & New Jersey
　Edition **(23558)**

OREGON
Portland
Portland Alliance **(26500)** ....(Combined) 7,000

PENNSYLVANIA
Horsham
CareerMagazine **(27056)**

King of Prussia
Nursing Spectrum—Philadelphia/Tri-State
　Edition **(27126)**

VIRGINIA
Falls Church
Nursing Spectrum—Washington D.C. & Baltimore
　Edition **(32050)**

WEST VIRGINIA
Pineville
Small Publisher **(33437)** ....(Paid) ‡1,000
　　　　　　　　　　　　　　(Free) ‡4,900

BRITISH COLUMBIA, CANADA
Burnaby
REALM Magazine **(34906)** ....(Combined) 185,000
Sphere Magazine **(34907)** ....(Combined) 185,000

CATS

See also Pets

ARIZONA
Phoenix
Cat World International **(798)** ....(Paid) 8,000
　　　　　　　　　　　　　　(Non-paid) 100

CALIFORNIA
Mission Viejo
Cat Fancy Magazine **(2549)** ....(Paid) 261,738

INDIANA
Indianapolis
Paws & Claws **(10159)** ....(Paid) 1,000
　　　　　　　　　　　　　　(Non-paid) 40,000

NEW JERSEY
Chatham
Animaltown News **(18727)** ....(Non-paid) 15,000

Manasquan
Cat Fanciers' Almanac **(19212)** ....(Paid) 5,386
　　　　　　　　　　　　　　(Free) 570

NEW YORK
Port Orange
CATS **(23122)** ....(Paid) 83,359

CHILDREN'S INTERESTS

See also Youths' Interests

CALIFORNIA
Beverly Hills
Toy Tips **(1578)** ....(Controlled) 3,000,000

Los Angeles
The Duckburg Times **(2254)** ....‡1,400

Santa Cruz
Stone Soup **(3690)** ....(Combined) 20,000

COLORADO
Colorado Springs
Clubhouse Jr. **(4241)** ....(Controlled) 88,000
Focus on the Family
　Clubhouse **(4246)** ....(Paid) 115,000

CONNECTICUT
Danbury
Peanut Butter **(4750)** ....‡150,000

East Haddam
KIND News **(4777)** 1,222,800

DELAWARE
Wilmington
Worddance **(5295)**

DISTRICT OF COLUMBIA
Washington
Children's Voice **(5410)** 15,000

ILLINOIS
Champaign
The Bulletin of the Center for Children's
　Books **(8182)** 5000

Chicago
America's Family Support Magazine **(8262)**

Des Plaines
Pack-O-Fun **(8766)** ....(Paid) ⊕105,000

Peru
Babybug **(9446)** 47,000
Cricket Magazine **(9447)** ....(Paid) ‡75,000
Ladybug **(9448)** ....(Paid) ‡130,000
Spider **(9450)** ....(Paid) 80,000

INDIANA
Chesterton
Guideposts for Kids **(9887)**

Indianapolis
Children's Digest **(10101)** ....(Paid) 91,165
Children's Playmate
　Magazine **(10102)** ....(Paid) 85,155
Humpty Dumpty's
　Magazine **(10119)** ....(Paid) 193,923
Indy's Child **(10135)** ....(Free) 60,000
　　　　　　　　　　　　　　(Paid) 20
Jack And Jill **(10138)** ....(Paid) 199,572
Turtle Magazine for Preschool
　Kids **(10177)** ....(Paid) 275,000
U.S. Kids **(10179)** ....(Paid) ‡225,000
　　　　　　　　　　　　　　(Non-paid) ‡2,000

MICHIGAN
Battle Creek
Children's Literature Association
　Quarterly **(14793)** ....‡850

Lansing
Michigan History for Kids **(15286)**

MINNESOTA
Duluth
New Moon **(15840)** ....(Paid) 22,500

Minneapolis
Surprises **(16135)** ....(Paid) 112,321

MISSOURI
Kansas City
College Outlook **(17163)** ....(Non-paid) 1,395,153

Circulation: ★ = ABC; △ = BPA; ♦ = CAC; • = CCAB; ❑ = VAC; ⊕ = PO Statement; ‡ = Publisher's Report; Boldface figures = sworn; Light figures = estimated.

2799

Magazines

Circ.   Circ.   Circ.

CHILDREN'S INTERESTS (continued)

NEW HAMPSHIRE
Peterborough
Appleseeds (18616)
California Chronicles (18618)
Faces (18623) 13,000
Footsteps (18624) 6,000
Odyssey (18626) 28,000

NEW JERSEY
Mountainside
Essex County
  Family (19316) ....(Controlled) 125,000
Middlesex County
  Family (19317) ....(Controlled) 125,000
Morris County
  Family (19318) ....(Controlled) 125,000

Newark
Jersey Journeys (19355) 9,500

Park Ridge
Kids Magazine (19409) ....(Non-paid) ‡30,000

NEW YORK
Congers
Inquest, The Gaming
  Magazine (20490) ....(Paid) 105,000
Toyfare, The Toy Magazine (20491)

Hamburg
Kids Courier (20704) ....(Non-paid) 385,117

Holbrook
Journal of Child-Care
  Administration (20749) ....(Paid) 1,000

Long Island City
Archaeology's Dig (20962)

New York
Kids Discover (22221)
Sports Illustrated for Kids (22777) ....(Paid) 613,157
                                    (Non-paid) 251,449
Time for Kids (22840) ....(Paid) 4,000,000

Yonkers
Zillions (23604) ....‡250,000

NORTH CAROLINA
Greensboro
Monkeyshines on America (23928)
Monkeyshines on Health and Science (23929)

OHIO
Bluffton
Boys' Quest (24683) ....(Paid) 10,000

Cincinnati
All About Kids (24768) ....(Free) 55,000
                                        (Paid) 50

Columbus
Wild Ohio Magazine (25069)

Dayton
Good News for Children (25118)
Promise (25124)
Seeds (25126)
Venture (25129)

Troy
Miami Valley Parents (25595)

PENNSYLVANIA
Honesdale
Highlights for Children (27048) ....‡3,000,000

Philadelphia
Metrokids Magazine (27568) ....(Free) 90,000

TENNESSEE
Nashville
Pockets Magazine (29481) ....(Paid) ‡96,000
                                  (Controlled) ‡3,000

TEXAS
Waco
Creative Kids (31245) 35,000

UTAH
Provo
Children's Book and Play Review (31401)

VIRGINIA
Reston
Ranger Rick (32412) ....‡550,000
Your Big Backyard (32424) ....(Combined) 1,100,000

WASHINGTON
Olympia
Young Voices Magazine (32864) 3,000

WISCONSIN
Madison
Telemedium (33976) ....(Combined) 600

Middleton
American Girl (34049) ....(Paid) 700,000

BRITISH COLUMBIA, CANADA
Victoria
YES Mag (35231) ....(Paid) 18,000

ONTARIO, CANADA
Aurora
Horsepower, Magazine for Young Horse
  Lovers (35650) ....(Paid) ‡8,000
                                  (Non-paid) ‡500

Guelph
CCL Canadian Children's Literature (Litterature
  Canadienne pour la Jeunesse) (35860) .....‡1,000

North York
Toys & Games (36132) ....(Combined) 5,000

Oakville
City Parent (36143) 260,000

Toronto
Chickadee (36548) ....(Paid) 66,645
                                  (Paid) 370
Kidsworld (36643) ....(Non-paid) 200,050
OWL (36693) ....(Paid) 63,059
                                  (Non-paid) 352

QUEBEC, CANADA
Saint-Lambert
Le Magazine Enfants
  Quebec (37359) ....(Combined) 72,102

CITY, HOTEL, RAILROAD, AND TRAVEL GUIDES

See also Travel and Tourism

CALIFORNIA
Palm Springs
Palm Springs Life's Desert
  Guide (2764) ....(Non-paid) 94,218

ILLINOIS
Moline
The Gold Book (9205)

INDIANA
Indianapolis
This is Indianapolis (10174) .....(Controlled) 300,000

NEW YORK
Bridgehampton
Dan's Paper (20243)

NORTH CAROLINA
Candler
Belize First Magazine (23682) ....(Paid) 5,050
                                  (Non-paid) 150,000

OHIO
Cleveland
This Week in Cleveland
  Magazine (24957) ....(Free) 10,000

WISCONSIN
Sturgeon Bay
Key to the
  Door...Illustrated (34351) .....(Non-paid) 140,000

CLUBS AND SOCIETIES

ALABAMA
Auburn University
Phi Kappa Phi Forum (50) ....(Paid) 110,000

Birmingham
Civitan Magazine (64) ....‡26,000

ARIZONA
Fountain Hills
American Amateur Journalist (710) ....(Paid) 300

CALIFORNIA
Los Angeles
Jonathan (2300) ....(Controlled) ‡3,800
Mercury (2329) ....‡5,000

Oakland
Almanac (2665) ....(Paid) 450

San Francisco
VIA (3459)

COLORADO
Aurora
Star Wars Insider (4150) ....(Paid) 250,000

Lakewood
American Penstemon Society
  Bulletin (4530) ....(Paid) 500

DISTRICT OF COLUMBIA
Washington
Club Director (5422) ....(Controlled) ⊕9,058
GFWC Clubwoman Magazine (5514) ....‡18,000

FLORIDA
Miami Springs
City & Country Club Life (6422) ....(Paid) 793
                                  (Non-paid) 13,903

ILLINOIS
Aurora
AAA—Chicago Motor Club Home & Away (8037)

Chicago
Ivy Leaf (8423) 40,000
The Zontian (8612) ....‡36,000

Urbana
Railroad History (9716) ....(Paid) 3,500

INDIANA
Indianapolis
The Columbian (10103) ....‡4,000
Indac Magazine (10120) ....‡2,500
Keynoter (10144) ....(Paid) 190,000

KANSAS
Manhattan
Kansas 4-H Journal (11624) ....‡13,500

MAINE
Augusta
The Christian Civic League
  Record (12890) ....(Paid) ‡2,500
                                  (Non-paid) ‡500

MARYLAND
Baltimore
Maryland Poetry Review (13215) ....(Paid) 500

MASSACHUSETTS
South Hamilton
Journal of the Evangelical Homiletics
  Society (14544) ....(Paid) 800

MICHIGAN
Detroit
D.A.C. News (14923) ....‡4,279

Warren
The Megarian (15659) ....(Paid) 52

MISSOURI
St. Louis
AAA Southern Traveler (17402) ......(Paid) ‡172,971
                                  (Non-paid) ‡939
Cherry Diamond (17421) 4,900

Midwest Traveler (17471) ....(Paid) 424,296
The Optimist Magazine (17478) ....‡118,500

NEW HAMPSHIRE
Nashua
The Clubhouse (18586)

NEW JERSEY
Vineland
The New Jersey
   Angler (19699) ....(Combined) 75,000

NEW YORK
Bronxville
The Villager (20294) ....(Paid) 450
                                     (Non-paid) 40

New York
Social Register Observer (22755)
The Winged Foot (22921) ....(Paid) ‡8,500
                                     (Non-paid) ‡400

Rye
Westchester Country Club News (23281) .....‡1,600

NORTH CAROLINA
Durham
Linking Ring (23834) ....(Controlled) 13,800

OHIO
Cleveland
CAC Journal (24864) ....‡1,800

OKLAHOMA
Norman
China Clipper (25933) ....(Controlled) 850

Oklahoma City
Vision (25997)

Tulsa
Jaycees Magazine (26119) ....‡135,000

OREGON
Salem
Slant 6 News (26572) ....(Paid) ‡1,950
                                  (Controlled) ‡50

TENNESSEE
Lawrenceburg
Yesterday and Today in Lawrence
   County (29317) ....(Paid) 200

TEXAS
Dallas
Private Clubs (30178) ....(Paid) 239,627

Randolph AFB
Daedalus Flyer (30969)

VIRGINIA
Blacksburg
4-H for Life (31871)

Reston
Teen Times (32421) ....‡215,000

Richmond
UDC Magazine (32458) ....(Paid) 9,000

WISCONSIN
Milwaukee
Marquette Magazine (34076) ....(Non-paid) ‡100,000

NOVA SCOTIA, CANADA
Dartmouth
The Torch (35551) ....(Non-paid) 30,000

ONTARIO, CANADA
Cambridge
Kin Mag (35726) ....(Paid) ISSN 002311436

Ottawa
Trail and Landscape (36277)

COLLECTING
See also Antiques; Art

ARIZONA
Surprise
Autograph Times (899) ....(Paid) 4,600
                                     (Non-paid) 1,800

CALIFORNIA
Anaheim
Knives Illustrated (1408) ....‡100,000

Corona
Pop Culture Collecting (1767)

El Cajon
Antique & Collectables (1843) ....(Combined) 25,000
Antique Journal for California &
   Nevada (1844) ....(Combined) 40,000
Antique Journal for the
   Northwest (1845) ....(Combined) 28,000

Pasadena
Firsts (2816)

San Anselmo
Western & Eastern Treasures (3085) ....‡60,000

Ventura
COINage (4002)

COLORADO
Colorado Springs
The Numismatist (4253) ....(Controlled) 27,300

Pueblo
American Breweriana (4597) .....(Controlled) 3,600

DELAWARE
Lewes
Decoy Magazine (5259) ....(Paid) ‡2,800
                                     (Non-paid) ‡100

FLORIDA
Hollywood
Fell's U.S. Coins Magazine (6194)

North Miami
Shekel (6466) ....(Combined) 3,800

Sarasota
Yesterday's Magazette (6670) ....(Paid) 1,500

ILLINOIS
Elgin
Aeronautica & Air Label Collectors
   Club (8822) ....(Controlled) 850

St. Charles
Crown Jewels of the Wire (9566) ......(Paid) ⊕1,670
                                  (Non-paid) ⊕15

IOWA
Grundy Center
Collectors News (10935) ....‡10,000

Lansing
Barr's Post Card News (11030) ....(Paid) ‡5,500
                                     (Non-paid) ‡550

Rockford
The American Revenuer (11183) ....(Paid) 1,300
                                     (Non-paid) 10

KANSAS
Topeka
Farm Collector (11818) ....(Paid) ‡40,000

MARYLAND
Arnold
The German Postal
   Specialist (13106) ....(Paid) ‡1,650
                                  (Controlled) ‡30

Bryantown
TAMS Journal (13397) ....‡1,200

Hunt Valley
The Vintage and Classic Baseball
   Collector (13583) ....(Controlled) 8,000

Riva
The Collectors Club Philatelist (13672) ....‡1,300

MASSACHUSETTS
Carlisle
Antique Radio
   Classified (14120) ....(Combined) 7,000

Ware
The New England Antiques
   Journal (14609) ....(Paid) 5,000
                                  (Controlled) 20,000

MICHIGAN
Muskegon
Contemporary Doll Collector (15387) ....‡22,000

MISSOURI
St. Louis
Allan Kaye's Sports Cards News & Price
   Guides (17408)

MONTANA
Helena
U.S. Toy Collector Magazine (17824) 2,800

NEW HAMPSHIRE
Hollis
Mekeel's Weekly Stamp
   News (18527) ....(Paid) ‡6,000
                                     (Non-paid) ‡1,000

Wolfeboro
Rare Coin Review (18655)

NEW YORK
Canandaigua
The New York-Pennsylvania
   Collector (20422) ....(Paid) 5,000
                                     (Non-paid) 2,500

Congers
Toyfare, The Toy Magazine (20491)

Hornell
Stamps (20752) ....‡14,500

New York
American Country Collectibles (21185)
The Antiquer (21223) ....(Controlled) 35,000
Collectibles, Flea Market
   Finds (21438) ....(Paid) 150,000

Northport
The Inside Collector (23017) ....(Paid) 30,000

Oceanside
Error Trends Coin Magazine (23030) 1,500

Westbury
Antiques & Collectibles
   Magazine (23551) ....(Non-paid) 6,000

NORTH DAKOTA
Bismarck
Vintage Guitar (24361) ....(Paid) ‡24,300
                                     (Non-paid) ‡400

OHIO
Marietta
Glass Collector's Digest (25345) ....‡6,500

New Philadelphia
The National Hobby News (25420)

Powell
Check the Oil! (25490) ....(Paid) 3,700

Sidney
Coin World (25516) ....(Paid) ‡83,051
                                     (Non-paid) ‡1,000
Linn's Stamp News (25518) ....‡48,000
Scott Stamp Monthly (25520) ....(Paid) ‡26,500
                                     (Non-paid) ‡50

OKLAHOMA
Norman
China Clipper (25933) ....(Controlled) 850

Tulsa
Collectors' Showcase (26109) .....(Combined) 10,000

PENNSYLVANIA
Harrisburg
Figurines & Collectibles (26990) ....(Paid) 54,085

Magazines

Circ.

Circ.

Circ.

COLLECTING (continued)

Lafayette Hill
Renninger's ANTIQUE
  GUIDE **(27132)** ....(Paid) ‡5,000
  (Non-paid) ‡45,000

Richboro
Glass Craftsman **(27933)** ....(Combined) 10,500

State College
The American Philatelist **(28016)** ....‡55,000
Philatelic Literature Review **(28020)** ....‡2,700

RHODE ISLAND
Cranston
The Village Chronicle **(28337)** ....(Paid) ‡13,000

Providence
Treasure Chest **(28428)** ....(Non-paid) ‡50,000
  (Paid) ‡250

SOUTH CAROLINA
Columbia
Manuscripts **(28557)** ....‡1,800

TENNESSEE
Mountain Home
Comics Revue **(29428)** ....(Paid) ‡1,200
  (Non-paid) ‡50

TEXAS
Dallas
Dragon Ball Z Collector **(30152)** ......(Paid) 300,000
Paper Money **(30175)** ....‡2,300

Fort Worth
Master Collector **(30347)** ....(Combined) 20,000

Fritch
The Trumpeter **(30374)** ....(Paid) ‡600
  (Controlled) ‡700

Mabank
The Horn Speaker **(30751)** ....(Paid) ‡1,225
  (Non-paid) ‡200

UTAH
Orem
The Doors Collectors Magazine **(31384)**

VERMONT
Williston
Mobilia Magazine **(31619)** ....(Paid) 29,000

VIRGINIA
Vienna
Topical Time **(32583)** ....‡6,000

WASHINGTON
Valleyford
Airpost Journal **(33173)** ....(Combined) 1,825

WISCONSIN
Iola
Arts & Crafts **(33801)** ....(Combined) 254,928
Bank Note Reporter **(33802)** ....(Paid) ‡6,509
Beans & Bears! **(33803)** ....(Combined) 169,433
Card Trade **(33807)** ....(Combined) 5,776
Coin Prices **(33809)** ....(Paid) 33,582
Coins Magazine **(33810)** ....‡31,977
Cotton & Quail Antique
  Gazette **(33815)** ....(Combined) 30,000
Craft Supply **(33816)** ....(Combined) 13,239
Discoveries **(33818)** ....(Combined) 13,388
EBay Magazine **(33824)** ....(Combined) 696,692
Goldmine **(33828)** ....(Paid) ‡27,758
Military Trader **(33837)** ....(Combined) 9,778
Numismatic News **(33839)** ....(Paid) ‡28,085
SCD's Price Guide Weekly **(33843)** ....(Paid) 835
Sports Collectors Digest **(33844)** ....(Paid) 35,000
Stamp Collector **(33845)** ....(Paid) 13,670
Stamp Wholesaler **(33846)** ....(Paid) 2,446
Trade Fax **(33850)** ....(Paid) 150
Tuff Stuff **(33852)** ....(Combined) 200,000
World Coin News **(33857)** ....(Paid) ‡6,434

Waukesha
Classic Toy Trains
  Magazine **(34398)** ....(Paid) ★62,788

ONTARIO, CANADA
Deep River
BNA Topics **(35761)** ....(Paid) 1,300

St. Catharines
Canadian Coin News **(36351)** ....(Paid) 7,500
The Canadian Stamp
  News **(36354)** ....(Paid) ‡5,300
Collectibles Canada **(36356)** ....(Paid) 20,200

Toronto
Canadian Philatelist **(36524)** ....(Paid) 3300

COMICS AND COMIC TECHNIQUE

CALIFORNIA
Daly City
Pro Tooner **(1804)** ....(Paid) 1,150

Pasadena
Bovine Gazette **(2811)**

Santa Ana
Cartoonist and Comic Artist
  Magazine **(3622)** ....(Paid) 5,000

CONNECTICUT
Fairfield
Cartoonist Profiles **(4786)**

Stamford
Archie Comics **(5140)** 1,021,809

GEORGIA
Atlanta
Hogan's Alley **(7016)** ....(Paid) 5000

Decatur
babysue **(7235)** ....(Controlled) 5,000

Marietta
Comic Shop News **(7410)** ....(Combined) 94,400

MICHIGAN
Detroit
Motorbooty **(14940)** ....(Paid) 25,000

MISSOURI
St. Louis
Snicker **(17511)** ....(Combined) 70,000

NEW JERSEY
Fairfield
Bits & Pieces **(18812)**

NEW YORK
Congers
Wizard **(20492)** ....(Paid) 197,000

New York
Comics Scene 2000 **(21453)**
Doctor Strange, Sorcerer Supreme **(21562)**
Ghost Rider **(21760)** ....(Paid) 3,000,000
The Hulk **(21827)** ....(Paid) 100,000
Morbius **(22365)** ....(Paid) 180,000

Rockville Centre
Heavy Metal **(23261)** ....(Paid) 100,000
  (Non-paid) 1,000

OHIO
Cleveland Heights
Funny Times **(24993)** ....⊕63,000

TENNESSEE
Mountain Home
Comics Revue **(29428)** ....(Paid) ‡1,200
  (Non-paid) ‡50

TEXAS
Dallas
Dragon Ball Z Collector **(30152)** ......(Paid) 300,000

WASHINGTON
Seattle
The Comedy Magazine **(32957)** ....(Paid) 15,000
The Comics Journal **(32958)** ....(Paid) ‡10,000

WISCONSIN
Iola
Comics Buyer's Guide **(33813)** ....(Paid) 11,218

Comics & Games
  Retailer **(33814)** ....(Non-paid) ‡4,434

ONTARIO, CANADA
Kitchener
Cerebus **(35959)** 12,000

Newmarket
Stitches **(36108)** ....(Non-paid) •36,336

QUEBEC, CANADA
Saint-Lambert
ARCHIE **(37357)** ....(Combined) ‡165,000

COMPUTERS

CALIFORNIA
Berkeley
Game Revolution **(1523)**

Brisbane
MacAddict **(1605)** ....(Paid) △196,000
Maximum PC **(1606)**
Next Generation **(1608)** ....(Paid) ‡115,613
PC Accelerator **(1609)**
PC Gamer **(1610)** ....(Paid) 357,718
PSM (PlayStation
  Magazine) **(1611)** ....(Paid) 304,458

Los Angeles
Afronet Magazine **(2202)**

San Diego
ComputorEdge **(3132)** ....(Controlled) 250,000
ComputorEdge **(3133)** ....(Non-paid) ‡80,000

San Francisco
IP Magazine **(3375)**
PC WORLD **(3413)** ....(Paid) 1,268,016
Wired **(3463)** ....(Paid) 507,816

COLORADO
Boulder
Iron Feather Journal **(4172)** ....(Combined) 3,500

Golden
Boardwatch Magazine **(4463)** ....(Paid) 20,764
  (Non-paid) 7,692

CONNECTICUT
Danbury
Family Computin- **(4740)**

DISTRICT OF COLUMBIA
Washington
Fast Forward **(5492)**

IDAHO
Sandpoint
MultiLingual Computing &
  Technology **(7979)** ....(Combined) 7,000

ILLINOIS
Chicago
GeoWorld **(8386)** ....(Paid) 21,575

KANSAS
Overland Park
KC Computer User **(11718)** ....(Paid) 60,000

MAINE
Portland
Interface Tech News **(13010)**

MASSACHUSETTS
Wayland
Popular Home Automation **(14615)** ....(Paid) ‡19,889

MICHIGAN
East Lansing
Communication Outlook **(14983)** ....(Paid) 1,500

Traverse City
Publishing Entrepreneur **(15601)**

MINNESOTA
Minneapolis
Game Informer Magazine **(16082)** .....(Paid) 217,653

Numbers cited after listings are entry numbers rather than page numbers.

NEBRASKA
Lincoln
PC Novice **(18111)** ....(Non-paid) 104,008
(Paid) 339,113
PC Today **(18112)** ....(Paid) 33,707
Smart Computing **(18120)** ....(Paid) 202,037

NEW JERSEY
Flemington
Children's Software Revue
(CSR) **(18818)** ....(Combined) ‡19,000

Medford
Searcher **(19232)** ....(Paid) 3,000
(Non-paid) 1,000

NEW YORK
Manhasset
Home PC **(21002)** ....(Paid) 512,474
Windows Magazine **(21018)** ....(Paid) 818,972

New York
ArtByte **(21254)**
Computer Life **(21476)** ....(Paid) 453,078
Computer Survival Guide **(21478)**
Computer Survival Journal **(21479)** ....(Paid) 100,000
Digital Coast Reporter **(21552)**
Family PC **(21680)** ....(Paid) 698,866
Internet User **(21942)** ....(Combined) 220,000
PC Magazine **(22534)** ....(Paid) 1,226,708
Silicon Alley Reporter **(22741)**
Window Sources **(22918)** ....(Paid) 400,738
Yahoo! Internet Life **(22947)** ....(Paid) 1,003,771
ZD Internet Magazine **(22955)**

Rochester
Computer Link Magazine **(23218)**
Inside the Internet **(23229)**

OREGON
Clackamas
Computer Bits **(26266)** ....(Non-paid) 35,000

TENNESSEE
Brentwood
Laptop Buyer's Guide & Handbook **(29063)**

VERMONT
West Topsham
Flash Magazine **(31616)**

WASHINGTON
Seattle
Be Magazine **(32947)** ....(Combined) 30,000

Spanaway
On Target Computing **(33091)**

WISCONSIN
Iola
EBay Magazine **(33824)** ....(Combined) 696,692

ONTARIO, CANADA
Nepean
Monitor **(36100)**

Toronto
Digital Journal.com **(36575)**

CONSUMER ELECTRONICS

ARIZONA
Glendale
Southwest Computer Monthly **(715)** ....(Paid) 18,000
(Non-paid) 32,000

CALIFORNIA
Anaheim
Auto Sound & Security **(1400)** ....(Paid) 27,330

Beverly Hills
Tips & Tricks **(1577)** ....(Paid) ★163,947

Los Angeles
Home Theater **(2293)** ....(Paid) 109,422

ILLINOIS
Lombard
NARDA Independent Retailer **(9117)** ....‡2,000

MASSACHUSETTS
Worcester
Home Automation **(14682)** ....(Non-paid) 4,200

NEBRASKA
Lincoln
Smart Computing **(18120)** ....(Paid) 202,037

NEW YORK
Hauppauge
Poptronics **(20721)**

New York
Mobile Entertainment **(22341)** ....(Paid) 102,992
Sony Style **(22763)**

ONTARIO, CANADA
Toronto
Digital Journal.com **(36575)**

CONSUMERISM

CALIFORNIA
Beverly Hills
Toy Tips **(1578)** ....(Controlled) 3,000,000

Santa Barbara
Freebies **(3640)** ....(Paid) ⊕356,815
(Non-paid) ⊕1,825

COLORADO
Fort Collins
Environ **(4430)** ....(Paid) 2,000
(Non-paid) 3,000

CONNECTICUT
Darien
Internet Shopper **(4773)** ....(Combined) 160,000

DISTRICT OF COLUMBIA
Washington
Consumer Comments **(5438)**
Consumers' Research **(5439)** ....‡7,200

ILLINOIS
Lincolnwood
Consumer Guide **(9092)**

Schaumburg
VANTAGE **(9592)** ....‡330,000

Skokie
CONSUMERS DIGEST **(9604)** ......(Paid) 1,000,033

Westmont
Editorial Pace **(9754)** ....(Controlled) ‡10,000

MISSOURI
St. Louis
Reviews Unlimited **(17488)** ....(Paid) 52,640

NEW YORK
Brooklyn
Consumer Info News **(20308)** 72,000

New York
Internet User **(21942)** ....(Combined) 220,000

Yonkers
Consumer Reports **(23598)** ....‡4,600,000
Refundle Bundle **(23600)** ....‡20,000

PENNSYLVANIA
Pittsburgh
FDA Consumer **(27787)**

ONTARIO, CANADA
Bath
Canadian MoneySaver **(35667)** ....‡19,100

QUEBEC, CANADA
Montreal
Lemon-Aid **(37174)** 20,000

CRAFTS, MODELS, HOBBIES, AND CONTESTS
See also Collecting; Photography

ARIZONA
Fountain Hills
American Amateur Journalist **(710)** ....(Paid) 300

CALIFORNIA
Canoga Park
Car Toy Collectibles **(1655)**
Kart Racer **(1657)**
Scale Ship Modeler **(1659)**

Concord
Tole World **(1755)** ....‡90,000
Weekend Woodcrafts **(1758)** ....(Paid) 33,000
Wood Strokes &
Woodcrafts **(1759)** ....(Paid) 102,090

Corona
Autograph Collector **(1766)** ....(Paid) 3,000
(Non-paid) 15,000

Corte Madera
The Crafts Fair Guide **(1770)** 3,500

Los Altos
Narrow Gauge and Short Line
Gazette **(2194)** ....(Paid) ‡16,300
(Non-paid) ‡219

Oakhurst
Horseless Carriage Gazette **(2658)** 5,000

Placentia
Kit Builders Magazine **(2847)** .....(Controlled) 10,000

Sacramento
Worldradio **(3023)** ....‡30,700

Salinas
American Squaredance **(3066)** ....‡18,000

San Anselmo
Western & Eastern Treasures **(3085)** ....‡60,000

Sierra Madre
Freshwater & Marine Aquarium
Magazine **(3765)** ....‡48,000
R/C Modeler **(3766)** ....‡220,000

COLORADO
Aurora
Model Railroading **(4147)** ....(Combined) ⊕12,860

Boulder
The Posthorn **(4184)** 1,000

CONNECTICUT
Newtown
Threads **(5046)** ....‡145,000

Ridgefield
Model Airplane News **(5099)** ....(Paid) 80,019
Radio Control Boat Modeler **(5100)** 25,000
Radio Control Car Action **(5101)** ....(Paid) 90,088

DELAWARE
Wilmington
The Crafts Report **(5289)** ....(Paid) ⊕23,000

FLORIDA
Miami
Mecanica Popular **(6369)** ....‡14,977

GEORGIA
Atlanta
Art Material Trade News **(6964)** ....(Paid) 168
(Non-paid) 8,100

Duluth
Shuttle Spindle & Dyepot **(7257)** 15,000

ILLINOIS
Des Plaines
Bridal Crafts **(8750)** ....(Paid) 52,066
Crafts 'N Things **(8756)** ....(Paid) 230,000
The Cross Stitcher **(8758)** ....(Paid) 107,208
Pack-O-Fun **(8766)** ....(Paid) ⊕105,000
Painting **(8767)** ....(Paid) ‡63,238

Forest Park
S Gaugian **(8893)** ....‡5,200

Magazines

Circ.

Circ.

Circ.

CRAFTS, MODELS, HOBBIES, AND CONTESTS (continued)

Sn3 Modeler (8894) ....(Paid) 2,000

St. Charles
Country Sampler (9564) ....(Paid) 434,323
Country Sampler Decorating
  Ideas (9565) ....(Paid) 200,469

INDIANA
Berne
Crazy for Cross Stitch (9803) ....(Combined) 60,000
Crazy for Cross Stitch (9804) 65,000
Crochet! (9806) ....(Combined) 56,000
Doll World (9808) ....‡39,030
Plastic Canvas Crafts (9815) ....‡60,541
Sewing Savvy (9819) ....(Paid) 57,000

IOWA
Des Moines
American Patchwork and
  Quilting (10770) ....(Paid) 236,304
WOOD (10815) ....(Paid) 551,121
Workbench (10817) ....(Paid) 352,470

Dubuque
Postcard Collector (10844) ....(Paid) ‡3,800

Grundy Center
Collectors News (10935) ....‡10,000

Lansing
Barr's Post Card News (11030) ....(Paid) ‡5,500
  (Non-paid) ‡550

Pleasant Hill
Jukebox Collector (11160) ....‡1,700

KANSAS
Topeka
Farm Collector (11818) ....(Paid) ‡40,000
Gas Engine Magazine (11820) ....(Paid) ‡22,000
Steam Traction (11837) ....‡6,500

KENTUCKY
Westport
Glass Patterns Quarterly (12437) .....(Paid) ⊕37,000

LOUISIANA
Bogalusa
SAC Newsmonthly (12534) ....(Paid) ‡2,000
  (Non-paid) ‡30

MASSACHUSETTS
Carlisle
Antique Radio
  Classified (14120) ....(Combined) 7,000

Newburyport
Nautical Research Journal (14380) ....‡1,700

MICHIGAN
Muskegon
Contemporary Doll Collector (15387) ....‡22,000
Soft Dolls & Animals (15389)
Stamping Arts & Crafts (15390)

Traverse City
Live Steam (15598) ....(Paid) ‡11,764
  (Non-paid) ‡107
Machinist's Workshop (15599) ....(Paid) ‡19,911
  (Non-paid) ‡91
Neil Knopf - Editor (15600) ....(Paid) ‡34,500
  (Non-paid) ‡92

Williamston
Out Your Backdoor (15685) ....(Paid) 1,000
  (Non-paid) 4,000

MINNESOTA
Eagan
American Woodworker (15861) ....(Paid) 332,911

Minneapolis
U.S. ART (16137) ....(Controlled) 55,000

St. Cloud
Interpretive Birding Bulletin (16342)

MONTANA
Helena
U.S. Toy Collector Magazine (17824) 2,800

NEW HAMPSHIRE
Nashua
The White Tops (18604) ....(Paid) ‡2,000
  (Controlled) ‡68

NEW JERSEY
Marlton
Lottery Player's Magazine (19216) ....(Paid) 170,000
  (Non-paid) 1,800

Morganville
Hobby Merchandiser (19286) ....(Paid) ‡2,200
  (Non-paid) ‡6,000

Newton
Creative Woodworks and
  Crafts (19370) ....(Combined) ⊕81,771
Flying Models (19371) ....⊕32,869
Paint Works (19373)
The Quilter (19374) ....⊕56,000
RailFan & Railroad (19375) ....‡56,000
Railroad Model Craftsman (19376) ....(Paid) ‡98,000
  (Non-paid) ‡500

Washington
Doll Castle News (19707) 7,500

NEW MEXICO
Los Alamos
Sport Rocketry (19894)

NEW YORK
Congers
Inquest, The Gaming
  Magazine (20490) ....(Paid) 105,000
Toyfare, The Toy Magazine (20491)

New York
Christmas Helps & Holiday
  Baking (21413) ....(Paid) 1,000,000
Crafts Magazine (21510) ....(Paid) 350,000
Martha Stewart Living (22287) ......(Paid) 2,436,422
This Old House (22831) ....(Paid) 663,345
TV Crosswords (22873) 207,638

Penfield
RollerCoaster! (23090) 6,000

NORTH CAROLINA
Asheville
FIBERARTS (23629) ....(Paid) ‡24,500
  (Non-paid) ‡300

Brasstown
Monitoring Times (23663) 25,000

OHIO
Cincinnati
Chip Chats (24781) ....‡35,000

Marietta
Bird Watcher's Digest (25343) ....‡90,000
Camp Chase
  Gazette (25344) ....(Combined) ⊕6,200
Glass Collector's Digest (25345) ....‡6,500

New Philadelphia
The National Hobby News (25420)

Westerville
Ceramics Monthly (25639) ....(Paid) 33,000
Pottery Making Illustrated (25644) .....(Paid) ‡13,000

OKLAHOMA
Grove
Lost Treasure (25848) ....‡45,000

OREGON
Hillsboro
Timbertimes (26373) 3,200

PENNSYLVANIA
Columbia
Bulletin of the National Association of Watch and
  Clock Collectors (26798) ....‡31,000

Harrisburg
Figurines & Collectibles (26990) ....(Paid) 54,085

Nazareth
O Guage Railroading (27311) ....(Paid) 39,000
  (Non-paid) 25

North East
Horn and Whistle (27339) ....(Paid) 194
  (Non-paid) 10

Richboro
Glass Craftsman (27933) ....(Combined) 10,500

RHODE ISLAND
Cranston
The Village Chronicle (28337) ....(Paid) ‡13,000

Providence
Treasure Chest (28428) ....(Non-paid) ‡50,000
  (Paid) ‡250

SOUTH DAKOTA
Sioux Falls
Knitter's (28964) ....‡70,000

TENNESSEE
Chattanooga
National Knife Magazine (29090) ......(Paid) ‡10,000
  (Non-paid) ‡350

TEXAS
Big Sandy
Hooked on Crochet (29921) ....(Paid) 85,000
Plastic Canvas Home &
  Holiday (29922) ....‡140,000
Quick & Easy Plastic Canvas (29923) ....‡75,000

Dallas
Dragon Ball Z Collector (30152) ......(Paid) 300,000

Houston
Turn For The Judges (TFTJ) (30537)

UTAH
Taylorsville
Seaways' Ships in Scale (31478) ......(Paid) ⊕6,700

VIRGINIA
Waterford
Clay Times (32609) ....(Paid) 15,500

WASHINGTON
Mukilteo
Mainline Modeler (32850) 13,405

Renton
Dragon Magazine (32923) 75,000

Seattle
Always Jukin' Magazine (32938) ....(Paid) 2,200
  (Non-paid) 250

Shelton
Char-Jay (33078)

WISCONSIN
Greendale
Crafting Traditions (33761) ....(Paid) ⊕700,000

Iola
Arts & Crafts (33801) ....(Combined) 254,928
Blade Magazine (33805) ....(Paid) ‡26,924
CNA (33808) ....(Combined) △30,791
Craft Supply (33816) ....(Combined) 13,239
The Doll Artisan (33819) ....‡13,000
Doll Costuming (33820)
Doll Crafter (33821) ....‡42,000
Dollmaking (33822) ....(Controlled) ⊕16,200
DOLLS (33823) ....‡81,724
Great American
  Crafts (33829) ....(Combined) 120,984
Memory Magic (33834) ....(Combined) 90,707
Michael's Create! (33836) ....(Combined) 200,000
Military Vehicles (33838) ....(Paid) ‡18,000
Teddy Bear Review (33847) ....(Paid) ‡55,045
Toy Cars & Models (33848) ....(Paid) 13,838
Toy Shop (33849) ....(Paid) ‡26,381

Waukesha
Bead and Button (34395) ....(Paid) ★140,878
Classic Trains (34399) ....(Paid) ★60,308
Dollhouse Miniatures
  Magazine (34404) ....(Paid) ★26,545
FineScale Modeler (34405) ....(Paid) 60,425
Garden Railways (34406) ....(Paid) ★38,215
Model Railroader (34407) ....(Paid) ★175,051
Model Retailer (34408) ....(Paid) ★4,320
Scale Auto Magazine (34411) ....(Paid) ★30,135
Trains (34413) ....(Paid) ★109,329

Numbers cited after listings are entry numbers rather than page numbers.

ONTARIO, CANADA
Burlington
Model Aviation
　Canada **(35717)** ....(Non-paid) ⊕12,000

Markham
Canadian Home
　Workshop **(36019)** ....(Paid) 110,743

DOGS
See also Pets

ARIZONA
Green Valley
German Shepherd Dog Review **(721)** ....‡4,000

CALIFORNIA
Berkeley
The Bark **(1494)**

Gilroy
The Rottweiler Quarterly **(2004)** 3,000
　　　　　　　　　　　　　　　　(Non-paid) 250

Midway City
The Royal Spaniels **(2539)** ....(Combined) 3,745

Mission Viejo
Dog Fancy Magazine **(2550)** ....(Paid) 293,273
Dog World **(2551)** ....(Paid) 55,771
Dogs USA **(2552)**

COLORADO
Wheat Ridge
Akita World **(4671)** ....(Paid) 1,000
　　　　　　　　　　　　　　　　(Non-paid) 100
The Boston Quarterly **(4672)** ....(Paid) 600
The Dalmatian Quarterly **(4674)** ....(Paid) 300
　　　　　　　　　　　　　　　　(Non-paid) 0
The German Shepherd.
　Quarterly **(4675)** ....(Paid) ‡600
　　　　　　　　　　　　　　　　(Non-paid) ‡0
The Irish Wolfhound Quarterly **(4677)** ....(Paid) ‡600
　　　　　　　　　　　　　　　　(Non-paid) ‡0
The Labrador Quarterly **(4678)** ....(Paid) 1,800
　　　　　　　　　　　　　　　　(Non-paid) ‡200
The Malamute Quarterly **(4679)** ....(Paid) ‡400
　　　　　　　　　　　　　　　　(Non-paid) ‡0
The Rhodesian Ridgeback
　Quarterly **(4681)** ....(Paid) 400
　　　　　　　　　　　　　　　　(Non-paid) 0
The Samoyed Quarterly **(4682)** ....(Paid) 400
　　　　　　　　　　　　　　　　(Non-paid) 0
The Siberian Quarterly **(4683)** ....(Paid) 700
　　　　　　　　　　　　　　　　(Controlled) 0

ILLINOIS
Chicago
American Field **(8256)** ....(Paid) ‡8,000
　　　　　　　　　　　　　　　　(Non-paid) ‡55

Sesser
American Cooner **(9597)** ....(Paid) 18,000
The Hunter's Horn **(9598)** ....‡8,500

Urbana
Poodle Review **(9715)** ....(Paid) 1,700
　　　　　　　　　　　　　　　　(Non-paid) 300

INDIANA
Indianapolis
Paws & Claws **(10159)** ....(Paid) 1,000
　　　　　　　　　　　　　　　　(Non-paid) 40,000

IOWA
Des Moines
You & Your Dog **(10819)**

KANSAS
Abilene
The Greyhound Review **(11334)** ....‡4,200

MICHIGAN
Kalamazoo
Bloodlines **(15232)** ....(Paid) ‡5,200
　　　　　　　　　　　　　　　　(Non-paid) ‡190
Coonhound Bloodlines **(15235)** ....(Paid) 20,700
Hunting Retriever **(15238)** ....(Paid) 5,000
　　　　　　　　　　　　　　　　(Non-paid) 50

Shelby Township
The Basenji **(15535)** ....‡1,450

MINNESOTA
Orr
Spaniels in the Field **(16244)** .....(Combined) ⊕1802

NEW JERSEY
Chatham
Animaltown News **(18727)** ....(Non-paid) 15,000

NORTH CAROLINA
Kittrell
Saint Fancier **(24032)** ....(Paid) 1,500

PENNSYLVANIA
Bradford
Hounds and Hunting **(26728)** ....‡7,917

ONTARIO, CANADA
Etobicoke
Dogs in Canada **(35814)** ....(Paid) 36,207
　　　　　　　　　　　　　　　　(Non-paid) 2,855

DRAMA AND THEATRE
See also Entertainment

CALIFORNIA
Los Angeles
Performing Arts **(2360)** ....(Controlled) 300,000
　　　　　　　　　　　　　　　　　　　600,000
Variety **(2427)** ....(Mon.) 34,293

Walnut Creek
Diablo Arts **(4053)**

COLORADO
Steamboat Springs
Vail International Dance
　Festival **(4635)** ....(Non-paid) ‡10,000

Westminster
Denver Arts Center Programs **(4662)** 2,600,000

MASSACHUSETTS
Amherst
Theatre Topics **(13806)** 2,300

Cambridge
TDR: The Drama Review **(14105)** 2,800

NEVADA
Henderson
ShowBiz Weekly **(18354)** ....(Non-paid) 150,216

NEW YORK
New York
American Theatre **(21207)** ....‡25,000
Models & Talent Contacts **(22345)** 50,000
Models & Talent Contacts **(22346)** ....‡180,000
The New Criterion **(22428)** 7,000
　　　　　　　　　　　　　　　　(Non-paid) 1,000
Ross Reports Television and
　Film **(22677)** ....(Combined) 15,103
Show Biz News & Model
　News **(22737)** ....(Combined) 75,000
Stages **(22783)** 10,000
TV & Film Extras **(22876)** 35,000

OHIO
Cincinnati
Dramatics Magazine **(24795)** ....(Paid) ‡34,497
　　　　　　　　　　　　　　　　(Non-paid) ‡321

PENNSYLVANIA
Allentown
ARTS ALIVE!
　Magazine **(26626)** ....(Controlled) ‡18,000

Philadelphia
Playbill **(27640)** ....(Non-paid) 180,000

TENNESSEE
Murfreesboro
Poems and Plays **(29431)** ....(Combined) 800

WASHINGTON
Seattle
ENCORE **(32963)** ....(Combined) ‡1,126,000

WISCONSIN
Waukesha
PLAYS **(34410)** ....‡9,000

ONTARIO, CANADA
Toronto
Opera Canada **(36688)** ....(Combined) ‡4,000

QUEBEC, CANADA
Montreal
Echos-Vedettes **(37111)** ....(Sat.) 76,119
Montreal Serai **(37191)**

DRESSMAKING, NEEDLEWORK, AND QUILTING
See also Fashion

ALABAMA
Birmingham
McCall's Needlework **(80)** ....(Non-paid) 500

Brownsboro
Sew Beautiful **(139)** ....‡80,000

COLORADO
Golden
Sew News **(4474)** ....(Paid) 166,734

CONNECTICUT
Newtown
Threads **(5046)** ....‡145,000

INDIANA
Berne
Crazy for Cross Stitch **(9803)** ....(Combined) 60,000
Creative Crafter **(9805)** ....‡179,650
Crochet! **(9806)** ....(Combined) 56,000
Crochet World **(9807)** ....‡68,000
Fast & Fun Crochet **(9809)** 59,000
Knitting Digest **(9813)** ....‡45,000
Old-Time Crochet **(9814)** ....‡47,000
Quick & Easy Quilting **(9817)** ....‡133,000
Quilt World **(9818)** ....‡66,042
Sewing Savvy **(9819)** ....(Paid) 57,000

IOWA
Ames
Needlework Retailer **(10592)**

Des Moines
American Patchwork and
　Quilting **(10770)** ....(Paid) 236,304
Embroidery Professional & Sewing Professional/Round
　Bobbin **(10784)** ....(Non-paid) ‡10,000

KENTUCKY
Paducah
American Quilter **(12337)** ....(Combined) 61,000

MICHIGAN
Muskegon
Soft Dolls & Animals **(15389)**

NEW YORK
Brooklyn
Vice **(20353)** ....(Non-paid) ‡75,000

New York
Butterick **(21363)**
Vogue Patterns Magazine **(22904)** .....(Paid) 66,172

OHIO
Zanesville
Cast On **(25716)** ....(Combined) 20,000

PENNSYLVANIA
Lemoyne
Rug Hooking Magazine **(27185)** 12,000

Montrose
Quiltworks Today **(27291)** ....‡85,000

SOUTH DAKOTA
Sioux Falls
Knitter's **(28964)** ....‡70,000

Circulation: ★ = ABC; △ = BPA; ♦ = CAC; ● = CCAB; ❑ = VAC; ⊕ = PO Statement; ‡ = Publisher's Report; Boldface figures = sworn; Light figures = estimated.

Magazines

Circ.

DRESSMAKING, NEEDLEWORK, AND QUILTING (continued)

TEXAS
Big Sandy
Plastic Canvas Home &
   Holiday **(29922)** ....‡140,000
Quick & Easy Plastic Canvas **(29923)** ....‡75,000

ONTARIO, CANADA
Toronto
KnitNet **(36645)** ....(Non-paid) 40,000

EDUCATION

See also Parenting

ARIZONA
Tucson
College & Career Guide News for College
   Students **(940)** ....(Non-paid) 10,000
Working Moms & Dads Magazine **(974)**

CALIFORNIA
Hollywood
The National Record **(2052)** ....(Paid) ‡12,000
                      (Non-paid) ‡41,600

Los Angeles
Rapport **(2377)** ....(Paid) 50,000

CONNECTICUT
Danbury
Junior Scholastic **(4743)** ....(Paid) 591,038
Let's Find Out **(4744)** ....‡600,000
The New York Times
   Upfront **(4746)** ....(Paid) 230,000
Scholastic Action **(4751)** 230,000
Scholastic News Citizen Edition **(4756)** 485,000
Scholastic News Explorer Edition **(4757)** 505,000
Scholastic News Newstime
   Edition **(4758)** 367,000
Scholastic News Pilot Edition **(4759)** 475,000
Scholastic News Ranger Edition **(4760)** 530,000
Scholastic News Trails Edition **(4761)** 530,000
Scholastic Scope **(4762)** ....(Paid) 438,662
Science World **(4763)** ....(Paid) 395,228

Stamford
Current Events **(5145)** ....‡257,402
Know Your World Extra **(5153)** ....‡172,109

DISTRICT OF COLUMBIA
Washington
Preventing School Failure **(5729)** ....(Paid) 635

FLORIDA
Gainesville
Florida Leader for High School
   Students **(6138)** 100
                        (Paid) 25,000

ILLINOIS
Champaign
Teaching Elementary Physical
   Education **(8220)** ....(Paid) ‡3,693

Chicago
Book Links: Connecting Books, Libraries and
   Classrooms **(8286)** ....(Paid) 24,265
                  (Non-paid) 5,735

Northbrook
Current Health 1 **(9314)** ....(Paid) 165,793
Current Health 2 **(9315)** ....(Paid) 229,274
Writing! **(9323)**

INDIANA
Indianapolis
Forensic Quarterly **(10112)** ....(Paid) 5000

MARYLAND
Hagerstown
Winner **(13571)** ....(Paid) 15,000

MASSACHUSETTS
Florence
Perspectiva **(14187)** 15,000

MISSOURI
Fenton
Practical
   Homeschooling **(17064)** ....(Paid) 25,000 copies

Kansas City
College Outlook **(17163)** ....(Non-paid) 1,395,153

NEW HAMPSHIRE
Peterborough
Appleseeds **(18616)**

NEW JERSEY
Caldwell
Children's House/Children's
   World **(18711)** ....‡47,500

Flemington
Children's Software Revue
   (CSR) **(18818)** ...:............(Combined) ‡19,000

Keyport
Careers & Colleges **(19155)** ....(Paid) ❏1,679
                  (Non-paid) ❏750,000

Trenton
New Jersey School Boards Association School
   Leader **(19664)**

NEW YORK
Chautauqua
Chautauquan Daily **(20453)** ....‡2,500

Great Neck
Making It! Careers
   Newsmagazine **(20692)** ....(Paid) 5,000
                    (Non-paid) 45,000

New York
Student Aid News **(22798)**
Women's Studies Quarterly **(22935)** ....‡1,500

Syracuse
News for You **(23414)** ....‡75,700

Victor
The Next Step
   Magazine **(23494)** ....(Non-paid) 440,000

TEXAS
Waco
Gifted Child Today
   Magazine **(31247)** ....(Paid) ‡15,000

VIRGINIA
Norfolk
Educational Technology Review **(32282)** ......‡7,500

Reston
DECA Dimensions **(32364)** ....(Paid) ⊕161,000
                 (Non-paid) ⊕500
Research Quarterly for Exercise and
   Sport **(32413)** ....(Paid) ‡7,000

WASHINGTON
Tonasket
Home Education
   Magazine **(33165)** ....(Paid) ‡12,700
                  (Non-paid) ‡12,400

ONTARIO, CANADA
Toronto
Chirp **(36549)** ....(Combined) 58,070
Kidsworld **(36643)** ....(Non-paid) 200,050
Owl Canadian Family **(36694)** ....(Non-paid) 154,519

QUEBEC, CANADA
Montreal
Nouvelles CEQ **(37197)** ....(Non-paid) 95,498

Saint-Lambert
Le Magazine Enfants
   Quebec **(37359)** ....(Combined) 72,102

ENTERTAINMENT

See also Drama and Theatre; Motion Pictures; Radio, Television, Cable, and Video

ALABAMA
Birmingham
LoMo Magazine **(79)**

ARIZONA
Bullhead City
Laughlin Nevada
   Entertainer **(665)** ....(Combined) 52,000

Glendale
Key Magazine
   Phoenix/Scottsdale **(714)** ....(Combined) 45,000

Phoenix
Phoenix New Times **(810)** ....(Non-paid) 130,979

Scottsdale
Key Magazine Palm
   Springs **(870)** ....(Combined) 45,000

CALIFORNIA
Beverly Hills
Inside Film Magazine **(1575)**
Tips & Tricks **(1577)** ....(Paid) ★163,947

Burbank
Action Pursuit Games **(1613)**
Entertainment Today **(1617)** ....‡215,000

Concord
BAM Magazine **(1750)** ....(Non-paid) △119,507

Inglewood
Gambling Times **(2071)** 125,000

La Jolla
Pre-Vue Entertainment
   Magazine **(2119)** ....(Paid) 2,609
                  (Non-paid) 200,000

Los Angeles
Blitz **(2222)** ....(Paid) ‡2,000
                (Controlled) ‡500
The Duckburg Times **(2254)** ....‡1,400
Femme Fatales **(2269)**
The Hollywood Reporter **(2291)** ....(Mon.-Fri.) 24,608
                  (Tues.) 32,799
Novedades **(2350)** ....(Combined) 50,000
Southern California Guide **(2395)**
Variety **(2427)** ....(Mon.) 34,293
Written By Magazine **(2442)** 15,000

Nevada City
Dream Magazine **(2615)**

North Hollywood
Emmy **(2642)** ....(Paid) ‡12,788
                (Non-paid) ‡2,331

San Diego
San Diego This Week **(3269)** .....(Combined) 30,000

San Francisco
The San Francisco and Bay Area
   Guide **(3428)** 1,800,000
SF Weekly **(3439)** ....(Non-paid) 123,462
*Surface **(3446)** ....(Paid) 112,000

San Ramon
The Nooner Magazine **(3607)** ....(Paid) 11
                  (Non-paid) 16,000

Seaside
Coast Weekly **(3750)**

South Lake Tahoe
Lake Tahoe Action
   Magazine **(3783)** ....(Paid) ‡10,000
                  (Free) ‡35,000

Temecula
Widescreen Review **(3843)** ....(Paid) ⊕50,000

Thousand Oaks
Elvis International
   Forum **(3866)** ....(Combined) 90,800

Universal City
Pratfall **(3972)** 1,500

Vacaville
Bingo and Gaming News **(3973)**

Walnut Creek
Diablo Arts (4053)

COLORADO
Aurora
Star Wars Insider (4150) ....(Paid) 250,000

Denver
5280 (4327) ....(Combined) 50,000
Interactive (4331)
Out Front Colorado (4346) ....(Free) 25,000

Littleton
Key Magazine
  Colorado (4550) ....(Combined) **38,000**

Steamboat Springs
Vail International Dance
  Festival (4635) ....(Non-paid) ‡10,000

CONNECTICUT
Norwalk
Good Time Fill-in Puzzles (5062)
Good Time Word Seek Puzzles (5063)

Orange
Beatles Fan Magazine (5090) ....(Paid) 5,200
                   (Non-paid) 800

Sandy Hook
Mayfair Magazine (5112)

Stamford
Club Modele Magazine (5143)

DISTRICT OF COLUMBIA
Washington
Fast Forward (5492)

FLORIDA
Geneva
Higher & Higher (6172) ....(Combined) 3,500

Miami
Bienvenidos a Miami (6341) ......(Non-paid) ‡16,000
Entertainment News &
  Views (6351) ....(Free) 125,000
Miami New Times (6370) ....(Non-paid) 106,692
                    (Paid) 33

Murdock
Country Grapevine (6437)

Naples
Naples Guide (6446) ....:...(Controlled) ‡270,000

Plantation
Loafer's Choice (6587) ....(Non-paid) 19,000

Tampa
World of Fandom (6783) ....(Controlled) 80,000

GEORGIA
Athens
Flagpole Magazine (6937) ....(Combined) 13,803

Atlanta
Hooters Magazine (7017) ....(Paid) 32,000

Sugar Hill
Key Magazine Atlanta (7573) .....(Combined) **15,000**

HAWAII
Kahului
Shemp! (7759) ....(Combined) 400

Kaneohe
Midweek Magazine (7774)

ILLINOIS
Chicago
Illinois Entertainer (8409) ....(Combined) 74,606

Fairbury
The Rocket (8879) ....(Non-paid) 80,000

Mount Prospect
Program (9249) ....(Combined) 28,000

INDIANA
Bloomington
The Ryder (9851) ....(Non-paid) 19,000

IOWA
Dubuque
The Dubuque Area
  Magazine (10843) ....(Combined) ‡40,000

KANSAS
Liberal
Leisure Times (11604)

Overland Park
Entertainment Design (11711) ....(Combined) 16,400

KENTUCKY
Lexington
Around the Town (12160) ....(Free) ‡10,000

LOUISIANA
New Orleans
This Week New
  Orleans (12757) ....(Combined) **5,500**

MAINE
Southwest Harbor
Face Magazine (13058) ....(Free) 17,500

MARYLAND
Baltimore
Baltimore City Paper (13131) ......(Non-paid) 86,113

Greenbelt
Recreation News (13559) ....(Non-paid) ‡130,000

Takoma Park
Sister 2 Sister (13752) ....(Paid) ★150,000

MASSACHUSETTS
Boston
J Magazine (13909) ....(Combined) 15,000

Cambridge
15 Minutes (14053) ....(Non-paid) ‡10,000

MICHIGAN
Ann Arbor
Ann Arbor Observer (14743) ....(Paid) 4,014
                (Non-paid) 56,974

FOUND (14750)

Ferndale
Real Detroit Weekly (15030) ....(Free) 65,000

Jenison
On the Town (15229) ....(Controlled) 36,500

Royal Oak
Cruise Entertainment
  Magazine (15479) ....(Non-paid) 5,000
HOUR Detroit (15481)

Troy
The Fear Finder (15625) ....(Combined) 500,000

MINNESOTA
Minneapolis
City Pages (16065) ....(Free) 116,697

St. Joseph
Music and Dance News (16357) ....(Paid) ‡2,000
                (Controlled) ‡12,000

St. Paul
Midwest Players (16389) ....(Free) 78,000

MISSOURI
Kansas City
eKC (17167) ....(Non-paid) 26,000

St. Louis
KETC Guide (17465) ....(Paid) 42,000

NEVADA
Henderson
ShowBiz Weekly (18354) ....(Non-paid) 150,216

Las Vegas
Key Magazine Las
  Vegas (18369) ....(Combined) ‡83,500
Magic (18377) ....(Controlled) 10,500
What's On, The Las Vegas
  Guide (18385) ....(Non-paid) 195,000
                (Paid) 3,200

NEW HAMPSHIRE
Nashua
The White Tops (18604) ....(Paid) ‡2,000
             (Controlled) ‡68

NEW JERSEY
Bridgewater
Strictly Hunterdon (18701) ....(Combined) 38,762

Clifton
Mortuary Times (18756)

Dover
Hot House (18778) ....(Non-paid) 13,000

Glen Rock
Scarlet Street (18848) ....(Paid) 26,000

Hackensack
Balloons & Parties Magazine (18851) ....‡7,000

Jersey City
Coming Up (19134) ....(Non-paid) 18,246
Go Out (19137) ....(Non-paid) 34,433

Ocean Grove
The Phantom of the Movies'
  Videoscope (19390) ....(Paid) 10,000

Pleasantville
Whoot Newspaper (19445) ....(Paid) 527
             (Free) 38,000

Somerset
Strictly Somerset (19567) ....(Non-paid) 68,283

Somerville
The Moneybook (19575) ....(Free) 112,500
TeeVee Moneysaver (Edition
  1) (19579) ....(Non-paid) 120,000

Westwood
Steppin' Out Magazine (19748) ....(Non-paid) 75,000

NEW YORK
East Rochester
Mobile Beat (20553)

Garden City
The Island-Ear (20643) 25,000

New York
Biography (21316) ....(Paid) 613,637
Buying & Dining
  Guide (21364) ....(Controlled) ‡500,000
Casting News (21378) ....(Paid) 100,000
             (Non-paid) 200,000
Cineaste (21419) 11,000
Circus Magazine (21420) ....(Paid) 307,092
            (Non-paid) 7,709
City Guide Magazine (21423) .....(Combined) 61,596
Daily Variety (21533) ....(Mon.-Fri.) 30,406
Entertainment Weekly (21609) ....(Paid) 1,520,463
The FADER (21675)
Flatiron Magazine (21706) ....(Controlled) 35,000
In Style (21857) ....(Paid) 1,584,691
Models & Talent Contacts (22345) 50,000
Models & Talent Contacts (22346) ....‡180,000
Modern Screen's Country
  Music (22352) ....(Paid) ‡100,000
Murray Hill News (22383) 15,000
Music Gigs & Auditions
  U.S.A. (22385) ....(Paid) ‡100,000
             (Non-paid) ‡200,000
Right On! (22667) ....(Paid) 77,247
Rolling Stone (22675) ....(Paid) 1,251,520
Ross Reports Television and
  Film (22677) ....(Combined) 15,103
Savoy (22707) ....(Combined) 200,000
Shift (22736) ....(Paid) ‡150,000
Show Biz News & Model
  News (22737) ....(Combined) 75,000
The Source (22764) ....(Paid) 454,726
SPIN (22772) ....(Paid) 540,063
Stages (22783) 10,000
talk (22814) ....
Teen People (22818) ....(Paid) 1,600,504
Tiger Beat Magazine (22835) 175,000
Time Out New York (22841) ......(Paid) 125,580
Travel, Food & Wine (22857)
TV & Film Extras (22876) 35,000
TV News (22877) ....(Free) ‡331,000
Us (22892) ....(Paid) 850,434
WNYC Program Guide (22923) ....(Paid) 55,000
             (Non-paid) 500

Magazines

Circulation: ★ = ABC; △ = BPA; ♦ = CAC; ♦ = CCAB; ❏ = VAC; ⊕ = PO Statement; ‡ = Publisher's Report; Boldface figures = sworn; Light figures = estimated.

2807

Circ.　　　　　　　　　　　Circ.　　　　　　　　　　　Circ.

ENTERTAINMENT (continued)

NORTH CAROLINA
Charlotte
Trend Magazine **(23757)**

Durham
Linking Ring **(23834)** ....(Controlled) 13,800

Fayetteville
Up & Coming Weekly **(23882)** .....(Non-paid) 15,000

Greenville
Campus Express **(23961)** ....(Free) ‡18,500

Shelby
TV Plus **(24228)** ....(Paid) 158,758

OHIO
Chagrin Falls
Currents **(24757)** 65,000

Cleveland
Northern Ohio LIVE **(24933)** ....(Paid) 15,724
(Non-paid) △14,846

Maineville
Key Magazine
　Cincinnati **(25327)** ....(Combined) ‡15,200

Troy
T.V. Week **(25598)**

OKLAHOMA
Oklahoma City
Oklahoma Entertainment
　News **(25978)** ....(Paid) 350
(Non-paid) 20,000

Shawnee
Frontier Country Key **(26063)** .....(Combined) 20,000

OREGON
Coos Bay
The Whole Shebang! **(26273)**

Eugene
Eugene Weekly **(26316)** ....(Free) 27,787

PENNSYLVANIA
Ambler
Easy Crosswords **(26647)**
Find the Word **(26649)**
Superb Crosswords **(26654)**

Clarks Summit
Happenings Magazine **(26786)** ....(Non-paid) ‡30,000

Pittsburgh
Grapevine Weekly **(27793)** ....(Paid) ‡300
(Free) ‡21,950
Key Magazine
　Pittsburgh **(27808)** ....(Combined) 10,000

Wilkes Barre
The Weekender **(28168)** ....(Non-paid) ‡42,000

RHODE ISLAND
North Scituate
The Northeast Square Dancer
　Magazine **(28378)** ....‡4,000

SOUTH DAKOTA
Sioux Falls
Sioux Falls Shopping News
　Informer **(28966)** ....(Free) ‡85,000

TENNESSEE
Memphis
Key Magazine
　Memphis **(29374)** ....(Combined) 23,000

Nashville
Nashville Scene **(29473)** ....(Non-paid) 52,500

TEXAS
Austin
Austin Chronicle **(29757)** ....(Free) 90,000
(Paid) 267
The Texas Review of Entertainment and Sports
　Law **(29846)**

Coppell
Facility Manager **(30073)** ....(Paid) ‡2,500
(Non-paid) ‡70

Dallas
Dragon Ball Z Collector **(30152)** ......(Paid) 300,000
Key Magazine
　Dallas **(30165)** ....(Controlled) ‡35,000

Fort Worth
Key Magazine Fort
　Worth **(30344)** ....(Combined) ‡11,740

Houston
Houston Press **(30488)** ....(Non-paid) 115,123
Key Magazine
　Houston **(30500)** ....(Combined) ‡41,505

UTAH
Salt Lake City
Salt Lake City Weekly **(31438)** ....(Paid) 210
(Non-paid) 48,761

WASHINGTON
Des Moines
Northwest Fun & Games **(32737)** ....(Paid) 1,500
(Controlled) 40,000

Seattle
The Comedy Magazine **(32957)** ....(Paid) 15,000
DirectGuide **(32960)** ....(Paid) 22,973
ENCORE **(32963)** ....(Combined) ‡1,126,000

WISCONSIN
Milwaukee
Key Milwaukee
　Magazine **(34072)** ....(Combined) ‡31,000
The Onion **(34091)** ....(Controlled) ‡240,000
(Paid) ❏20,489

ALBERTA, CANADA
Calgary
WHERE Calgary **(34659)** ....(Non-paid) 28,000

Edmonton
Satellite Entertainment
　Guide **(34727)** ....(Combined) 76,077
VU Magazine **(34733)** ....(Paid) 28,637

BRITISH COLUMBIA, CANADA
Vancouver
Georgia Straight **(35144)** ....(Free) 122,000
WHERE Vancouver **(35182)** ......(Non-paid) ‡52,000

NEWFOUNDLAND AND LABRADOR, CANADA
St. John's
The Newfoundland Herald **(35491)** .....(Paid) 27,383
(Non-paid) 544

NOVA SCOTIA, CANADA
Halifax
The Coast **(35562)** ....(Free) ❏19,276
(Paid) ❏11

ONTARIO, CANADA
Don Mills
Teen Tribune **(35778)** ....(Non-paid) •299,500

Guelph
Canadian Theatre Review **(35859)** 1,300

Thunder Bay
Thunder Bay Life **(36442)** ....‡3,000

Toronto
Campus.ca **(36486)** ....(Non-paid) •135,237
Digital Journal.com **(36575)**
Exclaim! **(36585)** ....(Non-paid) 102,302
Now **(36678)** ....(Paid) 55
(Free) 106,103
Performing Arts in Canada **(36701)** ....‡20,000
Toronto Events Calender **(36767)**

PRINCE EDWARD ISLAND, CANADA
Charlottetown
The Buzz **(36912)**

QUEBEC, CANADA
Montreal
Montreal Serai **(37191)**
Super Ecran **(37227)**

ENVIRONMENTAL AND NATURAL RESOURCES CONSERVATION

CALIFORNIA
Crescent City
The Kerf **(1787)** ....(Non-paid) 275

Oakland
California Coast &
　Ocean **(2673)** ....(Combined) 10,000
EarthLight Magazine **(2678)** ....(Paid) 6,500
(Non-paid) 500

Sacramento
Animal Issues **(2976)** ....(Paid) ‡30,000
(Non-paid) ‡1,000

San Francisco
Earth Island Journal **(3352)** ....(Combined) 18,000
Sierra **(3440)** ....(Paid) 728,000.

Torrance
Right of Way **(3941)** ....‡9,000

COLORADO
Denver
Colorado Outdoors **(4319)** ....(Paid) ‡43,576
(Controlled) ‡3,100

Fort Collins
Environ **(4430)** ....(Paid) 2,000
(Non-paid) 3,000

CONNECTICUT
East Haddam
KIND News **(4777)** 1,222,800

Norwalk
E **(5056)** 56,000

DISTRICT OF COLUMBIA
Washington
American Forests **(5329)** ....‡25,000
Atmosphere **(5371)**
Greenpeace Magazine **(5520)** ....(Paid) ‡400,000
Population Connection **(5723)** ....(Paid) 75,000

ILLINOIS
Ava
Illinois Audubon **(8045)** ....(Combined) 3,000

Chicago
Conscious Choice **(8342)** ....(Non-paid) 50,000

MARYLAND
Gaithersburg
Outdoor America **(13546)** 45,000

Lanham
Environmental Entomology **(13600)** 2,739

MASSACHUSETTS
Boston
AMC Outdoors **(13848)** ....(Paid) ‡94,000
(Non-paid) ‡1,000

Great Barrington
Orion **(14216)** ....(Paid) ‡20,000
(Controlled) ‡200

Woods Hole
Oceanus Magazine **(14673)** ..:.....(Controlled) 5,000

MICHIGAN
Charlevoix
The North Woods Call **(14865)** ....‡8,000

Ferndale
Fifth Estate **(15028)** ....(Paid) 5,000

Lansing
Michigan Out-of-Doors **(15289)** ....(Paid) △92,226
(Non-paid) △615

Okemos
Michigan Country Lines **(15416)** 240,000

MISSOURI
Jefferson City
Missouri Wildlife **(17130)** ....(Paid) ⊕23,000

MONTANA
Missoula
Bugle **(17865)** ....(Combined) 130,000

Numbers cited after listings are entry numbers rather than page numbers.

NEBRASKA
Lincoln
NEBRASKAland (18107) ....(Paid) ‡51,238
(Non-paid) ‡4,100

NEW HAMPSHIRE
Charlestown
Earth Work (18464) ....(Paid) 3,500

Concord
Forest Notes (18472) ....(Paid) ‡12,000
(Controlled) ‡400

NEW JERSEY
Far Hills
New Jersey
  Conservation (18817) ....(Combined) 5,000

Hoboken
Federal Facilities Environmental
  Journal (18947) 5985
International Journal of Energy Research (18982)
Journal of Applied Toxicology (19004)
Remediation (19097) 5985

Trenton
New Jersey
  Outdoors (19662) ....(Controlled) ⊕10,258

NEW YORK
Brooklyn
Satya (20344) ....(Combined) 10,000

Dolgeville
Vegetarian Voice (20533) ....(Combined) 11,000

LaFayette
Future Survey (20870) ....(Paid) 1,750

Lake George
Adirondac (20871) ....‡20,000

New York
Audubon (21272) ....(Paid) 454,885
Natural History Magazine (22405) .....(Paid) 300,000

Paul Smiths
Adirondack Journal of Environmental
  Studies (23083) ....(Combined) 350

OHIO
Columbus
Wild Ohio Magazine (25069)

OKLAHOMA
Oklahoma City
Outdoor Oklahoma (25990) ....‡20,000

OREGON
Eugene
Rain Magazine (26333) 700
(Non-paid) 1,300
Worm Digest (26335) ....(Paid) ‡6,200
(Non-paid) ‡800

Portland
The Bear Deluxe Magazine (26469) ....(Paid) 500
(Non-paid) 18,500
Cascadia Times (26472)
Portland Alliance (26500) ....(Combined) 7,000

PENNSYLVANIA
Coraopolis
RGS Magazine (26808) 23,000

Dingmans Ferry
Country Road
  Chronicles (26827) ....(Controlled) 51,000

Philadelphia
Toxicology & Ecotoxicology
  News/Reviews (27706) 600

SOUTH CAROLINA
Columbia
E2SC (28549) ....(Controlled) 3,177
South Carolina Wildlife (28568) ....‡60,000

Edgefield
Quail Unlimited (28601) ....(Paid) 50,000

TENNESSEE
Memphis
Ducks Unlimited (29370) ....(Paid) 661,171

Nashville
Tennessee Conservationist (29489) .....(Paid) 15,000

TEXAS
Austin
Indigenous Woman (29781) 4,000
(Non-paid) 1,000

College Station
Texas Shore Magazine (30054) ....(Combined) 5,500

Tyler
Both Sides Now (31196) ....‡200

VERMONT
Corinth
Northern Woodlands (31537) ....(Paid) ⊕14,000

VIRGINIA
Arlington
Nature Conservancy (31813) ....‡830,000

Reston
National Wildlife (32407) ....(Paid) 625,711

Richmond
Virginia Wildlife (32468) ....‡40,000

WASHINGTON
Renton
InterActions (32924)

WEST VIRGINIA
Harpers Ferry
Appalachian Trailway
  News (33333) ....(Paid) ‡29,000
(Non-paid) ‡500

WISCONSIN
Madison
Wisconsin Natural
  Resources (33988) ....(Paid) 128,000

ALBERTA, CANADA
St. Albert
The Alberta Game Warden (34841) ....‡11,000

BRITISH COLUMBIA, CANADA
Argenta
The Smallholder (34881) ....(Paid) 750

NEW BRUNSWICK, CANADA
St. Andrews
Atlantic Salmon Journal (35429) ....(Paid) ‡416
(Non-paid) ‡10,584

NOVA SCOTIA, CANADA
Dartmouth
Eastern Woods and
  Waters (35546) ....(Paid) 11,208
(Non-paid) 5,647

ONTARIO, CANADA
Don Mills
Seasons (35777) ....(Combined) ‡14,500

Ottawa
Canadian Geographic (36198) ....(Paid) 229,180
Trail and Landscape (36277)

Toronto
Women & Environments (36793) 2,000

QUEBEC, CANADA
Montreal
Sentier Chasse-Peche (37224) ....(Paid) ★45,091
(Non-paid) ★1,260

ETHNIC PUBLICATIONS

ALABAMA
Birmingham
Pure Heart Magazine (88)

ARIZONA
Tucson
Serb World U.S.A. (963) ....‡3,800

ARKANSAS
Forrest City
Home with Homeland (1138) 15,000

CALIFORNIA
Beverly Hills
The Ethiopian Mirror (1572) ....(Paid) 11,000
(Non-paid) 15,000

City of Industry
Travel & Recreation
  Magazine (1719) ....(Combined) 20,000

Daly City
Manila Mail (1803) ....(Combined) 15,000

El Monte
Chinese L.A. Daily
  News (1865) ....(Combined) 103,000

El Sobrante
Portuguese Journal (1869) ....‡9,000

Fontana
Pakistan (1919)

Glendale
California Courier (2007) ....(Paid) ‡2,800
(Free) ‡200
News Circle (2011) ....(Paid) ‡3,000
Weekend Balita (2013) ....(Combined) 80,000

Hayward
Voz de Portugal (2044) ....‡3,200

Irvine
Dan Chung News (2077) ....(Combined) 10,000

Los Angeles
Afronet Magazine (2202)
Al Talib (2204) ....(Controlled) 20,000
Beirut Times (2218) ....(Non-paid) 15,000
Black Lace (2220) ....(Paid) 9,000
(Non-paid) 200
Korean Sunday News (2309) .....(Combined) 22,000
Si Magazine (2387) ....(Paid) 50,000
U.S. Japan Business
  News (2422) ....(Combined) 40,000
World Reporter (2440) ....(Combined) 50,000

Mill Valley
Vestkusten (2542) ....(Paid) ‡1,800
(Free) ‡400

Montebello
Bayou Talk (2579) ....(Paid) 3,000
(Non-paid) 3,000

Monterey Park
Chinese American Daily
  News (2592) ....(Combined) 30,000

Riverside
Pasta Magazine (2942)

Rosemead
Saigon Times (2969) ....(Combined) 20,000

San Francisco
AsianWeek (3327) ....(Free) ‡50,000
(Paid) 4,066
Journal Francais (3381) ....‡20,000
Nichi Bei Times (3404) ....(Combined) 8,000
Swiss Journal (3447) ....‡10,000

San Jose
India Currents (3519) ....(Non-paid) ‡25,600
(Non-paid) ‡25,600

San Martin
The Filipino Monitor (3582) ....(Combined) 10,000

Santa Ana
The Hellenic Calendar (3626) .....(Combined) 10,000

Santa Barbara
SuperOnda (3660) ....(Combined) 102,016

Santa Clara
The Filipino-American
  Headliner (3670) ....(Combined) 5,000

Santa Monica
Fax Mainichi U.S.A. (3708) ....(Combined) 1,500

Sherman Oaks
Azerbaijan International (3760)

South San Francisco
Filipinas Magazine (3788) ....(Paid) 23,697
(Non-paid) 973

The Manila Bulletin
  USA (3790) ....(Combined) 50,000

Circulation: ★ = ABC; △ = BPA; ♦ = CAC; ● = CCAB; ❑ = VAC; ⊕ = PO Statement; ‡ = Publisher's Report; Boldface figures = sworn; Light figures = estimated.

2809

Magazines

Circ.

Circ.

Circ.

ETHNIC PUBLICATIONS (continued)
Torrance
Bridge U.S.A. **(3928)** ....(Combined) 35,000
Lighthouse **(3936)** ....(Combined) 31,200

COLORADO
Littleton
Democracy and Nature **(4546)** ....(Paid) 950
(Controlled) 50

FLORIDA
Dunedin
The Scottish Banner **(6062)** ....‡62,708

GEORGIA
Athens
Das Fenster Nach Druben **(6936)** .....(Paid) ‡15,000
(Free) ‡100

Atlanta
Korean Journal **(7025)** ....(Paid) 2,389
(Non-paid) 97,811

Doraville
Korean Southeast
News **(7242)** ....(Combined) 20,000

Mountain City
The Foxfire Magazine **(7449)** 3,000

Union City
The Atlanta Metro **(7613)** ....(Controlled) ‡29,000

HAWAII
Honolulu
East West Journal **(7687)** ....(Combined) 5,000
Hawaii Hochi **(7696)** ....(Combined) 8,000

ILLINOIS
Chicago
Chicago Shimpo **(8322)** ....(Combined) 5,000
Dawn **(8349)** ....(Paid) ‡4,800
(Controlled) ‡25
India Tribune **(8412)**
Prosveta **(8542)** ....‡21,000
Via Times
Newsmagazine **(8598)** ....(Combined) 60,000

Hoffman Estates
Danish Pioneer **(8999)** ....(Paid) ‡3,000
(Non-paid) ‡250

Joliet
Glasilo KSKJ (Americanski Slovenec) **(9033)**

Oak Park
Irish American News **(9376)** ....(Paid) ‡7,200
(Non-paid) ‡2,800

Skokie
Harmony **(9605)** ....‡25,000

INDIANA
Fort Wayne
Macedonian Tribune **(9972)** ....‡1,600

Hobart
Our Hope **(10064)** ....(Paid) ‡50
(Free) ‡3,500

MARYLAND
Baltimore
Vestnik **(13260)** ....(Combined) 10,000

Columbia
Korea Post **(13464)** ....(Combined) 13,000

Gaithersburg
China News Digest—Canada **(13533)**
China News Digest—Global **(13534)**
China News Digest—US **(13535)**
China News—Europe/Pacific **(13536)**
Hua Zia Wen Zhai **(13541)**

LaVale
German Life **(13615)** ....(Paid) 25,000
(Controlled) 15,000

MASSACHUSETTS
Boston
J Magazine **(13909)** ....(Combined) 15,000
Sampan **(13958)** ....(Controlled) 6,000

Cambridge
Dollars & Sense **(14049)** ....‡8,400

Watertown
The Armenian Mirror-Spectator **(14610)** 2,800
The Armenian Weekly **(14611)** ....(Paid) ‡2,200
(Free) ‡300

MICHIGAN
Westland
theIndian **(15681)**

MINNESOTA
St. Peter
Swedish-American Historical
Quarterly **(16431)** ....(Paid) ‡1,050
(Non-paid) ‡52

MISSOURI
Kansas City
Irish Families; Journal of **(17173)** ....(Paid) 2,000

NEW JERSEY
Basking Ridge
Ninnau **(18665)** ....(Paid) ‡2,500
(Non-paid) ‡500

Jersey City
El Nuevo Hudson **(19136)** ....(Non-paid) ♦55,525

Newark
Italian Tribune **(19354)** ....‡45,000
The Luso-Americano **(19358)**

Parsippany
The Ukrainian Weekly **(19415)** ....(Paid) ‡7,500
(Free) ‡500

NEW YORK
Baldwin
Polish American World **(20114)** ....(Paid) ‡10,000
(Free) ‡5,550

Boston
Polish-American Journal **(20239)** ....‡14,500

Brooklyn
Greenpoint Gazette **(20318)** 5,000

Cheektowaga
Am-Pol Eagle **(20455)** ....(Paid) 3,200

Flushing
Chosun Daily **(20607)**

Great Neck
New York Trend **(20693)** ....(Paid) 37,200
(Non-paid) 24,800

Jamaica
Bielarus/The Belarusan **(20831)** ....‡2,000

Long Island City
Kampana–Campana **(20964)** ....‡8,800
The Sae Gae Times **(20966)** .....(Combined) 40,000

New York
aMagazine **(21176)** ....(Paid) 210,250
Asahi Shimbun **(21259)** ....(Combined) 12,000
AUFBAU - The Transatlantic Jewish
Paper **(21273)** ....‡13,000
City Family **(21422)**
France-Amerique **(21733)** ....‡20,000
India in New York **(21863)** ....(Free) 21,781
Irish America Magazine **(21949)** 55,000
Irish Echo **(21950)** 58,000
Irish Voice Newspaper **(21951)** 65,000
The Japanese Daily Sun-Nikkan San **(21956)**
La Familia de la Ciudad **(22227)**
Little India **(22263)** ....(Controlled) ‡83,000
OCS News **(22483)** ....(Combined) 19,000
U.S. Frontline News **(22887)** ....(Combined) 29,000
Yomiuri America **(22951)** ....(Combined) 19,600

Utica
Y Drych (The Mirror) **(23469)** ....(Paid) ‡2,500
(Non-paid) ‡500

NORTH CAROLINA
Charlotte
La Noticia **(23747)** ....⊕26,000

OHIO
Dayton
Confrontation/Change
Review **(25112)** ....(Combined) ‡3,200

PENNSYLVANIA
Chalfont
HealthQuest **(26767)** ....(Paid) 1,000

Elkins Park
The Dong-A Daily
News **(26870)** ....(Combined) 23,000

Imperial
Voice of Youth **(27070)** ....‡4,000

Philadelphia
The Philadelphia Sunday
Sun **(27632)** ....(Paid) 20,000
South Philadelphia
American **(27691)** ....(Free) ‡20,000

Pittsburgh
American Srbobran **(27757)** ....‡12,000
Junior Magazine **(27806)** ....(Non-paid) 15,000
Sokol Polski (Polish
Falcon) **(27844)** ....(Free) ‡15,000
Zajednicar **(27856)** ....(Non-paid) 40,000

Scranton
Forum—A Ukrainian Review **(27959)** ....‡3,000
Polka—Polish Woman **(27961)** ....‡1,352

TEXAS
Dallas
But Viet Weekly
News **(30135)** ....(Combined) 27,500

Granger
Nasinec **(30409)** ....(Paid) ⊕300

Houston
Saudi Aramco World **(30527)** ....(Controlled) 180,000

VIRGINIA
Lorton
Hoa Thinh Don Viet
Bao **(32197)** ....(Combined) 6,000

Springfield
Albanian Times **(32538)**
Korean Weekly **(32548)** ....(Combined) 12,000

WASHINGTON
Seattle
ColorsNW Magazine **(32956)**
International Examiner **(32972)** ....(Paid) 2,000
(Free) 12,000

WISCONSIN
Hartland
J Desk International **(33779)** ....(Combined) 1,000

ALBERTA, CANADA
Calgary
Community Digest, Alberta
Edition **(34640)** ....(Free) 25,000

Edmonton
Alberta Sweetgrass **(34700)** ....(Combined) 7,000
Windspeaker **(34738)** ....(Combined) 18,000

BRITISH COLUMBIA, CANADA
Langley
The Windmill Herald **(35006)** ....‡11,500

Surrey
Charhdi Kala **(35107)** 15,000

Vancouver
Community Digest, BC
Edition **(35136)** ....(Free) ‡25,000
RicePaper **(35164)** ....(Combined) 4,000
Rungh **(35166)**
Scandinavian Press **(35167)**
Swedish Press **(35170)** ....(Paid) 4,000
(Non-paid) 1,000

MANITOBA, CANADA
Winnipeg
Promin **(35351)** ....‡1,637

NOVA SCOTIA, CANADA
Halifax
Celtic Heritage **(35560)** ....(Paid) ‡7,091
(Non-paid) ‡10,000

Numbers cited after listings are entry numbers rather than page numbers.

ONTARIO, CANADA
Downsview
Gujarat Vartman **(35784)** ....(Non-paid) 2,874

Hamilton
Canadian Serbian **(35878)** 1,000
Hellenic Hamilton News **(35881)** ....(Paid) ‡500
(Non-paid) ‡1,500

London
The Hellenic News **(35982)** ....(Paid) ‡850
(Non-paid) ‡4,150

North York
Bratstvo (Fraternity) **(36122)** ....(Paid) 1,500
(Controlled) 700

Oakville
The South Asian Voice **(36151)** ....(Paid) 35
(Non-paid) 8,000

Scarborough
Iranian Community Newspaper **(36377)**

Toronto
Satellite 1-416 **(36735)** ....(Combined) 1,500
Share **(36739)** ....(Combined) 153,000

West Hill
Macedonia **(36870)** ....(Paid) 1,800
(Free) 50

Willowdale
Fortnightly Al-Hilal **(36877)** ....(Paid) ‡4,000
(Free) ‡1,500

Windsor
The International Citizen **(36888)**

EXPORT CONSUMER MAGAZINES

NEW YORK
New York
Newsweek International - Latin America
Edition **(22461)** ....(Paid) 87,993
Time (Asia) **(22838)** ....(Paid) 315,753

ONTARIO, CANADA
Toronto
Time (Canada) **(36760)** ....(Paid) 240,684

FASHION

See also Dressmaking, Needlework, and Quilting

ARIZONA
Phoenix
Asian Sources Fashion Accessories &
Supplies **(787)**

Tempe
Java Magazine **(906)** ....(Controlled) 27,000

CALIFORNIA
Irvine
Mode **(2084)** ....(Paid) 615,436

Los Angeles
All About You **(2205)**
TEEN **(2410)** ....(Paid) 600,000

Palm Springs
JQ **(2762)**

San Francisco
*Surface **(3446)** ....(Paid) 112,000
XLR8R **(3465)** ....(Paid) 50,000

COLORADO
Golden
Sew News **(4474)** ....(Paid) 166,734

Longmont
Vows **(4561)**

CONNECTICUT
Stamford
Club Modele Magazine **(5143)**

DISTRICT OF COLUMBIA
Washington
LATINA Style **(5631)** ....(Paid) 150,000

FLORIDA
Altamonte Springs
Pageantry **(5902)** ....(Combined) 68,000

Miami
Tu Internacional **(6385)** ....‡11,452

GEORGIA
Roswell
Apparel Industry
International **(7512)** ....(Controlled) ‡13,750

KANSAS
Overland Park
Wearables Business **(11735)** ......(Combined) 14,723

MICHIGAN
Royal Oak
HOUR Detroit **(15481)**

NEW YORK
Brooklyn
Vice **(20353)** ....(Non-paid) ‡75,000

New York
Allure **(21174)** ....(Paid) 876,584
Elle **(21594)** ....(Paid) 1,000,638
Elle Canada **(21595)**
Embroidery Monogram Business **(21598)** 26,192
Esquire **(21627)** ....(Paid) 676,052
The FADER **(21675)**
Glamour **(21764)** ....(Paid) 2,147,263
GQ (Gentlemen's
Quarterly) **(21777)** ....(Paid) 898,508
Hair Cut and Style **(21787)**
Harper's Bazaar **(21790)** ....(Paid) 721,738
Honey **(21816)** ....(Combined) 200,000
Jane **(21955)** ....(Paid) 683,184
Lucky **(22269)**
Maxim **(22300)** ....(Paid) 2,458,150
more **(22366)** ....(Paid) 850,000
Savoy **(22707)** ....(Combined) 200,000
Show Biz News & Model
News **(22737)** ....(Combined) 75,000
Sportwear International **(22780)** ....‡26,000
Stuff Magazine **(22802)** ....(Paid) 812,079
Visionaire **(22902)** 5,000
Vogue **(22903)** ....(Paid) 1,174,183
Vogue Patterns Magazine **(22904)** .....(Paid) 66,172

TEXAS
Houston
Turn For The Judges (TFTJ) **(30537)**

VIRGINIA
Dillwyn
EGA Needle Arts
Magazine **(31996)** ....(Paid) 30,000

ONTARIO, CANADA
Toronto
FLARE **(36596)** ....(Paid) 160,220
Images **(36621)** ....(Non-paid) ‡490,000
Noise **(36675)**
Real You **(36723)**
Toronto Life Fashion
Magazine **(36769)** ....(Paid) 118,023
(Non-paid) 39,224

QUEBEC, CANADA
Dorval
Silk & Satin **(36988)**

FIREARMS

See also (Hunting, Fishing, and Game Management)

ARIZONA
Prescott
Rifle **(850)** ....‡95,000

CALIFORNIA
Auburn
Shotgun Sports **(1440)** ....‡108,000

Los Angeles
Guns & Ammo **(2284)** ....(Paid) ★496,648
Handguns **(2286)** ....(Paid) ★148,928
Petersen's Hunting **(2364)** ....(Paid) 380,798

San Diego
American Handgunner **(3111)** ....(Paid) 120,092
Guns Magazine **(3165)** ....(Paid) 85,487

San Luis Obispo
Command Magazine **(3564)** ....‡24,000
(Non-paid) ‡100

CONNECTICUT
Manchester
Precision Shooting **(4938)** 17,500

ILLINOIS
Peoria
Shooting Times **(9423)** ....(Paid) 202,611
Shotgun News **(9425)** ....(Controlled) 115,000

MONTANA
Belgrade
Trout Wrapper **(17724)**

NEW YORK
Buffalo
The New Gun Week **(20384)** ....(Paid) 19,641
(Non-paid) 390
Women and Guns **(20393)** ....‡18,000

New York
HandGunning **(21788)** ....‡80,000

TEXAS
San Antonio
Skeet Shooting Review **(31048)** 17,100

VERMONT
Tunbridge
The Artilleryman **(31607)** 1,800

VIRGINIA
Arlington
National Defense **(31810)** ....(Paid) 24,000
(Non-paid) 1,720

Fairfax
American Hunter **(32003)** ....(Paid) 1,203,693
American Rifleman **(32005)** ....(Paid) 1,608,439
America's 1st Freedom **(32006)** ....(Paid) 675,266
InSights **(32016)** ....(Paid) 33,000

WISCONSIN
Iola
Gun & Knife Show
Calendar **(33830)** ....(Paid) ‡4,648
Gun List **(33831)** ....(Paid) 62,514

FOOD AND COOKING

See also Home and Garden

ALABAMA
Huntsville
Old Huntsville **(271)**

ARIZONA
Tucson
Arizona Gourmet **(931)** ....(Combined) 29,353
Tucson Gourmet **(967)** ....(Combined) 31,776

CALIFORNIA
Concord
Veggie Life **(1756)** ....(Paid) 250,000

Los Angeles
Bon Appetit **(2224)** ....(Paid) 1,280,105

Riverside
Healthy Cooking **(2937)**
Pasta Magazine **(2942)**

San Francisco
Palate and Spirit **(3412)**

Santa Rosa
Wine X Magazine **(3736)** ....(Controlled) 50,000

CONNECTICUT
Newtown
Fine Cooking Magazine **(5040)** ....(Paid) 202,981
Kitchen Gardener **(5044)** ....‡95,000

Magazines

Circulation: ★ = ABC; △ = BPA; ♦ = CAC; • = CCAB; ▢ = VAC; ⊕ = PO Statement; ‡ = Publisher's Report; Boldface figures = sworn; Light figures = estimated.

Circ.

FOOD AND COOKING (continued)

DISTRICT OF COLUMBIA
Washington
The World & I **(5870)** ....(Paid) 20,056
(Non-paid) 2,781

FLORIDA
Coral Gables
The Wine News **(6015)** ....(Combined) 70,000

Hollywood
Specialty Cooking Magazine **(6198)**

INDIANA
Fowler
The Supermarket Gourmet **(9997)** ....(Paid) ‡200
(Free) ‡450

IOWA
Des Moines
Cuisine **(10779)**

LOUISIANA
New Orleans
New Orleans Menu **(12746)** ....(Combined) 3,000

MARYLAND
Baltimore
Vegetarian Journal **(13259)** 24,000

MASSACHUSETTS
Brookline
Cook's Illustrated **(14018)**

MINNESOTA
Minneapolis
Classic Cookbooks **(16067)** ....(Paid) 450,000
Pillsbury Classic
Cookbooks **(16119)** ....(Paid) 475,000
Pillsbury Fast & Healthy
Magazine **(16120)** ....(Paid) 152,514

St. Paul
American Cake Decorating **(16363)** ....(Paid) 10,000

NEVADA
Las Vegas
Kosher for Health **(18370)** ....(Paid) 25,000

NEW JERSEY
Bernardsville
New England Wine
Gazette **(18678)** ....(Non-paid) ♦18,418

Collingswood
Cuizine Magazine **(18767)** ....(Controlled) 35,350

Hoboken
Yeast **(19121)**

NEW YORK
Brooklyn
Kashrus Magazine **(20324)** ....‡10,000

Dolgeville
Vegetarian Voice **(20533)** ....(Combined) 11,000

Little Neck
Journal of Nutrition for the
Elderly **(20952)** ....(Controlled) ‡700

Melville
Energy Times **(21043)** ....(Controlled) 650,000

New York
Better Homes and Gardens Special Interest
Publications Low Calorie/Low Fat
Recipes **(21301)** ....(Paid) 184,500
Christmas Helps & Holiday
Baking **(21413)** ....(Paid) 1,000,000
Eating Well Magazine **(21579)** ....(Paid) 676,024
Food Arts **(21710)** ....(Non-paid) ‡55,581
(Paid) ‡1,513
Food & Wine **(21713)** ....(Paid) 860,254
Forbes FYI **(21720)**
Gourmet-The Magazine of Good
Living **(21776)** ....(Paid) 946,345
ICR: The International Cookbook
Revue **(21841)** 15,600
Martha Stewart Living **(22287)** ......(Paid) 2,436,422
Wine Spectator **(22919)** ....(Paid) 290,318

Woman's Day Eating Light **(22926)**
Woman's Day Holiday Baking **(22928)**

OREGON
Portland
Northwest Palate Magazine **(26488)** ....(Paid) 15,000

TEXAS
Fort Worth
Chile Pepper Magazine **(30332)** ....(Paid) 70,000
(Controlled) 30,000

VERMONT
Peacham
The Art of Eating **(31578)** ....(Paid) ⊕9,000

WASHINGTON
Seattle
Simply Seafood **(33031)**

WISCONSIN
Greendale
Taste of Home **(33764)** ....(Paid) 4,500,000

ONTARIO, CANADA
Concord
Enoteca Wine and Food Magazine **(35751)**

Don Mills
What's Cooking
Magazine **(35779)** ....(Non-paid) 1,300,000

Toronto
Food & Drink **(36598)** ....(Combined) 500,000

GAMES AND PUZZLES

CALIFORNIA
Berkeley
Game Revolution **(1523)**

Beverly Hills
Tips & Tricks **(1577)** ....(Paid) ★163,947

Brisbane
Next Generation **(1608)** ....(Paid) ‡115,613
PC Accelerator **(1609)**
PC Gamer **(1610)** ....(Paid) 357,718
PSM (PlayStation
Magazine) **(1611)** ....(Paid) 304,458

Foster City
PSExtreme **(1934)** ....(Paid) 125,000
(Non-paid) 250,000

Inglewood
Gambling Times **(2071)** 125,000

Vacaville
Bingo and Gaming News **(3973)**

CONNECTICUT
Norwalk
Easy & Fun Word Seek Puzzles **(5058)**
Family Word Seek Puzzles **(5059)**
Favorite Variety Puzzles and Games **(5060)**
Favorite Word Seek Puzzles **(5061)**

MARYLAND
Baltimore
The General **(13164)** ....(Paid) 48,500

MINNESOTA
Minneapolis
Game Informer Magazine **(16082)** .....(Paid) 217,653

NEW JERSEY
West Atlantic City
Casino Player **(19714)**
The Poker Digest Magazine **(19717)**
Strictly Slots **(19718)**

NEW YORK
Congers
Inquest, The Gaming
Magazine **(20490)** ....(Paid) 105,000

New Windsor
Chess Life **(21126)** ....‡80,000
SchoolMates **(21128)** ....(Paid) 30,000

New York
Super Easy-To-Do **(22807)**

PENNSYLVANIA
Ambler
All Crosswords Special **(26644)**
All Number-Finds **(26645)**
Easy Fill-Ins **(26648)**
Official's Cryptograms **(26652)**
Superior Fill-Ins **(26655)**

Philadelphia
High End **(27481)**

WASHINGTON
Des Moines
Northwest Fun & Games **(32737)** ....(Paid) 1,500
(Controlled) 40,000

WISCONSIN
Waukesha
Model Retailer **(34408)** ....(Paid) ★4,320

GAY AND LESBIAN INTERESTS

ARIZONA
Tucson
The Weekly Observer **(973)**

CALIFORNIA
Berkeley
Sinister Wisdom **(1559)** ....(Paid) ‡3,000
(Non-paid) ‡500

Hayward
Journal of Gay and Lesbian Social
Services **(2043)** ....(Paid) 422

Los Angeles
The Advocate **(2200)** ....(Paid) 103,129
Black Dates **(2219)**
Black Lace **(2220)** ....(Paid) 9,000
(Non-paid) 200
Blackfire **(2221)**
BLK **(2223)**
Freshmen **(2276)** 65,000
Kuumba **(2310)**
MEN **(2328)** 76,000
TenPercent **(2411)** 12,000

Sacramento
Mom Guess What Newspaper
(MGW) **(3010)** ....(Paid) ‡700
(Free) ‡21,000

San Diego
Update **(3285)** ....(Paid) ‡2,000
(Free) ‡25,000

San Francisco
Curve **(3348)** ....(Paid) 68,800
(Non-paid) 305
Journal of Homosexuality **(3382)** 1,298

Torrance
The Lesbian News **(3935)** ....‡110,000

West Hollywood
Frontiers **(4062)** ....(Combined) ‡46,000

CONNECTICUT
Stamford
Fairfield County Weekly **(5149)**
New Haven Advocate **(5156)**

DISTRICT OF COLUMBIA
Washington
Lambda Book Report **(5628)** ....(Paid) 8,000
(Non-paid) 150
The Washington Blade **(5842)** ....(Free) 41,446
(Paid) 1,346

FLORIDA
Daytona Beach
Our World **(6038)** ....‡75,000

Miami
The Weekly News **(6390)** ....(Free) ‡32,000

Tampa
The Gazette **(6766)** ....(Paid) 53,000

Numbers cited after listings are entry numbers rather than page numbers.

GEORGIA
Atlanta
Southern Voice **(7045)** ....(Non-paid) 20,634
(Paid) 161

ILLINOIS
Chicago
Gay Chicago Magazine **(8384)** ....(Paid) ‡750
(Free) ‡20,000
Libido **(8461)**
Nightlines Weekly **(8509)** ....(Non-paid) 12,000
Out! Resource Guide **(8520)** ....(Non-paid) 25,000
Outlines **(8522)** ....(Paid) 1,000
(Non-paid) 20,000

LOUISIANA
New Orleans
Ambush Magazine **(12726)** ....(Combined) 10,000

MARYLAND
Baltimore
Baltimore Gay Paper **(13132)** ....(Paid) ‡3,000
(Free) ‡10,000

MASSACHUSETTS
Boston
Bay Windows **(13852)** ....(Non-paid) 24,500
Fag Rag **(13891)** ....(Non-paid) 5,000
Gay and Lesbian Review Worldwide **(13895)**
Gayme **(13896)** ....(Paid) 600
(Non-paid) 6,400
The Guide **(13897)** ....(Combined) 30,000

Cambridge
Bad Attitude **(14040)** ....(Paid) ‡5,000

Great Barrington
Hikane: The Capable Woman **(14215)**

Jamaica Plain
Sojourner **(14262)** 30,000

Waltham
Transgender Tapestry **(14604)** .....(Combined) 8,000

MICHIGAN
Royal Oak
Cruise Entertainment
Magazine **(15479)** ....(Non-paid) 5,000

MINNESOTA
Minneapolis
Maize, A Lesbian Country Magazine **(16096)**

NEW YORK
Binghamton
Harrington Lesbian Fiction Quarterly **(20154)**

New York
Honcho Magazine **(21815)** ....(Paid) 100,000
HX Magazine **(21838)** ....(Free) 34,154
(Paid) 200
Journal of the Gay and Lesbian Medical
Association **(22076)**
LGNY **(22250)** ....‡35,000
Mandate Magazine **(22279)** 200,000
New York Blade News **(22438)** ....(Free) 40,000
(Paid) 83
Out Magazine **(22510)** ....(Paid) 100,126
Outyouth **(22514)**
Playguy Magazine **(22566)** 110,000

Rochester
Empty Closet **(23224)** ....(Non-paid) ⊕5,200

White Plains
Beau **(23570)** ....(Non-paid) 25,000

NORTH CAROLINA
Charlotte
Q-Notes **(23751)** ....(Non-paid) ‡10,000

Durham
GLQ **(23822)** ....(Combined) 1400

OHIO
Cleveland
Gay People's
Chronicle **(24902)** ....(Controlled) 15,000

PENNSYLVANIA
Philadelphia
Philadelphia Gay News **(27626)** 19,000

Wyoming
Checkmate Incorporating Dungeonmaster **(28198)**

TENNESSEE
Liberty
RFD **(29332)** ....(Paid) ‡2,900
(Non-paid) ‡900

UTAH
Salt Lake City
The Pillar **(31437)**

VIRGINIA
Hampton
Harrington Gay Men's Fiction Quarterly **(32129)**

QUEBEC, CANADA
Montreal
RG **(37220)** ....(Non-paid) ‡11,500

GENERAL EDITORIAL

CALIFORNIA
Carmel
Guest Life Monterey
Bay **(1672)** ....(Controlled) 20,000

Emeryville
The East Bay
Monthly **(1876)** ....(Controlled) ‡80,500
(Paid) ‡500

Hollywood
The National Record **(2052)** ....(Paid) ‡12,000
(Non-paid) ‡41,600

Los Angeles
FREEDOM Magazine **(2275)** ....‡150,000
Los Angeles Times
Magazine **(2327)** ....(Sun.) ‡1,531,527
National Lampoon **(2343)**

Pacifica
Social Policy **(2739)** ....‡2,000

Palm Desert
Saludos Hispanos **(2743)** 300,000

San Diego
Continental Newstime **(3136)** 600,000

San Francisco
Mother Jones **(3391)** ....(Paid) 165,663
NewsPort **(3403)**

DISTRICT OF COLUMBIA
Washington
American Visions **(5348)** ....(Paid) 125,000
(Controlled) 5,000
Insight **(5546)** 439,687
Kiplinger's Personal Finance
Magazine **(5625)** ....(Paid) 1,019,262
National Geographic **(5672)** .....(Paid) 7,828,642
National Geographic
WORLD **(5675)** ....(Paid) ‡1,246,210
(Free) ‡13,334
The New Republic **(5694)** ....(Paid) 98,328
Science News **(5781)** ....(Paid) 168,621
Smithsonian Magazine **(5794)** .....(Paid) 2,055,887
The Spotlight **(5803)** ....‡100,000
U.S. News & World
Report **(5836)** ....(Paid) 2,070,511
The Washington Post
Magazine **(5851)** ....(Paid) 80,077
The Wilson Quarterly **(5861)** ....(Paid) ‡60,000

FLORIDA
Coral Gables
Vista Magazine **(6014)** ....(Non-paid) 960,716

Miami
Harper's Bazaar en Espanol **(6357)** ....‡13,108

Palm Beach
Palm Beach Illustrated **(6543)** ....(Paid) 2,428
(Non-paid) 39,452

ILLINOIS
Chicago
Ebony **(8357)** ....(Paid) 1,728,986

EM: Ebony Man **(8367)** ....(Paid) 171,391
Jet **(8425)** ....(Paid) 944,073

Maywood
Aim—America's Intercultural
Magazine **(9163)** ....(Paid) ‡4,000
(Controlled) ‡3,000

Wheaton
The Quest **(9758)** 12,000

IOWA
Cedar Falls
The North American Review **(10659)** ....‡3,400

KANSAS
Topeka
Capper's **(11816)** ....(Paid) 215,175
Grit **(11821)** ....(Paid) 90,000
Lefthander Magazine **(11832)** 35,000

MASSACHUSETTS
Boston
The Atlantic Monthly **(13851)** ....(Paid) 458,667

MINNESOTA
Minneapolis
Utne **(16138)** ....(Paid) 232,629

MISSISSIPPI
Jackson
Mississippi Magazine **(16706)** ....(Paid) ‡34,000
(Non-paid) ‡500

NEW JERSEY
New Brunswick
Raritan **(19337)** ....(Paid) ‡3,000
(Non-paid) ‡500

NEW YORK
Brooklyn
The World at Large **(20357)** ....‡64,000

New York
Commentary **(21454)** ....(Paid) 26,000
(Non-paid) 600
Discover **(21555)** ....(Paid) 1,005,981
Editorials On File **(21586)** ....(Paid) ‡800
(Non-paid) ‡1,000
Forbes FYI **(21720)**
Harper's Magazine **(21791)** ....(Paid) 213,141
Interview **(21944)** ....(Paid) 185,612
Ladies' Home Journal **(22231)** .....(Paid) 4,101,550
Life Magazine **(22254)** ....(Paid) 1,590,397
The Nation **(22395)** ....(Paid) 94,003
The New Yorker **(22457)** ....(Paid) 843,151
Newsweek **(22459)** ....(Paid) 3,138,460
Newsweek International **(22460)**
Newsweek International - Latin America
Edition **(22461)** ....(Paid) 87,993
Oneworld **(22491)**
Parade **(22522)** 37,852,000
People Weekly **(22540)** ....(Paid) 3,525,250
Popular Mechanics **(22579)** ....(Paid) 1,224,960
Popular Science **(22582)** ....(Paid) 1,566,817
Redbook Magazine **(22639)** ....(Paid) 2,338,941
Rolling Stone **(22675)** ....(Paid) 1,251,520
Scientific American **(22714)** ....(Paid) 687,437
Temas **(22822)** ....(Paid) 107,000
(Non-paid) 6,200
Time **(22837)** ....(Paid) 4,056,150
Time International **(22839)**
Time for Kids **(22840)** ....(Paid) 4,000,000
Vanity Fair **(22895)** ....(Paid) 1,050,684
The Village Voice **(22900)** ....(Paid) 12,087
(Non-paid) 241,874
World News Digest **(22943)** ....(Paid) ‡5,600
World Press Review **(22945)** ....(Paid) 52,675

Pawling
Positive Thinking **(23086)** ....(Paid) ‡600,000
(Non-paid) ‡600,000

Pleasantville
Reader's Digest **(23112)** ....(Paid) 12,613,790

Valley Stream
U.S.A. Today **(23487)** ....‡254,000

NORTH CAROLINA
Burlington
City-County Magazine **(23671)** ....(Paid) ‡15,200

Circulation: ★ = ABC; △ = BPA; ◆ = CAC; • = CCAB; ❑ = VAC; ⊕ = PO Statement; ‡ = Publisher's Report; Boldface figures = sworn; Light figures = estimated.

Magazines

2813

Circ.

Circ.

Circ.

GENERAL EDITORIAL (continued)
Durham
Southern Exposure **(23846)** ....‡5,000

SOUTH CAROLINA
Mount Pleasant
Vital Speeches **(28695)**
Vital Speeches of the Day **(28696)** ....‡9,000

TEXAS
Austin
Texas Monthly **(29836)** ....(Paid) 300,991

VIRGINIA
Mc Lean
USA Weekend **(32259)** 23,700,000

WISCONSIN
Appleton
The New American **(33540)** ....‡55,000

Madison
The Progressive **(33972)** ....(Paid) ‡32,000
                                 (Non-paid) ‡1,000

ALBERTA, CANADA
Edmonton
Citizens Centre Report **(34705)** 45,000

ONTARIO, CANADA
Kingston
Queen's Quarterly **(35946)** ....‡3,750

Toronto
Maclean's **(36654)** ....(Paid) 506,428
Monarchy Canada **(36667)** ....‡2,000

QUEBEC, CANADA
L'Assomption
Ciao Magazine **(37034)** ....(Paid) ‡30,000
                             (Non-paid) ‡10,000

Montreal
L'actualite **(37080)** ....(Paid) 190,745
Reader's Digest
   Magazine **(37214)** ....(Paid) 1,025,256
Relations **(37215)** ....‡4,000
Selection du Reader's Digest (Canadian-French
   Edition) **(37223)** ....(Paid) 225,000

SASKATCHEWAN, CANADA
Regina
Briarpatch **(37525)** ....(Paid) ‡2,500
                             (Controlled) ‡1,400

HANDICAPPED
ARIZONA
Sun City West
Accent on Living **(897)** ....(Paid) ‡19,000
                             (Controlled) ‡300

CALIFORNIA
Costa Mesa
Ability Magazine **(1771)** ....‡165,000

Yucca Valley
Wheelers **(4129)**

DISTRICT OF COLUMBIA
Washington
Braille Book Review **(5381)** ....(Non-paid) ‡15,000
NICHCY News Digest **(5696)**

FLORIDA
Fort Lauderdale
The Voice Newspaper **(6086)**

IOWA
Council Bluffs
Daily Devotions for the
   Deaf **(10725)** ....(Non-paid) 20,000

Iowa City
Special Recreation Digest **(10988)**

KANSAS
Topeka
MOUTH **(11835)** ....(Paid) 6,540

KENTUCKY
Louisville
The Disability Rag's Ragged Edge
   Magazine **(12215)** 3,500

MARYLAND
Bethesda
Hearing Loss **(13343)** ....(Paid) 200,000

Riverdale
National Apostolate for Inclusion Ministry
   Quarterly **(13673)** ....(Paid) 500

Rockville
Challenge Magazine **(13676)** ....(Paid) 30,000

MASSACHUSETTS
Great Barrington
Hikane: The Capable Woman **(14215)**

Worcester
Home Automation **(14682)** ....(Non-paid) 4,200

MICHIGAN
East Lansing
Communication Outlook **(14983)** ....(Paid) 1,500

MISSOURI
Fulton
Missouri Record **(17077)**

NEW JERSEY
River Edge
Exceptional Parent **(19507)** ....(Paid) ‡35,000
                             (Controlled) ‡40,000

NEW YORK
Delmar
Access to Travel Magazine **(20527)** ....(Paid) 12,600

Levittown
PeopleNet **(20942)**

New York
Adult Lessons Quarterly **(21152)** ....(Non-paid) 2,350
Discovery Magazine **(21556)** ....(Non-paid) 1,200
John Milton Magazine **(21970)** .....(Non-paid) 3,591

Rochester
Deaf Life **(23221)** ....(Paid) 45,000

OHIO
Akron
Kaleidoscope **(24582)** ....(Paid) 1,500

Cincinnati
Silent Advocate **(24819)** ....(Non-paid) 30,000

TEXAS
Austin
Impact (Austin) **(29780)**

HEALTH
ALABAMA
Birmingham
Health **(73)** ....(Paid) 1,339,754

Montgomery
Alfa News **(360)** ....‡280,000

ARIZONA
Phoenix
Vim & Vigor Magazine **(813)** ....(Paid) 1,004,165

CALIFORNIA
Berkeley
Yoga Journal **(1566)** ....‡100,000

Concord
Veggie Life **(1756)** ....(Paid) 250,000

Los Angeles
Health Diet & Nutrition **(2287)** ....(Paid) 120,000
Let's Live **(2315)** ....(Combined) ‡1,250,000

Oakland
Diseased Pariah News **(2677)**

Oxnard
Ironman **(2730)** ....(Paid) 225,000

Riverside
Breastcare **(2932)**

San Anselmo
Common Ground **(3082)** ....(Paid) ‡2,000
                             (Non-paid) ‡103,000

San Diego
ACE FitnessMatters **(3105)** ....(Paid) 41,000

San Jose
Song Manh Magazine **(3538)** 10,000

Santa Barbara
Spa **(3658)** ....(Paid) ‡85,000

Santa Rosa
Share Guide **(3734)**

Woodland Hills
Fit Pregnancy **(4104)**
For Patients Only **(4106)** ....(Paid) 4,300
                             (Non-paid) 6,700
Shape **(4114)** ....(Paid) 1,538,192

COLORADO
Denver
NEXUS Magazine **(4344)** ....(Paid) 25,000
                             (Non-paid) 200

CONNECTICUT
Madison
Black Health **(4927)** ....(Paid) ‡2,340
                             (Free) ‡25,000

New Haven
Saint Raphael's Better
   Health **(5001)** ....(Non-paid) 124,442

Stamford
Vegetarian Times **(5162)** ....(Paid) 320,954

Westport
Remedy **(5216)** ....(Non-paid) 2,229,426

FLORIDA
Hollywood
Diet & Fitness **(6192)**
Specialty Cooking Magazine **(6198)**

Tampa
aakpRENALIFE **(6758)** ....(Paid) 20,000

GEORGIA
Atlanta
Women's Health Weekly **(7062)**

IDAHO
Dover
Alternative Medicine Review **(7852)** ....(Paid) ⊕7,500

ILLINOIS
Champaign
Journal of Aging and Physical
   Activity **(8193)** ....(Paid) 800

Chicago
Conscious Choice **(8342)** ....(Non-paid) 50,000

Evanston
Massage Therapy Journal **(8867)** ....(Paid) 68,000

Itasca
Family Safety & Health **(9013)** ....‡500,000

Lincolnwood
Consumer Guide **(9092)**

INDIANA
Indianapolis
Branches Magazine **(10099)** ......(Combined) 25,000
Child Life **(10100)** ....(Paid) 47,330

MARYLAND
Baltimore
Vegetarian Journal **(13259)** 24,000

Hagerstown
Vibrant Life **(13570)** ....‡35,000

Numbers cited after listings are entry numbers rather than page numbers.

MASSACHUSETTS
Grafton
Spirit of Change
    Magazine **(14213)** ....(Combined) 70,000

MICHIGAN
Detroit
The FORUM Magazine **(14932)** ....(Paid) ‡2,000
                                          (Non-paid) ‡8,000

MINNESOTA
Minnetonka
Today's Health & Wellness **(16177)** 200,000

MISSOURI
Columbia
Voice of the
    Diabetic **(17012)** ....(Non-paid) ‡320,097

St. Louis
Health Perspective **(17443)** ......(Non-paid) ‡125,000

NEVADA
Las Vegas
Kosher for Health **(18370)** ....(Paid) 25,000

NEW JERSEY
Hillside
Modern Nutrition News **(18879)**

Mahwah
Nutrition and Cancer **(19204)**

NEW MEXICO
Santa Fe
Mothering Magazine **(19936)** ....(Paid) ‡90,000
                                          (Non-paid) ‡500

NEW YORK
Binghamton
Journal of Consumer Health on the Internet **(20167)**

Dolgeville
Vegetarian Voice **(20533)** ....(Combined) 11,000

Ithaca
Human Ecology Forum **(20802)** ....(Paid) ‡600
                                          (Non-paid) ‡2,500

Melville
Energy Times **(21043)** ....(Controlled) 650,000

New York
Alzheimer's Care Quarterly **(21175)**
Eating Well Magazine **(21579)** ....(Paid) 676,024
Fitness Diet and Exercise Guide **(21704)**
Healthy Pregnancy **(21796)**
Inside MS **(21876)** 680,000
SELF Magazine **(22722)** ....(Paid) 1,190,707
Sports Tech **(22779)**
Studies in Family
    Planning **(22800)** ....(Non-paid) ‡4,400
                                          (Paid) ‡1,200

Stony Brook
New Living **(23373)** ....(Free) ‡100,000

NORTH CAROLINA
Greensboro
Monkeyshines on Health and Science **(23929)**

PENNSYLVANIA
Chalfont
HealthQuest **(26767)** ....(Paid) 1,000

Emmaus
Men's Health **(26877)** ....(Paid) 1,659,594
Prevention **(26880)** ....(Paid) 3,014,859

Haverford
Nutrition Health Review **(27029)** ....‡210,000

Honesdale
Himalayan Institute
    Quarterly **(27049)** ....(Non-paid) ‡35,000
Yoga International **(27052)** ....(Combined) 24,500

Levittown
CAPsule **(27187)** ....(Controlled) 2,000

Philadelphia
Toxicology & Ecotoxicology
    News/Reviews **(27706)** 600

Southampton
Philly Health & Fitness **(28007)** ....(Free) 60,000

Yardley
HEALTH & YOU **(28200)** ....‡1,700,000

PUERTO RICO
San Juan
Buena Vida **(28289)** ....(Paid) ‡39,500
                                          (Non-paid) ‡8,000

RHODE ISLAND
Providence
Medicine and Health Rhode
    Island **(28408)** ....(Paid) ‡1,900
                                          (Non-paid) ‡175

TENNESSEE
Franklin
Coping with Allergies and
    Asthma **(29196)** ....(Paid) ‡30,000
Coping with Cancer **(29197)** ....‡80,000

Seymour
Fitness Plus
    Magazine **(29597)** ....(Non-paid) 250,000

TEXAS
Austin
HerbalGram **(29778)**
Impact (Austin) **(29780)**

Dallas
Stroke Connection
    Magazine **(30183)** ....(Combined) 70,000

Houston
Health & Fitness Sports
    Magazine **(30478)** ....(Non-paid) 160,000

Sugar Land
Internet Journal of Health **(31146)**

Universal City
The American
    Wanderer **(31224)** ....(Combined) 7,500

UTAH
St. George
Total Health **(31418)** ....(Paid) ‡63,000
                                          (Controlled) ‡10,000

VIRGINIA
Alexandria
Diabetes Care **(31665)**

Glen Allen
Better Nutrition Magazine **(32111)** ....‡486,500

WISCONSIN
Madison
50 Plus Lifestyles **(33939)** ....‡5,300
                                          (Controlled) ‡34,300

Milwaukee
TOPS News **(34104)** ....(Paid) ‡292,827
                                          (Controlled) ‡4,803

NOVA SCOTIA, CANADA
Pictou
Total Health **(35603)**

ONTARIO, CANADA
Ottawa
Canadian Journal of Rural
    Medicine **(36218)** 6,300
Living Safety Magazine **(36260)** ....‡100,000

Toronto
Images **(36621)** ....(Non-paid) ‡490,000

PRINCE EDWARD ISLAND, CANADA
Kensington
Kindred Spirit **(36920)** ....(Paid) 1,800

HISTORY AND GENEALOGY

ALABAMA
Huntsville
Old Huntsville **(271)**

Tuscaloosa
Alabama Heritage **(483)** ....‡15,000

ARIZONA
Cave Creek
True West **(673)** ....(Paid) ‡23,267
                                          (Non-paid) ‡273

Phoenix
Arizona Highways **(779)** ....‡300,000,000

Williams
Route 66 Magazine **(1009)** ....(Paid) 5,000
                                          (Non-paid) 35,000

ARKANSAS
Batesville
Mid-America Folklore **(1041)** ....(Paid) 200

CALIFORNIA
Canoga Park
Sea Classics **(1660)** ....(Paid) ⊕57,346

Newport Beach
The Journal of Historical Review **(2629)** 1,500

Paradise
California Territorial
    Quarterly **(2805)** ....(Controlled) ‡3,000

Redlands
San Bernardino County Museum Association
    Quarterly **(2907)** ....(Paid) 2,800
                                          (Non-paid) 200

San Luis Obispo
Command Magazine **(3564)** ....‡24,000
                                          (Non-paid) ‡100

DISTRICT OF COLUMBIA
Washington
History **(5528)** ....(Paid) ‡460
Preservation **(5726)** ....(Paid) 204,149

FLORIDA
Sarasota
Yesterday's Magazette **(6670)** ....(Paid) 1,500

INDIANA
Berne
Good Old Days **(9810)** ....(Paid) ‡206,000
Good Old Days Specials **(9811)** ....(Paid) 46,000

Bloomington
The Journal of Women's
    History **(9844)** ....(Paid) ‡1,500
                                          (Non-paid) ‡50

Huntington
U.S. Catholic Historian **(10075)**

Indianapolis
Traces of Indiana and Midwestern
    History **(10175)** 11,000

Newburgh
Western Kentucky Journal **(10350)** ....(Paid) 400

IOWA
Iowa City
Iowa Heritage Illustrated **(10975)** ....‡3,300

KANSAS
Ellsworth
Kanhistique **(11427)** ....‡5,215

KENTUCKY
Bowling Green
Southern Folklore **(11949)** ....(Paid) ‡450
                                          (Non-paid) ‡20

Frankfort
Register of Kentucky Historical
    Society **(12075)** ....(Paid) ‡2,700

Jackson
The Kentucky Explorer **(12145)**

LOUISIANA
New Orleans
New Orleans Preservation in Print **(12747)**

Circ.   Circ.   Circ.

HISTORY AND GENEALOGY (continued)

MARYLAND
Germantown
The Journal of Afro-Latin American Studies and
    Literatures **(13554)**

Silver Spring
Labor's Heritage **(13735)** 5,000

MASSACHUSETTS
Edgartown
Martha's Vineyard
    Magazine **(14174)** ....(Paid) ‡7,600
    (Non-paid) ‡4,400

Newburyport
Nautical Research Journal **(14380)** ....‡1,700

MICHIGAN
Lansing
Michigan History **(15285)** 34,000
Michigan History for Kids **(15286)**

MINNESOTA
St. Peter
Swedish-American Historical
    Quarterly **(16431)** ....(Paid) ‡1,050
    (Non-paid) ‡52

MISSOURI
Kansas City
Irish Families; Journal of **(17173)** ....(Paid) 2,000

Kirbyville
The Ozarks Mountaineer **(17224)** .....(Paid) ‡32,000
    (Controlled) ‡1,500

St. Louis
Railroads of St. Louis
    Magazine **(17485)** ....(Paid) 600

MONTANA
Helena
Montana **(17819)** ....‡10,000

NEW HAMPSHIRE
Peterborough
California Chronicles **(18618)**
Calliope **(18619)** ....(Paid) ‡10,400
Footsteps **(18624)** 6,000

NEW MEXICO
Truth or Consequences
Chaparral Guide **(19967)** ....(Free) 7,300

NEW YORK
Cooperstown
Heritage **(20499)** 4,000
New York History **(20500)** ....(Paid) 4,350
    (Controlled) 69

Long Island City
Archaeology's Dig **(20962)**

New York
American Heritage **(21188)** ....(Paid) 340,000
Financial History **(21696)** ....(Paid) ‡2,100
    (Non-paid) ‡4,400
Women's Studies Quarterly **(22935)** ....‡1,500

NORTH CAROLINA
Cary
History Workshop **(23688)** ....(Paid) 2,100

OHIO
Cincinnati
Over the Front **(24812)** ....(Paid) 1,400

Columbus
Timeline **(25065)** ....‡20,000

Marietta
Camp Chase
    Gazette **(25344)** ....(Combined) ⊕6,200

Powell
Check the Oil! **(25490)** ....(Paid) 3,700

OKLAHOMA
Oklahoma City
Persimmon Hill **(25991)** ....‡15,000

OREGON
Hillsboro
Timbertimes **(26373)** 3,200

PENNSYLVANIA
Camp Hill
Early American Life **(26750)** ....(Paid) 100,000

Harrisburg
American History **(26982)** 120,000
British Heritage **(26984)** ....(Paid) 80,166
Civil War Times Illustrated **(26986)** 95,000
MHQ **(26998)** ....(Paid) ‡29,000

Marietta
Old News **(27221)** ....‡40,000

Philadelphia
The Journal of Presbyterian History **(27547)** ....‡800

State Line
Journal of the Johannes Schwalm Historical
    Association **(28033)**

UTAH
North Salt Lake
Heritage Quest Magazine **(31376)** .....(Paid) ‡16,000

VERMONT
Tunbridge
The Artilleryman **(31607)** 1,800
The Civil War News **(31608)** ....(Paid) 9,000
    (Free) 400

VIRGINIA
Leesburg
Aviation History **(32183)** ....(Controlled) 76,102

Richmond
UDC Magazine **(32458)** ....(Paid) 9,000

Roanoke
Blue Ridge Country **(32489)** 75,000

Williamsburg
Eighteenth-Century Life **(32616)** 800
Tidewater Virginia Families **(32619)**

WASHINGTON
Seattle
Pacific Northwest Quarterly **(33001)** 1,300

WEST VIRGINIA
Charleston
Goldenseal **(33270)** ....(Combined) ⊕22,000
The Southern Journal **(33272)** ....(Paid) 500
    (Non-paid) 100

WISCONSIN
Green Bay
Voyageur **(33742)** ....(Paid) 3,511

Greendale
Reminisce **(33763)** ....(Paid) ⊕1,750,000

MANITOBA, CANADA
Winnipeg
The Beaver **(35314)** ....(Paid) 51,000

ONTARIO, CANADA
Bowmanville
Epoch **(35693)** ....(Paid) ‡125
    (Non-paid) ‡100

Ottawa
Canadian Geographic **(36198)** ....(Paid) 229,180

Toronto
Family Chronicle **(36593)** ....(Paid) 25,000
Phoenix **(36706)** ....(Paid) 1,200

HOME AND GARDEN
ALABAMA
Birmingham
Southern Accents **(91)** ....(Paid) 376,340
Southern Living **(93)** ....(Paid) 2,537,485
Southern Living Garden Guide **(94)**
Southern Living Home for the Holidays **(95)**

ARIZONA
Scottsdale
Phoenix Home & Garden **(873)** ....(Paid) 73,539

CALIFORNIA
Los Angeles
Architectural Digest **(2214)** ....(Paid) 821,992
Home Magazine **(2292)** ....(Paid) 1,020,938

Menlo Park
Gentry Magazine and Northern California Home &
    Design **(2524)** ....(Non-paid) ‡32,500
    (Non-paid) ‡51,500
Sunset Magazine **(2527)** ....(Paid) 1,448,007

Pasadena
Journal of the Los Angeles International Fern
    Society **(2820)** ....(Combined) 400

Santa Monica
Unique Homes **(3719)** ....(Paid) 56,410

Sierra Madre
American Bungalow **(3764)**

COLORADO
Centennial
Mountain Living **(4225)** ....(Paid) 19,700
    (Non-paid) 11,300

Eldorado Springs
Rocky Mountain
    Gardener **(4411)** ....(Combined) 7,000

Lakewood
American Penstemon Society
    Bulletin **(4530)** ....(Paid) 500

CONNECTICUT
Glastonbury
Garlinghouse Home Plans
    Guide **(4868)** ....(Non-paid) ‡100,000

Newtown
Fine Gardening **(5041)** ....(Paid) 189,009
Kitchen Gardener **(5044)** ....‡95,000

Westport
Architectural Designs **(5211)** ....‡30,000

FLORIDA
Miami
Buenhogar **(6342)** ....‡18,449
Ideas para Su Hogar (Ideas for Your
    Home) **(6362)** ....‡10,848

Naples
Home & Condo **(6441)** ....(Paid) ‡6,000
    (Controlled) ‡29,000

St. Petersburg
The duPont Registry: A Buyer's Gallery of Fine
    Homes **(6625)** ....(Paid) 22,000
    (Controlled) 28,000

Winter Garden
Folkart Treasures **(6864)**

GEORGIA
Atlanta
Veranda **(7057)** ....(Paid) 393,270

IDAHO
Idaho Falls
Houseboat Magazine **(7864)** ....(Paid) 7,785
    (Non-paid) 24,172
The Mountain Gardener **(7866)**

ILLINOIS
Chicago
Outdoor Power Equipment **(8521)** ......(Paid) 1,089
    (Controlled) 16,930
Traditional Home **(8587)** ....(Paid) 831,580

Lake Forest
Chicago Home and
    Garden **(9061)** ....(Non-paid) 11,393
    (Paid) 29,964

St. Charles
Country Sampler **(9564)** ....(Paid) 434,323
Country Sampler Decorating
    Ideas **(9565)** ....(Paid) 200,469

IOWA
Des Moines
Better Homes and Gardens S.I.P.: Garden Ideas &
  Outdoor Living **(10771)** ....(Controlled) 500,000
Country Home **(10777)** ....(Paid) 1,045,729
Country Home Country
  Gardens **(10778)** ....(Paid) 353,973
Garden Gate **(10786)** ....(Paid) *not shown*
Workbench **(10817)** ....(Paid) 352,470

KANSAS
Prairie Village
Kansas City Homes &
  Gardens **(11762)** ....(Paid) ‡13,000
                                    (Non-paid) ‡2,800

LOUISIANA
Shreveport
American Rose **(12816)** ....(Paid) ‡22,109
                                    (Controlled) ‡150

MASSACHUSETTS
Boston
Horticulture **(13903)** ....(Paid) 210,000

Gloucester
Old-House Interiors **(14210)** .....(Paid) 120,000

Watertown
Bonsai Today **(14613)** ....‡8,012

Wayland
Popular Home Automation **(14615)** ....(Paid) ‡19,889

MINNESOTA
Falcon Heights
Northern Gardener **(15893)** ....‡60,000

Minneapolis
Midwest Home & Garden **(16097)** ...(Paid) 69,065

Minnetonka
Cooking Pleasures **(16168)** ....(Paid) 600,000
Gardening How-To **(16170)** ....(Paid) 550,000
Handy **(16171)** ....(Paid) 850,000

St. Paul
Country Style Homes Plans and
  Designs **(16372)** ....(Non-paid) 64,000
Distinguished Home
  Plans **(16374)** ....(Non-paid) 56,000
HomeStyles Home
  Plans **(16379)** ....(Non-paid) 53,000
New Country Homes **(16400)** ......(Non-paid) 53,000

MISSOURI
St. Louis
The National Gardener **(17475)** ....‡30,000

MONTANA
Billings
Montana Land
  Magazine **(17732)** ....(Controlled) ‡100,000

NEW HAMPSHIRE
Dublin
The Old Farmer's Almanac Gardener's
  Companion **(18499)** ....(Paid) 200,000

NEW JERSEY
Paramus
Contemporary Stone and Tile Design **(19401)**

Shrewsbury
Decks & Backyard
  Projects **(19549)** ....(Controlled) ‡168,830

NEW YORK
Brooklyn
Victorian Homes **(20354)** ....(Paid) 56,344

Melville
Kitchen and Bath Design Ideas **(21046)**

New York
American Homestyle and
  Gardening **(21189)** ....(Paid) 1,001,530
                                    (Non-paid) 23,382
Better Homes and Gardens Building
  Ideas **(21296)** ....(Paid) ‡450,000
Better Homes and Gardens Do It Yourself **(21297)**
Better Homes and Gardens: Garden, Deck and
  Landscape **(21298)** ....(Controlled) 459,000

Better Homes and Gardens Home Plan
  Ideas **(21299)**
Better Homes and Gardens Kitchen Plans **(21300)**
Better Homes and Gardens Special Interest
  Publications Low Calorie/Low Fat
  Recipes **(21301)** ....(Paid) 184,500
Christmas Helps & Holiday
  Baking **(21413)** ....(Paid) 1,000,000
Classic American Homes **(21427)**
Colonial Homes **(21441)** ....(Paid) 520,647
Country Accents **(21504)** ....‡350,000
Country Living **(21506)** ....(Paid) 1,673,792
Country Living Gardener **(21507)** ....(Paid) 360,000
Elle Decor **(21596)** ....(Paid) 467,367
Good Housekeeping **(21775)** ....(Paid) 4,558,524
Home Magazine **(21809)** ....(Paid) 1,010,623
Home Magazine's Home Plans **(21810)** ......‡70,013
Home Mechanix **(21811)** ....(Paid) 903,338
House Beautiful **(21821)** ....(Paid) 853,748
House Beautiful
  Kitchen/Baths **(21822)** ....(Paid) 350,000
In Style **(21857)** ....(Paid) 1,584,691
Log Homes Illustrated **(22265)** ....(Paid) 112,997
Martha Stewart at Home **(22286)**
Martha Stewart Living **(22287)** .....(Paid) 2,436,422
Metropolitan Home **(22328)** ....(Paid) 604,670
Midwest Living Magazine **(22335)** ....(Paid) 822,148
Mother Earth News **(22369)** ....(Paid) 366,793
This Old House **(22831)** ....(Paid) 663,345
Woman's Day Best Ideas for Christmas **(22925)**
Woman's Day Eating Light **(22926)**
Woman's Day Gardening & Outdoor Living **(22927)**
Woman's Day Holiday Baking **(22928)**
Woman's Day Home Decorating Ideas **(22929)**
Woman's Day Home Remodeling **(22930)**
Woman's Day Kitchens and Baths **(22931)**

Setauket
North Shore Homes **(23327)** ......(Non-paid) ‡42,000

NORTH CAROLINA
Fairview
Greenprints **(23876)** ....(Paid) 13,000
                                    (Non-paid) 2,000

Greensboro
Carolina Gardener **(23918)** ....(Paid) ‡21,625
                                    (Non-paid) ‡5,300

Hendersonville
Back Home **(23983)** ....‡29,414

OHIO
Troy
Miami Valley Home
  Finder **(25594)** ....(Combined) 20,000

OREGON
Ashland
Home Power **(26215)** 24,600
                                             45,000
                                             75,000

PENNSYLVANIA
Emmaus
Organic Gardening **(26879)** ....(Paid) 605,980

TEXAS
Austin
Austin Home and Living **(29760)** ....(Paid) ‡1,000
                                    (Controlled) ‡19,000

Dallas
Dallas/Fort Worth New Homes
  Guide **(30144)** ....(Controlled) ‡80,000

Mc Kinney
Neil Sperry's Gardens
  Magazine **(30779)** ....(Paid) 23,000
                                    (Non-paid) 633

San Antonio
San Antonio Homes &
  Gardens **(31046)** ....(Paid) ‡6,000
                                    (Non-paid) ‡29,000

Waco
Texas Gardener **(31253)** ....‡25,000

VERMONT
South Burlington
National Gardening **(31600)** ....(Paid) 279,705

WASHINGTON
Bellevue
Washington Magazine **(32670)** ....(Paid) 23,000
                                    (Non-paid) 31,000

Snohomish
Snohomish County
  Seniors **(33088)** ....(Non-paid) ‡10,000

WEST VIRGINIA
Martinsburg
House, Home and Garden **(33379)** ....‡10,000

WISCONSIN
Cedarburg
Wisconsin Home Gallery
  Magazine **(33621)** ....(Paid) ‡47,400
                                    (Controlled) ‡1,700

Fort Atkinson
Yard and Garden **(33723)** 17,500

Greendale
Country **(33758)**
Farm & Ranch Living **(33762)** 400,000

BRITISH COLUMBIA, CANADA
Argenta
The Smallholder **(34881)** ....(Paid) 750

Burnaby
Gardenwise Magazine **(34898)** ....(Paid) 18,038
                                    (Non-paid) 16,962

Vancouver
Gardens West **(35142)** ....(Paid) 39,318

ONTARIO, CANADA
Concord
Enoteca Wine and Food Magazine **(35751)**

Markham
Canadian Gardening **(36017)** ....(Paid) 142,135
Canadian Home and
  Country **(36018)** ....(Paid) ‡68,000
Canadian Home
  Workshop **(36020)** ....(Paid) 110,743

Ottawa
CMHC Housing Outlook, National Edition **(36237)**

Toronto
Canadian House & Home
  Magazine **(36503)** ....(Paid) 191,420
Cottage Life **(36563)** ....(Paid) 60,258
                                    (Non-paid) 9,876
Gardening Life **(36599)** ....(Combined) 99,082
Style at Home **(36752)** ....(Paid) 210,000

Unionville
Active Adult **(36827)**
Condo Life **(36828)**
Homes Magazine **(36829)** 100,000
Renovation & Decor **(36838)** .....(Controlled) 75,000

QUEBEC, CANADA
Outremont
Decoration Chez-Soi **(37263)** ....(Paid) 65,386
Les Idees de Ma Maison **(37267)** ......(Paid) 53,529
Renovation Bricolage **(37268)** ....(Paid) 35,576

Quebec
Fleurs, Plantes et Jardins **(37285)** .....(Paid) 54,340

Westmount
Residences **(37445)** ....(Combined) 70,278

IN-FLIGHT PUBLICATIONS

ARIZONA
Phoenix
America West Airlines
  Magazine **(773)** ....(Controlled) 130,000

FLORIDA
Cooper City
Lacja's World **(6003)** ....(Controlled) 20,000

Winter Park
Latitudes **(6882)** ....(Controlled) 105,000

HAWAII
Honolulu
Spirit of Aloha **(7719)** 100,000

Magazines

Circ.

IN-FLIGHT PUBLICATIONS (continued)
MASSACHUSETTS
Boston
Continental Magazine **(13884)** ....(Non-paid) 360,000

NORTH CAROLINA
Greensboro
Attacheair Magazine **(23916)** ....(Non-paid) ‡441,911
The Shuttle Sheet **(23937)**
SKY Magazine–(Delta Air
Lines) **(23938)** ....(Controlled) △489,315
United Hemispheres **(23942)** ....(Non-paid) ‡500,771

TEXAS
Fort Worth
American Way **(30329)** ....,....(Controlled) 344,375

WASHINGTON
Seattle
Alaska Airlines Magazines **(32937)** ....‡55,000
Horizon Air Magazine **(32971)** ....‡300,000

INTERCULTURAL INTERESTS

CALIFORNIA
La Mesa
Union Jack **(2124)** ....(Paid) 10,500
(Free) 70,000

Los Angeles
Amerasia Journal **(2207)** ....(Paid) 1,500
(Non-paid) 45
Brazzil **(2227)** ....-..12,000
Giant Robot **(2278)**
Korean Culture **(2308)** ....(Paid) 1,500
(Non-paid) 200
The New Korea **(2344)** ....(Paid) ‡3,000
(Non-paid) ‡100

San Francisco
France Today **(3363)** ....‡15,000
JINN Magazine **(3377)**
Ongaku Otaku **(3409)**

San Leandro
India West **(3562)** 25,000

CONNECTICUT
New Canaan
NordicReach **(4980)** ....(Paid) 16,000

DISTRICT OF COLUMBIA
Washington
France Magazine **(5502)** ....(Non-paid) 40,000

HAWAII
Honolulu
The Contemporary Pacific **(7685)** ....(Paid) 560
(Controlled) 15
Oceanic Linguistics **(7712)** ....(Paid) 400
(Controlled) 30

ILLINOIS
Chicago
Lithuanian Museum Review **(8467)** ......(Paid) ‡3500
(Controlled) ‡8950
Lituanus **(8468)** ....(Paid) 2,200

DeKalb
Crossroads **(8733)** ....(Paid) 300

Maywood
Aim–America's Intercultural
Magazine **(9163)** ....(Paid) ‡4,000
(Controlled) ‡3,000

LOUISIANA
Folsom
Whispering Wind **(12581)** ....‡28,000

MASSACHUSETTS
Hull
The Highlander **(14248)** 28,000

Newton
InterfaithFamily.com (IFF) **(14400)** 11,000

MISSOURI
St. Charles
Chinese American Forum **(17383)** ....(Paid) ‡500
(Non-paid) ‡750

Circ.

NEW YORK
New York
India Abroad **(21862)** ....(Fri.) 53,851
Midstream **(22334)** ....‡8,000
News India Times **(22458)**

PENNSYLVANIA
Ardmore
Halana **(26660)** ....(Paid) 2,000

Dingmans Ferry
Country Road
Chronicles **(26827)** ....(Controlled) 51,000

Levittown
Polish Heritage **(27189)** ....‡4,500

Scranton
Forum—A Ukrainian Review **(27959)** ....‡3,000

SOUTH DAKOTA
Rapid City
Well Nations
Magazine **(28934)** ....(Combined) 10,000

TEXAS
Austin
Indigenous Woman **(29781)** 4,000
(Non-paid) 1,000

WISCONSIN
Milwaukee
Viltis **(34106)** ....(Paid) ‡1,600
(Non-paid) ‡180

BRITISH COLUMBIA, CANADA
Vancouver
Scandinavian Press **(35167)**

ONTARIO, CANADA
Oakville
Pakeeza International **(36150)** ....(Paid) ‡35
(Non-paid) ‡8,000

Ottawa
Britannia **(36188)**

LIFESTYLE

ALABAMA
Birmingham
Coastal Living **(65)** ....(Paid) 435,473
Southern Living **(93)** ....(Paid) 2,537,485

Huntsville
Old Huntsville **(271)**

ARIZONA
Peoria
Sun Life Magazine **(770)** ....(Free) 40,000

Scottsdale
Arizona Trends **(867)** ....(Controlled) 34,000

Tucson
Tucson Lifestyle Magazine **(968)** ....(Paid) ‡6,000
(Controlled) ‡28,000

ARKANSAS
Little Rock
Arkansas Living **(1218)** ....(Controlled) 36,000

CALIFORNIA
Agoura
Biker **(1377)** ....(Paid) 48,033
Tailgate **(1380)** ....(Paid) ‡41,250
Tattoo **(1381)** ....(Paid) 117,346

Agoura Hills
In the Wind **(1386)** ....(Paid) 58,771

Beverly Hills
POPsmear **(1576)**

Los Angeles
BLK **(2223)**
Friendly Exchange **(2277)** ..:..(Controlled) ‡6,100,000
Situations Digest **(2389)**

Newport Beach
Coast Magazine **(2624)** ....(Combined) 45,000
Newport Beach 714 **(2632)** ....(Free) ‡52,000

Circ.

Oakland
Lifestyle **(2686)** ....(Paid) ‡3,000
(Non-paid) ‡90,000

Redding
After Five Magazine **(2886)** ....(Non-paid) ‡30,122

Redondo Beach
lovematters.com **(2910)**

Riverside
Inland Empire **(2939)** ....‡70,000
Pasta Magazine **(2942)**
Southern California Magazine **(2947)** ....‡20,000

Roseville
Single Again Magazine **(2972)** ....(Paid) 10,000

Sacramento
Sacramento Magazine **(3016)** ....(Paid) △33,132
(Non-paid) △4,107

San Anselmo
FAD Magazine **(3083)** ....(Paid) ‡69,843

San Francisco
*Surface **(3446)** ....(Paid) 112,000
The Urban Latino News **(3456)** ....(Non-paid) 20,000

San Ramon
The Nooner Magazine **(3607)** ....(Paid) 11
(Non-paid) 16,000

Santa Barbara
SuperOnda **(3660)** ....(Combined) 102,016

Ventura
WOODALL'S Camp-orama **(4017)** 35,000
WOODALL'S Camperways **(4018)** 40,000
WOODALL's Midwest RV Traveler **(4020)** 40,000

Walnut Creek
Diablo **(4052)** ....(Paid) 402
(Non-paid) 42,197

COLORADO
Aspen
Aspen Magazine **(4141)** ....(Paid) 5,500
(Non-paid) 10,500

Boulder
Loving More **(4177)** ....‡12,000

Denver
Colorado Country Life **(4312)** 160,000
5280 **(4327)** ....(Combined) 50,000
NEXUS Magazine **(4344)** ....(Paid) 25,000
(Non-paid) 200

Vail
Steamboat Magazine **(4653)** ....(Paid) ‡3,000
(Controlled) ‡17,000

CONNECTICUT
Trumbull
Connecticut Magazine **(5181)** ....(Paid) 86,820

Weston
Troika **(5209)** ....(Paid) 120,000

DISTRICT OF COLUMBIA
Washington
Caring People **(5395)**
LATINA Style **(5631)** ....(Paid) 150,000

FLORIDA
Aventura
Aventura Magazine **(5912)** ....(Combined) 30,000

Boca Raton
Boca Raton Magazine **(5928)** ....(Paid) ‡16,331
(Non-paid) ‡3,993

Clearwater
Tampa Bay Magazine **(5991)** ....(Paid) ‡17,371
(Controlled) ‡15,200

Gainesville
Relationships Today **(6156)** 160,000

Jacksonville
Jacksonville Magazine **(6214)** ....(Paid) 14,535
(Free) 6,613

Longboat Key
Black Tie **(6310)**

Naples
Gulfshore Life Magazine **(6440)** ....(Paid) ‡12,000
(Non-paid) ‡12,000

2818

Numbers cited after listings are entry numbers rather than page numbers.

Orlando
Florida Monthly Magazine **(6491)** ....(Paid) ‡207,390
(Non-paid) ‡5,284

Palm Beach
Bonkers? **(6541)** ....(Paid) 167,516
Palm Beach Illustrated **(6543)** ....(Paid) 2,428
(Non-paid) 39,452

St. Petersburg
The duPont Registry: A Buyer's Gallery of Fine
Homes **(6625)** ....(Paid) 22,000
(Controlled) 28,000

Tallahassee
Tallahassee Magazine **(6738)** .....(Controlled) 17,300

Venice
Wild Dog **(6832)** ....(Paid) ‡250
(Non-paid) ‡500

GEORGIA
Athens
Flagpole Magazine **(6937)** ....(Combined) 13,803

Atlanta
KNOW Atlanta
Magazine **(7024)** ....(Controlled) ⊕48,000

Macon
Macon Magazine **(7382)** ....(Paid) 7,000
(Non-paid) 3,000

HAWAII
Honolulu
Honolulu Magazine **(7701)** ....(Paid) 28,672

ILLINOIS
Chicago
AMA Alliance Today **(8251)** .....(Controlled) ‡40,000
The Baffler Magazine **(8280)** ....(Paid) 30,000
Chicago Life **(8315)** ....(Non-paid) 49,886
Chicago Magazine **(8316)** ....(Paid) 182,140
Chicago Tribune Magazine **(8328)**
Townsfolk **(8586)**

St. Charles
Country Sampler **(9564)** ....(Paid) 434,323

INDIANA
Indianapolis
Branches Magazine **(10099)** ......(Combined) 25,000
Indianapolis Monthly **(10131)** ....(Paid) 47,106

KANSAS
Prairie Village
Kansas City Homes &
Gardens **(11762)** ....(Paid) ‡13,000
(Non-paid) ‡2,800

KENTUCKY
Louisville
Louisville **(12227)** ....(Paid) 18,000
Today's Woman
Magazine **(12240)** ....(Non-paid) ‡46,000

MAINE
Portland
Portland **(13016)** ....(Paid) ‡10,000

MARYLAND
Baltimore
Baltimore City Paper **(13131)** ......(Non-paid) 86,113
Vegetarian Journal **(13259)** 24,000

Frederick
Frederick Magazine **(13512)** ......(Controlled) 16,000

Salisbury
The Metropolitan Magazine **(13710)** ....(Free) 28,603

MASSACHUSETTS
Edgartown
Martha's Vineyard
Magazine **(14174)** ....(Paid) ‡7,600
(Non-paid) ‡4,400

Newton
GenerationJ.com **(14396)**
Jewish Family & Life **(14402)**
JVibe.com **(14404)**

South Dartmouth
Hair to Stay **(14542)** ....(Paid) 10,000

Waltham
Transgender Tapestry **(14604)** .....(Combined) 8,000

MICHIGAN
Okemos
Michigan Country Lines **(15416)** 240,000

Royal Oak
HOUR Detroit **(15481)**

Traverse City
Traverse, Northern Michigan's
Magazine **(15603)** ....‡25,000

MINNESOTA
Edina
iAm Magazine! **(15875)** 50,000

Minneapolis
Minnesota Monthly **(16106)** ....(Paid) 68,922
MPLS.ST.PAUL **(16112)** ....(Paid) 72,305
Pillsbury Fast & Healthy
Magazine **(16120)** ....(Paid) 152,514

MONTANA
Kalispell
Montana Living **(17837)** ....(Combined) 120,000

NEVADA
Las Vegas
Your Life Matters **(18388)** ....(Controlled) 100,000

NEW HAMPSHIRE
Manchester
New Hampshire
Magazine **(18559)** ....(Combined) 26,000

Plymouth
Summer Week/Winter
Week **(18635)** ....(Non-paid) 18,000

NEW JERSEY
Basking Ridge
New Jersey Countryside
Magazine **(18664)** ....△30,000

Clayton
Homestead Hotline **(18750)** ....‡15,000

Englewood Cliffs
Hi Class Living **(18801)** ....(Controlled) ‡16,000

Hewitt
Journal America **(18872)** ....(Combined) ‡100,000

Pleasantville
Shoreeast Magazine **(19444)** ....‡75,000
‡100,000

West Atlantic City
The Poker Digest Magazine **(19717)** ·

NEW YORK
Delhi
Kaatskill Life **(20526)** ....(Paid) 8,000

Dolgeville
Vegetarian Voice **(20533)** ....(Combined) 11,000

Elmsford
Spotlight Magazine **(20584)** ....(Paid) 2,428
(Non-paid) 69,107

Westchester Spotlight **(20586)**

Ithaca
14850 Magazine **(20812)**

Levittown
PeopleNet **(20942)**

New York
Avenue **(21281)** ....(Non-paid) ‡81,000
Better Living **(21302)** ....‡200,000
Cigar Aficionado **(21418)** ....(Paid) 280,023
Country Accents **(21504)** ....‡350,000
Country Living **(21506)** ....(Paid) 1,673,792
Fit Magazine **(21703)** ....(Paid) 149,162
Flatiron News **(21706)** ....(Controlled) 35,000
Fresh From Sweden **(21736)** ....(Free) ‡3,500
Golf Magazine **(21774)** ....(Paid) 1,405,017
Gourmet-The Magazine of Good
Living **(21776)** ....(Paid) 946,345
In Style **(21857)** ....(Paid) 1,584,691
Marie Claire **(22281)** ....(Paid) 948,321
Midwest Living Magazine **(22335)** ....(Paid) 822,148

Mountain Sports &
Living **(22374)** ....(Paid) ‡400,000
(Non-paid) ‡112,346
New York Magazine **(22446)** ....(Paid) 440,308
O **(22481)**
Out Magazine **(22510)** ....(Paid) 100,126
Paper Magazine **(22520)** ....(Paid) 63,378
Punch in International Travel and Entertainment
Magazine **(22613)** ....(Non-paid) 100,000
Real Simple **(22636)** ....(Paid) ‡1,200,000
Savoy **(22707)** ....(Combined) 200,000
Shift **(22736)** ....(Paid) ‡150,000
SmartMoney **(22748)** ....(Paid) 822,436
SMOKE **(22749)**
Sportwear International **(22780)** ....‡26,000
Stuff Magazine **(22802)** ....(Paid) 812,079
Teen People **(22818)** ....(Paid) 1,600,504
Town & Country **(22849)** ....(Paid) 430,367
Travel, Food & Wine **(22857)**
W **(22905)** ....(Paid) 451,883

Niagara Falls
Natural Life **(23004)** ....(Combined) 35,000

Setauket
Prime Times **(23328)** ....(Free) 50,000

Westbury
R & R Shopper's
News **(23559)** ....(Controlled) ‡100,000

NORTH CAROLINA
Cary
Carolina Woman **(23685)** ....‡40,000

Durham
Fifty Plus **(23821)** ....(Paid) 1,500
(Non-paid) 135,000

Fayetteville
Up & Coming Weekly **(23882)** .....(Non-paid) 15,000

Hendersonville
Back Home **(23983)** ....‡29,414

NORTH DAKOTA
Bismarck
North Dakota
Horizons **(24355)** ....(Combined) 14,600

Mandan
North Dakota REC Magazine **(24498)** ....‡71,199

OHIO
Chagrin Falls
Currents **(24757)** 65,000

Chillicothe
Over the Back Fence **(24763)** ....(Paid) 15,000

OKLAHOMA
Oklahoma City
Oklahoma Living
Magazine **(25981)** ....(Paid) 240,440
(Non-paid) 1,200

OREGON
Coos Bay
The Whole Shebang! **(26273)**

Gold Beach
Backwoods Home Magazine **(26359)** ....‡45,000

PENNSYLVANIA
Camp Hill
Pennsylvania Magazine **(26753)** ....(Paid) ‡24,000
(Non-paid) ‡2,000

Harrisburg
Central PA **(26985)** ....(Paid) 38,350
Country Journal **(26989)** ....(Paid) 91,456
Penn Lines **(27004)** ....(Paid) 143,134

PUERTO RICO
San Juan
Imagen **(28295)** ....‡70,000

RHODE ISLAND
East Greenwich
The Rhode Island Gourmet
Guide **(28343)** ....(Controlled) 25,000

Circulation: ★ = ABC; △ = BPA; ♦ = CAC; • = CCAB; ❑ = VAC; ⊕ = PO Statement; ‡ = Publisher's Report; Boldface figures = sworn; Light figures = estimated.

Magazines

2819

Circ. | Circ. | Circ.

LIFESTYLE (continued)

SOUTH CAROLINA
Lexington
Sandlapper **(28685)**

SOUTH DAKOTA
Pierre
South Dakota Electric Cooperative
Connections **(28920)** ....‡103,000

Rapid City
Well Nations
Magazine **(28934)** ....(Combined) 10,000

TENNESSEE
Gainesboro
Rural Heritage **(29201)** ....‡6,000

TEXAS
Amarillo
Accent West **(29693)** ....‡8,500

Austin
New Texas **(29794)** ....(Non-paid) 25,000

Dallas
Cowboys & Indians **(30139)** ....(Paid) 101,225

San Antonio
San Antonio Homes &
Gardens **(31046)** ....(Paid) ‡6,000
(Non-paid) ‡29,000

Stafford
Houston Lifestyle & Homes
Magazine **(31127)** ....(Paid) 7,000
(Controlled) ⊕94,300

Wimberley
Hill Country Sun **(31302)** ....(Non-paid) ‡30,000

UTAH
Salt Lake City
Salt Lake Magazine **(31439)** ......(Combined) 25,000

VERMONT
Dorset
Stratton Magazine **(31539)** ....(Non-paid) 25,000

Troy
Naturist Life
International **(31606)** ....(Controlled) 1,700

VIRGINIA
Charlottesville
Albemarle **(31913)** ....(Paid) ⊕10,000

Glen Allen
Better Nutrition Magazine **(32111)** ....‡486,500

WASHINGTON
Bainbridge Island
Yes! A Journal of Positive
Futures **(32659)** ....(Paid) ‡20,000
(Non-paid) 3,000

Bellevue
Washington Magazine **(32670)** ....(Paid) 23,000
(Non-paid) 31,000

Seattle
Real Change **(33012)** ....(Paid) 30,000
Seattle Weekly **(33026)** ....(Free) ❑102,464
(Paid) ❑85

WISCONSIN
Eau Claire
Wisconsin West
Magazine **(33674)** ....(Combined) 5,000

Greendale
Country **(33758)**
Country Extra **(33759)** ....(Paid) ⊕325,000
Farm & Ranch Living **(33762)** 400,000

Mequon
Wisconsin in Motion **(34044)**

Oshkosh
Nude & Natural **(34225)** ....(Paid) 18,650
(Non-paid) 6,350

WYOMING
Sheridan
American Cowboy **(34587)** ....(Paid) 92,020

ALBERTA, CANADA
Edmonton
Western Living **(34736)** ....(Paid) •1,921
(Non-paid) •208,058

BRITISH COLUMBIA, CANADA
Vancouver
Georgia Straight **(35144)** ....(Free) 122,000
Watershed Sentinel **(35177)** ....(Combined) 4,000

NORTHWEST TERRITORIES, CANADA
Yellowknife
Up Here **(35527)** ....(Paid) 15,657
(Non-paid) 10,007

ONTARIO, CANADA
Don Mills
Hi-Rise **(35774)** ....(Controlled) ‡60,000

Hamilton
Hamilton Magazine **(35879)** ....(Paid) 1,000
(Non-paid) 38,000

Kingston
Profile Kingston **(35942)** ....(Controlled) 16,000

Thunder Bay
Thunder Bay Life **(36442)** ....‡3,000

Toronto
Campus.ca **(36486)** ....(Non-paid) •135,237
Cottage Life **(36563)** ....(Paid) 60,258
(Non-paid) 9,876
Del Condominium
Life **(36567)** ....(Controlled) 25,000
Elm Street **(36582)** ....(Paid) 44,842
(Non-paid) 597,736
Klublife **(36644)** ....(Combined) 40,000
Toronto Events Calender **(36767)**
Toronto Life **(36768)** ....(Paid) 92,574

QUEBEC, CANADA
Montreal
Coup de Pouce **(37106)** ....(Paid) 172,413
In Montreal **(37125)** ....(Paid) 30,000
Maison d'Aujourd'hui **(37181)** .....(Combined) 14,860
Voir **(37236)**

Montreal-Nord
Harrowsmith Country Life **(37251)** .....(Paid) 133,415

Westmount
Plaisirs de Vivre **(37444)** ....(Non-paid) 65,691
(Paid) 2,092

LITERATURE AND LITERARY REVIEWS

See also Science Fiction, Mystery, Adventure, and Romance

ALABAMA
Birmingham
Aura Literary/Arts Review **(56)** ....(Non-paid) ‡500

Mobile
Negative Capability **(327)** ....‡1,000

ARIZONA
Douglas
The Mirage **(687)** ....(Non-paid) 2,000

Flagstaff
American Indian Quarterly **(693)** 900

ARKANSAS
Little Rock
The Oxford American **(1235)** ....(Paid) 56,261

Russellville
Nebo **(1332)**

State University
Arkansas Review **(1348)** ....(Paid) 900

CALIFORNIA
Berkeley
Poetry Flash **(1551)** ....(Paid) ‡3,000
(Controlled) ‡22,000
The Threepenny Review **(1564)** ....(Paid) ‡8,000
(Non-paid) ‡2,000

Cedarville
Floating Island **(1681)**

Long Beach
Pearl **(2173)** ....(Combined) 550

Los Osos
Lynx Eye **(2482)** ....(Paid) 300
(Non-paid) 200

Marina del Rey
Storyette Magazine **(2510)** ....(Non-paid) ‡10,000

Nevada City
Dream Magazine **(2615)**
Wild Duck Review **(2616)** ....(Paid) ‡3,500

Paradise
Small Press Review **(2808)** ....(Paid) 2,800

Pasadena
Firsts **(2816)**
Iniquities **(2818)**

San Diego
Books **(3123)** ....‡422,000

San Francisco
Fourteen Hills **(3362)** ....(Paid) 600
Reader's Guide to the Underground
Press **(3420)** ....(Paid) 1,250
ZYZZYVA **(3467)** ....(Paid) ‡2,500
(Non-paid) ‡1,000

San Leandro
Five Fingers Review **(3561)** ....(Paid) 1,000

San Rafael
Whole Earth **(3603)** ....‡35,000

Santa Barbara
Short Fuse **(3656)** ....(Combined) 500

Sylmar
Avatar **(3835)**
Magic Realism **(3836)**
Strike Through The Mask **(3837)**
A Theater of Blood **(3838)** ....(Paid) 150
(Controlled) 50

COLORADO
Colorado Springs
Gauntlet **(4248)** ....(Paid) 20,000

Denver
The Bloomsbury Review **(4309)** ....(Paid) ‡10,000
(Controlled) ‡40,000

Edgewater
Pleiades Magazine **(4410)** ....(Combined) 10,000

CONNECTICUT
New Haven
The Yale Literary Magazine **(5008)** ....(Paid) 130
(Non-paid) 2,500
The Yale Review **(5009)** ....‡6,000

Southport
The Small Press Book Review **(5138)**

DISTRICT OF COLUMBIA
Washington
History **(5528)** ....(Paid) ‡460
Lambda Book Report **(5628)** ....(Paid) 8,000
(Non-paid) 150
The World & I **(5870)** ....(Paid) 20,056
(Non-paid) 2,781

FLORIDA
Gainesville
Counterpoise **(6135)**
Delos **(6136)** ....(Paid) 400
(Controlled) 25

Jacksonville
Kalliope **(6215)** ....(Paid) 1,500
(Non-paid) 100

Miami
Thoughts for All Seasons **(6384)** ...(Non-paid) 1,000

Pensacola
Half Tones to Jubilee **(6566)**

Tampa
Tampa Review **(6779)** ....(Paid) 650

GEORGIA
Dunwoody
The Chattahoochee Review **(7258)** ....(Paid) 185
(Non-paid) 1,250

Valdosta
Snake Nation Review **(7614)** ....(Controlled) 700

HAWAII
Honolulu
Bamboo Ridge **(7680)** ....‡500
Hawaii Pacific Review **(7698)** ....(Non-paid) 500
Manoa **(7709)** ....(Paid) 1,000
(Controlled) 65

ILLINOIS
Carol Stream
Books & Culture **(8134)** ....(Paid) 14,743
(Non-paid) 6,009

Chicago
Agnieszka's Dowry **(8248)**
Book Links: Connecting Books, Libraries and
  Classrooms **(8286)** ....(Paid) 24,265
(Non-paid) 5,735
Chicago Review **(8321)** ....(Paid) ‡2,700
(Non-paid) ‡100
Other Voices **(8519)** 1,300-1,700
Poetry **(8535)** ....(Paid) ‡9,800
(Non-paid) ‡60
Rain Crow **(8547)** ....(Paid) 300

Normal
The American Book Review **(9295)** ....(Paid) ‡1,200
(Non-paid) ‡1,000
Spoon River Poetry
  Review **(9306)** ....(Combined) 1,000

Peru
Babybug **(9446)** 47,000

Rockford
Chronicles **(9526)** ....‡8,000

INDIANA
Selma
Barnwood **(10447)**

Valparaiso
The Cresset **(10508)** ....‡4,700

West Lafayette
Modern Fiction Studies **(10550)** 3,000

IOWA
Anamosa
Wapsipinicon Almanac **(10602)** ......(Non-paid) 2,000

Cedar Falls
The North American Review **(10659)** ....‡3,400

Cedar Rapids
Coe Review **(10670)** ....(Controlled) 1,500

Des Moines
Yellowback Library **(10818)** ....‡650

KANSAS
Lawrence
Voodoo Souls Quarterly **(11569)**

KENTUCKY
Berea
Appalachian Heritage **(11936)** ....(Paid) 700
(Non-paid) 200

Covington
Diarist's Journal **(12026)** ....‡300

Louisville
Burroughs Bulletin **(12211)** ....(Paid) ‡800

Pikeville
Pikeville Review **(12358)** ....(Paid) 500

LOUISIANA
Metairie
Thema **(12679)** ....(Paid) 300
(Non-paid) 100

New Orleans
Fell Swoop **(12729)** ....‡500
New Laurel Review **(12743)**
New Orleans Review **(12748)** ....(Paid) ‡1,000
(Non-paid) ‡200

MAINE
Farmington
The Beloit Poetry Journal **(12959)** ......(Paid) ‡655
(Non-paid) ‡415

Portland
AudioFile **(13005)** ....(Combined) 20,000

MARYLAND
Baltimore
Anagram **(13122)**
Literature and Medicine **(13210)** 606
Shattered Wig Review **(13246)**
The Yale Journal of Criticism **(13264)** 606

Bethesda
Poet Lore **(13375)** ....(Paid) ‡600
(Non-paid) ‡10
Writer's Carousel **(13390)** ....(Paid) ‡3,000
(Non-paid) ‡3,500

Bowie
The Plastic Tower **(13393)** ....(Combined) 250

Edgewood
Companion in Zeor **(13492)**

Towson
Persuasions **(13762)**
Persuasions (Online Version) **(13763)**

MASSACHUSETTS
Amherst
Peregrine **(13804)**

Arlington
the new renaissance **(13821)** ....(Combined) 910

Boston
AGNI **(13847)** ....(Paid) 1,500
(Non-paid) 300
Bay Windows **(13852)** ....(Non-paid) 24,500
Gay and Lesbian Review Worldwide **(13895)**
The Horn Book Guide **(13901)** ....(Paid) 4,500
(Non-paid) 500
The Horn Book
  Magazine **(13902)** ....(Combined) 19,000
Ploughshares **(13950)**

Cambridge
Boston Review **(14042)** ....(Paid) ‡6,000
(Non-paid) ‡4,000
Harvard Advocate **(14055)** ....(Paid) ‡300
(Non-paid) ‡3,000

Edgartown
Martha's Vineyard
  Magazine **(14174)** ....(Paid) ‡7,600
(Non-paid) ‡4,400

Lawrence
The Long Story **(14267)** ....(Combined) 1,100

Lunenburg
Button **(14283)** ....(Combined) 1,200

Somerville
Double Take **(14534)** ....(Paid) 50,000

Spencer
Nostoc Magazine **(14549)** ....(Non-paid) 500

West Stockbridge
Lingo Magazine **(14627)** 3,500,000

MICHIGAN
Ann Arbor
Michigan Quarterly Review **(14768)** ....‡1,200

Detroit
Struggle **(14950)** ....(Combined) 600

Farmington Hills
Witness **(15021)** ....(Paid) ‡1,500
(Controlled) ‡1,500

Lansing
way station magazine **(15296)** .....(Combined) 1,040

MINNESOTA
Duluth
Lake Superior Magazine **(15839)** ......(Paid) ‡22,500

Frontenac
Mythos Journal **(15913)** ....(Paid) 500

Pine Island
Kumquat Meringue **(16271)** ....(Paid) 600

St. Joseph
Studio One/HCC **(16358)**

St. Paul
Ruminator Review **(16408)**

MISSISSIPPI
Hattiesburg
Mississippi Review **(16663)** ....(Combined) 1,500

MISSOURI
Columbia
The Missouri Review **(17003)** ....(Paid) 6,800
(Non-paid) 200

Florissant
The Lowell Review **(17069)** ....(Paid) 150
(Non-paid) 100

Kansas City
New Letters **(17188)** ....(Paid) ‡1,311
(Non-paid) ‡84
Thorny Locust **(17198)** ....(Paid) 200

Maryville
The Laurel Review
  (Maryville) **(17273)** ....(Controlled) 700

NEBRASKA
Lincoln
Legacy: A Journal of American Women
  Writers **(18089)**
Prairie Schooner **(18114)** ....(Paid) ‡2,800
(Non-paid) ‡300

NEVADA
Carson City
Cayo **(18326)**

Las Vegas
Art **(18360)** 100

NEW HAMPSHIRE
Warner
Color Wheel **(18647)** ....(Paid) 300

NEW JERSEY
Fanwood
Exit 13 Magazine **(18815)** ....(Paid) ‡200
(Non-paid) ‡100

Randolph
Journal of New Jersey Poets **(19495)** ....(Paid) ‡700
(Non-paid) ‡300

South Orange
The Chesterton Review **(19584)** ....(Paid) 1,600
(Non-paid) 30

NEW MEXICO
Albuquerque
Atom Mind **(19767)** ....(Paid) 800
(Non-paid) 350

Gallup
Paradoxism **(19857)** ....(Combined) 1000

NEW YORK
Binghamton
Gulp **(20153)** ....(Combined) 200
Harrington Lesbian Fiction Quarterly **(20154)**

Bronx
Book Review Digest **(20256)**

Bronxville
The Villager **(20294)** ....(Paid) 450
(Non-paid) 40

Brooklyn
Hanging Loose **(20319)** ....(Paid) ‡1,700
(Non-paid) ‡300
Matriarch's Way **(20330)**
Peep **(20336)** ....(Paid) 4,000

Chester
Heaven Bone **(20460)** ....(Paid) ‡500
(Controlled) ‡2,000

Magazines

Circ.　　　　　　　　　　Circ.　　　　　　　　　　Circ.

LITERATURE AND LITERARY REVIEWS
(continued)

Ithaca
14850 Magazine **(20812)**
Zuzu's Petals Quarterly Online **(20816)**

Jackson Heights
Editor's Choice **(20826)** ....(Paid) 3000
The Spirit That Moves Us **(20829)**

Mount Marion
ART TIMES **(21100)** ....(Paid) ‡1,000
　　　　　　　　　　　　　　(Non-paid) ‡25,000

New York
American Letters &
　Commentary **(21201)** ....(Controlled) 1,500
Bomb **(21331)** ....(Paid) ‡12,000
　　　　　　　　　　　　　　(Non-paid) ‡3,000
Book **(21334)**
Chelsea **(21398)** ....(Paid) 2,200
　　　　　　　　　　　　　　(Non-paid) 300
Fence **(21685)**
Grand Street **(21778)** ....‡8,000
Home Planet News **(21812)** ....(Paid) 700
　　　　　　　　　　　　　　(Non-paid) 200
The Hudson Review **(21826)** ....(Paid) ‡4,700
　　　　　　　　　　　　　　(Controlled) ‡100
Inspector 18 **(21878)** ....(Paid) 75
　　　　　　　　　　　　　　(Non-paid) 25
Joe Magazine **(21969)**
Literal Latté **(22260)** ....(Paid) ‡5,000
　　　　　　　　　　　　　　(Non-paid) ‡30,000
Meshuggah **(22317)** ....(Combined) 520
The New Criterion **(22428)** 7,000
　　　　　　　　　　　　　　(Non-paid) 1,000
The New York Review of
　Books **(22451)** ....(Paid) 117,221
The New York Times Book Review **(22454)**
Open City **(22493)**
Parabola **(22521)** ....(Paid) 40,000
　　　　　　　　　　　　　　(Non-paid) 520
The Paris Review **(22530)** ....(Paid) ‡5,500
　　　　　　　　　　　　　　(Non-paid) ‡500
The Quarterly **(22617)** ....(Paid) 10,000
Spinning Jenny **(22773)** ....(Paid) 1,000
Women's Studies Quarterly **(22935)** ....‡1,500

Niagara Falls
Slipstream **(23007)** ....(Paid) 500
　　　　　　　　　　　　　　(Non-paid) 40

Saratoga Springs
Salmagundi **(23302)** ....(Paid) ‡5,100
　　　　　　　　　　　　　　(Controlled) ‡200

NORTH CAROLINA
Asheville
Science Fiction Eye **(23633)** ....(Paid) 5,000

Chapel Hill
The Carolina Quarterly **(23701)** ......(Combined) 900
The Sun **(23727)** ....(Paid) 50,000

Durham
Boundary 2 **(23810)** ....(Paid) 850

Pembroke
Pembroke Magazine **(24115)** ....(Combined) 750

NORTH DAKOTA
Grand Forks
North Dakota Quarterly **(24456)** ....(Paid) 700
　　　　　　　　　　　　　　(Controlled) ‡200

OHIO
Akron
Kaleidoscope **(24582)** ....(Paid) 1,500

Berea
Grasslands Review **(24677)** ....(Paid) 200

Cleveland
Whiskey Island
　Magazine **(24965)** ....(Controlled) 1,500

Columbus
Narrative **(25033)**
Ohioana Quarterly **(25054)** ....(Paid) 1,100
　　　　　　　　　　　　　　(Non-paid) 1,000

Gambier
The Kenyon Review **(25212)** ....‡4,500

Kent
Luna Negra **(25276)**

Stow
Impetus **(25546)** ....(Paid) 500
　　　　　　　　　　　　　　(Non-paid) 500

Yellow Springs
The Antioch Review **(25690)** ....‡4,800

Youngstown
Pig Iron **(25698)** ....(Paid) 1,000

OKLAHOMA
Norman
Genre **(25934)** ....(Paid) 40,002
　　　　　　　　　　　　　　(Controlled) ‡15

Stillwater
Cimarron Review **(26076)** ....(Paid) ‡450
　　　　　　　　　　　　　　(Non-paid) ‡150

OREGON
Astoria
Nocturnal Lyric **(26226)** ....(Paid) 400

Eugene
Northwest Review **(26326)** ....(Controlled) 1,250

Portland
The Bear Deluxe Magazine **(26469)** ....(Paid) 500
　　　　　　　　　　　　　　(Non-paid) 18,500

PENNSYLVANIA
Gettysburg
The Gettysburg Review **(26938)** ....(Paid) ‡3,000

Lyndora
Poets at Work **(27208)** 300

Philadelphia
The American Poetry
　Review **(27374)** ....(Paid) ‡12,000
　　　　　　　　　　　　　　(Non-paid) ‡1,500

Pittsburgh
Creative Nonfiction **(27772)** ....(Paid) 4,500
Nite-Writer's International Literary Arts
　Journal **(27822)**

RHODE ISLAND
East Greenwich
Merlyn's Pen: Stories by American
　Students **(28341)** ....(Paid) ‡5,000
　　　　　　　　　　　　　　(Controlled) ‡1,000

Warwick
The Hunted News **(28450)**

SOUTH CAROLINA
Columbia
Manuscripts **(28557)** ....‡1,800

SOUTH DAKOTA
Vermillion
South Dakota Review **(29006)** ....(Paid) ‡400
　　　　　　　　　　　　　　(Non-paid) ‡150

TENNESSEE
Cookeville
Under the Sun **(29146)** ....(Paid) 500

Jonesborough
Storytelling Magazine **(29259)** ....‡10,000

Murfreesboro
Poems and Plays **(29431)** ....(Combined) 800

Sewanee
The Sewanee Review **(29595)** 3,560

TEXAS
Austin
Sulphur River Literary
　Review **(29810)** ....(Combined) 350

Dallas
Southwest Review **(30181)** ....(Paid) 1,000
　　　　　　　　　　　　　　(Non-paid) ‡400

Houston
Lucidity **(30504)** ....(Paid) ‡230
　　　　　　　　　　　　　　(Non-paid) ‡75

UTAH
Provo
BYU Studies **(31400)** ....(Paid) 4,000
　　　　　　　　　　　　　　(Non-paid) 250

VERMONT
Jericho
The Lyric **(31545)** ....(Paid) ‡700
　　　　　　　　　　　　　　(Non-paid) ‡28

Middlebury
Heron Dance **(31556)**

Randolph
Green World **(31580)** 200

VIRGINIA
Charlottesville
Belles Lettres **(31918)** ....(Paid) ‡6,000
　　　　　　　　　　　　　　(Controlled) ‡2,000
The Blue Penny Quarterly **(31919)**
Virginia Quarterly Review **(31947)**

Fredericksburg
Visions International **(32088)** ....(Paid) 750
　　　　　　　　　　　　　　(Non-paid) 80

Hampton
Harrington Gay Men's Fiction Quarterly **(32129)**

Lexington
Shenandoah **(32191)** ....‡1,200

Radford
Absolute Magnitude **(32344)** ....(Paid) 6,000
　　　　　　　　　　　　　　(Non-paid) 3,000

Winchester
Frogpond **(32628)** 1,000

WASHINGTON
Bainbridge Island
Gurukulam **(32658)** ....(Paid) ‡100
　　　　　　　　　　　　　　(Non-paid) ‡300

Bellevue
Arnazella **(32662)**

Nordland
Pangolin Papers **(32853)** ....(Paid) 500

Olympia
Young Voices Magazine **(32864)** 3,000

Pullman
ESQ **(32903)** ....(Paid) ‡588
　　　　　　　　　　　　　　(Non-paid) ‡43

Seattle
American Jones Building & Maintenance **(32940)**
Bellowing Ark **(32949)** ....(Paid) ‡450
　　　　　　　　　　　　　　(Non-paid) ‡100
Jack Mackerel Magazine **(32974)** .....(Non-paid) 500
PoetsWest Online **(33003)** ....(Free) 300

Vashon
PARA DOXA **(33183)** ....(Paid) 1,200
　　　　　　　　　　　　　　(Non-paid) 500

WEST VIRGINIA
Circleville
Combat **(33292)**

WISCONSIN
Beloit
Acorn Whistle **(33573)** ....(Paid) 400
　　　　　　　　　　　　　　(Non-paid) 100

Cambridge
Rosebud **(33615)** ....(Paid) ‡8000

Madison
Abraxas **(33915)** ....(Paid) ‡250
　　　　　　　　　　　　　　(Controlled) ‡300
L'Anello Che Non Tiene **(33919)**
Madison Review **(33960)**

River Falls
Literary Magazine Review **(34308)** ....(Paid) ‡265
　　　　　　　　　　　　　　(Non-paid) ‡40

ALBERTA, CANADA
Calgary
Filling Station **(34644)** ....(Paid) 625
　　　　　　　　　　　　　　(Non-paid) 75

　　　　　　　　　　Numbers cited after listings are entry numbers rather than page numbers.

BRITISH COLUMBIA, CANADA
Vancouver
B.C. Bookworld (35123) ....(Paid) 100,000
Canadian Literature (35133) ....(Paid) ‡1,500
(Non-paid) ‡150
Geist (35143) ....(Paid) 6,000
PRISM International (35159) ....(Paid) ‡1,200
(Non-paid) ‡100
Room of One's Own (35165) ....(Paid) ‡1,000
(Non-paid) ‡200
sub-TERRAIN Magazine (35169) ....(Paid) ⊕700
Victoria
The Claremont Review (35214) ....(Combined) 600
The Malahat Review (35221) ....(Paid) 1,000
(Controlled) 250

MANITOBA, CANADA
Winnipeg
Prairie Fire (35349) ....‡1,500

NEW BRUNSWICK, CANADA
Fredericton
The Fiddlehead (35394) ....(Paid) ‡900
(Non-paid) ‡50

NOVA SCOTIA, CANADA
Antigonish
The Antigonish Review (35536) ....(Paid) 700
(Non-paid) 200
Sydney
Pottersfield Portfolio (35609) ....(Combined) 2000

ONTARIO, CANADA
Kingston
Poetry Canada (35941) 1,600
Quarry Magazine (35943) ....‡600
Ottawa
Journal of Canadian
Poetry (36254) ....(Combined) 500
Palmerston
Country Charm Magazine (36304)
Toronto
Broken Pencil (36479) ....(Combined) 3,000
Descant (36570) ....(Paid) ‡1,025
(Non-paid) ‡75
Exile (36586) 1,100
Phoenix (36706) ....(Paid) 1,200
Word (36794) ....(Combined) 10,000
Waterloo
The New Quarterly (36856) ....(Paid) 600
(Non-paid) 100

QUEBEC, CANADA
Montreal
Montreal Serai (37191)

LOCAL, STATE, AND REGIONAL PUBLICATIONS

ALABAMA
Birmingham
Coastal Living (65) ....(Paid) 435,473
Huntsville
Old Huntsville (271)
Tuscaloosa
Alabama Heritage (483) ....‡15,000

ARIZONA
Bullhead City
Laughlin Nevada
Entertainer (665) ....(Combined) 52,000
Cave Creek
True West (673) ....(Paid) ‡23,267
(Non-paid) ‡273
Glendale
Key Magazine
Phoenix/Scottsdale (714) ....(Combined) 45,000
Parker
Arizona West (762) ....(Non-paid) 15,000
Phoenix
Phoenix Magazine (809) ....(Paid) 55,097
Scottsdale
Arizona Trends (867) ....(Controlled) 34,000

Key Magazine Palm
Springs (870) ....(Combined) 45,000
Sedona
Sedona Excentric (877) ....(Non-paid) ‡10,000
Tucson
Tucson Lifestyle Magazine (968) ....(Paid) ‡6,000
(Controlled) ‡28,000

ARKANSAS
Little Rock
Arkansas Living (1218) ....(Controlled) 36,000
Arkansas Times (1221) ....(Non-paid) 30,000
(Paid) 6,000

CALIFORNIA
Berkeley
News from Native California (1546) .....(Paid) 5,000
(Controlled) 500
Parents' Press (1550) ....(Combined) 75,000
Carmel
KEY Magazine, Carmel and Monterey
Peninsula (1673) ....(Non-paid) 40,000
La Verne
La Verne Magazine (2128) ....(Combined) 2,200
Lake Forest
Aliso Viejo News (2142)
Menlo Park
Gentry Magazine and Northern California Home &
Design (2524) ....(Non-paid) ‡32,500
(Non-paid) ‡51,500
Newport Beach
Coast Magazine (2624) ....(Combined) 45,000
Newport Beach 714 (2632) ....(Free) ‡52,000
Orange Coast (2634) ....(Paid) 29,118
Palm Springs
Palm Springs Life (2763) ....(Paid) 19,250
Paradise
California Territorial
Quarterly (2805) ....(Controlled) ‡3,000
Rancho Mirage
GOLF NEWS
Magazine (2878) ....(Controlled) ‡54,253
Riverside
Inland Empire (2939) ....‡70,000
Southern California Magazine (2947) ....‡20,000
Sacramento
Sacramento Magazine (3016) ....(Paid) △33,132
(Non-paid) △4,107
San Diego
San Diego Magazine (3265) ....(Paid) 46,545
San Diego This Week (3269) .....(Combined) 30,000
Today in San Diego (3280) ......(Non-paid) ‡80,000
San Francisco
Nob Hill Gazette (3405) ....(Combined) 75,000
San Francisco Magazine (3435) ....(Paid) 133,000
SF Weekly (3439) ....(Non-paid) 123,462
San Ramon
The Nooner Magazine (3607) ....(Paid) 11
(Non-paid) 16,000
Seaside
Coast Weekly (3750)
Sonoma
Valley of the Moon Visitor's
News (3779) ....(Free) 6,000
Valley Center
Valley Roadrunner (3985) ....(Combined) 3502
Vista
El Informador (4044) ....(Combined) 28,229
Good News Etc. (4045) ....(Combined) 42,000
Walnut Creek
Diablo (4052) ....(Paid) 402
(Non-paid) 42,197

COLORADO
Aspen
Aspen Magazine (4141) ....(Paid) 5,500
(Non-paid) 10,500
Centennial
Mountain Living (4225) ....(Paid) 19,700
(Non-paid) 11,300

Denver
Colorado Country Life (4312) 160,000
Colorado Outdoors (4319) ....(Paid) ‡43,576
(Controlled) ‡3,100
5280 (4327) ....(Combined) 50,000
Eldorado Springs
Rocky Mountain
Gardener (4411) ....(Combined) 7,000
Littleton
Key Magazine
Colorado (4550) ....(Combined) 38,000
Steamboat Springs
The Steamboat Whistle (4633) ....‡5,000
Vail-Beaver Creek
Magazine (4634) ....(Combined) 62,000
Vail
Steamboat Magazine (4653) ....(Paid) ‡3,000
(Controlled) ‡17,000

CONNECTICUT
Stamford
Links Magazine (5154) ....(Non-paid) 283,806
(Paid) 20,791
Trumbull
Connecticut Magazine (5181) ....(Paid) 86,820
Westport
Connecticut's County Kids (5212)

DELAWARE
Wilmington
Delaware Today (5292) ....(Paid) 23,138

DISTRICT OF COLUMBIA
Washington
Cathedral Age (5398) ....‡36,000
The Washington Post
Magazine (5851) ....(Paid) 80,077
Washingtonian Magazine (5856) ....(Paid) 157,701

FLORIDA
Aventura
Aventura Magazine (5912) ....(Combined) 30,000
Boca Raton
Boca Raton Magazine (5928) ....(Paid) ‡16,331
(Non-paid) ‡3,993
Clearwater
Tampa Bay Magazine (5991) ....(Paid) ‡17,371
(Controlled) ‡15,200
Jacksonville
Folio Weekly (6213) ....,......(Free) ❑43,401
(Paid) ❑9
Jacksonville Magazine (6214) ....(Paid) 14,535
(Free) 6,613
Miami
Entertainment News &
Views (6351) ....(Free) 125,000
Social (6380)
Naples
Gulfshore Life Magazine (6440) ....(Paid) ‡12,000
(Non-paid) ‡12,000
Orlando
Florida Monthly Magazine (6491) ....(Paid) ‡207,390
(Non-paid) ‡5,284
Palm Beach
Palm Beach Society
Magazine (6544) ....(Paid) 4,500
(Non-paid) 500
Sanibel
Island Life Magazine (6649) ....‡15,000
Tallahassee
Tallahassee Magazine (6738) .....(Controlled) 17,300
Venice
Florida Mariner (6830) ....(Paid) 332
(Free) 23,500

GEORGIA
Athens
Athens Magazine (6929) 6,500
Atlanta
Atlanta Homes and Lifestyles (6970) ....‡33,828

Circulation: ★ = ABC; △ = BPA; ◆ = CAC; ● = CCAB; ❑ = VAC; ⊕ = PO Statement; ‡ = Publisher's Report; Boldface figures = sworn; Light figures = estimated.

2823

	Circ.

LOCAL, STATE, AND REGIONAL PUBLICATIONS (continued)

WHERE Atlanta **(7061)** ....(Paid) ‡300
(Non-paid) 1,071,070

Blakely
Southern Festivals **(7131)** ....(Paid) 3,000
(Non-paid) 20,000

Macon
Macon Magazine **(7382)** ....(Paid) 7,000
(Non-paid) 3,000

Sugar Hill
Key Magazine Atlanta **(7573)** .....(Combined) **15,000**

Tucker
GEORGIA Magazine **(7610)** ....‡448,000

Union City
The Atlanta Metro **(7613)** ....(Controlled) ‡29,000

HAWAII
Honolulu
Honolulu Magazine **(7701)** ....(Paid) 28,672
Spotlight Big Island **(7720)** ....(Non-paid) 42,000
Spotlight Kauai **(7721)** ....(Non-paid) 42,000
Spotlight Oahu **(7722)** ....(Non-paid) 35,000
This Week Oahu **(7726)** ....(Non-paid) ‡42,000

Kaneohe
Midweek Magazine **(7774)**

IDAHO
Boise
Boise Family Magazine **(7803)** ....(Controlled) 18,000

ILLINOIS
Chicago
Chicago Life **(8315)** ....(Non-paid) 49,886
Chicago Magazine **(8316)** ....(Paid) 182,140
Home & Away **(8399)** 370,000
Townsfolk **(8586)**

DeKalb
Crossroads **(8733)** ....(Paid) 300

Edwardsville
Illinois Wildlife **(8813)** ....‡12,684

Glenview
North Shore Magazine **(8939)** ....(Paid) 51,340

Lake Forest
Chicago Home and
Garden **(9061)** ....(Non-paid) 11,393
(Paid) 29,964

Oak Brook
Business Ledger **(9343)** ....(Paid) 8,000

Springfield
Illinois Rural Electric News **(9630)** ....‡142,000

INDIANA
Indianapolis
Branches Magazine **(10099)** ......(Combined) 25,000
Electric Consumer **(10109)** ....(Paid) 250,000
(Non-paid) 172
Home & Away (Hoosier
Edition) **(10114)** ....‡221,977
Indianapolis Woman **(10134)** ....(Non-paid) 58,227
This is Indianapolis **(10174)** .....(Controlled) 300,000
Traces of Indiana and Midwestern
History **(10175)** 11,000

Kokomo
Kokomo Perspective **(10240)**

Michigan City
The Beacher **(10303)**

IOWA
Anamosa
Wapsipinicon Almanac **(10602)** ......(Non-paid) 2,000

Bettendorf
Home & Away (Minnesota
Edition) **(10621)** ....(Paid) 225,000
(Controlled) 400

Des Moines
Intro **(10788)** ....(Controlled) 170,000
The Iowan **(10798)** ....(Paid) ‡25,000
(Non-paid) ‡1,000

Dubuque
The Dubuque Area
Magazine **(10843)** ....(Combined) ‡40,000

Urbandale
Iowa REC News **(11276)** ....(Combined) ‡93,000

KANSAS
Ellsworth
Kanhistique **(11427)** ....‡5,215

Topeka
Kansas Country Living **(11827)** ....‡80,957

KENTUCKY
Berea
Appalachian Heritage **(11936)** ....(Paid) 700
(Non-paid) 200

Buckner
Fastline—Bluegrass Truck
Edition **(11968)** ....(Combined) 22,000
Fastline—Dakota Farm
Edition **(11969)** ....(Combined) 22,000
Fastline—Dixie Truck
Edition **(11970)** ....(Combined) 22,000
(Combined) 22,000
Fastline—Far West Farm
Edition **(11971)** ....(Combined) 22,000
Fastline—Florida Truck
Edition **(11972)** ....(Combined) 22,000
Fastline—Georgia Truck
Edition **(11973)** ....(Combined) 22,000
Fastline—Illinois Farm
Edition **(11974)** ....(Combined) 22,000
Fastline—Indiana Farm
Edition **(11975)** ....(Combined) 22,000
Fastline—Iowa Farm
Edition **(11976)** ....(Combined) 22,000
Fastline—Kansas Farm
Edition **(11977)** ....(Combined) 22,000
Fastline—Kentucky Farm
Edition **(11978)** ....(Combined) 22,000
Fastline—Mid-Atlantic Farm
Edition **(11979)** ....(Combined) 22,000
Fastline—Mid-South Farm
Edition **(11980)** ....(Combined) 22,000
Fastline—Mid-West Truck
Edition **(11981)** ....(Combined) 22,000
Fastline—Minnesota Farm
Edition **(11982)** ....(Combined) 22,000
Fastline—Missouri Farm
Edition **(11983)** ....(Combined) 22,000
Fastline—Nebraska Farm
Edition **(11984)** ....(Combined) 22,000
Fastline—Northeast Farm
Edition **(11985)** ....(Combined) 22,000
Fastline—Northland Truck
Edition **(11986)** ....(Combined) 22,000
Fastline—Northwest Farm
Edition **(11987)** ....(Combined) 22,000
Fastline—Ohio Farm
Edition **(11988)** ....(Combined) 22,000
Fastline—Oklahoma Farm
Edition **(11989)** ....(Combined) 22,000
Fastline—Ontario Farm
Edition **(11990)** ....(Combined) 22,000
Fastline—Rocky Mountain Farm
Edition **(11991)** ....(Combined) 22,000
Fastline—South Central Truck
Edition **(11992)** ....(Combined) 22,000
Fastline—Southeast Farm
Edition **(11993)** ....(Combined) 22,000
Fastline—Tennessee Farm
Edition **(11994)** ....(Combined) 22,000
Fastline—Tennessee Truck
Edition **(11995)** ....(Combined) 22,000
Fastline—Texas Farm
Edition **(11996)** ....(Combined) 22,000
Fastline—Tri-State Truck
Edition **(11997)** ....(Combined) 22,000
Fastline—Wisconsin Farm
Edition **(11998)** ....(Combined) 22,000

Frankfort
Kentucky Afield **(12066)** ....(Paid) ‡40,000
(Controlled) ‡4,000
Register of Kentucky Historical
Society **(12075)** ....(Paid) ‡2,700

Louisville
Kentucky Living **(12224)** ....(Paid) 479,791
Today's Woman
Magazine **(12240)** ....(Non-paid) ‡46,000

LOUISIANA
Baton Rouge
Louisiana Country **(12497)** ....‡130,000

Metairie
Louisiana Life Magazine **(12677)** ....‡40,001

New Orleans
New Orleans Magazine **(12745)** ....(Paid) 14,660
(Non-paid) 33,952
New Orleans Menu **(12746)** ....(Combined) 3,000
New Orleans Preservation in Print **(12747)**
This Week New
Orleans **(12757)** ....(Combined) 5,500

MAINE
Augusta
Maine Fish and Wildlife **(12893)** ....(Paid) 12,500
(Non-paid) 400

Camden
Down East Magazine **(12942)** 105,845
★112,677
Maine Boats &
Harbors **(12944)** ....(Combined) 20,000

Machias
Maine Magazine **(12987)** ....(Paid) 16,200

Portland
Portland **(13016)** ....(Paid) ‡10,000

MARYLAND
Baltimore
Baltimore Magazine **(13134)** ....(Paid) 50,186

Columbia
Columbia Magazine **(13458)** ......(Controlled) 33,000
The Official Guide to Howard
County **(13470)** ....‡35,000

Frederick
Frederick Magazine **(13512)** ......(Controlled) 16,000

Salisbury
The Metropolitan Magazine **(13710)** ....(Free) 28,603

MASSACHUSETTS
Edgartown
Martha's Vineyard
Magazine **(14174)** ....(Paid) ‡7,600
(Non-paid) ‡4,400

Nantucket
Nantucket Magazine **(14341)** ....(Combined) 8,864
Yesterday's Island **(14343)** ....(Non-paid) 350,000

Worcester
Worcester Magazine **(14693)** ....(Paid) 42
(Non-paid) 38,182

MICHIGAN
Ann Arbor
Ann Arbor Observer **(14743)** ....(Paid) 4,014
(Non-paid) 56,974

Grand Rapids
Grand Rapids Magazine **(15095)** ....(Paid) 8,600
(Non-paid) 8,000

Lansing
Michigan History **(15285)** 34,000
Michigan History for Kids **(15286)**
Michigan Traveler **(15293)** ....(Non-paid) 10,000
(Paid) 5,800

Royal Oak
HOUR Detroit **(15481)**

Saginaw
Review Magazine **(15490)** ....(Paid) 200
(Non-paid) 25,000

Southfield
Metro Parent
Magazine **(15545)** ....(Controlled) 66,000

Traverse City
Traverse, Northern Michigan's
Magazine **(15603)** ....‡25,000

Troy
The Fear Finder **(15625)** ....(Combined) 500,000

MINNESOTA
Duluth
North Coast Review **(15841)** ......(Controlled) 1,000

Edina
iAm Magazine! (15875) 50,000

Minneapolis
Minnesota Monthly (16106) ....(Paid) 68,922
MPLS.ST.PAUL (16112) ....(Paid) 72,305

MISSISSIPPI
Columbus
Mid-South Horse Review (16604) ......(Free) 12,500

Ridgeland
TODAY in Mississippi (16835) ....(Paid) ‡386,691
(Non-paid) ‡176

MISSOURI
Jefferson City
Rural Missouri (17132) ....‡388,000

Kansas City
eKC (17167) ....(Non-paid) 26,000

Kirbyville
The Ozarks Mountaineer (17224) .....(Paid) ‡32,000
(Controlled) ‡1,500

Perryville
MidAmerica Farmer
Grower (17337) ....(Paid) ‡14,379
(Non-paid) ‡10,451

Springfield
Springfield! Magazine (17611) ....‡51,600

MONTANA
Helena
Montana Magazine (17822) ....‡42,000

Kalispell
Montana Living (17837) ....(Combined) 120,000

NEBRASKA
Blair
Nebraska & Iowa Explorer (17957)

Lincoln
NEBRASKAland (18107) ....(Paid) ‡51,238
(Non-paid) ‡4,100

Omaha
Home & Away (18198) ....(Paid) 3,355,000

NEVADA
Carson City
Cayo (18326)
Nevada (18328) ....(Paid) ‡70,000
(Non-paid) ‡10,000
Range Magazine (18331) 150,000

Las Vegas
Key Magazine Las
Vegas (18369) ....(Combined) ‡83,500
What's On, The Las Vegas
Guide (18385) ....(Non-paid) 195,000
(Paid) 3,200

NEW HAMPSHIRE
Colebrook
Northern New Hampshire
Magazine (18469) ....(Paid) 3,000

Manchester
New Hampshire
Magazine (18559) ....(Combined) 26,000

NEW JERSEY
Bridgewater
Strictly Hunterdon (18701) ....(Combined) 38,762

Cinnaminson
Southern New Jersey Swapper (18745) 25,719

Collingswood
Cuizine Magazine (18767) ....(Controlled) 35,350

Englewood Cliffs
Hi Class Living (18801) ....(Controlled) ‡16,000

Far Hills
New Jersey
Conservation (18817) ....(Combined) 5,000

Jersey City
Coming Up (19134) ....(Non-paid) 18,246

Mountainside
Union County
Family (19319) ....(Controlled) 125,000

Pleasantville
Shoreeast Magazine (19444) ....‡75,000
‡100,000

Somerville
The Moneybook (19575) ....(Free) 112,500
TeeVee Moneysaver (Edition
1) (19579) ....(Non-paid) 120,000

Trenton
New Jersey
Outdoors (19662) ....(Controlled) ⊕10,258

NEW MEXICO
Santa Fe
Enchantment (19935) ....‡125,000
New Mexico Magazine (19938) ....(Paid) 117,718

Taos
Taos Magazine (19962) ....(Paid) ‡300
(Non-paid) ‡7,200

NEW YORK
Buffalo
Afro-Americans in New York Life and
History (20362) ....(Paid) 600

Cooperstown
New York History (20500) ....(Paid) 4,350
(Controlled) 69

Delhi
Kaatskill Life (20526) ....(Paid) 8,000

Elmsford
Spotlight Magazine (20584) ....(Paid) 2,428
(Non-paid) 69,107
Westchester Spotlight (20586)

Jay
Adirondack Life (20847) ....(Paid) ‡50,000
(Non-paid) ‡1,000

New York
Buying & Dining
Guide (21364) ....(Controlled) ‡500,000
City Guide Magazine (21423) .....(Combined) 61,596
The City Journal (21424) ....‡10,000
Midwest Living Magazine (22335) .....(Paid) 822,148
New York Magazine (22446) ....(Paid) 440,308
Time Out New York (22841) ....(Paid) 125,580
TV News (22877) ....(Free) ‡331,000

Niagara Falls
Natural Life (23004) ....(Combined) 35,000

Pittsford
Genesee Valley Parent
Magazine (23097) ....(Combined) 37,060

Poughkeepsie
Hudson Valley Magazine (23146) .....(Paid) ★24,610

Wappingers Falls
Hudson Valley Business
Journal (23502) ....(Paid) ‡4,000
(Free) ‡8,000

Williamsville
Buffalo Spree (23582) ....(Paid) ‡5,000
(Non-paid) ‡20,000

NORTH CAROLINA
Asheville
The Digest (23628) ....(Controlled) ‡225,000
This Week of Western North
Carolina (23634) ....(Paid) 25,000

Cary
Carolina Woman (23685) ....‡40,000

Chapel Hill
Triangle Pointer (23728) 45,000

Fayetteville
Up & Coming Weekly (23882) .....(Non-paid) 15,000

Greensboro
Our STATE (23932) 98,000

High Point
ESP Magazine (23996) ....(Non-paid) 17,000

Mount Airy
Simple Pleasures (24080) ....(Paid) ‡10,000
(Non-paid) ‡25,000

Raleigh
Carolina Country (24130) ....(Paid) 445,812
Piedmont Triad
Newcomer (24148) ....(Non-paid) 50,000
Piedmont Triad Newcomer (24149)
Triangle Newcomer (24157) ....(Non-paid) 50,000
Wildlife in North Carolina (24159) .....(Paid) ‡66,319
(Non-paid) ‡3,626

NORTH DAKOTA
Bismarck
Dakota Country (24351) ....(Paid) 12,199
(Non-paid) 2,150
North Dakota
Horizons (24355) ....(Combined) 14,600
North Dakota Outdoors (24356) ....(Paid) 24,000
(Non-paid) 2,000

Mandan
North Dakota REC Magazine (24498) ....‡71,199

OHIO
Chillicothe
Over the Back Fence (24763) ....(Paid) 15,000

Cincinnati
Cincinnati Magazine (24787) ....(Paid) ‡28,576
(Non-paid) ‡742

Cleveland
Cleveland Magazine (24872) 50,000
Northern Ohio LIVE (24933) ....(Paid) 15,724
(Non-paid) △14,846
Ohio Magazine (24937) ....(Paid) 90,425
This Week in Cleveland
Magazine (24957) ....(Free) 10,000

Columbus
Columbus Monthly (25009) ....(Paid) 34,280
Country Living (Ohio) (25012) ......(Paid) 282,050

Jefferson
The New Senior Life Styles
Vista (25264) ....(Non-paid) 5,000

Maineville
Key Magazine
Cincinnati (25327) ....(Combined) ‡15,200

Maumee
Bend of the River
Magazine (25368) ....(Paid) ‡7,500

Worthington
Home & Away (Ohio
Edition) (25679) ....(Controlled) 590,000

OKLAHOMA
Oklahoma City
Oklahoma Living
Magazine (25981) ....(Paid) 240,440
(Non-paid) 1,200
Oklahoma Today
Magazine (25988) ....(Paid) ‡44,000
(Non-paid) ‡2,000
Outdoor Oklahoma (25990) ....‡20,000

Shawnee
Frontier Country Key (26063) .....(Combined) 20,000

OREGON
Coos Bay
The Whole Shebang! (26273)

Eugene
Eugene Weekly (26316) ....(Free) 27,787

Florence
Oregon Coast (26352) ....‡36,700

Forest Grove
Ruralite (26357) ....‡281,400

Hillsboro
Timbertimes (26373) 3,200

Seaside
North Coast Tidings (26579) ....(Non-paid) 12,000

PENNSYLVANIA
Camp Hill
Pennsylvania Magazine (26753) ....(Paid) ‡24,000
(Non-paid) ‡2,000

Harrisburg
Central PA (26985) ....(Paid) 38,350
Pennsylvania Game News (27007) ....‡120,000

Circulation: ★ = ABC; △ = BPA; ♦ = CAC; ● = CCAB; ❑ = VAC; ⊕ = PO Statement; ‡ = Publisher's Report; Boldface figures = sworn; Light figures = estimated.

2825

Magazines

Circ.   Circ.   Circ.

LOCAL, STATE, AND REGIONAL PUBLICATIONS (continued)

Mount Joy
Where & When Pennsylvania's Travel Guide **(27299)** ....(Combined) ‡100,000

Philadelphia
The Philadelphia Spotlite **(27631)** ....(Controlled) 15,000

Pittsburgh
Key Magazine Pittsburgh **(27808)** ....(Combined) **10,000**
Pittsburgh Magazine **(27834)** ....(Paid) 48,575

State College
Town & Gown **(28021)** ....(Paid) ‡500
(Controlled) ‡19,500

Westtown
County Lines **(28153)** ....(Paid) ‡400
(Controlled) ‡15,600

SOUTH CAROLINA
Cayce
Living in South Carolina **(28503)** ....‡503,000

Columbia
South Carolina Wildlife **(28568)** ....‡60,000

Lexington
Sandlapper **(28685)**

Loris
Loris Times **(28686)** ....(Combined) 4,600

SOUTH DAKOTA
Pierre
Dakota Outdoors **(28916)** ....(Paid) 8,100
(Non-paid) 25
South Dakota Electric Cooperative Connections **(28920)** ....‡103,000

TENNESSEE
Franklin
Back Home in Kentucky **(29194)** ....‡11,000

Memphis
Key Magazine Memphis **(29374)** ....(Combined) **23,000**
The Memphis Flyer **(29375)** ......(Combined) 55,000
Memphis Magazine **(29376)** ....(Paid) 19,500

Nashville
Key Magazine Nashville **(29466)** 25,000
Nashville Scene **(29473)** ....(Non-paid) 52,500
Tennessee Magazine **(29492)** ....(Paid) 472,677

TEXAS
Amarillo
Accent West **(29693)** ....‡8,500

Austin
Impact (Austin) **(29780)**
Texas Co-op Power **(29813)** ....(Controlled) △825,000
Texas Highways **(29822)** ....(Paid) ‡262,438
(Controlled) ‡25,642
Texas Monthly **(29836)** ....(Paid) 300,991

Beaumont
Metropolitan Beaumont **(29899)** ....‡3000

Dallas
Cowboys & Indians **(30139)** ....(Paid) 101,225
D Magazine **(30140)** ....(Paid) 60,602
Key Magazine Dallas **(30165)** ....(Controlled) ‡35,000

Euless
DFW People **(30310)** ....(Controlled) ‡13,000

Fort Worth
Key Magazine Fort Worth **(30344)** ....(Combined) ‡11,740

Houston
Houston Press **(30488)** ......(Non-paid) 115,123
Inner-View **(30492)** ....‡50,000
Key Magazine Houston **(30500)** ....(Combined) ‡41,505

Marble Falls
101 Fun Things to Do **(30760)** ....(Non-paid) 20,000

Odessa
El Editor Permian Basin **(30871)** ....(Paid) 14,765

San Antonio
Que Pasa San Antonio **(31043)** ....(Combined) 125,000
RIO **(31044)** ....(Non-paid) ‡50,000

Stafford
Houston Lifestyle & Homes Magazine **(31127)** ....(Paid) 7,000
(Controlled) ⊕94,300

Wimberley
Hill Country Sun **(31302)** ....(Non-paid) ‡30,000

UTAH
Salt Lake City
Salt Lake City Weekly **(31438)** ....(Paid) 210
(Non-paid) 48,761

VERMONT
Burlington
Outdoors Magazine **(31516)** ......(Controlled) ⊕9,300
Seven Days **(31518)** ....(Free) ❑23,732
(Paid) ❑48

Dorset
Stratton Magazine **(31539)** .....(Non-paid) 25,000

Killington
The Mountain Times **(31547)** ....(Paid) ‡300
(Free) ‡10,300

Middlebury
Vermont Magazine **(31559)** 42,000

Montpelier
Vermont Life **(31565)** ....(Paid) ‡80,000
(Non-paid) ‡1,000

VIRGINIA
Glen Allen
Rural Living **(32112)** ....(Paid) 325,000

Richmond
Richmond Magazine **(32451)** ....(Paid) ‡25,000
(Controlled) ‡15,000
Style Weekly **(32456)** ....(Free) 39,601
Virginia Wildlife **(32468)** ....‡40,000

Roanoke
Blue Ridge Country **(32489)** 75,000
Roanoker Magazine **(32493)** ....(Paid) 9,850
(Non-paid) 2,450

Warrenton
Virginia Heritage **(32602)** ....(Paid) ‡10,000

WASHINGTON
Lynnwood
The Journal—Lynnwood Edition **(32823)** ....(Free) ‡82,000

Northgate
The Journal—Northgate Edition **(32855)** ....(Combined) ‡82,000

Renton
Northwest Baby & Child **(32925)** ......(Free) ‡27,000

Seattle
Pacific Northwest Quarterly **(33001)** 1,300
Puget Sound Parent **(33009)** ...(Combined) 30,000

WEST VIRGINIA
Charleston
Wonderful West Virginia **(33281)** 48,000

WISCONSIN
Black Earth
Wisconsin Trails **(33590)** 50,050

Cedarburg
Wisconsin Home Gallery Magazine **(33621)** ....(Paid) ‡47,400
(Controlled) ‡1,700

Chippewa Falls
Rural Minnesota News **(33628)** ....(Paid) 35,000

Eau Claire
Wisconsin West Magazine **(33674)** ....(Combined) 5,000

Madison
Madison Magazine **(33959)** ....(Combined) 18,000
Wisconsin Energy Cooperative News **(33981)** 153,000

Milwaukee
Key Milwaukee Magazine **(34072)** ....(Combined) ‡31,000
Life Without Limits **(34073)** ....(Non-paid) ⊕35,000
Milwaukee Magazine **(34086)** ....(Paid) 32,000
(Non-paid) 8,000

WYOMING
Casper
The WREN Magazine **(34484)** ....(Combined) 34,141

Cheyenne
Wyoming Wildlife **(34501)** ....(Paid) ‡35,000
(Controlled) ‡1,100

ALBERTA, CANADA
Calgary
WHERE Calgary **(34659)** ....(Non-paid) 28,000

Edmonton
Western Living **(34736)** ....(Paid) •1,921
(Non-paid) •208,058

St. Albert
The Alberta Game Warden **(34841)** ....‡11,000

BRITISH COLUMBIA, CANADA
Port Alberni
B.C. Waterfront & Island Magazine **(35049)**

Squamish
99 North Magazine **(35094)** ......(Non-paid) 100,000

Vancouver
Cottage **(35137)**
The Flag & Banner **(35141)** ....(Controlled) ⊕10,000
Vancouver Magazine **(35174)** ....(Paid) 5,627
(Non-paid) 49,125
Watershed Sentinel **(35177)** ....(Combined) 4,000
WHERE Vancouver **(35182)** ...(Non-paid) ‡52,000

Victoria
British Columbia Magazine **(35210)** ....(Paid) 125,000
(Non-paid) 1,000

NORTHWEST TERRITORIES, CANADA
Yellowknife
Up Here **(35527)** ....(Paid) 15,657
(Non-paid) 10,007

NOVA SCOTIA, CANADA
Halifax
Atlantic Progress Magazine **(35559)** ....(Controlled) •24,447
(Paid) •335
The Coast **(35562)** ....(Free) ❑19,276
(Paid) ❑11

ONTARIO, CANADA
Dresden
Grand Bend Sun **(35788)** ....(Non-paid) ‡22,000

Goderich
Focus Newsmagazine **(35850)** .....(Non-paid) 19,600

Hamilton
Hamilton Magazine **(35879)** ....(Paid) 1,000
(Non-paid) 38,000

Kingston
Profile Kingston **(35942)** ....(Controlled) 16,000

Ottawa
Ottawa Business Journal **(36264)** ....(Combined) •20,000

Thunder Bay
Thunder Bay Life **(36442)** ....‡3,000

Toronto
Coast Magazine—Ontario Edition **(36552)**
Del Condominium Life **(36567)** ....(Controlled) 25,000
Elm Street **(36582)** ....(Paid) 44,842
(Non-paid) 597,736
Eye **(36590)**
Toronto Events Calender **(36767)**
Toronto Life **(36768)** ....(Paid) 92,574
WHERE Toronto **(36791)** ....(Non-paid) ‡77,000

Unionville
Moving to Alberta **(36830)**
Moving to Montreal **(36831)**
Moving to Ottawa/Outaouais **(36832)**
Moving to Saskatchewan **(36833)**

Numbers cited after listings are entry numbers rather than page numbers.

Moving to Southwestern Ontario **(36834)**
Moving to Toronto **(36835)**
Moving to Vancouver & British Columbia **(36836)**
Moving to Winnipeg & Manitoba **(36837)**

Windsor
Room **(36889)** ....(Non-paid) 12,000

QUEBEC, CANADA
Montreal
In Montreal **(37125)** ....(Paid) 30,000
Montreal Scope **(37190)** ....(Non-paid) •**36,636**

Vanier
Pensez-Y Bien! **(37428)** ....(Non-paid) 134,609

Westmount
Plaisirs de Vivre **(37444)** ....(Non-paid) 65,691
(Paid) 2,092

MEN'S INTERESTS

CALIFORNIA
Los Angeles
Adam Film World Guide **(2197)** ....‡125,000
Adam Magazine **(2198)** 125,000
Players **(2370)** 50,000

CONNECTICUT
Sandy Hook
Club Confidential **(5108)**
Club International Magazine **(5109)**
Club Specials Magazine **(5111)**
Mayfair Magazine **(5112)**
Mayfair Specials **(5113)**

FLORIDA
Miami
Hombre Internacional **(6360)** ....‡12,749

ILLINOIS
Chicago
Playboy **(8533)** ....(Paid) 3,014,812

Glen Ellyn
Chicago Cigar Smoker
  Magazine **(8924)** ....(Paid) 5,000
(Controlled) 80,000

NEW JERSEY
Paramus
Genesis **(19403)**

NEW YORK
New York
Cigar Aficionado **(21418)** ....(Paid) 280,023
Esquire **(21627)** ....(Paid) 676,052
Exercise For Men Only **(21662)** ....(Paid) 89,163
Gallery Magazine **(21746)** ....‡362,863
GQ (Gentlemen's
  Quarterly) **(21777)** ....(Paid) 898,508
Men's Journal **(22315)** ....(Paid) 612,186
Penthouse
  Variations **(22539)** ....(Combined) 300,000
Stuff Magazine **(22802)** ....(Paid) 812,079

OHIO
Oxford
Journal of African American
  Men **(25455)** ....(Paid) ‡1,100

PENNSYLVANIA
Emmaus
Men's Health **(26877)** ....(Paid) 1,659,594

WISCONSIN
Iola
Military Vehicles **(33838)** ....(Paid) ‡18,000

MOTION PICTURES
**See also Photography; Radio, Television,
Cable, and Video**

CALIFORNIA
Beverly Hills
Inside Film Magazine **(1575)**

Burbank
Entertainment Today **(1617)** ....‡215,000

La Jolla
Pre-Vue Entertainment
  Magazine **(2119)** ....(Paid) 2,609
(Non-paid) 200,000

Los Angeles
Adam Film World Guide **(2197)** ....‡125,000
Cinefantastique **(2239)** ....‡70,000
Femme Fatales **(2269)**
Movieline **(2338)** ....(Paid) 315,873
Novedades **(2350)** ....(Combined) 50,000
Variety **(2427)** ....(Mon.) 34,293

Temecula
Widescreen Review **(3843)** ....(Paid) ⊕**50,000**

COLORADO
Aurora
Star Trek Communicator **(4149)** ....(Paid) 250,000
Star Wars Insider **(4150)** ....(Paid) 250,000

Boulder
Premiere **(4185)** ....(Paid) 603,998

CONNECTICUT
Sandy Hook
Mayfair Magazine **(5112)**

FLORIDA
Tampa
World of Fandom **(6783)** ....(Controlled) 80,000

INDIANA
Highland
The Midwest BEAT
  Magazine **(10063)** ....(Non-paid) ‡30,000

IOWA
Muscatine
Classic Images **(11102)** ....(Paid) 5,400
(Non-paid) 500

MARYLAND
Potomac
In-Motion **(13653)**

MICHIGAN
Roseville
Movie Collector's World **(15475)** ....(Paid) ‡4,800
(Controlled) ‡200

MINNESOTA
Mankato
Favorite Westerns & Serial World **(16025)** 2,000

NEW HAMPSHIRE
Peterborough
Take One **(18631)** ....‡1,325,538

NEW JERSEY
Montclair
Alternative Cinema **(19240)** ....(Controlled) 10,000

Ocean Grove
The Phantom of the Movies'
  Videoscope **(19390)** ....(Paid) 10,000

NEW YORK
New York
Bomb **(21331)** ....(Paid) ‡12,000
(Non-paid) ‡3,000
Casting News **(21378)** ....(Paid) 100,000
(Non-paid) 200,000
Cineaste **(21419)** 11,000
Film Bill **(21692)** ....(Controlled) 80,000
Ross Reports Television and
  Film **(22677)** ....(Combined) 15,103
talk **(22814)**
TV Executive Daily **(22875)** ....(Non-paid) ‡8,000

NORTH CAROLINA
Waynesville
Cliffhanger **(24277)** ....(Paid) 600
Under Western Skies **(24281)** ....(Paid) 800

VIRGINIA
Richmond
Burping Lula **(32431)** ....(Controlled) 5,000

WISCONSIN
Iola
The Big Reel **(33804)** ....(Paid) ‡5,256

ONTARIO, CANADA
Don Mills
Teen Tribune **(35778)** ....(Non-paid) •**299,500**

Mississauga
Marquee Magazine **(36076)** ....(Controlled) ‡312,000

QUEBEC, CANADA
Outremont
Le Lundi **(37266)** ....(Paid) 52,507

Sainte-Foy
Magazine Le Clap **(37374)** ....(Combined) 98,900

MOTORBIKES AND MOTORCYLES

ALABAMA
Montgomery
IronWorks **(367)** ....(Paid) ‡25,160
(Non-paid) ‡7,076

CALIFORNIA
Agoura
Biker **(1377)** ....(Paid) 48,033
Easyriders **(1378)** ....(Paid) 226,948
Tattoo **(1381)** ....(Paid) 117,346
V-Twin **(1383)**

Agoura Hills
In the Wind **(1386)** ....(Paid) 58,771

Anaheim
Hot Bike **(1406)** ....(Paid) 74,844

Lake Elsinore
Roadracing World & Motorcycle
  Technology **(2140)** ....(Paid) ‡20,000

Los Angeles
Dirt Rider **(2253)** ....(Paid) 201,432
Motorcyclist **(2336)** ....(Paid) 255,456

Newport Beach
Cycle World **(2625)** ....(Paid) 326,570

Santa Ana
Dealernews **(3624)** ....(Paid) △**105**
(Non-paid) △**15,477**

Valencia
Dirt Bike Magazine **(3977)** ....(Paid) 88,035
Dirt Wheels **(3978)** ....(Paid) 120,593
4-Wheel ATV Action **(3979)** ....(Paid) 36,826
Motocross Action **(3980)** ....(Paid) 82,266

CONNECTICUT
Huntington
The Motorcyclist's Post **(4918)** ....‡10,060

Stamford
Motorcycle Tour &
  Cruiser **(5155)** ....(Combined) 45,000

OHIO
Pickerington
American Motorcyclist **(25477)** ....(Paid) 245,772

SOUTH DAKOTA
Pierre
Motorcycle Events
  Magazine **(28917)** ....(Controlled) 60,000

TEXAS
Austin
Ride Texas
  Magazine **(29802)** ....(Combined) ‡15,000

WEST VIRGINIA
Buckhannon
Hack'd **(33263)** ....(Paid) 3000

BRITISH COLUMBIA, CANADA
Langley
MPH **(35004)** 2,000

Victoria
Canadian Biker **(35213)** ....(Paid) 6,900
(Non-paid) 4,600

Magazines

Circ.   Circ.   Circ.

MOTORBIKES AND MOTORCYLES (continued)

ONTARIO, CANADA
Toronto
Cycle Canada **(36566)** ....(Paid) 18,521
(Non-paid) 5,427

Motorsport Dealer &
Trade **(36670)** ....(Controlled) ‡5,000

QUEBEC, CANADA
Montreal
Moto Journal **(37192)** ....(Paid) 8,000
(Non-paid) 1,000

Motocycliste **(37193)** ....(Paid) 1,229
(Non-paid) 28,103

MUSIC AND MUSICAL INSTRUMENTS

ALABAMA
Birmingham
LoMo Magazine **(79)**

ARIZONA
Phoenix
Arizona Jazz Magazine **(781)**
Loud **(806)** 20,000

Tempe
Java Magazine **(906)** ....(Controlled) 27,000
Pool Dust **(912)** ....(Non-paid) ‡5,000

CALIFORNIA
Beverly Hills
POPsmear **(1576)**

Burbank
Preview Theater Magazine **(1623)** ....‡250,000

Concord
BAM Magazine **(1750)** ....(Non-paid) △119,507

Emeryville
Remix **(1881)**

Encinitas
Crawdaddy! **(1883)**

Gardena
Latin Beat Magazine **(2001)** ......(Combined) 50,000

Long Beach
The Jazz Review and Collectors Discography **(2169)**

Los Angeles
Blitz **(2222)** ....(Paid) ‡2,000
(Controlled) ‡500
Giant Robot **(2278)**
Option **(2353)** ....(Paid) ‡29,000
Rapport **(2377)** ....(Paid) 50,000
URB **(2424)** ....(Non-paid) 70,000

Lynwood
World of Pageantry **(2488)** ....(Paid) ⊕12,000

Malibu
Windplayer **(2497)**

Nevada City
Dream Magazine **(2615)**

San Anselmo
Acoustic Guitar Magazine **(3081)** ....(Paid) 50,000

San Francisco
BAST Music Magazine **(3328)**
ChinMusic Magazine **(3342)**
Ongaku Otaku **(3409)**
XLR8R **(3465)** ....(Paid) 50,000

San Jose
The Beethoven Journal **(3511)** 1,200

San Mateo
Bass Player **(3583)** 45,000

Thousand Oaks
Outburn **(3905)** 15,000

West Sacramento
Pulse! **(4066)** ....(Paid) 1,158
(Non-paid) 281,158

COLORADO
Boulder
Iron Feather Journal **(4172)** ....(Combined) 3,500

Recording **(4186)** ....(Paid) ‡24,679
(Non-paid) ‡2,857
Vibe Magazine **(4195)** ....(Paid) 760,152

Westminster
Denver Arts Center Programs **(4662)** 2,600,000

CONNECTICUT
Westport
Country Music **(5213)** ....(Paid) 306,415

DELAWARE
Wilmington
Yakuza **(5296)**

DISTRICT OF COLUMBIA
Washington
Musical Mainstream **(5665)** ....(Non-paid) ‡3,600
The Washington Opera
Magazine **(5849)** ....(Controlled) 80,000

FLORIDA
Boca Raton
Country Weekly **(5930)** ....(Paid) 455,086
Jazziz **(5935)** ....(Paid) ‡150,000
(Non-paid) ‡65,000

Geneva
Higher & Higher **(6172)** ....(Combined) 3,500

Miami
Reggae Report **(6377)**

Murdock
Country Grapevine **(6437)**

Orlando
Hinge Music Magazine **(6497)** .....(Non-paid) 15,000

Pompano Beach
Paul's Record Magazine **(6591)**

Tampa
World of Fandom **(6783)** ....(Controlled) 80,000

GEORGIA
Decatur
babysue **(7235)** ....(Controlled) 5,000

ILLINOIS
Chicago
Illinois Entertainer **(8409)** ....(Combined) 74,606
Roctober **(8559)**
The Sondheim Review **(8565)** .....(Controlled) 3,700

Elmhurst
Down Beat **(8834)** ....‡93,797
Music Inc. **(8836)** ....(Controlled) ‡8,900
Up Beat Daily **(8838)** ....(Non-paid) ‡10,000

Fairbury
The Rocket **(8879)** ....(Non-paid) 80,000

INDIANA
Highland
The Midwest BEAT
Magazine **(10063)** ....(Non-paid) ‡30,000

IOWA
Anita
Tradition Magazine **(10604)** ....(Paid) ‡3,500
(Controlled) ‡3,500

Fort Dodge
Musicians Hotline **(10905)** ....(Controlled) 15,000

Pleasant Hill
Jukebox Collector **(11160)** ....‡1,700

LOUISIANA
Lafayette
In Tune **(12617)** ....(Paid) ‡100
(Non-paid) ‡20

New Orleans
OffBeat Magazine **(12750)** ....(Combined) 50,000
The Second Line **(12752)** ....‡1,000

MARYLAND
Baltimore
Dirty Linen **(13157)** ....(Combined) 16,000

Lutherville
Music Monthly **(13626)** ....(Controlled) 35,000

Silver Spring
JazzTimes **(13728)** ....(Paid) ‡80,898
(Non-paid) ‡9,000
Pastoral Music **(13743)** 9000

Wheaton
Lexicon **(13780)**

MASSACHUSETTS
Billerica
Metronome Magazine **(13845)** ....(Controlled) 25,000

Boston
J Magazine **(13909)** ....(Combined) 15,000
The Noise **(13939)** ....(Paid) ‡5000

Jamaica Plain
Jamaica Plain Arts News **(14259)**

Waltham
Forced Exposure **(14599)**

MICHIGAN
Ferndale
Jam Rag **(15029)** ....(Non-paid) 13,000
Real Detroit Weekly **(15030)** ....(Free) 65,000

Royal Oak
Alarm Clock **(15476)** ....(Non-paid) 200
Big City Blues Magazine **(15477)**

MINNESOTA
Columbia Heights
Cake **(15810)** ....(Paid) 2,000
(Non-paid) 18,000

Minneapolis
The Mississippi Rag **(16111)** ....(Paid) ‡4,300
Profane Existence **(16124)** ....(Combined) 20,000

St. Joseph
Music and Dance News **(16357)** ....(Paid) ‡2,000
(Controlled) ‡12,000

MISSISSIPPI
University
Living Blues **(16866)** ....‡25,000

MISSOURI
St. Louis
Reviews Unlimited **(17488)** ....(Paid) 52,640

NEW HAMPSHIRE
Peterborough
CD Review **(18620)** ....(Paid) 95,635

NEW JERSEY
Cedar Grove
Modern Drummer Magazine **(18721)** ....‡103,000

Dover
Hot House **(18778)** ....(Non-paid) 13,000

Hoboken
BB Gun Magazine **(18900)**

Kingston
Keyboard Companion **(19156)**

Paramus
Hit Parader **(19404)** ....‡125,000

Sussex
The Dragon's Blood **(19607)** ....(Paid) 2,000

Tenafly
Fanfare **(19613)** ....(Paid) ‡9,000
(Controlled) ‡10,200

Weehawken
Jersey Beat **(19711)** ....(Combined) 2,500

NEW YORK
Bay Shore
The Music Paper **(20136)**

Bedford Hills
Piano Today **(20143)** ....‡20,000
Sheet Music Magazine **(20144)** 80,000

Brooklyn
Relix Magazine **(20341)** 70,000
Wax Poetics **(20356)**

East Rochester
Mobile Beat **(20553)**

New York
The Big Takeover **(21309)** ....(Paid) 12,000
Bomb **(21331)** ....(Paid) ‡12,000
(Non-paid) ‡3,000
Chamber Music **(21395)** ....(Paid) ‡10,000
(Non-paid) ‡2,000
Circus Magazine **(21420)** ....(Paid) 307,092
(Non-paid) 7,709
CMJ New Music Monthly **(21432)**
CMJ New Music Report **(21433)**
The FADER **(21675)**
Guitar World **(21783)** ....(Paid) 190,059
Kicks **(22218)**
Knotes **(22225)**
Metal Edge (TV Picture
Life) **(22320)** ....(Paid) 52,228
Modern Screen's Country
Music **(22352)** ....(Paid) ‡100,000
Opera News **(22497)** ....(Paid) 100,000
Paper Magazine **(22520)** ....(Paid) 63,378
Rolling Stone **(22675)** ....(Paid) 1,251,520
Seconds **(22717)** ....(Paid) 30,000
(Non-paid) 8,000
Skyscraper **(22744)**
The Source **(22764)** ....(Paid) 454,726
SPIN **(22772)** ....(Paid) 540,063

Redwood
Cadence Jazz and Blues Magazine **(23179)**

Snyder
Sensible Sound **(23342)** ....‡14,700

NORTH CAROLINA
Boone
The Singing News
Magazine **(23656)** ....(Paid) 150,000
(Controlled) 12,000

Chapel Hill
Tuba Frenzy **(23729)**

Durham
The Old-Time Herald **(23839)** ....(Paid) 3,000
(Non-paid) 2,000

NORTH DAKOTA
Bismarck
Vintage Guitar **(24361)** ....(Paid) ‡24,300
(Non-paid) ‡400

OHIO
Cincinnati
American Record Guide **(24772)** ....(Paid) ‡8,000
(Non-paid) ‡140

OREGON
Portland
Puncture **(26503)** ....(Paid) 11,000

PENNSYLVANIA
Ambler
Fly! **(26650)**

Ardmore
Halana **(26660)** ....(Paid) 2,000

Coatesville
The Lighthouse Electronic
Magazine **(26793)** ....(Free) 30,000

Philadelphia
MAGNET **(27560)** 35,000
Rocket Fuel Online **(27655)**

TENNESSEE
Nashville
Journal of Country Music **(29462)**

TEXAS
Austin
Latin American Music Review **(29791)** ....(Paid) 600

Houston
Angbase **(30456)**

Pflugerville
HM **(30931)** ....(Combined) ⊕15,000

UTAH
Orem
The Doors Collectors Magazine **(31384)**

VIRGINIA
Arlington
Early Music America **(31786)** .....(Combined) ⊕4,252

Richmond
Burping Lula **(32431)** ....(Controlled) 5,000
Easy Reeding **(32436)** ....(Combined) 18,000

Warrenton
Bluegrass Unlimited **(32599)** ....(Paid) ‡25,951
(Controlled) ‡133

WASHINGTON
Seattle
Heritage Music Review **(32970)**
Marlee Walker's Blues
To-Do's **(32985)** ....(Paid) 600
(Non-paid) 14,400

Tacoma
Victory Music Review **(33154)** .....(Combined) 3,500

WISCONSIN
Iola
Discoveries **(33818)** ....(Combined) 13,388
Goldmine **(33828)** ....(Paid) ‡27,758

Kenosha
The Harmonizer **(33870)** ....‡36,600

Madison
Drum Corps World **(33934)** ....‡3,582

BRITISH COLUMBIA, CANADA
Vancouver
Ralph **(35162)** ....(Controlled) 6,000

ONTARIO, CANADA
Dundas
Journal of the International Association of Jazz
Record Collectors **(35794)** ....‡2,000

Maple
Incursion Music Review **(36010)**

Mississauga
The Spill Magazine **(36087)** ....(Free) 5,000
UNRESTRAINED! **(36091)**

Ottawa
Country Music News **(36239)** ....(Paid) ‡4,200
(Controlled) ‡1,800

Toronto
Chart Magazine **(36546)** ....(Combined) 40,000
Coda Magazine **(36554)** ....(Paid) ‡3,000
(Non-paid) ‡100
Exclaim! **(36585)** ....(Non-paid) 102,302
Eye **(36590)**
Klublife **(36644)** ....(Combined) 40,000
Noise **(36675)**
Opera Canada **(36688)** ....(Combined) ‡4,000
RINSE **(36730)**

QUEBEC, CANADA
Longueuil
UHF Magazine **(37059)**

Outremont
Le Lundi **(37266)** ....(Paid) 52,507

NATIVE AMERICAN INTERESTS

ARIZONA
Flagstaff
American Indian Quarterly **(693)** 900

Window Rock
The Navajo Times **(1011)** 21,000

CALIFORNIA
Berkeley
News from Native California **(1546)** .....(Paid) 5,000
(Controlled) 500

Los Angeles
La Gente **(2311)** ....(Non-paid) 20,000

DISTRICT OF COLUMBIA
Washington
Cherokee Advocate **(5407)** 90,000

LOUISIANA
Folsom
Whispering Wind **(12581)** ....‡28,000

MONTANA
Pablo
Char-Koosta News **(17889)**

NEW MEXICO
Dulce
Jicarilla Chieftain **(19843)** ....‡1,000

NEW YORK
Ithaca
Native Americas **(20810)**

Rooseveltown
Akwesasne Notes **(23275)** ....‡10,000

NORTH CAROLINA
Cherokee
The Cherokee One
Feather **(23783)** ....(Paid) ‡2,750
(Free) ‡15

NORTH DAKOTA
Belcourt
Turtle Mountain Times **(24345)** ....(Combined) 2,070

OREGON
Portland
American Indian Basketry
Magazine **(26467)** ....‡5,000

PENNSYLVANIA
Turbotville
Indian Artifact Magazine **(28063)** ....(Paid) ‡4,000
(Non-paid) ‡42

WISCONSIN
Hayward
News from Indian Country **(33785)** ....‡7,000

Lac du Flambeau
Lac du Flambeau News **(33899)** ....(Paid) 500
(Non-paid) 10,000

ALBERTA, CANADA
Edmonton
Windspeaker **(34738)** ....(Combined) 18,000

Standoff
Kainai News **(34854)** ....(Paid) ‡1,250
(Free) ‡850

MANITOBA, CANADA
Winnipeg
Indian Life **(35333)** ....(Paid) ‡16,530
(Non-paid) ‡3,175

ONTARIO, CANADA
Sioux Lookout
Wawatay News **(36393)** ....‡9,200

QUEBEC, CANADA
Kahnawake
The Eastern Door **(37017)**

NEW AGE

See also Alternative and Underground

ARIZONA
Kingman
Kosmon Voice 2 **(730)** ....(Paid) 2,000

Tucson
Light of Consciousness **(955)** ....(Paid) 22,500

CALIFORNIA
Berkeley
American Spirit Newspaper **(1490)**
Psychic Reader **(1553)** ....(Free) 55,000

Circulation: ★ = ABC; △ = BPA; ♦ = CAC; ● = CCAB; ❑ = VAC; ⊕ = PO Statement; ‡ = Publisher's Report; Boldface figures = sworn; Light figures = estimated.

2829

Circ.   Circ.   Circ.

NEW AGE (continued)
SCP Journal (1557) ....(Paid) 15,000

Oceanside
Rays from the Rose
   Cross (2709) ....(Combined) ‡650

CONNECTICUT
Vernon
The Door Opener (5187) ....(Paid) 2,100
                                 (Non-paid) 400

FLORIDA
Miami
The New Times (6374) ....(Paid) ‡1,500
                               (Free) ‡21,500

GEORGIA
Decatur
Aurora Rising (7234) ....(Paid) 7,000
                            (Non-paid) 3,000

MASSACHUSETTS
Grafton
Spirit of Change
   Magazine (14213) ....(Combined) 70,000

Watertown
Body & Soul Magazine (14612) ....(Paid) 261,000
                          (Non-paid) 14,000

MICHIGAN
Southfield
phenomeNEWS (15547) ....(Free) 55,000

MINNESOTA
Frontenac
Mythos Journal (15913) ....(Paid) 500

Lakeville
FATE Magazine (15995) ....(Paid) 20,000
                              (Free) 200

NEW HAMPSHIRE
Warner
Color Wheel (18647) ....(Paid) 300

NEW JERSEY
Clifton
Christian New Age Quarterly (18752)

Sussex
The Dragon's Blood (19607) ....(Paid) 2,000

NEW YORK
Amityville
Moksha Journal (20050) ....(Controlled) 200

OREGON
Milwaukie
New Moon Rising (26438) 4,000

PENNSYLVANIA
Spring Mills
Universal Light Messenger (28010)

TEXAS
Tyler
Both Sides Now (31196) ....‡200

WASHINGTON
Bellingham
New Age Retailer (32677) ....(Non-paid) 10,000

Eastsound
NAPRA Review (32742) ....(Non-paid) 10,000

Spokane
Massage Magazine (33095)

PRINCE EDWARD ISLAND, CANADA
Kensington
Kindred Spirit (36920) ....(Paid) 1,800

PARAPSYCHOLOGY
See also Alternative and Underground

CALIFORNIA
Altadena
Skeptic (1393) ....(Controlled) 40,000

NEW MEXICO
Albuquerque
The Skeptical Inquirer (19786) ....(Paid) ‡34,091
                         (Non-paid) ‡1,598

NORTH CAROLINA
Durham
Journal of Parapsychology (23831) ....(Paid) ‡872
                        (Non-paid) ‡117

QUEBEC, CANADA
Laval
Horoscope Quotidien (37040) ....(Paid) ‡13,000
                        (Non-paid) ‡12,000

PARENTING
See also Babies; Children's Interests;
Youths' Interests

ARIZONA
Tucson
Good News Magazine (947) ......(Controlled) 29,500
Working Moms & Dads Magazine (974)

ARKANSAS
Little Rock
Little Rock Family (1233) ....(Free) ❑21,334

CALIFORNIA
Berkeley
Parents' Press (1550) ....(Combined) 75,000

Beverly Hills
Toy Tips (1578) ....(Controlled) 3,000,000

Canoga Park
Junior Baseball Magazine (1656) ....(Paid) 50,000

Encino
Los Angeles Family
   Magazine (1884) ....(Non-paid) 150,520
South Bay Family Magazine (1885)
Ventura Family Magazine (1886)

Los Gatos
Bay Area Parent—East Bay
   Edition (2477) ....(Free) 54,346
                        (Paid) 401

Woodland Hills
Fit Pregnancy (4104)

COLORADO
Centennial
Twins Magazine (4228) ....(Paid) ★25,624
                    (Non-paid) ★22,080

CONNECTICUT
Branford
Connecticut Parent
   Magazine (4708) ....(Non-paid) ‡49,500

Danbury
Parent & Chg- (4748) ....(Combined) 1,200,000

Darien
Lamaze Para Padres (4774) ....(Non-paid) △750,000
Lamaze Parents'
   Magazine (4775) ....(Non-paid) 2,700,000

Westport
Connecticut's County Kids (5212)

DELAWARE
Dover
The American Mother (5243) ....(Non-paid) 4,000

DISTRICT OF COLUMBIA
Washington
Parenting for High
   Potential (5715) ....(Combined) 15,000
Preventing School Failure (5729) ....(Paid) 635

FLORIDA
Jacksonville
North Florida FAMILIES
   Magazine (6216) ....(Controlled) 25,000

Orlando
Central Florida Family
   Magazine (6488) ....(Free) 70,000
                        (Paid) 2,789

GEORGIA
Atlanta
Atlanta Parent (6973) ....(Free) 85,000
                        (Paid) 30

Decatur
Young Horizons Indigo (7238) ....(Paid) 18,000
                        54,000

IDAHO
Boise
Boise Family Magazine (7803) ....(Controlled) 18,000

ILLINOIS
Carol Stream
Christian Parenting Today (8139) .....(Paid) ‡87,194
                    (Non-paid) ‡23,889

Chicago
America's Family Support Magazine (8262)

Oak Park
Chicago Parent Magazine (9373) .....(Free) 126,222
                        (Paid) 608

Schaumburg
Leaven (9585) ....(Paid) ⊕6,849
                    (Controlled) ⊕225
New Beginnings (9588) ....(Paid) ⊕29,463
                    (Controlled) ⊕300

INDIANA
Huntington
Catholic Parent (10068) ....(Paid) 20,000

Indianapolis
Child Life (10100) ....(Paid) 47,330
Indy's Child (10135) ....(Free) 60,000
                        (Paid) 20

IOWA
Des Moines
Iowa Parent & Family (10794) ....(Controlled) 26,000
                    (Non-paid) 25,680

MARYLAND
Annapolis
Chesapeake Family (13092) ....(Controlled) 40,000

Baltimore
Baltimore's Child (13137) ....(Controlled) ‡65,000

Hagerstown
Listen (13566) ....‡35,000

MASSACHUSETTS
East Longmeadow
Today's Family (14168) ....(Paid) 552
                        (Free) 20,000

Jamaica Plain
The Rhode Island Parents'
   Paper (14261) ....(Paid) 71
                        (Free) 35,000

Kingston
South Shore Baby
   Journal (14265) ....(Combined) 16,000

Newton
InterfaithFamily.com (IFF) (14400) 11,000
Jewish Family & Life (14402)

Northampton
FamilyFun (14428) ....(Paid) 1,450,000

MICHIGAN
Grand Rapids
Christian Home & School (15091) ......(Paid) ‡1,000
                    (Controlled) ‡69,000

Southfield
Metro Parent
   Magazine (15545) ....(Controlled) 66,000

MINNESOTA
Eagan
Minnesota Parent (15863) ....(Free) 58,500

MISSOURI
Fenton
Practical
Homeschooling (17064) ....(Paid) 25,000 copies

Springfield
Springfield Parent, Inc. (17612) ....:...(Free) ‡21,000

NEW JERSEY
Flemington
Children's Software Revue
(CSR) (18818) ....(Combined) ‡19,000

Hackensack
The Parent Paper (18853) ....(Combined) 50,409

Mountainside
Essex County
Family (19316) ....(Controlled) 125,000
Middlesex County
Family (19317) ....(Controlled) 125,000
Morris County
Family (19318) ....(Controlled) 125,000
Union County
Family (19319) ....(Controlled) 125,000

Park Ridge
Kids Magazine (19409) ....(Non-paid) ‡30,000

NEW MEXICO
Santa Fe
Mothering Magazine (19936) ....(Paid) ‡90,000
(Non-paid) ‡500

NEW YORK
Binghamton
Adoption Quarterly (20150)

Mamaroneck
New York Family (20987) ....(Paid) 266
(Free) 59,069
Westchester Family (20988) ....(Paid) 266
(Free) 59,069

New York
Adoptive Families (21150) ....(Paid) ‡25,000
Child (21409) ....(Paid) 921,332
(Non-paid) 100,185
Family Life (21679) ....(Paid) 510,826
(Non-paid) 101,162
Girl Scout Leader (21763) ....‡800,000
Healthy Pregnancy (21796)
offspring (22486) 200,000
Parenting Magazine (22524) ....(Paid) 1,415,855
Parenting's Healthy
Pregnancy (22525) ....(Paid) △67,166
(Non-paid) △2,255,258
Parents Baby (22526) ....(Controlled) $3,700,000
Parents Magazine (22528) ....(Paid) 2,004,929
(Non-paid) 142,708
Parents
Pregnancy (22529) ....:(Controlled) $2,000,000
Ser Padres (22732) ....(Controlled) 500,000

Pittsford
Genesee Valley Parent
Magazine (23097) ....(Combined) 37,060

NORTH CAROLINA
Charlotte
Charlotte Parent (23740) ....(Free) 54,000

Durham
Carolina Parent (23811) ....(Combined) 50,000

OHIO
Cincinnati
All About Kids (24768) ....(Free) 55,000
(Paid) 50

Troy
Miami Valley Parents (25595)

OREGON
Portland
Hip Mama (26480) ....(Paid) 5,000

PENNSYLVANIA
Fort Washington
Parents Express (26933) ......(Combined) ❑45,155

South Jersey Parents
Express (26934) ....(Combined) ❑14,845

Philadelphia
Family Times (27467) ....(Combined) 34,821

TENNESSEE
Summertown
Birth Gazette (29622) 2,500

TEXAS
Addison
DallasChild (29671)
FortWorthChild (29672)

Irving
Scouting (30608) ....(Paid) 1,000,000

San Antonio
Our Kids Magazine (31040) .....(Controlled) ‡35,000

Waco
Gifted Child Today
Magazine (31247) ....(Paid) ‡15,000

VIRGINIA
Harrisonburg
Living (32141) ....(Non-paid) 125,000

Herndon
Washington FAMILIES
Magazine (32166) ....(Controlled) 100,000

Richmond
The Journal of Perinatal
Education (32442) ....(Paid) ‡5,224
(Non-paid) ‡408

Virginia Beach
Tidewater Parent (32590) ....(Paid) ‡25
(Controlled) 40,000

WASHINGTON
Renton
Northwest Baby & Child (32925) ......(Free) ‡27,000

Seattle
Eastside Parent (32961)
Portland Parent (33004)
Puget Sound Parent (33009) .....(Combined) 30,000
Seattle's Child (33027) ....(Paid) ‡4,800
(Non-paid) ‡4,050
Seattle's Child (Snohomish County
Edition) (33028) ....(Combined) 8,850

Tonasket
Home Education
Magazine (33165) ....(Paid) ‡12,700
(Non-paid) ‡12,400

WISCONSIN
Madison
Dane County KIDS (33933) ....(Non-paid) 23,000
Fox Valley KIDS (33942) ....(Non-paid) 25,000
N.E.W. Kids (33965) ....(Non-paid) 24,000

Wauwatosa
Metro Parent (34443) ....(Free) 67,214
(Paid) 154

BRITISH COLUMBIA, CANADA
Vancouver
WestCoast Families (35179) ......(Combined) 50,000

ONTARIO, CANADA
Etobicoke
Best Wishes
Magazine (35812) ....(Non-paid) 153,239
Expecting (35815) ....(Non-paid) 143,041

Oakville
City Parent (36143) 260,000

Southampton
Adoption Helper (36399) ....(Paid) 700
Post-adoption Helper (36400) ....(Paid) 500

Toronto
Chirp (36549) ....(Combined) 58,070
Mere Nouvelle (36662) ....(Non-paid) 45,025
Owl Canadian Family (36694) ....(Non-paid) 154,519
Today's Parent (36762) ....(Paid) 121,000
(Non-paid) 52,000

Today's Parent
Newborn (36763) ....(Non-paid) 154,755

Today's Parent Pregnancy &
Birth (36764) ....(Non-paid) 199,575
Zellers Family (36797)

Windsor
Windsor Parent Magazine (36891)

QUEBEC, CANADA
Laval
C'est Pour Quand? (37035) ....(Non-paid) 44,000
Mon Bebe (37043) ....(Non-paid) 43,000

Montreal
Quebec Home & School
News (37211) ....(Paid) 5,850
(Free) 1,550

Saint-Lambert
Le Magazine Enfants
Quebec (37359) ....(Combined) 72,102

PERFORMING ARTS

ILLINOIS
Chicago
The Sondheim Review (8565) .....(Controlled) 3,700

NEW YORK
New York
Music Gigs & Auditions
U.S.A. (22385) ....(Paid) ‡100,000
(Non-paid) ‡200,000
Video Age Daily (22897) ....(Non-paid) ‡8,000

QUEBEC, CANADA
Montreal
Montreal Serai (37191)

PETS

See also Cats; Dogs

CALIFORNIA
Midway City
The Royal Spaniels (2539) ....(Combined) 3,745

Mission Viejo
Aquarium Fish Magazine (2546)
Bird Talk (2548) ....(Paid) 123,527
Dogs USA (2552)
Reptiles (2557) ....(Paid) 53,645

Monterey
Your World of Birds (2585)

Oakland
The Pet Companion (2694) ....(Controlled) 75,200

INDIANA
Indianapolis
Paws & Claws (10159) ....(Paid) 1,000
(Non-paid) 40,000

IOWA
Des Moines
You & Your Dog (10819)

MASSACHUSETTS
Boston
Animals Magazine (13850) ....(Paid) 70,000

MISSISSIPPI
Columbus
Mid-South Horse Review (16604) ......(Free) 12,500

NEW JERSEY
Chatham
Animaltown News (18727) ....(Non-paid) 15,000

Neptune
Tropical Fish Hobbyist (19320) ....‡60,000

NEW YORK
Brooklyn
Satya (20344) ....(Combined) 10,000

Smithtown
Modern Ferret (23338)

Circulation: ★ = ABC; △ = BPA; ◆ = CAC; • = CCAB; ❑ = VAC; ⊕ = PO Statement; ‡ = Publisher's Report; Boldface figures = sworn; Light figures = estimated.

2831

Circ.   Circ.   Circ.

PETS (continued)

TEXAS
Fort Worth
Petlife: Your Companion Animal
  Magazine **(30351)** ....(Paid) 120,000

WASHINGTON
Clinton
Animal People **(32719)** ....(Paid) 6,500
                       (Controlled) 8,500

Renton
InterActions **(32924)**

ONTARIO, CANADA
Richmond Hill
PETS Magazine **(36346)** ....(Paid) •44,038
                    (Non-paid) •1,756

PHOTOGRAPHY

CALIFORNIA
Los Angeles
Outdoor Photographer **(2354)** ....(Paid) 215,189

San Jose
ARTWEEK **(3510)** ....(Paid) ‡12,000
                    (Non-paid) ‡3,000

Santa Barbara
Photographer's Forum **(3650)** ....‡12,000

FLORIDA
Titusville
Shutterbug's Outdoor & Nature
  Photography **(6820)** ....(Combined) 37,200

ILLINOIS
Niles
Photo Techniques **(9293)** ....(Paid) 29,000

MASSACHUSETTS
Somerville
Double Take **(14534)** ....(Paid) 50,000

MINNESOTA
Minneapolis
Shots **(16126)** ....(Paid) 900
                    (Non-paid) 1,500

NEW MEXICO
Corrales
View Camera **(19839)** ....(Paid) ‡11,819
                  (Controlled) ‡225

NEW YORK
Bronx
Nueva Luz **(20279)** ....(Combined) 5,000

New York
American Photo **(21204)** ....(Paid) 255,971
Aperture **(21224)** ....‡17,000
Photography in New York **(22551)** 10,000
Popular Photography and
  Imaging **(22581)** ....(Paid) 458,714

Woodstock
Photography Quarterly **(23595)** ....(Paid) 10,000

NORTH CAROLINA
Lewisville
Today's Photographer
  Magazine **(24039)** ....(Paid) 80,000
                  (Controlled) 25,000

PENNSYLVANIA
New Wilmington
11 **(27322)**

WISCONSIN
Beloit
Acorn Whistle **(33573)** ....(Paid) 400
                  (Non-paid) 100

Waukesha
Birder's World **(34396)** ....(Paid) ★61,242

ONTARIO, CANADA
Toronto
Descant **(36570)** ....(Paid) ‡1,025
                (Non-paid) ‡75

POETRY

See also Literature and Literary Reviews

ALABAMA
Birmingham
Birmingham Poetry Review **(59)** ....(Paid) 700

ALASKA
Juneau
UAS Explorations **(598)** 650

ARKANSAS
Russellville
Nebo **(1332)**

CALIFORNIA
Cedarville
Floating Island **(1681)**

Claremont
Women's Studies **(1726)** ....(Paid) 500

Crescent City
The Kerf **(1787)** ....(Non-paid) 275

Irvine
The Ear **(2078)**

Kensington
Blue Unicorn **(2100)** ....(Combined) 475

Long Beach
Pearl **(2173)** ....(Combined) 550

Los Angeles
Kuumba **(2310)**

Los Gatos
Writing For Our Lives **(2480)** ....(Paid) 500

Oakland
Ruah **(2698)** ....(Combined) 300

Pearblossom
Silver Wings Mayflower Pulpit **(2833)** ......(Paid) 250

San Francisco
Poetry USA **(3415)** ....(Paid) 1,500

San Leandro
Five Fingers Review **(3561)** ....(Paid) 1,000

Sylmar
Avatar **(3835)**
A Theater of Blood **(3838)** ....(Paid) 150
                  (Controlled) 50

COLORADO
Edgewater
Pleiades Magazine **(4410)** ....(Combined) 10,000

Fort Collins
Colorado Review **(4428)** ....(Paid) 1,300

CONNECTICUT
Waterbury
Connecticut River Review **(5191)** ....(Paid) 250

FLORIDA
Miami
Thoughts for All Seasons **(6384)** ....(Non-paid) 1,000

Orlando
Florida Review **(6493)** ....(Controlled) 1,000

Pensacola
Half Tones to Jubilee **(6566)**

GEORGIA
Forest Park
Parnassus Literary Journal **(7277)** ....(Paid) 150

Savannah
Southern Poetry Review **(7539)** ....(Controlled) 1,000

Valdosta
Snake Nation Review **(7614)** ....(Controlled) 700

HAWAII
Honolulu
Hawaii Pacific Review **(7698)** ....(Non-paid) 500
Manoa **(7709)** ....(Paid) 1,000
                (Controlled) 65

ILLINOIS
Chicago
Agnieszka's Dowry **(8248)**
Another Chicago Magazine **(8264)** 2,000
Insects are People Too **(8415)**

Glenview
Free Lunch **(8935)** ....(Combined) ‡1,200

Gurnee
Children, Churches & Daddies **(8965)**

Highland Park
December **(8991)** ....(Paid) 1,000

Lincoln
Modern Haiku **(9083)** ....(Combined) 770

Loves Park
Rockford Review **(9120)** ....(Paid) 750

Normal
Spoon River Poetry
  Review **(9306)** ....(Combined) 1,000

Prospect Heights
Night Roses **(9471)** ....(Controlled) 300

INDIANA
Bloomington
Indiana Review **(9836)** ....(Combined) 2,000

Evansville
The Formalist **(9933)**

Terre Haute
Poet's Roundtable **(10488)** ....(Controlled) 1,000

IOWA
Cedar Rapids
Coe Review **(10670)** ....(Controlled) 1,500

Des Moines
Lyrical Iowa **(10803)**

KANSAS
Lawrence
First Intensity **(11551)** ....(Paid) ‡250
Voodoo Souls Quarterly **(11569)**

KENTUCKY
Pikeville
Pikeville Review **(12358)** ....(Paid) 500

LOUISIANA
New Orleans
New Laurel Review **(12743)**

MAINE
Portland
The Cafe Review **(13006)** ....(Controlled) 500

MARYLAND
Baltimore
Maryland Poetry Review **(13215)** ....(Paid) 500
Shattered Wig Review **(13246)**

Bowie
The Plastic Tower **(13393)** ....(Combined) 250

Waldorf
Cochran's Corner **(13771)** ....(Combined) 7,000

MASSACHUSETTS
Amherst
Peregrine **(13804)**

Arlington
the new renaissance **(13821)** ....(Combined) 910

Boston
AGNI **(13847)** ....(Paid) 1,500
                (Non-paid) 300

Cambridge
Harvard Review **(14066)** ....(Controlled) 2,300

Florence
Verse **(14188)**

Lawrence
The Long Story **(14267)** ....(Combined) 1,100

Lunenburg
Button **(14283)** ....(Combined) 1,200

Somerville
Double Take **(14534)** ....(Paid) 50,000

Spencer
Nostoc Magazine **(14549)** ....(Non-paid) 500

West Stockbridge
Lingo Magazine **(14627)** 3,500,000

MICHIGAN
Detroit
Struggle **(14950)** ....(Combined) 600

East Lansing
Red Cedar Review **(14992)**

Kalamazoo
Third Coast **(15245)** ....(Paid) 200

Lansing
way station magazine **(15296)** .....(Combined) 1,040

MINNESOTA
Duluth
North Coast Review **(15841)** ....(Controlled) 1,000

Minneapolis
Spout **(16133)** ....(Combined) 250
Xcp: Cross Cultural
 Poetics **(16142)** ....(Combined) 850

Pine Island
Kumquat Meringue **(16271)** ....(Paid) 600

St. Joseph
Studio One/HCC **(16358)**

MISSISSIPPI
Hattiesburg
Mississippi Review **(16663)** ....(Combined) 1,500

MISSOURI
Florissant
The Lowell Review **(17069)** ....(Paid) 150
                                        (Non-paid) 100

Maryville
The Laurel Review
 (Maryville) **(17273)** ....(Controlled) 700

MONTANA
Missoula
CutBank **(17866)** ....(Controlled) 1000

NEVADA
Carson City
Cayo **(18326)**

Las Vegas
Interim **(18364)** ....(Combined) 400

NEW HAMPSHIRE
Manchester
Red Brick Review **(18562)**

Portsmouth
Red Owl **(18638)** ....(Paid) 50
                                         (Non-paid) 50

NEW JERSEY
Fanwood
Exit 13 Magazine **(18815)** ....(Paid) ‡200
                                         (Non-paid) ‡100

Jersey City
Talisman **(19144)** ....(Paid) 1000

Ocean Grove
Sensations Magazine **(19391)** ....(Non-paid) 2,100

Paterson
The Paterson Literary
 Review **(19417)** ....(Controlled) 900

Randolph
Journal of New Jersey Poets **(19495)** ....(Paid) ‡700
                                         (Non-paid) ‡300

Spring Lake
Passaic Review **(19594)**

Sussex
The Dragon's Blood **(19607)** ....(Paid) 2,000

Teaneck
Bravo **(19608)** ....(Non-paid) 500

NEW MEXICO
Gallup
Paradoxism **(19857)** ....(Combined) 1000

Las Cruces
Whole Notes **(19878)** ....(Controlled) 300

Santa Fe
Countermeasures **(19933)** ....(Combined) 1,600

NEW YORK
Albany
The Little Magazine **(19994)**

Brooklyn
Poets on the Line **(20339)**

Buffalo
Earth's Daughters **(20378)** ....(Paid) 1,000

Flushing
Spring **(20613)** ....(Paid) 500

Garden City
Nassau Review **(20644)** ....(Non-paid) 1,200

Geneva
Seneca Review **(20655)** ....(Combined) 1000

Greenvale
Confrontation **(20698)** ....(Combined) 2,000

Jackson Heights
Editor's Choice **(20826)** ....(Paid) 3000
The Spirit That Moves Us **(20829)**

Mohegan Lake
The Iconoclast (Mohegan
 Lake) **(21088)** ....(Combined) 1,000

New York
American Letters &
 Commentary **(21201)** ....(Controlled) 1,500
American Poet **(21205)** ....(Paid) 10,000
Chelsea **(21398)** ....(Paid) 2,200
                                         (Non-paid) 300
Fence **(21685)**
Joe Magazine **(21969)**
Literal Latté **(22260)** ....(Paid) ‡5,000
                                         (Non-paid) ‡30,000
New York Quarterly **(22450)**
NYC Poetry Calendar **(22479)** ....(Combined) 30,000
Open City **(22493)**
Outerbridge **(22512)** ....(Non-paid) 500
Parnassus **(22531)** ....(Paid) 1,500
Spinning Jenny **(22773)** ....(Paid) 1,000

Niagara Falls
Slipstream **(23007)** ....(Paid) 500
                                         (Non-paid) 40

Potsdam
Blueline (Potsdam) **(23137)** ....(Combined) 600
Wallace Stevens Journal **(23141)** ....(Paid) 600
                                         (Non-paid) 100

Setauket
The Basement Magazine **(23325)**

Stony Brook
North Atlantic Review **(23374)** ....(Non-paid) 900

Water Mill
Literary Rocket **(23513)** 2,000

NORTH CAROLINA
Chapel Hill
The Carolina Quarterly **(23701)** ......(Combined) 900

Charlotte
Treewell **(23756)** ....(Paid) 150

Greensboro
Parting Gifts **(23933)**

Greenville
NCLR **(23966)** ....(Paid) 750
Tar River Poetry **(23970)** ....(Paid) 600

Pembroke
Pembroke Magazine **(24115)** ....(Combined) 750

OHIO
Berea
Grasslands Review **(24677)** ....(Paid) 200

Bowling Green
Mid-American Review **(24696)** .....(Controlled) 1,600

Burton
The Listening Eye **(24721)** ....(Paid) 250

Cleveland
Whiskey Island
 Magazine **(24965)** ....(Controlled) 1,500

Columbus
Lost and Found Times **(25029)** ......(Combined) 300
Pudding Magazine **(25057)**

Hiram
Hiram Poetry Review **(25247)** ....(Paid) 300
                                         (Non-paid) 100

Kent
Luna Negra **(25276)**

Lakewood
Taproot Reviews **(25288)** ....(Paid) 500
                                         (Non-paid) 2000

Oberlin
Field: Contemporary Poetry and
 Poetics **(25445)** ....(Paid) 1,500
                                         (Non-paid) 200

Youngstown
Pig Iron **(25698)** ....(Paid) 1,000

OREGON
Astoria
Nocturnal Lyric **(26226)** ....(Paid) 400

Portland
Hubbub **(26481)** ....(Combined) 350

PENNSYLVANIA
Ambridge
Taproot Literary
 Review **(26656)** ....(Controlled) 1,000

Doylestown
Matchbook **(26834)**

Lyndora
Poets at Work **(27208)** 300

Pittsburgh
Lilliput Review **(27811)**

RHODE ISLAND
Warwick
The Hunted News **(28450)**

TENNESSEE
Gallatin
Firefly Magazine **(29202)** ....(Controlled) 1,200

Memphis
River City **(29378)** ....(Controlled) 1,500

Murfreesboro
Poems and Plays **(29431)** ....(Combined) 800

Nashville
Cumberland Poetry Review **(29453)** ....(Paid) 500

TEXAS
Austin
Nerve Cowboy **(29793)** ....(Combined) 275
Sulphur River Literary
 Review **(29810)** ....(Combined) 350
William Carlos Williams Review **(29855)**

UTAH
Ogden
Weber Studies **(31379)** ....(Combined) 1,000

VERMONT
Jericho
The Lyric **(31545)** ....(Paid) ‡700
                                         (Non-paid) ‡28

Middlebury
Heron Dance **(31556)**

Randolph
Green World **(31580)** 200

Circulation: ★ = ABC; △ = BPA; ◆ = CAC; • = CCAB; ❑ = VAC; ⊕ = PO Statement; ‡ = Publisher's Report; Boldface figures = sworn; Light figures = estimated.

2833

Magazines

Circ.   Circ.   Circ.

POETRY (continued)

VIRGINIA
Abingdon
Sow's Ear Poetry
  Review **(31626)** ....(Combined) 650

Arlington
Bogg **(31782)** ....(Controlled) 850

Fairfax
Phoebe **(32026)** ....(Combined) 1,000
So to Speak **(32031)**

Fredericksburg
Visions International **(32088)** ....(Paid) 750
                                          (Non-paid) 80

Radford
Absolute Magnitude **(32344)** ....(Paid) 6,000
                                          (Non-paid) 3,000

Winchester
Frogpond **(32628)** 1,000

WASHINGTON
Olympia
Young Voices Magazine **(32864)** 3,000

Sammamish
Tundra **(32935)** ....(Combined) 700

Seattle
American Jones Building & Maintenance **(32940)**
PoetsWest Online **(33003)** ....(Free) 300
Raven Chronicles **(33011)** ....(Paid) 2,000

WEST VIRGINIA
Circleville
Combat **(33292)**

WISCONSIN
Beloit
Acorn Whistle **(33573)** ....(Paid) 400
                                          (Non-paid) 100
Magazine of Speculative
  Poetry **(33575)** ....(Combined) 150

Cambridge
Rosebud **(33615)** ....(Paid) ‡8000

Madison
Madison Review **(33960)**

Oshkosh
Wisconsin Review **(34228)** ....(Combined) ‡2,000

ALBERTA, CANADA
Calgary
Filling Station **(34644)** ....(Paid) 625
                                          (Non-paid) 75
The Prairie Journal of Canadian
  Literature **(34654)** ....(Paid) 600

BRITISH COLUMBIA, CANADA
Sardis
Teak Roundup **(35087)** ....(Controlled) 100

Vancouver
Ralph **(35162)** ....(Controlled) 6,000

NEW BRUNSWICK, CANADA
Fredericton
ellipse **(35393)** ....(Combined) 560

NOVA SCOTIA, CANADA
Glace Bay
Capers Aweigh Annual Anthology **(35554)**

Sydney
Pottersfield Portfolio **(35609)** ....(Combined) 2000

ONTARIO, CANADA
North York
Firm Noncommittal **(36127)** ....(Paid) 200

Ottawa
Journal of Canadian
  Poetry **(36254)** ....(Combined) 500

Toronto
Paperplates **(36696)**

Windsor
Windsor Review **(36892)** ....(Paid) 250

QUEBEC, CANADA
Montreal
Montreal Serai **(37191)**

SASKATCHEWAN, CANADA
Regina
Green's Magazine **(37530)** ....(Controlled) 250
Wascana Review of Contemporary Poetry and Short
  Fiction **(37535)** ....(Controlled) 278

PSYCHOLOGY AND PSYCHIATRY

CALIFORNIA
San Anselmo
Common Ground **(3082)** ....(Paid) ‡2,000
                                          (Non-paid) ‡103,000

DISTRICT OF COLUMBIA
Washington
Health Psychology **(5522)** 9,500
Neuropsychology **(5692)** 5,000
PsycSCAN: Behavior Analysis &
  Therapy **(5745)** ....(Paid) 1,200

MASSACHUSETTS
Boston
Community Support Network News **(13880)**

PENNSYLVANIA
Haverford
Nutrition Health Review **(27029)** ....‡210,000

RADIO, TELEVISION, CABLE, AND VIDEO

ALABAMA
Birmingham
Orchid Isle Television **(84)** 22,000

ARIZONA
Tempe
KAET Magazine **(910)** ....:....(Controlled) ‡55,000

CALIFORNIA
Anaheim
Audio/Video Interiors **(1399)** ....(Paid) 44,423

Beverly Hills
Tips & Tricks **(1577)** ....(Paid) ★163,947

Burbank
Preview Theater Magazine **(1623)** ....‡250,000

Chico
Videomaker Magazine **(1697)** ....(Paid) 90,460
                                          (Non-paid) 68

Fortuna
Satellite TV Week **(1930)** ....(Paid) 247,272
                                          (Non-paid) 6,174

Huntington Beach
KOCE Viewers Guide **(2063)** ....‡30,000

Los Angeles
Novedades **(2350)** ....(Combined) 50,000
Variety **(2427)** ....(Mon.) 34,293
Written By Magazine **(2442)** 15,000

Sacramento
Worldradio **(3023)** ....‡30,700

Temecula
Widescreen Review **(3843)** ....(Paid) ⊕50,000

COLORADO
Aurora
Star Trek Communicator **(4149)** ....(Paid) 250,000

CONNECTICUT
Newington
QST **(5037)** ....‡168,975

FLORIDA
Miami
TV y Novelas **(6386)** ....(Paid) 136,708

Tampa
World of Fandom **(6783)** ....(Controlled) 80,000

IDAHO
Idaho Falls
Cable Scene **(7862)** ....(Paid) 1,400

ILLINOIS
Mount Prospect
Program **(9249)** ....(Combined) 28,000

INDIANA
Highland
The Midwest BEAT
  Magazine **(10063)** ....(Non-paid) ‡30,000

MARYLAND
Potomac
In-Motion **(13653)**

MASSACHUSETTS
Boston
DVS Guide **(13887)** ....(Combined) 24,688

MICHIGAN
Detroit
Signal **(14946)** ....‡70,000

MINNESOTA
Minneapolis
Game Informer Magazine **(16082)** .....(Paid) 217,653

MISSOURI
St. Louis
KETC Guide **(17465)** ....(Paid) 42,000

NEW HAMPSHIRE
Peterborough
73 Amateur Radio Today **(18628)** 47,872
Take One **(18631)** ....‡1,325,538
Video Event **(18632)** ....(Paid) ‡1,098,659

NEW JERSEY
Englewood Cliffs
Soap Opera Update **(18803)** ....(Paid) 185,736

Ocean Grove
The Phantom of the Movies'
  Videoscope **(19390)** ....(Paid) 10,000

Westfield
Palmer Video News **(19745)**

NEW YORK
Farmingdale
TV Blueprint **(20597)** ....(Paid) ‡2,200,000

Hauppauge
Electronics Now **(20717)** ....(Paid) 76,889
Poptronics **(20722)** ....(Paid) 71,253

New York
AudioVideo
  International **(21271)** ....(Non-paid) ‡43,000
Casting News **(21378)** ....(Paid) 100,000
                                          (Non-paid) 200,000
Daytime TV **(21539)** ....‡102,010
TV News **(22877)** ....(Free) ‡331,000

Port Washington
CQ Amateur Radio **(23124)** ....(Paid) ‡90,000
                                          (Non-paid) ‡1,700
Micro Computer Journal **(23130)** ....‡50,000

NORTH CAROLINA
Brasstown
Monitoring Times **(23663)** 25,000

North Wilkesboro
The Record **(24109)** ....(Free) 23,081

Shelby
TV Plus **(24228)** ....(Paid) 158,758

Waynesville
Under Western Skies **(24281)** ....(Paid) 800

OHIO
Cincinnati
VIDEO WATCHDOG **(24826)**

Troy
T.V. Week **(25598)**

PENNSYLVANIA
Philadelphia
Applause **(27381)** ....(Controlled) 137,000

Radnor
TV Host Monthly **(27916)** ....(Paid) 1,024,472
(Non-paid) 209,485

TEXAS
Dallas
Dragon Ball Z Collector **(30152)** ......(Paid) 300,000

Tyler
Tyler Cableguide **(31200)** ....(Non-paid) ‡10,000

VIRGINIA
Arlington
WETA Magazine **(31841)** ....(Paid) ‡125,000
(Non-paid) ‡1,500

WASHINGTON
Seattle
DirectGuide **(32960)** ....(Paid) 22,973
KCTS Magazine **(32980)** ....(Paid) 130,000

WISCONSIN
Milwaukee
Fine Tuning **(34069)** 50,000

ALBERTA, CANADA
Edmonton
Satellite Entertainment
Guide **(34727)** ....(Combined) 76,077
VU Magazine **(34733)** ....(Paid) 28,637

BRITISH COLUMBIA, CANADA
Burnaby
TV Week Magazine **(34908)** ....(Paid) 67,816
(Non-paid) 1,457

Port Hardy
North Island Televiewer **(35052)** ....‡2,250

Vancouver
Adbusters **(35120)** ....(Paid) ‡20,000
(Non-paid) ‡5,000

NEWFOUNDLAND AND LABRADOR, CANADA
St. John's
The Newfoundland Herald **(35491)** .....(Paid) 27,383
(Non-paid) 544

ONTARIO, CANADA
Toronto
Starweek Magazine **(36747)** ....‡750,000
Stereo Video Guide **(36748)** ....‡35,000
TV Guide Canada **(36776)** ....(Paid) 500,629

QUEBEC, CANADA
Longueuil
UHF Magazine **(37059)**

Montreal
Echos-Vedettes **(37111)** ....(Sat.) 76,119
Feature **(37115)** ....(Combined) •900,000
Primeurs **(37209)** ....(Combined) 450,000
TV Hebdo **(37231)** ....(Paid) 190,123

Outremont
Le Lundi **(37266)** ....(Paid) 52,507

SASKATCHEWAN, CANADA
Yorkton
TV This Week **(37599)** ....(Paid) ‡11,316

SCIENCE

ARIZONA
Tucson
Paleoclimates **(958)**

CALIFORNIA
Altadena
Skeptic **(1393)** ....(Controlled) 40,000

Berkeley
Journal of Social and Evolutionary Systems **(1537)**

San Francisco
Mercury **(3390)** ....(Paid) ‡6,000
(Non-paid) ‡200

DISTRICT OF COLUMBIA
Washington
National Geographic **(5672)** ....(Paid) 7,828,642
The World & I **(5870)** ....(Paid) 20,056
(Non-paid) 2,781

ILLINOIS
Springfield
The Living Museum **(9639)** ....(Non-paid) ‡18,000

NEW JERSEY
East Windsor
Cycling Science **(18785)** ....(Paid) ‡8,800
(Non-paid) ‡6,500

Fairfield
Applied Mechanics Reviews **(18811)** ....‡1,000

Hoboken
Neuroscience Research Communications **(19073)**

NEW YORK
Ithaca
South American Explorer **(20814)** ....‡8,500

Long Island City
Archaeology's Dig **(20962)**

New York
Fullerene Science &
Technology **(21740)** ....(Paid) 250

NORTH CAROLINA
Greensboro
Monkeyshines on Health and Science **(23929)**

PENNSYLVANIA
Landisville
Bible and Spade **(27157)** ....(Paid) 1,500

Philadelphia
Toxicology & Ecotoxicology
News/Reviews **(27706)** 600

TEXAS
Austin
StarDate **(29809)** ....(Paid) 10,000

College Station
Food Additives and Contaminants **(30041)** 650

Houston
Maes National
Magazine **(30505)** ....(Combined) 10,000

WISCONSIN
Milwaukee
Moon Miners' Manifesto **(34089)** ....(Paid) 300

SCIENCE FICTION, MYSTERY, ADVENTURE, AND ROMANCE

ALABAMA
Tuscaloosa
Dreams and Nightmares **(486)** ....(Combined) 200

CALIFORNIA
Berkeley
Mystery Readers
Journal **(1544)** ....(Controlled) 2,000

Los Angeles
Cinefantastique **(2239)** ....‡70,000
Femme Fatales **(2269)**

Oakland
Affaire de Coeur **(2662)** ....(Paid) 50,000
(Non-paid) 100,000

COLORADO
Boulder
Soldier of Fortune **(4192)** ....‡60,000

IOWA
Des Moines
Yellowback Library **(10818)** ....‡650

KENTUCKY
Louisville
Burroughs Bulletin **(12211)** ....(Paid) ‡800

MARYLAND
Edgewood
Companion in Zeor **(13492)**

NEW JERSEY
Hoboken
The Magazine of Fantasy & Science
Fiction **(19055)** ....‡33,500

Scotch Plains
The Armchair Detective **(19533)** ....(Paid) 6,500
(Non-paid) 100

NEW YORK
Brooklyn
Romantic Times **(20343)** ....‡150,000

New York
Alfred Hitchcock's Mystery
Magazine **(21170)** ....(Paid) 48,424
Ellery Queen's Mystery Magazine **(21597)**
Modern Romances Presents True Life
Stories **(22351)**
New Mystery **(22432)** ....(Paid) 65,000
(Non-paid) 35,000
Space and Time Magazine **(22770)** ....(Paid) ‡1,500
(Non-paid) ‡200
Starlog **(22791)** ....(Paid) ⊕266,855
True Confessions **(22867)**
True Experience **(22868)** ....(Paid) ‡152,344
True Love **(22869)** ....(Paid) 220,000
True Romance **(22870)** 165,723

NORTH CAROLINA
Asheville
Science Fiction Eye **(23633)** ....(Paid) 5,000

PENNSYLVANIA
Hellertown
The Baker Street Journal **(27037)** ....‡1,800

RHODE ISLAND
Cranston
Haunts **(28334)** ....(Paid) 3,500
(Non-paid) 150

TEXAS
Austin
Nova Express **(29795)** ....(Combined) 500

UTAH
Provo
Leading Edge Magazine **(31405)** ....(Paid) ‡300

VIRGINIA
Radford
Absolute Magnitude **(32344)** ....(Paid) 6,000
(Non-paid) 3,000
Science Fiction Chronicle **(32346)** ....(Paid) 5,800
(Non-paid) 200

WASHINGTON
Renton
Dragon Magazine **(32923)** 75,000

Vashon
PARA DOXA **(33183)** ....(Paid) 1,200
(Non-paid) 500

WISCONSIN
Beloit
Magazine of Speculative
Poetry **(33575)** ....(Combined) 150

ALBERTA, CANADA
Edmonton
On Spec **(34722)** ....(Combined) 1,700

ONTARIO, CANADA
Colborne
The Mystery Review **(35747)** ....(Paid) ‡5,000

Orillia
Dreams and Visions **(36175)** ....(Paid) 200

Magazines

Circulation: ★ = ABC; △ = BPA; ♦ = CAC; • = CCAB; ☐ = VAC; ⊕ = PO Statement; ‡ = Publisher's Report; Boldface figures = sworn; Light figures = estimated.

2835

Circ.   Circ.   Circ.

SENIOR CITIZENS' INTERESTS

ALASKA
Anchorage
Senior Voice **(531)** ....(Combined) ‡10,000

ARIZONA
Tucson
Arizona Senior World **(934)** ....(Paid) 2,500
(Non-paid) 297,500

ARKANSAS
Little Rock
Aging Arkansas **(1208)** ....(Paid) 40,000

Malvern
La Villa News **(1262)** ....(Paid) 4,310
(Free) ‡400

CALIFORNIA
El Cajon
Southern California Senior
Life **(1848)** ....(Combined) ‡325,000

El Cerrito
Grand Times **(1861)** 400,000

La Canada
Not Born Yesterday **(2108)** ....(Paid) ‡2,100
(Controlled) ‡104,000

Los Angeles
Southern California Senior Life (Inland Empire
Edition) **(2398)** ....(Combined) 50,000
Southern California Senior Life (Los Angeles County
Edition) **(2399)** ....(Combined) 159,300
Southern California Senior Life (Orange County
Edition) **(2400)** ....(Combined) 45,700
Southern California Senior Life (Southern California
Edition) **(2401)** ....(Combined) 375,000
Southern California Senior Life (Southland
Edition) **(2402)** ....(Combined) 36,500

San Luis Obispo
Plus Magazine **(3568)** ....(Controlled) ‡34,000

Seal Beach
The Leisure World Golden Rain
News **(3749)** ....(Paid) 6705
(Free) 2295

Sun City
Sun City News **(3824)** ....(Fri.) 1,203

CONNECTICUT
Westport
Remedy **(5216)** ....(Non-paid) 2,229,426

DELAWARE
Dover
Better Years **(5244)** ....(Free) 24,000

DISTRICT OF COLUMBIA
Washington
AARP Bulletin **(5307)** ....(Paid) 21,068,515
Modern Maturity **(5657)** ....(Paid) 20,963,870

FLORIDA
Barefoot Bay
The Barefoot Tattler **(5915)** ......(Combined) ⊕6,850

Tallahassee
Elder Update **(6703)** ....(Free) ‡100,000

ILLINOIS
Schaumburg
VANTAGE **(9592)** ....‡330,000

INDIANA
Milford
Senior Life (Allen County
Edition) **(10310)** ....(Paid) 80
(Free) 27,950
Senior Life (El-Ko Edition) **(10311)** ....(Paid) 6
(Free) 18,500
Senior Life (Northwest
Edition) **(10312)** ....(Free) 32,000
(Paid) 39,000

KANSAS
Syracuse
Southwest Kansas Senior
Beacon **(11811)** ....(Free) ‡8,500

Wichita
Active Aging Publishing,
Inc. **(11880)** ....(Free) ‡45,500

MARYLAND
Baltimore
Serenity **(13245)** ....(Free) 67,000

MASSACHUSETTS
Boston
Boston Seniority **(13863)** ....(Free) ‡20
The Older American **(13943)** ....(Paid) ‡9,000
(Controlled) ‡3,000

Worcester
The Fifty Plus Advocate **(14679)** ....(Free) 80,000
(Paid) 1,303

MICHIGAN
Allegan
Senior Times **(14723)** ....(Free) 22,450
West Michigan Senior
Times **(14724)** ....(Free) 25,000

MISSOURI
Columbia
Journal of Housing for the Elderly **(16996)** 1,250

Springfield
East Tennessee Senior
Living **(17596)** ....(Combined) 25,000
4-States Senior Living **(17601)** ....(Combined) 25,000
Lake of the Ozarks Senior
Living **(17603)** ....(Combined) 25,000
Ozarks Senior Living **(17608)** .....(Combined) 25,000

NEVADA
Las Vegas
Nevada Senior World **(18380)** ....(Combined) 75,875

NEW JERSEY
Toms River
Senior Scoop **(19644)** ....(Combined) 42,851
Spirit +Plus **(19645)** ....(Non-paid) 50,000

NEW YORK
Brooklyn
The World at Large **(20357)** ....‡64,000

East Rochester
Golden Times **(20552)** ....(Paid) 20,000

New York
McCall's Prime Time **(22302)** 1,000,000

Saratoga Springs
The Duplex Planet **(23301)** ....(Paid) ‡1,000

Setauket
Prime Times **(23328)** ....(Free) 50,000

OHIO
Columbus
Ohio's Heritage **(25055)**

Jefferson
The New Senior Life Styles
Vista **(25264)** ....(Non-paid) 5,000

Troy
Miami Valley Fifty
Plus **(25593)** ....(Combined) 20,000

OREGON
Coos Bay
Prime Time **(26271)** ....(Free) ‡6,200

King City
The Regal Courier **(26381)** 4,500

Portland
Northwest Senior Life **(26489)** ....(Combined) 50,000

PENNSYLVANIA
Olyphant
CGA World **(27347)** ....‡200,000

TENNESSEE
Nashville
Mature Living **(29469)** ....‡330,000
Mature Years **(29470)** ....‡55,000

VIRGINIA
Alexandria
Adultspan Journal **(31630)**

Falls Church
American Guidance for
Seniors **(32040)** ....(Paid) 45,000

WASHINGTON
Longview
Cowlitz-Wahkiakum Senior
News **(32811)** ....(Free) ‡7,000

Olympia
The Thurston-Mason Senior
News **(32860)** ....(Free) 18,500

Spokane
Senior Times **(33099)** ....(Combined) 14,000

Tacoma
Senior Scene **(33150)** ....(Paid) ‡4,000
(Non-paid) ‡14,000

Vancouver
Senior Messenger **(33179)** ....(Non-paid) 13,000

WISCONSIN
Madison
50 Plus Lifestyles **(33939)** ....‡5,300
(Controlled) ‡34,300

Milwaukee
The Mature American **(34079)** ....(Controlled) 20,000

BRITISH COLUMBIA, CANADA
Vancouver
The Independent Times **(35149)** 60,000

Victoria
Ageing International **(35205)** ....(Paid) ‡900

MANITOBA, CANADA
Winnipeg
MSOS Journal **(35346)** ....(Paid) ‡14,000
(Free) ‡16,000

ONTARIO, CANADA
Cochrane
Vivre **(35745)** ....(Paid) ‡3,100
(Free) ‡600

Ottawa
Legion Magazine **(36258)** ....(Paid) 362,274

Petrolia
Mainly for Seniors
Lambton-Kent **(36326)** ....(Free) 16,000

Toronto
CARPNews Fifty
Plus **(36536)** ....(Combined) 210,244
Panthers' Plus, Canadian Grey Panthers **(36695)**

Unionville
Active Adult **(36827)**

QUEBEC, CANADA
Montreal
Le Bel Age **(37155)** ....(Paid) 149,754
Virage **(37235)** ....(Combined) 218,636

SEX/EROTICA

CALIFORNIA
Beverly Hills
Chic Magazine **(1570)** ....(Paid) 50,000
(Non-paid) 100
Hustler Busty Beauties **(1573)** ....‡205,000
Hustler Magazine **(1574)** 1,066,537

Los Angeles
Blackfire **(2221)**
Kuumba **(2310)**

COLORADO
Boulder
Loving More **(4177)** ....‡12,000

Denver
Rocky Mountain Oyster & National Oyster
　　Newspaper　**(4355)** ....(Paid) 100
　　　　　　　　　　　　　(Non-paid) 53,000

CONNECTICUT
Sandy Hook
Club Confidential　**(5108)**
Club International Magazine　**(5109)**
Club Magazine　**(5110)** ....‡355,000
Club Specials Magazine　**(5111)**
Mayfair Magazine　**(5112)**
Mayfair Specials　**(5113)**

ILLINOIS
Chicago
Libido　**(8461)**

MASSACHUSETTS
Newton
EIDOS　**(14393)** 12,000

NEW JERSEY
Paramus
Swank　**(19407)** ....(Paid) 250,000
　　　　　　　　　　　　　(Non-paid) 30,000

NEW YORK
New York
Forum　**(21729)** 251,795
Gallery Magazine　**(21746)** ....‡362,863
Penthouse　**(22538)** ....(Paid) 851,066
Penthouse
　　Variations　**(22539)** ....(Combined) 300,000
Playgirl　**(22565)** 350,000
The SandMUtopian
　　Guardian　**(22704)** ....(Paid) ‡4,000

PENNSYLVANIA
Wyoming
Checkmate Incorporating Dungeonmaster　**(28198)**

SOCIAL AND POLITICAL ISSUES
CALIFORNIA
Los Angeles
Street Scene　**(2406)** ....(Non-paid) 1,000

North Hollywood
Share International　**(2644)** ....(Paid) 5,000
　　　　　　　　　　　　　(Non-paid) 1,000

Oakland
Left Curve　**(2685)** ....(Paid) 1850
　　　　　　　　　　　　　　　　　　　　2000

Redondo Beach
lovematters.com　**(2910)**

San Francisco
JINN Magazine　**(3377)**

Stanford
Birth of Tragedy
　　Magazine　**(3794)** ....(Combined) 6,000

COLORADO
Colorado Springs
Gauntlet　**(4248)** ....(Paid) 20,000

Littleton
Democracy and Nature　**(4546)** ....(Paid) 950
　　　　　　　　　　　　　(Controlled) 50

CONNECTICUT
New Haven
Yale Journal of Law and
　　Feminism　**(5006)** ....(Paid) 1,100

DISTRICT OF COLUMBIA
Washington
Insight on the News　**(5547)**
National Right to Life News　**(5680)**
The New Republic　**(5694)** ....(Paid) 98,328
Population Connection　**(5723)** ....(Paid) 75,000
The Weekly
　　Standard　**(5859)** ....(Combined) ⊕85,895

FLORIDA
Gainesville
The Gainesville Iguana　**(6141)** ....(Paid) 700
　　　　　　　　　　　　　(Non-paid) 3,000

Orlando
Impact　**(6498)** ....(Non-paid) 12,000

GEORGIA
Americus
Habitat World　**(6921)** ....(Free) 1,050,000

ILLINOIS
Chicago
The Chicago Reporter　**(8320)** ....(Paid) 1,500
　　　　　　　　　　　　　(Non-paid) 4,000
The Neighborhood Works　**(8503)** ....(Paid) 2,500
　　　　　　　　　　　　　(Non-paid) 500

Glen Ellyn
Presidents & Prime Ministers　**(8932)** ......(Paid) 270
　　　　　　　　　　　　　(Non-paid) 5,200

IOWA
Hampton
Conservative Chronicle　**(10939)** ....(Paid) ⊕57,960
　　　　　　　　　　　　　(Free) 30

MAINE
Brooklin
Hope　**(12931)** 14,000

MARYLAND
Baltimore
Journal of Modern Greek Studies　**(13194)** ......‡700
Social Anarchism　**(13248)**

MASSACHUSETTS
Cambridge
Boston Review　**(14042)** ....(Paid) ‡6,000
　　　　　　　　　　　　　(Non-paid) ‡4,000
Catalyst　**(14044)** ....(Paid) 50,000
Peacework　**(14088)** ....(Combined) 2,000
Perspective　**(14089)** ....(Controlled) 4,000

Mattapan
Survival News　**(14313)** ....(Paid) 750
　　　　　　　　　　　　　(Free) ⊕9,000

Newton
SocialAction.com　**(14410)**

MICHIGAN
Dearborn Heights
The New Age Citizen　**(14909)** ....(Paid) 300
　　　　　　　　　　　　　(Non-paid) 4,000

Ferndale
Fifth Estate　**(15028)** ....(Paid) 5,000

MONTANA
Belgrade
Trout Wrapper　**(17724)**

NEW JERSEY
Somerset
Journal of Income
　　Distribution　**(19563)** ....(Combined) 200

NEW YORK
Binghamton
Celebrating Voices　**(20152)** 775

Bronx
Farming Uncle　**(20268)** ....(Paid) 400
　　　　　　　　　　　　　(Non-paid) 700

Brooklyn
Satya　**(20344)** ....(Combined) 10,000

Buffalo
Earth's Daughters　**(20378)** ....(Paid) 1,000

New York
The Activist　**(21148)**
Challenge New York　**(21394)**
City Limits　**(21425)** ....(Paid) 3,200
　　　　　　　　　　　　　(Non-paid) 1,000
Democratic Left　**(21543)**
FIRST THINGS　**(21701)** ....‡32,000
Out Magazine　**(22510)** ....(Paid) 100,126

Niagara Falls
New Internationalist　**(23005)** ....(Paid) ‡65,000

NORTH CAROLINA
Cary
History Workshop　**(23688)** ....(Paid) 2,100

Raleigh
North Carolina Insight　**(24145)** ....(Paid) ‡1,300

OHIO
Cleveland
Homeless Grapevine　**(24908)** ....(Paid) 10,000

OREGON
Eugene
Green Anarchy　**(26318)**

Portland
The Kithara　**(26484)** ....(Paid) 80

PENNSYLVANIA
Wayne
Breast Implant Litigation Reporter　**(28127)**

SOUTH CAROLINA
Mount Pleasant
Vital Speeches　**(28695)**

TENNESSEE
Nashville
The Bird Online　**(29445)**

TEXAS
Austin
The Progressive Populist　**(29798)** ......(Paid) ‡7,500
　　　　　　　　　　　　　(Non-paid) ‡10,000

VERMONT
Burlington
Seven Days　**(31518)** ....(Free) ❑23,732
　　　　　　　　　　　　　(Paid) ❑48

Middlebury
Heron Dance　**(31556)**

VIRGINIA
Alexandria
The Multiracial Activist　**(31712)**

Oakton
American Rennaissance　**(32315)**

Vienna
Sobran's　**(32582)** ....(Combined) ‡3,000

WASHINGTON
Clinton
Animal People　**(32719)** ....(Paid) 6,500
　　　　　　　　　　　　　(Controlled) 8,500

Langley
Alarming Cry News　**(32805)** ....(Combined) 1,500

Mill Creek
Sober Times　**(32832)** ....(Paid) 5,000
　　　　　　　　　　　　　(Non-paid) 45,000

Olympia
Works in Progress　**(32863)** ....(Free) 3,000

Port Townsend
Liberty　**(32893)** ....(Paid) ⊕13,000
　　　　　　　　　　　　　(Non-paid) ⊕100

Seattle
Voices of Experience　**(33038)** ....(Free) 28,000

WEST VIRGINIA
Hillsboro
Free Speech　**(33335)** ....(Paid) 3,800

BRITISH COLUMBIA, CANADA
Vancouver
RicePaper　**(35164)** ....(Combined) 4,000

Victoria
Last Rights　**(35219)** ....(Paid) 2,000
　　　　　　　　　　　　　(Non-paid) 500

Magazines

Circulation: ★ = ABC; △ = BPA; ♦ = CAC; ● = CCAB; ❑ = VAC; ⊕ = PO Statement; ‡ = Publisher's Report; Boldface figures = sworn; Light figures = estimated.

Circ.   Circ.   Circ.

SOCIAL AND POLITICAL ISSUES (continued)

NOVA SCOTIA, CANADA
Annapolis Royal
Gulf of Maine Times **(35534)** .....(Controlled) 13,000

ONTARIO, CANADA
North York
Bratstvo (Fraternity) **(36122)** ....(Paid) 1,500
(Controlled) 700

Ottawa
The Hill Times **(36248)**

Toronto
Catholic Missions in Canada **(36540)**

QUEBEC, CANADA
Montreal
Journal L'Itineraire **(37142)** ....(Paid) 20,000

SOCIETY

ARIZONA
Tucson
The Match! **(956)** 1,750

CALIFORNIA
Los Angeles
Situations Digest **(2389)**
Soldiers Today **(2391)**

COLORADO
Littleton
Democracy and Nature **(4546)** ....(Paid) 950
(Controlled) 50

FLORIDA
Palm Beach
Palm Beach Society
Magazine **(6544)** ....(Paid) 4,500
(Non-paid) 500

NEW YORK
LaFayette
Future Survey **(20870)** ....(Paid) 1,750

New York
Harper's Bazaar **(21790)** ....(Paid) 721,738

BRITISH COLUMBIA, CANADA
Vancouver
Rungh **(35166)**

SPORTS

CALIFORNIA
Mountain View
Track & Field News **(2609)** ....(Paid) 24,000
(Non-paid) 2,309

(ARCHERY)

CALIFORNIA
Orange
Bow and Arrow Hunting **(2721)** ....(Paid) ‡98,500
(Non-paid) ‡640

MINNESOTA
Maple Grove
Bowhunting World **(16037)** ....‡85,368

(AUTO RACING)

See also Automotive (Consumer)

CALIFORNIA
Agoura
Tailgate **(1380)** ....(Paid) ‡41,250

Anaheim
Off Road **(1412)**
Super Chevy **(1416)** ....(Paid) 190,480

Glendora
National Dragster **(2024)** ....(Paid) ‡82,666
(Non-paid) ‡2,627

Lake Elsinore
Roadracing World & Motorcycle
Technology **(2140)** ....(Paid) ‡20,000

Los Angeles
Car Craft **(2233)** ....(Paid) 375,186
Corvette Fever **(2247)**
JP **(2305)** ....(Combined) 80,000
Mopar Muscle **(2333)** ....(Paid) 69,621
Muscle Car Review **(2339)**
Mustang Monthly **(2341)**
Petersen's Circle Track **(2362)** ...(Paid) 130,212
Super Ford **(2408)** ....(Paid) 46,656

Newport Beach
Road & Track **(2635)** ....(Paid) 771,024

Pleasanton
MotoRacing **(2854)** ....(Combined) 2,200
North American Pylon **(2855)** ....(Paid) ‡1,300
(Free) ‡700

CONNECTICUT
Enfield
Dirt Late Model **(4780)**
Late Model Racer **(4781)**
Trackside **(4782)**

FLORIDA
Lakeland
Stock Car Racing **(6292)** ....(Paid) 225,117

GEORGIA
Alpharetta
Bracket Racing USA **(6917)** ....(Paid) ‡30,000

ILLINOIS
Evanston
Auto Racing Digest **(8850)** ....(Paid) ‡50,201

MASSACHUSETTS
North Easton
Speedway Scene **(14422)** ....‡64,000

MICHIGAN
Detroit
AutoWeek **(14916)** ....(Paid) 360,000

NEW JERSEY
Saddle Brook
Muscle Mustangs & Fast
Fords **(19529)** ....(Paid) 101,214

Trenton
Area Auto Racing News **(19653)** ....‡72,000

NORTH CAROLINA
Harrisburg
National Speed Sport News **(23978)** ....‡50,500

Winston-Salem
Southern MotoRacing **(24322)** ....‡12,000

PENNSYLVANIA
Mansfield
Christian Motorsports
Illustrated **(27217)** ....(Paid) 20,000

WASHINGTON
Vancouver
Racing WHEELS
Newspaper **(33178)** ....(Paid) 8,000
(Non-paid) 12,000

WISCONSIN
Milwaukee
Midwest Racing News **(34081)** ....‡7,000

Waukesha
Championship Racing Magazine **(34397)**

(BASEBALL)

ARIZONA
Tucson
Collegiate Baseball Newspaper **(941)** ....‡7,500

CALIFORNIA
Canoga Park
Junior Baseball Magazine **(1656)** ....(Paid) 50,000

San Francisco
ChinMusic Magazine **(3342)**

ILLINOIS
Evanston
Baseball Digest **(8851)** ....(Paid) 132,259

MARYLAND
Hunt Valley
The Vintage and Classic Baseball
Collector **(13583)** ....(Controlled) 8,000

MINNESOTA
Minneapolis
Let's Play Softball **(16092)** ....(Controlled) 6,533

St. Paul
Elysian Fields Quarterly **(16375)** ....(Paid) ‡2,000
(Non-paid) ‡150

NEW JERSEY
Trenton
Bullpen **(19654)** ....(Controlled) ‡33,000

NORTH CAROLINA
Durham
Baseball America **(23809)** ....‡68,000

OHIO
Cleveland
Baseball Research Journal **(24862)**

OKLAHOMA
Oklahoma City
Ballard Strikes Softball
Magazine **(25953)** ....(Controlled) ‡302,300

VIRGINIA
Mc Lean
USA TODAY Sports
Weekly **(32258)** ....(Paid) 213,598

(BASKETBALL)

GEORGIA
Lilburn
Coaching Women's
Basketball **(7371)** ....(Paid) 5,000
(Non-paid) 200

ILLINOIS
Evanston
Basketball Digest **(8852)** ....(Paid) ‡103,313

NEW YORK
New York
College Hoops Illustrated **(21439)**
NBA Hoop **(22412)**
NBA Inside Stuff **(22413)**

(BICYCLING)

CALIFORNIA
Canoga Park
Mountain Biking **(1658)**

Valencia
BMX Plus! **(3976)** ....‡47,615
Mountain Bike Action **(3981)** ....(Paid) 70,275

COLORADO
Boulder
VeloNews **(4194)** ....(Paid) 40,584

Colorado Springs
USA Cycling Magazine **(4259)** ....(Paid) ‡57,000
(Non-paid) ‡1,000

MICHIGAN
Williamston
Out Your Backdoor **(15685)** ....(Paid) 1,000
(Non-paid) 4,000

NEW JERSEY
East Windsor
Cycling Science **(18785)** ....(Paid) ‡8,800
(Non-paid) ‡6,500

NEW YORK
New York
Bicycle Retailer and Industry
　News (21308) 12,337

PENNSYLVANIA
Devon
O2 (26825) ....(Paid) 2,500
　　　　　　　　　　　　(Non-paid) 500

Emmaus
Bicycling (26874) ....(Paid) 280,218
　　　　　　　　　　　　(Non-paid) 6,704
Mountain Bike Magazine (26878) .....(Paid) 162,520

WASHINGTON
Port Townsend
Recumbent Cyclist News (32895) ....(Paid) 3,000
　　　　　　　　　　　　(Non-paid) 2,800

Seattle
The Bicycle Paper (32951) ....(Paid) 1,000
　　　　　　　　　　　　(Non-paid) 22,000

WISCONSIN
Waupaca
Silent Sports (34419) ....(Paid) 8,500
　　　　　　　　　　　　(Non-paid) 15,000

ONTARIO, CANADA
Toronto
Pedal Magazine (36700) ....(Paid) ‡5,000

QUEBEC, CANADA
Montreal
Bike, Boat & R.V. Trader/Moto, Bateau & Vehicules
　Recreatif Hebdo (37091)

(BOATING AND YACHTING)

See also (Water Sports)

ALABAMA
Montgomery
Bassmaster Magazine (361) ....(Paid) 600,000

CALIFORNIA
Canoga Park
Sea Classics (1660) ....(Paid) ⊕57,346

Carson
Trailer Boats Magazine (1677) ....(Paid) 75,398

Costa Mesa
Personal Watercraft
　Illustrated (1780) ....(Paid) ‡66,510
　　　　　　　　　　　　(Non-paid) ‡2,009

Foothill Ranch
Jet Sports (1921) ....(Paid) 44,332

Irvine
Sea Magazine (2090) ....(Paid) 18,693
　　　　　　　　　　　　(Non-paid) 30,693

Mill Valley
Latitude 38 (2540) ....(Combined) 48,000

Redondo Beach
Latitudes & Attitudes (2909) ....(Paid) ‡77,000

San Diego
The Log (Los Angeles/Ventura County
　Edition) (3224) ....(Combined) ⊕65,000
The Log (Orange County Edition) (3225)

Santa Ana
Dealernews (3624) ....(Paid) △105
　　　　　　　　　　　　(Non-paid) △15,477

Ventura
Powerboat Magazine (4008) 40,000

COLORADO
Colorado Springs
Currents (4244) ....(Paid) ‡4,500
　　　　　　　　　　　　(Non-paid) ‡2,000

CONNECTICUT
Essex
Soundings (4783) ....(Paid) ‡73,487

Norwalk
Yachting Magazine (5082) ....(Paid) 135,184

FLORIDA
Key Largo
Catamaran Sailor (6252) ....(Paid) 2,000
　　　　　　　　　　　　(Non-paid) 2,000

Miami
Pleasure Boatings Caribbean Sports & Travel
　Magazine (6376) ....(Paid) ‡21,775
　　　　　　　　　　　　(Non-paid) ‡3,475

St. Petersburg
The duPont Registry: A Buyer's Gallery of Fine
　Boats (6624) ....(Paid) 16,000
　　　　　　　　　　　　(Controlled) 38,000

Stuart
Florida Sportsman (6693) ....(Paid) 112,873

Venice
Florida Mariner (6830) ....(Paid) 332
　　　　　　　　　　　　(Free) 23,500

Winter Park
Boating Life (6877) ....(Paid) 100,000
Wake Boarding (6888) ....(Paid) 75,000

GEORGIA
Atlanta
Boating World (6981) ....(Paid) 106,854
　　　　　　　　　　　　(Non-paid) 21,193

IDAHO
Idaho Falls
Houseboat Magazine (7864) ....(Paid) 7,785
　　　　　　　　　　　　(Non-paid) 24,172
Pontoon & Deck Boat
　Magazine (7867) ....(Combined) 82,000

INDIANA
Indianapolis
USRowing (10180) 16,500

MAINE
Brooklin
WoodenBoat (12933) ....(Paid) 107,268

Camden
Maine Boats &
　Harbors (12944) ....(Combined) 20,000

Portland
Ocean Navigator (13015) ....(Paid) ‡43,000
　　　　　　　　　　　　(Non-paid) ‡2,000

MARYLAND
Annapolis
Chesapeake Bay Magazine (13091) ....(Paid) 44,991

Elkton
The Mariner (13496) ....(Combined) 35,000

MASSACHUSETTS
Boston
SAIL (13956) ....(Paid) ★170,000
　　　　　　　　　　　(Controlled) ★5,000

Newburyport
Nautical Research Journal (14380) ....‡1,700

MICHIGAN
Eastpointe
Propeller Magazine (14999) ....‡6,000

MINNESOTA
Maple Grove
Powersports
　Business (16039) ....(Controlled) ‡16,000

Minneapolis
Northern Breezes Sailing
　Magazine (16116) ....(Paid) ‡3,500
　　　　　　　　　　　　(Non-paid) ‡17,800

NEVADA
Reno
Bay and Delta Yachtsman (18418) ....‡30,000

NEW YORK
New York
Boating Magazine (21329) ....(Paid) 200,165
Motor Boating & Sailing (22371) ......(Paid) 127,664
　　　　　　　　　　　　(Non-paid) 31,612
Motorboating (22372)
Power and
　Motoryacht (22588) ....(Controlled) ‡119,424
　　　　　　　　　　　　(Paid) ‡37,746

NORTH CAROLINA
Raleigh
The Ensign (24134) ....(Paid) 38,572

OHIO
Cleveland Heights
Mid-America Boating (24994) .....(Combined) 30,084

RHODE ISLAND
East Greenwich
Rhode Island Boating (28342) ....(Paid) 50
　　　　　　　　　　　　(Non-paid) 20,000

Newport
Cruising World Magazine (28365) .....(Paid) 160,065
Sailing World (28373) ....(Paid) 57,388

SOUTH DAKOTA
Pierre
Dakota Outdoors (28916) ....(Paid) 8,100
　　　　　　　　　　　　(Non-paid) 25

TEXAS
Dallas
DIY Boat Owner (30151) ....(Controlled) 15,000

VIRGINIA
Alexandria
BoatU.S. Magazine (31648) ....(Paid) ★514,898

Springfield
Kayak Magazine (32547)

WASHINGTON
Seattle
Northwest Yachting (32996) ....(Paid) 1000
　　　　　　　　　　　　(Non-paid) 21,000
Nor'westing (32997) 19,000
Sea Kayaker Magazine (33017) ....(Paid) 30,000

WISCONSIN
Oconomowoc
Classic Boating (34201) ....(Controlled) 9,200

BRITISH COLUMBIA, CANADA
Vancouver
Pacific Yachting (35158) ....(Paid) 16,466
　　　　　　　　　　　　(Non-paid) 4,887

ONTARIO, CANADA
Mississauga
Canadian Yachting
　Magazine (36060) ....(Paid) 5,597
　　　　　　　　　　　　(Non-paid) 806

Scarborough
The Port Hole (Le
　Hublot) (36383) ....(Controlled) ‡35,000

QUEBEC, CANADA
Montreal
Bike, Boat & R.V. Trader/Moto, Bateau & Vehicules
　Recreatif Hebdo (37091)

(BOWLING)

CALIFORNIA
Burbank
California Bowling News (1615) ....‡14,000

ILLINOIS
Chicago
Bowlers Journal (8288) 20,000

Evanston
Bowling Digest (8853) ....(Paid) 86,147

Circulation: ★ = ABC; △ = BPA; ♦ = CAC; • = CCAB; ❏ = VAC; ⊕ = PO Statement; ‡ = Publisher's Report; Boldface figures = sworn; Light figures = estimated.

2839

Circ.

(BOWLING) (continued)

TEXAS
Arlington
Bowling Proprietor **(29731)** ....(Paid) ‡3,500
(Non-paid) ‡350

WISCONSIN
Greendale
Bowling Magazine **(33757)** ....‡45,000

(BOXING AND WRESTLING)

PENNSYLVANIA
Ambler
KO Magazine Superfight Color Special No.
1 **(26651)**
The Ring **(26653)** ....‡150,000

(FOOTBALL)

CALIFORNIA
Oakland
The Blitz **(2669)** ....(Controlled) 15,000

FLORIDA
Miami
Dolphin Digest **(6349)** ....(Paid) 30,000
(Non-paid) 500
Football News **(6355)** ....(Paid) 75,000
(Non-paid) 875

ILLINOIS
Evanston
Football Digest **(8859)** ....(Paid) 185,000
Mundelein
Bear Report **(9257)** ....(Paid) ⊕17,500
(Non-paid) ⊕2,000
Riverwoods
Pro Football Weekly **(9508)** ....(Paid) ‡55,000
(Non-paid) ‡342

INDIANA
Notre Dame
Blue & Gold Illustrated—Notre Dame
Football **(10368)** ....(Paid) 55,000

NEW YORK
New York
Touchdown Illustrated **(22848)** 2,800,000

(GENERAL SPORTS)

ARIZONA
Tempe
Pool Dust **(912)** ....(Non-paid) ‡5,000
SWEAT Magazine **(917)** ....(Free) 50,000
(Paid) 100
Tucson
Handball **(948)** ....‡10,000

ARKANSAS
Fayetteville
Hawgs Illustrated **(1120)** ....(Paid) 7,000
(Non-paid) 1,000

CALIFORNIA
Berkeley
Bay Sports Review **(1495)** ....(Paid) 1,000
(Non-paid) 49,000
Burbank
Paintball Magazine **(1622)**
Cardiff
Triathlete **(1663)** ....(Paid) 49,000
Inglewood
Gambling Times **(2071)** 125,000
Los Angeles
Mercury **(2329)** ....‡5,000
Oceanside
Snowboard Life **(2710)**
TransWorld Skateboarding
Magazine **(2711)** 100,000
TransWorld Snowboarding
Magazine **(2712)** ....(Paid) ‡180,000
(Non-paid) ‡109,000

Rosemead
American Sports **(2967)** ....(Paid) ‡544,389
(Non-paid) ‡3,912
San Francisco
THRASHER **(3452)** ....‡250,000
Solana Beach
City Sports **(3767)** ....(Non-paid) 75,000
Thousand Oaks
Journal of Sport & Social
Issues **(3901)** ....(Paid) 600
Woodland Hills
Men's Fitness **(4108)** ....(Paid) 607,738

COLORADO
Carbondale
Climbing Magazine **(4216)** ....(Paid) 50,598
Rock & Ice **(4217)** ....(Paid) 32,500
Colorado Springs
Coaching Volleyball **(4242)** ....(Paid) 3,250
Juco Review **(4251)** ....(Paid) 3,650
(Non-paid) 200
USA Table Tennis Magazine **(4260)** .....(Paid) 7,000
(Non-paid) 800
Telluride
Mountainfreak **(4644)** ....(Combined) 30,000

FLORIDA
Coral Gables
Entertainment & Sports Law Review **(6006)**
DeLand
Skydiving **(6056)** ....‡14,200
Wellington
Polo Players Edition **(6844)** ....‡7,000
Winter Park
Sport Diver **(6886)** ....(Combined) 175,000

GEORGIA
Atlanta
Net News **(7031)** ....(Paid) 56,000

ILLINOIS
Champaign
Athletic Therapy Today **(8181)** 3,000
Journal of the Philosophy of
Sport **(8197)** ....(Paid) 590
(Non-paid) 30
Journal of Sport Management **(8199)** ....(Paid) 1,250
Sociology of Sport Journal **(8216)** ....(Paid) ‡1,119
Sport History Review **(8217)** ....(Paid) ‡275
Teaching Elementary Physical
Education **(8220)** ....(Paid) ‡3,693
Chicago
Billiards Digest **(8283)** 20,000
Windy City Sports
Magazine **(8607)** ....(Controlled) ‡100,000
Evanston
Wrestling Digest **(8874)**

INDIANA
Indianapolis
Hoosier Outdoors **(10118)** ....(Non-paid) ‡120,000
U.S.A. Gymnastics **(10178)** ....‡80,000

KANSAS
Abilene
The Greyhound Review **(11334)** ....‡4,200

MARYLAND
Baltimore
Lacrosse **(13206)** ....(Paid) ‡15,000
(Non-paid) ‡1,000
Bethesda
SportsFan Magazine **(13382)** ....⊕80,000
Rockville
Challenge Magazine **(13676)** ....(Paid) 30,000

MASSACHUSETTS
Newton
JewishSports.com **(14403)**

MICHIGAN
Lansing
The Conservative News **(15274)** 13,000
Royal Oak
Sport Detroit **(15486)**
Williamston
Out Your Backdoor **(15685)** ....(Paid) 1,000
(Non-paid) 4,000

MINNESOTA
Minneapolis
Let's Play Softball **(16092)** ....(Controlled) 6,533
Minnesota Sports **(16108)**

MISSOURI
St. Louis
The Sporting News **(17515)** ....(Paid) 535,020

NEBRASKA
Lincoln
National Pastime **(18096)**
Nine **(18108)**

NEW MEXICO
Hobbs
Soaring **(19865)** 15,911
Santa Fe
Outside **(19940)** ....(Paid) 569,224

NEW YORK
Central Islip
New York Sportscene **(20449)** ....(Combined) 56,387
Ithaca
Training and
Conditioning **(20815)** ....(Controlled) 28,126
Lake George
Adirondac **(20871)** ....‡20,000
New York
American Cheerleader **(21184)** ....(Paid) ‡200,000
Esquire Sportman **(21628)**
India Abroad **(21862)** ....(Fri.) 53,851
Rugby **(22679)** ....(Paid) 10,000
Snowboarder **(22750)**
Sports Afield **(22775)** ....(Paid) 459,396
Sports Illustrated **(22776)** ....(Paid) 3,205,241
Sports Illustrated for Kids **(22777)** ...(Paid) 613,157
(Non-paid) 251,449
Sports Illustrated for Women **(22778)**
Sports Tech **(22779)**
Stony Brook
New Living **(23373)** ....(Free) ‡100,000

NORTH CAROLINA
Chapel Hill
ACC Sports Journal **(23697)**

OHIO
Cincinnati
Hacks 12Sports
Magazine **(24801)** ....(Combined) 20,000
Xenia
Athletes in Action **(25685)** ....(Paid) 13,700
(Free) 300

OKLAHOMA
Tulsa
Aggies Illustrated **(26106)** ....(Paid) 5,000
Sooners **(26132)** 16,000

OREGON
Monmouth
National Croquet Calendar **(26440)** ....‡373

PENNSYLVANIA
Devon
O2 **(26825)** ....(Paid) 2,500
(Non-paid) 500
Emmaus
Backpacker Magazine **(26873)** ....(Paid) 281,566

Numbers cited after listings are entry numbers rather than page numbers.

SOUTH CAROLINA
Mount Pleasant
The Water Log Maritime
Journal **(28697)** ....(Combined) 10,000

SOUTH DAKOTA
Sioux Falls
Deaf Sports Review **(28963)** ....‡3,000

TENNESSEE
Brentwood
Huskers Illustrated **(29062)** 14,000

TEXAS
Austin
Texas Coach **(29814)** ....(Paid) ‡16,000
(Non-paid) ‡253
The Texas Review of Entertainment and Sports
Law **(29846)**

Dallas
Beckett Sports Collectibles and
Autographs **(30130)** ....(Paid) ‡81,327
(Non-paid) ‡345

McKinney
American Cueist Magazine **(30801)** ......(Paid) 1,000
(Non-paid) 100

Universal City
The American
Wanderer **(31224)** ....(Combined) 7,500

VIRGINIA
Alexandria
Parachutist **(31721)** ....(Paid) ‡34,000
(Non-paid) ‡500

Charlottesville
Journal of Athletic Training **(31933)** ....‡13,500

Reston
AAHPERD Update **(32354)** ....(Paid) 24,165

WISCONSIN
Iola
Fantasy Sports **(33825)** ....(Combined) 70,000
SCD's Price Guide Weekly **(33843)** ....(Paid) 835
Sports Collectors Digest **(33844)** ....(Paid) 35,000
Trade Fax **(33850)** ....(Paid) 150
Tuff Stuff **(33852)** ....(Combined) 200,000

Waupaca
Silent Sports **(34419)** ....(Paid) 8,500
(Non-paid) 15,000

ONTARIO, CANADA
Markham
Outdoor Canada **(36029)** ....(Paid) 82,422

Toronto
explore **(36588)** ....(Paid) •24,575
Pedal Magazine **(36700)** ....(Paid) ‡5,000

QUEBEC, CANADA
Montreal
Bike, Boat & R.V. Trader/Moto, Bateau & Vehicules
Recreatif Hebdo **(37091)**

(GOLF)
CALIFORNIA
Irvine
Executive Golfer **(2081)** ....(Paid) 2,016
(Controlled) 99,778

Los Angeles
Golf Tips **(2279)** ....(Paid) 262,909

North Hollywood
Fore Magazine **(2643)** ....(Paid) 153,443
(Non-paid) 3,906

Rancho Mirage
GOLF NEWS
Magazine **(2878)** ....(Controlled) ‡54,253

Riverside
Southern California Golf **(2946)**

San Carlos
Golf Today **(3099)** ....(Free) ‡152,000

COLORADO
Steamboat Springs
Rocky Mountain Golf
Magazine **(4630)** ....(Combined) ‡60,000

CONNECTICUT
Stamford
Links Magazine **(5154)** ....(Non-paid) 283,806
(Paid) 20,791

Trumbull
Golf Digest **(5182)** ....(Paid) 1,563,476
Golf World **(5183)** ....(Paid) 147,492
(Non-paid) 9,716

FLORIDA
Orlando
GOLFWEEK **(6496)** 150,000

IDAHO
Idaho Falls
Idaho Golf **(7865)** ....(Combined) 30,000

ILLINOIS
Woodridge
Chicagoland Golf **(9771)** ....(Paid) ‡1,375
(Controlled) ‡51,125

MAINE
Yarmouth
Golf Course News **(13077)** ......(Controlled) ‡24,100

MASSACHUSETTS
Hubbardston
New England Golf **(14244)** ....(Paid) 38,000
(Controlled) 15,000

MICHIGAN
Ann Arbor
Michigan Golfer **(14763)** 18,000

MINNESOTA
Edina
Minnesota Golfer **(15876)** ....(Paid) ⊕69,345

Minnetonka
PGA Tour Partners **(16174)** ....(Paid) 500,000

NEW JERSEY
Far Hills
Golf Journal **(18816)** ....‡700,000

NEW YORK
New York
Golf Magazine **(21774)** ....(Paid) 1,405,017

Rochester
Rochester Golf Week
Newspaper **(23239)** ....‡26,000

OHIO
Cincinnati
HomeTown Golf Magazine **(24803)**

RHODE ISLAND
Cranston
Ocean State Golf **(28336)** ....(Paid) 1,000
(Non-paid) 25,000

TEXAS
Houston
Texas Golfer **(30534)** ....(Non-paid) 51,377

MANITOBA, CANADA
Winnipeg
Backspin **(35311)** ....(Non-paid) 10,000

ONTARIO, CANADA
Toronto
Canada's Golf Ranking
Magazine **(36489)** ....(Combined) 165,000
Score **(36736)** ....(Paid) •4,846
(Non-paid) •145,423
Scoregolf for Women **(36737)** ....(Paid) 1,000
(Non-paid) 59,000

(HOCKEY)
COLORADO
Colorado Springs
American Hockey
Magazine **(4234)** ....(Paid) 416,885

ILLINOIS
Evanston
Hockey Digest **(8861)** ....(Paid) ‡103,003

MINNESOTA
Minneapolis
Let's Play Hockey **(16091)** ....(Paid) 11,867

OKLAHOMA
Oklahoma City
Just Hockey **(25970)**

ONTARIO, CANADA
Peterborough
The Hockey Talk **(36315)** ....‡10,000

(HORSES AND HORSE RACING)
ARIZONA
Prescott Valley
Trail Blazer Horseback Trail
Riding **(856)** ....(Paid) 14,000
(Non-paid) 4,000

Scottsdale
National Horseman **(871)** ....(Paid) 3,800
(Non-paid) 1,000

CALIFORNIA
Arcadia
California Thoroughbred **(1427)** 5,500

Cambria
Arabian Horse World **(1648)** 10,000
Horse World **(1650)** ....‡3,500

Carlsbad
Horses USA **(1666)**

Mission Viejo
Horse Illustrated **(2554)** ....(Paid) 206,347
Young Rider **(2559)**

COLORADO
Aurora
International Arabian Horse **(4146)** ....‡30,000

Colorado Springs
Prorodeo Sports News **(4255)** ....‡37,972
Western Horseman **(4261)** ....(Paid) 226,134

Denver
NARHA Strides **(4341)** 4,100

GEORGIA
Augusta
SPUR MAGAZINE **(7103)** 25,000

IDAHO
Moscow
Appaloosa Journal **(7911)** 30,000

ILLINOIS
Downers Grove
Illinois Standardbred & Mid-America Harness
News **(8786)** 1,540

Kenilworth
Arabian Horse Express **(9043)** ....(Paid) ‡1,000

INDIANA
Fort Wayne
Hunter & Sport
Horse **(9970)** ....(Combined) ⊕29,435

Indianapolis
POA **(10161)** ....‡1,600

KENTUCKY
Lexington
The Blood-Horse **(12161)** ....(Paid) 22,000
Equestrian **(12164)** ....(Paid) 72,884
Horseman and Fair World **(12166)** ....‡7,500
Thoroughbred Times **(12178)** ....(Paid) 20,836

Magazines

Circ.　　　Circ.　　　Circ.

(HORSES AND HORSE RACING) (continued)

MARYLAND
Gaithersburg
Equus **(13538)** ....(Paid) 148,000

Timonium
Mid-Atlantic Thoroughbred **(13758)** ....(Paid) ‡10,500

MASSACHUSETTS
North Oxford
The Horsemen's Yankee Pedlar **(14425)**

MINNESOTA
Waseca
Arabian Horse Times **(16499)** ....(Paid) 22,000

MISSISSIPPI
Columbus
Mid-South Horse Review **(16604)** ......(Free) 12,500

MISSOURI
Bland
Mules and More **(16906)** ....(Combined) ⊕8,560

St. Louis
Saddle & Bridle Magazine **(17491)** .....(Paid) ‡5,500
(Controlled) ‡400

NEW YORK
Gouverneur
The Trottingbred **(20675)** ....‡500

Hicksville
Horse & Rider **(20739)** ....(Paid) 163,144

New York
Daily Racing Form **(21532)** ....(Mon.) 18,467
(Tues.) 10,481
(Fri.) 40,319
(Sat.) 63,430
(Sun.) 46,672

OHIO
Columbus
Hoof Beats **(25021)** ....(Paid) ‡14,803
(Controlled) ‡1,347

New London
The Horsemen's Corral **(25418)** 11,000

OKLAHOMA
Norman
Speedhorse Racing Report **(25943)** ....‡8,000

Tulsa
Palomino Horses **(26124)** ....⊕6663

OREGON
Beaverton
The Lariat **(26237)** ....(Paid) 4,500

PENNSYLVANIA
Harrisburg
TIMES: in harness **(27013)** 5,400

TENNESSEE
Gainesboro
Rural Heritage **(29201)** ....‡6,000

Lewisburg
Voice of the Tennessee Walking
Horse **(29326)** ....(Paid) ‡19,500
(Non-paid) ‡176

Shelbyville
Saddle Horse Report **(29599)** ....(Paid) ‡3,555
Walking Horse Report **(29601)** ....(Paid) ‡4,700

TEXAS
Amarillo
The American Quarter Horse
Journal **(29695)** ....(Paid) 70,052
The Quarter Racing Journal **(29697)** ....(Paid) 8,908

Fort Worth
Cutting Horse Chatter **(30336)** ....‡13,000
The Horsetrader **(30342)** ....‡20,452
Lone Star Horse Report **(30346)** ....(Paid) 1,000
(Controlled) 10,000
Paint Horse Journal **(30350)** ....(Paid) ‡35,038

Morgan Mill
Southwest Quarter Horse Track
Magazine **(30838)** ....‡8,800

Terrell
America's Barrel Racer **(31182)** ....(Paid) ‡2,800

VERMONT
Shelburne
The Morgan Horse **(31599)** ....‡8,000

VIRGINIA
Middleburg
The Chronicle of the
Horse **(32271)** ....(Paid) 21,652

WISCONSIN
Brookfield
American Farriers Journal **(33602)** .....(Paid) ‡7,000
(Non-paid) ‡200

ALBERTA, CANADA
Calgary
Canadian Rodeo News **(34639)** ....‡3,058
(Non-paid) ‡942

BRITISH COLUMBIA, CANADA
Vernon
Equinews **(35200)** ....(Paid) ‡17,492
(Non-paid) ‡800

NOVA SCOTIA, CANADA
Liverpool
Atlantic Horse & Pony **(35589)** ....(Paid) ‡3,000
(Controlled) ‡1,000

ONTARIO, CANADA
Ancaster
Rider **(35634)** ....‡8,000

Aurora
Canadian Thoroughbred **(35644)** ....‡4,500
The Corinthian Horse Sport **(35645)** .....(Paid) 6,500
(Non-paid) ‡200
Horse-Canada.com
Magazine **(35649)** ....(Paid) 20,000
Horsepower, Magazine for Young Horse
Lovers **(35650)** ....(Paid) ‡8,000
(Non-paid) ‡500

Mississauga
Trot **(36090)** ....(Paid) ‡20,000
(Non-paid) ‡2,000

Straffordville
The Canadian
Sportsman **(36408)** ....(Combined) •4,076

**(HUNTING, FISHING, AND GAME
MANAGEMENT)**

See also Firearms

ALABAMA
Montgomery
Bassmaster Magazine **(361)** ....(Paid) 600,000
Buckmasters Whitetail
Magazine **(362)** ....(Paid) 350,000
Guns&Gear **(366)** ....(Paid) 123,422

ARIZONA
Mesa
Arizona Hunter & Angler **(743)** ....(Paid) ‡57,927
(Non-paid) ‡842

Tucson
Safari Magazine **(962)** ....(Controlled) ‡39,000

ARKANSAS
Hartford
The Gamecock **(1170)** 14,300

Little Rock
Arkansas Wildlife **(1223)** ....(Paid) 31,000

CALIFORNIA
Auburn
Shotgun Sports **(1440)** ....‡108,000

Elk Grove
The Fish Sniffer **(1873)** ....(Paid) ‡20,500
(Controlled) ‡1,150

Los Angeles
Gun Dog **(2283)** ....(Paid) 43,501
Guns & Ammo **(2284)** ....(Paid) ★496,648
Petersen's Bowhunting **(2361)** ....(Paid) ★192,000
Petersen's Hunting **(2364)** ....(Paid) 380,798
Wildfowl **(2436)** ....(Paid) 40,553
Wing & Shot **(2438)** ....(Paid) 14,809

Newport Beach
Western Outdoors **(2637)** ....(Paid) 98,717

San Diego
Guns Magazine **(3165)** ....(Paid) 85,487

FLORIDA
Cedar Key
Cedar Key Beacon **(5979)** ....(Controlled) 1,500

Stuart
Florida Sportsman **(6693)** ....(Paid) 112,873

Winter Park
Marlin **(6883)** ....(Paid) 40,000
(Non-paid) 10,000
Sport Fishing **(6887)** ....(Paid) 153,255

GEORGIA
Augusta
Gray's Sporting Journal **(7099)** ....(Paid) 30,689

Marietta
Game & Fish Magazine **(7412)** ......(Paid) ★570,103
Georgia Sportsman **(7413)** 41,000

ILLINOIS
Boody
Full Cry **(8093)** ....(Paid) 19,029

Burr Ridge
Fishing Facts Magazine **(8102)** ....△29,494

Chicago
American Field **(8256)** ....(Paid) ‡8,000
(Non-paid) ‡55

Edwardsville
Illinois Wildlife **(8813)** ....‡12,684

Peoria
Shooting Times **(9423)** ....(Paid) 202,611

INDIANA
Indianapolis
Trap & Field **(10176)** ....(Paid) ‡15,500
(Non-paid) ‡500

IOWA
Goose Lake
Wildlife Harvest **(10926)** ....(Paid) ‡2,349
(Non-paid) ‡200

KENTUCKY
Lexington
The Chase **(12162)** ....‡3,400

MAINE
Camden
Fly Rod & Reel **(12943)** ....(Paid) 63,420

Yarmouth
The Maine Sportsman **(13082)** ....‡30,000

MASSACHUSETTS
Boston
Salt Water Sportsman **(13957)** ....(Paid) 163,857

MICHIGAN
Kalamazoo
Coonhound Bloodlines **(15235)** ....(Paid) 20,700

Lansing
Michigan Out-of-Doors **(15289)** ....(Paid) △92,226
(Non-paid) △615
Michigan Sportsman **(15292)**

MINNESOTA
Baxter
Walleye In-Sider **(15732)** ....(Paid) 67,642

Brainerd
In-Fisherman **(15767)** ....(Paid) 320,000

Ely
North Country Angler **(15881)** ....(Free) ‡8,000

Minnetonka
North American
Fisherman **(16172)** ....(Paid) 500,000
North American Hunter **(16173)** ....(Paid) 780,000

St. Paul
Pheasants Forever **(16404)** ....(Paid) ‡100,000

MONTANA
Missoula
Bugle **(17865)** ....(Combined) 130,000

NEW JERSEY
Shrewsbury
Aqua-Field Turkey Hunting
Guide **(19546)** ....(Controlled) ‡99,000
Blackpowder Hunter **(19547)** .....(Controlled) ‡97,100
Bowhunting **(19548)** ....(Controlled) ‡130,145
Deer Hunting North
America **(19550)** ....(Controlled) ‡124,500
Fishing Smart! **(19551)** ....(Controlled) ‡122,000
Fly Fishing Made Easy **(19552)** ....‡116,100
Fly Fishing
Quarterly **(19553)** ....(Controlled) ‡111,275
Fly Fishing in
Saltwater **(19554)** ....(Controlled) ‡104,350
Fly Fishing for
Trout **(19555)** ....(Controlled) ‡118,120

Somerdale
Discovering and Exploring New Jersey's Fishing
Streams and the Delaware
River **(19557)** ....(Paid) 3,000
New Jersey Lake Survey Fishing Maps
Guide **(19558)** ....(Paid) 4,000

Vineland
The New Jersey
Angler **(19699)** ....(Combined) 75,000

NEW YORK
New York
Field & Stream **(21691)** ....(Paid) 1,500,000

Shirley
The Fisherman **(23330)** ....(Paid) 92,000
The Fisherman-Long Island
Edition **(23331)** ....(Paid) ‡78,000
(Non-paid) ‡800

NORTH DAKOTA
Bismarck
Dakota Country **(24351)** ....(Paid) 12,199
(Non-paid) 2,150
North Dakota Outdoors **(24356)** ....(Paid) 24,000
(Non-paid) 2,000

OHIO
Columbus
FUR-FISH-GAME **(25018)** 107,313

OKLAHOMA
Bixby
Bassin' **(25762)** ....(Paid) 161,447
Crappie **(25764)** ....(Paid) 100,000

OREGON
Portland
Flyfishing & Tying Journal **(26478)** ....‡36,056
Salmon Trout Steelheader **(26506)** ....(Paid) ‡23,604
(Non-paid) ‡198

PENNSYLVANIA
Bradford
Hounds and Hunting **(26728)** ....‡7,917

Harrisburg
Fly Fisherman **(26991)** ....(Paid) 130,642
Pennsylvania Game News **(27007)** ....‡120,000

SOUTH CAROLINA
Columbia
South Carolina Wildlife **(28568)** ....‡60,000
SPORTING CLASSICS **(28569)** ....‡34,000

Gaffney
Grit and Steel **(28616)** ....‡6,000

SOUTH DAKOTA
Pierre
Dakota Outdoors **(28916)** ....(Paid) 8,100
(Non-paid) 25

TENNESSEE
Brownsville
Mid-South Hunting & Fishing
News **(29071)** ....(Paid) ‡18,000

Luttrell
Marine Fish Monthly **(29336)** ....(Paid) ‡33,600
(Non-paid) ‡475

Memphis
Ducks Unlimited **(29370)** ....(Paid) 661,171

TEXAS
San Antonio
Skeet Shooting Review **(31048)** 17,100

UTAH
Logan
Society & Natural Resources **(31351)** ....(Paid) ‡576

VERMONT
Bennington
American Angler **(31496)** ....(Paid) 62,564
Fly Tyer **(31498)** ....(Paid) 44,460
Saltwater Fly Fishing **(31501)** ....(Paid) ★18,412

Burlington
Outdoors Magazine **(31516)** ....(Controlled) ⊕9,300

VIRGINIA
Arlington
Trout **(31838)** ....(Paid) 65,000
(Non-paid) 1,000

Fairfax
American Hunter **(32003)** ....(Paid) 1,203,693
American Rifleman **(32005)** ....(Paid) 1,608,439
InSights **(32016)** ....(Paid) 33,000

WASHINGTON
Seattle
Fishing and Hunting
News **(32966)** ....(Paid) 100,186
(Non-paid) 7,169

Spokane
The Outdoor Press **(33096)** ....(Paid) ‡5,100
(Controlled) ‡200

WISCONSIN
Chilton
The Badger Sportsman **(33623)** ....‡26,200

Iola
Deer & Deer Hunting **(33817)** ....(Paid) 114,010
The Trapper & Predator
Caller **(33851)** ....(Paid) ‡38,241
Turkey and Turkey Hunting
Magazine **(33853)** ....(Paid) ‡44,268
Whitetail Business **(33855)** ....(Combined) 11,281
Wisconsin Outdoor Journal **(33856)** ....(Paid) 30,605

Mequon
Deer and Turkey Show
Previews **(34043)** ....(Controlled) 150,000

St. Germain
Musky Hunter **(34312)** 33,000

WYOMING
Cheyenne
Wyoming Wildlife **(34501)** ....(Paid) ‡35,000
(Controlled) ‡1,100

BRITISH COLUMBIA, CANADA
Vancouver
The Outdoor Edge **(35155)** ....(Paid) 48,915
Western Sportsman **(35180)** ....(Paid) 23,666

NEW BRUNSWICK, CANADA
St. Andrews
Atlantic Salmon Journal **(35429)** ....(Paid) ‡416
(Non-paid) ‡10,584

NOVA SCOTIA, CANADA
Dartmouth
Eastern Woods and
Waters **(35546)** ....(Paid) 11,208
(Non-paid) 5,647

ONTARIO, CANADA
Belleville
The Canadian Fly Fisher **(35677)**

Markham
Outdoor Canada **(36029)** ....(Paid) 82,422

Toronto
Ontario Out of Doors **(36686)** ....(Paid) •85,704
(Non-paid) •1,000

Waterdown
Canadian Sportfishing **(36844)** ....(Combined) 22,533

QUEBEC, CANADA
Gatineau
Info Plein Air **(36998)** ....(Non-paid) 75,000

Montreal
Sentier Chasse-Peche **(37224)** ....(Paid) ★45,091
(Non-paid) ★1,260

SASKATCHEWAN, CANADA
Saskatoon
Big Buck **(37548)** ....(Paid) 23,094

(MARTIAL ARTS)
CALIFORNIA
Burbank
Inside Kung-Fu **(1619)**
Martial Arts **(1620)**
Martial Arts Presents **(1621)** ....(Paid) 35,500

Claremont
Aikido Today Magazine **(1722)**

Fremont
Kung Fu/Qigong **(1939)** ....(Non-paid) 50000

Los Angeles
T'ai Chi **(2409)**

Santa Clarita
Black Belt Magazine **(3678)** ....‡105,000

PENNSYLVANIA
Erie
The Journal of Asian Martial
Arts **(26900)** ....(Paid) 1,500
(Non-paid) 7,500

(OUTDOORS)
CALIFORNIA
Anaheim
Knives Illustrated **(1408)** ....‡100,000

Ventura
Highways **(4004)** ....‡940,000
MotorHome **(4006)** ....(Paid) 142,073
Northeast Outdoors **(4007)** ....(Paid) ⊕9,394
(Non-paid) ⊕1,365
WOODALL'S Camp-orama **(4017)** 35,000
WOODALL'S Camperways **(4018)** 40,000
WOODALL's Midwest RV Traveler **(4020)** 40,000

COLORADO
Carbondale
Climbing Magazine **(4216)** ....(Paid) 50,598

Colorado Springs
Birding **(4236)** ....(Paid) 22,000
Christian Camp & Conference
Journal **(4240)** ....‡8,500

Denver
Colorado Outdoors **(4319)** ....(Paid) ‡43,576
(Controlled) ‡3,100

Telluride
Mountainfreak **(4644)** ....(Combined) 30,000

DISTRICT OF COLUMBIA
Washington
National Geographic Adventure **(5673)**

2843

Circ.   Circ.   Circ.

(OUTDOORS) (continued)

FLORIDA
Geneva
Florida Hiker Magazine **(6171)**

Stuart
Florida Sportsman **(6693)** ....(Paid) 112,873

INDIANA
Martinsville
Camping Magazine **(10293)** ....(Paid) ‡6,550
(Non-paid) ‡350

MARYLAND
Cumberland
Weekend Adventures
Magazine **(13475)** ....(Non-paid) 15,000

Gaithersburg
Outdoor America **(13546)** 45,000

MASSACHUSETTS
Boston
AMC Outdoors **(13848)** ....(Paid) ‡94,000
(Non-paid) ‡1,000

MICHIGAN
West Bloomfield
Michigan Natural Resources
Magazine **(15676)** ....(Paid) 67,459

Williamston
Out Your Backdoor **(15685)** ....(Paid) 1,000
(Non-paid) 4,000

MONTANA
Missoula
Bugle **(17865)** ....(Combined) 130,000

NEVADA
Carson City
Range Magazine **(18331)** 150,000

Incline Village
Adventure West **(18357)** ....(Paid) 83,716
(Non-paid) 66,530

NEW JERSEY
Califon
Women's Outdoor World
(WOW) **(18712)** ....(Paid) 30,000

Far Hills
New Jersey
Conservation **(18817)** ....(Combined) 5,000

Trenton
New Jersey
Outdoors **(19662)** ....(Controlled) ⊕10,258

NEW MEXICO
Santa Fe
Outside **(19940)** ....(Paid) 569,224

NEW YORK
New York
Outdoor Life **(22511)** ....(Paid) 1,369,094

NORTH CAROLINA
Raleigh
Great Expeditions **(24137)** ....(Paid) ‡5,500
(Non-paid) ‡10,000

OHIO
Port Clinton
Ohio Sportsman **(25483)** ....(Paid) ‡30,000

SOUTH DAKOTA
Pierre
Dakota Outdoors **(28916)** ....(Paid) 8,100
(Non-paid) 25

TEXAS
Austin
Texas Parks & Wildlife **(29838)** ....(Paid) 155,964

Frisco
Trailblazer **(30372)** ....(Paid) ‡79,000

VERMONT
Burlington
Outdoors Magazine **(31516)** ......(Controlled) ⊕9,300

Corinth
Northern Woodlands **(31537)** ....(Paid) ⊕14,000

VIRGINIA
Springfield
Kayak Magazine **(32547)**

WASHINGTON
Kirkland
Canoe and Kayak Magazine **(32797)** ....‡62,000

Seattle
Balloon Life **(32945)** ....(Paid) 4,000
Washington Trails **(33041)** ....‡5,000

WEST VIRGINIA
Harpers Ferry
Appalachian Trailway
News **(33333)** ....(Paid) ‡29,000
(Non-paid) ‡500

BRITISH COLUMBIA, CANADA
Gabriola Island
WaveLength Magazine **(34962)** ....(Paid) •319
(Non-paid) •21,054

New Westminster
B.C. Sport Fishing
Magazine **(35027)** ....(Paid) ‡19,481
(Non-paid) ‡982

Squamish
99 North Magazine **(35094)** ......(Non-paid) 100,000

Victoria
British Columbia
Magazine **(35210)** ....(Paid) 125,000
(Non-paid) 1,000

ONTARIO, CANADA
Hyde Park
Scope Camping
News **(35919)** ....(Controlled) ‡25,000

Markham
Outdoor Canada **(36029)** ....(Paid) 82,422

Mississauga
Camping Canada's RV Lifestyle
Magazine **(36056)** ....(Combined) ‡52,000

Rexdale
Canadian Camper **(36341)** ....(Controlled) ‡300

Toronto
Coast Magazine—Ontario Edition **(36552)**
Ontario Out of Doors **(36686)** ....(Paid) •85,704
(Non-paid) •1,000

Waterdown
Canadian Sportfishing **(36844)** ....(Combined) 22,533

QUEBEC, CANADA
Gatineau
Info Plein Air **(36998)** ....(Non-paid) •75,000

Montreal
Camping Caravaning **(37092)** ....(Paid) 4,046
(Non-paid) 23,176
Geo Plein Air **(37119)** ....(Paid) 12,333
(Non-paid) 8,959

(PHYSICAL FITNESS)

CALIFORNIA
Camarillo
Powerlifting USA Magazine **(1642)** ....(Paid) ‡16,200
(Non-paid) ‡99

Novato
Somatics **(2653)**

San Diego
ACE FitnessMatters **(3105)** ....(Paid) 41,000

Sherman Oaks
American Fitness **(3759)** ....(Paid) ‡34,708
(Non-paid) ‡7,292

Woodland Hills
Fit Pregnancy **(4104)**
Flex Magazines **(4105)** ....(Paid) 152,588
Muscle & Fitness **(4110)** ....(Paid) 454,177

Muscle & Fitness/Hers **(4111)**

CONNECTICUT
Wilton
Running Times **(5230)** ....(Paid) 61,259
(Non-paid) 15,235

DISTRICT OF COLUMBIA
Washington
National Geographic Adventure **(5673)**

FLORIDA
Hollywood
Diet & Fitness **(6192)**
Specialty Cooking Magazine **(6198)**

IOWA
Iowa City
Special Recreation Digest **(10988)**

NEW JERSEY
Hillside
Modern Nutrition News **(18879)**

NEW YORK
New York
Exercise For Men Only **(21662)** ....(Paid) 89,163
Fitness Magazine **(21705)** ....(Paid) 1,121,229
Iron Man **(21952)** 33,000

Setauket
Muscular Development **(23326)** ....‡140,000

PENNSYLVANIA
Emmaus
Rodale's Fitness Swimmer **(26881)**

TEXAS
Houston
Health & Fitness Sports
Magazine **(30478)** ....(Non-paid) 160,000

Universal City
The American
Wanderer **(31224)** ....(Combined) 7,500

UTAH
St. George
Total Health **(31418)** ....(Paid) ‡63,000
(Controlled) ‡10,000

VIRGINIA
Reston
Research Quarterly for Exercise and
Sport **(32413)** ....(Paid) ‡7,000

WISCONSIN
Mequon
Wisconsin in Motion **(34044)**

NOVA SCOTIA, CANADA
Pictou
Total Health **(35603)**

ONTARIO, CANADA
Toronto
Athletics Magazine **(36465)** ....‡5,000

(RUNNING)

CALIFORNIA
Mountain View
Track & Field News **(2609)** ....(Paid) 24,000
(Non-paid) 2,309

MASSACHUSETTS
Chilmark
California Track and Running
News **(14138)** ....(Combined) 22,000

Shutesbury
Running Wild **(14526)**

MICHIGAN
Ann Arbor
Michigan Runner & Fitness
Sports **(14769)** ....‡10,000

NEW YORK
New York
New York Runner **(22452)** ....‡40,000

OHIO
Westerville
Ohio Runner **(25643)** ....(Paid) ‡3,000

OREGON
Eugene
National Masters News **(26324)** ....(Paid) ‡6,775
(Free) ‡1,000

Lake Oswego
Youth Runner Magazine **(26406)** ....(Paid) 5,000
(Non-paid) 95,000

PENNSYLVANIA
Emmaus
Runner's World **(26882)** ....(Paid) 530,000

TEXAS
Houston
Inside Texas Running **(30493)** ....‡10,000

WASHINGTON
Seattle
Northwest Runner **(32995)** ....(Paid) 7,000

WISCONSIN
Waupaca
Silent Sports **(34419)** ....(Paid) 8,500
(Non-paid) 15,000

(SKATING)
CALIFORNIA
Sacramento
Heckler **(3001)** ....(Paid) 65,000

MASSACHUSETTS
Worcester
International Figure Skating **(14684)** ....(Paid) 60,000

NEBRASKA
Lincoln
U.S. Roller Skating **(18126)** ....(Paid) 5,500
(Non-paid) 200

OHIO
Columbus
Rinksider **(25059)** ....(Paid) ‡750
(Non-paid) ‡1,750

TEXAS
Dallas
Recreational Ice Skating **(30179)** .....(Paid) ⊕**59,000**
(Non-paid) ⊕**1,000**

(SKIING)
CALIFORNIA
Dana Point
POWDER **(1806)** ....‡112,000

Oceanside
FREEZE **(2707)** ....(Paid) 85,000
Snowboard Life **(2710)**

Sacramento
Heckler **(3001)** ....(Paid) 65,000

COLORADO
Boulder
Ski **(4187)** ....(Paid) 428,179
Ski Racing **(4188)** ....‡20,000
Skiing **(4189)** ....(Paid) 404,361
Skiing Trade News **(4190)** ....(Free) ‡16,875

CONNECTICUT
Woodbury
Ski Area Management **(5236)** ....(Paid) ‡4,056

FLORIDA
Winter Park
Waterski Magazine **(6889)** ....(Paid) 100,714

MICHIGAN
Boyne City
Snowscope **(14835)** ....(Paid) ‡3,354
(Non-paid) ‡13,646

NEW YORK
New York
Mountain Sports &
Living **(22374)** ....(Paid) ‡400,000
(Non-paid) ‡112,346

Snowboarder **(22750)**

WISCONSIN
Cable
Cross Country Skier **(33612)** ....‡75,000

ONTARIO, CANADA
Toronto
Ski Canada **(36741)** ....(Paid) •37,668
(Controlled) •10,106

QUEBEC, CANADA
McMasterville
Ski Presse **(37072)** ....(Paid) 423
(Non-paid) 150,577

(SNOWMOBILING)
IDAHO
Idaho Falls
SnoWest **(7870)** ....(Paid) 15,606
(Non-paid) 134,394

MICHIGAN
Boyne City
Snowscope **(14835)** ....(Paid) ‡3,354
(Non-paid) ‡13,646

East Jordan
Michigan Snowmobiler **(14980)** ....‡26,000

MINNESOTA
Bloomington
Supertrax International
Magazine **(15761)** ....(Paid) ‡14,122
(Non-paid) ‡189,908

Maple Grove
Powersports
Business **(16039)** ....(Controlled) ‡16,000
Snow Week **(16040)** 21,000

NEW BRUNSWICK, CANADA
Fredericton
Atlantic Snowmobiler **(35390)** .....(Combined) 18,193

ONTARIO, CANADA
Elliot Lake
The Trailrider **(35803)** ....(Controlled) 29,500

Markham
Snow Goer **(36032)** ....(Paid) 35,328
(Non-paid) 105,613

Newmarket
Ontario Snowmobiler **(36107)** ....(Paid) 85,000

(SOCCER)
CALIFORNIA
Berkeley
Soccer America **(1560)** ....(Paid) ‡35,000

Hawthorne
Soccer Now **(2040)**

ILLINOIS
Evanston
Soccer Digest **(8870)** ....‡36,000

NEW YORK
New York
Soccer Jr. **(22752)** ....(Paid) 110,000

(TRIATHLONS AND BIATHLONS)
COLORADO
Boulder
Inside Triathlon **(4171)** ....(Paid) 22,374

ILLINOIS
Skokie
Chicago's Amateur Athlete **(9602)** ....(Paid) 1,000
(Controlled) 54,000

(RACQUET SPORTS)
COLORADO
Colorado Springs
USA Table Tennis Magazine **(4260)** .....(Paid) 7,000
(Non-paid) 800

CONNECTICUT
Trumbull
Tennis USTA **(5186)** ....(Controlled) ‡360,000

NEW YORK
New York
Tennis **(22823)** ....(Paid) 711,855
Tennis Buyer's
Guide **(22824)** ....(Controlled) ‡10,836

Rye
Tennis Week **(23280)** ....‡103,296

TEXAS
Dallas
Black Tennis Magazine **(30133)** ....‡5,000

Houston
ADDvantage **(30454)**

ONTARIO, CANADA
Toronto
Ontario Tennis
Association **(36687)** ....(Controlled) ‡20,000

(WATER SPORTS)
See also (Boating and Yachting)

CALIFORNIA
Anaheim
Splash **(1413)** ....‡100,000
Surfing Magazine **(1417)** ....(Paid) 97,822

Dana Point
SURFER Magazine **(1807)** ....(Paid) 170,430

Foothill Ranch
Jet Sports **(1921)** ....(Paid) 44,332

Los Angeles
Skin Diver **(2390)** ....(Paid) ‡200,916

San Clemente
BodyBoarding Magazine **(3100)** ....(Paid) ‡44,757
(Controlled) ‡3,727

COLORADO
Boulder
Surfing Girl **(4193)**

FLORIDA
Polk City
The Water Skier **(6589)** ....(Paid) ‡40,000
(Non-paid) ‡500

Winter Park
Boating Life **(6877)** ....(Paid) 100,000
Sport Diver **(6886)** ....(Combined) 175,000
Wake Boarding **(6888)** ....(Paid) 75,000
Waterski Magazine **(6889)** ....(Paid) 100,714
Windsurfing **(6890)**

GEORGIA
Savannah
Rodale's SCUBA Diving **(7533)** ....(Paid) 152,716
(Non-paid) 40,085

IDAHO
Idaho Falls
Pontoon & Deck Boat
Magazine **(7867)** ....(Combined) 82,000

MISSOURI
Parkville
Dive Training **(17335)** ....(Paid) 18,000
(Non-paid) 83,000

Circulation: ★ = ABC; △ = BPA; ◆ = CAC; • = CCAB; ❑ = VAC; ⊕ = PO Statement; ‡ = Publisher's Report; Boldface figures = sworn; Light figures = estimated.

2845

Magazines

Circ.   Circ.   Circ.

(WATER SPORTS) (continued)
NEW YORK
New York
Motorboating **(22372)**

PENNSYLVANIA
Emmaus
Rodale's Fitness Swimmer **(26881)**

TEXAS
Austin
Sources **(29806)** ....(Paid) ‡14,000
(Controlled) ‡1,000

Sugar Land
Splash Magazine **(31164)**

VIRGINIA
Springfield
Kayak Magazine **(32547)**

BRITISH COLUMBIA, CANADA
Delta
Diver Magazine **(34946)** ....‡8,000

Gabriola Island
WaveLength Magazine **(34962)** ....(Paid) •319
(Non-paid) •21,054

ONTARIO, CANADA
Toronto
Windsport Magazine **(36792)** ....(Paid) ‡10,700
(Non-paid) ‡4,800

TRAVEL AND TOURISM
ALABAMA
Birmingham
Southern Living Vacations **(96)** ....‡200,000

ARIZONA
Glendale
Key Magazine
Phoenix/Scottsdale **(714)** ....(Combined) 45,000

Parker
Arizona West **(762)** ....(Non-paid) 15,000

Phoenix
Arizona Highways **(779)** ....‡300,000,000

Scottsdale
Key Magazine Palm
Springs **(870)** ....(Combined) 45,000
WHERE Phoenix/Scottsdale **(876)**

Sedona
Sedona Excentric **(877)** ....(Non-paid) ‡10,000

Williams
Route 66 Magazine **(1009)** ....(Paid) 5,000
(Non-paid) 35,000

CALIFORNIA
Carmel
KEY Magazine, Carmel and Monterey
Peninsula **(1673)** ....(Non-paid) 40,000

City of Industry
Travel & Recreation
Magazine **(1719)** ....(Combined) 20,000

Costa Mesa
Westways **(1781)** ....(Paid) 2,652,703
WHERE Orange County **(1782)**

Escondido
Inn Room Visitors Magazine **(1891)** ....(Paid) 58,344
(Controlled) 29,313

Foster City
National Motorist **(1933)** ....‡64,313

Los Angeles
Bon Appetit **(2224)** ....(Paid) 1,280,105
First Class Executive Travel **(2270)** 21,000
Southern California Guide **(2395)**
WHERE Los Angeles **(2435)**

Menlo Park
Sunset Magazine **(2527)** ....(Paid) 1,448,007

Mission Viejo
Hawaii **(2553)** ....(Paid) 80,000

Newport Beach
Coast Magazine **(2624)** ....(Combined) 45,000
Orange Coast **(2634)** ....(Paid) 29,118

Paso Robles
Paso Robles Press **(2831)** ....(Wed.) ‡12,500
(Fri.) ‡5,000

Sacramento
International Travel News **(3002)** 48,000

San Diego
Los Cabos Magazine **(3226)** ....(Combined) 150,000
San Diego This Week **(3269)** .....(Combined) 30,000
Today in San Diego **(3280)** ......(Non-paid) ‡80,000

San Francisco
VIA **(3458)** ....(Paid) 4,000,000
WHERE San Francisco **(3462)**

Santa Barbara
Islands Magazine **(3643)** ....(Paid) 66,000
Resorts & Great Hotels **(3653)** ......(Paid) ‡230,000
Spa **(3658)** ....(Paid) ‡85,000

Sonoma
Valley of the Moon Visitor's
News **(3779)** ....(Free) 6,000

Studio City
Ship to Shore **(3823)** ....(Controlled) 300

Truckee
North Tahoe/Truckee
Week **(3949)** ....(Controlled) ‡20,000

Ventura
MotorHome **(4006)** ....(Paid) 142,073
Trailer Life **(4011)** ....(Paid) 282,976
WOODALL's California RV
Traveler **(4016)** ....(Controlled) 25,000
WOODALL's Carolina RV
Traveler **(4019)** ....(Controlled) 22,000
WOODALL's Northeast
Outdoors **(4021)** ....(Paid) 10,000
(Non-paid) 10,000
WOODALL's Northeast
Summers **(4022)** ....(Controlled) 60,000
WOODALL'S Sunny
Destinations **(4024)** ....(Controlled) 55,000
WOODALL's Texas
RV **(4025)** ....(Controlled) 27,000

COLORADO
Boulder
Hawaii **(4170)**

Denver
Rocky Mountain
Motorist **(4353)** ....(Controlled) ‡265,000
WHERE Denver **(4367)** ....(Non-paid) 35,000

Littleton
Key Magazine
Colorado **(4550)** ....(Combined) 38,000

Steamboat Springs
The Steamboat Whistle **(4633)** ....‡5,000

CONNECTICUT
Hamden
Connecticut Traveler **(4880)** 258,000

Milford
JAX FAX Travel Marketing
Magazine **(4955)** ....(Paid) △13,587
(Controlled) △135,000

New Canaan
NordicReach **(4980)** ....(Paid) 16,000

West Hartford
Journeys **(5204)** 245,000

DELAWARE
Yorklyn
Britannia **(5305)**

DISTRICT OF COLUMBIA
Washington
National Geographic Adventure **(5673)**
National Geographic
Traveler **(5674)** ....(Paid) 724,094
WHERE Washington **(5860)** .....(Controlled) 100,000

FLORIDA
Cedar Key
Cedar Key Beacon **(5979)** ....(Controlled) 1,500

Cooper City
Lacja's World **(6003)** ....(Controlled) 20,000

Daytona Beach
Our World **(6038)** ....‡75,000

Fort Lauderdale
Porthole **(6083)**
Two-Lane Roads **(6085)**

Hollywood
Le Soleil de la Floride **(6195)** ....(Paid) 40,000
(Controlled) 10,000

Miami
Bienvenidos a Miami **(6341)** ......(Non-paid) ‡16,000
Geomundo **(6356)**
Pleasure Boatings Caribbean Sports & Travel
Magazine **(6376)** ....(Paid) ‡21,775
(Non-paid) ‡3,475
WHERE Miami **(6392)**

Naples
Naples Guide **(6446)** ....(Controlled) ‡270,000

North Miami Beach
Welcome to Miami and the
Beaches **(6469)** ....(Non-paid) △16,000

Orlando
WHERE Orlando **(6510)**

Sanibel
Island Life Magazine **(6649)** ....‡15,000

Sarasota
SEE Emerald Coast **(6665)** ....△545,000
SEE Florida Keys **(6666)** ....(Non-paid) △600,000
SEE Sarasota, Bradenton, Venice & Gulf Coast
Islands Magazine **(6667)** ....(Non-paid) 500,000

Tampa
AAA Going Places **(6757)** ....(Paid) 2,104,400

Winter Park
Caribbean Travel and Life **(6878)** .....(Paid) 155,868
Latitudes **(6882)** ....(Controlled) 105,000

GEORGIA
Atlanta
WHERE Atlanta **(7061)** ....(Paid) ‡300
(Non-paid) 1,071,070

Hampton
21st Century Adventures **(7320)**

Sugar Hill
Key Magazine Atlanta **(7573)** .....(Combined) 15,000

HAWAII
Honolulu
Spirit of Aloha **(7719)** 100,000
Spotlight Big Island **(7720)** ....(Non-paid) 42,000
Spotlight Kauai **(7721)** ....(Non-paid) 42,000
Spotlight Oahu **(7722)** ....(Non-paid) 35,000
This Week Big Island **(7724)** .....(Non-paid) 19,000
This Week Kauai **(7725)** ....(Non-paid) 480,000
This Week Oahu **(7726)** ....(Non-paid) ‡42,000

IDAHO
Montpelier
The Bear Laker **(7908)** ....‡5,300

ILLINOIS
Aurora
AAA—Chicago Motor Club Home & Away **(8037)**

Chicago
Adventure Road **(8244)** ....(Paid) 1,479,526
(Controlled) 250
Home & Away **(8399)** 370,000
Recreation Resources **(8553)** .....(Controlled) 51,100
WHERE Chicago **(8605)**

Evanston
Cruise Travel Magazine **(8855)** ....(Paid) 165,336
Travel America **(8871)**
TravelAmerica **(8872)** ....(Paid) 241,210

INDIANA
Carmel
Endless Vacation **(9879)** ....(Paid) 1,499,989

Indianapolis
Home & Away (Hoosier
Edition) **(10114)** ....‡221,977
This is Indianapolis **(10174)** .....(Controlled) 300,000

IOWA
Bettendorf
Home & Away (Minnesota
　Edition) **(10621)** ....(Paid) 225,000
　　　　　　　　　　　　(Controlled) 400

Des Moines
Intro **(10788)** ....(Controlled) 170,000
The Iowan **(10798)** ....(Paid) ‡25,000
　　　　　　　　　　　　(Non-paid) ‡1,000

KANSAS
Topeka
Kansas! **(11824)** ....(Combined) 46,000

KENTUCKY
Benton
Leisure Scene **(11932)** ....(Free) ‡20,000

Louisville
Kentucky Travel
　Guide **(12226)** ....(Non-paid) 300,000
Welcome to Greater
　Louisville **(12244)** ....(Controlled) 19,000

LOUISIANA
New Orleans
This Week New
　Orleans **(12757)** ....(Combined) **5,500**
WHERE New Orleans **(12761)**

MARYLAND
Baltimore
WHERE Baltimore **(13261)** ....(Non-paid) 33,000

Cumberland
Weekend Adventures
　Magazine **(13475)** ....(Non-paid) 15,000

MASSACHUSETTS
Boston
Boston Airport Journal **(13855)** ....(Non-paid) 21,000
Boston Seaport Journal **(13862)** ....(Non-paid) 6,000
The Guide **(13897)** ....(Combined) 30,000
Newbury Street and Back Bay
　Guide **(13938)** ....(Combined) 10,000
Panorama **(13946)** ....(Non-paid) ‡28,745
WHERE Boston **(13971)**

East Boston
Travel New England **(14166)** ....(Non-paid) 8,000

Falmouth
Enterprise Newspapers **(14182)** ....(Paid) 10,000
　　　　　　　　　　　　(Non-paid) 13,241

Nantucket
Yesterday's Island **(14343)** ....(Non-paid) 350,000

Orleans
Best Read Guide **(14454)** ...(Controlled) ‡1,050,000

MICHIGAN
Dearborn
Michigan Living **(14905)** ....(Paid) 1,037,811

Gaylord
Northern Lights **(15069)** ....(Non-paid) 15,000

Lansing
Michigan Traveler **(15293)** ....(Non-paid) 10,000
　　　　　　　　　　　　(Paid) 5,800

Warren
Chevy Outdoors **(15657)** ....(Paid) 80
　　　　　　　　　　　　(Non-paid) 999,950
Vista USA **(15664)** 572,102

MINNESOTA
Minneapolis
WHERE Indianapolis **(16140)**
WHERE Twin Cities **(16141)**

MISSOURI
St. Louis
AAA Southern Traveler **(17402)** ......(Paid) ‡172,971
　　　　　　　　　　　　(Non-paid) ‡939
Midwest Traveler **(17471)** ....(Paid) 424,296
WHERE St. Louis **(17532)** ....(Controlled) ‡34,000

MONTANA
Kalispell
Montana Living **(17837)** ....(Combined) 120,000

NEBRASKA
Blair
Nebraska & Iowa Explorer **(17957)**

Omaha
Home & Away **(18198)** ....(Paid) 3,355,000

NEVADA
Carson City
Nevada **(18328)** ....(Paid) ‡70,000
　　　　　　　　　　　　(Non-paid) ‡10,000
Nevada Events and
　Shows **(18330)** ....(Paid) ‡189,800
　　　　　　　　　　　　(Non-paid) ‡11,000

Incline Village
Adventure West **(18357)** ....(Paid) 83,716
　　　　　　　　　　　　(Non-paid) 66,530

Las Vegas
Key Magazine Las
　Vegas **(18369)** ....(Combined) ‡83,500
WHERE Las Vegas **(18386)**

NEW JERSEY
Voorhees
SJ First **(19703)** ....‡180,000

NEW MEXICO
Santa Fe
New Mexico Magazine **(19938)** ....(Paid) 117,718
The Santa Fean
　Magazine **(19945)** ....(Combined) 32,500

Truth or Consequences
Chaparral Guide **(19967)** ....(Free) 7,300

NEW YORK
Bridgehampton
Dan's Paper **(20243)**

Brooklyn
Travel National **(20351)** 114,000

Delmar
Access to Travel Magazine **(20527)** ....(Paid) 12,600

Flushing
TravLtips **(20614)** 25,000

Garden City
Car & Travel Monthly **(20635)** ....‡797,000

Ithaca
South American Explorer **(20814)** ....‡8,500

New York
Arthur Frommer's Budget
　Travel **(21255)** ....(Paid) ‡518,498
　　　　　　　　　　　　(Non-paid) ‡38,777
City Guide Magazine **(21423)** .....(Combined) 61,596
Conde Nast Traveler **(21481)** ....(Paid) 785,717
Gourmet-The Magazine of Good
　Living **(21776)** ....(Paid) 946,345
Inspector 18 **(21878)** ....(Paid) 75
　　　　　　　　　　　　(Non-paid) 25
Punch in International Travel and Entertainment
　Magazine **(22613)** ....(Non-paid) 100,000
SkyGuide **(22743)** ....(Paid) ‡129,957
Travel, Food & Wine **(22857)**
Travel Leisure **(22858)** ....(Paid) 960,485
WHERE New York **(22917)** .....(Non-paid) ‡570,619

Penfield
RollerCoaster! **(23090)** 6,000

Williamsville
The Motorist **(23584)** ....(Paid) 277,812

NORTH CAROLINA
Asheville
The Digest **(23628)** ....(Controlled) ‡225,000
This Week of Western North
　Carolina **(23634)** ....(Paid) 25,000

Chapel Hill
Journal of African
　Travel-Writing **(23709)** ....(Combined) 525
Triangle Pointer **(23728)** 45,000

Charlotte
GO Magazine **(23744)** ....‡750,000
Trend Magazine **(23757)**

Greensboro
Attacheair Magazine **(23916)** ....(Non-paid) ‡441,911
SKY Magazine—(Delta Air
　Lines) **(23938)** ....(Controlled) △489,315

Mount Airy
Simple Pleasures **(24080)** ....(Paid) ‡10,000
　　　　　　　　　　　　(Non-paid) ‡25,000

Raleigh
Great Expeditions **(24137)** ....(Paid) ‡5,500
　　　　　　　　　　　　(Non-paid) ‡10,000

NORTH DAKOTA
Minot
Going Places (Minot) **(24504)** ......(Non-paid) 39,760
　　　　　　　　　　　　(Paid) 240

OHIO
Cincinnati
Home and Away **(24802)** ....‡200,000

Cleveland
This Week in Cleveland
　Magazine **(24957)** ....(Free) 10,000

Independence
Ohio Motorist **(25252)** ....‡430,000

Maineville
Key Magazine
　Cincinnati **(25327)** ....(Combined) ‡15,200

Worthington
Home & Away (Ohio
　Edition) **(25679)** ....(Controlled) 590,000

OKLAHOMA
Oklahoma City
Oklahoma Today
　Magazine **(25988)** ....(Paid) ‡44,000
　　　　　　　　　　　　(Non-paid) ‡2,000

Shawnee
Frontier Country Key **(26063)** .....(Combined) 20,000

OREGON
Florence
Northwest Travel **(26351)** ....(Paid) ‡39,657
　　　　　　　　　　　　(Controlled) ‡1,950

Portland
Northwest Palate Magazine **(26488)** ....(Paid) 15,000

Seaside
North Coast Tidings **(26579)** ....(Non-paid) 12,000

PENNSYLVANIA
Allentown
AAA Traveler **(26624)** ....(Controlled) ‡150,000

Clarks Summit
Happenings Magazine **(26786)** ....(Non-paid) ‡30,000

Devon
O2 **(26825)** ....(Paid) 2,500
　　　　　　　　　　　　(Non-paid) 500

Edinboro
Heartland **(26861)** ....(Combined) 25,000

Lancaster
Big World **(27139)** ....(Paid) 15,000
　　　　　　　　　　　　(Non-paid) 200

Mount Joy
Where & When Pennsylvania's Travel
　Guide **(27299)** ....(Combined) ‡100,000

Philadelphia
AAA World **(27353)**
AAA World—Delaware **(27354)** 2,300,000
AAA World—Keystone **(27355)** 2,300,000
AAA World—Maryland **(27356)** 2,300,000
AAA World—Potomac **(27357)**
AAA World—Shore **(27358)** 2,300,000
AAA World—Valley **(27359)**
AAA World—Virginia **(27360)**
WHERE Philadelphia **(27720)**

Pittsburgh
Key Magazine
　Pittsburgh **(27808)** ....(Combined) **10,000**

York
Car & Travel **(28205)** ....(Non-paid) ‡151,936

PUERTO RICO
Guaynabo
WHERE Puerto Rico **(28246)**

Circulation: ★ = ABC; △ = BPA; ♦ = CAC; • = CCAB; ❑ = VAC; ⊕ = PO Statement; ‡ = Publisher's Report; Boldface figures = sworn; Light figures = estimated.

Circ.　　　　　　　　　Circ.　　　　　　　　　Circ.

TRAVEL AND TOURISM (continued)

SOUTH CAROLINA
Cayce
Living in South Carolina **(28503)** ....‡503,000

Myrtle Beach
Strand Magazine **(28703)** ......(Non-paid) ‡1,300,000

SOUTH DAKOTA
Pierre
Motorcycle Events
　Magazine **(28917)** ....(Controlled) 60,000

TENNESSEE
Memphis
Key Magazine
　Memphis **(29374)** ....(Combined) **23,000**

TEXAS
Austin
Texas Highways **(29822)** ....(Paid) ‡262,438
　　　　　　　　　　　　　　(Controlled) ‡25,642

Dallas
Key Magazine
　Dallas **(30165)** ....(Controlled) ‡35,000
TRAVELHOST **(30185)** ....(Non-paid) 521,215
WHERE Dallas **(30188)**

Fort Worth
American Way **(30329)** ....(Controlled) 344,375
Key Magazine Fort
　Worth **(30344)** ....(Combined) ‡11,740
WHERE Ft. Worth **(30356)**

Houston
Key Magazine
　Houston **(30500)** ....(Combined) ‡41,505
VACATIONS **(30540)** ....(Paid) 305,000

Marble Falls
101 Fun Things to Do **(30760)** ....(Non-paid) 20,000

San Antonio
Que Pasa San
　Antonio **(31043)** ....(Combined) 125,000
RIO **(31044)** ....(Non-paid) ‡50,000

VERMONT
Bennington
Transitions Abroad **(31495)** ....(Paid) ‡18,000

Killington
The Mountain Times **(31547)** ....(Paid) ‡300
　　　　　　　　　　　　　　(Free) ‡10,300

North Springfield
Vermont Green Mountain
　Guide **(31573)** ....(Free) 650,000

VIRGINIA
Fairfax
BYWAYS **(32011)** ....(Non-paid) ‡10,000

WASHINGTON
Bellevue
Motorist **(32667)** ....‡330,000
Washington Magazine **(32670)** ....(Paid) 23,000
　　　　　　　　　　　　　　(Non-paid) 31,000

Des Moines
Northwest Fun & Games **(32737)** ....(Paid) 1,500
　　　　　　　　　　　　　　(Controlled) 40,000

Eastsound
The San Juans Beckon **(32743)** ....(Free) 50,000

Lynnwood
RV Life **(32825)** ....(Controlled) 55,000

Seattle
Alaska Airlines Magazines **(32937)** ....‡55,000
Midwest Airlines
　Magazine **(32987)** ....(Non-paid) 33,000
Seattle Compass **(33018)** ....(Non-paid) 20,000
WHERE Seattle **(33044)** ....(Controlled) 40,000

Woodinville
Greater Seattle InfoGuide **(33213)** ......(Paid) 55,000
RV West Magazine **(33215)** ....‡40,000

WEST VIRGINIA
Bluefield
AAA Today **(33252)** ....‡14,695

Charleston
The Southern Journal **(33272)** ....(Paid) 500
　　　　　　　　　　　　　　(Non-paid) 100

WISCONSIN
Eagle River
Vacation Week **(33664)** ....(Non-paid) ‡14,000

Milwaukee
Key Milwaukee
　Magazine **(34072)** ....(Combined) ‡31,000

Sturgeon Bay
Key to the
　Door...Illustrated **(34351)** ......(Non-paid) 140,000

WYOMING
Sheridan
American Cowboy **(34587)** ....(Paid) 92,020

ALBERTA, CANADA
Calgary
WHERE Calgary **(34659)** ....(Non-paid) 28,000
WHERE Canadian
　Rockies **(34660)** ....(Non-paid) 375,000

Edmonton
WHERE Edmonton **(34737)** ....(Controlled) 240,000

BRITISH COLUMBIA, CANADA
Burnaby
Going Places **(34899)** ....(Paid) 106,654
Westworld **(34910)** ....(Paid) ‡853,237
　　　　　　　　　　　　(Controlled) ‡2,387
Westworld Alberta **(34911)** ....(Paid) 378,022

Port Alberni
B.C. Waterfront & Island Magazine **(35049)**

Squamish
99 North Magazine **(35094)** ......(Non-paid) 100,000

Vancouver
Cottage **(35137)**
Scandinavian Press **(35167)**
WHERE Alaska & The Yukon **(35181)**
WHERE Vancouver **(35182)** ......(Non-paid) ‡52,000

Victoria
British Columbia
　Magazine **(35210)** ....(Paid) 125,000
　　　　　　　　　　　　　　(Non-paid) 1,000
Island Visitor **(35217)** ....(Non-paid) 350,000
WHERE Victoria **(35230)** ....(Controlled) ‡281,000

NOVA SCOTIA, CANADA
Dartmouth
Saltscapes **(35550)**

Halifax
WHERE Halifax **(35572)**

ONTARIO, CANADA
Bracebridge
The Muskokan **(35696)** ....(Free) 20,000

Kingston
Key to Kingston **(35937)** ....(Non-paid) ‡18,000

Mississauga
Canadian Yachting
　Magazine **(36060)** ....(Paid) 5,597
　　　　　　　　　　　　　　(Non-paid) 806

Oakville
Tourist **(36152)**

Ottawa
Canadian Geographic **(36198)** ....(Paid) 229,180
WHERE Ottawa **(36279)** 35,000

Thunder Bay
Thunder Bay Guest
　Magazine **(36440)** ....(Controlled) ‡160,000

Toronto
Coast Magazine—Ontario Edition **(36552)**
explore **(36588)** ....(Paid) •24,575
Georgian Bay Today **(36600)** ....(Paid) 3,000
Journeywoman Online Magazine **(36640)**
The Student
　Traveller **(36750)** ....(Non-paid) ‡100,000
WHERE Toronto **(36791)** ....(Non-paid) ‡77,000

Unionville
Moving to Alberta **(36830)**
Moving to Montreal **(36831)**

Moving to Ottawa/Outaouais **(36832)**
Moving to Saskatchewan **(36833)**
Moving to Southwestern Ontario **(36834)**
Moving to Toronto **(36835)**
Moving to Vancouver & British Columbia **(36836)**
Moving to Winnipeg & Manitoba **(36837)**

Waterloo
Visitor **(36858)** ....(Non-paid) ‡50,000

QUEBEC, CANADA
Laprairie
Group Travel (Voyage en
　Groupe) **(37033)** ....(Paid) 415
　　　　　　　　　　　　　　(Controlled) 11,750

Laval
Touring **(37044)** ....(Paid) 540,672

Montreal
Doctor's Review **(37109)** ....(Combined) 38,500
Tourisme Jeunesse **(37228)** ......(Controlled) 75,000

Quebec
VOILA QUEBEC **(37297)** ....(Controlled) 88,766

VETERANS

DISTRICT OF COLUMBIA
Washington
The Jewish Veteran **(5563)** ....(Paid) 40,000
　　　　　　　　　　　　　　(Non-paid) 5,000

MINNESOTA
Pine Island
VietNow **(16272)** ....(Combined) 15,000

TEXAS
Fort Worth
Texan Veteran News **(30353)** ......(Non-paid) ‡1,000

WEST VIRGINIA
Circleville
Combat **(33292)**

YOUTHS' INTERESTS

**See also Children's Interests; Education;
Comics and Comic Technique; Parenting**

ALABAMA
Montgomery
Young Bucks Outdoors **(381)** ....(Paid) 50,000

CALIFORNIA
Agoura
Savage **(1379)**

Beverly Hills
Tips & Tricks **(1577)** ....(Paid) ★163,947

Canoga Park
Junior Baseball Magazine **(1656)** ....(Paid) 50,000

El Cajon
Youthworker **(1850)**

Los Angeles
All About You **(2205)**
The Duckburg Times **(2254)** ....‡1,400
Street Scene **(2406)** ....(Non-paid) 1,000
TEEN **(2410)** ....(Paid) 600,000

Pasadena
The REAL Girls Papers **(2826)**

Redondo Beach
lovematters.com **(2910)**

Sacramento
Heckler **(3001)** ....(Paid) 65,000

San Francisco
Slap **(3441)** ....(Paid) 70,000
THRASHER **(3452)** ....‡250,000
YO! **(3466)**

San Mateo
Junior Statement **(3588)** ....(Paid) 10,000

Santa Barbara
SuperOnda **(3660)** ....(Combined) 102,016

Santa Cruz
Stone Soup **(3690)** ....(Combined) 20,000

COLORADO
Boulder
Surfing Girl **(4193)**

Colorado Springs
Breakaway Magazine **(4237)** ....(Paid) 90,000
Clubhouse Jr. **(4241)** ....(Controlled) 88,000
Focus on the Family
     Clubhouse **(4246)** ....(Paid) 115,000

Loveland
Group Magazine **(4567)** ....‡55,000

CONNECTICUT
Stamford
Current Events **(5145)** ....‡257,402
Know Your World Extra **(5153)** ....‡172,109
Read **(5159)** ....‡250,000

DELAWARE
Wilmington
Worddance **(5295)**

DISTRICT OF COLUMBIA
Washington
National Geographic
     WORLD **(5675)** ....(Paid) ‡1,246,210
                                                 (Free) ‡13,334
Shofar **(5792)** ....‡30,000
World Around You **(5867)** 3,000

FLORIDA
Gainesville
Florida Leader
     Magazine **(6139)** ....(Controlled) ‡25,000

ILLINOIS
Carol Stream
Campus Life **(8135)** ....(Combined) 96,657
FFA New Horizons **(8143)** .....(Controlled) ‡512,644

Chicago
Book Links: Connecting Books, Libraries and
     Classrooms **(8286)** ....(Paid) 24,265
                                              (Non-paid) 5,735

Skokie
INsider Magazine **(9607)** ....(Paid) 1,000,000

INDIANA
Chesterton
Guideposts for Kids **(9887)**

Indianapolis
Forensic Quarterly **(10112)** ....(Paid) 5000
Keynoter **(10144)** ....(Paid) 190,000

KANSAS
Manhattan
Kansas 4-H Journal **(11624)** ....‡13,500

Newton
With **(11671)** 6,000

MARYLAND
Baltimore
Girls' Life (GL) **(13165)** ....(Paid) 315,905

Hagerstown
Listen **(13566)** ..../....‡35,000
Winner **(13571)** ....(Paid) 15,000

MASSACHUSETTS
Boston
My Friend **(13930)** ....‡11,500

MINNESOTA
Duluth
New Moon **(15840)** ....(Paid) 22,500

MISSOURI
St. Louis
Teen Time **(17522)**

Springfield
High Adventure **(17602)** ....‡88,000

NEW HAMPSHIRE
Nashua
The Clubhouse **(18586)**

Peterborough
Appleseeds **(18616)**
California Chronicles **(18618)**
Calliope **(18619)** ....(Paid) ‡10,400
Cobblestone **(18621)** ....(Paid) 30,000
Footsteps **(18624)** 6,000

NEW JERSEY
Flemington
Children's Software Revue
     (CSR) **(18818)** ....(Combined) ‡19,000

Keyport
Careers & Colleges **(19155)** ....(Paid) ❑1,679
                                           (Non-paid) ❑750,000

Mahwah
Journal of Research on Adolescence **(19199)**

Park Ridge
Kids Magazine **(19409)** ....(Non-paid) ‡30,000

Trenton
Bullpen **(19654)** ....(Controlled) ‡33,000

Washington
Hearts Aflame **(19708)** ....‡5,000

NEW YORK
Congers
Inquest, The Gaming
     Magazine **(20490)** ....(Paid) 105,000
Toyfare, The Toy Magazine **(20491)**
Wizard **(20492)** ....(Paid) 197,000

Hamburg
Kids Courier **(20704)** ....(Non-paid) 385,117

New York
The Activist **(21148)**
American Cheerleader **(21184)** ....(Paid) ‡200,000
Kidpreneurs News **(22220)** ....(Combined) 5,200
Kids Discover **(22221)**
NYC/New Youth
     Connections **(22478)** ....(Non-paid) ‡77,000
Right On! **(22667)** ....(Paid) 77,247
Seventeen **(22734)** ....(Paid) 2,369,734
Teen People **(22818)** ....(Paid) 1,600,504
Tiger Beat Magazine **(22835)** 175,000
YM **(22950)** ....(Paid) 2,202,979
Young Judaean **(22953)** ....(Paid) ‡5,000
                                             (Non-paid) ‡3,864

Victor
The Next Step
     Magazine **(23494)** ....(Non-paid) 440,000

OHIO
Bluffton
Boys' Quest **(24683)** ....(Paid) 10,000

Dayton
Visions **(25130)**

Troy
Miami Valley Parents **(25595)**

OREGON
Lake Oswego
Youth Runner Magazine **(26406)** ....(Paid) 5,000
                                              (Non-paid) 95,000

PENNSYLVANIA
Imperial
Voice of Youth **(27070)** ....‡4,000

RHODE ISLAND
Cumberland
Valley Breeze **(28339)** ....(Non-paid) ‡34,000

East Greenwich
Merlyn's Pen: Stories by American
     Students **(28341)** ....(Paid) ‡5,000
                                             (Controlled) ‡1,000

TEXAS
Irving
Boys' Life **(30604)** ....(Paid) 1,259,656

Waco
Creative Kids **(31245)** 35,000

UTAH
Provo
Children's Book and Play Review **(31401)**

VIRGINIA
Fairfax
InSights **(32016)** ....(Paid) 33,000

Harrisonburg
Living **(32141)** ....(Non-paid) 125,000

Reston
DECA Dimensions **(32364)** ....(Paid) ⊕161,000
                                          (Non-paid) ⊕500
Teen Times **(32421)** ....‡215,000

WASHINGTON
Olympia
Young Voices Magazine **(32864)** 3,000

WISCONSIN
Middleton
American Girl **(34049)** ....(Paid) 700,000

BRITISH COLUMBIA, CANADA
Victoria
The Claremont Review **(35214)** ......(Combined) 600
YES Mag **(35231)** ....(Paid) 18,000

MANITOBA, CANADA
Winnipeg
What! A Magazine **(35362)** ....(Non-paid) 247,249

ONTARIO, CANADA
Don Mills
Teen Tribune **(35778)** ....(Non-paid) •299,500

Ottawa
The Canadian Leader **(36222)** ....•37,825

Toronto
Canadian Guider **(36501)** ....(Paid) ‡300
                                           (Controlled) ‡40,000
Catch da Flava **(36538)** ....(Non-paid) 10,000
Exclaim! **(36585)** ....(Non-paid) 102,302
Kidsworld **(36643)** ....(Non-paid) 200,050
Klublife **(36644)** ....(Combined) 40,000
Noise **(36675)**
TG Magazine **(36757)**
Yunak **(36796)**

QUEBEC, CANADA
Montreal
In Montreal **(37125)** ....(Paid) 30,000
Le Magazine Jeunesse **(37168)** ....(Paid) 56,000
                                           (Non-paid) 3,000

Outremont
Filles d'Aujourd'hui **(37265)** ....(Paid) 56,532

Quebec
Adorable **(37279)** ....(Combined) 33,598

Saint-Lambert
Le Magazine Enfants
     Quebec **(37359)** ....(Combined) 72,102

Magazines

Circulation: ★ = ABC; △ = BPA; ◆ = CAC; • = CCAB; ❑ = VAC; ⊕ = PO Statement; ‡ = Publisher's Report; Boldface figures = sworn; Light figures = estimated.

2849

Daily Newspapers

Index entries are arranged geographically, first by states/provinces and then by cities. Within cities in this index, citations appear alphabetically by publication title. Citations in the index include publication title, entry number (given in parentheses immediately following the titles), street address, ZIP or Canadian Postal Code (in parentheses), phone number, and circulation figures.

Circ.

ALABAMA

Alexander City
Alexander City Outlook **(6)**
548 Cherokee Rd.
PO Box 999 (35010-0999)
Phone: (205)234-4281

Andalusia
The Andalusia Star News **(11)**
209 Dunson St.
PO Drawer 430 (36420-0430)
Phone: (334)222-2402

Anniston
The Anniston Star **(15)** ....(Mon.-Sat.) 25,668
PO Box 189 (36202) (Sun.) 27,019
Phone: (256)236-1551

Athens
Athens News Courier **(27)** ....(Tues.-Fri.) 7,549
410 W Green St. (Sun.) 8,393
PO Box 670 (35611-2518)
Phone: (256)232-2720

Birmingham
The Birmingham News **(58)** ......(Mon.-Thurs.) ★145,571
PO Box 2553 (35202) (Sun.) ★183,080
Phone: (205)325-2444 (Sat.) ★149,118
(Fri.) ★168,787

Birmingham Post-Herald **(60)** ....(Combined) ★156,012
2200 4th Ave. N. (35203)
Phone: (205)325-2344

Kilgore News Herald .**(78)** ....(Mon.-Fri.) ‡3,737
3800 Colonade Pkwy., (Sun.) ‡4,316
Ste. 450 (35243)
Phone: (205)298-7100

Moberly Monitor-Index & Evening
Democrat **(81)** ....(Mon.-Fri.) 6,395
3800 Colonnade Pkwy., (Sun.) 6,700
Ste. 450 (35243)
Phone: (205)298-7100

Cullman
The Cullman Times **(160)** ....(Mon.-Sat.) 10,759
300 4th Ave. SE (35055) (Sun.) 11,387
Phone: (256)734-2131

Decatur
Decatur Daily **(170)** ....(Mon.-Fri.) 25,459
PO Box 2213 (35609- (Sat.) 25,750
2213) (Sun.) 27,950

Dothan
The Dothan Eagle **(185)** ....(Mon.-Sat.) ★34,272
227 N. Oates St. (Sun.) ★36,180
PO Box 1968 (36302)
Phone: (334)792-3141

Enterprise
Enterprise Ledger **(201)**
PO Box 311130 (36331)
Phone: (334)347-9533

Fort Payne
The Times-Journal Midweek **(232)** ....‡7,100
PO Box 680349 (35968-1604)
Phone: (256)845-2550

Gadsden
Gadsden Times **(234)** ....(Mon.-Sat.) ★22,808
401 Locust St. (Sun.) ★24,547
PO Box 188 (35901-3737)
Phone: (205)549-2000

Huntsville
The Huntsville Times **(270)** ....(Mon.-Sat.) ★56,227
PO Box 1487, West Sta. (Sun.) ★75,622
(35807-0487)
Phone: (205)532-4000

Jasper
Jasper Mountain Eagle **(296)** ....(Mon.-Sat.) ★11,675
1301 Viking Dr. (Sun.) ★11,301
PO Box 1469 (35501)
Phone: (205)221-2840

Lanett
The Valley Times-News **(301)**
220 N 12th St.
PO Box 850 (36863)

Mobile
The Mobile Press **(324)** ....(Mon.-Fri.) 9,471
304 Government St.
PO Box 2488 (36630)
Phone: (334)433-1551

The Mobile Register **(325)** ....(Mon.-Fri.) ★95,547
304 Government St. (Sat.) ★89,647
PO Box 2488 (36602) (Sun.) ★113,040
Phone: (334)433-1551

Montgomery
The Montgomery Advertiser **(369)** ...(Mon.-Sat.) ★50,763
200 Washington Ave. (Sun.) ★62,137
PO Box 1000 (36101-1000)
Phone: (334)262-1611

Opelika
Opelika-Auburn News **(409)** ....(Mon.-Sat.) 13,438
3505 Pepperell Pkwy. (Sun.) 14,068
PO Box 2208 (36801)
Phone: (205)749-6271

Scottsboro
The Daily Sentinel **(445)** ....(Tues.-Fri.) ♦6,056
701 Veterans Dr. (35768- (Sun.) ♦6,741
2132)
Phone: (205)259-1020

Selma
The Selma Times-Journal **(452)** ....(Paid) 10,000
1018 Water Ave.
PO Box 611 (36701)
Phone: (334)875-2110

Talladega
The Daily Home **(465)** ....(Paid) 14,500
(35160) (Free) 16,923
Phone: (256)362-1903

Troy
Messenger **(473)** ....(Paid) 4,000
918 S Brundidge St. (Non-paid) 14,000
PO Box 727 (36081)
Phone: (334)566-4270

Tuscaloosa
The Tuscaloosa News **(492)** ....(Mon.-Sat.) ★34,613
6th St. & 20th Ave. (Sun.) ★36,897
PO Box 20587 (35401)
Phone: (205)345-0505

ALASKA

Anchorage
Anchorage Daily News **(523)** ....(Mon.-Sat.) 69,037
1001 Northway Dr. (Fri.) 79,378
PO Box 149001 (99514- (Sun.) 84,275
9001)
Phone: (907)257-4200

Fairbanks
Fairbanks Daily News-Miner **(567)** .....(Mon.-Sat.) 16,437
PO Box 70710 (99707) (Sun.) 21,329
Phone: (907)456-6661

Juneau
Juneau Empire **(596)** ....(Paid) 7,066
3100 Channel Dr. (Free) 190
(99801-7814)
Phone: (907)586-3740

Kenai
Peninsula Clarion **(607)** ....(Paid) ⊕5,710
PO Box 3009 (99611) (Non-paid) ⊕339
Phone: (907)283-7551

Ketchikan
Ketchikan Daily News **(611)** ....‡5,823
501 Dock St.
PO Box 7900 (99901)
Phone: (907)225-3157

Kodiak
Kodiak Daily Mirror **(616)** ....(Combined) 4,000
1419 Selig St. (99615)
Phone: (907)486-3227

Sitka
The Daily Sitka Sentinel **(638)** ....‡3,480
112 Barracks (99835)
Phone: (907)747-3219

ARIZONA

Casa Grande
Casa Grande Dispatch **(669)** ....(Mon.-Sat.) 9,579
PO Box 15002 (85230-5002)
Phone: (520)836-7461

Douglas
The Daily Dispatch **(686)** ....‡2,582
530 11th St.
PO Drawer H (85608)
Phone: (520)364-3424

Kingman
Kingman Daily Miner **(729)** ....(Mon.-Fri.) 8,500
3015 Stockton Hill Rd. (Sun.) 9,200
(86401)
Phone: (928)753-6397

Lake Havasu City
Today's News - Herald **(735)** ....(Tues.-Fri.) 9,475
2225 W Acoma Blvd. (Sun.) 11,645
(86403)
Phone: (928)855-2197

Mesa
The Tribune **(746)** ....(Mon.-Sat.) 109,786
120 W. 1st Ave. (85210) (Sun.) 110,679
Phone: (602)898-6500

Nogales
Herald **(754)**
159 W. Pajarito St.
(85621-2712)
Phone: (602)287-3622

Phoenix
The Arizona Republic **(782)** ....(Mon.-Fri.) 448,518
200 E. Van Buren St. (Sat.) 481,937
(85004-2238) (Sun.) 562,656
Phone: (602)444-8000

Prescott
The Prescott Courier **(848)** ....(Mon.-Fri.) 17,647
147 N Cortez (86301) (Sun.) 19,500
Phone: (520)445-3333

Scottsdale
Scottsdale Progress Tribune **(874)** .....(Mon.-Sat.) 18,387
7525 E. Camelback Rd. (Sun.) 18,429
PO Box 1150 (85252-1150)
Phone: (480)898-5680

Circulation: ★ = ABC; △ = BPA; ♦ = CAC; • = CCAB; ❑ = VAC; ⊕ = PO Statement; ‡ = Publisher's Report; Boldface figures = sworn; Light figures = estimated.

2851

Circ.   Circ.   Circ.

ARIZONA (continued)

Sierra Vista
Bisbee Daily Review **(885)** ....(Mon.-Fri.) 10,623
102 Fab Ave. (85635)   (Tues.) 7,173
Phone: (520)458-9440   (Sun.) 11,858

Sierra Vista Herald **(889)** ....(Mon.-Fri.) 10,978
102 Fab Ave. (85635)   (Sun.) 12,544
Phone: (520)458-9440

Sun City
Daily News-Sun **(895)** ....(Mon.-Sat.) 20,516
10102 Santa Fe Dr.
PO Box 1779 (85372)
Phone: (602)977-8351

Tucson
The Arizona Daily Star **(929)** ...(Mon.-Sat.) 102,960
4850 S. Park Ave.   (Sun.) 187,003
(85726-6807)
Phone: (520)573-4400

Tucson Citizen **(966)** ....(Mon.-Sat.) ★35,640
4850 S. Park Ave.
(85714)
Phone: (520)573-4561

Yuma
The Yuma Daily Sun **(1022)** ....(Mon.-Sat.) 22,249
2055 S Arizona Ave.   (Sun.) 26,670
PO Box 271 (85364)
Phone: (928)783-3333

ARKANSAS
Arkadelphia
Daily Siftings Herald **(1030)** ....(Paid) ‡3,100
205 S. 26th St.   (Non-paid) ‡125
PO Box 10 (71923)
Phone: (501)246-5525

Batesville
Batesville Guard **(1040)** ....(Paid) 8,973
258 W. Main St.   (Non-paid) ⊕121
Box 2036 (72501)
Phone: (870)793-2383

Benton
The Benton Courier **(1047)** ....(Mon.-Fri.) 7,788
321 N Market St.   (Sun.) 7,367
(72015)
Phone: (501)315-8228

Bentonville
Benton County Daily
Record **(1049)** ....(Mon.-Sat.) 11,264
104 SW A St.   (Sun.) 17,224
PO Box 1049 (72712)
Phone: (501)271-3700

Blytheville
Courier News **(1058)** ....(Mon.-Fri.) 4,308
PO Box 1108 (72316)
Phone: (870)763-4461

Conway
Log Cabin Democrat **(1083)** ....(Mon.-Fri.) 10,004
1058 Front St.   (Sun.) 11,019
PO Box 969 (72032)
Phone: (501)327-6621

Dardanelle
The Courier **(1097)**
107 Harrison St.
PO Box 270 (72834-
0270)
Phone: (501)229-2250

De Queen
De Queen Daily Citizen **(1100)** ....‡2,601
404 De Queen Ave.
PO Box 1000 (71832)
Phone: (870)642-2111

El Dorado
El Dorado News-Times **(1106)** ....(Mon.-Sat.) 10,020
111 N. Madison
PO Box 912 (71731-
0912)
Phone: (870)862-6611

Fayetteville
Northwest Arkansas Times **(1121)** ....(Sun.) ‡53,000
PO Box 1607 (72702)   (Mon.-Sat.) ‡38,000

Northwest Arkansas Times **(1122)** ....(Paid) ★17,102
212 N. East Ave.
PO Box 1607 (72702)
Phone: (479)442-1700

Forrest City
Times Herald **(1139)** ....(Paid) 4,800
222 N Izard St.
PO Box 1699 (72336)
Phone: (870)633-3130

Fort Smith
Southwest Times Record **(1143)** ....(Mon.-Sat.) 44,554
3600 Wheeler Ave.   (Sun.) 46,300
(72901)
Phone: (479)785-7700

Helena
The Daily World **(1174)**
417 York St.
PO Box 340 (72342)

Hope
Hope Star **(1178)** 5,068
PO Box 648 (71802)
Phone: (501)777-8841

Hot Springs
The Sentinel-Record **(1184)** ....(Mon.-Sat.) 17,774
PO Box 580 (71902)   (Sun.) 19,216
Phone: (501)623-7711

Jacksonville
Jacksonville Patriot **(1195)** ....(Paid) ‡2,000
9035 Pine   (Non-paid) ‡131
PO Box 1058 (72023)
Phone: (501)843-3534

Jonesboro
The Jonesboro Sun **(1197)** ....(Mon.-Sat.) ★24,783
PO Box 1249 (72403)   (Sun.) ★28,436
Phone: (501)935-5525

Little Rock
Arkansas
   Democrat-Gazette **(1216)** ....(Mon.-Sat.) 185,709
Capitol Ave. & Scott St.   (Sun.) 287,817
PO Box 2221 (72203)
Phone: (501)378-3400

Magnolia
Banner-News **(1258)** ....(Paid) ‡4,200
134 S. Washington
Box 100 (71753)
Phone: (870)234-5130

Malvern
Malvern Daily Record **(1263)** ....(Paid) ‡5,300
219 Locust St.   (Free) ‡3,100
PO Box 70 (72104-3721)
Phone: (501)337-7523

Mena
The Mena Star **(1275)** ....(Paid) 2,958
501-507 Mena St.   (Free) 80
PO Box 1307 (71953)
Phone: (479)394-1900

Mountain Home
The Baxter Bulletin **(1285)** ....(Mon.-Sat.) ★11,200
PO Drawer A (72653)
Phone: (870)425-3133

Newport
Newport Daily Independent **(1298)**
2408 Hwy., 367 N.
(72112)
Phone: (870)523-5855

Paragould
Paragould Daily Press **(1308)**
1401 W. Hunt St.
(72450)
Phone: (870)239-8562

Pine Bluff
Pine Bluff Commercial **(1314)** ....(Mon.-Sat.) 19,051
300 Beech St. (71601)   (Sun.) 19,749
Phone: (501)534-3400

Rogers
The Morning News of Northwest
   Arkansas **(1327)** ....(Mon.-Sat.) 35,035
313 S. 2nd St.   (Sun.) 36,443
PO Box 718 (72757)
Phone: (501)636-4411

Searcy
The Daily Citizen **(1337)** ....‡7,251
3000 E. Race Ave.   (Sun.) ‡7,833
(72143)
Phone: (501)268-8621

Stuttgart
The Stuttgart Daily Leader **(1352)** ....(Paid) 3,600
111 W. 6th St. (72160)   (Non-paid) 6,000
Phone: (501)673-8533

CALIFORNIA
Antioch
The Ledger Dispatch **(1425)** ....(Mon.-Sat.) 20,933
2640 Shadelands Dr.   (Sun.) 21,903
(94598-2513)
Phone: (925)935-2525

Auburn
Auburn Journal **(1436)** ....(Mon.-Fri.) ★11,674
1030 High St.   (Sun.) ★12,434
PO Box 5910 (95603-
4707)
Phone: (530)885-5656

Bakersfield
The Bakersfield
   Californian **(1447)** ....(Mon.-Sat.) ★71,495
PO Box BIN 440 (93302)   (Sun.) ★82,718
Phone: (661)395-7500

Banning
The Record-Gazette **(1478)** ....(Paid) 2,962
218 N Murray St.   (Free) 15,500
PO Box 727 (92220-
0005)
Phone: (909)849-4586

Barstow
Desert Dispatch **(1481)** ....(Mon.-Sat.) 5,338
130 Coolwater Ln.
(92311-3222)
Phone: (619)256-2257

Benicia
Benicia Herald **(1487)** ....(Free) 6,128
820 1st St. (94510-3216)   (Paid) 4,891
Phone: (707)745-0733

Chico
Chico Enterprise-Record **(1692)** ......(Mon.-Sat.) ★33,498
400 E. Park Ave.   (Sun.) ★33,341
(95928)
Phone: (916)891-1234

Danville
San Ramon Valley Times **(1809)** ....‡15,000
524 Hartz Ave.
PO Box 68 (94526)
Phone: (510)837-4267

Davis
Davis Enterprise **(1814)** ....(Mon.-Fri.) 9,857
315 G St. (95616)   (Sun.) 10,141
Phone: (530)756-0800

El Cajon
Madera Tribune **(1847)** ....(Mon.-Sat.) 8,585
150 Chambers St. #9
(92020-3366)

El Centro
Imperial Valley Press **(1851)** ....(Mon.-Fri.) 14,889
205 N. 8th St. (92243-   (Sun.) 15,855
2301)
Phone: (619)337-3400

Escondido
North County Times **(1892)** ....(Mon.-Sat.) ★92,490
207 E. Pennsylvania   (Sun.) ★93,337
Ave. (92025)
Phone: (619)745-6611

Eureka
Times-Standard **(1894)** ....(Mon.-Sat.) 18,826
PO Box 3580 (95502)   (Sun.) 20,728
Phone: (707)441-0500

Fairfield
Daily Republic **(1909)** ....(Mon.-Fri.) 20,000
1250 Texas St.   (Sat.) 21,000
PO Box 47 (94533-0747)
Phone: (707)425-4646

Fremont
The Argus **(1938)** ....(Mon.-Fri.) ★31,698
39737 Paseo Podue   (Sat.) ★27,185
   Parkway (94538)   (Sun.) ★31,898
Phone: (510)353-7001

Fresno
The Fresno Bee **(1950)** ....(Mon.-Sat.) ★158,286
1626 E St. (93786)   (Sun.) ★188,933
Phone: (559)441-6111

Fullerton
Daily Titan **(1989)** ....(Free) ‡6,000
College Park Building
2600 E. Nutwood Ave.,
Ste. 660 (92831-3110)
Phone: (714)278-2128

Gilroy
The Dispatch **(2003)** ....(Mon.-Fri.) 5,786
6400 Monterey Rd.
PO Box 22365 (95020)
Phone: (408)842-6400

Grass Valley
The Union **(2029)** ....(Mon.-Sat.) 17,000
464 Sutton Way (95945)
Phone: (530)273-9561

Hanford
The Hanford Sentinel **(2037)** ....(Mon.-Fri.) ★13,281
PO Box 9 (93232)   (Sun.) ★13,128
Phone: (559)582-0471

Hayward
The Daily Review **(2041)** ....(Mon.-Fri.) 38,218
116 W. Winton Ave.   (Sat.) 27,125
PO Box 5050 (94544)   (Sun.) 38,002
Phone: (510)783-6111

Hollister
The Free Lance **(2050)** ....(Mon.-Fri.) 4,500
350, 6th St. 1417
(95023)
Phone: (831)637-5566

Laguna Beach
The Laguna Journal **(2133)**
Village Business Center
301 Forest Ave. (92651)
Phone: (949)494-7121

Lakeport
Lake County Record-Bee **(2143)** ....(Tues.-Fri.) 6,614
PO Box 849 (95453)   (Sun.) 8,387
Phone: (707)263-5636

Livermore
Tri-Valley Herald **(2155)** ....(Mon.-Fri.) ★**45,591**
4770 Willow Rd., No.   (Sat.) ★**33,949**
  697 (94588-2762)   (Sun.) ★**44,134**
Phone: (925)416-4822

Lodi
Lodi News-Sentinel **(2158)** ....(Mon.-Sat.) 16,869
125 N. Church St.
  (95240-2102)
Phone: (209)369-2761

Lompoc
Lompoc Record **(2162)** ....(Mon.-Fri.) 8,098
115 N. H St. (93436)   (Sun.) 8,369
Phone: (805)737-9027

Los Angeles
Daily Commerce **(2251)** ....(Free) 279
915 E. 1st St. (90012-   (Paid) 2,829
  4050)
Phone: (213)229-5300

Investor's Business Daily **(2298)** ......(Mon.-Fri.) 303,581
12655 Beatrice St.
  (90066)
Phone: (310)448-6000

Korea Times **(2307)**
141 N Vermont Ave.
  (90004)
Phone: (213)368-4363

La Opinion **(2312)** ....(Mon.-Fri.) ★**126,189**
411 W. 5th St. (90013-   (Sat.) ★**102,473**
  1028)   (Sun.) ★**72,601**
Phone: (213)622-8332

Los Angeles Bulletin **(2319)** ....(Paid) 200
210 S. Spring St.   (Non-paid) 4,000
  (90012)
Phone: (213)628-4384

Los Angeles Daily Journal **(2321)** ....(Paid) 12,433
915 E. 1st St. (90012-   (Free) 514
  4050)
Phone: (213)229-5300

Los Angeles Times **(2326)** ....(Mon.-Fri.) ★**925,135**
202 W. 1st St. (90012)   (Sat.) ★**1,006,130**
Phone: (213)237-7811   (Sun.) ★**1,376,932**

Metropolitan News-Enterprise **(2331)** ....(Paid) ⊕**1,600**
210 S. Spring St.   (Non-paid) ⊕**40**
  (90012)
Phone: (213)628-4384

Manteca
Manteca Bulletin **(2502)** ....(Mon.-Sat.) 6,879
531 E. Yosemite Ave.   (Sun.) 6,879
PO Box 1958 (95336)
Phone: (209)249-3500

Martinez
Martinez News-Gazette **(2514)** ....(Paid) 3,070
615 Estudillo St. (94553)   (Free) 10,344
Phone: (925)228-6400

Marysville
Appeal Democrat **(2515)** ....(Mon.-Sat.) 21,969
1530 Ellis Lake Dr.   (Sun.) 22,217
PO Box 431 (95901-
  4269)
Phone: (916)741-2345

Modesto
The Modesto Bee **(2561)** ....(Mon.-Sat.) ★**84,751**
1325 H St. (95354)   (Sun.) ★**91,215**
Phone: (209)578-2028

Monterey
The Monterey County
  Herald **(2582)** ....(Mon.-Sat.) ★**34,813**
PO Box 271 (93942)   (Sun.) ★**38,330**
Phone: (831)372-3311

Monterey Park
Chinese Daily News,Inc **(2593)** ....‡**85,000**
1588 Corporate Center
  Dr. (91754)
Phone: (323)268-4982

International Daily News **(2594)** ....(Paid) 23,000
870 Monterey Pass Rd.   (Non-paid) 1,000
  (91754)
Phone: (213)265-1317

Napa
The Napa Valley Register **(2611)** ....(Mon.-Sat.) ★**18,808**
1615 2nd St.   (Sun.) ★**19,381**
PO Box 150 (94559)
Phone: (707)226-3711

Newport Beach
Newport Beach/Costa Mesa Daily
  Pilot **(2631)** ....(Free) 65,520
330 W. Bay St.   (Paid) 381
PO Box 1560 (92627)
Phone: (949)642-4321

Novato
Marin Independent Journal **(2651)** ......(Mon.-Fri.) 40,140
150 Alameda Del Prado   (Sat.) 38,019
  (94949)   (Sun.) 40,071
Phone: (415)883-8600

Oakland
The Inter-City Express **(2682)** ....(Paid) ‡1,023
1939 Harrison St., Ste.   (Non-paid) ‡14
  330 (94612-3532)

The Oakland Tribune **(2692)** ....(Mon.-Fri.) ★**69,079**
Tribune Tower   (Sat.) ★**51,683**
401 13th St. (94612)   (Sun.) ★**65,501**

Oceanside
The North County Times **(2708)** ....(Mon.-Sat.) 89,754
PO Box 90 (92049-0090)   (Sun.) 91,110
Phone: (714)433-7333

Ontario
Inland Valley Daily Bulletin **(2716)** ......(Mon.-Fri.) 68,073
2041 E. 4th St. (91761)   (Sat.) 69,370
Phone: (909)987-6397   (Sun.) 75,143

Palm Springs
The Desert Sun **(2758)** ....(Mon.-Sat.) 46,109
750 N. Gene Autry Tr.   (Sun.) 48,234
PO Box 190 (92263)
Phone: (619)332-8889

Palmdale
Antelope Valley Press **(2782)** ....(Mon.-Sat.) 35,326
PO Box 4050 (93590-   (Sun.) 41,284
  4050)
Phone: (661)273-2700

Palo Alto
Palo Alto Daily News **(2800)** ....(Paid) 25,000
324 High St. (94301)
Phone: (650)327-9090

Pasadena
Pasadena Star-News **(2823)** ....(Mon.-Fri.) 38,249
911 E. Colorado Blvd.   (Sat.) 39,738
  (91109)   (Sun.) 38,444
Phone: (818)578-6300

Petaluma
Petaluma Argus-Courier **(2836)** ....(Combined) 7,437
830 Petaluma Blvd. N
PO Box 1091 (94953)
Phone: (707)762-4541

Pleasanton
Valley Times **(2856)** ....(Mon.-Sat.) 44,354
127 Spring St.   (Sun.) 46,559
PO Box 607 (94566)
Phone: (510)847-2111

Porterville
Porterville Recorder **(2862)** ....(Mon.-Sat.) ★**10,080**
115 E. Oak
PO Box 151 (93257)
Phone: (209)784-5000

Red Bluff
Daily News **(2885)** ....(Mon.-Sat.) 7,256
545 Diamond Ave.
PO Box 220 (96080)
Phone: (530)527-2151

Redding
Record Searchlight **(2888)** ....(Mon.-Sat.) ★**34,706**
1101 Twin View Blvd.   (Sun.) ★**39,863**
  (96003)
Phone: (530)243-2424

Redlands
Facts **(2903)** ....(Mon.-Fri.) 7,042
700 Brookside Ave.   (Sun.) 6,939
PO Box 2240 (92373)
Phone: (909)793-3221

Redland's Daily Facts **(2905)** ......(Mon.-Fri.) ★**7,102**
700 Brookside Ave.   (Sun.) ★**7,151**
  (92373)
Phone: (909)793-3221

Riverside
The Press-Enterprise **(2943)** ....(Mon.-Sat.) ★**178,994**
3512 Fourteenth St.   (Sun.) ★**184,637**
  (92501)
Phone: (909)684-1200

Roseville
Press-Tribune **(2971)** ....(Combined) 8,424
188 Cirby Way (95678)
Phone: (916)786-8746

Sacramento
The Daily Recorder **(2995)** ....‡1,122
901 H St., Ste. 312
PO Box 1048 (95812-
  1048)
Phone: (916)444-2355

The Sacramento Bee **(3011)** ....(Mon.-Sat.) 296,482
2100 Q St.   (Sun.) 351,999
PO Box 15779 (95852)
Phone: (916)321-1000

Salinas
The Californian **(3067)** ....(Mon.-Fri.) ★**18,224**
123 W Alisal (93901)   (Sat.) ★**21,698**
Phone: (831)424-2221

San Bernardino
The San Bernardino County
  Sun **(3092)** ....(Mon.-Fri.) ★**74,540**
399 N. D St. (92401-   (Sat.) ★**72,625**
  1518)   (Sun.) ★**82,670**
Phone: (909)889-9666

San Diego
San Diego Daily Transcript **(3262)** .....(Mon.-Fri.) 15,000
2131 3rd Ave.
Box 85469 (92101)
Phone: (619)232-4381

The San Diego
  Union-Tribune **(3270)** ....(Mon.-Sat.) 374,133
PO Box 120191 (92112-   (Sun.) 444,649
  0191)
Phone: (619)299-3131

San Francisco
Chinese Times **(3341)** ....‡11,000
849 Kearny St. (94108-
  1303)
Phone: (415)982-0135

Hokubei Mainichi **(3371)** 10,000
1746 Post St. (94115)
Phone: (415)567-7323

Nichi Bei Times **(3404)** ....(Combined) 8,000
2211 Bush St. (94115)
Phone: (415)921-6820

San Francisco Chronicle **(3432)** .....(Mon.-Fri.) ★**512,129**
901 Mission St. (94103)   (Sun.) ★**539,563**
Phone: (415)777-1111   (Sat.) ★**479,433**

San Francisco Examiner **(3433)** .....(Mon.-Fri.) 107,129
901 Mission St. (94103)   (Sat.) 78,312
Phone: (415)777-1111

Wall Street Journal (Western
  Edition) **(3461)** ....(Mon.-Fri.) 398,205
201 California St., Ste.
  1350 (94111)
Phone: (415)986-6886

San Jose
Aberdeen American News **(3508)** ......(Mon.-Sat.) 17,160
50 W. San Fernando St.   (Sun.) 19,006
  (95113)
Phone: (408)938-7700

Akron Beacon Journal **(3509)** ....(Mon.-Sat.) 142,941
50 W. San Fernando St.   (Sun.) 193,641
  (95113)   (Sat.) ★**172,761**
Phone: (408)938-7700

Charlotte Observer **(3512)** ....(Mon.-Sat.) 241,071
50 W. San Fernando St.   (Sun.) 294,605
  (95113)
Phone: (408)938-7700

Columbus
  Ledger-Enquirer **(3513)** ......(Mon.-Thurs.) 47,763
50 W. San Fernando St.   (Fri.) 56,858
  (95113)   (Sat.) 55,506
Phone: (408)938-7700   (Sun.) 60,172

Duluth News Tribune **(3515)** ....(Mon.-Sat.) 47,718
50 W. San Fernando St.   (Sun.) 71,719
  (95113)
Phone: (408)938-7700

Grand Forks Herald **(3518)** ....(Mon.-Sat.) 34,275
50 W. San Fernando St.   (Sun.) 34,885
  (95113)
Phone: (408)938-7700

Lexington Herald-Leader **(3522)** ....(Mon.-Thurs.) 111,168
50 W. San Fernando St.   (Fri.) 134,774
  (95113)   (Sat.) 124,316
Phone: (408)938-7700   (Sun.) 149,614

The Macon Telegraph **(3523)** ....(Mon.-Thurs.) 68,191
50 W. San Fernando St.   (Fri.) 74,140
  (95113)   (Sat.) 70,920
Phone: (408)938-7700   (Sun.) 87,878

The Miami Herald **(3526)** ....(Mon.-Sat.) 611,315
50 W. San Fernando St.   (Sun.) 440,391
  (95113)
Phone: (408)938-7700

The News-Sentinel **(3528)** ....(Mon.-Sat.) 46,023
50 W. San Fernando St.
  (95113)
Phone: (408)938-7700

The Phoenix **(3531)** ....(Mon.-Sat.) ★**3,778**
411 E. Plumeria Dr.
  (95134)
Phone: (408)570-1000

Post-Tribune **(3532)** ....(Mon.-Sat.) 61,476
50 W. San Fernando St.   (Sun.) 67,343
  (95113)
Phone: (408)938-7700

Press-Telegram **(3533)** ....(Mon.-Fri.) 99,372
50 W. San Fernando St.   (Sat.) 87,688
  (95113)   (Sun.) 110,033
Phone: (408)938-7700

San Jose Mercury News **(3536)** ....(Mon.-Sat.) ★**272,682**
750 Ridder Park Dr.   (Sun.) ★**305,080**
  (95190-0001)
Phone: (408)920-5000

San Jose Post-Record **(3537)** 1,200
90 N. 1st St., Ste. 100
  (95113)
Phone: (408)287-4866

The Sun Herald **(3540)** ....(Mon.-Sat.) 48,844
50 W. San Fernando St.   (Sun.) 56,643
  (95113)
Phone: (408)938-7700

Circ.

CALIFORNIA (continued)

Tallahassee Democrat **(3542)** ....(Mon.-Sat.) 49,142
50 W. San Fernando St.   (Sun.) 66,199
(95113)
Phone: (408)938-7700

Vietnam Daily News **(3544)** 13,000
2350 S 10th St. (95112)
Phone: (408)292-3422

San Luis Obispo
The San Luis Obispo County Telegram
Tribune **(3569)** ....(Mon.-Sat.) 38,048
3825 S. Higuera St.   (Sun.) 43,213
PO Box 112 (93406-
0112)
Phone: (805)781-7902

San Mateo
San Mateo Times **(3589)** ....(Mon.-Fri.) ★34,918
1080 S Amphlett Blvd.   (Sat.) ★36,412
(94402)
Phone: (415)348-4321

Santa Ana
Orange County Register **(3630)** ......(Mon.-Sat.) 353,334
625 N. Grand Ave.   (Sun.) 410,207
(92701)

Santa Barbara
Santa Barbara News-Press **(3655)** .....(Mon.-Sat.) 44,600
715 Anacapa St. (93102-   (Sun.) 47,902
1359)
Phone: (805)564-5200

Santa Clarita
The Signal **(3679)** ....(Combined) 10,597
PO Box 801870 (91380-
1870)
Phone: (661)259-1000

Santa Cruz
Santa Cruz County
Sentinel **(3688)** ....(Mon.-Sat.) ★26,742
PO Box 638 (95061)   (Sun.) ★28,489
Phone: (408)423-4242

Santa Maria
Santa Maria Times **(3696)** ....(Mon.-Sat.) 18,062
3200 Skyway Dr.   (Sun.) 20,122
PO Box 400 (93455-
1896)
Phone: (805)925-2691

Santa Monica
Fax Mainichi U.S.A. **(3708)** ....(Combined) 1,500
2800 28th St., Ste. 103
(90405)
Phone: (310)664-1666

Santa Rosa
The Press Democrat **(3733)** ....(Mon.-Sat.) ★87,261
PO Box 910 (95402)   (Sun.) ★95,783
Phone: (707)526-8585

Sonora
Union-Democrat **(3780)** ....(Mon.-Sat.) 11,213
84 S. Washington St.
(95370)
Phone: (209)532-7151

South Lake Tahoe
Tahoe Daily Tribune **(3784)** ....(Paid) ‡9,134
3079 Harrison Ave.
(96150)
Phone: (530)541-3880

South San Francisco
Sing Tao Daily **(3791)**
215 Littlefield Ave.
(94080)
Phone: (650)872-1177

Stockton
The Record **(3807)** ....(Mon.-Thurs.) 66,277
530 E. Market St.   (Sun.) 77,704
PO Box 900 (95201-   (Fri.) 70,919
0900)   (Sat.) 70,919
Phone: (209)948-1702

Temecula
The Californian **(3841)** ....(Mon.-Sat.) 12,485
28765 Single Oak Dr.   (Sun.) 12,540
Ste. 100 (92590)
Phone: (909)676-4315

Torrance
Daily Breeze **(3932)** ....(Mon.-Sat.) 78,983
5215 Torrance Blvd.   (Sun.) 76,907
(90503-4077)
Phone: (310)540-5511

Tracy
Tracy Press **(3946)** ....(Mon.-Sat.) 10,827
145 W. 10th St.
PO Box 419 (95376-
3903)
Phone: (209)835-3030

Tulare
Advance-Register & Times **(3952)** ...(Mon.-Sat.) 8,319
PO Box 30 (93275-0030)
Phone: (209)688-0521

Circ.

Turlock
Turlock Journal **(3958)** ....(Mon.-Sat.) 6,500
138 S. Center St.
PO Box 800 (95380-
4508)
Phone: (209)634-9141

Ukiah
Ukiah Daily Journal **(3967)** ....(Mon.-Fri.) ★7,624
590 S. School St.   (Sun.) ★7,810
PO Box 749 (95482-
0749)
Phone: (707)468-0123

Vallejo
Vallejo Times-Herald **(3984)** ....(Mon.-Fri.) ★20,916
440 Curtola Pkwy.   (Sat.) ★18,632
PO Box 3188 (94590-   (Sun.) ★22,436
0660)
Phone: (707)644-1141

Ventura
Conejo Star **(4003)**
5250 Ralston St. (93003)

Ventura County Star **(4014)** ....(Mon.) ★93,480
5250 Ralston St. (93003)   (Sun.) ★106,876
     (Sat.) ★100,007
     (Tues.) ★75,408

Ventura County Star (Camarillo
Edition) **(4015)** ....(Mon.-Fri.) 94,836
5250 Ralston St. (93003)   (Sun.) 107,441

Victorville
The Daily Press **(4031)**
PO Box 1389 (92393-
1389)
Phone: (760)241-7744

Visalia
Visalia Times-Delta **(4040)** ....(Mon.-Fri.) 21,709
330 N West St. (93291-   (Sat.) 27,454
6010)
Phone: (559)735-3200

Walnut Creek
Contra Costa Times **(4050)** ....(Mon.-Sat.) ★182,196
2640 Shadelands Dr.   (Sun.) ★193,190
(94598-2513)
Phone: (925)935-2525

Watsonville
Register-Pajaronian **(4058)** ....(Mon.-Sat.) 7,435
1000 Main St.
PO Box 50055 (95077-
3732)
Phone: (408)761-0611

West Covina
San Gabriel Valley Tribune **(4060)** ....(Mon.-Fri.) ★48,817
1210 N. Azusa Canyon   (Sat.) ★48,332
Rd. (91790)   (Sun.) ★51,823

Whittier
Whittier Daily News **(4080)** ....(Mon.-Fri.) ★16,953
PO Box 581 (90608)   (Sat.) ★17,239
Phone: (310)698-0955   (Sun.) ★17,872

Willows
Colusa Sun-Herald **(4085)**
101 Airport Rd. (95988)
Phone: (530)934-6800

Woodland
The Daily Democrat **(4099)** ....(Mon.-Sat.) 9,887
711 Main St.   (Sun.) 10,259
PO Box 730 (95776)
Phone: (530)662-5421

Woodland Hills
Daily News **(4102)** ....(Mon.-Fri.) 190,010
PO Box 4200 (91365)   (Sat.) 164,684
Phone: (818)713-3000   (Sun.) 200,419

Yreka
Siskiyou Daily News **(4121)** ....‡6,000
PO Box 129 (96097-
0129)
Phone: (530)842-5777

COLORADO
Alamosa
The Valley Courier **(4132)** ....(Paid) 5,500
401 State Ave.   (Non-paid) 100
PO Box 1099 (81101)
Phone: (719)589-2553

Aspen
Aspen Daily News **(4140)** ....(Free) 14,500
517 E. Hopkins (81611-
1982)
Phone: (970)925-2220

Aspen Times **(4142)** ....‡11,000
310 E. Main St. (81611)
Phone: (303)925-3414

Boulder
Colorado Daily **(4161)** ....(Mon.-Thurs.) 17,000
2610 Pearl St. (80302)   (Fri.) 20,000
Phone: (303)443-6272

Daily Camera **(4163)** ....(Mon.-Sat.) 34,927
1048 Pearl (80302)   (Sun.) 43,572
Phone: (303)442-1202

Circ.

Daily Camera **(4164)**
1048 Pearl St.
PO Box 591 (80306)

Canon City
Daily Record **(4213)** ....(Mon.-Sat.) 8,523
701 S 9th St. (81212)
Phone: (719)275-7565

Castle Rock
Douglas County News Press/Highlands Ranch
Herald **(4222)** ....(Paid) ‡7,245
PO Box 1270 (80104)   (Free) ‡42,000
Phone: (303)688-3128

Colorado Springs
The Gazette **(4249)** ....(Mon.-Sat.) 98,416
1155 Kelly Johnson Blvd.   (Sun.) 117,971
(80903)
Phone: (719)265-2930

Craig
Craig Daily Press **(4295)** ....(Paid) 2,971
466 Yampa Ave. (81625)   (Free) 27
Phone: (970)824-7031

Denver
The Denver Post **(4324)** ....(Mon.-Sat.) 413,730
1560 Broadway (80202-   (Sun.) 558,560
1577)   (Sat.) ★621,221
Phone: (303)820-1010

Rocky Mountain News **(4354)** ......(Mon.-Sat.) 446,465
100 Gene Amole Way   (Sun.) 552,085
(80204)

Durango
Durango Herald **(4402)** ....(Mon.-Sat.) 8,438
PO Drawer A-0950   (Sun.) 9,545
(81302-0950)
Phone: (970)247-3504

Fort Collins
Fort Collins Coloradoan **(4431)** ....(Mon.-Sat.) 28,859
PO Box 1577 (80522)   (Sun.) 35,303
Phone: (970)224-7730

Fort Morgan
The Fort Morgan Times **(4446)** ....(Mon.-Sat.) ★4,395
329 Main St.
PO Box 4000 (80701)
Phone: (970)867-5651

Glenwood Springs
Glenwood Post **(4459)** ....(Paid) ⊕5,171
2014 Grand Ave. (81601)   (Free) ‡1,675
Phone: (970)945-8515

Grand Junction
The Daily Sentinel **(4478)** ....(Mon.-Sat.) 30,340
734 S. 7th St.   (Sun.) 35,654
PO Box 668 (81502-
0668)
Phone: (970)242-5050

Greeley
The Greenly Tribune **(4497)** ....(Mon.-Sat.) 24,751
501 8th Ave.   (Sun.) 24,597
PO Box 1690 (80632)
Phone: (970)352-0211

La Junta
La Junta Tribune-Democrat **(4527)** ....‡3,787
422 Colorado Ave.
PO Box 480 (81050)
Phone: (719)384-4475

Lamar
Lamar Daily News and Holly
Chieftain **(4537)** ....(Mon.-Fri.) ★2,797
310 S. 5th St.
PO Box 1217 (81052-
1217)
Phone: (719)336-2266

Longmont
Daily Times-Call **(4558)** ....(Mon.-Sat.) 22,085
350 Terry St.   (Sun.) 24,439
PO Box 299 (80502)
Phone: (303)776-2244

Loveland
Loveland Daily
Reporter-Herald **(4568)** ....(Mon.-Sat.) ★17,127
PO Box 59 (80539)   (Sun.) ★17,903
Phone: (970)669-5050

Montrose
Montrose Daily Press **(4580)** ...:.................‡6,600
535 S. 1st
PO Box 850 (81402)
Phone: (303)249-3444

Pueblo
The Pueblo Chieftain **(4599)** ....(Mon.-Sat.) ★50,950
PO Box 4040 (81003)   (Sun.) ★53,986
Phone: (719)544-3520

Rocky Ford
Rocky Ford Daily Gazette **(4616)** ....‡3,250
912 Elm Ave.
PO Box 430 (81067-
0430)
Phone: (719)254-3351

Numbers cited after listings are entry numbers rather than page numbers.

Salida
The Mountain Mail **(4620)** ....(Paid) ‡2,900
125 E. 2nd St.
PO Box 189 (81201-
0189)
Phone: (719)539-1455

Sterling
Journal-Advocate **(4639)** ....(Mon.-Sat.) ★5,608
504 N. 3rd St.
PO Box 1272 (80751)
Phone: (970)522-1990

Telluride
Telluride Daily Planet **(4645)** ....(Non-paid) 4,500
PO Box 2315 (81435)
Phone: (970)728-9788

Trinidad
Chronicle-News **(4648)** ....(Mon.-Fri.) 3,546
200 Church St.
PO Box 763 (81082-
0763)
Phone: (719)846-3311

Vail
Vail Daily **(4654)** ....(Mon.-Fri.) 13,645
PO Box 81 (81658)   (Sun.) 11,750
Phone: (970)949-0555

CONNECTICUT
Bridgeport
Connecticut Post **(4713)** ....(Mon.-Sat.) 78,455
410 State St. (06604-   (Sun.) 90,217
4501)

Bristol
The Bristol Press **(4721)** ....(Mon.-Sat.) ★12,634
99 Main St. (06010-
6579)
Phone: (203)584-0501

Danbury
News-Times **(4747)** ....(Mon.-Sat.) 33,743
333 Main St. (06810)   (Sun.) 39,024
Phone: (203)744-5100

Greenwich
Greenwich Time **(4874)** ....(Mon.-Fri.) ★12,260
20 E Elm St. (06830-   (Sat.) ★11,481
6529)   (Sun.) ★13,553
Phone: (203)625-4400

Hartford
The Hartford Courant **(4892)** ....(Mon.-Sat.) ★290,312
285 Broad St. (06115)   (Sun.) ★285,068
Phone: (860)241-6200   (Thurs.) ★240,046

Meriden
Record-Journal **(4940)** ....(Mon.-Sat.) 26,070
11 Crown St.   (Sun.) 26,287
PO Box 915 (06450)
Phone: (203)235-1661

Milford
Elm City Citizen Newspaper **(4954)** ......(Mon.-Fri.) 6,496
349 New Haven Ave.   (Sun.) 7,530
PO Box 5339 (06460)
Phone: (203)876-6800

Naugatuck
Naugatuck News **(4972)** 4,200
71 Weid Dr. (06770)
Phone: (203)729-2228

New Britain
The Herald **(4975)** ....(Mon.-Sat.) 22,756
1 Herald Square   (Sun.) 43,948
PO Box 2050 (06050)
Phone: (860)225-4601

New Haven
New Haven Register **(4999)** ....(Mon.-Fri.) 100,048
Long Wharf, 40 Sargent   (Sat.) 83,460
Dr. (06511)   (Sun.) 100,438
Phone: (203)789-5200

New London
The Day **(5018)** ....(Mon.-Sat.) ★40,745
47 Eugene O'Neill Dr.   (Sun.) ★45,567
(06320-1231)
Phone: (860)442-2200

Norwalk
The Hour **(5064)** ....(Mon.-Sat.) ★16,070
346 Main Ave. (06851)   (Sun.) ★15,590
Phone: (203)846-3281

Norwich
Norwich Bulletin **(5084)** ....(Mon.-Sat.) ★27,960
66 Franklin St. (06360)   (Sun.) ★32,304
Phone: (860)887-9211

Stamford
The Advocate **(5139)** ....(Mon.-Fri.) 28,514
75 Tresser Blvd.   (Sat.) 26,817
PO Box 9307 (06901-   (Sun.) 39,448
3304)
Phone: (203)964-3709

Torrington
The Register Citizen **(5179)** ....(Mon.-Sat.) 10,581
190 Water St.   (Sun.) 9,820
PO Box 58 (06790)
Phone: (860)489-3121

Waterbury
Republican-American **(5193)** ....(Mon.-Sat.) ★52,291
389 Meadow St. (06722)   (Sun.) ★67,544
Phone: (203)574-3636

Willimantic
The Chronicle **(5220)** ....(Mon.-Sat.) 11,000
PO Box 148
1 Chronicle Rd. (06226-
0148)
Phone: (203)423-8466

DELAWARE
Dover
Delaware State News **(5246)** ....(Mon.-Sat.) 17,693
PO Box 737 (19903)   (Sun.) 25,316
Phone: (302)674-3600

New Castle
The News Journal **(5267)** ....(Mon.-Sat.) 121,298
950 W. Basin Rd.   (Sun.) 142,858
PO Box 15505 (19720)
Phone: (302)324-2898

DISTRICT OF COLUMBIA
Washington
The Washington Post **(5850)** ....(Mon.-Fri.) ★746,724
1150 15th St. NW   (Sat.) ★694,624
(20071-2400)   (Sun.) ★1,048,122
Phone: (202)334-6000

The Washington Times **(5855)** ....(Mon.-Fri.) ★101,038
3600 New York Ave., NE   (Sat.) ★84,250
(20002)   (Sun.) ★46,619
Phone: (202)636-3000

FLORIDA
Bradenton
Bradenton Herald **(5956)** ....(Mon.-Sat.) 48,197
102 Manatee Ave. W.   (Sun.) 56,930
(34205)
Phone: (941)748-0411

Cape Coral
The Cape Coral Daily Breeze **(5971)** ....‡5,500
PO Box 151306 (33915-
1306)
Phone: (941)574-1110

Crystal River
Citrus County Chronicle **(6030)** .....(Mon.-Sat.) ★24,469
1624 N. Meadowcrest   (Sun.) ★27,310
Blvd. (34429)
Phone: (904)563-6363

Daytona Beach
The News-Journal **(6037)** ....(Mon.-Sat.) ★94,977
901 6th St. (32117-8099)   (Sun.) ★112,489
Phone: (386)252-1511

Florence
TimesDaily **(6071)** ....(Mon.-Sat.) 31,639
PO Box 797   (Sun.) 34,267

Fort Lauderdale
El Nuevo Herald **(6075)** ....(Mon.-Sat.) 90,543
1520 E Sunrise Blvd.   (Sun.) 97,705
(33304)
Phone: (954)462-3000

Sun-Sentinel **(6084)** ....(Mon.-Sat.) 267,677
200 E Las Olas Blvd.   (Sun.) 381,838
(33301-2293)
Phone: (954)356-4000

Fort Walton Beach
Northwest Florida Daily
News **(6121)** ....(Mon.-Sat.) 39,195
200 Racetrack Rd. NW   (Sun.) 51,226
(32548)

Gainesville
The Gainesville Sun **(6142)** ....(Mon.-Sat.) 51,407
2700 SW 13th St.   (Sun.) 58,238
(32608)
Phone: (352)378-1411

Homestead
South Dade News Leader **(6205)** ....(Combined) ‡12,514
15 NE 1st Rd. (33030)
Phone: (305)245-2311

Jacksonville
The Florida Times-Union **(6212)** ....(Mon.-Fri.) 182,136
1 Riverside Ave. (32202-   (Sat.) 208,916
4904)   (Sun.) 256,710
Phone: (904)359-4111

Key West
Key West Citizen **(6253)** ....(Mon.-Fri.) 10,031
3420 Northside Dr.   (Sun.) 11,835
(33040)
Phone: (305)292-7777

Lake City
Lake City Reporter **(6269)** ....(Mon.-Fri.) ★8,450
126 E. Duval St.
PO Box 1709 (32055-
4025)
Phone: (386)752-1293

Lakeland
The Ledger **(6289)** ....(Mon.-Fri.) ★70,726
33815 W Lime St.   (Sun.) ★86,067
PO Box 408 (33802)
Phone: (941)802-7000

Leesburg
Daily Commercial **(6301)** ....(Mon.-Sat.) 29,764
PO Box 490007 (34749-   (Sun.) 29,423
0007)
Phone: (352)365-8200

Marianna
Marianna Jackson County
Floridan **(6326)** ....(Tues.-Fri.) 5,968
4403 Constitution Ln.   (Sun.) 6,576
(32446)
Phone: (904)526-3614

Melbourne
Florida Today **(6334)** ....(Mon.-Fri.) 96,626
Gannett Plaza   (Sun.) 117,981
PO Box 419000 (32941-
9000)
Phone: (407)242-3500

Miami
Diario las Americas **(6348)** ....(Mon.-Fri.) ‡65,670
2900 NW 39th St.   (Sun.) ‡69,580
(33142)
Phone: (305)633-3341

Naples
Naples Daily News **(6445)** ....(Mon.-Sat.) 64,321
1075 Central Ave.   (Sun.) 77,198
(34102)
Phone: (239)262-3161

New Smyrna Beach
The Observer **(6458)** ....(Paid) 5,992
823 S. Dixie Hwy.
PO Box 10 (32170)
Phone: (386)427-1000

Ocala
Ocala Star-Banner **(6472)** ....(Mon.-Sat.) 51,358
2121 SW 19th Ave.   (Sun.) 55,234
PO Box 490 (34478)
Phone: (352)867-4010

Orlando
The Orlando Sentinel **(6503)** ....(Mon.-Sat.) ★247,674
633 N Orange Ave.   (Sun.) ★366,028
(32801-1300)
Phone: (407)420-5000

Palatka
Palatka Daily News **(6537)** ....(Mon.-Fri.) 11,372
1825 St. Johns Ave.
PO Box 777 (32178)

Palm Beach
Palm Beach Daily News **(6542)** ....(Paid) ‡5,458
265 Royal Poinciana   (Free) ‡2,101
Way (33480-4007)
Phone: (561)820-3800

Panama City
News Herald **(6556)** ....(Mon.-Sat.) 32,593
501 W. 11th St. (32402)   (Sun.) 37,399
Phone: (904)763-7621

Pensacola
Pensacola News Journal **(6568)** ......(Mon.-Fri.) ★63,342
1 News-Journal Plaza   (Sat.) ★63,291
(32501-5670)   (Sun.) ★81,220
Phone: (904)435-8500

Port Charlotte
The Charlotte Sun Herald **(6596)** ...(Mon.-Sat.) 30,359
23170 Harborview Rd.   (Sun.) 33,225
(33980)

St. Augustine
The St. Augustine Record **(6617)** ....(Mon.-Fri.) ★14,395
PO Box 1630 (32085-   (Sat.) ★15,171
1630)   (Sun.) ★16,377
Phone: (904)829-6562

St. Petersburg
St. Petersburg Times **(6633)** ....(Mon.-Sat.) ★314,337
490 1st Ave. S.   (Sun.) ★396,638
PO Box 1121 (33701)
Phone: (727)893-8111

Sanford
Sanford Herald **(6647)** ....(Paid) ‡9,500
300 N. French Ave.
(32771)
Phone: (407)322-2611

Sarasota
Sarasota Herald-Tribune **(6663)** ......(Mon.-Sat.) 94,912
801 S. Tamiami Trail   (Sun.) 118,785
(34236)
Phone: (941)953-7755

Stuart
The Stuart News **(6695)** ....(Mon.-Sat.) ★91,327
PO Box 9009 (34995-   (Sun.) ★103,253
9009)
Phone: (561)287-1550

Circulation: ★ = ABC; △ = BPA; ♦ = CAC; * = CCAB; ❑ = VAC; ⊕ = PO Statement; ‡ = Publisher's Report; Boldface figures = sworn; Light figures = estimated.

2855

Circ.

Circ.

Circ.

FLORIDA (continued)

Tampa
The Tampa Tribune **(6780)** ....(Mon.-Sat.) 211,055
202 S. Parker St.   (Sun.) 300,738
(33606)
Phone: (813)259-8010

Vero Beach
Press-Journal **(6836)** ....(Mon.-Sat.) 35,848
PO Box 1268 (32961)   (Sun.) 39,046
Phone: (561)562-2315

The Villages
The Villages Daily Sun **(6840)** ....(Paid) 15,236
1100 Main St. (32159)
Phone: (352)753-1119

West Palm Beach
The Palm Beach Post **(6848)** ....(Mon.-Sat.) 187,943
2751 S Dixie Hwy.   (Sun.) 238,334
(33405)
Phone: (561)820-4401

Winter Haven
Lake Wales Highlander **(6868)** ....(Paid) 2,798
PO Box 1440 (33882-
1440)
Phone: (863)294-1100

Winter Haven News Chief **(6873)** .....(Combined) 11,026
PO Box 1440 (33882)

GEORGIA
Albany
The Albany Herald **(6903)** ....(Mon.-Sat.) ★26,886
PO Box 48 (31702)   (Sun.) ★29,223

Americus
Americus Times-Recorder **(6920)** ....(Combined) 7,000
PO Box 1247 (31709)
Phone: (229)924-2751

Athens
Athens Banner Herald **(6928)** ......(Mon.-Thurs.) ★26,363
One Press Pl. (30601)   (Fri.) ★29,910
Phone: (706)549-0123   (Sun.) ★32,364
                                         (Sat.) ★28,263

Atlanta
The Atlanta Journal and
Constitution **(6972)** ....(Mon.-Thurs.) ★371,161
72 Marietta St. NW   (Fri.) ★424,521
PO Box 4689 (30303)   (Sat.) ★460,672
Phone: (404)577-5772   (Sun.) ★620,782

Augusta
The Augusta Chronicle **(7096)** ....(Mon.-Thurs.) 72,726
News Bldg.   (Fri.) 88,199
725 Broad St.   (Sat.) 85,652
PO Box 1928 (30903)   (Sun.) 97,488
Phone: (706)724-0851

Brainerd Daily Dispatch **(7098)** ...(Mon.-Fri.) 13,049
PO Box 936 (30903)   (Sun.) 16,990
Phone: (706)724-0851

Brunswick
The Brunswick News **(7139)** ....‡16,284
3011 Altama Ave.
PO Box 1557 (31521)
Phone: (912)265-8320

Carrollton
The Times-Georgian **(7157)** ....(Tues.-Fri.) ★9,324
PO Box 460 (30117-   (Sun.) ★9,504
0460)
Phone: (404)834-6631

Conyers
Rockdale Citizen **(7201)** ....(Paid) 10,232
969 Main St.   (Non-paid) 1,093
PO Box 136 (30012)
Phone: (770)483-7108

Cordele
Cordele Dispatch **(7203)** ....‡6,000
306 13th Ave. W.
PO Box 1058 (31015-
1058)
Phone: (912)273-2277

Dalton
The Daily Citizen-News **(7222)** ....(Mon.-Fri.) 14,443
308 S. Thornton   (Wed.) 13,714
PO Box 1167 (30720-   (Sun.) 12,691
8268)
Phone: (404)278-1011

Douglasville
Douglas County Sentinel **(7249)** ....(Tues.-Fri.) 6,138
6405 Fairbyrn Rd.   (Sat.) 6,138
PO Box 1586 (30134-   (Sun.) 5,465
6911)

Dublin
The Courier Herald **(7251)** ....(Mon.-Sat.) 11,056
PO Drawer B, Ct. Sq.
Sta. (31040-2449)
Phone: (912)272-5522

Gainesville
The Times **(7298)** ....(Mon.-Sat.) 21,153
PO Box 838 (30503)   (Sun.) 25,200
Phone: (770)532-1234

Griffin
Griffin Daily News **(7311)** ....(Mon.-Fri.) 10,090
323 E Solomon St.   (Sun.) 9,980
PO Box M (30224)
Phone: (770)227-3276

Jonesboro
Clayton News/Daily **(7351)** ....(Wed.) 21,625
138 Church St. (30236)

Milledgeville
The Union-Recorder **(7436)** 8,500
1 U-Recorder Plz.
PO Box 520 (31061)
Phone: (912)453-1450

Moultrie
Moultrie Observer **(7446)** 7,306
PO Box 889 (31776-
0889)
Phone: (229)985-4545

Rome
Rome News-Tribune **(7503)** ....(Mon.-Fri.) 16,118
PO Box 1633 (30162-   (Sun.) 19,472
1633)
Phone: (706)291-6397

Savannah
Savannah Morning News **(7536)** ....(Mon.-Sat.) 62,715
PO Box 1088 (31402-   (Sun.) 75,960
1088)
Phone: (912)236-0271

Statesboro
Statesboro Herald **(7564)** 8,000
1 Herald Sq.
PO Box 888 (30458)
Phone: (912)764-9031

Thomasville
Times-Enterprise **(7587)** ....(Tues.-Fri.) ★9,590
PO Box 650 (31792)   (Sun.) ★9,459
Phone: (912)226-2400

Tifton
The Tifton Gazette **(7599)** 9,880
211 N. Tift Ave.
PO Box 708 (31794)
Phone: (229)382-4321

Valdosta
The Valdosta Daily Times **(7616)** ....(Mon.-Sat.) ★18,496
PO Box 968 (31603)   (Sun.) ★20,585
Phone: (912)244-1880

Waycross
Waycross Journal Herald **(7644)** ....(Paid) ‡12,000
400 Isabella St.
PO Box 219 (31502)
Phone: (912)283-2244

HAWAII
Honolulu
The Honolulu Advertiser **(7700)** ....(Mon.-Sat.) 101,948
News Bldg.   (Sun.) 185,596
605 Kapiolani Blvd.
PO Box 3110 (96802)
Phone: (808)525-8090

Honolulu Star-Bulletin **(7702)** ....(Mon.-Sun.) 66,000
500 Ala Moana Blvd., 7-
210 (96813)
Phone: (808)529-4747

Kailua Kona
West Hawaii Today **(7766)** ....(Mon.-Thurs.) 10,810
PO Box 789 (96745-   (Fri.) 12,450
0789)   (Sun.) 14,636
Phone: (808)329-9311

Lihue
The Garden Island **(7779)** ....(Mon.-Sat.) ★8,047
3137 Kuhio Hwy.   (Sun.) ★8,998
PO Box 231 (96766)
Phone: (808)245-3681

Wailuku
Maui News **(7795)** ....(Mon.-Thurs.) 17,090
100 Mahalani St. (96793)   (Fri.) 19,286
                                         (Sun.) 24,035

IDAHO
Blackfoot
The Morning News **(7800)** ....‡5,000
34 N. Ash
PO Box 70 (83221)
Phone: (208)785-1100

Boise
The Idaho Statesman **(7811)** ....(Mon.-Sat.) ‡64,526
1200 N. Curtis Rd.   (Sun.) ‡87,188
PO Box 40 (83707)
Phone: (208)377-6200

Burley
South Idaho Press **(7839)** ....(Mon.-Fri.) 4,463
230 E Main St. (83318)   (Sun.) 4,677
Phone: (208)678-2201

Coeur d'Alene
Coeur d'Alene Press **(7844)** ....(Mon.-Sat.) ‡14,500
201 N. 2nd St. (83814)   (Sun.) ‡28,200
Phone: (208)664-8176

Idaho Falls
The Post-Register **(7868)** ....(Mon.-Sat.) 23,746
333 Northgate Mile   (Sun.) 25,386
PO BOX 1800 (83401)
Phone: (208)522-1800

Lewiston
Lewiston Morning Tribune **(7891)** ....(Mon.-Sun.) ‡26,330
PO Box 957 (83501)   (Sun.) ‡27,608
Phone: (208)743-9411

Moscow
Daily News **(7912)** ....‡9,800
409 S. Jackson St.
(83843)
Phone: (208)882-5561

Nampa
Idaho Press Tribune **(7930)** ....(Mon.-Sat.) 20,488
1618 N Midland Blvd.   (Sun.) 20,653
PO Box 9399 (83652)
Phone: (208)467-9251

Post Falls
Post Falls Press **(7958)** ....(Combined) 4,000
PO Box 39 (83877)
Phone: (208)773-7502

Sandpoint
The Daily Bee **(7978)**
310 Church St.
PO Box 159 (83864)
Phone: (208)263-9534

Twin Falls
Times-News **(7988)** ....(Mon.-Sat.) ★22,656
132 3rd St. W.   (Sun.) ★23,103
Box 548 (83303)
Phone: (208)733-0931

ILLINOIS
Alton
The Telegraph **(8009)** ....(Mon.-Sat.) 27,134
111 E. Broadway   (Sun.) 29,010
PO Box 278 (62002-
0278)
Phone: (618)463-2563

Arlington Heights
Daily Herald **(8022)** ....(Mon.-Sat.) 145,902
PO Box 280 (60006)   (Sun.) 144,218
Phone: (847)427-4300

Aurora
The Beacon-News **(8040)** ....(Mon.-Sat.) ★28,394
101 S River St. (60506)   (Sun.) ★30,972
Phone: (630)844-5844

Belleville
Belleville News-Democrat **(8060)** .....(Mon.-Sat.) ★53,878
120 S. Illinois St.   (Sun.) ★64,241
PO Box 427 (62222-
0427)
Phone: (618)234-1000

Belvidere
Belvidere Daily Republican **(8062)**
401 Whitney Blvd.
(61008)
Phone: (815)547-0084

Benton
News **(8072)**
111 E Church (62812-
2238)
Phone: (618)438-5611

Bloomington
The Pantagraph **(8079)** ....(Mon.-Sat.) 47,919
301 W. Washington St.   (Sun.) 52,247
PO Box 2907 (61702-
2907)
Phone: (309)829-9000

Canton
The Daily Ledger **(8110)** ....‡7,183
53 W. Elm St.
PO Box 540 (61520)
Phone: (309)647-5100

Carbondale
Southern Illinoisan **(8121)** ....(Mon.-Sat.) ★28,267
710 N Illinois (62901)   (Sun.) ★36,381
Phone: (618)529-5454

Carmi
Carmi Times **(8131)** 3,350
323-325 E. Main St.
PO Box 190 (62821)
Phone: (618)382-4176

Centralia
Centralia Sentinel **(8174)** ....(Paid) ♦14,313
232 E. Broadway   (Non-paid) ♦348
PO Box 627 (62801)
Phone: (618)532-5604

Morning Sentinel **(8175)** ....(Combined) 15,319
232 E. Broadway
PO Box 627 (62801)
Phone: (618)532-5604

2856

Numbers cited after listings are entry numbers rather than page numbers.

Newspapers

Champaign
The News-Gazette **(8205)** ....(Mon.-Fri.) 43,149
15 Main St. (Sat.) 45,625
PO Box 677 (61820) (Sun.) 49,180
Phone: (217)351-5252

Charleston
Times-Courier **(8236)** ....(Mon.-Sat.) 7,029
2110 Woodfall Dr., No.
10 (61920-3058)
Phone: (217)345-7085

Chicago
Chicago Sun-Times **(8326)** ....(Mon.-Fri.) ★479,584
401 N. Wabash Ave. (Sat.) ★313,692
(60611-3593) (Sun.) ★371,257
Phone: (312)321-3000

Chicago Tribune **(8327)** ....(Sat.) 558,466
435 N. Michigan Ave. (Sun.) 1,001,662
(60611-4041) (Paid) ★1,012,240
Phone: (312)222-4150 (Sat.) ★573,328

El Manana News **(8362)** ....(Combined) ‡140
6140 W Deamak Rd.
(60804)
Phone: (708)652-5841

Polish Daily News **(8536)** ....(Paid) ‡10,847
5711 N. Milwaukee (Free) ‡203
(60646)
Phone: (773)763-3343

The Wall Street Journal (Midwest
Edition) **(8602)** ....(Mon.-Fri.) 492,514
1 S. Wacker Dr., Ste.
2100 (60606)
Phone: (312)750-4000

Clinton
Clinton Daily Journal **(8682)** ....(Paid) ‡3,500
PO Box 615 (Non-paid) ‡250
Rte. 54 W. (61727)
Phone: (217)935-3171

Crystal Lake
Northwest Herald **(8695)** ....(Mon.-Sat.) ★35,649
7717 South Rt. 31 (Sun.) ★37,817
(60014)

Danville
Commercial-News **(8701)** .....,.......(Mon.-Sat.) 17,733
17 W. North St. (61833) (Sun.) 19,629
Phone: (217)446-1000

Decatur
Herald & Review **(8711)** ....(Mon.-Fri.) 33,688
601 E. William St. (Sat.) 40,277
(62525) (Sun.) 41,052
Phone: (217)429-5151

DeKalb
The Daily Chronicle **(8734)** ....(Mon.-Fri.) 10,616
1586 Barber Green Rd. (Sun.) 11,365
PO Box 587 (60115)
Phone: (815)756-4841

Dixon
The Telegraph **(8776)** ....(Mon.-Sat.) ★9,250
113-115 S Peoria Ave.
(61021)
Phone: (815)284-2222

Edwardsville
Edwardsville Intelligencer **(8812)** ....(Mon.-Sat.) ★5,515
117 N 2nd St.
PO Box 70 (62025-1938)
Phone: (618)656-4700

Effingham
Effingham Daily News **(8816)** ....(Mon.-Sat.) ★13,205
201 N Banker St.
PO Box 370 (62401-
2304)
Phone: (217)347-7151

Elgin
The Courier News **(8823)** ....(Mon.-Sat.) 16,121
300 Lake St. (60120) (Sun.) 17,331
Phone: (708)888-7800

Flora
Daily Clay County Advocate-Press **(8890)** ....(Paid) 3,750
105 W. North Ave. (Free) 50
PO Box 519 (62839-
1613)
Phone: (618)662-2108

Freeport
Freeport Journal-Standard **(8898)** ....(Mon.-Sat.) ★13,693
27 S State Ave. (Sun.) ★14,003
PO Box 330 (61032)
Phone: (815)232-1171

Galesburg
The Register-Mail **(8906)** ....(Mon.-Sat.) 15,573
140 S Prairie St. (Sun.) 14,734
PO Box 310 (61402-
0310)
Phone: (309)343-7181

Geneva
Kane County Chronicle **(8918)** ....(Mon.-Sat.) 14,440
1000 Randall Rd.
(60134)
Phone: (630)232-9222

Harrisburg
The Daily Register **(8972)** ....(Combined) 5,201
35 S. Vine St. (62946-
1725)
Phone: (618)253-7146

Joliet
Herald-News **(9034)** ....(Mon.-Sat.) 37,723
300 Caterpillar Dr. (Sun.) 41,286
(60436)
Phone: (815)729-6161

The Joliet Herald News **(9035)** ....(Mon.-Sat.) 37,462
300 Caterpillar Dr. (Sun.) 42,902
(60436)
Phone: (815)729-6161

Kankakee
The Daily Journal **(9039)** ....(Mon.-Fri.) 29,038
8 Dearborn Sq. (60901) (Sun.) 33,331
Phone: (815)937-3300

Kewanee
Star-Courier **(9045)** ....(Mon.-Sat.) 5,872
105 E. Central Blvd.
(61443-0836)
Phone: (309)852-2181

La Salle
News-Tribune **(9056)** ....(Mon.-Sat.) 18,953
426 2nd St. (61301)
Phone: (815)223-3200

Lawrenceville
Daily Record **(9068)** ....(Paid) 4,005
1209 State St.
PO Box 559 (62439)
Phone: (618)943-2331

Lincoln
Courier **(9082)** ....(Mon.-Sat.) 6,940
601 Pulaski St. (62656-
2825)
Phone: (217)732-2101

Litchfield
Litchfield News-Herald **(9113)** ....‡5,800
112 E Ryder St.
PO Box 160 (62056)
Phone: (217)324-2121

Macomb
Macomb Journal **(9130)** 7,800
203 N. Randolph (61455) (Sun.) 8,500
Phone: (309)833-2114

Marion
Harrison Daily Times **(9142)** ....(Paid) 11,011
606 N. Van Buren (Controlled) 127
(62959)
Phone: (618)993-1711

Marion Daily Republican **(9143)** ....(Paid) 3,958
502 W Jackson St.
PO Box 490 (62959)
Phone: (618)993-2626

Mattoon
Journal-Gazette **(9159)** ....(Mon.-Sat.) 11,386
100 Broadway (61938)
Phone: (217)235-5656

McHenry
Northwest Herald **(9166)**
1111 N Green St., No.
200 (60050)
Phone: (815)385-0170

Moline
The Dispatch and the Rock Island
Argus **(9204)** ....(Mon.-Sat.) ‡41,203
1720 5th Ave. (61265) (Sun.) 34,144
Phone: (309)764-4344

Monmouth
The Daily American **(9214)** ....(Combined) 3,297
PO Box 650 (61462)
Phone: (309)734-3176

Daily Journal **(9215)** ....(Combined) 1,159
PO Box 650 (61462)
Phone: (309)734-3176

Daily Review Atlas **(9216)** ....‡4,000
400 S. Main St. (61462)
Phone: (309)734-3176

Morris
Morris Daily Herald **(9225)** ....‡7,800
1804 N Division St.
(60450)
Phone: (815)942-3221

Mount Carmel
Daily Republican Register **(9231)** ....(Paid) ⊕4,094
115 E 4th St. (Free) ⊕63
PO Box 550 (62863-
0550)
Phone: (618)262-5144

Mount Vernon
Register-News **(9253)** ....(Mon.) 11,821
118 N 9th St. (Tues.-Fri.) 10,688
PO Box 489 (62864) (Sat.) 10,688
Phone: (618)242-0113

Olney
Olney Daily Mail **(9384)**
206 Whittle Ave.
PO Box 340 (62450)
Phone: (618)393-2931

Ottawa
The Daily Times **(9390)** ....(Mon.-Sat.) 12,654
110 W. Jefferson (61350)
Phone: (815)433-2000

Paris
Beacon-News **(9399)** ....(Mon.-Sat.) 28,389
PO Box 100 (61944) (Sun.) 31,710
Phone: (217)465-6424

Paxton
Paxton Daily Record **(9411)** ....‡1,229
218 N. Market
PO Box 73 (60957)
Phone: (217)379-2356

Pekin
Pekin Daily Times **(9414)** ....(Mon.-Sat.) 12,610
20 S. 4th St.
PO Box 430 (61554)
Phone: (309)346-1111

Peoria
Journal Star **(9419)** ....(Mon.-Fri.) ★68,439
1 News Plaza (61643) (Sat.) ★79,938
Phone: (309)686-3000 (Sun.) ★89,705

Pontiac
Daily Leader **(9464)** ....‡6,800
318 N. Main St.
PO Box 170 (61764)
Phone: (815)842-1153

Quincy
The Quincy Herald Whig **(9474)** .....(Mon.-Sat.) ★22,956
130 S 5th St. (Sun.) ★27,543
PO Box 909 (62306-
0909)
Phone: (217)223-5100

Robinson
Robinson Daily News **(9512)** ....(Paid) ⊕6,825
302 S Cross St.
PO Box 639 (62454)
Phone: (618)544-2101

Rock Island
Rock Island Argus **(9519)** ....(Mon.-Sat.) ★29,631
1724 4th Ave. (61201- (Sun.) ★34,469
8713)
Phone: (309)786-6441

Rockford
Rockford Register Star **(9532)** ....(Mon.-Sat.) ★68,015
99 E. State St. (61104) (Sun.) ★80,692
Phone: (815)987-1200

Shelbyville
Union **(9599)**
100 W Main St.
PO Box 347 (62565)
Phone: (217)774-2161

Springfield
State Journal-Register **(9642)** ....(Mon.-Sat.) ★57,384
1 Copley Plz. (Sun.) ★66,708
PO Box 219 (62701-
1927)
Phone: (217)788-1300

Sterling
The Daily Gazette **(9663)** 14,639
PO Box 498 (61081)
Phone: (815)625-3600

Streator
Times-Press **(9669)** ....(Mon.-Sat.) 8,387
115 Oak St. (61364-
2805)
Phone: (815)673-3771

Taylorville
Breeze-Courier **(9678)** ....(Mon.-Fri.) 6,382
212 S Main St. (Sun.) 6,456
PO Box 440 (62568)
Phone: (217)824-2233

Tinley Park
Daily Southtown **(9685)** ....(Mon.-Fri.) 52,567
6901 W 159th St. (Sat.) 41,841
(60477-1604) (Sun.) 58,678
Phone: (708)633-6880

Watseka
Iroquois County's Times-Republic **(9739)** 2,700
1492 E. Walnut St.
PO Box 250 (60970)
Phone: (815)432-5227

Circulation: ★ = ABC; △ = BPA; ♦ = CAC; ◆ = CCAB; □ = VAC; ⊕ = PO Statement; ‡ = Publisher's Report; Boldface figures = sworn; Light figures = estimated.

Circ.

Circ.

Circ.

ILLINOIS (continued)

West Frankfort
West Frankfort Daily American **(9749)**
PO Box 617 (62896)
Phone: (618)937-2146

INDIANA

Anderson
Anderson Herald-Bulletin **(9783)** ......(Mon.-Sat.) ★**25,401**
1133 Jackson St. (Sun.) ★**27,204**
(46016-1466)
Phone: (317)643-5371

Auburn
The Evening Star **(9789)** ....‡7,391
118 W. 9th St.
PO Box 431 (46706-
2225)

Bedford
The Times-Mail **(9798)** ....(Mon.-Sat.) 13,681
813 16th St.
PO Box 849 (47421)
Phone: (812)275-3355

Bloomfield
The Evening World **(9821)** ....(Paid) 3,000
31 W Main St. (Free) 125
PO Box 311 (47424)
Phone: (812)384-3501

Bloomington
Herald-Times **(9827)** ....(Mon.-Sat.) ★**27,272**
1900 S Walnut St. (Sun.) ★**44,496**
PO Box 909 (47402)
Phone: (812)332-4401

Brazil
The Brazil Times **(9869)** ....(Paid) ‡5,242
100 N Meridian St.
PO Box 429 (47834)
Phone: (812)446-2216

Chesterton
Chesterton Tribune **(9886)** ....⊕**5,000**
193 S Calumet Rd.
PO Box 919 (46304)
Phone: (219)926-1131

Clinton
The Daily Clintonian **(9891)** ....(Paid) ⊕**5,385**
422 S. Main St. (47842) (Free) ⊕24
Phone: (765)832-2443

Columbia City
The Post & Mail **(9893)** ....‡4,867
PO Box 128 (46725)
Phone: (260)248-5112

Columbus
The Republic **(9895)** ....(Mon.-Sat.) ♦**21,291**
333 2nd St. (47201- (Sun.) ♦**23,830**
6795)
Phone: (812)372-7811

Connersville
Connersville News-Examiner **(9900)** ....(Paid) 8,362
406 Central Ave.
PO Box 287 (47331-
0287)
Phone: (765)825-0585

Crawfordsville
Journal Review **(9909)** ....(Mon.-Sat.) 10,084
119 N. Green St.
PO Box 512 (47933)
Phone: (317)362-1200

Decatur
Decatur Daily Democrat **(9922)** ....‡5,939
141 S 2nd St.
PO Box 1001 (46733)
Phone: (260)724-2121

Elkhart
The Truth **(9924)** ....(Mon.-Sat.) 27,761
421 S. 2nd St. (Sun.) 31,438
Box 487 (46516-3227)
Phone: (219)294-1661

Elwood
The Call-Leader **(9932)** ....(Paid) ‡3,400
317 S. Anderson St.
PO Box 85 (46036-2018)
Phone: (765)552-3355

Fort Wayne
Fort Wayne Journal-Gazette **(9968)**
600 W. Main St. (46802-
1498)
Phone: (260)461-8853

The Journal Gazette **(9971)** ....(Mon.-Sat.) 57,995
600 W Main St. (Sun.) 130,347
PO Box 88 (46801-0088)
Phone: (260)461-8444

Frankfort
Times **(9999)** ....(Paid) 7,000
251 E. Clinton St., No. 9
(46041-1906)
Phone: (765)659-4622

Franklin
Daily Journal **(10005)** ....(Mon.-Fri.) ♦**18,356**
2575 N. Morton St. (Sat.) ♦**19,267**
(46131)
Phone: (317)736-7101

The Republic **(10008)** ....(Combined) 21,912
2575 N. Morton St.
(46131)
Phone: (317)736-7101

Goshen
The Goshen News **(10024)** ....(Mon.-Sat.) ★**16,517**
PO Box 569 (46526- (Sun.) ★**16,246**
0569)
Phone: (219)533-2151

Greencastle
Banner-Graphic **(10033)** 6,181
100 N Jackson St.
(46135-1240)
Phone: (317)653-5151

Greenfield
Daily Reporter **(10040)** ....(Paid) 11,400
22 W. New Rd. (Non-paid) 87
PO Box 279 (46140)
Phone: (317)462-5528

Greensburg
The Greensburg Daily News **(10043)** ....‡6,750
135 S Franklin St.
PO Box 106 (47240)
Phone: (812)663-3111

Hammond
The Times **(10053)** ....(Mon.-Sat.) 85,506
601 W 45th Ave. (Sun.) 93,201
(46321)
Phone: (219)933-3200

Hartford City
Hartford City News Times **(10060)** ....‡2,800
123 S. Jefferson St.
(47348)
Phone: (317)348-0110

Huntington
Herald-Press **(10069)** ....(Mon.-Fri.) ‡7,200
7 N. Jefferson St. (Sun.) ‡8,300
(46750-2839)
Phone: (260)356-6700

Indianapolis
The Indianapolis Star **(10133)** ....(Mon.-Sat.) 251,601
307 N. Pennsylvania St. (Sun.) 365,546
(46204)
Phone: (317)444-4000

Jasper
The Herald **(10219)** ....(Paid) ‡12,865
216 E. 4th
PO Box 31 (47547)
Phone: (812)482-2424

Jeffersonville
The Evening News **(10225)** ....(Paid) 10,500
221 Spring St.
PO Box 867 (47131-
0867)
Phone: (812)283-6636

Kendallville
News-Sun **(10228)** ....(Mon.-Sat.) 9,953
102 N. Main St.
PO Box 39 (46755)
Phone: (219)347-0400

Kokomo
Kokomo Tribune **(10241)** ....(Mon.-Sat.) ★**22,049**
300 N. Union St. (46901) (Sun.) ★**24,753**
Phone: (317)459-3121

La Porte
La Porte Herald-Argus **(10246)** ....(Mon.-Sat.) ★**12,133**
701 State St. (46350)
Phone: (219)362-2161

LaPorte Herald-Argus **(10247)** ....(Paid) ★**11,949**
701 State. St. (46350)
Phone: (219)362-2161

Lafayette
Journal and Courier **(10251)** ....(Mon.-Sat.) 37,370
217 N 6th St. (47901- (Sun.) 43,641
1448)
Phone: (317)423-5511

Lebanon
The Lebanon Reporter **(10270)** 7,200
117 E. Washington St.
(46052)
Phone: (765)482-5400

Logansport
Pharos-Tribune **(10275)** ....(Mon.-Fri.) 11,588
517 E. Broadway (Sun.) 12,340
PO Box 210 (46947)
Phone: (219)722-5000

Madison
The Madison Courier **(10283)** ....(Paid) 9,596
310 Courier Sq. (47250) (Free) 56
Phone: (812)265-3641

Marion
Chronicle-Tribune **(10287)** ....(Mon.-Sat.) 19,656
PO Box 309 (46952- (Sun.) 21,322
0309)

Martinsville
Reporter-Times **(10294)** ....(Paid) 7,695
dba Reporter-Times
60 S. Jefferson St.
PO Box 1636 (46151)
Phone: (765)342-3311

Merrillville
Post-Tribune **(10299)** ....(Mon.-Sat.) ★**64,862**
1433 E. 83rd Ave. (Sun.) ★**69,877**
(46410-6307)
Phone: (219)648-3000

Michigan City
The News-Dispatch **(10304)** ....(Mon.-Sat.) 12,887
121 W. Michigan Blvd. (Sun.) 13,591
(46360-3274)
Phone: (219)874-7211

Monticello
Monticello Herald Journal **(10320)**
114 S Main St.
PO Box 409 (47960-
2328)
Phone: (574)583-5121

Mount Vernon
Mt. Vernon Democrate **(10323)** ....(Paid) 3,746
502 E 4th St. (Free) 285
PO Box 767 (47620)
Phone: (812)838-4811

Muncie
The Star Press **(10328)** ....(Mon.-Sat.) 33,625
PO Box 2408 (47307- (Sun.) 37,504
0408)
Phone: (765)213-5700

New Albany
The New Albany Tribune **(10339)** ......(Mon.-Fri.) 11,919
303 Scribner St.
PO Box 997 (47150)
Phone: (812)944-6481

New Castle
Courier-Times **(10342)** 12,000
201 S 14th St. (47362-
3328)
Phone: (765)529-1111

Notre Dame
The Observer **(10375)** 12,500
PO Box Q (46556)
Phone: (219)631-7471

Peru
Peru Daily Tribune **(10396)** ....(Paid) 6,975
26 W 3rd St. (Non-paid) 33
PO Box 87 (46970-2155)
Phone: (317)473-6641

Portland
The Commercial Review **(10403)** 5,922
309 W Main
PO Box 1049 (47371)
Phone: (219)726-8141

Princeton
Princeton Daily Clarion **(10409)** ....‡6,623
100 N Gibson
PO Box 30 (47670)
Phone: (812)385-2525

Rensselaer
Rensselaer Republican **(10414)** ....‡3,600
PO Box 298 (47978-
0298)
Phone: (219)866-5111

Richmond
Palladium-Item **(10420)** ....(Mon.-Sat.) ★**19,263**
1175 N A St. (Sun.) ★**22,790**
PO Box 308 (47374-
3226)
Phone: (765)962-1575

Rochester
The Rochester Sentinel **(10431)**
118 E 8th St.
PO Box 260 (46975)
Phone: (574)223-2111

Rushville
Rushville Republican **(10437)** ....‡3,983
PO Box 189 (46173-
0189)
Phone: (765)932-2222

Seymour
Seymour Daily Tribune **(10448)** ....(Mon.-Sat.) 10,235
100 St. Louis Ave.
PO Box 447 (47274)
Phone: (812)522-4871

Shelbyville
The Shelbyville News **(10452)** ....(Mon.-Sat.) 10,409
123 E. Washington St.
PO Box 750 (46176)
Phone: (317)398-6631

Numbers cited after listings are entry numbers rather than page numbers.

South Bend
Hometown News **(10455)**
225 W. Colfax Ave.
(46626)
Phone: (219)235-6161

South Bend Tribune **(10458)** ....(Mon.-Sat.) ‡63,441
225 W. Colfax Ave.   (Sun.) ‡82,748
(46626)
Phone: (574)235-6161

Spencer
World **(10472)** ....(Paid) ‡3,550
114 E. Franklin St.
(47460)
Phone: (812)829-2255

Sullivan
Daily Times **(10474)** ....‡4,700
PO Box 130 (47882)
Phone: (812)268-6356

Terre Haute
Tribune-Star **(10490)** ....(Mon.-Sat.) 30,954
222 S. 7th St.   (Sun.) 38,813
PO Box 149 (47808)
Phone: (812)231-4200

Tipton
Tipton Tribune **(10506)** ....(Paid) ⊕2,761
110 W. Madison   (Free) ⊕128
PO Box 248 (46072)
Phone: (317)675-2115

Vincennes
Vincennes Sun-Commercial **(10522)** ....(Mon.-Fri.) 12,195
PO Box 396 (47591)   (Sun.) 13,887
Phone: (812)886-9955

Wabash
Plain Dealer **(10529)** ....(Paid) 6,204
123 W Canal St.   (Non-paid) 51
Box 379 (46992)
Phone: (219)563-2131

Warsaw
Times-Union **(10537)** ....(Mon.-Sat.) 11,650
PO Box 1448 (46581-
1448)
Phone: (219)267-3111

Washington
Washington Times-Herald **(10540)** ......(Mon.-Sat.) 9,005
102 E. Van Trees St.
PO Box 471 (47501-
4701)
Phone: (812)254-0480

Winchester
The News Gazette **(10566)** ....(Paid) 4,906
PO Box 429 (47394)
Phone: (317)584-4501

IOWA
Ames
The Tribune **(10594)** ....‡9,851
317 5th St. (50010)
Phone: (515)232-2160

Atlantic
Atlantic News-Telegraph **(10610)** ....(Paid) 6,154
410 Walnut St.   (Free) 18,800
PO Box 230 (50022)
Phone: (712)243-2624

Bloomfield
The Bloomfield Democrat **(10622)**
PO Box 10 (52537)

Boone
Boone News-Republican **(10625)** ....‡3,149
Box 100 (50036)
Phone: (515)432-1234

Burlington
Hawk Eye **(10638)** ....(Mon.-Sat.) ★19,342
PO Box 10 (52601)   (Sun.) ★21,127
Phone: (319)754-6824

Carroll
The Times Herald **(10652)** ....(Paid) ‡6,051
508 N. Court St. (51401)   (Free) ‡22,320
Phone: (712)792-3573

Centerville
Iowegian **(10688)** ....(Paid) 3,197
105 N. Main St. (52544)   (Non-paid) 17
Phone: (515)856-6336

Charles City
Charles City Press **(10695)** ....‡2,833
801 Riverside
PO Box 397 (50616-
0397)
Phone: (641)228-3211

Cherokee
Cherokee Daily Times **(10699)** ....(Paid) 3,100
111 S. 2nd St.   (Free) 25
PO Box 281 (51012)
Phone: (712)225-5111

Clinton
Clinton Herald **(10710)** ....(Mon.-Sat.) ★12,254
221 6th Ave. S (52732-
4305)
Phone: (319)242-7101

Council Bluffs
The Daily Nonpareil **(10726)** ....(Mon.-Sat.) 17,012
117 Pearl St. (51503)   (Sun.) 18,704
Phone: (712)328-1811

Creston
Creston News Advertiser **(10732)** ....‡5,590
503 W. Adams St.
PO Box 126 (50801)
Phone: (641)782-2141

Davenport
The Ledger-Independent **(10736)** ....‡8,200
215 Main St. (52801-
1924)
Phone: (563)383-2100

Quad-City Times **(10738)** ....(Mon.-Fri.) ★51,385
500 E. 3rd St.   (Sat.) ★62,672
PO Box 3828 (52801)   (Sun.) ★71,239

Des Moines
The Business Daily **(10772)** ....(Combined) 500
The Depot at Fourth
100 4th St. (50309)
Phone: (515)288-3336

The Des Moines Register **(10781)** ....(Mon.-Sat.) 153,792
PO Box 957 (50304)   (Sun.) 235,211
Phone: (515)284-8000

Dubuque
Telegraph Herald **(10845)** ....(Mon.-Sat.) 28,725
Box 688 (52004-0668)   (Sun.) 34,086
Phone: (563)588-5687

Fairfield
The Fairfield Ledger **(10882)** ....‡4,910
112 E Broadway Ave.
Box 171 (52556-3202)
Phone: (641)472-4129

Fort Dodge
The Messenger **(10903)** ....(Mon.-Sat.) 19,162
PO Box 659 (50501)   (Sun.) 21,483
Phone: (515)573-2141

Fort Madison
Ft. Madison Daily Democrat **(10916)** ....‡7,148
1226 Ave. H (52627-
4544)
Phone: (319)372-6421

Iowa City
Iowa City Press Citizen **(10974)** ......(Mon.-Fri.) ★15,733
1725 N. Dodge St.   (Sat.) ★17,482
(52245)
Phone: (319)337-3181

Keokuk
Daily Gate City **(11013)** ....(Combined) 23,300
c/o Daily Gate City
1016 Main St.
PO Box 430 (52632)
Phone: (319)524-8300

Le Mars
The Daily Sentinel **(11033)** ....‡4,025
PO Box 930 (51031)
Phone: (712)546-7031

Daily Sentinel **(11034)**
41 1st Ave. N.E. (51031)
Phone: (712)546-7031

Marshalltown
Times-Republican **(11066)** ....(Mon.-Sat.) ★10,400
(50158)   (Sun.) ★10,761

Mason City
Globe-Gazette **(11071)** ....(Mon.-Sat.) ★19,005
300 N Washington Ave.   (Sun.) ★23,005
PO Box 271 (50401-
3222)
Phone: (515)421-0500

Mount Pleasant
Mt. Pleasant News **(11094)** ....(Paid) ‡3,050
215 W Monroe St.
PO Box 240 (52641-
0240)
Phone: (319)385-3131

Muscatine
Muscatine Journal **(11103)** ....(Mon.-Sat.) ★7,998
301 E 3rd St. (52761)
Phone: (319)263-2331

Newton
The Newton Daily News **(11115)** 5,500
200 1st Ave. E (50208)
Phone: (641)792-3121

Oelwein
Register **(11123)** 6,067
PO Box 511
25 1st St. SE (50662-
2306)
Phone: (319)283-2144

Oskaloosa
The Oskaloosa Herald **(11134)**
1901 A Ave. W. (52577)
Phone: (515)672-2581

Ottumwa
The Ottumwa Courier **(11140)** ....(Mon.-Sat.) 16,000
213 E. 2nd St. (52501)
Phone: (641)684-4611

Shenandoah
Valley News Today **(11199)** ....‡3,598
702 W. Sheridan Ave.
(51601)

Sioux City
Sioux City Journal **(11213)** ....(Mon.-Sat.) ★41,577
515 Pavonia St. (51102)   (Sun.) ★42,243
Phone: (712)279-5026

Spencer
The Daily Reporter **(11230)** ....‡4,000
310 E. Milwaukee
PO Box 197 (51301)
Phone: (712)262-6610

Vinton
Cedar Valley Times **(11282)** ....‡2,000
108 E. 5th St.
PO Box 468 (52349)
Phone: (319)472-2311

Washington
The Washington Evening Journal **(11286)** ....‡4,117
111 North Marion Ave.
(52353)

Waterloo
Waterloo-Cedar Falls
Courier **(11289)** ....(Mon.-Fri.) 44,948
501 Commercial St.   (Sun.) 51,795
(50701)
Phone: (319)291-1400

Webster City
Daily Freeman-Journal **(11313)** 3,908
7 22nd St.
PO Box 490 (50595)
Phone: (515)832-4350

KANSAS
Abilene
Abilene Reflector Chronicle **(11332)** ....(Paid) 4,088
303 N Broadway   (Free) 175
PO Box 8 (67410)
Phone: (785)263-1000

Arkansas City
Traveler **(11341)** ....‡6,300
200 E 5th Ave.
Box 988 (67005-2606)

Atchison
Atchison Daily Globe **(11345)** ....(Mon.-Fri.) 5,126
1015-25 Main St.   (Sun.) 5,282
PO Box 247 (66002)
Phone: (913)367-0583

Augusta
Augusta Daily Gazette **(11350)** ....‡2,972
204 E 5th St.
PO Box 9 (67010)
Phone: (316)775-2218

Chanute
The Chanute Tribune **(11377)** ....(Paid) 4,644
15 N Evergreen   (Free) 26
PO Box 559 (66720)
Phone: (620)431-4100

Coffeyville
Coffeyville Journal **(11386)** ....(Mon.-Fri.) 6,983
Eight & Elm Sts.   (Sun.) 8,105
PO Box 847 (67337)

Colby
Colby Free Press **(11388)** 3,300
155 W 5th St.
Box 806 (67701-2312)
Phone: (785)462-3963

Columbus
Columbus Daily Advocate **(11395)** ....(Paid) ⊕2,460
215 S Kansas Ave.   (Free) ⊕38
PO Box 231 (66725)
Phone: (316)429-2773

Council Grove
Council Grove Republican **(11404)** ....(Paid) 2,103
208 W Main   (Free) 37
PO Box 237 (66846)
Phone: (620)767-5123

Derby
The Daily Reporter **(11407)** ....(Paid) ‡2,000
PO Box 190 (67037)
Phone: (316)788-2835

Dodge City
Dodge City Daily Globe **(11414)** ....‡9,185
705 2nd (67801)

Circulation: ★ = ABC; △ = BPA; ♦ = CAC; ● = CCAB; ❑ = VAC; ⊕ = PO Statement; ‡ = Publisher's Report; Boldface figures = sworn; Light figures = estimated.

Circ. Circ. Circ.

KANSAS (continued)

El Dorado
El Dorado Times **(11421)** ....‡4,768
PO Box 694 (67042)
Phone: (316)321-1120

Emporia
The Emporia Gazette **(11429)** ....(Mon.-Sat.) ★8,379
517 Merchant St.
(66801)
Phone: (316)342-4800

Fort Scott
The Fort Scott Tribune **(11443)** ....(Paid) ⊕3,406
6 E Wall St. (Free) ⊕153
PO Box 150 (66701)
Phone: (620)223-1460

Garden City
The Garden City
Telegram **(11449)** ....(Mon.-Sat.) ★9,924
PO Box 958 (67846)
Phone: (316)275-8500

Goodland
The Goodland Daily News **(11464)** ....(Paid) 2,297
1205 Main St. (67735- (Free) ‡50
2946)
Phone: (785)899-2338

Great Bend
Great Bend Tribune **(11468)** ....(Mon.-Fri.) 7,048
2012 Forest Ave. (Sun.) 7,362
Box 228 (67530)
Phone: (316)792-1211

Hays
The Hays Daily News **(11480)** ....(Mon.-Fri.) 12,249
507 Main St. (67601) (Sun.) 13,255
Phone: (785)628-1081

Hiawatha
Hiawatha Daily World **(11491)** ....(Paid) ‡2,143
607 Utah (66434) (Free) ‡47
Phone: (785)742-2111

Hutchinson
The Hutchinson News **(11501)** ....(Mon.-Sat.) ★33,169
PO Box 190 (Sun.) ★38,075
300 W. 2nd St (67504-
0190)
Phone: (620)694-5740

Independence
Independence Daily
Reporter **(11509)** ....(Mon.-Fri.) 7,992
320 N 6th St. (Sun.) 8,547
PO Box 869 (67301)
Phone: (316)331-3550

Iola
The Iola Register **(11513)** ....(Paid) 4,200
302 S Washington Ave. (Free) 85
PO Box 767 (66749)
Phone: (316)365-2111

Junction City
Daily Union **(11519)** ....(Mon.-Fri.) 6,455
222 W. 6th St. (66441) (Sun.) 7,099
Phone: (785)762-5000

Kansas City
Kansas City Kansan **(11527)** ....(Mon.-Fri.) ‡11,027
901 N 8th St. (66101) (Sun.) ‡12,100
Phone: (913)371-4300

Lawrence
Journal-World **(11560)** ....(Mon.-Sat.) 19,202
609 New Hampshire St. (Sun.) 20,307
PO Box 888 (66044)
Phone: (785)843-1000

The Lawrence
Journal-World **(11563)** ....(Mon.-Sat.) ★19,122
PO Box 888 (66044) (Sun.) ★19,476
Phone: (785)832-1000

Leavenworth
Leavenworth Times **(11580)** ....(Mon.-Fri.) 6,300
PO Box 144 (66048) (Sun.) 7,294

Liberal
Southwest Daily Times **(11605)** ....(Paid) 6,829
16 S. Kansas Ave. (Non-paid) 328
(67901-3732)

Lyons
Lyons Daily News **(11616)** ....‡2,278
210 W Commercial
PO Box 560 (67554-
2716)
Phone: (316)257-2368

Manhattan
Mercury **(11629)** ....(Mon.-Fri.) ★10,125
PO Box 787 (66502) (Sun.) ★11,450
Phone: (785)776-8805

McPherson
McPherson Sentinel **(11642)** ....(Paid) ‡4,615
301 S Main (67460) (Free) ‡4,214
Phone: (620)241-2422

Newton
Newton Kansan **(11669)** ....(Paid) 7,750
121 W. 6th St.
PO Box 268 (67114)
Phone: (316)283-1500

Norton
Norton Daily Telegram **(11678)** ....(Free) 1,915
215 S. Kansas Ave.
(67654-0320)
Phone: (785)877-3361

Olathe
The Olathe Daily News **(11683)** ....(Mon.-Fri.) 6,477
Box 130 (66051) (Sat.) 6,450
Phone: (913)764-2211

Ottawa
Ottawa Herald **(11689)** ....(Paid) ‡6,098
104 S Cedar (66067) (Non-paid) ‡7,123
Phone: (785)242-4700

Parsons
Parsons Sun **(11744)** 7,189
220 S. 18th
PO Box 836 (67357-
0836)
Phone: (620)421-2000

Pittsburg
Morning Sun **(11754)** ....(Paid) 11,300
PO Drawer H (66762) (Free) 242
Phone: (316)231-2600

Pratt
The Pratt Tribune **(11764)** ....‡2,500
320 S Main (67124)
Phone: (620)672-5511

Russell
Russell Daily News **(11772)**
802 N Maple St.
PO Box 513 (67665-
1937)
Phone: (785)483-2116

Salina
The Salina Journal **(11784)** ....(Mon.-Sat.) 29,501
333 S. 4th St. (Sun.) 31,725
PO Box 740 (67402-
0740)
Phone: (785)823-6363

Topeka
The Topeka
Capital-Journal **(11838)** ....(Mon.-Sat.) 57,474
616 SE Jefferson St. (Sun.) 65,020
(66607)
Phone: (785)295-1111

Wellington
Wellington Daily News **(11866)** ....(Paid) 3,800
113 W Harvey Ave.
PO Box 368 (67152-
3840)
Phone: (620)326-3326

Wichita
Wichita Eagle **(11891)** ....(Mon.-Thurs.) ★87,411
PO Box 820 (67201) (Fri.) ★96,033
Phone: (316)268-6351 (Sat.) ★92,721
(Sun.) ★148,624

Winfield
Winfield Daily Courier **(11910)** ....(Mon.-Sat.) 5,445
201 E. 9th Ave. (67156)
Phone: (620)221-1050

KENTUCKY

Ashland
The Daily Independent **(11917)** ....(Mon.-Sat.) 22,532
22417th St., No. 311 (Sun.) 25,888
(41101-7606)

Bowling Green
Daily News **(11943)** ....(Mon.-Sat.) 21,884
813 College St. (Sun.) 26,449
PO Box 90012 (42102)
Phone: (270)781-1700

Corbin
Times-Tribune **(12020)** 8,500
201 N. Kentucky Ave.
PO Box 516 (40701-
1529)
Phone: (606)528-2464

Covington
The Kentucky Post **(12027)** ....‡47,742
421 Madison Ave.
PO Box 2678 (41011)
Phone: (606)292-2600

Danville
Advocate-Messenger **(12036)** ....(Mon.-Fri.) ★10,690
330 S 4th St. (40422- (Sun.) ★12,432
2033)
Phone: (606)236-2551

Elizabethtown
The Virginian Pilot **(12044)** ....(Mon.-Fri.) 192,924
408 W. Dixie (42701) (Sat.) 218,940
Phone: (502)769-2312 (Sun.) 231,845

Frankfort
State Journal **(12076)** ....(Mon.-Fri.) ★8,944
1216 Wilkinson Blvd. (Sun.) ★10,505
(40601-1200)

Glasgow
Glasgow Daily Times **(12090)** ....(Mon.-Fri.) ★9,332
100 Commerce Dr. (Sun.) ★9,836
(42141)
Phone: (502)678-5171

Harlan
The Harlan Daily Enterprise **(12104)** 6,766
1548 S. U.S. Hwy. 421
PO Box E (40831)
Phone: (606)573-4510

Hopkinsville
Kentucky New Era **(12132)** ....(Mon.-Sat.) ★11,967
1618 E. 9th St.
PO Box 1087 (42240)
Phone: (270)886-4444

Louisville
The Courier-Journal **(12213)** ....(Mon.-Sat.) ★217,396
525 W. Broadway St. (Sun.) ★282,072
(40202-7431)
Phone: (502)582-4011

Madisonville
The Messenger **(12271)** ....(Tues.-Fri.) 9,162
221 S. Main St. (42431) (Sat.) 9,162
Phone: (270)824-3300 (Sun.) 8,905

Mayfield
Mayfield Messenger **(12284)**
201 N 8th St.
Box 709 (42066-1825)
Phone: (270)247-5223

Middlesboro
Daily News **(12293)** ....(Mon.-Fri.) 7,200
PO Box 579 (40965)
Phone: (606)248-1010

Murray
Murray Ledger and Times **(12316)** ....(Paid) ‡7,500
1001 Whitnell Ave. (Free) ‡7,500
Box 1040 (42071)
Phone: (270)753-1916

Owensboro
Messenger-Inquirer **(12327)** ....(Mon.-Sat.) ★29,866
1401 Frederica St. (Sun.) ★32,781
PO Box 1480 (42301)
Phone: (270)926-0123

Paducah
The Paducah Sun **(12339)** ....(Mon.-Sat.) ★25,827
PO Box 2300 (42002- (Sun.) ★28,554
2300)
Phone: (502)443-1771

Somerset
Commonwealth-Journal **(12403)** 8,663
110-112 E. Mount (Sun.) 8,904
Vernon St.
PO Box 859 (42502)
Phone: (606)678-8191

Winchester
The Winchester Sun **(12454)** 7,300
PO Box 4300 (40392)
Phone: (859)744-3123

LOUISIANA

Abbeville
Abbeville Meridional **(12455)** ....(Mon.-Fri.) 5,457
318 N Main St. (Sun.) 5,860
PO Box 400 (70510)
Phone: (337)893-4223

Alexandria
Alexandria Daily Town
Talk **(12456)** ....(Mon.-Sat.) 35,314
1201 3rd St. (Sun.) 41,167
P.O. Box 7558 (71306)
Phone: (318)487-6397

Bastrop
Bastrop Daily Enterprise **(12483)**
119 E. Hickory
PO Box 311 (71221)
Phone: (318)281-2691

Baton Rouge
The Advocate **(12484)** ....(Mon.-Fri.) 96,239
525 Lafayette St. (70802- (Sat.) 109,897
5410) (Sun.) 129,706
Phone: (225)388-0216

Bogalusa
The Bogalusa Daily News **(12533)** ....(Paid) 6,237
525 Ave. V
PO Box 820 (70427-
4413)
Phone: (985)732-2565

Crowley
The Crowley Post-Signal **(12557)** 4,950
602 N Parkerson Ave.
Box 1589 (70526)
Phone: (337)783-3450

2860

Numbers cited after listings are entry numbers rather than page numbers.

Franklin
Franklin Banner-Tribune **(12582)** ....(Paid) 3,280
115 Wilson St.   (Non-paid) 1,720
PO Box 566 (70538-
6150)
Phone: (337)828-3706

Hammond
Hammond Daily Star **(12590)** ....(Mon.-Fri.) 12,172
725 S. Morrison Blvd.   (Sun.) 14,325
(70404)

Houma
The Courier **(12601)** ....(Mon.-Sat.) 19,471
3030 Barrow St.   (Sun.) 21,350
PO Box 2717 (70361)

Jennings
Jennings Daily News **(12606)** ....‡5,600
238 Market St.
PO Box 910 (70546)

Lake Charles
Lake Charles American
Press **(12637)** ....(Mon.-Sat.) ★36,520
PO Box 2893 (70602)   (Sun.) ★40,725
Phone: (318)433-3000

Leesville
Leesville Daily Leader **(12658)** ....(Paid) ‡6,460
206 E Texas   (Free) ‡9,153
PO Box 619 (71446)
Phone: (337)239-3444

Minden
Minden Press-Herald **(12687)** ....(Paid) 4,844
203 Gleason St.   (Free) 275
PO Box 1339 (71055)
Phone: (318)377-1866

Monroe
The News-Star **(12692)** ....(Mon.-Sat.) 37,180
411 N. 4th St., No. 1502   (Sun.) 42,163
(71201)
Phone: (318)322-5161

Morgan City
The Daily Review **(12707)** ....‡6,374
1014 Front St.
PO Box 948 (70381)
Phone: (985)384-8370

New Iberia
Daily Iberian **(12722)** ....(Mon.-Sat.) 15,000
PO Box 9290 (70562-   (Sun.) 16,000
9290)
Phone: (337)365-6773

New Orleans
The Times-Picayune **(12758)** ....(Mon.-Sat.) ★255,994
3800 Howard Ave.   (Sun.) ★285,602
(70125-1429)
Phone: (504)826-3729

Opelousas
Daily World **(12791)** ....(Mon.-Fri.) 12,558
2781 F49 S Service Rd.   (Sun.) 14,000
PO Box 1179 (70571-
1179)
Phone: (337)942-4971

Ruston
Ruston Daily Leader **(12806)** ....(Paid) ‡6,990
212 W Park Ave.,   (Non-paid) ‡7,000
PO Box 520 (71270-
4314)
Phone: (318)255-4353

Shreveport
The Times **(12820)** ....(Mon.-Sat.) 77,323
222 Lake St. (71101)   (Sun.) 95,275
Phone: (318)459-3200

Sulphur
Southwest Daily News **(12852)** ....(Combined) ‡16,000
716 E. Napoleon
PO Box 1999 (70664-
1999)
Phone: (318)527-7075

Thibodaux
Daily Comet **(12858)** ....(Mon.-Fri.) 11,971
705 W 5th Ave.
PO Box 5238 (70302)
Phone: (504)447-4055

MAINE
Augusta
Kennebec Journal **(12892)** ....(Mon.-Sat.) ★15,097
274 Western Ave.   (Sun.) ★14,196
PO Box 1052 (04330-
4976)
Phone: (207)623-3811

Bangor
Bangor Daily News **(12903)** ....(Mon.-Fri.) ★63,797
491 Main St.   (Sun.) ★75,806
PO Box 1329 (04402-
1329)
Phone: (207)990-8000

Biddeford
Journal Tribune **(12922)** ....(Mon.-Fri.) 9,148
PO Box 627 (04005)   (Sat.) 10,827
Phone: (207)282-1535

Brunswick
Brunswick Times
Record **(12935)** ....(Mon.-Thurs.) ★10,845
6 Industry Rd.   (Fri.) ★13,159
PO Box 10 (04011)
Phone: (207)729-3311

Lewiston
Lewiston Sun-Journal **(12976)** ....(Mon.-Sat.) ★34,830
104 Park St. (04240)   (Sun.) ★36,431
Phone: (207)784-5411

Portland
Maine Sunday Telegram **(13012)** ....(Paid) 145,000
PO Box 1460 (04104)
Phone: (207)791-6650

Portland Press Herald **(13017)** .....(Mon.-Sat.) ★76,833
PO Box 1460 (04104)   (Sun.) ★124,060
Phone: (207)791-6650

MARYLAND
Annapolis
The Capital **(13090)** ....(Mon.-Sat.) ★45,538
2000 Capital Dr. (21401)   (Sun.) ★48,730
Phone: (410)268-5000

Baltimore
The Baltimore Sun **(13135)** ....(Mon.) ★253,439
501 N. Calvert St.   (Sun.) ★465,513
(21278-0001)   (Tues.-Fri.) ★300,410
Phone: (410)332-6000

Cumberland
Cumberland Times News **(13474)** .....(Mon.-Sat.) 31,026
19 Baltimore St.   (Sun.) 33,553
PO Box 1662 (21502)
Phone: (301)722-4600

Easton
Star-Democrat & Sunday
Star **(13489)** ....(Mon.-Fri.) 17,042
PO Box 600 (21601)   (Sun.) 18,813
Phone: (410)822-1500

Elkton
Cecil Whig **(13495)** ....(Mon.-Fri.) ♦14,266
601 Bridge St.   (Sun.) ♦15,941
PO Box 429 (21922-
0429)
Phone: (410)398-3311

Frederick
The Frederick-News
Post **(13513)** ....(Combined) ★41,920
200 E. Patrick St.
PO Box 578 (21705-
0578)
Phone: (301)662-1177

Hagerstown
The Daily-Mail **(13563)** ....(Mon.-Fri.) 34,484
PO Box 439 (21741)   (Sat.) 35,208
Phone: (301)733-5131   (Sun.) 39,368

The Morning Herald **(13568)** ....(Mon.-Fri.) 21,348
PO Box 439 (21741)   (Sat.) 35,725
Phone: (301)733-5131   (Sun.) 39,849

Rockville
The Montgomery Journal **(13688)** ......(Mon.-Fri.) 30,184
5706 Frederick Ave.
(20852-1818)
Phone: (301)670-1400

Salisbury
The Daily Times **(13707)** ....(Mon.-Sat.) 27,263
115 E. Carroll St.   (Sun.) 30,894
(21802)
Phone: (410)749-7171

Westminster
Carroll County Times **(13776)** ....(Mon.-Sat.) 22,936
201 Railroad Ave.   (Sun.) 24,047
PO Box 346 (21157-
4823)
Phone: (410)848-4400

MASSACHUSETTS
Athol
Athol Daily News **(13824)** ....‡5,684
225 Exchange St.
(01331)
Phone: (978)249-3535

Attleboro
The Sun Chronicle **(13825)** ....(Mon.-Sat.) ★20,810
34 S Main St. (02703)   (Sun.) ★21,572
Phone: (508)222-7000

Beverly
Salem Evening News **(13842)** ....(Mon.-Sat.) 34,413
32 Dunham Rd. (01915)
Phone: (978)922-1234

Boston
The Boston Globe **(13857)** ....(Mon.-Fri.) ★463,113
135 Morrissey Blvd.   (Sat.) ★448,044
PO Box 2378 (02107-   (Sun.) ★703,053
3310)
Phone: (617)929-2935

Boston Herald **(13858)** ....(Mon.-Fri.) ★242,957
One Herald Sq.   (Sat.) ★192,277
PO Box 2096 (02106-   (Sun.) ★158,786
2096)
Phone: (617)426-3000

The Christian Science
Monitor **(13875)** ....(Mon.-Fri.) 65,277
One Norway St. (02115)
Phone: (617)450-2000

Brockton
The Enterprise **(14012)** ....(Mon.-Fri.) 41,197
60 Main St.   (Sat.) 40,762
PO Box 1450 (02303)   (Sun.) 40,212
Phone: (508)586-6200

Dedham
Daily Transcript **(14154)** ....(Combined) 36,984
254 2nd Ave. (02494)
Phone: (781)433-6700

Fall River
Herald News **(14181)** ....(Mon.-Sat.) 23,854
207 Pocasset St.   (Sun.) 26,211
Box 2410 (02722)
Phone: (508)676-8211

Fitchburg
Sentinel & Enterprise **(14184)** ....(Mon.-Sat.) ★16,761
808 Main St. (01420)   (Sun.) ★17,445
Phone: (978)343-6911

Framingham
The MetroWest Daily News **(14199)**
33 New York Ave.
(01701)

Gardner
The Gardner News **(14209)** ....(Mon.-Sat.) 7,818
309 Central St. (01440)
Phone: (978)632-8000

Gloucester
Times **(14211)** ....(Mon.-Sat.) 11,806
Whittemore St. (01930)
Phone: (508)283-7000

Greenfield
The Recorder **(14222)** ....(Mon.-Sat.) 14,261
14 Hope St.
PO Box 1367 (01302-
1367)
Phone: (413)772-0261

Haverhill
The Haverhill Gazette **(14232)** 7,500
447 W Lowell Ave.
PO Box 991 (01831)
Phone: (978)374-0321

Hyannis
Cape Cod Times **(14250)** ....(Mon.-Sat.) ★53,014
319 Main St. (02601)   (Sun.) ★64,028
Phone: (508)775-1200

Lawrence
The Eagle-Tribune **(14266)** ....(Mon.-Sat.) ★51,940
PO Box 100 (01842)   (Sun.) ★57,731
Phone: (978)946-2000

Lowell
Lowell Sun **(14278)** ....(Mon.-Fri.) ★48,538
15 Kearney Sq. (01853)   (Sat.) ★46,180
                       (Sun.) ★50,382

Lynn
Daily Evening Item **(14284)** ....(Mon.-Fri.) 18,816
38 Exchange St.   (Sat.) 17,652
PO Box 951 (01903)
Phone: (617)593-7700

Malden
Malden Evening News **(14296)** ....‡15,000
277 Commercial St.
(02148)
Phone: (617)321-8000

Marlborough
Hudson Daily Sun **(14306)** ....(Combined) 6,227
40 Mechanic St. (01752-
4425)
Phone: (508)490-7450

Marlborough Enterprise **(14307)** ....(Combined) 36,984
40 Mechanic St. (01752-
4425)

Medford
Daily Mercury **(14320)** ....‡4,995
800 Hingham St.
PO Box 309 (02370)
Phone: (781)878-1111

Needham
Milford Daily News **(14362)** ....(Mon.-Sat.) 12,679
254 2nd Ave. (02494)
Phone: (781)433-6700

New Bedford
The Standard-Times **(14377)** ....(Mon.-Sat.) ★34,873
25 Elm St. (02740)   (Sun.) ★39,044
Phone: (508)997-7411

Circulation: ★ = ABC; △ = BPA; ♦ = CAC; • = CCAB; ❑ = VAC; ⊕ = PO Statement; ‡ = Publisher's Report; Boldface figures = sworn; Light figures = estimated.

2861

Circ.

MASSACHUSETTS (continued)

Newburyport
Newburyport Daily News **(14381)** ....(Mon.-Sat.) ★**14,087**
23 Liberty St. (01950)
Phone: (508)462-6666

North Adams
Transcript **(14418)** ....(Mon.-Fri.) ★**6,874**
Box 473 (01247)   (Sat.) ★**8,040**
Phone: (413)663-3741

Northampton
Daily Hampshire Gazette **(14427)** ......(Mon.-Sat.) 19,851
PO Box 299 (01061)

Pittsfield
The Berkshire Eagle **(14468)** ....(Mon.-Sat.) 31,363
Clocktower Business   (Sun.) 35,146
  Park
75 S. Church St. (01201)
Phone: (413)496-6355

Quincy
The Patriot Ledger **(14491)** ....(Mon.-Fri.) ★**66,578**
PO Box 699159 (02269-   (Sat.) ★**80,091**
  9159)
Phone: (617)786-7000

Reading
Daily Chronicle **(14498)** ....(Paid) ‡**14,215**
PO Box 240 (01867)   (Controlled) 2,092
Phone: (781)944-2200

Salem
Salem News **(14514)** ....(Mon.-Sat.) 34,133
155 Washington St.
  (01970)
Phone: (508)744-0600

Southbridge
The Southbridge Evening News **(14547)** ....(Paid) ‡**5,400**
25 Elm St. (01550)
Phone: (508)764-6102

Springfield
Union-News & Sunday
  Republican **(14552)** ....(Mon.-Sat.) ★**94,699**
1860 Main St. (01101)   (Sun.) ★**133,023**
Phone: (413)788-1000

Taunton
Taunton Daily Gazette **(14584)** ....(Mon.-Sat.) 13,013
5 Cohannet St. (02780-   (Sun.) 12,486
  3903)
Phone: (508)880-9000

Wakefield
Item **(14593)**
26 Albion St. (01880)
Phone: (781)245-0080

Waltham
News Tribune **(14602)** ....(Combined) 36,984
254 2nd Ave. (02494)
Phone: (781)433-6700

Westfield
The Westfield Evening News **(14643)**
62 School St., No. 64
  (01085-2835)
Phone: (413)568-4921

Woburn
Daily Times Chronicle **(14669)** ....(Paid) 10,077
1 Arrow Dr. (01801-   (Non-paid) 354
  3514)
Phone: (781)933-3700

Worcester
Telegram & Gazette **(14690)** ....(Mon.-Sat.) ★**102,978**
20 Franklin St.   (Sun.) ★**122,645**
PO Box 15012 (01615)
Phone: (508)793-9100

MICHIGAN
Adrian
The Daily Telegram **(14708)** ....(Mon.-Sat.) 15,361
133 N. Winter St.   (Sun.) 16,489
PO Box 647 (49221)
Phone: (517)265-5111

Albion
Albion Recorder **(14715)** ....(Paid) 3,100
111 W. Center St.   (Non-paid) 10,000
  (49224-1755)
Phone: (517)629-3984

Alpena
Alpena News **(14735)** ....(Mon.-Sat.) ★**11,261**
130 Park Pl.
PO Box 367 (49707)
Phone: (989)354-3111

Ann Arbor
The Ann Arbor News **(14742)** ....(Mon.-Sat.) ★**52,943**
340 E. Huron St., PO   (Sun.) ★**66,934**
  Box 1147 (48104-
  1147)
Phone: (734)994-6989

Bad Axe
Huron Daily Tribune **(14785)** ....(Mon.-Fri.) ★**7,304**
211 N. Heisterman St.   (Sun.) ★**7,791**
  (48413)
Phone: (989)269-6461

Battle Creek
Battle Creek Enquirer **(14791)** ....(Mon.-Sat.) 25,741
155 W. Van Buren St.   (Sun.) 34,416
  (49017-3093)
Phone: (616)964-0299

Bay City
The Bay City Times **(14802)** ....(Mon.-Sat.) ★**35,565**
311 5th St. (48708)   (Sun.) ★**46,393**
Phone: (989)895-8551

Big Rapids
The Pioneer **(14818)** ....(Paid) 5,859
502 N. State St. (49307)   (Free) 24
Phone: (231)796-4831

Cadillac
Cadillac News **(14842)** ....(Mon.-Fri.) ‡1,0218
130 N. Mitchell St.   (Sat.) ‡11,500
  (49601-1865)   (Free) ‡2,0225
Phone: (231)775-6565

Cheboygan
Daily Tribune **(14872)** ....(Paid) 4,550
308 N Main   (Non-paid) 450
PO Box 290 (49721)
Phone: (231)627-7144

Coldwater
Coldwater Daily Reporter **(14887)** ....‡6,000
15 W. Pearl St. (49036-
  1912)
Phone: (517)278-2318

Detroit
Detroit Free Press **(14924)** ....(Mon.-Fri.) ★**611,230**
600 W. Fort St. (48226)   (Sat.) ★**547,506**
Phone: (313)222-6600   (Sun.) ★**738,709**

The Detroit News **(14927)** ....(Mon.-Fri.) 237,991
615 W. Lafayette Blvd.   (Sat.) 546,342
  (48226-3197)   (Sun.) 738,248
Phone: (313)222-2300

Dowagiac
Dowagiac Daily News **(14977)**
205 Spaulding St.
Box 30 (49047-1474)
Phone: (269)782-2101

East Lansing
The State News **(14993)** ....‡33,000
343 Student Service
  Bldg. (48824)
Phone: (517)355-3447

Escanaba
The Daily Press **(15007)** 11,842
600 Ludington St.
  (49829)
Phone: (906)786-2021

Flint
The Flint Journal **(15033)** ....(Mon.-Sat.) ★**84,437**
200 E. 1st St. (48502-   (Sun.) ★**103,720**
  1925)

Grand Haven
Tribune **(15085)** ....(Mon.-Sat.) 10,135
301 N 3rd St. (49417)
Phone: (616)847-3493

Grand Rapids
The Grand Rapids
  Press **(15096)** ....(Mon.-Sat.) ★**140,135**
155 Michigan St. NW   (Sun.) ★**192,477**
  (49503-2302)
Phone: (616)459-1400

Greenville
The Daily News **(15135)** ....(Paid) 8,649
109 N. Lafayette St.
  (48838-9998)
Phone: (616)754-9301

Hillsdale
Hillsdale Daily News **(15163)** ....(Combined) ⊕7,373
33 McCollum St.
PO Box 287 (49242-
  0287)
Phone: (517)437-7351

Holland
The Holland Sentinel **(15174)** ....(Mon.-Sat.) ★**18,984**
54 W 8th St. (49423)   (Sun.) ★**20,366**
Phone: (616)392-2311

Houghton
The Daily Mining
  Gazette **(15183)** ....(Mon.-Sat.) ★**10,567**
PO Box 368 (49931)
Phone: (906)482-1500

Ionia
Sentinel-Standard **(15206)**
114 N. Depot St.
  (48846)
Phone: (616)527-2100

Iron Mountain
The Daily News **(15208)** ....(Mon.-Sat.) 9,858
215 E. Ludington St.
PO Box 460 (49801-
  2917)
Phone: (906)774-2772

Ironwood
Ironwood Daily Globe **(15213)** ....‡8,585
118 E McLeod Ave.
  (49938)
Phone: (906)932-2211

Jackson
The Jackson Citizen
  Patriot **(15221)** ....(Mon.-Sat.) ★**35,237**
214 S Jackson St.   (Sun.) ★**40,423**
  (49201-2282)
Phone: (517)781-2300

Kalamazoo
Kalamazoo Gazette **(15242)** ....(Mon.-Fri.) ★**55,761**
401 S. Burdick St.   (Sat.) ★**63,375**
  (49007)   (Sun.) ★**74,759**
Phone: (269)345-3511

Lansing
Lansing State Journal **(15277)** ....(Mon.-Sat.) ★**71,727**
120 E. Lenawee (48919)   (Sun.) ★**90,957**

Ludington
Ludington Daily News **(15322)** ....(Mon.-Sat.) ★**8,943**
202 N. Rath St.
PO Box 340 (49431-
  0340)
Phone: (231)845-5181

Manistee
Manistee News Advocate **(15329)** ....‡5,898
75 Maple St.
PO Box 317 (49660)
Phone: (616)723-3592

Marquette
The Mining Journal **(15338)** ....(Mon.-Sat.) ★**15,977**
PO Box 430 (49855)   (Sun.) ★**17,971**
Phone: (906)228-2500

Midland
Midland Daily News **(15355)** ....(Mon.-Sat.) ★**16,615**
PO Box 432 (48640-   (Sun.) ★**18,335**
  5161)
Phone: (517)835-7171

Monroe
The Monroe Evening News/The Monroe Sunday
  News **(15364)** ....(Mon.-Sat.) 22,325
20 W. 1st St. (48161)   (Sun.) 24,891
Phone: (734)242-1100

Mount Clemens
The Macomb Daily **(15372)** ....(Mon.-Sat.) ★**46,523**
100 Macomb Daily Dr.   (Sun.) ★**70,351**
PO Box 707 (48046)   (Thurs.) ★**61,655**
Phone: (810)469-4510

Mount Pleasant
The Morning Sun **(15379)** ....(Mon.-Fri.) ★**11,652**
PO Box 447 (48804-   (Sun.) ★**12,866**
  0447)
Phone: (989)779-6050

Muskegon
The Muskegon Chronicle & The Sunday
  Chronicle **(15388)** ....(Mon.-Sat.) ★**46,505**
981 3rd St.   (Sun.) ★**51,534**
PO Box 59 (49443)
Phone: (616)722-3161

Niles
Niles Daily Star **(15404)**
217 N. 4th St. (49120-
  2301)

Owosso
The Argus-Press **(15428)** ....(Paid) ‡**12,000**
201 E. Exchange St.
PO Box 399 (48867)
Phone: (989)725-5136

Petoskey
Petoskey News-Review **(15436)** ....(Mon.-Fri.) ★**11,322**
  (49770-0528)
Phone: (231)347-5461

Pontiac
Oakland Press **(15450)** ....(Mon.-Sat.) ★**66,645**
48 W. Huron St., No.   (Sun.) ★**83,900**
  436009   (Thurs.) ★**83,180**
PO Box 9 (48342-2101)
Phone: (248)332-8181

Port Huron
Times Herald **(15451)** ....(Mon.-Sat.) 30,987
911 Military St. (48060)   (Sun.) 43,096
Phone: (810)985-7171

Royal Oak
The Daily Tribune **(15480)** ....(Mon.-Fri.) 16,148
210 E. 3rd St. (48067-   (Sun.) 19,342
  2603)
Phone: (248)414-9500

Numbers cited after listings are entry numbers rather than page numbers.

Saginaw
The Saginaw News **(15491)** .... (Mon.-Sat.) ★47,100
203 S. Washington Ave.   (Sun.) ★57,711
(48607)

St. Joseph
The Herald-Palladium **(15512)** .... (Mon.-Sat.) 28,179
3450 Hollywood Rd.   (Sun.) 30,065
PO Box 128 (49085)
Phone: (269)429-2400

Sault Sainte Marie
Evening News **(15526)** 9,213
109 Arlington St. (49783-
1901)
Phone: (906)632-2235

Sault Ste. Marie Evening News **(15527)**
109 Arlington St. (49783)
Phone: (906)632-2235

Sturgis
Sturgis Journal **(15580)** .... ‡7,687
209 John St.
Box 660 (49091-1459)

Three Rivers
Three Rivers Commercial-News **(15592)** ..... (Paid) 4,503
124 N Main St. (49093)   (Free) ‡17,100
Phone: (269)279-7488

Traverse City
Traverse City
Record-Eagle **(15602)** .... (Mon.-Sat.) ★29,341
120 W Front St.   (Sun.) ★40,199
PO Box 632 (49685-
4968)
Phone: (616)946-2000

MINNESOTA
Albert Lea
Tribune **(15706)** .... (Mon.-Fri.) 7,708
808 W Front St., No. 60   (Sun.) 7,940
(56007)
Phone: (507)373-1411

Austin
Austin Daily Herald **(15723)** .... (Mon.-Fri.) 8,500
310 Second St. NE   (Sun.) 8,440
PO Box 578 (55912-
0578)
Phone: (507)433-8851

Bemidji
The Pioneer **(15739)** .... (Mon.-Fri.) 10,270
Box 455 (56619)   (Sun.) 10,838
Phone: (218)751-3740

Brainerd
Dispatch **(15766)** .... (Mon.-Fri.) 13,994
506 James St.   (Sun.) 18,261
PO Box 974 (56401)
Phone: (218)829-4705

Crookston
Crookston Daily Times **(15819)** .... (Paid) 4,195
124 S Broadway   (Free) 250
PO Box 615 (56716)
Phone: (218)281-2730

Fairmont
Sentinel **(15890)** .... (Mon.-Sat.) 8,336
64 Downtown Plaza
PO Box 681 (56031)
Phone: (507)235-3303

Faribault
News **(15894)** .... ‡7,772
PO Box 249 (55021)
Phone: (507)334-1853

Fergus Falls
Fergus Fall Daily Journal **(15897)** .... (Mon.-Sat.) 9,409
914 E Channing Ave.
PO Box 506 (56537)
Phone: (218)736-7511

Hibbing
Hibbing Daily Tribune **(15954)** .... (Sun.) 6,747
2142 1st Ave.   (Mon.-Fri.) 6,048
PO Box 38 (55746-1805)
Phone: (218)262-1011

International Falls
The Daily Journal **(15968)** 4,456
1602 Hwy. 71 (56649-
2161)
Phone: (218)285-7411

Mankato
Free Press **(16026)** .... (Mon.-Sat.) 24,058
PO Box 3287 (56002-
3287)
Phone: (507)625-4451

Marshall
Marshall Independent **(16042)** .... (Mon.-Sat.) 8,174
508 W Main
PO Box 411 (56258)
Phone: (507)537-1551

Minneapolis
Star Tribune **(16134)** .... (Mon.-Sat.) ★342,780
425 Portland Ave.   (Sun.) ★674,343
(55488)
Phone: (612)673-4000

New Ulm
Journal **(16213)** .... (Mon.-Sat.) 9,282
303 N. Minnesota St.   (Sun.) 9,770
Box 487 (56073)
Phone: (507)359-2911

Owatonna
Owatonna People's Press **(16254)** ....(Tues.-Fri.) ★6,859
Box 346   (Sun.) ★7,103
135 W. Pearl St. (55060-
0346)
Phone: (507)451-2840

Red Wing
Republican-Eagle **(16293)** .... (Mon.-Sat.) 7,852
2760 No. Service Dr.
Box 82 (55066)
Phone: (651)388-8235

Rochester
Post-Bulletin **(16311)** .... (Mon.-Fri.) ★43,351
18 1st Ave. SE   (Sat.) ★46,688
PO Box 6118 (55903-
6118)
Phone: (507)285-7600

St. Cloud
St. Cloud Times **(16345)** .... (Mon.-Sat.) ★27,999
3000 N 7th St. (56301)   (Sun.) ★37,410
Phone: (320)255-8700

St. Paul
St. Paul Pioneer Press **(16409)** .... (Mon.-Fri.) 201,583
345 Cedar St. (55101)   (Sat.) 174,117
Phone: (651)222-5011   (Sun.) 255,067

Virginia
Mesabi Daily News **(16485)** .... (Mon.-Sat.) ◆9,766
704 7th Ave. S. (55792)   (Sun.) ◆11,415
Phone: (218)741-5544

Willmar
West Central Tribune **(16518)** .... (Paid) 17,134
PO Box 839 (56201)
Phone: (320)235-1150

Winona
Winona Daily News **(16527)** .... (Mon.-Sat.) ★11,545
601 Franklin St.   (Sun.) ★12,258
PO Box 5147 (55987-
3822)
Phone: (507)453-3510

Worthington
Daily Globe **(16539)** .... (Paid) 12,330
300 11th St.   (Free) 15,200
PO Box 639 (56187)
Phone: (507)376-9711

Worthington Globe **(16540)** .... (Combined) 12,647
PO Box 639 (56187)
Phone: (507)376-9711

MISSISSIPPI
Brookhaven
Daily Leader **(16578)** .... (Mon.-Fri.) 7,485
128 N. Railroad Ave.   (Sun.) 7,492
PO Box 551 (39601)
Phone: (601)833-6961

Clarksdale
The Clarksdale Press
Register **(16588)** .... (Mon.-Sat.) 6,307
123 2nd St.
PO Box 1119 (38614)
Phone: (662)627-2201

Cleveland
Bolivar Commercial **(16590)** .... (Mon.-Fri.) ★6,964
PO Box 1050 821 N.
Chrisman Ave. (38732)
Phone: (601)843-4241

Columbus
The Commercial Dispatch **(16603)** ......(Mon.-Fri.) 13,635
PO Box 511 (39703-   (Sun.) 15,279
0511)
Phone: (601)328-2424

Corinth
The Daily Corinthian **(16615)** ....(Tues.-Fri.) 7,500
1607 S Harper Rd.   (Sat.) 7,500
PO Box 1800 (38834)   (Sun.) 7,610
Phone: (601)287-6111

Greenville
Delta Democrat Times **(16631)** ....(Mon.-Fri.) 12,346
988 N. Broadway   (Sun.) 13,521
PO Box 1618 (38702)
Phone: (601)335-1155

Greenwood
Greenwood Commonwealth **(16644)** .....(Mon.-Fri.) 7,915
329 Hwy. 82 W   (Sun.) 8,259
PO Box 8050 (38930)
Phone: (662)453-5312

Hattiesburg
Hattiesburg American **(16661)** .... (Mon.-Sat.) 22,741
825 N. Main St.   (Sun.) 26,958
PO Box 1111 (39401)
Phone: (601)582-4321

Jackson
The Clarion Ledger **(16695)** .... (Mon.-Sat.) ★95,806
201 S. Congress   (Sun.) ★110,142
PO Box 40 (39205)
Phone: (601)961-7000

Laurel
Laurel Leader Call **(16741)** .... (Mon.-Sat.) ★7,834
PO Box 728 (39441-   (Sun.) ★7,659
0728)
Phone: (601)428-0551

McComb
Enterprise-Journal **(16762)** ....(Mon.-Fri.) ★11,492
PO Box 2009 (39649)   (Sun.) ★12,083
Phone: (601)684-2421

Meridian
Meridian Star **(16769)** .... (Mon.-Sat.) 17,701
814 22nd Ave.   (Sun.) 19,532
Box 1591 (39301)
Phone: (601)693-1551

Natchez
The Natchez Democrat **(16793)** .....(Mon.-Sat.) ❏10,022
PO Box 1447 (39121)   (Sun.) ❏10,082
Phone: (601)442-9101

Oxford
The Oxford Eagle **(16807)** ....(Paid) ‡4,982
PO Box 866 (38655)   (Free) ‡13,000
Phone: (662)234-4331   (Free) 11,000

Pascagoula
Mississippi Press **(16811)** .... (Mon.-Fri.) 20,108
405 Delmas Ave.   (Sun.) 21,038
PO Box 849 (39567)
Phone: (601)762-1111

Picayune
Picayune Item **(16819)** .... ‡13,585
PO Box 580 (39466-
0580)
Phone: (601)798-4766

Starkville
The Starkville Daily News **(16845)** .... ‡6,500
316 University Dr.
PO Drawer 1068 (39759)

Tupelo
Northeast Mississippi Daily
Journal **(16849)** .... (Mon.-Sat.) 36,032
PO Box 909 (38802-   (Sun.) 36,052
0909)
Phone: (601)842-2611

Vicksburg
Vicksburg Evening Post **(16871)** .....(Mon.-Sat.) ★14,070
PO Box 821668 (39182-   (Sun.) ★14,350
1668)

West Point
Daily Times Leader **(16875)**
227 Court St.
PO Box 1176 (39773)
Phone: (662)494-1422

MISSOURI
Blue Springs
Blue Springs Examiner (Daily
Edition) **(16908)** ....(Combined) 4,868
PO Box 1057 (64013)
Phone: (816)229-9161

Boonville
News & Advertiser **(16914)** ....(Paid) 2,973
412 High St. (65233)
Phone: (816)882-5335

Brookfield
The Daily News-Bulletin **(16927)** .... ‡5,100
107 N Main
PO Box 40 (64628)

Camdenton
The Lake Sun Leader **(16937)**
450 N. Highway 5
(65020)
Phone: (573)346-2132

Cape Girardeau
Southeast Missourian **(16945)** .... (Mon.-Fri.) 16,211
301 Broadway   (Sun.) 25,833
PO Box 699 (63701)   (Wed.) 29,984
Phone: (573)335-6611   (Sat.) 15,198

Southeast Missourian Plus **(16946)** ....(Combined) 17,215
301 Broadway
PO Box 699 (63701)
Phone: (573)335-6611

Carrollton
Carrollton Daily Democrat **(16955)** 2,700
Highway 65 S
PO Box 69 (64633)
Phone: (660)542-0881

Circulation: ★ = ABC; △ = BPA; ◆ = CAC; ● = CCAB; ❏ = VAC; ⊕ = PO Statement; ‡ = Publisher's Report; Boldface figures = sworn; Light figures = estimated.

2863

Circ.   Circ.   Circ.

MISSOURI (continued)

Carthage
The Carthage Press **(16959)** ....(Paid) ‡5,600
527 S. Main St.
PO Box 678 (64836)
Phone: (417)358-2191

Chillicothe
Constitution-Tribune **(16977)** 6,240
818 Washington St.
PO Box 707 (64601)

Clinton
The Clinton Daily Democrat **(16983)** ....‡3,989
212 S. Washington
PO Box 586 (64735)
Phone: (816)885-2281

Columbia
Columbia Daily Tribune **(16990)** ......(Mon.-Sat.) ★18,682
101 N. Fourth St.   (Sun.) ★23,739
PO Box 798 (65205-0798)
Phone: (573)815-1500

Columbia Missourian **(16991)** ....(Mon.-Fri.) 6,188
221 S. 8th St.   (Sun.) 5,065
PO Box SM7 (65205)
Phone: (573)882-5700

Dexter
The Daily Statesman **(17032)** ....(Tues.) 9,747
133 S. Walnut   (Sun.) 3,656
PO Box 579 (63841)
Phone: (314)624-4545

Excelsior Springs
The Daily Standard **(17050)** ....‡3,500
417 Thompson Ave.
PO Box 7 (64024)
Phone: (816)637-3147

Fulton
The Fulton Sun **(17076)** ....‡5,200
115 E. 5th St.
PO Box 550 (65251-0541)
Phone: (573)642-7272

Hannibal
Hannibal Courier-Post **(17090)** ....(Mon.-Fri.) ★8,416
PO Box A (63401)   (Sat.) ★8,350
Phone: (573)221-2800

Independence
Blue Springs & Independence Examiner Extra (Daily
Edition) **(17108)** ....(Wed.) 67,000
410 S Liberty St.   (Paid) 15,500
(64050-3805)
Phone: (816)254-8600

The Examiner **(17110)** 10,068
410 S Liberty St.   (Wed.) 35,180
PO Box 459 (64051)
Phone: (816)254-8600

Independence Examiner (Daily
Edition) **(17113)** ....(Free) 146
410 S Liberty St.   (Paid) 10,621
(64050-3805)
Phone: (816)254-8600

Jefferson City
Jefferson City News Tribune **(17122)** .....(Sun.) ★23,959
210 Monroe (65101)   (Mon.-Sat.) ★17,377
Phone: (573)636-3131

Joplin
The Joplin Globe **(17141)** ....(Mon.-Sat.) 30,903
117 E. 4th St.   (Sun.) 39,793
Box 7 (64801)
Phone: (417)623-3480

Kansas City
Blade-Empire **(17157)** ....‡3,500
4800 Main St., Ste. 100
(64112-2513)
Phone: (816)756-1000

The Kansas City Star **(17180)** ......(Mon.-Sat.) ★269,188
1729 Grand Blvd.   (Sun.) ★379,971
(64108-1413)
Phone: (816)234-4141

Kennett
The Daily Dunklin Democrat **(17217)** ....(Wed.) 10,078
203 1st St. (63857)   (Sun.) 3,316
Phone: (314)888-4505   (Tues.-Fri.) 3,224

Kirksville
Kirksville Daily Express and
News **(17227)** ....(Mon.-Fri.) ‡7,600
110 E McPherson   (Sun.) ‡8,000
PO Box 809 (63501)
Phone: (660)665-4663

Lebanon
The Lebanon Daily Record **(17238)** ....(Paid) 4,528
PO Box 192 (65536)   (Free) 285
Phone: (417)532-9131

Macon
Macon Chronicle-Herald **(17259)** ....‡3,218
204 W. Bourke St.
PO Box 7 (63552-1503)
Phone: (816)385-3121

Marshall
The Marshall Democrat-News **(17265)** ....(Paid) 3,980
121 N. Lafayette   (Free) 8,370
PO Box 100 (65340)
Phone: (660)886-2233

Maryville
Maryville Daily Forum **(17274)** ....‡3,983
111 E. Jenkins
PO Box 188 (64468)
Phone: (660)562-2424

Mexico
The Mexico Ledger **(17284)** ....(Mon.-Sat.) 7,615
PO Box 8 (65265-0008)

Monett
Monett Times **(17293)**
505 E Broadway St.
(65708)
Phone: (417)235-3135

Neosho
Neosho Daily News **(17304)** ....(Paid) 5,100
1006 W Harmony   (Wed.) 7,800
PO Box 848 (64850)
Phone: (417)451-1520

Nevada
Nevada Daily Mail/Herald **(17308)** ....(Mon.-Fri.) 2,542
131 S Cedar   (Sun.) 2,964
PO Box 247 (64772)
Phone: (417)667-3344

Park Hills
The Daily Journal **(17334)** ....(Mon.-Fri.) 8,792
1513 St. Joe Dr.   (Sun.) 8,851
PO Box A (63601)
Phone: (573)431-2010

Poplar Bluff
Daily American Republic **(17357)** ....(Mon.-Fri.) 13,138
208 Poplar St.   (Sun.) 13,988
PO Box 7 (63901)   (Wed.) 17,034
Phone: (573)785-1414

Richmond
The Daily News **(17375)** ....‡3,000
204 W North Main St.,
No. 100
PO Box 100 (64085-1743)
Phone: (816)776-5454

Rolla
Rolla Daily News **(17380)** 5,800
101 W 7th St.
PO Box 808 (65401-0808)
Phone: (573)364-2468

St. Joseph
St. Joseph News-Press **(17394)** ......(Mon.-Sat.) ★38,391
825 Edmond   (Sun.) ★41,366
PO Box 29 (64501)
Phone: (816)271-8500

St. Louis
The Daily Herald **(17431)** ....(Mon.-Sat.) 30,960
900 N. Tucker Blvd.   (Sun.) 32,578
PO Box 717 (63101)
Phone: (314)340-8000

Saint Charles Watchman **(17492)** ...(Combined) ‡20,000
200 S Bemiston, Ste.
212 (63105-1915)
Phone: (314)725-1515

St. Louis Post-Dispatch **(17506)** ....(Mon.-Sat.) ★287,424
1 Metropolitan Sq., Ste.   (Sun.) ★468,134
1300 (63102)
Phone: (314)340-8000

Sedalia
The Sedalia Democrat **(17570)** ....(Mon.-Sat.) 11,911
7th & Massachusetts   (Sun.) 12,425
Ave.
PO Box 848 (65302)
Phone: (660)826-1000

Sikeston
The Standard Democrat **(17581)** ......(Mon.-Sat.) ◆6,582
205 S New Madrid St.   (Sun.) ◆7,776
(63801)   (Wed.) ◆20,776
Phone: (314)471-1137

Trenton
Republican-Times **(17652)** ....(Paid) ‡3,435
122 E 8th St.   (Non-paid) ‡72
PO Box 548 (64683-0548)
Phone: (816)359-2212

Warrensburg
The Daily Star-Journal **(17666)** ....(Mon.-Fri.) 5,464
135 E Market
PO BOX 68 (64093)
Phone: (816)747-8123

Warrenton
News Democrat Journal **(17689)** ....(Sun.) 22,769
220 E Main (63383)   (Wed.) 23,372
Phone: (636)456-3481   (Fri.) 22,769

Waynesville
Daily Guide **(17709)**
PO Box 578 (65583)
Phone: (314)336-3711

West Plains
West Plains Daily Quill **(17716)** ....(Paid) 9,484
125 N Jefferson St.   (Free) 6
PO Box 110 (65775-0110)
Phone: (417)256-9191

MONTANA

Billings
The Billings Gazette **(17729)** ....(Mon.-Sat.) ★46,588
401 N Broadway   (Sun.) ★52,199
PO Box 36300 (59107)
Phone: (406)657-1200

Bozeman
Bozeman Daily Chronicle **(17751)** ....(Mon.-Sat.) ★15,258
PO Box 1190 (59771-1190)   (Sun.) ★16,504
Phone: (406)587-4491

Butte
Montana Standard **(17761)** ....(Mon.-Sat.) 14,383
PO Box 627 (59703)   (Sun.) 14,760
Phone: (406)496-5500

Great Falls
Great Falls Tribune **(17799)** ....(Mon.-Sat.) ★33,390
PO Box 5468 (59403)   (Sun.) ★37,776
Phone: (406)791-1444

Hamilton
Ravalli Republic **(17808)** ....‡5,626
232 Main St. (59840)
Phone: (406)363-3300

Havre
Havre Daily News **(17813)** ....(Paid) ⊕4,348
PO Box 431 (59501)
Phone: (406)265-6795

Helena
Independent Record **(17818)** ....(Mon.-Sat.) ★13,713
PO Box 4249   (Sun.) ★14,610
317 Cruse Ave. (59601-5003)
Phone: (406)442-7190

Kalispell
The Daily Inter Lake **(17836)** ....(Mon.-Fri.) 15,600
727 E Idaho   (Sun.) 18,300
PO Box 7610 (59904)
Phone: (406)755-7000

Livingston
Livingston Enterprise **(17856)** ....‡3,600
PO Box 2000 (59047)
Phone: (406)222-2000

Miles City
Miles City Star **(17861)**
818 Main St.
PO Box 1216 (59301)
Phone: (406)232-0450

Missoula
Missoulian **(17869)** ....(Mon.-Sat.) ★30,066
PO Box 8029 (59807)   (Sun.) ★34,998
Phone: (406)523-5200

NEBRASKA

Alliance
Alliance Times-Herald **(17927)** ....(Combined) ⊕3,117
114 E 4th St.
PO Box G (69301)
Phone: (308)762-3060

Beatrice
Beatrice Daily Sun **(17947)** ....(Mon.-Sat.) ★7,983
200 N 7th St.
PO Box 847 (68310-3916)
Phone: (402)223-5233

Columbus
Columbus Telegram **(17981)** ....(Mon.-Fri.) 10,100
1254 27th Ave.   (Sun.) 10,970
PO Box 648 (68601)
Phone: (402)563-7547

Falls City
Journal **(18009)** ....(Paid) 3,914
Box 128 (68355)
Phone: (402)245-2431

Grand Island
Grand Island Independent **(18025)** .....(Mon.-Sat.) 23,842
422 W 1st St.   (Sun.) 25,673
PO Box 1208 (68802)
Phone: (308)382-1000

Hastings
The Hastings Tribune **(18037)** ....(Mon.-Sat.) 12,002
908 W 2nd St.   12,032
Box 788 (68902-0788)
Phone: (402)462-2131

Holdrege
Holdrege Daily Citizen **(18049)** .... (Mon.-Fri.) 3,199
PO Box 344 (68949)
Phone: (308)995-4441

Kearney
Kearney Hub **(18059)** .... (Mon.-Fri.) ★12,574
PO Box 1988 (68848)   (Sat.) ★13,876
Phone: (308)237-2152

Lincoln
Daily Nebraskan **(18083)** 14,000
PO Box 880448 (68588-
0448)

Lincoln Journal **(18090)** .... (Mon.-Fri.) 38,303
PO Box 81609 (68508-   (Sat.) 84,258
1609)   (Sun.) 85,071
Phone: (402)475-4200

Lincoln Journal Star **(18091)** .... (Mon.-Sat.) ★74,506
926 P St.   (Sun.) ★83,387
PO Box 81609 (68508)
Phone: (402)475-4200

McCook
McCook Daily Gazette **(18153)** .... (Paid) 10,061
W 1st & E Sts.   (Free) 14,000
PO Box 1268 (69001)
Phone: (308)345-4500

Nebraska City
Nebraska City News-Press **(18166)** .....(Mon.-Fri.) ‡2,100
806 Central Ave. (68410)

Norfolk
Norfolk Daily News **(18170)** .... (Mon.-Sat.) ★17,617
525 Norfolk Ave.
Box 977 (68702-0977)
Phone: (402)371-1020

North Platte
North Platte Telegraph **(18176)** ......(Mon.-Sat.) ★13,454
621 N. Chestnut (69101)   (Sun.) ★13,847

Omaha
Omaha World-Herald **(18206)** .... (Mon.-Fri.) 214,651
1334 Dodge St. (68102-   (Sat.) 206,764
1122)   (Sun.) 261,036
Phone: (402)444-1000

Scottsbluff
Star-Herald **(18265)** .... (Tues.-Fri.) 15,765
1405 Broadway   (Sat.) 15,765
PO Box 1709 (69363-   (Sun.) 16,539
1709)
Phone: (308)632-9000

Sidney
Sidney Sun Telegraph **(18278)** .... (Paid) ‡2518
1136 Illinois
PO Box 193 (69162)
Phone: (308)254-2818

York
York News-Times **(18321)** 5,000
327 Platte Ave.
PO Box 279 (68467-
3547)
Phone: (402)362-4478

NEVADA
Carson City
Nevada Appeal **(18329)** .... (Mon.-Fri.) 14,481
200 Bath St.   (Sun.) 15,008
PO Box 2288 (89703-
2405)
Phone: (702)882-2111

Elko
Elko Daily Free Press **(18335)** .... ‡8,000
(89801)
Phone: (775)753-8082

Ely
Ely Daily Times **(18340)** .... ⊕2,585
297 Eleventh St. E.
PO Box 150820 (89315-
0820)
Phone: (775)289-4491

Fallon
Lahontan Valley News/Fallon Eagle
Standard **(18345)** .... (Paid) 5,200
562 N Maine St.
PO Box 1297 (89406-
2813)
Phone: (775)423-6041

Las Vegas
Las Vegas
Review-Journal **(18374)** .... (Mon.-Fri.) ★164,848
1111 W. Bonanza Rd.   (Sat.) ★188,051
PO Box 70 (89125)   (Sun.) ★220,398
Phone: (702)383-0211

Reno
Reno Gazette-Journal **(18423)** .... (Mon.-Sat.) ★66,073
PO Box 22000 (89520-   (Sun.) ★83,752
2000)
Phone: (702)788-6397

Sparks
Daily Sparks Tribune **(18445)** .... ‡6,320
1002 C St.
PO Box 887 (89431-
4929)
Phone: (775)358-8061

NEW HAMPSHIRE
Claremont
Eagle Times **(18465)** .... (Mon.-Fri.) 8,691
RR 2, Box 301 (03743-   (Sun.) 9,096
9308)
Phone: (603)543-3100

Concord
Concord Monitor **(18471)** .... (Mon.-Fri.) ★20,514
1 Monitor Dr.   (Sun.) ★23,580
PO Box 1177 (03302-   (Sat.) ★22,047
1177)
Phone: (603)224-5301

Dover
Foster's Democrat **(18491)** .... (Mon.-Sat.) ★23,694
333 Central Ave. (03820-   (Sun.) ★27,916
4127)
Phone: (603)742-4455

Hudson
The Telegraph **(18529)** .... (Mon.-Sat.) 26,442
17 Executive Dr. (03051)   (Sun.) 32,529
Phone: (603)882-2741

Keene
The Keene Sentinel **(18530)** .... (Mon.-Sat.) ★13,991
60 West St.   (Sun.) ★13,291
PO Box 546 (03431-
0546)
Phone: (603)352-1234

Laconia
Citizen **(18536)** .... (Mon.-Sat.) 9,168
171 Fair St. (03246)   (Sun.) 29,976
Phone: (603)524-8300

Manchester
The Union Leader **(18565)** .... (Mon.-Fri.) ★62,677
100 William Loeb Dr.   (Sat.) ★60,486
PO Box 9555 (03109-   (Sun.) ★84,560
5309)
Phone: (603)668-4321

Nashua
The Telegraph **(18601)** .... (Mon.-Sat.) 26,890
PO Box 1008 (03061)   (Sun.) 33,183
Phone: (603)882-2741

North Conway
The Conway Daily Sun **(18614)**
PO Box 1940 (03860)
Phone: (603)356-3456

Portsmouth
Portsmouth Herald **(18637)** .... (Mon.-Sat.) ★14,961
111 Maplewood Ave.   (Sun.) ★21,395
(03801)
Phone: (603)436-1800

West Lebanon
Valley News **(18650)** .... (Mon.-Sat.) 17,544
7 Interchange Dr.   (Sun.) 17,534
(03784)
Phone: (603)298-8711

NEW JERSEY
Atlantic City
The Press of Atlantic
City **(18658)** .... (Mon.-Sat.) ★77,795
11 Devins Ln. (08232-   (Sun.) ★97,108
3806)
Phone: (609)272-1234

Bridgeton
Bridgeton Evening News **(18690)** ......(Mon.-Sat.) ★7,142
100 Commerce
PO Box 596 (08302-
2602)
Phone: (609)451-1000

Cherry Hill
Courier-Post **(18733)** .... (Mon.-Sat.) ★79,574
301 Cuthbert Blvd.   (Sun.) ★96240
(08002)
Phone: (609)486-2411

East Brunswick
Asbury Park Press **(18779)** .... (Mon.-Sat.) ★63,126
35 Kennedy Blvd.   (Sun.) ★69,489
(08816)
Phone: (732)246-5500

The Home News &
Tribune **(18781)** .... (Mon.-Sat.) 66,311
35 Kennedy Blvd.   (Sun.) 74,186
(08816)
Phone: (732)246-5500

Hackensack
The Record **(18854)** .... (Mon.-Sat.) ★178,962
150 River St. (07601-   (Sun.) ★226,091
7172)
Phone: (201)646-4000

Jersey City
The Hudson Dispatch **(19139)** .... ‡30,077
30 Journal Sq. (07306)
Phone: (201)653-1000

Jersey Journal **(19141)** .... (Mon.-Sat.) 50,386
30 Journal Sq. (07306)
Phone: (201)653-1000

Newark
Star-Ledger **(19366)** .... (Mon.-Fri.) 407,592
1 Star-Ledger Plaza   (Sat.) 332,586
(07102-1200)   (Sun.) 606,462
Phone: (973)877-4040

Newton
New Jersey Herald **(19372)** .... (Mon.-Fri.) 16,999
2 Spring St.   (Sun.) 23,643
PO Box 10 (07860-0010)
Phone: (973)383-1500

Parsippany
Daily Record **(19411)** .... (Mon.-Sat.) 50,958
800 Jefferson Rd.   (Sun.) 56,338
PO Box 217 (07054)
Phone: (973)428-6200

SVOBODA **(19414)** .... (Paid) ‡12,500
2200 Route 10   (Free) ‡300
PO Box 280 (07054)
Phone: (973)292-9800

Salem
Today's Sunbeam **(19532)** .... (Mon.-Fri.) ★9,767
93 5th St. (08079)   (Sun.) ★9,522
Phone: (609)935-1500   (Sat.) ★8,840

Somerville
The Courier-News **(19572)** .... (Mon.-Sat.) ★40,885
1201 Rte. 22 W   (Sun.) ★35,593
PO Box 6600 (08807)
Phone: (908)722-8800

Toms River
Ocean County Observer **(19642)** .... (Mon.-Fri.) 9,757
8 Robbins St. (08753)   (Sun.) 9,4052
Phone: (732)349-3000

Trenton
The Times **(19668)** .... (Mon.-Sat.) 78,202
500 Perry St. (08605)   (Sun.) 87,471
Phone: (609)989-5454

The Trentonian **(19670)** .... (Mon.-Sat.) 50,980
Southand at Perry St.   (Sat.) 45,698
(08602)   (Sun.) 40,527
Phone: (609)989-7800

Vineland
The Daily Journal **(19698)** .... (Mon.-Sat.) 17,614
891 E Oak Rd. (08360)
Phone: (609)691-5000

Willingboro
Burlington County Times **(19753)** .....(Mon.-Fri.) 39,239
4284 Rte. 130 (08046)   (Sun.) 44,338
Phone: (609)871-8000

Woodbury
Gloucester County Times **(19756)** ...(Mon.-Fri.) ★22,791
309 S Broad St. (08096)   (Sat.) ★20,455
Phone: (609)845-3300   (Sun.) ★26,296

NEW MEXICO
Alamogordo
Alamogordo Daily News **(19758)** .... (Mon.-Fri.) ★7,306
518 24th St. (88310)   (Sun.) ★8,401
Phone: (505)437-7120

Albuquerque
Albuquerque Journal **(19763)** .... (Mon.-Sat.) 108,931
7777 Jefferson NE   (Sun.) 153,560
(87109)
Phone: (505)823-3393

The Albuquerque Tribune **(19764)** .....(Mon.-Sat.) 18,919
7777 Jefferson NE
(87109)
Phone: (505)823-7777

Artesia
Artesia Daily Press **(19817)** 3,446
PO Box 190 (88211-
0190)

Carlsbad
Carlsbad Current-Argus **(19822)** ....(Tues.-Fri.) ★8,185
PO Box 1629 (88220)   (Sun.) ★8,376
Phone: (505)887-5501

Clovis
Clovis News Journal **(19830)** .... (Mon.-Thurs.) ★7,779
PO Box 1689 (88102)   (Fri.) ★8,427
Phone: (505)763-3431   (Sun.) ★8,820

Deming
Deming Headlight **(19840)** .... (Paid) 3650
219 E. Maple   (Free) ‡7000
PO Box 881 (88031)
Phone: (505)546-2611

Farmington
The Daily Times **(19846)** .... (Mon.-Sat.) 17,440
201 N. Allen Ave.   (Sun.) 19,102
PO Box 450 (87401-
6212)
Phone: (505)325-4545

Circulation: ★ = ABC; △ = BPA; ◆ = CAC; • = CCAB; ❏ = VAC; ⊕ = PO Statement; ‡ = Publisher's Report; Boldface figures = sworn; Light figures = estimated.

2865

Newspapers

Circ.   Circ.   Circ.

NEW MEXICO (continued)

Gallup
The Independent (19856) ....(Mon.-Fri.) 16,998
500 N. 9th St. (Sat.) 19,450
PO Box 1210 (87305)
Phone: (505)863-6811

Grants
Beacon (19862) ....(Tues.) ‡7,200
523 W. Santa Fe Ave. (Fri.) 3,200
PO Box 579 (87020)
Phone: (505)287-4411

Hobbs
Hobbs News-Sun (19864) ....(Mon.-Fri.) 9,218
PO Box 850 (88241) (Sun.) 9,801
Phone: (505)393-2123

Las Cruces
The Las Cruces
    Sun-News (19873) ....(Mon.-Fri.) ★22,274
256 W Las Cruces Ave. (Sun.) ★25,434
    (88004) (Sat.) ★20,920
Phone: (505)541-5400

Sun-News (19876) ....(Mon.-Fri.) 22,432
256 W. Las Cruces (Sat.) 21,803
    (88005) (Sun.) 25,164

Las Vegas
Las Vegas Optic (19889) ....‡5,986
PO Box 2670 (87701)

Los Alamos
Los Alamos Monitor (19893) ....(Paid) 4,966
256 O.P. Rd. (Free) 12
PO Box 1268 (87544)
Phone: (505)662-4185

Lovington
The Lovington Daily Leader (19897) ....(Paid) 2,390
14 W Ave B (Free) 50
PO Box 1717 (88260)
Phone: (505)396-2844

Roswell
Roswell Daily Record (19913) ....(Mon.-Fri.) ‡13,864
2301 N. Main St. (Sun.) ‡13,864
PO Box 1897 (88201-
6452)
Phone: (505)622-7710

Santa Fe
The Santa Fe New
    Mexican (19943) ....(Mon.-Sat.) ★25,336
202 E. Marcy St. (Sun.) ★27,343
    (87501-2021)
Phone: (505)986-3075

Silver City
Silver City Daily Press (19953) ....(Paid) 8,025
300 W Market St. (Free) 150
PO Box 740 (88062)
Phone: (505)388-1576

NEW YORK

Albany
The Times Union (20006) ....(Mon.-Sat.) ★99,242
Box 15000, News Plz. (Sun.) ★145,357
    (12212)
Phone: (518)454-5694

Amsterdam
The Recorder (20056) ....(Mon.-Sat.) 10,124
PO Box 309 (12010) (Sun.) 10,369
Phone: (518)843-1100

Auburn
The Citizen (20105) ....(Mon.-Fri.) 12,540
25 Dill St. (13021) (Sat.) 11,823
Phone: (315)253-5311 (Sun.) 14,171

Batavia
News (20121) ....(Mon.-Sat.) 15,427
2 Apollo Dr. (14021)
Phone: (716)343-8000

Binghamton
Press & Sun-Bulletin (20211) ....(Mon.-Sat.) ★57,576
Binghamton Press Co. (Sun.) ★72,962
Vestal Pkwy. E.
PO Box 1270 (13902)
Phone: (607)798-1151

Brooklyn
Daily Challenge (20310) 79,000
1360 Fulton St. (11216)
Phone: (718)636-9500

Buffalo
The Buffalo News (20368) ....(Mon.-Sat.) ★223,957
1 News Plz. (14203- (Sun.) ★306,102
2994)
Phone: (716)849-3434

Canandaigua
The Daily Messenger (20420) ....(Mon.-Fri.) 13,686
73 Buffalo St. (14424) (Sun.) 14,647
Phone: (716)394-0770

Catskill
Daily Mail (20438) 3,579
PO Box 484 (12414)
Phone: (518)943-2100

Corning
Leader (20503) ....(Mon.-Sat.) 14,594
34 W. Pulteney St. (Sun.) 14,286
    (14830)
Phone: (607)936-4651

Cortland
Cortland Standard (20512) ....(Paid) ‡11,202
PO Box 5548 (13045)
Phone: (607)756-5665

Dunkirk
Observer (20537) ....(Mon.-Sat.) 12,483
10 E. 2nd St. (14048) (Sun.) 12,670
Phone: (716)366-3000

Elmira
Star-Gazette (20573) ....(Mon.-Sat.) ★29,169
PO Box 285 (14902) (Sun.) ★40,270
Phone: (607)734-5151

Flushing
Chosun Daily (20607)
35-11 Farrington St.
    (11354)
Phone: (718)463-1400

Geneva
Finger Lakes Times (20653) ....(Mon.-Sat.) ★16,902
218 Genesee St. (Sun.) ★19,539
PO Box 393 (14456)
Phone: (315)789-3376

Glens Falls
The Post-Star (20669) ....(Mon.-Sat.) ★34,202
Lawrence & Cooper St. (Sun.) ★37,650
    (12801)
Phone: (518)792-3131

Gloversville
The Leader-Herald (20671) ....(Mon.-Sat.) ★11,179
8-10 E Fulton St. (Sun.) ★12,525
    (12078-3283)
Phone: (518)725-8616

Herkimer
The Evening Telegram (20732) ....(Mon.-Sat.) 6,900
111 Green St. (13350)
Phone: (315)866-2220

Hornell
The Evening Tribune (20751) ....(Paid) ‡9,500
85 Canisteo St. (14843-
1544)
Phone: (607)324-1425

Hudson
Register-Star (20767) ....(Mon.-Fri.) 6,444
364 Warren St. (12534) (Sun.) 6,688
Phone: (518)828-1616

Ithaca
The Ithaca Journal (20807) ....(Mon.-Fri.) ★18,791
123-125 W. State St. (Sat.) ★22,860
PO Box 430 (14850-
0430)
Phone: (607)272-2321

Jamestown
The Post-Journal (20842) ....(Mon.-Sat.) ★20,258
15 W. 2nd St. (14701) (Sun.) ★20,796
Phone: (716)487-1111

Kingston
Daily & Sunday Freeman (20860) ....(Mon.-Fri.) 21,515
79 Hurley Ave. (12401) (Sat.) 20,562
Phone: (914)331-5000 (Sun.) 28,564

Little Falls
The Evening Times (20951) ....‡4,350
PO Box 1007 (13365)
Phone: (315)823-3680

Long Island City
Noticias del Mundo (20965) ....(Paid) 37,000
38-42 9th St., 3rd Fl.
    (11101)
Phone: (718)786-4343

The Sae Gae Times (20966) ....(Combined) 40,000
38-42 9th St. (11101)
Phone: (718)361-2600

Mamaroneck
Mamaroneck Daily Times (20986) ....(Mon.-Sat.) 4,897
1 Gannett Dr. (10604- (Sun.) 5,102
3406)
Phone: (914)694-9300

Massena
The Daily Courier Observer (21027) ....‡11,500
PO Box 300 (13662)
Phone: (315)393-1002

Medina
The Journal-Register (21036) ....(Mon.-Fri.) 4,311
409 Main St., No. 13
    (14103-1416)
Phone: (716)798-1400

Melville
Newsday (21051) ....(Mon.-Fri.) 576,692
235 Pinelawn Rd. (Sat.) 417,949
    (11747-4250) (Sun.) 663,220
Phone: (516)843-2700

Middletown
Times Herald-Record (21081) ....(Mon.-Sat.) ★84,277
40 Mulberry St. (10940) (Sun.) ★95,531
Phone: (914)343-2181

Mount Vernon
Mount Vernon Daily Argus (21103) .....(Mon.-Sat.) 6,020
1 Gannett Dr. (10604- (Sun.) 6,740
3406)
Phone: (914)694-9300

New York
American Banker (21180) ....(Mon.-Fri.) 14,611
1 State St. Plz. (10004)
Phone: (212)803-8200

Asahi Shimbun (21259) ....(Combined) 12,000
845 3rd Ave. (10022)
Phone: (212)755-3900

Daily Variety (21533) ....(Mon.-Fri.) 30,406
249 W. 17th St. (10011-
5322)
Phone: (212)337-6900

El Diario/La Prensa (21590) ....(Mon.-Fri.) 53,843
345 Hudson St. (10014) (Sat.) 46,090
Phone: (212)807-4600 (Sun.) 36,152

New Russian Word (22434)
252 W. 37th St., 9th Fl.
    (10018)
Phone: (212)387-0299

New York Daily News (22440) ....(Mon.-Fri.) 716,095
450 W 33rd St. (10001) (Sat.) 548,380
Phone: (212)210-2100 (Sun.) 821,080

The New York Law
    Journal (22445) ....(Mon.-Fri.) 13,745
345 Park Ave. S (10010)
Phone: (212)779-9200

New York Post (22448) ....(Mon.-Fri.) 487,219
1211 6th Ave. (10036) (Sat.) 376,871
Phone: (212)930-8000 (Sun.) 368,636

The New York Times (22453) .....(Mon.-Fri.) ★1,113,000
229 W. 43rd St. (10036- (Sat.) ★1,055,512
3913) (Sun.) ★1,6671,865
Phone: (212)556-1234

Polish Daily News (22571) ....(Paid) 39,000
333 W 38th St. (10018) (Free) 450
Phone: (212)594-2266

Wall Street Journal (22906) ....(Mon.-Fri.) ★1,800,607
200 Liberty St. (10281)
Phone: (212)416-2000

Women's Wear Daily (22936) ....(Mon.-Fri.) 44,015
7 W. 34th St. (10001)
Phone: (212)630-4000

Niagara Falls
Niagara Gazette (23006) ....(Mon.-Sat.) 24,182
310 Niagara St. (Sun.) 46,766
PO Box 549 (14302-
0549)
Phone: (716)282-2311

North Tonawanda
Tonawanda News (23016) ....(Mon.-Sat.) ★11,219
435 River Rd. (14120-
6809)
Phone: (716)693-1000

Norwich
The Evening Sun (23020) 5,614
18-20 Mechanic St.
PO Box 111 (13815-
2038)
Phone: (607)334-4714

Ogdensburg
Advance-News (23032)
PO Box 409 (13669)
Phone: (315)393-1002

Journal (23033)
PO Box 409 (13669)
Phone: (315)393-1002

Olean
Olean Times-Herald (23040) ....(Mon.-Sat.) ★16,556
639 Norton Dr. (14760) (Sun.) ★16,966
Phone: (716)372-3121

Oneida
The Oneida Daily
    Dispatch (23045) ....(Mon.-Sat.) ★6,729
130 Broad St.
PO Box 120 (13421)
Phone: (315)363-5100

Oneonta
The Daily Star (23049) ....(Mon.-Sat.) 18,181
PO Box 250 (13820)
Phone: (607)432-1000

Oswego
The Palladium-Times (23062) ....(Mon.-Sat.) 9,049
140 W 1st St. (13126)
Phone: (315)343-3800

Plattsburgh
Press-Republican (23103) ....(Mon.-Sat.) 22,685
170 Margaret St., PO (Sun.) 23,584
    Box 459 (12901)
Phone: (518)561-2300

Poughkeepsie
Poughkeepsie Journal **(23149)** ....(Mon.-Sat.) ★**39,984**
85 Civic Center Plaza   (Sun.) ★**51,067**
(12601-2410)
Phone: (914)454-2000

Rochester
The Daily Record **(23220)** ....(Paid) ‡2,860
11 Centre Park   (Free) ‡150
PO Box 30006 (14603-
3006)
Phone: (585)232-6920

Democrat and
Chronicle **(23222)** ....(Mon.-Sat.) ★**172,124**
55 Exchange Blvd.   (Sun.) ★**232,193**
(14614-2001)
Phone: (716)232-7100

Rome
Daily Sentinel **(23264)** ....(Mon.-Sat.) 15,030
333 W. Dominick St.
PO Box 471 (13442-
0471)

Salamanca
Press **(23293)**
36 River St., No. 42
(14779)
Phone: (716)945-1644

Saranac Lake
Adirondack Daily Enterprise **(23297)** ....(Paid) 5,100
POB 318
61 Broadway (12983)
Phone: (518)891-2600

Saratoga Springs
The Saratogian **(23303)** ....(Mon.-Sat.) ★**11,461**
20 Lake Ave. (12866-   (Sun.) ★**12,932**
2314)
Phone: (518)584-4242

Schenectady
The Daily Gazette **(23314)** ....(Mon.-Sat.) 53,787
2345 Maxon Rd. Ext.   (Sun.) 54,764
PO Box 1090 (12301-
1090)
Phone: (518)374-4141

Staten Island
Staten Island Advance **(23361)** ......(Mon.-Sat.) ★**65,287**
950 Fingerboard Rd.   (Sun.) ★**84,446**
(10305)

Syracuse
The Post-Standard **(23419)** ....(Mon.-Sat.) ★**123,836**
PO Box 4915 (13221)   (Sun.) ★**178,132**
Phone: (315)470-0011

Syracuse Herald-Journal **(23426)** ......(Mon.-Sat.) 33,069
Clinton Sq.
PO Box 4915 (13221)
Phone: (315)470-0011

Troy
The Record **(23457)** ....(Mon.-Sat.) 22,291
501 Broadway (12181)   (Sun.) 23,908
Phone: (518)270-1200

Utica
Observer-Dispatch **(23466)** ....(Mon.-Sat.) ★**45,916**
221 Oriskany Plz.   (Sun.) ★**53,629**
(13501)
Phone: (315)792-5000

Watertown
Watertown Daily Times **(23514)** ......(Mon.-Sat.) ★**31,800**
260 Washington St.   (Sun.) ★**36,970**
Times Bldg. (13601)
Phone: (315)782-1000

Wellsville
The Wellsville Daily Reporter **(23533)** ....(Paid) ‡4,000
159 N. Main St. (14895-
1149)
Phone: (716)593-5300

White Plains
The Item **(23571)** ....(Mon.-Sat.) 8,712
1 Gannett Dr. (10604-   (Sun.) 9,200
3406)
Phone: (914)694-9300

NORTH CAROLINA
Asheboro
The Courier-Tribune **(23621)** ....(Mon.-Sat.) 16,327
500 Sunset Ave.   (Sun.) 17,500
PO Box 340 (27203-
5330)
Phone: (336)625-2101

Asheville
Asheville Citizen-Times **(23627)** ....(Mon.-Sat.) 55,245
14 O. Henry Ave.   (Sun.) 68,751
(28801)
Phone: (828)252-5611

Burlington
Times-News **(23672)** ....(Mon.-Sat.) ★**27,418**
707 S Main St.   (Sun.) ★**29,203**
PO Box 481 (27216)
Phone: (336)227-0131

Clinton
The Sampson
Independent **(23789)** ....(Combined) 17,048
303 Elizabeth St.
Box 110 (28328)
Phone: (910)592-8137

Dunn
The Daily Record **(23803)** ....(Mon.-Fri.) 9,870
99 W. Broad St.
PO Box 1448 (28335)

Durham
The Herald-Sun **(23824)** ....(Mon.-Sat.) ★**50,015**
2828 Picket Rd. (27705)   (Sun.) ★**56,612**

Eden
Eden Daily News **(23855)**
804 Washington St.
PO Box 308 (27288-
6031)
Phone: (919)623-2155

Elizabeth City
The Daily Advance **(23860)** ....(Mon.-Fri.) 11,193
216 S Poindexter St.   (Sun.) 11,792
PO Box 588 (27909-
4835)
Phone: (919)335-0841

Elizabethtown
Bladen Journal **(23864)** 4,100
PO Box 67 (28337)
Phone: (919)862-4163

Fayetteville
The Fayetteville Observer **(23879)** ....(Mon.-Fri.) ★**66,423**
(28302)   (Sat.) ★**71,369**
Phone: (910)486-3504   (Sun.) ★**73,636**

Gastonia
Gaston Gazette **(23907)** ....(Mon.-Sat.) ★**30,770**
2500 E. Franklin Blvd.   (Sun.) ★**34,614**
PO Box 1538 (28053)
Phone: (704)864-3291

Goldsboro
Goldsboro News-Argus **(23910)** ....(Mon.-Fri.) ★**21,228**
310 N Berkeley Blvd.   (Sun.) ★**24,096**
(27534)
Phone: (919)778-2211

Greensboro
News & Record **(23930)** ....(Mon.-Fri.) 86,241
200 E. Market St.   (Sat.) 101,618
PO Box 20848 (27401-   (Sun.) 112,259
2910)
Phone: (336)373-7000

Greenville
The Daily Reflector **(23962)** ....(Mon.-Sat.) 20,359
PO Box 1967 (27835)   (Sun.) 23,550
Phone: (252)752-6166

Henderson
Henderson Daily Dispatch **(23981)** ......(Tues.-Fri.) 8,562
PO Box 908 (27536-   (Sat.) 8,562
0908)   (Sun.) 9,099
Phone: (919)492-4001

Hendersonville
The Times-News **(23984)** ....(Mon.-Sat.) ★**19,536**
PO Box 490 (28793-   (Sun.) ★**19,833**
0490)
Phone: (704)692-0505

High Point
High Point Enterprise **(23998)** ......(Mon.-Sat.) ★**28,987**
210 Church Ave.   (Sun.) ★**30,573**
PO Box 1009 (27261)
Phone: (336)888-3500

Jacksonville
Daily News **(24011)** ....(Mon.-Sat.) 20,906
724 Bell Fork Rd.   (Sun.) 23,217
PO Box 196 (28546)
Phone: (910)353-1171

Kannapolis
The Independent Tribune **(24016)** ......(Mon.-Fri.) 20,538
924 Cloverleaf Plz.   (Sun.) 22,887
(28082)
Phone: (704)782-3155

Kinston
The Free Press **(24027)** ....(Mon.-Fri.) 12,573
2103 N. Queen St.   (Sun.) 14,202
(28501)
Phone: (252)527-3191

Lenoir
Lenoir News-Topic **(24035)** ....(Tues.-Fri.) ★**9,461**
PO Box 1110 (28645)   (Sat.) ★**9,238**
Phone: (704)758-7381   (Sun.) ★**9,730**

Lexington
The Dispatch **(24040)** ....(Mon.-Sat.) 12,864
30 E. 1st Ave.
PO Box 908 (27293)
Phone: (336)249-3981

Lumberton
The Robesonian **(24051)** ....(Mon.-Sat.) ★**12,877**
121 W 5th St.   (Sun.) ★**15,662**
PO Box 1028 (28359)
Phone: (910)739-4322

Marion
McDowell News **(24056)** ....(Paid) ‡6,769
26 N. Logan St.   (Non-paid) ‡254
PO Box 610 (28752-
3944)
Phone: (704)652-3313

Monroe
The Enquirer-Journal **(24066)** ....(Tues.-Fri.) 9,428
500 W Jefferson St.   (Sat.) 9,428
PO Box 5040 (28111-   (Sun.) 11,540
4657)
Phone: (704)289-1541

Morganton
The News Herald **(24073)** ....(Mon.-Fri.) 11,918
301 Collett St.   (Sun.) 12,523
PO Box 280 (28655-
3322)
Phone: (828)328-8725

Mount Airy
Mount Airy News **(24079)** ....(Mon.-Fri.) 9,556
319 N Renfro St.   (Sun.) 10,285
PO Box 808 (27030-
0808)
Phone: (336)786-4141

New Bern
Sun Journal **(24097)** ....(Mon.-Sat.) ★**15,348**
3200 Wellons Blvd.   (Sun.) ★**16,658**
PO Box 1149 (28562)
Phone: (919)638-8101

Newton
Observer-News-Enterprise **(24106)** ....‡4,031
309 N. College Ave.
PO Box 48 (28658-0048)
Phone: (828)464-0221

Raleigh
The News and Observer **(24141)** ....(Mon.-Fri.) ★**163,295**
215 S. McDowell St.   (Sat.) ★**182,783**
PO Box 191 (27602)   (Sun.) ★**208,290**
Phone: (919)829-4700

Reidsville
The Reidsville Review **(24180)** ....(Paid) 6,979
225 Turner Dr.
PO Box 2157 (27320-
5736)

Roanoke Rapids
Daily Herald **(24195)** ....(Mon.-Fri.) 12,291
916 Roanoke Ave.   (Sun.) 12,951
(27870)
Phone: (919)537-2505

Rockingham
Richmond County Daily
Journal **(24201)** ....(Mon.-Fri.) ★**8,767**
105 E. Washington St.   (Sun.) ★**8,956**
(28379)
Phone: (919)997-3111

Rocky Mount
The Evening Telegram **(24204)** ....(Mon.-Sat.) 14,530
150 Howard St.   (Sun.) 16,747
PO Box 1080 (27802-
1080)
Phone: (919)446-5161

Rocky Mount Telegram **(24205)** ......(Mon.-Sat.) ★**14,210**
Tiffany Office Building   (Sun.) ★**16,633**
800 Tiffany Blvd.
PO Box 1080 (27802)
Phone: (252)446-5161

Salisbury
The Salisbury Post **(24215)** ....(Mon.-Sat.) 24,178
131 W. Innes St.   (Sun.) 25,874
PO Box 4639 (28145-
4639)
Phone: (704)633-8950

Sanford
The Sanford Herald **(24219)** ....(Tues.-Fri.) 12,220
PO Box 100 (27330-   (Sat.) 12,220
0100)   (Sun.) 12,047
Phone: (919)708-9000

Shelby
The Shelby Star **(24227)** ....(Mon.-Sat.) ★**14,487**
315 E Graham St.   (Sun.) ★**14,416**
PO Box 48 (28150)
Phone: (704)484-7000

Statesville
Statesville Record and
Landmark **(24247)** ....(Mon.-Fri.) ★**14,714**
222 E Broad St.   (Sat.) ★**16,059**
PO Box 1071 (28677-   (Sun.) ★**15,416**
5325)
Phone: (704)873-1451

Tarboro
The Daily Southerner **(24254)** ....(Paid) **6300**
504 W. Wilson St.   (Non-paid) 5280
PO Box 1199 (27886)
Phone: (919)823-3106

Thomasville
The Times **(24256)** ....(Combined) 6,555
512 Turner St.
PO Box 549 (27360)
Phone: (910)472-9500

Circulation: ★ = ABC; △ = BPA; ♦ = CAC; • = CCAB; ❑ = VAC; ⊕ = PO Statement; ‡ = Publisher's Report; Boldface figures = sworn; Light figures = estimated.

2867

Newspapers

        Circ.   Circ.   Circ.

NORTH CAROLINA (continued)

Tryon
The Tryon Daily Bulletin **(24259)** ....‡5,200
16 N Trade St. (28782)
Phone: (828)859-9151

Washington
Washington Daily News **(24273)** ....(Mon.-Sat.) 10,019
217 N Market St. (Sun.) 10,200
PO Box 1788 (27889)
Phone: (252)946-2144

Wilmington
Wilmington Morning Star **(24298)** ...(Mon.-Sat.) ★53,909
PO Box 840 (28402) (Sun.) ★61,164
Phone: (910)343-2000

Wilson
Wilson Daily Times **(24312)** ....(Mon.-Sat.) ★16,400
2001 Downing St.
PO Box 2447 (27894)
Phone: (252)243-5151

Winston-Salem
Winston-Salem Journal **(24324)** ......(Mon.-Sat.) ★85,670
PO Box 3159 (27102- (Sun.) ★96,785
3159)
Phone: (336)727-7211

NORTH DAKOTA

Bismarck
The Bismarck Tribune **(24349)** ....(Mon.-Sat.) ★27,531
707 E. Front Ave. (Sun.) ★31,120
(58504)
Phone: (701)223-2500

Devils Lake
Journal **(24390)**
516 4th St.
PO Box 1200 (58301)
Phone: (701)662-2127

Dickinson
The Dickinson Press **(24394)** ....(Mon.-Fri.) 7,713
1815 W 1st St. (Sun.) 7,996
PO Box 1367 (58601)
Phone: (701)225-8111

Fargo
The Forum **(24411)** ....(Mon.-Sat.) 51,312
Box 2020 (Sun.) 64,0101
101 5th St. N. (58102-
4826)
Phone: (701)241-5402

Jamestown
The Jamestown Sun **(24476)** ....‡7,236
PO Box 1760 (58402-
1760)

Minot
The Minot Daily News **(24505)** ......(Mon.-Sat.) ★22,136
301 4th St. SE (58701) (Sun.) ★22,975
Phone: (701)857-1900

Valley City
Valley City Times-Record **(24544)** ....(Paid) ‡3,300
146 3rd St. NE
PO Box 697 (58072)
Phone: (701)845-0463

Wahpeton
Daily News **(24549)** ....(Paid) 4,927
PO Box 760 (58074-
0760)
Phone: (701)642-8585

Williston
Williston Daily Herald **(24560)** ....(Paid) 5,890
PO Box 1447 (58801) (Free) 35
Phone: (701)572-2165

OHIO

Akron
The Akron Legal News **(24573)** ....‡5,000
60 S Summit St. (44308)
Phone: (330)376-0917

Alliance
The Review **(24605)** ....(Mon.-Sat.) ★12,733
40 S. Linden Ave.
PO Box 2180 (44601)
Phone: (330)821-1200

Ashland
Ashland Times-Gazette **(24617)** ......(Mon.-Sat.) ★12,358
40 E 2nd St. (44805)
Phone: (419)281-0581

Ashtabula
Ashtabula Star-Beacon **(24623)** ......(Mon.-Sat.) ★20,010
4626 Park Ave. (Sun.) ★21,460
PO Box 2100 (44004)
Phone: (440)994-3241

The Star Beacon **(24624)** ....(Mon.-Sat.) 20,607
PO Box 2100 (44005- (Sun.) 21,977
2100)
Phone: (216)593-1166

Athens
The Athens Messenger **(24628)** ......(Mon.-Fri.) ★10,767
Rte. 33 N. & Johnson (Sun.) ★13,353
Rd.
PO Box 4210 (45701)
Phone: (614)592-6612

Bellefontaine
The Bellefontaine
Examiner **(24666)** ....(Mon.-Sat.) ★9,062
127 E. Chillicothe Ave.
(43311)
Phone: (937)592-3060

Bellevue
The Bellevue Gazette **(24669)** 3,200
107 N. Sandusky St.
(44811)
Phone: (419)483-4190

Bowling Green
Sentinel-Tribune **(24701)** ....(Mon.-Sat.) 12,119
300 E. Poe Rd.
PO Box 88 (43402)
Phone: (419)352-4611

Bryan
The Bryan Times **(24714)** ....(Mon.-Sat.) ★10,733
127 S. Walnut St.
PO Box 471 (43506)
Phone: (419)636-1111

Bucyrus
The Bucyrus
Telegraph-Forum **(24718)** ....(Mon.-Sat.) ★7,196
PO Box 471 (44820)
Phone: (419)562-3333

Cambridge
The Daily Jeffersonian **(24724)** ....(Mon.-Fri.) ★12,687
831 Wheeling Ave. (Sun.) ★13,201
PO Box 10 (43725)
Phone: (740)439-3531

Canton
The Repository **(24731)** ....(Mon.-Sat.) ★65,129
500 Market Ave. S (Sun.) ★81,290
(44702-2112)
Phone: (216)454-5611

Celina
The Daily Standard **(24749)** ....(Paid) ‡10,200
123 E Market St. (Free) ‡50
PO Box 140 (45822)
Phone: (419)586-2371

Chillicothe
Chillicothe Gazette **(24761)** ....(Mon.-Fri.) ★16,436
50 West Main St. (Sat.) ★16,485
(45601) (Sun.) ★16,221

Cincinnati
The Cincinnati Enquirer **(24785)** ....(Mon.-Thurs.) 195,360
312 Elm St. (45202) (Fri.) 218,667
Phone: (513)721-2700 (Sat.) 210,217
(Sun.) 311,425

The Cincinnati Post **(24788)** ....(Mon.-Fri.) 55,807
125 E. Court St. (45202) (Sat.) 79,903
Phone: (513)352-2000

Circleville
Circleville Herald **(24850)** ....(Mon.-Sat.) ★6,577
PO Box 498
210 N. Court St. (43113)
Phone: (614)474-3131

Cleveland
Plain Dealer **(24943)** ....(Mon.-Sat.) ★363,750
1801 Superior Ave. (Sun.) ★481,126
(44114)
Phone: (216)999-6000

Columbus
The Columbus Dispatch **(25008)** ....(Mon.-Sat.) ★251,557
34 S. 3rd St. (43215) (Sun.) ★372,474
Phone: (614)461-5000

Coshocton
Coshocton Tribune **(25096)** ....(Mon.-Sat.) ★7,184
550 Main St. (Sun.) ★7,528
PO Box 10 (43812)
Phone: (740)622-1122

Dayton
Dayton Daily News **(25113)** ....(Thurs.) ★188,272
45 S. Ludlow St. (45402) (Fri.) ★147,412
Phone: (973)225-7479 (Sat.) ★141,594
(Sun.) ★199,286

Defiance
Crescent-News **(25157)** ....(Mon.-Fri.) ★17,615
624 W Second St. (Sun.) ★18,524
PO Box 249 (43512)
Phone: (419)784-5441

Delaware
Gazette **(25160)** ....(Paid) ⊕8,534
18 E. William St.
PO Box 100 (43015)
Phone: (740)363-1161

East Liverpool
The Review **(25171)** ....(Mon.-Sat.) 9,838
210 E. 4th St. (43920)
Phone: (330)385-4545

Elyria
Chronicle-Telegram **(25178)** ....(Mon.-Sat.) ★25,136
225 East Ave. (Fri.) ★28,203
PO Box 4010 (44036) (Sun.) ★26,924
Phone: (216)329-7000

Fairborn
Fairborn Daily Herald **(25187)** ....(Paid) 4,197
PO Box 1352 (45324-
1352)

Findlay
The Courier **(25194)** ....(Mon.-Sat.) 23,052
701 W. Sandusky St.
(45840)
Phone: (419)422-5151

Fremont
The News-Messenger **(25202)** ....(Mon.-Sat.) 13,800
1700 Cedar St.
PO Box 1230 (43420)
Phone: (419)332-5511

Gallipolis
The Daily Sentinel **(25208)** ....(Mon.-Fri.) ★4,044
825 3rd Ave. (45631)
Phone: (740)446-2342

Gallipolis Daily Tribune **(25209)** ....(Mon.-Fri.) 5,014
825 3rd Ave. (45631)
Phone: (740)446-2342

Greenfield
The Review Times **(25225)** ....(Paid) ‡7,487
345 Jefferson St. (Free) ‡1,620
PO Box 118 (45123)
Phone: (513)981-2141

Greenville
The Daily Advocate **(25227)** ....(Mon.-Sat.) 7,327
PO Box 220 (45331)
Phone: (513)548-3151

Hamilton
Journal-News **(25235)** ....(Mon.-Sat.) ★22,437
228 Court St. & Journal (Sun.) ★23,436
Sq. (45011)
Phone: (513)863-8200

Ironton
Tribune **(25253)** ....(Mon.-Fri.) 6,200
PO Box 647 (45638) (Sun.) 7,200
Phone: (614)532-1441

Kenton
KentonTimes **(25281)** ....(Paid) 8,000
201 E. Columbus St.
(43326)
Phone: (419)673-1102

Lancaster
Eagle-Gazette **(25289)** ....(Mon.-Sat.) ★15,243
138 W. Chestnut St. (Sun.) ★15,526
(43130)
Phone: (740)681-4344

Lima
The Lima News **(25297)** ....(Mon.-Sat.) 35,266
3515 Elida Rd. (Sun.) 43,525
PO Box 690 (45807-
0690)
Phone: (419)223-1010

Lisbon
Morning Journal **(25308)** ....(Mon.-Sat.) 13,732
308 W Maple St. (Sun.) 13,332
(44432)
Phone: (330)424-9541

Logan
Logan Daily News **(25312)** ....(Mon.-Sat.) 4,533
72 E. Main St.
PO Box 758 (43138-
0758)

Lorain
The Morning Journal **(25315)** ....(Mon.-Sat.) 34,311
1657 Broadway (44052) (Sun.) 38,106
Phone: (216)245-6901

Madison
Madison Press **(25326)** ....(Paid) ‡6,500
30 S Oak St. ⊕10,800
PO Box 390 (43140-
1079)
Phone: (740)852-1616

Mansfield
News Journal **(25332)** ....(Mon.-Sat.) ★32,966
70 W. 4th St. (Sun.) ★42,490
PO Box 25 (44903)
Phone: (419)522-3311

Marietta
The Marietta Times **(25347)** ....(Mon.-Sat.) ★11,506
700 Channel Ln.
PO Box 635 (45750)
Phone: (614)373-2121

Marion
The Marion Star **(25351)** ....(Mon.-Sat.) ★14,349
150 Ct. St. (43302) (Sun.) ★14,745
Phone: (614)387-0400

Martins Ferry
The Times Leader **(25356)** ....(Mon.-Fri.) 18,355
200 S. 4th St. (43935)   (Sun.) 21,037
Phone: (740)633-1131

Marysville
Marysville Journal-Tribune **(25357)** ....‡6,337
207 N. Main St.
Box 226 (43040)
Phone: (937)644-9111

Massillon
The Independent **(25360)** ....(Mon.-Sat.) ‡15,216
50 North Ave. NW   (Sun.) ‡14,559
(44647)
Phone: (330)833-2631

Medina
Medina County Gazette **(25373)** ....(Mon.-Sat.) 15,356
885 W Liberty St.
(44258)
Phone: (216)725-4166

Middletown
Middletown Journal **(25378)** ....(Mon.-Sat.) ★21,189
52 S. Broad St.   (Sun.) ★22,487
PO Box 490 (45044)
Phone: (513)422-3611

Mount Vernon
Mt. Vernon News **(25399)** ....(Mon.-Sat.) 9,634
18 E. Vine (43050)
Phone: (614)397-5333

Napoleon
Northwest Signal **(25402)** ....‡5,704
595 E. Riverview
PO Box 567 (43545)
Phone: (419)592-5055

New Philadelphia
Times-Reporter **(25421)** ....(Mon.-Sat.) ★23,344
629 Wabash Ave. NW   (Sun.) ★24,827
PO Box 667 (44663)
Phone: (330)364-5577

Newark
The Advocate **(25424)** ....(Mon.-Sat.) 21,764
22 N. 1st St. (43055-   (Sun.) 22,687
5608)
Phone: (740)345-4053

Norwalk
Norwalk Reflector **(25441)** ....(Mon.-Sat.) ★8,701
61 E. Monroe St.
(44857)
Phone: (419)668-3771

Port Clinton
News Herald **(25482)** ....(Mon.-Sat.) 6,164
115 W. 2nd St.
PO Box 550 (43452)
Phone: (419)734-3141

Portsmouth
Portsmouth Daily Times **(25484)** ....(Mon.-Sat.) 15,944
637 6th St. (45662)   (Sun.) 15,830
Phone: (614)353-3101

Ravenna
Record-Courier **(25493)** ....(Mon.-Sat.) ★18,168
126 N. Chestnut St.   (Sun.) ★19,441
PO Box 1201 (44266)
Phone: (330)296-9657

St. Marys
The Evening Leader **(25504)** 6,600
102 E Spring St. (45885)
Phone: (419)394-7414

Salem
Salem News **(25506)** ....(Mon.-Sat.) ★7,509
161 N. Lincoln Ave.   (Sun.) ★6,785
(44460)
Phone: (330)332-4601

Sandusky
Sandusky Register **(25510)** ....(Mon.-Sat.) ★23,263
314 W. Market St.   (Sun.) ★27,591
(44870-2410)
Phone: (419)625-5500

Shelby
Shelby Daily Globe **(25514)** ....(Paid) ⊕4,035
37 W Main St.   (Non-paid) ⊕20
PO Box 647 (44875)
Phone: (419)342-4276

Sidney
The Sidney Daily News **(25521)** ....(Mon.-Sat.) 13,638
911 Vandemark Rd.
PO Box 150 (45365-
0150)
Phone: (937)498-2111

Springfield
Springfield News-Sun **(25532)** ....(Mon.-Sat.) ★30,848
202 N. Limestone St.   (Sun.) ★37,398
(45501)
Phone: (937)328-0300

Steubenville
Herald-Star **(25539)** ....(Mon.-Sat.) ★15,415
401 Herald Sq. (43952)   (Sun.) ★23,181
Phone: (740)283-4711

Tiffin
Advertiser-Tribune **(25559)** ....(Mon.-Sat.) ★10,944
320 Nelson St.   (Sun.) ★11,520
PO Box 778 (44883-
0778)
Phone: (419)448-3200

Toledo
The Blade **(25564)** ....(Mon.-Sat.) ‡140,000
541 N. Superior St.   (Sun.) ‡194,000
(43660-1000)
Phone: (419)724-6000

Troy
Troy Daily News **(25597)** ....(Mon.-Sat.) 10,838
224 S Market St.
(45373-3300)
Phone: (937)335-5634

Upper Sandusky
Chief-Union **(25604)** ....‡4,700
111 W Wyandot Ave.
PO Box 180 (43351)
Phone: (419)294-2332

Urbana
Urbana Daily Citizen **(25607)** ....(Mon.-Sat.) ★6,174
220 E. Court St.
PO Box 191 (43078)
Phone: (513)652-1331

Van Wert
Van Wert Times-Bulletin **(25609)**
PO Box 271
700 Fox Rd. (45891-
0271)
Phone: (419)238-2285

Wapakoneta
Wapakoneta Daily News **(25615)**
8 Willipie St.
PO Box 389 (45895)
Phone: (419)738-2120

Warren
Tribune Chronicle **(25617)** ....(Mon.-Sat.) ★34,443
240 Franklin St. SE   (Sun.) ★39,065
PO Box 1431 (44482)
Phone: (216)841-1600

Washington Court House
Record-Herald **(25619)** ....(Paid) ‡6,000
138 S. Fayette St.
(43160)
Phone: (740)335-3611

Willoughby
The News-Herald **(25662)** ....(Mon.-Sat.) 48,033
7085 Mentor Ave.   (Sun.) 59,506
(44094)
Phone: (440)951-0000

Wilmington
Wilmington News-Journal **(25667)** ....‡7,500
47 S. South St. (45177)
Phone: (937)382-2574

Wooster
The Daily Record **(25672)** ....(Mon.-Sat.) 22,374
212 E. Liberty St.   (Sun.) 23,177
PO Box 918 (44691-
4348)
Phone: (216)264-1125

Xenia
The Xenia Daily Gazette **(25687)** ....(Mon.-Sat.) 7,516
(45385-3580)

Youngstown
The Vindicator **(25699)** ....(Mon.-Sat.) 70,231
Vindicator Sq. No. 107   (Sun.) 100,736
PO Box 780 (44501)
Phone: (330)747-1471

Zanesville
The Times Recorder **(25717)** ....(Mon.-Sat.) ★21,203
34 S. 4th St. (43701)   (Sun.) ★20,729
Phone: (614)452-4561

OKLAHOMA
Ada
Ada Evening News **(25723)** ....(Mon.-Fri.) 9,375
116 N Broadway   (Sun.) 9,483
PO Box 489 (74820)
Phone: (580)332-4433

Altus
Altus Times **(25730)** ....‡6,600
PO Box 578 (73521)
Phone: (405)482-1221

Alva
Alva Review-Courier **(25737)** ....‡2,200
620 Choctaw (73717)
Phone: (405)327-2200

Ardmore
The Daily Ardmoreite **(25745)** ....(Mon.-Fri.) 10,995
PO Box 1328 (73402-   (Sun.) 13,087
1328)
Phone: (580)221-6500

Blackwell
Blackwell Journal-Tribune **(25765)** ....(Mon.-Fri.) ‡2,540
PO Box 760 (74631-   (Sun.) ‡2,690
0760)
Phone: (405)363-3370

Chickasha
Express-Star **(25785)** ....(Mon.-Fri.) ‡5,500
P.O. Box E (73023)   (Sun.) ‡6,400
Phone: (405)224-2600

Claremore
Claremore Daily Progress **(25788)** ......(Tues.-Fri.) 6,018
315 W. Will Rogers Blvd.   (Sun.) 6,881
(74017)
Phone: (918)341-1101

Clinton
The Clinton Daily News **(25790)** ....(Paid) ‡5,243
522 Avant Ave. (73601-   (Free) ‡21
3431)
Phone: (580)323-5151

Duncan
The Duncan Banner **(25800)** ....(Mon.-Fri.) 8,996
1001 Elm St.   (Sun.) 10,300
PO Box 1268 (73534-
1268)
Phone: (580)255-5354

Durant
The Bonham Daily Favorite **(25803)**
200 Beech St. (74701)

Durant Daily Democrat **(25804)** ....(Paid) 6,440
200 W. Beech   (Free) 604
PO Box 250 (74701)
Phone: (405)924-4388

El Reno
The El Reno Daily Tribune **(25816)** ....(Mon.-Fri.) ‡4,235
201 N. Rock Island   (Sun.) ‡4,606
PO Box 9 (73036)
Phone: (405)262-9000

Enid
News and Eagle **(25822)** ....(Mon.-Sat.) ★19,530
227 W Broadway   (Sun.) ★21,728
PO Box 1192 (73702)
Phone: (405)233-6600

Frederick
Frederick Leader **(25839)** ....(Paid) 2,100
304 W. Grand   (Free) 30
PO Box 190 (73542)
Phone: (580)335-2188

Guthrie
Guthrie News Leader **(25853)** ....(Tues.-Fri.) 2,849
107 W. Harrison   (Sun.) 3,158
PO Box 879 (73044)
Phone: (405)282-2222

Guymon
Guymon Daily Herald **(25855)** ....(Paid) 3,600
PO Box 19 (73942)   (Non-paid) 150
Phone: (405)338-3355

Holdenville
Holdenville Daily News **(25869)** ....(Paid) ‡3,270
1112 South Creek   (Free) ‡410
PO Box 751 (74848)
Phone: (405)379-5411

Hugo
The Hugo Daily News **(25872)**
128 E. Jackson St.
(74743)
Phone: (580)326-3311

Idabel
McCurtain Daily Gazette **(25875)** ......(Tues.-Fri.) ‡6,400
PO Box 179 (74745)   (Sun.) ‡8,400
Phone: (580)286-3321

Lawton
The Lawton Constitution **(25887)** .....(Mon.-Sat.) ★20,595
3rd & A Ave.   (Sun.) ★24,268
PO Box 2068 (73502-
0848)
Phone: (580)353-0620

Press **(25888)** ....(Paid) ‡14,818
3rd & A Ave.   (Free) ‡164
PO Box 2068 (73502-
0848)
Phone: (580)353-0620

McAlester
The McAlester NEWS-CAPITAL &
Democrat **(25909)** ....(Mon.-Fri.) 11,380
500 Second St.   (Sun.) 11,502
PO Box 987 (74502)
Phone: (918)423-1700

Muskogee
Phoenix &
Times-Democrat **(25923)** ....(Mon.-Sat.) 19,660
214 Wall St. (74401)   (Sun.) 20,656
Phone: (918)684-2900

Norman
The Norman Transcript **(25937)** .....(Mon.-Sat.) 15,475
PO Drawer 1058 (73070-   (Sun.) 17,241
1058)
Phone: (405)321-1800

Newspapers

Circulation: ★ = ABC; △ = BPA; ◆ = CAC; ● = CCAB; ❑ = VAC; ⊕ = PO Statement; ‡ = Publisher's Report; Boldface figures = sworn; Light figures = estimated.

2869

Circ.   Circ.   Circ.

OKLAHOMA (continued)

Oklahoma City
Oklahoman **(25989)** ....(Mon.-Sat.) ★199,581
9000 N. Broadway   (Sun.) ★289,605
PO Box 25125 (73114)
Phone: (405)475-3311

Pauls Valley
Pauls Valley Daily
  Democrat **(26029)** ....(Tues.-Fri.) ‡3,800
108 S. Willow   (Sun.) ‡4,800
PO Box 790 (73075)
Phone: (405)238-6464

Perry
The Perry Daily Journal **(26032)** ....‡3,260
714 Delaware St.
PO Box 311 (73077-
0311)
Phone: (405)336-2222

Ponca City
The Ponca City News **(26037)** ....(Mon.-Fri.) 10,201
300 N. 3rd St.   (Sun.) 11,585
PO Box 191 (74602)
Phone: (580)765-3311

Poteau
Poteau Daily News & Sun **(26045)** ....‡5,550
804 N. Broadway St.
PO Box 1237 (74953-
3535)
Phone: (918)647-3188

Pryor
Times **(26049)**
PO Box 308 (74362)
Phone: (918)825-3292

Sapulpa
Sapulpa Daily Herald **(26056)** ....(Paid) ⊕7,075
PO Box 1370 (74067-   (Free) ⊕25
1370)
Phone: (918)224-5185

Seminole
The Seminole Producer **(26058)** ......(Tues.-Fri.) ‡5,626
121 N Main   (Sun.) ‡6,250
PO Box 431 (74868)
Phone: (405)382-1100

Shawnee
The Shawnee News-Star **(26065)** ......(Tues.-Fri.) 10,288
PO Box 1688 (74801)   (Sat.) 19,288
Phone: (405)273-4200   (Sun.) 11,396

Stillwater
The News Press **(26079)** ....(Mon.-Sat.) ★9,105
PO Box 2288 (74076)   (Sun.) ★9,764
Phone: (405)372-5000

Tulsa
Tulsa World **(26139)** ....(Mon.-Sat.) 143,582
315 S. Boulder Ave.   (Sun.) 206,801
PO Box 1770 (74103)
Phone: (918)581-8300

Vinita
The Vinita Daily Journal **(26176)** ....(Paid) 4,150
138 S Wilson   (Free) 6,000
PO Box 328 (74301-
0328)
Phone: (918)256-6422

Weatherford
Weatherford Daily News **(26186)** ....‡4,300
118, S.Broadway (73096-
0919)
Phone: (580)772-3301

Westville
Tahlequah Daily Press **(26191)**
PO Box 550 (74965)
Phone: (919)723-5445

Wewoka
Wewoka Daily Times **(26194)** ....‡1,250
210 S Wewoka
PO Box 61 (74884)
Phone: (405)257-3341

Woodward
Woodward News **(26198)** ....(Paid) 6,411
904 Oklahoma Ave.   (Free) 10,019
PO Box 928 (73801)
Phone: (580)256-2200

OREGON
Albany
Albany Democrat-Herald **(26206)** .....(Mon.-Sat.) ★17,989
600 Lyon St. SW
PO Box 130 (97321-
0041)
Phone: (541)926-2211

Ashland
The Tidings **(26218)** ....(Mon.-Sat.) ★5,010
PO Box 7 (97520)
Phone: (503)482-3456

Astoria
The Daily Astorian **(26224)** ....(Mon.-Fri.) ★8,429
PO Box 210 (97103)
Phone: (503)325-3211

Baker City
Baker City Herald **(26232)** ....(Mon.-Thurs.) 3,173
1915 1st St.   (Fri.) 3,470
PO Box 807 (97814)
Phone: (503)523-3673

Bend
The Bulletin **(26241)** ....(Mon.-Fri.) 27,663
1777 SW Chandler Ave.   (Sun.) 29,007
PO Box 6020 (97708)
Phone: (541)382-1181

Coos Bay
The World **(26274)** ....(Mon.-Fri.) 14,192
350 Commercial   (Sat.) 15,747
PO Box 1840 (97420-
0147)
Phone: (503)269-1222

Corvallis
The Corvallis
  Gazette-Times **(26286)** ....(Mon.-Sat.) 12,245
600 SW Jefferson Ave.   (Sun.) 14,713
PO Box 368 (97333)
Phone: (541)753-2641

Eugene
The Register-Guard **(26334)** ....(Mon.-Fri.) ★72,28
3500 Chad Dr., 97408   (Sat.) ★81,056
PO Box 10188 (97440-   (Sun.) ★77,191
2188)
Phone: (541)485-1234

Grants Pass
Grants Pass Daily Courier **(26362)** ....(Mon.-Sat.) 16,987
409 SE 7th St.
PO Box 1468 (97526)
Phone: (541)474-3700

Klamath Falls
Herald and News **(26384)** ....(Mon.-Fri.) 17,200
PO Box 788 (97601-   (Sun.) 17,800
0320)
Phone: (541)885-4410

La Grande
The Observer **(26399)** ....(Mon.-Sat.) 6,768
PO Box 3170 (97850)
Phone: (503)963-3161

Medford
The Mail Tribune **(26418)** ....(Mon.-Thurs.) ★26,737
Fir & 6th St.   (Fri.) ★35,148
PO Box 1108 (97501)   (Sun.) ★31,838
Phone: (503)776-4422   (Sat.) ★26,737

Ontario
Argus Observer **(26453)** ....(Mon.-Fri.) 7,144
1160 SW 4th S.   (Sun.) 8,292
PO Box 130 (97914-
4365)
Phone: (541)889-5387

Pendleton
East Oregonian **(26458)** ....(Mon.-Sat.) 11,107
211 S.E. Byers   (Sun.) 11,989
PO Box 1089 (97801)
Phone: (541)276-2211

Portland
The Oregonian **(26495)** ....(Mon.-Fri.) ★342,789
1320 SW Broadway   (Sat.) ★330,636
(97201-3469)   (Sun.) ★423,033
Phone: (503)221-8327

Roseburg
The News-Review **(26555)** ....(Mon.-Fri.) ★19,281
345 NE Winchester   (Sun.) ★20,294
PO Box 1248 (97470)
Phone: (541)672-3321

Salem
Statesman Journal **(26573)** ....(Mon.-Sat.) ★55,886
280, Church St. NE   (Sun.) ★63,255
PO Box 13009 (97301)
Phone: (503)399-6611

PENNSYLVANIA
Allentown
The Morning Call **(26629)** ....(Mon.-Sat.) 127,175
101 N. 6th St., No. 1260   (Sun.) 170,744
(18101-1403)
Phone: (610)820-6500

Altoona
Altoona Mirror **(26635)** ....(Mon.-Sat.) ★32,185
PO Box 2008 (16603-   (Sun.) ★38,738
2008)
Phone: (814)946-7411

Beaver
Beaver County Times **(26684)** ....(Mon.-Fri.) ★42,778
400 Fair Ave.   (Sun.) ★48,875
PO Box 400 (15009-
0400)
Phone: (412)775-3200

Bedford
Bedford Daily Gazette **(26688)** ....‡10,200
PO Box 671 (15522)
Phone: (814)623-1151

Bloomsburg
Press Enterprise **(26718)** ....(Mon.-Sat.) 20,990
3185 Lackawanna Ave.   (Sun.) 20,347
(17815-3398)
Phone: (717)784-2121

Bradford
The Bradford Era **(26727)** ....(Mon.-Sat.) 10,937
43 Main St.
PO Box 365 (16701)
Phone: (814)368-3173

Butler
Butler Eagle **(26743)** ....(Mon.-Fri.) ★28,784
PO Box 271 (16003)   (Sun.) ★30,677

Carlisle
Sentinel **(26761)** ....(Mon.-Sat.) 15,287
457 E North St.   (Sun.) 15,497
PO Box 130 (17013)
Phone: (717)243-2611

Chambersburg
Public Opinion **(26769)** ....(Mon.-Sat.) 21,448
77 N. 3rd St.
PO Box 499 (17201)
Phone: (717)264-6161

Clearfield
The Progress **(26788)** ....(Mon.-Sat.) 13,911
206 E. Locust St.
PO Box 291 (16830)
Phone: (814)765-5581

Connellsville
The Daily Courier **(26801)** ....(Mon.-Sat.) 9,686
127 N. Apple St. (15425-
3196)
Phone: (724)628-2000

Corry
Corry Journal **(26809)** ....(Paid) 4,184
28 W South St. (16407)   (Free) 200
Phone: (814)665-8291

Danville
The Danville News **(26817)** ....‡3,839
PO Box 200 (17821)
Phone: (717)275-3235

Doylestown
The Intelligencer
  Record **(26832)** ....(Mon.-Thurs.) ★43,819
333 N Broad St., No.   (Fri.) ★51,384
858 (18901-0858)   (Sun.) ★52,197
Phone: (215)345-3000

Easton
The Express-Times **(26850)** ....(Mon.-Fri.) ★48,641
30 N. 4th St.   (Sat.) ★45,213
PO Box 391 (18044)   (Sun.) ★48,882
Phone: (610)258-7171

Elkins Park
The Dong-A Daily News **(26870)** ......(Combined) 23,000
7300 Old York Rd., No.
213 (19027)
Phone: (215)935-5000

Ellwood City
Ellwood City Ledger **(26871)** ....‡6,991
835 Lawrence Ave.
(16117)
Phone: (724)758-5573

Erie
Erie Daily Times **(26896)** ....(Mon.-Fri.) 8,513
205 W. 12th St. (16534-
0001)
Phone: (814)453-4691

Erie Times-News **(26897)** ....(Sat.) ★59,928
205 W. 12th St. (16534-   (Sun.) ★87,913
0001)   (Mon.-Fri.) ★58,101
Phone: (814)453-4691

Morning News **(26901)** ....(Mon.-Fri.) 35,912
205 W. 12th St. (16534-   (Sat.) 61,625
0001)   (Sun.) 93,645
Phone: (814)453-4691

Gettysburg
Gettysburg Times **(26939)** ....(Mon.-Sat.) 9,775
PO Box 3669
1570 Fairfield Rd.
(17325)
Phone: (717)334-1131

Greensburg
Standard-Observer **(26955)** ....(Mon.-Sat.) 7,428
622 Cabin Hill Dr.
(15601)
Phone: (724)834-1151

Tribune-Review **(26956)** ....(Mon.) ★107,395
622 Cabin Hill Dr.   (Tues.-Fri.) ★119,338
(15601)   (Sat.) ★119,338
Phone: (724)834-1151   (Sun.) ★179,567

Greenville
Record-Argus **(26958)** ....(Mon.-Sat.) 5,443
10 Penn Ave.
PO Box 711 (16125-
0711)
Phone: (724)588-5000

Hanover
The Evening Sun (26974) ....(Mon.-Sat.) 19,348
135 Baltimore St. (Sun.) 20,242
(17331)
Phone: (717)637-3736

Harrisburg
The Patriot-News (27002) ....(Mon.-Sat.) ★101,598
812 Market St. (17105) (Sun.) ★153,351
Phone: (717)255-8100

Hazleton
Standard-Speaker (27035) ....(Mon.-Sat.) ★21,394
PO Box 578 (18201) (Sun.) ★20,988
Phone: (717)455-3636

Honesdale
The Wayne Independent (27051) 8,500
220 8th St., No. 122
(18431-1854)
Phone: (570)253-3055

Horsham
The Record (27063) ....(Mon.-Fri.) ‡44,729
145 N. Easton Rd. (Sun.) ‡52,143
(19044)
Phone: (215)957-8100

Huntingdon
The Daily News (27068) ....‡10,227
325 Penn St. (16652)
Phone: (814)643-4040

Indiana
Gazette (27073) ....(Mon.-Sat.) 17,012
899 Water St. (Sun.) 9,068
PO Box 10 (15701-1705)
Phone: (724)465-5555

Johnstown
Tribune-Democrat (27089) ....(Mon.-Sat.) ★42,622
425 Locust St. (15907) (Sun.) ★47,757
Phone: (814)532-5199

Kane
Kane Republican (27103) ....(Combined) ⊕2,850
200 N Fraley St. (16735)
Phone: (814)837-6000

Lancaster
Intelligencer Journal (27141) ....(Mon.-Sat.) ★45,424
8 W. King St.
PO Box 1328 (17608-
1328)
Phone: (717)291-8811

Lancaster New Era (27143) ....(Mon.-Sat.) ★43,194
8 W. King St.
PO Box 1328 (17608-
1328)
Phone: (717)291-8811

Lansdale
The Reporter (27159) 18,602
307 Derstine Ave.
(19446-3532)
Phone: (215)855-8440

Latrobe
The Latrobe Bulletin (27165) ....(Mon.-Sat.) 7,900
1211 Ligonier St.
PO Box 111 (15650-
0111)
Phone: (724)537-3351

Lebanon
Lebanon Daily News (27172) ....(Mon.-Sat.) 20,484
718 Poplar St. (Sun.) 20,801
PO Box 600 (17042)
Phone: (717)272-5611

Lehighton
The Times News (27183) ....(Mon.-Sat.) 14,387
PO Box 239 (18235-
0239)
Phone: (610)826-2554

Levittown
Bucks County Courier
Times (27186) ....(Mon.-Fri.) ★67,094
8400 Rte. 13 (19057) (Sun.) ★73,252
Phone: (215)949-4000

Lock Haven
The Express (27204) ....(Mon.-Sat.) 9,754
9-11 W. Main St.
PO Box 208 (17745-
1217)
Phone: (717)748-6791

Mc Keesport
The Daily News (27228) ....(Mon.-Sat.) 22,079
409 Walnut St. (15132)
Phone: (412)664-9161

Meadville
The Meadville Tribune (27235) ....(Mon.-Sat.) ★14,746
947 Federal Ct. (16335- (Sun.) ★14,636
3234)
Phone: (814)724-6370

Milton
The Milton Daily Standard/The Lewisburg Daily
Journal (27270) ....(Paid) ‡4,500
21 Arch St. (17847-0259)
Phone: (717)742-9671

Monessen
The Valley Independent (27273) .....(Mon.-Sat.) ★15,462
Eastgate 19 (15062)
Phone: (724)684-5200

New Castle
New Castle News (27314) ....(Mon.-Sat.) ★18,707
2735 N. Mercer St.
PO Box 60 (16105-1728)
Phone: (412)654-6651

Norristown
The Times Herald (27337) ....(Mon.-Sat.) 22,601
410 Markley St. (Sun.) 19,050
PO Box 591 (19404)
Phone: (610)272-2500

Oil City
The Derrick (27346) ....‡18,096
PO Box 928 (16301)
Phone: (814)676-7444

Philadelphia
Philadelphia Daily News (27625) ......(Mon.-Fri.) 152,037
400 N. Broad St. (Sat.) 75,981
(19130-4015)
Phone: (215)854-5900

Philadelphia Inquirer (27627) ....(Mon.-Fri.) ★373,892
400 N. Broad St. (Sat.) ★321,253
(19130) (Sun.) ★747,969
Phone: (215)854-2000

Pittsburgh
Post-Gazette (27837) ....(Mon.-Fri.) ★246,091
34 Blvd. of the Allies (Sat.) ★233,356
(15222) (Sun.) ★406,930
Phone: (412)263-1100

Pottstown
The Mercury (27899) ....(Mon.-Sat.) 25,350
24 N. Hanover St. (Sun.) 26,173
(19464)
Phone: (215)323-3000

Pottsville
Pottsville Republican (27903) ....(Mon.-Fri.) 29,563
111 Mahantongo St. (Sat.) 32,100
(17901-3008) (Sun.) 32,100
Phone: (717)622-3456

Primos
The Daily Times (27907) ....(Mon.-Fri.) 51,098
500 Mildred Ave. (19018) (Sat.) 42,431
Phone: (610)622-8800 (Sun.) 49,218

Punxsutawney
The Spirit (27909) ....(Paid) 5,862
510 Pine St. (Free) 44
PO Box 444 (15767-
0444)
Phone: (814)938-8740

Reading
Reading Eagle (27919) ....(Mon.-Sat.) ★63,199
PO Box 582 (19603- (Sun.) ★92,111
0582)

Reading Times (27920) ....(Mon.-Fri.) ★51,222
PO Box 582 (19603-
0582)

Ridgway
The Ridgway Record (27935) ....‡3,112
20 Main St.
PO Box T (15853-0366)
Phone: (814)773-3161

St. Marys
The Daily Press (27942) ....‡5,489
245 Brussels St.
PO Box 353 (15857-
0353)
Phone: (814)781-1596

Sayre
The Evening Times (27945) 7,841
201 N. Lehigh Ave. (Free) 42
(18840)
Phone: (570)888-9643

Scranton
The Scranton Times (27963) ....(Mon.-Fri.) ★33,226
149 Penn Ave. (Sat.) ★58,702
PO Box 3311 (18505- (Sun.) ★75,675
3311)
Phone: (570)348-9154

Shamokin
News-Item (27984) ....(Mon.-Sat.) ★10,985
707 N. Rock St.
PO Box 587 (17872)
Phone: (570)644-6397

Sharon
The Herald (27986) ....(Mon.-Sat.) 21,603
PO Box 51 (16146) (Sun.) 23,019
Phone: (412)981-6100

Somerset
Daily American (28002) ....(Mon.-Sat.) 13,676
334 W. Main St.
PO Box 638 (15501)
Phone: (814)444-5900

State College
Centre Daily Times (28018) ....(Mon.-Fri.) 25,503
3400 E. College Ave. (Sat.) 26,447
(16801-7528) (Sun.) 32,633
Phone: (814)238-5000

Stroudsburg
Pocono Record (28035) ....(Mon.-Sat.) 20,447
511 Lenox St. (18360) (Sun.) 26,023
Phone: (570)421-3000

Sunbury
The Daily Item (28038) ....(Mon.-Sat.) 23,947
200 Market St. (Sun.) 27,556
PO Box 607 (17801-
0607)
Phone: (717)286-5671

Tarentum
Valley News Dispatch (28048) ....(Mon.-Sat.) ★30,572
210 4th Ave. (15084) (Sun.) ★30,604
Phone: (724)226-4666

Titusville
The Titusville Herald (28050) 4,833
209 W Spring St.
PO Box 328 (16354)
Phone: (814)827-3634

Towanda
The Daily Review (28053) ....(Mon.-Sat.) ♦9,263
116 Main St. (18848) (Sun.) ♦10,342
Phone: (570)265-2151

Tyrone
The Daily Herald (28064) ....‡2,300
1067 Pennsylvania Ave (Sat.) 7,000
(16686)
Phone: (814)684-4000

Uniontown
Herald-Standard (28067) ....(Mon.-Fri.) ★28,128
8-18 E Church St. (Sun.) ★30,536
PO Box 848 (15401-
3563)
Phone: (412)439-7500

Warren
Warren Times Observer (28105) ...(Mon.-Sat.) ★11,385
205 Pennsylvania Ave.
W
PO Box 188 (16365-
2412)
Phone: (814)723-8200

Washington
Observer-Reporter (28115) ....(Mon.-Sat.) ★36,399
122 S. Main St. (15301) (Sun.) ★38,817
Phone: (724)222-2200

Waynesboro
Record Herald (28138) ....(Mon.-Sat.) 8,789
PO Box 271 (17268-
2156)
Phone: (717)762-2151

West Chester
Daily Local News (28146) ....(Mon.-Fri.) 30,451
250 N Bradford Ave. (Sat.) 27,275
(19382-2800) (Sun.) 30,022
Phone: (610)696-1776

Wilkes Barre
Citizens' Voice (28164) ....(Mon.-Sat.) ★32,335
75 N. Washington St. (Sun.) ★30,472
(18711)
Phone: (570)821-2000

The Times Leader (28167) ....(Mon.-Sat.) 44,131
15 N. Main St. (18711) (Sun.) 62,738
Phone: (570)829-7100

York
York Daily Record (28207) ....(Mon.-Fri.) ★43,845
122 S George St. (Sat.) ★70,986
PO Box 15122 (17405-
7122)
Phone: (717)771-2000

The York Dispatch (28208) ....(Mon.-Fri.) ★39,150
1517 E Philadelphia, Ste.
2807 (17403-1234)
Phone: (717)854-1575

PUERTO RICO
San Juan
El Nuevo Dia (28292) ....(Mon.-Sat.) 200,484
PO Box 9067512 (Sun.) 239,494
(00906-7512)
Phone: (787)641-8000

El Vocero de Puerto Rico (28294) ....(Mon.-Fri.) 181,168
PO Box 9023831 (Sat.) 156,051
(00902-3831)
Phone: (809)721-2300

RHODE ISLAND
Newport
The Newport Daily News (28368) .....(Mon.-Sat.) 12,680
PO Box 420
101 Malbone Rd.
(02840)
Phone: (401)849-3300

Circulation: ★ = ABC; △ = BPA; ♦ = CAC; ● = CCAB; ❑ = VAC; ⊕ = PO Statement; ‡ = Publisher's Report; Boldface figures = sworn; Light figures = estimated.

Newspapers

Circ.　　　　　　　　　　　Circ.　　　　　　　　　　　Circ.

RHODE ISLAND (continued)
Pawtucket
The Times **(28379)** ....(Mon.-Sat.) 13,763
23 Exchange St.
PO Box 307 (02862)
Phone: (401)722-4000

West Warwick
The Kent County Daily
Times **(28455)** ....(Mon.-Sat.) ★4,101
1353 Main St. (02893)
Phone: (401)821-7400

Westerly
The Westerly Sun **(28458)** ....(Mon.-Sat.) ★9,977
PO Box 520 (02891-　　　　　　　　(Sun.) ★10,658
0520)
Phone: (401)596-7791

Woonsocket
The Call **(28460)** ....(Mon.-Sat.) ★14,009
75 Main St.　　　　　　　　　　　　(Sun.) ★18,915
PO Box A (02895)
Phone: (401)762-3000

SOUTH CAROLINA
Aiken
Aiken Standard **(28467)** ....(Mon.-Sat.) ★13,364
326 Rutland Dr.　　　　　　　　　　(Sun.) ★14,066
PO Box 456 (29801-
4006)
Phone: (803)648-2311

Anderson
Anderson
Independent-Mail **(28473)** ....(Mon.-Sat.) ★38,576
1000 Williamston Rd.　　　　　　　　(Sun.) ★44,194
PO Box 2507 (29622)
Phone: (864)224-4321

Beaufort
The Beaufort Gazette **(28487)** ......(Mon.-Sat.) ★11,879
1556 Salem Rd.　　　　　　　　　　(Sun.) ★11,535
PO Box 399 (29901)
Phone: (843)524-3183

Charleston
The Post and Courier **(28517)** ......(Mon.-Sat.) ★101,288
134 Columbus St.　　　　　　　　　(Sun.) ★113,999
(29403)
Phone: (843)577-7111

Columbia
The State **(28570)** ....(Mon.-Sat.) 118,783
C/O Mark Lett　　　　　　　　　　(Sun.) 156,165
PO Box 1333 (29202)
Phone: (803)771-6161

Florence
Florence Morning News **(28602)** ....(Mon.-Sat.) ★32,800
PO Box 100528 (29501-　　　　　　(Sun.) ★35,344
0528)
Phone: (803)317-6397

Greenville
The Greenville News **(28623)** ....(Mon.-Fri.) ★88,870
PO Box 1688 (29602)　　　　　　　(Sat.) ★97,274
Phone: (864)298-4100　　　　　　　(Sun.) ★119,410

Greenwood
Index-Journal **(28646)** ....(Mon.-Sat.) 14,575
PO Box 1018 (29648)　　　　　　　　(Sun.) 16,172

Hilton Head Island
The Island Packet **(28661)** ....(Mon.-Sat.) ★17,536
PO Box 5727 (29938)　　　　　　　(Sun.) ★19,052
Phone: (843)706-8100

Orangeburg
The Times & Democrat **(28733)** .....(Mon.-Sat.) ★17,970
(29115)　　　　　　　　　　　　　(Sun.) ★18,375
Phone: (803)534-1060

Rock Hill
The Herald **(28744)** ....(Mon.-Sat.) 31,050
132 W. Main St.　　　　　　　　　　(Sun.) 32,918
PO Box 11707 (29730)
Phone: (803)329-4000

Spartanburg
Herald-Journal **(28759)** ....(Mon.-Sat.) ★51,376
PO Box 1657 (29304)　　　　　　　(Sun.) ★59,637
Phone: (864)582-4511

Sumter
The Item **(28768)** ....(Mon.-Fri.) ★29,820
20 N. Magnolia　　　　　　　　　　(Sun.) ★34,242
PO Box 1677 (29150)
Phone: (803)775-6331

Union
Union Daily Times **(28776)** ....(Paid) ‡7,400
PO Box 749
100 Times Blvd. (29379-
0749)
Phone: (864)427-1234

SOUTH DAKOTA
Brookings
The Brookings Register **(28812)** ....(Mon.-Fri.) 5,483
312 5th St.　　　　　　　　　　　　(Sat.) 5,678
PO Box 177 (57006-
0177)
Phone: (605)692-6271

Madison
Madison Daily Leader **(28886)** ....‡3,551
214 S. Egan Ave.
PO Box 348 (57042)
Phone: (605)256-4555

Mitchell
The Daily Republic **(28900)** ....(Mon.-Fri.) ❑12,243
120 S. Lawler　　　　　　　　　　(Sat.) ❑12,485
PO Box 1288 (57301)
Phone: (605)996-5514

Pierre
Pierre Capital Journal **(28918)**
333 W Dakota
PO Box 878 (57501)
Phone: (605)224-7301

Rapid City
Rapid City Journal **(28931)** ....(Mon.-Sat.) ★29,820
507 Main St.　　　　　　　　　　(Sun.) ★34,242
PO Box 450 (57701)
Phone: (605)394-8383

Spearfish
Black Hills Pioneer **(28993)** ....‡5,000
315 Seaton Cir.
PO Box 7 (57783)
Phone: (605)642-2761

Watertown
Watertown Public Opinion **(29019)** ....(Mon.-Sat.) 13,558
120 3rd Ave. NW
Box 10 (57201)
Phone: (605)886-6901

Yankton
Yankton Daily Press & Dakotan **(29040)** ....‡10,180
319 Walnut St.
PO Box 56 (57078)
Phone: (605)665-7811

TENNESSEE
Athens
Daily Post-Athenian **(29052)** ....(Mon.-Fri.) 10,807
PO Box 340 (37371-　　　　　　　(Sat.) 11,958
0340)　　　　　　　　　　　　　(Sun.) 11,958

Chattanooga
Chattanooga Times & Free
Press **(29087)** ....(Mon.-Sat.) 72,449
400 E. 11th St.　　　　　　　　　(Sun.) 100,997
PO Box 1447 (37401)
Phone: (423)756-1234

Cleveland
The Cleveland Daily
Banner **(29121)** ....(Mon.-Fri.) 15,370
PO Box 3600 (37320-　　　　　　　(Sun.) 17,024
3600)
Phone: (423)472-5041

Columbia
The Daily Herald **(29136)** ....(Mon.-Fri.) 11,769
1115 S. Main　　　　　　　　　　(Sun.) 13,452
PO Box 1425 (38401)
Phone: (615)388-6464

Cookeville
Herald-Citizen Plus **(29143)** ....(Mon.-Fri.) ★11,151
555 S Old Kentucky Rd.　　　　　　(Sun.) ★13,773
PO Box 2729 (38502)
Phone: (931)526-9715

Dyersburg
State Gazette **(29175)** ....(Mon.-Fri.) 7,696
PO Box 808
Hwy. 51 By-Pass
(38025)
Phone: (901)285-4091

Elizabethton
Elizabethton Star **(29179)** ....(Mon.-Fri.) 8,315
300 Sycamore St.　　　　　　　　(Sun.) 9,963
PO Box 1960 (37644-
1960)
Phone: (423)542-4151

Greeneville
The Greeneville Sun **(29212)** ....(Mon.-Sat.) ★14,613
121 W Summer St.
PO Box 1630 (37743-
4923)
Phone: (615)638-4181

Johnson City
Johnson City Press **(29251)** ....(Mon.-Sat.) 30,365
204 W Main St.　　　　　　　　　(Sun.) 34,413
PO Box 1717 (37601)
Phone: (423)929-3111

Kingsport
Kingsport Times News **(29260)** ....(Mon.-Fri.) ★41,396
701 Lynn Garden Dr.　　　　　　　(Sat.) ★39,998
PO Box 479 (37662)　　　　　　　(Sun.) ★44,648
Phone: (423)246-8121

Knoxville
The Knoxville
News-Sentinel **(29280)** ....(Mon.-Thurs.) 119,901
2332 News Sentinel Dr.　　　　　　(Fri.) 133,856
(37921)　　　　　　　　　　　　(Sat.) 130,890
Phone: (865)523-3131　　　　　　　(Sun.) 159,109

Maryville
The Daily Times **(29347)** ....(Mon.-Sat.) 20,811
307 E. Harper St.　　　　　　　　(Sun.) 19,963
PO Box 9740 (37802)
Phone: (423)981-1100

Memphis
The Commercial Appeal **(29362)**
495 Union Ave. (38103)
Phone: (901)529-2211

The Daily News **(29367)** ....‡2,000
193 Jefferson Ave.
(38103)
Phone: (901)523-1561

Morristown
Citizen Tribune **(29418)** ....(Mon.-Fri.) ★18,236
PO Box 625 (37815-　　　　　　　(Sun.) ★24,441
0625)
Phone: (423)581-5630

Murfreesboro
Daily News-Journal **(29430)** ....(Mon.-Sat.) 15,465
224 N Walnut St.　　　　　　　　(Sun.) 18,235
PO Box 68 (37133-0068)
Phone: (615)893-5860

Oak Ridge
The Oak Ridger **(29551)** ....(Mon.-Thurs.) 8,500
785 Oak Ridge Turnpike　　　　　　(Fri.) 9,500
Box 3446 (37831-3446)
Phone: (423)482-1021

Paris
The Paris Post-Intelligencer **(29559)** ....(Paid) 7,900
208 E Wood St.　　　　　　　　(Non-paid) 105
PO Box 310 (38242-
0310)
Phone: (731)642-1162

Sevierville
Mountain Press **(29589)** ....‡9,787
119 Riverbend Dr.
(37876)
Phone: (865)428-0746

Shelbyville
Shelbyville Times-Gazette **(29600)** ....‡8,458
323 E. Depot St.
PO Box 380 (37162)
Phone: (931)684-1200

Union City
Union City Daily Messenger **(29635)** ....‡8,700
613 E. Jackson St.
Box 430 (38261)
Phone: (731)885-0744

TEXAS
Abilene
Abilene Reporter-News **(29652)** ....(Mon.-Sat.) ★34,007
101 Cypress St.　　　　　　　　　(Sun.) ★43,855
PO Box 30 (79604)
Phone: (915)673-4271

Amarillo
Amarillo Globe-News **(29694)** ....(Sun.) ★64,013
PO Box 2091 (79166)　　　　　　(Mon.-Sat.) 51,623
Phone: (806)376-4488

Angleton
Angleton Times **(29725)** ....(Paid) ♦2,593
700 Western Ave.　　　　　　　(Non-paid) ♦111
(77515)
Phone: (979)849-8581

Athens
Athens Daily Review **(29746)** ....‡7,250
201 S. Prairieville St.
PO Box 32 (75751-0032)
Phone: (903)675-5626

Austin
Austin
American-Statesman **(29755)** .....(Mon.-Sat.) ★183,288
Austin360　　　　　　　　　　(Sun.) ★233,608
305 S. Congress Ave.
(78701)
Phone: (512)912-2591

Bay City
The Daily Tribune **(29891)** ....(Paid) 5,739
PO Box 2450 (77404)　　　　　　(Free) 1,413
Phone: (979)245-5555

Numbers cited after listings are entry numbers rather than page numbers.

Baytown
The Baytown Sun **(29894)** ....(Mon.-Fri.) 9,976
1301 Memorial Dr.　　　　　　　(Sun.) 10,954
PO Box 90 (77520)
Phone: (281)422-8302

Beaumont
Beaumont Enterprise **(29897)** ....(Mon.-Sat.) ★55,553
380 Main St.　　　　　　　　　(Sun.) ★62,784
PO Box 3071 (77704-
3071)
Phone: (409)833-3311

Big Spring
Big Spring Herald **(29924)** ....(Mon.-Fri.) ★4,337
710 Scurry　　　　　　　　　　(Sun.) ★5,364
PO Box 1431 (79720)
Phone: (915)263-7331

Borger
Borger News-Herald **(29937)** ....(Mon.-Fri.) 6,448
207 N. Main St.　　　　　　　　(Sun.) 7,321
PO Box 5130 (79008-
5130)
Phone: (806)273-5611

Brenham
The Banner Press **(29948)** ....(Mon.-Fri.) 5,627
PO Box 585 (77834)　　　　　　(Sun.) 5,587

Brownsville
Brownsville Herald **(29959)** ....(Mon.-Fri.) 16,632
PO Box 351 (78522-　　　　　　(Sun.) 18,349
0351)
Phone: (210)542-4301

Brownwood
Brownwood Bulletin **(29965)** ......(Mon.-Fri.) ‡9,000
700 Carnegie St.　　　　　　　(Sun.) ‡11,000
PO Box 1189 (76801)
Phone: (915)646-2541

Bryan
Bryan-College Station
Eagle **(29973)** ....(Mon.-Sat.) ★24,875
1729 Briarcrest Dr.　　　　　　(Sun.) ★28,329
PO Box 3000 (77802)
Phone: (979)776-4444

Cleburne
Cleburne Times-Review **(30025)** ....(Mon.-Fri.) ‡7,850
PO Box 1569 (76033-　　　　　　(Sun.) ‡9,200
1569)
Phone: (817)645-2441

Clute
Brazosport Facts **(30033)** ....(Mon.-Sat.) 16,727
PO Box 549　　　　　　　　　(Sun.) 17,861
720 S. Main
PO Box 549 (77531)
Phone: (409)265-7411

Conroe
Conroe Courier **(30070)** ....(Mon.-Sat.) ★11,207
100 Ave. A　　　　　　　　　(Sun.) ★12,269
PO Box 609 (77301)
Phone: (409)756-6671

Corpus Christi
Corpus Christi
Caller-Times **(30076)** ....(Mon.-Thurs.) ★63,260
820 N. Lower Broadway　　　　(Fri.) ★64,524
PO Box 9136 (78469)　　　　　(Sun.) ★80,321
Phone: (361)884-2011　　　　　(Sat.) ★61,837

Corsicana
Corsicana Daily Sun **(30101)** ....(Mon.-Sat.) ‡10,444
405 E. Collin　　　　　　　　(Sun.) ‡10,996
PO Box 622 (75151-
9006)
Phone: (214)872-3931

Dalhart
Dalhart Daily Texan **(30119)** ....(Tues.-Fri.) ‡2,600
410 Denrock Ave.　　　　　　(Sun.) ‡2,600
(79022)
Phone: (806)244-4511

Dallas
The Dallas Morning
News **(30147)** ....(Mon.-Thurs.) ★505,724
508 Young St.　　　　　　　　(Fri.) ★586,886
PO Box 655237 (75265)　　　　(Sat.) ★543,411
Phone: (214)977-8222　　　　　(Sun.) ★784,905

Del Rio
Del Rio News-Herald **(30224)** ....(Mon.-Sat.) 5,116
PO Box 4020 (78840)　　　　　(Sun.) 5,550
Phone: (512)775-1551

Denton
Denton Record Chronicle **(30235)** .....(Mon.-Fri.) 16,272
314 E. Hickory　　　　　　　(Wed.) 40,428
PO Box 369 (76201)　　　　　(Sun.) 19,403
Phone: (940)387-3811

El Paso
El Paso Times **(30280)** ....(Mon.-Sat.) ★72,398
Times Plaza (79901-　　　　　(Sun.) ★89,669
1470)
Phone: (915)546-6104

Ennis
Ennis Daily News **(30309)** ....(Mon.-Fri.) ‡4,050
213 N Dallas St.　　　　　　　(Sun.) ‡4,050
PO Box 100 (75120)
Phone: (972)875-3801

Fort Worth
Fort Worth
Star-Telegram **(30338)** ....(Mon.-Thurs.) ★218,975
PO Box 1870 (76101)　　　　　(Fri.) ★261,418
Phone: (817)390-7400　　　　　(Sat.) ★254,046
　　　　　　　　　　　　(Sun.) ★321,354

Gainesville
Gainesville Daily Register **(30376)** ....(Paid) 7,500
306 E. California St.　　　　　(Free) 45
PO Box 309 (76241)
Phone: (817)665-5511

Galveston
The Galveston County Daily
News **(30380)** ....(Mon.-Sat.) 24,025
8522 Teichman Rd.　　　　　　(Sun.) 24,875
PO Box 628 (77553)
Phone: (409)683-5200

Greenville
Greenville Herald Banner **(30413)** ....(Mon.-Sat.) 8,935
2305 King St.　　　　　　　　(Sun.) 10,138
PO Box 1047 (75403-
1047)
Phone: (903)455-4220

Harlingen
Valley Morning Star **(30425)** ....(Mon.-Sat.) 23,492
1310 S Commerce　　　　　　(Sun.) 25,577
PO Box 511 (78551)
Phone: (956)430-6200

Henderson
Henderson Daily News **(30440)** ....(Paid) ⊕6,600
1711 S Hwy. 79
PO Box 30 (75653-0030)
Phone: (903)657-2501

Hereford
The Hereford Brand **(30443)** ....‡4,300
PO Box 673 (79045)
Phone: (806)364-2030

Houston
Houston Chronicle **(30481)** ....(Mon.-Sat.) ★552,052
801 Texas Ave. (77002)　　　　(Sun.) ★744,935
Phone: (713)220-7171

Huntsville
The Huntsville Item **(30595)** ....(Mon.-Fri.) 6,276
PO Box 539 (77342-　　　　　　(Sun.) 6,588
0534)

Kerrville
Kerrville Daily Times **(30639)** ....(Mon.-Fri.) 8,627
429 Jefferson St. (78028)　　　(Sun.) 10,437
Phone: (830)896-7000

Laredo
Laredo Morning Times **(30670)** ....(Mon.-Sat.) 21,256
111 Esperanza Dr., No.　　　　(Sun.) 23,593
2129 (78041-2607)
Phone: (210)728-2500

Longview
Longview News-Journal **(30704)** ......(Mon.-Sat.) ★28,758
320 Methvin St. (75601)　　　　(Sun.) ★35,967
Phone: (903)757-3311

Lubbock
Lubbock
Avalanche-Journal **(30715)** ......(Mon.-Sat.) ★52,486
710 Ave. J, No. 491　　　　　(Sun.) ★62,259
(79401-1808)
Phone: (806)762-8844

Lufkin
The Lufkin Daily News **(30739)** ....(Mon.-Fri.) 14,608
PO Box 1089 (75902-　　　　　(Sat.) 14,852
1089)　　　　　　　　　　　(Sun.) 16,600
Phone: (409)632-6631

Nacogdoches Daily Sentinel **(30740)** .....(Mon.-Fri.) 8,825
PO Box 1089 (75902-　　　　　(Sat.) 9,146
1089)　　　　　　　　　　　(Sun.) 10,904
Phone: (409)632-6631

Marshall
Marshall News Messenger **(30766)** ......(Mon.-Sat.) ★6,731
PO Box 730 (75671-　　　　　　(Sun.) ★7,505
0730)
Phone: (903)935-7914

Mc Kinney
McKinney Courier Gazette **(30776)** ......(Mon.-Fri.) 6,802
PO Box 400 (75071)　　　　　(Sun.) 7,530
Phone: (972)542-2631

McAllen
The Monitor **(30785)** ....(Mon.-Sat.) 36,796
PO Box 760 (78505-　　　　　　(Sun.) 43,623
0760)
Phone: (210)686-4343

Mexia
The Mexia Daily News **(30811)** ....(Paid) ‡3,051
214 N Railroad St.
PO Box 431 (76667)
Phone: (254)562-2868

Midland
Midland
Reporter-Telegram **(30814)** ....(Mon.-Sat.) ★19,605
201 E. Illinois St.　　　　　　(Sun.) ★23,583
PO Box 1650 (79701-
4852)
Phone: (915)682-5311

Mineral Wells
Index **(30832)** ....(Paid) ‡5,300
PO Box 370 (76067)　　　　　(Free) ‡12,000
Phone: (817)325-4466

Mount Pleasant
Mount Pleasant Daily Tribune **(30840)** ......(Paid) ⊕5,500
1705 Industrial　　　　　　　(Non-paid) ⊕175
PO Box 1177 (75456-
1177)
Phone: (903)572-1705

Nacogdoches
The Daily Sentinel **(30849)** ....(Mon.-Fri.) ‡9,000
4920 Colonial Dr.　　　　　　(Sun.) ‡11,950
(75963)
Phone: (936)564-8361

Odessa
Odessa American **(30872)** ....(Mon.-Sat.) ★25,593
222 E. 4th　　　　　　　　　(Sun.) ★28,256
PO Box 2952 (79760)
Phone: (915)337-6262

Orange
The Orange Leader **(30888)** ....(Mon.-Fri.) 8,616
200 W. Front Ave.　　　　　　(Sat.) 8,616
PO Box 1028 (77630-　　　　　(Sun.) 9,620
0128)
Phone: (409)883-3571

Palestine
Palestine Herald-Press **(30897)** ....(Mon.-Sat.) 8,505
519 N. Elm St.　　　　　　　(Sun.) 8,930
PO Box 379 (75802-
0379)
Phone: (903)729-0281

Pampa
The Pampa News **(30900)** ....(Mon.-Fri.) 6,614
403 W Atchison　　　　　　　(Sun.) 7,358
PO Box 2198 (79066)
Phone: (806)669-2525

Paris
The Paris News **(30905)** ....(Mon.-Fri.) 10,314
PO Box 1078 (75461)　　　　　(Sun.) 11,318
Phone: (903)785-8744

Pasadena
Pasadena Citizen **(30914)** ....(Combined) 6,174
PO Box 6192 (77506)　　　　　(Sun.) 11,111
Phone: (713)477-0221

Pearland
Texas City Sun **(30919)** ....(Mon.-Sat.) 5,870
2404 S Park (77581)　　　　　(Sun.) 6,191
Phone: (409)945-3441

Pecos
Pecos Enterprise **(30923)** 2,300
324 S Cedar St.
PO Box 2057 (79772)
Phone: (915)445-5475

Plainview
Plainview Daily Herald **(30939)** ....(Mon.-Fri.) 6,000
820 Broadway (79072)　　　　　(Sun.) 6,500
Phone: (806)296-1300

Port Arthur
Port Arthur News **(30953)** ....(Mon.-Sat.) 18,726
549 4th St.　　　　　　　　　(Sun.) 19,299
PO Box 789 (77641)
Phone: (409)985-5541

Rosenberg
The Herald Coaster **(30992)** ....(Mon.-Fri.) 7,724
1902 S. Fourth St.　　　　　　(Sun.) 7,967
(77471-4998)
Phone: (281)342-4474

San Angelo
San Angelo
Standard-Times **(31010)** ....(Mon.-Sat.) ★27,933
PO Box 5111 (76902)　　　　　(Sun.) ★33,219
Phone: (915)653-1221

San Antonio
The Daily Commercial Recorder **(31028)**
17400 Judson Rd.
(78247)
Phone: (210)453-3300

Express-News **(31029)** ....(Mon.-Thurs.) ★220,998
PO Box 2171 (78297-　　　　　(Fri.) ★263,581
2171)　　　　　　　　　　　(Sat.) ★356,377
Phone: (210)250-3000　　　　　(Sun.) ★251,460

San Marcos
San Marcos Daily Record **(31085)** ......(Tues.-Fri.) 4,856
1910 S. Interstate Hwy.　　　　(Sun.) 6,982
35
PO Box 1109 (78666-
5901)
Phone: (512)392-2458

Circ. · · · Circ. · · · Circ.

TEXAS (continued)

Seguin
The Seguin
  Gazette-Enterprise **(31096)** ....(Tues.-Fri.) 4,790
1012 Schriewer (78155) · · · · · · · · · · (Sun.) 6,526
Phone: (830)379-5402

Sherman
Herald Democrat **(31103)** ....(Mon.-Fri.) 23,866
603 Sam Rayburn Fwy. · · · · · · · · · · (Sun.) 26,745
S. (75090)
Phone: (903)893-8181

Snyder
Snyder Daily News **(31114)** ....(Mon.-Fri.) ‡5,050
3600 College Ave. · · · · · · · · · · (Sun.) ‡6,100
PO Box 949 (79549)
Phone: (915)573-5486

Stephenville
Stephenville Empire-Tribune **(31130)** 5,800
590 South Loop
PO Box 958 (76401-
  4224)
Phone: (254)965-3124

Sulphur Springs
News-Telegram **(31166)** ....(Paid) 6,879
PO Box 598 (75483)
Phone: (903)885-8663

Sweetwater
Sweetwater Reporter **(31170)** ....(Paid) 3,600
PO Box 750 (79556) · · · · · · · · · · (Non-paid) 115
Phone: (915)236-6677

Temple
Temple Daily Telegram **(31179)** ....(Mon.-Fri.) 21,749
PO Box 6114 (76503- · · · · · · · · · · (Sun.) 24,772
  6114)

Texarkana
Texarkana Gazette **(31184)** ....(Mon.-Sat.) ★31,354
315 Pine St. (75501) · · · · · · · · · · (Sun.) ★34,676
Phone: (903)794-3311

Tyler
Tyler Morning Telegraph **(31203)** ....(Mon.-Sat.) ★43,479
410 W. Erwin St.
PO Box 2030 (75710)
Phone: (903)597-8111

Victoria
The Victoria Advocate **(31236)** ....(Mon.-Sat.) ★37,460
311 E. Constitution · · · · · · · · · · (Sun.) ★39,134
PO Box 1518 (77901)
Phone: (361)575-1451

Waco
Waco Tribune-Herald **(31257)** ....(Mon.-Sat.) 40,863
900 Franklin Ave. · · · · · · · · · · (Sun.) 51,519
(76701-1906)
Phone: (254)757-5757

Waxahachie
Waxahachie Daily Light **(31271)** ....(Mon.-Fri.) ‡5,313
200 W. Marvin · · · · · · · · · · (Sun.) ‡5,313
PO Box 877 (75165-
  3040)
Phone: (214)937-3310

Weatherford
Weatherford Democrat **(31273)** 5,935
512 Palo Pinto St. · · · · · · · · · · 7,473
(76086)
Phone: (817)594-7447

Wichita Falls
Times Record News **(31293)** ...(Mon.-Sat.) 35,505
1301 Lamar (76301) · · · · · · · · · · (Sun.) 40,141
Phone: (940)767-8341

UTAH
Logan
The Herald Journal **(31350)** ....(Mon.-Sat.) ★14,963
75 W. 300 N. · · · · · · · · · · (Sun.) ★15,122
PO Box 487 (84323-
  0487)
Phone: (435)752-2121

Ogden
Standard-Examiner **(31378)** ....(Mon.-Sat.) ★58,464
332 Standard Way · · · · · · · · · · (Sun.) ★64,191
PO Box 12790 (84412-
  2790)
Phone: (801)625-4200

St. George
The Spectrum **(31417)** ....(Mon.) 22,091
275 E. St. George Blvd. · · · · (Tues.-Fri.) 20,948
(84770-2954) · · · · · · · · · · (Sat.) 20,948
Phone: (801)674-6200 · · · · · · · · · · (Sun.) 22,144

Salt Lake City
Deseret News **(31426)** ....(Mon.-Sat.) ★68,297
30 East 100 South · · · · · · · · · · (Sun.) ★68,852
(84111)

The Salt Lake Tribune **(31440)** .....(Mon.-Sat.) ★134,777
143 S. Main St. (84111) · · · · · · · · · · (Sun.) ★152,147
Phone: (801)257-8742

VERMONT
Barre
The Times-Argus **(31488)** ....(Mon.-Sat.) ★11,045
540 N. Main St. · · · · · · · · · · (Sun.) 12,682
PO Box 707 (05641)
Phone: (802)479-0191

Bennington
The Bennington Banner **(31497)** ....(Mon.-Fri.) ★7,737
425 Main St. (05201) · · · · · · · · · · (Sat.) ★8,233
Phone: (802)447-7567

Brattleboro
Brattleboro Reformer **(31508)** ....(Mon.-Fri.) ★10,429
Black Mountain Rd. · · · · · · · · · · (Sat.) ★11,655
PO Box 802 (05301- · · · · · · · · · · (Sun.) ★12,212
  0802)
Phone: (802)254-2311

Burlington
The Burlington Free Press **(31514)** ....(Mon.-Sat.) 49,559
191 College St. (05402- · · · · · · · · · · (Sun.) 60,265
  0010)
Phone: (802)863-3441

Newport
The Newport Daily Express **(31572)** ....(Paid) ‡4,600
PO Box 347 (05855) · · · · · · · · · · (Free) ‡5,001
Phone: (802)334-6568

Rutland
Rutland Herald **(31585)** ....(Mon.-Sat.) ★22,096
27 Wales St. · · · · · · · · · · (Sun.) ★22,739
PO Box 668 (05702-
  0668)
Phone: (802)747-6121

St. Albans
The St. Albans Messenger **(31590)** ....(Paid) 4,989
281 N. Main St. · · · · · · · · · · (Free) 140
PO Box 1250 (05478)
Phone: (802)524-9771

St. Johnsbury
Caledonian-Record **(31593)** ....(Mon.-Sat.) ★10,654
25 Federal St. (05819)

VIRGINIA
Alexandria
The Alexandria Journal **(31634)** ......(Mon.-Fri.) 5,792
6408 Edsall Rd. (22312)
Phone: (703)560-4000

Fairfax Journal **(31671)** ....(Mon.-Fri.) 52,358
6408 Edsall Rd. (22312)
Phone: (703)560-4000

Arlington
The Arlington Journal **(31779)** ....(Mon.-Fri.) 8,462
6408 Edsall Rd. (22312)
Phone: (703)560-4000

Bristol
Herald-Courier/Virginia-Tennessean **(31897)**.(Mon.-Sat.)★40,905
320 Morrison Blvd. · · · · · · · · · · (Sun.) ★42,591
(24201-3812)
Phone: (540)669-2181

Charlottesville
The Cavalier Daily **(31921)** ....(Free) ‡10,000
PO Box 400703 (22904-
  4703)
Phone: (434)924-1086

The Daily Progress **(31926)** ....(Mon.-Sat.) 30,189
685 W Rio Rd. · · · · · · · · · · (Sun.) 34,328
PO Box 9030 (22906)
Phone: (804)978-7200

Christiansburg
The News-Messenger **(31972)** ....(Paid) ‡5,907
PO Box 419 (24068) · · · · · · · · · · (Free) ‡4,200
Phone: (540)382-6171

Covington
Virginian Review **(31982)** ....(Mon.-Sat.) 7,808
128 N. Maple Ave.
PO Box 271 (24426)
Phone: (540)962-2121

Culpeper
Culpeper Star-Exponent **(31987)** 7,800
122 W Spencer St.
PO Box 111 (22701)
Phone: (540)825-0771

Danville
Danville Register & Bee **(31991)** .....(Mon.-Sat.) ★21,233
PO Box 331 (24543) · · · · · · · · · · (Sun.) ★24,745

Fredericksburg
The Free Lance-Star **(32085)** ....(Mon.-Sat.) ★47,708
616 Amelia St. (22401) · · · · · · · · · · (Sun.) ★52,523

Harrisonburg
Daily News-Record **(32138)** ....(Mon.-Sat.) ★32,350
231 S. Liberty St.
PO Box 193 (22803)
Phone: (540)574-6200

Lynchburg
The News & Daily
  Advance **(32207)** ....(Mon.-Sat.) 37,245
101 Wyndale Dr. · · · · · · · · · · (Sun.) 42,879
PO Box 10129 (24506-
  0129)
Phone: (804)385-5450

Manassas
Manassas Journal
  Messenger **(32223)** ....(Mon.-Fri.) 5,600
9009 Church St. (20110) · · · · · · · · · · (Sat.) 18,820
Phone: (703)368-3101 · · · · · · · · · · (Sun.) 18,602

Martinsville
Martinsville Bulletin **(32233)** ....(Mon.-Fri.) ★17,653
204 Broad St. (24115- · · · · · · · · · · (Sun.) ★19,712
  3199)
Phone: (276)638-8801

Mc Lean
Argus Leader **(32240)** ....(Mon.-Sat.) 52,531
7950 Jones Branch Dr. · · · · · · · · · · (Sun.) 74,519
  (22107)
Phone: (703)854-6000

The Bellingham Herald **(32242)** ....(Mon.-Sat.) 24,710
7950 Jones Branch Dr. · · · · · · · · · · (Sun.) 31,478
  (22107)
Phone: (703)854-6000

The Herald-Dispatch **(32245)** ....(Mon.-Sat.) 35,503
7950 Jones Branch Dr. · · · · · · · · · · (Sun.) 41,041
  (22107)
Phone: (703)854-6000

The Jackson Sun **(32247)** ....(Mon.-Sat.) 37,311
7950 Jones Branch Dr. · · · · · · · · · · (Sun.) 40,000
  (22107)
Phone: (703)854-6000

The Olympian **(32251)** ....(Mon.-Sat.) 37,968
7950 Jones Branch Dr. · · · · · · · · · · (Sun.) 45,291
  (22107)
Phone: (703)854-6000

Ossining Citizen Register **(32252)** ....(Mon.-Sat.) 5,876
7950 Jones Branch Dr. · · · · · · · · · · (Sun.) 6,675
  (22107)
Phone: (703)854-6000

Rockland Journal-News **(32254)** ....(Mon.-Fri.) 40,387
7950 Jones Branch Dr. · · · · · · · · · · (Sun.) 52,844
  (22107)
Phone: (703)854-6000

The Tennessean **(32256)** ....(Mon.-Fri.) 181,702
7950 Jones Branch Dr. · · · · · · · · · · (Sat.) 213,019
  (22107) · · · · · · · · · · (Sun.) 260,992
Phone: (703)854-6000

USA Today **(32257)** ....(Mon.-Thurs.) ★2,136,068
7950 Jones Branch Dr. · · · · · · · · · · (Fri.) ★2,610,225
  (22107)
Phone: (703)854-6000

Wausau Daily Herald **(32261)** ....(Mon.-Fri.) 22,942
7950 Jones Branch Dr. · · · · · · · · · · (Sat.) 24,226
  (22107) · · · · · · · · · · (Sun.) 30,640
Phone: (703)854-6000

White Plains Reporter
  Dispatch **(32262)** ....(Mon.-Sat.) 46,715
7950 Jones Branch Dr. · · · · · · · · · · (Sun.) 55,276
  (22107)
Phone: (703)854-6000

Yonkers Herald
  Statesman **(32263)** ....(Mon.-Sat.) 20,7187
7950 Jones Branch Dr. · · · · · · · · · · (Sun.) 25,3002
  (22107)
Phone: (703)854-6000

Newport News
Daily Press **(32279)** ....(Mon.-Sat.) ★92,434
7505 Warwick Blvd, · · · · · · · · · · (Sun.) ★115985
  (23607)

Norfolk
The Virginian-Pilot **(32296)** ....(Mon.-Fri.) 199,335
150 W. Brambleton Ave. · · · · · · · · · · (Sat.) 228,919
  (23510-2018) · · · · · · · · · · (Sun.) 235,267
Phone: (757)446-2000

Petersburg
The Progress-Index **(32330)** ....(Mon.-Sat.) 17,878
15 Franklin St. (23803) · · · · · · · · · · (Sun.) 18,406
Phone: (804)732-3456

Richmond
Richmond
  Times-Dispatch **(32452)** ....(Mon.-Sat.) ★187,409
300 E. Franklin St. · · · · · · · · · · (Sun.) ★228,262
PO Box 85333 (23293)

Roanoke
The Roanoke Times **(32491)** ....(Mon.-Sat.) 98,552
PO Box 2491 (24010- · · · · · · · · · · (Sun.) 116,207
  2491)
Phone: (703)981-3257

Staunton
The Daily News Leader **(32555)** ....(Mon.-Sat.) 18,354
St. 11 N. Central Ave. · · · · · · · · · · (Sun.) 21,517
PO Box 59 (24402)
Phone: (540)885-7281

The News-Leader **(32556)** ....(Mon.-Sat.) ★62,158
11 N. Central Ave. · · · · · · · · · · (Sun.) ★90,893
PO Box 59 (24402)

Numbers cited after listings are entry numbers rather than page numbers.

Strasburg
Northern Virginia Daily **(32563)** ....(Mon.-Sat.) 15,191
152 N Holliday St.
PO Box 69 (22657-0069)
Phone: (540)465-5137

Suffolk
Suffolk News-Herald **(32566)** ....(Mon.-Fri.) 4,240
PO Box 1220 (23434)   (Sun.) 4,318
Phone: (757)539-3437

Tarrytown
Tarrytown Daily News **(32569)** ....(Mon.-Sat.) 3,172
7950 Jones Branch Dr.   (Sun.) 3,625
(22107)
Phone: (703)854-6000

Waynesboro
The News-Virginian **(32610)** ....(Mon.-Sat.) ★8,283
544 W. Main St.   (Sun.) ★7,988
PO Box 1027 (22980)
Phone: (540)949-8213

Winchester
The Winchester Star **(32630)** ....(Mon.-Fri.) ★21,564
2 N. Kent St. (22601)   (Sat.) ★25,615
Phone: (540)667-3200

Woodbridge
Potomac News **(32637)** ....(Mon.-Fri.) 15,086
14010 Smoketown Rd.   (Sat.) 18,820
PO Box 2470 (22192)   (Sun.) 18,602
Phone: (703)878-8000

WASHINGTON

Aberdeen
The Daily World **(32647)** ....(Mon.-Sat.) 15,721
315 S. Michigan   (Sun.) 15,795
PO Box 269 (98520)
Phone: (206)532-4000

Bellevue
Eastside Journal **(32665)** ....(Mon.-Sat.) ★25,408
1705 132nd Ave. NE   (Sun.) ★25,166
PO Box 90130 (98009)
Phone: (425)455-2222

Bremerton
The Sun **(32695)** ....(Mon.-Sat.) 33,552
545 5th St. (98337)   (Sun.) 36,786
Phone: (360)377-3711

Centralia
The Chronicle **(32704)** ....(Mon.-Sat.) 14,126
PO Box 580 (98531)
Phone: (360)736-3311

Ellensburg
Daily Record **(32748)** ....‡5,525
401 North Main (98926)
Phone: (509)925-1414

Everett
The Herald **(32761)** ....(Mon.-Sat.) 52,361
1213 Grand & California   (Sun.) 60,467
Sts.
PO Box 930 (98206)
Phone: (425)339-3000

Kent
South County Journal **(32796)** ....(Mon.-Sat.) ★21,696
PO Box 130 (98035)   (Sun.) ★23,219
Phone: (253)872-6600

Longview
The Daily News **(32812)** ....(Mon.-Sun.) 24,975
770 11th Ave.
PO Box 189 (98632)

Moses Lake
Columbia Basin Herald **(32838)**
813 W 3rd Ave. (98837-
2008)
Phone: (509)765-4561

Mount Vernon
Skagit Valley Herald **(32845)** ....(Mon.-Sat.) 19,419
1000 E. College Way   (Sun.) 20,441
PO Box 578 (98273-
0578)
Phone: (360)424-3251

Pasco
Tri-City Herald **(32877)** ....(Mon.-Sat.) ★40,993
PO Box 2608 (99302-   (Sun.) ★44,782
2608)
Phone: (509)582-1500

Port Angeles
Peninsula Daily News **(32888)** ....(Mon.-Fri.) ★16,564
305 W. 1st St. (98362)   (Sun.) ★18,077
Phone: (360)452-2345

Seattle
InternationalTimes.com **(32973)**
1916 Pike Pl., Ste. 831
(98101)

Seattle Post-Intelligencer **(33021)** ....(Mon.-Fri.) ★157,558
101 Elliott Ave. W.   (Sat.) ★144,484
(98119)   (Sun.) ★473,010
Phone: (206)448-8000

Seattle Times **(33023)** ....(Mon.-Fri.) 225,222
1120 John St.   (Sat.) 214,501
PO Box 70 (98111-0070)   (Sun.) 482,978
Phone: (206)464-2132

Spokane
The Spokesman-Review **(33101)** ......(Mon.-Fri.) 105,550
999 W Riverside Ave.   (Sat.) 125,966
PO Box 2160 (99210)   (Sun.) 137,568
Phone: (509)459-5000

Sunnyside
Daily Sun News **(33142)** ....(Paid) 3,914
PO Box 878 (98944)   (Free) 11,474
Phone: (509)837-4500

Tacoma
The News Tribune **(33147)** ....(Mon.-Sat.) 127,629
PO Box 11000 (98411-   (Sun.) 144,333
0008)
Phone: (253)597-8688

Vancouver
The Columbian **(33175)** ....(Mon.-Sat.) ★51,263
PO Box 180 (98666)   (Sun.) ★61,254
Phone: (360)694-3391

Walla Walla
Walla Walla
   Union-Bulletin **(33188)** ....(Mon.-Fri.) ★14,478
112 S. 1st Ave. (99362)   (Sun.) ★15,949
Phone: (509)525-3300

Wenatchee
The Wenatchee World **(33196)** ....(Mon.-Fri.) ★25,041
14 N. Mission (98801)   (Sun.) ★27,570
Phone: (509)663-5761

Yakima
Yakima Herald-Republic **(33223)** .....(Mon.-Sat.) ★38,772
114 N 4th St.   (Sun.) ★40,386
PO Box 9668 (98909)
Phone: (509)248-1251

WEST VIRGINIA

Beckley
Register-Herald **(33241)** ....(Mon.-Sat.) ★28,906
PO Box 2398 (25802)   (Sun.) ★30,240
Phone: (304)255-4400

Bluefield
Daily Telegraph **(33255)** ....(Mon.-Sat.) 21,573
928 Bluefield Ave.   (Sun.) 23,402
(24701-2744)
Phone: (304)327-2800

Charleston
Charleston Daily Mail **(33267)** ....(Mon.-Sat.) ★35,855
1001 Virginia St. E.   (Sun.) ★92,233
(25331)
Phone: (304)348-5140

Charleston Gazette **(33268)** ....(Mon.-Sat.) ★51,020
1001 Virginia St. E   (Sun.) ★92,233
PO Box 2993 (25301)
Phone: (304)348-5100

Clarksburg
Clarksburg Exponent **(33293)** ....(Mon.-Sat.) ★16,066
324 Hewes Ave. (26301-   (Sun.) ★20,262
2744)
Phone: (304)624-6411

Clarksburg Telegram **(33294)** ....(Mon.-Sat.) ★16,066
324 Hewes Ave. (26301-   (Sun.) ★20,262
2744)
Phone: (304)624-6411

Fairmont
Times-West Virginian **(33313)** ....(Mon.-Sat.) ★11,871
PO Box 2530 (26555-   (Sun.) ★12,828
2530)
Phone: (304)363-5000

Keyser
Mineral Daily News-Tribune **(33352)** 4,200
24 Armstrong St.
PO Box 879 (26726)
Phone: (304)788-3333

Lewisburg
West Virginia Daily News **(33367)** ....(Paid) ⊕3,860
PO Box 471 (24901)   (Free) ⊕62
Phone: (304)645-1206

Logan
The Logan Banner **(33370)** ....(Mon.-Fri.) 9,609
PO Box 720 (25601)   (Sun.) 9,733
Phone: (304)752-6950

Martinsburg
The Journal **(33380)** ....(Mon.-Sat.) 18,582
207 W King St. (25401)   (Sun.) 19,665
Phone: (304)263-8931

Morgantown
Dominion Post **(33393)** ....(Mon.-Sat.) ★19,253
Greer Bldg.   (Sun.) 20,869
1251 Earl L Core Rd.
(26505)
Phone: (304)292-6301

Moundsville
Moundsville Daily Echo **(33408)** ....‡4,200
713 Lafayette Ave.
PO Box 369 (26041)
Phone: (304)845-2660

Parkersburg
The Parkersburg News **(33420)** ....(Mon.-Sat.) 20,811
PO Box 1787 (26102-   (Sun.) 34,522
1787)
Phone: (304)485-1891

The Parkersburg Sentinel **(33421)** ......(Mon.-Sat.) 6,419
519 Juliana St.
PO Box 1788 (26102)
Phone: (304)485-1891

Point Pleasant
Point Pleasant Register **(33439)** ......(Mon.-Sat.) 4,656
200 Main St., No. 237
(25550-1030)
Phone: (304)675-1333

Weirton
The Daily Times **(33489)** ....(Mon.-Sat.) ★6,023
114 Lee Ave. (26062-
4619)
Phone: (304)748-0606

Welch
The Welch Daily News **(33492)** ....‡7,000
125 Wyoming St.
PO Box 569 (24801)
Phone: (304)436-3144

Wheeling
Intelligencer **(33502)** ....(Mon.-Fri.) ★20,971
1500 Main St. (26003)   (Sat.) ★35,657
Phone: (304)233-0100

News-Register **(33503)** ....(Mon.-Fri.) ★15,802
1500 Main St. (26003)   (Sun.) ★40,574
Phone: (304)233-0100

Williamson
News **(33512)** 10,627
PO Box 1660 (25661)
Phone: (304)235-4242

WISCONSIN

Antigo
Antigo Daily Journal **(33531)** ....(Paid) ⊕6,841
612 Superior St. (54409)   (Free) 17
Phone: (715)623-4191

Appleton
The Post-Crescent **(33542)** ....(Mon.-Fri.) 56,218
PO Box 59 (54912)   (Sat.) 67,587
Phone: (920)733-4411   (Sun.) 74,804

Ashland
The Daily Press **(33554)** ....(Paid) ♦6,418
122 3rd St. W. (54806-   (Non-paid) ♦29
1620)
Phone: (715)682-2313

Baraboo
Baraboo News Republic **(33562)** ......(Mon.-Sat.) ★3,975
219 1st St.
PO Box 9 (53913)
Phone: (608)356-4808

Beaver Dam
Daily Citizen **(33567)** ....(Mon.-Fri.) ★10,593
805 Park Ave. (53916)   (Sat.) ★12,835
Phone: (920)885-7800

Beloit
Beloit Daily News **(33574)** ....(Paid) ‡14,411
149 State St. (53511)   (Non-paid) ‡382
Phone: (608)365-8811

Chippewa Falls
Chippewa Herald **(33626)** ....‡7,541
321 Frenette Drive
PO Box 69 (54729)
Phone: (715)723-5515

Chippewa Herald Telegram **(33627)** ....(Paid) 7,325
321 Frenette Dr.   (Free) 31
PO Box 69 (54729-0069)
Phone: (715)723-9104

Eau Claire
Leader-Telegram **(33672)** ....(Mon.-Fri.) ★27,959
PO Box 570 (54702)   (Sat.) ★33,194
Phone: (715)833-9200   (Sun.) ★39,002

Fond du Lac
The Reporter (Fond du
   Lac) **(33697)** ....(Mon.-Fri.) 19,000
PO Box 630 (54936-   (Sun.) 20,807
0630)

Fort Atkinson
Daily Jefferson County Union **(33706)**
28 W Milwaukee Ave.
(53538)
Phone: (920)563-5553

Green Bay
Green Bay News-Chronicle **(33740)** ....‡10,500
133 S. Monroe St.   7,400
PO Box 2467 (54306)
Phone: (920)432-2941

Circulation: ★ = ABC; △ = BPA; ♦ = CAC; • = CCAB; ❑ = VAC; ⊕ = PO Statement; ‡ = Publisher's Report; Boldface figures = sworn; Light figures = estimated.

2875

Circ. Circ. Circ.

WISCONSIN (continued)

Green Bay Press-Gazette **(33741)** ....(Mon.-Fri.) ★**56,943**
PO Box 23430 (54305- (Sat.) ★**67,405**
3430) (Sun.) ★**83,821**

Janesville
The Janesville Gazette **(33858)** ......(Mon.-Sat.) ★**23,497**
PO Box 5001 (53547- (Sun.) ★**26,792**
5001)
Phone: (608)754-3311

Kenosha
Kenosha News **(33872)** ....(Mon.-Sat.) 26,441
715 58th St. (53140) (Sun.) 28,722
Phone: (262)657-1000

La Crosse
La Crosse Tribune **(33885)** ....(Mon.-Fri.) ★**31,903**
401 N. 3rd St. (54601) (Sat.) ★**39,007**
Phone: (608)782-9710 (Sun.) ★**40,879**

Madison
The Capital Times **(33925)** ....(Mon.-Fri.) 19,408
1901 Fish Hatchery Rd. (Sat.) 21,956
PO Box 8060 (53708)
Phone: (608)252-6400

Wisconsin State Journal **(33990)** ....(Mon.-Fri.) ★**89,569**
1901 Fish Hatchery Rd. (Sat.) ★**100,187**
PO Box 8058 (53713) (Sun.) ★**154,427**
Phone: (608)252-6100

Manitowoc
Herald-Times Reporter **(34013)** ....(Mon.-Sat.) 17,771
902 Franklin St. (Sun.) 17,495
PO Box 790 (54221-
0790)
Phone: (920)684-4433

Marinette
Marinette Eagle-Star **(34018)** ....‡8,800
PO Box 77 (54143)
Phone: (715)735-6611

Marshfield
Marshfield News-Herald **(34027)** ......(Mon.-Fri.) ★**13,712**
111 W 3rd St. (Sat.) ★**14,512**
PO Box 70 (54449-2811)
Phone: (715)384-3131

Milwaukee
Milwaukee Journal
Sentinel **(34084)** ....(Mon.-Fri.) ★**242,234**
PO Box 661 (53201) (Sat.) ★**232,652**
Phone: (414)224-2000 (Sun.) ★**434,023**

Monroe
The Monroe Times **(34151)** ....(Paid) 6,400
1065 4th Ave. W
PO Box 230 (53566)
Phone: (608)328-4202

Oshkosh
Northwestern **(34224)** ....(Mon.-Sat.) 24,291
224 State St. (Sun.) 27,884
PO Box 2926 (54901-
4839)
Phone: (920)235-7700

Portage
Daily Register **(34255)** ....(Free) 16
PO Box 470 (53901) (Paid) 4,829
Phone: (608)742-2111

Portage Daily Register **(34259)** ....(Mon.-Sat.) ★**4,850**
PO Box 470 (53901)
Phone: (608)742-2111

Racine
The Journal Times **(34273)** ....(Mon.-Sat.) ★**29,217**
212 4th St. (53403-1066) (Sun.) ★**31,336**
Phone: (262)634-3322

Shawano
Shawano Leader **(34317)** ....(Paid) 6,700
1464 E. Green Bay St.
(54166)
Phone: (715)526-2121

Sheboygan
The Sheboygan Press **(34321)** ....(Mon.-Sat.) 27,055
632 Center Ave. (53081) (Sun.) 28,678
Phone: (920)457-7711

Spooner
Spooner Advocate **(34337)** ....(Paid) ◆**4,726**
509 Front St. (Non-paid) ◆**24**
PO Box 338 (54801)
Phone: (715)635-2181

Superior
The Daily Telegram **(34359)** ....(Paid) ◆**7,621**
1226 Ogden Ave. (Non-paid) ◆**272**
(54880)
Phone: (715)394-4411

Watertown
Watertown Daily Times **(34392)**
115 W Main St.
PO Box 140 (53094-
0140)
Phone: (920)261-4949

Waukesha
Waukesha County
Freeman **(34414)** ....(Mon.-Sat.) ★**15,492**
PO Box 7 (53187)
Phone: (414)542-2501

West Bend
The Daily News **(34445)** ....(Mon.-Fri.) 10,501
PO Box 478 (53095)
Phone: (262)306-5000

Wisconsin Rapids
The Daily Tribune **(34463)** ....(Mon.-Sat.) 13,278
220 1st Ave. S. (54495)
Phone: (715)423-7200

WYOMING
Casper
Casper Star-Tribune **(34482)** ....(Mon.-Sat.) ★**30,646**
170 Star Ln. (Sun.) ★**33,369**
PO Box 80 (82602)
Phone: (307)266-0500

Cheyenne
Wyoming Tribune-Eagle **(34500)** .....(Mon.-Sat.) ★**15,923**
702 W Lincolnway (Sun.) ★**17,485**
(82001-4359)
Phone: (307)634-3361

Gillette
The News Record **(34527)** ....(Mon.-Fri.) ‡6,869
1201 W. 2nd St. (Sun.) ‡7,735
PO Box 3006 (82716)
Phone: (307)682-9306

Laramie
Laramie Daily Boomerang **(34549)** ....(Tues.-Fri.) ★**5,511**
320 E. Grand Ave (Sat.) ★**5,511**
(82070) (Sun.) ★**5,877**
Phone: (307)742-2176

Rawlins
Daily Times **(34572)** ....‡3,780
6th & Buffalo
PO Box 370 (82301)
Phone: (307)324-3411

Riverton
The Riverton Ranger **(34577)** ....(Paid) ‡6,970
421 E. Main St.
PO Box 993 (82501)
Phone: (307)856-2244

Rock Springs
Daily Rocket-Miner **(34581)** ....(Tues.-Fri.) ★**7,538**
PO Box 98 (82902-0098) (Sat.) ★**7,538**
Phone: (307)362-3736

Sheridan
The Sheridan Press **(34588)** ....(Mon.-Sat.) 6,232
144 Grinnell St.
PO Box 2006 (82801)
Phone: (307)672-2431

Worland
Northern Wyoming Daily
News **(34604)** ....(Tues.-Fri.) 3,667
201 N. 8th (82401) (Sat.) 3,667
Phone: (307)347-3241

ALBERTA, CANADA
Calgary
Calgary Herald **(34631)** ....(Mon.-Thurs.) ★**110,583**
215-16 St. SE (Fri.) ★**141,095**
(T2P 0W8) (Sat.) ★**125,040**
Phone: (403)235-7433 (Sun.) ★**113,020**

The Calgary Sun **(34633)** ....(Mon.-Sat.) ★**65,968**
2615 12th St. NE (Sun.) ★**97,239**
(T2E 7W9)
Phone: (403)250-4200

Edmonton
The Edmonton Journal **(34711)** ....(Mon.-Thurs.) 141,193
PO Box 2421 (T5J 0S1) (Fri.) 168,900
Phone: (780)429-5200 (Sat.) 141,193
(Sun.) 139,164

The Edmonton Sun **(34712)** ....(Mon.-Sat.) 74,367
4990 92nd Ave., Ste. (Sun.) 112,133
250 (T6B 3A1)
Phone: (780)468-0100

Fort McMurray
Fort McMurray Today **(34767)** ....(Mon.-Thurs.) 4,398
8550 Franklin Ave. (Fri.) 6,246
(T9H 3G1)
Phone: (780)743-8186

Grande Prairie
Daily Herald-Tribune **(34774)**
10604 100th St., Bag
3000 (T8V 6V4)
Phone: (780)532-1110

Lethbridge
The Lethbridge Herald **(34795)** ....(Mon.-Thurs.) ★**19,737**
504 - 7th St. S. (Fri.) ★**23,213**
PO Box 670 (T1J 3Z7) (Sat.) ★**20,386**
Phone: (403)328-4411 (Sun.) ★**18,818**

Medicine Hat
The Medicine Hat News **(34810)** .....(Mon.-Sat.) ★**13,994**
3257 Dunmore Rd. S.E.
PO Box 10 (T1A 7E6)
Phone: (403)527-1101

Red Deer
Red Deer Advocate **(34830)** ....(Mon.-Sat.) ★**17,930**
2950 Bremner Ave. (Fri.) ★**21,381**
PO Bag 5200 (T4N 5G3)
Phone: (403)343-2400

BRITISH COLUMBIA, CANADA
Cranbrook
Cranbrook Daily Townsman **(34934)** .....(Mon.-Fri.) 4,433
822 Cranbrook St. N.
(V1C 3R9)
Phone: (604)426-5201

Dawson Creek
Peace River Block News **(34941)** ....‡2,548
901 100 Ave (V1G 1W2)

Kamloops
The Kamloops News **(34977)** ....(Mon.-Sat.) ★**14,389**
393 Seymour St.
(V2C 6P6)
Phone: (250)372-2381

Kelowna
The Daily Courier **(34988)** ....(Mon.-Fri.) 16,798
550 Doyle Ave. (Sat.) 18,886
PO Box 40 (V1Y 7V1) (Sun.) 16,118
Phone: (604)762-4445

Kimberley
The Daily Bulletin **(34997)** ....(Paid) 2,400
335 Spokane St.
(V1A 1Y9)
Phone: (250)427-5333

Nanaimo
Nanaimo Daily News **(35020)** ....(Mon.-Sat.) ★**9,334**
2575 McCullough Rd.,
Ste. B1 (V9S 5W5)
Phone: (250)729-4200

Nelson
Nelson Daily News **(35024)** ....(Mon.-Fri.) 3,746
266 Baker St. (V1L 4H3)
Phone: (250)352-3552

Penticton
Penticton Herald **(35044)** ....(Mon.-Fri.) 8,866
186 Nanaimo Ave. W.
(V2A 1N4)
Phone: (604)492-4002

Port Alberni
Alberni Valley Times **(35048)** ....(Mon.-Fri.) 6,121
4918 Napier St.
Box 400 (V9Y 7N1)
Phone: (604)723-8171

Prince George
The Prince George Citizen **(35057)** ....(Mon.-Sat.) 17,080
150 Brunswick St. (Fri.) 19,192
PO Box 5700 (V2L 5K9)
Phone: (250)562-2441

Prince Rupert
The Daily News **(35064)** ....(Mon.-Fri.) 3,024
801 2nd Ave. W.
(V8J 1A6)
Phone: (250)624-6781

Trail
Trail Daily Times **(35115)** ....(Mon.-Fri.) 5,350
1163 Cedar Ave.
(V1R 4B8)
Phone: (250)368-8551

Vancouver
The Province **(35160)** ....(Mon.-Fri.) 157,485
1-200 Granville St. (Sun.) 196,367
(V6C 3N3)
Phone: (604)605-2111

The Vancouver Sun **(35175)** ....(Mon.-Thurs.) 186,665
1-200 Granville St. (Fri.) 220,757
(V6C 3N3) (Sat.) 249,861
Phone: (604)605-2111

Victoria
Times Colonist **(35226)** ....(Mon.-Sat.) 75,072
2621 Douglas St. (Sun.) 75,213
PO Box 300 (V8T 4M2)
Phone: (250)380-5211

MANITOBA, CANADA
Brandon
Brandon Sun **(35254)** ....(Mon.-Fri.) ★**15,297**
501 Rosser Ave. (Sat.) ★**19,928**
(R7A 0K4) (Sun.) ★**13,309**
Phone: (204)727-2451

Flin Flon
The Reminder **(35266)** ....(Paid) 3,800
10 North Ave. (R8A 0T2)
Phone: (204)687-3454

Numbers cited after listings are entry numbers rather than page numbers.

Portage La Prairie
The Daily Graphic (35281) ....(Mon.-Sat.) 3,900
1941 Saskatchewan Ave.
W.
PO Box 130 (R1N 3B4)
Phone: (204)857-3427

Winnipeg
The Winnipeg Free
   Press (35363) ....(Mon.-Fri.) ★120,489
1355 Mountain Ave.   (Sat.) ★174,299
(R2X 3B6)   (Sun.) ★119,466
Phone: (204)697-7001

The Winnipeg Sun (35364) ....(Mon.-Fri.) ★44,602
1700 Church Ave.   (Sat.) ★44,305
(R2X 3A2)   (Sun.) ★55,830
Phone: (204)632-2768

NEW BRUNSWICK, CANADA
Bathurst
Jacksonville
   Journal-Courier (35377) ....(Mon.-Sat.) 14,994
355 King Ave.   (Sun.) 14,598
PO Box 416 (E2A 1P4)
Phone: (506)546-4491

Fredericton
The Daily Gleaner (35392) ....(Mon.-Sat.) 28,172
984 Prospect St. W.
PO Box 3370 (E3B 2T8)
Phone: (506)452-6671

Moncton
The Times-Transcript (35413) ....(Mon.-Fri.) 37,286
939 Main St.   (Sat.) 49,616
PO Box 1001 (E1C 8P3)
Phone: (506)859-4900

St. John
The Telegraph Journal (35431) ....(Mon.-Fri.) 41,300
210 Crown St.   (Sat.) 46,500
PO Box 2350 (E2L 3V8)
Phone: (506)632-8888

NEWFOUNDLAND AND LABRADOR, CANADA
Corner Brook
The Western Star (35447) ....(Mon.-Sat.) 8,796
106 West St.
PO Box 460 (A2H 6E7)
Phone: (709)634-4348

St. John's
The Telegram (35494) ....(Mon.-Fri.) 33,065
Columbus Dr.   (Sat.) 58,887
PO Box 5970 (A1C 5X7)   (Sun.) 33,693

NOVA SCOTIA, CANADA
Amherst
Amherst Daily News (35532) ....(Mon.-Fri.) 3,956
10 Lawrence St.
PO Box 280 (B4H 3Z2)
Phone: (902)667-5102

Dartmouth
The Daily News (35545) ....(Mon.-Sat.) 29,152
11 Thornhill Dr.   (Sun.) 45,408
(B3B 1R9)

Halifax
The Chronicle Herald (35561) ....(Mon.-Sat.) 90,052
1650 Argyle St.
(B3J 2T2)
Phone: (902)426-2811

The Daily News Worldwide (35563)
PO Box 8330, Sta. A
(B3K 5M1)
Phone: (902)461-6161

The Halifax Herald (35566) ....(Sun.) 54,249
1650 Argyle St.
(B3J 2T2)
Phone: (902)426-2811

Sydney
Cape Breton Post (35607) ....(Mon.-Sat.) 26,500
255 George St.
PO Box 1500 (B1P 6K6)
Phone: (902)564-5451

Truro
Truro Daily News (35616) ....(Mon.-Fri.) 7,200
6 Louise St.   (Sat.) 9,200
PO Box 220 (B2N 5C3)
Phone: (902)893-9405

ONTARIO, CANADA
Barrie
The Barrie Examiner (35658) ....(Mon.-Sat.) 11,446
16 Bayfield St.
PO Box 370 (L4M 4T6)
Phone: (705)726-6537

Belleville
The Intelligencer (35678) ....(Mon.-Fri.) 16,825
45 Bridge St. E.   (Sun.) 16,235
PO Box 5600 (K8N 1L5)
Phone: (613)962-9171

Brampton
The Brampton Guardian (35698) ....(Wed.) 67,646
685 Queen St. W   (Fri.) 67,025
(L6V 1A1)   (Sun.) 67,063
Phone: (905)454-4344

Brantford
The Brantford Expositor (35703) ....(Mon.-Sat.) 23,590
53 Dalhousie St.
(N3T 5S8)
Phone: (519)756-2020

Brockville
The Brockville Recorder and
   Times (35708) ....(Mon.-Sat.) 13,479
1600 California Ave.
Bag 10 (K6V 5T8)

Cambridge
Cambridge Daily Reporter (35723) ......(Mon.-Sat.) 9,239
26 Ainslie St. S.
PO Box 1510 (N1R 3K1)
Phone: (519)621-3810

Chatham
Chatham Daily News (35729) ....(Mon.-Sat.) 14,926
45 4th St.
PO Box 2007
   (N7M 2G4)
Phone: (519)354-2000

Cobourg
Cobourg Daily Star (35741) 5,552
99 King St. W.
PO Box 400 (K9A 4L1)

Cornwall
Standard-Freeholder (35755) ....(Mon.-Sat.) 15,036
44 Pitt St. (K6J 3P3)
Phone: (613)933-3160

Don Mills
National Post (35776) ....(Mon.-Fri.) 336,150
1450 Don Mills Rd.   (Sat.) 399,032
   (M3B 2X7)
Phone: (416)445-6641

Fort Frances
The Daily Bulletin (35840) ....(Paid) **3,013**
116 1st St
PO Box 339 (P9A 3M7)
Phone: (807)274-5373

Guelph
Guelph Mercury (35864) ....(Mon.-Sat.) 14,500
8-14 Macdonnell St.
PO Box 3604 (N1H 6P7)
Phone: (519)822-4310

Hamilton
The Spectator (35890) ....(Mon.-Fri.) 103,915
44 Frid St.   (Sat.) 129,867
PO Box 300 (L8N 3G3)
Phone: (905)526-3333

Kenora
Daily Miner & News (35929) ....(Mon.-Fri.) 3,825
33 Main St. S
PO Box 1620 (P9N 3X7)
Phone: (807)468-5555

Kingston
The Kingston Whig-Standard (35939)
6 Cataraqui St.
PO Box 2300 (K7L 4Z7)
Phone: (613)544-5000

Whig-Standard (35948) ....(Mon.-Fri.) 27,169
306 King St. E.   (Sat.) 34,517
PO Box 2300 (K7L 4Z7)
Phone: (613)544-5000

Kirkland Lake
The Northern Daily News (35957) ......(Mon.-Sat.) 5,626
8 Duncan Ave.
PO Box 1030 (P2N 3L4)
Phone: (705)567-5321

Kitchener
Kitchener-Waterloo Record (35961) .....(Mon.-Fri.) 66,172
225 Fairway Rd. S.   (Sat.) 83,785
   (N2G 4E5)
Phone: (519)894-2231

Lindsay
The Lindsay Daily Post (35971) ......(Combined) ★4,793
15 William St. N.
   (K9V 3Z8)
Phone: (705)324-2113

London
The London Free Press (35987) ......(Mon.-Fri.) ★91,526
369 York St. (N6A 4G1)   (Sat.) ★114,081
Phone: (519)679-1111

Niagara Falls
The Review (36110) ....(Mon.-Sat.) 17,788
PO Box 270 (L2E 6T6)

North Bay
The North Bay Nugget (36116) ....(Mon.-Thurs.) 17,306
(P1B 8J6)   (Fri.) 19,740
Phone: (705)475-2182   (Sat.) 19,740

Orillia
Daily Packet and Times (36174) ....(Mon.-Sat.) 8,583
31 Colborne St. E.
PO Box 220 (L3V 6J5)
Phone: (705)325-1355

Ottawa
Le Droit (36257) ....(Mon.-Fri.) ★34,968
P O Box (K1G 3J9)   (Sat.) ★39,843
Phone: (613)562-0111

The Ottawa Citizen (36265) ....(Mon.-Fri.) ★133,977
1101 Baxter Rd.   (Sat.) ★171,231
PO Box 5020 (K2C 3M4)   (Sun.) ★130,499
Phone: (613)596-3664

Owen Sound
The Sun Times (36299) ....(Mon.-Thurs.) 18,156
290 9th St. E.   (Fri.) 21,951
(N4K 1N7)   (Sat.) 18,156
Phone: (519)372-4328

Pembroke
Observer (36308) ....(Mon.-Sat.) 6,867
186 Alexander St.
PO Box 190 (K8A 4L9)
Phone: (613)732-3691

Pembroke Daily News (36309) ....(Wed.) 18,794
186 Alexander St.   (Sun.) 28,146
PO Box 190 (K8A 6X3)
Phone: (613)735-3141

Peterborough
The Peterborough (36317)
730 The Kingsway
PO Box 3890 (K9J 8L4)
Phone: (705)745-4641

Port Hope
Port Hope Evening Guide (36334) 3,243
95 Walton St.
PO Box 296 (L1A 3W4)
Phone: (905)885-2471

St. Catharines
The Standard (36357) ....(Mon.-Fri.) 33,673
17 Queen St. (L2R 5G5)   (Sat.) 42,010
Phone: (905)684-7251

St. Thomas
St. Thomas Times-Journal (36363) ......(Mon.-Sat.) 8,412
16 Hincks St. (N5R 5Z2)
Phone: (519)631-2790

Sarnia
The Sarnia Observer (36365) ....(Mon.-Sat.) 21,917
140 Front St. S.
PO Box 3009 (N7T 7M8)
Phone: (519)344-3641

Sault Sainte Marie
The Sault Star (36370) ....(Mon.-Sat.) 22,525
145 Old Garden River
Rd.
PO Box 460 (P6A 5M5)
Phone: (705)759-3030

Simcoe
The Simcoe Reformer (36391) ....(Mon.-Fri.) 9,618
105 Donly Dr. S.
   (N3Y 4L2)
Phone: (519)426-5710

Stratford
The Beacon Herald (36409) ....(Mon.-Sat.) 12,269
108 Ontario St.
PO Box 430 (N5A 6T6)
Phone: (519)271-2220

Sudbury
The Sudbury Star (36420) ....(Mon.-Sat.) 21,547
33 McKenzie St.   (Sun.) 25,405
   (P3C 4Y1)
Phone: (705)674-5271

Thunder Bay
The Chronicle-Journal (36438) ....(Mon.-Fri.) 32,981
75 Cumberland St. S.   (Sat.) 38,752
   (P7B 1A3)   (Sun.) 32,075
Phone: (807)343-6200

Timmins
The Daily Press (36453) ....(Mon.-Sat.) 10,343
187 Cedar St. S.   (Sat.) 10,457
PO Box 560 (P4N 7G1)
Phone: (705)268-5050

Toronto
El Popular (36581) ....‡10,500
2413 Dundas St W.
   (M6P 1X3)
Phone: (416)531-2495

The Financial Post (36594) ....(Tues.-Fri.) 77,757
333 King St. E.   (Sat.) 155,475
   (M5A 3X5)
Phone: (416)947-2257

The Globe and Mail (36606) ....(Mon.-Fri.) 354,574
444 Front St. W.   (Sat.) 416,457
   (M5V 2S9)
Phone: (416)585-5406

The Korea Times (36646) ....(Paid) ‡8,200
287 Bridgeland Ave.   (Free) ‡1,500
   (M6H 1X2)
Phone: (416)787-1111

Newspapers

Circulation: ★ = ABC; △ = BPA; ♦ = CAC; ● = CCAB; ❏ = VAC; ⊕ = PO Statement; ‡ = Publisher's Report; Boldface figures = sworn; Light figures = estimated.

Circ.

Circ.

Circ.

ONTARIO, CANADA (continued)
The Toronto Star **(36770)** ....(Mon.-Fri.) ★462,985
1 Yonge St., 5th Fl.   (Sat.) ★673,663
  (M5E 1E6)   (Sun.) ★430,089
Phone: (416)367-2000

Welland
The Tribune **(36867)** ....(Mon.-Sat.) 17,693
228 E. Main St.
PO Box 278 (L3B 5P5)
Phone: (905)732-2411

Windsor
The Windsor Star **(36893)** ....(Mon.-Fri.) ★75,114
167 Ferry St. (N9A 4M5)   (Sat.) ★85,447
Phone: (519)255-5711

Woodstock
The Daily Sentinel-Review **(36907)** 9,324
16-18 Brock St.
PO Box 1000 (N4S 8A5)
Phone: (519)537-2341

PRINCE EDWARD ISLAND, CANADA
Charlottetown
The Guardian **(36915)** ....(Mon.-Sat.) 20,260
165 Prince St.
PO Box 760 (C1A 4R7)
Phone: (902)629-6000

Summerside
Journal-Pioneer **(36924)** ....(Mon.-Sat.) 10,226
4 Queen St. (C1N 4K5)
Phone: (902)436-2121

QUEBEC, CANADA
Chicoutimi
Le Quotidien du
  Saguenay-Lac-Saint-Jean **(36965)**.(Mon.-Sat.)28,914
1051, boul. Talbot
  (G7H 5C1)
Phone: (418)545-4474

Granby
La Voix de l'Est **(37000)** ....(Mon.-Fri.) 15,281
76 Dufferin St.   (Sat.) 18,668
  (J2G 9L4)
Phone: (450)375-4555

Montreal
The Gazette **(37118)** ....(Mon.-Fri.) 141,137
250 St-Antoine St. W.   (Sat.) 197,532
  (H2Y 3R7)   (Sun.) 129,791
Phone: (514)987-2350

La Presse **(37150)** ....(Mon.-Fri.) 170,362
7, rue St-Jacques   (Sat.) 268,420
  (H2Y 1K9)   (Sun.) 180,426
Phone: (514)285-7272

Le Devoir **(37159)** ....(Mon.-Fri.) 25,080
2050 De Bleury St., 9th   (Sat.) 38,236
  Fl. (H3A 3M9)
Phone: (514)985-3399

Le Journal de Montreal **(37163)** .....(Mon.-Fri.) ★259,594
4545, rue Frontenac   (Sat.) ★312,153
  (H2H 2R7)   (Sun.) ★266,656
Phone: (514)521-4545

The Montreal Gazette **(37188)** ....(Mon.-Fri.) ★142,091
250 St-Antoine St. W.   (Sat.) ★169,933
  (H2Y 3R7)   (Sun.) ★139,323
Phone: (514)987-2350

Quebec
Le Journal de Quebec **(37288)** ....(Mon.-Fri.) ★96,646
450, rue Bechard, Vanier   (Sat.) ★120,743
  (G1M 2E9)   (Sun.) ★99,094
Phone: (418)683-1573

Le Soleil **(37290)** ....(Mon.-Fri.) ★81,045
925 Chemin St. Louis   (Sat.) ★112,951
PO Box 1547 (G1K 7J6)   (Sun.) ★90,304
Phone: (418)686-3394

Sherbrooke
La Tribune **(37393)** ....(Mon.-Fri.) 30,731
1950 Roy St. (J1K 2X8)   (Sat.) 38,741
Phone: (819)564-5450

The Record **(37395)** ....(Mon.-Fri.) 5,260
1195 Galt E. (J1G 1Y7)
Phone: (819)569-9525

Trois-Rivieres
Le Nouvelliste **(37416)** ....(Mon.-Fri.) 44,094
1920 Bellefeuille St.   (Sat.) 48,256
CP 668 (G9A 3Y2)
Phone: (819)376-2501

SASKATCHEWAN, CANADA
Moose Jaw
The Moose Jaw Times-Herald **(37502)** ....(Paid) 9,100
44 Fairford St. W.
  (S6H 1V1)
Phone: (306)692-6441

Prince Albert
Prince Albert Daily Herald **(37517)** ......(Mon.-Sat.) 8,675
30 10th St. E.
PO Box 550 (S6V 5R9)
Phone: (306)764-4276

Regina
Leader-Post **(37532)** ....(Mon.-Thurs.) 52,503
1964 Park St. (S4P 3G4)   (Fri.) 65,114
Phone: (306)565-8211   (Sat.) 62,634

YUKON TERRITORY, CANADA
Whitehorse
The Whitehorse Star **(37605)** ....(Mon.-Thurs.) 2,621
2149 2nd Ave.   (Fri.) 4,402
  (Y1A 1C5)

Paid Community Newspapers

Index entries are arranged geographically, first by states/provinces and then by cities. Within cities in this index, citations appear alphabetically by publication title. Citations include publication title, entry number (given in parentheses immediately following the title), and circulation figures.

Circ.

ALABAMA
Abbeville
The Abbeville Herald (1) 2,080

Albertville
The Sand Mountain Reporter (3) ....(Paid) 10,492

Alexander City
The Dadeville Record (7) 1,988

Andalusia
The Butler County News (12) 2,200

Arab
The Arab Tribune (23) ....‡6,980

Atmore
Atmore Advance (33) 4,213

Bay Minette
Baldwin Times (51) ....‡4,800

Birmingham
Birmingham Times (61) ....(Paid) ‡10,000
(Free) ‡350
Birmingham World (62) ....(Paid) ‡12,600
Deep South Jewish Voice (67) ....(Combined) 3,200

Brewton
The Brewton Standard & The Plus (136) .....‡4,100

Butler
Choctaw Advocate (140) ....‡4,400

Camden
Wilcox Progressive Era (143)

Carrollton
Pickens County Herald (146) ....(Paid) ‡4,500

Centre
Cherokee County Herald (148) ....(Paid) 5,000

Centreville
Centreville Press (151) 4,200

Chatom
Washington County News (152) ....‡4,000
6,780

Clanton
Chilton County News (154) ....(Paid) 2,000

Clayton
The Clayton Record (158) ....‡2,500

Columbiana
Shelby County Reporter (159) ....(Paid) 9,588

Cullman
The Cullman Tribune (161) ....‡15,000

Demopolis
The Demopolis Times (178) ....‡2,750

Dothan
The Headland Observer (187) ....(Paid) ‡1,683
(Free) ‡67

Elba
The Elba Clipper (197) 3,200

Eufaula
The Cuthbert Times & News
Record (204) ....‡2,100
The Eufaula Tribune (205) 6,350

Eutaw
Greene County Democrat (208) ....‡3,500

Flomaton
Tri-City Ledger (216) ....‡5,300

Fort Payne
Dekalb Advertiser (230) ....(Paid) ⊕6,172
(Non-paid) ⊕60

Geneva
Geneva County Reaper (239) 3,300
Hartford News-Herald (240) 1,400
Ledger (241) ....(Paid) 1,100
(Free) 35

Greensboro
The Greensboro Watchman (243) 3,050

Grove Hill
Clarke County Democrat (247) ....‡5,000

Gulf Shores
Islander (252)

Guntersville
The Advertiser-Gleam (254) ....(Paid) 11,401

Haleyville
Northwest Alabamian (257) ....‡7,200

Hamilton
The Journal-Record (261) 8,500

Hanceville
The Hanceville Herald (263) 1,600

Hartselle
Hartselle Enquirer (264) ....(Paid) 7,650
(Free) 7,980

Heflin
The Cleburne News (266) ....(Paid) ‡3,500

Huntsville
Speakin' Out News (274) ....‡24,000

Jackson
North Jackson Progress (290) 3,500
The South Alabamian (291) ....‡4,900

Jacksonville
The Jacksonville News (294) .....(Combined) ‡3,300

Lafayette
Lafayette Sun (300) 3,000

Linden
The Democrat-Reporter (303) ....‡7,125

Lineville
The Clay Times Journal (304) 3,700

Livingston
Sumter County Record-Journal (306) 4,000

Marion
Marion Times-Standard (312) 2,100

Mobile
Mobile Beacon (323) ....‡4,952
National Inner City (326) ....‡8,000
The New Times (328) ....(Paid) ‡5,000
(Free) ‡150

Monroeville
The Monroe Journal (351) ....‡6,700

Montgomery
Montgomery Independent (370) ....(Paid) ‡4,700
(Free) ‡2,300
The Prattville Progress (376) ....‡5,800

Moulton
The Moulton Advertiser (396) 5,500

Oneonta
The Blount Countian (404) 7,100

Opp
The Opp News (410)

Oxford
The Oxford Independent (415)

Ozark
The Southern Star (419) 5,000

Phenix City
The Phenix Citizen (424) ....‡5,000

Piedmont
The Journal Independent (427) ....‡3,450

Rainsville
The Weekly Post (429) ....(Paid) ‡2,250
(Free) ‡200

Red Bay
The Red Bay News (431) 5,300

Robertsdale
Fairhope Courier (436) ....‡4,400
The Independent (437) 4,500

Rogersville
East Lauderdale News (440) ....‡4,400

Russellville
Franklin County Times (441) ....(Paid) 4,200
(Free) 8,125

St. Clair
St. Clair News-Aegis (443) ....(Paid) 5,167

Sulligent
Lamar Leader (460) ....‡3,500

Tallassee
The Tallassee Tribune (467) 4,200

Thomasville
The Thomasville Times (470) ....(Paid) 4,000

Tuskegee
The Tuskegee News (508) ....(Paid) 4,800

Union Springs
Union Springs Herald (510) 3,000

Vernon
The Lamar Democrat (512) ....‡3,400

Wetumpka
The Wetumpka Herald (515) ....‡5,300

ALASKA
Anchor Point
The Bush Blade (519) ....(Controlled) 6,000

Anchorage
Senior Voice (531) ....(Combined) ‡10,000

Circulation: ★ = ABC; △ = BPA; ♦ = CAC; • = CCAB; ❏ = VAC; ⊕ = PO Statement; ‡ = Publisher's Report; Boldface figures = sworn; Light figures = estimated.

2879

Circ.　　　　　　　　　　Circ.　　　　　　　　　　Circ.

ALASKA (continued)

Bethel
Tundra Drums (554) ....‡6,800

Cordova
The Cordova Times (558) ....‡1,800

Delta Junction
Alaska Highway News (560) ....(Mon.-Fri.) 3,593
Delta Wind (561) ....(Paid) ‡950
(Free) ‡125

Dillingham
The Bristol BayTimes (562) ......(Controlled) ⊕2,076

Dutch Harbor
The Dutch Harbor Fisherman (564) ....(Paid) ⊕1,002
(Controlled) 1,046

Eagle River
Alaska Star (565) ....(Paid) ‡7,380
(Free) ‡1,200

Fort Richardson
Alaska Post (581) ....(Controlled) 10,000

Haines
Chilkat Valley News (584) ....‡1,300

Homer
Homer News (588) ....(Paid) 3,707

Kotzebue
The Arctic Sounder (621) ....(Paid) 2,185

Petersburg
Petersburg Pilot (631) ....‡1,800

Seward
The Seward Phoenix LOG (637) ....(Paid) 1,838
(Free) 56

Skagway
The Skagway News (641) ....‡950

Thorne Bay
Island News (643) ....(Paid) ‡1,700
(Free) ‡100

Tok
Mukluk News (644) ....(Paid) 700

Wasilla
Frontiersman (649) ....(Fri.) 7,013

Wrangell
Wrangell Sentinel (653) ....(Paid) ‡1,475
(Free) ‡25

ARIZONA
Ajo
Ajo Copper News (655) ....‡2,100

Benson
San Pedro Valley News-Sun (658) 2,900

Bisbee
The Bisbee Observer (659) ....(Controlled) ‡2,200

Buckeye
Buckeye Valley News (662) 2,600

Bullhead City
Mohave Valley Daily
News (666) ....(Mon.-Fri.) 7,841
(Sun.) 9,327

Camp Verde
The Camp Verde Journal (668) ....(Combined) 2,126

Coolidge
Coolidge Examiner (677) ....‡2,364

Cottonwood
Verde Independent (680) ....(Paid) ⊐3,672

Eagar
The Apache County Reporter (691) ......(Paid) 450
(Non-paid) 450

Eloy
Eloy Enterprise (692) ....‡1,154

Flagstaff
Navajo-Hopi Observer (698) ......(Non-paid) 13,500

Florence
Florence Reminder & Blade-Tribune (707) ....‡1,700

Fountain Hills
The Fountain Hills Times (711) 5,200

Glendale
The Glendale Star (713) ....‡10,000

Globe
Arizona Silver Belt (717) ....‡7,336

Green Valley
Green Valley News & Sun (722) 11,500

Holbrook
Holbrook Tribune-News (724) ....(Paid) ‡3,700
(Free) ‡2,600

Kearny
Copper Basin News (727) ....‡2,600

Litchfield Park
West Valley View (742) ....(Controlled) 36,228

Nogales
Nogales International (755) 5,000

Parker
Parker Pioneer (763) 5,149

Payson
Payson Roundup and Advisor (767) ......(Paid) 7,300

Peoria
Peoria Times (769) ....‡6,200

Phoenix
Ahwatukee Foothills
News (772) ....(Controlled) 54,500
Arizona Informant (780) ....‡1,800
The Business Journal of
Phoenix (795) ....(Paid) 13,677
Jewish News of Greater Phoenix (805) ....‡6,500

Safford
Eastern Arizona Courier (860) 8,742

San Manuel
San Manuel Miner (865) 3,200

Scottsdale
Arizona Trends (867) ....(Controlled) 34,000

Sedona
Sedona Excentric (877) ....(Non-paid) ‡10,000
Sedona Red Rock News (878) ....(Paid) 6,786
(Free) 85

Show Low
White Mountain Independent (881) .....(Paid) ⊕8,661
(Non-paid) ⊕17

Sierra Vista
The Copper Era (886) ....‡2,450
The Huachuca Scout (887) 13,500

Superior
Superior Sun (898) ....‡1,300

Tucson
Arizona Jewish Post (932) 6,800
The Weekly Observer (973)

Wickenburg
The Wickenburg Sun (1005) ....‡3,749

Willcox
Arizona Range News (1008) 3,200

Williams
Williams-Grand Canyon News (1010) ....‡5,000

Window Rock
The Navajo Times (1011) 21,000

Yuma
Foothills Sentinel (1017) ....(Paid) 3,071
(Non-paid) 14,000

ARKANSAS
Ashdown
Little River News (1036) 3,700

Atkins
Chronicle (1037) 2,400

Bald Knob
Bald Knob Banner (1038) ....‡3,500

Beebe
Beebe News (1045) ....‡2,500

Bella Vista
The Weekly Vista (1046) ....(Paid) ‡5,000

Bentonville
The Herald-Leader (1050) ....(Paid) 4,358
(Non-paid) 60

Berryville
Star Tribune (1054) ....‡4,007

Blytheville
Blytheville Courier
News (1057) ....(Mon.-Fri.) ♦3,617
(Wed.) ♦11,107

Booneville
Booneville Democrat (1063)

Cabot
Cabot Star-Herald (1067) ....(Paid) 6,250
(Free) 250

Camden
Camden News (1069) 350

Carlisle
Carlisle Independent (1074) ....(Paid) 1,515
(Free) 109

Charleston
Charleston Express (1076) ....(Paid) 2,250
(Free) 25

Cherokee Village
Villager Journal (1077) ....(Paid) 3,373

Clarendon
Monroe County Sun (1079) 1,600

Clarksville
Johnson County Graphic (1080) ....‡8,200

Clinton
Van Buren County
Democrat (1082) ....(Paid) ‡4,700

Corning
Clay County Courier (1090) 3,400

Crossett
Ashley News Observer (1092) 4,950

Danville
Yell County Record (1096) 4,700

Dardanelle
Post Dispatch (1098) ....(Paid) ‡2,462
(Free) ‡96

De Queen
De Queen Bee (1099) ....‡1,677

De Witt
De Witt Era-Enterprise (1103) 3,300

Decatur
Decatur Herald (1104) ....(Combined) 509

Dumas
Dumas Clarion (1105) ....‡3,400

England
The England Democrat (1111) ....‡1,426

Eudora
Eudora Enterprise (1112) ....‡800

Flippin
Mountain Echo (1134) ....‡2,300

Fordyce
News-Advocate (1135) ....‡3,286

Forrest City
Home with Homeland (1138) 15,000

Greenwood
Greenwood Democrat (1162) ....(Paid) 2,680
(Non-paid) 12

Gurdon
The Gurdon Times (1163) ....‡2,132

Hamburg
Ashley County Ledger (1164) ....‡3,000

Hampton
South Arkansas Accent (1165) ....‡1,600

Harrisburg
The Modern News (1166) ....(Paid) 2,100
(Free) 30

Hazen
The DeValls Bluff Times (1171) ....(Paid) 486
(Free) 14
Grand Prairie Herald (1172) ....(Paid) 1,650
(Free) 50

Heber Springs
Sun Times (1173) ....(Wed.) 4,962
(Fri.) 5,140

Huntsville
Madison County Record (1192) 5,200

2880

Numbers cited after listings are entry numbers rather than page numbers.

Imboden
The Ozark Journal **(1194)** ....‡1800

Jasper
Newton County Times **(1196)** ....‡3,000

Lake Village
Chicot County Spectator **(1205)** ....‡2,000

Lewisville
Lafayette County Democrat **(1206)** 1,500
28,000

Lincoln
Lincoln Leader **(1207)** ....(Paid) ‡1,700
(Free) ‡100

Little Rock
Aging Arkansas **(1208)** ....(Paid) 40,000
Arkansas Times **(1221)** ....(Non-paid) 30,000
(Paid) 6,000

Lonoke
Lonoke Democrat **(1257)** ....(Paid) 2,600
(Free) 100

Malvern
La Villa News **(1262)** ....(Paid) 4,310
(Free) ‡400

Manila
The Town Crier **(1266)** ....(Paid) 3,000
(Free) 4,400

Marianna
Courier-Index **(1267)** ....‡2,500

Marked Tree
Tri-City Tribune **(1268)** ....‡2,500

Marshall
Mountain Wave **(1269)** ....‡4,450

McCrory
McCrory Monitor-Leader-Advocate **(1271)** ......‡1,800

McGehee
Times-News **(1272)** ....‡3,400

Melbourne
The Times **(1274)** 1,200

Monticello
Advance-Monticellonian **(1278)** ....‡5,000

Mount Ida
Montgomery County News **(1283)** ....‡1,950

Mountain View
Stone County Leader **(1291)** ....‡4,339

Murfreesboro
Murfreesboro Diamond **(1293)** ....‡1,800

Nashville
The Nashville News **(1294)**

North Little Rock
The Times **(1300)** ....‡8,091

Osceola
Osceola Times **(1304)** 6,500

Ozark
Ozark Spectator **(1305)** 5,800

Paragould
NE AR Tribune **(1307)** ....(Paid) 4,650
(Non-paid) 350

Paris
Paris Express **(1311)** 3,800

Pea Ridge
The Times of Northeast Benton
County **(1312)** ....‡1,690

Piggott
The Piggott Times **(1313)** ....(Paid) 3,100

Pocahontas
Pocahontas Star Herald **(1316)** ....‡6,100

Prairie Grove
Prairie Grove Enterprise **(1322)** ......(Paid) ‡2,200
(Free) ‡100

Prescott
Nevada County Picayune **(1323)** 2,000

Rector
Clay County Democrat **(1324)** 2,000

Rison
Cleveland County Herald **(1325)** 2,800

Rogers
Rogers Hometown News **(1328)** ....(Wed.) 3,600

Salem
The News **(1335)** 3,550

Sheridan
Sheridan Headlight **(1343)** ....‡4,050

Smackover
Smackover Journal **(1346)** 1,200

Star City
Lincoln Ledger **(1347)** ....(Paid) ‡2,225
(Free) ‡75

Trumann
Trumann Democrat **(1358)** ....‡2,500

Waldron
Waldron News **(1361)** 2,250
The Waldron News -
Bulletin **(1362)** ....(Paid) ⊕**1,600**
(Non-paid) ⊕**5,400**

Walnut Ridge
The Times Dispatch **(1363)** ....(Paid) ‡5,700
(Free) ‡39

Warren
Warren Eagle Democrat **(1365)** 4,700

Wynne
Wynne Progress **(1372)** ....‡3,500

CALIFORNIA
Alameda
Alameda County Observer **(1387)** ....‡30,000

Alpine
Alpine Sun **(1392)** ....(Paid) ‡2,200

Alturas
Modoc County Record **(1394)** 4,500

Atascadero
Atascadero News **(1435)** ....‡6,450

Auburn
Sentinel **(1439)** ....(Controlled) 10,000

Avalon
The Catalina Islander **(1443)** ....(Paid) ‡4,000
(Free) ‡2,000

Bakersfield
Bakersfield News Observer **(1448)**
El Mexicalo **(1450)** ....(Paid) ‡9,676
(Free) ‡5,563
El Popular **(1451)** 25,000
Wasco Tribune **(1454)** ....(Controlled) 5,600

Bell
Bell/Maywood/Cudahy Industrial
Post **(1482)** ....(Paid) 134
(Free) 21,662

Berkeley
Psychic Reader **(1553)** ....(Free) 55,000

Beverly Hills
The Beverly Hills Courier **(1569)** ......(Paid) ‡2,930
(Free) ‡46,000

Big Bear Lake
Big Bear Life & the Grizzly **(1580)** ....‡9,000

Bishop
Inyo Register **(1583)** 7,590
Review-Herald **(1584)** 5,329

Blythe
Palo Verde Valley Times **(1587)** ....‡4,200

Bodega Bay
The Bodega Bay Navigator **(1590)** ......(Paid) 1,400
(Non-paid) 400

Bolinas
Coastal Post **(1591)** ....(Combined) 14,500

Boonville
The Anderson Valley Advertiser **(1592)** 4,000

Borrego Springs
Borrego Sun **(1593)** ....‡4,200

Burbank
Burbank Leader **(1614)** ....(Wed.) 25,110
(Sat.) 32,263

Burlingame
Independent News Group **(1632)** ....‡17,000

Burney
Intermountain News **(1635)** ....‡3,254

California City
The Mojave Desert News **(1639)** ....(Paid) ‡6,000
(Free) ‡200

Calistoga
The Weekly Calistogan **(1641)** ....‡3,000

Cambria
The Cambrian **(1649)** 4,100

Camp Pendleton
The Scout **(1652)**

Campbell
Campbell Express **(1653)** ....‡1,562

Carmichael
Carmichael Times **(1675)**

Cathedral City
Desert Post WEEKLY **(1679)** ....‡40,000

Chester
Chester Progressive **(1691)** 2,390

Chino
Chino Champion **(1708)** ....(Combined) 39,700
Chino Hills Champion **(1709)** .....(Combined) 39,700

Chowchilla
The Chowchilla News **(1711)** 3,300

Chula Vista
Star-News **(1715)** ....(Mon.-Fri.) ★35,126
(Mon.-Sat.) ★35,064
(Sun.) ★36,763

Clearlake
Clear Lake Observer-American **(1728)** ....‡3,363

Clipper Mills
Rabbit Creek Journal **(1729)** ....‡2,000

Cloverdale
Cloverdale Reveille **(1730)** ....(Paid) ‡2,400

Clovis
The Clovis Independent **(1733)** ....(Paid) ‡7,400
(Free) ‡21,600

Coalinga
Coalinga Record **(1735)** ....‡7,500

Colfax
Colfax Record **(1739)** 1,830

Colton
Colton City News **(1740)**
Colton Courier **(1741)** ....(Free) ‡16,000
(Paid) ‡1,000
Grand Terrace City News **(1742)**
Loma Linda City News **(1743)**

Compton
Carson Bulletin **(1746)** ....(Paid) 8,000
(Free) 9,000
Compton Bulletin **(1747)** ....(Paid) 12,000
(Free) 10,000

Copperopolis
Copperopolis Herald **(1763)** ....(Non-paid) 1,000
The Linden Herald **(1764)** ....(Paid) ‡1,200

Corcoran
The Corcoran Journal **(1765)** ....(Paid) 2,500
(Free) 26

Costa Mesa
Daily Pilot **(1774)** 40,000

Crescent City
The Triplicate **(1788)** ....(Tues.-Fri.) 4,894
(Sat.) 6,070

Delano
Delano Record **(1821)** ....‡4,650

Denair
Denair Dispatch **(1824)** ....‡3,300

Dinuba
Dinuba Sentinel **(1828)** ....(Paid) 3,693
(Free) 9

Dixon
The Dixon Tribune **(1831)** ....(Paid) ‡4,400
(Free) ‡1,000
Dixon's Independent
Voice **(1832)** ....(Combined) ⊕5,980

Dorris
Butte Valley Star **(1833)** ....‡3,000

Circ.　　　　　　　　　　　　Circ.　　　　　　　　　　　　Circ.

CALIFORNIA (continued)

Downieville
The Mountain Messenger **(1837)** ....(Paid) ‡3,000

El Cajon
Amador
Ledger-Dispatch **(1842)** ....(Combined) ‡6,874
Los Banos Enterprise **(1846)** ....(Paid) ‡4,500
(Free) ‡7,300

El Dorado
El Dorado Gazette/Georgetown Gazette and Town
Crier **(1863)** ....‡1,500

El Monte
Chinese L.A. Daily
News **(1865)** ....(Combined) 103,000

Elk Grove
Elk Grove-Laguna
Neighbors **(1872)** ....(Controlled) 45,000

Escalon
Escalon Times **(1888)** 4,700

Exeter
The Exeter Sun **(1907)** ....‡3,099

Fall River Mills
Mountain Echo **(1911)** ....(Paid) ‡2,554
(Free) ‡444

Felton
The Valley Press **(1913)** ....(Combined) ‡8,500

Ferndale
The Ferndale Enterprise **(1914)** 1,600

Fillmore
The Fillmore Herald **(1915)** ....‡3,000

Firestone Park
Firestone Park News/Southeast News
Press **(1916)** ....(Paid) ‡18,000
(Free) ‡6,000

Fontana
Fontana Herald-News **(1918)** ....(Paid) 5,263
(Free) 14,737
Pakistan **(1919)**

Fort Bragg
Fort Bragg Advocate-News **(1922)** .....(Thurs.) 5,400

Fort Jones
Pioneer Press **(1926)** 3,900

Frazier Park
The Mountain
Enterprise **(1936)** ....(Combined) 3,000

Fresno
California Advocate **(1944)** 22,500
Neighbors **(1952)**

Galt
The Galt Herald **(1994)** ....(Wed.) 10,400

Garden Grove
Orange County News **(1998)** ....(Paid) ‡10,000
(Free) ‡20,000

Gardena
Gardena Valley News **(2000)** ....(Paid) ‡5,700

Glendale
California Courier **(2007)** ....(Paid) ‡2,800
(Free) ‡200
KaMai Forum **(2010)** ....‡12,000
Weekend Balita **(2013)** ....(Combined) 80,000

Gridley
The Gridley Herald **(2032)** ....‡3,400

Gualala
Independent Coast Observer **(2034)** ....‡3,100

Half Moon Bay
Half Moon Bay Review and Pescadero
Pebble **(2036)** ....‡7,500

Hayward
Hayward & Castro Valley
Observer **(2042)** ....‡30,000

Healdsburg
The Healdsburg Tribune **(2046)** ....‡4,100
(Free) 3,000

Holtville
Calexico Chronicle **(2055)**
Holtville Tribune **(2056)**

Hughson
Hughson Chronicle **(2058)** ....‡4,200

Idyllwild
Idyllwild Town Crier **(2069)** 3,800

Imperial
Imperial Valley Weekly **(2070)**

Jackson
Calaveras Ledger
Dispatch **(2095)** ....(Controlled) 6,037

Julian
Julian News **(2098)** ....(Controlled) 2,500

Kerman
The Kerman News **(2101)** ....‡2,000

Kingsburg
Recorder **(2106)** 3,300

La Canada
La Canada Valley Sun **(2107)** ....‡5,500

La Jolla
La Jolla Light **(2115)** ....‡26,000

La Mesa
San Diego Jewish Times **(2123)** ......(Paid) ⊕15,663
(Non-paid) ⊕510
Union Jack **(2124)** ....(Paid) 10,500
(Free) 70,000

Laguna Hills
Leisure World News **(2134)** ....‡11,555

Lake Arrowhead
Crestline Courier-News **(2137)** ....‡2,850
Mountain News **(2138)** ....‡7,500

Lamont
Lamont Reporter **(2145)** 6,000

Laytonville
Mendocino County
Observer **(2150)** ....(Controlled) 2,500

Lemoore
The Lemoore Advance **(2152)** ....‡15,020

Lockeford
A Touch of Country **(2156)** 10,000

Loomis
Loomis News **(2180)** 1,500

Los Altos
Los Altos Town Crier **(2193)** .....(Combined) 16,500

Los Angeles
California Staats-Zeitung **(2232)** 18,700
Central Star/Journal
Wave **(2234)** ....(Combined) 37,210
El Sereno Star **(2263)** ....(Paid) 250
(Free) 7,400
Herald Dispatch **(2288)** ....‡35,000
Heterodoxy **(2289)** ....(Paid) 11,000
Hollywood Independent **(2290)** ....(Controlled) 30,460
Korean Sunday News **(2309)** ......(Combined) 22,000
Northeast Sun Commerce
Comet **(2349)** ....(Controlled) ♦104,000
Novedades **(2350)** ....(Combined) 50,000
The Rafu Shimpo **(2376)** ....(Paid) 15,500
U.S. Japan Business
News **(2422)** ....(Combined) 40,000
Watts Star Review **(2431)** ....‡30,000
Wilshire Independent **(2437)** ......(Combined) 33,000

Loyalton
Sierra Booster **(2484)** ....(Paid) ‡2,26
(Free) ‡930

Lucerne Valley
The Leader **(2485)** ....(Paid) ‡1,550
(Free) ‡50

Lynwood
Lynwood Journal **(2486)**
Lynwood Press **(2487)** 12,500
World of Pageantry **(2488)** ....(Paid) ⊕12,000

Malibu
The Malibu Times **(2492)** ....‡12,000

Mariposa
Mariposa Gazette and Miner **(2512)** ...(Paid) ‡5,300
The Mariposa Guide **(2513)**

Mendocino
Mendocino Beacon **(2519)** ....(Thurs.) ⊕2,278

Merced
The Signal **(2528)** ....(Free) ‡1,500

Middletown
Middletown Times Star **(2538)** ....‡3,000

Mill Valley
Vestkusten **(2542)** ....(Paid) ‡1,800
(Free) ‡400

Montebello
Bayou Talk **(2579)** ....(Paid) 3,000
(Non-paid) 3,000

Monterey Park
Monterey Park Progress **(2596)** ....(Free) 17,788

Moreno Valley
Valley Times **(2600)** ....(Combined) 634

Mount Shasta
Mount Shasta Herald, Weed Press, Dunsmuir
News **(2605)** ....(Combined) ‡15,075

Napa
The Napa County Record **(2610)** ....‡5,501

Newman
The West Side Index **(2620)** 1,850

Novato
Novato Advance **(2652)** ....(Paid) 7,220
(Free) 7,400

Oakdale
Oakdale Leader **(2656)** ....(Paid) ‡4,899
(Free) ‡5,911

Oakland
Oakland Bay Area Observer **(2690)** ....‡30,000
The Pet Companion **(2694)** ....(Controlled) 75,200
San Leandro Observer **(2699)** ....‡30,000

Ojai
Ojai Valley News **(2714)** ....‡4,940

Oxnard
Ventura County Vida Newspaper **(2731)** 35,000

Pacific Palisades
Palisadian-Post **(2736)** ....(Paid) 4,564
(Free) 145

Pacifica
Pacifica Tribune **(2738)** ....(Wed.) 7,248

Palm Springs
Coachella Valley Sun **(2756)** 174,000

Palmdale
Desert Mailer News **(2784)** ....(Tues.) 11,677

Palos Verdes Peninsula
Palos Verdes Peninsula
News **(2804)** ....(Thurs.) 15,000
(Sat.) 6,200

Paradise
The Paradise Post **(2807)** ....(Sat.) 8,040

Paramount
The Paramount Journal **(2810)** ....‡4,500

Paso Robles
Central Coast Times **(2830)** ....(Paid) ‡4,717
(Free) ‡1,200

Patterson
Patterson Irrigator **(2832)** ....(Paid) 2,550

Perris
The Perris Progress **(2835)** ....(Paid) ‡4,000

Phelan
Mountaineer Progress **(2837)** ....‡4,900

Piedmont
Piedmont & Berkeley Observer **(2842)** ....‡20,000
Piedmont Press **(2843)** ....(Paid) ‡4
(Non-paid) ‡26,996

Placerville
Mountain Democrat **(2848)** ....(Mon.) 12,566
(Thurs.) 11,991
(Fri.) 14,358

Point Reyes Station
Point Reyes Light **(2859)** ....‡4,300

Portola
Portola Reporter **(2864)** ....‡1,950

Poway
Poway News Chieftain **(2867)** ....(Paid) 1,414
(Free) 12,107

Quincy
Feather River Bulletin **(2869)** ....‡3,380

Indian Valley Record **(2870)** 1,205

Ramona
Ramona Sentinel **(2872)** ....(Paid) 6,100
           (Free) 135

Rancho Cordova
Grapevine Independent **(2874)** ....(Paid) 7,000
         (Non-paid) 4,000

Rancho Mirage
Rancho Mirage Post **(2879)** ....‡6,000

Redondo Beach
Easy Reader/Redondo Beach Hometown
 News **(2908)** ....(Combined) 61,198

Reedley
Reedley Exponent **(2916)** ....(Paid) ‡3,650
         (Free) ‡16,400

Reseda
California Hungarians **(2917)** ....‡2,000

Rialto
Rialto Record **(2919)** ....(Free) ‡16,000
         (Paid) ‡1,000

Rio Vista
River News Herald & Isleton
 Journal **(2927)** ....‡4,000

Ripon
The Ripon Record **(2928)** ....(Paid) ‡2,600

Riverbank
The Riverbank News **(2929)**

Riverside
Black Voice News **(2931)** ....‡7,500

Rosamond
Acton/Aqua Dulce News **(2966)** ....(Controlled) 4,700

Sacramento
El Hispano **(2998)** ....(Paid) ‡3,250
         (Free) ‡17,000
Gold River News **(3000)** ....(Non-paid) 4,500
The Sacramento Gazette **(3014)** ....(Paid) 1,480
Sacramento News &
 Review **(3017)** ....(Combined) 93,000
Sacramento Observer **(3018)** ....‡49,090

St. Helena
St. Helena Star **(3065)** ....‡12,000

San Andreas
The Calaveras Enterprise **(3079)** ....(Paid) 5,300
Calaveras Prospect (Weekly, Citizen &
 Chronicle) **(3080)** ....‡11,315

San Bernardino
El Chicano **(3086)** ....(Free) ‡16,000
Precinct Reporter **(3089)** ....‡55,000
The San Bernardino American
 News **(3090)** 5,000

San Bruno
San Bruno Herald **(3097)** 11,495

San Diego
La Prensa San Diego **(3220)** ....‡30,000
San Diego Commerce **(3259)** ....(Paid) 670
         (Free) 209
The San Diego Voice and
 Viewpoint **(3271)** 13,000

San Fernando
The San Fernando Sun Newspaper and Valley
 View **(3322)**

San Francisco
East Bay Guardian **(3353)** ....(Paid) 2,000
        (Non-paid) 70,000
El Bohemio News **(3357)** ....(Free) 60,000
El Latino **(3358)** ....(Non-paid) 28,500
         (Paid) 11,500
Irish Focus News **(3376)** ....⊕4,000
        (Non-paid) ⊕15,000
San Francisco **(3425)** ....(Combined) ‡108,895
Sun-Reporter **(3445)** ....‡11,249
Texas Lawyer **(3451)** ....(Paid) 10,200

San Jose
La Oferta Review **(3521)** 54,915
Metro **(3525)**
Thoi Bao **(3543)** ....(Combined) 12,000

San Leandro
India West **(3562)** 25,000

San Marino
San Marino Tribune **(3581)** ......(Combined) 4,400

San Mateo
Enterprise-Journal **(3586)** ....(Paid) 2,764
        (Free) 13,986

San Rafael
News Pointer **(3602)** ....(Combined) ‡10,500

Sanger
The Fowler Ensign **(3615)** ....‡1,809
Sanger Herald **(3617)** ....‡3,200

Santa Ana
Aliso Viejo News **(3618)** ....(Controlled) 3,997
        (Paid) 2,100
The Hellenic Calendar **(3626)** .....(Combined) 10,000

Santa Cruz
Metro Santa Cruz **(3687)**

Santa Monica
The Good Life **(3710)** ....(Combined) 40,000
World Tribune **(3720)** ....(Paid) 29,000

Sausalito
Marinscope Community
 Newspaper **(3747)** ....(Combined) 45,000

Scotts Valley
Scotts Valley Banner **(3748)** ....(Paid) ‡3,700
        (Non-paid) ‡2,800

Seaside
Coast Weekly **(3750)**

Sebastopol
Sonoma West Times & News **(3754)** 6,000

Selma
The Selma Enterprise **(3755)** ....‡4,603

Shafter
Arvin Tiller **(3756)** ....(Paid) 2,500
Shafter Press **(3757)** ....(Paid) 2,300
        (Non-paid) 4,000

Soledad
Gonzales Tribune **(3768)** ....‡705
King City Rustler **(3769)** ....‡3,225
Soledad Bee **(3770)** 1,125

Solvang
Santa Ynez Valley News **(3771)** ......(Tues.) 13,500
        (Thurs.) 7,500

Sonoma
Rohnert Park Community
 Voice **(3775)** ....(Free) 18,000
The Sonoma Index-Tribune **(3777)** .....(Paid) 10,531

Sun City
Sun City News **(3824)** ....(Fri.) 1,203

Susanville
Lassen County Times **(3832)** ....(Paid) 6,252
        (Free) 3,705

Tehachapi
Tehachapi News **(3840)** ....‡8,013

Temecula
Rancho News **(3842)** ....(Fri.) 412

Tiburon
The Ark **(3926)** ....(Paid) ‡3,500
        (Free) ‡40

Trona
Trona Argonaut **(3948)** ....‡1,200

Truckee
The Sierra Sun **(3950)** 6,000

Twentynine Palms
The Desert Trail **(3964)** ....‡3,700

Ventura
Los Angeles Times—Ventura County Edition **(4005)**

Walnut Creek
Rossmoor News **(4056)** ....‡6700

Waterford
The Waterford News **(4057)** ....‡5,200

Weaverville
Trinity Journal **(4059)** ....‡4,700

West Sacramento
News-Ledger **(4065)** 2,100

Westminster
Viet Bao Kinh Te **(4075)**
Westminister Herald **(4076)** ....⊕4,300

Willits
The Willits News **(4083)** 3,100

Willow Creek
The Kourier **(4084)** ....‡3,000

Willows
Corning Observer **(4086)** ....‡2,350
Orland Press-Register **(4087)** 7,500
The Willows Journal **(4088)**

Wilmington
Wilmington Beacon **(4090)**

Winters
Winters Express **(4094)** ....‡2,480

Winton
Hilmar Times **(4096)** ....‡4,000
Winton Times **(4098)** ....‡2,700

Yankee Hill
Feather River Canyon News **(4118)**

Yucca Valley
Hi-Desert Star **(4128)** ....‡10,100

COLORADO
Akron
The Akron News-Reporter **(4130)** ......(Paid) ‡2,500
        (Free) ‡30

Bailey
Park County Republican and The Fairplay
 Flume **(4152)** ....‡3,500

Berthoud
The Old Berthoud Recorder **(4153)** ....(Paid) ‡3,000

Boulder
Boulder Planet **(4158)**

Brighton
Standard Blade **(4202)** ....(Paid) 6,593
        (Non-paid) 25,227

Brush
Brush News-Tribune **(4209)** ....⊕1,832

Burlington
Burlington Record & Plains Dealer **(4210)** 7,500

Carbondale
The Valley Journal **(4218)**

Center
Center Post-Dispatch **(4229)** ....(Paid) 556
        (Free) 9

Central City
Weekly Register-Call **(4231)** ....(Paid) 1,294
        (Non-paid) 23

Cheyenne Wells
The Range-Ledger & Cheyenne
 Records **(4232)** 1,300

Colorado City
Greenhorn Valley-News **(4233)** ....(Paid) 1,240
        (Non-paid) 10

Cortez
Cortez Journal **(4289)** ....‡6,685
Sentinel **(4290)** ....‡6,200

Crested Butte
Crested Butte Chronicle &
 Pilot **(4298)** ....(Paid) ‡4,900
        (Free) ‡40

Deer Trail
Tri-County Tribune **(4301)** ....‡400

Delta
Delta County Independent **(4302)** 7,300

Denver
The Colorado Leader **(4316)** ....‡2,065
Denver Herald-Dispatch **(4322)** 8,600
Intermountain Jewish News **(4332)** .....(Paid) ‡9,750
        (Free) ‡165
Out Front Colorado **(4346)** ....(Free) 25,000

Dove Creek
Dove Creek Press **(4400)** ....(Paid) ‡1,100
        (Free) ‡58

Durango
Dolores Star **(4401)** ....(Paid) ‡1,400
        (Free) ‡10

Eads
Kiowa County Press **(4407)** ....(Paid) ‡1,100
        (Free) ‡50

Newspapers

Circulation: ★ = ABC; △ = BPA; ♦ = CAC; • = CCAB; ⊡ = VAC; ⊕ = PO Statement; ‡ = Publisher's Report; Boldface figures = sworn; Light figures = estimated.

2883

| | Circ. | | Circ. | | Circ. |

COLORADO (continued)

Eagle
The Eagle Valley Enterprise **(4408)** ......(Paid) 3000
(Free) 300

Eaton
North Weld Herald **(4409)** 1,700

Estes Park
Trail-Gazette **(4424)** ....‡5,877

Evergreen
Canyon Courier **(4425)** ....(Paid) ‡8,000
(Free) ‡400

Flagler
The Flagler News & Mile Save
Shopper **(4426)** 1,400

Florence
Florence Citizen **(4427)** ....‡1,500

Fort Collins
The Northern Colorado Business
Report **(4436)** ....(Combined) 12,000

Fort Lupton
Ft. Lupton Press **(4445)** ....(Paid) ‡1,100
(Non-paid) ‡4,400

Fountain
El Paso County Advertiser &
News **(4451)** ....(Paid) 1,663
Fountain Valley News **(4452)** ....(Paid) 3,000

Fowler
Fowler Tribune **(4454)** ....‡1,400

Frederick
Farmer and Miner **(4455)** ....‡1,300

Fruita
Fruita Times **(4458)** ....(Paid) ⊕1,335
(Free) ⊕104

Golden
Golden Transcript **(4468)** ....(Paid) 3,843
(Free) 913

Granby
Sky-Hi News **(4475)** ....(Paid) 3,800
(Free) 7,500
Winter Park Manifest **(4476)** ....(Paid) 2,900
(Free) 800

Gunnison
Gunnison Country Times **(4509)** ....‡3,800

Haxtun
The Haxtun-Fleming Herald **(4514)** ....‡1,250

Holyoke
Holyoke Enterprise **(4517)** ....(Paid) 2,000
(Free) 20

Hugo
Eastern Colorado Plainsmen **(4518)** ....(Paid) ‡1,315
(Free) ‡45

Johnstown
Johnstown Breeze **(4522)** 1,600

Julesburg
Julesburg Advocate **(4523)** ....(Paid) 1,850
(Free) 30

Kersey
The Voice **(4524)** 1,125

Kremmling
Middle Park Times **(4525)** ....(Paid) ‡1,500
(Free) ‡20

La Junta
Ag Journal **(4526)** ....‡10,300

Lake City
Silver World **(4529)** ....(Paid) ‡1,450
(Free) ‡10

Las Animas
Bent County Democrat **(4542)** ....(Paid) ‡1,200
(Non-paid) ‡800

Limon
The Limon Leader **(4544)** ....‡2,225

Littleton
Littleton Independent **(4551)** ....‡10,500

Lyons
The Old Lyons Recorder **(4570)** ....(Paid) ‡2,750

Mancos
The Mancos Times **(4571)** ....‡992

Meeker
The Meeker Herald **(4573)** ....(Paid) ‡1,800
(Free) ‡20

Monte Vista
The Del Norte Prospector **(4574)** ....(Paid) ‡630
(Free) ‡5
The Monte Vista Journal **(4575)** ....(Paid) 2,000
(Free) 33

Monument
The Tribune **(4584)** ....(Paid) ‡4,444
(Free) ‡145

Nucla
San Miguel Basin Forum **(4588)** ....‡1,500

Ordway
The Ordway New Era **(4589)** ....(Paid) ‡1,200
(Free) ‡200

Pagosa Springs
The Pagosa Springs Sun **(4590)** ....‡4,500

Palisade
The Palisade Tribune and Valley
Report **(4593)** ....(Paid) ‡1,721
(Free) ‡2,500

Rangely
Rangely Times **(4613)** 1,250

Ridgway
Ouray County Plaindealer **(4614)** ......(Paid) ‡1,025
(Free) ‡41
The Ridgway Sun **(4615)** 1,005

Saguache
Saguache Crescent **(4617)** ....‡665

Salida
Chaffee County Times **(4618)** ....‡3,000
The Herald Democrat **(4619)**

San Luis
Costilla County Free Press **(4623)** ....(Paid) ‡275
(Free) ‡25

Silverton
The Silverton Standard and The
Miner **(4626)** ....(Paid) ‡1,400
(Free) ‡6

Simla
Ranchland News **(4627)**

South Fork
South Fork Times **(4628)** ....(Paid) 770
(Free) 7

Steamboat Springs
Hayden Valley Press **(4629)** ....‡571
Steamboat Pilot **(4631)** ....‡6,900

Strasburg
Eastern Colorado News **(4643)** 1,978

Walden
Jackson County Star **(4655)** ....(Paid) ‡1,370
(Free) ‡30

Walsenburg
Huerfano World **(4656)** ....(Paid) ‡2,975
(Free) ‡25

Westcliffe
Wet Mountain Tribune **(4658)** ....‡2,820

Westminster
Westminster Window **(4669)** ....(Paid) 5,200
(Non-paid) 109

Windsor
Windsor Beacon **(4687)** ....(Paid) ‡3,000

Woodland Park
The Gold Rush **(4690)** ....‡1,200
Ute Pass Courier **(4691)** 3,750
13,100

Wray
The Wray Gazette **(4692)** ....(Paid) 3,125
(Free) 40

Yuma
Yuma Pioneer **(4694)** ....‡2,850

CONNECTICUT
Avon
Avon News **(4696)** ....(Paid) 1,883
(Non-paid) 160

Bloomfield
Bloomfield Journal **(4700)** ....(Paid) 2,008
(Non-paid) 414

Branford
Branford Review **(4707)** ....(Wed.) ‡7,000
(Sat.) ‡6,000

Bridgeport
Bridgeport News **(4711)** ....(Non-paid) ♦9,252

Bristol
Rocky Hill Post **(4722)** ....(Paid) 1,585
(Non-paid) 34
West Hartford News **(4723)** ....(Paid) 9,122
(Non-paid) 270
Wethersfield Post **(4724)** ....(Paid) 3,817
(Non-paid) 188

Brookfield
Brookfield Journal **(4725)** ....(Paid) ♦9,704
(Non-paid) ♦33,884

Canton
Canton News **(4732)** ....(Paid) 1,246
(Non-paid) 169

Cheshire
The Cheshire Herald **(4733)** ....‡7,200

Clinton
Clinton Recorder **(4734)** ....(Paid) 4,292

East Hartford
The Gazette **(4778)** ....(Paid) ‡209
(Free) ‡19,497

Fairfield
Fairfield Citizen-News **(4787)** ....(Paid) 8,409

Farmington
Farmington Valley Herald **(4822)** ....‡6,000

Glastonbury
The Glastonbury
Citizen **(4869)** ....(Combined) ‡9,200

Hartford
Hartford Advocate **(4891)** ....(Paid) 55,000
Hartford Inquirer **(4893)** 125,000

Kent
Kent Good Times Dispatch **(4920)** ....(Paid) 793
(Non-paid) 1

Lakeville
Lakeville Journal **(4921)** ....(Paid) 4,493
(Non-paid) 47

Lewisboro
The Lewisboro Ledger **(4923)** ....(Paid) ♦2,117
(Non-paid) ♦53

Madison
The Sound **(4936)** ....(Combined) 20,000

Milford
The Advertiser **(4951)** ....‡17,500

New Canaan
New Canaan Advertiser **(4979)** ....(Thurs.) 6,462

New Haven
Shore Line Times **(5002)** ....(Wed.) ‡9,548
(Fri.) ‡9,548

New Milford
Bethel Beacon **(5027)** ....(Paid) 1,278
(Non-paid) 1
Housatonic Weekend **(5030)** ......(Non-paid) 19,805
New Milford Times **(5032)** ....(Paid) 4,575
(Non-paid) 5
The Patent Trader **(5033)** ....(Paid) 6,702
(Non-paid) 1,830
The Putnam County Courier **(5034)** .....(Paid) 4,875
(Free) 207

Newington
The Newington Town Crier **(5036)** ......(Paid) 2,993
(Non-paid) 32

Newtown
The Newtown Bee **(5045)** ....(Paid) ♦6,936
(Non-paid) ♦61

Norwalk
Inside FC **(5065)**
New Canaan Lifestyles **(5071)** 90,177
Norwalk Citizen-News **(5072)**
Westport News **(5080)** ....(Paid) 8,953
Wilton Lifestyles **(5081)** ....(Combined) 90,177

Old Saybrook
Pictorial-Gazette **(5088)** ....(Paid) ‡8,500

2884

Numbers cited after listings are entry numbers rather than page numbers.

Ridgefield
The Redding Pilot **(5102)** ....(Paid) ♦**2,287**
(Non-paid) ♦63
The Ridgefield Press **(5103)** ....(Paid) ♦**6,892**
(Non-paid) ♦163

Shelton
Monroe Courier **(5127)** ....(Paid) ♦**3,841**
(Non-paid) ♦475
Trumbull Times **(5128)** ....(Paid) ♦**6,402**
(Non-paid) ♦638

Simsbury
Simsbury News **(5130)** ....(Paid) 2,506
(Non-paid) 46

Southington
The Observer **(5134)** ....(Paid) 5,755
(Non-paid) 42

Stamford
Fairfield County Weekly **(5149)**
New Haven Advocate **(5156)**
Valley Advocate **(5161)**
Westchester County Weekly **(5164)**

Stratford
Stratford Star **(5173)** ....(Non-paid) ♦**15,176**

Thomaston
Thomaston Express **(5174)** ....‡**1,900**

Watertown
Town Times **(5201)** ....(Paid) 260
(Non-paid) 9,119

West Hartford
Connecticut Jewish Ledger **(5202)** ....‡**30,000**

West Haven
West Haven News **(5207)** ....(Paid) ‡**550**
(Free) ‡**8,600**

Weston
The Weston Forum **(5210)** ....(Paid) ♦**15,706**
(Non-paid) ♦**9,618**

Wilton
Wilton Bulletin **(5231)** ....(Paid) ♦**3,202**
(Non-paid) ♦152

Windsor
Windsor Locks Journal **(5234)** ....(Paid) 1,594
(Non-paid) 32

DELAWARE
Dover
Better Years **(5244)** ....(Free) 24,000
Brandywine Community
News **(5245)** ....(Paid) 12,955
Greenville Community
News **(5248)** ....(Combined) 9,500
Hockessin Community
News **(5249)** ....(Combined) 14,600
Mill Creek Community News **(5250)** ....(Paid) 10,800

Georgetown
Sussex Countian **(5253)** ....‡**4,740**

Harrington
Harrington Journal **(5257)** ....‡**2,300**

Lewes
Cape Gazette **(5258)** ....(Combined) ⊕**7,300**

Middletown
Middletown Transcript **(5261)** ....(Paid) 5,500

New Castle
New Castle Weekly **(5266)** ....‡**1,200**

Seaford
Leader & State Register **(5285)** 10,000

DISTRICT OF COLUMBIA
Washington
Chemical Regulation Reporter **(5404)**
The Washington Informer **(5846)** ....‡**27,000**

FLORIDA
Apopka
The Apopka Chief **(5908)** ....(Paid) 3,700

Barefoot Bay
The Barefoot Tattler **(5915)** ......(Combined) ⊕**6,850**

Bartow
The Polk County
Democrat **(5918)** ....(Combined) ⊕**4,393**

Belleview
Voice of South Marion **(5923)** 2,800

Blountstown
The County Record **(5925)** 3,000

Boca Raton
National Examiner **(5937)** ....(Paid) 432,886
Weekly World News **(5941)**

Branford
The Branford News **(5962)** ....(Paid) ‡**2,000**

Bristol
The Calhoun-Liberty Journal **(5963)** 5,050

Bronson
Levy County Journal **(5964)** ....(Paid) 1,100

Brooksville
Hernando Today **(5965)** ....(Free) ‡**12,000**
(Paid) ‡**15,000**

Bunnell
Flagler/Palm Coast News-Tribune **(5967)** ......‡**7,828**

Bushnell
Sumter County Times **(5969)** ....‡**5,000**

Callahan
Nassau County Record **(5970)** ....‡**5,000**

Cedar Key
Cedar Key Beacon **(5979)** ....(Controlled) 1,500

Chattahoochee
Twin City News **(5980)** ....‡**1,800**

Chiefland
Chiefland Citizen **(5981)** 4,200

Chipley
Washington County News **(5984)**

Clearwater
Jewish Press of Pinellas
County **(5987)** ....(Controlled) 4,967
Jewish Press of Tampa **(5988)** ....(Controlled) 6,984

Clermont
South Lake Press **(5995)** ....(Paid) 2,800
(Free) 300
Zephyrhills Shopper **(5996)** ....(Paid) ‡**5,500**

Clewiston
Clewiston News **(5997)** ....‡**3,500**

Coral Springs
Coral Springs/Parkland
Forum **(6017)** ....(Combined) 30,600

Crawfordville
The Leon County News **(6020)** ....‡**100**
The Wakulla News **(6021)** ....‡**5,400**

Crescent City
Courier Journal **(6022)** ....(Paid) 2,250

Crestview
Crestview News Bulletin **(6023)** ....(Combined) 3,014

Cross City
Dixie County Advocate **(6029)** ....‡**3,500**

Dade City
Pasco News **(6031)** ....‡**5,000**

Daytona Beach
Daytona Times **(6036)** ....‡**20,150**

Deerfield Beach
Observer Community Newspaper **(6051)** 25,000

DeFuniak Springs
DeFuniak Herald **(6052)** 7,500
The Herald Breeze **(6053)** ....(Paid) 877
(Free) 3,500

DeLand
The New Volusian **(6055)** ....‡**4,500**

Destin
The Destin Log **(6059)** ....(Paid) 9,181
(Non-paid) 285
The Walton Log **(6060)** ....(Combined) 1,408

Everglades City
Everglades Echo **(6068)** 1,000

Fernandina Beach
News-Leader **(6069)** ....(Wed.) 10,068

Fort Lauderdale
New Times Broward-Palm Beach **(6081)**

Fort Meade
The Fort Meade Leader **(6092)** ....‡**1,285**

Fort Myers Beach
Fort Myers Beach Bulletin **(6117)** .....(Paid) ‡**16,000**
(Free) ‡**14,500**

Frostproof
Frostproof News **(6127)** ....‡**2,000**

Gainesville
The Record Farm & Ranch **(6154)** ....‡**5,000**
The Record-Local **(6155)** ....‡**5,000**

Graceville
The Graceville News **(6173)** ....‡**1750**

Gulf Breeze
The Gulf Breeze Sentinel **(6177)** ....‡**5,500**

Havana
Havana Herald **(6185)** ....(Paid) ⊕**2,600**
(Free) ⊕**25**

Hialeah
El Sol de Hialeah **(6187)** ....(Non-paid) ‡**24,000**

High Springs
The High Springs Herald **(6190)** ......(Paid) ‡**5,000**

Jacksonville Beach
Beaches Leader/Ponte Vedra
Leader **(6247)** ....‡**12,000**

Jupiter
The Jupiter Courier **(6249)** ....(Paid) ‡**8,000**
(Free) ‡**17,000**

Key Biscayne
The Islander News **(6251)** ....(Paid) ‡**3,100**
(Free) ‡**600**

Kissimmee
Osceola News-Gazette **(6262)** ...(Non-paid) 27,568
(Paid) 990

Lake Placid
Journal **(6285)** 4,900

Lake Wales
The Lake Wales News **(6286)** ....(Paid) ‡**3,300**
(Free) ‡**25**

Lantana
Amerikan Uutiset **(6298)** 5,000

Live Oak
The Jasper News **(6305)** ....(Paid) 2,100
(Free) 300
Live Oak Suwannee Democrat **(6306)** 5,500

Macclenny
The Baker County Press **(6316)** ....‡**5,000**

Madison
Madison County Carrier **(6317)** ....‡**4,100**
Madison Enterprise-Recorder **(6318)** ....‡**2,475**

Marathon
Florida Keys Keynoter **(6321)** ....(Wed.) 9,730
(Sat.) 10,539

Margate
Margate/Coconut Creek
Forum **(6325)** ....(Combined) 21,070

Mayo
The Mayo Free Press **(6332)** ....‡**1,650**

Miami
El Nuevo Patria **(6350)** ....(Paid) ‡**12,910**
(Free) ‡**17,090**
The Florida Newspaper **(6353)** ....(Paid) ‡**8,000**
(Free) ‡**200**
La Voz Catolica **(6367)** ....(Free) ❏**58,025**
The Miami Times **(6372)** ....(Wed.) 22,050
Miami Today **(6373)** ....(Controlled) △**32,146**
(Paid) △**601**
South Miami News **(6381)** ....‡**8,000**
Vida Social **(6389)** ....(Combined) 277,385

Milton
Santa Rosa Press Gazette **(6425)** ....‡**7,500**

Monticello
Monticello News **(6435)** ....‡**3,000**

Moore Haven
Glades County Democrat **(6436)** ....‡**1,500**

Naples
Golden Gate Gazette **(6439)** ....(Combined) 7,000
Marco Island Eagle **(6444)** ....(Wed.) 8,838

Circulation: ★ = ABC; △ = BPA; ♦ = CAC; • = CCAB; ❏ = VAC; ⊕ = PO Statement; ‡ = Publisher's Report; Boldface figures = sworn; Light figures = estimated.

2885

Newspapers

Circ.   Circ.   Circ.

FLORIDA (continued)
New Port Richey
Suncoast News **(6455)** ....(Wed.) 134,488
    (Sat.) 127,730
West Pasco Press **(6456)** ....(Paid) ⊕712

Niceville
Bay Beacon **(6460)** ....(Paid) 2,200
Beacon Express **(6461)** ....‡14,000

North Port
North Port Sun Herald **(6471)** ....(Paid) 3,200
    (Free) 5,000

Okeechobee
Okeechobee News **(6481)** ....(Sun.) ‡4,000

Orlando
Florida Sun Review **(6494)**
La Semana **(6500)** ....(Non-paid) 66,390
    (Paid) 10
The Orlando Times **(6504)** 11,000
Orlando Weekly **(6505)**

Palm Coast
National Enquirer **(6548)** ....(Paid) 2,075,063

Pensacola
The Escambia Sun-Press **(6565)** 3,500
Pensacola Voice **(6569)** ....‡35,896

Perry
Perry News-Herald **(6581)** 9,000
Perry Taco Times **(6582)** ....‡5,000

Pompano Beach
The Pompano Ledger **(6592)** ....(Paid) ‡5,000

Port St. Joe
The Star **(6601)** ....‡4,950

Quincy
Gadsden County Times **(6612)** ....(Paid) ⊕5,120
    (Free) ⊕380

Ruskin
The Observer News **(6615)** ....(Free) 35,000

St. Petersburg
Pinellas News **(6632)**
The Weekly Challenger **(6635)** 45,000

Sanibel
Island Reporter **(6650)** 8,500
The Islander **(6651)** ....‡6,000

Sarasota
The Bulletin **(6655)** ....(Paid) 16,500
New Yorker Staats Zeitung **(6661)** 14,450

Sebring
The News-Sun **(6679)** ....(Wed.) 11,625
    (Fri.) 11,200
    (Sun.) 12,685

Starke
Bradford County Telegraph **(6689)** 6,000
Lake Region Monitor **(6690)** 2,250
Union County Times **(6691)** ....(Paid) 2,250
    (Free) 300

Tallahassee
Capital Outlook **(6702)** 11,333
Florida Medical Association **(6735)**
The Tallahassee Advertiser **(6737)** ......(Paid) 8,120
    (Free) 1,880

Tampa
Florida Sentinel-Bulletin **(6763)** ....‡23,345
Free Press **(6765)** ....‡1,040
The Gazette **(6766)** ....(Paid) 53,000
La Gaceta **(6773)** ....‡18,079

Trenton
Gilchrist County Journal **(6824)** 4,000

Venice
Englewood Sun Herald **(6829)** ....‡4,500
The Venice Gondolier **(6831)** ....(Wed.) 10,603
    (Sat.) 11,189

Wauchula
The Herald-Advocate **(6841)** ....⊕5,470

Wellington
Greenacres/Lantana/Lake Worth
  Forum **(6843)** ....(Combined) 23,000

Williston
Williston Sun-Suwannee Valley
  News **(6863)** ....‡2,300

Winter Garden
West Orange Times **(6865)** 7,000

Winter Haven
Newschief **(6869)** ....(Combined) 2,104

Winter Park
Winter Park/Maitland
  Observer **(6891)** ....(Thurs.) 10,000

GEORGIA
Adel
Adel News-Tribune **(6899)** 3,200
Quitman Free Press **(6900)** 3,400

Alamo
The Wheeler County Eagle **(6901)** ....‡1,081

Albany
The Albany Journal **(6904)** ....(Fri.) 12,000

Alma
Alma Times **(6914)** ....‡3,100

Ashburn
The Wiregrass Farmer **(6927)** 3,000

Athens
Berkeley Democrat **(6931)** ....(Combined) 11,806

Atlanta
Atlanta Daily World **(6968)** ....‡10,000
The Atlanta Inquirer **(6971)** ....(Paid) 61,082
The Atlanta Voice **(6974)** 50,000
Daily Report **(6997)** ....(Paid) ◆5,541
    (Non-paid) ◆321

Augusta
Augusta Focus **(7097)** ....(Paid) ‡19,500
    (Free) ‡1,000
The Metro Courier **(7101)** ....‡28,760

Bainbridge
The Post-Searchlight **(7118)** ....‡7,000

Barnesville
The Herald-Gazette **(7121)** ....‡5,000

Baxley
The Baxley News-Banner **(7123)** ....‡4,600

Blackshear
Times **(7128)** 3,000

Blakely
Early County News **(7130)** ....‡3,900

Blue Ridge
The News Observer **(7133)** 10,200

Bremen
The Haralson Gateway Beacon **(7137)** ....‡6,500

Butler
Taylor County News **(7146)** 2,500

Cairo
Cairo Messenger **(7148)** 6,200

Calhoun
The Calhoun Times **(7149)** ....(Paid) 9,200

Camilla
The Camilla Enterprise & The Pelham
  Journal **(7152)** ....‡4,000

Carrollton
Bowdon Bulletin **(7155)** ....(Paid) 1,400

Cedartown
The Cedartown Standard **(7165)** ....(Paid) ‡3,400

Chatsworth
Chatsworth Times **(7168)** ....(Paid) 5,400

Claxton
The Enterprise **(7171)** ....‡3,500

Cochran
The Cochran Journal **(7178)** ....‡3,600
Twiggs County New Era **(7181)** ....(Paid) 2,009
    (Free) 50

Colquitt
Miller County Liberal **(7182)** ....‡2,900

Columbus
The Columbus Times **(7183)** ....‡20,000

Comer
The Comer News **(7197)** ....‡1,700

Commerce
The Commerce News **(7198)** ....‡4,600

Cornelia
The Northeast Georgian **(7207)** 9,500

Covington
Covington News **(7210)** ....‡7,450

Crawfordville
Crawfordville
  Advocate-Democrat **(7214)** ....(Paid) 790
    (Free) 10

Dahlonega
The Dahlonega Nugget **(7219)** ....‡6,550

Dallas
Dallas New Era **(7221)** ....(Paid) 6,900
    (Free) 125

Danielsville
Monitor **(7227)** ....‡1,800

Darien
The Darien News **(7228)** ....‡3,464

Dawson
The Dawson News **(7229)** ....‡2,800

Dawsonville
Dawson News & Advertiser **(7232)** ....‡5,500

Donalsonville
Donalsonville News **(7240)** ....‡3,500

Douglas
The Douglas Enterprise & Bonus **(7244)** ......‡8,500

Eastman
Times Journal Spotlight **(7261)** ....‡4,950

Eatonton
The Eatonton Messenger **(7264)** ....(Paid) ‡4,000

Elberton
The Elberton Star &
  Examiner **(7267)** ....(Paid) ‡5,700
    (Free) ‡140

Ellijay
Times-Courier **(7270)** ....(Paid) 7,350
    (Non-paid) 35

Fayetteville
Fayette Daily News **(7271)** ....‡9,100

Fitzgerald
The Herald-Leader **(7272)** ....‡5,341

Folkston
Charlton County Herald **(7274)** 3,000

Forsyth
Monroe County Reporter **(7279)** 4,000

Fort Gordon
The Signal **(7283)** ....‡16,000

Fort Valley
Fort Valley Herald **(7286)** ....‡6,000
Leader-Tribune **(7287)** 4,200

Franklin
The News & Banner **(7292)** 1,100

Glennville
Glennville Sentinel **(7305)** ....(Paid) ⊕4,300

Gordon
Wilkinson County News **(7307)** ....(Paid) ‡2,650

Gray
The Jones County News **(7308)** 5,500

Greensboro
The Herald-Journal **(7309)** ....‡5,000

Hartwell
The Hartwell Sun **(7321)** ....‡7,085

Hawkinsville
Hawkinsville Dispatch and
  News **(7323)** ....(Paid) ‡2,910
    (Non-paid) ‡50

Hazlehurst
Jeff Davis Ledger **(7325)** ....‡3,800

Hiawassee
Towns County Herald **(7329)** ....‡3,500

Hinesville
The Coastal Courier **(7330)** 5,500

Hogansville
The Hogansville Herald **(7337)** ....‡1,150

Jackson
Jackson Progress-Argus (7339) ....‡4,100

Jasper
Pickens County Progress (7341) ....‡7,000

Jefferson
Banks County News (7345) 6,700
The Jackson Herald (7346) ....‡7,800

Jesup
The Press-Sentinel (7347) 7,200

Kennesaw
Bright Side (7353) ....(Combined) 47,000

La Fayette
Walker County Messenger (7360) ......(Paid) ‡4,170

Lakeland
Lanier County News (7366) ....‡1,200

Lawrenceville
Gwinnett Daily Post (7368) ....(Paid) 61,738
(Non-paid) 126

Leesburg
Lee County Ledger (7370) ....(Paid) ‡2,650
(Free) ‡25

Lincolnton
Lincolnton Journal (7375) 2,300

Louisville
News & Former & Wadley Herald/The Jefferson
Reporter (7376) ....(Paid) ‡4,800
(Free) ‡65

Manchester
Harris County Journal (7407) 4,300

Marietta
The Truth at Last (7421) ....(Paid) ‡30,000
(Free) ‡12,000

Martinez
Columbia County News
Times (7426) ....(Wed.) 18,000
(Sun.) 26,000

Mc Rae
Telfair Enterprise (7427) ....‡3,400

McDonough
The Daily Herald (7429) ....‡7,000

Metter
The Metter Advertiser (7431) ....‡2,966

Millen
Millen News (7441) 2,000

Monroe
Walton Tribune/Advertiser (7442) ....(Paid) 6,122
(Non-paid) 16,000

Monticello
The Monticello News (7445) ....‡3,000

Nahunta
Brantley Enterprise (7451) 2,300

Nashville
The Berrien Press (7452) ....‡4,200

Newnan
The Newnan Times-Herald (7453) 14,000

Norcross
The Weekly (7472)

Ocilla
Star (7476) 2,300

Oglethorpe
Oglethorpe Echo (7477)

Pearson
Atkinson County Citizen (7482) ....(Paid) ‡1,400
(Free) ‡53

Perry
The Houston Home Journal (7483) 8,900

Pine Mountain
Harris County Herald (7485)

Reidsville
The Tattnall Journal (7488) ....‡4,100

Richland
Manchester Star-Mercury (7493) ....(Paid) ‡3,650
(Free) ‡26
Meriwether-Vindicator (7494) ....‡1,700
Patriot-Citizen (7495) ....‡1250

Rincon
Effingham Herald (7496) 5,300

Ringgold
Catoosa County News (7497) 4,700

Royston
The News Leader (7521) ....‡3,300

St. Marys
The Southeast Georgian (7523) ....‡5,000
Tribune & Georgian (7524) ....‡7,800

St. Simons Island
The Islander (7525) 4,000

Sandersville
Sandersville Progress (7526) 5,300
The Wrightsville Headlight (7527) ....‡2,200

Savannah
The Savannah Herald (7534) ....(Paid) 8,500
The Savannah Tribune (7538) ....(Paid) ‡8,000
(Free) ‡8,000

Soperton
The Montgomery Monitor (7558) 1,950
The Soperton News (7559) 2,050

Stewart
Stewart-Webster Journal (7569) ....‡1950

Summerville
The Summerville News (7575) ....‡7,850

Swainsboro
The Blade (7578) ....(Paid) 6,000
(Free) 8,388

Sylvania
Sylvania Telephone (7581) 5,061

Sylvester
The Sylvester Local News (7582) ....‡3,800

Talbotton
Talbotton New Era (7583) ....‡1,000

Thomaston
Thomaston Times (7585) 6,700

Thomson
McDuffie Progress (7592) 4,500

Toccoa
The Toccoa Record (7605) ....(Paid) 7,300
(Free) 125

Trenton
The Dade County Sentinel (7608) ....‡3,850

Vidalia
The Advance Progress (7628) 6,500

Vienna
The News Observer (7633) ....(Paid) 1,843
(Free) 87

Villa Rica
Villa Rican (7634) 2,500

Warrenton
The Warrenton Clipper (7639) 3,300

Washington
News-Reporter (7640) 4,900

Watkinsville
Oconee Enterprise (7643) ....(Thurs.) 4,031

Waynesboro
The True Citizen (7649) ....‡5,200

Winder
The Barrow County News (7652) ....(Wed.) 5,883
(Sun.) 5,713
The Barrow County
News (7653) ....(Combined) 5,732

Zebulon
Pike County Journal-Reporter (7658) ....‡3,000

HAWAII

Honolulu
Downtown Planet (7686)
East West Journal (7687) ....(Combined) 5,000
Hawaii Hochi (7696) ....(Combined) 8,000

Maunaloa
The Dispatch (7788) ....(Controlled) ⊕5,150

IDAHO

Aberdeen
The Aberdeen Times (7797) ....(Paid) ⊕1,000
(Free) ⊕18

American Falls
The Power County Press (7798) ....‡2,000

Arco
The Arco Advertiser (7799) ....‡2,185

Bonners Ferry
Bonners Ferry Herald (7836) ....‡3,200

Buhl
Buhl Herald (7838) ....(Paid) ‡2,700
(Free) ‡45

Cambridge
Upper Country
News-Reporter (7841) ....(Paid) ‡1,056
(Free) ‡50

Challis
The Challis Messenger (7842) ....‡1,900

Cottonwood
Cottonwood Chronicle (7849) ....‡1,150

Council
Adams County Record (7850) 2,600

Driggs
Teton Valley News (7853) ....‡2,300

Eagle
Valley Times (7854)

Emmett
Messenger Index (7855) 7,000

Garden Valley
The Idaho World (7856) 1,200

Grangeville
Idaho County Free Press (7857) ....(Paid) ‡4,100
(Free) ‡10,100

Idaho Falls
Freemont Current (7863)

Jerome
North Side News (7881) ....‡1,600

Kamiah
The Clearwater Progress (7885) ....‡1,600

Kendrick
Gazette News (7886) ....(Paid) ‡860
(Free) ‡50

Malad City
Malad City Idaho Enterprise (7904) ....‡1,500

McCall
The Star-News (7905) ....‡4,000

Montpelier
The News-Examiner (7909) ....(Paid) 1,975
(Free) 50

Moscow
Talk of the Town (7921)

Mountain Home
Mountain Home News (7926) ....‡4,000

Nezperce
Lewis County Herald (7935) ....‡1,050

Orofino
Clearwater Tribune (7938) ....‡3,000

Payette
Independent-Enterprise (7943) ....(Paid) 1,852
(Free) 63

Post Falls
Post Falls Tribune (7959) 1,200

Preston
Preston Citizen (7960) ....(Paid) 2,044
(Non-paid) 88

Priest River
The Priest River Times (7962) ....(Free) ‡6,800

Rexburg
Rexburg Standard Journal (7963) ....‡6,200

Rigby
Jefferson Star (7967) ....‡1,750

St. Anthony
Fremont County Herald-Chronicle (7971) ......‡2,200

Circulation: ★ = ABC; △ = BPA; ♦ = CAC; • = CCAB; ▢ = VAC; ⊕ = PO Statement; ‡ = Publisher's Report; Boldface figures = sworn; Light figures = estimated.

2887

Circ.

IDAHO (continued)

St. Maries
St. Marie's Gazette-Record (7972) ....‡3,507

Salmon
The Recorder-Herald (7974) ....(Paid) 2,975
(Non-paid) 158

Sandpoint
The Bonner County Daily Bee (7977)

Shelley
The Shelley Pioneer (7980) ....‡1,850

Shoshone
Lincoln County Journal (7981) ....‡1,000

Soda Springs
Caribou County Sun (7982) ....‡3,000

Weiser
Weiser Signal American (7998) ....(Paid) ‡2,500

ILLINOIS
Albion
Journal-Register (8003) ....‡3,162

Aledo
The Times-Record (8005) ....(Paid) 3,500
(Non-paid) 8,600

Algonquin
Algonquin Countryside (8007) .....(Combined) 49,572

Altamont
The Altamont News (8008) ....‡1,972

Amboy
The Amboy News (8012) 2,400

Anna
Gazette-Democrat (8013) ....(Thurs.) 4,558

Antioch
Antioch News (8016) 4,132

Arcola
Arcola Record Herald (8018) 2,100

Arlington Heights
Arlington Heights Post (8021) .....(Combined) 49,572

Arthur
Arthur Graphic Clarion (8027) ....‡3,100

Ashland
Ashland Sentinel (8028) ....‡850

Ashton
The Ashton Gazette (8029) ....(Paid) ‡900
(Free) ‡10

Assumption
Golden Prairie News (8030) ....‡2,200

Atwood
Atwood Herald (8031) ....‡1,150

Auburn
Auburn Citizen (8032) ....‡1,600
Chatham Clarion (8033) 1,850
Pawnee Post (8034) ....‡800

Augusta
Eagle-Scribe (8035) ....(Paid) ‡960
Eagles Scribe (8036) ....‡552

Avon
Avon Sentinel (8047) ....(Paid) ‡650
(Free) ‡100

Barrington
Barrington Courier-Review (8048) ......(Thurs.) 7,604

Barry
The Paper (8049) ....‡2,000

Bartlett
Bartlett Examiner (8050) 11,000

Bartonville
Limestone Independent News (8051) ....(Paid) 2,300
(Free) 200

Beardstown
Cass County
Star-Gazette (8055) ....(Combined) 3,300

Beecher
Beecher Herald (8057) 1,700

Beecher City
Beecher City Journal (8058) 1,600

Circ.

Berwyn
Berwyn/Stickney/Forest View
LIFE (8075) ....(Paid) 11,500
Cicero Life (8076) ....(Paid) 11,500

Blue Island
Aslip/Crestwood/Blue Island
Star (8087) ....(Thurs.) 54,309
(Sun.) 56,355

Blue Mound
Blue Mound Leader (8088) ....(Paid) 850
(Free) 50

Bluffs
Bluffs Times (8089) ....‡2,850
Meredosia Budget (8090) ....‡1,000
Triopia Tribune (8091) ....‡1,000

Breese
Breese Journal (8097) 6,165

Brighton
The Southwestern Journal (8098) 1,550

Bunker Hill
The Bunker Hill Gazette-News (8101) ....‡1,650

Bushnell
The McDonough Democrates (8103) ....‡2,500

Cairo
Herald (8105)

Calumet City
Burnham/Calumet City
Star (8107) ....(Thurs.) 54,209
(Sun.) 56,355

Cambridge
Chronicle (8108) ....(Paid) ‡1,264

Camp Point
Camp Point Journal (8109) 800

Carlinville
Carlinville Democrat (8125) ....‡2,300
The Enquirer-Democrat (8126) .....(Combined) 5,000

Carlyle
Union Banner (8129) ....(Paid) ‡4,931
(Free) ‡89

Carol Stream
Carol Stream Examiner (8136) ....(Paid) 7,800

Carrollton
Gazette-Patriot (8159) ....(Paid) ⊕1,588
(Free) ⊕60
Greene Prairie Press (8161) 2,900

Carthage
Hancock County Journal
Pilot (8165) ....(Paid) ‡4,000

Cary
Cary-Grove
Countryside (8167) ....(Combined) 49,572

Casey
Reporter (8173) ....(Paid) ‡2,500

Cerro Gordo
The News-Record (8176) ....‡1,500

Chester
Randolph County Herald Tribune (8239) 3,500

Chicago
Back of the Yards
Journal (8279) ....(Combined) 44,000
The Beverly Review (8282) ....‡6,500
Chatham-Southeast Citizen (8304) ....(Paid) ‡20,597
(Free) ‡9,365
Chicago Crusader (8310) ....(Paid) ‡57,000
Chicago Shimpo (8322) ....(Combined) 5,000
The New #Chicago Shoreland
News (8323) 38,000
(Paid) 9,880
Chicago Weekend (8329) ....(Paid) ‡22,583
(Free) ‡2,053
Edison-Norwood Times
Review (8360) ....(Combined) 37,449
Exito! (8371) ....(Free) 83,497
Hi-Riser (8397) ....(Combined) 18,575
Hyde Park Citizen (8402) ....‡17,000
In These Times (8410) ....‡20,000
Independent Bulletin (8411) 60,000
India Tribune (8412)
La Raza (8453) ....(Paid) ♦12,159
(Non-paid) ♦130,686
Metro EXTRA (8486) ....‡4,709

Circ.

Near North News (8502) ....(Paid) 7,265
(Free) 80
Northwest Leader (8511) 25,000
People's Tribune (8528)
Pilsen/Little Village/Cicero/Berwyn
EXTRA (8531) ....‡13,297
The Revolutionary Worker (8556)
South End Citizen (8566) ....(Free) ‡19,586
(Paid) ‡9,121
South Suburban Citizen (8567) ....(Free) ‡12,750
(Paid) 8,750
Southwest EXTRA (8568) ....‡4,926
Southwest News-Herald (8569) ....‡23,083
Suburban Leader (8573) 11,000
Suburban Post (8574) 11,000
West Suburban Extra (8604)
Windy City Times (8608) ....(Non-paid) 1,800

Chicago Heights
Chicago Standard News (8666) 16,000
South Suburban Standard (8669) 15,000

Chillicothe
Chillicothe Times-Bulletin (8670) ....(Paid) 2,050

Christopher
The Progress (8672) ....‡1,400

Cicero
El Dia Newspaper (8673) ....(Paid) 3,000
(Free) 27,000
Tele Guia de Chicago (8676) ....(Paid) 9,516
(Non-paid) 11,121

Cissna Park
Cissna Park News (8678) ....(Paid) 1,500
News/Independent (8679) ....‡1,992
Rankin Independent (8680) ....(Paid) 400

Clifton
Advocate (8681) ....(Paid) ‡2,000

Coal City
The Braidwood Journal (8686) 1,125

Collinsville
Madison county journals (8687) ....‡7,800

Country Club Hills
Country Club Hills/Hazel Crest
Star (8688) ....(Thurs.) 54,209
(Sun.) 56,355

Crete
Crete Record (8693) 2,100

Decatur
Decatur Voice of the Black
Community (8710) ....(Paid) ‡16,000
(Non-paid) ‡3,000

Deerfield
Deerfield Review (8723) ....(Combined) 38,946

Delavan
The Delavan Times (8746) ....‡1,500

Des Plaines
Des Plaines Times (8759) ....(Combined) 37,449

Divernon
Divernon News (8775) 400

Dongola
Dongola Tri-County Record (8778) ....‡909

Downers Grove
Bolingbrook/Romeoville
Reporter (8780) ....(Combined) 9,200
Darien Du Page
Progress (8782) ....(Combined) 8,089
Downers Grove Reporter (8784) ....(Wed.) 5,146
(Fri.) 23,570
Lemont
Reporter/Metropolitan (8788) .....(Combined) 6,000
Lisle Reporter (8789) ....(Combined) 9,200
Naperville Reporter (8791) ....(Combined) 9,200
SE DuPage Suburban
LIFE/Reporter (8794) ....(Paid) 15,100
Westmont Progress (8797) ....(Combined) 10,400
Willowbrook Progress (8798) ....(Combined) 2,218

Dwight
Dwight Star & Herald (8801) ....(Paid) 2,384
(Free) 15

Earlville
The Earlville Leader (8802) ....‡1,300

East Dubuque
Register (8803) ....‡1,300

2888

Numbers cited after listings are entry numbers rather than page numbers.

East St. Louis
East St. Louis Monitor **(8807)** ....‡22,500

Edgebrook
Edgebrook Times
  Review **(8809)** ....(Combined) 37,449

Edinburg
The Herald-Star **(8810)** ....(Paid) ‡630
(Free) ‡20

Edwardsville
Command Post **(8811)** ....‡14,100

Elburn
The Elburn Herald **(8821)** 4,000

Elizabethtown
Hardin County Independent **(8830)** .....(Paid) ⊕2,240

Elk Grove Village
Elk Grove Times **(8831)** ....(Combined) 49,572

Elmwood
Elmwood Gazette **(8843)** ....‡550

Erie
The Review **(8846)** 2,000

Eureka
Woodford County Journal-Eureka
  Edition **(8847)** ....‡1,700

Evanston
Evanston Review **(8858)** ....(Combined) 43,110

Fairbury
Blade **(8878)** ....‡3,500

Fairfield
Wayne County Press **(8880)** ....‡7,850

Farina
Farina News **(8884)**

Farmer City
Farmer City Journal **(8885)** ....(Combined) ‡1,700

Farmington
Farmington Bugle **(8888)** ....‡375

Fisher
Fisher Reporter **(8889)** ....‡1,150

Forreston
Journal **(8895)** 1,175

Franklin
The Franklin Times **(8896)** ....‡600

Fulton
Fulton Press **(8902)** ....(Combined) 5,500

Galena
Galena Gazette and Advertiser **(8904)** ....‡5,100

Galesburg
The Zephyr **(8907)** ....(Paid) 2,000

Galva
Galva News **(8911)** 2,314

Gardner
Gardner Chronicle **(8913)** ....(Paid) 760
(Free) 200

Geneseo
Geneseo Republic **(8914)** 3,821
Orion Gazette **(8916)**

Gillespie
Gillespie Area News **(8920)** ....‡2,715

Gilman
Star **(8921)** 2,800

Girard
The Girard Gazette **(8922)** ....(Paid) ⊕1,300
(Free) ⊕30

Glasford
The Glasford Gazette **(8923)** ....‡1,100

Glen Ellyn
Glen Ellyn News **(8927)** ....(Combined) 11,250

Glenview
Glencoe News **(8936)** ....(Combined) 43,110
Glenview
  Announcements **(8937)** ....(Combined) 43,110
Northbrook Star **(8940)** ....(Combined) 43,110
Wilmette Life **(8942)** ....(Combined) 43,110

Golconda
Herald-Enterprise **(8945)** ....‡2,100

Golden
Golden-Clayton New Era **(8946)** 800

Goreville
Goreville Gazette **(8948)** ....(Paid) 800
(Free) 100

Grant Park
Grant Park Gazette **(8950)** 880

Granville
Putnam County Record **(8951)** 3,400

Grayslake
Fox Lake Press **(8954)** ....‡4,856
Grayslake Review **(8955)** ....(Combined) 38,946
Grayslake Times **(8956)** ....‡4,712
Mundelein News **(8958)** ....‡3,020

Greenup
Greenup Press **(8960)** ....(Paid) 1,703
(Paid) 57

Greenville
The Greenville Advocate **(8961)** ....‡5,100

Gurnee
Gurnee Press **(8966)** 4,618
Gurnee Review **(8967)** ....(Combined) 38,946

Hampshire
Hampshire Register News **(8969)** ....(Paid) 1,654
(Free) 23

Hanover Park
Hanover Park Examiner **(8970)** 7,000

Hardin
Calhoun News-Herald **(8971)** ....‡4,000

Harvey
Harvey/Markham Star **(8976)** ....(Thurs.) 54,209
(Sun.) 56,355

Harwood Heights
Norridge-Harwood Heights
  News **(8978)** ....(Combined) 37,449

Havana
Havana Mason County
  Democrat **(8979)** ....(Combined) 6,300

Henry
Henry News-Republican **(8981)** 2,850
Wenona Index **(8982)** 1,000

Herrin
The Spokesman **(8983)** ....(Paid) 2,000

Herscher
Herscher Press **(8985)** ....(Paid) 882
(Free) 10

Heyworth
The Heyworth Star **(8986)** ....‡1,025

Highland
Highland News Leader **(8988)** ....(Paid) 6,500
(Free) ‡8,500
Highland Park News **(8989)** ......(Combined) 38,946

Hillsboro
M & M Journal **(8995)** ....(Combined) 6,393
Montgomery County News **(8996)** 6,700

Hinsdale
The Doings **(8997)** ....(Paid) 25,467

Hoffman Estates
Hoffman Estates Review **(9000)** ....(Thurs.) 2,682

Homer Township
Homer Township Star **(9002)** ....(Thurs.) 54,209
(Sun.) 56,355

Homewood
Homewood/Flossmoor Star **(9003)** ....(Thurs.) 54,209
(Sun.) 56,355

Hoopeston
Extra Shopping Guide **(9004)** 1,935
8,056

Huntley
The Farmside: Huntley,
  Marengo **(9006)** ....(Combined) 2,250

Illiopolis
County Line Observer **(9007)** ....‡575
Illiopolis Sentinel **(9008)** ....(Paid) ‡675
(Free) ‡50

Joliet
Farmers' Weekly Review **(9032)** **11,500**

Kewanee
Atkinson-Annawan News **(9044)** ....‡475

Kinmundy
Kinmundy Express **(9049)**

La Fayette
Prairie Times **(9051)** ....(Paid) ‡1140

Lacon
Lacon Home Journal **(9060)** ....‡2,400

Lake Forest
Lake Forester **(9062)** ....(Combined) 38,946

Lake Villa
Lake Villa Record **(9064)** 2,513

Lake Zurich
Lake Zurich Courier **(9065)** ....(Combined) 49,572

Lansing
Lansing/Lynwood Star **(9067)** ....(Thurs.) 54,209
(Sun.) 56,355

Lawrenceville
Lawrence County News **(9069)** ....(Paid) 401

Le Roy
The Le Roy Journal **(9072)** ....(Paid) ‡1,350

Lebanon
Advertiser **(9073)** 1,750

Liberty
Liberty Bee-Times **(9076)** ....‡1,400

Libertyville
Libertyville News **(9080)** 2,652
Libertyville Review **(9081)** ....(Combined) 38,946

Lincolnwood
The Booster **(9090)** ....(Paid) 4,188
Lincolnwood Life **(9097)** ....(Paid) ♦1,607
North Town News-Star **(9102)** ....(Paid) ♦6,403
Rogers Park/Edgewater/Uptown
  News-Star **(9103)** ....(Combined) 6,333
Uptown News Star **(9106)** ....(Paid) 6,806
(Free) 1,641

Lindenhurst
Lindenhurst News **(9107)** 2,231
The Review of Lake
  Villa/Lindenhurst **(9108)** ....(Combined) 38,946

Lombard
Lombardian **(9116)** ....‡21,500
Villa Park Review/Lombardian **(9118)** ....‡21,500
13,500

Louisville
Louisville Clay County Republican **(9119)** .....‡2,250

Machesney Park
News Gazette **(9126)** ....‡7,400
Northern Ogle Tempo **(9127)** ....(Paid) 6,488
(Free) 71

Macomb
Abingdon Argus **(9128)** ....(Paid) 1,750
(Free) 15
Roseville Independent **(9132)** ....(Paid) ‡750
(Free) ‡25

Mahomet
Mahomet Citizen **(9138)** 2,600

Manteno
The Manteno News **(9140)** ....‡2,000

Marion
Chariton Courier **(9141)** ....‡550

Marissa
Journal-Messenger **(9149)** 2,600

Mascoutah
Fairview Heights Tribune **(9151)**
Herald Scott Flyer **(9153)**
Lebanon Herald **(9154)**
Mascoutah Herald **(9155)**

Matteson
Matteson/Richton Star **(9158)** ....(Thurs.) 54,209
(Sun.) 56,355

Maywood
Maywood Herald **(9164)** ....(Combined) 31,238

Melrose Park
Melrose Park Herald **(9170)** ......(Combined) 31,238

Melvin
Ford County Press **(9171)** ....(Paid) 983
(Free) 29

Circulation: ★ = ABC; △ = BPA; ♦ = CAC; • = CCAB; ❑ = VAC; ⊕ = PO Statement; ‡ = Publisher's Report; Boldface figures = sworn; Light figures = estimated.

Circ.   Circ.   Circ.

ILLINOIS (continued)

Mendon
Mendon Dispatch-Times (9173) 1,000

Mendota
Mendota Reporter (9174) ....(Paid) ‡4,400
(Free) ‡8,000

Metamora
Herald (9177) 5,000

Metropolis
Metropolis Planet (9178) ....(Paid) 4,700
(Free) 50

Midlothian
Bridgeview Independent (9184) ....(Paid) ‡2,600
(Free) ‡800
Palos Citizen (9193) ....(Paid) ‡4,500
(Free) ‡500

Milford
Milford Herald-News (9196) ....‡1,050

Minonk
Woodford County Journal-Minonk
Edition (9200) ....‡612

Mokena
Frankfort/Mokena Star (9201) ....(Thurs.) 54,209
(Sun.) 56,355

Momence
Momence Progress-Reporter (9211) ....‡2,150

Monee
Monee Monitor (9212) 1,200

Monmouth
Murphysboro American (9217) .,...(Combined) 8,770

Monticello
Piatt County
Journal-Republican (9222) ....(Paid) 3,608
(Non-paid) 98

Morrison
Whiteside News Sentinel (9227) ....‡3,000

Morrisonville
Morrisonville Times (9228) 1,000

Morton
Morton Times News (9229) ....(Paid) 2,600

Morton Grove
Morton Grove Champion
Review (9230) ....(Combined) 43,110

Mount Carroll
Carroll County
Mirror-Democrat (9235) ....(Paid) ‡2,000

Mount Morris
Mt. Morris Times (9241) ....‡1,945

Mount Olive
The Mt. Olive Herald (9246) 1,500

Mount Prospect
Mount Prospect Times (9247) ....(Combined) 37,449

Mount Pulaski
Mt. Pulaski Weekly News (9251) 1,650

Mount Sterling
The Democrat-Message (9252) ....(Paid) 2,900

Mount Zion
Region News (9254) ....‡1,650

Mundelein
Mundelein Review (9258) ....(Combined) 38,946

Naperville
Batavia Sun (9260) ....(Combined) 280,876
The Bolingbrook Sun (9261) .....(Combined) 280,786
Geneva Sun (9264) ....(Combined) 280,786
Homer/Lockport/Lemont
Sun (9266) ....(Combined) 280,786
Lincoln-Way Sun (9268) ....(Combined) 280,786
The Lisle Sun (9269) ....(Combined) 280,786
The Naperville Sun (9270) ....(Sun.) 20,828
(Wed.) 21,234
(Fri.) 21,234
Plainfield Sun (9272) ....(Combined) 280,786
St. Charles Sun (9273) ....(Combined) 280,786
Sun Publications (9274) ....‡13,000
Wheaton Sun (9275) ....(Combined) 280,786

Nashville
The Nashville News (9277) ....‡5,300

Nauvoo
The New Independent (9279) 446

New Baden
Clinton County News (9280) ....‡1,500

New Berlin
New Berlin Bee (9281) ....‡575

New Lenox
New Lenox Community Reporter (9282) 950

Newman
Newman Independent (9283) 400

Newton
Newton Press-Mentor (9284) ....‡4,000

Niles
Niles Herald-Spectator (9292) .....(Combined) 37,449

Nokomis
Free Press-Progress (9294) ....‡2,350

Normal
Normal Normalite (9301) ....‡1,817

Norris City
Norris City Banner (9311) ....(Paid) ‡1,330
(Free) ‡14

O Fallon
O'Fallon Progress (9334) 4,000

Oak Brook
Addison Press (9336) ....(Combined) 6,000
Bensenville/Wood Dale
Press (9341) ....(Combined) 6,000
Bloomingdale/Glendale Heights
Press (9342) ....(Combined) 11,200
Carol Stream Press (9344) ....(Combined) 11,200
Countryside/Indian Head Park/Willow Springs/Burr
Ridge/Pleasantdale Suburban
Life (9346) ....(Paid) 20,850
Darien Metropolitan (9348)
Elmhurst Press (9349) ....(Combined) 15,000
Hillside/Broadview/Berkeley/Westchester Suburban
Life (9352) ....(Paid) 20,850
Itasca/Roselle Press: Serving Bartlett/Hanover Park/
Steamwood Press (9354) ......(Combined) 11,200
Lombard Suburban LIFE (9359)
North Riverside/Riverside/Riverside Lawn Suburban
Life (9361) ....(Paid) 20,850
Roselle Press (9364)
Suburban LIFE Citizen (9367) ....(Paid) 24,119
Villa Park/Oakbrook Terrace
Argus (9368) ....(Combined) 15,000
Villa Park Suburban LIFE (9369)
Western Springs Suburban
Life (9370) ....(Paid) 20,850

Oak Forest
Oak Forest/Midlothian Star (9371) ....(Thurs.) 54,209
(Sun.) 56,355

Oak Lawn
Oak Lawn Star (9372) ....(Thurs.) 52,209
(Sun.) 56,355

Oak Park
Forest Park Review (9375) 2,900
Tri-City Journal (9377) 50,000
Wednesday Journal of Oak Park & River
Forest (9378) ....(Paid) 8,500
(Free) 3,000

Oblong
Oblong Gem (9381) ....(Paid) 1,750

Okawville
Times (9383)

Oquawka
Oquawka Current (9386) ....(Paid) 1,957
(Free) 24

Oregon
Ogle County Life (9387) ....(Paid) ‡1,324
(Free) ‡11,535
Republican-Reporter (9388) ....(Paid) 1,300
(Free) 2,000

Orland Park
Orland Park Star (9389) ....(Thurs.) 54,209
(Sun.) 56,355

Palatine
Palatine Countryside (9395) ....(Combined) 49,572

Palos Heights
Regional News (9397) ....(Paid) ⊕187,820
(Free) ⊕100

The Reporter (9398) ....(Paid) ⊕17,986
(Free) ⊕100

Park Forest
Park Forest Star (9402) ....(Thurs.) 54,209
(Sun.) 56,255

Park Ridge
Park Ridge
Herald-Advocate (9407) ....(Combined) 37,449

Paxton
Loda Times (9410) ....‡326

Peoria
El Paso Times-Journal (9418) ....(Paid) 1,150
Peoria Times Observer (9422) ....(Free) 20,000
(Paid) 150

Peotone
Manhattan American (9443) 1,350
Peotone Vedette (9444) 2,600

Percy
The County Journal (9445) 7,000

Petersburg
The Petersburg Observer (9454) ....‡3,150

Pittsfield
Pike Press (9455) ....‡7,900

Plainfield
The Enterprise (9458) 6,500

Pleasant Plains
The Pleasant Press (9460) ....‡450

Polo
Tri-County Press (9463) ....(Combined) 7,500

Pontiac
The Flanagan Home Times (9465) .....(Paid) ‡1,050
(Free) ‡50

Princeton
Bureau County Republican (9467) 7,000

Prophetstown
The Prophetstown Echo (9470) 2,300

Proviso
West Proviso Herald (9472) ......(Combined) 31,238

Ramsey
Ramsey News-Journal (9484) 1,847

Rancho Santa Fe
Rancho Santa Fe Sun (9486) ....‡1,000

Rantoul
Gibson City Courier (9487) ....(Paid) ◆1,587
(Non-paid) ◆40
Rantoul Press (9488) ....(Paid) ◆7,459
(Non-paid) ◆18,508

Raymond
The Panhandle Press (9489) ....‡1,200
The Raymond News (9490) ....(Paid) 600
(Non-paid) 25

Reddick
Reddick-Essex Courier/Herscher
Press (9491) ....(Paid) 700
(Free) 25

Riverton
Buffalo Tri City Register (9499)
Williamsville Sun (9500)

Roanoke
Woodford County Journal-Roanoke
Edition (9511) ....(Paid) ‡988

Rochelle
News-Leader (9514) ....(Paid) ‡4,850
(Non-paid) ‡150

Rockford
The Post-Journal and Metro Rockford
Journal (9529) ....‡21,855

Rolling Meadows
Rolling Meadows
Review (9550) ....(Combined) 49,572

Romeoville
The Romeoville Sun (9553) ....(Paid) 1,467
(Free) 131

Round Lake
Round Lake News (9557) ....‡4,410

Rushville
Times (9558) ....(Paid) ‡3,325
(Free) ‡50

St. Anne
Record (9560) ....‡400

St. Charles
Geneva Republican (9569) ....(Combined) 17,300
St. Charles Republican (9571) ....(Combined) 17,300
Warrenville Post (9572) ....(Combined) 7,800
West Chicago Press (9573) ....(Combined) 7,800
Winfield Press (9575) ....(Combined) 7,800

St. Elmo
Banner (9576) ....‡1,300

Salem
Salem Times-Commoner (9577) ....(Paid) 5,264
(Free) 123

Savanna
Times-Journal (9581) ....‡2,100

Schaumburg
Schaumburg Review (9591) ....(Combined) 49,572

Sidell
Sidell Reporter (9601) ....‡817

Skokie
Harmony (9605) ....‡25,000
Skokie Life (9611) ....(Paid) ♦1,807
Skokie Review (9612) ....(Combined) 43,110

South Holland
South Holland/Dolton Star (9617) .....(Thurs.) 54,209
(Sun.) 56,355

Staunton
Staunton Star-Times (9661) ....(Paid) ‡3,891

Steeleville
Steeleville Ledger (9662) ....(Paid) ‡1,758
(Non-paid) ‡202

Streamwood
Streamwood Examiner (9668) ....(Paid) 7,000

Stronghurst
Hancock County Quill (9671) ....‡1,250
The Henderson County Quill (9672) ....‡1,700

Sullivan
News Progress (9673) ....(Paid) ‡3,800
(Free) ‡154

Summit
Des Plaines Valley News (9674) ....‡8,000

Sumner
The Sumner Press (9676) ....‡2,150

Teutopolis
Teutopolis Press and Dieterich Special
Gazette (9682) ....(Paid) 1,070

Thomson
Carroll County Review (9683) ....‡2,253

Tinley Park
Chicago Heights Star (9684) ....(Thurs.) 54,209
(Sun.) 56,355
Palos Area Star (9687) ....(Thurs.) 54,209
(Sun.) 56,255
Tinley Park Star (9689) ....(Thurs.) 54,209
(Sun.) 56,355
Worth/Chicago Ridge Star (9690) .....(Thurs.) 54,209
(Sun.) 56,355

Toledo
Toledo Democrat (9691) 1,250

Tolono
County Star (9692) ....(Paid) ⊕1,850

Tonica
The Tonica News (9693) ....‡1,000

Trenton
Sun (9694) ....(Paid) ‡1,450
(Free) ‡50

Tuscola
Review (9695) ....‡7,000

University Park
Crete/University Park Star (9696) .....(Thurs.) 54,209
(Sun.) 56,355

Vandalia
Vandalia Leader Union (9725) 5,300

Vienna
The Vienna Times (9729) ....‡2,600

Villa Grove
Villa Grove News (9730) ....‡1,675

Walnut
The Walnut Leader (9732) ....‡2,300

Warren
Wadsworth News (9733) 1,862

Washburn
Leader (9734) 1,000

Waterloo
Republic Times (9736) ....‡5,629

Wauconda
Wauconda Leader (9743) ....‡3,615

Waukegan
Vernon Hills Review (9744) ....(Combined) 38,946

Waverly
Waverly Journal (9748) ....‡1,350

West Salem
Times Advocate (9751) ....(Paid) 2,400
(Free) 6,500

Wheaton
Wheaton Leader (9760) ....(Combined) 11,250

Wheeling
Wheeling Countryside (9762) .....(Combined) 49,572

Williamsfield
Williamsfield Times (9763) ....‡625

Wilmington
The Coal City Courant (9765) 22,500

Winchester
Campbell Publication (9766) ....‡1,800

Windsor
Shelby County
News-Gazette (9767) ....(Combined) 1,035

Winnetka
Winnetka Talk (9768) ....(Combined) 43,110

Woodstock
The Woodstock
Independent (9772) ....(Paid) ⊕3,000

Worden
Madison County Chronicle (9773) ....‡1,100

Yates City
Yates City Banner (9774) ....‡350

Yorkville
Kendall County Record (9776) ....‡3,600
Ledger-Sentinel (9777) ....‡3,100
Tri County Today (9778) 3,735

Zion
Zion Benton News (9780) ....‡3,500

INDIANA
Albion
Albion New Era (9781) ....‡2,200

Alexandria
Alexandria Times-Tribune (9782) ....(Paid) 2,400

Attica
The Neighbor (9788) ....(Paid) 1,928

Avon
Hendrick County Flyer/Weekend
Edition (9793) ....(Combined) 30,500
Westside Flyer (9795) 13,500

Batesville
The Herald-Tribune (9796) ....‡4,500

Bloomfield
The Bloomfield News (9820) ....(Paid) ‡357

Bloomington
The Bloomington Independent (9824)

Bluffton
Bluffton News-Banner (9863) ....(Paid) ‡5,640

Boonville
Boonville Standard (9866) ....(Paid) 4,219

Bourbon
Bourbon News-Mirror (9868) ....‡1,300

Bremen
Bremen Enquirer (9872) ....‡1,900

Brookville
Democrat (9874) ....‡5,900

Brownstown
The Jackson County Banner (9875) .....(Paid) 3,800
(Free) 5

Butler
The Butler Bulletin (9876) ....(Paid) 1000

Cayuga
Herald News (9883) ....‡850

Churubusco
Churubusco News (9889) ....(Paid) ⊕1,766

Clay City
The News (9890) 2,000

Corydon
The Clarion (9904) ....(Paid) 12,569
(Free) 170
The Corydon Democrat (9905) 8,289

Crothersville
Crothersville Times (9913) ....‡2,800

Crown Point
Cedar Lake-Lowell Star (9914) ....⊕520
Crown Point Star (9915) ....⊕2,224

Culver
Culver Citizen (9916) ....(Paid) ⊕1,538
(Non-paid) ⊕30

Dale
Spencer County Leader (9917) ....‡2,000

Danville
The Republican (9921) ....‡1,350

Ellettsville
Journal (9931) 2,500

Ferdinand
The Ferdinand News (9955) ....(Wed.) ‡3,500

Flora
Carroll County Comet (9962) ....(Paid) ‡5,000
(Free) ‡35

Fort Branch
South Gibson Star-Times (9963) ....(Paid) ⊕2,650

Fort Wayne
Frost Illustrated (9969) ....(Paid) ‡1,342
(Free) ‡32

Fowler
Benton Review (9996) ....(Paid) ‡2,859
(Free) ‡76

Francesville
Francesville Tribune (9998) 850

Franklin
Franklin Challenger (10006) ....(Paid) ‡3,000
Herald Republican (10007) ....‡7,200

French Lick
Springs Valley Herald (10011) ....‡3,000

Garrett
The Garrett Clipper (10014) ....‡1,800

Gary
Gary New Crusader (10015) ....‡27,000
Info (10016) ....(Paid) ‡18,640
(Free) ‡2,415

Gas City
Twin City Journal-Reporter (10020) ....‡2,150

Goshen
El Puente (10022) ....(Combined) 6,050

Greenfield
Ad News (10038) ....‡17,000

Greensburg
Greensburg Times (10044) ....‡446

Greenwood
The Greenwood and Southside
Challenger (10046) ....‡4,000

Hagerstown
The Hagerstown Exponent (10048) ....‡2,500

Hamilton
The Hamilton News (10049) ....‡1,050

Highland
The Calumet Press (10062) ....(Free) 40,340

Newspapers

Circ.

Circ.

Circ.

INDIANA (continued)

Hope
The Hope Star-Journal **(10065)** ....(Paid) 1,312
(Free) 102

Indianapolis
Court & Commercial
Record **(10105)** ....(Controlled) ⊕1,127
The Criterion **(10106)** ....(Combined) 72,500
Indiana Herald **(10126)**
The Indiana Jewish Post and Opinion **(10127)**
The Indianapolis Herald **(10130)** ....(Paid) 20
(Non-paid) 3,100
The Indianapolis Recorder **(10132)** 13,300
Lawrence Community
Journal **(10146)** ....(Paid) 4,700
(Non-paid) 8,500
The Word **(10184)** ....(Paid) 15,000

Jasonville
Jasonville Leader **(10218)** ....(Paid) ‡840
(Free) ‡20

Jeffersonville
Clark County Journal **(10224)** 12,500

Kentland
Newton County Enterprise **(10231)** ......(Paid) 1,730

Kewanna
The Observer **(10232)** ....‡685

Knightstown
Knightstown Banner **(10236)** ....‡1,600

Knox
The Leader **(10238)** ....‡4,237

Lafayette
Lafayette Business
Digest **(10252)** ....(Controlled) 1,500
The Lafayette Leader **(10253)** ....‡5,000

LaGrange
La Grange Countian **(10264)** ....‡4,700
La Grange News **(10265)** ....‡4,710
La Grange Standard **(10266)** ....‡5,706

Lawrenceburg
Dearborn County Register **(10268)** .....(Paid) ‡7,861
(Free) ‡32
The Journal Press **(10269)** ....(Paid) 6,391
(Free) 35

Liberty
Liberty Herald **(10271)** ....‡2,400

Ligonier
Advance Leader **(10272)** ....‡1,081

Loogootee
Loogootee Tribune **(10278)** 3,300

Lowell
Lowell Tribune **(10280)** ....‡4,650
The Northern Star **(10281)** ....(Paid) ‡1,300

Middlebury
Middlebury Independent **(10307)** 780

Middletown
Middletown News **(10308)** ....‡1,950

Milford
The Mail-Journal **(10309)** ....(Paid) 3,300
(Free) 40

Mitchell
The Mitchell Tribune **(10319)** ....(Paid) ‡3,000

Montpelier
The Montpelier Herald **(10321)** ....(Paid) 406
(Free) 6

Mooresville
The Times **(10322)** ....(Paid) ⊕7,200

Nappanee
Nappanee Advance-News **(10336)** ....(Paid) 2,750
(Free) 150

Nashville
Brown County Democrat **(10337)** ....‡4,406

New Palestine
New Palestine Press **(10346)** ....(Paid) 2,500

Newburgh
Newburgh Chandler Register **(10349)** ....‡2,638

Noblesville
Noblesville Times **(10355)** 350

North Manchester
The News Journal **(10360)** ....(Paid) ‡2,000

North Vernon
North Vernon Plain Dealer **(10362)** 6,657
North Vernon Sun **(10363)** 6,000

Oakland City
Oakland City Journal **(10381)** ....(Wed.) ‡1,823

Odon
Journal **(10383)** 2,782

Orleans
Progress-Examiner **(10384)** ....‡2,000

Ossian
The Ossian Journal **(10385)** ....(Paid) ‡600

Paoli
News **(10387)** 3,200
Republican **(10389)** 3,200

Pekin
Austin Chronicle **(10392)** 4,784

Petersburg
The Press-Dispatch **(10400)** 5,472

Portland
Dunkirk News & Sun **(10404)** ....‡1,547

Poseyville
Posey County News **(10407)** ....‡4,800

Rensselaer
Kankakee Valley Post News **(10412)** ....‡3,192

Rising Sun
Ohio County News **(10428)** ....(Paid) ‡647
(Free) ‡8
Rising Sun Recorder **(10429)** ....(Paid) 1,785
(Free) 15

Rockport
The Spencer County
Journal-Democrat **(10434)** 5,625

Rockville
Parke County Sentinel **(10435)** ....‡4,500

Royal Center
Royal Center Record **(10436)** ....‡1,200

Salem
The Salem Democrat **(10439)** ....(Paid) 6,100
(Free) 176

Scottsburg
Scott County Journal **(10445)** 5000

South Bend
Morresville/Decatur
Times **(10457)** ....(Combined) 6,144
Tri-County News **(10459)** ....‡1,000

South Whitley
Tribune News **(10469)** ....‡2,145

Spencer
Spencer Owen Leader **(10471)** ....(Paid) 549
(Free) 25

Swayzee
Oak Hill Times **(10478)** ....‡1,700

Tell City
The Perry County News **(10482)** 7,490

Versailles
Osgood Journal **(10516)** ....(Paid) ‡4,900
(Free) ‡41
The Versailles Republican **(10518)** ....‡5,200

Vevay
The Switzerland Democrat **(10519)** ....‡800
Vevay Reveille-Enterprise **(10520)** ....‡2,842

Wabash
The Paper **(10528)** ....(Tues.) 16,225

Wakarusa
Wakarusa Tribune **(10533)** ....(Paid) ‡1,400
(Free) ‡90

Walkerton
The Independent-News **(10534)** ....‡2,400

Westville
Regional News **(10560)** ....(Paid) ‡550
Westville Indicator **(10561)** ....‡5,200

Williamsport
The Review-Republican **(10562)** ....‡3,750

Winamac
Pulaski County Journal **(10564)** 3600

Winchester
News & Advertiser **(10565)** ....‡18,688

Wolcott
The New Wolcott Enterprise **(10567)** .....(Paid) ‡896
(Free) ‡37

Worthington
Worthington Times **(10568)** ....‡1,000

Zionsville
Zionsville Times Sentinel **(10569)** ....‡4,000

IOWA
Adair
The Adair News **(10571)** ....(Paid) ‡1,427

Afton
Afton Star-Enterprise **(10573)** ....‡1185

Akron
Akron Register-Tribune **(10574)** ....(Paid) 1,400
(Free) 1,450

Albia
Monroe County News **(10575)** ....(Paid) 3,500
(Free) 300
Union Republican **(10576)** ....(Paid) 3,500
(Free) 300

Algona
The Algona Upper Des Moines **(10579)** ....‡4,950

Allison
Butler County Tribune Journal **(10584)** ....‡1,545

Alta
Alta Advertiser **(10585)** ....‡900

Altoona
Altoona Herald-Mitchellville Index **(10586)** .....‡3,000

Anamosa
Anamosa Journal-Eureka **(10601)** ....(Paid) 2,600

Anita
Anita Tribune **(10603)** ....‡1,500

Armstrong
The Armstrong Journal **(10607)** 915
The Ringsted Dispatch **(10608)** ....(Paid) 600
(Free) 50

Audubon
Audubon County Advocate
Journal **(10614)** ....(Paid) 2,172

Avoca
Avoca Journal-Herald **(10615)** 1,750

Bancroft
The Bancroft Register **(10616)** ....(Paid) 1,104
(Free) ‡30

Bayard
News Gazette **(10617)** ....‡2600
Scranton Journal **(10618)** ....‡1,100

Bellevue
Herald-Leader **(10619)** ....‡2,800

Belmond
Belmond Independent **(10620)** ....‡2,000

Breda
Breda News **(10630)** 600

Britt
The Britt News-Tribune **(10631)** ....‡2,000

Brooklyn
Brooklyn Chronicle **(10633)** ....(Paid) 1,900
(Free) ‡22

Buffalo Center
Tribune **(10635)** ....(Paid) ‡1,500

Calmar
Calmar Courier **(10647)** 2,000

Carlisle
The Carlisle Citizen **(10649)** ....‡1,550
Marion County News **(10650)** 1,300

Carroll
Carroll Today **(10651)** 2,000

Cascade
Cascade Pioneer **(10655)** ....‡2,400

Central City
Linn News-Letter **(10691)** ....‡2,450

Chariton
The Chariton Leader **(10692)** ....‡3,000
Herald-Patriot **(10693)** ....‡3,650

Clarinda
The Herald-Journal **(10702)** ....(Paid) ‡3,900
(Free) ‡250

Clarion
Wright County Monitor **(10704)** ....⊕2,000

Clarksville
Clarksville Star **(10705)** 1,200

Clear Lake
Clear Lake Mirror Reporter **(10706)**
Clear Lake Reporter **(10707)** ....‡2,200

Clearfield
Chronicle **(10709)** ....(Paid) 684
(Free) 15

Colfax
Jasper County Tribune **(10717)** 2,000

Columbus Junction
The Columbus Gazette **(10718)** ....‡1,600

Conrad
The Record **(10719)** ....‡1,250

Coon Rapids
Coon Rapids Enterprise **(10720)** 1,500

Corning
Adams County Free Press **(10722)** ......(Paid) 2,645
(Free) 66

Correctionville
Sioux Valley News **(10723)** ....‡1,300

Corydon
Times-Republican **(10724)** ....‡3,320

Dayton
Dayton Review **(10753)** ....‡845

De Witt
The Observer **(10755)** ....(Paid) ‡4,622
(Free) ‡2,387

Decorah
Journal **(10756)** ....‡6,400
Public Opinion **(10758)** ....(Paid) ‡6,100

Denison
Bulletin **(10765)** ....(Paid) ‡4,383
(Free) ‡4,352

Des Moines
Cityview **(10776)** ....(Non-paid) 33,000

Diagonal
The Diagonal Progress **(10839)** ....(Paid) 465

Doon
Doon Press **(10840)** ....‡3,300

Dunlap
The Dunlap Reporter **(10857)** ....‡1,400

Durant
Wilton-Durant Advocate
News **(10858)** ....(Paid) 2,628
(Free) 32

Dyersville
Dyersville Commercial **(10859)** .....(Combined) 4,000

Dysart
The Dysart Reporter **(10862)** ....‡800

Eagle Grove
Eagle Grove Eagle **(10863)** ....‡2,500

Eddyville
Eddyville Tribune **(10865)** 500

Edgewood
Edgewood Reminder **(10867)** ....‡1,500

Eldora
Hardin County Index **(10868)** ....‡3,020
Herald-Ledger **(10869)** ....‡3,020

Eldridge
The North Scott Press **(10870)** ....(Paid) ‡5,800

Elgin
The Elgin Echo **(10871)** 1,700

Elk Horn
The Danish Villages Voice **(10872)** 1,100

Elkader
The Clayton County
Register **(10873)** ....(Paid) ‡2,350
(Free) ‡102
7,000

Emmetsburg
Democrat **(10876)** ....‡2,279
Reporter **(10877)** ....‡2,286

Essex
The Essex Independent **(10878)** ....‡400

Everly
Everly-Royal News **(10881)** ....(Paid) 859
(Free) 30

Farmington
Van Buren County Leader-Record **(10887)** ....‡1,784

Fayette
Fayette Leader **(10889)** ....‡2,000

Fontanelle
Fontanelle Observer **(10890)** ....‡1,100

Forest City
Forest City Summit **(10891)** ....(Paid) ‡3,573
(Free) ‡7,564

Fremont
Batavia Beacon **(10917)**
Forum **(10918)**

George
Lyon County News **(10920)** 900

Gladbrook
Northern Sun Print **(10922)** 1,209

Glidden
Glidden Graphic **(10924)** 1,054

Gowrie
The Gowrie News **(10927)** ....‡1,400

Graettinger
The Graettinger Times **(10928)** ....(Paid) ‡741
(Free) ‡100

Greene
The Greene Recorder **(10929)** 1,300

Greenfield
Adair County Free Press **(10930)** ....‡2,426

Grinnell
Grinnell Herald-Register **(10931)** ....(Paid) 3,450
(Free) 355

Griswold
Griswold American **(10934)** 1,722

Grundy Center
The Grundy Register **(10936)** 3,200

Guthrie Center
Guthrie Center Times **(10937)** ....(Paid) 2,022
(Non-paid) 17

Guttenberg
The Guttenberg Press **(10938)** ....(Paid) 2,543
(Non-paid) 18

Hampton
Hampton Chronicle **(10940)** ....(Paid) 3,049
(Free) 2,400

Harlan
News-Advertiser **(10942)** ....‡4,725
Tribune **(10945)** ....‡4,725

Hartley
Hartley Sentinel **(10948)** ....(Paid) 1,433
(Free) 45

Hawarden
The Independent **(10950)** 1,400

Holstein
The Advance **(10951)** ....‡1,300

Hospers
Siouxland Press **(10952)** ....(Paid) ‡1,785
(Free) ‡50

Hubbard
South Hardin
Signal-Review **(10953)** ....(Paid) ‡1,361
(Free) ‡31

Hudson
Hudson Herald **(10954)** ....‡1,300

Hull
Sioux County Index-Reporter **(10956)** ....‡1,200

Humboldt
Humboldt Independent **(10957)** ....‡5,000

Humeston
The Humeston New Era **(10960)** ....‡1,000

Ida Grove
Ida County Courier-Reminder **(10961)** 3,000

Indianola
Record-Herald and Indianola
Tribune **(10965)** ....(Paid) ‡5,056
(Free) ‡154

Inwood
West Lyon Herald **(10967)** ....(Paid) ‡1,700
(Free) ‡3,450

Iowa City
The Daily Iowan **(10972)** ....‡20,500

Iowa Falls
Times-Citizen **(11001)** ....(Paid) ‡4,200
(Free) ‡9,000

Ireton
Ireton Examiner **(11004)** 625

Jefferson
The Bee **(11005)** ....(Paid) 200
(Free) 7,100
The Jefferson Herald **(11006)** ....⊕2,821

Jesup
Citizen Herald **(11007)** ....(Paid) ‡1,192

Jewell
South Hamilton Record News **(11008)** 950

Kalona
The Kalona News **(11010)** 3,000

Kanawha
The Kanawha Reporter **(11011)** ....(Paid) 750
(Free) 50

Keosauqua
Van Buren County Register **(11016)** ....‡2,987

Keota
The Keota Eagle **(11017)** ....‡1,350

Knoxville
Journal-Express **(11019)** 3500

La Porte City
Progress Review **(11022)** ....(Paid) 1,400
1,500

Lake City
Lake City Graphic **(11023)** ....‡1,800

Lake Mills
Graphic **(11024)** 2,187

Lake View
Lake View Resort and Green
Saver **(11026)** ....‡1,650

Lamoni
Chronicle **(11028)**

Laurens
The Laurens Sun **(11032)** ....‡1,350

Lenox
Time Table **(11036)** ....(Paid) 1,000
(Free) 15

Leon
Journal-Reporter **(11038)** ....‡2,150

Lime Springs
Lime Springs Herald **(11039)** ....‡850

Logan
Logan Herald-Observer **(11040)** ....(Paid) 2,095
(Free) 35

Lone Tree
Lone Tree Reporter **(11041)** ....‡1,100

Lowden
Sun-News **(11042)** ....‡1,190

Madrid
Madrid Register-News **(11043)** 1,400

Malvern
The Leader **(11044)** ....(Paid) ‡1,200
(Free) ‡50

Newspapers

Circ.   Circ.   Circ.

IOWA (continued)

Manchester
The Manchester Press (11045) ....‡5,188

Manilla
The Manilla Times (11047) ....‡1,200

Manly
Signal (11048) ....‡1,000

Manning
The Manning Monitor (11049) ....‡1,700

Manson
Calhoun County Journal'herald (11050) 2,085

Mapleton
Charter Oak-Ute Newspaper (11051)
Schleswig Leader (11053) 1,175

Maquoketa
Maquoketa Sentinel-Press (11055) ....‡5,200

Marcus
Marcus News (11058) 1,600

Marengo
The Belle Plaine Union (11059) 3,465
Journal-Tribune (11062) 4,800
Pioneer Republican (11063) ....‡2,675
South Benton Star-Press (11064) 2,500

Mediapolis
Mediapolis News (11082) 1,600

Missouri Valley
Missouri Valley Times News (11085) 2,100

Monroe
Monroe Legacy (11087) 840

Montezuma
Montezuma Republican (11088) 1,900

Monticello
The Monticello Express (11089) ....‡3,400

Moravia
Moravia Union (11090) ....‡1,000
Moulton Tribune (11091) ....‡900

Morning Sun
Morning Sun News-Herald (11092) ....‡900

Mount Ayr
Mt. Ayr Record-News (11093) ....‡2,550

Mount Vernon
The Hillsboro Star-Journal (11097) .....(Paid) ‡2,757
(Free) ‡150
The Sun (11098) ....‡2,203

Moville
Moville Record (11101) ....‡1,475

Nashua
Nashua Reporter and Weekly
Post (11107) ....(Paid) ‡1,100
(Free) ‡20

Nevada
Nevada Journal (11109) ....‡3,200

New Hampton
New Hampton Tribune (11111) ....(Paid) 3,500

New London
The New London Journal (11112) 1,092

New Sharon
New Sharon Star (11113) ....(Paid) 633

Newell
Buena Vista County
Journal (11114) ....(Paid) ‡1,071
(Free) ‡63

North English
The North English Record (11118) ....‡900

Norwalk
North Warren Town and County
News (11119) ....(Combined) 1,445

Oakland
The Herald (11120) ....(Paid) ‡1,814
(Free) ‡22

Ocheyedan
Ocheyedan Press and Melvin
News (11121) ....‡1,524

Odebolt
The Chronicle (11122) ....‡3,000

Ogden
Ogden Reporter (11125) 2,000

Onawa
Onawa Democrat (11126) ....(Paid) ‡2,950
Sentinel (11127) 2,400

Orange City
Sioux County
Capital-Democrat (11130) ....(Paid) ‡1,800
(Free) ‡50

Osage
Mitchell County Press-News (11131) ....(Paid) 3,496
(Free) 61

Osceola
Osceola Sentinel-Tribune (11133) ......(Paid) ‡3,843
(Free) ‡75

Ossian
The Ossian Bee (11139) ....‡1,230

Panora
Guthrie County Vedette (11147) 1,400

Parkersburg
Eclipse-News-Review (11149) ....(Paid) ‡2,335
(Free) ‡52

Paullina
The Paullina Times (11150) ....(Paid) 1,250
(Free) 15

Pella
The Chronicle (11151) ....‡3,350

Perry
Perry Chief (11156) ....(Paid) 2,722
(Free) 36

Peterson
Peterson Patriot (11159) ....‡580

Pocahontas
Pocahontas Record Democrat (11162) 1,950

Pomeroy
Journal Herald (11164) 1,400

Postville
The Postville Herald-Leader (11165) .....(Paid) 1,800
(Free) 14

Prairie City
Prairie City News (11166) ....(Paid) 964
(Free) 48

Preston
Preston Times (11167) 1,000

Primghar
O'Brien County Bell (11168) ....‡1,042

Red Oak
The Red Oak Express (11170) 4,950

Reinbeck
Courier (11174) ....(Paid) ‡1,750

Remsen
Remsen Bell-Enterprise (11175) ....‡1,200

Riceville
Riceville Recorder (11176) ....‡1,350

Richland
Plainsman-Clarion (11177) ....‡1,656

Riverside
Riverside Current (11178) ....‡620

Rock Rapids
Lyon County Reporter (11179) ....(Paid) ‡2,542
(Free) ‡50

Rockford
Advertiser-Register (11182) 1,900

Rockwell City
Calhoun County Advocate (11184) 2,187

Sac City
Sac Sun (11187) 1,900

Sanborn
Sanborn Pioneer (11188) ....(Paid) 800

Schaller
Schaller Herald (11189) 850

Seymour
The Seymour Herald (11191) 1,600

Shelby
Gazette (11192) ....‡1,850

Sheldon
N'West Iowa Review (11194) ....(Paid) ⊕4,491
(Non-paid) ⊕100
Sheldon Mail-Sun (11195) ....(Paid) ⊕2,011
(Free) ⊕17

Sibley
Osceola County Gazette-Tribune (11202) ......‡1,800

Sidney
The Sidney Argus-Herald (11203) ......(Paid) ‡1,200

Sigourney
Sigourney News-Review (11204) ....(Paid) ‡3,000
(Free) ‡48

Sioux Center
The Sioux Center News (11207) ......(Paid) 2,473
(Free) 71

Sioux Rapids
Sioux Rapids Bulletin-Press (11227) ....‡1,200

Slater
Tri County Times (11228) 4,500

Solon
Solon Economist (11229)

Spirit Lake
The Beacon (11236) ....(Paid) ‡3,458
(Free) ‡10
Milford Mail and Terril
Record (11237) ....(Paid) 1,148
(Free) 25
News (11238) 660

Stacyville
The Monitor Review (11241) ....‡1,475

State Center
Mid Iowa Enterprise (11242) ....‡1,500

Storm Lake
The Pilot-Tribune (11244) ....‡3,200

Story City
The Story City Herald (11251) ....(Paid) ‡2,200

Strawberry Point
Press Journal (11253) 1,876

Stuart
The Stuart Herald (11255) ....(Paid) ‡1,350
(Free) ‡50

Sully
Diamond Trail News (11257) ....(Paid) 1,850
(Free) 18

Sumner
Sumner Gazette (11258) ....(Paid) 1808
(Free) 65

Sutherland
Courier (11259) ....(Paid) ‡764
(Free) ‡30

Swea City
Swea City Herald-Press (11260) ....‡837

Tabor
Fremont-Mills Beacon Enterprise (11261)

Tama
The Tama News-Herald (11263) ....(Paid) 3,200

Thompson
The Thompson Courier-Rake
Register (11266) ....(Paid) ‡900
(Free) ‡20

Thornton
Southern County News (11267) ....(Paid) 1,000

Tipton
Clarence-Lowden Sun News (11268) ....‡1,250

Titonka
Titonka Topic (11270) ....(Paid) 600
50

Toledo
Toledo Chronicle (11272) ....‡3200

Traer
Star-Clipper (11273) 2,300

Tripoli
Tripoli Leader (11274) 1,512

Vail
The Observer (11280) ....‡1,114

Wapello
The Wapello Republican **(11285)** ....‡2,450

Waukon
Waukon Standard **(11303)**

Waverly
Bremer County Independent **(11306)** 6,350
Waverly Democrat **(11309)** 6,326

Wellman
Wellman Advance **(11317)** 1,300

West Branch
West Branch Times **(11318)** ....‡1,450

West Burlington
Des Moines County News **(11319)** 1,800

West Liberty
West Liberty Index **(11323)** ....‡2,000

West Point
Donnellson Star **(11324)**
West Point Bee **(11325)**

West Union
Fayette County Union **(11326)**

What Cheer
What Cheer Paper **(11327)** ....‡1,455

Winfield
Winfield Beacon & Wayland
News **(11328)** ....‡1,850

Winthrop
The Winthrop News **(11329)** ....‡2,000

Wyoming
Midland Times **(11331)** ....(Paid) ‡1,000
(Free) ‡20

KANSAS
Alma
The Signal-Enterprise **(11337)** ....(Paid) ‡1,650
(Free) ‡50

Andover
The Andover Journal
Advocate **(11338)** ....(Paid) ⊕2,408
(Free) ⊕47

Anthony
The Anthony Republican **(11339)** ....(Paid) 2,700
(Free) 30

Ashland
Clark County Clipper **(11344)** 1,345

Attica
Attica Independent **(11347)** 800

Atwood
The Rawlins County Square
Deal **(11348)** ....(Paid) ‡1,840

Baldwin City
The Baldwin City Signal **(11351)**

Belle Plaine
The Belle Plaine News **(11354)** ....(Paid) ⊕895
(Free) ⊕50
The Oxford Register **(11355)** ....(Paid) ⊕371
(Free) ⊕24

Belleville
Belleville Telescope **(11356)** ....‡4,669
Scandia Journal **(11358)** ....(Paid) 650
(Free) 15

Beloit
Beloit Call **(11361)**

Bird City
Bird City Times **(11362)** 628

Bonner Springs
Chieftain **(11363)** ....(Paid) ‡5,200
(Non-paid) ‡7,800
Sentinel **(11365)** ....(Paid) ‡5,200
(Non-paid) ‡7,800

Burden
The Cowley County Reporter **(11368)** ....(Paid) ‡465
(Free) ‡20

Burlingame
Osage County Chronicle **(11369)** ....⊕5,029

Burlington
Coffey County Republican **(11370)** ......(Paid) 3,318
(Free) 41

Caldwell
The Caldwell Messenger **(11372)** ....(Paid) ‡1,498
(Free) ‡30

Caney
Montgomery County Chronicle **(11374)** 3,100

Cawker City
Cawker City Ledger **(11375)** ....‡1,200

Chetopa
The Chetopa Advance **(11380)** 1,300

Cimarron
Bucklin Banner **(11381)** 1,100
Haskell County
Monitor-Chief **(11382)** ....(Paid) ‡1,600
(Free) ‡10
Jacksonian **(11383)** 1,250

Clyde
Clyde Republican **(11385)** ....‡1,000

Coldwater
The Western Star **(11394)** ....‡1,250

Columbus
The Modern Light **(11396)** ....(Paid) ‡220
(Non-paid) ‡10

Conway Springs
Conway Springs Star and the Argonia
Argosy **(11400)** 1,600
The South Haven New Era **(11401)** ....‡500

Cottonwood Falls
Chase County Leader-News **(11402)** 1700

Courtland
Courtland Journal-Empire **(11405)** 800

Derby
The Record/Journal **(11408)** 375
Wichita Journal **(11410)** 350

Dighton
The Dighton Herald **(11412)** 1,303

Downs
Downs News and Times **(11420)** ....(Paid) ‡1,250

Elkhart
Elkhart Tri-State News **(11422)** ....(Paid) 1,525
(Free) 50

Ellinwood
The Ellinwood Leader **(11424)** ....‡1,400

Ellis
The Ellis Review **(11425)** ....(Paid) 1,054
(Free) 33

Ellsworth
The Ellsworth Reporter **(11426)** ....‡3,050
Marquette Tribune **(11428)** ....‡659

Erie
The Erie Record **(11436)** ....‡1,249

Eureka
Eureka Herald **(11437)** 3,600

Fairview
Fairview Enterprise **(11439)** 600

Frankfort
Frankfort Area News **(11446)** ....(Paid) 700

Fredonia
Wilson County Citizen **(11447)** ....(Paid) ‡3,990
(Free) ‡40

Galena
Galena Sentinel-Times **(11448)** 1,350

Gardner
Gardner News **(11455)** 2,000

Garnett
Eastern Kansas Senior Star **(11458)** 8,521
Review **(11459)** 4,074

Girard
The Girard Press **(11460)** ....(Paid) 2,300

Glasco
The Delphos Republican **(11461)** 384
The Glasco Sun **(11462)** 870

Greensburg
Kiowa County Signal **(11475)** ....(Paid) 1,600
(Free) 50

Gypsum
Gypsum Advocate **(11476)** ....(Paid) ‡2,940
(Non-paid) ‡107

Harper
Harper Advocate **(11478)** 1,910

Hays
Ellis County Star **(11479)** ....‡2,000

Herington
The Herington Times **(11488)** ....(Paid) 2,250
(Free) 25

Hesston
The Hesston Record **(11490)** ....(Paid) ‡1,000

Hill City
The Hill City Times **(11494)** ....(Paid) 2,600
(Free) 50

Holton
The Holton Recorder **(11495)** ....‡4,900

Horton
Everest World **(11496)** ....(Paid) 245
(Non-paid) 14
Horton Headlight **(11497)** 2,200

Hoxie
The Hoxie Sentinel **(11498)** ....‡1,800

Hugoton
The Hugoton Hermes **(11499)** ....(Paid) 2,350
(Free) 50

Jetmore
The Jetmore Republican **(11516)** ....(Paid) ‡1,110
(Free) ‡20

Johnson
The Johnson Pioneer **(11518)** ....‡1,100

Kansas City
Kansas City Wyandotte Echo **(11528)** 1,600
The Piper Press **(11531)** ....(Free) ‡606
The Record **(11532)** ....‡1,100
The Wyandotte West **(11536)** **2,185**

Kingman
Kingman Journal **(11539)** 3,700
Kingman Leader-Courier **(11540)** 3,700

Kiowa
News **(11541)** 1,650

La Crosse
The Rush County News **(11542)** ....(Paid) ‡2,100
(Free) ‡200

Lakin
Independent **(11544)** ....‡1,705

Lawrence
The Baldwin Ledger **(11548)** ....(Paid) ‡3,500

Lebanon
The Lebanon Times **(11587)** ....‡650

Leoti
Leoti Standard **(11600)** ....‡1,650

Lewis
The Edwards County Sentinel **(11601)** ....‡1,958
Lewis Press **(11602)** 400

Lincoln
Lincoln Sentinel-Republican **(11608)** ....(Paid) ‡2,100
(Free) ‡30

Lindsborg
Lindsborg News-Record **(11611)** ....‡3,100

Logan
The Logan Republican **(11612)** ....‡912

Longton
The Elk County Citizen-Advance
News **(11613)** ....(Paid) 1,550
(Free) 200

Louisburg
Louisburg Herald **(11614)** 2,000

Lucas
Lucas-Sylvan News **(11615)** ....‡890

Madison
The Madison News **(11618)** ....(Paid) ‡740
(Free) ‡25

Mankato
Jewell County News **(11637)** ....‡3,700
Jewell County Record **(11638)** ....(Paid) ‡1,095
(Free) ‡50

	Circ.		Circ.		Circ.

KANSAS (continued)

Marysville
The Marysville Advocate **(11639)** ....(Paid) 5,534
(Free) 61

Meade
Meade County News **(11646)** ....‡1,900

Medicine Lodge
Barber County Index **(11649)** ....(Paid) 2,350

Miltonvale
Record **(11652)** ....(Paid) 650
(Free) 10

Minneapolis
The Minneapolis
Messenger **(11654)** ....(Paid) ‡2,543
(Free) ‡60

Minneola
The Minneola Record **(11655)** 558

Montezuma
Montezuma Press **(11658)** 1,100

Moundridge
The Ledger **(11659)** 1,800

Mount Hope
The Mount Hope Clarion **(11661)** 1,600

Mulvane
The Mulvane News **(11664)** 1,750

Natoma
Natoma-Luray Independent **(11665)** ....‡1,750

Neodesha
Neodesha Derrick **(11666)** ....‡1,800

Ness City
Ness County News **(11667)** ....‡2,425

Oakley
The Oakley Graphic **(11680)** ....(Paid) ‡1,500
(Free) ‡30

Oberlin
The Oberlin Herald **(11681)** ....(Paid) ‡2,426

Onaga
Onaga Herald **(11685)** ....‡1,100

Osborne
Osborne County Farmer **(11686)** ....‡2,755

Oskaloosa
The Oskaloosa Independent **(11687)** ....(Paid) 2,281

Oswego
Oswego Independent-Observer **(11688)** 1,500

Ottawa
Ottawa Times Shopper **(11691)** ....(Paid) 1,200
(Free) 14,475

Overland Park
California-Arizona Farm Press **(11701)**
Kansas City Jewish Chronicle **(11717)**

Paola
Miami County Republic **(11741)** ....(Paid) 5,277
Osawatomie Graphic **(11742)** 3,490
(Combined) 7000

Peabody
Peabody Gazette-Bulletin **(11747)** 1,400

Phillipsburg
Phillips County Review **(11748)** ....(Paid) ‡2,000

Plainville
Plainville Times **(11759)** ....(Paid) ‡2,450
(Free) ‡40

Pleasanton
Linn County News **(11760)** 3,000

Pretty Prairie
Ninnescah Valley News **(11767)** ....‡750

Quinter
Gove County Advocate **(11768)** 1,900

Riley
The Riley Countian **(11769)** 1,200

Russell
The Russell Record **(11773)**

Sabetha
The Sabetha Herald **(11776)** ....(Paid) ‡3,000

St. John
St. John News **(11778)** ....‡1,350

St. Marys
St. Marys Star **(11779)** ....(Paid) ‡1,815
(Free) ‡10

Salina
The Chapman Advertiser & Enterprise
Journal **(11781)** ....(Paid) ‡1,075

Sedan
Sedan **(11796)**
Sedan Times-Star **(11797)** ....(Paid) 2,100

Seneca
Courier Tribune **(11798)** ....‡3,200

Sharon Springs
Western Times **(11799)** ....‡1,353

Shawnee
Shawnee Journal Herald **(11801)** ....(Paid) 350
(Non-paid) 10,000

Smith Center
Smith County Pioneer **(11806)** 3,989

Spearville
The Spearville News **(11807)** ....(Paid) 975

Stafford
The Stafford Courier **(11808)** ....‡1,750

Sterling
Sterling Bulletin **(11809)** ....(Paid) 1,200

Syracuse
Syracuse Journal **(11812)** ....(Paid) 1,600

Tonganoxie
Tonganoxie Mirror **(11813)** 2,500

Tribune
Greeley County Republican **(11848)** ......(Paid) 1,500
(Free) 16

Troy
The Highland Vidette **(11850)** ....‡900
Kansas Chief **(11851)** ....(Paid) 1,495

Turon
The Record **(11852)** ....‡800

Ulysses
The Ulysses News **(11854)** ....‡2,600

Valley Center
Ark Valley News **(11857)** ....‡2,100

Valley Falls
Valley Falls Vindicator **(11858)** 2,435

Wa Keeney
Western Kansas World **(11859)** 2,050

Wamego
Wamego Times **(11862)** 2,200

Washington
Washington County News **(11863)** .....(Paid) ‡3,050

Wathena
The Wathena Times **(11865)** ....‡1,800

Westmoreland
Westmoreland Recorder **(11870)** ....‡1,000

White City
Prairie Post **(11878)** ....(Paid) 840
(Controlled) 21

Wilson
Wilson World **(11908)** ....(Paid) 926

Yates Center
The Yates Center News **(11913)** ....(Paid) ‡1,998
(Free) ‡100

KENTUCKY

Albany
Clinton County News **(11914)** ....‡3,650

Bardstown
Kentucky Standard **(11926)** 9,650

Beaver Dam
Ohio County Messenger **(11930)** ....‡2,100

Bedford
The Trimble Banner **(11931)** ....(Paid) 1,800

Benton
Tribune Courier **(11933)** ....(Paid) 7,400
(Free) 200

Berea
Berea Citizen **(11937)** ....‡3,600

Booneville
Booneville Sentinel **(11940)** ....‡2,100

Brandenburg
The Meade County Messenger **(11963)** 5,686

Brooksville
Bracken County News **(11966)** ....‡3,000

Burkesville
Cumberland County News **(11999)** 2,900

Cadiz
The Cadiz Record **(12002)** ....‡4,800
Herald Ledger **(12003)** ....‡3,000

Campbellsville
Central Kentucky
News-Journal **(12006)** ....(Paid) ‡7,115
(Free) ‡20

Campton
Wolfe County News **(12010)** ....(Paid) 2,800

Carrollton
The News-Democrat **(12011)** 3,615

Central City
Central City Times-Argus **(12014)** 3,000

Clinton
Hickman County Gazette **(12016)** ......(Paid) ‡2,150
(Free) ‡50

Covington
The Suspension Press **(12028)** ....(Paid) ‡38,000
(Free) ‡3,200

Cumberland
Tri-City News **(12031)** ....‡2,200

Dawson Springs
The Dawson Springs Progress **(12042)** 2,600

Edmonton
Herald-News **(12043)** ....(Paid) 3,167

Elkton
Todd County Standard **(12051)** ....‡2,300

Flemingsburg
The Fleming Gazette **(12057)** 3,600

Fort Thomas
Campbell County Recorder **(12063)** .....(Paid) 1,694
(Non-paid) 12

Frankfort
The Kentucky Journal **(12071)** ....(Paid) 5,000
(Non-paid) 400

Fulton
The Fulton Leader **(12084)** ....‡3,150

Georgetown
The Georgetown-News Graphic **(12088)** 5,000

Glasgow
Glasgow Republican **(12091)** 1,500

Grayson
Grayson Journal-Enquirer **(12093)** ......(Paid) ‡3,542

Greensburg
Record-Herald **(12097)** 4,587

Greenup
The Greenup News **(12098)** ....‡3,768

Hardinsburg
Breckinridge County
Herald-News **(12103)** ....(Paid) ‡5,600

Harrodsburg
The Harrodsburg Herald **(12111)** ......(Thurs.) 6,024

Hartford
Ohio County Times-News **(12112)** ....‡6,700

Hawesville
Hancock Clarion **(12114)** ....‡4,100

Hazard
Hazard Herald **(12115)** ....‡5,126

Hickman
The Hickman Courier **(12126)** ....‡2,250

Hindman
Troublesome Creek Times **(12128)** ....(Paid) ⊕4,185
(Free) ⊕207

Hodgenville
LaRue County Herald News **(12131)** ....‡4,667

Horse Cave
Hart County News-Herald **(12137)** ......(Paid) ‡8,600
The Progress (KY) **(12138)** ....(Paid) ‡5,155
(Free) ‡3,389

Hyden
The Leslie County News **(12139)** 5,600

Inez
The Mountain Citizen **(12140)** ....‡5,800

Irvine
Citizen Voice & Times **(12141)** ....(Paid) ‡4,750
(Free) ‡9,700

Jackson
Beattyville Enterprise **(12143)** 3,000
Jackson Times **(12144)** 6,000

Jenkins
Letcher County Community
News-Press **(12149)** ....‡2,000

La Grange
The Oldham Era **(12151)** ....‡6,900

Lancaster
Central Record **(12152)** ....‡4,700

Lawrenceburg
The Anderson News **(12154)** ....‡5,755

Leitchfield
Grayson County News-Gazette **(12157)** ....‡6,220

Liberty
The Casey County News **(12200)**

London
The Sentinel-Echo **(12203)** ....‡7,500

Louisa
The Big Sandy News **(12208)** ....‡4,200

Louisville
Louisville Defender **(12229)** ....(Non-paid) ♦536
(Paid) ♦2,689
The Voice-Tribune **(12243)** ....(Paid) ‡11,859
(Free) ‡1,571

Manchester
Enterprise **(12278)** 7,200

Marion
The Crittenden Press **(12281)** ....‡4,250

Mc Kee
The Jackson County Sun **(12291)** ....(Paid) 3,650
(Free) 12

Monticello
Wayne County Outlook **(12298)** 6,000

Morehead
Menifee County News **(12302)** ....⊕797
The Morehead News **(12303)** ....(Paid) ⊕5,629

Morganfield
The Union County Advocate **(12307)** ....(Paid) 5,300
(Free) 200

Morgantown
The Butler County and Green River Republican
Banner **(12310)** ....‡5,300

Mount Sterling
Mt. Sterling Advocate **(12311)** 6,350

Mount Vernon
Mt. Vernon Signal **(12314)** ....‡5,400

New Castle
Henry County Local **(12321)** ....‡4,770
Henry County Local &
Shopper **(12322)** ....(Paid) ⊕4,500
(Controlled) ⊕35

Nicholasville
The Jessamine Journal **(12325)** 6,600

Olive Hill
Olive Hill Times **(12326)** ....(Paid) ‡2,905

Owenton
The News-Herald **(12334)** ....‡3,600

Paducah
Carlisle County News **(12338)** ....‡3,500

Paintsville
The Paintsville Herald **(12349)** ....‡5,200

Paris
Bourbon County Citizen **(12353)** ....‡4,100

Pikeville
Appalachian News Express **(12357)** ....‡10,800

Pineville
The Pineville Sun **(12367)** 3,000

Prestonsburg
The Floyd County Times **(12370)** 11,400

Princeton
Times Leader **(12374)** ....‡5,700

Providence
The Journal-Enterprise **(12378)** ....‡4,500

Radcliff
The Sentinel **(12379)** ....(Paid) ⊕3,133
(Non-paid) ⊕305

Russell Springs
The Times Journal **(12387)** ....(Paid) ‡4,015
(Free) ‡235

Russellville
News-Democrat & Leader **(12389)** .....(Paid) ‡6,621

Salyersville
Salyersville Independent **(12390)** ....‡4,200

Scottsville
The Citizen-Times **(12394)** ....‡5,900

Sebree
The Sebree Banner **(12397)** ....‡3,800

Shelbyville
Community Times **(12398)** ....(Paid) 1,294
(Free) 9,706
Sentinel-News **(12399)** ....(Paid) ‡8,003

Shepherdsville
Pioneer News Extra **(12401)** ....(Paid) ⊕6,324
(Controlled) ⊕11,132

Smithland
The Livingston Ledger **(12402)** ....‡2,500

Somerset
Somerset Pulaski News Journal **(12406)** ......‡7,500

Springfield
The Springfield Sun **(12415)** ....(Paid) ‡4,350
(Free) ‡16

Stanford
The Interior Journal **(12416)** 4,314

Sturgis
The Sturgis News **(12420)** 3,200

Tompkinsville
Tompkinsville News **(12422)** ....(Paid) ‡4,365
(Free) ‡216

Vanceburg
Lewis County Herald **(12423)** ....‡4,500

Versailles
Woodford Sun **(12429)** 6,000

Warsaw
Gallatin County News **(12432)** ....(Paid) 2,500

Whitesburg
The Mountain Eagle **(12438)**

Whitley City
McCreary County Record **(12442)** ....‡4,984

Williamsburg
The Whitley Republican News
Journal **(12445)** 8,107

Williamstown
Grant County News **(12448)** ....(Paid) ⊕5,925
(Non-paid) ⊕40

LOUISIANA
Alexandria
The Alexandria News Weekly **(12457)** ....‡13,750

Amite
Amite Tangi-Digest **(12470)** ....‡2,500

Arabi
Saint Bernard Voice **(12474)** ....(Paid) ⊕2,600

Arcadia
Bienville Democrat/Ringgold
Record **(12476)** ....‡2,700

Baker
Baker Observer **(12478)** ....‡779

Basile
The Basile Weekly **(12482)** ....(Paid) ‡1,300
(Free) ‡36

Baton Rouge
Baton Rouge Weekly Press **(12485)** .....(Paid) 7,500
Louisiana Market Bulletin **(12500)** ....‡16,800

Belle Chasse
The Plaquemines Gazette **(12528)** ....‡3,000
The Plaquemines Watchman **(12529)** ....‡3,000

Bernice
Bernice Banner News **(12532)** ....(Paid) ⊕1,000

Bossier City
Bossier Banner-Progress **(12536)** ....‡500
Bossier Press Tribune **(12537)** ....(Paid) 2,000
(Free) 300

Boutte
St. Charles Herald-Guide **(12540)** ....‡4,400

Bunkie
The Bunkie Record **(12542)** 1,300

Cameron
Cameron Parish Pilot **(12544)** ....‡2,300

Church Point
Church Point News **(12545)** 1,600

Clinton
Clinton/East Feliciana Watchman **(12546)** .....‡2,250

Colfax
The Chronicle **(12547)** ....‡3,000

Columbia
Caldwell Watchman
Progress **(12548)** ....(Wed.) 1,200

Coushatta
The Coushatta Citizen **(12551)** ....‡2,900

Covington
The News Banner **(12554)** ....(Controlled) 22,500
St. Tammany Farmer **(12555)** ....(Paid) ⊕3,330
(Free) ⊕350

Crowley
Lake Arthur Sun-Times **(12558)** 1,000

Denham Springs
News **(12562)**

DeQuincy
The DeQuincy News **(12563)** ....‡3,500

Dodson
The Piney Woods
Journal **(12567)** ....(Combined) 15,000

Donaldsonville
Donaldsonville Chief **(12569)** ....(Paid) ‡3,000
(Non-paid) ‡3,000

Farmerville
The Gazette **(12578)** ....‡4,200

Ferriday
The Concordia Sentinel **(12579)** ....‡5,500

Franklinton
Franklinton Era-Leader **(12583)** 3,485

Gonzales
Gonzales Weekly **(12587)** ....‡8,700

Greensburg
St. Helena Echo **(12589)** ....‡1,900

Haynesville
The Haynesville News **(12598)** ....(Paid) ‡2,754
(Free) ‡35

Homer
The Guardian-Journal **(12600)** ....(Paid) 2,400
(Free) 1,100

Jeanerette
Enterprise **(12605)** 4,500

Jonesboro
Jackson Independent **(12608)** 3,500

Jonesville
Catahoula News-Booster **(12610)** ....‡3,600

Kaplan
Kaplan Herald **(12611)** ....‡3,500

Circulation: ★ = ABC; △ = BPA; ♦ = CAC; ● = CCAB; ❑ = VAC; ⊕ = PO Statement; ‡ = Publisher's Report; Boldface figures = sworn; Light figures = estimated.

2897

Circ.   Circ.   Circ.

LOUISIANA (continued)

Kentwood
The Kentwood News-Ledger **(12612)** .... ‡2,300
Louisiana News **(12613)** .... ‡2,100

Kinder
Kinder Courier-News **(12614)** 1,600

Lake Providence
Banner-Democrat **(12652)** .... ‡2,200

LaPlace
L'Observateur **(12655)** ....(Paid) 5,000
(Non-paid) 21,580

Lutcher
The Enterprise **(12664)** 1,900
News Examiner **(12665)** .... (Combined) 10,703

Mansfield
The Interstate Progress **(12667)** .... ‡1,800
Mansfield Enterprise-Progress **(12668)** .... ‡4,200

Many
Sabine Index **(12669)** .... ‡6,100

Marksville
Louisiana Roots **(12674)** .... ‡5,000

Metairie
New Orleans
  CityBusiness **(12678)** .... (Combined) 12,800

Natchitoches
The Natchitoches Times **(12718)** 8,000

New Orleans
Louisiana Weekly **(12740)** 20,000
New Orleans Data News
  Weekly **(12744)** ....(Paid) ‡380
(Free) ‡20,000

New Roads
The Pointe Coupee Banner **(12787)** 5,200

Oak Grove
West Carroll Gazette **(12788)** .... ‡2,300

Oakdale
Oakdale Journal **(12790)** 3,000

Plaquemine
Plaquemine Post-South **(12795)** ....(Paid) 5,500
(Non-paid) 146

Ponchatoula
The Enterprise **(12796)** ....(Paid) ‡2,100
(Free) ‡250
The Ponchatoula Times **(12797)** ......(Paid) ‡7,100

Port Allen
West Side Journal **(12799)** 3,000

Rayne
The Rayne Independent **(12801)** .... ‡3,800

Rayville
Richland Beacons News **(12804)** .... ‡1,400

St. Francisville
St. Francisville Democrat **(12812)** .... ‡1,900

St. Joseph
The Tensas Gazette **(12813)** 3,000

St. Martinville
Teche News **(12814)** ....(Paid) ⊕5,852
(Non-paid) ⊕56

Shreveport
The Shreveport Sun **(12819)** ....(Paid) 4,968
(Free) 102

Springhill
Springhill Press & News Journal **(12847)** ..... ‡4,000

Sulphur
The Iowa News **(12851)** ....(Controlled) 4,100

Tallulah
The Madison Journal **(12855)** .... ‡3,400

Ville Platte
Ville Platte Gazette **(12865)** .... ‡4,000

Vinton
The Vinton News **(12869)** .... ‡2,260

Vivian
Caddo Citizen **(12871)** .... ‡3,600

Welsh
Welsh Citizen **(12873)**

West Monroe
The Ouachita Citizen **(12874)** .... ‡6,000

Westlake
Westlake/Moss Bluff News **(12879)** .... ‡2,091

Winnfield
Winn Parish Enterprise **(12880)** .... ‡4,200

Winnsboro
The Franklin Sun **(12883)** .... ‡6,200

Zachary
Zachary Plainsman-News **(12884)** 2,163

MAINE
Augusta
Capital Weekly **(12889)** ....(Paid) ‡5,573
(Non-paid) ‡260

Bangor
Maine Times **(12904)** ....(Paid) ‡11,000

Bar Harbor
The Bar Harbor Times **(12917)** ....(Paid) ‡8,266
(Free) ‡121

Belfast
The Republican Journal **(12920)** ....(Paid) 7,450

Bethel
The Bethel Oxford County Citizen **(12921)** 3,100

Blue Hill
The Weekly Packet **(12924)** ....(Paid) 1,984
(Free) 53

Boothbay Harbor
Boothbay Register **(12925)** 5,467

Bridgton
The Bridgton News **(12930)** .... ⊕6,783

Calais
The Calais Advertiser **(12938)** 4,350

Camden
The Camden Herald **(12941)** 5,000

Cape Elizabeth
The Cape Courier **(12945)** ....(Combined) 4,000

Caribou
Aroostook Republican &
  News **(12946)** ....(Paid) 5,075

Castine
Castine Patriot **(12949)** 1,000

Damariscotta
Lincoln County News **(12950)** ....(Paid) 7,800
(Non-paid) 58

Dexter
The Eastern Gazette **(12951)** .... ‡17,250

Dover Foxcroft
The Piscataquis Observer **(12952)** .... ‡5,500

Eastport
The Quoddy Tides **(12954)** .... ‡4,805

Ellsworth
The Ellsworth American **(12955)** ......(Paid) ⊕10,979
(Free) ⊕190

Falmouth
The Forecaster—Northern
  Edition **(12957)** ....(Non-paid) 23,000
The Forecaster—Southern
  Edition **(12958)** ....(Non-paid) 17,000

Farmington
Franklin Journal and Farmington
  Chronicle **(12960)** ....(Tues.) ⊕4,590
(Fri.) ⊕5,290

Fort Fairfield
Fort Fairfield Review **(12963)** ....(Paid) 2,103
(Free) 70

Houlton
Houlton Pioneer Times **(12968)** .... ‡5,700

Kennebunk
York County Coast Star **(12973)** ....(Paid) 9,5827
(Non-paid) 100

Lincoln
Lincoln News **(12981)** ....(Paid) ‡5,439
(Free) ‡20

Livermore Falls
Livermore Falls Advertiser **(12984)** ....(Paid) ⊕3,060
(Non-paid) ⊕10

Machias
County Wide Newspaper **(12985)** ....(Paid) 4,800
(Free) 300
Machias Valley News
  Observer **(12986)** ....(Paid) 3,200
(Non-paid) 100

Millinocket
The Katahdin Times **(12990)** ....(Paid) 4,200
(Free) 160

New Gloucester
New Gloucester News **(12991)** 3,300

Norway
Advertiser-Democrat **(12993)** .... ‡7,500

Old Town
Penobscot Times, Inc. **(12997)** ....(Paid) ‡3,900
(Free) ‡200

Presque Isle
Star-Herald **(13035)** .... ‡7475

Rockland
The Courier-Publications **(13044)** 9,129
Lincoln County Weekly **(13045)** ....(Free) 34,054

Sanford
The Sanford News **(13049)** ....(Paid) ‡6,500

Stonington
Island Ad-Vantages **(13064)** 2,491

Westbrook
American Journal **(13074)** ....(Paid) 6,700
(Free) 122

Windham
The Suburban News **(13076)** ....(Combined) 8000

York
The York Weekly **(13083)** ....(Paid) ‡4,918
(Free) ‡175

MARYLAND
Aberdeen
Harford Business Ledger,
  Inc. **(13085)** ....(Controlled) 5,954

Baltimore
Baltimore Afro-American **(13128)** ....(Sat.) 9,947

Bel Air
Aegis **(13289)** ....(Wed.) 30,580
(Fri.) 27,565
The Weekender **(13291)** .... ‡10,000

Berlin
Maryland Coast Dispatch **(13293)** .....(Paid) ‡25,000

Bowie
Blade-News **(13391)** ....(Thurs.) 13,402

Brunswick
The Brunswick Citizen **(13395)** 3,500

Centreville
Record Observer **(13404)** ....(Paid) 2,829
(Non-paid) 76

Chestertown
Kent County News **(13405)** ....(Paid) 7,641
(Non-paid) 55

Columbia
Arbutus Times **(13452)** ....(Paid) 4,207
(Non-paid) 1,060
Catonsville Times **(13456)** ....(Paid) 6,991
(Non-paid) 4,108
Howard County Times **(13461)** ....(Paid) 24,406
Jeffersonian **(13463)** ....(Paid) 6,783
(Non-paid) 869
Laurel Leader **(13465)** ....(Paid) 318
(Non-paid) 1,060
Northeast Booster **(13467)** ....(Paid) 11
(Non-paid) 21,444
Northeast Reporter **(13468)** ....(Non-paid) 16,978
(Paid) 14
Towson Times **(13472)** ....(Paid) 190
(Non-paid) 37,724

Crisfield
Crisfield Times **(13473)** ....(Combined) 1,884

Denton
Times/Record **(13482)** ....(Paid) 2,882
(Non-paid) 139

Dundalk
Dundalk Eagle (13484) ....(Paid) ‡20,000
(Free) ‡1,030

Easton
The Calvert County
Recorder (13486) ....(Paid) 9,250
(Non-paid) 101

Gaithersburg
China News Digest—Global (13534)

Glen Burnie
The Maryland Gazette (13555) 36,573

Hancock
The Hancock News (13579) ....‡2,600

Lexington Park
St. Mary's Enterprise (13616) ....(Paid) 14,776
(Non-paid) 554

Middletown
The Middletown Valley
Citizen (13628) ....(Paid) ‡2,000
(Non-paid) ‡35

Oakland
The Republican (13635) ....(Thurs.) 11,425

Ocean City
Maryland Times-Press (13638) ....(Paid) 5,500

Pocomoke City
Worcester County
Messenger (13645) ....(Paid) 3,200

Princess Anne
Somerset Herald (13669) ....(Paid) 3,000
(Free) 3,000

Salisbury
The Wave (13711) ....(Paid) 378
(Non-paid) 13,783

Silver Spring
Prensa Hispana (13744)

Upper Marlboro
Enquirer Gazette (13768) ....(Paid) 3,866
(Non-paid) 1,002

Waldorf
Maryland Independent (13772) ....(Paid) 21,677
(Non-paid) 321

Westminster
The Carroll County
Times (13775) ....(Paid) 23,000 Daily
24,000 Sunday

Wheaton
The Washington
Diplomat (13782) ....(Combined) 35,000

MASSACHUSETTS
Abington
Abington/Rockland Mariner (13785) ......(Paid) 2,461
(Non-paid) 86

Amherst
Amherst Bulletin (13791) ....(Controlled) 13,000
Amherst Student (13792) ....(Controlled) 2,500

Andover
The Andover Townsman (13811) ....⊕8,401

Arlington
Arlington Advocate (13817) ....(Combined) 69,131

Avon
Avon Messenger (13827) ....‡1,213

Ayer
The Public Spirit (13829) 12,000

Barre
Barre Gazette (13833) ....‡2,500

Bedford
Bedford Minuteman (13835) ......(Combined) 69,131

Belmont
Belmont
Citizen-Herald (13839) ....(Combined) 69,131

Boston
The Boston Jewish Times (13859) ....‡11,000
The Boston Phoenix (13861) ....(Paid) 68,000
(Free) 50,000
El Mundo (13888) 27,000
The Jewish Advocate (13910) 22,000
Newbury Street and Back Bay
Guide (13938) ....(Combined) 10,000

Post-Gazette (13951) ....(Paid) 15,900
Syndicated Columnists
Weekly (13967) ....(Combined) 1,500
The Worcester Phoenix (13972)

Bourne
Bourne Courier (14001) ....(Paid) 2,114
(Free) 482

Braintree
Braintree Gazette (14003) ....‡1,605

Bridgewater
Bridgewater Independent (14006) ....‡3,942
Bridgewater Townsman (14007) ....(Paid) 1,566
(Non-paid) 125
East Bridgewater Star (14008) ....(Paid) ‡2,345

Brockton
Brockton News Tribune (14011) ....‡3,150

Cambridge
Harvard University Gazette (14068) 30,150

Canton
Canton Register (14118) ....‡1,102

Carver
Carver Reporter (14122) ....(Combined) 2,559

Charlestown
Charlestown Patriot & Somerville
Chronicle (14123) ....‡4,500

Chatham
The Cape Cod Chronicle (14124)

Clinton
The Item (14139) ....‡5,700

Cohasset
Cohasset Mariner (14141) ....(Paid) 1,756
(Non-paid) 86

Concord
The Beacon (14144) ....(Paid) 5,669
(Non-paid) 44
Chelmsford
Independent (14145) ....(Combined) 69,131
Lexington Minuteman (14147) .....(Combined) 69,131
Woburn Advocate (14149) ....(Non-paid) 9,624
(Paid) 75

Danvers
Advertiser (14152) 5,800

Dedham
The Dedham Times (14155) ....(Paid) ⊕2,400

Dorchester
Dorchester Argus-Citizen (14159) ....‡7,350

Dracut
The Dispatch News (14161) ....(Paid) ‡1,000
(Free) ‡19,000

Duxbury
Duxbury Clipper (14162) ....(Paid) ‡4,500
(Free) ‡150

Easton
Easton Bulletin (14173) ....‡2,144

Edgartown
Vineyard Gazette (14175) 13,478

Fairhaven
The Advocate (14177) ....(Paid) ‡2,900

Fitchburg
Pioneer (14183) ....‡2,000

Foxboro
The Foxboro Reporter (14189) ....‡5,200

Great Barrington
Berkshire Record (14214) ....‡4,500

Halifax
Halifax/Plympton
Reporter (14224) ....(Combined) 1,616

Hamilton
Hamilton-Wenham
Chronicle (14225) ....(Combined) 60,253

Hanover
Hanover Branch (14227) ....‡1,750
Hanover Mariner (14228) ....(Paid) 2,381
(Non-paid) 124

Hanson
Hanson Town Crier (14229) ....‡2,171

Hingham
Hingham Mariner (14234) ....(Paid) 4,038
(Non-paid) 166

Holbrook
Holbrook Sun (14235) ....(Paid) 1,871
(Non-paid) 173
Holbrook Times (14236) ....(Paid) ‡1,446

Holden
The Landmark (14237) ....⊕9,244

Hyannis
The Barnstable Patriot (14249) ....‡4,614

Hyde Park
Hyde Park Mattapan
Tribune (14255) ....(Paid) ‡5,330
(Free) ‡539

Jamaica Plain
Jamaica Plain/Roxbury Citizen (14260) ....‡3,700

Kingston
Kingston Independent Voice (14263) ....‡3,000

Lexington
Winchester Star (14275) .....(Combined) 69,131

Littleton
Littleton Independent (14276) .....(Combined) 69,131

Lynnfield
The Lynnfield Villager (14288) ....(Paid) 1,467
(Non-paid) 151

Malden
The Malden Milestone (14297)

Manchester
The Manchester Cricket (14302) ....‡2,376

Mansfield
Mansfield Reporter (14303) ....(Paid) ‡1,425

Marshfield
South Look (14309) ....(Paid) 54,000
(Free) 2,500

Maynard
Maynard Beacon (14315) ....(Combined) 69,131

Medfield
Medfield Suburban
Press (14317) ....(Combined) 3,091

Medford
Saugus Advertiser (14324) ....(Combined) 60,253

Melrose
Melrose Free Press (14328) ......(Combined) 60,253

Middleboro
Middleboro Gazette (14331) 5,860

Milton
Milton Record Transcript (14336) ....‡5,900
Milton Townsman (14337) 1,640

Nantucket
The Inquirer and Mirror (14340) ......(Paid) ♦10,609
(Non-paid) ♦187

Needham
Billerica Minuteman (14349) ....(Combined) 69,131
Braintree Forum (14350) ....(Paid) 4,508
(Non-paid) 189
Burlington Union (14351) ....(Combined) 69,131
Cambridge Chronicle (14352) ....(Paid) 8,106
(Non-paid) 1,589
Cape Codder (14353) ....(Paid) 14,988
Danvers Herald (14354) ....(Combined) 60,253
Hingham Journal (14355)
Ipswich Chronicle (14356) ....(Combined) 60,253
Lincoln Journal (14358) ....(Combined) 69,131
Marshfield Mariner (14359) ....‡4,399
(Non-paid) 175
Metro West Daily
News (14361) ....(Non-paid) ‡73,928
North Andover Citizen (14368) ....(Combined) 60,253
Sharon Advocate (14370) ....(Combined) 36,984
Stoughton Journal (14371) ....(Combined) 36,984
The Wellesley
Townsman (14372) ....(Combined) 32,287

North Reading
North Reading Transcript (14426) ....(Paid) 4,345
(Non-paid) 193

Norton
Norton Courier (14437) 1,500

Newspapers

Circulation: ★ = ABC; △ = BPA; ♦ = CAC; ● = CCAB; ❑ = VAC; ⊕ = PO Statement; ‡ = Publisher's Report; Boldface figures = sworn; Light figures = estimated.

2899

Circ.

Circ.

Circ.

MASSACHUSETTS (continued)

Norwell
Norwell Mariner **(14444)** ....(Paid) 2,188
(Non-paid) 104

Palmer
Journal Register **(14456)** 5,200
Ware River News **(14457)** ....‡4,600

Pembroke
Pembroke Mariner **(14465)** ....(Paid) 1,531
(Non-paid) 178
Pembroke Reporter **(14466)** ....(Paid) 1,441

Pepperell
Times-Free Press **(14467)** 9,700

Pittsfield
Berkshire Summer **(14469)**
Pittsfield Gazette **(14472)**

Plymouth
Old Colony Memorial **(14479)** .....(Combined) 12,437
The Sentinel **(14481)** ....(Combined) 2,551
Wareham Courier **(14482)** ....(Combined) 4,717

Provincetown
The Provincetown Advocate **(14485)** 8,398

Quincy
Sun **(14492)** ....(Paid) ‡6,150
(Free) ‡440

Randolph
Randolph Herald **(14495)** ....(Paid) ‡1,421
Randolph Mariner **(14496)** ....(Paid) 1,565
(Non-paid) 88

Raynham
Raynham Journal **(14497)** ....(Paid) 1,774

Revere
Chelsea Record **(14499)** ....(Paid) ♦2,852
(Non-paid) ♦300
Revere Journal **(14502)** ....(Paid) 7,494
(Non-paid) 75
Winthrop Sun Transcript **(14503)** ....(Paid) 3,902
(Non-paid) 66

Rockland
Abington Standard **(14506)** ....‡1,694
Rockland Standard **(14507)** ....(Paid) 2,284
Stoughton Chronicle **(14508)** ....(Paid) 3,173

Scituate
Scituate Mariner **(14518)** ....(Paid) 3,777
(Non-paid) 130

Sharon
Sharon Sentinel **(14519)** ....⊕3,172

Shelburne Falls
Shelburne Falls and West County
News **(14521)** ....‡2,800

Sherborn
Dover-Sherborn Suburban
Press **(14523)** ....(Combined) 2,077

Somerset
The Spectator **(14527)** ....(Paid) ♦5,414
(Non-paid) ♦355

South Boston
South Boston Tribune **(14540)** ....‡8,000

South Dartmouth
The Chronicle **(14541)** 6,150

Southborough
Southborough Villager **(14546)** ....(Combined) 36,984

Spencer
The New Leader **(14548)** 4,000

Stoneham
The Stoneham Independent **(14569)** .....(Paid) 3,800
(Non-paid) 14

Sudbury
The Sudbury Town
Crier **(14579)** ....(Combined) 36,984

Swampscott
Swampscott Reporter **(14583)** ....(Combined) 60,253

Tewksbury
Wilmington-Tewksbury Town
Crier **(14588)** ....(Paid) 5,486
(Non-paid) 343

Vineyard Haven
Martha's Vineyard Times **(14591)**

Walpole
The Walpole Times **(14594)** ....(Paid) 5,700
(Free) 121

Watertown
The Armenian Mirror-Spectator **(14610)** 2,800

West Bridgewater
West Bridgewater Times **(14624)** 1,067

West Springfield
West Springfield Record **(14625)** 5,600

Westborough
The Westborough News **(14639)** ....(Paid) 4,300

Westfield
The Longmeadow News **(14641)** ....‡1,930

Westford
The Westford Eagle **(14646)** ......(Combined) 69,131

Weymouth
Weymouth Dispatch **(14653)** 1,288
Weymouth News **(14654)** ....(Paid) 4,692
(Non-paid) 208

Whitinsville
Blackstone Valley Tribune **(14656)** .....(Wed.) ‡5,300
(Fri.) ‡12,996

Whitman
Whitman/Hanson Mariner **(14657)** ....(Paid) 1,730
(Non-paid) 39
Whitman Times **(14658)** ....⊕2,166

Winchendon
The Winchendon Courier **(14664)** 2,000

Wollaston
Campus Camera **(14671)**

Worcester
Hanover News **(14681)** 1,000
Jewish Chronicle **(14685)** ....‡4000

Yarmouth Port
The Register **(14704)** ....‡8,900
The Register **(14705)** ....‡9,274

MICHIGAN

Ada
Ada/Cascade/Forest Hills
Advance **(14706)** ....(Free) 14,900
(Paid) 669

Allegan
The Allegan County News **(14719)** 5,500

Armada
Armada Times **(14782)** 2,500

Atlanta
Montmorency County Tribune **(14783)** ....‡5,350

Bellaire
Antrim County News **(14805)** ....‡5,600

Belleville
The Belleville
Enterprise **(14806)** ....(Combined) 2,068
The View **(14807)** ....(Paid) ♦1,059
(Non-paid) ♦216

Berrien Springs
The Journal Era **(14812)** ....‡2,000

Big Rapids
Manistee County Pioneer Press **(14816)** ......‡1,500

Birmingham
Birmingham Eccentric **(14824)** ....(Sun.) 11,562
(Thurs.) 11,600
Northeast Detroiter Harper Woods
Herald **(14826)** ....‡12,604

Blissfield
The Advance **(14827)** ....(Paid) 2,395
(Free) 176

Boyne City
The Citizen **(14832)** ....(Paid) ‡2,700

Bronson
The Bronson Journal **(14837)** ....‡2,250

Brown City
The Brown City Banner **(14839)**

Buchanan
Berrien County Record **(14840)** ....(Paid) 2,600
(Free) 350

Caledonia
Grand Valley East
Advance **(14851)** ....(Free) 18,520
(Paid) 11

Canton
Canton Eagle **(14853)** ....(Combined) 4,798

Caro
Tuscola County Advertiser **(14858)** .....(Wed.) 8,423
(Sat.) 7,709

Cass City
Cass City Chronicle **(14862)** ....‡3,454

Charlevoix
Charlevoix Courier **(14864)** 2,513

Chelsea
The Chelsea Standard **(14876)** ....(Paid) ♦3,758
(Non-paid) ♦30

Clare
The Clare Sentinel **(14879)** ....‡3,200

Clarkston
Clarkston Eccentric **(14880)** ....(Sun.) 0
(Thurs.) 6,347
The Clarkston News **(14881)** ....(Paid) 3,400

Climax
Crescent **(14882)** ....‡850

Clinton
The Clinton Local **(14883)** ....‡1,700

Clio
The Clio Messenger **(14885)** ......(Combined) 8,889

Coopersville
Ottawa Advance **(14891)** ....(Free) 10,600
(Paid) 60

Croswell
Jeffersonian **(14892)** ....(Combined) ‡8,500

Davison
The Davison Flagstaff **(14896)** .....(Combined) 8,808
The Davison Index **(14897)** 11,000

Dearborn
Dearborn Heights Press & Guide **(14900)**
Dearborn Press & Guide **(14901)** ....(Paid) ♦15,274
(Non-paid) ♦15,567
Warrendale-West Detroit Press & Guide **(14907)**

Dearborn Heights
Times-Herald **(14910)** ....‡27,000

Decatur
Decatur Republican **(14911)** 1,600

Deckerville
The Deckerville Recorder **(14912)** ....‡2,189

Detroit
The Citizen **(14918)** ....‡10,242
Michigan Chronicle **(14938)** ....‡47,428

Dexter
The Dexter Leader **(14976)** ....(Paid) ♦2,904
(Non-paid) ♦21

East Tawas
Iosco County News Herald **(14997)** ....‡7,790

Edwardsburg
Argus **(15004)** 1,800

Elk Rapids
The Town Meeting **(15005)** ....(Paid) 2,000

Escanaba
The Delta Reporter **(15008)** 3,420

Evart
Evart Review **(15013)** ....‡2,183

Farmington
Farmington Observer **(15014)** ....(Sun.) 11,362
(Thurs.) 11,507

Flint
The Flint Township
News **(15034)** ....(Combined) 10,779

Flushing
The Flushing Observer **(15050)** ....‡7,500

Frankenmuth
Frankenmuth News **(15052)** ....‡5,100

Frankfort
Benzie County Record-Patriot **(15053)** ....‡4,427

Numbers cited after listings are entry numbers rather than page numbers.

Freeport
Freeport News (15055)
Record (15056) 600

Fremont
Times-Indicator (15058) 7,500

Garden City
Garden City Observer (15064) ....(Sun.) 4,823
(Thurs.) 4,343

Gaylord
Gaylord Herald Times (15068) ....(Paid) ‡7,010
(Free) ‡140

Grand Blanc
The Grand Blanc
News (15083) ....(Combined) 13,935

Grand Rapids
East Grand Rapids
Cadence (15093) ....(Free) 5,125
(Paid) 669
Grand Rapids Advance (15094) ....(Free) 12,375
(Paid) 32
The Grand Rapids Times (15097)
Northfield Advance (15098) ....(Free) 19,775
(Paid) 87

Grayling
Crawford County Avalanche (15131) ....‡5,000

Grosse Ile
The Ile Camera (15138) ....(Paid) ♦3,059
(Non-paid) ♦10

Grosse Pointe Farms
The Connection (15139) ....(Combined) 5,000
Grosse Pointe News (15140) ....(Thurs.) 14,693

Hamtramck
The Polish Weekly (15141) ....‡2,000

Harbor Beach
Times (15143)

Harbor Springs
Harbor Springs Harbor Light (15144) ....‡2,000

Harrisville
Alcona County Review (15146) ....‡3,400

Hart
Oceana's Herald-Journal (15147) ....‡7,560

Hastings
The Hastings Banner (15152) ....‡7,000

Highland Park
Michigan Citizen (15161) ....(Paid) 51,442
(Free) 918

Homer
The Homer Index (15181) 1,900

Honor
Ad-Visor (15182) 8,500

Houghton Lake
The Houghton Lake
Resorter (15188) ....(Paid) ⊕7,635
(Non-paid) ⊕50

Howell
Brighton Argus (15190) ....(Paid) 11,065
(Non-paid) 485
Holly Herald (15192) ....(Combined) 41,300
Home Town News (15193) ....(Paid) 10,503
(Free) 11,321
Livingston County Press and
Argus (15196) ....(Mon.-Sat.) ♦15,335
(Sun.) ♦16,801

Hudson
Hudson Post Gazette (15201) 2,000

Imlay City
Tri-City Times (15202) 6,200

Indian River
Straitsland Resorter (15203) ....‡3,200

Inkster
Inkster Ledger Star (15204) ....(Paid) 1,695
(Non-paid) 889

Iron River
Iron River Reporter (15211) ....‡7,200

Ithaca
Gratiot County Herald (15219) ....‡7,100

Jackson
Blazer News (15220) ....‡2,000

The Spectator (15224)

Jenison
Cadence (15227) ....‡5,400
Grand Valley West
Advance (15228) ....(Free) 17,160
(Paid) 6,028
Sparta/Kent City
Advance (15230) ....(Controlled) 12,526
(Paid) 125

Jonesville
Jonesville Independent (15231) 1,200

Kalkaska
The Leader and the Kalkaskian (15261) 3,900

Kentwood
Kentwood Advance (15263) ....(Free) 16,075
(Paid) 669

Lake Leelanau
Leelanau Enterprise & Tribune (15267) 8,005

Lake Odessa
Lakewood News (15268) ....(Paid) 70
(Free) 6,000

Lake Orion
Lake Orion Eccentric (15270) ....(Sun.) 0
(Thurs.) 4,460
Lake Orion Review (15271) 3,400

Lakeview
Lakeview Enterprise (15272) ....‡1,685

Lanse
L'Anse Sentinel (15273) ....‡4,241

Lapeer
County Press (15308) ....(Wed.) 16,865
(Sun.) 18,100

Livonia
Livonia Observer (15317)

Lowell
Lowell Ledger (15320) 2,200

Mackinac Island
The Mackinac Island Town Crier (15325) .....‡3,600

Mancelona
The Torch (15327) 2,050

Manchester
Manchester Enterprise (15328) ....(Paid) ♦1,775
(Non-paid) ♦23

Manistique
Pioneer-Tribune (15333) 4,000

Marcellus
Marcellus News (15335) 1,400

Marlette
Leader (15336) ....‡2,000

Mayville
Mayville Monitor (15352) ....(Paid) 1,200

Minden City
Minden City Herald (15361) ....(Paid) 1450
(Free) 100

Monroe
The Monroe Guardian (15365) ....(Paid) ♦1,013
(Non-paid) ♦5,959

Morenci
The Morenci Observer (15369) ....(Paid) ‡2,370

Mount Morris
Genesee County Herald (15373) 2,000

Munising
The Munising News (15386) ....(Paid) ‡3,075
(Free) ‡65

New Buffalo
New Buffalo Times (15399) ....‡5,000

Newberry
Newberry News (15400) 3,600

Northville
The Northville Record (15405) .....(Combined) 5,405

Novi
Novi News (15410) ....(Combined) 4,954

Oak Park
The Michigan Post (15413) ....(Paid) 10,000

Onaway
The Onaway Outlook (15420) ....‡2,400

Presque Isle County Advance (15421) 4,400

Ontonagon
The Ontonagon Herald (15422) 3,750

Oscoda
Oscoda Press (15425) 5,900

Owosso
The Durand Express (15429) ....(Paid) 2,133
(Non-paid) 65

Oxford
Oxford Eccentric (15431) ....(Sun.) 0
(Thurs.) 3,048
The Oxford Leader (15432) ....(Paid) ‡3,297
(Free) ‡36

Paw Paw
The Courier-Leader (15433) ....(Paid) ⊕4,069
(Free) 45

Pinconning
Pinconning Journal (15444) 1,950

Plainwell
The Union Enterprise (15446) ....(Paid) 755

Plymouth
Plymouth Observer (15448) ....(Sun.) 6,187
(Thurs.) 5,882

Redford
Redford Observer (15462) ....(Sun.) 7,224
(Thurs.) 6,608

Reed City
The Herald-News (15464)

Rochester
Rochester Eccentric (15466) ....(Sun.) 15,276
(Thurs.) 15,190

Romeo
The Romeo Observer (15473) ....(Paid) 6,971
(Free) 6,650

Romulus
Romulus Roman (15474) ....(Paid) 1,084
(Non-paid) 2,758

Royal Oak
Clawson Mirror (15478) ....(Combined) 5,953
Royal Oak Courier (15484)

Saginaw
The Saginaw Press (15492) ....(Paid) ⊕462
(Free) ⊕6

St. Ignace
The St. Ignace News (15508) 7,000

Saline
Milan News-Leader (15517) ....(Paid) ♦1,924
(Non-paid) ♦66
The Saline Reporter (15519) ....(Paid) ♦4,517
(Non-paid) ♦94

Saugatuck
The Commercial Record (15525) ....(Paid) 2,068
(Free) 33

Sebewaing
Huron County Press &
Newsweekly (15533) ....(Paid) 4,500

Seney
Grand Marais Pilot & Pictured Rocks
Review (15534) ....‡35,000

Shelby Township
Macomb County Legal News (15536) 1,279

Shepherd
Shepherd Argus (15538) 2,000

South Lyon
The South Lyon Herald (15540) ....(Paid) 6,200
(Non-paid) 102

Southfield
Southfield Eccentric (15548) ....(Sun.) 8,120
(Thurs.) 8,029

Southgate
Heritage Sunday (15565) ....(Paid) ♦64,432
(Non-paid) ♦16,069
The News-Herald (15566) ....(Wed.) ♦69,722

Sparta
South Advance (15569) ....(Controlled) 17,000
(Paid) 125

Springport
Signal (15574)

Circulation: ★ = ABC; △ = BPA; ♦ = CAC; ♦ = CCAB; ☐ = VAC; ⊕ = PO Statement; ‡ = Publisher's Report; Boldface figures = sworn; Light figures = estimated.

Circ.

Circ.

Circ.

MICHIGAN (continued)

Standish
Arenac County Independent (15575) .... ‡6,156

Sunfield
The Sunfield Sentinel (15583) .... ‡900

Swartz Creek
The Swartz Creek
News (15584) .... (Combined) 10,779

Tecumseh
The Tecumseh Herald (15590) .... ‡5,800

Three Rivers
Your Community News (15593) .... ‡17,100

Troy
The Fear Finder (15625) .... (Combined) 500,000
Troy Eccentric (15642) .... (Sun.) 10,415
(Thurs.) 10,309

Union City
Register-Tribune (15646) .... (Paid) ‡1,256
(Free) ‡20

Vanderbilt
Our Home Town (15650) .... (Paid) ‡1,200
(Free) ‡100

Vassar
Vassar Pioneer Times (15652) 1,500

Vicksburg
Commercial-Express (15654) 2,350

Warren
Warren Weekly (15666) .... (Non-paid) 60,514

Watervliet
Tri-City Record (15669) .... ‡2,800

Wayland
Penasee Globe (15670) .... ‡18,500
Wayland-Weston Town Crier (15671) ... (Paid) 4,951
(Non-paid) 169

Wayne
Wayne Eagle (15673) .... (Combined) 2,396
Westland Eagle (15674) .... (Combined) 7,185

West Bloomfield
West Bloomfield Eccentric (15677) ..... (Sun.) 10,403
(Thurs.) 10,404

West Branch
Ogemaw County Herald (15680)

Westland
Westland Observer (15682) .... (Sun.) 7,706
(Thurs.) 6,832

Wyoming
Wyoming Advance (15687) .... (Free) 22,500
(Paid) 669

Yale
Yale Expositor (15689) 3,000

Zeeland
Zeeland Record (15694) .... ‡1,200

MINNESOTA
Ada
Norman County Index (15696) .... ‡2,350

Adrian
Nobles County Review (15699) .... ‡1,400

Aitkin
Aitkin Independent Age (15700) .... ‡6,175

Albany
Stearns-Morrison Enterprise (15704) 4,500

Alden
The Alden Advance (15711) .... ‡1,080

Alexandria
The Echo/Press (15712) .... (Fri.) 10,167
(Wed.) 9,388

Annandale
Annandale Advocate (15717)

Appleton
Appleton Press (15719) 2,950

Arlington
Arlington Enterprise (15721) 1,550

Askov
Askov American (15722) .... ‡2,000

Babbitt
Babbitt Weekly News (15726) 1,800

Bagley
Farmers Independent (15727) .... ‡2,600

Balaton
Balaton-Press-Tribune (15729) .... ‡1,000

Battle Lake
Battle Lake Review (15730) .... (Paid) ‡2,215
(Free) ‡70

Baudette
The Baudette Region (15731) .... (Paid) ‡2,195
(Free) ‡5

Beardsley
Valley News (15734) .... (Paid) 1,375
(Free) 30

Belgrade
Belgrade Observer (15735) 1,200

Belle Plaine
Belle Plaine Herald (15736) 3,500

Benson
Swift County Monitor-News (15747) 3,200

Biwabik
Biwabik Times (15752) 1,200

Blackduck
The American (15753) 1,021

Blaine
Blaine Spring Lake Park Life (15756) .... ‡2,251

Blooming Prairie
Blooming Prairie Times (15757) .... ‡1,600

Blue Earth
Faribault County Register (15762)

Brownton
The Bulletin (15776) .... ‡1,026

Burnsville
Dakota County Tribune (15782) .... ‡1,084

Caledonia
Caledonia Argus (15783) .... (Paid) 2,900

Cambridge
Cambridge Star (15784) .... (Free) 13,065
(Paid) 603
County News (15785) 10,600

Cannon Falls
Beacon (15788) .... ‡4,400

Cass Lake
Cass Lake Times (15790) .... (Paid) 1,340

Champlin
Champlin Dayton Press (15791) .... (Paid) 1,922
(Free) 4,715

Chaska
Chaska Herald (15793) .... (Free) 400
(Paid) 4,200

Chisholm
The Chisholm Tribune-Press (15796) .... ‡2,700

Chokio
Chokio Review (15797) .... ‡1,000

Clara City
Clara City Herald (15798) .... ‡1,490

Clarissa
Independent News Herald (15799) 2,700

Clinton
Northern Star (15800) .... (Paid) 1,990
(Non-paid) 20

Cloquet
Cloquet Journal (15801) .... (Paid) ♦2,780
(Non-paid) ♦37
The Pine Knot (15802) .... (Paid) ♦3,221
(Non-paid) ♦40

Cold Spring
Cold Spring Record (15803) .... (Paid) ‡3,600
(Free) ‡25

Comfrey
The Comfrey Times (15811) .... ‡950
The Times (15812)

Cook
Cook News-Herald (15813) 3,652

Coon Rapids
Anoka County Union (15815) .... ‡5,329
Coon Rapids Herald (15816) .... ‡3,430

Cottage Grove
South Washington County
Bulletin (15817) .... ⊕11,048

Cottonwood
Tri-County News (15818) 2,200

Crosby
Crosby-Ironton Courier (15822) .... (Paid) 4,282
(Free) 51

Crystal
Crystal Robbinsdale Sun
Post (15823) .... (Paid) ♦707
(Non-paid) ♦10,250

Dassel
Enterprise Dispatch (15824) 3,500

Dawson
Sentinel (15825) .... (Paid) ‡2,150
(Free) ‡15

Deer River
Western Itasca Review (15826) .... (Paid) 1,622
(Free) 27

Delano
Delano Eagle (15827) .... (Paid) 1,331
(Free) 3,598

Detroit Lakes
Detroit Lakes Tribune (15829) .... (Paid) 52
(Non-paid) 5,796

Dodge Center
Dodge Center Star-Record (15833) ...... (Paid) 1,450
(Free) 50

East Grand Forks
Exponent (15865) .... ‡2,300

Eden Prairie
Eden Prairie News (15868) .... (Free) 11,000

Eden Valley
Journal (15871) .... ‡1,375
Watkins Patriot (15872) 600

Edgerton
The Edgerton Enterprise (15873) .... (Paid) 1,970
(Free) 32

Ely
Ely Echo (15880) 4,900

Elysian
The Elysian Enterprise (15883) .... (Paid) ‡480
(Free) ‡27

Erskine
Erskine Echo (15884) .... ‡1,030

Fairfax
Fairfax Standard (15888) .... ‡1,760

Floodwood
The Forum (15904) .... (Paid) ‡1,000
(Free) ‡60

Fosston
The Thirteen Towns (15908) .... (Paid) ‡2,800

Fulda
Fulda Free Press (15914) .... ‡1,400

Gaylord
Hub (15915) .... ‡2,260

Gibbon
The Gibbon Gazette (15916) .... (Paid) 950
(Free) 20

Glencoe
The Glencoe Enterprise (15917) .... ‡3,200
McLeod County Chronicle (15918) ..... (Paid) ‡3,181
(Free) 56

Glenwood
Pope County Tribune (15920) .... (Paid) ‡4,000
(Free) ‡100

Gonvick
Leader-Record (15924) .... (Paid) 2,000

Grand Marais
Cook County News-Herald (15926) .... (Paid) ♦3,857
(Non-paid) ♦10

Grand Rapids
Herald-Review (15928) ....(Paid) ◆7,703
(Non-paid) ◆128

Grygla
The Grygla Eagle (15936) ....‡750

Hallock
Kittson County Enterprise (15937) ......(Paid) ‡1,885

Hanska
The Hanska Herald (15939) ....(Paid) ⊕772
(Free) ⊕28

Hastings
Hastings Star Gazette (15941) ....‡5,600

Hawley
Hawley Herald (15943) ....(Paid) ‡2,400
(Free) ‡50

Hayfield
Hayfield Herald (15944) ....‡1,750

Hector
Bird Island Union (15945) ....‡1,100
News Mirror (15946) ....(Paid) 2,500
(Free) 200

Henderson
Henderson Independent (15947) ....(Paid) 1,000

Hendricks
Hendricks Pioneer (15948) ....(Paid) 900

Henning
The Henning Advocate (15949) ....‡1,511

Herman
Grant County Herald (15950) ....(Controlled) ⊕2,150
Herman Review (15951) ....‡1,275

Hermantown
Hermantown Star (15952) ....(Paid) 1,767
(Free) 97

Heron Lake
Tri County News (15953) ....(Paid) ‡1,000
(Free) ‡25

Hills
The Hills Crescent (15961) ....‡800

Hinckley
The Hinckley News (15962) ....‡2,000

Howard Lake
Howard Lake-Waverly Montrose Herald
Journal (15966) ....‡1,300

Hutchinson
Hutchinson Leader (15967) ....(Paid) ‡5,564

Isle
Mille Lacs Messenger (15972) 5,600

Ivanhoe
Ivanhoe Times (15973) ....(Paid) 1,100
(Non-paid) 55

Jackson
Jackson County Pilot (15974) ....(Paid) ‡2,426
(Free) ‡100

Janesville
Janesville Argus (15978) 1,300

Jasper
Jasper Journal (15979) ....‡1,010

Jordan
Jordan Independent (15980) ....(Paid) ⊕1,500
(Free) 67

Karlstad
North Star News (15981) ....(Paid) ‡2,487
(Free) ‡75

Kasson
Dodge County Independent (15982) ....‡2,300

Kenyon
The Kenyon Leader (15983) ....(Paid) 1,887
(Free) 49

Kerkhoven
The Kerkhoven Banner (15984) 1,500

Kiester
The Courier-Sentinel (15985) 1,778

Kimball
Tri-County News (15986) ....(Paid) 1,375
(Free) 25

La Crescent
Houston County News (15987) 2,400

Lafayette
Lafayette-Nicollet Ledger (15989) 1,240

Lake Benton
Lake Benton Valley Journal (15990) 960

Lake City
Lake City Graphic (15991) ....‡3,200

Lakefield
Lakefield Standard (15993) ....(Paid) ‡1,950
(Free) ‡12

Lamberton
Lamberton News (15997) ....(Paid) 1,703
(Free) 50

Le Center
Le Center Leader (15998) ....(Paid) 2,000
(Free) 20

Le Roy
Le Roy Independent (15999) ....‡1,300

Le Sueur
Le Sueur News-Herald (16000) ....‡2,600

Lindstrom
Chicago County Press (16002) ....(Paid) ‡3,835
(Free) ‡30

Litchfield
Litchfield Independent-Review (16004) 3,800

Little Falls
Morrison County Record (16006) ....(Free) 18,405
(Paid) 543

Long Prairie
Long Prairie Leader (16009) 3,500

Luverne
Rock County Star Herald (16014) 3,000

Mabel
News-Record (16017) ....‡1,900

Madelia
Times-Messenger (16019) ....(Paid) ‡2,100

Madison
Western Guard (16020) ....‡3,500

Madison Lake
Lake Region Times (16022) ....(Paid) 855
(Free) 30
100

Mahnomen
Pioneer (16023) ....‡2,800

Maple Lake
Maple Lake Messenger (16041) ....‡1,750

Melrose
Beacon (16051) 3,000

Milaca
Mille Lacs County Times (16053)

Milan
Milan Standard-Watson Journal (16054) ....‡950

Minneapolis
The Circle (16064) ....(Paid) 1,000
(Non-paid) 14,000
Minnesota Christian
Chronicle (16101) ....(Paid) 23,000
Minnesota Spokesman (16107) ....(Paid) ‡3,790
(Free) ‡517
Northeaster &
Northnews (16115) ....(Non-paid) ‡34,500
Southwest Farm Press (16130) ....(Paid) 25,009
(Non-paid) 21,666

Minneota
Minneota Mascot (16165) 1,400

Minnesota Lake
Tribune (16166) ....‡900

Montevideo
American News (16180) ....(Paid) 4,566
(Free) 30

Montgomery
Montgomery Messenger (16183) ....‡2,500

Monticello
Times (16186) ....‡3,450

Moose Lake
Star-Gazette (16194) ....(Paid) 2,850

Morris
Sun-Tribune (16198) ....(Paid) ‡3,568
(Free) ‡62

Mound
The Laker (16201) ....‡9,200

Mountain Lake
Mountain Lake/Butterfield
Observer/Advocate (16202) ....‡1,856

Nashwauk
Eastern Itascan (16203) ....(Paid) 1,757

Nevis
Northwoods Press (16204) ....(Paid) 1,620
(Free) 40

New Prague
New Prague Times (16209) 4,300

New Richland
New Richland Star (16212) ....(Paid) 2,000

New York Mills
Herald (16220) ....‡2,000

North Branch
ECM Post-Review (16221) ....(Paid) ‡2,495

North St. Paul
Maplewood Review (16227) ....(Paid) 1,077
(Free) 192
Oakdale-Lake Elmo Review (16228) ....(Paid) 910
(Free) 128
Ramsey County Review (16229) ....(Wed.) 1,335

Northfield
Northfield News (16236) ....(Paid) 5,790
(Free) 375

Norwood
Norwood-Young America
Times (16241) ....(Paid) ‡2,272
(Free) ‡138

Oklee
The Oklee Herald (16242) 906

Olivia
Olivia Times-Journal (16243) ....(Paid) ‡1,507
(Non-paid) ‡445

Ortonville
The Ortonville Independent (16245) ....‡3,650

Osseo
North Crow River News (16248) ....(Paid) 2,805
(Free) 5,233
Osseo-Maple Grove Press (16249) .....(Paid) 4,690
(Free) 9,391
Rockford Area News Leader (16250) ....(Paid) **1,189**
(Free) **2,812**
South Crow River News (16251) ....(Paid) **1,189**
(Free) **2,812**

Parkers Prairie
The Independent (16259) 1,800

Pelican Rapids
Pelican Rapids Press (16261) ....(Paid) 3,369
(Free) 26

Perham
Perham Enterprise Bulletin (16265) 3,450

Pine City
Pine City Pioneer (16268) ....‡3,532

Pine River
Pine River Journal (16274) ....‡2,410

Pipestone
Pipestone County Star (16275) ....(Paid) 3,714
(Non-paid) 99

Plainview
Plainview News (16278) 3,380

Princeton
Princeton Union-Eagle (16284) ....(Paid) 3,666
(Free) 70

Prior Lake
Prior Lake American (16288) ....⊕7,300

Proctor
Proctor Journal (16289) ....(Paid) 1,950
(Free) 50

Raymond
The Raymond-Prinsburg News (16291) ....‡943

Circulation: ★ = ABC; △ = BPA; ◆ = CAC; ◆ = CCAB; ❑ = VAC; ⊕ = PO Statement; ‡ = Publisher's Report; Boldface figures = sworn; Light figures = estimated.

2903

Circ. | Circ. | Circ.

MINNESOTA (continued)

Red Lake Falls
Gazette **(16292)** ....‡1,599

Redwood Falls
Redwood Gazette **(16295)** ....‡5,100

Roseau
Roseau Times-Region **(16328)** ....‡3,950

Rushford
Tri-County Record **(16337)** 1,700

Ruthton
Buffalo Ridge Gazette **(16339)** ....(Paid) 481
(Free) 20

St. Charles
Press **(16341)** 2,000

St. James
Plaindealer **(16355)** ....‡2,790

Sandstone
Pine County Courier **(16435)** ....‡2,000

Sauk Centre
Herald **(16436)** 3,500
Sauk Rapids Herald **(16437)** 1,100

Savage
Savage Pacer **(16441)** ....(Paid) 5,440

Sebeka
Review-Messenger **(16442)** ....‡3,421

Shakopee
Shakopee Valley News **(16445)** ....(Paid) 5,450
(Free) 344

Silver Lake
Silver Lake Leader **(16448)** ....(Paid) ‡1,475
(Free) ‡25

Sleepy Eye
Sleepy Eye
Herald-Dispatch **(16451)** ....(Paid) ‡3,600
(Free) ‡310

Spicer
Kandiyohi County Times **(16454)** 6,500

Spring Grove
Herald **(16455)** ....‡1,500

Spring Valley
Spring Valley Tribune **(16458)** ....‡1,900

Springfield
Springfield Advance-Press **(16459)** .....(Paid) ‡2,742

Staples
Staples World **(16460)** ....⊕2,569

Starbuck
Starbuck Times **(16462)** ....(Paid) ‡1,800
(Free) ‡25

Stephen
The Messenger **(16463)** 2,200

Thief River Falls
Thief River Falls Times **(16468)** ....‡5,400

Tower
Tower News **(16475)** 2,041

Tracy
Headlight Herald **(16476)**

Truman
The Truman Tribune **(16478)** ....‡1,100

Twin Valley
Twin Valley Times/Gary Graphic **(16479)** ......‡1,515

Two Harbors
Lake County
News-Chronicle **(16480)** ....(Paid) ◆3,259
(Non-paid) ◆68

Tyler
The Tyler Tribune **(16482)** ....‡1,500

Ulen
The Ulen Union **(16483)** ....(Paid) 1,250
(Free) 25

Verndale
The Verndale Sun **(16484)** ....(Paid) ‡1,000
(Free) ‡26

Wabasha
Wabasha County Herald **(16486)** ....‡3,200

Wabasso
Wabasso Standard **(16487)** 1,400

Waconia
Waconia Patriot **(16488)**

Wadena
Pioneer Journal **(16490)** ....(Combined) 3,875

Walker
The Pilot-Independent **(16494)** ....(Paid) ◆2,712
(Non-paid) ◆43

Wanamingo
The News Record **(16495)** 700

Warren
Sheaf **(16496)** ....(Paid) 3,133
(Non-paid) 129

Warroad
The Warroad Pioneer **(16497)** ....‡2,400

Waseca
Waseca County News **(16500)** ....(Paid) ‡3,727

Watertown
Carver County News **(16503)** ....(Paid) 1,920
(Non-paid) 50

Waterville
Lake Region Life **(16504)** ....‡1,603

Wells
The Wells Mirror **(16505)** 2,050

Westbrook
Westbrook Sentinel & Tribune **(16507)** 1,700

Wheaton
Wheaton Gazette **(16508)** ....(Combined) 27,127

White Bear Lake
Shoreview Press **(16512)** ....(Paid) 212
(Non-paid) 9,701

Williams
The Northern Light **(16516)** ....‡1,400

Windom
Cottonwood County Citizen **(16523)** ....‡3,806

Winsted
Winsted-Lester Prairie Herald
Journal **(16537)** ....(Paid) 1,400

Woodbury
Woodbury Bulletin **(16538)** ....(Paid) 10,396

Zumbrota
News-Record **(16542)** ....(Combined) 4403

MISSISSIPPI

Aberdeen
Aberdeen Examiner **(16543)** ....‡7,000

Ackerman
Choctaw Plaindealer **(16544)** ....(Paid) ‡2,700
(Free) ‡89

Amory
The Amory Advertiser **(16545)** ....‡7,000

Ashland
Southern Advocate **(16548)** 1,400

Baldwyn
The Baldwyn News **(16549)** ....(Paid) 2,650

Batesville
The Panolian **(16550)** ....‡9,675

Bay St. Louis
The Sea Coast Echo **(16552)** ....‡6,630

Bay Springs
Jasper County News **(16554)** ....(Paid) ‡3,046
(Free) ‡350

Belmont
Belmont-Tishomingo Journal **(16557)** ....‡2,100

Belzoni
The Belzoni Banner **(16558)** ....‡1,800

Booneville
Banner Independent **(16571)** 5,304

Brandon
Rankin County News **(16575)** ....‡7,000

Bruce
Calhoun County Journal **(16581)** 3,450

Calhoun City
The Monitor-Herald **(16582)** ....‡4,000

Canton
Madison County Herald **(16583)** ....‡4,500

Carthage
Carthaginian **(16586)** ....‡5,400

Charleston
Charleston Sun-Sentinel **(16587)** ....(Paid) ‡2,479
(Free) ‡105

Collins
The News-Commercial **(16598)** ....(Paid) ⊕3,217
(Free) ⊕23

Columbia
Columbian-Progress/Marion County
Advertiser **(16599)** ....(Thurs.) ‡12,200
(Sun.) ‡11,636

Crystal Springs
Meteor **(16620)** ....‡5,000

De Kalb
Kemper County Messenger **(16621)** ....‡2,400

Eupora
Webster Progress-Times **(16622)** ....(Paid) ‡2638
(Free) ‡90

Fayette
The Fayette Chronicle **(16623)** ....(Paid) ‡2,500
(Free) ‡100

Forest
Scott County Times **(16625)** 5,000

Fulton
Itawamba County Times **(16628)** ....‡5,500

Grenada
Grenada Lake Herald **(16653)** 8,050

Hattiesburg
Lamar County News **(16662)** 600

Hazlehurst
Copiah County Courier **(16678)** ....(Paid) ‡4,450
(Free) ‡2,500

Hernando
DeSoto Times Today **(16679)** ....(Paid) ‡8,138

Holly Springs
The South Reporter **(16681)** ....‡6,200

Houston
The Times Post **(16685)** 4,500

Indianola
Enterprise-Tocsin **(16687)**

Iuka
Tishomingo County News **(16691)** ....‡6,000

Jackson
Jackson Advocate **(16696)** ....(Paid) ‡20,000
(Free) ‡3,000

Kosciusko
The Star-Herald **(16734)** ....‡8,500

Leakesville
Greene County Herald **(16744)** 3,000

Leland
The Leland Progress **(16745)** 1,280

Lexington
Holmes County Herald **(16746)** ....(Paid) ⊕3,813

Liberty
The Southern Herald **(16748)** ....(Paid) ‡1,300
(Free) ‡30

Macon
Macon Beacon **(16754)** 4,500

Magee
The Magee Courier **(16755)** ....‡3,700
Simpson County News **(16756)** ....‡6108

Magnolia
Magnolia Gazette **(16758)** ....(Paid) ‡1,100

Marks
Quitman County Democrat **(16759)** 2,100

Meadville
Franklin Advocate **(16766)** ....‡3,700
Wilk-Amite Record **(16767)** ....(Paid) ‡1,900
(Free) ‡25

Numbers cited after listings are entry numbers rather than page numbers.

Monticello
Lawrence County Press **(16788)** ....(Paid) ‡3,450

Natchez
The Aquaculture News **(16791)** ....(Paid) ‡5,000

New Albany
New Albany Gazette **(16798)** ....(Paid) ‡6,095
                                        (Free) ‡12,112

Newton
The Newton Record **(16800)** ....‡2,700

Okolona
Okolona Messenger **(16803)** 2,400

Picayune
The Swap Shop **(16820)** 18,000

Pontotoc
The Pontotoc Progress **(16823)**

Poplarville
Poplarville Democrat **(16824)** ....‡2,400

Port Gibson
The Port Gibson Reveille **(16826)** ....(Paid) 2,222
                                        (Free) ‡49

Raleigh
Smith County Reformer **(16832)** 3,859

Richton
The Richton Dispatch **(16833)** ....(Paid) ‡1,750
                                        (Free) ‡10

Rolling Fork
Deer Creek Pilot **(16838)** ....‡1,500

Sardis
The Southern Reporter **(16840)** ....‡2,311

Senatobia
The Democrat **(16841)** ....‡5,200
The Democrat **(16842)** ....(Combined) 15,300

Tunica
The Tunica Times **(16848)** ....(Paid) ‡1,907

Tylertown
The Tylertown Times **(16862)** ....‡3,294

Waynesboro
The Wayne County News **(16872)** ....‡5,202

Wiggins
Stone County Enterprise **(16877)** 3,600

Winona
Conservative **(16879)** ....(Paid) ‡1,183
The Winona Times **(16880)** ....(Paid) ‡2,979

Woodville
The Woodville Republican **(16882)** 2,551

Yazoo City
The Yazoo Herald **(16883)** ....‡4,000

MISSOURI
Adrian
The Adrian Journal **(16886)** ....‡1,500
The Archie News **(16887)** ....‡300

Albany
The Albany Ledger Headlight **(16889)** ....‡1,600

Alma
The Santa Fe Times **(16890)** ....(Paid) 820
                                        (Non-paid) 900

Ash Grove
Commonwealth **(16892)** ....‡1,645

Ashland
Boone County Journal **(16893)** ....‡1,750

Aurora
The Aurora Advertiser **(16894)** ....‡3,850

Ava
Douglas County Herald **(16896)** ....‡4,800

Belle
The Belle Banner **(16899)** ....‡2,278
Bland Courier **(16900)** 900

Belton
The Star Herald **(16901)** ....(Paid) 4,500

Bethany
Bethany Republican-Clipper **(16902)** ....‡3,800

Bloomfield
The North Stoddard Countian **(16907)** ....‡3,200

Blue Springs
Blue Springs Examiner (Wednesday
   Edition) **(16909)** ....(Combined) 22,724

Bolivar
Bolivar Herald-Free Press **(16911)** ....‡7,400

Bowling Green
The Bowling Green Times **(16915)** 3,352
Democrat **(16916)** 1,337

Braymer
Braymer Bee **(16926)** 1,300

Brunswick
The Brunswicker **(16928)** ....‡1,800

Buffalo
Buffalo Reflex **(16929)** ....‡4,700
County Courier **(16930)** ....‡1,550

Cabool
The Cabool Enterprise **(16934)** 2,100

California
Democrat **(16935)** ....‡4,000

Cameron
Cameron Citizen Observer **(16938)** ......(Paid) 2,500
                                        (Free) 58

Canton
Press-News Journal **(16942)** ....‡3,500

Caruthersville
The Democrat-Argus **(16963)** ....(Paid) ‡2,802
                                        (Free) ‡33

Cassville
Cassville Democrat **(16965)** 5,000
Wheaton Journal **(16967)** ....(Paid) 500

Chaffee
Scott County Signal **(16971)** ....‡7,000

Charleston
The Enterprise-Courier **(16972)** ....‡3,400

Clarence
The Clarence Courier **(16980)** ....‡1,600

Clinton
The Kayo **(16984)** ....‡14,700

Concordia
The Concordian **(17026)** ....(Paid) ‡2,695
                                        (Free) ‡64

Crane
The Crane Chronicle/Stone County
   Republican **(17027)** ....(Paid) 2,750
                                        (Non-paid) 15

Cuba
Cuba Free Press **(17029)** 3,950
Steelville Star/Crawford Mirror **(17030)** ....‡3,450

Dixon
Pilot **(17035)** ....‡2,650

Doniphan
Prospect-News **(17036)** 5,500

Drexel
Drexel Star **(17039)** 700

East Prairie
East Prairie Eagle **(17040)** ....‡2,500

Edina
Sentinel **(17041)**

El Dorado Springs
El Dorado Springs Sun **(17042)** ....(Mon.-Sat.) 9,904
                                        (Sun.) 16,420

Eldon
The Eldon Advertiser **(17045)** ....‡4,625
Miller County
   Autogram-Sentinel **(17046)** ....(Paid) 2,000

Ellington
Reynolds County Courier **(17047)** ....‡2,300

Elsberry
Elsberry Democrat **(17048)** 1,500

Eminence
The Current Wave **(17049)** ....‡2,000

Fairfax
The Fairfax Forum **(17053)** ....‡920

Fayette
The Democrat-Leader **(17058)** 2,410

The Fayette Advertiser **(17059)** ....(Paid) 2,310
                                        (Free) 92

Fredericktown
Democrat-News **(17074)** ....‡3,200

Gainesville
Ozark County Times **(17080)** ....(Paid) 3,400

Gallatin
North Missourian **(17081)** ....‡2,575

Glasgow
The Glasgow Missourian **(17083)** ....‡1,650

Granby
Newton County News **(17085)** ....‡1,500

Grandview
Jackson County Advocate **(17086)** 6,200

Grant City
The Grant City Times-Tribune **(17087)** 1,650

Greenfield
Greenfield Vedette **(17088)** 2,500

Hamilton
Hamilton Advocate **(17089)** 1,973

Harrisonville
Cass County
   Democrat-Missourian **(17093)** ....(Paid) 6,165

Hermann
Advertiser-Courier **(17096)**

Hermitage
The Index **(17097)** 4,509

Higginsville
Higginsville Advance **(17098)** ....‡2,200

Holden
The Holden
   Image-Progress **(17099)** ....(Paid) ‡2,150
                                        (Free) ‡5,600

Hollister
Branson Daily News **(17100)** 10,000

Hopkins
The Hopkins Journal **(17101)** ....‡900

Houston
Houston Herald **(17102)** ....‡4,200

Independence
Blue Springs & Independence Examiner Suburban
   Life (Wednesday
   Edition) **(17109)** ....(Combined) 67,135
Independence Examiner (Wednesday
   Edition) **(17114)** ....(Combined) 43,634

Jamesport
Tri-County Weekly **(17119)** ....‡1,550

Kahoka
Media **(17151)** ....(Paid) ‡2,600

Kansas City
Call **(17159)** ....(Fri.) 17,310
Dos Mundos Bilingual Newspaper **(17165)** 20,000
The Pitch **(17193)** ....(Free) 80,000

Kearney
The Kearney Courier **(17216)** ....‡3,940

King City
Tri-County News **(17223)** 1,850

Knob Noster
Knob Noster Item **(17233)** ....‡1,200

La Belle
The La Belle Star **(17234)** ....‡1,000

Lamar
Lamar Democrat **(17235)** ....(Paid) ‡3,850
                                        (Free) ‡600

Lancaster
The Excelsior **(17236)** ....‡1,800

Lawson
The Lawson Review **(17237)** ....‡1,700

Lees Summit
Lees Summit Journal **(17243)** ....(Paid) 4,679
                                        (Non-paid) 224

Lexington
The Lexington News **(17246)** ....‡3,000

Liberal
Liberal News **(17247)** 1,083

Circulation: ★ = ABC; △ = BPA; ♦ = CAC; ● = CCAB; ❑ = VAC; ⊕ = PO Statement; ‡ = Publisher's Report; Boldface figures = sworn; Light figures = estimated.

Newspapers

2905

	Circ.		Circ.		Circ.

MISSOURI (continued)

Licking
Licking News **(17252)** ....‡2,500

Lincoln
Lincoln New Era **(17254)** ....(Paid) ‡400

Linn
Unterrified Democrat **(17255)** 4,800

Louisiana
The Louisiana Press-Journal **(17256)** 3,263

Malden
Delta News-Journal **(17260)** ....‡1,262

Mansfield
Mirror-Republican **(17261)** ....‡2,300

Marble Hill
The Banner-Press **(17262)** ....(Paid) 4,600
(Free) 16

Marceline
The Marceline Press **(17264)** ....‡1,787

Marshfield
The Marshfield Mail **(17271)** ....(Paid) 5,500

Marthasville
The Marthasville
Record **(17272)** ....(Combined) 1,700

Maysville
DeKalb County
Record-Herald **(17280)** ....(Paid) 18,000

Memphis
Memphis Democrat **(17281)** 2,400

Mexico
Monroe City News **(17285)** ....‡1,500

Milan
The Milan Standard **(17289)** ....‡3,862

Miller
The Miller Press **(17290)** 525

Montgomery City
Montgomery Standard **(17296)** ....(Paid) ‡3,700

Mound City
Mound City News **(17298)** 2,600

Mountain Grove
News Journal **(17300)** 3,800

Mountain View
Standard News **(17303)**

New Haven
New Haven Leader **(17313)** ....‡1,300

New London
Ralls County Herald-Enterprise **(17314)** ....‡1,300

New Madrid
The Weekly Record **(17315)** ....‡1150

Norborne
Norborne Democrat-Leader **(17317)** ....‡1,350

Odessa
The Odessan **(17319)** 4,700

Oregon
Times Observer **(17320)** ....‡1,438

Osceola
Humansville Star-Leader **(17323)** 1,785
St. Clair County Courier **(17325)** ....(Paid) 2,165
(Free) 4,000

Owensville
Gasconade County Republican **(17329)** ....‡3,408

Ozark
Christian County Headliners News **(17330)** ....‡5,000

Palmyra
Palmyra Spectator **(17331)** 2,800

Paris
Monroe County Appeal **(17332)** ....‡2,200

Perryville
The Perry County
Republic-Monitor **(17339)** ....(Paid) 5,800
Perryville Sun Times **(17340)**

Piedmont
Wayne County Journal-Banner **(17343)** ....‡5,150

Pineville
McDonald County News-Gazette **(17346)** ......‡2,000

McDonald County Press **(17347)** 6,127

Platte City
The Landmark **(17349)** ....‡2,500
Platte County Citizen **(17350)** ....(Paid) ‡3,800
(Free) ‡4,000

Plattsburg
The Leader **(17351)** ....‡2,280

Pleasant Hill
Pleasant Hill Times **(17352)** ....‡6,000

Portageville
Missourian News **(17363)** ....‡1,800

Potosi
The Independent-Journal **(17364)** ....‡5,600

Princeton
Post-Telegraph **(17366)** ....‡2,670

Puxico
Puxico Weekly Press **(17367)** 2,300

Republic
Republic Monitor **(17371)** 3,500

Rich Hill
Rich Hill Mining Review **(17372)** 1,850

Richland
The Richland Mirror **(17373)** ....(Paid) ‡2,000

Rock Port
The Atchison County Mail **(17377)** .....(Paid) ‡2,550
(Free) ‡23

Ste. Genevieve
Ste. Genevieve Herald **(17387)** ....‡4,700

St. James
Leader-Journal **(17388)** ....‡2,900

St. Joseph
The St. Joseph Telegraph **(17395)** 1,000

St. Louis
Franklin County
Watchman **(17439)** ....(Combined) ‡20,000
Missouri Lawyers Weekly **(17473)** ......(Paid) ‡2,960
(Non-paid) ‡91
St. Louis American **(17493)** ....(Paid) 393
(Non-paid) 62,880
St. Louis Argus **(17494)** 33,000
St. Louis Crusader **(17500)** ....(Paid) ‡9,000
(Controlled) ‡150
The St. Louis Metro Evening
Whirl **(17504)** ....‡49,500
West End-Clayton Word **(17531)**

Salem
The Salem News **(17563)** ....(Combined) ‡8,300

Salisbury
Salisbury Press-Spectator **(17565)** ....‡2,285

Sarcoxie
Pierce City Leader-Journal **(17566)** 900
The Sarcoxie Record **(17567)** ....‡1,400

Savannah
Savannah Reporter and Andrew County
Democrat **(17568)** ....‡3,200

Sedalia
Central Missouri News **(17569)**

Senath
Dunklin County Press **(17575)** ....‡1,700

Seneca
Seneca News-Dispatch **(17576)** 1,790

Seymour
Webster County
Citizen **(17577)** ....(Controlled) 2,408

Shelbina
Shelbina Democrat **(17578)** 2,100

Shelbyville
Shelby County Herald **(17579)** ....(Paid) 2,105
(Free) 40

Sheridan
Quad River News **(17580)** ....(Paid) 750

Slater
Slater Main Street
News **(17590)** ....(Combined) 1,650

Smithville
The Smithville Lake
Herald **(17591)** ....(Paid) ⊕2,600
(Free) ⊕75

Steele
The Steele Enterprise **(17638)** ....(Paid) ‡1,894
(Free) ‡383

Stockton
Cedar County Republican **(17639)** ....‡3,300

Stover
Morgan County Press **(17640)** ....‡1,500

Sullivan
The Sullivan Independent News **(17641)** ......‡7,000

Sweet Springs
Sweet Springs Herald **(17644)** ....‡1,990

Tarkio
The Tarkio Avalanche **(17646)** 1,800

Thayer
The South Missourian News **(17648)** ....‡1,632

Tipton
The Tipton Times **(17651)** ....‡1,947

Troy
Troy Free Press **(17656)** ....(Paid) ‡3,000

Unionville
Unionville Republican & Putnam County
Journal **(17658)** ....(Paid) ‡2,200
(Free) ‡200

Van Buren
The Current Local **(17661)** ....‡2,200

Vandalia
Vandalia Leader-Press **(17662)** ....‡2,400

Versailles
Leader-Statesman **(17663)** 3,700

Vienna
Maries County Gazette **(17665)** 2,399

Warrenton
Chesterfield Journal **(17676)** ....(Sun.) 16,525
(Wed.) 16,826
(Fri.) 16,525
Citizen Journal **(17677)** ....(Sun.) 18,492
(Wed.) 18,779
County Star Journal West **(17680)** .....(Sun.) 11,636
(Wed.) 11,762
Mid County Journal **(17687)** ....(Sun.) 11,064
(Wed.) 11,507
North County Journal East **(17690)** ....(Sun.) 40,072
(Wed.) 41,025
St. Peters Journal **(17694)** ....(Sun.) 33,296
(Wed.) 34,159
(Fri.) 33,246
South City Journal **(17695)** ....(Wed.) 16,850
Southwest City Journal **(17698)** ....(Sun.) 24,346
(Wed.) 24,960

Warsaw
Benton County Enterprise **(17703)** ....(Paid) 4,500
(Free) 200

Washington
Washington Missourian **(17705)** ....(Wed.) 15,494
(Sat.) 13,771

Webb City
Webb City Sentinel **(17712)** ....‡2,000

Wellsville
Wellsville Optic-News **(17715)** ....‡2,000

Weston
Weston Chronicle **(17718)** ....(Paid) ‡1,800
(Free) ‡50

Windsor
Cole Camp Courier **(17720)** ....‡1,250

MONTANA
Anaconda
The Anaconda Leader **(17721)** ....(Paid) 3,800
(Free) 60

Baker
Fallon County Times **(17722)** 1,650

Belgrade
High Country Independent Press **(17723)** .....‡2,500

Numbers cited after listings are entry numbers rather than page numbers.

Big Sandy
Big Sandy Mountaineer (17726) ....(Paid) ‡912
(Free) ‡43

Bigfork
Bigfork Eagle (17728) ....(Paid) ‡1,600
(Free) ‡4,500

Billings
The Billings Times (17731) ....(Paid) ‡1,700
(Free) ‡50

Boulder
Boulder Monitor (17750) ....‡1,000

Broadus
Powder River Examiner (17759) 1,100

Browning
Glacier Reporter (17760) ....‡2,600

Cascade
Cascade Courier (17768) ....(Paid) ‡600
(Free) ‡15

Chester
Liberty County Times (17769) 1,852

Chinook
The Chinook Opinion (17770) ....‡1,800

Choteau
Choteau Acantha (17771) ....‡2,150

Columbia Falls
Hungry Horse News (17773) ....‡7,400

Columbus
Carbon County News (17774) 3,200
Stillwater County News (17775) ....‡2,100

Conrad
Independent-Observer (17776) ....‡2,760

Cut Bank
Cut Bank Pioneer Press (17778) ....(Paid) ‡1,825
(Free) ‡18
Western Breeze (17779) ....(Paid) 1,800
(Free) 80

Deer Lodge
Banner (17780) ....‡1,100
Silver State Post (17781) ....‡1,800

Dillon
Dillon Tribune (17782) ....(Paid) ‡2,764
(Free) ‡20

Ekalaka
Eagle (17786) 1,035

Ennis
The Madisonian (17787) ....‡2,300

Eureka
Tobacco Valley News (17788) 2,200

Forsyth
The Independent Enterprise (17790) 1,900

Fort Benton
The River Press (17791) 2,052

Glendive
Ranger-Review (17795) ....‡4,400

Hardin
Big Horn County News (17811) ....‡3,550

Harlowton
Times-Clarion (17812) ....‡1,300

Huntley
Yellowstone County News, Inc. (17834) ....‡3,500

Laurel
Laurel Outlook (17846) ....(Paid) ‡3,587
(Free) ‡55

Lewistown
Lewistown News-Argus (17848) ....‡4,874

Libby
Western News (17852) 4,550

Malta
The Phillips County News (17858) ....‡2,925

Pablo
Char-Koosta News (17889)

Philipsburg
The Philipsburg Mail (17890) 1,482

Plains
Valley Press (17893) 1,800

Polson
Lake County Leader (17899) ....‡5,600

Poplar
Wotanin-Wowapi (17901) ....(Paid) 800
(Non-paid) 2,000

Roundup
Roundup Record-Tribune and Winnett
Times (17902) ....‡2,800

Scobey
Daniels County Leader (17903) ....‡5,000

Seeley Lake
The Seeley Swan
Pathfinder (17905) ....(Paid) ⊕1,300

Shelby
The Shelby Promoter (17906) ....‡2,700

Sidney
The Sidney Herald-Leader (17910) 3,900

Stanford
Judith Basin Press (17912) 1,000

Terry
Terry Tribune (17913) ....‡900

Thompson Falls
Sanders County Ledger (17914) ....‡2,900

Three Forks
Herald (17915) ....(Paid) 1,350

Townsend
The Townsend Star (17916) ....‡1,500

Valier
The Valierian (17917) ....‡600

White Sulphur Springs
The Meagher County News (17918) ....‡1,200

Whitefish
Whitefish Pilot (17919) ....(Paid) ‡4,300

Wibaux
The Wibaux Pioneer-Gazette (17921) ....‡1,000

Wolf Point
Herald-News (17922) 2,200

NEBRASKA

Ainsworth
Star-Journal (17923) 3,056

Albion
Albion News (17926) ....‡3,200

Alma
Harlan County Journal (17933) ....‡2,280

Arapahoe
Arapahoe Public Mirror (17934) 1,250

Arlington
Arlington Citizen (17935) ....(Paid) ‡726

Arthur
Arthur Enterprise (17936) ....‡500

Ashland
The Ashland Gazette (17937) ....⊕1,870

Atkinson
The Atkinson Graphic (17938) 2,165

Auburn
Auburn Press-Tribune (17939) ....(Paid) ‡3,267
(Free) ‡95
Nemaha County Herald (17940) ......(Paid) ‡3,275
(Free) ‡87

Bassett
Rock County Leader (17943) ....‡1,687

Battle Creek
Battle Creek Enterprise (17945) 700

Bayard
The Bayard Transcript (17946) ....‡1,300

Beaver City
Times-Tribune (17950) ....(Paid) ‡820
(Free) ‡13

Bellevue
Bellevue Leader (17951) ....(Combined) ‡25,629

Benkelman
Benkelman Post and
News-Chronicle (17952) ....(Paid) ‡1,276
(Non-paid) ‡30

Bertrand
The Bertrand Herald (17953) ....(Paid) ‡600

Blair
Blair Enterprise (17954) ....‡4,100

Bloomfield
Bloomfield Monitor (17961) ....‡1,640

Blue Hill
Blue Hill Leader (17962) ....‡1,440

Bridgeport
Bridgeport News-Blade (17964) 1,600

Broken Bow
Custer County Chief (17965) 3,200

Butte
The Butte Gazette (17968) 622

Cairo
Cairo Record (17969) ....‡750

Callaway
The Callaway Courier (17970) ....(Paid) ‡850
(Free) ‡18

Cedar Rapids
Cedar Rapids Press (17971) ....‡350

Central City
Republican Nonpareil (17972) ....(Paid) ‡2,350
(Free) ‡50

Chadron
Chadron Record (17973) ....(Paid) ‡2,100
(Free) ‡7,700

Chappell
The Chappell Register (17977) ....‡1,200

Clarkson
The Colfax County Press (17978) ....‡1,944

Coleridge
Coleridge Blade (17979) 1,000

Cozad
Tri-City Trib (17986) 3,350

Crawford
The Crawford Clipper/Harrison
Sun (17989) ....(Paid) ‡1,300
(Non-paid) ‡100

Creighton
The Creighton News (17991) ....‡1,500

Crete
The Crete News (17993) ....‡4,167

Crofton
Crofton Journal (17995) ....‡1,200

Dodge
Dodge Criterion (17999) ....‡1,100

Doniphan
The Doniphan Herald (18000) ....(Paid) 742
(Free) 26

Elkhorn
Douglas County Post-Gazette (18002) ....‡9,600

Elwood
Elwood Bulletin (18003) 850

Exeter
Fillmore County News (18004) ....‡690

Fairbury
Fairbury Journal-News (18005) ....‡6,881

Fullerton
Nance County Journal (18015) 1,700

Geneva
The Nebraska Signal (18016) ....(Paid) ‡3,250

Genoa
Genoa Leader-Times (18017) 947

Gering
Gering Courier (18018) ....‡2,681

Gibbon
The Gibbon Reporter (18021) ....(Paid) ‡1,121
(Free) ‡13

Gordon
Gordon Journal (18022) ....‡2,600

Gothenburg
The Gothenburg Times (18024) ....‡2,500

Circulation: ★ = ABC; △ = BPA; ◆ = CAC; ● = CCAB; ❏ = VAC; ⊕ = PO Statement; ‡ = Publisher's Report; Boldface figures = sworn; Light figures = estimated.

Circ.

Circ.

Circ.

NEBRASKA (continued)

Grant
Grant Tribune Sentinel (18032) ....(Paid) 2,000
(Non-paid) 100

Gretna
Gretna Guide & News (18033) ....‡3,890

Hartington
Cedar County News (18034) ....(Paid) 2,280

Hayes Center
Times-Republican (18043) ....‡936

Hebron
Hebron Journal Register (18045) 3,400

Hemingford
The Ledger (18046) ....(Paid) ‡1,214
(Free) ‡31

Henderson
The Henderson News (18047) ....‡800

Hickman
The VOICE News (18048) ....‡2,500

Howells
Howells Journal (18052) ....‡1,250

Humboldt
The Humboldt Standard (18053) ....‡1,363

Imperial
The Imperial Republican (18054) ....(Paid) ‡2,242
(Free) ‡50
Wauneta Breeze (18055) ....‡1,123

Indianola
The Indianola News (18056) ....‡500

Kimball
Western Nebraska
Observer (18068) ....(Paid) ‡1,910
(Free) ‡15

Laurel
Laurel Advocate (18069) ....‡950

Lawrence
Locomotive (18070) ....‡871

Leigh
Leigh World (18071) ....‡1,027

Lexington
Clipper-Herald (18072) ....‡3,000

Lincoln
Chester Herald (18078) 1,800

Loup City
Sherman County Times (18150) ....‡1,541

Lyons
Lyons Mirror Sun (18151) ....‡1,100

Madison
Star-Mail (18152) ....‡1,400

Meadow Grove
Meadow Grove News (18160) 790

Milford
The Milford Times (18162) ....(Paid) 5,259
(Non-paid) 8

Minden
The Minden Courier (18163) ....‡2,800

Mitchell
The Index (18164) 2,075

Mullen
Hooker County Tribune (18165) 875

Neligh
Neligh News and Leader (18168) ....‡2,564

Nelson
Nelson Gazette (18169) ....‡700

North Bend
North Bend Eagle (18175) ....‡1,500

Oakland
Oakland Independent (18186) ....‡1,980

Ogallala
Keith County News (18188) ....(Paid) ⊕3,950

Omaha
Jewish Press (18199) 3,800

Oneill
Frontier and Holt County
Independent (18232) 5,225

Orchard
Orchard News (18235) ....‡750

Osceola
The Polk County News (18239) ....‡1,015

Oshkosh
Garden County News (18240) 1,884

Osmond
Osmond Republican (18241) ....‡1,037

Overton
The Beacon-Observer (18242) ....‡1,650

Oxford
Oxford Standard (18243) 1,000

Pawnee City
The Pawnee Republican (18244) ......(Paid) 1,834
(Free) 52

Pender
The Pender Times (18245) ....‡1,500

Petersburg
Petersburg Press (18246) 600

Pierce
Pierce County Leader (18248) ....‡2,075

Plainview
Plainview News (18249) ....‡1757

Plattsmouth
Plattsmouth Journal (18250) ....‡5,234

Ponca
Nebraska Journal-Leader (18252) 1,300

Ralston
The Ralston Recorder (18253) 1,850

Ravenna
The Ravenna News (18254) ....‡1,700

Red Cloud
Red Cloud Chief (18255) 1,850

St. Edward
The St. Edward Advance (18257) ....‡900

St. Paul
St. Paul Phonograph-Herald (18258) ....‡2,502

Sargent
Burwell Tribune (18259) ....(Paid) ‡2,100
Sargent Leader (18260) ....(Paid) ‡750
(Free) ‡50
Wheeler County Independent (18261) 325

Scottsbluff
Business Farmer (18262) ....(Paid) 2,750

Scribner
Rustler Sentinel (18274) ....(Paid) 2,000
(Free) 13

Seward
Seward County Independent (18276) ...(Paid) 4,048
(Free) 107

Shelton
The Shelton Clipper (18277) ....(Paid) ‡1,006
(Free) ‡8

Sidney
Sidney Sun Telegraph (18278) ....(Paid) ‡2518

South Sioux City
South Sioux City Star (18280) ....‡3,400

Spalding
Spalding Enterprise (18281) ....‡725

Spencer
The Spencer Advocate (18282) 1,082

Springview
Springview Herald (18283) ....‡850

Stanton
The Register (18284) ....‡1,624

Stapleton
Arnold Sentinel (18285) ....‡1,000
The Graphic (18286) 467
The Stapleton Enterprise (18287) ....‡725

Stromsburg
The Polk County News (18288) ....‡1,281

Superior
The Superior Express (18289) ....(Paid) ⊕3,700

Sutherland
Courier-Times (18291) ....‡1,400

Sutton
Clay County News (18292) ....(Paid) 2,805
(Free) 50

Syracuse
Syracuse Journal-Democrat (18293) ....‡2,694

Taylor
Taylor Clarion (18294) ....(Paid) 375
(Non-paid) 25

Tecumseh
Chieftain (18295) 2,613

Tekamah
Burt County Plaindealer (18296) ....‡2,300

Tilden
Tilden Citizen (18298) 1,300

Trenton
The Hitchcock County News (18299) ....‡1,126

Verdigre
Verdigre Eagle (18301) ....‡1,500

Wahoo
Wahoo Newspaper (18302) ....⊕4,329

Wakefield
The Wakefield Republican (18303) ....‡1,150

Wausa
The Wausa Gazette (18304) ....‡1,025

Waverly
Waverly News (18305) ....⊕1,704

Wayne
The Wayne Herald (18306) ....(Paid) 2,600
(Free) 9,300

West Point
West Point News (18312) 4,150

Wilber
De Witt Times-News (18315) 800
The Wilber Republican (18316) 1,500

Wisner
Wisner News-Chronicle (18317) ....(Paid) 1,957
(Free) ‡38

Wood River
The Wood River Sunbeam (18318) 1,200

Wymore
Wymore Arbor State (18319) 1,700

NEVADA
Boulder City
Boulder City News (18325) ....‡5,400

Gardnerville
The Record-Courier (18349)

Hawthorne
Mineral County
Independent-News (18352) ....(Paid) 2,900

Henderson
Henderson Home News (18353) ....‡15,000

Incline Village
North Lake Tahoe Bonanza (18358)

Las Vegas
Las Vegas Business
Press (18371) ....(Controlled) 12,500
Las Vegas CityLife (18372) ......(Combined) 238,000
Las Vegas Sentinel-Voice (18375) 5,000
Las Vegas Weekly (18376) ....(Free) 56,290
Nevada Senior World (18380) ....(Combined) 75,875

Lovelock
Lovelock Review-Miner (18412) ....(Paid) ‡1,400
(Free) ‡15

Pahrump
Pahrump Valley Times (18414)

Pioche
Lincoln County Record (18415) ....⊕1,700

Reno
Ahora Spanish News (18416) ....(Paid) 620
(Free) 11,380
Tahoe World (18425) 6,000

Numbers cited after listings are entry numbers rather than page numbers.

Tonopah
Eureka Sentinel **(18446)** ....‡550
Times Bonanza and Goldfield
    News **(18447)** ....‡2,600

Winnemucca
The Humboldt Sun **(18450)** ....‡4,000

Yerington
Fernley Leader/Dayton
    Courier **(18453)** ....(Paid) 3,100

NEW HAMPSHIRE

Berlin
Berlin Reporter **(18455)** 5,300

Center Ossipee
Carroll County Independent and
    Pioneer **(18463)** ....‡3859

Colebrook
The News and Sentinel **(18468)** 5,000

Derry
Derry News **(18488)** ....‡11,000

Exeter
The Hampton Union **(18506)** ....(Combined) 6,252
The Rockingham News **(18507)** ......(Paid) 6,235

Hillsboro
The Messenger **(18524)** ....(Paid) 10,000
The Messenger **(18525)** ....(Free) ‡22,506

Lancaster
Coos County Democrat **(18541)** ....‡6,500

Littleton
The Courier **(18548)** ....‡6,925

Meredith
The Meredith News **(18575)** ....(Paid) 4,000
                                                              (Free) 21

Milford
Bedford Journal **(18576)** ....(Combined) 7,500
The Cabinet **(18577)** 8,000
Hollis Brookline Journal **(18578)** ....(Non-paid) 5,000
Merrimack Journal **(18579)** ....(Non-paid) 10,000

Newbury
Argus-Champion **(18613)** ....‡5,400

North Sutton
InterTown Record **(18615)**

Peterborough
The Monadnock Ledger **(18625)** ....(Paid) 8,265
                                                              (Free) 49
The Peterborough Transcript **(18627)** 5,900

Plymouth
The Record Enterprise **(18634)** ....(Paid) ⊕5,942

Salem
Salem Observer **(18645)** ....‡5,000

Warner
Warner's New Paper **(18648)** 1,000

Windham
Windham Independent **(18653)** ....(Paid) ‡2,300
                                                              (Free) ‡50

Wolfeboro
Granite State News **(18654)** ....‡5,500

NEW JERSEY

Belvidere
News **(18671)** ....(Paid) ♦854

Berlin
The Journal **(18674)** ....‡15,000

Bernardsville
The Bernards Township Community
    News **(18675)** ....(Non-paid) ♦1,135
The Bernardsville
    News **(18676)** ....(Combined) 8,880
The Progress **(18679)** ....!...(Non-paid) 7,685
                                                              (Paid) 274

Blackwood
News Report **(18681)** ....(Paid) ‡3,854
                                                              (Free) ‡5,000
Plain Dealer **(18682)** ....‡3,040
Record Breeze **(18683)** ....‡3,667

Bloomfield
Belleville Post **(18685)** ....(Combined) 572
The Glen Ridge Paper **(18686)** ....(Combined) 1,211

The Independent Press **(18687)** ....(Paid) 2,284
                                                              (Non-paid) 670

Bridgewater
Strictly Hunterdon **(18701)** ....(Combined) 38,762

Cape May
Star and Wave **(18719)** ....‡6,000

Cedar Grove
Verona-Cedar Grove Times **(18722)** .....(Paid) 3,250

Chester
Observer-Tribune **(18742)** ....(Combined) 7,115

Cinnaminson
Riverside Reporter **(18743)**
Town News **(18746)**

Clark
The Clark/Cranford Eagle **(18747)** ....(Paid) ♦28,202
                                                              (Non-paid) ♦1,035

Clifton
North Jersey Prospector **(18757)** ......(Paid) ‡30,100
                                                              (Free) ‡51,000
Post Eagle **(18758)** ....‡14,000

Collingswood
The Retrospect **(18768)**

Cranford
Cranford Chronicle **(18771)** ....(Paid) 4,320

Dayton
Central Post **(18776)** ....(Paid) 4,316

Denville
The Citizen of Morris County **(18777)**

East Orange
East Orange Record **(18782)** ......(Combined) 1,903

Edison
Metuchen Edison Review **(18787)** ....(Paid) 3,632

Elizabeth
La Voz **(18790)** ....⊕38,000

Elmer
Elmer Times **(18793)** 2,021

Englewood
Press Journal/Valley Star **(18797)** ....‡10,160

Fair Lawn
The News Beacon **(18808)** 4,000

Flemington
Delaware Valley News **(18819)** ....(Thurs.) 3,622
Hunterdon County
    Democrat **(18820)** ....(Thurs.) 23,355

Florham Park
Florham Park Eagle **(18826)** ....(Combined) 1,828

Forked River
Lacey Beacon **(18829)** ....(Thurs.) 2,359

Franklinville
Gloucester County Sentinel **(18837)** .....(Paid) 4,400

Freehold
Sentinel **(18840)** ....‡45,000
Suburban **(18841)** ....‡45,000

Garfield
The Messenger **(18843)** ....‡1,430

Gloucester City
Gloucester City News **(18849)** ....(Paid) ‡5,000
                                                              (Free) ‡100

Hackettstown
The Blairstown Press **(18855)** ....(Paid) ♦2,328
Star Gazette **(18857)** ....(Paid) ♦3,014

Hammonton
Atlantic County Record **(18862)** ....‡928
Egg Harbor News **(18863)** ....‡1,200
Hammonton News **(18864)** ....‡5,400
Mainland Journal **(18865)** ....‡2,000

Hasbrouck Heights
The Observer **(18867)** ....‡2,322
The Weekly News **(18868)** ....(Paid) ‡1,590
                                                              (Free) ‡1,410

Hawthorne
Hawthorne Press **(18871)** 9,000

Highland Park
Highland Park Herald **(18873)** ....(Paid) 1,155

Hightstown
The Messenger-Press **(18875)** ....(Paid) 4,650

Hillside
Modern Nutrition News **(18879)**

Hopewell
Hopewell Valley News **(19124)** 3829

Irvington
Irvington Herald **(19125)** ....(Combined) 904

Kenilworth
Freie Zeitung **(19153)** ....‡3,000

Lakehurst
Advance News **(19157)** ....(Paid) ⊕22,000

Lawrenceville
The Lawrence Ledger **(19162)** 3,283

Ledgewood
Star Journal **(19167)** ....‡2,700
West Morris Star Journal **(19168)** ....(Paid) 501

Linden
Spectator Leader **(19171)** ....(Paid) 1,339

Livingston
West Essex Tribune **(19178)** ....(Thurs.) 6,860

Madison
Hanover Eagle & Weekly Regional
    News **(19181)** ....(Paid) 2,626
                                                              (Non-paid) 32

Manahawkin
Manahawkin Newspaper **(19210)** ....(Paid) 22,000
                                                              (Free) 50,400

Manasquan
The Coast Star **(19213)** 14,200

Maywood
Ale Street News **(19218)** ....(Combined) 110,000
Our Town **(19219)** ....‡3,650

Medford
The Central Record **(19222)** ....(Paid) 13,912
                                                              (Non-paid) 74

Middletown
The Courier **(19234)** ....‡7,000

Netcong
News-Leader **(19323)** ....(Combined) 397

New Egypt
The New Egypt Press **(19346)** ....‡2,600

New Providence
Summit Herald **(19349)** ....(Paid) 1,751
                                                              (Non-paid) 158

Newark
Italian Tribune **(19354)** ....‡45,000
The Luso-Americano **(19358)**

North Brunswick
Central Post Tempo **(19380)** ....‡3,391

Nutley
Nutley Journal **(19385)** ....(Paid) 1,040

Ocean City
Ocean City Sentinel **(19388)** 10,888

Ocean Grove
The Times At The Jersey Shore **(19392)** 7,200

Orange
Orange Transcript **(19396)** ....(Paid) 1,046
West Orange Chronicle **(19397)** ....(Paid) 3,771

Palisades Park
Bergen News **(19398)** ....(Non-paid) 29,939

Parsippany
The Ukrainian Weekly **(19415)** ......(Paid) ‡7,500
                                                              (Free) ‡500

Phillipsburg
Free Press **(19421)** ....‡3,000

Piscataway
Piscataway Review **(19430)** ....(Paid) 2,258

Princeton
Cranbury Press **(19458)** ....‡4,616
Franklin News Record **(19460)** ....(Paid) 5,148
The Manville News **(19464)** ....‡1,261
The Princeton Packet **(19471)** 13,087

Rahway
The Citizen **(19485)** ....(Paid) ‡2,100
Rahway Progress **(19486)** ....(Combined) 633

Circulation: ★ = ABC; △ = BPA; ♦ = CAC; • = CCAB; ❏ = VAC; ⊕ = PO Statement; ‡ = Publisher's Report; Boldface figures = sworn; Light figures = estimated.

2909

Newspapers

Circ.   Circ.   Circ.

NEW JERSEY (continued)

Ridgewood
Berger County Newspapers,
  Inc. **(19502)** ....(Paid) ‡3,751
                            (Free) ‡2,500
The Town Journal **(19504)** ....(Non-paid) ♦6,924
The Wyckoff Suburban
  News **(19506)** ....(Wed.) 5,702

Riverton
Newsweekly **(19521)** ....(Paid) 6,000

Roxbury Township
Roxbury Register **(19525)** ....(Paid) ♦2,012
                            (Non-paid) ♦362

Scotch Plains
Scotch Plains-Fanwood
  Press **(19534)** ....(Paid) 2,084
                            (Non-paid) 5

Secaucus
Home News **(19538)** ....‡3,500

Somerset
Somerset Messenger
  Gazette **(19565)** ....(Paid) 5,807

Somerville
Bound Brook Chronicle **(19571)** ....(Paid) 3,960
The Journal (Greenbrook-North Plainfield
  Edition) **(19573)** ....(Paid) 1,474
Middlesex Chronicle **(19574)** ....(Free) 15,292
Record-Press **(19576)** ....(Paid) 3,427
The Review **(19577)** ....(Paid) 3,478

South Plainfield
South Plainfield Reporter **(19590)** ....(Paid) 1,729

Springfield
Echo Leader **(19595)** ....(Paid) 1,717
                            (Non-paid) 53

Stanhope
The Chronicle **(19597)** ....(Paid) 3,742
The Journal **(19598)** ....(Paid) 1,312
The Sussex County Chronicle **(19599)** ....(Paid) 905

Stirling
Chatham Courier **(19600)** ....(Combined) 3,532
Echoes-Sentinel **(19601)** ....(Combined) 5,264
Hunterdon Review **(19602)** ....(Combined) 3,288
The Madison Eagle **(19603)** ....(Combined) 3,175
Morris News Bee **(19604)** ....(Combined) 1,946

Toms River
Weekend Reporter **(19647)** ....(Non-paid) 60,124

Trenton
The Colonial **(19655)** ....(Combined) 3,862
Glenside News **(19656)** ....(Combined) 3,817
Main Line Life **(19657)** ....(Combined) 12,288
Montgomery Life **(19660)** ....(Combined) 2,952
The Spring-ford
  Reporter **(19666)** ....(Combined) 3,490
Springfield Sun **(19667)** ....(Combined) 3,712
Times Chronicle **(19669)** ....(Combined) 9,645
Willow Grove Guide **(19671)** .....(Combined) 1,373

Tuckerton
Tuckerton Beacon **(19681)** ....(Thurs.) 4,305

Union
The Leader **(19683)** ....(Combined) 1,360
News-Record **(19685)** ....(Combined) 5,078
News-Record of Maplewood and South
  Orange **(19686)** ....(Paid) 5,127
                            (Non-paid) 78
Summit Observer **(19687)** ....(Combined) 917
Union Leader **(19688)** ....(Paid) 3,607

Union City
AVANCE Weekly **(19689)** 25,000
El Especial **(19690)** ....(Paid) 71,250
                            (Free) 1,400

Vailsburg
Vailsburg Leader **(19696)** ....(Paid) 74

Waretown
Ocean County Journal **(19705)**

West Caldwell
Parsippany News **(19719)** ....(Paid) 20,000

West Paterson
Belleville Times **(19726)** ....(Paid) 45,524
Bloomfield Life **(19727)** ....(Thurs.) 3,000
Glen Ridge Voice **(19729)** ....(Thurs.) 45,524
The Item of Millburn- and Sho-
  Hills **(19730)** ....(Paid) 45,524
The Montclair Times **(19732)** ...(Thurs.) 45,524

Nutley Sun **(19734)** ....(Paid) 45,524
The Ridgewood News **(19737)** ....(Fri.) 45,524
                            (Sun.) 7,115
Suburban Trends **(19739)** ....(Wed.) 45,524
                            (Sun.) 11,029

Westfield
The Times of Scotch
  Plains-Fanwood **(19746)** ....‡7,500
The Westfield Leader **(19747)** ....(Paid) 7,500

Whippany
New Jersey Jewish News—Central
  Edition **(19749)** ....(Paid) 7,000
New Jersey Jewish News—Metrowest
  Edition **(19750)** ....(Paid) 28,186

Wildwood
Gazette Leader **(19751)** ....(Paid) 728
                            (Non-paid) 1

NEW MEXICO
Albuquerque
Health City Sun **(19772)** ....(Paid) ⊕1,500
                            (Free) ⊕500
New Mexico Jewish
  Link **(19779)** ....(Combined) 20,000
Weekly Alibi **(19789)** ....(Free) ❑41,276

Angel Fire
Sangre de Cristo Chronicle **(19816)** ....‡2,800

Belen
Valencia County
  News-Bulletin **(19820)** ....(Paid) 6,000
                            (Free) 17,000

Carrizozo
Lincoln County News **(19827)** ....(Paid) 1,823
                            (Free) 93

Clayton
Union County Leader **(19828)** ....(Paid) ⊕2,602
                            (Free) ⊕31

Espanola
Rio Grande Sun **(19844)** ....‡11,079

Fort Sumner
De Baca County News **(19855)** ....‡1,400

Hobbs
Gaines County News **(19863)** ....(Paid) 1,000
                            (Free) 10

Jal
The Jal Record **(19871)** 1,575

Ruidoso
The Ruidoso News **(19928)** ....(Paid) ⊕4,854
                            (Non-paid) ⊕154

Santa Rosa
Santa Rosa News **(19951)** ....‡2,200

Socorro
EL Defensor Chieftain **(19958)** ....‡3,117

Taos
The Taos News **(19963)** ....(Thurs.) 10,553

Truth or Consequences
The Herald **(19968)** ....‡4,300
Sierra County Sentinel **(19969)** ....‡4,137

Tucumcari
Quay County Sun **(19971)** ....(Paid) ‡3,200

NEW YORK
Adams
Jefferson County Journal **(19976)** 3,000

Akron
Akron Bugle **(19977)** ....(Paid) ‡1,797
                            (Non-paid) ‡33

Albany
The Jewish World **(19990)** ....(Paid) ‡3,311

Albion
Albion Advertiser **(20019)** ....‡1,850

Alden
Alden Advertiser **(20021)** ....(Paid) ‡3,345
                            (Free) ‡108

Alexandria Bay
Thousand Islands Sun **(20022)** ....(Paid) ‡6,397

Alfred
The Alfred Sun **(20023)** ....(Paid) ‡950
                            (Free) ‡50

Altamont
Altamont Enterprise and Albany County
  Post **(20027)** ....‡7,300

Amenia
Harlem Valley Times **(20029)** ....‡3,476

Amityville
Amityville Record **(20035)** ....(Paid) 2,850
                            (Free) 150

Amsterdam
Hamilton County News **(20055)** ....‡4,285

Arkville
Catskill Mountain News **(20063)** ....‡4,000

Astoria
Queens Gazette **(20102)**

Baldwin
Baldwin Herald **(20113)** ....(Paid) ‡2,738
                            (Free) ‡1,704

Ballston Spa
Ballston Journal **(20119)** ....(Paid) 2,142

Bayside
The Bayside Times **(20138)** ....(Paid) 10,950

Beacon
Beacon Light **(20139)** 2,700

Bellerose
Free Sons Reporter **(20145)** ....(Controlled) 4,600

Bellmore
Bellmore/Merrick Observer **(20146)** ....‡5,000
Seaford/Wantagh Observer **(20147)** ....‡5,000

Bethpage
Bethpage Newsgram **(20149)** ....(Paid) ‡2,740

Boonville
Boonville Herald & Adirondack
  Tourist **(20237)** ....(Paid) 2,937
                            (Free) 233

Brewster
Brewster Times **(20242)** 8,200

Brockport
Brockport Post **(20244)** ....(Paid) ♦1,884
                            (Non-paid) ♦477

Bronx
Bronx Press Blue **(20258)** ...(Non-paid) 10,000
Bronx Press Gold **(20259)** ....(Non-paid) 10,000
Bronx Press Red **(20260)** ...(Non-paid) 10,000
Bronx Press-Review **(20261)** ....‡50,000
Co-Op City News **(20263)** ....‡16,000
Inner City Press **(20273)**
The Riverdale Press **(20284)** ....(Paid) 13,000
                            (Free) 2,000

Bronxville
Review Press **(20293)**

Brooklyn
Afro-American Times **(20295)** 55,000
Arts and Leisure Times **(20296)** ....(Paid) 98,000
Bay News **(20299)** ....(Mon.) 21,420
Bay Ridge Courier **(20300)** 10,225
Brooklyn Heights Press **(20301)** 19,200
The Brooklyn Paper/Brooklyn's Weekly
  Newspaper **(20303)** ....(Combined) ‡81,000
Brooklyn Record **(20304)** ....‡8,500
Canarsie Courier **(20305)** 8,500
Canarsie Digest **(20306)** 10,135
Downtown News **(20315)** ....(Combined) 81,000
Entertainment Lifestyles **(20316)** 119,000
Flatbush Life **(20317)** 12,350
Greenpoint Gazette **(20318)** 5,000
Home Reporter & Sunset News **(20320)** ......‡8,941
The Jewish Herald **(20322)** ....‡312,000
Jewish Press **(20323)** ....(Paid) ⊕105,203
                            (Free) ⊕1,930
Kings Courier **(20325)** 19,430
Laiks (Time) **(20329)** 10,500
Metropolitan News **(20331)** 142,600
New York Entertainment Scene **(20333)** 116,000
Park Slope Paper **(20335)** ....(Combined) ‡81,000
Restaurant/Food Review **(20342)** 101,000
Travel International **(20350)** 116,000

Buffalo
Buffalo Criterion **(20364)**
Buffalo Jewish Review **(20365)** ....‡4,100
BuffaloBeat **(20370)** ....(Combined) 50,000
The Challenger **(20372)** ....‡10,000
Ken-Ton Bee **(20383)** ....(Paid) ♦1,731
                            (Free) ⊕42

Callicoon
Sullivan County Democrat **(20415)** ..... (Paid) ‡8,050
(Free) ‡225

Cambridge
The Eagle **(20416)** .... (Paid) 4,550
(Free) 35

Camillus
The Camillus Advocate **(20417)** .... (Paid) ‡2,215
(Free) 378

Canandaigua
Brighton Pittsford Post **(20419)** .... (Paid) ♦8,212
(Non-paid) ♦1,030

The New York-Pennsylvania
Collector **(20422)** .... (Paid) 5,000
(Non-paid) 2,500

Penfield Post Republican **(20423)** ...... (Paid) ♦3,250
(Non-paid) ♦913

Canastota
Canastota Bee-Journal **(20425)** .... (Paid) 1,632
(Free) 171

Chittenango-Bridgeport
Times **(20426)** .... (Paid) 1,551
(Free) 239

Carmel
Carmel Times **(20436)** 12,000

Carthage
Carthage Republican
Tribune **(20437)** .... (Paid) ‡2,584
(Free) ‡39

Cazenovia
Cazenovia Republican **(20441)** .... (Paid) 2,245
(Free) 279

Hamilton/Morrisville Tribune **(20442)** ..... (Paid) 1,202
(Free) 160

Central Square
Central Square Citizen Outlet **(20451)** 5,600

Chatham
The Chatham Courier-Rough
Notes **(20452)** .... (Paid) ‡5,306
(Free) ‡500

Cheektowaga
Am-Pol Eagle **(20455)** .... (Paid) 3,200
Cheektowaga Bee **(20456)** .... (Paid) ⊕1,572
(Free) ⊕23
Cheektowaga Times **(20457)** .... (Paid) ‡4,000

Clarence
Clarence Bee **(20461)** .... (Paid) ⊕4,067
(Free) ⊕54

Clinton
The Clinton Courier **(20470)** .... ‡2,300

Cobleskill
Times-Journal **(20479)** .... (Paid) 7,400

Cold Spring
Putnam County News & Recorder **(20483)** .... ‡4,500

Colonie
Colonie Spotlight **(20485)** .... ‡6,000

Commack
Commack News **(20487)** 4,500

Conklin
The Country Courier **(20493)** .... (Paid) 1,500
The Vestal Town Crier **(20495)** 1,050
The Windsor Standard **(20496)** 1,450

Cooperstown
The CoopersTown Crier **(20497)**

Croton On Hudson
The Gazette **(20515)** .... (Controlled) ‡2,825

Cuba
Patriot & Free Press **(20517)** .... ‡4,400

Dansville
Genessee Country Express **(20519)** .... ‡2,936

Delhi
Delaware County
Times **(20525)** .... (Mon.-Fri.) 50,746
(Sat.) 42,355
(Sun.) 48,178

Delmar
The Spotlight **(20528)** .... ‡16,000

Deposit
Deposit Courier **(20529)** .... (Paid) ‡2,100

DeWitt
DeWitt Times **(20531)** .... (Paid) 1,375
(Free) 197

Dundee
The Dundee Observer **(20534)** 3,200

East Aurora
East Aurora Advertiser **(20539)** .... ‡4,400
East Aurora Bee **(20540)** .... (Paid) ⊕2,000
(Free) ⊕163

East Fishkill
East Fishkill Record **(20544)** 3,100

East Hampton
The East Hampton Star **(20545)** ..... (Thurs.) 31,237

East Meadow
East Meadow Beacon **(20549)** 5,400
Meadowbrook Times **(20550)** .... (Paid) ‡1,422
(Free) ‡225

East Rochester
East Rochester Post Herald **(20551)** ...... (Paid) 977
(Non-paid) 87
Golden Times **(20552)** .... (Paid) 20,000

East Setauket
Three Village Herald **(20556)** .... ‡8,000
The Village Times **(20557)** .... ‡9,188

Eastchester
The Eastchester
Record **(20562)** .... (Combined) ⊕4,058

Elizabethtown
The Valley News **(20568)** .... (Paid) 2,171
(Non-paid) 101

Ellenville
The Ellenville Press **(20569)** .... (Paid) 2,000

Elma
Elma Review **(20570)** .... ‡1,200

Elmont
Elmont Herald **(20581)** .... (Paid) 4,000
(Free) 600
The Three Village Times **(20582)** .... ‡1,849

Fairport
Perinton-Fairport Post **(20590)** .... (Paid) ♦4,350
(Non-paid) ♦796

Far Rockaway
Rockaway Journal **(20591)** .... (Paid) ‡1,410
(Free) ‡318
The Wave **(20592)** .... ‡12,300

Farmingdale
Farmingdale Observer **(20595)** .... ‡4,174

Fishkill
Fishkill Standard **(20601)** 6,200

Floral Park
The Floral Park Bulletin **(20603)** .... (Paid) 8,000
(Free) 100
Floral Park Dispatch **(20604)** .... ‡1,452
The Gateway **(20605)** .... (Paid) ‡12,000
(Free) ‡200

Flushing
The Flushing Times **(20608)** .... (Paid) 4,966
Resumen Newspaper **(20612)** .... ‡27,500

Forest Hills
The Forest Hills Ledger **(20616)** .... (Paid) 2,357

Fort Plain
Courier-Standard-Enterprise **(20618)** .... ‡4,778

Franklin Square
The Franklin Square
Bulletin **(20619)** .... (Paid) ‡8,700
(Free) ‡200

Freeport
Long Island Graphic **(20625)** .... (Paid) ‡820
(Free) ‡192

Fresh Meadows
The Fresh Meadows Times **(20628)** ..... (Paid) 1,606
Queens Tribune **(20629)** .... (Paid) 2,000
(Free) 144,000

Fulton
The Fulton Patriot **(20630)** 5,500
The Valley News **(20631)** .... (Paid) ‡7,870

Garden City
Garden City Life **(20641)** .... (Paid) ‡3,261
(Free) ‡500

Garden City News **(20642)** .... (Paid) 7,490
(Non-paid) 100

Glen Cove
Glen Cove Record Pilot **(20660)** .... (Paid) ‡6,520

Glen Oaks
The Glen Oaks Ledger **(20666)** .... (Paid) 1,684

Glendale
Glendale Register **(20667)** 10,000

Goshen
Independent Republican **(20673)** .... (Paid) ‡3,800
(Free) ‡100

Gouverneur
Gouverneur Tribune-Press **(20674)** .... ‡4,680

Grand Island
Island Dispatch **(20678)** .... (Paid) 2,900

Granville
Sentinel **(20682)** .... ‡3,200
Whitehall Times **(20683)** .... (Paid) ⊕1,900

Great Neck
Great Neck Record **(20688)** .... (Paid) ‡7,109

Greece
The Greece Post **(20696)** .... (Paid) ♦6,669
(Non-paid) ♦1,020

Greene
Chenango American, Whitney Point Reporter, and
Oxford Review Times **(20697)** .... ‡3,500

Greenville
Greenville Local **(20700)** .... ‡1,600

Greenwich
The Journal-Press **(20701)** .... (Paid) ⊕1,606
(Non-paid) ⊕71

Greenwood Lake
Greenwood Lake and West Milford
News **(20702)** .... ‡4,000

Hamburg
Sun & Erie County Independent **(20705)** ..... ‡10,349

Hamilton
Mid-York Weekly **(20708)** .... (Combined) 9,300

Hancock
Hancock Herald **(20710)** .... ‡2,625

Harrison
The Harrison
Independent **(20712)** .... (Combined) ⊕4,300
Women's News **(20713)** .... ‡250,000

Hastings on Hudson
The Enterprise **(20716)** .... (Paid) ‡6,100
(Free) ‡250

Hempstead
Hempstead Beacon **(20728)** .... ‡5,400
La Tribuna Hispana-USA **(20729)** .... (Paid) 2,000
(Non-paid) 58,000

Henrietta
Henrietta Post **(20731)** .... (Paid) ♦2,319
(Non-paid) ♦499

Hicksville
Hicksville Illustrated News **(20738)** ..... (Paid) ‡5,434
Mid-Island Times **(20741)** .... (Paid) 1,840
(Non-paid) 150

Highland Falls
News of the Highlands **(20747)** 2,800

Hillsdale
The Independent **(20748)** .... (Tues.) 8,500
(Fri.) 9,000

Huntington
The Long Islander **(20774)** .... ‡8,473
The Record Northport **(20775)** .... ‡9,222

Hyde Park
Hyde Park Townsman **(20779)** 2,500

Irondequoit
Irondequoit Post **(20783)** .... (Paid) ♦6,093
(Non-paid) ♦731

Islip
Islip News **(20786)** .... ‡2,187

Jackson Heights
El Tiempo de New York **(20827)** ..... (Paid) ‡48,000
(Free) ‡500

Circulation: ★ = ABC; △ = BPA; ♦ = CAC; ● = CCAB; ❑ = VAC; ⊕ = PO Statement; ‡ = Publisher's Report; Boldface figures = sworn; Light figures = estimated.

Circ.   Circ.   Circ.

NEW YORK (continued)

Jamaica
Leader Observer **(20837)** ....‡7,500
The New York Voice/Harlem
U.S.A. **(20839)** ....(Paid) ‡70,000

Jericho
Jericho News Journal **(20849)** ....(Paid) 690
(Non-paid) 50
Syosset/Jericho Tribune **(20850)** ....(Paid) ‡4,114

Kingston
The Mountain Eagle **(20861)** 5,000
Woodstock Times **(20862)**

La Grange
La Grange Independent **(20866)** 2,600

Lackawanna
The Front Page **(20867)** ....(Combined) ‡9,500
South Buffalo News **(20868)** ....‡5,300

Lake Placid
The Lake Placid News **(20875)** ....(Paid) ‡4,500

Lancaster
Lancaster Bee/Depew Bee **(20883)** ....(Paid) ⊕3,775
(Free) ⊕39

Laurelton
The Laurelton Times **(20939)** ....(Paid) 1,647

Levittown
Levittown Tribune **(20941)** ....‡4,457

Little Neck
The Little Neck Ledger **(20953)** ....(Paid) 3,119

Liverpool
Liverpool Review **(20954)** ....(Paid) 4,005
(Free) ⊕573
The Review **(20955)** ....‡4,005

Locust Valley
Leader **(20959)** ....‡3,875

Long Beach
Long Beach Herald **(20960)** ....(Paid) ‡4,451
(Free) ‡1,883

Long Island City
Kampana–Campana **(20964)** ....‡8,800

Lowville
Journal and Republican **(20968)** ......(Paid) ‡3,798

Lynbrook
East Rockaway/Lynbrook
Observer **(20973)** ....(Paid) 2,635
(Free) 250
Long Beach Independent Voice **(20974)** .....‡12,000
Lynbrook USA **(20975)** ....‡9,000
The MAILeader **(20976)** ....‡9,000
Village Herald **(20978)** ....(Paid) ‡3,369
(Free) ‡1,902

Lyons
Wayne County Star **(20979)** 4,819

Mahopac
Mahopac Press **(20980)** 3,200

Malverne
Malverne Times **(20983)**

Manhasset
Manhasset Press **(21006)** ....(Paid) ‡4,961

Marcellus
Marcellus Observer **(21021)** ....(Paid) ‡1,288
(Free) ‡98

Massapequa
Massapequan Observer **(21025)** ....(Paid) ‡2,898

Mattituck
The News-Review **(21031)** ....(Paid) ‡6,105
The Suffolk Times **(21032)** ....(Paid) ‡11,236
(Free) ‡441

Merrick
Bellmore Life **(21070)** 3,728
The Freeport-Baldwin
Leader **(21071)** ....(Thurs.) 2,232
Merrick Beacon **(21072)** ....‡4,500
Merrick Life **(21073)** ....(Thurs.) 5,344
Wantagh-Seaford Citizen **(21074)** ......(Thurs.) 3,398

Mexico
Independent Mirror **(21076)** 3,600
Salmon River News **(21077)** 7,500

Millbrook
Millbrook Round Table **(21083)** ....‡2,400

Pine Plains Register Herald **(21084)** ....‡1,800

Mineola
Mineola American **(21086)** ....(Paid) ‡4,280

Monroe
The Warwick Advertiser **(21091)** ....(Free) ⊕9,000

Moravia
Republican-Register **(21096)** ....‡5,500

Mt. Kisco
Patent Trader **(21099)**

Mount Vernon
The Mt. Vernon
Independent **(21104)** ....(Combined) 6,000

Narrowsburg
The River Reporter **(21107)** ....(Paid) ⊕3,332
(Non-paid) ⊕330

Nassau
Nassau Herald **(21108)** ....(Paid) ‡9,505
(Free) ‡1,144

New Hyde Park
The Illustrated News **(21110)** ....‡4,098
New Hyde Park Herald
Courier **(21111)** ....(Paid) 2,258
(Non-paid) 120

New Paltz
The Herald **(21112)** ....(Paid) 3,000

New Rochelle
New Rochelle
Standard-Star **(21120)** ....(Mon.-Sat.) 9,787
(Sun.) 10,450
Parkchester News **(21121)** ....(Free) ‡12,500
Town and Village **(21123)** ....‡12,000

New York
Amsterdam News **(21211)** ....(Wed.) 51,133
The Asian Wall Street Journal Weekly
Edition **(21265)** ....‡11,000
Challenge New York **(21394)**
Chelsea Clinton News **(21399)** ....‡9,162
Cong Thuong **(21482)** ....‡5,000
Impacto Latin News **(21855)** 128,000
Irish Echo **(21950)** 58,000
The Japanese Daily Sun-Nikkan San **(21956)**
The Jerusalem Post, International
Edition **(21959)** 4,200
Jewish Forward **(21963)** 25,000
Jewish Post of New
York **(21965)** ....(Controlled) 18,000
The Jewish Week **(21966)** ....(Paid) ★72,421
La Voz Hispana **(22228)** 60,082
The New York Beacon **(22437)** 71,750
New York Blade News **(22438)** ....(Free) 40,000
(Paid) 83
The New York Evening
Express **(22442)** ....(Paid) 1,200
New York Generator **(22444)**
The New York Times Large Type
Weekly **(22455)** ....(Paid) 15,000
News India Times **(22458)**
Nordstjernan (Swedish
News) **(22468)** ....(Paid) ‡5,000
(Free) ‡100
NY Carib News **(22477)** ....(Paid) ‡67,000
(Free) ‡4,500
OCS News **(22483)** ....(Combined) 19,000
Our Town **(22509)** ....‡70,000
Tevyne **(22825)** ....‡3,500
The Thomas Tribune **(22832)** ....(Paid) 1,550
Vaba Eesti Sona (Free Estonian
Word) **(22893)** ....‡2,750
The Villager **(22901)**
The Westsider **(22915)** ....(Paid) 8,983
(Free) 3,000
Workers World **(22938)** ....(Paid) 3000 Approx.
Yomiuri America **(22951)** ....(Combined) 19,600

Newark
Courier-Gazette **(22994)** ....‡3,500

Newburgh
Hudson Valley Black Press **(23001)** ....‡42,500

North Bellmore
Jewish Singles News/Single News & Views/Singles
Style **(23010)**

North Castle
The North Castle
News **(23011)** ....(Combined) ⊕3,300

North Creek
The North Creek News-Enterprise **(23012)** ....‡2,100

North Syracuse
North Syracuse Star-News **(23014)** ......(Paid) 3,725
(Non-paid) 772

Northport
The Northport Journal **(23018)** ....‡1,820

Norwich
The Gazette **(23021)** 2,750

Oceanside
Oceanside-Island Park
Herald **(23031)** ....(Paid) ‡4,163
(Free) ‡1,105

Old Bethpage
Able Newspaper **(23036)** 35,000

Owego
Owego Pennysaver **(23067)** ....(Paid) 6
(Non-paid) 17,787

Oyster Bay
Oyster Bay Enterprise Pilot **(23069)** ....(Paid) ‡3,358
Oyster Bay-Syosset Guardian **(23070)** ....‡3,200

Palatine Bridge
Farm Chronicle **(23074)** ....(Paid) 22,000

Patchogue
Long Island Advance **(23076)** 10,500

Pawling
Pawling News Chronicle **(23085)** ....(Paid) 4,984
(Free) 312

Peekskill
The Star **(23088)** ....(Mon.-Sat.) 6,396
(Sun.) 8,054

Pelham
The Pelham Sun **(23089)** ....‡2,360

Penn Yan
The Chronicle-Express **(23092)** ....(Paid) 3,860
(Free) 31

Perry
Perry Herald **(23094)** ....(Paid) 920
(Free) 36

Phoenix
Phoenix Register **(23096)** ....(Mon.-Fri.) 482,259
(Sat.) 508,025
(Sun.) 599,450

Plainview
Plainview Herald **(23098)** ....‡2,178

Plattsburgh
The North Countryman **(23102)** ....(Paid) 17
(Non-paid) 1,675

Pleasant Valley
Voice Ledger **(23109)** 2,600

Port Chester
Westmore News **(23115)** ....(Paid) 2,600
(Free) 700

Port Jefferson
The Village Beacon Record **(23117)** ....‡7,000

Port Jefferson Station
Port Times Record **(23118)** ....‡6,659

Port Jervis
Gazette **(23119)** ....‡9,400

Port Washington
Port Washington News **(23133)** ....(Paid) ‡7,668
(Free) ‡500

Queens
Queens Ledger **(23169)** ....(Paid) 18,000

Queens Village
The Queens Village Times **(23170)** .....(Paid) 2,043

Randolph
The Randolph Register **(23176)** ....(Paid) 1,400

Ravena
News-Herald **(23177)** ....‡2,850

Red Creek
Post Herald **(23178)** ....‡2,100

Rhinebeck
Gazette-Advertiser **(23184)** ....‡3,700

Richmond Hill
The Richmond Hill Times **(23188)** ....(Paid) 1,906

Ridgewood
The Steuben News **(23197)** .....(Controlled) ‡10,000

Numbers cited after listings are entry numbers rather than page numbers.

Times Newsweekly **(23198)** ....(Paid) 23,095
(Free) 325

Riverhead
Suffolk County Life **(23205)** ....(Wed.) 516,251

Rochester
Campus Times **(23214)** ....(Controlled) 5,000
Communicade **(23217)** ....(Paid) 2,800
(Free) 200
Courier Journal **(23219)** 3,000

Rockville
Rockville Centre Herald **(23260)** ....(Paid) ‡3,160
(Non-paid) ‡2,011

Rockville Centre
Rockville Centre News and Owl **(23262)**

Ronkonkoma
Ronkonkoma Review **(23272)** ....(Paid) 4,800
(Free) 600

Roslyn
The Roslyn News **(23278)** ....(Paid) ‡4,788
(Free) ‡500

Rye
Rye Chronicle **(23279)** ....⊕3,966

Sag Harbor
The Sag Harbor Express **(23283)**

Saugerties
Saugerties Post Star **(23308)** ....‡5,000

Sayville
Suffolk County News **(23311)** ....(Paid) 15,000

Scarsdale
The Scarsdale Inquirer **(23313)** ....(Paid) 6,410
(Free) 425

Seneca Falls
Reveille/Between the
Lakes **(23324)** ....(Paid) ‡1,925
(Free) ‡305

Sherburne
Sherburne News **(23329)** ....‡1,850

Sidney
Tri-Town News **(23332)** ....‡6,300

Smithtown
Brookhaven Review **(23336)** ....(Paid) 5,000
Mid Island News **(23337)** ....(Paid) ⊕2,149
Observer **(23339)** 8,750
Smithtown Messenger **(23340)** 7,820
The Smithtown News **(23341)** ....‡9,957

Southampton
Shelter Island Reporter **(23345)** ....(Paid) ‡2,995
(Free) ‡200

Southold
The Traveler-Watchman **(23347)** ......(Paid) ‡20,500
(Free) ‡500

Spencer
Random Harvest Weekly **(23349)** ....(Paid) 789
(Free) 29

Springville
Springville Journal **(23354)** ....(Paid) 3,999
(Free) 1,004

Staten Island
Staten Island Register **(23363)** 20,300

Syosset
Syosset Advance **(23382)** ....(Paid) 2,100
(Non-paid) 150
Syosset Tribune **(23383)** ....‡5,600

Syracuse
Baldwinsville Messenger **(23388)** ....(Paid) 6,200
(Non-paid) 433
Cortland Sunday/Democrat **(23397)** ....(Paid) ‡9,965
Fayetteville Eagle Bulletin **(23403)** ....(Paid) 6,050
(Free) 786
Marcellus Observer **(23410)** ....(Paid) ‡1,425
(Free) ‡140
The Messenger **(23412)** ....‡6,200
News for You **(23414)** ....‡75,700
Syracuse New Times **(23428)** ....(Paid) 400
(Controlled) 46,200

Troy
Lafayette News **(23453)** ....‡2,400
Tri-County Times **(23459)** ....(Paid) 24,284
(Non-paid) 9,218

Trumansburg
Finger Lake Community
Newspaper **(23461)** 5,400
Ovid Gazette **(23462)**
Trumansburg Free Press **(23463)** ....‡5,400

Uniondale
Uniondale Beacon **(23465)** ....‡5,200

Valley Stream
The Courier **(23486)** ....(Paid) ‡5,400
(Free) ‡1,000
Valley Stream Herald **(23488)** ....(Paid) ‡6,671
(Free) ‡1,399

Vestal
Wyoming Valley Jewish
Reporter **(23489)** ....(Paid) ⊕2,000

Walden
Wallkill Valley Times **(23496)** ....(Paid) ‡4,352
(Free) ‡100

Walton
The Walton Reporter **(23497)** ....(Paid) ‡7,100
(Free) ‡175

Wappingers Falls
Southern Dutchess News **(23503)** ......(Paid) ‡8,000
(Free) ‡200

Warrensburg
The Adirondack Journal **(23504)** ....(Paid) 168
(Non-paid) 11,447
The Warrensburg-Lake George
News **(23505)** ....(Combined) ‡14,800

Warwick
Warwick Valley Dispatch **(23508)** ....‡2,650

Washingtonville
Orange County Post **(23512)** ....‡2,842

Waterville
The Waterville Times **(23523)** ....‡2,670

Watkins Glen
Watkins Review & Express **(23525)** ....‡3,200

Webster
Wayne County Mail **(23527)** ....‡1,837
Webster Herald **(23528)** ....(Paid) ‡4,782
The Webster Post **(23530)** ....(Paid) ♦3,746
(Non-paid) ♦871

West Coxsackie
Greene County News **(23540)**

West Hempstead
West Hempstead Beacon **(23542)** ....‡5,400

West Seneca
West Seneca Bee **(23547)** ....(Paid) ⊕3,608
(Free) ⊕25

West Winfield
Star **(23550)**

Westbury
The Westbury Times **(23560)** ....(Paid) ‡3,975
(Free) ‡500

Westfield
Chautauqua News **(23561)** ....(Paid) ‡702
(Free) ‡93
Mayville Sentinel **(23562)** ....(Paid) ‡687
(Free) ‡63
Westfield Republican **(23565)** ....‡1,690

Westhampton Beach
Southampton Press-Western
Edition **(23567)** ....(Thurs.) 6,556

White Plains
The Sound Shore Review **(23574)** ......(Paid) 2,000
(Free) 8,000

Whitestone
The Whitestone Times **(23581)** ....(Paid) 3,886

Williston Park
Williston Times **(23585)** 2,600

Windham
The Windham Journal **(23587)** ....‡2,100

Woodbury
Monroe Woodbury Photo
News **(23592)** ....(Free) 9,000

Woodstock
Ulster County Townsman **(23596)** ......(Paid) ‡4,870
(Free) ‡32

Yonkers
The Sound View News **(23601)** ....(Combined) 6,000
The Yonkers Home News &
Times **(23603)** ....(Combined) 20,100

Yorktown Heights
North County News **(23609)** 10,086

NORTH CAROLINA
Ahoskie
Roanoke Chowen News-Herald **(23614)** ....‡8,800

Albemarle
Stanly News and Press **(23618)** ....(Sun.) 9,664
(Tues.) 9,268
(Thurs.) 9,268

Andrews
The Andrews Journal **(23619)** 2,600

Asheboro
The Randolph Guide **(23622)** ....(Paid) ‡2,332

Belmont
Belmont Banner **(23642)** ....(Combined) 6,150

Benson
The Clayton News-Star **(23644)** ....(Combined) 3,250
Four Oaks-Benson News in
Review **(23645)** ....‡4,500

Black Mountain
The Black Mountain News **(23646)** 3,850

Blowing Rock
The Blowing Rocket **(23650)** ....(Paid) ‡3,500
(Free) ‡200

Boone
Watauga Democrat **(23657)** ....(Paid) 6,848

Brevard
The Transylvania Times **(23664)**

Bryson City
Smoky Mountain Times **(23666)** ....(Paid) ‡3,000
(Free) ‡25

Burgaw
Pender Post **(23670)** 5,100

Burnsville
The Yancey Journal **(23678)** ....(Paid) ‡6,000
(Free) ‡360

Carolina Beach
Island Gazette **(23684)**

Cary
The Cary News **(23686)** ....‡12,347

Cashiers
Crossroads Chronicle **(23694)** ....‡2,400

Chapel Hill
Chapel Hill News **(23702)** ....(Wed.) ♦20,538
(Sun.) ♦20,608

Charlotte
The Charlotte Post **(23741)** ....‡11,500
The Charlotte World **(23742)** ....(Paid) ‡1,800
(Non-paid) ‡8,200
La Noticia **(23747)** ....⊕26,000
Q-Notes **(23751)** ....(Non-paid) ‡10,000

Cherokee
The Cherokee One
Feather **(23783)** ....(Paid) ‡2,750
(Free) ‡15

Cherryville
Cherryville Eagle **(23784)** 3,800

Clemmons
Clemmons Courier **(23787)** ....‡3,200
Davie County Enterprise-Record **(23788)** 7,500

Columbus
Polk County News Journal **(23792)** 2,500

Creedmoor
Butner-Creedmoor News **(23794)** ....‡5,000

Durham
Carolina Parent **(23811)** ....(Combined) 50,000
The Carolina Times **(23812)** ....‡5,800

Edenton
The Chowan Herald **(23856)** 4,700

Elkin
The Tribune **(23867)** ....(Paid) ‡6,000

Circulation: ★ = ABC; △ = BPA; ♦ = CAC; ● = CCAB; ❏ = VAC; ⊕ = PO Statement; ‡ = Publisher's Report; Boldface figures = sworn; Light figures = estimated.

2913

Circ.

Circ.

Circ.

NORTH CAROLINA (continued)

Farmville
Farmville Enterprise **(23877)** ....‡3,050

Franklin
The Franklin Press **(23898)** ....‡9,200

Fuquay Varina
Fuquay Varina Independent **(23903)** ....(Paid) ‡5,000
(Free) ‡125

Garner
Garner News **(23904)** ....‡5,750

Gatesville
Gates County Index **(23909)** 2,700

Graham
Alamance News **(23912)** ....(Thurs.) 6,065

Greensboro
Carolina Peacemaker **(23919)** ....‡6,400

Grifton
The Times-Leader **(23977)** ....(Paid) 2,250

Hayesville
The Clay County Progress **(23980)** ....‡3,850

Hertford
Perquimans Weekly **(23986)** 2,000

Hickory
Hickory News **(23988)** ....‡6,200

Highlands
The Highlander **(24008)** ....‡3,750

Jamestown
Jamestown News **(24015)** 4,000

Kenansville
Duplin Times Progress **(24019)** 13,000

Kenly
Kenly News **(24020)** ....‡3,200

King
Times-News **(24023)** ....‡6,100

Kings Mountain
Kings Mountain
Herald **(24025)** ....(Combined) 15,000

Laurinburg
The Laurinburg Exchange **(24033)** ....(Paid) 8,450

Liberty
The Liberty News **(24043)** ....(Paid) 2,500
(Free) 91

Lillington
Harnett County News **(24044)** ....‡3,100

Lincolnton
Lincoln Times-News **(24045)** **10,903**

Littleton
The Littleton Observer **(24048)** ....(Paid) 2,800

Louisburg
Franklin Times **(24049)** ....‡8,569

Madison
The Messenger **(24052)** 7,310

Manteo
Coastland Times **(24053)** ....(Paid) 9,285
(Free) 140

Marshall
The News Record **(24059)** ....(Paid) 4,500
(Free) 100

Marshville
The Home News **(24060)** 2,950

Mebane
Mebane Enterprise **(24063)** 6,600

Mooresville
Mooresville Tribune **(24068)** 7,650

Morehead City
Carteret County
News-Times **(24070)** ....(Wed.) 10,218
(Fri.) 10,218
(Sun.) 11,702

Morganton
Valdese News **(24074)** ....(Paid) 555
(Free) 8,300

Mount Olive
Mount Olive Tribune **(24086)** ....‡4,965

Murphy
Cherokee Scout **(24088)** ....‡8,000

Nags Head
Outer Banks Sentinel **(24092)** ....(Paid) ⊕7,610

Nashville
The Nashville Graphic **(24094)** ....(Paid) ‡4,200

Newland
Avery Journal **(24103)** ....(Paid) 7,800
(Free) 250

North Wilkesboro
Journal-Patriot **(24108)** ....‡16,000

Oxford
Oxford Public Ledger **(24111)** ....‡6,500

Pembroke
The Carolina Indian Voice **(24114)** ....‡6,700

Pineville
Suburban News **(24116)** ....(Non-paid) 60,000

Pittsboro
Chatham Record **(24118)** 3,100

Plymouth
Roanoke Beacon **(24119)** ....‡4,691

Raeford
News-Journal **(24121)** ....‡4,500

Red Springs
The Red Springs Citizen **(24177)** 2,400

Robbinsville
Graham Star **(24200)** ....(Paid) ‡3,900
(Free) ‡50

Roxboro
Courier-Times **(24209)** ....‡9,000

St. Pauls
The St. Pauls Review **(24213)** ....‡3,200

Shallotte
Brunswick Beacon **(24223)** ....‡17,000

Smithfield
The Smithfield Herald **(24232)** ....(Tues.) ★15,080
(Fri.) ★15,080

Snow Hill
Snow Hill Standard-Laconic **(24234)** 3,250

Southern Pines
The Pilot **(24235)** ....(Paid) ⊕14,500

Southport
The State Port Pilot **(24239)** ....(Paid) 9,100

Sparta
The Alleghany News **(24240)** ....(Paid) ‡4,540
(Free) ‡100

Spring Hope
Spring Hope Enterprise/Bailey
News **(24244)** 3,000

Spruce Pine
Mitchell News Journal **(24245)** ....‡6,500

Statesville
County News **(24246)** ....(Paid) ‡2,500
(Free) ‡2,500

Swansboro
Tideland News **(24250)** ....(Paid) 2,500
(Free) 400

Sylva
The Sylva Herald & Ruralite **(24251)** 7,195

Tabor City
Tabor-Loris Tribune **(24253)** ....‡3,972

Taylorsville
The Taylorsville Times **(24255)** ....(Paid) ‡6,570
(Free) ‡105

Troy
Montgomery Herald **(24257)** ....‡6,700

Wadesboro
Anson Record-Messenger &
Intelligencer **(24260)** ....‡6,700

Wake Forest
Wake Weekly **(24262)** 8,500

Wallace
Pender Chronicle **(24264)** 5,418
Wallace Enterprise **(24265)** 7,500

Walnut Cove
Danbury Reporter **(24267)** 5,600

Warsaw
Warsaw-Faison News **(24271)** 5,200

Waynesville
The Enterprise **(24278)** ....(Paid) 2,000
(Free) 25
The Mountaineer **(24280)** ....(Combined) 12,231

Wendell
Wendell Clarion **(24282)** ....‡3,880

West Jefferson
The Jefferson Post **(24283)** ....(Paid) ‡6,500
(Free) ‡5,000

Whiteville
The News Reporter **(24285)** ....(Paid) ‡10,241

Williamston
The Enterprise **(24290)** ....(Paid) ⊕**4,526**
(Free) ⊕**30**
The Weekly Herald **(24291)** ....(Paid) ⊕**845**
(Free) ⊕**25**

Wilmington
The Wilmington Journal **(24297)** 9,000

Windsor
Bertie Ledger-Advance **(24316)** ....‡4,375
4,175
4,150

Winston-Salem
Winston-Salem Chronicle **(24323)** ....(Paid) 5,292
(Non-paid) 497

Yadkinville
Yadkin Ripple **(24339)** 5,800

Yanceyville
The Caswell Messenger **(24340)** ....‡4,900

Zebulon
Eastern Wake News **(24341)** 7,700

NORTH DAKOTA

Beach
Billings County Pioneer **(24343)** ....‡440
Golden Valley News **(24344)** ....(Paid) ‡1,317
(Free) ‡45

Belcourt
Turtle Mountain Times **(24345)** ....(Combined) 2,070

Beulah
Beulah Beacon **(24347)** ....(Paid) 2,398
(Free) 39

Bismarck
Oakes Times **(24358)** ....(Paid) 1,500

Bottineau
Courant **(24376)** ....‡3,900

Bowbells
Burke County Tribune **(24379)** ....‡1,500

Bowman
Bowman County Pioneer **(24380)** 1,600

Cando
Towner County Record Herald **(24383)** ....‡2,840

Casselton
Cass County Reporter **(24386)** ....(Paid) ⊕**3,106**
(Free) ⊕**50**

Cavalier
The Cavalier Chronicle **(24387)** ....‡3,100

Cooperstown
Griggs County Sentinel-Courier **(24388)** ....‡1,700

Crosby
The Journal **(24389)** 2,800

Drayton
Valley News & Views **(24403)** ....‡945

Elgin
Carson Press **(24405)** ....‡1,000
Grant County News **(24406)** ....⊕**1,700**

Ellendale
The Dickey County Leader **(24407)** ....‡1269

Enderlin
Enderlin Independent **(24410)** ....‡1,000

Finley
Steele County Press **(24437)** ....‡1,500

Fordville
Aneta Star **(24439)** ....‡375
The Express **(24441)** ....‡100
Hatton Free Press **(24442)** ....(Paid) ‡430
Larimore Leader **(24443)** ....‡125
McVille Messenger **(24444)** ....‡275
Nelson County Arena **(24445)** ....‡535

Garrison
McLean County Independent **(24448)** ....(Paid) 3,616
(Free) 59

Glen Ullin
Glen Ullin Times **(24449)** 900

Grafton
The Record **(24450)** ....‡4,000

Hankinson
Richland County News-Monitor **(24467)** ....‡1,800

Harvey
The Herald-Press **(24468)** 3,350

Hazen
Hazen Star **(24470)** ....(Paid) 2,108
(Free) 49

Hebron
Hebron Herald **(24471)** ....(Paid) ‡1,225
(Free) ‡65

Hettinger
Adams County Record **(24472)** ....‡2,000

Hillsboro
Hillsboro Banner **(24474)** ....‡1,500

Kenmare
Kenmare News **(24484)** ....‡2,100

Killdeer
Dunn County Herald **(24485)** 1,400

Kulm
The Kulm Messenger **(24486)** ....(Paid) ‡992
(Free) ‡48

La Moure
La Moure Chronicle **(24487)** ....‡1,350

Lakota
Lakota American **(24488)** 1,600

Langdon
Cavalier County Republican **(24489)** ....‡2,800

Linton
Emmons County Record **(24492)** ....‡2,900

Lisbon
Ransom County Gazette **(24493)** 2,950

Litchville
Bulletin **(24496)** ....‡1,200

McClusky
McClusky Gazette **(24502)**

Mohall
Renville County Farmer **(24520)** ....‡1,700

Napoleon
Homestead **(24521)** ....‡1,850

New England
The Herald **(24522)** ....‡1,750

New Salem
New Salem Journal **(24525)** ....‡1,500

New Town
New Town News **(24526)** ....(Paid) 1,112
(Free) 33

Northwood
Gleaner **(24527)** 1,600

Park River
Walsh County Press **(24529)** ....‡2,800

Parshall
Mountrail County Record **(24530)**

Pembina
New Era **(24531)** ....‡800

Rolla
Turtle Mountain Star **(24534)** ....(Paid) 3,400

Rugby
Pierce County Tribune **(24535)** 2,700

Stanley
Mountrail County Promoter, Inc. **(24537)** .....‡2,400

Steele
Ozone-Press **(24538)** 1,425

Tioga
Tioga Tribune **(24539)** 2,200

Towner
Mouse River Journal **(24541)** 2,000

Turtle Lake
McLean County Journal **(24542)** ....(Paid) 846
(Free) 56

Underwood
Underwood News **(24543)** ....(Paid) 662
(Free) 19

Walhalla
Walhalla Mountaineer **(24552)** 1,400

Washburn
Center Republican **(24553)** ....(Paid) 680
(Free) 18
The Leader-News **(24554)** ....(Paid) 2,500
(Non-paid) 50

Watford City
McKenzie County Farmer **(24555)** ....‡2,300

West Fargo
West Fargo Pioneer **(24557)** 3,000

Westhope
Standard **(24558)** ....‡800

Wishek
The Wishek Star **(24568)** ....‡1,450

OHIO

Ada
The Ada Herald **(24570)** ....‡2,700

Akron
The Akron Reporter **(24574)** 17,000
West Side Leader **(24593)** ....(Combined) 43,600

Andover
Pymatuning Area News **(24611)** ....(Paid) ‡2,100

Antwerp
Antwerp Bee-Argus **(24612)** ....(Paid) 1,500

Archbold
Archbold Buckeye **(24613)** ....(Paid) ⊕3,029
(Free) ⊕80
Farmland News **(24614)** 7,107

Attica
Attica Hub **(24638)** ....(Paid) ‡3,000
(Free) ‡43

Avon Lake
The Press **(24640)** ....‡10,000

Barberton
Barberton Herald **(24641)** ....‡7,900

Barnesville
Barnesville Enterprise **(24642)** 4,825

Batavia
The Clermont Sun **(24643)** 3,800

Bay Village
Lorain County Times **(24645)**

Beachwood
Cleveland Jewish News **(24651)** ....(Paid) 16,000
The Sun Messenger **(24658)** ....(Paid) 13,625
The Sun Press **(24659)** ....(Paid) 19,901

Bedford
Bedford Sun Banner **(24660)** ....(Paid) 5,007
Bedford Times-Register **(24661)** ....‡3,674

Bellville
The Bellville Star & Tri Forks
Press **(24673)** 2,000

Berea
The News Sun **(24678)** ....(Paid) 16,271

Bloomville
Bloomville Gazette **(24681)** ....(Paid) ‡340
(Free) ‡14

Bluffton
Bluffton News **(24682)** 2,900

Boardman
Boardman News **(24684)** ....‡9,000

Brecksville
The Sun Courier **(24706)** ....(Paid) 7,235

Brooklyn
Brooklyn Sun Journal **(24711)** ....(Paid) 6,889

Brookville
Star **(24712)** ....(Paid) 300
(Free) 6,000

Brunswick
Brunswick Sun Times **(24713)** ....(Paid) 6,167

Cadiz
Harrison News Herald **(24722)** ....‡6,400

Caldwell
Journal & Noble County Leader **(24723)** ......‡5,000

Cambridge
The New Concord Area Leader **(24726)** ......‡1,250

Canton
Stark Jewish News **(24732)** ....(Controlled) 2,000

Carey
The Progressor-Times **(24741)** ....(Combined) ‡4,000

Carrollton
The Free Press-Standard **(24742)** ....⊕**7,414**

Centerville
The Centerville-Bellbrook
Times **(24753)** ....(Wed.) 21,766
(Sat.) 2,548

Chagrin Falls
Chagrin Herald Sun **(24755)** ....(Paid) 17,889
The Chagrin Valley Times **(24756)** .....(Paid) ‡14,000
(Free) 4,000

Cincinnati
Cincinnati CityBeat **(24784)** ....(Free) 40,287
(Paid) 25
The Cincinnati Herald **(24786)** ....(Paid) ‡24,500
Valley Courier **(24825)** ....(Paid) ‡3,000
(Free) ‡200

Cleveland
Call and Post **(24865)** ....‡43,283
Gay People's
Chronicle **(24902)** ....(Controlled) 15,000
Homeless Grapevine **(24908)** ....(Paid) 10,000
The Montrose Sun **(24928)** .....(Combined) ‡22,741
The Sun **(24954)** ....(Combined) ★**3,409**
West Akron Sun **(24963)** ......(Combined) ‡22,741
West Geauga Sun **(24964)** ....(Paid) 17,164

Cleveland Heights
Mid-America Boating **(24994)** .....(Combined) 30,084

Clyde
The Clyde Enterprise **(24996)** 1,700

Coldwater
Mercer County Chronicle **(24997)** ......(Paid) ‡2,400

Columbus
The Times **(25066)** 10,835

Columbus Grove
Putnam County Vidette/Pandora
Times **(25091)** ....‡1,400

Continental
News-Review **(25094)** 1,050

Crestline
The Crestline Advocate **(25101)** ....(Paid) ‡2,200

Dalton
The Dalton Gazette & Kidron
News **(25105)** ....‡1,385
1,495

Delta
The Delta Atlas **(25164)** ....(Paid) ‡2,000
(Non-paid) ‡200

Dresden
Dresden Transcript **(25167)** 5,800

Eaton
Eaton Register-Herald **(25174)** 6,800

Edgerton
The Edgerton Earth **(25176)** ....‡1,475

Edon
The Edon Commercial **(25177)** ....(Paid) 850
(Free) 150

Euclid
Euclid Sun Journal **(25184)** ....(Paid) 14,401
Sun Scoop Journal **(25185)** ....(Paid) 14,401

Circulation: ★ = ABC; △ = BPA; ♦ = CAC; ● = CCAB; ❑ = VAC; ⊕ = PO Statement; ‡ = Publisher's Report; Boldface figures = sworn; Light figures = estimated.

2915

Newspapers

Circ.   Circ.   Circ.

OHIO (continued)

Forest Hills
Forest Hills Journal-Press (25199) ....(Paid) 7,923
(Non-paid) 5,276

Fredericktown
The Knox County Citizen (25201) 1,400

Georgetown
The News Democrat (25216) ....(Paid) 4,500
(Free) 200

Germantown
The Germantown Press (25218) 2,700

Granville
Community Booster (25220) ....(Non-paid) 28,000
Granville Sentinel (25223) ....(Controlled) 2,200

Grove City
Grove City Record (25233) ....(Paid) ‡3,587

Harrison
Harrison Press (25238) ....(Paid) 5,509
(Non-paid) 40
(Paid) ⊕5,875
(Non-paid) ⊕41

Hartville
The Hartville News (25239) ....(Paid) ⊕2,736
(Free) ⊕27

Heath
Ace News (25240) ....(Paid) ‡5,000
(Free) ‡1,000

Hicksville
The News Tribune (25241) ....(Paid) 2,450
(Non-paid) 50

Hillsboro
Press-Gazette (25243) ....(Paid) ‡6,500

Huber Heights
Huber Heights Courier (25249) 11,250

Jackson
Times Journal (25257) ....(Tues.) 5,325
(Thurs.) 5,325
(Sun.) 5,492

Jefferson
The Courier (Conneaut) (25261) ....(Paid) 2,800
The Gazette (25262) ....(Paid) ‡4,200
The Lake County
Gazette (25263) ....(Combined) 12,000
The Sentinel (25265) ....(Free) ‡13,000
The Tribune (25266) ....(Paid) 4,500
The Valley News (25267) ....(Paid) ‡1,365
(Free) ‡35

Johnstown
Johnstown Independent (25271) ....(Paid) 2,128

Kettering
Kettering-Oakwood Times (25284) .....(Wed.) 28,867
(Sat.) 2,144

Lakewood
Lakewood Sun Post (25287) ....(Paid) 9,592

Lebanon
Western Star (25295) ....(Paid) 7,000
(Free) 245

Liberty Center
The Liberty Press (25296) ....(Paid) ‡1,300
(Free) ‡173

Louisville
The Louisville Herald (25319) ....(Paid) ‡3,100

Loveland
The Bethel Journal (25321) ....(Combined) 1,691
Community Journal (North) (25323) ......(Paid) 1,771
(Non-paid) 5,116

Malvern
The News Leader (25328) ....‡4,400

Manchester
The Manchester Signal (25329) ....(Paid) ‡3,500

Maple Heights
Garfield-Maple Sun (25342) ....(Paid) 8,369

McConnelsville
Morgan County Herald (25369) ....‡4,582

Mechanicsburg
Mechanicsburg Telegram (25371) ....(Paid) ‡750

Medina
The Medina Sun (25374) ....(Thurs.) 11,777

Miamisburg
Miamisburg/West Carrollton News (25375)

Milford
Milford Advertiser-Press (25384) ....(Non-paid) 4,282
(Paid) 4,108

Millersburg
Holmes County Hub (25388) ....‡4,500

Minerva
The News Leader (25392) ....‡4,400
West Virginia Hillbilly (25393) ....(Paid) 4,500
(Free) 500

Minster
Community Post (25394) ....(Paid) 2,250

Montpelier
The Leader-Enterprise (25395) ....‡1,800

New Carlisle
New Carlisle Sun (25408) ....(Paid) 2,700

New Lexington
Perry County Tribune (25414) ....‡4,400

New London
Firelands Farmer (25417) ....‡5,870
New London Record (25419) ....‡2,200

New Philadelphia
The National Hobby News (25420)

New Washington
New Washington Herald (25423) ....‡1,516

Newcomerstown
The Newcomerstown News (25431) ....‡3,500

North Baltimore
The North Baltimore News (25432) ....‡1,300

North Olmsted
The Sun Herald (25438) ....(Paid) 15,905
West Side Sun News (25439) ....(Paid) 15,434

Northfield
Nordonia Hills Sun (25440) ....(Combined) 2,854

Oak Harbor
The Ottawa County Exponent (25442) 3,000

Oberlin
News-Tribune (25446) ....‡2,680

Ontario
Tribune-Courier (25451) ....(Paid) ⊕2,085
(Free) ⊕150

Ottawa
Putnam County Sentinel (25452) ....‡8,800

Oxford
The Oxford Press (25458) ....‡4,400

Parma
Parma Sun Post (25467) ....(Paid) 24,103

Pataskala
Pataskala Standard (25470) ....(Paid) 5,000
(Free) 12

Paulding
Paulding Progress (25471) ....‡4,300

Perrysburg
Perrysburg Messenger
Journal (25475) ....(Paid) 5,600
(Free) ‡7,500

Plain City
Plain City Advocate (25479) ....(Paid) ‡1,900

Richwood
The Richwood Gazette (25496) ....‡2,800

Ripley
The Ripley Bee (25498) ....‡2,000

Roaming Shores
Shores News (25500) ....(Paid) ‡1,129
(Non-paid) ‡200

Rocky River
Westlaker Times (25502)

Rossford
Rossford Record Journal (25503) ....‡1,800

Sandusky
The North Ridgeville Press & Light (25508) 7,000

Sidney
Enon Messenger (25517)

Solon
Solon Herald Sun (25527) ....(Paid) 17,889
The Solon Times (25528) ....‡6,000

Spencerville
The Journal-News (25530) ....‡2,035

Springboro
The Star Press (25531) ....(Paid) 2,744
(Free) 9,321

Stow
Stow Sentry (25547) ....(Paid) ‡14,182

Strongsville
The Sun Star (25550) ....(Paid) 12,432

Struthers
The Journal (25551) ....‡4,000

Sunbury
News (25552) ....‡3,250

Swanton
The Swanton
Enterprise (25553) ....(Combined) ‡10,000

Sylvania
Sylvania Herald (25554) 3,500
Toledo Herald (25555) ....(Paid) 316
(Non-paid) 33,000
Toledo Jewish News (25556) ......(Controlled) 3,000

Tipp City
Troy Advocate (25562)
West Milton Record (25563) ....(Paid) ‡1,716
(Free) ‡150

Toledo
La Prensa Nacional (25568) ....(Paid) 6,000
Maumee Valley Herald (25569) ....(Paid) 1,500
The Toledo Journal (25570) 19,000

Troy
Miami Valley Sunday
News (25596) ....(Sun.) ★10,465

Twinsburg
The Twinsburg Sun (25599) ....(Combined) 2,854

Urbana
Star Republican (25606) ....(Paid) ‡200
(Free) ‡21,400

Utica
The Utica Herald (25608) 2,100

Vandalia
Vandalia Drummer News (25611) ....‡5,200

Vermilion
Vermilion Photo Journal (25612) 6,500

Versailles
The Versailles Policy (25613) ....‡2,200

Wadsworth
Sun Banner Pride (25614) ....(Paid) 3,578

Warren
The Times (25616) ....(Free) ‡7,700

Waynesburg
Press-News (25627) ....‡3,000

Wellington
Wellington Enterprise (25628) ....‡2,800

West Alexandria
Twin Valley News & Advisor (25631) ....(Paid) ‡600
(Free) ‡8,000

West Unity
Advance-Reporter (25635)

Westlake
West Life (25649) ....‡15,200

Wheelersburg
The Scioto Voice (25650) ....(Paid) ⊕2,168
(Free) ⊕165

Willard
Willard Times Junction (25654) ....(Paid) ⊕4,200

Woodsfield
Monroe County Beacon (25670) ....‡4,900

Worthington
Rocky Fork
Enterprise (25681) ....(Combined) 12,211

Yellow Springs
Yellow Springs News (25692) ....(Paid) ‡1,800
(Free) ‡50

Youngstown
The Buckeye Review (25694) ....(Paid) ‡5,000
(Free) ‡100

OKLAHOMA

Allen
Advocate (25729) 1,300

Antlers
Antlers American (25743) 3,000

Apache
Apache News (25744) ....(Paid) ‡1,200
(Free) ‡20

Arnett
Ellis County Capital (25750) ....(Paid) ⊕1,100
(Free) ⊕35
The Gage Record (25751) ....(Paid) ⊕390
(Free) ⊕15

Barnsdall
Barnsdall Times (25753) 1,400

Beaver
The Herald-Democrat (25757) ....‡2,000

Bethany
The Tribune (25761) 3,500

Bixby
Bixby Bulletin (25763) ....(Paid) ‡2,197

Boise City
The Boise City News (25766) ....(Paid) 1,800
(Free) 60

Bristow
The Bristow News (25767) ....‡3,225
The Record-Citizen (25768) ....‡3,125

Broken Arrow
The Ledger (25771) ....(Paid) ‡3,812
(Free) 30,500

Broken Bow
Broken Bow News (25774)

Buffalo
Harper County Journal (25777) ....(Paid) 1,200
(Free) 400

Canton
The Canton Times (25778) 800

Carnegie
Carnegie Herald (25779) ....‡1,795

Chandler
The Lincoln County News (25780) .....(Paid) ‡3,899
(Free) ‡134

Checotah
McIntosh County Democrat (25781) ....(Paid) ‡2,995
(Free) ‡205

Chelsea
Chelsea Reporter (25782) ....‡1,889

Cherokee
Cherokee Messenger &
 Republican (25783) ....‡2,450

Cheyenne
Cheyenne Star (25784) ....‡2,100

Coalgate
Coalgate Record-Register (25793) 2,192

Corn
Washita County Enterprise (25794) ....‡1,000

Covington
Covington Record (25795) ....‡850

Davenport
The New Era (25797) ....‡1200

Durant
The Honey Grove
 Signal-Citizen (25806) ....(Paid) 1,637
(Free) 45

Eufaula
Indian Journal (25829) ....‡3,600
⊕503

Fairfax
Fairfax Chief (25831) ....(Paid) 1,550
(Free) 50

Fairview
Fairview Republican (25833) ....‡3,341

Fletcher
Fletcher Herald (25835) 1,000

Frederick
The Frederick Press (25840) ....‡3,000

Garber
Garber-Billings News (25842) ....(Paid) ‡678
(Free) ‡177

Geary
Star (25843) ....(Paid) ‡865
(Free) ‡150

Grandfield
Big Pasture News (25845) ....(Paid) ‡700

Grove
Grove Sun (25847) ....(Paid) 6,271
The South Grand
 Laker (25849) ....(Combined) 2,260

Hartshorne
Hartshorne Sun (25858) ....‡1,671

Haskell
Haskell News (25859) ....‡2,100

Healdton
The Healdton Herald (25860) ....(Paid) ‡1,461
(Free) ‡12

Heavener
The Heavener Ledger (25861) ....‡3,600

Hennessey
Clipper (25862) 800

Henryetta
Henryetta Daily
 Free-Lance (25863) ....(Controlled) ‡2,212

Hinton
Hinton Record (25864) ....(Paid) 950

Hobart
Hobart Democrat-Chief (25865) ....‡3,200

Hominy
News Progress (25870) ....(Paid) 1,445
(Non-paid) 35

Jay
Delaware County Journal (25878) ....(Paid) 1,800
3,000

Kingfisher
Kingfisher Times and Free Press (25879) .....‡3,800

Konawa
Konawa Leader (25880) 1,200

Laverne
Leader Tribune (25883) ....‡1,650

Lawton
Cache Times Weekly (25884) ....‡1,108

Lindsay
Lindsay News (25899) ....(Paid) ⊕2,500

Madill
The Madill Record (25902) ....(Paid) 4,448
(Free) 100

Marietta
Monitor (25904) 3,550

Marlow
Marlow Review (25905) ....‡3,400

Maysville
The Maysville News (25908) ....(Paid) 1,100
(Free) 25

McLoud
The McLoud News (25914) ....(Combined) 1,374

Medford
Medford Patriot-Star and Grant County
 Journal (25915) ....(Paid) ⊕1,500

Meeker
The Meeker News (25916) ....‡1,400

Newcastle
The Newcastle Pacer (25929) ....‡1,400

Newkirk
Newkirk Herald-Journal (25930) ....(Paid) ‡1,510
(Free) ‡200

Nichols Hills
Friday (25931) ....(Paid) 8,290

Nowata
Nowata Star (25949) ....‡2,700

Okarche
Okarche Chieftain (25950) 700

Okeene
The Okeene Record (25951) ....‡1,300

Okemah
Okemah News Leader (25952) ....‡3,000

Oklahoma City
The Black Chronicle (25955) ....(Paid) ‡28,927
The Harrah News (25965) ....‡2,600
The Oklahoma Observer (25983) ....‡7,500

Oologah
Oologah Lake Leader (26027) ....(Paid) ‡2,857

Owasso
Owasso Reporter (26028) ....‡7,500

Pawhuska
Pawhuska Journal-Capital (26030) 2,000

Pawnee
The Pawnee Chief (Division of American-Chief
 Co.) (26031) ....‡3,001

Picher
Tri-State Tribune (26034) ....‡2,607

Piedmont
Piedmont-Surrey Gazette (26035) 1,200

Prague
The Prague Times-Herald (26048) ....‡2,450

Purcell
Purcell Register (26050) ....(Paid) 4,746
(Free) 25

Ringling
The Ringling Eagle (26051) ....‡1171

Ryan
The Ryan Leader (26052) ....(Paid) ‡560
(Free) ‡20

Sallisaw
Sequoyah County Times (26053) ....‡7,000

Sand Springs
Sand Springs Leader (26054) ....(Paid) 4,500
(Non-paid) 5,500

Sentinel
Sentinel Leader (26059) 1,350

Shattuck
Northwest Oklahoman and Ellis County
 News (26060) ....‡1,491

Shawnee
The County Democrat Publishing
 Co. (26061) ....‡230

Shidler
The Review (26071) ....‡1,100

Skiatook
Skiatook Journal (26072) ....(Paid) ‡2,373

Snyder
Kiowa County Democrat (26073) ....‡1,475

Stigler
News-Sentinel (26075) ....‡3,906

Stilwell
Democrat-Journal (26088) ....‡6,500

Stroud
Stroud American (26089) ....‡2,500

Sulphur
Times-Democrat (26090) 3,900

Tahlequah
The Tahlequah Times Journal (26095)

Talihina
Talihina American (26098) ....‡2,074

Tecumseh
Countywide News (26099) ....⊕1,783

Tishomingo
Johnston County Capital
 Democrat (26100) ....‡3,150

Tonkawa
Tonkawa News (26102) ....‡1,900

Circulation: ★ = ABC; △ = BPA; ♦ = CAC; ● = CCAB; ❏ = VAC; ⊕ = PO Statement; ‡ = Publisher's Report; Boldface figures = sworn; Light figures = estimated.

Newspapers

2917

Circ.

OKLAHOMA (continued)

Tulsa
The Oklahoma Eagle (26122) ....‡12,800
Tulsa County News (26135) ....(Paid) ‡1,177
Urban Tulsa (26140) ....(Free) 30,000

Wagoner
Wagoner Tribune (26178) ....‡3,800

Wakita
The Wakita Herald (26179) ....‡650

Walters
Walters Herald (26180) ....‡3,150

Waukomis
The Oklahoma Hornet (26182) ....(Paid) ‡500
(Free) ‡40

Waurika
Waurika News-Democrat (26183) ....‡1,600

Waynoka
Woods County Enterprise (26184) ......(Paid) ‡1,000
(Free) ‡34

Weleetka
The Weleetkan (26190) 1,000

Westville
The Westville Reporter (26192) ....(Paid) 2,600

Wetumka
Hughes County Times (26193) 2,650

Wilburton
Latimer County News-Tribune (26195) ....‡3,400
Latimer County Today (26196) ....‡5,026

Wilson
The Wilson Post-Democrat (26197) ....‡617

Wynnewood
Wynnewood Gazette (26202) 1,700

Yukon
Review (26205)

OREGON
Baker City
The Record-Courier (26233) ....‡3,950

Bandon
Western World (26236) ....(Paid) ⊕2,414
(Free) ⊕32

Brookings
Curry Coastal Pilot (26255) ....‡7,150

Brownsville
Times (26258) 1,800

Burns
Burns Times-Herald (26259) ....‡3,000

Cave Junction
Illinois Valley News (26264) ....‡3,500

Clatskanie
Clatskanie Chief (26268) ....(Paid) 2000

Condon
The Times-Journal (26270) ....‡1,680

Coquille
Coquille Valley Sentinel (26281) ....(Paid) ‡2,200
(Free) ‡2,495

Creswell
Country Mile Media, Inc. (26297) ....‡3,700

Dallas
Polk County Itemizer Observer (26300) ....‡6,800

Dayton
The Dayton Tribune (26305) ....‡424

Drain
The Drain Enterprise (26306) ....‡1,300

Eagle Point
Upper Rogue Independent (26307) .....(Paid) ‡2,000
(Free) ‡11,000

Enterprise
Wallowa County Chieftain (26310) 4,196

Estacada
Clackamas County News (26313) ....‡2,400

Eugene
Northwest Comic
News (26325) ....(Controlled) 20,000

Circ.

Florence
The Siuslaw News (26353) 6,913

Forest Grove
News-Times (26355) ....(Paid) ‡5,600

Gold Beach
Curry County Reporter (26360) ....(Wed.) 3,036

Gresham
The Gresham Outlook (26365) ....(Paid) 9,780
(Free) 1,050

Heppner
Gazette-Times (26367) ....‡1,850

Hermiston
The Hermiston Herald (26369) ....(Paid) 4,100
(Free) 6,900

Hillsboro
Hillsboro Argus (26372) ....‡16,075

John Day
Blue Mountain Eagle (26378) 4,000

Junction City
Tri-County News (26379) 2,700

Keizer
Keizertimes (26380) 3,400

Lake Oswego
Lake Oswego Review (26404) ....(Paid) ‡8,478

Lincoln City
The News Guard (26411) ....(Paid) ‡5,648
(Free) ‡173

Madras
The Madras Pioneer (26412) ....(Paid) 3,800
(Free) 75

McKenzie Bridge
McKenzie River Reflections (26413) ....(Paid) 922

McMinnville
The Linfield Review (26414) ....(Combined) 1,500
News-Register (26415) ....‡9,000
News-Register (26416) 4,096

Merrill
Lost River Star (26434)

Milton-Freewater
Milton-Freewater Valley Times (26435)

Myrtle Point
Myrtle Point Herald (26442) ....(Paid) ‡2,100
(Free) ‡100

Newberg
The Newberg Graphic (26444) ....‡5,500

Newport
News-Times (26445) ....‡10,500

Oakridge
Dead Mountain Echo (26452) ....‡1,200

Pendleton
The Pendleton Record (26460) ....‡1,050

Port Orford
Port Orford News (26465) ....‡1,250

Portland
Cascadia Times (26472)
The Community Ear (26474) ....(Paid) 10,000
Portland Alliance (26500) ....(Combined) 7,000
The Portland Skanner (26502) ....(Paid) ‡20,000

Prineville
Central Oregonian (26548) ....‡4,342

Redmond
The Redmond Spokesman (26552) .....(Paid) ‡5,010
(Free) ‡40

Reedsport
The Courier (26553) ....‡2,800

St. Helens
Chronicle/Sentinel-Mist (26563) ....(Paid) ‡6,200
(Free) 11,700

Salem
Oregon Peaceworker (26570) .....(Controlled) 17,000
West Side (26574) ....‡8,000

Scappoose
The South County Spotlight (26578) .....(Paid) 4,370

Seaside
Seaside Signal (26580) ....‡3,000

Circ.

Sheridan
The Sun (26582) ....(Paid) ‡2,500

Silverton
Appeal Tribune/Mt. Angel
News (26584) ....(Combined) 7,700

Springfield
The Springfield News (26586) ....(Paid) 11,200

Sutherlin
The Sun-Tribune (26591) ....(Paid) 900
(Free) 100

Sweet Home
New Era (26593) ....‡3,000

Tillamook
Headlight-Herald (26597) ....⊕8,229

Umpqua
Umpqua Free Press (26601) 3,000

Vale
Malheur Enterprise (26602) ....(Paid) ‡2,350
(Free) ‡40

Veneta
West-Lane News (26605) ....‡2,000

Warrenton
The Columbia Press (26610) ....‡1,500

Wilsonville
The Canby Herald (26613) ....(Paid) ‡5,680

Woodburn
Woodburn Independent (26619) 5,000

PENNSYLVANIA
Albion
Albion News (26623) ....(Paid) 3,850

Allentown
East Penn Press (26627) ....(Paid) ‡5,023
(Free) ‡815

Ardmore
Main Line Life (26661) ....(Combined) 12,158
Main Line Times (26662) ....(Thurs.) 11,433

Aspinwall
The Herald (26666) ....(Paid) 5,944
(Free) 50

Bath
Home News (26683) ....(Paid) ‡4,500
(Free) ‡85

Bedford
Inquirer (26689) ....‡585

Blairsville
Dispatch (26714) ....(Paid) ♦1,735
(Non-paid) ♦20,106

Boyertown
The Boyertown Area Times (26726) .....(Paid) 6,217
(Free) 285

Brookville
Tri-County Sunday (26733) ....(Paid) ‡5,011

Canton
Independent-Sentinel (26755) ....‡2,300

Carbondale
Carbondale News (26756) ....‡6,300

Clarion
Clarion News (26780) ....(Paid) 6,900
(Free) 200

Clarks Summit
Abington Journal (26785) ....(Paid) 3,820
(Free) 178

Claysville
Weekly Recorder (26787) 3,500

Cochranton
Conneautville Courier (26795) ....‡1,200

Collegeville
Independent and Montgomery
Transcript (26797) ....‡4,300

Conshohocken
The Coshohocken
Recorder (26803) ....(Paid) ‡8,000
(Free) ‡300

2918

Numbers cited after listings are entry numbers rather than page numbers.

Coudersport
The Potter Leader
  Enterprise **(26811)** ....(Paid) ‡9,800
                                    (Free) ‡225

Dallas
The Dallas Post **(26816)** ....⊕2,917

Delta
Star **(26822)** ....‡3,995

Dillsburg
Dillsburg Banner **(26826)** ....(Paid) 3,500
                                    (Non-paid) 500

Drexel Hill
Marcus Hook Press **(26835)** ....‡3,500
Upper Darby Press **(26836)** ....‡4,100

Du Bois
Courier Express **(26837)** ....(Mon.-Fri.) ★10,491
                                    (Sun.) ★15,582

Duncannon
Duncannon Record **(26842)** ....‡2,600

Dushore
Sullivan Review **(26844)** ....(Paid) 6,974
                                    (Free) 61

Ebensburg
The Cresson/Gallitzin Mainliner **(26855)** 3,425
The Ebensburg News Leader **(26856)** 2,110
The Mountaineer-Herald **(26857)** 3,200
The Nanty Glo Journal **(26858)** 3,088

Edinboro
Heartland **(26861)** ....(Combined) 25,000
The Independent-Enterprise **(26862)** .....(Free) 5,934
                                    (Paid) 2,311

Elizabethtown
Elizabethtown Chronicle **(26865)** ....(Paid) ‡3,200

Ephrata
The Ephrata Review **(26887)** ....‡9,246
Lancaster Farming **(26888)** ....(Paid) ⊕51,000
                                    (Free) ⊕1,000

Folsom
Ridley Press **(26921)** ....⊕7,000

Forest City
The Forest City News **(26923)** ....(Paid) ‡3,021
                                    (Free) ‡166

Fort Washington
Ambler Gazette **(26924)** ....(Combined) 11,255

Girard
Cosmopolite Herald **(26943)** ....(Paid) ‡2,589
                                    (Free) ‡5,722

Glen Mills
Garnet Valley Press **(26945)** ....(Controlled) 2,500

Greencastle
Echo-Pilot **(26949)** 2,500

Hamburg
Item **(26971)** ....(Mon.-Sat.) ★5,083
                                    (Sun.) ★27,463

Hatboro
Hatboro Progress **(27027)** 17,500

Hawley
The News Eagle **(27032)** ....(Paid) ⊕7,169
                                    (Free) ⊕203

Hershey
Hershey Chronicle **(27041)** 7,700

Hummelstown
The Sun **(27066)** ....(Paid) 6,352
                                    (Free) 722

Johnsonburg
The Johnsonburg Press **(27085)** ....(Paid) ‡2,200

Kennett Square
The Kennett Paper **(27106)**

Kutztown
The Patriot **(27130)** ....‡6,100

Lancaster
Lancaster Sunday News **(27144)** ......(Sun.) 102,457

Leechburg
Apollo News-Record **(27180)** ....‡2,600
Leechburg Advance **(27181)** ....(Paid) ‡1,313
                                    (Non-paid) ‡15

Lititz
Lititz Record-Express **(27203)** ....(Paid) ‡6,910
                                    (Free) ‡190

Martinsburg
Morrisons Cove Herald **(27222)** ....(Paid) 6,500
                                    (Free) 125

Mc Kees Rocks
Suburban Gazette **(27227)** ....‡8,300

McConnellsburg
Fulton County News **(27230)** ....‡6,820

Meyersdale
The New Republic **(27248)** ....‡5,000

Middleburg
Snyder County
  Times **(27249)** ....(Combined) ‡25,000

Middletown
Press & Journal **(27260)** ....‡9,900

Mifflinburg
Mifflinburg Telegraph **(27262)** ....(Paid) 650

Mifflintown
Juniata Sentinel **(27263)** ....‡7,900

Millersburg
Upper Dauphin Sentinel **(27265)** ....(Paid) 9,129
                                    (Free) 2,000

Monroeville
Advance Leader Star **(27274)** ....(Paid) ‡4,708
                                    (Free) ‡170

Coraopolis Record
  Star **(27276)** ....(Combined) 1,389
Cranberry Star **(27277)** ....(Paid) 322
                                    (Non-paid) 12,555
Moon Record Star **(27278)** ....(Paid) 1,790
                                    (Non-paid) 98
Murrysville Star **(27279)** ....(Paid) 774
                                    (Non-paid) 3,539
Oakmont Advance
  Leader **(27281)** ....(Combined) 1,578
Penn Hills Progress Star **(27282)** ....(Paid) 2,777
                                    (Non-paid) 166
Plum Advance Leader
  Star **(27283)** ....(Combined) 4,612
The Progress Star **(27284)** ....(Paid) ‡5,367
                                    (Free) ‡325
Sewickley Herald Star **(27285)** .....(Combined) 2,922
Signal Item Star **(27286)** ....(Combined) 2,471
Times-Express Star **(27287)** ....(Paid) 4,370
                                    (Non-paid) 221

Montrose
Susquehanna County
  Independent **(27292)** ....(Paid) 4,000
                                    (Free) 300

Moon
The Record Star **(27295)** ....(Paid) 4,047
                                    (Non-paid) 401

Moscow
Villager **(27297)** ....‡5,000

Mount Jewett
Bradford
  Journal/Miner **(27298)** ....(Combined) 14,000

Mount Pleasant
The Mount Pleasant Journal **(27301)** ....⊕5,492

Mountain Top
Mountaintop Eagle **(27304)** ....(Paid) ⊕2,708
                                    (Free) ⊕33

Muncy
The Luminary **(27306)** 1,500

Murrysville
Penn Franklin News **(27307)** 6,500

New Bethlehem
The Leader-Vindicator **(27312)** 5,400

New Bloomfield
Perry County Times **(27313)** ....‡5,300

New Hope
New Hope Gazette **(27320)** ....‡4,000

New Wilmington
Globe **(27323)**

Newtown
The Advance of Bucks County **(27327)** ....‡6,000

Newtown Square
County Press **(27328)** ....(Paid) ‡5,031
                                    (Free) ‡533
Haverford Press **(27329)** ....(Paid) ‡2,340
                                    (Non-paid) ‡206
Upper Darby and Drexel Hill
  Press **(27334)** ....(Paid) ‡1,516
                                    (Non-paid) ‡113

North East
North East Breeze **(27340)** ....(Paid) ‡2,628
                                    (Free) ‡4,977

Northern Cambria
The Star Courier **(27344)**
Star Courier **(27345)** ....‡4,500

Oxford
Chester County Press **(27348)** ....‡15,438

Paoli
Suburban Advertiser **(27350)** ....(Paid) ◆4
                                    (Non-paid) ◆16,446

Perkasie
Perkasie News-Herald **(27352)**

Philadelphia
In Pittsburgh
  Newsweekly **(27490)** ....(Non-paid) 71,821
The Philadelphia Tribune **(27633)** .....(Tues.) 13,196
                                    (Fri.) 9,269

Pine Grove
The Press Herald **(27752)** ....‡3,795

Pittsburgh
The Herald **(27796)** ....(Paid) 6,090
                                    (Free) 779
New Pittsburgh Courier **(27821)** ....‡30,000
South Hills Record **(27845)** ....(Paid) 4,394
                                    (Non-paid) 354

Pittston
Sunday Dispatch **(27885)** 8,5000

Port Allegany
Port Allegany
  Reporter-Argus **(27897)** ....(Paid) ‡2,295
                                    (Free) ‡305

Portage
The Portage Dispatch **(27898)** 5,272

Punxsutawney
County Neighbors **(27908)** ....‡5,000

Quakertown
The Free Press **(27914)** ....(Wed.) 3,440

Red Hill
The Hearthstone Town and
  Country **(27926)** ....(Paid) 5,175

Renovo
The Record **(27931)** 2,750

Saxton
Broad Top Bulletin **(27944)** ....‡3,250

Schuylkill Haven
The Call **(27951)** ....(Paid) 4,047

Scottdale
The Independent-Observer **(27952)** ....⊕3,470
The Ligonier Echo **(27953)** ....‡4,692

Scranton
Narodna Volya Ukrainian **(27960)** ......(Paid) ‡3,000
                                    (Free) ‡200
Triboro Banner **(27964)** ....‡5,500

Shippensburg
The News-Chronicle **(27989)** ....‡6,200
Valley Times-Star **(27991)** ....‡3,500

Souderton
News-Herald **(28004)** ....(Combined) 8,263
Souderton Independent **(28005)** ....(Combined) 8,592

Springfield
Springfield Press **(28012)** ....‡6,360

State College
Voices of Central
  Pennsylvania **(28022)** ....(Non-paid) ‡10,000

Strasburg
Strasburg Weekly News **(28034)** ....(Paid) ‡782
                                    (Free) ‡84

Susquehanna
County Transcript **(28041)** ....‡13,000

Newspapers

Circulation: ★ = ABC; △ = BPA; ◆ = CAC; ◆ = CCAB; ❑ = VAC; ⊕ = PO Statement; ‡ = Publisher's Report; Boldface figures = sworn; Light figures = estimated.

2919

Circ.

Circ.

Circ.

PENNSYLVANIA (continued)

Swarthmore
The Swarthmorean (28046) ....‡2,010

Tionesta
The Forest Press (28049) ....‡4,800

Tower City
West Schuylkill Herald (28054) ....‡2,000

Troy
Troy Gazette Register (28058) ....‡1,250

Tunkhannock
The New Age-Examiner (28062) ....(Paid) 3,720
(Free) 35

Union City
Times-Leader (28066) ....(Paid) ‡3,030
(Free) ‡7,170

Valley View
Citizen-Standard (28093) 4,500

Vandergrift
The Vandergrift News (28095) ....‡2,856

Wayne
The Suburban (28136) ....(Thurs.) 8,463

West Newton
The Times Sun (28151) 3,268

White Haven
The Journal Herald (28155) ....(Paid) ‡1,298
Journal of the Pocono
Plateau (28156) ....(Controlled) 14,000
Journal Valley News (28157) ......(Controlled) 6,500

Williamsport
Williamsport
Sun-Gazette (28182) ....(Mon.-Sat.) ★27,916
(Sun.) ★35,936

Yardley
Yardley News (28202) ....‡5,500

Yeadon
Yeadon Times (28204) ....‡2,500

York
York Sunday News (28210)

PUERTO RICO
Hato Rey
La Estrella De Puerto
Rico (28248) ....(Combined) 123,300

RHODE ISLAND
Barrington
Barrington Times (28324) ....(Paid) ♦4,988
(Non-paid) ♦110

Bristol
Bristol Phoenix (28326) ....(Paid) ♦5,828
(Non-paid) ♦150
Sakonnet Times (28327) ....(Paid) ♦6,486
(Non-paid) ♦431

Cranston
Cranston Herald (28332) ....(Paid) ♦2,651
(Non-paid) ♦80
The Cranston Mirror (28333) 9,970

East Greenwich
The East Greenwich Pendulum
Times (28340) ....(Paid) ♦2,675
(Non-paid) ♦27

East Providence
East Providence Post (28344) 10,000

Greenville
North Providence North
Star (28355) ....(Non-paid) ♦192
(Paid) ♦743
The Observer (28356) ....(Paid) ♦4,271
(Non-paid) ♦351

Jamestown
Rhode Island Senior Times (28357) .....(Paid) 2,100
(Non-paid) 32,900

Newport
Newport Mercury (28370) ....‡1,471

North Kingstown
The Standard Times (28376) ......(Combined) 5,657

Providence
The Providence
Journal (28415) ....(Mon.-Sat.) 160,610
(Sun.) 229,271
Rhode Island Herald (28422) ....(Paid) ‡5,600
(Non-paid) ‡20,000

Wakefield
The Coventry Courier (28444) ....(Paid) ♦1,077
(Non-paid) ♦28
The Narragansett Times (28445) ......(Paid) ♦5,761
(Non-paid) ♦120
North-East Independent (28446) ......(Paid) ♦2,576
(Non-paid) ♦15
South County
Independent (28447) ....(Combined) ♦4,741

Warren
Warren Times-Gazette (28448) ....(Paid) ♦2,861
(Non-paid) ♦121

Warwick
Warwick Beacon (28453) ....(Paid) ♦8,489
(Non-paid) ♦172

Wyoming
The Chariho Times (28463) ....(Paid) ♦2,124
(Non-paid) ♦57

SOUTH CAROLINA
Abbeville
The Press and Banner (28464) ....‡5,400

Aynor
Aynor Journal (28478) ....(Combined) 2,000

Bamberg
Advertiser-Herald (28479) ....(Paid) ⊕2,504
(Non-paid) ⊕496
North Trade Journal (28480) ....(Paid) ⊕905
(Non-paid) ⊕395
The Santee Striper (28481) 1,500

Barnwell
People-Sentinel (28482) ....‡6,000

Batesburg-Leesville
The Twin-City News (28485) ....‡4,800

Belton
The News Chronicle (28492) ....‡4400

Bennettsville
Malboro Herald-Advocate (28493) ....‡6,800

Bishopville
Lee County Observer (28494) ....‡4,000

Blacksburg
Blacksburg Times (28496) ....‡1,990

Camden
Chronicle-Independent (28499) ....(Paid) ⊕8,436
(Non-paid) ⊕87

Charleston
Charleston Black Times (28509) 6,883
The Charleston Chronicle (28510) .....(Paid) 3,000
(Free) 3,000
The Charleston City Paper (28511)

Cheraw
The Cheraw Chronicle (28527) ....‡8,050

Chesnee
Chesnee Tribune (28530) ....(Paid) ‡1,850
(Free) ‡100

Chester
Chester News and Reporter (28531) ...(Paid) 6,900
(Free) 80

Clinton
Clinton Chronicle (28539) ....‡4,100

Clover
Clover Herald (28542) ....‡3,000

Columbia
Benedict Tiger (28543) ....(Non-paid) 2,500
The Black News (28544)
Point (28562)

Conway
The Horry Independent (28589) ....(Paid) ‡5,600
(Non-paid) ‡400
The Loris Scene (28591) ....(Free) ‡6,200

Cowpens
Cowpens/Pacolet Tribune (28594) ....‡1,125

Darlington
News and Press (28596) ....‡6,000

Dillon
The Dillon Herald (28597) ....(Paid) ‡6,565
(Free) ‡506

Easley
The Easley
Progress (28598) ....(Controlled) ⊕10,000

Edgefield
Advertiser (28599) 500
The Citizen-News (28600) ....‡4,900

Fort Mill
Fort Mill Times (28612) ....‡6,500

Gaffney
The Gaffney Ledger (28615) ....(Paid) 8,500
(Free) 116

Goose Creek
The Goose Creek Gazette (28620) ....‡15,000

Greenville
GSA Business (28624) ....(Controlled) 10,500

Greer
The Greer Citizen (28652) ....(Paid) ‡10,500

Hampton
Hampton County Guardian (28655) 4,800

Hartsville
Messenger (28657) ....(Mon.) 4,986
(Wed.) 6,719

Hemingway
The Weekly Observer (28659) ....‡2,800

Inman
Inman Times (28667) ....‡3,000

Kershaw
News Era (28671)

Kingstree
The News (28674) 5,000
The News (28675) ....(Paid) ⊕4,800

Lancaster
The Lancaster News (28680) ....‡12,606

Landrum
The News Leader (28681) 4,000

Laurens
Laurens County Advertiser (28682) .....(Paid) ‡7,600
(Free) ‡200

Manning
The Manning Times (28687) ....‡4,500

Marion
Lake City News & Post (28688) ....(Paid) ⊕4,000
Marion Star and Mullins
Enterprise (28689) ....(Paid) ‡7,000

Mc Cormick
McCormick Messenger (28690) ....‡2,700

Mount Pleasant
Charleston Regional Business
Journal (28692) ....(Combined) 8,200
Journal (28693) ....(Combined) ‡4,000

North Augusta
The Star (28719) ....(Combined) ⊕3,500

North Myrtle Beach
North Myrtle Beach Times (28730) ....‡13,400

Orangeburg
Orangeburg Black Voice (28731) 5,365

Pageland
The Pageland Progressive-Journal (28739) ....‡4,400

Pawleys Island
Coastal Observer (28742) ....(Combined) 4,700

Pickens
The Pickens Sentinel (28743) ....‡7,000

St. George
The Eagle-Record (28750) 3,200

St. Matthews
The Calhoun Times (28752) ....(Paid) 2,100

Saluda
Saluda Standard Sentinel (28753) ....‡4,500

Seneca
Daily Journal
Messenger (28754) ....(Combined) 8,943

Numbers cited after listings are entry numbers rather than page numbers.

Simpsonville
Tribune-Times (28756) ....‡7,200

Spartanburg
Dispatch-News (28758) 6,500

Summerville
Journal-Scene (28765) 11,000

Walhalla
Keowee Courier (28778) ....‡2,400

Walterboro
The Press and Standard (28781) ....‡7,000

Westminster
The Westminster News (28784) ....‡2,500

Whitmire
The Whitmire News (28785) ....‡1,500

Williamston
The Journal (28786) ....‡5,600

Winnsboro
Herald-Independent (28787) ....(Paid) ‡5,295
(Free) ‡145

Woodruff
The Woodruff News (28788) ....(Paid) ⊕4,200

York
Yorkville Enquirer (28790) ....⊕3,700

SOUTH DAKOTA
Alcester
Alcester Union (28801) ....‡976

Alexandria
The Alexandria Herald (28802) ....‡685

Arlington
Arlington Sun (28803) 1,500

Armour
Armour Chronicle (28804) ....‡882
Delmont Record (28805) ....‡250

Bowdle
The Bowdle Pioneer (28808) ....‡650

Britton
Journal (28810) ....(Paid) ‡1,946
Langford Bugle (28811) ....‡476

Buffalo
Nation's Center News (28826) ....(Paid) 1,744
(Free) 50

Burke
Burke Gazette (28827) ....‡1,613

Canistota
The Canova Herald (28828) ....(Paid) 590
(Free) 10

Castlewood
Estelline Journal (28829) ....(Paid) 800
Hamlin County Republican (28830) ....‡800

Chamberlain
Chamberlain-Oacoma Register (28831) 3,125

Clark
Clark County Courier (28832) ....‡2,600

Clear Lake
Clear Lake Courier (28833) ....(Paid) ‡1,487
(Free) ‡98

Custer
Custer County
Chronicle (28836) ....(Controlled) 2,150
Hill City Prevailer-News (28837) ....‡1,100

De Smet
The De Smet News (28841) ....‡1,405

Doland
Conde News (28844) ....(Paid) 570
Doland Times Record (28845) ....(Paid) 570

Dupree
West River Progress (28846) 721

Eagle Butte
Eagle Butte News (28847) ....‡2,139

Edgemont
Edgemont Herald-Tribune (28849)

Elk Point
The Leader-Courier (28850) ....(Paid) ‡1,807
(Free) ‡35

Elkton
The Elkton Record (28851) ....‡800

Emery
The Emery Enterprise (28852) ....‡538

Eureka
The Northwest-Blade (28853) ....‡1,456

Faulkton
Faulk County Record (28854) ....(Paid) ⊕1,702
(Free) ⊕5

Flandreau
Moody County Enterprise (28855) ....‡2,800

Freeman
Courier (28857) ....‡2,400

Garretson
Garretson Weekly (28858) ....‡1,000

Geddes
Charles Mix County News (28860) ....‡700

Gregory
Gregory Times Advocate (28861) .,.......2,500

Groton
Brown County Independent (28862) ....‡1,100
Groton Regional Independent (28863) ....‡1,375

Hayti
Hamlin County Herald-Enterprise (28865) .....‡1,000

Highmore
The Highmore Herald (28866) ....‡1,450

Hot Springs
The Hot Springs Star (28867) 2,500

Hoven
Hoven Review (28870) ....(Paid) ‡760
(Free) ‡20

Howard
Miner County Pioneer (28871) ....‡1,700

Ipswich
The Ipswich Tribune (28873) 1,000
Roscoe-Hosmer Independent (28874) 650

Irene
The Tri-County News (28875) ....‡567

Isabel
The Isabel Dakotan (28876) ....(Paid) ‡521
(Free) ‡79

Kadoka
Kadoka Press (28877) 1,091

Kimball
Brule-Buffalo County News (28879) ....‡1,000

Lake Preston
Times (28880) ....(Controlled) ‡1,122
(Non-paid) ‡35

Lead
The Lawrence County Centennial (28881) .....‡2,700

Lemmon
Leader (28882) ....(Paid) ‡1,950

Lennox
Lennox Independent (28884) 2,000

Marion
The Marion Record (28889) ....‡1025

Menno
Hutchinson Herald (28892) ....(Paid) ‡1,076

Milbank
Grant County Review (28893) ....‡4,100

Miller
The Miller Press (28896) 2,081

Mission
Mellette County News (28897) 500
Todd County Tribune (28898) ....‡2,000

Mobridge
The Mobridge Tribune (28905) ...,......(Paid) ‡3,021

Murdo
The Murdo Coyote (28909) ....‡830

Newell
Butte County Valley
Irrigator (28910) ....(Paid) ‡1,135

Onida
The Onida Watchman (28911) 1,200

Parker
The New Era (28912) 1,300

Parkston
The Tripp Star-Ledger (28913)

Philip
Pioneer Review (28914) 1,740

Pierre
The Times (28923) ....(Paid) ‡1069
(Non-paid) ‡27

Platte
Enterprise (28928) ....(Paid) ‡2,014
(Free) ‡25

Pollock
Prairie Pioneer (28929) 1,900

Presho
Lyman County Herald (28930) ....(Paid) 1,000

Redfield
The Redfield Press (28953) ....‡1,950

Rosholt
The Rosholt Review (28958) ....(Paid) ‡1,280
(Free) ‡32

Scotland
Scotland Journal (28959) 1,000

Selby
Selby Record (28960) ....(Paid) 1,243
(Free) 24

Sisseton
Courier (28991) 3,950

South Shore
South Shore Gazette (28992) ....‡500

Springfield
Times (28997) 600

Stickney
The Stickney Argus (28998) ....(Paid) ‡665
(Free) ‡22

Sturgis
Black Hills Press (28999) ....‡4,800
Meade County Times-Tribune (29000) ....‡4,800

Timber Lake
Timber Lake Topic (29003) 1,500

Tyndall
Tyndall Tribune & Register (29004) 1,500

Vermillion
Plain Talk (29005) ....‡2,500

Volga
Volga Tribune (29012) ....‡800

Wagner
The Wagner Post and Announcer (29014) 1800

Wakonda
Wakonda Times (29015) ....‡400

Wall
Pennington County Courant (29016) ....‡1,000
(Free) 6,570

Webster
Reporter and Farmer (29027) ....‡3,830

Wessington
Wessington Times Enterprise (29028) 600

White
Tri-City Star (29030) ....‡700

Wilmot
The Wilmot Enterprise (29031) ....‡700

Winner
Winner Advocate (29032) ....‡3,080

Woonsocket
Woonsocket News (29035) ....‡1,370

Yankton
Missouri Valley Observer (29036) 2,950

TENNESSEE
Ashland City
Ashland City Times (29051) ....(Combined) 5,601

Benton
Polk County News-Citizen Advance (29054) 3,800

Newspapers

Circulation: ★ = ABC; △ = BPA; ♦ = CAC; ● = CCAB; ❑ = VAC; ⊕ = PO Statement; ‡ = Publisher's Report; Boldface figures = sworn; Light figures = estimated.

2921

Circ.   Circ.   Circ.

TENNESSEE (continued)

Bolivar
Bulletin Times **(29057)** ....(Paid) 4,800
(Free) 11,000

Brownsville
Brownsville States-Graphic **(29070)** .....(Paid) ‡5,000

Byrdstown
Pickett County Press **(29076)** ....‡2,000

Camden
The Camden Chronicle **(29078)** 5700

Carthage
Carthage Courier **(29081)** ....‡4,800

Celina
Citizen-Statesman **(29084)** ....(Paid) 2,600

Chattanooga
Hamilton County Herald **(29089)**

Clinton
The Courier-News **(29129)** ....‡5,500

Collierville
The Collierville Herald **(29133)** ....‡7,000
Independent **(29135)** ....(Free) 10,000

Covington
The Covington Leader **(29153)** ....(Paid) ‡8,930

Crossville
Crossville Chronicle **(29157)** ....‡7,000
‡10,600

Dayton
The Herald-News **(29163)** ....(Combined) ‡18,000

Dickson
The Dickson Herald **(29165)** ....(Paid) 7,236
(Non-paid) 271

Dresden
Dresden Enterprise **(29170)** ....‡5,200

Dunlap
The Dunlap Tribune **(29171)** ....(Paid) 3,335
(Free) 15

Dyer
Tri-City Reporter **(29173)** ....‡3,250

Dyersburg
Dyersburg News **(29174)** ....(Non-paid) 16,070
(Paid) 114

Erin
The Stewart-Houston Times **(29182)** ....‡5,800

Erwin
The Erwin Record **(29184)** 4,920

Fayetteville
Elk Valley Times **(29188)** 8,400

Franklin
Brentwood Journal **(29195)**

Gallatin
The News-Examiner **(29203)** ....(Paid) 10,800
(Free) 169

Hartsville
The Hartsville Vidette **(29218)** ....‡2,152

Hohenwald
Lewis County Herald **(29223)** ....‡3,750

Humboldt
The Chronicle **(29224)** ....‡4,100

Jefferson City
Standard Banner **(29247)** ....(Paid) 5,746
(Non-paid) 109

Jonesborough
Herald and Tribune **(29258)** ....‡4,500

Kingston
Roane County News **(29269)** 9,369

La Follette
La Follette Press **(29308)**

Lafayette
Macon County Times **(29312)** ....‡6,000

Lawrenceburg
Democrat-Union **(29315)** ....⊕7,600

Lebanon
The Wilson World **(29321)** ....(Paid) 5,200
(Free) 625

Lenoir City
News-Herald **(29323)** ....‡7,823

Livingston
Overton County News **(29333)**

Lynchburg
The Moore County News **(29337)** ......(Paid) ‡1,600
(Free) ‡13

Madisonville
The Democrat-Observer **(29340)** ....‡19,500

Maynardville
The News Leader **(29351)** ....‡3,000

Mc Kenzie
McKenzie Banner **(29352)** ....(Free) ‡200

Mc Minnville
Southern Standard **(29353)** ....‡8,300

Memphis
The Bartlett Express **(29358)** ....‡6,790
Tri-State Defender **(29383)** ....‡15,000

Milan
Milan Mirror-Exchange **(29414)** ....‡5,400

Millington
The Millington Star **(29416)** ....‡4,000

Mountain City
The Tomahawk **(29426)** ....‡5,600

Nashville
The News Herald **(29476)** ....‡25,000
The Tennessee Tribune **(29495)** ......(Paid) ‡25,000
WESTVIEW **(29502)** ....‡5,000

Newport
Newport Plain Talk **(29544)** ....‡9250

Oneida
Independent Herald **(29553)** ....‡4,600
Scott County News **(29554)** 7,000

Pigeon Forge
The Weekly Star **(29566)** ....(Paid) ‡3,500
(Free) ‡5,000

Pikeville
The Bledsonian Banner **(29567)** ....(Paid) 3,197
(Free) 87

Pulaski
Giles Free Press **(29571)** ....‡8,247
Pulaski Citizen **(29572)** ....‡8,561

Ripley
The Lauderdale Voice **(29576)** ....‡4,500

Rogersville
Rogersville Review **(29580)** ....(Wed.) ‡5,600
(Sat.) ‡12,000

Savannah
Courier **(29584)** ....(Paid) 8,805

Selmer
Independent-Appeal **(29588)** ....‡6,800

Seymour
Tri-County News **(29598)** ....(Paid) ‡2,500

Smithville
Smithville Review **(29604)** ....(Paid) 4,114
(Free) 406

Smyrna
The Rutherford Courier **(29605)** ....(Paid) ‡5,000

Somerville
Fayette County Review **(29607)** ....(Paid) ‡3,600
Fayette Falcon **(29608)** ....‡3,310

South Pittsburg
South Pittsburg Hustler **(29610)** 2,500

Sparta
The Expositor **(29613)** ....(Paid) 5,500
(Non-paid) 5,000

Springfield
Robertson County
Times **(29618)** ....(Combined) 8,470

Sweetwater
Monroe County
Advocate/Democrat **(29624)** ....(Paid) 15,100
(Non-paid) 1

Tazewell
Claiborne Progress **(29625)** ....‡7,076

Tiptonville
Lake County Banner **(29627)** ....‡3,300

Tracy City
Grundy County Herald **(29628)** ....‡5,000

Trenton
The Herald-Gazette **(29629)** ....(Paid) 3,500
(Free) 8,500

Tullahoma
The Tullahoma News and
Guardian **(29633)** ....‡9,500

Wartburg
Morgan County News **(29639)** ....‡4,574

Waverly
News-Democrat **(29642)** ....(Paid) 3,318
(Free) 264

Waynesboro
The Wayne County News **(29644)** ....‡7,000

Winchester
Herald-Chronicle **(29647)** ....(Paid) ‡9100
(Free) ‡43

Woodbury
Cannon Courier **(29649)** 3,000

TEXAS

Abernathy
Abernathy Weekly Review **(29651)** ....(Paid) ‡850
(Free) ‡11

Albany
The Albany News **(29676)** 1,800

Aledo
The Community News **(29677)** ....(Paid) ⊕2,328

Alpine
Alpine Avalanche **(29682)** 4,500

Alvin
The Alvin Sun **(29690)** ....(Paid) 2,450
(Free) 20

Amarillo
El Mensajero **(29696)** ....(Paid) 500
(Non-paid) 14,500

Anahuac
Anahuac Progress **(29721)** ....(Free) 636
(Paid) 1,468
The Progress **(29722)** ....(Paid) 2,245
(Free) 211

Andrews
Andrews County News **(29723)** ....‡3,900

Aransas Pass
Aransas Pass Progress **(29727)** ....(Paid) ⊕2,876
Index **(29728)** ....‡972
The Ingleside Index **(29729)** ....(Paid) ⊕1,111

Austin
The Progressive Populist **(29798)** ......(Paid) ‡7,500
(Non-paid) ‡10,000
Texas Observer **(29837)** 6,000
Westlake Picayune **(29854)** ....‡3,000

Azle
Azle News **(29886)** ....(Paid) ⊕4,914
(Non-paid) ⊕225

Ballinger
The Ballinger Ledger **(29887)** ....(Thurs.) ‡2,300

Bandera
Bulletin **(29888)** ....(Paid) ‡5,500

Bartlett
Tribune-Progress **(29889)** ....(Paid) 1,550

Bastrop
The Bastrop Advertiser **(29890)** ....‡5,000

Bellville
Times **(29914)** ....‡4,250

Belton
The Belton Journal **(29916)** ....‡4,000

Big Lake
The Big Lake Wildcat **(29919)** ....‡1,300

Big Sandy
The Big Sandy & Hawkins Journal and Tri Area
News **(29920)** ....‡1,450

Blanco
Blanco County News **(29927)** Media.............2,900

Blossom
Blossom Times **(29929)** 375

Boerne
Hill Country Recorder **(29930)** ....(Paid) ‡6,100

Booker
The Booker News **(29936)** ....‡1,147

Bowie
The Bowie News **(29939)** ....‡4,500

Brady
The Brady Herald **(29943)** ....(Paid) 3,219
(Free) 62

Breckenridge
Breckenridge American **(29946)** ....(Paid) ‡3,702
(Free) ‡42

Bremond
Bremond Press **(29947)** ....‡1,250

Brownfield
Brownfield News **(29953)** ....(Paid) ‡3,100

Brownsboro
Chandler & Brownsboro
Statesman **(29955)** ....(Paid) ‡1,500

Buda
The Free Press **(29985)** ....(Paid) ⊕4,795

Buffalo
Buffalo Press **(29986)** ....(Paid) 2,000
(Non-paid) 3,600

Burkburnett
Informer Star **(29987)** ....‡2,750

Burleson
Burleson Star **(29988)** ....‡7,211

Burnet
Burnet Bulletin **(29991)** ....‡4,200
Citizen Gazette **(29992)** ....(Paid) 1,100

Caldwell
Burleson County Citizen-Tribune **(29994)** ......‡4,200

Canadian
The Canadian Record **(29997)** ....‡2,000

Canton
Canton Herald **(29998)** 6,800

Canyon
The Canyon News **(30000)** .....:.......(Paid) ‡3,950
(Free) ‡300

Canyon Lake
Canyon Lake Times
Guardian **(30002)** ....(Paid) ‡2,860
(Free) ‡140

Carrollton
Metrocrest News **(30004)** ....(Paid) 41,600

Castroville
Medina Valley Times **(30008)** ....(Paid) 3,800

Cedar Creek
Cedar Creek Pilot **(30009)** ....‡5,444

Cedar Hill
Cedar Hill Today **(30011)** ....(Paid) ❏2,269
(Free) ❏100

Center
Light & Champion **(30012)** ....‡5,500

Centerville
Centerville News **(30015)** ....(Paid) ‡1,906
(Free) ‡394

Chico
Chico Texan **(30016)** 680

Childress
The Childress Index **(30017)** ....(Paid) ‡3,047
(Sun.) ‡3,181

Cisco
The Cisco Press **(30020)** ....‡2,050

Clarendon
The Clarendon Enterprise **(30021)** ....‡1,600

Clarksville
The Clarksville Times **(30022)** 3,500

Cleveland
Cleveland Advocate **(30028)** ....‡2,900
Spring Observer **(30030)** ....(Paid) 6,173
(Free) 62

Clifton
The Clifton Record **(30031)** ....‡3,010

Clyde
Journal **(30034)** 2,500

Coleman
Chronicle & Democrat-Voice **(30035)** 3,250

Colorado City
Colorado City Record **(30063)** ....‡3,600

Columbus
The Banner Press
Newspaper **(30064)** ....(Paid) ‡5,000
Colorado County Citizen **(30065)** ....(Paid) ‡4,000

Commerce
Commerce Journal **(30067)** ....(Paid) ‡2,740
(Free) ‡4,300

Copperas Cove
Copperas Cove Leader-Press **(30074)** ....‡3,200

Corrigan
The Corrigan Times **(30100)** ....‡1,400

Crane
The Crane News **(30105)** ....‡1,800

Crockett
Houston County Courier **(30106)** ....‡5,435

Crosbyton
Crosby County News & Chronicle **(30109)** ......‡950

Cross Plains
Review **(30110)** 1,650

Crowell
The Foard County News **(30111)** ....‡1,400

Crowley
Crowley Review **(30112)** ....(Paid) ⊕3,000

Crystal City
Zavala County Sentinel **(30114)** ....‡2,300

Cuero
The Cuero Record **(30115)** ....‡3,550

Daingerfield
The Bee **(30118)** 3,200

Dallas
African Herald **(30121)** ....(Paid) 12,500
Dallas Post Tribune **(30149)** ....‡20,000
Park Cities People **(30176)** ....(Combined) 7,719
The White Rocker **(30189)** ....‡4,500

Decatur
Wise County Messenger **(30221)** ....(Mon.-Fri.) 8,026
(Sun.) 5,900

Dell City
Hudspeth County Herald-Dell Valley
Review **(30231)** ....(Paid) ‡738
(Free) ‡10

Deport
Deport Times **(30245)** ....‡1,675

DeSoto
DeSoto Today **(30246)** ....(Paid) ❏2,878
(Free) ❏100

Devine
The Devine News **(30247)** ....‡3,215

Diboll
Free Press **(30248)** 3,500

Dimmitt
Castro County News **(30249)** ....(Paid) ‡2,103
(Free) ‡73

Dumas
Moore County News-Press **(30251)** ....⊕3,800

Duncanville
Duncanville Today **(30254)** ....(Paid) ❏4,387
(Free) ❏100

Eagle Lake
Eagle Lake Headlight **(30256)** ....(Paid) ‡2,450
(Free) ‡46

Eagle Pass
News-Guide **(30257)** ....‡3,250

Earth
Earth Weekly News **(30262)** ....(Paid) ‡850
(Free) ‡100

East Bernard
East Bernard Tribune **(30263)** ....‡1,200

Eastland
Eastland Telegram **(30264)** ....‡2,500
The Rising Star **(30265)** ....(Combined) 1,000

Eden
The Eden Echo **(30269)** ....‡1,200

Edgewood
Edgewood Enterprise **(30270)** ....‡1,120

Edna
Jackson County Herald-Tribune **(30275)** ....‡4,000

El Campo
El Campo Leader-News **(30276)** ....‡6,100

Electra
Electra Star-News **(30306)** ....(Paid) ‡2,000
(Free) ‡100

Emory
Rains County Leader **(30307)** ....‡2,467

Ennis
Ellis County News **(30308)** ....‡5,000

Fairfield
The Fairfield Recorder **(30311)** 3,800

Falfurrias
Falfurrias Facts **(30313)** ....(Paid) ⊕2,500

Farwell
State Line Tribune **(30315)** ....‡1,228

Floresville
Floresville Chronicle-Journal **(30318)** ....‡4,000
Wilson County News **(30319)** ......(Combined) 11,000

Flower Mound
Flower Mound Leader **(30321)**

Floydada
Floyd County
Hesperian-Beacon **(30322)** ....(Paid) 2,485
(Free) 31

Forney
Forney Messenger **(30325)** ....‡2,300

Fort Stockton
Fort Stockton Pioneer **(30326)** ....(Paid) 3,500

Fort Worth
Fort Worth Business Press **(30337)**

Franklin
Franklin News Weekly **(30362)** ....‡1,400
Review-Appeal **(30363)** ....(Paid) 8,883
(Free) 11,870

Frankston
The Frankston Citizen **(30364)** ....‡1,224

Fredericksburg
Standard-Radio Post **(30365)** ....(Paid) ‡9,485
(Free) ‡60

Freer
The Freer Press **(30367)** ....(Paid) ‡856
(Free) ‡13

Friona
The Friona Star **(30370)** ....‡2,250

Frisco
The Frisco Enterprise **(30371)**

Fritch
The Eagle Press **(30373)**

Gail
The Borden Star **(30375)** ....(Paid) 500
(Free) 10

Garland
The Garland News **(30384)** ....(Paid) 8,411
(Non-paid) 338
Vietnam Weekly
News **(30385)** ....(Combined) 12,000

Gatesville
Messenger and Star-Forum **(30388)** 4,500

Georgetown
Sunday Sun **(30392)** ....‡10,019
Williamson County Sun **(30393)** ....‡9,829

Giddings
Giddings Times and News **(30395)** ....‡7,100

Gilmer
The Gilmer Mirror **(30396)** ....(Paid) 4,777
(Free) 25

Newspapers

Circulation: ★ = ABC; △ = BPA; ♦ = CAC; • = CCAB; ❏ = VAC; ⊕ = PO Statement; ‡ = Publisher's Report; Boldface figures = sworn; Light figures = estimated.

2923

Circ. Circ. Circ.

TEXAS (continued)

Glen Rose
Glen Rose Reporter (30398) ....‡2,938

Goliad
The Texan Express (30399) ....(Paid) ‡2,196
(Free) ‡26

Gonzales
The Gonzales Inquirer (30400) ....‡3,585

Gorman
The Gorman Progress (30401) ....‡1,005

Graham
The Graham Leader (30402) ....(Paid) ⊕4,384

Granbury
Hood County News (30404) 10,953

Grandview
Grandview Tribune (30408) ....‡1,200

Granger
Nasinec (30409) ....(Paid) ⊕300

Grapeland
The Grapeland Messenger (30410) .....(Paid) ‡2,000
(Free) ‡300

Groesbeck
Journal (30417) ....‡4,300

Groveton
Groveton News (30418) ....(Paid) 1,583
(Free) 40

Hamilton
The Hamilton Herald-News (30420) 3,700

Hamlin
Hamlin Herald (30422) 1,500

Hart
The Hart Beat (30432) ....(Paid) ‡400
(Non-paid) ‡50

Haskell
The Haskell Free Press (30433) ....‡2,100

Hearne
The Hearne Democrat (30435) ....‡3,750

Hemphill
Sabine County Reporter and the
Rambler (30437) ....(Paid) 3,132
(Non-paid) 59

Hempstead
The Waller County
News-Citizen (30439) ....(Paid) ‡2,551

Henrietta
Clay County Leader (30442) ....(Paid) 3,400
(Non-paid) 59

Highlands
Highland Star/Crosby
Courier (30448) ....(Paid) ‡7,500

Hillsboro
Reporter (30449) ....(Paid) ‡5,000
(Free) ‡2,800

Hondo
Hondo Anvil Herald (30451) ....‡4,762

Houston
Houston Defender (30482) ....(Paid) ‡23,000
(Free) ‡4,000
Houston Forward Times (30484) ....‡64,580
Houston Tribune (30489) ....(Controlled) 22,500
The Informer & Texas Freeman (30491) 30,000
Jewish Herald-Voice (30494) ....(Paid) ‡7,000
(Free) ‡53
La Informacion (30501) 84,000
La Voz de Houston
Newspaper (30503) ....(Non-paid) 96,780

Howe
Texoma Enterprise (30591) ....(Paid) ⊕638
(Free) ⊕53

Jacksboro
Jack County Herald (30614) ....(Paid) ⊕2,111
Jacksboro Gazette-News (30615) ......(Paid) ⊕2,111

Jasper
The Jasper News Boy (30619) 21,160

Jefferson
Jefferson Jimplecute (30624) 2,700

Jewett
The Jewett Messenger (30625) 1,800

Johnson City
Johnson City Record Courier (30626) 1,500

Joshua
Joshua Tribune (30629) ....‡1,400

Junction
The Junction Eagle (30630) ....(Paid) 2,400

Karnes City
The Countywide (30632) ....‡3,016

Kaufman
The Kaufman Herald (30633) ....(Paid) 3,677

Kerens
Kerens Tribune (30637) 800

Kermit
The Winkler County News (30638) ......(Paid) 3,700

Kerrville
Kerrville Mountain Sun (30640) ....(Paid) ‡5,700
(Free) ‡20

Killeen
Killeen Daily Herald (30644) .....(Mon.-Sat.) ★18,674
(Sun.) ★24,964

Kingsville
Kingsville Record (30647) ....(Wed.) 5,125
(Sun.) 4,848

Knox City
Knox County News (30653) ....‡1,500

Kress
Kress Chronicle (30654) ....(Combined) ⊕480

La Feria
La Feria News (30655) ....(Paid) 3,200

La Grange
The Fayette County Record (30656) ......‡6,200

La Porte
The Bayshore Sun (30658) ....(Paid) 2,560

La Vernia
La Vernia News (30660) ....(Paid) ‡1,400
(Free) ‡30

Lake Dallas
Denton County Express (30661) 4,000
The Lake Cities Sun (30662) ....(Paid) ‡2,200
(Free) ‡200

Lamesa
Lamesa Press-Reporter (30663) ....(Paid) ‡3,779

Lampasas
Lampasas Dispatch Record (30665) ....‡4,238

Lancaster
Lancaster Today (30668) ....(Paid) ❏2,126
(Free) ❏100

Leakey
Real American (30680) ....‡2,250

Leonard
Leonard Graphic (30681) ....‡2,200

Levelland
Levelland & Hockley County News
Press (30682) ....‡4,875

Lewisville
The Colony Leader (30685) ......(Combined) 10,278
Lewisville Leader (30687) ....(Wed.) 29,372
(Sat.) 28,034

Liberty
Liberty Vindicator (30690) ....(Paid) 2,831
(Free) 1,761

Lindale
The Lindale News (30693) ....(Paid) 2,500
(Free) 25

Linden
Cass County Sun (30694) ....‡2,200

Little Elm
The Little Elm Journal (30695)

Littlefield
Amherst Press (30696) ....(Paid) ‡187
Lamb County
Leader-News (30697) ....(Combined) ‡2,425

Livingston
Lake Livingston Progress (30699) ....⊕5,898

Polk County Enterprise (30700) ....(Combined) 8,400

Llano
Llano News (30702) ....‡3,600

Lockhart
Lockhart Post-Register (30703) ....(Paid) 3,908
(Free) 28

Luling
The Luling Newsboy & Signal (30749) ....‡2,009

Madisonville
The Madisonville Meteor and
Times (30752) ....(Paid) 3,400
(Non-paid) 25

Malakoff
The Malakoff News (30755) ....(Paid) ‡1,254
(Free) ‡246

Mansfield
News-Mirror (30757) ....(Paid) 3,968
(Non-paid) 29

Marble Falls
The Highlander News (30759)
River Cities Tribune (30762) .....(Combined) ⊕4,650

Marfa
The Big Bend Sentinel (30764) ....(Paid) 2,106
(Free) 54

Marlin
Marlin Democrat (30765) ....‡3,000

Mart
The Mart Herald (30770) ....‡2,200

Mason
Mason County News (30771) ....(Paid) 2,683
(Free) 5

Matador
Motley County Tribune (30772) ....‡1,200

Mathis
The Mathis News (30773) ....(Paid) ‡2,071
(Free) ‡50

Mc Camey
Mc Camey News (30774) 1,100

Mc Gregor
The Mc Gregor Mirror and Crawford
Sun (30775) 2,229

Mc Kinney
McKinney Messenger (30778)

McAllen
Pharr Advance News (30786) ....(Paid) ‡8,411
(Free) ‡3,000

Memphis
The Memphis Democrat (30802) ....(Paid) ‡845
(Free) ‡78

Menard
News and Messenger (30804) ....‡1,205

Mercedes
The Mercedes Enterprise (30805) ....(Paid) 1,724
(Free) 6

Merkel
The Merkel Mail (30806) ....‡1,538

Mesquite
The Mesquite News (30808) ......(Combined) 30,247

Mexia
Hubbard City News (30810)

Miami
The Miami Chief (30813) ....‡630

Midland
Nueva Vista (30815)

Midlothian
The Midlothian Mirror (30826) ....‡2,200

Miles
The Concho Herald (30828) 200
Messenger (30829) ....‡600

Mineola
Mineola Monitor (30830) ....‡3,100

Mission
Progress-Times (30833) ....‡6,500

Monahans
The Monahans News (30835) ....‡3,200

Moody
The Moody Courier (30837) ....(Paid) 800
(Free) 200

Morton
Morton Tribune (30839) ....‡1,200

Mount Vernon
Optic-Herald (30843) ....‡3,100

Muenster
Muenster Enterprise (30844) .....(Paid) 1,800
(Free) 20

Muleshoe
Bailey County Journal (30845) 1,800
Muleshoe and Baily County
Journal (30846) ....‡1,800

Munday
The Munday Courier (30848) ....(Paid) 1,403
(Free) 41

Naples
The Monitor (30855) ....(Paid) 2,188
(Free) 49

Navasota
Navasota Examiner (30856) ....(Paid) 5,535
(Free) 73

Needville
Gulf Coast Tribune (30859) ....‡1,400

New Boston
Bowie County Citizens
Tribune (30860) ....(Paid) ‡6,500
(Free) ‡3,500

New Ulm
Enterprise (30866) ....‡1,486

Newton
Newton County News (30867) .....(Controlled) 2,400

Nocona
News (30868) 2,000

Normangee
The Normangee Star (30869) ....‡1,400

Odem
The Odem-Edroy Times (30870) ....‡600

Odonnell
O'Donnell Index-Press (30884) ....(Combined) 495

Olney
The Olney Enterprise (30885) ....‡2,528

Olton
The Olton Enterprise (30886) ....(Paid) 1,100
(Free) 35

Overton
The Overton Press (30890) ....(Paid) ‡1,800
(Free) ‡700

Ozona
The Ozona Stockman (30891) ......(Paid) 1,755

Paducah
The Paducah Post (30893) ....‡1,645

Palacios
Palacios Beacon (30894) ....(Paid) ‡2,000

Palestine
The Clarion (30896) ....(Paid) 1,000

Panhandle
Panhandle Herald (30903) ....(Paid) ‡1,700
(Free) ‡42

Panola
Panola Watchman (30904) ....(Paid) 4,500
(Non-paid) 6,200

Pearland
Friendswood Journal (30916) 3,200
Pearland Journal (30917) ....‡3500

Pearsall
Frio-Nueces Current (30920) 2,700

Perryton
The Perryton Herald (30927) 4,200

Petersburg
Petersburg Post (30930) ....(Paid) ‡642
(Free) ‡40

Pflugerville
The Pflugerville Pflag (30932) ....‡4,000

Pharr
Advance News Journal (30933)

Picayune
Beeville Bee–Picayune (30934) ....(Paid) ‡4,898
(Free) ‡125

Pilot Point
Post Signal (30935) 2,000

Pittsburg
The Pittsburg Gazette (30936) ....(Paid) ‡3,396
(Free) ‡50

Plano
Plano Star Courier (30948) 8,312
(Sun.) 10,049

Pleasanton
Express (30952) ....‡7,200

Port Isabel
Port Isabel/South Padre
Press (30954) ....(Paid) 5,000
(Non-paid) 150

Port Lavaca
The Port Lavaca Wave & Calhoun County WAVE
EXTRA (30956) ....‡5,392

Post
The Post Dispatch (30961) 1,800

Quanah
Quanah Tribune-Chief (30963) 1500

Quinlan
The Tawakoni News (30966) ....‡3,600

Quitaque
Valley Tribune (30967) ....‡1,000

Quitman
Wood County Democrat (30968) ....‡4,200

Raymondville
Raymondville Chronicle and Willacy County
News (30970) ....(Paid) ⊕3,210
(Non-paid) ⊕15

Refugio
Refugio County Press (30973) ....(Paid) ‡2,461
(Free) ‡34

Richardson
Richardson News (30978) ....(Paid) 7,024
(Non-paid) 200

Riesel
The Riesel Rustler (30982) ....‡1,000

Robert Lee
Observer/Enterprise (30984) 2,000

Robstown
Nueces County Record Star (30985) ....‡6,000

Rockdale
The Rockdale Reporter &
Messenger (30987) ....(Paid) ⊕4,832
(Free) ⊕130

Rockport
The Rockport Pilot (30988) ....(Paid) ⊕5,300

Rocksprings
The Texas Mohair Weekly (30989) 1,200

Roma
The South Texas Reporter (30990) 3,000

Rosebud
The Rosebud News (30991) 2,074

Rotan
Advance Star Record (30994) ....‡1,550

Round Rock
The Round Rock Leader (30995) ......(Paid) ⊕6,093
(Free) ⊕450

Rowena
Rowena Press (30997) ....‡200

Rowlett
The Rowlett Lakeshore Times (30998)

Rusk
Cherokeean/Herald (30999) ....(Paid) 3,809

St. Jo
The Saint Jo Tribune (31003) ....‡991

San Antonio
Bulverde Community News (31027)

San Antonio
San Antonio Register (31047) ....(Paid) ‡7,800
(Non-paid) ‡200

San Augustine
San Augustine Tribune (31080) ....(Paid) ‡5,000

San Benito
San Benito News (31081) ....(Paid) 4,612
(Free) 125

San Jacinto
San Jacinto News Times (31082) 2,486

San Saba
San Saba News and Star (31089) ....‡3,100

Sanderson
The Sanderson Times (31092) ....(Paid) ‡900
(Free) ‡12

Schulenburg
The Schulenburg Sticker (31093) ......(Paid) ⊕2,720
(Free) ⊕138

Seagoville
Seagoville Suburbia News (31094) 1,000

Sealy
The Sealy News (31095) ....‡5,195

Seminole
The Seminole Sentinel (31098) ....‡2,300

Seymour
The Baylor County Banner (31102) ......(Paid) 2,518
(Free) 45

Shiner
The Shiner Gazette (31105) ....(Paid) 2,748
(Free) 98

Silsbee
The Silsbee Bee (31106) ....(Paid) 5,800

Sinton
Portland News (31110) ....‡2,500
San Patricio County News (31111) ....‡2,500

Slaton
The Slatonite (31112) ....‡2,450

Smithville
The Smithville Times (31113) ....(Paid) 2,900
(Free) 100

Sonora
Devil's River News (31119) ....‡1,400

Southlake
Colleyville News and
Times (31122) ....(Paid) ‡3,878
(Non-paid) ‡1,142
Southlake Times (31123)

Spearman
The Hansford County
Reporter-Statesman (31124) ....‡1,700

Spur
The Texas Spur (31125) 2,000

Stamford
Stamford American (31128) ....‡2,845

Sterling City
Sterling City News-Record (31134) ....(Paid) ‡530
(Free) ‡530

Stratford
Stratford Star (31135) 1,500

Sugar Land
The Fort Bend Mirror (31137) ....(Paid) 350
(Free) 155

Sulphur Springs
Hopkins County Echo (31165) ....‡930

Sweetwater
Nolan County Shopper (31169) ....‡6,000

Taft
The Taft Tribune (31173) ....‡1,200

Tahoka
Lynn County News (31174) ....(Paid) 1,400
(Free) 40

Talco
Talco Times (31175) ....‡400

Teague
The Teague Chronicle (31176) ....‡2,650

Circulation: ★ = ABC; △ = BPA; ◆ = CAC; ● = CCAB; ❑ = VAC; ⊕ = PO Statement; ‡ = Publisher's Report; Boldface figures = sworn; Light figures = estimated.

2925

Circ.

Circ.

Circ.

TEXAS (continued)

Three Rivers
The Progress (31191) ....(Paid) ‡3,173
(Free) ‡13

Throckmorton
Tribune (31192)

Trenton
Tribune (31193) ....(Paid) 1,300

Tulia
The Tulia Herald (31195) ....(Paid) 2,776

Tyler
Tyler
Courier-Times-Telegraph (31201) ......(Sun.) 50,418

Uvalde
Uvalde Leader-News (31225) 6,410

Van Alstyne
Van Alstyne Leader (31229) 1,500

Van Horn
The Van Horn Advocate (31230) 1,000

Vega
The Vega Enterprise (31231) ....‡600

Vidor
Vidorian (31243) ....(Paid) 1,473
(Free) 27

Waco
TIEMPO (31254)
Waco Citizen Newspaper (31256) ....(Paid) 3,000
(Free) 600

Wallis
Wallis News-Review (31268) ....‡1,100

Weimar
Weimar Mercury (31276) ....(Paid) ‡3,328
(Free) ‡234

Wellington
Wellington Leader (31277) ....(Paid) 2,350
(Free) 95

West
The West News (31282) ....(Paid) ‡3,100

Wharton
Wharton Journal-Spectator (31284) .....(Paid) ‡4,773
(Free) ‡40

Wheeler
Times (31287) 1,350

White Deer
White Deer News (31289) 1,900

Whitesboro
Whitesboro News-Record (31291) 2,900

Whitewright
The Whitewright Sun (31292) ....‡1,100

Wills Point
Van Zandt News (31300) ....(Paid) ‡7,000
Wills Point Chronicle (31301) 4,600

Wimberley
The Wimberley View (31304) ....(Sat.) 1,500
(Wed.) 3,300

Winnsboro
The Winnsboro News (31305) ....(Paid) 4,114
(Free) 4

Wolfe City
The Wolfe City Mirror (31307) ....‡1000

Wylie
The Wylie News (31310) ....(Combined) ‡4,302

Yoakum
Yoakum Herald-Times (31311) ....(Paid) 3,000

Yorktown
The Yorktown News (31312) ....‡2,000
Yorktown News-View (31313)

Zapata
Zapata County News (31314) ....(Combined) ⊕2,992

UTAH
American Fork
Citizen (31316) ....(Paid) ‡3,300
New Utah! Lindon Edition (31317) ....(Paid) 500
New Utah! Lone Peak
Edition (31318) ....(Paid) 1,900

Beaver
The Beaver Press (31320) 1,300

Bountiful
Eagle Newspaper (31323) ....(Combined) ‡83,000

Brigham City
Box Elder News Journal (31324) ....(Paid) ‡5,500
(Free) ‡5,300

Coalville
Summit County Bee (31330) ....‡1,800

Delta
Millard County Chronicle Progress (31331) ....‡3,000

Emery County
Emery County Progress (31333) ....(Paid) 2,100

Heber City
Wasatch Wave (31337) 2,950

Kanab
Southern Utah News (31342) ....‡2,200

Lehi
Lehi Free Press (31345) ....(Paid) ‡2,800

Logan
The Cache Citizen (31347) 18,500

Magna
Magna Times & West Valley News (31364) 5,500

Manti
The Messenger Enterprise (31366) ....‡950

Moab
The Times Independent (31369) 3,000

Monticello
The San Juan Record (31370) ....(Paid) 2,550

Morgan
Morgan County News (31371) ....(Paid) ‡1,000
(Free) ‡100

Mount Pleasant
The Pyramid (31372) ....(Paid) 2,600

Nephi
Nephi Times-News (31375) ....‡1,200

Pleasant Grove
Pleasant Grove Review (31390) ....(Paid) ‡2,500

Price
Sun Advocate (31393) ....‡5,450

Richfield
The Richfield Reaper (31414) 6,000

Roosevelt
Uintah Basin Standard (31415) ....(Paid) ‡4,500

Salt Lake City
The Pillar (31437)

Spanish Fork
Spanish Fork Press (31474) ....‡3,100

Springville
Eureka Reporter (31476) 512
Springville Herald (31477) ....‡2,874

Tooele
Tooele Transcript-Bulletin (31480) ......(Paid) ‡7,500
(Free) ‡70

Tremonton
Leader Garland Times (31481) ....(Paid) ‡3,100
(Free) ‡3,900

Tropic
Garfield County News (31482) ....(Paid) ‡2,000

Vernal
Vernal Express (31483) ....(Paid) ⊕4,883
(Free) ⊕27

West Valley City
West Valley Eagle (31486)

VERMONT
Barton
the Chronicle (31493) ....(Paid) ⊕7,863
(Free) 215

Bradford
Journal Opinion (31506) ....(Paid) ‡4,700

Enosburg
County Courier (31541) 3,500

Fairfax
The Fairfax News (31543)

Hardwick
The Hardwick Gazette (31544) ....(Paid) 2,700
(Free) 20

Ludlow
Black River Tribune (31549) ....‡3,500

Middlebury
Addison County Independent (31555) ....(Paid) 7,500

Morrisville
News and Citizen (31569) ....(Paid) ‡3,800

Northfield
Northfield News (31574) ....(Paid) ‡1,750

Randolph
The Herald of Randolph (31581) 6,278

Springfield
Springfield Reporter (31603) ....(Paid) 1,700
(Non-paid) 100

Stowe
The Stowe Reporter (31604) ....(Paid) ‡5,485
(Free) ‡50

Waitsfield
The Valley Reporter (31610) ....(Paid) 3,500
(Free) 78

West Dover
Deerfield Valley News (31615) ....‡3,900

Woodstock
The Vermont Standard (31624) ....‡4,200

VIRGINIA
Abingdon
Abingdon Virginian (31625) ....(Paid) ‡5,500
(Free) ‡1,000
Washington County News (31627) .....(Paid) ‡4,964
(Free) ‡27

Alexandria
Alexandria Gazette
Packet (31633) ....(Combined) 12,508
Journal of Counseling and
Development (31692) ....(Paid) 59,000
The Journal Friday Home
Report (31696) ....(Paid) 150,000
(Free) 50,000
Prince William
Journal (31724) ....(Combined) 10,599

Altavista
The Altavista Journal (31756) ....‡6,600

Amherst
Nelson County Times (31760) ....(Thurs.) 3,887
New Era-Progress (31761) ....(Thurs.) 4,414

Appomattox
Times-Virginian (31764) ....(Paid) 3,900
(Free) 3,200

Ashburn
Loudoun Easterner (31853) ....(Non-paid) ‡44,000

Ashland
Herald-Progress (31856) ....(Mon.) 8,000
(Thurs.) 8,000

Bedford
Bedford Bulletin (31861) ....‡8,500

Berryville
Clarke Times-Courier (31864) ....‡3,160

Big Stone Gap
The Post (31865) ....⊕4,394

Blackstone
Courier-Record (31892) ....(Paid) ‡7,150
(Free) ‡200

Bowling Green
The Caroline Progress/Caroline
Express (31895) ....(Paid) ‡4,595
(Free) ‡4,650

Brookneal
The Union Star (31905) ....‡3,000

Charlottesville
The Observer (31936) ....(Combined) 20,000
Rural Virginian (31940) ....(Non-paid) 12,000
Tribune (31943) ....(Paid) ‡12,000
(Free) ‡125

2926

Numbers cited after listings are entry numbers rather than page numbers.

Chase City
The News-Progress (31959) ....(Paid) ‡6,500

Chatham
Star-Tribune (31962) ....‡8,372
8,532

Clarksville
The Mecklenberg Sun (31974) ....(Paid) 4,000
(Free) 14,333
The News Progress (31975) ....‡7,100

Culpeper
Culpeper News (31986) ....(Paid) 5,800
(Free) 300

Dinwiddie
Dinwiddie Monitor (31997) ....(Paid) 3,690
(Non-paid) 1,550

Drakes Branch
Charlotte Gazette (31998) 3,200

Elkton
The Valley Banner (32001) ....(Thurs.) 4,372

Farmville
The Farmville Herald (32067) ....‡8,600

Fincastle
The Fincastle Herald and Botetourt County
News (32075) ....‡5,900

Floyd
Press (32076) 4,700

Franklin
Independent-Messenger (32079) ....‡6,540
The Tidewater News (32080) ....(Paid) ‡9,325

Front Royal
Warren Sentinel (32096) ....(Thurs.) 5,482

Galax
The Gazette (32099) ....‡8,800

Gate City
Scott County Virginia Star (32108) ......(Paid) 6,700

Gloucester
Gloucester-Mathews
Gazette-Journal (32115) ....(Thurs.) 11,463

Grundy
The Virginia Mountaineer (32121) ......(Paid) ‡8,270
(Free) ‡125

Heathsville
The Northumberland Echo (32158) .....(Paid) ‡3,100
(Free) ‡75

Herndon
Rappahannock News (32165) ....(Paid) ‡2,751
(Free) ‡106

Hillsville
The Carroll News (32167) ....‡6,700

Independence
The Declaration & Blue Ridge
Sun (32172) ....‡5,000

Lawrenceville
Brunswick Times-Gazette (32178) ....‡5,990

Lebanon
The Lebanon News (32179)

Leesburg
The New Federalist (32186) ....(Paid) 93,000
(Non-paid) 1,105

Lexington
The News-Gazette (32190) ....(Wed.) 8,861

Loudoun
Loudoun Times-Mirror (32199) ....(Paid) ‡17,173
(Free) ‡3,627

Louisa
The Central Virginian (32200) ....(Paid) ‡7,800
(Free) ‡100

Luray
Page News and Courier (32203) ......(Thurs.) 7,646

Lynchburg
The News Advance (32206) ....(Mon.-Sat.) 37,177
(Sun.) 42,344

Madison
Madison County Eagle (32220) ....‡4,300

Marion
Smyth County News &
Messenger (32226) ....(Wed.) 6,600
(Sat.) 6,600

Mechanicsville
Goochland Gazette (32267) ....(Paid) 2,915
(Non-paid) 10

Merrifield
Northern Virginia Sun (32269) ....(Paid) 245
(Non-paid) 68,678

Moneta
Smith Mountain Eagle (32273) ....‡3,900

Monterey
The Recorder (32274) ....‡5,200

Montross
Westmoreland News (32275) ....(Paid) ‡4,152
(Free) ‡118

New Castle
The New Castle Record (32278) ....‡1,870

Norfolk
New Journal & Guide (32291) ....(Combined) 25,000

Norton
The Coalfield Progress (32310) ....(Tues.) 7,373
(Thurs.) 7,731

Onley
The Eastern Shore News (32318) ....‡13,800

Orange
Orange County Review (32321) ....‡7,400
Richlands News Press (32322) ....‡8,300

Pennington Gap
Powell Valley News (32326) 7,471

Purcellville
Blue Ridge Leader (32339) ....(Controlled) 14,000

Richmond
Virginia Farm Bureau News (32461) ....‡136,000

Roanoke
Roanoke Tribune (32492) 5,200

Rocky Mount
Franklin News-Post (32512) ....‡8,500

Rustburg
The Lynchburg Ledger (32519)

St. Paul
Clinch Valley Times (32520) ....‡2,500

Salem
Salem Times-Register (32521) ....‡5,000

Smithfield
The Smithfield Times (32526) ....‡5,100

South Boston
Gazette Virginian (32530) ....‡11,400

South Hill
The South Hill Enterprise (32534) 8,400

Springfield
Air Force Times (32537) ....(Paid) 61,846

Stanardsville
Greene County Record (32552) ....‡3,000

Stuart
The Enterprise (32564) ....(Paid) ‡5,750
(Free) ‡150

Suffolk
Sun (32567) ....‡21,204

Tappahannock
Rappahannock Times (32568) ....‡5,400

Tazewell
Clinch Valley News (32570) ....(Paid) 3,462
(Free) 36

Urbanna
Southside Sentinel (32572) ....(Paid) 5,400
(Free) 75

Victoria
Kenbridge-Victoria Dispatch (32576) ....‡3,300

Vinton
The Vinton Messenger (32586) 3,000

Wakefield
Sussex-Surry Dispatch (32598) ....(Paid) ‡3,500
(Free) ‡5,600

Warrenton
The Fauquier Citizen (32600) ....(Paid) 9,545
Fauquier Times-Democrat (32601) ....‡15,300

Warsaw
Northern Neck News (32606) 7,286

Williamsburg
The Virginia Gazette (32620) ....‡16,500

Woodstock
The Shenandoah
Valley-Herald (32640) ....(Wed.) 5,587

Wytheville
Southwest Virginia Enterprise (32643) 7,500

Yorktown
The Poquoson Post (32645) ....(Paid) 4,000
York Town Crier (32646) ....(Combined) ⊕17,000

WASHINGTON
Arlington
Arlington Times (32654) ....(Free) ‡11,109
(Paid) ‡2,308

Bainbridge Island
The Bainbridge Island
Review (32657) ....(Paid) ♦4,586
(Non-paid) ♦40

Bremerton
Bremerton Patriot (32692) ....(Paid) ♦272
(Non-paid) ♦11,698

Brewster
Brewster Quad-City Herald (32696) 2,000

Burien
Des Moines News (32699) ....(Paid) 33,000
(Free) 38,000

Cashmere
Cashmere Valley Record (32702) 1,600

Cathlamet
The Wahkiakum County Eagle (32703) ....‡1,617

Chelan
Lake Chelan Mirror (32713) 3,000

Cheney
Cheney Free Press (32714) ....‡3,200

Chewelah
The Independent (32716) ....‡2,350

Cle Elum
Northern Kittitas County Tribune (32718) ......‡3,044

Colfax
Whitman County Gazette (32720) 4,450

Connell
Franklin County Graphic (32730) ....(Free) 2,808
(Paid) 170

Coulee City
News-Standard (32731) ....‡800

Davenport
Davenport Times (32733) 2,100

Dayton
Dayton Chronicle (32734) ....‡1,800

Deer Park
Deer Park Tribune (32735) ....(Paid) ‡3,500
(Free) ‡10,000

Eastsound
The Islands' Sounder (32741) ....(Paid) ♦2,388
(Non-paid) ♦6

Eatonville
South Pierce County
Dispatch (32744) ....(Paid) 5,213
(Free) 18,425

Enumclaw
Enumclaw Courier-Herald (32754) 6,000

Ephrata
Grant County Journal (32756) ....(Paid) 3,160
(Free) 60

Federal Way
Federal Way Mirror (32764) ....(Paid) ♦904
(Non-paid) ♦29,243

Ferndale
Westside Record-Journal (32769) ......(Paid) ‡3,000
(Free) 4,559

Newspapers

Circulation: ★ = ABC; △ = BPA; ♦ = CAC; ● = CCAB; ❏ = VAC; ⊕ = PO Statement; ‡ = Publisher's Report; Boldface figures = sworn; Light figures = estimated.

2927

Circ.

Circ.

Circ.

WASHINGTON (continued)

Friday Harbor
The Journal of the San Juan
Islands **(32772)** ....(Paid) ♦**3,253**
(Non-paid) ♦**216**

Gig Harbor
Peninsula Gateway **(32774)** .....(Combined) ‡12,000

Goldendale
The Goldendale Sentinel **(32776)** 3,250

Grand Coulee
The Star **(32779)** 1,990

Grandview
Grandview Herald **(32783)** ....‡2,550

Issaquah
The Issaquah Press **(32784)** ....‡7,700

Kirkland
Kirkland Courier **(32798)** ....(Free) ‡13,000

La Conner
Channel Town Press **(32801)** 2,000

Langley
South Whidbey Record **(32806)** ....(Paid) ♦**4,521**
(Non-paid) ♦**15**
South Whidbey Record **(32807)** ....(Paid) ♦**4,521**
(Non-paid) ♦**15**

Leavenworth
The Leavenworth Echo **(32809)** 2,800

Long Beach
Chinook Observer **(32810)** ....‡7,200

Longview
The Enterprise **(32813)** ....(Combined) ‡6,000

Lynden
Lynden Tribune **(32820)** ....,......(Paid) ‡7,000
(Free) ‡7,500

Mercer Island
Mercer Island Reporter **(32829)** ....‡5,100

Monroe
The Cascade County
Billboard **(32833)** ....(Controlled) ‡11,500
Monroe Monitor/Valley News **(32834)** ....‡3,436

Montesano
The Montesano Vidette **(32835)** ....(Combined) 3,000

Morton
East County Journal **(32836)** ....(Paid) ‡3,007

Newport
The Newport Miner & Gem State
Miner **(32851)** ....‡6,000

North Seattle
The Journal—North Seattle
Edition **(32854)** ....(Paid) 82,000

Oak Harbor
Whidbey News-Times **(32857)** ....(Paid) ♦**7,049**
(Free) ♦**22**

Odessa
The Odessa Record **(32858)** ....‡1,250

Olympia
Works in Progress **(32863)** ....(Free) 3,000

Omak
The Omak-Okanogan County
Chronicle **(32872)** ....(Combined) ‡18,000

Oroville
Okanogan Valley
Gazette-Tribune **(32873)** ....(Paid) 2,700

Othello
The Othello Outlook **(32875)** ....‡2,000

Pomeroy
East Washingtonian **(32887)** ....‡1,550

Port Orchard
The Port Orchard
Independent **(32891)** ....(Paid) ♦**1,346**
(Non-paid) ♦**14,415**

Port Townsend
Port Townsend/Jefferson County
Leader **(32894)** ....‡9,970

Poulsbo
North Kitsap Herald **(32898)** ....(Paid) ♦**1,496**
(Non-paid) ♦**9,013**

North Kitsap Herald **(32899)** ....(Paid) ♦**1,496**
(Free) ♦**9,013**

Prosser
Prosser Record-Bulletin **(32900)** ....‡3,250

Puyallup
Puyallup Herald **(32918)** ....(Paid) 23,000
(Free) 590

Quincy
Quincy Valley Post-Register **(32919)** ....‡2,100

Raymond
The Willapa Harbor Herald **(32922)** ....‡3,800

Renton
Northwest Christian
Journal **(32926)** ....(Controlled) ‡27,000

Ritzville
The Ritzville Adams County
Journal **(32932)** ....‡1,911

Seattle
The Beacon Hill News **(32948)** ....(Paid) 15,300
Capitol Hill Times **(32953)** ....(Paid) 15,000
The Jewish Transcript **(32975)** ....‡4,500
North American Post **(32991)** ....(Fri.) 5,000
(Combined) 8,000
Northwest Asian Weekly **(32993)** ......(Paid) ‡9,000
(Free) ♦**6,000**
Queen Anne/Magnolia News **(33010)** ....‡21,000
Seattle Medium **(33020)** 37,000
West Seattle Herald/White Center
News **(33042)** ....‡10,000
Western Viking **(33043)** ....‡3,000

Sequim
The Sequim Gazette **(33077)** ....(Wed.) 7,350

Shelton
Shelton-Mason County Journal **(33079)** ....‡9,359

Silverdale
Central Kitsap Reporter **(33083)** ....(Paid) ♦**422**
(Non-paid) ♦**16,855**

Snohomish
Everett News Tribune **(33085)** ......(Non-paid) 3,200
(Paid) 12,800
The Monroe Tribune **(33086)** ....(Paid) ‡14,000
Mukilteo Tribune **(33087)** ....(Non-paid) 8,000
The Snohomish County Tribune **(33089)** .....‡14,000

Snoqualmie
Snoqualmie Valley Record **(33090)** 5000

Spokane
Spokane, Washington, Official
Gazette **(33100)** ....(Combined) 190
The Valley News Herald **(33102)** ....(Paid) ‡9,100

Sprague
The Sprague Advocate **(33139)** 500

Stanwood
Stanwood/Camano News **(33140)** 3,750

Stevenson
Skamania County Pioneer **(33141)** 2,600

Tacoma
The Northwest Dispatch **(33148)** ....(Paid) ‡7,700
(Free) ‡3,900
Tacoma True Citizen **(33152)** 13,500

Tenino
The Tenino Independent & Sun
News **(33163)** ....(Paid) ‡1,700

Toppenish
Review Independent **(33167)** 1,700

Twisp
Methow Valley News **(33171)** 3,000

Vancouver
Vancouver Business
Journal **(33180)** ....(Controlled) 5,793

Vashon
Lakewood Journal **(33182)** ....(Paid) 1,973
(Non-paid) 6,355
The Vashon Beachcomber **(33184)** ....(Paid) ♦**3,126**
(Non-paid) ♦**155**

Waitsburg
The Times **(33186)** ....‡1,800

White Salmon
The Enterprise **(33206)** ....(Paid) 2,800
(Free) 30

Wilbur
The Wilbur Register **(33207)** ....‡1,670

Woodinville
The Northlake News **(33214)**
Valley View **(33216)**
Woodinville WEEKLY **(33217)**

Yelm
Nisqually Valley News **(33239)** ....‡4,000

WEST VIRGINIA
Berkeley Springs
The Morgan Messenger **(33247)** ....⊕**5,500**

Charles Town
Spirit of Jefferson-Advocate **(33266)** ....‡5,000

Charleston
Sunday Gazette-Mail **(33273)** ....(Sun.) 102,089

Clay
Clay County Free Press **(33297)** ....‡4,250

Culloden
Putnam Democrat **(33299)** 1,300

Elizabeth
Wirt County Journal **(33304)** ....(Paid) 2,300

Franklin
Pendleton Times **(33320)** 1,800

Glenville
The Glenville Democrat **(33322)** ....(Paid) 2,000
(Free) 100
The Glenville Pathfinder **(33323)** ....(Paid) ‡1,500
(Non-paid) ‡30

Grafton
Mountain Statesman **(33325)** ....‡3,500

Grantsville
Calhoun Chronicle **(33328)** 3,300

Hamlin
Hamlin Weekly News
Sentinel **(33330)** ....(Controlled) 5,620
Lincoln Journal **(33331)** ....‡12,433

Hinton
Hinton News **(33337)** 3,000

Hurricane
The Hurricane Breeze **(33348)** 1,675

Iaeger
The Industrial News **(33351)** ....‡2,510

Keyser
The Weekender Mountain Echo-News
Tribune **(33355)** 4,400

Kingwood
Preston County Journal **(33359)** 5,400

Lewisburg
Greenbrier Valley
Ranger **(33364)** ....(Non-paid) 27,011
Mountain Messenger
Newspaper **(33366)** ....(Paid) 4,776
(Non-paid) 300

Madison
Coal Valley News **(33374)** ....‡5,300

Marlinton
The Pocahontas Times **(33376)** ....‡6,325

Montgomery
The Montgomery Herald **(33386)** 5,100

Moorefield
The Moorefield Examiner **(33389)** ....‡4,762

Mullens
The Mullens Advocate **(33410)** ....‡5,000

New Cumberland
Hancock County Courier **(33412)** ....(Paid) ‡2,253
(Free) ‡30

New Martinsville
Wetzel Chronicle **(33413)** ....‡5,400

Oak Hill
Fayette Tribune **(33417)** ....(Paid) 4,200

Pennsboro
The Pennsboro News **(33428)** ....‡5,200

Petersburg
Grant County Press **(33429)** ....‡5,325

Numbers cited after listings are entry numbers rather than page numbers.

Philippi
Barbour Democrat (**33431**) ....‡5,300

Piedmont
The Piedmont Herald (**33435**) ....‡2,700

Princeton
Princeton Times (**33441**) ....(Paid) ‡2,175
(Free) ‡15

Richwood
Nicholas County News Leader (**33447**) ....‡5,400

Ripley
The Jackson Herald (**33448**) ....‡6,500
Jackson Star News (**33449**) ....‡4,884

Romney
Hampshire Review (**33452**) ....‡6100

St. Marys
Pleasants County Leader (**33460**) ....‡2,200
The St. Marys Oracle (**33461**) ....‡3,500

Shinnston
The Shinnston News/The Harrison County
Journal (**33466**) ....‡4,000

Sistersville
Tyler Star-News (**33467**) ....‡3,400

Spencer
Roane County Reporter (**33470**) ....‡2,321
Times Record (**33471**) ....‡3,776

Summersville
The Nicholas Chronicle (**33473**) ....(Paid) ‡6,000
(Free) ‡200

Sutton
Braxton Citizens' News (**33475**) ....‡6,500
Braxton Democrat-Central (**33476**) ....‡4,200

Union
The Monroe Watchman (**33479**) 4,200

Wayne
Wayne County Publication Inc (**33484**) 5,860

Webster Springs
Webster Echo (**33485**) 3,200
Webster Republican (**33486**) 1,515

Wellsburg
The Brooke County Review (**33494**) ....‡2,000

West Union
The Herald Record (**33496**) ....‡2,900

Weston
The Weston Democrat (**33497**) ....‡8,126

Williamson
Williamson Sun and Sentinel (**33513**)

WISCONSIN
Abbotsford
Record-Review (**33516**) 2,700
Tribune-Phonograph (**33517**) 2,600

Adams
Adams County Times (**33518**)
Times Reporter (**33519**) 2,124

Algoma
Algoma Record-Herald (**33520**) 5,500

Amery
Amery Free Press (**33527**) ....(Paid) 4,969
(Non-paid) 34

Arcadia
The Arcadia News-Leader (**33553**) ....‡2,500

Augusta
Augusta Area Times (**33559**) ....‡1,500

Baldwin
Bulletin (**33560**) ....‡3,000

Balsam Lake
County Ledger-Press (**33561**) 8,716

Barron
Barron News Shield (**33565**) 3,000

Belleville
Belleville Recorder (**33572**) ....(Combined) ‡8,500

Berlin
Berlin Journal (**33580**) ....‡4,000
The Fox Lake Representative (**33582**) ....‡450
Green Lake County Reporter (**33583**) ....‡1,100
Omro Herald (**33584**) ....‡1,200

Princeton
Princeton Times-Republic (**33585**) ....‡1,400

Black Earth
Allamakee Journal (**33587**)

Black River Falls
Banner Journal (**33591**) ....‡4,560

Blair
The Blair Press (**33594**) ....‡1,500

Blanchardville
Pecatonica Valley Leader (**33595**) ....(Paid) 1,600

Bloomer
Bloomer Advance (**33596**) ....‡3,850

Boscobel
The Boscobel Dial (**33598**) ....(Paid) ‡5,900

Brillion
The Brillion News (**33599**) ....‡1,948

Brodhead
Independent-Register (**33601**) ....‡8,790

Burlington
Burlington Standard Press (**33608**) .....(Paid) ‡5,600
(Free) ‡11,000
The East Troy News (**33609**) ....‡1,600

Cadott
Cadott Sentinel (**33613**) ....(Paid) ‡1,250

Cambridge
The Cambridge News (**33614**) ....‡2,025

Campbellsport
Campbellsport News (**33616**) 2,000

Cashton
The Cashton Record (**33618**) ....(Paid) ‡1,550
(Free) ‡50

Cedarburg
News Graphic (**33619**) ....(Mon.) 8,237
(Thurs.) 8,237

Chetek
The Chetek Alert (**33622**) ....‡3,600

Chilton
Times-Journal (**33625**) ....‡5,400

Clinton
The Clinton Topper (**33635**) ....(Paid) ‡1,300
(Free) ‡50

Clintonville
Clintonville Tribune-Gazette (**33637**) ....‡3,279

Cochrane
Buffalo County Journal (**33640**) 2,000

Colfax
Messenger (**33641**) 1410

Columbus
Columbus Journal-Republican (**33642**) 2,800

Cornell
The Cornell & Lake Holcombe
Courier (**33644**) ....(Paid) ‡3,200

Cottage Grove
Monona Community Herald (**33646**) ....‡1,209

Cuba City
Tri-County Press (**33647**) ....‡3,100

Cumberland
Cumberland Advocate (**33648**) ....‡3,200

Darlington
Republican Journal (**33649**) 3,316

De Forest
De Forest Times-Tribune (**33650**) 2,825

De Pere
De Pere Journal (**33651**) 3,750

Deerfield
The Independent (**33652**) ....(Paid) ‡2,000

Delavan
The Delavan Enterprise (**33653**) ....‡4,752

Denmark
The Denmark Press (**33657**) ....‡2,600

Dodgeville
The Dodgeville Chronicle (**33658**) ......(Paid) 4,700
(Free) 200

Durand
The Courier-Wedge (**33661**) 4,300

Eagle River
The Three Lakes News (**33663**) ......(Paid) ⊕10,200
Vilas County News
Review (**33665**) ....(Paid) ⊕10,200

Edgerton
The Edgerton Reporter (**33687**) ....‡4,000

Elkhorn
The Elkhorn Independent (**33688**) ....‡2,750

Ellsworth
Pierce County Herald (**33689**) 4,500

Elmwood
Elmwood Argus (**33690**) ....‡500

Evansville
Evansville Review (**33692**) 1,600

Fennimore
Fennimore Times (**33693**) 2,000

Fitchburg
Ftichburg Star (**33694**) ....(Free) ‡6,600

Florence
The Florence Mining
News (**33695**) ....(Combined) 2,021

Frederic
Inter-County Leader (**33727**) ....‡4,478

Galesville
Galesville Republican (**33732**) ....(Paid) ‡1,850
(Non-paid) ‡25

Gays Mills
Crawford County Independent
Scout (**33733**) ....‡2,250

Glenwood City
Tribune Press Reporter (**33734**) ....‡3,100

Glidden
Enterprise (**33735**) 1,480

Grantsburg
Burnett County
Sentinel (**33737**) ....(Combined) 3,750

Hammond
Central St. Croix News (**33773**) 1,450

Hartland
The Index (**33778**) 2,004
Lake Country Reporter (**33780**) 8,690

Hayward
Sawyer County Record (**33786**) ....(Paid) ♦6,680
(Non-paid) ♦41

Hillsboro
Hillsboro Sentry-Enterprise (**33791**) ....‡1,800

Horicon
The Horicon Reporter (**33793**) ....‡1,750

Hudson
Hudson Star-Observer (**33795**) 7,500

Hurley
Iron County Miner (**33797**) ....‡2,827

Iola
Amherst Tomorrow River
Times (**33799**) ....(Controlled) ⊕400
Iola Herald (**33832**) 1,120
The Manawa Advocate (**33833**) ......(Controlled) 550
Waupaca County News (**33854**)

Juneau
Dodge County Independent News (**33869**) 1,200

Kenosha
The Labor Paper (**33873**) 15,000

Kewaskum
Kewaskum Statesman (**33879**) ....‡3,125

Kewaunee
Kewaunee Enterprise (**33880**) 2,500

Kiel
Tri-County News (**33882**) ....(Paid) 4,000
(Free) 200

La Farge
Epitaph News (**33897**) 1,800

Ladysmith
Ladysmith News (**33900**) ....(Paid) 5,750

Circulation: ★ = ABC; △ = BPA; ♦ = CAC; • = CCAB; ❑ = VAC; ⊕ = PO Statement; ‡ = Publisher's Report; Boldface figures = sworn; Light figures = estimated.

2929

Newspapers

Circ.

WISCONSIN (continued)

Lake Geneva
Lake Geneva Regional News **(33903)** ....‡7,000
Peach & Leisure **(33904)** ....‡35,000

Lake Mills
The Lake Mills Leader **(33906)** ....‡3,000

Lancaster
Grant County Herald Independent **(33907)** ....‡4,000

Lodi
The Lodi Enterprise **(33911)** ....‡2,000

Loyal
Tribune-Record-Gleaner **(33913)** ....‡3,569

Luxemburg
Luxemburg News **(33914)** 2,000

Marion
Marion Advertiser **(34023)** 2,700

Markesan
Neighbors **(34025)** ....(Paid) ‡7,960

Mayville
The Mayville News **(34032)** 4,085
4,120

Medford
The Star News **(34034)** ....(Paid) ‡6,231
(Free) ‡68

Melrose
Melrose Chronicle **(34037)** ....‡4,300

Menomonie
Dunn County News, Shopper, and
Reminder **(34038)** ....(Wed.) 4,273
(Sun.) 4,273

Middleton
Middleton Times-Tribune **(34051)** ....(Paid) ⊕3,300
(Non-paid) ⊕15,000

Milton
The Milton Courier **(34054)** ....‡3,104

Milwaukee
Milwaukee Courier **(34083)** 40,000
Milwaukee Times **(34088)** ....(Non-paid) ‡7,500
The Onion **(34091)** ....(Controlled) ‡240,000
(Paid) ❏20,489

Mineral Point
Democrat-Tribune **(34145)** 1,259

Minocqua
Lakeland Times **(34146)** 10,500

Mondovi
Mondovi Herald-News **(34149)** ....(Paid) ‡3,460
(Free) ‡48

Montello
Marquette County Tribune **(34154)** .....(Paid) ‡4,585
(Free) ‡44

Mosinee
The Mosinee Times **(34155)** ....‡2,575

Mount Horeb
Mt. Horeb Mail **(34156)** ....(Paid) 2,900
(Non-paid) 9,209

Mukwonago
The Mukwonago Chief **(34158)**

Neillsville
The Clark County Press **(34163)** ....(Paid) 3,650

New Berlin
The Bay Viewer **(34166)** 1,529
Brookfield News **(34167)** 6,340
Brown Deer Herald **(34168)** 1,596
Cudahy Reminder/Enterprise **(34169)** 3,434
Elm Grove Elm Leaves **(34170)** 1,596
Fox Point-Bayside-River Hills
Herald **(34171)** 1,966
Franklin-Hales Corners Hub **(34172)** 4,324
Germantown Banner Press **(34173)** 2,310
Glendale Herald **(34174)** 1,840
Greendale Village Life **(34175)** 2,947
Greenfield Observer **(34176)** 3,469
Menomonee Falls News **(34177)** 1,468
Mequon-Thiensville Courant **(34178)** 1,468
Muskego Sun **(34179)** 3,574
New Berlin Citizen **(34180)** 4,309
Oak Creek Pictorial **(34182)** 4,566
Shorewood Herald **(34185)** 1,811
South Milwaukee Voice Graphic **(34186)** 3,645
Sussex-Lannon-Lisbon News **(34187)** 596

Circ.

Wauwatosa News-Times **(34188)** 6,286
West Allis Star **(34189)** 4,926
Whitefish Bay Herald **(34190)** 2,988

New London
New London Press-Star **(34192)** ....(Paid) ‡3,117

New Richmond
The News **(34193)** ....(Paid) 5,000

Niagara
The Niagara Journal **(34196)** ....‡1,100

Oconomowoc
Oconomowoc Enterprise **(34203)** 5,000

Oconto
Oconto County Reporter **(34204)** 4,300

Oconto Falls
Oconto County
Times-Herald **(34208)** ....(Paid) ‡4,729
(Free) ‡150

Onalaska
Holmen Courier **(34210)** ....(Paid) ⊕1,225
Onalaska Community Life **(34211)** .....(Paid) ⊕1,243

Oregon
Oregon Observer **(34218)** ....(Paid) ‡2,500

Orfordville
Orfordville Journal and Footville
News **(34220)** 966

Palmyra
Palmyra Enterprise **(34232)** 1,400

Park Falls
The Park Falls Herald **(34233)** ....(Paid) ◆3,024
(Non-paid) ◆2

Peshtigo
The Peshtigo Times **(34236)** ....‡10,817

Phillips
The Bee **(34237)** ....(Paid) ◆4,405
(Non-paid) ◆10

Platteville
Platteville Journal **(34242)** ....(Paid) ‡4,200

Plymouth
The Review **(34249)** ....‡6,968
Sheboygan Falls News **(34250)** ....‡2,083

Portage
Elroy Wonewoc Keystone
Tribune **(34256)** ....(Combined) 1,045
Keystone Reporter **(34257)** 2,000
Mauston Star Times **(34258)** ....(Combined) 3000
West Salem Coulee
News **(34261)** ....(Combined) 1,998

Poynette
Poynette Press **(34264)** 1,549

Prairie du Chien
Courier-Press **(34266)** ....(Combined) ‡20,000

Random Lake
The Sounder **(34280)** 2,852

Reedsburg
Reedsburg
Times-Press **(34281)** ....(Combined) 1,582

Rice Lake
Rice Lake Chronotype **(34294)** ....(Paid) 9,400
(Free) 152

Richland Center
Richland Observer **(34298)** 4,000

Ripon
The Ripon Commonwealth
Express **(34302)** ....‡3,700

River Falls
River Falls Journal **(34309)** ....‡4,600

Sauk City
Sauk-Prairie Star **(34313)** 4,000

Sharon
The Sharon Reporter **(34316)** ....‡850

Shell Lake
Washburn County Register **(34326)** ....(Paid) ‡1,566
(Free) ‡20

Sparta
Monroe County Democrat **(34331)** 5,200
The Sparta Herald **(34332)** 5,000
Triad **(34333)** ....(Free) ‡4,000

Circ.

Spring Green
The Weekly Home News **(34339)** 2,000

Spring Valley
Spring Valley Sun **(34340)** ....(Paid) ‡700

Stanley
The Stanley Republican **(34342)** 2,500

Stoughton
Stoughton Courier Hub **(34349)** ....⊕4,600

Sturgeon Bay
Door County Advocate **(34350)** ....(Paid) 12,600
(Combined) 21,500

Sun Prairie
The Star **(34358)** ....‡5,200

Sussex
Sussex Sun **(34364)** 3,093

Thorp
Thorp Courier **(34367)** ....‡2,464

Tomah
Journal and Monitor-Herald **(34369)** 5,300

Tomahawk
Tomahawk Leader **(34373)** ....(Paid) ‡4,150

Turtle Lake
Turtle Lake Times **(34376)** 1,250

Valders
The Valders Journal **(34379)** ....‡2,301

Verona
The Verona Press **(34380)** ....(Paid) ‡1,937
(Free) ‡6,000

Viroqua
Vernon County Broadcaster **(34383)** ....‡5,950

Walworth
Times **(34386)** ....‡3,942

Washburn
The County Journal **(34388)** 4,200

Waterford
The Waterford Post **(34390)** 2,350

Waterloo
The Courier **(34391)** ....‡2,700

Waunakee
Waunakee Tribune **(34418)** 2,000

Waupaca
Waupaca County Post **(34421)** 7,200

Waupun
Neighbors **(34427)** ....‡3,000

Wautoma
Waushara Argus **(34442)** 6,500

West Salem
Economy Shopper **(34449)** 2,100

Westby
The Times **(34450)** 2,000

Weyauwega
The Chronicle **(34451)** ....(Paid) ‡3,015
(Free) ‡9,700

Whitehall
News-Wave **(34452)** 1,074
Whitehall Times **(34454)** ....(Paid) 2,734
(Free) 70

Whitewater
Whitewater Register **(34458)** ....(Paid) ‡2900

Winter
Sawyer County Gazette **(34461)** 2,000

Wisconsin Dells
Wisconsin Dells
Events **(34462)** ....(Combined) 2,078

Wittenberg
Wittenberg Enterprise and Birnamwood
News **(34471)** ....(Paid) 1,700
(Free) 300

Wonewoc
Wonewoc Reporter **(34472)** 1,000

Woodville
Woodville Leader **(34473)** ....‡850

Numbers cited after listings are entry numbers rather than page numbers.

WYOMING

Afton
Star Valley Independent **(34474)** 3,350

Basin
Republican-Rustler **(34477)** ....‡1,264

Buffalo
Buffalo Bulletin **(34478)** ....‡4,350

Casper
Casper Journal **(34481)** ....(Paid) ‡4,800
(Combined) 30,000

Cody
Cody Enterprise **(34513)** ....(Paid) ‡6,869
(Free) ‡288

Douglas
Douglas Budget **(34519)** ....‡3,701

Dubois
The Dubois Frontier **(34520)** ....(Paid) ‡1,300
(Free) ‡20

Evanston
Uinta County Herald **(34521)** ....‡4,700

Glenrock
Glenrock Independent **(34531)** 912

Green River
Green River Star **(34532)** ....‡3,200

Greybull
Greybull Standard **(34534)** ....(Paid) ‡1,575
(Free) ‡800

Jackson
Jackson Hole Guide **(34535)** ....‡7,500
6,000
Jackson Hole News & Guide **(34536)** 11,500

Kemmerer
Kemmerer Gazette **(34541)** ....(Paid) ‡2,000
(Free) ‡50

Lander
The Lander Wyoming State
Journal **(34543)** 4,100

Lingle
Guernsey Gazette **(34559)** ....(Paid) ‡720
(Free) ‡8
Lingle Guide **(34560)** ....(Paid) ‡640
(Free) ‡12

Lovell
The Lovell Chronicle **(34561)** ....(Paid) ‡2,164
(Free) ‡40

Lusk
The Lusk Herald **(34562)** 1,350

Lyman
Bridger Valley Pioneer **(34563)** ....(Paid) ‡1,800
(Free) ‡123

Newcastle
News Letter Journal **(34564)** ....(Paid) ‡2,500
(Free) ‡40

Pine Bluffs
Pine Bluffs Post **(34566)** 1,800

Pinedale
Pinedale Roundup **(34568)** ....‡3,400

Powell
The Powell Tribune **(34569)** ....‡4,200

Saratoga
Saratoga Sun **(34586)** 1,850

Shoshoni
Shoshoni Pioneer **(34593)** 780

Sundance
The Sundance Times **(34594)** ....‡1,850

Thermopolis
Independent Record **(34595)** ....(Paid) 2,495
(Free) 19

Torrington
Torrington Telegram **(34597)** ....‡3,200

Upton
Weston County Gazette **(34600)** 800

Wheatland
Platte County Record Times **(34601)** ....‡2,900

ALBERTA, CANADA

Airdrie
Airdrie Echo **(34608)** ....(Paid) 10,780

Banff
Banff Crag and Canyon **(34612)** ....‡3,323

Barrhead
Barrhead Leader **(34614)** 4,010

Bashaw
The Bashaw Star **(34615)** ....‡612

Bassano
The Bassano Times **(34616)** 800

Beaverlodge
The Advertiser **(34617)** ....(Wed.) 1,611

Blairmore
The Crowsnest Pass
Promoter **(34618)** ....(Paid) ‡2,600
(Free) ‡100
The Pass Herald **(34619)** ....(Paid) 2,153
(Free) 110

Bonnyville
Bonnyville Nouvelle **(34621)** ....‡3,942

Bow Island
The 40-Mile County Commentator **(34622)** ....‡5,891

Brooks
Brooks Bulletin **(34623)** ....(Combined) ‡5,537

Canmore
Canmore Leader **(34678)** ....‡3,845

Cardston
The Star **(34680)** 3,500

Castor
Castor Advance **(34682)** ....‡1,168

Claresholm
Claresholm Local Press **(34683)** ....‡2,041

Coaldale
Sunny South News **(34684)** 4025

Cochrane
Cochrane Times **(34685)** ....‡2,523

Cold Lake
Cold Lake Sun **(34687)** ....(Paid) ‡6,819
(Free) ‡124

Consort
Consort Enterprise **(34689)** ....‡1,293

Coronation
Coronation Review **(34690)** ....(Paid) 1,220

Devon
Beaumont Nouvelle **(34692)** 4,722
Devon Dispatch **(34693)** ....(Paid) ‡2,049

Didsbury
The Didsbury Review **(34694)** ....‡1603

Drayton Valley
Drayton Valley Western Review **(34695)** 5,000

Drumheller
The Drumheller Mail **(34696)** ....‡4,833

Edmonton
Alberta Sweetgrass **(34700)** ....(Combined) 7,000
Beverly Page **(34702)** 15,000
Le Franco-Albertain **(34720)** ....(Paid) 4,300
(Free) 50
Ukrainian News **(34732)** ....(Paid) 4,487
(Non-paid) 2,000
Windspeaker **(34738)** ....(Combined) 18,000

Edson
Edson Leader **(34758)**

Elk Point
Elk Point Review **(34763)** ....(Paid) ‡589

Fairview
The Fairview Post **(34764)** 3,400

Falher
Smoky River Express **(34765)** ....‡2,050

Fort Macleod
The Macleod Gazette **(34766)** ....‡1,544

Fort Saskatchewan
The Fort Saskatchewan Record **(34771)**
The Record **(34772)** ....(Paid) 1,862
(Free) 2,217

Grande Cache
Grande Cache Mountaineer **(34773)** .....(Paid) 1,217

Grimshaw
Mile Zero News **(34778)** ....‡1,375

Hanna
The Hanna Herald **(34779)** 3,200

High Level
The Echo **(34780)** 1,908

High Prairie
South Peace News **(34781)** 2,500

High River
High River Times **(34783)** ....(Paid) 3,130
(Free) 199

Innisfail
Innisfail Province **(34787)** ....‡7,535

Jasper
Jasper Booster **(34789)** 1,661

Lac La Biche
Lac La Biche Post **(34790)** 2,800

Lacombe
The Lacombe Globe **(34791)** ....(Paid) ‡3,800
(Free) ‡200

Lloydminster
Lloydminster Daily Times **(34802)**
Meridian Booster **(34803)** ....(Non-paid) 15,000

Manning
Banner Post **(34806)** 1,217
The Northern Pioneer **(34807)** 1,081

Mayerthorpe
Mayerthorpe Freelancer **(34808)** ....(Paid) 1,455

Nanton
The Nanton News **(34817)** 1,353

Olds
Olds Gazette **(34819)** 3,990
5,000

Oyen
The Oyen Echo **(34821)** ....(Paid) ‡1,439
(Free) ‡35

Peace River
Record-Gazette **(34822)** ....(Paid) 3,156

Pincher Creek
Pincher Creek Echo **(34824)** 2,450

Provost
The Provost News **(34826)** ....(Paid) 1,941
(Free) 106

Rocky Mountain House
The Mountaineer **(34839)** ....(Wed.) 4,861

Rycroft
The Central Peace Signal **(34840)** 2,480

St. Albert
St. Albert Gazette **(34842)** ....(Wed.) 23,860
(Free) 15,500

St. Michael
The Triangle **(34843)** ....‡1,600

Sedgewick
Community Press **(34846)** ....‡3,577

Smoky Lake
Smoky Lake Signal **(34851)** ....(Paid) 1,500
(Free) 1,200

Stony Plain
The Reporter **(34857)** ....‡11,320

Strathmore
The Strathmore Standard **(34858)** ....‡4,241

Sundre
Round-Up **(34859)** 2,127
2110

Swan Hills
Swan Hills Grizzly Gazette **(34860)** ....‡700

Three Hills
Capital **(34861)** 3,709

Tofield
Tofield Mercury **(34862)** ....‡2,144

Valleyview
Valleyview Valley Views **(34863)** 1500

Newspapers

Circ.　　　　　　Circ.　　　　　　Circ.

ALBERTA, CANADA (continued)

Vegreville
Vegreville Observer (34865) ....(Free) 5,700

Viking
The Weekly Review (34866) ....‡1,856

Vulcan
The Vulcan Advocate (34867) ....‡3,317
　　　　　　　　　　　　　　　　　　　‡2,408

Westlock
Westlock News (34871) 6,000

Wetaskiwin
Wetaskiwin Times Advertiser (34873) ....‡11,415

Whitecourt
Whitecourt Star (34875) ....‡3,025

BRITISH COLUMBIA, CANADA

Aldergrove
The Afro News (34879)
Aldergrove Star (34880) 8,886

Armstrong
Armstrong Advertiser (34882) ....(Paid) 1,800
　　　　　　　　　　　　　　　　(Non-paid) 10

Ashcroft
Ashcroft Journal (34883) ....(Paid) ‡1,780
　　　　　　　　　　　　　　　　　(Free) ‡2,550

Big White
Big White Mountaineer (34885) ....(Paid) 764

Bowen Island
The Bowen Island Undercurrent (34886) ......‡6,000

Burns Lake
Lakes District News (34915) ....‡1,950

Campbell River
Campbell River
　Courier-Islander (34917) ....(Paid) 16,350

Chetwynd
Chetwynd Echo (34924) ....(Paid) ‡1,300

Chilliwack
The Chilliwack Progress (34926) ......(Tues.) 27,451
　　　　　　　　　　　　　　　　　(Fri.) 27,256

Creston
Creston Valley Advance (34939) 4,179

Fernie
The Free Press (34953) ....(Paid) 2,800

Fort Nelson
Fort Nelson News (34956) ....‡2,500

Fort St. James
Caledonia Courier (34958) ....(Paid) ‡1,147

Gold River
The Record (34964) ....(Combined) 1,300

Golden
The Golden Star (34966) ....‡2,225

Grand Forks
Gazette (34971) ....‡3,198

Greenwood
Boundary Creek Times
　Mountaineer (34973) ....(Paid) 764

Hagensborg
Coast Mountain News (34974) ....‡1,000

Houston
Houston Today (34975) 1,257

Invermere
The Valley Echo (34976) ....‡3,580
　　　　　　　　　　　　　　　　　　　3400

Kelowna
Kelowna Capital News (34989) ....(Sun.) 50,947
　　　　　　　　　　　　　　　(Wed.) 51,009
　　　　　　　　　　　　　　　　(Fri.) 49,541

Keremeos
Keremeos Review (34996) ....(Combined) ‡1,735

Kitimat
Northern Sentinel (34998) 2,500

Ladysmith
Ladysmith-Chemainus Chronicle (35001) .....‡2,533

Lake Cowichan
The Lake News (35002) ....(Paid) 1,579
　　　　　　　　　　　　　　　　　(Free) 1,080

Langley
The Windmill Herald (35006) ....‡11,500

Lazo
CFB Comox Totem
　Times (35008) ....(Combined) 2,150

Lillooet
Bridge River-Lillooet
　News (35010) ....(Combined) 2,652

Merritt
Merritt Herald (35014) ....‡2,094

Mission
Fraser Valley Record (35015) ....(Non-paid) 10
　　　　　　　　　　　　　　　　　(Paid) 5,138
The Mission City
　Record (35016) ....(Combined) 9,734

Nakusp
Arrow Lakes News (35017) ....‡2,249

Okanagan Falls
Okanagan Falls Review (35037) ....‡1,735

Oliver
Oliver Chronicle (35038) 2,471

100 Mile House
Free Press (35040) 5,068

Osoyoos
Osoyoos Times (35042) ....‡2,650

Penticton
Penticton Western
　News (35045) ....(Non-paid) 20,062

Port Hardy
North Island Gazette (35051) ....‡3,167

Powell River
The Powell River Peak (35054) ....(Paid) ‡4,296
　　　　　　　　　　　　　　　　(Non-paid) ‡7,975

Princeton
Princeton-Similkameen Spotlight (35066) 1,800

Queen Charlotte
Queen Charlotte Islands Observer (35068) ....‡1,850

Revelstoke
Revelstoke Times Review (35071)

Salmon Arm
Salmon Arm Observer (35081) ....‡4,775

Salt Spring Island
Gulf Islands Driftwood (35086) ....‡4,372

Sicamous
Eagle Valley News (35089) ....‡1,208

Smithers
The Interior News (35090) ....‡4,877

Summerland
Summerland Review (35103) ....‡2,854

Surrey
Akal Guardian (35105) ....(Non-paid) 15,000
Charhdi Kala (35107) 15,000

Terrace
Terrace Review (35111) ....‡2,000

Ucluelet
The Westerly News (35117) ....‡1,500

Valemount
The Valley Sentinel (35118) ....(Paid) ‡1,182
　　　　　　　　　　　　　　　　　(Free) ‡12

Vancouver
The Flag & Banner (35141) ....(Controlled) ⊕10,000
The Jewish Western
　Bulletin (35151) ....(Combined) 2,587

Vanderhoof
Omineca Express (35198) ....‡2,600

Victoria
The Lookout (35220) ....‡5,000
Saanich News (35225) 32,800

Williams Lake
The Tribune (35243) ....‡6,130

MANITOBA, CANADA

Altona
The Red River Valley Echo (35247) ....‡6,423

Baldur
Gazette-News (35251) 1,300

Boissevain
Boissevain Recorder (35252) ....‡1,650

Carberry
Carberry News-Express (35259) ....‡1,277

Carman
Carman Valley
　Leader (35260) ....(Combined) ‡7,100

Cartwright
Southern Manitoba Review (35261) ....(Paid) ‡1,033
　　　　　　　　　　　　　　　　　(Free) ‡34

Dauphin
Dauphin Herald (35263) ....‡6,300

Deloraine
Times & Star (35265) ....(Paid) 1,125
　　　　　　　　　　　　　　　　　(Free) 50

Glenboro
The Glenboro Gazette (35268) ....‡1,200

Grandview
Grandview Exponent (35269) ....‡1,330

Killarney
Guide (35270) 2,054

Lac du Bonnet
Lac du Bonnet Leader (35271) ....(Paid) ‡1,816

Manitou
The Western Canadian (35272) ....(Paid) ‡1,850
　　　　　　　　　　　　　　　　　(Free) ‡10

Melita
Melita New Era (35273) ....‡1,600

Minnedosa
The Minnedosa Tribune (35274) ....‡3,691

Neepawa
The Gladstone Enterprise (35276) ......(Paid) ‡1,772
Heartland Shopper (35277) ....‡5,860

The Pas
Opasquia Times (35278) ....‡3,637

Pilot Mound
The Sentinel Courier (35280) ....(Paid) 1,379
　　　　　　　　　　　　　　　　　(Free) 25

Portage La Prairie
Herald Leader Press (35282) ....‡6,500

Reston
The Reston Recorder (35285) ....(Paid) ‡1,131
　　　　　　　　　　　　　　　　　(Free) ‡1,169

Rivers
Rivers Banner (35286) ....(Paid) ‡1,850

Roblin
Roblin Review (35287) ....‡2,023

Russell
Banner (35288) 2,350

St. Boniface
La Liberte (35289) 6,000

Shoal Lake
Crossroads This Week (35292) ....(Paid) ‡3,533

Souris
The Souris Plaindealer (35293) ....(Paid) ‡1,427

Steinbach
The Carillon (35294) ....(Thurs.) 11,004

Stonewall
The Selkirk Journal (35297) ......(Combined) 17,128
Stonewall Argus & Teulon
　Times (35298) ....(Combined) ‡4,689

Swan River
Star & Times (35299) 4,500

Thompson
The Citizen (35300) ....(Paid) ‡3,320
　　　　　　　　　　　　　　　　(Free) ‡200
Thompson Nickel Belt News (35301) ....‡6,721

Treherne
The Times (35305) 3,000

Virden
Virden Empire-Advance (35306) ....‡2,928

Winnipeg
Czas (Times) (35325) ....(Paid) 3,000
(Free) 1,000
The Jewish Post & News (35334) ......(Paid) •2,306
(Non-paid) •755
KANADA KURIER (35335) ......(Combined) ‡25,000
Ukrainian Voice (35354) ....(Paid) 1,880
(Free) 50

NEW BRUNSWICK, CANADA
Bathurst
The Northern Light (35378) ....(Wed.) 6,786

Campbellton
L'Aviron (35382) ....‡8,000
The Tribune (35383) ....(Wed.) 5,238

Edmundston
Journal Le Madawaska
Ltee (35385) ....(Wed.) ‡7,724

Grand Falls
The Cataract (35406) ....‡4,875

Miramichi
Miramichi Leader (35408) ....(Tues.) ★7,668
Miramichi Weekend (35409) ....(Sat.) 8,046

Moncton
The Moncton Provider (35412) ....‡700

Sackville
The Sackville Tribune-Post (35427) .....(Wed.) 3,344

St. Stephen
Courier Weekend (35436) ....‡3,197
Saint Croix Courier (35437) 4,579

Woodstock
The Bugle (35440) ....(Paid) 6,310

NEWFOUNDLAND AND LABRADOR, CANADA
Corner Brook
Humber Log (35446) ....(Paid) ‡5,835
(Free) ‡125

Gander
The Beacon (35455) ....(Paid) ‡6,200

Happy Valley
Labradorian (35465) ....(Paid) ‡3,184
(Free) ‡250
Northern Reporter (35466) ....‡1,500

Harbour Breton
The Coaster (35468) ....‡1,476

Labrador City
The Aurora (35469) ....‡3,480

Lewisporte
The Pilot (35470) ....(Paid) 4,841
(Free) ‡125

Marystown
The Southern Gazette (35472) ....(Paid) ‡4,850
(Free) ‡550

Port-aux-Basques
The Gulf News (35477) ....‡3,317

St. Anthony
Northern Pen (35482) 6,316

St. John's
Express (35486) ....(Non-paid) 50,515

Springdale
Nor'Wester (35507) ....(Paid) ‡3,989
(Free) ‡4,700

Stephenville
The Georgian (35508) ....‡2,956

NORTHWEST TERRITORIES, CANADA
Fort Smith
Slave River Journal (35514) ....‡2,193

Hay River
The Hub (35515) ....(Paid) 1,826
(Controlled) 1,163

Iqaluit
Nunatsiaq News (35519) ....(Combined) ‡9,800

Yellowknife
L'Aquilon (35522) ....‡1,000
Deh Cho Drum (35523) ....(Combined) 1,244

Inuvik Drum (35524) ....(Combined) 1,462
News/North (35525) ....(Paid) 6,783
(Controlled) 3,344
The Press Independent (35526) ....‡4,724
Yellowknifer (35528) ....(Paid) 4,486
(Controlled) 555

NOVA SCOTIA, CANADA
Annapolis Royal
The Spectator (35535) ....(Paid) ‡1,954
(Free) ‡100

Antigonish
The Casket (35537) 8,000

Berwick
The Register (35541) 2,948

Bridgewater
Bulletin/Progress
Enterprise (35542) ....(Paid) ‡12,334
(Free) ‡267

Digby
The Digby Courier (35552) ....(Paid) ‡4,700
(Free) ‡185

Inverness
The Inverness Oran (35581) ....(Paid) 5,073
(Free) 5,154

Liverpool
Advance (35586) 3,500

Lunnegburg
Progress Enterprise 1 Bulletin (35593) ....‡14,000

Middleton
The Mirror-Examiner (35594) ....(Paid) ‡2,296
(Free) ‡135

New Glasgow
The Evening News (35596) ....(Combined) 18,200

New Minas
The Kentville Advertiser (35599) ....(Tues.) 6,630
(Fri.) 5,349

Oxford
The Oxford Journal (35600) ....‡3,550

Pictou
Pictou Advocate (35602) ....‡4,021

Shelburne
The Coast Guard (35604) 5,600

Springhill
Springhill-Parrsboro Record (35606) ....‡4,800

Yarmouth
Yarmouth Vanguard (35624) ....(Tues.) 6,305
(Fri.) 4,586

ONTARIO, CANADA
Alexandria
The Glengarry News (35629) ....(Wed.) 6,596

Alliston
The Herald (35630) ....(Wed.) 4,300

Almonte
Gazette (35631) ....(Wed.) 2,539

Amherstburg
The Amherstburg Echo (35632)

Arnprior
Chronicle-Guide (35635) ....(Wed.) 2,756

Atikokan
The Atikokan Progress (35639) ....(Paid) 1,769

Aylmer
The Aylmer Express (35654) 3,977

Ayr
Ayr News (35656) ....(Paid) 3,850

Barry's Bay
Barry's Bay This Week (35666) 5,700

Beamsville
Lincoln Post Express (35670) ....‡3,500

Beansville
The Grimsby Independent (35671) ....‡5,261

Beaverton
Brock Citizen (35672) ....(Paid) 1,600

Beeton
The Beeton Record Sentinel (35673) ....‡3,900

Belle River
Lakeshore News (35675) ....(Paid) ‡2,336
(Free) ‡164

Blenheim
Blenheim News-Tribune (35686) ....(Wed.) 2,917

Bobcaygeon
Independent (35689) 2,400

Bolton
The Enterprise (35690) 11,815

Bracebridge
Bracebridge Examiner Limited (35694) 4,750

Brighton
Brighton Independent (35707) ....(Paid) 439
(Controlled) 14,091

Burks Falls
The Almaguin News (35712) 6,000

Caledonia
The Grand River Sachem (35721) ....‡2,400
Regional News This Week (35722) 17,500

Cambridge
The Cambridge Reporter (35724)

Carleton Place
Carleton Place Canadian (35728) ....(Wed.) 3,246

Chesley
The Chesley Enterprise (35734) 3,077

Chesterville
Chesterville Record (35735) ....(Paid) 2,700
(Non-paid) 300

Clinton
Clinton News-Record (35737) ....(Paid) 3,460
(Free) 163

Cobden
The Cobden Sun (35740) ....‡1,600

Cobourg
Northumberland News (35742) ....(Combined) 21,500

Cochrane
Pinewood Country Creations (35744) ....(Paid) 1,978

Colborne
Colborne Chronicle (35746) 1,300

Collingwood
The Enterprise-Bulletin (35748) ....(Wed.) 4,190
(Sat.) 17,565

Cornwall
Le Journal de Cornwall (35753) ....(Paid) ‡1,023
(Free) ‡1,077

Deep River
North Renfrew Times (35762) ....‡2,338
★2,294

Dorchester
Signpost (35782) ....‡2,600

Downsview
Giornale di Sicilia (35783)
Toronto Jewish Press (35785)

Drayton
Eramosa Community News (35786) 3,500

Dresden
The Bothwell Times (35787) 1,650

Dryden
The Dryden Observer (35790) ....(Tues.) 5,500

Dundalk
Dundalk Herald (35793) ....‡3,500

Dunnville
The Dunnville Chronicle (35795) 3,800

Durham
The Durham Chronicle (35798) 1,038

Dutton
Dutton Advance (35799) 1,600

Eganville
The Eganville Leader (35800) 6,000

Elmira
The Elmira Independent (35805) 4,554

Elmvale
Elmvale Lance (35806) ....‡1,500

Circulation: ★ = ABC; △ = BPA; ♦ = CAC; ● = CCAB; ❏ = VAC; ⊕ = PO Statement; ‡ = Publisher's Report; Boldface figures = sworn; Light figures = estimated.

Circ.

ONTARIO, CANADA (continued)

Erin
The Erin Advocate (35807) ....‡2,463

Espanola
Mid-North Monitor (35808) 3,400

Essex
Free Press (35809) ....(Paid) ‡3,000
(Free) ‡700

Exeter
Times-Advocate (35828) 4,900

Flesherton
Flesherton Advance (35832) ....‡1,500

Forest
The Forest Standard (35838) ....(Paid) ‡3,437
(Free) ‡41

Fort Frances
Ft. Frances Times and Rainy Lake
Herald (35841) ....(Wed.) 6,114

Gananoque
The Reporter (35844) ....(Wed.) 3,469

Geraldton
Geraldton-Longlac Times-Star (35846) ....‡1,780

Glencoe
Transcript & Free Press (35848) ....(Paid) 2,500
(Free) ‡56

Goderich
The Goderich Signal-Star (35851) 5,512
The Teeswater News (35852) ....‡1,650

Grand Bend
The Lakeshore Advance (35854) 2,000

Grand Valley
Star and Vidette (35855) ....(Paid) ‡1,150
(Free) ‡200

Gravenhurst
Gravenhurst Banner (35856) ....‡3,250

Hagersville
Haldimand Press (35871) 4,307

Haliburton
Haliburton County Echo & Minden
Recorder (35872) ....‡5,000
The Times (35873) ....(Paid) ‡3,028
(Free) ‡25

Hanover
The Hanover Post (35900) ....(Tues.) 3,600

Harriston
The Harriston Review (35902) ....‡1,700

Harrow
Harrow & Colchester South This
Week (35903) ....(Paid) ‡1,400
The Harrow News (35904) ....‡1,450

Hawkesbury
Le Carillon (35907) ....(Free) ‡16,000
(Paid) ‡450

Hearst
Le Nord (35911) ....(Paid) 3,455
(Free) 45

Hornepayne
Bear News (35916) ....(Paid) 500

Huntsville
Huntsville Forester (35917) ....(Wed.) 6,515

Ingersoll
Ingersoll Times (35921) 3,400

Innisfil
Innisfil Scope (35922) ....(Paid) ‡1,625

Iroquois
The Chieftain (35923) ....‡1,900

Iroquois Falls
The Enterprise (35924) ....(Wed.) 2,296

Kapuskasing
Northern Times (35926) ....‡4,600
10,829

Kemptville
The Advance (35928) ....‡4,900

Kent
North Kent Leader (35931) ....‡3,300

Circ.

Keswick
Georgina Advocate (35932) ....(Paid) ‡200
(Free) ‡15,309

Kincardine
The Independent (35933) ....(Paid) ‡2,000
Kincardine News (35934) ....‡4,003

Kingsville
The Kingsville Reporter (35956) ....‡2,254

Leamington
Leamington Shopper (35969) ....(Paid) 5,000

Lindsay
Lindsay Performer (35972) ....‡23,452

Listowel
The Listowel Banner (35975) ....(Paid) ‡3,844
(Free) ‡71

Little Current
Manitoulin Expositor (35977) ....(Wed.) 5,385

London
The Shoreline News (35992) ....(Combined) 3,200

Lucknow
The Lucknow Sentinel (36004) ....(Paid) 1,867

Manitoulin Usland
Manitoulin Recorder (36008) ....(Fri.) 2,650

Manotick
MANOTICK Messenger (36009) 1,600

Marathon
Mercury (36011) ....‡1403

Markdale
The Markdale Standard (36013) ....(Paid) 1,024

Markham
Economist & Sun (36024) ....(Tues.) 37,137
(Thurs.) 37,333
(Sat.) 37,248
Flamborough Review (36025) ....‡12,223

Mattawa
The Mattawa Recorder (36035) ....‡1,000

Meaford
The Express (36036) ....(Combined) 2,551

Midland
Ajax-Pickering News
Advertiser (36038) ....(Fri.) 49,831
(Sun.) 43,090
(Wed.) 44,355
The Collingwood Connection (36040)
The Free Press (36041) ....(Paid) 4,311
The Midland Mirror (36043) ....(Combined) 18,200
Orillia Today (36044) ....(Combined) 18,500

Mildmay
Mildmay Town & Country Crier (36046) 2,000

Millbrook
Millbrook Times (36047) ....‡1,151

Mississauga
Kanadske Listy (Canadian Pages) (36072) ....‡2,800
Teviskes Ziburiai (The Lights of
Homeland) (36089) ....(Paid) ‡3,286
(Free) ‡142

Mitchell
The Mitchell Advocate (36094)

Morrisburg
The Leader (36096) ....(Paid) 2,013

Mount Forest
The Mount Forest Confederate (36097) ....‡2,614

Napanee
Napanee Beaver (36098) ....(Fri.) 14,188
(Wed.) 4,128

New Liskeard
Temiskaming Speaker (36105) .....(Combined) 7,400

Nipigon
Nipigon-Red Rock Gazette (36115) .....(Paid) ‡1,992
(Free) ‡55

Norwich
Norwich Gazette (36134) 2,000

Oakville
Oakville Beaver (36147) ....(Paid) 562
(Non-paid) 38,750
Oakville Today (36149) 22,000
The South Asian Voice (36151) ....(Paid) 35
(Non-paid) 8,000

Circ.

Ohsweken
Tekawennake (36155) 2500

Orangeville
The Orangeville Banner (36172) ....(Paid) •346
(Non-paid) •20,860

Orono
Orono Weekly Times (36179) 1,100

Oshawa
Oshawa-Whitby-Clarington-Port Perry This
Week (36181) ....(Wed.) 84,313
(Tues.) 87,990
(Fri.) 88,846
(Sun.) 100,611

Ottawa
The Hill Times (36248)
Ottawa Jewish Bulletin (36266) ....(Controlled) 9,200
Ottawa Sun (36268) ....(Mon.-Fri.) ★51,958
(Sat.) ★46,198
(Sun.) ★54,375

Palmerston
Palmerston Observer (36305) 1,400

Paris
Paris Star (36306) 4,481

Parkhill
The Parkhill Gazette (36307) ....‡1,765

Perth
The Perth Courier (36312) ....(Wed.) 5,415

Peterborough
Arthur (36313) ....(Free) ‡3,000
Peterborough
Examiner (36318) ....(Controlled) 71,600
Peterborough This Week (36319) ......(Wed.) 45,082
(Sat.) 46,769

Picton
Picton Gazette (36329) ....(Wed.) 3,033
(Fri.) 10,000

Port Dover
Port Dover Maple Leaf (36332) ....(Paid) ‡4,250

Port Elgin
Shoreline Beacon Times (36333) ....‡2,995

Port Perry
Port Perry Star (36335) ....(Tues.) 5,000
(Fri.) 23,000

Prescott
Journal (36337) 3,285

Rainy River
Rainy River Record (36338) ....‡1,500

Renfrew
Mercury (36339) ....(Wed.) 4,885

St. Mary's
Journal-Argus (36360) 4,190

Sarnia
Lambton Shopping News (36364) 43,000
Sarnia This Week (36366) ....(Paid) 23,000
(Free) 6,500

Sault Sainte Marie
Sault Ste. Marie This Week (36369) 34,500

Scarborough
Iranian Community Newspaper (36377)
Parry Sound Beacon-Star (36381) 6,000
Parry Sound North Star (36382) 7,000

Seaforth
Huron Expositor (36388) ....(Paid) ‡2,658

Shelburne
Free Press & Economist (36389) ....‡2,800

Sioux Lookout
Wawatay News (36393) ....‡9,200

Smiths Falls
The Record News (36395) ....(Wed.) 2,709

Smithville
West Lincoln Review (36398) ....‡1,922

Stayner
Stayner Sun (36401) 1,200

Stittsville
The Stittsville News (36404) ....‡3,598

Stouffville
Stouffville Sun (36407) ....‡6,500

Numbers cited after listings are entry numbers rather than page numbers.

Strathroy
The Age Dispatch (36412) ....(Paid) 5,400

Sturgeon Falls
Tribune (36414) ....(Paid) 2,653

Sudbury
Journal Le Voyageur (36416) 10,000
Sudbury Northern Life (36419) ....(Paid) 44,335

Tavistock
Tavistock Gazette (36430) 1,300

Thamesville
Thamesville Herald (36432) ....(Paid) ‡900
(Non-paid) ‡100

Thessalon
The North Shore Sentinel (36433) 3,300

Thornbury
Courier-Herald (36434) ....‡1,300

Thorold
Thorold News (36435) ....(Paid) 2,415
(Non-paid) 235

Thunder Bay
Thunder Bay Post (36443) ....‡48,000

Tillsonburg
Delhi News-Record (36449) 3,719
The Tillsonburg News (36450) 7,694

Timmins
Moosonee Freighter (36455) 1,000
The Timmins Times (36456) ....(Paid) 13
(Non-paid) 18,772

Toronto
Canadian Free Press (36499)
Corriere Canadese/Canadian
Courier (36560) ....(Controlled) ‡32,630
Deutsche Presse (German
Press) (36572) ....‡30,000
L'Express (36589) ....(Paid) 20,000
(Non-paid) 5,000
Georgian Bay Today (36600) ....(Paid) 3,000
Latvija Amerika (36649) ....‡3,000
Le Courrier d'Oshawa (36650)
Magyar Naplo (36655) ....(Paid) ‡5,000
(Free) ‡4,000
Meie Elu (36661) ....‡2,500
MetroToday (36664)
Polish Canadian Courier/Nowy
Kurier (36713) 20,000
Satellite 1-416 (36735) ....(Combined) 1,500
Shing Wah News (36740) ....(Paid) 1,000
(Free) 9,000
Toronto East End Express (36766)

Tottenham
The Tottenham Times (36823) ....‡3,900

Trenton
Trentonian and Tri-County News (36825) 7,958

Tweed
Tweed News (36826) ....(Paid) ‡1,263

Uxbridge
Uxbridge Times-Journal (36839) ....‡9,000

Vankleek Hill
The Review (36840) ....‡4,338

Virgil
The Niagara Advance (36841) ....‡6,000

Walkerton
Herald-Times (36842) ....‡2,943

Waterloo
Waterloo Chronicle (36859) 24,500

Watford
Watford Guide-Advocate (36864) ....(Paid) 1,373

Wawa
Algoma News Review (36865) ....(Paid) ‡1,400
(Free) ‡50

Westport
The Review Mirror (36871) ....‡2,400

Wheatley
Wheatley Journal (36872) ....(Paid) 1,300

Wiarton
The Wiarton Echo (36874) ....‡4,542

Willowdale
Fortnightly Al-Hilal (36877) ....(Paid) ‡4,000
(Free) ‡1,500

North York Mirror (36881) ....(Non-paid) 99,028
The Scarborough
Mirror (36883) ....(Non-paid) 108,216

Winchester
The Winchester Press (36885) 4,200

Windsor
The International Citizen (36888)

PRINCE EDWARD ISLAND, CANADA
Alberton
West Prince Graphic (36911) ....(Wed.) 2,155

Charlottetown
The Buzz (36912)

Montague
The Eastern Graphic (36921) ....(Wed.) 5,645

Summerside
EDT (36922) ....‡1,000
The First Informer (36923) ....(Paid) ‡588
(Free) ‡12
La Voix Acadienne (36925) ....(Controlled) 1,050

QUEBEC, CANADA
Abitibiens
L'Echo Abitibien (36928) ....(Wed.) 15,000

Amos
L'Echo d'Amos (36932) ....‡3,921

Arthabaska
Union (36941) ....‡25,000

Beauport
Beauport Express (36948) 38,287

Cap-aux-Meules
Le Radar (36954) ....(Fri.) 2,300

Chibougamau
La Sentinelle (36964) ....(Tues.) 2,394

Farnham
L'Avenir de Brome Missisquoi (36994) ......‡8,733

Hudson
Hudson Gazette (37001) ....‡8,000

Huntingdon
Gleaner (37008) ....(Wed.) 3,534

Kahnawake
The Eastern Door (37017)

La Sarre
L'Echo d'Abitibi Ouest (37022) ....‡3,212

Lachute
Tribune Express Progres
Watchman (37030) ....(Combined) ‡13,100

Lennoxville
The Townships Sun (37047) ....‡750

Longueuil
La Terre de Chez Nous (37052) ....(Paid) 40,400

Louiseville
L'Echo de Louiseville (37060) ....(Wed.) 5,387

Malartic
L'Echo de Malartic (37064) ....‡914

Matane
La Voix du Dimanche (37068) 9,800
La Voix Gaspesienne (37069) ....(Wed.) 4,979

Mont-Tremblant
L'Information du Nord
L'Annonciation (37075) ....(Paid) ‡7,500

Montreal
Il Cittadino Canadese (37124) ....‡48,320

New Carlisle
Gaspe Spec (37255) 2,818

Plessisville
L'avenir De L'erable (37269) ....(Tues.) 11,093

Richelain
Servir (37306) 3,300

Riviere-du-Loup
Le Saint Laurent/Portage (37314) ......(Paid) 27,693

Rouyn-Noranda
La Frontiere (37321) ....(Wed.) 5,614

Saint-Bruno
Le Journal de Saint-Bruno (37329) 17,573

Ste.-Foy
Quebec Chronicle
Telegraph (37338) ....(Paid) ‡1,981

Saint-Hubert
Le Journal de Saint-Hubert (37345) ....‡28,800

Saint-Hyacinthe
Le Clairon Regional de St.
Hyacinthe (37350) 33,926

Saint-Jean
Le Canada Francais (37354) ....(Wed.) 14,431

Saint-Jerome
Journal Le Nord (37356) 39,725

Saint-Lambert
St. Lambert Journal (37360) 5,000

Saint-Laurent
Abaka (37361) ....(Paid) ‡875
(Free) ‡75

Shawville
The Equity (37392) ....(Wed.) 4,300

Sorel
La Voix (37404) ....(Non-paid) 28,185

Stanstead
The Stanstead Journal (37408) ....‡3,500

Trois-Pistoles
Le Courrier (37414) 11,725

Victoriaville
La Nouvelle (37431) 40,000

Wakefield
The Low Down to Hull & Back
News (37439) 2,000

Windsor
L'Etincelle (37450) ....(Free) ‡8,700

SASKATCHEWAN, CANADA
Assiniboia
The Assiniboia Times (37451) ....‡4,300

Biggar
The Independent (37452) ....‡2,347

Broadview
Broadview Express (37453) 805

Canora
Canora Courier (37455) ....‡2,300
Norquay North Star (37456) ....‡860
Preeceville Progress (37457) ....‡1,1675

Carlyle
Carlyle Observer (37458) ....‡2,098

Carnduff
Gazette-Post-News (37459) ....‡1,335

Craik
Craik Weekly News (37461) 1,800

Cut Knife
Highway 40 Courier (37462) ....(Combined) ‡576

Davidson
Davidson Leader (37463) ....‡1,972

Esterhazy
Potashville-Miner Journal (37464) ....‡1,900

Estevan
The Estevan Mercury (37465) 5,059

Eston
The Eston Press Review (37467) ....‡1,300

Foam Lake
Foam Lake Review (37468) 2,000
Ituna News (37469) 1,000

Fort Qu'Appelle
Ft. Qu'Appelle Times (37470) 1,650

Gravelbourg
Tribune (37471) ....(Paid) 1,400

Grenfell
Grenfell Sun (37472) ....‡1,285

Gull Lake
Gull Lake Advance (37473) ....‡1,514

Herbert
The Herald (37474) 1,700

Circulation: ★ = ABC; △ = BPA; ◆ = CAC; ● = CCAB; ▢ = VAC; ⊕ = PO Statement; ‡ = Publisher's Report; Boldface figures = sworn; Light figures = estimated.

Newspapers

2935

Circ.

Circ.

Circ.

SASKATCHEWAN, CANADA (continued)

Hudson Bay
Hudson Bay Post-Review **(37475)** ....‡1,800

Humboldt
Journal **(37476)** 4,631

Indian Head
Indian Head-Wolseley News **(37477)**

Kamsack
Kamsack Times **(37478)** ....‡1,790

Kerrobert
Kerrobert Citizen-Dispatch **(37480)** 950

Kindersley
Kindersley Clarion **(37481)** 3,039
The Leader News **(37482)** 1,135

Kipling
The Citizen **(37485)** 1,847

La Ronge
The La Ronge Northerner **(37486)** ......(Paid) 2,000

Langenburg
The Four-Town Journal **(37488)** ....(Paid) 1,664

Lanigan
Lanigan Advisor **(37489)** 1,429

Lumsden
The New Waterfront Press **(37491)** 1,750

Macklin
Macklin Mirror **(37492)** ....‡970

Maidstone
Mirror **(37493)** ....(Paid) 1,343

Maple Creek
Maple Creek News **(37494)** 2,500

Meadow Lake
Meadow Lake Progress **(37495)** 3,933

Melfort
Kinistino—Birch Hills
   Post—Gazette **(37497)** ....‡1,620
The Melfort Journal **(37498)** ....‡3,760

Melville
Advance **(37500)** ....‡3,500

Moosomin
World Spectator **(37504)** 3,023

Nipawin
Nipawin Journal **(37506)** 4,000
Nipawin N.E. Region Community
   Booster **(37507)** ....(Paid) ‡16,046

North Battleford
News-Optimist **(37508)** ....‡3,414
The Riverbend Review **(37510)** ....(Paid) 756
Sunday Edition News-Optimist **(37511)** 3,143

Outlook
The Outlook **(37514)** ....‡2,540

Oxbow
Oxbow Herald **(37515)** 1,500

Radville
The Radville Star **(37523)** 1,350

Redvers
Optimist **(37524)** 1,921

Regina
Journal L'Eau Vive **(37531)** ....(Paid) ‡1,400
(Free) ‡100

Rosetown
Rosetown Eagle **(37545)** 2,382

Rosthern
Saskatchewan Valley News **(37547)** ....‡3,102

Shaunavon
Shaunavon Standard **(37569)** 3,100

Shellbrook
Shellbrook Chronicle **(37571)** ....‡2,683
Spiritwood Herald **(37572)** ....‡1,148

Strasbourg
Last Mountain Times **(37574)** ....‡1,826

Tisdale
Tisdale Recorder **(37580)** ....‡2,667

Unity
Northwest Herald **(37581)** ....(Paid) 1,926
(Free) 300

Wadena
Kelvington Radio **(37582)** ....(Paid) 1,155
The Wadena News **(37583)** ....(Paid) 3,232
(Free) 53

Wakaw
Recorder **(37584)** 2,000

Watrous
The Watrous Manitou **(37585)** ....(Paid) ‡1,632

Watson
East Central Connection **(37586)** ....‡12,642
The Naicam News **(37587)** ....(Paid) 702
(Free) 10
The Watson Witness **(37588)** ....‡450

Weyburn
Weyburn Review **(37591)** ....‡5,260

Whitewood
Whitewood Herald **(37594)** 1,400

Wilkie
The Wilkie Press **(37595)** ....(Paid) 833
(Free) 150

Wynyard
Wynyard Advance/Gazette **(37597)** 3,245

Yorkton
Yorkton This Week & Enterprise **(37600)** 9,272

YUKON TERRITORY, CANADA
Whitehorse
Yukon News **(37606)** ....(Mon.) 5,740
(Wed.) 6,384
(Fri.) 7,796

Numbers cited after listings are entry numbers rather than page numbers.

Free Newspapers

Index entries are arranged geographically, first by states/provinces and then by cities. Within cities in this index, citations appear alphabetically by publication title. Citations include publication title, entry number (given in parentheses immediately following the title), and circulation figures.

Circ.

ALABAMA
Auburn
The Auburn Bulletin (38) ....(Paid) 3,200
(Free) 7,000

Clanton
The Clanton Advertiser (155) ....(Paid) ‡4,000
(Free) ‡8,500

Dothan
The Dothan Progress (186) ....(Paid) 361

Enterprise
Daleville Sun Courier (200) ....,....(Free) 5,960
(Paid) 67
The Southeast Sun (202) ....(Free) 12,905
(Paid) 66

Haleyville
The Times-Record (258) ....(Paid) ‡4,600
(Free) ‡9,196

Leeds
The Leeds News (302) ....(Combined) 2,998

Madison
Madison County Record (310) ....(Paid) ‡4,000

Samson
Samson Ledger (444) ....(Paid) ‡5,700
(Free) ‡9,400

ALASKA
Anchorage
Sourdough Sentinel (532) ....(Free) 7,500

Kenai
Dispatch (606) ....(Non-paid) 8,500

Wasilla
Valley Sun (650) ....(Paid) 42
(Free) 9,750

ARIZONA
Apache Junction
Apache Junction
Independent (656) ....(Combined) ‡21,000
East Mesa
Independent (657) ....(Combined) ‡35,000

Bullhead City
Colorado River
Weekender (664) ....(Combined) 29,146
Laughlin Nevada
Entertainer (665) ....(Combined) 52,000

Cave Creek
Sonoran News (672) ....(Combined) 24,500

Chandler
Chandler Independent (674) .....(Combined) ‡27,000

Cottonwood
Cottonwood Journal
Extra (679) ....(Combined) 7,013

Flagstaff
Canyon Shopper (695) ....(Free) ‡25,000

Gilbert
Gilbert Independent (712) ....(Combined) ‡25,000

Glendale
Thunderbolt (716) ....(Free) ‡11,500

Circ.

Globe
Copper Country News (718) ......(Controlled) ‡9,000

Kingman
The Prospector (731) ....(Free) 9,749

Lake Havasu City
River Extra (734) ....(Free) 6,400

Paradise Valley
Paradise Valley
Independent (761) ....(Combined) ‡23,000

Prescott
Chino Valley Review (846) ....(Free) 2,678
(Paid) 341
Prescott Valley Tribune (849) ....(Free) 8,196
(Paid) 202

Scottsdale
Arizona Pennysaver (866) ....(Free) 604,000
North Scottsdale
Independent (872) ....(Combined) ‡13,000

Sierra Vista
The Mountain View News (888) ......(Free) ‡22,000

Sun City
Sun Cities
Independent (896) ....(Combined) ‡25,000

Tempe
SWEAT Magazine (917) ....(Free) 50,000
(Paid) 100

Tucson
Tucson Weekly (970) ....(Free) 55,000
(Paid) 52

Winslow
The Winslow Mail (1014) ....(Wed.) ‡5,360
(Fri.) ‡1,700

Yuma
The Sun Visitor (1019) ....(Controlled) 22,000

ARKANSAS
Blytheville
Village News (1059) ....(Free) 9,348

CALIFORNIA
Agoura Hills
Acorn (1385) ....(Paid) ‡200
(Free) ‡26,600

Alhambra
Alhambra Post Advocate (1388) ....(Paid) 701
(Free) 24,210

Anaheim
Anaheim Hills News (1398) ....(Paid) 25
(Free) 10,200

Anderson
The Valley Post (1423) ....(Paid) ‡3,500
(Free) ‡10,000

Arcata
North Coast Journal (1430) ....(Free) ❑13,428
(Paid) ❑168

Bakersfield
Bakersfield's Shopper (1449) ....(Free) 103,560

Circ.

Bell Gardens
Bell Gardens Review (1483) ....(Paid) 70

Belvedere
E.L.A. Brooklyn-Belvedere
Comet (1485) ....(Paid) ♦26
(Free) ♦5,300

Berkeley
American Spirit Newspaper (1490)
Berkeley Tri City Post (1499) ....(Free) ‡20,000

Camp Pendleton
Flight Jacket (1651) ....(Free) ‡13,000

Carmel
Carmel Pine Cone (1670) ....(Paid) ‡25,000

Carpinteria
Coastal View (1676) ....(Non-paid) 7,000
(Paid) 250

Ceres
The Ceres Courier (1682) ....(Free) 19,500

Chico
Chico News & Review (1693) ....(Free) 40,682
(Paid) 52

Chula Vista
California Weekly (1713) ....(Free) 48,298
(Paid) 2,623

Compton
Compton/Carson Wave (1748) .....(Non-paid) 40,365
Compton Metropolitan
Gazette (1749) ....(Free) 60,000

Costa Mesa
O.C. Weekly (1779) ....(Non-paid) 70,000
(Paid) 2

Culver City
Culver City Chronicle (1791) ....(Paid) 7
(Non-paid) 10,770
Culver City Star (1792) ....(Non-paid) 29,109

Daly City
Daly City Record (1802) ....(Paid) 1,070
(Free) 23,180
Manila Mail (1803) ....(Combined) 15,000

Dana Point
Dana Point News (1805) ....(Paid) 7,783
(Controlled) 3,605

Downey
Downey Herald American (1834) ....(Paid) 291
(Free) 25,500

East Los Angeles
East Los Angeles Commerce
Tribune (1840) ....(Paid) 1,325
(Free) 17,349

Edwards AFB
Desert Wings (1841) ....(Non-paid) 10,000

El Segundo
Astro News (1867) ....(Non-paid) 5,500
El Segundo Herald (1868) ....(Paid) ‡266
(Free) ‡15,000

Escondido
Escondido News-Reporter (1889) ....(Paid) 200
(Non-paid) 1,000

Circulation: ★ = ABC; △ = BPA; ♦ = CAC; • = CCAB; ❑ = VAC; ⊕ = PO Statement; ‡ = Publisher's Report; Boldface figures = sworn; Light figures = estimated.

2937

Circ.　　　　　Circ.　　　　　Circ.

CALIFORNIA (continued)

Fallbrook
Enterprise (1912) ....(Free) ‡6,950

Fortuna
Humboldt Beacon &
　Advance (1928) ....(Paid) ‡4,750
　　　　　　　　　　　　　　　　(Free) ‡12,000

Foster City
Foster City Islander (1932) ....(Free) ‡6,175

Fountain Valley
Huntington Beach/Fountain Valley
　Independent (1935) ....(Combined) 34,828

Fresno
Vida En El Valle (1959) ....(Free) 29,190
　　　　　　　　　　　　　　　　(Paid) 46

Galt
Elk Grove Citizen (1993) ....(Wed.) 9,700
　　　　　　　　　　　　　　　　(Fri.) 9,700
Laguna Citizen (1995) ....(Thurs.) 12,700

Glendora
OCB Tracker (2025) ....(Combined) 10,000

Hesperia
Hesperia Resorter (2048) ....(Paid) ‡2,200
　　　　　　　　　　　　　　　　(Free) ‡12,000

Huntington Beach
The Sun Journal (2065) ....(Free) 32,000
　　　　　　　　　　　　　　　　(Paid) 50

Huntington Park
Huntington Park Bulletin (2068) ....(Paid) 54
　　　　　　　　　　　　　　　　(Free) 12,850

Inglewood
Inglewood/Hawthorne
　Wave (2072) ....(Non-paid) 45,453
Inglewood Tribune (2073) ....(Paid) 1,000
　　　　　　　　　　　　　　　　(Free) 9,000

Irvine
Dan Chung News (2077) ....(Combined) 10,000
Waterfront Southern California
　News (2092) ....(Paid) 10,000
　　　　　　　　　　　　　　(Non-paid) 30,000

Kerman
West Side Advance (2102) ....(Free) ‡10,325

Lafayette
Contra Costa Sun (2131) ....(Paid) 8,000

Laguna Beach
Laguna Beach News (2132) ....‡13,223

Laguna Niguel
Laguna Niguel News (2136) ....‡17,877

Lompoc
Space and Missile Times (2163) ....(Free) ‡8,500

Long Beach
Downtown Gazette (2166) ....(Free) 20,501
El Economico (2167) ....(Free) 100,000
Grunion Gazette (2168) ....(Free) 36,408
　　　　　　　　　　　　　　　　(Paid) 60
Long Beach Express (2171) ....(Free) 60,000

Los Alamitos
News-Enterprise (2191) ....(Paid) ‡350
　　　　　　　　　　　　　　　　(Free) ‡30,300

Los Angeles
City Terrace Comet (2240) ....(Paid) ♦211
　　　　　　　　　　　　　　　　(Free) ♦4,528
Civic Center NewSource (2241) ....(Paid) 200
　　　　　　　　　　　　　　(Non-paid) 7,000
Eagle Rock Sentinel (2255) ....(Wed.) 8,600
　　　　　　　　　　　　　　　　(Sat.) 8,600
Eastside Journal (2257) ....(Controlled) 16,075
Eastside Sun (2258) ....(Paid) ♦24,000
　　　　　　　　　　　　　　　　(Free) ‡22,500
Edicion Bilingue Independent (2260) ....(Paid) 7
　　　　　　　　　　　　　　(Non-paid) 22,735
El Clasificado (2262) ....(Non-paid) 130,000
L.A. Weekly (2313) ....(Non-paid) 210,240
　　　　　　　　　　　　　　　　(Paid) 1,667
Lincoln Heights
　Bulletin-News (2318) ....(Wed.) 9,125
　　　　　　　　　　　　　　　　(Sat.) 9,125
Los Angeles Downtown
　News (2322) ....(Free) 47,000
Los Angeles Independent (2323) ......(Free) 162,146
　　　　　　　　　　　　　　　　(Paid) 68
Mesa Tribune Wave (2330) 31,609

Mexican American Sun (2332) ....(Paid) ♦104,000
　　　　　　　　　　　　　　　　(Free) ♦13,770
Mount Washington
　Star-Review (2337) ....(Controlled) 5,135
News-Herald and Journal (2347)
Park Labrea News and Beverly
　Press (2358) ....(Free) ‡11,000
Riverside Bulletin (2380) ....(Non-paid) 1,000
South Gate Press (2392) ....(Paid) 61
　　　　　　　　　　　　　　　　(Free) 24,076
Southwest News Wave (2403) 38,932
Street Scene (2406) ....(Non-paid) 1,000
20 de Mayo (2417) 25,000
Vida Nueva (2430) ....(Free) ❑63,584
West Hollywood Independent (2432) ....(Paid) 9
　　　　　　　　　　　　　　(Non-paid) 31,680
Westchester Star (2433) ....(Non-paid) 9,956
The Westsider (2434) ....(Paid) 11
　　　　　　　　　　　　　　(Non-paid) 20,650
World Reporter (2440) ....(Combined) 50,000
Wyvernwood Chronicle (2443) ....(Paid) ♦2
　　　　　　　　　　　　　　　　(Free) ♦1,948

Los Gatos
Los Gatos Weekly Times (2478) ....(Free) 17,506
　　　　　　　　　　　　　　　　(Paid) 1,667
Saratoga News (2479) ....(Combined) ‡9,500

Malibu
The Malibu Surfside News (2491) ....(Paid) 4,000
　　　　　　　　　　　　　　　　(Free) 8,000

Mammoth Lakes
Mammoth Times (2498) ....(Free) ‡300
　　　　　　　　　　　　　　　　(Paid) ‡6,520

Manhattan Beach
The Beach Reporter (2500) ....(Free) 50,915

March Air Force Base
The Beacon (2503) ....(Free) 9,100

Marina del Rey
The Argonaut (2504) ....(Free) 42,000

Menlo Park
The Almanac (2522) ....(Free) ‡17,500

Mill Valley
Pacific Sun (2541) ....(Paid) ❑167
　　　　　　　　　　　　　　　　(Free) ❑38,707

Millbrae
Millbrae Sun (2543) ....(Paid) 1,441
　　　　　　　　　　　　　　　　(Free) 17,824
Pennisula Reporter (2544) ....(Paid) 27
　　　　　　　　　　　　　　　　(Free) 7,473

Milpitas
Milpitas Post (2545) ....(Paid) 3,050
　　　　　　　　　　　　　　　　(Free) 15,300

Montebello
Montebello Comet (2580) ....(Paid) ♦10
　　　　　　　　　　　　　　　　(Free) ♦15,657

Monterey Park
Chinese American Daily
　News (2592) ....(Combined) 30,000
Monterey Park Comet (2595) ....(Paid) 23
　　　　　　　　　　　　　　　　(Free) 104,000

Newman
The Gustine Standard (2619) ....(Free) 5,300

Norwalk
Norwalk Herald American (2648) ....(Paid) 74
　　　　　　　　　　　　　　　　(Free) 24,405

Oakland
Argus Enterprise (2666) ....(Controlled) 41,349
El Mundo (2680) ....(Free) ‡31,864
The Journal (2683) 11,519
Oakland Post (2691) ....(Free) ‡62,496

Pacoima
San Fernando Gazette
　Express (2742) ....(Free) 60,000

Palm Springs
The Public Record (2766) ....(Paid) ‡500
　　　　　　　　　　　　　　　　(Free) ‡500

Palmdale
Cover Story (2783) ....(Non-paid) 48,831

Palo Alto
Palo Alto Weekly (2801) ....(Paid) 5,501
　　　　　　　　　　　　　　　　(Free) 41,499

Paramount
Paramount/Bellflower Herald
　American (2809) ....(Paid) 24
　　　　　　　　　　　　　　　　(Free) 24,800

Pasadena
Pasadena Gazette (2822) ....(Free) 60,000
Pasadena Weekly (2824) ....(Paid) 29
　　　　　　　　　　　　　　　　(Free) 35,935

Pico Rivera
Pico Rivera/Santa Fe Springs
　News (2840) ....(Free) 19,461

Pomona
La Voz (2860) ....(Paid) 200
　　　　　　　　　　　　　　　　(Free) 19,800

Poway
Corridor News (2866) ....(Paid) 521
　　　　　　　　　　　　　　　　(Free) 10,980

Rancho Bernardo
Rancho Bernardo News
　Journal (2873) ....(Paid) 509
　　　　　　　　　　　　　　　　(Free) 14,182

Rancho Santa Fe
Rancho Santa Margarita
　News (2881) ....(Free) ‡6,177

Redlands
Globetrotter (2904) ....(Free) 10,000

Richmond
Richmond Post (2921) ....(Free) ‡21,900

Ridgecrest
News-Review (2923) ....(Paid) 2,006
　　　　　　　　　　　　　　　　(Free) 6,200

Riverside
Lake Elsinore Valley
　Sun-Tribune (2940) ....(Fri.) 458

Rocklin
Placer Herald (2956) ....(Paid) 1,316
　　　　　　　　　　　　　　　　(Free) 10,277

Rohnert Park
The Community Voice (2961)

Rosemead
Rosemead/South San Gabriel
　Progress (2968) ....(Free) ‡14,447
Saigon Times (2969) ....(Combined) 20,000

Sacramento
Sacramento Bulletin (3012) ....(Non-paid) 1,000

San Bernardino
San Bernardino Bulletin (3091) ......(Non-paid) 1,000

San Clemente
San Clemente Sun-Post News (3102) ....‡16,322
Sun Post News (3103) ....(Mon.-Fri.) ‡7,500

San Diego
Ahora Now (3109) ....(Paid) 100
　　　　　　　　　　　　　　　　(Free) 20,000
Beach & Bay Press (3119) ....(Free) 20,000
　　　　　　　　　　　　　　　　(Paid) 51
La Jolla Village News (3219) ....(Free) 35000
San Diego Bulletin (3257) ....(Non-paid) 1,000
San Diego Parent (3267) ....(Free) 80,000
　　　　　　　　　　　　　　　　(Paid) 61
San Diego Reader (3268) ....(Free) 160,000
Update (3285) ....(Paid) ‡2,000
　　　　　　　　　　　　　　　　(Free) ‡25,000
USIU Envoy (3286) ....(Controlled) 2,000

San Francisco
Bay Area Reporter (3329) ....(Non-paid) 34,735
California Voice (3339) ....(Free) 37,325
North Beach Now (3407) ....(Free) ‡40,000
The San Francisco Bay
　Guardian (3429) ....(Non-paid) 160,758
San Francisco Bay View (3430) ....(Paid) ‡500
　　　　　　　　　　　　　　(Non-paid) ‡19,500
San Francisco
　Independent (3434) ....(Tues.) ❑212,702
　　　　　　　　　　　　　　　　(Wed.) ❑167,252
San Francisco Observer (3437) ....(Paid) 121
　　　　　　　　　　　　　　　　(Free) 40,000
San Francisco Post (3438) ....(Free) ‡18,289
The Urban Latino News (3456) ....(Non-paid) 20,000
The Urban Latino News (3457) 20,000-25,000

San Jose
El Observador (3516) ....(Paid) 451
　　　　　　　　　　　　　　　　(Free) 75,549
Metro (3524) ....(Free) 85,000

San Juan Capistrano
Capistrano Valley News **(3559)** ....(Controlled) 5,493
(Paid) 3,283

San Luis Obispo
New Times **(3567)** ....(Free) ❑37,981
(Paid) ❑28

San Martin
The Filipino Monitor **(3582)** ....(Combined) 10,000

San Mateo
Coastside Chronicle **(3584)** ....(Paid) 24
(Free) 7,401

San Pedro
Random Lengths/Harbor Independent
News **(3595)** ....(Free) ‡20,000

Santa Ana
Azteca News **(3620)** ....(Free) ‡33,000
Farandula USA **(3625)** ....(Free) 40,588
Miniondas **(3629)** ....(Free) 40,877
(Paid) 5
Saddleback Valley News **(3632)** .....(Free) ‡53,411
Union Hidpana **(3634)** ....(Non-paid) 35,000

Santa Barbara
Santa Barbara
Independent **(3654)** ....(Free) ❑38,700

Santa Clara
The Filipino-American
Headliner **(3670)** ....(Combined) 5,000

Santa Maria
Central Coast This Week **(3695)** ....(Free) 14,500

Seal Beach
The Leisure World Golden Rain
News **(3749)** ....(Paid) 6705
(Free) 2295

South San Francisco
The Manila Bulletin
USA **(3790)** ....(Combined) 50,000

Springville
The Tule Times **(3793)** ....(Paid) ‡2,200
(Free) ‡100

Stockton
Record Weekly **(3808)** ....(Free) 88,246

Torrance
Lighthouse **(3936)** ....(Combined) 31,200
South Bay Extra **(3944)** ....(Non-paid) 109,515

Vacaville
Bingo and Gaming News **(3973)**

Van Nuys
La Guia Familiar **(3991)** ....(Free) ‡242,375
Mundo L.A. **(3992)** ....(Free) 540,000

Ventura
Ventura Bulletin **(4012)** ....(Non-paid) 1,000
Ventura County Reporter **(4013)** ....(Paid) ‡250
(Free) ‡35,000

Victorville
Daily Press Preview **(4032)** ....(Tues.) 34,000

Vista
El Informador **(4044)** ....(Combined) 28,229

West Whittier
Whittier Independent **(4070)** ....(Free) ‡19,115

Whittier
Mean Street **(4078)** ....(Free) 70,000

Woodland Hills
The Valley Vantage **(4115)** ....(Free) 20,000
Vecinos del Valle **(4116)** ....(Free) 48,371

COLORADO
Boulder
Boulder Weekly **(4159)** ....(Non-paid) 25,000

Colorado Springs
Colorado Springs
Independent **(4243)** ....(Combined) 36,300
Mountaineer **(4252)** ....(Free) ‡15,000
Space Observer **(4257)** ....(Free) ‡7,500

Frisco
Summit Daily **(4456)** ....(Mon.-Fri.) 9,725
(Sun.) 8,821

Golden
The Jefferson County
Transcript **(4469)** ....(Free) ‡9,000

Grand Junction
The Nickel Want Ads **(4480)** .....(Combined) 22,000

Greenwood Village
The Villager **(4507)** ....(Paid) 3,500
(Free) 2,000

The Villager Office Park
News **(4508)** ....(Non-paid) 4,500

Monte Vista
SLV Midweek **(4576)** ....(Free) 15,000
SLV Saturday Want Ads **(4577)** ......(Free) ‡14,500

Steamboat Springs
Steamboat Today **(4632)** ....(Mon.-Fri.) ❑10,209
(Sat.) ❑8,394

USAF Academy
Academy Spirit **(4651)** ....(Free) ‡7,500

CONNECTICUT
Black Rock
Weston Voice **(4699)** ....(Free) 3,250

Easton
Easton Courier **(4779)** ....(Paid) ◆1,487
(Non-paid) ◆187

Glastonbury
Rivereast News Bulletin **(4870)** ......(Free) 24,000

Litchfield
Litchfield Enquirer **(4924)** ....(Paid) 1,875
(Non-paid) 2

Milford
The Bulletin **(4953)** ....(Free) ‡9,600
Milford Reporter **(4956)** ....(Free) ‡11,300
Stratford Bard **(4958)** ....(Free) ‡17,000

New Haven
The Inner City Newspaper **(4991)** .....(Free) ‡35,000
New Haven Advocate **(4998)** ....(Free) 55,000

New Milford
Business Digest **(5028)** ....(Non-paid) 4,907
Fairfield Minuteman **(5029)** ....(Non-paid) 21,652
Litchfield Weekend **(5031)** ....(Non-paid) 6,592
Westport Minuteman **(5035)** ....(Non-paid) 15,217

North Haven
The Advisor **(5047)** ....(Free) ‡31,500

Norwalk
Norwalk Lifestyles **(5073)** ....(Free) 15,059

Putnam
Putnam Courier Trader **(5093)** ......(Non-paid) 9,994
(Paid) 1,326

Ridgefield
The Darien Times **(5096)** ....(Paid) ◆1,026
(Non-paid) ◆5,437

Shelton
The Amity Observer **(5120)** ......(Non-paid) ◆8,394
The Hamden Journal **(5122)** .....(Non-paid) ◆13,306
The Milford Mirror **(5126)** .....(Non-paid) ◆14,122
The Valley Gazette **(5129)** ......(Non-paid) ◆12,296

Southbury
Southbury Voices **(5133)** ....(Wed.) ◆27,233
(Sun.) ◆22,048

Wallingford
CT LIFE **(5188)** ....(Combined) 74,363

Wilton
The Wilton Villager **(5232)** ....(Non-paid) 8,338
(Paid) 35

Woodbury
Voices **(5237)** ....(Paid) 373
(Non-paid) 27,198
(Sun.) 22,028
VOICES Sunday-Weekly Star **(5238)** ....(Paid) 72
(Non-paid) 22,141

DELAWARE
Dover
The Airlifter **(5242)** ....(Free) 7,000
Dover Post **(5247)** ....(Free) 24,615
(Paid) 1,917

Rehoboth Beach
Delaware Coast Press **(5284)** ....(Paid) 342
(Non-paid) 14,137

Smyrna
Smyrna/Clayton Sun-Times **(5287)** ....(Paid) 3,700

DISTRICT OF COLUMBIA
Washington
The Georgetown
Current **(5509)** ....(Combined) ‡40,250
The InTowner Newspaper **(5560)** ....(Paid) 100
(Free) 32,000
Mississippi Monitor **(5653)** ....(Non-paid) 16,000
The Northwest
Current **(5697)** ....(Combined) ‡40,250

FLORIDA
Alachua
Hare Krishna World **(5898)** ....(Paid) ⊕8,000

Apollo Beach
East Bay Breeze **(5907)** ....(Free) 17,000

Apopka
The Planter Newspaper **(5911)** ....(Free) 10,000

Avon Park
Prensa Hispana (Hispanic
Press) **(5913)** ....(Free) 30,000

Bonifay
Holmes County Advertiser **(5945)** ......(Free) ‡4,200

Bonita Springs
Bonita Banner **(5946)** ....(Free) 33,000

Boynton Beach
Boynton Beach Times **(5948)** ....(Free) 40,750

Cape Coral
The Pine Island Eagle **(5974)** ....(Free) ‡8,500

Carrollwood
Carrollwood News **(5976)** ....(Free) 31,951

Coral Gables
Coral Gables News **(6005)** ....(Free) ‡12,000

Coral Springs
Tamarac/North Lauderdale
Forum **(6018)** ....(Non-paid) 18,165

Crestview
News Extra **(6024)** ....(Free) 12,169

Deerfield Beach
Eastsider **(6049)** ....(Controlled) 30,875
Jewish Journal Dade **(6050)** ......(Combined) 22,315

Dunedin
The Dunedin Times/The Palm Harbor
Sounder **(6061)** ....(Paid) 250
(Free) 24,750

Fort Lauderdale
City Link **(6074)** ....(Non-paid) 51,798
Hometown Herald **(6076)** ....(Paid) ‡42,200
Waterfront News **(6087)** ....(Paid) ‡750
(Free) ‡39,000
Westside Gazette **(6088)** ....(Paid) ‡7,000
(Free) ‡14,500

Fort Myers
Community Voice **(6095)** ....(Non-paid) 10,000
Lehigh Acres News Star **(6096)** ....(Paid) 8,393
(Free) 6,889

Gulf Breeze
Perido Pelican **(6179)** ....(Non-paid) ‡8,000

Hallandale
The Digest **(6184)** ....(Free) ‡48,000

Homestead
Palmetto Bay News **(6204)** ....(Free) 6,000

Islamorada
Free Press **(6208)** ....(Free) ‡13,000
12,000

Jacksonville Beach
Sun-Times **(6248)** ....(Free) ‡23,500

Kendall
Kendall News **(6250)** ....(Free) ‡15,000

Kissimmee
Osceola Shopper **(6263)** ....(Non-paid) 35,500
South Orange News **(6264)** ....(Non-paid) 21,900

La Belle
Caloosa Belle **(6267)** ....(Free) 7,500
Immokalee Bulletin **(6268)** ....(Free) ‡3,500

Lake Worth
Lake Worth Herald **(6288)** ....(Paid) 2,000
(Free) 36,000

Circulation: ★ = ABC; △ = BPA; ◆ = CAC; • = CCAB; ❑ = VAC; ⊕ = PO Statement; ‡ = Publisher's Report; Boldface figures = sworn; Light figures = estimated.

2939

Circ.

Circ.

Circ.

FLORIDA (continued)

Longboat Key
The Longboat Observer **(6311)** ....(Free) 17,472
(Paid) 1,325

Lutz
The Lutz Community News **(6315)** ......(Free) 9,500

Marathon
Marathon/Big Pine Key Free
Press **(6322)** ....(Free) 11,300

Mayport
The Mirror **(6333)** ....(Free) ‡9,700

Miami
Hialea-Opa Locka News **(6359)** ......(Free) ‡7,000
Libre **(6368)** ....(Paid) 2,000
(Free) 8,000
Miami New Times **(6370)** ....(Non-paid) 106,692
(Paid) 33
Miami Shores News **(6371)** ....(Free) ‡4,000
Pinecrest Tribune **(6375)**
The Weekly News **(6390)** ....(Free) ‡32,000

Miami Beach
The Sun Post **(6417)** ....(Paid) ‡2,000
(Free) ‡45,000

Milton
Santa Rosa Free Press **(6424)** ....(Free) ‡21,500

North Miami Beach
North Miami Beach News **(6468)** .....(Free) ‡13,000

Plant City
The Courier **(6585)**

Sarasota
Pelican Press **(6662)** ....(Paid) ‡800
(Free) ‡23,500

Stuart
Fort Pierce News **(6694)** ....(Non-paid) 22,950

Sun City Center
The Sun **(6698)** ....(Combined) 11,500

Sunrise
The Broward Informer **(6699)** ....(Paid) ‡2,000
(Free) ‡80,000
South Florida
Parenting **(6700)** ....(Combined) 108,309

Tallahassee
Rental Guide **(6731)** ....(Non-paid) 128,926

Tampa
The Laker **(6774)** ....(Free) ‡21,500
Spectator Magazine **(6778)** ....(Non-paid) 52,740
Town'n Country News **(6781)** ....(Free) 22,000

Temple Terrace
The Temple Terrace
Beacon **(6815)** ....(Free) 10,000

Titusville
Star Advocate **(6821)** ....(Free) 22,500

Wewahitchka
The Gulf County Breeze **(6862)** ....(Paid) ‡1,300
(Free) ‡200

Winter Haven
La Prensa Newspaper **(6867)** ....(Free) ‡19,828

GEORGIA
Acworth
Acworth Neighbor **(6896)** ....(Non-paid) 22,262
(Paid) 14

Adairsville
North Bartow News **(6898)** ....(Free) ‡7,000

Alpharetta
Alpharetta Neighbor **(6916)** ....(Combined) 23,943

Athens
Athens Star **(6930)** ....(Free) ‡30,185

Atlanta
Creative Loafing **(6996)** ....(Free) 140,000
(Paid) 124
Korean Journal **(7025)** ....(Paid) 2,389
(Non-paid) 97,811
Mundo Hispanico **(7029)** ....(Combined) 57,500
Northside Neighbor/Sandy Springs
Neighbor **(7033)** ....(Paid) 37
(Non-paid) 21,519

Austell
Austell Neighbor **(7115)** ....(Combined) 43,222

Blairsville
North Georgia News **(7129)** ....(Paid) ‡9,700
(Free) ‡5,000

Brunswick
Harbor Sound **(7140)** ....(Free) ‡28,000

Chamblee
Chamblee De Kalb
Neighbor **(7167)** ....(Combined) 21,344

Cherokee
Cherokee Plus **(7169)** ....(Non-paid) ♦19,500

Cobb
The East Cobb Neighbor **(7177)** ....(Paid) 5
(Non-paid) 42,474

Covington
Multi-County Star **(7211)** ....(Free) ‡26,300

Cumming
Forsyth County News **(7215)** ....(Mon.-Fri.) 12,701
(Sun.) 14,202

Decatur
Decatur De Kalb
Neighbor **(7236)** ....(Combined) 45,551

Doraville
Doraville De Kalb Neighbor **(7241)** ....(Paid) 13
(Non-paid) 21,344
Korean Southeast
News **(7242)** ....(Combined) 20,000

Dunwoody
Dunwoody De Kalb Neighbor **(7259)** ....(Paid) ♦9
(Non-paid) ♦21,886

Forest Park
The Clayton Neighbor **(7275)** ....(Paid) 11
(Non-paid) 42,683

Fort Benning
The Benning Leader **(7280)** ....(Free) 25,000

Griffin
The Fayette Neighbor **(7310)** ....(Paid) 7
(Non-paid) 22,701

Henry
The Henry Neighbor **(7328)** ....(Paid) 7
(Non-paid) 29,909

Kennesaw
Kennesaw Neighbor **(7354)** ....(Non-paid) 22,262
(Paid) 14

Marietta
The Douglas Neighbor **(7411)** ....(Paid) 13
(Non-paid) 21,115
Mableton Neighbor **(7414)** ....(Combined) 42,814
Roswell Neighbor **(7416)** ....(Paid) ♦16
(Non-paid) ♦18,879
Sandy Springs Neighbor **(7417)** ....(Free) 27,259
(Paid) 215
The South De Kalb
Neighbor **(7418)** ....(Non-paid) 17,575
The South Fulton Neighbor **(7419)** ....(Paid) 11
(Non-paid) 27,489
Tucker De Kalb
Neighbor **(7422)** ....(Combined) 45,551
Vinings Neighbor **(7423)** ....(Combined) 10,992

Norcross
Gwinnett Extra **(7461)** ....(Sun.) 41,230
(Wed.) 48,758

Powder Springs
Powder Springs
Neighbor **(7486)** ....(Combined) 42,814

Roberta
The Georgia Post **(7498)** ....(Paid) 2,050
(Free) 3

Rockdale
Rockdale Neighbor **(7500)** ....(Paid) 5
(Non-paid) 16,096

Savannah
Savannah Jewish News **(7535)** ....‡1,700

Smyrna
The Smyrna Neighbor **(7555)** ......(Non-paid) 10,992
(Paid) 9

Stone Mountain
The Stone Mountain De Kalb
Neighbor **(7571)** ....(Combined) 45,551

Summerville
Chattooga Press **(7574)** ......(Free) 11,100

Warner Robins
Robins Rev-Up **(7637)** ....(Free) ‡20,000

HAWAII
Honolulu
Honolulu Weekly **(7703)** ....(Free) 43,786
(Paid) 48

Kaneohe
Central Sun-Press **(7768)** ....(Combined) 12,286
Hawaii Army Weekly **(7769)** ....(Free) 13,489
Hawaii Kai/East Oahu Sun
Press **(7770)** ....(Combined) 7,193
Hawaii Marine **(7771)** ....(Free) 9,000
Hawaii Navy News **(7772)** ....(Free) 15,873
Hawaiian Falcon **(7773)** ....(Free) 7,315
Military Sun Press **(7775)** ....(Free) ‡7,374
Windward Sun-Press **(7776)** ....(Combined) 23,030

Lahaina
Lahaina News **(7777)** ....(Paid) ‡350
(Free) ‡8,607

Makawao
Haleakala Times **(7786)** ....(Combined) 17,000
Kihei Times **(7787)** ....(Combined) 10,000

IDAHO
Boise
Boise Weekly **(7804)** ....(Non-paid) 15,719
Gunfighter **(7808)** ....(Free) ‡5,400

Coeur d'Alene
NIC Sentinel **(7845)** ....(Non-paid) 4,000

Hailey
Wood River Journal **(7860)** ....(Free) 10,310
(Paid) 2,000

Ketchum
Idaho Mountain Express **(7887)** .....(Paid) ‡2,200
(Free) ‡11,300

ILLINOIS
Alton
Today's Advantage **(8010)** ....(Free) ‡42,216

Antioch
Lakes Area Advertiser **(8017)** ....(Free) ❏186,123
(Paid) ❏79

Belleville
Belleville Journal **(8059)** ....(Sun.) 27,301
(Wed.) 28,310

Bloomington
The Twin City Community
News **(8081)** ....(Free) 32,500

Boca Raton
Boca Raton Community
News **(8092)** ....(Combined) 37,775

Bourbonnais
The Herald/Country Market **(8094)** .....(Paid) ‡5,100
(Free) ‡26,000

Buffalo Grove
Buffalo Grove
Countryside **(8100)** ....(Combined) 49,572

Cahokia
The Herald **(8104)** ....(Paid) ‡100
(Free) ‡12,500

Casey
The Marketplace for Greenup &
Toledo **(8172)** ....(Free) ⊕3,300

Champaign
The Octopus **(8207)** ....(Combined) 22,000

Chicago
Bridgeport News **(8290)** ....(Combined) 4,680
Brighton Park-McKinley Park
Life **(8292)** ....(Free) ‡30,000
Broward Jewish Journal **(8293)** ....(Free) 72,000
Chicago Reader **(8319)** ....(Non-paid) 133,158
(Paid) 291
Chicago South Shore Scene **(8324)** ....(Paid) ‡1,000
(Free) ‡19,000
Chicago's Northwest Side
Press **(8330)** ....(Paid) ‡9,000
(Free) ‡38,000
Deerfield Beach Times **(8350)** ....(Free) 19,133
Edgebrook Reporter **(8359)** ......(Free) ‡12,000
Harlem-Irving Times **(8390)** ....(Paid) ♦2,715
Hyde Park Herald **(8403)** ....(Paid) ‡9,000
(Free) ‡17,600
Inside **(8416)** ....(Free) ‡49,500

Journal **(8427)** ....(Free) ‡1,000
Logan Square Extra **(8469)** ....(Free) ‡16,000
N'DIGO **(8501)** ....(Combined) 125,000
New City **(8505)** ....(Free) 70,000
(Paid) 40
Northwest Extra **(8510)** ....(Free) 10,000
The Other Side of the Lake **(8518)** 16,000
Palm Beach Jewish Journal
North **(8525)** ....(Combined) 21,575
Pro-Life Action News **(8539)** ....(Paid) ⊕8,000
West Boca Community
News **(8603)** ....(Non-paid) 30,240
Wicker Park/West Town EXTRA **(8606)**

Cicero
El Imparcial **(8674)** ....(Free) 30,000

DeKalb
The MidWeek **(8737)** ....(Free) ‡30,000

Delray Beach
Delray Beach Community
News **(8747)** ....(Combined) 31,300

Downers Grove
Clarendon Hills Progress **(8781)** .....(Combined) 560
Downers Grove
Progress **(8783)** ....(Combined) 10,400
Southeast DuPage
Progress **(8795)** ....(Non-paid) 31,800
Woodridge Progress **(8799)** ....(Combined) 10,400

Gibson City
Target **(8919)** ....(Non-paid) 12,520

Glen Ellyn
Glen Ellyn Press **(8928)** ....(Paid) ‡219
(Free) ‡4,252
North DuPage Press **(8930)** ......(Combined) 10,285

Granite City
Sunday Home Journal **(8949)** ....(Free) 23,000

Itasca
Control Isa Show Reporter **(9012)**

Jacksonville
Murrayville Gazette **(9023)** ....(Free) 600

Lanark
Prairie Advocate **(9066)** ....(Free) 10,300
(Paid) 2,300

Lewistown
Fulton Democrat **(9075)** ....(Free) 4,800

Lincolnwood
Elmwood Park/River Grove
Times **(9093)** ....(Paid) ♦1,497
Harlem-Foster Times **(9094)** ....(Paid) ♦2,807
Jefferson Park/Portage Park
Times **(9095)** ....(Paid) ♦4,385
Lincoln-Belmont Booster **(9096)** ....(Paid) 1,188
Morton Grove-Niles Life **(9098)** ......(Paid) ♦570
The Niles Life **(9099)** ....(Paid) ♦518
Norridge Times **(9100)** ....(Paid) ♦3,130
North Center-Irving Park
Booster **(9101)** ....(Paid) 396
(Free) 12,997
Schiller Park **(9104)** ....(Paid) 341
(Free) 7,345
Skyline **(9105)** ....(Paid) ♦40
(Non-paid) ♦16,610

Mason City
Manito Review **(9156)** ....(Free) 3,250
Mason City Banner Times **(9157)** ....(Paid) 2,100
(Free) 7,500

Midlothian
Beverly News **(9183)** ....(Paid) ‡4,080
(Free) ‡100
Burbank Stickney
Independent **(9185)** ....(Paid) ‡5,700
(Free) ‡200
Chicago Ridge Citizen **(9186)** ....(Paid) ‡3,600
(Free) ‡300
Evergreen Park Courier **(9187)** ....(Paid) ‡4,410
(Free) ‡500
Hickory Hills Citizen **(9188)** ....(Paid) ‡3,530
(Free) ‡400
Midlothian-Bremen
Messenger **(9189)** ....(Paid) ‡10,200
(Free) ‡500
Mount Greenwood Express **(9190)** .....(Paid) ‡7,471
(Free) ‡300
Oak Lawn Independent **(9191)** ....(Paid) ‡12,000
(Free) ‡1,800
Orland Township Messenger **(9192)** ....(Paid) ‡3,788
(Free) ‡200

Scottsdale Ashburn
Independent **(9194)** ....(Free) ‡5,800
Worth Citizen **(9195)** ....(Paid) ‡2,600
(Free) ‡300

Minier
Olympia Review **(9199)** ....(Free) ‡6,900

Moline
The Leader **(9206)** ....(Free) 48,161
(Paid) 110

Naperville
The Fox Valley Villages/60504
Sun **(9263)** ....(Combined) 280,786

Niles
The Niles Bugle **(9291)** ....(Paid) ‡2,500
(Free) ‡17,000

Oak Brook
Ad ExPress **(9335)**
Elmhurst Suburban LIFE **(9350)** ....(Free) 30,986
Lombard Spectator **(9358)** ......(Combined) 15,000

Ogden
Ogden Leader **(9382)** ....(Free) 7,800

Ottawa
Thrif-T-Nickel Weekly
News-Tab **(9391)** ....(Paid) ‡12
(Free) ‡14,539

Peoria
East Peoria Times-Courier **(9417)** ....(Paid) 100
(Free) 8,380
Washington Times-Reporter **(9428)** ....(Paid) 10
(Free) 8,800

Rockford
The Rock River Times **(9531)** ....(Free) ‡20,000

Rockton
The Herald **(9546)** ....(Paid) 3,680
(Free) 29,482

St. Charles
West DuPage Press **(9574)** ....(Combined) 10,094

Savanna
Northwestern Illinois
Dispatch **(9580)** ....(Free) ‡10,000

Seneca
Town & Country **(9596)** ....(Paid) ‡29
(Free) ‡6,403

Springfield
Illinois Times **(9632)** ....(Free) 29,940
(Paid) 60

Swansea
Fairview Heights/O'Fallon
Journal **(9677)** ....(Sun.) 9,940
(Wed.) 9,760

Washington
Courier **(9735)** ....(Paid) ‡500
(Free) ‡18,000

West Palm Beach
Palm Beach Jewish Journal
South **(9750)** ....(Combined) 26,500

INDIANA
Avon
The Hendricks County
Flyer **(9794)** ....(Combined) 35,100

Beech Grove
The Southside Times **(9801)** ....(Free) ‡22,500

Brookville
American **(9873)** ....(Paid) 1175

Charlestown
The Leader **(9885)** ....(Free) 12,027
(Paid) 28

Fairmount
News-Sun **(9954)** ....(Mon.-Sat.) 8,176

Fishers
Center Grove Gazette **(9956)** ......(Non-paid) 8,756
(Paid) 10
The Daily Ledger **(9957)** ....(Paid) 11,963
Fishers Sun-Herald **(9958)** ....(Non-paid) 14,240
(Paid) 82
Lawrence Topics **(9959)** ....(Non-paid) 15,834
(Paid) 25
Westfield Enterprise **(9960)** ......(Non-paid) 4,869
(Paid) 60
White River Gazette **(9961)** ....(Combined) 8,768

Fort Wayne
Waynedale News **(9974)** ....(Free) ‡6,000

Geist
Geist Gazette **(10021)** ....(Non-paid) 5,417
(Paid) 22

Goshen
The Paper (Elkhart County
Edition) **(10027)** ....(Free) 34,020
The Paper (Goshen
Edition) **(10028)** ....(Free) 29,759

Grabill
East Allen Courier **(10032)** ....(Paid) ‡400
(Free) ‡6,600

Greenfield
Indy Suburban
Newspapers **(10041)** ....(Free) ‡49,000
Westside Enterprise **(10042)** ....(Non-paid) 12,000

Indianapolis
Cumberland Courier **(10107)** ....(Non-paid) 15,200
The East Side Herald **(10108)** ....(Paid) 50
(Free) 20,000
The Northeast Herald **(10156)** ....(Paid) 101
(Free) 5,000
Speedway Town Press **(10172)** ....(Free) 7,000
The Spotlight **(10173)** ....(Wed.) 24,609
West Side Messenger **(10183)** ....(Combined) ‡7,000

Lowell
Cedar Lake Journal **(10279)** ....(Paid) ‡1,550

Noblesville
Carmel News Tribune **(10353)** ....(Combined) 21,200
Lawrence Times **(10354)** ....(Non-paid) 7,560
(Paid) 143
Northside Topics **(10356)** ....(Non-paid) 18,323
(Paid) 65
Pike Topics **(10357)** ....(Combined) 8,913

Pekin
The Banner-Gazette **(10393)** ....(Free) 16,560
(Paid) 86

Rensselaer
Morocco Courier **(10413)** ....(Paid) ‡1,455
(Free) ‡23

Salem
The Salem Leader **(10440)** ....(Paid) 6,100
(Free) 176
The Washington County
Edition **(10441)** ....(Free) 10,730

Scottsburg
The Giveaway **(10444)** ....(Free) 16,873
(Paid) 90

South Bend
Tribune Business Weekly **(10460)** ....(Paid) ‡658
(Non-paid) ‡7,973

Warsaw
The Paper (Kosciusko
Edition) **(10536)** ....(Free) 22,100
Times-Union **(10537)** ....(Mon.-Sat.) 11,650

Westfield
Icon **(10559)** ....(Combined) 14,400

IOWA
Ackley
World Journal **(10570)** ....(Paid) 2,570
(Free) 1,800

Boone
Boone County Shopping
News **(10624)** ....(Free) 11,408

Cedar Rapids
Iowa Farmer Today **(10674)** .....(Controlled) ‡71,228

Cresco
Times-Plain Dealer **(10730)** ....(Paid) ‡3,450
(Free) ‡7,650

Denison
Review **(10766)** ....(Paid) ‡4,286
(Free) ‡4,261

Des Moines
Iowa Parent & Family **(10794)** ....(Controlled) 26,000
(Non-paid) 25,680

Garner
Garner Leader and Signal **(10919)** .....(Paid) ‡2,250
(Free) ‡5,600

Circulation: ★ = ABC; △ = BPA; ♦ = CAC; • = CCAB; □ = VAC; ⊕ = PO Statement; ‡ = Publisher's Report; Boldface figures = sworn; Light figures = estimated.

2941

Newspapers

Circ.   Circ.   Circ.

IOWA (continued)

Mapleton
Mapleton Press **(11052)** ....(Paid) 2,338
(Free) 75

Rock Valley
The Rock Valley Bee **(11181)** ....(Paid) ‡1,600
(Free) ‡4,750

Storm Lake
Storm Lake Times **(11245)** ....(Paid) 3,200
(Non-paid) 10,000

KANSAS
Caney
Good News **(11373)** ....(Free) ‡42,578

Fort Riley
Fort Riley Post **(11442)** ....(Paid) ‡250
(Free) ‡7,391

Gardner
La Latina Presencia **(11456)** ....(Non-paid) 5,000
The Spring Hill New Era **(11457)** ....(Paid) 1,000
(Free) 3,000

Independence
The Independence News **(11510)** ....(Paid) ‡650
(Free) ‡350

Lake Quivera
Leawood Sun, Blue Valley
Edition **(11543)** ....(Combined) ‡112,441

Leavenworth
Fort Leavenworth Lamp **(11579)** ....(Non-paid) **7,500**

Leawood
Leawood Sun **(11586)** ....(Combined) 112,441

Merriam
Northeast Johnson County
Sun **(11651)** ....(Combined) ‡112,441

Mission
Mission Sun **(11656)** ....(Combined) 137,000

Olathe
Olathe Sun **(11684)** ....(Combined) 112,441

Overland Park
College Boulevard News **(11706)** ....(Paid) ‡100
(Free) ‡30,000
Johnson County
Sun **(11716)** ....(Combined) 112,441
Lenexa Sun **(11720)** ....(Combined) 112,441
Overland Park Sun **(11723)** ....(Combined) 112,441
Overland Park Sun, Blue Valley
Edition **(11724)** ....(Combined) 112,441

Prairie Village
Prairie Village Sun **(11763)** ......(Combined) 112,441

Roeland Park
Roeland Park Sun **(11770)** ......(Combined) 103,679

Shawnee
Shawnee-Merriam
Sun **(11802)** ....(Combined) ‡112,441

Stillwell
Sun Newspaper **(11810)** ....(Combined) 103,679

Wamego
The Smoke Signal **(11861)** ....(Free) ‡10,700

Wichita
Active Aging Publishing,
Inc. **(11880)** ....(Free) ‡45,500

KENTUCKY
Florence
Dixie News **(12059)** ....(Paid) 500
(Free) 23,700

Fort Campbell
Ft. Campbell Courier **(12060)** ....(Free) 23,000

Fort Knox
Inside the Turret **(12062)** ....(Free) ‡20,000

Louisville
Louisville Eccentric Observer
(LEO) **(12230)** ....(Combined) 45,000

Paris
Citizen-Advertiser **(12354)** ....(Free) ‡11,700

Pendleton
The Falmouth Outlook **(12355)** ....(Paid) ⊕3,916
(Free) ⊕20

Shepherdsville
Pioneer News **(12400)** ....(Paid) 6,500
(Free) 17,000

Tompkinsville
Monroe County Citizen **(12421)** ....(Non-paid) ‡5,169

LOUISIANA
Arcadia
The Arcadia Progress **(12475)** ....(Free) ‡9,133
The Ringgold Progress **(12477)** ....(Free) ‡6,630

Bunkie
Avoyelles Journal **(12541)** ....(Free) 17,600

Columbia
News Journal **(12549)**

Covington
St. Tammany News-Banner **(12556)** .....(Paid) 5,000
(Non-paid) 17,500

Deridder
Beauregard Daily News **(12564)** ....(Paid) ‡8,400
(Free) ‡5,400
Guardian **(12565)** ....(Free) ‡15,000

Lafayette
The Times of
Acadiana **(12620)** ....(Non-paid) 32,785

Larose
The Lafourche Gazette **(12656)** ....(Free) ‡14,000

Mamou
Mamou Acadian Press **(12666)** ....(Paid) 64
(Free) 2,500

Morgan City
St. Mary Journal **(12708)** ....(Free) ‡10,500

New Orleans
Gambit Weekly **(12731)** ....(Free) 44,714
(Paid) 76

Slidell
Slidell Sentry-News **(12843)** ....(Free) 247
(Paid) 4,797

Springhill
The Advertiser **(12846)** ....(Free) 9,100

MAINE
Bath
Coastal Journal **(12918)** ....(Free) 19,000

Gray
The Gray News **(12966)**

Madawaska
St. John Valley Times **(12989)** ....(Paid) 6,500
(Free) 20

Portland
Casco Bay Weekly **(13007)** ....(Combined) 30,000

MARYLAND
Baltimore
Annapolis Times **(13124)** ....(Non-paid) 5,000
Avenue News **(13127)** ....(Wed.) 33,663
(Thurs.) 39,927
The Baltimore Chronicle **(13130)** ....(Paid) ‡450
(Free) ‡14,000
Baltimore City Paper **(13131)** ......(Non-paid) 86,113
The Baltimore Guide **(13133)** ....(Paid) 159
(Non-paid) 39,398
Baltimore Times **(13136)** ....(Non-paid) ♦42,978
Prince George's
Times **(13239)** ....(Non-paid) ‡10,000
Shore Times **(13247)** ....(Non-paid) 5,000

Bethesda
Parent & Child **(13371)** ....(Free) 51,122
(Paid) 337

Cambridge
The Dorchester Star **(13399)** .....(Non-paid) ♦12,058

Chevy Chase
Potomac Children **(13408)** ....(Free) 33,988
(Paid) 72

Columbia
The Baltimore
Messenger **(13453)** ....(Non-paid) 13,793
(Paid) 43
Columbia Flier **(13457)** ....(Non-paid) 38,394
Korea Post **(13464)** ....(Combined) 13,000
North County News **(13466)** ....(Non-paid) 17,525
(Paid) 12

Northeast Times Booster **(13469)** ....(Paid) 21
(Non-paid) 18,793
Owings Mills Times **(13471)** ....(Paid) 133
(Non-paid) 34,914

Damascus
Damascus
Courier-Gazette **(13481)** ....(Combined) 7,392

Ellicott City
The View from Ellicott
City **(13500)** ....(Non-paid) 21,230

Fort Meade
Soundoff **(13504)** ....(Non-paid) 11,841
(Paid) 8

Frederick
Aspen Hill Gazette **(13506)** ....(Combined) 8,324
Burtonsville Gazette **(13507)** ......(Controlled) 17,653
(Paid) 6
Business Gazette **(13508)** ....(Non-paid) 28,191
College Park Gazette **(13509)** ....(Combined) 17,460
Frederick Gazette **(13511)** ....(Combined) 68,000
Kensington Gazette **(13515)** ......(Combined) 7,158
Montgomery Village
Gazette **(13516)** ....(Combined) 9,888
New Market/Urbana
Gazette **(13517)** ....(Combined) 8,905
North Potomac
Gazette **(13518)** ....(Combined) 4,079
Poolesville Gazette **(13519)** ......(Combined) 4,144
Silver Spring Gazette **(13521)** ....(Combined) 24,558
Takoma Park **(13522)** ....(Combined) 5,720
Walkersville/Thurmont
Gazette **(13525)** ....(Combined) 9,961

Gaithersburg
China News Digest—Canada **(13533)**
China News Digest—US **(13535)**
China News—Europe/Pacific **(13536)**
The Gaithersburg
Gazette **(13540)** ....(Combined) 31,522

Germantown
The Germantown
Gazette **(13553)** ....(Combined) 20,099

Greenbelt
Greenbelt News Review **(13558)** ....(Paid) ‡100
(Free) ‡10,900

Kingsville
Times-Herald **(13593)** 32,000

Potomac
Potomac/Bethesda
Almanac **(13658)** ....(Combined) 12,400

Rockville
Montgomery County Sentinel **(13687)** ....(Paid) 6,100

MASSACHUSETTS
Ashland
Ashland TAB **(13822)** ....(Combined) 32,287

Ayer
Fort Devens Dispatch **(13828)** ....(Free) 5,200

Boston
The Beacon Hill Times **(13853)** ....(Paid) 100
(Non-paid) 14,000
Boston Seniority **(13863)** ....(Free) ‡20
Boston TAB **(13864)** ....(Free) 18,633
Sampan **(13958)** ....(Controlled) 6,000
The South End News **(13961)** ....(Paid) 300
(Free) 18,500

Bourne
The Bourne Enterprise **(14002)** ....(Paid) 10,087

Brewster
Brewster Oracle **(14005)** ....(Non-paid) 1,666

Brookline
Brookline TAB **(14017)** ....(Free) 14,391

Cambridge
Cambridge TAB **(14043)** ....(Free) 9,579

Cape Cod
Cape Cod News **(14119)**

Carlisle
Carlisle Mosquito **(14121)** ....(Free) ‡1,850

Chatham
Chatham Current **(14125)** ....(Non-paid) 1,677

Concord
About Action
Unlimited **(14142)** ....(Combined) 72,011

2942

Numbers cited after listings are entry numbers rather than page numbers.

Danvers
North Shore Sunday (14153) .....(Combined) 60,253

Dover
Dover-Sherborn TAB (14160) ....(Free) 4,094

Duxbury
Duxbury Reporter (14163) ....(Combined) 2,540

East Boston
East Boston Times (14165) ....(Free) ‡15,500

East Longmeadow
The Reminder (14167) ....(Free) ‡30,000

Eastham
Eastham-Wellfleet
    Oracle (14172) ....(Non-paid) 1,659

Everett
Leader-Herald and News
    Gazette (14176) ....(Free) ‡15,000

Framingham
Framingham TAB (14196) ....(Free) 11,680

Greenfield
The Athol/Orange Town
    Crier (14219) ....(Free) 11,166
The Greenfield Town Crier (14220) ....(Free) 19,119

Harwich
Harwich Oracle (14230) ....(Non-paid) 3,425

Holliston
Holliston TAB (14238) ....(Combined) 32,287

Kingston
Kingston Reporter (14264) ....(Combined) 3,953

Marblehead
Marblehead Reporter (14304) .....(Combined) 60,253

Marshfield
Marshfield Reporter (14308) ....(Combined) 3,030

Mashpee
Mashpee Messenger (14311) ....(Non-paid) 2,290

Mattapan
Survival News (14313) ....(Paid) 750
                                                  (Free) ⊕9,000

Mattapoisett
The Wanderer (14314)

Medford
Malden Observer (14323) ....(Combined) 60,253

Milford
Neighbors (14332) ....(Free) ‡25,581

Natick
Natick TAB (14348) ....(Free) 7,647

Needham
Needham TAB (14365) ....(Free) 10,811
Needham Times (14366) ....(Free) 11,700
Newton TAB (14367) ....(Free) 29,853
Parkway Transcript (14369) ....(Combined) 32,287
West Roxbury Transcript (14373) ....(Paid) 4,032
                                                  (Free) 190

Newton
Newton Graphic (14407) ....(Paid) 323
                                                  (Free) 28,018

North Adams
The Advocate (14416) ....(Non-paid) 20,500
The Advocate (14417) ....(Paid) ‡62
                                                  (Free) ‡20,500

Peabody
Lynnfield-Peabody
    Edition (14462) ....(Non-paid) 4,528
Peabody-Lynnfield
    Edition (14464) ....(Non-paid) 19,330

Revere
East Boston Sun
    Transcript (14500) ....(Non-paid) 10,300
The Everett
    Independent (14501) ....(Non-paid) ‡7,500

Somerville
The Somerville
    News (14538) ....(Combined) ‡14,000

Stoughton
Suburban News (14570) ....(Free) 30,000

Tewksbury
Tewksbury Advertiser (14587) ....(Combined) 69,131

Wayland
Wayland Town Crier &
    TAB (14616) ....(Combined) 36,984

Wellesley
Wellesley Townsman (14618) ....(Non-paid) 5,622

Wellfleet
Wellfleet Oracle (14622) ....(Paid) 97
                                                  (Free) 1,417

Weston
Weston Town Crier &
    TAB (14652) ....(Non-paid) 2,424

Woburn
Middlesex East Update (14670) ....(Non-paid) 5,011

Worcester
The Fifty Plus Advocate (14679) ....(Free) 80,000
                                                  (Paid) 1,303

Yarmouth Port
Orleans Oracle (14703) ....(Free) 1,094

MICHIGAN
Allegan
Senior Times (14723) ....(Free) 22,450
West Michigan Senior
    Times (14724) ....(Free) 25,000

Battle Creek
Battle Creek Shopper
    News (14792) ....(Free) ‡51,855

Brooklyn
The Exponent (14838) ....(Paid) ‡6,000

Cadillac
Northern Michigan News (14843) ....(Paid) ‡9,747
                                                  (Free) ‡16,638

Canton
Canton Observer (14854) ....(Sun.) 10,518
                                                  (Thurs.) 9,864

Carson City
Carson City Gazette (14861) ....(Paid) ‡273
                                                  (Free) ‡9,730

Charlotte
Charlotte Shopping Guide (14866) ....(Paid) 46
                                                  (Non-paid) 15,107
Delta Waverly Community
    News (14867) ....(Paid) 56
                                                  (Non-paid) 8,565
DeWitt Bath Review (14868) .....(Non-paid) 7,746
                                                  (Paid) 28
Eaton Rapids Community
    News (14869) ....(Paid) ♦1,305
                                          (Non-paid) ♦120,193
The Grand Ledge
    Independent (14870) ....(Paid) 259
                                                  (Non-paid) 13,314

Clare
Clare County Review (14878) ....(Paid) ‡918
                                                  (Non-paid) ‡9,082

Commerce
Commerce Spinal Column
    Newsweekly (14890) ....(Free) ‡9,800

Detroit
EL CENTRAL
    Newspaper (14930) ....(Combined) 14,000
Metro Times (14936) ....(Non-paid) 106,805
The Monitor (14939) ....(Free) ‡47,000

Eastpointe
The Advisor (14998) ....(Free) ‡43,822

Gaylord
Charlevoix Co. Star (15067) ....(Non-paid) 10,146

Gladwin
Gladwin County Record and Beaverton
    Clarion (15080) ....(Paid) ‡8,200
                                                  (Free) ‡60

Hastings
Hastings Reminder (15153) ....(Free) 28,450
Maple Valley News (15154) ....(Free) ‡3,200
The Sun & News (15155) ....‡8,000

Highland
Highland Spinal Column
    Newsweekly (15160) ....(Free) ‡3,950

Howell
The Fenton Independent (15191) ....(Sun.) 12,193
                                                  (Thurs.) 12,148

Leslie
Leslie Local Independent (15313) ......(Paid) ‡1,600
                                                  (Free) ‡7,000

Marquette
Action Shopper (15337) ....(Free) ‡28,000

Marshall
Marshall Community
    Advisor (15351) ....(Free) 18,791

Milford
Milford Spinal Column
    Newsweekly (15358) ....(Free) ‡2,500
Milford Times (15359) ....(Combined) 7,500

Mount Clemens
The Advisor (15370) ....(Non-paid) 43,313

New Baltimore
The Voice News (15398) ....(Free) 62,024

Niles
Hometown News (15403) ....(Free) ‡27,000

Novi
Novi Spinal Column
    Newsweekly (15411) ....(Free) ‡4,150

Petoskey
The Graphic (15435) ....(Free) 17,000

Plymouth
The Community Crier (15447) ....(Paid) ‡5,687
                                                  (Free) ‡14,128

Rockford
Rockford/Cedar Springs
    Advance (15469) ....(Free) 16,450
                                                  (Paid) 97

Romeo
The Countryman (15472) ....(Non-paid) ‡6,650

Royal Oak
Huntington Woods/Berkley
    Mirror (15482) ....(Combined) 9,038
Pleasant Ridge/Ferndale
    Mirror (15483) ....(Combined) 11,307
Royal Oak Mirror (15485) ....(Combined) 28,345
The Weekly Tribune Plus (15487)

St. Johns
The Clinton County
    News (15509) ....(Combined) 14,115

Sandusky
Sanilac County News (15522) ....(Paid) ‡9,400
                                                  (Free) ‡23,900

Shelby Township
Romeo-Washington
    Source (15537) ....(Non-paid) 8,086

Southfield
phenomeNEWS (15547) ....(Free) 55,000

Southgate
The Suburban News (15567) ....(Paid) ♦693
                                          (Non-paid) ♦63,965

Sterling Heights
Sterling Heights
    Source (15576) ....(Non-paid) 34,706

Stockbridge
Stockbridge Town Crier (15579) ....(Paid) 1,808
                                          (Non-paid) 8,383287

Three Oaks
South County Gazette and
    Shopper (15591) ....(Combined) ‡11,002

Troy
Troy-Somerset Gazette (15643) ....(Free) ‡24,500

Union City
Tribune (15647) ....(Free) 2,456

Walker
Walker/Westside Advance (15655) .....(Free) 23,500
                                                  (Paid) 669

Warren
Renaissance Times—New Center
    News (15661) ....(Free) 8,000
Tech Center News (15662) ......(Controlled) ‡16,000
Warren Advisor (15665) ....(Non-paid) 12,672

Waterford
Waterford Spinal Column
    Newsweekly (15668) ....(Free) ‡13,600

Circulation: ★ = ABC; △ = BPA; ♦ = CAC; ♠ = CCAB; ❑ = VAC; ⊕ = PO Statement; ‡ = Publisher's Report; Boldface figures = sworn; Light figures = estimated.

2943

Circ.

MICHIGAN (continued)

Wayne
Eyewitness **(15672)** ....(Combined) 17,960

West Bloomfield
West Bloomfield Spinal Column
 Newsweekly **(15678)** ....(Free) ‡9,900

White Lake
White Lake Spinal Column
 Newsweekly **(15683)** ....(Free) ‡5,900

Whitehall
White Lake Beacon **(15684)** ....(Paid) ‡815
 (Free) ‡9,885

MINNESOTA
Apple Valley
Apple Valley/Rosemount Sun
 Current **(15718)** ....(Paid) ♦256
 (Non-paid) ♦14,869

Big Lake
Clearwater Tribune **(15750)** ....(Non-paid) 4,476
West Sherburne Tribune **(15751)** ....(Paid) 188
 (Non-paid) 13,536

Blaine
Blaine Banner **(15755)** ....(Non-paid) ‡10,000

Brooklyn Center
Brooklyn Center Sun-Post **(15774)** ....(Paid) ♦736
 (Non-paid) ♦5,831

Burnsville
Burnsville/Savage Sun
 Current **(15781)** ....(Paid) ♦298
 (Non-paid) ♦29,312

Chanhassen
The Chanhassen Villager **(15792)** ....(Paid) ‡85
 (Free) ‡4,290

Detroit Lakes
Becker County Record **(15828)** ....(Free) 13,346
 (Paid) 227
Lake Area Press **(15830)** ....(Free) 18,792

Duluth
Duluth Budgeteer News **(15836)** ....(Paid) ♦260
 (Non-paid) ♦43,785

Eagan
Eagan Sun Current **(15862)** ....(Paid) ♦166
 (Non-paid) ♦32,102

Eden Prairie
Brooklyn Park Sun-Post **(15867)** ....(Paid) ♦513
 (Non-paid) ♦19,170
Eden Prairie Sun Current **(15869)** ....(Free) ♦12,361
 (Paid) ♦379

Edina
Edina Sun Current **(15874)** ....(Paid) ♦1,337
 (Non-paid) ♦17,301

Elk River
Elk River Star News **(15878)** ....(Paid) ‡16,718

Excelsior
Excelsior/Shorewood/Chanhassen
 Sun-Sailor **(15887)** ....(Paid) ♦546
 (Non-paid) ♦5,482

Fairmont
Fairmont Photo Press **(15889)** ....(Free) 11,800

Granite Falls
The Advocate-Tribune **(15934)** ....(Paid) ‡3,700
 (Free) ‡100

Greenbush
New River Record **(15935)** ....(Paid) ‡540
 (Free) ‡25

Hopkins
Hopkins/East Minnetonka
 Sailor-Sun **(15963)** ....(Paid) ♦13,803

Lakeville
This Week Life & Times **(15996)** ......(Free) 23,597

Le Sueur
Valley **(16001)** ....(Free) ‡7,500

Longville
Pine Cone Press-Citizen **(16012)** ....(Paid) ‡384
 (Non-paid) ‡6,609

Minneapolis
City Pages **(16065)** ....(Free) 116,697
Skyway News **(16127)** ....(Free) 44,546
Southwest Journal **(16131)** ....(Non-paid) 40,000

Minnetonka
Wayzata Sun-Sailor **(16178)** ....(Non-paid) 4,461
 (Paid) 272
West Minnetonka/Deephaven
 Sun-Sailor **(16179)** ....(Paid) ♦407
 (Non-paid) ♦5,935

Mora
Kanabec County Times **(16195)** ....(Paid) ‡3,000
 (Free) ‡11,000

New Brighton
New Brighton-Mounds View
 Bulletin **(16205)** ....(Paid) 129
 (Free) 9,425

New Hope
New Hope/Golden Valley
 Sun-Post **(16207)** ....(Paid) ♦1,106
 (Non-paid) ♦10,092

North St. Paul
East Side Review **(16225)** ....(Free) 20,128
Roseville Review **(16230)** ....(Free) 15,866
South-West Review **(16231)** ....(Free) 23,389
Woodbury-South Maplewood
 Review **(16232)** ....(Free) 12,674

Owatonna
Owatonna Area Shopper **(16253)** ......(Free) 14,167

Park Rapids
Park Rapids Enterprise **(16256)** ....(Combined) 5,767

Plymouth
Wayzata/Orono/Long Lake
 Sun-Sailor **(16280)** ....(Paid) 23,000

Richfield
Richfield Sun Current **(16304)** ....(Paid) ♦1,113
 (Non-paid) ♦8,611

St. Anthony
The St. Anthony Bulletin **(16340)** ....(Paid) 47
 (Free) 2,150

St. Louis Park
St. Louis Park Sun-Sailor **(16361)** ....(Paid) ♦807
 (Non-paid) ♦12,070

St. Paul
Villager **(16413)** ....(Paid) ‡400
 (Free) ‡49,600
The Voice of
 Agriculture **(16414)** ....(Combined) 35,000

Shoreview
Shoreview-Arden Hills Bulletin **(16447)** ......(Paid) 56
 (Free) 13,425

South St. Paul
South St. Paul/Inver Grove Heights Sun
 Current **(16453)** ....(Paid) ♦224
 (Non-paid) ♦14,362

Storden
Village Insight **(16464)** ....(Paid) ‡100
 (Free) ‡1,900

Thief River Falls
Northern Watch **(16467)** ....(Combined) ‡23,200

Wadena
Intercom **(16489)** ....(Non-paid) 14,883

West St. Paul
West Saint Paul/Mendota Heights Sun
 Current **(16506)** ....(Paid) ♦200
 (Non-paid) ♦9,552

White Bear Lake
Quad Community Press **(16510)** ....(Paid) 2,291
 (Free) 6,894
St. Croix Valley Press **(16511)** ....(Free) 10,247
 (Paid) 181
Vadnais Heights Press **(16514)** ....(Paid) 316
 (Non-paid) 3,833
White Bear Press **(16515)** ....(Free) 13,929
 (Paid) 4,784

Winona
Winona Post **(16528)** ....(Free) ‡24,440

MISSISSIPPI
Columbus
Silver Wings **(16605)** ....(Free) 3,000

Holly Springs
Pigeon Roost News **(16680)** ....(Free) 6,500

Jackson
Northside Sun **(16711)** ....(Paid) ‡8,430
 (Free) ‡595

Olive Branch
DeSoto County Tribune **(16804)** ....(Paid) ‡9,897
 (Free) ‡8,100

Pearl
The Weekly Leader **(16815)** ....(Free) ‡14,800

Prentiss
The Prentiss Headlight **(16827)** ....(Paid) 2,366
 (Free) 5,482

MISSOURI
Cassville
Barry County Advertiser **(16964)** ....(Paid) ‡300
 (Non-paid) ‡11,200

Centralia
Fireside Guard **(16969)** ....(Paid) 3,700
 (Free) 1,100

Farmington
Farmington Press **(17054)** ....(Combined) ‡4,600

Festus
Courier Journal **(17065)** ....(Free) 46,438

Kansas City
Clay & Platte
 Dispatch-Tribune **(17162)** ....(Paid) 7,229
 (Free) 35,221
Northland News **(17190)** ....(Free) 19,270
The Wednesday Magazine **(17202)** ....(Paid) 136
 (Free) 23,010

Kirksville
The Crier **(17225)** ....(Paid) 105
 (Free) 20,455

Liberty
Liberty Tribune **(17248)** ....(Combined) 2,659
 (Free) 10,306
Platte County Sun Gazette **(17249)** ....(Paid) 158
 (Free) 13,055

Macon
The Journal **(17258)** ....(Free) 11,000

Mount Vernon
Lawrence County Record **(17299)** ......(Paid) ‡3,812
 (Free) ‡3,450

Owensville
East Central Ad Mart **(17328)** ....(Free) ‡6,812

Raytown
Raytown
 Dispatch-Tribune **(17368)** ....(Combined) 11,442
Raytown Post **(17369)** ....(Free) ‡18,000

St. Louis
Cadenza **(17419)** ....(Non-paid) ‡8,000
Community News **(17425)** ....(Free) ‡30,000
Neighborhood Journal **(17476)** ....(Free) ‡18,467
The Riverfront Times **(17490)** ....(Paid) 219
 (Free) 101,914
South County Times **(17514)** ....(Free) 35,210

Springfield
East Tennessee Senior
 Living **(17596)** ....(Combined) 25,000
4-States Senior Living **(17601)** ....(Combined) 25,000
Lake of the Ozarks Senior
 Living **(17603)** ....(Combined) 25,000
Ozarks Senior Living **(17608)** .....(Combined) 25,000

Warrenton
Cahokia-Dupo Journal **(17674)** ....(Sun.) 11,125
 (Wed.) 11,515
Central West End Journal **(17675)** ....(Wed.) 6,093
Collinsville Herald-Journal **(17678)** .....(Sun.) 18,923
 (Wed.) 19,598
County Journal **(17679)** ....(Wed.) 6,790
East St. Louis Journal **(17681)** ....(Wed.) 15,855
Edwardsville Journal **(17682)** ....(Wed.) 13,782
Granite City Journal **(17684)** ....(Sun.) 21,201
 (Wed.) 21,760
Jefferson County Journal **(17685)** ....(Sun.) 22,745
 (Wed.) 23,234
 (Fri.) 22,745
Meramec Journal **(17686)** ....(Sun.) 15,514
 (Wed.) 16,051
 (Fri.) 15,514
Monroe County Clarion
 Journal **(17688)** ....(Sun.) 14,094
 (Wed.) 14,094
North Side Journal **(17691)** ....(Wed.) 31,605

Press Journal **(17692)** ....(Sun.) 35,048
(Wed.) 35,954
(Fri.) 34,048
St. Charles Journal **(17693)** ....(Sun.) 24,347
(Wed.) 25,092
(Fri.) 24,247
South County Journal **(17696)** ....(Sun.) 22,011
(Wed.) 22,586
(Fri.) 22,011
South Side Journal **(17697)** ....(Sun.) 28,665
(Wed.) 29,425
Southwest County Journal **(17699)** .....(Sun.) 28,959
(Wed.) 29,952
(Fri.) 28,959
Warrenton Journal **(17700)** ....(Wed.) 13,736
West County Journal **(17701)** ....(Sun.) 24,921
(Wed.) 25,600
(Fri.) 23,914

Webster Groves
Webster-Kirkwood Times **(17714)** ....(Free) 30,484

MONTANA
Big Timber
The Big Timber Pioneer **(17727)** ....(Paid) ‡1,900

Billings
The Billings Outpost **(17730)** ....(Free) ‡20,000

Fairfield
Fairfield Sun Times **(17789)** ....(Paid) 1,150
(Free) 20

Glasgow
The Courier Express **(17792)** ....(Free) ‡11,000
The Glasgow Courier **(17793)** ....(Paid) ‡4,300

Libby
The Montanian **(17851)** ....(Combined) 4,000

Missoula
Missoula Independent **(17868)** ....(Combined) 25,000

NEBRASKA
Deshler
The Deshler Rustler **(17998)** ....(Paid) ‡1,700

North Platte
Telegraph Happenings **(18177)** ....(Free) ‡12,554

Offutt A F B
The Air Pulse **(18187)** ....(Free) ‡13,000

Ord
The Ord Quiz **(18236)** ....(Paid) ‡2,650
(Free) ‡85

NEVADA
Las Vegas
El Tiempo Libre **(18362)** ....(Free) 32,000
The Jewish Reporter **(18365)** .....(Controlled) 13,000

NEW HAMPSHIRE
Bradford
The Bradford Bridge **(18460)**

Conway
The Mount Washington Valley Mountain
Ear **(18483)** ....‡‡15,000
o
Northern Light **(18484)** ....(Non-paid) 34,759

Exeter
The Exeter
News-Letter **(18505)** ....(Combined) 6,010

Hudson
Hudson Litchfield News **(18528)** ......(Free) ⊕11,600

Nashua
1590 Broadcaster **(18598)** ....(Free) ‡50,000

NEW JERSEY
Bayonne
Bayonne Community News **(18666)** ....(Free) 28,525

Bedminster
Hills-Bedminster Press **(18668)** ......(Non-paid) 3,558
(Paid) 143

Bergen
The North
Bergen/Reporter **(18672)** ....(Non-paid) 18,660

Bernardsville
The Hills Community
News **(18677)** ....(Non-paid) ♦1,770
New England Wine
Gazette **(18678)** ....(Non-paid) ♦18,418

Burlington
Bensalem Express **(18704)** ....(Free) ‡9,325
Bristol Express **(18705)** ....(Non-paid) ‡5500
Burlington Mail **(18706)** ....(Non-paid) ‡7000
Croydon Express **(18707)** ....(Non-paid) ‡3250
Fairless Hills Express **(18708)** ......(Non-paid) ‡5000
Levittown Express **(18709)** ....(Free) ‡9,325
Mount Holly Mail **(18710)** ....(Non-paid) ‡7000

Chester
Mount Olive Chronicle **(18741)** .....(Combined) 2,683

Cinnaminson
South Jersey Advisor **(18744)** ....(Free) ‡35,000

Clark
Elizabeth City News **(18748)** ....(Non-paid) 93,757

Clifton
Dateline Journal **(18754)** ....(Thurs.) 30,175

Cresskill
Twin-Boro News **(18774)** ....(Free) ♦19,689

Elizabeth
Mensaje **(18791)** ....(Paid) 52,000

Fair Lawn
The Shopper News **(18809)** ......(Non-paid) ♦74,422
The Week Ahead **(18810)** ....(Free) ‡37,949

Flemington
Today in Hunterdon **(18821)** ....(Free) ‡30,000

Fort Dix
The Fort Dix Post **(18830)** ....(Free) 9,263

Franklin
Franklin Focus **(18835)** ....(Non-paid) 556
(Paid) 1,595

Freehold
Bayshore Independent **(18838)** .....(Non-paid) 15,715
The News
Transcript **(18839)** ....(Combined) ‡140,000

Hackensack
The Parent Paper **(18853)** .....(Combined) 50,409

Hackettstown
Community Forum **(18856)** ....(Non-paid) ♦51,784
Suburban News **(18858)** ....(Combined) 93,817

Hamilton
Tempo-Mercer **(18861)** ....(Free) 14,000

Hoboken
The Current **(18924)** ....(Free) ‡10,000
The Hoboken Reporter **(18964)** ....(Non-paid) 16,135

Jersey City
Coming Up **(19134)** ....(Non-paid) 18,246
El Nuevo Hudson **(19136)** ......(Non-paid) ♦55,525
Go Out **(19137)** ....(Non-paid) 34,433
The Jersey City
Reporter **(19140)** ....(Non-paid) 16,296
This Week in Bayonne **(19146)** ....(Non-paid) 20,061
This Week in Jersey
City **(19147)** ....(Non-paid) 77,880

Kearny
The Observer **(19151)** ....(Free) 30,000

Kenilworth
The Leader **(19154)** ....(Paid) 1,299
(Non-paid) 21

Manahawkin
Beacon Mailbag **(19209)** ....(Fri.) 51,593

Middletown
Middletown
Independent **(19235)** ....(Non-paid) 17,985

New Providence
Independent Press **(19347)** ....(Paid) 196
(Free) 34,813

Newton
A Shopper's Guide **(19377)** ....(Non-paid) 39,708

Palisades Park
Sun Bulletin **(19399)** ....(Paid) 1,558
(Free) 7,783

Pleasantville
At the Shore **(19443)** ....(Fri.) 180,000
Whoot Newspaper **(19445)** ....(Paid) 527
(Free) 38,000

Princeton
Town Topics **(19475)** ....(Paid) ‡7,218
(Free) ‡4,497
U.S. 1 Newspaper **(19477)** ....(Free) ‡19,000

Ramsey
The Home and Store
News **(19489)** ....(Free) 33,316

Randolph
Randolph Reporter **(19496)** ....(Combined) 4,029

Ridgewood
Town News **(19505)** ....(Non-paid) ♦15,178

Rockaway
Neighbor News **(19522)** ....(Non-paid) 33,207
Suburban Life **(19523)** ....(Non-paid) 16,430

Secaucus
The Secaucus Reporter **(19541)** ....(Non-paid) 6,050

Somerset
Somerset Spectator **(19566)** ....(Paid) ‡4,600
(Free) ‡500

Surf City
The Sandpaper **(19606)** ....(Non-paid) 35,000

Teaneck
Teaneck Suburbanite **(19610)** ...(Non-paid) ♦11,443

Toms River
Ocean County
Reporter **(19643)** ....(Combined) 97,113

Weehawken
The Weehawken
Reporter **(19712)** ....(Non-paid) 5,050

West Paterson
Lakeland Today **(19731)** ....(Non-paid) 15,387
Northern Valley
Suburbanite **(19733)** ....(Non-paid) 45,524
Pascack Valley Community
Life **(19735)** ....(Non-paid) 45,524
Passaic Valley Today **(19736)** ....(Non-paid) 10,263
South - Bergenite **(19738)** ....(Non-paid) 45,524
Today Newspapers **(19740)** ....(Non-paid) ♦41,692
Wayne Today **(19741)** ....(Combined) ♦45,524

Willingboro
Airtides **(19752)** ....(Non-paid) ♦9,291
The Post **(19754)** ....(Non-paid) ♦9,196

NEW MEXICO
Albuquerque
Focus KAFB Newspaper **(19771)** .....(Free) ‡15,000

Las Cruces
Las Cruces Bulletin **(19872)** ....(Paid) 500
(Free) 21,000

Raton
The Raton Range **(19910)** ....(Paid) ‡2,700
(Free) ‡11,300

Santa Fe
Buzz'n **(19932)** ....(Non-paid) 20,000
Santa Fe Reporter **(19944)** ....(Paid) 105
(Free) 20,000

White Sands Missile Range
White Sands Missile
Ranger **(19974)** ....(Free) ‡6,000

NEW YORK
Adams
The Empire State Farmer **(19975)** .....(Free) ‡6,000

Amityville
Amityville Suffolk Life **(20036)** ....(Wed.) 16,921
Massapequa Post **(20049)** ....(Paid) 4,200
(Free) 100

Babylon
Photo News **(20111)** ....(Paid) ‡5,200
(Free) ‡27,000
West Babylon Suffolk Life **(20112)** ....(Wed.) 19,349

Bath
Steuben Courier-Advocate **(20125)** .....(Free) 10,760

Bay Shore
Bay Shore Suffolk Life **(20135)** ....(Free) 154,464

Bellport
Bellport/East Patchogue Suffolk
Life **(20148)** ....(Wed.) 11,078

Brentwood
Brentwood Suffolk Life **(20240)** ....(Wed.) 14,324

Bridgehampton
Dan's Paper **(20243)**

Newspapers

Circ.   Circ.   Circ.

NEW YORK (continued)

Bronx
Riverdale Review **(20285)** ....(Combined) 20,000

Brooklyn
Caribbean Life **(20307)** ....(Non-paid) ♦126,108
Spring Creek Sun **(20348)** ....(Non-paid) 10,000

Buffalo
Artvoice **(20363)** ....(Free) ❏52,922
The Buffalo Rocket **(20369)** ....(Free) ‡14,000
Depew Bee **(20377)** ....(Paid) 1,572
(Free) 22
Riverside Review **(20387)** ....(Free) ‡14,300
West Side Times **(20391)** ....(Free) ‡13,000

Canandaigua
Gates Chili Post **(20421)** ....(Paid) ♦5,895
(Non-paid) ♦1,290

Centereach
Centereach/Lake Grove Suffolk
Life **(20445)** ....(Wed.) 12,488

Central Islip
Central Islip/Hauppauge Suffolk
Life **(20448)** ....(Wed.) 13,860

Cheektowaga
Metro Community News **(20458)** ......(Free) 306,143

Clifton Park
Community News **(20464)** ....(Free) ‡26,000

Commack
Commack/Kings Park Suffolk
Life **(20486)** ....(Wed.) 17,559

Coram
Coram/Middle Island Suffolk
Life **(20501)** ....(Wed.) 18,554

Cortland
Consumer News **(20511)** ....(Free) ‡11,337

East Hampton
Hampton East Suffolk Life **(20546)** ....(Wed.) 17,019

East Islip
East Islip Suffolk Life **(20548)** ....(Wed.) 13,908

Elizabethtown
North Country Free
Trader **(20564)** ....(Free) ‡31,591
Times of Ticonderoga **(20566)** ......(Non-paid) 7,317
(Paid) 456

Garden City
The Island-Ear **(20643)** 25,000

Grand Island
Lewiston-Porter Sentinel **(20679)** ....(Free) 10,600
Niagara-Wheatfield Tribune **(20680)** ....(Paid) 10,100

Hamburg
Kids Courier **(20704)** ....(Non-paid) 385,117

Hicksville
Franklin Square Shopper's Guide **(20736)**
Freeport Shopper's Guide **(20737)**
Merrick/Bellmore South Shopper's Guide **(20740)**
Rockville Centre Shopper's Guide **(20745)**
Valley Stream Shopper's Guide **(20746)**

Huntington
Huntington Suffolk Life **(20772)** ....(Wed.) 17,315

Huntington Station
Huntington Station Suffolk
Life **(20778)** ....(Wed.) 17,890

Jamaica
Jamaica Shopping & Entertainment
Guide **(20836)** ....(Free) ‡30,000

Lindenhurst
Lindenhurst Suffolk Life **(20949)** ....(Wed.) 14,538
South Bay's Shopping
Newspaper **(20950)** ....(Free) ‡103,100

Mamaroneck
Connecticut Family **(20984)** ....(Free) 34,976
(Paid) 42

Mastic
Mastic/Shirley Suffolk Life **(21030)** ....(Wed.) 16,048

Medford
Holbrook/Bohemia Suffolk
Life **(21033)** ....(Wed.) 14,337
Medford/Holtsville Suffolk
Life **(21034)** ....(Wed.) 13,269

Medina
Medina Daily Journal-Register–Eastern Niagara
Edition **(21037)** ....(Mon.-Fri.) ★4,301

Melville
Dix Hills/Melville Suffolk
Life **(21042)** ....(Wed.) 13,429

Monroe
The Chronicle **(21089)** ....(Non-paid) 9,000

Moriches
Moriches Suffolk Life **(21097)** ....(Wed.) 11,100

New Paltz
Huguenot Herald **(21113)** ....(Paid) 3,500
(Free) 10,000

New York
Action **(21146)** ....(Paid) 5,000
(Free) 2,000
The Antiquer **(21222)**
Cleveland Free Times **(21428)**
Downtown Express **(21567)** ....(Free) ‡56,897
Hungarian Word (Amerikai Magyar
SZO) **(21836)** ....(Paid) ‡1,000
(Free) ‡150
Manhattan Spirit **(22280)** ....(Free) ‡76,000
New York Press **(22449)** ....(Non-paid) 115,059
The Upper East Side
Resident **(22888)** ....(Non-paid) 200,000
The Upper West Side
Resident **(22889)** ....(Free) ‡50,000

North Tonawanda
Record Advertiser **(23015)** ....(Non-paid) 32,635
(Paid) 14

Northport
Northport Suffolk Life **(23019)** ....(Wed.) 17,262

Orchard Park
Orchard Park Bee **(23057)** ....(Free) 42
(Paid) 2,100

Ozone Park
Forum of Queens **(23072)** ....(Free) 22,000

Patchogue
Patchogue Suffolk Life **(23077)** ....(Wed.) 12,212

Port Jefferson
Port Jefferson Suffolk Life **(23116)** ....(Wed.) 14,538

Potsdam
North Country This Week **(23138)** ....(Paid) 12
(Non-paid) 9,769

Rego Park
Queens Chronicle **(23180)** ......(Non-paid) ⊕160,000

Riverhead
Deer Park Suffolk Life **(23199)** ....(Wed.) 19,889
Mid-Hampton Suffolk Life **(23200)** .....(Wed.) 16,132
North Fork Suffolk Life **(23201)** ......(Wed.) 13,441
Riverhead Suffolk Life **(23202)** ....(Wed.) 18,153
Smithtown Suffolk Life **(23203)** ....(Wed.) 14,629

Rochester
City Newspaper **(23216)** ....(Paid) 200
(Free) 42,000
Empty Closet **(23224)** ....(Non-paid) ⊕5,200

Rocky Point
Rocky Point Suffolk Life **(23263)** ......(Wed.) 15,770

Ronkonkoma
Ronkonkoma Suffolk Life **(23273)** ....(Wed.) 13,496

St. James
St. James/Nesconset Suffolk
Life **(23290)** ....(Wed.) 9,694

Salamanca
The Independent Olean
Press **(23292)** ....(Free) ‡11,900

Sayville
Sayville/Oakdale Suffolk
Life **(23310)** ....(Wed.) 12,320

Selden
Selden/Farmingville Suffolk
Life **(23323)** ....(Wed.) 12,301

Spencerport
Hamlin Clarkson Herald **(23350)** ....(Paid) 11
(Non-paid) 6,094
Suburban News (North
Edition) **(23351)** ....(Non-paid) 6,705
(Paid) 7
Suburban News (South Edition) **(23352)** ....(Paid) 80
(Non-paid) 11,274

Suburban News West **(23353)** ......(Non-paid) 8,590

Stony Brook
Stony Brook/Setauket Suffolk
Life **(23377)** ....(Wed.) 13,014

Syracuse
Onondaga Valley
News **(23416)** ....(Non-paid) ‡8,154
Pennywise/Villager **(23418)** ....(Non-paid) ‡9,311

Wading River
Community Journal **(23495)** ....(Free) ‡7,000

Wappingers Falls
Beacon Free Press **(23501)** ....(Paid) ‡247
(Free) ‡8,550

Warsaw
Warsaw Penny Saver **(23506)** .....(Non-paid) 9,301

West Islip
West Islip Suffolk Life **(23544)** ....(Wed.) 8,543

Westhampton
Hampton West Suffolk
Life **(23566)** ....(Wed.) 16,408

Williamsville
East Aurora Bee **(23583)** ....(Paid) 10,530
(Non-paid) 5

NORTH CAROLINA
Asheville
Good News **(23630)** ....(Non-paid) 41,302
Mountain Xpress **(23632)** ....(Combined) 24,877

Black Mountain
Creations **(23647)** ....(Combined) 50,000

Boone
The Mountain Times **(23654)** .....(Combined) 30,842

Chadbourn
News-Times **(23695)** ....(Free) 8,656

Charlotte
The Leader **(23748)** ....(Paid) 1,000
(Non-paid) 36,000

Durham
Independent Weekly **(23828)** ....(Paid) 81
(Free) 40,184

Fairmont
The Times-Messenger **(23872)** ....(Paid) ‡1,409
(Free) ‡466

Fayetteville
Spring Lake News **(23881)** ....(Free) ‡8,500
Up & Coming Weekly **(23882)** .....(Non-paid) 15,000

Forest City
County News-Enterprise **(23893)** .....(Free) ‡17,000
The Daily Courier **(23894)** ....(Paid) 11,937
(Free) 129

Hickory
Extra **(23987)** ....(Free) ‡16,500

Marion
The Express **(24055)** ....(Free) ‡8,350

Mount Airy
Surry Scene **(24081)** ....(Free) ‡21,500

Raeford
Fort Bragg Paraglide **(24120)** ....(Free) 25,000

Raleigh
The Carolinian **(24131)** ....(Paid) ‡12,000
(Free) ‡225

Siler City
The Chatham News **(24230)** ....(Paid) ‡4,733
(Free) ‡191

NORTH DAKOTA
Bismarck
Dakota Catholic Action **(24350)** ....(Non-paid) 16,800

New Rockford
Transcript **(24524)** ....(Paid) ‡2,000
(Free) ‡1,000

Williston
Plains Reporter **(24559)** ....(Free) ‡14,200

OHIO
Akron
Akron Jewish News **(24572)** ....(Non-paid) 3,200

Numbers cited after listings are entry numbers rather than page numbers.

Athens
The Athens News **(24629)** ......(Combined) ❏**17,375**

Aurora
Aurora Advocate **(24639)** ....(Free) ‡5,680

Bedford
Twinsburg Bulletin **(24662)** ....(Paid) 687
(Free) 7,765

Bellevue
Bellevue RFD News **(24670)** ....(Paid) 400
(Non-paid) 9,500

Bexley
Bexley News **(24680)** ....(Paid) ◆**330**
(Non-paid) ◆**9,160**

Cardington
Morrow County
Independent **(24739)** ....(Paid) ‡1,000
(Free) ‡100

Cincinnati
Downtowner Newspaper **(24794)** ......(Free) ‡18,000

Cleveland
Scene **(24952)**

Columbia Station
Rural-Urban Record **(24998)** ....(Free) ‡17,000

Columbus
Booster **(25001)** ....(Paid) 3,389
(Free) 14,979
Columbus Alive **(25007)** ....(Combined) 50,000
Eastside Messenger **(25016)** ....(Non-paid) 49,491
German Village Gazette **(25020)** ....(Paid) ◆**30**
(Non-paid) ◆**4,418**
Northland News **(25037)** ....(Paid) 3,830
(Non-paid) 17,553
Northwest Columbus News **(25038)** ....(Paid) 880
(Non-paid) 6,065
Southeast Messenger **(25062)** ....(Non-paid) 32,188
Southwest Messenger **(25063)** ....(Non-paid) 18,976
Tri-Village News **(25067)** ....(Paid) 368
(Non-paid) 4,112
Westside Messenger **(25068)** ......(Non-paid) 45,031

Covington
Stillwater Valley
Advertiser **(25100)** ....(Combined) 9,539

Cuyahoga Falls
Cuyahoga Falls
News-Press **(25103)** ....(Paid) ‡2,335
(Free) ‡24,571

Dayton
Oakwood Register **(25123)** ....(Paid) ‡500
(Non-paid) ‡6,500

Delta
The Delta Atlas **(25164)** ....(Paid) ‡2,000
(Non-paid) ‡200

Dublin
Dublin News **(25168)** ....(Paid) ◆**4,370**
(Non-paid) ◆**13,534**

Fairfield
Fairfield Echo **(25188)** ....(Free) ‡19,500
Fairfield Leader **(25189)** ....(Paid) ‡2,800
(Free) ‡125

Gahanna
Gahanna News **(25206)** ....(Paid) ◆**1,286**
(Free) ◆**12,121**

Greenville
The Early Bird **(25228)** ....(Paid) 42
(Non-paid) 27,376

Grove City
Grove City News **(25232)** ....(Paid) ◆**41**
(Non-paid) ◆**10,521**

Hilliard
Hilliard Northwest News **(25242)** ....(Paid) 3,585
(Non-paid) 15,774

Hudson
Hudson Hub-Times **(25250)** ....(Paid) ‡468
(Free) ‡9,296

Jefferson
The New Senior Life Styles
Vista **(25264)** ....(Non-paid) 5,000

Loveland
Clermont Community
Journal **(25322)** ....(Combined) 23,199

Community Press of
Mason **(25324)** ....(Non-paid) 11,419

Madison
Madison Messenger **(25325)** .....(Non-paid) ◆**12,649**

Mantua
Record-News **(25341)** ....(Paid) ‡100
(Free) ‡10,367

Millbury
The Press, Metro Edition **(25385)** ....(Free) ‡20,175
The Press, Suburban Edition **(25386)** ....‡0
‡17,349
16,224

Millersburg
The Holmes County Bargain
Hunter **(25387)** ....(Free) 18,000
Tuscarawas Bargain
Hunter **(25389)** ....(Free) 32,000
The Wayne Journal **(25390)** ....(Free) 28,000

Mount Orab
Brown County Press **(25396)** ....(Free) ‡16,350

Mount Sterling
The Tribune **(25398)** ....(Free) ‡6,750

Perrysburg
Point and Shoreland Journal **(25476)** ....(Free) 7,800

Port Clinton
The Beacon **(25480)** ....(Free) ‡13,500
Lake Front News **(25481)** ....(Free) ‡16,500

Powell
Olentangy Valley News **(25492)** .....(Non-paid) 6,029
(Paid) 1,389

Sidney
Miamisburg Sun **(25519)**

Tallmadge
Tallmadge Express **(25557)** ....(Paid) ‡6,674
(Free) ‡5,281

University Heights
The Carroll News **(25602)** ....(Free) ‡5,000

Upper Arlington
Upper Arlington News **(25603)** ....(Paid) 6,174
(Non-paid) 9,718

Wauseon
Heartland Trader **(25623)** ....(Free) 15,053

Wellston
The Telegram **(25630)** ....(Paid) ‡6,400

West Carrollton
West Carrollton Times **(25632)** ....(Free) ‡6,650

Westerville
Westerville News & Public
Opinion **(25646)** ....(Paid) 7,697
(Non-paid) 13,087

Whitehall
Whitehall News **(25652)** ....(Paid) 76
(Non-paid) 10,179

Willoughby
Lake County Business Journal **(25661)** ....(Paid) 400
(Non-paid) 5,300

Willshire
Photo Star **(25666)** ....(Paid) 200
(Free) 11,300

Worthington
Worthington News **(25682)** ....(Paid) 5,856
(Non-paid) 12,569

Wright Patterson AFB
Skywrighter **(25684)** ....(Free) ‡35,000

Xenia
Green County Spectrum **(25686)** ......(Free) ‡13,600

OKLAHOMA
Altus
Patriot **(25731)** ....(Free) 5,000

Bethany
Northwest Metro Times **(25759)** .....(Non-paid) 7,000

Davis
The Davis News **(25799)** ....(Paid) ‡1,800

Eldorado
Eldorado Courier **(25818)** ....(Paid) ‡500
(Free) ‡19

Fairland
The Afton-Fairland American **(25832)** ....(Paid) 1,200
(Free) 37

Fort Sill
The Cannoneer **(25837)** ....(Free) ‡14,500

Moore
Moore American **(25921)** ....(Combined) 3530
South OKC Leader **(25922)** ....(Combined) 15,756

Oklahoma City
Capitol Hill Beacon **(25957)** ....(Paid) 921
(Free) 50,845
Oklahoma Gazette **(25979)** ....(Non-paid) 54,709

Spiro
Spiro Graphic **(26074)** ....(Paid) ‡3,000
(Free) ‡50

Tulsa
Catoosa Times **(26108)** ....(Paid) ‡1,500

Woodward
Woodward News **(26198)** ....(Paid) 6,411
(Free) 10,019

Yale
News **(26203)** ....(Paid) ‡1,472
(Free) ‡52

OREGON
Coos Bay
Prime Time **(26271)** ....(Free) ‡6,200

Hood River
Hood River News **(26376)** ....(Paid) 5,760
(Free) 62

Lebanon
Lebanon Express **(26408)** ....(Paid) 3,000

Molalla
Molalla Pioneer **(26439)** ....(Paid) ‡3,050
(Free) ‡2,950

Newberg
Christian News
Northwest **(26443)** ....(Non-paid) 30,000

Port Orford
Port Orford Today **(26466)** 1,100

Portland
Beaverton Valley Times **(26470)** ....(Paid) 7,905
(Free) 10,000
Willamette Week **(26515)** ....(Paid) ❏**124**
(Free) ❏**83,105**

Stayton
Stayton Mail **(26589)** ....(Paid) 3,500
(Free) 5,880

Tigard
Tigard Times **(26596)** ....(Paid) 4,937
(Free) 7,863

Waldport
South Lincoln County News **(26606)** ....(Free) 6,400

West Linn
West Linn Tidings **(26611)** ....(Paid) 3,995
(Free) 1,075

Wilsonville
Wilsonville Spokesman **(26617)** ....(Free) ‡7,800

PENNSYLVANIA
Ardmore
Germantown Courier **(26659)** ....(Paid) ◆**11**
(Non-paid) ◆**19,192**

Bakerstown
Pittsburgh Parent **(26668)** ....(Non-paid) 49,385
(Paid) 37

Brookville
Jeffersonian Democrat **(26732)** ....(Wed.) 3,894

Cranberry
Cranberry Eagle/The News
Weekly **(26815)** ....(Wed.) 12,108
(Sun.) 14,392

Doylestown
Bucks County Telegraph **(26831)** ....(Paid) ‡140
(Free) ‡8,360

Emlenton
The Progress News **(26872)** ....(Free) ‡15,000

Circulation: ★ = ABC; △ = BPA; ◆ = CAC; • = CCAB; ❏ = VAC; ⊕ = PO Statement; ‡ = Publisher's Report; Boldface figures = sworn; Light figures = estimated.

2947

Circ.

Circ.

Circ.

PENNSYLVANIA (continued)
Everett
The Shoppers Guide **(26914)** ....(Paid) 56
(Free) 26,027

Feasterville
Bucks County Tribune **(26919)** ....(Paid) ‡1,350
(Free) ‡14,900

Fort Washington
North Penn Life **(26931)** ....(Combined) 11,515

Grove City
Allied News **(26963)** ....(Paid) ‡4,152
(Free) ‡10,927

Hanover
The Community Sun **(26973)** ......(Non-paid) 28,529
Sun Marketplace **(26977)** ....(Non-paid) ♦28,489

Harleysville
Courier News Weekly **(26981)** ....(Free) ‡46,000

Harrisburg
Mode Weekly **(26999)** ....(Free) 14,149

Havertown
News of Delaware
County **(27030)** ....(Paid) ♦13,817
(Non-paid) ♦18,212

Horsham
Far Northeast Citizen Sentinel **(27060)** ....(Paid) 250
(Free) 14,250
Progress of Montgomery
County **(27062)** ....(Paid) ‡251
(Free) ‡17,000

King of Prussia
King of Prussia
Courier **(27125)** ....(Non-paid) ♦6,486

Lansdale
This Week **(27160)** ....‡18,602

McMurray
The Almanac **(27231)** ....(Paid) ♦281
(Non-paid) ♦56,607

Media
Town Talk **(27243)** ....(Free) ‡90,000

Mercersburg
Mercersburg Journal/Ad
Journal **(27246)** ....(Paid) 2,700
(Free) 5,295

Middleburg
Union County Times **(27250)** ....‡25,000

Monroeville
Norwin Star Star **(27280)** ....(Paid) 12,000
(Non-paid) 13,983
Woodland Hills Progress **(27288)** ....(Paid) 1,811
(Non-paid) 147

Mount Pleasant
The Advisor - Youngwood **(27300)** ....(Free) ⊕3,426

Mountain Top
Mountaintop Journal **(27305)** ....(Non-paid) 4,000

New Castle
Weekly Bargain Bulletin **(27315)** ......(Free) ‡20,000

Philadelphia
City Paper **(27405)** ....(Free) 97,555
Community Focus **(27424)** ....(Free) ‡16,000
25,000
Juniata News **(27556)** ....(Free) ‡10,000
Mt. Airy Times
Express **(27575)** ....(Non-paid) ♦13,507
(Paid) ♦13
News Gleaner (Bustleton-Somerton
Edition) **(27581)** ....(Combined) 93,923
News Gleaner (Far Northeast
Edition) **(27582)** ....(Combined) 93,923
News Gleaner (Frankford Juniata
Edition) **(27583)** ....(Combined) 93,923
News Gleaner (Mayfair-Northeast
Edition) **(27584)** ....(Combined) 93,923
News Gleaner (Six
Editions) **(27585)** ....(Non-paid) ♦78,796
(Paid) ♦353
Northeast Breeze
Edition **(27586)** ....(Non-paid) ♦17,800
(Paid) ♦18
Olney Times **(27597)** ....(Free) ♦18,785
Philadelphia New
Observer **(27630)** ....(Paid) ‡10,303
(Free) ‡70,697

The Philadelphia Tribune Metro
Edition **(27634)** ....(Sun.) ♦47,408
(Tues.) ♦20,250
(Wed.) ♦34,000
(Thurs.) ♦64,000
(Fri.) ♦10,643
Philadelphia Weekly **(27635)** ....(Free) 111,613
The Review **(27653)** ....(Paid) ‡12,500
(Free) ‡11,000
South Philadelphia
American **(27691)** ....(Free) ‡20,000
Southwest Globe Times **(27692)** ......(Free) ‡25,000
The Spirit of Philadelphia **(27694)**

Pittsburgh
Griffin's Tri-State Food
News **(27794)** ....(Paid) ‡15,000
Pittsburgh City Paper **(27832)** ....(Combined) 77,500
Pittsburgh Renaissance
News **(27835)** ....(Free) ‡30,000
South Pittsburgh Reporter **(27846)** ....(Free) 18,000
The Valley Mirror **(27854)** ....(Paid) ‡7,000

Punxsutawney
The Spirit Extra **(27910)** ....(Paid) 3,188
(Free) 10,769

Shippensburg
The Slate **(27990)** ....(Non-paid) 4,000

Slippery Rock
Slippery Rock Eagle **(27998)** .....(Combined) 12,000
Tri-County News **(27999)** ....(Paid) 20
(Free) ‡21,047

Trevose
Northeast Times **(28057)** ....(Combined) 114,332

Upper Darby
El Hispano **(28088)** ....(Paid) 1,000
(Non-paid) 47,000

Wilkes Barre
The Weekender **(28168)** ....(Non-paid) ‡42,000

Wyalusing
The Rocket-Courier **(28196)** .....(Controlled) ‡5,400

York
Weekly Record **(28206)** ....(Free) 38,400

PUERTO RICO
Arecibo
El Norte **(28223)** ....(Combined) 50,000

Fajardo
Periodico Horizonte **(28242)** ......(Combined) 45,000

Humacao
Periodico El Oriental **(28249)** .....(Combined) 59,500
Periodico El Regional de
Guayama **(28250)** ....(Non-paid) 39,800
Periodico La Opinion Del
Sur **(28251)** ....(Paid) 49,500

Mayaguez
Vision **(28258)** ....(Non-paid) 53,895
(Paid) 6

Mercedita
La Perla Del Sur **(28271)** ....(Non-paid) ♦76,650

RHODE ISLAND
Cumberland
Valley Breeze **(28339)** ....(Non-paid) ‡34,000

Greenville
Johnston Sunrise **(28354)** ....(Non-paid) ♦6,892

Newport
The Newport Navalog **(28371)** ....(Free) ‡6,000
Newport This Week **(28372)** ....(Paid) 600
(Free) 14,000

Providence
Providence Phoenix **(28416)** ....(Free) ‡64,000

Warwick
East Side Monthly **(28449)** ....(Free) ♦14,247

SOUTH CAROLINA
Bluffton
Hilton Head News **(28497)** ....‡19,500

Camden
Mall in Your Mailbox **(28500)** ....⊕20,200

Columbia
Free Times **(28550)** ....(Combined) ⊕30,000

Florence
The News Journal **(28603)** ....(Free) ‡35,053

Georgetown
Georgetown Time **(28618)** ....(Free) 13,000

Hanahan
The Hanahan News **(28656)** ....(Paid) 1,225
(Free) 19,925

Mount Pleasant
Moultrie News **(28694)** ....(Free) ‡21,000

Myrtle Beach
Strand Magazine **(28703)** ....(Non-paid) ‡1,300,000

SOUTH DAKOTA
Brandon
Brandon Valley Challenger **(28809)** ......(Paid) 1,100
(Free) 4,600

Corsica
Corsica Globe **(28834)** ....(Paid) ‡1,365
(Free) ‡15

Wessington Springs
Wessington Springs True
Dakotan **(29029)** ....(Paid) 1,500
(Free) 50

TENNESSEE
Clarksville
Montgomery County
News **(29115)** ....(Combined) ‡500

Cleveland
Bradley News Weekly **(29120)** .....(Non-paid) 21,674
(Paid) 6

Germantown
Shelby Sun Times **(29206)** ....(Non-paid) 35,000

Hendersonville
Star News **(29220)** 13,000

Huntingdon
Carroll County News **(29229)** ....(Paid) ‡6,650
(Free) ‡4,850

Lawrenceburg
Lawrence County Advocate **(29316)** ....(Paid) 267
(Wed.) 16,000
(Sun.) 14,500

Madison
The Messenger **(29338)** ....(Free) 8,000

Memphis
Southaven Press **(29381)** ....(Free) 16,000

Mount Juliet
The Chronicle of Mt. Juliet **(29425)** ....(Paid) 150
(Free) 11,600

Nashville
Franklin Journal **(29456)** ....(Free) ‡12,000
The News Beacon **(29475)** ....(Free) ‡25,000

Ripley
Lauderdale County
Enterprise **(29575)** ....(Paid) ‡4,427
(Free) ‡22

Somerville
East Shelby Review **(29606)** ....(Free) 4,800

Sparta
Expositor **(29612)** ....(Paid) ‡5,400
(Free) ‡11,400

TEXAS
Angleton
The Bulletin **(29726)** ....(Combined) 6000

Argyle
The Argyle Sun **(29730)** ....(Free) 2,100

Atlanta
Citizens Journal **(29748)** ....(Paid) ‡6,200
(Free) ‡14,500

Austin
The Villager **(29853)** ....(Free) ‡6,000

Benbrook
Benbrook News **(29918)** ....(Free) ‡7,500

Bryan
The Press of Bryan-College
Station **(29975)** ....(Free) ‡38,000

2948

Numbers cited after listings are entry numbers rather than page numbers.

Cameron
The Cameron Herald **(29995)** ....(Paid) ‡3,763
(Free) ‡3,000

Cedar Hill
Cedar Hill Sentinel **(30010)**

The Colony
The Colony Courier-Leader **(30062)** .....(Free) 9,500
(Paid) 2,915

Coppell
Coppell Gazette **(30072)** ....(Paid) 1,091
(Free) 6,852

Dallas
Auto Revista **(30125)** ....(Free) 41,000
But Viet Weekly
News **(30135)** ....(Combined) 27,500
Community Quest **(30138)** ....(Non-paid) 5,000
Dallas Observer **(30148)** ....(Non-paid) 110,684
The Dallas Weekly Newspaper **(30150)** ....(Paid) 78
(Free) 15,258
The Met **(30167)** ....(Non-paid) 54,193
Northside People **(30170)** ....(Free) 9,124
(Paid) 2,022
Oak Cliff Tribune **(30173)** ....(Paid) ‡4,100

Deer Park
Deer Park
Broadcaster/Progress **(30223)** ....(Paid) 200
(Free) 11,000

Eagle Pass
Sunday News **(30258)** ....(Free) ‡47,413

Friendswood
Friendswood Reporter News & Pearland Reporter
News **(30369)** ....(Paid) 2,500
(Free) 8,000

Grapevine
The Grapevine Sun **(30412)** ......(Combined) 20,127

Horizon City
West Texas County Courier **(30453)** .....(Paid) ‡150
(Free) ‡10,000

Houston
African-American News &
Issues **(30455)** ....(Combined) 350,000
Bay Area Sun **(30460)** ....(Free) 29,640
(Paid) 20
Houston Press **(30488)** ....(Non-paid) 115,123
The North Freeway Leader **(30510)** ....(Free) 84,459
Northeast News **(30511)** ....(Free) 32,500
The 1960 Sun **(30519)** ....(Non-paid) 75,584
(Paid) 33
Semana **(30528)** ....(Non-paid) 109,768

Keller
The Keller Citizen **(30635)** ....(Paid) 252
(Free) 26,168

Kingwood
Kingwood Observer **(30650)** .....(Non-paid) ❏25,000
Observer Newspapers **(30651)** ....(Free) 47,415

Lewisville
Lewisville News **(30688)** ....(Combined) 19,346

Liberty
The Liberty Gazette **(30689)** ....(Free) ‡9,000
Pony Express Mail **(30691)** ....(Free) ⊕9,682

Lubbock
Lubbock Southwest Digest **(30716)** .....(Paid) ‡3,137
(Free) ‡1,243

Marble Falls
The Picayune **(30761)** ....(Controlled) 22,250

Mc Kinney
McKinney Courier Gazette
Pennysaver **(30777)** ....(Combined) 31,844
North Texas Life **(30780)** ....(Non-paid) 13,200
North Texas Life **(30781)** ....(Non-paid) ❏12,983

McAllen
El Periodico, U.S.A. **(30783)** ....(Free) ‡35,000
Enlace, U.S.A. **(30784)** ....(Free) 30,000
Sunshine **(30788)** ....(Free) ‡25,000
Valley Town Crier **(30789)** ....(Free) ❏97,710
Winter Texan **(30790)** ....(Free) 12,572

Midlothian
Midlothian Today **(30827)** ....(Paid) ❏1,437
(Free) ❏100

Nederland
Mid County Chronicle **(30857)** ....(Free) ‡23,500

Orange
Opportunity Valley News **(30887)** ....(Free) 24,485

Pasadena
Fort Bend/Southwest
Sun **(30910)** ....(Combined) 69,535
The Lake Houston
Sun **(30911)** ....(Combined) 10,848
The North Channel
Sun **(30912)** ....(Combined) 32,142

Pearland
Pearland Reporter News **(30918)** ....(Paid) ‡892
(Free) ‡14,108

River Oaks
River Oaks News **(30983)** ....(Free) ‡4,500

Round Top
The Round Top
Register **(30996)** ....(Combined) ‡30,000

Sabinal
Sabinal Sampler **(31002)** ....(Free) ‡800

San Angelo
Goodfellow Monitor **(31004)** ....(Controlled) 5,000

San Antonio
Herald **(31032)** ....(Paid) 143
(Free) 27,657

Temple
Fort Hood Sentinel **(31177)** ....‡22,500

Trinity
The Trinity Standard **(31194)** ....(Paid) ‡2,145
(Free) ‡15

Tyler
Smith County News **(31198)** ....(Free) ‡63,250

Waco
The Lariat **(31251)** ....(Paid) 500
(Non-paid) 7,000

Weslaco
Mid-Valley Town Crier **(31278)** ....(Wed.) ♦25,960
(Sun.) ♦17,960

West Columbia
The Brazoria County News **(31283)** ....‡11,000
‡10,300

White Settlement
White Settlement Bomber
News **(31290)** ....(Free) ‡7,000

Wimberley
Hill Country Sun **(31302)** ....(Non-paid) ‡30,000

UTAH
Bountiful
Davis County Clipper **(31322)** ....(Paid) 12,000
(Free) 8,000

Delta
Millard County Gazette **(31332)** ....(Free) ‡4,800

Gunnison
The Salina Sun **(31336)** ....(Paid) ‡600
(Free) ‡980

Layton
Lakeside Review **(31343)** ....(Free) 37,500

Ogden
Hilltop Times **(31377)** ....(Free) ‡20,000

Orem
Orem-Geneva Times **(31385)** ....(Paid) ‡4,000
(Free) ‡1,400

Park City
Park Record Newspaper **(31387)** ....(Paid) ‡8,200
(Free) ‡100

Tooele
Shopper's Guide (UT) **(31479)** ....(Free) ‡3,500

VERMONT
Barre
The World (Vermont) **(31490)** .....(Combined) 28,941

Bellows Falls
The Bellows Falls Town
Crier **(31494)** ....(Free) 9,301

Brattleboro
The Brattleboro Town Crier **(31509)** ....(Free) 11,443

Colchester
Essex Reporter **(31531)**

Killington
The Mountain Times **(31547)** ....(Paid) ‡300
(Free) ‡10,300

Manchester Center
The Manchester Journal **(31553)** 15,000

Milton
Milton Independent **(31563)**

Morrisville
The Transcript **(31570)** ....(Free) ‡13,500

South Hero
Islander **(31601)** ....(Non-paid) 6,500

VIRGINIA
Alexandria
Arlington Sun Gazette **(31642)** ....(Combined) 32,073
Mt. Vernon Gazette **(31710)** ....(Non-paid) 13,100

Amelia Court House
Amelia Bulletin Monitor **(31759)** ....(Paid) ‡6,692
(Free) ‡2,798

Arlington
El Tiempo Latino **(31787)** ....(Controlled) ★27,423
Pentagram **(31816)** ....(Free) 26,000

Burke
The Burke/Fairfax Station
Connection **(31908)** ....(Free) 14,006

Centreville
CentreView **(31910)** ....(Free) ❏19,223

Fairfax
Broadside **(32010)** ....(Free) ‡5,000
The Fairfax Connection **(32015)** ....(Free) ❏8,508

Great Falls
The Great Falls
Connection **(32118)** ....(Free) ❏6,024

Hampton
Casemate **(32126)** ....(Free) ‡5,000
The Flyer **(32127)** ....(Controlled) ‡13,500
Hampton Script **(32128)** ....(Combined) 5,000

Herndon
Centerville Times **(32161)** ....(Paid) 189
(Free) 10,929
Herndon Times **(32163)** ....(Free) 12,525
(Paid) 220
The Observer **(32164)** ....(Combined) 31,492

Leesburg
Eastern Loudoun Times **(32184)** ....(Paid) 35
(Non-paid) 23,682
Leesburg Today **(32185)** ....(Free) 34,100

Lexington
The Weekender **(32193)** ....(Controlled) 15,500

Lorton
Hoa Thinh Don Viet
Bao **(32197)** ....(Combined) 6,000

Mc Lean
The Herndon Connection **(32246)** ......(Free) ❏9,942
The Loudoun Connection **(32248)** ....(Free) ❏10,880
The Mc Lean Connection **(32249)** ....(Free) ❏9,361
The Reston Connection **(32253)** ......(Free) ❏10,640
Valley Scene **(32260)** ....(Free) ‡138,500

Mechanicsville
The Mechanicsville
Local **(32268)** ....(Non-paid) 22,537
(Paid) 143

Merrifield
Sun Gazette **(32270)** ....(Paid) 85
(Non-paid) 37,738

Newport News
The Wheel **(32280)** ....(Free) ‡10,500

Norfolk
Soundings **(32294)** ....(Free) ‡40,000

Pearisburg
Virginian-Leader **(32325)** ....(Paid) 5,868
(Free) 21

Reston
Reston/Herndon Times-Mirror **(32414)** .....(Paid) 499
(Non-paid) 14,321
Virginia Parent News **(32423)** ....(Paid) 100
(Free) 35,000

Richlands
Tazewell County Free
Press **(32426)** ....(Free) 13,500

Newspapers

Circ.

VIRGINIA (continued)
Richmond
Richmond Free Press **(32450)** ....(Free) 24,903
(Paid) 167

Springfield
Korean Weekly **(32548)** ....(Combined) 12,000
The Springfield Connection **(32551)** ....(Free) ❏9,703

Vienna
The Vienna/Oakton
Connection **(32584)** ....(Free) ❏9,574
Vienna Times **(32585)** ....(Paid) 180
(Non-paid) 10,766

Woodbridge
Belvoir Eagle **(32636)** ....(Free) 19,000
Quantico Sentry **(32638)** ....(Free) ‡11,000

WASHINGTON
Battle Ground
The Reflector (WA) **(32661)** ....(Free) 23,400
(Paid) 942

Bellevue
Bothell-Kenmore Reporter **(32664)** ......(Free) 29,000

Bothell
Apartments for Rent Magazine **(32690)**

Bremerton
North Kitsap
Neighbors **(32693)** ....(Combined) 12,562
South Kitsap Neighbors **(32694)** .....(Tues.) ◆30,787
(Non-paid) ◆39,502

Camas
Camas-Washougal
Post-Record **(32701)** ....(Paid) ‡4,200
(Free) ‡3,600

Colville
Statesman-Examiner & The
Sun **(32726)** ....(Paid) ‡5,519
(Free) ‡17,629
The Sun **(32727)** ....(Free) 17,629

Enumclaw
Muttmatchers Messenger **(32755)** 25,000

Kelso
The Nickel-Kelso **(32786)**

Langley
Southend Neighborhood
Classifieds **(32808)** ....(Non-paid) ◆1,648

Longview
Cowlitz-Wahkiakum Senior
News **(32811)** ....(Free) ‡7,000

Lynnwood
The Journal—Lynnwood
Edition **(32823)** ....(Free) ‡82,000

Marysville
The Marysville Globe **(32828)** ....(Paid) 2,659
(Free) 16,081

Northgate
The Journal—Northgate
Edition **(32855)** ....(Combined) ‡82,000

Oak Harbor
Crosswind **(32856)** ....(Non-paid) ◆7,041

Olympia
The Thurston-Mason Senior
News **(32860)** ....(Free) 18,500

Orting
Country Gazette **(32874)** ....(Free) ‡6,000

Seattle
Ballard News Tribune **(32944)** ....(Combined) 10,000
Belltown Dispatch **(32950)** ....(Paid) 200
(Non-paid) 6,000
Facts Newspaper **(32964)** ....(Paid) 13,000
(Free) 29,650
International Examiner **(32972)** ....(Paid) 2,000
(Free) 12,000
Madison Park Times **(32983)** ....‡7,100
neo **(32989)**
North Seattle
Herald-Outlook **(32992)** ....(Paid) ‡10,000
Redmond Sammamish Valley
News **(33013)** ....(Controlled) 16,010
(Paid) 287
The Seattle Press **(33022)** ....(Paid) 300
(Non-paid) 32,000
The Stranger **(33033)** ....(Non-paid) 79,167
(Paid) 53

Circ.

The Voice Newspaper **(33037)** 12,400
Voices of Experience **(33038)** ....(Free) 28,000

Silverdale
N.W. Navigator **(33084)** ....(Combined) ◆6,696

Spokane
The Pacific Northwest
Inlander **(33097)** ....(Free) 32,155
(Paid) 45
Senior Times **(33099)** ....(Combined) 14,000

Tacoma
The Ranger **(33149)** ....(Free) ‡24,700
Tacoma Reporter **(33151)** 35,000

Toppenish
Review Independent **(33166)** ....(Paid) 4,400
(Free) 4,000
Viva **(33168)** ....(Non-paid) 15,000

Wenatchee
El Mundo **(33193)** ....(Paid) ❏235
(Non-paid) ❏14,643

WEST VIRGINIA
Parsons
The Parsons Advocate **(33427)** ....(Paid) ‡3,900
(Free) ‡66

Pineville
The Independent Herald **(33436)** ....(Paid) ‡3,484
(Free) ‡1,507

Ripley
Star Herald **(33450)** ....(Non-paid) 12,500

WISCONSIN
Appleton
The Scene **(33544)**

Baraboo
News Republic Cent
Saver **(33563)** ....(Combined) 15,054

Beaver Dam
Tri County Citizen **(33568)** ....(Free) ‡29,000

Black Earth
North Iowa Times **(33589)** ....(Paid) ‡2,600
(Free) ‡200

Delavan
The Week **(33655)** ....(Non-paid) ◆32,346
(Paid) ◆202

Denmark
Country Chronicle **(33656)** ....(Paid) 381
(Free) 14,631

Green Bay
Community News E/W **(33738)** ....(Non-paid) 44,000

Hartland
J Desk International **(33779)** ....(Combined) 1,000
Oconomowoc Buyers
Guide **(33782)** ....(Non-paid) 11,754

Janesville
The Janesville Sunday
Messenger **(33859)** ....(Free) 28,360

Lake Geneva
Resorter **(33905)** ....(Combined) ‡14,000

Madison
Isthmus **(33949)** ....(Paid) 519
(Free) 60,508

Merrill
Foto News **(34045)** 251
(Free) 16,500

Milwaukee
Milwaukee Community
Journal **(34082)** ....(Paid) 4,960
(Free) 35,000
Milwaukee Star **(34087)** ....(Free) 20,000
Shepherd Express **(34101)** ....(Free) 60,845
(Paid) 76
Welfare Warriors **(34107)** ....(Paid) 250
(Non-paid) 16,000

Phillips
Phillips Bee **(34239)** ....(Paid) 4,346

Rhinelander
Rhinelander Our Town **(34285)** ....(Free) ‡12,048

Twin Lakes
Westosha Report **(34377)** ....(Paid) ‡6,300
(Free) ‡6,000

Circ.

Waupun
Action Advertiser **(34425)** ....(Wed.) 34,853
(Sun.) 46,659

ALBERTA, CANADA
Athabasca
The Advocate **(34609)** ....(Paid) ‡4,471

Banff
Banff Crag & Canyon **(34613)** ....(Free) 13,817

Calgary
The Calgary Mirror (Northside and
Southside) **(34632)** ....(Free) ‡160,000

Calmar
Calmar Community Voice **(34674)** ....(Free) ‡2,000

Camrose
The Camrose Booster **(34675)** ....(Paid) ‡23
(Free) ‡12,884
Camrose Canadian **(34676)** ....‡13,071

Carstairs
Carstairs Courier **(34681)** ....(Free) 3,000

Cochrane
Rocky View Times **(34686)** ....(Free) ‡10,400
(Free) ‡10,622

Coldlake
Canadian Forces Base Cold Lake
Courier **(34688)** ....(Free) ‡3,000

Edmonton
The Edmonton
Examiner **(34708)** ....(Non-paid) 172,804
(Paid) 162
Sealandair **(34728)** ....(Paid) 21
(Free) 3,200

Grande Prairie
Peace Country Extra **(34775)** ....(Free) 11,000

Hinton
Parklander **(34785)** ....(Paid) 3,350

Irricana
Crossfield/Irricana Rocky View/Five Village
Weekly **(34788)** ....(Free) 15,832

Leduc
Leduc Representative **(34792)** ....(Free) ‡13,704

Morinville
Morinville Mirror **(34816)** ....(Paid) ‡1,200
(Free) ‡3,300

Okotoks
Okotoks Western Wheel **(34818)** ....(Paid) 8,600

Onoway
Onoway Community Voice **(34820)** .....(Free) ‡4,000

Ponoka
Ponoka News & Advertiser **(34825)** ....(Paid) ‡25
(Free) ‡6,300

Red Deer
Central Alberta Adviser **(34828)** ....(Free) ‡27,865
Central Alberta Life **(34829)** ....(Non-paid) 37,663
The Red Deer Express **(34831)** ....(Free) ‡23,709
Red Deer Life **(34832)** ....(Non-paid) 26,880

Redwater
Redwater Tribune **(34838)** ....(Paid) 2,000
(Free) 1,500

St. Paul
St. Paul Journal **(34844)** ....(Paid) ‡6,500
(Free) ‡842

Sherwood Park
Sherwood Park News **(34847)** ....(Free) ‡18,085

Slave Lake
Lakeside Leader **(34848)** ....(Paid) 3,291
(Free) 1,020

Spruce Grove
The Grove Examiner **(34852)** ....(Free) 6,047
Wabamun Community
Voice **(34853)** ....(Free) ‡3,500

Standoff
Kainai News **(34854)** ....(Paid) ‡1,250
(Free) ‡850

Wainwright
Wainwright Edge **(34868)** ....(Free) 9,800
Wainwright Star Chronicle **(34869)** .....(Paid) ‡2,956

BRITISH COLUMBIA, CANADA

Abbotsford
Abbotsford Times **(34876)** ....(Non-paid) 40,970
Abbotsford Times **(34877)** ....(Non-paid) 40,970

Barriere
North Thompson Star/Journal **(34884)** ....(Paid) ‡221
(Free) ‡4143

Burnaby
The Burnaby-New Westminster News
Leader **(34893)** ....(Combined) 62,034
Burnaby Now **(34894)** ....(Non-paid) 47,544

Campbell River
Campbell River/Comox Valley North
Islander **(34916)** ....(Non-paid) ‡41,506
Campbell River Mirror **(34918)** ....(Wed.) ‡10,775
(Fri.) ‡13,500

Chilliwack
Chilliwack Progress Weekender
Edition **(34927)** ....(Free) 24,488
Chilliwack Times **(34928)** ....(Non-paid) 26,500
(Paid) 20

Coquitlam
Coquitlam Now **(34930)** ....(Non-paid) 51,312

Courtenay
Comox Valley Record **(34931)** ....(Free) ‡21,364

Cranbrook
The Kootenay
Advertiser **(34935)** ....(Non-paid) ‡31,753

Delta
The Delta Optimist **(34945)** ....(Non-paid) 16,460
North Delta Sentinel **(34947)** ....(Free) ‡12,320

Duncan
The Citizen **(34949)** ....(Free) ‡24,000
Cowichan News Leader **(34950)** .....(Free) ‡19,576
The Pictorial **(34951)** ....(Free) ‡22,475

Grand Forks
Boundary Bulletin **(34970)** ....(Free) ‡5,270

Kamloops
Kamloops This Week **(34978)** ....(Non-paid) 29,581

Langley
The Langley Times **(35003)** ....(Non-paid) 33,406
(Paid) 26

Lantzville
The Log **(35007)** ....(Free) ‡2,743

Lazo
Totem Times **(35009)** ....(Free) 2,100

Mackenzie
The Times **(35011)** ....(Free) 1,000

Maple Ridge
Maple Ridge-Pitt Meadows
News **(35012)** ....(Non-paid) 27,450
The Tri-City News **(35013)** ....(Non-paid) 45,854

Nanaimo
Harbor City Star **(35019)** ....(Paid) ‡65
(Free) ‡97,381

New Westminster
Other Press **(35030)** ....(Free) 5,000
The Record **(35031)** ....(Free) 16,800

North Vancouver
North Shore News **(35036)** ....(Non-paid) 65,430
(Paid) 557

Parksville
Parksville-Qualicum Beach
News **(35043)** ....(Free) ‡16,300

Quesnel
Quesnel Cariboo Observer **(35069)** ......(Paid) 5,000
(Free) 9,000

Richmond
Pazifische Rundschau (Pacific
Review) **(35075)** ....(Combined) ‡12,390
(Free) ‡110
Richmond News **(35076)** ....(Non-paid) 46,937
The Richmond Review **(35077)** ....(Thurs.) 45,500

Salmon Arm
Shuswap Market News **(35082)** ....(Paid) ‡14,900

Sooke
Sooke Mirror **(35093)** ....(Free) 3,000

Summerland
The Bulletin **(35102)** ....(Free) 5,500

Surrey
The Now
Newspaper **(35109)** ....:......(Combined) •109,792

Vancouver
The Calgary Straight **(35129)** ......(Non-paid) 26,034
East Side Revue **(35139)** ....(Free) ‡2,300
The Vancouver Courier **(35173)** ....(Sun.) 106,950
(Wed.) 132,650
West Side Revue **(35178)** ....(Free) ‡7,500

Vernon
The Morning Star **(35201)** ....(Non-paid) 31,422
(Paid) 110
Sun Review **(35202)** ....(Non-paid) 29,388

Williams Lake
The Tribune Weekender **(35244)** ....(Non-paid) 9,800

MANITOBA, CANADA

Morris
Crow Wing Warrior **(35275)** ....(Free) ‡15,300

Stonewall
Interlake Spectator **(35296)** ....(Free) ‡13,316

Winkler
The Winkler Times **(35307)** 7,264

Winnipeg
The Herald **(35331)** ....(Free) ‡38,505
The Lance **(35336)** ....(Free) 48,231
The Metro **(35344)** ....(Free) 50,595
MSOS Journal **(35346)** ....(Paid) ‡14,000
(Free) ‡16,000
The Times **(35352)** ....(Free) ‡32,815
Voxair **(35357)** ....(Free) 4,850

NEW BRUNSWICK, CANADA

Oromocto
The Oromocto
Post-Gazette **(35424)** ....(Paid) ‡3,240
(Free) ‡540

Sussex
Kings County Record **(35438)** ....(Tues.) 4,524

NEWFOUNDLAND AND LABRADOR, CANADA

St. John's
Advertiser **(35484)** ....(Combined) ‡5,050
The Express **(35487)** ....(Non-paid) 40,500
Packet **(35493)** ....(Paid) ‡6,022
(Free) ‡170

NOVA SCOTIA, CANADA

Annapolis Royal
Gulf of Maine Times **(35534)** .....(Controlled) 13,000

Bridgewater
Lighthouse Log **(35543)** ....(Paid) ‡16
(Controlled) ‡21,834

Greenwood
Aurora **(35556)** ....(Free) ‡5,800

Windsor
The Hants Journal **(35619)** ....(Paid) 3,946
(Free) 64

ONTARIO, CANADA

Ancaster
Ancaster News-Journal **(35633)** ....(Free) 6,311

Arnprior
Chronicle Weekender **(35636)** ......(Non-paid) 13,300
West Carleton Review **(35638)** ......(Non-paid) 6,300

Barrie
The Barrie Examiner This
Week **(35659)** ....(Tues.) 39,728
(Thurs.) 40,981

Borden
Borden Citizen **(35691)** ....(Paid) ‡300
(Free) ‡3,700

Bowmanville
Clarington / Courtice **(35692)** ....(Free) 21,000

Bracebridge
Muskoka Advance **(35695)** ....(Free) 21,491

Brampton
Guardian **(35700)** ....(Paid) ‡3,000
(Free) ‡57,000

Burlington
Burlington Post **(35714)** ....(Wed.) 46,635
(Fri.) 47,123
(Sun.) 47,124

Cambridge
Cambridge Times **(35725)** ....(Free) ‡31,400

Chatham
Chatham This Week **(35730)** ......(Non-paid) 19,949

Cochrane
Vivre **(35745)** ....(Paid) ‡3,100
(Free) ‡600

Creemore
Creemore Echo **(35760)** ....(Combined) 16,000

Durham
The Citizen (Mount Forest
Citizen) **(35797)** ....(Free) 4,204

Elliot Lake
The Standard **(35802)** ....(Paid) **4,902**

Essex
Voice of the Essex Farmer **(35810)** ....(Free) ‡4,360

Fergus
Fergus-Elora News Express **(35829)** ......(Paid) 4,392

Gananoque
PIC Press **(35843)** ....(Non-paid) 9,000

Hastings
Hastings Star **(35905)** ....(Free) ‡1,899
(Paid) 6

Havelock
Havelock Citizen **(35906)** ....(Free) ‡2,321
(Paid) 10

Hawkesbury
The Tribune/Express **(35908)** ....(Free) 23,200

Hornel Heights
The Shield **(35915)** ....(Free) ‡1,000

Ignace
Ignace Driftwood **(35920)** ....(Paid) 720

Kanata
Kanata Kourier-Standard **(35925)** ....(Paid) 50
(Non-paid) 24,800

Kingston
Kingston This Week **(35938)** ....(Tues.) 47,769
(Fri.) 47,769

Lambton
Voice of the Lambton
Farmer **(35967)** ....(Free) ‡7,070

LaSalle
LaSalle Silhouette **(35968)** ....(Non-paid) 9,500

Lindsay
Lindsay This Week **(35973)** ....(Paid) ‡101
(Free) ‡27,400

London
The Herald **(35983)** ....(Free) ‡20,000
University of Western Ontario,
Gazette **(35994)** 10,000

Madoc
Madoc Review **(36005)** ....(Paid) ‡16
(Free) ‡2,708

Marmora
Marmora Herald **(36034)** ....(Paid) ‡14
(Free) ‡2,008

Middlesex
Voice of the Middlesex
Farmer **(36037)** ....(Free) ‡6,350

Midland
Barrie Advance **(36039)** ....(Sun.) 45,740
(Tues.) 25,962
(Wed.) 45,754
(Fri.) 45,747

The Free Press This
Week **(36042)** ....(Non-paid) 14,211

Mississauga
The Mississauga Booster **(36079)** ......(Free) 32,000
(Free) 36,000
The Mississauga News **(36081)** ......(Wed.) 123,049
(Fri.) 121,435
(Sun.) 121,390
(Thurs.) 44,733

Circulation: ★ = ABC; △ = BPA; ♦ = CAC; • = CCAB; ❑ = VAC; ⊕ = PO Statement; ‡ = Publisher's Report; Boldface figures = sworn; Light figures = estimated.

2951

Newspapers

	Circ.

ONTARIO, CANADA (continued)

New Hamburg
New Hamburg Independent **(36103)** .....(Paid) 4,200

Niagara Falls
The Times **(36111)** ....(Paid) ‡69
(Free) ‡10,500

North York
York Gazette **(36133)**

Ontario
Baldwin Shopper's Guide **(36157)**
Bellmore/Merrick North Shopper's Guide **(36159)**
Cedarhurst/Lawrence Shopper's Guide **(36160)**
Douglaston/Little Neck Shopper's Guide **(36161)**
East Meadow Shopper's Guide **(36162)**
Elmont Shopper's Guide **(36163)**
Hempstead Shopper's Guide **(36164)**
Hewlett/Woodmere Shopper's Guide **(36165)**
Long Beach Shopper's Guide **(36166)**
Lynbrook/East Rockaway/Malverne Shopper's
Guide **(36167)**
Queens Village Shopper's Guide **(36168)**
Uniondale/Roosevelt Shopper's Guide **(36169)**
West Hempstead Shopper's Guide **(36170)**
Westbury Shopper's Guide **(36171)**

Orangeville
Orangeville Citizen **(36173)** ....(Free) 11,600

Orillia
The Packet & Times This
Week **(36176)** ....(Non-paid) 13,113

Orleans
The Star **(36178)** ....(Free) 35,088

Ottawa
Centretown News **(36233)** ....(Free) ‡14,000
The Ottawa X Press **(36269)** ....(Free) ❑27,464
(Paid) ❑3

Pembroke
Pembroke Daily News **(36309)** ....(Wed.) 18,794
(Sun.) 28,146

Petrolia
Mainly for Seniors
Lambton-Kent **(36326)** ....(Free) 16,000

Renfrew
The Renfrew Weekend
News **(36340)** ....(Non-paid) 14,352

Richmond Hill
The Liberal **(36343)** ....(Sun.) 75,359
(Tues.) 75,312
(Thurs.) 61,277
The Liberal Newspaper **(36344)** ....(Tues.) 70,000
(Thurs.) 92,000
(Sun.) 92,000
Vaughan Liberal **(36347)** ....(Free) 78,000

Simcoe
Simcoe and Nanticoke
Times **(36390)** ....(Wed.) ‡16,680
(Sat.) ‡16,680

Stirling
The Community Press **(36402)** ....(Paid) 360
(Free) 54,000

Stoney Creek
Hamilton Mountain News **(36405)** .....(Free) ‡43,500
Stoney Creek News **(36406)** ....(Free) ‡24,000

Stratford
Marketplace **(36410)** ....(Free) 16,419

Timmins
The Daily Press,
E.M.C. **(36454)** ....(Non-paid) 19,663

Toronto
Bayview Post **(36472)** ....(Free) ❑27,643
Eye Weekly **(36591)** ....(Free) 102,484
(Paid) 3
Kerala Express **(36641)** ....(Paid) ‡120
(Free) ‡2,000
The New Pathway **(36673)** ....(Paid) ‡4,500
(Free) ‡110
North Toronto Post **(36676)** ....(Free) ❑28,222
Now **(36678)** ....(Paid) 55
(Free) 106,103
Richmond Hill Post **(36729)** ....(Free) ❑29,824
Share **(36739)** ....(Combined) 153,000
Thornhill Post **(36759)** ....(Free) ❑25,220
The Town Crier **(36771)** ....(Free) ‡213,900
University of Toronto
Bulletin **(36778)** ....(Controlled) **14,051**

Vapaa Sana **(36784)** ....(Paid) 1,707
(Non-paid) 107
Village Post **(36787)** ....(Free) ❑25,373
The Villager **(36788)** ....(Paid) ‡300
(Free) ‡43,200

Trenton
CONTACT **(36824)** ....(Free) ‡3,500

Wallaceburg
The Courier Press **(36843)** ....(Free) ‡11,600

Wingham
The Wingham
Advance-Times **(36902)** ....(Paid) ‡2,306

QUEBEC, CANADA

Acton Vale
La Pensee de
Bagot **(36929)** ....(Controlled) ‡13,333

Alma
Superintendent's Profile Product-Service
Directory **(36930)** ....(Free) 19,957

Amqui
L'Avant-Poste **(36935)** ....(Controlled) 8,542

Bedford
Journal des Rivieres **(36949)** ....(Free) 6,650

Beloeil
L'Oeil Regional **(36950)** ....(Controlled) 29,350

Brossard
Brossard-Eclair **(36951)** ....(Controlled) ‡24,635

Buckingham
Le Bulletin **(36952)** ....(Controlled) 10,892

Cabano
Le Touladi **(36953)** ....(Free) ‡9,600

Cap-de-la-Madeleine
L'Hebdo-Journal **(36956)** ....(Controlled) 44,691

Chambly
Le Journal de Chambly
Inc. **(36959)** ....(Controlled) ‡20,700

Chandler
Le Havre **(36960)** ....(Controlled) ‡7,493

Coaticook
Le Progres de
Coaticook **(36976)** ....(Controlled) 7,578

Cookshire
Le Haut St-Francois **(36978)** ....(Free) ‡8,300

Cote St.-Luc
The Suburban **(36979)** ....(Free) 103,962

Dolbeau-Mistassini
Le Point **(36986)** 11,466

Donnacona
Le Courrier de
Portneuf **(36987)** ....(Controlled) ‡23,917

Drummondville
L'Express **(36989)** ....(Controlled) 43,876
La Parole **(36990)** ....(Controlled) ‡35,435

Gaspe
Le Pharillon **(36997)** ....(Controlled) 9,188

Gatineau
La Revue de
Gatineau **(36999)** ....(Controlled) ‡37,180

Hull
Le Regional Hull-Aylmer **(37002)** ......(Free) ‡35,516

Joliette
L'Action **(37010)** ....(Controlled) 45,140
Le Regional de Lanaudiere-Jolliette
Journal **(37011)** ....(Free) ‡40,500

Lac Etchemin
La Voix du Sud **(37027)** ....(Controlled) ‡19,144

Lac Megantic
L'Echo de Frontenac **(37028)** ....(Paid) 4,580
(Free) 3,992
(Non-paid) 4,089

Lachute
L'Argenteuil **(37029)** ....(Combined) ‡13,500

Laval
Le Courrier des
Moulins **(37041)** ....(Controlled) ‡38,792

Levis
Le Peuple Tribune **(37049)** ....(Free) ‡26,033

Longueuil
Le Courrier du Sud (The South Shore
Courier) **(37053)** ....(Free) 120,000
Longueuil Extra **(37056)** ....(Controlled) 54,200

Louiseville
Salut Dimanche **(37061)** ....(Combined) 17,377

Maniwaki
La Gatineau **(37065)** ....(Free) ‡9,000

Mont-Joli
L'Information **(37073)** ....(Free) ‡11,920

Mont-Laurier
L'Echo de la Lievre **(37074)** ....(Free) ‡11,600

Mont-Tremblant
L'Information de Ste.
Agathe **(37076)** ....(Free) ‡14,700

Montmagny
Le Peuple de la Cote du
Sud **(37077)** ....(Free) ‡16,250

Montreal
ADSUM **(37083)** ....(Free) ‡5,000
L'Artisan **(37087)** ....(Controlled) ‡47,722
L'Avenir de l'Est **(37090)** ....(Controlled) ‡44,070
Courier Laval du Jeudi **(37107)** ....(Free) 106,877
Guide de
Montreal-Nord **(37121)** ......(Controlled) 32,869
L'Hebdo Rive-Nord **(37122)** ....(Controlled) 45,118
L'Infomateur **(37129)** ....(Controlled) 17,448
INSIEME **(37132)** ....(Paid) ‡18,000
(Free) ‡20,000
Journal de St. Michel **(37146)** .....(Free) ‡22,500
La Tribune Canadienne
Grecque **(37153)** ....(Paid) 200
(Free) 13,500
Le Courrier Laval du
Dimanche **(37158)** ....(Controlled) 106,877
Le Flambeau de l'Est **(37160)** ...(Controlled) 50,671
Le Journal de Rosemont et Petite
Patrie **(37164)** ....(Controlled) 58,741
Le Journal St-Louis & Mile
End **(37165)** ....(Combined) 20,000
Le Journal de
St-Michel **(37166)** ....(Controlled) 22,500
Le/The Monitor **(37172)** ....(Combined) 29,500
Les Nouvelles de
l'Est **(37178)** ....(Controlled) 27,338
Montreal Mirror **(37189)** ....(Combined) 74,188
Progres de St.
Leonard **(37210)** ....(Controlled) 30,054
A Voz de Portugal **(37237)** ....(Paid) ‡3,755
(Free) ‡6,245

Napierville
Coup d'Oeil **(37254)** ....(Controlled) ‡13,350

New Richmond
L'Echo de la Baie **(37258)** ....(Paid) ‡1,152
(Free) ‡16,842

Nicolet
Le Courrier-Sud **(37259)** ....(Controlled) ‡20,047

Outremont
L'Express
d'Outremont **(37264)** ....(Controlled) 16,000

Quebec
Le Peuple de Lotbiniere **(37289)** ......(Free) ‡11,900

Rimouski
Le Rimouskois **(37307)** ....(Free) 23,463
Progres-Echo **(37308)** ....(Free) 29,868

Riviere-du-Loup
Info Dimanche **(37313)** ....(Controlled) 29,118

Roberval
L'Etoile du Lac **(37319)** ....(Controlled) 12,800

Saint-Andre-Avellin
Journal La Petite-Nation **(37325)** ....(Free) ‡8,002

Saint-Eustache
L'Eveil **(37331)** ....(Controlled) 37,925
La Concorde **(37332)** ....(Controlled) ‡28,650

Saint-Georges-de-Beauce
L'Eclaireur-Progres/Beauce
Nouvelle **(37341)** ....(Paid) 1,000
(Free) 25,000

Saint-Jean
Le Richelieu
 Dimanche **(37355)** ....(Controlled) 35,500
          (Paid) 9

Saint-Laurent
Nouvelles Saint-Laurent
 News **(37365)** ....(Free) 26,300

Saint-Pascal
Le Placoteux **(37367)** ....(Paid) ‡60
        (Non-paid) ‡17,142

Ste.-Therese
La Voix des Mille Iles **(37368)** ....(Free) ‡42,650

Sainte-Anne-des-Monts
Le Riverain **(37372)** ....(Free) 5,894

Sainte-Julie
L'Information de Ste.
 Julie **(37381)** ....(Controlled) 21,082

Sainte-Therese
Le Nord Info **(37384)** ....(Controlled) 48,775

Sept-Iles
Le Nord-Est Plus **(37386)** ....(Controlled) 14,022

Shawinigan
L'Hebdo Mekinac/des
 Chenaux **(37390)** ....(Free) 12,716

Sorel
Journal La Voix **(37403)** ....(Free) ‡28,185
Les Deux Rives **(37405)** ....(Free) ‡28,000

Terrebonne
La Revue **(37409)** ....(Free) ‡45,100

Thetford Mines
Le Courrier Frontenac **(37410)** ....(Free) 20,572

Trois-Rivieres
La Gazette Populaire **(37415)** ....(Paid) ‡70
         (Free) ‡71,000

Valleyfield
Le Journal St. Francois
 Inc. **(37424)** ....(Free) ‡29,800
Le Saint Francois **(37425)** ....(Free) ‡29,800
Le Soleil du St.
 Laurent **(37426)** ....(Controlled) 26,275

Ville-Marie
Le Temiscamien **(37437)** ....(Controlled) ‡8,380

Westmount
The Westmount
 Examiner **(37446)** ....(Controlled) ‡9,800

SASKATCHEWAN, CANADA
Bushell Park
The Prarie Flyer II **(37454)** ....(Free) ‡500

Coronach
Triangle News **(37460)** ....(Paid) 550
         (Free) 450

Kelvington
The View From Here **(37479)** ....(Paid) ‡1,326
         (Free) ‡200

Lanigan
Lanigan Advisor **(37490)** ....(Non-paid) 2,000

Moose Jaw
Moose Jaw This Week **(37501)** ....(Free) ‡19,478

Southey
Market Connection **(37573)** ....(Non-paid) ⊕**10,700**

Weyburn
Estevan This Week **(37590)** ....(Free) **11,071**
Weyburn This Week **(37592)** .....(Controlled) ‡9,315

Yorkton
This Week Marketplace **(37598)** ....(Free) 38,000

Newspapers

Shopping Guides

Index entries are arranged geographically, first by states/provinces and then by cities. Within cities in this index, citations appear alphabetically by publication title. Citations include publication title, entry number (given in parentheses immediately following the title), and circulation figures.

Circ.

ALABAMA
Fort Payne
Times-Journal (231) ....(Mon.-Fri.) 4,648
(Sun.) 5,442

Hartselle
Hartselle Shopping Guide (265) ....(Paid) ‡7,019
(Free) ‡7,980

Oneonta
The Blount County Shopping
Guide (405) ....(Free) ‡7,300

ALASKA
Anchorage
GreatLander Bush Mailer (526) ....(Free) 36,343

ARIZONA
Bullhead City
Booster Advertiser (663) ....(Combined) 14,751

Casa Grande
Wampum Saver (670)

Cornville
Measure for Measure (678) ....‡3,200

Lake Havasu City
White Sheet-The Lake Havasu City
Advertiser (736) ....(Free) ‡14,000

Parker
White Sheet-The Parker
Advertiser (764) ....(Free) ‡12,500

Scottsdale
Arizona Pennysaver (866) ....(Free) 604,000

Sierra Vista
The Mountain View News (888) ......(Free) ‡22,000

Tucson
Tucson Shopper (969) ....(Free) ‡293,400

Yuma
Bajo El Sol (1016) ....(Non-paid) ♦20,369
The Prospector (1018) ....(Non-paid) ♦33,858
Super Shopper (1020) ....(Non-paid) ♦45,384

ARKANSAS
Bentonville
Neighbor Shopper (1051) ....(Free) 12,059

Monticello
Drew County Shopper's Guide (1279) 9,800

Pocahontas
Randco Trading Post (1317) ....(Free) ‡8,000

Searcy
Mailbox News Packet (1338) ....(Free) ‡27,600

Warren
Shoppers Guide Weekly (1364) ....(Free) 6,500

Wynne
East Arkansas News Leader (1371) 21,340

CALIFORNIA
Arroyo Grande
Five Cities Times Press
Recorder (1433) ....(Free) ‡8,575

Banning
The Record-Gazette TMC (1479) ....(Free) 17,600

Blythe
White Sheet-The Blythe
Advertiser (1588) ....(Free) ‡7,400

Brea
The Original
Pennysaver (1599) ....(Free) ‡4,710,500
Pennysaver (1600) 220,000
PennySaver (1601) ....(Free) ‡2,036,000
PennySaver/San Diego
South (1602) ....(Non-paid) 1,057,000

Brentwood
The Value News (1604) ....(Non-paid) 20,721

Delano
Market Shopper (1822) ....(Free) ‡11,350

Dinuba
The Sentinel-Advertiser (1829) ....(Free) 16,041

El Centro
Valley Shopper-The El Centro
Advertiser (1852) ....(Paid) ‡19,525

Eureka
Tri-City Weekly (1895) ....(Combined) ❑45,818
Tri-City Weekly (Southern
Edition) (1896) ....(Combined) 13,438

Foothill
Cover Story (1920) ....(Non-paid) 4,200

Hanford
Sentinel Plus (2038) ....(Mon.-Sat.) 12,779
(Sun.) 12,738

Hemet
Dollarsaver (2047) ....(Free) ‡41,000

Lake Arrowhead
Mountain Shopper (2139)

Lodi
Lodi News-Merchandiser (2157) ....(Free) ‡9,338

Mariposa
Gazette Mountain Life (2511) ....(Paid) ‡5,100

Marysville
CoverStory (2516) ....(Free) ‡29,000

Morongo Basin
White Sheet-The Morongo Basin
Advertiser (2602) ....(Free) ‡9,000

Norco
Corona-Norco Independent (2641) ....(Fri.) 814

Oakdale
Oakdale Advertiser (2655) ....(Free) 4,223

Oakhurst
Sierra Home Advertiser (2659) ....(Free) ‡12,500

Oakland
The Classified Flea
Market (2676) ....(Combined) 100,000

Ojai
Ojai Valley Shopper (2715)

Ontario
Ontario Green Sheet (2718) ....(Free) 22,800

Oroville
The Digger Shopper &
News (2728) ....(Free) ‡17,600
Oroville Shopping News (2729) ....(Free) 10,200

Pacific Palisades
Post Shopper (2737) ....(Free) 5,700

Pacifica
The Wave, The Buyer's Guide for the
Coastside (2740) ....(Free) 5,900
(Wed.) 7,912

Palm Desert
Victorville Green Sheet (2744) ....(Free) 15,500
White Sheet-The Indio
Advertiser (2745) ....(Free) ‡10,000
White Sheet-The Palm Desert
Advertiser (2746) ....(Free) ‡30,000
White Sheet-The Tri-State
Advertiser (2747) ....(Non-paid) ‡10,500

Palm Springs
White Sheet-The Palm Springs
Advertiser (2770) ....(Free) ‡10,000

Redlands
Redlands Green Sheet (2906) ....(Free) 20,400

Riverside
Riverside Green Sheet (2944) ....(Free) 13,400

San Bernardino
North San Bernardino Green
Sheet (3088) ....(Free) 19,800
West San Bernardino Green
Sheet (3093) ....(Non-paid) 18,300

San Rafael
Classified Gazette (3599) ....(Free) ‡60,000

Sanger
Herald Advertiser (3616) ....(Free) ‡14,100

Sebastopol
Sonoma West Exchange (3753) ....(Free) 11,300

Shafter
Shafter Shopper (3758) ....(Free) ‡4,000

Sonoma
The Classified Gazette (Sonoma County
Edition) (3773) ....(Free) ‡26,854
Headliner (3774) ....(Non-paid) 14,117
Shopping News/Penny
Pincher (3776) ....(Free) 6,800
Sonoma Valley News (3778) ....(Free) ‡5,000

Vacaville
The Weekly Star (3974) ....(Free) ‡8,869

Visalia
Weekly Visalia Times-Daily (4041) .....(Free) 28,000

Winton
Atwater's New Times (4095) ....(Paid) 2,800
Merced County Times (4097) ....(Paid) 5,600

Woodland Hills
Mission Valley Review (4109) ....(Free) 8,048

Circ.

COLORADO
Brighton
The Free Advertiser **(4201)**

Lamar
The Tri State Trader **(4538)** ....(Free) ‡14,000

CONNECTICUT
Derby
Shopping News **(4776)** ....(Non-paid) 18,189

Middlebury
Consumer Connection **(4942)** ....(Free) 15,000

Rockville
The Broadcaster **(5105)** ....(Free) 28,762

Southington
The Step Saver **(5135)** ....(Non-paid) ‡90,330

Torrington
Foothills Trader **(5178)** ....(Paid) ‡25
(Free) ‡42,000

DELAWARE
Rehoboth Beach
Delaware Beachcomber **(5283)** ....(Free) ‡25,000

FLORIDA
Bartow
Bartow Shopper **(5916)** ....(Combined) 6,671

Bradenton
Bradenton Shopping
Guide **(5957)** ....(Non-paid) 63,960

Bunnell
Flagler Pennysaver **(5968)** ....(Free) ‡7,480

Cape Coral
Lee County Shopper **(5973)** ....(Free) 105,000

Dade City
Pasco Shopper **(6032)** ....(Free) ‡223,167

De Land
West Volusia
Pennysaver **(6047)** ....(Non-paid) 50,000

Fruitland Park
Sumter Shopper **(6128)** ....(Free) ‡13,044

Gainesville
Buyers' Guide **(6132)** ....(Free) ‡40,000

Lake City
News Advertiser **(6270)** ....(Paid) ‡3,265
(Free) ‡22,519

Miami
Herald Values **(6358)** ....(Combined) 729,186

Naples
Naples Times **(6447)** ....‡16,000

New Smyrna Beach
New Smyrna Pennysaver **(6457)** ......(Free) ‡26,000

Okeechobee
Okeechobee Shoppers
Guide **(6482)** ....(Free) 14,000

Ormond Beach
Daytona Pennysaver **(6532)** ....(Free) ‡57,660

Palatka
Putnam Pennysaver **(6538)** ....(Free) ‡26,015

Plant City
Plant City Shopper **(6586)** ....(Free) 26,800

Plantation
Pennysaver **(6588)** ....(Free) 62,500

Punta Gorda
Charlotte Shopping Guide **(6607)** .....(Free) ‡38,000

St. Augustine
St. John's Pennysaver **(6618)** ....(Free) **25,222**

Sarasota
Venice Weekly **(6668)** ....(Non-paid) 29,349

Sebring
Sebring Shopping
Guide **(6680)** ....(Non-paid) 18,687

Stuart
Flashes Shopping Guide **(6692)** ....(Free) 61,300

Tampa
The Flyer **(6764)** ....(Free) 815,000

Circ.

Venice
The Advertiser **(6828)** ....(Free) 131,900

Winter Haven
North Lakeland
Shopper **(6870)** ....(Combined) 28,339
Shopper **(6871)** ....(Free) 16,000
South Lakeland Shopper **(6872)** ......(Free) 28,152
Winter Haven Shopper **(6874)** ....(Free) ‡33,000

GEORGIA
Albany
Albany Area Advertiser **(6902)** ....(Free) 38,000

Bainbridge
The Post-Searchlight Extra **(7119)** ......(Paid) ‡6,000
(Free) ‡15,500

Conyers
East Metro Plus **(7200)** ....(Free) ‡22,000

Cordele
Cover Story **(7204)** ....(Free) ‡3,000

Dawson
Southern Connection **(7230)** ....(Free) ‡12,898

Douglas
The Douglas Shopper **(7245)** ....(Free) ‡18,700

Eatonton
Messenger Plus **(7265)** ....(Non-paid) ‡8,300

Fort Oglethorpe
Busy Shopper **(7284)** ....(Non-paid) 32,900

Hinesville
Tri-County Penny Saver **(7331)** ....(Free) 21,500

Savannah
Savannah Pennysaver **(7537)** ....(Free) ‡79,500

Thomson
Dollar Saver **(7591)** ....(Free) 15,500

Tifton
Gazette Shopping Guide **(7595)** ....(Free) ‡15,850
Tiftarea Shopper **(7598)** ....(Free) 16,500

Vidalia
The Advantage **(7629)** ....(Free) 20,400

Warner Robins
The Warner Robins Buyers Guide **(7638)**

Winder
The Barrow County
Shopper **(7654)** ....(Free) 11,421

Woodstock
News Shopper **(7656)** ....(Non-paid) 19,190

HAWAII
Bellmore
Bellmore South This
Week/Pennysaver **(7659)** ....(Free) ‡14,348

Cedarhurst
Cedarhurst Pennysaver **(7661)** ....(Free) 10,000

Elmont
Elmont Pennysaver **(7663)** ....(Free) 14,988

Far Rockaway
Far Rockaway Pennysaver **(7664)** ......(Free) 11,440

Franklin Square
Franklin Square Pennysaver **(7665)** .....(Free) 8,321

Hewlett
Hewlett/Woodmere
Pennysaver **(7669)** ....(Free) 10,536

Honolulu
This Week **(7723)** ....(Paid) ♦332,402
(Non-paid) ♦637,286

Long Beach
Long Beach Pennysaver **(7784)** ....(Free) 18,966

Lynbrook
Lynbrook Pennysaver **(7785)** ....(Free) 16,288

Oceanside
Oceanside Pennysaver **(7790)** ....(Free) 11,326

Rockville Centre
Rockville Centre Pennysaver **(7792)** ....(Free) 10,280

Valley Stream
Valley Stream Pennysaver **(7793)** .....(Free) 14,591

Circ.

IDAHO
Coeur d'Alene
Nickel's Worth **(7846)** 38,000

Lewiston
Moneysaver (Lewiston) **(7892)** ....(Free) 47,584

Moscow
Idaho Moneysaver **(7917)** ....(Non-paid) 12,000
Moscow Moneysaver **(7919)** ....(Non-paid) 10,000

ILLINOIS
Anna
Monday's Pub **(8014)** ....(Free) ‡12,000

Antioch
The Advertiser **(8015)** ....(Paid) ‡234
(Free) ‡200,000

Beardstown
Star Gazette Extra **(8056)** ....(Free) ‡8,700

Belvidere
Boone County Shopper, Inc. **(8063)** ....(Paid) ‡70
(Free) ‡17,515

Brighton
Southwestern Shoppers
Guide **(8099)** ....(Free) ‡4,044

Carlinville
The Enquirer Express **(8127)** ....(Free) 15,000

Carrollton
Greene County Shopper **(8160)** ....(Free) 11,700
Jersey County Shopper **(8162)** ....(Free) 13,500

Chicago
Clear-Ridge Reporter **(8334)** 22,900
Pompano Times **(8537)** ....(Combined) 22,130

Cuba
Buyer's Guide Shopper **(8700)** ....(Paid) ‡0
(Free) ‡4,838

Elmwood
The Advertiser **(8842)** ....(Free) ‡5,500
Home Shopper **(8844)** ....(Free) ‡7,635

Eureka
Woodford Star **(8848)** ....(Free) ‡13,746

Freeburg
The Freeburg Tribune **(8897)** ....(Free) ‡2,900

Freeport
Freeport Shopping
News **(8899)** ....(Non-paid) 22,861

Fulton
Whiteside Shopper **(8903)**

Geneseo
Henry County Advertizer
Shopper **(8915)** ....(Free) 19,200

Geneva
Chronicle Extra **(8917)** ....(Free) ‡10,500

Grayslake
Market Journal **(8957)** ....(Free) 82,387

La Fayette
Prairie Shopper **(9050)** ....(Free) 5,900

Lacon
Illinois Valley Peach **(9059)** ....(Free) ⊕10,000

Machesney Park
Journal **(9125)** ....(Paid) 43,000

Mendota
Mendota Shopping Guide **(9175)** ......(Free) ‡11,500

Monmouth
Pennysaver **(9218)** ....(Free) ‡14,019

Tinley Park
The Penny Saver **(9688)** 450,000

Waterloo
The Shopper **(9737)** ....(Free) ‡7,548

Watseka
Illinois Spirit Shopping
Guide **(9738)** ....(Free) ‡9,362

Yorkville
Fox Valley Shopping News **(9775)** ....(Paid) 228
(Free) 21,773

Zion
The Bargaineer **(9779)** ....(Non-paid) 35,000
(Paid) 5,000

Numbers cited after listings are entry numbers rather than page numbers.

INDIANA
Attica
The Messenger **(9787)** ....(Free) ‡11,669

Bluffton
The Echo **(9864)** ....(Controlled) ‡13,930

Brazil
Times Advantage **(9870)** ....(Free) ‡4,700
(Paid) 500

Cloverdale
The Hoosier Topics **(9892)** ....(Combined) 15,092

Connersville
Whitewater Valley Market
Guide **(9902)** ....(Free) 8,747

DeMotte
Action Plus Shopper **(9923)** ....(Free) ‡14,750

Evansville
Thrifty Nickel Want Ads **(9936)** ....(Free) ‡40,500

Greenfield
The Advertiser **(10039)** ....(Non-paid) ‡18,000

Kentland
Indiana Spirit Shopping
Guide **(10230)** ....(Free) ‡6,409

Ligonier
The Monday Leader **(10273)** ....(Free) 14,900

Lowell
South Lake Advertiser **(10282)** ....(Free) ‡2,670

Madison
The Weekly Herald **(10284)** ....‡386

Michigan City
The Town Crier **(10305)** ....(Free) 72,000

Muncie
The Advertiser **(10325)** ....(Controlled) 20,000

Nappanee
Farm and Home News **(10335)** ....(Free) 18,500

Oakland City
Oakland City Journal Dollar
Saver **(10382)** ....(Free) ‡3,850

Ossian
The Sunriser News **(10386)** .....(Controlled) ‡12,242

Paoli
Orange Countian **(10388)** ....(Free) 10,573

Peru
The Good Times **(10395)** ....(Free) 138,442

Princeton
Gibson County Today **(10408)** ....(Free) ‡5,534

Rensselaer
Shoppers News **(10415)** ....(Free) ‡13,500

Rochester
Shopping Guide News **(10432)** ....(Free) 8,682
(Paid) 37

Tell City
Lincolnland Shopping
Guide **(10481)** ....(Non-paid) 7,759

Versailles
Spotlight - Advertiser **(10517)** .....(Combined) 12,500

Wabash
The $hopper **(10530)** ....(Non-paid) 8,955

IOWA
Adel
The Round-up **(10572)** ....(Free) 9,200

Algona
The Reminder **(10580)** ....(Free) ‡13,100
The Weekend
Express **(10581)** ....(Non-paid) ‡13,100

Ames
The Advertiser **(10587)** ....(Free) ‡25,623

Auburn
Tri-County Special **(10613)** ....(Free) 7,800

Britt
Town & County Advertiser **(10632)** .....(Free) ‡4,500

Cedar Falls
Hometowner, Inc. **(10656)** ....(Free) ‡61,650

Cedar Rapids
Penny Saver **(10676)** ....(Free) 78,081

Centerville
Ad Express **(10687)** ....(Free) 10,200

Clear Lake
The Clear Lake
Reporter/Advertiser **(10708)** ....(Free) ‡2,500

Denison
Ad-Visor **(10764)** ....(Free) ‡8,500

Des Moines
Central Shopper **(10774)** ....(Free) 11,137
Leetown Shopper **(10802)** ....(Free) 14,045
Northcentral Shopper **(10805)** ......(Free) 17,045
Northeast Shopper **(10806)** ....(Free) 14,440
Northwest Shopper **(10807)** ......(Non-paid) 22,034
Shopper-News
Network **(10809)** ....(Non-paid) 145,764
Southside Shopper **(10810)** ....(Free) 19,635
Valley Shopper **(10813)** ....(Free) 21,380

Dubuque
The Dubuque Advertiser **(10842)** ......(Free) ‡36,500

Dyersville
Eastern Iowa Shopping News **(10860)** 19,000

Eagle Grove
Wright County Shopper's
Guide **(10864)** ....(Free) ‡2,900

Harlan
PennySaver **(10943)** ....(Free) ‡8,921
Rocket Common Supplement
Shopper **(10944)** ....(Free) 34,559

Humboldt
Humboldt Reminder **(10958)** ....(Free) 13,017

Indianola
EXTRA **(10964)** ....(Free) 11,500

Iowa City
The Community News
Advertisers **(10971)** ....(Free) 35,638

Iowa Falls
The Advertiser **(10999)** ....(Free) 9,000

Knoxville
The Reminder **(11020)** ....(Free) 12,600

Laurens
The Laurens Reminder **(11031)** ....(Free) 5,600

Marengo
The 4-County Market **(11060)** ....(Free) ‡7450

Marshalltown
Pennysaver **(11065)** ....(Free) ‡22,213

Mason City
The Mason City Shopper **(11073)** ......(Free) 28,204

Missouri Valley
Missouri Valley
Merchandiser **(11084)** ....(Non-paid) ⊕4,900
(Paid) ⊕2,100

Mount Vernon
The SUNlight **(11099)** ....(Free) ‡4,000

Muscatine
The Post **(11104)** ....(Free) 20,850

Nevada
Money Saver **(11108)** ....(Free) 7,448

New Hampton
Impact Advertiser
Shopper **(11110)** ....(Non-paid) 6,800

Orange City
Ad-Visor **(11128)** ....(Free) 8,000

Oskaloosa
Oskaloosa Shopper **(11135)** ....(Free) 20,500

Perry
Chiefland Shopper **(11155)** ....(Free) 17,400

Pocahontas
Pocahontas County
Advertiser **(11161)** ....(Free) 4,700

Polk City
Ankeny Press Citizen **(11163)** ....(Free) 16,847

Rockwell City
Calhoun County Reminder **(11185)** ....(Free) ‡6,200

Sac City
Sac City Reminder **(11186)** ....(Free) 6,500

Sheldon
Golden Shopper **(11193)** ....(Free) ‡21,242

Sioux Center
Sioux Center Shopper **(11208)** ....(Free) ‡12,500

Spencer
Northwest Iowa Shopper **(11231)** .....(Free) ‡25,500

Story City
The Story City Reminder **(11252)** ......(Free) ‡3,100

Stuart
The 5 x 80 Bulletin **(11254)** ....(Free) ‡9,023

Tama
Tama County
Shopper-Advisor **(11262)** ....(Free) ‡13,500

Vinton
Vinton Livewire **(11283)** ....(Free) ‡10,350

KANSAS
Abilene
Central Marketplace **(11333)**

Bonner Springs
Chieftain Shopper **(11364)** ....(Paid) ‡5,200
(Non-paid) ‡7,800

Concordia
Advertiser **(11397)** ....(Free) 11,804

Derby
The Weekly Shopper **(11409)** ...(Non-paid) ‡14,100

Goodland
Country Advocate **(11463)** ....(Free) ‡16,000

Hiawatha
Penny Press 4 **(11492)** ....(Free) ‡14,225

Junction City
Daily Union Extra **(11520)** ....(Free) ‡7,300

Kansas City
The Suburban Advertiser **(11533)** ....(Free) 2,185
Wyandotte County
Shopper **(11535)** ....(Free) ‡46,000

Leavenworth
The Chronicle Shopper **(11578)** ....(Non-paid) 22,000

Mulvane
Bandwagon **(11663)** ....(Free) 5,650

Newton
Prairie Advisor **(11670)** ....(Free) 8,000

Rose Hill
The Rose Hill Reporter **(11771)**

Salina
The Buyer's Guide **(11780)** ....(Free) 25,800
Country Roads **(11782)**

Wichita
Wichita Pennypower
News **(11892)** ....(Combined) ♦76,687

KENTUCKY
Bowling Green
Country Peddler **(11942)** ....(Free) ‡33,700
Daily News Express **(11944)** ....(Wed.) 11,500
(Sun.) 20,000

Daily News Shopping
Guide **(11945)** ....(Mon.-Sun.) 21,000
(Sun.) 26,800

Maysville
Advertiser **(12288)** ....(Free) ‡20,133

Mount Sterling
Mt. Sterling
Advocate-Advertiser **(12312)** ....(Free) 17,400

Pendleton
The Shopper's Outlook **(12356)** ....(Free) ‡9,013

Somerset
Lake Cumberland Shopper **(12404)** ....(Free) 30,000

LOUISIANA
Coushatta
The Coushatta Citizen
Shopper **(12552)** ....(Free) ‡3,900

Gonzales
Community Mirror **(12586)** ....(Free) ‡27,000

Circulation: ★ = ABC; △ = BPA; ♦ = CAC; ● = CCAB; ▢ = VAC; ⊕ = PO Statement; ‡ = Publisher's Report; Boldface figures = sworn; Light figures = estimated.

2957

Circ.

LOUISIANA (continued)
Hammond
Star Shopping Guide (12593) ....(Wed.) ‡16,800
(Sun.) ‡15,900

Rayne
Tribune Plus (12802) ....(Free) 4572

Westlake
Builder News Extra (12878) ....(Free) ‡6,909

MARYLAND
Aberdeen
The Bargaineer (13084) ....(Free) ◆33,224

Bel Air
Impulse (13290) ....(Non-paid) 87,798

Hanover
Pennysaver (13580) ....(Free) ‡1,200,000

Princess Anne
Somerset/Crisfield Express (13668) .....(Free) ‡1,700

MASSACHUSETTS
Clinton
Item Extra (14140) ....(Free) ‡7,000

Great Barrington
Southern Berkshire Shopper's
Guide (14217) ....(Controlled) ‡20,000
(Free) $5,000

Lee
The Berkshire Penny
Saver (14269) ....(Free) ‡14,500

Randolph
Moneysaver (14494) ....(Free) ‡18,500

Somerville
Dollar Saver (14533)
Newsweekly (14537) ....(Free) ‡12,435

Westfield
The Wallace Pennysaver (14642) .....(Free) ‡26,837

MICHIGAN
Adrian
Access (14707) ....(Free) 37,435

Albion
Morning Star: The Shopping
Guide (14716) ....(Free) 9,366

Allegan
Allegan Flashes (14720) ....(Free) 16,340
(Paid) 7
Kalamazoo Flashes (14721) ......(Combined) 79,850
Lakeshore Flashes Shopping
Guide (14722) ....(Controlled) 9,128
(Paid) 2
Zeeland Flashes Shopping
Guide (14725) ....(Controlled) 9,853
(Paid) 2

Alma
Alma Reminder (14728) ....(Free) 19,975
Carson City Reminder (14729) ....(Free) 10,680
Clare County Buyers
Guide (14730) ....(Free) ‡12,470
The Edmore Advertiser (14731) ......(Free) 13,997
Hemlock Shoppers Guide (14732) ......(Free) 10,630

Bad Axe
The Thumb Blanket (14786) ....(Non-paid) 18,859

Baldwin
Lake County Star (14790) ....(Free) ‡4,154

Benton Harbor
Twin City Trade Lines Shopper's
Guide (14809) ....(Free) 32,266

Big Rapids
Tri-County Shoppers
Guide (14819) ....(Free) ‡10,990

Caro
Shoppers Advantage (14856) ....(Non-paid) ◆23,023
Shopper's Guide (14857) ....(Combined) 42,600

Cheboygan
Shoppers Fair (14873) ....(Free) ‡24,000

Eaton Rapids
Flashes Shoppers Guide &
News (15000) ....(Free) ‡10,000

Eau Claire
Central County (15001) ....(Non-paid) 13,633

Central County Trade Lines Shopper's
Guide (15002) ....(Free) 14,324
Twin City (15003) ....(Non-paid) 32,107

Fowlerville
Fowlerville Shopper (15051) ....(Non-paid) 9,919

Fremont
Hi-Lites Shoppers Guide (15057) ....(Free) 20,000

Gaylord
Alpena Star (15066) ....(Combined) 19,424
Charlevoix Co. Star (15067) ....(Non-paid) 10,146
Northern Star (15070) ....(Non-paid) 18,460
Petoskey Star
Advertiser (15071) ....(Non-paid) 13,161
Presque Isle Star (15072) ....(Free) 7,522
Star Advertiser (15073) ....(Free) 14,731
Star Buyer's Guide (15074) ....(Free) 30,293
Straits Area Star (15075) ....(Free) 15,767

Gladwin
Gladwin Buyers Guide (15079) ....(Free) 17,200

Greenville
The Buy Line (15134) ....(Free) ‡37,605

Hartland
Hartland Shopper (15149) ....(Non-paid) 9,002

Highland
Highland Shopping Guide (15159) ....(Free) ‡14,121

Holland
Holland Flashes Shopping
Guide (15173) ....(Free) 27,540

Howard City
River Valley News
Shopper (15189) ....(Free) ‡20,600

Howell
The Lakes Area
Shopper (15195) ....(Non-paid) 10,442
Monday Green Sheet (15198) .....(Non-paid) 66,174

Hudson
Bi-County Herald (15200) ....(Free) ‡11,500

Ironwood
North Country Sun (15214) ....(Non-paid) 16,430

Kalamazoo
Flashes Kalamazoo
Shopper (15236) ....(Free) 84,950

Lapeer
Lapeer Buyer's Guide (15309) ....(Free) 30,775

Livonia
Dollar Saver (15314)

Manistee
West Shore Shoppers
Guide (15330) ....(Free) 17,700

Mount Pleasant
Buyers Guide (15374) ....(Free) ‡28,259
Midland Buyer's Guide (15378) ....(Free) 27,901

Munising
The Alger County Shopper (15385) ....‡5,000

Otsego
Shoppers Guide (15426) ....(Free) ‡12,500

Petoskey
The AD-vertiser (15434) ....(Free) ‡18,592
Super Shopper (15437) ....‡27,500

Pinckney
The Pinckney Shopper (15443) ...(Non-paid) 13,350
(Paid) 115

Reed City
Freeway Shoppers Guide (15463) ......(Free) ‡9,971

St. Johns
St. Johns Reminder (15510) ....(Free) 17,600

Saline
Mr. Mazoo (15518) ....(Free) ‡15,065

Sandusky
Sanilac County Buyer's
Guide (15521) ....(Free) 19,086

Sault Sainte Marie
Tri-County Buyers' Guide (15528) .....(Free) ‡19,770

Tawas City
The Northeastern
Shopper (15585) ....(Free) ‡40,252

Vassar
Cass River Trader (15651) ....(Free) 18,000

Vicksburg
The Broadcast (15653) ....(Free) ‡10,500

MINNESOTA
Aitkin
Bargain Hunter (15701) ....(Free) ‡21,500

Alexandria
Lakeland Shopping Guide (15713) .....(Free) 31,000

Buffalo
The Drummer (15777) ....(Non-paid) 40,100

Cambridge
Scotsman (15786) ....(Paid) ‡508
(Free) ‡60,000

Cannon Falls
Cannon Shopper (15789) ....(Free) ‡8,900

Coon Rapids
Anoka County Shopper (15814) ....(Free) 62,553

Elk River
Elk River Star Shopper (15879)

Ely
North Country Saver (15882) ....(Free) 9,000

Fairmont
Fairmont Photo Press (15889) ....(Free) 11,800

Fergus Falls
The Heartland Shopping
News (15898) ....(Non-paid) 13,971
The Midweek (15899) ....(Non-paid) 20,853

Forest Lake
St. Croix Valley Peach (15906) ....(Free) ‡31,865

Goodhue
The Country Shopper (15925)

Grand Rapids
Itasca Shopper (15929) ....(Non-paid) ◆10,289

Halstad
The Shopper Diversified (15938) ......(Free) ‡40,220

Howard Lake
Herald Journal Shopper (15965) ....(Free) ‡6,000

Jackson
Livewire (15975) ....(Paid) 321
(Free) 10,333

Lake City
Lake City Shopper (15992) ....(Free) ‡7,500

Lindstrom
Search Shopper (16003) ....(Free) ‡18,277

Little Falls
Morrison County Record (16006) ....(Free) 18,405
(Paid) 543

Luverne
Luverne Announcer (16013) ....(Free) 10,122

Madelia
Southern Minnesota
Peach (16018) ....(Non-paid) ‡15,500

Mankato
Home Magazine (16027) ....(Combined) 39,153

Marshall
Shoppers Review (16043) ....(Free) ‡13,103

Melrose
Bargain Searchlight (16050) ....(Free) 1,600

Monticello
Monticello Shopper (16185) ....(Paid) ‡200
(Free) ‡21,600

Mora
Mora Advertisers (16196) ....(Paid) ‡192
(Free) ‡10,554

North St. Paul
Lillie Suburban Shopping
Review (16226) ....(Mon.) 23,353

Northfield
Northfield Shopper (16237) ....(Free) 12,000

Pequot Lakes
Echoland Shopper (16262) ....(Free) ‡22,373

Perham
Contact (16264) ....(Free) 10,000

Numbers cited after listings are entry numbers rather than page numbers.

Princeton
Town and Country
Shopper **(16285)** ....(Free) ‡13,420
(Free) 12,098

Roseau
The Borderline **(16327)** ....(Free) 11,125

Rushford
Tri-County Record Special
Edition **(16338)** ....(Paid) 1,700

St. Cloud
The Shopping News **(16347)** .....(Combined) 44,309

St. James
Town and Country
Shopper **(16356)** ....(Free) ‡12,860

Sebeka
Total Shopper **(16443)** ....(Free) 4,900

Slayton
Murray County Wheel/Herald **(16449)** ....(Paid) ‡960
(Free) ‡6,200

Spring Valley
River Valley Shopper **(16457)** ....(Free) ‡13,815

Staples
Sunday Square Shooter **(16461)** ....(Free) ‡9,500

Two Harbors
Two Harbors Manney
Shopper **(16481)** ....(Free) ‡7,981

Walker
The Co-Pilot **(16493)** ....(Non-paid) ♦7,007

Willmar
The Sunday Reminder **(16517)** ....(Non-paid) 28,800

MISSISSIPPI
Brookhaven
Buyers Guide **(16577)** ....(Free) ‡15,000

Laurel
Impact of Hattiesburg **(16739)** .....(Non-paid) 61,402
Impact of Laurel **(16740)** ....(Wed.) 46,695
(Sun.) 53,854

Magee
The Simpson Shopper **(16757)** ......(Non-paid) 6,700

McComb
Southwest Sun **(16763)** ....(Free) 8,000

Natchez
Miss-Lou Guide **(16792)** ....(Free) ❑13,180

MISSOURI
Adrian
Star Lite Shoppers Guide **(16888)** ......(Free) ‡4600

Bethany
Pony Express **(16903)** ....(Free) ‡16,000

Blue Springs
Town & Country
News **(16910)** ....(Controlled) 26,600

Cameron
The Cameron Shopper **(16939)** ....(Free) 15,600

Excelsior Springs
Town & Country Leader **(17051)** ....(Paid) ‡245
(Free) ‡20,100

Gladstone
Gladstone News **(17082)** ....(Free) ‡60,210

Harrisonville
Cass County Shopper **(17094)** ....(Free) 19,032

Ironton
Mountain Echo/X-Tra **(17117)** ....(Paid) 3,000
(Free) 3,900

Kirksville
The Marketplace **(17228)** ....(Free) ‡6,000
(Paid) ‡8,000

Lees Summit
Lees Summit Journal-Extra **(17244)** .....(Paid) 4,308
(Free) 20,026

Marshfield
The Country Mailbox **(17270)** ....‡10,612
5,500

Maryville
Penny Press 2 **(17276)** ....‡19,100
Weekly Bargain Shopper **(17277)** .....(Free) ‡11,500

Mexico
Mark Twain Regional
News **(17283)** ....(Free) ‡15,500

Osceola
St. Clair County Buyer's
Guide **(17324)** ....(Free) ‡4,000

Owensville
East Central Ad Mart **(17328)** ....(Free) ‡6,812

Perryville
The Republic-Monitor Shopping
Guide **(17341)** ....(Free) ‡8,400

Richmond
The Advantage **(17374)** ....(Free) 9,000

Springfield
Pennypower Shopping
News **(17609)** ....(Wed.) 147,400

Warrensburg
Warrensburg Gazette **(17670)** ....(Paid) ‡800

Webb City
Wise Buyer **(17713)** ....(Non-paid) ‡10,000

Windsor
Benton County Shopper **(17719)** ....(Free) 8,100

MONTANA
Culbertson
The Searchlight **(17777)** ....(Combined) ‡1,000

Dillon
Tribune Advertiser **(17783)** ....(Free) ‡4,600

Great Falls
Consumers Press **(17798)** ....(Combined) 32,720

Hamilton
Post Script **(17807)** ....(Free) ‡12,000

Helena
The Adit **(17816)** ....(Free) ‡25,000

Plentywood
The Greeter **(17894)** ....(Free) ‡3,000

Polson
Lake County
Advertiser **(17898)** ....(Non-paid) 12,000

NEBRASKA
Beatrice
Penny Press 5 **(17948)** ....(Free) ‡18,500

Blair
Clipper **(17955)** ....(Paid) 4,366
(Free) 9,483
Clipper Shopper **(17956)** ....(Combined) ‡8,750
Sarpy County Extra **(17958)** ....(Free) ‡2,800

Columbus
Columbus Area Choice **(17980)** ....(Non-paid) 24,940

Fremont
HomeFront Buyer's
Guide **(18011)** ....(Non-paid) 22,300

Grand Island
Mighty Nickel **(18026)** ....(Free) ‡25,950

Nebraska City
Penny Press 1 **(18167)** ....(Free) ‡20,850

Scottsbluff
Express Shopper **(18264)** ....(Free) 10,000

Seward
The Connection **(18275)** ....(Free) ‡4,100

Tekamah
Midwest Messenger **(18297)** ....(Free) ‡154,380

West Point
Elkhorn Valley Shopper **(18311)** ......(Free) ‡10,010

York
Trade & Transactions **(18320)** ....(Paid) 46
(Free) 24,094

NEVADA
Las Vegas
Nifty Nickel **(18382)** ....(Non-paid) 60,000

Reno
Pennysaver **(18422)** ....(Free) 148,000

NEW HAMPSHIRE
Keene
The Monadnock Shopper
News **(18531)** ....(Free) ‡39,500

Plymouth
The Penny Saver **(18633)** ....(Free) ‡18,748

NEW JERSEY
Cherry Hill
South Jersey Shoppers
Guide **(18738)** ....(Free) 416,200

Cinnaminson
Southern New Jersey Swapper **(18745)** 25,719

Fair Lawn
Fair Lawn-Elmwood Park-Saddle Brook
Shopper **(18806)** ....(Free) ‡28,195

Garfield
Garfield-Wallington-South Hackensack
Shopper **(18842)** ....(Free) ‡15,473

Hawthorne
Hawthorne-Glen Rock-Haledon-North Haledon-
Prospect Park Shopper **(18870)** ....(Free) ‡19,086

Lodi
Lodi-Hasbrouck Heights-Woodridge-Maywood-Rochelle
Park Shopper **(19179)** ....(Free) ‡21,434

New Brunswick
Middlesex Buyer's
Guide **(19335)** ....(Non-paid) 11,858

Somerville
Somerset County Buyer's
Guide **(19578)** ....(Non-paid) 24,493
Value Shopper **(19580)** ....(Non-paid) 36,464

NEW YORK
Akron
Akron-Corfu Pennysaver **(19978)** ....(Non-paid) 7,394

Albion
Lake Country Pennysaver **(20020)** ....(Paid) 9
(Non-paid) 19,643

Arcade
Arcade Pennysaver **(20062)** ....(Non-paid) 13,102

Attica
Attica Pennysaver **(20104)** ....(Non-paid) 6,764

Avon
Genesee Valley **(20109)** ....(Combined) 131,888

Ballston
Ballston-Malta Pennysaver **(20118)** ......(Free) 6,485

Batavia
The Drummer
Pennysaver **(20120)** ....(Non-paid) 23,015

Blasdell
Blasdell Lackawanna
Pennysaver **(20234)** ....(Non-paid) 13,808

Bolivar
Moneysaver Shopping Guide **(20235)** ....(Paid) 10
(Non-paid) 5,325
Moneysaver Shopping News **(20236)** ....(Paid) 31
(Non-paid) 8,362

Boonville
North Country
Pennysaver **(20238)** ....(Combined) 5,280

Brockport
Tri-County Advertiser **(20247)** ......(Non-paid) 15,924

Canandaigua
Shopping News **(20424)** ....(Free) ‡53,000

Canisteo
Dansville-Wayland
Pennysaver **(20427)** ....(Non-paid) 8,816
Hornell-Canisteo
Penn-E-Saver **(20428)** ....(Non-paid) 13,518
(Paid) 16

Catskill
Mountain Pennysaver **(20439)** ....(Free) 20,669

Clifton Park
Clifton Park North
Pennysaver **(20462)** ....(Non-paid) ♦17,669
Clifton Park South
Pennysaver **(20463)** ....(Non-paid) ♦17,955
Latham Pennysaver **(20466)** ......(Non-paid) ♦15,309
Moneysaver **(20467)** ....(Free) ‡18,103

Circulation: ★ = ABC; △ = BPA; ♦ = CAC; • = CCAB; ❑ = VAC; ⊕ = PO Statement; ‡ = Publisher's Report; Boldface figures = sworn; Light figures = estimated.

2959

Circ.

NEW YORK (continued)

Clifton Springs
The Merchandiser **(20468)** ....(Combined) 7,770

Clinton
Farm and Home
  Pennysaver **(20471)** ....(Combined) 8,197
Pennysaver (Oneida
  Edition) **(20473)** ....(Free) 14,000

Cobleskill
My Shopper **(20478)** ....(Paid) 10
  (Non-paid) 24,178

Conklin
Rural Pennysaver, Inc. **(20494)** ....(Free) ‡26,000

Cooperstown
Hall of Fame Pennysaver **(20498)** ....(Paid) 7
  (Non-paid) 8,848

Corinth
Pennysaver/News **(20502)** ....(Free) ‡15,000

Cornwall
Cornwall Local **(20510)** ....‡3,300

Dansville
Geneseeway Shopper **(20518)** ....(Free) ‡11,700

Delhi
County Shopper—Catskill Park
  Edition **(20523)** ....(Non-paid) 6,665
County Shopper—Delaware
  Edition **(20524)** ....(Non-paid) 12,041

East Aurora
East Aurora/Elma
  Pennysaver **(20541)** ....(Non-paid) 15,928

East Rochester
Shopping Bag &
  Advertiser **(20554)** ....(Free) 261,407

Elizabethtown
Plattsburgh Free
  Trader **(20565)** ....(Non-paid) 25,134
Tri Lakes Free Trader **(20567)** ....(Non-paid) 11,267

Elmsford
The Pennysaver **(20583)** ....(Non-paid) 375,000

Farmingdale
Pennysaver **(20596)** ....(Free) 16,889

Franklinville
Franklinville Pennysaver **(20620)** ....(Non-paid) 5,460

Fredonia
Dunkirk-Fredonia-Westfield
  Pennysaver **(20621)** ....(Non-paid) 18,880
Lakeshore Pennysaver **(20622)** ......(Non-paid) 5,342

Freeville
Suburban Cortland-Ithaca
  Shopper **(20627)** ....(Free) 23,225

Fulton
The Valley Shopper **(20632)** ....(Non-paid) 4,400

Grand Island
Grand Island PennySaver **(20677)** ....(Free) 6,800

Great Neck
Car Buyer's Market **(20687)**

Hamburg
Hamburg Pennysaver **(20703)** .....(Non-paid) 25,100

Harriman
The Marketplace
  Pennysaver **(20711)** ....(Controlled) 99,000

Herkimer
Herkimer Pennysaver **(20733)** ....(Combined) 14,341

Hicksville
Results Media Shopper's
  Guide **(20744)** ....(Non-paid) 966,536

Horseheads
Corning Pennysaver **(20759)** ....(Non-paid) 29,340
The Shopper **(20760)** ....(Free) **27,000**

Interlaken
Tri-Village Pennysaver **(20782)** ....(Paid) 200
  (Non-paid) 6,000

Ithaca
Ithaca Pennysaver **(20808)** ....(Paid) 200
  (Non-paid) 27,000

Lawrence
Prime Time **(20940)** ....(Free) 108,240

Circ.

Liberty
Catskill Shopper-Sullivan & Ulster County
  Editions **(20943)** ....(Non-paid) 42,711

Lindenhurst
Babylon South Bay's
  Shopper **(20946)** ....(Free) 18,511
Deer Park South Bay's
  Shopper **(20947)** ....(Free) 18,156
Lindenhurst/South Bay's Shopping
  Newspaper **(20948)** ....(Free) ‡23,498

Lockport
Metro Retailer **(20957)** ....(Non-paid) 33,576

Lynbrook
South Shore Record **(20977)** 18,000

Manlius
Jamesville/Dewitt/Fayetteville/Manlius
  Pennysaver **(21020)** ....(Non-paid) ‡17,536

Massena
County Pennysaver **(21026)** ....(Non-paid) 30,420
  (Paid) 89

Medina
Orleans Shopper **(21038)** ....(Free) 16,800

Middletown
Big Saver **(21079)** ....(Free) ‡60,000

Newark
Lyons Shopping Guide **(22995)** .....(Non-paid) 5,882
Newark Pennysaver **(22996)** ....(Non-paid) 6,985
Sodus Pennysaver **(22997)** ....(Non-paid) 8,440

Norwich
Norwich Pennysaver **(23022)** ....(Non-paid) 17,418
Sidney Pennysaver **(23023)** ....(Non-paid) 11,897

Oneida
Pennysaver (Chittenango
  Edition) **(23046)** ....(Free) 4,870

Orchard Park
Orchard Park
  Pennysaver **(23058)** ....(Non-paid) 61,717

Owego
Broome Pennysaver **(23065)** ......(Non-paid) 37,283

Penn Yan
Chronicle Ad-Viser **(23091)** ....(Free) ‡12,925

Perry
Perry Shopper **(23095)** ....(Combined) 7,350

Plainview
Plainview/Jericho Pennysaver **(23099)**

Port Byron
Port Byron Shopping
  Guide **(23114)** ....(Free) ‡10,523

Richfield Springs
Turnpike Pennysaver **(23187)** ....(Paid) 11
  (Non-paid) 5,883

Rochester
Greece Pennysaver **(23227)** ....(Free) ‡30,000
Irondequoit Shopper **(23231)** .....(Non-paid) 16,488
Timesaver **(23241)** ....(Free) 10,372

Rome
Rome Pennysaver **(23266)** ....(Combined) 16,857

Saugerties
Mohawk Valley
  Pennysaver **(23307)** ....(Free) ‡16,108

Springville
Springville PennySaver **(23355)** .....(Non-paid) 9,900

Staten Island
Staten Island Pennysaver **(23362)** ....(Free) ‡75,000

Syosset
North Shore Today **(23380)** .....(Wed.) ◆187,740
North Shore Today's Elite **(23381)** .....(Free) 20,108
Syosset/Woodbury Pennysaver **(23384)**

Syracuse
Auburn Pennysaver **(23387)** ......(Non-paid) ‡19,731
Baldwinsville
  Pennysaver **(23389)** ....(Non-paid) ‡12,960
Bellevue-Geddes
  Pennysaver **(23390)** ....(Non-paid) ‡11,487
City Edition
  Pennysaver **(23394)** ....(Non-paid) ‡5,290
Court-Butternut
  Pennysaver **(23398)** ....(Non-paid) ‡10,705
East Syracuse/Minoa/Kirkville/Bridgeport
  Pennysaver **(23401)** ....(Non-paid) ‡11,024

Circ.

Eastwood Pennysaver **(23402)** .....(Non-paid) ‡8,655
Fulton Pennysaver **(23404)** ......(Non-paid) ‡16,335
Geneva Pennysaver **(23405)** .....(Non-paid) ‡11,112
Liverpool-Phoenix
  Pennysaver **(23408)** ....(Non-paid) ‡20,688
Lyncourt Pennysaver **(23409)** ......(Non-paid) ‡6,535
Mattydale-North Syracuse
  Pennysaver **(23411)** ....(Non-paid) ‡21,791
Moravia Pennysaver **(23413)** ....(Non-paid) ‡10,053
North Area
  Pennysaver **(23415)** ....(Non-paid) ‡8,583
Seneca Falls
  Pennysaver **(23421)** ....(Non-paid) ‡11,822
Skaneateles-Marcellus
  Pennysaver **(23422)** ....(Non-paid) ‡7,404
Solvay-Camillus
  Pennysaver **(23423)** ....(Non-paid) ‡19,475
Strathmore-Onondaga Hill
  Pennysaver **(23424)** ....(Non-paid) ‡4,822
Syracuse East
  Pennysaver **(23425)** ....(Non-paid) ‡9,595
Town & Country
  Pennysaver **(23431)** ....(Non-paid) ‡15,442

Utica
Utica Pennysaver **(23468)** ....(Combined) 16,954

Warsaw
Warsaw Penny Saver **(23506)** ......(Non-paid) 9,301

Watkins Glen
The Hi-Lites **(23524)** ....(Non-paid) 8,500

Webster
Webster-Ontario-Walworth
  Pennysaver **(23529)** ....(Free) 20,349

Wellsville
The Allegany County.
  Pennysaver **(23532)** ....(Free) 25,000

West Seneca
West Seneca
  Pennysaver **(23548)** ....(Non-paid) 19,200

Westfield
Westfield/Corry Quality
  Guide **(23563)** ....(Free) ‡13,186
Westfield Quality Guide **(23564)** ......(Free) ‡14,893

Whitesboro
Suburban Pennysaver **(23577)** ....(Combined) 14,019

Yorktown Heights
Yorktown Pennysaver
  Corp. **(23610)** ....(Combined) 341,675

NORTH CAROLINA
Ahoskie
Commonwealth Progress **(23613)** ....(Paid) ‡1,815
  (Free) ‡5,000

Albemarle
The Advantage **(23617)** ....(Free) ‡8,300

Asheville
Iwanna **(23631)** ....(Paid) 32,000
  (Free) 3,000

Chapel Hill
Chapel News **(23703)** ....(Free) ‡19,384
Village Advocate **(23730)** ....(Wed.) ◆17,848
  (Sun.) ◆17,735

Elkin
The Yadkin Valley
  Advertiser **(23868)** ....(Non-paid) ⊕16,850

Garner
Southside Shopper, Inc. **(23906)** ......(Free) ‡44,000

New Bern
The New Bern Shopper **(24096)** ....(Free) 37,200

Raleigh
The AD-PAK (Raleigh
  Edition) **(24123)** ....(Non-paid) 78,063

Waynesville
Mid-Week Messenger **(24279)** ....(Free) 9,000

Wilmington
The AD-PAK (Wilmington
  Edition) **(24294)** ....(Free) ‡44,000

NORTH DAKOTA
Bowman
The Finder - Bowman
  Edition **(24381)** ....(Free) 11,000

Jamestown
The Prairie Post **(24477)** ....(Free) 18,639

Mandan
The Finder (Mandan) **(24497)** ....(Free) 37,800

Minot
The Trading Post **(24506)** ....(Free) 18,000

West Fargo
The Midweek **(24556)** ....(Free) 55,000

OHIO
Bryan
The Countyline **(24715)** ....(Free) ‡24,650

Cambridge
The Guernsey-Noble
Advertiser **(24725)** ....(Non-paid) ♦12,855

Chillicothe
County Line
Advertiser **(24762)** ....(Non-paid) ♦3,881
The Ross County
Advertiser **(24764)** ....(Non-paid) ♦23,543

Circleville
The Pickaway County
Advertiser **(24852)** ....(Non-paid) ♦19,847

Coshocton
The Coshocton County
Advertiser **(25095)** ....(Non-paid) ♦14,257

Covington
Penny Saver **(25099)** ....(Combined) 10,021
Stillwater Valley
Advertiser **(25100)** ....(Combined) 9,539

Geneva, Perry
The Free Enterprise **(25215)** ....(Free) 17,269

Germantown
Booster **(25217)** ....(Free) 6,500

Greenwich
The Shopper's Helper **(25230)** ....(Free) 13,550

Jackson
The Jackson County
Advertiser **(25256)** ....(Non-paid) ♦11,103
The Vinton County
Advertiser **(25258)** ....(Non-paid) ♦3,690

Lancaster
Lancaster Fairfield
Advertiser **(25290)** ....(Free) ♦33,734

Lisbon
Central Shopper **(25307)** ....(Free) ‡43,588

Logan
Hocking Valley
Advertiser **(25311)** ....(Non-paid) ♦9,506

Loudonville
The Loudonville Times and The Loudonville Mohican
Area Shopper **(25317)** ....(Free) ‡13,800

Napoleon
Spotlite **(25403)** ....(Free) ‡12,000

New Lexington
The Buckeye Lake
Advertiser **(25411)** ....(Non-paid) 6,643
The Morgan County
Advertiser **(25412)** ....(Non-paid) ♦5,101
The Perry County
Advertiser **(25413)** ....(Non-paid) ♦12,380
Tribune Shopping News **(25415)** ......(Free) ‡15,200

Newark
The Newark-Licking
Advertiser **(25425)** ....(Non-paid) ♦36,971

Oberlin
The Shopping News **(25449)** ....(Free) ‡9,600

Paulding
The Weekly Reminder **(25472)** ....(Free) ‡9,100

Rittman
The Trading Post **(25499)** ....(Non-paid) 43,273

Rocky River
Tradin' Times **(25501)** ....(Free) 55,043

Springfield
Tri-County Shoppers
News **(25533)** ....(Non-paid) 66,533

Troy
Miami County
Advocate **(25592)** ....(Non-paid) ♦24,833

Washington Court House
South Central Ohio Shopper's
Guide **(25620)** ....(Non-paid) ‡24,000

Waverly
The Pike County
Advertiser **(25624)** ....(Non-paid) ♦10,062

West Alexandria
Twin Valley News & Advisor **(25631)** ....(Paid) ‡600
(Free) ‡8,000

Zanesville
Times-Recorder
Midweek **(25718)** ....(Mon.-Sat.) 21,806

OKLAHOMA
Bethany
Northwest Metro Times **(25759)** .....(Non-paid) 7,000

Bristow
Zanesville Muskingum
Advertiser **(25769)** ....(Non-paid) ♦35,072

Durant
Grayson County Shopper **(25805)** .....(Free) ‡44,149
The Shopper (Zone I) **(25808)** ....(Free) ‡14,239
The Shopper (Zone II) **(25809)** ....(Free) ‡9,191

Enid
Shopper's Edge **(25823)** ....(Non-paid) 25,000

Lindsay
Shopper News Note **(25900)** ....(Paid) ⊕210
(Free) ⊕6,168

Newcastle
Early Bird Express **(25928)** ....‡8,500

Sapulpa
Sapulpa Herald Extra **(26057)** ....(Free) ‡10,294

OREGON
Albany
This Week **(26207)** ....(Free) 18,000

Coos Bay
South Coast Shopper **(26272)** ....(Free) ‡15,000

Hillsboro
West Valley Courier **(26374)** ....(Free) 19,957

Ontario
Treasure Valley Reminder **(26454)** .....(Free) 15,000

Prineville
X-TRA **(26549)** ....(Free) 2,500

Sutherlin
The Umpqua Shopper **(26592)** ....(Free) ‡27,000

Veneta
Tri-County Shopper **(26604)** ....(Free) 13,500

PENNSYLVANIA
Bellefonte
Bargain Sheet **(26694)** ....(Free) ‡40,000

Chambersburg
The Franklin Shopper **(26768)** .....(Non-paid) 40,517

Cochranton
Area Shopper **(26794)** ....(Free) ‡103,000

Coopersburg
Penny Power **(26807)** ....(Non-paid) 63,337
(Paid) 9

Ebensburg
Pennysaver **(26859)** ....(Free) ‡15,000
Traders Guide **(26860)** ....(Paid) 9,980

Edinboro
The Independent-Enterprise **(26862)** .....(Free) 5,934
(Paid) 2,311

Emlenton
The Progress News **(26872)** ....(Free) ‡15,000

Ephrata
Shopping News of Lancaster
County **(26889)** ....(Paid) 43
(Non-paid) 35,785

Hamburg
East Penn Valley Merchandiser **(26970)** ....(Paid) 24
(Non-paid) 34,757
Northern Berks Merchandiser **(26972)** ......(Paid) 30
(Non-paid) 30,201

Hanover
Hanover Area
Merchandiser **(26975)** ....(Combined) 76,590

Harrisburg
The Guide News **(26994)** ....(Free) ‡161,543

Hughesville
East Lycoming Shopper and
News **(27065)** ....(Free) 18,800

Lebanon
Dauphin Schuylkill Area
Merchandiser **(27169)** ....(Combined) 97,201
Gettysburg Area Merchandiser **(27170)**
Hershey Area
Merchandiser **(27171)** ....(Combined) 97,201
Lebanon Valley Area
Merchandiser **(27173)** ....(Combined) 97,201
Myerstown Area
Merchandiser **(27174)** ....(Combined) 97,201
Northern Adams-York Area
Merchandiser **(27175)** ....(Combined) 76,590

Mansfield
Penny-Saver **(27219)** ....(Free) ‡10,000

Meadville
The Fast Track **(27233)** ....(Free) ‡12,000

Mercersburg
Mercersburg Journal/Ad
Journal **(27246)** ....(Paid) 2,700
(Free) 5,295

Pottstown
Mercury Tri-County Market
Place **(27900)** ....(Free) ‡33,500

Reading
Greater Reading Area
Merchandiser **(27918)** ....(Free) 96,825

Red Hill
Upper Perk Shoppers
Guide **(27927)** ....(Free) 19,220

Ridgway
Shop-Right 1 **(27936)** ....(Free) ‡19,086
Shop-Right 1 & 2 **(27937)** ....(Free) ‡32,492

Somerset
The Sunday Shopper **(28003)** ....(Free) ‡34,100

Southampton
Carrier Pigeon **(28006)** ....(Free) ‡160,000
(Controlled) ‡500

Trevose
Bucks County
Midweek **(28055)** ....(Non-paid) 145,598

West Chester
The Village News **(28149)** ....(Free) 21,301
(Paid) 77

Wilkes Barre
The Expressline **(28166)** ....(Non-paid) ♦57,096

RHODE ISLAND
Bristol
Shopping News South **(28328)** ....(Non-paid) ♦7,290

Coventry
The Reminder **(28330)** ....(Free) ‡30,000

Warwick
Pennysaver **(28451)** ....(Free) ♦4,615

SOUTH CAROLINA
Cheraw
Chesterfield County
Shopper **(28528)** ....(Free) ‡12,976

Greenville
Food Extra **(28622)** ....(Free) 84,652

Rock Hill
Star Watch **(28745)** ....(Free) ⊕9,000

Seneca
Golden Corner
Shopper **(28755)** ....(Non-paid) 11,067

Walterboro
Colleton Shopper **(28780)** ....(Free) ‡18,000

SOUTH DAKOTA
Brookings
Prairie Profile **(28815)** ....(Free) 11,000

Circulation: ★ = ABC; △ = BPA; ♦ = CAC; • = CCAB; ❑ = VAC; ⊕ = PO Statement; ‡ = Publisher's Report; Boldface figures = sworn; Light figures = estimated.

2961

Circ.

SOUTH DAKOTA (continued)

Town and Country
Shopper (28817) ....(Free) ‡15,500

Custer
Western Trader (28838) ....(Free) 3,800

Mitchell
Advisor (28899) ....(Free) ❑17,983

Mobridge
The Monday Reminder (28906) ....,...(Free) ‡6,095

Pierre
The Reminder Plus (28919) ....(Free) ‡19,800

Sioux Falls
Sioux Falls Shopping
News (28965) ....(Non-paid) 85,000

Wagner
Wagner Announcer (29013) ....(Free) ‡4,650

Watertown
Coteau Shopper (29017) ....(Free) ‡25500

Yankton
Missouri Valley Shopper (29037) ......(Free) ‡23,220

TENNESSEE
Clarksville
The Peddler (29116) ....(Free) ‡27,000

Columbia
Middle Tennessee
Shopper (29137) ....(Free) ⊕31,500
31,486

Cookeville
The Peddler (29145) ....(Free) ‡15,000

Dayton
Herald-News Sunrise
Edition (29164) ....(Free) ‡13,000

Fayetteville
Exchange (29189) ....(Free) ‡20,300

Millington
South Tipton Star (29417) ....(Free) ‡2,000

Pikeville
The Sequatchie Valley
Shopper (29568) ....(Free) 14,980

Rockwood
The Roane County
News/Record (29578) ....(Free) ‡15,000

South Pittsburg
Sequatchie Valley
Purchase (29609) ....(Free) ‡13,300

Sweetwater
Advocate Penny Saver (29623) ....(Free) ‡15,100

Waverly
The Shopper's Guide (29643) ....(Free) 9,500

White House
Bargain Browser (29646) ....(Free) 20,136

TEXAS
Abilene
Thrifty Nickel Want Ads (29655) ......(Free) ‡39,000

Alvin
The Alvin Advertiser (29689) ....(Free) 16,794

Athens
The Advertiser (29745) ....(Free) ‡8,150

Austin
Austin Greensheet (29759) ....(Free) ❑38,949

Bonham
Fannin County Special (29933) ......(Free) ‡14,686

Brenham
Bargain Hunter (29949) ....(Free) 12,394

Brownsville
Bargain Book (Central) (29956) ....(Free) 20,109
Bargain Book (North) (29957) ....(Free) 37,120
Bargain Book (South) (29958) ....(Free) 47,072

Burleson
Star Review (29990) ....(Free) ‡6,000

Center
The Merchandiser (30013) ....(Free) 9,000

Cleveland
Eastex News-Shopper (30029) ....(Free) ‡12,275

Corpus Christi
Ad Sack (30075) ....(Free) ‡50,000

Corsicana
Navarro County Sun
Extra (30102) ....(Free) ‡25,250

Dallas
Dallas Greensheet (30145) ....(Free) ❑185,938
El Extra (30154) ....(Free) ❑27,298

Georgetown
Sun Advertiser (30391) ....(Free) ‡8,650

Greenville
Hunt County Shopper (30414) ....(Free) ‡25,020

Houston
Clear Lake Citizen & Exchange
News (30462) 26,700
Houston Greensheet (30485) ....(Free) ❑353,667

La Porte
Bayshore Sun Extra (30659) ....(Free) 8,416

Lubbock
Thrifty Nickel Want Ads (30719) ......(Free) ‡45,000

Pasadena
Pasadena Broadcaster (30913) ....(Free) 16,000

Pecos
Pecos Free Press (30924) ....(Free) 4,000

Rosenberg
Herald Coaster Extra (30993) ....(Free) 13,435

Vidor
Vidorian Shopper (31244) ....(Free) ‡11,000

Weatherford
Parker County Shopper (31272) ......(Free) ‡22,731

UTAH
American Fork
New Utah! Shopper (31319) ....(Paid) 1,900

Kanab
Color Country Shopper (31341) ....(Free) ‡2,000

Mount Pleasant
The Pyramid Shopper (31373) .....(Combined) 8,600

Richfield
Reaper Extra (31413) ....(Free) ‡6,600

VERMONT
Bennington
Pennysaver Press (31500) ....(Non-paid) 27,212

Manchester Center
Vermont News Guide (31554) ....(Free) 15,600
(Paid) 400

VIRGINIA
Bedford
Bedford Bullet (31860) ....(Free) ‡24,300

Chincoteague
The Chincoteague
Beachcomber (31971) ....(Free) ‡11,000

Clarksville
Super Shopper (31976) ....(Free) ‡9,100

Covington
Alleghany Highlander (31981) ....(Free) ‡6,000

Falls Church
Thrifty Nickel (32058) ....(Free) ‡125,000

Independence
The Declaration Dynamo (32173) .....(Free) 3,000

Petersburg
The Progress-Index Extra (32331) ...(Free) ‡20,040

South Boston
Gazette/Virginia Shopper (32529) ....(Free) 4,274

Wytheville
Enterprise Buyers'
Catalogue (32642) ....(Free) 7,350

WASHINGTON
Arlington
Arlington Times (32654) ....(Free) ‡11,109
(Paid) ‡2,308

Camas
At Your Leisure (32700) ....(Free) ‡3,400

Duvall
Jubilee (32740)

Grand Coulee
Star Buyer's Guide (32780) ....(Free) ‡3400

Lynnwood
Little Nickel
Classifieds (32824) ....(Non-paid) ‡320,000

Moses Lake
Nickel Saver (32839) ....(Free) ‡20,000

Mount Vernon
Skagit Weekly (32846) ....(Free) 12,500

Seattle
The Shopper (33030) ....(Free) ‡18,000

Shelton
The Shopper's Weekly (33080) ....(Non-paid) 16,000

Yelm
Nisqually Valley Shopper (33240) .....(Free) ‡19,750

WEST VIRGINIA
Charleston
Jefferson Buyers Guide (33271) ....(Free) 14,964

Culloden
The Putnam - Cabell Post (33298) ......(Paid) ‡125
(Free) ‡50,500

Hamlin
Lincoln Times (33332) ....(Non-paid) ⊕12,400

Keyser
Today's Shopper (33354) ....(Free) 35,000

Lewisburg
Greenbrier Valley Trader (33365) 9,500

Martinsburg
Buyers Guide (33378) ....(Free) 43,930

Moundsville
Green Tab-Northern
Valley (33407) ....(Combined) 17,865

New Martinsville
Wetzel Green Tab (33414) ....(Non-paid) 19,923

Ripley
Star Herald (33450) ....(Non-paid) 12,500

WISCONSIN
Algoma
The Kewaunee County
Star (33521) ....(Free) ‡12,300
Kewaunee County Sunday
Chronicle (33522) ....(Non-paid) 9,600

Antigo
Antigo Area Shoppers Guide (33530) ....(Paid) 25
(Non-paid) 13,174
The Journal Express (33533) ....(Free) ‡5,400

Appleton
The Bargain Bulletin (33535) ....(Wed.) 54,152
Neenah/Menasha Buyers'
Guide (33539) ....(Non-paid) 23,030

Ashland
Evergreen Country
Shopper (33555) ....(Non-paid) 14,760

Beldenville
Shopper (33571) ....(Paid) 62
(Free) 60,727

Beloit
Stateline Shopping News (33577) .....(Wed.) 34,585
(Sun.) 51,868

Berlin
Berlin/Ripon Buyers'
Guide (33581) ....(Free) ‡22,400

Brillion
Lake to Lake Shopper (33600) ....(Free) ‡8,373

Burlington
Wisconsin Hi-Liter (33610) ....(Free) 33,450
(Paid) 10

Cedarburg
The Sunday Post-Ozaukee
County (33620) ....(Combined) 28,648

Chilton
Calumet County Shopper (33624) .....(Free) ‡20,400

Chippewa Falls
Stoplight (33629) ....(Controlled) 13,538
Your Family Shopper (33630) ......(Non-paid) 30,699

Clintonville
Clintonville Shopper's
Guide (33636) ....(Free) 13,948

Columbus
Shopping Reminder (33643) ....(Non-paid) 8,926

Delavan
Walworth County Shopper Advertiser & Shopper
Sunday (33654) ....(Wed.) 37,827
(Sun.) 37,959

Eagle River
North Woods Trader (33662) ......(Free) ‡20,300

Edgerton
Advertiser (33685) ....(Free) ‡2,450

Ettrick
Arrow Shopper (33691) ....(Free) ‡25,350

Frederic
Indianhead Advertiser (33726) ....(Free) ‡20,188
Tri-County North
Advertiser (33728) ....(Free) ‡16,513
Tri-County South Advisor (33729) ....(Free) ‡19,836
Wild Rivers Advertiser -
North (33730) ....(Free) ‡18,305
Wild Rivers Advertiser -
South (33731) ....(Free) ‡20,551

Greenfield
Greenfield/Greendale
Enterprise (33765) ....(Free) ‡84,490

Hales Corners
Franklin/Hales Corners
Enterprise (33768) ....(Free) ‡84,490

Hartland
Lake County Buyer's
Guide (33781) ....(Free) 17,902

Hayward
Four Seasons
Shopper (33784) ....(Non-paid) ♦9,286

Hudson
Hot Sheet Shopper TMC (33794) .....(Free) ‡19,000

Janesville
The Jotter (33860) ....(Free) 28,864

Jefferson
Advertiser - North and South Edition (33867) 234
(Free) 42,125
Jefferson County
Advertiser (33868) ....(Non-paid) 32,324

Kenosha
Kenosha Bulletin (33871) ....(Free) ‡70,000

Kiel
Tempo (33881) ....(Free) ‡20,000

La Crosse
Buyers Express (33884) ....(Free) ‡20,000

Lodi
Prairie/Valley Shopping
News (33912) ....(Free) ‡12,000

Markesan
Monday Marketeer (34024) ....(Free) ‡19,000

Marshfield
Marshfield Buyers'
Guide (34026) ....(Combined) 22,086

Menomonie
Dunn County Reminder (34039) ......(Free) ‡24,850

Milwaukee
Ads Express (34055) ....(Free) ‡189,600

Monroe
Monroe Area Shopping
News (34150) ....(Non-paid) 15,945

Mukwonago
KMA Chief II (34157) ....(Free) ‡9,600
Times-Record/Bulletin (34159) ....(Free) ‡13,050

Neillsville
Black River County
Shopper (34162) ....(Free) 17,300

New Berlin
New Berlin Enterprise (34181) ....(Free) ‡84,490

New London
New London Buyers'
Guide (34191) ....(Combined) 13,859

Oconomowoc
Lake Area Sunday
Post (34202) ....(Combined) 32,313

Oconto Falls
The Bonus Paper (34207) ....(Free) ‡17,658

Oregon
Great Dane Shopping
News (34216) ....(Free) ‡26,750

Oshkosh
Oshkosh Buyers'
Guide (34227) ....(Combined) 25,236

Oxford
Rural Rambler (34231) ....‡14,926

Phillips
The Extra Shopper (34238) ......(Non-paid) ♦11,150

Platteville
Grant, Iowa, Lafayette Shopping
News (34241) ....(Paid) 102
(Free) 37,158

Portage
Cent Saver Buyer's
Guide (34252) ....(Non-paid) 12,460
Cent Saver Extra (34253) ....(Non-paid) 16,500
Cent Saver Reminder (34254) ....(Non-paid) 22,065
Shopper Stopper (34260) ....(Paid) 27
(Free) 125,790

Prairie du Chien
Courier-Press (34267) ....(Non-paid) 12,000
(Paid) 3,950
Wisconsin-Iowa Shopping News (34268) ....(Paid) 54
(Non-paid) 19,564

Racine
Pennysaver (34274) ....(Free) ‡59,321

Rhinelander
Rhinelander/Hodag Buyers'
Guide (34284) ....(Combined) 19,438

Rice Lake
Early Bird (34293) ....(Free) ‡34,400

Richland Center
Richland Center Shopping
News (34297) ....(Free) ‡12,828

Seymour
Seymour Buyers' Guide and Times
Press (34315) ....(Combined) 12,100

Shawano
The Shawano Shopper (34318) ....(Non-paid) 23,112

Sheboygan
Shoreline Chronicle (34322) ....(Non-paid) 18,379

Sister Bay
Door Reminder (34329) ....(Non-paid) 15,544

Sparta
Foxxy Shopper (34330) ....(Free) 15,284

Spooner
The Evergreen Shopping
Guide (34336) ....(Non-paid) ♦18,056

Spring Valley
Valley Values Shopper (34341) ....(Free) 4,800

Stevens Point
Stevens Point Buyers'
Guide (34344) ....(Combined) 23,754

Sun Prairie
The Hometown Advertiser (34357) ....(Free) 32,473

Superior
Superior Manney Shopper (34361) ....(Free) ‡20,933

Waukesha
This Week Publications (34412) ....(Free) 242,182

Waupaca
Waupaca Buyers'
Guide (34420) ....(Combined) 16,062

Waupun
Action Advertiser (34425) ....(Wed.) 34,853
(Sun.) 46,659
Action Shopper (34426) ....(Wed.) 15,414

Wausau
Wausau Buyers'
Guide (34430) ....(Combined) 40,624

West Bend
The Sunday Post (Washington
County) (34446) ....(Free) ‡48,100

Whitehall
Tri-County Tab (34453) ....(Free) ‡14,683

Whitewater
Good Morning
Advertiser (34456) ....(Combined) 18,332

Wisconsin Rapids
Wisconsin Rapids Buyers'
Guide (34464) ....(Combined) 22,711

Wittenberg
Shopping News Northerner (34470)

WYOMING
Cheyenne
Trader's Shopper's Guide (34496) ....(Free) ‡25,000

Cody
Buyer's Guide (34512) ....(Free) ‡21,000

Evanston
Uinta County Herald Shoppers
Guide (34522) ....(Free) ‡7,700

Gillette
The Gillette Area
Advertiser (34526) ....(Free) ‡12,500

Riverton
The ADvertiser (34575) ....(Free) 17,500

ALBERTA, CANADA
Innisfail
Innisfail Booster (34786) ....(Free) ‡9,671

Leduc
Leduc Representative (34792) ....(Free) ‡13,704

Lethbridge
The Lethbridge Shopper (34796) ......(Free) ‡32,500

Medicine Hat
The Medicine Hat Shopper (34811) ....(Free) 23,688

Stettler
The Stettler Independent (34855) ....‡3,701

Vegreville
The Vegreville News Advertiser (34864)

BRITISH COLUMBIA, CANADA
Kaslo
Cast Logan/Slocan Valley
Pennywise (34984) ....(Free) 6,156
Kaslo Pennywise (34985) ....(Free) 3,093
Nelson Pennywise (34986) ....(Free) 4,560
Trail/Beaver Valley/Salmo
Pennywise (34987) ....(Free) 8655

Kitimat
Weekend Advertiser (34999) ....(Free) ‡15,800

New Westminster
Vancouver Buy and Sell
Press (35032) ....(Thurs.) 41,052

Williams Lake
The Tribune Weekender (35244) ....(Non-paid) 9,800

NOVA SCOTIA, CANADA
Truro
Colchester Sunday (35615) ....(Free) 20,000

ONTARIO, CANADA
Bayside
Bayside South/Oakland Gardens
Pennysaver (35668) ....(Free) ‡13,395
Bayside West Pennysaver (35669) ....(Free) ‡12,439

Beeton
Woodbridge Advertiser (35674) ....‡6,200

Belleville
Shopper's Market (35679) ....(Free) ‡50,000

Brampton
Brampton Pennysaver (35699) ....(Free) 55,447
Mississauga Pennysaver (35701) ......(Free) ‡65,300
Rexdale Pennysaver (35702) ....(Free) 15,780

Circulation: ★ = ABC; △ = BPA; ♦ = CAC; ● = CCAB; ▢ = VAC; ⊕ = PO Statement; ‡ = Publisher's Report; Boldface figures = sworn; Light figures = estimated.

2963

Newspapers

Circ.

Circ.

Circ.

ONTARIO, CANADA (continued)

Brantford
Brantford Pennysaver **(35704)** ....(Free) 42,600

Cornwall
Smart Shoppers **(35754)** ....(Free) ‡10,000

Dunnville
Dunnville Shoppers Guide **(35796)**

Elliot Lake
The Marketplace **(35801)** ....(Controlled) 8,000

Fergus
The Wellington Advertiser **(35830)** .....(Free) 32,000

Floral Park
Floral Park Bellerose North
  Pennysaver **(35833)** ....(Free) ‡10,665
Floral Park Bellerose South
  Pennysaver **(35834)** ....(Free) ‡10,155

Flushing
East Flushing Pennysaver **(35835)** ....(Free) ‡15,195
Flushing Pennysaver **(35836)** ....(Free) ‡14,280
North Flushing
  Pennysaver **(35837)** ....(Free) ‡11,750

Garden City
Garden City Pennysaver **(35845)** ....(Free) ‡8,272

Guelph
Guelph Pennysaver **(35865)** ....(Free) ‡42,900

Herricks
Herricks-Searingtown
  Pennysaver **(35913)** ....(Free) ‡12,040

Kitchener
Kitchener-Waterloo Pennysaver **(35960)** 90,000
KW Real Estate News **(35962)** ....(Free) 10,000

Malton
Malton Pennysaver **(36007)** ....(Free) 8,360

Mineola
Mineola Pennysaver **(36052)** ....(Free) ‡11,898

New Hyde Park
New Hyde Park
  Pennysaver **(36104)** ....(Free) ‡12,204

Niagara Falls
Niagara Shopping News **(36109)** ......(Free) ‡30,000

Oakville
Milton Shopping News **(36146)** ....(Free) 17,048
Oakville Shopping News **(36148)** ....(Free) **37,000**

Ontario
Bayside-North Pennysaver **(36158)** ....(Free) ‡16,255

Petrolia
Petrolia Topic **(36327)** ....(Paid) 3,500

St. Thomas
Elgin County Market **(36361)** ....(Free) ‡29,300

Stirling
Stirling News-Argus **(36403)** ....(Free) ‡5,080
                                          (Paid) 9

Whitestone
Whitestone Pennysaver **(36873)** ....(Free) ‡12,375

Woodstock
Oxford Shopping News **(36908)** ....(Free) ‡27,580

QUEBEC, CANADA
Chateauguay
L'Information Regionale **(36962)** ....(Free) ‡27,105

Montreal
Journal do Emigrante **(37140)** ....(Free) 10,000

SASKATCHEWAN, CANADA
Estevan
Trader Express **(37466)** ....(Free) 11,484

Kindersley
West-Central Crossroads **(37483)** .....(Free) ⊕**14,300**

North Battleford
Regional
  Optimist/Advertiser-Post **(37509)** ....(Free) ‡19,605

Swift Current
The Southwest Booster **(37575)** ....(Free) 19,100

Tisdale
The Parkland Review **(37579)** ....(Free) ‡15,769

Weyburn
Booster **(37589)** ....(Free) ‡12,508

2964

Numbers cited after listings are entry numbers rather than page numbers.

Radio Station Formats

Citations in this index are grouped by industry-defined formats (included in the Index to Subject Terms). Within subject categories, entries appear geographically by states/provinces and alphabetically within cities. Citations include the station call letters and frequencies; references are to entry numbers, which appear in parentheses.

ADULT ALBUM ALTERNATIVE

ALASKA
Juneau
KSUP-FM - 106.3 **(602)**

ARIZONA
Flagstaff
KFLX-FM - 105.1; 97.1 **(699)**

ARKANSAS
Barling
KERX-FM - 95.3 **(1039)**

Camden
KCAC-FM - 89.5 **(1072)**

CALIFORNIA
Fort Bragg
KOZT-FM - 95.3 **(1923)**

Fresno
KFSR-FM - 90.7 **(1967)**

San Francisco
KLLC-FM - 97.3 **(3490)**

San Marcos
KKSM-AM - 1320 **(3579)**

COLORADO
Aspen
KSPN-FM - 103.1, 97.3, and 98.3 **(4143)**

Avon
KTUN-FM - 101.5 **(4151)**

Boulder
KBCO-FM - 97.3 **(4196)**

Frisco
KYSL-FM - 93.9 **(4457)**

Steamboat Springs
KFMU-FM - 104.1, 104.9, and 105.5 **(4638)**

CONNECTICUT
Sharon
WKZE-FM - 98.1 **(5116)**

DELAWARE
Selbyville
WOCM-FM - 98.1 **(5286)**

FLORIDA
Estero
WJBX-FM - 99.3 **(6065)**

INDIANA
Gary
WGVE-FM - 88.7 **(10019)**

KENTUCKY
Highland Heights
WNKU-FM - 89.7 **(12127)**

Lexington
WUKY-FM - 91.3 **(12197)**

Louisville
WFPK-FM - 91.9 **(12250)**

Paducah
WPAD-AM - 1560 **(12347)**

LOUISIANA
Deridder
KROK-FM - 92.1 **(12566)**

MAINE
Portland
WCLZ-FM - 98.9 **(13022)**

MARYLAND
Cumberland
WTBO-AM - 1450 **(13480)**

MASSACHUSETTS
Holyoke
WRNX-FM - 100.9 FM **(14243)**

MICHIGAN
Detroit
WDVD-FM - 96.3 **(14961)**

Novi
WOVI-FM - 89.5 **(15412)**

MISSOURI
Columbia
KBXR-FM - 102.3 **(17014)**

Warrensburg
KTBG-FM - 90.9 **(17673)**

NEBRASKA
Omaha
KCTY-FM - 106.9 **(18214)**

NEW HAMPSHIRE
Conway
WMWV-FM - 93.5 **(18486)**

NEW JERSEY
Upper Montclair
WMSC-FM - 90.3 **(19695)**

NEW MEXICO
Albuquerque
KTZO-FM - 103.3 **(19814)**

Taos
KTAO-FM - 101.9 **(19966)**

NORTH CAROLINA
Charlotte
WGWG-FM - 88.3 **(23771)**

Manteo
WVOD-FM - 99.1 **(24054)**

Wilkesboro
WSIF-FM - 90.9 **(24289)**

OHIO
Akron
WAPS-FM - 91.3 **(24595)**

OKLAHOMA
Stillwater
KSPI-FM - 93.7 **(26086)**

TENNESSEE
Nashville
WRLG-FM - 94.1 **(29528)**

TEXAS
Austin
KGSR-FM - 107.1 **(29863)**

Dallas
KERA-FM - 90.1 **(30203)**

Johnson City
KFAN-FM - 107.9 **(30627)**

UTAH
Park City
KPCW-FM - 91.9 **(31388)**

VERMONT
Montpelier
WNCS-FM - 104.7 **(31567)**

Northfield
WNUB-FM - 88.3 **(31577)**

Wilmington
WMTT-FM - 100.7 **(31621)**

VIRGINIA
Norfolk
WKOC-FM - 93.7 **(32302)**

WASHINGTON
Seattle
KMTT-FM - 103.7 **(33062)**

WISCONSIN
Burlington
WBSD-FM - 89.1 **(33611)**

Clintonville
WFCL-AM - 1380 **(33638)**

Milwaukee
WUWM-FM - 89.7 **(34137)**

WYOMING
Laramie
KUWR-FM - 91.9 **(34557)**

ONTARIO, CANADA
Sudbury
CJRQ-FM - 92.7 **(36426)**

Circulation: ★ = ABC; △ = BPA; ◆ = CAC; ● = CCAB; ❑ = VAC; ⊕ = PO Statement; ‡ = Publisher's Report; Boldface figures = sworn; Light figures = estimated.

2965

ADULT CONTEMPORARY

ALABAMA
Anniston
WDNG-AM - 1450　**(19)**

Atmore
WYDH-FM - 105.9　**(37)**

Birmingham
WMJJ-FM - 96.5　**(124)**
WYSF-FM - 94.5　**(132)**

Centre
WAGC-AM - 1560　**(149)**

Dadeville
WZLM-FM - 97.3　**(168)**

Enterprise
WKMX-FM - 106.7　**(203)**

Eufaula
WULA-FM - 92.7　**(207)**

Florence
WQLT-FM - 107.3　**(224)**

Gulf Shores
WCSN-FM - 105.7　**(253)**

Guntersville
WGSV-AM - 1270　**(255)**

Huntsville
WAHR-FM - 99.1　**(280)**

Jackson
WHOD-FM - 94.5　**(293)**

Mobile
WMXC-FM - 99.9　**(346)**

Montgomery
WBAM-FM - 98.9　**(384)**

Ozark
WRJM-FM - 93.7　**(422)**

Scottsboro
WMXN-AM - 98.3　**(449)**

Sylacauga
WAWV-FM - 98.3　**(462)**

Tallassee
WACQ-FM - 99.9　**(469)**

Tuscaloosa
WTBC-AM - 1230　**(499)**

ALASKA
Anchorage
KMXS-FM - 103.1　**(545)**

Bethel
KYUK-AM - 640　**(556)**

Fairbanks
KWLF-FM - 98.1　**(580)**

Homer
KWVV-FM - 105　**(592)**

Juneau
KINY-AM - 800　**(599)**

Kenai
KSRM-AM - 920　**(609)**

Ketchikan
KTKN-AM - 930　**(614)**

Kodiak
KRXX-FM - 101.1　**(619)**

Wasilla
KMBQ-FM - 99.7　**(651)**

ARIZONA
Claypool
KIKO-FM - 106.1　**(675)**

Cottonwood
KYBC-AM - 1600　**(683)**

Flagstaff
KVNA-FM - 97.5　**(705)**

Lake Havasu City
KZUL-FM - 104.5　**(741)**

Page
KXAZ-FM - 93.3　**(760)**

Phoenix
KESZ-FM - 99.9　**(817)**
KKLT-FM - 98.7　**(825)**
KMXP-FM - 96.9　**(827)**
KPHX-AM - 1480　**(833)**
KSUN-AM - 1400　**(838)**

Prescott
KGCB-FM - 90.9　**(851)**

Prescott Valley
KPPV-FM - 106.7　**(857)**

Show Low
KQAZ-FM - 101.7　**(882)**
KVWM-AM - 970　**(883)**
KVWM-FM - 93.5　**(884)**

Sierra Vista
KZMK-FM - 100.9　**(893)**

Tucson
KMXZ-FM - 94.9　**(986)**
KZPT-FM - 104.1　**(1003)**

ARKANSAS
Arkadelphia
KDEL-FM - 100.9　**(1031)**

Batesville
KZLE-FM - 93.1　**(1044)**

Brinkley
KBRI-AM - 1570　**(1064)**

Conway
KCON-AM - 1230　**(1085)**

El Dorado
KLBQ-FM - 99.3　**(1110)**

Harrison
KHOZ-AM - 900　**(1168)**

Hot Springs
KYDL-FM - 96.7　**(1189)**

Jonesboro
KOCY-FM - 105.3　**(1201)**

Magnolia
KVMA-FM - 107.9　**(1260)**

Mountain Home
KKTZ-FM - 93.5　**(1287)**

North Little Rock
KMZX-FM - 106.3　**(1303)**

Paragould
KDRS-FM - 107.1　**(1310)**

Pocahontas
KPOC-FM - 103.9　**(1319)**

CALIFORNIA
Bakersfield
KLLY-FM - 95.3　**(1468)**

Blythe
KJMB-FM - 100.3　**(1589)**

Burbank
KYSR-FM - 98.7　**(1630)**

Calexico
KQVO-FM - 97.7　**(1638)**

Chico
KMXI-FM - 95.1　**(1703)**

Chula Vista
XLTN-FM - 104.5　**(1718)**

El Centro
KGBA-FM - 100.1　**(1854)**
KXO-FM - 107.5　**(1858)**

Eureka
KFMI-FM - 96.3　**(1900)**

Fort Bragg
KSAY-FM - 98.5　**(1924)**

Fullerton
KBPK-FM - 90.1　**(1991)**

Jackson
KNGT-FM - 94.3　**(2096)**

Joshua Tree
KCDZ-FM - 107.7　**(2097)**

King City
KRKC-FM - 102.1　**(2105)**

La Verne
KULV-AM - 550　**(2129)**

Lancaster
KBET-AM - 1220　**(2149)**

Los Angeles
KOST-FM - 103.5　**(2465)**

Merced
KIBG-FM - 106.3　**(2532)**

Modesto
KJSN-FM - 102.3　**(2568)**

Monterey
KWAV-FM - 96.9　**(2588)**

Napa
KVYN-FM - 99.3　**(2613)**

Oakhurst
KAAT-FM - 103.1 & translators 104.3　**(2660)**

Palm Desert
KEZN-FM - 103.1　**(2750)**

Palm Springs
KPSI-FM - 100.5　**(2780)**

Palmdale
KGMX-FM - 106.3　**(2785)**

Pleasanton
KKIQ-FM - 101.7　**(2857)**

Redding
KNNN-FM - 99.3　**(2891)**

Reseda
KOJJ-FM - 100.5　**(2918)**

Sacramento
KGBY-FM - 92.5　**(3031)**
KYMX-FM - 96.1　**(3059)**

Salinas
KRAY-FM - 103.5　**(3074)**

San Diego
KFMB-FM - 100.7　**(3299)**
KMCG-FM - 95.7　**(3304)**
KOCL-FM - 94.1　**(3306)**
KYXY-FM - 96.5　**(3317)**

San Francisco
KABL-AM - 960　**(3468)**
KBLX-FM - 102.9　**(3471)**
KISQ-FM - 98.1　**(3487)**
KKSF-FM - 103.7　**(3489)**
KLLC-FM - 97.3　**(3490)**
KOIT-AM - 1260　**(3494)**
KOIT-FM - 96.5　**(3495)**

San Jose
KARA-FM - 105.7　**(3545)**
KBAY-FM - 94.5　**(3547)**

San Luis Obispo
KKJL-AM - 1400　**(3571)**

Santa Barbara
KSBL-FM - 101.7　**(3667)**

Santa Maria
KBOX-FM - 104.1　**(3697)**

Santa Paula
KKZZ-AM - 1400　**(3723)**

Santa Rosa
KZST-FM - 100.1　**(3743)**

Solvang
KSYV-FM - 96.7　**(3772)**

Temecula
KATY-FM - 101.3　**(3844)**

Ukiah
KWNE-FM - 94.5　**(3971)**

Vacaville
KUIC-FM - 95.3　**(3975)**

Victorville
KZXY-FM - 102.3　**(4039)**

Visalia
KSEQ-FM - 97.1　**(4043)**

Yuba City
KUBA-AM - 1600　**(4124)**
KXCL-FM - 103.9　**(4125)**

Numbers cited in bold after listings are entry numbers rather than page numbers.

COLORADO
Alamosa
KALQ-FM - 93.5 **(4133)**

Colorado Springs
KKLI-FM - 106.3 **(4272)**
KRDO-FM - 95.1 **(4277)**
KRMH-FM - 93.5 **(4280)**

Cortez
KRTZ-FM - 98.7 **(4292)**

Denver
KALC-FM - 105.9 **(4369)**
KOSI-FM - 101.1 **(4386)**

Durango
KIQX-FM - 101.3 **(4403)**

Fort Morgan
KBRU-FM - 101.7 **(4447)**
KPRB-FM - 106.3 **(4449)**

Grand Junction
KMGJ-FM - 93.1 **(4490)**

Gunnison
KPKE-AM 1490 1KW - 98.3 **(4512)**

Lamar
KSNZ-FM - 93.3 **(4540)**

Longmont
KCDC-FM - 90.7 **(4563)**

Pagosa Springs
KWUF-FM - 106.3 **(4592)**

Pueblo
KVUU-FM - 99.9 **(4611)**

Salida
KVRH-FM - 92.3 **(4621)**
KVRH-FM - 92.3 **(4622)**

Sterling
KPMX-FM - 105.7 **(4641)**

Trinidad
KCRT-FM - 92.5 **(4650)**

CONNECTICUT
Bridgeport
WEBE-FM - 107.9 **(4717)**
WICC-AM - 600 **(4719)**

Danbury
WDAQ-FM - 98.3 **(4765)**

Farmington
WRCH-FM - 100.5 **(4866)**
WZMX-FM - 93.7 **(4867)**

Lakeville
WQQQ-FM - 103.3 **(4922)**

Litchfield
WZBG-FM - 97.3 **(4925)**

Milford
WEZN-FM - 99.9 **(4959)**

Putnam
WINY-AM - 1350 **(5095)**

Sharon
WKZE-AM - 1020 **(5115)**

Waterbury
WWCO-AM - 1240 **(5198)**

Willimantic
WILI-AM - 1400 **(5222)**
WILI-FM - 98.3 **(5223)**

DELAWARE
Milford
WAFL-FM - 97.7 **(5262)**

Wilmington
WJBR-FM - 99.5 **(5300)**
WSTW-FM - 93.7 **(5303)**

DISTRICT OF COLUMBIA
Washington
WASH-FM - 97.1 **(5878)**
WHUR-FM - 96.3 **(5884)**
WKYS-FM - 93.9 **(5888)**
WRQX-FM - 107.3 **(5894)**

FLORIDA
Belle Glade
WBGF-FM - 93.5 **(5921)**

Big Pine Key
WWUS-FM - 104.1 **(5924)**

Fort Myers
WINK-FM - 96.9 **(6107)**
WTLT-FM - 93.5 **(6114)**

Gainesville
WKTK-FM - 98.5 **(6163)**

Gulf Breeze
WMEZ-FM - 94.1 **(6183)**

Hollywood
WFLC-FM - 97.3 **(6201)**

Homosassa
WXCV-FM - 95.3 **(6207)**

Jacksonville
WEJZ-FM - 96.1 **(6221)**
WMXQ-FM - 102.9 **(6233)**
WSOL-FM - 101.5 **(6240)**

Key West
WKEY-FM - 93.5 **(6257)**

Lake City
WNFB-FM - 94.3 **(6273)**

Marathon
WAVK-FM - 105.5 **(6323)**

Melbourne
WLRQ-FM - 99.3 **(6338)**

Miami
WAXY-AM - 709 **(6396)**
WLYF-FM - 101.5 **(6405)**
WQAM-AM - 560 **(6413)**

Miramar
WLVE-FM - 93.9 **(6431)**
WPLL-FM - 103.5 **(6432)**

Naples
WSGL-FM - 103.1 **(6454)**

Ocala
WMFQ-FM - 92.9 **(6475)**

Orlando
WCFB-FM - 94.5 **(6514)**
WMMO-FM - 98.9 **(6523)**
WOMX-FM - 105.1 **(6525)**

St. Augustine
WSOS-FM - 94.1 **(6621)**

St. Petersburg
WHPT-FM - 102.5 **(6638)**
WWRM-FM - 94.9 **(6644)**

Sanford
WSDO-AM - 1400 **(6648)**

Sebring
WWLL-FM - 105.7 **(6681)**

Tallahassee
WBZE-FM - 98.9 **(6743)**

Tampa
WMTX-FM - 100.7 **(6798)**
WSSR-FM - 95.7 **(6803)**

Vero Beach
WGYL-FM - 93.7 **(6837)**

West Palm Beach
WEAT-FM - 104.3 **(6851)**
WMBX-FM - 102.3 **(6855)**

Winter Haven
WSIR-AM - 1490 **(6876)**

GEORGIA
Albany
WQVE-FM - 105.5 **(6913)**

Americus
WDEC-FM - 94.7 **(6924)**

Atlanta
WSB-FM - 98.5 **(7086)**

Brunswick
WWSN-FM - 103.3 **(7144)**

Cedartown
WGAA-AM - 1340 **(7166)**

Clayton
WRBN-FM - 104.1 **(7175)**

Columbus
WCGQ-FM - 107.3 **(7186)**
WGSY-FM - 100.1 **(7189)**

Dalton
WYYU-FM - 104.5 **(7226)**

Dublin
WKKZ-FM - 92.7 **(7252)**

Grovetown
WJDS-FM - 620 **(7318)**

Hinesville
WCGN /Fm - 106.3 **(7334)**

Jackson
WJGA-FM - 92.1 **(7340)**

Lagrange
WMGP-FM - 98.1 **(7363)**
WTRP-AM - 620 **(7365)**

Macon
WPEZ-FM - 93.7 **(7401)**

McDonough
WKKP-AM - 1410 **(7430)**

Peachtree City
WMKJ-FM - 96.7 **(7480)**

Rome
WKCX-FM - 97.7 **(7504)**

Savannah
WAEV-FM - 97.3 **(7542)**

Statesboro
WMCD-FM - 100.1 **(7566)**

Tifton
WBHB-AM - 1240 **(7600)**
WJYF-FM - 95.3 **(7601)**

Valdosta
WQPW-FM - 95.7 **(7623)**
WSTI-FM - 105.3 **(7624)**

Vidalia
WTCQ-FM - 97.7 **(7631)**

Washington
WXKT-FM - 100.1 **(7642)**

HAWAII
Hilo
KKBG-FM - 97.9 **(7676)**
KWXX-FM - 94.7 **(7678)**

Honolulu
KISA-AM - 1540 **(7742)**
KRTR-FM - 96.3 **(7750)**
KSSK-AM - 590 **(7751)**
KSSK-FM - 92.3 **(7752)**

Kahului
KMVI-AM - 550 **(7760)**
KNUI-AM - 900 **(7761)**
KNUI-FM - 99.9 **(7762)**

Lihue
KFMN-FM - 96.9 **(7781)**

IDAHO
Boise
KBOI-AM - 670 **(7817)**
KCIX-FM - 105.9 **(7821)**
KXLT-FM - 107.9 **(7834)**
KZMG-FM - 93.1 **(7835)**

Jerome
KMVX-FM - 102.9 **(7884)**

Ketchum
KSKI-FM - 103.7 **(7889)**

Lewiston
KATW-FM - 101.5 **(7893)**

McCall
KMCL-FM - 101.1 **(7907)**

Moscow
KRPL-AM - 1400 **(7923)**

Orofino
KLER-FM - 95.3 **(7940)**

Rexburg
KADQ-FM - 94.3 **(7965)**

Radio Station Formats

ADULT CONTEMPORARY (continued)

Salmon
KSRA-AM - 92.7 **(7975)**

ILLINOIS
Bloomington
WBNQ-FM - 101.5 **(8082)**

Canton
WBYS-FM - 1560 **(8112)**

Champaign
WHMS-FM - 97.5 **(8228)**
WLRW-FM - 94.5 **(8231)**

Chicago
WEJM-FM - 106.3 **(8620)**
WLIT-FM - 93.9 **(8637)**
WNND-FM - 100.3 **(8646)**
WVAZ-FM - 102.7 **(8657)**

Crest Hill
WJTW-FM - 93.5 **(8691)**

Crystal Lake
WAIT-AM - 850 **(8697)**
WZSR-FM - 105.5 **(8698)**

Danville
WDNL-FM - 102.1 **(8706)**
WITY-AM - 980 **(8708)**

Decatur
WSOY-FM - 102.9 **(8721)**

DeKalb
WDKB-FM - 94.9 **(8742)**

Du Quoin
WDQN-AM - 1580 **(8800)**

Effingham
WCBH-FM - 104.3 **(8818)**

Fairfield
WFIW-FM - 104.9 **(8882)**

Freeport
WFRL-AM - 1570 **(8901)**

Galva
WGEN-AM - 1500 **(8912)**

Harrisburg
WEBQ-FM - 102.3 **(8974)**

Jacksonville
WEAI-FM - 107.1 **(9025)**
WLDS-AM - 1180 **(9028)**

Kankakee
WKAN-AM - 1320 **(9041)**

La Salle
WAJK-FM - 99.3 **(9057)**

Lawrenceville
WAKO-AM - 910 **(9070)**
WAKO-FM - 103.1 **(9071)**

Litchfield
WAOX-FM - 105.3 **(9114)**

Mattoon
WLBH-FM - 96.9 **(9161)**

Metropolis
WRIK-FM - 98.3 **(9182)**

Monmouth
WMOI-FM - 97.7 **(9220)**

Mount Zion
WXFM-FM - 99.3 **(9255)**

Nashville
WNSV-FM - 104.7 **(9278)**

Newton
WIKK-FM - 103.5 **(9285)**

Paxton
WPXN-FM - 104.9 **(9412)**

Peoria
WQEZ-FM - 94.3 **(9438)**

Plano
WSPY-FM - 107.1 **(9459)**

Pontiac
WJEZ-FM - 93.7 **(9466)**

Quincy
KGRC-FM - 92.9 **(9475)**

Rockford
WGFB-FM - 103.1 **(9536)**

Rushville
WKXQ-FM - 92.5 **(9559)**

Salem
WJBD-AM - 1350 **(9578)**
WJBD-FM - 100.1 **(9579)**

Springfield
WNNS-FM - 98.7 **(9653)**
WVEM-FM - 101.9 **(9659)**

Sterling
WSSQ-FM - 94.3 **(9665)**

Urbana
WBCP-AM - 1580 **(9721)**

Watseka
WGFA-FM - 94.1 **(9741)**

INDIANA
Anderson
WQME-FM - 98.7 FM **(9785)**

Bloomington
WBWB-FM - 96.7 **(9856)**

Bluffton
WNUY-FM - 100.1 **(9865)**

Chesterton
WDSO-FM - 88.3 **(9888)**

Columbus
WRZQ-FM - 107.3 **(9898)**
WWWY-FM - 104.9 **(9899)**

Crawfordsville
WIMC-FM - 103.9 **(9912)**

Daleville
WHTI-FM - 96.7 **(9919)**

Evansville
WDKS-FM - 106.1 **(9938)**
WIKY-FM - 104.1 **(9944)**

Fort Wayne
WAJI-FM - 95.1 **(9976)**
WGL-FM - 102 **(9987)**

Frankfort
WSHW-FM - 99.7 **(10003)**

Goshen
WKAM-AM - 1460 **(10030)**

Hammond
WWJY-FM - 103.9 **(10058)**

Indianapolis
WXXP-FM - 97.9 **(10217)**

Jasper
WITZ-AM - 990 **(10221)**
WITZ-FM - 104.7 **(10222)**

Kokomo
WZWZ-FM - 92.5 **(10245)**

Logansport
WLHM-FM - 102.3 **(10276)**

Madison
WORX-FM - 96.7 **(10285)**

Marion
WMRI-FM - 106.9 **(10292)**

Michigan City
WEFM-FM - 95.9 **(10306)**

Muncie
WLBC-FM - 104.1 **(10333)**

Paoli
WUME-FM - 95.3 **(10391)**

Portland
WPGW-AM - 1440 **(10405)**

Richmond
WFMG-FM - 101.3 **(10423)**

Rochester
WROI-FM - 92.1 **(10433)**

Seymour
WZZB-AM - 1390 **(10451)**

South Bend
WNSN-FM - 101.5 **(10465)**

Tell City
WTCJ-AM - 1230 **(10483)**

Terre Haute
WLEZ-FM - 102.7 **(10497)**

Valparaiso
WNWI-AM - 1080 **(10514)**

Vincennes
WZDM-FM - 92.1 **(10527)**

Washington
WAMW-FM - 107.9 **(10542)**

IOWA
Algona
KLGA-AM - 1600 **(10582)**
KLGA-FM - 92.7 **(10583)**

Burlington
KBUR-AM - 1490 **(10641)**
KGRS-FM - 107.3 **(10644)**
KKMI-FM - 93.5 **(10645)**

Carroll
KKRL-FM - 93.7 **(10654)**

Cedar Falls
KUNI-FM - 90.9 **(10668)**

Centerville
KCOG-AM - 1400 **(10689)**

Chariton
KELR-FM - 105.3 **(10694)**

Charles City
KCHA-AM - 1580 **(10696)**
KCHA-FM - 95.9 **(10697)**
KCZE-FM - 95.1 **(10698)**

Cresco
KCZQ-FM - 102.3 **(10731)**

Davenport
KMXG-FM - 96.1 **(10744)**

Decorah
KDEC-FM - 100.5 **(10760)**

Denison
KDSN-FM - 107.1 **(10769)**

Des Moines
KLTI-FM - 104.1 **(10827)**
KMXD-FM - 100.3 **(10829)**
KSTZ-FM - 102.5 **(10832)**

Dubuque
KATF-FM - 92.9 **(10847)**
KDTH-AM - 1370 **(10848)**
KLYV-FM - 105.3 **(10852)**

Elkader
KADR-AM - 1400 **(10874)**

Forest City
KIOW-FM - 107.3 **(10892)**

Fort Dodge
KUEL-FM - 92.1 **(10913)**

Grinnell
KGRN-AM - 1410 **(10933)**

Hampton
KLMJ-FM - 104.9 **(10941)**

Independence
KQMG-AM - 1220 **(10962)**
KQMG-FM - 95.3 **(10963)**

Iowa City
KCJJ-AM - 1630 **(10991)**

Iowa Falls
KIFG-FM - 95.3 **(11003)**

Maquoketa
KMAQ-FM - 95.1 **(11057)**

Mason City
KGLO-AM - 1300 **(11075)**

Muscatine
KWPC-AM - 860 **(11106)**

Osage
KWMM-FM - 98.7 **(11132)**

Ottumwa
KTWA-FM - 92.7 **(11145)**

Sioux Center
KSOU-FM - 93.9 **(11211)**

Sioux City
KGLI-FM - 95.5 (11215)
KSFT-FM - 107.1 (11220)

Spencer
KLLT-FM - 104.9 (11235)

Spirit Lake
KUOO-FM - 103.9 (11239)

Storm Lake
KAYL-FM - 101.7 (11248)

Washington
KCII-AM - 106.1 (11287)
KCII-FM - 106.1 (11288)

Waverly
KWAY-FM - 99.3 (11312)

KANSAS
Burlington
KSNP-FM - 95.3 (11371)

Chanute
KKOY-FM - 105.5 (11379)

Clay Center
KCLY-FM - 100.9 (11384)

Concordia
KCKS-FM - 94.9 (11398)

Dodge City
KOLS-FM - 95.5 (11418)

Emporia
KRWV-FM - 99.5 (11434)

Garden City
KKJQ-FM - 97.3 (11453)

Goodland
KKCI-FM - 102.5 (11466)

Hays
KJLS-FM - 103.3 (11486)

Independence
KIND-FM - 102.9 (11512)

Iola
KIKS-FM - 99.3 (11515)

Junction City
KQLA-FM - 103.5 (11523)

Lawrence
KLWN-AM - 1320 (11575)

Manhattan
KBLS-FM - 102.5 (11631)

Norton
KQNK-AM - 106.7 (11679)

Parsons
KLKC-AM - 1540 (11745)
KLKC-FM - 93.5 (11746)

Phillipsburg
KKAN-AM - 1490 (11749)
KQMA-FM - 92.5 (11750)

Russell
KRSL-AM - 990 (11774)

Topeka
KMAJ-FM - 107.7 (11842)

Ulysses
KFXX-FM - 106.7 (11855)

Westwood
KRBZ-FM - 96.5 (11874)

KENTUCKY
Ashland
WCMI-AM - 1340 (11919)

Barbourville
WKKQ-FM - 96.1 (11923)

Bardstown
WOKH-FM - 96.7 (11928)

Bowling Green
WUHU-FM - 107.1 (11962)

Campbellsville
WCKQ-FM - 104.1 (12008)

Corbin
WCTT-FM - 107.3 (12023)

Elizabethtown
WQXE-FM - 98.3 (12049)

Frankfort
WKED-FM - 103.7 (12082)

Grayson
WUGO-FM - 102.3 (12096)

Harlan
WTUK-FM - 105.1 (12108)

Hopkinsville
WHOP-AM - 1230 (12133)

Lexington
WGKS-FM - 96.9 (12184)

Maysville
WFTM-FM - 95.9 (12290)

Middlesboro
WFXY-AM - 1490 (12294)

Owensboro
WVJS-AM - 1420 (12333)

Paducah
WDXR-FM - 94.3 (12344)

Prestonsburg
WQHY-FM - 95.5 (12373)

Richmond
WEKY-AM - 1340 (12386)

Somerset
WWZB-FM - 93.9 (12414)

West Liberty
WQXX-FM - 106.1 (12435)

Whitesburg
WIFX-FM - 94.3 (12440)

LOUISIANA
Alexandria
KKST-FM - 98.7 (12464)
KSYL-AM - 970 (12468)

Baker
WQCK-FM - 92.7 (12480)

Baton Rouge
KRVE-FM - 96.1 (12510)
WBBE-FM - 103.3 (12513)

Lake Charles
KHLA-FM - 99.5 (12645)
KVEE-FM - 107.5 (12649)

Many
KZBL-FM - 100.7 (12673)

Metairie
WLMG-FM - 101.9 (12683)
WLTS-FM - 105.3 (12684)
WMXZ-FM - 95.7 (12685)

Monroe
KNOE-AM - 101.9 (12699)
KNOE-FM - 101.9 (12700)

Moreauville
KLIL-FM - 92.1 (12706)

New Orleans
WBSN-FM - 89.1 (12768)

Shreveport
KSYR-FM - 95.7 (12836)
KVKI-FM - 96.5 (12840)

Winnfield
KVCL-AM - 1270 (12881)

MAINE
Auburn
WMWX-FM - 99.9 (12888)

Augusta
WFAU-AM - 1280 (12899)
WTVL-AM - 1490 (12902)

Bangor
WKSQ-FM - 94.5 (12911)
WPBC-FM - 99.5 (12914)

Caribou
WCXU-FM - 97.7 (12947)
WCXX-FM - 102.3 (12948)

Dover Foxcroft
WDME-FM - 103.1 (12953)

Farmington
WKTJ-FM - 99.3 (12962)

Houlton
WHOU-FM - 100.1 (12972)

Presque Isle
WQHR-FM - 96.1 (13041)

South Portland
WMGX-FM - 93.1 (13055)

MARYLAND
Annapolis
WNAV-AM - 1430 (13101)

Baltimore
WTMD-FM - 89.7 (13285)
WWMX-FM - 106.5 (13288)

Chestertown
WCTR-AM - 1530 (13406)

Cumberland
WCBC-AM - 1270 (13476)
WKGO-FM - 106.1 (13477)

Easton
WCEI-FM - 96.7 (13490)

Frostburg
WLIC-FM - 97.1 (13530)

Hunt Valley
WZBA-FM - 100.7 (13584)

La Plata
WSMD-AM - 1560 (13595)

Laurel
WILC-AM-VIVA900 - 900 (13614)

Middletown
WAFY-FM - 103.1 (13629)

Mountain Lake Park
WKHJ-FM - 104.5 (13633)

Salisbury
WDIH-FM - 90.3 (13714)
WQHQ-FM - 104.7 (13718)

Worton
WKHS-FM - 90.5 (13784)

MASSACHUSETTS
Beverly
WNSH-AM - 1570 (13844)

Boston
WAAF-AM - 1440 (13974)

Cambridge
WJIB-AM - 740 (14115)

Fitchburg
WEIM-AM - 1280 (14185)

Great Barrington
WSBS-AM - 860 (14218)

Hamilton
WGAW-AM - 1340 (14226)

Hyannis
WOCN-FM - 103.9 (14252)
WQRC-FM - 99.9 (14254)

Marshfield
WATD-FM - 95.9 (14310)

Milford
WMRC-AM - 1490 (14333)

North Adams
WNAW-AM - 1230 (14421)

Orange
WCAT-FM - 99.9 (14453)

Paxton
WSRS-FM - 96.1 (14459)

Pittsfield
WBRK-AM - 1340 (14475)
WUPE-FM - 95.9 (14478)

Roxbury
WILD-AM - 1090 (14510)

Salem
WESX-AM - 1230 (14516)

Springfield
WAIC-FM - 91.9 (14555)
WMAS-FM - 94.7 (14560)

ADULT CONTEMPORARY (continued)

West Yarmouth
WCOD-FM - 106.1 (14628)
WTWV-FM - 101.1 (14633)

Worcester
WXLO-FM - 104.5 (14702)

MICHIGAN
Adrian
WLEN-FM - 103.9 (14712)

Alpena
WHSB-FM - 107.7 (14741)

Ann Arbor
WQKL-FM - 107.1 (14779)

Bad Axe
WLEW-FM - 102.1 (14789)

Battle Creek
WBXX-FM - 95.3 (14795)
WBXX-FM - 95.3 (14796)

Benton Harbor
WHFB-FM - 99.9 (14811)

Big Rapids
WBRN-FM - 100.9 (14821)

Bingham Farms
CIDR-FM - 93.9 (14822)

Cadillac
WLXV-FM - 96.7 (14849)

Caro
WIDL-FM - 92.1 (14859)

Coldwater
WTVB-AM - 1590 (14888)

Detroit
WMXD-FM - 92.3 (14973)

Dowagiac
WDOW-FM - 92.1 (14979)

Farmington Hills
WNIC-FM - 100.3 (15025)

Flint
WCRZ-FM - 107.9 (15039)

Frankfort
WBNZ-FM - 99.3 (15054)

Grand Blanc
WSNL-AM - 600 (15084)

Grand Haven
WGHN-AM - 1370 (15086)
WGHN-FM - 92.1 (15087)

Grand Rapids
WBMX-AM - 640 (15104)
WLHT-FM - 95.7 (15114)
WOOD-FM - 105.7 (15119)
WOOD-FM - 105.7 (15120)
WTRV-FM - 100.5 (15124)

Hart
WCXT-FM - 105.3 (15148)

Hillsdale
WCSR-AM - 1340 (15166)
WCSR-FM - 92.1 (15167)

Holland
WEVS-FM - 92.7 (15175)

Houghton
WOLV-FM - 97.7 (15187)

Ironwood
WIMI-FM - 99.7 (15215)
WUPM-FM - 106.9 (15217)

Kalamazoo
WFAT-FM - 96.5 (15248)
WQLR-FM - 106.5 (15257)

Lansing
WILS-AM - 1320 (15299)
WXLA-AM - 1180 (15307)

Ludington
WKLA-FM - 106.3 (15324)

Marquette
WKQS-FM - 101.9 (15344)
WMQT-FM - 107.7 (15345)
WQXO-AM - 1400 (15348)

Monroe
WTWR-FM - 98.3 (15368)

Muskegon
WSHZ-FM - 107.9 (15396)

Oak Park
WKQI-FM - 95.5 (15414)

Petoskey
WLXT-FM - 96.3 (15439)

Port Huron
WBTI-FM - 96.9 (15453)
WGRT-FM - 102.3 (15454)

Prudenville
WUPS-FM - 98.5 (15461)

Saginaw
WIOG-FM - 102.5 (15499)

Sault Sainte Marie
WSOO-AM - 1230 (15530)

South Haven
WCSY-FM - 98.3 (15539)

Traverse City
WLDR-FM - 101.9 (15609)

MINNESOTA
Albert Lea
KCPI-FM - 94.9 (15709)

Baxter
WJJY-FM - 106.7 (15733)

Benson
KSCR-FM - 93.5 (15749)

Brainerd
KLLZ-AM - 1600 (15770)

Breezy Point
KLKS-FM - 104.3 (15772)

Crookston
KROX-AM - 1260 (15821)

Detroit Lakes
KDLM-AM - 1340 (15832)

Duluth
KDAL-AM - 610 (15845)
WWAX-FM - 92.1 (15858)

Eveleth
WEVE-FM - 97.9 (15886)

Fairmont
KFMC-FM - 106.5 (15891)

Fosston
KKEQ-FM - 107.1 (15912)

Glenwood
KSTQ-FM - 99.3 (15921)

Grand Marais
WTIP-FM - 90.7 (15927)

Grand Rapids
KMFY-FM - 96.9 (15931)

Little Falls
KFML-FM - 94.1 (16007)
KLTF-AM - 960 (16008)

Luverne
KQAD-AM - 800 (16016)

Mankato
KEEZ-FM - 99.1 (16032)
KTOE-AM - 1420 (16035)

Minneapolis
KSTP-FM - 94.5 (16154)
WLTE-FM - 102.9 (16163)
WXPT-FM - 104.1 (16164)

New Ulm
KNUJ-FM - 107.3 (16218)

Northfield
KYMN-AM - 1080 (16239)

Perham
KPRW-FM - 99.5 (16267)

Redwood Falls
KLGR-FM - 97.7 (16300)

Sleepy Eye
BRAT-FM - 107.3 (16452)

Winona
KAGE-FM - 95.3 (16533)

MISSISSIPPI
Biloxi
WMJY-FM - 93.7 (16568)

Cleveland
WMJW-FM - 107.5 (16595)

Clinton
WHJT-FM - 96.3 (16597)

Columbia
WCJU-AM - 1450 (16600)
WFFF-FM - 96.7 (16602)

Hattiesburg
WJMG-FM - 92.1 (16673)
WMFM-FM - 106.3 (16675)

Indianola
WNLA-FM - 105.5 (16689)

Laurel
WQIS-AM - 890 (16743)

Meridian
WJDQ-FM - 101.3 (16774)

Oxford
WQLJ-FM - 93.7 (16810)

Starkville
WLZA-FM - 96.1 (16847)

Tupelo
WFTA-FM - 101.9 (16853)
WSYE-FM - 93.3 (16856)

Wesson
WCLL-FM - 90.7 (16874)

MISSOURI
Carrollton
KRLI-FM - 97.5 (16958)

Carthage
KMXL-FM - 95.1 (16961)

Columbia
KPLA-FM - 101.5 (17022)

El Dorado Springs
KESM-AM - 1580 (17043)
KESM-FM - 105.5 (17044)

Joplin
KOBC-FM - 90.7 (17145)

Kaiser
KLOZ-FM - 92.7 (17153)

Liberty
KWJC-FM - 91.9 (17251)

Mexico
KXEO-AM - 1340 (17288)

Montgomery City
KMCR-FM - 103.9 (17297)

St. Charles
KCLC-FM - 89.1 (17385)

St. Joseph
KGNM-AM - 1270 (17396)
KKJO-FM - 105.5 (17397)

St. Louis
KEZK-FM - 102.5 (17539)
KYKY-FM - 98.1 (17555)

Sedalia
KSDL-FM - 92.1 (17573)

Sikeston
KMAL-FM - 92.9 (17585)

Springfield
KGBX-FM - 105.9 (17620)

MONTANA
Belgrade
KGVW-AM - 640 (17725)

Billings
KBBB-FM - 103.7 (17736)
KYYA-FM - 93.3 (17747)

Butte
KOPR-FM - 94.1 (17764)

Dillon
KBEV-FM - 98.3　**(17784)**

Havre
KOJM-AM - 610　**(17814)**

Helena
KMTX-FM - 105.3　**(17830)**

Lewistown
KLCM-FM - 95.9　**(17849)**

Libby
KTNY-FM - 101.7　**(17855)**

Miles City
KATL-AM - 770　**(17862)**

Missoula
KMSO-FM - 102.5　**(17883)**

Shelby
KSEN-AM - 1150　**(17907)**

Sidney
KTHC-FM - 95.1　**(17911)**

NEBRASKA
Ainsworth
KBRB-AM - 1400　**(17924)**
KBRB-FM - 92.7　**(17925)**

Alliance
KCOW-AM - 1400　**(17929)**
KPNY-FM - 102.1　**(17930)**

Beatrice
KWBE-AM - 1450　**(17949)**

Fairbury
KGMT-AM - 1310　**(18006)**

Grand Island
KRGI-AM - 1430　**(18029)**
KSYZ-FM - 107.7　**(18031)**

Hastings
KHAS-AM - 1230　**(18039)**

Holdrege
KMTY-FM - 97.7　**(18050)**

Lincoln
KBBK-FM - 107.3　**(18130)**
KFOR-AM - 1240　**(18133)**

McCook
KICX-FM - 96.1　**(18155)**

Norfolk
KEXL-FM - 106.7　**(18171)**

North Platte
KELN-FM - 97.1　**(18178)**

Omaha
KCTY-FM - 106.9　**(18214)**
KEFM-FM - 96.1　**(18215)**
KKCD-FM - 92.3 KEZO, 105.9 KKLD, 104.5 KRSZ,
　97.7 KQLH, 94.1 KMXM,KBBX　**(18222)**
KSRZ-FM - 104.5　**(18227)**

Plattsmouth
KOTD-AM - 1020　**(18251)**

York
KTMX-FM - 104.9　**(18323)**

NEVADA
Ely
KCLS-FM - 101.7　**(18341)**

Fallon
KVLV-FM - 99.3　**(18347)**

Gardnerville
KGVM-FM - 99.3　**(18350)**

Las Vegas
KDOX-AM - 1280　**(18393)**

Tonopah
KHWK-FM - 92.7　**(18448)**

NEW HAMPSHIRE
Berlin
WBRL-AM - 1400　**(18457)**

Claremont
WHDQ-FM - 106.1　**(18466)**

Conway
WBNC-AM - 1050　**(18485)**
WVMJ-FM - 104.5　**(18487)**

Dover
WBYY-FM - 98.7　**(18492)**
WWNH-AM - 1340　**(18497)**

Franklin
WFTN-FM - 94.1　**(18510)**

Keene
WKNE-FM - 103.7　**(18534)**

Laconia
WLNH-AM - 1350　**(18539)**
WLNH-FM - 98.3　**(18540)**

Lebanon
WCFR-FM - 93.5　**(18544)**

Littleton
WLTN-FM - 96.7　**(18552)**

Manchester
WZID-FM - 95.7　**(18573)**

NEW JERSEY
Bridgeton
WSNJ-AM - 1240　**(18691)**
WSNJ-FM - 107.7　**(18692)**

Camden
WSSJ-AM - 1310　**(18717)**

Lincroft
WBJB-FM - 90.5　**(19170)**

Linwood
WTKU-FM - 98.3　**(19175)**

New Brunswick
WMGQ-FM - 98.3　**(19343)**

Newton
WSUS-FM - 102.3　**(19379)**

Northfield
WFPG-FM - 96.9　**(19383)**

Pleasantville
WBNJ-FM - 96.1　**(19446)**
WMID-AM - 1340　**(19447)**

Princeton
WHWH-AM - 1350　**(19480)**

Vineland
WMIZ-AM - 1270　**(19701)**

NEW MEXICO
Carlsbad
KCDY-FM - 104.1　**(19826)**

Clovis
KTQM-FM - 99.9　**(19836)**

Deming
KDEM-FM - 94.3　**(19841)**

Farmington
KNMI-FM - 88.9　**(19849)**
KWYK-FM - 94.9　**(19853)**

Hobbs
KZOR-FM - 94.1　**(19870)**

Las Cruces
KMVR-FM - 104.9　**(19883)**

Las Vegas
KLVF-FM - 100.7　**(19892)**

Lovington
KLEA-AM - 630　**(19899)**

Roswell
KBIM-FM - 94.9　**(19916)**
KCRX-AM - 1430　**(19918)**
KINF-AM - 1020　**(19920)**

Ruidoso Downs
KRUI-AM - 1490　**(19931)**

Santa Fe
KSFQ-FM - 101.1　**(19949)**

Silver City
KSCQ-FM - 92.9　**(19957)**

Tucumcari
KQAY-FM - 92.7　**(19972)**

NEW YORK
Albany
WRVE-FM - 99.5　**(20015)**

Amagansett
WBAZ-FM - 102.5　**(20028)**

Baldwinsville
WBXL-FM - 90.5　**(20115)**

Batavia
WXOX-FM - 101.7　**(20124)**

Bath
WVIN-FM - 98.3　**(20134)**

Beacon
WHUD-FM - 100.7　**(20140)**

Brentwood
WXBA-FM - 88.1　**(20241)**

Buffalo
WEDG-FM - 103.3　**(20398)**
WJYE-FM - 96.1　**(20404)**
WUFO-AM - 1080　**(20412)**

Canton
WVNC-FM - 96.7　**(20434)**

Center Moriches
WHFM-FM - 95.3　**(20444)**

Corning
WCBA-FM - 98.7　**(20505)**

Dansville
WDNY-FM - 93.9　**(20521)**

Dundee
WFLR-FM - 95.9　**(20536)**

Farmingdale
WKJY-FM - 98.3　**(20599)**
WMJC-FM - 94.3　**(20600)**

Fredonia
WBKX-FM - 96.5　**(20623)**

Glens Falls
WWSC-AM - 1450　**(20670)**

Hartsdale
WFAS-FM - 103.9　**(20715)**

Hornell
WHHO-AM - 1320　**(20756)**

Hudson
WCTW-FM - 98.5　**(20769)**

Ithaca
WYXL-FM - 97.3　**(20825)**

Jamestown
WWSE-FM - 93.3　**(20846)**

Kingston
WKNY-AM - 1490　**(20864)**

Lake Placid
WLPW-FM - 105.5　**(20877)**
WRGR-FM - 102.3　**(20878)**

Liberty
WVOS-FM - 95.9　**(20945)**

Massena
WMSA-AM - 1340　**(21028)**
WYBG-AM - 1050　**(21029)**

Monticello
WSUL-FM - 98.3　**(21094)**

Nanuet
WRCR-AM - 1300　**(21106)**

New York
WBMB-AM - 590　**(22964)**
WPAT-FM - 93.1　**(22984)**
WWPR-FM - 105.1　**(22993)**

Newburgh
WGNY-FM - 103.1　**(23003)**

Norwich
WKXZ-FM - 93.9　**(23024)**

Olean
WMXO-FM - 101.5　**(23043)**

Oneida
WMCR-AM - 1600　**(23047)**
WMCR-FM - 106.3　**(23048)**

Oneonta
WSRK-FM - 103.9　**(23055)**

Patchogue
WALK-AM - 1370　**(23078)**
WALK-FM - 97.5　**(23079)**

ADULT CONTEMPORARY (continued)

Penn Yan
WYLF-AM - 850 **(23093)**

Plattsburgh
WIRY-AM - 1340 **(23106)**

Port Jervis
WTSX-FM - 96.7 **(23121)**

Potsdam
WPDM-AM - 1470 **(23142)**
WSNN-FM - 99.3 **(23143)**

Poughkeepsie
WBWZ-FM - 93.3 **(23154)**
WCZX-FM - 97.7 **(23155)**

Rochester
WVOR-FM - 100.5 **(23256)**

Saranac Lake
WYZY-FM - 106.3 **(23300)**

Schenectady
WKRD-FM - 93.7 **(23316)**

Sidney
WCDO-AM - 1490 **(23333)**
WCDO-FM - 100.9 **(23334)**

Southold
WBSQ-FM - 102.5 **(23348)**

Springville
WSPQ-AM - 1330 **(23356)**

Stillwater
WQAR-FM - 101.3 **(23368)**

Syracuse
WLTI-FM - 105.9 **(23439)**
WYYY-FM - 94.5 **(23449)**
WZUN-FM - 102.1 **(23450)**

Utica
WRFM-FM - 93.5 **(23478)**

Vestal
WLTB-FM - 101.7 **(23492)**

Watertown
WTOJ-FM - 103.1 **(23520)**

Wellsville
WJQZ-FM - 103.5 **(23534)**

Whitesboro
WLZW-FM - 98.7 **(23580)**

NORTH CAROLINA
Boone
WATA-AM - 1450 **(23660)**
WECR-FM - 102.3 **(23661)**

Charlotte
WLNK-FM - 107.9 **(23773)**
WRCM-FM - 91.9 **(23778)**

Elkin
WIFM-FM - 100.9 **(23870)**

Fayetteville
WAZZ-AM - 1490 **(23884)**
WQSM-FM - 98.1 **(23891)**

Greensboro
WKSI-FM - 98.7 **(23950)**
WQMG-FM - 97.1 **(23957)**

Greenville
WNCT-FM - 107.9 **(23973)**

Laurinburg
WLNC-AM - 1300 **(24034)**

Newton
WNNC-AM - 1230 **(24107)**

Raleigh
WRAL-FM - 101.5 **(24169)**
WRSN-FM - 93.9 **(24174)**

Rockingham
WAYN-AM - 900 **(24202)**

Shallotte
WLTT-FM - 103.7 **(24225)**

Siler City
WNCA-AM - 1570 **(24231)**

Wanchese
WYND-FM - 92.3 **(24270)**

Wilmington
WGNI-FM - 102.7 **(24300)**

Winston-Salem
WAAA-AM - 980 **(24326)**
WBFJ-AM - 1550 **(24328)**
WBFJ-FM - 89.3 **(24329)**

NORTH DAKOTA
Belcourt
KEYA-FM - 88.5 **(24346)**

Devils Lake
KDVL-FM - 102.5 **(24392)**

Dickinson
KDIX-AM - 1230 **(24398)**
KZRX-FM - 92.1 **(24402)**

Fargo
KLTA-FM - 105.1 **(24424)**
KRVI-FM - 95.1 **(24428)**

Grand Forks
KZLT-FM - 104.3 **(24464)**

Minot
KMXA-FM - 99.9 **(24512)**

Valley City
KQDJ-FM - 101.1 **(24546)**

OHIO
Akron
WKDD-FM - 98.1 **(24598)**

Ashtabula
WREO-FM - 97.1 **(24626)**
WZOO-FM - 102.5 **(24627)**

Athens
WXTQ-FM - 105.5 **(24637)**

Bellaire
WOMP-FM - 100.5 **(24664)**

Cambridge
WCMJ-FM - 96.7 **(24727)**

Canton
WHBC-FM - 94.1 **(24735)**
WRCW-AM - 1060 **(24737)**

Castalia
WGGN-FM - 97.7 **(24743)**

Celina
WCSM-AM - 1350 **(24750)**
WCSM-FM - 96.7 **(24751)**
WKKI-FM - 94.3 **(24752)**

Cleveland
WMVX-FM - 106.5 **(24982)**
WQAL-FM - 104.1 **(24984)**

Columbus
WSNY-FM - 94.7 **(25085)**

Coshocton
WTNS-FM - 99.3 **(25098)**

Dayton
WIZE-AM - 1340 **(25145)**
WMMX-FM - 107.7 **(25147)**
WONE-AM - 980 **(25148)**

Defiance
WDFM-FM - 98.1 **(25158)**

Englewood
WLPM-AM - 1450 **(25183)**

Findlay
WKXA-FM - 100.5 **(25197)**

Fremont
WFRO-AM - 900 **(25204)**
WFRO-FM - 99.1 **(25205)**

Greenfield
WVNU-FM - 97.5 **(25226)**

Jackson
WKOV-FM - 96.7 **(25259)**

Kenton
WKTN-FM - 95.3 **(25282)**

Lima
WZOQ-FM - 92.1 **(25306)**

Mansfield
WRGM-AM - 1440 **(25336)**
WYHT-FM - 105.3 **(25340)**

Marietta
WMOA-AM - 1490 **(25349)**

Marion
WDIF-FM - 94.3 **(25353)**
WMRN-AM - 1490 **(25354)**

McConnelsville
WJAW-FM - 100.9 **(25370)**

Milan
WLKR-FM - 95.3 **(25382)**

Millersburg
WKLM-FM - 95.3 **(25391)**

Napoleon
WNDH-FM - 103.1 **(25404)**

Piketon
WXZQ-FM - 100.1 **(25478)**

Portsmouth
WNXT-FM - 99.3 **(25486)**

Sandusky
WCPZ-FM - 102.7 **(25512)**

Sidney
WMVR-AM - 1080 **(25522)**
WMVR-FM - 105.5 **(25523)**

Tiffin
WTTF-AM - 1600 **(25561)**

Toledo
WLQR-AM - 1470 **(25581)**
WRVF-FM - 101.5 **(25584)**
WWWM-FM - 105.5 **(25590)**

Upper Sandusky
WYNT-FM - 95.9 **(25605)**

Van Wert
WERT-AM - 1220 **(25610)**

Youngstown
WMXY-FM - 98.9 **(25708)**

Zanesville
WCVZ-FM - 92.7 **(25719)**
WHIZ-FM - 102.5 **(25721)**

OKLAHOMA
Bartlesville
KYFM-FM - 100.1 **(25756)**

Duncan
KRHD-FM - 102.3 **(25802)**

Durant
KSEO-AM - 750 **(25811)**

Frederick
KYBE-FM - 95.9 **(25841)**

Grove
KGND-FM - 107.5 **(25851)**

Hugo
KIHN-AM - 1340 **(25873)**

Lawton
KBZQ-FM - 99.5 **(25890)**

Oklahoma City
KOCC-FM - 88.9 **(26008)**
KQSR-FM - 94.7 **(26014)**

Ponca City
KIXR-FM - 104.7 **(26039)**
KLOR-FM - 99.3 **(26040)**
KOKB-AM - 1580 **(26042)**
WBBZ-AM - 1230 **(26044)**

Shawnee
KGFF-AM - 1450 **(26066)**

Tulsa
KGTO-AM - 1050 **(26147)**
KRAV-FM - 96.5 **(26162)**

Woodward
KMZE-FM - 92.1 **(26199)**

OREGON
Albany
KFLY-FM - 101.5 **(26208)**

Astoria
KCBZ-FM - 96.5 **(26229)**

Bend
KLRR-FM - 01.75 **(26245)**
KWPK-FM - 104.1 **(26253)**

                                      Numbers cited in bold after listings are entry numbers rather than page numbers.

Coos Bay
KACW-FM - 107.3 **(26275)**

The Dalles
KMCQ-FM - 104.5 **(26303)**

Eugene
KMGE-FM - 94.5 **(26342)**

Gold Beach
KGBR-FM - 92.7 **(26361)**

Grants Pass
KROG-FM - 96.9 **(26364)**

Klamath Falls
KKRB-FM - 106.9 **(26394)**

La Grande
KWRL-FM - 99.9 **(26403)**

Medford
KRTA-AM - 610 **(26426)**

Newport
KYTE-FM - 102.7 **(26451)**

Pendleton
KUMA-FM - 107.7 **(26462)**

Roseburg
KQEN-AM - 1240 **(26558)**

Tillamook
KTIL-FM - 94.1 **(26599)**

PENNSYLVANIA
Allentown
WFMZ-FM - 100.7 **(26630)**

Bala Cynwyd
WBEB-FM - 101.1 **(26671)**
WDAS-FM - 105.3 **(26672)**
WFNI-FM - 104.5 **(26673)**
WTEL-AM - 860 **(26680)**

Bedford
WAYC-FM - 100.9 **(26690)**

Bradford
WESB-AM - 1490 **(26730)**

Chambersburg
WIKZ-FM - 95.1 **(26772)**

Clarion
WCCR-FM - 92.7 **(26782)**

Clearfield
WOKW-FM - 102.9 **(26790)**
WQYX-FM - 93.1 **(26791)**

Connellsville
WLSW-FM - 103.9 **(26802)**

Corry
WWCB-AM - 1370 **(26810)**

Emporium
WLEM-AM - 1250 **(26884)**
WQKY-FM - 99.3 **(26885)**

Erie
WXKC-FM - 99.9 **(26913)**

Folsom
WRSD-FM - 94.9 **(26922)**

Franklin
WOXX-FM - 99.3 **(26936)**

Gettysburg
WGET-AM - 1320 **(26941)**

Greenville
WGRP-AM - 940 **(26961)**

Harrisburg
WRVV-FM - 97.3 **(27024)**

Honesdale
WDNH-FM - 95.3 **(27053)**

Indiana
WCCS-AM - 1160 **(27079)**
WDAD-AM - 1450 **(27080)**

Johnstown
WKYE-FM - 95.5 **(27094)**
WSRA-FM - 101.7 **(27098)**

Lafayette Hill
KWFT-AM - 990 **(27136)**

Lansford
WMGH-FM - 105.5 **(27164)**

Lebanon
WLBR-AM - 1270 **(27177)**

Lehigh Valley
WLEV-FM - 96.1 **(27182)**

Lincoln University
WLIU-FM - 88.7 **(27201)**

Lock Haven
WSNU-FM - 92.1 **(27206)**

Louistown
WLAK-FM - 103.5 **(27207)**

Masontown
WRIJ-FM - 106.9 **(27225)**

Millersburg
WQLV-FM - 98.9 **(27267)**

Mount Union
WXMJ-FM - 99.5 **(27303)**

New Castle
WJST-FM - 92.1 **(27317)**

New Wilmington
WWNW-FM - 88.9 **(27326)**

Philadelphia
WRDR-FM - 104.9 **(27743)**

Pittsburgh
WLTJ-FM - 92.9 **(27867)**
WZPT-FM - 100.7 **(27884)**

Pittston
WAMT-FM - 103.1 **(27886)**
WDMT-FM - 102.3 **(27887)**

Pottsville
WPPA-AM - 1360 **(27906)**

Punxsutawney
WPXZ-FM - 104.1 **(27912)**

Renovo
WZYY-FM - 106.9 **(27932)**

Sayre
WATS-AM - 960 **(27946)**
WAVR-FM - 102.1 **(27947)**

Scranton
WWDL-FM - 104.9 **(27973)**

Selinsgrove
WHLM-FM - 106.5 **(27976)**

Shamokin
WSPI-FM - 99.7 **(27985)**

Slippery Rock
WSRU-FM - 90.1 **(28001)**

State College
WMAJ-AM - 1450 **(28025)**
WZWW-FM - 95.3 **(28031)**

Stroudsburg
WSBG-FM - 93.5 **(28036)**

Sunbury
WKOK-AM - 1070 **(28039)**
WQKX-FM - 94.1 **(28040)**

Uniontown
WMBS-AM - 590 **(28068)**

Warren
WNAE-AM - 1310 **(28107)**
WRLP-FM - 103.1 **(28108)**

Wellsboro
WNBT-AM - 1490 **(28143)**

Wilkes Barre
WEMR-FM - 107.7 **(28176)**

Williamsport
WISL-AM - 1590 **(28186)**
WISL-FM - 95.3 **(28187)**
WKSB-FM - 102.7 **(28188)**
WSFT-FM - 107.9 **(28192)**

PUERTO RICO
Arecibo
WMIA-AM - 1070 **(28226)**

Barranquitas
WOLA-AM - 1380 **(28230)**

Cabo Rojo
WEKO-AM - 930 **(28234)**

Caguas
WVJP-AM - 1110 **(28236)**

Gavco
WENA-AM - 1330 **(28245)**

Mayaguez
WTIL-AM - 1300 **(28269)**

Ponce
WIOC-FM - 105.1 **(28277)**

San Sebastian
WLRP-AM - 1460 **(28314)**
WRSS-AM - 1410 **(28315)**

RHODE ISLAND
East Providence
WWLI-FM - 105 **(28351)**

Narragansett
WPJB-FM - 102.7 **(28364)**

Providence
WSNE-FM - 93.3 **(28438)**

Woonsocket
WNRI-AM - 1380 **(28462)**

SOUTH CAROLINA
Aiken
WAJY-FM - 102.7 **(28470)**

Barnwell
WBAW-AM - 99.1 **(28483)**
WBAW-FM - 99.1 **(28484)**

Camden
WPUB-FM - 94.3 **(28502)**

Charleston
WSSX-FM - 95.1 **(28524)**

Columbia
WTCB-FM - 106.7 **(28585)**

Greenville
WMYI-FM - 102.5 **(28637)**

Greenwood
WZSN-FM - 103.5 **(28651)**

Mt. Pleasant
WALC-FM - 100.5 **(28698)**

Myrtle Beach
WYAV-FM - 104.1 **(28716)**

Newberry
WKDK-AM - 1240 **(28718)**

North Augusta
WSLT-FM - 98.3 **(28724)**

North Charleston
WSUY-FM - 96.9 **(28727)**

Pamplico
WMXT-FM - 102.1 **(28741)**

Rock Hill
WRHI-AM - 1340 **(28748)**

Spartanburg
WSPA-FM - 98.9 **(28763)**

SOUTH DAKOTA
Aberdeen
KBFO-FM - 106.7 **(28793)**
KGIM-AM - 1420 **(28795)**
KSDN-AM - 930 **(28798)**

Brookings
KBRK-FM - 93.7 **(28819)**

Madison
KJAM-FM - 103.1 **(28888)**

Mitchell
KQRN-FM - 107.3 **(28904)**

Rapid City
KKMK-FM - 93.9 **(28944)**
KTOQ-AM - 1340 **(28951)**

Sioux Falls
KELO-FM - 92.5 **(28975)**

Watertown
KIXX-FM - 96.1 **(29021)**
KWAT-AM - 950 **(29025)**

Winner
KWYR-FM - 93.7 **(29034)**

Circulation: ★ = ABC; △ = BPA; ◆ = CAC; ● = CCAB; ❑ = VAC; ⊕ = PO Statement; ‡ = Publisher's Report; Boldface figures = sworn; Light figures = estimated.

ADULT CONTEMPORARY (continued)

Yankton
KVHT-FM - 106.3 **(29042)**
KYNT-AM - 1450 **(29044)**

TENNESSEE
Brownsville
WTNE-AM - 1500 **(29075)**

Camden
WRJB-FM - 98.3 **(29080)**

Chattanooga
WDEF-AM - 1370 **(29097)**
WDEF-FM - 92.3 **(29098)**
WLMR-AM - 1450 **(29106)**
WSKZ-FM - 106.5 **(29109)**

Cleveland
WAYA-FM - 93.9 **(29124)**

Columbia
WKRM-AM - 1340 **(29140)**

Cookeville
WGIC-FM - 98.5 **(29149)**

Covington
WKBQ-FM - 93.5 **(29155)**

Dyersburg
WASL-FM - 100.1 **(29177)**

Fayetteville
WYTM-FM - 105.5 **(29192)**

Jackson
WFKX-FM - 95.7 **(29235)**
WHHM-FM - 107.7 **(29236)**
WMXX-FM - 103.1 **(29237)**

Knoxville
WJXB-FM - 97.5 **(29293)**
WKCS-FM - 91.1 **(29294)**
WQBB-AM - 1040 **(29298)**

Martin
WCMT-FM - 101.7 **(29345)**

Memphis
WDIA-AM - 1070 **(29390)**
WEZI-FM - 94.3 **(29393)**
WMC-FM - 99.7 **(29404)**
WQOX-FM - 88.5 **(29409)**
WRVR-FM - 104.5 **(29412)**

Morristown
WMXK-FM - 94.1 **(29424)**

Nashville
WJXA-FM - 92.9 **(29513)**
WLAC-AM - 105.9 **(29517)**
WNAZ-FM - 89.1 **(29522)**
WNRZ-FM - 91.5 **(29524)**

Oneida
WBNT-FM - 105.5 **(29556)**

Paris
WLZK-FM - 94.1 **(29561)**

Savannah
WXOQ-FM - 105.5 **(29587)**

TEXAS
Amarillo
KAEZ-FM - 105.7 **(29702)**
KMXJ-FM - 94.1 **(29714)**

Austin
KAMX-FM - 94.7 **(29858)**
KHHL-FM - 98.9 **(29865)**
KKMJ-FM - 95.5 **(29869)**

Brownwood
KBWD-AM - 1380 **(29968)**
KPSM-FM - 99.3 **(29970)**

Bryan
KKYS-FM - 104.7 **(29980)**
KVJM-FM - 103.1 **(29983)**

Center
KDXI-FM - 1360 **(30014)**

Dallas
KDMX-FM - 102.9 **(30200)**

El Campo
KULP-FM - 96.9 **(30278)**

Fort Stockton
KFST-AM - 860 **(30327)**

Grapeland
KBHT-FM - 93.5 **(30411)**

Houston
KODA-FM - 99.1 **(30568)**
KPFT-FM - 90.1 **(30569)**

Jacksonville
KOOI-FM - 106.5 **(30618)**

Jasper
KJAS-FM - 107.3 **(30621)**

Laredo
KRRG-FM - 98.1 **(30677)**

Liberty
KSHN-FM - 99.9 **(30692)**

Longview
KJTX-FM - 104.5 **(30706)**

Lubbock
KMMX-FM - 100.3 **(30732)**

Lufkin
KAFX-FM - 95.5 **(30742)**
KUEZ-FM - 100.1 **(30747)**

Madisonville
KMVL-FM - 100.5 **(30754)**

McAllen
KVLY-FM - 107.9 **(30799)**

Memphis
KLSR-FM - 105.3 **(30803)**

Midland
KODM-FM - 97.9 **(30823)**

Odessa
KCRS-FM - 103.3 **(30874)**

Pampa
KGRO-AM - 1230 **(30901)**

Paris
KPLT-FM - 107.7 **(30909)**

Pecos
KPTX-FM - 98.3 **(30926)**

Perryton
KEYE-FM - 96.1 **(30929)**

Plainview
KVOP-FM - 106.9 **(30945)**

San Antonio
KQXT-FM - 101.9 **(31067)**
KSJL-AM - 760 **(31071)**
KSLR-AM - 630 **(31072)**
KSMG-FM - 105.3 **(31073)**

Tyler
KTYL-FM - 93.1 **(31218)**
KVNE-FM - 89.5 **(31219)**
WHYN-FM - 93.1 **(31223)**

Victoria
KVIC-FM - 95.1 **(31240)**

Waco
KEYR-FM - 92.9 **(31259)**

UTAH
Fillmore
KZEZ-FM - 95.7 **(31335)**

St. George
KSNN-FM - 93.5 **(31421)**

Salt Lake City
KBEE-FM - 98.7 **(31444)**
KSFI-FM - 100.3 **(31456)**

VERMONT
Brattleboro
WTSA-FM - 96.7 **(31513)**

Burlington
WEZF-FM - 92.9 **(31523)**
WEZF-FM - 92.9 **(31524)**

East Poultney
WNYV-FM - 94.1 **(31540)**

Lyndonville
WGMT-FM - 97.7 **(31550)**

Middlebury
WFAD-AM - 1490 **(31560)**

Montpelier
WSKI-AM - 1240 **(31568)**

Randolph Center
WVTC-FM - 90.7 **(31583)**

Rutland
WJJR-FM - 98.1 **(31587)**
WZRT-FM - 97.1 **(31589)**

VIRGINIA
Bedford
WBLT-AM - 1350 **(31863)**

Charlottesville
WQMZ-FM - 95.1 **(31954)**

Clifton Forge
WXCF-FM - 103.9 **(31977)**

Emporia
WEVA-AM - 860 **(32002)**

Farmville
WFLO-FM - 95.7 **(32071)**

Fredericksburg
WBQB-FM - 101.5 **(32090)**

Gloucester
WXGM-AM - 1420 **(32116)**
WXGM-FM - 99.1 **(32117)**

Grundy
WMJD-FM - 97.7 **(32122)**

Hampden Sydney
WWHS-FM - 92.1 **(32125)**

Harrisonburg
WQPO-FM - 100.7 **(32152)**

Lynchburg
WZZY-FM - 97.9 **(32219)**

Manassas
WPLC-FM - 94.3 **(32225)**

Martinsville
WMVA-AM - 1450 **(32238)**

Norton
WNVA-FM - 106.3 **(32313)**

Onley
WESR-FM - 103.3 **(32320)**

Pennington Gap
WSWV-FM - 105.5 **(32328)**

Richlands
WRIC-FM - 100.7 **(32429)**

Richmond
WMXB-FM - 103.7 **(32480)**

Roanoke
WTOY-AM - 1480 **(32506)**

Salem
WSLQ-FM - 99.1 **(32524)**

Smithfield
WYCS-FM - 91.5 **(32528)**

South Boston
WJLC-FM - 98.3 **(32532)**

Staunton
WTON-FM - 94.3 **(32561)**

Virginia Beach
WPTE-FM - 94.9 **(32596)**
WWDE-FM - 101.3 **(32597)**

Winchester
WINC-FM - 92.5 **(32632)**

WASHINGTON
Aberdeen
KJET-FM - 105.7 **(32650)**
KXRO-AM - 1320 **(32652)**

Bellevue
KLSY-FM - 92.5 **(32673)**

Centralia
KITI-FM - 95.1 **(32708)**

Colville
KCRK-FM - 92.1 **(32728)**

Ellensburg
KQBE-FM - 103.1 **(32751)**

Forks
KLLM-FM - 103.9 **(32770)**
KVAC-AM - 1490 **(32771)**

Kelso
KLOG-AM - 1490 **(32787)**

Moses Lake
KDRM-FM - 99.3 **(32842)**

Olympia
KXXO-FM - 96.1 **(32871)**

Othello
KZLN-FM - 97.5 **(32876)**

Pasco
KEYW-FM - 98.3 **(32879)**
KONA-AM - 610 **(32883)**
KONA-FM - 105.3 **(32884)**

Seattle
KPLZ-FM - 101.5 **(33068)**

Shelton
KMAS-AM - 1030 **(33081)**

Spokane
KAAK-FM - 98.9 **(33104)**
KISC-FM - 98.1 **(33118)**

Wenatchee
KPQ-FM - 102.1 **(33202)**

Yakima
KQSN-FM - 92.9 **(33233)**
KRSE-FM - 105.7 **(33234)**

WEST VIRGINIA
Charleston
WVAF-FM - 99.9, repeater 95.3 **(33286)**
WVSR-FM - 102.7 **(33291)**

Elkins
WDNE-AM - 1240 **(33308)**

Fairmont
WGYE-FM - 102.7 **(33314)**

Kingwood
WFSP-FM - 107.7 **(33361)**

Logan
WVOW-AM - 1290 **(33371)**
WVOW-FM - 101.9 **(33372)**

Petersburg
WQWV-FM - 103.7 **(33430)**

Philippi
WQAB-FM - 91.3 **(33434)**

Ronceverte
WRON-AM - 1400 **(33455)**

St. Marys
WRRR-FM - 93.9 **(33462)**

Summersville
WCWV-FM - 92.9 **(33474)**

Welch
WELC-AM - 1150 **(33493)**

WISCONSIN
Appleton
WEMI-FM - 91.9 **(33548)**

Black River Falls
WWIS-FM - 99.7 **(33593)**

Fond du Lac
KFIZ-AM - 1450 **(33699)**
KFIZ-FM - 107.1 **(33700)**
WFDL-FM - 97.7 **(33701)**

Green Bay
WKSZ-FM - 95.9 **(33750)**

Hales Corners
WAMG-FM - 103.7 **(33770)**
WMYX-FM - 99.1 **(33772)**

Hayward
WHSM-FM - 101.1 **(33788)**
WRLS-FM - 92.3 **(33790)**

Kenosha
WLIP-AM - 1050 **(33878)**

Marinette
WAGN-AM - 1340 **(34019)**
WLST-FM - 95.1 **(34021)**

Mauston
WRJC-AM - 1270 **(34031)**

Medford
WKEB-FM - 99.3 **(34036)**

Menomonie
WJRV-FM - 95.9 **(34041)**

Merrill
WJMT-AM - 730 **(34046)**

Milwaukee
WKTI-FM - 94.5 **(34124)**
WLTQ-FM - 97.3 **(34125)**

Portage
WPDR-AM - 1350 **(34263)**

Racine
WEZY-FM - 92.1 **(34277)**

Reedsburg
WRDB-AM - 1400 **(34283)**

Rhinelander
WRHN-FM - 100.1 **(34291)**

Rice Lake
WAQE-FM - 97.7 **(34296)**

Richland Center
WRCO-AM - 1450 **(34300)**
WRCO-FM - 100.9 **(34301)**

River Falls
WEVR-AM - 1550 **(34310)**
WEVR-FM - 106.3 **(34311)**

Stevens Point
WSPT-FM - 97.9 **(34346)**

Sturgeon Bay
WDOR-AM - 910 **(34354)**

Tomah
WXYM-FM - 96.1 **(34372)**

Tomahawk
WJJQ-FM - 92.5 **(34375)**

Waupaca
WDUX-FM - 92.7 **(34424)**

Wausau
WYCO-FM - 107.9 **(34441)**

WYOMING
Casper
KMGW-FM - 94.5 **(34489)**

Cheyenne
KLEN-FM - 106.3 **(34507)**

Cody
KTAG-FM - 97.9 **(34516)**

Evanston
KEVA-AM - 1240 **(34524)**

Jackson
KZJH-FM - 95.3 **(34540)**

Laramie
KIMX-FM - 105.5 **(34555)**

Newcastle
KASL-AM - 1240 **(34565)**

Rawlins
KIQZ-FM - 92.7 **(34573)**

Riverton
KTRZ-FM - 93.1 **(34580)**

Sheridan
KWYO-AM - 1410 **(34590)**

Thermopolis
KTHE-AM - 1240 **(34596)**

Wheatland
KZEW-FM - 101.7 **(34603)**

ALBERTA, CANADA
Calgary
CKMX-AM - 1060 **(34671)**

Canmore
CHMN-FM - 106.5 **(34679)**

Edmonton
CHQT-AM - 880 **(34749)**
CJCA-AM - 930 **(34752)**

Edson
YR Radio - 96.7 FM, 970 AM, 1230 AM, 1450 AM **(34762)**

Fort McMurray
CKYX-FM - 97.9 **(34769)**

Grande Prairie
CFGP-FM - 97.7 **(34776)**

Lethbridge
CFRV-FM - 107.7 **(34799)**

Medicine Hat
CJCY-AM - 1390 **(34814)**

Red Deer
CHUB-FM - 105.5 **(34833)**

BRITISH COLUMBIA, CANADA
Chilliwack
CHWK-AM - 1270 **(34929)**

Courtenay
CFCP-FM - 98.9 **(34933)**

Crawford Bay
CKKC-FM - 101.9 **(34938)**

Creston
CFKC-AM - 1340 **(34940)**

Fernie
CFEK-AM - 1240 **(34954)**

Gold River
CJGR-FM - 100 **(34965)**

Golden
CKGR-AM - 1400 **(34968)**
CKIR-AM - 870 **(34969)**

Kamloops
CHNL-AM - 610 **(34980)**
CKRV-FM - 97.5 **(34983)**

Kelowna
CILK-FM - 101.5 **(34992)**
CKOV-AM - 630 **(34994)**

Kitimat
CKTK-AM - 1230 **(35000)**

Nanaimo
CHWF-FM - 106.9 **(35021)**

Nelson
CKKC-AM - 880 **(35026)**

Penticton
CKOR-AM - 800 **(35047)**

Port Alberni
CJAV-AM - 1240 **(35050)**

Port Hardy
CFNI-AM - 1240 **(35053)**

Prince George
CKPG-AM - 550 **(35062)**

Prince Rupert
CHTK-AM - 560 **(35065)**

Revelstoke
CKCR-AM - 1340 **(35072)**

Salmon Arm
CKXR-AM - 580 **(35083)**
CKXR-FM - 102.1 **(35084)**

Squamish
CIEG-FM - 107.5 **(35095)**
CIPN-FM - 104.7 **(35096)**
CISC-FM - 107.5 **(35097)**
CISE-FM - 104.7 **(35098)**
CISP-FM - 104.5 **(35099)**
CISQ-FM - 107.1 **(35100)**

Terrace
CFTK-AM - 590 **(35112)**

Trail
CJAT-FM - 95.7 **(35116)**

Vancouver
CHQM-FM - 103.5 **(35187)**
CKKS-FM - 96.9 **(35193)**
CKST-AM - 1040 **(35195)**

Vernon
CICF-AM - 1050 **(35203)**
CJIB-AM - 940 **(35204)**

Whistler
CISW-FM - 102.1 **(35239)**

Circulation: ★ = ABC; △ = BPA; ♦ = CAC; ● = CCAB; ❑ = VAC; ⊕ = PO Statement; ‡ = Publisher's Report; Boldface figures = sworn; Light figures = estimated.

2975

ADULT CONTEMPORARY (continued)

MANITOBA, CANADA
Brandon
CKX-FM - 96.1 **(35258)**

Flin Flon
CFAR-AM - 590 **(35267)**

The Pas
CJAR-AM - 1240 **(35279)**

Thompson
CHTM-AM - 610 **(35303)**

NEW BRUNSWICK, CANADA
Bathurst
CKBC-AM - 1360 **(35381)**

Campbellton
CKNB-AM - 950 **(35384)**

Edmundston
CJEM-FM - 92.7 **(35387)**

Fredericton
CFXYFM - 105.3 **(35402)**

Grand Falls
CKMV-AM - 1490 **(35407)**

Miramichi
CFAN-FM - 99.3 **(35410)**

Moncton
CFQM-FM - 103.9 **(35418)**
CHOY-FM - 99.9 **(35419)**

St. John
CIOK-FM - 100.5 **(35434)**

Sussex
CJCW-AM - 590 **(35439)**

Woodstock
CJCJ-FM - 104.1 **(35441)**

NEWFOUNDLAND AND LABRADOR, CANADA
Clarenville
CKVO-AM - 710 **(35445)**

Corner Brook
CFCB-AM - 570 **(35451)**

Deer Lake
CFDL-FM - 97.9 **(35454)**

Gander
CKGA-AM - 650 **(35457)**

Port au Choix
CFNW-AM - 790 **(35480)**

St. Anthony
CFNN-FM - 97.9 **(35483)**

Stephenville
CFSX-AM - 870 **(35509)**

NORTHWEST TERRITORIES, CANADA
Hay River
CJCD-FM - 100.1 **(35516)**

Rankin Inlet
CBQR-FM - 105.1 **(35521)**

Yellowknife
CFYK-AM - 1340 **(35529)**

NOVA SCOTIA, CANADA
Amherst
CKDH-AM - 900 **(35533)**

Antigonish
CJFX-AM - 98.9 **(35540)**

Kentville
CKWM-FM - 97.7 **(35585)**

New Glasgow
CKEC-AM - 1320 **(35597)**

Shelburne
CJLS-FM - 96.3 **(35605)**

Sydney
CHER-AM - 950 **(35611)**

Truro
CKTO-FM - 100.9 **(35618)**

Yarmouth
CJLS-FM - 95.5 **(35626)**

ONTARIO, CANADA
Barrie
CFJB-FM - 95.7 **(35660)**
CIQB-FM - 101.1 **(35662)**

Belleville
CJOJ-FM - 95.5 **(35683)**

Blind River
CKNR-FM - 94.1 **(35687)**

Brockville
CFJR-FM - 104.9 FM **(35710)**

Chatham
CKSY-FM - 94.3 **(35732)**

Cobourg
CHUC-AM - 1450 **(35743)**

Collingwood
CKCB-FM - 95.1 **(35749)**

Cornwall
CFLG-FM - 104.5 mhz **(35757)**

Dryden
CKDR-AM - 800 **(35791)**

Fort Francis
CFOB-FM - 640 **(35842)**

Guelph
CIMJ-FM - 106.1 **(35869)**

Hamilton
CKLH-FM - 102.9 **(35897)**

Hawkesbury
CHPR-FM - 102.1 **(35909)**

Huntsville
MORE-FM - 105.5 **(35918)**

Kenora
CJRL-AM - 1220 **(35930)**

Kingston
CFLY-FM - 98.3 **(35951)**

Kirkland Lake
CJKL-FM - 101.5 FM **(35958)**

Kitchener
CHYM-FM - 96.7 **(35964)**

Lindsay
CKLY-AM - 910 **(35974)**

New Liskeard
CJTT-FM - 104.5 FM **(36106)**

Orillia
CICX-FM - 105.9 **(36177)**

Oshawa
CKDO-AM - 1350 **(36182)**
CKGE-FM - 94.9 **(36183)**

Ottawa
CBOF-FM - 90.7 **(36285)**
CFRA-AM - 580 **(36289)**

Ottawa Falls
CIOX-FM - 101.1 **(36298)**

Owen Sound
CIXK-FM - 106.5 **(36302)**

Peterborough
CKWF-FM - 101.5 **(36325)**

Sault Sainte Marie
CHAS-FM - 100.5 **(36371)**

Simcoe
CHCD-FM - 106.7 **(36392)**

Sudbury
CHYC-AM - 900 **(36423)**
CJMX-FM - 105.3 **(36425)**

Timmins
CHYK-FM - 104.1 **(36457)**

Toronto
CHFI-FM - 98.1 **(36807)**
CHUM-FM - 104.5 **(36812)**
CJEZ-FM - 97.3 **(36819)**
CKFM-FM - 99.9 **(36821)**

Waterloo
CKWR-FM - 98.5 **(36863)**

Wawa
CJWA-AM - 1240 **(36866)**

Wingham
CKNX-FM - 101.7 **(36904)**

Woodstock
CKDK-FM - 103.9 **(36909)**

QUEBEC, CANADA
L'Annonciation
CFLO-FM - 104.7 **(36940)**

Asbestos
CJAN-FM - 99.3 **(36942)**

Cap-aux-Meules
CFIM-FM - 92.7 **(36955)**

Carleton
CIEU-FM - 94.9 **(36958)**

Chicoutimi
CBJ-FM - 93.7 **(36969)**
CFIX-FM - 96.9 **(36972)**

Drummondville
CJDM-FM - 92.1 **(36993)**

Kahnawake
CKRK-FM - 103.7 **(37019)**

La Tuque
CFLM-AM - 1240 **(37024)**

Lachute
CJLA-FM - 104.9 **(37031)**

Laval
CFGL-FM - 105.7 **(37045)**

Maniwaki
CHGA-FM - 97.3 **(37066)**

Montreal
CBF-FM - 100.7 **(37240)**
CIBL-FM - 101.5 **(37244)**
CITE-FM - 107.3 **(37246)**
CJFM-FM - 95.9 **(37248)**

New Carlisle
CHNC-AM - 1150 **(37256)**
CHNC-AM - 610 **(37257)**

Noranda
CKRN-AM - 1400 **(37261)**

Plessisville
CKYQ-FM - 95.7 **(37270)**

Port-Cartier
CIPC-FM - 99.1 **(37278)**

Quebec
CHVD-AM - 1230 **(37299)**
CHVD-FM - 92.1 **(37300)**
CITF-FM - 107.5 **(37301)**

Roberval
CHRL-FM - 99.5 **(37320)**

Saint-Gabriel
CFNJ-FM - 99.1 **(37340)**

Saint-Georges-de-Beauce
CKRB-FM - 103.3 **(37343)**

Saint-Hyacinthe
CFEI-FM - 106.5 **(37352)**

Sainte-Marie
CHEQ-FM - 101.3 **(37382)**

Seneterre
CIBO-FM - 100.5 **(37385)**

Sorel-Tracy
CJSO-FM - 101.7 **(37406)**

Val d'Or
CKVD-AM - 900 **(37423)**

Valleyfield
CKOD-FM - 103.1 **(37427)**

Ville-Marie
CKVM-AM - 710 **(37438)**

SASKATCHEWAN, CANADA
Kindersley
CFYM-AM - 1210 **(37484)**

Prince Albert
CHQX-FM - 101.5 **(37520)**

Regina
CHMX-FM - 92.1 **(37540)**

Numbers cited in bold after listings are entry numbers rather than page numbers.

Rosetown
CJYM-AM - 1330 **(37546)**

Saskatoon
CKOM-AM - 650 **(37566)**

Swift Current
CIMG-FM - 94.1 **(37576)**

YUKON TERRITORY, CANADA
Whitehorse
CHON-FM - 98.1 **(37607)**

AGRICULTURAL

ALABAMA
Andalusia
WAAO-FM - 103.7 **(14)**

Atmore
WASG-AM - 550 **(34)**

Dothan
WTVY-FM - 95.5 **(193)**

ARKANSAS
Brinkley
KBRI-AM - 1570 **(1064)**
KQMC-FM - 102.3 **(1065)**

Helena
KFFA-FM - 103.1 **(1177)**

CALIFORNIA
El Centro
KXO-AM - 1230 **(1857)**

King City
KRKC-AM - 1490 **(2104)**

Merced
KUBB-FM - 96.3 **(2534)**

Porterville
KTIP-AM - 1450 **(2863)**

Yuba City
KUBA-AM - 1600 **(4124)**

COLORADO
Alamosa
KGIW-AM - 1450 **(4135)**

Fort Morgan
KSIR-AM - 1010 **(4450)**

FLORIDA
Wauchula
WAUC-AM - 1310 **(6842)**

IDAHO
Boise
KKIC-AM - 950 **(7826)**

Grangeville
KORT-FM - 92.7 **(7859)**

ILLINOIS
Canton
WBYS-AM - 1560 **(8111)**

Carthage
WCAZ-AM - 990 **(8166)**

Effingham
WCRC-FM - 95.7 **(8820)**

Galva
WGEN-AM - 1500 **(8912)**

Harrisburg
WEBQ-AM - 1240 **(8973)**

Highland
WCBW-AM - 880 **(8990)**

Jacksonville
WLDS-AM - 1180 **(9028)**

Jerseyville
WJBM-AM - 1480 **(9029)**

Litchfield
WSMI-FM - 106.1 **(9115)**

Macomb
WLRB-AM - 1510 **(9136)**

McLeansboro
WMCL-AM - 1060 **(9168)**

Monmouth
WMOI-FM - 97.7 **(9220)**
WRAM-AM - 1330 **(9221)**

Quincy
WGEM-FM - 105.1 **(9479)**

Sterling
WSDR-AM - 1240 **(9664)**

Urbana
WILL-AM - 580 **(9723)**

INDIANA
Crawfordsville
WCVL-AM - 1550 **(9911)**

Frankfort
WILO-AM - 1570 **(10002)**
WSHW-FM - 99.7 **(10003)**

Rushville
WKWH-FM - 94.3 **(10438)**

Salem
WSLM-AM - 1220 **(10442)**
WSLM-FM - 97.9 **(10443)**

IOWA
Carroll
KCIM-AM - 1380 **(10653)**

Cedar Rapids
WMT-AM - 600 **(10685)**

Clinton
KCLN-AM - 1390 **(10712)**
KROS-AM - 1340 **(10713)**

Dubuque
KDTH-AM - 1370 **(10848)**

Ottumwa
KBIZ-AM - 1240 **(11141)**

Shenandoah
KMA-AM - 960 **(11200)**

Sioux Center
KDCR-FM - 88.5 **(11209)**

Webster City
KQWC-AM - 1570 **(11315)**

KANSAS
Brewster
KGCR-FM - 107.7 **(11366)**

Garden City
KBUF-AM - 1030 **(11451)**

Hiawatha
KNZA-FM - 103.9 **(11493)**

Pittsburg
KKOW-AM - 860 **(11755)**

Pratt
KWLS-AM - 1290-AM **(11766)**

Salina
KSAL-AM - 1150 **(11789)**

Topeka
WIBW-AM - 580 **(11846)**

KENTUCKY
Albany
WANY-AM - 1390 **(11915)**
WANY-FM - 106.3 **(11916)**

Morganfield
WMSK-FM - 95.3 **(12309)**

Paducah
WKYQ-FM - 93.3 **(12345)**

Richmond
WEKY-AM - 1340 **(12386)**

LOUISIANA
Lake Providence
KLPL-AM - 1050 **(12653)**

Opelousas
KSLO-AM - 1230 **(12793)**

Tallulah
KBYO-FM - 104.9 **(12856)**

MARYLAND
Chestertown
WCTR-AM - 1530 **(13406)**

Westminster
WTTR-AM - 1470 **(13779)**

MICHIGAN
Caro
WKYO-AM - 1360 **(14860)**

Three Rivers
WLKM-FM - 95.9 **(15596)**

MINNESOTA
Albany
KASM-AM - 1150 **(15705)**

Alexandria
KIKV-FM - 100.7 **(15715)**

Fairmont
KSUM-AM - 1370 **(15892)**

Fergus Falls
KBRF-AM - 1250 **(15900)**

Luverne
KLQL-FM - 101.1 **(16015)**
KQAD-AM - 800 **(16016)**

Marshall
KMHL-AM - 1400 **(16047)**

Morris
KMRS-AM - 1230 **(16199)**

New Ulm
KNUJ-AM - 860 **(16217)**

Park Rapids
KPRM-AM - 870 **(16258)**

Pipestone
KLOH-AM - 1050 **(16277)**

Redwood Falls
KLGR-AM - 1490 **(16299)**
KLGR-FM - 97.7 **(16300)**

Rochester
KMFX-AM - 1190 **(16314)**
KWEB-AM - 1270 **(16321)**

Willmar
KWLM-AM - 1340 **(16522)**

MISSISSIPPI
Natchez
WQNZ-FM - 95.1 **(16796)**

Tupelo
WWMS-FM - 97.5 **(16860)**

MISSOURI
Ava
KKOZ-AM - 1430 **(16897)**
KKOZ-FM - 92.1 **(16898)**

Butler
KMAM-AM - 1530 **(16932)**

Cape Girardeau
KZIM-AM - 960 **(16954)**

Carrollton
KAOL-AM - 1430 **(16956)**
KMZU-FM - 100.7 **(16957)**

Marshall
KMMO-AM - 102.9 **(17266)**
KMMO-FM - 102.9 **(17267)**

Mexico
KWWR-FM - 95.7 **(17287)**
KXEO-AM - 1340 **(17288)**

Springfield
KTTS-FM - 94.7 **(17630)**

Thayer
KALM-AM - 1290 **(17649)**

Warrenton
KWRE-AM - 730 **(17702)**

MONTANA
Glasgow
KLTZ-AM - 1240 **(17794)**

Great Falls
KMON-AM - 560 **(17802)**

AGRICULTURAL (continued)

Plentywood
KATQ-AM - 1070 **(17895)**
KATQ-FM - 100.1 **(17896)**

Scobey
KCGM-FM - 95.7 **(17904)**

NEBRASKA
Alliance
KCOW-AM - 1400 **(17929)**

Broken Bow
KCNI-AM - 1280 **(17967)**

Hastings
KHAS-AM - 1230 **(18039)**

Lexington
KRVN-AM - 880 **(18075)**

North Platte
KOOQ-AM - 1410 **(18183)**

Scottsbluff
KNEB-AM - 960 **(18270)**
KNEB-FM - 94.1 **(18271)**

Sidney
KSID-AM - 1340 **(18279)**

Superior
KRFS-AM - 1600 **(18290)**

West Point
KTIC-AM - 840 **(18313)**

NEW MEXICO
Clayton
KLMX-AM - 1450 **(19829)**

NEW YORK
Warsaw
WCJW-AM - 1140 **(23507)**

NORTH CAROLINA
Greenville
WNCT-AM - 1070 **(23972)**

Roanoke Rapids
WPTM-FM - 102.3 **(24196)**

Rose Hill
WEGG-AM - 710 **(24208)**

NORTH DAKOTA
Bowman
KPOK-AM - 1340 **(24382)**

Fargo
KFGO-AM - 790 **(24419)**

Grand Forks
KKXL-AM - 1440 **(24461)**
KNOX-AM - 1310 **(24462)**
KZLT-FM - 104.3 **(24464)**

Oakes
KDDR-AM - 1220 **(24528)**

OHIO
Coshocton
WTNS-FM - 99.3 **(25098)**

Marion
WMRN-AM - 1490 **(25354)**

Napoleon
WNDH-FM - 103.1 **(25404)**

Springfield
WKSW-FM - 101.7 **(25537)**

Van Wert
WERT-AM - 1220 **(25610)**

Wilmington
WKFI-AM - 1090 **(25668)**

OKLAHOMA
Alva
KALV-AM - 1430 **(25739)**

Guymon
KKBS-FM - 92.7 **(25857)**

Hobart
KTJS-AM - 1420 **(25868)**

Weatherford
KWEY-AM - 1590 **(26188)**

OREGON
The Dalles
KYYT-FM - 102.3 **(26304)**

SOUTH DAKOTA
Aberdeen
KGIM-AM - 1420 **(28795)**
KKAA-AM - 1560 **(28796)**

Belle Fourche
KBFS-AM - 1450 **(28807)**

Huron
KOKK-AM - 1210 **(28872)**

Lemmon
KBJM-AM - 1400 **(28883)**

Milbank
KDIO-AM - 1350 **(28894)**

Mitchell
KMIT-FM - 105.9 **(28902)**

Pierre
KGFX-AM - 1060 **(28925)**

Sturgis
KBHB-AM - 810 **(29002)**

Winner
KWYR-AM - 1260 **(29033)**

Yankton
WNAX-AM - 570 **(29045)**

TENNESSEE
Dickson
WDKN-AM - 1260 **(29166)**

Jamestown
WDEB-AM - 1500 **(29245)**
WDEB-FM - 103.9 **(29246)**

TEXAS
Amarillo
KGNC-AM - 710 **(29709)**

Bridgeport
KBOC-FM - 98.3 **(29952)**

Carrizo Springs
KBEN-AM - 1450 **(30003)**

College Station
WTAW-AM - 1620 **(30061)**

Edinburg
KURV-AM - 710 **(30274)**

El Campo
KULP-AM - 1390 **(30277)**

Hamilton
KCLW-AM - 900 **(30421)**

Haskell
KVRP-FM - 95.5 **(30434)**

Hemphill
KPBL-AM - 1240 **(30438)**

Plainview
KKYN-AM - 1090 **(30941)**

Robstown
KROB-AM - 1510 **(30986)**

San Antonio
WOAI-AM - 1200 **(31079)**

Uvalde
KVOU-AM - 1400 **(31226)**

VERMONT
Waterbury
WDEV-AM - 550 **(31612)**

VIRGINIA
Wytheville
WYVE-AM - 1280 **(32644)**

WEST VIRGINIA
Fisher
WELD-AM - 690 **(33317)**

WISCONSIN
Beaver Dam
WBEV-AM - 1430 **(33569)**
WXRO-FM - 95.3 **(33570)**

Dodgeville
WDMP-AM - 810 **(33659)**
WDMP-FM - 99.3 **(33660)**

Hartford
WTKM-AM - 1540 **(33774)**
WTKM-FM - 104.9 **(33775)**

Marshfield
WDLB-AM - 1450 **(34028)**

Reedsburg
WNFM-FM - 104.9 **(34282)**

Waupaca
WDUX-AM - 800 **(34423)**

WYOMING
Powell
KLVY-AM - 1260 **(34570)**

Sheridan
KROE-AM - 930 **(34589)**

ALBERTA, CANADA
High River
CHRB-AM - 1140 **(34784)**

Stettler
CKSQ-AM - 1400 **(34856)**

MANITOBA, CANADA
Altona
CFAM-AM - 950 **(35248)**
CHSM-AM - 1250 **(35249)**

Boissevain
CJRB-AM - 1220 **(35253)**

Dauphin
CKDM-AM - 730 **(35264)**

Portage La Prairie
CFRY-AM - 920 **(35284)**

NOVA SCOTIA, CANADA
New Glasgow
CKEC-AM - 1320 **(35597)**

ONTARIO, CANADA
Simcoe
CHCD-FM - 106.7 **(36392)**

SASKATCHEWAN, CANADA
Kindersley
CFYM-AM - 1210 **(37484)**

Yorkton
CJGX-AM - 940 **(37602)**

ALBUM-ORIENTED ROCK (AOR)

ALABAMA
Auburn
WEGL-FM - 91.1 **(48)**

ALASKA
Anchorage
KWHL-FM - 106.5 **(549)**

Juneau
KSUP-FM - 106.3 **(602)**

McGrath
KSKO-AM - 870 **(623)**

St. Paul Island
KUHB-FM - 91.9 **(634)**

ARIZONA
Mesa
KDKB-FM - 93.3 **(750)**

Tempe
KUPD-FM - 97.9 **(923)**

Tucson
KLPX-FM - 96.1 **(984)**

ARKANSAS
Fayetteville
KKEG-FM - 92.1 **(1129)**

Russellville
KXRJ-FM - 91.9 **(1334)**

CALIFORNIA
Burbank
KROQ-FM - 106.7 **(1629)**

Concord
KFJO-FM - 92.1 **(1760)**

Fort Bragg
KOZT-FM - 95.3 **(1923)**

Los Angeles
KLOS-FM - 95.5 **(2459)**

Marysville
KSXX-FM - 99.9 **(2518)**

Merced
KBRE-FM - 92.5 **(2531)**

Modesto
KHOP-FM - 95.1 **(2567)**

Palm Springs
KCLB-FM - 93.7 **(2772)**

Redding
KRRX-FM - 106.1 **(2896)**

Ridgecrest
KSSI-FM - 102.7 **(2926)**

Sacramento
KRXQ-FM - 93.7 **(3047)**

San Francisco
KFOG-FM - 104.5 **(3481)**

San Jose
KLEL-FM - 89.3 **(3549)**
KSJO-FM - 92.7 **(3553)**

San Luis Obispo
KZOZ-FM - 93.3 **(3576)**

San Rafael
KSRH-FM - 88.1 **(3606)**

Santa Rosa
KXFX-FM - 101.7 **(3742)**

COLORADO
Colorado Springs
KILO-FM - 94.3 **(4268)**

Longmont
KCDC-FM - 90.7 **(4563)**

Montrose
KSTR-FM - 96.1 **(4582)**

Pueblo
KTSC-FM - 89.5 **(4609)**

CONNECTICUT
Brookfield
WRKI-FM - 95.1 **(4731)**

Milford
WPLR-FM - 99.1 **(4961)**

New Haven
WAVZ-AM - 1300 **(5011)**

Somers
WDJW-FM - 89.7 **(5131)**

FLORIDA
Big Pine Key
WWUS-FM - 104.1 **(5924)**

Fort Walton Beach
WKSM-FM - 99.5 **(6124)**

Key West
WOZN-FM - 98.7 **(6258)**

Maitland
WJRR-FM - 101.1 **(6319)**

Orlando
WHTQ-FM - 96.5 **(6519)**

Panama City
WTBB-FM - 97.7 **(6562)**

St. Petersburg
WHPT-FM - 102.5 **(6638)**

Sarasota
WYNF-FM - 105.9 **(6678)**

Tampa
WXTB-FM - 97.8 **(6811)**

GEORGIA
Atlanta
WKLS-FM - 96.1 **(7075)**

Bogart
WPUP-FM - 103.7 **(7135)**

Macon
WQBZ-FM - 106.3 **(7403)**

Valdosta
WWRQ-FM - 107.7 **(7627)**

HAWAII
Hilo
KHWI-FM - 101.5 **(7674)**

Wailuku
KAOI-FM - 103.7 **(7796)**

IDAHO
Lewiston
KLHS-FM - 88.9 **(7897)**
KOZE-FM - 96.5 **(7900)**

ILLINOIS
Champaign
WEVX-FM - 95.3 **(8227)**

Chicago
WIIT - 88.9 **(8629)**
WLUP-FM - 97.9 **(8640)**
WXRT-FM - 93.1 **(8661)**

Crest Hill
WLLI-FM - 96.7 **(8692)**

Elmhurst
WRSE-FM - 88.7 **(8841)**

Flossmoor
WHFH-FM - 88.5 **(8892)**

Joliet
WYKT-FM - 105.5 **(9038)**

Rockford
WXRX-FM - 104.9 **(9543)**

Springfield
WQLZ-FM - 92.7 **(9654)**

INDIANA
Chesterton
WDSO-FM - 88.3 **(9888)**

Evansville
WGBF-FM - 103.1 **(9943)**

Fort Wayne
WBYR-FM - 98.9 **(9981)**
WEXI-FM - 102.9 **(9983)**
WXKE-FM - 103.9 **(9994)**

Franklin
WFCI-FM - 89.5 **(10009)**

Hammond
WABT-FM - 103.9 **(10055)**

Indianapolis
WRZX-FM - 103.3 **(10209)**

Lafayette
WKHY-FM - 93.5 **(10260)**

IOWA
Davenport
WXLP-FM - 96.9 **(10752)**

Fort Dodge
KKEZ-FM - 94.5 **(10910)**

Pella
KFMG-FM - 103.3 **(11154)**

Waterloo
KFMW-FM - 107.9 **(11292)**

KANSAS
Baldwin City
KNBU-FM - 89.7 **(11352)**

Fort Scott
KOMB-FM - 103.9 **(11445)**

Manhattan
KMKF-FM - 101.5 **(11634)**

Westwood
KQRC-FM - 98.9 **(11873)**

Wichita
KICT-FM - 95.1 **(11898)**
KRZZ-FM - 96.3 **(11902)**

KENTUCKY
Louisville
WTFX-FM - 100.5 **(12266)**

Somerset
WSCC-FM - 92.1 **(12408)**

LOUISIANA
Metairie
WCKW-FM - 92.3 **(12680)**

Morgan City
KMRC-AM - 1430 **(12712)**

Shreveport
KTAL-FM - 98.1 **(12837)**

MAINE
Portland
WBLM-FM - 102.9 **(13021)**

MARYLAND
Baltimore
WIYY-FM - 97.9 **(13275)**

Rockville
WWDC-FM - 101.1 **(13705)**

MASSACHUSETTS
Boston
WAAF-FM - 107.3 **(13975)**

Concord
WIQH-FM - 88.3 **(14150)**

Deerfield
WGAJ-FM - 91.7 **(14158)**

Franklin
WGAO-FM - 88.3 **(14208)**

Hyannis
WPXC-FM - 102.9 **(14253)**

Tisbury
WMVY-FM - 92.7 **(14589)**

Topsfield
WBMT-FM - 88.3 **(14590)**

Walpole
WSRB-FM - 91.5 **(14595)**

West Yarmouth
WKPE-AM - 1170 **(14631)**
WKPE-FM - 104.7 **(14632)**

Worcester
WWFX-FM - 100.1 **(14700)**

MICHIGAN
Ann Arbor
WIQB-FM - 102.9 **(14778)**

Bay City
WCHW-FM - 91.3 **(14804)**

Burton
WWBN-FM - 101.5 **(14841)**

Canton
WSDP-FM - 88.1 **(14855)**

Detroit
WDZR-FM - 102.7 **(14963)**

Ferndale
WRIF-FM - 101.1 **(15032)**

Kalamazoo
WRKR-FM - 107.7 **(15259)**

Kalkaska
WKAL-AM - 1420 **(15262)**

Lapeer
WRXF-FM - 103.1 **(15312)**

Circulation: ★ = ABC; △ = BPA; ♦ = CAC; ● = CCAB; ❏ = VAC; ⊕ = PO Statement; ‡ = Publisher's Report; Boldface figures = sworn; Light figures = estimated.

2979

ALBUM-ORIENTED ROCK (AOR) (continued)

Muskegon
WMRR-FM - 101.7 **(15393)**

Saginaw
WKQZ-FM - 93.3 **(15502)**

St. Joseph
WIRX-FM - 107.1 **(15515)**

MINNESOTA
Bemidji
KBSB-FM - 89.7 **(15742)**

Minneapolis
KTCZ-FM - 97.1 **(16155)**
KXXR-FM - 93.7 **(16157)**

Sauk Rapids
WHMH-FM - 101.7 **(16440)**

Winona
KSMR-FM - 92.5 **(16535)**

MISSOURI
Cape Girardeau
KCGQ-FM - 99.3 **(16949)**

Marshall
KMVC-FM - 91.7 **(17268)**

Poplar Bluff
KJEZ-FM - 95.5 **(17358)**

St. Louis
KSHE-FM - 94.7 **(17549)**
WVRV-FM - 101.1 **(17561)**

Springfield
KZRQ-FM - 104.1 **(17636)**

MONTANA
Butte
KMBR-FM - 95.5 **(17763)**

NEBRASKA
Omaha
KKCD-FM - 92.3 KEZO, 105.9 KKLD, 104.5 KRSZ, 97.7 KQLH, 94.1 KMXM,KBBX **(18222)**

Wayne
KWSC-FM - 91.9 **(18310)**

NEVADA
Las Vegas
KOMP-FM - 92.3 **(18403)**
KUNV-FM - 91.5 **(18406)**

Tonopah
KHWK-FM - 92.7 **(18448)**

NEW HAMPSHIRE
Hanover
WFRD-FM - 99.3 **(18521)**

Manchester
WGIR-FM - 101.1 **(18570)**

Plymouth
WPCR-FM - 91.7 **(18636)**

Portsmouth
WHEB-FM - 100.3 **(18641)**

NEW JERSEY
Cedar Knolls
WDHA-FM - 105.5 **(18723)**

Flemington
WCVH-FM - 90.5 **(18822)**

Franklin Lakes
WRRH-FM - 88.7 **(18836)**

Lincroft
WBJB-FM - 90.5 **(19170)**

Madison
WMNJ-FM - 88.9 **(19183)**

Morristown
WJSV-FM - 90.5 **(19315)**

South Belmar
WRAT-FM - 95.9 **(19581)**

South Orange
WSOU-FM - 89.5 **(19587)**

NEW MEXICO
Albuquerque
KPEK-FM - 100.3 **(19809)**

Farmington
KNMI-FM - 88.9 **(19849)**

Taos
KKIT-AM - 1340 **(19964)**

NEW YORK
Alfred
WETD-FM - 90.9 **(20026)**

Batavia
WGCC-FM - 90.7 **(20123)**

Brockport
WBSU-FM - 89.1 **(20249)**

Cazenovia
WITC-FM - 88.9 **(20443)**

Clinton
WHCL-FM - 88.7 **(20475)**

Corning
WPHD-FM - 94.7, 95.3, 99.5 **(20509)**

Garden City
WLIR-FM - 92.7 **(20646)**

Ithaca
WICB-FM - 91.7 **(20819)**
WICB.FM - 105.9 **(20820)**
WVBR-FM - 93.5 & 105.5 **(20823)**

New York
WNEW-FM - 102.7 **(22976)**

Plainview
WPOB-FM - 88.5 **(23101)**

Poughkeepsie
WRRV-FM - 92.7 **(23163)**

Queensbury
WGFR-FM - 92.7 **(23174)**

Rochester
WNVE-FM - 95.1 **(23250)**

Rooseveltown
CKON-FM - 97.3 **(23276)**

St. Bonaventure
WSBU-FM - 88.3 **(23288)**

Staten Island
WSIA-FM - 88.9 **(23367)**

Syracuse
WAQX-FM - 95.7 **(23435)**

Valhalla
WARY-FM - 88.1 **(23485)**

West Babylon
WBAB-FM - 102.3 **(23537)**

NORTH CAROLINA
Boone
WASU-FM - 90.5 **(23659)**

Edenton
WERX-FM - 102.5 **(23858)**

Fairmont
WSTS-FM - 100.9 **(23874)**

Raleigh
WRDU-FM - 106.1 **(24173)**

NORTH DAKOTA
Belcourt
KEYA-FM - 88.5 **(24346)**

Fargo
KQWB-FM - 98.7 **(24426)**

OHIO
Akron
WONE-FM - 97.5 **(24600)**

Alliance
WRMU-FM - 91.1 **(24607)**

Canton
WRQK-FM - 106.9 **(24738)**

Cincinnati
WEBN-FM - 102.7 **(24838)**

Cleveland
WMMS-FM - 100.7 **(24981)**

Columbus
WBZX-FM - 99.7 **(25075)**
WLVQ-FM - 96.3 **(25080)**

Crestline
WYXZ-FM - 98.7 **(25102)**

Dayton
WTUE-FM - 104.7 **(25153)**
WXEG-FM - 103.9 **(25155)**

Findlay
WLFC-FM - 88.3 **(25198)**

Toledo
WIOT-FM - 104.7 **(25579)**

OKLAHOMA
Oklahoma City
KATT-FM - 100.5 **(25999)**

Tonkawa
KAYE-FM - 90.7 **(26103)**

Tulsa
KMOD-FM - 97.5 **(26151)**
KSTM-FM - 99.5 **(26164)**

OREGON
Medford
KZZE-FM - 106.3 **(26432)**

Portland
KUFO-FM - 101.1 **(26541)**

PENNSYLVANIA
Bloomsburg
WBUQ-FM - 91.1 **(26720)**

California
WVCS-FM - 91.9 **(26747)**

Chester
WDNR-FM, Widener University - 89.5 **(26776)**

Harrisburg
WTPA-FM - 93.5 **(27025)**

Johnstown
WQKK-FM - 99.1 **(27097)**

Lewisburg
WVBU-FM - 90.5 **(27195)**

North East
WRKT-FM - 100.9 **(27341)**

Pittsburgh
WDVE-FM - 102.5 **(27864)**
WRRK-FM - 96.9 **(27878)**

Schnecksville
WXLV-FM - 90.3 **(27950)**

Shippensburg
WSYC-FM - 88.7 **(27994)**

Slippery Rock
WSRU-FM - 90.1 **(28001)**

Whitehall
WZZO-FM - 95.1 **(28162)**

Wilkes Barre
WBSX-FM - 93.7 **(28173)**
WXAR-FM - 95.7 **(28180)**

RHODE ISLAND
Providence
WHJY-FM - 94.1 **(28435)**

SOUTH CAROLINA
Myrtle Beach
WKZQ-AM - 1450 **(28708)**

North Augusta
WRXR-FM - 96.3 **(28723)**

TENNESSEE
Chattanooga
WAWL-FM - 91.5 **(29096)**
WDOD-FM - 96.5 **(29100)**

Henderson
WFHC-FM - 91.5 **(29219)**

Knoxville
WIMZ-FM - 103.5 **(29290)**

Numbers cited in bold after listings are entry numbers rather than page numbers.

WUTK-FM - 90.3 **(29305)**

Memphis
WMFS-FM - 92.9 **(29405)**

Sparta
WRKK-FM - 105.5 **(29614)**

TEXAS
Abilene
KEYJ-FM - 107.9 **(29661)**

Alvin
KACC-FM - 89.7 **(29691)**

Amarillo
KACV-FM - 89.9 **(29700)**

Austin
KLBJ-FM - 93.7 **(29871)**
KROX-FM - 101.5 **(29876)**

Corpus Christi
KNCN-FM - 101.3 **(30090)**

Dallas
KEGL-FM - 97.1 **(30202)**

El Paso
KLAQ-FM - 95.5 **(30296)**

Harker Heights
KLFX-FM - 107.3 **(30424)**

Houston
KLOL-FM - 101.1 **(30563)**

Lufkin
KTBQ-FM - 107.7 **(30745)**

McAllen
KFRQ-FM - 94.5 **(30795)**

Odessa
KFZX-FM - 102.1 **(30875)**

San Antonio
KISS-FM - 99.5 **(31059)**
KSAQ-FM - 96.1 **(31069)**

VIRGINIA
Hampden Sydney
WWHS-FM - 92.1 **(32125)**

Radford
WVMJ-FM - 105.3 **(32352)**

Roanoke
WROV-AM - 1240 **(32504)**

WASHINGTON
Newport
KUBS-FM - 91.5 **(32852)**

Pasco
KXRX-FM - 97.1 **(32886)**

Spokane
KEZE-FM - 105.7 **(33113)**
KSFC-FM - 91.9 **(33126)**

Yakima
KYSC-FM - 88.5 **(33235)**

WEST VIRGINIA
Elkins
WCDE-FM - 90.3 **(33307)**

Fairmont
WRLF-FM - 94.3 **(33315)**

Morgantown
WCLG-FM - 100.1 **(33402)**

WISCONSIN
Eau Claire
WISM-FM - 98.1 **(33681)**

Kenosha
WIIL-FM - 95.1 **(33877)**

La Crosse
WRQT-FM - 95.7 **(33896)**

Merrill
WMZK-FM - 104.1 **(34047)**

Milwaukee
WLZR-FM - 102.9 **(34127)**

WYOMING
Jackson
KMTN-FM - 1290 **(34538)**

ALBERTA, CANADA
Edmonton
CFBR-FM - 100.3 **(34744)**

BRITISH COLUMBIA, CANADA
Kamloops
CIFM-FM - 98.3 **(34981)**

Penticton
CJMG-FM - 97.1 **(35046)**

Prince George
CIRX-FM - 94.3 **(35059)**

Williams Lake
CFFM-FM - 97.5 **(35245)**

MANITOBA, CANADA
Winnipeg
CJKR-FM - 97.5 **(35371)**

NEWFOUNDLAND AND LABRADOR, CANADA
Bonavista Bay
CJOZ-FM - 92.1 **(35442)**

Corner Brook
CHOZ-FM - 94.3 **(35452)**

Gander
CHOZ-FM - 99.9 **(35456)**

Grand Falls
CHOS-FM - 95.9 **(35462)**

Marystown
CIOZ-FM - 94.7 **(35474)**

St. John's
VOCM-FM - 97.5 **(35505)**

Stephenville
CIOS-FM - 98.5 **(35510)**

ONTARIO, CANADA
Hamilton
CJXY-FM - 107.9 **(35896)**

London
CFPL-FM - 95.9 **(35997)**

Ottawa
CKQB-FM - 106.9 **(36295)**

St. Catharines
CHTZ-FM - 97.7 **(36358)**

Sarnia
CHKS-FM - 106.3 **(36368)**

Timmins
CJQQ-FM - 92.1 **(36458)**

QUEBEC, CANADA
Sillery
CHOI-FM - 98.1 **(37402)**

Westmount
CHOM-FM - 97.7 **(37448)**

SASKATCHEWAN, CANADA
Regina
CIZL-FM - 98.9 **(37541)**

Saskatoon
CFMC-FM - 95.1 **(37562)**

YUKON TERRITORY, CANADA
Whitehorse
CHON-FM - 98.1 **(37607)**

ALTERNATIVE/NEW MUSIC/ PROGRESSIVE

ALABAMA
Auburn
WEGL-FM - 91.1 **(48)**

Birmingham
WRAX-FM - 107.7 **(127)**

Jacksonville
WLJS-FM - 91.9 **(295)**

Tuscaloosa
WVUA-FM - 90.7 **(504)**

ALASKA
Anchorage
KRUA-FM - 88.1 **(546)**

Fairbanks
KSUA-FM - 91.5 **(575)**

ARIZONA
Phoenix
KZON-FM - 101.5 **(845)**

Tempe
KASC-AM - 1260 **(920)**
KUKQ-AM - 1060 **(922)**

ARKANSAS
Arkadelphia
KSWH-FM - 91.9 **(1033)**

Conway
KHDX-FM - 93.1 **(1088)**

CALIFORNIA
Arcata
KRFH-AM - 610 **(1432)**

Berkeley
KALX-FM - 90.7 **(1567)**

Burbank
KROQ-FM - 106.7 **(1629)**

Claremont
KSPC-FM - 88.7 **(1727)**

Concord
KVHS-FM - 90.5 **(1762)**

Fresno
KALZ-FM - 102.7 **(1962)**

Fullerton
KFCR-FM - 93.5 **(1992)**

La Jolla
KSDT-FM - 95.5 **(2122)**

La Verne
KULV-AM - 550 **(2129)**
KULV-FM - 107.9 **(2130)**

Los Angeles
KXLU-FM - 88.9 **(2472)**

Palo Alto
KZSU-FM - 90.1 **(2803)**

Pebble Beach
KSPB-FM - 91.9 **(2834)**

Riverside
KUCR-FM - 88.3 **(2954)**

Rohnert Park
KSUN-FM - 95 **(2964)**

Sacramento
KSSU-AM - 1580 **(3050)**
KWOD-FM - 106.5 **(3055)**

San Bernardino
KCXX-FM - 103.9 **(3094)**

San Diego
KCR-FM - 98.9 **(3297)**

San Francisco
KDNZ-FM - 88.7 **(3478)**
KITS-FM - 105.3 **(3488)**
KUSF-FM - 90.3 **(3503)**

San Juan Capistrano
KMRJ-FM - 99.5 **(3560)**

San Luis Obispo
KCPR-FM - 91.3 **(3570)**

Santa Barbara
KCSB-FM - 91.9 **(3662)**

Santa Clara
KSCU-FM - 103.3 **(3677)**

Turlock
KCSS-FM - 91.9 **(3960)**

COLORADO
Boulder
KVCU-AM - 1190 **(4198)**

ALTERNATIVE/NEW MUSIC/
PROGRESSIVE (continued)

Colorado Springs
KEPC-FM - 89.7 **(4266)**

Cortez
KSJD-FM - 91.5 **(4293)**

Denver
KTCL-FM - 93.3 **(4390)**

Fort Collins
KCSU-FM - 90.5 **(4441)**

Grand Junction
KMSA-FM - 91.3 **(4491)**

Greeley
KUNC-FM - 91.5 **(4503)**

USAF Academy
KAFA-FM - 104.5 **(4652)**

CONNECTICUT
Danbury
WXCI-FM - 91.7 **(4768)**

Hartford
WRTC-FM - 89.3 **(4911)**

New London
WAXK-FM - 102.3 **(5021)**

Sharon
WKZE-FM - 98.1 **(5116)**

Storrs
WHUS-FM - 91.7 **(5170)**

West Haven
WNHU-FM - 88.7 **(5208)**

DELAWARE
Georgetown
WDTS-AM - 620 **(5254)**

FLORIDA
Coral Gables
WVUM-FM - 90.5 **(6016)**

Jacksonville
WPLA-FM - 93.3 **(6237)**

Key West
WIIS-FM - 107.1 **(6255)**

Orlando
WOCL-FM - 105.9 **(6524)**

St. Petersburg
WECX-FM - 99.9 **(6637)**

Tampa
WUTZ-AM - 1080 **(6809)**

GEORGIA
Atlanta
WNNX-FM - 99.7 **(7078)**
WRAS-FM - 88.5 **(7082)**

Milledgeville
WGUR-FM - 88.9 **(7437)**

Statesboro
WVGS-FM - 91.9 **(7567)**

Tifton
WPLH-FM - 103.1 **(7603)**

Valdosta
WVVS-FM - 90.9 **(7626)**

HAWAII
Honolulu
KPOI-FM - 97.5 **(7749)**
KUCD-FM - 101.9 **(7754)**

ILLINOIS
Bloomington
WESN-FM - 88.1 **(8084)**

Champaign
WPGU-FM - 107.1 **(8233)**

Chicago
WCRX-FM - 88.1 **(8619)**
WHPK-FM - 88.5 **(8628)**
WIIT - 88.9 **(8629)**
WKIE-FM - 92.7 **(8633)**
WKQX-FM - 101.1 **(8635)**

WLUW-FM - 88.7 **(8641)**
WXAV-FM - 88.3 **(8659)**

Decatur
WJMU-FM - 89.5 **(8719)**

Elmhurst
WRSE-FM - 88.7 **(8841)**

Elsah
WTPC-FM - 105.3 **(8845)**

Evanston
WNUR-FM - 89.3 **(8876)**

Flossmoor
WHFH-FM - 88.5 **(8892)**

Glenview
WGBK-FM - 88.5 **(8943)**

Mattoon
WLKL-FM - 89.9 **(9162)**

Monmouth
WMCR-FM - 88.9 **(9219)**

Mount Carmel
WVJC-FM - 89.1 **(9233)**

Naperville
WONC-FM - 89.1 **(9276)**

Normal
WZND-FM - 106.1 **(9310)**

Quincy
WQUB-FM - 90.3 **(9482)**

River Grove
WRRG-FM - 88.9 **(9497)**

INDIANA
Bloomington
WIUS-AM - 1570 **(9859)**
WTTS-FM - 92.3 **(9861)**

Carmel
WHJE-FM - 91.3 **(9882)**

Chesterton
WDSO-FM - 88.3 **(9888)**

Columbia City
WJHS-FM - 91.5 **(9894)**

Evansville
WUEV-FM - 91.5 **(9951)**

Fort Wayne
WEJE-FM - 96.3 **(9982)**
WXKE-FM - 103.9 **(9994)**

Franklin
WFCI-FM - 89.5 **(10009)**

Greencastle
WGRE-FM - 91.5 **(10037)**

Indianapolis
WRZX-FM - 103.3 **(10209)**

Notre Dame
WVFI-AM - 640 **(10380)**

Terre Haute
WMHD-FM - 90.5 **(10499)**

IOWA
Ames
KURE-FM - 88.5 **(10598)**

Council Bluffs
KIWR-FM - 89.7 **(10727)**

Davenport
KALA-FM - 88.5 **(10740)**

Decorah
KWLC-AM - 1240 **(10762)**

Dubuque
KLCR-FM - 96.9 **(10851)**

Forest City
KZOW-FM - 91.9 **(10893)**

Fort Dodge
KICB-FM - 88.1 **(10909)**

Iowa City
KRUI-FM - 89.7 **(10993)**

Oskaloosa
KIGC-FM - 88.7 **(11138)**

Pella
KCUI-FM - 89.1 **(11153)**

Sioux City
KMSC-FM - 88.3 **(11218)**

Storm Lake
KBVU-FM - 97.5 **(11249)**

Waverly
KWAR-FM - 89.1 **(11310)**

West Des Moines
KWDM-FM - 88.7 **(11321)**

KANSAS
Baldwin City
KNBU-FM - 89.7 **(11352)**

Dodge City
KONQ-FM - 91.9 **(11419)**

Lawrence
KJHK-FM - 90.7 **(11574)**

Manhattan
KSDB-FM - 91.9 **(11635)**

North Newton
KBCU-FM - 88.1 **(11677)**

Winfield
KSWC-FM - 100.3 **(11912)**

KENTUCKY
Lexington
WRFL-FM - 88.1 **(12194)**

LOUISIANA
Baton Rouge
KLSU-FM - 91.1 **(12508)**

Natchitoches
KNWD-FM - 91.7 **(12720)**

New Orleans
KKND-FM - 106.7 **(12765)**

Shreveport
KSCL-FM - 91.3 **(12834)**

Thibodaux
KNSU-FM - 91.5 **(12861)**

MAINE
Bangor
WHSN-FM - 89.3 **(12909)**

Brunswick
WBOR-FM - 91.1 **(12937)**

Portland
WCYI-FM - 93.9 **(13024)**
WNHQ-FM - 92.1 **(13030)**

Presque Isle
WUPI-FM - 92.1 **(13042)**

Waterville
WMHB-FM - 89.7 **(13073)**

MARYLAND
Annapolis
WRNR-FM - 103.1 **(13102)**

Baltimore
WHSR-AM - 530 **(13273)**

Catonsville
WUMD-FM - 560 **(13403)**

College Park
WMUC-FM - 88.1 **(13447)**

Emmitsburg
WMTB-FM - 89.9 **(13502)**

Frostburg
WFWM-FM - 91.9 **(13529)**

MASSACHUSETTS
Boston
WBCN-FM - 104.1 **(13976)**

Bridgewater
WBIM-FM - 91.5 **(14009)**

Chestnut Hill
WZBC-FM - 90.3 **(14135)**

Concord
WIQH-FM - 88.3 **(14150)**

Deerfield
WGAJ-FM - 91.7 **(14158)**

Fitchburg
WXPL-FM - 91.3 **(14186)**

Framingham
WDJM-FM - 91.3 **(14202)**

Franklin
WGAO-FM - 88.3 **(14208)**

Haverhill
WXRV-FM - 92.5 **(14233)**

Lowell
WJUL-FM - 91.5 **(14282)**

Lynn
WFNX-FM - 101.7 **(14286)**

Milton
WMLN-FM - 91.5 **(14338)**

Northampton
WOZQ-FM - 91.9 **(14434)**

Northfield
WNMH-FM - 91.5 **(14436)**

Salem
WMWM-FM - 91.7 **(14517)**

Sheffield
WBSL-FM - 91.7 **(14520)**

Sudbury
WYAJ-FM - 97.7 **(14582)**

Walpole
WSRB-FM - 91.5 **(14595)**

West Yarmouth
WDVT-FM - 1240 **(14629)**

Westfield
WSKB-FM - 89.5 **(14645)**

Williamstown
WCFM-FM - 91.9 **(14662)**

Winchester
WHSR-FM - 91.9 **(14668)**

Worcester
WCHC-FM - 88.1 **(14695)**

MICHIGAN
Canton
WSDP-FM - 88.1 **(14855)**

Dearborn
WHFR-FM - 89.3 **(14908)**

Detroit
WDET-FM - 101.9 **(14957)**

Farmington Hills
WORB-FM - 90.3 **(15026)**

Holland
WTHS-FM - 89.9 **(15179)**

Kalamazoo
WIDR-FM - 89.1 **(15249)**

Kalkaska
WKAL-AM - 1420 **(15262)**

Marquette
WUPX-FM - 91.5 **(15349)**

Mount Pleasant
WMHW-FM - 91.5 **(15383)**

Traverse City
WNMC-FM - 90.7 **(15612)**

MINNESOTA
Bemidji
KBSB-FM - 89.7 **(15742)**

Collegeville
KJNB-FM - 99.9 **(15807)**

Duluth
KUMD-FM - 103.3 **(15852)**

Minneapolis
KUOM-AM - 770 **(16156)**

Morris
KUMM-FM - 89.7 **(16200)**

St. Cloud
KVSC-FM - 88.1 **(16352)**

St. Louis Park
KDXL-FM - 106.5 **(16362)**

MISSISSIPPI
Jackson
WMPR-FM - 90.1 **(16726)**

University
WUMS-FM - 92.1 **(16869)**

MISSOURI
Columbia
KCOU-FM - 88.1 **(17015)**
KFMZ-FM - 98.3 **(17016)**

Marshall
KMVC-FM - 91.7 **(17268)**

Maryville
KDLX-FM - 106.7 **(17278)**

Poplar Bluff
KLID-AM - 1340 **(17359)**

St. Louis
KCFV-FM - 89.5 **(17534)**
KPNT-FM - 105.7 **(17546)**
KWUR-FM - 90.3 **(17554)**

MONTANA
Missoula
KBGA-FM - 89.9 **(17878)**

NEBRASKA
Kearney
KLPR-FM - 91.3 **(18065)**

Lincoln
KRNU-FM - 90.3 **(18143)**

NEVADA
Reno
KDOT-FM - 104.5 **(18429)**

NEW HAMPSHIRE
Durham
WUNH-FM - 91.3 **(18504)**

Exeter
WPEA-FM - 90.5 **(18508)**

Hanover
WDCR-AM - 1340 **(18520)**

Henniker
WNEC-FM - 91.7 **(18523)**

Keene
WKNH-FM - 91.3 **(18535)**

Nashua
WHOB-FM - 106.3 **(18607)**

NEW JERSEY
Blackwood
WDBK-FM - 91.5 **(18684)**

Flemington
WCVH-FM - 90.5 **(18822)**

Jersey City
WGKR-AM - 540 **(19150)**

Lawrenceville
WRRC-FM - 107.7 **(19166)**

Madison
WMNJ-FM - 88.9 **(19183)**

Neptune
WHTG-FM - 106.3 **(19322)**

New Brunswick
WRSU-FM - 88.7 **(19345)**

Piscataway
WVPH-FM - 90.3 **(19432)**

Princeton
WPRB-FM - 103.3 **(19481)**

Randolph
WCCM-AM - 640 **(19499)**

Somers Point
WJSE-FM - 102.7 **(19559)**

Teaneck
WFDQ-FM - 91.9 **(19611)**
WFDU-FM - 89.1 **(19612)**

Upper Montclair
WMSC-FM - 90.3 **(19695)**

Wayne
WPSC-FM - 88.7 **(19710)**

West Long Branch
WMCX-FM - 88.9 **(19723)**

NEW MEXICO
Albuquerque
KTEG-FM - 104.7 **(19813)**
KTZO-FM - 103.3 **(19814)**

Farmington
KNMI-FM - 88.9 **(19849)**

Portales
KZIA-AM - 1610 **(19909)**

NEW YORK
Albany
WCDB-FM - 90.9 **(20010)**
WHRL-FM - 103.1 **(20012)**

Annandale On Hudson
WXBC-AM - 540 **(20061)**

Auburn
WDWN-FM - 89.1 **(20108)**

Batavia
WGCC-FM - 90.7 **(20123)**

Binghamton
WHRW-FM - 90.5 **(20223)**

Brockport
WBSU-FM - 89.1 **(20249)**

Buffalo
WBNY-FM - 91.3 **(20396)**

Cazenovia
WITC-FM - 88.9 **(20443)**

Cortland
WSUC-FM - 90.5 **(20514)**

Fredonia
WCVF-FM - 88.9 **(20624)**

Garden City
WLIR-FM - 92.7 **(20646)**

Geneseo
WGSU-FM - 89.3 **(20651)**

Hamilton
WRCU-FM - 90.1 **(20709)**

Ithaca
WICB-FM - 91.7 **(20819)**
WVIC-FM - 105.9 **(20824)**

New York
WBMB-AM - 590 **(22964)**
WFIT-AM - 530 **(22969)**
WKCR-FM - 89.9 **(22972)**
WNYU-FM - 89.1 **(22981)**
WPUB-AM - 640 **(22987)**

Old Westbury
WNYT-AM - 550 **(23038)**

Oneonta
WONY-FM - 90.9 **(23053)**
WRHO-FM - 89.7 **(23054)**

Oswego
WNYO-FM - 88.9 **(23063)**

Potsdam
WTSC-FM - 91.1 **(23144)**

Rochester
WIRQ-FM - 94.3 **(23249)**
WRUR-FM - 88.5 **(23254)**

Saratoga Springs
WSPN-FM - 91.1 **(23305)**

Schenectady
WRUC-FM - 89.7 **(23322)**

Troy
WRPI-FM - 91.5 **(23460)**

Woodstock
WDST-FM - 100.1 **(23597)**

Circulation: ★ = ABC; △ = BPA; ♦ = CAC; ● = CCAB; ❑ = VAC; ⊕ = PO Statement; ‡ = Publisher's Report; Boldface figures = sworn; Light figures = estimated.

Radio Station Formats

2983

ALTERNATIVE/NEW MUSIC/ PROGRESSIVE (continued)

NORTH CAROLINA
Charlotte
WEND-FM - 106.5 (23768)

Durham
WXDU-FM - 88.7 (23854)

Elon
WSOE-FM - 89.3 (23871)

Greensboro
WQFS-FM - 90.9 (23956)
WUAG-FM - 103.1 (23960)

Greenville
WZMB-FM - 91.3 (23976)

High Point
WWIH-FM - 90.3 (24007)

Mars Hill
WVMH-FM - 90.5 (24058)

Raleigh
WKNC-FM - 88.1 (24164)

Sanford
WDCC-FM - 90.5 (24220)

Winston-Salem
WAKE-FM - 89.5 (24327)

NORTH DAKOTA
Bismarck
KXUM-AM - 670 (24373)

Grand Forks
KFJM-FM - 90.7 (24459)

OHIO
Ashland
WRDL-FM - 88.9 (24622)

Berea
WBWC-FM - 88.3 (24679)

Centerville
WCWT-FM - 101.5 (24754)

Columbus
WCBE-FM - 90.5 (25076)

Dayton
WGXM-FM - 98.1 (25140)

Granville
WDUB-FM - 91.1 (25224)

Hamilton
WHSS-FM - 89.5 (25236)

Oxford
WOXY-FM - 97.7 (25464)

Streetsboro
WSTB-FM - 88.9 (25549)

Tiffin
WHEI-FM - 88.9 (25560)

Westerville
WOBN-FM - 101.5 (25647)
WUFM-FM - 88.7 (25648)

Wheelersburg
WRAU-FM - 94.9 (25651)

OKLAHOMA
Oklahoma City
KOKF-FM - 90.9 (26011)

Stillwater
KSPI-FM - 93.7 (26086)

Tulsa
KMYZ-FM - 104.5 (26154)

OREGON
Ashland
KSMF-FM - 89.1 (26222)

Eugene
KWVA-FM - 88.1 (26349)

Portland
KRRC-FM - 104.1 (26539)
KSTE-FM - 105.9 (26540)

PENNSYLVANIA
Bloomsburg
WBUQ-FM - 91.1 (26720)

Chester
WDNR-FM, Widener University - 89.5 (26776)

Clarion
WCCB-AM - 1610 (26781)

Conshohocken
WPLY-FM - 100.3 (26805)

East Stroudsburg
WESS-FM - 90.3 (26848)

Erie
WERG-FM - 89.9 (26903)

Greenville
WTGP-FM - 88.1 (26962)

Lewisburg
WVBU-FM - 90.5 (27195)

Meadville
WARC-FM - 90.3 (27236)

Middletown
WMSS-FM - 91.1 (27261)

Millersville
WIXQ-FM - 91.7 (27268)

Nanticoke
WSFX-FM - 105.7 FM (27309)

Philadelphia
WKDU-FM - 91.7 (27737)
WQHS-AM - 730 (27742)
WXPN-FM - 88.5 (27747)

Pittsburgh
WPPJ-AM - 670 (27871)
WXDX-FM - 105.9 (27882)

Reading
WXAC-FM - 91.3 (27925)

Schnecksville
WXLV-FM - 90.3 (27950)

Shippensburg
WSYC-FM - 88.7 (27994)

Slippery Rock
WRSK-FM - 88.1 (28000)

State College
WGMR-FM - 101.1 (28024)

Swarthmore
WSRN-FM - 91.5 (28047)

Wilkes Barre
WCLH-FM - 90.7 (28174)

Williamsport
WPTC-FM - 88.1 (28189)
WRLC-FM - 91.7 (28191)

York
WVYC-FM - 99.7 (28218)

RHODE ISLAND
Bristol
WQRI-FM - 88.3 (28329)

Coventry
WCVY-FM - 91.5 (28331)

Providence
WDOM-FM - 91.3 (28433)
WRBU-FM - 95.5 (28437)
WWRX-FM - 103.7 (28440)

Smithfield
WJMF-FM - 88.7 (28443)

SOUTH CAROLINA
Charleston
WAVF-FM - 96.1 (28520)

Clemson
WSBF-FM - 88.1 (28538)

Columbia
WARQ-FM - 93.5 (28572)

Greenville
WPLS-FM - 96.7 (28640)

Hemingway
WLGI-FM - 90.9 (28660)

SOUTH DAKOTA
Brookings
KSDJ-FM - 90.7 (28824)

Rapid City
KTEQ-FM - 91.3 (28950)

Sioux Falls
KCFS-FM - 94.5 (28970)
KRRO-FM - 103.7 (28981)

Spearfish
KBHU-FM - 89.1 (28995)

Vermillion
KAOR-FM - 91.1 (29008)

TENNESSEE
Chattanooga
WAWL-FM - 91.5 (29096)

Cookeville
WTTU-FM - 88.5 (29151)

Kingsport
WRZK-FM - 95.9 (29267)

Knoxville
WUTK-FM - 90.3 (29305)

Murfreesboro
WMTS-FM - 88.3 (29438)

Nashville
WRLT-FM - 100.1 (29529)
WRVU-FM - 91.1 (29530)

Springfield
WDBL-FM - 94.3 (29620)

TEXAS
Amarillo
KACV-FM - 89.9 (29700)

Austin
KAMX-FM - 94.7 (29858)
KROX-FM - 101.5 (29876)
KVRX-FM - 91.7 (29881)

Canyon
KWTS-FM - 91.1 (30001)

College Station
KANM-FM - 99.9 (30058)

Houston
KTBZ-FM - 94.5 (30575)
KTRU-FM - 91.7 (30581)

Huntsville
KSHU-FM - 90.5 (30601)

Lubbock
KTXT-FM - 88.1 (30735)

Nacogdoches
KSAU-FM - 90.1 (30854)

Plainview
KWLD-FM - 91.5 (30946)

San Antonio
KSYM-FM - 90.1 (31074)

San Marcos
KTSW-FM - 89.9 MAZ (31087)

UTAH
Cedar City
KSUU-FM - 91.1 (31329)

Orem
KOHS-FM - 91.7 (31386)

Salt Lake City
KXRK-FM - 96.3 (31469)

Spanish Fork
KHQN-AM - 1480 (31475)

VERMONT
Castleton
WIUV-FM - 91.3 (31529)

Colchester
WWPV-FM - 88.7 (31535)

Lyndonville
WWLR-FM - 91.5 (31551)

Manchester
WEQX-FM - 102.7 (31552)

Northfield
WNUB-FM - 88.3 (31577)

Plainfield
WGDR-FM - 91.1 (31579)

Vergennes
WBTZ-FM - 99.9 (31609)

VIRGINIA
Blacksburg
WTJY-FM - 89.5 (31889)

Bridgewater
WGMB-AM - 640 (31896)

Charlottesville
WTJU-FM - 91.1 (31955)

Farmville
WMLU - 91.3 (32072)

Hampden Sydney
WWHS-FM - 92.1 (32125)

Harrisonburg
WXJM-FM - 88.7 (32156)

Norfolk
WODU-AM - 1630 (32304)
WROX-FM - 96.1 (32305)

WASHINGTON
Auburn
KGRG-FM - 89.9 (32656)

Bellevue
KASB-FM - 89.3 (32671)

Bellingham
KUGS-FM - 89.3 (32685)

Centralia
KCED-FM - 91.3 (32705)

Kennewick
KTCV-FM - 88.1 (32793)

Pullman
KZUU-FM - 90.7 (32917)

Seattle
KCMU-FM - 90.3 (33050)
KNDD-FM - 107.7 (33063)

Spokane
KAGU-FM - 88.7 (33107)
KWRS-FM - 90.3 (33132)

WEST VIRGINIA
Elkins
WCDE-FM - 90.3 (33307)

Morgantown
WWVU-FM - 91.7 (33406)

Shepherdstown
WSHC-FM - 89.7 (33465)

WISCONSIN
La Crosse
WFBZ-FM - 105.5 (33888)

Madison
WMMM-FM - 105.5 (34001)

Milwaukee
WLUM-FM - 102.1 (34126)
WMSE-FM - 91.7 (34130)

Platteville
WSUP-FM - 90.5 (34248)

Sheboygan
WSHS-FM - 91.7 (34325)

Stevens Point
WWSP-FM - 89.9 (34347)

Superior
KUWS-FM - 91.3 (34362)

Whitewater
WSUW-FM - 91.7 (34460)

ALBERTA, CANADA
Calgary
CBR-FM - 102.1 (34662)
CJSW-FM - 90.9 (34670)

Edmonton
CJSR-FM - 88.5 (34753)

BRITISH COLUMBIA, CANADA
Victoria
CKMO-FM - 103.1 (35236)

NEW BRUNSWICK, CANADA
Fredericton
CHSR-FM - 97.9 (35403)

NEWFOUNDLAND AND LABRADOR, CANADA
St. John's
CHMR-FM - 93.5 (35498)

NOVA SCOTIA, CANADA
Antigonish
CFXU-AM - 690 (35539)

ONTARIO, CANADA
Hamilton
CFMU-FM - 93.3 (35893)

London
CHRW-FM - 94.7 (35999)

Ottawa
CHUO-FM - 89.1 (36291)

Toronto
CFNY-FM - 102.1 (36804)
CHRY-FM - 105.5 (36810)
CIUT-FM - 89.5 (36816)
CKLN-FM - 88.1 (36822)

Windsor
CIMX-FM - 88.7 (36898)

QUEBEC, CANADA
Montreal
CKUT-FM - 90.3 (37250)

Quebec
CKRL-FM - 89.1 (37304)

Verdun
CKOI-FM - 96.9 (37429)

BIG BAND/NOSTALGIA

ALABAMA
York
WYLS-AM - 670 (518)

ALASKA
Anchorage
KHAR-AM - 590 (542)

ARIZONA
Phoenix
KOY-AM - 101.5 (830)

Prescott
KNOT-AM - 1450 (852)

Tucson
KRQ-FM - 93.7 (991)

ARKANSAS
Benton
KAKI-FM - 107.1 (1048)

CALIFORNIA
Cathedral City
KWXY-FM - 98.5 (1680)

Hesperia
KRAK-AM - 1470 (2049)

Lakeport
KXBX-AM - 1270 (2144)

Modesto
KBEE-AM - 970 (2564)

Oakhurst
KAAT-FM - 103.1 & translators 104.3 (2660)

Palm Springs
KCMJ-AM - 1140 (2773)

Pasadena
KPCC-FM - 89.3 (2829)

San Diego
KPOP-AM - 1360 (3311)

Twentynine Palms
KQYN-AM - 1250 (3966)

COLORADO
Colorado Springs
KCMN-AM - 1530 (4265)
KTWK-AM - 1300 (4284)

Denver
KEZW-AM - 1430 (4377)

CONNECTICUT
Bloomfield
WJMJ-FM - 88.9 (4705)

Monroe
WGRS-FM - 91.5 (4964)
WGSK-FM - 90.1 (4965)
WMNR-FM - 88.1 (4966)
WRXC-FM - 90.1 (4967)

DELAWARE
Claymont
WJBR-AM - 1290 (5239)

Georgetown
WJWL-AM - 900 (5255)

FLORIDA
Delray Beach
WDBF-AM - 1420 (6058)

Hernando
WRZN-AM - 720 (6186)

Jacksonville
WJAX-AM - 1220 (6224)

Orlando
WHOO-AM - 990 (6518)

Palm Harbor
WGUL-AM - 860 (6553)
WGUL-FM - 106.3 (6554)

West Palm Beach
WRMS-FM - 97.9 (6860)

GEORGIA
Macon
WALJ-FM - 107.1 (7388)

Manchester
WFDR-AM - 1370 (7408)

HAWAII
Honolulu
KZOO-AM - 1210 (7758)

IDAHO
Idaho Falls
KUPI-AM - 980 (7878)

Ketchum
KEZQ-FM - 92.9 (7888)

ILLINOIS
Mount Carmel
WVMC-AM - 1360 (9234)

Watseka
WGFA-AM - 1360 (9740)

INDIANA
Indianapolis
WHUT-AM - 1470 (10198)

IOWA
Cedar Rapids
KMRY-AM - 1450 (10683)

Clinton
KCLN-AM - 1390 (10712)

Creston
KITR-FM - 101.3 (10733)
KSIB-AM - 1520 (10734)

Davenport
WKBF-AM - 1270 (10748)

Des Moines
KRNT-AM - 1350 (10831)

Keokuk
KOKX-AM - 1310 (11014)

Circulation: ★ = ABC; △ = BPA; ◆ = CAC; • = CCAB; ❑ = VAC; ⊕ = PO Statement; ‡ = Publisher's Report; Boldface figures = sworn; Light figures = estimated.

2985

BIG BAND/NOSTALGIA (continued)

Storm Lake
KAYL-AM - 990 **(11247)**

Waterloo
KWLO-AM - 1330 **(11297)**

KANSAS
Abilene
KABI-AM - 1560 **(11335)**

Independence
KIND-AM - 1010 **(11511)**

KENTUCKY
Lexington
WBBE-AM - 1580 **(12181)**

LOUISIANA
Houma
KJIN-AM - 1490 **(12603)**

MAINE
Auburn
WLAM-AM - 870 **(12885)**

Brewer
WDEA-AM - 1370 **(12927)**

MARYLAND
Easton
WEMD-AM - 1460 **(13491)**

Princess Anne
WESM-FM - 91.3 **(13670)**

MASSACHUSETTS
Medford
WXKS-AM - 1430 **(14326)**

Salem
WESX-AM - 1230 **(14516)**

MICHIGAN
Owosso
WOAP-AM - 1090 **(15430)**

Rogers City
WMLQ-FM - 96.7 **(15470)**

Saginaw
WCEN-AM - 1150 **(15495)**

MINNESOTA
Albany
KASM-AM - 1150 **(15705)**

Hibbing
WHLB-AM - 1400 **(15956)**

Minneapolis
KLBB-AM - 1400 **(16150)**

New Ulm
KNUJ-AM - 860 **(16217)**

MISSOURI
Branson
KOMC-FM - 100.1 **(16923)**

Carthage
KDMO-AM - 1490 **(16960)**

Maryville
KXCV-FM - 90.5 **(17279)**

Springfield
KTOZ-AM - 1060 **(17629)**

MONTANA
Missoula
KLCY-AM - 930 **(17882)**

NEW HAMPSHIRE
Lebanon
WCFR-AM - 1480 **(18543)**

NEW JERSEY
Bayville
WOBM-AM - 1160 **(18667)**

NEW MEXICO
Silver City
KNFT-AM - 950 **(19954)**

NEW YORK
Baldwinsville
WFBL-AM - 1050 **(20116)**

Buffalo
WHLD-AM - 1270 **(20401)**

Cheektowaga
WECK-AM - 1230 **(20459)**

Corning
WCBA-AM - 1350 **(20504)**

Farmingdale
WHLI-AM - 1100 **(20598)**

Johnstown
WIZR-AM - 930 **(20852)**

New Rochelle
WRTN-FM - 93.5 **(21124)**

Patchogue
WLIM-AM - 1580 **(23080)**

Rochester
WEZO-AM - 950 **(23246)**

Salamanca
WGGO-AM - 1590 **(23295)**

Utica
WADR-AM - 1480 **(23471)**
WRNY-AM - 1350 **(23479)**
WUTQ-AM - 1550 **(23481)**

NORTH CAROLINA
Dallas
WSGE-FM - 91.7 **(23797)**

Fayetteville
WAZZ-AM - 1490 **(23884)**

High Point
WISC-FM - 98.3 **(24004)**

Southern Pines
WIOZ-AM - 550 **(24238)**

Sparta
WCOK-AM - 1060 **(24241)**

NORTH DAKOTA
Bismarck
KLXX-AM - 1270 **(24369)**

OHIO
Ashland
WNCO-AM - 1340 **(24620)**

Chagrin Falls
WKHR-FM - 88.3 **(24758)**

Cincinnati
WMKV-FM - 89.3 **(24844)**

Youngstown
WRTK-AM - 1390 **(25711)**
WSOM-AM - 600 **(25712)**

OREGON
Coos Bay
KHSN-AM - 1230 **(26279)**

Eugene
KKXO-AM - 1450 **(26340)**

Grants Pass
KAJO-AM - 1270 **(26363)**

PENNSYLVANIA
Easton
WEST-AM - 1400 **(26852)**

Elizabethtown
WQXA-AM - 1250 **(26867)**

Erie
WRIE-AM - 1260 **(26911)**

Greencastle
WCBG-AM - 1590 **(26951)**

Harrisburg
WKBO-AM - 1230 **(27020)**

Lancaster
WLAN-AM - 1390 **(27152)**

Linesville
WVCC-FM - 101.7 **(27202)**

Monroeville
WXVX-AM - 1510 **(27289)**

Selinsgrove
WJMW-AM - 550 **(27977)**

Warminster
WLBS-FM - 91.7 **(28103)**

Whitehall
WKAP-AM - 1470 **(28161)**

PUERTO RICO
Bayamon
WLUZ-AM - 1600 **(28232)**

Caguas
WNEL-AM - 1430 **(28235)**

Mayaguez
WTIL-AM - 1300 **(28269)**

RHODE ISLAND
East Providence
WPRL-FM - 790 **(28347)**

SOUTH CAROLINA
Camden
WCAM-AM - 1590 **(28501)**

Hilton Head Island
WLOW-FM - 107.9 **(28665)**

North Charleston
WTMZ-AM - 910 **(28729)**

TENNESSEE
Donelson
WAMB-FM - 98.7 **(29169)**

Nashville
WAMB-AM - 1160 **(29506)**

TEXAS
Carrizo Springs
KBEN-AM - 1450 **(30003)**

Dallas
KAAM-AM - 1310 **(30192)**

Huntsville
KMHT-AM - 1450 **(30599)**

Killeen
KNCT-FM - 91.3 **(30645)**

San Antonio
KLUP-AM - 930 **(31062)**

San Saba
KBAL-AM - 1410 **(31090)**

Stephenville
KSTV-AM - 1510 **(31132)**

Terrell
KPYK-AM - 1570 **(31183)**

Uvalde
KVOU-AM - 1400 **(31226)**

UTAH
Logan
KLGN-AM - 1390 **(31359)**

VERMONT
Burlington
WJOY-AM - 1230 **(31525)**

VIRGINIA
Charlottesville
WKAV-AM - 1400 **(31953)**

Urbanna
WNDJ-FM - 104.9 **(32573)**

Williamsburg
WMBG-AM - 740 **(32626)**

Woodstock
WAZR-FM - 93.7 **(32641)**

Numbers cited in bold after listings are entry numbers rather than page numbers.

WASHINGTON
Lynnwood
KSER-FM - 90.7 **(32826)**

Olympia
KBRD-AM - 680 **(32868)**

WEST VIRGINIA
Buckhannon
WBUC-AM - 1460 **(33265)**

Wheeling
WBBD-AM - 1400 **(33505)**

WISCONSIN
Appleton
WRJQ-AM - 1570 **(33552)**

Madison
WNWC-AM - 1190 **(34004)**

Neenah
WNAM-AM - 1280 **(34160)**

Neillsville
WCCN-AM - 1370 **(34164)**

Tomah
WTMB-AM - 1460 **(34371)**

Waupun
WFDL AM - 1170 **(34428)**

ONTARIO, CANADA
Peterborough
CKPT-AM - 1420 **(36322)**

Windsor
CKWW-AM - 580 **(36900)**

BLUEGRASS

ALABAMA
Sumiton
WRSM-AM - 1540 **(461)**

ARKANSAS
State University
KASU-FM - 91.9 **(1351)**

DISTRICT OF COLUMBIA
Washington
WAMU-FM - 88.5 **(5877)**

FLORIDA
Bartow
WBAR-AM - 1460 **(5919)**

Chiefland
WLQH-AM - 940 **(5982)**
WLQH-FM - 97.3 **(5983)**

GEORGIA
Mountain City
WALH-AM - 1340 **(7450)**

ILLINOIS
Farmer City
WWHP-FM - 98.3 **(8886)**

INDIANA
New Albany
WXLM-FM - 105.7 **(10340)**

IOWA
Decorah
KWLC-AM - 1240 **(10762)**

KANSAS
North Newton
KBCU-FM - 88.1 **(11677)**

KENTUCKY
Albany
WANY-AM - 1390 **(11915)**
WANY-FM - 106.3 **(11916)**

Jackson
WEKG-AM - 810 **(12146)**

Leitchfield
WMTL-AM - 870 **(12158)**

Lexington
WRFL-FM - 88.1 **(12194)**

Manchester
WTBK-FM - 105.7 **(12280)**

Renfro Valley
WRVK-AM - 1460 **(12381)**

Stanton
WSKV-FM - 104.9 **(12419)**

Vanceburg
WKKS-AM - 1570 **(12425)**

MASSACHUSETTS
Provincetown
WOMR-FM - 92.1 **(14487)**

Worcester
WICN-FM - 90.5 **(14698)**

MICHIGAN
Kalamazoo
WMUK-FM - 102.1 **(15256)**

MINNESOTA
Bemidji
KBSB-FM - 89.7 **(15742)**

MISSISSIPPI
Booneville
WMAE-FM - 91.3 **(16574)**

Jackson
WTWZ-AM - 1120 **(16731)**

MISSOURI
Point Lookout
KCOZ-FM - 91.7 **(17355)**

Rolla
KUMR-FM - 88.5 **(17382)**

St. Charles
KCLC-FM - 89.1 **(17385)**

NEW HAMPSHIRE
Henniker
WNEC-FM - 91.7 **(18523)**

NEW YORK
New York
WKCR-FM - 89.9 **(22972)**

Pulaski
WSCP-FM - 101.7 **(23167)**

NORTH CAROLINA
Durham
WXDU-FM - 88.7 **(23854)**

Lenoir
WKGX-AM - 1080 **(24038)**

Mocksville
WDSL-AM - 1520 **(24065)**

Mount Airy
WPAQ-AM - 740 **(24082)**

Roanoke Rapids
WPTM-FM - 102.3 **(24196)**

Sparta
WCOK-AM - 1060 **(24241)**

OREGON
Gresham
KMHD-FM - 89.1 **(26366)**

PENNSYLVANIA
Lebanon
WADV-AM - 940 **(27176)**

TENNESSEE
Bristol
WOPI-AM - 1490 **(29069)**

Camden
WFWL-AM - 1220 **(29079)**

Jefferson City
WJFC-AM - 1480 **(29248)**

La Follette
WLAF-AM - 1450 **(29310)**

Loudon
WLOD-AM - 1140 **(29335)**

Shelbyville
WLIJ-AM - 1580 **(29602)**

Tazewell
WNTT-AM - 1250 **(29626)**

TEXAS
Bridgeport
KBOC-FM - 98.3 **(29952)**

VIRGINIA
Blacksburg
WKEX-AM - 1430 **(31887)**

Duffield
WDUF-AM - 1120 **(32000)**

Galax
WBRF-FM - 98.1 **(32100)**

Harrisonburg
WEMC-FM - 91.7 **(32143)**

Rocky Mount
WYTI-AM - 1570 **(32513)**

South Boston
WSBV-AM - 1560 **(32533)**

Triangle
WPWC-AM - 1480 **(32571)**

WASHINGTON
Bellevue
KBCS-FM - 91.3 **(32672)**

Lynnwood
KSER-FM - 90.7 **(32826)**

WEST VIRGINIA
Fisher
WELD-AM - 690 **(33317)**

Weston
WHAW-AM - 980 **(33499)**

NOVA SCOTIA, CANADA
New Glasgow
CKEC-AM - 1320 **(35597)**

BLUES

ALABAMA
Birmingham
WJLD-AM - 1400 **(118)**

Demopolis
WVFG-FM - 107.5 **(180)**

Normal
WJAB-FM - 90.9 **(402)**

Tuscaloosa
WTSK-AM - 790 **(501)**

Tuscumbia
WZZA-AM - 1410 **(506)**

Wetumpka
WAPZ-AM - 1250 **(516)**

York
WSLY-FM - 104.9 **(517)**

ALASKA
Bethel
KYUK-AM - 640 **(556)**

Unalaska
KIAL-AM - 1450 **(645)**

ARKANSAS
Helena
KFFA-AM - 1360 **(1176)**

State University
KASU-FM - 91.9 **(1351)**

CALIFORNIA
Fresno
KFSR-FM - 90.7 **(1967)**

BLUES (continued)

Long Beach
KLON-FM - 88.1 **(2179)**

Mission Viejo
KSBR-FM - 88.5 **(2560)**

Riverside
KUCR-FM - 88.3 **(2954)**

San Diego
KSDS-FM - 88.3 **(3314)**

Santa Clara
KSCU-FM - 103.3 **(3677)**

Turlock
KCSS-FM - 91.9 **(3960)**

COLORADO
Alamosa
KRZA-FM - 88.7 **(4136)**

Pagosa Springs
KWUF-FM - 106.3 **(4592)**

CONNECTICUT
Hartford
WQTQ-FM - 89.9 **(4909)**

Sharon
WKZE-FM - 98.1 **(5116)**

FLORIDA
Lakeland
WWAB-AM - 1330 **(6297)**

GEORGIA
Irwinton
WVKX-FM - 103.7 **(7338)**

Savannah
WHCJ-FM - 90.3 **(7544)**

Tifton
WPLH-FM - 103.1 **(7603)**

ILLINOIS
Chicago
WGCI-AM - 1390 **(8623)**
WUBT-FM - 103.5 **(8655)**

East St. Louis
WESL-AM - 1490 **(8808)**

Farmer City
WWHP-FM - 98.3 **(8886)**

Normal
WGLT-FM - 89.1-FM **(9308)**
WZND-FM - 106.1 **(9310)**

INDIANA
Bloomington
WTTS-FM - 92.3 **(9861)**

Evansville
WNIN-FM - 88.3 **(9947)**

Terre Haute
WISU-FM - 89.7 **(10496)**

IOWA
Cedar Rapids
KCCK-FM - 88.3 **(10678)**

Waterloo
KBBG-FM - 88.1 **(11290)**

KANSAS
Dodge City
KONQ-FM - 91.9 **(11419)**

LOUISIANA
Morgan City
KBZE-FM - 105.9 **(12710)**

New Orleans
WODT-AM - 1280 **(12772)**
WODT-FM - 1280 **(12773)**
WWOZ-FM - 90.7 **(12783)**

Ruston
KRUS-AM - 1490 **(12810)**

MARYLAND
Annapolis
WYRE-AM - 810 **(13103)**

Princess Anne
WESM-FM - 91.3 **(13670)**

MASSACHUSETTS
Provincetown
WOMR-FM - 92.1 **(14487)**

MICHIGAN
Detroit
WCHB-AM - 1200 **(14956)**
WDET-FM - 101.9 **(14957)**
WQBH-AM - 1400 **(14974)**

Farmington Hills
WXDX AM - 1310 **(15027)**

Lansing
WLNZ-FM - 89.7 **(15303)**

Mount Pleasant
WCMU-FM - 89.5 **(15380)**

Traverse City
WNMC-FM - 90.7 **(15612)**

MISSISSIPPI
Greenwood
WKXG-AM - 1540 **(16650)**

Hattiesburg
WORV-AM - 1580 **(16676)**

Holly Springs
WURC-FM - 88.1 **(16684)**

Ridgeland
WKXI-FM - 107.5 **(16836)**

MISSOURI
Springfield
KTOZ-AM - 1060 **(17629)**

NEBRASKA
Kearney
KLPR-FM - 91.3 **(18065)**

NEVADA
Las Vegas
KCEP-FM - 88.1 **(18392)**
KUNV-FM - 91.5 **(18406)**

NEW HAMPSHIRE
Henniker
WNEC-FM - 91.7 **(18523)**

NEW JERSEY
Cedar Knolls
WDHA-FM - 105.5 **(18723)**

Teaneck
WFDQ-FM - 91.9 **(19611)**
WFDU-FM - 89.1 **(19612)**

NEW MEXICO
Albuquerque
KSYU-FM - 95.1 **(19812)**

NEW YORK
New York
WPUB-AM - 640 **(22987)**

Rochester
WDKX-FM - 103.9 **(23245)**

Rooseveltown
CKON-FM - 97.3 **(23276)**

NORTH CAROLINA
Dallas
WSGE-FM - 91.7 **(23797)**

Durham
WXDU-FM - 88.7 **(23854)**

Greenville
WOOW-AM - 1340 **(23975)**

New Bern
WIKS-FM - 101.9 **(24099)**

OHIO
Columbus
WCBE-FM - 90.5 **(25076)**

Englewood
WLPM-AM - 1450 **(25183)**

OKLAHOMA
Norman
KGOU-FM - 106.3 **(25945)**
KROU-FM - 105.7 **(25947)**

PENNSYLVANIA
Lincoln University
WLIU-FM - 88.7 **(27201)**

Philadelphia
WXPN-FM - 88.5 **(27747)**

SOUTH CAROLINA
Columbia
WLXC-FM - 98.5 **(28580)**

North Charleston
WPAL-AM - 730 **(28726)**

TENNESSEE
Chattanooga
WUTC-FM - 88.1 **(29112)**

Henderson
WFHC-FM - 91.5 **(29219)**

TEXAS
Amarillo
KACV-FM - 89.9 **(29700)**
KBZD-FM - 99.7 **(29705)**

Huntsville
KMHT-FM - 103.9 **(30600)**

Prairie View
KPVU-FM - 91.3 **(30962)**

San Antonio
KCJZ-FM - 106.7 **(31052)**

VIRGINIA
Hampton
WARR-AM - 1520 **(32131)**

Petersburg
WVST-FM - 91.3 **(32333)**

South Hill
WJWS-AM - 1370 **(32535)**

WASHINGTON
Bellevue
KBCS-FM - 91.3 **(32672)**

WEST VIRGINIA
Elkins
WCDE-FM - 90.3 **(33307)**

WISCONSIN
Eau Claire
WUEC-FM - 89.7 **(33684)**

Milwaukee
WNOV-AM - 860 **(34134)**
WYMS-FM - 88.9 **(34144)**

Ripon
WBJZ-FM - 104.7 **(34304)**

MANITOBA, CANADA
Winnipeg
CBW-AM - 990 **(35366)**
CBW-FM - 98.3 **(35367)**

QUEBEC, CANADA
Kahnawake
CKRK-FM - 103.7 **(37019)**

Quebec
CKRL-FM - 89.1 **(37304)**

CAJUN

LOUISIANA
Donaldsonville
KKAY-AM - 1590 **(12570)**

Numbers cited in bold after listings are entry numbers rather than page numbers.

WKAY-AM - 1590 (12571)

Eunice
KEUN-AM - 1490 (12576)

Larose
KLEB-AM - 1600 (12657)

New Iberia
KANE-AM - 1240 (12723)

CLASSIC ROCK

ALABAMA
Birmingham
WJSR-FM - 91.1 (120)

Decatur
WTAK-FM - 106.1 (175)

Jacksonville
WLJS-FM - 91.9 (295)

Mobile
WRKH-FM - 96.1 (350)

Tuscaloosa
WLXY-FM - 100.7 (497)
WRTR-FM - 105.5 (498)

ARIZONA
Douglas
KEAL-FM - 95.3 (690)

Tucson
KHYT-FM - 107.5 (982)

ARKANSAS
Fayetteville
KKEG-FM - 92.1 (1129)

Harrison
KCWD-FM - 96.7 (1167)

Little Rock
KKPT-FM - 94.1 (1245)

Monticello
KHBM-FM - 93.5 (1281)

Van Buren
KLSZ-FM - 102.7 (1360)

CALIFORNIA
Big Pine
KWTY-FM - 102.9 (1582)

Chico
KZAP-FM - 96.7 (1706)

Eureka
KXGO-FM - 93.1 (1906)

Fort Bragg
KOZT-FM - 95.3 (1923)

Fresno
KJFX-FM - 95.7 (1973)

Los Angeles
KCBS-FM - 93.1 (2449)

Modesto
KHKK-FM - 104.1 (2566)

Palm Springs
KCMJ-FM - 92.7 (2774)

Ridgecrest
KSSI-FM - 102.7 (2926)

San Diego
KGB-FM - 101.5 (3301)
KPLN-FM - 103.7 (3310)

San Jose
KUFX-FM - 98.5 (3558)

San Rafael
KSRH-FM - 88.1 (3606)

Santa Barbara
KTYD-FM - 99.9 (3668)

COLORADO
Colorado Springs
KKFM-FM - 98.1 (4271)
KYZX-FM - 103.9 (4287)

Denver
KALC-FM - 105.9 (4369)

KKHK-FM - 99.5 (4383)
KRFX-FM - 103.5 (4388)

Fort Collins
KPAW-FM - 107.9 (4443)

Grand Junction
KKNN-FM - 95.1 (4489)

Steamboat Springs
KFMU-FM - 104.1, 104.9, and 105.5 (4638)

CONNECTICUT
Hartford
WHCN-FM - 105.9 (4903)

DELAWARE
Claymont
WRDX-FM - 94.7 (5240)

FLORIDA
Fort Myers
WARO-FM - 94.5 (6099)

Jacksonville
WFYV-FM - 104.5 (6222)

Miramar
WBGG-FM - 105.9 (6428)

Tallahassee
WGLF-FM - 104.1 (6749)

Tavernier
WFKZ-FM - 103.1 (6814)

West Palm Beach
WKGR-FM - 98.7 (6853)

GEORGIA
Atlanta
WKLS-FM - 96.1 (7075)
WWUF-FM - 97.7 (7091)
WZGC-FM - 92.9 (7094)

Augusta
WEKL-FM - 102.3 (7107)

Douglas
WDMG-AM - 860 (7247)
WDMG-FM - 99.5 (7248)

Metter
WHCG-AM - 1360 (7433)

Tifton
WPLH-FM - 103.1 (7603)

HAWAII
Pukalani
KMVI-FM - 98.3 (7791)

IDAHO
Boise
KKGL-FM - 96.9 (7825)
KQFC-FM - 97.9 (7829)

Lewiston
KVAB-FM - 102.9 (7902)

Pocatello
KMGI-FM - 102.5 (7951)

ILLINOIS
Aurora
WKKD-AM - 1580 (8043)

Champaign
WPCD-FM - 88.7 (8232)

Chicago
WZZN-FM - 94.7 (8665)

Naperville
WONC-FM - 89.1 (9276)

Normal
WIHN-FM - 96.7 (9309)

Springfield
WYMG-FM - 100.5 (9660)

Sterling
WZZT-FM - 95.1 (9666)

INDIANA
Angola
WEAX-FM - 88.3 (9786)

Bloomington
WTTS-FM - 92.3 (9861)

Carmel
WHJE-FM - 91.3 (9882)

Daleville
WWWO-FM - 93.5 (9920)

Fort Wayne
WEXI-FM - 102.9 (9983)
WXKE-FM - 103.9 (9994)

Lafayette
WKHY-FM - 93.5 (10260)

Mishawaka
WAOR-FM - 95.3 (10315)
WRBR-FM - 103.9 (10318)

Peru
WARU-AM - 1600 (10398)
WARU-FM - 101.9 (10399)

Vincennes
WBTO-FM - 102.3 (10525)

IOWA
Dubuque
KGGY-FM - 102.3 (10850)

Eddyville
KKSI-FM - 101.5 (10866)

Humboldt
KHBT-FM - 97.7 (10959)

Tama
KZAT-FM - 95.5 (11264)

Waterloo
KCRR-FM - 97.7 (11291)
KFMW-FM - 107.9 (11292)

KANSAS
Baldwin City
KNBU-FM - 89.7 (11352)

Fort Scott
KOMB-FM - 103.9 (11445)

Great Bend
KVGB-FM - 104.3 (11474)

Lawrence
KLZR-FM - 105.9 (11576)

Pratt
KDGB-FM - 93.1 (11765)

Westwood
KYYS-FM - 99.7 (11876)

Wichita
KRZZ-FM - 96.3 (11902)

Winfield
KSWC-FM - 100.3 (11912)

KENTUCKY
Elizabethtown
WRZI-FM - 101.5 (12050)

Glasgow
WPTQ-FM - 103.7 (12092)

Harold
WXLR-FM - 104.9 (12110)

Lexington
WKQQ-FM - 98.1 (12187)

Louisville
WQMF-FM - 95.7 (12262)

Madisonville
WKTG-FM - 93.9 (12276)

Manchester
WTBK-FM - 105.7 (12280)

Monticello
WKYM-FM - 101.7 (12301)

Paducah
WDDJ-FM - 96.9 (12342)

LOUISIANA
Alexandria
KZMZ-FM - 96.9 (12469)

Baton Rouge
WDGL-FM - 98.1 (12516)

Circulation: ★ = ABC; △ = BPA; ♦ = CAC; • = CCAB; ❏ = VAC; ⊕ = PO Statement; ‡ = Publisher's Report; Boldface figures = sworn; Light figures = estimated.

2989

CLASSIC ROCK (continued)

Houma
KXOR-FM - 106.3 **(12604)**

Natchitoches
KNWD-FM - 91.7 **(12720)**

MAINE
Portland
WBLM-FM - 102.9 **(13021)**

Sanford
WCDQ-FM - 92.1 **(13050)**

MARYLAND
Baltimore
WOCT-FM - 104.3 **(13282)**

Mechanicsville
WSMD-FM - 98.3 **(13627)**

Oakland
WXIE-FM - 92.3 **(13637)**

Rockville
WARW-FM - 94.7 **(13701)**

MASSACHUSETTS
Boston
WZLX-FM - 100.7 **(14000)**

Deerfield
WGAJ-FM - 91.7 **(14158)**

East Longmeadow
WAQY-FM - 102.1 **(14169)**
WAQY-FM - 102.1 **(14170)**

Franklin
WGAO-FM - 88.3 **(14208)**

Hyannis
WCIB-FM - 101.9 **(14251)**
WPXC-FM - 102.9 **(14253)**

Topsfield
WBMT-FM - 88.3 **(14590)**

Walpole
WSRB-FM - 91.5 **(14595)**

MICHIGAN
Bad Axe
WLEW-FM - 102.1 **(14789)**

Big Rapids
WBRN-FM - 100.9 **(14821)**

Fremont
WEFG-FM - 97.5 **(15059)**

Grand Rapids
WBFX-FM - 101.3 **(15103)**
WKLQ-FM - 94.5 **(15112)**
WLAV-FM - 96.9 **(15113)**

Holland
WEVS-FM - 92.7 **(15175)**

Holt
WVIC-FM - 94.1 **(15180)**

Kalamazoo
WRKR-FM - 107.7 **(15259)**

Lansing
WMMQ-FM - 94.9 **(15304)**

Saginaw
WILZ-FM - 104.5 **(15498)**
WKQZ-FM - 93.3 **(15502)**
WYLZ-FM - 100.9 **(15507)**

Sault Sainte Marie
WSUE-FM - 101.3 **(15531)**

Southfield
WCSX-FM - 94.7 **(15557)**

MINNESOTA
Duluth
KDDS-AM - 1490 **(15847)**
KQDS-FM - 94.9 **(15850)**

Hibbing
KMFG-FM - 102.9 **(15955)**

International Falls
KGHS-AM - 1230 **(15969)**

Minneapolis
WLOL-FM - 100.3 **(16162)**

North Mankato
KXLP-FM - 93.1 **(16222)**

Rochester
KRCH-FM - 101.7 **(16317)**

MISSISSIPPI
Cleveland
WRKG-FM - 95.3 **(16596)**

Jackson
WTYX-FM - 94.7 **(16732)**

Meridian
WKZB-FM - 93.5 **(16775)**

MISSOURI
Kirksville
KRXL-FM - 94.5 **(17231)**

Poplar Bluff
KJEZ-FM - 95.5 **(17358)**

Springfield
KKLH-FM - 104.7 **(17623)**
KWTO-FM - 98.7 **(17634)**

MONTANA
Billings
KRKX-FM - 94.1 **(17742)**

Black Eagle
KTZZ-FM - 93.7 **(17749)**

Butte
KMBR-FM - 95.5 **(17763)**

Great Falls
KLFM-FM - 92.9 **(17801)**

Helena
KZMT-FM - 101.1 **(17832)**

Missoula
KZOQ-FM - 100.1 **(17888)**

NEBRASKA
Broken Bow
KBBN-FM - 98.3 **(17966)**

Columbus
KKOT-FM - 93.5 **(17982)**

Lincoln
KTGL-FM - 92.9 **(18145)**

McCook
KRKU-FM - 98.5 **(18158)**

Ogallala
KOGA-FM - 99.7 **(18191)**

NEVADA
Elko
KLKO-FM - 93.7 **(18338)**

Reno
KNHK-FM - 92.9 **(18432)**
KOZZ-FM - 105.7 **(18435)**

NEW HAMPSHIRE
Concord
WNHI-FM - 93.3 **(18479)**

Dover
WSAK-FM - 102.1 **(18495)**
WXBB-FM - 105.3 **(18498)**

Gilford
WBHG-FM - 101.5 **(18511)**

Hillsboro
WRCI-FM - 107.7 **(18526)**

Lebanon
WVRR-FM - 101.7 **(18546)**

Littleton
WMTK-FM - 106.3 **(18553)**

NEW JERSEY
Glassboro
WGLS-FM - 89.7 **(18845)**

Lawrenceville
WRRC-FM - 107.7 **(19166)**

Linwood
WMGM-FM - 103.7 **(19172)**

Pleasantville
WZXL-FM - 100.7 **(19448)**

NEW MEXICO
Albuquerque
KLSK-FM - 98.1 **(19802)**

Clovis
KICA-FM - 98.3 **(19834)**

Farmington
KRWN-FM - 93 **(19852)**

Gallup
KXXI-FM - 93.7 **(19861)**

Roswell
KSFX-FM - 100.5 **(19927)**

NEW YORK
Albany
WPYX-FM - 106.5 **(20014)**

Alfred
WETD-FM - 90.9 **(20026)**

Buffalo
WGRF-FM - 96.9 **(20399)**
WUFX-FM - 103.3 **(20413)**

Corning
WPHD-FM - 94.7, 95.3, 99.5 **(20509)**

New York
WAXQ-FM - 104.3 **(22962)**

Oneonta
WZOZ-FM - 103.1 **(23056)**

Poughkeepsie
WPDH-FM - 101.5 **(23160)**

Salamanca
WQRT-FM - 98.3 **(23296)**

Saratoga Springs
WSPN-FM - 91.1 **(23305)**

Washington Mills
WRCK-FM - 107.3 **(23510)**

Watertown
WCIZ-FM - 93.3 **(23517)**
WOTT-FM - 100.7 **(23519)**

NORTH CAROLINA
Concord
WEGO-AM - 1410 **(23793)**

Dallas
WSGE-FM - 91.7 **(23797)**

Greensboro
WKRR-FM - 92.3 **(23949)**

Raleigh
WRDU-FM - 106.1 **(24173)**

Sparta
WCOK-AM - 1060 **(24241)**

Wanchese
WOBR-FM - 95.3 **(24269)**

Washington
WERO-FM - 93.3 **(24275)**

NORTH DAKOTA
Bismarck
KBYZ-FM - 96.5 **(24365)**

Fargo
KFGO-FM - 101.9 **(24420)**
KQWB-FM - 98.7 **(24426)**

Minot
KRRZ-AM - 1390 **(24513)**

OHIO
Bucyrus
WQEL-FM - 92.7 **(24720)**

Cincinnati
WOFX-FM - 92.5 **(24845)**

Crestline
WYXZ-FM - 98.7 **(25102)**

Numbers cited in bold after listings are entry numbers rather than page numbers.

Dayton
WING-FM - 102.9 (25144)

Granville
WDUB-FM - 91.1 (25224)

Ironton
WMLV-FM - 107.1 (25254)

Youngstown
WYFM-FM - 102.9 (25713)

OKLAHOMA
Ada
KTLS-FM - 106.5 (25727)

Altus
KRKZ-FM - 93.5 (25735)

Lawton
KZCD-FM - 94.1 (25897)

Tonkawa
KAYE-FM - 90.7 (26103)

Tulsa
KJSR-FM - 103.3 (26150)
KMOD-FM - 97.5 (26151)

OREGON
Coquille
KBDN-FM - 96.5 (26282)

Medford
KBOY-FM - 95.7 (26420)

Newport
KCRF-FM - 96.7 (26447)

Portland
KGON-FM - 92.3 (26527)

PENNSYLVANIA
Altoona
WBRX-FM - 94.3 (26637)
WBXQ-FM - 94.7 (26638)

Bala Cynwyd
WMGK-FM - 102.9 (26675)

Bedford
WBVE-FM - 107.5 (26692)

Bloomsburg
WBUQ-FM - 91.1 (26720)
WCNR-AM - 930 (26721)

Chester
WDNR-FM, Widener University - 89.5 (26776)

Erie
WQHZ-FM - 102.3 (26908)

Greencastle
WSRT-FM - 92.1 (26952)

Greenville
WEXC-FM - 107.1 (26960)

Halfway
WQCM-FM - 96.7 (26969)

Indiana
WQMU-FM - 103.1 (27082)

Lewisburg
WVBU-FM - 90.5 (27195)

Millersville
WIXQ-FM - 91.7 (27268)

North East
WRKT-FM - 100.9 (27341)

Pottsville
WPAM-AM - 1450 (27905)

Scranton
WEZX-FM - 106.9 (27967)

State College
WQWK-FM - 97.1 (28028)

Wilkes Barre
WXAR-FM - 95.7 (28180)
WXBE-FM - 97.9 (28181)

PUERTO RICO
San Juan
WCAD-FM - 105.7 (28298)

RHODE ISLAND
Coventry
WCVY-FM - 91.5 (28331)

SOUTH CAROLINA
Charleston
WYBB-FM - 98.1 (28526)

Greenville
WROQ-FM - 101.1 (28641)

Myrtle Beach
WWSK-FM - 107.1 (28712)

SOUTH DAKOTA
Aberdeen
KSDN-FM - 94.1 (28799)

Brookings
KKQQ-FM - 102.3 (28823)

Rapid City
KFXS-FM - 100.3 (28939)

Sioux Falls
KRRO-FM - 103.7 (28981)

Watertown
KPHR-FM - 106.3 (29022)

TENNESSEE
Chattanooga
WFXS-FM - 102.3 (29104)

Gray
WQUT-FM - 101.5 (29211)

Jackson
WYNU-FM - 92.3 (29242)
WYNU-FM - 92.3 (29243)

Memphis
WEGR-FM - 102.7 (29391)

Union City
WWUC-FM - 105.7 (29637)

TEXAS
Abilene
KEYJ-FM - 107.9 (29661)

Austin
KPEZ-FM - 102.3 (29875)

College Station
KTSR-FM - 92.1 (30060)

Houston
KKRW-FM - 93.7 (30560)

Huntsville
KSHU-FM - 90.5 (30601)

Lubbock
KONE-FM - 101.1 (30734)

McAllen
KFRQ-FM - 94.5 (30795)

Mesquite
KEOM-FM - 88.5 (30809)

Nacogdoches
KSAU-FM - 90.1 (30854)

Odessa
KFZX-FM - 102.1 (30875)

Paris
KBUS-FM - 101.9 (30906)

Rusk
KWRW-FM - 97.7 (31001)

San Angelo
KWFR-FM - 101.9 (31023)

South Padre Island
KVPA-FM - 101.1 (31120)

Stephenville
KPAR-AM - 1420 (31131)

Tyler
KKTX-AM - 1240 (31214)

UTAH
Salt Lake City
KRSP-FM - 103.5 (31455)

VERMONT
Brattleboro
WKVT-FM - 92.7 (31511)

Middlebury
WGTK-FM - 100.9 (31561)

Randolph Center
WCVR-FM - 102.1 (31582)

VIRGINIA
Charlottesville
WWWV-FM - 97.5 (31958)

Farmville
WMLU - 91.3 (32072)

Hampden Sydney
WWHS-FM - 92.1 (32125)

Radford
WVMJ-FM - 105.3 (32352)

Richmond
WRXL-FM - 102.1 (32485)

Roanoke
WPVR-FM - 94.9 (32501)

Winchester
WWRE-FM - 105.5 (32634)

WASHINGTON
Aberdeen
KDUX-FM - 104.7 (32649)
KSWW-FM - 102.1 (32651)

Bellingham
KISM-FM - 92.9 (32683)

Colfax
KRAO-FM - 102.5 (32723)

Grand Coulee
KEYG-AM - 1490 (32781)
KEYG-FM - 98.5 (32782)

Kennewick
KEGX-FM - 106.5 (32790)

Seattle
KMTT-FM - 103.7 (33061)

Spokane
KAEP-FM - 105.7 (33106)
KKZX-FM - 98.9 (33119)
KTSL-FM - 101.9 (33130)
KWHK-FM - 103.9 (33131)
KZPH-FM - 106.7 (33137)

Tacoma
KBTC-FM - 91.7 (33155)

Yakima
KATS-FM - 94.5 (33225)
KJOX-AM - 980 (33231)
KYSC-FM - 88.5 (33235)

WEST VIRGINIA
Elkins
WCDE-FM - 90.3 (33307)

Keyser
WQZK-FM - 94.1 (33358)

St. Albans
WKLC-FM - 105.1 (33458)
WKLC FM - 105.1 (33459)

Vienna
WRZZ-FM - 106.1 (33483)

Weston
WHAW-AM - 980 (33499)

WISCONSIN
Appleton
WAPL-FM - 105.7 (33546)
WOZZ-FM - 93.5 (33551)

Ashland
WJJH-FM - 96.7, 102.3 (33558)

Eau Claire
WISM-FM - 98.1 (33681)

Fond du Lac
WTCX-FM - 96.1 (33702)

Madison
WIBA-FM - 101.5 (33997)

CLASSIC ROCK (continued)

Manitowoc
WQTC-FM - 102.3 **(34017)**

Neillsville
WCCN-FM - 107.5 **(34165)**

Sheboygan
WSHS-FM - 91.7 **(34325)**

Shell Lake
WGMO-FM - 95.3 **(34328)**

Wisconsin Rapids
WGLX-FM - 103.3 **(34467)**

WYOMING
Cody
KCGL-FM - 104.1 **(34514)**

Jackson
KMTN-FM - 1290 **(34538)**
KZJH-FM - 95.3 **(34540)**

Lander
KDLY-FM - 97.5 **(34544)**

Sheridan
KZWY-FM - 94.9 **(34592)**

ALBERTA, CANADA
Calgary
CJAY-FM - 92.1 **(34669)**

Edmonton
CFBR-FM - 100.3 **(34744)**

BRITISH COLUMBIA, CANADA
Fort Nelson
CFNL-AM - 590 **(34957)**

Kelowna
CKLZ-FM - 104.7 **(34993)**

NEW BRUNSWICK, CANADA
Fredericton
CIBX-FM - 106.9 **(35404)**

Moncton
CJMO-FM - 103.1 **(35420)**

NEWFOUNDLAND AND LABRADOR, CANADA
Churchill Falls
CFLC-FM - 97.9 **(35444)**

Wabush
CFLW-AM - 1340 **(35512)**

ONTARIO, CANADA
London
CFHK-FM - 103.1 **(35995)**

Toronto
CILQ-FM - 107.1 **(36813)**

QUEBEC, CANADA
Quebec
CKRL-FM - 89.1 **(37304)**

Thetford Mines
CFJO-FM - 97.3 **(37411)**

SASKATCHEWAN, CANADA
La Ronge
MBC-FM - 89.9 **(37487)**

CLASSICAL

ALABAMA
Dora
WPYK-AM - 1010 **(184)**

Gadsden
WSGN-FM - 91.5 **(237)**

Huntsville
WLRH-FM - 89.3 **(284)**

Mobile
WHIL-FM - 91.3 **(340)**

Muscle Shoals
WQPR-FM - 88.7 **(400)**

Robertsdale
WDXZ-AM - 1000 **(438)**

Troy
WRWA-FM - 88.7 **(475)**
WTJB-FM - 91.7 **(478)**
WTSU-FM - 89.9 **(479)**

Tuscaloosa
WUAL-FM - 91.5 **(503)**

ALASKA
Anchorage
KLEF-FM - 98.1 **(544)**

Bethel
KYUK-AM - 640 **(556)**

Fairbanks
KUAC-FM - 89.9 **(578)**

Juneau
KTOO-FM - 104.3 **(604)**

ARIZONA
Flagstaff
KNAU-FM - 88.7 **(700)**

Mesa
KBAQ-FM - 89.5 **(749)**

Yuma
KAWC-FM - 88.9 **(1023)**

ARKANSAS
Fayetteville
KUAF-FM - 91.3 **(1131)**

Little Rock
KLRE-FM - 90.5 **(1247)**

Russellville
KXRJ-FM - 91.9 **(1334)**

State University
KASU-FM - 91.9 **(1351)**

CALIFORNIA
Carlsbad
KFSD-AM - 1450 **(1669)**

Los Angeles
KMZT-FM - 105.1 **(2463)**
KUSC-FM - 91.5 **(2470)**
KXLU-FM - 88.9 **(2472)**

Monterey
KBOQ-FM - 95.5 **(2586)**

Northridge
KCSN-FM - 88.5 **(2647)**

Palm Springs
KPSC-FM - 88.5 **(2778)**

Philo
KZYX-FM - 90.7 **(2838)**

Riverside
KUCR-FM - 88.3 **(2954)**

Sacramento
KXPR-FM - 90.9 **(3056)**

San Bernardino
KVCR-FM - 91.9 **(3095)**

San Francisco
KDFC-FM - 102.1 **(3477)**

San Rafael
KKHI-FM - 100.7 **(3605)**

Santa Barbara
KDB-FM - 93.7 **(3663)**
KFAC-FM - 88.7 **(3665)**

Thousand Oaks
KCPB-FM - 91.1 **(3925)**

Turlock
KCSS-FM - 91.9 **(3960)**

COLORADO
Alamosa
KRZA-FM - 88.7 **(4136)**

Denver
KVOD-FM - 92.5 **(4393)**
KVOD-FM - 90.1 FM **(4394)**

Grand Junction
KPRN-FM - 89.5 **(4492)**

Greeley
KUNC-FM - 91.5 **(4503)**

Westminster
KPOF-AM - 910 **(4670)**

CONNECTICUT
Bloomfield
WJMJ-FM - 88.9 **(4705)**

Fairfield
WSHU-FM - 91.1 **(4792)**

Hartford
WPKT-FM - 90.5 **(4906)**
WTMI-AM - 1290 **(4913)**

Monroe
WGRS-FM - 91.5 **(4964)**
WGSK-FM - 90.1 **(4965)**
WMNR-FM - 88.1 **(4966)**
WRXC-FM - 90.1 **(4967)**

New Canaan
WSLX-FM - 91.9 **(4981)**

Norwich
WNPR-FM - 89.1 **(5087)**

Sharon
WKZE-FM - 98.1 **(5116)**

DISTRICT OF COLUMBIA
Washington
WGMS-FM - 103.5 **(5883)**

FLORIDA
Boynton Beach
WXEL-FM - 90.7 **(5954)**

Fort Myers
WGCU-FM - 90.1 **(6104)**

Fort Pierce
WQCS-FM - 88.9 **(6120)**

Gainesville
WUFT-FM - 89.1 **(6168)**

Pensacola
WUWF-FM - 88.1 **(6579)**

Tallahassee
WFSQ-FM - 91.5 **(6746)**

Tampa
WBVM-FM - 90.5 **(6785)**
WUSF-FM - 89.7 **(6807)**

GEORGIA
Atlanta
WABE-FM - 90.1 **(7064)**
WUNV-FM - 91.7 **(7089)**

Augusta
WACG-FM - 90.7 **(7104)**

Claxton
WCLA-FM - 107.3 **(7173)**

Gainesville
WBCX-FM - 89.1 **(7300)**

Savannah
WSVH-FM - 91.1 **(7549)**

Warm Springs
WJSP-FM - 88.1 **(7636)**

HAWAII
Honolulu
KHPR-FM - 88.1 **(7737)**
KIPO-FM - 89.3 **(7741)**
KKUA-FM - 90.7 **(7745)**

IDAHO
Boise
KBSU-FM - 90.3 **(7818)**

McCall
KBSM-FM - 91.7 **(7906)**

Rexburg
KBYI-FM - 100.5 **(7966)**

Twin Falls
KBSW-FM - 91.7 **(7991)**

ILLINOIS
Carbondale
WSIU-FM - 91.9 **(8123)**

Chicago
WHPK-FM - 88.5 **(8628)**

DeKalb
WNIU-FM - 89.5 **(8745)**

Macomb
WIUM-FM - 91.3 **(9134)**

Peoria
WCBU-FM - 89.9 **(9430)**

Quincy
WQUB-FM - 90.3 **(9482)**

Rock Island
WVIK-FM - 90.3 **(9525)**

Rockford
WYHY-FM - 95.3 **(9544)**

Springfield
WUIS-FM - 91.9 **(9658)**

INDIANA
Bloomington
WFIU-FM - 103.7 **(9857)**

Evansville
WNIN-FM - 88.3 **(9947)**

Fort Wayne
WBNI-FM - 89.1 **(9979)**

Goshen
WGCS-FM - 91.1 **(10029)**

Indianapolis
WFYI-FM - 90.1 **(10195)**
WICR-FM - 88.7 **(10199)**
WSYW-AM - 810 **(10210)**
WSYW-FM - 107.1 **(10211)**

Muncie
WBST-FM - 92.1 **(10330)**

West Lafayette
WBAA-AM - 920 **(10556)**
WBAA-FM - 101.3 **(10557)**

IOWA
Ames
WOI-FM - 90.1 **(10600)**

Cedar Falls
KHKE-FM - 89.5 **(10667)**
KUNI-FM - 90.9 **(10668)**

Decorah
KLSE-FM - 91.7 **(10761)**
KWLC-AM - 1240 **(10762)**

Dubuque
KLCR-FM - 96.9 **(10851)**

Fairfield
KHOE-FM - 90.5 **(10884)**

Fort Dodge
KTPR-FM - 91.1 **(10912)**

Iowa City
KSUI-FM - 91.7 **(10994)**

Sioux City
KWIT-FM - 90.3 **(11225)**

KANSAS
Hutchinson
KHCC-FM - 90.1 **(11505)**

Mission
KXTR-FM - 96.5 **(11657)**

Salina
KHCD-FM - 89.5 **(11786)**

Westwood
KXTR-AM - 1660 **(11875)**

Wichita
KMUW-FM - 89.1 **(11899)**

KENTUCKY
Bowling Green
WDNS-FM - 93.3 **(11956)**

Hazard
WEKH-FM - 90.9 **(12117)**

Murray
WKMS-FM - 91.3/92.1 Paducah, KY; 99.5 Paris, TN **(12319)**

Richmond
WEKU-FM - 88.9 **(12385)**

LOUISIANA
Coushatta
KRRP-AM - 950 **(12553)**

Lake Providence
KLPL-AM - 1050 **(12653)**

Monroe
KEDM-FM - 90.3 **(12694)**

New Orleans
KTLN-FM - 90.5 **(12766)**
WWNO-FM - 89.9 **(12782)**

Shreveport
KDAQ-FM - 89.9 **(12823)**
KLSA-FM - 90.7 **(12827)**

MARYLAND
Baltimore
WBJC-FM - 91.5 **(13268)**

Frostburg
WFWM-FM - 91.9 **(13529)**

Salisbury
WSCL-FM - 89.5 **(13719)**
WSDL-FM - 90.7 **(13720)**

MASSACHUSETTS
Amherst
WFCR-FM - 88.5 **(13809)**

Boston
WGBH-FM - 89.7 **(13985)**

Provincetown
WOMR-FM - 92.1 **(14487)**

Tisbury
WMVY-FM - 92.7 **(14589)**

Waltham
WCRB-FM - 102.5 **(14607)**

West Yarmouth
WFCC-FM - 107.5 **(14630)**

MICHIGAN
Alpena
WCML-FM - 91.7 **(14739)**

Dearborn
WHFR-FM - 89.3 **(14908)**

Flint
WFUM-FM - 91.1 **(15044)**

Houghton
WGGL-FM - 91.1 **(15186)**

Interlochen
WIAA-FM - 88.7 **(15205)**

Kalamazoo
WMUK-FM - 102.1 **(15256)**

Marquette
WNMU-FM - 90.1, 107.1, 91.9, 91.3, 91.1, 107.3 **(15346)**

Mount Pleasant
WCMU-FM - 89.5 **(15380)**

Twin Lake
WBLV-FM - 90.3 **(15645)**

Warren
WPHS-FM - 89.1 **(15667)**

MINNESOTA
Aitkin
KKIM-FM - 94.3 **(15702)**

Bemidji
KCRB-FM - 88.5 **(15744)**

Brainerd
KBPR-FM - 90.7 **(15768)**

Buhl
WIRR-FM - 90.9 **(15780)**

Collegeville
KSJR-FM - 90.1 **(15809)**

Duluth
WSCD-FM - 92.9 **(15857)**

Marshall
KARZ-FM - 107.5 **(16045)**

Moorhead
KCCM-FM - 91.1 **(16191)**
KQMN-FM - 91.1 **(16193)**

Northfield
WCAL-FM - 89.3 **(16240)**

Rochester
KLCD-FM - 89.5 **(16313)**

St. Paul
KSJN-FM - 99.5 **(16422)**

MISSISSIPPI
Biloxi
WMAH-FM - 90.3 **(16566)**

Booneville
WMAE-FM - 91.3 **(16574)**

Greenwood
WMAO-FM - 90.9 **(16651)**

Jackson
WKNP-FM - 90.1 **(16721)**
WMPN-FM - 91.3 **(16724)**

Meadville
WMAU-FM - 88.9 **(16768)**

Mississippi State
WMAB-FM - 89.9 **(16786)**

Oxford
WMAV-FM - 90.3 **(16808)**

MISSOURI
Columbia
KBIA-FM - 91.3 **(17013)**

Maryville
KXCV-FM - 90.5 **(17279)**

Point Lookout
KCOZ-FM - 91.7 **(17355)**

Rolla
KUMR-FM - 88.5 **(17382)**

St. Louis
KFUO-FM - 99.1 **(17540)**

Springfield
KSMU-FM - 91.1 **(17627)**

MONTANA
Kalispell
KALS-FM - 97.1 **(17839)**

NEBRASKA
Alliance
KTNE-FM - 91.1 **(17931)**

Hastings
KHNE-FM - 89.1 **(18041)**

Lexington
KLNE-FM - 88.7 **(18073)**

Lincoln
KCNE-FM - 91.9 **(18131)**
KMNE-FM - 90.3 **(18139)**
KPNE-FM - 91.7 **(18141)**
KRNE-FM - 91.5 **(18142)**
KUCV-FM - 91.1 FM **(18146)**

Norfolk
KXNE-FM - 89.3 **(18172)**

Omaha
KVNO-FM - 90.7 **(18228)**

NEVADA
Reno
KUNR-FM - 88.7 **(18442)**

Tonopah
KTPH-FM - 91.7 **(18449)**

NEW HAMPSHIRE
Concord
WEVO-FM - 89.1 **(18476)**

Henniker
WNEC-FM - 91.7 **(18523)**

Radio Station Formats

Circulation: ★ = ABC; △ = BPA; ♦ = CAC; • = CCAB; ❑ = VAC; ⊕ = PO Statement; ‡ = Publisher's Report; Boldface figures = sworn; Light figures = estimated.

2993

CLASSICAL (continued)

NEW JERSEY
Flemington
WCVH-FM - 90.5 **(18822)**

Princeton
WPRB-FM - 103.3 **(19481)**

Trenton
WWFM-The Classical Network - 89.1 **(19679)**
WWNJ-FM - 91.1 **(19680)**

NEW MEXICO
Albuquerque
KHFM-FM - 96.3 **(19799)**

Las Cruces
KRWG-FM - 90.7 **(19885)**

Maljamar
KMTH-FM - 98.7 **(19902)**

Portales
KENW-FM - 89.5 **(19905)**

NEW YORK
Binghamton
WSKG-FM - 89.3 **(20228)**
WSQE-FM - 91.1 **(20230)**
WSQG-FM - 89.3 **(20231)**
WSQX-FM - 88.7 **(20232)**

Buffalo
WNJA-FM - 89.7 **(20410)**

New York
WKCR-FM - 89.9 **(22972)**
WNYC-FM - 93.9 **(22980)**
WQXR-FM - 96.3 **(22990)**

Rochester
WRUR-FM - 88.5 **(23254)**

Schenectady
WBKK-FM - 97.7 **(23315)**
WMHT-FM - 89.1 **(23317)**
WRHV-FM - 88.7 **(23321)**

Southampton
WPBX-FM - 88.3 **(23346)**

Syracuse
WCNY-FM - 91.3 **(23436)**

Ticonderoga
WANC-FM - 103.9 **(23451)**

NORTH CAROLINA
Asheville
WCQS-FM - 88.1 **(23635)**
WFQS-FM - 91.3 **(23636)**

Chapel Hill
WUNC-FM - 91.5 **(23732)**

Davidson
WDAV-FM - 89.9 **(23800)**

New Bern
WTEB-FM - 89.3 **(24102)**

Wake Forest
WCPE-FM - 89.7 **(24263)**

Winston-Salem
WFDD-FM - 88.5 **(24330)**

NORTH DAKOTA
Bismarck
KCND-FM - 90.5 **(24366)**
KDPR-FM - 89.9 **(24367)**

Fargo
KDSU-FM - 91.9 **(24417)**

Grand Forks
KFJM-FM - 90.7 **(24459)**
KUND-AM - 1370 **(24463)**

Minot
KMPR-FM - 88.9 **(24510)**

Williston
KPPR-FM - 90.5 **(24563)**

OHIO
Athens
WOUB-FM - 91.3 **(24633)**
WOUC-FM - 89.1 **(24635)**

Cincinnati
WGUC-FM - 90.9 **(24839)**

Cleveland
WCLV-FM - 104.9 **(24969)**

Columbus
WOSU-FM - 89.7 **(25083)**

Dayton
WDPR-FM - 88.1 **(25135)**

Ironton
WOUL-FM - 89.1 **(25255)**

Kent
WKSU-FM - 89.7 **(25279)**

Lima
WGLE-FM - 90.7 **(25300)**

Nelsonville
WAIS-AM - 770 **(25406)**

Painesville
WBKC-AM - 1460 **(25465)**

Toledo
WGBE-FM - 90.9 **(25576)**
WGTE-FM - 91.3 **(25577)**

Youngstown
WYSU-FM - 88.5 **(25714)**

OKLAHOMA
Edmond
KCSC-FM - 90.1 **(25815)**

Lawton
KCCU-FM - 89.3 **(25891)**
KLCU-FM - 90.3 **(25893)**

Madill
KMAD-AM - 1550 **(25903)**

Stillwater
KOSU-FM - 91.7 **(26084)**

OREGON
Ashland
KSOR-FM - 90.1 **(26223)**

Baker City
KKBC-FM - 95.3 **(26235)**

Milton-Freewater
KHSS-FM - 100.7 **(26436)**

Portland
KBPS-AM - 1450 **(26520)**
KBPS-FM - 89.9 **(26521)**

PENNSYLVANIA
Danville
WPGM-AM - 1570 **(26820)**
WPGM-FM - 96.7 **(26821)**

Erie
WQLN-FM - 91.3 **(26909)**

Grove City
WSAJ-FM - 91.1 **(26967)**

Philadelphia
WRTI-FM - 90.1 **(27744)**

Pittsburgh
WQED-FM - 89.3 **(27874)**

Pittston
WVIA-FM - 89.9 **(27893)**

Slippery Rock
WSRU-FM - 90.1 **(28001)**

Williamsport
WPTC-FM - 88.1 **(28189)**

PUERTO RICO
Mayaguez
WTPM-FM - 92.9 **(28270)**

San Juan
WRTU-FM - 89.7 **(28309)**

RHODE ISLAND
Providence
WDOM-FM - 91.3 **(28433)**

SOUTH CAROLINA
Beaufort
WJWJ-FM - 89.9 **(28489)**

Columbia
WEPR-FM - 90.1 **(28575)**

SOUTH DAKOTA
Brookings
KESD-FM/South Dakota Public Broadcasting - 88.3 **(28820)**

Pierpont
KDSD-FM - 90.9 **(28915)**

Reliance
KTSD-FM - 91.1 **(28956)**

Sioux Falls
KCSD-FM - 90.9 **(28971)**
KRSD-FM - 88.1 **(28982)**

Vermillion
KUSD-FM - 89.7 **(29010)**

TENNESSEE
Collegedale
WSMC-FM - 90.5 **(29132)**

Henderson
WFHC-FM - 91.5 **(29219)**

Johnson City
WETS-FM - 89.5 **(29256)**

Knoxville
WUOT-FM - 91.9 **(29303)**

Memphis
WKNO-FM - 91.1 **(29399)**

Nashville
WGFX-FM - 104.5 **(29511)**
WHRS-FM - 91.7 **(29512)**
WPLN-FM - 90.3 **(29525)**

TEXAS
Abilene
KACU-FM - 89.7 **(29657)**

Amarillo
KACV-FM - 89.9 **(29700)**

Austin
KMFA-FM - 89.5 **(29873)**

College Station
KAMU-FM - 90.9 **(30056)**

Corpus Christi
KEDT-FM - 90.3 **(30082)**

Dallas
WRR-FM - 101.1 **(30220)**

Harlingen
KHID-FM - 88.1 **(30427)**
KMBH-FM - 88.9 **(30429)**

Henderson
KWRD-AM - 1470 **(30441)**

Houston
KRTS-FM - 92.1 **(30573)**
KUHF-FM - 88.7 **(30583)**

Huntsville
KSHU-FM - 90.5 **(30601)**

Kilgore
KTPB-FM - 88.7 **(30643)**

Killeen
KNCT-FM - 91.3 **(30645)**

Levelland
KLVT-FM - 105.3 **(30684)**

Lubbock
KOHM-FM - 89.1 **(30733)**

Odessa
KRIL-AM - 1410 **(30883)**

San Angelo
KGKL-AM - 960 **(31015)**

San Antonio
KPAC-FM - 88.3 **(31066)**

Tyler
KGLY-FM - 91.3 **(31213)**

Numbers cited in bold after listings are entry numbers rather than page numbers.

Waco
KWBU-FM - 103.3 **(31261)**

UTAH
Logan
KUSU-FM - 89.5, 91.5 **(31361)**

Provo
KBYU-FM - 89.1, 89.5 **(31410)**

VERMONT
Colchester
WRVT-FM - 88.7 **(31532)**
WVPS-FM - 107.9 **(31534)**

Windsor
WVPR-FM - 89.5 **(31622)**

VIRGINIA
Arlington
WETA-FM - 90.9 **(31845)**
WETH-FM - 89.1 **(31847)**

Blacksburg
WVTW-FM - 88.5 **(31890)**

Charlottesville
WTJU-FM - 91.1 **(31955)**
WVTU-FM - 89.3 **(31957)**

Harrisonburg
WEMC-FM - 91.7 **(32143)**
WMRA-FM - 90.7 **(32148)**
WMRL-FM - 89.9 **(32149)**
WMRY-FM - 103.5 **(32150)**

Norfolk
WHRO-FM - 90.3 **(32299)**

Richmond
WCVE-FM - 88.9 **(32474)**

Roanoke
WVTF-FM - 89.1 **(32507)**
WVTR-FM - 91.9 **(32508)**

Wise
WISE-FM - 90.5 **(32635)**

WASHINGTON
Lynnwood
KSER-FM - 90.7 **(32826)**

Olympia
KLDY-AM - 1280 **(32870)**

Pullman
KFAE-FM - 89.1 **(32910)**
KRFA-FM - 91.7 **(32913)**

Seattle
KING-FM - 98.1 **(33054)**

Spokane
KPBX-FM - 91.1 **(33123)**

WEST VIRGINIA
Charleston
WVNP-FM - 89.9 **(33287)**
WVPB-FM - 91.7 **(33288)**
WVPN-FM - 88.5 **(33289)**

Parkersburg
WVPG-FM - 90.3 **(33426)**

WISCONSIN
Eau Claire
WUEC-FM - 89.7 **(33684)**

Kenosha
WGTD-FM - 91.1 **(33876)**

La Crosse
WLSU-FM - 88.9 **(33894)**

Madison
WORT-FM - 89.9 **(34007)**

Milwaukee
WFMR-FM - 106.9 **(34116)**

WYOMING
Laramie
KUWR-FM - 91.9 **(34557)**

ALBERTA, CANADA
Calgary
CBR-FM - 102.1 **(34662)**

MANITOBA, CANADA
Boissevain
CJRB-AM - 1220 **(35253)**

Winnipeg
CBW-AM - 990 **(35366)**
CBW-FM - 98.3 **(35367)**

NEW BRUNSWICK, CANADA
Fredericton
CBZ-FM - 101.5 **(35400)**

ONTARIO, CANADA
Ottawa
CBOF-FM - 90.7 **(36285)**

Toronto
CFMX-FM - 96.3 **(36803)**

Windsor
CBC-FM - 89.9 **(36895)**

QUEBEC, CANADA
Chicoutimi
CBJX-FM - 100.9 **(36971)**

Quebec
CKRL-FM - 89.1 **(37304)**

Sainte-Foy
CBV-FM - 95.3, 106.3 **(37377)**

CONTEMPORARY CHRISTIAN

ALABAMA
Anniston
WGRW-FM - 90.7 **(20)**

Birmingham
WLJR-FM - 88.5 **(122)**
WRRS-FM - 101.1 **(128)**

Dadeville
WELL-FM - 88.7 **(167)**

Mobile
WBHY-FM - 88.5 **(336)**

ALASKA
Nome
KICY-FM - 100.3 **(627)**

Petersburg
KRSA-AM - 580 **(633)**

ARIZONA
Phoenix
KRDS-FM - 1190 **(836)**

Yuma
KCFY-FM - 88.1 **(1025)**

ARKANSAS
Fort Smith
KZKZ-FM - 106.3 **(1159)**

Russellville
KMTC-FM - 91.1 **(1333)**

West Memphis
KSUD-AM - 730 **(1370)**

CALIFORNIA
Glendale
KKLA-FM - 99.5 **(2016)**

Lancaster
KAVC-AM - 1340 **(2148)**

Merced
KAMB-FM - 101.5 **(2530)**

Rocklin
KLVW-FM - 99.1 **(2959)**
KYLV-FM - 88.9 **(2960)**

Sacramento
KFYE-FM - 106.3 **(3030)**
KLOV-FM - 89.3 **(3033)**
KLVA-FM - 105.5 **(3034)**
KLVB-AM - 730 **(3035)**
KLVC-FM - 88.3 **(3036)**
KLVG-FM - 103.7 **(3037)**
KLVJ-FM - 100.1 **(3038)**
KLVN-FM - 100.1 **(3039)**
KLVP-FM - 88.7 **(3040)**
KLVR-FM - 91.9 **(3041)**

KLVS-FM - 99.3 **(3042)
KLVU-FM - 107.1 **(3043)**
KLVY-FM - 91.1 **(3044)**
KZLV-FM - 91.3 **(3061)**

San Luis Obispo
KLFF-FM - 89.3 **(3572)**

Van Nuys
KTLW-FM - 88.9 **(3998)**

Yucaipa
KADU-FM - 90.1 **(4126)**

COLORADO
Denver
KLZ-AM - 560 **(4384)**

Grand Junction
KEXO-AM - 1230 **(4484)**
KJOL-FM - 90.3 **(4486)**

Pueblo
KFEL-AM - 970 **(4604)**
KNKN-FM - 107.1 **(4606)**

DELAWARE
Milford
WXPZ-FM - 101.3 **(5263)**

FLORIDA
Bradenton
WJIS-FM - 88.1 **(5959)**

Crestview
WXEI-FM - 95.3 **(6028)**

Fort Myers
WAYJ-FM - 88.7 **(6100)**

Fort Walton Beach
WPSM-FM - 91.1 **(6126)**

Jacksonville
WIOJ-AM - 1010 **(6223)**
WNCM-FM - 88.1 **(6234)**

Lakeland
WTWB-AM - 1570 **(6296)**

Miami
WMCU-FM - 89.7 **(6406)**

Orlando
WRLZ-AM - 1270 **(6527)**

Port Richey
WLPJ-FM - 91.5 **(6599)**

Vero Beach
WSCF-FM - 91.9 **(6838)**

GEORGIA
Cumming
WWEV-FM - 91.5 **(7217)**

Marietta
WFTD-AM - 1080 **(7424)**

Peachtree City
WVFJ-FM - 93.3 **(7481)**

Rossville
WJOC-AM - 1490 **(7511)**

Thomasville
WJEP-AM - 1020 **(7589)**

Waycross
WGIA-AM - 1350 **(7647)**

HAWAII
Honolulu
KAIM-FM - 95.5 **(7730)**

IDAHO
Boise
KBXL-FM - 94.1 **(7820)**

ILLINOIS
Carlinville
WIBI-FM - 91.1 **(8128)**

Dennison
WKZI-AM - 800 **(8748)**

Elgin
WJKL-FM - 94.3 **(8828)**

Circulation: ★ = ABC; △ = BPA; ♦ = CAC; ● = CCAB; ❑ = VAC; ⊕ = PO Statement; ‡ = Publisher's Report; Boldface figures = sworn; Light figures = estimated.

2995

CONTEMPORARY CHRISTIAN (continued)

Greenville
WGRN-FM - 89.5 **(8964)**

Loves Park
WQFL-FM - 100.9 **(9122)**

Morris
WCFL-FM **(9226)**

Peoria
WCIC-FM - 91.5 **(9431)**

Wheaton
WETN-FM - 88.1 **(9761)**

INDIANA
Anderson
WQME-FM - 98.7 FM **(9785)**

Bloomington
WVNI-FM - 95.1 **(9862)**

Elkhart
WFRN-FM - 104.7 **(9926)**

Fort Wayne
WLAB-FM - 88.3 **(9989)**

Indianapolis
WEDM-FM - 91.1 **(10193)**
WXIR-FM - 98.3 **(10216)**

South Bend
WHME-FM - 103.1 **(10463)**

Terre Haute
WMGI-FM - 100.7 **(10498)**

IOWA
Sioux Center
KSOU-AM - 1090 **(11210)**

Waterloo
KWOF-AM - 850 & 89.1 FM **(11298)**
KWOF-FM - 88.1 **(11299)**

KANSAS
Clay Center
KCLY-FM - 100.9 **(11384)**

Emporia
KNGM-FM - 91.9 **(11433)**

Kansas City
KCNW-AM - 1380 **(11537)**

Leavenworth
KKLO-AM - 1410 **(11582)**

Manhattan
KHCA-FM - 95.3 **(11632)**

Meade
KJIL-FM - 99.1 **(11648)**

Ottawa
KRBW-FM - 90.5 **(11693)**

KENTUCKY
Grayson
WKCC-FM - 96.7 **(12095)**

London
WWLT-FM - 103.1 **(12206)**

Louisville
WJIE-FM - 88.5 **(12255)**
WRVI-FM - 105.9 **(12264)**

Middlesboro
WMIK-FM - 92.7 **(12296)**

Pippa Passes
WWJD-FM - 91.7 **(12369)**

Whitesburg
WEZC-AM - 1480 **(12439)**

LOUISIANA
Minden
KBEF 104.5 FM - 104.5 **(12690)**

New Orleans
WSHO-AM - 800 **(12776)**

MAINE
Bangor
WJCX-FM - 99.5 **(12910)**

Freeport
WMSJ-FM - 89.3 **(12965)**

MARYLAND
Grantsville
WAIJ-FM - 90.3 **(13557)**

Potomac
WCTN-AM - 950 **(13666)**

MASSACHUSETTS
Franklin
WGAO-FM - 88.3 **(14208)**

MICHIGAN
Coleman
WPRJ-FM - 101.7 **(14889)**

Detroit
WMUZ-FM - 103.5 **(14972)**

Holland
WJQK-FM - 99.3 **(15177)**

Spring Arbor
WSAE-FM - 106.9 **(15573)**

MINNESOTA
Duluth
WNCB-FM - 89.5 **(15856)**

Forest Lake
WLKX-FM - 95.9 **(15907)**

Osakis
KCGN-FM - 101.5 **(16247)**

Sauk Rapids
KKJM-FM - 92.9 **(16438)**

MISSISSIPPI
Clinton
WHJT-FM - 96.3 **(16597)**

Columbus
WJWF-AM - 1400 **(16610)**

Pascagoula
WZZJ-AM - 1580 **(16814)**

MISSOURI
Joplin
KOBC-FM - 90.7 **(17145)**

Mountain Grove
KELE-AM - 1360 **(17301)**

St. Joseph
KGNM-AM - 1270 **(17396)**

MONTANA
Glendive
KGLE-AM - 590 **(17796)**

Kalispell
KALS-FM - 97.1 **(17839)**

NEVADA
Carson City
KNIS-FM - 91.3 **(18332)**

Las Vegas
KKVV-AM - 1060 AM **(18398)**

NEW HAMPSHIRE
Derry
WDER-AM - 1320 **(18489)**

NEW JERSEY
Ocean City
WIBG-AM - 1020 **(19389)**

NEW MEXICO
Albuquerque
KLYT-FM - 88.3 **(19804)**

Carlsbad
KAMQ-AM - 1240 **(19823)**

Farmington
KPCL-FM - 95.7 **(19851)**

NEW YORK
Brockport
WASB-AM - 1590 **(20248)**

Cohoes
WBAR-FM - 94.7 **(20480)**

East Syracuse
WVOA-FM - 103.9 **(20561)**

Lake Katrine
WLJP-FM - 89.3 **(20872)**
WPGL-FM - 90.7 **(20873)**
WRPJ-FM - 88.9 **(20874)**

New Hartford
WVVC-FM - 100.7 **(21109)**

NORTH CAROLINA
Charlotte
WGAS-AM - 1420 **(23770)**
WGWG-FM - 88.3 **(23771)**
WRCM-FM - 91.9 **(23778)**

Dallas
WSGE-FM - 91.7 **(23797)**

Durham
WRTP-AM - 1530 **(23850)**

Franklin
WPFJ-AM - 1480 **(23901)**

Mayodan
WLOE-AM - 1490 **(24061)**
WMYN-AM - 1420 **(24062)**

Raleigh
WDTF-AM - 570 **(24163)**

Wilmington
WWIL-FM - 90.5 **(24308)**

Wilson
WVOT-AM - 1420 **(24315)**

Winston-Salem
WBFJ-FM - 89.3 **(24329)**

NORTH DAKOTA
Fargo
KFBN-FM - 88.7 **(24418)**

Mandan
KNDR-FM - 104.7 **(24499)**

Minot
KHRT-FM - 106.9 **(24508)**

OHIO
Belpre
WMBP-FM - 91.9 **(24675)**

Castalia
WGGN-FM - 97.7 **(24743)**

Cincinnati
WAKW-FM - 93.3 **(24831)**
WVMX-FM - 101.9 **(24848)**

Fairfield
WNLT-FM - 104.3 **(25191)**
WVRB-FM - 95.3 **(25192)**

Mount Vernon
WNZR-FM - 90.9 **(25401)**

Westerville
WUFM-FM - 88.7 **(25648)**

OKLAHOMA
Elk City
KXOO-FM - 94.3 **(25821)**

Oklahoma City
KOCC-FM - 88.9 **(26008)**

Ponca City
KLVV-FM - 88.7 **(26041)**

OREGON
Albany
KHPE-FM - 107.9 **(26209)**

Bend
KNLR-FM - 97.5 **(26248)**

Coos Bay
KYTT-FM - 98.7 **(26280)**

Portland
KBVM-FM - 88.3 **(26522)**

Numbers cited in bold after listings are entry numbers rather than page numbers.

KLVP-AM - 1040 **(26532)**

PENNSYLVANIA
Brookhaven
WVCH-AM - 740 **(26731)**

Chester
WDNR-FM, Widener University - 89.5 **(26776)**

Du Bois
WDBA-FM - 107.3 **(26840)**

Grantham
WVMM-FM - 90.7 **(26947)**

Lafayette Hill
KWFT-AM - 990 **(27136)**
WZZD-AM - 990 **(27138)**

Lewisburg
WGRC-FM - 91.3 **(27194)**

Millersville
WIXQ-FM - 91.7 **(27268)**

Pittsburgh
WORD-FM - 101.5 **(27868)**

Sellersville
WBYO-FM - 88.9 **(27983)**

SOUTH CAROLINA
Greenville
WLFJ-FM - 89.3 **(28634)**

Lake City
WVLC-AM - 1260 **(28679)**

Summerville
WYFH-FM - 90.7 **(28767)**

SOUTH DAKOTA
Rapid City
KSLT-FM - 107.3 **(28949)**

TENNESSEE
Bristol
WHGG-FM - 90.1 **(29068)**

Columbia
WMRB-AM - 910 **(29142)**

Humboldt
WLSZ-FM - 105.3 **(29228)**

Knoxville
WRJZ-AM - 620 **(29299)**

Milligan College
WZMC-AM - 870 **(29415)**

Nashville
WNAZ-FM - 89.1 **(29522)**
WNRZ-FM - 91.5 **(29524)**
WYYB-FM - 93.7 **(29540)**

Tullahoma
WJIG-AM - 740 **(29634)**

TEXAS
Abilene
KGNZ-FM - 88.1 **(29662)**

Amarillo
KAEZ-FM - 105.7 **(29702)**
KLMN-FM - 89.1 **(29712)**
KRGN-FM - 103.1 **(29716)**

Bryan
KAGC-AM - 1510 **(29976)**

Edinburg
KOIR-FM - 88.5 **(30272)**
KRIO-AM - 910 **(30273)**

Garland
KXVI-AM - 91.1 **(30387)**

Humble
KSBJ-FM - 89.3 **(30592)**

Keene
KJCR-FM - 88.3 **(30634)**

McAllen
KEPI-FM - 88.7 **(30793)**
KEPX-FM - 89.5 **(30794)**

Plainview
KWLD-FM - 91.5 **(30946)**

Sweetwater
KXOX-AM - 1240 **(31171)**

Wichita Falls
KMOC-FM - 89.5 **(31298)**

VERMONT
Essex
WGLY-FM - 93.5 **(31542)**

VIRGINIA
Blacksburg
SPIRIT-FM - 90.9 **(31881)**

Broadway
WLTK-FM - 103.3 **(31904)**

Churchville
WNLR-AM - 1150 **(31973)**

Lynchburg
WWMC-FM - 90.9 **(32217)**

Spotsylvania
WJYJ-FM - 90.5 **(32536)**

Virginia Beach
WODC-FM - 88.5 - 103.7 - 103.9 - 97.9 **(32595)**

WASHINGTON
Chehalis
KACS Christian Radio - 90.5 **(32712)**

Lynden
KWPZ-FM - 106.5 **(32822)**

Pullman
KRLF-FM - 88.5 **(32914)**

Seattle
KCMS-FM - 105.3 **(33049)**
KGNW-AM - 820 **(33053)**

Spokane
KAAR-FM - 95.3 **(33105)**

WEST VIRGINIA
Lewisburg
WRLB-FM - 95.3 **(33368)**
WRRL-AM - 1130 **(33369)**

Moundsville
WRKP-FM - 96.5 **(33409)**

South Charleston
WJYP-FM - 100.9 **(33468)**

WISCONSIN
Chippewa Falls
WOGO-AM - 680 **(33632)**
WWIB-FM - 103.7 **(33633)**

Milwaukee
WJYI-AM - 1340 **(34122)**

Schofield
WCLQ-FM - 89.5 **(34314)**

Sturgeon Bay
WPFF-FM - 90.5 **(34356)**

WYOMING
Casper
KCSP-FM - 90.3 **(34487)**

MANITOBA, CANADA
Winnipeg
CKJS-AM - 810 **(35373)**

ONTARIO, CANADA
Barrie
CJLF-FM - 100.3 **(35663)**

Oakville
CJYE-AM - 1250 **(36154)**

Ottawa
CHRI-FM - 99.1 **(36290)**

Sudbury
CJTK-FM - 95.5 **(36427)**

Thunder Bay
CJOA-FM - 95.1 **(36447)**

CONTEMPORARY COUNTRY

ALABAMA
Albertville
WQSB-FM - 105.1 **(5)**

Birmingham
WZZK-AM - 610 **(133)**
WZZK-FM - 104.7 **(134)**

Clanton
WEZZ-FM - 97.7 **(156)**

Cullman
WKUL-FM - 92.1 **(166)**

Decatur
WDRM-FM - 102.1 **(172)**

Dothan
WTVY-FM - 95.5 **(193)**

Elba
WZTZ-FM - 101.1 **(199)**

Fayette
WLDX-AM - 990 **(215)**

Florence
WXFL-FM - 96.1 **(226)**

Jasper
WARF-AM - 95.3 **(297)**
WFFN-FM - 95.3 **(298)**

Mobile
WKSJ-FM - 94.9 **(343)**

Montgomery
WLWI-FM - 92.3 **(387)**

Roanoke
WELR-FM - 102.3 **(435)**

Scottsboro
WKEA-FM - 98.3 **(448)**

Selma
WDXX-FM - 100.1 **(453)**

ALASKA
Anchorage
KBYR-AM - 700 **(538)**

Fairbanks
KIAK-AM - 970 **(573)**

Kenai
KWHQ-FM - 100.1 **(610)**

ARIZONA
Holbrook
KZUA-FM - 92.1 **(726)**

Miami
KQSS-FM - 98.3 **(753)**

Parker
KLPZ-AM - 1380 **(765)**

Phoenix
KWCY-FM - 103.5 **(843)**

Safford
KXKQ-FM - 94.1 **(864)**

Sierra Vista
KWCD-FM - 92.3 **(891)**

Tucson
KIIM-FM - 99.5 **(983)**

Window Rock
KTNN-AM - 660 **(1013)**

ARKANSAS
Arkadelphia
KVRC-AM - 1240 **(1034)**

Camden
KAMD-FM - 97.1 **(1071)**
KCXY-FM - 95.3 **(1073)**

Conway
KTOD-FM - 92.7 **(1089)**

Crossett
KAGH-AM - 800 **(1093)**
KAGH-FM - 104.9 **(1094)**

De Queen
KDQN-FM - 92.1 **(1102)**

Circulation: ★ = ABC; △ = BPA; ♦ = CAC; • = CCAB; ❑ = VAC; ⊕ = PO Statement; ‡ = Publisher's Report; Boldface figures = sworn; Light figures = estimated.

Radio Station Formats

2997

CONTEMPORARY COUNTRY (continued)

Fort Smith
KTCS-AM - 1410 **(1155)**

Hope
KHPA-FM - 104.9 **(1179)**

Jonesboro
KFIN-FM - 107.9 **(1200)**

Little Rock
KSSN-FM - 95.7 **(1251)**
KVLO-FM - 102.9 **(1254)**

Mena
KENA-FM - 102.1 **(1277)**

Mountain Home
KPFM-FM - 105.5 **(1288)**

Ozark
KDYN-AM - 1540 **(1306)**

Searcy
KAPZ-AM - 710 **(1340)**
KKSY-FM - 107.1 **(1342)**

Stuttgart
KWAK-AM - 1240 **(1353)**

Texarkana
KKYR-AM - 790 **(1355)**
KKYR-FM - 102.5 **(1356)**

CALIFORNIA
Bakersfield
KUZZ-FM - 107.9 **(1474)**

Chico
KHSL-FM - 103.5 **(1700)**

Eureka
KEKA-FM - 101.5 **(1899)**

Lemoore
KJOP-AM - 1240 **(2153)**

Redding
KNCQ-FM - 97.3 **(2890)**
KNRO-AM - 1670 **(2892)**

Rohnert Park
KRPQ-FM - 104.9 **(2963)**

Salinas
KTOM-AM - 1380 **(3076)**
KTOM-FM - 100.7 **(3077)**

Tulare
KJUG-FM - 106.7 **(3956)**

Twentynine Palms
KDHI-FM - 92.1 **(3965)**

Victorville
KATJ-FM - 100.7 **(4034)**

COLORADO
Colorado Springs
KBZC-AM - 1300 **(4263)**
KKCS-FM - 101.9 **(4270)**

Denver
KYGO-FM - 98.5 **(4396)**

Grand Junction
KEKB-FM - 99.9 **(4483)**

Montrose
KKXK-FM - 94.1 **(4581)**

FLORIDA
Chiefland
WLQH-AM - 940 **(5982)**

Clewiston
WAFC-FM - 99.5 **(5998)**

Lakeland
WPCV-FM - 97.5 **(6295)**

Ocala
WTRS-FM - 102.3 **(6479)**

Orlando
WWKA-FM - 92.3 **(6530)**

Palatka
WIYD-AM - 1260 **(6539)**

Tallahassee
WTNT-FM - 94.9 **(6753)**

Tampa
WQYK-FM - 99.5 **(6801)**

Trenton
WDFL-AM - 1240 **(6825)**
WDFL-FM - 106.3 **(6826)**

GEORGIA
Cedartown
WGAA-AM - 1340 **(7166)**

Dublin
WXLI-AM - 1230 **(7256)**

Elberton
WWRK-FM - 92.1 **(7268)**

Gainesville
WLBA-AM - 1130 **(7303)**

Macon
WDEN-FM - 99.1 **(7394)**

Mountain City
WALH-AM - 1340 **(7450)**

Quitman
WSFB-AM - 1490 **(7487)**

Swainsboro
WXRS-FM - 100.5 **(7580)**

Valdosta
WAAC-FM - 92.9 **(7618)**

West Point
WCJM-FM - 100.9 **(7651)**

IDAHO
Blackfoot
KECN-AM - 690 **(7801)**

Boise
KIZN-FM - 92.3 **(7824)**
KQFC-FM - 97.9 **(7828)**

Jerome
KKMV-FM - 92.5 **(7883)**

Oldtown
KMJY-AM - 700 **(7936)**
KMJY-FM - 104.5 **(7937)**

Pocatello
KZBQ-AM - 1290 **(7956)**
KZBQ-FM - 93.7 **(7957)**

Twin Falls
KEZJ-AM - 1450 **(7993)**

ILLINOIS
Decatur
WDZQ-FM - 95.1 **(8717)**

Farmer City
WWHP-FM - 98.3 **(8887)**

Galesburg
WAAG-FM - 94.9 **(8909)**

Greenville
WGEL-FM - 101.7 **(8963)**

Joliet
WCCQ-FM - 98.3 **(9036)**

McLeansboro
WMCL-AM - 1060 **(9168)**

Pittsfield
WBBA-FM - 97.5 **(9457)**

Springfield
WFMB-FM - 104.5 **(9648)**
WMHX-FM - 93.9 **(9652)**

INDIANA
Aurora
WSCH-FM - 99.3 **(9792)**

Columbus
WKKG-FM - 101.5 **(9897)**

Evansville
WKDQ-FM - 99.5 **(9946)**
WYNG-FM - 105.3 **(9953)**

Fort Wayne
WBTU-FM - 93.3 **(9980)**

Greensburg
WTRE-AM - 1330 **(10045)**

La Porte
WCOE-FM - 96.7 **(10248)**

Marion
WCJC-FM - 99.3 **(10290)**

North Vernon
WIKI-FM - 95.3 **(10364)**

Salem
WSLM-AM - 1220 **(10442)**

Scottsburg
WMPI-FM - 105.3 **(10446)**

Sullivan
WNDI-AM - 1550 **(10475)**
WNDI-FM - 95.3 **(10476)**

Terre Haute
WTHI-FM - 99.9 **(10503)**

IOWA
Davenport
WLLR-FM - 103.7-FM **(10750)**

Forest City
KIOW-FM - 107.3 **(10892)**

Hampton
KLMJ-FM - 104.9 **(10941)**

Marshalltown
KXIA-FM - 101.1 **(11069)**

Oskaloosa
KBOE-AM - 740 **(11136)**

Ottumwa
KRKN-FM - 104.3 **(11144)**

Perry
KDLS-AM - 1310 **(11157)**

Red Oak
KCSI-FM - 95.3 **(11171)**
KOAK-AM - 1080 **(11173)**

Shenandoah
KMA-AM - 960 **(11200)**

Waukon
KNEI-AM - 1140 **(11304)**

KANSAS
Colby
KXXX-AM - 790 **(11393)**

Junction City
KJCK-AM - 1420 **(11521)**

Liberal
KSLS-FM - 101.5 **(11606)**

Marysville
KNDY-FM - 95.5 **(11641)**

Pittsburg
KKOW-FM - 96.9 **(11756)**

Salina
KYEZ-FM - 93.7 **(11791)**

Topeka
WIBW-FM - 97.3 **(11847)**

Ulysses
KULY-AM - 1420 **(11856)**

KENTUCKY
Burkesville
WKYR-AM - 1570 **(12000)**
WKYR-FM - 107.9 **(12001)**

Catlettsburg
WTCR-AM - 1420 **(12012)**
WTCR-FM - 103.3 **(12013)**

Louisville
WAMZ-FM - 97.5 **(12245)**

Owingsville
WKCA-FM - 107.7 **(12336)**

Paducah
WKYQ-FM - 93.3 **(12345)**

Richmond
WCYO-FM - 100.7 **(12384)**

Salyersville
WRLV-FM - 97.3 **(12393)**

Somerset
WSEK-FM - 97.1 **(12409)**

Vanceburg
WKKS-AM - 1570 (12425)

Williamsburg
WEZJ-FM - 104.3 (12447)

LOUISIANA
Houma
KCIL-FM - 107.5 (12602)

Lake Charles
KYKZ-FM - 96.1 (12651)

New Iberia
KXKC-FM - 99.1 (12725)

New Orleans
WNOE-FM - 101.1 (12771)

Opelousas
KSLO-AM - 1230 (12793)

Shreveport
KRMD-FM - 101.1 (12831)

MAINE
Augusta
WEBB-FM - 98.5 (12898)
WKCG-FM - 101.3 (12900)

Brewer
WBFB-FM - 104.7 (12926)

Norway
WOXO-FM - 92.7 (12995)

Skowhegan
WCME-FM - 93.5 (13052)

MARYLAND
Havre de Grace
WXCY-FM - 103.7 (13581)

Salisbury
WICO-FM - 97.5 (13716)

MICHIGAN
Adrian
WQTE-FM - 95.3 (14713)

Alpena
WATZ-FM - 99.3 (14737)

Bad Axe
WLEW-AM - 1340 (14788)

Battle Creek
WNWN-FM - 98.5 (14797)

Houghton
WCCY-AM - 1400 (15185)

Ironwood
WJMS-AM - 590 (15216)

Muskegon
WMUS-AM - 1090 (15394)
WMUS-FM - 106.9 (15395)

Port Huron
WSAQ-FM - 107.1 (15458)

MINNESOTA
Bemidji
KBHP-FM - 101.1 (15741)

Blue Earth
KBEW-FM - 98.1 (15764)

Fairmont
KSUM-AM - 1370 (15892)

Fergus Falls
KBRF-AM - 1250 (15900)

Jackson
KKOJ-AM - 1190 (15977)

Park Rapids
KPRM-AM - 870 (16258)

Pine City
WCMP-FM - 100.9 (16270)

Preston
KFIL-AM - 1060 (16282)

Princeton
WQPM-AM - 1300 (16286)
WQPM-FM - 106.1 (16287)

Rochester
KWWK-FM - 96.5 (16322)

St. Cloud
WWJO-FM - 98.1 (16354)

Thief River Falls
KKAQ-AM - 1460 (16470)

Wadena
KWAD-AM - 920 (16492)

MISSISSIPPI
Brookhaven
WBKN-FM - 92.1 (16579)

Corinth
WADI-FM - 95.3 (16616)

Greenville
KUUZ-FM - 95.9 (16632)
WDMS-FM - 100.7 (16638)

Iuka
WVOM-AM - 1270 (16693)

Kosciusko
WBKJ-FM - 105.1 (16736)

Natchez
WQNZ-FM - 95.1 (16796)

Prentiss
WJDR-FM - 98.3 (16828)

Tupelo
WWMS-FM - 97.5 (16860)

MISSOURI
Clinton
KDKD-FM - 95.3 (16986)

Dexter
KDEX-AM - 1590 (17033)
KDEX-FM - 102.3 (17034)

Flat River
KFMO-AM - 1240 (17068)

Fulton
KFAL-AM - 900 (17078)

Louisiana
KJFM-FM - 102.1 (17257)

Marshall
KMMO-AM - 102.9 (17266)
KMMO-FM - 102.9 (17267)

St. Louis
WKKX-FM - 106.5 (17558)

Springfield
KTTS-FM - 94.7 (17630)

Thayer
KAMS-FM - 95.1 (17650)

MONTANA
Billings
KCTR-FM - 102.9 (17739)

Helena
KHKR-FM - 104.1 (17829)

Kalispell
KOFI-FM - 103.9 (17843)

Livingston
KPRK-AM - 1340 (17857)

Missoula
KYSS-FM - 94.9 (17887)

Scobey
KCGM-FM - 95.7 (17904)

NEBRASKA
Ainsworth
KBRB-AM - 1400 (17924)
KBRB-FM - 92.7 (17925)

Broken Bow
KCNI-AM - 1280 (17967)

Chadron
KQSK-FM - 97.5 (17976)

Fairbury
KUTT-FM - 99.5 (18007)

Grand Island
KRGI-FM - 96.5 (18030)

McCook
KIOD-FM - 105.3 (18156)

North Platte
KXNP-FM - 103.5 (18185)

Ogallala
KMCX-FM - 106.5 (18189)

Scottsbluff
KNEB-FM - 94.1 (18271)

Sidney
KSID-AM - 1340 (18279)

NEVADA
Las Vegas
KWNR-FM - 95.5 (18408)

NEW HAMPSHIRE
Dover
WPKQ-FM - 103.7 (18494)

Lebanon
WXXK-FM - 100.5 (18547)

NEW JERSEY
Northfield
WPUR-FM - 107.3 (19384)

NEW MEXICO
Clayton
KLMX-AM - 1450 (19829)

Las Vegas
KFUN-AM - 1230 (19891)

Roswell
KEND-FM - 106.5 (19919)

Ruidoso
KWES-FM - 93.5 (19930)

NEW YORK
Binghamton
WHWK-FM - 98.1 (20224)

Clintondale
WRWD-FM - 107.3 (20476)

Elmira
WPGI-FM - 100.9 (20578)

Hawthorne
WRGX-FM - 107.1 (20726)

Ithaca
WQNY-FM - 103.7 (20821)

Latham
WGNA-FM - 107.7 (20937)

Malone
WVNV-FM - 96.5 (20982)

Olean
WPIG-FM - 95.7 (23044)

Patterson
WPUT-AM - 1510 (23082)

Walton
WDLA-FM - 92.1 (23499)

Whitesboro
WFRG-FM - 104.3 (23578)

NORTH CAROLINA
Asheville
WKSF-FM - 99.9 (23638)

Bryson City
WBHN-AM - 1590 (23667)

Burnsville
WKYK-AM - 940 (23679)

Charlotte
WSOC-FM - 103.7 (23779)

Murphy
WCVP-FM - 95.9 (24091)

Raleigh
WQDR-FM - 94.7 (24167)

Roanoke Rapids
WPTM-FM - 102.3 (24196)

Sparta
WCOK-AM - 1060 (24241)

CONTEMPORARY COUNTRY (continued)

Wilmington
WWQQ-FM - 101.3 **(24309)**

NORTH DAKOTA
Beulah
KHOL-AM - 1410 **(24348)**

Bismarck
KQDY-FM - 94.5 **(24370)**

Carrington
KDAK-AM - 1600 **(24385)**

Fargo
KVOX-FM - 99.9 **(24431)**

Harvey
KHND-AM - 1470 **(24469)**

Hettinger
KNDC-AM - 1490 **(24473)**

Williston
KDSR-FM - 101.1 **(24561)**

OHIO
Cincinnati
WBBI-FM - 107.5 **(24833)**

Coshocton
WTNS-AM - 1560 **(25097)**

Dayton
WHKO-FM - 99.1 **(25142)**

Middleport
WMPO-AM - 1390 **(25376)**

New Philadelphia
WTUZ-FM - 99.9 **(25422)**

Springfield
WKSW-FM - 101.7 **(25537)**

Toledo
WKKO-FM - 99.9 **(25580)**

Washington Court House
WCHO-FM - 105.5 **(25622)**

OKLAHOMA
Ada
KADA-AM - 1230 **(25725)**
KADA-FM - 99.3 **(25726)**

Bristow
KREK-FM - 104.9 **(25770)**

Broken Bow
KKBI-FM - 106.1 **(25776)**

Cushing
KUSH-AM - 1600 **(25796)**

Grove
KGVE-FM - 99.3 **(25852)**

Guymon
KGYN-AM - 1210 **(25856)**

Marlow
KFXI-FM - 92.1 **(25906)**

McAlester
KMCO-FM - 101.3 **(25910)**

Shawnee
KWSH-AM - 1260 **(26069)**

Tulsa
KVOO-FM - 98.5 **(26169)**
KWEN-FM - 95.5 **(26170)**

Woodward
KWOX-FM - 101.1 **(26200)**

OREGON
Albany
KRKT-FM - 99.9 **(26212)**
KXPC-FM - 103.7 **(26214)**

Coos Bay
KBBR-AM - 1340 **(26276)**

Eugene
KKNU-FM - 93.1 **(26339)**

Gold Beach
KGBR-FM - 92.7 **(26361)**

Klamath Falls
KKJX-AM - 960 **(26393)**

KLAD-FM - 92.5 **(26395)**

Medford
KRWQ-FM - 100.3 **(26427)**

Newport
KPPT-FM - 100.7 **(26450)**

Roseburg
KRSB-FM - 103.1 **(26560)**

St. Helens
KOHI-AM - 1600 **(26564)**

PENNSYLVANIA
Bala Cynwyd
WXTU-FM - 92.5 **(26682)**

Bethlehem
WCTO-FM - 96.1 **(26709)**

Corry
WWCB-AM - 1370 **(26810)**

Emporium
WLEM-AM - 1250 **(26884)**
WQKY-FM - 99.3 **(26885)**

Gettysburg
WGTY-FM - 107.7 **(26942)**

Hershey
WRKZ-FM - 106.7 **(27045)**

Selinsgrove
WLGL-FM - 92.3 **(27978)**
WWBE-FM - 98.3 **(27980)**
WYGL-AM - 1240 **(27981)**
WYGL-FM - 100.5 **(27982)**

Shenandoah
WMBT-AM - 1530 **(27987)**

Waynesburg
WANB-AM - 1580 **(28139)**
WANB-FM - 103.1 **(28140)**

SOUTH CAROLINA
Florence
WHSC-AM - 1450 **(28606)**

Greenwood
WSCZ-FM - 96.7 **(28650)**

Myrtle Beach
WYAK-AM - 1270 **(28714)**
WYAK-FM - 103.1 **(28715)**

Orangeburg
WIGL-FM - 102.9 **(28734)**

Rock Hill
WRHM-FM - 107.1 **(28749)**

Union
WBCU-AM - 1460 **(28777)**

SOUTH DAKOTA
Huron
KOKK-AM - 1210 **(28872)**

Madison
KJAM-AM - 1390 **(28887)**

Pierre
KPLO-FM - 94.5 **(28927)**

Watertown
KDLO-FM - 96.9 **(29020)**

Yankton
KKYA-FM - 93.1 **(29041)**

TENNESSEE
Carthage
WUCZ-FM - 104.1 **(29083)**

Centerville
WNKX-FM - 96.7 **(29086)**

Dunlap
WSDQ-AM - 1190 **(29172)**

Fayetteville
WYTM-FM - 105.5 **(29192)**

Greeneville
WIKQ-FM - 103.1 **(29214)**

Jackson
WTNV-FM - 104.1 **(29240)**

Jamestown
WDEB-AM - 1500 **(29245)**
WDEB-FM - 103.9 **(29246)**

Lenoir City
WLIL-AM - 730 **(29324)**
WLIL-FM - 93.5 **(29325)**

Lexington
WZLT-FM - 99.3 **(29331)**

Livingston
WLIV-AM - 920 **(29334)**

Maryville
WGAP-AM - 1400 **(29349)**
WGAP-FM - 95.7 **(29350)**

Nashville
WSM-FM - 95.5 **(29534)**

Parsons
WKJQ-FM - 97.3 **(29565)**

St. Joseph
WJOR-FM - 101.5 **(29583)**

Savannah
WKWX-FM - 93.5 **(29586)**

Springfield
WDBL-AM - 1590 **(29619)**

Union City
WYVY-FM - 104.9 **(29638)**

TEXAS
Abilene
KEAN-AM - 1280 **(29659)**
KEAN-FM - 105.1 **(29660)**

Alpine
KALP-FM - 92.7 **(29686)**

Amarillo
KBUY-FM - 94.1 **(29704)**

Beaumont
KAYD-FM - 101.7 **(29901)**

Carrizo Springs
KBEN-AM - 1450 **(30003)**

Childress
KSRW-FM - 96.1 **(30019)**

Dallas
KPLX-FM - 99.5 **(30211)**

Johnson City
KNAF-AM - 910 **(30628)**

Livingston
KETX-AM - 1440 **(30701)**

Lubbock
KLLL-AM - 1590 **(30730)**
KLLL-FM - 96.3 **(30731)**

Lufkin
KYKS-FM - 105.1 **(30748)**

Memphis
KLSR-FM - 105.3 **(30803)**

Mexia
KYCX-FM - 104.9 **(30812)**

Mount Pleasant
KSCN-FM - 96.9 **(30842)**

Muleshoe
KMUL-AM - 1380 **(30847)**

Pampa
KOMX-FM - 100.3 **(30902)**

Paris
KOYN-FM - 93.9 **(30907)**

Perryton
KEYE-AM - 1400 **(30928)**

Robstown
KROB-AM - 1510 **(30986)**

San Antonio
KAJA-FM - 97.3 **(31051)**

Stephenville
KSTV-FM - 93.1 **(31133)**

Sweetwater
KXOX-AM - 1240 **(31171)**

Tyler
KNUE-FM - 101.5 **(31216)**

Numbers cited in bold after listings are entry numbers rather than page numbers.

Uvalde
KYUF-FM - 104.9 **(31227)**

Vernon
KVWC-AM - 1490 **(31232)**

Weatherford
KYXS-FM - 95.9 **(31275)**

UTAH
Cedar City
KSSD-FM - 92.5 **(31327)**

Manti
KMTI-AM - 650 **(31367)**

Salt Lake City
KKAT-FM - 101.9 **(31451)**
KSOP-FM - 104.3 **(31459)**

Vernal
KLCY-FM - 105.9 **(31484)**

VERMONT
East Poultney
WNYV-FM - 94.1 **(31540)**

St. Johnsbury
WKXH-FM - 105.5 **(31595)**

VIRGINIA
Bristol
WXBQ-FM - 96.9 **(31901)**

Castlewood
WXLZ-AM - 1140 **(31909)**

Chase City
WFXQ-FM - 99.9 **(31960)**

Danville
WAKG-FM - 103.3 **(31992)**

Grundy
WNRG-AM - 940 **(32123)**

Lebanon
WXLZ-FM - 107.3 **(32181)**

Radford
WPSK-FM - 107.1 **(32350)**

Rural Retreat
WCRR-AM - 660 **(32517)**
WCRR-FM - 95.3 **(32518)**

Virginia Beach
WCMS-AM - 1050 **(32591)**
WCMS-FM - 100.5 **(32592)**

Warsaw
WNNT-FM - 100.9 **(32607)**
WNNT-FM - 100.9 **(32608)**

Wytheville
WYVE-AM - 1280 **(32644)**

WASHINGTON
Ephrata
KULE-FM - 92.3 **(32758)**

Spokane
KDRK-FM - 93.7 **(33110)**

WEST VIRGINIA
Beckley
WTNJ-FM - 105.9 **(33245)**

Fisher
WELD-AM - 690 **(33317)**

Morgantown
WKKW-FM - 97.9 **(33403)**

Ripley
WCEF-FM - 98.3 **(33451)**

Vienna
WNUS-FM - 107.1 **(33482)**

WISCONSIN
Beaver Dam
WXRO-FM - 95.3 **(33570)**

Madison
WYZM-FM - 105.1 **(34011)**

Menomonie
WRDN-AM - 1430 **(34042)**

Milwaukee
WMIL-FM - 106.1 **(34129)**

Neenah
WWWX-FM - 96.9 **(34161)**

Portage
WDDC-FM - 100.1 **(34262)**

Rhinelander
WHDG-FM - 97.5 **(34288)**

Stevens Point
WYTE-FM - 96.7 **(34348)**

Viroqua
WVRQ-FM - 102.3 **(34385)**

WYOMING
Evanston
KOTB-FM - 106.1 **(34525)**

Wheatland
KYCN-AM - 1340 **(34602)**

ALBERTA, CANADA
Calgary
CKRY-FM - 105.1 **(34672)**

Edmonton
CISN-FM - 103.9 **(34750)**

Fort McMurray
CJOK-FM - 93.3 **(34768)**

Grande Prairie
CJXX-FM - 93.1 **(34777)**

High Prairie
CKVH-AM - 1020 **(34782)**

High River
CHRB-AM - 1140 **(34784)**

Medicine Hat
CHAT-AM - 1270 **(34812)**

Red Deer
CKGY-FM - 95.5 **(34835)**

Stettler
CKSQ-AM - 1400 **(34856)**

Wetaskiwin
CKJR-AM - 1440 **(34874)**

BRITISH COLUMBIA, CANADA
Campbell River
CFWB-AM - 1490 **(34920)**

Dawson Creek
CJDC-FM - 92.7 **(34943)**

Kamloops
CKB2-FM - 100.1 MHZ **(34982)**

Nanaimo
CKEG-AM - 1570 **(35022)**

Port Alberni
CJAV-AM - 1240 **(35050)**

Vancouver
CJJR-FM - 93.7 **(35190)**

MANITOBA, CANADA
Thompson
CHTM-AM - 610 **(35303)**

NEWFOUNDLAND AND LABRADOR, CANADA
Carbonear
CHVO-AM - 560 **(35443)**

Gander
CKXD-AM - 1010 **(35458)**

Musgravetown
CKXB-AM - 670 **(35476)**

NORTHWEST TERRITORIES, CANADA
Yellowknife
CKLB-FM - 101.9 **(35530)**

NOVA SCOTIA, CANADA
Sydney
CJCB-AM - 1270 **(35612)**

Truro
CKCL-AM - 600 **(35617)**

ONTARIO, CANADA
Ajax
CJKX-FM - 95.9 **(35628)**

Hamilton
CHAM-AM - 820 **(35894)**

Leamington
CHYR-FM - 96.7 **(35970)**

London
CJBX-FM - 92.7 **(36003)**

Marathon
CFNO-FM - 93.1 **(36012)**

Ottawa
CBOF-FM - 90.7 **(36285)**

Owen Sound
CKYC-FM - 93.7 **(36303)**

Wingham
CKNX-AM - 920 **(36903)**

SASKATCHEWAN, CANADA
Meadow Lake
CJNS-AM - 1240 **(37496)**

Melfort
CJVR-AM - 750 **(37499)**

North Battleford
CJNB-AM - 1050 **(37513)**

Shaunavon
CJSN-AM - 1490 **(37570)**

Yorkton
CJGX-AM - 940 **(37602)**

CONTEMPORARY HIT RADIO (CHR)

ALABAMA
Mobile
WABB-FM - 97.5 **(333)**

Oxford
WVOK-FM - 97.9 **(418)**

ALASKA
Fairbanks
KWLF-FM - 98.1 **(580)**

McGrath
KSKO-AM - 870 **(623)**

ARIZONA
Lake Havasu City
KBBC-FM - 101.1 **(738)**

Sedona
KAZM-AM - 780 **(879)**

Tucson
KOHT-FM - 98.3 **(989)**
KRQQ-FM - 93.7 **(992)**

ARKANSAS
Fort Smith
KZBB-FM - 97.9 **(1158)**

Hot Springs
KLAZ-FM - 105.9 **(1185)**

CALIFORNIA
Bakersfield
KKXX-FM - 105.3 **(1467)**
KSPL-FM - 102.9 **(1470)**

Burbank
KPWR-FM - 105.9 **(1628)**

Fremont
KOHL-FM - 89.3 **(1940)**

Joshua Tree
KCDZ-FM - 107.7 **(2097)**

Riverside
KGGI-FM - 99.1 **(2951)**

Sacramento
KSFM-FM - 102.5 **(3048)**
KYDS-FM - 91.5 **(3058)**

Salinas
KDON-FM - 102.5 **(3070)**

CONTEMPORARY HIT RADIO
(CHR) (continued)

San Diego
XHTZ-FM - 90.3　**(3319)**

San Francisco
KMEL-FM - 106.1　**(3491)**
KYLD-FM - 94.9　**(3505)**

San Rafael
KSRH-FM - 88.1　**(3606)**

San Ysidro
XEBG-AM - 1550　**(3608)**

Ventura
KCAQ-FM - 104.7　**(4028)**

Yucaipa
KLRD-FM - 90.1　**(4127)**

COLORADO
Colorado Springs
KKMG-FM - 98.9　**(4273)**

Cortez
KSJD-FM - 91.5　**(4293)**

CONNECTICUT
Hamden
WKCI-FM - 101.3　**(4882)**

Hartford
WKSS-FM - 95.7　**(4904)**

New Britain
WFCS-FM - 107.7　**(4977)**

New London
WQGN-FM - 105.5　**(5024)**

Willimantic
WILI-FM - 98.3　**(5223)**

DELAWARE
Georgetown
WOCQ-FM - 103.9　**(5256)**

Wilmington
WSTW-FM - 93.7　**(5303)**

DISTRICT OF COLUMBIA
Washington
WKYS-FM - 93.9　**(5888)**
WPGC-FM - 95.5　**(5892)**

FLORIDA
Gainesville
WYKS-FM - 105.3　**(6170)**

Jacksonville
WAPE-FM - 95.1　**(6219)**

Key West
WEOW-FM - 92.7　**(6254)**

Melbourne
WAOA-FM - 107.1　**(6335)**

Panama City
WFSY-FM - 98.5　**(6559)**
WILN-FM - 105.9　**(6560)**

Pensacola
WJLQ-FM - 100.7　**(6575)**

Tampa
WFLZ-FM - 93.3　**(6791)**

GEORGIA
Albany
WMGR-FM - 97.3　**(6911)**

Atlanta
WSTR-FM - 94.1　**(7088)**

Carrollton
WCKS-FM - 102.7　**(7159)**

Macon
WMGB-FM - 93.7　**(7399)**

Rome
WQTU-FM - 102.3　**(7506)**

HAWAII
Hilo
KKBG-FM - 97.9　**(7676)**

Honolulu
KDDB-FM - 102.7　**(7732)**
KIKI-AM - 990　**(7738)**
KIKI-FM - 93.9　**(7739)**

Lihue
KQNG-FM - 93.5　**(7783)**

Wailuku
KAOI-FM - 103.7　**(7796)**

IDAHO
Idaho Falls
KFTZ-FM - 103.3　**(7873)**

Moscow
KZFN-FM - 106.1　**(7924)**

ILLINOIS
Champaign
WLRW-FM - 94.5　**(8231)**

Chicago
WBBM-FM - 96.3　**(8614)**
WKIE-FM - 92.7　**(8633)**

Rockford
WZOK-FM - 97.5　**(9545)**

INDIANA
Chesterton
WDSO-FM - 88.3　**(9888)**

Evansville
WDKS-FM - 106.1　**(9938)**

Fort Wayne
WMEE-FM - 97.3　**(9990)**

Indianapolis
WBDG-FM (Giant 90.0) - 90.9　**(10190)**
WHHH-FM - 96.3　**(10197)**

Lafayette
WAZY-FM - 96.5　**(10258)**
WXXB-FM - 102.9　**(10263)**

Warsaw
WRSW-AM - 1480　**(10539)**

IOWA
Atlantic
KXKT-FM - 103.7　**(10612)**

Davenport
WHTS-FM - 98.9　**(10747)**

Oskaloosa
KIGC-FM - 88.7　**(11138)**

Ottumwa
KOTM-FM - 97.7　**(11143)**

Waterloo
KFMW-FM - 107.9　**(11292)**
KOKZ-FM - 105.7　**(11296)**

KANSAS
Colby
KTCC-FM - 91.9　**(11392)**

Dodge City
KONQ-FM - 91.9　**(11419)**

Fort Scott
KOMB-FM - 103.9　**(11445)**

Junction City
KJCK-FM - 94.5　**(11522)**

Ottawa
KTJO-FM - 88.9　**(11694)**

Salina
KQNS-FM - 95.5　**(11787)**

KENTUCKY
Elizabethtown
WRZI-FM - 101.5　**(12050)**

Hazard
WKIC-AM - 1390　**(12120)**

Louisville
WDJX-FM - 99.7　**(12248)**

Owensboro
WQXQ-FM - 101.9　**(12332)**

Paducah
WDDJ-FM - 96.9　**(12342)**

Pikeville
WPKE-AM - 1240　**(12365)**
WPKE-FM - 103.1　**(12366)**

LOUISIANA
Baton Rouge
WLSS-FM - 102.5　**(12521)**

Morgan City
KFXY-FM - 96.7　**(12711)**

Shreveport
KRUF-FM - 94.5　**(12832)**

MAINE
Augusta
WMME-FM - 92.3　**(12901)**

Portland
WJBQ-FM - 97.9　**(13027)**
WRED-FM - 95.9　**(13031)**

Standish
WSJB-FM - 91.5　**(13059)**

MARYLAND
Baltimore
WERQ-FM - 92.3　**(13272)**

MASSACHUSETTS
East Sandwich
WSDH-FM - 91.5　**(14171)**

Fairhaven
WFHN-FM - 107.1　**(14179)**

Medford
WXKS-FM - 107.9　**(14327)**

Northampton
WHMP-FM - 99.3　**(14433)**

Northfield
WNMH-FM - 91.5　**(14436)**

Pittsfield
WBEC-FM - 105.5　**(14474)**
WRCZ-FM - 101.7　**(14476)**

Winchendon
WINQ-FM - 97.7　**(14665)**

MICHIGAN
Detroit
WDRQ-FM - 93.1　**(14959)**

Flint
WWCK-AM - 105.5　**(15048)**

Grand Rapids
WSNX-FM - 104.5　**(15122)**
WVTI-FM - 96.1　**(15126)**

Lansing
WHZZ-FM - 101.7　**(15298)**

Marquette
WKQS-FM - 101.9　**(15344)**

Monroe
WTWR-FM - 98.3　**(15368)**

Oak Park
WKQI-FM - 95.5　**(15414)**

Sault Sainte Marie
WYSS-FM - 99.5　**(15532)**

MINNESOTA
Bemidji
KBSB-FM - 89.7　**(15742)**

Fairmont
KFMC-FM - 106.5　**(15891)**

Mankato
KDOG-FM - 96.7　**(16031)**

Minneapolis
KDWB-FM - 101.3　**(16147)**

Rochester
KROC-FM - 106.9　**(16319)**

St. Cloud
KCLD-FM - 104.7　**(16350)**

MISSISSIPPI
Greenville
WIQQ-FM - 102.3　**(16641)**

Gulfport
WZKX-FM - 107.9 (16660)

Tupelo
WWKZ-FM - 105.3 (16859)

MISSOURI
Columbia
KOQL-FM - 106.1 (17021)

Joplin
KSYN-FM - 92.5 (17150)

Monett
KKBL-FM - 95.9 (17294)

NEBRASKA
Hastings
KCNT-FM - 88.1 (18038)

Lincoln
KFRX-FM - 102.7 (18134)

Omaha
KQKQ-FM - 98.5 (18226)

Scottsbluff
KMOR-FM - 92.9 (18269)

NEVADA
Reno
KWNZ-FM - 97.3 (18443)

Tonopah
KHWK-FM - 92.7 (18448)

NEW JERSEY
Newton
WHCY-FM - 106.3 (19378)

Princeton
WPST-FM - 97.5 (19482)

NEW MEXICO
Albuquerque
KKSS-FM - 97.3 (19801)

Gallup
KKOR-FM - 94.5 (19860)

Las Cruces
KHQT-FM - 103.1 (19881)

Roswell
KBCQ-FM - 97.1 (19914)

NEW YORK
Albany
WKKF-FM - 102.3 (20013)

Alfred
WETD-FM - 90.9 (20026)

Baldwinsville
WBXL-FM - 90.5 (20115)

Beacon
WSPK-FM - 104.7 (20142)

Brockport
WBSU-FM - 89.1 (20249)

Buffalo
WKSE-FM - 98.5 (20406)

Cortland
WSUC-FM - 90.5 (20514)

Elmira
WLVY-FM - 94.3 (20577)

Endwell
WMRV-FM - 105.7 (20589)

Homer
WXHC-FM - 101.5 (20750)

Hornell
WKPQ-FM - 105.3 (20757)

New York
WKDM-AM - 1380 (22973)
WQHT-FM - 97.1 (22989)

Poughkeepsie
WALL-AM - 1340 (23152)
WEOK-AM - 1390 (23157)
WPKF-FM - 96.1 (23161)

Syracuse
WNTQ-FM - 93.1 (23442)

WWHT-FM - 107.9 (23448)

Utica
WOWB-FM - 105.5 (23476)
WOWZ-FM - 97.9 (23477)
WSKS-FM - 102.5 (23480)

Watertown
WBDR-FM - 102.7 (23516)

West Babylon
WBLI-FM - 106.1 (23538)
WNYG-AM - 1440 (23539)

Windham
WRIP-FM - 97.9 (23588)

NORTH CAROLINA
Cullowhee
WWCU-FM - 90.5 (23796)

Greensboro
WJMH-FM - 102.1 (23948)
WKZL-FM - 107.5 (23951)

Hendersonville
WHKP-AM - 1450 (23985)

New Bern
WLOJ-AM - 1490 (24100)
WRHT-FM - 96.3 (24101)

NORTH DAKOTA
Bismarck
KYYY-FM - 92.9 (24374)

Jamestown
KSJZ-FM - 93.3 (24482)

OHIO
Athens
WXTQ-FM - 105.5 (24637)

Brookfield
WAKZ-FM - 95.9 (24708)

Dayton
WGTZ-FM - 92.9 (25139)

Greenville
WTGR-FM - 97.5 (25229)

Lima
WZOQ-FM - 92.1 (25305)

Piketon
WXZQ-FM - 100.1 (25478)

Uhrichsville
WNPQ-FM - 95.9 (25601)

Youngstown
WHOT-FM - 101.1 (25706)

OKLAHOMA
Durant
KSSU-FM - 91.9 (25812)

Lawton
KMGZ-FM - 95.3 (25894)

Oklahoma City
KKWD-FM - 97.9 (26006)
KOKF-FM - 90.9 (26011)
KYIS-FM - 98.9 (26022)

Tulsa
KHTT-FM - 106.9 (26148)
KMYZ-AM - 1570 (26153)

OREGON
Eugene
KDUK-FM - 104.7 (26336)

La Grande
KUBQ-FM - 98.7 (26402)

Medford
KIFS-FM - 107.5 (26423)
KTMT-FM - 93.7 (26430)

Portland
KKRZ-FM - 100.3 (26530)

PENNSYLVANIA
Altoona
WPRR-FM - 100.1 (26640)

Bala Cynwyd
WIOQ-FM - 102.1 (26674)

Clarion
WCUC-FM - 91.7 (26783)

Concordville
WZZE-FM - 97.3 (26800)

Harrisburg
WNNK-FM - 104.1 (27023)

Johnstown
WGLU-FM - 92.1 (27091)

Lafayette Hill
KNIN-FM - 92.9 (27133)

Lancaster
WJTL-FM - 90.3 (27151)
WLAN-FM - 96.9 (27153)

Lewistown
WMRF-FM - 95.9 (27198)

Middletown
WMSS-FM - 91.1 (27261)

Pittsburgh
WBZZ-FM - 93.7 (27861)

Reading
WRFY-FM - 102.5 (27923)

Slippery Rock
WSRU-FM - 90.1 (28001)

State College
WBHV-FM - 103.1 (28023)

Whitehall
WAEB-FM - 104.1 (28160)

Wilkes Barre
WBHT-FM - 97.1 (28171)

Williamsport
WHTO-FM - 93.3 (28185)

PUERTO RICO
Bayamon
WXLX-FM - 103.7 (28233)

Gavco
WENA-AM - 1330 (28245)

Guaynabo
WMEG-FM - 106.9 (28247)

Manati
WBQN-AM - 1160 (28257)

Mayaguez
WAEL-FM - 96.1 (28259)
WOYE-FM - 94.1 (28267)

RHODE ISLAND
East Providence
WZRA-FM - 99.7 (28352)
WZRI-FM - 100.3 (28353)

Pawtucket
WWKX-FM - 106.3 (28380)

SOUTH CAROLINA
Columbia
WNOK-FM - 104.7 (28581)

Greenville
WFBC-FM - 93.7 (28630)

Hilton Head Island
WAVE-FM - 106.9 (28664)

Myrtle Beach
WWXM-FM - 97.7 (28713)

SOUTH DAKOTA
Rapid City
KRCS-FM - 93.1 (28948)

Sioux Falls
KKLS-FM - 104.7 (28977)
KMXC-FM - 97.3 (28978)

TENNESSEE
Crossville
WXVL-FM - 99.3 (29162)

Erwin
WXIS-FM - 103.9 (29186)

Harrogate
WLMU-FM - 91.3 (29217)

CONTEMPORARY HIT RADIO
(CHR) (continued)
Humboldt
WLSQ-FM - 94.3　**(29227)**
WLSZ-FM - 105.3　**(29228)**

Martin
WUTM-FM - 90.3　**(29346)**

Nashville
WRVW-FM - 107.5　**(29531)**

Paris
WAKQ-FM - 105.5　**(29560)**

TEXAS
Abilene
KORQ-FM - 96.1　**(29664)**

Alamo
KBFM-FM - 104.1　**(29673)**

Amarillo
KPRF-FM - 98.7　**(29715)**

Austin
KHFI-FM - 96.7　**(29864)**

Beaumont
KZZB-AM - 990　**(29911)**

Bryan
KKYS-FM - 104.7　**(29980)**

Corpus Christi
KZFM-FM - 95.5　**(30097)**

Dallas
KRBV-FM - 100.3　**(30212)**

El Paso
KHPX-FM - 98.3　**(30293)**
KPRR-FM - 102.1　**(30298)**

Houston
KRBE-FM - 104　**(30572)**

Laredo
KRRG-FM - 98.1　**(30677)**

San Angelo
KIXY-FM - 94.7　**(31018)**

San Antonio
KTFM-FM - 102.7　**(31075)**

Waco
KWTX-FM - 97.5　**(31264)**

UTAH
Cedar City
KBRE-FM - 94.9　**(31326)**

Ogden
KWCR-FM - 88.1　**(31382)**

Salt Lake City
KISN-FM - 97.1　**(31449)**
KUTQ-FM - 99.5　**(31467)**
KZHT-FM - 94.9　**(31470)**

VERMONT
Colchester
WXXX-FM - 95.5　**(31536)**

VIRGINIA
Abingdon
WABN-FM - 92.7　**(31628)**

Arlington
WWVZ-FM - 103.9　**(31848)**
WWZZ-FM - 104.1　**(31849)**

Bristol
WAEZ-FM - 99.3　**(31898)**

Lynchburg
WLYK-FM - 100.1　**(32215)**

Marion
WZVA-FM - 103.5　**(32232)**

Richmond
WRVQ-FM - 94.5　**(32484)**
WRXL-FM - 102.1　**(32485)**

Roanoke
WXLK-FM - 92.3　**(32511)**

WASHINGTON
Longview
KLYK-FM - 105.5　**(32818)**

Mercer Island
KMIH-FM - 104.5　**(32830)**

Pullman
KHTR-FM - 104.3　**(32911)**

Seattle
KNHC-FM - 89.5　**(33064)**
KPLZ-FM - 101.5　**(33068)**
KUBE-FM - 93.3　**(33071)**

Spokane
KXLY-FM - 99.9　**(33135)**

Yakima
KFFM-FM - 107.3　**(33228)**
KYSC-FM - 88.5　**(33235)**

WEST VIRGINIA
Bluefield
WHAJ-FM - 104.5　**(33256)**

Huntington
WKEE-FM - 100.5　**(33341)**

Martinsburg
WKMZ-FM - 95.9　**(33382)**

Morgantown
WVAQ-FM - 101.9　**(33405)**

WISCONSIN
Altoona
WIAL-FM - 94.1　**(33526)**

Eau Claire
WBIZ-FM - 100.7　**(33677)**

Green Bay
WQLH-FM - 98.5　**(33754)**

Milwaukee
WKTI-FM - 94.5　**(34124)**

Onalaska
WLXR-FM - 104.9　**(34215)**

WYOMING
Casper
KTRS-FM - 104.7　**(34490)**

ALBERTA, CANADA
Edmonton
CKNG-FM - 92.5　**(34755)**

Fort McMurray
CKYX-FM - 97.9　**(34769)**

Lloydminster
CKSA-AM - 1080　**(34805)**

Red Deer
CIZZ-FM - 98.9　**(34834)**

BRITISH COLUMBIA, CANADA
Dawson Creek
CJDC-AM - 890　**(34942)**
CJDC-FM - 92.7　**(34943)**

Richmond
CKZZ-FM - 95.3　**(35078)**

MANITOBA, CANADA
Brandon
CKX-FM - 96.1　**(35258)**

NEW BRUNSWICK, CANADA
Moncton
CKCW-FM - 94.5　**(35421)**

Woodstock
CJCJ-FM - 104.1　**(35441)**

NEWFOUNDLAND AND LABRADOR, CANADA
Churchill Falls
CFLC-FM - 97.9　**(35444)**

Corner Brook
CHOZ-FM - 94.3　**(35452)**

Gander
CHOZ-FM - 99.9　**(35456)**

Grand Falls
CHOS-FM - 95.9　**(35462)**

Marystown
CIOZ-FM - 94.7　**(35474)**

St. John's
CHOZ-FM - 94.7　**(35499)**

Stephenville
CIOS-FM - 98.5　**(35510)**

Wabush
CFLW-AM - 1340　**(35512)**

ONTARIO, CANADA
Barrie
CHAY-FM - 93.1　**(35661)**

Brockville
CJPT-FM - 103.7　**(35711)**

London
CIXX-FM - 106.9　**(36000)**

Ottawa
CKTF-FM - 104.1　**(36296)**
KOOL-FM - 93.9　**(36297)**

Sarnia
CFGX-FM - 99.9　**(36367)**

QUEBEC, CANADA
Chicoutimi
CJAB-FM - 94.5　**(36973)**

Montreal
CKMF-FM - 94.3　**(37249)**

Port-Cartier
CIPC-FM - 99.1　**(37278)**

Quebec
CHIK-FM - 98.9　**(37298)**

Verdun
CKVL-AM - 850　**(37430)**

YUKON TERRITORY, CANADA
Whitehorse
CKRW-AM - 610　**(37608)**

COUNTRY

ALABAMA
Alexander City
WDLK-AM - 1450　**(9)**

Anniston
WHMA-FM - 100.5　**(22)**

Arab
WRAB-AM - 1380　**(24)**

Ashland
WASZ-FM - 95.5　**(25)**
WZZX-AM - 780　**(26)**

Atmore
WASG-AM - 550　**(34)**

Butler
WPRN-FM - 107.7　**(141)**

Calera
WBYE-AM - 1370　**(142)**

Centre
WEIS-AM - 990　**(150)**

Citronelle
WHXT-FM - 102.1　**(153)**

Clanton
WEZZ-FM - 97.7　**(156)**

Cullman
WFMH-FM - 95.5　**(165)**
WKUL-FM - 92.1　**(166)**

Decatur
WDRM-FM - 102.1　**(173)**

Dora
WPYK-AM - 1010　**(184)**

Dothan
WDJR-FM - 96.9　**(191)**
WTVY-FM - 95.5　**(193)**

Evergreen
WPGG-FM - 93.3　**(211)**

Florala
WKWL-AM - 1230 **(217)**

Fort Payne
WZOB-AM - 1250 **(233)**

Geneva
WGEA-AM - 1150 **(242)**

Greenville
WQZX-FM - 94.3 **(246)**

Guntersville
WTWX-FM - 95.9 **(256)**

Haleyville
WJBB-FM - 92.7 **(260)**

Hamilton
WERH-AM - 970 **(262)**

Huntsville
WTKI-AM - 1450 **(287)**

Luverne
WLVN-AM - 1080 **(309)**

Mobile
WKSJ-AM - 1270 **(342)**

Moulton
WHIY-AM - 1190 **(397)**

Muscle Shoals
WLAY-AM - 100.3 **(399)**

Oneonta
WKLD-FM - 97.7 **(408)**

Opp
WAMI-AM - 860 **(412)**
WAMI-FM - 102.3 **(413)**
WOPP-AM - 1290 **(414)**

Ozark
WOAB-FM - 104.9 **(420)**

Pell City
WFHK-AM - 1430 **(423)**

Red Bay
WRMG-AM - 1430 **(432)**

Robertsdale
WDXZ-AM - 1000 **(438)**

Scottsboro
WWIC-AM - 1050 **(450)**

Sumiton
WRSM-AM - 1540 **(461)**

Talladega
WEYY-FM - 92.7 **(466)**

Thomasville
WJDB-FM - 95.5 **(472)**

ALASKA
Bethel
KYUK-AM - 640 **(556)**

Fairbanks
KIAK-FM - 102.5 **(574)**

Glennallen
KCAM-AM - 790 **(583)**

Homer
KGTL-AM - 620 **(590)**
KPEN-FM - 101.7 **(591)**

Ketchikan
KGTW-FM - 106.7 **(612)**

Kodiak
KVOK-AM - 560 **(620)**

McGrath
KSKO-AM - 870 **(623)**

St. Paul Island
KUHB-FM - 91.9 **(634)**

Sitka
KSBZ-FM - 103.1 **(640)**

Unalaska
KIAL-AM - 1450 **(645)**

Valdez
KVAK-AM - 1230 **(648)**

ARIZONA
Bullhead City
KFLG-FM - 94.7 **(667)**

Flagstaff
KOLT-FM - 105.7 **(702)**
KSED-FM - 107.5 **(703)**

Kingman
KGMN-FM - 99.9 **(733)**

Page
KPGE-AM - 1340 **(759)**

Payson
KMOG-AM - 1420 **(768)**

Prescott
KNOT-FM - 99.1 **(853)**

Quartzsite
KBUX-FM - 94.3 **(859)**

Safford
KCUZ-AM - 1490 **(862)**
KFMM-FM - 99.1 **(863)**

Tucson
KCUB-AM - 1290 **(976)**

Wickenburg
KSWG-FM - 96.3 **(1007)**

Winslow
KINO-AM - 1230 **(1015)**

ARKANSAS
Berryville
KTHS-AM - 1480 **(1055)**
KTHS-FM - 107.1 **(1056)**

Blytheville
KHLS-FM - 96.3 **(1061)**

Brinkley
KQMC-FM - 102.3 **(1065)**

Clarksville
KLYR-AM - 1360 **(1081)**

Conway
KTOD-FM - 92.7 **(1089)**

Corning
KCCB-AM - 1260 **(1091)**

De Queen
KDQN-FM - 92.1 **(1102)**

El Dorado
KIXB-FM - 103.3 **(1109)**

Fayetteville
KAMO-FM - 94.3 **(1126)**

Fordyce
KQEW-FM - 102.3 **(1137)**

Forrest City
KBFC-FM - 93.5 **(1141)**

Fort Smith
KMAG-FM - 99.1 **(1152)**

Glenwood
KWXE-FM - 104.5 **(1160)**
KWXI-AM - 670 **(1161)**

Harrison
KHOZ-FM - 102.9 **(1169)**

Helena
KFFA-FM - 103.1 **(1177)**

Hope
KTPA-AM - 1370 **(1180)**
KXAR-AM - 1490 **(1181)**

Hot Springs
KQUS-FM - 97.5 **(1186)**

Magnolia
KVMA-AM - 630 **(1259)**
KZHE-FM - 100.5 **(1261)**

Malvern
KBOK-AM - 1310 **(1264)**

Mountain Home
KPFM-FM - 105.5 **(1288)**
KTLO-AM - 1240 **(1289)**

Nashville
KBHC-AM - 1260 **(1295)**
KMTB-FM - 99.5 **(1296)**

Pocahontas
KRLW-FM - 106.3 **(1321)**

Salem
KSAR-FM - 92.3 **(1336)**

Texarkana
KLLI-FM - 95.9 **(1357)**

Warren
KWRF-AM - 860 **(1366)**
KWRF-FM - 105.5 **(1367)**

Wynne
KWYN-AM - 1400 **(1373)**
KWYN-FM - 92.5 **(1374)**

Yellville
KCTT-FM - 101.7 **(1375)**

CALIFORNIA
Alturas
KCNO-FM - 94.5 **(1395)**

Anaheim
KIKF-FM - 94.3 **(1421)**

Bakersfield
KCWR-FM - 107.1 **(1459)**
KUZZ-AM - 550 **(1473)**

Bishop
KIBS-FM - 100.7 **(1586)**

Brawley
KROP-AM - 1300 **(1597)**

Chico
KHSL-FM - 103.5 **(1700)**

Chula Vista
XHCR-FM - 99.3 **(1717)**

Colton
KFRG-FM - 95.1 **(1744)**
KVFG-FM - 103.1 **(1745)**

Crescent City
KPOD-AM - 1240 **(1789)**
KPOD-FM - 97.9 **(1790)**

Eureka
KRED-FM - 92.3 **(1904)**

Fresno
KSKS-FM - 93.7 **(1983)**

Grass Valley
KNCO-FM - 94.1 **(2031)**

Kernville
KCNQ-FM - 102.5 **(2103)**

King City
KRKC-AM - 1490 **(2104)**

Los Angeles
KZLA-FM - 93.9 **(2474)**

Merced
KUBB-FM - 96.3 **(2534)**

Modesto
KATM-FM - 103.3 **(2563)**

Palm Springs
KPLM-FM - 106.1 **(2777)**

Ridgecrest
KLOA-FM - 104.9 **(2925)**

Sacramento
KRAK-FM - 98.5 **(3046)**

San Diego
KSON-FM - 97.3 **(3315)**

San Jose
KRTY-FM - 95.3 **(3552)**

San Ysidro
XEMMM-AM - 800 **(3610)**

Santa Maria
KSNI-FM - 102.5 **(3700)**

Santa Rosa
KFGY-FM - 92.9 **(3738)**

Sonora
KKBN-FM - 93.5 **(3781)**

Susanville
KJDX-FM - 93.3 **(3833)**

Tulare
KJUG-AM - 1270 **(3955)**

Ukiah
KUKI-FM - 103.3 **(3970)**

Ventura
KKBE-FM - 105.5 **(4029)**

COUNTRY (continued)

Victorville
KIXW-AM - 960 **(4036)**
KROY-AM - 1590 **(4037)**

Yreka
KSYC-FM - 103.9 **(4123)**

COLORADO
Alamosa
KGIW-AM - 1450 **(4135)**

Burlington
KNAB-FM - 104.1 **(4212)**

Canon City
KSTY-FM - 104.5 **(4215)**

Colorado Springs
KCCY-FM - 96.9 **(4264)**
KRMH-AM - 1230 **(4279)**

Cortez
KISZ-FM - 97.9 **(4291)**

Craig
KRAI-AM - 550 **(4296)**

Denver
KCKK-AM - 1600 **(4374)**

Durango
KRSJ-FM - 100.5 **(4406)**

Glenwood Springs
KMTS-FM - 99.1 **(4461)**

Grand Junction
KRYD-FM - 105 **(4495)**

La Junta
KTHN-FM - 92.1 **(4528)**

Lamar
KLMR-AM - 920 **(4539)**
KVAY-FM - 105.7 **(4541)**

Monte Vista
KSLV-AM - 1240 **(4578)**

Pagosa Springs
KWUF-AM - 1400 **(4591)**

Silt
KKGD-AM - 810 **(4624)**

Steamboat Springs
KBCR-FM - 96.9 **(4637)**

Sterling
KNNG-FM - 104.7 **(4640)**

Trinidad
KCRT-AM - 1240 **(4649)**

Walsenburg
KSPK-FM - 102.3, 103.5 **(4657)**

Windsor
KUAD-FM - 99.1 **(4688)**

Wray
KRDZ-AM - 1440 **(4693)**

CONNECTICUT
Hartford
WWYZ-FM - 92.5 **(4915)**

Norwich
WCTY-FM - 97.7 **(5085)**

DELAWARE
Dover
WDSD-FM - 92.9 **(5252)**

FLORIDA
Apalachicola
WOCX-FM - 106.5 **(5906)**

Blountstown
WPHK-FM - 102.3 **(5926)**
WYBT-AM - 1000 **(5927)**

Brooksville
WWJB-AM - 1450 **(5966)**

Chiefland
WLQH-AM - 940 **(5982)**
WLQH-FM - 97.3 **(5983)**

Crestview
WAAZ-FM - 104.9 **(6025)**
WJSB-AM - 1050 **(6026)**

Dade City
WDCF-AM - 1350 **(6033)**

DeFuniak Springs
WZEP-AM - 1460 **(6054)**

Fort Myers
WWGR-FM - 101.9 **(6115)**

Fort Pierce
WAVW-FM - 101.7 **(6119)**

Gretna
WGWD-FM - 93.3 **(6176)**

Jacksonville
WROO-FM - 107.3 **(6238)**

Lake City
WGRO-AM - 960 **(6272)**

Miami
WKIS-FM - 99.9 **(6401)**

Ocala
WOGK-FM - 93.7 **(6478)**
WTRS-FM - 102.3 **(6479)**

Ormond Beach
WGNE-FM - 99.9 **(6535)**

Palatka
WIYD-AM - 1260 **(6539)**
WPLK-AM - 800 **(6540)**

Perry
WNFK-FM - 105.5 **(6583)**

Punta Gorda
WIKX-FM - 92.9 **(6610)**

St. Augustine
WAOC-AM - 1420 **(6619)**

Sarasota
WCTQ-FM - 106.5 **(6672)**

Sebring
WWOJ-FM - 99.1 **(6682)**

Tallahassee
WAIB-FM - 103.1 **(6741)**

Tampa
WRBQ-FM - 104.7 **(6802)**

Tavares
WHDM-AM - 1440 **(6812)**

GEORGIA
Albany
WOBB-FM - 100.3 **(6912)**

Americus
WISK-FM - 98.7 **(6926)**

Athens
WNGC-FM - 106.1 **(6957)**

Atlanta
WKHX-FM - 101.5 **(7074)**

Barnesville
WBAF-AM - 1090 **(7122)**

Baxley
WBYZ-FM - 94.5 **(7125)**

Blue Ridge
WPPL-FM - 103.9 **(7134)**

Calhoun
WJTH-AM - 900 **(7151)**

Carrollton
WBTR-FM - 92.1 **(7158)**

Cedartown
WGAA-AM - 1340 **(7166)**

Cleveland
WRWH-AM - 1350 **(7176)**

Columbus
WSTH-FM - 106.1 **(7194)**

Commerce
WJJC-AM - 1270 **(7199)**

Cornelia
WCON-AM - 1450 **(7208)**
WCON-FM - 99.3 **(7209)**

Dahlonega
WKHC-FM - 104.3 **(7220)**

Dalton
WQMT-FM - 98.9 **(7225)**

Dublin
WMCG-FM - 104.9 **(7253)**
WQZY-FM - 95.9 **(7255)**

Eastman
WUFF-AM - 710 **(7262)**
WUFF-FM - 92.1 **(7263)**

Fort Valley
WKXK-FM - 97.9 **(7290)**

Griffin
WEKS-FM - 92.5 **(7313)**
WHIE-AM - 1320 **(7314)**

Hartwell
WKLY-AM - 980 **(7322)**

Hazlehurst
WVOH-AM - 920 **(7326)**
WVOH-FM - 93.5 **(7327)**

Jasper
WLJA-FM - 93.5 **(7342)**
WPGHY-AM - 1560 **(7343)**
WYYZ-AM - 1490 **(7344)**

Jesup
WIFO-FM - 105.5 **(7349)**
WLOP-AM - 1370 **(7350)**

Kingsland
WKBX-FM - 106.3 **(7358)**

La Fayette
WQCH-AM - 1590 **(7361)**

Louisville
WPEH-AM - 1420 **(7377)**
WPEH-FM - 92.1 **(7378)**

Macon
WDEN-AM - 1500 **(7393)**
WPGA-AM - 980 **(7402)**
WVMG-AM - 1440 **(7404)**
WVMG-FM - 96.7 **(7405)**

Madison
WYTH-AM - 1250 **(7406)**

Milledgeville
WKZR-FM - 102.3 **(7439)**

Newnan
WCOH-AM - 1400 **(7454)**

Rome
WTSH-FM - 107.1 **(7510)**

Sandersville
WSNT-FM - 99.9 **(7529)**

Savannah
WJCL-FM - 96.5 **(7545)**
WNMT-AM - 1520 **(7547)**

Summerville
WGTA-AM - 950 **(7577)**

Tallapoosa
WKNG-AM - 1060 **(7584)**

Thomson
WTHO-FM - 101.7 **(7593)**

Tifton
WPLH-FM - 103.1 **(7603)**
WTIF-AM - 1340 **(7604)**

Valdosta
WJEM-AM - 1150 **(7622)**

Waycross
WKUB-FM - 105.1 **(7648)**

West Point
WCJM-FM - 100.9 **(7651)**

IDAHO
Boise
KFXD-AM - 580 **(7822)**
KKIC-AM - 950 **(7826)**

Coeur d'Alene
KVNI-AM - 1080 **(7848)**

Idaho Falls
KUPI-FM - 99.1 **(7879)**

Lewiston
KCLK-FM - 94.1 **(7895)**

Numbers cited in bold after listings are entry numbers rather than page numbers.

Montpelier
KVSI-AM - 1450 **(7910)**

Mountain Home
kMHI-AM - 1240 **(7927)**

Oldtown
KMJY-AM - 700 **(7936)**

Orofino
KLER-AM - 1300 **(7939)**

Osburn
KWAL-AM - 620 **(7941)**

Payette
KIOV-AM - 1450 **(7944)**

St. Maries
KOFE-AM - 1240 **(7973)**

Salmon
KSRA-AM - 92.7 **(7975)**

Soda Springs
KBRV-AM - 790 **(7983)**
KFIS-FM - 100.1 **(7984)**

Twin Falls
KEZJ-FM - 95.7 **(7994)**

ILLINOIS
Aledo
WRMJ-FM - 102.3 **(8006)**

Cairo
WKRO-AM - 1490 **(8106)**

Carmi
WRUL-FM - 97.3 **(8133)**

Carthage
WCAZ-AM - 990 **(8166)**

Chicago
WUSN-FM - 99.5 **(8656)**

Clinton
WHOW-AM - 1520 **(8684)**

Danville
WIAI-FM - 99.1 **(8707)**

Effingham
WCRC-FM - 95.7 **(8820)**

Fairfield
WOKZ-FM - 105.9 **(8883)**

Farmer City
WWHP-FM - 98.3 **(8886)**

Freeport
WFPS-FM - 92.1 **(8900)**

Harrisburg
WEBQ-AM - 1240 **(8973)**

Jacksonville
WJVO-FM - 105.5 **(9027)**

Joliet
WCCQ-FM - 98.3 **(9036)**

Kankakee
WKAN-FM - 1320 **(9042)**

Litchfield
WSMI-FM - 106.1 **(9115)**

Marion
WDDD-FM - 107.3 **(9146)**

Mendota
WGLC-FM - 100.1 **(9176)**

Metropolis
WIBH-AM - 1440 **(9179)**
WMOK-AM - 920 **(9180)**

Monmouth
WRAM-AM - 1330 **(9221)**

Monticello
WCZQ-FM - 105.5 **(9223)**

Paris
WACF-FM - 98.5 **(9400)**

Peoria
WOAM-AM - 1350 **(9435)**
WXCL-FM - 104.9 **(9442)**

Peru
WALS-FM - 102.1 **(9451)**

Savanna
WCCI-FM - 100.3 **(9582)**

Taylorville
WMKR-FM - 94.3 **(9679)**

INDIANA
Batesville
WRBI-FM - 103.9 **(9797)**

Boonville
WBNL-AM - 1540 **(9867)**

Connersville
WIFE-FM - 100.3 **(9903)**

Covington
WKZS-FM - 103.1 **(9908)**

Fort Wayne
WQHK-AM - 1380 **(9993)**

Frankfort
WILO-AM - 1570 **(10002)**

French Lick
WFLQ-FM - 100.1 **(10012)**

Indianapolis
WCKN-AM - 1260 **(10192)**
WFMS-FM - 95.5 **(10194)**
WIRE-FM - 100.9 **(10201)**

Jasper
WBDC-FM - 100.9 **(10220)**

Jeffersonville
WAVG-AM - 1450 **(10227)**

Knightstown
WKPW-FM - 90.7 **(10237)**

Kokomo
WWKI-FM - 100.5 **(10244)**

Lafayette
WKOA-FM - 105.3 **(10261)**
WLFF-FM - 95.3 **(10262)**

LaGrange
WTHD-FM - 105.5 **(10267)**

Martinsville
WCBK-FM - 102.3 **(10295)**
WMCB-AM - 1540 **(10297)**

Mishawaka
WBYT-FM - 100.7 **(10316)**

New Castle
WMDH-FM - 102.5 **(10345)**

Plymouth
WNZE-FM - 94.3 **(10401)**

Portland
WPGW-FM - 100.9 **(10406)**

Rushville
WKWH-FM - 94.3 **(10438)**

Seymour
WQKC-FM - 93.7 **(10450)**

Spencer
WSKT-FM - 92.7 **(10473)**

Valparaiso
WLJE-FM - 105.5 **(10513)**

Wabash
WKUZ-FM - 95.9 **(10532)**

Washington
WWBL-FM - 106.5 **(10543)**

IOWA
Albia
KLBA-AM - 1370 **(10577)**
KLBA-FM - 96.7 **(10578)**

Burlington
KDMG-FM - 103.1 **(10643)**

Carroll
KCIM-AM - 1380 **(10653)**

Cedar Rapids
KHAK-FM - 98.1 **(10682)**

Centerville
KMGO-FM - 98.7 **(10690)**

Clinton
KZEG-FM - 94.7 **(10714)**

Creston
KITR-FM - 101.3 **(10733)**
KSIB-AM - 1520 **(10734)**

Davenport
KBOB-FM - 99.7 **(10741)**
WLLR-AM - 1230 **(10749)**

Denison
KDSN-AM - 1530 **(10768)**

Dyersville
KDST-FM - 99.3 **(10861)**

Elkader
KCTN-FM - 100.1 **(10875)**

Estherville
KILR-FM - 95.9 **(10880)**

Fort Dodge
KIAQ-FM - 96.9 **(10908)**
KWMT-AM - 540 **(10915)**

Grinnell
KGRN-AM - 1410 **(10933)**

Iowa Falls
KIFG-AM - 95.3 **(11002)**

Maquoketa
KMAQ-AM - 1320 **(11056)**

Mason City
KIA-FM - 93.9 **(11076)**

Muscatine
KWCC-FM - 93.1 **(11105)**

Newton
KCOB-AM - 1280 **(11116)**
KCOB-FM - 95.9 **(11117)**

Oskaloosa
KBOE-FM - 104.9 **(11137)**

Ottumwa
KLEE-AM - 1480 **(11142)**

Perry
KDLS-AM - 1310 **(11157)**
KDLS-FM - 105.5 **(11158)**

Sheldon
KIWA-AM - 1550 **(11196)**
KIWA-FM - 105.3 **(11197)**

Sioux City
KSUX-FM - 105.7 **(11222)**

Spencer
KICD-FM - 107.7 **(11234)**

Stuart
KGRA-FM - 98.9 **(11256)**

Waterloo
KOEL-FM - 92.3 **(11295)**

Waukon
KNEI-FM - 103.5 **(11305)**

KANSAS
Atchison
KAIR-FM - 93.7 **(11346)**

Belleville
KREP-FM - 92.1 **(11360)**

Burlington
KSNP-FM - 95.3 **(11371)**

Clay Center
KCLY-FM - 100.9 **(11384)**

Emporia
KVOE-FM - 101.7 **(11435)**

Eureka
KOTE-FM - 93.5 **(11438)**

Garden City
KBUF-AM - 1030 **(11451)**
KKJQ-FM - 97.3 **(11453)**

Goodland
KLOE-AM - 730 **(11467)**

Hays
KHAZ-FM - 99.5 **(11485)**

Herington
KDMM-FM - 105.7 **(11489)**

Hiawatha
KNZA-FM - 103.9 **(11493)**

Circulation: ★ = ABC; △ = BPA; ♦ = CAC; • = CCAB; ❑ = VAC; ⊕ = PO Statement; ‡ = Publisher's Report; Boldface figures = sworn; Light figures = estimated.

3007

COUNTRY (continued)

Hutchinson
KHUT-FM - 102.9 (11506)
KXKU-FM - 97.1 (11508)

Iola
KALN-AM - 1370 (11514)

Marysville
KNDY-AM - 1570 (11640)

Ottawa
KOFO-AM - 1220 (11692)

Pittsburg
KKOW-AM - 860 (11755)

Pratt
KWLS-AM - 1290-AM (11766)

Salina
KSKG-FM - 99.9 (11790)

Topeka
KTPK-FM - 106.9 (11844)

Westwood
WDAF-AM - 610 (11877)

Wichita
KFDI-FM - 101.3 (11895)

KENTUCKY
Albany
WANY-AM - 1390 (11915)

Barbourville
WYWY-AM - 950 (11924)

Bardstown
WBRT-AM - 1320 (11927)

Benton
WCBL-AM - 1290 (11934)

Bowling Green
WBVR-FM - 96.7 (11953)
WGGC-FM - 95.1 (11957)

Brandenburg
WMMG-AM - 1140 (11964)
WMMG-FM - 93.5 (11965)

Cadiz
WKDZ-FM - 106.5 (12005)

Columbia
WAIN-FM - 93.5 (12019)

Corbin
WKDP-FM - 99.5 (12025)

Cumberland
WCPM-AM - 1280 (12032)
WSEH-FM - 102.7 (12033)

Cynthiana
WCYN-FM - 102.3 (12035)

Danville
WHBN-AM - 1420 (12040)

Elkton
WEKT-AM - 1070 (12052)

Flemingsburg
WFLE-AM - 1060 (12058)

Franklin
WFKN-AM - 1220 (12083)

Fulton
WKZT-AM - 1270 (12085)

Grayson
WGOH-AM - 1370 (12094)

Greenup
WLGC-FM - 105.7 (12100)

Greenville
WKYA-FM - 105.5 (12101)

Harlan
WFSR-AM - 970 (12106)

Hazard
WSGS-FM - 101.1 (12121)

Hopkinsville
WHOP-FM - 98.7 (12134)

Jamestown
WJRS-FM - 104.9 (12148)

Lexington
WFLE-FM - 95.1 (12183)
WRFL-FM - 88.1 (12194)
WVLK-FM - 92.9 (12199)

Liberty
WKDO-AM - 1560 (12201)
WKDO-FM - 98.7 (12202)

London
WWEL-FM - 103.9 (12205)

Louisville
WIBL-FM - 101.7 (12254)

Madisonville
WFMW-AM - 730 (12273)
WHRZ-FM - 97.7 (12274)

Manchester
WKLB-AM - 1290 (12279)

Marion
WMJL-AM - 1500 (12282)

Martin
WMDJ-FM - 101.1 (12283)

Mayfield
WLLE-FM - 94.7 (12286)

Mc Kee
WWAG-FM - 107.9 (12292)

Morganfield
WMSK-AM - 1550 (12308)
WMSK-FM - 95.3 (12309)

Murray
WFGE-FM - 103.7 (12318)

Paintsville
WSIP-FM - 98.9 (12352)

Pikeville
WDHR-FM - 93.1 (12361)

Prestonsburg
WDOC-AM - 1310 (12372)

Renfro Valley
WRVK-AM - 1460 (12381)

Salyersville
WRLV-AM - 1140 (12392)

Scottsville
WVLE-FM - 99.3 (12396)

Stanford
WRSL-FM - 95.9 (12418)

Stanton
WSKV-FM - 104.9 (12419)

Vanceburg
WKKS-AM - 1570 (12425)
WKKS-FM - 104.9 (12426)

West Liberty
WMOR-AM - 1330 (12434)

Wickliffe
WGKY-FM - 95.9 (12444)

LOUISIANA
Alexandria
KRRV-FM - 100.3 (12467)

Baton Rouge
WTCE-FM - 100.7 (12525)

Crowley
KSIG-AM - 1450 (12561)

Eunice
KBAZ-FM - 102.1 (12575)
KEUN-AM - 1490 (12576)
KJJB-FM - 105.5 (12577)

Franklinton
WFCG-AM - 1110 (12584)
WFCG-FM - 98.9 (12585)

Hammond
WHMD-FM - 107.1 (12596)

Jennings
KJEF-FM - 92.9 (12607)

Lake Providence
KLPL-AM - 1050 (12653)

Leesville
KJAE-FM - 93.5 (12659)
KVVP-FM - 105.7 (12661)

Logansport
KJVC-FM - 92.7 (12662)
KORI-FM - 104.7 (12663)

Many
KWLV-FM - 107.1 (12672)

Marksville
KAPB-FM - 97.7 (12676)

Monroe
KJLO-FM - 104.1 (12695)

Morgan City
KQKI-FM - 95.3 (12713)

Natchitoches
KSBH-FM - 94.9 (12721)

Opelousas
KSLO-AM - 1230 (12793)

Ruston
KXKZ-FM - 107.5 (12811)

Shreveport
KXKS-FM - 93.7 (12842)

Tallulah
KBYO-FM - 104.9 (12856)

Vidalia
KVLA-AM - 1400 (12864)

Winnfield
KVCL-FM - 92.1 (12882)

MAINE
Brewer
WQCB-FM - 106.5 (12928)

Ellsworth
WLKE-FM - 99.1 (12956)

Machias
WALZ-FM - 95.3 (12988)

Portland
WTHT-FM - 107.5 (13032)

MARYLAND
Baltimore
WPOC-FM - 93.1 (13283)

Cambridge
WAAI-FM - 100.9 (13400)

Cumberland
WROG-FM - 102.9 (13479)

La Plata
WKIK-FM - 102.9 (13594)

Lexington Park
WMDM-FM - 97.7 (13618)

Mountain Lake Park
WMSG-AM - 1050 (13634)

Rockville
WMZQ-FM - 98.7 (13703)

Salisbury
WWFG-FM - 99.9 (13721)

MASSACHUSETTS
Palmer
WARE-AM - 1250 (14458)

Pittsfield
WUHN-AM - 1110 (14477)

MICHIGAN
Alma
WMLM-AM - 1520 AM (14734)

Caro
WKYO-AM - 1360 (14860)

Escanaba
WYKX-FM - 104.7 (15012)

Fremont
WSHN-FM - 100.1 (15062)

Gladwin
WGDN-FM - 103.1 (15082)

Grayling
WGRY-FM - 100.3 (15133)

Greenville
WSTG-AM - 1380 (15137)

Hastings
WBCH-FM - 100.1 **(15157)**

Ironwood
WJMS-AM - 590 **(15216)**

Ontonagon
WUPY-FM - 101.1 **(15424)**

Saginaw
WCEN-FM - 94.5 **(15496)**
WKCQ-FM - 98.1 **(15500)**

Tawas City
WKJC-FM - 104.7 **(15587)**

Three Rivers
WLKM-AM - 1520 **(15595)**

Traverse City
WBCM-FM - 93.5 **(15606)**

Ypsilanti
WSDS-AM - 1480 **(15693)**

MINNESOTA
Aitkin
KKIM-FM - 94.3 **(15702)**

Albany
KASM-AM - 1150 **(15705)**

Alexandria
KIKV-FM - 100.7 **(15715)**

Bemidji
KBHP-FM - 101.1 **(15741)**

Faribault
KDHL-AM - 920 **(15895)**

Forest Lake
WLKX-FM - 95.9 **(15907)**

Fosston
KKCQ-AM - 1480 **(15910)**
KKCQ-FM - 96.7 **(15911)**

International Falls
KSDM-FM - 104.1 **(15970)**

Little Falls
KLTF-AM - 960 **(16008)**

Long Prairie
KEYL-AM - 1400 **(16010)**

Luverne
KLQL-FM - 101.1 **(16015)**

Madison
KLQP-FM - 92.1 **(16021)**

Marshall
KMHL-AM - 1400 **(16047)**

Minneapolis
KEEY-FM - 102.1 **(16148)**

Montevideo
KDMA-AM - 1460 **(16181)**

New Ulm
KNSG-FM - 94.7 **(16216)**
KNUJ-AM - 860 **(16217)**

North Mankato
KYSM-FM - 103.5 **(16224)**

Owatonna
KRUE-FM - 92.1 **(16255)**

Park Rapids
KPRM-AM - 870 **(16258)**

Pipestone
KLOH-AM - 1050 **(16277)**

Preston
KFIL-FM - 103.1 **(16283)**

Red Wing
KCUE-AM - 1250 **(16294)**

Redwood Falls
KLGR-AM - 1490 **(16299)**

Rochester
KMFX-AM - 1190 **(16314)**

St. Peter
KRBI-AM - 1310 **(16432)**

Slayton
KJOE-FM - 106.1 **(16450)**

Wadena
KKWS-FM - 105.9 **(16491)**

Warroad
KKWQ-FM - 92.5 **(16498)**

Willmar
KDJS-FM - 95.3 **(16521)**

Winona
KAGE-AM - 1380 **(16532)**

MISSISSIPPI
Batesville
WJBI-AM - 1290 **(16551)**

Bay Springs
WIZK-FM - 94.3 **(16556)**

Belzoni
WELZ-AM - 1460 **(16561)**

Biloxi
WKNN-FM - 99.1 **(16564)**

Cleveland
WDTL-FM - 92.9 **(16594)**

Columbia
WFFF-AM - 1360 **(16601)**

Columbus
WMBC-FM - 103.1 **(16612)**

Corinth
WCMA-AM - 1230 **(16617)**

Greenville
WGVM-AM - 1260 **(16640)**

Greenwood
WABG-AM - 960 **(16647)**

Hattiesburg
WKNZ-FM - 107.1 **(16674)**

Houston
WCPC-AM - 940 **(16686)**

Iuka
WFXO-FM - 104.9 **(16692)**

Jackson
WMSI-FM - 102.9 **(16727)**

Laurel
WBBN-FM - 95.9 **(16742)**

Louisville
WLSM-FM - 107.1 **(16752)**

McComb
WAKH-FM - 105.7 **(16764)**

Meridian
WOKK-FM - 97.1 **(16779)**
WYYW-FM - 95.1 **(16781)**

Philadelphia
WHOC-AM - 1490 **(16817)**

Picayune
WRJW-AM - 1320 **(16821)**

Quitman
WYKK-FM - 98.9 **(16831)**

Tupelo
WFTO-AM - 1330 **(16854)**

Wiggins
WLUN-FM - 95.3 **(16878)**

MISSOURI
Ava
KKOZ-AM - 1430 **(16897)**
KKOZ-FM - 92.1 **(16898)**

Bethany
KAAN-AM - 870 **(16904)**
KAAN-FM - 95.5 **(16905)**

Bolivar
KYOO-AM - 1200 **(16913)**

Bowling Green
KPCR-FM - 1530 **(16918)**
KPCR-FM - 94.1 **(16919)**

Branson
KRZK-FM - 106.3 **(16924)**

Buffalo
KBFL-FM - 99.9 **(16931)**

Butler
KMAM-AM - 1530 **(16932)**
KMOE-FM - 92.1 **(16933)**

California
KREL-AM - 1420 **(16936)**

Cape Girardeau
KEZS-FM - 102.9 **(16950)**

Carrollton
KAOL-AM - 1430 **(16956)**
KMZU-FM - 100.7 **(16957)**

Doniphan
KOEA-FM - 97.5 **(17038)**

El Dorado Springs
KESM-AM - 1580 **(17043)**
KESM-FM - 105.5 **(17044)**

Houston
KBTC-AM - 1250 **(17103)**
KUNQ-FM - 99.3 **(17104)**

Joplin
KIXQ-FM - 102.5 **(17144)**

Kennett
KCRV-AM - 1370 **(17219)**

Lebanon
KCLQ-FM - 107.9 **(17240)**
KLWT-AM - 1230 **(17241)**

Memphis
KMEM-FM - 100.5 **(17282)**

Mexico
KWWR-FM - 95.7 **(17287)**

Monett
KRMO-AM - 990 **(17295)**

Mountain Grove
KELE-FM - 92.5 **(17302)**

Neosho
KBTN-AM - 1420 **(17305)**
KBTN-FM - 99.7 **(17306)**
KNEO-FM - 91.7 **(17307)**

Nevada
KNEM-AM - 1240 **(17309)**
KNMO-FM - 97.5 **(17310)**

Perryville
KBDZ-FM - 93.1 **(17342)**

Piedmont
KPWB-FM - 104.9 **(17345)**

Potosi
KYRO-AM - 1280 **(17365)**

Sedalia
KDRO-AM - 1490 **(17572)**

Springfield
KGMY-FM - 100.5 **(17622)**

Sullivan
KTUI-FM - 100.9 **(17643)**

Tarkio
KTRX-FM - 93.5 **(17647)**

Thayer
KAMS-FM - 95.1 **(17650)**

Trenton
KTTN-FM - 92.3 **(17655)**

Warrenton
KWRE-AM - 730 **(17702)**

Warsaw
KAYQ-FM - 97.7 **(17704)**

Waynesville
KJPW-AM - 1390 **(17710)**
KJPW-FM - 102.3 **(17711)**

West Plains
KKDY-FM - 102.5 **(17717)**

MONTANA
Billings
KGHL-AM - 790 **(17740)**

Black Eagle
KEIN-AM - 1310 **(17748)**

Bozeman
KBOZ-AM - 1090 **(17754)**

Circulation: ★ = ABC; △ = BPA; ◆ = CAC; ● = CCAB; ❑ = VAC; ⊕ = PO Statement; ‡ = Publisher's Report; Boldface figures = sworn; Light figures = estimated.

3009

COUNTRY (continued)

Dillon
KDBM-AM - 1490 (17785)

Glasgow
KLTZ-AM - 1240 (17794)

Great Falls
KMON-AM - 560 (17802)
KMON-FM - 94.5 (17803)

Hamilton
KLYQ-AM - 1240 (17810)

Helena
KBLL-FM - 99.5 (17826)
KHKR-AM (17828)

Lewistown
KXLO-AM - 1230 (17850)

Libby
KLCB-AM - 1230 (17853)

Miles City
KKRY-FM - 92.5 (17863)

Missoula
KGGL-FM - 93.3 (17880)

Plentywood
KATQ-AM - 1070 (17895)
KATQ-FM - 100.1 (17896)

Polson
KERR-AM - 750 (17900)

Scobey
KCGM-FM - 95.7 (17904)

Shelby
KZIN-FM - 96.3 (17908)

NEBRASKA
Alliance
KAAQ-FM - 105.9 (17928)

Chadron
KCSR-AM - 610 (17975)

Columbus
KZEN-FM - 100.3 (17985)

Cozad
KAMI-FM - 104.5 (17988)

Johnson
KCOE-FM - 105.5 (18057)

Lexington
KRVN-AM - 880 (18075)

Oneill
KBRX-FM - 102.9 (18234)

Ord
KNLV-AM - 1060 (18237)
KNLV-FM - 103.9 (18238)

Scottsbluff
KNEB-AM - 960 (18270)
KOLT-AM - 1320 (18273)

Superior
KRFS-AM - 1600 (18290)

Wayne
KTCH-AM - 1590 (18308)

NEVADA
Elko
KRJC-FM - 95.3 (18339)

Ely
KDSS-FM - 92.7 (18342)

Fallon
KVLV-AM - 980 (18346)

Las Vegas
KIWD FM - 101.9 (18396)

Reno
KHIT-AM - 1450 (18431)

Winnemucca
KWNA-FM - 92.7 (18452)

NEW HAMPSHIRE
Dover
WOKQ-FM - 97.5 (18493)

Franklin
WFTN-AM - 1240 (18509)

NEW JERSEY
Stirling
WKMB-AM - 1070 (19605)

Teaneck
WFDU-FM - 89.1 (19612)

Toms River
WJRZ-FM - 100.1 (19650)

NEW MEXICO
Alamogordo
KRSY-FM - 92.7 (19761)

Albuquerque
KBQI-FM - 107.9 (19795)
KRST-FM - 92.3 (19810)

Artesia
KTZA-FM - 92.9 (19819)

Belen
KARS-AM - 860 (19821)

Carlsbad
KATK-FM - 92.1 (19824)

Clayton
KLMX-AM - 1450 (19829)

Clovis
KCLV-AM - 1240 (19831)
KCLV-FM - 99.1 (19832)

Deming
KOTS-AM - 1230 (19842)

Farmington
KNDN-AM - 960 (19848)

Gallup
KGLX-FM - 99.1 (19859)

Hobbs
KPER-FM - 95.7 (19868)

Las Cruces
KGRT-FM - 103.9 (19880)

Pinehill
KTDB-FM - 89.7 (19904)

Portales
KSEL-FM - 95.3 (19908)

Silver City
KNFT-AM - 950 (19954)
KNFT-FM - 102.9 (19955)

Socorro
KMXQ-FM - 92.9 (19960)

Taos
KKIT-AM - 1340 (19964)

Truth or Consequences
KCHS-AM - 1400 (19970)

Tucumcari
KTNM-AM - 1400 (19973)

NEW YORK
Buffalo
WYRK-FM - 106.5 (20414)

Clintondale
WRWD-FM - 107.3 (20476)

Dundee
WFLR-AM - 1570 (20535)

Elmira
WQIX-AM - 820 (20579)

Jamestown
WHUG-FM - 101.7 (20843)

Lancaster
WXRL-AM - 1300 (20885)

Latham
WGNA-AM - 1460 (20936)

Liberty
WVOS-AM - 1240 (20944)

Lowville
WBRV-AM - 900 (20970)
WBRV-FM - 101.3 (20971)
WLLG-FM - 99.3 (20972)

Malone
WVNV-FM - 96.5 (20982)

Pulaski
WSCP-FM - 101.7 (23167)

Rochester
WBEE-FM - 92.5 (23244)

Rooseveltown
CKON-FM - 97.3 (23276)

Springville
WSPQ-AM - 1330 (23356)

Utica
WBUG-AM - 1570 (23472)
WBUG-FM - 101.1 (23473)

Walton
WDLA-AM - 1270 (23498)

Warsaw
WCJW-AM - 1140 (23507)

Wellsville
WLSV-AM - 790 (23535)
WZKZ-FM - 101.9 (23536)

NORTH CAROLINA
Ahoskie
WQDK-FM - 99.3 (23615)

Asheboro
WKXR-AM - 1260 (23624)

Asheville
WWNC-AM - 570 (23640)

Boone
WZJS-FM - 100.7 (23662)

Burlington
WKIX-FM - 96.1 (23675)
WKXU-FM - 101.1 (23676)
WPCM-AM - 920 (23677)

Canton
WPTL-AM - 920 (23683)

Cherryville
WCSL-AM - 1590 (23785)

Claremont
WCXN-AM - 1170 (23786)

Dallas
WSGE-FM - 91.7 (23797)

Durham
WAGR-AM - 1340 (23847)
WJSK-FM - 102.3 (23848)

Fayetteville
WKML-FM - 95.7 (23890)

Forest City
WAGY-AM - 1320 (23895)

Greenville
WNCT-AM - 1070 (23972)

Henderson
WIZS-AM - 1450 (23982)

Hickory
WIRC-AM - 630 (23993)

King
WKTE-AM - 1090 (24024)

Kings Mountain
WKMT-AM - 1220 (24026)

Kinston
WBSY-FM - 104.7 (24028)
WZBR-FM - 97.7 (24031)

Lenoir
WKGX-AM - 1080 (24038)

Lincolnton
WLON-AM - 1050 (24046)

Marion
WBRM-AM - 1250 (24057)

Mocksville
WDSL-AM - 1520 (24065)

Monroe
WIXE-AM - 1190 (24067)

Morganton
WMNC-AM - 1430 (24077)

Mount Airy
WSYD-AM - 1300 (24083)

Murphy
WCVP-AM - 600 (24090)
WCVP-FM - 95.9 (24091)

Numbers cited in bold after listings are entry numbers rather than page numbers.

Newland
WECR-AM - 1130 (24104)

Roanoke Rapids
WPTM-FM - 102.3 (24196)

Roxboro
WKRX-FM - 96.7 (24210)

Rutherfordton
WCAB-AM - 590 (24212)

Shallotte
WCCA-FM - 106.3 (24224)

Smithfield
WMPM-AM - 1270 (24233)

Statesville
WNBR-FM - 94.1 (24249)

Troy
WJRM-AM - 1390 (24258)

Wallace
WLSE-AM - 1400 (24266)

Wanchese
WNHW-FM - 92.3 (24268)

West Jefferson
WKSK-AM - 580 (24284)

Zebulon
WETC-AM - 540 (24342)

NORTH DAKOTA
Belcourt
KEYA-FM - 88.5 (24346)

Bismarck
KBMR-AM - 1130 (24363)
KSSS-FM - 101.5 (24371)

Bottineau
KBTO-FM - 101.9 (24377)

Bowman
KPOK-AM - 1340 (24382)

Devils Lake
KDLR-AM - 1240 (24391)
KZZY-FM - 103.5 (24393)

Dickinson
KCAD-FM - 99.1 (24396)

Grafton
KXPO-AM - 1340 (24452)

Grand Forks
KKXL-AM - 1440 (24461)

Jamestown
KSJB-AM - 600 (24481)

Langdon
KNDK-AM - 1080 (24490)

Lisbon
KQLX-AM - 890 (24494)
KQLX-FM - 106.1 (24495)

Mayville
KMAV-AM - 1520 (24500)
KMAV-FM - 105.5 (24501)

Minot
KCJB-AM - 910 (24507)
KYYX-FM - 97.1 (24516)
KZPR-FM - 105.3 (24517)

Oakes
KDDR-AM - 1220 (24528)

Rugby
KZZJ-AM - 1450 (24536)

Tioga
KTGO-AM - 1090 (24540)

Valley City
KOVC-AM - 1490 (24545)

Wahpeton
KBMW-AM - 1450 (24551)

Williston
KDSR-FM - 101.1 (24561)
KEYZ-AM - 660 (24562)

OHIO
Akron
WQMX-FM - 94.9 (24601)
WSLR-AM - 1350 (24602)

Ashland
WNCO-FM - 101.3 (24621)

Brookfield
WICT-FM - 95.1 (24709)

Cambridge
WWKC-FM - 104.9 (24729)

Chillicothe
WKKJ-FM - 93.3 (24766)

Cincinnati
WBBI-FM - 107.5 (24833)

Cleveland
WGAR-FM - 99.5 (24974)

Columbus
WCOL-FM - 92.3 (25078)

Conneaut
WWOW-AM - 1360 (25093)

Dayton
WGXM-FM - 98.1 (25140)

Delphos
WDOH-FM - 107.1 (25163)

Findlay
WCKY-FM - 103.7 (25195)

Geneva
WKKY-FM - 104.7 (25214)

Hillsboro
WSRW-FM - 106.7 (25246)

Lancaster
WHOK-FM - 95.5 (25292)

Logan
WLGN-AM - 98.3 (25313)

Middletown
WPFB-FM - 105.9 (25380)

Milan
WKFM-FM - 96.1 (25381)

Nelsonville
WAIS-AM - 770 (25406)

Newark
WCLT-FM - 100.3 (25428)

Oberlin
WOBL-AM - 1320 (25450)

Portsmouth
WPAY-FM - 104.1 (25488)

Steubenville
WOGH-FM - 103.5 (25542)

Toledo
WTOD-AM - 1560 (25586)

Upper Sandusky
WYNT-FM - 95.9 (25605)

Washington Court House
WCHO-FM - 105.5 (25622)

Waverly
WXIC-AM - 660 (25625)
WXIZ-FM - 100.9 (25626)

West Union
WRAC-FM - 103.1 (25634)

Wilmington
WSWO-FM - 102.3 (25669)

Wooster
WQKT-FM - 104.5 (25677)

Xenia
WBZI-AM - 1500 (25688)
WBZI-FM - 95.3 (25689)

Youngstown
WQXK-FM - 105.1 (25709)

OKLAHOMA
Altus
KEYB-FM - 107.9 (25733)
KWHW-AM - 1450 (25736)

Alva
KALV-AM - 1430 (25739)

Anadarko
KRMP-AM - 103.5 (25741)
KRMT-FM - 103.7 (25742)

Ardmore
KICM-FM - 93.7 (25747)
KKAJ-FM - 95.7 (25748)

Broken Arrow
KULM-FM - 98.3 (25773)

Durant
KLBC-FM - 106.3 (25810)

Elk City
KECO-FM - 96.5 (25820)

Enid
KNID-FM - 99.7 (25827)

Eufaula
KTNT-FM - 102.5 (25830)

Frederick
KYBE-FM - 95.9 (25841)

Grove
KGND-AM - 1470 (25850)

Hobart
KTJS-AM - 1420 (25868)

Hugo
KIHN-AM - 1340 (25873)
KITX-FM - 95.5 (25874)

Idabel
KBEL-FM - 96.7 (25877)

Lawton
KLAW-FM - 101.3 (25892)

Lindsay
KBLP-FM - 105.1 (25901)

Madill
KMAD-AM - 1550 (25903)

Marlow
KFXT-FM - 100.9 (25907)

McAlester
KNED-AM - 1150 (25911)

Muskogee
KMMY-FM - 97.1 (25924)
KTFX-FM - 102.1 (25925)

Oklahoma City
KTST-FM - 101.9 (26018)
KXXY-FM - 96.1 (26021)

Perry
KVCS-AM - 1020 (26033)

Ponca City
KPNC-FM - 100.9 (26043)

Shawnee
KIRC-FM - 105.9 (26067)
KWSH-FM - 104.7 (26070)

Sulphur
KGOK-FM - 97.7 (26091)
KVLH-AM - 1470 (26092)

Tahlequah
KEOK-FM - 101.7 (26096)

Tulsa
KVOO-AM - 1170 (26168)

Vinita
KITO-FM - 96.1 (26177)

Watonga
KIMY-FM - 93.9 (26181)

Weatherford
KCDL-FM - 99.3 (26187)
KWEY-AM - 1590 (26188)
KWEY-FM - 97.3 (26189)

OREGON
Albany
KRKT-AM - 990 (26211)

Astoria
KVAS-AM - 1230 (26231)

Bend
KSJJ-FM - 102.9 (26250)
KWLZ-FM - 96.5 (26252)

Burns
KZZR-AM - 1230 (26261)

Cottage Grove
KNND-AM - 1400 (26296)

COUNTRY (continued)

The Dalles
KYYT-FM - 102.3 (26304)

Enterprise
KWVR-AM - 1340 (26311)
KWVR-FM - 92.1 (26312)

Eugene
KUGN-FM - 97.9 (26347)

Hermiston
KOHU-AM - 1360 (26370)

Hood River
KIHR-AM - 1340 (26377)

Medford
KAKT-FM - 105.1 (26419)

Milton-Freewater
KTEL-AM - 1490 (26437)

Newport
KPPT-AM - 1230 (26449)

Pendleton
KWHT-FM - 103.5 (26463)

Portland
KUPL-AM - 970 (26542)
KUPL-FM - 98.7 (26543)

Prineville
KRCO-AM - 690 (26551)

Reedsport
KDUN-AM - 1030 (26554)

Roseburg
KRNR-AM - 1490 (26559)

Sweet Home
KFIR-AM - 720 (26594)

Tillamook
KTIL-FM - 94.1 (26599)

PENNSYLVANIA

Bala Cynwyd
KVLE-FM - 102.3 (26670)

Carlisle
WIOO-AM - 1000 (26764)

Chambersburg
WCHA-AM - 800 (26770)
WIHR-FM - 94.3 (26771)

Clarion
WWCH-AM - 1300 (26784)

Du Bois
WOWQ-FM - 102.1 (26841)

Edinboro
WXTA-FM - 97.9 (26864)

Ephrata
WIOV-FM - 105.1 (26892)

Everett
WSKE-AM - 1040 (26915)
WSKE-FM - 104.3 (26916)

Greencastle
WAYZ-FM - 104.7 (26950)

Greenville
WEXC-FM - 107.1 (26960)

Honesdale
WPSN-AM - 1590 (27054)

Johnstown
WJAC-AM - 850 (27092)
WMTZ-FM - 96.5 (27095)

Kane
WLMI-FM - 103.9 (27105)

Lafayette Hill
KWFS-AM - 1290 (27134)
KWFS-FM - 103.3 (27135)

Lebanon
WADV-AM - 940 (27176)
WWSM-AM - 1510 (27179)

Meadville
WGYI-FM - 98.5 (27237)
WGYY-FM - 100.3 (27238)

Millersville
WIXQ-FM - 91.7 (27268)

Mount Union
WHUN-AM - 1150 (27302)

Philipsburg
WPHB-AM - 1260 (27750)
WPHB-AM - 1260 (27751)

Pittsburgh
WDSY-FM - 107.9 (27862)

Pittston
WGGY-FM - 101.3 (27889)

Ridgway
WDDH-FM - 97.5 (27939)

Roaring Spring
WKMC-AM - 1370 (27940)

Troy
WHGL-AM - 1310 (28060)
WHGL-FM - 100.3 (28061)

Tyrone
WTRN-AM - 1340 (28065)

Warren
WKNB-FM - 104.3 (28106)

RHODE ISLAND

Westerly
WJJF-AM - 95.9 (28459)

SOUTH CAROLINA

Allendale
WDOG-AM - 1460 (28471)
WDOG-FM - 93.5 (28472)

Anderson
WRIX-FM - 103.1 (28477)

Bishopville
WAGS-AM - 1380 (28495)

Charleston
WALI-FM - 93.7 (28519)

Columbia
WCOS-FM - 97.5 (28574)

Greenville
WESC-FM - 92.5 (28629)

Holly Hill
WJBS-AM - 1440 (28666)

Kingstree
WDKD-AM - 1310 (28677)

Mount Pleasant
WEZL-FM - 103.5 (28699)

North Augusta
WKBG-FM - 107.7 (28722)

North Charleston
WNKT-FM - 107.5 (28725)

Summerville
WAZS-AM - 980 (28766)

Walhalla
WGOG-FM - 96.3 (28779)

SOUTH DAKOTA

Aberdeen
KGIM-AM - 1420 (28795)

Belle Fourche
KBFS-AM - 1450 (28807)

Hot Springs
KZMX-AM - 580 (28868)
KZMX-FM - 96.7 (28869)

Lemmon
KBJM-AM - 1400 (28883)

Mitchell
KMIT-FM - 105.9 (28902)

Pierre
KGFX-AM - 1060 (28925)

Rapid City
KIMM-AM - 1150 (28940)
KIQK-FM - 104.1 (28941)

Redfield
KQKD-AM - 1380 (28954)

Sioux Falls
KTWB-FM - 101.9 (28986)
KXRB-AM - 1000 (28988)

Sturgis
KBHB-AM - 810 (29002)

Watertown
KSDR-FM - 92.9 (29024)

Winner
KWYR-AM - 1260 (29033)

Yankton
WNAX-AM - 570 (29045)

TENNESSEE

Alamo
WCTA-AM - 810 (29047)

Ardmore
WSLV-AM - 1110 (29050)

Bolivar
WMOD-FM - 96.7 (29059)

Bristol
WOPI-AM - 1490 (29069)

Brownsville
WTBG-FM - 95.3 (29074)

Byrdstown
WSBI-AM - 1210 (29077)

Camden
WFWL-AM - 1220 (29079)

Centerville
WNKX-AM - 1570 (29085)

Clinton
WYSH-AM - 1380 (29130)

Columbia
WMCP-AM - 1280 (29141)

Covington
WKBL-AM - 1250 (29154)

Cowan
WZYX-AM - 1440 (29156)

Crossville
WEGE-FM - 102.5 (29161)

Dickson
WDKN-AM - 1260 (29166)

Elizabethton
WBEJ-AM - 1240 (29180)

Erwin
WEMB-AM - 1420 (29185)

Fayetteville
WYTM-FM - 105.5 (29192)

Gallatin
WHIN-AM - 1010 (29204)

Gray
WGOC-AM - 640 (29208)

Greeneville
WGRV-AM - 1340 (29213)
WIKQ-FM - 103.1 (29214)

Jackson
WWYN-FM - 106.9 (29241)

Jefferson City
WJFC-AM - 1480 (29248)

Knoxville
WIVK-FM - 107.7 (29292)

La Follette
WQLA-FM - 104.9 (29311)

Lafayette
WEEN-AM - 1460 (29313)
WLCT-FM - 102.1 (29314)

Lawrenceburg
WDXE-AM - 1370 (29318)
WWLX-AM - 590 (29320)

Lebanon
WJKM-AM - 1090 (29322)

Lewisburg
WAXO-AM - 1220 (29327)
WJJM-AM - 1490 (29328)
WJJM-FM - 94.3 (29329)

Lexington
WDXL-AM - 1490 (29330)

Mc Minnville
WBMC-AM - 960 (29355)

Numbers cited in bold after listings are entry numbers rather than page numbers.

Memphis
WOGY-FM - 94.1 **(29408)**

Morristown
WJDT-FM - 106.5 **(29422)**

Mountain City
WMCT-AM - 1390 **(29427)**

Nashville
WBUZ-FM - 102.9 **(29507)**
WKDF-FM - 103.3 **(29515)**
WSIX-FM - 97.9 **(29532)**
WSM-AM - 650 **(29533)**
WZUS-FM - 100.9 **(29542)**

Oneida
WBNT-FM - 105.5 **(29556)**

Paris
WMUF-AM - 1000 **(29562)**

Pulaski
WKSR-AM - 1420 **(29573)**
WKSR-FM - 98.3 **(29574)**

Ripley
WTRB-AM - 1570 **(29577)**

Rogersville
WEYE-FM - 104.3 **(29581)**
WRGS-AM - 1370 **(29582)**

Sevierville
WDLY-FM - 105.5 **(29591)**
WSEV-AM - 930 **(29592)**

Shelbyville
WLIJ-AM - 1580 **(29602)**

South Pittsburg
WEPG-AM - 910 **(29611)**

Springfield
WSGI-AM - 1100 **(29621)**

Tazewell
WNTT-AM - 1250 **(29626)**

Union City
WYVY-FM - 104.9 **(29638)**

Wartburg
WECO-FM - 101.3 **(29641)**

Winchester
WCDT-AM - 1340 **(29648)**

TEXAS
Abilene
KBCY-FM - 99.7 **(29658)**

Alamo
KTEX-FM - 100.3 **(29675)**

Alice
KOPY-FM - 92.1 **(29680)**

Amarillo
KATP-FM - 101.9 **(29703)**
KGNC-FM - 97.9 **(29710)**
KLCJ-AM - 1360 **(29711)**
KMML-FM - 96.9 **(29713)**

Andrews
KACT-FM - 105.5 **(29724)**

Arlington
KSCS-FM - 96.3 **(29741)**

Atoka
KHKC-FM - 103.1 **(29749)**

Austin
KASE-FM - 100.7 **(29859)**
KVET-AM - 1300 **(29880)**

Bay City
KIOX-AM - 1270 **(29892)**
KMKS-FM - 102.5 **(29893)**

Beaumont
KYKR-FM - 95.1 **(29910)**

Big Spring
KBST-AM - 1490 **(29925)**

Bonham
KFYN-AM - 1420 **(29934)**
KFYZ-FM - 98.3 **(29935)**

Borger
KQTY-AM - 1490 **(29938)**

Bowie
KNTX-AM - 1410 **(29942)**

Brady
KNEL-FM - 95.3 **(29945)**

Brenham
KWHI-AM - 1280 **(29951)**

Bridgeport
KBOC-FM - 98.3 **(29952)**

Brownwood
KOXE-FM - 101.3 **(29969)**

Bryan
KAGG-FM - 96.1 **(29977)**
KORA-FM - 98.3 **(29981)**

Carthage
KGAS-FM - 104.3 **(30007)**

Clarksville
KCAR-AM - 1350 **(30023)**

Cleburne
KCLE-AM - 1140 **(30026)**
KTFW-AM - 1460 **(30027)**

Comanche
KCOM-AM - 1550 **(30066)**

Conroe
KVST-FM - 103.7 **(30071)**

Corpus Christi
KFTX-FM - 97.5 **(30085)**
KOUL-FM - 103.7 **(30092)**
KRYS-FM - 99.1 **(30094)**

Corsicana
KAND-AM - 1340 **(30103)**

Crockett
KIVY-FM - 92.7 **(30108)**

Cuero
KTXC-AM - 1600 **(30116)**

Dallas
KCWW-AM - 1580 **(30195)**
KYNG-FM - 105.3 **(30217)**

Del Rio
KDLK-FM - 94.1 **(30226)**
KWMC-AM - 1490 **(30229)**

Dumas
KDDD-FM - 95.3 **(30253)**

Duncanville
KVMX-FM - 96.7 **(30255)**

Eagle Pass
KINL-FM - 92.7 **(30259)**

Eastland
KATX-FM - 97.7 **(30266)**
KEAS-AM - 1590 **(30267)**

El Campo
KULP-AM - 1390 **(30277)**

El Paso
KHEY-FM - 96.3 **(30292)**

Fairfield
KNES-FM - 99.1 **(30312)**

Floydada
KFLP-FM - 106.1 **(30324)**

Fort Stockton
KFST-FM - 94.3 **(30328)**

Freeport
KBRZ-AM - 1460 **(30366)**

Gainesville
KGAF-AM - 1580 **(30377)**

Greenville
KGVL-AM - 1400 **(30415)**
KIKT-FM - 93.5 **(30416)**

Hallettsville
KHLT-AM - 1520 **(30419)**

Hamilton
KCLW-AM - 900 **(30421)**

Haskell
KVRP-FM - 95.5 **(30434)**

Hemphill
KPBL-AM - 1240 **(30438)**

Henderson
KWRD-AM - 1470 **(30441)**

Hereford
KPAN-AM - 860 **(30446)**
KPAN-FM - 106.3 **(30447)**

Hillsboro
KHBR-AM - 1560 **(30450)**

Hondo
KCWM-AM - 1460 **(30452)**

Houston
KIKK-AM - 650 **(30555)**
KIKK-FM - 95.7 **(30556)**
KILT-FM - 100.3 **(30558)**

Jasper
KWYX-FM - 102.7 **(30623)**

Junction
KMBL-AM - 1450 **(30631)**

La Grange
KBUK-FM - 104.9 **(30657)**

Lamesa
KPET-AM - 690 **(30664)**

Lampasas
KCYL-AM - 1450 **(30667)**

Levelland
KLVT-FM - 105.3 **(30684)**

Liberty
KSHN-FM - 99.9 **(30692)**

Longview
KYKX-FM - 105.7 **(30707)**

Lubbock
KFYO-AM - 790 **(30725)**

Lufkin
KRBA-AM - 1340 **(30743)**

Malakoff
KCKL-FM - 95.9 **(30756)**

Midland
KTXC-FM - 104.7 **(30824)**

Mineola
KMOO-FM - 99.9 **(30831)**

Mount Pleasant
KIMP-AM - 960 **(30841)**

New Braunfels
KNBT-FM - 92.1 **(30863)**

Orange
KOGT-AM - 1600 **(30889)**

Palestine
KYYK-FM - 98.3 **(30899)**

Pearsall
KVWG-AM - 1280 **(30921)**
KVWG-FM - 95.3 **(30922)**

Pecos
KIUN-AM - 1400 **(30925)**

Plainview
KKYN-FM - 106.9 **(30942)**
KOYL-AM - 1310 **(30943)**

Plano
KHYI-FM - 95.3 **(30949)**

Raymondville
KSOX-AM - 1240 **(30971)**
KSOX-FM - 107.1 **(30972)**

Robstown
KROB-AM - 1510 **(30986)**

San Angelo
KGKL-AM - 960 **(31015)**
KGKL-FM - 97.5 **(31016)**

San Antonio
KCYY-FM - 100.3 **(31054)**
KKYX-AM - 680 **(31060)**

San Saba
KBAL-FM - 106.1 **(31091)**

Seguin
KWED-AM - 1580 **(31097)**

Seminole
KIKZ-AM - 1250 **(31099)**
KSEM-FM - 106.3 **(31100)**

Silsbee
KWDX-FM - 101.7 **(31109)**

Circulation: ★ = ABC;　△ = BPA;　◆ = CAC;　● = CCAB;　❑ = VAC;　⊕ = PO Statement;　‡ = Publisher's Report;　Boldface figures = sworn;　Light figures = estimated.

Radio Station Formats

3013

COUNTRY (continued)

Snyder
KSNY-FM - 101.5 (31117)

Stephenville
KSTV-FM - 93.1 (31133)

Sulphur Springs
KSCH-FM - 95.9 (31167)

Sweetwater
KXOX-AM - 1240 (31171)
KXOX-FM - 96.7 (31172)

Texarkana
KFYX-FM - 107.1 (31188)

Vernon
KVWC-FM - 103.1 (31233)

Victoria
KIXS-FM - 107.9 (31239)
KZAM-FM - 104.7 (31242)

Waco
WACO-FM - 99.9 (31267)

Weatherford
KJSA-AM - 1140 (31274)

Wharton
KANI-AM - 1500 (31286)

UTAH
Logan
KNFL-FM - 104.9 (31360)

Magna
KRGO-FM - 107.9 (31365)

Price
KARB-FM - 98.3 (31394)

Roosevelt
KNEU-AM - 1250 (31416)

St. George
KONY-FM - 99.9 (31420)

Salt Lake City
KMRI-AM - 1550 (31453)
KSOP-FM - 104.3 (31459)
KUBL-FM - 93.3 (31463)

VERMONT
Barre
WSNO-AM - 1450 (31492)

Burlington
WOKO-FM - 98.9 (31526)

St. Albans
WLFE-FM - 102.3 (31591)

Wells River
WYKR-FM - 101.3 (31614)

VIRGINIA
Altavista
WKDE-FM - 105.5 (31758)

Blacksburg
WBGS-AM - 1030 (31883)
WBYG-FM - 99.5 (31884)

Bristol
WXBQ-FM - 96.9 (31901)

Charlottesville
WCYK-AM - 810 (31950)
WCYK-FM - 99.7 (31951)

Clintwood
WDIC-AM - 1430 (31978)

Covington
WIQO-FM - 100.9 (31983)

Crewe
WSVS-AM - 800 (31985)

Farmville
WFLO-AM - 870 (32070)

Franklin
WLQM-AM - 1250 (32082)
WLQM-FM - 101.7 (32083)

Fredericksburg
WFLS-FM - 93.3 (32091)

Galax
WBRF-FM - 98.1 (32100)

Gate City
WGAT-AM - 1050 (32109)

Gretna
WMNA-AM - 730 (32119)
WMNA-FM - 106.3 (32120)

Hampton
WBYM-AM - 1490 (32132)

Harrisonburg
WKCY-FM - 104.3 (32147)

Lebanon
WLRV-AM - 1380 (32180)

Leesburg
WAGE-AM - 1200 (32188)

Lexington
WREL-FM - 96.7 (32196)

Louisa
WLSA-FM - 105.5 (32201)

Luray
WRAA-AM - 1330 (32204)

Lynchburg
WYYD-FM - 107.9 (32218)

Marion
WMEV-FM - 93.9 (32228)

Martinsville
WHEE-AM - 1370 (32237)

Mount Jackson
WSIG-FM - 96.9 (32277)

Norton
WAXM-FM - 93.5 (32311)
WNVA-AM - 1350 (32312)
WNVA-FM - 106.3 (32313)

Orange
WJMA-AM - 1340 (32323)
WJMA-FM - 96.7 (32324)

Pound
WDXC-FM - 102.3 (32336)

Radford
WRIQ-FM - 101.7 (32351)

Richmond
WJMO-FM - 105.7 (32479)

Rocky Mount
WYTI-AM - 1570 (32513)

Salem
WSLC-AM - 610 (32523)

Staunton
WKDW-AM - 900 (32558)
WTON-AM - 1240 (32560)

Stuart
WHEO-AM - 1270 (32565)

Triangle
WPWC-AM - 1480 (32571)

Virginia Beach
WGH-FM - 97.3 (32594)

Warrenton
WKCW-AM - 1420 (32604)

WASHINGTON
Bellingham
KIXT-AM - 930 (32684)

Centralia
KMNT-FM - 102.9 (32709)

Colfax
KCLX-AM - 1450 (32722)
KZZL-FM - 99.5 (32724)

Colville
KCVL-AM - 1240 (32729)

Dunmore
WCHG-FM - 107.1 (32739)

Grand Coulee
KEYG-AM - 1490 (32781)

Kelso
KUKN-FM - 105.5 (32788)

Kennewick
KIOK-FM - 94.9 (32791)

Longview
KBAM-AM - 1270 (32815)

Moses Lake
KWIQ-AM - 100.3 (32843)
KWIQ-FM - 100.3 (32844)

Mount Vernon
KAPS-AM - 660 (32847)

Olympia
KGY-FM - 96.9 (32869)

Pasco
KORD-FM - 102.7 (32885)

Seattle
KMPS-AM - 1090 (33059)
KMPS-FM - 94.1 FM (33060)

Spokane
KGA-AM - 1510 (33114)

Wenatchee
KKRV-AM - 104.7 (33199)
KYSN-FM - 97.7 (33205)

WEST VIRGINIA
Beckley
WJLS-FM - 99.5 (33244)

Berkeley Springs
WCST-AM - 1010 (33248)
WCST-FM - 93.5 (33249)

Buckhannon
WBRB-FM - 101.3 (33264)

Charleston
WQBE-FM - 97.5 (33285)

Danville
WZAC-AM - 92.5 (33300)

Dunmore
WVLS-FM - 89.7 (33302)
WVMR-FM - 89.7 (33303)

Elkins
WDNE-FM - 98.9 (33309)
WVUC-FM - 93.1 (33311)

Fisher
WELD-FM - 101.7 (33318)

Grafton
WTBZ-FM - 95.9 (33327)

Huntington
WDGG-FM - 93.7 (33339)

Kingwood
WKMM-FM - 96.7 (33362)

Martinsburg
WEPM-AM - 1340 (33381)

Montgomery
WMON-AM - 1340 (33388)

Morgantown
WAJR-AM - 1440 (33400)

New Martinsville
WETZ-FM - 103.9 (33416)

Parkersburg
WHBR-FM - 103.1 (33424)

Rupert
WYKM-AM - 1250 (33457)

Spencer
WVRC-AM - 1400 (33472)

Sutton
WDBS-FM - 97.1 (33477)

Webster Springs
WAFD-FM - 100.3 (33488)

Weston
WHAW-AM - 980 (33499)

Wheeling
WOVK-FM - 98.7 (33507)

Williamson
WXCC-FM - 96.5 (33515)

WISCONSIN
Berlin
WISS-AM - 1090 (33586)

Dodgeville
WDMP-AM - 810 (33659)

Numbers cited in bold after listings are entry numbers rather than page numbers.

WDMP-FM - 99.3 **(33660)**

Eau Claire
WAXX-FM - 104.5 **(33675)**

Hartford
WTKM-AM - 1540 **(33774)**
WTKM-FM - 104.9 **(33775)**

Janesville
WJVL-FM - 99.9 **(33865)**

La Crosse
WQCC-FM - 106.3 **(33895)**

Ladysmith
WLDY-AM - 1340 **(33902)**

Lancaster
WGLR-FM - 97.7 **(33909)**

Madison
WWQM-FM - 106.3 **(34010)**

Manitowoc
WCUB-AM - 980 **(34014)**

Marinette
WHYB-FM - 103.7 **(34020)**

Marshfield
WOSQ-FM - 92.3 **(34030)**

New Richmond
WIXK-AM - 1590 **(34194)**
WIXK-FM - 107.1 **(34195)**

Oconto
WOCO-AM - 1260 **(34205)**

Oshkosh
WPCK-FM - 104.9 **(34229)**
WPKR-FM - 99.5 **(34230)**

Park Falls
WCQM-FM - 98.3 **(34234)**

Prairie du Chien
WQPC-FM - 94.3 **(34271)**

Reedsburg
WNFM-FM - 104.9 **(34282)**

Rice Lake
WAQE-AM - 1090 **(34295)**

Richland Center
WRCO-AM - 1450 **(34300)**
WRCO-FM - 100.9 **(34301)**

Shawano
WTCH-AM - 960 **(34320)**

Sheboygan
WBFM-FM - 93.7 **(34323)**

Tomahawk
WJJQ-FM - 92.5 **(34375)**

Washburn
WEGZ-FM - 105.9 **(34389)**

Watertown
WTTN-AM - 1580 **(34393)**

Waupaca
WDUX-AM - 800 **(34423)**

Wausau
WDEZ-FM - 101.9 **(34432)**

West Bend
WBWI-FM - 92.5 **(34448)**

Whitehall
WHTL-FM - 102.3 **(34455)**

Whitewater
WSLD-FM - 104.5 **(34459)**

WYOMING
Afton
KRSV-AM - 1210 **(34475)**
KRSV-FM - 98.7 **(34476)**

Casper
KTWO-AM - 1030 **(34491)**

Cheyenne
KKWY-AM - 1630 **(34506)**
KPIN-FM - 101.1 **(34508)**

Cody
KZMQ-AM - 1140 **(34517)**
KZMQ-FM - 100.3 **(34518)**

Gillette
KIML-AM - 1270 **(34530)**

Jackson
KSGT-AM - 1340 **(34539)**

Lander
KOVE-AM - 1330 **(34546)**

Laramie
KCGY-FM - 95.1 **(34554)**

Newcastle
KASL-AM - 1240 **(34565)**

Powell
KLVY-AM - 1260 **(34570)**

Rock Springs
KQSW-FM - 96.5 **(34583)**

Sheridan
KYTI-FM - 93.7 **(34591)**

Torrington
KERM-FM - 98.3 **(34598)**
KGOS-AM - 1490 **(34599)**

ALBERTA, CANADA
Blairmore
CJEV-AM - 1340 **(34620)**

Crowsnest Pass
CJPR-AM - 1490 **(34691)**

Drumheller
CKDQ-AM - 910 **(34697)**

Edmonton
CFCW-AM - 790 **(34745)**

Edson
CFYR-AM - 1400 **(34759)**
CIYR-AM - 1230 **(34760)**
CJYR-AM - 970 **(34761)**

Lethbridge
CHLB-FM - 95.5 **(34800)**

Peace River
CKYL-AM - 610 **(34823)**

St. Paul
CHLW-AM - 1310 **(34845)**

Wainwright
CKKY-AM - 830 **(34870)**

Westlock
CFOK-AM - 1370 **(34872)**

BRITISH COLUMBIA, CANADA
Dawson Creek
CJDC-AM - 890 **(34942)**

Fort Nelson
CFNL-AM - 590 **(34957)**

Fort St. James
CIFJ-AM - 1480 **(34959)**

Fraser Lake
CIFL-AM - 1450 **(34961)**

Golden
CKGR-AM - 1400 **(34968)**
CKIR-AM - 870 **(34969)**

100 Mile House
CKBX-AM - 840 **(35041)**

Port Alberni
CJAV-AM - 1240 **(35050)**

Powell River
CHQB-AM - 1280 **(35055)**

Prince George
CIOI-FM - 101.3 **(35058)**
CJCI-AM - 620 **(35060)**

Revelstoke
CKCR-AM - 1340 **(35072)**

Terrace
CJFW-FM - 103.1 **(35114)**

Vanderhoof
CIVH-AM - 1340 **(35199)**

Williams Lake
CKWL-AM - 570 **(35246)**

MANITOBA, CANADA
Brandon
CKLQ-AM - 880 **(35256)**

Portage La Prairie
CFRY-AM - 920 **(35284)**

Winkler
CKMW-AM - 1570 **(35308)**

NEW BRUNSWICK, CANADA
Campbellton
CKNB-AM - 950 **(35384)**

Fredericton
CKHJ-FM - 105.3 **(35405)**

St. John
CHSJ-FM - 94.1 **(35433)**

Woodstock
CJCJ-FM - 104.1 **(35441)**

NEWFOUNDLAND AND LABRADOR, CANADA
Churchill Falls
CFLC-FM - 97.9 **(35444)**

Corner Brook
CKXX-FM - 103.9 **(35453)**

Gander
CKXD-AM - 1010 **(35458)**

Grand Falls
CKCM-AM - 620 **(35463)**

Marystown
CHCM-AM - 740 **(35473)**

St. John's
VOCM-AM - 590 **(35504)**

Stephenville
CFSX-AM - 870 **(35509)**

Wabush
CFLW-AM - 1340 **(35512)**

NORTHWEST TERRITORIES, CANADA
Yellowknife
CFYK-AM - 1340 **(35529)**

NOVA SCOTIA, CANADA
Bridgewater
CKBW-AM - 1000 **(35544)**

Kentville
CKDY-AM - 1420 **(35583)**
CKEN-AM - 97.7 **(35584)**

Liverpool
CKBW-FM - 98.1 **(35592)**

Middleton
CKAD-AM - 1350 **(35595)**

New Glasgow
CKEC-AM - 1320 **(35597)**

Windsor
CFAB-AM - 1450 **(35620)**

ONTARIO, CANADA
Cornwall
CJSS-AM - 1220 **(35758)**

Kingston
CFMK-FM - 96.3 **(35952)**

North Bay
CKAT-AM - 600 **(36119)**

Pembroke
CHVR-FM - 96.7 **(36310)**

Peterborough
CKQM-FM - 105.1 **(36323)**

Sault Sainte Marie
CJQM-FM - 104.3 **(36372)**

Smiths Falls
CJET-AM - 630 **(36396)**

Timmins
CKGB-FM - 750 **(36459)**

Welland
CHOW-FM - 91.7 **(36868)**

Circulation: ★ = ABC; △ = BPA; ✦ = CAC; ● = CCAB; ❑ = VAC; ⊕ = PO Statement; ‡ = Publisher's Report; Boldface figures = sworn; Light figures = estimated.

3015

COUNTRY (continued)

PRINCE EDWARD ISLAND, CANADA
Charlottetown
CFCY-AM - 630 (36918)

QUEBEC, CANADA
Fort Coulonge
CHIP-FM - 101.7 (36996)

Kahnawake
CKRK-FM - 103.7 (37019)

Noranda
CKRN-AM - 1400 (37261)

SASKATCHEWAN, CANADA
La Ronge
MBC-FM - 89.9 (37487)

Moose Jaw
CHAB-AM - 800 (37503)

Prince Albert
CKBI-AM - 900 (37522)

Regina
CKRM-AM - 620 (37543)

Saskatoon
CJWW-AM - 600 (37565)

Swift Current
CKSW-AM - 570 (37578)

Weyburn
CFSL-AM - 1190 (37593)

Yorkton
CJGX-AM - 940 (37602)

YUKON TERRITORY, CANADA
Whitehorse
CHON-FM - 98.1 (37607)

EASY LISTENING

ALABAMA
Auburn
WAUD-AM - 1230 (47)

Huntsville
WRSA-FM - 96.9 (286)

Ozark
WOZK-AM - 900 (421)

Selma
WMRK-AM - 1340 (456)

ALASKA
Bethel
KYKD-FM - 100.1 (555)

ARIZONA
Colorado City
KCCA-FM - 107.1 (676)

Quartzsite
KBUX-FM - 94.3 (859)

ARKANSAS
Fort Smith
KFPW-AM - 1230 (1147)

Hot Springs
KXOW-AM - 1420 (1188)

CALIFORNIA
Cathedral City
KWXY-FM - 98.5 (1680)

Palm Springs
KWXY-AM - 1340 (2781)

COLORADO
Grand Junction
KJYE-FM - 92.3 (4487)

Greeley
KSIR-FM - 107.1 (4502)

CONNECTICUT
Bloomfield
WJMJ-FM - 88.9 (4705)

FLORIDA
Lakeland
WONN-AM - 1230 (6294)

Miami
WRHC-AM - 1560 (6414)

Naples
WAVV-FM - 101.1 (6452)

Palm Harbor
WGUL-AM - 860 (6553)
WGUL-FM - 106.3 (6554)

Tampa
WDUV-FM - 105.5 (6787)

GEORGIA
Covington
WGFS-AM - 1430 (7213)

Kingsland
WATY-FM - 91.3 (7357)

Quitman
WSFB-AM - 1490 (7487)

HAWAII
Honolulu
KUMU-FM - 94.7 (7755)
KZOO-AM - 1210 (7758)

Kailua
KLEI-AM - 1130 (7765)

IDAHO
Nampa
KJHY-FM - 101.9 (7933)

ILLINOIS
Clinton
WHOW-FM - 95.9 (8685)

Shelbyville
WRAN-FM - 98.3 (9600)

Springfield
WLUJ-FM - 89.7 (9651)

Watseka
WGFA-AM - 1360 (9740)

INDIANA
Jasper
WITZ-AM - 990 (10221)
WITZ-FM - 104.7 (10222)

IOWA
Cedar Rapids
KMRY-AM - 1450 (10683)

Mason City
KCMR-FM - 97.9 (11074)

KANSAS
Newton
KOEZ-FM - 92.3 (11673)

KENTUCKY
Central City
WNES-AM - 1050 (12015)

LOUISIANA
Haynesville
KWHN-FM - 105.5 (12599)

MAINE
Machias
WALZ-FM - 95.3 (12988)

MARYLAND
Baltimore
WLIF-FM - 101.9 (13278)

Easton
WEMD-AM - 1460 (13491)

Hagerstown
WJEJ-AM - 1240 (13577)

MASSACHUSETTS
Greenfield
WGAM-AM - 1520 (14223)

North Adams
WMNB-FM - 100.1 (14420)

Plymouth
WPLM-FM - 99.1 (14484)

MICHIGAN
Grand Rapids
WTRV-FM - 100.5 (15124)

Newberry
WNBY-AM - 93.7 (15401)

Tawas City
WIOS-AM - 1480 (15586)

MINNESOTA
Park Rapids
KDKK-FM - 97.5 (16257)

MISSISSIPPI
Greenville
WBAQ-FM - 97.9 (16637)

MISSOURI
Bowling Green
KBMX-FM - 101.9 (16917)

Springfield
KTXR-FM - 101.3 (17631)

MONTANA
Kalispell
KALS-FM - 97.1 (17839)

Libby
KTNY-FM - 101.7 (17855)

NEW HAMPSHIRE
Laconia
WEZS-AM - 1350 (18538)

NEW MEXICO
Maljamar
KMTH-FM - 98.7 (19902)

Pinehill
KTDB-FM - 89.7 (19904)

Portales
KENW-FM - 89.5 (19905)

Taos
KKIT-AM - 1340 (19964)

NEW YORK
Hartsdale
WFAS-AM - 1230 (20714)

NORTH CAROLINA
Mount Airy
WPAQ-AM - 740 (24082)

Sylva
WRGC-AM - 680 (24252)

Wanchese
WYND-FM - 92.3 (24270)

OHIO
Alliance
WDPN-AM - 1310 (24606)

Brookfield
WWSY-FM - 95.9 (24710)

Dayton
WPTW-AM - 1570 (25151)

Eaton
WCTM-AM - 1130 (25175)

Mansfield
WRGM-AM - 1440 (25336)

OKLAHOMA
Hobart
KTJS-AM - 1420 (25868)

Lawton
KCCU-FM - 89.3 (25891)

Numbers cited in bold after listings are entry numbers rather than page numbers.

OREGON
Coos Bay
KHSN-AM - 1230 **(26279)**

Portland
KEUG-FM - 105.5 **(26524)**

Waldport
KORC-AM - 820 **(26608)**

PENNSYLVANIA
Harrisburg
WNCE-FM - 92.1 **(27022)**

Montrose
WPEL-AM - 1250 **(27293)**
WPEL-FM - 96.5 **(27294)**

Nanticoke
WNAK-AM - 730 **(27308)**

St. Marys
WKBI-AM - 1400 **(27943)**

PUERTO RICO
Caguas
WVJP-AM - 1110 **(28236)**

Mayaguez
WIOB-FM - 97.5 **(28261)**
WKJB-FM - 99.1 **(28263)**
WTPM-FM - 92.9 **(28270)**

Ponce
WEUC-FM - 88.9 **(28276)**

San Juan
WORO-FM - 92.5 **(28306)**
WRSJ-AM - 1560 **(28308)**
WRTU-FM - 89.7 **(28309)**

SOUTH CAROLINA
Greenville
WMUU-FM - 94.5 **(28636)**

TENNESSEE
Germantown
WPLX-AM - 1170 **(29207)**

TEXAS
Abilene
KZQQ-AM - 1560 **(29669)**

Austin
KOKE-AM - 1370 **(29874)**

Carrizo Springs
KBEN-AM - 1450 **(30003)**

Corpus Christi
KLUX-FM - 89.5 **(30089)**

Crockett
KIVY-AM - 1290 **(30107)**

Hereford
KNNK-FM - 100.5 **(30445)**

Killeen
KNCT-FM - 91.3 **(30645)**

Terrell
KPYK-AM - 1570 **(31183)**

UTAH
Manti
KMXU-FM - 105.1 **(31368)**

Salt Lake City
KFAM-AM - 700 **(31446)**

VIRGINIA
Virginia Beach
WWDE-FM - 101.3 **(32597)**

WASHINGTON
Wenatchee
KAAP-FM - 99.5 **(33197)**

WEST VIRGINIA
Huntington
WMEJ-FM - 91.9 **(33342)**

WISCONSIN
Baraboo
WRPQ-AM - 740 **(33564)**

Hales Corners
WAMG-FM - 103.7 **(33770)**

Marshfield
WLJY-FM - 106.5 **(34029)**

Monroe
WEKZ-FM - 93.7 **(34153)**

Park Falls
WNBI-AM - 980 **(34235)**

Poynette
WIBU-AM - 900 **(34265)**

ALBERTA, CANADA
Calgary
CBR-FM - 102.1 **(34662)**

BRITISH COLUMBIA, CANADA
Summerland
CHOR-AM - 1450 **(35104)**

Vancouver
CKBD-AM - 600 **(35192)**

ONTARIO, CANADA
Tillsonburg
CKOT-FM - 101.3 **(36452)**

PRINCE EDWARD ISLAND, CANADA
Charlottetown
CHLQ-FM - 93.1 **(36919)**

QUEBEC, CANADA
Noranda
CHOA-FM - 103.5/96.5/103.9 **(37260)**

Sept-Iles
CBSI-FM - 98.1 FM **(37387)**

ECLECTIC

ALABAMA
Atmore
WBCA-AM - 1110 **(35)**

Birmingham
WBFR-FM - 89.5 **(105)**

Tuscaloosa
WAPR-FM - 88.3 **(496)**

ALASKA
Anchorage
KSKA-FM - 91.1 **(547)**

Barrow
KBRW-AM - 680 **(552)**

Bethel
KYUK-AM - 640 **(556)**

Cordova
KLAM-AM - 1450 **(559)**

Galena
KIYU-AM - 910 **(582)**

Haines
KHNS-FM - 102.3 **(586)**

Ketchikan
KRBD-FM - 105.9 **(613)**

Kotzebue
KOTZ-AM - 89.9 **(622)**

Petersburg
KFSK-FM - 100.9 **(632)**

Talkeetna
KTNA-FM - 88.5 **(642)**

Valdez
KCHU-AM - 770 **(646)**
KCHU-FM - 88.1 **(647)**

ARIZONA
Phoenix
KPHX-AM - 1480 **(833)**

Whiteriver
KNNB-FM - 88.1 **(1004)**

ARKANSAS
Fayetteville
KREB-AM - 1190 **(1130)**

CALIFORNIA
Berkeley
KALX-FM - 90.7 **(1567)**
KPFA-FM - 94.1 **(1568)**

Cupertino
KKUP-FM - 91.5 **(1800)**

Davis
KDVS-FM - 90.3 **(1819)**

Fresno
KFCF-FM - 88.1 **(1964)**
KFSR-FM - 90.7 **(1967)**

Hoopa
KIDE-FM - 91.3 **(2057)**

La Jolla
KSDT-FM - 95.5 **(2122)**

Mendocino
KMFB-FM - 92.7 **(2520)**

Moraga
KSMC-FM - 89.5 **(2598)**

North Hollywood
KPFK-FM - 90.7 **(2645)**

Northridge
KCSN-FM - 88.5 **(2647)**

Philo
KZYX-FM - 90.7 **(2838)**

Riverside
KUCR-FM - 88.3 **(2954)**

Sacramento
KYDS-FM - 91.5 **(3058)**

San Diego
KCR-AM - 1620 **(3296)**
KCR-FM - 98.9 **(3297)**

San Francisco
KALW-FM - 91.7 **(3469)**

San Jose
KSJS-FM - 90.5 **(3554)**

Santa Barbara
KCSB-FM - 91.9 **(3662)**

Santa Monica
KCRW-FM - 89.9 **(3722)**

Stockton
KSJC-FM - 89.5 **(3816)**
KUOP-FM - 91.3 **(3819)**

COLORADO
Alamosa
KASF-FM - 90.9 **(4134)**

Boulder
KGNU-FM - 88.5 **(4197)**
KVCU-AM - 1190 **(4198)**

Denver
KTCL-FM - 93.3 **(4390)**

Gunnison
KWSB-FM - 91.1 **(4513)**

Ignacio
KSUT-FM - 91.3 **(4520)**

CONNECTICUT
Bridgeport
WPKN-FM - 89.5 **(4720)**

Fairfield
WVOF-FM - 88.5 **(4793)**

Hartford
WRTC-FM - 89.3 **(4911)**

Middletown
WESU-FM - 88.1 **(4948)**

New London
WCNI-FM - 91.1 **(5022)**

Storrs
WHUS-FM - 91.7 **(5170)**

West Hartford
WWUH-FM - 91.3 **(5206)**

Circulation: ★ = ABC; △ = BPA; ♦ = CAC; ● = CCAB; ❑ = VAC; ⊕ = PO Statement; ‡ = Publisher's Report; Boldface figures = sworn; Light figures = estimated.

3017

ECLECTIC (continued)

Westport
WWPT-FM - 90.3 **(5218)**

Willimantic
WECS-FM - 90.1 **(5221)**

DELAWARE
Newark
WVUD-FM - 91.3 **(5282)**

FLORIDA
Daytona Beach
WERU-FM - 104.7 **(6043)**

Port Charlotte
WVIJ-FM - 91.7 **(6597)**

Tallahassee
WVFS-FM - 89.7 **(6756)**

Tampa
WMNF-FM - 88.5 **(6796)**

Winter Park
WPRK-FM - 91.5 **(6894)**

GEORGIA
Athens
WUOG-FM - 90.5 **(6958)**

Atlanta
WREK-FM - 91.1 **(7083)**
WRFG-FM - 89.3 **(7084)**

Marietta
WGHR-FM - 100.7 **(7425)**

HAWAII
Honolulu
KZOO-AM - 1210 **(7758)**

ILLINOIS
Canton
WBYS-AM - 1560 **(8111)**

Carbondale
WDBX-FM - 91.1 **(8122)**

Carthage
WCAZ-AM - 990 **(8166)**

Chicago
WHPK-FM - 88.5 **(8627)**
WHPK-FM - 88.5 **(8628)**
WZRD-FM - 88.3 **(8664)**

Elgin
WEPS-FM - 88.9 **(8827)**

Lake Forest
WMXM-FM - 88.9 **(9063)**

Macomb
WIUM-FM - 91.3 **(9134)**
WIUS-FM - 88.3 **(9135)**

Park Ridge
WMTH-FM - 90.5 **(9409)**

Quincy
WQUB-FM - 90.3 **(9482)**

Rock Island
WAUG-AM - 570 **(9522)**
WAUG-FM - 97.9 **(9523)**

Romeoville
WLRA-FM - 88.1 **(9554)**

Springfield
WQNA-FM - 88.3 **(9655)**

Summit
WARG-FM - 88.9 **(9675)**

INDIANA
Howe
WHWE-FM - 89.7 **(10066)**

Indianapolis
WRFT-FM - 91.5 **(10207)**

Muncie
WCRD-AM - 540 **(10331)**

Richmond
WECI-FM - 91.5 **(10422)**

South Bend
WETL-FM - 91.7 **(10461)**

Valparaiso
WVUR-FM - 95.1 **(10515)**

West Lafayette
WBAA-AM - 920 **(10556)**

IOWA
Ames
KURE-FM - 88.5 **(10598)**

Cedar Falls
KGRK-AM - 970 **(10666)**
KUNI-FM - 90.9 **(10668)**

Des Moines
KDPS-FM - 88.1 **(10823)**

Mason City
KRNI-AM - 1010 **(11078)**
KUNY-FM - 91.5 **(11079)**

Mount Vernon
KRNL-FM - 89.7 **(11100)**

Sioux Center
KDCR-FM - 88.5 **(11209)**

KANSAS
Manhattan
KSDB-FM - 91.9 **(11635)**

Phillipsburg
KKAN-AM - 1490 **(11749)**
KQMA-FM - 92.5 **(11750)**

KENTUCKY
Georgetown
WRVG-FM - 89.9 **(12089)**

Lexington
WRFL-FM - 88.1 **(12194)**

Owensboro
WKWC-FM - 90.3 **(12330)**

Whitesburg
WMMT-FM - 88.7 **(12441)**

LOUISIANA
Baton Rouge
WRKF-FM - 89.3 **(12523)**

Lake Providence
KLPL-FM - 92.7 **(12654)**

Shreveport
KDAQ-FM - 89.9 **(12823)**

MAINE
Lewiston
WRBC-FM - 91.5 **(12980)**

Portland
WMPG-FM - 90.9 **(13029)**

Standish
WSJB-FM - 91.5 **(13059)**

MARYLAND
Baltimore
WHSR-AM - 530 **(13273)**

Brunswick
WTRI-AM - 1520 **(13396)**

MASSACHUSETTS
Acton
WHAB-FM - 89.1 **(13786)**

Amherst
WMUA-FM - 91.1 **(13810)**

Andover
WPAA-FM - 91.7 **(13815)**

Boston
WBUR-FM - 90.9 **(13978)**
WERS-FM - 88.9 **(13983)**
WRBB-FM - 104.9 **(13993)**
WTBU-FM - 89.3 **(13997)**

Franklin
WGAO-FM - 88.3 **(14208)**

Harwich
WCCT-FM - 90.3 **(14231)**

Holliston
WHHB-FM - 99.9 **(14240)**

North Adams
WJJW-FM - 91.1 **(14419)**

North Easton
WSHL-FM - 91.3 **(14424)**

Northampton
WOZQ-FM - 91.9 **(14434)**
WRSI-FM - 93.9 **(14435)**

Provincetown
WOMR-FM - 92.1 **(14487)**

South Hadley
WMHC-FM - 91.5 **(14543)**

Springfield
WSCB-FM - 89.9 **(14563)**
WTCC-FM - 90.7 **(14564)**

Wellesley
WZLY-FM - 91.5 **(14620)**

West Barnstable
WKKL-FM - 90.7 **(14623)**

Worcester
WCUW-FM - 91.3 **(14696)**
WWPI-FM - 90.1 **(14701)**

MICHIGAN
Dearborn
WHFR-FM - 89.3 **(14908)**

East Lansing
WDBM-FM - 88.9 **(14994)**

Farmington Hills
WORB-FM - 90.3 **(15026)**

Flint
WFBE-FM - 95.1 **(15041)**

Garden City
WCAR-AM - 1090 **(15065)**

Harrison
WVXH-FM - 92.1 **(15145)**

Monroe
WEJY-FM - 97.5 **(15367)**
WTWR-FM - 98.3 **(15368)**

Olivet
WOCR-FM - 89.7 **(15419)**

Port Huron
WSGR-FM - 91.3 **(15459)**

Rochester
WXOU-FM - 88.3 **(15468)**

West Bloomfield
WBLD-FM - 89.3 **(15679)**

Ypsilanti
WEMU-FM - 89.1 **(15692)**

MINNESOTA
Grand Rapids
KAXE-FM - 91.7 **(15930)**

Mankato
KMSU-FM - 89.7 **(16034)**

Minneapolis
KFAI-FM - 90.3 & 106.7 **(16149)**

Montevideo
KMGM-FM - 105.5 **(16182)**

St. Paul
WMCN-FM - 91.7 **(16428)**

Winona
KQAL-FM - 89.5 **(16534)**

MISSISSIPPI
Hattiesburg
WUSM-FM - 88.5 **(16677)**

Houston
WCPC-AM - 940 **(16686)**

Itta Bena
WVSD-FM - 91.7 **(16690)**

MISSOURI
Charleston
KCHR-AM - 1350 **(16973)**

Numbers cited in bold after listings are entry numbers rather than page numbers.

Chesterfield
KYMC-FM - 89.7 **(16976)**

Kansas City
KKFI-FM - 90.1 **(17209)**

Point Lookout
KCOZ-FM - 91.7 **(17355)**

Rolla
KMNR-FM - 89.7 **(17381)**
KUMR-FM - 88.5 **(17382)**

St. Louis
KDHX-FM - 88.1 **(17535)**

MONTANA
Bozeman
KGLT-FM - 91.9 **(17757)**

NEBRASKA
Blair
KDCV-FM - 91.1 **(17960)**

Crookston
KINI-FM - 96.1 **(17996)**

Lincoln
KZUM-FM - 89.3 **(18148)**

NEVADA
Reno
KUNR-FM - 88.7 **(18442)**

NEW HAMPSHIRE
Plymouth
WPCR-FM - 91.7 **(18636)**

NEW JERSEY
Hackettstown
WNTI-FM - 91.9 **(18859)**

Jersey City
WFMU-FM - 91.1 **(19149)**

Lawrence Township
WLCR-FM - 89.7 **(19161)**

Lawrenceville
WRRC-FM - 107.7 **(19166)**

Mahwah
WRPR-FM - 90.3 **(19208)**

Pemberton
WBZC-FM - 88.9 and 95.1 **(19419)**

Pomona
WLFR-FM - 91.7 **(19449)**

Teaneck
WFDQ-FM - 91.9 **(19611)**

NEW MEXICO
Albuquerque
KUNM-FM - 89.9 **(19815)**

Las Vegas
KEDP-FM - 91.1 **(19890)**

Portales
KZIA-AM - 1610 **(19909)**

Raton
KRTN-AM - 1490 **(19911)**

Socorro
KTEK-FM - 88.7 **(19961)**

NEW YORK
Brookville
WCWP-FM - 88.1 **(20361)**

Canton
WSLO-FM - 90.9 **(20432)**
WSLU-FM - 89.5 **(20433)**

Corning
WCEB-FM - 91.9 **(20506)**

Elmira
WECW-FM - 107.7 **(20574)**

Geneva
WEOS-FM - 89.7 **(20657)**

Hempstead
WRHU-FM - 88.7 **(20730)**

Kingston
WAMK-FM - 90.9 **(20863)**

New Paltz
WFNP-FM - 88.7 **(21115)**

New Rochelle
WVOX-AM - 1460 **(21125)**

New York
WBMB-AM - 590 **(22964)**

Ossining
WOSS-FM - 91.1 **(23060)**

Oswego
WNYO-FM - 88.9 **(23063)**

Plattsburgh
WPLT-FM - 93.9 **(23107)**

Potsdam
WTSC-FM - 91.1 **(23144)**

Poughkeepsie
WVKR-FM - 91.3 **(23164)**

Saranac Lake
WSLL-FM - 90.5 **(23299)**

Stony Brook
WUSB-FM - 90.1 **(23378)**

NORTH CAROLINA
Greensboro
WNAA-FM - 90.1 **(23954)**

Greenville
WZMB-FM - 91.3 **(23976)**

Roanoke Rapids
WZRU-FM - 99.5 **(24199)**

Wilmington
WHQR-FM - 91.3 **(24301)**

Winston-Salem
WSNC-FM - 90.5 **(24333)**

NORTH DAKOTA
Belcourt
KEYA-FM - 88.5 **(24346)**

Four Bears
KMHA-FM - 91.3 **(24447)**

OHIO
Athens
WOUB-AM - 1340 **(24632)**

Bellefontaine
WPKO-FM - 98.3 **(24668)**

Cincinnati
WVXU-FM - 91.7 **(24849)**

Cleveland
WCSB-FM - 89.3 **(24972)**

Dayton
WDPS-FM - 89.5 **(25136)**
WWSU-FM - 106.9 **(25154)**

New Concord
WMCO-FM - 90.7 **(25410)**

Oxford
WMSR-FM - 89.1 **(25462)**

Springfield
WUSO-FM - 89.1 **(25538)**

Wooster
WCWS-FM - 90.9 **(25675)**

Yellow Springs
WYSO-FM - 91.3 **(25693)**

OKLAHOMA
Goodwell
KPSU-FM - 91.7 **(25844)**

Oklahoma City
KEBC-AM - 1340 **(26001)**

OREGON
Ashland
KSKF-FM - 90.9 **(26221)**

Corvallis
KBVR-FM - 88.7 **(26292)**

Eugene
KLCC-FM - 89.7 **(26341)**
KRVM-FM - 91.9 **(26345)**

Klamath Falls
KTEC-FM - 89.5 **(26397)**

La Grande
KEOL-FM - 91.7 **(26400)**

Portland
KBPS-AM - 1450 **(26520)**
KPSU-AM - 1450 **(26537)**

Warm Springs
KWSO-FM - 91.9 **(26609)**

PENNSYLVANIA
Allentown
WMUH-FM - 91.7 **(26633)**

Carlisle
WDCV-FM - 88.3 **(26763)**

Greenville
WTGP-FM - 88.1 **(26962)**

Grove City
WSAJ-AM - 1340 **(26966)**

Havertown
WHHS-FM - 107.9 **(27031)**

Indiana
WIUP-FM - 90.1 **(27081)**

Lancaster
WFNM-FM - 89.1 **(27149)**
WLCH-FM - 91.3 **(27154)**

Levittown
WBCB-AM - 1490 **(27190)**

Millersville
WIXQ-FM - 91.7 **(27268)**

Pittsburgh
WPTS-FM - 92.1 **(27872)**
WRCT-FM - 88.3 **(27877)**

Pittston
WVIA-FM - 89.9 **(27893)**

Scranton
WUSR-FM - 99.5 **(27971)**
WVMW-FM - 91.5 **(27972)**

Washington
WNJR-FM - 91.7 **(28122)**

Wilkes Barre
WRKC-FM - 88.5 **(28178)**

PUERTO RICO
Arecibo
WMSW-AM - 1120 **(28227)**
WNIK-AM - 1230 **(28228)**

RHODE ISLAND
Kingston
WRIU-FM - 90.3 **(28361)**

Portsmouth
WJHD-FM - 90.7 **(28383)**

Providence
WBSR-FM - 88.1 **(28432)**
WXIN-FM - 90.7 **(28441)**

SOUTH CAROLINA
Rock Hill
WRHI-AM - 1340 **(28748)**

SOUTH DAKOTA
Rapid City
KTEQ-FM - 91.3 **(28950)**

Sioux Falls
KRSD-FM - 88.1 **(28982)**

TENNESSEE
Bluff City
WHCB-FM - 91.5 **(29056)**

Chattanooga
WUTC-FM - 88.1 **(29112)**

Gallatin
WVCP-FM - 88.5 **(29205)**

Radio Station Formats

ECLECTIC (continued)

Kingsport
WCSK-FM - 90.3 (29264)

TEXAS
College Station
KANM-FM - 99.9 (30058)

Houston
KTRU-FM - 91.7 (30581)

Mesquite
KEOM-FM - 88.5 (30809)

Plains
KPHS-FM - 90.3 (30937)

VERMONT
Burlington
WRUV-FM - 90.1 (31527)

Colchester
WWPV-FM - 88.7 (31535)

Johnson
WJSC-FM - 90.7 (31546)

VIRGINIA
Ferrum
WFFC-FM - 89.9 (32074)

Hampden Sydney
WWHS-FM - 92.1 (32125)

Hampton
WHOV-FM - 88.1 (32133)

Lexington
WLUR-FM - 91.5 (32194)

Norfolk
WHRV-FM - 89.5 (32301)
WODU-AM - 1630 (32304)

Radford
WVRU-FM - 89.9 (32353)

Roanoke
WVTF-FM - 89.1 (32507)

Williamsburg
WCWM-FM - 90.7 (32625)

WASHINGTON
Bellingham
KUGS-FM - 89.3 (32685)

Gig Harbor
KGHP-FM - 89.9 (32775)

Mount Vernon
KSVR-FM - 90.1 (32849)

Olympia
KAOS-FM - 89.3 (32866)

Pullman
KZUU-FM - 90.7 (32917)

Tacoma
KUPS-FM - 90.1 (33159)

WEST VIRGINIA
Bethany
WVBC-FM - 88.1 (33251)

Fort Gay
WFGH-FM - 90.7 (33319)

Huntington
WMUL-FM - 88.1 (33343)

Pineville
WWYO-AM - 970 (33438)

South Charleston
WJYP-FM - 100.9 (33468)

WISCONSIN
Hayward
WOJB-FM - 88.9 (33789)

Madison
WRFW-FM - 88.7 (34008)
WSUM-FM - 91.7 (34009)

Milwaukee
WMUR-FM - 96 (34131)

ALBERTA, CANADA
Calgary
CBR-AM - 1010 (34661)

Edmonton
CBX-FM - 90.9 (34741)
CKUA-AM - 580 (34756)

BRITISH COLUMBIA, CANADA
Burnaby
CJSF-FM - 90.1 FM (34914)

Vancouver
CBUFT-FM - 97.7 (35183)
CHKG-FM - 96.1 (35186)

Victoria
CFUV-FM - 101.9 (35233)

MANITOBA, CANADA
Churchill
CHFC-AM - 1230 (35262)

Winnipeg
CKUW-FM - 95.9 FM (35376)

NEW BRUNSWICK, CANADA
Fredericton
CBZF-FM - 102.3 (35401)

Moncton
CBAF-AM - 1300 (35414)
CBAF-FM - 88.5, 105.7 (35415)

Sackville
CHMA-FM - 106.9 (35428)

NEWFOUNDLAND AND LABRADOR, CANADA
St. John's
VOWR-AM - 800 (35506)

NORTHWEST TERRITORIES, CANADA
Inuvik
CHAK-AM - 860 (35518)

Yellowknife
CFYK-AM - 1340 (35529)
CKLB-FM - 101.9 (35530)

NOVA SCOTIA, CANADA
Eskasoni First Nation
CICU-FM - 94.1 (35553)

Halifax
CKDU-FM - 97.5 (35578)

Yarmouth
CIFA-FM - 104.1 (35625)

ONTARIO, CANADA
Kingston
CFRC-FM - 101.9 (35953)

Moosonee
CHMO-AM - 1450 (36095)

Ohsweken
CKRZ-FM - 100.3 (36156)

Peterborough
CFFF-FM - 92.7 (36320)

Simcoe
CHCD-FM - 106.7 (36392)

Sudbury
CBCS-FM (36421)

Thunder Bay
CBQ-FM - 88.3 (36445)

Toronto
CBL-AM - 1927 (36799)
CIUT-FM - 89.5 (36816)

QUEBEC, CANADA
Amqui
CFVM-AM - 99.9 (36936)

Montreal
CBM-FM - 93.5 (37241)
CINQ-FM - 102.3 (37245)

Plessisville
CKYQ-FM - 95.7 (37270)

Quebec
CKIA-FM - 96.1 (37303)

SASKATCHEWAN, CANADA
Saskatoon
CFCR-FM - 90.5 (37561)

Wollaston Lake
CKUT-AM - 1600 (37596)

EDUCATIONAL

ALABAMA
Dothan
WVOB-FM - 91.3 (195)

Gadsden
WSGN-FM - 91.5 (237)

Huntsville
WYFD-FM - 91.7 (288)

ALASKA
Barrow
KBRW-AM - 680 (552)
KBRW-FM - 91.9 (553)

Nome
KNOM-AM - 780 (628)
KNOM-FM - 96.1 (629)

ARIZONA
Sierra Vista
KWRB-FM - 90.9 (892)

Tempe
KASC-AM - 1260 (920)

ARKANSAS
Cave City
KZIG-FM - 89.9 (1075)

Mountain Home
KCMH-FM - 91.5 (1286)

CALIFORNIA
Burney
KIBC-FM - 90.5 (1636)

Chico
KZFR-FM - 90.1 (1707)

Hayward
KCRH-FM - 89.9 (2045)

Le Grand
KEFR-FM - 89.9 (2151)

Los Angeles
KDIS-AM - 1110 (2453)

Oakland
KEAR-FM - 106.9 (2704)

Riverside
KUCR-FM - 88.3 (2954)

Salinas
KHDC-FM - 90.9 (3071)

San Francisco
KDNZ-FM - 88.7 (3478)

Santa Cruz
KZSC-FM - 88.1 (3693)

Turlock
KBDG-FM - 90.9 (3959)

COLORADO
Fort Collins
KCSU-FM - 90.5 (4441)

CONNECTICUT
Hartford
WQTQ-FM - 89.9 (4909)

GEORGIA
Kingsland
WATY-FM - 91.3 (7357)

IDAHO
Twin Falls
KCIR-FM - 90.7 (7992)

ILLINOIS
Elgin
WEPS-FM - 88.9 (8827)

Springfield
WQNA-FM - 88.3 **(9655)**

Wheaton
WETN-FM - 88.1 **(9761)**

INDIANA
Gary
WGVE-FM - 88.7 **(10019)**

North Manchester
WBKE-FM - 89.5 **(10361)**

IOWA
Ames
KURE-FM - 88.5 **(10598)**

Fairfield
KHOE-FM - 90.5 **(10884)**

Waterloo
KBBG-FM - 88.1 **(11290)**

KANSAS
Topeka
KJTY-FM - 88.1 **(11840)**

KENTUCKY
Keavy
WVCT-FM - 91.5 **(12150)**

Somerset
WWOG-FM - 90.9 **(12413)**

LOUISIANA
Dry Prong
KVDP-FM - 89.1 **(12572)**

Lafayette
KDYS-AM - 1520 **(12624)**

Port Allen
KPAE-FM - 91.5 **(12800)**

MASSACHUSETTS
Springfield
WNEK-FM - 105.1 **(14561)**

Winchester
WHSR-FM - 91.9 **(14668)**

MICHIGAN
Auburn Hills
WAHS-FM - 89.5 **(14784)**

Bloomfield Hills
WBFH-FM - 88.1 **(14831)**

Detroit
WDTR-FM - 90.9 **(14960)**

Harrison
WVXH-FM - 92.1 **(15145)**

Ontonagon
WOAS-FM - 88.5 **(15423)**

Rogers City
WVXA-FM - 96.7 **(15471)**

MINNESOTA
Thief River Falls
KSRQ-FM - 90.1 **(16472)**

MONTANA
Missoula
KBGA-FM - 89.9 **(17878)**

NEBRASKA
Hastings
KCNT-FM - 88.1 **(18038)**

NEW HAMPSHIRE
New London
WSCS-FM - 90.9 **(18612)**

NEW JERSEY
Franklin Lakes
WRRH-FM - 88.7 **(18836)**

NEW MEXICO
Maljamar
KMTH-FM - 98.7 **(19902)**

Portales
KENW-FM - 89.5 **(19905)**

NEW YORK
Brentwood
WXBA-FM - 88.1 **(20241)**

Brooklyn
WNYE-FM - 91.5 **(20358)**

Islandia
WFRS-FM - 88.9 **(20785)**

NORTH CAROLINA
Durham
WNCU-FM - 90.7 **(23849)**

Wilmington
WRQR-AM - 104.5 **(24304)**

OHIO
Batavia
WCNE-FM - 88.7 **(24644)**

Cincinnati
WJVS-FM - 88.3 **(24840)**
WMKV-FM - 89.3 **(24844)**

De Graff
WDEQ-FM - 103.3 **(25156)**

Jefferson
WCVJ-FM - 90.9 **(25268)**

OREGON
Eagle Point
KEPO-FM - 92.9 **(26308)**

Portland
KBPS-AM - 1450 **(26520)**

PENNSYLVANIA
Allentown
WMUH-FM - 91.7 **(26633)**

PUERTO RICO
Ponce
WEUC-FM - 88.9 **(28276)**

San Juan
WBMJ-AM - 1190 **(28297)**
WIVV-AM - 1370 **(28301)**

Trujillo Alto
WVID-FM - 90.3 **(28318)**

SOUTH CAROLINA
Greenville
WLFJ-FM - 89.3 **(28634)**

Orangeburg
WSSB-FM - 90.3 **(28738)**

TENNESSEE
Mc Minnville
WCPI-FM - 91.3 **(29356)**

Savannah
WDNX-FM - 89.1 **(29585)**

TEXAS
Bryan
KEOS-FM - 89.1 **(29979)**

UTAH
St. George
KOEZ 105.1 FM - 91.7, 105.1 **(31419)**

WASHINGTON
Ellensburg
KCWU-FM - 88.1 **(32750)**

Yakima
KDNA-FM - 91.9 **(33227)**

WEST VIRGINIA
Bethany
WVBC-FM - 88.1 **(33251)**

WISCONSIN
Lancaster
WJTY-FM - 88.1 **(33910)**

BRITISH COLUMBIA, CANADA
Victoria
CKMO-FM - 103.1 **(35236)**

NEW BRUNSWICK, CANADA
Moncton
CBAL-FM - 98.3 **(35417)**

ETHNIC

ALASKA
Unalaska
KIAL-AM - 1450 **(645)**

ARIZONA
Douglas
KDAP-AM - 1450 **(689)**

Globe
KJAA-AM - 1240 **(720)**

Tuba City
KGHR-FM - 91.5 **(926)**

Whiteriver
KNNB-FM - 88.1 **(1004)**

Window Rock
KTNN-AM - 660 **(1013)**

ARKANSAS
Little Rock
KITA-AM - 1440 **(1244)**

CALIFORNIA
Bakersfield
KSPL-FM - 102.9 **(1470)**
KTQX-FM - 90.1 **(1471)**

Camarillo
KMRO-FM **(1646)**

El Centro
KUBO-FM - 88.7 **(1855)**

Fresno
KTRB-AM - 860 **(1985)**

Inglewood
KTYM-AM - 1460 **(2075)**

Los Angeles
KIRN-AM - 670 **(2457)**
KMAX-FM - 107.1 **(2461)**
KXLU-FM - 88.9 **(2472)**
KXOL-FM - 96.3 **(2473)**

Los Banos
KLBS-AM - 1330 **(2476)**

Palm Desert
KUNA-FM - 96.7 **(2752)**

Philo
KZYX-FM - 90.7 **(2838)**

Sacramento
KZCO-FM - 97.7 **(3060)**

Salinas
KHDC-FM - 90.9 **(3071)**

San Francisco
KALW-FM - 91.7 **(3469)**
KBLX-FM - 102.9 **(3472)**
KEST-AM - 1450 **(3480)**
KTVO-AM - 1400 **(3502)**
KUTO-AM - 1400 **(3504)**

San Jose
KSJX-AM - 1500 **(3555)**

Stockton
KSJC-FM - 89.5 **(3816)**

Tulare
KGEN-FM - 94.5 **(3954)**

COLORADO
Denver
KJME-AM - 1390 **(4381)**

CONNECTICUT
West Hartford
WWUH-FM - 91.3 **(5206)**

West Haven
WNHU-FM - 88.7 **(5208)**

Circulation: ★ = ABC; △ = BPA; ♦ = CAC; ● = CCAB; ❑ = VAC; ⊕ = PO Statement; ‡ = Publisher's Report; Boldface figures = sworn; Light figures = estimated.

3021

ETHNIC (continued)

DISTRICT OF COLUMBIA
Washington
WPFW-FM - 89.3 **(5890)**

FLORIDA
Davie
WAVS-AM - 1170 **(6035)**

Fort Myers
WCRM-AM - 1350 **(6102)**

Homestead
WOIR-AM - 1430 **(6206)**

North Miami
WLQY-AM - 1320 **(6467)**

Oldsmar
WPSO-AM - 1500 **(6485)**

Orlando
WRLZ-AM - 1270 **(6527)**

Tallahassee
WAMF-FM - 90.5 **(6742)**

GEORGIA
Atlanta
WRFG-FM - 89.3 **(7084)**

Fort Valley
WXKO-AM - 1150 **(7291)**

Hinesville
WGML-AM - 990 **(7335)**

Scottdale
WATB-AM - 1420 **(7553)**

HAWAII
Eleele
KUAI-AM - 720 **(7662)**

Hilo
KAHU-AM - 1060 **(7672)**

Honolulu
KISA-AM - 1540 **(7742)**
KKEA-AM - 1420 **(7744)**
KNDI-AM - 1270 **(7747)**
KZOO-AM - 1210 **(7758)**

Kahului
KMVI-AM - 550 **(7760)**
KPOA-FM - 93.5 **(7763)**

ILLINOIS
Chicago
WSBC-AM - 1240 **(8651)**

Cicero
WCEV-AM - 1450 AM **(8677)**

Evanston
WONX-AM - 1590 **(8877)**

Highland Park
WEEF-AM - 1430 **(8994)**

Northbrook
WNVR-AM - 1030 **(9324)**

Oak Park
WPNA-AM - 1490 **(9379)**

IOWA
Cedar Falls
KUNI-FM - 90.9 **(10668)**

LOUISIANA
Hammond
KSLU-FM - 90.9 **(12595)**

Morgan City
KQKI-FM - 95.3 **(12713)**

Shreveport
KSCL-FM - 91.3 **(12834)**

MARYLAND
Glen Burnie
WJRO-AM - 1590 **(13556)**

MASSACHUSETTS
Beverly
WNSH-AM - 1570 **(13844)**

Boston
WUNR-AM - 1600 **(13999)**

Cambridge
WRCA-AM - 1330 **(14117)**

Marblehead
WLYN-AM - 101.7 **(14305)**

New Bedford
WJFD-FM - 97.3 **(14379)**

Newton
WNTN-AM - 1550 **(14413)**

Somerset
WHTB-AM - 1400 **(14528)**

Worcester
WCUW-FM - 91.3 **(14696)**

MICHIGAN
Saginaw
WTLZ-FM - 107.1 **(15506)**

Traverse City
WNMC-FM - 90.7 **(15612)**

MINNESOTA
Albany
KASM-AM - 1150 **(15705)**

Minneapolis
KFAI-FM - 90.3 & 106.7 **(16149)**

MISSISSIPPI
Lexington
WXTN-AM - 1000 **(16747)**

NEVADA
Las Vegas
KUNV-FM - 91.5 **(18406)**

NEW JERSEY
New Brunswick
WRSU-FM - 88.7 **(19345)**

Teaneck
WFDU-FM - 89.1 **(19612)**

NEW MEXICO
Farmington
KNDN-AM - 960 **(19848)**

Magdalena
KABR-AM - 1500 **(19901)**

Pinehill
KTDB-FM - 89.7 **(19904)**

Santa Fe
KSWV-AM - 810 **(19950)**

Taos
KKIT-AM - 1340 **(19964)**

NEW YORK
Bronx
WFUV-FM - 90.7 **(20292)**

Buffalo
WHLD-AM - 1270 **(20401)**

New Rochelle
WVOX-AM - 1460 **(21125)**

New York
WKCR-FM - 89.9 **(22972)**
WNJR-AM - 1430 **(22977)**
WNWK-FM - 105.9 **(22978)**

Rochester
WRUR-FM - 88.5 **(23254)**
WWWG-AM - 1460 **(23257)**

NORTH CAROLINA
Durham
WTIK-AM - 1310 **(23852)**

Greensboro
WJMH-FM - 102.1 **(23948)**

OHIO
Athens
WOUB-AM - 1340 **(24632)**

OREGON
Warm Springs
KWSO-FM - 91.9 **(26609)**

Woodburn
KWBY-AM - 940 **(26620)**

PENNSYLVANIA
Allentown
WMUH-FM - 91.7 **(26633)**

Bala Cynwyd
WNWR-AM - 1540 **(26676)**

Chester
WDNR-FM, Widener University - 89.5 **(26776)**

Monroeville
WXVX-AM - 1510 **(27289)**

New Castle
WKST-AM - 1200 **(27318)**

Philadelphia
WKDU-FM - 91.7 **(27737)**

White Oak
WEDO-AM - 810 **(28158)**

PUERTO RICO
Naguabo
WYQE-FM - 92.9 **(28273)**

SOUTH DAKOTA
Mc Laughlin
KLND-FM - 89.5 **(28891)**

TEXAS
Corpus Christi
KBNJ-FM - 91.7 **(30080)**

El Paso
KHPX-FM - 98.3 **(30293)**
KINT-FM - 93.9 **(30294)**

Houston
KHCB-AM - 1400 **(30547)**
KTEK-AM - 1110 **(30576)**

Lufkin
KRBA-AM - 1340 **(30743)**

Odessa
KQLM-FM - 107.9 **(30882)**

VIRGINIA
Falls Church
WUST-AM - 1120 **(32065)**

WASHINGTON
Lynnwood
KSER-FM - 90.7 **(32826)**

Seattle
KXPH-AM - 1540 **(33074)**

Washougal
KMUZ-AM - 1230 **(33192)**

Wenatchee
KWWX-AM - 1340 **(33204)**

WISCONSIN
Appleton
WRJQ-AM - 1570 **(33552)**

Hartford
WTKM-AM - 1540 **(33774)**
WTKM-FM - 104.9 **(33775)**

Milwaukee
WYMS-FM - 88.9 **(34144)**

Sheboygan
WSHS-FM - 91.7 **(34325)**

Sturgeon Bay
WAUN-FM - 92.7 **(34352)**

ALBERTA, CANADA
Edmonton
CKER-FM - 101.9 **(34754)**

MANITOBA, CANADA
Winnipeg
CKJS-AM - 810 **(35373)**

Numbers cited in bold after listings are entry numbers rather than page numbers.

NEW BRUNSWICK, CANADA
Moncton
CBAL-FM - 98.3 **(35417)**

NORTHWEST TERRITORIES, CANADA
Baker Lake
CKQN-FM - 99.3 **(35513)**

Yellowknife
CKLB-FM - 101.9 **(35530)**

ONTARIO, CANADA
Hamilton
CFMU-FM - 93.3 **(35893)**

Leamington
CHYR-FM - 96.7 **(35970)**

Oakville
CJMR-AM - 1320 **(36153)**

Toronto
CHIN-AM - 1540 **(36808)**
CHIN-FM - 100.7 **(36809)**
CIRV-FM - 88.7 **(36814)**

Waterloo
CKWR-FM - 98.5 **(36863)**

QUEBEC, CANADA
Fort Coulonge
CHIP-FM - 101.7 **(36996)**

Montreal
CINQ-FM - 102.3 **(37245)**

Quebec
CKIA-FM - 96.1 **(37303)**
CKRL-FM - 89.1 **(37304)**

Westmount
CFMB-AM - 1280 **(37447)**

FOLK

ARKANSAS
State University
KASU-FM - 91.9 **(1351)**

CONNECTICUT
Fairfield
WSHU-FM - 91.1 **(4792)**

Monroe
WGRS-FM - 91.5 **(4964)**
WGSK-FM - 90.1 **(4965)**

West Hartford
WWUH-FM - 91.3 **(5206)**

West Haven
WNHU-FM - 88.7 **(5208)**

DISTRICT OF COLUMBIA
Washington
WAMU-FM - 88.5 **(5877)**

ILLINOIS
Macomb
WIUM-FM - 91.3 **(9134)**

Quincy
WQUB-FM - 90.3 **(9482)**

INDIANA
Elkhart
WVPE-FM - 88.1 **(9930)**

Evansville
WNIN-FM - 88.3 **(9947)**

Goshen
WGCS-FM - 91.1 **(10029)**

IOWA
Decorah
KWLC-AM - 1240 **(10762)**

KANSAS
North Newton
KBCU-FM - 88.1 **(11677)**

MASSACHUSETTS
Amherst
WFCR-FM - 88.5 **(13809)**

Boston
WGBH-FM - 89.7 **(13985)**
WUMB-FM - 91.9 **(13998)**

Provincetown
WOMR-FM - 92.1 **(14487)**

Sheffield
WBSL-FM - 91.7 **(14520)**

Worcester
WICN-FM - 90.5 **(14698)**

MICHIGAN
Detroit
WDET-FM - 101.9 **(14957)**

Traverse City
WNMC-FM - 90.7 **(15612)**

MINNESOTA
Albert Lea
KATE-FM - 1450 **(15708)**

MISSISSIPPI
Booneville
WMAE-FM - 91.3 **(16574)**

NEVADA
Las Vegas
KUNV-FM - 91.5 **(18406)**

NEW HAMPSHIRE
Concord
WEVO-FM - 89.1 **(18476)**

Henniker
WNEC-FM - 91.7 **(18523)**

NEW JERSEY
Teaneck
WFDU-FM - 89.1 **(19612)**

NEW YORK
Albany
WAMC-FM - 90.3 **(20009)**

Binghamton
WSKG-FM - 89.3 **(20228)**
WSQE-FM - 91.1 **(20230)**
WSQG-FM - 89.3 **(20231)**
WSQX-FM - 88.7 **(20232)**

Bronx
WFUV-FM - 90.7 **(20292)**

Canajoharie
WCAN-FM - 93.3 **(20418)**

Rooseveltown
CKON-FM - 97.3 **(23276)**

Ticonderoga
WANC-FM - 103.9 **(23451)**

NORTH CAROLINA
Asheville
WFQS-FM - 91.3 **(23636)**

Chapel Hill
WUNC-FM - 91.5 **(23732)**

PENNSYLVANIA
Grove City
WSAJ-FM - 91.1 **(26967)**

PUERTO RICO
San Juan
WRTU-FM - 89.7 **(28309)**

SOUTH CAROLINA
Bishopville
WAGS-AM - 1380 **(28495)**

SOUTH DAKOTA
Sioux Falls
KCSD-FM - 90.9 **(28971)**

TEXAS
Corpus Christi
KEDT-FM - 90.3 **(30082)**

UTAH
Logan
KUSU-FM - 89.5, 91.5 **(31361)**

VIRGINIA
Charlottesville
WTJU-FM - 91.1 **(31955)**

Harrisonburg
WMRA-FM - 90.7 **(32148)**
WMRL-FM - 89.9 **(32149)**
WMRY-FM - 103.5 **(32150)**

WASHINGTON
Bellevue
KBCS-FM - 91.3 **(32672)**

Pullman
KFAE-FM - 89.1 **(32910)**
KRFA-FM - 91.7 **(32913)**

Spokane
KPBX-FM - 91.1 **(33123)**

WEST VIRGINIA
Weston
WHAW-AM - 980 **(33499)**

WISCONSIN
Eau Claire
WUEC-FM - 89.7 **(33684)**

Madison
WORT-FM - 89.9 **(34007)**

FRENCH

LOUISIANA
Jennings
KJEF-FM - 92.9 **(12607)**

Morgan City
KQKI-FM - 95.3 **(12713)**

Opelousas
KSLO-AM - 1230 **(12793)**

ALBERTA, CANADA
Calgary
CBRF-FM - 103.9 **(34663)**

Edmonton
CBXY-AM - 1490 **(34743)**
CHFA-AM - 680 **(34748)**

MANITOBA, CANADA
Winnipeg
CKSB-AM - 1050 **(35375)**

NEW BRUNSWICK, CANADA
Bathurst
CKBC-AM - 1360 **(35381)**

Campbellton
CKNB-AM - 950 **(35384)**

Edmundston
CJEM-FM - 92.7 **(35387)**

Moncton
CBAL-FM - 98.3 **(35417)**
CHOY-FM - 99.9 **(35419)**

Pokemouche
Radio Peninsule, Inc. - 97.1 **(35425)**

ONTARIO, CANADA
Hearst
CINN-FM - 91.1 **(35912)**

London
CJBC-FM - 90.3 **(36001)**

Penetanguishene
CFRH-FM - 88.1 **(36311)**

Timmins
CHYK-FM - 104.1 **(36457)**

Toronto
CJBC-AM - 860 **(36817)**

Circulation: ★ = ABC; △ = BPA; ♦ = CAC; ● = CCAB; ❏ = VAC; ⊕ = PO Statement; ‡ = Publisher's Report; Boldface figures = sworn; Light figures = estimated.

3023

FRENCH (continued)

Windsor
CBEF-AM - 540 **(36896)**

QUEBEC, CANADA
L'Annonciation
CFLO-FM - 104.7 **(36940)**

Cap-aux-Meules
CFIM-FM - 92.7 **(36955)**

Chicoutimi
CBJ-FM - 93.7 **(36969)**
CBJX-FM - 100.9 **(36971)**

Fort Coulonge
CHIP-FM - 101.7 **(36996)**

La Sarre
CKLS-AM - 1240 **(37023)**

La Tuque
CFLM-AM - 1240 **(37024)**

Lachute
CJLA-FM - 104.9 **(37031)**

Maniwaki
CHGA-FM - 97.3 **(37066)**

Montmagny
CFEL-FM - 102.1 **(37078)**

Plessisville
CKYQ-FM - 95.7 **(37271)**

Quebec
CHVD-AM - 1230 **(37299)**
CHVD-FM - 92.1 **(37300)**

Saint-Gabriel
CFNJ-FM - 99.1 **(37340)**

Sainte-Foy
CHRC-AM - 800 **(37379)**

Seneterre
CIBO-FM - 100.5 **(37385)**

Sept-Iles
CKCN-FM - 94.1 **(37388)**

Sherbrooke
CHLT-AM - 630 **(37397)**
CIMO-FM - 106.1 **(37398)**

Sillery
CHOI-FM - 98.1 **(37402)**

Thetford Mines
CJLP-FM - 107.1 **(37412)**
CKLD-FM - 105.5 **(37413)**

Trois-Rivieres
CHLN-AM - 550 **(37418)**

Verdun
CKVL-AM - 850 **(37430)**

SASKATCHEWAN, CANADA
Regina
CBKF-FM - 97.7 **(37537)**

FULL SERVICE

ALABAMA
Birmingham
WATV-AM - 900 **(104)**

ALASKA
Dillingham
KDLG-AM - 670 **(563)**

Homer
KBBI-AM - 890 **(589)**

Juneau
KINY-AM - 800 **(599)**

Kenai
KDLL-FM - 91.9 **(608)**

Kodiak
KMXT-FM - 100.1 **(617)**

Petersburg
KRSA-AM - 580 **(633)**

Sand Point
KSDP-AM - 830 **(635)**

Wrangell
KSTK-FM - 101.7 **(654)**

ARIZONA
Green Valley
KGVY-AM - 1080 **(723)**

Tucson
KXCI-FM - 91.3 **(1001)**

ARKANSAS
McGehee
KVSA-AM - 1220 **(1273)**

Warren
KWRF-AM - 860 **(1366)**

CALIFORNIA
Berkeley
KPFA-FM - 94.1 **(1568)**

Los Altos
KFJC-FM - 89.7 **(2196)**

Los Angeles
KIRN-AM - 670 **(2457)**
KLSX-FM - 97.1 **(2460)**

Palm Desert
WNRK-AM - 1260 **(2753)**

Palo Alto
KZSU-FM - 90.1 **(2803)**

Redway
KMUD-FM - 91.1 **(2912)**

San Diego
KFMB-AM - 760 **(3298)**

San Francisco
KPOO-FM - 89.5 **(3497)**

Santa Cruz
KUSP-FM - 88.9 **(3692)**

Susanville
KSUE-AM - 1240 **(3834)**

COLORADO
Boulder
KWAB-AM - 1490 **(4199)**

Burlington
KNAB-AM - 1140 **(4211)**
KNAB-FM - 104.1 **(4212)**

Carbondale
KDNK-FM - 90.5 **(4219)**

Crested Butte
KBUT-FM - 90.3 **(4299)**

Greeley
KUNC-FM - 91.5 **(4503)**

Gunnison
KPKE-AM - 1490 **(4511)**

Salida
KVRH-FM - 92.3 **(4621)**
KVRH-FM - 92.3 **(4622)**

Telluride
KOTO-FM - 91.7 **(4646)**

CONNECTICUT
Danbury
WLAD-AM - 800 **(4766)**

Fairfield
WVOF-FM - 88.5 **(4793)**

Hamden
WQAQ-FM - 98.1 **(4883)**

Middletown
WMRD-AM - 1150 **(4949)**
WMRD-AM - 1150 **(4950)**

Old Saybrook
WLIS-AM - 1420 **(5089)**

Sharon
WKZE-AM - 1020 **(5115)**

Wallingford
WWEB-FM - 89.9 **(5189)**

Willimantic
WILI-AM - 1400 **(5222)**

Windsor
WKND-AM - 1480 **(5235)**

DELAWARE
Lewes
WGMD-FM - 92.7 **(5260)**

Newark
WVUD-FM - 91.3 **(5282)**

DISTRICT OF COLUMBIA
Washington
WMAL-AM - 630 **(5889)**

FLORIDA
DeFuniak Springs
WZEP-AM - 1460 **(6054)**

Jacksonville
WJCT-FM - 89.9 **(6225)**

Oldsmar
WPSO-AM - 1500 **(6485)**

GEORGIA
Albany
WGPC-AM - 1450 **(6909)**
WGPC-FM - 104.5 **(6910)**

Dalton
WBLJ-AM - 1230 **(7223)**

HAWAII
Eleele
KUAI-AM - 720 **(7662)**

Honolulu
KTUH-FM - 90.3 **(7753)**

IDAHO
Boise
KBOI-AM - 670 **(7817)**

Grangeville
KORT-FM - 92.7 **(7859)**

Idaho Falls
KID-AM - 590 **(7874)**

Rexburg
KBYI-FM - 100.5 **(7966)**

ILLINOIS
Bloomington
WJBC-AM - 1230 **(8085)**

Canton
WBYS-AM - 1560 **(8111)**

Charleston
WEIU-FM - 88.9 **(8237)**

Chicago
WHPK-FM - 88.5 **(8627)**
WKKC-FM - 89.3 **(8634)**

Galva
WGEN-AM - 1500 **(8912)**

Highland
WCBW-AM - 880 **(8990)**

Peoria
WMBD-AM - 1470 **(9433)**

Salem
WJBD-AM - 1350 **(9578)**

INDIANA
Evansville
WPSR-FM - 90.7 **(9948)**
WUEV-FM - 91.5 **(9951)**

Logansport
WSAL-AM - 1230 **(10277)**

Rushville
WKWH-FM - 94.3 **(10438)**

Warsaw
WRSW-AM - 1480 **(10539)**

IOWA
Ames
KASI-AM - 1430 **(10596)**

Burlington
KBUR-AM - 1490 **(10641)**

Carroll
KCIM-AM - 1380 **(10653)**

Forest City
KIOW-FM - 107.3 **(10892)**

Grinnell
KDIC-FM - 88.5 **(10932)**
KGRN-AM - 1410 **(10933)**

Le Mars
KLEM-AM - 1410 **(11035)**

Manchester
KMCH-FM - 94.7 **(11046)**

Mason City
KGLO-AM - 1300 **(11075)**

KANSAS
Dodge City
KGNO-AM - 1370 **(11417)**

Fort Scott
KMDO-AM - 1600 **(11444)**

Garden City
KIUL-AM - 1240 **(11452)**

Goodland
KLOE-AM - 730 **(11467)**

Hays
KAYS-AM - 1400 **(11483)**

McPherson
KBBE-FM - 96.7 **(11644)**
KNGL-AM - 1540 **(11645)**

Phillipsburg
KKAN-AM - 1490 **(11749)**

KENTUCKY
Lexington
WVLK-AM - 590 **(12198)**

LOUISIANA
Amite
WABL-AM - 1570 **(12471)**

Angola
KLSP-FM - 91.7 **(12473)**

New Orleans
WTUL-FM - 91.5 **(12778)**

MAINE
Calais
WQDY-FM - 92.7 **(12940)**

MARYLAND
Annapolis
WNAV-AM - 1430 **(13101)**

Bel Air
WHFC-FM - 91.1 **(13292)**

Brunswick
WTRI-AM - 1520 **(13396)**

College Park
WMUC-FM - 88.1 **(13448)**

Hagerstown
WJEJ-AM - 1240 **(13577)**

Westminster
WTTR-AM - 1470 **(13779)**

MASSACHUSETTS
Amherst
WAMH-FM - 89.3 **(13808)**

Beverly
WNSH-AM - 1570 **(13844)**

Boston
WQLL-FM - 96.5 **(13992)**

Cambridge
WHRB-FM - 95.3 **(14114)**
WMBR-FM - 88.1 **(14116)**

Great Barrington
WSBS-AM - 860 **(14218)**

Hyannis
WQRC-FM - 99.9 **(14254)**

Medford
WMFO-FM - 91.5 **(14325)**

Milford
WMRC-AM - 1490 **(14333)**

Pittsfield
WBEC-AM - 1420 **(14473)**

Sheffield
WBSL-FM - 91.7 **(14520)**

Springfield
WNEK-FM - 105.1 **(14561)**

Sudbury
WYAJ-FM - 97.7 **(14582)**

MICHIGAN
Adrian
WVAC-FM - 107.9 **(14714)**

Ann Arbor
WCBN-FM - 88.3 **(14776)**

Caro
WKYO-AM - 1360 **(14860)**

Flint
WFBE-FM - 95.1 **(15041)**

Grand Rapids
WOOD-AM - 1300 **(15118)**

Holland
WHTC-AM - 1450 **(15176)**

Iron Mountain
WMIQ-AM - 1450 **(15209)**

Kalamazoo
WKDS-FM - 89.9 **(15250)**

Marquette
WNMU-FM - 90.1, 107.1, 91.9, 91.3, 91.1,
 107.3 **(15346)**

Sandusky
WMIC-AM - 660 **(15523)**

Southfield
WSHJ-FM - 88.3 **(15560)**

MINNESOTA
Ada
KRJB-FM - 106.3 **(15697)**

Buffalo
KRWC-AM - 1360 **(15779)**

Cambridge
WREV-FM - 105.3 **(15787)**

Litchfield
KLFD-AM - 1410 **(16005)**

Long Prairie
KEYL-AM - 1400 **(16010)**

Minneapolis
KFAI-FM - 90.3 & 106.7 **(16149)**
WCCO-AM - 830 **(16159)**

Pine City
WCMP-AM - 1350 **(16269)**

Pipestone
KLOH-AM - 1050 **(16277)**

Roseau
KCAJ-FM - 102.1 **(16329)**

St. Cloud
WJON-AM - 1240 **(16353)**

Thief River Falls
KTRF-AM - 1230 **(16473)**

Winona
KQAL-FM - 89.5 **(16534)**

MISSISSIPPI
Canton
WMGO-AM - 1370 **(16585)**

Meridian
WMAW-FM - 88.1 **(16776)**

Natchez
WNAT-AM - 1450 **(16795)**

MISSOURI
Bowling Green
WBOW-AM - 640 **(16920)**

Cape Girardeau
KRCU-FM - 90.9 **(16953)**

Kansas City
KKFI-FM - 90.1 **(17209)**

Kirksville
KIRX-AM - 1450 **(17230)**

Moberly
KWIX-AM - 1230 **(17291)**

Overland
KRHS-FM - 90.1 **(17327)**

Salem
KSMO-AM - 1340 **(17564)**

Versailles
KTKS-FM - 95.1 **(17664)**

MONTANA
Bozeman
KBOZ-AM - 1090 **(17754)**

Lewistown
KXLO-AM - 1230 **(17850)**

Plentywood
KATQ-AM - 1070 **(17895)**
KATQ-FM - 100.1 **(17896)**

NEBRASKA
Broken Bow
KCNI-AM - 1280 **(17967)**

Lincoln
KFOR-AM - 1240 **(18133)**

West Point
KTIC-AM - 840 **(18313)**
KWPN-FM - 107.9 **(18314)**

York
KAWL-AM - 1370 **(18322)**

NEW HAMPSHIRE
Durham
WUNH-FM - 91.3 **(18504)**

NEW JERSEY
Bridgeton
WSNJ-AM - 1240 **(18691)**
WSNJ-FM - 107.7 **(18692)**

Hackettstown
WRNJ-AM - 1510 **(18860)**

Jersey City
WFMU-FM - 91.1 **(19149)**

Pomona
WLFR-FM - 91.7 **(19449)**

Princeton
WHWH-AM - 1350 **(19480)**

NEW MEXICO
Albuquerque
KUNM-FM - 89.9 **(19815)**

Clovis
KWKA-AM - 680 **(19837)**

NEW YORK
Amsterdam
WCSS-AM - 1490 **(20058)**

Batavia
WBTA-AM - 1490 **(20122)**

Canton
WSLU-FM - 89.5 **(20433)**
WVNC-FM - 96.7 **(20434)**

Dansville
WDNY-AM - 1400 **(20520)**
WDNY-FM - 93.9 **(20521)**

Dunkirk
WDOE-AM - 1410 **(20538)**

Garden City
WHPC-FM - 90.3 **(20645)**

Geneva
WEOS-FM - 89.7 **(20657)**
WGVA-AM - 1240 **(20659)**

Glens Falls
WWSC-AM - 1450 **(20670)**

Gloversville
WENT-AM - 1340 **(20672)**

FULL SERVICE (continued)

Hornell
WLEA-AM - 1480 **(20758)**

Massena
WMSA-AM - 1340 **(21028)**

Patterson
WPUT-AM - 1510 **(23082)**

Pomona
WRKL-AM - 910 **(23113)**

Syosset
WKWZ-FM - 88.5 **(23385)**

NORTH CAROLINA
Asheville
WWNC-AM - 570 **(23640)**

Buies Creek
WCCE-FM - 90.1 **(23669)**

Chapel Hill
WXYC-FM - 89.3 **(23733)**

Greenville
WZMB-FM - 91.3 **(23976)**

Hendersonville
WHKP-AM - 1450 **(23985)**

Mars Hill
WVMH-FM - 90.5 **(24058)**

Mount Airy
WPAQ-AM - 740 **(24082)**

Rockingham
WLWL-AM - 770 **(24203)**

Rocky Mount
WEED-AM - 1390 **(24206)**

Salisbury
WSAT-AM - 1280 **(24217)**

Spindale
WNCW-FM - 88.7 **(24243)**

Sylva
WRGC-AM - 680 **(24252)**

Winston-Salem
WFDD-FM - 88.5 **(24330)**

OHIO
Akron
WAKR-AM - 1590 **(24594)**

Bryan
WBNO-FM - 100.9 **(24716)**

Canton
WHBC-AM - 1480 **(24734)**

Chillicothe
WBEX-AM - 1490 **(24765)**

Cleveland
WJCU-FM - 88.7 **(24975)**
WRUW-FM - 91.1 **(24985)**

Dover
WJER-AM - 1450 **(25165)**

Hamilton
WMOH-AM - 1450 **(25237)**

Wilberforce
WCSU-FM - 88.9 **(25653)**

Zanesville
WHIZ-AM - 1240 **(25720)**

OKLAHOMA
Okmulgee
KOKL-AM - 1240 **(26025)**

OREGON
Astoria
KMUN-FM - 91.9 **(26230)**

Coos Bay
KBBR-AM - 1340 **(26276)**

Grants Pass
KAJO-AM - 1270 **(26363)**

Newport
KBCH-AM - 1400 **(26446)**

Portland
KBOO-FM - 90.7 **(26519)**
KEX-AM - 1190 **(26525)**

PENNSYLVANIA
Aston
WPWA-AM - 1590 **(26667)**

Butler
WBUT-AM - 1050 **(26745)**

Franklin
WOYL-AM - 1340 **(26937)**

Indiana
WCCS-AM - 1160 **(27079)**

Meadville
WMGW-AM - 1490 **(27239)**

New Castle
WKST-AM - 1200 **(27318)**

North Versailles
WKHB-AM - 620 **(27343)**

Reading
WEEU-AM - 830 **(27921)**

Slippery Rock
WSRU-FM - 90.1 **(28001)**

State College
WPSU-FM - 91.5 **(28026)**

Uniontown
WMBS-AM - 590 **(28068)**

PUERTO RICO
Ponce
WLEO-AM - 1170 **(28278)**

San Juan
WKVM-AM - 810 **(28304)**

Yauco
WKFE-AM - 1550 **(28323)**

SOUTH DAKOTA
Aberdeen
KGIM-AM - 1420 **(28795)**

Pierre
KCCR-AM - 1240 **(28924)**

Sioux Falls
KSOO-AM - 1140 **(28984)**

TENNESSEE
Clarksville
WAPX-FM - 91.7 **(29117)**

Jamestown
WDEB-AM - 1500 **(29245)**
WDEB-FM - 103.9 **(29246)**

Memphis
WEVL-FM - 89.9 **(29392)**

Mountain City
WMCT-AM - 1390 **(29427)**

Paris
WTPR-AM - 710 **(29563)**

Sewanee
WUTS-FM - 91.3 **(29596)**

Winchester
WCDT-AM - 1340 **(29648)**

TEXAS
Abilene
KBCY-FM - 99.7 **(29658)**

Cameron
KMIL-AM - 1330 **(29996)**

Dallas
KERA-FM - 90.1 **(30203)**
KNON-FM - 89.3 **(30210)**

Floydada
KFLP-FM - 106.1 **(30324)**

Fort Worth
KTCU-FM - 88.7 **(30358)**

Jacksonville
KOOI-FM - 106.5 **(30618)**

Lampasas
KCYL-AM - 1450 **(30667)**

New Braunfels
KGNB-AM - 1420 **(30862)**

Seminole
KIKZ-AM - 1250 **(31099)**

Sulphur Springs
KSST-AM - 1230 **(31168)**

VERMONT
Bennington
WBTN-AM - 1370 **(31503)**

Middlebury
WFAD-AM - 1490 **(31560)**
WRMC-FM - 91.1 **(31562)**

Warren
WDEV-FM - 96.1 **(31611)**

Waterbury
WDEV-AM - 550 **(31612)**

VIRGINIA
Amherst
WAMV-AM - 1420 **(31762)**

Blacksburg
WVTW-FM - 88.5 **(31890)**

Danville
WBTM-AM - 1330 **(31993)**

Floyd
WGFC-AM - 1030 **(32077)**

Fredericksburg
WFVA-AM - 1230 **(32092)**

Galax
WBRF-FM - 98.1 **(32100)**

Gretna
WMNA-AM - 730 **(32119)**
WMNA-FM - 106.3 **(32120)**

Hillsville
WHHV-AM - 1400 **(32168)**

Leesburg
WAGE-AM - 1200 **(32188)**

Onley
WESR-FM - 103.3 **(32320)**

Roanoke
WKBA-AM - 1550 **(32500)**
WVTR-FM - 91.9 **(32508)**
WVZN-AM - 1170 **(32509)**

WASHINGTON
Aberdeen
KXRO-AM - 1320 **(32652)**

Bellevue
KBCS-FM - 91.3 **(32672)**

Bellingham
KGMI-AM - 790 **(32682)**

Moses Lake
KBSN-AM - 1470 **(32841)**

Tacoma
KUPS-FM - 90.1 **(33159)**

Walla Walla
KWCW-FM - 90.5 **(33190)**

WEST VIRGINIA
Fisher
WELD-FM - 101.7 **(33318)**

Kingwood
WFSP-FM - 107.7 **(33361)**

WISCONSIN
Appleton
WHBY-AM - 1150 **(33549)**

Beloit
WBCR-FM - 90.3 **(33578)**

Black River Falls
WWIS-FM - 99.7 **(33593)**

Manitowoc
WOMT-AM - 1240 **(34016)**

Numbers cited in bold after listings are entry numbers rather than page numbers.

Monroe
WEKZ-AM - 1260 (34152)

Ripon
WRPN-AM - 1600 (34305)

Sturgeon Bay
WDOR-AM - 910 (34354)

WYOMING
Newcastle
KASL-AM - 1240 (34565)

ALBERTA, CANADA
Calgary
CHQR-AM - 770 (34667)

Edmonton
CBX-AM - 740 (34740)

Medicine Hat
CHAT-AM - 1270 (34812)

Slave Lake
CKWA-AM - 1210 (34850)

BRITISH COLUMBIA, CANADA
Fort St. John
CKNL-AM - 560 (34960)

Vancouver
CITR-FM - 101.9 (35189)
CKNW-AM - 980 (35194)

Victoria
CFAX-AM - 1070 (35232)

MANITOBA, CANADA
Winnipeg
CKSB-AM - 1050 (35375)

NEWFOUNDLAND AND LABRADOR, CANADA
St. John's
CBN-AM - 640 (35495)
CBN-FM - 106.9 (35496)
CHMR-FM - 93.5 (35498)

NORTHWEST TERRITORIES, CANADA
Iqaluit
CFFB-AM - 1230 (35520)

ONTARIO, CANADA
Bancroft
CHMS-FM - 97.7 (35657)

Belleville
CJLX-FM - 92.3 (35682)

Cornwall
CJSS-AM - 1220 (35758)

Guelph
CFRU-FM - 93.3 (35868)

Ottawa
CKCU-FM - 93.1 (36293)

Thunder Bay
CBQ-FM - 88.3 (36445)

Waterloo
CKMS-FM - 100.3 (36862)

PRINCE EDWARD ISLAND, CANADA
Summerside
CJRW-AM - 102.1 (36926)

QUEBEC, CANADA
Amqui
CFVM-AM - 99.9 (36936)

Asbestos
CJAN-FM - 99.3 (36942)

Jonquiere
CHOC-FM - 92.5 (37015)

Plessisville
CKYQ-FM - 95.7 (37270)

Sainte-Foy
CBV-AM - 980 (37376)

SASKATCHEWAN, CANADA
Melfort
CJVR-AM - 750 (37499)

GOSPEL

ALABAMA
Anniston
WANA-AM - 1490 (18)

Ashland
WASZ-FM - 95.5 (25)
WZZX-AM - 780 (26)

Atmore
WPHG-AM - 1620 (36)

Birmingham
WJLD-AM - 1400 (118)

Boaz
WBSA-AM - 1300 (135)

Calera
WBYE-AM - 1370 (142)

Camden
WCOX-AM - 1450 (144)
WCOX-FM - 102.3 (145)

Carrollton
WRAG-AM - 590 (147)

Cullman
WFMH-AM - 1460 (164)

Decatur
WJRA-AM - 1310 (174)

Eva
WRJL-AM - 1170 (209)

Hamilton
WERH-AM - 970 (262)

Huntsville
WDJL-AM - 1000 (281)

Moody
WURL-AM - 760 (395)

Russellville
WKAX-AM - 1500 (442)

Sheffield
WBTG-FM - 106.3 (458)

Sylacauga
WYEA-AM - 1290 (464)

Tuscaloosa
WACT-AM - 1420 (495)
WWPG-AM - 1280 (505)

Tuscumbia
WZZA-AM - 1410 (506)

Wetumpka
WAPZ-AM - 1250 (516)

ARKANSAS
Fordyce
KBJT-AM - 1570 (1136)

North Little Rock
KLRG-AM - 1150 (1301)
KMTL-AM - 760 (1302)

COLORADO
Fountain
KWYD-AM - 1580 (4453)

CONNECTICUT
Danbury
WRNE-AM - 980 (4767)

Hartford
WQTQ-FM - 89.9 (4909)

DELAWARE
Wilmington
WFAI-AM - 1510 (5298)

DISTRICT OF COLUMBIA
Washington
WPGC-AM - 1580 (5891)

FLORIDA
Blountstown
WYBT-AM - 1000 (5927)

Chiefland
WLQH-AM - 940 (5982)

WLQH-FM - 97.3 (5983)

Fort Myers
WCRM-AM - 1350 (6102)

Jacksonville
WZAZ-AM - 1400 (6245)

Miami Beach
WMBM-AM - 1490 (6418)

Milton
WECM-AM - 1490 (6427)

Port Charlotte
WVIJ-FM - 91.7 (6597)

Stuart
WRBD-AM - 1470 (6697)

Tallahassee
WHBT-AM - 1410 (6750)

Zolfo Springs
WZTK-AM - 1480 (6895)

GEORGIA
Athens
WBKZ-AM - 880 (6955)

Augusta
WFAM-AM - 1050 (7108)
WKZK-AM - 1600 (7111)
WTHB-AM - 1550 (7114)

Bainbridge
WMGR-AM - 930 (7120)

Baxley
WUFE-AM - 1260 (7126)

Claxton
WCLA-AM - 1470 (7172)

Columbus
WEAM-AM - 1580 (7188)

Conyers
WPBS-AM - 1040am (7202)

Cornelia
WCON-AM - 1450 (7208)

Douglasville
WDCY-AM - 1520 (7250)

Jasper
WLJA-FM - 93.5 (7342)
WYYZ-AM - 1490 (7344)

Macon
WBML-AM - 900 (7390)
WDDO-AM - 1240 (7392)
WVMG-AM - 1440 (7404)
WVMG-FM - 96.7 (7405)

Monroe
WKUN-AM - 1580 (7444)

Moultrie
WMTM-AM - 1300 (7447)

Mountain City
WALH-AM - 1340 (7450)

Quitman
WSFB-AM - 1490 (7487)

Rockmart
WZOT-AM - 1220 (7501)

Sandersville
WSNT-AM - 1490 (7528)

Savannah
WHCJ-FM - 90.3 (7544)

Summerville
WGTA-AM - 950 (7577)

West Point
WCJM-FM - 100.9 (7651)

ILLINOIS
Ava
WXAN-FM - 103.9 (8046)

INDIANA
Elkhart
WFRN-AM - 1270 (9925)

French Lick
WFLQ-FM - 100.1 (10012)

GOSPEL (continued)

Salem
WSLM-FM - 97.9 **(10443)**

South Bend
WUBS-FM - 89.7 **(10468)**

Washington
WAMW-AM - 1580 **(10541)**

IOWA
Sioux City
KTFC-FM - 103.3 **(11223)**

Waterloo
KBBG-FM - 88.1 **(11290)**

KANSAS
Meade
KHYM-FM - 103.9 **(11647)**

KENTUCKY
Barbourville
WYWY-AM - 950 **(11924)**

Cadiz
WKDZ-AM - 1110 **(12004)**

Falmouth
WIOK-FM - 107.5 **(12056)**

Garrison
WOKE-FM - 98.3 **(12086)**

Latonia
WCVG-AM - 1320 **(12153)**

Louisville
WLLV-AM - 1240 **(12259)**

Morganfield
WMSK-AM - 1550 **(12308)**

Paintsville
WSIP-AM - 1490 **(12351)**

Williamsburg
WEKC-AM - 710 **(12446)**

LOUISIANA
Baton Rouge
WNDC-AM - 910 **(12522)**

Bogalusa
WIKC-AM - 1490 **(12535)**

Buras
KAGY-AM - 1510 **(12543)**

Columbia
KCTO-AM - 1540 **(12550)**

Lafayette
KNEK-AM - 1190 **(12629)**

Lake Charles
KLCL-AM - 1470 **(12646)**

Lake Providence
KLPL-AM - 1050 **(12653)**

New Orleans
WYLD-AM - 940 **(12785)**

Shreveport
KIOU-AM - 1480 **(12826)**

MARYLAND
Baltimore
WCAO-AM - 600 **(13269)**
WEAA-FM - 88.9 **(13270)**
WWIN-AM - 1400 **(13286)**

Braddock Heights
WJTM-FM - 88.1 **(13394)**

Mountain Lake Park
WMSG-AM - 1050 **(13634)**

Princess Anne
WESM-FM - 91.3 **(13670)**

MICHIGAN
Detroit
WMKM-AM - 1440 **(14971)**

Flint
WFLT-AM - 1420 **(15043)**

Midland
WUGN-FM - 99.7 **(15357)**

MISSISSIPPI
Belzoni
WELZ-AM - 1460 **(16561)**

Brandon
WRKN-AM - 970 **(16576)**

Brookhaven
WCHJ-AM - 1470 **(16580)**

Columbia
WCJU-AM - 1450 **(16600)**

Corinth
WKCU-AM - 1350 **(16618)**

Greenwood
WGRM-AM - 1240 **(16648)**
WGRM-FM - 93.9 **(16649)**
WKXG-AM - 1540 **(16650)**

Hattiesburg
WAML-AM - 1340 **(16667)**
WEEZ-FM - 99.3 **(16670)**
WORV-AM - 1580 **(16676)**

Holly Springs
WKRA-AM - 1110 **(16682)**

Houston
WCPC-AM - 940 **(16686)**

Indianola
WNLA-AM - 1380 **(16688)**

Jackson
WMPR-FM - 90.1 **(16726)**
WRTM-AM - 1490 **(16730)**
WZRX-AM - 1590 **(16733)**

Lorman
WPRL-FM - 91.7 **(16749)**

Meridian
WNBN-AM - 1290 **(16778)**

Natchez
WMIS-AM - 1240 **(16794)**

Picayune
WRJW-AM - 1320 **(16821)**

Senatobia
WSAO-AM - 1140 **(16844)**

West Point
WROB-AM - 1450 **(16876)**

Wiggins
WLUN-FM - 95.3 **(16878)**

Yazoo City
WJNS-FM - 92.1 **(16884)**

MISSOURI
Branson
KOMC-AM - 1220 **(16922)**

Kansas City
KPRT-AM - 1590 **(17213)**

Neosho
KNEO-FM - 91.7 **(17307)**

Piedmont
KPWB-AM - 1140 **(17344)**

St. Charles
KIRL-AM - 1460 **(17386)**

Sikeston
KRHW-AM - 1520 **(17586)**

Trenton
KTTN-FM - 92.3 **(17655)**

NEW HAMPSHIRE
Dover
WWNH-AM - 1340 **(18497)**

NEW JERSEY
Linwood
WUSS-AM - 1490 **(19176)**

NEW MEXICO
Truth or Consequences
KCHS-AM - 1400 **(19970)**

NEW YORK
Buffalo
WMNY-AM - 1120 **(20407)**
WUFO-AM - 1080 **(20412)**

East Syracuse
WSIV-AM - 1540 **(20560)**

Mineola
WTHE-AM - 1520 **(21087)**

Rochester
WWWG-AM - 1460 **(23257)**

NORTH CAROLINA
Ahoskie
WRCS-AM - 970 **(23616)**

Asheboro
WZOO-AM - 710 **(23625)**

Asheville
WKJV-AM - 1380 **(23637)**

Charlotte
WBAV-AM - 1600 **(23763)**

Dobson
WYZD-AM - 1560 **(23802)**

Dunn
WCKB-AM - 780 **(23804)**

Edenton
WBXB-FM - 100.1 **(23857)**

Elizabeth City
WGAI-AM - 560 **(23862)**

Farmville
WGHB-AM - 1250 **(23878)**

Fayetteville
WIDU-AM - 1600 **(23888)**

Goldsboro
WFMC-AM - 730 **(23911)**

Greensboro
WNAA-FM - 90.1 **(23954)**

Greenville
WOOW-AM - 1340 **(23975)**

High Point
WOKX-AM - 1590 **(24006)**

Jacksonville
WJCV-AM - 1290 **(24012)**

King
WKTE-AM - 1090 **(24024)**

Kings Mountain
WKMT-AM - 1220 **(24026)**

Kinston
WELS-AM - 1010 **(24029)**
WELS-FM - 102.9 **(24030)**

Morganton
WCIS-AM - 760 **(24076)**

Mount Airy
WSYD-AM - 1300 **(24083)**

New Bern
WLOJ-AM - 1490 **(24100)**

Oxford
WCBQ-AM - 1340 **(24112)**
WHNC-AM - 890 **(24113)**

Pisgah Forest
WGCR-AM - 720 **(24117)**

Roanoke Rapids
WSMY-AM - 1400 **(24197)**

St. Pauls
WKKE-AM - 1080 **(24214)**

Sanford
WXKL-AM - 1290 **(24222)**

Smithfield
WMPM-AM - 1270 **(24233)**

Whiteville
WENC-AM - 1220 **(24286)**

Wilmington
WWIL-AM - 1490 **(24307)**

Wilson
WGTM-AM - 590 **(24313)**

NORTH DAKOTA
Belcourt
KEYA-FM - 88.5 **(24346)**

Numbers cited in bold after listings are entry numbers rather than page numbers.

OHIO
Cleveland
WABQ-AM - 1540 (24967)

Columbus
WVKO-AM - 1580 (25089)

Dayton
WGNZ-AM - 1110 (25138)

Englewood
WLPM-AM - 1450 (25183)

Steubenville
WDIG-AM - 950 (25541)

Wilmington
WKFI-AM - 1090 (25668)

Youngstown
WGFT-FM - 101.1 (25705)

OKLAHOMA
Tulsa
KMSI-FM - 88.1 (26152)

PENNSYLVANIA
Lafayette Hill
KWFT-AM - 990 (27136)

Norristown
WNAP-AM - 1110 (27338)

PUERTO RICO
Santurce
WNRT-FM - 96.9 (28316)

SOUTH CAROLINA
Charleston
WMCJ-AM - 950 (28523)

Cheraw
WCRE-AM - 1420 (28529)

Clemson
WAHT-AM - 1560 (28536)

Greenville
WGVL-AM - 1440 (28632)

Hemingway
WLGI-FM - 90.9 (28660)

Kershaw
WKSC-AM - 1300 (28672)

St. George
WQIZ-AM - 810 (28751)

Walterboro
WALD-AM - 1080 (28782)

West Columbia
WGCV-AM - 620 (28783)

SOUTH DAKOTA
Sioux Falls
KNWC-AM - 1270 (28979)
KNWC-FM - 96.5 (28980)

TENNESSEE
Bristol
WBCV-AM - 1550 (29067)

Chattanooga
WFLI-AM - 1070 (29102)

Cowan
WZYX-AM - 1440 (29156)

Crossville
WAEW-AM - 1330 (29160)

Erwin
WEMB-AM - 1420 (29185)

Jamestown
WDEB-AM - 1500 (29245)
WDEB-FM - 103.9 (29246)

Jellico
WJJT-AM - 1540 (29249)

La Follette
WLAF-AM - 1450 (29310)

Lafayette
WEEN-AM - 1460 (29313)

Loudon
WLOD-AM - 1140 (29335)

Memphis
WLOK-AM - 1340 (29402)

Mountain City
WMCT-AM - 1390 (29427)

Nashville
WFSK-FM - 88.1 (29510)
WMDB-AM - 880 (29520)
WNAH-AM - 1360 (29521)

Parsons
WKJQ-AM - 1550 (29564)

Rockwood
WOFE-AM - 580 (29579)

Rogersville
WRGS-AM - 1370 (29582)

Shelbyville
WLIJ-AM - 1580 (29602)

Tazewell
WNTT-AM - 1250 (29626)

Wartburg
WECO-AM - 940 (29640)

TEXAS
Austin
KAZI-FM - 88.7 (29860)

Beaumont
KQHN-AM - 1510 (29908)

Bridgeport
KBOC-FM - 98.3 (29952)

Carthage
KGAS-AM - 1590 (30006)

Dallas
KHVN-AM - 970 (30207)

Fairfield
KNES-FM - 99.1 (30312)

Hereford
KNNK-FM - 100.5 (30445)

Levelland
KLVT-AM - 1230 (30683)

Longview
KJTX-FM - 104.5 (30706)

Marshall
KBWC-FM - 91.1 (30767)

Midland
KJBC-AM - 1150 (30818)

New Boston
KNBO-AM - 1530 (30861)

Prairie View
KPVU-FM - 91.3 (30962)

Waco
KRZI-AM - 1580 (31260)

VIRGINIA
Blacksburg
WBGS-AM - 1030 (31883)

Broadway
WBTX-AM - 1470 (31903)

Chester
WROU-AM - 1240 (31969)

Danville
WILA-AM - 1580 (31994)
WVOV-AM - 970 (31995)

Duffield
WDUF-AM - 1120 (32000)

Fairlawn
WKNV-AM - 890 (32038)

Farmville
WAMF-AM - 1490 (32069)

Franklin
WLQM-AM - 1250 (32082)

Galax
WWWJ-AM - 1360 (32101)

Hampton
WHOV-FM - 88.1 (32133)
WTJZ-AM - 1270 (32135)

Marion
WOLD-AM - 1330 (32230)

Pound
WKVG-AM - 1000 (32337)

Richmond
WFTH-AM - 1590 (32477)

Rocky Mount
WYTI-AM - 1570 (32513)

Triangle
WPWC-AM - 1480 (32571)

WASHINGTON
Blaine
KARI-AM - 550 (32689)

Pasco
KGSG-FM - 93.7 (32881)

WEST VIRGINIA
Kingwood
WFSP-AM - 1560 (33360)

Lost Creek
WOTR-FM - 96.3 (33373)

Point Pleasant
WPCN-FM - 88.1 (33440)

WISCONSIN
Milwaukee
WGLB-AM - 1560 (34118)
WNOV-AM - 860 (34134)

ALBERTA, CANADA
Edmonton
CJCA-AM - 930 (34752)

NEWFOUNDLAND AND LABRADOR, CANADA
Mount Pearl
VOAR-AM - 1210 (35475)

HAWAIIAN

HAWAII
Hilo
KAHU-AM - 1060 (7672)
KWXX-FM - 94.7 (7678)

HEAVY METAL

CONNECTICUT
West Haven
WNHU-FM - 88.7 (5208)

IOWA
Dubuque
KLCR-FM - 96.9 (10851)

NEW HAMPSHIRE
Hanover
WDCR-AM - 1340 (18520)

NEW JERSEY
Flemington
WCVH-FM - 90.5 (18822)

Upper Montclair
WMSC-FM - 90.3 (19695)

NEW YORK
Cortland
WSUC-FM - 90.5 (20514)

Ithaca
WICB-FM - 105.9 (20820)

Rooseveltown
CKON-FM - 97.3 (23276)

NORTH CAROLINA
Mars Hill
WVMH-FM - 90.5 (24058)

Raleigh
WKNC-FM - 88.1 (24164)

Circulation: ★ = ABC; △ = BPA; ♦ = CAC; • = CCAB; ❑ = VAC; ⊕ = PO Statement; ‡ = Publisher's Report; Boldface figures = sworn; Light figures = estimated.

3029

Radio Station Formats

HEAVY METAL (continued)

PENNSYLVANIA
Bloomsburg
WBUQ-FM - 91.1 **(26720)**

Millersville
WIXQ-FM - 91.7 **(27268)**

Wilkes Barre
WCLH-FM - 90.7 **(28174)**

VERMONT
Lyndonville
WWLR-FM - 91.5 **(31551)**

HIP HOP

ALABAMA
Wetumpka
WAPZ-AM - 1250 **(516)**

CALIFORNIA
Fresno
KFSR-FM - 90.7 **(1967)**

COLORADO
Denver
KQKS-FM - 107.5 **(4387)**

CONNECTICUT
Hartford
WQTQ-FM - 89.9 **(4909)**

NEW HAMPSHIRE
Henniker
WNEC-FM - 91.7 **(18523)**

NEW JERSEY
Teaneck
WFDQ-FM - 91.9 **(19611)**

NEW MEXICO
Farmington
KNMI-FM - 88.9 **(19849)**

NEW YORK
New York
WPUB-AM - 640 **(22987)**

NORTH CAROLINA
Raleigh
WKNC-FM - 88.1 **(24164)**

NORTH DAKOTA
Minot
KMSU - 19 **(24511)**

OHIO
Alliance
WRMU-FM - 91.1 **(24607)**

OKLAHOMA
Langston
KALU-FM - 89.3 **(25882)**

TEXAS
Austin
KAZI-FM - 88.7 **(29860)**

Houston
KPTY-FM - 104.9 **(30571)**

QUEBEC, CANADA
Kahnawake
CKRK-FM - 103.7 **(37019)**

HISPANIC

ARIZONA
Douglas
KAPR-AM - 930 **(688)**
KDAP-AM - 1450 **(689)**

Globe
KJAA-AM - 1240 **(720)**

Phoenix
KIDR-AM - 740 **(822)**
KPHX-AM - 1480 **(833)**
KSUN-AM - 1400 **(838)**

Tucson
KHRR-AM - 101.7 **(980)**

ARKANSAS
De Queen
KDQN-AM - 1390 **(1101)**

Fayetteville
KZRA-AM - 1590 **(1132)**

Van Buren
KAYR-AM - 1060 **(1359)**

CALIFORNIA
Bakersfield
KCHJ-AM - 1010 **(1458)**
KIWI-FM - 92.1 **(1466)**
KSPL-FM - 102.9 **(1470)**
KWAC-AM - 1490 **(1475)**

Brawley
KMXX-FM - 99.3 **(1596)**

Calexico
KICO-AM - 1490 **(1637)**
KQVO-FM - 97.7 **(1638)**

Camarillo
KEYQ-AM - 980 **(1644)**
KGZO-FM - 90.9 **(1645)**
KMRO-FM - 90.3 **(1647)**

Chula Vista
XLTN-FM - 104.5 **(1718)**

Corona
KWRM-AM - 1370 **(1769)**

Fresno
KHOT-AM - 1250 **(1971)**
KOQO-AM - 790 **(1979)**
KOQO-FM - 101.9 **(1980)**
KQEQ-AM - 1210 **(1981)**
KTRB-AM - 860 **(1985)**

Glendale
KLTX-AM - 1390 **(2018)**
KTNQ-AM - 1020 **(2021)**

Hanford
KIGS-AM - 620 **(2039)**

Hollywood
KWKW-AM - 1330 **(2054)**

Lemoore
KJOP-AM - 1240 **(2153)**

Los Angeles
KVCA-AM - 670 **(2471)**

Merced
KLOQ-FM - 98.7 **(2533)**

Oxnard
KMLA-FM - 103.7 **(2733)**
KOXR-AM - 910 **(2734)**

Palm Desert
KESQ-AM - 1400 **(2748)**
KUNA-FM - 96.7 **(2752)**

Palm Springs
KCLB-AM - 970 **(2771)**

Reseda
KOJJ-FM - 100.5 **(2918)**

Riverside
KDIF-AM - 1440 **(2950)**
KVAR-AM - 1160 **(2955)**

Sacramento
KZCO-FM - 97.7 **(3060)**

Salinas
KDBV-AM - 980 **(3069)**
KRAY-FM - 103.5 **(3074)**

San Francisco
KIQI-AM - 1010 **(3486)**
KSOL-FM - 98.9 **(3501)**

San Jose
KAZA-AM - 1290 **(3546)**

San Ysidro
XEBG-AM - 1550 **(3608)**
XEMBC-AM - 1190 **(3609)**

XEMMM-AM - 800 **(3610)**
XEWV-AM - 940 **(3611)**
XEWV-FM - 106.7 **(3612)**
XEYX-AM - 820 **(3613)**

Santa Ana
KWIZ-FM - 96.7 **(3638)**

Santa Maria
KTAP-AM - 1600 **(3702)**

Santa Rosa
KBBF-FM - 89.1 **(3737)**
KRRS-AM - 1460 **(3740)**

Stockton
KLOC-AM - 920 **(3812)**
KMIX-AM - 1390 **(3813)**
KMIX-FM - 100.9 **(3814)**

Tulare
KGEN-AM - 1370-AM **(3953)**
KGEN-FM - 94.5 **(3954)**

Victorville
KWRN-AM - 1550 **(4038)**

COLORADO
Alamosa
KRZA-FM - 88.7 **(4136)**

Denver
KBNO-AM - 1280 **(4372)**
KJME-AM - 1390 **(4381)**

Pueblo
KRMX-AM - 107.1 **(4608)**

Windsor
KVVS-AM - 1170 **(4689)**

CONNECTICUT
Bridgeport
WCUM-AM - 1450 **(4716)**

Hartford
WLAT-AM - 910 **(4905)**
WPRX-AM - 1120 **(4908)**

Newington
WRYM-AM - 840 **(5038)**

DELAWARE
Milford
WYUS-AM - 930 **(5264)**

FLORIDA
Avon Park
WAVP-AM - 1390 **(5914)**

Casselberry
WONQ-AM - 1030 **(5977)**
WRMQ-AM - 1140 **(5978)**

Homestead
WOIR-AM - 1430 **(6206)**

Kissimmee
WFIV-AM - 1080 **(6266)**

Miami
WKAT-AM - 1360 **(6400)**
WOCN-AM - 1450 **(6409)**
WSUA-AM - 1260 **(6415)**

North Miami
WLQY-AM - 1320 **(6467)**

Orlando
WXTO-AM - 1600 **(6531)**

Tampa
WAMA-AM - 1550 **(6784)**

West Palm Beach
WWRF-AM - 1380 **(6861)**

Winter Haven
WSIR-AM - 1490 **(6876)**

GEORGIA
Athens
WBKZ-AM - 880 **(6955)**

Austell
WAOS-AM - 1460 **(7116)**

Smyrna
WAZX-AM - 1550 **(7556)**

Numbers cited in bold after listings are entry numbers rather than page numbers.

IDAHO
Boise
KWEI-FM - 99.5 **(7833)**

ILLINOIS
Chicago
WIND-AM - 560 **(8630)**
WLEY-FM - 107.9 **(8636)**
WOJO-FM - 105.1 **(8648)**
WRZA-FM - 99.9 **(8650)**

Evanston
WONX-AM - 1590 **(8877)**

IOWA
Sioux City
KWIT-FM - 90.3 **(11225)**

LOUISIANA
New Orleans
KGLA-AM - 1540 **(12764)**

MARYLAND
Laurel
WILC-AM-VIVA900 - 900 **(13614)**

MASSACHUSETTS
Cambridge
WRCA-AM - 1330 **(14117)**

Methuen
WHAV-AM - 1490 **(14330)**

West Springfield
WACM-AM - 1490 **(14626)**

MICHIGAN
Wyoming
WYGR-AM - 1530 **(15688)**

MINNESOTA
Chaska
KSMM-AM - 1530 **(15795)**

NEVADA
Las Vegas
KDOX-AM - 1280 **(18393)**
KLSQ-AM - 870 **(18400)**

Reno
KXEQ-AM - 1340 **(18444)**

NEW HAMPSHIRE
Salem
WNNW-AM - 1110 **(18646)**

NEW JERSEY
Paterson
WWRV-AM - 1330 **(19418)**

Vineland
WMIZ-AM - 1270 **(19701)**

NEW MEXICO
Albuquerque
KEXT-FM - 104.7 **(19798)**
KRZY-FM - 105.9 **(19811)**

Belen
KARS-AM - 860 **(19821)**

Deming
KOTS-AM - 1230 **(19842)**

Espanola
KDCE-AM - 950 **(19845)**

Hobbs
KLMA-FM - 96.5 **(19867)**
KPZA-FM - 103.7 **(19869)**

Las Vegas
KFUN-AM - 1230 **(19891)**

Roswell
KPSA-AM - 1230 **(19923)**
KPSA-FM - 106.1 **(19924)**

Santa Fe
KSWV-AM - 810 **(19950)**

Taos
KKIT-AM - 1340 **(19964)**

NEW YORK
New York
WHCR-FM - 90.3 **(22970)**
WKDM-AM - 1380 **(22973)**
WPAT-FM - 93.1 **(22984)**
WSKQ-FM - 97.9 **(22992)**

Poughkeepsie
WALL-AM - 1340 **(23152)**
WEOK-AM - 1390 **(23157)**

NORTH CAROLINA
Charlotte
WNOW-AM - 1030 **(23776)**

Claremont
WCXN-AM - 1170 **(23786)**

Dallas
WSGE-FM - 91.7 **(23797)**

OKLAHOMA
El Reno
KZUE-AM - 1460 **(25817)**

OREGON
Medford
KRTA-AM - 610 **(26426)**

PENNSYLVANIA
Allentown
WHOL-AM - 1600 **(26632)**

Bala Cynwyd
WTEL-AM - 860 **(26680)**

Lafayette Hill
KWFS-AM - 1290 **(27134)**

Lancaster
WLCH-FM - 91.3 **(27154)**

PUERTO RICO
Arecibo
WMIA-AM - 1070 **(28226)**
WNIK-FM - 106.5 **(28229)**

Bayamon
WLUZ-AM - 1600 **(28232)**

Caguas
WVJP-AM - 1110 **(28236)**
WVJP-FM - 103.3 **(28237)**

Cidra
WBRQ-FM - 97.7 **(28240)**

Fajardo
WDOY-FM - 96.5 **(28243)**
WMDD-AM - 1480 **(28244)**

Isabela
WISA-AM - 1390 **(28252)**

Lares
WGDL-AM - 1200 **(28254)**

Luquillo
WZOL-FM - 92.1 **(28256)**

Mayaguez
WAEL-FM - 96.1 **(28259)**
WIOB-FM - 97.5 **(28261)**
WORA-AM - 760 **(28265)**
WPRA-AM - 990 **(28268)**
WTIL-AM - 1300 **(28269)**
WTPM-FM - 92.9 **(28270)**

Naguabo
WYQE-FM - 92.9 **(28273)**

Ponce
WEUC-AM - 1420 **(28275)**
WEUC-FM - 88.9 **(28276)**
WLEO-AM - 1170 **(28278)**
WOQI-FM - 93.3 **(28279)**
WPAB-AM - 550 **(28280)**
WPRP-AM - 910 **(28282)**
WZAR-FM - 101.9 **(28284)**

Salinas
WHOY-AM - 1210 **(28288)**

San Juan
WCAD-FM - 105.7 **(28298)**
WIPR-FM - 91.3 **(28300)**
WKAQ-AM - 580 **(28302)**
WKAQ-FM - 104.7 **(28303)**
WQII-AM - 1140 **(28307)**
WRSJ-AM - 1560 **(28308)**

WUNO-AM - 1320 **(28311)**
WZNT-FM - 93.7 **(28313)**

San Sebastian
WLRP-AM - 1460 **(28314)**

Vega Baja
WEGA-AM - 1350 **(28320)**

Vieques
WSAN-FM - 98.9 **(28321)**

Yabucoa
WXEW-AM - 840 **(28322)**

TENNESSEE
Brownsville
WNWS-AM - 1520 **(29073)**

Franklin
WHEW-AM - 1380 **(29200)**

Memphis
WGSF-AM - 1210 **(29394)**

Nashville
WKDA-AM - 1200 **(29514)**

TEXAS
Alamo
KJAV-FM - 104.9 **(29674)**

Alice
KOPY-AM - 1070 **(29679)**

Arlington
KTNO-AM - 1540 **(29742)**

Austin
KELG-AM - 1440 **(29861)**

Brownfield
KKUB-AM - 1300 **(29954)**

Brownsville
KBNR-FM - 88.3 **(29961)**
KBOR-AM - 1700 **(29962)**
KTJN-FM - 106 **(29963)**

Brownwood
KXYL-AM - 1240 **(29971)**

Bryan
KTAM-AM - 1240 **(29982)**

Carrizo Springs
KBEN-AM - 1450 **(30003)**

College Station
KBMA-FM - 99.5 **(30059)**

Comanche
KCOM-AM - 1550 **(30066)**

Corpus Christi
KCCT-AM - 1150 **(30081)**
KEDT-FM - 90.3 **(30082)**
KSAB-FM - 99.9 **(30095)**

Corsicana
KICI-FM - 107.9 **(30104)**

Dallas
KESS-AM - 1270 **(30205)**
KXEB-AM - 910 **(30215)**

Dumas
KDDD-AM - 800 **(30252)**

Eagle Pass
XEMU-AM - 580 **(30261)**

Edinburg
KRIO-AM - 910 **(30273)**

El Paso
KBNA-AM - 920 **(30285)**
KBNA-FM - 97.5 **(30286)**
KINT-FM - 93.9 **(30294)**
KVER-FM - 91.1 FM **(30303)**

Fort Stockton
KFST-FM - 94.3 **(30328)**

Fort Worth
KFJZ-AM - 870 **(30357)**

Houston
KLAT-AM - 1010 **(30561)**
KXYZ-AM - 1320 **(30586)**

Laredo
KBNL-FM - 89.9 **(30671)**
KDOS-AM - 1490 **(30672)**

Radio Station Formats

HISPANIC (continued)

Lubbock
KLFB-AM - 1420 (30729)

Mc Kinney
KTCY-FM - 104.9 (30782)

McAllen
KCZO-FM - 92.1 (30792)
KEPX-FM - 89.5 (30794)
KIRT-AM - 1580 (30796)
KKPS-FM - 99.5 (30797)
KQXX-FM - 98.5 (30798)

Odessa
KNDA-AM - 1000 (30877)
KOZA-AM - 1230 (30880)

Pearsall
KVWG-AM - 1280 (30921)
KVWG-FM - 95.3 (30922)

Pecos
KIUN-AM - 1400 (30925)

Plainview
KVOP-AM - 1090 (30944)

Port Lavaca
KGUL-AM - 1560 (30959)

Quanah
KVDL-AM - 1150 (30965)

San Angelo
KSJT-FM - 107.5 (31021)

San Antonio
KCOR-AM - 1350 (31053)
KEDA-AM - 1540 (31056)
KSAH-AM - 720 (31068)

Seminole
KIKZ-AM - 1250 (31099)

Waco
KRZI-AM - 1580 (31260)

Weslaco
KRGE-AM - 1290 (31279)

UTAH
Hooper
KSVN-AM - 730 (31339)

Ogden
KYFO-AM - 1490 (31383)

VIRGINIA
Fredericksburg
WYSK-AM - 1350 (32093)

WASHINGTON
Aberdeen
KBKW-AM - 1450 (32648)

Mount Vernon
KSVR-FM - 90.1 (32849)

Wenatchee
KWWX-AM - 1340 (33203)

Yakima
KDNA-FM - 91.9 (33227)
KZTB-FM - 96.7 (33237)
KZTS-AM - 1210 (33238)

WYOMING
Rawlins
KRAL-AM - 1240 (34574)

HOT COUNTRY

ALABAMA
Anniston
WHMA-FM - 100.5 (22)

ALASKA
Anchorage
KBRJ-FM - 104.1 (537)

Juneau
KTKU-FM - 105.1 (603)

ARIZONA
Cottonwood
KVRD-FM - 105.7 (682)

ARKANSAS
Bryant
KCDI-FM - 93.3 (1066)

Fort Smith
KTCS-FM - 99.9 (1156)

COLORADO
Longmont
KLMO-AM - 1060 (4564)

Yuma
KATR-FM - 98.3 (4695)

FLORIDA
Live Oak
WQHL-FM - 98.1 (6309)

GEORGIA
Savannah
WJCL-FM - 96.5 (7545)

IDAHO
Grangeville
KORT-AM - 1230 (7858)
KORT-FM - 92.7 (7859)

Idaho Falls
KID-FM - 96.1 (7875)

Lewiston
KMOK-FM - 106.9 (7898)

ILLINOIS
Bloomington
WBWN-FM - 104.1 (8083)

Mount Carmel
WSJD-FM - 100.5 (9232)

INDIANA
Frankfort
KFAV-FM - 99.9 (10001)

Princeton
WRAY-AM - 1250 (10410)
WRAY-FM - 98.1 (10411)

Richmond
WQLK-FM - 96.1 (10427)

IOWA
Fort Dodge
KIAQ-FM - 96.9 (10908)

Storm Lake
KKIA-FM - 92.9 (11250)

KANSAS
Great Bend
KHOK-FM - 100.7 (11470)

Phillipsburg
KKAN-AM - 1490 (11749)
KQMA-FM - 92.5 (11750)

KENTUCKY
Jackson
WEKG-AM - 810 (12146)
WJSN-FM - 106.5 (12147)

West Liberty
WLKS-FM - 102.9 (12433)

MAINE
Presque Isle
WBPW-FM - 96.9 (13038)

MICHIGAN
Hastings
WBCH-AM - 1220 (15156)

MINNESOTA
Detroit Lakes
KBOT-FM - 104.1 (15831)

Fergus Falls
KJJK-FM - 96.5 (15902)

Spring Grove
KQYB-FM - 98.3 (16456)

Winona
KWNO-FM - 99.3 (16536)

MISSISSIPPI
Bay St. Louis
WBSL-AM - 1190 (16553)

Tupelo
WZLQ-FM - 98.5 (16861)

MISSOURI
Farmington
KYLS-FM - 95.9 (17057)

Trenton
KGOZ-FM - 101.7 (17653)

MONTANA
Billings
KIDX-FM - 98.5 (17741)

NEBRASKA
Gordon
KSDZ-FM - 95.5 (18023)

Lincoln
KFGE-FM - 98.1 (18132)

NEW MEXICO
Clovis
KKYC-FM - 102.3 (19835)

Roswell
KMOU-FM - 104.7 (19921)

Taos
KKIT-FM - 99.9 (19965)

NEW YORK
Geneva
WFLK-FM - 101.7 (20658)

Newark
WUUF-FM - 103.5 (23000)

Wellsville
WZKZ-FM - 101.9 (23536)

NORTH CAROLINA
Franklin
WNCC-FM - 96.7 (23900)

Greensboro
WHSL-FM - 100.3 (23947)

Morganton
WMNC-FM - 92.1 (24078)

Nags Head
WRSF-FM - 105.7 (24093)

NORTH DAKOTA
Dickinson
KCAD-FM - 99.1 (24397)

Langdon
KNDK-FM - 95.7 (24491)

Williston
KYYZ-FM - 96.1 (24567)

OHIO
East Liverpool
WELA-FM - 104.3 (25172)

Jackson
WKOV-FM - 96.7 (25259)

Logan
WLGN-FM - 98.3 (25314)

Marion
WMRN-FM - 106.9 (25355)

Nelsonville
WSEO-FM - 107.7 (25407)

OKLAHOMA
Enid
KOFM-FM - 103.1 (25828)

Hobart
KQTZ-FM - 105.9 (25867)

OREGON
Coquille
KSHR-FM - 97.3 (26283)

PENNSYLVANIA
Brownsville
WOGG-FM - 94.9 **(26738)**

Waynesburg
WCYJ-FM - 88.7 **(28141)**

SOUTH CAROLINA
Greenville
WSSL-FM - 100.5 **(28642)**

SOUTH DAKOTA
Mobridge
KOLY-FM - 99.5 **(28908)**

TENNESSEE
Dickson
WFGZ-FM - 94.5 **(29167)**

Knoxville
WOKI-FM - 100.3 **(29297)**

Savannah
WKWX-FM - 93.5 **(29586)**

TEXAS
Bay City
KMKS-FM - 102.5 **(29893)**

Kenedy
KAML-AM - 990 **(30636)**

UTAH
Logan
KBLQ-FM - 92.9 **(31357)**

VIRGINIA
Blackstone
WBBC-FM - 93.5 **(31893)**

Culpeper
WCUL-FM - 103.1 **(31988)**

Wytheville
WYVE-AM - 1280 **(32644)**

WASHINGTON
Bellingham
KIXT-AM - 930 **(32684)**

Ellensburg
KXLE-FM - 95.3 **(32753)**

Olympia
KAYO-FM - 99.3 **(32867)**

WEST VIRGINIA
Charleston
WKWS-FM - 96.1 **(33283)**

WISCONSIN
Ashland
WBSZ-FM - 93.3 **(33557)**

Clintonville
WJMQ-FM - 92.3 **(33639)**

Kenosha
WEXT-FM - 104.7 **(33875)**

Sparta
WCOW-FM - 97.1 **(34334)**

WYOMING
Buffalo
KLGT-FM - 92.9 **(34480)**

Cody
KZMQ-FM - 100.3 **(34518)**

Gillette
KGWY-FM - 100.7 **(34529)**

ALBERTA, CANADA
Athabasca
CKBA-AM - 850 **(34611)**

BRITISH COLUMBIA, CANADA
Fort St. John
CKNL-AM - 560 **(34960)**

Quesnel
CKCQ-AM - 920 **(35070)**

Victoria
CKXM-AM - 1200 **(35237)**

MANITOBA, CANADA
Brandon
CKX-AM - 1150 **(35257)**

NEWFOUNDLAND AND LABRADOR, CANADA
St. John's
CKIX-FM - 99.1 **(35502)**

NOVA SCOTIA, CANADA
Halifax
CHFX-FM - 101.9 **(35573)**

ONTARIO, CANADA
Belleville
CJBQ-AM - 800 **(35681)**

Midland
KICX-FM - 104.1 **(36045)**

Sudbury
CIGM-AM - 790 **(36424)**

Tillsonburg
CKOT-AM - 1510 **(36451)**

INFORMATION

ALABAMA
Gadsden
WSGN-FM - 91.5 **(237)**

Mobile
WABB-AM - 1480 **(332)**

ARIZONA
Flagstaff
KNAU-FM - 88.7 **(700)**

ARKANSAS
Conway
KFCA-AM - 1330 **(1087)**

Helena
KFFA-AM - 1360 **(1176)**

Little Rock
KUAR-FM - 89.1 **(1253)**

Wynne
KWYN-AM - 1400 **(1373)**

CALIFORNIA
San Francisco
KCBS-AM - 740 **(3474)**

Santa Maria
KSMA-AM - 1240 **(3699)**

Ukiah
KWNE-FM - 94.5 **(3971)**

West Sacramento
KJAY-AM - 1430 **(4067)**

COLORADO
Longmont
KLMO-AM - 1060 **(4564)**

CONNECTICUT
Hamden
WQUN-AM - 1220 **(4884)**

Plantsville
WNTY-AM - 990 **(5091)**

DISTRICT OF COLUMBIA
Washington
WAMU-FM - 88.5 **(5877)**

FLORIDA
Boca Raton
WSBR-AM - 740 **(5943)**

Fort Walton Beach
WFTW-AM - 1260 **(6123)**

Ocala
WHOF-AM - 640 **(6474)**

Tallahassee
WFSU-FM - 88.9 **(6747)**

GEORGIA
Savannah
WSVH-FM - 91.1 **(7549)**

Tucker
WGUN-AM - 1010 **(7612)**

HAWAII
Hilo
KPUA-AM - 670 **(7677)**

Honolulu
KHPR-FM - 88.1 **(7737)**
KIPO-FM - 89.3 **(7741)**

IDAHO
Boise
KBSY-FM - 88.5 **(7819)**

ILLINOIS
Chicago
WVAZ-FM - 102.7 **(8657)**

Crest Hill
WJOL-AM - 1340 **(8690)**

Decatur
WSOY-AM - 1340 **(8720)**

Quincy
WGEM-AM - 1440 **(9478)**

Waukegan
WKRS-AM - 1220 **(9746)**

INDIANA
Fort Wayne
WBNI-FM - 89.1 **(9979)**

Indianapolis
WBRI-AM - 1500 **(10191)**

South Bend
WETL-FM - 91.7 **(10461)**

IOWA
Boone
KWBG-AM - 1590 **(10629)**

Cedar Rapids
KCCK-FM - 88.3 **(10678)**

Decorah
KWLC-AM - 1240 **(10762)**

Spencer
KDWD-FM - 100.1 **(11232)**

KANSAS
Overland Park
KCCV-AM - 760 **(11739)**

KENTUCKY
Bowling Green
WKCT-AM - 930 **(11958)**

Murray
WKMS-FM - 91.3/92.1 Paducah, KY; 99.5 Paris, TN **(12319)**

LOUISIANA
Opelousas
KSLO-AM - 1230 **(12793)**

MAINE
Dover Foxcroft
WDME-FM - 103.1 **(12953)**

MARYLAND
Cumberland
WNTR-AM - 1230 **(13478)**

MASSACHUSETTS
Boston
WBUR-FM - 90.9 **(13978)**

MICHIGAN
Ann Arbor
WUOM-FM - 91.7 **(14781)**

Radio Station Formats

INFORMATION (continued)

Battle Creek
WBCK-AM - 930 **(14794)**

Detroit
WDTR-FM - 90.9 **(14960)**

East Lansing
WKAR-AM - 870 **(14995)**

Grand Rapids
WGVU-AM - 1480 **(15109)**
WGVU-FM - 88.5 **(15110)**

Manistee
WMTE-AM - 1340 **(15332)**

Pittsford
WPCJ-FM - 91.1 **(15445)**

Rogers City
WVXA-FM - 96.7 **(15471)**

MINNESOTA
Albert Lea
KATE-AM - 1450 **(15707)**

Blue Earth
KBEW-AM - 1560 **(15763)**

Collegeville
KNSR-FM - 88.9 **(15808)**

Detroit Lakes
KDLM-AM - 1340 **(15832)**

Duluth
KDAL-AM - 610 **(15845)**
KUMD-FM - 103.3 **(15852)**

Faribault
KDHL-AM - 920 **(15895)**

Fergus Falls
KBRF-AM - 1250 **(15900)**

Marshall
KMHL-AM - 1400 **(16047)**

Minneapolis
KBEM-FM - 88.5 **(16145)**

Montevideo
KDMA-AM - 1460 **(16181)**

Moorhead
KCCD-FM - 90.3 **(16190)**
KNTN-FM - 102.7 **(16192)**

Pipestone
KLOH-AM - 1050 **(16277)**

Rochester
KXLC-FM - 91.1 **(16323)**
KZSE-FM - 90.7 **(16326)**

Worthington
KWOA-AM - 730 **(16541)**

MISSISSIPPI
Columbus
WKOR-AM - 980 **(16611)**

Lorman
WPRL-FM - 91.7 **(16749)**

Mississippi State
WMAB-FM - 89.9 **(16786)**

MISSOURI
Farmington
KREI-AM - 800 **(17055)**

Kirksville
KIRX-AM - 1450 **(17230)**

Thayer
KALM-AM - 1290 **(17649)**

Trenton
KTTN-FM - 92.3 **(17655)**

NEBRASKA
Hastings
KHAS-AM - 1230 **(18039)**

Omaha
KIOS-FM - 91.5 **(18220)**

NEW HAMPSHIRE
Nashua
WSMN-AM - 1590 **(18608)**

NEW JERSEY
Millville
WMVB-AM - 1440 **(19237)**

Pemberton
WBZC-FM - 88.9 and 95.1 **(19419)**

Toms River
WOBM-FM - 92.7 **(19651)**

NEW YORK
Binghamton
WSQX-FM - 91.5 **(20233)**

Fulton
WZZZ-AM - 1300 **(20633)**

New York
WNYC-AM - 820 **(22979)**

NORTH CAROLINA
Durham
WNCU-FM - 90.7 **(23849)**

Hickory
WIRC-AM - 630 **(23993)**

Mayodan
WLOE-AM - 1490 **(24061)**
WMYN-AM - 1420 **(24062)**

Newton
WNNC-AM - 1230 **(24107)**

Raleigh
WSHA-FM - 88.9 **(24175)**

NORTH DAKOTA
Devils Lake
KDLR-AM - 1240 **(24391)**

Grand Forks
KUND-AM - 1370 **(24463)**

Jamestown
KQDJ-AM - 1400 **(24480)**

Langdon
KNDK-AM - 1080 **(24490)**

Oakes
KDDR-AM - 1220 **(24528)**

OHIO
Cleveland
WCPN-FM - 90.3 **(24970)**

Columbus
WOSU-AM - 820 **(25082)**

Lima
WGLE-FM - 90.7 **(25300)**

Portsmouth
WNXT-AM - 1260 **(25485)**

Toledo
WGTE-FM - 91.3 **(25577)**

OKLAHOMA
Norman
KNOR-AM - 1400 **(25946)**

OREGON
Burns
KZZR-AM - 1230 **(26261)**

Coquille
KWRO-AM - 630 **(26284)**

Corvallis
KOAC-AM - 550 **(26293)**

Hillsboro
KUIK-AM - 1360 **(26375)**

PENNSYLVANIA
Beaver Falls
WMBA-AM - 1460 **(26687)**

Bethlehem
WGPA-AM - 1100 **(26711)**

Levittown
WBCB-AM - 1490 **(27190)**

Monroeville
WXVX-AM - 1510 **(27289)**

Philadelphia
WHYY-FM - 90.9 **(27733)**

Punxsutawney
WECZ-AM - 1540 **(27911)**

RHODE ISLAND
Providence
WBSR-FM - 88.1 **(28432)**

SOUTH CAROLINA
Orangeburg
WSSB-FM - 90.3 **(28738)**

Union
WBCU-AM - 1460 **(28777)**

TENNESSEE
Collegedale
WSMC-FM - 90.5 **(29132)**

Jackson
WDXI-AM - 1310 **(29234)**

Nashville
WFSK-FM - 88.1 **(29510)**

TEXAS
Dallas
KERA-FM - 90.1 **(30203)**

Jacksonville
KEBE-AM - 1400 **(30617)**

Midland
KJBC-AM - 1150 **(30818)**

UTAH
Logan
KUSU-FM - 89.5, 91.5 **(31361)**

VERMONT
St. Johnsbury
WSTJ-AM - 1340 **(31596)**

VIRGINIA
Lebanon
WLRV-AM - 1380 **(32180)**

Spotsylvania
WJYJ-FM - 90.5 **(32536)**

WASHINGTON
Aberdeen
KBKW-AM - 1450 **(32648)**

Ellensburg
KCWU-FM - 88.1 **(32750)**

Longview
KEDO-AM - 1400 **(32816)**

Port Angeles
KONP-AM - 1450 **(32889)**

Seattle
KUOW-FM - 94.9 **(33072)**

Spokane
KXLY-AM - 920 **(33134)**

Yakima
KDNA-FM - 91.9 **(33227)**

WEST VIRGINIA
Bluefield
WHIS-AM - 1440 **(33257)**

WISCONSIN
Eau Claire
WUEC-FM - 89.7 **(33684)**

Madison
WIBA-AM - 1310 **(33996)**

Tomahawk
WJJQ-FM - 92.5 **(34375)**

BRITISH COLUMBIA, CANADA
Victoria
CFAX-AM - 1070 **(35232)**

Numbers cited in bold after listings are entry numbers rather than page numbers.

MANITOBA, CANADA
Portage La Prairie
CFRY-AM - 920 **(35284)**

NEW BRUNSWICK, CANADA
St. John
CBD-FM - 91.3 **(35432)**

NEWFOUNDLAND AND LABRADOR, CANADA
Corner Brook
CBY-AM - 990 **(35449)**

Mount Pearl
VOAR-AM - 1210 **(35475)**

ONTARIO, CANADA
Belleville
CJLX-FM - 92.3 **(35682)**

Ottawa
CBO-FM - 91.5 **(36284)**

Toronto
CFRB-AM - 1010 **(36805)**

QUEBEC, CANADA
Montreal
CJAD-AM - 800 **(37247)**

JAZZ

ALABAMA
Birmingham
WVSU-FM - 91.1 **(130)**

Huntsville
WLRH-FM - 89.3 **(284)**

Jacksonville
WLJS-FM - 91.9 **(295)**

Montgomery
WVAS-FM - 90.7 **(394)**

Muscle Shoals
WQPR-FM - 88.7 **(400)**

Normal
WJAB-FM - 90.9 **(402)**

Troy
WTJB-FM - 91.7 **(478)**
WTSU-FM - 89.9 **(479)**

Tuscaloosa
WUAL-FM - 91.5 **(503)**

ALASKA
Bethel
KYUK-AM - 640 **(556)**

Fairbanks
KUAC-FM - 89.9 **(578)**

Juneau
KTOO-FM - 104.3 **(604)**

Unalaska
KIAL-AM - 1450 **(645)**

ARIZONA
Phoenix
KYOT-FM - 95.5 **(844)**

Tempe
KJZZ-FM - 91.5 **(921)**

Tucson
KOAZ-FM - 97.5 **(988)**
KUAZ-AM - 1550 **(997)**
KUAZ-FM - 89.1 **(998)**

Yuma
KAWC-FM - 88.9 **(1023)**

ARKANSAS
Russellville
KXRJ-FM - 91.9 **(1334)**

State University
KASU-FM - 91.9 **(1351)**

CALIFORNIA
Carmel
KRML-AM - 1410 **(1674)**

Culver City
KTWV-FM - 94.7 **(1796)**

Fortuna
KQEX-FM - 100.3 **(1931)**

Fresno
KEZL-FM - 96.7 **(1963)**
KFSR-FM - 90.7 **(1967)**

Long Beach
KLON-FM - 88.1 **(2179)**

Los Angeles
KMZT-FM - 105.1 **(2463)**
KXLU-FM - 88.9 **(2472)**

Mission Viejo
KSBR-FM - 88.5 **(2560)**

Modesto
KRVR-FM - 105.5 **(2570)**

Moraga
KSMC-FM - 89.5 **(2598)**

Riverside
KUCR-FM - 88.3 **(2954)**

San Diego
KSDS-FM - 88.3 **(3314)**

San Francisco
KBLX-FM - 102.9 **(3471)**
KKSF-FM - 103.7 **(3489)**

San Mateo
KCSM-FM - 91.1 **(3592)**

Santa Clara
KSCU-FM - 103.3 **(3677)**

Thousand Oaks
KCLU-FM - 88.3 Ventura County, 102.3 FM Santa Barbara County **(3924)**

Turlock
KCSS-FM - 91.9 **(3960)**

COLORADO
Alamosa
KRZA-FM - 88.7 **(4136)**

Colorado Springs
KSKX-FM - 105.5 **(4281)**

Denver
KHIH-FM - 95.7 **(4378)**
KJCD-FM - 104.3 **(4380)**
KUVO-FM - 89.3 **(4392)**

Greeley
KUNC-FM - 91.5 **(4503)**

CONNECTICUT
Hartford
WQTQ-FM - 89.9 **(4909)**
WRTC-FM - 89.3 **(4911)**

Monroe
WRXC-FM - 90.1 **(4967)**

Sharon
WKZE-FM - 98.1 **(5116)**

West Hartford
WWUH-FM - 91.3 **(5206)**

West Haven
WNHU-FM - 88.7 **(5208)**

DISTRICT OF COLUMBIA
Washington
WDCU-FM - 90.1 **(5881)**
WJZW-FM - 105.9 **(5887)**
WPFW-FM - 89.3 **(5890)**

FLORIDA
Delray Beach
WDBF-AM - 1420 **(6058)**

Fort Myers
WDRR-FM - 98.5 **(6103)**
WGCU-FM - 90.1 **(6104)**

Gainesville
WUFT-FM - 89.1 **(6168)**

Jacksonville
WMXQ-FM - 102.9 **(6233)**

Melbourne
WFIT-FM - 89.5 **(6337)**

Miami
WDNA-FM - 88.9 **(6399)**

Miramar
WLVE-FM - 93.9 **(6431)**
WWLV-FM - 93.9 **(6433)**

Orlando
WUCF-FM - 89.9 **(6529)**

Palm Harbor
WGUL-AM - 860 **(6553)**
WGUL-FM - 106.3 **(6554)**

Pensacola
WUWF-FM - 88.1 **(6579)**

South Daytona
WPUL-AM - 1590 **(6685)**

Tallahassee
WAMF-FM - 90.5 **(6742)**

Tampa
WUSF-FM - 89.7 **(6807)**

Vero Beach
WGYL-FM - 93.7 **(6837)**

Winter Park
WLOQ-FM - 103.1 **(6892)**

GEORGIA
Atlanta
WCLK-FM - 91.9 **(7070)**
WUNV-FM - 91.7 **(7089)**

Augusta
WACG-FM - 90.7 **(7104)**

Gainesville
WBCX-FM - 89.1 **(7300)**

Macon
WALJ-FM - 107.1 **(7388)**

Savannah
WHCJ-FM - 90.3 **(7544)**
WSVH-FM - 91.1 **(7549)**

HAWAII
Honolulu
KIPO-FM - 89.3 **(7741)**

IDAHO
Nampa
KJHY-FM - 101.9 **(7933)**

ILLINOIS
Carbondale
WSIU-FM - 91.9 **(8123)**

Chicago
WHPK-FM - 88.5 **(8628)**
WNUA-FM - 95.5 **(8647)**
WSBC-AM - 1240 **(8651)**

DeKalb
WNIJ-FM - 90.5 **(8744)**

Edwardsville
WSIE-FM - 88.7 **(8815)**

Elmhurst
WRSE-FM - 88.7 **(8841)**

Glen Ellyn
WDCB-FM - 90.9 **(8933)**

Harvey
WBEE-AM - 1570 **(8977)**

Macomb
WIUM-FM - 91.3 **(9134)**

Normal
WGLT-FM - 89.1-FM **(9308)**

Quincy
WQUB-FM - 90.3 **(9482)**

Rock Island
WVIK-FM - 90.3 **(9525)**

INDIANA
Bloomington
WFIU-FM - 103.7 **(9857)**

Elkhart
WVPE-FM - 88.1 **(9930)**

Circulation: ★ = ABC; △ = BPA; ♦ = CAC; • = CCAB; ❑ = VAC; ⊕ = PO Statement; ‡ = Publisher's Report; Boldface figures = sworn; Light figures = estimated.

3035

JAZZ (continued)

Fort Wayne
WBNI-FM - 89.1 **(9979)**

Indianapolis
WICR-FM - 88.7 **(10199)**

Terre Haute
WISU-FM - 89.7 **(10496)**

West Lafayette
WBAA-AM - 920 **(10556)**

IOWA
Cedar Falls
KHKE-FM - 89.5 **(10667)**

Cedar Rapids
KCCK-FM - 88.3 **(10678)**

Davenport
KALA-FM - 88.5 **(10740)**

Decorah
KWLC-AM - 1240 **(10762)**

Des Moines
KLYF-FM - 106.3 **(10828)**

Fort Dodge
KTPR-FM - 91.1 **(10912)**

Oskaloosa
KIGC-FM - 88.7 **(11138)**

Sioux City
KWIT-FM - 90.3 **(11225)**

Waterloo
KBBG-FM - 88.1 **(11290)**

KANSAS
Lawrence
KJHK-FM - 90.7 **(11574)**

Westwood
KCIY-FM - 106.5 **(11871)**

Wichita
KMUW-FM - 89.1 **(11899)**

KENTUCKY
Lexington
WRFL-FM - 88.1 **(12194)**

Murray
WKMS-FM - 91.3/92.1 Paducah, KY; 99.5 Paris,
   TN **(12319)**

LOUISIANA
Lafayette
KJCB-AM - 770 **(12626)**

Monroe
KEDM-FM - 90.3 **(12694)**

New Orleans
WWNO-FM - 89.9 **(12782)**
WWOZ-FM - 90.7 **(12783)**

Shreveport
KDAQ-FM - 89.9 **(12823)**
KLSA-FM - 90.7 **(12827)**
KSCL-FM - 91.3 **(12834)**

Winnfield
KVCL-AM - 1270 **(12881)**

MARYLAND
Annapolis
WYRE-AM - 810 **(13103)**

Baltimore
WEAA-FM - 88.9 **(13270)**
WJHU-FM - 88.1 **(13276)**
WTMD-FM - 89.7 **(13285)**

Frostburg
WFWM-FM - 91.9 **(13529)**

Princess Anne
WESM-FM - 91.3 **(13670)**

MASSACHUSETTS
Amherst
WFCR-FM - 88.5 **(13809)**

Beverly
WBOQ-FM - 104.9 **(13843)**

Boston
WGBH-FM - 89.7 **(13985)**
WSJZ-FM - 96.9 **(13996)**

Deerfield
WGAJ-FM - 91.7 **(14158)**

Provincetown
WOMR-FM - 92.1 **(14487)**

Sheffield
WBSL-FM - 91.7 **(14520)**

Springfield
WAIC-FM - 91.9 **(14555)**

Tisbury
WMVY-FM - 92.7 **(14589)**

Worcester
WICN-FM - 90.5 **(14698)**

MICHIGAN
Alpena
WCML-FM - 91.7 **(14739)**

Dearborn
WHFR-FM - 89.3 **(14908)**

Detroit
WDET-FM - 101.9 **(14957)**
WJZZ-FM - 105.9 **(14969)**
WQBH-AM - 1400 **(14974)**

Farmington Hills
WLLZ-FM - 98.7 **(15024)**

Flint
WFUM-FM - 91.1 **(15044)**

Grand Rapids
WGVU-FM - 88.5 **(15110)**
WYBN-FM - 93.1 **(15128)**

Highland Park
WHPR-FM - 88.1 **(15162)**

Kalamazoo
WMUK-FM - 102.1 **(15256)**

Lansing
WLNZ-FM - 89.7 **(15303)**

Marquette
WNMU-FM - 90.1, 107.1, 91.9, 91.3, 91.1,
   107.3 **(15346)**

Mount Pleasant
WCMU-FM - 89.5 **(15380)**

Saginaw
WTLZ-FM - 107.1 **(15506)**

Traverse City
WNMC-FM - 90.7 **(15612)**

Twin Lake
WBLV-FM - 90.3 **(15645)**

Ypsilanti
WEMU-FM - 89.1 **(15692)**

MINNESOTA
Albert Lea
KATE-FM - 1450 **(15708)**

Minneapolis
KBEM-FM - 88.5 **(16145)**

MISSISSIPPI
Holly Springs
WURC-FM - 88.1 **(16684)**

Jackson
WMPR-FM - 90.1 **(16726)**

Lorman
WPRL-FM - 91.7 **(16749)**

MISSOURI
Columbia
KWWC-FM - 90.5 **(17024)**

Jefferson City
KJLU-FM - 88.9 **(17136)**

Kansas City
KCUR-FM - 89.3 **(17208)**

Maryville
KXCV-FM - 90.5 **(17279)**

Point Lookout
KCOZ-FM - 91.7 **(17355)**

St. Charles
KIRL-AM - 1460 **(17386)**

St. Louis
KATZ-FM - 100.3 **(17533)**
KWMU-FM - 90.7 **(17553)**

Springfield
KTOZ-AM - 1060 **(17629)**

NEBRASKA
Hastings
KHNE-FM - 89.1 **(18041)**

Kearney
KLPR-FM - 91.3 **(18065)**

Lexington
KLNE-FM - 88.7 **(18073)**

Norfolk
KXNE-FM - 89.3 **(18172)**

Omaha
KIOS-FM - 91.5 **(18220)**
KVNO-FM - 90.7 **(18228)**

NEVADA
Reno
KUNR-FM - 88.7 **(18442)**

NEW HAMPSHIRE
Concord
WEVO-FM - 89.1 **(18476)**

Hanover
WDCR-AM - 1340 **(18520)**

Henniker
WNEC-FM - 91.7 **(18523)**

NEW JERSEY
Atlantic City
WSAX-FM - 102.3 **(18659)**

Flemington
WCVH-FM - 90.5 **(18822)**

New Brunswick
WRSU-FM - 88.7 **(19345)**

Newark
WBGO-FM - 88.3 **(19368)**

Princeton
WPRB-FM - 103.3 **(19481)**

Teaneck
WFDU-FM - 89.1 **(19612)**

NEW MEXICO
Las Cruces
KRWG-FM - 90.7 **(19885)**

Maljamar
KMTH-FM - 98.7 **(19902)**

Portales
KENW-FM - 89.5 **(19905)**

NEW YORK
Albany
WAMC-FM - 90.3 **(20009)**

Binghamton
WSKG-FM - 89.3 **(20228)**
WSQE-FM - 91.1 **(20230)**
WSQG-FM - 89.3 **(20231)**
WSQX-FM - 88.7 **(20232)**
WSQX-FM - 91.5 **(20233)**

Buffalo
WBFO-FM - 88.7 **(20395)**

Canajoharie
WCAN-FM - 93.3 **(20418)**

Clinton
WHCL-FM - 88.7 **(20475)**

Herkimer
WVHC-FM - 91.5 **(20734)**

Lake Ronkonkoma
WSHR-FM - 91.9 **(20879)**

New Rochelle
WRTN-FM - 93.5 **(21124)**

Numbers cited in bold after listings are entry numbers rather than page numbers.

New York
WBMB-AM - 590 **(22964)**
WKCR-FM - 89.9 **(22972)**
WQCD-FM - 101.9 **(22988)**

North Greece
WGMC-FM - 90.1, 105.1 **(23013)**

Rochester
WDKX-FM - 103.9 **(23245)**
WRUR-FM - 88.5 **(23254)**
WXXI-AM - 1370 **(23258)**

Rooseveltown
CKON-FM - 97.3 **(23276)**

Saratoga Springs
WSPN-FM - 91.1 **(23305)**

Southampton
WPBX-FM - 88.3 **(23346)**

Staten Island
WSIA-FM - 88.9 **(23367)**

Syracuse
WAER-FM - 88.3 **(23434)**
WCNY-FM - 91.3 **(23436)**

NORTH CAROLINA
Durham
WNCU-FM - 90.7 **(23849)**
WXDU-FM - 88.7 **(23854)**

Fayetteville
WFSS-FM - 91.9 **(23887)**

Greensboro
WNAA-FM - 90.1 **(23954)**

Greenville
WOOW-AM - 1340 **(23975)**

Raleigh
WAB-FM - 99.9 **(24161)**
WAHD-FM - 90.5 **(24162)**
WSHA-FM - 88.9 **(24175)**

Winston-Salem
WSNC-FM - 90.5 **(24333)**

NORTH DAKOTA
Bismarck
KCND-FM - 90.5 **(24366)**
KDPR-FM - 89.9 **(24367)**

Fargo
KDSU-FM - 91.9 **(24417)**

Minot
KMPR-FM - 88.9 **(24510)**

Williston
KPPR-FM - 90.5 **(24563)**

OHIO
Alliance
WRMU-FM - 91.1 **(24607)**

Athens
WOUB-FM - 91.3 **(24633)**
WOUC-FM - 89.1 **(24635)**

Bowling Green
WBGU-FM - 88.1 **(24703)**

Cleveland
WCPN-FM - 90.3 **(24970)**

Columbus
WCBE-FM - 90.5 **(25076)**

Dublin
WZJZ-FM - 104.3 **(25170)**

Elyria
WNWV-FM - 107.3 **(25182)**

Ironton
WOUL-FM - 89.1 **(25255)**

Oxford
WMUB-FM - 88.5 **(25463)**

Toledo
WXTS-FM - 88.3 **(25591)**

Youngstown
WYSU-FM - 88.5 **(25714)**

OKLAHOMA
Langston
KALU-FM - 89.3 **(25882)**

Lawton
KCCU-FM - 89.3 **(25891)**

Norman
KROU-FM - 105.7 **(25947)**

OREGON
Ashland
KSKF-FM - 90.9 **(26221)**
KSMF-FM - 89.1 **(26222)**

Bend
KMJZ-FM - 95.1 **(26247)**

Gresham
KMHD-FM - 89.1 **(26366)**

Portland
KKJZ-FM - 106.7 **(26529)**

PENNSYLVANIA
Bloomsburg
WBUQ-FM - 91.1 **(26720)**

Chester
WDNR-FM, Widener University - 89.5 **(26776)**

Erie
WQLN-FM - 91.3 **(26909)**

Grove City
WSAJ-FM - 91.1 **(26967)**

Lincoln University
WLIU-FM - 88.7 **(27201)**

Philadelphia
WJJZ-FM - 106.1 **(27736)**
WKDU-FM - 91.7 **(27737)**
WRTI-FM - 90.1 **(27744)**

Pittsburgh
WDUQ-FM - 90.5 **(27863)**

Pittston
WVIA-FM - 89.9 **(27893)**

Slippery Rock
WSRU-FM - 90.1 **(28001)**

Williamsport
WPTC-FM - 88.1 **(28189)**

PUERTO RICO
San Juan
WORO-FM - 92.5 **(28306)**
WRTU-FM - 89.7 **(28309)**

Trujillo Alto
WVID-FM - 90.3 **(28318)**

RHODE ISLAND
Newport
WADK-AM - 1540 **(28374)**
WOTB-FM - 100.3 **(28375)**

Providence
WDOM-FM - 91.3 **(28433)**
WRBU-FM - 95.5 **(28437)**

SOUTH CAROLINA
Hemingway
WLGI-FM - 90.9 **(28660)**

Orangeburg
WSSB-FM - 90.3 **(28738)**

Sumter
WRJA-FM - 88.1 **(28774)**

SOUTH DAKOTA
Brookings
KESD-FM/South Dakota Public Broadcasting -
88.3 **(28820)**

Pierpont
KDSD-FM - 90.9 **(28915)**

Reliance
KTSD-FM - 91.1 **(28956)**

Sioux Falls
KCSD-FM - 90.9 **(28971)**

Vermillion
KUSD-FM - 89.7 **(29010)**

TENNESSEE
Chattanooga
WUTC-FM - 88.1 **(29112)**

Henderson
WFHC-FM - 91.5 **(29219)**

Knoxville
WSMJ-FM - 98.7 **(29301)**
WUOT-FM - 91.9 **(29303)**

Memphis
WUMR-FM - 91.7 **(29413)**

Murfreesboro
WMOT-FM - 89.5 **(29437)**

Nashville
WFSK-FM - 88.1 **(29510)**
WMDB-AM - 880 **(29520)**
WRLT-FM - 100.1 **(29529)**
WRVU-FM - 91.1 **(29530)**

TEXAS
Amarillo
KACV-FM - 89.9 **(29700)**

Austin
KAZI-FM - 88.7 **(29860)**

College Station
KAMU-FM - 90.9 **(30056)**

Commerce
KETR-FM - 88.9 **(30069)**

Corpus Christi
KEDT-FM - 90.3 **(30082)**

Denton
KNTU-FM - 88.1 **(30243)**

Harlingen
KHID-FM - 88.1 **(30427)**
KMBH-FM - 88.9 **(30429)**

Houston
KTSU-FM - 90.9 **(30582)**

Huntsville
KSHU-FM - 90.5 **(30601)**

Killeen
KNCT-FM - 91.3 **(30645)**

Lubbock
KOHM-FM - 89.1 **(30733)**

Marshall
KBWC-FM - 91.1 **(30767)**

Nacogdoches
KSAU-FM - 90.1 **(30854)**

Prairie View
KPVU-FM - 91.3 **(30962)**

San Antonio
KSYM-FM - 90.1 **(31074)**

South Padre Island
KZSP-FM - 95.3 **(31121)**

UTAH
Salt Lake City
KUER-FM - 90.1 **(31465)**

VERMONT
Colchester
WRVT-FM - 88.7 **(31532)**
WVPS-FM - 107.9 **(31534)**

Lyndonville
WWLR-FM - 91.5 **(31551)**

Waterbury
WDEV-AM - 550 **(31612)**

Windsor
WVPR-FM - 89.5 **(31622)**

VIRGINIA
Charlottesville
WTJU-FM - 91.1 **(31955)**

Fairfax
WJFK-AM - 1300 **(32035)**

Hampton
WARR-AM - 1520 **(32131)**
WHOV-FM - 88.1 **(32133)**

Harrisonburg
WEMC-FM - 91.7 **(32143)**

Petersburg
WVST-FM - 91.3 **(32333)**

Circulation: ★ = ABC; △ = BPA; ◆ = CAC; ● = CCAB; ❑ = VAC; ⊕ = PO Statement; ‡ = Publisher's Report; Boldface figures = sworn; Light figures = estimated.

3037

Radio Station Formats

JAZZ (continued)

Richmond
WCVE-FM - 88.9 **(32474)**

Wise
WISE-FM - 90.5 **(32635)**

WASHINGTON
Bellevue
KBCS-FM - 91.3 **(32672)**

Cheney
KEWU-FM - 89.5 **(32715)**

Lynnwood
KSER-FM - 90.7 **(32826)**

Pullman
KFAE-FM - 89.1 **(32910)**
KRFA-FM - 91.7 **(32913)**

Spokane
KPBX-FM - 91.1 **(33123)**

Tacoma
KPLU-FM - 88.5 **(33158)**

WEST VIRGINIA
Charleston
WVNP-FM - 89.9 **(33287)**
WVPB-FM - 91.7 **(33288)**
WVPN-FM - 88.5 **(33289)**

Elkins
WCDE-FM - 90.3 **(33307)**

Parkersburg
WVPG-FM - 90.3 **(33426)**

WISCONSIN
Eau Claire
WUEC-FM - 89.7 **(33684)**

La Crosse
WLSU-FM - 88.9 **(33894)**

Madison
WORT-FM - 89.9 **(34007)**

Milwaukee
WYMS-FM - 88.9 **(34144)**

Ripon
WBJZ-FM - 104.7 **(34304)**

Superior
KUWS-FM - 91.3 **(34362)**

WYOMING
Riverton
KCWC-FM - 88.1 **(34578)**

ALBERTA, CANADA
Calgary
CBR-FM - 102.1 **(34662)**
CJSW-FM - 90.9 **(34670)**

MANITOBA, CANADA
Winnipeg
CBW-AM - 990 **(35366)**
CBW-FM - 98.3 **(35367)**

ONTARIO, CANADA
Hamilton
CFMU-FM - 93.3 **(35893)**

Ottawa
CBOF-FM - 90.7 **(36285)**

Toronto
CJRT-FM - 91.1 **(36820)**

QUEBEC, CANADA
Quebec
CKRL-FM - 89.1 **(37304)**

MIDDLE-OF-THE-ROAD (MOR)

ALABAMA
Alexander City
WRFS-AM - 1050 **(10)**

Ozark
WOZK-AM - 900 **(421)**

York
WYLS-AM - 670 **(518)**

ARIZONA
Tucson
KFLT-AM - 830 **(978)**

ARKANSAS
Bentonville
KJEM-FM - 93.3 **(1053)**

Mountain Home
KTLO-FM - 97.9 **(1290)**

CALIFORNIA
Sacramento
KCTC-AM - 1320 **(3025)**

San Diego
KPOP-AM - 1360 **(3311)**

Victorville
KWRN-AM - 1550 **(4038)**

COLORADO
Burlington
KNAB-AM - 1140 **(4211)**

Durango
KIUP-AM - 930 **(4404)**

FLORIDA
Crestview
WJSB-AM - 1050 **(6026)**

Gainesville
WLUS-AM - 980 **(6164)**

Hernando
WRZN-AM - 720 **(6186)**

New Smyrna Beach
WSBB-AM - 1230 **(6459)**

Punta Gorda
WKII-AM - 1070 **(6611)**

Rockledge
WRFB-AM - 860 **(6614)**

Tampa
WLVU-FM - 106.3 **(6794)**

Winter Haven
WHNR-AM - 1360 **(6875)**

GEORGIA
Bainbridge
WMGR-AM - 930 **(7120)**

Brunswick
WMOG-AM - 1490 **(7142)**

Griffin
WKEU-AM - 1450 **(7315)**

Manchester
WFDR-AM - 1370 **(7408)**

McDonough
WKKP-AM - 1410 **(7430)**

Thomson
WTWA-AM - 1240 **(7594)**

Winder
WYFW-FM - 89.5 **(7655)**

HAWAII
Hilo
KIPA-AM - 620 **(7675)**

ILLINOIS
DeKalb
WLBK-AM - 1360 **(8743)**

Harvard
WMCW-AM - 1600 **(8975)**

Mount Carmel
WVMC-AM - 1360 **(9234)**

Paris
WPRS-AM - 1440 **(9401)**

Springfield
WLUJ-FM - 89.7 **(9651)**

Vandalia
WPMB-AM - 1500 **(9726)**

INDIANA
Mount Vernon
WYFX-FM - 106.7 **(10324)**

South Bend
WHLY-AM - 1620 **(10462)**

IOWA
Atlantic
KJAN-AM - 1220 **(10611)**

Cherokee
KCHE-AM - 1440 **(10700)**

Fort Dodge
KVFD-AM - 1400 **(10914)**

Grinnell
KGRN-AM - 1410 **(10933)**

KANSAS
Garden City
KIUL-AM - 1240 **(11452)**

Great Bend
KNNS-AM - 1510 **(11471)**

KENTUCKY
Henderson
WSON-AM - 860 **(12125)**

Mayfield
WYMC-AM - 1430 **(12287)**

MASSACHUSETTS
Beverly
WNSH-AM - 1570 **(13844)**

Springfield
WMAS-AM - 1450 **(14559)**

MICHIGAN
Ann Arbor
WAAM-AM - 1600 **(14774)**

Cheboygan
WCBY-AM - 1240 **(14874)**

Grand Rapids
WBMX-AM - 640 **(15104)**

Ionia
WION-AM - 1430 **(15207)**

Kalamazoo
WKPR-AM - 1420 **(15253)**

Muskegon
WMHG-AM - 1600 **(15392)**

Saginaw
WSAM-AM - 1400 **(15504)**

Sandusky
WTGV-FM - 97.7 **(15524)**

MINNESOTA
Albert Lea
KATE-AM - 1450 **(15707)**

Cambridge
WREV-FM - 105.3 **(15787)**

Morris
KMRS-AM - 1230 **(16199)**

Pine City
WCMP-AM - 1350 **(16269)**

MISSISSIPPI
Gulfport
WROA-AM - 1390 **(16658)**

MISSOURI
Creve Coeur
WIL-AM - 1430 **(17028)**

Doniphan
KDFN-AM - 1500 **(17037)**

MONTANA
Malta
KMMR-FM - 100.1 **(17859)**

Numbers cited in bold after listings are entry numbers rather than page numbers.

NEBRASKA
Fremont
KHUB-AM - 1340 **(18014)**

Holdrege
KUVR-AM - 1380 **(18051)**

Kearney
KKPR-AM - 1460 **(18063)**

Valentine
KVSH-AM - 940 **(18300)**

NEW HAMPSHIRE
Wolfeboro
WASR-AM - 1420 **(18656)**

NEW JERSEY
Cedar Knolls
WMTR-AM - 1250 **(18724)**

NEW MEXICO
Las Cruces
KSNM-AM - 570 **(19887)**

NEW YORK
Amsterdam
WCSS-AM - 1490 **(20058)**

Endwell
WINR-AM - 680 **(20588)**

New Rochelle
WRTN-FM - 93.5 **(21124)**

Riverhead
WRIV-AM - 1390 **(23206)**

NORTH CAROLINA
Charlotte
WGAS-AM - 1420 **(23770)**

Elizabeth City
WCNC-AM - 1240 **(23861)**

High Point
WISC-FM - 98.3 **(24004)**

OHIO
Akron
WAKR-AM - 1590 **(24594)**

Cambridge
WILE-AM - 1270 **(24728)**

Fostoria
WFOB-AM - 1430 **(25200)**

OKLAHOMA
Norman
KNOR-AM - 1400 **(25946)**

Tulsa
KNYD-FM - 90.5 **(26155)**
KOZO-FM - 89.7 **(26159)**

OREGON
Brookings
KURY-FM - 95.3 **(26257)**

Coos Bay
KHSN-AM - 1230 **(26279)**

Florence
KCST-AM - 1250 **(26354)**

Grants Pass
KAJO-AM - 1270 **(26363)**

Lebanon
KSHO-AM - 920 **(26410)**

Salem
KBZY-AM - 1490 **(26575)**

PENNSYLVANIA
Hanover
WHVR-AM - 1280 **(26979)**

Lansford
WLSH-AM - 1410 **(27163)**

Latrobe
WQTW-AM - 1570 **(27166)**

Linesville
WVCC-FM - 101.7 **(27202)**

Stroudsburg
WVPO-AM - 840 **(28037)**

Titusville
WTIV-AM - 1230 **(28051)**

PUERTO RICO
Isabela
WISA-AM - 1390 **(28252)**

San Juan
WQII-AM - 1140 **(28307)**

Yabucoa
WXEW-AM - 840 **(28322)**

SOUTH CAROLINA
Camden
WCAM-AM - 1590 **(28501)**

Greenwood
WCRS-AM - 1450 **(28647)**

SOUTH DAKOTA
Brookings
KBRK-AM - 1430 **(28818)**

TENNESSEE
Donelson
WAMB-FM - 98.7 **(29169)**

Kingsport
WKPT-AM - 1400 **(29265)**

Knoxville
WRJZ-AM - 620 **(29299)**

Nashville
WQDQ-AM - 1200 **(29526)**

TEXAS
Madisonville
KMVL-AM - 1220 **(30753)**

McAllen
KBRN-AM - 1500 **(30791)**

Paris
KPLT-AM - 1490 **(30908)**

San Antonio
KLUP-AM - 930 **(31062)**

Tyler
KDOK-FM - 92.1 **(31209)**

VERMONT
Waterbury
WDEV-AM - 550 **(31612)**

VIRGINIA
Grundy
WMJD-FM - 97.7 **(32122)**

WASHINGTON
Spokane
KAQQ-AM - 590 **(33108)**

WEST VIRGINIA
Parkersburg
WADC-AM - 1050 **(33423)**

Wheeling
WBBD-AM - 1400 **(33505)**

WISCONSIN
Chippewa Falls
WCFW-FM - 105.7 **(33631)**

Greenfield
WOKY-AM - 920 **(33767)**

Platteville
WPVL-AM - 1590 **(34246)**

River Falls
WEVR-FM - 106.3 **(34311)**

Tomah
WTMB-AM - 1460 **(34371)**

ALBERTA, CANADA
Crowsnest Pass
CJPR-AM - 1490 **(34691)**

Edson
CFYR-AM - 1400 **(34759)**
CIYR-AM - 1230 **(34760)**
CJYR-AM - 970 **(34761)**

BRITISH COLUMBIA, CANADA
Fort Nelson
CFNL-AM - 590 **(34957)**

Golden
CKGR-AM - 1400 **(34968)**
CKIR-AM - 870 **(34969)**

Revelstoke
CKCR-AM - 1340 **(35072)**

Smithers
CFBV-AM - 870 **(35091)**

MANITOBA, CANADA
Altona
CFAM-AM - 950 **(35248)**

Boissevain
CJRB-AM - 1220 **(35253)**

NEWFOUNDLAND AND LABRADOR, CANADA
Goose Bay
CFLN-AM - 1230 **(35459)**

Port-aux-Basques
CFGN-AM - 1230 **(35479)**

NORTHWEST TERRITORIES, CANADA
Hay River
CKHR-FM - 107.3 **(35517)**

ONTARIO, CANADA
Marathon
CFNO-FM - 93.1 **(36012)**

QUEBEC, CANADA
Amos
CHAD-AM - 1340 **(36933)**

Chateauguay
CHAI-FM - 101.9 **(36963)**

Drummondville
CHRD-FM - 105.3 **(36992)**

Fermont
CFMF-FM - 103.1 **(36995)**

Matane
CBGA-AM - 1250 **(37070)**
CHRM-FM - 105.3 **(37071)**

Noranda
CKRN-AM - 1400 **(37261)**

Plessisville
CKYQ-FM - 95.7 **(37270)**

Rimouski
CJBR-FM - 101.5 **(37310)**
CJOI-FM - 109.8 **(37311)**

Riviere-du-Loup
CIEL-FM - 103.7 **(37315)**

Sainte-Anne-des-Monts
CJMC-AM - 1490 **(37373)**

Thetford Mines
CJLP-FM - 107.1 **(37412)**
CKLD-FM - 105.5 **(37413)**

Val d'Or
CKVD-AM - 900 **(37423)**

Victoriaville
CFDA-FM - 101.9 FM **(37434)**

SASKATCHEWAN, CANADA
Yorkton
CJGX-AM - 940 **(37602)**

MUSIC OF YOUR LIFE

ARIZONA
Green Valley
KGVY-AM - 1080 **(723)**

Circulation: ★ = ABC; △ = BPA; ◆ = CAC; ● = CCAB; ❏ = VAC; ⊕ = PO Statement; ‡ = Publisher's Report; Boldface figures = sworn; Light figures = estimated.

3039

MUSIC OF YOUR LIFE (continued)

ARKANSAS
Helena
KFFA-AM - 1360 **(1176)**

CALIFORNIA
Alturas
KKFJ-AM - 570 **(1396)**

Oakhurst
KTNS-AM - 1060 **(2661)**

CONNECTICUT
Waterbury
WATR-AM - 1320 **(5197)**

FLORIDA
Daytona Beach
WROD-AM - 1340 **(6045)**

Palm Harbor
WGUL-AM - 860 **(6553)**
WGUL-FM - 106.3 **(6554)**

Rockledge
WRFB-AM - 860 **(6614)**

INDIANA
Valparaiso
WAKE-AM - 1500 **(10512)**

KENTUCKY
Lebanon
WLBN-AM - 1590 **(12155)**

LOUISIANA
Minden
KASO-AM - 1240 **(12689)**

MARYLAND
Rockfield
WWDC-AM - 101.1 **(13674)**

MASSACHUSETTS
Springfield
WMAS-AM - 1450 **(14559)**

MICHIGAN
Fremont
WUBR-AM - 1490 **(15063)**

MINNESOTA
Aitkin
KKIN-AM - 930 **(15703)**

Benson
KBMO-AM - 1290 **(15748)**

MISSOURI
Columbia
KOPN-FM - 89.5 **(17020)**

Springfield
KGMY-AM - 1400 **(17621)**

NEW YORK
Binghamton
WKOP-AM - 1360 **(20226)**

Dansville
WDNY-AM - 1400 **(20520)**

Deer Park
WLIE-AM - 540 **(20522)**

Hudson
WHUC-AM - 1230 **(20770)**

Poughkeepsie
WKIP-AM - 1450 **(23159)**

OHIO
Canton
WINW-AM - 1520 **(24736)**

OKLAHOMA
McAlester
KTMC-AM - 1400 **(25912)**

OREGON
Brookings
KURY-AM - 910 **(26256)**

PENNSYLVANIA
Harrisburg
WKBO-AM - 1230 **(27020)**

Johnstown
WUZZ-FM - 105.7 **(27099)**

New Castle
WBZY-AM - 1280 **(27316)**

Stroudsburg
WVPO-AM - 840 **(28037)**

Wilkes Barre
WARM-AM - 590 **(28169)**

SOUTH CAROLINA
Murrells Inlet
WJXY-AM - 1050 **(28701)**

TENNESSEE
Henderson
WFHC-FM - 91.5 **(29219)**

Knoxville
WVOZ-AM - 1180 **(29307)**

Morristown
WCRK-AM - 1150 **(29421)**

Nashville
WNAZ-FM - 89.1 **(29522)**
WNRZ-FM - 91.5 **(29524)**

TEXAS
Abilene
KZQQ-AM - 1560 **(29669)**

VIRGINIA
Culpeper
WCVA-AM - 1490 **(31989)**

Harrisonburg
WMXH-FM - 105.7 **(32151)**

WASHINGTON
Anacortes
KLKI-AM - 1340 **(32653)**

Kennewick
KALE-AM - 960 **(32789)**

WEST VIRGINIA
Keyser
WKLP-AM - 1390 **(33357)**

WISCONSIN
Hayward
WHSM-AM - 910 **(33787)**

Ladysmith
WLDY-AM - 1340 **(33902)**

Poynette
WIBU-AM - 900 **(34265)**

QUEBEC, CANADA
Quebec
CJMF-FM - 93.3 **(37302)**

NEW AGE

ALABAMA
Troy
WRWA-FM - 88.7 **(475)**

ARKANSAS
State University
KASU-FM - 91.9 **(1351)**

CALIFORNIA
San Francisco
KEST-AM - 1450 **(3480)**

CONNECTICUT
Fairfield
WSHU-FM - 91.1 **(4792)**

West Haven
WNHU-FM - 88.7 **(5208)**

KANSAS
Hutchinson
KHCC-FM - 90.1 **(11505)**

Salina
KHCD-FM - 89.5 **(11786)**

LOUISIANA
Monroe
KEDM-FM - 90.3 **(12694)**

MARYLAND
Baltimore
WTMD-FM - 89.7 **(13285)**

MICHIGAN
Grand Rapids
WYBN-FM - 93.1 **(15128)**

MISSISSIPPI
Mississippi State
WMAB-FM - 89.9 **(16786)**

MISSOURI
Columbia
KBIA-FM - 91.3 **(17013)**

NEW MEXICO
Albuquerque
KKOB-AM - 770 **(19800)**

NORTH CAROLINA
Mars Hill
WVMH-FM - 90.5 **(24058)**

PENNSYLVANIA
Lincoln University
WLIU-FM - 88.7 **(27201)**

Pittsburgh
WQED-FM - 89.3 **(27874)**

Pittston
WVIA-FM - 89.9 **(27893)**

UTAH
Ogden
KBZN-FM - 97.9 **(31380)**

WISCONSIN
Milwaukee
WYMS-FM - 88.9 **(34144)**

NEWS

ALABAMA
Andalusia
WAAO-FM - 103.7 **(14)**

Athens
WVNN-AM - 770 **(30)**

Atmore
WASG-AM - 550 **(34)**
WBCA-AM - 1110 **(35)**

Auburn
WANI-AM - 1400 **(46)**
WAUD-AM - 1230 **(47)**

Birmingham
WAPI-AM - 1070 **(103)**
WERC-AM - 960 **(115)**

Bridgeport
WBTS-AM - 1480 **(138)**

Eufaula
WULA-AM - 1240 **(206)**

Florence
WBCF-AM - 1240 **(221)**

Foley
WHEP-AM - 1310 **(229)**

Greenville
WGYV-AM - 1380 **(244)**

Numbers cited in bold after listings are entry numbers rather than page numbers.

Haleyville
WJBB-AM - 1230 **(259)**

Huntsville
WLRH-FM - 89.3 **(284)**

Jackson
WHOD-AM - 1230 **(292)**

Mobile
WABB-AM - 1480 **(332)**
WDLT-AM - 660 **(338)**
WNTM-AM - 710 **(348)**

Muscle Shoals
WQPR-FM - 88.7 **(400)**

Roanoke
WELR-AM - 1360 **(434)**

Selma
WHBB-AM - 1490 **(454)**

Sylacauga
WFEB-AM - 1340 **(463)**

Troy
WTBF-FM - 94.7 **(477)**
WTJB-FM - 91.7 **(478)**
WTSU-FM - 89.9 **(479)**

Tuscaloosa
WTBC-AM - 1230 **(500)**
WUAL-FM - 91.5 **(503)**

Tuscumbia
WZZA-AM - 1410 **(506)**

ALASKA
Anchorage
KENI-AM - 650 **(540)**
KFQD-AM - 750 **(541)**
KSKA-FM - 91.1 **(547)**

Bethel
KYUK-AM - 640 **(556)**

Cordova
KLAM-AM - 1450 **(559)**

Fairbanks
KFAR-AM - 660 **(572)**
KUAC-FM - 89.9 **(578)**

Juneau
KINY-AM - 800 **(599)**
KTOO-FM - 104.3 **(604)**

Kenai
KSRM-AM - 920 **(609)**

Ketchikan
KTKN-AM - 930 **(614)**

Kodiak
KVOK-AM - 560 **(620)**

Kotzebue
KOTZ-AM - 89.9 **(622)**

McGrath
KSKO-AM - 870 **(623)**

Petersburg
KFSK-FM - 100.9 **(632)**

ARIZONA
Bullhead City
KFLG-FM - 94.7 **(667)**

Flagstaff
KNAU-FM - 88.7 **(700)**
KVNA-AM - 600 **(704)**

Globe
KJAA-AM - 1240 **(720)**

Holbrook
KDJI-AM - 1270 **(725)**

Kingman
KAAA-AM - 1230 **(732)**

Miami
KIKO-AM - 1340 **(752)**

Parker
KLPZ-AM - 1380 **(765)**

Phoenix
KFNN-AM - 1510 **(819)**
KFYI-AM - 910 **(820)**
KIDR-AM - 740 **(822)**
KMYL-AM - 1190 **(828)**
KPHX-AM - 1480 **(833)**

KTAR-AM - 620 **(839)**

Prescott
KYCA-AM - 1490 **(855)**

Prescott Valley
KQNA-AM - 1130 **(858)**

Safford
KATO-AM - 1230 **(861)**
KCUZ-AM - 1490 **(862)**
KFMM-FM - 99.1 **(863)**

Sedona
KAZM-AM - 780 **(879)**

Sierra Vista
KTAN-AM - 1420 **(890)**

Tempe
KJZZ-FM - 91.5 **(921)**

Tucson
KFLT-AM - 830 **(978)**
KNST-AM - 790 **(987)**
KTKT-AM - 990 **(993)**
KUAZ-AM - 1550 **(997)**
KUAZ-FM - 89.1 **(998)**

Winslow
KINO-AM - 1230 **(1015)**

Yuma
KAWC-FM - 88.9 **(1023)**

ARKANSAS
Bentonville
KESE-AM - 1190 **(1052)**

Blytheville
KLCN-AM - 910 **(1062)**

Brinkley
KBRI-AM - 1570 **(1064)**
KQMC-FM - 102.3 **(1065)**

Conway
KCON-AM - 1230 **(1085)**
KFCA-AM - 1330 **(1087)**

El Dorado
KELD-AM - 1400 **(1108)**

Fayetteville
KFAY-AM - 1030 **(1127)**
KKEG-FM - 92.1 **(1129)**
KREB-AM - 1190 **(1130)**
KUAF-FM - 91.3 **(1131)**

Fordyce
KBJT-AM - 1570 **(1136)**
KQEW-FM - 102.3 **(1137)**

Fort Smith
KFSA-AM - 950 **(1148)**
KWHN-AM - 1650 **(1157)**

Helena
KFFA-FM - 103.1 **(1177)**

Hot Springs
KZNG-AM - 1340 **(1190)**

Little Rock
KARN-AM - 920 **(1240)**
KKRN-FM - 102.5 **(1246)**
KUAR-FM - 89.1 **(1253)**

Malvern
KBOK-AM - 1310 **(1264)**

Marshall
KCGS-AM - 960 **(1270)**

Mena
KENA-FM - 102.1 **(1277)**

Ozark
KDYN-AM - 1540 **(1306)**

Paragould
KDRS-AM - 1490 **(1309)**

Pocahontas
KPOC-AM - 1420 **(1318)**

Rogers
KURM-AM - 790 **(1329)**

Russellville
KXRJ-FM - 91.9 **(1334)**

Salem
KSAR-FM - 92.3 **(1336)**

State University
KASU-FM - 91.9 **(1351)**

Stuttgart
KWAK-AM - 1240 **(1353)**

CALIFORNIA
Bakersfield
KERN-AM - 1410 **(1461)**
KGEO-AM - 1230 **(1463)**
KNZR-AM - 1560 **(1469)**

Berkeley
KALX-FM - 90.7 **(1567)**

Carlsbad
KCEO-AM - 1000 **(1668)**

Chico
KPAY-AM - 1290 **(1704)**

Costa Mesa
XBACH-AM - 540 **(1785)**

Davis
KDVS-FM - 90.3 **(1819)**

El Centro
KXO-AM - 1230 **(1857)**

Eureka
KINS-AM - 980 **(1903)**

Fort Bragg
KSAY-FM - 98.5 **(1924)**

Fresno
KMJ-AM - 580 **(1974)**
KMPH-FM - 107.5 **(1975)**

Glendale
KTNQ-AM - 1020 **(2021)**

Grass Valley
KNCO-AM - 830 **(2030)**

Inglewood
KTYM-AM - 1460 **(2075)**

King City
KRKC-AM - 1490 **(2104)**

Los Angeles
KFWB-AM - 980 **(2456)**
KNX-AM - 1070 **(2464)**
KXLU-FM - 88.9 **(2472)**

Merced
KYOS-AM - 1480 **(2536)**

Modesto
KFIV-AM - 1360 **(2565)**

Napa
KVON-AM - 1440 **(2612)**

Palm Springs
KDES-AM - 920 **(2775)**
KPSI-AM - 920 **(2779)**

Pasadena
KPCC-FM - 89.3 **(2829)**

Porterville
KTIP-AM - 1450 **(2863)**

Redding
KQMS-AM - 1400 **(2893)**

Ridgecrest
KLOA-AM - 1240 **(2924)**

Sacramento
KFBK-AM - 1530 **(3029)**
KXPR-FM - 90.9 **(3056)**

San Bernardino
KVCR-FM - 91.9 **(3095)**

San Diego
KOGO-AM - 600 **(3307)**
KPBS-FM - 89.5 **(3308)**

San Francisco
KALW-FM - 91.7 **(3469)**
KCBS-AM - 740 **(3474)**
KCSF-FM - 90.9 **(3476)**
KGO-AM - 810 **(3484)**

San Jose
KLIV-AM - 1590 **(3550)**

San Mateo
KCSM-FM - 91.1 **(3592)**

NEWS (continued)

San Ysidro
XEBG-AM - 1550 **(3608)**
XEYX-AM - 820 **(3613)**

Sand City
KNRY-AM - 1240 **(3614)**

Santa Cruz
KSCO-AM - 1080 **(3691)**

Santa Maria
KSMA-AM - 1240 **(3699)**

Santa Rosa
KSRO-AM - 1350 **(3741)**

Solvang
KSYV-FM - 96.7 **(3772)**

Sonora
KVML-AM - 1450 **(3782)**

South Lake Tahoe
KOWL-AM - 1490 **(3785)**

Susanville
KSUE-AM - 1240 **(3834)**

Ukiah
KDAC-AM - 1230 **(3968)**
KUKI-AM - 1400 **(3969)**
KWNE-FM - 94.5 **(3971)**

Yreka
KSYC-AM - 1490 **(4122)**

Yuba City
KUBA-AM - 1600 **(4124)**

COLORADO
Alamosa
KGIW-AM - 1450 **(4135)**
KRZA-FM - 88.7 **(4136)**

Boulder
KGNU-FM - 88.5 **(4197)**

Canon City
KRLN-AM - 1400 **(4214)**

Colorado Springs
KRCC-FM - 91.5 **(4275)**
KVOR-AM - 740 **(4285)**

Cortez
KVFC-AM - 740 **(4294)**

Denver
KOA-AM - 850 **(4385)**
KVOD-FM - 90.1 FM **(4394)**
KXKL-FM - 105.1 **(4395)**

Fort Collins
KCOL-AM - 600 **(4440)**

Grand Junction
KPRN-FM - 89.5 **(4492)**

Longmont
KLMO-AM - 1060 **(4564)**

Pueblo
KCSJ-AM - 590 **(4603)**

Windsor
KVVS-AM - 1170 **(4689)**

CONNECTICUT
Bloomfield
WDRC-AM - 1360 **(4703)**

Brookfield
WINE-AM - 940 **(4730)**

Danbury
WRNE-AM - 980 **(4767)**

Fairfield
WSHU-FM - 91.1 **(4792)**

Farmington
WRCH-AM - 910 **(4865)**

Greenwich
WGCH-AM - 1490 **(4878)**

Hamden
WELI-AM - 960 **(4881)**
WQUN-AM - 1220 **(4884)**

New London
WSUB-AM - 980 **(5025)**

Norwich
WNPR-FM - 89.1 **(5087)**

Old Saybrook
WLIS-AM - 1420 **(5089)**

Plantsville
WNTY-AM - 990 **(5091)**

Waterbury
WATR-AM - 1320 **(5197)**

West Hartford
WWUH-FM - 91.3 **(5206)**

DELAWARE
Dover
WDOV-AM - 1410 **(5251)**

Wilmington
WDEL-AM - 1150 **(5297)**
WFAI-AM - 1510 **(5298)**
WILM-AM - 1450 **(5299)**

DISTRICT OF COLUMBIA
Washington
WAMU-FM - 88.5 **(5877)**
WPFW-FM - 89.3 **(5890)**
WTOP-AM - 1500 **(5895)**

FLORIDA
Boca Raton
WSBR-AM - 740 **(5943)**
WWNN-AM - 980 **(5944)**

Boynton Beach
WXEL-FM - 90.7 **(5954)**

Chiefland
WLQH-AM - 940 **(5982)**

Crestview
WXEI-FM - 95.3 **(6028)**

Daytona Beach
WNDB-AM - 1150 **(6044)**
WXVQ-AM - 1490 **(6046)**

DeFuniak Springs
WZEP-AM - 1460 **(6054)**

DeLand
WYND-AM - 1310 **(6057)**

Englewood
WENG-AM - 1530 **(6063)**

Fort Myers
WGCU-FM - 90.1 **(6104)**
WINK-AM - 1200 **(6106)**
WNOG-AM - 1270 **(6110)**

Fort Walton Beach
WFTW-AM - 1260 **(6123)**

Gainesville
WRUF-AM - 850 **(6165)**
WSKY-FM - 97.3 **(6167)**
WUFT-FM - 89.1 **(6168)**

Jacksonville
WJCT-FM - 89.9 **(6225)**
WZNZ-AM - 1460 **(6246)**

Lake Wales
WIPC-AM - 1280 **(6287)**

Lakeland
WLKF-AM - 1430 **(6293)**

Marianna
WTOT-AM - 980 **(6329)**
WTYS-AM - 1340 **(6330)**

Melbourne
WTAI-AM - 1560 **(6339)**

Miami
WLRN-FM - 91.3 **(6402)**
WMRZ-AM - 790 **(6407)**

Milton
WEBY-AM - 1330 **(6426)**
WECM-AM - 1490 **(6427)**

Miramar
WINZ-AM - 940 **(6429)**

Ocala
WOCA-AM - 1370 **(6477)**

Orlando
WDBO-AM - 580 **(6515)**

Ormond Beach
WELE-AM - 1380 **(6534)**

Pensacola
WSWL-AM - 790 **(6577)**
WUWF-FM - 88.1 **(6579)**

Port Charlotte
WVIJ-FM - 91.7 **(6597)**

Port St. Lucie
WAXE-AM - 1370 **(6602)**

St. Augustine
WFOY-AM - 1240 **(6620)**

Sarasota
WSPB-AM - 1450 **(6674)**

Tallahassee
WFSU-FM - 88.9 **(6747)**

Tampa
WFLA-AM - 970 **(6789)**
WUSF-FM - 89.7 **(6807)**

Tavares
WKIQ-AM - 1240 **(6813)**

Titusville
WAMT-AM - 1060 **(6822)**
WPGS-AM - 840 **(6823)**

Vero Beach
WTTB-AM - 1490 **(6839)**

West Palm Beach
WEAT-AM - 850 **(6850)**
WLVJ-AM - 640 **(6854)**

Winter Haven
WHNR-AM - 1360 **(6875)**

Zolfo Springs
WZTK-AM - 1480 **(6895)**

GEORGIA
Americus
WISK-AM - 1390 **(6925)**

Athens
WGAU-AM - 1340 **(6956)**

Atlanta
WABE-FM - 90.1 **(7064)**
WAOK-AM - 1380 **(7068)**
WSB-AM - 750 **(7085)**
WUNV-FM - 91.7 **(7089)**

Augusta
WACG-FM - 90.7 **(7104)**

Bogart
WRFC-AM - 960 **(7136)**

Brunswick
WMOG-AM - 1490 **(7142)**

Calhoun
WEBS-AM - 1030 **(7150)**

Canton
WCHK-AM - 1290 **(7153)**

Cartersville
WYXC-AM - 1270 **(7163)**

Cedartown
WGAA-AM - 1340 **(7166)**

Dalton
WBLJ-AM - 1230 **(7223)**
WDAL-AM - 1430 **(7224)**
WYYU-FM - 104.5 **(7226)**

Douglas
WDMG-AM - 860 **(7247)**
WDMG-FM - 99.5 **(7248)**

Dublin
WMLT-AM - 1330 **(7254)**

Gainesville
WDUN-AM - 550 **(7301)**

Griffin
WHIE-AM - 1320 **(7314)**

Kingsland
WKBX-FM - 106.3 **(7358)**

LaGrange
WTRP-AM - 620 **(7365)**

Macon
WBNM-AM - 1120 **(7391)**

WMAC-AM - 940 **(7397)**

Madison
WYTH-AM - 1250 **(7406)**

McDonough
WKKP-AM - 1410 **(7430)**

Milledgeville
WKGQ-AM - 1060 **(7438)**
WMVG-AM - 1450 **(7440)**

Rome
WLAQ-AM - 1410 **(7505)**
WRGA-AM - 1470 **(7507)**
WTSH-AM - 1360 **(7509)**

Savannah
WSVH-FM - 91.1 **(7549)**

Swainsboro
WXRS-AM - 1590 **(7579)**

Thomson
WTHO-FM - 101.7 **(7593)**

Valdosta
WJEM-AM - 1150 **(7622)**

Warm Springs
WJSP-FM - 88.1 **(7636)**

West Point
WCJM-FM - 100.9 **(7651)**

HAWAII
Hilo
KPUA-AM - 670 **(7677)**

Honolulu
KKUA-FM - 90.7 **(7745)**
KZOO-AM - 1210 **(7758)**

Kahului
KNUI-AM - 900 **(7761)**

Lihue
KQNG-AM - 570 **(7782)**

IDAHO
Boise
KBSU-FM - 90.3 **(7818)**
KBSY-FM - 88.5 **(7819)**
KIDO-AM - 580 **(7823)**
KWEI-AM - 1260 **(7832)**

Coeur d'Alene
KVNI-AM - 1080 **(7848)**

Idaho Falls
KID-AM - 590 **(7874)**

McCall
KBSM-FM - 91.7 **(7906)**

Pocatello
KPKY-FM - 94.9 **(7952)**
KWIK-AM - 1240 **(7955)**

Rexburg
KADQ-FM - 94.3 **(7965)**

Rupert
KBAR-AM - 1230 **(7968)**

Salmon
KSRA-AM - 92.7 **(7975)**

Soda Springs
KBRV-AM - 790 **(7983)**

Twin Falls
KBSW-FM - 91.7 **(7991)**
KLIX-AM - 1310 **(7995)**

ILLINOIS
Alton
WBGZ-AM - 1570 **(8011)**

Aurora
WBIG-AM - 1280 **(8042)**
WKKD-AM - 1580 **(8043)**

Carbondale
WSIU-FM - 91.9 **(8123)**

Carmi
WROY-AM - 1460 **(8132)**
WRUL-FM - 97.3 **(8133)**

Carterville
WJPF-AM - 1020 **(8163)**

Carthage
WCAZ-AM - 990 **(8166)**

Champaign
WDWS-AM - 1400 **(8225)**

Chicago
WBBM-AM - 780 **(8613)**
WGN-AM - 720 **(8625)**
WLS-AM - 890 **(8638)**
WMAQ-AM - 670 **(8642)**

Crest Hill
WJOL-AM - 1340 **(8690)**

Danville
WDAN-AM - 1490 **(8705)**

Decatur
WDZ-AM - 1050 **(8716)**
WSOY-AM - 1340 **(8720)**

DeKalb
WLBK-AM - 1360 **(8743)**
WNIJ-FM - 90.5 **(8744)**

Edwardsville
WSIE-FM - 88.7 **(8815)**

Effingham
WCRA-AM - 1090 **(8819)**
WCRC-FM - 95.7 **(8820)**

Elgin
WRMN-AM - 1410 **(8829)**

Fairfield
WFIW-AM - 1390 **(8881)**

Galesburg
WGIL-AM - 1400 **(8910)**

Glen Ellyn
WDCB-FM - 90.9 **(8933)**

Herrin
WJPF-AM - 1340 **(8984)**

Highland
WCBW-AM - 880 **(8990)**

Jacksonville
WJIL-AM - 1550 **(9026)**
WLDS-AM - 1180 **(9028)**

Kewanee
WKEI-AM - 1450 **(9047)**

Macomb
WIUM-FM - 91.3 **(9134)**
WLRB-AM - 1510 **(9136)**

Marion
WDDD-AM - 810 **(9145)**

McLeansboro
WMCL-AM - 1060 **(9168)**

Metropolis
WNPX-AM - 750 **(9181)**

Monmouth
WMOI-FM - 97.7 **(9220)**
WRAM-AM - 1330 **(9221)**

Murphysboro
WINI-AM - 1420 **(9259)**

Normal
WGLT-FM - 89.1-FM **(9308)**
WZND-FM - 106.1 **(9310)**

Olney
WVLN-AM - 740 **(9385)**

Park Ridge
WMTH-FM - 90.5 **(9409)**

Peoria
WCBU-FM - 89.9 **(9430)**

Pittsfield
WBBA-AM - 1580 **(9456)**

Plano
WSPY-FM - 107.1 **(9459)**

Princeton
WZOE-AM - 1490 **(9468)**

Quincy
WGEM-AM - 1440 **(9478)**
WGEM-FM - 105.1 **(9479)**
WTAD-AM - 930 **(9483)**

Rock Island
WVIK-FM - 90.3 **(9525)**

Rockford
WROK-AM - 1440 **(9541)**

Salem
WJBD-FM - 100.1 **(9579)**

Sparta
WHCO-AM - 1230 **(9618)**

Spaulding
WMAY-AM - 970 **(9619)**

Springfield
WUIS-FM - 91.9 **(9658)**

Sterling
WSDR-AM - 1240 **(9664)**

Streator
WSPL-AM - 1250 **(9670)**

Taylorville
WTIM-FM - 97.3 **(9680)**

Urbana
WILL-AM - 580 **(9723)**

Waukegan
WKRS-AM - 1220 **(9746)**

Winnetka
WNTH-FM - 88.1 **(9769)**

INDIANA
Bloomington
WFIU-FM - 103.7 **(9857)**
WGCL-AM - 1370 **(9858)**

Columbus
WCSI-AM - 1010 **(9896)**

Daleville
WHBU-AM - 1240 **(9918)**

Elkhart
WTRC-AM - 1340 **(9929)**
WVPE-FM - 88.1 **(9930)**

Evansville
WGBF-AM - 1280 **(9942)**
WNIN-FM - 88.3 **(9947)**

Fort Wayne
WBNI-FM - 89.1 **(9979)**
WOWO-AM - 1190 **(9991)**

Indianapolis
WBRI-AM - 1500 **(10191)**
WFYI-FM - 90.1 **(10195)**

Linton
WBTO-FM - 93.3 **(10274)**

Madison
WORX-FM - 96.7 **(10285)**
WXGO-AM - 1270 **(10286)**

Marion
WGOM-AM - 860 **(10291)**

Merrillville
WLTH-AM - 1370 **(10301)**

Muncie
WBST-FM - 92.1 **(10330)**

North Vernon
WNVI-AM - 1460 **(10365)**

Richmond
WHON-AM - 930 **(10424)**
WKBV-AM - 1490 **(10425)**

Rushville
WKWH-FM - 94.3 **(10438)**

Seymour
WZZB-AM - 1390 **(10451)**

South Bend
WSBT-AM - 960 **(10466)**

Terre Haute
WTHI-AM - 1480 **(10502)**

Valparaiso
WNWI-AM - 1080 **(10514)**

Vincennes
WAOV-AM - 1450 **(10524)**

West Lafayette
WBAA-AM - 920 **(10556)**

Circulation: ★ = ABC; △ = BPA; ♦ = CAC; • = CCAB; ❑ = VAC; ⊕ = PO Statement; ‡ = Publisher's Report; Boldface figures = sworn; Light figures = estimated.

3043

NEWS (continued)

IOWA

Ames
WOI-AM - 640 (10599)

Atlantic
KJAN-AM - 1220 (10611)

Burlington
KCPS-AM - 1150 (10642)

Cedar Falls
KCNZ-AM - 1250 (10665)

Cedar Rapids
KCRG-AM - 1600 (10679)
WMT-AM - 600 (10685)

Clinton
KROS-AM - 1340 (10713)

Davenport
WOC-AM - 1420 (10751)

Decorah
KDEC-AM - 1240 (10759)

Des Moines
WHO-AM - 1040 (10837)

Dubuque
KDTH-AM - 1370 (10848)
WDBQ-AM - 1490 (10854)

Dyersville
KDST-FM - 99.3 (10861)

Estherville
KILR-AM - 1070 (10879)

Fairfield
KMCD-AM - 1570 (10886)

Fort Dodge
KTPR-FM - 91.1 (10912)

Hampton
KLMJ-FM - 104.9 (10941)

Iowa City
KCJJ-AM - 1630 (10991)
KXIC-AM - 800 (10995)
WSUI-AM - 910 (10998)

Keokuk
KOKX-AM - 1310 (11014)

Marshalltown
KFJB-AM - 1230 (11068)

Mason City
KGLO-AM - 1300 (11075)

Muscatine
KWPC-AM - 860 (11106)

Oelwein
KOEL-AM - 950 (11124)

Ottumwa
KBIZ-AM - 1240 (11141)
KLEE-AM - 1480 (11142)

Red Oak
KCSI-FM - 95.3 (11171)
KOAK-AM - 1080 (11173)

Shenandoah
KMA-AM - 960 (11200)

Sioux Center
KDCR-FM - 88.5 (11209)

Sioux City
KSCJ-AM - 1360 (11219)
KWIT-FM - 90.3 (11225)
KWSL-AM - 1470 (11226)

Spencer
KDWD-FM - 100.1 (11232)
KICD-AM - 1240 (11233)

Stuart
KGRA-FM - 98.9 (11256)

Waterloo
KXEL-AM - 1540 (11301)

Webster City
KQWC-AM - 1570 (11315)
KQWC-FM - 95.7 (11316)

KANSAS

Abilene
KABI-AM - 1560 (11335)

Brewster
KGCR-FM - 107.7 (11366)

Chanute
KKOY-AM - 1460 (11378)

Concordia
KNCK-AM - 1390 (11399)

Goodland
KLOE-AM - 730 (11467)

Great Bend
KVGB-AM - 1590 (11473)

Hiawatha
KNZA-FM - 103.9 (11493)

Hutchinson
KHCC-FM - 90.1 (11505)
KWBW-AM - 1450 (11507)

Lawrence
KLWN-AM - 1320 (11575)

Manhattan
KMAN-AM - 1350 (11633)

Overland Park
KCCV-AM - 760 (11739)

Pratt
KWLS-AM - 1290-AM (11766)

Salina
KHCD-FM - 89.5 (11786)
KSAL-AM - 1150 (11789)

Topeka
WIBW-AM - 580 (11846)

Westwood
KMBZ-AM - 980 (11872)

Wichita
KMUW-FM - 89.1 (11899)
KNSS-AM - 1240 (11900)

Winfield
KKLE-AM - 1550 (11911)

KENTUCKY

Albany
WANY-AM - 1390 (11915)
WANY-FM - 106.3 (11916)

Bowling Green
WBGN-AM - 1340 (11951)
WKCT-AM - 930 (11958)

Columbia
WAIN-AM - 1270 (12018)

Corbin
WKDP-AM - 1330 (12024)

Danville
WHIR-AM - 1230 (12041)

Elizabethtown
WIEL-AM - 1400 (12047)

Elkton
WEKT-AM - 1070 (12052)

Harlan
WFSR-AM - 970 (12106)

Hartford
WSNR-AM - 1600 (12113)

Hazard
WEKH-FM - 90.9 (12117)

Henderson
WSON-AM - 860 (12125)

Highland Heights
WNKU-FM - 89.7 (12127)

Hopkinsville
WHOP-AM - 1230 (12133)

Lexington
WLAP-AM - 630 (12190)
WRFL-FM - 88.1 (12194)
WUKY-FM - 91.3 (12197)

London
WFTG-AM - 1400 (12204)

Louisville
WFPL-FM - 89.3 (12251)
WHAS-AM - 840 (12252)
WNAI-AM - 680 (12261)

Marion
WMJL-AM - 1500 (12282)

Maysville
WFTM-AM - 1240 (12289)

Middlesboro
WFXY-AM - 1490 (12294)

Morehead
WMKY-FM - 90.3 (12306)

Murray
WKMS-FM - 91.3/92.1 Paducah, KY; 99.5 Paris, TN (12319)
WNBS-AM - 1340 (12320)

Owensboro
WOMI-AM - 1490 (12331)

Paducah
WKYQ-FM - 93.3 (12345)
WKYX-AM - 570 (12346)

Prestonsburg
WDOC-AM - 1310 (12372)

Richmond
WEKU-FM - 88.9 (12385)

Somerset
WSFC-AM - 1240 (12410)
WTLO-AM - 1480 (12412)

Vancleve
WMTC-AM - 730 (12427)
WMTC-FM - 99.9 (12428)

LOUISIANA

Alexandria
KDBS-AM - 1410 (12462)

Baton Rouge
WJBO-AM - 1150 (12518)

Bogalusa
WIKC-AM - 1490 (12535)

Eunice
KEUN-AM - 1490 (12576)

Lake Providence
KLPL-AM - 1050 (12653)

Metairie
WGSO-AM - 990 (12681)

Monroe
KEDM-FM - 90.3 (12694)
KMLB-AM - 1440 (12698)

Natchitoches
KNOC-AM - 1450 (12719)

New Orleans
WSMB-AM - 1350 (12777)
WWL-AM - 870 (12780)
WWNO-FM - 89.9 (12782)

Opelousas
KSLO-AM - 1230 (12793)

Shreveport
KBCL-AM - 1070 (12822)
KEEL-AM - 710 (12824)
KLSA-FM - 90.7 (12827)

Slidell
WSLA-AM - 1560 (12845)

Thibodaux
KTIB-AM - 640 (12862)

Ville Platte
KVPI-AM - 1050 (12866)

MAINE

Auburn
WLAM-FM-1470 - 106.7 (12886)

Augusta
WFAU-AM - 1280 (12899)

Bangor
WZON-AM - 620 (12916)

Dover Foxcroft
WDME-FM - 103.1 (12953)

Portland
WLOB-AM - 1310 (13028)

Sanford
WSME-AM - 1220 (13051)

South Portland
WGAN-AM - 560 **(13054)**

Waterville
WMHB-FM - 89.7 **(13073)**

MARYLAND
Annapolis
WBIS-AM - 1190 **(13098)**

Baltimore
WBAL-AM - 1090 **(13265)**
WJHU-FM - 88.1 **(13276)**

Chestertown
WCTR-AM - 1530 **(13406)**

College Park
WMUC-FM - 88.1 **(13447)**

Cumberland
WCBC-AM - 1270 **(13476)**
WNTR-AM - 1230 **(13478)**

Frostburg
WFWM-FM - 91.9 **(13529)**

Gaithersburg
WMET-AM - 1150 **(13552)**

Hagerstown
WHAG-AM - 1410 **(13575)**

Lanham
WOL-AM - 1450 **(13611)**

Lexington Park
WMDM-AM - 1690 **(13617)**

Mechanicsville
WSMD-FM - 98.3 **(13627)**

Princess Anne
WESM-FM - 91.3 **(13670)**

Salisbury
WICO-AM - 1320 **(13715)**
WSCL-FM - 89.5 **(13719)**
WSDL-FM - 90.7 **(13720)**

Thurmont
WTHU-AM - 1450 **(13756)**

MASSACHUSETTS
Amherst
WFCR-FM - 88.5 **(13809)**

Boston
WBUR-FM - 90.9 **(13978)**
WBZ-AM - 1030 **(13979)**
WGBH-FM - 89.7 **(13985)**
WTBU-FM - 89.3 **(13997)**

Brockton
WBET-AM - 1460 **(14014)**

Fairhaven
WBSM-AM - 1420 **(14178)**

Fitchburg
WEIM-AM - 1280 **(14185)**

Harwich
WCCT-FM - 90.3 **(14231)**

Lowell
WCAP-AM - 980 **(14281)**

Methuen
WCCM-AM - 1490 **(14329)**
WHAV-AM - 1490 **(14330)**

Milton
WMLN-FM - 91.5 **(14338)**

North Adams
WNAW-AM - 1230 **(14421)**

Northampton
WHMP-AM - 1400 **(14432)**

Northfield
WNMH-FM - 91.5 **(14436)**

Orange
WCAT-AM - 700 **(14452)**

Pittsfield
WBEC-AM - 1420 **(14473)**

Plymouth
WPLM-AM - 1390 **(14483)**

Quincy
WJDA-AM - 1300 **(14493)**

Salem
WESX-AM - 1230 **(14516)**

Somerset
WSAR-AM - 1480 **(14529)**

Taunton
WPEP-AM - 1570 **(14585)**

West Yarmouth
WXTK-FM - 95.1 **(14634)**

Woods Hole
WCAI-FM - 90.1 **(14674)**

Worcester
WCUW-FM - 91.3 **(14696)**
WGFP-AM - 940 **(14697)**
WICN-FM - 90.5 **(14698)**

MICHIGAN
Adrian
WABJ-AM - 1490 **(14711)**

Alpena
WATZ-AM - 1450 **(14736)**
WCML-FM - 91.7 **(14739)**

Ann Arbor
WAAM-AM - 1600 **(14774)**
WTKA-AM - 1050 **(14780)**
WUOM-FM - 91.7 **(14781)**

Battle Creek
WBCK-AM - 930 **(14794)**

Big Rapids
WBRN-AM - 1460 **(14820)**

Cadillac
WATT-AM - 1240 **(14844)**

Detroit
WDET-FM - 101.9 **(14957)**
WJR-AM - 760 **(14968)**

East Lansing
WKAR-AM - 870 **(14995)**

Flint
WFDF-AM - 910 **(15042)**

Frankfort
WBNZ-FM - 99.3 **(15054)**

Fremont
WSHN-AM - 1550 **(15061)**

Grand Rapids
WBMX-AM - 640 **(15104)**
WGVU-AM - 1480 **(15109)**
WGVU-FM - 88.5 **(15110)**
WNWZ-AM - 1410 **(15116)**
WVGR-FM - 104.1 **(15125)**

Hancock
WMPL-AM - 920 **(15142)**

Houghton
WGGL-FM - 91.1 **(15186)**

Ionia
WION-AM - 1430 **(15207)**

Iron Mountain
WMIQ-AM - 1450 **(15209)**

Ishpeming
WIAN-AM - 1240 **(15218)**

Jackson
WKHM-AM - 970 **(15226)**

Kalamazoo
WKZO-AM - 590 **(15254)**
WMUK-FM - 102.1 **(15256)**

Lansing
WJIM-AM - 1240 **(15300)**

Ludington
WKLA-AM - 1450 **(15323)**

Manistee
WMTE-AM - 1340 **(15332)**

Marquette
WDMJ-AM - 1320 **(15340)**
WNMU-FM - 90.1, 107.1, 91.9, 91.3, 91.1,
  107.3 **(15346)**
WZAM-AM - 970 **(15350)**

Monroe
WTWR-FM - 98.3 **(15368)**

Mount Pleasant
WCMU-FM - 89.5 **(15380)**
WMMI-AM - 830 **(15384)**

Ontonagon
WUPY-FM - 101.1 **(15424)**

Petoskey
WJML-AM - 1110 **(15438)**
WWKK-AM - 750 **(15442)**

Pittsford
WPCJ-FM - 91.1 **(15445)**

Rogers City
WVXA-FM - 96.7 **(15471)**

Saginaw
WCEN-AM - 1150 **(15495)**
WSGW-AM - 790 **(15505)**

St. Joseph
WSJM-AM - 1400 **(15516)**

Sault Sainte Marie
WKNW-AM - 1400 **(15529)**

Southfield
WWJ-AM - 950 **(15561)**

Three Rivers
WLKM-FM - 95.9 **(15596)**

Traverse City
WTCM-AM - 580 **(15614)**

Twin Lake
WBLV-FM - 90.3 **(15645)**

Ypsilanti
WEMU-FM - 89.1 **(15692)**

MINNESOTA
Albert Lea
KATE-AM - 1450 **(15707)**
KATE-FM - 1450 **(15708)**

Brainerd
KLIZ-AM - 1380 **(15769)**
WWWI-AM - 1270 **(15771)**

Collegeville
KJNB-FM - 99.9 **(15807)**
KNSR-FM - 88.9 **(15808)**

Crookston
KROX-AM - 1260 **(15821)**

Detroit Lakes
KDLM-AM - 1340 **(15832)**

Duluth
KDAL-AM - 610 **(15845)**
KUMD-FM - 103.3 **(15852)**
WDSM-AM - 710 **(15855)**

Fairmont
KSUM-AM - 1370 **(15892)**

Faribault
KDHL-AM - 920 **(15895)**

Fergus Falls
KBRF-AM - 1250 **(15900)**

Forest Lake
WLKX-FM - 95.9 **(15907)**

Grand Rapids
KOZY-AM - 1320 **(15932)**

Hastings
KDWA-AM - 1460 **(15942)**

Hibbing
WHLB-AM - 1400 **(15956)**
WNMT-AM - 650 **(15960)**

International Falls
KGHS-AM - 1230 **(15969)**

Luverne
KQAD-AM - 800 **(16016)**

Madison
KLQP-FM - 92.1 **(16021)**

Mankato
KEEZ-FM - 99.1 **(16032)**
KTOE-AM - 1420 **(16035)**

Marshall
KMHL-AM - 1400 **(16047)**

Montevideo
KDMA-AM - 1460 **(16181)**

NEWS (continued)

Moorhead
KCCD-FM - 90.3 **(16190)**
KNTN-FM - 102.7 **(16192)**

New Ulm
KNUJ-AM - 860 **(16217)**

Northfield
KYMN-AM - 1080 **(16239)**

Park Rapids
KDKK-FM - 97.5 **(16257)**
KPRM-AM - 870 **(16258)**

Red Wing
KCUE-AM - 1250 **(16294)**

Redwood Falls
KLGR-AM - 1490 **(16299)**
KLGR-FM - 97.7 **(16300)**

Rochester
KNFX-AM - 970 **(16315)**
KROC-AM - 1340 **(16318)**
KWEB-AM - 1270 **(16321)**
KXLC-FM - 91.1 **(16323)**
KZSE-FM - 90.7 **(16326)**

St. Cloud
KNSI-AM - 1450 **(16351)**
WJON-AM - 1240 **(16353)**

St. Peter
KRBI-AM - 1310 **(16432)**

Waseca
KOWZ-AM - 1170 **(16501)**

Willmar
KWLM-AM - 1340 **(16522)**

Worthington
KWOA-AM - 730 **(16541)**

MISSISSIPPI

Biloxi
WMAH-FM - 90.3 **(16566)**
WVMI-AM - 570 **(16570)**

Booneville
WMAE-FM - 91.3 **(16574)**

Cleveland
WDSK-AM - 1410 **(16593)**

Columbus
WKOR-AM - 980 **(16611)**

Greenwood
WMAO-FM - 90.9 **(16651)**

Gulfport
WROA-AM - 1390 **(16658)**
WZKX-FM - 107.9 **(16660)**

Houston
WCPC-AM - 940 **(16686)**

Jackson
WJNT-AM - 1180 **(16719)**
WKNP-FM - 90.1 **(16721)**
WMPN-FM - 91.3 **(16724)**

Lorman
WPRL-FM - 91.7 **(16749)**

Meadville
WMAU-FM - 88.9 **(16768)**

Mississippi State
WMAB-FM - 89.9 **(16786)**

Natchez
WQNZ-FM - 95.1 **(16796)**

Oxford
WMAV-FM - 90.3 **(16808)**

Pascagoula
WGUD-AM - 1490 **(16813)**

Philadelphia
WHOC-AM - 1490 **(16817)**

Senatobia
WKNA-FM - 88.9 **(16843)**

Tupelo
WELO-AM - 580 **(16851)**
WWMS-FM - 97.5 **(16860)**

MISSOURI

Ava
KKOZ-AM - 1430 **(16897)**
KKOZ-FM - 92.1 **(16898)**

Butler
KMAM-AM - 1530 **(16932)**

Cameron
KMRN-AM - 1360 **(16940)**

Cape Girardeau
KZIM-AM - 960 **(16954)**

Clinton
KDKD-AM - 1280 **(16985)**

Columbia
KBIA-FM - 91.3 **(17013)**
KFRU-AM - 1400 **(17017)**
KOPN-FM - 89.5 **(17020)**

Farmington
KREI-AM - 800 **(17055)**

Festus
KJFF-AM - 1400 **(17066)**

Hannibal
KHMO-AM - 1070 **(17091)**

Jefferson City
KLIK-AM - 1240 **(17139)**

Joplin
KQYX-AM - 1450 **(17148)**

Kansas City
KCUR-FM - 89.3 **(17208)**

Kennett
KMIS-AM - 1050 **(17222)**

Kirksville
KIRX-AM - 1450 **(17230)**

Lebanon
KBNN-AM - 750 **(17239)**
KTTK-FM - 90.7 **(17242)**

Marshall
KMMO-AM - 102.9 **(17266)**
KMMO-FM - 102.9 **(17267)**

Maryville
KXCV-FM - 90.5 **(17279)**

Mexico
KWWR-FM - 95.7 **(17287)**
KXEO-AM - 1340 **(17288)**

Monett
KRMO-AM - 990 **(17295)**

Osage Beach
KRMS-AM - 1150 **(17322)**

Perryville
KBDZ-FM - 93.1 **(17342)**

Piedmont
KPWB-AM - 1140 **(17344)**

Point Lookout
KCOZ-FM - 91.7 **(17355)**

Potosi
KYRO-AM - 1280 **(17365)**

Richmond
KAYX-FM - 92.5 **(17376)**

Rolla
KUMR-FM - 88.5 **(17382)**

St. Charles
KCLC-FM - 89.1 **(17385)**

St. Louis
KMOX-AM - 1120 **(17543)**
KTRS-AM - 550 **(17551)**
KWMU-FM - 90.7 **(17553)**

Sedalia
KSIS-AM - 1050 **(17574)**

Sikeston
KMAL-FM - 92.9 **(17585)**
KSIM-AM - 1400 **(17587)**
KTCB-AM - 1470 **(17588)**

Springfield
KTTS-FM - 94.7 **(17630)**
KWTO-AM - 560 **(17633)**

Sullivan
KTUI-AM - 1560 **(17642)**

Thayer
KAMS-FM - 95.1 **(17650)**

Warrensburg
KTBG-FM - 90.9 **(17673)**

Warrenton
KWRE-AM - 730 **(17702)**

Washington
KLPW-AM - 1220 **(17708)**

MONTANA

Billings
KBLG-AM - 910 **(17737)**
KBUL-AM - 970 **(17738)**

Butte
KXTL-AM - 1370 **(17767)**

Havre
KOJM-AM - 610 **(17814)**

Helena
KBLL-AM - 1240 **(17825)**
KCAP-AM - 1340 **(17827)**

Kalispell
KALS-FM - 97.1 **(17839)**
KOFI-AM - 1180 **(17842)**

Laurel
KBSR-AM - 1490 **(17847)**

NEBRASKA

Alliance
KCOW-AM - 1400 **(17929)**
KTNE-FM - 91.1 **(17931)**

Crookston
KINI-FM - 96.1 **(17996)**

Falls City
KTNC-AM - 1230 **(18010)**

Fremont
KHUB-AM - 1340 **(18014)**

Hastings
KHNE-FM - 89.1 **(18041)**

Johnson
KCOE-FM - 105.5 **(18057)**

Kearney
KGFW-AM - 1340 **(18061)**

Lexington
KLNE-FM - 88.7 **(18073)**
KRVN-AM - 880 **(18075)**
KRVN-FM - 93.1 **(18076)**

Lincoln
KCNE-FM - 91.9 **(18131)**
KLCV-FM - 88.5 **(18135)**
KLIN-AM - 1400 **(18136)**
KMNE-FM - 90.3 **(18139)**
KPNE-FM - 91.7 **(18141)**
KRNE-FM - 91.5 **(18142)**
KUCV-FM - 91.1 FM **(18146)**
KZUM-FM - 89.3 **(18148)**

McCook
KSWN-FM - 93.9 **(18159)**

Norfolk
KEXL-FM - 106.7 **(18171)**
KXNE-FM - 89.3 **(18172)**
WJAG-AM - 780 **(18174)**

North Platte
KODY-AM - 1240 **(18182)**
KOOQ-AM - 1410 **(18183)**

Ogallala
KMCX-FM - 106.5 **(18189)**

Omaha
KFAB-AM - 1110 **(18217)**
KIOS-FM - 91.5 **(18220)**
KKAR-AM - 1290 **(18221)**
KVNO-FM - 90.7 **(18228)**

Sidney
KSID-AM - 1340 **(18279)**

NEVADA

Las Vegas
KDWN-AM - 720 **(18394)**
KENO-AM - 1460 **(18395)**
KNUU-AM - 970 **(18402)**
KSHP-AM - 1400 **(18404)**
KXNT-AM - 840 **(18409)**

       Numbers cited in bold after listings are entry numbers rather than page numbers.

Reno
KPLY-AM - 1230 (18436)
KPTT-AM - 630 (18437)
KUNR-FM - 88.7 (18442)

Tonopah
KTPH-FM - 91.7 (18449)

NEW HAMPSHIRE
Concord
WEVO-FM - 89.1 (18476)
WKXL-AM - 1450 (18478)
WTPL-FM - 107.7 (18481)

Dover
WTSN-AM - 1270 (18496)

Gilford
WEMJ-AM - 1490 (18512)

Keene
WKNE-AM - 1290 (18533)

Littleton
WLTN-AM - 1400 (18551)

Manchester
WGIR-AM - 610 (18569)

Portsmouth
WGIN-AM - 930 (18639)
WGIP-AM - 1540 (18640)

Winchester
WKBK-AM - 1290 (18651)

Wolfeboro
WASR-AM - 1420 (18656)

NEW JERSEY
Lincroft
WBJB-FM - 90.5 (19170)

Linwood
WOND-AM - 1400 (19174)

Millville
WMVB-AM - 1440 (19237)

New Brunswick
WCTC-AM - 1450 (19342)

Newton
WSUS-FM - 102.3 (19379)

Pompton Lakes
WGHT-AM - 1500 (19450)

Toms River
WOBM-FM - 92.7 (19651)

Trenton
WKOE-FM - 106.3 (19675)
WKXW-FM - 101.5 (19676)

NEW MEXICO
Alamogordo
KINN-AM - 1270 (19759)
KRSY-AM - 1230 (19760)

Artesia
KSVP-AM - 990 (19818)

Carlsbad
KCCC-AM - 930 (19825)

Clayton
KLMX-AM - 1450 (19829)

Clovis
KICA-AM - 980 (19833)
KWKA-AM - 680 (19837)

Farmington
KENN-AM - 1390 (19847)

Las Cruces
KOBE-AM - 1450 (19884)
KRWG-FM - 90.7 (19885)

Los Alamos
KRSN-AM - 1490 (19895)

Magdalena
KABR-AM - 1500 (19901)

Maljamar
KMTH-FM - 98.7 (19902)

Pinehill
KTDB-FM - 89.7 (19904)

Portales
KENW-FM - 89.5 (19905)

Raton
KRTN-AM - 1490 (19911)

Roswell
KBIM-AM - 910 (19915)

Taos
KKIT-AM - 1340 (19964)

Truth or Consequences
KCHS-AM - 1400 (19970)

NEW YORK
Albany
WAMC-FM - 90.3 (20009)
WGY-AM - 810 (20011)

Avon
WYSL-AM - 1030 (20110)

Batavia
WBTA-AM - 1490 (20122)

Binghamton
WNBF-AM - 1290 (20227)
WSKG-FM - 89.3 (20228)
WSQE-FM - 91.1 (20230)
WSQG-FM - 89.3 (20231)
WSQX-FM - 88.7 (20232)
WSQX-FM - 91.5 (20233)

Brockport
WBSU-FM - 89.1 (20249)

Buffalo
WBFO-FM - 88.7 (20395)
WNED-AM - 970 (20408)

Canajoharie
WCAN-FM - 93.3 (20418)

Clinton
WHCL-FM - 88.7 (20475)

Clintondale
WRWD-FM - 107.3 (20476)

Crown Point
WIPS-AM - 1250 (20516)

Elmira
WQIX-AM - 820 (20579)
WWLZ-AM - 820 (20580)

Fredonia
WBKX-FM - 96.5 (20623)

Gouverneur
WGIX-FM - 95.3 (20676)

Hartsdale
WFAS-AM - 1230 (20714)

Horseheads
WENY-AM - 1230 (20761)

Ithaca
WHCU-AM - 870 (20818)

Jamestown
WJTN-AM - 1240 (20844)

Jeffersonville
WJFF-FM - 90.5 (20848)

Kingston
WAMK-FM - 90.9 (20863)

Massena
WYBG-AM - 1050 (21029)

Monticello
WDNB-FM - 102.1 (21093)

Nanuet
WRCR-AM - 1300 (21106)

New Rochelle
WVOX-AM - 1460 (21125)

New York
WABC-AM - 770 (22960)
WCBS-AM - 880 (22965)
WEVD-AM - 1050 (22968)
WHCR-FM - 90.3 (22970)
WINS-AM - 1010 (22971)
WKCR-FM - 89.9 (22972)
WNWK-FM - 105.9 (22978)
WNYC-AM - 820 (22979)
WPAT-FM - 93.1 (22984)

Newark
WACK-AM - 1420 (22998)

Newburgh
WGNY-AM - 1200 (23002)

Ogdensburg
WPAC-FM - 92.7 (23034)

Olean
WMNS-AM - 1360 (23042)

Ossining
WOSS-FM - 91.1 (23060)

Oswego
WNYO-FM - 88.9 (23063)
WRVO-FM - 89.9 (23064)

Owego
WEBO-AM - 1330 (23068)

Pomona
WRKL-AM - 910 (23113)

Rochester
WDKX-FM - 103.9 (23245)
WHAM-AM - 1180 (23247)
WXXI-AM - 1370 (23258)

Saranac Lake
WNBZ-AM - 1240 (23298)

Schenectady
WRCZ-FM - 94.5 (23319)

Sidney
WCDO-AM - 1490 (23333)
WCDO-FM - 100.9 (23334)

Southampton
WPBX-FM - 88.3 (23346)

Syracuse
WAER-FM - 88.3 (23434)
WSYR-AM - 570 (23445)

Ticonderoga
WANC-FM - 103.9 (23451)

Walton
WDLA-FM - 92.1 (23499)

Watertown
WATN-AM - 1240 (23515)

Woodstock
WDST-FM - 100.1 (23597)

NORTH CAROLINA
Aberdeen
WQNX-AM - 1350 (23612)

Asheville
WFQS-FM - 91.3 (23636)

Belmont
WCGC-AM - 1270 (23643)

Burlington
WBAG-AM - 1150 (23674)

Chapel Hill
WUNC-FM - 91.5 (23732)

Charlotte
WBT-AM - 1110 (23764)
WBT-FM - 99.3 (23765)

Durham
WNCU-FM - 90.7 (23849)
WSRC-AM - 1410 (23851)

Edenton
WZBO-AM - 1260 (23859)

Elizabeth City
WGAI-AM - 560 (23862)

Elkin
WIFM-AM - 100.9 (23869)

Fayetteville
WFNC-AM - 640 (23886)

Graham
WSML-AM - 1200 (23913)

Greenville
WCZI-FM - 98.3 (23971)
WNCT-AM - 1070 (23972)

High Point
WMFR-AM - 1230 (24005)

Jacksonville
WLAS-AM - 910 (24014)

Lexington
WLXN-AM - 1440 (24041)

Lincolnton
WLON-AM - 1050 (24046)

Circulation: ★ = ABC; △ = BPA; ♦ = CAC; • = CCAB; ❑ = VAC; ⊕ = PO Statement; ‡ = Publisher's Report; Boldface figures = sworn; Light figures = estimated.

3047

NEWS (continued)

Mars Hill
WVMH-FM - 90.5 **(24058)**

New Bern
WTEB-FM - 89.3 **(24102)**

Newport
WTKF-FM - 107.3 **(24105)**

Pisgah Forest
WGCR-AM - 720 **(24117)**

Rockingham
WAYN-AM - 900 **(24202)**

Rutherfordton
WCAB-AM - 590 **(24212)**

Salisbury
WSAT-AM - 1280 **(24217)**
WSTP-AM - 1490 **(24218)**

Sanford
WFJA-FM - 105.5 **(24221)**
WXKL-AM - 1290 **(24222)**

Shelby
WOHS-AM - 730 **(24229)**

Southern Pines
WEEB-AM - 990 **(24237)**

Washington
WDLX-AM - 930 **(24274)**

Whiteville
WTXY-AM - 1540 **(24287)**

Williamston
WIAM-AM - 900 **(24292)**

Wilmington
WAAV-FM - 94.1 **(24299)**
WHQR-FM - 91.3 **(24301)**
WMFD-AM - 630 **(24303)**

Winston-Salem
WFDD-FM - 88.5 **(24330)**
WSJS-AM - 600 **(24332)**
WSNC-FM - 90.5 **(24333)**
WXII-AM - 830 **(24336)**

NORTH DAKOTA

Beulah
KHOL-AM - 1410 **(24348)**

Bismarck
KCND-FM - 90.5 **(24366)**
KYYY-FM - 92.9 **(24374)**

Devils Lake
KDLR-AM - 1240 **(24391)**

Fargo
KDSU-FM - 91.9 **(24417)**
KFGO-AM - 790 **(24419)**
KVOX-AM - 1280 **(24430)**
WDAY-AM - 970 **(24434)**

Grand Forks
KNOX-AM - 1310 **(24462)**
KUND-AM - 1370 **(24463)**
KZLT-FM - 104.3 **(24464)**

Jamestown
KSJB-AM - 600 **(24481)**

Minot
KMPR-FM - 88.9 **(24510)**

Oakes
KDDR-AM - 1220 **(24528)**

Williston
KEYZ-AM - 660 **(24562)**
KPPR-FM - 90.5 **(24563)**

OHIO

Akron
WNIR-FM - 100.1 **(24599)**

Ashtabula
WFUN-AM - 970 **(24625)**

Athens
WOUB-AM - 1340 **(24632)**
WOUB-FM - 91.3 **(24633)**
WOUC-FM - 89.1 **(24635)**

Bellaire
WOMP-AM - 1290 **(24663)**

Bellefontaine
WBLL-AM - 1390 **(24667)**

Belpre
WCVV-FM - 89.5 **(24674)**

Boardman
WKBN-AM - 570 **(24685)**

Chillicothe
WBEX-AM - 1490 **(24765)**

Cincinnati
WKRC-AM - 550 **(24841)**
WLW-AM - 700 **(24843)**
WVXU-FM - 91.7 **(24849)**

Cleveland
WCPN-FM - 90.3 **(24970)**
WTAM-AM - 1100 **(24986)**

Columbus
WCBE-FM - 90.5 **(25076)**
WFII-AM - 1230 **(25079)**
WOSU-AM - 820 **(25082)**
WTVN-AM - 610 **(25088)**

Dayton
WHIO-AM - 1210 **(25141)**
WING-AM - 1410 **(25143)**

Dover
WJER-FM - 101.7 **(25166)**

East Liverpool
WOHI-AM - 1490 **(25173)**

Elyria
WEOL-AM - 930 **(25180)**

Findlay
WFIN-AM - 1330 **(25196)**

Fostoria
WFOB-AM - 1430 **(25200)**

Ironton
WOUL-FM - 89.1 **(25255)**

Kent
WKSU-FM - 89.7 **(25279)**

Lima
WCIT-AM - 940 **(25299)**
WGLE-FM - 90.7 **(25300)**
WIMA-AM - 1150 **(25301)**

Mansfield
WMAN-AM - 1400 **(25335)**

Marion
WDIF-FM - 94.3 **(25353)**
WMRN-AM - 1490 **(25354)**

Middletown
WPFB-AM - 910 **(25379)**

Napoleon
WNDH-FM - 103.1 **(25404)**

Newark
WCLT-AM - 1430 **(25427)**
WNKO-FM - 101.7 **(25430)**

Painesville
WBKC-AM - 1460 **(25465)**

Portsmouth
WNXT-AM - 1260 **(25485)**
WPAY-AM - 1400 **(25487)**

Springfield
WBLY-AM - 1600 **(25535)**

Steubenville
WSTV-AM - 1340 **(25543)**

Toledo
WGBE-FM - 90.9 **(25576)**
WGTE-FM - 91.3 **(25577)**
WSPD-AM - 1370 **(25585)**

Uhrichsville
WBTC-AM - 1540 **(25600)**

Van Wert
WERT-AM - 1220 **(25610)**

Youngstown
WYSU-FM - 88.5 **(25714)**

OKLAHOMA

Ada
KADA-AM - 1230 **(25725)**
KADA-FM - 99.3 **(25726)**

Alva
KALV-AM - 1430 **(25739)**

Ardmore
KICM-FM - 93.7 **(25747)**

Bartlesville
KWON-AM - 1400 **(25755)**

Duncan
KRHD-AM - 1350 **(25801)**

Enid
KCRC-AM - 1390 **(25825)**
KGWA-AM - 960 **(25826)**

Hobart
KTJS-AM - 1420 **(25868)**

Lawton
KCCU-FM - 89.3 **(25891)**

Norman
KGOU-FM - 106.3 **(25945)**
KNOR-AM - 1400 **(25946)**
KROU-FM - 105.7 **(25947)**

Oklahoma City
KTOK-AM - 1000 **(26017)**

Ponca City
KLOR-FM - 99.3 **(26040)**
WBBZ-AM - 1230 **(26044)**

Stillwater
KOSU-FM - 91.7 **(26084)**
KSPI-AM - 780 **(26085)**

Tulsa
KHTT-FM - 106.9 **(26148)**
KRMG-AM - 740 **(26163)**

OREGON

Ashland
KAGI-AM - 930 **(26219)**
KCMX-AM - 580 **(26220)**
KSKF-FM - 90.9 **(26221)**
KSMF-FM - 89.1 **(26222)**
KSOR-FM - 90.1 **(26223)**

Astoria
KAST-AM - 1370 **(26227)**

Baker City
KBKR-AM - 1490 **(26234)**

Bend
KBND-AM - 1110 **(26244)**

Burns
KZZR-AM - 1230 **(26261)**

Coos Bay
KACW-FM - 107.3 **(26275)**

Coquille
KWRO-AM - 630 **(26284)**

Corvallis
KOAC-AM - 550 **(26293)**

Cottage Grove
KNND-AM - 1400 **(26296)**

Eugene
KPNW-AM - 1120 **(26344)**
KUGN-AM - 590 **(26346)**

Hillsboro
KUIK-AM - 1360 **(26375)**

Klamath Falls
KAGO-AM - 1150 **(26389)**
KFLS-AM - 1450 **(26392)**

La Grande
KLBM-AM - 1450 **(26401)**

Lebanon
KGAL-AM - 1580 **(26409)**

Medford
KMED-AM - 1440 **(26424)**
KTMT-AM - 580 **(26429)**

Newport
KNPT-AM - 1310 **(26448)**

Ontario
KSRV-AM - 1380 **(26456)**

Portland
KFXX-AM - 910 **(26526)**
KWJJ-FM - 99.5 **(26545)**

Roseburg
KQEN-AM - 1240　(26558)
KRNR-AM - 1490　(26559)

Salem
KYKN-AM - 1430　(26576)

PENNSYLVANIA
Altoona
WRTA-AM - 1240　(26641)
WVAM-AM - 1430　(26643)

Beaver Falls
WBVP-AM - 1230　(26686)
WMBA-AM - 1460　(26687)

Bethlehem
WGPA-AM - 1100　(26711)

Bloomsburg
WCNR-AM - 930　(26721)

Butler
WISR-AM - 680　(26746)

Carnegie
WOHZ-AM - 1600　(26765)

Erie
WPSE-AM - 1450　(26907)
WQLN-FM - 91.3　(26909)

Gettysburg
WGET-AM - 1320　(26941)

Harrisburg
WHP-AM - 580　(27016)

Johnstown
WNTJ-AM - 96.5　(27096)

Kittanning
WTYM-AM - 1380　(27128)

Lafayette Hill
KWFS-AM - 1290　(27134)

Lancaster
WLCH-FM - 91.3　(27154)

Lansdale
WNPV-AM - 1440　(27161)

Lincoln University
WLIU-FM - 88.7　(27201)

New Castle
WKST-AM - 1200　(27318)

Philadelphia
KYW-AM - 1060　(27728)
WHYY-FM - 90.9　(27733)
WPHE-AM - 690　(27738)

Philipsburg
WPHB-AM - 1260　(27751)

Pittsburgh
KDKA-AM - 1020　(27858)
KQV-AM - 1410　(27860)
WDUQ-FM - 90.5　(27863)
WEAE-AM - 1250　(27865)
WESA-AM - 940　(27866)
WRCT-FM - 88.3　(27877)

Pittston
WGBI-AM - 910　(27888)
WILK-AM - 980　(27890)
WOGY-AM - 1300　(27892)
WVIA-FM - 89.9　(27893)

Pottstown
WPAZ-AM - 1370　(27902)

Pottsville
WPPA-AM - 1360　(27906)

Punxsutawney
WECZ-AM - 1540　(27911)
WPXZ-FM - 104.1　(27912)

State College
WMAJ-AM - 1450　(28025)
WRSC-AM - 1390　(28029)
WZWW-FM - 95.3　(28031)

Uniontown
WMBS-AM - 590　(28068)

Washington
WJPA-AM - 1450　(28120)
WJPA-FM - 95.3　(28121)

White Oak
WEDO-AM - 810　(28158)

Whitehall
WAEB-AM - 790　(28159)

Williamsport
WRAK-AM - 1400　(28190)

York
WSBA-AM - 910　(28216)
WSOX-FM - 96.1　(28217)

PUERTO RICO
Arecibo
WCMN-AM - 1280　(28224)
WMIA-AM - 1070　(28226)

Cabo Rojo
WEKO-AM - 930　(28234)

Camuy
WCHQ-AM - 1360　(28239)

Juana Diaz
WCGB-AM - 1060　(28253)

Lares
WGDL-AM - 1200　(28254)

Mayaguez
WKJB-AM - 710　(28262)
WKJB-FM - 99.1　(28263)
WTIL-AM - 1300　(28269)
WTPM-FM - 92.9　(28270)

Ponce
WEUC-AM - 1420　(28275)
WPAB-AM - 550　(28280)

San Juan
WKAQ-AM - 580　(28302)
WRTU-FM - 89.7　(28309)
WSKN-AM - 630　(28310)
WUNO-AM - 1320　(28311)

RHODE ISLAND
East Providence
WPRO-AM - 630　(28348)

Newport
WADK-AM - 1540　(28374)

Providence
WHJJ-AM - 920　(28434)
WXIN-FM - 90.7　(28441)

Woonsocket
WNRI-AM - 1380　(28462)

SOUTH CAROLINA
Anderson
WAIM-AM - 1230　(28476)

Barnwell
WBAW-AM - 99.1　(28483)

Columbia
WEPR-FM - 90.1　(28575)
WISW-AM - 1320　(28577)
WVOC-AM - 560　(28586)

Florence
WJMX-AM - 970　(28607)

Fountain Inn
WFIS-AM - 1600　(28614)

Greenville
WORD-AM - 1330　(28639)

Newberry
WKDK-AM - 1240　(28718)

North Augusta
WGUS-AM - 1380　(28721)

North Charleston
WTMA-AM - 1250　(28728)

Rock Hill
WRHI-AM - 1340　(28748)

Spartanburg
WSPA-AM - 950　(28762)

Sumter
WDXY-AM - 1240　(28770)
WRJA-FM - 88.1　(28774)

Union
WBCU-AM - 1460　(28777)

SOUTH DAKOTA
Aberdeen
KKAA-AM - 1560　(28796)
KQAA-FM - 94.9　(28797)
KSDN-AM - 930　(28798)

Brookings
KBRK-AM - 1430　(28818)
KESD-FM/South Dakota Public Broadcasting - 88.3　(28820)

Deadwood
KDSJ-AM - 980　(28842)

Huron
KOKK-AM - 1210　(28872)

Lemmon
KBJM-AM - 1400　(28883)

Madison
KJAM-AM - 1390　(28887)
KJAM-FM - 103.1　(28888)

Milbank
KDIO-AM - 1350　(28894)

Mitchell
KMIT-FM - 105.9　(28902)
KORN-AM - 1490　(28903)

Pierpont
KDSD-FM - 90.9　(28915)

Pierre
KGFX-AM - 1060　(28925)

Rapid City
KOTA-AM - 1380　(28946)

Reliance
KTSD-FM - 91.1　(28956)

Sioux Falls
KCSD-FM - 90.9　(28971)
KELO-AM - 1320　(28974)
KRSD-FM - 88.1　(28982)
KWSN-AM - 1230　(28987)

Vermillion
KUSD-FM - 89.7　(29010)

Winner
KWYR-AM - 1260　(29033)
KWYR-FM - 93.7　(29034)

Yankton
KYNT-AM - 1450　(29044)
WNAX-AM - 570　(29045)

TENNESSEE
Athens
WYXI-AM - 1390　(29053)

Bolivar
WBOL-AM - 1560　(29058)

Bristol
WHGG-FM - 90.1　(29068)

Chattanooga
WGOW-AM - 1150　(29105)
WUTC-FM - 88.1　(29112)

Cleveland
WDNT-AM - 1280　(29126)
WXQK-AM - 970　(29128)

Collegedale
WSMC-FM - 90.5　(29132)

Cookeville
WATX-AM - 1590　(29147)
WPTN-AM - 780　(29150)

Cowan
WZYX-AM - 1440　(29156)

Crossville
WAEW-AM - 1330　(29160)

Fayetteville
WYTM-FM - 105.5　(29192)

Gray
WJCW-AM - 910　(29209)

Jackson
WDXI-AM - 1310　(29234)
WNWS-FM - 101.5　(29238)
WTJS-AM - 1390　(29239)
WWYN-FM - 106.9　(29241)

Johnson City
WETS-FM - 89.5　(29256)

Knoxville
WNOX-AM - 990　(29296)
WUTK-AM - 850　(29304)

Circulation: ★ = ABC; △ = BPA; ♦ = CAC; ● = CCAB; ❑ = VAC; ⊕ = PO Statement; ‡ = Publisher's Report; Boldface figures = sworn; Light figures = estimated.

3049

NEWS (continued)

Martin
WCMT-AM - 1410 **(29344)**
WCMT-FM - 101.7 **(29345)**

Maryville
WGAP-AM - 1400 **(29349)**
WGAP-FM - 95.7 **(29350)**

Mc Minnville
WBMC-AM - 960 **(29355)**

Memphis
WGSF-AM - 1210 **(29394)**
WKNO-FM - 91.1 **(29399)**
WKNQ-FM - 90.7 **(29401)**
WLOK-AM - 1340 **(29402)**
WMC-AM - 790 **(29403)**
WNWZ-AM - 1430 **(29406)**
WREC-AM - 600 **(29410)**

Morristown
WMTN-AM - 1300 **(29423)**

Murfreesboro
WGNS-AM - 1450 **(29436)**
WMOT-FM - 89.5 **(29437)**

Nashville
WHRS-FM - 91.7 **(29512)**
WKDA-AM - 1200 **(29514)**
WLAC-AM - 1510 **(29518)**
WPLN-FM - 90.3 **(29525)**
WSM-AM - 650 **(29533)**
WWTN-FM - 99.7 **(29538)**

Paris
WMUF-AM - 1000 **(29562)**

Portland
WQKR-AM - 1270 **(29570)**

Winchester
WCDT-AM - 1340 **(29648)**

Woodbury
WBRY-AM - 1540 **(29650)**

TEXAS

Abilene
KACU-FM - 89.7 **(29657)**

Amarillo
KGNC-AM - 710 **(29709)**
KTNZ-AM - 1010 **(29717)**

Arlington
KRLD-AM - 1080 **(29740)**
WBAP-AM - 820 **(29744)**

Atoka
KHKC-FM - 103.1 **(29749)**

Austin
KLBJ-AM - 590 **(29870)**
KROX-FM - 101.5 **(29876)**
KTAE-AM - 1260 **(29877)**

Beaumont
KLVI-AM - 560 **(29906)**
KOLE-AM - 1340 **(29907)**

Big Spring
KBST-AM - 1490 **(29925)**

Bridgeport
KBOC-FM - 98.3 **(29952)**

Brownfield
KKUB-AM - 1300 **(29954)**

Brownwood
KXYL-FM - 96.9 **(29972)**

Carrizo Springs
KBEN-AM - 1450 **(30003)**

Center
KDXI-FM - 1360 **(30014)**

College Station
KAMU-FM - 90.9 **(30056)**
WTAW-AM - 1620 **(30061)**

Corpus Christi
KEDT-FM - 90.3 **(30082)**
KEYS-AM - 1440 **(30083)**
KKTX-AM - 1360 **(30087)**
KSIX-AM - 1230 **(30096)**

Crockett
KIVY-AM - 1290 **(30107)**

Dallas
KERA-FM - 90.1 **(30203)**

Del Rio
KTJK-AM - 1230 **(30228)**
KWMC-AM - 1490 **(30229)**

Eagle Pass
KINL-FM - 92.7 **(30259)**

Edinburg
KURV-AM - 710 **(30274)**

El Campo
KULP-AM - 1390 **(30277)**

El Paso
KROD-AM - 600 **(30299)**

Floresville
KWCB-FM - 89.7 **(30320)**

Freer
KBRA-FM - 95.9 **(30368)**

Galveston
KGBC-AM - 1540 **(30383)**

Garland
KXVI-AM - 91.1 **(30387)**

Hamilton
KCLW-AM - 900 **(30421)**

Harlingen
KHID-FM - 88.1 **(30427)**
KMBH-FM - 88.9 **(30429)**

Haskell
KVRP-FM - 95.5 **(30434)**

Hillsboro
KHBR-AM - 1560 **(30450)**

Houston
KSEV-AM - 700 **(30574)**
KTRH-AM - 740 **(30579)**
KUHF-FM - 88.7 **(30583)**
KXYZ-AM - 1320 **(30586)**

Jacksonville
KEBE-AM - 1400 **(30617)**

Jasper
KTXJ-AM - 1350 **(30622)**

Kenedy
KAML-AM - 990 **(30636)**

Laredo
KLAR-AM - 1300 **(30675)**

Liberty
KSHN-FM - 99.9 **(30692)**

Lubbock
KFYO-AM - 790 **(30725)**
KJTV-AM - 950 **(30727)**

Lufkin
KSFA-AM - 860 **(30744)**

Marshall
KCUL-AM - 1410 **(30768)**

Mesquite
KEOM-FM - 88.5 **(30809)**

Midland
KJBC-AM - 1150 **(30818)**
KMND-AM - 1510 **(30822)**

Mount Pleasant
KIMP-AM - 960 **(30841)**

Odessa
KRIL-AM - 1410 **(30883)**

Pampa
KOMX-FM - 100.3 **(30902)**

Paris
KPLT-AM - 1490 **(30908)**

Plainview
KKYN-AM - 1090 **(30941)**

Robstown
KROB-AM - 1510 **(30986)**

San Angelo
KKSA-AM - 1260 **(31019)**
KSJT-FM - 107.5 **(31021)**

San Antonio
KTSA-AM - 550 **(31076)**
WOAI-AM - 1200 **(31079)**

Snyder
KSNY-FM - 101.5 **(31117)**

Sweetwater
KXOX-AM - 1240 **(31171)**

Temple
KTEM-AM - 1400 **(31181)**

Texarkana
KTFS-AM - 940 **(31190)**

Tyler
KTBB-AM - 600 **(31217)**

Uvalde
KVOU-AM - 1400 **(31226)**

Victoria
KAMG-AM - 1340 **(31237)**

Waco
KRZI-AM - 1580 **(31260)**
KWTX-AM - 1230 **(31263)**

UTAH

Blanding
KUTA-AM - 790 **(31321)**

Cedar City
KSUB-AM - 590 **(31328)**

Hooper
KSVN-AM - 730 **(31339)**

Logan
KUSU-FM - 89.5, 91.5 **(31361)**
KVNU-AM - 610 **(31363)**

Ogden
KLO-AM - 1430 **(31381)**

Park City
KPCW-FM - 91.9 **(31388)**

Salt Lake City
KCNR-AM - 860 **(31445)**
KFNZ-AM - 1320 **(31447)**
KISN-AM - 570 **(31448)**
KSL-AM - 1160 **(31457)**
KUER-FM - 90.1 **(31465)**

South Jordan
KTKK-AM - 630 **(31473)**

Vernal
KVEL-AM - 920 **(31485)**

West Valley City
KALL-AM - 910 **(31487)**

VERMONT

Barre
WSNO-AM - 1450 **(31492)**

Bennington
WBTN-AM - 1370 **(31503)**

Brattleboro
WKVT-AM - 1490 **(31510)**

Colchester
WRVT-FM - 88.7 **(31532)**
WVMT-AM - 620 **(31533)**
WVPS-FM - 107.9 **(31534)**

St. Johnsbury
WSTJ-AM - 1340 **(31596)**

Waterbury
WDEV-AM - 550 **(31612)**

Windsor
WVPR-FM - 89.5 **(31622)**

VIRGINIA

Arlington
WETA-FM - 90.9 **(31845)**
WETH-FM - 89.1 **(31847)**

Blacksburg
WVTW-FM - 88.5 **(31890)**

Bristol
WXBQ-AM - 980 **(31900)**

Broadway
WBTX-AM - 1470 **(31903)**

Charlottesville
WINA-AM - 1070 **(31952)**
WVTU-FM - 89.3 **(31957)**

Danville
WBTM-AM - 1330 **(31993)**

Emporia
WEVA-AM - 860 **(32002)**

Farmville
WFLO-AM - 870 **(32070)**

Gloucester
WXGM-AM - 1420 **(32116)**

Hampden Sydney
WWHS-FM - 92.1 **(32125)**

Harrisonburg
WHBG-AM - 1360 **(32144)**
WMRA-FM - 90.7 **(32148)**
WMRL-FM - 89.9 **(32149)**
WMRY-FM - 103.5 **(32150)**
WSVA-AM - 550 **(32153)**

Lebanon
WLRV-AM - 1380 **(32180)**

Lexington
WLUR-FM - 91.5 **(32194)**
WREL-AM - 1450 **(32195)**

Lynchburg
WBRG-AM - 1050 **(32211)**

Norfolk
WHRV-FM - 89.5 **(32301)**

Onley
WESR-AM - 1330 **(32319)**

Petersburg
WVST-FM - 91.3 **(32333)**

Pulaski
WBLB-AM - 1340 **(32338)**

Radford
WFNR-AM - 710 **(32348)**
WNNI-AM - 1260 **(32349)**

Richmond
WCVE-FM - 88.9 **(32474)**
WVNZ-AM - 990 **(32487)**

Roanoke
WFIR-AM - 960 **(32497)**
WVTR-FM - 91.9 **(32508)**

South Boston
WSBV-AM - 1560 **(32533)**

Staunton
WINF-AM - 970 **(32557)**

Winchester
WINC-AM - 1400 **(32631)**

Wise
WISE-FM - 90.5 **(32635)**

WASHINGTON
Aberdeen
KBKW-AM - 1450 **(32648)**
KSWW-FM - 102.1 **(32651)**

Bellingham
KGMI-AM - 790 **(32682)**

Centralia
KELA-AM - 1470 **(32706)**

Ellensburg
KXLE-AM - 1240 **(32752)**

Ephrata
KULE-AM - 730 **(32757)**

Forks
KVAC-AM - 1490 **(32771)**

Kennewick
KTCR-AM - 1340 **(32792)**

Longview
KEDO-AM - 1400 **(32816)**

Moses Lake
KBSN-AM - 1470 **(32841)**

Mount Vernon
KAPS-AM - 660 **(32847)**
KBRC-AM - 1430 **(32848)**

Pasco
KONA-AM - 610 **(32883)**
KONA-FM - 105.3 **(32884)**

Port Angeles
KONP-AM - 1450 **(32889)**

Pullman
KFAE-FM - 89.1 **(32910)**
KQQQ-AM - 1150 **(32912)**
KRFA-FM - 91.7 **(32913)**
KWSU-AM - 1250 **(32915)**

Quincy
KWNC-AM - 1370 **(32920)**

Seattle
KIRO-AM - 710 **(33056)**
KNWX-AM - 1210 **(33065)**
KOMO-AM - 1000 **(33066)**
KUOW-FM - 94.9 **(33072)**

Shelton
KMAS-AM - 1030 **(33081)**

Spokane
KPBX-FM - 91.1 **(33123)**
KQDI-AM - 1450 **(33124)**
KXLY-AM - 920 **(33134)**

Tacoma
KPLU-FM - 88.5 **(33158)**

Wenatchee
KPQ-AM - 560 **(33201)**

Yakima
KIT-AM - 1280 **(33230)**

WEST VIRGINIA
Beckley
WWNR-AM - 620 **(33246)**

Berkeley Springs
WCST-FM - 93.5 **(33249)**

Bluefield
WHIS-AM - 1440 **(33257)**
WTZE-AM - 1470 **(33260)**

Buckhannon
WBUC-AM - 1460 **(33265)**

Charleston
WCHS-AM - 580 **(33282)**
WQBE-AM - 97.5 **(33284)**
WVNP-FM - 89.9 **(33287)**
WVPB-FM - 91.7 **(33288)**
WVPN-FM - 88.5 **(33289)**

Elkins
WDNE-AM - 1240 **(33308)**

Fairmont
WTCS-AM - 1490 **(33316)**

Fisher
WELD-AM - 690 **(33317)**

Huntington
WRVC-AM - 930 **(33344)**

Kingwood
WFSP-AM - 1560 **(33360)**

Martinsburg
WEPM-AM - 1340 **(33381)**
WRNR-AM - 740 **(33383)**

Morgantown
WAJR-AM - 1440 **(33400)**

New Martinsville
WETZ-AM - 1330 **(33415)**

Parkersburg
WVPG-FM - 90.3 **(33426)**

South Charleston
WJYP-FM - 100.9 **(33468)**

Vienna
WLTP-AM - 1450 **(33481)**

WISCONSIN
Altoona
WAYY-AM - 790 **(33524)**

Amery
WXCE-AM - 1260 **(33528)**

Appleton
WHBY-AM - 1150 **(33549)**

Beaver Dam
WBEV-AM - 1430 **(33569)**
WXRO-FM - 95.3 **(33570)**

Eau Claire
WUEC-FM - 89.7 **(33684)**

Fond du Lac
KFIZ-AM - 1450 **(33699)**

Janesville
WCLO-AM - 1230 **(33864)**

Kenosha
WGTD-FM - 91.1 **(33876)**
WLIP-AM - 1050 **(33878)**

La Crosse
WIZM-AM - 1410 **(33889)**

Lancaster
WGLR-FM - 97.7 **(33909)**

Madison
WIBA-AM - 1310 **(33996)**
WORT-FM - 89.9 **(34007)**

Marshfield
WDLB-AM - 1450 **(34028)**

Milwaukee
WMCS-AM - 1290 **(34128)**
WTMJ-AM - 620 **(34135)**
WUWM-FM - 89.7 **(34137)**

New Richmond
WIXK-AM - 1590 **(34194)**
WIXK-FM - 107.1 **(34195)**

Racine
WRJN-AM - 1400 **(34278)**

Reedsburg
WNFM-FM - 104.9 **(34282)**

Ripon
WRPN-AM - 1600 **(34305)**

Shawano
WTCH-AM - 960 **(34320)**

Sheboygan
WHBL-AM - 1330 **(34324)**

Sparta
WCOW-FM - 97.1 **(34334)**
WKLJ-AM - 1290 **(34335)**

Stevens Point
WSPT-AM - 1010 **(34345)**

Superior
KUWS-FM - 91.3 **(34362)**

Tomahawk
WJJQ-FM - 92.5 **(34375)**

Waupaca
WDUX-AM - 800 **(34423)**
WDUX-FM - 92.7 **(34424)**

Wausau
WRIG-AM - 1390 **(34437)**
WSAU-AM - 550 **(34438)**

West Bend
WBKV-AM - 1470 **(34447)**

Wisconsin Rapids
WFHR-AM - 1320 **(34466)**

WYOMING
Cheyenne
KFBC-AM - 1240 **(34502)**

Laramie
KOWB-AM - 1290 **(34556)**
KUWR-FM - 91.9 **(34557)**

Sheridan
KROE-AM - 930 **(34589)**

ALBERTA, CANADA
Calgary
CHQR-AM - 770 **(34667)**
CJSW-FM - 90.9 **(34670)**

BRITISH COLUMBIA, CANADA
Cranbrook
CHDR-FM - 104.7 **(34937)**

Kamloops
CHNL-AM - 610 **(34980)**

Kelowna
CBTK-FM - 88.9 **(34990)**

Port Alberni
CJAV-AM - 1240 **(35050)**

NEWS (continued)
Quesnel
CKCQ-AM - 920 **(35070)**

Vancouver
CFRO-FM - 102.7 **(35185)**
CKNW-AM - 980 **(35194)**
CKWX-AM - 1130 **(35197)**

Victoria
CFAX-AM - 1070 **(35232)**

MANITOBA, CANADA
Altona
CFAM-AM - 950 **(35248)**

Dauphin
CKDM-AM - 730 **(35264)**

Winnipeg
CJOB-AM - 680 **(35372)**

NEW BRUNSWICK, CANADA
Fredericton
CBZ-AM - 970 **(35399)**

St. John
CBD-FM - 91.3 **(35432)**

NEWFOUNDLAND AND LABRADOR, CANADA
Corner Brook
CBY-AM - 990 **(35449)**

Happy Valley
CFGB-FM - 89.5 **(35467)**

Port-aux-Basques
CFCV-FM - 97.7 **(35478)**

NORTHWEST TERRITORIES, CANADA
Yellowknife
CFYK-AM - 1340 **(35529)**
CKLB-FM - 101.9 **(35530)**

NOVA SCOTIA, CANADA
Halifax
CJCH-AM - 920 **(35576)**
CKDU-FM - 97.5 **(35578)**

New Glasgow
CKEC-AM - 1320 **(35597)**

ONTARIO, CANADA
Hamilton
CHML-AM - 900 **(35895)**

Kingston
CFRC-FM - 101.9 **(35953)**

Kitchener
CKGL-AM - 570 **(35966)**

London
CFPL-AM - 980 **(35996)**

Niagara Falls
CJRN-AM - 710 **(36112)**

Ottawa
CBOF-FM - 90.7 **(36285)**

Owen Sound
CFOS-AM - 560 **(36300)**
CFPS-AM - 1490 **(36301)**

Peterborough
CKRU-AM - 980 **(36324)**

St. Catharines
CKTB-AM - 610 **(36359)**

Sarnia
CFGX-FM - 99.9 **(36367)**

Simcoe
CHCD-FM - 106.7 **(36392)**

Sioux Lookout
WRN-FM - 89.1 **(36394)**

Toronto
CFRB-AM - 1010 **(36805)**
CFTR-AM - 680 **(36806)**

Windsor
CBC-AM - 1550 **(36894)**
CBEF-AM - 540 **(36896)**
CKLW-AM - 800 **(36899)**

QUEBEC, CANADA
Chicoutimi
CBJ-FM - 93.7 **(36969)**
CBJE-FM - 102.7 **(36970)**

La Sarre
CKLS-AM - 1240 **(37023)**

Montreal
CINQ-FM - 102.3 **(37245)**
CJAD-AM - 800 **(37247)**

Noranda
CKRN-AM - 1400 **(37261)**

Quebec
CKIA-FM - 96.1 **(37303)**
CKRL-FM - 89.1 **(37304)**

Sainte-Foy
CHRC-AM - 800 **(37379)**

Sept-Iles
CKCN-FM - 94.1 **(37388)**

Sherbrooke
CHLT-AM - 630 **(37397)**

Thetford Mines
CJLP-FM - 107.1 **(37412)**
CKLD-FM - 105.5 **(37413)**

Trois-Rivieres
CHLN-AM - 550 **(37418)**

Westmount
CKAM-AM - 990 **(37449)**

SASKATCHEWAN, CANADA
Regina
CJME-AM - 980 **(37542)**

OLDIES

ALABAMA
Athens
WKAC-AM - 1080 **(28)**

Birmingham
WODL-FM - 106.9 **(125)**

Brewton
WEBJ-AM - 1240 **(137)**

Demopolis
WZNJ-FM - 106.5 **(182)**

Elba
WELB-AM - 1350 **(198)**

Gadsden
WGAD-AM - 1350 **(235)**

Greenville
WGYV-AM - 1380 **(244)**

Huntsville
WAFN-FM - 92.7 **(279)**

Monroeville
WMFC-AM - 1360 **(352)**
WMFC-FM - 99.3 **(353)**

Muscle Shoals
WKGL-FM - 97.7 **(398)**

Oneonta
WCRL-AM - 1570 **(407)**

Opp
WOPP-AM - 1290 **(414)**

Ozark
WOZK-AM - 900 **(421)**

Tallassee
WACQ-AM - 1130 **(468)**

ALASKA
Bethel
KYUK-AM - 640 **(556)**

ARIZONA
Flagstaff
KWMX-FM - 96.7 **(706)**

Holbrook
KDJI-AM - 1270 **(725)**

Lake Havasu City
KFWJ-AM - 980 **(739)**

Miami
KIKO-AM - 1340 **(752)**

Phoenix
KOOL-FM - 94.5 **(829)**

Quartzsite
KBUX-FM - 94.3 **(859)**

Springerville
KRVZ-AM - 1400 **(894)**

Tucson
KWFM-FM - 92.9 **(1000)**

Wickenburg
KBSZ-AM - 1250 **(1006)**

Yuma
KBLU-AM - 560 **(1024)**
KJOK-AM - 1400 **(1026)**

ARKANSAS
Batesville
KBTA-AM - 1340 **(1043)**

Cave City
KZIG-FM - 89.9 **(1075)**

Cherokee Village
KFCM-FM - 98.3 **(1078)**

Crossett
KWLT-FM - 102.7 **(1095)**

Fort Smith
KBBQ-FM - 100.7 **(1146)**

Malvern
KISI-FM - 101.5 **(1265)**

Nashville
KNAS-FM - 105.5 **(1297)**

Pocahontas
KRLW-AM - 1320 **(1320)**

Searcy
KAWW-FM - 100.7 **(1341)**

Stuttgart
KWAK-FM - 105.5 **(1354)**

CALIFORNIA
Bishop
KBOV-AM - 1230 **(1585)**

California City
KCEL-FM - 106.9 **(1640)**

El Centro
KXO-AM - 1230 **(1857)**

Fresno
KFSO-FM - 92.9 **(1966)**

Los Angeles
KRLA-AM - 1110 **(2466)**
KRTH-FM - 101.1 **(2467)**

Mendocino
KMFB-FM - 92.7 **(2520)**

Merced
KABX-FM - 97.5 **(2529)**

National City
XHRM-FM - 92.5 **(2614)**

Palm Desert
WNRK-AM - 1260 **(2753)**

Palm Springs
KCMJ-AM - 1140 **(2773)**
KCMJ-FM - 92.7 **(2774)**
KDES-FM - 104.7 **(2776)**

Palmdale
KWJL-AM - 1470 **(2787)**

Redding
KRDG-FM - 105.3 **(2895)**

Sacramento
KSMJ-AM - 1380 **(3049)**
KZZOKY-FM - 100.5 **(3062)**

Salinas
KOCN-FM - 105.1 **(3073)**

San Diego
KBZT-FM - 94.9 **(3295)**
KOCL-FM - 94.1 **(3306)**

San Francisco
KFRC-AM - 610 **(3482)**

KFRC-FM - 99.7 (3483)
KISQ-FM - 98.1 (3487)
KSFO-AM - 560 (3500)

Santa Barbara
KIST-AM - 1340 (3666)

Santa Maria
KUHL-AM - 1410 (3704)
KXFM-FM - 99.1 (3705)

Stockton
KQOD-FM - 100.1 (3815)
KSTN-AM - 1420 (3817)

Susanville
KSUE-AM - 1240 (3834)

Yreka
KSYC-AM - 1490 (4122)

COLORADO
Canon City
KRLN-AM - 1400 (4214)

Colorado Springs
KSPZ-FM - 92.9 (4282)

Cortez
KVFC-AM - 740 (4294)

Fort Morgan
KFTM-AM - 1400 (4448)

Glenwood Springs
KGLN-AM - 980 (4460)

Gunnison
KPKE-AM - 1490 (4511)

Steamboat Springs
KBCR-AM - 1230 (4636)

Sterling
KSTC-AM - 1230 (4642)

Wray
KRDZ-AM - 1440 (4693)

CONNECTICUT
Bloomfield
WDRC-FM - 102.9 (4704)

Hartford
WQTQ-FM - 89.9 (4909)

New London
WKWL-FM - 100.9 (5023)

Sharon
WKZE-AM - 1020 (5115)

Westport
WMMM-AM - 1260 (5217)

FLORIDA
Bartow
WWBF-AM - 1130 (5920)

Belle Glade
WBGF-FM - 93.5 (5921)

Chipley
WBGC-AM - 1240 (5985)

DeFuniak Springs
WZEP-AM - 1460 (6054)

Fort Myers
WOLZ-FM - 95.3 (6111)

Fort Walton Beach
WMMK-FM - 92.1 (6125)

Jacksonville
WKQL-FM - 96.9 (6231)

Live Oak
WLVO-FM - 106.1 (6307)

Maitland
WSHE-FM - 100.3 (6320)

Miami
WAXY-AM - 709 (6396)
WMXJ-FM - 102.7 (6408)
WQAM-AM - 560 (6413)

New Smyrna Beach
WSBB-AM - 1230 (6459)

Pensacola
WYCL-FM - 107.3 (6580)

Perry
WPRY-AM - 1400 (6584)

Port St. Lucie
WQOL-FM - 103.7 (6605)

Punta Gorda
KII-FM - 98.9 (6608)

St. Petersburg
WYUU-FM - 92.5 (6645)

Sarasota
WSRZ-FM - 107.9 (6675)

South Daytona
WPUL-AM - 1590 (6685)

West Palm Beach
WOLL-FM - 105.5 (6856)

GEORGIA
Atlanta
WFOX-FM - 97.1 (7072)

Augusta
WGOR-FM - 93.9 (7109)

Brunswick
WMOG-AM - 1490 (7142)

Buford
WLKQ-FM - 102.3 (7145)

Calhoun
WEBS-AM - 1030 (7150)

Canton
WCHK-AM - 1290 (7153)

Columbus
WRLD-FM - 95.3 (7193)

Dublin
WMLT-AM - 1330 (7254)

Gainesville
WMJE-FM - 102.9 (7304)

Griffin
WQUL-FM - 97.7 (7316)

Grovetown
WJDS-FM - 620 (7318)

Kingsland
WOKF-FM - 92.5 (7359)

Macon
WAYS-FM - 99.1 (7389)

Mc Rae
WYIS-AM - 1410 (7428)

McDonough
WKKP-AM - 1410 (7430)

Metter
WBMZ-FM - 103.7 (7432)

Moultrie
WMTM-FM - 93.9 (7448)

Savannah
WGCO-FM - 98.3 (7543)

Tifton
WKAA-FM - 97.7 (7602)

Trenton
WKWN-AM - 1420 (7609)

Vidalia
WVOP-AM - 970 (7632)

HAWAII
Hilo
KHLO-AM - 850 (7673)

IDAHO
Boise
KLTB-FM - 104.3 (7827)

Ketchum
KWYS-AM - 920 (7890)

Lewiston
KOZE-AM - 950 (7899)

Moscow
KRPL-AM - 1400 (7923)

Pocatello
KPKY-FM - 94.9 (7952)

Preston
KACH-AM - 1340 (7961)

Twin Falls
KLIX-FM - 96.5 (7996)

ILLINOIS
Aurora
WKKD-FM - 95.9 (8044)

Benton
WQRL-FM - 106.3 (8073)

Carmi
WROY-AM - 1460 (8132)

Champaign
WKIO-FM - 92.5 (8230)

Chicago
WGCI-AM - 1390 (8623)
WJMK-FM - 104.3 (8632)
WUBT-FM - 103.5 (8655)

Dixon
WIXN-AM - 1460 (8777)

Jacksonville
WEAI-FM - 107.1 (9025)

Jerseyville
WJBM-AM - 1480 (9029)

La Salle
WLPO-AM - 1220 (9058)

Peoria
WPBG-FM - 93.3 (9436)

Princeton
WZOE-FM - 98.1 (9469)

Rockford
WLUV-FM - 96.7 (9538)

Vandalia
WPMB-AM - 1500 (9726)

INDIANA
Bedford
WBIW-AM - 1340 (9799)
WQRK-FM - 105.5 (9800)

Chesterton
WDSO-FM - 88.3 (9888)

Corydon
WOCC-AM - 1550 (9906)

Crawfordsville
WCVL-AM - 1550 (9911)

Elkhart
WTRC-AM - 1340 (9929)

Evansville
WJPS-AM - 1400 (9945)

Fort Wayne
WYSR-FM - 94.1 (9995)

Kendallville
WAWK-AM - 1140 (10229)

Knox
WKVI-AM - 1520 (10239)

Kokomo
WIOU-AM - 1350 (10242)

Lafayette
WJEF-FM - 91.9 (10259)

Madison
WXGO-AM - 1270 (10286)

Marion
WBAT-AM - 1400 (10289)

Michigan City
WEFM-FM - 95.9 (10306)

Mishawaka
WNIL-AM - 1290 (10317)

Paoli
WSEZ-AM - 1560 (10390)

Pendleton
WEEM-FM - 91.7 (10394)

Plymouth
WTCA-AM - 1050 (10402)

Rensselaer
WRIN-AM - 1560 (10419)

Circulation: ★ = ABC; △ = BPA; ♦ = CAC; • = CCAB; ❑ = VAC; ⊕ = PO Statement; ‡ = Publisher's Report; Boldface figures = sworn; Light figures = estimated.

3053

OLDIES (continued)

Seymour
WZZB-AM - 1390 (10451)

Terre Haute
WSDM-FM - 97.7 (10500)

Valparaiso
WNWI-AM - 1080 (10514)

Wabash
WJOT-AM - 1510 (10531)

IOWA
Albia
KLBA-AM - 1370 (10577)
KLBA-FM - 96.7 (10578)

Burlington
KKMI-FM - 93.5 (10645)

Clarinda
KKBZ-FM - 99.3 (10703)

Clinton
KCLN-AM - 1390 (10712)

Davenport
KUUL-FM - 103.7 (10745)

Des Moines
KIOA-FM - 93.3 (10826)
KXTX-AM - 940 (10835)

Dubuque
WDBQ-FM - 107.5 (10855)

Fairfield
KIIK-FM - 95.9 (10885)

Harlan
KNOD-FM - 105.3 (10947)

Keokuk
KOKX-FM - 95.3 (11015)

Mount Pleasant
KILJ-AM - 1130 (11095)

Ottumwa
KBIZ-AM - 1240 (11141)

Sioux City
KKMA-FM - 99.5 (11216)

KANSAS
Burlington
KSNP-FM - 95.3 (11371)

Dodge City
KGNO-AM - 1370 (11417)
KONQ-FM - 91.9 (11419)

Emporia
KANS-FM - 92.9 (11432)

Fort Scott
KOMB-FM - 103.9 (11445)

Great Bend
KGTR-FM - 96.7 (11469)

Hutchinson
KGGG-FM - 94.7 (11504)

Parsons
KLKC-AM - 1540 (11745)
KLKC-FM - 93.5 (11746)

Salina
KSAJ-FM - 98.5 (11788)

KENTUCKY
Benton
WCBL-FM - 99.1 (11935)

Campbellsville
WTCO-AM - 1450 (12009)

Cynthiana
WCYN-AM - 1400 (12034)

Elizabethtown
WASE-FM - 103.5 (12046)

Frankfort
WCND-AM - 940 (12079)
WFKY-AM - 1490 (12080)

Harlan
WHLN-AM - 1410 (12107)

Hopkinsville
WHVO-AM - 1480 (12135)

Irvine
WIRV-AM - 1550 (12142)

Jackson
WEKG-AM - 810 (12146)

Lexington
WTKT-FM - 103.3 (12195)

Louisville
WRKA-FM - 103.1 (12263)

Monticello
WKYM-FM - 101.7 (12301)

Paducah
WKYX-AM - 570 (12346)

Prestonsburg
WQHY-FM - 95.5 (12373)

Richmond
WEKY-AM - 1340 (12386)

Somerset
WTLO-AM - 1480 (12412)

Vanceburg
WKKS-AM - 1570 (12425)

LOUISIANA
Alexandria
KFAD-FM - 93.9 (12463)

Lafayette
KJCB-AM - 770 (12626)

Leesville
KLLA-AM - 1570 (12660)

Many
KWLA-AM - 1400 (12671)

Moreauville
KLIL-FM - 92.1 (12706)

Oak Grove
KWCL-FM - 96.7 (12789)

Opelousas
KOGM-FM - 107.1 (12792)

Ruston
KPCH-FM - 97.7 (12809)

Shreveport
KRVQ-FM - 102.1 (12833)

Springhill
KBSF-AM - 1460 (12848)
KTKC-FM - 92.7 (12849)

Thibodaux
KTIB-AM - 640 (12862)

Ville Platte
KVPI-FM - 92.5 (12867)

MAINE
Augusta
WABK-FM - 104.3 (12897)

Brewer
WWMJ-FM - 95.7 (12929)

Newport
WGUY-FM - 102.1 (12992)

Presque Isle
WOZI-FM - 101.9 (13040)

South Portland
WYNZ-FM - 100.9 (13056)

MARYLAND
Aberdeen
WAMD-AM - 970 (13087)

Annapolis
WYRE-AM - 810 (13103)

Cumberland
WCBC-AM - 1270 (13476)

Hagerstown
WARK-AM - 1490 (13573)
WARX-FM - 106.9 (13574)
WJEJ-AM - 1240 (13577)

Rockville
WTOP-FM - 94.3 (13704)

Westminster
WTTR-AM - 1470 (13779)

MASSACHUSETTS
Beverly
WNSH-AM - 1570 (13844)

Boston
WQLL-FM - 96.5 (13992)

Brighton
WODS-FM - 103.3 (14010)

North Adams
WNAW-AM - 1230 (14421)

Provincetown
WOMR-FM - 92.1 (14487)

Salem
WESX-AM - 1230 (14516)

Sheffield
WBSL-FM - 91.7 (14520)

Worcester
WORC-FM - 98.9 (14699)

MICHIGAN
Battle Creek
WWKN-FM - 104.9 (14801)

Ferndale
WOMC-FM - 104.3 (15031)

Fremont
WLCS-FM - 98.3 (15060)

Gaylord
WSNQ-AM - 900 (15078)

Grand Rapids
WODJ-FM - 107.3 (15117)

Holland
WEVS-FM - 92.7 (15175)

Iron Mountain
WOBE-FM - 101.5 (15210)

Iron River
WIKB-AM - 1230 (15212)

Lansing
WJIM-FM - 97.5 (15301)

Manistique
WTIQ-AM - 1490 (15334)

Marquette
WFXD-FM - 103.3 (15341)
WHCH-FM - 98.3 (15342)

Newberry
WNBY-FM - 93.7 (15402)

Otsego
WQXC-FM - 100.9 (15427)

Petoskey
WMBN-AM - 1340 (15440)

Port Huron
WHLX-AM - 1590 (15456)

Rochester
WPON-AM - 1460 (15467)

Saginaw
WHNN-FM - 96.1 (15497)
WKNX-AM - 1250 (15501)

Sturgis
WMSH-AM - 1230 (15581)
WMSH-FM - 99.3 (15582)

Traverse City
WAIR-FM - 92.5 (15605)
WCCW-FM - 107.5 (15607)

MINNESOTA
Albert Lea
KATE-FM - 1450 (15708)
KYTC-FM - 102.7 (15710)

Blue Earth
KBEW-AM - 1560 (15763)

Faribault
KDHL-AM - 920 (15895)

Fergus Falls
KJJK-AM - 1020 (15901)

Grand Rapids
KOZY-AM - 1320 (15932)

Hastings
KDWA-AM - 1460 (15942)

Hibbing
WMFG-FM - 106.3 **(15959)**

Little Falls
KFML-FM - 94.1 **(16007)**

Long Prairie
KXDL-FM - 99.7 **(16011)**

Mahnomen
KRJM-FM - 101.5 **(16024)**

Minneapolis
KQQL-FM - 107.9 **(16152)**

New Prague
KCHK-AM - 1350 **(16210)**
KCHK-FM - 95.5 **(16211)**

North Mankato
KYSM-AM - 1230 **(16223)**

Park Rapids
KDKK-FM - 97.5 **(16257)**

Pipestone
KISD-FM - 98.7 **(16276)**

Thief River Falls
KSNR-FM - 100.3 **(16471)**

Willmar
KDJS-AM - 1590 **(16520)**

MISSISSIPPI
Amory
WAFM-FM - 95.3 **(16546)**

Corinth
WXRZ-FM - 94.3 **(16619)**

Greenville
KZYQ-FM - 103.5 **(16633)**
WNIX-AM - 1330 **(16642)**

Gulfport
WGCM-FM - 102.3 **(16656)**

Hattiesburg
WHER-FM - 103.7 **(16672)**

Holly Springs
WKRA-FM - 92.7 **(16683)**

Jackson
WQJQ-FM - 105.1 **(16728)**

Kosciusko
WKOZ-AM - 1340 **(16738)**

Natchez
WQNZ-FM - 95.1 **(16796)**

New Albany
WNAU-AM - 1470 **(16799)**

Tupelo
WELO-AM - 580 **(16851)**

MISSOURI
Chillicothe
KCHI-AM - 1010 **(16978)**
KCHI-FM - 98.5 **(16979)**

Farmington
KYLS-AM - 1450 **(17056)**

Jefferson City
KKCA-FM - 100.5 **(17138)**

Kansas City
KMJK-FM - 107.3 **(17212)**

Kennett
KCRV-AM - 1370 **(17219)**
KCRV-FM - 105.1 **(17220)**

Kirksville
KIRX-AM - 1450 **(17230)**

Moberly
KZZT-FM - 105.5 **(17292)**

Poplar Bluff
KLID-AM - 1340 **(17359)**

St. Joseph
KSFT-AM - 1550 **(17399)**

St. Louis
KRJY-FM - 96.3 **(17547)**

Springfield
KOSP-FM - 105.1 **(17625)**

Warrensburg
KOKO-AM - 1450 **(17672)**

MONTANA
Butte
KXTL-AM - 1370 **(17767)**

Great Falls
KLFM-FM - 92.9 **(17801)**

Kalispell
KGEZ-AM - 600 **(17841)**
KOFI-AM - 1180 **(17842)**

Missoula
KYLT-AM - 1340 **(17886)**

NEBRASKA
Ainsworth
KBRB-AM - 1400 **(17924)**

Falls City
KTNC-AM - 1230 **(18010)**

Gordon
KSDZ-FM - 95.5 **(18023)**

Kearney
KKPR-FM - 98.9 **(18064)**

McCook
KBRL-AM - 1300 **(18154)**

North Platte
KOOQ-AM - 1410 **(18183)**

Ogallala
KOGA-AM - 930 **(18190)**

Omaha
KGOR-FM - 99.9 **(18219)**

Oneill
KBRX-AM - 1350 **(18233)**

Scottsbluff
KOAQ-AM - 690 **(18272)**

Wayne
KTCH-FM - 104.9 **(18309)**

York
KAWL-AM - 1370 **(18322)**

NEVADA
Carson City
KPTL-AM - 1300 **(18333)**

Ely
KELY-AM - 1230 **(18343)**

Reno
KGVN-FM - 93.7 **(18430)**

NEW HAMPSHIRE
Berlin
WMOU-AM - 1230 **(18458)**

Bow
WNNH-FM - 99.1 **(18459)**

Gilford
WLKZ-FM - 104.9 **(18513)**

Lebanon
WMXR-FM - 93.9 **(18545)**

Winchester
WXOD-FM - 98.7 **(18652)**

NEW JERSEY
Camden
WSSJ-AM - 1310 **(18717)**

Hackettstown
WRNJ-AM - 1510 **(18860)**

Linwood
WTKU-FM - 98.3 **(19175)**

Neptune
WHTG-AM - 1410 **(19321)**

Toms River
WJRZ-FM - 100.1 **(19650)**

Trenton
WKXW-FM - 101.5 **(19676)**

Vineland
WVLT-FM - 92.1 **(19702)**

NEW MEXICO
Clovis
KWKA-AM - 680 **(19837)**

Farmington
KNDN-AM - 960 **(19848)**

Hobbs
KHOB-AM - 1390 **(19866)**

Lovington
KLEA-FM - 101.7 **(19900)**

Ruidoso
KBUY-AM - 1360 **(19929)**

Santa Fe
KBOM-FM - 106.7 **(19947)**
KSWV-AM - 810 **(19950)**

NEW YORK
Alfred
WETD-FM - 90.9 **(20026)**

Baldwinsville
WSEN-FM - 92.1 **(20117)**

Bath
WABH-AM - 1380 **(20126)**
WVIN-FM - 98.3 **(20134)**

Binghamton
WCDW-FM - 100.5 **(20222)**

Buffalo
WHTT-FM - 104.1 **(20402)**

Corning
WCBA-AM - 1350 **(20504)**
WGMM-FM - 97.7 **(20508)**

Crown Point
WIPS-AM - 1250 **(20516)**

Farmingdale
WHLI-AM - 1100 **(20598)**

Fulton
WZZZ-AM - 1300 **(20633)**

Gouverneur
WGIX-FM - 95.3 **(20676)**

Hornell
WLEA-AM - 1480 **(20758)**

Hudson
WZCR-FM - 93.5 **(20771)**

Ilion
WXUR-FM - 92.7 **(20781)**

Ithaca
WTKO-AM - 1470 **(20822)**

Jamestown
WKSN-AM - 1340 **(20845)**

Johnstown
WSRD-FM - 104.9 **(20853)**

Latham
WTRY-AM - 980 **(20938)**

Malone
WICY-AM - 1490 **(20981)**

Marcy
WODZ-FM - 96.1 **(21022)**

Massena
WYBG-AM - 1050 **(21029)**

New York
WCBS-FM - 101.1 **(22966)**

Ogdensburg
WPAC-FM - 92.7 **(23034)**
WSLB-AM - 1400 **(23035)**

Olean
WHDL-AM - 1450 **(23041)**

Patterson
WAXB-FM - 105.5 **(23081)**

Port Jervis
WDLC-AM - 1490 **(23120)**

Potsdam
WPDM-AM - 1470 **(23142)**
WSNN-FM - 99.3 **(23143)**

Poughkeepsie
WBPM-FM - 94.3 **(23153)**
WCZX-FM - 97.7 **(23155)**

Circulation: ★ = ABC; △ = BPA; ♦ = CAC; ● = CCAB; ❑ = VAC; ⊕ = PO Statement; ‡ = Publisher's Report; Boldface figures = sworn; Light figures = estimated.

3055

Radio Station Formats

OLDIES (continued)

Rochester
WBBF-FM - 98.9 **(23243)**

Rooseveltown
CKON-FM - 97.3 **(23276)**

Sag Harbor
WLNG-AM - 1600 **(23284)**
WLNG-FM - 92.1 **(23285)**

Sidney
WCDO-AM - 1490 **(23333)**
WCDO-FM - 100.9 **(23334)**

Windham
WRIP-FM - 97.9 **(23588)**

Woodside
WWRL-AM - 1600 **(23594)**

NORTH CAROLINA
Burlington
WPCM-AM - 920 **(23677)**

Chapel Hill
WCHL-AM - 1360 **(23731)**

Charlotte
WWMG-FM - 96.1 **(23782)**

Clinton
WCLN-AM - 1170 **(23790)**

Elizabethtown
WBLA-AM - 1440 **(23865)**
WGQR-FM - 105.7 **(23866)**

Fairmont
WFMO-AM - 860 **(23873)**

Fayetteville
WFLB-FM - 96.5 **(23885)**

Gastonia
WGNC-AM - 1450 **(23908)**

Greensboro
WMQX-FM - 93.1 **(23953)**

Greenville
WNCT-FM - 107.9 **(23973)**

Jacksonville
WKOO-FM - 98.7 **(24013)**

Laurinburg
WLNC-AM - 1300 **(24034)**

Lenoir
WJRI-AM - 1340 **(24037)**

Mooresville
WHIP-AM - 1350 **(24069)**

Raleigh
WTRG-FM - 100.7 **(24176)**

Salisbury
WSAT-AM - 1280 **(24217)**

Sanford
WFJA-FM - 105.5 **(24221)**

Shelby
WOHS-AM - 730 **(24229)**

Washington
WERO-FM - 93.3 **(24275)**

Whiteville
WTXY-AM - 1540 **(24287)**

Winston-Salem
WPOL-AM - 1340 **(24331)**
WSNC-FM - 90.5 **(24333)**

NORTH DAKOTA
Belcourt
KEYA-FM - 88.5 **(24346)**

Dickinson
KDIX-AM - 1230 **(24398)**

Grafton
KAUJ-FM - 100.9 **(24451)**

Jamestown
KXGT-FM - 95.5 **(24483)**

Wahpeton
KBMW-AM - 107.1 **(24550)**

OHIO
Akron
WJMP-AM - 1520 **(24597)**

Alliance
WRMU-FM - 91.1 **(24607)**

Ashland
WGLN-FM - 102.3 **(24619)**

Bucyrus
WBCO-AM - 1540 **(24719)**

Chillicothe
WBEX-AM - 1490 **(24765)**

Cleveland
WJMO-AM - 1490 **(24976)**
WMJI-FM - 105.7 **(24980)**

Columbus
WBNS-FM - 97.1 **(25073)**

Dayton
WCLR-FM - 95.7 **(25134)**
WHIO-AM - 1210 **(25141)**
WIZE-AM - 1340 **(25145)**

East Liverpool
WOHI-AM - 1490 **(25173)**

Mansfield
WSWR-FM - 100.1 **(25337)**

Marion
WMRN-AM - 1490 **(25354)**

North Baltimore
WPFX-FM - 107.7 **(25433)**

Streetsboro
WSTB-FM - 88.9 **(25549)**

Willoughby
WELW-AM - 1330 **(25665)**

Wooster
WKVX-AM - 960 **(25676)**

Youngstown
WBBG-FM - 93.3 **(25702)**

OKLAHOMA
Clinton
KCLI-AM - 1320 **(25792)**

Durant
KSEO-AM - 750 **(25811)**

Hugo
KIHN-AM - 1340 **(25873)**

Poteau
KPRV-AM - 1280 **(26047)**

Stillwater
KVRO-FM - 98.1 **(26087)**

Tulsa
KQLL-FM - 106.1 **(26161)**
KTSO-FM - 94.1 **(26166)**

OREGON
Bend
KQAK-FM - 105.7 **(26249)**

Burns
KQHC-FM - 92.7 **(26260)**

Coos Bay
KDCO-FM - 93.5 **(26278)**

The Dalles
KACI-AM - 1300 **(26301)**
KACI-FM - 97.7 **(26302)**

Eugene
KODZ-FM - 99.1 **(26343)**

Hermiston
KQFM-FM - 100.5 **(26371)**

McMinnville
KLYC-AM - 1260 **(26417)**

PENNSYLVANIA
Bala Cynwyd
KVLE-FM - 102.3 **(26670)**

Bedford
WBFD-AM - 1310 **(26691)**

Bethlehem
WGPA-AM - 1100 **(26711)**

Butler
WBUT-AM - 1050 **(26745)**

Chester
WDNR-FM, Widener University - 89.5 **(26776)**

Corry
WWCB-AM - 1370 **(26810)**

Easton
WODE-FM - 99.9 **(26854)**

Emporium
WLEM-AM - 1250 **(26884)**
WQKY-FM - 99.3 **(26885)**

Greenville
WEXC-FM - 107.1 **(26960)**

Harrisburg
WKBO-AM - 1230 **(27020)**
WWKL-FM - 99.3 **(27026)**

Hermitage
WWIZ-FM - 103.9 **(27038)**

Hollidaysburg
WALY-FM - 103.9 **(27047)**

Honesdale
WYCY-FM - 105.3 **(27055)**

Johnstown
WJAC-AM - 850 **(27092)**
WUZZ-FM - 105.7 **(27099)**
WVSC-AM - 990 **(27100)**

Kittanning
WTYM-AM - 1380 **(27128)**

Latrobe
WQTW-AM - 1570 **(27166)**

Lehighton
WYNS-AM - 1160 **(27184)**

Lewistown
WIEZ-AM - 670 **(27196)**
WKVA-AM - 920 **(27197)**

Lock Haven
WBPZ-AM - 1230 **(27205)**

Manheim
WHBO-FM - 92.7 **(27216)**

Millersville
WIXQ-FM - 91.7 **(27268)**

Pittsburgh
WESA-AM - 940 **(27866)**
WWSW-AM - 970 **(27880)**
WWSW-FM - 94.5 **(27881)**

Sayre
WTTC-AM - 1550 **(27948)**
WTTC-FM - 95.3 **(27949)**

Scranton
WICK-AM - 1400 **(27968)**
WQFM-FM - 92.1 **(27969)**
WQFN-FM - 100.1 **(27970)**
WYCK-AM - 1340 **(27974)**

Shenandoah
WQIN-AM - 1290 **(27988)**

State College
WZWW-FM - 95.3 **(28031)**

Warren
WRRN-FM - 92.3 **(28109)**

Washington
WJPA-AM - 1450 **(28120)**
WJPA-FM - 95.3 **(28121)**

White Oak
WEDO-AM - 810 **(28158)**

York
WSOX-FM - 96.1 **(28217)**

PUERTO RICO
Coamo
WCPR-AM - 1450 **(28241)**

Mayaguez
WCTA-FM - 95.1 **(28260)**
WKJB-AM - 99.1 **(28263)**

San Juan
WCAD-FM - 105.7 **(28298)**
WVIS-FM - 106.1 **(28312)**

RHODE ISLAND
Providence
WWBB-FM - 101.5 (28439)

SOUTH CAROLINA
Abbeville
WZLA-FM - 92.9 (28466)

Beaufort
WVGB-AM - 1490 (28491)

Cheraw
WCRE-AM - 1420 (28529)

Columbia
WOMG-FM - 103.1 (28583)

Greenwood
WCZZ-AM - 1090 (28648)

Hemingway
WLGI-FM - 90.9 (28660)

Johnston
WJES-AM - 1190 (28669)
WKSX-FM - 92.7 (28670)

Mount Pleasant
WXLY-FM - 102.5 (28700)

Murrells Inlet
WSYN-FM - 106.5 (28702)

Myrtle Beach
WVCO-FM - 94.9 (28711)

Newberry
WKDK-AM - 1240 (28718)

Sumter
WIBZ-FM - 95.5 (28771)

SOUTH DAKOTA
Aberdeen
KQAA-FM - 94.9 (28797)

Brookings
KJJQ-AM - 910 (28822)

Custer
KAWK-FM - 105.1 (28839)

Deadwood
KDSJ-AM - 980 (28842)

Milbank
KMSD-AM - 1510 (28895)

Pierre
KCCR-AM - 1240 (28924)

Rapid City
KKLS-AM - 920 (28943)

Sturgis
KBHB-AM - 810 (29002)

TENNESSEE
Athens
WYXI-AM - 1390 (29053)

Cleveland
WDNT-FM - 104.9 (29127)

Columbia
WKOM-FM - 101.7 (29139)

Cookeville
WPTN-AM - 780 (29150)

Dunlap
WSDQ-AM - 1190 (29172)

Dyersburg
WTRO-AM - 1450 (29178)

Gray
WKOS-FM - 104.9 (29210)

Humboldt
WIRJ-AM - 740 (29226)

Jackson
WMXX-FM - 103.1 (29237)

Knoxville
WMYU-FM - 102.1 (29295)

Memphis
WJCE-AM - 680 (29398)
WODZ-AM - 680 (29407)

Morristown
WMTN-AM - 1300 (29423)

Nashville
WGFX-FM - 104.5 (29511)
WMAK-FM - 96.3 (29519)

Newport
WLIK-AM - 1270 (29545)

Paris
WTPR-AM - 710 (29563)

Sparta
WTZX-AM - 860 (29616)

Trenton
WTKB-FM - 93.7 (29631)

TEXAS
Beaumont
KCOL-FM - 92.5 (29904)

Big Spring
KBYG-AM - 1400 (29926)

Brady
KNEL-AM - 1490 (29944)

Childress
KCTX-AM - 1510 (30018)

Clarksville
KGAP-FM - 98.5 (30024)

Corpus Christi
KLTG-FM - 96.5 (30088)

Cuero
KVCQ-FM - 97.7 (30117)

Dallas
KLUV-FM - 98.7 (30209)

Del Rio
KWMC-AM - 1490 (30229)

El Paso
KOFX-FM - 92.3 (30297)

Grand Prairie
KKDA-AM - 730 (30406)

Hamilton
KCLW-AM - 900 (30421)

Houston
KLDE-FM - 107.5 (30562)
KTSU-FM - 90.9 (30582)

Huntsville
KHVL-AM - 1490 (30598)
KMHT-AM - 1450 (30599)

Liberty
KSHN-FM - 99.9 (30692)

Lufkin
KUEZ-FM - 100.1 (30747)

Marshall
KCUL-FM - 92.3 (30769)

Midland
KMCM-FM - 96.9 (30819)

Monahans
KLBO-AM - 1330 (30836)

Odessa
KCHX-FM - 106.7 (30873)

Palestine
KNET-AM - 1450 (30898)

Prairie View
KPVU-FM - 91.3 (30962)

Quanah
KIXC-FM - 100.9 (30964)

Rusk
KTLU-AM - 1580 (31000)

San Angelo
KELI-FM - 98.7 (31014)

San Antonio
KCJZ-FM - 106.7 (31052)
KONO-AM - 860 (31064)
KONO-FM - 101.1 (31065)

Silsbee
KSET-AM - 1300 (31108)

Texarkana
KEWL-AM - 1400 (31186)
KEWL-FM - 95.1 (31187)

Tyler
KGLD-AM - 1330 (31212)

Vernon
KVWC-AM - 1490 (31232)
KVWC-FM - 103.1 (31233)

UTAH
Blanding
KUTA-AM - 790 (31321)

Cedar City
KBRE-AM - 940 (31325)

Logan
KGNT-FM - 103.9 (31358)

Price
KPRQ-FM - 100.9 (31396)
KRPX-AM - 1080 (31397)

Salt Lake City
KTCE-FM - 92.3 (31461)

VERMONT
Brattleboro
WTSA-FM - 96.7 (31513)

East Poultney
WNYV-FM - 94.1 (31540)

Randolph Center
WWWT-AM - 1320 (31584)

St. Johnsbury
WSTJ-AM - 1340 (31596)

VIRGINIA
Blacksburg
WBZK-AM - 980 (31885)
WCBX-AM - 900 (31886)

Brookneal
WODI-AM - 1230 (31906)

Charlottesville
WCHV-AM - 1260 (31949)
WCYK-FM - 99.7 (31951)

Clintwood
WDIC-FM - 92.1 (31979)

Covington
WKEY-AM - 1340 (31984)

Front Royal
WZRV-FM - 95.3 (32098)

Kilmarnock
WKWI-FM - 101.7 (32175)

Marion
WOLD-FM - 102.5 (32231)

Radford
WNNI-AM - 1260 (32349)

Staunton
WSVO-FM - 93.1 (32559)

Warrenton
WINX-FM - 94.3 (32603)

WASHINGTON
Centralia
KITI-AM - 1420 (32707)

Goldendale
KLCK-AM - 1400 (32777)

Longview
KEDO-AM - 1400 (32816)

Mount Vernon
KBRC-AM - 1430 (32848)

Newport
KUBS-FM - 91.5 (32852)

Olympia
KBRD-AM - 680 (32868)

Seattle
KBSG-AM - 1210 (33046)
KBSG-FM - 97.3 (33047)

Spokane
KEYF-FM - 101.1 (33112)
KXAA-FM - 99.5 (33133)

Yakima
KMWX-AM - 1460 (33232)

OLDIES (continued)

WEST VIRGINIA
Beckley
WIWS-AM - 1070 **(33242)**

Bluefield
WKQY-FM - 100.1 **(33258)**

Elkins
WBTQ-FM - 93.5 **(33306)**

Fisher
WELD-AM - 690 **(33317)**

Huntington
WRVC-FM - 92.7 **(33345)**
WVHU-AM - 800 **(33347)**

Keyser
WCBC-FM - 107.1 **(33356)**

Morgantown
WCLG-AM - 1300 **(33401)**

Princeton
WKOY-FM - 100.9 **(33442)**

Ravenswood
WFYZ-AM - 1360 **(33445)**
WMOV-AM - 1360 **(33446)**

Ronceverte
WRON-FM - 97.7 **(33456)**

Vienna
WDMX-FM - 100.1 **(33480)**

Weirton
WCDK-FM - 106.3 **(33490)**

Williamson
WBTH-AM - 1400 **(33514)**

WISCONSIN
Altoona
WECL-FM - 92.9 **(33525)**

Appleton
WECB-FM - 104.3 **(33547)**

Ashland
WATW-AM - 1400 **(33556)**

Beaver Dam
WBEV-AM - 1430 **(33569)**

Beloit
WGEZ-AM - 1490 **(33579)**

Black River Falls
WWIS-AM - 1260 **(33592)**

Eagle River
WERL-AM - 950 **(33666)**

Fort Atkinson
WFAW-AM - 940 **(33724)**
WKCH-FM - 106.5 **(33725)**

Hales Corners
WEMP-AM - 1250 **(33771)**

Ladysmith
WJBL-FM - 93.1 **(33901)**

Madison
WOLX-FM - 94.9 **(34006)**

Manitowoc
WLTU-FM - 92.1 **(34015)**

Marshfield
WDLB-AM - 1450 **(34028)**

Mayville
WMDC-FM - 98.7 **(34033)**

Oconto
WOCO-FM - 107.1 **(34206)**

Onalaska
WLFN-AM - 1490 **(34214)**

Platteville
WPVL-FM - 107.1 **(34247)**

Port Washington
WGLB-FM - 100.1 **(34251)**

Prairie du Chien
WPRE-AM - 980 **(34270)**

Shawano
WOWN-FM - 99.3 **(34319)**

Tomah
WBOG-FM - 94.5 **(34370)**

Tomahawk
WJJQ-FM - 92.5 **(34375)**

Two Rivers
WTRW-AM - 1590 **(34378)**

Viroqua
WVRQ-AM - 1360 **(34384)**

Wausau
WIZD-FM - 99.9 **(34435)**
WOFM-FM - 94.7 **(34436)**

Whitehall
WHTL-FM - 102.3 **(34455)**

WYOMING
Buffalo
KBBS-AM - 1450 **(34479)**

Cheyenne
KPIN-FM - 101.1 **(34508)**
KRAE-AM - 1480 **(34509)**
KRRR-FM - 104.9 **(34510)**

Cody
KZMQ-AM - 1140 **(34517)**

Kemmerer
KMER-AM - 950 **(34542)**

Newcastle
KASL-AM - 1240 **(34565)**

Rock Springs
KRKK-AM - 1360 **(34584)**

Sheridan
KROE-AM - 930 **(34589)**

Wheatland
KZEW-FM - 101.7 **(34603)**

Worland
KWOR-AM - 1340 **(34606)**

ALBERTA, CANADA
Calgary
CFFR-AM - 660 **(34666)**

Canmore
CHMN-FM - 106.5 **(34679)**

Edmonton
CFRN-AM - 1260 **(34746)**

BRITISH COLUMBIA, CANADA
Gold River
CJGR-FM - 100 **(34965)**

Kamloops
CHNL-AM - 610 **(34980)**

Port Alberni
CJAV-AM - 1240 **(35050)**

Vancouver
CISL-AM - 650 **(35188)**

MANITOBA, CANADA
Winnipeg
CFRW-AM - 1290 **(35369)**

NEW BRUNSWICK, CANADA
Woodstock
CJCJ-FM - 104.1 **(35441)**

NEWFOUNDLAND AND LABRADOR, CANADA
St. John's
CJYQ-AM - 930 **(35501)**

NOVA SCOTIA, CANADA
Amherst
CKDH-AM - 900 **(35533)**

Halifax
CHNS-AM - 960 **(35574)**

Sydney
CHER-AM - 950 **(35611)**

ONTARIO, CANADA
Cobourg
CHUC-AM - 1450 **(35743)**

Elliot Lake
CKNR-AM - 1340 **(35804)**

Guelph
CJOY-AM - 1460 **(35870)**

Hamilton
CKOC-AM - 1150 **(35898)**

Kenora
CJRL-AM - 1220 **(35930)**

Kingston
CFFX-AM - 960 **(35950)**

Niagara Falls
CJRN-AM - 710 **(36112)**

North Bay
CHUR-FM - 100.5 **(36118)**

Ottawa
CFRA-AM - 580 **(36289)**

Owen Sound
CFOS-AM - 560 **(36300)**
CFPS-AM - 1490 **(36301)**

Stratford
CJCS-AM - 1240 **(36411)**

Toronto
CHUM-AM - 1050 **(36811)**

Waterloo
CKKW-AM - 1090 **(36861)**

QUEBEC, CANADA
Levis
CFOM-FM - 102.9 **(37050)**

SASKATCHEWAN, CANADA
Melfort
CJVR-AM - 750 **(37499)**

Rosetown
CJYM-AM - 1330 **(37546)**

POLKA

MARYLAND
Glen Burnie
WJRO-AM - 1590 **(13556)**

MICHIGAN
Elsie
WOES-FM - 91.3 **(15006)**

MINNESOTA
Albany
KASM-AM - 1150 **(15705)**

NEBRASKA
Columbus
KTTT-AM - 1510 **(17984)**

PENNSYLVANIA
Bethlehem
WGPA-AM - 1100 **(26711)**

Shiremanstown
WWII-AM - 720 **(27995)**

WISCONSIN
Hartford
WTKM-AM - 1540 **(33774)**
WTKM-FM - 104.9 **(33775)**

Sturgeon Bay
WAUN-FM - 92.7 **(34352)**

PUBLIC RADIO

ALABAMA
Birmingham
WBHM-FM - 90.3 **(107)**

Huntsville
WLRH-FM - 89.3 **(284)**

Mobile
WHIL-FM - 91.3 **(340)**

Muscle Shoals
WQPR-FM - 88.7 **(400)**

Troy
WRWA-FM - 88.7 **(475)**
WTJB-FM - 91.7 **(478)**
WTSU-FM - 89.9 **(479)**

Tuscaloosa
WAPR-FM - 88.3 **(496)**
WUAL-FM - 91.5 **(503)**

ALASKA
Anchorage
KSKA-FM - 91.1 **(547)**

Barrow
KBRW-AM - 680 **(552)**
KBRW-FM - 91.9 **(553)**

Dillingham
KDLG-AM - 670 **(563)**

Fairbanks
KFAR-AM - 660 **(572)**
KUAC-FM - 89.9 **(578)**

Galena
KIYU-AM - 910 **(582)**

Haines
KHNS-FM - 102.3 **(586)**

Homer
KBBI-AM - 890 **(589)**

Juneau
KTOO-FM - 104.3 **(604)**

Ketchikan
KRBD-FM - 105.9 **(613)**

Kodiak
KMXT-FM - 100.1 **(617)**

Kotzebue
KOTZ-AM - 89.9 **(622)**

McGrath
KSKO-AM - 870 **(623)**

Sitka
KCAW-FM - 104.7 **(639)**

Unalaska
KIAL-AM - 1450 **(645)**

Valdez
KCHU-AM - 770 **(646)**

Wrangell
KSTK-FM - 101.7 **(654)**

ARIZONA
Flagstaff
KNAU-FM - 88.7 **(700)**

Tempe
KJZZ-FM - 91.5 **(921)**

Tucson
KUAZ-AM - 1550 **(997)**
KUAZ-FM - 89.1 **(998)**

ARKANSAS
Fayetteville
KUAF-FM - 91.3 **(1131)**

CALIFORNIA
Arcata
KHSU-FM - 90.5 **(1431)**

Fresno
KXEX-AM - 1550 **(1988)**

Los Angeles
KUSC-FM - 91.5 **(2470)**
KXLU-FM - 88.9 **(2472)**

Monterey
KXDC-FM - 101.7 **(2589)**

Northridge
KCSN-FM - 88.5 **(2647)**

Pacific Grove
KAZU-FM - 90.3 **(2735)**

Palm Springs
KPSC-FM - 88.5 **(2778)**

Pasadena
KPCC-FM - 89.3 **(2829)**

Philo
KZYX-FM - 90.7 **(2838)**

Redway
KMUD-FM - 91.1 **(2912)**

Sacramento
KXPR-FM - 90.9 **(3056)**

San Bernardino
KVCR-FM - 91.9 **(3095)**

San Diego
KPBS-FM - 89.5 **(3308)**

San Francisco
KALW-FM - 91.7 **(3469)**
KQED-FM - 88.5 **(3498)**

San Luis Obispo
KXTZ-FM - 95.3 **(3575)**

San Mateo
KCSM-FM - 91.1 **(3592)**

Santa Barbara
KFAC-FM - 88.7 **(3665)**

Santa Cruz
KUSP-FM - 88.9 **(3692)**

Santa Monica
KCRW-FM - 89.9 **(3722)**

Stockton
KUOP-FM - 91.3 **(3819)**

Thousand Oaks
KCLU-FM - 88.3 Ventura County, 102.3 FM Santa
  Barbara County **(3924)**
KCPB-FM - 91.1 **(3925)**

COLORADO
Alamosa
KRZA-FM - 88.7 **(4136)**

Boulder
KGNU-FM - 88.5 **(4197)**

Carbondale
KDNK-FM - 90.5 **(4219)**

Colorado Springs
KRCC-FM - 91.5 **(4275)**

Denver
KUVO-FM - 89.3 **(4392)**

Grand Junction
KPRN-FM - 89.5 **(4492)**

Greeley
KUNC-FM - 91.5 **(4503)**

Ignacio
KSUT-FM - 91.3 **(4520)**

CONNECTICUT
Fairfield
WSHU-FM - 91.1 **(4792)**

Hartford
WPKT-FM - 90.5 **(4906)**

Norwich
WNPR-FM - 89.1 **(5087)**

DISTRICT OF COLUMBIA
Washington
WDCU-FM - 90.1 **(5881)**

FLORIDA
Boynton Beach
WXEL-FM - 90.7 **(5954)**

Fort Myers
WGCU-FM - 90.1 **(6104)**

Fort Pierce
WQCS-FM - 88.9 **(6120)**

Gainesville
WAJD-AM - 1390 **(6161)**
WUFT-FM - 89.1 **(6168)**

Melbourne
WFIT-FM - 89.5 **(6337)**

Miami
WDNA-FM - 88.9 **(6399)**
WLRN-FM - 91.3 **(6402)**

Pensacola
WUWF-FM - 88.1 **(6579)**

Tallahassee
WFSU-FM - 88.9 **(6747)**

Tampa
WUSF-FM - 89.7 **(6807)**

GEORGIA
Atlanta
WABE-FM - 90.1 **(7064)**
WCLK-FM - 91.9 **(7070)**
WUNV-FM - 91.7 **(7089)**

Augusta
WACG-FM - 90.7 **(7104)**

Carrollton
WWGC-FM - 90.7 **(7160)**

Savannah
WSVH-FM - 91.1 **(7549)**

Smyrna
WAZX-AM - 1550 **(7556)**

Warm Springs
WJSP-FM - 88.1 **(7636)**

HAWAII
Hanalei
KAQA-FM - 91.9 **(7666)**
KKCR-FM - 90.9 **(7667)**

Honolulu
KKUA-FM - 90.7 **(7745)**
KORL-AM - 690 **(7748)**

IDAHO
Boise
KBSU-FM - 90.3 **(7818)**

McCall
KBSM-FM - 91.7 **(7906)**

Rexburg
KBYI-FM - 100.5 **(7966)**

Rupert
KFTA-AM - 970 **(7969)**

Twin Falls
KBSW-FM - 91.7 **(7991)**

ILLINOIS
Carbondale
WSIU-FM - 91.9 **(8123)**

Champaign
WEFT-FM - 90.1 **(8226)**

Chicago
WXEX-FM - 107.9 **(8660)**

DeKalb
WNIJ-FM - 90.5 **(8744)**
WNIU-FM - 89.5 **(8745)**

Edwardsville
WSIE-FM - 88.7 **(8815)**

Glen Ellyn
WDCB-FM - 90.9 **(8933)**

Macomb
WIUM-FM - 91.3 **(9134)**

Peoria
WCBU-FM - 89.9 **(9430)**

Quincy
WQUB-FM - 90.3 **(9482)**

Rock Island
WVIK-FM - 90.3 **(9525)**

Romeoville
WLRA-FM - 88.1 **(9554)**

Springfield
WUIS-FM - 91.9 **(9658)**

Winnetka
WNTH-FM - 88.1 **(9769)**

INDIANA
Elkhart
WVPE-FM - 88.1 **(9930)**

Evansville
WNIN-FM - 88.3 **(9947)**

Fort Wayne
WBNI-FM - 89.1 **(9979)**

PUBLIC RADIO (continued)

Indianapolis
WFYI-FM - 90.1 **(10195)**

Muncie
WBST-FM - 92.1 **(10330)**

West Lafayette
WBAA-AM - 920 **(10556)**

IOWA
Ames
WOI-AM - 640 **(10599)**
WOI-FM - 90.1 **(10600)**

Cedar Falls
KHKE-FM - 89.5 **(10667)**
KUNI-FM - 90.9 **(10668)**

Council Bluffs
KIWR-FM - 89.7 **(10727)**

Decorah
KLSE-FM - 91.7 **(10761)**

Iowa City
KSUI-FM - 91.7 **(10994)**
WSUI-AM - 910 **(10998)**

Mason City
KRNI-AM - 1010 **(11078)**
KUNY-FM - 91.5 **(11079)**

Sioux City
KWIT-FM - 90.3 **(11225)**

KANSAS
Garden City
KANZ-FM - 91.1 **(11450)**

Hutchinson
KHCC-FM - 90.1 **(11505)**

Lawrence
KANU-FM - 91.5 **(11573)**

Salina
KHCD-FM - 89.5 **(11786)**

KENTUCKY
Bowling Green
WDCL-FM - 89.7 **(11955)**
WKYU-FM - 88.9 **(11960)**

Hazard
WEKH-FM - 90.9 **(12117)**

Louisville
WFPL-FM - 89.3 **(12251)**

Murray
WKMS-FM - 91.3/92.1 Paducah, KY; 99.5 Paris,
TN **(12319)**

Richmond
WEKU-FM - 88.9 **(12385)**

LOUISIANA
Baton Rouge
WBRH-FM - 90.3 **(12514)**
WRKF-FM - 89.3 **(12523)**

Hammond
KSLU-FM - 90.9 **(12595)**

New Orleans
KTLN-FM - 90.5 **(12766)**
WRBH-FM - 88.3 **(12775)**
WTUL-FM - 91.5 **(12778)**
WWNO-FM - 89.9 **(12782)**

Shreveport
KDAQ-FM - 89.9 **(12823)**

MAINE
Houlton
WHOU-FM - 100.1 **(12972)**

MARYLAND
Baltimore
WBJC-FM - 91.5 **(13268)**
WEAA-FM - 88.9 **(13270)**

MASSACHUSETTS
Amherst
WFCR-FM - 88.5 **(13809)**

Boston
WGBH-FM - 89.7 **(13985)**

Rockland
WRPS-FM - 88.3 **(14509)**

Sheffield
WBSL-FM - 91.7 **(14520)**

MICHIGAN
Flint
WFBE-FM - 95.1 **(15041)**
WFUM-FM - 91.1 **(15044)**

Grand Rapids
WGVU-FM - 88.5 **(15110)**
WVGR-FM - 104.1 **(15125)**
WYBN-FM - 93.1 **(15128)**

Harrison
WVXH-FM - 92.1 **(15145)**

Houghton
WGGL-FM - 91.1 **(15186)**

Kalamazoo
WMUK-FM - 102.1 **(15256)**

Mount Pleasant
WCMU-FM - 89.5 **(15380)**

Twin Lake
WBLV-FM - 90.3 **(15645)**

Ypsilanti
WEMU-FM - 89.1 **(15692)**

MINNESOTA
Albert Lea
KATE-FM - 1450 **(15708)**

Bemidji
KCRB-FM - 88.5 **(15744)**

Brainerd
KBPR-FM - 90.7 **(15768)**

Buhl
WIRR-FM - 90.9 **(15780)**

Collegeville
KNSR-FM - 88.9 **(15808)**
KSJR-FM - 90.1 **(15809)**

Duluth
KUMD-FM - 103.3 **(15852)**
WSCD-FM - 92.9 **(15857)**

Grand Rapids
KAXE-FM - 91.7 **(15930)**

Mankato
KMSU-FM - 89.7 **(16034)**

Moorhead
KCCM-FM - 91.1 **(16191)**

Northfield
WCAL-FM - 89.3 **(16240)**

St. Paul
KSJN-FM - 99.5 **(16422)**

Winona
KQAL-FM - 89.5 **(16534)**

MISSISSIPPI
Jackson
WKNP-FM - 90.1 **(16721)**
WMPR-FM - 90.1 **(16726)**

Lorman
WPRL-FM - 91.7 **(16749)**

Meridian
WMAW-FM - 88.1 **(16776)**

Senatobia
WKNA-FM - 88.9 **(16843)**

MISSOURI
Cape Girardeau
KRCU-FM - 90.9 **(16953)**

Columbia
KBIA-FM - 91.3 **(17013)**

Kansas City
KCUR-FM - 89.3 **(17208)**
KKFI-FM - 90.1 **(17209)**

Maryville
KXCV-FM - 90.5 **(17279)**

Point Lookout
KCOZ-FM - 91.7 **(17355)**

Rolla
KUMR-FM - 88.5 **(17382)**

St. Charles
KCLC-FM - 89.1 **(17385)**

St. Louis
KWMU-FM - 90.7 **(17553)**

Springfield
KSMU-FM - 91.1 **(17627)**

Warrensburg
KTBG-FM - 90.9 **(17673)**

Warrenton
KWRE-AM - 730 **(17702)**

NEBRASKA
Alliance
KTNE-FM - 91.1 **(17931)**

Hastings
KHNE-FM - 89.1 **(18041)**

Lexington
KLNE-FM - 88.7 **(18073)**

Norfolk
KXNE-FM - 89.3 **(18172)**

NEW JERSEY
Trenton
WNJS-FM - 88.1 **(19677)**
WWFM-The Classical Network - 89.1 **(19679)**
WWNJ-FM - 91.1 **(19680)**

NEW MEXICO
Albuquerque
KRZY-FM - 105.9 **(19811)**
KUNM-FM - 89.9 **(19815)**

Las Cruces
KRWG-FM - 90.7 **(19885)**

Pinehill
KTDB-FM - 89.7 **(19904)**

NEW YORK
Albany
WAMC-FM - 90.3 **(20009)**

Binghamton
WSKG-FM - 89.3 **(20228)**
WSQE-FM - 91.1 **(20230)**
WSQX-FM - 88.7 **(20232)**
WSQX-FM - 91.5 **(20233)**

Bronx
WFUV-FM - 90.7 **(20292)**

Buffalo
WBFO-FM - 88.7 **(20395)**
WNED-AM - 970 **(20408)**

Canajoharie
WCAN-FM - 93.3 **(20418)**

Canton
WSLO-FM - 90.9 **(20432)**
WSLU-FM - 89.5 **(20433)**

Cortland
WSUC-FM - 90.5 **(20514)**

Fredonia
WCVF-FM - 88.9 **(20624)**

Geneva
WEOS-FM - 89.7 **(20657)**

Hamilton
WRCU-FM - 90.1 **(20709)**

Kingston
WAMK-FM - 90.9 **(20863)**

New Paltz
WFNP-FM - 88.7 **(21115)**

New York
WHCR-FM - 90.3 **(22970)**
WNYC-AM - 820 **(22979)**
WNYC-FM - 93.9 **(22980)**

Oneonta
WRHO-FM - 89.7 **(23054)**

Oswego
WRVO-FM - 89.9 **(23064)**

Numbers cited in bold after listings are entry numbers rather than page numbers.

Potsdam
WTSC-FM - 91.1 **(23144)**

Rochester
WXXI-AM - 1370 **(23258)**

St. Bonaventure
WSBU-FM - 88.3 **(23288)**

Saranac Lake
WSLL-FM - 90.5 **(23299)**

Schenectady
WMHT-FM - 89.1 **(23317)**
WRHV-FM - 88.7 **(23321)**

Southampton
WPBX-FM - 88.3 **(23346)**

Syracuse
WAER-FM - 88.3 **(23434)**
WCNY-FM - 91.3 **(23436)**
WOLF-AM - 1490 **(23443)**

Ticonderoga
WANC-FM - 103.9 **(23451)**

Troy
WRPI-FM - 91.5 **(23460)**

Utica
WOUR-FM - 96.9 **(23475)**

NORTH CAROLINA
Asheville
WFQS-FM - 91.3 **(23636)**

Davidson
WDAV-FM - 89.9 **(23800)**

Durham
WNCU-FM - 90.7 **(23849)**
WXDU-FM - 88.7 **(23854)**

Fayetteville
WFSS-FM - 91.9 **(23887)**

Mars Hill
WVMH-FM - 90.5 **(24058)**

New Bern
WTEB-FM - 89.3 **(24102)**

Spindale
WNCW-FM - 88.7 **(24243)**

Wilmington
WHQR-FM - 91.3 **(24301)**

Winston-Salem
WFDD-FM - 88.5 **(24330)**

NORTH DAKOTA
Bismarck
KCND-FM - 90.5 **(24366)**
KDPR-FM - 89.9 **(24367)**

Fargo
KDSU-FM - 91.9 **(24417)**

Minot
KMPR-FM - 88.9 **(24510)**

Williston
KPPR-FM - 90.5 **(24563)**

OHIO
Athens
WOUB-AM - 1340 **(24632)**
WOUB-FM - 91.3 **(24633)**
WOUC-FM - 89.1 **(24635)**

Cincinnati
WGUC-FM - 90.9 **(24839)**
WJVS-FM - 88.3 **(24840)**
WMKV-FM - 89.3 **(24844)**
WVXU-FM - 91.7 **(24849)**

Cleveland
WCPN-FM - 90.3 **(24970)**

Columbus
WCBE-FM - 90.5 **(25076)**

Ironton
WOUL-FM - 89.1 **(25255)**

Kent
WKSU-FM - 89.7 **(25279)**

Lima
WGLE-FM - 90.7 **(25300)**

Oxford
WMUB-FM - 88.5 **(25463)**

Toledo
WGBE-FM - 90.9 **(25576)**
WGTE-FM - 91.3 **(25577)**

Yellow Springs
WYSO-FM - 91.3 **(25693)**

OKLAHOMA
Edmond
KCSC-FM - 90.1 **(25815)**

Stillwater
KOSU-FM - 91.7 **(26084)**

OREGON
Ashland
KSKF-FM - 90.9 **(26221)**
KSMF-FM - 89.1 **(26222)**
KSOR-FM - 90.1 **(26223)**

Corvallis
KOAC-AM - 550 **(26293)**

Eugene
KLCC-FM - 89.7 **(26341)**

Portland
KBPS-AM - 1450 **(26520)**

Warm Springs
KWSO-FM - 91.9 **(26609)**

PENNSYLVANIA
Bethlehem
WDIY-FM - 88.1 **(26710)**

East Stroudsburg
WESS-FM - 90.3 **(26848)**

Erie
WQLN-FM - 91.3 **(26909)**

Lincoln University
WLIU-FM - 88.7 **(27201)**

Philadelphia
WHYY-FM - 90.9 **(27733)**
WRTI-FM - 90.1 **(27744)**
WXPN-FM - 88.5 **(27747)**

Pittsburgh
WDUQ-FM - 90.5 **(27863)**
WQED-FM - 89.3 **(27874)**

Schnecksville
WXLV-FM - 90.3 **(27950)**

State College
WPSU-FM - 91.5 **(28026)**

Swarthmore
WSRN-FM - 91.5 **(28047)**

SOUTH CAROLINA
Beaufort
WJWJ-FM - 89.9 **(28489)**

Columbia
WEPR-FM - 90.1 **(28575)**

Sumter
WRJA-FM - 88.1 **(28774)**

SOUTH DAKOTA
Sioux Falls
KCSD-FM - 90.9 **(28971)**
KRSD-FM - 88.1 **(28982)**

TENNESSEE
Chattanooga
WUTC-FM - 88.1 **(29112)**

Johnson City
WETS-FM - 89.5 **(29256)**

Knoxville
WUOT-FM - 91.9 **(29303)**

Memphis
WKNO-FM - 91.1 **(29399)**

Nashville
WHRS-FM - 91.7 **(29512)**
WPLN-FM - 90.3 **(29525)**

TEXAS
Abilene
KACU-FM - 89.7 **(29657)**

Austin
KUT-FM - 90.5 **(29879)**

Beaumont
KVLU-FM - 91.3 **(29909)**

Canyon
KWTS-FM - 91.1 **(30001)**

Commerce
KETR-FM - 88.9 **(30069)**

Corpus Christi
KEDT-FM - 90.3 **(30082)**

Dallas
KERA-FM - 90.1 **(30203)**

Floresville
KWCB-FM - 89.7 **(30320)**

Houston
KUHF-FM - 88.7 **(30583)**
KYND-AM - 1520 **(30587)**

Killeen
KNCT-FM - 91.3 **(30645)**

Lubbock
KOHM-FM - 89.1 **(30733)**

San Angelo
KUTX-FM - 90.1 **(31022)**

San Antonio
KPAC-FM - 88.3 **(31066)**

Waco
KWBU-FM - 103.3 **(31261)**

UTAH
Cedar City
KSUU-FM - 91.1 **(31329)**

Logan
KUSU-FM - 89.5, 91.5 **(31361)**

Provo
KBYU-FM - 89.1, 89.5 **(31410)**

Salt Lake City
KUER-FM - 90.1 **(31465)**

VERMONT
Colchester
WRVT-FM - 88.7 **(31532)**
WVPS-FM - 107.9 **(31534)**

Johnson
WJSC-FM - 90.7 **(31546)**

Lyndonville
WWLR-FM - 91.5 **(31551)**

Randolph Center
WVTC-FM - 90.7 **(31583)**

Windsor
WVPR-FM - 89.5 **(31622)**

VIRGINIA
Arlington
WETA-FM - 90.9 **(31845)**
WETH-FM - 89.1 **(31847)**

Harrisonburg
WMRA-FM - 90.7 **(32148)**
WMRL-FM - 89.9 **(32149)**
WMRY-FM - 103.5 **(32150)**

Norfolk
WHRO-FM - 90.3 **(32299)**
WHRV-FM - 89.5 **(32301)**

Richmond
WCVE-FM - 88.9 **(32474)**

Wise
WISE-FM - 90.5 **(32635)**

WASHINGTON
Pullman
KFAE-FM - 89.1 **(32910)**
KRFA-FM - 91.7 **(32913)**

Seattle
KUOW-FM - 94.9 **(33072)**
KVI-AM - 570 **(33073)**

PUBLIC RADIO (continued)

Spokane
KPBX-FM - 91.1 **(33123)**

Tacoma
KPLU-FM - 88.5 **(33158)**

WISCONSIN
Appleton
WLFM-FM - 91.1 **(33550)**

Green Bay
WHID-FM - 88.1 **(33749)**

Kenosha
WGTD-FM - 91.1 **(33876)**

La Crosse
WLSU-FM - 88.9 **(33894)**

Madison
WHWC-FM - 88.3 **(33995)**
WORT-FM - 89.9 **(34007)**
WRFW-FM - 88.7 **(34008)**

Milwaukee
WUWM-FM - 89.7 **(34137)**

Rhinelander
WXPR-FM - 91.7 **(34292)**

Sturgeon Bay
WBDK-FM - 96.7 **(34353)**

Superior
KUWS-FM - 91.3 **(34362)**

Wausau
WIFC-FM - 95.5 **(34434)**

BRITISH COLUMBIA, CANADA
Vancouver
CFRO-FM - 102.7 **(35185)**

MANITOBA, CANADA
Altona
CILT-FM - 96.7 **(35250)**

NORTHWEST TERRITORIES, CANADA
Iqaluit
CFFB-AM - 1230 **(35520)**

ONTARIO, CANADA
Chatham
CFCO-AM - 630 **(35731)**

Windsor
CBC-AM - 1550 **(36894)**
CBEF-AM - 540 **(36896)**

RAP

CALIFORNIA
Santa Clara
KSCU-FM - 103.3 **(3677)**

Turlock
KCSS-FM - 91.9 **(3960)**

CONNECTICUT
Hartford
WQTQ-FM - 89.9 **(4909)**

West Haven
WNHU-FM - 88.7 **(5208)**

GEORGIA
Statesboro
WVGS-FM - 91.9 **(7567)**

IOWA
Dubuque
KLCR-FM - 96.9 **(10851)**

MARYLAND
Emmitsburg
WMTB-FM - 89.9 **(13502)**

MINNESOTA
St. Louis Park
KDXL-FM - 106.5 **(16362)**

NEW JERSEY
Flemington
WCVH-FM - 90.5 **(18822)**

NEW MEXICO
Farmington
KNMI-FM - 88.9 **(19849)**

TEXAS
Austin
KAZI-FM - 88.7 **(29860)**

REGGAE

CALIFORNIA
Fresno
KFSR-FM - 90.7 **(1967)**

CONNECTICUT
Hartford
WQTQ-FM - 89.9 **(4909)**

FLORIDA
Fort Lauderdale
WSRF-AM - 1580 **(6091)**

NORTH CAROLINA
Durham
WXDU-FM - 88.7 **(23854)**

Raleigh
WKNC-FM - 88.1 **(24164)**

TEXAS
Austin
KAZI-FM - 88.7 **(29860)**

Prairie View
KPVU-FM - 91.3 **(30962)**

RELIGIOUS

ALABAMA
Alabaster
WGTT-AM - 1500 **(2)**

Arab
WRAB-AM - 1380 **(24)**

Birmingham
WBFR-FM - 89.5 **(105)**
WDJC-FM - 93.7 **(114)**
WGIB-FM - 91.9 **(116)**
WLPH-AM - 1480 **(123)**
WRRS-FM - 101.1 **(128)**

Bridgeport
WBTS-AM - 1480 **(138)**

Camden
WCOX-AM - 1450 **(144)**
WCOX-FM - 102.3 **(145)**

Clanton
WKLF-AM - 980 **(157)**

Dadeville
WELL-FM - 88.7 **(167)**

Decatur
WJRA-AM - 1310 **(174)**

Demopolis
WXAL-AM - 1400 **(181)**

Dixons Mills
WMBV-FM - 91.9 **(183)**

Dora
WPYK-AM - 1010 **(184)**

Dothan
WGTF-FM - 89.5 **(192)**
WVOB-FM - 91.3 **(195)**

Evergreen
KDKO-AM - 1510 **(210)**

Florala
WKWL-AM - 1230 **(217)**

Gadsden
WJBY-AM - 930 **(236)**

Huntsville
WOCG-FM - 90.1 **(285)**

WYFD-FM - 91.7 **(288)**

Montgomery
WLBF-FM - 89.1 **(386)**
WMGY-AM - 800 **(389)**

Oxford
WTBJ-FM - 91 **(417)**

Phenix City
WFRC-FM - 90.5 **(426)**

Red Bay
WRMG-AM - 1430 **(432)**

Sumiton
WRSM-AM - 1540 **(461)**

Sylacauga
WYEA-AM - 1290 **(464)**

ALASKA
Anchorage
KATB-FM - 89.3 **(535)**

Bethel
KYKD-FM - 100.1 **(555)**

Glennallen
KCAM-AM - 790 **(583)**

Naknek
KAKN-FM - 100.9-FM **(624)**

Nenana
KIAM-AM - 630 **(625)**

Nome
KICY-AM - 850 **(626)**
KNOM-FM - 96.1 **(629)**

ARIZONA
Lake Havasu City
KNLB-FM - 91.1 **(740)**

Parker
KWFH-FM - 90.1 **(766)**

Phoenix
KASA-AM - 1540 **(816)**
KFLR-FM - 90.3 **(818)**
KPHX-AM - 1480 **(833)**
KPXQ-AM - 1360 **(835)**

Prescott
KGCB-FM - 90.9 **(851)**

Tuba City
KTBA-AM - 1050 **(927)**

Tucson
KFLT-AM - 830 **(978)**

Window Rock
KHAC-AM - 880 **(1012)**

ARKANSAS
Berryville
KTHS-AM - 1480 **(1055)**

Brinkley
KBRI-AM - 1570 **(1064)**

Cave City
KZIG-FM - 89.9 **(1075)**

Hot Springs
KSBC-FM - 90.1 **(1187)**

Little Rock
KAAY-AM - 1090 **(1238)**
KITA-AM - 1440 **(1244)**

Marshall
KCGS-AM - 960 **(1270)**

Monticello
KHBM-AM - 1430 **(1280)**

Mountain Home
KCMH-FM - 91.5 **(1286)**

Nashville
KBHC-AM - 1260 **(1295)**

Pine Bluff
KCAT-AM - 1340 **(1315)**

Siloam Springs
KLRC-FM - 101.1 **(1344)**

West Memphis
KKLV-FM - 94.7 **(1369)**

Numbers cited in bold after listings are entry numbers rather than page numbers.

CALIFORNIA
Angwin
KNDL-FM - 89.9 (1424)

Bakersfield
KAXL-FM - 88.3 (1456)
KERI-AM - 1180 (1460)
KHIS-AM - 800 (1465)

Burney
KIBC-FM - 90.5 (1636)

Camarillo
KEYQ-AM - 980 (1644)
KGZO-FM - 90.9 (1645)
KMRO-FM (1646)
KMRO-FM - 90.3 (1647)

Ceres
KADV-FM - 90.5 (1683)

Chico
KKXX-AM - 930 (1702)

Costa Mesa
KBRT-AM - 740 (1784)

Dinuba
KRDU-AM - 1130 (1830)

El Centro
KGBA-FM - 100.1 (1854)

Fresno
KIRV-AM - 1510 (1972)

Glendale
KKLA-AM - 1240 (2015)

Inglewood
KTYM-AM - 1460 (2075)

Le Grand
KEFR-FM - 89.9 (2151)

Long Beach
KFRN-AM - 1280 (2178)

Los Angeles
KFSG-FM - 93.5 (2455)

Merced
KAMB-FM - 101.5 (2530)

Modesto
KUYL-AM - 1280 (2571)

Mount Bullion
KCIV-FM - 99.9 (2603)

Oakland
KEAR-FM - 106.9 (2704)

Oxnard
KDAR-FM - 98.3 (2732)

Palm Desert
KESQ-AM - 1400 (2748)

Redding
KVIP-AM - 540 (2898)
KVIP-FM - 98.1 (2899)

Riverside
KPRO-AM - 1570 (2952)
KSGN-FM - 89.7 (2953)

Sacramento
KEBR-AM - 88.1 (3027)
KEBR-FM - 88.1 (3028)
KLVG-FM - 103.7 (3037)

San Diego
KPRZ-AM - 1210 (3312)

Santa Ana
KWVE-FM - 107.9 (3639)

Stockton
KCJH-FM - 89.1 (3811)
KYCC-FM - 90.1 (3820)

Sun City
KAEH-FM - 100.9 (3825)

Visalia
KARM-FM - 89.7 (4042)

West Sacramento
KJAY-AM - 1430 (4067)

Yucaipa
KLRD-FM - 90.1 (4127)

COLORADO
Alamosa
KGIW-AM - 1450 (4135)

Breen
KLLV-AM - 550 (4200)

Brighton
KLTT-AM - 670 (4203)

Colorado Springs
KGFT-FM - 100.7 (4267)
KTLF-FM - 90.5 (4283)

Fountain
KWYD-AM - 1580 (4453)

Grand Junction
KCIC-FM - 88.5 (4482)

Westminster
KPOF-AM - 910 (4670)

CONNECTICUT
Hartford
WRTC-FM - 89.3 (4911)

Milford
WFIF-AM - 1500 (4960)

FLORIDA
Altamonte Springs
WHIM-AM - 1520 (5904)
WTLN-AM - 950 (5905)

Boynton Beach
WRMB-FM - 89.3 (5953)

Cocoa
WMIE-FM - 91.5 (6001)
WWBC-AM - 1510 (6002)

Crestview
WTJT-FM - 90.1 (6027)

Daytona Beach
WAPN-FM - 91.5 (6041)

DeLand
WYND-AM - 1310 (6057)

Englewood
WSEB-FM - 91.3 (6064)

Fort Lauderdale
WEXY-AM - 1520 (6090)

Fort Myers
WAYJ-FM - 88.7 (6100)
WSOR-FM - 90.9 (6112)

Green Cove Springs
WAYR-AM - 550 (6174)

Jacksonville
WIOJ-AM - 1010 (6223)
WJFR-FM - 88.7 (6227)
WNCM-FM - 88.1 (6234)
WROS-AM - 1050 (6239)
WSVE-AM - 1280 (6241)

Key West
WJIR-FM - 90.9 (6256)

Keystone Heights
WYFB-FM - 90.5 (6259)

Marianna
WJNF-FM - 88.3 (6328)

Melbourne
WCIF-FM - 106.3 (6336)

North Miami
WLQY-AM - 1320 (6467)

Ocala
WHOF-AM - 640 (6474)

Oldsmar
WPSO-AM - 1500 (6485)

Orlando
WRLZ-AM - 1270 (6527)

Port Orange
WMFJ-AM - 1450 (6598)

Port Richey
WYFE-FM - 88.9 (6600)

St. Petersburg
WTIS-AM - 1110 (6641)

Stuart
WCNO-FM - 89.9 (6696)

Tallahassee
WCVC-AM - 1330 (6745)
WHBT-AM - 1410 (6750)

Tampa
WBVM-FM - 90.5 (6785)

Tavares
WHDM-AM - 1440 (6812)

Titusville
WPGS-AM - 840 (6823)

Vero Beach
WSCF-FM - 91.9 (6838)

West Palm Beach
WLVJ-AM - 640 (6854)

GEORGIA
Albany
WANL-AM - 1250 (6907)

Atlanta
WAEC-AM - 860 (7065)
WAFS-AM - 920 (7066)

Augusta
WFAM-AM - 1050 (7108)

Barnesville
WBAF-AM - 1090 (7122)

Bloomingdale
WYFS-FM - 89.5 (7132)

Cartersville
WCCV-FM - 91.7 (7162)

Cataula
WYFK-FM - 89.5 (7164)

Cedartown
WGAA-AM - 1340 (7166)

Covington
WGFS-AM - 1430 (7213)

Cumming
WWEV-FM - 91.5 (7217)

East Point
WTJH-AM - 1260 (7260)

Ellenwood
WSSA-AM - 1570 (7269)

Fort Valley
WXKO-AM - 1150 (7291)

Hartwell
WKLY-AM - 980 (7322)

Hazlehurst
WVOH-AM - 920 (7326)

Hinesville
WGML-AM - 990 (7335)

LaGrange
WOAK-FM - 90.9 (7364)

Macon
WBML-AM - 900 (7390)
WVMG-FM - 96.7 (7405)

Perry
WCOP-FM - 99.9 (7484)

Rome
WROM-AM - 710 (7508)

Royston
WBIC-AM - 810 (7522)

Thomasville
WJEP-AM - 1020 (7589)

Toccoa Falls
WRAF-FM - 90.9 & 88.5 (7607)

Trenton
WKWN-AM - 1420 (7609)

Valdosta
WAFT-FM - 101.1 (7619)

Vidalia
WGPH-FM - 91.5 (7630)

Waycross
WACL-AM - 570 (7645)
WGIA-AM - 1350 (7647)

Circulation: ★ = ABC; △ = BPA; ♦ = CAC; ● = CCAB; ❑ = VAC; ⊕ = PO Statement; ‡ = Publisher's Report; Boldface figures = sworn; Light figures = estimated.

3063

Radio Station Formats

RELIGIOUS (continued)

Waynesboro
WYFA-FM - 107.1 **(7650)**

Winder
WYFW-FM - 89.5 **(7655)**

Young Harris
WZCM-AM - 770 **(7657)**

HAWAII
Honolulu
KGU-AM - 760 **(7734)**
KLHT-AM - 1040 **(7746)**
KNDI-AM - 1270 **(7747)**
KZOO-AM - 1210 **(7758)**

Kahului
KMVI-AM - 550 **(7760)**

IDAHO
Boise
KSPD-AM - 790 **(7830)**

Caldwell
KBGN-AM - 1060 **(7840)**

Twin Falls
KCIR-FM - 90.7 **(7992)**

ILLINOIS
Bourbonnais
WONU-FM - 89.7 **(8096)**

Champaign
WBGL-FM - 91.7 **(8223)**

Chicago
WJCG-FM - 89.9 **(8631)**
WMBI-AM - 1110 **(8644)**
WMBI-FM - 90.1 **(8645)**
WYLL-AM - 1160 **(8663)**

East Moline
WDLM-AM - 960 **(8804)**
WDLM-FM - 89.3 **(8805)**

Greenville
WGRN-FM - 89.5 **(8964)**

Highland
WCBW-AM - 880 **(8990)**

Joliet
WJCH-FM - 91.9 **(9037)**

Loves Park
WGSL-FM - 91.1 **(9121)**
WQFL-FM - 100.9 **(9122)**

Marion
WBVN-FM - 104.5 **(9144)**

Pekin
WBNH-FM - 88.5 **(9415)**

Peoria
WPEO-AM - 1020 **(9437)**

Quincy
WGCA-FM - 88.5 **(9477)**

Sparta
WHCO-AM - 1230 **(9618)**

Springfield
WLGM-FM - 97.7 **(9650)**
WLUJ-FM - 89.7 **(9651)**

Wheaton
WETN-FM - 88.1 **(9761)**

INDIANA
Covington
WFOF-FM - 90.3 **(9907)**

Evansville
WVHI-AM - 1330 **(9952)**

Fort Wayne
WBCL-FM - 90.3 **(9978)**
WFCV-AM - 1090 **(9984)**
WLAB-FM - 88.3 **(9989)**

Hammond
WYCA-FM - 92.3 **(10059)**

Haubstadt
WBGW-FM - 101.5 **(10061)**

Indianapolis
WNTS-AM - 1590 **(10206)**

New Albany
WXLN-AM - 1570 **(10341)**

South Bend
WHME-FM - 103.1 **(10463)**
WUBS-FM - 89.7 **(10468)**

IOWA
Boone
KFGQ-AM - 1260 **(10627)**
KFGQ-FM - 99.3 **(10628)**

Brooklyn
KSKB-FM - 99.1 **(10634)**

Council Bluffs
KLNG-AM - 1560 **(10728)**

Decorah
KWLC-AM - 1240 **(10762)**

Des Moines
KDFR-FM - 91.3 **(10821)**
KWKY-AM - 1150 **(10833)**

Mason City
KCMR-FM - 97.9 **(11074)**

Shenandoah
KYFR-AM - 920 **(11201)**

Sioux Center
KDCR-FM - 88.5 **(11209)**

Waterloo
KNWS-AM - 101.9 **(11293)**
KNWS-FM - 101.9 **(11294)**
KWOF-AM - 850 & 89.1 FM **(11298)**
KWOF-FM - 88.1 **(11299)**

KANSAS
Brewster
KGCR-FM - 107.7 **(11366)**

Derby
KYFW-FM - 88.3 **(11411)**

Dodge City
KONQ-FM - 91.9 **(11419)**

Emporia
KNGM-FM - 91.9 **(11433)**

Hays
KPRD-FM - 88.9 **(11487)**

Hutchinson
KCVW-FM - 94.3 **(11503)**

Leavenworth
KKLO-AM - 1410 **(11582)**

Newton
KJRG-AM - 950 **(11672)**

Overland Park
KCCV-AM - 760 **(11739)**
KCCV-FM - 92.3 **(11740)**

Scott City
KFLA-AM - 1310 **(11795)**

Topeka
KJTY-FM - 88.1 **(11840)**

Wichita
KSGL-AM - 900 **(11904)**
KZZD-FM - 90.7 **(11907)**

KENTUCKY
Albany
WANY-AM - 1390 **(11915)**
WANY-FM - 106.3 **(11916)**

Ashland
WOKT-AM - 1040 **(11921)**

Bowling Green
WCVK-FM - 90.7 **(11954)**

Cumberland
WCPM-AM - 1280 **(12032)**

Danville
WDFB-AM - 1170 **(12038)**
WDFB-FM - 88.1 **(12039)**

Grayson
WKCC-FM - 96.7 **(12095)**

Harlan
WFSR-AM - 970 **(12106)**

Hazard
WJMD-FM - 104.7 **(12118)**

Hopkinsville
WNKJ-FM - 89.3 **(12136)**

Jackson
WEKG-AM - 810 **(12146)**

Keavy
WVCT-FM - 91.5 **(12150)**

Liberty
WKDO-FM - 98.7 **(12202)**

London
WYGE-FM - 92.3 **(12207)**

Louisville
WLSY-FM - 94.7 **(12260)**
WSOH-FM - 88.3 **(12265)**

Madisonville
WSOF-FM - 89.9 **(12277)**

Middlesboro
WMIK-FM - 92.7 **(12296)**

Pikeville
WJSO-FM - 90.1 **(12362)**
WLSI-AM - 900 **(12364)**

Scottsville
WLCK-AM - 1250 **(12395)**

Somerset
WWOG-FM - 90.9 **(12413)**

Vancleve
WMTC-AM - 730 **(12427)**
WMTC-FM - 99.9 **(12428)**

Versailles
WJMM-FM - 99.3 **(12430)**
WJMM-FM - 99.3 **(12431)**

Wickliffe
WBCE-AM - 1200 **(12443)**

LOUISIANA
Baker
WQCK-FM - 92.7 **(12480)**

Ball
KWDF-AM - 840 **(12481)**

Baton Rouge
WJFM-FM - 88.5 **(12519)**

Crowley
KAJN-FM - 102.9 **(12560)**

Dry Prong
KVDP-FM - 89.1 **(12572)**

Lafayette
KJCB-AM - 770 **(12626)**

Metairie
WVOG-AM - 600 **(12686)**

New Orleans
WBOK-AM - 1230 **(12767)**
WBSN-FM - 89.1 **(12768)**
WSHO-AM - 800 **(12776)**
WYLD-AM - 940 **(12785)**

Rayville
KTJC-FM - 92.3 **(12805)**

Shreveport
KBCL-AM - 1070 **(12822)**
KFLO-AM - 1300 **(12825)**

MAINE
Bangor
WHCF-FM - 88.5 **(12908)**

Topsham
WBCI-FM - 105.9 **(13067)**

MARYLAND
Annapolis
WFSI-FM - 107.9 **(13099)**

Baltimore
WRBS-FM - 95.1 **(13284)**
WWIN-AM - 1400 **(13286)**

Denton
WKDI-AM - 840 **(13483)**

Elkton
WOEL-FM - 89.9 **(13497)**

Frostburg
WFRB-AM - 560 (13528)

Glen Burnie
WJRO-AM - 1590 (13556)

Potomac
WCTN-AM - 950 (13666)

Princess Anne
WOLC-FM - 102.5 (13671)

Takoma Park
WGTS-FM - 91.9 (13753)

Towson
WBMD-AM - 750 (13767)

Williamsport
WCRH-FM - 90.5 (13783)

MASSACHUSETTS
Boston
WEZE-AM - 590 (13984)

Chicopee
WACE-AM - 730 (14137)

Springfield
WAIC-FM - 91.9 (14555)
WVNE-AM - 760 (14565)

MICHIGAN
Albion
WUFN-FM - 96.7 (14717)
WUNN-AM - 1,100 khz (14718)

Ann Arbor
WDEO-AM - 990 (14777)

Battle Creek
WOLY-AM - 1500 (14798)

Charlotte
WLCM-AM - 1390 (14871)

Detroit
WCHB-AM - 1200 (14956)
WMUZ-FM - 103.5 (14972)

Flint
WFLT-AM - 1420 (15043)

Gaylord
WOLW-FM - 91.1 (15076)
WPHN-FM - 90.5 (15077)

Grand Blanc
WSNL-AM - 600 (15084)

Grand Rapids
WCSG-FM - 91.3 (15105)
WFUR-AM - 1570 (15106)

Holland
WJQK-FM - 99.3 (15177)
WPNW AM - 1260 (15178)

Kalamazoo
WKPR-AM - 1420 (15253)

Kingsford
WEUL-FM - 98.1 (15266)

Lapeer
WMPC-AM - 1230 (15311)

Livonia
WLQV-AM - 1500 (15319)

Marquette
WHWL-FM - 95.7 (15343)

Midland
WUGN-FM - 99.7 (15357)

Milford
WEXL-AM - 1340 (15360)

Ontonagon
WUPY-FM - 101.1 (15424)

Owosso
WOAP-AM - 1090 (15430)

Pittsford
WPCJ-FM - 91.1 (15445)

Port Huron
WNFA-FM - 88.3 (15457)

Saginaw
WTLZ-FM - 107.1 (15506)

Spring Arbor
KTGG-AM - 1540 (15572)

Traverse City
WLJN-AM - 1400 (15610)
WLJN-FM - 89.9 (15611)

Zeeland
WGNB-FM - 89.3 (15695)

MINNESOTA
Blue Earth
KJLY-FM - 104.5 (15765)

Duluth
KDNW-FM - 97.3 (15849)
WWJC-AM - 850 (15859)

Fosston
KKEQ-FM - 107.1 (15912)

Osakis
KBHL-FM - 103.9 (16246)
KCGN-FM - 101.5 (16247)

Park Rapids
KDKK-FM - 97.5 (16257)
KPRM-AM - 870 (16258)

Pequot Lakes
KTIG-FM - 102.7 (16263)

Plymouth
WCTS-AM - 1030 (16281)

Roseville
KTIS-AM - 900 (16335)

St. Cloud
KCFB-FM - 91.5 (16349)

St. Paul
KNOF-FM - 95.3 (16421)

MISSISSIPPI
Belzoni
WELZ-AM - 1460 (16560)

Columbus
WACR-AM - 1050 (16607)
WJWF-AM - 1400 (16610)

Greenville
WESY-AM - 1580 (16639)

Hattiesburg
WEEZ-FM - 99.3 (16670)

Holly Springs
WURC-FM - 88.1 (16684)

Houston
WCPC-AM - 940 (16686)

Jackson
WTWZ-AM - 1120 (16731)

Lexington
WXTN-AM - 1000 (16747)

Meridian
WNBN-AM - 1290 (16778)

Natchez
WMIS-AM - 1240 (16794)

Senatobia
WSAO-AM - 1140 (16844)

MISSOURI
Branson
KLFC-FM - 88.1 (16921)

Butler
KMAM-AM - 1530 (16932)
KMOE-FM - 92.1 (16933)

Centralia
KMFC-FM - 92.1 (16970)

Clayton
KFUO-AM - 850 (16982)

Cuba
KGNN-FM - 90.3 (17031)

Joplin
KOCR-AM - 1310 (17146)

Kansas City
KLJC-FM - 88.5 (17210)

Kennett
KCRV-AM - 1370 (17219)

New Bloomfield
KNLG-FM - 90.3 (17311)

Piedmont
KPWB-AM - 1140 (17344)

Richmond
KAYX-FM - 92.5 (17376)

St. Charles
KCLC-FM - 89.1 (17385)

St. Louis
KSIV-AM - 1320 (17550)
WRYT-AM - 1080 (17559)

Springfield
KWFC-FM - 89.1 (17632)

Trenton
KTTN-FM - 92.3 (17655)

Warrenton
KWRE-AM - 730 (17702)

MONTANA
Belgrade
KGVW-AM - 640 (17725)

Billings
KURL-AM - 730 (17746)

NEBRASKA
Columbus
KTLX-FM - 91.9 (17983)

Doniphan
KROA-FM - 95.7 (18001)

Holdrege
KUVR-AM - 1380 (18051)

Lincoln
KLCV-FM - 88.5 (18135)

McCook
KNGN-AM - 1360 (18157)

North Platte
KJLT-AM - 970 (18179)
KJLT-FM - 94.9 (18180)

Omaha
KCRO-AM - 660 (18213)
KGBI-FM - 100.7 (18218)

Scottsbluff
KCMI-FM - 96.9 (18267)

NEVADA
Carson City
KNIS-FM - 91.3 (18332)

NEW HAMPSHIRE
Derry
WDER-AM - 1320 (18489)

NEW JERSEY
Camden
WKDN-FM - 106.9 (18715)
WTMR-AM - 800 (18718)

Cherry Hill
WSJI-FM - 89.5 (18740)

Hasbrouck Heights
WWDJ-AM - 970 (18869)

Paterson
WWRV-AM - 1330 (19418)

West Orange
WFME-FM - 94.7 (19725)

Zarephath
WAWZ-FM - 99.1 (19757)

NEW MEXICO
Clayton
KLMX-AM - 1450 (19829)

NEW YORK
Bath
WCID-FM - 89.1 (20127)
WCIH-FM - 90.3 (20128)
WCII-FM - 88.5 (20129)
WCIK-FM - 103.1 (20130)
WCIY-FM - 88.9 (20131)
WCOT-FM - 103.1 (20132)
WCOU-FM - 88.3 (20133)

Radio Station Formats

Circulation: ★ = ABC; △ = BPA; ◆ = CAC; ● = CCAB; ❑ = VAC; ⊕ = PO Statement; ‡ = Publisher's Report; Boldface figures = sworn; Light figures = estimated.

RELIGIOUS (continued)

Buffalo
WDCX-FM - 99.5 **(20397)**
WHLD-AM - 1270 **(20401)**

Cohoes
WBAR-FM - 94.7 **(20480)**
WHAZ-AM - 1330 **(20481)**
WMNV-FM - 104.1 **(20482)**

East Syracuse
WSIV-AM - 1540 **(20560)**

Horseheads
WLNL-AM - 1000 **(20764)**
WMKB-FM - 96.9 **(20765)**

Houghton
WJSL-FM - 90.3 **(20766)**

Islandia
WFRS-FM - 88.9 **(20785)**

Lake Katrine
WPGL-FM - 90.7 **(20873)**

Mineola
WTHE-AM - 1520 **(21087)**

New Hartford
WVVC-FM - 100.7 **(21109)**

New York
WMCA-AM - 570 **(22974)**
WNWK-FM - 105.9 **(22978)**

Newark
WFRW-FM - 88.1 **(22999)**

Rochester
WWWG-AM - 1460 **(23257)**

Syracuse
WMHI-FM - 102.9 **(23440)**
WMHR-FM - 102.9 **(23441)**

Webster
WMHN-FM - 89.3 **(23531)**

NORTH CAROLINA

Asheville
WKJV-AM - 1380 **(23637)**

Black Mountain
WMIT-FM - 106.9 **(23649)**

Canton
WPTL-AM - 920 **(23683)**

Charlotte
WAVO-AM - 1150 **(23761)**
WGAS-AM - 1420 **(23770)**
WNMX-FM - 1240 **(23775)**
WOGR-AM - 1540 **(23777)**

Durham
WSRC-AM - 1410 **(23851)**

Forest City
WAGY-AM - 1320 **(23895)**
WWOL-AM - 780 **(23896)**

Hickory
WPIR-FM - 88.1 **(23994)**

High Point
WHPE-FM - 95.5 **(24003)**

Kannapolis
WRKB-AM - 1460 **(24017)**
WRNA-AM - 1140 **(24018)**

Morganton
WCIS-AM - 760 **(24076)**

Raeford
WMFA-AM - 1400 **(24122)**

Raleigh
WDTF-AM - 570 **(24163)**
WPJL-AM - 1240 **(24166)**

Red Springs
WYRU-AM - 1160 **(24179)**

Roanoke Rapids
WPTM-FM - 102.3 **(24196)**

Sparta
WCOK-AM - 1060 **(24241)**

Spindale
WGMA-AM - 1520 AM **(24242)**

Winston-Salem
WBFJ-AM - 1550 **(24328)**

WTOB-AM - 1380 **(24334)**

NORTH DAKOTA

Fargo
KFNW-AM - 1200 **(24422)**
KFNW-FM - 97.9 **(24423)**

Minot
KHRT-FM - 106.9 **(24508)**

OHIO

Archbold
WBCY-FM - 89.5 **(24615)**

Belpre
WCVV-FM - 89.5 **(24674)**

Castalia
WGGN-FM - 97.7 **(24743)**

Cedarville
WCDR-FM - 90.3 **(24746)**
WOHC-FM - 90.1 **(24747)**
WOHP-FM - 88.3 **(24748)**

Cincinnati
WTSJ-AM - 1050 **(24847)**

Cleveland
WCCD-AM - 1000 **(24968)**
WVMN-FM - 90.1 **(24989)**

Conneaut
WGOJ-FM - 105.5 **(25092)**

Fairfield
WCNW-AM - 1560 **(25190)**

Gahanna
WCVO-FM - 104.9 **(25207)**

Gallipolis
WJEH-AM - 990 **(25211)**

Holland
WPOS-FM - 102.3 **(25248)**

Jefferson
WCVJ-FM - 90.9 **(25268)**

Lima
WTGN-FM - 97.7 **(25303)**

Mansfield
WVMC-FM - 90.7 **(25338)**

Marietta
WJAW-AM - 630 **(25348)**

Peninsula
WCUE-AM - 1150 **(25473)**

Springfield
WEEC-FM - 100.7 **(25536)**

Toledo
WOTL-FM - 90.3 **(25583)**

OKLAHOMA

Ada
KADA-AM - 1230 **(25725)**

Alva
KALV-AM - 1430 **(25739)**

Atoka
KEOR-AM - 1110 **(25752)**

Hobart
KTJS-AM - 1420 **(25868)**

Langston
KALU-FM - 89.3 **(25882)**

Miami
KGLC-FM - 100.9 **(25917)**

Midwest City
KTLV-AM - 1220 **(25919)**

Oklahoma City
KQCV-AM - 800 **(26013)**

Shawnee
KQCV-FM - 95.1 **(26068)**

Taft
KHJM-FM - 100.3 **(26093)**

Tulsa
KCFO-AM - 970 **(26145)**
KDKR-FM - 91.3 **(26146)**
KMSI-FM - 88.1 **(26152)**
KNYD-FM - 90.5 **(26155)**

KOZO-FM - 89.7 **(26159)**
KXOJ-FM - 100.9 **(26172)**
WOFN-FM - 88.7 **(26175)**

OREGON

Albany
KHPE-FM - 107.9 **(26209)**
KWIL-AM - 790 **(26213)**

Bend
KNLR-FM - 97.5 **(26248)**

Coos Bay
KYTT-FM - 98.7 **(26280)**

Portland
KKSL-AM - 1290 **(26531)**
KPDQ-AM - 800 **(26535)**
KPDQ-FM - 93.7 **(26536)**

Springfield
KORE-AM - 1050 **(26588)**

Winston
KGRV-AM - 700 **(26618)**

PENNSYLVANIA

Allentown
WHOL-AM - 1600 **(26632)**

Apollo
WAVL-AM - 910 **(26658)**

Brookhaven
WVCH-AM - 740 **(26731)**

Cashtown
WFKJ-AM - 890 **(26766)**

Danville
WBGM-FM - 88.1 **(26819)**
WPGM-AM - 1570 **(26820)**
WPGM-FM - 96.7 **(26821)**

Hunlock Creek
WRGN-FM - 88.1 **(27067)**

Jersey Shore
WJSA-AM - 1600 **(27084)**

Lafayette Hill
WFIL-AM - 560 **(27137)**
WZZD-AM - 990 **(27138)**

Lancaster
WDAC-FM - 94.5 **(27148)**
WJTL-FM - 90.3 **(27151)**
WLCH-FM - 91.3 **(27154)**

Lewisburg
WGRC-FM - 91.3 **(27194)**

Lincoln University
WLIU-FM - 88.7 **(27201)**

Masontown
WRIJ-FM - 106.9 **(27225)**

Monroeville
WXVX-AM - 1510 **(27289)**

Montrose
WPEL-AM - 1250 **(27293)**
WPEL-FM - 96.5 **(27294)**

Norristown
WNAP-AM - 1110 **(27338)**

Philadelphia
WKDU-FM - 91.7 **(27737)**
WPHE-AM - 690 **(27738)**

Red Lion
WGCB-AM - 1440 **(27928)**
WGCB-FM - 96.1 **(27929)**

Sellersville
WBYO-FM - 88.9 **(27983)**

Shiremanstown
WWII-AM - 720 **(27995)**

State College
WQJU-FM - 107.1 **(28027)**
WTLR-FM - 89.9 **(28030)**

Waterford
WCTL-FM - 106.3 **(28123)**

Wellsboro
WLIH-FM - 107.1 **(28142)**

White Oak
WEDO-AM - 810 **(28158)**

Numbers cited in bold after listings are entry numbers rather than page numbers.

Windber
WFRJ-FM - 88.9 FM **(28195)**

Yardley
WCHR-AM - 920 **(28203)**

PUERTO RICO
Juana Diaz
WCGB-AM - 1060 **(28253)**

Mayaguez
WTPM-FM - 92.9 **(28270)**

Ponce
WPPC-AM - 1570 **(28281)**

San Juan
WBMJ-AM - 1190 **(28297)**
WERR-FM - 104.1 **(28299)**
WIVV-AM - 1370 **(28301)**
WORO-FM - 92.5 **(28306)**
WRSJ-AM - 1560 **(28308)**

RHODE ISLAND
Warwick
WARV-AM - 1590 **(28454)**

SOUTH CAROLINA
Beaufort
WVGB-AM - 1490 **(28491)**

Cowpens
WYFG-FM - 91.1 **(28595)**

Florence
WOLS-AM - 1230 **(28610)**

Gaffney
WFGN-AM - 1180 **(28617)**

Greenville
WLFJ-FM - 89.3 **(28634)**
WMUU-AM - 1260 **(28635)**
WTBI-AM - 1540 **(28643)**

Greer
WPJM-AM - 800 **(28654)**

Ladson
WKCL-FM - 91.5 **(28678)**

Lake City
WVLC-AM - 1260 **(28679)**

Orangeburg
WPJK-AM - 1580 **(28735)**

Pageland
WRML-FM - 102.3 **(28740)**

Summerville
WYFH-FM - 90.7 **(28767)**

Sumter
WLJI-FM - 98.3 **(28773)**

Woodruff
WDRF-AM - 1510 **(28789)**

SOUTH DAKOTA
Rapid City
KLMP-FM - 97.9 **(28945)**
KSLT-FM - 107.3 **(28949)**

Sioux Falls
KCFS-FM - 94.5 **(28970)**
KNWC-AM - 1270 **(28979)**
KNWC-FM - 96.5 **(28980)**

TENNESSEE
Bluff City
WHCB-FM - 91.5 **(29056)**

Bristol
WHGG-FM - 90.1 **(29068)**

Chattanooga
WDYN-FM - 89.7 **(29101)**
WMBW-FM - 88.9 **(29107)**

Church Hill
WMCH-AM - 1260 **(29113)**

Cleveland
WAYB-FM - 95.7 **(29125)**

Englewood
WENR-AM - 1090 **(29181)**

Fayetteville
WBXR-AM - 1140 **(29191)**
WYTM-FM - 105.5 **(29192)**

Jellico
WJJT-AM - 1540 **(29249)**

Kingsport
WCQR-FM - 88.3 **(29263)**

Knoxville
WITA-AM - 1490 **(29291)**
WRJZ-AM - 620 **(29299)**

La Follette
WGLH-AM - 960 **(29309)**

Madison
WYFN-AM - 980 **(29339)**

Mc Minnville
WAKI-AM - 1230 **(29354)**
WBMC-AM - 960 **(29355)**

Memphis
WBBP-AM - 1480 **(29387)**
WBPB-AM - 1480 **(29388)**
WCRV-AM - 640 **(29389)**

Nashville
WENO-AM - 760 **(29509)**
WNAZ-FM - 89.1 **(29522)**
WNQM-AM - 1300 **(29523)**
WNRZ-FM - 91.5 **(29524)**

Newport
WLIK-AM - 1270 **(29545)**

Oneida
WOCV-AM - 1310 **(29557)**

St. Joseph
WJOR-FM - 101.5 **(29583)**

TEXAS
Abilene
KGNZ-FM - 88.1 **(29662)**

Alamo
KJAV-FM - 104.9 **(29674)**

Amarillo
KXRI-FM - 91.9 **(29719)**

Arlington
KTNO-AM - 1540 **(29742)**

Austin
KIXL-AM - 970 **(29866)**

Baytown
KWWJ-AM - 1360 **(29896)**

Belton
KTON-AM - 940 **(29917)**

Brownsville
KBNR-FM - 88.3 **(29961)**

Brownwood
KBUB-FM - 90.3 **(29967)**
KPSM-FM - 99.3 **(29970)**

Bryan
KAGC-AM - 1510 **(29976)**

Canton
KVCI-AM - 1510 **(29999)**

Carrizo Springs
KBEN-AM - 1450 **(30003)**

Comanche
KCOM-AM - 1550 **(30066)**

Corpus Christi
KBNJ-FM - 91.7 **(30080)**
KFGG-FM - 88.7 **(30084)**
KLUX-FM - 89.5 **(30089)**

El Paso
KELP-AM - 1590 **(30289)**
KVER-FM - 91.1 FM **(30303)**

Farwell
KIJN-AM - 1060 **(30316)**
KIJN-FM - 92.3 **(30317)**

Hamilton
KCLW-AM - 900 **(30421)**

Hemphill
KPBL-AM - 1240 **(30438)**

Houston
KANJ-FM - 91.5 **(30545)**
KHCB-AM - 1400 **(30547)**
KHCB-FM - 105.7 **(30548)**
KHCH-AM - 1400 **(30549)**
KHCL-FM - 92.5 **(30550)**

KHOP-FM - 89.3 **(30551)**
KHTA-FM - 92.5 **(30553)**
KJOJ-FM - 103.3 **(30559)**
KMAT-FM - 105.1 **(30565)**
KTEK-AM - 1110 **(30576)**
KTSU-FM - 90.9 **(30582)**

Humble
KSBJ-FM - 89.3 **(30592)**

Irving
KWRD-FM - 100.7 **(30612)**

Jacksonville
KBJS-FM - 90.3 **(30616)**

Laredo
KBNL-FM - 89.9 **(30671)**
KHOY-FM - 88.1 **(30674)**

Lubbock
KJAK-FM - 92.7 **(30726)**

Lufkin
KRBA-AM - 1340 **(30743)**

Marshall
KCUL-AM - 1410 **(30768)**

McAllen
KCZO-FM - 92.1 **(30792)**

Mission
KCAS-FM - 91.5 **(30834)**

Odessa
KKKK-FM - 101.3 **(30876)**

Robstown
KROB-AM - 1510 **(30986)**

San Angelo
KCRN-AM - 1340 **(31012)**
KCRN-FM - 93.9 **(31013)**

San Antonio
KDRY-AM - 1100 **(31055)**
KSLR-AM - 630 **(31072)**

Seminole
KIKZ-AM - 1250 **(31099)**
KSEM-FM - 106.3 **(31100)**

Snyder
KSNY-AM - 1450 **(31116)**

Tyler
KGLY-FM - 91.3 **(31213)**

Waco
KBBW-AM - 1010 **(31258)**

Weslaco
KRGE-AM - 1290 **(31279)**

Wharton
KANI-AM - 1500 **(31286)**

Wichita Falls
KMOC-FM - 89.5 **(31298)**

UTAH
Hooper
KSVN-AM - 730 **(31339)**

VERMONT
Essex
WGLY-FM - 93.5 **(31542)**

Rutland
WFTF-FM - 90.5 **(31586)**

VIRGINIA
Appomattox
WTTX-AM - 1280 **(31765)**
WTTX-FM - 107.1 **(31766)**

Arlington
WABS-AM - 780 **(31844)**

Ashland
WYFJ-FM - 100.1 **(31859)**

Big Stone Gap
WLSD-AM - 1220 **(31866)**

Blacksburg
SPIRIT-FM - 90.9 **(31881)**
WAMN-AM - 1050 **(31882)**
WPIN-AM - 810 **(31888)**

Bristol
WZAP-AM - 690 **(31902)**

Circulation: ★ = ABC; △ = BPA; ● = CAC; ◆ = CCAB; ❑ = VAC; ℗ = PO Statement; ‡ = Publisher's Report; Boldface figures = sworn; Light figures = estimated.

3067

RELIGIOUS (continued)

Broadway
WLTK-FM - 103.3 **(31904)**

Chase City
WMEK-AM - 980 **(31961)**

Chatham
WKBY-AM - 1080 **(31963)**

Chesapeake
WPMH-AM - 1010 **(31966)**
WYFI-FM - 99.7 **(31967)**

Chester
WGGN-AM - 820 **(31968)**

Chesterfield
WGGM-AM - 820 **(31970)**

Churchville
WNLR-AM - 1150 **(31973)**

Clintwood
WDIC-AM - 1430 **(31978)**

Danville
WVOV-AM - 970 **(31995)**

Dublin
WPIN-FM - 91.5 **(31999)**

Falls Church
KFAX-AM - 1220 **(32061)**
WFAX-AM - 1220 **(32062)**

Galax
WBRF-FM - 98.1 **(32100)**

Hampton
WARR-AM - 1520 **(32131)**
WTJZ-AM - 1270 **(32135)**

Luray
WYFT-FM - 103.9 **(32205)**

Martinsville
WPIM-FM - 90.5 **(32239)**

Norton
WNVA-AM - 1350 **(32312)**

Pennington Gap
WSWV-AM - 1570 **(32327)**

Petersburg
WVST-FM - 91.3 **(32333)**

Quinque
WKTR-AM - 840 **(32343)**

Richlands
WGTH-FM - 105.5 **(32428)**

Roanoke
WRIS-AM - 1410 **(32503)**
WVZN-AM - 1170 **(32509)**

Salem
WPAR-FM - 91.3 **(32522)**

Smithfield
WKGM-AM - 940 **(32527)**

South Boston
WSBV-AM - 1560 **(32533)**

Warrenton
WPRZ-AM - 1250 **(32605)**

WASHINGTON
College Place
KGTS-FM - 91.3 **(32725)**

Dishman
KSPO-FM - 106.5 **(32738)**

Kirkland
KARR-AM - 1460 **(32800)**

Longview
KJVH-FM - 89.5 **(32817)**
KZOE-FM - 90.3 **(32819)**

Lynden
KWPZ-FM - 106.5 **(32822)**

Pasco
KOLU-FM - 90.1 **(32882)**

Seattle
KCIS-AM - 630 **(33048)**
KCMS-FM - 105.3 **(33049)**
KGNW-AM - 820 **(33053)**

Spokane
KAAR-FM - 95.3 **(33105)**
KGDN-FM - 101.3 **(33115)**
KGER-FM - 95.9 **(33116)**
KMBI-AM - 1330 **(33120)**
KMBI-FM - 107.9 **(33121)**
KMLW-FM - 88.3 **(33122)**
KTAC-FM - 93.9 **(33129)**

Tumwater
KVSN-AM - 1340 **(33170)**

Wenatchee
KPLW-FM - 89.9 **(33200)**

Yakima
KBBO-AM - 1390 **(33226)**

WEST VIRGINIA
Beckley
WJLS-AM - 560 **(33243)**

Bluefield
WPIB-FM - 90.9 **(33259)**

Fairmont
WTCS-AM - 1490 **(33316)**

Fisher
WELD-AM - 690 **(33317)**

Grafton
WTBZ-AM - 1260 **(33326)**

Huntington
WMEJ-FM - 91.9 **(33342)**

Hurricane
WOKU-AM - 1080 **(33349)**

Moundsville
WRKP-FM - 96.5 **(33409)**

Oak Hill
WOAY-AM - 860 **(33418)**

Rupert
WYKM-AM - 1250 **(33457)**

South Charleston
WJYP-FM - 100.9 **(33468)**
WSCW-AM - 1410 **(33469)**

Summersville
WCWV-FM - 92.9 **(33474)**

Welch
WELC-AM - 1150 **(33493)**

WISCONSIN
Appleton
WEMI-FM - 91.9 **(33548)**

Brookfield
WRRD-AM - 540 **(33607)**

Chippewa Falls
WWIB-FM - 103.7 **(33633)**

Lancaster
WJTY-FM - 88.1 **(33910)**

Madison
WNWC-FM - 102.5 **(34005)**

Milladore
WGNV-FM - 88.5 **(34053)**

Milwaukee
KCVS-FM - 91.7 **(34111)**
KVCX-FM - 101.5 **(34112)**
WVCF-FM - 90.5 **(34138)**
WVCX-FM - 98.9 **(34139)**
WVCY-AM - 690 **(34140)**
WVCY-FM - 107.7 **(34141)**

Sturgeon Bay
WPFF-FM - 90.5 **(34356)**

Suring
WRVM-FM - 102.7 **(34363)**

WYOMING
Casper
KUYO-AM - 830 **(34493)**

ALBERTA, CANADA
Edmonton
CKER-FM - 101.9 **(34754)**

High River
CHRB-AM - 1140 **(34784)**

Stettler
CKSQ-AM - 1400 **(34856)**

Wetaskiwin
CKJR-AM - 1440 **(34874)**

NEWFOUNDLAND AND LABRADOR, CANADA
Mount Pearl
VOAR-AM - 1210 **(35475)**

ONTARIO, CANADA
Barrie
CJLF-FM - 100.3 **(35663)**

Ottawa
CHRI-FM - 99.1 **(36290)**

Sudbury
CJTK-FM - 95.5 **(36427)**

Thunder Bay
CJOA-FM - 95.1 **(36447)**

SASKATCHEWAN, CANADA
Melfort
CJVR-AM - 750 **(37499)**

SOFT ROCK

ALABAMA
Huntsville
WAHR-FM - 99.1 **(280)**

Montgomery
WMXS-FM - 103.3 **(391)**

Ozark
WRJM-FM - 93.7 **(422)**

ALASKA
Ketchikan
KTKN-AM - 930 **(614)**

McGrath
KSKO-AM - 870 **(623)**

ARIZONA
Tucson
KOAZ-FM - 97.5 **(988)**

ARKANSAS
Jonesboro
KOZY-FM - 105.3 **(1202)**

CALIFORNIA
Bakersfield
KGFM-FM - 101.5 **(1464)**

Chico
KFMF-FM - 93.9 **(1699)**
KPPL-FM - 107.5 **(1705)**

Fresno
KFSR-FM - 90.7 **(1967)**
KSOF-FM - 92.9 **(1984)**

Oakhurst
KAAT-FM - 103.1 & translators 104.3 **(2660)**

Redding
KSHA-FM - 104.3 **(2897)**

COLORADO
Monte Vista
KSLV-FM - 95.3 **(4579)**

FLORIDA
Gulf Breeze
WMEZ-FM - 94.1 **(6183)**

Miami
WLYF-FM - 101.5 **(6405)**

Ocala
WMFQ-FM - 92.9 **(6475)**

Orlando
WMMO-FM - 98.9 **(6523)**

West Palm Beach
WEAT-FM - 104.3 **(6851)**

Numbers cited in bold after listings are entry numbers rather than page numbers.

GEORGIA
Atlanta
WPCH-FM - 94.9 **(7080)**

Hawkinsville
WQSY-FM - 103.9 **(7324)**

Quitman
WSFB-AM - 1490 **(7487)**

Valdosta
WDDQ-FM - 92.1 **(7620)**

IDAHO
Boise
KXLT-FM - 107.9 **(7834)**

ILLINOIS
Kewanee
WJRE-FM - 93.9 **(9046)**

Peoria
WQEZ-FM - 94.3 **(9438)**
WSWT-FM - 106.9 **(9439)**

Pontiac
WJEZ-FM - 93.7 **(9466)**

Springfield
WVEM-FM - 101.9 **(9659)**

INDIANA
Rochester
WROI-FM - 92.1 **(10433)**

Tell City
WTCJ-AM - 1230 **(10483)**

Terre Haute
WLEZ-FM - 102.7 **(10497)**

IOWA
Sioux City
KSFT-FM - 107.1 **(11220)**

KANSAS
Emporia
KRWV-FM - 99.5 **(11434)**

Fort Scott
KOMB-FM - 103.9 **(11445)**

KENTUCKY
Princeton
WAVJ-FM - 104.9 **(12375)**
WPKY-AM - 1580 **(12376)**

LOUISIANA
Monroe
KRVV-FM - 100.1 **(12702)**

MAINE
Augusta
WTVL-AM - 1490 **(12902)**

MICHIGAN
Detroit
WDVD-FM - 96.3 **(14961)**

Mount Pleasant
WCZY-FM - 104.3 **(15382)**

Three Rivers
WLKM-FM - 95.9 **(15596)**

MINNESOTA
Glenwood
KSTQ-FM - 99.3 **(15921)**

Rochester
KYBA-FM - 105.3 **(16325)**

MISSISSIPPI
Philadelphia
WWSL-FM - 102.3 **(16818)**

MISSOURI
Trenton
KTTN-AM - 1600 **(17654)**

MONTANA
Bozeman
KBOZ-FM - 97.5 **(17755)**

NEW JERSEY
Toms River
WOBM-FM - 92.7 **(19651)**

NEW MEXICO
Roswell
KINF-AM - 1020 **(19920)**

NEW YORK
Amagansett
WBAZ-FM - 102.5 **(20028)**

Batavia
WBTA-AM - 1490 **(20122)**

Horseheads
WENY-FM - 92.7 **(20762)**

Kingston
WKNY-AM - 1490 **(20864)**

Poughkeepsie
WRNQ-FM - 92.1 **(23162)**

Rochester
WRMM-FM - 101.3 **(23252)**

Utica
WRFM-FM - 93.5 **(23478)**

Vestal
WMXW-FM - 103.3 **(23493)**

NORTH CAROLINA
Charlotte
WLYT-FM - 102.9 **(23774)**

Laurinburg
WLNC-AM - 1300 **(24034)**

Murfreesboro
WDLZ-FM - 98.3 **(24087)**

Murphy
WCNG-FM - 102.7 **(24089)**

Raleigh
WRSN-FM - 93.9 **(24174)**

NORTH DAKOTA
Fargo
KRVI-FM - 95.1 **(24427)**
KRVI-FM - 95.1 **(24428)**

OHIO
Dayton
WGXM-FM - 98.1 **(25140)**

Mansfield
WVNO-FM - 106.1 **(25339)**

McConnelsville
WJAW-FM - 100.9 **(25370)**

Middleport
WMPO-FM - 92.1 **(25377)**

OKLAHOMA
Grove
KGND-FM - 107.5 **(25851)**

Oklahoma City
KQSR-FM - 94.7 **(26014)**

OREGON
Astoria
KAST-FM - 92.9 **(26228)**

Bend
KMGX-FM - 100.7 **(26246)**

PENNSYLVANIA
Johnstown
WSRA-FM - 101.7 **(27098)**

Lancaster
WROZ-FM - 101.3 **(27156)**

Lebanon
WQIC-FM - 100.1 **(27178)**

Milton
WVLY-FM - 100.9 **(27272)**

Shamokin
WSPI-FM - 99.7 **(27985)**

Sunbury
WQKX-FM - 94.1 **(28040)**

York
WARM-FM - 103.3 **(28213)**

PUERTO RICO
Mayaguez
WKJB-FM - 99.1 **(28263)**

SOUTH CAROLINA
Columbia
WLTY-FM - 96.7 **(28579)**

Myrtle Beach
WKZQ-FM - 101.7 **(28709)**

TENNESSEE
Greeneville
WSMG-AM - 1450 **(29215)**

Kingsport
WTFM-FM - 98.5 **(29268)**

Knoxville
WKCS-FM - 91.1 **(29294)**

Morristown
WBGQ-FM - 100.7 **(29420)**

Nashville
WJXA-FM - 92.9 **(29513)**

Trenton
WWEZ-FM - 97.5 **(29632)**

TEXAS
Dallas
KBFB-FM - 97.9 **(30193)**

Hamilton
KCLW-AM - 900 **(30421)**

Jacksonville
KOOI-FM - 106.5 **(30618)**

Jasper
KJAS-FM - 107.3 **(30621)**

Lufkin
KUEZ-FM - 100.1 **(30747)**

UTAH
Fillmore
KMGR-FM - 95.7 **(31334)**

Salt Lake City
KMUT-FM - 105.7 **(31454)**

VIRGINIA
Marion
WOLD-FM - 102.5 **(32231)**

Virginia Beach
WWDE-FM - 101.3 **(32597)**

WASHINGTON
Bellingham
KAFE-FM - 104.3 **(32680)**

Olympia
KXXO-FM - 96.1 **(32871)**

Wenatchee
KAAP-FM - 99.5 **(33197)**

WEST VIRGINIA
Summersville
WCWV-FM - 92.9 **(33474)**

Wheeling
WKWK-FM - 97.3 **(33506)**

WISCONSIN
Minocqua
WMQA-FM - 95.9 **(34148)**

Rhinelander
WRHN-FM - 100.1 **(34291)**

Sturgeon Bay
WDOR-FM - 93.9 **(34355)**

ALBERTA, CANADA
Lethbridge
CJRX-FM - 106.7 **(34801)**

Circulation: ★ = ABC; △ = BPA; ♦ = CAC; ♣ = CCAB; ⊔ = VAC; ⊕ = PO Statement; ‡ = Publisher's Report; Boldface figures = sworn; Light figures = estimated.

3069

SOFT ROCK (continued)

BRITISH COLUMBIA, CANADA
Castlegar
CHNV-FM - 103.5 (34921)
CKQR-AM - 99.3 (34922)

Grand Forks
CKGF-AM - 1340 (34972)

Kelowna
CILK-FM - 101.5 (34992)

Prince Rupert
CHTK-AM - 560 (35065)

Vancouver
CKKS-FM - 96.9 (35193)

MANITOBA, CANADA
The Pas
CJAR-AM - 1240 (35279)

NEW BRUNSWICK, CANADA
Edmundston
CFAI-FM - 101.1 (35386)

Fredericton
CIBX-FM - 106.9 (35404)

Pokemouche
Radio Peninsule, Inc. - 97.1 (35425)

NEWFOUNDLAND AND LABRADOR, CANADA
Grand Falls
CKCM-AM - 620 (35463)

NOVA SCOTIA, CANADA
Amherst
CKDH-AM - 900 (35533)

Antigonish
CJFX-AM - 98.9 (35540)

Halifax
CIOO-FM - 100.1 (35575)

Sydney
CKPE-FM - 94.9 (35614)

ONTARIO, CANADA
Bracebridge
CFBG-FM - 99.5 (35697)

Chatham
CKUE-FM - 95.1 (35733)

Cobourg
CHUC-AM - 1450 (35743)

Huntsville
MORE-FM - 105.5 (35918)

Timmins
CHYK-FM - 104.1 (36457)

QUEBEC, CANADA
Hull
CIMF-FM - 94.9 (37007)

Lachute
CJLA-FM - 104.9 (37031)

Quebec
CKRL-FM - 89.1 (37304)

Rimouski
CIKI-FM - 98.7 (37309)

Riviere-du-Loup
CIEL-FM - 103.7 (37315)

Saint-Hilarion
CIHO-FM - 96.3 (37344)

Trois-Rivieres
CHEY-FM - 94.7 (37417)

SASKATCHEWAN, CANADA
Prince Albert
CHQX-FM - 101.5 (37520)

SOUTHERN GOSPEL

ALABAMA
Albertville
WAVU-AM - 630 (4)

Boaz
WBSA-AM - 1300 (135)

Butler
WPRN-FM - 107.7 (141)

Carrollton
WRAG-AM - 590 (147)

Centre
WEIS-AM - 990 (150)

Clanton
WKLF-AM - 980 (157)

Cullman
WFMH-AM - 1460 (164)

Dadeville
WELL-FM - 88.7 (167)

Eva
WRJL-AM - 1170 (209)

Geneva
WGEA-AM - 1150 (242)

Haleyville
WJBB-AM - 1230 (259)

Mobile
WLPR-AM - 960 (344)

Rainsville
WVSM-AM - 1500 (430)

Russellville
WKAX-AM - 1500 (442)

Scottsboro
WZCT-AM - 1330 (451)

Sheffield
WBTG-FM - 106.3 (458)

Thomasville
WJDB-AM - 105.5 (471)

Tuscaloosa
WACT-AM - 1420 (495)

Vernon
WJEC-FM - 106.5 (513)

ALASKA
Nome
KICY-AM - 850 (626)

ARKANSAS
Fort Smith
KFSA-AM - 950 (1148)

Marshall
KCGS-AM - 960 (1270)

Mena
KENA-AM - 1450 (1276)

FLORIDA
Jacksonville
WOBS-AM - 1530 (6236)

Marianna
WTYS-FM - 94.1 (6331)

Port Charlotte
WVIJ-FM - 91.7 (6597)

Tallahassee
WCVC-AM - 1330 (6745)

GEORGIA
Bremen
WGMI-AM - 1440 (7138)

Clarkesville
WCHM-AM - 1490 (7170)

Columbus
WPNX-AM - 1460 (7191)

Commerce
WJJC-AM - 1270 (7199)

Douglasville
WDCY-AM - 1520 (7250)

Ellenwood
WSSA-AM - 1570 (7269)

Reidsville
WRBX-FM - 104.1 (7491)
WTNL-AM - 1390 (7492)

Rome
WROM-AM - 710 (7508)

Royston
WBIC-AM - 810 (7522)

ILLINOIS
Marion
WGGH-AM - 1150 (9147)

INDIANA
Indianapolis
WBRI-AM - 1500 (10191)

IOWA
Bloomfield
KOJY-FM - 106.9 (10623)

KENTUCKY
Elkton
WEKT-AM - 1070 (12052)

Hazard
WJMD-FM - 104.7 (12118)

Lexington
WCGW-AM - 770 (12182)

Middlesboro
WMIK-AM - 560 (12295)

Monticello
WFLW-AM - 1360 (12300)

Richmond
WCBR-AM - 1110 (12383)

Somerset
WKEQ-AM - 910 (12407)

Stanford
WRSL-AM - 1520 (12417)

Vancleve
WMTC-AM - 730 (12427)
WMTC-FM - 99.9 (12428)

LOUISIANA
Ball
KWDF-AM - 840 (12481)

Monroe
KLIC-AM - 1230 (12696)

MARYLAND
Frostburg
WLIC-FM - 97.1 (13530)

Grantsville
WAIJ-FM - 90.3 (13557)

MICHIGAN
Gladwin
WGDN-AM - 1350 (15081)

MISSISSIPPI
Batesville
WJBI-AM - 1290 (16551)

Bay Springs
WIZK-AM - 1570 (16555)

Booneville
WBIP-FM - 99.3 (16573)

Brookhaven
WBKN-FM - 92.1 (16579)

Hattiesburg
WBKH-AM - 950 (16668)
WFOR-AM - 1400 (16671)

Holly Springs
WKRA-AM - 1110 (16682)

Kosciusko
WJTA-FM - 91.7 (16737)

Ocean Springs
WOSM-FM - 103.1 (16802)

Poplarville
WRPM-AM - 1530 (16825)

MISSOURI
Excelsior Springs
KEXS-AM - 1090 (17052)

Lebanon
KTTK-FM - 90.7 **(17242)**

Marble Hill
KMHM-FM - 104.1 **(17263)**

Mexico
KJAB-FM - 88.3 **(17286)**

Poplar Bluff
KLUH-FM - 90.3 **(17360)**
KOKS-FM - 89.5 **(17361)**

Sikeston
KTCB-AM - 1470 **(17588)**

Springfield
KWFC-FM - 89.1 **(17632)**

NORTH CAROLINA
Clinton
WCLN-AM - 1170 **(23790)**

Granite Falls
WYCV-AM - 900 **(23914)**

Greensboro
WPET-AM - 950 **(23955)**

Kannapolis
WRKB-AM - 1460 **(24017)**
WRNA-AM - 1140 **(24018)**

Kinston
WELS-AM - 1010 **(24029)**

Rose Hill
WEGG-AM - 710 **(24208)**

Williamston
WIAM-FM - 98.9 **(24293)**

Wilson
WLLY-AM - 1350 **(24314)**

OHIO
Gallipolis
WJEH-AM - 990 **(25211)**

Waverly
WXIC-AM - 660 **(25625)**

West Union
WRAC-FM - 103.1 **(25634)**

OKLAHOMA
Atoka
KEOR-AM - 1110 **(25752)**

Miami
KVIS-AM - 910 **(25918)**

Oklahoma City
KKMG-FM - 93.3 **(26005)**

Taft
KHJM-FM - 100.3 **(26093)**

Tahlequah
KTLQ-AM - 1350 **(26097)**

Tulsa
KDKR-FM - 91.3 **(26146)**
WOFN-FM - 88.7 **(26175)**

PENNSYLVANIA
Lebanon
WADV-AM - 940 **(27176)**

Martinsburg
WJSM-FM - 92.7 **(27224)**

Masontown
WRIJ-FM - 106.9 **(27225)**

SOUTH CAROLINA
Greer
WCKI-AM - 1300 **(28653)**

Pageland
WRML-FM - 102.3 **(28740)**

Summerville
WAZS-AM - 980 **(28766)**

Woodruff
WDRF-AM - 1510 **(28789)**

TENNESSEE
Bolivar
WBOL-AM - 1560 **(29058)**

Bristol
WHGG-FM - 90.1 **(29068)**

Camden
WFWL-AM - 1220 **(29079)**

Jamestown
WCLC-FM - 105.1 **(29244)**

Johnson City
WETB-AM - 790 **(29255)**

Knoxville
WATO-AM - 1290 **(29287)**

Sparta
WSMT-AM - 1050 **(29615)**

TEXAS
Athens
KLVQ-AM - 1410 **(29747)**

Borger
KQTY-AM - 1490 **(29938)**

Dallas
KDFT-AM - 540 **(30198)**

Houston
KALT-AM - 900 **(30544)**

Midland
KJBC-AM - 1150 **(30818)**

New Boston
KNBO-AM - 1530 **(30861)**

Texarkana
KPYN-FM - 100.1 **(31189)**

Winnsboro
KWNS-FM - 104.7 **(31306)**

VIRGINIA
Blacksburg
WXRI-FM - 91.3 **(31891)**

Danville
WVOV-AM - 970 **(31995)**

Gate City
WGAT-AM - 1050 **(32109)**

Marion
WMEV-AM - 1010 **(32227)**

Pulaski
WBLB-AM - 1340 **(32338)**

Richlands
WGTH-AM - 540 **(32427)**
WGTH-FM - 105.5 **(32428)**

Roanoke
WWWR-AM - 910 **(32510)**

Winchester
WTRM-FM - 91.3 **(32633)**

WEST VIRGINIA
Beckley
WJLS-AM - 560 **(33243)**

Huntington
WEMM-FM - 107.9 **(33340)**

Princeton
WPVO-AM - 1490 **(33443)**

South Charleston
WSCW-AM - 1410 **(33469)**

Webster Springs
WAFD-FM - 100.3 **(33488)**

SPORTS

ALABAMA
Andalusia
WAAO-FM - 103.7 **(14)**

Anniston
WHMA-AM - 1390 **(21)**

Athens
WUMP-AM - 730 **(29)**

Auburn
WANI-AM - 1400 **(46)**
WAUD-AM - 1230 **(47)**

Bessemer
WSMQ-AM - 1450 **(53)**

Birmingham
WJOX-AM - 690 **(119)**

Bridgeport
WBTS-AM - 1480 **(138)**

Calera
WBYE-AM - 1370 **(142)**

Decatur
WWTM-AM - 1400 **(176)**

Florence
WYTK-FM - 93.9 **(227)**

Foley
WHEP-AM - 1310 **(229)**

Greenville
WQZX-FM - 94.3 **(246)**

Jackson
WHOD-AM - 1230 **(292)**

Mobile
WABB-AM - 1480 **(332)**
WNSP-FM - 105.5 **(347)**

Montgomery
WMGY-AM - 800 **(389)**
WMSP-AM - 740 **(390)**

Roanoke
WELR-AM - 1360 **(434)**

Sylacauga
WFEB-AM - 1340 **(463)**

Troy
WTBF-AM - 970 **(476)**

Tuscaloosa
WTBC-AM - 1230 **(500)**

Vernon
WVSA-AM - 1380 **(514)**

ALASKA
Anchorage
KAXX-AM - 1020 **(536)**

Bethel
KYUK-AM - 640 **(556)**

Fairbanks
KCBF-AM - 820 **(571)**

Juneau
KJNO-AM - 630 **(600)**

Ketchikan
KTKN-AM - 930 **(614)**

ARIZONA
Flagstaff
KVNA-AM - 600 **(704)**

Globe
KJAA-AM - 1240 **(720)**

Holbrook
KDJI-AM - 1270 **(725)**

Miami
KIKO-AM - 1340 **(752)**

Phoenix
KGME-AM - 1360 **(821)**
KIDR-AM - 740 **(822)**
KPHX-AM - 1480 **(833)**
KTAR-AM - 620 **(839)**

Prescott
KYCA-AM - 1490 **(855)**

Prescott Valley
KQNA-AM - 1130 **(858)**

Safford
KATO-AM - 1230 **(861)**
KCUZ-AM - 1490 **(862)**
KFMM-FM - 99.1 **(863)**

Sedona
KAZM-AM - 780 **(879)**

Sierra Vista
KTAN-AM - 1420 **(890)**

Tucson
KFFN-AM - 1490 **(977)**
KNST-AM - 790 **(987)**

Winslow
KINO-AM - 1230 **(1015)**

SPORTS (continued)

ARKANSAS
Berryville
KTHS-FM - 107.1 (1056)

Conway
KCON-AM - 1230 (1085)
KFCA-AM - 1330 (1087)

Fayetteville
KFAY-AM - 1030 (1127)
KKEG-FM - 92.1 (1129)

Fort Smith
KHGG-AM - 1580 (1151)
KPBI-AM - 1510 (1153)
KWHN-AM - 1650 (1157)

Helena
KFFA-AM - 1360 (1176)

Jonesboro
KOZY-FM - 105.3 (1202)

Mena
KENA-FM - 102.1 (1277)

Ozark
KDYN-AM - 1540 (1306)

Paragould
KDRS-AM - 1490 (1309)

Pocahontas
KPOC-AM - 1420 (1318)

West Memphis
KSUD-AM - 730 (1370)

CALIFORNIA
Berkeley
KALX-FM - 90.7 (1567)

El Centro
KXO-AM - 1230 (1857)

Eureka
KATA-AM - 1340 (1897)
KINS-AM - 980 (1903)

Fresno
KWRU-AM - 940 (1987)

Glendale
KLAC-AM - 570 (2017)

Hollywood
KWKW-AM - 1330 (2054)

Napa
KVON-AM - 1440 (2612)

Porterville
KTIP-AM - 1450 (2863)

Quincy
KNLF-FM - 95.9 (2871)

Redding
KMCA-AM - 1450 (2889)

Sacramento
KCTC-AM - 1320 (3025)
KHTK-AM - 1140 (3032)

San Diego
KOGO-AM - 600 (3307)
XTRA-AM - 690 (3320)

San Francisco
KNBR-AM - 680 (3493)
KSFO-AM - 560 (3500)

San Ysidro
XEBG-AM - 1550 (3608)
XEYX-AM - 820 (3613)

Sand City
KNRY-AM - 1240 (3614)

Santa Maria
KSMA-AM - 1240 (3699)

Solvang
KSYV-FM - 96.7 (3772)

South Lake Tahoe
KOWL-AM - 1490 (3785)

COLORADO
Colorado Springs
KRDO-AM - 1240 (4276)

Cortez
KVFC-AM - 740 (4294)

Denver
KKFN-AM - 950 (4382)
KOA-AM - 850 (4385)

Englewood
KXPK-FM - 92.1 (4420)
KYBG-AM - 1090 (4421)

Fort Collins
KIIX-AM - 1410 AM (4442)

Fort Morgan
KSIR-AM - 1010 (4450)

Grand Junction
KEKB-FM - 99.9 (4483)
KRGS-AM - 690 (4494)
KTMM-AM - 1340 (4496)

Pagosa Springs
KWUF-AM - 1400 (4591)

Pueblo
KCSJ-AM - 590 (4603)
KGHF-AM - 1350 (4605)

Steamboat Springs
KBCR-AM - 1230 (4636)

CONNECTICUT
Bloomfield
WDRC-AM - 1360 (4703)

Greenwich
WGCH-AM - 1490 (4878)

Hartford
WPOP-AM - 1410 (4907)

New London
WSUB-AM - 980 (5025)

Plantsville
WNTY-AM - 990 (5091)

DISTRICT OF COLUMBIA
Washington
WTOP-AM - 1500 (5895)

FLORIDA
Boca Raton
WSBR-AM - 740 (5943)

Daytona Beach
WNDB-AM - 1150 (6044)
WXVQ-AM - 1490 (6046)

Englewood
WENG-AM - 1530 (6063)

Gainesville
WRUF-AM - 850 (6165)

Jacksonville
WNZS-AM - 930 (6235)
WVOJ-AM - 970 (6244)

Lake City
WDSR-AM - 1340 (6271)

Lake Wales
WIPC-AM - 1280 (6287)

Miami
WQAM-AM - 560 (6413)

Ocala
WMOP-AM - 900 (6476)

Orlando
WDBO-AM - 580 (6515)
WHTQ-FM - 96.5 (6519)

Ormond Beach
WELE-AM - 1380 (6534)

Pensacola
WTKX-FM - 101.5 (6578)

St. Augustine
WFOY-AM - 1240 (6620)

St. Petersburg
WSUN-AM - 620 (6640)

Tallahassee
WNLS-AM - 1270 (6752)

Tampa
WDAE-AM - 620 (6786)

Tavares
WKIQ-AM - 1240 (6813)

Titusville
WPGS-AM - 840 (6823)

Venice
WAMR-AM - 1320 (6833)

Vero Beach
WTTB-AM - 1490 (6839)

Wauchula
WAUC-AM - 1310 (6842)

West Palm Beach
WEAT-AM - 850 (6850)

Zolfo Springs
WZTK-AM - 1480 (6895)

GEORGIA
Athens
WGAU-AM - 1340 (6956)

Atlanta
WQXI-AM - 790 (7081)

Augusta
WRDW-AM - 1480 (7112)

Bogart
WRFC-AM - 960 (7136)

Brunswick
WMOG-AM - 1490 (7142)
WSFN-AM - 790 (7143)

Columbus
WDAK-AM - 540 (7187)

Commerce
WJJC-AM - 1270 (7199)

Dalton
WYYU-FM - 104.5 (7226)

Douglas
WDMG-AM - 860 (7247)
WDMG-FM - 99.5 (7248)

Gainesville
WDUN-AM - 550 (7301)

LaGrange
WLAG-AM - 1240 (7362)
WTRP-AM - 620 (7365)

Macon
WMAC-AM - 940 (7397)
WVMG-AM - 1440 (7404)
WVMG-FM - 96.7 (7405)

Milledgeville
WMVG-AM - 1450 (7440)

Rome
WLAQ-AM - 1410 (7505)
WTSH-AM - 1360 (7509)

Swainsboro
WXRS-AM - 1590 (7579)

Thomson
WTHO-FM - 101.7 (7593)

Washington
WLOV-AM - 1370 (7641)
WXKT-FM - 100.1 (7642)

HAWAII
Hilo
KPUA-AM - 670 (7677)

Honolulu
KGU-AM - 760 (7734)
KWAI-AM - 1080 (7756)

Kahului
KNUI-AM - 900 (7761)

IDAHO
Idaho Falls
KID-AM - 590 (7874)
KUPI-AM - 980 (7878)

Lewiston
KCLK-AM - 1430 (7894)

Pocatello
KBRV-AM - 790 (7949)
KSEI-AM - 930 (7954)
KWIK-AM - 1240 (7955)

Rexburg
KADQ-FM - 94.3　**(7965)**

Soda Springs
KBRV-AM - 790　**(7983)**

ILLINOIS
Alton
WBGZ-AM - 1570　**(8011)**

Aurora
WBIG-AM - 1280　**(8042)**
WKKD-AM - 1580　**(8043)**

Carmi
WROY-AM - 1460　**(8132)**
WRUL-FM - 97.3　**(8133)**

Champaign
WDWS-AM - 1400　**(8225)**

Chicago
WKIE-FM - 92.7　**(8633)**
WSBC-AM - 1240　**(8651)**
WSCR-AM - 670　**(8652)**

Crest Hill
WJOL-AM - 1340　**(8690)**

Danville
WDAN-AM - 1490　**(8705)**

Decatur
WDZ-AM - 1050　**(8716)**

Galesburg
WGIL-AM - 1400　**(8910)**

Galva
WGEN-AM - 1500　**(8912)**

Highland
WCBW-AM - 880　**(8990)**

Jerseyville
WJBM-AM - 1480　**(9029)**

Marion
WDDD-AM - 810　**(9145)**

Monmouth
WMOI-FM - 97.7　**(9220)**
WRAM-AM - 1330　**(9221)**

Normal
WZND-FM - 106.1　**(9310)**

Peoria
WWSS-AM - 1290　**(9441)**

Quincy
WGEM-AM - 1440　**(9478)**

Salem
WJBD-FM - 100.1　**(9579)**

Savanna
WCCI-FM - 100.3　**(9582)**

Sparta
WHCO-AM - 1230　**(9618)**

Springfield
WFMB-AM - 1450　**(9647)**

Sterling
WSDR-AM - 1240　**(9664)**

Taylorville
WTIM-FM - 97.3　**(9680)**

Waukegan
WKRS-AM - 1220　**(9746)**

Winnetka
WNTH-FM - 88.1　**(9769)**

INDIANA
Columbia City
WJHS-FM - 91.5　**(9894)**

Columbus
WCSI-AM - 1010　**(9896)**

Crawfordsville
WCVL-AM - 1550　**(9911)**

Daleville
WHBU-AM - 1240　**(9918)**

Elkhart
WTRC-AM - 1340　**(9929)**

Frankfort
WILO-AM - 1570　**(10002)**

French Lick
WFLQ-FM - 100.1　**(10012)**

Indianapolis
WNDE-AM - 1260　**(10203)**

Kokomo
WIOU-AM - 1350　**(10242)**

Madison
WORX-FM - 96.7　**(10285)**
WXGO-AM - 1270　**(10286)**

Marion
WGOM-AM - 860　**(10291)**

Muncie
WXFN-AM - 1340　**(10334)**

New Castle
WMDH-AM - 1550　**(10344)**

Richmond
WKBV-AM - 1490　**(10425)**

Rushville
WKWH-FM - 94.3　**(10438)**

Salem
WSLM-FM - 97.9　**(10443)**

Terre Haute
WBOW-AM - 1300　**(10495)**
WSDX-AM - 1130　**(10501)**

Vincennes
WAOV-AM - 1450　**(10524)**

IOWA
Burlington
KCPS-AM - 1150　**(10642)**

Cedar Falls
KCNZ-AM - 1250　**(10665)**

Cedar Rapids
WMT-AM - 600　**(10685)**

Clinton
KROS-AM - 1340　**(10713)**

Davenport
KJOC-AM - 1170　**(10742)**
WLLR-AM - 1230　**(10749)**

Des Moines
KPSZ-AM - 940　**(10830)**
KRNT-AM - 1350　**(10831)**
KWKY-AM - 1150　**(10833)**
KXNO-AM - 1460　**(10834)**
WHO-AM - 1040　**(10837)**

Hampton
KLMJ-FM - 104.9　**(10941)**

Iowa City
KCJJ-AM - 1630　**(10991)**

Marshalltown
KXIA-FM - 101.1　**(11069)**

Ottumwa
KBIZ-AM - 1240　**(11141)**

Red Oak
KCSI-FM - 95.3　**(11171)**
KOAK-AM - 1080　**(11173)**

Sioux Center
KDCR-FM - 88.5　**(11209)**

Sioux City
KSCJ-AM - 1360　**(11219)**

Spencer
KDWD-FM - 100.1　**(11232)**

Washington
KCII-AM - 106.1　**(11287)**
KCII-FM - 106.1　**(11288)**

KANSAS
Abilene
KABI-AM - 1560　**(11335)**

Concordia
KNCK-AM - 1390　**(11399)**

Great Bend
KVGB-AM - 1590　**(11473)**

Hays
KAYS-AM - 1400　**(11483)**

Hiawatha
KNZA-FM - 103.9　**(11493)**

Hutchinson
KWBW-AM - 1450　**(11507)**

Manhattan
KMAN-AM - 1350　**(11633)**

Pratt
KWLS-AM - 1290-AM　**(11766)**

Salina
KSAL-AM - 1150　**(11789)**

Topeka
WIBW-AM - 580　**(11846)**

Westwood
KMBZ-AM - 980　**(11872)**

Wichita
KFH-AM - 1330　**(11896)**

Winfield
KKLE-AM - 1550　**(11911)**

KENTUCKY
Albany
WANY-AM - 1390　**(11915)**
WANY-FM - 106.3　**(11916)**

Bowling Green
WBGN-AM - 1340　**(11951)**

Danville
WHIR-AM - 1230　**(12041)**

Greenup
WLGC-AM - 1520　**(12099)**

Harlan
WFSR-AM - 970　**(12106)**

Hartford
WSNR-AM - 1600　**(12113)**

Henderson
WSON-AM - 860　**(12125)**

Lexington
WLXG-AM - 1300　**(12192)**

Louisville
WNAI-AM - 680　**(12261)**
WTMT-AM - 620　**(12267)**
WXXA-AM - 790　**(12268)**

Manchester
WTBK-FM - 105.7　**(12280)**

Marion
WMJL-AM - 1500　**(12282)**

Mayfield
WKJM-AM - 1320　**(12285)**

Maysville
WFTM-AM - 1240　**(12289)**

Murray
WNBS-AM - 1340　**(12320)**

Paducah
WDXR-AM - 1450　**(12343)**
WKYX-AM - 570　**(12346)**

Richmond
WEKY-AM - 1340　**(12386)**

LOUISIANA
Alexandria
KDBS-AM - 1410　**(12462)**

Baton Rouge
WSKR-AM - 1210　**(12524)**

Eunice
KEUN-AM - 1490　**(12576)**

Lafayette
KVOL-AM - 1330　**(12633)**
KVOL-FM - 105.9　**(12634)**

New Orleans
WWL-AM - 870　**(12780)**

Ruston
KPCH-FM - 97.7　**(12809)**

Shreveport
KFLO-AM - 1300　**(12825)**
KRMD-AM - 1340　**(12830)**
KWKH-AM - 1130　**(12841)**

Circulation: ★ = ABC; △ = BPA; ✦ = CAC; • = CCAB; ❑ = VAC; ⊕ = PO Statement; ‡ = Publisher's Report; Boldface figures = sworn; Light figures = estimated.

3073

SPORTS (continued)
Slidell
WSLA-AM - 1560 **(12845)**

Sulphur
KEZM-AM - 1310 **(12854)**

MAINE
Dover Foxcroft
WDME-FM - 103.1 **(12953)**

Norway
WKTQ-AM - 1450 **(12994)**
WTME-AM - 780 **(12996)**

MARYLAND
Baltimore
WBAL-AM - 1090 **(13265)**

Cambridge
WCEM-AM - 1240 **(13401)**

Chestertown
WCTR-AM - 1530 **(13406)**

College Park
WMUC-FM - 88.1 **(13447)**

Cumberland
WCBC-AM - 1270 **(13476)**
WNTR-AM - 1230 **(13478)**

Frostburg
WFRB-AM - 560 **(13528)**

Hagerstown
WHAG-AM - 1410 **(13575)**

Mechanicsville
WSMD-FM - 98.3 **(13627)**

Salisbury
WICO-AM - 1320 **(13715)**

Silver Spring
WTEM-AM - 980 **(13748)**

Westminster
WTTR-AM - 1470 **(13779)**

MASSACHUSETTS
Boston
WEEI-AM - 850 **(13982)**
WTBU-FM - 89.3 **(13997)**

Fitchburg
WEIM-AM - 1280 **(14185)**

Lowell
WCAP-AM - 980 **(14281)**

Methuen
WCCM-AM - 1490 **(14329)**

Milton
WMLN-FM - 91.5 **(14338)**

Paxton
WTAG-AM - 580 **(14460)**

Quincy
WJDA-AM - 1300 **(14493)**

Salem
WESX-AM - 1230 **(14516)**

Somerset
WSAR-AM - 1480 **(14529)**

MICHIGAN
Alma
WFYC-AM - 1280 **(14733)**

Alpena
WATZ-AM - 1450 **(14736)**

Ann Arbor
WTKA-AM - 1050 **(14780)**

Big Rapids
WBRN-AM - 1460 **(14820)**

Cheboygan
WIDG-AM - 940 **(14875)**

Dowagiac
WDOW-AM - 1440 **(14978)**

Farmington Hills
WDFN-AM - 1130 **(15023)**

Flint
WFDF-AM - 910 **(15042)**

Frankfort
WBNZ-FM - 99.3 **(15054)**

Fremont
WSHN-AM - 1550 **(15061)**

Grand Rapids
WBBL-AM - 1340 **(15102)**

Greenville
WSTG-AM - 1380 **(15137)**

Hancock
WMPL-AM - 920 **(15142)**

Ishpeming
WIAN-AM - 1240 **(15218)**

Jackson
WIBM-AM - 1450 **(15225)**
WKHM-AM - 970 **(15226)**

Kalamazoo
WQSN-AM - 1660 **(15258)**

Lansing
WVFN-AM - 730 **(15306)**

Lapeer
WLSP-AM - 1530 **(15310)**

Marquette
WDMJ-AM - 1320 **(15340)**

Ontonagon
WUPY-FM - 101.1 **(15424)**

St. Joseph
WSJM-AM - 1400 **(15516)**

Sault Sainte Marie
WKNW-AM - 1400 **(15529)**

Southfield
WWJ-AM - 950 **(15561)**
WXYT-AM - 1270 **(15563)**

Tawas City
WIOS-AM - 1480 **(15586)**
WKJC-FM - 104.7 **(15587)**

MINNESOTA
Bemidji
KBUN-AM - 1450 **(15743)**

Brainerd
WWWI-AM - 1270 **(15771)**

Collegeville
KJNB-FM - 99.9 **(15807)**

Detroit Lakes
KDLM-AM - 1340 **(15832)**

Duluth
WDSM-AM - 710 **(15855)**

Fairmont
KSUM-AM - 1370 **(15892)**

Forest Lake
WLKX-FM - 95.9 **(15907)**

Hastings
KDWA-AM - 1460 **(15942)**

Hibbing
WMFG-AM - 1240 **(15958)**
WNMT-AM - 650 **(15960)**

Luverne
KQAD-AM - 800 **(16016)**

Mankato
KEEZ-FM - 99.1 **(16032)**

Marshall
KMHL-AM - 1400 **(16047)**

Montevideo
KDMA-AM - 1460 **(16181)**

New Ulm
KNUJ-AM - 860 **(16217)**

Northfield
KYMN-AM - 1080 **(16239)**

Redwood Falls
KLGR-AM - 1490 **(16299)**
KLGR-FM - 97.7 **(16300)**

Rochester
KWEB-AM - 1270 **(16321)**

St. Cloud
WJON-AM - 1240 **(16353)**

St. Paul
WDGY-AM - 630 **(16427)**

St. Peter
KRBI-AM - 1310 **(16432)**

Willmar
KWLM-AM - 1340 **(16522)**

MISSISSIPPI
Amory
WAMY-AM - 1580 **(16547)**

Booneville
WBIP-AM - 1400 **(16572)**
WBIP-FM - 99.3 **(16573)**

Cleveland
WCLD-AM - 1490 **(16591)**

Columbus
WSSO-AM - 1230 **(16614)**

Gulfport
WROA-AM - 1390 **(16658)**

Houston
WCPC-AM - 940 **(16686)**

Jackson
WJDX-AM - 620 **(16718)**

Lorman
WPRL-FM - 91.7 **(16749)**

Louisville
WLSM-AM - 1270 **(16751)**

McComb
WAPF-AM - 980 **(16765)**

Meridian
WFFX-AM - 1450 **(16773)**

Monticello
WMLC-AM - 1270 **(16790)**

New Albany
WNAU-AM - 1470 **(16799)**

Oxford
WQLJ-FM - 93.7 **(16810)**

Pascagoula
WGUD-AM - 1490 **(16813)**

Tupelo
WTUP-AM - 1490 **(16857)**

MISSOURI
Ava
KKOZ-AM - 1430 **(16897)**
KKOZ-FM - 92.1 **(16898)**

Cape Girardeau
KGIR-AM - 1220 **(16952)**
KZIM-AM - 960 **(16954)**

Columbia
KFRU-AM - 1400 **(17017)**

Independence
KCTE-AM - 1510 **(17116)**

Kirksville
KIRX-AM - 1450 **(17230)**

Lebanon
KTTK-FM - 90.7 **(17242)**

Marshall
KMMO-AM - 102.9 **(17266)**
KMMO-FM - 102.9 **(17267)**

Mexico
KXEO-AM - 1340 **(17288)**

Piedmont
KPWB-AM - 1140 **(17344)**

St. Louis
KMOX-AM - 1120 **(17543)**

Salem
KSMO-AM - 1340 **(17564)**

Sikeston
KMAL-FM - 92.9 **(17585)**

Springfield
KWTO-AM - 560 **(17633)**

Sullivan
KTUI-FM - 100.9 **(17643)**

Numbers cited in bold after listings are entry numbers rather than page numbers.

Thayer
KALM-AM - 1290 **(17649)**
KAMS-FM - 95.1 **(17650)**

MONTANA
Billings
KBLG-AM - 910 **(17737)**

Butte
KXTL-AM - 1370 **(17767)**

Helena
KCAP-AM - 1340 **(17827)**

Kalispell
KALS-FM - 97.1 **(17839)**

Missoula
KGRZ-AM - 1450 **(17881)**

NEBRASKA
Alliance
KCOW-AM - 1400 **(17929)**

Broken Bow
KBBN-FM - 98.3 **(17966)**

Falls City
KTNC-AM - 1230 **(18010)**

Hastings
KHAS-AM - 1230 **(18039)**

Kearney
KKPR-AM - 1460 **(18063)**

Lexington
KRVN-AM - 880 **(18075)**
KRVN-FM - 93.1 **(18076)**

Norfolk
KEXL-FM - 106.7 **(18171)**

Omaha
KAZP-AM - 1620 **(18211)**
KKAR-AM - 1290 **(18221)**

Sidney
KSID-AM - 1340 **(18279)**

NEVADA
Elko
KRJC-FM - 95.3 **(18339)**

Las Vegas
KBAD-AM - 920 **(18390)**
KDWN-AM - 720 **(18394)**

Reno
KPLY-AM - 1230 **(18436)**
KPTT-AM - 630 **(18437)**

NEW HAMPSHIRE
Claremont
WTSV-AM - 1230 **(18467)**

Concord
WKXL-AM - 1450 **(18478)**
WTPL-FM - 107.7 **(18481)**

Dover
WTSN-AM - 1270 **(18496)**

Gilford
WEMJ-AM - 1490 **(18512)**

Littleton
WLTN-AM - 1400 **(18551)**

Nashua
WSMN-AM - 1590 **(18608)**

Portsmouth
WGIN-AM - 930 **(18639)**
WGIP-AM - 1540 **(18640)**

NEW JERSEY
Pompton Lakes
WGHT-AM - 1500 **(19450)**

Princeton
WPRB-FM - 103.3 **(19481)**

NEW MEXICO
Alamogordo
KRSY-AM - 1230 **(19760)**

Clayton
KLMX-AM - 1450 **(19829)**

Las Cruces
KOBE-AM - 1450 **(19884)**

Truth or Consequences
KCHS-AM - 1400 **(19970)**

NEW YORK
Astoria
WFAN-AM - 660 **(20103)**

Brockport
WBSU-FM - 89.1 **(20249)**

Canton
WVNC-FM - 96.7 **(20434)**

Clinton
WHCL-FM - 88.7 **(20475)**

Elmira
WELM-AM - 1410 **(20575)**
WWLZ-AM - 820 **(20580)**

Gouverneur
WGIX-FM - 95.3 **(20676)**

Ilion
WNRS-AM - 1420 **(20780)**

Lake Placid
WIRD-AM - 920 **(20876)**

Massena
WYBG-AM - 1050 **(21029)**

New Rochelle
WVOX-AM - 1460 **(21125)**

Newark
WACK-AM - 1420 **(22998)**

Newburgh
WGNY-AM - 1200 **(23002)**

Ogdensburg
WPAC-FM - 92.7 **(23034)**

Owego
WEBO-AM - 1330 **(23068)**

Queensbury
WMML-AM - 1230 **(23175)**

Rochester
WDKX-FM - 103.9 **(23245)**

Springville
WSPQ-AM - 1330 **(23356)**

Syracuse
WAER-FM - 88.3 **(23434)**
WHEN-AM - 620 **(23438)**
WSYR-AM - 570 **(23445)**

Trumansburg
WPIE-AM - 1160 **(23464)**

Vestal
WENE-AM - 1430 **(23490)**

Wellsville
WLSV-AM - 790 **(23535)**

NORTH CAROLINA
Belmont
WCGC-AM - 1270 **(23643)**

Burlington
WBAG-AM - 1150 **(23674)**

Charlotte
WFNZ-AM - 610 **(23769)**

Cherryville
WCSL-AM - 1590 **(23785)**

Concord
WEGO-AM - 1410 **(23793)**

Durham
WSRC-AM - 1410 **(23851)**
WXDU-FM - 88.7 **(23854)**

Edenton
WZBO-AM - 1260 **(23859)**

Elizabeth City
WGAI-AM - 560 **(23862)**

Farmville
WGHB-AM - 1250 **(23878)**

Fayetteville
WFNC-AM - 640 **(23886)**

Forest City
WAGY-AM - 1320 **(23895)**

Gastonia
WGNC-AM - 1450 **(23908)**

Greensboro
WPET-AM - 950 **(23955)**
WTCK-AM - 1320 **(23958)**

Henderson
WIZS-AM - 1450 **(23982)**

Jacksonville
WLAS-AM - 910 **(24014)**

Lexington
WLXN-AM - 1440 **(24041)**

Lincolnton
WLON-AM - 1050 **(24046)**

Mars Hill
WVMH-FM - 90.5 **(24058)**

New Bern
WLOJ-AM - 1490 **(24100)**

Newport
WTKF-FM - 107.3 **(24105)**

Raleigh
WRBZ-AM - 850 **(24171)**

Rockingham
WAYN-AM - 900 **(24202)**

Rocky Mount
WRMT-AM - 1490 **(24207)**

Salisbury
WSAT-AM - 1280 **(24217)**

Shelby
WOHS-AM - 730 **(24229)**

Southern Pines
WEEB-AM - 990 **(24237)**

Sylva
WRGC-AM - 680 **(24252)**

Whiteville
WTXY-AM - 1540 **(24287)**

Williamston
WIAM-AM - 900 **(24292)**

Wilmington
WAAV-FM - 94.1 **(24299)**

Winston-Salem
WSNC-FM - 90.5 **(24333)**

NORTH DAKOTA
Beulah
KHOL-AM - 1410 **(24348)**

Bismarck
KLXX-AM - 1270 **(24369)**

Devils Lake
KDLR-AM - 1240 **(24391)**

Fargo
KFGO-AM - 790 **(24419)**
KVOX-AM - 1280 **(24430)**

Grand Forks
KZLT-FM - 104.3 **(24464)**

Minot
KRRZ-AM - 1390 **(24513)**

Oakes
KDDR-AM - 1220 **(24528)**

OHIO
Ashtabula
WFUN-AM - 970 **(24625)**

Bellaire
WOMP-AM - 1290 **(24663)**

Bellefontaine
WBLL-AM - 1390 **(24667)**

Chardon
WATJ-AM - 1560 **(24759)**

Cincinnati
WCKY-AM - 1360 **(24836)**

Cleveland
WKNR-AM - 850 **(24978)**
WTAM-AM - 1100 **(24986)**

Circulation: ★ = ABC; △ = BPA; ♦ = CAC; • = CCAB; ❏ = VAC; ⊕ = PO Statement; ‡ = Publisher's Report; Boldface figures = sworn; Light figures = estimated.

3075

SPORTS (continued)

Columbus
WBNS-AM - 1460 **(25072)**

Coshocton
WTNS-FM - 99.3 **(25098)**

Dover
WJER-FM - 101.7 **(25166)**

East Liverpool
WOHI-AM - 1490 **(25173)**

Elyria
WEOL-AM - 930 **(25180)**

Fostoria
WFOB-AM - 1430 **(25200)**

Mansfield
WMAN-AM - 1400 **(25335)**

Marietta
WMOA-AM - 1490 **(25349)**

Marion
WDIF-FM - 94.3 **(25353)**
WMRN-AM - 1490 **(25354)**

Massillon
WTIG-AM - 990 **(25362)**

McConnelsville
WJAW-FM - 100.9 **(25370)**

Portsmouth
WNXT-AM - 1260 **(25485)**

Springfield
WBLY-AM - 1600 **(25535)**

Steubenville
WSTV-AM - 1340 **(25543)**

Toledo
WSPD-AM - 1370 **(25585)**

Uhrichsville
WBTC-AM - 1540 **(25600)**

Van Wert
WERT-AM - 1220 **(25610)**

Youngstown
WBBW-AM - 1240 **(25703)**
WRBP-AM - 1440 **(25710)**

OKLAHOMA
Ada
KADA-AM - 1230 **(25725)**
KADA-FM - 99.3 **(25726)**

Alva
KALV-AM - 1430 **(25739)**

Ardmore
KICM-FM - 93.7 **(25747)**
KVSO-AM - 1240 **(25749)**

Bartlesville
KWON-AM - 1400 **(25755)**

Enid
KCRC-AM - 1390 **(25825)**

Hobart
KTJS-AM - 1420 **(25868)**

Idabel
KBEL-AM - 1240 **(25876)**

Lawton
KRX-AM - 1050 **(25895)**

Oklahoma City
WWLS-FM - 104.9 **(26024)**

Ponca City
WBBZ-AM - 1230 **(26044)**

Tulsa
KQLL-AM - 1430 **(26160)**
KRMG-AM - 740 **(26163)**

OREGON
Astoria
KAST-AM - 1370 **(26227)**

Bend
KBND-AM - 1110 **(26244)**

Coos Bay
KACW-FM - 107.3 **(26275)**

Eugene
KPNW-AM - 1120 **(26344)**

Hillsboro
KUIK-AM - 1360 **(26375)**

Klamath Falls
KFLS-AM - 1450 **(26392)**

Lebanon
KGAL-AM - 1580 **(26409)**

Medford
KTMT-AM - 580 **(26429)**

Newport
KNPT-AM - 1310 **(26448)**

Portland
KFXX-AM - 910 **(26526)**

Roseburg
KRNR-AM - 1490 **(26559)**

Salem
KYKN-AM - 1430 **(26576)**

PENNSYLVANIA
Beaver Falls
WBVP-AM - 1230 **(26686)**
WMBA-AM - 1460 **(26687)**

Bloomsburg
WCNR-AM - 930 **(26721)**

Du Bois
WCED-AM - 1420 **(26839)**

Dunmore
WKQV-FM - 95.7 **(26843)**

Easton
WODE-AM - 1230 **(26853)**

Elizabethtown
WPDC-AM - 1600 **(26866)**

Ephrata
WIOV-AM - 1240 **(26891)**

Erie
WPSE-AM - 1450 **(26907)**

Lancaster
WLPA-AM - 1490 **(27155)**

Mexico
WJUN-AM - 1220 **(27247)**

New Castle
WJST-FM - 92.1 **(27317)**
WKST-AM - 1200 **(27318)**

Philadelphia
WIP-AM - 610 **(27735)**

Pittsburgh
WEAE-AM - 1250 **(27865)**
WESA-AM - 940 **(27866)**
WRCT-FM - 88.3 **(27877)**

Pittston
WGBI-AM - 910 **(27888)**

Pottstown
WPAZ-AM - 1370 **(27902)**

Pottsville
WPPA-AM - 1360 **(27906)**

Punxsutawney
WPXZ-FM - 104.1 **(27912)**

Scranton
WBAX-AM - 1240 **(27965)**
WEJL-AM - 630 **(27966)**

Slippery Rock
WSRU-FM - 90.1 **(28001)**

State College
WMAJ-AM - 1450 **(28025)**
WRSC-AM - 1390 **(28029)**

Washington
WJPA-AM - 1450 **(28120)**
WJPA-FM - 95.3 **(28121)**

Whitehall
WAEB-AM - 790 **(28159)**

Williamsport
WRAK-AM - 1400 **(28190)**

York
WOYK-AM - 1350 **(28214)**

PUERTO RICO
Camuy
WCHQ-AM - 1360 **(28239)**

RHODE ISLAND
East Providence
WSKO-AM - 790 **(28350)**

Providence
WBSR-FM - 88.1 **(28432)**
WDOM-FM - 91.3 **(28433)**

SOUTH CAROLINA
Barnwell
WBAW-AM - 99.1 **(28483)**

Clemson
WCCP-FM - 104.9 **(28537)**

Clinton
WPCC-AM - 1410 **(28541)**

Columbia
WCOS-AM - 1400 **(28573)**

Fountain Inn
WFIS-AM - 1600 **(28614)**

Greenville
WORD-AM - 1330 **(28639)**

Newberry
WKDK-AM - 1240 **(28718)**

Orangeburg
WSPX-FM - 94.5 **(28737)**

Rock Hill
WRHM-FM - 107.1 **(28749)**

Sumter
WDXY-AM - 1240 **(28770)**

SOUTH DAKOTA
Belle Fourche
KBFS-AM - 1450 **(28807)**

Brookings
KBRK-AM - 1430 **(28818)**

Crooks
KSFS-AM - 1520 **(28835)**

Milbank
KDIO-AM - 1350 **(28894)**

Mitchell
KMIT-FM - 105.9 **(28902)**

Winner
KWYR-FM - 93.7 **(29034)**

Yankton
KVTK-AM - 1570 **(29043)**
WNAX-AM - 570 **(29045)**

TENNESSEE
Carthage
WRKM-AM - 1350 **(29082)**

Cleveland
WDNT-AM - 1280 **(29126)**
WXQK-AM - 970 **(29128)**

Dickson
WDKN-AM - 1260 **(29166)**

Dyersburg
WTRO-AM - 1450 **(29178)**

Erwin
WEMB-AM - 1420 **(29185)**

Fayetteville
WYTM-FM - 105.5 **(29192)**

Humboldt
WHMT-AM - 1190 **(29225)**

Jackson
WDXI-AM - 1310 **(29234)**
WTJS-AM - 1390 **(29239)**

Knoxville
WIMZ-AM - 1240 **(29289)**

Martin
WCMT-AM - 1410 **(29344)**
WCMT-FM - 101.7 **(29345)**

Memphis
WHBQ-AM - 560 **(29395)**
WREC-AM - 600 **(29410)**

Numbers cited in bold after listings are entry numbers rather than page numbers.

Murfreesboro
WGNS-AM - 1450 (29436)

Nashville
WAMB-AM - 1160 (29506)
WLAC-AM - 1510 (29518)
WWTN-FM - 99.7 (29538)

Paris
WMUF-AM - 1000 (29562)

Portland
WQKR-AM - 1270 (29570)

Trenton
WTKB-FM - 93.7 (29631)

Winchester
WCDT-AM - 1340 (29648)

TEXAS
Abilene
KWKC-AM - 1340 (29668)

Amarillo
KGNC-AM - 710 (29709)

Austin
KLBJ-AM - 590 (29870)
KTAE-AM - 1260 (29877)

Carrizo Springs
KBEN-AM - 1450 (30003)

College Station
WTAW-AM - 1620 (30061)

Corpus Christi
KEYS-AM - 1440 (30083)

Crockett
KIVY-AM - 1290 (30107)

Del Rio
KTJK-AM - 1230 (30228)
KWMC-AM - 1490 (30229)

Eagle Pass
KINL-FM - 92.7 (30259)

Edinburg
KURV-AM - 710 (30274)

El Campo
KULP-AM - 1390 (30277)
KULP-FM - 96.9 (30278)

El Paso
KHEY-AM - 1380 (30291)
KROD-AM - 600 (30299)

Freer
KBRA-FM - 95.9 (30368)

Galveston
KGBC-AM - 1540 (30383)

Haskell
KVRP-FM - 95.5 (30434)

Houston
KILT-AM - 610 (30557)
KSEV-AM - 700 (30574)
KTRH-AM - 740 (30579)
KXYZ-AM - 1320 (30586)

Kenedy
KAML-AM - 990 (30636)

Liberty
KSHN-FM - 99.9 (30692)

Lufkin
KSFA-AM - 860 (30744)

Nederland
KAYC-AM - 1450 (30858)

Pampa
KOMX-FM - 100.3 (30902)

Paris
KPLT-AM - 1490 (30908)

Plano
KHYI-FM - 95.3 (30949)

Robstown
KROB-AM - 1510 (30986)

San Angelo
KKSA-AM - 1260 (31019)

San Antonio
WOAI-AM - 1200 (31079)

Silsbee
KSET-AM - 1300 (31108)
KWDX-FM - 101.7 (31109)

Snyder
KSNY-FM - 101.5 (31117)

Sweetwater
KXOX-AM - 1240 (31171)

Tyler
KTBB-AM - 600 (31217)

Uvalde
KYUF-FM - 104.9 (31227)

UTAH
Blanding
KUTA-AM - 790 (31321)

Cedar City
KSUB-AM - 590 (31328)

Hooper
KSVN-AM - 730 (31339)

Logan
KVNU-AM - 610 (31363)

Ogden
KLO-AM - 1430 (31381)

St. George
KZNU-AM - 1450 (31422)

Spanish Fork
KHQN-AM - 1480 (31475)

Vernal
KVEL-AM - 920 (31485)

West Valley City
KALL-AM - 910 (31487)

VERMONT
Bennington
WBTN-AM - 1370 (31503)

Brattleboro
WTSA-AM - 1450 (31512)

Colchester
WVMT-AM - 620 (31533)

Waterbury
WDEV-AM - 550 (31612)

VIRGINIA
Blackstone
WKLV-AM - 1440 (31894)

Broadway
WBTX-AM - 1470 (31903)

Fairfax
WJFK-FM - 106.7 (32036)

Franklin
WLQM-FM - 101.7 (32083)

Gate City
WGAT-AM - 1050 (32109)

Gloucester
WXGM-AM - 1420 (32116)

Grundy
WNRG-AM - 940 (32123)

Hampden Sydney
WWHS-FM - 92.1 (32125)

Lebanon
WLRV-AM - 1380 (32180)

Lexington
WLUR-FM - 91.5 (32194)
WREL-AM - 1450 (32195)

Lynchburg
WBRG-AM - 1050 (32211)

Martinsville
WMVA-AM - 1450 (32238)

Petersburg
WVST-FM - 91.3 (32333)

Radford
WFNR-AM - 710 (32348)

Richmond
WRNL-AM - 910 (32483)
WVNZ-AM - 990 (32487)

Salem
WSLC-AM - 610 (32523)

Staunton
WTON-AM - 1240 (32560)

Virginia Beach
WGH-AM - 1310 (32593)

WASHINGTON
Bellevue
KASB-FM - 89.3 (32671)

Centralia
KELA-AM - 1470 (32706)

Ellensburg
KXLE-AM - 1240 (32752)

Ephrata
KULE-AM - 730 (32757)

Everett
KRKO-AM - 1380 (32762)

Forks
KVAC-AM - 1490 (32771)

Kelso
KLOG-AM - 1490 (32787)

Moses Lake
KBSN-AM - 1470 (32841)

Mount Vernon
KBRC-AM - 1430 (32848)

Pasco
KFLD-AM - 870 (32880)

Port Angeles
KONP-AM - 1450 (32889)

Pullman
KQQQ-AM - 1150 (32912)

Quincy
KWNC-AM - 1370 (32920)

Seattle
KIRO-AM - 710 (33056)

Spokane
KXLY-AM - 920 (33134)

Wenatchee
KKRT-AM - 900 (33198)
KPQ-AM - 560 (33201)

Yakima
KIT-AM - 1280 (33230)

WEST VIRGINIA
Berkeley Springs
WCST-FM - 93.5 (33249)

Charleston
WCHS-AM - 580 (33282)
WQBE-AM - 97.5 (33284)
WVSR-AM - 1240 (33290)

Clarksburg
WXKX-AM - 1340 (33296)

Elkins
WDNE-AM - 1240 (33308)

Fairmont
WTCS-AM - 1490 (33316)

Martinsburg
WEPM-AM - 1340 (33381)
WRNR-AM - 740 (33383)

New Martinsville
WETZ-AM - 1330 (33415)

South Charleston
WJYP-FM - 100.9 (33468)

Sutton
WSGB-AM - 1490 (33478)

Vienna
WLTP-AM - 1450 (33481)

Weirton
WEIR-AM - 1430 (33491)

WISCONSIN
Appleton
WHBY-AM - 1150 (33549)

Ashland
WATW-AM - 1400 (33556)

SPORTS (continued)

Beaver Dam
WBEV-AM - 1430   (33569)

Chippewa Falls
WOGO-AM - 680   (33632)

Eau Claire
WBIZ-AM - 1400   (33676)
WEAQ-AM - 1150   (33678)

Fond du Lac
KFIZ-AM - 1450   (33699)

Green Bay
WDUZ-AM - 1400   (33746)

Hayward
WRLS-FM - 92.3   (33790)

La Crosse
WKBH-AM - 1570   (33891)

Lancaster
WGLR-FM - 97.7   (33909)

Madison
WHIT-AM - 1550   (33994)
WIBA-AM - 1310   (33996)

Marinette
WMAM-AM - 570   (34022)

Marshfield
WDLB-AM - 1450   (34028)

Reedsburg
WNFM-FM - 104.9   (34282)

Rhinelander
WOBT-AM - 1240   (34290)

Richland Center
WRCO-AM - 1450   (34300)

Ripon
WRPN-AM - 1600   (34305)

River Falls
WEVR-AM - 1550   (34310)
WEVR-FM - 106.3   (34311)

Shawano
WTCH-AM - 960   (34320)

Sheboygan
WHBL-AM - 1330   (34324)

Sparta
WCOW-FM - 97.1   (34334)

Sturgeon Bay
WDOR-FM - 93.9   (34355)

Tomahawk
WJJQ-AM - 810   (34374)

Waukesha
WAUK-AM - 1510   (34416)

Waupaca
WDUX-AM - 800   (34423)
WDUX-FM - 92.7   (34424)

Wausau
WSAU-AM - 550   (34438)
WXCO-AM - 1230   (34440)

West Bend
WBKV-AM - 1470   (34447)

WYOMING
Cheyenne
KFBC-AM - 1240   (34502)

Laramie
KOWB-AM - 1290   (34556)

Powell
KLVY-AM - 1260   (34570)

Sheridan
KROE-AM - 930   (34589)

BRITISH COLUMBIA, CANADA
Cranbrook
CHDR-FM - 104.7   (34937)

Kamloops
CHNL-AM - 610   (34980)

Vancouver
CKNW-AM - 980   (35194)

MANITOBA, CANADA
Dauphin
CKDM-AM - 730   (35264)

Winnipeg
CJOB-AM - 680   (35372)

ONTARIO, CANADA
Kingston
CKLC-AM - 1380   (35954)

London
CFPL-AM - 980   (35996)
CJBK-AM - 1290   (36002)

Niagara Falls
CJRN-AM - 710   (36112)

Ottawa
CBOF-FM - 90.7   (36285)
CFGO-AM - 1200   (36288)

Peterborough
CKRU-AM - 980   (36324)

Simcoe
CHCD-FM - 106.7   (36392)

Toronto
CJCL-AM - 590   (36818)

Windsor
CBEF-AM - 540   (36896)

QUEBEC, CANADA
Asbestos
CJAN-FM - 99.3   (36942)

TALK

ALABAMA
Anniston
WHMA-AM - 1390   (21)

Ashland
WZZX-AM - 780   (26)

Athens
WUMP-AM - 730   (29)
WVNN-AM - 770   (30)

Atmore
WASG-AM - 550   (34)

Auburn
WANI-AM - 1400   (46)

Bessemer
WSMQ-AM - 1450   (53)

Birmingham
WAPI-AM - 1070   (103)
WERC-AM - 960   (115)
WJLD-AM - 1400   (118)

Camden
WCOX-AM - 1450   (144)
WCOX-FM - 102.3   (145)

Cullman
WKUL-FM - 92.1   (166)

Decatur
WYAM-AM - 890   (177)

Demopolis
WXAL-AM - 1400   (181)

Dora
WPYK-AM - 1010   (184)

Eufaula
WULA-AM - 1240   (206)

Florence
WBCF-AM - 1240   (221)
WYTK-FM - 93.9   (227)

Foley
WHEP-AM - 1310   (229)

Geneva
WGEA-AM - 1150   (242)

Greenville
WGYV-AM - 1380   (244)

Jackson
WHOD-AM - 1230   (292)

Jasper
WZPQ-AM - 1360   (299)

Mobile
WABB-AM - 1480   (332)
WBHY-AM - 840   (335)
WNTM-AM - 710   (348)

Selma
WHBB-AM - 1490   (454)

Sheffield
WBTG-AM - 1290   (457)

Sylacauga
WFEB-AM - 1340   (463)

Troy
WTBF-AM - 970   (476)

Tuscaloosa
WTBC-AM - 1230   (500)
WWPG-AM - 1280   (505)

Tuscumbia
WZZA-AM - 1410   (506)

Vernon
WVSA-AM - 1380   (514)

ALASKA
Anchorage
KABN-AM - 840   (533)
KENI-AM - 650   (540)

Bethel
KYUK-AM - 640   (556)

Fairbanks
KFAR-AM - 660   (572)

Juneau
KJNO-AM - 630   (600)

Kenai
KSRM-AM - 920   (609)

Kodiak
KVOK-AM - 560   (620)

ARIZONA
Flagstaff
KVNA-AM - 600   (704)

Globe
KJAA-AM - 1240   (720)

Kingman
KAAA-AM - 1230   (732)

Mesa
KXAM-AM - 1310   (751)

Oro Valley
KVOI-AM - 690   (757)

Parker
KLPZ-AM - 1380   (765)

Phoenix
KFNN-AM - 1510   (819)
KFYI-AM - 910   (820)
KIDR-AM - 740   (822)
KMYL-AM - 1190   (828)
KPXQ-AM - 1360   (835)
KTAR-AM - 620   (839)

Prescott
KYCA-AM - 1490   (855)

Prescott Valley
KQNA-AM - 1130   (858)

Safford
KATO-AM - 1230   (861)

Sedona
KAZM-AM - 780   (879)

Sierra Vista
KTAN-AM - 1420   (890)

Tucson
KFFN-AM - 1490   (977)
KFLT-AM - 830   (978)
KNST-AM - 790   (987)

ARKANSAS
El Dorado
KELD-AM - 1400   (1108)

Fayetteville
KFAY-AM - 1030   (1127)
KREB-AM - 1190   (1130)

Fordyce
KBJT-AM - 1570   (1136)

Numbers cited in bold after listings are entry numbers rather than page numbers.

Fort Smith
KHGG-AM - 1580　(1151)
KPBI-AM - 1510　(1153)
KWHN-AM - 1650　(1157)

Harrison
KHOZ-AM - 900　(1168)

Helena
KFFA-AM - 1360　(1176)

Hope
KXAR-AM - 1490　(1181)

Hot Springs
KZNG-AM - 1340　(1190)

Little Rock
KARN-AM - 920　(1240)
KITA-AM - 1440　(1244)
KKRN-FM - 102.5　(1246)

Marshall
KCGS-AM - 960　(1270)

Ozark
KDYN-AM - 1540　(1306)

Paragould
KDRS-AM - 1490　(1309)

Rogers
KURM-AM - 790　(1329)

Siloam Springs
KUOA-AM - TER0　(1345)

West Memphis
KSUD-AM - 730　(1370)

Wynne
KWYN-AM - 1400　(1373)

CALIFORNIA
Alturas
KKFJ-AM - 570　(1396)

Bakersfield
KERI-AM - 1180　(1460)
KERN-AM - 1410　(1461)
KGEO-AM - 1230　(1463)
KNZR-AM - 1560　(1469)

Calexico
KICO-AM - 1490　(1637)

Carlsbad
KCEO-AM - 1000　(1668)

Chico
KPAY-AM - 1290　(1704)

Costa Mesa
KBRT-AM - 740　(1784)

Eureka
KINS-AM - 980　(1903)

Fresno
KMJ-AM - 580　(1974)
KWRU-AM - 940　(1987)

Glendale
KKLA-AM - 1240　(2015)
KKLA-FM - 99.5　(2016)
KRLA-AM - 870　(2019)
KTNQ-AM - 1020　(2021)

Grass Valley
KNCO-AM - 830　(2030)

Hollywood
KWKW-AM - 1330　(2054)

Lancaster
KAVC-AM - 1340　(2148)

Los Angeles
KABC-AM - 790　(2446)
KFI-AM - 640　(2454)
KVCA-AM - 670　(2471)

Marysville
KMYC-AM - 1410　(2517)

Merced
KYOS-AM - 1480　(2536)

Modesto
KFIV-AM - 1360　(2565)

Napa
KVON-AM - 1440　(2612)

North Hollywood
KPFK-FM - 90.7　(2645)

Oxnard
KDAR-FM - 98.3　(2732)

Palm Springs
KDES-AM - 920　(2775)
KPSI-AM - 920　(2779)

Porterville
KTIP-AM - 1450　(2863)

Quincy
KNLF-FM - 95.9　(2871)

Redding
KMCA-AM - 1450　(2889)
KQMS-AM - 1400　(2893)

Ridgecrest
KLOA-AM - 1240　(2924)

Sacramento
KFBK-AM - 1530　(3029)
KHTK-AM - 1140　(3032)
KSTE-AM - 650　(3051)

San Diego
KFMB-AM - 760　(3298)
KOGO-AM - 600　(3307)
KPRZ-AM - 1210　(3312)
KSDO-AM - 1130　(3313)

San Francisco
KALW-FM - 91.7　(3469)
KEST-AM - 1450　(3480)
KGO-AM - 810　(3484)

San Ysidro
XEMBC-AM - 1190　(3609)

Sand City
KNRY-AM - 1240　(3614)

Santa Cruz
KSCO-AM - 1080　(3691)

Santa Maria
KSMA-AM - 1240　(3699)

Santa Rosa
KSRO-AM - 1350　(3741)

Sonora
KVML-AM - 1450　(3782)

South Lake Tahoe
KOWL-AM - 1490　(3785)

Susanville
KSUE-AM - 1240　(3834)

Ukiah
KDAC-AM - 1230　(3968)
KUKI-AM - 1400　(3969)

Van Nuys
KTLW-FM - 88.9　(3998)

Yreka
KSYC-AM - 1490　(4122)

COLORADO
Alamosa
KGIW-AM - 1450　(4135)

Canon City
KRLN-AM - 1400　(4214)

Colorado Springs
KKCS-AM - 1460　(4269)
KRDO-AM - 1240　(4276)
KVOR-AM - 740　(4285)

Denver
KBCO-AM - 1190　(4370)
KHOW-AM - 630　(4379)
KOA-AM - 850　(4385)
KXKL-FM - 105.1　(4395)

Englewood
KXPK-FM - 92.1　(4420)
KYBG-AM - 1090　(4421)

Fort Collins
KCOL-AM - 600　(4440)

Fort Morgan
KSIR-AM - 1010　(4450)

Fountain
KWYD-AM - 1580　(4453)

Grand Junction
KBZS-AM - 620　(4481)
KTMM-AM - 1340　(4496)

Longmont
KLMO-AM - 1060　(4564)

Pagosa Springs
KWUF-AM - 1400　(4591)

Pueblo
KCSJ-AM - 590　(4603)

CONNECTICUT
Bloomfield
WDRC-AM - 1360　(4703)

Danbury
WRNE-AM - 980　(4767)

Greenwich
WGCH-AM - 1490　(4878)

Hamden
WELI-AM - 960　(4881)

Milford
WFIF-AM - 1500　(4960)

New London
WSUB-AM - 980　(5025)

Old Saybrook
WLIS-AM - 1420　(5089)

Plantsville
WNTY-AM - 990　(5091)

Waterbury
WATR-AM - 1320　(5197)

West Hartford
WWUH-FM - 91.3　(5206)

Westport
WMMM-AM - 1260　(5217)

DELAWARE
Dover
WDOV-AM - 1410　(5251)

Wilmington
WDEL-AM - 1150　(5297)
WFAI-AM - 1510　(5298)

DISTRICT OF COLUMBIA
Washington
WAMU-FM - 88.5　(5877)

FLORIDA
Brooksville
WWJB-AM - 1450　(5966)

Clearwater
WTAN-AM - 1340　(5994)

Crestview
WXEI-FM - 95.3　(6028)

Daytona Beach
WNDB-AM - 1150　(6044)
WXVQ-AM - 1490　(6046)

DeLand
WYND-AM - 1310　(6057)

Englewood
WENG-AM - 1530　(6063)

Fort Myers
WINK-AM - 1200　(6106)
WNOG-AM - 1270　(6110)
WTLQ-AM - 1240　(6113)

Fort Walton Beach
WFTW-AM - 1260　(6123)

Gainesville
WLUS-AM - 980　(6164)
WRUF-AM - 850　(6165)
WSKY-FM - 97.3　(6167)

Jacksonville
WVOJ-AM - 970　(6244)

Lake City
WDSR-AM - 1340　(6271)

Lake Wales
WIPC-AM - 1280　(6287)

Lakeland
WLKF-AM - 1430　(6293)
WTWB-AM - 1570　(6296)

Marianna
WTOT-AM - 980　(6329)

TALK (continued)
WTYS-AM - 1340 (6330)

Melbourne
WTAI-AM - 1560 (6339)

Miami
WLRN-FM - 91.3 (6402)
WMRZ-AM - 790 (6407)
WQAM-AM - 560 (6413)

Milton
WEBY-AM - 1330 (6426)

Ocala
WMOP-AM - 900 (6476)
WOCA-AM - 1370 (6477)

Orlando
WDBO-AM - 580 (6515)

Ormond Beach
WELE-AM - 1380 (6534)

Pensacola
WTKX-FM - 101.5 (6578)

Port St. Lucie
WAXE-AM - 1370 (6602)
WPSL-AM - 1590 (6604)
WZZR-FM - 92.7 (6606)

Punta Gorda
WCCF-AM - 1580 (6609)

St. Augustine
WFOY-AM - 1240 (6620)

St. Petersburg
WSUN-AM - 620 (6640)

Sarasota
WSPB-AM - 1450 (6674)
WTMY-AM - 1280 (6676)

Sebring
WWTK-AM - 730 (6683)

Tallahassee
WNLS-AM - 1270 (6752)

Tampa
WFLA-AM - 970 (6789)
WHNZ-AM - 1250 (6793)
WQYK-AM - 1010 (6800)

Tavares
WKIQ-AM - 1240 (6813)

Titusville
WAMT-AM - 1060 (6822)
WPGS-AM - 840 (6823)

Vero Beach
WTTB-AM - 1490 (6839)

West Palm Beach
WPBR-AM - 1340 (6857)

Winter Haven
WHNR-AM - 1360 (6875)

Zolfo Springs
WZTK-AM - 1480 (6895)

GEORGIA
Albany
WALG-AM - 1590 (6906)

Americus
WISK-AM - 1390 (6925)

Athens
WGAU-AM - 1340 (6956)

Atlanta
WAOK-AM - 1380 (7068)
WLTA-AM - 1400 (7076)
WNIV-AM - 970 (7077)
WQXI-AM - 790 (7081)
WSB-AM - 750 (7085)
WUNV-FM - 91.7 (7089)

Augusta
WFAM-AM - 1050 (7108)

Bainbridge
WMGR-AM - 930 (7120)

Bogart
WRFC-AM - 960 (7136)

Cartersville
WYXC-AM - 1270 (7163)

Cleveland
WRWH-AM - 1350 (7176)

Columbus
WDAK-AM - 540 (7187)

Dalton
WBLJ-AM - 1230 (7223)
WDAL-AM - 1430 (7224)

Douglas
WDMG-AM - 860 (7247)
WDMG-FM - 99.5 (7248)

Gainesville
WDUN-AM - 550 (7301)

Griffin
WHIE-AM - 1320 (7314)

Hartwell
WKLY-AM - 980 (7322)

Jasper
WPGHY-AM - 1560 (7343)

Kingsland
WOKF-FM - 92.5 (7359)

LaGrange
WTRP-AM - 620 (7365)

Macon
WBNM-AM - 1120 (7391)
WMAC-AM - 940 (7397)

Madison
WYTH-AM - 1250 (7406)

Marietta
WFTD-AM - 1080 (7424)

Milledgeville
WKGQ-AM - 1060 (7438)

Rome
WLAQ-AM - 1410 (7505)
WRGA-AM - 1470 (7507)

Statesboro
WWNS-AM - 1240 (7568)

Swainsboro
WXRS-AM - 1590 (7579)

Valdosta
WJEM-AM - 1150 (7622)

HAWAII
Hilo
KPUA-AM - 670 (7677)

Honolulu
KAIM-AM - 870 (7729)
KWAI-AM - 1080 (7756)
KZOO-AM - 1210 (7758)

Lihue
KQNG-AM - 570 (7782)

IDAHO
Boise
KBXL-FM - 94.1 (7820)
KIDO-AM - 580 (7823)
KSPD-AM - 790 (7830)
KWEI-AM - 1260 (7832)

Chubbuck
KRCD-FM - 1490 (7843)

Idaho Falls
KID-AM - 590 (7874)

Lewiston
KCLK-AM - 1430 (7894)

Pocatello
KBRV-AM - 790 (7949)
KSEI-AM - 930 (7954)

Rupert
KBAR-AM - 1230 (7968)

St. Maries
KOFE-AM - 1240 (7973)

Salmon
KSRA-AM - 92.7 (7975)

Soda Springs
KBRV-AM - 790 (7983)

Twin Falls
KCIR-FM - 90.7 (7992)
KEZJ-AM - 1450 (7993)

KLIX-AM - 1310 (7995)

ILLINOIS
Alton
WBGZ-AM - 1570 (8011)

Aurora
WBIG-AM - 1280 (8042)

Berkeley
WJJG-AM - 1530 (8074)

Champaign
WDWS-AM - 1400 (8225)

Chicago
WCKG-FM - 105.9 (8618)
WGN-AM - 720 (8625)
WKIE-FM - 92.7 (8633)
WLS-AM - 890 (8638)
WVON-AM - 1450 (8658)
WYLL-AM - 1160 (8663)

Crest Hill
WJOL-AM - 1340 (8690)

Danville
WDAN-AM - 1490 (8705)

Decatur
WDZ-AM - 1050 (8716)
WSOY-AM - 1340 (8720)

Effingham
WCRA-AM - 1090 (8819)

Elgin
WRMN-AM - 1410 (8829)

Fairfield
WFIW-AM - I390 (8881)

Galesburg
WGIL-AM - 1400 (8910)

Herrin
WJPF-AM - 1340 (8984)

Highland
WCBW-AM - 880 (8990)

Jacksonville
WJIL-AM - 1550 (9026)
WLDS-AM - 1180 (9028)

Kewanee
WKEI-AM - 1450 (9047)

Marion
WDDD-AM - 810 (9145)

Metropolis
WNPX-AM - 750 (9181)

Monmouth
WRAM-AM - 1330 (9221)

Murphysboro
WINI-AM - 1420 (9259)

Olney
WVLN-AM - 740 (9385)

Pittsfield
WBBA-AM - 1580 (9456)

Plano
WSPY-FM - 107.1 (9459)

Princeton
WZOE-AM - 1490 (9468)

Quincy
WTAD-AM - 930 (9483)

Rockford
WROK-AM - 1440 (9541)

Sparta
WHCO-AM - 1230 (9618)

Sterling
WSDR-AM - 1240 (9664)

Streator
WSPL-AM - 1250 (9670)

Taylorville
WTIM-FM - 97.3 (9680)

Urbana
WILL-AM - 580 (9723)

Winnetka
WNTH-FM - 88.1 (9769)

INDIANA
Auburn
WGLL-AM - 1570 **(9790)**

Bloomington
WGCL-AM - 1370 **(9858)**

Columbus
WCSI-AM - 1010 **(9896)**

Daleville
WHBU-AM - 1240 **(9918)**

Elkhart
WFRN-AM - 1270 **(9925)**

Evansville
WGBF-AM - 1280 **(9942)**

Fort Wayne
WOWO-AM - 1190 **(9991)**

Gary
WGVE-FM - 88.7 **(10019)**

Hammond
WIMS-AM - 1420 **(10056)**
WJOB-AM - 1230 **(10057)**

Indianapolis
WBRI-AM - 1500 **(10191)**
WFYI-FM - 90.1 **(10195)**
WNDE-AM - 1260 **(10203)**

Linton
WBTO-FM - 93.3 **(10274)**

Marion
WGOM-AM - 860 **(10291)**

Merrillville
WLTH-AM - 1370 **(10301)**

New Albany
WXLN-AM - 1570 **(10341)**

New Castle
WMDH-AM - 1550 **(10344)**

North Vernon
WNVI-AM - 1460 **(10365)**

Richmond
WHON-AM - 930 **(10424)**
WKBV-AM - 1490 **(10425)**

Salem
WSLM-FM - 97.9 **(10443)**

South Bend
WETL-FM - 91.7 **(10461)**
WSBT-AM - 960 **(10466)**

Terre Haute
WBOW-AM - 1300 **(10495)**
WSDX-AM - 1130 **(10501)**
WTHI-AM - 1480 **(10502)**

Valparaiso
WNWI-AM - 1080 **(10514)**

Vincennes
WAOV-AM - 1450 **(10524)**

West Lafayette
WBAA-AM - 920 **(10556)**

IOWA
Ames
KASI-AM - 1430 **(10596)**

Burlington
KCPS-AM - 1150 **(10642)**

Cedar Falls
KCNZ-AM - 1250 **(10665)**

Cedar Rapids
WMT-AM - 600 **(10685)**

Clinton
KROS-AM - 1340 **(10713)**

Council Bluffs
KLNG-AM - 1560 **(10728)**

Davenport
WOC-AM - 1420 **(10751)**

Des Moines
KWKY-AM - 1150 **(10833)**
WHO-AM - 1040 **(10837)**

Dubuque
KDTH-AM - 1370 **(10848)**
WDBQ-AM - 1490 **(10854)**

Estherville
KILR-AM - 1070 **(10879)**

Fairfield
KMCD-AM - 1570 **(10886)**

Iowa City
WSUI-AM - 910 **(10998)**

Keokuk
KOKX-AM - 1310 **(11014)**

Marshalltown
KFJB-AM - 1230 **(11068)**

Ottumwa
KLEE-AM - 1480 **(11142)**

Sheldon
KIWA-AM - 1550 **(11196)**
KIWA-FM - 105.3 **(11197)**

Sioux City
KSCJ-AM - 1360 **(11219)**
KWSL-AM - 1470 **(11226)**

Spencer
KDWD-FM - 100.1 **(11232)**
KICD-AM - 1240 **(11233)**

Waterloo
KXEL-AM - 1540 **(11301)**

Webster City
KQWC-AM - 1570 **(11315)**
KQWC-FM - 95.7 **(11316)**

KANSAS
Chanute
KKOY-AM - 1460 **(11378)**

Garden City
KBUF-AM - 1030 **(11451)**

Goodland
KLOE-AM - 730 **(11467)**

Great Bend
KVGB-AM - 1590 **(11473)**

Hutchinson
KWBW-AM - 1450 **(11507)**

Kansas City
KCNW-AM - 1380 **(11537)**

Lawrence
KLWN-AM - 1320 **(11575)**

Manhattan
KMAN-AM - 1350 **(11633)**

Overland Park
KCCV-AM - 760 **(11739)**
KCCV-FM - 92.3 **(11740)**

Parsons
KLKC-AM - 1540 **(11745)**
KLKC-FM - 93.5 **(11746)**

Salina
KSAL-AM - 1150 **(11789)**

Topeka
KMAJ-AM - 1440 **(11841)**
WIBW-AM - 580 **(11846)**

Wellington
KLEY-AM - 1130 **(11867)**

Westwood
KMBZ-AM - 980 **(11872)**

Wichita
KFH-AM - 1330 **(11897)**
KNSS-AM - 1240 **(11900)**

KENTUCKY
Bowling Green
WBGN-AM - 1340 **(11951)**
WKCT-AM - 930 **(11958)**

Columbia
WAIN-AM - 1270 **(12018)**

Corbin
WKDP-AM - 1330 **(12024)**

Danville
WHIR-AM - 1230 **(12041)**

Elizabethtown
WIEL-AM - 1400 **(12047)**

Elkton
WEKT-AM - 1070 **(12052)**

Lexington
WLAP-AM - 630 **(12190)**

London
WFTG-AM - 1400 **(12204)**

Louisville
WFPL-FM - 89.3 **(12251)**
WHAS-AM - 840 **(12252)**
WKJK-AM - 1080 **(12256)**
WLSY-FM - 94.7 **(12260)**
WNAI-AM - 680 **(12261)**
WSOH-FM - 88.3 **(12265)**

Manchester
WTBK-FM - 105.7 **(12280)**

Murray
WNBS-AM - 1340 **(12320)**

Owensboro
WOMI-AM - 1490 **(12331)**

Paducah
WKYX-AM - 570 **(12346)**

Pikeville
WJSO-FM - 90.1 **(12362)**

Somerset
WSFC-AM - 1240 **(12410)**
WTLO-AM - 1480 **(12412)**

LOUISIANA
Baton Rouge
WJBO-AM - 1150 **(12518)**

Lafayette
KPEL-FM - 105.1 **(12630)**
KVOL-AM - 1330 **(12633)**
KVOL-FM - 105.9 **(12634)**

Metairie
WGSO-AM - 990 **(12681)**
WVOG-AM - 600 **(12686)**

Monroe
KLIC-AM - 1230 **(12696)**
KMLB-AM - 1440 **(12698)**

Natchitoches
KNOC-AM - 1450 **(12719)**

New Orleans
WSHO-AM - 800 **(12776)**
WSMB-AM - 1350 **(12777)**
WWL-AM - 870 **(12780)**

Shreveport
KBCL-AM - 1070 **(12822)**
KEEL-AM - 710 **(12824)**

Slidell
WSLA-AM - 1560 **(12845)**

Vidalia
KVLA-AM - 1400 **(12864)**

Winnfield
KVCL-AM - 1270 **(12881)**

MAINE
Bangor
WHCF-FM - 88.5 **(12908)**
WJCX-FM - 99.5 **(12910)**
WZON-AM - 620 **(12916)**

Norway
WKTQ-AM - 1450 **(12994)**
WTME-AM - 780 **(12996)**

Portland
WLOB-AM - 1310 **(13028)**

Sanford
WSME-AM - 1220 **(13051)**

South Portland
WGAN-AM - 560 **(13054)**
WZAN-AM - 970 **(13057)**

Topsham
WBCI-FM - 105.9 **(13067)**

MARYLAND
Annapolis
WBIS-AM - 1190 **(13098)**

Baltimore
WBAL-AM - 1090 **(13265)**

Circulation: ★ = ABC; △ = BPA; ♦ = CAC; • = CCAB; □ = VAC; ⊕ = PO Statement; ‡ = Publisher's Report; Boldface figures = sworn; Light figures = estimated.

3081

TALK (continued)

WEAA-FM - 88.9 (13270)
WJHU-FM - 88.1 (13276)

Chestertown
WCTR-AM - 1530 (13406)

Cumberland
WCBC-AM - 1270 (13476)
WNTR-AM - 1230 (13478)

Easton
WEMD-AM - 1460 (13491)

Frostburg
WFRB-AM - 560 (13528)

Hagerstown
WARK-AM - 1490 (13573)
WHAG-AM - 1410 (13575)

Lanham
WOL-AM - 1450 (13611)

Lexington Park
WMDM-AM - 1690 (13617)

Salisbury
WICO-AM - 1320 (13715)

Silver Spring
WTEM-AM - 980 (13748)

Thurmont
WTHU-AM - 1450 (13756)

MASSACHUSETTS
Boston
WBZ-AM - 1030 (13979)
WEZE-AM - 590 (13984)
WRKO-AM - 680 (13994)

Brockton
WBET-AM - 1460 (14014)

Chicopee
WACE-AM - 730 (14137)

Fairhaven
WBSM-AM - 1420 (14178)

Fitchburg
WEIM-AM - 1280 (14185)

Lowell
WCAP-AM - 980 (14281)

Methuen
WCCM-AM - 1490 (14329)
WHAV-AM - 1490 (14330)

Newton
WNTN-AM - 1550 (14413)

Northampton
WHMP-AM - 1400 (14432)

Orange
WCAT-AM - 700 (14452)

Paxton
WTAG-AM - 580 (14460)

Pittsfield
WBEC-AM - 1420 (14473)

Salem
WESX-AM - 1230 (14516)

Somerset
WHTB-AM - 1400 (14528)
WSAR-AM - 1480 (14529)

Springfield
WNNZ-AM - 640 (14562)
WVNE-AM - 760 (14565)

Taunton
WPEP-AM - 1570 (14585)

West Yarmouth
WXTK-FM - 95.1 (14634)

Woods Hole
WCAI-FM - 90.1 (14674)

Worcester
WGFP-AM - 940 (14697)

MICHIGAN
Adrian
WABJ-AM - 1490 (14711)

Alpena
WATZ-AM - 1450 (14736)

Ann Arbor
WAAM-AM - 1600 (14774)
WDEO-AM - 990 (14777)
WTKA-AM - 1050 (14780)
WUOM-FM - 91.7 (14781)

Battle Creek
WBCK-AM - 930 (14794)

Big Rapids
WBRN-AM - 1460 (14820)

Cadillac
WATT-AM - 1240 (14844)

Detroit
WJR-AM - 760 (14968)
WMUZ-FM - 103.5 (14972)

Dowagiac
WDOW-AM - 1440 (14978)

East Lansing
WKAR-AM - 870 (14995)

Escanaba
WCHT-AM - 600 (15009)

Flint
WFDF-AM - 910 (15042)

Fremont
WSHN-AM - 1550 (15061)

Grand Rapids
WMFN-AM - 640 (15115)
WOOD-AM - 1300 (15118)
WTKG-AM - 1230 (15123)
WVGR-FM - 104.1 (15125)

Hancock
WMPL-AM - 920 (15142)

Holland
WPNW AM - 1260 (15178)

Iron Mountain
WMIQ-AM - 1450 (15209)

Ironwood
WJMS-AM - 590 (15216)

Ishpeming
WIAN-AM - 1240 (15218)

Jackson
WKHM-AM - 970 (15226)

Kalamazoo
WKMI-AM - 1360 (15252)
WKZO-AM - 590 (15254)

Lansing
WJIM-AM - 1240 (15300)
WVFN-AM - 730 (15306)

Lapeer
WLSP-AM - 1530 (15310)

Ludington
WKLA-AM - 1450 (15323)

Manistee
WMTE-AM - 1340 (15332)

Marquette
WDMJ-AM - 1320 (15340)

Mount Pleasant
WMMI-AM - 830 (15384)

Petoskey
WJML-AM - 1110 (15438)
WMKT-AM - 1270 (15441)
WWKK-AM - 750 (15442)

Rochester
WPON-AM - 1460 (15467)

Rogers City
WVXA-FM - 96.7 (15471)

Saginaw
WCEN-AM - 1150 (15495)
WKNX-AM - 1250 (15501)
WSGW-AM - 790 (15505)

St. Joseph
WSJM-AM - 1400 (15516)

Sault Sainte Marie
WKNW-AM - 1400 (15529)

Southfield
WKRK-FM - 97.1 (15559)

Sterling Heights
WUFL-AM - 1030 (15578)

Tawas City
WIOS-AM - 1480 (15586)

Traverse City
WNMC-FM - 90.7 (15612)
WTCM-AM - 580 (15614)

MINNESOTA
Albany
KASM-AM - 1150 (15705)

Albert Lea
KATE-AM - 1450 (15707)

Bemidji
KBUN-AM - 1450 (15743)
KKBJ-AM - 1360 (15745)

Brainerd
KLIZ-AM - 1380 (15769)
WWWI-AM - 1270 (15771)

Crookston
KROX-AM - 1260 (15821)

Duluth
WDSM-AM - 710 (15855)

Eveleth
KRBT-AM - 1340 (15885)

Fergus Falls
KBRF-AM - 1250 (15900)

Forest Lake
WLKX-FM - 95.9 (15907)

Hastings
KDWA-AM - 1460 (15942)

Hibbing
WHLB-AM - 1400 (15956)
WNMT-AM - 650 (15960)

Little Falls
KLTF-AM - 960 (16008)

Mankato
KTOE-AM - 1420 (16035)

New Ulm
KNUJ-AM - 860 (16217)

Park Rapids
KPRM-AM - 870 (16258)

Red Wing
KCUE-AM - 1250 (16294)

Rochester
KOLM-AM - 1520 (16316)
KROC-AM - 1340 (16318)
KWEB-AM - 1270 (16321)

St. Cloud
KNSI-AM - 1450 (16351)
WJON-AM - 1240 (16353)

St. Paul
WDGY-AM - 630 (16427)

St. Peter
KRBI-AM - 1310 (16432)

Waseca
KOWZ-AM - 1170 (16501)

Willmar
KWLM-AM - 1340 (16522)

Worthington
KWOA-AM - 730 (16541)

MISSISSIPPI
Amory
WAMY-AM - 1580 (16547)

Belzoni
WELZ-AM - 1460 (16560)

Biloxi
WVMI-AM - 570 (16570)

Cleveland
WDSK-AM - 1410 (16593)

Columbia
WCJU-AM - 1450 (16600)

Columbus
WKOR-AM - 980 (16611)

Numbers cited in bold after listings are entry numbers rather than page numbers.

Greenwood
WABG-AM - 960 (16647)

Holly Springs
WURC-FM - 88.1 (16684)

Jackson
WJDX-AM - 620 (16718)
WJNT-AM - 1180 (16719)

Meridian
WALT-AM - 910 (16772)
WFFX-AM - 1450 (16773)

Monticello
WMLC-AM - 1270 (16790)

Philadelphia
WHOC-AM - 1490 (16817)

Senatobia
WKNA-FM - 88.9 (16843)

Tupelo
WELO-AM - 580 (16851)

MISSOURI
Ava
KKOZ-AM - 1430 (16897)
KKOZ-FM - 92.1 (16898)

Cameron
KMRN-AM - 1360 (16940)

Cape Girardeau
KZIM-AM - 960 (16954)

Clinton
KDKD-AM - 1280 (16985)

Columbia
KFRU-AM - 1400 (17017)
KOPN-FM - 89.5 (17020)

Farmington
KREI-AM - 800 (17055)

Festus
KJFF-AM - 1400 (17066)

Hannibal
KHMO-AM - 1070 (17091)

Jefferson City
KLIK-AM - 1240 (17139)

Joplin
KQYX-AM - 1450 (17148)

Kansas City
KCUR-FM - 89.3 (17208)

Kirksville
KIRX-AM - 1450 (17230)

Lebanon
KBNN-AM - 750 (17239)

Liberty
KCXL-AM - 1140 (17250)

Mexico
KJAB-FM - 88.3 (17286)

Mountain Grove
KELE-AM - 1360 (17301)

Osage Beach
KRMS-AM - 1150 (17322)

Richmond
KAYX-FM - 92.5 (17376)

St. Louis
KEZK-FM - 98.1 (17538)
KMOX-AM - 1120 (17543)
KSIV-AM - 1320 (17550)
KTRS-AM - 550 (17551)
WGNU-AM - 920 (17556)

Sedalia
KSIS-AM - 1050 (17574)

Sikeston
KSIM-AM - 1400 (17587)

Springfield
KWTO-AM - 560 (17633)

Sullivan
KTUI-AM - 1560 (17642)

Washington
KLPW-AM - 1220 (17708)

MONTANA
Billings
KBLG-AM - 910 (17737)

Havre
KOJM-AM - 610 (17814)

Helena
KBLL-AM - 1240 (17825)
KCAP-AM - 1340 (17827)

Kalispell
KOFI-AM - 1180 (17842)

Laurel
KBSR-AM - 1490 (17847)

Missoula
KGRZ-AM - 1450 (17881)

NEBRASKA
Alliance
KCOW-AM - 1400 (17929)

Columbus
KTTT-AM - 1510 (17984)

Cozad
KAMI-AM - 1580 (17987)

Fremont
KHUB-AM - 1340 (18014)

Holdrege
KUVR-AM - 1380 (18051)

Kearney
KGFW-AM - 1340 (18061)

Lincoln
KLCV-FM - 88.5 (18135)
KLIN-AM - 1400 (18136)

McCook
KSWN-FM - 93.9 (18159)

Norfolk
WJAG-AM - 780 (18174)

North Platte
KODY-AM - 1240 (18182)

Omaha
KFAB-AM - 1110 (18217)
KKAR-AM - 1290 (18221)

NEVADA
Carson City
KPTL-AM - 1300 (18333)

Las Vegas
KDWN-AM - 720 (18394)
KKVV-AM - 1060 AM (18398)
KNUU-AM - 970 (18402)
KSHP-AM - 1400 (18404)
KXNT-AM - 840 (18409)

Reno
KPTT-AM - 630 (18437)
KUNR-FM - 88.7 (18442)

NEW HAMPSHIRE
Claremont
WTSV-AM - 1230 (18467)

Concord
WKXL-AM - 1450 (18478)
WTPL-FM - 107.7 (18481)

Dover
WTSN-AM - 1270 (18496)

Gilford
WEMJ-AM - 1490 (18512)

Keene
WKNE-AM - 1290 (18533)

Littleton
WLTN-AM - 1400 (18551)

Manchester
WGIR-AM - 610 (18569)

Nashua
WSMN-AM - 1590 (18608)

New London
WNTK-AM - 1020 (18610)
WNTK-FM - 99.7 (18611)

Portsmouth
WGIN-AM - 930 (18639)
WGIP-AM - 1540 (18640)

Winchester
WKBK-AM - 1290 (18651)

NEW JERSEY
Glassboro
WGLS-FM - 89.7 (18845)

Hackettstown
WRNJ-AM - 1510 (18860)

Jersey City
WFMU-FM - 91.1 (19149)

Linwood
WOND-AM - 1400 (19174)

Millville
WMVB-AM - 1440 (19237)

New Brunswick
WCTC-AM - 1450 (19342)

Northfield
WFPG-AM - 1450 (19382)

Pompton Lakes
WGHT-AM - 1500 (19450)

Trenton
WKXW-FM - 101.5 (19676)

NEW MEXICO
Alamogordo
KINN-AM - 1270 (19759)
KRSY-AM - 1230 (19760)

Albuquerque
KDAZ-AM - 730 (19796)

Artesia
KSVP-AM - 990 (19818)

Carlsbad
KCCC-AM - 930 (19825)

Clovis
KICA-AM - 980 (19833)

Farmington
KENN-AM - 1390 (19847)

Hobbs
KHOB-AM - 1390 (19866)

Las Cruces
KOBE-AM - 1450 (19884)

Los Alamos
KRSN-AM - 1490 (19895)

Pinehill
KTDB-FM - 89.7 (19904)

Roswell
KBIM-AM - 910 (19915)

Silver City
KNFT-AM - 950 (19954)

Tucumcari
KTNM-AM - 1400 (19973)

NEW YORK
Albany
WGY-AM - 810 (20011)

Avon
WYSL-AM - 1030 (20110)

Batavia
WBTA-AM - 1490 (20122)

Binghamton
WNBF-AM - 1290 (20227)

Brentwood
WXBA-FM - 88.1 (20241)

Clinton
WHCL-FM - 88.7 (20475)

Corning
WCLI-AM - 1450 (20507)

Deer Park
WLIE-AM - 540 (20522)

Elmira
WQIX-AM - 820 (20579)
WWLZ-AM - 820 (20580)

Fulton
WZZZ-AM - 1300 (20633)

Circulation: ★ = ABC; △ = BPA; ♦ = CAC; • = CCAB; ❑ = VAC; ⊕ = PO Statement; ‡ = Publisher's Report; Boldface figures = sworn; Light figures = estimated.

Radio Station Formats

3083

TALK (continued)

Hartsdale
WFAS-AM - 1230 **(20714)**

Hornell
WHHO-AM - 1320 **(20756)**
WLEA-AM - 1480 **(20758)**

Horseheads
WENY-AM - 1230 **(20761)**

Ithaca
WHCU-AM - 870 **(20818)**

Jamestown
WJTN-AM - 1240 **(20844)**

Lockport
WLVL-AM - 1340 **(20958)**

Massena
WYBG-AM - 1050 **(21029)**

Nanuet
WRCR-AM - 1300 **(21106)**

New Rochelle
WVOX-AM - 1460 **(21125)**

New York
WABC-AM - 770 **(22960)**
WEVD-AM - 1050 **(22968)**
WNWK-FM - 105.9 **(22978)**
WNYC-AM - 820 **(22979)**
WOR-AM - 710 **(22983)**

Newark
WACK-AM - 1420 **(22998)**

Newburgh
WGNY-AM - 1200 **(23002)**

Olean
WMNS-AM - 1360 **(23042)**
WMXO-FM - 101.5 **(23043)**

Ossining
WOSS-FM - 91.1 **(23060)**

Oswego
WRVO-FM - 89.9 **(23064)**

Pomona
WRKL-AM - 910 **(23113)**

Rochester
WHAM-AM - 1180 **(23247)**
WXXI-AM - 1370 **(23258)**

Springville
WSPQ-AM - 1330 **(23356)**

Syracuse
WSYR-AM - 570 **(23445)**

Trumansburg
WPIE-AM - 1160 **(23464)**

Vestal
WENE-AM - 1430 **(23490)**

Walton
WDLA-FM - 92.1 **(23499)**

Warsaw
WCJW-AM - 1140 **(23507)**

Watertown
WATN-AM - 1240 **(23515)**

NORTH CAROLINA
Aberdeen
WQNX-AM - 1350 **(23612)**

Belmont
WCGC-AM - 1270 **(23643)**

Burlington
WBAG-AM - 1150 **(23674)**

Chapel Hill
WUNC-FM - 91.5 **(23732)**

Charlotte
WBT-AM - 1110 **(23764)**
WBT-FM - 99.3 **(23765)**

Clinton
WRRZ-AM - 880 **(23791)**

Dallas
WZRH-AM - 960 **(23798)**

Durham
WTIK-AM - 1310 **(23852)**

Edenton
WZBO-AM - 1260 **(23859)**

Elizabeth City
WGAI-AM - 560 **(23862)**

Elkin
WIFM-AM - 100.9 **(23869)**

Fayetteville
WFNC-AM - 640 **(23886)**

Graham
WSML-AM - 1200 **(23913)**

Greensboro
WTCK-AM - 1320 **(23958)**

Greenville
WCZI-FM - 98.3 **(23971)**
WOOW-AM - 1340 **(23975)**

Hickory
WHKY-AM - 1290 **(23991)**
WIRC-AM - 630 **(23993)**

High Point
WGOS-AM - 1070 **(24002)**
WMFR-AM - 1230 **(24005)**

Jacksonville
WLAS-AM - 910 **(24014)**

King
WKTE-AM - 1090 **(24024)**

Lexington
WLXN-AM - 1440 **(24041)**

Mayodan
WLOE-AM - 1490 **(24061)**
WMYN-AM - 1420 **(24062)**

Monroe
WIXE-AM - 1190 **(24067)**

New Bern
WLOJ-AM - 1490 **(24100)**

Newport
WTKF-FM - 107.3 **(24105)**

Newton
WNNC-AM - 1230 **(24107)**

Pisgah Forest
WGCR-AM - 720 **(24117)**

Raleigh
WRBZ-AM - 850 **(24171)**

Roanoke Rapids
WPTM-FM - 102.3 **(24196)**

Rutherfordton
WCAB-AM - 590 **(24212)**

Salisbury
WSTP-AM - 1490 **(24218)**

Southern Pines
WEEB-AM - 990 **(24237)**

Washington
WDLX-AM - 930 **(24274)**

Whiteville
WTXY-AM - 1540 **(24287)**

Williamston
WIAM-AM - 900 **(24292)**

Wilmington
WAAV-FM - 94.1 **(24299)**
WMFD-AM - 630 **(24303)**

Winston-Salem
WSJS-AM - 600 **(24332)**
WSNC-FM - 90.5 **(24333)**
WTOB-AM - 1380 **(24334)**

NORTH DAKOTA
Fargo
KFGO-AM - 790 **(24419)**
KVOX-AM - 1280 **(24430)**
WDAY-AM - 970 **(24434)**

Grand Forks
KNOX-AM - 1310 **(24462)**
KZLT-FM - 104.3 **(24464)**

Jamestown
KSJB-AM - 600 **(24481)**

OHIO
Akron
WNIR-FM - 100.1 **(24599)**

Ashtabula
WFUN-AM - 970 **(24625)**

Athens
WOUB-AM - 1340 **(24632)**

Bellaire
WOMP-AM - 1290 **(24663)**

Bellefontaine
WBLL-AM - 1390 **(24667)**

Boardman
WKBN-AM - 570 **(24685)**
WNIO-AM - 1540 **(24687)**

Bucyrus
WBCO-AM - 1540 **(24719)**

Canton
WRCW-AM - 1060 **(24737)**

Cincinnati
WCKY-AM - 1360 **(24836)**
WKRC-AM - 550 **(24841)**
WLW-AM - 700 **(24843)**
WTSJ-AM - 1050 **(24847)**

Cleveland
WCCD-AM - 1000 **(24968)**
WTAM-AM - 1100 **(24986)**

Columbus
WFII-AM - 1230 **(25079)**
WOSU-AM - 820 **(25082)**
WTVN-AM - 610 **(25088)**

Coshocton
WTNS-FM - 99.3 **(25098)**

Dayton
WING-AM - 1410 **(25143)**

East Liverpool
WOHI-AM - 1490 **(25173)**

Findlay
WFIN-AM - 1330 **(25196)**

Fostoria
WFOB-AM - 1430 **(25200)**

Lima
WCIT-AM - 940 **(25299)**
WIMA-AM - 1150 **(25301)**

Mansfield
WMAN-AM - 1400 **(25335)**

Marion
WMRN-AM - 1490 **(25354)**

Middletown
WPFB-AM - 910 **(25379)**

Newark
WCLT-AM - 1430 **(25427)**
WHTH-AM - 790 **(25429)**
WNKO-FM - 101.7 **(25430)**

Oxford
WMUB-FM - 88.5 **(25463)**

Painesville
WBKC-AM - 1460 **(25465)**

Portsmouth
WPAY-AM - 1400 **(25487)**

Springfield
WBLY-AM - 1600 **(25535)**

Steubenville
WSTV-AM - 1340 **(25543)**

Toledo
WCWA-AM - 1230 **(25575)**
WSPD-AM - 1370 **(25585)**

Uhrichsville
WBTC-AM - 1540 **(25600)**

Willoughby
WELW-AM - 1330 **(25665)**

Youngstown
WBBW-AM - 1240 **(25703)**
WGFT-FM - 101.1 **(25705)**

OKLAHOMA
Ada
KADA-FM - 99.3 **(25726)**

Numbers cited in bold after listings are entry numbers rather than page numbers.

Altus
KKVO-FM - 90.9 (25734)

Alva
KALV-AM - 1430 (25739)

Ardmore
KVSO-AM - 1240 (25749)

Bartlesville
KWON-AM - 1400 (25755)

Chickasha
KWCO-AM - 105.5 (25786)

Duncan
KRHD-AM - 1350 (25801)

Enid
KCRC-AM - 1390 (25825)
KGWA-AM - 960 (25826)

Hugo
KITX-FM - 95.5 (25874)

Idabel
KBEL-AM - 1240 (25876)

Lawton
KRX-AM - 1050 (25895)

Norman
KGOU-FM - 106.3 (25945)
KROU-FM - 105.7 (25947)

Oklahoma City
KQCV-AM - 800 (26013)
KTOK-AM - 1000 (26017)

Ponca City
KOKB-AM - 1580 (26042)

Stillwater
KSPI-AM - 780 (26085)

Tulsa
KQLL-AM - 1430 (26160)
KRMG-AM - 740 (26163)

OREGON
Albany
KLOO-AM - 1340 (26210)

Ashland
KAGI-AM - 930 (26219)
KCMX-AM - 580 (26220)

Astoria
KAST-AM - 1370 (26227)

Baker City
KBKR-AM - 1490 (26234)

Bend
KBND-AM - 1110 (26244)

Clackamas
KKGT-AM - 1150 (26267)

Coquille
KWRO-AM - 630 (26284)

The Dalles
KACI-AM - 1300 (26301)

Eugene
KPNW-AM - 1120 (26344)
KUGN-AM - 590 (26346)

Hillsboro
KUIK-AM - 1360 (26375)

Klamath Falls
KAGO-AM - 1150 (26389)

La Grande
KLBM-AM - 1450 (26401)

Lebanon
KGAL-AM - 1580 (26409)

Medford
KMED-AM - 1440 (26424)

Newport
KNPT-AM - 1310 (26448)

Ontario
KSRV-AM - 1380 (26456)

Pendleton
KUMA-AM - 1290 (26461)

Portland
KFXX-AM - 910 (26526)
KKSL-AM - 1290 (26531)
KPDQ-AM - 800 (26535)

KPDQ-FM - 93.7 (26536)
KWJJ-AM - 1080 (26544)

Roseburg
KQEN-AM - 1240 (26558)
KTBR-AM - 950 (26561)
KTBR-FM - 94.1 (26562)

Salem
KYKN-AM - 1430 (26576)

Tillamook
KMBD-AM - 1590 (26598)
KTIL-FM - 94.1 (26599)

PENNSYLVANIA
Allentown
WHOL-AM - 1600 (26632)

Altoona
WRTA-AM - 1240 (26641)
WVAM-AM - 1430 (26643)

Bala Cynwyd
WPHT-AM - 1210 (26678)
WWDB-FM - 96.5 (26681)

Beaver Falls
WBVP-AM - 1230 (26686)
WMBA-AM - 1460 (26687)

Bloomsburg
WBUQ-FM - 91.1 (26720)
WCNR-AM - 930 (26721)

Butler
WISR-AM - 680 (26746)

Carnegie
WOHZ-AM - 1600 (26765)

Du Bois
WCED-AM - 1420 (26839)

Harrisburg
WHP-AM - 580 (27016)

Johnstown
WNTJ-AM - 96.5 (27096)

Lafayette Hill
WFIL-AM - 560 (27137)

Lancaster
WLCH-FM - 91.3 (27154)

Lansdale
WNPV-AM - 1440 (27161)

Millersville
WIXQ-FM - 91.7 (27268)

Milton
WMLP-AM - 1380 (27271)

New Castle
WKST-AM - 1200 (27318)

North Versailles
WKHB-AM - 620 (27343)

Philadelphia
WHAT-AM - 1340 (27732)
WHYY-FM - 90.9 (27733)
WPHE-AM - 690 (27738)

Philipsburg
WPHB-AM - 1260 (27751)

Pittsburgh
KDKA-AM - 1020 (27858)
WEAE-AM - 1250 (27865)
WESA-AM - 940 (27866)
WORD-FM - 101.5 (27868)
WPIT-AM - 730 (27870)

Pittston
WGBI-AM - 910 (27888)
WILK-AM - 980 (27890)
WOGY-AM - 1300 (27892)

Pottstown
WPAZ-AM - 1370 (27902)

Reading
WEEU-AM - 830 (27921)

Shiremanstown
WWII-AM - 720 (27995)

State College
WRSC-AM - 1390 (28029)

Uniontown
WMBS-AM - 590 (28068)

White Oak
WEDO-AM - 810 (28158)

Whitehall
WAEB-AM - 790 (28159)

Williamsport
WRAK-AM - 1400 (28190)

York
WSBA-AM - 910 (28216)

PUERTO RICO
Arecibo
WCMN-AM - 1280 (28224)
WMIA-AM - 1070 (28226)

Cabo Rojo
WEKO-AM - 930 (28234)

Juana Diaz
WCGB-AM - 1060 (28253)

Mayaguez
WKJB-AM - 710 (28262)
WTPM-FM - 92.9 (28270)

Ponce
WEUC-AM - 1420 (28275)
WPAB-AM - 550 (28280)

San Juan
WKAQ-AM - 580 (28302)
WQII-AM - 1140 (28307)
WSKN-AM - 630 (28310)

Utuado
WUPR-AM - 1530 (28319)

Yabucoa
WXEW-AM - 840 (28322)

Yauco
WKFE-AM - 1550 (28323)

RHODE ISLAND
East Providence
WPRO-AM - 630 (28348)

Newport
WADK-AM - 1540 (28374)

Providence
WALE-AM - 990 (28431)
WDOM-FM - 91.3 (28433)
WHJJ-AM - 920 (28434)
WXIN-FM - 90.7 (28441)

Woonsocket
WNRI-AM - 1380 (28462)

SOUTH CAROLINA
Anderson
WAIM-AM - 1230 (28476)
WRIX-FM - 103.1 (28477)

Burnettown
WKRU-AM - 1510 (28498)

Columbia
WVOC-AM - 560 (28586)

Florence
WJMX-AM - 970 (28607)

Fountain Inn
WFIS-AM - 1600 (28614)

Greenville
WORD-AM - 1330 (28639)

North Augusta
WGUS-AM - 1380 (28721)

North Charleston
WTMA-AM - 1250 (28728)
WTMZ-AM - 910 (28729)

Rock Hill
WRHI-AM - 1340 (28748)

Spartanburg
WSPA-AM - 950 (28762)

Sumter
WDXY-AM - 1240 (28770)

SOUTH DAKOTA
Aberdeen
KKAA-AM - 1560 (28796)
KSDN-AM - 930 (28798)

Circulation: ★ = ABC; △ = BPA; ◆ = CAC; ● = CCAB; ❑ = VAC; ⊕ = PO Statement; ‡ = Publisher's Report; Boldface figures = sworn; Light figures = estimated.

3085

TALK (continued)

Milbank
KDIO-AM - 1350 (28894)

Mitchell
KORN-AM - 1490 (28903)

Rapid City
KLMP-FM - 97.9 (28945)
KOTA-AM - 1380 (28946)

Sioux Falls
KELO-AM - 1320 (28974)
KWSN-AM - 1230 (28987)

Watertown
KSDR-AM - 1480 (29023)
KWAT-AM - 950 (29025)

Yankton
KYNT-AM - 1450 (29044)

TENNESSEE
Alcoa
WBCR-AM - 1470 (29048)

Athens
WYXI-AM - 1390 (29053)

Bluff City
WHCB-FM - 91.5 (29056)

Bolivar
WBOL-AM - 1560 (29058)

Chattanooga
WGOW-AM - 1150 (29105)

Cookeville
WATX-AM - 1590 (29147)

Crossville
WAEW-AM - 1330 (29160)

Erwin
WEMB-AM - 1420 (29185)

Fayetteville
WYTM-FM - 105.5 (29192)

Gray
WJCW-AM - 910 (29209)

Jackson
WDXI-AM - 1310 (29234)
WNWS-FM - 101.5 (29238)
WTJS-AM - 1390 (29239)
WWYN-FM - 106.9 (29241)

Johnson City
WETS-FM - 89.5 (29256)

Knoxville
WNOX-AM - 990 (29296)

Lebanon
WJKM-AM - 1090 (29322)

Martin
WCMT-AM - 1410 (29344)

Memphis
WCRV-AM - 640 (29389)
WKNQ-FM - 90.7 (29401)
WLOK-AM - 1340 (29402)
WMC-AM - 790 (29403)
WREC-AM - 600 (29410)

Murfreesboro
WGNS-AM - 1450 (29436)

Nashville
WENO-AM - 760 (29509)
WFSK-FM - 88.1 (29510)
WKDA-AM - 1200 (29514)
WLAC-AM - 1510 (29518)
WTN-FM - 99.7 (29536)
WWTN-FM - 99.7 (29538)

Portland
WQKR-AM - 1270 (29570)

Shelbyville
WZNG-AM - 1400 (29603)

Union City
WQAK-FM - 105.7 (29636)

Winchester
WCDT-AM - 1340 (29648)

TEXAS
Abilene
KWKC-AM - 1340 (29668)

Amarillo
KGNC-AM - 710 (29709)
KTNZ-AM - 1010 (29717)

Arlington
WBAP-AM - 820 (29744)

Austin
KJCE-AM - 1370 (29867)
KLBJ-AM - 590 (29870)
KTAE-AM - 1260 (29877)

Beaumont
KLVI-AM - 560 (29906)
KOLE-AM - 1340 (29907)

Big Spring
KBYG-AM - 1400 (29926)

Brownwood
KXYL-FM - 96.9 (29972)

College Station
WTAW-AM - 1620 (30061)

Corpus Christi
KEYS-AM - 1440 (30083)
KKTX-AM - 1360 (30087)

Crockett
KIVY-AM - 1290 (30107)

Dallas
KLIF-AM - 570 (30208)

Del Rio
KWMC-AM - 1490 (30229)

Edinburg
KURV-AM - 710 (30274)

El Paso
KELP-AM - 1590 (30289)
KROD-AM - 600 (30299)
KSVE-AM - 1150 (30301)

Freer
KBRA-FM - 95.9 (30368)

Galveston
KGBC-AM - 1540 (30383)

Garland
KXVI-AM - 91.1 (30387)

Harlingen
KVJY-AM - 840 (30431)

Houston
KCOH-AM - 1430 AM (30546)
KSEV-AM - 700 (30574)
KTEK-AM - 1110 (30576)
KTRH-AM - 740 (30579)
KXYZ-AM - 1320 (30586)

Irving
KWRD-FM - 100.7 (30612)

Jacksonville
KEBE-AM - 1400 (30617)

Johnson City
KNAF-AM - 910 (30628)

Laredo
KLAR-AM - 1300 (30675)

Lubbock
KFYO-AM - 790 (30725)
KJTV-AM - 950 (30727)

Lufkin
KSFA-AM - 860 (30744)

Marshall
KCUL-AM - 1410 (30768)

Midland
KJBC-AM - 1150 (30818)
KMND-AM - 1510 (30822)

Muleshoe
KMUL-AM - 1380 (30847)

Paris
KPLT-AM - 1490 (30908)

Plainview
KKYN-AM - 1090 (30941)

San Angelo
KKSA-AM - 1260 (31019)

San Antonio
KSLR-AM - 630 (31072)
KTSA-AM - 550 (31076)
WOAI-AM - 1200 (31079)

Seguin
KWED-AM - 1580 (31097)

Silsbee
KSET-AM - 1300 (31108)

Temple
KTEM-AM - 1400 (31181)

Terrell
KPYK-AM - 1570 (31183)

Texarkana
KEWL-AM - 1400 (31186)
KTFS-AM - 940 (31190)

Tyler
KEES-AM - 1430 (31210)
KTBB-AM - 600 (31217)
KYZS-AM - 1490 (31220)

Victoria
KAMG-AM - 1340 (31237)

Waco
KRZI-AM - 1580 (31260)
KWTX-AM - 1230 (31263)

Wharton
KANI-AM - 1500 (31286)

UTAH
Blanding
KUTA-AM - 790 (31321)

Cedar City
KSUB-AM - 590 (31328)

Heber City
KTMP-AM - 1340 (31338)

Hooper
KSVN-AM - 730 (31339)

Logan
KVNU-AM - 610 (31363)

Ogden
KLO-AM - 1430 (31381)

Price
KOAL-AM - 750 (31395)

Salt Lake City
KSL-AM - 1160 (31457)

South Jordan
KTKK-AM - 630 (31473)

Spanish Fork
KHQN-AM - 1480 (31475)

Vernal
KVEL-AM - 920 (31485)

West Valley City
KALL-AM - 910 (31487)

VERMONT
Barre
WSNO-AM - 1450 (31492)

Bennington
WBTN-AM - 1370 (31503)

Brattleboro
WKVT-AM - 1490 (31510)

Colchester
WVMT-AM - 620 (31533)

St. Albans
WWSR-AM - 1420 (31592)

VIRGINIA
Ashland
WHAN-AM - 1430 (31858)

Bedford
WBLT-AM - 1350 (31863)

Blacksburg
WCBX-AM - 900 (31886)
WVTW-FM - 88.5 (31890)

Bristol
WXBQ-AM - 980 (31900)

Brookneal
WODI-AM - 1230 (31906)

Charlottesville
WINA-AM - 1070 (31952)
WVTU-FM - 89.3 (31957)

Chase City
WMEK-AM - 980　(31961)

Danville
WVOV-AM - 970　(31995)

Emporia
WEVA-AM - 860　(32002)

Fairfax
WJFK-AM - 1300　(32035)

Farmville
WAMF-AM - 1490　(32069)
WFLO-AM - 870　(32070)

Front Royal
WFTR-AM - 1450　(32097)

Harrisonburg
WHBG-AM - 1360　(32144)
WKCY-AM - 1300　(32146)
WSVA-AM - 550　(32153)

Lexington
WREL-AM - 1450　(32195)

Lynchburg
WBRG-AM - 1050　(32211)
WLLL-AM - 930　(32213)

Martinsville
WMVA-AM - 1450　(32238)

Norfolk
WTAR-AM - 850　(32306)

Norton
WNVA-AM - 1350　(32312)

Onley
WESR-AM - 1330　(32319)

Radford
WFNR-AM - 710　(32348)
WNNI-AM - 1260　(32349)

Richmond
WVNZ-AM - 990　(32487)

Roanoke
WFIR-AM - 960　(32497)
WVTR-FM - 91.9　(32508)

South Boston
WSBV-AM - 1560　(32533)

Stuart
WHEO-AM - 1270　(32565)

Winchester
WINC-AM - 1400　(32631)

WASHINGTON
Aberdeen
KBKW-AM - 1450　(32648)

Bellingham
KGMI-AM - 790　(32682)

Centralia
KELA-AM - 1470　(32706)

Ellensburg
KXLE-AM - 1240　(32752)

Ephrata
KULE-AM - 730　(32757)

Everett
KRKO-AM - 1380　(32762)

Kennewick
KTCR-AM - 1340　(32792)

Lynnwood
KSER-FM - 90.7　(32826)

Moses Lake
KBSN-AM - 1470　(32841)

Mount Vernon
KSVR-FM - 90.1　(32849)

Newport
KUBS-FM - 91.5　(32852)

Port Angeles
KONP-AM - 1450　(32889)

Pullman
KQQQ-AM - 1150　(32912)

Seattle
KGNW-AM - 820　(33053)
KIRO-AM - 710　(33056)
KLFE-AM - 1590　(33058)

KOMO-AM - 1000　(33066)
KVI-AM - 570　(33073)

Spokane
KQDI-AM - 1450　(33124)
KXLY-AM - 920　(33134)

Tacoma
KLAY-AM - 1180　(33157)

Wenatchee
KPQ-AM - 560　(33201)

Yakima
KIT-AM - 1280　(33230)

WEST VIRGINIA
Beckley
WWNR-AM - 620　(33246)

Bluefield
WHIS-AM - 1440　(33257)
WTZE-AM - 1470　(33260)

Charleston
WCHS-AM - 580　(33282)
WQBE-AM - 97.5　(33284)

Elkins
WDNE-AM - 1240　(33308)

Huntington
WRVC-AM - 930　(33344)

Kingwood
WFSP-AM - 1560　(33360)

Martinsburg
WRNR-AM - 740　(33383)

Morgantown
WAJR-AM - 1440　(33400)

New Martinsville
WETZ-AM - 1330　(33415)

Sutton
WSGB-AM - 1490　(33478)

Vienna
WLTP-AM - 1450　(33481)

Wheeling
WWVA-AM - 1170　(33510)

WISCONSIN
Altoona
WAYY-AM - 790　(33524)

Appleton
WHBY-AM - 1150　(33549)

Beaver Dam
WBEV-AM - 1430　(33569)

Black River Falls
WWIS-AM - 1260　(33592)

Brookfield
WRRD-AM - 540　(33607)

Eau Claire
WMEQ-AM - 880　(33682)

Fond du Lac
KFIZ-AM - 1450　(33699)

Fort Atkinson
WFAW-AM - 940　(33724)

Green Bay
WHID-FM - 88.1　(33749)
WNFL-AM - 1440　(33752)

Janesville
WCLO-AM - 1230　(33864)

Madison
WHIT-AM - 1550　(33994)
WHWC-FM - 88.3　(33995)
WORT-FM - 89.9　(34007)

Marshfield
WDLB-AM - 1450　(34028)

Medford
WIGM-AM - 1490　(34035)

Merrill
WJMT-AM - 730　(34046)

Milwaukee
WISN-AM - 1130　(34119)
WMCS-AM - 1290　(34128)
WTMJ-AM - 620　(34135)

Portage
WPDR-AM - 1350　(34263)

Racine
WRJN-AM - 1400　(34278)

Ripon
WRPN-AM - 1600　(34305)

Sheboygan
WHBL-AM - 1330　(34324)

Shell Lake
WCSW-AM - 940　(34327)

Sparta
WKLJ-AM - 1290　(34335)

Stevens Point
WSPT-AM - 1010　(34345)

Superior
KUWS-FM - 91.3　(34362)

Tomahawk
WJJQ-AM - 810　(34374)

Wausau
WSAU-AM - 550　(34438)
WXCO-AM - 1230　(34440)

West Bend
WBKV-AM - 1470　(34447)

Wisconsin Rapids
WFHR-AM - 1320　(34466)

WYOMING
Cheyenne
KFBC-AM - 1240　(34502)

Cody
KODI-AM - 1400　(34515)

Laramie
KOWB-AM - 1290　(34556)

ALBERTA, CANADA
Calgary
CHQR-AM - 770　(34667)

BRITISH COLUMBIA, CANADA
Crawford Bay
CKKC-FM - 101.9　(34938)

Creston
CFKC-AM - 1340　(34940)

Kelowna
CBTK-FM - 88.9　(34990)

Nelson
CKKC-AM - 880　(35026)

Port Alberni
CJAV-AM - 1240　(35050)

Trail
CJAT-FM - 95.7　(35116)

Vancouver
CKNW-AM - 980　(35194)
CKST-AM - 1040　(35195)

Victoria
CFAX-AM - 1070　(35232)

MANITOBA, CANADA
Thompson
CBWK-FM - 100.9　(35302)

Winnipeg
CJOB-AM - 680　(35372)

NEW BRUNSWICK, CANADA
Fredericton
CBZ-AM - 970　(35399)

NEWFOUNDLAND AND LABRADOR, CANADA
St. John's
VOCM-AM - 590　(35504)

NORTHWEST TERRITORIES, CANADA
Rankin Inlet
CBQR-FM - 105.1　(35521)

Yellowknife
CFYK-AM - 1340　(35529)
CKLB-FM - 101.9　(35530)

Radio Station Formats

TALK (continued)

NOVA SCOTIA, CANADA
Halifax
CJCH-AM - 920   (35576)
CKDU-FM - 97.5   (35578)

ONTARIO, CANADA
Kingston
CFRC-FM - 101.9   (35953)
CKLC-AM - 1380   (35954)

Kitchener
CKGL-AM - 570   (35966)

London
CFPL-AM - 980   (35996)
CJBK-AM - 1290   (36002)

Ottawa
CBOF-FM - 90.7   (36285)
CFGO-AM - 1200   (36288)

Owen Sound
CFOS-AM - 560   (36300)
CFPS-AM - 1490   (36301)

Peterborough
CFFF-FM - 92.7   (36320)
CKRU-AM - 980   (36324)

St. Catharines
CKTB-AM - 610   (36359)

Toronto
CBL-AM - 1927   (36799)
CFRB-AM - 1010   (36805)

Windsor
CBC-AM - 1550   (36894)
CKLW-AM - 800   (36899)

QUEBEC, CANADA
Amqui
CFVM-AM - 99.9   (36936)

Chicoutimi
CBJ-FM - 93.7   (36969)
CBJE-FM - 102.7   (36970)

La Sarre
CKLS-AM - 1240   (37023)

Montreal
CBF-AM - 690   (37239)
CINQ-FM - 102.3   (37245)
CJAD-AM - 800   (37247)

Plessisville
CKYQ-FM - 95.7   (37270)

Quebec
CJMF-FM - 93.3   (37302)

Roberval
CHRL-FM - 99.5   (37320)

Sainte-Foy
CHRC-AM - 800   (37379)

Sept-Iles
CBSI-FM - 98.1 FM   (37387)
CKCN-FM - 94.1   (37388)

Sherbrooke
CHLT-AM - 630   (37397)

Trois-Rivieres
CHLN-AM - 550   (37418)

Westmount
CKAM-AM - 990   (37449)

SASKATCHEWAN, CANADA
Regina
CJME-AM - 980   (37542)

TEJANO

ARIZONA
Tucson
KXEW-AM - 1600   (1002)

TEXAS
Austin
KKLB-FM - 92.5   (29868)

Big Spring
KBYG-AM - 1400   (29926)

Del Rio
KTJK-AM - 1230   (30228)

Hereford
KPAN-AM - 860   (30446)
KPAN-FM - 106.3   (30447)

Lubbock
KXTQ-FM - 93.7   (30738)

Victoria
KVLT-FM - 92.3   (31241)

TOP 40

ALABAMA
Athens
WZYP-FM - 104.3   (32)

Montgomery
WBAM-FM - 98.9   (384)

ALASKA
Unalaska
KIAL-AM - 1450   (645)

ARIZONA
Lake Havasu City
KBBC-FM - 101.1   (738)

Phoenix
KPHX-AM - 1480   (833)
KZON-FM - 101.5   (845)

ARKANSAS
El Dorado
KLBQ-FM - 99.3   (1110)

Little Rock
KQAR-FM - 100.3   (1250)

CALIFORNIA
Brawley
KSIQ-FM - 96.1   (1598)

Burbank
KIIS-AM - 102.7   (1625)
KIIS-FM - 102.7   (1626)

Hanford
KIGS-AM - 620   (2039)

San Francisco
KDNZ-FM - 88.7   (3478)

San Luis Obispo
KSLY-FM - 96.1   (3574)

COLORADO
Windsor
KVVS-AM - 1170   (4689)

CONNECTICUT
Somers
WDJW-FM - 89.7   (5131)

FLORIDA
Miami
WPOW-FM - 96.5   (6412)

Wauchula
WAUC-AM - 1310   (6842)

GEORGIA
Milledgeville
WGUR-FM - 88.9   (7437)

Savannah
WAEV-FM - 97.3   (7542)

IDAHO
Payette
KIOV-AM - 1450   (7944)

Rupert
KZDX-FM - 99.9   (7970)

Salmon
KSRA-AM - 92.7   (7975)

ILLINOIS
Mattoon
WLKL-FM - 89.9   (9162)

Peru
WIVQ-FM - 103.3   (9453)

Sterling
WSSQ-FM - 94.3   (9665)

Waukegan
WXLC-FM - 102.3   (9747)

INDIANA
Jasper
WITZ-AM - 990   (10221)
WITZ-FM - 104.7   (10222)

IOWA
Ames
KCCQ-FM - 105.1   (10597)

Bloomfield
KOJY-FM - 106.9   (10623)

Dubuque
KLYV-FM - 105.3   (10852)

Iowa City
KKRQ-FM - 100.7   (10992)

Spencer
KDWD-FM - 100.1   (11232)

KANSAS
Baldwin City
KNBU-FM - 89.7   (11352)

KENTUCKY
Harlan
WTUK-FM - 105.1   (12108)

Manchester
WTBK-FM - 105.7   (12280)

Whitesburg
WIFX-FM - 94.3   (12440)

LOUISIANA
Lafayette
KSMB-FM - 94.5   (12632)

Monroe
KXUL-FM - 91.1   (12703)

MASSACHUSETTS
Beverly
WNSH-AM - 1570   (13844)

North Adams
WNAW-AM - 1230   (14421)

Walpole
WSRB-FM - 91.5   (14595)

Winchester
WHSR-FM - 91.9   (14668)

MICHIGAN
Bloomfield Hills
WBFH-FM - 88.1   (14831)

Kalamazoo
WKFR-FM - 103.3   (15251)

MINNESOTA
Marshall
KKCK-FM - 99.7   (16046)

St. Louis Park
KDXL-FM - 106.5   (16362)

MISSISSIPPI
Jackson
WDBT-FM - 95.5   (16717)

MISSOURI
Poplar Bluff
KJEZ-FM - 95.5   (17358)

St. Louis
WKBQ-FM - 104.1   (17557)

NEBRASKA
Kearney
KQKY-FM - 105.9   (18066)

Lincoln
KSLI-FM - 104.1   (18144)

NEW HAMPSHIRE
Concord
WJYY-FM - 105.5 **(18477)**

NEW JERSEY
Atlantic City
WZBZ-FM - 99.3 **(18661)**

Camden
WSSJ-AM - 1310 **(18717)**

Franklin Lakes
WRRH-FM - 88.7 **(18836)**

Lawrenceville
WRRC-FM - 107.7 **(19166)**

Manahawkin
WBBO-FM - 98.5 **(19211)**

NEW MEXICO
Clayton
KLMX-AM - 1450 **(19829)**

NEW YORK
Endwell
WMRV-FM - 105.7 **(20589)**

New York
WPLJ-FM - 95.5 **(22986)**

Paul Smiths
WPSA-FM - 98.3 **(23084)**

NORTH CAROLINA
Cullowhee
WWCU-FM - 90.5 **(23796)**

Mars Hill
WVMH-FM - 90.5 **(24058)**

New Bern
WRHT-FM - 96.3 **(24101)**

Sylva
WRGC-AM - 680 **(24252)**

NORTH DAKOTA
Fargo
WDAY-AM - 970 **(24435)**

OHIO
Alliance
WZKL-FM - 92.5 **(24608)**

Athens
WOUB-AM - 1340 **(24632)**

Bellevue
WNRR-FM - 92.1 **(24672)**

Boardman
WMXY-FM - 98.9 **(24686)**

OKLAHOMA
Oklahoma City
KJYO-FM - 102.7 **(26004)**

OREGON
Seaside
KSWB-AM - 840 **(26581)**

PENNSYLVANIA
Greenville
WEXC-FM - 107.1 **(26960)**

Hanover
WYCR-FM - 98.5 **(26980)**

New Wilmington
WWNW-FM - 88.9 **(27326)**

North East
WRTS-FM - 103.7 **(27342)**

Pittsburgh
WPPJ-AM - 670 **(27871)**
WZKT-FM - 98.3 **(27883)**

Pittston
WKRZ-FM - 98.5 **(27891)**

Schnecksville
WXLV-FM - 90.3 **(27950)**

Tyrone
WTRN-AM - 1340 **(28065)**

Wilkes Barre
WBHD-FM - 94.3 **(28170)**

PUERTO RICO
Arecibo
WCMN-FM - 107.3 **(28225)**

Cidra
WBRQ-FM - 97.7 **(28240)**

Coamo
WCPR-AM - 1450 **(28241)**

Fajardo
WDOY-FM - 96.5 **(28243)**
WMDD-AM - 1480 **(28244)**

Lares
WGDL-AM - 1200 **(28254)**

Mayaguez
WORA-AM - 760 **(28265)**
WPRA-AM - 990 **(28268)**

Ponce
WPRP-AM - 910 **(28282)**
WZAR-FM - 101.9 **(28284)**
WZBS-AM - 1490 **(28285)**

San Juan
WKAQ-FM - 104.7 **(28303)**
WZNT-FM - 93.7 **(28313)**

Utuado
WUPR-AM - 1530 **(28319)**

RHODE ISLAND
East Providence
WPRO-FM - 92.3 **(28349)**

SOUTH CAROLINA
Florence
WJMX-FM - 103.3 **(28608)**

SOUTH DAKOTA
Winner
KWYR-FM - 93.7 **(29034)**

Yankton
KVHT-FM - 106.3 **(29042)**

TENNESSEE
Dickson
WQZQ-FM - 102.5 **(29168)**

Fayetteville
WYTM-FM - 105.5 **(29192)**

Harrogate
WLMU-FM - 91.3 **(29217)**

Humboldt
WLSQ-FM - 94.3 **(29227)**

Nashville
WMDB-AM - 880 **(29520)**

Waynesboro
WWON-AM - 930 **(29645)**

TEXAS
Dallas
KHKS-FM - 106.1 **(30206)**

UTAH
Pleasant Grove
KPGR-FM - 88.1 **(31391)**

VERMONT
Barre
WORK-FM - 107.1 **(31491)**

VIRGINIA
Farmville
WMLU - 91.3 **(32072)**

Grundy
WMJD-FM - 97.7 **(32122)**

Richmond
WCDX-FM - 92.10 **(32473)**

WASHINGTON
Mercer Island
KMIH-FM - 104.5 **(32830)**

Tacoma
KVTI-FM - 90.9 **(33160)**

WEST VIRGINIA
Elkins
WELK-FM - 94.7 **(33310)**

Wheeling
WPHP-FM - 91.9 **(33508)**

WISCONSIN
La Crosse
WIZM-FM - 93.3 **(33890)**

WYOMING
Worland
KKLX-FM - 96.1 **(34605)**

BRITISH COLUMBIA, CANADA
Prince George
CKKN-FM - 101.3 **(35061)**

Vernon
CJIB-AM - 940 **(35204)**

Victoria
CIOC-FM - 98.5 **(35235)**

NEW BRUNSWICK, CANADA
Edmundston
CFAI-FM - 101.1 **(35386)**

NEWFOUNDLAND AND LABRADOR, CANADA
Grand Falls
CKIM-AM - 1240 **(35464)**

ONTARIO, CANADA
Belleville
CJOJ-FM - 95.5 **(35683)**

Ottawa
CKKL-FM - 93.9 **(36294)**

Sudbury
CHNO-FM - 103.9 **(36422)**

Toronto
CDIC-FM - 103.5 **(36801)**

QUEBEC, CANADA
Degelis
CFVD-FM - 95.5 **(36985)**

Montreal
CKMF-FM - 94.3 **(37249)**

Riu-Du-Loup
CIBM-FM - 107.1 **(37312)**

Sherbrooke
CIMO-FM - 106.1 **(37398)**

SASKATCHEWAN, CANADA
Prince Albert
CFMM-FM - 99.1 **(37519)**

URBAN CONTEMPORARY

ALABAMA
Birmingham
WBHK-FM - 98.7 **(106)**

Carrollton
WRAG-AM - 590 **(147)**

Decatur
WAJF-AM - 1490 **(171)**

Evergreen
KDKO-AM - 1510 **(210)**

Florence
WSBM-AM - 1340 **(225)**

Greenville
WKXN-FM - 95.9 **(245)**

Huntsville
WDJL-AM - 1000 **(281)**
WEUP-AM - 1600 **(282)**

Mobile
WBLX-FM - 92.9 **(337)**

Oxford
WARB-AM - 1580 **(416)**

Circulation: ★ = ABC; △ = BPA; ♦ = CAC; • = CCAB; ❑ = VAC; ⊕ = PO Statement; ‡ = Publisher's Report; Boldface figures = sworn; Light figures = estimated.

3089

URBAN CONTEMPORARY (continued)

Selma
WJUS-AM - 1310 **(455)**

Spanish Fort
WMMV-FM - 105.5 **(459)**

Tuscaloosa
WTUG-FM - 92.9 **(502)**

York
WSLY-FM - 104.9 **(517)**

ARIZONA
Phoenix
KISO-AM - 1230 **(823)**

ARKANSAS
Hope
KXAR-FM - 101.7 **(1182)**

Little Rock
KIPR-FM - 92.3 **(1243)**
KOKY-FM - 102.1 **(1249)**

North Little Rock
KLRG-AM - 1150 **(1301)**
KMZX-FM - 106.3 **(1303)**

Pine Bluff
KCAT-AM - 1340 **(1315)**

West Helena
KCLT-FM - 104.9 **(1368)**

CALIFORNIA
Inglewood
KJLH-FM - 102.3 **(2074)**

San Francisco
KDNZ-FM - 88.7 **(3478)**

San Rafael
KSRH-FM - 88.1 **(3606)**

Whittier
KACD-FM - 103.1 **(4081)**

COLORADO
Colorado Springs
KKMG-FM - 98.9 **(4273)**

CONNECTICUT
Danbury
WRNE-AM - 980 **(4767)**

Hartford
WQTQ-FM - 89.9 **(4909)**

New Haven
WYBC-FM - 94.3 **(5015)**

Windsor
WKND-AM - 1480 **(5235)**

DELAWARE
Wilmington
WJKS-FM - 101.7 **(5301)**

DISTRICT OF COLUMBIA
Washington
WHUR-FM - 96.3 **(5884)**
WPGC-FM - 95.5 **(5892)**

FLORIDA
Belle Glade
WSWN-AM - 900 **(5922)**

Fort Lauderdale
WEXY-AM - 1520 **(6090)**

Hollywood
WEDR-FM - 99.1 **(6200)**

Lakeland
WWAB-AM - 1330 **(6297)**

Naples
WPJS-AM - 1330 **(6453)**

St. Petersburg
WRXB-AM - 1590 **(6639)**

South Daytona
WPUL-AM - 1590 **(6685)**

Stuart
WRBD-AM - 1470 **(6697)**

Tallahassee
WAMF-FM - 90.5 **(6742)**
WHBX-FM - 96.1 **(6751)**

Tampa
WTMP-AM - 1150 **(6804)**

GEORGIA
Athens
WBKZ-AM - 880 **(6955)**

Augusta
WAKB-FM - 96.9 **(7106)**

Fort Valley
WFXM-FM - 100.1 **(7289)**

Hinesville
WSGA-FM - 104.7 **(7336)**

Irwinton
WVKX-FM - 103.7 **(7338)**

Jackson
WJGA-FM - 92.1 **(7340)**

Statesboro
WVGS-FM - 91.9 **(7567)**

Thomasville
WHGH-AM - 840 **(7588)**

Valdosta
WGOV-AM - 950 **(7621)**
WVVS-FM - 90.9 **(7626)**

ILLINOIS
Champaign
WPCD-FM - 88.7 **(8232)**

Chicago
WEJM-FM - 106.3 **(8620)**
WGCI-FM - 107.5 **(8624)**
WIIT - 88.9 **(8629)**
WVAZ-FM - 102.7 **(8657)**

Urbana
WBCP-AM - 1580 **(9721)**

INDIANA
Franklin
WIJY-FM - 95.9 **(10010)**

Indianapolis
WSYW-AM - 810 **(10210)**

IOWA
Cedar Falls
KUNI-FM - 90.9 **(10668)**

Davenport
KALA-FM - 88.5 **(10740)**

Iowa City
KRUI-FM - 89.7 **(10993)**

Oskaloosa
KIGC-FM - 88.7 **(11138)**

KANSAS
Winfield
KSWC-FM - 100.3 **(11912)**

LOUISIANA
Alexandria
KBCE-FM - 102.3 **(12461)**

Baton Rouge
KQXL-FM - 106.5 **(12509)**
WEMX-FM - 94.1 **(12517)**

Belle Chasse
KMEZ-FM - 102.9 **(12530)**

Grambling
KGRM-FM - 91.5 **(12588)**

Lafayette
KFXZ-FM - 106.3 **(12625)**
KJCB-AM - 770 **(12626)**
KRRQ-FM - 95.5 **(12631)**

Monroe
KRVV-FM - 100.1 **(12702)**
KYEA-FM - 98.3 **(12704)**

Natchitoches
KNWD-FM - 91.7 **(12720)**

New Orleans
WQUE-FM - 93.3 **(12774)**

WYLD-FM - 98.5 **(12786)**

Shreveport
KSCL-FM - 91.3 **(12834)**

MARYLAND
Baltimore
WEAA-FM - 88.9 **(13270)**
WWIN-FM - 95.9 **(13287)**

MASSACHUSETTS
Brockton
WBOT-FM - 97.7 **(14015)**

Deerfield
WGAJ-FM - 91.7 **(14158)**

Roxbury
WILD-AM - 1090 **(14510)**

Springfield
WAIC-FM - 91.9 **(14555)**

Waltham
WJMN-FM - 94.5 **(14608)**

Worcester
WCHC-FM - 88.1 **(14695)**

MICHIGAN
De Witt
WQHH-FM - 96.5 **(14899)**

Detroit
WGPR-FM - 107.5 **(14964)**
WJLB-FM - 97.9 **(14967)**
WMXD-FM - 92.3 **(14973)**
WQBH-AM - 1400 **(14974)**

Flint
WDZZ-FM - 92.7 **(15040)**

Highland Park
WHPR-FM - 88.1 **(15162)**

Kentwood
WJNZ-AM - 1680 **(15265)**

Lansing
WXLA-AM - 1180 **(15307)**

Saginaw
WTLZ-FM - 107.1 **(15506)**

Traverse City
WNMC-FM - 90.7 **(15612)**

MINNESOTA
Minneapolis
KMOJ-FM - 89.9 **(16151)**
KSGS-AM - 950 **(16153)**

MISSISSIPPI
Clarksdale
WAID-FM - 106.5 **(16589)**

Cleveland
WCLD-FM - 103.9 **(16592)**

Columbus
WACR-AM - 1050 **(16607)**
WACR-FM - 103.9 **(16608)**
WMXU-FM - 106.1 **(16613)**

Greenville
WBAD-FM - 94.3 **(16636)**
WESY-AM - 1580 **(16639)**

Greenwood
WKXG-AM - 1540 **(16650)**

Gulfport
WQFX-FM - 96.7 **(16657)**

Hattiesburg
WJMG-FM - 92.1 **(16673)**
WORV-AM - 1580 **(16676)**

Holly Springs
WKRA-FM - 92.7 **(16683)**

Jackson
WRJH-FM - 97.7 **(16729)**

Meridian
WNBN-AM - 1290 **(16778)**

Natchez
WTYJ-FM - 97.7 **(16797)**

Quitman
WBFN-AM - 1500 **(16830)**

Tupelo
WESE-FM - 92.5 (16852)

MISSOURI
Jefferson City
KJLU-FM - 88.9 (17136)

Marshall
KMVC-FM - 91.7 (17268)

St. Charles
KIRL-AM - 1460 (17386)

St. Louis
KMJM-FM - 104.9 (17541)

NEBRASKA
Omaha
KBBX-AM - 1420 (18212)

NEVADA
Las Vegas
KCEP-FM - 88.1 (18392)

NEW HAMPSHIRE
Concord
WSPS-FM - 90.5 (18480)

NEW JERSEY
Lawrenceville
WRRC-FM - 107.7 (19166)

NEW YORK
Cortland
WSUC-FM - 90.5 (20514)

Latham
WFLY-FM - 92.3 (20935)

New York
WBLS-FM - 107.5 (22963)
WHCR-FM - 90.3 (22970)
WRKS-FM - 98.7 (22991)

Oswego
WNYO-FM - 88.9 (23063)

Poughkeepsie
WPKF-FM - 96.1 (23161)

Woodside
WWRL-AM - 1600 (23594)

NORTH CAROLINA
Durham
WXDU-FM - 88.7 (23854)

Elizabeth City
WRVS-FM - 89.9 (23863)

Fayetteville
WIDU-AM - 1600 (23888)
WZFX-FM - 99.1 (23892)

Goldsboro
WFMC-AM - 730 (23911)

Greensboro
WJMH-FM - 102.1 (23948)
WNAA-FM - 90.1 (23954)

Raleigh
WQOK-FM - 97.5 (24168)

Roanoke Rapids
WSMY-AM - 1400 (24197)

Winston-Salem
WSNC-FM - 90.5 (24333)

OHIO
Cleveland
WZAK-FM - 93.1 (24992)

Elyria
WJTB-AM - 1040 (25181)

Toledo
WLQR-AM - 1470 (25581)

Youngstown
WRBP-AM - 1440 (25710)

OKLAHOMA
Langston
KALU-FM - 89.3 (25882)

Oklahoma City
KOKF-FM - 90.9 (26011)
KVSP-AM - 1140 (26019)

Tulsa
KYAL-AM - 1550 (26173)

PENNSYLVANIA
Bala Cynwyd
WDAS-FM - 105.3 (26672)

Bloomsburg
WBUQ-FM - 91.1 (26720)

Chester
WDNR-FM, Widener University - 89.5 (26776)

Conshohocken
WPHI-FM - 103.9 (26804)

Lincoln University
WLIU-FM - 88.7 (27201)

Millersville
WIXQ-FM - 91.7 (27268)

Philadelphia
WHAT-AM - 1340 (27732)
WKDU-FM - 91.7 (27737)
WUSL-FM - 98.9 (27746)

Pittsburgh
WPPJ-AM - 670 (27871)

RHODE ISLAND
Providence
WDOM-FM - 91.3 (28433)
WRBU-FM - 95.5 (28437)

SOUTH CAROLINA
Allendale
WDOG-AM - 1460 (28471)
WDOG-FM - 93.5 (28472)

Barnwell
WBAW-AM - 99.1 (28483)

Columbia
WWDM-FM - 103.1 (28587)

Laurens
WLBG-AM - 860 (28684)

North Augusta
WFXA-FM - 103.1 (28720)

Orangeburg
WQKI-FM - 93.9 (28736)

Spartanburg
WASC-AM - 1530 (28760)

Sumter
WKHT-FM - 93.7 (28772)

TENNESSEE
Bolivar
WBOL-AM - 1560 (29058)

Clarksville
WJMR-AM - 1370 (29119)

Jackson
WFKX-FM - 95.7 (29235)

Memphis
WDIA-AM - 1070 (29390)
WHRK-FM - 97.1 (29397)

Nashville
WFSK-FM - 88.1 (29510)
WMDB-AM - 880 (29520)
WQQK-FM - 92.1 (29527)

Springfield
WDBL-AM - 1590 (29619)

TEXAS
Austin
KAZI-FM - 88.7 (29860)

Grand Prairie
KKDA-FM - 104.5 (30407)

Harker Heights
KIIZ-AM - 1050 (30423)

Houston
KCOH-AM - 1430 AM (30546)
KMJQ-FM - 102.1 (30567)

Huntsville
KMHT-FM - 103.9 (30600)
KSHU-FM - 90.5 (30601)

San Antonio
KSJL-AM - 760 (31071)

Tyler
KZEY-AM - 690 (31221)

UTAH
Logan
KLGN-AM - 1390 (31359)

Ogden
KWCR-FM - 88.1 (31382)

VERMONT
Lyndonville
WWLR-FM - 91.5 (31551)

VIRGINIA
Charlottesville
WCHV-AM - 1260 (31949)

Farmville
WAMF-AM - 1490 (32069)

Hampden Sydney
WWHS-FM - 92.1 (32125)

Hampton
WARR-AM - 1520 (32131)
WHOV-FM - 88.1 (32133)

Lynchburg
WJJS-AM - 1320 (32212)

Norfolk
WMYK-FM - 92.1 (32303)

Richmond
WCDX-FM - 92.10 (32473)

WASHINGTON
Seattle
KRIZ-AM - 1420 (33069)

Tacoma
KZIZ-AM - 1420 (33161)

WISCONSIN
Janesville
WKPO-FM - 105.9 (33866)

Superior
KUWS-FM - 91.3 (34362)

QUEBEC, CANADA
Montreal
CKMF-FM - 94.3 (37249)

Quebec
CKRL-FM - 89.1 (37304)

Rouyn-Noranda
CJMM-FM - 99.1 (37323)

Val d'Or
CJMV-FM - 102.7 (37422)

WORLD BEAT

CALIFORNIA
San Diego
KSDS-FM - 88.3 (3314)

San Francisco
KCSF-FM - 90.9 (3476)

Turlock
KCSS-FM - 91.9 (3960)

CONNECTICUT
Sharon
WKZE-FM - 98.1 (5116)

IOWA
Fairfield
KHOE-FM - 90.5 (10884)

LOUISIANA
New Orleans
WWOZ-FM - 90.7 (12783)

Circulation: ★ = ABC; △ = BPA; ♦ = CAC; • = CCAB; ❏ = VAC; ⊖ = PO Statement; ‡ = Publisher's Report; Boldface figures = sworn; Light figures = estimated.

3091

WORLD BEAT (continued)

MASSACHUSETTS
Provincetown
WOMR-FM - 92.1 **(14487)**

NEVADA
Las Vegas
KUNV-FM - 91.5 **(18406)**

NEW HAMPSHIRE
Henniker
WNEC-FM - 91.7 **(18523)**

VIRGINIA
Harrisonburg
WEMC-FM - 91.7 **(32143)**

WASHINGTON
Bellevue
KBCS-FM - 91.3 **(32672)**

ZYDECO

LOUISIANA
Donaldsonville
KKAY-AM - 1590 **(12570)**
WKAY-AM - 1590 **(12571)**

Trade, Technical, and Professional Publications

Index entries are arranged by subject (please refer to the Index to Subject Terms). Within the subject groupings, entries appear geographically by states/provinces and alphabetically within cities. Citations in this index include publication title, entry numbers (given in parentheses), and circulation figures.

Circ.

ACCOUNTANTS AND ACCOUNTING

See also Banking, Finance, and Investments

ALABAMA
Tuscaloosa
Accounting Historians Journal **(480)**

CALIFORNIA
Berkeley
The International Journal of Accounting **(1529)**

Redwood City
California CPA **(2913)** ....‡29,000
(Controlled) ‡500

DISTRICT OF COLUMBIA
Washington
Bank Marketing **(5373)**
Community Banker **(5428)**

FLORIDA
Gainesville
Business & Professional Ethics
Journal **(6131)** 700
Professional Ethics **(6153)** ....(Paid) 700

Sarasota
Accounting Horizons **(6652)**
Accounting Review **(6653)** 10,000
Issues in Accounting Education **(6657)**

Tallahassee
Florida CPA Today **(6709)** ....(Controlled) 19,400

GEORGIA
Atlanta
Auditing **(6976)** ....(Paid) 2,400

HAWAII
Honolulu
Hawaii CPA News **(7693)** ....(Paid) 1,750

ILLINOIS
Chicago
Illinois CPA Insight **(8408)** ....‡25,000
Insight (Chicago) **(8417)** ....(Controlled) ⊕27,000
Journal of Accounting Research **(8428)**

Riverwoods
Federal Audit Guides **(9504)**

KANSAS
Pittsburg
Journal of Managerial
Issues **(11752)** ....(Controlled) 1,000

MARYLAND
Greenbelt
Spectrum (Greenbelt) **(13560)** ......(Controlled) 2,750

MICHIGAN
East Lansing
Behavioral Research in
Accounting **(14982)** ....(Paid) 1,800

Kalamazoo
Journal of International Accounting, Auditing and
Taxation **(15239)**

NEW JERSEY
Hoboken
The Journal of Corporate Accounting and
Finance **(19020)** 5985

Jersey City
CPA Client Bulletin **(19135)**
Journal of Accountancy **(19142)** ....(Paid) 371,491

Montvale
Strategic Finance **(19275)** ....(Paid) 63,750

NEW YORK
New York
Accounting Technology **(21135)** ....‡30,000
Bank Investment Marketing **(21286)**
The CPA Journal **(21509)** ....(Paid) 33,000
Journal of Accounting, Auditing &
Finance **(21973)** ....(Paid) 1,000
Journal of Construction Accounting and
Taxation **(22038)**
The Practical Accountant **(22589)** ....‡40,000
Practical Tax Strategies **(22591)** ....(Paid) ‡8831
(Non-paid) ‡115
Review of Accounting Studies **(22655)**

OHIO
Dublin
The Ohio CPA Journal **(25169)** ....‡18,500

OKLAHOMA
Shawnee
CPA Software News **(26062)** ....(Paid) 51,411

PENNSYLVANIA
Philadelphia
Pennsylvania CPA
Journal **(27621)** ....(Paid) ‡20,000
(Non-paid) ‡2,500

TEXAS
Austin
American Taxation Association
Journal **(29752)** ....(Paid) 1,500

Houston
Art Law & Accounting
Reporter **(30459)** ....(Paid) 1,500

VIRGINIA
Alexandria
National Public Accountant **(31713)** ....‡20,000

Arlington
The Exempt Organization Tax
Review **(31792)** ....‡1,000
Highlights and Documents **(31795)**
State Tax Notes **(31833)**

Springfield
The Cooperative Accountant **(32541)** ....‡2,500

WISCONSIN
Appleton
TAXPRO Quarterly Journal **(33545)** ....(Paid) 16,000
(Non-paid) 1,000

Circ.

BRITISH COLUMBIA, CANADA
Vancouver
Beyond Numbers **(35127)** ....(Controlled) ‡9,200
CGA Magazine **(35135)** ....(Combined) 56,863

ONTARIO, CANADA
Markham
The Bottom Line **(36015)** ....(Paid) ‡4,974
(Controlled) ‡25,399

Toronto
CA Magazine **(36483)** ....(Paid) 71,448
(Non-paid) 3,386
Contemporary Accounting
Research **(36559)** ....(Controlled) 1,225

Waterloo
Journal of Management Accounting
Research **(36853)** ....(Paid) 2,300

ACQUIRED IMMUNE DEFICIENCY SYNDROME

See also Medicine and Surgery; Health and Healthcare

CALIFORNIA
San Francisco
BETA (Bulletin of Experimental Treatments for
AIDS) **(3330)** ....(Non-paid) 25,000
Journal of Neuro-AIDS **(3383)** ....(Paid) 74

Thousand Oaks
Journal of the Association of Nurses in AIDS
Care **(3880)** ....(Paid) ‡3,000

CONNECTICUT
West Hartford
Journal of HIV/AIDS Prevention and Education for
Adolescents & Children **(5203)** ....(Paid) 125

GEORGIA
Atlanta
AIDS Weekly Plus **(6961)**

MARYLAND
Baltimore
Journal of Acquired Immune Deficiency Syndrome
(JAIDS) **(13177)** ....(Non-paid) ‡2,621

NEW YORK
Larchmont
AIDS PATIENT CARE and STDs **(20886)**
AIDS Research and Human Retroviruses **(20887)**

New York
Body Positive **(21330)** ....(Paid) 5,000
(Controlled) 10,000

PENNSYLVANIA
Philadelphia
AIDS **(27365)** ....(Paid) ‡2,804

WISCONSIN
Madison
Wisconsin AIDS Update **(33977)**

Circulation: ★ = ABC; △ = BPA; ◆ = CAC; ● = CCAB; ❏ = VAC; ⊕ = PO Statement; ‡ = Publisher's Report; Boldface figures = sworn; Light figures = estimated.

3093

Circ.   Circ.   Circ.

ADVERTISING AND MARKETING

See also Public Relations; Selling and Salesmanship

ALABAMA
Montgomery
Journal of Nonprofit & Public Sector
  Marketing **(368)** 451

ARIZONA
Phoenix
Exhibitor Times **(803)** ....(Combined) 13,623

CALIFORNIA
Berkeley
Journal of Relationship
  Marketing **(1536)** ....(Paid) 148
Services Marketing
  Quarterly **(1558)** ....(Controlled) ‡453

Los Angeles
Variety's on Production **(2428)** ....(Paid) ‡200
  (Controlled) ‡28,000

Menlo Park
Communication Arts **(2523)** ....(Paid) ‡70,189

Rocklin
Web Commerce Today **(2957)**
Web Marketing Today **(2958)**

Santa Ana
InfoText **(3628)** ....(Controlled) ‡18,000
Response TV **(3631)** ....(Paid) 700
  (Non-paid) 21,000

Santa Barbara
The Journal of Services Marketing **(3648)**

COLORADO
Centennial
Healthcare Advertising
  Review **(4224)** ....(Paid) ‡1,000

Golden
Advertising & Marketing
  Review **(4462)** ....(Combined) 3,300

Greenwood Village
Cable Avails **(4504)**

CONNECTICUT
Hartford
Industrial Marketing Management **(4895)** 1,304
The Journal of Private Enterprise **(4896)**

Norwalk
Telemarketing & Call Center
  Solutions **(5076)** ....(Paid) 2,170
  (Non-paid) 28,331

Stamford
Catalog Age **(5141)** ....(Paid) ★769
  (Non-paid) ★15,864
Direct **(5148)** ....(Combined) 36,582
Operations and Fulfillment **(5157)** .....(Paid) ‡13,000
PROMO **(5158)** ....(Paid) 3,710
  (Non-paid) 21,632

DISTRICT OF COLUMBIA
Washington
ABA Bank Marketing
  Magazine **(5310)** ....(Paid) ‡4,003
ASMC Sales & Marketing
  Magazine **(5369)** ....‡4,000
Bank Marketing **(5373)**
Gallup Poll Tuesday Briefing **(5504)** ....(Paid) 400
Sales & Marketing Ideas **(5776)** 14,000

FLORIDA
Boca Raton
Medical Marketing &
  Media **(5936)** ....(Controlled) ‡10,000

Coral Gables
Journal of the Academy of Marketing
  Science **(6009)** ....‡1,500

Fort Myers
SignCraft **(6098)** ....(Paid) ★12,947

Gainesville
Marketing Science **(6151)** ....‡1,960

Miami
The Flyer **(6354)** ....(Non-paid) ‡1,018,449

St. Petersburg
Maddux Report **(6630)** ....(Paid) 1,040
  (Controlled) 13,180

GEORGIA
Atlanta
Healthcare Marketing Report **(7015)**

Roswell
Point Of Purchase **(7516)** ....(Controlled) 19,500

ILLINOIS
Chicago
Advertising Age **(8245)** ....(Paid) ★64,018
Adweek/Midwest **(8246)** ....(Combined) 33,396
BtoB Magazine **(8294)** ....(Controlled) 45,000
Journal of Marketing
  Research **(8444)** ....(Paid) ‡8,000
Journal of Public Policy &
  Marketing **(8449)** ....(Paid) ‡472
Link **(8466)** ....(Paid) 2,022
  (Non-paid) 9,971
Marketing Health Services **(8477)** ......(Paid) ‡3781
  (Non-paid) ‡179
Marketing Management **(8478)** ....(Paid) ‡3118
  (Non-paid) ‡73
Marketing News **(8479)** ....(Paid) 25,030
  (Non-paid) 409
Marketing Research **(8480)** ....(Paid) ‡3305
  (Non-paid) ‡59
NPN International **(8513)** ....(Controlled) ‡7,500
Velocity **(8597)** ....(Controlled) 2,500
  4,000

Des Plaines
Consumer Magazine Advertising
  Source **(8754)** ....(Paid) 2,381

Skokie
P-O-P Design **(9608)** ....(Non-paid) △18,005
P-O-P Times **(9609)** ....(Non-paid) △19,379

Tinley Park
Money Maker's Monthly **(9686)** ......(Paid) ‡125,000
  (Non-paid) ‡125,000

IOWA
Ames
Journal of Advertising **(10590)**

Burlington
Ad Trends **(10636)**

KANSAS
Pittsburg
Journal of Managerial
  Issues **(11752)** ....(Controlled) 1,000

MARYLAND
Baltimore
NAD KARU Case Reports **(13223)**

Salisbury
Art Calendar **(13706)** ....(Paid) 12,000

MASSACHUSETTS
Boston
Adweek/New England **(13846)** ....(Paid) ‡3925

Sudbury
The WANT ADvertiser **(14580)** 65,000

MICHIGAN
Detroit
The Adcrafter **(14913)** ....‡3,000

MINNESOTA
Maple Grove
Format Magazine **(16038)** ....(Non-paid) 3,000

Minneapolis
Potentials **(16122)** ....(Non-paid) ★50,000
Quirk's Marketing Research
  Review **(16125)** ....(Non-paid) 16,000

NEW HAMPSHIRE
Littleton
Media Market Guide **(18549)** ....(Paid) ‡1,000
  (Controlled) ‡100

NEW JERSEY
Florham Park
Exhibit Marketing
  Magazine **(18824)** ....(Non-paid) 124,000

Hoboken
Journal of Direct and Interactive
  Marketing **(19021)** 7,000

West Long Branch
Health Marketing Quarterly **(19721)**

West Trenton
Med Ad News **(19742)** ....(Controlled) ‡13,000
  (Paid) ‡3,000
Medical Advertising **(19743)** .....(Combined) △14,000

NEW YORK
Auburn
The Finger Lakes Business
  Almanac **(20106)** ....(Paid) 1,100
  (Non-paid) 900

Binghamton
Journal of Promotion Management **(20193)** 305

Garden City
Direct Marketing Magazine **(20637)** ......(Paid) 7,660
  (Controlled) 932
Fund Raising Management
  Magazine **(20640)** ....(Paid) ‡6,705
  (Controlled) ‡1,715

Great Neck
Journal of Business Forecasting
  Methods **(20691)** ....(Paid) 3,500

New York
Adweek **(21157)** ....(Paid) 30,000
Adweek Western Edition **(21158)** ......(Paid) ‡40,441
Bank Investment Marketing **(21286)**
Brand Marketing **(21337)** ....△22,000
Card Marketing **(21373)**
Creative **(21512)** 15,500
DM News **(21561)** ....(Controlled) ‡40,000
Drop Shipping News **(21570)**
Editor & Publisher **(21585)** ....(Paid) 14,278
  (Non-paid) 3,905
Journal of Advertising
  Research **(21976)** ....(Paid) ‡4,200
Journal of Business-to-Business
  Marketing **(22016)** 473
Journal of Strategic Marketing **(22194)**
Lurzer's International
  Archive **(22271)** ....(Paid) 9,600
  (Non-paid) 100
Sales & Marketing Management **(22701)** ...‡70,000
Warehousing
  Management **(22908)** ....(Combined) 50,066

OHIO
Cincinnati
Journal of Marketing for Higher
  Education **(24806)** ....(Controlled) ‡248
Signs of the Times **(24817)** ....(Paid) 9,299
  (Non-paid) 8,358
Visual Merchandising and Store
  Design **(24827)** ....(Paid) 7,132
  (Non-paid) 20,103

Fairborn
Contractor Marketing **(25186)** ......(Controlled) 4,500

Marion
American Demographics **(25350)** ....(Paid) 26,310

OREGON
Terrebonne
Topicator **(26595)** ....‡160

PENNSYLVANIA
Middletown
Journal of International Consumer
  Marketing **(27257)** ....(Paid) 371

Philadelphia
Advertising/Communications Times **(27364)**
Journal of Food Products Marketing **(27528)** 480

Trevose
The Counselor **(28056)** ....(Paid) 10,400

SOUTH CAROLINA
Myrtle Beach
Today's $85,000 Freelance
  Writer **(28704)** ....(Non-paid) 4,000

TENNESSEE
Nashville
Journal of Service Research **(29464)**

TEXAS
Dallas
Retailer and Marketing
  News **(30180)** ....(Controlled) ‡7,500

Denton
Journal of Marketing Channels **(30238)** 393

Hurst
Self-Employed America **(30602)** ......(Paid) ‡250,000

Irving
Promotional Products
    Business **(30607)** ....(Paid) 12,000
                                       (Non-paid) 384

Sugar Land
Asia Pacific Journal of Tourism
    Research **(31136)** ....(Paid) 400

VIRGINIA
Falls Church
Inside Direct Mail **(32048)**
Promotional
    Marketing **(32055)** ....(Combined) ‡20,300
Target Marketing **(32057)** ....(Controlled) ‡35,469

McLean
H.S.M.A.I. Marketing
    Review **(32265)** ....(Controlled) 7,000

Richmond
What's New in Advertising and Marketing **(32470)**

WASHINGTON
Seattle
Media Inc. **(32986)**

WISCONSIN
Appleton
Marketplace Magazine **(33537)** ....(Paid) 15,000

ONTARIO, CANADA
Markham
Pool & Spa Marketing **(36030)** ....(Paid) ‡2,000
                                (Non-paid) ‡7,000

Toronto
Adnews **(36461)** ....(Combined) 6,625
Canadian Advertising Rates &
    Data **(36490)** ....(Combined) •1,901
Marketing Magazine **(36657)** ....(Paid) 12,761
Strategy **(36749)** ....(Combined) 16,700

QUEBEC, CANADA
Montreal
Info Presse Communications **(37127)** ....(Paid) 5,500
                                (Controlled) 2,500

Westmount
The Image News **(37443)** 1,500

AIR CONDITIONING AND REFRIGERATION

See also Plumbing and Heating

ALABAMA
Birmingham
Associated Plumbing Heating &
    Cooling **(55)** ....(Non-paid) ‡2,000

CALIFORNIA
Laguna Hills
Reeves Journal **(2135)** ....(Controlled) ‡13,500

FLORIDA
Altamonte Springs
Ohio Perspective **(5901)** ....(Controlled) ‡8,000
Wisconsin Perspective **(5903)** .....(Controlled) ‡7,200

Boca Raton
HVAC/R Distribution Today **(5932)** ....(Paid) 500
                               (Non-paid) 250

Winter Park
Florida Forum **(6879)** ....(Controlled) ‡4,500

GEORGIA
Atlanta
ASHRAE Journal **(6966)** ....(Paid) 49,200
                             (Non-paid) 11,157
International Journal of Heating, Ventilating, Air-
    Conditioning and Refrigeration Research (HVAC &
    R Research) **(7018)**

ILLINOIS
Elgin
Service and Contracting (S &
    C) **(8826)** ....(Paid) 14,233
                               (Non-paid) 42

Springfield
Illinois Master Plumber **(9626)** ....‡2,000

INDIANA
Indianapolis
Indiana Contractor **(10125)** ....(Controlled) ‡5,579

MICHIGAN
Troy
Air Conditioning, Heating and Refrigeration
    News **(15616)** ....(Paid) 25,938
                              (Non-paid) 4,706
Engineered Systems **(15623)** ....(Paid) 100
                              (Controlled) 58,000
Snips Magazine **(15640)** ....(Paid) 1,151
                              (Controlled) 22,000

NEW YORK
New York
Consulting-Specifying
    Engineer **(21490)** ....(Controlled) ‡47,508

NORTH CAROLINA
Garner
North Carolina Plumbing-Heating-Cooling
    Forum **(23905)** ....(Non-paid) ‡1,000

Greensboro
Southern PHC
    Magazine **(23939)** ....(Non-paid) ‡12,274

OHIO
Cleveland
Contracting Business **(24875)** .....(Controlled) 52,000
Heating/Piping/Air Conditioning Engineering
    (HPAC) **(24906)** ....(Paid) 1,250
                              (Non-paid) 56,000

SOUTH CAROLINA
Beaufort
Refrigeration **(28488)**

Columbia
Palmetto Piper **(28559)** ....‡2,700

ONTARIO, CANADA
Toronto
Heating, Plumbing, Air Conditioning Buyers'
    Guide **(36613)** ....(Controlled) 15,528
HPAC (Heating-Plumbing-Air Conditioning
    Magazine) **(36620)** ....(Combined) 16,528

ANTHROPOLOGY AND ETHNOLOGY

ARIZONA
Tucson
Kiva **(952)** ....(Paid) ‡1,200
                                (Non-paid) ‡25

CALIFORNIA
Berkeley
Classical Antiquity **(1508)**
Measurement **(1541)**

Los Osos
Rapa Nui Journal **(2483)** 400

San Diego
Journal of Anthropological Archaeology **(3179)**

Santa Barbara
Journal of Linguistic
    Anthropology **(3647)** ....(Paid) 900

Sebastopol
KMT **(3751)** ....(Paid) ⊕14,793

Thousand Oaks
Cross-Cultural Research **(3861)** ....(Paid) ‡500
Journal of Contemporary
    Ethnography **(3885)** ....(Paid) ‡700

CONNECTICUT
Putnam
Spring Journal **(5094)** ....(Paid) ‡2000

DISTRICT OF COLUMBIA
Washington
Anthropological Quarterly **(5354)** ....(Paid) ‡794
                              (Non-paid) ‡91
The Journal of Indo-European
    Studies **(5598)** ....(Paid) ‡856
                              (Non-paid) ‡56
The Journal of Social
    Psychology **(5616)** ....(Paid) ‡1,700
The Mankind Quarterly **(5643)** ....(Paid) ‡1,075
                              (Non-paid) ‡60
Mediterranean Quarterly **(5646)** ....(Paid) 650

Paleobiology **(5713)**

FLORIDA
Orlando
The Journal of Human Performance in Extreme
    Environments **(6499)** ....(Paid) 200

Thonotosassa
The Florida Anthropologist **(6816)** ....‡950

IDAHO
Moscow
Northwest Anthropological Research
    Notes **(7920)** ....(Paid) 350

ILLINOIS
Chicago
Public Culture **(8544)** ....(Combined) 1000

DeKalb
Crossroads **(8733)** ....(Paid) 300
Names **(8739)** ....(Paid) 850

Normal
Pan-Japan **(9302)** ....‡500
Personal Relationships **(9303)** ....(Paid) ‡567
                              (Non-paid) ‡74

Springfield
The Living Museum **(9639)** ....(Non-paid) ‡18,000

Urbana
Steward Anthropological Society
    Journal **(9718)** ....(Paid) 150

INDIANA
Bloomington
Journal of Folklore Research **(9841)**

West Lafayette
Anthrozoos **(10544)** ....(Paid) 850
                              (Non-paid) 50

KANSAS
Topeka
The Kansas Anthropologist **(11825)** ....(Paid) 350

KENTUCKY
Lexington
Journal of Caribbean Studies **(12167)** 1,000

Wilmore
Missiology **(12453)** ....‡2,000

LOUISIANA
Baton Rouge
Journal of Mayan Linguistics **(12490)** ......(Paid) 100

MAINE
Blue Hill
Mammoth Trumpet **(12923)** ....(Paid) 1,300

MARYLAND
Bethesda
Entomology Abstracts **(13334)**

Cheverly
Romani Studies **(13407)** ....(Paid) 272

MASSACHUSETTS
Boston
Central European History **(13871)**

Cambridge
Cultural Survival Quarterly **(14047)** ....(Paid) 10,000

MICHIGAN
Ann Arbor
Comparative Studies in Society &
    History **(14745)** ....(Paid) ‡2028

MISSOURI
Columbia
Missouri Archaeologist **(16998)** ....(Paid) 825

NEW HAMPSHIRE
Peterborough
Faces **(18623)** 13,000

NEW JERSEY
Hoboken
American Journal of Physical
    Anthropology **(18888)** 18,200
Evolutionary Anthropology **(18946)** 5985
Geoarchaeology **(18952)** 3850
International Journal of Osteoarchaeology **(18993)**

Circ.   Circ.   Circ.

ANTHROPOLOGY AND ETHNOLOGY (continued)

Mahwah
Mind, Culture, and Activity (19202)

NEW MEXICO
Albuquerque
Human Nature (19773)
Journal of Anthropological
  Research (19774) ....(Paid) 1,200
                    (Non-paid) ‡50

NEW YORK
Amityville
Abstracts in Anthropology (20034)

Armonk
Anthropology & Archeology of
  Eurasia (20065) ....(Paid) ⊕322
Chinese Sociology and
  Anthropology (20071) ....(Paid) ⊕199

Ithaca
Cornell Science & Technology
  Magazine (20799) ....‡3,000
Indonesia (20803) ....(Combined) 500

New York
Journal of Cultural Heritage (22044)
Polar Record (22570) 800
Social Anthropology (22753) ....(Paid) ‡1263
                    (Non-paid) ‡41

NORTH CAROLINA
Durham
Comparative Studies of South Asia, Africa, and the
  Middle East (23815) ....(Paid) 450

OHIO
Cleveland
Explorer (24894) ....‡11,000

OKLAHOMA
Oklahoma City
Human Organization (25966) ....‡3,999

PENNSYLVANIA
Mc Keesport
Latin America Indian Literatures
  Journal (27229) ....(Combined) 260

Pittsburgh
Ethnology (27786) ....‡2,000

TENNESSEE
Murfreesboro
Tennessee Folklore Society
  Bulletin (29434) ....(Paid) ‡380
                    (Non-paid) ‡47

TEXAS
Austin
Journal of the History of Sexuality (29787) 1,000

VERMONT
Benson
Central Asia Monitor (31504) 235

VIRGINIA
Arlington
American Anthropologist (31770) ....‡13,500
American Ethnologist (31771) ....‡3,500
Anthropology of Consciousness (31774)
Anthropology and Education
  Quarterly (31775) ....‡1,500
Anthropology and Humanism (31776) 600
Cultural Anthropology (31784) ....‡1,400
Ethos (31789) ....(Paid) ‡1,200
Journal of Latin American Anthropology (31802)
Medical Anthropology
  Quarterly (31807) ....(Paid) 2,000
Museum Anthropology (31809)
Political and Legal Anthropological Review (31818)
SACC Notes—Teaching Anthropology (31826)
Transforming Anthropology (31837)

WISCONSIN
Madison
Arctic Anthropology (33922) ....(Paid) 700
Ethnohistory (33936) ....‡1,300

ONTARIO, CANADA
Hamilton
Nexus (35887)

Ottawa
Beads (36186) ....(Paid) 1,000
                    (Controlled) 50

Toronto
Journal of Cognition and Development (36633)

QUEBEC, CANADA
Montreal
Canadian Review of Sociology and
  Anthropology (37100)

Ste.-Foy
Anthropologie et Societes (37335)

APPLIANCES

ILLINOIS
Lombard
NARDA Independent Retailer (9117) ....‡2,000

Oak Brook
Appliance (9337) ....(Non-paid) △33,500
Appliance China Edition (9338) ....(Non-paid) 13,000
Appliance European
  Edition (9339) ....(Non-paid) 8,000
Appliance Latin America
  Edition (9340) ....(Non-paid) 8,000

St. Charles
Appliance Service
  News (9561) ....(Combined) ‡32,000
Appliance Service News (9562)

MASSACHUSETTS
Wayland
Electronic House (14614) ....‡80,000

OHIO
Solon
Appliance
  Manufacturer (25524) ....(Non-paid) ‡36,040

ONTARIO, CANADA
Toronto
Housewares Canada (36619) ....‡14,000

ARCHAEOLOGY

ARIZONA
Tucson
Arizona Archaeologist (928) ....(Controlled) 780
Kiva (952) ....(Paid) ‡1,200
                    (Non-paid) ‡25

CALIFORNIA
Berkeley
Classical Antiquity (1508)
PaleoBios (1549)

Los Osos
Rapa Nui Journal (2483) 400

San Diego
Journal of Anthropological Archaeology (3179)

Sebastopol
KMT (3751) ....(Paid) ⊕14,793

COLORADO
Denver
Southwestern Lore (4357) ....‡1,000

DELAWARE
Wilmington
Archaeological Society of Delaware
  Bulletin (5288) ....(Paid) 100

DISTRICT OF COLUMBIA
Washington
American Antiquity (5324) ....‡6,400
The Journal of Indo-European
  Studies (5598) ....(Paid) ‡856
                    (Non-paid) ‡56
Latin American Antiquity (5630) ....‡1,500
Paleobiology (5713)
The SAA Archaeological Record (5774)

FLORIDA
Thonotosassa
The Florida Anthropologist (6816) ....‡950

HAWAII
Honolulu
Asian Perspectives (7679) ....(Paid) 550
                    (Controlled) 25

IDAHO
Moscow
Northwest Anthropological Research
  Notes (7920) ....(Paid) 350

ILLINOIS
Normal
International Journal of Historical Archaeology (9299)

Urbana
Illinois Archaeology (9707) ....(Controlled) 200
Steward Anthropological Society
  Journal (9718) ....(Paid) 150

IOWA
Ames
Aeon (10588) ....(Paid) 500
                    (Non-paid) 100

Iowa City
Midcontinental Journal of Archeology (10981)

MAINE
Blue Hill
Mammoth Trumpet (12923) ....(Paid) 1,300

MASSACHUSETTS
Somerville
Technology & Conservation of Art, Architecture &
  Antiquities (14539) ....(Non-paid) ‡15,000

MICHIGAN
Ann Arbor
University of Michigan Museums of Art and
  Archaeology Bulletin (14771)

MISSOURI
Chesterfield
Central States Archaeological
  Journal (16974) ....‡5,700

Columbia
Missouri Archaeologist (16998) ....(Paid) 825
Muse (17007) ....(Controlled) 660
                    (Paid) 1,200

NEW JERSEY
Hoboken
Archaeological Prospection (18896)
Geoarchaeology (18952) 3850
International Journal of Osteoarchaeology (18993)

Princeton
Hesperia (19461) ....(Paid) ‡785
                  (Controlled) ‡217

NEW MEXICO
Santa Fe
Pottery Southwest (19941) ....(Paid) 170

NEW YORK
Amityville
Abstracts in Anthropology (20034)
North American Archaeologist (20052)

Armonk
Anthropology & Archeology of
  Eurasia (20065) ....(Paid) ⊕322

Long Island City
Archaeology (20961) ....(Paid) 227,499

New York
African Archaeological Review (21163)
Cambridge Archaeological
  Journal (21366) ....(Paid) ‡750
                  (Non-paid) ‡99
Journal of Archaeological Method and
  Theory (21997)
Journal of Archaeological Research (21998)
Journal of World Prehistory (22214)
Rural History (22681) 500

Rochester
The Bulletin (23212)

OHIO
Cleveland
Explorer (24894) ....‡11,000

Numbers cited after listings are entry numbers rather than page numbers.

PENNSYLVANIA
Landisville
Bible and Spade **(27157)** ....(Paid) 1,500

RHODE ISLAND
Portsmouth
Journal of Roman
   Archaeology **(28381)** ....(Non-paid) 1,250

TENNESSEE
Nashville
Ancient Mesoamerica **(29442)** ....(Paid) ‡800
                                   (Non-paid) ‡65

TEXAS
Alpine
Journal of Big Bend Studies **(29683)**

College Station
American Association of Stratigraphic Palynologists
   Contributions Series **(30036)** ....(Combined) 952
Palynology **(30047)** ....(Controlled) 952

WISCONSIN
Milwaukee
Wisconsin Archeologist **(34108)** ....‡527

WYOMING
Casper
Wyoming Archeologist **(34485)** ....(Combined) 400

NEWFOUNDLAND AND LABRADOR, CANADA
St. John's
Mouseion **(35490)** ....(Paid) 800

ONTARIO, CANADA
Ottawa
Beads **(36186)** ....(Paid) 1,000
                                   (Controlled) 50

Richmond Hill
Ontario Archaeology **(36345)** ....(Paid) 700

SASKATCHEWAN, CANADA
Saskatoon
Saskatchewan Archaeology **(37553)** ....(Paid) 200

ARCHITECTURE

See also Construction, Contracting,
Building, and Excavating

ARIZONA
Phoenix
Southwest Contractor **(811)** ....(Combined) 6,000

Scottsdale
Frank Lloyd Wright
   Quarterly **(869)** ....(Controlled) 10,000

Tucson
Environment and Behavior **(946)** ....(Paid) ‡1,600
                                 (Non-paid) ‡152

CALIFORNIA
Berkeley
Design Book Review **(1513)** ....‡7,000

Orinda
Tradeline's Exclusive Reports Online **(2727)** 7,000

Sacramento
arcCa **(2977)** 10,000

San Luis Obispo
Design Methods **(3565)**

Sierra Madre
American Bungalow **(3764)**

COLORADO
Boulder
Masonry Society Journal **(4179)** .....(Controlled) 850

CONNECTICUT
Newtown
Fine Homebuilding **(5042)** ....(Paid) 296,467

DISTRICT OF COLUMBIA
Washington
ASID ICON **(5367)** ....(Controlled) 33,000
Builder **(5386)** ....(Paid) 194,000
                            (Controlled) 30,000
Building Products **(5387)** ....(Controlled) ‡70,000
Custom Home **(5456)** ....‡40,000
Kitchen & Bath Showroom **(5626)**

Preservation **(5726)** ....(Paid) 204,149
Seniors' Housing News **(5789)**

FLORIDA
Coral Gables
International Journal for Housing Science and Its
   Applications **(6007)** ....(Controlled) 700

Gainesville
Art Reference Services Quarterly **(6130)** 321

Tampa
Design Cost Data **(6761)** ....(Controlled) ‡15,000
                       (Controlled) ‡15,000

GEORGIA
Alpharetta
CE News **(6918)** ....(Controlled) 49,610

Atlanta
Best Sellers Collection **(6977)** ......(Combined) 5,200

Norcross
Construction Market Data, A/E/C
   Magazine **(7457)** ....(Combined) 8,000

ILLINOIS
Chicago
Form & Function **(8380)** ....(Controlled) 120,000
Inland Architect **(8414)** ....(Paid) ‡6,000
                             (Non-paid) ‡500
Journal of Architectural and Planning
   Research **(8433)**
Journal of the Society of Architectural Historians
   (JSAH) **(8450)** ....(Controlled) ‡3,450
Manufactured Home
   Merchandiser **(8476)** ....(Controlled) ‡18,452
Realty and Building **(8552)** ....(Paid) ‡13,280
                            (Controlled) ‡1,130

Des Plaines
Professional Builder **(8768)** 122,000
                        (Controlled) 140,018

Elmhurst
Marquee **(8835)** ....(Controlled) ‡1,000

Northbrook
Plumbing Engineer **(9320)** ....(Free) ‡25,600

IOWA
Des Moines
Country Home **(10777)** ....(Paid) 1,045,729

MARYLAND
Baltimore
Quicks Professional
   Journal **(13240)** ....(Non-paid) ‡6,500

MASSACHUSETTS
Cambridge
Appendx **(14038)**
Harvard Design Magazine **(14057)** 12,000

Somerville
Technology & Conservation of Art, Architecture &
   Antiquities **(14539)** ....(Non-paid) ‡15,000

MICHIGAN
Detroit
Place **(14944)** ....(Controlled) 3,500

Troy
Environmental Design and
   Construction **(15624)** ....(Non-paid) △15,500

MINNESOTA
Minneapolis
Architectural Research Quarterly **(16057)** 500
Architecture Minnesota **(16058)** ....(Paid) ‡3,000
                           (Controlled) ‡4,000

Roseville
Fabric Architecture **(16331)** ....(Paid) 621
                          (Controlled) 12,400

MISSOURI
St. Louis
St. Louis Construction News &
   Review **(17498)** ....(Paid) ‡2,415
                            (Non-paid) ‡8,970

NEVADA
Reno
Architectural West **(18417)** ....(Controlled) 20,200

NEW JERSEY
Paramus
Contemporary Stone and Tile Design **(19401)**

Red Bank
Today's Facility
   Manager **(19501)** ....(Controlled) ❑50,000

NEW MEXICO
Albuquerque
The Adobe Journal **(19762)** ....(Paid) 1,400
                         (Non-paid) 3,100
Conceptions Helpless **(19770)** ....(Controlled) 700

Santa Fe
Designer/Builder **(19934)** ....(Controlled) 4,000

NEW YORK
Albany
Association for Preservation
   Technology **(19982)** ....(Paid) 1,700

Brooklyn
PLACES **(20337)** ....(Paid) ‡9,000
                         (Controlled) ‡200
Traditional Building **(20349)** ....(Paid) 11,240
                       (Non-paid) 11,760

Elbridge
Structural Mover **(20563)**

New York
Architectural Lighting **(21242)** ......(Non-paid) 25,000
Architectural Record **(21243)** ......(Paid) 104,301
Better Homes and Gardens Building
   Ideas **(21296)** ....(Paid) ‡450,000
Contract **(21497)** ....(Paid) 354
                        (Controlled) 30,087
Contract **(21498)** 30,000
House Beautiful **(21821)** ....(Paid) 853,748
House Beautiful's Houses and Plans **(21823)**
INTERIORS **(21891)** ....(Paid) 11,009
                       (Non-paid) 15,351
The Magazine Antiques **(22274)** ....(Paid) 70,605
Metropolis Magazine **(22327)** ....(Combined) 47,000

NORTH CAROLINA
Durham
North Carolina Architecture **(23837)** ......(Paid) ‡150
                       (Controlled) ‡3,500

OHIO
Woodville
Metal Architecture **(25671)** ....(Controlled) 31,483

OREGON
Portland
Journal of the American Planning Association
   (JAPA) **(26483)** ....(Paid) ⊕11,400

TEXAS
Austin
Texas Architect **(29811)** ....(Paid) ‡7,181
                       (Non-paid) ‡4,735
Texas Construction **(29815)** ....(Controlled) ‡6,500

Dallas
Builder Insider **(30134)** ....(Non-paid) 8,500

VIRGINIA
Garrisonville
Architects' Guide to Glass, Metal &
   Glazing **(32103)** ....(Controlled) 20,000

Reston
Journal of Architectural Engineering **(32370)**

WISCONSIN
Madison
Wisconsin Architect **(33978)** ....‡3,536

ALBERTA, CANADA
Calgary
International Journal of Parallel and Distributed
   Systems and Networks **(34647)**
Onsite Review **(34652)** ....(Paid) 500

BRITISH COLUMBIA, CANADA
Burnaby
Award Magazine **(34889)** ....(Combined) 7,657

ONTARIO, CANADA
Etobicoke
Info-Link **(35816)** ....(Combined) •44,168

Mississauga
CAD Systems **(36054)** ....(Combined) 21,211

Circ.   Circ.   Circ.

ARCHITECTURE (continued)

Ottawa
Wood Design & Building **(36281)** ....(Paid) 8,000
(Non-paid) 25,000
Wood Lebois **(36282)** ....(Combined) 67,000

Toronto
Azure Magazine **(36469)** ....(Combined) •10,566
Canadian Architect **(36491)** ....(Non-paid) 6,117
(Paid) 4,127

QUEBEC, CANADA
Montreal
Fifth Column **(37116)**

Sainte-Adele
ARQ, La revue
d'architecture **(37370)** ....(Controlled) 3,485

SASKATCHEWAN, CANADA
Saskatoon
The Structurist **(37558)** ....(Paid) 1,000

ART AND ART HISTORY

ALABAMA
Montgomery
Alabama Arts **(355)**

CALIFORNIA
Claremont
Women's Studies **(1726)** ....(Paid) 500

Los Angeles
African Arts **(2201)** 4,000

Oakland
California Coast &
Ocean **(2673)** ....(Combined) 10,000

Rancho Palos Verdes
Friends of French Art **(2880)**

Rancho Santa Fe
Silver Magazine **(2882)** ....‡6,000

San Francisco
San Francisco Art Institute
Magazine **(3426)** ....(Combined) 6,500

San Jose
Switch **(3541)**

Santa Rosa
Wine X Magazine **(3736)** ....(Controlled) 50,000

Sebastopol
KMT **(3751)** ....(Paid) ⊕14,793

Ventura
Art/Life **(4000)**

West Hollywood
Art Issues **(4061)** ....(Non-paid) 9,000

COLORADO
Colorado Springs
Journal of Regional Criticism **(4250)**

Pueblo
Southeastern College Art Conference Review **(4601)**

CONNECTICUT
Danbury
Art & Man **(4735)** ....‡180,000
Scholastic Ars- **(4752)**

DELAWARE
Winterthur
Winterthur Portfolio **(5304)** ....(Paid) ‡1,600

DISTRICT OF COLUMBIA
Washington
American Institute for Conservation of Historic and
Artistic Works Journal **(5331)** ....(Paid) 3,700
American Studies International **(5345)** ....‡800
Arts Education Policy Review **(5362)** ....‡1,061
Crisis Magazine **(5449)** ....(Paid) 20,000
(Non-paid) 3,000
The Textile Museum Journal **(5821)** 5,000
1,000
400
Washington Review **(5853)** ....(Controlled) 800
Women in the Arts **(5862)**

FLORIDA
Gainesville
Art Reference Services Quarterly **(6130)** 321

Orlando
Sunshine Artist **(6508)** ....(Combined) ⊕30,000

Tallahassee
Studies in Art Education **(6736)** ....(Paid) ‡4,197
(Non-paid) ‡30

GEORGIA
Atlanta
Art Papers Magazine **(6965)** ....(Paid) 135,000

ILLINOIS
Champaign
Visual Arts Research **(8222)** ....(Paid) 500

Chicago
Art Institute of Chicago Museum
Studies **(8275)** ....(Paid) 1,500
Lenox Avenue **(8460)**

Evanston
Arsenal **(8849)**

Mundelein
Art Therapy **(9256)** 4,700

Urbana
The Communication Review **(9702)**

INDIANA
Valparaiso
The Cresset **(10508)** ....‡4,700

MARYLAND
Baltimore
Modernism/Modernity **(13220)** ....(Combined) 637

Salisbury
Art Calendar **(13706)** ....(Paid) 12,000

Silver Spring
Uno Mas Magazine **(13747)**

MASSACHUSETTS
Deerfield
Historic Deerfield **(14157)**

Greenfield
Markers **(14221)** ....(Paid) 200

Malden
The Journal of Aesthetics and Art
Criticism **(14292)** ....‡2,500
The Russian Review **(14299)** ....(Paid) ‡1,700
(Non-paid) ‡100

Provincetown
Provincetown Arts **(14486)** ....(Combined) 10,000

Somerville
Technology & Conservation of Art, Architecture &
Antiquities **(14539)** ....(Non-paid) ‡15,000

West Stockbridge
Lingo Magazine **(14627)** 3,500,000

MICHIGAN
Ann Arbor
University of Michigan Museums of Art and
Archaeology Bulletin **(14771)**

Birmingham
Lightworks **(14825)** ....(Combined) 2,000

Detroit
Bulletin of the Detroit Institute of
Arts **(14917)** ....(Combined) 5,500

MINNESOTA
Eagan
Wildlife Art **(15864)** ....‡65,000

Minneapolis
Illustrator **(16085)**
U.S. ART **(16137)** ....(Controlled) 55,000

MISSOURI
Columbia
Muse **(17007)** ....(Controlled) 660
(Paid) 1,200

Kansas City
Forum **(17170)** ....(Paid) 600
(Non-paid) 10,000

St. Louis
DECOR **(17432)** ....(Paid) 24,245
(Non-paid) 785
Saint Louis Art Museum Bulletin **(17495)**

Springfield
Explorations in Renaissance
Culture **(17598)** ....(Combined) 314

NEBRASKA
Lincoln
Uncoverings **(18125)** ....(Paid) 1,500

NEW JERSEY
Englewood
Surface Design
Journal **(18798)** ....(Combined) 5,700

Lambertville
Modernism Magazine **(19159)** ....(Paid) ‡7,500
Style 1900 **(19160)** ....(Paid) 16,500

Morganville
Picture Framing
Magazine **(19287)** ....(Paid) △24,000

Princeton
Hesperia **(19461)** ....(Paid) ‡785
(Controlled) ‡217

NEW MEXICO
Albuquerque
Conceptions Helpless **(19770)** ....(Controlled) 700

NEW YORK
Binghamton
Ijele **(20155)**

Bronx
Art Index **(20253)**
Viewfinder Journal of Focal Point
Gallery **(20289)** 4000

East Hampton
2wice **(20547)** ....(Paid) ‡2,500

New York
American Art Journal **(21177)**
American Artist **(21178)** ....(Paid) 180,471
American Craft **(21186)** ....(Paid) 40,000
Aristos **(21248)**
Art, Antiquity and Law **(21250)**
Art Business News **(21252)**
Arton Paper **(21258)**
I.F.A.R. Journal **(21851)**
The Magazine Antiques **(22274)** ....(Paid) 70,605
Master Drawings **(22289)** ....(Combined) 1,500
The Metropolitan Museum of Art
Bulletin **(22329)** ....(Paid) ‡3,000
(Non-paid) ‡108,000
PIX **(22555)**
Pixel Vision **(22556)**
Renaissance Quarterly **(22646)** ....‡3,500
Sculpture Review **(22715)** 7,000
Trans **(22852)** ....(Paid) ⊕453
Watercolor **(22911)** 38,868

Rochester
Porticus **(23236)** ....(Controlled) 2,000

Rosendale
Binnewater Tides **(23277)** ....(Paid) ‡1,000
(Non-paid) ‡6,000

NORTH CAROLINA
Boone
Albion **(23651)** ....(Paid) ‡1,574
(Non-paid) ‡47

Greensboro
Letter Arts Review **(23927)** ....(Paid) 5,000
(Non-paid) 800

Winston-Salem
Journal of Early Southern Decorative
Arts **(24319)** ....(Paid) 1,500

OHIO
Cincinnati
North Light **(24811)** ....(Non-paid) 68,635

Mansfield
The Carousel News & Trader
Magazine **(25330)** ....(Paid) 3,000
(Non-paid) 200

Oberlin
Allen Memorial Art Museum Bulletin **(25443)**

OKLAHOMA
Tulsa
Gilcrease Journal **(26117)** ....(Controlled) 5,000

OREGON
Corvallis
CALYX (26285) ....(Paid) 4,500
(Non-paid) 500

PENNSYLVANIA
Philadelphia
The Classical World (27406) ....‡3,000
Philadelphia Museum of Art
Bulletin (27629) ....(Paid) ‡4,000
(Non-paid) ‡4,000

Pittsburgh
Carnegie Magazine (27764) ....(Paid) 28,679

University Park
Art Education (28070) ....(Paid) ‡18,000
(Non-paid) ‡63

TEXAS
Houston
Art Law & Accounting
Reporter (30459) ....(Paid) 1,500

VIRGINIA
Charlottesville
Imprint (31930) ....(Paid) 550

Fairfax
So to Speak (32031)

Front Royal
Sacred Music (32095) ....‡1,000

Waterford
Clay Times (32609) ....(Paid) 15,500

WASHINGTON
Seattle
Glass Art Society Journal (32968)
Jack Mackerel Magazine (32974) .....(Non-paid) 500

WISCONSIN
La Farge
Xerolage (33898) ....(Combined) 110

MANITOBA, CANADA
Winnipeg
Border Crossings Magazine (35317) 6,500

NOVA SCOTIA, CANADA
Halifax
Arts Atlantic (35558) ....(Combined) 2,200

ONTARIO, CANADA
North York
Applied Arts
Magazine (36120) ....(Combined) 13,000

Ottawa
Inuit Art Quarterly (36252) ....(Controlled) **1,500**
(Paid) 1,600

Toronto
C Magazine (36482)
Poiesis (36712)

QUEBEC, CANADA
Montreal
Scrivener (37222) ....(Combined) 500

SASKATCHEWAN, CANADA
Saskatoon
The Structurist (37558) ....(Paid) 1,000

ASTRONAUTICS

See also Nuclear Engineering

CALIFORNIA
Lancaster
Aerotech News &
Review (2146) ....(Non-paid) 15,000

San Diego
Advances in Astronautical Sciences (3108) 400

DISTRICT OF COLUMBIA
Washington
Air Jobs Digest (5317) ....(Combined) 40,000

INDIANA
West Lafayette
The Journal of the Astronautical
Sciences (10548) ....‡1,800

NEW YORK
Hauppauge
International Journal of Space Research (20718)

New York
Journal of Reducing Space Mission Cost (22178)
NASA Tech Briefs (22393) .....(Controlled) ‡200,000

VIRGINIA
Reston
Aerospace America (32355) ....(Paid) 23,432
(Controlled) 43,600
AIAA Journal (32357) ....‡4,100
International Aerospace Abstracts (32366)
Journal of Spacecraft and
Rockets (32395) ....‡2,700

ASTRONOMY AND METEOROLOGY

ARIZONA
Tempe
Publication of the Astronomical Society of the
Pacific (914) ....‡2,500

Tucson
Astrophysical Journal Supplement
Series (936) ....(Paid) ‡1,800

CALIFORNIA
Los Angeles
The Griffith Observer (2281) ....(Paid) 2,400
(Controlled) 80
Planetarian (2368) ....(Paid) 700

Palo Alto
Annual Review of Astronomy and
Astrophysics (2788)
Annual Review of Earth and Planetary
Sciences (2789)

San Diego
Icarus (3169)

San Francisco
Mercury (3390) ....(Paid) ‡6,000
(Non-paid) ‡200

Spring Valley
Geocosmic Magazine (3792) ....(Paid) 3,000

DISTRICT OF COLUMBIA
Washington
Bulletin of the American Astronomical
Society (5388) ....‡1,665

MASSACHUSETTS
Boston
Bulletin of the AMS (13867) ....‡12,585
Journal of Atmospheric and Oceanic
Technology (13913) ....‡1,588
Journal of Climate (13914) ....‡2,481
Monthly Weather Review (13929) ....‡2,972
Weather and Forecasting (13970) ....‡2,985

Cambridge
Journal of the American Association of Variable Star
Observers (14073)
Sky & Telescope (14100) ....(Paid) 132,726

Littleton
Meteorological & Geoastrophysical
Abstracts (14277) ....‡350

Needham
NCGR Journal (14364) ....(Paid) 3,100

NEW HAMPSHIRE
Peterborough
Odyssey (18626) 28,000

NEW YORK
New York
Astrophysics (21268)
Cosmic Research (21502)
Experimental Astronomy (21665)
Solar System Research (22761)

TEXAS
Austin
StarDate (29809) ....(Paid) 10,000

WASHINGTON
Seattle
The Amateur Telescope Making Journal (32939)
The Astronomical Journal (32943) ....‡1,929

WISCONSIN
Waukesha
Astronomy (34394) ....(Paid) ★152,821

ONTARIO, CANADA
Toronto
Journal of the Royal Astronomical Society of Canada
(R.A.S.C.) (36638) ....‡5,000

AUTOMATION

See also Computers

ARIZONA
Scottsdale
Visual Developer (875)

CALIFORNIA
Los Alamitos
Computing in Science & Engineering (2182)
IT Professional (2190) ....(Combined) ‡8,557

COLORADO
Broomfield
Digital Graphics (4204) ....(Paid) △72
(Non-paid) △18,513

Longmont
Robotics World (4560) ....(Combined) ‡22,500

Westminster
AIX Update (4659)
MQ Update (4664)
RACF Update (4667)

GEORGIA
Atlanta
TechLINKS (7051) ....‡23,000

Marietta
OR/MS Today (7415) ....(Combined) 14,268

ILLINOIS
Chicago
Card Technology (8298) ....(Combined) ‡25,047

MAINE
Portland
Interface Tech News (13010)

MASSACHUSETTS
Boston
Boston University Journal of Science & Technology
Law (13865)

Brookline
Server/Workstation Expert (14025)
WebServer OnLine (14026)

Cambridge
Journal of Machine Learning Research (14078)

Framingham
Application Development Trends (14191)
SC Magazine (14200) ....(Controlled) 43,100

Stow
Technology Meetings (14576)

Wayland
Electronic House (14614) ....‡80,000

MICHIGAN
Dearborn
Technology and Culture (14906)

NEW HAMPSHIRE
Nashua
Wireless Integration (18605)

NEW JERSEY
Hoboken
Journal of Robotic Systems (19046)

Medford
Marketing Library Services (19230)

Montvale
ColdFusion Developer's Journal
(CFDJ) (19247) ....(Combined) 30,000
Linux Business Week (19261) ....(Combined) 60,000
PowerBuilder Developer's
Journal (19273) ....(Combined) 37,000
Web Services Journal (19279)
WebLogic Developers
Journal (19280) ....(Combined) 25,000

Circulation: ★ = ABC; △ = BPA; ♦ = CAC; ● = CCAB; ❑ = VAC; ⊕ = PO Statement; ‡ = Publisher's Report; Boldface figures = sworn; Light figures = estimated.

3099

Circ.   Circ.   Circ.

AUTOMATION (continued)

WebSphere Developer's
   Journal **(19281)** ....(Combined) 25,000
Wireless Business &
   Technology **(19282)** ....(Combined) 130,000
XML-Journal **(19283)**

Morris Plains
Scientific -Computing &
   -Automation **(19306)** ....(Non-paid) ‡45,027

NEW YORK
Melville
Workforce Diversity for Engineering and IT
   Professionals **(21067)** ....(Combined) 15,046

New York
Annals of Operations Research **(21218)**
Annals of Software Engineering **(21219)**
Automation and Remote Control **(21275)**
Autonomous Agents and Multi-Agent
   Systems **(21279)**
Autonomous Robots **(21280)**
BT Technology Journal **(21345)**
Computational & Mathematical Organization
   Theory **(21470)**
Computer-Human Interaction (TOCHI) **(21474)**
Design Automation for Embedded Systems **(21546)**
Ethics and Information Technology **(21632)**
Executive Technology **(21661)** .....(Non-paid) 47,000
Formal Methods in System Design **(21726)**
Genetic Programming and Evolvable
   Machines **(21750)**
Information Systems Frontiers **(21870)**
Information and Systems Security (TISSEC) **(21871)**
International Journal of Computer Vision **(21903)**
Journal of Automated Reasoning **(22004)**
Journal of Intelligent Information Systems **(22099)**
Journal of Intelligent Manufacturing **(22100)**
Journal of Intelligent and Robotic Systems **(22101)**
Journal of Supercomputing **(22197)**
Journal of Systems Integration **(22200)**
Machine Learning **(22272)**
Managing
   Automation **(22278)** ....(Non-paid) △100,174
Minds and Machines **(22337)**
Modeling and Computer Simulation
   (TOMACS) **(22344)**
Multidimensional Systems and Signal
   Processing **(22379)**
Multimedia Tools and Applications **(22380)**
NETNOMICS **(22418)**
Networking (TON) **(22420)**
Networks and Spatial Economics **(22421)**
Photonic Network Communications **(22552)**
Real-Time Systems **(22637)**
Robotica **(22673)** 600
StandardView **(22789)**

OKLAHOMA
Tulsa
Utility Automation **(26141)** ....(Controlled) ‡25,000

PENNSYLVANIA
Hershey
Annals of Cases on Information Technology
   (ACIT) **(27039)** ....(Paid) 200

Philadelphia
Cybernetics and
   Systems **(27447)** ....(Combined) ‡341

VIRGINIA
Falls Church
Government E-Business **(32047)**

WASHINGTON
Seattle
Linux Gazette **(32981)**

ONTARIO, CANADA
Mississauga
CAD Systems **(36054)** ....(Combined) 21,211

Toronto
EDGE **(36577)** ....(Combined) 16,361
Technology in
   Government **(36756)** ....(Combined) 18,318

QUEBEC, CANADA
Montreal
Journal Industriel du
   Quebec **(37141)** ....(Combined) 20,431

AUTOMOTIVE (TRADE)

**See also Transportation, Traffic, and
Shipping; Trailers and Accessories; Trucks
and Trucking**

CALIFORNIA
Agoura
V-Twin News **(1384)**

Anaheim
The Automotive Booster of
   California **(1401)** ....(Non-paid) ‡4,700
O & A Marketing News **(1411)** ....(Paid) ‡4,522
                                            (Free) ‡2,732
Turbo & Hi-Tech Performance **(1419)** ....‡120,000

Brentwood
Packard Cormorant **(1603)** ....(Combined) 5,000

Los Angeles
Kit Car **(2306)** ....(Paid) ⊕60,000
Petersen's 4 Wheel & Off
   Road **(2363)** ....(Paid) 451,260

Torrance
Automotive Fleet **(3927)** ....(Paid) 252
                                        (Non-paid) 21,706
LCT **(3934)** ....(Paid) ‡10,000
                                         (Non-paid) ‡200
Mobile Electronics Magazine **(3939)** ....(Paid) 76
                                        (Non-paid) 22,576

Van Nuys
Import Automotive Parts &
   Accessories **(3990)** ....(Paid) △30
                                      (Controlled) △30,981
Specialty Automotive
   Magazine **(3995)** ....(Controlled) ‡24,947
                                            (Paid) ‡22

COLORADO
Broomfield
Restyling Magazine **(4207)**

Denver
Parts & People **(4347)** ....(Combined) 40,000

CONNECTICUT
Bridgeport
Auto Merchandising
   News **(4710)** ....(Controlled) ‡27,936

Enfield
Dirt Late Model **(4780)**
Late Model Racer **(4781)**
Trackside **(4782)**

Norwalk
Advanced Transportation Technology News **(5049)**

DISTRICT OF COLUMBIA
Washington
Parking Magazine **(5716)** 5,000

FLORIDA
Boynton Beach
Eastern Aftermarket
   Journal **(5949)** ....(Controlled) 10,150

Miami
Mecanica Popular **(6369)** ....‡14,977

GEORGIA
Roswell
Automotive & Transportation
   Interiors **(7514)** ....(Controlled) ‡13,093
Truck Accessory
   News **(7520)** ....(Controlled) ‡10,000

ILLINOIS
Cary
Fleet Equipment **(8168)** ....(Controlled) ‡63,000

Chicago
American Clean Car **(8253)** ....‡13,500
Chilton's Motor Age **(8331)** ....(Paid) 1,111
                                        (Non-paid) 142,036
Motor Service **(8495)** ....(Controlled) ‡175,000

INDIANA
Centerville
Vintage Ford **(9884)** ....(Controlled) 8,500

Terre Haute
Automotive Contact **(10484)** ....(Non-paid) 4,000

IOWA
Cedar Falls
Trucking Times & Sport Utility
   News **(10663)** ....(Combined) 13,500

KANSAS
Overland Park
Automobile Red Book **(11698)** ....(Paid) ‡1,540

KENTUCKY
Louisville
Tire Retreading/Repair Journal **(12239)** 2,300

MARYLAND
Bethesda
Aftermarket Insider **(13296)**

Lanham
Nozzle & Wrench **(13608)** ....(Controlled) ‡3,000

MASSACHUSETTS
Boston
Tomorrow Magazine **(13968)**

Franklin
Collision Magazine **(14204)** ....(Paid) ‡7,900
                                         (Controlled) ‡3,000
Motoring Road Magazine **(14206)**
Wheelings -New England
   Mechanic **(14207)** ....(Paid) ‡8,000
                                         (Controlled) ‡1,000

MICHIGAN
Detroit
Automotive News **(14915)** ....(Paid) ★80,614

Farmington Hills
Supercharger **(15020)** ....(Paid) 17,988

Southfield
ActionLINE Magazine **(15541)** ....(Combined) 30,000
Ward's Auto World **(15550)** ......(Controlled) 100,541
Ward's Automotive International **(15551)**
Ward's Automotive International Focus on
   China **(15552)**
Ward's Automotive Reports **(15553)**
Ward's Automotive
   Yearbook **(15554)** ....(Paid) 5,000
Ward's Engine and Vehicle Technology
   Update **(15555)**

Warren
U.S. Auto Scene **(15663)** 8,000

MINNESOTA
Bloomington
Motor Magazine **(15760)** ....(Non-paid) ★141,084
                                            (Paid) ★3,311

MISSOURI
Hazelwood
The Automotive Messenger **(17095)** ....‡14,000

Independence
Army Motors **(17105)** ....(Controlled) 10,000

Springfield
Transmission Digest **(17616)** ....(Paid) 1,360
                                         (Controlled) 17,162
Undercar Digest **(17617)** ....(Paid) 226
                                         (Controlled) ‡40,108

NEBRASKA
Lincoln
Marketer **(18095)** ....(Combined) ‡1,400

NEW JERSEY
Fort Lee
Auto Laundry News **(18831)** ....(Paid) 708
                                         (Controlled) 16,269

Iselin
NAFA Fleet Executive **(19126)** ....(Paid) 4,000
                                         (Controlled) 3,900

NEW YORK
Hicksville
New York Auto Repair
   News **(20742)** ....(Controlled) ‡11,321

Latham
Professional Carwashing &
   Detailing **(20933)** ....(Paid) 3,330
                                         (Controlled) 13,817

New York
Auto Interiors **(21274)** 13,642

Numbers cited after listings are entry numbers rather than page numbers.

Automotive Body Repair
News **(21276)** ....(Controlled) 60,488
(Controlled) 60,488

Automotive
Industries **(21277)** ....(Non-paid) ‡105,000
Automotive Marketing **(21278)** ....(Paid) 174
(Non-paid) 40,034
Glass Digest **(21766)** ....(Paid) 10,790
(Non-paid) 3,945

NORTH CAROLINA
Charlotte
GO Magazine **(23744)** ....‡750,000

OHIO
Akron
BodyShop Business **(24575)** ......(Controlled) 60,107
Counterman **(24578)** ....(Controlled) 50,062
Engine Builder **(24579)** ....(Controlled) 19,064
Import Car **(24581)** ....(Controlled) 29,209
Tire Business **(24589)** ....(Paid) ★**7,001**
(Non-paid) ★**15,092**
Tire Review **(24590)** ....(Controlled) 32,050
Underhood Service **(24591)** ....(Controlled) 40,558

Cincinnati
Automotive Design and Production **(24776)**
Automotive Finishing **(24778)**

Cleveland
Aftermarket Business **(24853)** ....(Paid) 319
(Non-paid) 40,129
Aftermarket Business AAIW Show
Daily **(24854)** 40,439

OKLAHOMA
Moore
Midwestern States Salvage
Guide **(25920)** ....(Paid) ‡250
(Non-paid) ‡14,000

PENNSYLVANIA
East Greenville
Automotive Cooling Journal **(26846)** ....(Paid) ‡2,644
(Non-paid) ‡7,556

Philadelphia
Vehicle Leasing Today **(27716)**

Pittsburgh
Automotive Market Report **(27760)** 10,000

Warrendale
Automotive Engineering
International **(28111)** ....(Combined) 124,500
SAE Off-Highway
Engineering **(28114)** ....(Controlled) 16,772

Wayne
Automotive Litigation Reporter **(28125)**

TEXAS
Arlington
ServiceInsights **(29735)** ....(Non-paid) 30,661
Used Car Dealer **(29738)** ....(Paid) ‡15,537
(Non-paid) ‡358

Austin
Dealers' Choice **(29774)** ....(Paid) 1,250
(Controlled) 550

Bedford
AutoInc **(29913)** ....‡13,000

Dallas
Auto Revista **(30125)** ....(Free) 41,000

Houston
Trailer/Body Builders **(30535)** ....(Controlled) ‡14,110

VIRGINIA
Alexandria
Utility Fleet Management **(31748)** ....‡22,014

Arlington
Composites Fabrication **(31783)** ....(Combined) 8,000

Fairfax
Automotive Recycling **(32007)** ......(Non-paid) ‡2,000

Falls Church
Lube Report **(32049)** ....(Controlled) 10,000

Garrisonville
USGlass, Metal & Glazing **(32106)** ....△27,826

Mc Lean
AutoGlass **(32241)** ....(Paid) 7,000
NADA's AutoExec
Magazine **(32250)** ....(Paid) 21,804

WASHINGTON
Seattle
Northwest Motor **(32994)** ....‡11,500

WISCONSIN
Fort Atkinson
Fleet Maintenance
Supervisor **(33710)** ....(Controlled) △44,018
Professional Tool & Equipment
News **(33718)** ....(Non-paid) ‡110,143

BRITISH COLUMBIA, CANADA
Burnaby
Collision Quarterly **(34895)** ....(Controlled) 6,179
Westworld British
Columbia **(34912)** ....(Paid) 489,123

ONTARIO, CANADA
Etobicoke
Automotive Parts &
Technology **(35811)** ....(Combined) •**34,605**

Mississauga
Canadian Auto World **(36057)** ....(Combined) ‡5,763

Toronto
L'Automobile **(36468)** ....(Combined) •**12,087**
Bodyshop **(36476)** ....(Combined) •**11,834**
Jobber News **(36631)** ....(Combined) 11,127
Service Station and Garage
Management **(36738)** ....(Combined) •**30,360**
Specialty & Performance
Magazine **(36745)** ....(Controlled) 10,000

QUEBEC, CANADA
Longueuil
Le Garagiste **(37054)** ....(Combined) 16,363

Montreal
Auto Trader/Auto Hebdo **(37089)**

AVIATION

ALABAMA
Maxwell AFB
Air and Space Power Journal **(315)** ....(Paid) ‡1,200
(Controlled) ‡20,000

Montgomery
Civil Air Patrol News **(363)** ....‡60,000

ARIZONA
Tucson
Contact! (Tucson) **(942)** ....(Combined) 1,290

ARKANSAS
Little Rock
Air Medical Journal **(1209)** ....(Paid) ‡5,250

CALIFORNIA
Moffett Field
ASRS Directline **(2573)**
Callback **(2574)** ....(Combined) 85,000

Palm Springs
GEO Europe **(2760)**

Woodland Hills
Airpower **(4100)**

COLORADO
Grand Junction
Navioneer **(4479)** 1,200

CONNECTICUT
Greenwich
Flying **(4872)** ....(Paid) 313,246

Monroe
Army Aviation Magazine **(4962)** ....‡14,500

DISTRICT OF COLUMBIA
Washington
Agricultural Aviation **(5316)** ....(Controlled) 6,000
Air Jobs Digest **(5317)** ....(Combined) 40,000
Air Transport World **(5318)** ......(Controlled) ‡43,300
Airport Equipment &
Technology **(5319)** ....(Combined) 19,958
FAA Aviation News **(5489)** ....(Paid) 18,000
(Controlled) 13,000

FLORIDA
Orlando
Flying Physician **(6495)**

GEORGIA
Atlanta
Commuter Air International **(6988)** ....(Paid) 650
(Controlled) 32,000

IOWA
Fort Dodge
Aviators Hot Line **(10894)** ....(Combined) ‡30,000
Business Air Today **(10895)** ......(Non-paid) ‡27,000

KANSAS
Wichita
ABS Magazine **(11879)** 10,000
International Flying
Farmer **(11882)** ....(Controlled) ‡1,900

MARYLAND
Frederick
AOPA Pilot **(13505)** ....(Paid) 341,339
Flight Training **(13510)** ....(Paid) 28,000
(Controlled) 40,000

Potomac
Aviation
Maintenance **(13646)** ....(Controlled) ‡40,000
Avionics Magazine **(13647)** ......(Controlled) 21,300
Rotor & Wing **(13660)** ....(Paid) 7,738
(Non-paid) 31,786

MASSACHUSETTS
Burlington
Journal of Air Transport Management **(14028)**

MICHIGAN
Ann Arbor
Great Lakes Pilot
News **(14752)** ....(Non-paid) 14,000

MINNESOTA
Mayer
Annals of Balloon History and Museology **(16048)**

MISSOURI
Independence
Avionics News **(17107)** ....(Non-paid) 7,200

St. Louis
Missouri Botanical Garden Annals **(17472)**

NEBRASKA
Lincoln
Controller **(18082)**

NEW JERSEY
Midland Park
Aviation International
News **(19236)** ....(Non-paid) ‡30,256

Montclair
ACCA Express **(19239)** ....(Non-paid) ‡1,475

Pitman
General Aviation Accident Report **(19434)**

NEW YORK
Jamaica
Airport Press **(20830)** ....(Free) 18,000

Mount Kisco
ABD **(21098)** ....(Combined) ‡20,000

New York
Air Space and Law **(21169)**
Aviation Week & Space
Technology **(21282)** ....(Paid) 104,546
IEEE Aerospace and Electronic Systems
Magazine **(21843)** ....(Paid) ‡11,500
(Non-paid) ‡500
Journal of Elasticity **(22057)**
Journal of Navigation **(22139)** ....(Paid) 455
(Non-paid) 3,346
REVISTA AEREA **(22665)** ....(Controlled) 11,200

Poughkeepsie
WW1 Aero **(23151)** ....(Paid) ‡1,500

Queens
Air Cargo News **(23168)** ....(Paid) 153
(Non-paid) 29,252

Rye Brook
A/C FLYER **(23282)** 39,525

White Plains
Aviation Monthly **(23569)** ....‡10,000
NTSB Reporter **(23572)**

Circulation: ★ = ABC; △ = BPA; ♦ = CAC; • = CCAB; ❑ = VAC; ⊕ = PO Statement; ‡ = Publisher's Report; Boldface figures = sworn; Light figures = estimated.

Trade, Technical, and Professional Publications

Circ.   Circ.   Circ.

AVIATION (continued)

OHIO
Akron
Buoyant Flight (24577) ....‡1,000

Johnstown
The International Journal of Aviation
   Psychology (25270)

Wright Patterson AFB
DISAM Journal (25683)

OREGON
Eugene
GPS World (26317) 38,000

PENNSYLVANIA
Johnstown
The Pennsylvania
   Geographer (27088) ....(Combined) 450

Pittsburgh
The Mobility Forum (27815)
Naval Aviation News (27819)
United States Army Aviation Digest (27852)

Warrendale
Aerospace Engineering (28110) 32,238

TEXAS
Dallas
Journal of Air Law and
   Commerce (30163) ....‡2,000

Del Rio
Volando (30225) ....(Paid) ‡1,840
                              (Non-paid) ‡4,816

Randolph AFB
Daedalus Flyer (30969)

VIRGINIA
Alexandria
Airport Magazine (31632) 7,000
Aviation Mechanics Bulletin (31644) 2,700
Flight Safety Digest (31673)
Journal of the American Helicopter
   Society (31686) ....‡6,400
Professional Pilot (31728) ....(Controlled) ‡40,000
ROTOR (31734) ....(Controlled) 17,000
Vertiflite (31749) ....‡8,500
Wings of Gold (31753) ....(Paid) ‡9,200
                              (Non-paid) ‡905

Arlington
Air Force Magazine (31768) ....(Paid) 182,330
                              (Non-paid) 6,165
Journal of Air Traffic Control (31800) ....‡4,000

Fairfax
Skyways (32030) ....(Paid) 1,200

Herndon
Air Line Pilot (32159) ....‡95,000

Reston
Aerospace America (32356)
AIAA Journal (32357) ....‡4,100
AIAA Student Journal (32358)
Finding Guide to AIAA Meeting Papers (32365)
Journal of Aerospace Engineering (32368)
Journal of Aircraft (32369) ....‡2,700
Journal of Guidance, Control, and
   Dynamics (32380) ....‡2,700
Journal of Propulsion and Power (32392) .....‡2,000
Journal of Thermophysics and Heat
   Transfer (32398) ....‡1,600

WASHINGTON
Lakewood
General Aviation News (32804) ....(Paid) ‡35,000
                              (Controlled) ‡8,000

WISCONSIN
Fort Atkinson
Aircraft Maintenance
   Technology (33703) ....(Controlled) △42,000
Airport Business (33704) ....(Controlled) ‡17,500

Oregon
World Airshow News (34219) ....(Paid) ‡2,000
                              (Non-paid) ‡1,500

ONTARIO, CANADA
Mississauga
Helicopters Magazine (36070) ......(Controlled) 5,846
Wings Magazine (36092) ....(Combined) •12,832

Ottawa
Canadian Flight Annual (36196) ....‡23,000
Canadian Journal of Remote Sensing (36216)

Willowdale
C.A.H.S. Journal (36875) ....‡1,300

QUEBEC, CANADA
Alouette
Phare/Beacon (36931) ....(Controlled) 2,500

Montreal
The ICAO Journal (37123) 58,482

BAKING

See also Confectionaries and Frozen Dairy Products

CALIFORNIA
Oakland
Pacific Bakers News (2693) ....(Controlled) 3,000

ILLINOIS
Des Plaines
Modern Baking (8763) ....(Controlled) ‡27,300

INDIANA
Berne
Home Cooking (9812) ....‡84,266

KANSAS
Manhattan
American Institute of Baking Technical
   Bulletin (11619)

MARYLAND
Kensington
BCTGM News (13590) ....(Controlled) 135,000

MISSOURI
Kansas City
Baking Buyer (17155) ....(Non-paid) 30,000
Baking & Snack (17156) ....(Controlled) ‡11,379
Milling & Baking News (17185) ....(Paid) 4,163

NEW JERSEY
Hoboken
Yeast (19121)

NEW YORK
New York
Pastry Art & Design (22532) .....(Combined) 27,000

OHIO
Cleveland
Baking Management (24859) ....(Combined) 9,700

ONTARIO, CANADA
Delhi
Bakers Journal (35763) ....(Controlled) •6,433

BANKING, FINANCE, AND INVESTMENTS

See also Accountants and Accounting; Commerce and Industry; Savings and Loan

ALABAMA
Birmingham
International Review of Financial Analysis (74)

ALASKA
Anchorage
Journal of Energy, Finance and Development (527)

ARKANSAS
Little Rock
Arkansas Banker (1212) ....‡2,000

CALIFORNIA
Claremont
North American Journal of Economics and
   Finance (1725) ....(Paid) 300
                              (Non-paid) 50

Los Angeles
Investor's Business
   Daily (2298) ....(Mon.-Fri.) 303,581

Mission Viejo
Barter News (2547) ....(Controlled) 30,000

Newport Beach
The Investment
   Reporter (2628) ....(Controlled) 35,000

Palm Springs
Commodity Price Charts (2757)
Investor Direct (2761)

San Diego
Business Opportunities Journal (3126) ......‡132,000
Journal of Financial Intermediation (3195)
Journal of Housing Economics (3198)
Mortgage Originator
   Magazine (3238) ....(Combined) 16,522

San Francisco
The Red Herring (3422) ....(Paid) 162,666
                              (Non-paid) 5,611
Research (3424) ....(Paid) 80
                              (Non-paid) 85,300

Santa Barbara
Journal of IS Financial
   Management (3645) ....(Controlled) 925
Journal of IT Financial Management (3646)

South Pasadena
The Business Picture (3786)

Thousand Oaks
Public Finance Review (3909) ....(Paid) ‡700

Walnut Creek
REITStreet Magazine (4055) ....(Non-paid) 4,000

COLORADO
Denver
Journal of Financial
   Planning (4337) ....(Controlled) ‡50,000

Englewood
MGMA Connexion (4414) ....(Controlled) 19,000

CONNECTICUT
Greenwich
Global Custodian (4873)
Plan Sponsor (4875) ....(Non-paid) 35,000

Waterbury
Secondary Marketing
   Executive (5194) ....(Controlled) ‡21,000
Servicing
   Management (5195) ....(Controlled) ‡22,000

DISTRICT OF COLUMBIA
Washington
ABA Bank Marketing
   Magazine (5310) ....(Paid) ‡4,003
ABA Consumer Credit Delinquency Bulletin (5311)
Bank Marketing (5373)
Brookings Papers on Economic Activity (5384)
Capital Idea$ (5393)
Community Banker (5428)
EBRI Quarterly Pension Investment
   Report (5470) ....‡350
Finance &
   Development (5495) ....(Controlled) 95,000
The IDB (5540) ....(Paid) 1,000
Independent Banker (5542) ....(Paid) ‡7,045
                              (Non-paid) ‡2,329
International Journal of Government Auditing (5554)
International Monetary Fund Staff Papers (5557)
Journal of Agricultural Lending (5568) .....(Paid) 580
Journal of Housing
   Research (5597) ....(Non-paid) 6,200
The Journal of Structured and Project
   Finance (5617)
Mortgage Banking Magazine (5662) ....‡6,800
OECD Journal on Budgeting (5701)
SEC Docket (5785)
Strategic Investor Relations (5806)

FLORIDA
Apopka
Moneyworld (5910) ....(Paid) 40,000
                              (Free) 260,000

Coral Gables
Public Budgeting and
   Finance (6011) ....(Non-paid) ‡2,100
                              (Paid) ‡900

Longwood
Bull & Bear Financial
   Report (6312) ....(Paid) 50,000
                              (Non-paid) 17,000

St. Petersburg
Florida Trend (6628) ....(Paid) 50,000
                              (Non-paid) 10,371

Sarasota
Accounting Horizons **(6652)**
Intermarket Review **(6656)**
Journal of Information Systems **(6658)**

Tallahassee
Florida Banking **(6706)**

Tampa
Financial Management **(6762)** ....‡12,000

GEORGIA
Atlanta
Economic Review **(7000)** ....(Controlled) ‡23,000
Financial Services Review **(7007)** ....(Paid) 500
PENSION
  Management **(7037)** ....(Combined) 28,927

Norcross
Georgia Trend **(7460)** ....(Paid) 13,374
                       (Non-paid) 36,635

ILLINOIS
Champaign
Journal of Education
  Finance **(8196)** ....(Paid) ⊕1,200
The Quarterly Review of Economics and
  Finance **(8214)** 2,000

Chicago
AAII Journal **(8240)** ....‡170,000
Banking Strategies **(8281)** ....(Paid) 32,000
Business Insurance **(8296)** ....(Paid) 25,386
                 (Controlled) 20,339
Collections & Credit
  Risk **(8335)** ....(Controlled) △24,548
Commercial Investment Real
  Estate **(8337)** ....(Paid) ‡600
                (Controlled) ‡11,000
Computerized Investing **(8341)** ....‡42,000
Crain's Chicago Business **(8346)** ...(Paid) ★43,316
                (Non-paid) ★6,710
Futures Magazine **(8383)** ....(Paid) 18,077
                (Controlled) 46,924
Government Finance Review **(8388)** 14,000
Investment News **(8419)**
Mutual Funds **(8498)**
Realty and Building **(8552)** ....(Paid) ‡13,280
               (Controlled) ‡1,130

Riverwoods
Bankruptcy Law Reports **(9501)** ....‡500
Financial and Estate Planning **(9505)**

Schaumburg
North American Actuarial
  Journal **(9589)** ....(Non-paid) 17,000

Skokie
Your Money **(9613)** ....(Paid) 403,712

Springfield
Illinois Banker **(9621)** ....‡2,200

INDIANA
Hammond
Dow Theory Forecasts **(10050)** ....(Paid) 16,000

Indianapolis
Hoosier Banker **(10115)** ....‡3,800

South Bend
The Journal of Private Equity **(10456)**

KANSAS
Shawnee Mission
Bank News **(11803)** ....(Paid) 1,931
                (Non-paid) 5,170
Texas Banking **(11805)** ....(Paid) ‡5,000
                (Controlled) ‡300

Topeka
The Kansas Banker **(11826)** ....‡1,100

KENTUCKY
Louisville
Kentucky Banker **(12223)** ....(Combined) 1,600
UMI's Banking Information
  Index **(12241)** ....(Paid) 410
                (Non-paid) 20

MARYLAND
Bethesda
AFP Exchange **(13295)** ....(Paid) 14,000
                (Non-paid) 200

Columbia
Business Credit **(13455)** ....(Paid) △25,960

Rockville
First Call/Thomson Financial Insiders'
  Chronicle **(13679)**
Mutual Funds Update **(13689)** .....(Combined) 2,500

MASSACHUSETTS
Amherst
The Journal of Alternative Investments **(13796)**

Boston
The Commercial Record **(13879)** 3,200
                (Free) 408
Professional Collector Magazine **(13952)**
Stages **(13962)**

Concord
Bank Accounting & Finance **(14143)** ....(Paid) 1,000
Commercial Lending Review **(14146)** ....(Paid) 1,000

Winchester
Real Estate Finance **(14667)** 2,600

MICHIGAN
Lansing
Michigan Banker Magazine **(15280)** ......(Paid) ‡650

Madison Heights
Better Investing **(15326)** ....(Paid) 350,000

Troy
Detroit Legal News **(15618)** ....⊕1,850
Leaders' Edge **(15628)**

MINNESOTA
Minneapolis
Collector **(16068)** ....‡6,100
Federal Reserve Bank of Minneapolis Quarterly
  Review **(16080)**
Northwestern Financial
  Review **(16117)** ....(Paid) 2,000

MISSISSIPPI
Jackson
The Mississippi Banker **(16699)** ....‡1,300

MISSOURI
Kansas City
Economic Review **(17166)** ....(Free) ‡26,000

St. Louis
St. Louis Watchman
  Advocate **(17509)** ....(Combined) ‡40,000

Springfield
Traders World **(17615)** ....(Paid) 11,000

NEBRASKA
Lincoln
Quarterly Journal of Business &
  Economics **(18116)** ....(Paid) 500
                (Non-paid) 100

NEW JERSEY
Florham Park
Financial Executive **(18825)** 18,000

Hoboken
Banks in Insurance Report **(18899)** 5985
The Journal of Futures Markets **(19024)** 7700
Strategic Management
  Journal **(19108)** ....(Paid) 28,000

Jersey City
CPA Client Bulletin **(19135)**
Mansfield Stock Chart Service **(19143)**
Tax Adviser **(19145)**

Mahwah
The Journal of Behavioral Finance **(19195)**

Princeton
Bloomberg Markets
  Magazine **(19454)** ....(Non-paid) ‡150,537
C.F.M.A. Building Profits **(19456)** ....(Paid) 7,000
              (Combined) 12,000
Dowline **(19459)** 110,000

Princeton Junction
Card Manufacturing **(19483)** ....(Paid) 3,000

Shrewsbury
Investment Advisor
  Magazine **(19556)** ....(Controlled) ‡75,000

NEW YORK
Buffalo
Buffalo Law Journal **(20366)** ....(Paid) 700
                (Non-paid) 30

Huntington
Institutional Holding of Oil Stocks **(20773)**

Lake Success
The Market Guide–Select Over the Counter Stock
  Edition **(20880)**

Manhasset
Wall Street and Technology **(21017)**

New York
ABA Banking Journal **(21130)** 31,119
American Banker **(21180)** ....(Mon.-Fri.) 14,611
American Business **(21182)** ....‡110,000
Angel Advisor **(21214)**
Asia-Pacific Financial Markets **(21261)**
Asset Protection Journal **(21267)**
Bank Investment Marketing **(21286)**
Bank Technology
  News **(21287)** ....(Non-paid) ‡36,043
Banking & Financial Services Policy Report **(21288)**
Banking Law Journal **(21289)** ....(Paid) 2,500
Barron's **(21292)** ....(Paid) 300,158
The Bond Buyer **(21332)**
Bond Guide **(21333)** ....(Paid) 70,000
Broker Magazine **(21344)**
The Bulletin **(21348)** ....(Controlled) 2,800
Card Marketing **(21373)**
Compensation & Benefits Management **(21466)**
Corporate Business Taxation Monthly **(21500)**
Credit Card Management **(21513)** ....(Paid) 3,252
               (Non-paid) 8,524
Credit Memo **(21514)** ....(Non-paid) 3,000
Credit Union Journal **(21515)**
CreditWeek **(21516)**
Derivatives Quarterly **(21544)**
Earnings Guide **(21575)**
Energy in the News **(21604)** ......(Controlled) 30,000
European Finance Review **(21636)**
European Financial Law Review **(21637)**
Federal Reserve Bank of New York Economic Policy
  Review **(21682)**
Financial Crime Review **(21695)**
Financial History **(21696)** ....(Paid) ‡2,100
               (Non-paid) ‡4,400
Financial History Review **(21697)** 550
Financial Planning **(21698)** ....(Paid) 25,000
              (Controlled) 75,000
Financial Services Marketing **(21699)**
Financing Operations **(21700)** ....(Paid) 1,247
Future Banker **(21743)**
Global Finance **(21770)** ....(Paid) 350
              (Controlled) 50,000
Global Finance Journal **(21771)**
Global Investment
  Magazine **(21772)** ....(Controlled) △20,000
Infrastructure Finance **(21873)** ...(Controlled) 16,353
Insights **(21877)**
Institutional Investor **(21880)** ....(Paid) 8,000
              (Controlled) 95,000
Institutional Investor (International
  Edition) **(21881)** ....(Non-paid) 36,394
International Journal of Health Care Finance and
  Economics **(21908)**
The International Tax Journal **(21938)**
International Tax and Public Finance **(21939)**
Investment Dealers' Digest **(21946)** ....(Paid) ‡3,848
Investment Management Weekly **(21947)**
Journal of Applied Corporate Finance **(21989)**
Journal of Cost Management **(22040)**
Journal of Deferred Compensation **(22047)**
The Journal of Derivatives **(22048)**
The Journal of Investment Compliance **(22108)**
Journal of Pension Benefits **(22152)**
Journal of Pension Planning and
  Compliance **(22153)**
The Journal of Portfolio
  Management **(22164)** 4,500
Journal of Property Tax Management **(22166)**
The Journal of Risk Finance **(22180)**
Journal of State Taxation **(22192)**
Mergers & Acquisitions **(22316)** ....(Paid) ‡3,445
              (Non-paid) ‡400
Money **(22360)** ....(Paid) 1,906,352
Mortgage Servicing News **(22367)** ......(Free) 20,000
Mortgage Technology **(22368)** ....(Paid) 600
              (Controlled) 21,314
Municipal Finance Journal **(22382)**
National Mortgage News **(22399)** ....(Paid) 10,097
On Wall Street **(22489)**
Operation Update **(22498)**
Origination News **(22503)**
Pensions & Investments **(22537)** ....(Paid) 9,555
              (Non-paid) 40,231
Private Equity Week **(22594)**
The Real Estate Finance Journal **(22631)** 2,500
Review of Derivatives Research **(22658)**

Circ.   Circ.   Circ.

BANKING, FINANCE, AND INVESTMENTS
(continued)

The Review of Income and
  Wealth **(22659)** ....‡1,400
The Review of Securities & Commodities
  Regulation **(22662)**
The Secured Lender **(22718)** .....(Controlled) ‡8,600
Securities Industry News **(22719)**
Securities Regulation Law
  Journal **(22720)** ....(Paid) 1,074
                    (Non-paid) 107
Small Business Banker **(22745)**
Standard & Poor's A.S.E. Stock
  Reports **(22784)** ....‡4,287
Standard & Poor's Corporation Records, Current
  News Edition **(22785)** ....‡5,600
Standard & Poor's Dividend Record **(22786)**
Standard & Poor's Nasdaq and Regional Exchange
  Stock Reports **(22787)** ....‡4,673
Standard & Poor's N.Y.S.E. Stock
  Reports **(22788)** ....‡5,368
Stock Guide **(22793)** ....(Paid) 300,000
Treasury and Risk Management
  Magazine **(22860)** 46,000
Trendline Current Market
  Perspectives **(22861)** ....(Paid) 3,000
Trendline Daily Action Stock Charts **(22862)**
Trusts and Estates **(22872)** ....(Paid) △10,035
                (Non-paid) △4,485
U.S. Banker **(22886)** ....(Paid) 1,679
              (Controlled) 38,621
Web Finance **(22912)**
World Banking Abstracts **(22940)**
Worth Magazine **(22946)** ....(Paid) 501,071

St. James
Professional Check Casher **(23289)** 5,731

Scarsdale
Equities Magazine Co. **(23312)** ....(Paid) ‡10,017
               (Non-paid) ‡6,595

Yonkers
The Stock Market Magazine **(23602)**

NORTH CAROLINA
Cary
The Review of Financial
  Studies **(23693)** ....(Paid) ‡2,025

Chapel Hill
The Journal of Fixed Income **(23712)**

Raleigh
Carolina Banker **(24129)** ....(Non-paid) ‡6,500

OHIO
Columbus
Journal of Money, Credit, and
  Banking **(25025)** ....‡4,000
Ohio Record **(25048)** ....(Controlled) 5,500

OKLAHOMA
Oklahoma City
Oklahoma Banker **(25973)** ....‡2,500

PENNSYLVANIA
Bryn Mawr
Journal of Financial Service
  Professionals **(26741)** ....‡28,000

Philadelphia
Business Review **(27390)** ....(Non-paid) 10,000
Federal Reserve Bank of Philadelphia Business
  Review **(27469)** ....(Non-paid) 10,000
The RMA Journal **(27654)** ....(Paid) ‡2,500
             (Non-paid) ‡17,500

Pittsburgh
Official Summary of Security Transactions and
  Holdings **(27823)**

Wayne
Bank and Lender Liability Litigation Reporter **(28126)**
Securities Litigation & Regulation Reporter **(28135)**

SOUTH CAROLINA
Columbia
Journal of Financial Research **(28552)**

TENNESSEE
Brentwood
Bank Director **(29060)** ....(Paid) 8,200
             (Non-paid) 23,780

Nashville
The Tennessee Banker **(29488)** ....‡2,350

TEXAS
Austin
The Bank Quarterly **(29762)**

Dallas
Bankers Digest **(30126)** ....‡3,200
Economic and Financial Policy Review **(30153)**

Houston
MRI Banker's Guide to Foreign
  Currency **(30509)** ....(Paid) 12,000
             (Non-paid) 400
Oil and Gas Investor **(30515)** ....(Paid) 3,765
             (Non-paid) 356

Plano
The Journal of Investing **(30947)**

Waco
Journal of Entrepreneurial and Small Firm
  Finance **(31250)**

VIRGINIA
Alexandria
Armed Forces Comptroller **(31643)** ....‡20,000
Journal of Government Financial
  Management **(31697)**

Arlington
The Federal Credit Union **(31793)** ......(Paid) 11,136
             (Controlled) 1,400
Washington Techway **(31840)**

Charlottesville
CFA Digest **(31922)** ....(Combined) ⊕45,000

Falls Church
GAMA International
  Journal **(32046)** ....(Controlled) 6,000

Langley AFB
Statistics of Income - SOI Bulletin **(32177)**

Richmond
Federal Reserve Bank of Richmond Economic
  Quarterly **(32437)**

WASHINGTON
Seattle
Journal of Financial and Quantitative
  Analysis **(32977)** ....‡3,200
Technical Analysis of Stocks &
  Commodities **(33035)** 65,000
Working Money **(33045)** ....(Paid) 165,000

WISCONSIN
Hartland
Bank Financial Quarterly **(33776)**
Credit Union Financial Profiles **(33777)**
S & L—Savings Bank Financial Quarterly **(33783)**

Madison
Credit Union Magazine **(33929)** ....(Paid) 39,000
Credit Union National Association GAC, Governmental
  Affairs Conference **(33930)** 2,000
50 Plus Lifestyles **(33939)** ....‡5,300
             (Controlled) ‡34,300

BRITISH COLUMBIA, CANADA
Vancouver
Enterprise **(35140)** ....(Paid) 2,000
             (Non-paid) 1,000

MANITOBA, CANADA
Winnipeg
Trade and Commerce **(35353)** ....(Paid) 221
             (Non-paid) 9,745

ONTARIO, CANADA
Bath
Canadian MoneySaver **(35667)** ....‡19,100

Ottawa
Insolvency Bulletin **(36251)** ....(Non-paid) 3,500

Toronto
Bank Facts **(36470)**
Banking and Finance Law Review **(36471)**
Benefits and Pensions
  Monitor **(36475)** ....(Combined) 20,108
Canadian Banker **(36493)**
Canadian Business **(36494)** ....(Paid) 81,377
Canadian Shareowner **(36530)** ....(Paid) ‡20,000
             (Non-paid) ‡200
Canadian Tax Journal (Revue fiscale
  canadienne) **(36531)** ....‡8,300
C.D. Howe Institute Commentary **(36543)**
The Financial Post **(36594)** ......(Tues.-Fri.) 77,757
             (Sat.) 155,475

Investment Executive **(36624)** .....(Controlled) 45,600
Investor's Digest of
  Canada **(36625)** ....(Paid) 25,700
             (Non-paid) 28,000
Money Digest **(36668)**

QUEBEC, CANADA
Montreal
The Insurance
  Journal **(37133)** ....(Combined) 18,000
Magazine Finance **(37180)** ....(Combined) 40,000

BEVERAGES, BREWING, AND BOTTLING

ARIZONA
Phoenix
Arizona Beverage Analyst **(774)** ....(Paid) ‡135
             (Controlled) ‡4,417

CALIFORNIA
Palm Springs
Beverage Dynamics **(2754)** ....(Non-paid) △50,037

Pleasant Hill
Beverage Industry News **(2852)** ....(Paid) ‡11,250
             (Non-paid) ‡5,618

San Rafael
Wines & Vines **(3604)** ....‡4,185

Santa Rosa
The Food & Beverage Industry **(3725)**
The Food & Beverage
  Journal **(3726)** ....(Combined) 27,000
Wine X Magazine **(3736)** ....(Controlled) 50,000

COLORADO
Denver
Colorado Beverage Analyst **(4311)** ....(Paid) ‡345
             (Controlled) ‡1,743

Pueblo
American Breweriana **(4597)** ....(Controlled) 3,600

CONNECTICUT
Norwalk
Beverage & Food
  Dynamics **(5050)** ....(Controlled) △65,081
Cheers **(5052)** ....(Controlled) 90,000
Modern Brewery Age **(5068)** ....(Paid) ‡1,915
Modern Brewery Age Tabloid
  Edition **(5069)** ....‡5,181
StateWays **(5074)** ....(Controlled) ‡10,000

DISTRICT OF COLUMBIA
Washington
Washington DC Beverage
  Journal **(5844)** ....(Paid) ‡473
             (Controlled) ‡977

FLORIDA
Miami
Southern Beverage Journal **(6382)** ....‡23,000

Tallahassee
Grape Times **(6723)** 200

HAWAII
Honolulu
Hawaii Beverage Guide **(7690)** ....‡2,000

ILLINOIS
Bensenville
Food Engineering (North American
  Edition) **(8067)** ....(Paid) 662
             (Non-paid) 50,000

KANSAS
Wichita
Kansas Beverage News **(11884)** 2,300

MARYLAND
Elkridge
Maryland Beverage Journal **(13493)** ....(Paid) ‡4,600
             (Controlled) ‡1,800

MASSACHUSETTS
Boston
Massachusetts Beverage
  Business **(13926)** ....(Paid) ‡7,485
             (Non-paid) ‡560

Winchester
The Quarterly Review of
　Wines　**(14666)** ....(Paid) ‡81,540
　　　　　　　　　　　(Non-paid) ‡54,900

NEBRASKA
Lincoln
Nebraska Beverage Analyst　**(18098)** .....(Paid) ‡141
　　　　　　　　　　　(Non-paid) ‡2,634

NEVADA
Las Vegas
Cocktails Magazine　**(18361)** ....(Paid) 25,000

NEW JERSEY
Liberty Corner
Bartender
　Magazine　**(19169)** ....(Controlled) ‡148,250

Maywood
Ale Street News　**(19218)** ....(Combined) 110,000

Union
New Jersey Beverage
　Journal　**(19684)** ....(Paid) 4,972
　　　　　　　　　　　(Non-paid) 2,414

NEW MEXICO
Santa Fe
New Mexico Beverage
　Analyst　**(19937)** ....(Paid) ‡704
　　　　　　　　　　　(Non-paid) ‡154

NEW YORK
Elmsford
Wine Enthusiast Magazine　**(20587)** 110,000

New York
Beverage Aisle　**(21303)** ....(Non-paid) 22,012
Beverage Media　**(21304)** ....(Paid) 7,473
　　　　　　　　　　　(Controlled) 3,473
Beverage World　**(21305)** ....(Non-paid) ‡34,000
Beverage World en
　Espanol　**(21306)** ....(Combined) ‡11,100
Beverage World International　**(21307)** ....‡22,500
Chain Leader　**(21392)**
Food Engineering (International
　Edition)　**(21711)** ....(Paid) ‡734
　　　　　　　　　　　(Non-paid) ‡15,043
ID: The Information Source for Managers and
　DSRs　**(21842)**
Impact　**(21854)**
Market Watch　**(22285)** ....‡51,760
Wine Spectator　**(22919)** ....(Paid) 290,318
Wine & Spirits Magazine　**(22920)** ....‡82,000

Rochester
American Wine Society Journal　**(23209)** ....‡5,500

OHIO
Louisville
The Friends of Wine　**(25318)**

OKLAHOMA
Oklahoma City
Oklahoma Beverage News　**(25975)** 1,325

OREGON
Portland
Fresh Cup Magazine　**(26479)**

PENNSYLVANIA
Lancaster
Wine East　**(27146)**

RHODE ISLAND
Providence
Rhode Island Beverage Journal　**(28421)** 1,300

VIRGINIA
Alexandria
American Brewer　**(31635)** ....(Combined) 3,000
Bottled Water Reporter　**(31649)** ....(Paid) ‡3,200
　　　　　　　　　　　(Non-paid) ‡150

WEST VIRGINIA
Wheeling
Atlantic Control States Beverage
　Journal　**(33500)** ....(Paid) 3,675
　　　　　　　　　　　(Controlled) 7,159
Ohio Beverage Journal　**(33504)** ......(Paid) ‡2,072
　　　　　　　　　　　(Controlled) ‡4,876

WISCONSIN
Madison
Wisconsin Beverage Business　**(33979)** ....‡6,000

Thiensville
The Brewers Bulletin　**(34365)** 600
Brewers Digest　**(34366)** ....(Paid) ‡2,759
　　　　　　　　　　　(Non-paid) ‡119

MANITOBA, CANADA
Winnipeg
Bar & Beverage Business
　Magazine　**(35313)** ....(Combined) 16,077

ONTARIO, CANADA
Ottawa
BiereMag　**(36187)** ....(Paid) 500
　　　　　　　　　　　(Non-paid) 1,000

Toronto
Food in Canada　**(36597)** ....(Combined) 9,065

QUEBEC, CANADA
Montreal
Wine Tidings　**(37238)** ....(Combined) 19,300

BIOLOGY

ALABAMA
Birmingham
Nucleosides & Nucleotides & Nucleic
　Acids　**(82)** 400
Paleontological Journal　**(85)** 425

ARIZONA
Tempe
Copeia　**(902)**

CALIFORNIA
Berkeley
Historical Studies in the Physical and Biological
　Sciences　**(1525)**
Journal of Lipid Research　**(1535)** ....(Paid) ‡2,029
Journal of Social and Evolutionary Systems　**(1537)**

Davis
Pesticide Biochemistry and Physiology　**(1817)**

Irvine
Biomedical Optics　**(2076)**

Los Angeles
Clinical Immunology　**(2242)**

Palo Alto
Annual Review of Genetics　**(2790)**
Annual Review of Microbiology　**(2792)**

San Diego
Anaerobe　**(3112)**
Analytical Biochemistry　**(3113)**
Archives of Biochemistry and Biophysics　**(3116)**
Biochemical and Biophysical Research
　Communications　**(3120)**
Biological Control　**(3121)**
Blood Cells, Molecules, & Diseases　**(3122)**
Brain, Behavior, and Immunity　**(3124)**
Cell Biology International　**(3128)**
Cryobiology　**(3137)**
Cytokine　**(3138)**
Developmental Biology　**(3140)**
Experimental Cell Research　**(3147)** 1,986
Experimental Neurology　**(3150)**
Experimental Parasitology　**(3151)**
Food Microbiology　**(3156)**
Frontiers in Neuroendocrinology　**(3157)**
Fungal Genetics and Biology　**(3158)**
Fungal Genetics and Biology　**(3159)**
General and Comparative Endocrinology　**(3161)**
Hormones and Behavior　**(3168)**
ImmunoMethods　**(3173)**
Journal of Colloid and Interface Science　**(3181)**
Journal of Invertebrate Pathology　**(3199)**
Journal of Magnetic Resonance　**(3201)**
Journal of Magnetic Resonance　**(3202)**
Journal of Magnetic Resonance　**(3203)**
Metabolic Engineering　**(3228)**
Methods　**(3229)**
Methods　**(3230)**
Methods in Immunology and
　Immunochemistry　**(3231)**
Microvascular Research　**(3232)**
Molecular and Cellular Neurosciences　**(3234)**
Molecular Genetics and Metabolism　**(3235)**
Molecular Phylogenetics and Evolution　**(3236)**
Neurobiology of Learning and Memory　**(3240)**
NeuroImage　**(3241)**
Nitric Oxide　**(3242)**
Plasmid　**(3246)**
Protein Expression and Purification　**(3250)**
Seminars in Cell & Developmental Biology　**(3273)**

Theoretical Population Biology　**(3278)**
Virology　**(3288)**

Santa Cruz
Invertebrate Biology　**(3684)**

CONNECTICUT
Farmington
Brain, Behavior and Evolution　**(4801)** 1,000
Journal of Biomedical Science　**(4836)**
Pathobiology　**(4853)** 1,050
Tumor Biology　**(4862)** 1,000

New Haven
Quarterly Review of Biophysics　**(5000)** 700

Shelton
American Biotechnology
　Laboratory　**(5117)** ....(Non-paid) ‡70,792

DELAWARE
Newark
Journal of Foraminiferal Research　**(5276)**

DISTRICT OF COLUMBIA
Washington
Applied and Environmental
　Microbiology　**(5358)** ....(Paid) ‡8,932
　　　　　　　　　　　(Non-paid) ‡35
ASM News　**(5368)** ....(Paid) ‡42,684
　　　　　　　　　　　(Non-paid) ‡50
Biomacromolecules　**(5376)** 2000
BioScience　**(5378)** ....(Paid) ‡10,000
　　　　　　　　　　　(Non-paid) ‡402
Clinical Microbiology Reviews　**(5421)** ....‡6,693
Crystal Growth & Design　**(5451)** 1,300
Family Systems　**(5490)** ....(Combined) 680
Journal of Bacteriology　**(5575)** ....(Combined) ‡4,833
Journal of Clinical
　Microbiology　**(5577)** ....(Combined) ‡9,101
Journal of Virology　**(5618)** ....(Paid) ‡5,663
　　　　　　　　　　　(Non-paid) ‡30
Microbiology and Molecular Biology
　Reviews　**(5648)** ....(Paid) ‡9,905
Molecular and Cellular
　Biology　**(5658)** ....(Combined) ‡4,104

FLORIDA
Boynton Beach
Journal of Immunoassay and
　Immunochemistry　**(5951)** 350
Preparative Biochemistry &
　Biotechnology　**(5952)** 300

Seminole
Journal of Crustacean Biology　**(6684)** ...(Paid) ‡952

GEORGIA
Athens
Plant Molecular Biology
　Reporter　**(6948)** ....(Paid) ‡2,200

Atlanta
BioWorld Magazine　**(6978)** ....(Controlled) ‡10,000

HAWAII
Honolulu
Pacific Science　**(7715)** ....(Paid) ‡680
　　　　　　　　　　　(Controlled) ‡30

ILLINOIS
Carbondale
The Bryologist　**(8115)** ....(Paid) ‡900

Chicago
Physiological and Biochemical Zoology　**(8530)**

Evanston
Journal of Biological Rhythms　**(8863)** ....(Paid) ‡478
　　　　　　　　　　　(Non-paid) ‡77

INDIANA
Lafayette
Protein Science　**(10254)**

Notre Dame
American Midland
　Naturalist　**(10366)** ....(Paid) ‡1,137
　　　　　　　　　　　(Controlled) ‡54

Terre Haute
Issues in Law & Medicine　**(10487)** ......(Paid) 1,000
　　　　　　　　　　　(Controlled) 2,000

KANSAS
Emporia
Kansas Biology Teacher　**(11430)** ....(Combined) 300

Circulation: ★ = ABC; △ = BPA; ♦ = CAC; ● = CCAB; ▢ = VAC; ⊕ = PO Statement; ‡ = Publisher's Report; Boldface figures = sworn; Light figures = estimated.

3105

Trade, Technical, and Professional Publications

Circ.   Circ.   Circ.

BIOLOGY (continued)

MAINE
Salsbury Cove
MDIBL Bulletin (13048)

MARYLAND
Baltimore
Journal of Immunotherapy (13193) ....(Paid) 696
Maryland Naturalist (13213) ....(Paid) 250
(Controlled) 40
Molecular Medicine (13221) ....(Combined) 500

Bethesda
Agricultural and Environmental Biotechnology
Abstracts (13297)
Algology, Mycology & Protozoology: Microbiology
Abstracts, Section C (13299)
American Journal of Physiology
(Consolidated) (13304) ....(Combined) ‡2,639
ASFA Aquaculture Abstracts (13315)
ASFA/Aquatic Sciences & Fisheries Abstracts Part 1:
Biological Sciences & Living Resources (13316)
ASFA Marine Biotechnology Abstracts (13317)
Bacteriology: Microbiology Abstracts, Section
B (13319)
Biophysical Journal (13321)
Calcium and Calcified Tissue Abstracts (13322)
Cellular Immunology (13323)
Chemoreception Abstracts (13324)
CSA Neurosciences Abstracts (13328)
The FASEB Journal (13335) 6,000
Immunology Abstracts (13344)
Industrial and Applied Microbiology: Microbiology
Abstracts, Section A (13345)
The Journal of Biological
Chemistry (13350) ....‡5,000
The Journal of Molecular
Diagnostics (13352) ....(Paid) 3,000
Medical and Pharmaceutical Biotechnology
Abstracts (13359)
Nucleic Acids Abstracts (13368)
Virology and AIDS Abstracts (13387)

College Park
Virtual Journal of Biological Physics
Research (13444)

Gaithersburg
Experimental Aging Research (13539) 1,000

Largo
InVitro Cellular & Developmental Biology -
PLANT (13612) ....‡2,500

Rockville
The Plant Cell (13694) ....‡5,000

MASSACHUSETTS
Burlington
The Knee (14031) ....‡2,250
Supramolecular Science (14033)

Cambridge
AJOB (14036)
Cell (14045) ....(Combined) ‡12,000
Neuron (14085) ....(Combined) ‡4,146
Q (14092)

Malden
Journal of Neurochemistry (14295) 2333

Norwell
Journal of Agricultural and Environmental
Ethics (14441) ....(Paid) 211
(Non-paid) 27

Waltham
Journal of Neurogenetics (14600)

Westborough
BioTechniques (14635) 62,000
Peptide Research (14638) 3,000

Woods Hole
The Biological Bulletin (14672) .....(Controlled) 1,690

MICHIGAN
Kalamazoo
Journal of Investigative
Surgery (15240) ....(Paid) ‡571

MINNESOTA
Minneapolis
Journal of Andrology (16086) ....‡1,200

MISSOURI
St. Louis
Analytical and Quantitative Cytology and
Histology (17413) ....(Paid) ‡3,090

NEBRASKA
Lincoln
Photochemistry and Photobiology (18113) 815
(Non-paid) 1,600

NEW JERSEY
Hoboken
American Journal of Human
Biology (18885) 5600
The Anatomical Record (18890) 8400
Biopolymers (18906) 7000
Biotechnology & Bioengineering (18907) 11,900
Catheterization and Cardiovascular
Diagnosis (18908) 23,800
Cell Biochemistry and Function (18909)
Cell Motility and the Cytoskeleton (18910) 4900
Complexity (18920) 14,000
Developmental Dynamics (18927) 8750
Environmetrics (18942)
GLIA (18954) 4200
Hematological Oncology (18961)
Human Mutation (18967) 4900
Hydrobiological Journal (18970) 325
Journal of Biomedical Materials
Research (19007) 17,500
Journal of Cellular Biochemistry (19008) 5950
Journal of Chemical Technology and
Biotechnology (19010)
Journal of Labelled Compounds and
Radiopharmaceuticals (19028) ....(Paid) 4,900
Journal of Molecular
Recognition (19032) ....(Paid) 4,200
Journal of Morphology (19033) 6300
Journal of Peptide Science (19040)
Journal of Raman Spectroscopy (19044)
Journal of the Science of Food and
Agriculture (19047)
The Journal of Trace Elements in Experimental
Medicine (19051) 2800
Luminescence (19054)
Magnetic Resonance in Chemistry (19056)
Microscopy Research and
Technique (19062) 5600
Neuroscience Research Communications (19073)
NMR in Biomedicine (19074)
Radiation Oncology Investigations (19094) 3500
Reviews in Medical Virology (19099) ....(Paid) 3,500
Teratogenesis, Carcinogenesis and
Mutagenesis (19117) ....(Paid) 3,850
Teratology (19118) 11,550
Yeast (19121)
Zoo Biology (19122) 3850

Mahwah
International Journal of Behavioral Medicine (19192)

Medford
Biology Digest (19221) 1,900

Morris Plains
Biomedical Products (19288) ....(Controlled) ‡71,000

Totowa
Molecular Biotechnology (19652) ....(Paid) 350

West Orange
Zygote (19724) ....(Paid) ‡252
(Non-paid) ‡88

NEW YORK
Bronx
Biological & Agricultural Index (20255)

Ithaca
Geomicrobiology
Journal (20801) ....(Controlled) ‡281

Larchmont
Antioxidants and Redox Signaling (20889)
Astrobiology (20891)
Cloning and Stem Cells (20894)
DNA and Cell Biology (20897) ....‡1,200

New York
Applied Biochemistry and Microbiology (21228)
Artificial Cells, Blood Substitutes and Immobilization
Biotechnology (21256) 325
Biochemistry (Moscow) (21310)
BioComplexity (21311)
BioControl (21312)
Biodiversity and Conservation (21313)
Biogerontology (21315)
Biological Invasions (21317)
Biological Reviews of the Cambridge Philosophical
Society (21318)
Biology Bulletin (21319)
Biomedical Engineering (21320)
Biomedical Microdevices (21321)
BioMetals (21323)

Bioscience Reports (21325)
Biotechnology Letters (21326)
Bulletin of Experimental Biology and
Medicine (21350)
Cellular and Molecular Neurobiology (21387)
Cellulose (21388)
Chromosome Research (21414)
Current Microbiology (21525) ....(Combined) 700
Doklady Biological Sciences (21563)
Dreaming (21569)
European Journal of Phycology (21647)
Genetical Research (21752) 800
Glycoconjugate (21773)
The Histochemical Journal (21804)
Integrated Pest Management (21886)
JMBA: Journal of the Marine Biological
Association (21967) 1600
Journal of Applied Phycology (21993)
Journal of Bioeconomics (22008)
Journal of Bioenergetics and Biomembranes (22009)
Journal of Biological Physics (22010)
The Journal of Biomedical Informatics (22012)
Journal of Biomolecular NMR (22013)
The Journal of Cell Biology (22019) ....‡3,524
Journal of Computer-Aided Molecular Design (22036)
Journal of Evolutionary Biochemistry and
Physiology (22066)
Journal of the History of Biology (22089)
Journal of Mammary Gland Biology and
Neoplasia (22119)
Journal of Membrane
Biology (22132) ....(Combined) 800
Journal of Molecular
Evolution (22136) ....(Combined) 1,000
Journal of Neurocytology (22142)
Journal of Paleolimnology (22150)
Letters in Peptide Science (22248)
Mammalian Genome (22276) ....(Combined) 925
Microbiology (22331)
Molecular Biology (22353)
Molecular Biology Reports (22354)
Molecular Breeding (22355)
Molecular and Cellular Biochemistry (22356)
Molecular Diversity (22357)
Molecular Engineering (22358)
Mycological Research (22387) 1750
Mycopathologia (22389)
Nature (22409) ....(Non-paid) 681
Nature Biotechnology (22410) ....(Paid) 11,000
(Controlled) 5,000
Nature Genetics (22411) ....(Paid) 6,100
Origins of Life and Evolution of the
Biosphere (22504)
Parasitology (22523) 900
Plant Cell, Tissue and Organ Culture (22557)
Plant Ecology (22558)
Plant Foods for Human Nutrition (22560)
Reviews in Fish Biology and Fisheries (22664)
Russian Journal of Biorganic Chemistry (22684)
Russian Journal of Developmental Biology (22686)
Russian Journal of Marine Biology (22691)
Sensory Systems (22728)
Somatic Cell and Molecular Genetics (22762)

Stony Brook
The Quarterly Review of
Biology (23375) ....(Paid) ‡3,100
(Non-paid) ‡200

NORTH CAROLINA
Winston-Salem
The Journal of Parasitology (24320)

OHIO
Columbus
Ohio Biological Survey Miscellaneous
Contributions (25040) ....(Paid) 80

PENNSYLVANIA
Media
Age (27241)

Philadelphia
Annals of Human Biology (27378)
International Journal of Hyperthermia (27499)
International Journal of Radiation Biology (27506)
Journal of Natural History (27538) ....(Paid) 333,180
Medical Informatics & The Internet in
Medicine (27566)
Molecular Cancer Research (27572) .....(Paid) 2,400
Molecular Diagnosis (27573)
Molecular Membrane Biology (27574)
Xenobiotica (27724)

TENNESSEE
Knoxville
Journal of Nematology (29277) ....‡1,000

Numbers cited after listings are entry numbers rather than page numbers.

Memphis
Journal of Biomolecular Techniques **(29371)**

TEXAS
Austin
Bioorganic Chemistry **(29765)**

Galveston
International Journal of Developmental
Neuroscience **(30381)** ....(Paid) 700
(Non-paid) 300

San Antonio
Pharmacology Biochemistry and Behavior **(31041)**

UTAH
Provo
Western North American
Naturalist **(31409)** ....(Paid) 225

VIRGINIA
Reston
The American Biology
Teacher **(32359)** ....(Paid) ‡11,000
(Controlled) ‡100

WISCONSIN
Madison
Biology of
Reproduction **(33924)** ....(Controlled) 3,200

Waukesha
Birder's World **(34396)** ....(Paid) ★61,242

BRITISH COLUMBIA, CANADA
Victoria
Archaea **(35206)** ....(Paid) 500
(Non-paid) 500

MANITOBA, CANADA
Winnipeg
Biochemistry and Cell Biology (Biochimie et Biologie
Cellulaire) **(35316)** ....‡1,225

ONTARIO, CANADA
Ottawa
Canadian Association of Radiologists
Journal **(36189)** 1,600
Canadian Journal of Microbiology (Revue Canadienne
de Microbiologie) **(36208)** ....‡1,725
CMAJ/JAMC (Canadian Medical Association Journal)/
(Journal de l'Association Medicale
Canadienne) **(36236)** ....(Combined) •62,008

Thunder Bay
Alices **(36436)**

Waterloo
Biotechnology Advances **(36846)** 1,000

BOATS AND MARINE

See also Ships and Shipping

CONNECTICUT
Essex
Soundings Trade Only **(4784)** ....(Paid) 1,098
(Free) 32,007

Mystic
Log of Mystic Seaport **(4968)** ....(Paid) 22,000
(Controlled) 300

FLORIDA
Fort Lauderdale
Marine Business Journal **(6080)** ....(Paid) 27,000
(Controlled) 1,426
Waterfront News **(6087)** ....(Paid) ‡750
(Free) ‡39,000

St. Petersburg
The duPont Registry: A Buyer's Gallery of Fine
Boats **(6624)** ....(Paid) 16,000
(Controlled) 38,000

ILLINOIS
Niles
Boat and Motor Dealer **(9286)** ....(Paid) 34
(Controlled) 31,706
Marina/Dock Age **(9290)** ....(Controlled) ‡17,090

MAINE
Brooklin
Professional
BoatBuilder **(12932)** ....(Controlled) 23,688

Portland
National Fisherman **(13013)** ....(Paid) 40,034

MASSACHUSETTS
Indian Orchard
Titanic Commutator **(14256)**

MINNESOTA
St. Paul
Marine Textiles **(16386)** ....(Paid) ‡3,000
(Non-paid) ‡5,000

NEW YORK
New York
Journal of Navigation **(22139)** ....(Paid) 455
(Non-paid) 3,346

RHODE ISLAND
East Greenwich
Rhode Island Boating **(28342)** ....(Paid) 50
(Non-paid) 20,000

SOUTH CAROLINA
Mount Pleasant
The Water Log Maritime
Journal **(28697)** ....(Combined) 10,000

QUEBEC, CANADA
Montreal
Bike, Boat & R.V. Trader/Moto, Bateau & Vehicules
Recreatif Hebdo **(37091)**

BOOK TRADE AND AUTHOR NEWS

CALIFORNIA
Los Angeles
Rapport **(2377)** ....(Paid) 50,000

Oakland
Locus **(2687)** ....‡10,000

San Diego
Writers' Monthly **(3289)**

San Francisco
Feminist Bookstore News **(3360)** ....(Paid) ‡800
(Non-paid) ‡50

Sunnyvale
Speculations **(3831)**

COLORADO
Aurora
Authorship **(4145)** ....‡4,000

Colorado Springs
CBA Marketplace **(4239)** ....(Paid) ‡8,514
(Non-paid) ‡567

CONNECTICUT
Westport
MultiCultural Review **(5214)** ....(Paid) ‡5,000

DISTRICT OF COLUMBIA
Washington
Inter-American Review of
Bibliography **(5548)** ....(Paid) ‡400
(Non-paid) ‡400

FLORIDA
Gainesville
Librarians at Liberty **(6150)**

Sarasota
New Writer's Magazine **(6660)** ....‡5,000
Writer's Guidelines Magazine **(6669)** .....(Paid) ‡750
(Non-paid) ‡250

ILLINOIS
Champaign
The Bulletin of the Center for Children's
Books **(8182)** 5000

Chicago
Black Books Bulletin: Words Work **(8284)**
Booklist **(8287)** ....(Paid) ‡26,119
(Non-paid) ‡2,385

MAINE
Bangor
The Write Markets Report **(12905)** ......(Paid) 1,000

MASSACHUSETTS
Cambridge
The Boston Book
Review **(14041)** ....(Combined) ‡10,000

MICHIGAN
Traverse City
Independent Publisher Online **(15597)** 30,000

MINNESOTA
Dundas
Dime Novel Roundup **(15860)** ....‡250

St. Paul
Technical Communication
Quarterly **(16410)** ....(Combined) 2,000

NEW JERSEY
Bridgewater
Books for Growing
Minds **(18693)** ....(Non-paid) 12,500
Books and More for Growing
Minds **(18694)** ....(Non-paid) 14,200
Forecast **(18695)** ....(Non-paid) 22,400
Hot Picks **(18696)** ....(Non-paid) 15,500
Now Hear This **(18697)** ....(Non-paid) 13,900
Paper Clips **(18698)** ....(Non-paid) 16,800
School Selection
Guide **(18699)** ....(Non-paid) 50,000
Spirit **(18700)** ....(Non-paid) 10,000
Travel Guide **(18703)** ....(Non-paid) 12,500

NEW YORK
New York
Bookseller **(21335)** 11,050
Kirkus Reviews **(22223)** ....(Paid) ‡4,000
Poets & Writers Magazine **(22568)** ....‡60,000
Publishers Weekly **(22610)** ....(Paid) 32,863
Publishing Research
Quarterly **(22611)** ....(Paid) ‡800

NORTH CAROLINA
Raleigh
Bulletin of Bibliography **(24127)** 1,600

OHIO
Cincinnati
Writer's Digest **(24829)** 215,000

OREGON
Cottage Grove
Book Dealers World **(26294)** ....‡20,000

Portland
Reference & Research Book News **(26504)**
Sci Tech Book News **(26507)**

SOUTH CAROLINA
Charleston
Against the Grain **(28504)** ....(Paid) 2,000
(Non-paid) 200

Columbia
Papers of the Bibliographical Society of
America **(28561)** ....‡1,250

Myrtle Beach
Today's $85,000 Freelance
Writer **(28704)** ....(Non-paid) 4,000

TEXAS
Fort Worth
Book News & Book Business
Mart **(30330)** ....(Controlled) 50,000

VIRGINIA
Radford
Science Fiction Chronicle **(32346)** ....(Paid) 5,800
(Non-paid) 200

WASHINGTON
Bellingham
New Age Retailer **(32677)** ....(Non-paid) 10,000

Eastsound
NAPRA Review **(32742)** ....(Non-paid) 10,000

Seattle
The Comics Journal **(32958)** ....(Paid) ‡10,000

WISCONSIN
Iola
Comics & Games
Retailer **(33814)** ....(Non-paid) ‡4,434

Waukesha
The Writer Magazine **(34415)** ....(Paid) ★35,627

Circulation: ★ = ABC; △ = BPA; ♦ = CAC; • = CCAB; ❑ = VAC; ⊕ = PO Statement; ‡ = Publisher's Report; Boldface figures = sworn; Light figures = estimated.

3107

Trade, Technical, and Professional Publications

Circ.   Circ.   Circ.

BOOK TRADE AND AUTHOR NEWS (continued)

ONTARIO, CANADA
Cornwall
Writer's Lifeline (35756) ....(Paid) ‡1,200
(Non-paid) ‡300

Ottawa
Writer's Block (36283)

Toronto
Journal of Scholarly Publishing (36639) 1,500
Quill & Quire (36721) ....(Combined) 6,000

BOTANY

ALASKA
Juneau
Primroses (597) ....(Paid) ‡600
(Non-paid) ‡10

ARIZONA
Phoenix
Agave (771) ....(Paid) 2,000

Tucson
Desert Plants (945) ....(Combined) 1,000

ARKANSAS
Little Rock
American Fern Journal (1211) ....‡1,200

CALIFORNIA
Auburn
Bromeliad Society
Journal (1437) ....(Combined) 1700

Berkeley
The Four Seasons (1522) ....(Combined) 431

Claremont
Aliso (1723) ....(Combined) 300

Monrovia
Cactus and Succulent
Journal (2576) ....(Paid) ‡3,500

Oakland
Almanac (2665) ....(Paid) 450

COLORADO
Lakewood
American Penstemon Society
Bulletin (4530) ....(Paid) 500

GEORGIA
Athens
Journal of Plant Nutrition (6946) 500
Plant Molecular Biology
Reporter (6948) ....(Paid) ‡2,200

Palmetto
Tipularia (7478) ....(Paid) 450

HAWAII
Waianae
Hawaii Orchid Journal (7794) ....‡750

ILLINOIS
Carbondale
The Bryologist (8115) ....(Paid) ‡900

Rolling Meadows
Greenhouse Business (9547) ......(Non-paid) 18,000

KANSAS
Lawrence
Journal of the Torrey Botanical
Society (11559) ....(Combined) ‡1,483
Mycologia (11564) ....‡2,100

MAINE
Orono
Journal of Phycology (13001) ....‡1,900

MARYLAND
Baltimore
Maryland Naturalist (13213) ....(Paid) 250
(Controlled) 40

Rockville
Plant Physiology (13695) ....‡5,000

MASSACHUSETTS
Amherst
The Herb, Spice, and Medicinal Plant
Digest (13794) 600

Jamaica Plain
Arnoldia (14258) 4,450

Watertown
Bonsai Today (14613) ....‡8,012

MINNESOTA
St. Paul
Molecular Plant-Microbe Interactions
(MPMI) (16397) ....(Paid) 1,500
(Non-paid) 7
Phytopathology (16405) ....(Paid) 3,200
(Non-paid) 17
Plant Disease (16406) ....(Paid) ‡4,000
(Non-paid) ‡31

MISSOURI
St. Louis
Novon (17477)

NEW HAMPSHIRE
Durham
Rhodora (18501) ....(Paid) 800
(Non-paid) 15

Manchester
Tree Care Industry (18564) ......(Controlled) ‡28,000

NEW JERSEY
Hoboken
Pest Management Science (19081)

NEW YORK
Bronx
Advances in Economic Botany (20251)
The Botanical Review (20257) ....‡1,800
Economic Botany (20266) ....‡2,200
Flora Neotropica (20269)
North American Flora (20278)

Brooklyn
Plants & Gardens News (20338) ....‡18,000

Ithaca
American Journal of Botany (20789) ....‡4,693

New York
Cellulose (21388)
Edinburgh Journal of Botany (21584) 500
Environmental & Experimental
Botany (21616) 800
European Journal of Plant Pathology (21648)
Evolutionary Ecology (21660)
Field Mycology (21689)
Journal of Plant Growth
Regulation (22160) ....(Combined) 825
Molecular Breeding (22355)
The Mycologist (22388) 2700
The New Phytologist (22433)
Photosynthesis Research (22553)
Plant Foods for Human Nutrition (22560)
Russian Journal of Plant Physiology (22694)

NORTH CAROLINA
Charlotte
CASTANEA (23738) ....(Paid) ‡1,100

OHIO
Kirtland
Leaves Class and Events
Magazine (25285) ....‡9,000

PENNSYLVANIA
Philadelphia
International Journal of Pest Management (27504)
Xenobiotica (27724)

Pittsburgh
Huntia (27797) ....(Combined) 250

TEXAS
College Station
American Association of Stratigraphic Palynologists
Contributions Series (30036) ....(Combined) 952
Palynology (30047) ....(Controlled) 952

WISCONSIN
Oshkosh
Michigan Botanist (34223) ....(Combined) ⊕800

BRITISH COLUMBIA, CANADA
Victoria
Tree Physiology (35227) ....(Controlled) 1,000

ONTARIO, CANADA
London
Canadian Plant Disease
Survey (35980) ....(Controlled) 500

Ottawa
Canadian Journal of Plant
Science (36212) ....‡1,100

BROOM, BRUSHES, AND MOPS

ILLINOIS
Arcola
Broom Brush and Mop (8019)

VIRGINIA
Huddleston
Brushware (32171) ....‡2,200

BUILDING MANAGEMENT AND MAINTENANCE
See also Real Estate

CALIFORNIA
Garden Grove
Apartment News (1997) ....‡3700

Huntington Beach
Apartment Management
Magazine (2059) ....(Paid) 500
(Non-paid) 60,000

Los Angeles
The Economic Home
Owner (2259) ....(Paid) 100,000

Woodland Hills
ICS Cleaning Specialist (4107) 27,000

DISTRICT OF COLUMBIA
Washington
Boma (5380) ....(Paid) 17,500
The Corridor Real Estate
Journal (5443) ....(Paid) ‡5,000
(Controlled) ‡3,000

FLORIDA
St. Petersburg
Maddux Report (6630) ....(Paid) 1,040
(Controlled) 13,180

GEORGIA
Snellville
Fencepost Magazine (7557) ......(Non-paid) ⊕13,000

HAWAII
Honolulu
Building Management
Hawaii (7682) ....(Non-paid) 4,700

ILLINOIS
Bensenville
SECURITY (8071) ....(Controlled) 40,541

Chicago
Journal of Property Management (8448) .....‡23,000

Country Club Hills
International Code Council (8689) ....‡14,000

KANSAS
Overland Park
American School &
University (11696) ....(Controlled) 63,000

MARYLAND
Olney
EH & S Solutions (Environmental Health & Safety
Solutions) (13641) ....(Paid) ‡1,600
(Non-paid) 9,000

Housing Operations
Manager (13642) ....(Paid) ‡1,600
(Non-paid) ‡7,400

Silver Spring
Manager's Source Guide (13737) 10,000

MASSACHUSETTS
Millers Falls
Old Mill Marketing **(14335)** ....‡8,000,000

MICHIGAN
Farmington Hills
Building Business & Apartment
   Management **(15016)** ....(Paid) ‡12,000
                                 (Controlled) ‡100

NEW JERSEY
Morris Plains
Industrial Maintenance and Plant
   Operation **(19293)** ....(Controlled) 107,000

NEW YORK
Latham
Cleaning and Maintenance Management
   Magazine **(20932)** ....(Non-paid) 36,936
                                 (Paid) 6,472

Melville
Maintenance Supplies **(21048)** ....(Non-paid) ‡16,500

New York
Facilities Design &
   Management **(21673)** ....(Non-paid) 35,000

OHIO
Cleveland
Pest Control **(24940)** ....(Controlled) ‡16,668
                                 (Paid) ‡3,386
Pest Control Technology **(24941)** ....(Paid) 4,500
                                 (Non-paid) 15,500
Properties Magazine **(24945)** ....(Paid) 1,500
                                 (Free) 1,500

Westerville
Executive Housekeeping
   Today **(25640)** ....(Paid) ‡5,000
                                 (Non-paid) ‡168

PENNSYLVANIA
Ardmore
Tourist Attractions & Parks
   Magazine **(26665)** ....(Combined) ‡31,424

TEXAS
Houston
Facility Management Journal **(30472)** 14,600

VIRGINIA
Alexandria
Security Management **(31736)** ....(Paid) 28,697
                                 (Non-paid) 356

Fairfax
Services **(32028)** ....(Paid) 4,499
                                 17,916

Reston
Journal of Professional Issues in Engineering
   Education and Practice **(32391)**

WISCONSIN
Milwaukee
Building Operating
   Management **(34059)** ....(Paid) 155
                                 (Non-paid) 66,966
Maintenance Solutions **(34075)**
Sanitary Maintenance **(34099)** ....(Paid) 521
                                 (Non-paid) 16,071

ONTARIO, CANADA
Burlington
PEM Plant Engineering and
   Maintenance **(35718)** ....(Combined) 18,089

Mississauga
Homes & Cottages **(36071)** ....(Non-paid) 67,000

QUEBEC, CANADA
Montreal
Inter-Mecanique du
   Batiment **(37134)** ....(Combined) •6,350

BUILDING MATERIALS, CONCRETE, BRICK, AND TILE

CALIFORNIA
Berkeley
Home Energy **(1526)** ....(Combined) ‡4,091

Newport Beach
Building Products
   Digest **(2623)** ....(Controlled) ‡12,750

The Merchant Magazine **(2630)** ....(Paid) ‡3,798
                                 (Controlled) 269

CONNECTICUT
Bethel
Experimental Mechanics **(4697)** 4,500

ILLINOIS
Addison
Concrete Cunstruction **(8000)** ....(Paid) △57,658
                                 (Non-paid) △12,376
Masonry Construction **(8002)** ....(Paid) 608
                                 (Non-paid) 31,639

Chicago
PCI Journal **(8527)** ....(Paid) ‡6,131
                                 (Non-paid) ‡500

Des Plaines
Concrete Repair
   Bulletin **(8753)** ....(Controlled) 12,000

Springfield
ILMDA Advantage **(9633)** ....(Combined) ‡918

INDIANA
Indianapolis
MC Magazine **(10151)** ....(Non-paid) ‡8,000

IOWA
Hull
Hardware Trade **(10955)** ....(Non-paid) 32,327

KANSAS
Overland Park
Concrete Products **(11707)** ....(Non-paid) 20,084

MICHIGAN
Farmington Hills
ACI Structural Journal **(15015)** ....‡16,400
Concrete Abstracts **(15017)** ....‡676
Concrete International **(15018)** ....(Paid) 697
                                 (Controlled) 15,625

Troy
Floor Covering Installer **(15626)**
Walls & Ceilings **(15644)** ....(Controlled) ‡30,600
                                 (Paid) ‡243

MINNESOTA
Minneapolis
Building Material
   Dealer **(16062)** ....(Controlled) ‡29,242

NEVADA
Reno
Architectural West **(18417)** ....(Controlled) 20,200
Western
   Roofing/Insulation/Siding **(18426)** .....(Paid) ‡3,017
                                 (Controlled) ‡20,345

NEW YORK
New York
Building Supply Home
   Centers **(21347)** ....(Non-paid) ‡51,305
Contract **(21498)** 30,000
Fenestration **(21686)** ....(Paid) ★122
                                 (Non-paid) ★18,408
National Home Center News **(22396)** ....(Paid) 5,665
                                 (Non-paid) 46,210
New York Construction
   News **(22439)** ....(Paid) ‡6,100
Tile & Decorative Surfaces **(22836)** .....(Paid) 1,137
                                 (Non-paid) 20,441

PENNSYLVANIA
Blooming Glen
Journal of Applied Asphalt Binder
   Technology **(26716)**

Erie
Builder/Dealer **(26893)** ....(Non-paid) ‡28,829

TEXAS
Houston
Underground Construction **(30538)**

VIRGINIA
Alexandria
Insulation Outlook **(31684)** ....(Paid) 2,100
                                 (Controlled) 4,700

Arlington
Composites Fabrication **(31783)** ....(Combined) 8,000

Garrisonville
USGlass, Metal & Glazing **(32106)** ....△27,826

Herndon
CM News **(32162)** ....(Non-paid) ‡3,500

Mc Lean
Cast Polymer Connection **(32243)** ....(Paid) 3,000

WISCONSIN
Iola
Metal Roofing Magazine **(33835)**

BRITISH COLUMBIA, CANADA
Surrey
BSDA News Magazine **(35106)** ....(Non-paid) ‡1,200

ONTARIO, CANADA
Toronto
Centre **(36544)** ....(Controlled) 15,749
Hardware
   Merchandising **(36611)** ....(Combined) •15,037
Home Improvement
   Retailing **(36616)** ....(Combined) 15,356

QUEBEC, CANADA
Longueuil
Quart de Rond **(37058)** ....(Combined) 3,000

Westmount
Aggregates & Roadbuilding
   Magazine **(37441)** ....(Combined) •12,175

BUSINESS

See also Accountants and Accounting; Advertising and Marketing; Banking, Finance, and Investments; Chambers of Commerce and Boards of Trade; Commerce and Industry; Economics; International Business and Economics; Management and Administration; Purchasing; Selling and Salesmanship; Taxation and Tariff

ALABAMA
Birmingham
Birmingham Business Journal **(57)** ....(Paid) 10,000
                                 (Controlled) 8,000

Gulf Shores
ConventionSouth **(250)**

Montgomery
Southern Business & Economic
   Journal **(377)** ....(Combined) 950

ARIZONA
Glendale
Southwest Computer Monthly **(715)** ....(Paid) 18,000
                                 (Non-paid) 32,000

Phoenix
Arizona Business Gazette **(775)** ....(Paid) 10,208
                                 (Free) 5,744
Arizona Capitol Times **(776)** ....(Combined) 5,000
Business Journal - Serving Phoenix and the Valley of
   the Sun **(796)**
Business Law Today **(797)** ....(Paid) △50,664

Tempe
Inside Supply Management **(905)** .....(Paid) ‡45,000
                                 (Non-paid) ‡300

Tucson
Arizona's Economy **(935)**
The Daily Territorial **(944)** ....(Paid) 892
                                 (Free) 100

ARKANSAS
Fayetteville
Arkansas Business & Economic
   Review **(1115)** ....(Controlled) 4,000

Little Rock
Arkansas Business **(1213)** ....(Paid) 6,500
                                 (Controlled) 2,000

CALIFORNIA
Berkeley
California Management Review
   (CMR) **(1503)** ....‡5,500

Fresno
The Business Journal **(1943)** ....‡8,000
Vegetable **(1958)** ....(Controlled) ‡8,371

Circulation: ★ = ABC; △ = BPA; ♦ = CAC; • = CCAB; ❑ = VAC; ⊕ = PO Statement; ‡ = Publisher's Report; Boldface figures = sworn; Light figures = estimated.

3109

Circ.   Circ.   Circ.

BUSINESS (continued)

Fullerton
Structural Equation Modeling (1990)

Huntington Beach
Home Business (2062)

Irvine
Entrepreneur's Bizstartups.com (2080)
Knowledge Management (2082)
Orange County Business
    Journal (2086) ....(Paid) 13,456
         (Non-paid) 599

Los Angeles
Business Forum (2229)
ETCetera (2266) ....(Paid) 300
The Los Angeles Business
    Journal (2320) ....(Paid) ★20,956
San Fernando Valley Business Journal (2383)
Southern California Business Trends (2394)
Tradeshow Week (2414)

Newport Beach
The Investment
    Reporter (2628) ....(Controlled) 35,000
OC Metro (2633) ....(Combined) 90,000

Oakland
California Business Law Reporter (2672)
Journal of Employee Ownership Law and
    Finance (2684) ....(Combined) 550

Palm Springs
Beverage Dynamics (2754) ....(Non-paid) △50,037
Candy Business (2755)
Commodity Price Charts (2757)
Professional Candy Buyer (2765)
The Public Record (2766) ....(Paid) ‡500
         (Free) ‡500

Pleasanton
Easy Bay Business
    Times (2853) ....(Combined) 12,000

Redwood City
Profit (2915) ....(Controlled) ‡115,854

Rocklin
Web Commerce Today (2957)

Sacramento
The Business Journal (2978) ....(Paid) 12,727
California Manufacturer (2985) ....‡10,000
Comstock's Business
    Magazine (2993) ....(Controlled) 20,000

San Diego
Access VB- SQL Advisor (3104) ....(Paid) 20,000
IDEA Personal Trainer (3172) ....(Combined) 10,000
Latin American Business Review (3221)
Mobile Business Advisor (3233) ....(Paid) 20,000
San Diego Business Journal (3258) ....‡22,500
San Diego Commerce (3259) ....(Paid) 670
         (Free) 209
San Diego Daily
    Transcript (3262) ....(Mon.-Fri.) 15,000

San Francisco
Business Valuation Review (3332) .....(Paid) ‡1,100
         (Controlled) ‡700
Consulting Rates and Business Practices Annual
    Survey (3345)
eCompany Now (3354)
The Red Herring (3422) ....(Paid) 162,666
         (Non-paid) 5,611
San Francisco Business
    Times (3431) ....(Paid) 19,929
Wall Street Journal (Western
    Edition) (3461) ....(Mon.-Fri.) 398,205
World Trade (3464)

San Jose
Franchise UPDATE (3517)
San Jose Business Journal (3535) .....(Paid) 16,000
San Jose Post-Record (3537) 1,200

Santa Barbara
Hispanic Business (3641) ....(Paid) 65,000
         (Controlled) 165,000
Journal of IT Financial Management (3646)

Santa Rosa
North Bay Biz (3731) ....(Paid) ⊕8,515
         (Non-paid) ⊕5,485

Saratoga
EC.COM Magazine (3744) ......(Controlled) △40,522

Torrance
Minority Business Entrepreneur (3938) 40,000

Van Nuys
Dayspa (3986) ....(Controlled) 32,564

Walnut Creek
Contra Costa News Register (4049) ....‡500

Winchester
Diversity Magazine (4092)
Hispanic Times Magazine (4093) ....(Paid) ‡628
         (Controlled) ‡60,000

COLORADO
Castle Rock
Clayton-Fillmore Report (4221)

Centennial
ColoradoBiz (4223)

Denver
The Denver Business
    Journal (4321) ....(Paid) 17,397

Golden
CLEC Magazine (4464)

Grand Junction
The Business Times of Western Colorado (4477)

Littleton
International Business & Economics Research
    Journal (4548) ....(Paid) ‡200
         (Controlled) ‡200
Review of Business Information
    Systems (4554) ....(Paid) ‡300
         (Controlled) ‡50

CONNECTICUT
Bridgeport
Business Woman (4712) ....(Combined) 15,000

Hartford
Industrial Marketing Management (4895) 1,304

Middlebury
Business Digest of Greater
    Waterbury (4941) 6,000

New Haven
Business Times (4984) ....(Non-paid) ‡22,400
Fairfield County Business Times (4988) ....‡7,400

Norwalk
Business Geographics (5051) .....(Controlled) 30,185

Southport
Private Power Executive (5137)

Stamford
Customer Support
    Management (5147) ....(Combined) 42,000
Direct (5148) ....(Combined) 36,582

DELAWARE
Newark
Business Ledger (5269) ....(Paid) ♦954
         (Non-paid) ♦9,126

DISTRICT OF COLUMBIA
Washington
Bank & Corporate Governance Law Reporter (5372)
Brookings Papers on Economic Activity (5384)
The Business Advocate (5389) 200,000
Business Ethics Quarterly (5391) ....(Paid) 1,000
BusinessWoman
    Magazine (5392) ....(Controlled) ‡70,000
Capital Idea$ (5393)
Community Banker (5428)
Cooperative Business Journal (5442)
EDP Weekly's IT Monitor (5472)
Franchising World (5503) ....(Paid) ‡233
         (Controlled) ‡10,200
International Monetary Fund Staff Papers (5557)
International Trade by Commodities, Series C (5558)
Nabe News (5666)
Nabe Quarterly Surveys (5667)
Nation's Business (5685) ....(Paid) 858,718
The NFIB Foundation Small Business Economic
    Trends (5695) 1,000
PPI Detailed Report (5725)
Salary Survey (5775)
Securities Reform Act Litigation Reporter (5787)
The Tax Executive (5811) ....(Combined) 5,556
Washington Business
    Journal (5843) ....(Paid) 20,208
Washington
    Technology (5854) ....(Controlled) 40,000
World Economic Outlook (5869)

FLORIDA
Altamonte Springs
Internal Auditor (5900) 50,000

Brandon
New Media Magazine (5960)

Fort Lauderdale
Business in Broward (6073) ....(Paid) ‡14,200
         (Controlled) ‡5,800

Gainesville
Business & Professional Ethics
    Journal (6131) 700
Professional Ethics (6153) ....(Paid) 700

Gulf Breeze
Mexico Business Journal (6178)

Miami
Daily Business Review (6347) ....(Paid) 10,184
         (Controlled) 286
Hombre Internacional (6360) ....‡12,749
Miami Today (6373) ....(Controlled) △32,146
         (Paid) △601

Naples
Emergence (6438)

Orlando
Orlando Business Journal (6502) ....(Paid) 11,536

St. Petersburg
Maddux Report (6630) ....(Paid) 1,040
         (Controlled) 13,180

Sarasota
Sarasota Magazine (6664) ....(Combined) ‡13,000

Winter Haven
Financial Studies of the Small Business (6866)

GEORGIA
Athens
Georgia Business and Economic
    Conditions (6938) ....(Free) ‡2,000

Atlanta
Atlanta Business Chronicle (6967) ......(Paid) 30,367
Business Atlanta (6982) ....(Paid) 1,694
         (Controlled) 35,759
TechLINKS (7051) ....‡23,000

Marietta
APICS-The Performance
    Advantage (7409) ....(Paid) ‡82,000

Norcross
Engineering Economist (7459)
Industrial Management (7466)

Savannah
The Business Report &
    Journal (7531) ....(Mon.) 20,000

Thomasville
South Georgia Business
    Journal (7586) ....(Paid) ⊕1,000
         (Controlled) ⊕7,000

HAWAII
Honolulu
Hawaii Business (7691) ....(Paid) ‡3,057
         (Non-paid) ‡10,197
Pacific Business News (7713) ....(Paid) 15,381
Pacific Magazine with Islands Business (7714)

IDAHO
Boise
The Idaho Business Review (7809) ......(Paid) 3,100
         (Free) 450

Sandpoint
MultiLingual Computing &
    Technology (7979) ....(Combined) 7,000

ILLINOIS
Carol Stream
Your Church (8158) ....(Controlled) 150,000

Chicago
American International College Journal of
    Business (8257)
Card Technology (8298) ....(Combined) ‡25,047
Chicago Business (8307) ....(Paid) ‡300
         (Non-paid) ‡2,500
Crain's Chicago Business (8346) .....(Paid) ★43,316
         (Non-paid) ★6,710
Investment News (8419)
Northwestern Journal of International Law &
    Business (8512) ....(Combined) 598

Numbers cited after listings are entry numbers rather than page numbers.

The Wall Street Journal (Midwest
  Edition) **(8602)** ....(Mon.-Fri.) 492,514
Zacks Analyst Watch **(8609)** ....(Paid) 500+
Zacks Earnings Forecaster **(8610)**
Zacks Profit Guide **(8611)**

Lincolnshire
Salon Today Magazine **(9088)** ....‡30,000

Millstadt
Kansas City
  Commerce **(9197)** ....(Controlled) ⊕8,170

Northbrook
On the Mark **(9319)** ....(Non-paid) 80,000

Oak Brook
The Illinois Manufacturers **(9353)** ....(Paid) 6,000

Riverwoods
Federal Audit Guides **(9504)**

St. Charles
Country Business **(9563)** ....(Combined) 30,000

Tinley Park
Money Maker's Monthly **(9686)** ......(Paid) ‡125,000
                                 (Non-paid) ‡125,000

Urbana
International Journal of Expert Systems **(9711)**

Vernon Hills
Legal Management **(9728)** ....(Controlled) ‡25,200

INDIANA
Bloomington
Indiana Business
  Review **(9831)** ....(Controlled) 2,000

Evansville
Indiana Journal of Commerce &
  Industry **(9934)** ....(Paid) 8,000

Indianapolis
Indiana Business
  Magazine **(10124)** ....(Controlled) 3,175
                                 (Non-paid) 26,622
                                          2,619

IOWA
Ames
Journal of Advertising **(10590)**
Needlework Retailer **(10592)**

Carlisle
Business & Industry **(10648)** ....(Controlled) ‡12,100

Des Moines
The Business Daily **(10772)** ....(Combined) 500
Des Moines Business
  Record **(10780)** ....(Paid) ‡3,932
Iowa Business & Technology Resource
  Guide **(10789)** ....(Combined) 15,000

Fort Dodge
Packaging and Converting
  Hotline **(10906)** ....(Combined) 10,000

Mason City
The Business Journal **(11070)** ......(Non-paid) 3,000

KANSAS
Pittsburg
Journal of Managerial
  Issues **(11752)** ....(Controlled) 1,000

KENTUCKY
Frankfort
Workforce Professional **(12077)** ....(Paid) ‡16,000

Lexington
The Lane Report **(12172)** ....(Paid) 157
                                 (Non-paid) 12,763

Murray
Journal of Business and Public Affairs **(12315)**

LOUISIANA
Baton Rouge
Greater Baton Rouge Business
  Report **(12489)** ....(Paid) ‡2,657
                                 (Non-paid) ‡6,001

Monroe
Journal of Internet Commerce **(12691)**

MARYLAND
Baltimore
Baltimore Business Journal **(13129)** .....(Paid) 9,089

Frederick
Troubled Company Prospector **(13523)**
Troubled Company Reporter **(13524)**

Gaithersburg
EA Journal **(13537)** 10,000

Linthicum
Information Systems Research (ISR) **(13620)**
INFORMS Journal on Computing **(13621)**
Management Science **(13622)** ....(Paid) 4,300
M&SOM (Manufacturing & Service Operations
  Management) **(13623)**
OR/MS Today **(13624)**

Potomac
Card News **(13648)**
Diesel Fuel News **(13651)**
ISP Business News **(13654)**
Wireless Business & Technology **(13663)**

Rockville
First Call/Thomson Financial Insiders'
  Chronicle **(13679)**
Mutual Funds Update **(13689)** .....(Combined) 2,500

Silver Spring
INFORM **(13727)** ....(Non-paid) ‡40,000

Towson
Research in Healthcare Financial
  Management **(13765)**

MASSACHUSETTS
Boston
Boston Business Journal **(13856)** .....(Paid) ★15,734
Business History Review **(13869)** ....(Paid) 2,000
                                 (Non-paid) 300
DMI Academic Review **(13886)**
Fast Company **(13892)** ....(Paid) 708,251
Federal Reserve Bank of Boston Regional
  Review **(13893)** ....(Controlled) 20,000
Harvard Business Review **(13898)** ....(Paid) 249,100
Inc. **(13904)** ....(Paid) 660,960
Inc. Technology **(13905)** ....(Paid) 640,000
Massachusetts CPA Review Online **(13927)**
New England Economic
  Review **(13933)** ....(Non-paid) ‡15,000

Cambridge
eWeek **(14052)**
MIT Sloan Management Review **(14082)**
Operations Research **(14087)** ....(Paid) ‡5,300
Reflections **(14097)**
Sloan Management Review **(14101)** ....‡25,000
Training Media Review **(14108)**
Worldprofit Online
  Magazine **(14112)** ....(Non-paid) 600,000

Framingham
Application Development Trends **(14191)**
CIO Magazine **(14192)** ....(Paid) ‡5,052
                                 (Controlled) ‡125,000
CIO Web Business **(14193)** ....(Paid) 150,000
SC Magazine **(14200)** ....(Controlled) 43,100

Lexington
CryoGas International **(14271)**

Newton
Electronic Business Asia **(14395)**
Supply Chain Management Review **(14411)**

Norwell
New England Real Estate
  Journal **(14442)** ....(Paid) ‡8,000
                                 (Free) ‡1,200

Plymouth
Plymouth County Business
  Review **(14480)** ....(Non-paid) 5,000

Stow
Religious Conference Manager **(14575)**
Technology Meetings **(14576)**

Worcester
Worcester Business
  Journal **(14692)** ....(Combined) 11,000

MICHIGAN
Boyne City
Outstate Business **(14833)** ....(Non-paid) ‡10,000

Detroit
Crain's Detroit Business **(14920)** ......(Paid) ★34,685
Detroiter **(14929)** ....(Paid) 18,535
                                 (Controlled) 2,000

Flint
The Journal of Business
  Communication **(15035)** 2,550
Journal of Leadership and Organizational
  Studies **(15036)**

Hemlock
Business Monthly **(15158)** ....(Combined) 15,000

Howell
Insider Business Journal **(15194)** ....(Paid) 1,600
                                 (Non-paid) 6,400
                                 (Non-paid) 13,000

Kalamazoo
Business Outlook for West
  Michigan **(15233)** ....(Paid) 100
                                 (Controlled) 25

Lansing
Journal of Small
  Business **(15276)** ....(Non-paid) 9,000

Troy
CircuiTree **(15617)**
Leaders' Edge **(15628)**
Process Cooling and Equipment **(15637)**

MINNESOTA
Duluth
The Duluthian **(15837)** ....‡1,800

Minneapolis
Business Ethics **(16063)** ....(Paid) 5,000
                                 (Non-paid) 6,000
CityBusiness **(16066)** ....(Paid) 11,278
Collector **(16068)** ....‡6,100
Federal Reserve Bank of Minneapolis Quarterly
  Review **(16080)**
Finance and Commerce **(16081)** ....‡1,500
Presentations
  Magazine **(16123)** ....(Controlled) ‡75,000

St. Paul
Gaming Products and
  Services **(16377)** ....(Paid) 10,000

MISSISSIPPI
Jackson
Mississippi Business
  Journal **(16700)** ....(Paid) ‡8,620
                                 (Non-paid) ‡2,460

MISSOURI
Fort Leonard Wood
America's Insider **(17070)**

Kansas City
Ingram's **(17172)** ....(Controlled) 20,439
                                 (Paid) 3,301
Kansas City Business
  Journal **(17178)** ....(Paid) 10,941
Women in Business **(17204)** ....(Paid) 50,000

St. Louis
Agri Marketing **(17407)** ....(Paid) 212
                                 (Controlled) 8,325
Disaster Recovery Journal **(17434)**
St. Louis Business Journal **(17496)** ....(Paid) 18,400
St. Louis Countian **(17499)** 1,300

Springfield
Springfield Business Journal **(17610)** ....(Paid) 6,200
                                 (Non-paid) 800

NEBRASKA
Omaha
The Lincoln Business Journal **(18202)**
The Midlands Business Journal **(18203)**
The Omaha Business Journal **(18205)**

NEVADA
Las Vegas
Nevada Business Journal **(18378)** ......(Paid) ‡6,000
                                 (Controlled) ‡9,000
New Age Networking
  Magazine **(18381)** ....(Combined) 125,000

NEW HAMPSHIRE
Hampton
Midrange Enterprise **(18514)** ......(Combined) 45,000

Manchester
Business NH Magazine **(18556)** ....(Paid) ‡600
                                 (Controlled) ‡13,850
New Hampshire Business Review **(18558)** 15,000
Northeast Export
  Magazine **(18561)** ....(Controlled) 11,750

	Circ.

BUSINESS (continued)

Peterborough
Consulting **(18622)**
Shareholder Value **(18629)**

NEW JERSEY
Fairfield
New Jersey Business **(18814)** ....‡20,000

Hoboken
International Journal of Intelligent Systems in
Accounting, Finance, and Management **(18987)**
Journal of Behavioral Decision Making **(19005)**
Journal of Forecasting **(19023)** ....(Paid) 9,800
Natural Gas **(19069)** 5,985
Strategic Management
Journal **(19108)** ....(Paid) 28,000
Thunderbird International Business
Review **(19119)** 5950

Montvale
Business & Health **(19243)** ....(Paid) 3,100
(Controlled) 47,479
Linux Business Week **(19261)** ....(Combined) 60,000
Medical Economics **(19262)** ....(Paid) 94,000
(Controlled) 64,000
Medical Economics for
Surgeons **(19265)** ....(Paid) 1,202
(Controlled) 48,300
Web Services Journal **(19279)**
Wireless Business &
Technology **(19282)** ....(Combined) 130,000
XML-Journal **(19283)**
XML Journal **(19284)**

Morris Plains
Medical Design
Technology **(19298)** ....(Non-paid) 35,450

Morristown
New Jersey Monthly **(19313)** ....(Paid) 94,000

Paramus
Microwaves & RF
Magazine **(19405)** ....(Controlled) 35,000

Parsippany
Non-profit Times **(19412)**

Princeton
Business Today
(Princeton) **(19455)** ....(Controlled) 200,000

South Orange
Mid-Atlantic Journal of Business **(19585)** 700

Trenton
Mercer Business Magazine **(19658)** ....(Paid) ‡5,431
(Non-paid) ‡3,169

West Atlantic City
Casino Journal **(19713)**

NEW MEXICO
Albuquerque
Business & Society **(19768)**
SourceBook **(19787)**
SourceMex Economic News and Analysis on
Mexico **(19788)**

NEW YORK
Binghamton
Journal of African Business **(20160)**
Journal of Convention & Exhibition
Management **(20168)**
Journal of End User Computer Support **(20170)**

Bronx
Business Periodicals Index **(20262)**

Brooklyn
Daily Bulletin **(20309)** ....‡5,200

Buffalo
Business First of Buffalo **(20371)** ....(Paid) 9,696

Commack
Long Island **(20489)** ....(Paid) 10,000

Jamaica
Review of Business **(20840)**

LaFayette
Future Survey **(20870)** ....(Paid) 1,750

Latham
Capital District Business
Review **(20931)** ....(Paid) 9,273

Mamaroneck
Ethikos **(20985)**

Manhasset
Printed Circuit Fabrication **(21011)**
VARBUSINESS **(21016)** ....(Non-paid) ‡107,500
Wall Street and Technology **(21017)**

Melville
Photo Trade News **(21054)**

New York
The Asian Wall Street Journal Weekly
Edition **(21265)** ....‡11,000
Back Stage West **(21284)** 95,011
Black Enterprise **(21328)** ....(Paid) 421,169
Brand Marketing **(21337)** ....△22,000
Business Communication
Quarterly **(21353)** ....(Combined) 1,875
Business Eastern Europe **(21354)**
Business Europe **(21356)**
Business Latin America **(21358)**
Business & Society Review **(21359)** ....‡2,355
2,000
The Business Torts Reporter **(21360)**
Business Week **(21362)** ....(Paid) 949,860
Card Marketing **(21373)**
CED **(21385)**
Compensation & Benefits Management **(21466)**
Computer Survival Guide **(21478)**
Corporate Business Taxation Monthly **(21500)**
Crain's New York
Business **(21511)** ....(Paid) ★42,420
(Non-paid) ★21,574
Credit Memo **(21514)** ....(Non-paid) 3,000
Credit Union Journal **(21515)**
The Deal **(21541)**
Derivatives Quarterly **(21544)**
Development Business **(21547)**
Dispute Resolution Journal **(21558)** ....(Paid) ‡2,000
(Controlled) ‡13,000
Earnings Guide **(21575)**
Entrepreneurship, Innovation and Change **(21610)**
Executive Technology **(21661)** .....(Non-paid) 47,000
Facilities & Event
Management **(21674)** ....(Controlled) 30,582
Federal Reserve Bank of New York Economic Policy
Review **(21682)**
Financial Services Marketing **(21699)**
Financing Operations **(21700)** ....(Paid) 1,247
Forbes **(21718)** ....(Paid) 884,201
Forbes ASAP **(21719)**
Fortune **(21727)** ....(Paid) 853,267
FSB **(21739)**
Future Banker **(21743)**
FUTURIFIC **(21744)**
Group Decision and Negotiation **(21781)**
HR Executive Review **(21825)**
Insights **(21877)**
International Journal of Franchising and Distribution
Law **(21907)**
International Studies of Management &
Organization **(21937)** ....(Paid) ⊕415
The International Tax Journal **(21938)**
Investment Management Weekly **(21947)**
Journal of Business Strategy **(22015)**
Journal of Cost Management **(22040)**
Journal of Deferred Compensation **(22047)**
Journal of Heuristics **(22088)**
Journal of Industry, Competition and Trade **(22094)**
Journal of Management and Governance **(22120)**
Journal of Market-Focused Management **(22122)**
Journal of Pension Benefits **(22152)**
Journal of Pension Planning and
Compliance **(22153)**
Journal of Property Tax Management **(22166)**
Journal of State Taxation **(22192)**
Journal of Technology Transfer **(22203)**
McKinsey Quarterly **(22303)**
MSI Europe **(22376)**
Municipal Finance Journal **(22382)**
NAFTA **(22392)**
The Nikkei Weekly **(22463)**
On Wall Street **(22489)**
Origination News **(22503)**
PC Computing **(22533)** ....(Paid) 1,026,034
Private Equity Week **(22594)**
Registered Rep. **(22642)** ....(Controlled) 93,800
Retail Merchandiser **(22653)** .....(Controlled) ‡35,000
Retail Tech **(22654)**
Risk Management **(22671)** ....(Paid) △8,672
(Non-paid) △6,500
Securities Industry News **(22719)**
Small Business Banker **(22745)**
Small Business Opportunities **(22746)** 250,000
Soap and Cosmetics **(22751)**
strategy + business **(22796)** ....(Paid) 38,936
(Non-paid) 51,641
Television Europe **(22820)**
Transform Magazine **(22853)**
Transnational Corporations **(22854)**

Variety and General Merchandise
TradeNews **(22896)**
Wall Street
Journal **(22906)** ....(Mon.-Fri.) ★1,800,607
Web Finance **(22912)**
Ziff Davis Smart Business for the New
Economy **(22956)**

Oakdale
Journal of Business and Economic
Studies **(23029)** ....(Paid) 700

Oneonta
New York Economic Review **(23051)** ......(Paid) 150

Potsdam
Northern New York Business
Journal **(23139)** ....(Free) 5,000

Rochester
Business Strategies
Newspaper **(23213)** ....(Paid) ‡10,000
The Daily Record **(23220)** ....(Paid) ‡2,860
(Free) ‡150
Rochester Business
Journal **(23238)** ....(Combined) 70,000

Ronkonkoma
LI Business News **(23270)**
Long Island Business News **(23271)** ....(Paid) 8,500
(Non-paid) 3,500

Syracuse
The Business
Record **(23391)** ....(Controlled) ‡17,500

Wappingers Falls
Hudson Valley Business
Journal **(23502)** ....(Paid) ‡4,000
(Free) ‡8,000

NORTH CAROLINA
Cary
Journal of Law, Economics, and
Organization **(23692)**

Charlotte
The Business Journal of
Charlotte **(23736)** ....(Paid) 13,922
Business Journal - Serving Metropolitan Kansas
City **(23737)**
Minneapolis-St. Paul CityBusiness **(23750)**
Sacramento Business
Journal **(23752)** ....(Paid) 12,981
Silicon Valley/San Jose Business Journal **(23753)**

Greensboro
Business Life
Magazine **(23917)** ....(Combined) ‡15,000
Southern Purchaser **(23940)** ....(Non-paid) ‡9,500
Triad Business News **(23941)** ....(Paid) 3,117
(Non-paid) 6,917

New Bern
Carolina Business **(24095)** ....(Non-paid) 20,000

Raleigh
Piedmont Triad
Newcomer **(24148)** ....(Non-paid) 50,000

OHIO
Akron
Plastics News **(24585)** ....(Paid) 21,350
(Non-paid) 39,920

Chesterland
Organization Development
Journal **(24760)** ....(Combined) 720

Cincinnati
Cincinnati Business Courier **(24783)** ....(Paid) 12,701
The Small Business Journal **(24820)**

Cleveland
Behavioral Health Management **(24863)** 21,802
Cleveland Enterprise
Magazine **(24871)** ....(Controlled) ‡30,669
Cleveland Small Business
News **(24874)** ....(Controlled) 188,200
Crain's Cleveland
Business **(24877)** ....(Paid) ★21,109
FLOW Manufacturing
Report **(24895)** ....(Combined) 45,000
Inside Business **(24912)** ....(Non-paid) 30,000
Research Studies **(24949)**
Supply Chain Technology
News **(24955)** ....(Non-paid) 45,000
Transportation & Distribution **(24958)**

Columbus
Batelle Solutions
  Update **(25000)** ....(Non-paid) 40,000
Business First-Columbus **(25003)** ......(Paid) ‡10,612
COMMUNIQUE **(25011)** ....(Paid) ‡42,000
                                                                    (Controlled) ‡1,000

Dayton
The Business News **(25108)** ....(Paid) 12,300
                                                                    (Non-paid) 453
College Planning and Management **(25111)**

Fairborn
Contractor Marketing **(25186)** ......(Controlled) 4,500

OKLAHOMA
Norman
Oklahoma Business Bulletin **(25938)** ....‡500

Tulsa
Tulsa Daily Commerce & Legal
  News **(26136)** ....‡450

OREGON
Portland
Daily Journal of Commerce **(26475)** .....(Paid) 3,341
                                                                    (Controlled) 809
Pacific Marketer **(26498)**
Portland Business Journal **(26501)** .....(Paid) 13,936

PENNSYLVANIA
Blue Bell
EXEC **(26724)** ....(Controlled) 40,000

Hershey
Annals of Cases on Information Technology
  (ACIT) **(27039)** ....(Paid) 200
Information Resources Management
  Journal **(27042)** ....(Controlled) 700
Journal of End User
  Computing **(27043)** ....(Controlled) 450
Journal of Global Information
  Management **(27044)** ....(Controlled) 600

Indiana
Advances in Competitiveness Research **(27071)**
Competitveness Review **(27072)** .....(Combined) 700

King of Prussia
Smart Business Now
  Magazine **(27127)** ....(Combined) 27,000

Middletown
Journal of East-West Business **(27254)** 250

Philadelphia
Philadelphia Business
  Journal **(27624)** ....(Paid) 11,506
Top Producer **(27705)** ....(Non-paid) 178,085

Pittsburgh
Current Business Reports **(27774)**
Current Business Reports: Monthly Wholesale Trade,
  Sales, and Inventories **(27775)**
Health Care Financing Review **(27795)**
Pittsburgh Business Times **(27830)** .....(Paid) 16,731

Spring House
Office Systems 96 **(28009)** ......(Controlled) 100,225

RHODE ISLAND
Providence
Providence Business News **(28414)** ....(Paid) 5,785

SOUTH CAROLINA
Charleston
Commerce Magazine **(28512)**

Columbia
Business & Economic Review **(28546)** ....‡6,100
Journal of Financial Research **(28552)**
Journal of Management **(28553)**

Greenville
GSA Business **(28624)** ....(Controlled) 10,500

Mount Pleasant
Charleston Regional Business
  Journal **(28692)** ....(Combined) 8,200

TENNESSEE
Johnson City
Journal of Asia-Pacific Business **(29252)**

Martin
Journal of Business and Economic
  Perspectives **(29342)**

Memphis
Business Perspectives **(29359)** .....(Non-paid) ‡4,100

Murfreesboro
Tennessee's Business **(29435)** ......(Non-paid) 4,500

Nashville
Amusement Business **(29441)** ....(Paid) 8,981
California Medicine **(29448)**
Healthcare Business
  Month **(29457)** ....(Combined) 38,109
Journal of Service Research **(29464)**
Nashville Business Journal **(29472)** ......(Paid) 6,200

TEXAS
Austin
Austin Business Journal **(29756)** ....(Paid) ★7,027
Journal of Organizational Computing and Electronic
  Commerce **(29789)**
Texas Journal of Business
  Law **(29827)** ....(Paid) 4,000

Dallas
Daily Commercial Record **(30142)**
Economic and Financial Policy Review **(30153)**

Fort Worth
Code One **(30334)**

Houston
Houston Business Journal **(30480)** .....(Paid) 19,214
Houston Economic Highlights **(30483)**
OfficeSolutions **(30512)**

Huntsville
Journal of Business Strategies **(30596)**

Hurst
Self-Employed America **(30602)** ......(Paid) ‡250,000

Irving
Lamp (New York) **(30606)**

McAllen
The South Texas Business
  Journal **(30787)** ....(Paid) ‡3,500
                                                                    (Controlled) ‡3,000

San Antonio
The San Antonio Business
  Journal **(31045)** ....(Paid) 11,932

Stafford
Fort Bend Business Journal **(31126)** 6,287

Waco
Entrepreneurship Theory and
  Practice **(31246)** ....‡1,600
Journal of Entrepreneurial and Small Firm
  Finance **(31250)**

VERMONT
Burlington
Vermont Business
  Magazine **(31519)** ....(Paid) ‡1,697
                                                                    (Non-paid) ‡4,037

Williston
Business People
  Vermont **(31618)** ....(Controlled) ⊕6,000

VIRGINIA
Alexandria
American Brewer **(31635)** ....(Combined) 3,000
Business Products Industry
  Report **(31650)** ....(Paid) ‡11,000
                                                                    (Non-paid) ‡101
Journal of Business & Economic Statistics **(31689)**

Arlington
Journal of Research Administration **(31805)**
Management Quarterly **(31806)**
Washington Techway **(31840)**

Ashburn
Business Today Egypt **(31850)**
Egypt Today **(31851)**

Falls Church
Catalog Success
  Magazine **(32042)** ....(Combined) 15,245

Harrisonburg
Journal of Global Business **(32139)**

Langley AFB
Statistics of Income - SOI Bulletin **(32177)**

Oakton
ASBA Today **(32316)** ....(Non-paid) 5,000

Reston
Business Education Forum **(32362)** ....‡15,873
DECA Dimensions **(32364)** ....(Paid) ⊕161,000
                                                                    (Non-paid) ⊕500

P.B.L. Business Leader (32409)

Richmond
Virginia Business **(32460)** ....(Controlled) 32,500
What's New in Advertising and Marketing **(32470)**

Springfield
OfficePRO **(32550)** ....(Paid) 35,000

Virginia Beach
The Shilling **(32589)**

Williamsburg
Business and Economic
  History **(32614)** ....(Combined) 650

WASHINGTON
Bellevue
Washington CEO **(32669)** ....(Controlled) 37,000

Seattle
Asia Pacific Economic
  Review **(32942)** ....(Combined) 30,500
Horizon Air Magazine **(32971)** ....‡300,000
Puget Sound Business
  Journal **(33007)** ....(Paid) 20,000
Seattle Daily Journal of
  Commerce **(33019)** ....‡5,500
Technical Analysis of Stocks &
  Commodities **(33035)** 65,000

Sequim
Peninsula Business Journal **(33076)** ....(Paid) 200
                                                                    (Non-paid) 4,600

Tacoma
The Business
  Examiner **(33144)** ....(Combined) 10,000

Wenatchee
Everett Business Journal **(33194)**
Wenatchee Business
  Journal **(33195)** ....(Paid) ‡1,900
                                                                    (Non-paid) ‡2,300

Woodinville
China Markets for Melamine **(33208)**
China Paints and Coatings: Market and
  Opportunities **(33209)**
China Synthetic Rubber Markets **(33210)**

WISCONSIN
Appleton
Marketplace Magazine **(33537)** ....(Paid) 15,000

Black Earth
Corporate Report Wisconsin **(33588)** ....(Paid) 71
                                                                    (Controlled) 30,000

Madison
AQUA Magazine **(33921)** ....(Controlled) 15,000

Milwaukee
American Business Law Journal **(34058)**
The Business Journal Serving Greater
  Milwaukee **(34060)** ....(Paid) 10,100
Contracting Profits **(34064)** ....(Paid) 50
                                                                    (Controlled) 35,000
Small Business
  Times **(34102)** ....(Combined) 20,000

ALBERTA, CANADA
Edmonton
Commerce News **(34706)** ....(Non-paid) 36,000
Edmonton and Homersham Commerce &
  Industry **(34709)** ....(Non-paid) ‡5,000

BRITISH COLUMBIA, CANADA
Bowen Island
OFFICE@Home **(34887)**

Burnaby
B. C. Business **(34890)**

Cranbrook
Kootenay Business Magazine **(34936)** ......(Paid) 24
                                                                    (Controlled) ‡9,100

Vancouver
Beyond Numbers **(35127)** ....(Controlled) ‡9,200
Business in Vancouver Media
  Group **(35128)** ....(Paid) 10,000

NEW BRUNSWICK, CANADA
Fredericton
Journal of Comparative International
  Management **(35396)**

Moncton
The Atlantic
  Co-operator **(35411)** ....(Combined) 21,000

Circ.   Circ.   Circ.

BUSINESS (continued)

NEWFOUNDLAND AND LABRADOR, CANADA
St. John's
Atlantic Business
  Magazine (35485) ....(Non-paid) 30,500

ONTARIO, CANADA
Aurora
Canadian Business Law Journal (35641)

Hamilton
B12-Hamilton/Halton Business
  Report (35875) ....(Controlled) ‡23,375

London
London Business Monthly
  Magazine (35986) ....(Paid) ‡1,020
                  (Non-paid) ‡13,467

Mississauga
Charitable Business
  Magazine (36061) ....(Controlled) 12,000
Mississauga Business
  Times (36080) ....(Controlled) ‡19,500

Oakville
Business Executive (36136) ....(Non-paid) 30,000

Scarborough
Northern Ontario
  Business (36379) ....(Controlled) ‡10,500

Thunder Bay
Thunder Bay
  Business (36439) ....(Controlled) ‡7,500

Toronto
Association (36464) ....(Combined) 15,000
Canadian Business (36494) ....(Paid) 81,377
Canadian Treasurer (36534) ....(Controlled) 5,000
EDGE (36577) ....(Combined) 16,361
Italy Canada Trade (36627)
Ivey Business Journal (36628)
Ivey Business Quarterly (36629) ....(Paid) ‡8,500
                (Non-paid) ‡6,500
Profit (36719) ....(Non-paid) 59,8624
Rob Magazine (36731) ....(Paid) 276,000
Toronto Business Journal (36765)

QUEBEC, CANADA
Laval
Entreprendre (37037) ....(Combined) ‡60,000

Montreal
Journal de
  l'Assurance (37143) ....(Controlled) 26,000
Le Magazine PME (37169) ......(Combined) •39,764
LES AFFAIRES (37175)
Meetings Monthly (37185) ....(Controlled) 13,600
Revue Commerce (37217) ....(Paid) 43,111

Quebec
Le Journal Economique de
  Quebec (37287) ....(Combined) 11,234

CARPENTRY

ILLINOIS
Chicago
Manufactured Home
  Merchandiser (8476) ....(Controlled) ‡18,452

WISCONSIN
Iola
Frame Building News (33827) 19,991

CEMETERIES AND MONUMENTS

ILLINOIS
Chicago
The Cremationist of North America (8347) ....‡1,600

Des Plaines
Catholic Cemetery (8752) ....‡2,000

OHIO
Mount Sterling
Stone in America (25397) ....‡2,200

SOUTH CAROLINA
Beaufort
Alliance (28486) ....(Controlled) 8,000

VIRGINIA
Reston
International Cemetery and Funeral
  Management (32367) ....(Paid) ‡4,100
              (Non-paid) 2,000

ONTARIO, CANADA
Delhi
Turf & Recreation (35771) ....(Combined) 15,000

CERAMICS

See also Glass and China

NEW MEXICO
Santa Fe
Pottery Southwest (19941) ....(Paid) 170

NEW YORK
New York
American Ceramics (21183)
Glass and Ceramics (21765)

OHIO
Materials Park
Advanced Materials &
  Processes (25363) ....(Paid) 30,000

Westerville
American Ceramic Society
  Bulletin (25636) 15,000
Ceramic Engineering and Science
  Proceedings (25637) ....(Paid) 1,519
              (Non-paid) 16
Ceramic Source (25638) ....(Paid) 14,500
             (Non-paid) 6,000
Journal of the American Ceramic
  Society (25641) ....(Paid) ‡2,600

VIRGINIA
Waterford
Clay Times (32609) ....(Paid) 15,500

WISCONSIN
Iola
Dollmaking (33822) ....(Controlled) ⊕16,200
Fired Arts & Crafts (33826) ....‡16,500

ONTARIO, CANADA
Willowdale
Canadian Ceramics Quarterly (36876) ....‡1,200

CHAMBERS OF COMMERCE AND BOARDS OF TRADE

FLORIDA
Sarasota
Sarasota Magazine (6664) ....(Combined) ‡13,000

Tallahassee
On Track (6726) 300

ILLINOIS
Chicago
Chamber Way
  Germany/Midwest (8303) ....:(Controlled) 6,000
Italian American Chamber of Commerce of Chicago
  Bulletin (8422) ....(Paid) 800

MICHIGAN
Detroit
Detroiter (14929) ....(Paid) 18,535
             (Controlled) 2,000

MINNESOTA
Duluth
The Duluthian (15837) ....‡1,800

MISSOURI
St. Louis
St. Louis Commerce (17497) ....(Paid) 7,154
            (Non-paid) 2,826

NEW JERSEY
Trenton
Mercer Business Magazine (19658) ....(Paid) ‡5,431
            (Non-paid) ‡3,169

OKLAHOMA
Oklahoma City
The Point! (25993) ....‡5,800

ALBERTA, CANADA
Edmonton
Commerce News (34706) ....(Non-paid) 36,000

ONTARIO, CANADA
Toronto
German American Trade (36603) 2,400
Italy Canada Trade (36627)

QUEBEC, CANADA
Montreal
Italian Commerce of Commerce of
  Canada (37136) ....(Non-paid) ‡8,000

CHEMISTRY, CHEMICALS, AND CHEMICAL ENGINEERING

ALABAMA
Birmingham
Geochemistry International (72) 675

ARIZONA
Phoenix
For Formulation Chemists Only (804)

CALIFORNIA
Berkeley
Experimental Heat Transfer (1520) ....(Paid) ‡267
Journal of Catalysis (1531)

Davis
Pesticide Biochemistry and Physiology (1817)

Fresno
Agribusiness Fieldman (1941) .....(Controlled) ‡8,058

San Diego
Analytical Biochemistry (3113)
Archives of Biochemistry and Biophysics (3116)
Biochemical and Biophysical Research
  Communications (3120)
Journal of Colloid and Interface Science (3181)
Journal of Food Composition and Analysis (3196)
Journal of Magnetic Resonance (3203)
Journal of Molecular Spectroscopy (3206)
Molecular Genetics and Metabolism (3235)
Nitric Oxide (3242)

COLORADO
Denver
Technometrics (4362) ....(Combined) ⊕6,377

Wheat Ridge
Composites
  Technology (4673) ....(Controlled) ‡25,000
High-Performance
  Composites (4676) ....(Controlled) ‡20,000

CONNECTICUT
Norwalk
Journal of Radiation Curing (5066) ....(Paid) 690
            (Non-paid) 1,810
Nanoparticle News (5070)

Storrs
Spectroscopy Letters (5168) ....(Paid) 325

DISTRICT OF COLUMBIA
Washington
Antimicrobial Agents and
  Chemotherapy (5355) ....(Paid) ‡5,810
            (Non-paid) ‡30
Biomacromolecules (5376) 2000
Chemical Regulation Reporter (5404)
ChemMatters (5406) ....(Paid) ⊕40,000
Crystal Growth & Design (5451) 1,300
Journal of Combinatorial Chemistry (5578) 2,650
Journal of Natural Products (5604) 2,400
Journal of Pharmaceutical
  Sciences (5612) ....(Paid) ‡5,000
            (Non-paid) ‡120
Modern Drug Discovery (5656)
Organic Letters (5711) 3,500

FLORIDA
Boynton Beach
Instrumentation Science & Technology (5950) 325

GEORGIA
Athens
Molecular Physics (6947)

IDAHO
Boise
The Chemical Educator (7805)

ILLINOIS

Argonne
Solvent Extraction and Ion
Exchange **(8020)** ....(Paid) 325

Carol Stream
Cosmetics & Toiletries **(8142)** ....(Paid) 3,278
Perfumer and Flavorist **(8152)** ....‡1,774

Champaign
Journal of the American Oil Chemists'
Society **(8194)** ....(Paid) ‡3,000
(Non-paid) ‡50

Chicago
Numerical Heat Transfer, Part A:
Applications **(8515)** ....‡586

Itasca
Chemical Processing **(9009)** ......(Non-paid) ‡65,000
Processing **(9016)** ....(Paid) 105,000

Niles
Journal of Analytical
Toxicology **(9287)** ....(Paid) ‡1,250
(Non-paid) ‡64
Journal of Chromatographic
Science **(9288)** ....(Paid) ‡1,581
(Non-paid) ‡63

Northbrook
RadTech Report **(9321)** ....(Non-paid) 1,750

INDIANA
West Lafayette
International Reviews in Physical Chemistry **(10547)**

KANSAS
Lawrence
Chemical Times & Trends **(11549)** ....‡7,500

LOUISIANA
Lake Charles
Applied Spectroscopy Reviews **(12635)** ....(Paid) 400
Microchemical Journal **(12639)**

MARYLAND
Bethesda
American Journal of Physiology
(Consolidated) **(13304)** ....(Combined) ‡2,639
BioEngineering Abstracts **(13320)**
Chemoreception Abstracts **(13324)**
The Journal of Biological
Chemistry **(13350)** ....‡5,000

College Park
CHAOS **(13414)**
The Journal of Chemical Physics **(13425)** ....‡N/A
Journal of Physical and Chemical Reference
Data **(13430)**

Gaithersburg
Journal of AOAC International **(13544)** ....‡2,300

MASSACHUSETTS
Boston
Organic Preparations and Procedures
International **(13944)**

Burlington
Supramolecular Science **(14033)**
Ultrasonics Sonochemistry **(14035)**

Lexington
CryoGas International **(14271)**

Medford
Applied Biochemistry and Biotechnology **(14319)**

Newton
CPI Purchasing **(14385)** ....(Non-paid) ‡40,007

MICHIGAN
Michigan
Journal of Solid State Chemistry **(15354)**

MINNESOTA
St. Paul
Cereal Chemistry **(16368)** ....(Paid) ‡3,260
(Controlled) ‡26
Cereal Foods World **(16369)** ....(Paid) ‡4,231
(Controlled) ‡303
Journal of the American Society of Brewing
Chemists **(16381)** ....(Controlled) 1,000
Powder and Bulk
Engineering **(16407)** ....(Free) ‡35,005

MISSOURI
Fort Leonard Wood
CML Army Chemical Review **(17071)**

St. Louis
Synthesis and Reactivity in Inorganic and Metal-
Organic Chemistry **(17519)** 300

MONTANA
Missoula
Journal of Carbohydrate Chemistry **(17867)** 550

NEBRASKA
Lincoln
Comments on Toxicology **(18081)**
Photochemistry and Photobiology **(18113)** 815
(Non-paid) 1,600

NEW HAMPSHIRE
Durham
Structural Chemistry **(18502)** ....(Paid) ‡200
(Non-paid) ‡50

NEW JERSEY
Hoboken
Abstract Bulletin of the Institute of Paper Science
and Technology **(18880)** ....(Paid) ‡660
(Controlled) ‡90
Advanced Functional Materials **(18881)**
Applied Organometallic Chemistry **(18893)**
Biomedical Chromatography **(18904)**
Biopolymers **(18906)** 7000
Cell Biochemistry and Function **(18909)**
Flavour and Fragrance Journal **(18949)**
GLIA **(18954)** 4200
Heteroatom Chemistry **(18962)**
International Journal of Chemical
Kinetics **(18977)** 4550
International Journal of Quantum
Chemistry **(18995)** 5950
Journal of Biochemical and Molecular
Toxicology **(19006)**
Journal of Chemical Technology and
Biotechnology **(19010)**
Journal of Chemometrics **(19011)** ....(Paid) 4,200
Journal of Computational Chemistry **(19019)** 8400
Journal of Mass Spectrometry **(19029)**
Journal of Microcolumn
Separations **(19031)** 5,985
Journal of Molecular
Recognition **(19032)** ....(Paid) 4,200
Journal of Peptide Science **(19040)**
Journal of Physical Organic
Chemistry **(19041)** ....(Paid) 3,500
Journal of Polymer Science **(19042)** 12,950
Journal of Raman Spectroscopy **(19044)**
Journal of Thermal Analysis and Calorimetry **(19050)**
Luminescence **(19054)**
Magnetic Resonance in Chemistry **(19056)**
Microscopy Research and
Technique **(19062)** 5600
Neuroscience Research Communications **(19073)**
NMR in Biomedicine **(19074)**
Packaging Technology and
Science **(19078)** 2,800
Pest Management Science **(19081)**
Phytochemical Analysis **(19083)** 3,500
Phytotherapy Research **(19084)** 4,200
Rapid Communications in Mass
Spectrometry **(19096)** ....(Paid) 4,900
Surface and Interface
Analysis **(19112)** ....(Paid) 5,950
X-Ray Spectrometry **(19120)**
Yeast **(19121)**

Morris Plains
Chemical
Equipment **(19289)** ....(Non-paid) ‡1,03,050
Powder/Bulk Solids **(19302)** ....(Non-paid) ‡40,020

Newark
Advances in Polymer Technology **(19350)** 3850
Polymer Preprints **(19363)** ....(Controlled) 9,000

Ramsey
Happi Household & Personal Products
Industry **(19488)** ....(Paid) 700
(Controlled) 15,905
Ink World **(19491)**

NEW YORK
Melville
Physiological Chemistry and Physics and Medical
NMR **(21057)** ....(Combined) 353
Soap/Cosmetics/Chemical
Specialties **(21064)** ....(Paid) 1,187
(Controlled) 15,662

New York
Adsorption **(21151)**
AICHE Journal **(21166)** 3,025
Analytical Letters **(21212)** ....(Paid) 550
Applied Biochemistry and Microbiology **(21228)**
Aquatic Geochemistry **(21238)**
Artificial Cells, Blood Substitutes and Immobilization
Biotechnology **(21256)** 325
Biochemistry (Moscow) **(21310)**
BioMetals **(21323)**
Catalysis Letters **(21379)**
CATTECH **(21384)**
Cellulose **(21388)**
Chemical Engineering **(21400)** ....(Paid) 25,929
(Non-paid) 32,469
Chemical Engineering
Progress **(21401)** ....(Paid) 39,881
Chemical Market Reporter **(21402)** ....‡16,801
Chemical and Petroleum Engineering **(21403)**
Chemical Specialties **(21404)**
Chemistry of Heterocyclic Compounds **(21405)**
Chemistry of Natural Compounds **(21406)**
Colloid Journal **(21440)**
Computational Geosciences **(21469)**
Current Topics in Chinese Science Section B:
Chemistry **(21526)**
Doklady Chemistry **(21564)**
Doklady Physical Chemistry **(21565)**
Drying Technology **(21572)** 350
Ecotoxicology **(21583)**
Environmental Geochemistry and Health **(21618)**
Eurotec **(21658)** 11,000
Fibre Chemistry **(21688)**
Foundations of Chemistry **(21730)**
Fullerene Science &
Technology **(21740)** ....(Paid) 250
Glycoconjugate **(21773)**
Heat Exchanger Design
Update **(21798)** ....(Paid) 100
High Energy Chemistry **(21800)**
The Histochemical Journal **(21804)**
Hyperfine Interactions **(21840)**
Integrated Pest Management **(21886)**
Interface Science **(21890)**
Journal of Analytical Chemistry **(21987)**
Journal of Applied Electrochemistry **(21990)**
Journal of Atmospheric Chemistry **(22002)**
Journal of Chemical Crystallography **(22020)**
Journal of Chemical Ecology **(22021)**
Journal of Computer-Aided Materials Design **(22035)**
Journal of Computer-Aided Molecular Design **(22036)**
Journal of Elasticity **(22057)**
Journal of Electroceramics **(22058)**
Journal of Evolutionary Biochemistry and
Physiology **(22066)**
Journal of Fluid Mechanics **(22070)** 1700
Journal of Inclusion Phenomena and Macrocyclic
Chemistry **(22092)**
Journal of Liquid Chromatography & Related
Technologies **(22114)** ....(Paid) 800
Journal of Materials Science **(22123)**
Journal of Materials Science Letters **(22124)**
Journal of Materials Synthesis and
Processing **(22125)**
Journal of Polymers and the Environment **(22162)**
Journal of Porous Materials **(22163)**
Journal of Protein Chemistry **(22167)**
Journal of Radioanalytical and Nuclear
Chemistry **(22175)**
Journal of Solution Chemistry **(22190)**
The Journal of Supercritical
Fluids **(22199)** ....(Paid) 229
(Controlled) 34
Journal of Trace and Microprobe
Techniques **(22206)** ....(Paid) 225
Letters in Peptide Science **(22248)**
Lubricants World **(22268)**
Molecular and Cellular Biochemistry **(22356)**
Molecular Diversity **(22357)**
Molecular Engineering **(22358)**
Pharmaceutical Chemistry Journal **(22546)**
Photosynthesis Research **(22553)**
Plasmas and Polymers **(22563)**
Radiochemistry **(22622)**
Reaction Kinetics and Catalysis Letters **(22627)**
Russian Chemical Bulletin **(22682)**
Russian Journal of Applied Chemistry **(22683)**
Russian Journal of Biorganic Chemistry **(22684)**
Russian Journal of Coordination Chemistry **(22685)**
Russian Journal of Electrochemistry **(22688)**
Russian Journal of General Chemistry **(22689)**
Russian Journal of Organic Chemistry **(22693)**
Soviet Metal Technology **(22768)**
Theoretical and Experimental Chemistry **(22826)**
Theoretical Foundations of Chemical
Engineering **(22827)**

Circulation: ★ = ABC; △ = BPA; ♦ = CAC; • = CCAB; ▢ = VAC; ⊕ = PO Statement; ‡ = Publisher's Report; Boldface figures = sworn; Light figures = estimated.

3115

Trade, Technical, and Professional Publications

Circ.   Circ.   Circ.

CHEMISTRY, CHEMICALS, AND CHEMICAL ENGINEERING (continued)

Pearl River
Synthetic Communications **(23087)** 1,200

Staten Island
Journal of Inorganic and Organometallic
 Polymers **(23359)**

Syracuse
Journal of Wood Chemistry and
 Technology **(23406)** 300

Troy
Separation Science and
 Technology **(23458)** ....(Paid) 600

OHIO
Akron
Rubber Chemistry and
 Technology **(24586)** ....‡3,000

Cincinnati
Automotive Finishing **(24778)**

Columbus
CA Selects **(25004)**
Organic Process Research &
 Development **(25056)** 2,500

Materials Park
Engineered Materials Abstracts **(25365)**

OKLAHOMA
Stillwater
Heat Transfer Engineering: An International
 Quarterly **(26078)** ....‡688

PENNSYLVANIA
Blooming Glen
Journal of Applied Asphalt Binder
 Technology **(26716)**

Philadelphia
The Chemical Engineer **(27397)**
Chemical Engineering Research and Design **(27398)**
International Journal of Radiation Biology **(27506)**
Journal of Automatic Chemistry **(27517)**
Molecular Membrane Biology **(27574)**
Particulate Science and Technology **(27612)** ....‡150

Pittsburgh
Journal of Research of the National Institute of
 Standards and Technology **(27804)**

TENNESSEE
Memphis
Journal of Biomolecular Techniques **(29371)**

TEXAS
Austin
Bioorganic Chemistry **(29765)**

Galveston
International Journal of Developmental
 Neuroscience **(30381)** ....(Paid) 700
        (Non-paid) 300

Houston
Environmental Toxicology and
 Chemistry **(30471)** 5,500
Materials Performance **(30506)** ....(Paid) ‡15,835

VIRGINIA
Charlottesville
Clinical Chemistry **(31924)** ....(Combined) 12,000
HYLE **(31929)**

Richmond
Polymer-Plastics Technology and
 Engineering **(32446)** 325

WASHINGTON
Woodinville
China Markets for Melamine **(33208)**
China Paints and Coatings: Market and
 Opportunities **(33209)**
China Synthetic Rubber Markets **(33210)**
China Wood Preservatives **(33211)**
Chinese Markets for Dimethylacetamide **(33212)**

WISCONSIN
Milwaukee
Aldrichimica Acta **(34056)** ....(Non-paid) 140,000

WYOMING
Laramie
Energy Sources **(34548)** ....(Controlled) ‡345

ALBERTA, CANADA
Calgary
Energy
 Processing/Canada **(34643)** ......(Combined) 9,800

ONTARIO, CANADA
Ottawa
Canadian Association of Radiologists
 Journal **(36189)** 1,600
Canadian Chemical News (L'Actualite Chimique
 Canadienne) **(36191)** ....(Paid) 4,171
        (Non-paid) 814
Canadian Journal of Chemistry (Revue Canadienne
 de Chimie) **(36202)** ....‡1,700
CMAJ/JAMC (Canadian Medical Association Journal)/
 (Journal de l'Association Medicale
 Canadienne) **(36236)** ....(Combined) •62,008
Physics Essays **(36272)** ....‡171

Toronto
Canadian Process Equipment & Control
 News **(36527)** ....(Combined) 25,000

Waterloo
Biotechnology Advances **(36846)** 1,000
Chem 13 News **(36848)** ....(Paid) 4,000

QUEBEC, CANADA
Montreal
Canadian Journal of Chemical
 Engineering **(37096)** ....‡1,050
Journal of Pulp & Paper
 Science **(37145)** ....(Combined) 13,150

CHIROPRACTIC

CALIFORNIA
Huntington Beach
Dynamic Chiropractic **(2060)** ......(Controlled) 68,000

Los Angeles
Chiropractic Products **(2238)** ......(Controlled) 40,000

MARYLAND
Towson
JNMS: Journal of the Neuromusculoskeletal
 System **(13760)** ....(Paid) 7,000

MISSOURI
St. Louis
Managed Care/Innovations **(17469)** ....‡24,000

NEW JERSEY
Hoboken
Arthritis Care and Research **(18898)** ....‡1,575

TEXAS
Austin
Texas Journal of
 Chiropractic **(29828)** ....(Controlled) ‡2,300

VIRGINIA
Arlington
ICA Review **(31796)** ....(Paid) ‡8,000

Richlands
Chiropractic History **(32425)** ....(Paid) ‡523
        (Non-paid) ‡250

ONTARIO, CANADA
Toronto
Journal of the Canadian Chiropractic
 Association **(36632)** ....(Combined) •5,539

CIVIL RIGHTS

See also Ethnic and Minority Studies

CALIFORNIA
Culver City
Turning the Tide **(1795)** ....(Paid) ‡750
        (Non-paid) ‡9,250

DISTRICT OF COLUMBIA
Washington
Civil Rights Journal **(5416)**

KANSAS
Topeka
MOUTH **(11835)** ....(Paid) 6,540

KENTUCKY
Louisville
The Disability Rag's Ragged Edge
 Magazine **(12215)** 3,500

LOUISIANA
New Orleans
Human Rights Review **(12733)** ....(Paid) ‡600

MASSACHUSETTS
Cambridge
Q Journal **(14093)**

Chestnut Hill
Massachusetts Discrimination Law Reporter **(14130)**

MICHIGAN
Ann Arbor
Michigan Journal of Gender &
 Law **(14764)** ....(Paid) 230

NEW YORK
New York
Asia-Pacific Journal on Human Rights and the
 Law **(21263)**
Human Rights Case Digest **(21834)**
International Children's Rights Monitor **(21893)**
The International Journal of Children's
 Rights **(21901)**
International Journal on Minority and Group
 Rights **(21911)**

TENNESSEE
Nashville
Journal of Intergroup
 Relations **(29463)** ....(Paid) ‡1,150
        (Non-paid) ‡25

TEXAS
Austin
Texas Forum on Civil Liberties and Civil
 Rights **(29821)** ....(Combined) 400

WASHINGTON
Seattle
Prison Legal News **(33006)** ....(Paid) 4,000
        (Non-paid) 230

ONTARIO, CANADA
Ottawa
Human Rights Tribune/Tribune Des Droits
 Humains **(36249)** ....(Controlled) 1,500

CLOTHING

See also General Merchandise; Fashion

ARIZONA
Phoenix
Asian Sources Fashion Accessories &
 Supplies **(787)**
Swim Fashion Quarterly **(812)**

CALIFORNIA
Los Angeles
Apparel News South **(2212)** 19,248
California Apparel News **(2230)** 15,872
        (Non-paid) 6,000
New York Apparel News **(2346)** 10,049

Palm Springs
JQ **(2762)**

COLORADO
Greenwood Village
Stitches Magazine **(4505)** ....(Combined) 18,302

Longmont
Vows **(4561)**

DISTRICT OF COLUMBIA
Washington
The Custom Tailor **(5457)** ....‡500

GEORGIA
Atlanta
Textile World Latina **(7055)** ....(Combined) 12,500

Roswell
Apparel Industry
 International **(7512)** ....(Controlled) ‡13,750

ILLINOIS
Chicago
Chicago Apparel News **(8306)** 10,764

Highland Park
Made to Measure (8993) ....(Controlled) ⊕25,000

KANSAS
Overland Park
Wearables Business (11735) ......(Combined) 14,723

MARYLAND
Earleville
Dress (13485)

MINNESOTA
Minnetonka
Tack'n Togs
　Merchandising (16176) ....(Controlled) ‡14,264

NEW JERSEY
South Plainfield
Imprinting Business (19589) ....(Paid) 988
　　　　　　　　　　　　　　(Controlled) 24,000

NEW YORK
New York
APPAREL
　Merchandising (21226) ....(Non-paid) ‡38,650
Children's Business (21410) ......(Non-paid) ‡14,083
Daily News Record (21531) ....(Paid) 17,069
Earnshaw's Review (21576) ....(Paid) 3,132
　　　　　　　　　　　　　　(Non-paid) 8,784
Embroidery Monogram Business (21598) 26,192
Femme-Lines (21684) ....(Paid) 3,900
　　　　　　　　　　　　　　(Non-paid) 7,000
MascuLines (22288)
Outerwear Magazine (22513) ....‡17,000
Women's Wear Daily (22936) ......(Mon.-Fri.) 44,015

TEXAS
Dallas
Dallas Apparel News (30143) 21,023

VIRGINIA
Dillwyn
EGA Needle Arts
　Magazine (31996) ....(Paid) 30,000

ONTARIO, CANADA
Ottawa
Canadian Home Economics Journal (Revue
　Canadienne d'Economie
　Familiale) (36199) ....…......(Controlled) ‡2,000

Toronto
Style (36751)

QUEBEC, CANADA
Montreal
KIDS CREATIONS (37147) ....(Non-paid) 7,571

COMMERCE AND INDUSTRY

**See also Banking, Finance, and
Investments; Chambers of Commerce and
Boards of Trade; International Business
and Economics**

ALABAMA
Montgomery
Developing Alabama (364) ....(Non-paid) 7,000

ARIZONA
Flagstaff
Journal of the Flagstaff
　Institute (697) ....(Combined) 150

CALIFORNIA
San Francisco
Processed World (3416) ....(Paid) 1,200
　　　　　　　　　　　　　　(Non-paid) 800

Santa Monica
Ergonomics in Design (3707) ....(Paid) 5,300

CONNECTICUT
Prospect
Job Shop Technology
　(JST) (5092) ....(Controlled) ‡32,000

FLORIDA
Nokomis
Modern Applications News
　(MAN) (6464) ....(Controlled) ‡85,001
　　　　　　　　　　　　　　(Free) ‡118
　　　　　　　　　　　　　　(Paid) ‡17

St. Petersburg
Florida Trend (6628) ....(Paid) 50,000
　　　　　　　　　　　　　　(Non-paid) 10,371
Maddux Report (6630) ....(Paid) 1,040
　　　　　　　　　　　　　　(Controlled) 13,180

GEORGIA
Atlanta
Adhesives Age (6960) ....(Paid) 1,727
　　　　　　　　　　　　　　(Controlled) 24,962

Norcross
IIE Solutions (7462) ....(Paid) 17,000
Industrial Management (7466)
Site Selection
　Magazine (7469) ....(Combined) 45,000

ILLINOIS
Bensenville
Industrial Paint and
　Powder (8068) ....(Controlled) 38,300

Chicago
The Surplus Record (8578) ....(Non-paid) ‡167,907
　　　　　　　　　　　　　　(Paid) ‡604
Utillaje (8596) ....(Paid) 500
　　　　　　　　　　　　　　(Controlled) 30,250

Decatur
Milling Journal (8713) ....…....(Controlled) 1,700

Des Plaines
Contractor Magazine (8755) ......(Controlled) 48,504
　　　　　　　　　　　　　　(Controlled) 48,504

Elk Grove Village
Gear Technology (8832) ....(Paid) 500
　　　　　　　　　　　　　　(Controlled) 9,000
　　　　　　　　　　　　　　　　　3,000

Flossmoor
Adhesives & Sealants
　Industry (8891) ....(Controlled) 16,500

Itasca
Control Ad-Lits (9011)

Skokie
Computer Listing Service's Machinery & Equipment
　Guide (9603) ....(Non-paid) ‡4,000

IOWA
Carlisle
Business & Industry (10648) ....(Controlled) ‡12,100

Davenport
Quality Control and Applied Statistics (10739)

LOUISIANA
Monroe
Journal of Internet Commerce (12691)

MARYLAND
Linthicum
M&SOM (Manufacturing & Service Operations
　Management) (13623)

MASSACHUSETTS
Burlington
European Journal of Purchasing and Supply
　Management (14027)

Newton
Global Design News (14397)
Industrial Distribution (14398) .....(Non-paid) ‡41,500
Modern Materials
　Handling (14406) ....(Non-paid) ‡105,841

MICHIGAN
Dearborn
Forming &
　Fabricating (14902) ....(Controlled) 65,496
Journal of Manufacturing
　Systems (14903) ....(Paid) 1,500

Novi
Filtration News (15408) ....(Controlled) ‡31,555

Troy
Energy User News (15622) ....(Paid) 894
　　　　　　　　　　　　　　(Non-paid) 50,027

MINNESOTA
Plymouth
Precision Manufacturing (16279) ....(Non-paid) 6,535

NEW HAMPSHIRE
Hampton
Midrange Enterprise (18514) ......(Combined) 45,000

NEW JERSEY
Hoboken
Managerial and Decision Economics (19058)

Morris Plains
Industrial Maintenance and Plant
　Operation (19293) ....(Controlled) 107,000
Industrial Product
　Bulletin (19294) ....(Non-paid) ‡170,000
Product Design and
　Development (19303) ....(Controlled) 160,000

Princeton Junction
Card Manufacturing (19483) ....(Paid) 3,000

Randolph
Consumer Goods
　Technology (19494) ....(Controlled) 25,000

Red Bank
Business Facilities (19500) ....(Free) 43,500

NEW YORK
Great Neck
American Industry (20685) ....(Controlled) ‡25,000
Asian Industrial
　Reporter (20686) ....(Non-paid) ‡26,141
Industrial Purchasing
　Agent (20689) ....(Controlled) ‡25,000
World Industrial Reporter (Reportero
　Industrial) (20695) ....(Non-paid) ‡71,101

Ithaca
Industrial and Labor Relations
　Review (20804) ....(Paid) ‡2,400
　　　　　　　　　　　　　　(Non-paid) ‡165

Melville
The Commerical
　Image (21041) ....(Non-paid) ‡22,607

New York
Industrial Equipment
　News (21865) ....(Controlled) ‡208,174
Industry and Environment (21867)
Journal of Heat Transfer (22086) 2,737
Journal of Industry, Competition and Trade (22094)
Journal of Network Industries (22140)
Journal of Pressure Vessel
　Technology (22165) 1,864
The Licensing Book (22252) ....‡20,711
MSI (22375) ....(Non-paid) ‡105,500
MSI Europe (22376)
Plastics Technology (22564) ....(Paid) ⊕46,530
　　　　　　　　　　　　　　(Non-paid) ⊕3,728
Review of Industrial Organization (22660)
Treasury and Risk Management
　Magazine (22860) 46,000

Westbury
Area Development
　Magazine (23552) ....(Controlled) ‡40,000

OHIO
Cincinnati
Applied Occupational & Environmental
　Hygiene (24774) ....(Paid) ‡6,278
　　　　　　　　　　　　　　(Non-paid) ‡225

Cleveland
DesignMart (24881) ....(Combined) 112,000
FLOW Manufacturing
　Report (24895) ....(Combined) 45,000

Columbus
The Daily Reporter (25015) ....(Paid) 5,300
　　　　　　　　　　　　　　(Free) 64
Finer Points Magazine (25017) ....(Controlled) 4,500
Materials Evaluation (25030) ....(Paid) 10,000
　　　　　　　　　　　　　　(Non-paid) 0

Solon
Tooling &
　Production (25529) ....(Controlled) ‡80,845

OKLAHOMA
Tulsa
Control Solutions (26111) ....(Controlled) ‡92,608

PENNSYLVANIA
Butler
Abrasive Users News Fax (26742) .....(Non-paid) 10

Newtown Square
Powder Diffraction (27331) ....(Paid) 750
　　　　　　　　　　　　　　(Non-paid) 57

Norristown
Industrial Safety and Hygiene
　News (27335) ....(Controlled) ‡62,057

Circulation: ★ = ABC; △ = BPA; ◆ = CAC; ● = CCAB; ❑ = VAC; ⊕ = PO Statement; ‡ = Publisher's Report; Boldface figures = sworn; Light figures = estimated.

Trade, Technical, and Professional Publications

3117

Circ.

COMMERCE AND INDUSTRY (continued)

Pittsburgh
Journal of Law & Commerce (27802)

RHODE ISLAND
Newport
Early American Industries Association
Chronicle (28366) ....(Combined) 3,200

Westerly
Manufacturer's Mart (28457) ....(Non-paid) 46,000

SOUTH CAROLINA
Charleston
Commerce Magazine (28512)

TEXAS
El Paso
Twin Plant News (30283) ....(Controlled) 9,600

Fort Worth
Commercial Recorder (30335) ....‡600

VIRGINIA
Alexandria
Compoundings (31657) ....(Paid) 2,175

Arlington
Composites Fabrication (31783) ....(Combined) 8,000

Fairfax
Materials & Manufacturing
Processes (32025) ....(Paid) 325

WASHINGTON
Poulsbo
Export Leads (32897)

WISCONSIN
Fort Atkinson
OEM Off-Highway (33715) ....(Controlled) ‡17,500

BRITISH COLUMBIA, CANADA
Burnaby
Journal of Commerce (34904) .....(Combined) 2,537

MANITOBA, CANADA
Winnipeg
Commerce &
Industry (35323) ....(Combined) •18,000
Trade and Commerce (35353) ....(Paid) 221
(Non-paid) 9,745

ONTARIO, CANADA
Markham
Produits Pour L'Industrie
Quebecoise (36031) ....(Combined) 15,074

Mississauga
Alliance Magazine (36053) ....(Paid) 823
(Non-paid) 7,171

Oakville
Industrial Process Products and
Technology (36145) ....(Combined) 23,775

Toronto
Canadian Industrial Equipment
News (36506) ....(Combined) 22,363
Italy Canada Trade (36627)
Plant (36709) ....(Non-paid) •23,681
(Paid) •4,596

QUEBEC, CANADA
Jonquiere
Le Lingot (37012) ....‡16,000

Montreal
Le Journal Industriel du
Quebec (37162) ....(Combined) 19,652

Quebec
Magazine Circuit
Industriel (37291) ....(Controlled) 17,652

COMMUNICATIONS

See also Journalism and Publishing; Public Relations; Radio, Television, Cable, and Video; Telecommunications

ALABAMA
Tuscaloosa
American Journalism (484) ....(Paid) 800
Media Psychology (488)

Circ.

ARKANSAS
State University
Southwestern Mass Communication
Journal (1350) ....(Paid) 500

CALIFORNIA
Concord
ETC: A Review of General
Semantics (1753) 1,500

Fresno
Western Journal of Communication (1960) 2,600

Los Angeles
Amass (2206) ....(Paid) 6,000

Menlo Park
Communication Arts (2523) ....(Paid) ‡70,189

Rancho Santa Margarita
The Toastmaster (2883) 170,000

San Diego
Journal of Visual Communication and Image
Representation (3216)
Optical Fiber Technology (3244)

San Francisco
IABC Communication World (3374) .....(Paid) 14,506
(Non-paid) 657
MediaFile (3389) 15,000

Thousand Oaks
Communication Abstracts (3855) ....(Paid) 600
Communication Research (3856) ....(Paid) 800
Journal of Business and Technical
Communications (3883) ....(Paid) 500
Journal of Communication Inquiry (3884)
Journal of Language and Social
Psychology (3894) ....(Paid) 300
Management Communication
Quarterly (3902) ....(Paid) ‡600
Written Communication (3922) ....(Paid) ‡700

COLORADO
Denver
Newspapers &
Technology (4343) ....(Non-paid) ‡17,822

CONNECTICUT
Tolland
International Journal of Instructional Media
(IJIM) (5176) 2000

Wilton
EMedia Magazine (5227)

DELAWARE
Newark
Communication Quarterly (5270) ....‡2,700

DISTRICT OF COLUMBIA
Washington
The Howard Journal of Communications (5532)
Journal of Applied Communication Research (5571)
Journal of the Association for Communication
Administration (JACA) (5574) ....‡400
Journal of Broadcasting & Electronic
Media (5576) ....(Paid) ‡2,230
(Non-paid) ‡120
Journal of Health Communication (5595)
Quarterly Journal of Speech (5754) ....(Paid) ‡5,695
(Non-paid) ‡100
Text and Performance Quarterly (5820)

FLORIDA
Daytona Beach
Public Safety
Communications (6039) ....(Paid) ‡14,000
(Controlled) ‡135

Miami
Hora de Cierre (6361) ....(Controlled) 10,000

St. Petersburg
Journal of Mass Media Ethics (6629)

GEORGIA
Athens
Communication Education (6933) ....‡4,000
Critical Studies in Media
Communication (6935) ....‡4,000
Women's Studies in Communication (6953)

Atlanta
Defense & Security
Electronics (6999) ....(Paid) 1,681
(Non-paid) 43,000

Circ.

ILLINOIS
Carbondale
American Journal of Semiotics (8114) ....‡600

Urbana
College Composition and
Communication (9700) ....(Paid) 11,500
The Communication Review (9702)

Westmont
Business Communications
Review (9753) ....(Paid) 10,510
(Non-paid) 4,020

INDIANA
Bloomington
Federal Communications Law
Journal (9826) ....(Paid) ‡4,000

KANSAS
Overland Park
Cellular & Mobile
International (11704) ....(Combined) 10,000

MAINE
Bangor
The Write Markets Report (12905) ......(Paid) 1,000

MARYLAND
Bethesda
Electronics & Communications Abstracts
Journal (13333)

Linthicum
Information Systems Research (ISR) (13620)

Potomac
Communications Today (13650)
Wireless Data News (13664) ....(Controlled) ‡28,000

MASSACHUSETTS
Boston
Design Management Journal (13885)
DMI Academic Review (13886)

MICHIGAN
Flint
The Journal of Business
Communication (15035) 2,550

Michigan
Brain and Language (15353)

MINNESOTA
Maple Grove
Format Magazine (16038) ....(Non-paid) 3,000

MISSOURI
Warrensburg
Missouri Speech & Theatre
Journal (17667) ....(Controlled) 300

NEW HAMPSHIRE
Amherst
oemagazine (18454) ....(Controlled) ‡25,000

NEW JERSEY
Hoboken
International Journal of Communication
Systems (18980)
International Journal of Network
Management (18988)
International Journal of Satellite Communications
Networking (18997)
Journal of the American Society for Information
Science (19001) 33,600
Journal of Communications Technology and
Electronics (19016)

NEW YORK
Amityville
Journal of Collective Negotiations in the Public
Sector (20042)
Journal of Technical Writing and
Communication (20048)

Geneseo
Journal of Speech and Hearing
Research (20649) ....‡46,805

Manhasset
Call Center Magazine (20991) ....(Paid) 60,795
(Non-paid) 37,179
Internet Week (21005) ....(Non-paid) 200,000

New York
Business Communication
Quarterly **(21353)** ....(Combined) 1,875
CED **(21385)**
Personal Communications Magazine **(22543)**
Release 1.0 **(22643)**

NORTH CAROLINA
Cary
Journal of Communication **(23689)** .....(Paid) ‡5,000

Chapel Hill
Mass Communication and
Society **(23715)** ....(Paid) 1,100

OHIO
Akron
Ohio Speech Journal **(24583)**

Dayton
Health Communication **(25120)**

OKLAHOMA
Ada
Communication Studies **(25724)**

Bartlesville
Community Relations Report **(25754)** ......(Paid) 700

PENNSYLVANIA
Levittown
North American Shortwave Association (NASWA)—
The Journal **(27188)** ....(Paid) 1,200

Philadelphia
Behavior & Information Technology **(27387)**
Communication Monographs **(27423)** ....‡4,000

Pittsburgh
Social Epistemology **(27842)**

TEXAS
Denton
The Journal of Media Economics **(30239)**

UTAH
Provo
Journal of Media and Religion **(31404)**
Rhetoric Society Quarterly **(31407)** ....(Paid) 900

VIRGINIA
Annandale
Communication Booknotes Quarterly **(31763)**

Blacksburg
Communication Law and Policy **(31868)**

Fairfax
Women and Language **(32034)** ......(Combined) 400

Vienna
Foundation Update **(32577)**

WASHINGTON
Tacoma
Forensic **(33145)** ....(Controlled) 660

ALBERTA, CANADA
Calgary
Canadian Journal of
Communication **(34636)** ....(Paid) 405
(Controlled) 40

ONTARIO, CANADA
Aurora
CANADIAN SECURITY **(35643)** ....‡14,832

Ottawa
Radio Aids to Marine Navigation **(36274)**

Toronto
Direction Informatique **(36576)** ....(Combined) 20,585
Poiesis **(36712)**

Windsor
Informal Logic **(36887)** ....(Controlled) 400

COMPUTERS

ALABAMA
Birmingham
Russian Journal of Mathematical
Physics **(89)** 5985

ARIZONA
Glendale
Southwest Computer Monthly **(715)** ....(Paid) 18,000
(Non-paid) 32,000

Phoenix
Asian Sources Computer Products **(784)**
Computer Literature Index **(800)** .....(Controlled) 500
PC AI **(808)** ....(Combined) 10,000

Scottsdale
Document
Management **(868)** ....(Controlled) ⊕45,000
Visual Developer **(875)**

CALIFORNIA
Aliso Viejo
Computing News &
Reviews **(1390)** ....(Controlled) 30,000

Beverly Hills
Computer Technology
Review **(1571)** ....(Controlled) 72,552

Brisbane
The Net **(1607)**

Chatsworth
Enterprise Systems Journal **(1686)** .....(Paid) 80,000
The Industry Standard **(1687)**
InfoWorld Direct **(1688)** ....(Paid) 100,000

Chico
Smart TV & Sound
Magazine **(1696)** ....(Combined) 50,000

Costa Mesa
Law Office Computing **(1776)**

Dublin
Sybase Magazine **(1839)** ....(Controlled) 64,672

El Cerrito
Computer Currents **(1860)** ....(Paid) 1,000
(Non-paid) 670,000

Elk Grove
Delphi Informant **(1871)** ....(Paid) ‡22,500
(Non-paid) ‡500

Web Publisher **(1874)**

Folsom
Converge **(1917)**

Los Alamitos
Computer Magazine **(2181)** ....(Combined) 90,000
Computing in Science & Engineering **(2182)**
IEEE Computer Graphics and
Applications **(2183)** ....(Paid) 10,519
(Non-paid) 77
IEEE Design and Test of
Computers **(2184)** ....(Paid) 4,051
(Non-paid) 45
IEEE Intelligent Systems **(2185)** ....‡3,612
IEEE Internet Computing **(2186)** ....(Paid) 14,455
IEEE Micro **(2187)** ....(Paid) 12,000
IEEE Multimedia **(2188)**
IEEE Software Magazine **(2189)** ....(Paid) 16,982
IT Professional **(2190)** ....(Combined) ‡8,557

Menlo Park
AI Magazine **(2521)** 7,000
SCO World Magazine **(2526)** .....(Controlled) 50,000

Morgan Hill
Computer Fair Show
Program **(2601)** ....(Non-paid) ‡11,000

Mountain View
Global Technology Business **(2606)**

Palo Alto
Java Pro **(2796)**
Microsoft Interactive Developer **(2799)**

Redlands
Arc News **(2900)** ....(Non-paid) 380,000

Redwood City
Oracle Magazine **(2914)** ....(Free) ‡271,152
Profit **(2915)** ....(Controlled) ‡115,854

Rocklin
Web Commerce Today **(2957)**

San Diego
Access VB- SQL Advisor **(3104)** ....(Paid) 20,000
Computer Speech & Language **(3130)**
Computer Vision and Image Understanding **(3131)**
e-Business Advisor **(3144)** ....(Paid) 60,000
Graphical Models **(3163)**
Graphical Models **(3164)**

Journal of Computer and System Sciences **(3186)**
Journal of Network and Computer
Applications **(3208)**
Journal of Parallel and Distributed Computing **(3210)**
Lotus Advisor
Magazine **(3227)** ....(Combined) 15,000
Mobile Business Advisor **(3233)** ....(Paid) 20,000
Real-Time Imaging **(3253)**
San Diego Computer
Journal **(3260)** ....(Combined) 40,000
Simulation **(3275)** ....‡3,800
Transactions of the Society for Computer Simulation
International **(3283)** 1,000

San Francisco
CADENCE **(3333)** ....(Paid) 21,078
(Controlled) 78,943
Consulting Rates and Business Practices Annual
Survey **(3345)**
DV Media Group **(3351)** ....‡60,000
eCompany Now **(3354)**
Game Developer **(3364)**
Macworld **(3388)** ....(Paid) 459,267
(Non-paid) 167,877
The Red Herring **(3422)** ....(Paid) 162,666
(Non-paid) 5,611

San Jose
Switch **(3541)**

San Mateo
Dr. Dobb's Journal **(3585)** ....△120,195
InfoWorld **(3587)** ....(Controlled) 370,000
Windows Developer's
Journal **(3591)** ....(Paid) ‡23,057
(Non-paid) ‡263

Santa Ana
CADALYST **(3621)** ....(Paid) 20,204
(Non-paid) 61,395

Santa Barbara
Journal of IS Financial
Management **(3645)** ....(Controlled) 925

Santa Clara
CONNECT **(3669)** ....(Paid) 110
(Non-paid) 52,637

Saratoga
EC.COM Magazine **(3744)** ......(Controlled) △40,522

Sunnyvale
Interact **(3829)** ....(Paid) ‡7,615
(Controlled) ‡4,000

Thousand Oaks
Simulation & Gaming **(3916)** ....(Paid) ‡600

Westlake Village
MacTech Magazine **(4071)** ......(Combined) ‡15,488

COLORADO
Boulder
MSDN Magazine **(4180)**

Broomfield
Digital Graphics **(4204)** ....(Paid) △72
(Non-paid) △18,513

Englewood
Webcom Communication Corp **(4416)**

Golden
Boardwatch Magazine **(4463)** ....(Paid) 20,764
(Non-paid) 7,692

Longmont
Robotics World **(4560)** ....(Combined) ‡22,500

Loveland
NEWS/400 **(4569)** ....(Paid) 22,285

Westminster
AIX Update **(4659)**
CICS Update **(4660)**
DB2 Update **(4661)**
Mainframe Market Monitor **(4663)**
MQ Update **(4664)**
MVS Update **(4665)**
News IS **(4666)**
RACF Update **(4667)**
TCP/SNA Update **(4668)**

CONNECTICUT
Danbury
Computing Software Review **(4738)**
Electronic Learning **(4739)** ....(Paid) 8,060
(Controlled) 62,167

Home-Office Computing **(4741)** ....(Paid) 504,203

Circulation: ★ = ABC; △ = BPA; ◆ = CAC; ● = CCAB; ❑ = VAC; ⊕ = PO Statement; ‡ = Publisher's Report; Boldface figures = sworn; Light figures = estimated.

Trade, Technical, and Professional Publications

3119

Circ.   Circ.   Circ.

COMPUTERS (continued)

Darien
Internet Shopper **(4773)** ....(Combined) 160,000

Fairfield
MacII Review **(4791)** 18,700

Norwalk
Business Geographics **(5051)** .....(Controlled) 30,185
CTI **(5053)**

Wilton
EContent **(5225)** ....‡12,000
EMedia **(5226)** ....(Combined) △30,277
EMedia Magazine **(5227)**
IE Magazine **(5228)** ....(Controlled) ‡36,000

DISTRICT OF COLUMBIA
Washington
Computer Law Reporter '**(5431)**
Washington
   Technology **(5854)** ....(Controlled) 40,000

FLORIDA
Brandon
New Media Magazine **(5960)**
NewMedia **(5961)** ....(Combined) 250,000

Fort Myers
AFSM International Professional
   Journal **(6093)** 20,000

Hollywood
Electronic Commerce
   World **(6193)** ....(Paid) ‡44,000

Oldsmar
Mac Design Magazine **(6484)**

Sarasota
Journal of Information Systems **(6658)**

GEORGIA
Atlanta
Defense & Security
   Electronics **(6999)** ....(Paid) 1,681
                              (Non-paid) 43,000
Health Management
   Technology **(7014)** ....(Paid) 3,000
                              (Non-paid) 35,000
TechLINKS **(7051)** ....‡23,000

Marietta
OR/MS Today **(7415)** ....(Combined) 14,268

Norcross
MicroTimes **(7467)** ....(Free) 230,036

HAWAII
Honolulu
Language Learning and
   Technology **(7708)** ....(Non-paid) 3,944

ILLINOIS
Chicago
AS/400 Systems
   Management **(8276)** ....(Controlled) ‡45,000
Card Technology **(8298)** ....(Combined) ‡25,047
The Chicago Computer
   Guide **(8309)** ....(Controlled) 54,000
Upstart **(8594)** ....(Combined) 65,000

Itasca
Control **(9010)** ....(Non-paid) ‡72,217

Lombard
NARDA Independent Retailer **(9117)** ....‡2,000

Urbana
International Journal of Expert Systems **(9711)**

IOWA
Fairfield
Pocket PC **(10883)** ....(Paid) 18108

KANSAS
Lawrence
Sys Admin **(11565)** ....(Paid) ‡21,138

Manhattan
Journal of Research on Computing in
   Education **(11622)** 2,500

Topeka
Hi-Tech Home **(11822)** ....(Controlled) ‡45,000

KENTUCKY
Bardstown
Computer Times **(11925)** ...(Combined) 100,000

Prospect
Rainbow-Pcar Reviews
   On-Line **(12377)** ....(Paid) ‡87,046
                              (Controlled) ‡351

LOUISIANA
Monroe
Journal of Internet Commerce **(12691)**

MAINE
Portland
Computers in Nursing **(13009)** ....(Paid) 3,100
Interface Tech News **(13010)**

Yarmouth
IT Support News **(13080)** ....(Controlled) ‡45,100

MARYLAND
Bethesda
Computer and Information Systems Abstracts
   Journal **(13326)**

Columbia
IEEE Circuits and Devices **(13462)** ......(Paid) **7,500**

Linthicum
Information Systems Research (ISR) **(13620)**
INFORMS Journal on Computing **(13621)**
M&SOM (Manufacturing & Service Operations
   Management) **(13623)**

Potomac
ISP Business News **(13654)**
Wireless Networks **(13665)**

Silver Spring
INFORM **(13727)** ....(Non-paid) ‡40,000

MASSACHUSETTS
Amherst
Journal of Computing in Higher
   Education **(13797)** ....(Paid) 200
                              (Non-paid) 200

Boston
The Bulletin of Symbolic Logic **(13868)** ....‡2,500
Game Pro **(13894)** ....(Paid) 55,000

Brookline
Server/Workstation
   Expert **(14024)** ....(Controlled) 85,000
Server/Workstation Expert **(14025)**
WebServer OnLine **(14026)**

Cambridge
Computer Music Journal **(14046)** 2,193
eWeek **(14052)**
Information and Computation **(14070)**
Journal of Machine Learning Research **(14078)**
Presence **(14090)** ....(Paid) 1000
Sm@rt Partner **(14102)**

Framingham
Application Development Trends **(14191)**
CIO Web Business **(14193)** ....(Paid) 150,000
Computerworld **(14194)** ....(Paid) 170,031
Java Report **(14198)** ....(Paid) 30,000
SC Magazine **(14200)** ....(Controlled) 43,100

Newton
Datamation **(14386)** ....(Paid) 2,168
                              (Non-paid) 160,052
Digital News &
   Review **(14388)** ....(Controlled) ‡90,000

Southborough
IntraNet Magazine **(14545)**

Stow
Technology Meetings **(14576)**

Wellesley Hills
Contingency Planning and Recovery Journal
   (CPR-J) **(14621)**

Westborough
Client/Server
   Computing **(14636)** ....(Controlled) 95,000

Worcester
Science & Engineering Network News **(14688)**

MICHIGAN
Troy
CircuiTree **(15617)**

MINNESOTA
Minneapolis
Computer User **(16069)** ....(Non-paid) ‡50,000

MISSOURI
St. Louis
Disaster Recovery Journal **(17434)**

NEBRASKA
Lincoln
Journal of Database
   Management **(18087)** ....(Controlled) 300
Processor **(18115)**

NEVADA
Reno
Computers in the Schools **(18419)** ....(Paid) 542

NEW HAMPSHIRE
Amherst
oemagazine **(18454)** ....(Controlled) ‡25,000

Hanover
Circuit Cellar INK **(18515)** ....(Paid) ‡34,000
                              (Non-paid) ‡6,800

Nashua
BackOffice Magazine **(18582)** ....(Combined) ‡80,000
Computer Design **(18587)** .....(Non-paid) ‡113,000
Computer Graphics World **(18588)** ....(Paid) 9,706
                              (Non-paid) 54,961
Electronic Publishing **(18589)** 70,000
Integrated Communications
   Design **(18593)** ....‡23,406
Portable Design **(18599)**
Wireless Integration **(18605)**

Peterborough
Supply Chain Systems
   Magazine **(18630)** ....(Non-paid) 67,500

Rye
Personal Engineering & Instrumentation
   News **(18643)** ....(Paid) ‡250
                              (Controlled) ‡50,000

NEW JERSEY
Flemington
Children's Software Revue
   (CSR) **(18818)** ....(Combined) ‡19,000

Hoboken
Applied Stochastic Models in Business and
   Industry **(18894)**
Complexity **(18920)** 14,000
Concurrency and Computation: Practice and
   Experience **(18923)**
GPS Solutions **(18955)**
International Journal of Imaging Systems and
   Technology **(18985)** 3500
International Journal of Intelligent
   Systems **(18986)** ....(Combined) 3,675
Journal of Software Maintenance **(19048)**
Journal of Visualization and Computer
   Animation **(19052)**
Networks **(19071)** 1,000
Numerical Linear Algebra with Applications **(19075)**
Progress in Photovoltaics **(19087)** ......(Paid) 17,500
Random Structures & Algorithms **(19095)** 3850
Scientific Programming **(19102)** 3850
Software **(19104)**
Software Process **(19105)**
Systems and Computers in Japan **(19115)** ......‡300
Systems Research and Behavioral Science **(19116)**

Mahwah
Human-Computer Interaction **(19191)**
International Journal of Human Computer
   Interaction **(19194)** ....‡500
Neural Computing Surveys **(19203)**

Medford
BBS Magazine **(19220)**
Information Today **(19225)** ....(Paid) ‡5,000
                              (Non-paid) ‡5,000
Internet & Personal Computing Abstracts **(19226)**
KMWorld **(19227)** ....(Non-paid) △60,000
Link-Up **(19228)** ....(Paid) ‡4,000
                              (Non-paid) ‡6,000
Marketing Asst. **(19229)** ....(Paid) 5,000
                              (Non-paid) 5,000
MultiMedia Schools **(19231)** 15,000

Montvale
ColdFusion Developer's Journal
   (CFDJ) **(19247)** ....(Combined) 30,000
Java Developer's Journal **(19258)**
Linux Business Week **(19261)** ....(Combined) 60,000
PowerBuilder Developer's
   Journal **(19273)** ....(Combined) 37,000
Web Services Journal **(19279)**
WebLogic Developers
   Journal **(19280)** ....(Combined) 25,000

WebSphere Developer's
Journal **(19281)** ....(Combined) 25,000
Wireless Business &
Technology **(19282)** ....(Combined) 130,000
XML-Journal **(19283)**
XML Journal **(19284)**

Morris Plains
Scientific -Computing &
-Automation **(19306)** ....(Non-paid) ‡45,027

Newark
Rutgers Computer and Technology Law
Journal **(19364)**

Paramus
Wireless Systems Design **(19408)** ....△**37,200**

Randolph
Retail Info Systems
News **(19497)** ....(Controlled) ‡18,500

River Edge
International Journal on Artificial Intelligence
Tools **(19508)**
International Journal of Intelligent and Cooperative
Information Systems **(19510)**
International Journal of Software Engineering and
Knowledge Engineeg **(19513)**
Parallel Processing Letters **(19520)**

NEW MEXICO
Santa Fe
PRO/E **(19942)** ....(Controlled) 7,000
SOLID Solutions
Magazine **(19946)** ....(Controlled) 7,000

NEW YORK
Amityville
Journal of Educational Computing Research **(20044)**

Armonk
International Journal of Electronic
Commerce **(20079)** ....(Paid) 254

Binghamton
Journal of Consumer Health on the Internet **(20167)**
Journal of End User Computer Support **(20170)**
Journal of Internet Cataloging **(20185)**
Journal of Technology in Human
Services **(20203)** ....(Combined) 750

Bronx
Computer Living/New
York **(20264)** ....(Paid) ‡22,000
(Non-paid) ‡10,000

Great Neck
International Instrumentation and
Controls **(20690)** ....(Non-paid) ‡31,098

Hauppauge
Electronics Now **(20717)** ....(Paid) 76,889
Poptronics **(20722)** ....(Paid) 71,253

Manhasset
Computer Retail Week **(20993)**
CRN **(20994)** ....(Free) 117,500
Database Programming &
Design **(20995)** ....(Paid) 25,427
(Non-paid) 1,683
Embedded Systems Programming **(21000)** 60,000
Imaging Magazine **(21003)** 83,000
InformationWEEK **(21004)** ....(Non-paid) ‡440,000
Network Computing **(21007)** ....(Paid) 220,000
Network Magazine **(21008)** ....(Paid) ‡125,000
Performance
Computing **(21009)** ....(Controlled) ‡89,000
Software Development **(21013)** ....‡72,000
Technology & Learning **(21014)** ......(Paid) 12,924
(Non-paid) 68,188
Wall Street and Technology **(21017)**

Melville
Advanced Imaging **(21039)** ......(Controlled) ‡55,009
Workforce Diversity for Engineering and IT
Professionals **(21067)** ....(Combined) 15,046

Middle Island
The Hacker Quarterly **(21078)**

New York
Accounting Technology **(21135)** ....‡30,000
ACM Computing Surveys **(21136)** ....‡18,036
ACM Transactions on Computer
Systems **(21137)** 4,100
ACM Transactions on Database
Systems **(21138)** 6,433
ACM Transactions on Graphics **(21139)** 6,104
ACM Transactions on Information
Systems **(21140)** 4,573

ACM Transactions on Mathematical
Software **(21141)** 2,500
ACM Transactions on Programming Languages and
Systems **(21142)** 5,000
ACM Transactions on Software Engineering and
Methodology **(21143)**
Algorithmica **(21173)** ....(Combined) **700**
Annals of Operations Research **(21218)**
Annals of Software Engineering **(21219)**
Autonomous Agents and Multi-Agent
Systems **(21279)**
Autonomous Robots **(21280)**
BT Technology Journal **(21345)**
CATTECH **(21384)**
Cluster Computing **(21431)**
Combinatorics, Probability and
Computing **(21451)** 300
Communications of the
ACM **(21459)** ....(Paid) ‡80,370
Computational Geosciences **(21469)**
Computational & Mathematical Organization
Theory **(21470)**
Computational Mathematics and Modeling **(21471)**
Computer Bulletin **(21472)**
Computer Buyer's Guide &
Handbook **(21473)** ....‡40,240
Computer-Human Interaction (TOCHI) **(21474)**
Computer Shopper **(21477)** ....(Paid) 504,352
Computing Reviews **(21480)** ....‡1,900
Constraints **(21486)**
Data Mining and Knowledge Discovery **(21538)**
Design Automation of Electronic Systems
(TODAES) **(21545)**
Design Automation for Embedded Systems **(21546)**
Education and Information Technologies **(21587)**
Empirical Software Engineering **(21599)**
Formal Methods in System Design **(21726)**
Genetic Programming and Evolvable
Machines **(21750)**
Higher-Order and Symbolic Computation **(21803)**
IEEE Communications
Magazine **(21844)** ....(Paid) 50,000
(Non-paid) 1,000
IEEE Computational Science and
Engineering **(21845)**
IEEE Potentials **(21847)** ....(Paid) 48,252
(Non-paid) 866
Information Display **(21869)** ....(Paid) ‡3,000
(Non-paid) ‡10,000
Information Systems Frontiers **(21870)**
Information and Systems Security (TISSEC) **(21871)**
Information Technology and
Disabilities **(21872)** ....(Non-paid) 1,900
Insurance Networking **(21884)**
interactions **(21889)** ....(Paid) 10,000
International Journal of Computer Vision **(21903)**
International Journal of Computers for Mathematical
Learning **(21904)**
International Journal of Parallel
Programming **(21913)**
International Journal of Technology and Design
Education **(21922)**
Internet Health Care **(21941)**
Journal of Algebraic Combinatorics **(21980)**
Journal of the Association for Computing
Machinery **(22001)** ....‡11,400
Journal of Automated Reasoning **(22004)**
Journal of Automation and Information
Sciences **(22005)**
The Journal of Biomedical Informatics **(22012)**
Journal of Combinatorial Optimization **(22030)**
Journal of Computational Analysis and
Applications **(22034)**
Journal of Computer-Aided Materials Design **(22035)**
Journal of Experimental Algorithmics (JEA) **(22067)**
Journal of Functional Programming **(22073)** 400
Journal of Intelligent Information Systems **(22099)**
Journal of Intelligent Manufacturing **(22100)**
Journal of Intelligent and Robotic Systems **(22101)**
Journal of Internet Law **(22106)**
Journal of Nanoparticle Research **(22138)**
Journal of Scientific Computing **(22184)**
Journal of Supercomputing **(22197)**
Journal of Systems Integration **(22200)**
Journal of Thermal Analysis and Calorimetry **(22204)**
Learning Environments Research **(22243)**
Machine Learning **(22272)**
Machine Translation **(22273)**
Mathematical Structures in Computer
Science **(22298)** 350
Methodology and Computing in Applied
Probability **(22326)**
Mobile Networks and Applications **(22342)**
Modeling and Computer Simulation
(TOMACS) **(22344)**
Multibody System Dynamics **(22378)**

Multidimensional Systems and Signal
Processing **(22379)**
Multimedia Tools and Applications **(22380)**
NETNOMICS **(22418)**
netWorker **(22419)**
Networking (TON) **(22420)**
Networks and Spatial Economics **(22421)**
On **(22487)**
Optical Networks Magazine **(22499)**
PC Computing **(22533)** ....(Paid) 1,026,034
PC Week **(22535)** ....(Controlled) 128,277
Photonic Network Communications **(22552)**
Pixel Vision **(22556)**
Problems of Information Transmission **(22596)**
Programming and Computer Software **(22599)**
Queueing Systems **(22619)**
Real-Time Systems **(22637)**
Release 1.0 **(22643)**
Reliable Computing **(22644)**
Rhizome Digest **(22666)** ....(Combined) 6,600
Robotica **(22673)** 600
STACKS **(22781)**
StandardView **(22789)**
Transform Magazine **(22853)**
Wireless & Mobility **(22922)**
Yahoo! Internet Life **(22947)** ....(Paid) 1,003,771
Year/2000 Journal **(22948)**

Port Washington
Micro Computer Journal **(23130)** ....‡50,000

Rochester
Computer Link Magazine **(23218)**
Inside the Internet **(23229)**

Salamanca
Electronic Retailer **(23291)** ....(Controlled) ‡18,000

Stony Brook
Journal of Educational Technology Systems **(23370)**

Syracuse
American Journal of Mathematical and Management
Sciences **(23386)** ....‡1,000

West Henrietta
The IP.com Journal **(23543)**

Yorktown Heights
IBM Systems
Journal **(23607)** ....(Combined) ‡35,000
Natural Language
Engineering **(23608)** ....(Paid) ‡245
(Non-paid) ‡59

NORTH CAROLINA
Raleigh
Social Science Computer Review **(24153)** 1,000

OHIO
Cincinnati
Content Networking Journal **(24790)**

Cleveland
Frontline Solutions **(24900)** ....(Paid) 83
(Controlled) 75,000
Journal of Systems
Management **(24917)** ....(Paid) ‡8,000
Supply Chain Technology
News **(24955)** ....(Non-paid) 45,000

OKLAHOMA
Shawnee
CPA Software News **(26062)** ....(Paid) 51,411

OREGON
Eugene
Journal of Research on Technology in
Education **(26319)**
Learning and Leading with
Technology **(26322)** ....(Paid) ‡10,000
(Free) ‡2,000

PENNSYLVANIA
Blue Bell
ComputerTalk for the
Pharmacist **(26723)** ....(Paid) 400
(Non-paid) 32,500
EXEC **(26724)** ....(Controlled) 40,000

Erie
Business Solutions **(26894)** ....(Non-paid) ‡40,000

Exton
Enterprise Engineering Modeling
World **(26917)** ....(Combined) 125,000

Fort Washington
ENT **(26927)**

Circulation: ★ = ABC; △ = BPA; ◆ = CAC; ● = CCAB; □ = VAC; ⊕ = PO Statement; ‡ = Publisher's Report; Boldface figures = sworn; Light figures = estimated.

3121

Circ.   Circ.   Circ.

COMPUTERS (continued)

Enterprise Linux **(26928)**
Enterprise Systems **(26929)** ......(Non-paid) ‡83,500

Hershey
Annals of Cases on Information Technology
   (ACIT) **(27039)** ....(Paid) 200
Information Resources Management
   Journal **(27042)** ....(Controlled) 700
Journal of End User
   Computing **(27043)** ....(Controlled) 450
Journal of Global Information
   Management **(27044)** ....(Controlled) 600

Holland
Cryptosystems Journal **(27046)**

Philadelphia
Applied Artificial
   Intelligence **(27382)** ....(Combined) ‡453
Behavior & Information Technology **(27387)**
Cybernetics and
   Systems **(27447)** ....(Combined) ‡341
International Journal of Computer Integrated
   Manufacturing **(27495)**
International Journal of Geographical Information
   Science **(27498)**
SIAM Journal on Computing **(27679)** ....‡2,076
SIAM Journal on Optimization **(27685)** ....‡1,736
SIAM Journal on Scientific
   Computing **(27686)** ....‡2,152

Pittsburgh
Journal of Research of the National Institute of
   Standards and Technology **(27804)**

Spring House
Office Systems 96 **(28009)** ......(Controlled) 100,225

Wayne
Computer & Online Industry Litigation
   Reporter **(28130)**

RHODE ISLAND
Providence
Real Estate Software
   Guide **(28419)** ....(Paid) 63,000

SOUTH CAROLINA
Anderson
Online **(28474)** ....‡7,500
+online user **(28475)**

TENNESSEE
Knoxville
Information Management Journal **(29272)** 11,000

Memphis
Discourse Processes **(29369)**

TEXAS
Arlington
Journal of Technology in Human
   Services **(29733)** ....(Controlled) ‡513

Austin
Cisco World **(29767)** ....(Non-paid) ‡20,000
Corel **(29771)** ....(Controlled) ‡58,000
Journal of Organizational Computing and Electronic
   Commerce **(29789)**
Severworld **(29804)** ....(Controlled) ‡20,000

San Marcos
CALICO **(31083)** ....‡1,020

Waco
The HP Chronicle **(31248)** ....(Combined) ‡17,000
UNISYS World **(31255)** ....‡12,500

UTAH
Provo
Genealogical Computing **(31403)** ....(Paid) ‡8,700
                                        (Controlled) ‡50

VIRGINIA
Fairfax
SIGNAL **(32029)** ....(Paid) △26,483
                                        (Non-paid) △2,046

Falls Church
Federal Computer Week **(32044)** .....(Free) ‡86,000
Government E-Business **(32047)**

Norfolk
Information Technology in Childhood Education
   Annual **(32283)**
Journal of Educational Multimedia and
   Hypermedia **(32285)** ....(Paid) ‡1,000
WebNet Journal **(32297)**

Reston
Journal of Computing in Civil Engineering **(32374)**
Technology and Children **(32419)**

WASHINGTON
Bellingham
Optical Engineering **(32678)** ....(Paid) 10,000

Seattle
Be Magazine **(32947)** ....(Combined) 30,000
Embedded Linux Journal **(32962)**
Linux Gazette **(32981)**
Linux Journal **(32982)** ....(Combined) 30,000
Puget Sound Computer
   User **(33008)** ....(Non-paid) 208,768
Technical Analysis of Stocks &
   Commodities **(33035)** 65,000

WISCONSIN
Eau Claire
Computer Science Education **(33667)** ....‡500
International Journal of Computer Simulation **(33670)**

Oak Creek
Technical Support **(34199)** ....(Controlled) 44,113

ALBERTA, CANADA
Calgary
International Journal of Computers and
   Applications **(34646)**
International Journal of Parallel and Distributed
   Systems and Networks **(34647)**

BRITISH COLUMBIA, CANADA
Vancouver
Canadian Computer
   Wholesaler **(35130)** ....(Combined) 14,709

ONTARIO, CANADA
Hamilton
Text Technology **(35891)** ....(Paid) 200

Mississauga
CAD Systems **(36054)** ....(Combined) 21,211

North York
Market News **(36129)** ....(Combined) 11,200

Scarborough
CIO Canada **(36374)** ....(Controlled) •8,000
Computerworld
   Canada **(36376)** ....(Controlled) 40,000
Network World
   Canada **(36378)** ....(Controlled) 14,538

Toronto
AutoCAD User **(36467)** ....(Controlled) 15,000
Channel Business **(36545)** ....(Controlled) •16,150
Computer Dealer News **(36556)** 18,418
Computing Canada **(36557)** 40,703
Direction Informatique **(36576)** ....(Combined) 20,585
EDGE **(36577)** ....(Combined) 16,361
IT Magazine **(36626)** 20,000
Technology in
   Government **(36756)** ....(Combined) 18,318

CONFECTIONARIES AND FROZEN DAIRY PRODUCTS
See also Baking

CALIFORNIA
Marina del Rey
Candy World Illustrated **(2505)** ....(Paid) ‡500
                                        (Non-paid) ‡1,500
Lott's 3—in—1 Buyer's Guide **(2509)** ....(Paid) ‡300
                                        (Controlled) ‡1,700

Oakland
Pacific Bakers News **(2693)** ....(Controlled) 3,000

DISTRICT OF COLUMBIA
Washington
Distribution Channels **(5465)** ....(Paid) 3,754
                                        (Controlled) 8,323

ILLINOIS
Deerfield
Candy Industry **(8722)** ....(Paid) 1,197
                                        (Non-paid) 5,003
Refrigerated and Frozen Foods **(8727)**

MARYLAND
Kensington
BCTGM News **(13590)** ....(Controlled) 135,000

NEW JERSEY
Glen Rock
The Manufacturing
   Confectioner **(18846)** ....(Paid) 2,446
                                        (Non-paid) 2,407

NEW YORK
New York
Chocolatier **(21412)** ....(Paid) ‡150,000

ONTARIO, CANADA
Delhi
Bakers Journal **(35763)** ....(Controlled) •6,433

CONGRESSIONAL AND FEDERAL GOVERNMENT AFFAIRS

CALIFORNIA
Los Angeles
Government Programs **(2280)** ....(Paid) 100,000
National Auctions and
   Sales **(2342)** ....(Paid) 120,000
U.S. Immigration **(2421)** ....(Paid) 100,000

DISTRICT OF COLUMBIA
Washington
Annual Energy Review 2000 **(5352)**
The Brookings Review **(5385)** ....(Paid) ‡6,000
                                        (Controlled) ‡10,000
Congress in Print **(5432)**
CongressDaily/A.M. **(5433)**
Congressional Digest **(5434)**
CovertAction Quarterly **(5446)** ....‡12,000
CQ Weekly **(5448)** ....(Paid) 8,009
                                        (Non-paid) 1,385
Federal Mine Safety and Health Review **(5494)**
Governing Magazine **(5517)** ....(Controlled) 86,000
The Hill **(5526)** 22,500
International Journal of Government Auditing **(5554)**
The Journal of International Security Affairs **(5600)**
National Alliance **(5668)** ....‡14,700
Regulation **(5760)** ....(Paid) 1,500
                                        (Controlled) 15,000
The Republican
   Woman **(5762)** ....(Controlled) 100,000
Roll Call **(5771)** ....(Paid) 5,161
                                        (Non-paid) 12,244
U.S. Medicine **(5835)** ....(Paid) 70
                                        (Free) 40,192

FLORIDA
Coral Gables
Public Budgeting and
   Finance **(6011)** ....(Non-paid) ‡2,100
                                        (Paid) ‡900

Tallahassee
Government Information Quarterly **(6722)**

MARYLAND
Potomac
The Public Manager **(13659)** ....‡4,000

MASSACHUSETTS
Boston
Journal of Aging and Social Policy **(13911)** 448

MISSISSIPPI
Jackson
Mississippi Municipalities **(16707)**

OHIO
Cleveland
Government PROcurement
   Magazine **(24904)** ....(Controlled) 23,000
Government Product
   News **(24905)** ....(Controlled) ‡85,054

PENNSYLVANIA
Easton
Publius: The Journal of
   Federalism **(26851)** ....(Paid) ‡1,200
                                        (Non-paid) ‡100

Pittsburgh
Code of Federal Regulations **(27766)**
Congressional Record **(27768)**
Customs Bulletin and Decisions **(27778)**
Decisions of the Department of the Interior **(27779)**
Diplomatic List **(27781)**
Federal Register **(27788)**
Monthly Catalog of U.S. Government
   Publications **(27816)**
Treasury Bulletin **(27849)** 594

Treaties and Other International Acts
Series **(27850)** 126

VIRGINIA
Alexandria
Journal of Government Financial
Management **(31697)**

WASHINGTON
Seattle
Voices of Experience **(33038)** ....(Free) 28,000

ONTARIO, CANADA
Mississauga
Government
Business **(36068)** ....(Controlled) ‡20,661

Toronto
Behind the Headlines **(36473)** ....(Paid) 1,200

CONSTRUCTION, CONTRACTING, BUILDING, AND EXCAVATING

See also Architecture; Building Materials, Concrete, Brick, and Tile; Engineering (Various branches); Roads and Streets; Wood and Woodworking

ALABAMA
Birmingham
Southern Building **(92)** ....‡16,200

Mobile
Elevator World **(319)** ....(Paid) ‡6,200
(Non-paid) ‡162

Tuscaloosa
Equipment World
Magazine **(487)** ....(Controlled) ‡84,300

ARIZONA
Phoenix
Southwest Contractor **(811)** ....(Combined) 6,000

ARKANSAS
Little Rock
Construction News **(1227)** ....(Paid) 168
(Controlled) 6,279

CALIFORNIA
Downey
ECA Magazine **(1835)** ....(Non-paid) ‡1,800

Los Angeles
Earth **(2256)** ....(Controlled) ‡6,000

Riverside
California Builder &
Engineer **(2933)** ....(Controlled) ‡11,281

San Rafael
Correctional News **(3600)** ....(Combined) 13,218

Torrance
Right of Way **(3941)** ....‡9,000

Ventura
Automated Builder **(4001)** ....(Controlled) 24,739

Woodland Hills
Scaffold Industry Association Magazine **(4113)**

COLORADO
Boulder
Masonry Society Journal **(4179)** .....(Controlled) 850

Colorado Springs
American Painting Contractor **(4235)** ....‡30,736

Denver
The Daily Journal **(4320)** ....(Paid) ‡1,206
(Controlled) ‡3,859

Longmont
Flooring Magazine **(4559)** ....(Combined) 18,800

CONNECTICUT
Bethel
Experimental Mechanics **(4697)** 4,500

Hartford
Connecticut Housing Production and Permit
Authorized Construction **(4887)**

Newtown
Fine Homebuilding **(5042)** ....(Paid) 296,467

DISTRICT OF COLUMBIA
Washington
Building Products **(5387)** ....(Controlled) ‡70,000
The Carpenter **(5396)** 473,104
Construction & Modernization Report **(5436)**
Custom Home **(5456)** ....‡40,000
Journal of Housing and Community
Development **(5596)** ....(Non-paid) 13,000
Journal of the International Union of Bricklayers &
Allied Craftworkers **(5601)** ....(Paid) ‡2,000
(Controlled) ‡110,000
Kitchen & Bath Showroom **(5626)**
Nation's Building News **(5684)** 150,000
Old-House Journal **(5707)** ....(Paid) 145,141
ProSales **(5734)** ....(Controlled) 40,000
Remodeling **(5761)** ....(Paid) 1,056
(Controlled) 80,000
Sales & Marketing Ideas **(5776)** 14,000
Seniors' Housing News **(5789)**

FLORIDA
Altamonte Springs
Florida Plumbing
Prospective **(5899)** ....(Combined) 8,000

Coral Gables
International Journal for Housing Science and Its
Applications **(6007)** ....(Controlled) 700

Tampa
Design Cost Data **(6761)** ....(Controlled) ‡15,000
(Controlled) ‡15,000

GEORGIA
Alpharetta
CE News **(6918)** ....(Controlled) 49,610

Atlanta
Access Control & Security Systems
Integration **(6959)** ....(Paid) ‡262
(Controlled) ‡31,000
Best Sellers Collection **(6977)** ......(Combined) 5,200
Swimming Pool/Spa
Age **(7048)** ....(Controlled) 17,064
(Controlled) 17,064

Norcross
Construction Market Data
Inc. **(7458)** ....(Combined) ‡3,000

Roswell
Retail Operations &
Construction **(7518)** ....(Controlled) 25,500

ILLINOIS
Addison
Concrete Cunstruction **(8000)** ....(Paid) △57,658
(Non-paid) △12,376

Bensenville
Contractors Guide **(8065)** ....(Paid) 148
(Non-paid) 23,434

Chicago
Dodge Construction News (Illinois, Indiana, Wisconsin
Edition) **(8356)** ....(Paid) ‡650
Modern Steel
Construction **(8493)** ....(Controlled) ‡40,000
Realty and Building **(8552)** ....(Paid) ‡13,280
(Controlled) ‡1,130

Des Plaines
Professional Builder **(8768)** 122,000
(Controlled) 140,018

Roads & Bridges
Magazine **(8770)** ....(Controlled) ‡65,000

Northbrook
Plumbing Engineer **(9320)** ....(Free) ‡25,600

Oak Brook
Construction Equipment Distribution **(9345)** ....‡4,000
Professional Remodeler **(9362)**

St. Charles
Interior Construction **(9570)** ....(Controlled) ‡8,300

INDIANA
Berne
Proven Home Plans For
Today **(9816)** ....(Paid) 60,000

Indianapolis
Construction Digest **(10104)** ....(Paid) 496
(Non-paid) 12,576

Spencer
Indiana Builder
Magazine **(10470)** ....(Non-paid) 12,500

IOWA
Cedar Rapids
Buildings **(10669)** ....(Non-paid) ★57,010
Construction Equipment Operation and
Maintenance **(10672)** ....(Controlled) ‡63,487

Fort Dodge
Contractors Hot Line **(10896)** ....(Paid) ‡3,658
(Non-paid) ‡36,342
Contractors Hot Line Monthly Equipment
Guide **(10897)** ....(Paid) 10,000

KANSAS
Overland Park
CEE News **(11703)** ....(Controlled) ‡105,221
Electrical Construction and Maintenance
(EC&M) **(11708)** ....(Controlled) 102,521
(Paid) 1,214
International Construction **(11715)** ....△25,000

LOUISIANA
Baton Rouge
Louisiana Contractor **(12496)** ....⊕4,575

New Orleans
Daily Journal of Commerce **(12728)**

MARYLAND
Baltimore
Mid-Atlantic Builder **(13218)** ....‡3,000
Quicks Professional
Journal **(13240)** ....(Non-paid) ‡6,500

Bethesda
Lead Detection and Abatement
Contractor **(13356)** ....(Paid) 10,000

MASSACHUSETTS
Needham Heights
Contractors Equipment Guide **(14376)** ....‡26,262

Norwood
CIM Construction Journal **(14445)** ....‡3,200

MICHIGAN
Bloomfield Hills
CAM Magazine **(14828)** ....(Paid) 4,461
(Non-paid) 389

Farmington Hills
Building Business & Apartment
Management **(15016)** ....(Paid) ‡12,000
(Controlled) ‡100
Concrete International **(15018)** ....(Paid) 697
(Controlled) 15,625

Troy
Environmental Design and
Construction **(15624)** ....(Non-paid) △15,500
Floor Covering Installer **(15626)**
National Driller **(15630)**
PM Engineer **(15633)** ....(Non-paid) 25,005
Roofing Contractor **(15638)**

MINNESOTA
New Hope
Construction Bulletin
Magazine **(16206)** ....(Paid) 2,496
(Non-paid) 722

MISSISSIPPI
Vicksburg
Dredging Research **(16870)** ....(Non-paid) 2200

MISSOURI
Independence
Lift Equipment **(17115)** ....(Combined) 16,500

Kansas City
Midwest Contractor **(17184)** ....(Paid) 283
(Controlled) 7,496

St. Louis
St. Louis Construction News &
Review **(17498)** ....(Paid) ‡2,415
(Non-paid) ‡8,970

NEVADA
Reno
Architectural West **(18417)** ....(Controlled) 20,200

NEW JERSEY
Montclair
Shelterforce **(19241)** ....(Combined) ⊕5,000

Princeton
C.F.M.A. Building Profits **(19456)** ....(Paid) 7,000
(Combined) 12,000

Circulation: ★ = ABC; △ = BPA; ♦ = CAC; • = CCAB; ❑ = VAC; ⊕ = PO Statement; ‡ = Publisher's Report; Boldface figures = sworn; Light figures = estimated.

3123

Trade, Technical, and Professional Publications

Circ.   Circ.   Circ.

CONSTRUCTION, CONTRACTING, BUILDING, AND EXCAVATING (continued)

NEW MEXICO
Santa Fe
Designer/Builder (19934) ....(Controlled) 4,000

NEW YORK
Brooklyn
Traditional Building (20349) ....(Paid) 11,240
(Non-paid) 11,760

Elbridge
Structural Mover (20563)

New York
Better Homes and Gardens Building
Ideas (21296) ....(Paid) ‡450,000
Building Design &
Construction (21346) ....(Non-paid) ‡78,300
Construction
Equipment (21487) ....(Controlled) ‡80,021
Construction Products (21488) ....(Non-paid) 101,000
(Non-paid) 101,000
Contract (21498) 30,000
ENR: Engineering
News-Record (21607) ....(Paid) 75,706
Fenestration (21686) ....(Paid) ★122
(Non-paid) ★18,408
House Beautiful (21821) ....(Paid) 853,748
Infrastructure Finance (21873) ....(Controlled) 16,353
Journal of Construction Accounting and
Taxation (22038)
Kitchen and Bath Business (22224) .....(Paid) 9,740
(Controlled) 38,532
Multi-Housing News (22377) .....(Controlled) ‡30,000
New York Construction
News (22439) ....(Paid) ‡6,100
The Punch List (22614)
Store Equipment &
Design (22795) ....(Controlled) 22,244

Palatine Bridge
Hard Hat News (23075) 54,094

OHIO
Bowling Green
Equipment Echoes (24691) ....(Paid) 4,300

Cleveland
R.S.I. Magazine (24951) ....(Paid) 1,247
(Non-paid) 21,890

Columbus
Ohio Contractor (25041) ....(Paid) ‡850
(Non-paid) ‡5,500

Fairborn
Contractor Marketing (25186) ......(Controlled) 4,500

Woodville
Metal Architecture (25671) ....(Controlled) 31,483

OKLAHOMA
Oklahoma City
Central Oklahoma Home
Builder (25959) ....(Controlled) 3,000

PENNSYLVANIA
Erie
Builder/Dealer (26893) ....(Non-paid) ‡28,829

Fort Washington
Construction Equipment
Guide-Northeast (26925) ....(Paid) ‡171
(Non-paid) ‡30,585

Pittsburgh
Construction Reports: Housing Starts (C20) (27769)
Construction Reports: Housing Units Authorized by
Building Permits & Contracts (C40) (27770)
Construction Reports: Value of New Construction Put
in Place (C30) (27771)
Current Housing Reports (27776)

Wayne
Asbestos Property Litigation Reporter (28124)

RHODE ISLAND
East Providence
The Rhode Island Builder
Report (28345) ....(Non-paid) 2,300

TEXAS
Austin
Texas Construction (29815) ....(Controlled) ‡6,500

Dallas
Builder Insider (30134) ....(Non-paid) 8,500

Foundation Drilling (30158) ....(Controlled) 1,700
Houston
Drilling Contractor (30470) ....(Paid) 130
(Non-paid) 29,000
Underground Construction (30538)

UTAH
Provo
Permanent Buildings &
Foundations (31406) ....(Paid) ‡2,824
(Non-paid) ‡26,653

Salt Lake City
Intermountain Contractor (31431) ....(Paid) ‡2,600
Utah Building Magazine (31441)

VERMONT
Newbury
Timber Framing (31571) ....(Paid) 1,800

VIRGINIA
Alexandria
The Construction Specifier (31658) .....(Paid) 19,752
CONSTRUCTOR (31659) ....(Paid) ⊕38,072
(Non-paid) ⊕41,026

Arlington
ABC Today (31767) ....(Paid) ‡20,000
(Non-paid) ‡2,000
The National Utility
Contractor (31812) ....(Non-paid) △23,000

Herndon
CM News (32162) ....(Non-paid) ‡3,500

Moon
Virginia Builder (32276) ....(Non-paid) ‡5,000

Reston
Civil Engineering-ASCE (32363) ....(Paid) 95,459
(Controlled) 7,686
Journal of Composites for Construction (32373)
Journal of Construction Engineering and
Management (32375)
Journal of Performance of Constructed
Facilities (32389)
Journal of Structural Engineering (32396)
Practice Periodical on Structural Design and
Construction (32411) ....(Paid) 2,500

Richmond
Lifting & Transportation
International (32443) ....(Combined) ‡16,854

WASHINGTON
Kirkland
Pacific Builder & Engineer (32799) ....(Paid) 251
(Controlled) 12,274

Seattle
Seattle Daily Journal of
Commerce (33019) ....‡5,500

WEST VIRGINIA
Charleston
West Virginia Construction
News (33275) ....(Paid) ‡30
(Non-paid) ‡1,130

WISCONSIN
Brookfield
Western Builder (33606) ....(Paid) 2,825
(Non-paid) 445

Fort Atkinson
Equipment Today (33707) ....(Controlled) ‡80,000
OEM Off-Highway (33715) ....(Controlled) ‡17,500
Pavement (33716) ....(Controlled) 20,000
Qualified Remodeler
Magazine (33719) ....(Controlled) 84,500

Iola
Frame Building News (33827) 19,991
Metal Roofing Magazine (33835)
Rural Builder (33842) ....(Paid) ‡28,683

Madison
Wisconsin Architect (33978) ....‡3,536

Milwaukee
Building Operating
Management (34059) ....(Paid) 155
(Non-paid) 66,966

Spooner
Underground Focus (34338) ......(Combined) 18,200

ALBERTA, CANADA
Edmonton
Construction Alberta News (34707)

BRITISH COLUMBIA, CANADA
Burnaby
Award Magazine (34889) ....(Combined) 7,657
Journal of Commerce (34904) .....(Combined) 2,537

ONTARIO, CANADA
Etobicoke
Info-Link (35816) ....(Combined) •44,168

Nepean
The Ottawa Construction
News (36101) ....(Non-paid) 5,393

North York
Daily Commercial News and Construction
Record (36126) 3,500

Ottawa
Wood Design & Building (36281) ....(Paid) 8,000
(Non-paid) 25,000
Wood Lebois (36282) ....(Combined) 67,000

Toronto
Heavy Construction
News (36614) ....(Combined) 26,981
Home Improvement
Retailing (36616) ....(Combined) 15,356

QUEBEC, CANADA
Anjou
Construire (36937) ....(Combined) 27,400

Montreal
Inter-Mecanique du
Batiment (37134) ....(Combined) •6,350

Saint-Laurent
Journal Constructo (37363) ....(Combined) 3,345

CONSUMERISM

ILLINOIS
Chicago
Journal of Marketing (8443) ....(Paid) ‡9028
(Free) 65

IOWA
Ames
Journal of Consumer Affairs (10591)

NEW JERSEY
Mahwah
Journal of Consumer Psychology (19197)

NEW YORK
New York
Home Mechanix (21811) ....(Paid) 903,338

Rhinebeck
The Trends Journal (23186)

CONVENTIONS, MEETINGS, AND TRADE FAIRS

ALABAMA
Gulf Shores
ConventionSouth (250)

CALIFORNIA
Los Angeles
Association News (2215) ....(Controlled) ‡40,000
Tradeshow Week (2414)

Santa Monica
TradeShow & Exhibit Manager (3718) 18,500

Woodland Hills
Exhibit Builder (4103) 15,000

FLORIDA
Boca Raton
Corporate & Incentive
Travel (5929) ....(Non-paid) 40,123

ILLINOIS
Chicago
Convene (8343) ....(Paid) ‡4,000
(Controlled) ‡35,010

KANSAS
Overland Park
Expo **(11712)** ....(Controlled) 7,500

MASSACHUSETTS
Stow
Association Meetings **(14571)** ....(Controlled) ‡22,000
Corporate Meetings &
   Incentives **(14572)** ....(Controlled) ‡36,776
Medical Meetings **(14574)** ....(Controlled) ‡12,500

NEW JERSEY
Chatham
Physicians' Travel & Meeting
   Guide **(18732)** ....(Paid) 6,929
                                          (Non-paid) 135,367

Secaucus
Meetings &
   Conventions **(19540)** ....(Controlled) ‡80,511

NEW YORK
Hornell
Stamps Auction News **(20753)** ....(Paid) ‡750
                                             (Non-paid) ‡500

New York
Meeting News **(22313)** ....(Non-paid) ‡65,000
Successful Meetings **(22805)** ....(Controlled) ‡75,000

WISCONSIN
Milwaukee
Reunions Magazine **(34098)** ....(Paid) ‡3,000
                                             (Non-paid) ‡9,000

ONTARIO, CANADA
Toronto
Meetings & Incentive
   Travel **(36660)** ....(Combined) •10,422

COSMETICS AND TOILETRIES
See also Hairstyling

ARIZONA
Phoenix
For Formulation Chemists Only **(804)**

CALIFORNIA
Van Nuys
Nailpro **(3994)** ....(Paid) △**19,041**
                                          (Non-paid) △**37,604**

COLORADO
Broomfield
Natural Business **(4205)** ....(Paid) 900

ILLINOIS
Carol Stream
Cosmetics & Toiletries **(8142)** ....(Paid) 3,278
Global Cosmetic Industry **(8144)**
Skin Inc. **(8155)** ....(Paid) ‡6,006
                                          (Controlled) ‡3,401

Lincolnshire
Modern Salon **(9086)** ....(Paid) ★**60,437**
                                          (Non-paid) ★**58,588**
Salon Today Magazine **(9088)** ....‡30,000

MARYLAND
Chevy Chase
The Rose Sheet **(13409)**

NEW JERSEY
Morris Plains
Pharmaceutical
   Processing **(19301)** ....(Non-paid) ‡30,025

NEW YORK
Melville
Soap/Cosmetics/Chemical
   Specialties **(21064)** ....(Paid) 1,187
                                          (Controlled) 15,662

New York
SalonNews **(22703)**
Soap and Cosmetics **(22751)**

WASHINGTON
Silvana
The Saponifier **(33082)** ....(Paid) 2,000

ONTARIO, CANADA
Toronto
Cosmetics **(36561)** ....(Combined) •9,904

Cosmetics **(36562)** ....(Controlled) ‡5,640

QUEBEC, CANADA
Montreal
Spa Management **(37226)** ....(Paid) ‡28,623

DENTISTRY

CALIFORNIA
Sacramento
CDA Update **(2992)** ....(Paid) ‡17,447
                                          (Non-paid) ‡104
Journal of the California Dental
   Association **(3003)** ....(Paid) ‡18,000
                                          (Non-paid) ‡1,200

San Diego
Journal of the American College of
   Dentists **(3178)** ....(Controlled) ‡5,000

San Francisco
Contact Point **(3346)** ....(Non-paid) ‡6,500

COLORADO
Boulder
Journal of Clinical
   Orthodontics **(4174)** ....(Paid) ‡10,445

CONNECTICUT
Farmington
Caries Research **(4803)** 1,450

Monroe
LMT **(4963)** ....‡19,627

FLORIDA
Tallahassee
Today's FDA **(6740)** 7,500

GEORGIA
Byron
Flossline **(7147)**

HAWAII
Honolulu
Hawaii Dental Journal **(7695)** ....(Paid) 1,100

ILLINOIS
Arlington Heights
Journal of the History of
   Dentistry **(8024)** ....(Paid) 750

Carol Stream
Journal of Orofacial Pain **(8146)** ....(Paid) ⊕**2,800**
QDT **(8153)** ....(Paid) 3,000
Quintessence International **(8154)** .....(Paid) ‡16,000

Chicago
ADA News **(8242)** 140,000
AGD Impact **(8247)** ....‡37,000
ASDA News **(8277)** 15,000
CDS Review **(8302)** ....‡8,500
Chicago Dental Society
   News **(8312)** ....(Non-paid) 8,000
The Dental Assistant **(8352)** ....(Paid) ‡14,800
General Dentistry **(8385)** ....(Paid) ‡39,000
                                          (Non-paid) ‡26,000
Journal of the American Dental
   Association **(8430)** ....(Paid) 135,456
                                          (Non-paid) 2,723
Journal of Dental Hygiene **(8436)** ....(Paid) ‡36,000
                                          (Non-paid) ‡2,000
Journal of Dentistry for
   Children **(8437)** ....(Paid) ‡4,265
                                          (Controlled) ‡29
Journal of Periodontology **(8447)** 8,664
Mouth **(8496)** ....(Paid) 16,000
Special Care in Dentistry **(8570)** ....‡2,500

Northfield
Dental Lab Products **(9327)** ....(Non-paid) 18,827
Dental Products
   Report **(9328)** ....(Controlled) 150,271

Springfield
Illinois Dental Journal **(9623)** .....(Controlled) ‡6,300

INDIANA
Indianapolis
Operative Dentistry **(10157)** ......(Controlled) ⊕**1,890**

KENTUCKY
Lexington
Journal of Oral and Maxillofacial
   Surgery **(12168)** ....‡10,037

MARYLAND
Hagerstown
Journal of Endodontics **(13564)** ....(Paid) ‡6,050
                                          (Non-paid) ‡75

MICHIGAN
Lansing
Journal of the Michigan Dental
   Association **(15275)** ....(Paid) 6,300

MINNESOTA
St. Paul
Northwest Dentistry **(16402)** ....(Combined) 3,180

MISSOURI
Jefferson City
Focus MDA **(17121)** ....‡2,200

St. Louis
American Journal of Orthodontics and Dentofacial
   Orthopedics **(17411)** ....(Paid) ‡15,309
The Journal of Evidence-Based Dental
   Practice **(17454)**
The Journal of Prosthetic
   Dentistry **(17460)** ....(Paid) ‡6,619
Oral Surgery, Oral Medicine, Oral Pathology, Oral
   Radiology, and
   Endodontics **(17480)** ....(Paid) ‡6,529

NEW JERSEY
Jamesburg
The Compendium of Continuing Education in
   Dentistry **(19128)** ....(Combined) 120,000

Mahwah
The Journal of Practical Hygiene **(19198)**
Practical Procedures & Aesthetic Dentistry **(19205)**

North Brunswick
Journal of the New Jersey Dental
   Association **(19381)** ....(Paid) ‡4,500
                                          (Non-paid) ‡500

NEW YORK
Albany
New York State Dental Journal **(19998)** 14,000

NORTH CAROLINA
Chapel Hill
Journal of Public Health
   Dentistry **(23713)** ....(Controlled) ‡1,300

OKLAHOMA
Tulsa
Dental Economics **(26112)** .....(Controlled) ‡110,019
Dental Equipment & Materials **(26113)**
Proofs **(26130)** ....‡5409
RDH **(26131)** ....(Paid) 310
                                          (Non-paid) 66,856

PENNSYLVANIA
Harrisburg
Pennsylvania Dental
   Journal **(27006)** ....(Paid) ‡5,000
                                          (Non-paid) ‡200

Philadelphia
Dental Clinics **(27449)**
Journal of Prosthodontics **(27549)** ....(Paid) 3,312
Penn Dental Journal **(27620)** ......(Controlled) 8,000

TENNESSEE
Chattanooga
CRANIO **(29088)** ....(Paid) ‡1,638
                                          (Non-paid) ‡308

Nashville
Tennessee Dental Association
   Journal **(29490)** ....(Combined) 2,300

TEXAS
Austin
Texas Dental Journal **(29816)** 7,800

Dallas
Baylor Dental Journal **(30129)** .....(Controlled) 7,500

Houston
The Journal of the Greater Houston Dental
   Society **(30496)** ....(Non-paid) 1,700

San Antonio
Journal of Dental
   Education **(31033)** ....(Paid) ‡3,900
                                          (Controlled) ‡195

Circ.   Circ.   Circ.

DENTISTRY (continued)

VIRGINIA
Alexandria
Advances in Dental
  Research (31631) ....(Paid) ‡1,100
Journal of Dental Research (31693) ....‡6,500

Winchester
The Functional
  Orthodontist (32629) ....(Controlled) ‡7,000

WASHINGTON
Seattle
The Journal of the Seattle-King County Dental
  Society (32979) ....‡2,000

WEST VIRGINIA
Charleston
West Virginia Dental Journal (33276) ....‡1,100

WISCONSIN
Milwaukee
International Journal of
  Orthodontics (34071) ....(Paid) ⊕4,100

ONTARIO, CANADA
Hamilton
Biological Therapies in
  Dentistry (35874) ....(Paid) ⊕500
Journal of Esthetic and Restorative
  Dentistry (35885) 50,000

Ottawa
Journal of the Canadian Dental Association (Journal
  de l'Association Dentaire
  Canadienne) (36253) ....(Combined) •19,897

Toronto
Dental Guide (Don Mills) (36568)
Dental Practice Management (36569) ....‡17,399
Ontario Dentist (36682) ....(Paid) 6,800
                                      (Non-paid) 400
Oral Health (36690) ....(Controlled) •17,524

QUEBEC, CANADA
Montreal
Journal Dentaire du Quebec
  (JDQ) (37139) ....‡5,300

DRAMA AND THEATRE

See also Performing Arts

ALABAMA
Auburn University
Bulletin of the Comediantes (49) ....(Paid) 500

ARIZONA
Tempe
Stage of the Art (915)
Youth Theatre Journal (918)

COLORADO
Boulder
On-Stage Studies (4183)

Steamboat Springs
Vail International Dance
  Festival (4635) ....(Non-paid) ‡10,000

CONNECTICUT
New Haven
Theater (5003) ....(Combined) 2,400

DISTRICT OF COLUMBIA
Washington
The World & I (5870) ....(Paid) 20,056
                                      (Non-paid) 2,781

IOWA
Pella
Theatre History Studies (11152) ....(Paid) 1,000

KANSAS
Lawrence
Journal of Dramatic Theory and Criticism (11555)
Latin American Theatre
  Review (11562) ....(Paid) 1,100

KENTUCKY
Louisville
Theatre Design &
  Technology (12238) ....(Paid) ‡4,250
                                      (Non-paid) ‡250

MICHIGAN
Kalamazoo
Comparative Drama (15234) ....(Paid) ‡850
                                      (Controlled) ‡50

MINNESOTA
Minneapolis
Xcp: Cross Cultural
  Poetics (16142) ....(Combined) 850

NEVADA
Las Vegas
Magic (18377) ....(Controlled) 10,500

NEW YORK
Brooklyn
Asian Theater Journal (20297) ....(Paid) 550
                                      (Controlled) 40

East Hampton
2wice (20547) ....(Paid) ‡2,500

New York
Art Bulletin (21251)
Art Journal (21253)
Back Stage West (21284) 95,011
The Dramatist (21568) ....(Paid) 8,000
Entertainment Design Magazine (21608) 17,255
Independent Shavian (21861)
New Theatre Quarterly (22436) 1,250
Opera News (22497) ....(Paid) 100,000
Ross Reports Television and
  Film (22677) ....(Combined) 15,103
Stage Directions (22782) ....(Paid) ‡4,000
                                      (Non-paid) ‡3,500

OHIO
Cincinnati
America Drama (24769)
Teaching Theatre (24822) 4,000

TENNESSEE
Nashville
National Drama Service (29474) ....(Paid) 6,000

BRITISH COLUMBIA, CANADA
Vancouver
Dance International (35138) ....(Paid) 3,500

MANITOBA, CANADA
Winnipeg
Ovation (35348) 22,000

ONTARIO, CANADA
Guelph
Canadian Theatre Review (35859) 1,300
Essays in Theatre/Etudes
  Theatrales (35862) ....(Combined) 350

Toronto
C Magazine (36482)
Modern Drama (36665) 2,177
Performing Arts and Entertainment in
  Canada (36702) ....(Paid) 44,630
Theatre Research in Canada/Recherches Theatrales
  Au Canada (36758)

DRUGS AND PHARMACEUTICALS

ARKANSAS
Little Rock
Drug Metabolism Reviews (1228) 800

CALIFORNIA
Loma Linda
Clinical Research and Regulatory Affairs (2159)

Los Angeles
Journal of Intravenous Therapy (2302) ....‡1,000
Pharmaceutical Research (2366)

Mission Viejo
Medical Industry Information
  Report (2555) ....(Controlled) 16,500

Sacramento
California Pharmacist (2986) ....‡6,000

San Diego
Drug Delivery (3143)
Regulatory Toxicology and Pharmacology (3254)
Toxicology and Applied Pharmacology (3282)

San Francisco
Journal of Psychoactive Drugs (3384) ....‡800

Thousand Oaks
Journal of Pharmacy Practice (3897) ......(Paid) 200

COLORADO
Lakewood
Community
  Pharmacist (4531) ....(Controlled) ‡46,000
HealthCare Distributor (4532) ....‡9,500

Littleton
The Journal of Pediatric Pharmacology and
  Therapeutics (4549)

CONNECTICUT
Farmington
Pharmacology (4855) 1,150

Rocky Hill
Connecticut Pharmacist (5106) .....(Controlled) 1,500

DELAWARE
Newark
Drug and Chemical Toxicology (5272) 350

DISTRICT OF COLUMBIA
Washington
Journal of the American Pharmaceutical
  Association (5570) ....(Paid) ‡50,000
Journal of Pharmaceutical
  Sciences (5612) ....(Paid) ‡5,000
                                      (Non-paid) ‡120
Pharmacy Today (5719) 117,000

FLORIDA
Boca Raton
Medical Marketing &
  Media (5936) ....(Controlled) ‡10,000

Tallahassee
Florida Pharmacy Today (6717) ....‡3,000

Tampa
Pharmaceutical Engineering (6776) .....(Paid) 17,500

GEORGIA
Augusta
American Journal of Pharmaceutical
  Education (7095) ....(Paid) ‡3,000
                                      (Non-paid) ‡200

ILLINOIS
Chicago
New Product News (8506) ....(Paid) ‡800

Northfield
Pharmaceutical Representative (9332) 42,000

Springfield
Illinois Pharmacist (9629) ....‡2,610

INDIANA
Bloomington
Pharmaceutical Development and Technology (9847)

Indianapolis
Indiana Pharmacist (10129) ....‡1,500

IOWA
Des Moines
The Journal (10799) ....(Paid) 1,300
                                      (Non-paid) 50

Iowa City
The PDA Journal of Pharmaceutical Science &
  Technology (10983) ....(Controlled) 9,266

KANSAS
Topeka
Journal of Kansas
  Pharmacy (11823) ....(Paid) 1,250
                                      (Controlled) 147

KENTUCKY
Frankfort
The Kentucky Pharmacist (12073) ......(Paid) ‡1,800
                                      (Non-paid) ‡100

LOUISIANA
Baton Rouge
The Louisiana Pharmacist (12502) ....‡1,500

MARYLAND
Baltimore
Addictive Disorders & Their Treatment (13107)
Journal of Cardiovascular
  Pharmacology (13181) 1451
Maryland Pharmacist (13214) 1,100

Therapeutic Drug Monitoring **(13254)** 813

Bethesda
American Journal of Health-System
Pharmacy **(13300)** ....(Paid) ‡28,765
(Non-paid) ‡10,505

International Pharmaceutical
Abstracts **(13346)** ....(Paid) ‡376
(Non-paid) ‡55

Journal of Pharmacology & Experimental
Therapeutics **(13355)** ....(Paid) ‡2,320
(Non-paid) ‡221

Molecular Pharmacology **(13362)** ....(Paid) ‡1,218
(Non-paid) ‡64

Potomac
Immunopharmacology and
Immunotoxicology **(13652)** ....(Paid) 325

Rockville
Pharmacopeial Forum **(13693)** ....(Paid) ‡2,000
(Non-paid) ‡200

Silver Spring
Journal of Ethnomedicine and Drug
Development **(13730)**

MASSACHUSETTS
Amherst
The Herb, Spice, and Medicinal Plant
Digest **(13794)** 600

Andover
Journal of Toxicology, Cutaneous and Ocular
Toxicology **(13812)** ....(Paid) 425

Boston
Journal of Clinical
Psychopharmacology **(13915)** ....(Paid) ‡8,614
(Non-paid) ‡163
Pharmacotherapy **(13948)** ....‡8,000

MICHIGAN
Lansing
Michigan Pharmacist **(15290)** ....‡3,900

MINNESOTA
Minneapolis
Journal of Toxicology Toxin
Reviews **(16090)** ....(Paid) 225

MISSISSIPPI
Jackson
Journal of Pharmacoepidemiology **(16698)** 175
Mississippi Pharmacist **(16708)** 1,600

University
Journal of Pharmacy
Teaching **(16865)** ....(Paid) 272

MISSOURI
Jefferson City
Missouri Pharmacist **(17129)** ....(Paid) 1,300

St. Louis
Clinical Pharmacology and
Therapeutics **(17423)** ....(Combined) ‡3,800
Facts and Comparisons **(17437)**
Hospital Pharmacy **(17445)** ....(Paid) ‡33,500
Pharmacy Practice Management
Quarterly **(17483)** ....(Paid) 1,213
(Non-paid) 78

NEBRASKA
Omaha
Pharmacological Reviews **(18207)** ......(Paid) ‡2,042
(Non-paid) ‡71

NEW JERSEY
Bloomfield
U.S. Pharmacist **(18689)** ....(Combined) 120,874

Chatham
P & T **(18731)** ....(Controlled) 54,025

Fort Lee
Private Label **(18833)** ....(Paid) ‡961
(Non-paid) ‡28,080

Hoboken
Biopharmaceutics and Drug Disposition **(18905)**
Drug Development Research **(18932)** 3500
Human Psychopharmacology **(18968)**
Journal of Mass Spectrometry **(19029)**
Journal of Peptide Science **(19040)**
Magnetic Resonance in Chemistry **(19056)**
Pharmacoepidemiology and Drug
Safety **(19082)** 2,800
Phytochemical Analysis **(19083)** 3,500

Phytotherapy Research **(19084)** 4,200
Rapid Communications in Mass
Spectrometry **(19096)** ....(Paid) 4,900
Teratology **(19118)** 11,550

Jamesburg
Pharmacy Times **(19131)** ....(Paid) 480
(Non-paid) 120,000

Montvale
Drug Topics **(19252)** ....(Paid) 1,847
(Controlled) 100,000
Hospital Pharmacist Report **(19255)** ....(Paid) 78
(Non-paid) 27,706

Morris Plains
Pharmaceutical Laboratory **(19300)** 30,050
Pharmaceutical
Processing **(19301)** ....(Non-paid) ‡30,025

Piscataway
Rutgers Center of Alcohol
Studies **(19431)** ....(Combined) ⊕2,100

Princeton
New Jersey Journal of
Pharmacy **(19466)** ....(Controlled) ‡1,500

West Trenton
Medical Advertising **(19743)** .....(Combined) △14,000

NEW YORK
Albany
New York State
Pharmacist **(19999)** ....(Paid) ‡2,700

Binghamton
Journal of Ethnicity in Substance Abuse **(20172)**
Journal of Herbs, Spices & Medicinal Plants **(20178)**
Journal of Managed Pharmaceutical
Care **(20188)** ....(Paid) 2,200
Journal of Pharmaceutical Marketing &
Management **(20191)** ....(Paid) 886
Journal of Research in Pharmaceutical
Economics **(20197)** 405
Journal of Social Work Practice in the
Addictions **(20200)**
Journal of Teaching in the Addictions **(20201)**

Larchmont
Journal of Ocular Pharmacology and
Therapeutics **(20918)**
Natural Pharmacy **(20922)**

Mineola
Journal of Toxicology: Clinical Toxicology **(21085)**

New York
Chain Drug Review **(21391)** ....(Paid) 902
(Non-paid) 42,898
Chain Store Age **(21393)** ....(Paid) 2,253
(Non-paid) 33,398
Critical Reviews in Therapeutic Drug Carrier
Systems **(21520)** ....(Paid) 500
Drug Store News **(21571)** ....(Paid) 2,644
(Non-paid) 43,720
International Journal of Rehabilitation and
Health **(21916)**
Investigational New Drugs **(21945)**
Journal of Liposome
Research **(22113)** ....(Paid) 400
Journal of Pharmacokinetics and
Pharmacodynamics **(22156)**
Lippincott's Hospital Pharmacy **(22259)** 33,000
Monthly Prescribing
Reference **(22363)** ....(Controlled) 150,638
Nature Biotechnology **(22410)** ....(Paid) 11,000
(Controlled) 5,000
Pharmaceutical Chemistry Journal **(22546)**
Pharmacy Practice News **(22547)** ....(Paid) ‡189
(Non-paid) ‡46,827
Pharmacy World & Science **(22548)**
Vaccine **(22894)**

NORTH CAROLINA
Chapel Hill
North Carolina Pharmacist **(23718)** .....(Paid) ‡3,819

OHIO
Cincinnati
The Annals of Pharmacotherapy **(24773)** ......‡7,200
The Journal of Pharmacy
Technology **(24807)** ....(Paid) ‡1,200
(Non-paid) ‡100

Cleveland
Formulary **(24898)** ....(Controlled) 45,000

OKLAHOMA
Oklahoma City
Oklahoma Pharmacist **(25984)** ....‡1,400

OREGON
Eugene
BioPharm **(26314)** ....(Paid) 222
(Non-paid) 18,910
Pharmaceutical Executive **(26330)** ....(Paid) 1,920
(Controlled) 12,502
Pharmaceutical Technology **(26331)** .....(Paid) 1,208
(Controlled) 35,000

Wilsonville
Oregon Pharmacist **(26616)** ....‡1,350

PENNSYLVANIA
Blue Bell
ComputerTalk for the
Pharmacist **(26723)** ....(Paid) 400
(Non-paid) 32,500

Harrisburg
Pennsylvania Pharmacist **(27011)** ....‡2,750

Philadelphia
Drug Metabolism and
Disposition **(27454)** ....(Paid) ‡925
(Non-paid) ‡93
Journal of Microencapsulation **(27535)**
Journal of Pharmacy Practice **(27546)** ....‡781

Pittsburgh
FDA Consumer **(27787)**

RHODE ISLAND
Providence
Psychopharmacology Update **(28418)**

Warwick
Rhode Island Pharmacist **(28452)** ....(Paid) 503

SOUTH CAROLINA
Columbia
Palmetto Pharmacist **(28558)** ....(Paid) 1,800

SOUTH DAKOTA
Pierre
South Dakota Pharmacist **(28922)** ....(Paid) 1,650

TEXAS
Austin
Drug Development and Industrial
Pharmacy **(29775)** 875
Texas Pharmacy **(29840)** ....‡2,800

Dallas
Home Health Products **(30161)**

San Antonio
Pharmacology Biochemistry and Behavior **(31041)**

UTAH
Salt Lake City
Journal of Pain and Palliative Care
Pharmacotherapy **(31435)** ....(Paid) 3,000

VIRGINIA
Alexandria
America's Pharmacist **(31639)** ....(Paid) ‡15,176
(Non-paid) ‡8,646
The Consultant
Pharmacist **(31660)** ....(Paid) ‡11,000
(Controlled) ‡11,450

WASHINGTON
Renton
Washington Pharmacist **(32927)** ....(Paid) 2,000
(Non-paid) 100

WEST VIRGINIA
Charleston
West Virginia Pharmacists
Association **(33280)** ....‡1,000

WISCONSIN
Madison
Journal of the Pharmacy Society of
Wisconsin **(33954)** ....(Paid) ‡1,800
(Non-paid) 150
Pharmacy in History **(33968)** ....(Paid) ‡1,100
(Non-paid) ‡100

BRITISH COLUMBIA, CANADA
Vancouver
BC Pharmacy **(35124)** ....(Non-paid) 3,800

Trade, Technical, and Professional Publications

Circ.   Circ.   Circ.

DRUGS AND
PHARMACEUTICALS (continued)

ONTARIO, CANADA
Oakville
Canadian Journal of Clinical
  Pharmacology (36138) ....(Controlled) 7,000

Ottawa
Canadian Journal of Hospital
  Pharmacy (36206) ....(Paid) 2,513
    (Controlled) 741
Canadian Journal of Physiology and Pharmacology
  (Revue Canadienne de Physiologie et
  Pharmacologie) (36211) ....‡1,000
Canadian Pharmaceutical
  Journal (36225) ....(Non-paid) 8,298
    (Paid) 9,600

Port Burwell
The Canadian Journal of
  Herbalism (36331) 1,000

Toronto
Pharmacy Connection (36703) 12,200
Pharmacy Post (36704) ....(Combined) 18,529
Pharmacy Practice (36705) ......(Combined) 20,077

QUEBEC, CANADA
Montreal
L'Actualite
  Pharmaceutique (37082) ....(Non-paid) 6,311
    (Paid) 381
Quebec Pharmacie (37212) ....(Controlled) 7,422

ECOLOGY AND CONSERVATION

**See also Forestry; Natural History and
Nature Study; Waste Management and
Recycling; Water Supply and Sewage
Disposal; (Hunting, Fishing, and Game
Management)**

ALABAMA
Birmingham
Eurasian Soil Science (71)

Montgomery
Outdoor Alabama (372) ....‡12,000

CALIFORNIA
Berkeley
Ecology Law Quarterly (1515)
Ecology Terrain (1516) ....(Paid) 5,000
Environmental News
  Network (1517) ....(Controlled) 125,000
The Four Seasons (1522) ....(Combined) 431
Home Energy (1526) ....(Combined) ‡4,091

Carmel
Community Spirit Magazine
  (Carmel) (1671) ....(Combined) 125,000

Davis
California Water Resources Center
  Contribution (1812) ....(Non-paid) 450

Los Angeles
UCLA Journal of Environmental Law and
  Policy (2418)

Nevada City
Wild Duck Review (2616) ....(Paid) ‡3,500

Oakland
Urban Ecology (2702)

Sacramento
Journal of Environmental Hydrology (3004)

San Diego
Environmental Research (3145)
Journal of Environmental Economics and
  Management (3190)
Journal of Environmental Management (3191)
Journal of Environmental Psychology (3192)

San Francisco
Biodynamics (3331) ....‡1,500

COLORADO
Boulder
Journal of Energy and
  Development (4175) ....(Combined) 1,000

Denver
Journal of Environmental
  Health (4336) ....(Controlled) 7,000

Lakewood
Journal of Range Management (4533) 3,400

Paonia
High Country News (4594) ....(Combined) 22,500

CONNECTICUT
Hartford
Ecological Psychology (4890)

Norwalk
E (5057)

DISTRICT OF COLUMBIA
Washington
DEFENDERS Magazine (5460) ....‡275,000
Environment (5480) ....(Combined) 5,851
The Environmental
  Forum (5481) ....(Controlled) 3,900
Environmental Science & Technology (5482)
EPA Administrative Law Reporter (5484)
The Journal of Environmental
  Education (5586) ....(Paid) ‡1,300
National Environmental Enforcement
  Journal (5670) ....(Controlled) 750
National Parks (5679) ....(Paid) 348,951
World Watch (5871) ....(Paid) ‡15,000
    (Non-paid) ‡1,200
Worldwatch Paper Series (5872) ....(Paid) ‡14,000
    (Non-paid) ‡1,000

FLORIDA
Boynton Beach
Instrumentation Science & Technology (5950) 325

Sparr
The International Permaculture Solutions
  Journal (6687)
Permaculture Review, Overview and Digest (6688)

Winter Park
Florida Specifier (6881) ....(Paid) ‡1,000
    (Controlled) ‡11,000

GEORGIA
Lilburn
Strategic Planning for Energy and the
  Environment (7374) ....(Paid) 8,600

IDAHO
Moscow
Electronic Green Journal
  (EGJ) (7913) ....(Non-paid) 20,000
Women in Natural Resources (7922)

ILLINOIS
Edwardsville
Illinois Wildlife (8813) ....‡12,684

Springfield
Illinois Parks & Recreation
  Magazine (9628) 6,000

IOWA
Ankeny
Conservation Voices (10605) .....(Combined) 12,032
Journal of Soil and Water
  Conservation (10606) 9,358

Des Moines
Iowa Conservationist (10790) ....(Paid) 50,000
    (Controlled) 4,000

Fort Dodge
Land & Water (10902) ....(Paid) 4,000
    (Non-paid) 16,000

KENTUCKY
Frankfort
Kentucky Afield (12066) ....(Paid) ‡40,000
    (Controlled) ‡4,000

Louisville
American Conchologist (12210) ....(Combined) 1,700

LOUISIANA
Hammond
Journal of Herpetology (12591) ....(Combined) 2,550

MAINE
Augusta
Maine Fish and Wildlife (12893) ....(Paid) 12,500
    (Non-paid) 400

Steuben
The Northeastern Naturalist (13060)
The Southeastern Naturalist (13061)

MARYLAND
Bethesda
Ecology Abstracts (13329)
EIS: Digests of Environmental Impact
  Statements (13331)
North American Journal of Fisheries
  Management (13366) ....‡3,200
Pollution Abstracts (13376)
Transactions of the American Fisheries
  Society (13385) ....‡3,700

Rockville
Hazard Technology (13681) ....‡55,000

Takoma Park
Endangered Species & Wetlands Report (13751)

MASSACHUSETTS
Boston
Animals Magazine (13850) ....(Paid) 70,000
Conservation Matters (13883)

Cambridge
Journal of Industrial
  Ecology (14076) ....(Combined) 1,100

Newton
Boston College Environmental Affairs Law
  Review (14384) ....(Paid) 800

MICHIGAN
Ann Arbor
Endangered Species
  Update (14748) ....(Controlled) 1,450
Journal of Great Lakes Research (14756)
Wetlands (14772)

Charlevoix
The North Woods Call (14865) ....‡8,000

Lansing
TRACKS MAGAZINE (15295) 62,000

Troy
Pollution Engineering (15635) ....(Controlled) ‡58,000

MINNESOTA
St. Louis Park
EI Digest (16360)

St. Paul
Minnesota Conservation
  Volunteer (16390) 125,000

MISSISSIPPI
Ocean Springs
Current (16801) ....(Paid) 1,200
    (Non-paid) 200

University
Estuaries (16864)

MISSOURI
Jefferson City
Missouri
  Conservationist (17124) ....(Combined) 440,000

North Kansas City
AFA Watchbird (17318) ....(Paid) 10,000
    (Non-paid) 100

St. Louis
Synthesis/Regeneration (17520)

MONTANA
Helena
AERO Sun-Times (17817) ....(Paid) 630
    (Controlled) 50

NEW HAMPSHIRE
Nashua
CleanRooms International (18585)

NEW JERSEY
Hoboken
Aquatic Conservation (18895)
Environmental Quality Management (18941)
Environmetrics (18942)
River Research and Applications (19100)

NEW MEXICO
Albuquerque
Natural Resources Journal (19776) .....(Paid) ‡1,400

New Mexico
Ecotoxicology and Environmental Safety (19903)

NEW YORK
Albany
New York State
Conservationist **(19997)** ....(Paid) ‡120,000
(Non-paid) ‡5,000

Amityville
Journal of Environmental
Systems **(20045)** ....(Paid) 1,200

Ithaca
Ecological Applications **(20800)** ....‡4,500

Kings Point
International Journal of Environmental Studies:
Sections A & B **(20859)**

Mineola
Journal of Toxicology: Clinical Toxicology **(21085)**

New York
The Air Pollution Consultant **(21168)**
Archives of Environmental Contamination and
Toxicology **(21245)** ....(Combined) **800**
Art Bulletin **(21251)**
Art Journal **(21253)**
Biodiversity and Conservation **(21313)**
Bird Conservation International **(21327)** 500
Columbia Journal of Environmental
Law **(21446)** ....(Paid) 1,200 Approx.
Conservation Genetics **(21484)**
The Earth Times **(21577)**
Ecotoxicology **(21583)**
Environment, Development and Sustainability **(21611)**
Environment (News) **(21612)**
Environmental Biology of Fishes **(21613)**
Environmental Claims Journal **(21614)**
Environmental and Ecological Statistics **(21615)**
Environmental Fluid Mechanics **(21617)**
Environmental Geochemistry and Health **(21618)**
Environmental
Management **(21619)** ....(Combined) **1,000**
Environmental Modeling & Assessment **(21620)**
Environmental Monitoring and Assessment **(21621)**
Environmental Nutrition **(21622)**
The Environmentalist **(21623)**
European Environmental Law Review **(21635)**
European Journal of Phycology **(21647)**
Industry and Environment **(21867)**
International Environmental Agreements **(21896)**
JMBA: Journal of the Marine Biological
Association **(21967)** 1600
Journal of Aquatic Ecosystem Stress and
Recovery **(21996)**
Journal of Insect Conservation **(22097)**
Journal of Tropical Ecology **(22209)** 700
Landscape Ecology **(22232)**
Microbial Ecology **(22330)** ....(Combined) 1,350
Mitigation and Adaption Strategies for Global
Change **(22339)**
Natural Hazards **(22404)**
New Forests **(22429)**
On Earth **(22488)** ....‡135,000
OnEarth **(22490)**
Plant Ecology **(22558)**
Russian Journal of Ecology **(22687)**

Paul Smiths
Adirondack Journal of Environmental
Studies **(23083)** ....(Combined) 350

Syracuse
Clearwaters **(23395)** ....(Paid) ‡2,400
(Non-paid) ‡300

NORTH CAROLINA
Durham
Duke Environmental Law and Policy Forum **(23816)**
Environmental History **(23820)** ....‡1,900

Raleigh
Wildlife in North Carolina **(24159)** .....(Paid) ‡66,319
(Non-paid) ‡3,626

OHIO
Cleveland
Energy & Environmental
Management **(24892)** ....(Combined) 30,000
Energy Journal **(24893)** ....(Controlled) 4,000

Columbus
Critical Reviews in Environmental Science and
Technology **(25013)** ....(Controlled) 700

OREGON
Ashland
Pulse of the Planet **(26216)** ....(Paid) 2,000

Bend
Natural Areas Journal **(26243)** .....(Combined) 2,250

Eugene
Worm Digest **(26335)** ....(Paid) ‡6,200
(Non-paid) ‡800

Portland
Environmental Law
(Portland) **(26476)** ....(Combined) 849
Wings **(26516)** ....(Paid) 5,500

PENNSYLVANIA
Chester
Journal of Solid Waste Technology and
Management **(26775)** ....(Combined) 175

Emmaus
Compost Science & Utilization **(26876)** ....(Paid) 800

Harrisburg
Pennsylvania Game News **(27007)** ....‡120,000

Mechanicsburg
Pennsylvania Forests **(27240)** ....(Paid) ‡2,500
(Non-paid) ‡500

Philadelphia
International Journal of Pest Management **(27504)**
Journal of Toxicology and Environmental
Health **(27553)** 855

Pittsburgh
EM **(27783)** ....‡10,000
Pollution Equipment
News **(27836)** ....(Controlled) 90,600

TENNESSEE
Knoxville
FORUM for Applied Research and Public
Policy **(29271)**

TEXAS
Austin
Texas Environmental Law Journal **(29818)**

College Station
Palynology **(30047)** ....(Controlled) 952

Denton
Environmental Ethics **(30237)** ....(Paid) 2,000

Houston
Environmental Toxicology and
Chemistry **(30471)** 5,500

UTAH
Logan
Society & Natural Resources **(31351)** ....(Paid) ‡576

VIRGINIA
Alexandria
The American Gardener **(31636)** 28,000
Water Environment Research **(31751)** ....‡8,500
Water Environment & Technology **(31752)**

Arlington
Endangered Species Bulletin **(31788)**

Chesapeake
Calypso Log **(31964)** ....‡100,000

Fairfax
Journal of Environmental Science and Health, Part A:
Toxic/Hazardous Substances & Environmental
Engineering **(32020)** ....(Paid) 300
Journal of Environmental Science and Health, Part B:
Pesticides, Food Contaminants, and Agricultural
Wastes **(32021)** ....(Paid) 325
Synergist **(32032)**

Ivy
World Climate Report **(32174)** .....(Combined) 3,000

Middleburg
Journal of the American Water Resources
Association **(32272)** 3,000

Reston
Journal of Water Resources Planning and
Management **(32401)** ....(Paid) ⊕1,500

Springfield
Environmental Carcinogenesis & Ecotoxicology
Reviews **(32543)** ....(Paid) ‡250

WISCONSIN
Appleton
Progress in Paper
Recycling **(33543)** ....(Combined) 700

Madison
Ecological Restoration **(33935)** ....(Paid) 2,700
Journal of Environmental Quality **(33951)** 3,400

Waukesha
Birder's World **(34396)** ....(Paid) ★61,242

WYOMING
Cheyenne
Wyoming Wildlife **(34501)** ....(Paid) ‡35,000
(Controlled) ‡1,100

ALBERTA, CANADA
Athabasca
The Trumpeter **(34610)** ....(Paid) ‡600
(Non-paid) ‡200

BRITISH COLUMBIA, CANADA
Langley
Supply Post **(35005)** ....(Combined) ‡18,000

Vancouver
Recycling Product
News **(35163)** ....(Combined) 16,631

Victoria
Tree Physiology **(35227)** ....(Controlled) 1,000

ONTARIO, CANADA
Aurora
Environmental Science &
Engineering **(35647)** ....(Combined) 19,095

Burlington
Water Quality Research Journal of
Canada **(35719)** ....(Paid) 300

Ottawa
Nature Canada **(36263)** 31,400

Peterborough
Environmental Reviews (Dossiers
Environnement) **(36314)**

Toronto
Accident Prevention **(36460)** ......(Combined) 11,173
Green Teacher **(36609)** ....(Controlled) 7,400
Journal of Environmental Law and Practice **(36635)**
Kick It Over **(36642)** ....(Paid) ‡1,500
(Non-paid) ‡500

Waterloo
Alternatives Journal **(36845)** 4,500
Environments **(36850)** ....(Combined) 400

QUEBEC, CANADA
Ste.-Foy
Ecoscience **(37336)**

ECONOMICS

**See also Banking, Finance, and
Investments**

ALABAMA
Florence
Journal of Legal Economics **(219)** ....(Paid) 570
(Controlled) 35

Tuscaloosa
Alabama Economic Outlook **(482)**

ARIZONA
Tucson
Arizona's Economy **(935)**

ARKANSAS
Fayetteville
Arkansas Business & Economic
Review **(1115)** ....(Controlled) 4,000

CALIFORNIA
Berkeley
Bad Subjects **(1493)**
China Economic Review **(1507)**

Claremont
North American Journal of Economics and
Finance **(1725)** ....(Paid) 300
(Non-paid) 50

Fullerton
Structural Equation Modeling **(1990)**

Huntington Beach
Economic Inquiry **(2061)** ....(Paid) 3,300
(Non-paid) 25

Circulation: ★ = ABC; △ = BPA; ♦ = CAC; ● = CCAB; ❑ = VAC; ⊕ = PO Statement; ‡ = Publisher's Report; Boldface figures = sworn; Light figures = estimated.

3129

Circ.   Circ.   Circ.

ECONOMICS (continued)

Irvine
Knowledge Management (2082)

La Jolla
Abstracts of Working Papers in Economics
(AWPE) (2111)

Los Angeles
REASON (2378) ....(Paid) 55,000

San Diego
Explorations in Economic History (3152)
Games and Economic Behavior (3160)
Journal of Economic Theory (3189)
Journal of Environmental Economics and
Management (3190)
Journal of Housing Economics (3198)
Journal of the Japanese and International
Economics (3200)
Journal of Urban Economics (3215)
Research in Economics (3255)
Review of Economic Dynamics (3256)

Santa Monica
RAND Journal of Economics (3714) ....(Paid) ‡3,000
(Non-paid) ‡80

Stanford
Journal of Economic Literature (3796) ....‡27,000

Thousand Oaks
Economic Development
Quarterly (3862) ....(Paid) ‡1,300
(Non-paid) ‡164
Indian Economic and Social History Review (3874)
Politics & Society (3908) ....(Paid) 800

COLORADO
Fort Collins
Journal of Agricultural & Resource Economics (4434)

CONNECTICUT
Hartford
The Journal of Private Enterprise (4896)

Middletown
Journal of Comparative Economics (4944)

New Haven
Econometric Theory (4987) 1000

DISTRICT OF COLUMBIA
Washington
Brookings Papers on Economic Activity (5384)
The Brookings Review (5385) ....(Paid) ‡6,000
(Controlled) ‡10,000
The Business Advocate (5389) 200,000
Business Economics (5390) ....‡3,600
Current (5453) ....‡2,174
The DAC Journal (5458)
Economia (5471)
Executive Intelligence
Review (5485) ....(Combined) ⊕15,000
Finance &
Development (5495) ....(Controlled) 95,000
The International Economy (5550) ....(Paid) 2,000
International Trade by Commodities, Series C (5558)
The Journal of Economic
Education (5581) ....(Paid) ‡1,100
Journal of Social, Political & Economic
Studies (5615) ....(Paid) ‡1,150
(Non-paid) ‡55
National Tax Journal (5681)
OECD Economic Surveys (5700)
The Public Interest (5750) 8,000
Today's Internist (5825) ....(Paid) ‡20,979
(Non-paid) ‡15,013
TransCaucasus, A Chronology (5828) 2,000
The World Bank Economic
Review (5868) ....(Paid) 1,800
(Non-paid) 10,000
World Economic Outlook (5869)

FLORIDA
Tallahassee
On Track (6726) 300

Vero Beach
Antitrust Law and Economics Review (6834)

GEORGIA
Athens
Georgia Business and Economic
Conditions (6938) ....(Free) ‡2,000

Atlanta
Economic Review (7000) ....(Controlled) ‡23,000
EconSouth (7001)

ILLINOIS
Champaign
The Quarterly Review of Economics and
Finance (8214) 2,000

Chicago
Economic Perspectives (8358)
Law Practice Management (8459) 16,024
Mathematical Finance (8482) ....‡800

Evanston
Journal of Economics and Management
Strategy (8864) 1,000

Rockford
Chronicles (9526) ....‡8,000

KANSAS
Prairie Village
Expansion Management (11761) ....(Paid) 500
(Non-paid) 45,000

Wichita
Kansas Economic Report (11885) 700

LOUISIANA
Baton Rouge
Louisiana Rural
Economist (12503) ....(Controlled) ‡1,265

MARYLAND
Lanham
Journal of Economic Entomology (13604) 1,800

MASSACHUSETTS
Belmont
IDB America (13840)

Boston
Business History Review (13869) ....(Paid) 2,000
(Non-paid) 300
Connection (13882) ....(Controlled) 13,500
Federal Reserve Bank of Boston Regional
Review (13893) ....(Controlled) 20,000
New England Economic
Indicators (13932) ....(Free) 7000
New England Economic
Review (13933) ....(Non-paid) ‡15,000

Cambridge
Dollars & Sense (14049) ....‡8,400
Econometrica (14050) ....‡7,000
NBER Reporter (14083)
The Quarterly Journal of
Economics (14094) ....‡4,900
Review of Economics and
Statistics (14098) 3,500

Malden
American Journal of Agricultural
Economics (14289) 4,300

MINNESOTA
Minneapolis
Journal of Economic
Perspectives (16087) ....(Paid) 27,000

MISSOURI
Kansas City
Journal of Forensic Economics (17174)

St. Louis
Atlantic Economic Journal (17417)
Forum for Social
Economics (17438) ....(Controlled) 450
International Advances in Economic
Research (17446)
Social Justice Review (17512) ....(Paid) 4,600
(Non-paid) 500

MONTANA
Missoula
The Montana Business
Quarterly (17870) ....(Paid) ‡1,300
(Non-paid) ‡200

NEBRASKA
Lincoln
Quarterly Journal of Business &
Economics (18116) ....(Paid) 500
(Non-paid) 100

NEW HAMPSHIRE
Durham
Journal of the History of Economic Thought (18500)

NEW JERSEY
Hoboken
Applied Stochastic Models in Business and
Industry (18894)
Health Economics (18959)
Journal of Applied Econometrics (19002)
Journal of Forecasting (19023) ....(Paid) 9,800
Journal of International
Development (19027) ....(Paid) 2,800
Managerial and Decision Economics (19058)

New Brunswick
Comparative Economic Studies (19328) ....‡950

Princeton
American Economic Review (19452) ....‡27,000

Somerset
Journal of Income
Distribution (19563) ....(Combined) 200
The Review of Black Political
Economy (19564) ....(Paid) ‡1,000

NEW YORK
Armonk
Challenge (20066) ....‡3,000
China Briefing (20067)
The Chinese Economy (20068) ....(Paid) ⊕224
India Briefing (20078)
International Journal of Electronic
Commerce (20079) ....(Paid) 254
Korea Briefing (20088)
Problems of Economic
Transition (20091) ....(Paid) ⊕360

Irvington on Hudson
The Freeman (20784) ....(Mon.-Fri.) 22,451
(Sun.) 29,888

Ithaca
Cornell Political Forum (20798) .....(Non-paid) 8,000

New York
Cepal Review (21390)
Economics and Philosophy (21581) 1,100
European Journal of Law and Economics (21645)
Experimental Economics (21666)
Extremes (21671)
Federal Reserve Bank of New York Economic Policy
Review (21682)
Georgist Journal (21757) ....(Paid) ‡600
(Non-paid) ‡50
India Abroad (21862) ....(Fri.) 53,851
Journal of American Studies (21986) .....(Paid) ‡455
(Non-paid) ‡3,346
Journal of Asian Economics (21999)
Journal of Bioeconomics (22008)
Journal of Cultural Economics (22043)
Journal of Economic Growth (22054)
The Journal of Economic History (22055) 3250
Journal of Modern African Studies (22135) 1600
The Journal of Socio-Economics (22188)
Journal of Technology Transfer (22203)
Journal of Thermal Analysis and Calorimetry (22204)
Journal of World Trade (22215)
Legal Issues of Economic Integration (22245)
McKinsey Quarterly (22303)
Mitigation and Adaption Strategies for Global
Change (22339)
MOCT-MOST (22343)
Monthly Review (22364) ....(Paid) ‡5,321
(Non-paid) ‡97
Open Economies Review (22494)
Quarterly Journal of Austrian
Economics (22618) ....(Combined) 1,000
The Review of Austrian Economics (22656)
Review of Derivatives Research (22658)
Review of Industrial Organization (22660)
Treasury and Risk Management
Magazine (22860) 46,000
The Urban League Review (22890) 500

Oneonta
New York Economic Review (23051) ......(Paid) 150

NORTH CAROLINA
Cary
Journal of Law, Economics, and
Organization (23692)

Durham
History of Political Economy (23825) ....‡1,350

Raleigh
Social Science Computer Review (24153) 1,000

Research Triangle Park
Southern Growth Magazine (24187)

3130

OHIO
Cleveland
Economic Commentary **(24885)** ....(Non-paid) ‡6,200
Economic Review **(24886)** ....(Non-paid) ‡6,400
Economic Trends **(24887)** ....(Non-paid) 8,800

Dayton
International Review of Economics and
   Finance **(25121)**

OKLAHOMA
Stillwater
Southern Economic Journal **(26081)** 3,000

PENNSYLVANIA
Easton
Eastern Economic Journal **(26849)** 1,000

Philadelphia
Entrepreneurship and Regional Development **(27461)**
Ergonomics **(27463)**
Ergonomics Abstracts **(27464)**
International Economic Review **(27494)** ....‡2,400
International Journal of Remote Sensing **(27507)**

Pittsburgh
Employment and Earnings **(27784)**

SOUTH CAROLINA
Columbia
Business & Economic Review **(28546)** ....‡6,100

TENNESSEE
Knoxville
FORUM for Applied Research and Public
   Policy **(29271)**
J E I **(29274)** ....(Combined) ⊕1,999
Journal of Post Keynesian
   Economics **(29278)** ....(Paid) 1850

Memphis
Business Perspectives **(29359)** .....(Non-paid) ‡4,100

TEXAS
College Station
Contemporary Economic
   Policy **(30039)** ....(Paid) ‡3,200
                                                       (Non-paid) ‡75

Dallas
Economic and Financial Policy Review **(30153)**

Denton
The Journal of Media Economics **(30239)**

Houston
Houston Economic Highlights **(30483)**

VIRGINIA
Alexandria
Family Economics and Nutrition
   Review **(31672)** ....(Paid) 900
                                                      (Non-paid) 3,500
Journal of Business & Economic Statistics **(31689)**
Journal of Cost Analysis and
   Management **(31691)** ....(Combined) 4,000

Harrisonburg
Journal of Global Business **(32139)**

Langley AFB
Statistics of Income - SOI Bulletin **(32177)**

WASHINGTON
Ferndale
The North American Technocrat **(32768)** 1,500

Seattle
Nonprofit and Voluntary Sector
   Quarterly **(32990)** 1,700

WISCONSIN
Madison
Journal of Human
   Resources **(33952)** ....(Controlled) 2,000
Land Economics **(33956)** 2,000

BRITISH COLUMBIA, CANADA
Burnaby
B. C. Business **(34890)**

Victoria
British Columbia Business Indicators **(35208)**
British Columbia Origin Exports **(35211)**
British Columbia Regional Index **(35212)**
Economic Accounts **(35215)**
Labour Force Survey **(35218)**

ONTARIO, CANADA
Ottawa
Canadian Economic Observer **(36192)** ....‡3,600
Canadian Journal of Agricultural
   Economics **(36200)** ....(Paid) 1,000

Toronto
C.D. Howe Institute Commentary **(36543)**

QUEBEC, CANADA
Montreal
Canadian Journal of Economics (Revue Canadienne
   d'Economique) **(37097)**
Italian Commerce of Commerce of
   Canada **(37136)** ....(Non-paid) ‡8,000
LES AFFAIRES **(37175)**
Policy Options Politiques **(37207)** ....(Paid) 3,100
                                                         (Non-paid) 3,100
Revue Commerce **(37217)** ....(Paid) 43,111

Mount Royal
Economic Planning in Free Societies **(37252)**

EDUCATION

See also Vocational Education

ALABAMA
Auburn
Professional Educator **(44)** ....(Combined) 200

Auburn University
Phi Kappa Phi Forum **(50)** ....(Paid) 110,000

Birmingham
Journal of the National Collegiate Honors Council
   (JNCHC) **(76)** ....(Non-paid) 990

Livingston
Alabama Counseling Association
   Journal **(305)** ....(Non-paid) 2000

Mobile
College Student Journal **(318)** ....‡800
Journal of Instructional Psychology **(321)** ....‡450
Reading Improvement **(329)** ....‡2,500

ARIZONA
Phoenix
Current Index to Journals in Education **(801)**

Tempe
Education and Training in Developmental
   Disabilities **(903)** ....‡7,500
General Music Today **(904)**
Journal of Historical Research in Music
   Education **(907)** ....(Combined) 227
Stage of the Art **(915)**
Youth Theatre Journal **(918)**

ARKANSAS
Fayetteville
The Arkansas Traveler **(1118)** .....(Non-paid) ‡6,000
Rehabilitation Education **(1124)** ....(Paid) ‡700
                                                            (Non-paid) ‡50

Little Rock
Arkansas Educator **(1217)** ....‡18,268

CALIFORNIA
Berkeley
Issues in Education **(1530)**

Burlingame
California Educator **(1631)** ....‡330,000

Chatsworth
Syllabus Magazine **(1690)**

Chula Vista
Education **(1714)** ....‡3,500

Concord
CMEA News **(1751)** ....(Paid) ‡3,250
ETC: A Review of General
   Semantics **(1753)** 1,500

Emeryville
Mathematics in Education and Research **(1878)**

Folsom
Converge **(1917)**

Los Angeles
Educational Assessment **(2261)**

Monterey
Applied Language
   Learning **(2581)** ....(Non-paid) 4,500

Oakland
The Black Scholar **(2668)** ....(Paid) 10,000
                                                      (Non-paid) 60,000

Playa del Rey
Cancer Victors Journal **(2851)** ....(Paid) ‡20,000

Redondo Beach
School Transportation News **(2911)** ....(Paid) ‡1,756
                                                            (Non-paid) ‡21,403

Sacramento
Education California
   (EDCAL) **(2996)** ....(Paid) 17,117
                                                         (Controlled) 200
Leadership Magazine **(3005)** ....(Paid) 16,205
                                                            (Non-paid) 294

San Bernardino
Journal of Latinos and Education **(3087)**

San Diego
Arts & Activities **(3117)** ....(Combined) 18,268
Contemporary Educational Psychology **(3135)**
San Diego Family
   Magazine **(3263)** ....(Free) ‡119,862
                                                        (Paid) ‡143
S.D.T.A. Teacher
   Advocate **(3272)** ....(Non-paid) ‡8,000

San Francisco
Educational Foundations **(3355)** 800
Educational Leadership and
   Administration **(3356)** ....(Paid) 125
Journal of Critical Inquiry into Curriculum and
   Instruction **(3379)** ....(Paid) 200
Journal of Curriculum
   Theorizing **(3380)** ....(Paid) 500
Journal of Thought **(3385)** ....‡400
Mercury **(3390)** ....(Paid) ‡6,000
                                                     (Non-paid) ‡200
Multicultural Education **(3392)** ....(Paid) 900
New Directions for Adult and Continuing
   Education **(3396)** ....‡812
New Directions for Community
   Colleges **(3398)** ....(Paid) 827
                                                     (Non-paid) 178
New Directions for Higher
   Education **(3400)** ....(Paid) 1,927
                                                     (Non-paid) 63
New Directions for Institutional
   Research **(3401)** ....(Paid) 1,033
                                                     (Non-paid) 70
Notes and Abstracts in American and International
   Education **(3408)** ....(Paid) 125
Summer Academe **(3444)** ....(Paid) 800
Taboo **(3449)** ....(Paid) 125
Teacher Education Quarterly **(3450)** 900
Vitae Schololasticae **(3460)** ....(Paid) 125

San Jose
Newslink **(3529)** ....(Controlled) ‡156,000

San Mateo
Junior Statement **(3588)** ....(Paid) 10,000

Santa Monica
RAND Review **(3715)** ....(Controlled) 15,000

Thousand Oaks
Education and Urban Society **(3863)**
Educational Administration
   Abstracts **(3864)** ....(Paid) 300
Educational and Psychological
   Measurement **(3865)** ....(Paid) ‡1,250
Urban Education **(3919)** ....(Paid) ‡862
                                                     (Non-paid) ‡111

West Sacramento
California Schools **(4064)** ....(Paid) ‡7,840
                                                     (Non-paid) ‡465

COLORADO
Boulder
American Suzuki Journal **(4156)** ....‡9,000
EDUCAUSE Quarterly **(4166)** ....(Paid) 7,600
                                                        (Free) ⊕170

Colorado Springs
Coaching Volleyball **(4242)** ....(Paid) 3,250

Denver
Focus on Exceptional Children **(4328)**
State Education Leader **(4360)** ....(Paid) 1,000
                                                        (Controlled) 4,000

Fort Collins
English Journal **(4429)** ....(Paid) 31,000
Statement (Fort Collins) **(4439)** ....(Paid) 850

Circulation: ★ = ABC; △ = BPA; ♦ = CAC; • = CCAB; ▢ = VAC; ⊕ = PO Statement; ‡ = Publisher's Report; Boldface figures = sworn; Light figures = estimated.

3131

Circ.   Circ.   Circ.

EDUCATION (continued)

Las Vegas
Learning and Individual Differences **(4543)**

Loveland
Children's Ministry Magazine **(4566)** ....(Paid) 55,000
(Non-paid) 5,000

Mancos
Tribal College Journal of American Indian Higher
Education (TCJ) **(4572)**

Pueblo
Radical Pedagogy **(4600)**

CONNECTICUT
Danbury
Choices **(4736)** ....‡200,000
Instructor **(4742)** ....(Paid) 208,319
Junior Scholastic **(4743)** ....(Paid) 591,038
Let's Find Out **(4744)** ....‡600,000
Literary Cavalcade **(4745)** ....(Paid) 147,480
The New York Times
Upfront **(4746)** ....(Paid) 230,000
Scholastic Action **(4751)** 230,000
Scholastic Ars- **(4752)**
Scholastic DynaMath **(4754)** ....‡235,000
Scholastic News Citizen Edition **(4756)** 485,000
Scholastic News Explorer Edition **(4757)** 505,000
Scholastic News Newstime
Edition **(4758)** 367,000
Scholastic News Pilot Edition **(4759)** 475,000
Scholastic News Ranger Edition **(4760)** 530,000
Scholastic News Trails Edition **(4761)** 530,000
Science World **(4763)** ....(Paid) 395,228
Storyworks **(4764)**

East Haddam
KIND News **(4777)** 1,222,800

Hartford
The Journal of Private Enterprise **(4896)**

Middletown
Choice **(4943)** ....(Paid) ‡3,500
(Controlled) ‡141

Mystic
Matrix: The Magazine for Leaders in Higher
Education **(4969)**

New Britain
Multicultural Perspectives **(4976)**

Norwalk
Curriculum
Administrator **(5054)** ....(Controlled) △69,000
Teaching/K-8 **(5075)** ....(Paid) 102,130
(Non-paid) 3,736
University Business **(5079)** ....(Controlled) 34,000

Stamford
Current Science **(5146)** ....‡357,583
Read **(5159)** ....‡250,000
Weekly Reader (Pre-K
edition) **(5163)** ....(Paid) 508,153

Storrs
UConn Traditions **(5169)** ....(Controlled) 160,000

Tolland
International Journal of Instructional Media
(IJIM) **(5176)** 2000

DELAWARE
Newark
Journal of Adolescent & Adult
Literacy **(5275)** ....‡15,000
The Reading Teacher **(5279)** ....‡64,000
Reading Today **(5280)** ....(Paid) 80,000

DISTRICT OF COLUMBIA
Washington
AAUW in Action **(5308)** ....(Non-paid) 150,000
Academe: Bulletin of the AAUP **(5312)** ......‡46,000
American Educational Research
Journal **(5326)** ....‡19,800
American Educator **(5327)** ....‡630,000
American Teacher **(5346)** ....(Paid) 850,000
Arts Education Policy Review **(5362)** ....‡1,061
ASEE Prism **(5364)** ....‡12,000
ASHE-ERIC Higher Education
Reports **(5365)** ....‡4,000
Change **(5403)** ....(Combined) ‡15,000
ChemMatters **(5406)** ....(Paid) ⊕40,000
Children & Schools **(5409)** 2,400
The Chronicle of Higher
Education **(5413)** ....(Paid) 90,509
The Clearing House **(5418)** ....‡2,000
College Mathematics Journal **(5424)**

College Teaching **(5425)** ....(Paid) ‡1,945
Community Colleges
Journal **(5429)** ....(Paid) ‡12,800
(Controlled) ‡21
C.U.A. Magazine **(5452)** ....(Non-paid) 50,000
Currents **(5455)** ....‡15,000
Educational Evaluation and Policy
Analysis **(5473)** ....‡6,000
Educational Researcher **(5474)** ....‡23,800
Gifted Child Quarterly **(5515)** ....(Paid) 6,500
Higher Education Management **(5525)**
The International Journal of Action
Methods **(5552)** ....(Combined) 351
The Journal of Economic
Education **(5581)** ....(Paid) ‡1,100
Journal of Education for
Business **(5582)** ....(Paid) ‡1,297
Journal of Educational Psychology **(5584)** .....‡5,100
The Journal of Educational
Research **(5585)** ....(Paid) ‡2,900
The Journal of Experimental
Education **(5587)** ....(Paid) ‡1,100
The Journal of Negro
Education **(5605)** ....(Paid) ‡2,300
(Controlled) ‡100
Liberal Education **(5636)** ....(Paid) ‡900
(Controlled) ‡4,000
Lincoln Review **(5637)** ....(Non-paid) ‡7,000
Momentum **(5659)** ....(Paid) ‡24,500
The Presidency **(5727)** ....(Paid) ‡1150
(Non-paid) ‡6350
Preventing School Failure **(5729)** ....(Paid) 635
Quarterly Journal of Speech **(5754)** ....(Paid) ‡5,695
(Non-paid) ‡100
RE:view **(5758)** ....(Combined) ‡4,850
Review of Educational Research **(5765)** .....‡18,400
Science Activities **(5779)** 1,042
Science Books & Films **(5780)** ....(Paid) ‡4,500
(Non-paid) ‡600
The Social Studies **(5795)** ....(Paid) 1,727
Sociology of Education **(5798)** ....‡3,000
Teaching Sociology **(5815)** ....‡2,400
Thought & Action **(5823)** ....(Paid) 80,000
Trusteeship **(5832)** 32,000
The Volta Review **(5840)** ....‡4,400
Young Children **(5873)** ....‡104,790

FLORIDA
Gainesville
Journal of College and University Student
Housing **(6146)**

Holmes Beach
School Intervention Report **(6202)** ......(Paid) ‡1,700
(Non-paid) ‡1,000

Lake Park
Kidstuff **(6284)** 10,000

Sarasota
Issues in Accounting Education **(6657)**

Tallahassee
Research in Review **(6732)**
Studies in Art Education **(6736)** ....(Paid) ‡4,197
(Non-paid) ‡30

GEORGIA
Athens
Communication Education **(6933)** ....‡4,000
Journal of Higher Education Outreach and
Engagement (JHEOE) **(6944)**
Journal of Learning Disabilities **(6945)** .....‡8,500
Southeastern Journal of Music
Education **(6951)** ....(Paid) 300

Atlanta
Black Employment and Education
Magazine **(6979)** ....(Paid) ‡25,000
(Controlled) ‡150,000
The Journal of the Learning Sciences **(7021)**

Decatur
Young Horizons Indigo **(7238)** ....(Paid) 18,000
54,000

Kennesaw
Teaching of Psychology **(7355)**

Lilburn
Coaching Women's
Basketball **(7371)** ....(Paid) 5,000
(Non-paid) 200

Macon
Mercer University Discoveries **(7385)**
URSA **(7387)**

HAWAII
Honolulu
Chinese Language Teachers Association
Journal **(7684)** 650
Language Learning and
Technology **(7708)** ....(Non-paid) 3,944

IDAHO
Boise
IEA Reporter **(7812)** ....(Paid) ‡11,500
(Non-paid) ‡600

ILLINOIS
Carbondale
French Review **(8117)** 12,000

Champaign
The Journal of Aesthetic
Education **(8192)** ....(Paid) 1,000
(Non-paid) 50
Journal of Education
Finance **(8196)** ....(Paid) ⊕1,200
Visual Arts Research **(8222)** ....(Paid) 500

Chicago
American Libraries **(8259)** ....(Combined) ‡59,300
Chicago Business **(8307)** ....(Paid) ‡300
(Non-paid) ‡2,500
Journal of the Medical Library
Association **(8445)** ....(Non-paid) ‡5,000
(Paid) ‡800

DeKalb
Journal of Emotional and Behavioral
Disorders **(8736)** ....(Paid) ‡1,782
(Non-paid) ‡94
Thresholds in Education **(8741)** ....‡250

Evanston
Journal of Secondary Gifted Education **(8865)**

Lincolnshire
Salon Today Magazine **(9088)** ....‡30,000

Macomb
Journal of Elementary Science Education **(9129)**

Naperville
Learning Point **(9267)**
Pathways to School Improvement **(9271)**

Normal
Illinois English Bulletin **(9297)**
Journal of Management
Education **(9300)** ....(Paid) 1,000

Northbrook
Career World **(9313)** ....(Paid) 87,000
Current Health 1 **(9314)** ....(Paid) 165,793
Current Health 2 **(9315)** ....(Paid) 229,274
In Motion **(9317)** ....(Non-paid) 1,000,000
Writing! **(9323)**

River Forest
Lutheran Education Journal **(9492)** ....‡4,200

Skokie
School Social Work Journal **(9610)**

Springfield
Illinois School Board Journal **(9631)** ....(Paid) ‡7,737
(Non-paid) ‡690
Teaching and Learning in Medicine **(9643)**

Urbana
Bulletin of the Council for Research in Music
Education **(9698)** ....(Paid) ‡1,000
(Non-paid) ‡100
College Composition and
Communication **(9700)** ....(Paid) 11,500
College English **(9701)** ....(Paid) 16,000
The Council Chronicle **(9703)** ....(Paid) 77,000
English Education **(9704)** ....(Paid) 4,000
Illinois Classical Studies **(9708)** ...(Controlled) 260
Language Arts **(9714)** ....(Paid) 20,000
Research in the Teaching of
English **(9717)** ....(Paid) 5,000
Teaching English in the Two-Year
College **(9720)** ....(Paid) 5,000

Wheaton
Journal of Outcome Measurement **(9756)**

INDIANA
Bloomington
Educational Horizons **(9825)** ....(Paid) ⊕11,553
Phi Delta Kappan **(9848)** ....‡95,000
TechTrends: for Leaders in Education &
Training **(9853)** ....‡8,000

Indianapolis
ISBA Journal **(10136)** ....(Paid) ‡2,800
ISTA Advocate **(10137)** ....(Controlled) ‡50,000
Kappa Delta Pi Record **(10143)** ....(Paid) 60,000

Muncie
Indiana Musicator **(10327)** ....(Paid) 2,000
The Teacher Educator **(10329)** ......(Combined) 740

IOWA
Ames
New Directions for Student
   Services **(10593)** ....(Paid) 1,200
                                          (Controlled) 95

Decorah
Luther Alumni
   Magazine **(10757)** ....(Non-paid) 35,000

Des Moines
The Iowa School Board
   Dialogue **(10795)** ....(Paid) 4,086
                                          (Non-paid) 682
Journal of Teacher
   Education **(10801)** ....(Paid) 3,000
                                        (Controlled) 5,200
                                          (Non-paid) 86

Iowa City
Midwest Modern Language Association
   Journal **(10982)** ....(Paid) 2,000

KANSAS
Emporia
Kansas Biology Teacher **(11430)** ....(Combined) 300

Kansas City
Topics in Early Childhood Special
   Education **(11534)** ....(Paid) 1,700

Manhattan
Jazz Education Journal **(11621)** ....(Paid) 7,500
                                          (Non-paid) 300
Journal of Research on Computing in
   Education **(11622)** 2,500

Overland Park
Learning Disability Quarterly **(11719)**

Pittsburg
The Midwest Quarterly **(11753)** ....(Paid) ‡800
                                          (Non-paid) ‡150

KENTUCKY
Bowling Green
Kentucky English Bulletin **(11947)** ....(Paid) 600

Frankfort
KEA News **(12065)** ....(Free) 39,000

Murray
Journal of Business and Public Affairs **(12315)**

Russellville
Bluegrass Music News **(12388)** ....‡2,100

LOUISIANA
Baton Rouge
Journal for Research in Music
   Education **(12491)** ....(Paid) ‡3,500
                                         (Controlled) ‡9
LAE News **(12492)** ....‡21,000
The Louisiana Boardmember **(12495)** ....‡1,000
Update **(12507)**

Lake Charles
National Forum of Applied Educational Research
   Journal **(12640)** 7,500
National Forum of Education Administration and
   Supervision Journal **(12641)** 7,500
National Forum of Special Education
   Journal **(12642)** 7,500
National Forum of Teacher Education
   Journal **(12643)** 7,500

Natchitoches
College Student Affairs
   Journal **(12715)** ....(Paid) 1,200

New Orleans
Journal for Minority Medical
   Students **(12735)** ....(Non-paid) 10,000
The Keepsake **(12736)** ....(Paid) ‡10,000
SENGA **(12753)**

MARYLAND
Annapolis Junction
NEA Today **(13104)** ....(Paid) 2,140,876

Baltimore
The Journal of the Association for Persons with
   Severe Handicaps **(13179)** .....(Controlled) ‡4,000
Journal of Education for Students Placed at
   Risk **(13188)**
School Library Media Activities
   Monthly **(13244)** ....(Paid) ⊕11,500
UMBC Review **(13257)**

Bethesda
Advances in Physiology
   Education **(13294)** ....(Combined) ‡9,739
Communique **(13325)**
Education Week **(13330)** ....(Paid) 52,665
School Psychology Review **(13378)**
Teacher Magazine **(13383)** ....(Paid) 22,769
                                         (Non-paid) 100,000

College Park
Science Communication **(13439)** ....(Paid) ‡418
                                          (Non-paid) ‡12

Lanham
International Journal of Educational
   Reform **(13602)** ....(Controlled) 300
Voice of Youth
   Advocates **(13609)** ....(Combined) 6,000

Olney
Journal of Research in Childhood Education **(13643)**

Silver Spring
The Journal of Adventist
   Education **(13729)** ....(Paid) ‡7,500
                                          (Non-paid) ‡250
Montessori News **(13740)** ....(Paid) ‡550
Social Education **(13746)** ....(Paid) ‡29,000

Thurmont
Maryland Music
   Educator **(13755)** ....(Combined) 1,400

Towson
The IN-REPORT **(13759)** ....‡2,200

MASSACHUSETTS
Amherst
American Journal of Physics **(13789)** 8,100
Journal of Computing in Higher
   Education **(13797)** ....(Paid) 200
                                          (Non-paid) 200

Boston
Cable in the Classroom **(13870)** ......(Paid) 120,941
Connection **(13882)** ....(Controlled) 13,500

Cambridge
Harvard Educational Review **(14058)** ....‡10,000
Q Journal **(14093)**
Radical Teacher **(14096)** 2,000

Chestnut Hill
Educational Policy **(14127)** ....(Paid) 700
                                          (Non-paid) 30
The Review of Higher
   Education **(14133)** ....(Combined) 1,660
Teaching Exceptional Children **(14134)** 56,814

Cummaquid
TIE (The International Educator) **(14151)** 14,000

MICHIGAN
Ann Arbor
The Education Digest **(14747)** ....‡14,000
Learning Disabilities Research and
   Practice **(14758)** 12,500

Bloomfield Hills
Roeper Review **(14829)** ....(Paid) 2,200
                                          (Non-paid) 200

Detroit
The FORUM Magazine **(14932)** ....(Paid) ‡2,000
                                          (Non-paid) ‡8,000

East Lansing
MEA Voice **(14988)** ....‡160,000

Grand Rapids
Christian Home & School **(15091)** ......(Paid) ‡1,000
                                        (Controlled) ‡69,000
Pedagogy **(15100)**

Kalamazoo
Reading Horizons **(15244)**

Lansing
Media Spectrum **(15278)** 1,350

Southfield
Lawrence Technological University
   Magazine **(15544)** ....(Non-paid) 32,000

Troy
Student Assistance Journal **(15641)** ....(Paid) ‡3,000
                                         (Controlled) ‡7,000

Ypsilanti
Educational Studies **(15691)**

MINNESOTA
Minneapolis
Illustrator **(16085)**
NST (Nature, Society and Thought) **(16118)** 500

St. Cloud
Journal of Geography **(16343)** ....‡4,500

St. Paul
Minnesota Educator **(16391)** ....‡78,000
Technical Communication
   Quarterly **(16410)** ....(Combined) 2,000

MISSISSIPPI
Jackson
The Mississippi Educator **(16701)** ....‡13,000

MISSOURI
Columbia
The Counseling
   Psychologist **(16992)** ....(Paid) ‡5,400
                                          (Non-paid) ‡128
School and Community **(17008)** ....‡43,000

Fulton
Missouri Record **(17077)**

Jefferson City
Something Better **(17134)** ....(Paid) ‡30,000
                                          (Non-paid) ‡1,000

Point Lookout
Teaching History: A Journal of Methods **(17354)**

Warrenton
Evangelizing Today's Child **(17683)** ....‡14,000

NEBRASKA
Lincoln
Nebraska Music Educator **(18104)** ....(Paid) 1,650
NSEA Voice **(18110)** ....‡24,350
School Psychology Quarterly **(18118)** ....(Paid) 3,000

Omaha
Journal of Alcohol and Drug
   Education **(18200)** ....(Paid) 1,000

NEVADA
Las Vegas
Journal of Special Education
   Technology **(18367)** ....(Paid) 1,700
Reading Research Quarterly **(18383)** ....‡11,000

NEW HAMPSHIRE
Lebanon
Dartmouth Medicine **(18542)** ....(Non-paid) 25,000

NEW JERSEY
Bloomfield
On the Green **(18688)** ....(Non-paid) 8,000

Bridgewater
School Selection
   Guide **(18699)** ....(Non-paid) 50,000
TopCats! **(18702)** ....(Non-paid) 50,000

Caldwell
Children's House/Children's
   World **(18711)** ....‡47,500

Cherry Hill
Die Unterrichtspraxis/Teaching
   German **(18734)** ....(Combined) 4,100

Englewood
Employment Opportunities (Englewood) **(18795)**

Englewood Cliffs
Educational Technology **(18799)** ....‡3,000

Ewing
TIES Magazine **(18805)**

Flemington
Children's Software Revue
   (CSR) **(18818)** ....(Combined) ‡19,000

Hoboken
Computer Applications in Engineering
   Education **(18921)** 4550
Dyslexia **(18933)**
Journal of Research in Science
   Teaching **(19045)** 19,950
Software **(19104)**

Circulation: ★ = ABC; △ = BPA; ♦ = CAC; • = CCAB; ❑ = VAC; ⊕ = PO Statement; ‡ = Publisher's Report; Boldface figures = sworn; Light figures = estimated.

Circ.   Circ.   Circ.

EDUCATION (continued)

Little Falls
Curriculum Review **(19177)** ....‡2,200

Mahwah
Applied Measurement in Education **(19186)**
Mathematical Thinking and Learning **(19201)**

Medford
MultiMedia Schools **(19231)** 15,000

Monroe
Educational Viewpoints **(19238)**

New Brunswick
African Studies Review **(19324)**

Piscataway
Journal of Applied School
Psychology **(19428)** 800

Princeton
Academic Questions **(19451)** ....(Paid) ‡4,500

Trenton
NJEA Review **(19665)** ....(Paid) 148,000

NEW YORK
Albany
The New York Teacher **(20001)** ......(Paid) 337,000

Amityville
Journal of Drug Education **(20043)**
Journal of Educational Computing Research **(20044)**

Armonk
Chinese Education &
Society **(20069)** ....(Paid) ⊕151
European Education **(20077)** ....(Paid) ⊕169
Russian Education and
Society **(20093)** ....(Paid) ⊕211

Binghamton
Journal of Library & Information Services for Distance
Learning **(20187)**
Journal of Teaching in the Addictions **(20201)**
Journal of Teaching in Travel & Tourism **(20202)**

Bronx
Education Index **(20267)**

Buffalo
Child Study Journal **(20374)**

Canton
St. Lawrence **(20431)** ....(Controlled) ‡27,000

Flushing
Journal of Educational and Psychological
Consultation **(20609)**
Reading and Writing Quarterly: Overcoming Learning
Difficulties **(20611)**

Hauppauge
NAEB Journal **(20719)** ....(Paid) 2,600

Holbrook
Journal of Child-Care
Administration **(20749)** ....(Paid) 1,000

Long Island City
Community Review **(20963)**

Manhasset
Technology & Learning **(21014)** ....(Paid) 12,924
(Non-paid) 68,188

Monroe
Smith University Funding Report **(21090)**

New York
ADE Bulletin **(21149)** ....(Controlled) 2,000
American Artist **(21178)** ....(Paid) 180,471
Biomimetics **(21324)**
Children's Literature in Education **(21411)**
City Family **(21422)**
Education and Information Technologies **(21587)**
Education Update **(21588)** ....(Free) 60,000
English Digest **(21605)** ....(Controlled) 50,000
European Journal for Education Law and
Policy **(21642)**
Functional and Developmental Morphology **(21742)**
Innovative Higher Education **(21874)**
Instructional Science **(21882)**
International Journal for the Advancement of
Counseling **(21899)**
International Review of Education **(21935)**
Journal of Behavioral Education **(22006)**
Journal of Educational Change **(22056)**
Journal of Mathematics Teacher Education **(22129)**
Journal of Medical Humanities **(22130)**

Journal of Personnel Evaluation in
Education **(22155)**
Journal of Science Teacher Education **(22183)**
Journal of Teaching in Social
Work **(22202)** ....(Controlled) 327
Kidpreneurs News **(22220)** ....(Combined) 5,200
La Familia de la Ciudad **(22227)**
Music Alive! **(22384)**
Nursing Education
Perspectives **(22473)** ....(Paid) 3,000
(Controlled) 12,000
P S C Clarion **(22516)**
Reading and Writing **(22628)**
Research in Higher Education **(22648)**
School Library Journal **(22710)** ....(Paid) 38,021
Science & Education **(22712)**
Special Education Report **(22771)**
Student Aid News **(22798)**
Teachers College Record **(22817)** ......(Paid) ‡3,500
(Non-paid) ‡300
Teenpreur **(22819)** ....(Combined) 8200
The Wall Street Journal—Classroom Edition **(22907)**

Rensselaerville
Innovating Magazine **(23182)** ....(Paid) ‡800
(Non-paid) ‡27

Stony Brook
Journal of Educational Technology Systems **(23370)**

Stuyvesant Falls
Academic Exchange
Quarterly **(23379)** ....(Paid) 2,500

Syracuse
Laubach Litscape **(23407)** ....(Paid) 60,000

Yonkers
Foreign Language Annals **(23599)** ....‡8,000

NORTH CAROLINA
Boone
Journal of Developmental
Education **(23653)** ....(Controlled) 3,500
The Physics Teacher **(23655)** 10,000

Chapel Hill
The High School Journal **(23708)** ....(Paid) 1,500
Journal of Early Intervention **(23711)** ....(Paid) 6,500
(Controlled) 10

Greensboro
Learning **(23926)** ....(Controlled) 150,000

Raleigh
Community College Review **(24133)** 1,350
1,200
Exceptionality **(24135)**
Tar Heel Junior
Historian **(24155)** ....(Non-paid) 9,000

NORTH DAKOTA
Bismarck
North Dakota Education
News **(24353)** ....(Non-paid) ‡8,500

Grand Forks
Teaching & Learning **(24457)**

Wahpeton
American Technical Education Association
Journal **(24547)**

OHIO
Bowling Green
Inquiry **(24692)**

Cincinnati
American Music Teacher **(24771)** .....(Paid) ‡24,000
(Free) ‡300
Teacher Education and Special
Education **(24821)** ....(Paid) 3,100
Teaching Theatre **(24822)** 4,000
Weekly Bible Reader **(24828)** ....‡104,000

Columbus
The Journal of Higher Education **(25024)** .....‡4,000
Journal of Music Teacher Education **(25026)**
Ohio Schools **(25049)** ....‡128,400
School Science and Mathematics **(25061)** .....‡3500
Theory into Practice **(25064)** ....(Paid) 1,500
(Non-paid) ‡200

Dayton
American Educational History
Journal **(25106)** ....(Paid) ‡110
College Planning and Management **(25111)**
School Planning and Management **(25125)**
Today's Catholic Teacher **(25127)** .....(Paid) ‡48,000
(Non-paid) ‡2,000

Oxford
Journal on Excellence in College
Teaching **(25456)** ....(Paid) 965
Teaching Philosophy **(25461)** ....(Paid) ‡1,110
(Non-paid) ‡47

Westerville
Middle School Journal **(25642)** ....(Paid) ‡33,000
(Controlled) ‡50

Worthington
The Book Report **(25678)** ....‡15,000
Library Talk **(25680)** 10,000

Youngstown
Contributions to Music
Education **(25696)** ....(Paid) 400

OKLAHOMA
Lawton
Choral Journal **(25885)** ....‡18,500

Norman
Journal of Music Theory
Pedagogy **(25936)** ....(Paid) 500
The Rural Educator Journal **(25942)** .....(Paid) 1,200

Oklahoma City
Focus on Members **(25964)** ....‡25,000

OREGON
Eugene
Journal of Research on Technology in
Education **(26319)**
Learning and Leading with
Technology **(26322)** ....(Paid) ‡10,000
(Free) ‡2,000

Portland
Today's OEA **(26512)**

PENNSYLVANIA
Bethlehem
Journal of Career Planning &
Employment **(26701)** 4,237

Camp Hill
Journal of Educational
Relations **(26752)** ....(Paid) ‡800

Harrisburg
The VOICE for Education **(27014)** ....‡140,000

Horsham
Counterpoint **(27057)** ....(Paid) 100,000
Early Childhood Law and Policy Reporter **(27059)**

King of Prussia
ADVANCE for Occupational Therapy
Practitioners **(27117)** ....(Non-paid) ‡60,000

Kutztown
School Arts Magazine **(27131)** ....(Paid) 23,829
(Non-paid) 441

Middletown
Journal of Teaching in International
Business **(27259)** 245

New Cumberland
PSBA Bulletin **(27319)** ....‡13,400

Philadelphia
Communication Monographs **(27423)** ....‡4,000
History of Education **(27482)**
International Journal of Lifelong Education **(27500)**
International Journal of Mathematical Education in
Science and Technology **(27501)**
International Journal of Science Education **(27508)**
Journal of Curriculum Studies **(27523)**
Journal of Education Policy **(27526)**
Maritime Policy & Management **(27561)**
Media and Methods Magazine **(27563)** 72,000
Nurse Educator **(27587)** ....(Paid) 2,950
Word & Image **(27721)**

Pittsburgh
Resources in Education **(27840)**

University Park
Art Education **(28070)** ....(Paid) ‡18,000
(Non-paid) ‡63
Journal of General Education **(28078)** ....‡1300
Research/Penn State **(28083)** .....(Controlled) 25,000

West Chester
College Literature **(28145)** ....(Combined) 700

SOUTH CAROLINA
Charleston
Assessment for Effective
Information **(28505)** 1,700

Clinton
Presbyterian College
Magazine **(28540)** ....(Non-paid) 14,000

Columbia
Programming Magazine **(28563)** ....(Paid) 5,000

Orangeburg
Psychology and Education **(28732)**

SOUTH DAKOTA
Lennox
Reclaiming Children and Youth **(28885)**

TENNESSEE
Knoxville
Journal for the Education of the
Gifted **(29275)** ....(Paid) 2,600
(Non-paid) 65
Journal of Industrial Teacher Education **(29276)**
Journalism and Mass Communication
Educator **(29279)** ....‡3,718
Soundings **(29281)** ....‡1,700

Nashville
Cognition and Instruction **(29452)**
The Journal of Special
Education **(29465)** ....(Paid) ‡3,268
(Non-paid) ‡108
Leader in Christian Education
Ministries **(29467)** ....(Paid) 3,000
(Controlled) 1,000
Peabody Journal of Education **(29479)** ....‡1,000

TEXAS
Austin
Infancy **(29783)**
International Journal of Qualitative Studies in
Education **(29785)**
Social Studies and the Young
Learner **(29805)** ....(Paid) 6,000
The Southwestern Musician **(29808)** ....‡10,500
Texas Coach **(29814)** ....(Paid) ‡16,000
(Non-paid) ‡253
Texas Lone Star **(29834)** ....(Combined) 11,000
TSTA Advocate **(29852)** 90,000

College Station
Reading Psychology **(30048)**

Dallas
Notes on Literacy **(30172)** ....‡500

Denton
Community/Junior College Journal of Research and
Practice **(30234)** ....(Paid) ‡440
(Non-paid) ‡63
Educational Gerontology **(30236)**

Marathon
The Five Owls **(30758)** ....(Paid) 1,500
(Non-paid) 2,000

San Antonio
Journal of Dental
Education **(31033)** ....(Paid) ‡3,900
(Controlled) ‡195
Journal of Language, Identity, and
Education **(31034)**

San Marcos
CALICO **(31083)** ....‡1,020

UTAH
Murray
UEA Action **(31374)** ....(Paid) ‡18,800
(Controlled) ‡917

VERMONT
Brandon
Paths of Learning **(31507)** ....(Paid) 800

Montpelier
Vermont-NEA Today **(31566)** ....‡8,800

VIRGINIA
Alexandria
The American School Board
Journal **(31637)** ....(Paid) ‡36,064
Career Development
Quarterly **(31651)** ....(Paid) ‡5,500
(Non-paid) ‡70
Children and Families **(31654)** ....(Paid) 17,000

Counseling Today **(31661)** ....(Paid) ‡56,000
(Free) ‡59
Counselor Education and
Supervision **(31663)** ....(Paid) 3,500
Educational Leadership **(31669)** ....‡180,000
INFO-LINE **(31683)** 4,200
Journal of Counseling and
Development **(31692)** ....(Paid) 59,000
Journal of Humanistic Counseling &
Development **(31698)** ....(Paid) ‡1,700
Journal of Multicultural Counseling and
Development **(31699)** ....(Paid) ‡3,000
Journal of Social Work Education **(31702)**
Journal of Statistics
Education **(31703)** ....(Non-paid) 2,230
Measurement and Evaluation in Counseling and
Development **(31708)** ....(Paid) 1,900
Principal **(31725)** ....‡30,000
Professional School Counseling **(31729)** .....‡15,500
TESOL Journal **(31742)** ....(Combined) 15,000
TESOL Quarterly **(31743)** ....‡10,000

Arlington
Exceptional Child Education
Resources **(31790)** ....(Paid) ‡643
(Non-paid) ‡2
Exceptional Children **(31791)** ....‡59,244
Journal of College Science
Teaching **(31801)** ....(Paid) ‡5,200
(Non-paid) ‡500
NSTA Reports! **(31815)** ....(Paid) 53,000
Physical Disabilities—Education & Related
Services **(31817)** ....(Non-paid) 1,300
Quantum **(31822)**
The School Administrator **(31827)** ......(Paid) 14,500
Science Scope **(31828)** ....(Paid) ‡15,000
(Non-paid) ‡26,000
The Science Teacher **(31829)** ....‡27,000

Charlottesville
College Services **(31925)** ....(Controlled) 2,850
Questions **(31939)**

Fairfax
Black Issues in Higher Education **(32009)**
Intervention in School and
Clinic **(32017)** ....(Paid) 3,000

Lynchburg
Remedial and Special Education
(RASE) **(32209)** ....(Paid) 2,587
(Non-paid) 97

Norfolk
Information Technology in Childhood Education
Annual **(32283)**
International Journal of Educational
Telecommunications **(32284)**
Journal of Educational Multimedia and
Hypermedia **(32285)** ....(Paid) ‡1,000
Journal of Interactive Learning Research **(32288)**
Journal of Technology & Teacher
Education **(32289)** ....(Paid) ‡650

Radford
National Honors Report **(32345)** ....(Paid) 1,300

Reston
AAHPERD Update **(32354)** ....(Paid) 24,165
The American Biology
Teacher **(32359)** ....(Paid) ‡11,000
(Controlled) ‡100
Business Education Forum **(32362)** ....‡15,873
Journal of Health Education **(32381)** ....‡10,000
Journal of Physical Education, Recreation & Dance
(JOPERD) **(32390)** ....(Paid) 20,000
Journal for Research in Mathematics
Education **(32393)** ....‡11,844
Journal of Research in Music Education **(32394)**
The Mathematics Teacher **(32403)** ......(Paid) 49,000
Mathematics-Teaching in the Middle
School **(32404)** ....(Paid) 36,000
Music Educators Journal **(32405)** ......(Paid) ‡80,000
NASSP Bulletin **(32406)** ....‡37,500
Strategies **(32415)** ....‡10,000
Strategies **(32416)** 7,460
Teaching Children Mathematics **(32417)** 48,000
Teaching Music **(32418)** ....(Paid) 80,000
Technology and Children **(32419)**
The Technology Teacher **(32420)** ....‡5,000
Update: Applications of Research in Music
Education **(32422)**

Richmond
Virginia Journal of Education **(32463)** ....‡58,000

Williamsburg
Al-Arabiyya **(32612)**

Journal of Psychoeducational
Assessment **(32618)** ....(Paid) ‡865
(Controlled) ‡74

WASHINGTON
Edmonds
Voice of Washington Music
Educators **(32747)** ....(Controlled) 1,500

Federal Way
WEA Action **(32765)** ....(Paid) 74,000

Pullman
International Education Forum **(32904)**

Seabeck
Video Librarian **(32936)** ....(Paid) 2,000
(Non-paid) 100

Seattle
Teacher Librarian **(33034)** ....(Combined) 9,700

Tonasket
Home Education
Magazine **(33165)** ....(Paid) ‡12,700
(Non-paid) ‡12,400

Walla Walla
Whitman Academic Journal **(33189)**

WEST VIRGINIA
Morgantown
Rural Special Education
Quarterly **(33396)** ....(Paid) 370

WISCONSIN
Eau Claire
Computer Science Education **(33667)** ....‡500
Feminist Teacher **(33669)** ....(Paid) 900

Edgerton
Career Directions **(33686)** ....(Non-paid) ‡70,000

Madison
Monatshefte **(33963)** ....‡1,000

Milwaukee
Education Administration
Quarterly **(34066)** ....(Paid) 1,751
(Non-paid) 81
Rethinking Schools **(34097)** ....(Paid) ‡7,000
(Non-paid) ‡25,000

River Falls
Argumentation and
Advocacy **(34306)** ....(Paid) 1,000
LERN Magazine **(34307)**

ALBERTA, CANADA
Edmonton
The Alberta Journal of Educational
Research **(34699)** ....‡450
The ATA Magazine **(34701)** ....‡42,000
Journal of Distance
Education **(34718)** ....(Controlled) 700
Past Imperfect **(34723)** ....(Paid) 75

BRITISH COLUMBIA, CANADA
Burnaby
Educational Psychologist **(34897)**

Prince George
Journal of College Reading and Learning **(35056)**

Vancouver
International Journal of Testing **(35150)**

MANITOBA, CANADA
Winnipeg
English Quarterly **(35327)** ....(Paid) 450

NEWFOUNDLAND AND LABRADOR, CANADA
Pouch Cove
Resource Links **(35481)**

St. John's
Newfoundland Studies **(35492)** ....(Controlled) 300

NOVA SCOTIA, CANADA
Dartmouth
Kodaly Society of Canada, Alla
Breve **(35548)** ....(Paid) 400

Halifax
Dalhousie Alumni
Magazine **(35564)** ....(Controlled) 46,000

ONTARIO, CANADA
Belleville
The Canadian **(35676)** ....‡1,000

Circulation: ★ = ABC; △ = BPA; ♦ = CAC; • = CCAB; ❑ = VAC; ⊕ = PO Statement; ‡ = Publisher's Report; Boldface figures = sworn; Light figures = estimated.

3135

Trade, Technical, and Professional Publications

Circ.   Circ.   Circ.

EDUCATION (continued)

London
Journal of Systemic
    Therapies **(35985)** ....(Paid) ‡2,500
Ontario Mathematics
    Gazette **(35991)** ....(Paid) 1,200

Mississauga
School Business
    Magazine **(36086)** ...:...........(Controlled) ‡10,000

Ottawa
Caravan **(36231)** ....(Paid) ‡1,000
                                        (Non-paid) ‡100
CAUT (ACPPU) Bulletin **(36232)** ....‡34,500
Crux Mathematicorum with Mathematical
    Mayhem **(36240)** 800
University Affairs (Affaires
    Universitaires) **(36278)** ....(Combined) 22,480

Toronto
Canadian Shareowner **(36530)** ....(Paid) ‡20,000
                                        (Non-paid) ‡200
Curriculum Inquiry **(36565)** 10,000
Education Canada **(36578)** ....(Paid) ‡3,500
                                        (Controlled) ‡250
Education Forum **(36579)** ....(Combined) 37,919
Education & Law Journal **(36580)**
Green Teacher **(36609)** ....(Controlled) 7,400
Kidsworld **(36643)** ....(Non-paid) 200,050
OTF (FEO)
    Interaction **(36692)** ....(Non-paid) ‡130,000
Professionally Speaking/Pour Parler
    Profession **(36717)** ....(Combined) 170,000
                                                        10,000
The Register **(36724)** ....(Combined) 5,000
TEACH Magazine **(36754)** ....(Paid) 1,100
                                        (Controlled) 22,000
Teaching Librarian **(36755)** ....(Paid) 1,374
University of Toronto
    Bulletin **(36778)** ....(Controlled) 14,051
University of Toronto
    Magazine **(36781)** ....(Controlled) 240,441

Waterloo
Chem 13 News **(36848)** ....(Paid) 4,000

PRINCE EDWARD ISLAND, CANADA
Charlottetown
Exceptionality Education Canada (EEC) **(36914)**

QUEBEC, CANADA
L'Ancienne-Lorett
Les Enseignants **(37032)** ....‡5,000

Montreal
Education Libraries **(37112)** ....(Combined) 400
L'Infomane **(37128)** 1,500
Journal CAJLE **(37137)**
Les Debrouillards **(37176)** ....(Controlled) 37,500
Quebec Home & School
    News **(37211)** ....(Paid) 5,850
                                        (Free) 1,550
Revue Canadienne de Psycho-Education **(37216)**
Universites **(37232)**

Quebec City
Recueil des Sentences de l'Education **(37305)**

SASKATCHEWAN, CANADA
Regina
School Trustee **(37534)**

ELECTRICAL ENGINEERING

**See also Electronics Engineering; Lighting;
Power and Power Plants; Radio, Television,
Cable, and Video; Telecommunications**

ARIZONA
Dewey
World Scanner Report **(684)** ....(Paid) 800
                                        (Non-paid) 50

CALIFORNIA
Arcadia
Electrical News **(1428)** ....(Paid) ‡1,100
                                        (Free) ‡41,000

La Jolla
IEEE Antennas &
    Propogation **(2113)** ....(Controlled) 10,400

San Diego
Graphical Models **(3163)**

COLORADO
Boulder
The Boulder County Business
    Report **(4157)** ....,.......(Paid) 10,000

Morrison
NETA World **(4587)** ....(Controlled) 6,000

FLORIDA
Largo
The Battery Man **(6299)** 4,100

GEORGIA
Atlanta
The Complete European Trade Digest Electrical
    Edition **(6989)**
The Complete European Trade Digest Machinery
    Edition **(6990)**
The Complete European Trade Digest Medical
    Edition **(6991)**
The Complete European Trade Digest Semiconductor
    Equipment & Materials Edition **(6992)**
EMC Test & Design **(7002)**

Norcross
Engineering Economist **(7459)**

ILLINOIS
Grayslake
Connector Specifier **(8953)** ......(Controlled) △35,013

Northbrook
Semiconductor
    Magazine **(9322)** ....(Non-paid) 43,000

Oak Brook
Semiconductor International **(9365)** ......(Paid) 1,015
                                        (Non-paid) 45,541

KANSAS
Overland Park
CEE News **(11703)** ....(Controlled) ‡105,221
Electrical Construction and Maintenance
    (EC&M) **(11708)** ....(Controlled) 102,521
                                                (Paid) 1,214
Electrical Wholesaling **(11709)** ....(Paid) 12,515
                                        (Non-paid) 12,471

MARYLAND
Bethesda
Electrical Contractor **(13332)** .....(Non-paid) △87,000

MASSACHUSETTS
Cambridge
NBER Reporter **(14083)**

Newton
EDN Europe **(14390)**
Electronic Business Asia **(14395)**

MISSOURI
St. Louis
TED The Electrical Distributor
    Magazine **(17521)** ....(Combined) △30,160

NEW JERSEY
Hoboken
Electrical Engineering in Japan **(18936)**
Engineering Design and Automation **(18939)** 5985
International Journal of Circuit Theory and
    Applications **(18978)**
International Journal of Energy Research **(18982)**
Optimal Control Applications and Methods **(19077)**
Progress in Photovoltaics **(19087)** ......(Paid) 17,500

Piscataway
IEEE Electrical Insulation
    Magazine **(19423)** ....(Paid) 8,000
                                        (Non-paid) 1,000
IEEE Industry Applications
    Magazine **(19425)** ....(Paid) 12,000
IEEE Transactions on Components, Packaging &
    Manufacturing Technology, Part B **(19426)**
IEEE Transactions on Components, Packaging &
    Manufacturing Technology, Part C **(19427)**

River Edge
International Journal of High Speed
    Electronics **(19509)** ....(Paid) 200
                                        (Non-paid) 100

NEW YORK
Manhasset
Printed Circuit Fabrication **(21011)**

New York
Consulting-Specifying
    Engineer **(21490)** ....(Controlled) ‡47,508

IEEE Network **(21846)** ....(Paid) 12,385
                                        (Non-paid) 82
IEEE Potentials **(21847)** ....(Paid) 48,252
                                        (Non-paid) 866
International Private Power Quarterly **(21931)**
Journal of Electronic Testing **(22059)**
Journal of VLSI Signal Processing-Systems for
    Signal, Image, and Video Technology **(22213)**

OHIO
Cleveland
EE Product News **(24888)** 116,000
Energy Journal **(24893)** ....(Controlled) 4,000

PENNSYLVANIA
Philadelphia
International Journal of Control **(27496)**
International Journal of Optoelectronics **(27502)**

TEXAS
Richardson
IAEI News **(30974)** ....‡24,000

VIRGINIA
Arlington
Management Quarterly **(31806)**

Falls Church
Dealerscope: The Business of CE Retailing **(32043)**

Reston
Journal of Energy Engineering **(32376)**

Rosslyn
Electrical Standards and Product
    Guide **(32514)** ....(Non-paid) ‡26,000
ElectroIndustry (ei) **(32515)** ....(Non-paid) 26,000

WYOMING
Laramie
Energy Sources **(34548)** ....(Controlled) ‡345

ALBERTA, CANADA
Calgary
International Journal of Power and Energy
    Systems **(34648)**

ONTARIO, CANADA
Ajax
Electricity Today **(35627)** ....(Non-paid) 12,000
                                        (Paid) 37

Mississauga
Electrical Business **(36064)** ......(Combined) •18,028

QUEBEC, CANADA
Montreal
Electricite Quebec **(37113)** ....(Controlled) 9,670

ELECTRONICS ENGINEERING

See also Electrical Engineering; Computers

CALIFORNIA
Carlsbad
Fiber and Integrated Optics **(1664)** ....‡443

Los Alamitos
IEEE Multimedia **(2188)**

San Diego
Digital Signal Processing **(3142)**

COLORADO
Highlands Ranch
CED (Communications Engineering &
    Design) **(4516)** ....(Non-paid) ‡22,500

CONNECTICUT
Wilton
EMedia Magazine **(5227)**

FLORIDA
Hollywood
Electronic Commerce
    World **(6193)** ....(Paid) ‡44,000

Nokomis
EE Evaluation
    Engineering **(6463)** ....(Non-paid) ‡76,049

GEORGIA
Atlanta
Circuits Assembly **(6984)** ....(Combined) ‡42,371
PC Fab **(7035)** 37,000

ILLINOIS
Bensenville
Assembly (8064) ....(Controlled) ‡60,000

Chicago
Electrical Apparatus (8363) ....(Paid) 873
(Controlled) 15,183
Electromagnetics (8364) ....(Combined) ‡361

Grayslake
Connector Specifier (8953) ....(Controlled) △35,013
SMT (8959) ....(Controlled) 46,017

Northbrook
Semiconductor
Magazine (9322) ....(Non-paid) 43,000

Rolling Meadows
Journal of The Institute of Environmental Sciences
and Technology (9548) ....‡5,000

KANSAS
Overland Park
Electrical Construction and Maintenance
(EC&M) (11708) ....(Controlled) 102,521
(Paid) 1,214
PCIM Power Electronic Systems (11725)
RF Design (11729) ....(Paid) 200
(Non-paid) 40,000
Seguridad Latina (11730) ....(Combined) 16,000

MARYLAND
Bethesda
Electronics & Communications Abstracts
Journal (13333)

College Park
IEEE Transactions on Components, Packaging &
Manufacturing Technology, Part A (13420)

Columbia
IEEE Circuits and Devices (13462) ......(Paid) 7,500

Potomac
Avionics Magazine (13647) ....(Controlled) 21,300

MASSACHUSETTS
Brookline
IEEE Transactions on Automatic Control (14020)

Cambridge
R.L.E. Currents (14099) ....(Non-paid) ‡4,000

Framingham
EOS/ESD Technology (14195) ....(Non-paid) ‡31,000

Newton
EDN China (14389) ....(Controlled) 20,400
EDN Europe (14390)
EDN Magazine
Edition (14391) ....(Non-paid) 161,523
(Paid) 3,131
EDN Products and
Careers (14392) ....(Controlled) ‡131,000
Electronic Business (14394) ....(Combined) ‡52,000
Electronic Business Asia (14395)
Test & Measurement
World (14412) ....(Controlled) ‡65,000

Norwood
Journal of Electronic
Defense (14447) ..:.............(Paid) ‡15,084
Microwave Journal (14450) ....(Paid) 869
(Controlled) 53,681

Wayland
Popular Home Automation (14615) ....(Paid) ‡19,889

MICHIGAN
Troy
Security Distributing & Marketing
(SDM) (15639) ....(Combined) ‡28,003

MINNESOTA
St. Paul
Powder and Bulk
Engineering (16407) ....(Free) ‡35,005

MISSOURI
Independence
Avionics News (17107) ....(Non-paid) 7,200

NEVADA
Carson City
MOTION (18327) ....(Non-paid) 33,000

NEW HAMPSHIRE
Nashua
Advanced
Packaging (18581) ....(Controlled) △26,523
Computer Design (18587) ....(Non-paid) ‡113,000
Industrial Laser Solutions (18591) .....(Paid) ‡12,505
Integrated Communications
Design (18593) ....‡23,406
Laser Focus World (18594) ....‡69,203
Lightwave (18595) 37,000
Microlithography World (18596) ....(Paid) ‡4,000
Military & Aerospace
Electronics (18597) ....(Paid) 200
(Controlled) 48,000
Solid State
Technology (18600) ....(Non-paid) ‡44,050

Peterborough
audioXpress (18617) ....(Paid) 15,000

NEW JERSEY
Hoboken
Electronics and Communications in
Japan (18937) 425
Engineering Design and Automation (18939) ...5985
International Journal of Adaptive Control and Signal
Processing (18975)
International Journal of Circuit Theory and
Applications (18978)
International Journal of Numerical Modelling (18992)
Journal of Software Maintenance (19048)
Quality and Reliability Engineering
International (19093)
Scientific Programming (19102) 3850

Medford
STAR TECH Journal (19233) ....‡2,500

Morris Plains
Lasers & Optronics (19296) 60,000
(Controlled) 50,069

Paramus
Electronic Design (19402) ....(Non-paid) ‡165,000

Pennington
The Electrochemical Society
Interface (19420) ....(Paid) 8,500

Piscataway
IEEE Engineering in Medicine and Biology
Magazine (19424) ....(Paid) ‡8,779
IEEE Industry Applications
Magazine (19425) ....(Paid) 12,000
IEEE Transactions on Components, Packaging &
Manufacturing Technology, Part B (19426)
IEEE Transactions on Components, Packaging &
Manufacturing Technology, Part C (19427)

Sparta
Printed Circuit Network (19593) 12,500

NEW YORK
Garden City
Electronic Products (20638) ....(Controlled) ‡123,788

Hauppauge
Electronics Now (20717) ....(Paid) 76,889
Poptronics (20722) ....(Paid) 71,253

Manhasset
EBN (20998) ....(Non-paid) ‡57,100
Electronic Engineering
Times (20999) ....(Free) ‡127,087
Printed Circuit Design &
Manufacture (21010) ....(Paid) 246
(Controlled) 25,111
Printed Circuit Fabrication (21011)

Melville
Advanced Imaging (21039) ......(Controlled) ‡55,009

New York
AES Daily (21159)
Design Automation of Electronic Systems
(TODAES) (21545)
Design Automation for Embedded Systems (21546)
ECN (Electronic Component
News) (21580) ....(Controlled) ‡143,050
Electronic Packaging &
Production (21593) ....(Controlled) ‡42,000
IEEE Aerospace and Electronic Systems
Magazine (21843) ....(Paid) ‡11,500
(Non-paid) ‡500
IEEE Computational Science and
Engineering (21845)
IEEE Network (21846) ....(Paid) 12,385
(Non-paid) 82
IEEE Signal Processing Letters (21848)

IEEE Transactions on Industrial
Electronics (21850) ....(Paid) 6,000
Information Display (21869) ....(Paid) ‡3,000
(Non-paid) ‡10,000
Journal of Electronic Testing (22059)
Journal of Microelectronic Systems
Integration (22133)
Personal Communications Magazine (22543)
Radiophysics and Quantum Electronics (22623)
Russian Microelectronics (22696)
STACKS (22781)

Port Washington
Electronic Servicing & Technology (23126) 12,000
EQ (23127) ....(Paid) 13,197
(Non-paid) 24,945
Micro Computer Journal (23130) ....‡50,000

White Plains
Tape/Disc Business (23575) ....(Paid) 400
(Non-paid) 11,600

NORTH CAROLINA
Raleigh
Robotics & Automation
Magazine (24152) ....(Paid) ‡7,500

OHIO
Cleveland
EE Product News (24888) 116,000
The Electron (24889) ....‡25,000

PENNSYLVANIA
Philadelphia
Electric Machines Components and
Systems (27456) ....(Combined) ‡376
International Journal of Control (27496)
International Journal of Electronics (27497)
International Journal of Optoelectronics (27502)

Valley Forge
U.S. Tech (28092) 40,000

West Conshohocken
Item-Interference Technology Engineers
Master (28150) ....(Non-paid) 25,000

TEXAS
College Station
Electronic Imaging (30040)

VIRGINIA
Arlington
Management Quarterly (31806)

Fairfax
SIGNAL (32029) ....(Paid) △26,483
(Non-paid) △2,046

Falls Church
Dealerscope: The Business of CE Retailing (32043)

ONTARIO, CANADA
Markham
Canadian Electronics (36016) ....(Combined) •22,120

Mississauga
EP&T (Electronic Products and
Technology) (36066) ....(Controlled) •24,108

North York
Marketnews (36130) ....(Combined) •10,538

QUEBEC, CANADA
Montreal
Electronique Industrielle et Commerciale
(EIC) (37114) ....(Controlled) 9,202

EMPLOYMENT AND HUMAN RESOURCES

See also Labor

CALIFORNIA
Berkeley
California Public Employee Relations (1505)

Costa Mesa
Workforce (1783) ....‡32,000

Los Angeles
Current Employment (2249) ....(Paid) 120,000

Marina del Rey
HR/PC (2508)

San Francisco
Advances in Developing Human Resources (3324)

Circulation: ★ = ABC; △ = BPA; ♦ = CAC; • = CCAB; ❏ = VAC; ⊕ = PO Statement; ‡ = Publisher's Report; Boldface figures = sworn; Light figures = estimated.

3137

Trade, Technical, and Professional Publications

Circ.   Circ.   Circ.

EMPLOYMENT AND HUMAN RESOURCES
(continued)

Human Resource Development
    Quarterly **(3373)** 17,000

Santa Clara
High Technology Careers
    Magazine **(3671)** ....(Non-paid) ‡166,500

Thousand Oaks
Human Resources Abstracts **(3873)** ......(Paid) ‡500
Work and Occupations **(3921)** ....(Paid) ‡700

Van Nuys
Entertainment Employment Journal **(3989)**

Winchester
Hispanic Times Magazine **(4093)** ....(Paid) ‡628
                                     (Controlled) ‡60,000

DISTRICT OF COLUMBIA
Washington
Air Jobs Digest **(5317)** ....(Combined) 40,000
EBRI Issue Brief **(5469)**
EBRI Quarterly Pension Investment
    Report **(5470)** ....‡350
Employee Benefit Notes **(5477)**
Mobility **(5655)** ....(Paid) ‡11,970
                                     (Non-paid) ‡498
Occupational Outlook
    Quarterly **(5698)** ....(Paid) ⊕15,500
The Public Employee
    Magazine **(5749)** ....‡1,400,000
Quarterly Labour Force Statistics **(5755)**

FLORIDA
Tallahassee
Review of Public Personnel
    Administration **(6733)** ....(Paid) 863
                                     (Non-paid) 60

GEORGIA
Atlanta
PENSION
    Management **(7037)** ....(Combined) 28,927

ILLINOIS
Champaign
Perspectives on Work **(8211)**

Chicago
Employee Benefit Plan
    Review **(8368)** ....(Paid) 2,624
                                     (Non-paid) 19,236
IHRIM Journal **(8405)**
IHRIM.link **(8406)**
IHRIM.Wire **(8407)**

Evanston
Graduating Engineer & Computer
    Careers **(8860)** ....(Non-paid) 65,000

Oak Brook
Employee Services
    Management **(9351)** ....(Paid) ‡4,000
                                     (Non-paid) ‡600

Riverwoods
Pension Plan Guide **(9507)** ....‡5,000

KENTUCKY
Louisville
Unique Opportunities **(12242)** .....(Controlled) 80,000

MASSACHUSETTS
Andover
Work **(13814)**

Cambridge
Training Media Review **(14108)**

Cummaquid
TIE (The International Educator) **(14151)** 14,000

Waltham
Careers and the Technology
    Undergrad **(14598)** ....(Non-paid) 30,000

MICHIGAN
Troy
EAP Digest **(15621)** ....(Paid) ‡3,000
                                     (Controlled) ‡7,000

MISSOURI
Aurora
The NADE Advocate **(16895)** ....(Paid) ‡2,500
                                     (Non-paid) ‡100

St. Louis
Affirmative Action Register **(17405)** ....(Paid) ‡950
                                     (Controlled) ‡62,500
Employment
    Marketplace **(17436)** ....(Controlled) 18,000

NEW HAMPSHIRE
Charlestown
Earth Work **(18464)** .:......................(Paid) 3,500

NEW JERSEY
Englewood
Employment Opportunities (Englewood) **(18795)**

Hoboken
Employment Relations Today **(18938)** 5985
Human Factors in Ergonomics and
    Manufacturing **(18966)** ....(Combined) 3,325
Human Resource Management **(18969)** 5950
Journal of Organizational
    Excellence **(19038)** 5985

Montvale
JobWatch **(19259)**
Nursing Opportunities **(19267)**

NEW YORK
Albany
Employment Review **(19984)** ....(Non-paid) ‡600

Armonk
Working USA **(20101)** ....(Paid) 1,271

Binghamton
Journal of Human Resources in Hospitality &
    Tourism **(20182)**

Great Neck
Making It! Careers
    Newsmagazine **(20692)** ....(Paid) 5,000
                                     (Non-paid) 45,000

Melville
Workforce Diversity **(21066)** ....(Non-paid) 52,608

New York
Academic Physician & Scientist **(21132)**
Benefits Law Journal **(21295)** 5,985
Compensation & Benefits
    Review **(21467)** ....(Paid) 3000
                                     (Non-paid) 800
Employee Benefit
    News **(21600)** ....(Combined) ‡61,000
Employee Benefits Report **(21601)**
Employee Relations Law Journal **(21602)** 5985
Employee Responsibilities and Rights
    Journal **(21603)**
HR Executive Review **(21825)**
Human Resource Planning **(21833)**
Journal of Compensation and
    Benefits **(22033)** ....(Paid) 2816
                                     (Non-paid) 1509
Journal of Occupational Rehabilitation **(22148)**

OHIO
Bowling Green
Personnel Psychology **(24698)** ....(Paid) 2,300

Cleveland
SERB Official Reporter **(24953)**

PENNSYLVANIA
Bethlehem
Journal of Career Planning &
    Employment **(26701)** 4,237

Horsham
Human Resource Executive **(27061)** .....(Paid) 7,049
                                     (Controlled) 52,981

Pittsburgh
Employment and Earnings **(27784)**

TEXAS
Irving
The Journal of African Human Resources and
    Business Issues **(30605)**

UTAH
South Jordan
Classical Singer
    Magazine **(31472)** ....(Combined) 4000

VERMONT
Bennington
Transitions Abroad **(31495)** ....(Paid) ‡18,000

VIRGINIA
Alexandria
Career Development
    Quarterly **(31651)** ....(Paid) ‡5,500
                                     (Non-paid) ‡70
Counseling Today **(31661)** ....(Paid) ‡56,000
                                     (Free) ‡59
HR News **(31680)** ....(Paid) 170,000
HRMagazine **(31681)** 78,446
Journal of Employment
    Counseling **(31694)** ....(Paid) ‡1,400
                                     (Non-paid) ‡60
NSBE Magazine **(31716)** ....(Paid) ‡8,000
                                     (Non-paid) ‡14,934
Public Personnel Management **(31732)** ....‡7,000
T+D Magazine **(31740)** ....(Paid) 35,229
                                     (Non-paid) 82

Norfolk
Profile (Norfolk) **(32292)** ....(Non-paid) 30,000

WISCONSIN
Brookfield
Benefits Quarterly **(33603)** ....(Paid) ‡2,800
                                     (Non-paid) ‡14,800
Employee Benefits Journal **(33605)** .....(Paid) ‡1,200
                                     (Non-paid) ‡37,000

Milwaukee
National Ad Search **(34090)**

ONTARIO, CANADA
Mississauga
The Classified News **(36063)** ....(Free) 174,000

Toronto
Benefits Canada **(36474)** ....(Combined) •17,212
Canadian HR Reporter **(36504)** ....(Paid) ‡5,088
                                     (Non-paid) ‡4,646

QUEBEC, CANADA
Quebec
Revue Relations Industrielles/Industrial
    Relations **(37296)** ....(Paid) 1,500
                                     (Non-paid) 150

ENGINEERING (VARIOUS BRANCHES)

**See also Chemistry, Chemicals, and
Chemical Engineering; Electrical
Engineering; Electronics Engineering;
Nuclear Engineering**

ALABAMA
Auburn
Noise Control Engineer
    Journal **(43)** ....(Paid) ‡2,000
                                     (Controlled) ‡100

Birmingham
Russian Journal of Mathematical
    Physics **(89)** 5985

CALIFORNIA
Berkeley
California Engineer **(1501)** ....(Controlled) ‡10,000
Experimental Heat Transfer **(1520)** ....(Paid) ‡267
Probability in the Engineering and Informational
    Sciences **(1552)** 350

Covina
SAMPE Journal **(1786)** ....(Paid) ‡5,000

Cupertino
International Journal of Offshore and Polar
    Engineering **(1797)** ....(Combined) 1400

Davis
Mechanics of Structures and Machines **(1816)**

Downey
ECA Magazine **(1835)** ....(Non-paid) ‡1,800

Los Alamitos
Computing in Science & Engineering **(2182)**

Los Angeles
Earth **(2256)** ....(Controlled) ‡6,000
Journal of Materials Engineering and
    Performance **(2303)** ....(Paid) ⊕541
                                     (Non-paid) ⊕141

Oakland
TEST Engineering &
    Management **(2700)** ....(Non-paid) ‡8,772

Orinda
Tradeline's Exclusive Reports Online **(2727)** 7,000

Riverside
California Builder &
  Engineer **(2933)** ....(Controlled) ‡11,281

San Diego
Applied and Computational Harmonic Analysis **(3115)**
Journal of Colloid and Interface Science **(3181)**
Optical Fiber Technology **(3244)**
Quality Assurance **(3251)**

Santa Clara
High Technology Careers
  Magazine **(3671)** ....(Non-paid) ‡166,500

Santa Monica
Human Factors **(3711)** ....(Combined) 6,300

Santa Rosa
The California Surveyor **(3724)** ....(Non-paid) ‡5,000

Thousand Oaks
Public Works Management &
  Policy **(3910)** ....(Paid) 4,000

Torrance
Right of Way **(3941)** ....‡9,000

COLORADO
Boulder
Colorado Engineer **(4162)** ....(Non-paid) ‡5,000
                               (Non-paid) ‡5,000

Denver
Technometrics **(4362)** ....(Combined) ⊕6,377

Englewood
www.industry.net **(4417)** ....(Non-paid) 500,000

Golden
Mines Magazine **(4470)** ....‡20,000

Littleton
Mining Engineering **(4553)** ....(Paid) 17,057

Wheat Ridge
High-Performance
  Composites **(4676)** ....(Controlled) ‡20,000

CONNECTICUT
Bethel
Experimental Mechanics **(4697)** 4,500
Experimental Techniques **(4698)** ....‡4,380

Brookfield
Plastics Engineering **(4727)** 32,035
Polymer Engineering and Science **(4728)** 1,400

Southport
Gas Turbine World **(5136)** ....(Paid) 910
                               (Controlled) 9,666

DISTRICT OF COLUMBIA
Washington
ASEE Prism **(5364)** ....‡12,000
The Bridge **(5383)**
Engineers **(5479)** ....(Controlled) 1,200
Navy Civil Engineer **(5690)** ....(Paid) ‡200
                               (Non-paid) ‡16,000
Today's Engineer **(5824)** ....(Combined) 5,000

FLORIDA
Gainesville
Professional Ethics **(6153)** ....(Paid) 700

Orlando
The Journal of Human Performance in Extreme
  Environments **(6499)** ....(Paid) 200

Tallahassee
Florida Engineering Society
  Journal **(6710)** ....(Paid) ‡4,500

Tampa
Pharmaceutical Engineering **(6776)** .....(Paid) 17,500

GEORGIA
Alpharetta
CE News **(6918)** ....(Controlled) 49,610
Structural Engineer **(6919)** ....(Non-paid) 34,000

Atlanta
The Complete European Trade Digest Electrical
  Edition **(6989)**
The Complete European Trade Digest Machinery
  Edition **(6990)**
The Complete European Trade Digest Medical
  Edition **(6991)**

The Complete European Trade Digest Semiconductor
  Equipment & Materials Edition **(6992)**
International Journal of Heating, Ventilating, Air-
  Conditioning and Refrigeration Research (HVAC &
  R Research) **(7018)**

Flowery Branch
Certified Engineering
  Technician **(7273)** ....(Controlled) 2,000

Lilburn
Cogeneration and Competitive Power
  Journal **(7372)** ....(Paid) 2,200
Energy Engineering **(7373)** ....(Paid) 9,000
Strategic Planning for Energy and the
  Environment **(7374)** ....(Paid) 8,600

Norcross
IIE Solutions **(7462)** ....(Paid) 17,000
IIE Transactions on Design &
  Manufacturing **(7463)** ....(Paid) 2,500
IIE Transactions on Operations Engineering **(7464)**
IIE Transactions on Scheduling &
  Logistics **(7465)** ....(Paid) 2,500

ILLINOIS
Bensenville
Assembly **(8064)** ....(Controlled) ‡60,000

Champaign
Illinois Technograph **(8189)** ....(Paid) ‡800
                               (Non-paid) ‡4,000

Chicago
Engineering Journal **(8369)** ....‡6,500
Midwest Engineer **(8489)** ....‡1,000
Numerical Heat Transfer, Part A:
  Applications **(8515)** ....‡586
PCI Journal **(8527)** ....(Paid) ‡6,131
                               (Non-paid) ‡500
SWE **(8579)** ....‡15,000

Des Plaines
Water Engineering &
  Management **(8773)** ....(Paid) 3,648
                               (Non-paid) 37,442

Dorsey
Weight Engineering **(8779)** ....(Controlled) ‡1,000

Elk Grove Village
Gear Technology **(8832)** ....(Paid) 500
                               (Controlled) 9,000
                               3,000

Evanston
Graduating Engineer & Computer
  Careers **(8860)** ....(Non-paid) 65,000
IIE Transactions **(8862)** ....(Paid) 1,000

Itasca
Plant Services **(9015)** ....(Controlled) ‡110,000

Northbrook
Plumbing Engineer **(9320)** ....(Free) ‡25,600

Park Ridge
Lubrication Engineering **(9406)** ....(Paid) ‡7,000

Rosemont
Die Casting Engineer **(9555)** ....(Paid) ‡3,400
                               (Non-paid) ‡350

Springfield
Illinois Engineer **(9624)** ....(Paid) 3,200
                               (Non-paid) 100

INDIANA
Notre Dame
Notre Dame Technical Review **(10374)** 1,700

West Lafayette
Engineering Design Graphics
  Journal **(10546)** ....(Controlled) 575

KANSAS
Manhattan
Kansas State Engineer **(11627)** ....(Paid) ‡100
                               (Non-paid) ‡3,000
Maintenance Engineering Bulletins **(11628)**

Overland Park
Broadcast
  Engineering **(11699)** ....(Controlled) ‡32,000

KENTUCKY
Frankfort
Kentucky Engineer **(12069)** ....(Paid) ⊕5,593

LOUISIANA
Baton Rouge
Louisiana Engineer & Surveyor
  Journal **(12498)** ....(Paid) 30,000

MARYLAND
Baltimore
Hispanic Engineer **(13168)** ....‡15,000
Quicks Professional
  Journal **(13240)** ....(Non-paid) ‡6,500
USBE & Information
  Technology **(13258)** ....(Non-paid) 35,000

Bethesda
BioEngineering Abstracts **(13320)**
Mechanical Engineering Abstracts **(13358)**
PE & RS Photogrammetric Engineering & Remote
  Sensing **(13372)** ....‡9,500

Frederick
Professional
  Surveyor **(13520)** ....(Controlled) ‡52,000

Gaithersburg
ACSM Bulletin **(13531)** 10,000
Cartography and Geographic Information
  Science **(13532)** 3,500
Machining Science and
  Technology **(13545)** ....(Paid) 250
Surveying and Land Information
  Science **(13548)** ....(Paid) 8,500

Waldorf
Accident Investigation
  Quarterly **(13769)** ....(Combined) 1,800
Accident Reconstruction
  Journal **(13770)** ....(Combined) 2800

MASSACHUSETTS
Boston
Civil Engineering Practice **(13878)** ....(Paid) 3,000
Design Management Journal **(13885)**

Cambridge
Technology Review **(14107)** ....(Paid) 221,784

Chicopee
National Engineer **(14136)** ....(Paid) ‡5,422
                               (Controlled) ‡56

Framingham
EOS/ESD Technology **(14195)** ....(Non-paid) ‡31,000

Newton
Design News **(14387)** ....(Non-paid) ‡182,000
Global Design News **(14397)**

Pittsfield
Photonics Spectra **(14471)** ....(Controlled) ‡86,500

Waltham
Careers and the Technology
  Undergrad **(14598)** ....(Non-paid) 30,000

Westborough
District Energy **(14637)** ....‡3,520

Worcester
AI EDAM **(14675)** ....(Paid) ‡350
                               (Non-paid) ‡67
Science & Engineering Network News **(14688)**

MICHIGAN
Detroit
Wayne State
  Magazine **(14953)** ....(Non-paid) 18,000

Farmington Hills
Concrete International **(15018)** ....(Paid) 697
                               (Controlled) 15,625

St. Joseph
Applied Engineering in
  Agriculture **(15511)** ....(Paid) ‡700
Resource **(15513)** ....‡9,000
Transactions of the ASAE **(15514)** ....‡1,200

Troy
P.O.B. (Point of
  Beginning) **(15634)** ....(Controlled) ‡40,030
Process Cooling and Equipment **(15637)**

MINNESOTA
Minneapolis
Engineering and Mining
  Journal **(16074)** ....(Non-paid) 14,082
Engineering Minnesota **(16075)** ....(Non-paid) ‡4,000

Roseville
Geotechnical Fabrics Report **(16332)** ...(Paid) 2,061
                               (Controlled) 13,939

Circulation: ★ = ABC; △ = BPA; ♦ = CAC; ◆ = CCAB; ❑ = VAC; ⊕ = PO Statement; ‡ = Publisher's Report; Boldface figures = sworn; Light figures = estimated.

3139

Circ.   Circ.   Circ.

ENGINEERING (VARIOUS BRANCHES)
(continued)

MISSOURI
Fort Leonard Wood
Engineer: The Professional Bulletin for Army
Engineers **(17073)**

Jefferson City
The Missouri Engineer **(17125)** ....(Paid) 2,600
(Non-paid) 900

NEW HAMPSHIRE
Amherst
oemagazine **(18454)** ....(Controlled) ‡25,000

NEW JERSEY
Fairfield
Applied Mechanics Reviews **(18811)** ....‡1,000
Heat Transfer-Recent
Contents **(18813)** ....(Paid) ⊕400

Hoboken
Communications in Numerical Methods in
Engineering **(18918)**
Complexity **(18920)** 14,000
Computer Applications in Engineering
Education **(18921)** 4550
Earthquake Engineering and Structural
Dynamics **(18935)**
Electrical Engineering in Japan **(18936)**
Engineering Design and Automation **(18939)** 5985
Heat Transfer - Japanese Research **(18960)** 400
International Journal of Adaptive Control and Signal
Processing **(18975)**
International Journal of Circuit Theory and
Applications **(18978)**
International Journal of Energy Research **(18982)**
International Journal of Imaging Systems and
Technology **(18985)** 3500
International Journal of Network
Management **(18988)**
International Journal for Numerical and Analytical
Methods in Geomechanics **(18989)**
International Journal for Numerical Methods in
Engineering **(18990)**
International Journal for Numerical Methods in
Fluids **(18991)**
International Journal of Robust and Nonlinear
Control **(18996)**
International Journal of Satellite Communications
Networking **(18997)**
Journal of Communications Technology and
Electronics **(19016)**
Microwave and Optical Technology
Letters **(19064)** 4900
Numerical Linear Algebra with Applications **(19075)**
Optimal Control Applications and Methods **(19077)**
Packaging Technology and
Science **(19078)** 2,800
Permafrost and Periglacial
Processes **(19080)** 3,500
Quality and Reliability Engineering
International **(19093)**
Remediation **(19097)** 5985
The Structural Design of Tall Buildings **(19110)**

Mahwah
Transportation Human Factors **(19206)**

Morris Plains
Medical Design
Technology **(19298)** ....(Non-paid) 35,450
Product Design and
Development **(19303)** ....(Controlled) 160,000
R & D Magazine **(19305)** ....(Controlled) 90,230

Piscataway
IEEE Engineering in Medicine and Biology
Magazine **(19424)** ....(Paid) ‡8,779

NEW MEXICO
Santa Fe
PRO/E **(19942)** ....(Controlled) 7,000
SOLID Solutions
Magazine **(19946)** ....(Controlled) 7,000

NEW YORK
Bronx
Applied Science & Technology Index **(20252)**

Brooklyn
The Knowledge Engineering Review **(20327)** 400

Hauppauge
International Journal of Space Research **(20718)**

Ithaca
Cornell Science & Technology
Magazine **(20799)** ....‡3,000

Manhasset
Printed Circuit Fabrication **(21011)**

Melville
Workforce Diversity for Engineering and IT
Professionals **(21067)** ....(Combined) 15,046

New York
AICHE Journal **(21166)** 3,025
ASME News **(21266)** ....(Paid) ‡120,000
Atomization and Sprays **(21270)** ....(Paid) 500
Aviation Week & Space
Technology **(21282)** ....(Paid) 104,546
Chemical Engineering **(21400)** .....(Paid) 25,929
(Non-paid) 32,469
Chemical Engineering
Progress **(21401)** ....(Paid) 39,881
Chemical and Petroleum Engineering **(21403)**
Computational Geosciences **(21469)**
Critical Reviews in Therapeutic Drug Carrier
Systems **(21520)** ....(Paid) 500
ENR: Engineering
News-Record **(21607)** ....(Paid) 75,706
Environmental Fluid Mechanics **(21617)**
Eurotec **(21658)** 11,000
Extremes **(21671)**
Flow, Turbulence and Combustion **(21707)**
Fluid Dynamics **(21708)**
Geotechnical and Geological Engineering **(21758)**
Heat Exchanger Design
Update **(21798)** ....(Paid) 100
Hydrotechnical Construction **(21839)**
IEEE Spectrum **(21849)** ....(Paid) 3,39,000
(Non-paid) 30,699
Infrastructure Finance **(21873)** ....(Controlled) 16,353
International Applied Mechanics **(21892)**
International Journal of Fracture **(21906)**
Journal of Applied Mechanics **(21991)** 3,679
Journal of the Audio Engineering
Society **(22003)** ....‡13,561
Journal of Biomechanical
Engineering **(22011)** 1,312
Journal of Dynamic Systems, Measurement, and
Control **(22051)** 2,091
Journal of Elasticity **(22057)**
Journal of Energy Resources
Technology **(22060)** 1,493
Journal of Engineering for Gas Turbines and
Power **(22061)** 2,224
Journal of Engineering for Industry **(22062)** ...2,192
Journal of Engineering Mathematics **(22063)**
Journal of Fluids Engineering **(22071)** 2,450
Journal of Heuristics **(22088)**
Journal of Materials Science **(22123)**
Journal of Materials Science Letters **(22124)**
Journal of Pressure Vessel
Technology **(22165)** 1,864
Journal of Tribology **(22208)** 1,702
Journal of Turbomachinery **(22210)**
LD+A **(22240)** ....‡10,000
Mechanical Engineering **(22305)** ....(Paid) 95,414
(Non-paid) 6,300
Mechanical Engineering-CIME **(22306)**
Mechanics of Time-Dependent Materials **(22308)**
Melts **(22314)**
Mitigation and Adaption Strategies for Global
Change **(22339)**
Nonlinear Dynamics **(22465)**
Open Systems & Information Dynamics **(22495)**
Optimization and Engineering **(22500)**
Plant Engineering **(22559)** ......(Controlled) ‡116,700
Plasma Chemistry and Plasma Processing **(22562)**
Polymer Reaction Engineering **(22578)**
Power **(22587)** ....(Paid) 5,977
(Non-paid) 60,463
Proceedings of the IEEE **(22597)** ....‡21,000
Queueing Systems **(22619)**
Russian Journal of Nondestructive Testing **(22692)**
Soil Mechanics and Foundation Engineering **(22760)**
Strength of Materials **(22797)**

Rome
RAC Journal **(23265)** ....(Controlled) 25,000

Stony Brook
Journal of Thermal Spray
Technology **(23371)** ....(Paid) ⊕481
(Non-paid) 199

Yorktown Heights
IBM Journal of Research and
Development **(23606)** ....(Combined) ‡14,000

NORTH CAROLINA
Raleigh
The Professional Engineer **(24150)** ....‡3,200

Research Triangle Park
INTECH **(24185)** ....(Paid) 41,977
(Non-paid) 8,623

OHIO
Bay Village
Sound and Vibration **(24646)** ....(Controlled) ‡12,356

Cincinnati
AFE Facilities Engineering
Journal **(24767)** ....(Paid) 8,000
(Non-paid) 100

Cleveland
Hydraulics &
Pneumatics **(24910)** ....(Controlled) ‡49,878
Machine Design **(24923)** ....(Non-paid) ‡180,619
Mechanical Solutions **(24926)** ....(Combined) 100,000
Motion Systems
Consultant **(24930)** ....(Combined) 10,000
PT Design **(24947)** ....(Controlled) ‡56,050
Welding Innovation **(24962)** ....(Controlled) ‡78,000

Columbus
The News in
Engineering **(25035)** ....(Combined) 30,000
Ohio County Engineer **(25042)** .....(Non-paid) ‡2,600
Ohio Engineer **(25043)** ....(Paid) 3,551
(Non-paid) 259

Materials Park
Alloy Digest **(25364)** 250
Engineered Materials Abstracts **(25365)**

Solon
Designfax **(25525)** ....(Non-paid) 108,919

Woodville
Metal Architecture **(25671)** ....(Controlled) 31,483

OKLAHOMA
Oklahoma City
Oklahoma Professional Engineer **(25985)** ......‡2,000

Stillwater
Heat Transfer Engineering: An International
Quarterly **(26078)** ....‡688

Tulsa
Control Solutions **(26111)** ....(Controlled) ‡92,608
Power Engineering **(26127)** ....(Controlled) 58,000

PENNSYLVANIA
Butler
Abrasive Users News Fax **(26742)** .....(Non-paid) 10

Chester
Journal of Solid Waste Technology and
Management **(26775)** ....(Combined) 175

Exton
Enterprise Engineering Modeling
World **(26917)** ....(Combined) 125,000

Lewisburg
Progressive Engineer **(27192)**

Philadelphia
International Journal of Production Research **(27505)**
Journal of Medical Engineering &
Technology **(27534)**
Mechanics of Advanced Materials and
Structures **(27562)**
Particulate Science and Technology **(27612)** ....‡150
SIAM Journal on Optimization **(27685)** ....‡1,736

Pittsburgh
AISE Steel Technology **(27754)** ....(Paid) ‡12,034
(Non-paid) ‡589
Journal of Research of the National Institute of
Standards and Technology **(27804)**

University Park
Earth and Mineral
Sciences **(28075)** ....(Controlled) ‡18,500
Journal of Wave-Material Interaction **(28080)**

Valley Forge
U.S. Tech **(28092)** 40,000

Warrendale
Aerospace Engineering **(28110)** 32,238
SAE Off-Highway
Engineering **(28114)** ....(Controlled) 16,772

TENNESSEE
Knoxville
The Bent of Tau Beta Pi **(29270)** .....(Paid) ‡89,138

TEXAS
Austin
Corel **(29771)** ....(Controlled) ‡58,000
Texas Construction **(29815)** ....(Controlled) ‡6,500
Texas Professional
　Engineer **(29842)** ....(Paid) ‡6,200
　　　　　　　　　　　　　(Non-paid) ‡500
The Texas Surveyor **(29848)** ....‡2,500

Dallas
Better Roads **(30131)** ....(Non-paid) 39,424

Houston
Corrosion **(30466)** ....‡3,500
Hart's Lubricants
　World **(30477)** ....(Controlled) 10,240
Materials Performance **(30506)** ....(Paid) ‡15,835
Offshore Engineer **(30514)** ......(Combined) △31,269
Pipeline News **(30520)**
Power & Gas
　Marketing **(30521)** ....(Combined) 20,000
Rehabilitation
　Technology **(30523)** ....(Combined) 32,000

Richardson
Journal of Petroleum
　Technology **(30976)** ....(Paid) 51,000
　　　　　　　　　　　　(Non-paid) 4,000
SPE Drilling and Completion **(30979)** ....‡5,800
SPE Production and Facilities **(30980)** ....‡5,000
SPE Reservoir Evaluation &
　Engineering **(30981)** ....‡5,000

VIRGINIA
Alexandria
Engineering Times **(31670)** ....(Paid) 58,000
　　　　　　　　　　　　(Non-paid) 12,996
The Military Engineer **(31709)** ....(Paid) 20,066
NSBE Magazine **(31716)** ....(Paid) ‡8,000
　　　　　　　　　　　　(Non-paid) ‡14,934

Arlington
Air Traffic Control Quarterly **(31769)** 2800
Sea Technology **(31831)** ....(Paid) 250
　　　　　　　　　　　　(Controlled) 20,500

Blacksburg
Engineering Now **(31869)** ....(Controlled) 15,000
Engineers' Forum **(31870)**
Wood & Fiber Science **(31880)** ....‡800

Glen Allen
The Virginia Engineer **(32113)** ....(Paid) ‡3,100
　　　　　　　　　　　　(Controlled) ‡753

Reston
Aerospace America **(32355)** ....(Paid) 23,432
　　　　　　　　　　　　(Controlled) 43,600
ASCE News **(32361)** ....(Paid) ‡100,000
Civil Engineering-ASCE **(32363)** ....(Paid) 95,459
　　　　　　　　　　　　(Controlled) 7,686
Journal of Aerospace Engineering **(32368)**
Journal of Architectural Engineering **(32370)**
Journal of Bridge
　Engineering **(32371)** ....(Paid) 2,300
Journal of Cold Regions Engineering **(32372)**
Journal of Composites for Construction **(32373)**
Journal of Computing in Civil Engineering **(32374)**
Journal of Engineering
　Mechanics **(32377)** ....(Paid) ⊕2200
Journal of Environmental
　Engineering **(32378)** ....(Paid) ⊕5000
Journal of Geotechnical and Geoenvironmental
　Engineering **(32379)**
Journal of Hydraulic
　Engineering **(32382)** ....(Paid) ⊕1,500
Journal of Hydrologic Engineering **(32383)**
Journal of Infrastructure Systems **(32384)**
Journal of Irrigation and Drainage
　Engineering **(32385)**
Journal of Management in Engineering **(32386)**
Journal of Materials in Civil Engineering **(32387)**
Journal of Performance of Constructed
　Facilities **(32389)**
Journal of Structural Engineering **(32396)**
Journal of Surveying Engineering **(32397)**
Journal of Transportation Engineering **(32399)**
Journal of Urban Planning and
　Development **(32400)** ....(Paid) ⊕1,800
Journal of Waterway, Port, Coastal, and Ocean
　Engineering **(32402)**
Natural Hazards Review **(32408)**
Practice Periodical of Hazardous, Toxic, and
　Radioactive Waste Management **(32410)**

Practice Periodical on Structural Design and
　Construction **(32411)** ....(Paid) 2,500

WASHINGTON
Kirkland
Pacific Builder & Engineer **(32799)** ....(Paid) 251
　　　　　　　　　　　　(Controlled) 12,274

Lacey
Quality Engineering **(32803)**

WEST VIRGINIA
Charleston
West Virginia Construction
　News **(33275)** ....(Paid) ‡30
　　　　　　　　　　　　(Non-paid) ‡1,130

Morgantown
Cost Engineering **(33391)** ....‡6,000

WISCONSIN
Fort Atkinson
Pavement **(33716)** ....(Controlled) 20,000

Madison
Wisconsin Engineer **(33982)** ....(Paid) 1,300
　　　　　　　　　　　　(Non-paid) 2,300

Oak Creek
Engineering Professional **(34198)** ....‡10,000

Waukesha
Diesel & Gas Turbine
　Worldwide **(34401)** ....(Paid) ‡675
　　　　　　　　　　　　(Controlled) ‡20,050
Diesel Progress International
　Edition **(34402)** ....(Paid) ‡91
　　　　　　　　　　　　(Controlled) ‡13,247
Diesel Progress North American
　Edition **(34403)** ....(Paid) 255
　　　　　　　　　　　　(Controlled) 27,462

ALBERTA, CANADA
Calgary
Control and Intelligent Systems **(34641)**
International Journal of Robotics and
　Automation **(34649)**
Journal of Advanced
　Transportation **(34650)** ....(Combined) 355

Edmonton
The PEGG **(34724)** ....(Controlled) 31,647

BRITISH COLUMBIA, CANADA
Burnaby
Innovation **(34902)** ....(Combined) •19,500

ONTARIO, CANADA
Aurora
Environmental Science &
　Engineering **(35647)** ....(Combined) 19,095

Burlington
PEM Plant Engineering and
　Maintenance **(35718)** ....(Combined) 18,089

Etobicoke
The Ontario Technologist **(35818)** .....(Paid) ‡21,800

Markham
Design Product News **(36023)** ....(Combined) 19,416

Mississauga
Manufacturing
　Automation **(36075)** ....(Combined) 21,295

Ottawa
Canadian Journal of Civil Engineering (Revue
　Canadienne de Genie Civil) **(36203)** ....‡2,885
Geomatica **(36246)** ....(Paid) ‡1,046
　　　　　　　　　　　　(Controlled) ‡43

Toronto
Cabling Systems **(36485)** ....(Combined) 11,000
Canadian Consulting
　Engineer **(36495)** ....(Combined) •8,991
Design Engineering **(36571)** .....(Combined) •19,190
Engineering
　Dimensions **(36583)** ....(Combined) •67,233
The Ontario Land Surveyor **(36683)** ....‡1,650

QUEBEC, CANADA
Montreal
Canadian Journal of Chemical
　Engineering **(37096)** ....‡1,050
L'Ingenieur **(37131)** ....‡17,500
Plan **(37206)** ....(Combined) 48,000

ENTOMOLOGY
See also Natural History and Nature Study

ALABAMA
Birmingham
Entomological Review **(70)** 425

CALIFORNIA
San Diego
Biological Control **(3121)**

San Jose
The Pan-Pacific Entomologist **(3530)** ....‡750

DISTRICT OF COLUMBIA
Washington
Proceedings of the Entomological Society of
　Washington **(5730)** ....‡800

FLORIDA
Gainesville
Contributions on Entomology International **(6134)**
Holarctic Lepidoptera **(6143)** ....(Combined) 425
Oriental Insects **(6152)**
Tropical Lepidoptera **(6159)** ....(Combined) 805

Homestead
Florida Entomologist **(6203)** ....‡1,000

LOUISIANA
Baton Rouge
The Coleopterists Bulletin **(12487)** ....‡850

MARYLAND
Lanham
American Entomologist **(13597)** ....(Paid) 8300
Annals of the Entomological Society of
　America **(13598)** 2,100
Environmental Entomology **(13600)** 2,739
Environmental Entomology **(13601)**
Journal of Economic Entomology **(13604)** 1,800
Journal of Medical Entomology **(13605)** 1,100

MASSACHUSETTS
Cambridge
Psyche **(14091)** 700

MICHIGAN
Ann Arbor
Great Lake Entomologist **(14751)** ....(Combined) 715

Lansing
YES Quarterly **(15297)** ....(Paid) 700

NEW JERSEY
Hoboken
Archives of Insect Biochemistry and
　Physiology **(18897)**

Vincentown
Entomological News **(19697)** ....‡750

NEW YORK
Larchmont
Vector-Borne and Zoonotic Diseases **(20929)**

New York
BioControl **(21312)**
Experimental and Applied Acarology **(21664)**
Journal of Insect Behavior **(22096)**
Journal of Insect Conservation **(22097)**

OREGON
Portland
Wings **(26516)** ....(Paid) 5,500

PENNSYLVANIA
Philadelphia
Transactions of the American Entomological
　Society **(27708)** ....‡500

TEXAS
College Station
Southwestern Entomologist **(30051)** ....(Paid) 491

VIRGINIA
Martinsville
Virginia Explorer **(32234)**

ONTARIO, CANADA
Ottawa
The Canadian Entomologist **(36193)** ....‡1,100

Circulation: ★ = ABC; △ = BPA; ♦ = CAC; • = CCAB; ❑ = VAC; ⊕ = PO Statement; ‡ = Publisher's Report; Boldface figures = sworn; Light figures = estimated.

3141

Circ.   Circ.   Circ.

ETHNIC AND MINORITY STUDIES

ARIZONA
Tempe
Bilingual Review/Revista Bilingue **(900)**

Tucson
Perspectives in Mexican American
 Studies **(959)** ....(Paid) 500
Studies in Latin American Popular Culture **(965)**

CALIFORNIA
Berkeley
Mexican Studies-Estudios
 Mexicanos **(1542)** ....(Paid) ❑1,400

Irvine
Mexican Studies/Estudios Mexicanos **(2083)**

Los Angeles
American Indian Culture and Research
 Journal **(2208)** ....(Combined) 1,200
Aztlan **(2216)** ....(Paid) ‡600
Chicano-Latin Law Review **(2237)** 340
Sinorama/Kuang Hua Hua Pao **(2388)**

Mountain View
La Red—The Net **(2607)** ....(Combined) 5,000

San Francisco
Chinese America **(3340)**

Thousand Oaks
Journal of Health Care for the Poor and
 Underserved **(3891)** ....(Paid) ‡742
                                      (Non-paid) ‡101

COLORADO
Mancos
Tribal College Journal of American Indian Higher
 Education (TCJ) **(4572)**

DELAWARE
Newark
MACLAS Latin American Essays **(5278)**

DISTRICT OF COLUMBIA
Washington
Chemical Waste Litigation Reporter **(5405)**
Civil Rights Journal **(5416)**
Minority Health Today **(5652)**

GEORGIA
Decatur
Young Horizons Indigo **(7238)** ....(Paid) 18,000
                                            54,000

HAWAII
Honolulu
Chinese Language Teachers Association
 Journal **(7684)** 650
Korean Studies **(7707)** ....(Paid) 160
                                       (Controlled) 60

ILLINOIS
Lisle
ABNF Journal **(9109)** ....(Combined) 562
Journal of Cultural
 Diversity **(9110)** ....(Combined) 1,000

INDIANA
Bloomington
Israel Studies **(9838)** 400

Lafayette
Voices in Italian
 Americana **(10255)** ....(Combined) 300

KANSAS
Lawrence
Latin American Theatre
 Review **(11562)** ....(Paid) 1,100

LOUISIANA
Baton Rouge
Journal of Mayan Linguistics **(12490)** ......(Paid) 100

New Orleans
Journal for Minority Medical
 Students **(12735)** ....(Non-paid) 10,000
The Keepsake **(12736)** ....(Paid) ‡10,000

MARYLAND
Adelphi
NABJ Journal **(13088)** ....(Paid) 3,000

Baltimore
Flower of the Forest Black Genealogical
 Journal **(13161)**

MICHIGAN
Detroit
Journal of Aging and
 Ethnicity **(14933)** ....(Combined) 150

MINNESOTA
Bemidji
Oshkaabewis Native Journal **(15738)**

Minneapolis
Akademiska Dzive/Academic
 Life **(16055)** ....(Controlled) 800
The Sons of Norway
 Viking **(16128)** ....(Combined) ‡56,000
Xcp: Cross Cultural
 Poetics **(16142)** ....(Combined) 850

Rapid City
Wicazo Sa Review **(16290)**

MISSOURI
St. Louis
Snicker **(17511)** ....(Combined) 70,000

NEW JERSEY
New Brunswick
African Studies Review **(19324)**

Somerset
The Review of Black Political
 Economy **(19564)** ....(Paid) ‡1,000

South River
Bielaruskaya Dumka **(19592)** ....(Combined) 500

NEW YORK
Binghamton
Journal of Ethnic & Cultural Diversity in Social
 Work **(20171)** 732

Brooklyn
International Journal of Kurdish
 Studies **(20321)** ....(Combined) 500

Chautauqua
Journal of Multicultural Nursing and Health
 (JMCNH) **(20454)**

Ithaca
Indonesia **(20803)** ....(Combined) 500

New York
Critical Survey **(21521)**
French Politics, Culture and Society **(21735)**
Journal of Immigrant Health **(22091)**
Nomadic Peoples **(22464)**
Scandinavian Review **(22708)** ....(Paid) 6,000
Sephardic Scholar **(22729)** ....(Paid) 5,000
The Urban League Review **(22890)** 500

Stony Brook
Forum Italicum **(23369)** ....(Paid) 800

NORTH CAROLINA
Durham
Hopscotch **(23826)** ....(Combined) 2,500

OHIO
Oxford
Journal of African American
 Men **(25455)** ....(Paid) ‡1,100

OKLAHOMA
Norman
American Indian Law
 Review **(25932)** ....(Combined) 630

PENNSYLVANIA
Melrose Park
Contemporary Jewry **(27245)** ....(Paid) 500

Pittsburgh
Critica Hispanica **(27773)**
Latin American Literary
 Review **(27809)** ....(Combined) 1,250

Swarthmore
Latin American Jewish Studies **(28042)**

RHODE ISLAND
Cranston
Inti **(28335)** ....(Controlled) 1,000

TEXAS
Houston
Saudi Aramco World **(30527)** ....(Controlled) 180,000

VERMONT
Benson
Central Asia Monitor **(31504)** 235

VIRGINIA
Charlottesville
Dieciocho **(31928)** ....(Combined) 270

Fairfax
Black Issues Book
 Review **(32008)** ....(Combined) ★54,853
Black Issues in Higher Education **(32009)**

Norfolk
Scotia **(32293)** ....(Paid) 100

Williamsburg
Al-Arabiyya **(32612)**
Chasqui **(32615)** ....(Combined) 385

WASHINGTON
Longview
Swedish American
 Genealogist **(32814)** ....(Controlled) 1,100

ALBERTA, CANADA
Calgary
Canadian Ethnic Studies
 Journal **(34634)** ....(Combined) 2,400

NEW BRUNSWICK, CANADA
Bathurst
Ven'd'Est **(35379)** ....(Paid) ⊕3,874
                                 (Non-paid) ⊕1,126

ONTARIO, CANADA
Guelph
Scottish Tradition **(35867)**

London
Canadian Journal of Latin American and Caribbean
 Studies **(35978)** ....(Controlled) 500

Toronto
Diaspora **(36574)** 500

Willowdale
Journal of Asian and African Studies **(36880)**

PRINCE EDWARD ISLAND, CANADA
Charlottetown
Canadian Review of Studies in
 Nationalism **(36913)** ....(Controlled) 600

QUEBEC, CANADA
Montreal
Centre D'Etudes de L'Asie de
 L'Est/Cahiers **(37101)** ....(Controlled) 300

Quebec
Continuite **(37282)** ....⊕5,000
                                            ⊕3,920

FIRE FIGHTING

CALIFORNIA
Auburn
FPC/Fire Protection
 Contractor **(1438)** ....(Controlled) 2,300

Bellflower
American Fire Journal **(1484)** ....‡5,800

Sacramento
California Fire Service **(2981)** ....(Paid) ‡26,000

COLORADO
Denver
Public Safety Product
 News **(4350)** ....(Non-paid) 14,292

DISTRICT OF COLUMBIA
Washington
International Fire
 Fighter **(5551)** ....(Non-paid) 195,000

FLORIDA
Pompano Beach
Florida Fireman **(6590)** ....‡5,900

ILLINOIS
Chicago
Firewatch! **(8377)**

IOWA
Des Moines
Iowa Smoke-Eater **(10796)** ....‡8,000

MASSACHUSETTS
Quincy
Fire Technology **(14489)** ....‡4,000
NFPA Journal **(14490)** ....‡66,000

MINNESOTA
St. Paul
Minnesota Smoke-Eater **(16395)** ....‡12,000

NEBRASKA
Pierce
Nebraska Smoke-Eater **(18247)** ....‡9,000

NEW JERSEY
Fair Lawn
Fire Engineering **(18807)** ....(Paid) 44,264

Hoboken
Fire and Materials **(18948)**

NEW YORK
Amityville
Journal of Applied Fire Science **(20041)**

Melville
Firehouse Magazine **(21044)** ....(Paid) 90,000
(Non-paid) 24,743

NORTH CAROLINA
Raleigh
National Fire &
Rescue **(24140)** ....(Controlled) 36,777

PENNSYLVANIA
Pittsburgh
Fire Management Today **(27789)**

TEXAS
College Station
Industrial Fire World **(30043)** ....(Paid) 18,000

Dallas
Sprinkler Age **(30182)** ....(Non-paid) ‡3,926

ONTARIO, CANADA
Delhi
Fire Fighting in
Canada **(35768)** ....(Controlled) •5,083

Toronto
The Canadian
Firefighter **(36498)** ....(Controlled) 11,200

FIREARMS

ARIZONA
Prescott
Handloader **(847)** ....‡150,000

CALIFORNIA
San Diego
Shooting Industry **(3274)** ....(Paid) ‡893
(Non-paid) ‡16,462

ILLINOIS
Aledo
The Gun Report **(8004)** ....‡5,000

INDIANA
Friendship
Muzzle Blasts **(10013)** ....‡22,000

RHODE ISLAND
Lincoln
Man at Arms **(28362)** ....(Paid) ‡21,000
(Non-paid) ‡80

VIRGINIA
Fairfax
American Rifleman **(32005)** ....(Paid) 1,608,439

Harrisonburg
Journal of Mine Action **(32140)**

ALBERTA, CANADA
Medicine Hat
Demining Technology Information Forum
Journal **(34809)**

FISH AND COMMERCIAL FISHERIES

ALASKA
Juneau
Alaska Fishery Research
Bulletin **(594)** ....(Controlled) 750

IDAHO
Moscow
Women in Natural Resources **(7922)**

MAINE
Portland
Alaska Fisherman's
Journal **(13004)** ....(Paid) △1,865
(Non-paid) △7,589
National Fisherman **(13013)** ....(Paid) 40,034
Seafood Business **(13019)** ....(Paid) 1,175
(Controlled) 15,087

Stonington
Commercial Fisheries News **(13062)** 8,500
Fish Farming News **(13063)** ....(Controlled) 8,500
Marine Performance and Fisheries Product
News **(13065)** ....(Controlled) 14,525

MARYLAND
Bethesda
ASFA Aquaculture Abstracts **(13315)**
ASFA/Aquatic Sciences & Fisheries Abstracts Part 1:
Biological Sciences & Living Resources **(13316)**
Fisheries **(13336)** ....‡9,300
Journal of Aquatic Animal
Health **(13349)** ....(Paid) 1,500
North American Journal of
Aquaculture **(13365)** ....‡2,200
North American Journal of Fisheries
Management **(13366)** ....‡3,200
Transactions of the American Fisheries
Society **(13385)** ....‡3,700

MISSOURI
Jefferson City
Missouri
Conservationist **(17124)** ....(Combined) 440,000

NEW YORK
New York
Environmental Biology of Fishes **(21613)**
Fish Physiology and Biochemistry **(21702)**
Fly Fishing Retailer **(21709)**
Reviews in Fish Biology and Fisheries **(22664)**

NORTH CAROLINA
Asheville
Aquaculture Magazine **(23626)** ....(Paid) 4,975

PENNSYLVANIA
Pittsburgh
Fishery Bulletin **(27790)**

TEXAS
Port Lavaca
Gulf Coast Fisherman **(30955)** ....(Paid) ‡19,500
(Non-paid) ‡200

WASHINGTON
Olympia
The Trout & Salmon Leader **(32861)**

Seattle
Pacific Fishing **(33000)** ....(Paid) 6,413

BRITISH COLUMBIA, CANADA
Courtenay
Northern Aquaculture Magazine **(34932)** ....‡4,000

New Westminster
The Fisherman **(35029)** ....(Paid) 5,000
(Free) 350

NOVA SCOTIA, CANADA
Dartmouth
Journal of Northwest Atlantic Fishery
Science **(35547)**

ONTARIO, CANADA
Ottawa
Canadian Journal of Fisheries & Aquatic
Science **(36205)** 2,000

FLOORING AND FLOOR COVERING

CALIFORNIA
Woodland Hills
Commercial Floor Care **(4101)**

COLORADO
Longmont
Flooring Magazine **(4559)** ....(Combined) 18,800

MINNESOTA
Bloomington
Midwest Retailer **(15759)** ....(Non-paid) ‡5,500

NEW YORK
Garden City
Floor Covering Weekly **(20639)** ....(Paid) 10,470
(Non-paid) 8,304

Hicksville
Floor Covering News **(20735)** ....(Paid) ‡2,855
(Controlled) ‡12,906

Pound Ridge
Floor Focus **(23165)** 14,500

NORTH CAROLINA
Arden
Rug News **(23620)** ....(Controlled) 4,500

ONTARIO, CANADA
Picton
Coverings **(36328)** ....(Controlled) 7,200

FLORISTS AND FLORICULTURE

See also Landscape Architecture; Seed and
Nursery Trade

CALIFORNIA
Los Angeles
Flowers **(2272)** ....(Combined) △35,000

San Diego'
California Garden **(3127)** 2,100

FLORIDA
Boca Raton
Produce Business **(5939)** ....(Paid) ‡7,706
(Non-paid) ‡12,170

ILLINOIS
Batavia
FloraCulture International
Magazine **(8052)** ....(Combined) 13,500
Green Profit Magazine **(8053)** .....(Non-paid) 25,000
Grower Talks **(8054)** ....(Paid) 9,230

Chicago
Flora Magazine **(8378)** ....‡17,100
Flower News **(8379)** ....(Non-paid) ‡11,188
(Paid) ‡5,941

Downers Grove
Florist **(8785)** ....(Paid) ‡25,713

Northfield
Floral & Nursery Times **(9329)** ....(Paid) ‡4,276
(Controlled) ‡12,500

Rolling Meadows
Greenhouse Business **(9547)** ......(Non-paid) 18,000

KANSAS
Lenexa
Floral Retailing
Magazine **(11591)** ....(Controlled) ‡15,000

Topeka
Florists' Review Magazine **(11819)** .....(Paid) 24,054
(Non-paid) 4,008

MICHIGAN
Haslett
Michigan Florist **(15150)** ....(Controlled) ‡10,000

Livonia
The Extra Touch Online **(15315)**

Trade, Technical, and Professional Publications

Circ.   **Circ.**   **Circ.**

FLORISTS AND FLORICULTURE (continued)

OHIO
Columbus
Ohio Florists Association
  Bulletin **(25044)** ....(Paid) 3,500

TEXAS
Fort Worth
Greenhouse Management and
  Production **(30341)** ....(Combined) ‡15,548
Nursery Management and
  Production **(30349)** ....(Combined) △15,207

VIRGINIA
Alexandria
Floral Management **(31674)** ....(Paid) 23,200
  (Non-paid) 1,800

QUEBEC, CANADA
Quebec
Fleur Design **(37284)** ....‡1,850
Option Serre **(37294)** ....‡1,580

FOOD AND GROCERY TRADE

**See also Baking; Confectionaries and
Frozen Dairy Products; Fruit, Fruit
Products, and Produce Trade; Milk and
Dairy Products**

ARIZONA
Phoenix
Arizona Food Industry Journal **(778)** ....‡3,000

CALIFORNIA
Fresno
Vegetable **(1958)** ....(Controlled) ‡8,371

Marina del Rey
Cracker/Snack World **(2507)** ....(Paid) ‡500
  (Controlled) ‡1,500

Palm Springs
Beverage Dynamics **(2754)** ....(Non-paid) △50,037
Candy Business **(2755)**
Professional Candy Buyer **(2765)**

San Francisco
The Culinarian **(3347)** ....‡1,500

San Rafael
Grocers Report **(3601)** ....(Controlled) ‡15,000

Santa Rosa
The Food & Beverage Industry **(3725)**
The Food & Beverage
  Journal **(3726)** ....(Combined) 27,000

COLORADO
Boulder
Delicious Living! **(4165)** ....(Paid) 458,974
Natural Foods
  Merchandiser **(4181)** ....(Paid) △15,003

Broomfield
Natural Business **(4205)** ....(Paid) 900

CONNECTICUT
Stamford
Vegetarian Times **(5162)** ....(Paid) 320,954

Trumbull
Journal of Texture Studies **(5185)**

DISTRICT OF COLUMBIA
Washington
Amber Waves **(5321)**
ASMC Sales & Marketing
  Magazine **(5369)** ....‡4,000
Catering Industry Employee **(5397)** ....‡215,000
Food Marketing Industry Speaks **(5498)**

FLORIDA
Miami Springs
Airline, Ship & Catering ONBOARD SERVICES
  Magazine **(6421)** ....(Paid) 19
  (Non-paid) 3,890

South Miami
Today's Grocer **(6686)** ....(Controlled) ‡19,500

GEORGIA
Acworth
Food People **(6897)** ....(Paid) 309
  (Non-paid) 44,097

Atlanta
Southeast Food Service
  News **(7044)** ....(Paid) ‡2,076
  (Controlled) ‡22,414

Gainesville
Shelby Report of the
  Southeast **(7295)** ....(Paid) 2,059
  (Controlled) 23,077
Shelby Report of the
  Southwest **(7296)** ....(Paid) ‡1,846
  (Controlled) ‡20,357
  (Non-paid) ‡3,638
Sunbelt Foodservice **(7297)** ....(Paid) 1,533
  (Controlled) 28,573

Smyrna
Georgia Food Connection **(7554)**

ILLINOIS
Bensenville
Food Engineering (North American
  Edition) **(8067)** ....(Paid) 662
  (Non-paid) 50,000
Prepared Foods **(8069)**

Chicago
CarneTec **(8299)** ....(Non-paid) 6,200
Chef **(8305)** ....(Paid) 1,500
  (Controlled) 42,000
Equipment Solutions **(8370)** ....(Paid) ‡1,265
  (Non-paid) ‡29,054
Fancy Food & Culinary
  Products **(8374)** ....(Paid) 3,060
  (Non-paid) 22,000
FEDA News and Views **(8375)** ....(Controlled) 1,600
Grocery Headquarters **(8389)** ...(Controlled) ‡63,207
IGA Grocergram **(8404)** ....(Paid) ‡17,976
Meat Marketing &
  Technology **(8483)** ....(Combined) 20,058
New Product News **(8506)** ....(Paid) ‡800
NPN International **(8513)** ....(Controlled) ‡7,500

Deerfield
Industria Alimenticia **(8725)** ....△18,000
Refrigerated and Frozen Foods **(8727)**
Snack Food and Wholesale Bakery **(8728)**

Itasca
Food Processing **(9014)** ....(Combined) △65,031

Millstadt
Meat Business
  Magazine **(9198)** ....(Non-paid) ‡9,100

Mount Morris
Meat Processing **(9240)** ....(Paid) 361
  (Non-paid) 20,913

Northbrook
Food Product Design **(9316)** ....(Combined) △29,200

IOWA
Des Moines
Iowa Grocer **(10791)** ....‡2,500
Journal of Food Protection **(10800)** ....‡3,100

Iowa City
Prairie News **(10985)** ....(Paid) ‡20,000

KANSAS
Shawnee Mission
Kansas Food Dealers Bulletin **(11804)**

KENTUCKY
Louisville
Pizza Today **(12234)** ....(Paid) 11,376
  (Non-paid) 28,616

MAINE
Portland
Seafood Business **(13019)** ....(Paid) 1,175
  (Controlled) 15,087

Yarmouth
Gourmet News **(13078)** ....(Non-paid) 23,100

MARYLAND
Bethesda
Military Grocer **(13360)** ....(Controlled) 8,000

Columbia
Food World **(13460)** ....(Non-paid) ‡22,000

Rockville
Inspection Monitor **(13682)**

Timonium
Food Production Management **(13757)** ....(Paid) 214
  (Non-paid) 4,030

MASSACHUSETTS
Malden
Choices **(14290)** ....(Combined) 6,100

MICHIGAN
Lansing
Michigan Food News **(15283)** ......(Controlled) 9,000

MINNESOTA
St. Paul
Cereal Chemistry **(16368)** ....(Paid) ‡3,260
  (Controlled) ‡26
Cereal Foods World **(16369)** ....(Paid) ‡4,231
  (Controlled) ‡303
Minnesota Grocer **(16392)** ....‡1,500

MISSOURI
Kansas City
Meat & Poultry **(17182)** ....(Controlled) ‡18,249

Springfield
Missouri Grocer **(17606)** ....‡1,750

MONTANA
Helena
The Montana Food
  Distributor **(17821)** ....(Paid) ‡1,000
  (Non-paid) ‡100

NEBRASKA
Lincoln
The Voice **(18127)** ....‡1,200

NEVADA
Las Vegas
Journal of Restaurant and Foodservice
  Marketing **(18366)** ....(Paid) 500

NEW HAMPSHIRE
Manchester
News & Food Report **(18560)** ....‡1,300

NEW JERSEY
Elmwood Park
Food Institute Report **(18794)** ....(Paid) 3,000

Fort Lee
Private Label **(18833)** ....(Paid) ‡961
  (Non-paid) ‡28,080
Quick Frozen Foods
  International **(18834)** ....(Paid) ‡6,011
  (Controlled) ‡5,528

Hackensack
Modern Grocer **(18852)** ....(Paid) 3,000
  (Non-paid) 12,000

Hoboken
Journal of the Science of Food and
  Agriculture **(19047)**
Packaging Technology and
  Science **(19078)** 2,800

Morris Plains
Food Manufacturing **(19291)** 40,043
Food Products and
  Equipment **(19292)** ....(Controlled) ‡48,000

Morristown
Art Culinaire **(19310)** ....‡14,500

South Plainfield
Whole Foods **(19591)** ....(Paid) 303
  (Controlled) 16,203

NEW YORK
Albany
Food Industry Advocate **(19987)** ....(Paid) ‡7,700
  (Non-paid) ‡2,000

Binghamton
Journal of Herbs, Spices & Medicinal Plants **(20178)**

Melville
Health Products Business **(21045)** ....(Paid) 12
  (Non-paid) 18,463

New York
Chain Leader **(21392)**
Chocolatier **(21412)** ....(Paid) ‡150,000
Environmental Nutrition **(21622)**
Food Arts **(21710)** ....(Non-paid) ‡55,581
  (Paid) ‡1,513
Food Engineering (International
  Edition) **(21711)** ....(Paid) ‡734
  (Non-paid) ‡15,043
Food Logistics **(21712)**
Foodservice Equipment and Supplies **(21715)**

Frozen Food Digest Magazine **(21738)** ....‡13,500
ID: The Information Source for Managers and
   DSRs **(21842)**
Institutional
   Distribution **(21879)** ....(Non-paid) ‡39,018
Supermarket
   Business **(22808)** ....(Controlled) ‡62,739
Supermarket News **(22809)** ....(Paid) 40,234
Tea and Coffee Trade
   Journal **(22816)** ....(Combined) 11,178

Nyack
Cucinazte **(23026)** 4,000
   6,000

Skaneateles
Empire State Food Service
   News **(23335)** ....(Controlled) 15,500

Westbury
Government Food
   Service **(23555)** ....(Controlled) 10,500

OHIO
Cleveland
Convenience Store Decisions **(24876)** ....‡41,800
Food Management **(24896)** .....(Combined) ‡117,740

Louisville
The Friends of Wine **(25318)**

North Canton
ECO Communicator **(25434)** ....‡750

OKLAHOMA
Oklahoma City
Oklahoma Grocers Journal **(25980)** ......(Paid) 1,500

OREGON
Salem
Hospitality News for the Western United
   States **(26568)** ....(Non-paid) 40,000

Wilsonville
Oregon Grocery Line **(26615)** ......(Controlled) ‡400

PENNSYLVANIA
Broomall
Food Trade News **(26736)** ......(Controlled) ‡23,000

Camp Hill
The Food Industry Advisor **(26751)** ....(Paid) 10,000
   (Non-paid) 1,000

Middletown
Journal of International Food and Agribusiness
   Marketing **(27258)** 380

Philadelphia
Journal of Food Products Marketing **(27528)** 480

Pittsburgh
FDA Consumer **(27787)**

TEXAS
Austin
Texas Food Merchant **(29820)** ....(Paid) ‡1500
   (Controlled) ‡814

College Station
Journal of Agricultural and Food
   Information **(30044)** ....(Paid) 200

Lewisville
Food Herald **(30686)** ....(Paid) ‡1,000
   (Non-paid) ‡250

UTAH
Salt Lake City
The Intermountain Retailer **(31432)** ....‡1,200

VIRGINIA
Alexandria
School Foodservice &
   Nutrition **(31735)** ....(Paid) 58,000
   (Non-paid) 5,000

Blacksburg
Journal of College and University
   Foodservice **(31873)** ....(Paid) 139
Journal of Nutrition in Recipe and Menu
   Development **(31876)** ....(Paid) 159

Falls Church
Food Distributor **(32045)** ....(Controlled) 8,600

WISCONSIN
Fond du Lac
Cooking for Profit **(33696)** ....‡70,000

Madison
The Cheese Reporter **(33926)** ....(Paid) 1,665
   (Free) 170
Food Reviews International **(33940)** 350
Wisconsin Grocer **(33983)** ....‡1,500

Milwaukee
Outpost Exchange **(34092)** ....(Non-paid) ‡31,000

BRITISH COLUMBIA, CANADA
Burnaby
Grocer Today
   Magazine **(34900)** ....(Combined) 14,355

MANITOBA, CANADA
Winnipeg
Western Grocer **(35359)** ....(Combined) •16,200
Western Restaurant News **(35361)** 13,148

ONTARIO, CANADA
Delhi
Canadian Pizza Magazine **(35765)** 10,000

Toronto
Canadian Grocer **(36500)** ....(Non-paid) •18,054
   (Paid) •2,341
L'Epicier **(36584)** ....(Controlled) 12,806
Food in Canada **(36597)** ....(Combined) 9,065

QUEBEC, CANADA
Saint-Etienne-de-Lauzon
Le Chef du Service
   Alimentaire **(37330)** ....(Controlled) •20,629

FOOD PRODUCTION

CALIFORNIA
Palm Springs
Candy Business **(2755)**
Professional Candy Buyer **(2765)**

San Diego
Food Microbiology **(3156)**

Santa Rosa
The Food & Beverage Industry **(3725)**
The Food & Beverage
   Journal **(3726)** ....(Combined) 27,000

DISTRICT OF COLUMBIA
Washington
Amber Waves **(5321)**
Food Chemical News **(5497)**
Rural Cooperatives **(5773)** ....(Paid) 8,000

FLORIDA
St. Augustine
The National Culinary Review **(6616)**

ILLINOIS
Bensenville
Prepared Foods **(8069)**

Chicago
CarneTec **(8299)** ....(Non-paid) 6,200
Equipment Solutions **(8370)** ....(Paid) ‡1,265
   (Non-paid) ‡29,054
Meat Marketing &
   Technology **(8483)** ....(Combined) 20,058

Deerfield
Industria Alimenticia **(8725)** ....△18,000
Refrigerated and Frozen Foods **(8727)**
Snack Food and Wholesale Bakery **(8728)**

Itasca
Processing **(9016)** ....(Paid) 105,000

Northbrook
Food Product Design **(9316)** ....(Combined) △29,200

MAINE
Yarmouth
Gourmet News **(13078)** ....(Non-paid) 23,100

MARYLAND
Rockville
Inspection Monitor **(13682)**

NEW JERSEY
Elmwood Park
Food Institute Report **(18794)** ....(Paid) 3,000

Hoboken
Journal of the Science of Food and
   Agriculture **(19047)**
Pest Management Science **(19081)**

Morris Plains
Food Manufacturing **(19291)** 40,043

NEW YORK
Binghamton
Journal of Herbs, Spices & Medicinal Plants **(20178)**
Journal of New Seeds **(20190)**

New York
Chain Leader **(21392)**
Food Logistics **(21712)**
Foodservice Equipment and Supplies **(21715)**
ID: The Information Source for Managers and
   DSRs **(21842)**
International Journal of Food Properties **(21905)**
Pastry Art & Design **(22532)** .....(Combined) 27,000

Skaneateles
Empire State Food Service
   News **(23335)** ....(Controlled) 15,500

NORTH DAKOTA
Fargo
Valley Potato Grower **(24415)** ....(Paid) 200
   (Non-paid) 11,620

OREGON
Astoria
Journal of Aquatic Food Product
   Technology **(26225)** 170

PENNSYLVANIA
Hazleton
Journal of Nutraceuticals, Functional & Medical
   Foods **(27034)** ....(Paid) ‡97
   (Non-paid) ‡23

SOUTH DAKOTA
Rapid City
South Dakota Stock Grower **(28932)** ....(Paid) 1,309
   (Controlled) 40

TEXAS
College Station
Food Additives and Contaminants **(30041)** 650

UTAH
Provo
Benson Institute Review **(31398)**

ONTARIO, CANADA
Guelph
Agri-Food Research in Ontario/Recherche Agro-
   alimentaire en
   Ontario **(35858)** ....(Combined) 7,500

FORESTRY

ALABAMA
Montgomery
Alabama Forests **(357)** ....‡3,500
Southern Loggin' Times **(378)** ....(Controlled) 13,416
Timber Harvesting **(379)** ....(Controlled) 20,409
Timber Processing **(380)** ....(Controlled) 20,497

COLORADO
Fort Collins
Human Dimensions of Wildlife **(4432)**
RMRScience **(4437)** ....(Controlled) 2,000

CONNECTICUT
New Haven
Journal of Sustainable Forestry **(4996)** 148

DISTRICT OF COLUMBIA
Washington
American Forests **(5329)** ....‡25,000
Tree Farmer **(5830)** ....(Non-paid) 8,000
   (Paid) 8,000
   65,000

GEORGIA
Atlanta
Forest Landowner **(7008)** 10,500

Norcross
TOPS **(7470)** ....(Paid) ‡4,800

Wadley
Logger and Lumberman **(7635)** ....(Non-paid) 18,677

IDAHO
Moscow
Women in Natural Resources **(7922)**

Circulation: ★ = ABC; △ = BPA; • = CAC; ◦ = CCAB; ❑ = VAC; ⊕ = PO Statement; ‡ = Publisher's Report; Boldface figures = sworn; Light figures = estimated.

3145

	Circ.

FORESTRY (continued)

LOUISIANA
Alexandria
Forests & People (12458) ....(Combined) 5,600

Dodson
The Piney Woods
Journal (12567) ....(Combined) 15,000

MARYLAND
Bethesda
Forest Science (13337) 2,000
Journal of Forestry (13351) 20,000
Northern Journal of Applied
Forestry (13367) 2,000
Southern Journal of Applied
Forestry (13381) 2,000
Western Journal of Applied
Forestry (13388) 1,000

MASSACHUSETTS
Peabody
City Trees (14461) ....(Controlled) 5,000

MICHIGAN
Howell
Michigan Christmas Tree Journal (15197) 1,200

MISSOURI
St. Louis
American Christmas Tree Journal (17409) ....‡1,600

NEW HAMPSHIRE
Concord
Forest Notes (18472) ....(Paid) ‡12,000
(Controlled) ‡400

NEW YORK
New York
New Forests (22429)

Old Forge
Northern Logger and Timber
Processor (23037) ....(Paid) 13,052

Rensselaer
The Lumber Co-Operator (23181) ....(Paid) 3,800
(Controlled) 262

NORTH CAROLINA
Durham
Environmental History (23820) ....‡1,900

OREGON
Portland
Export Report (26477) 275
Injury and Illness Incidence (26482) 275
Monthly F.O.B. Price Summary, Past Sales (Coast
Mills) (26485) 280
Monthly F.O.B. Price Summary, Past Sales (Inland
Mills) (26486) 300
Western Lumber Facts (26514) 380

PENNSYLVANIA
Mechanicsburg
Pennsylvania Forests (27240) ....(Paid) ‡2,500
(Non-paid) ‡500

TENNESSEE
Franklin
Southern Lumberman (29199) ....(Paid) ‡4,000
(Controlled) ‡11,000

UTAH
Logan
Society & Natural Resources (31351) ....(Paid) ‡576

VIRGINIA
Richmond
Virginia Forests (32462) ....(Paid) 3,250

WASHINGTON
Chehalis
Log Trucker (32710) ....(Combined) ‡12,000
Loggers World (32711) ....‡16,000

Edmonds
Timber West (32746) ....(Paid) 135
(Controlled) 10,500

WISCONSIN
Rhinelander
The Timber Producer (34286) ....(Combined) ‡3,500

BRITISH COLUMBIA, CANADA
Argenta
The Smallholder (34881) ....(Paid) 750

Langley
Supply Post (35005) ....(Combined) ‡18,000

North Vancouver
Logging & Sawmilling
Journal (35035) ....(Combined) •16,889

Vancouver
Specialty Wood
Journal (35168) ....(Combined) 9,942

Victoria
Tree Physiology (35227) ....(Controlled) 1,000

NOVA SCOTIA, CANADA
Liverpool
Atlantic Forestry Review (35588) ....(Paid) 3,500
(Controlled) 3,500

ONTARIO, CANADA
Ottawa
The Forestry Chronicle (36243) ....‡3,000

QUEBEC, CANADA
Baie D'urfe'
Canadian Forest
Industries (36944) ....(Combined) 14,218
Operations Forestieres et de
Scierie (36946) ....(Non-paid) •5,615

FRUIT, FRUIT PRODUCTS, AND PRODUCE TRADE
See also Food and Grocery Trade

CALIFORNIA
Fresno
Grape Grower
Magazine (1951) ....(Non-paid) 11,276
Tree Fruit (1957) ....(Controlled) ‡11,008

FLORIDA
Bartow
The Citrus Industry (5917) ....‡10,000

Boca Raton
Produce Business (5939) ....(Paid) ‡7,706
(Non-paid) ‡12,170

Tampa
Citrus and Vegetable
Magazine (6760) ....(Controlled) △12,000

KANSAS
Lenexa
Fresh Trends (11592)
The Packer (11594) ....(Paid) 14,000
Produce Merchandising (11596) 12,057

NEW JERSEY
Englewood Cliffs
The Produce News (18802) ....(Paid) 2,014
(Non-paid) 8,465

WASHINGTON
Yakima
Carrot Country (33218) ....(Controlled) ‡2,650
Potato Country (33221) ....(Controlled) ‡7,544
The Tomato
Magazine (33222) ....(Controlled) ‡6,742

ONTARIO, CANADA
Delhi
Fruit and Vegetable
Magazine (35769) ....(Paid) ‡3,000

FUNERAL DIRECTORS

CALIFORNIA
Monterey
Mortuary Management (2583) ....(Paid) ⊕8,500

FLORIDA
Tallahassee
Florida Funeral Director (6712) ....(Paid) 1,000
(Non-paid) 50
Thanatos (6739) ....(Paid) ‡7,000
(Non-paid) ‡200

ILLINOIS
Chicago
The Cremationist of North America (8347) ....‡1,600

OHIO
Youngstown
YB News (25700) ....(Paid) 1,555
(Non-paid) 17,266

SOUTH CAROLINA
Beaufort
Alliance (28486) ....(Controlled) 8,000

TEXAS
Austin
Texas Director (29817) ....(Non-paid) 1,150

WISCONSIN
Brookfield
The Director (33604) ....(Paid) 13,222
(Non-paid) 787

FUR TRADE AND FUR FARMING

WYOMING
Riverton
American Trapper (34576) ....‡11,500

FURNITURE AND FURNISHINGS

CALIFORNIA
Woodland Hills
ICS Cleaning Specialist (4107) 27,000
National Floor Trends Magazine (4112) 27,000

ILLINOIS
Des Plaines
udm/Upholstery Design and
Management (8772) ....(Non-paid) 8,600

Lincolnshire
Accessory Merchandising (9084) 21,000

Lombard
NARDA Independent Retailer (9117) ....‡2,000

MARYLAND
Millersville
Cleaning & Restoration (13630) ....‡2,600

MASSACHUSETTS
Newton
Interior Design (14401) ....(Paid) 54,584

MINNESOTA
St. Paul
Fine Furnishings International
(FFI) (16376) ....(Paid) 664
(Controlled) 20,467
Upholstery Journal (16412) ....(Paid) 3,000
(Non-paid) 5,000

NEW HAMPSHIRE
Laconia
Hearth & Home
Magazine (18537) ....(Non-paid) ‡17,000

NEW JERSEY
Ramsey
Carpet and Rug Industry (19487) ....(Paid) 319
(Non-paid) 4,807

NEW YORK
New Rochelle
Furniture World
Magazine (21116) ....(Controlled) 21,285

New York
Small World (22747) ....(Non-paid) 6,588
(Paid) 485

NORTH CAROLINA
High Point
Casual Living (23995) 13,000
Furniture Today (23997) ....(Paid) 17,326
(Non-paid) 4,708
High Points (23999)
Home Furnishings
Retailer (24000) ....(Non-paid) 14,500

RHODE ISLAND
Providence
Bedroom (28388) ....(Controlled) 21,700

Futon Life **(28397)** ....(Controlled) 21,500

VIRGINIA
Alexandria
BEDTimes **(31647)** ....‡3,600

WISCONSIN
Fort Atkinson
Laminating Design and
   Technology **(33712)** ....(Controlled) 40,000
Wood Digest **(33722)** ....(Controlled) ‡51,010

QUEBEC, CANADA
Victoriaville
2x4 (All About Wood) **(37433)** ....(Controlled) ‡7,569

GENERAL MERCHANDISE

**See also Retail; Clothing; Cosmetics and
Toiletries; Drugs and Pharmaceuticals**

ARIZONA
Phoenix
Asian Sources Electronic Components **(785)**
Asian Sources Electronics **(786)**
Asian Sources Gifts & Home Products **(788)**
Asian Sources Timepieces **(791)**

CALIFORNIA
Los Angeles
Closeout News Magazine **(2243)** ......(Paid) ‡84,000
           (Controlled) ‡14,650

Marina del Rey
Cigar / Tobacco World **(2506)** ....(Paid) ‡300
          (Non-paid) ‡1,700

CONNECTICUT
Trumbull
The Bargain News **(5180)** ....(Paid) 42,000

DISTRICT OF COLUMBIA
Washington
Stores **(5805)** ....(Paid) 15,776
        (Non-paid) 19,966

FLORIDA
Clearwater
Value Retail News **(5992)** ....‡5,000

Lake Mary
Inspirational Giftware **(6277)**

ILLINOIS
St. Charles
Country Business **(9563)** ....(Combined) 30,000

KANSAS
Overland Park
The Auctioneer **(11697)** ....‡5,800
Wearables Business **(11735)** ......(Combined) 14,723

MASSACHUSETTS
Babson Park
Journal of Retailing **(13832)** ....(Paid) 2,500

Burlington
Journal of Retailing and Consumer Services **(14029)**

MINNESOTA
Minnetonka
Tack'n Togs
   Merchandising **(16176)** ....(Controlled) ‡14,264

MISSOURI
Kansas City
Discover Mid-America **(17164)** .....(Non-paid) 30,000

NEBRASKA
Omaha
Heartland Retailer **(18197)** ....(Free) ‡15,250

NEW JERSEY
Florham Park
Exhibit Marketing
   Magazine **(18824)** ....(Non-paid) 124,000

Fort Lee
Private Label **(18833)** ....(Paid) ‡961
        (Non-paid) ‡28,080

NEW YORK
Centerport
Swap Meet Magazine **(20447)** .....(Non-paid) 72,000

Melville
Army-Navy Store and Outdoor
   Merchandiser **(21040)** ....(Paid) ‡12,000

New York
Chain Store Age **(21393)** ....(Paid) 2,253
        (Non-paid) 33,398
Home Furnishings News (HFN) **(21808)**
MMR **(22340)** ....(Paid) 6,498
        (Non-paid) 28,123
Small World **(22747)** ....(Non-paid) 6,588
        (Paid) 485

Port Washington
Retail Roundup **(23135)**

NORTH CAROLINA
Oriental
Shop Talk! **(24110)** ....(Paid) 3,500

OKLAHOMA
Oklahoma City
Oklahoma Retailer **(25987)** ....(Controlled) ‡4,400

PENNSYLVANIA
Philadelphia
International Journal of Geographical Information
   Science **(27498)**

MANITOBA, CANADA
Winnipeg
C Store Canada **(35318)**

NEW BRUNSWICK, CANADA
Moncton
The Atlantic
   Co-operator **(35411)** ....(Combined) 21,000

GENETICS

See also Science (General)

CALIFORNIA
Palo Alto
Annual Review of Genetics **(2790)**

San Diego
Genomics **(3162)**
Molecular Therapy **(3237)**
Plasmid **(3246)**
Protein Expression and Purification **(3250)**

CONNECTICUT
Farmington
Cytogenetics and Cell Genetics **(4810)** 1,800
Human Heredity **(4833)** 1,000

DISTRICT OF COLUMBIA
Washington
The Journal of Genetic
   Psychology **(5593)** ....(Paid) 795

KANSAS
Lawrence
Evolution **(11550)** 3,878
Human Biology **(11552)** 1,800

MARYLAND
Bethesda
ASFA Marine Biotechnology Abstracts **(13317)**
Genetics Abstracts **(13340)**
Physiological Genomics **(13373)**

Gaithersburg
Experimental Aging Research **(13539)** 1,000

MASSACHUSETTS
Waltham
Journal of Neurogenetics **(14600)**

MINNESOTA
Minneapolis
Genetics in Medicine **(16083)** ....(Paid) ‡1,405

NEW JERSEY
Hoboken
American Journal of Medical
   Genetics **(18887)** 9800
Developmental Genetics **(18928)** 3850
Developmental Psychobiology **(18929)** 5600
Genetic Epidemiology **(18951)** 6300
Human Mutation **(18967)** 4900
Proteins: Structure, Function, and
   Genetics **(19089)** 8400
Yeast **(19121)**

NEW YORK
Larchmont
Biotechnology Law Report **(20892)**
Cloning and Stem Cells **(20894)**
Genetic Engineering News **(20901)**

New York
Annals of Human Genetics **(21217)**
Behavior Genetics **(21293)**
Conservation Genetics **(21484)**
Familial Cancer **(21676)**
Genetic Resources and Crop Evolution **(21751)**
Genetical Research **(21752)** 800
Journal of Genetic Counseling **(22079)**
Mammalian Genome **(22276)** ....(Combined) 925
Nature Genetics **(22411)** ....(Paid) 6,100
Russian Journal of Genetics **(22690)**

PENNSYLVANIA
Philadelphia
Annals of Human Biology **(27378)**

Pittsburgh
Genetics **(27791)** ....‡5,200

TEXAS
Austin
Biochemical Genetics **(29764)**

Galveston
International Journal of Developmental
   Neuroscience **(30381)** ....(Paid) 700
        (Non-paid) 300

ONTARIO, CANADA
North York
Genome **(36128)** ....‡1,400

Waterloo
Biotechnology Advances **(36846)** 1,000

GEOGRAPHY

ALASKA
Anchorage
Alaska Geographic **(521)** ....(Paid) 4,001

CALIFORNIA
Redlands
Arc News **(2900)** ....(Non-paid) 380,000

San Diego
The Professional Geographer **(3249)** 8,000

DISTRICT OF COLUMBIA
Washington
Annals of the Association of American
   Geographers **(5351)** ....‡8,750
Computational Seismology **(5430)**
National Geographic **(5672)** ....(Paid) 7,828,642
Reviews of Geophysics **(5767)**

FLORIDA
Miami
Geomundo **(6356)**

GEORGIA
Athens
Southeastern Geographer **(6950)** ....(Combined) 900

ILLINOIS
DeKalb
Names **(8739)** ....(Paid) 850

MARYLAND
Gaithersburg
ACSM Bulletin **(13531)** 10,000
Cartography and Geographic Information
   Science **(13532)** 3,500
Surveying and Land Information
   Science **(13548)** ....(Paid) 8,500

Silver Spring
Demography **(13724)** ....(Paid) 3,000

MASSACHUSETTS
Worcester
Economic Geography **(14678)** ....‡1,750

MINNESOTA
St. Cloud
Journal of Geography **(16343)** ....‡4,500

Circ.   Circ.   Circ.

GEOGRAPHY (continued)
NEW HAMPSHIRE
Peterborough
Faces (18623) 13,000

NEW JERSEY
Hoboken
International Journal of Population
   Geography (18994)
River Research and Applications (19100)

NEW YORK
New York
Geographical Review (21753)
GeoJournal (21754)
Journal of American Studies (21986) .....(Paid) ‡455
                                       (Non-paid) ‡3,346
Landscape Ecology (22232)
Polar Record (22570) 800

OHIO
Bowling Green
Journal of Cultural Geography (24694)

Columbus
Geographical Analysis (25019) ....‡800

PENNSYLVANIA
Johnstown
The Pennsylvania
   Geographer (27088) ....!........(Combined) 450

Topton
Special Libraries Association, Geography & Map
   Division (28052) ....(Paid) ‡700
                                       (Controlled) ‡39

ONTARIO, CANADA
Toronto
Cartographica (36537) 950

Waterloo
Environments (36850) ....(Combined) 400

QUEBEC, CANADA
Montreal
The Canadian Geographer (37093)

GEOLOGY

ALABAMA
Birmingham
Doklady Earth Sciences (69) ....‡500
Geochemistry International (72) 675

ARIZONA
Tucson
Paleoclimates (958)

CALIFORNIA
El Cerrito
Bulletin (1859) ....(Paid) ‡2,737
Seismological Research Letters (1862)

Palo Alto
Annual Review of Earth and Planetary
   Sciences (2789)

Sacramento
California Geology Magazine (2982) 7,000
Journal of Environmental Hydrology (3004)

San Diego
Icarus (3169)
Quaternary Research (3252)

COLORADO
Boulder
Abstracts with Programs (4154) 6,000
Geological Society of America
   Bulletin (4168) ....‡5,000
Geology (4169) ....(Paid) ‡6,500

Denver
Mountain Geologist (4340) ....(Paid) 2,200

Littleton
Economic Geology (4547) 5,000

CONNECTICUT
New Haven
American Journal of Science (4982) 2,500

DELAWARE
Newark
Journal of Foraminiferal Research (5276)

DISTRICT OF COLUMBIA
Washington
American Mineralogist (5336) ....(Paid) 3,200
EOS (5483) 41,000
International Journal of Geomagnetism and
   Aeronomy (5553)
Journal of Geophysical Research (5594)
Paleobiology (5713)
Rocks & Minerals (5770) ....(Paid) ‡3,100
                                       (Controlled) 1,000
Tectonics (5817)

FLORIDA
Boca Raton
International Journal of Geomechanics (5934)

HAWAII
Honolulu
Marine Georesources and Geotechnology (7711)

KANSAS
Lawrence
Journal of Paleontology (11557) ....‡2,500

MASSACHUSETTS
Cambridge
Journal of Sedimentary Research (14079) 6,000

MISSISSIPPI
Jackson
Mississippi Geology (16703) ....(Non-paid) 1,100

NEW JERSEY
Hoboken
Archaeological Prospection (18896)
Earthquake Engineering and Structural
   Dynamics (18935)
Environmetrics (18942)
Geoarchaeology (18952) 3850
Geological Journal (18953)
Hydrological Processes (18971)
Journal of Quaternary
   Science (19043) ....(Paid) 4,200
Permafrost and Periglacial
   Processes (19080) 3,500
River Research and Applications (19100)
X-Ray Spectrometry (19120)

NEW MEXICO
Socorro
New Mexico Geology (19959) ....(Combined) 650

NEW YORK
Ithaca
Geomicrobiology
   Journal (20801) ....(Controlled) ‡281

New York
American Museum Novitates (21202)
Computational Geosciences (21469)
Environmental Geochemistry and Health (21618)
Geological Magazine (21755) 850
Geotechnical and Geological Engineering (21758)
Journal of Atmospheric Chemistry (22002)
Journal of Paleolimnology (22150)
Journal of Seismology (22185)
Marine Geophysical Researches (22282)
Mathematical Geology (22293)
Polar and Glaciological Abstracts (22569) 300
Polar Record (22570) 800
Studia Geophysica et Geodaetica (22799)

Troy
Carbonates and Evaporites (23452)
Northeastern Geology and Environmental
   Sciences (23454) ....(Paid) 400

NORTH CAROLINA
Durham
Southeastern Geology (23845) ....‡500

OKLAHOMA
Norman
Oklahoma Geology
   Notes (25940) ....(Combined) 1,000

Tulsa
AAPG Bulletin (26104) ....‡30,000
AAPG Explorer (26105) ....(Paid) ‡30,000
                                       (Controlled) ‡300
Geophysics (26116) ....‡16,530

OREGON
Klamath Falls
Radio Science (26385)

Portland
Oregon Geology (26491) ....(Controlled) ‡1,350

TEXAS
College Station
American Association of Stratigraphic Palynologists
   Contributions Series (30036) ....(Combined) 952
Palynology (30047) ....(Controlled) 952

UTAH
Logan
Arid Land Research and Management (31346)

VIRGINIA
Alexandria
Geotimes (31675) ....(Paid) 10,092
                                       (Non-paid) 502

Reston
Journal of Geotechnical and Geoenvironmental
   Engineering (32379)
Journal of Waterway, Port, Coastal, and Ocean
   Engineering (32402)

WISCONSIN
Madison
Ground Water (33944)

ALBERTA, CANADA
Calgary
Arctic (34627)

Edmonton
Canadian Journal of Earth Sciences (Revue
   Canadienne des Sciences de la
   Terre) (34703) ....‡2,200
The PEGG (34724) ....(Controlled) 31,647

NOVA SCOTIA, CANADA
Wolfville
Atlantic Geology (35623)

ONTARIO, CANADA
Mississauga
Canadian Geotechnical Journal (Revue Canadienne
   de Geotechnique) (36059) ....‡2,700

GERONTOLOGY

ARKANSAS
Little Rock
Geriatric Nursing (1230) ....(Paid) ‡6,050

CALIFORNIA
Redlands
Clinical Gerontologist (2902) ....(Paid) 540

San Francisco
Aging Today (3325) ....(Paid) ‡12,500
                                       (Free) ‡1,500
Generations, Journal of the American Society on
   Aging (3365) ....(Paid) 14,200
                                       (Controlled) 300

Thousand Oaks
Abstracts in Social Gerontology (3845) ....‡350
Journal of Aging and Health (3877) ......(Paid) ‡600

CONNECTICUT
Farmington
Gerontology (4827) 1,250

DISTRICT OF COLUMBIA
Washington
The Gerontologist (5513) ....(Paid) ‡7,400
Innovations (5545) ....(Paid) 5,000
The Journals of Gerontology; Psychological Sciences
   & Social Sciences (5621) ....(Paid) ‡5,600

FLORIDA
Sarasota
Journal of Women and Aging (6659) 467

Tampa
Journal of Mental Health and
   Aging (6771) ....(Combined) 300

ILLINOIS
Wheaton
Journal of Religious Gerontology (9757) 691

KENTUCKY
Louisville
Developmental Neuropsychology **(12214)**

MARYLAND
Baltimore
Caring for the Ages **(13143)** ....(Paid) 47,946

Gaithersburg
Experimental Aging Research **(13539)** 1,000

MASSACHUSETTS
Malden
Journal of the American Geriatrics
    Society **(14293)** ....‡9,228

Worcester
Gerontology & Geriatrics Education **(14680)** .....‡407

MICHIGAN
Detroit
Journal of Aging and
    Ethnicity **(14933)** ....(Combined) 150

MISSOURI
Columbia
Journal of Aging Studies **(16994)**

NEW JERSEY
Thorofare
Journal of Gerontological
    Nursing **(19621)** ....(Paid) ‡10,000

NEW YORK
Amityville
International Journal of Aging and Human
    Development **(20038)**

Binghamton
Journal of Elder Abuse and
    Neglect **(20169)** 1,193

Bronx
Physical & Occupational Therapy in
    Geriatrics **(20280)** ....(Combined) 890

Little Neck
Journal of Nutrition for the
    Elderly **(20952)** ....(Controlled) ‡700

New York
Ageing and Society **(21164)** ....(Paid) ‡948
    (Non-paid) ‡102
Biogerontology **(21315)**
Contemporary
    Gerontology **(21494)** ....(Controlled) 1,000
International
    Psychogeriatrics **(21932)** ....(Combined) 1,400
Journal of Aging and Identity **(21978)**
Journal of Clinical Geropsychology **(22025)**
Journal of Cross-Cultural Gerontology **(22041)**
Journal of Gerontological Social
    Work **(22081)** 998
Topics in Geriatric
    Rehabilitation **(22845)** ....(Paid) 1,768
    (Non-paid) 70

NORTH CAROLINA
Durham
Research on Aging **(23842)** ....(Paid) ‡1,350
    (Non-paid) ‡84

OHIO
Cleveland
Geriatrics **(24903)** ....(Controlled) ‡77,000

Dayton
Ethics, Law and Aging
    Review **(25115)** ....(Combined) 1,000

Kettering
Journal of Nutrition, Health & Aging **(25283)**

OKLAHOMA
Stillwater
Southwest Journal on
    Aging **(26082)** ....(Controlled) 750

PENNSYLVANIA
Levittown
CAPsule **(27187)** ....(Controlled) 2,000

Philadelphia
Clinics in Geriatric Medicine **(27415)**

TEXAS
Denton
Educational Gerontology **(30236)**

BRITISH COLUMBIA, CANADA
Victoria
Ageing International **(35205)** ....(Paid) ‡900

ONTARIO, CANADA
Hamilton
Canadian Journal on Aging (La Revue Canadienne
    du vieillissement) **(35876)** ....(Paid) 1,935
    (Non-paid) 27

Toronto
Geriatric Medicine Quarterly **(36601)**
Geriatrics Today **(36602)** ....(Combined) 18,000

GIFTS, TOYS, AND NOVELTIES

CALIFORNIA
Tarzana
RePlay Magazine **(3839)** ....(Combined) 4,000

ILLINOIS
Chicago
Giftware News **(8387)** ....(Paid) 15,239
    (Non-paid) 21,766

NEW JERSEY
Goshen
Selling Christmas
    Decorations **(18850)** ....(Controlled) 17,500

Morganville
Hobby Merchandiser **(19286)** ....(Paid) ‡2,200
    (Non-paid) ‡6,000

NEW YORK
New York
Children's Business **(21410)** ......(Non-paid) ‡14,083
Gifts & Decorative
    Accessories **(21761)** ....(Paid) 25,726
Giftware Business **(21762)** ....(Paid) 4,285
    (Controlled) 30,114
The Toy Book **(22850)** ....(Non-paid) 14,584
    (Paid) 617

PENNSYLVANIA
Ardmore
Souvenirs, Gifts, & Novelties
    Magazine **(26664)** ....(Controlled) ‡41,871

WISCONSIN
Waukesha
Model Retailer **(34408)** ....(Paid) ★4,320

ONTARIO, CANADA
North York
Toys & Games **(36132)** ....(Combined) 5,000

Toronto
Gifts & Tablewares **(36604)** ....(Paid) 1,796
    (Non-paid) 14,065

GLASS AND CHINA

See also Ceramics

ILLINOIS
Chicago
Giftware News **(8387)** ....(Paid) 15,239
    (Non-paid) 21,766

KENTUCKY
Westport
Glass Patterns Quarterly **(12437)** .....(Paid) ⊕37,000

MARYLAND
Baltimore
International Chinese Snuff Bottle Society
    Journal **(13172)** 600

MASSACHUSETTS
Franklin
Glass New England **(14205)** ....(Non-paid) 2,150

MISSOURI
Raytown
Stained Glass Magazine **(17370)** ......(Paid) ‡9,000
    (Non-paid) ‡140

NEW YORK
New York
Giftware Business **(21762)** ....(Paid) 4,285
    (Controlled) 30,114

Glass and Ceramics **(21765)**

Glass Digest **(21766)** ....(Paid) 10,790
    (Non-paid) 3,945
Glass Industry **(21767)** ....(Paid) 1,641
    (Non-paid) 970
Glass Physics and Chemistry **(21768)**

OKLAHOMA
Oklahoma City
The China Painter **(25960)** ....‡9,500

PENNSYLVANIA
East Greenville
Antique Bottle and Glass
    Collector **(26845)** ....(Controlled) ⊕3,700

VIRGINIA
Garrisonville
AGRR: AutoGlass Repair and
    Replacement **(32102)** ....(Non-paid) 10,190
Architects' Guide to Glass, Metal &
    Glazing **(32103)** ....(Controlled) 20,000
Plastics Fabricating &
    Forming **(32104)** ....(Paid) ‡25,000
Shelter **(32105)**
USGlass, Metal & Glazing **(32106)** ....△27,826
Window Film **(32107)** ....(Paid) ‡6,831

Mc Lean
AutoGlass **(32241)** ....(Paid) 7,000
Glass Magazine **(32244)** ....(Paid) △4,375
    (Non-paid) △19,363

WASHINGTON
Seattle
Glass Art Society Journal **(32968)**

ONTARIO, CANADA
Exeter
Glass Canada **(35826)** ....(Non-paid) ‡5,200

GOLF COURSE MANAGEMENT

See also Turf and Turf Maintenance

CONNECTICUT
New Canaan
Golf Range Magazine **(4978)** ....(Paid) 810
    (Controlled) 5,820

Trumbull
Golf World Business **(5184)** .....(Controlled) ‡18,500

FLORIDA
Clearwater
Southern Golf **(5990)**

ILLINOIS
Chicago
California Fairways **(8297)**

MAINE
Yarmouth
Golf Course News **(13077)** ......(Controlled) ‡24,100

MISSOURI
St. Louis
Resort Management & Operations **(17486)**

VERMONT
St. Johnsbury
TURF **(31594)** ....(Controlled) ‡68,600

ONTARIO, CANADA
Delhi
Turf & Recreation **(35771)** ....(Combined) 15,000

GRAPHIC ARTS AND DESIGN

CALIFORNIA
Agoura
Tattoo Industry **(1382)**

Menlo Park
Communication Arts **(2523)** ....(Paid) ‡70,189

Roseville
Before & After **(2970)** ....(Paid) ‡33,000

FLORIDA
Oldsmar
Mac Design Magazine **(6484)**

Ponte Vedra Beach
Digital Output **(6594)** 30,000

Circ.   Circ.   Circ.

GRAPHIC ARTS AND DESIGN (continued)

ILLINOIS
Chicago
Visible Language (8599) ....‡1,300

Skokie
P-O-P Design (9608) ....(Non-paid) △18,005

South Holland
IPA Bulletin (9615) ....‡1,600

INDIANA
West Lafayette
Engineering Design Graphics
   Journal (10546) ....(Controlled) 575

KANSAS
Overland Park
Entertainment Design (11711) ....(Combined) 16,400

MASSACHUSETTS
Boston
DMI Academic Review (13886)

Natick
Journal of Graphics Tools (14347) 2,000

NEW HAMPSHIRE
Nashua
Electronic Publishing (18589) 70,000

NEW JERSEY
Lambertville
Modernism Magazine (19159) ....(Paid) ‡7,500

NEW YORK
New York
Gain (21745)
International Journal of Technology and Design
   Education (21922)
Rhizome Digest (22666) ....(Combined) 6,600
Trace: AIGA Journal of
   Design (22851) ....(Controlled) 17,000

NORTH CAROLINA
Greenville
Sign Builder
   Illustrated (23969) ....(Non-paid) ‡12,000

OHIO
Cincinnati
HOW (24804) ....(Paid) 37,008

Cleveland
DesignMart (24881) ....(Combined) 112,000
Mechanical Solutions (24926) ....(Combined) 100,000
Motion Systems
   Consultant (24930) ....(Combined) 10,000

TEXAS
Leakey
Fine Print (30679) 2000

WASHINGTON
Seattle
Media Inc. (32986)

ONTARIO, CANADA
Toronto
AutoCAD User (36467) ....(Controlled) 15,000

HAIRSTYLING

See also Cosmetics and Toiletries

CALIFORNIA
Van Nuys
Dayspa (3986) ....(Controlled) 32,564

CONNECTICUT
Milford
American Salon (4952) 133,000

ILLINOIS
Lincolnshire
Modern Salon (9086) ....(Paid) ★60,437
   (Non-paid) ★58,588

NEW YORK
New York
Salon News (22702) ....(Combined) 77,000
SalonNews (22703)

OKLAHOMA
Tulsa
State of the Art (26133) ....(Paid) 40,000

ONTARIO, CANADA
Toronto
Salon Magazine (36734) ....(Controlled) 25,000

HANDICAPPED

ARIZONA
Sun City West
Accent on Living (897) ....(Paid) ‡19,000
   (Controlled) ‡300

Tucson
Quest (960) ....(Non-paid) 115,000

CALIFORNIA
Oakland
Impact! (2681) ....(Non-paid) 3,000

San Francisco
Disability Statistics Report (3349)

COLORADO
Denver
NARHA Strides (4341) 4,100

DISTRICT OF COLUMBIA
Washington
American Rehabilitation (5341) 4,700
Braille Forum (5382) ....(Non-paid) 22,000
Mental Retardation (5647) ....(Paid) 10,000
Musical Mainstream (5665) ....(Non-paid) ‡3,600
RE:view (5758) ....(Combined) ‡4,850
Section 504 Compliance Handbook (5786)
Talking Book Topics (5810) ....(Free) ‡286,000
Update (Library of
   Congress) (5837) ....(Non-paid) 7,600
World Around You (5867) 3,000

FLORIDA
Fort Lauderdale
Journal of Developmental and Physical
   Disabilities (6078)

Hollywood
Reach Out Magazine (6197) ....(Paid) ‡3,000

GEORGIA
Athens
Journal of Learning Disabilities (6945) ....‡8,500

ILLINOIS
Champaign
Adapted Physical Activity
   Quarterly (8177) ....(Paid) ‡977
   ‡26

Chicago
Disability Studies Quarterly (8354) ....(Paid) 500

Macomb
PALAESTRA (9131) ....(Combined) ‡5000

MARYLAND
Baltimore
The Journal of the Association for Persons with
   Severe Handicaps (13179) .....(Controlled) ‡4,000

Bethesda
Hearing Loss (13343) ....(Paid) 200,000

Landover Hills
Vision (13596) ....‡1,000

Lusby
JADARA (13625) ....(Paid) 1,200

Silver Spring
The Arc's Government Report (13723)
Mental Health Report (13738)

MISSOURI
Fulton
Missouri Record (17077)

NEW JERSEY
New Brunswick
Journal of Religion, Disability &
   Health (19334) ....(Paid) 335

Springfield
Progress in Research (19596) .....(Non-paid) 25,000

Thorofare
O&P Business News (19628)
O&P World (19629)

NEW YORK
Buffalo
Technology and Disability (20390)

New York
Information Technology and
   Disabilities (21872) ....(Non-paid) 1,900
International Rehabilitation
   Review (21934) ....(Paid) 5,000
Open World for Disability and Mature
   Travel (22496) ....(Paid) 1,500
   (Non-paid) 8,500

PENNSYLVANIA
Horsham
Counterpoint (27057) ....(Paid) 100,000
Early Childhood Law and Policy Reporter (27059)

King of Prussia
ADVANCE for Occupational Therapy
   Practitioners (27117) ....(Non-paid) ‡60,000

Pittsburgh
Journal for Vocational Special Needs
   Education (27805)

TEXAS
Austin
Journal of Disability Policy
   Studies (29786) ....(Paid) 400

VIRGINIA
Alexandria
Journal of Rehabilitation (31701) 15,000

Arlington
Assistive Technology (31781)
Physical Disabilities—Education & Related
   Services (31817) ....(Non-paid) 1,300

HARDWARE

ARIZONA
Phoenix
Asian Sources Hardwares (789)

FLORIDA
Naples
Link (6443) ....(Paid) 13,000

IOWA
Hull
Hardware Trade (10955) ....(Non-paid) 32,327

MISSOURI
Kansas City
Southwestern Retailer (17197) ....(Paid) ‡1,100
   (Controlled) ‡420

NEW YORK
New York
Hardware Age's Home Improvement
   Market (21789) ....(Paid) 2,600
   (Non-paid) 66,895

VIRGINIA
Chantilly
Doors and Hardware (31911) ....(Paid) ‡13,000
   (Non-paid) ‡200

MANITOBA, CANADA
Winnipeg
WRLA Yardstick (35365) ....(Controlled) 1,650

ONTARIO, CANADA
Toronto
Hardware and Home Centre
   Magazine (36610) ....(Combined) •16,036
Hardware
   Merchandising (36611) ....(Combined) •15,037
Home Improvement
   Retailing (36616) ....(Combined) 15,356

QUEBEC, CANADA
Longueuil
Quart de Rond (37058) ....(Combined) 3,000

HEALTH AND FITNESS

ALABAMA
Birmingham
COOKING LIGHT　**(66)** ....(Paid) 1,574,194

COLORADO
Boulder
Delicious Living!　**(4165)** ....(Paid) 458,974

Colorado Springs
Strength and Conditioning
　Journal　**(4258)** ....(Paid) 26,000

CONNECTICUT
Danbury
Coach and Athletic Director　**(4737)** 2,50,000

ILLINOIS
Champaign
Exercise Immunology Review　**(8187)** .....(Paid) ‡170

Springfield
Illinois Parks & Recreation
　Magazine　**(9628)** 6,000

MASSACHUSETTS
Concord
Perspective　**(14148)** ....‡6,700

MICHIGAN
Birmingham
Balance　**(14823)**

MINNESOTA
St. Paul
Melpomene　**(16388)** ....(Paid) 1,700
　　　　　　　　　　　　　　　(Non-paid) 173

NEVADA
Las Vegas
ACSM's Health & Fitness
　Journal　**(18359)** ....‡10,700
Healing Arts Quarterly　**(18363)** ....(Paid) 25,000

NEW JERSEY
South Plainfield
Whole Foods　**(19591)** ....(Paid) 303
　　　　　　　　　　　　　　(Controlled) 16,203

NEW YORK
Brooklyn
Awake!　**(20298)** ....‡20,682,000

Westbury
Government Recreation and
　Fitness　**(23556)** ....(Paid) 10,500

VIRGINIA
Reston
American Journal of Health Education　**(32360)**

BRITISH COLUMBIA, CANADA
Burnaby
alive　**(34888)** ....‡240,000

ONTARIO, CANADA
Hamilton
Healthy Weight Journal　**(35880)** ....(Paid) 892
　　　　　　　　　　　　　　(Non-paid) 892

Ottawa
Physical & Health Education Journal　**(36270)**

QUEBEC, CANADA
Montreal
Dietetique en Action　**(37108)**
Spa Management　**(37226)** ....(Paid) ‡28,623

HEALTH AND HEALTHCARE

See also Hospitals and Healthcare
Institutions; Medicine and Surgery; Nursing

ALABAMA
Birmingham
Nutrition Reviews　**(83)** ....‡6,500

ARKANSAS
Little Rock
Air Medical Journal　**(1209)** ....(Paid) ‡5,250
AJIC (American Journal of Infection
　Control)　**(1210)** ....(Paid) ‡11,136
The Case Manager　**(1226)** ....(Combined) 20,000

Journal of Registry
　Management　**(1232)** ....(Non-paid) 2,600

CALIFORNIA
Berkeley
Cambridge Quarterly of Healthcare
　Ethics　**(1506)** 950
HSR　**(1527)**

Burbank
Home Health Care Services Quarterly　**(1618)**

Davis
Clinical Reviews in Allergy & Immunology　**(1813)**

Encinitas
Alternative Therapies in Health and
　Medicine　**(1882)** ....(Paid) 14,000

Los Angeles
The American Senior　**(2209)** ....(Paid) 120,000
Contemporary Long Term
　Care　**(2246)** ....(Paid) 2,529
　　　　　　　　　　　　　(Non-paid) 38,337
Fitness Management Magazine　**(2271)** ....(Paid) 243
　　　　　　　　　　　　　(Controlled) 26,000
Physical Therapy
　Products　**(2367)** ....(Controlled) 40,000
Respiratory Therapy
　Products　**(2379)** ....(Controlled) 30,000

Malibu
HomeCare Magazine　**(2490)** .....(Controlled) ‡17,069

Monrovia
Health Freedom News　**(2577)**

Sacramento
California Community Care News/Senior Citizens
　Today　**(2980)** ....(Paid) 5,000
California Journal of Health-System Pharmacy　**(2984)**
Sierra Sacramento Valley
　Medicine　**(3019)** ....(Controlled) 2,000

San Diego
IDEA Health & Fitness
　Source　**(3171)** ....(Paid) 23,000
JEMS　**(3175)** ....(Paid) 28,000
　　　　　　　　　　　　　(Controlled) 12,000
Preventive Medicine　**(3248)**
San Diego County Physician　**(3261)** .....(Paid) 3,000

San Francisco
BETA (Bulletin of Experimental Treatments for
　AIDS)　**(3330)** ....(Non-paid) 25,000
Journal of Cardiac Failure　**(3378)**
Pain Management Nursing　**(3411)**

Santa Monica
RAND Review　**(3715)** ....(Controlled) 15,000

Santa Rosa
Northwesterner　**(3732)** ....(Non-paid) 700

Sherman Oaks
Spondylitis Plus　**(3763)**

Thousand Oaks
AWHONN Lifelines　**(3851)** ....(Paid) 21,500
Evaluation & the Health
　Professions　**(3867)** ....(Paid) ‡500
Journal of Adolescent
　Research　**(3876)** ....(Paid) ‡600
Journal of Aging and Health　**(3877)** ......(Paid) ‡600
Journal of the Association of Nurses in AIDS
　Care　**(3880)** ....(Paid) ‡3,000
Journal of Health Care for the Poor and
　Underserved　**(3891)** ....(Paid) ‡742
　　　　　　　　　　　　　(Non-paid) ‡101

Van Nuys
Dayspa　**(3986)** ....(Controlled) 32,564

COLORADO
Boulder
Nutrition Science News　**(4182)** ....(Combined) 21,000

Broomfield
Natural Business　**(4205)** ....(Paid) 900

Colorado Springs
Physician Magazine　**(4254)** ....‡71,000

Denver
American Journal of Bariatric
　Medicine　**(4304)** ....(Controlled) 1,800
Primary Care Case Reviews　**(4349)**
Public Safety Product
　News　**(4350)** ....(Non-paid) 14,292
SSM　**(4358)** ....(Combined) 14,000

CONNECTICUT
Farmington
Community Genetics　**(4809)** ....(Combined) 1,000
Forschende Komplementarmedizin und Klassische
　Naturheilkunde　**(4826)** ....(Combined) 4,000
HeartDrug　**(4830)**

Hebron
Radiation Protection
　Management　**(4916)** ....(Paid) 750
RSO Magazine　**(4917)** ....(Paid) 950

Madison
Depression and Stress　**(4928)**
Journal of Developmental and Learning
　Disorders　**(4932)**

New Haven
Journal of Health Politics, Policy and
　Law　**(4994)** ....‡2500

New London
Medical Benefits　**(5019)**

Ridgefield
Medicina Y Cultura　**(5098)** ....(Controlled) 35,000

Vernon
The Door Opener　**(5187)** ....(Paid) 2,100
　　　　　　　　　　　　　(Non-paid) 400

Wilton
Critical Care
　International　**(5224)** ....(Controlled) ‡26,000

DISTRICT OF COLUMBIA
Washington
American Journal on Mental
　Retardation　**(5333)** ....(Combined) 10,000
American Journal of Public Health　**(5334)** ....‡33,000
Archives of Environmental
　Health　**(5360)** ....(Paid) ‡1,600
Caring　**(5394)** ....(Paid) 7,000
Good Medicine Magazine　**(5516)**
Health & Social Work　**(5523)** 6,500
Healthplan　**(5524)** ....(Paid) ‡6,700
Journal of American College
　Health　**(5569)** ....(Combined) ‡2,700
Journal of Health Communication　**(5595)**
Journals of Gerontology　**(5620)**
Minority Health Today　**(5652)**
The Nation's Health　**(5687)** ....(Paid) ‡29,300
　　　　　　　　　　　　　(Non-paid) ‡1,000
Provider　**(5735)** 44,778
Quality Matters　**(5753)** ....(Paid) 1,500
State Health Monitor　**(5804)**
Youth Today　**(5874)** ....(Combined) 58,000

FLORIDA
Boca Raton
Your Health　**(5942)** ....(Paid) 47,288

Deerfield Beach
Counselor　**(6048)** ....(Paid) 30,000

Fort Lauderdale
The Voice Newspaper　**(6086)**

Fort Myers
Children's Health Care　**(6094)**

Naples
Operative Techniques in Thoracic and Cardiovascular
　Surgery　**(6448)**

Tampa
Cancer Control Journal　**(6759)**
Health Science　**(6768)** 6,000
Journal of Behavioral Health Services &
　Research　**(6769)** ....(Paid) 3,500
　　　　　　　　　　　　　(Non-paid) 100
Journal of Mental Health and
　Aging　**(6771)** ....(Combined) 300

GEORGIA
Atlanta
Club Industry　**(6987)** ....(Combined) 30,107
Emerging Infectious Diseases　**(7003)**
Healthcare Marketing Report　**(7015)**
Morbidity and Mortality Weekly
　Report　**(7028)** ....(Combined) 44,000
Stem Cell Week　**(7046)**
Women's Health Weekly　**(7062)**

Augusta
Journal of PeriAnesthesia Nursing　**(7100)**

IDAHO
Dover
Alternative Medicine Review　**(7852)** ....(Paid) ⊕7,500

Circulation: ★ = ABC; △ = BPA; ✦ = CAC; ● = CCAB; ❑ = VAC; ⊕ = PO Statement; ‡ = Publisher's Report; Boldface figures = sworn; Light figures = estimated.

3151

Circ.   Circ.   Circ.

HEALTH AND HEALTHCARE (continued)

ILLINOIS

Arlington Heights
FacilityCare (8023) ....(Paid) 37,000

Aurora
Advances in Wound Care (8038) ....(Paid) ‡4,500
(Non-paid) ‡2,000

Carol Stream
Skin Inc. (8155) ....(Paid) ‡6,006
(Controlled) ‡3,401

Champaign
Adapted Physical Activity
Quarterly (8177) ....(Paid) ‡977
‡26

Chicago
AIDS Book Review
Journal (8250) ....(Non-paid) 5,000
Business Insurance (8296) ....(Paid) 25,386
(Controlled) 20,339
Frontiers of Health Services
Management (8382) ....‡2,500
Health Data Management (8392)
Health Data Management (8393)
Healthcare Executive (8396) ....(Paid) 20,832
(Non-paid) 406
Hospitals & Health Networks (8401)
Journal of AHIMA (8429) ....(Paid) 45,000
(Non-paid) 450
Journal of the American Dietetic
Association (8431) ....(Paid) 70,980
(Non-paid) 582
Journal of Healthcare Risk
Management (8440) ....(Paid) 4,300
Journal of the Medical Library
Association (8445) ....(Non-paid) ‡5,000
(Paid) ‡800
Marketing Health Services (8477) ....(Paid) ‡3781
(Non-paid) ‡179
Materials Management in Health
Care (8481) ....(Non-paid) 30,000
Modern Healthcare (8490) ....(Paid) 2,828
(Non-paid) 76,894
Modern Physician (8492)
The PMA (8534) 22,000

Elgin
International Journal of Dermatology (8824)

Evanston
Patient Care and Nursing
Products (8868) ....(Controlled) ‡75,171

Itasca
Safety+Health (9018) ....(Controlled) 51,000

Lisle
ABNF Journal (9109) ....(Combined) 562

Northbrook
AWHP's Worksite
Health (9312) ....(Controlled) 2,900
Current Health 1 (9314) ....(Paid) 165,793
Current Health 2 (9315) ....(Paid) 229,274

Oak Brook
Employee Services
Management (9351) ....(Paid) ‡4,000
(Non-paid) ‡600

Oak Park
Doody's Health Sciences Book Review
Journal (9374) ....(Paid) 750
(Non-paid) 100

Oakbrook Terrace
The Joint Commission Journal on Quality
Improvement (9380) ....‡5,300

Park Ridge
AMT Events (9404) ....(Controlled) 26,000

St. Charles
Dietary Manager Magazine (9567) 17,000

Westchester
Sleep (9752) ....(Paid) 4,051

Wheaton
Journal of Outcome Measurement (9756)

INDIANA

Indianapolis
Journal of Nursing Scholarship (10140) 115,000
Medical Care (10152) ....(Paid) 2,293
The Saturday Evening
Post (10169) ....(Paid) 385,123
Seminars in Pediatric Surgery (10170)

Seminars in Respiratory Infections (10171)

KANSAS

Kansas City
Focus on Autism and Other Developmental
Disabilities (11526) ....(Paid) ‡1600

Leawood
Family Practice Management (11584) ....‡97,348

Overland Park
Home Care Magazine (11714)

KENTUCKY

Louisville
Journal of Cardiothoracic and Vascular
Anesthesia (12220)
Unique Opportunities (12242) .....(Controlled) 80,000

LOUISIANA

New Orleans
The Keepsake (12736) ....(Paid) ‡10,000
The Ochsner Journal (12749) ......(Combined) 9,496

MAINE

Augusta
Fatal Occupational Injuries in
Maine (12891) ....(Non-paid) 1,000

MARYLAND

Baltimore
The Annals of Dyslexia (13123) 12,000
Caring for the Ages (13143) ....(Paid) 47,946
Journal of Health Care Law and
Policy (13191) ....(Paid) 250
Journal of Voice (13205) 2178
World Federation for Mental Health Annual
Report (13263) ....(Paid) 2500

Bethesda
Health Affairs (13341) ....(Paid) ‡11,500
Health and Safety Science Abstracts (13342)
OT Practice (13370)

College Park
Medical Dosimetry (13434)

Columbia
American Journal of Dance Therapy (13451)

Ellicott City
International Journal of Emergency Mental
Health (13498)

Gaithersburg
Quality Management in Health
Care (13547) ....(Paid) 1,400
Topics in Clinical Nutrition (13549) ......(Paid) 1,400
(Non-paid) 86

Hyattsville
Advance Data (13585) ....(Non-paid) 15,000

Rockville
Internal Medicine News (13684) ....(Paid) 101,608
Journal of Speech, Language, and Hearing
Research (13685)
Prevention Pipeline (13696)

Towson
Research in Healthcare Financial
Management (13765)

MASSACHUSETTS

Amherst
International Quarterly of Community Health
Education (13795)

Boston
Health and Human Rights (13899) ....(Paid) ‡970
Living Healthy Magazine (13923)
Nutrition Today (13941) ....(Paid) 15,200
Obesity Research (13942) ....(Paid) 1,200
Public Health Reports (13954) 7,500
Seminars in Thoracic & Cardiovascular
Surgery (13959)

Malden
Journal of Experimental Therapeutics and
Oncology (14294)

Natick
Clinical Excellence for Nurse Practitioners (14345)

Newton
Innovations in End-of-Life Care (14399)

Sudbury
The Cancer Journal (14578)

Weston
American Journal of Alzheimers
Disease (14648) ....(Paid) ‡2,200
Healing Ministry (14650) 1,100
Journal of Healthcare Safety, Compliance & Infection
Control (14651) ....(Paid) ‡2,200

MICHIGAN

Detroit
Clinical Journal of Women's Health (14919)
Outcomes Management (14942) ....(Paid) ‡1,100

Southfield
Health Care Weekly Review (15543)

Troy
EAP Digest (15621) ....(Paid) ‡3,000
(Controlled) ‡7,000

MINNESOTA

Minneapolis
Journal of Andrology (16086) ....‡1,200

Rochester
Operative Techniques in General Surgery (16310)

MISSOURI

Kansas City
Journal of Rural Health (17177) ....(Paid) 2,400

Rolla
Original Internist (17378) 7,500

St. Louis
Diabetes (17433)
Issues (17448)
Journal of the American Psychiatric Nurses
Association (17453) ....(Paid) ‡5,733
Journal of Hand Surgery (17455)
Managed Care/Innovations (17469) ....‡24,000
Topics in Stroke
Rehabilitation (17525) ....(Paid) 1,000

MONTANA

Missoula
St. Patrick Hospital Health
Update (17876) ....(Controlled) 30,000

NEVADA

Las Vegas
Healing Arts Quarterly (18363) ....(Paid) 25,000

Reno
Journal of Renal Nutrition (18420)

NEW HAMPSHIRE

Concord
WomenWise (18475) ....(Paid) 600
(Non-paid) 1,400

Nashua
Healthcare Review (18590) .....(Combined) ❏52,503

NEW JERSEY

Chatham
CUTIS (18728)
Hospital Therapy (18730) ....(Non-paid) ‡45,080

Clifton
Clinician Reviews (18753)

Cranford
Safety Briefs (18772) ....(Non-paid) ‡8,000

Edison
Applied Clinical
Trials (18786) ....(Combined) △14,972

Hoboken
Biopharmaceutics and Drug Disposition (18905)
Health Care Analysis (18958)
Health Economics (18959)
International Journal of Health Planning and
Management (18984)
Pharmacoepidemiology and Drug
Safety (19082) 2,800
Phytochemical Analysis (19083) 3,500
Statistics in Medicine (19106) ....(Paid) 12,600

Jamesburg
Internal Medicine World
Report (19130) ....(Controlled) 100,423

Lawrenceville
New Jersey Medicine (19163) 9,200

Montvale
Business & Health (19243) ....(Paid) 3,100
(Controlled) 47,479

Clinical Cardiology Alert (19245)

Contraceptive Technology Update **(19251)**
ED Nursing **(19253)**
Infectious Disease Alert **(19256)**
Internal Medicine Alert **(19257)**
Journal of the American Academy of Physician
  Assistants (JAAPA) **(19260)** ....(Controlled) **40,500**
Medical Economics—Obstetrics/Gynecology
  Edition **(19263)** ....(Non-paid) 30,000
OB/GYN Clinical Alert **(19268)**
Strategic Medicine **(19276)**
Trauma Reports **(19277)**

New Brunswick
Journal of Religion, Disability &
  Health **(19334)** ....(Paid) 335

Newark
Healthstate **(19353)** ....(Non-paid) ‡52,000

Piscataway
Rutgers Center of Alcohol
  Studies **(19431)** ....(Combined) ⊕2,100

Pitman
MedSurg Nursing **(19435)**

Plainsboro
Home Healthcare
  Consultant **(19441)** ....(Paid) 65,000
The Journal of Gender-Specific Medicine **(19442)**

Princeton
International Journal of Occupational Medicine,
  Immunology and Toxicology **(19462)**

Thorofare
Hem/Onc Today **(19616)** ....(Controlled) ⊕33,000
Journal of Spirochetal and Tick-borne
  Diseases **(19627)**
O&P Business News **(19628)**
O&P World **(19629)**
Today in Cardiology **(19641)**

West Long Branch
Health Marketing Quarterly **(19721)**

Wood Ridge
Journal of Community Health Nursing **(19755)**

NEW MEXICO
Santa Fe
OR Manager **(19939)** ....(Combined) 3,500

NEW YORK
Amityville
International Journal of Health Services **(20039)**
New Solutions **(20051)**

Binghamton
Journal of Aggression, Maltreatment &
  Trauma **(20162)**
Journal of Cannabis Therapeutics **(20165)**
Journal of Consumer Health on the Internet **(20167)**
Journal of Health Care
  Chaplaincy **(20176)** ....(Controlled) 417
Journal of Herbal Pharmacotherapy **(20177)**
Journal of Herbs, Spices & Medicinal Plants **(20178)**
Journal of HIV/AIDS & Social Services **(20179)**
Journal of Managed Pharmaceutical
  Care **(20188)** ....(Paid) 2,200
Journal of Neurotherapy **(20189)**
Journal of Social Work in Long-Term Care **(20199)**
Journal of Technology in Human
  Services **(20203)** ....(Combined) 750
Journal of Whiplash & Related Disorders **(20207)**
Occupational Therapy in Mental
  Health **(20209)** 906
Physical and Occupational Therapy in
  Pediatrics **(20210)** ....(Controlled) ‡1,178

Buffalo
Techniques in Regional Anesthesia and Pain
  Management **(20389)**

Chautauqua
Journal of Multicultural Nursing and Health
  (JMCNH) **(20454)**

Clifton Park
Infant—Toddler Intervention **(20465)** ....(Paid) 780

Glen Head
International Journal of Surgical
  Pathology **(20663)** ....(Combined) 2,865
Trends in Amplification **(20664)** ....(Combined) 1,865

Jamaica
International Chinese Sexology Journal **(20835)**

Larchmont
Alternative & Complementary Therapies **(20888)**

Disease Management **(20896)**
Journal of Men's Health **(20916)**
Viral Immunology **(20930)**

Little Neck
Journal of Nutrition for the
  Elderly **(20952)** ....(Controlled) ‡700

Melville
Health Products Business **(21045)** ....(Paid) 12
                              (Non-paid) 18,463

Mineola
Journal of Toxicology: Clinical Toxicology **(21085)**

New York
Advanced in Renal Replacement Therapy **(21153)**
Advances in Health Sciences Education **(21155)**
Aesthetic Surgery
  Journal **(21161)** ....(Combined) ‡5,389
Alzheimer's Care Quarterly **(21175)**
American Journal of Preventive
  Medicine **(21198)** ....(Paid) ‡2,500
                              (Non-paid) ‡18
Annals of Vascular
  Surgery **(21220)** ....(Combined) **2,300**
Biomedical Safety and Standards **(21322)**
Body Positive **(21330)** ....(Paid) 5,000
                              (Controlled) 10,000
Care Management Journals **(21377)** .....(Paid) 1000
                              (Non-paid) 66
Complementary Health Practice
  Review **(21468)** ....(Controlled) 350
Epidemiology and Infection **(21624)** 1000
European Journal of Epidemiology **(21643)**
European Journal of Health Law **(21644)**
Familial Cancer **(21676)**
Family & Community Health **(21678)** ....(Paid) 1,327
                              (Non-paid) 106
Fit Magazine **(21703)** ....(Paid) 149,162
Global Change & Human Health **(21769)**
Guttmacher Report on Public Policy **(21784)**
Health Care Management Science **(21793)**
The Health Care Manager **(21794)** ......(Paid) 1,899
                              (Free) 66
Health Services and Outcomes Research
  Methodology **(21795)**
Inside MS **(21876)** 680,000
International Journal of Cardiovascular
  Imaging **(21900)**
International Journal of Health Care Finance and
  Economics **(21908)**
International Journal of Obstetric Anesthesia **(21912)**
International Journal of Stress Management **(21920)**
International Urology and Nephrology **(21940)**
Internet Health Care **(21941)**
Journal of Controversial Medical Claims **(22039)**
Journal of Cutaneous
  Medicine **(22045)** ....(Combined) 2,500
Journal of the Gay and Lesbian Medical
  Association **(22076)**
Journal of Gender, Culture, and Health **(22077)**
Journal of Genetic Couseling **(22079)**
Journal of Health Care Compliance **(22084)**
Journal of Health Care
  Finance **(22085)** ....(Paid) 2,034
                              (Non-paid) 73
Journal of Immigrant Health **(22091)**
Journal of Inherited Metabolic Disease **(22095)**
Journal of Insurance Coverage **(22098)**
Kidney **(22219)** ....(Combined) 700
Loss, Grief and Care **(22267)**
Managed Care Quarterly **(22277)** 2200
Medicine and Health **(22311)**
Nursing Education
  Perspectives **(22473)** ....(Paid) 3,000
                              (Controlled) 12,000
NUTRITION **(22476)**
Osteoporosis International **(22507)**
Pain Digest **(22518)** ....(Combined) 1,000
Quality of Life Research **(22615)**
Reviews in Endocrine & Metabolic Disorders **(22663)**
Sepsis **(22730)**
SIECUS Report **(22740)** ....(Paid) ‡2,700
Social Work in Health Care **(22757)** 1,608
Topics in Clinical Chiropractic **(22844)** 1,037
Topics in Health Information
  Management **(22846)** 1,500
Vaccine **(22894)**
Women and Health **(22932)** ......(Controlled) ‡1,010

Port Washington
International Journal of Fertility and Women's
  Medicine **(23129)**

Rhinebeck
FOCUS: Journal for Respiratory Care Managers and
  Educators **(23183)**

Rochester
Families, Systems &
  Health **(23225)** ....(Controlled) ⊕1,250

NORTH CAROLINA
Chapel Hill
Seminars in Radiation Oncology **(23722)**

Durham
Journal of Bone and Mineral
  Research **(23829)** 5,000

Greenville
Occupational Therapy in Health Care **(23968)** 650

Wilmington
Health Care for Women
  International **(24295)** ....‡696

Winston-Salem
Arthroscopy **(24318)**

OHIO
Cincinnati
Applied Occupational & Environmental
  Hygiene **(24774)** ....(Paid) ‡6,278
                              (Non-paid) ‡225

Cleveland
Behavioral Health Management **(24863)** 21,802
Journal of Law and Health **(24915)**
Managed Healthcare **(24924)** ....(Paid) △**2,937**
                              (Controlled) △**35,221**
Occupational
  Hazards **(24936)** ....(Controlled) ‡65,000

Dayton
Health Communication **(25120)**

Kent
Journal of School Health **(25274)** 5,000

Kettering
Journal of Nutrition, Health & Aging **(25283)**

OKLAHOMA
Stillwater
Southwest Journal on
  Aging **(26082)** ....(Controlled) 750

OREGON
Eugene
Dendron News **(26315)** ....(Paid) 20,000

PENNSYLVANIA
Hanover
Revista Panamericana de Salud
  Publica **(26976)** ....‡12,000

Hazleton
Journal of Nutraceuticals, Functional & Medical
  Foods **(27034)** ....(Paid) ‡97
                              (Non-paid) ‡23

King of Prussia
ADVANCE for Directors in Rehabilitation **(27109)**
ADVANCE for Health Information Executives **(27110)**
ADVANCE for Health Information
  Professionals **(27111)**
ADVANCE for Managers of Respiratory
  Care **(27113)** ....(Controlled) ‡21,000
ADVANCE for
  Nurses **(27116)** ....(Combined) 510,000
ADVANCE for Physical Therapists and PT
  Assistants **(27118)** ....(Controlled) ‡75,000
ADVANCE for Physician
  Assistants **(27119)** ....(Non-paid) ‡31,900
ADVANCE for Providers of Post-Acute Care **(27120)**

Malvern
Extended Care Product
  News **(27211)** ....(Controlled) ‡46,464
Ostomy/Wound Management **(27215)** 20,201

Norristown
Industrial Safety and Hygiene
  News **(27335)** ....(Controlled) ‡62,057

Philadelphia
Advances in Skin & Wound
  Care **(27363)** ....(Controlled) 20,389
Archives of Family Medicine **(27383)**
AUA News **(27386)** ....(Combined) 12,405
Cancer Epidemiology, Biomarkers &
  Prevention **(27391)** ....(Controlled) 1,421
Cardiology Clinics: Annual of Drug Therapy **(27394)**
Chest Surgery Clinics **(27399)**
Clinical Pediatric Emergency Medicine **(27409)**
Clinical Perspectives in Gastroenterology **(27410)**
Clinics in Family Practice **(27414)**

Circulation: ★ = ABC; △ = BPA; ♦ = CAC; • = CCAB; ❏ = VAC; ⊕ = PO Statement; ‡ = Publisher's Report; Boldface figures = sworn; Light figures = estimated.

3153

Trade, Technical, and Professional Publications

Circ.   Circ.   Circ.

HEALTH AND HEALTHCARE (continued)

Clinics in Liver Disease (27417)
Clinics in Perinatology (27418)
Complementary Medicine for the Physician (27425)
Critical Care Clinics (27429)
CRNA (27431)
Foot and Ankle Clinics (27471)
Gastroenterology Clinics (27474)
Gastrointestinal Endoscopy Clinics (27475)
Growth Hormone and IGF Research (27477)
Hematology/Oncology Clinics (27480)
Home Care Manager (27485)
Home Healthcare Nurse Manager (27486)
Immunology and Allergy Clinics (27489)
Infectious Disease Clinics (27491)
Journal of Cardiovascular Pharmacology and
  Therapeutics (27519)
Journal of Child and Family Nursing (27521)
Journal of Gynecologic Techniques (27529)
Journal of Nuclear
  Cardiology (27539) ....(Combined) ‡6,499
Journal of Pain (27542)
Journal of Pediatric Orthopaedics, Part
  B. (27544) ....(Paid) 1,000
Journal of Professional Nursing (27548)
Journal of the Society of Pediatric
  Nurses (27550) ....‡3,000
Journal of Toxicology and Environmental
  Health (27553) 855
Journal of Trauma Nursing (27554)
Molecular Diagnosis (27573)
Neurology Network Commentary (27578)
Operative Techniques in Gynecologic
  Surgery (27601)
Operative Techniques in Neurosurgery (27602)
Operative Techniques in Orthopaedics (27604)
Operative Techniques in Plastic and Reconstructive
  Surgery (27606)
Operative Techniques in Sports Medicine (27607)
Physical Therapy Case Reports (27639)
Seizure (27657)
Seminars in Breast Disease (27661)
Seminars in Cardiothoracic and Vascular
  Anesthesia (27662)
Seminars in Cutaneous Medicine and
  Surgery (27663)
Seminars in Diagnostic Pathology (27665)
Seminars in Gastrointestinal Disease (27666)
Seminars in Neonatology (27667)
Seminars in Oncology Nursing (27668)
Seminars in Pediatric Neurology (27669)
Seminars in Urologic Oncology (27676)
Sports Chiropractic &
  Rehabilitation (27695) ....(Paid) 2121
Techniques in Gastrointestinal Endoscopy (27698)
Techniques in Vascular and Interventional
  Radiology (27700)
Transplantation Reviews (27710)

Pittsburgh
Alcohol, Health and Research World (27755)
Clinical Journal of Oncology
  Nursing (27765) ....(Combined) ‡30,000
Environmental Health Perspectives (27785)
Health Care Financing Review (27795)
Industrial Hygiene
  News (27800) ....(Controlled) 62,000
Pittsburgh Hospital News (27833) 30,000

Spring City
For the Record (28008) ....(Controlled) 58,000

Wayne
Clinical Leadership and Management
  Review (28129) ....(Paid) ‡7,500
                                      (Non-paid) ‡200
Occupational Therapy
  Forum (28134) ....,....(Controlled) ‡25,000

Yardley
Managed Care (28201) ....(Controlled) 60,000

RHODE ISLAND
Providence
Allergy and Asthma
  Proceedings (28385) ....(Combined) 3,000
Healthcare Technology
  Management (28399) ....(Controlled) 21,748
Medical Imaging (28406) ....(Controlled) 21,195
Medical Law's Regan Report (28407)
24x7 (28429) ....(Controlled) 15,766

SOUTH CAROLINA
Charleston
Health Physics (28513) 6,897
Journal of Agromedicine (28514) ....(Paid) 218

Fort Mill
Aquatic Therapy Journal (28611)

SOUTH DAKOTA
Sioux Falls
South Dakota Journal of
  Medicine (28967) ....(Controlled) 1,940

TENNESSEE
Nashville
California Medicine (29448)
Healthcare Business
  Month (29457) ....(Combined) 38,109
X-Ray News (29504)

TEXAS
Dallas
Home Health Products (30161)
Occupational Health &
  Safety (30174) ....(Combined) △81,000

Houston
Clinical Cancer
  Research (30463) ....(Combined) ⊕4,552
Research Initiative/Treatment
  Action! (30524) 1,200

San Antonio
Journal of Musculosketal
  Pain (31035) ....(Paid) 1,588

Sugar Land
Internet Journal of Academic Physician
  Assistants (31138)
Internet Journal of Advanced Nursing
  Practice (31139)
The Internet Journal of Anesthesiology (31140)
Internet Journal of Asthma, Allergy and
  Immunology (31141)
Internet Journal of Emergency and Intensive Care
  Medicine (31142)
Internet Journal of Family Practice (31143)
Internet Journal of Gastroenterology (31144)
Internet Journal of Gynecology and
  Obstetrics (31145)
Internet Journal of Health (31146)
Internet Journal of Healthcare Administration (31147)
Internet Journal of Infectious Disease (31148)
Internet Journal of Internal Medicine (31149)
Internet Journal of Law, Healthcare and
  Ethics (31150)
Internet Journal of Neuromonitoring (31151)
Internet Journal of Neurosurgery (31152)
Internet Journal of Ophthalmology and Visual
  Science (31153)
Internet Journal of Orthopedic Surgery (31154)
Internet Journal of Pain, Symptom Control and
  Palliative Care (31155)
Internet Journal of Pathology (31156)
Internet Journal of Pediatrics and
  Neonatology (31157)
Internet Journal of Perfusionists (31158)
Internet Journal of Pulmonary Medicine (31159)
Internet Journal of Radiology (31160)
Internet Journal of Rescue and Disaster
  Medicine (31161)
Internet Journal of Surgery (31162)
Internet Journal of Thoracic and Cardiovascular
  Surgery (31163)

VIRGINIA
Alexandria
Balance (31646) ....(Combined) 6,900
Diabetes Care (31665)
Family Economics and Nutrition
  Review (31672) ....(Paid) 900
                                      (Non-paid) 3,500
PT, Magazine of Physical
  Therapy (31731) ....(Paid) 65,000

Ashburn
Therapeutic Recreation
  Journal (31855) ....(Paid) ‡3,500
                                      (Controlled) ‡100

Blacksburg
Journal of Health & Social
  Behavior (31875) ....‡3,500

Buckingham
Integral Yoga Magazine (31907) 1,500

Fairfax
American Industrial Hygiene Association
  Journal (32004) ....(Paid) ‡10,750
Synergist (32032)

Norfolk
Journal of Health and Social
  Policy (32287) ....(Controlled) ‡265

Reston
American Journal of Health Education (32360)
Journal of Health Education (32381) ....‡10,000

Richmond
Infection Control & Sterilization
  Technology (32438) ....(Paid) △25,000
The Journal of Perinatal
  Education (32442) ....(Paid) ‡5,224
                                      (Non-paid) ‡408

Springfield
Journal of Environmental Science and Health, Part C:
  Environmental Carcinogenesis and Ectoxicology
  Reviews (32545) 250

WASHINGTON
Issaquah
Journal of Heart-Centered Therapies (32785)

Port Townsend
Townsend Letter for Doctors &
  Patients (32896) ....(Controlled) 6,000

Seattle
Journal of the American Board of Family
  Practice (32976) ....(Paid) 64,644
Outlook (32999) ....(Non-paid) 20,000
Regional Anesthesia and Pain Medicine (33014)
Seminars in Clinical Neuropsychiatry (33029)
The Washington Nurse (33040) ....(Controlled) 7,600

Spokane
Massage Magazine (33095)

WEST VIRGINIA
Charleston
West Virginia Nurse (33279) ....(Paid) ⊕32,000

Green Bank
American Journal of Electroneurodiagnostic
  Technology (33329) ....(Paid) ‡3,024
                                      (Non-paid) ‡69

WISCONSIN
Hudson
Neurology & Clinical Neurophysiology (33796)

Madison
Food Reviews International (33940) 350
Wisconsin AIDS Update (33977)

Milwaukee
Outpost Exchange (34092) ....(Non-paid) ‡31,000
Sanitary Maintenance (34099) ....(Paid) 521
                                      (Non-paid) 16,071

ALBERTA, CANADA
Edmonton
Health Law Journal (34715)
Health Law Review (34716)
Qualitative Health Research (34726) .....(Paid) 1,100
                                      (Non-paid) 118

BRITISH COLUMBIA, CANADA
Burnaby
alive (34888) ....‡240,000

Vancouver
Healthcare Product
  News (35146) ....(Combined) 15,388

White Rock
Canadian Nursing Home
  Journal (35240) ....(Paid) 1,730
                                                3,000
Occupational Therapy
  NOW (35242) ....(Combined) 6,500

MANITOBA, CANADA
Winnipeg
Bibliotheca Medica Canadiana (35315)

ONTARIO, CANADA
Arnprior
Long Term Care (35637) ....(Controlled) 5,600

Burlington
Canadian Occupational
  Safety (35716) ....(Combined) 12,528

Hamilton
International Journal of Infectious
  Diseases (35882) ....(Paid) 2,769
Journal of the American Academy of
  Audiology (35883) ....(Paid) 9,065

Journal of Continuing Education in the Health
  Professions **(35884)** ....(Paid) 2,790
Journal of Travel Medicine **(35886)** ....(Paid) ‡2,486
Seminars in Headache Management **(35889)**
Transfusion Medicine Reviews **(35892)**

Markham
Canadian Journal of Dietetic Practice and
  Research **(36021)** ....(Combined) 6,000

Milton
Peritoneal Dialysis
  International **(36050)** ....(Paid) ‡4,000

Newmarket
Stitches **(36108)** ....(Non-paid) •36,336

Oakville
Canadian Respiratory
  Journal **(36141)** ....(Controlled) 15,500

Ottawa
Canadian Journal of Public Health **(36215)** ....‡3000
Canadian Journal of Respiratory
  Therapy **(36217)** 2,900
Canadian Journal of Rural
  Medicine **(36218)** 6,300
CMA News **(36235)** ....‡45,600
Compendium of Pharmaceuticals and
  Specialties **(36238)**
Healthcare Management
  Forum **(36247)** ....(Controlled) **3,270**
Provincial Drug Benefit Programs **(36273)**

Port Burwell
The Canadian Journal of
  Herbalism **(36331)** 1,000

Sudbury
Canadian Journal of Program Evaluation/Revue
  Canadienne D'evaluation de
  Programme **(36415)** 1,525

Toronto
Benefits and Pensions
  Monitor **(36475)** ....(Combined) 20,108
Canadian Journal of Human Sexuality **(36509)**
Canadian Occupational Health and Safety News
  (COHSN) **(36521)** ....‡1,100
Geriatrics Today **(36602)** ....(Combined) 18,000
Health Watch
  Canada **(36612)** ....(Non-paid) 569,150
Journal of Critical Care **(36634)**
Journal of Orthomolecular Medicine **(36636)**
Mere Nouvelle **(36662)** ....(Non-paid) 45,025
OH&S Canada **(36680)** ....(Paid) 8,271
                                   (Non-paid) 2,405
Today's Parent
  Newborn **(36763)** ....(Non-paid) 154,755
Vitality Magazine **(36789)** ....(Paid) 50,000

QUEBEC, CANADA
Montreal
Artere **(37086)** ....(Paid) ‡6,661
Ascent Magazine **(37088)** ....(Controlled) 10,000

Saint-Laurent
Canadian Journal of Allergy & Clinical
  Immunology **(37362)** 5,730

HEARING AND SPEECH

ARIZONA
Flagstaff
Annual Review of Applied Linguistics **(694)**

COLORADO
Henderson
Paws for Silence **(4515)**

DISTRICT OF COLUMBIA
Washington
American Annals of the Deaf **(5323)** ....‡3,500
Text and Performance Quarterly **(5820)**
The Volta Review **(5840)** ....‡4,400
Volta Voices **(5841)** ....(Paid) ⊕**4,400**

ILLINOIS
Urbana
Studies in the Linguistic
  Sciences **(9719)** ....(Controlled) 260

KENTUCKY
Lexington
Aphasiology **(12159)**

LOUISIANA
Lafayette
Clinical Linguistics and Phonetics **(12615)**

MARYLAND
Bethesda
Hearing Loss **(13343)** ....(Paid) 200,000

Burtonsville
Sign Language Studies **(13398)**

Landover Hills
Vision **(13596)** 1,000

Rockville
Asha **(13675)** ....‡94,000
Language, Speech, and Hearing Services in
  Schools **(13686)** ....‡49,000

Silver Spring
NADmag **(13741)** 7,000

MICHIGAN
Detroit
Southern Communication
  Journal **(14949)** ....(Paid) ‡2,650
                                    (Non-paid) ‡50

Hillsdale
IMPRIMIS **(15164)**

Livonia
The Hearing
  Professional **(15316)** ....(Controlled) ‡3,300

MISSOURI
Fulton
Missouri Record **(17077)**

NEBRASKA
Lincoln
AAC **(18077)** ....(Paid) 1,700
                                    (Non-paid) 200

NEW YORK
Geneseo
Journal of Speech and Hearing
  Research **(20649)** ....‡46,805

Glen Head
Trends in Amplification **(20664)** ....(Combined) 1,865

New York
International Journal of Speech Technology **(21919)**
Seminars in Speech and
  Language **(22726)** ....‡1,733
Topics in Language
  Disorders **(22847)** ....(Paid) 3,278
                                    (Non-paid) 78

Rochester
Deaf Life **(23221)** ....(Paid) 45,000

NORTH CAROLINA
Cary
The Journal of Deaf Studies and Deaf
  Education **(23690)** ....(Paid) 396

OHIO
Cincinnati
Silent Advocate **(24819)** ....(Non-paid) 30,000

ONTARIO, CANADA
Hamilton
Journal of the American Academy of
  Audiology **(35883)** ....(Paid) 9,065

Windsor
Informal Logic **(36887)** ....(Controlled) 400

HISTORY AND GENEALOGY

ALABAMA
Auburn University
Bulletin of the Comediantes **(49)** ....(Paid) 500

Florence
Journal of Muscle Shoals
  History **(220)** ....(Paid) 1,000

Huntsville
Oral History Review **(272)**

Mobile
Gulf South Historical
  Review **(320)** ....(Combined) 750

Scottsboro
Jackson County Chronicles **(446)** ....(Paid) 400

Tuscaloosa
Accounting Historians Journal **(480)**
American Journalism **(484)** ....(Paid) 800

ALASKA
Anchorage
Alaska History **(522)** ....(Paid) 500

ARIZONA
Tombstone
The National Tombstone Epitaph **(925)** ....‡8,500

Tucson
Journal of Arizona
  History **(950)** ....(Controlled) 2,300
Journal of the Southwest **(951)** ....(Paid) 1,000
Kiva **(952)** ....(Paid) ‡1,200
                                   (Non-paid) ‡25
Vietnam War Generation Journal **(971)**

ARKANSAS
Batesville
Mid-America Folklore **(1041)** ....(Paid) 200

Fayetteville
Arkansas Historical Quarterly **(1116)** ....‡1,600
Flashback **(1119)** ....(Paid) 850

Fort Smith
Fort Smith Historical Society
  Journal **(1142)** ....(Paid) 450

Helena
Phillips County Historical Review **(1175)**

Hot Springs
Arkansas Family Historian **(1183)** ....(Paid) 1,000

Rogers
Backtracker **(1326)** ....(Combined) 240

Searcy
White County Heritage **(1339)** 400

CALIFORNIA
Bakersfield
Historic Kern **(1452)** ....(Controlled) 450
Strategy & Tactics **(1453)** ....(Paid) ⊕**5,200**

Berkeley
Agricultural History **(1488)** ....‡1,050
Classical Antiquity **(1508)**
Early China **(1514)** ....(Controlled) 350
Historical Studies in the Physical and Biological
  Sciences **(1525)**
The Public Historian **(1554)** 1,600

Claremont
Women's Studies **(1726)** ....(Paid) 500

Davis
French Historical Studies **(1815)** ....(Paid) 1,800

Escondido
Hidden Valley Journal **(1890)**

Goleta
Ancestors West **(2027)** ....(Combined) 640

Los Angeles
Comitatus **(2244)** ....(Paid) 750
ETCetera **(2266)** ....(Paid) 300
Southern California Quarterly **(2397)** ......(Paid) 1,200
Urban History **(2425)** 750

Oakland
The Nugget and CGS News **(2689)** 850

Paradise
Genealogical Goldmine **(2806)** ....(Combined) 200

Rancho Cucamonga
Skinner Kinsmen Update **(2877)** .....(Combined) 200

Riverside
Central European History **(2934)**

San Diego
Explorations in Economic History **(3152)**
Historia Mathematica **(3167)**
Journal of San Diego
  History **(3212)** ....(Combined) 3,500

San Francisco
Chinese America **(3340)**

San Pedro
Sudden Enlightenment Digest **(3596)**

Trade, Technical, and Professional Publications

HISTORY AND GENEALOGY (continued)

Sebastopol
KMT (3751) ....(Paid) ⊕14,793

Studio City
Ship to Shore (3823) ....(Controlled) 300

Thousand Oaks
Indian Economic and Social History Review (3874)

Yorba Linda
Theosophical History (4119) ....(Combined) 205

COLORADO
Arvada
The Plantagenet
Connection (4138) ....(Combined) 1,150

Denver
Nuestras Raices/Our
Roots (4345) ....(Controlled) 550

Golden
Dayspring (4466) ....(Paid) 726

CONNECTICUT
Brookfield
ROTA.GENE (4729) ....(Paid) ‡300
(Non-paid) ‡150

Mystic
Log of Mystic Seaport (4968) ....(Paid) 22,000
(Controlled) 300

Stamford
Connecticut Ancestry (5144) ....(Combined) 340

Stonington
Historical Footnotes (5165) ....(Paid) 900

Tolland
Connecticut Maple Leaf (5175) 700

DELAWARE
Newark
The History of the Family (5273)

Wilmington
Delaware Genealogical Society
Journal (5290) ....(Paid) 700

DISTRICT OF COLUMBIA
Washington
Afro-American Historical and Genealogical Society
Journal (5315) ....(Paid) 910
American Studies International (5345) ....‡800
The Catholic Historical
Review (5400) ....(Paid) ‡1,926
(Non-paid) ‡166
Cold War International History Project (5423)
Daughters of the American Revolution
Magazine (5459) ....‡40,000
Historical Methods (5527) ....(Paid) 547
Journal of Winston Churchill (5619)
National Genealogical Society
Quarterly (5671) ....‡18,000
National Trust Forum (5682) ....(Paid) 4,000
Presidential Studies Quarterly (5728)
Washington History (5845) ....(Paid) 3,000

FLORIDA
Jacksonville
Southern Genealogists Exchange
Quarterly (6217) ....(Controlled) 300

Miami
Tequesta (6383) ....(Paid) 3,600

Pensacola
Pensacola History
Illustrated (6567) ....(Controlled) 700

West Palm Beach
Ancestry (6845) ....(Combined) 400

GEORGIA
Atlanta
Atlanta History Center (6969) ....(Paid) 5,500
Journal of American Ethnic
History (7019) ....(Paid) ‡1,000

Demorest
The American Genealogist (7239) ....‡1,880

Savannah
Georgia Historical Quarterly (7532) ....‡3,500

HAWAII
Honolulu
Hawaiian Journal of
History (7699) ....(Combined) ⊕1,800
Journal of World History (7705) ....(Paid) 1,575
(Controlled) 50

IDAHO
Boise
Genealogical Journal of Jefferson County, New
York (7806) ....(Paid) ‡200
Genealogical Journal of Oneida County, New
York (7807) ....(Paid) 300

Moscow
Latah Legacy (7918)

Rexburg
Snake River Echoes (7964) ....(Controlled) 250

ILLINOIS
Bloomington
The Historical Messenger (8078) ....(Paid) ‡290
(Non-paid) ‡140

Bourbonnais
The-A-Ki-Ki (8095)

Champaign
Sport History Review (8217) ....(Paid) ‡275

Chicago
The American Archivist (8252) 4,634
Chicago History (8313) ....(Paid) 8,500
(Non-paid) 1,000
Law and History Review (8458)
Mid-America (Chicago) (8488) ....(Paid) 500
Osiris (8517)
Swiss-American Historical
Society (8580) ....(Paid) 400
Ukrainian Philatelist (8589) ....(Controlled) 415

Clinton
Dewitt County Genealogical Society
Quarterly (8683) ....(Controlled) 200

Danville
Heritage of Vermilion
County (8702) ....(Controlled) ⊕1,500

DeKalb
Crossroads (8733) ....(Paid) 300

Evanston
Eighteenth-Century Studies (8857) ....‡4400

McHenry
Lynn—Linn Lineage
Quarterly (9165) ....(Combined) 150

Peoria
The Short Line (9424) ....(Paid) 1,100
(Non-paid) 20

Springfield
Journal of the Abraham Lincoln Association (9635)
Journal of Illinois History (9636) ....(Paid) 1,800

Urbana
Champaign County Genealogical Society
Quarterly (9699) ....(Controlled) 250
Railroad History (9716) ....(Paid) 3,500

Wauconda
The Classical Bulletin (9742) ....(Paid) ‡520
(Non-paid) ‡480

INDIANA
Bloomington
The American Historical
Review (9823) ....(Controlled) ‡18,000
History & Memory (9828) 500
Indiana Magazine of History (9835) 9,600
Jewish Social Studies (9839) 600
The Journal of American History (9840) 12,000
Victorian Studies (9854) 2,300

Fort Wayne
CLIO (9965)

Gosport
Owen County History &
Genealogy (10031) ....(Paid) 380

Indianapolis
Religion and American Culture (10166)

Rochester
Fulton County Images (10430) ....(Controlled) 700

Vincennes
Northwest Trail Tracer (10521)

West Lafayette
Journal of the Early
Republic (10549) ....(Combined) 1,450

IOWA
Clarinda
The Civil War Lady (10701)

Des Moines
Hawkeye Heritage (10787) ....(Controlled) 3,000

Iowa City
Annals of Iowa (10968) ....‡1,000

KANSAS
Manhattan
Journal of the West (11623) 4,500

Topeka
The Kansas Anthropologist (11825) ....(Paid) 350
Topeka Genealogical Society
Quarterly (11839) ....(Controlled) 1,095

KENTUCKY
Bowling Green
Southern Folklore (11949) ....(Paid) ‡450
(Non-paid) ‡20

Campbellsville
Central Kentucky
Researcher (12007) ....(Controlled) 315

Frankfort
Kentucky Ancestors (12067) ....(Paid) 3,200

Lexington
Journal of Caribbean Studies (12167) 1,000

Louisville
Filson History
Quarterly (12216) ....(Controlled) 4,100
Ohio Valley History (12233) ....(Controlled) 2,000

LOUISIANA
Baton Rouge
The Southern Review (12506) ....‡2,500

Lafayette
Louisiana History (12618) ....‡1,200

Shreveport
North Louisiana History (12817) ....(Paid) 500

MAINE
Farmington
Maine Genealogist (12961) ....(Combined) 2,000

Orono
Northeast Folklore (13002)

Portland
Maine History (13011) 2,800

MARYLAND
Baltimore
Bulletin of the History of Medicine (13140) ....‡2,394
English Literary History (ELH) (13159) ....‡1,908
Flower of the Forest Black Genealogical
Journal (13161)
Late Imperial China (13207) ....(Combined) 553
Maryland Historical Magazine (13211) ....‡4,500
Reviews in American History (13242) ....‡3,205

College Park
The Hispanic American Historical
Review (13419) ....‡2,200
Prologue (13438) ....(Combined) 2,400

Elkton
Cecil Historical Journal (13494)

Frostburg
Journal of the Alleghenies (13527) ....(Paid) 200

Gaithersburg
Western Maryland
Genealogy (13551) ....(Controlled) 704

Silver Spring
Demography (13724) ....(Paid) 3,000
Journal of Negro History (13732) ....(Paid) ‡3,700
(Non-paid) ‡300

Towson
Journal of Colonialism & Colonial
History (13761) ....(Paid) 850

MASSACHUSETTS
Boston
Business History Review (13869) ....(Paid) 2,000
(Non-paid) 300

International Journal of the Classical
  Tradition **(13907)** ....(Paid) ‡800
New England Ancestors **(13931)** ......(Paid) 20,000
New England Historical and Genealogical
  Register **(13934)** ....‡18,500
The New England
  Quarterly **(13937)** ....(Paid) ‡2,000
                  (Non-paid) ‡400

Brookline
Journal of Modern
  Hellenism **(14021)** ....(Combined) 650

Cambridge
Harvard Journal of Asiatic
  Studies **(14061)** ....(Paid) 1,100
Journal of Cold War
  Studies **(14075)** ....(Combined) 2,300
The Journal of Interdisciplinary
  History **(14077)** 2,000
Speculum, A Journal of Medieval
  Studies **(14104)** ....‡6,000

Duxbury
Journal of Turkish Studies/Turkluk Bilgisi
  Arastirmalari **(14164)**

Greenfield
Markers **(14221)** ....(Paid) 200

Indian Orchard
Titanic Commutator **(14256)**

Lynnfield
Essex Genealogist **(14287)** ....(Paid) 800

Nantucket
Renaissance Magazine **(14342)** ....(Paid) ‡24,000
                (Non-paid) ‡2,000

Newton Centre
American Jewish History **(14414)** ....‡3,550

Westfield
Historical Journal of
  Massachusetts **(14640)** ....(Paid) 1000

Williamstown
Gastronomica **(14659)**

MICHIGAN
Ann Arbor
Comparative Studies in Society &
  History **(14745)** ....(Paid) ‡2028
Journal of American Folklore **(14754)** 3,000
Journal of Cuneiform Studies **(14755)** .....(Paid) 500

Dearborn
Technology and Culture **(14906)**

Detroit
Detroit Society for Genealogical Research
  Magazine **(14928)** ....‡900

East Lansing
The Historian **(14984)** ....(Combined) 16,000
Northeast African Studies **(14991)**

Kalamazoo
Medieval Prosopography at Medieval Institute
  Publications **(15243)**

Kentwood
Old Mill News **(15264)** ....‡2,000

Mount Pleasant
Michigan Historical Review **(15376)**

MINNESOTA
Duluth
Lake Superior Magazine **(15839)** ......(Paid) ‡22,500

Mayer
Annals of Balloon History and Museology **(16048)**

Northfield
German Studies
  Review **(16234)** ....(Combined) 2,100
Norwegian-American Studies **(16238)**

Roseville
Minnesota Genealogical Journal **(16334)**

St. Paul
Dakota Collector **(16373)** ....(Combined) 70
Minnesota History **(16393)** ....‡18,500

MISSISSIPPI
Jackson
The Journal of Mississippi History **(16697)** ....‡1,500

Tupelo
Northeast Mississippi Historical and Genealogical
  Society Quarterly **(16850)** ....(Combined) 475

MISSOURI
Cape Girardeau
Big Muddy **(16943)**

Columbia
Missouri Historical Review **(16999)** ....‡6,400
Missouri State Genealogical Association
  Journal **(17005)** ....(Paid) 705

Kansas City
Family Records, TODAY **(17168)** ....(Paid) ‡210
Kansas City Genealogist **(17179)** ....(Paid) ‡400
                (Non-paid) ‡150

Point Lookout
Teaching History: A Journal of Methods **(17354)**

Rolla
Phelps County Genealogical Society
  Quarterly **(17379)** ....(Paid) 190

St. Louis
Gateway Heritage **(17441)** ....(Paid) ‡6,500
               (Controlled) ‡500
Journal of Policy History **(17459)** ....(Paid) 700
Manuscripta **(17470)** ....(Combined) 500
Social Justice Review **(17512)** ....(Paid) 4,600
               (Non-paid) 500

Springfield
Explorations in Renaissance
  Culture **(17598)** ....(Combined) 314

NEBRASKA
Lincoln
Great Plains Quarterly **(18085)** ......(Controlled) 600
National Pastime **(18096)**
Nebraska History **(18101)** ....‡3,800
Nine **(18108)**

NEW HAMPSHIRE
Durham
Journal of the History of Economic Thought **(18500)**

Milton
Chips from Many Trees and Growing
  Roots **(18580)** ....(Combined) 225

Peterborough
Cobblestone **(18621)** ....(Paid) 30,000

NEW JERSEY
Bergenfield
Avotaynu **(18673)** ....(Combined) 3,400

Marmora
The Mayflower Quarterly **(19217)** ....(Paid) 26,000

New Brunswick
American Journal of Ancient
  History **(19325)** ....(Paid) 600
Journal of the History of
  Ideas **(19333)** ....(Paid) ‡3,300
               (Controlled) ‡140

Newark
Jersey Journeys **(19355)** 9,500
New Jersey History **(19360)** ....(Paid) 2,000

Princeton
Princeton History **(19470)** 1,500

Upper Montclair
Bulletin of the American Society of
  Papyrologists **(19692)** 500

NEW MEXICO
Albuquerque
Colonial Latin America Historical
  Review **(19769)** ....(Combined) 400
New Mexico Historical
  Review **(19778)** ....(Paid) 1,200

NEW YORK
Alfred
Historical Reflections/Reflexions
  Historiques **(20024)** ....(Combined) 540

Annandale-on-Hudson
Hudson Valley Regional
  Review **(20060)** ....(Paid) 350

Armonk
Chinese Studies in History **(20072)** ......(Paid) ⊕252
Russian Studies in History **(20096)** ......(Paid) ⊕256

Bronx
Biography Index **(20254)**
Current Biography **(20265)** ....‡11,000

Brooklyn
International Journal of Kurdish
  Studies **(20321)** ....(Combined) 500

Canton
The Quarterly **(20430)** ....(Paid) 950
               (Non-paid) 75

Clinton
American Journal of Philology **(20469)** ....‡1,517

Elmira
Chemung Historical Journal **(20572)**

Elmsford
Westchester Historian **(20585)** ....(Combined) 725

Hauppauge
White House Studies **(20723)**

Lowville
Lewis County Historical Society Journal **(20969)**

New York
Anglo-Saxon England **(21216)** 500
Art, Antiquity and Law **(21250)**
Art Bulletin **(21251)**
Camden Fifth Series **(21369)**
Charioteer **(21397)** ....(Paid) 800
Chronos **(21415)**
Contemporary European History **(21492)** 650
Continuity and Change **(21496)** 650
de Halve Maen **(21540)**
Early Music History **(21574)** 550
The Historical Journal **(21806)** 1500
Indo-Iranian Journal **(21864)**
International Labor and Working-Class
  History **(21926)** 900
International Review of Social
  History **(21936)** 970
               (Non-paid) 199
The Journal of African
  History **(21977)** ....(Paid) ‡1,601
              (Non-paid) ‡67
Journal of American Studies **(21986)** .....(Paid) ‡455
             (Non-paid) ‡3,346
Journal of Cultural Heritage **(22044)**
The Journal of Ecclesiastical
  History **(22053)** 1250
The Journal of Economic History **(22055)** 3250
Journal of the History of Biology **(22089)**
Journal of the History of International Law **(22090)**
Journal of Modern African Studies **(22135)** 1600
The Journal of Psychohistory **(22168)** ....‡7,000
The Legal History Review **(22244)**
Modern Asian Studies **(22347)** 1150
The New York Genealogical and Biographical
  Record **(22443)** ....‡3,625
Niepodleglosc/Independence **(22462)** .(Combined)1,500
Radical History Review **(22621)** ....(Paid) 1,200
Renaissance Quarterly **(22646)** ....‡3,500
Royal Historical Society Transactions **(22678)**
Rural History **(22681)** 500
Science & Society **(22713)** 1,923

Oyster Bay
Theodore Roosevelt Association
  Journal **(23071)** ....(Paid) 2,200

Port Washington
Cow Neck Peninsula Historical Society
  Journal **(23123)**

Poughkeepsie
WW1 Aero **(23151)** ....(Paid) ‡1,500

Rochester
About...Time **(23207)** ....(Paid) ‡56,000
Fifteenth Century Studies **(23226)** 400
Rochester History **(23240)** ....(Paid) 1,000

Syracuse
Tree Talks **(23432)** ....(Paid) 800

Woodbury
Long Island Forum **(23591)** ....‡5,850

NORTH CAROLINA
Boone
Albion **(23651)** ....(Paid) ‡1,574
               (Non-paid) ‡47
Appalachian Journal **(23652)** ....(Paid) 500

Cary
Journal of the History of Medicine and Allied
  Sciences **(23691)** 1,100

Circ.   Circ.   Circ.

HISTORY AND GENEALOGY (continued)

Chapel Hill
Southern Cultures **(23724)** ....(Paid) 2,400

Charlotte
Journal of Urban History **(23746)** ....(Paid) 1,400
                                     (Non-paid) 144

Durham
Environmental History **(23820)** ....‡1,900
Greek, Roman, and Byzantine
   Studies **(23823)** ....(Paid) ‡750
                                (Non-paid) ‡20
History of Political Economy **(23825)** ....‡1,350
Journal of Medieval and Early Modern
   Studies **(23830)** ....(Combined) 1,000
Southern Exposure **(23846)** ....‡5,000

Fairview
Exemplaria **(23875)** ....(Paid) 600

Greenville
North Carolina Genealogical Society
   Journal **(23967)** ....(Controlled) 2,000

Horse Shoe
A Lot of Bunkum **(24010)** ....(Controlled) 750

Mount Holly
Footprints in Time **(24084)**

Raleigh
North Carolina Historical Review **(24144)** ......‡1,500
Tar Heel Junior
   Historian **(24155)** ....(Non-paid) 9,000

Shelby
Eswau Huppeday **(24226)** ....(Controlled) 500

NORTH DAKOTA
Bismarck
North Dakota History **(24354)** ......(Combined) 1,700

OHIO
Amherst
Inland Seas **(24610)** ....‡2,250

Bowling Green
Equipment Echoes **(24691)** ....(Paid) 4,300
Journal of Cultural Geography **(24694)**

Cincinnati
American Jewish Archives **(24770)**

Columbus
Bandwagon **(24999)** ....‡1,400
Ohio History **(25046)**

Dayton
American Educational History
   Journal **(25106)** ....(Paid) ‡110
The Gettysburg Magazine **(25117)**

Kent
Civil War History **(25272)** ....‡1,850

Lakewood
Hubbell Family Historical Society Annual **(25286)**

Mansfield
Ohio Records & Pioneer
   Families **(25333)** ....(Controlled) 1,605

North Jackson
Bushong Bulletin **(25436)** ....(Controlled) 80

OKLAHOMA
Durant
Red River Valley Historical Journal **(25807)**

Lawton
Tree Tracers **(25889)** ....(Combined) 400

Oklahoma City
The Chronicles of Oklahoma **(25962)** ....‡6,100

OREGON
Klamath Falls
Shaw Historical Library
   Journal **(26386)** ....(Combined) 240

Phoenix
Rogue Digger **(26464)** ....(Paid) 413

Portland
Oregon Historical Quarterly **(26492)** ....(Paid) 7,000
                                 (Non-paid) 250
Pacific Historical Review **(26497)** ....‡1,465

Roseburg
Umpqua Trapper **(26556)** ....(Paid) 340

PENNSYLVANIA
Harrisburg
Pennsylvania Heritage **(27008)** ....‡13,500

Lancaster
Pennsylvania Mennonite
   Heritage **(27145)** ....(Combined) 3,000

Laureldale
Berks County Genealogical Society
   Journal **(27167)** ....(Paid) 1,200

Media
Voices **(27244)** ....(Controlled) 500

Philadelphia
Germantown Crier **(27476)** ....‡600
Nursing History Review **(27592)**
Pennsylvania Magazine of History and
   Biography **(27623)** ....‡2000
Proceedings of the American Philosophical
   Society **(27648)** ....(Paid) ‡650
                               (Non-paid) ‡1,200

Pittsburgh
Ancient Philosophy **(27758)** ....(Combined) 750
Social Science History **(27843)** ....‡1,500

Ridgway
Elk Horn **(27934)**

State College
Centre County Heritage **(28017)** .....(Controlled) 500
Pennsylvania History **(28019)** ....‡1,000

State Line
Johannes Schwalm Historical Association
   Journal **(28032)**

Warren
Stepping Stones **(28104)**

Washington
Topic (Washington) **(28117)** ....(Combined) 500

RHODE ISLAND
Manville
Je Me Souviens **(28363)** ....(Combined) 1,700

Newport
Newport History **(28369)** ....(Controlled) 1,400

North Providence
Rhode Island Postal History Journal **(28377)** 80

Portsmouth
Journal of Roman
   Archaeology **(28381)** ....(Non-paid) 1,250

SOUTH CAROLINA
Charleston
South Carolina Historical
   Magazine **(28518)** ....‡5,000

Conway
Independent Republic
   Quarterly **(28590)** ....(Combined) 400

SOUTH DAKOTA
Pierre
South Dakota History **(28921)** ....(Paid) 1,600

TENNESSEE
Lawrenceburg
Yesterday and Today in Lawrence
   County **(29317)** ....(Paid) 200

Memphis
Ansearchin' News **(29357)**

Murfreesboro
Border States **(29429)**
Tennessee Folklore Society
   Bulletin **(29434)** ....(Paid) ‡380
                               (Non-paid) ‡47

Nashville
History News **(29458)** ....(Paid) ‡5,100
                               (Non-paid) ‡828
Tennessee Historical
   Quarterly **(29491)** ....(Combined) 2,700

Normandy
Bedford Historical
   Quarterly **(29546)** ....(Combined) 196

Sevierville
Smoky Mountain Historical Society
   Journal **(29590)** ....(Combined) 725

TEXAS
Alpine
Journal of Big Bend Studies **(29683)**

Austin
Anglican & Episcopal History **(29753)** ....‡1,500
Austin Genealogical Society Quarterly **(29758)**
Folk Dance Problem
   Solver **(29776)** ....(Combined) 650
Journal of the History of Sexuality **(29787)** 1,000
Southwestern Historical Quarterly **(29807)** .....‡3,300
Texas Historian **(29824)** ....‡1,800

College Station
Helios (Lubbock) **(30042)**
Seventeenth-Century News **(30049)** 1,200

Dallas
Arthuriana **(30124)** ....(Paid) ‡750
Dallas Journal **(30146)** ....(Paid) ⊕1275

Denton
Military History of the
   West **(30242)** ....(Combined) 550

Houston
Journal of Southern
   History **(30499)** ....(Controlled) 5,000

Lubbock
Eighteenth Century **(30710)**

Nacogdoches
East Texas Historical Journal **(30850)** .....(Paid) 535

Richardson
Mexican War Journal **(30977)** ....(Combined) 135

Woodville
The Booster **(31309)** ....(Paid) ‡4,500
                               (Non-paid) ‡10,500

UTAH
Logan
Everton's Family History
   Magazine **(31348)** ....‡48,000
Genealogical Helper **(31349)**
Western Historical
   Quarterly **(31355)** ....(Paid) ⊕2,500

Provo
Genealogical Computing **(31403)** ....(Paid) ‡8,700
                               (Controlled) ‡50

Salt Lake City
Utah Genealogical Association **(31442)** 1,000

VERMONT
Barre
Vermont History **(31489)** ....(Controlled) 2,600

VIRGINIA
Arlington
Arlington Historical
   Magazine **(31778)** ....(Controlled) 600

Charlottesville
Augustinian Studies **(31917)**

Fairfax
Journal of Social
   History **(32024)** ....(Combined) 1,500
Skyways **(32030)** ....(Paid) 1,200

Falmouth
The Virginia Genealogist **(32066)** ....‡800

Leesburg
Vietnam **(32187)**

Lexington
The Journal of Military
   History **(32189)** ....(Paid) ‡2,900
                               (Non-paid) ‡30

Lorton
Journal of the Lincoln
   Assassination **(32198)** ....(Combined) 90

Norfolk
Scotia **(32293)** ....(Paid) 100

Richmond
The Journal of the Jamestown Rediscovery
   Center **(32441)**
Magazine of Virginia
   Genealogy **(32444)** ....(Paid) 2,900
Virginia Magazine of History and
   Biography **(32465)** ....(Non-paid) ‡8,500

Roanoke
Journal **(32490)** ....(Paid) 900

Staunton
Augusta Historical
  Bulletin (32553) ....(Controlled) 500

Williamsburg
Business and Economic
  History (32614) ....(Combined) 650
William and Mary
  Quarterly (32623) ....(Combined) ⊕3,600

WASHINGTON
Longview
Swedish American
  Genealogist (32814) ....(Controlled) 1,100

Olympia
Olympia Genealogical Society
  Quarterly (32859) ....(Controlled) 200

Valleyford
Airpost Journal (33173) ....(Combined) 1,825

WEST VIRGINIA
Lewisburg
Greenbrier Historical Society
  Journal (33363) ....(Controlled) 1,000

WISCONSIN
Green Bay
Voyageur (33742) ....(Paid) 3,511

Madison
Historic Madison (33946) ....(Controlled) 900
Pharmacy in History (33968) ....(Paid) ‡1,100
                        (Non-paid) ‡100
Wisconsin Magazine of History (33986) ......‡11,500

Milwaukee
The SAR Magazine (34100) ....‡26,000

WYOMING
Laramie
Quidditas (34552)

ALBERTA, CANADA
Edmonton
Past Imperfect (34723) ....(Paid) 75

Lethbridge
Victorian Review (34798) ....(Paid) 350

BRITISH COLUMBIA, CANADA
Burnaby
International History
  Review (34903) ....(Controlled) 900

Nanaimo
Canadian Bulletin of Medical History/Bulletin Canadien
  D'historie de la Medecine (35018) ......(Paid) 300

Richmond
British Columbia Genealogist (35074) ....(Paid) 1,000

Vancouver
BC Studies (35125) ....(Paid) ‡600
                        (Controlled) ‡50

MANITOBA, CANADA
Winnipeg
Generations (35329) ....(Controlled) 800
Manitoba History (35338)

NEW BRUNSWICK, CANADA
Fredericton
Acadiensis (35388) ....(Controlled) 850

ONTARIO, CANADA
Deep River
BNA Topics (35761) ....(Paid) 1,300

Hamilton
Russell: The Journal of Bertrand Russell
  Studies (35888) ....(Paid) 360

Ottawa
Canadian Review of American
  Studies (36227) ....(Paid) 475
RCMP Veterans' Association Quarterly/Association
  des anciens de la GRC
  Trimestrialle (36275) 13,000

Thunder Bay
Thunder Bay Historical Museum Society, Papers and
  Records (36441) ....(Controlled) 800

Toronto
Canadian Historical Review (36502) 2,100
Families (36592) ....(Combined) 5,150
Historical Studies (36615)

Loyalist Gazette (36652) ....(Paid) 2,000
Onomastica Canadiana (36681) ....(Paid) 250
Renaissance and Reformation/Renaissance et
  Reforme (36726) ....(Combined) 700
Urban History Review (36783) ....(Paid) 400
York Pioneer (36795) ....(Controlled) 400

Willowdale
Ontario History (36882) ....‡1,700

QUEBEC, CANADA
Chicoutimi
Saguenayensia (36968)

Montreal
Canadian Rail/Rail
  Canadien (37099) ....(Combined) 1,050
Folk-Lore (37117) ....(Controlled) 2,500
Revue d'histoire de l'Amerique
  francaise (37218) ....(Controlled) 1,100

Quebec
Continuite (37282) ....⊕5,000
                        ⊕3,920

Saint-Hyacinthe
La Rivardiere (37349)

Sillery
Le Journal des Blais (37400)

Stanstead
Stanstead Historical Society Journal (37407)

SASKATCHEWAN, CANADA
Regina
Saskatchewan Genealogical
  Society (37533) ....(Controlled) 1,550

Saskatoon
Canadian Journal of History/Annales canadiennes
  d'histoire (37550) ....(Combined) 690
Lumen (37552) ....(Paid) 300
Saskatchewan History (37554) .....(Combined) ⊕700
Saskatoon History
  Review (37555) ....(Combined) 400

HOME ECONOMICS

CALIFORNIA
Thousand Oaks
Family and Consumer Sciences Research
  Journal (3869) ....(Paid) 1,000

CONNECTICUT
Danbury
Choices (4736) ....‡200,000

VIRGINIA
Alexandria
AAFCS Action (31629) ....(Paid) 23,073
                        (Controlled) 100
Journal of Family and Consumer Sciences: From
  Research to Practice (31695) ....(Paid) 14,500
                        (Non-paid) 150

ONTARIO, CANADA
Ottawa
Canadian Home Economics Journal (Revue
  Canadienne d'Economie
  Familiale) (36199) ....(Controlled) ‡2,000

HOME FURNISHINGS, CURTAINS, DRAPERIES

See also Furniture and Furnishings; Glass
and China; Lighting

DISTRICT OF COLUMBIA
Washington
ASID ICON (5367) ....(Controlled) 33,000

FLORIDA
West Palm Beach
Draperies and Window
  Coverings (6846) ....(Paid) 5,265
                        (Non-paid) 20,006

ILLINOIS
Lincolnshire
Accessory Merchandising (9084) 21,000

MASSACHUSETTS
Newton
Interior Design (14401) ....(Paid) 54,584

Wayland
Electronic House (14614) ....‡80,000

MINNESOTA
Hopkins
Mirror News Magazine (15964) ....(Paid) ‡42,230
                        (Non-paid) ‡5,660

St. Paul
Window Fashions (16417) ....(Paid) 4,400
                        (Controlled) 24,400

NEBRASKA
Omaha
Heartland Retailer (18197) ....(Free) ‡15,250

NEW HAMPSHIRE
Laconia
Hearth & Home
  Magazine (18537) ....(Non-paid) ‡17,000

NEW YORK
Melville
Wall & Window
  Trends (21065) ....(Combined) 22,011

New York
Colonial Homes (21441) ....(Paid) 520,647
Weekend Decorating Projects (22913)

HOSPITALS AND HEALTHCARE INSTITUTIONS

See also Health and Healthcare; Medicine
and Surgery; Nursing

ARIZONA
Phoenix
Assisted Living Success (792) ....(Combined) 15,000

CALIFORNIA
Berkeley
Journal of Hospital
  Marketing (1534) ....(Controlled) ‡250

Glendale
Administrative Radiology
  Journal (2006) ....(Paid) 11,380

Los Angeles
Contemporary Long Term
  Care (2246) ....(Paid) 2,529
                        (Non-paid) 38,337

Torrance
Emergency (3933) 29,000

COLORADO
Centennial
Healthcare Advertising
  Review (4224) ....(Paid) ‡1,000

Littleton
Activities, Adaptation & Aging (4545) 737

CONNECTICUT
Shelton
European Clinical
  Laboratory (5121) ....(Non-paid) ‡18,072

DISTRICT OF COLUMBIA
Washington
Clinical Laboratory
  News (5420) ....(Controlled) 25,000
Hospital Topics (5529) ....(Paid) 670

FLORIDA
Tampa
Physician Executive (6777) ....(Paid) ‡300
                        (Controlled) ‡13,000

GEORGIA
Atlanta
Health Management
  Technology (7014) ....(Paid) 3,000
                        (Non-paid) 35,000

Journal of Nursing
  Measurement (7023) ....(Combined) 400

ILLINOIS
Chicago
AHA News (8249) ....(Paid) 20,000
Health Facilities Management (8394) ....(Paid) 1,722
                        (Controlled) 27,000

Circ.   Circ.   Circ.

HOSPITALS AND HEALTHCARE INSTITUTIONS (continued)

Health Forum Journal (8395) ....(Paid) ‡2,400
(Non-paid) ‡0

Journal of Healthcare
Management (8439) ....(Paid) ‡1,500
(Controlled) ‡27,000

Journal of Healthcare Risk
Management (8440) .....,......,.....(Paid) 4,300
Trustee (8588) ....‡25,000

Glenview
Journal for Healthcare Quality (8938) ....(Paid) 8,000
(Controlled) 500

Highland Park
Healthcare Purchasing News (8992) ....(Paid) 80
(Non-paid) 33,000

Northfield
McKnight's Long-Term Care
News (9331) ....(Paid) ‡850
(Controlled) ‡50,025

Schaumburg
Outpatient Care Technology (9590) ....△37,700

MASSACHUSETTS
Shrewsbury
Journal of Intensive Care
Medicine (14524) ....‡2,200

Weston
American Journal of Hospice and Palliative
Care (14649) ....(Paid) ‡2,931
(Non-paid) ‡107

MICHIGAN
Lansing
Michigan Health and Hospitals (15284) ....‡2,000

MISSOURI
St. Louis
Health Progress (17444) ....(Paid) ‡11,000
(Controlled) ‡9,300
Journal of WOCN (Wound, Ostomy, and Continence
Nursing) (17464) ....(Paid) ‡4,855
Pharmacy Practice Management
Quarterly (17483) ....(Paid) 1,213
(Non-paid) 78

NEW HAMPSHIRE
Nashua
Healthcare Review (18590) .....(Combined) ❑52,503

NEW JERSEY
Chatham
Hospital Therapy (18730) ....(Non-paid) ‡45,080
P & T (18731) ....(Controlled) 54,025

Hoboken
Health Care Analysis (18958)
Health Economics (18959)
International Journal of Health Planning and
Management (18984)
Statistics in Medicine (19106) ....(Paid) 12,600
Teratogenesis, Carcinogenesis and
Mutagenesis (19117) ....(Paid) 3,850

Jamesburg
Resident & Staff Physician (19132)

Montvale
Hospital Pharmacist Report (19255) ....(Paid) 78
(Non-paid) 27,706
Patient Care for the Nurse Practitioner (19271)

Morris Plains
Patient Management (19299) .....(Controlled) 60,100

NEW YORK
Binghamton
Journal of Hospital Librarianship (20180)

New York
Health Care Management
Review (21792) ....(Paid) ‡4,429
International Journal of Health Care Finance and
Economics (21908)
International Journal of Technology Assessment in
Health Care (21921) 1500
Journal of Ambulatory Care
Management (21981) ....(Paid) 2,598
(Non-paid) 123
Managed Care Quarterly (22277) 2200
Medicine and Health (22311)
Nursing Leadership Forum (22474) ....(Paid) 240
(Free) 50

Research and Theory for Nursing
Practice (22649) ....(Paid) 600
Restaurants & Institutions (22652) ....(Paid) 1,807
(Non-paid) 171,525

OHIO
Cincinnati
EI Hospital (24796) ....(Controlled) ‡15,500

Cleveland
Formulary (24898) ....(Controlled) 45,000
Managed Healthcare (24924) ....(Paid) △2,937
(Controlled) △35,221

Nursing Homes (24934)

Dayton
Ethics, Law and Aging
Review (25115) ....(Combined) 1,000

PENNSYLVANIA
Philadelphia
Academic Emergency
Medicine (27361) ....(Paid) 5,600
Heart and Lung (27479) ....(Combined) ‡3,899

Pittsburgh
Health Care Financing Review (27795)

TEXAS
Sugar Land
Internet Journal of Emergency and Intensive Care
Medicine (31142)

BRITISH COLUMBIA, CANADA
Vancouver
Healthcare Product
News (35146) ....(Combined) 15,388

White Rock
Canadian Nursing Home
Journal (35240) ....(Paid) 1,730
3,000

ONTARIO, CANADA
Toronto
Hospital News Canada (36618) ....(Non-paid) 38,000

QUEBEC, CANADA
Montreal
Artere (37086) ....(Paid) ‡6,661

Saint-Etienne-de-Lauzon
Le Chef du Service
Alimentaire (37330) ....(Controlled) •20,629

HOTELS, MOTELS, RESTAURANTS, AND CLUBS

CALIFORNIA
Santa Ana
Hospitality Product
News (3627) ....(Non-paid) 34,000

CONNECTICUT
Norwalk
Cheers (5052) ....(Controlled) 90,000

DISTRICT OF COLUMBIA
Washington
Catering Industry Employee (5397) ....‡215,000
Construction & Modernization Report (5436)
Lodging Magazine (5640) ....(Paid) 4,885
(Non-paid) 52,000

FLORIDA
North Miami
FIU Hospitality Review (6465) .....(Controlled) 7,000

Tallahassee
Florida Hotel & Motel
Journal (6713) ....(Controlled) ‡8,350

GEORGIA
Gainesville
Sunbelt Foodservice (7297) ....(Paid) 1,533
(Controlled) 28,573

ILLINOIS
Chicago
Chef (8305) ....(Paid) 1,500
(Controlled) 42,000
Convene (8343) ....(Paid) ‡4,000
(Controlled) ‡35,010
Equipment Solutions (8370) ....(Paid) ‡1,265
(Non-paid) ‡29,054

FEDA News and Views (8375) ....(Controlled) 1,600

IOWA
Des Moines
Entree (10785) ....(Non-paid) ‡650

KENTUCKY
Louisville
Pizza Today (12234) ....(Paid) 11,376
(Non-paid) 28,616

MASSACHUSETTS
Cambridge
Foodservice East (14054) ....‡23,000

MICHIGAN
East Lansing
Journal of Hospitality and Leisure
Marketing (14986) 396

MISSISSIPPI
Oxford
Nightclub & Bar Magazine (16806) ......(Paid) 2,603
(Non-paid) 21,135

MISSOURI
St. Louis
Club Management (17424) ....(Paid) 9,957
(Controlled) 3,355
Resort Management & Operations (17486)

NEW JERSEY
Liberty Corner
Bartender
Magazine (19169) ....(Controlled) ‡148,250

Secaucus
Hotel & Travel Index–International
Edition (19539) ....(Paid) 57,000

West Atlantic City
Casino Journal (19713)
Nevada Hospitality (19715)

NEW YORK
Binghamton
International Journal of Hospitality & Tourism
Administration (20157)
Journal of Human Resources in Hospitality &
Tourism (20182)
Journal of Quality Assurance in Hospitality &
Tourism (20194)

East Setauket
Hotel Business (20555)

Ithaca
The Cornell Hotel and Restaurant Administration
Quarterly (20794) ....‡3,500

New York
Hospitality Design (21819) ....(Paid) 1376
(Controlled) 28,000
HOTELS (21820) ....(Non-paid) 60,000
(Non-paid) 60,000
Institutional
Distribution (21879) ....(Non-paid) ‡39,018
Nation's Restaurant News (22402) .....(Paid) 81,202
Restaurant Business (22651) ....(Controlled) 129,000
Restaurants & Institutions (22652) ....(Paid) 1,807
(Non-paid) 171,525
Trends in the Hotel Industry (22863)
Western Itasca Review & Deerpath
Shopper (22914) ....(Paid) ‡86,801
(Free) ‡4,307

Nyack
Cucinazte (23026) 4,000
6,000

Westbury
Military Club & Hospitality (23557) ....(Paid) ‡61
‡9,079

OHIO
Cleveland
Food Management (24896) .....(Combined) ‡117,740
Hotel & Motel Management (24909) .....(Paid) 1,019
(Controlled) 58,144
LH (Lodging
Hospitality) (24920) ....(Controlled) ‡51,600
Restaurant
Hospitality (24950) ....(Non-paid) ‡120,838

Columbus
Midwest Foodservice
News (25031) ....(Controlled) ‡40,000

Ohio Tavern News (25053) ....(Paid) ‡4,000
(Controlled) ‡4,500

OKLAHOMA
Oklahoma City
Midsouthwest Restaurant (25972) ....‡2,500

OREGON
Salem
Hospitality News for the Western United
States (26568) ....(Non-paid) 40,000

TEXAS
Austin
Food & Service News (29777) ....‡10,000

Dallas
TRAVELHOST (30185) ....(Non-paid) 521,215

Fort Worth
Southwest Airlines Spirit (30352) 371,020

VIRGINIA
McLean
H.S.M.A.I. Marketing
Review (32265) ....(Controlled) 7,000

Richmond
Journal of Hospitality & Tourism Research (32440)

WASHINGTON
Bothell
Vacation Ownership World (32691) ....‡3,000

WISCONSIN
Fond du Lac
Cooking for Profit (33696) ....‡70,000

Madison
On Premise (33966) ....(Paid) 4,600
(Controlled) 400
Wisconsin Restaurateur (33989) ....‡4,200

BRITISH COLUMBIA, CANADA
Burnaby
Hospitality Today (34901) ....(Combined) 6,814

MANITOBA, CANADA
Winnipeg
Bar & Beverage Business
Magazine (35313) ....(Combined) 16,077
Western Hotelier (35360) ....(Combined) 4,342

ONTARIO, CANADA
Don Mills
Foodservice and Hospitality
Magazine (35773) ....(Controlled) 25,051
Hotelier (35775) ....(Controlled) 9,044

Mississauga
Ontario Restaurant News (36083) 16,500
Patron Magazine (36084) ....(Controlled) 40,000

QUEBEC, CANADA
Saint-Etienne-de-Lauzon
Le Chef du Service
Alimentaire (37330) ....(Controlled) •20,629

HOUSEWARES

MAINE
Yarmouth
Kitchenware News (13081) ......(Combined) ‡12,122

NEW YORK
New York
LDB Interior Textiles (22241) ....(Paid) ‡146
(Free) ‡12,253

HUMANITIES

ALABAMA
Huntsville
Oral History Review (272)

ARIZONA
Flagstaff
International Journal of Humanities and
Peace (696) ....(Paid) 2000

Tucson
Arizona Quarterly (933) ....(Paid) ‡350
(Non-paid) ‡300

CALIFORNIA
Berkeley
Evaluation Practice (1519) 1500
Mexican Studies-Estudios
Mexicanos (1542) ....(Paid) ❑1,400

La Mirada
Journal of Psychology and
Theology (2126) ....‡1,350

Pasadena
Journal of Interdisciplinary
Studies (2819) ....(Non-paid) 1,000

San Diego
Legal Theory (3223) 600

San Marino
Huntington Library Quarterly (3580) ......(Paid) ‡700
(Non-paid) ‡150

DISTRICT OF COLUMBIA
Washington
The American Scholar (5343) ....‡25,000
Humanitas (5538)
Kennedy Institute of Ethics Journal (5623) 2,000

ILLINOIS
Chicago
Signs (8564) ....‡3,149

INDIANA
Valparaiso
The Cresset (10508) ....‡4,700

KANSAS
Topeka
The Social Science Journal (11836) ....‡1,400

LOUISIANA
Lake Charles
McNeese Review (12638) ....(Combined) 200

MARYLAND
Baltimore
Configurations (13150) ....(Paid) 781
Modernism/Modernity (13220) ....(Combined) 637
Postmodern Culture (13238)

MASSACHUSETTS
Amherst
The Massachusetts Review (13803) ....(Paid) ‡1,400
(Non-paid) ‡300

Cambridge
DAEDALUS (14048) ....‡20,000

Malden
The Journal of Aesthetics and Art
Criticism (14292) ....‡2,500
The Russian Review (14299) ....(Paid) ‡1,700
(Non-paid) ‡100

Williamstown
Gastronomica (14659)

MICHIGAN
Ann Arbor
Michigan Academician (14759) ....(Paid) ⊕850

MINNESOTA
Minneapolis
NST (Nature, Society and Thought) (16118) 500

MISSISSIPPI
Hattiesburg
Southern Quarterly (16664) ....‡950

MISSOURI
St. Louis
Manuscripta (17470) ....(Combined) 500
Thalia (17523) 450

NEBRASKA
Lincoln
Great Plains Quarterly (18085) ......(Controlled) 600

NEW JERSEY
New Brunswick
Journal of the History of
Ideas (19333) ....(Paid) ‡3,300
(Controlled) ‡140

NEW YORK
Albany
13th Moon (20005)

Bronx
Humanities Index (20271)

Farmingdale
Aitia/Humanities
Magazine (20593) ....(Controlled) 5,000

New York
Journal of Adult Development (21975)
Journal of American Studies (21986) .....(Paid) ‡455
(Non-paid) ‡3,346
Journal of Cultural Economics (22043)
Prospects (22600) 600
Theoria (22829)

NORTH CAROLINA
Boone
Albion (23651) ....(Paid) ‡1,574
(Non-paid) ‡47

Durham
Nepantla (23835)

OHIO
Bowling Green
Clues: A Journal of Detection (24690)
Journal of Popular Culture (24695) ....‡3,500

PENNSYLVANIA
Indiana
Works and Days (27078) 350

Philadelphia
Proceedings of the American Philosophical
Society (27648) ....(Paid) ‡650
(Non-paid) ‡1,200

Pittsburgh
Carnegie Magazine (27764) ....(Paid) 28,679

TENNESSEE
Knoxville
Soundings (29281) ....‡1,700

TEXAS
College Station
Helios (Lubbock) (30042)

UTAH
Ogden
Weber Studies (31379) ....(Combined) 1,000

Salt Lake City
Western Humanities Review (31443) ....‡1,033

VIRGINIA
Front Royal
Sacred Music (32095) ....‡1,000

Hollins College
The Hollins Critic (32169) ....‡500

WISCONSIN
Madison
Substance (33975) ....(Paid) 500

ONTARIO, CANADA
Kingston
Queen's Quarterly (35946) ....‡3,750

Ottawa
Humanist in Canada (36250) 1,500

Peterborough
Journal of Canadian Studies (Revue d'Etudes
Canadiennes) (36316) ....‡1,350

Toronto
Poiesis (36712)

INDEXES, ABSTRACTS, REPORTS, PROCEEDINGS, AND BIBLIOGRAPHIES

ARIZONA
Phoenix
Computer Literature Index (800) .....(Controlled) 500
Current Index to Journals in Education (801)

CALIFORNIA
Glendale
Cumulative Index to Nursing & Allied Health
Literature (Print Index) (2008) ....‡1,800

Circulation: ★ = ABC; △ = BPA; ♦ = CAC; • = CCAB; ❑ = VAC; ⊕ = PO Statement; ‡ = Publisher's Report; Boldface figures = sworn; Light figures = estimated.

3161

Circ.   Circ.   Circ.

INDEXES, ABSTRACTS, REPORTS, PROCEEDINGS, AND BIBLIOGRAPHIES (continued)

La Jolla
Abstracts of Working Papers in Economics (AWPE) **(2111)**

Los Altos
The Psychoanalytic Quarterly **(2195)** ....‡3,200

Thousand Oaks
Abstracts in Social Gerontology **(3845)** ....‡350
Communication Abstracts **(3855)** ....(Paid) 600
Criminal Justice Abstracts **(3859)** ....‡800
Educational Administration
    Abstracts **(3864)** ....(Paid) 300
Human Resources Abstracts **(3873)** ......(Paid) ‡500
Journal of Planning Literature **(3898)** ......(Paid) ‡500
Peace Research Abstracts
    Journal **(3906)** ....(Paid) 200
Sage Family Studies
    Abstracts **(3912)** ....(Paid) ‡300
Sage Public Administration
    Abstracts **(3913)** ....(Paid) ‡300
Sage Urban Studies Abstracts **(3914)** .....(Paid) ‡300

DISTRICT OF COLUMBIA
Washington
Bulletin of the American Astronomical
    Society **(5388)** ....‡1,665
Current Antarctic
    Literature **(5454)** ....(Controlled) ‡1,100
Gallup Poll Tuesday Briefing **(5504)** ....(Paid) 400
Inter-American Review of
    Bibliography **(5548)** ....(Paid) ‡400
                                          (Non-paid) ‡400
The Journal of Consulting and Clinical
    Psychology **(5579)** ....‡9,650
Psychological Abstracts **(5738)** ....‡1,000
PsycSCAN: Applied Psychology **(5744)** ....‡1,400
PsycSCAN: Clinical Psychology **(5746)** ....‡3,600
PsycSCAN: LD/MR **(5747)** ....‡900
Review of Metaphysics **(5766)** ....‡2,500
Social Work Research **(5797)** ....(Paid) 2,200

FLORIDA
Homestead
Florida Entomologist **(6203)** ....‡1,000

ILLINOIS
Des Plaines
gasLine **(8762)**

KENTUCKY
Louisville
UMI's Banking Information
    Index **(12241)** ....(Paid) 410
                                          (Non-paid) 20

MARYLAND
Baltimore
A.J.N. International Nursing Index **(13110)**
Alternative Press Index **(13111)** ....(Paid) ‡550
                                          (Controlled) ‡200

Bethesda
Agricultural and Environmental Biotechnology
    Abstracts **(13297)**
Algology, Mycology & Protozoology: Microbiology
    Abstracts, Section C **(13299)**
Animal Behavior Abstracts **(13311)**
ASFA 2: Ocean Technology, Policy & Non-Living
    Resources **(13313)**
ASFA Aquaculture Abstracts **(13315)**
ASFA/Aquatic Sciences & Fisheries Abstracts Part 1:
    Biological Sciences & Living Resources **(13316)**
Bacteriology: Microbiology Abstracts, Section
    B **(13319)**
Calcium and Calcified Tissue Abstracts **(13322)**
Chemoreception Abstracts **(13324)**
Computer and Information Systems Abstracts
    Journal **(13326)**
Conference Papers Index **(13327)**
CSA Neurosciences Abstracts **(13328)**
Ecology Abstracts **(13329)**
Electronics & Communications Abstracts
    Journal **(13333)**
Genetics Abstracts **(13340)**
Health and Safety Science Abstracts **(13342)**
Immunology Abstracts **(13344)**
Industrial and Applied Microbiology: Microbiology
    Abstracts, Section A **(13345)**
International Pharmaceutical
    Abstracts **(13346)** ....(Paid) ‡376
                                          (Non-paid) ‡55

Linguistics and Language Behavior
    Abstracts **(13357)** ....‡900
Mechanical Engineering Abstracts **(13358)**
Medical and Pharmaceutical Biotechnology
    Abstracts **(13359)**
Nucleic Acids Abstracts **(13368)**
Oceanic Abstracts **(13369)**
Pollution Abstracts **(13376)**
Sociological Abstracts **(13379)** ....‡1,900
Solid State and Superconductivity Abstracts **(13380)**
Toxicology Abstracts **(13384)**
Virology and AIDS Abstracts **(13387)**

College Park
Bulletin of the American Physical
    Society **(13413)** ....‡39,757
Current Physics Index **(13415)** ....‡279

MASSACHUSETTS
Littleton
Meteorological & Geoastrophysical
    Abstracts **(14277)** ....‡350

MICHIGAN
Chelsea
Personnel Management Abstracts **(14877)** ......‡645

Farmington Hills
Concrete Abstracts **(15017)** ....‡676

Warren
The Music Index **(15660)** ....‡750

NEW JERSEY
Bridgewater
Books and More for Growing
    Minds **(18694)** ....(Non-paid) 14,200
Forecast **(18695)** ....(Non-paid) 22,400
Hot Picks **(18696)** ....(Non-paid) 15,500
Now Hear This **(18697)** ....(Non-paid) 13,900
Paper Clips **(18698)** ....(Non-paid) 16,800

Hoboken
Abstract Bulletin of the Institute of Paper Science
    and Technology **(18880)** ....(Paid) ‡660
                                          (Controlled) ‡90

Medford
Information Science Abstracts **(19224)**
Internet & Personal Computing Abstracts **(19226)**

Somerset
Women Studies Abstracts **(19570)** .....(Paid) ‡1,000

NEW YORK
Albany
Film Literature Index **(19986)** ....‡525

Amityville
Abstracts in Anthropology **(20034)**

Bronx
Abridged Readers' Guide to Periodical
    Literature **(20250)**
Applied Science & Technology Index **(20252)**
Art Index **(20253)**
Biography Index **(20254)**
Biological & Agricultural Index **(20255)**
Business Periodicals Index **(20262)**
Education Index **(20267)**
General Science Index **(20270)**
Humanities Index **(20271)**
Index to Legal Periodicals & Books **(20272)**
Library Literature & Information Science **(20275)**
Readers' Guide to Periodical Literature **(20283)**
Social Sciences Index **(20287)**
Vertical File Index **(20288)**

New York
City of New York Council Digest **(21426)**
Current Bibliographical Information **(21523)**
Journal of Rheology **(22179)**
Monthly Bibliography, Part II **(22361)**
Proceedings of the IEEE **(22597)** ....‡21,000
RILM Abstracts of Music
    Literature **(22668)** ....‡1,200
Semigroup Forum **(22723)** ....(Combined) 500
UNDOC **(22883)**
World Banking Abstracts **(22940)**
World News Digest **(22943)** ....(Paid) ‡5,600

NORTH CAROLINA
Raleigh
Bulletin of Bibliography **(24127)** 1,600

OHIO
Beachwood
Alloys Index **(24647)**
Metals Abstracts **(24653)**

Nonferrous Alert **(24654)**
Polymers/Ceramics/Composites Alert **(24655)**
Steels Alert **(24657)**

Bowling Green
The Philosopher's Index **(24699)** ....(Paid) ‡1,322
                                          (Non-paid) ‡175

Columbus
CA Selects **(25004)**
Ohio Biological Survey Miscellaneous
    Contributions **(25040)** ....(Paid) 80

Materials Park
Engineered Materials Abstracts **(25365)**

OKLAHOMA
Tulsa
Petroleum Abstracts **(26125)**

OREGON
Terrebonne
Topicator **(26595)** ....‡160

PENNSYLVANIA
Philadelphia
Proceedings of the American Philosophical
    Society **(27648)** ....(Paid) ‡650
                                          (Non-paid) ‡1,200
Transactions and Studies of the College of
    Physicians of
    Philadelphia **(27709)** ....(Combined) 1,900

Pittsburgh
Abridged Index Medicus **(27753)**
Answers **(27759)** ....‡5,000
Index Medicus **(27798)**
Monthly Catalog of U.S. Government
    Publications **(27816)**

RHODE ISLAND
Providence
Abstracts of Papers Presented to the American
    Mathematical Society **(28384)** ....(Paid) ‡2,640
Current Mathematical
    Publications **(28394)** ....(Paid) ‡1,180
Mathematical Reviews **(28404)** ....(Paid) ‡1,500

SOUTH CAROLINA
Columbia
Papers of the Bibliographical Society of
    America **(28561)** ....‡1,250

TENNESSEE
Nashville
Television News Index and
    Abstracts **(29487)** ....‡200

Oak Ridge
Concentrating Solar Power **(29547)**
Geothermal Energy Technology **(29548)**

VIRGINIA
Reston
International Aerospace Abstracts **(32366)**

WASHINGTON
Seattle
Glass Art Society Journal **(32968)**

WISCONSIN
Madison
Feminist Periodicals **(33938)** 1,000

INSURANCE

ARKANSAS
Little Rock
The Case Manager **(1226)** ....(Combined) 20,000

CALIFORNIA
Burbank
California Broker **(1616)** ....‡25,000

San Diego
The Insurance Journal of the
    West **(3174)** ....(Controlled) 11,000

CONNECTICUT
Hartford
Managers Handbook **(4897)** ....‡8,000

DISTRICT OF COLUMBIA
Washington
Contingencies **(5441)** ....(Paid) ‡13,000
(Controlled) ‡10,000

FLORIDA
Boca Raton
Insurance Meetings
Management **(5933)** ....(Non-paid) 5,075

Ponte Vedra Beach
Actuarial Digest **(6593)** ....(Controlled) 16,100

GEORGIA
Atlanta
LOMA Resource **(7026)** ....(Non-paid) 27,000
Resource **(7040)** ....(Non-paid) 27,000

ILLINOIS
Chicago
Business Insurance **(8296)** ....(Paid) 25,386
(Controlled) 20,339
Defense Counsel Journal **(8351)**
Employee Benefit Plan
Review **(8368)** ....(Paid) 2,624
(Non-paid) 19,236

Park Ridge
Round the Table **(9408)**

Schaumburg
North American Actuarial
Journal **(9589)** ....(Non-paid) 17,000

Springfield
Broker News **(9620)** ....(Controlled) 500,000
Insurance Insight **(9634)** ....(Controlled) 2,500

INDIANA
Indianapolis
NAMIC National Affairs Insider **(10155)**
Property/Casualty Insurance **(10163)**
Property/Casualty Insurance
Magazine **(10164)** ....(Paid) 11,000

KANSAS
Overland Park
Broker World **(11700)** ....(Paid) ‡25,552
(Non-paid) ‡1902

Topeka
Kansas Insurance Agent and
Broker **(11829)** ....(Paid) ‡934
(Non-paid) ‡106

KENTUCKY
Erlanger
National Underwriter Life and Health-Financial
Services Edition **(12053)**
National Underwriter Property and Casualty/Risk and
Benefits Management **(12054)** ....(Paid) 18,564
(Non-paid) 27,550
Who Writes What in Life and Health
Insurance **(12055)**

Lexington
Leader's Magazine **(12173)** ....‡6,249

LOUISIANA
New Orleans
Surplus Line Reporter & Insurance
News **(12755)** ....(Non-paid) ‡4,008
Texas Surplus Line Reporter **(12756)** ....(Paid) ‡835
(Non-paid) ‡5,110

MASSACHUSETTS
Boston
The Standard **(13963)** 5,123

Stow
Insurance Conference
Planner **(14573)** ....(Controlled) ‡8,500

MICHIGAN
Adrian
The National Gleaner Forum **(14710)** ....⊕31,000

Port Huron
Woman's Life **(15452)** ....(Non-paid) 32,000

MINNESOTA
Chaska
Minnesota Insurance **(15794)** ......(Non-paid) ‡3,987

MISSOURI
St. Louis
Life Insurance Selling **(17466)** ....(Paid) 41,734

NEW JERSEY
Hoboken
Banks in Insurance Report **(18899)** 5985
Health Care Analysis **(18958)**

Oldwick
Best's Review **(19395)** ....‡62,977

NEW YORK
Glenmont
Professional Insurance Agents **(20668)** ....‡5,400

New York
The Bulletin **(21348)** ....(Controlled) 2,800
Financial Crime Review **(21695)**
Insurance Networking **(21884)**
International Insurance Law Journal **(21898)**
Risk Management **(22671)** ....(Paid) △8,672
(Non-paid) △6,500
S & P's Insurance Digest/Life Insurance
Edition **(22699)**
S & P's Insurance Digest/Property-Casualty &
Reinsurance Edition **(22700)**

OHIO
Cincinnati
Home and Away **(24802)** ....‡200,000

OKLAHOMA
Tulsa
Today's Insurance Woman **(26134)** ....‡15,000

PENNSYLVANIA
Berwyn
The Mutual Magazine **(26697)** ....‡8,500

Bryn Mawr
Journal of Financial Service
Professionals **(26741)** ....‡28,000

Horsham
Risk & Insurance **(27064)** ....(Paid) 3,141
(Controlled) 43,527

Malvern
CPCU Journal **(27210)** ....(Paid) 29,000
The Journal of Risk and
Insurance **(27213)** ....‡1,500

Philadelphia
AAA World—Keystone **(27355)** 2,300,000
AAA World—Shore **(27358)** 2,300,000

TEXAS
Austin
The Insurance Journal of
Texas **(29784)** ....(Controlled) 5,600

VERMONT
Ludlow
The Appraisers Standard **(31548)** ....(Combined) 700

VIRGINIA
Alexandria
Independent Agent **(31682)** ....(Controlled) 45,000
Professional Agent **(31727)** ....(Paid) ‡33,000

Arlington
The Insurance Tax Review **(31797)**
Public Risk **(31821)** ....(Paid) ‡3,000

Falls Church
Advisor Today **(32039)** ....(Controlled) 89,870
GAMA International
Journal **(32046)** ....(Controlled) 6,000

WASHINGTON
Brier
CLAIMS **(32698)** ....(Paid) ‡7,000
(Non-paid) ‡3,000

WISCONSIN
Madison
Journal of Insurance
Regulation **(33953)** ....(Paid) 1,950
(Non-paid) 15

Milwaukee
Catholic Knight
Magazine **(34062)** ....(Controlled) ‡60,000
The Family Friend **(34068)** ....(Non-paid) 33,000

ONTARIO, CANADA
Don Mills
Canadian Underwriter **(35772)** ....(Paid) 5,126
(Non-paid) 4,709

North York
CAIFA Forum **(36123)** ....(Paid) ‡1,500
(Controlled) ‡18,000

Toronto
Canadian Independent Adjuster **(36505)**
Canadian Insurance X Canadian Insurance
Magazine **(36507)** ....(Paid) •4,058
(Non-paid) •7,569

QUEBEC, CANADA
Montreal
The Insurance
Journal **(37133)** ....(Combined) 18,000
Journal de
l'Assurance **(37143)** ....(Controlled) 26,000

INTERCULTURAL INTERESTS

ALABAMA
Auburn University
Bulletin of the Comediantes **(49)** ....(Paid) 500

ALASKA
Anchorage
First Alaskans **(525)**

CALIFORNIA
Berkeley
Early China **(1514)** ....(Controlled) 350
Mexican Studies-Estudios
Mexicanos **(1542)** ....(Paid) ❑1,400

Los Angeles
Polish Music Journal **(2372)**
Ufahamu **(2420)** ....(Combined) 250

San Bernardino
Journal of Latinos and Education **(3087)**

San Mateo
Slavic & East European Information
Resources **(3590)** 150

Santa Barbara
Sino-Japanese Studies **(3657)**

COLORADO
Boulder
Journal of the American Oriental
Society **(4173)** ....‡2,300
Many Mountains Moving **(4178)** ....(Paid) 1,800
(Non-paid) 200

CONNECTICUT
New Britain
Multicultural Perspectives **(4976)**

DELAWARE
Newark
MACLAS Latin American Essays **(5278)**

DISTRICT OF COLUMBIA
Washington
American Review of Canadian Studies **(5342)**
The Americas **(5349)** ....‡1,000
The Journal of Indo-European
Studies **(5598)** ....(Paid) ‡856
(Non-paid) ‡56
Journal of Palestine Studies **(5610)** .....(Paid) 3,500

FLORIDA
Bradenton
East European Quarterly **(5958)** ....‡1,000

Gainesville
African Studies Quarterly **(6129)**

Miami
Caribbean Review **(6344)** ....(Paid) ‡5,000
(Non-paid) ‡2,000

Japan Studies Review **(6364)**

GEORGIA
Mountain City
The Foxfire Magazine **(7449)** 3,000

Statesboro
SECOLAS Annals **(7562)**

ILLINOIS
Chicago
The Journal of Comparative Asian
Development **(8434)**
Metmenys **(8484)** ....(Paid) 700

Circulation: ★ = ABC; △ = BPA; ♦ = CAC; • = CCAB; ❑ = VAC; ⊕ = PO Statement; ‡ = Publisher's Report; Boldface figures = sworn; Light figures = estimated.

3163

Circ.   Circ.   Circ.

INTERCULTURAL INTERESTS (continued)
Swiss-American Historical
Society **(8580)** ....(Paid) 400

Rockford
Chronicles **(9526)** ....‡8,000

INDIANA
bloomington
Africa Today **(9822)** ....(Paid) 1,800
(Controlled) 66
Journal of Japanese Linguistics **(9842)**
Mongolian Studies **(9845)**

MARYLAND
Baltimore
Journal of Asian American
Studies **(13178)** ....(Combined) 857

MASSACHUSETTS
Boston
International Journal of the Classical
Tradition **(13907)** ....(Paid) ‡800

Brookline
Journal of Modern
Hellenism **(14021)** ....(Combined) 650

Cambridge
Asian American Policy
Review **(14039)** ....(Combined) 700
Transition **(14109)** ....(Paid) 1,100
(Non-paid) 200

Duxbury
Journal of Turkish Studies/Turkluk Bilgisi
Arastirmalari **(14164)**

Malden
The Russian Review **(14299)** ....(Paid) ‡1,700
(Non-paid) ‡100

MICHIGAN
Ann Arbor
Early Modern Japan **(14746)**
International Journal of Middle East
Studies **(14753)** ....(Paid) ‡3456
(Non-paid) ‡29

Cedar
Bulletin of Concerned Asian
Scholars **(14863)** ....‡1,500

East Lansing
Northeast African Studies **(14991)**

MINNESOTA
Bemidji
Germanic Notes and Reviews **(15737)**

Minneapolis
Xcp: Cross Cultural
Poetics **(16142)** ....(Combined) 850

NEW JERSEY
Cherry Hill
German Quarterly **(18735)** ....(Combined) 3,200

Morristown
Eire-Ireland **(19312)** ....(Paid) ‡5,000
(Controlled) ‡500

New Brunswick
African Studies Review **(19324)**
East Asia **(19331)** ....(Paid) ‡700
Italian Quarterly **(19332)** ....(Paid) 1,050

Princeton Junction
Card Manufacturing **(19483)** ....(Paid) 3,000

NEW MEXICO
Albuquerque
Colonial Latin America Historical
Review **(19769)** ....(Combined) 400

NEW YORK
Armonk
The Chinese Economy **(20068)** ....(Paid) ⊕224
Chinese Education &
Society **(20069)** ....(Paid) ⊕151
Chinese Law and
Government **(20070)** ....(Paid) ⊕227
Chinese Sociology and
Anthropology **(20071)** ....(Paid) ⊕199
Chinese Studies in History **(20072)** ......(Paid) ⊕252
Contemporary Chinese
Thought **(20073)** ....(Paid) ⊕154
European Education **(20077)** ....(Paid) ⊕169

International Journal of
Sociology **(20082)** ....(Paid) ⊕302

Binghamton
African Philosophy **(20151)**
Ijele **(20155)**
Jenda **(20159)**
Journal of Ethnicity in Substance Abuse **(20172)**
Journal of Immigrant & Refugee Services **(20183)**
West Africa Review **(20220)**

Brooklyn
International Journal of Kurdish
Studies **(20321)** ....(Combined) 500

Nanuet
Wazobia News **(21105)**

New York
Charioteer **(21397)** ....(Paid) 800
Columbia Journal of Asian
Law **(21445)** ....(Paid) ‡270
European Judaism **(21654)**
French Politics, Culture and Society **(21735)**
German Politics and Society **(21759)**
Indo-Iranian Journal **(21864)**
Journal of the Hellenic
Diaspora **(22087)** ....(Paid) ‡600
(Non-paid) ‡100
Journal of Modern African Studies **(22135)** 1600
Modern Asian Studies **(22347)** 1150
New German Critique **(22430)**
The Polish Review **(22572)** ....(Paid) ‡1,500
(Controlled) ‡200
Scandinavian Review **(22708)** ....(Paid) 6,000

NORTH CAROLINA
Chapel Hill
Annali D'Italianistica **(23698)** 600

Durham
Comparative Studies of South Asia, Africa, and the
Middle East **(23815)** ....(Paid) 450

PENNSYLVANIA
Glenolden
Journal of Scotch-Irish Studies **(26946)**

Harrisburg
German Policy Studies **(26992)**

Philadelphia
Middle East Quarterly **(27569)** ....(Paid) ‡2,100

Pittsburgh
Latin American Research Review **(27810)**

PUERTO RICO
San Juan
Caribbean Studies **(28291)**

TENNESSEE
Harriman
Journal of Men's Studies **(29216)** ....(Paid) 400

Johnson City
Journal of Asia-Pacific Business **(29252)**

Nashville
Acquerello Italiano **(29439)**
Champs-Elysees **(29449)**
Puerta del Sol **(29482)**
Schau ins Land **(29485)**

TEXAS
San Antonio
Journal of Language, Identity, and
Education **(31034)**

UTAH
Salt Lake City
The Journal of Asian Studies **(31433)** ....‡10,000

VIRGINIA
Arlington
Anthropology of Consciousness **(31774)**

WASHINGTON
Seattle
Journal of Japanese Studies **(32978)** ....(Paid) 1,900
positions **(33005)** ....(Combined) 950

WISCONSIN
Milwaukee
Digest of Middle East Studies
(DOMES) **(34065)** ....(Paid) 1,000

ALBERTA, CANADA
Edmonton
Canadian Slavonic Papers/Revue Canadienne des
Slavistes **(34704)** ....(Paid) 750
(Non-paid) 50
Seminar **(34729)** 825

ONTARIO, CANADA
Guelph
Scottish Tradition **(35867)**

London
Canadian Journal of Latin American and Caribbean
Studies **(35978)** ....(Controlled) 500

Waterloo
Germano-Slavica **(36851)** ....(Paid) ‡200

Willowdale
Journal of Asian and African Studies **(36880)**

QUEBEC, CANADA
Montreal
Canadian Jewish Studies/Etudes Juives
Canadiennes **(37094)** ....(Paid) 354
Interculture **(37135)**
Journal CAJLE **(37137)**
Revue d'histoire de l'Amerique
francaise **(37218)** ....(Controlled) 1,100

INTERIOR DESIGN/DECORATING
See also Paint and Wallcoverings

DISTRICT OF COLUMBIA
Washington
ASID ICON **(5367)** ....(Controlled) 33,000

ILLINOIS
St. Charles
Interior Construction **(9570)** ....(Controlled) ‡8,300

MINNESOTA
St. Paul
Fine Furnishings International
(FFI) **(16376)** ....(Paid) 664
(Controlled) 20,467
Window Fashions **(16418)** ....(Paid) 27,000
(Non-paid) 27,000

NEW JERSEY
Hackensack
Balloons & Parties Magazine **(18851)** ....‡7,000

NEW YORK
Melville
Kitchen and Bath Design
News **(21047)** ....(Non-paid) ‡55,837

New York
Architectural Lighting **(21242)** ......(Non-paid) 25,000
Contract **(21497)** ....(Paid) 354
(Controlled) 30,087
Facilities Design &
Management **(21673)** ....(Non-paid) 35,000
Hospitality Design **(21819)** ....(Paid) 1376
(Controlled) 28,000
House Beautiful's Houses and Plans **(21823)**
INTERIORS **(21891)** ....(Paid) 11,009
(Non-paid) 15,351
Metropolitan Home **(22328)** ....(Paid) 604,670

BRITISH COLUMBIA, CANADA
Burnaby
Award Magazine **(34889)** ....(Combined) 7,657

ONTARIO, CANADA
Etobicoke
Info-Link **(35816)** ....(Combined) •44,168

INTERNATIONAL AFFAIRS

CALIFORNIA
Berkeley
Berkeley Journal of International Law **(1497)**
Studies in Comparative International
Development **(1563)** ....(Paid) ‡600

Irvine
Mexican Studies/Estudios Mexicanos **(2083)**

Oakland
Asian Survey **(2667)** ....‡3,300

Palo Alto
U.S. - Japan Women's Journal **(2802)**

Riverside
Latin American Perspectives **(2941)** ....(Paid) ‡1,550
(Non-paid) ‡83

Santa Monica
RAND Review **(3715)** ....(Controlled) 15,000

Stanford
Stanford Journal of International Relations **(3800)**

Thousand Oaks
China Report **(3853)** ....(Paid) 1,700
International Studies **(3875)**
Modern China **(3903)** ....(Paid) ‡700

COLORADO
Boulder
Latin American Politics and
Society **(4176)** ....(Paid) 1,300
(Controlled) 202

CONNECTICUT
Milford
National Development/Desarrollo
Nacional **(4957)** ....(Controlled) ‡21,000

New Haven
Journal of Conflict
Resolution **(4993)** ....(Paid) ‡2,363
(Non-paid) ‡114

DISTRICT OF COLUMBIA
Washington
American Journal of International
Law **(5332)** ....‡6,800
American Review of Canadian Studies **(5342)**
Arms Control Today **(5361)** ....‡3,000
Asian Affairs **(5366)** 364
The Brookings Review **(5385)** ....(Paid) ‡6,000
(Controlled) ‡10,000
Demokratizatsiya **(5461)** ....(Paid) 300
Foreign Policy **(5499)** ....(Paid) 34,000
(Non-paid) 40,000
(Combined) 70,000
Foreign Service
Journal **(5500)** ....(Combined) ‡15,000
George Washington Journal of International Law and
Economics **(5507)**
International Journal of Legal
Information **(5555)** ....(Paid) 600
International Legal Materials **(5556)** ......(Paid) 2,111
The Journal of International Security Affairs **(5600)**
Journal of Social, Political & Economic
Studies **(5615)** ....(Paid) ‡1,150
(Non-paid) ‡55
Law and Policy in International Business **(5633)**
The Middle East Journal **(5650)** ....‡3,500
Middle East Research & Information
Project **(5651)** 4,000
Multinational Monitor **(5663)** ....(Paid) ‡10,000
(Non-paid) ‡2,000
The National Interest **(5677)** .....(Combined) ‡20,000
OECD Observer **(5703)**
Perspectives on Political
Science **(5717)** ....(Paid) 467
Sister City News **(5793)** ....(Paid) ‡11,312
(Free) ‡2,000
Washington Report on Middle East Affairs **(5852)**
World Affairs **(5866)** ....(Paid) ‡600
World Watch **(5871)** ....(Paid) ‡15,000
(Non-paid) ‡1,200

FLORIDA
Gulf Breeze
Russia & Eurasia Documents Annual **(6180)**

GEORGIA
Americus
Journal of Third World Studies **(6922)** ....(Paid) 815

ILLINOIS
Chicago
Bulletin of the Atomic Scientists **(8295)** ......‡10,000

River Forest
World Libraries **(9493)** ....(Controlled) 298

INDIANA
Notre Dame
Review of Politics **(10378)** 1,700

MAINE
Orono
Canadian-American Public Policy **(12999)**

MARYLAND
Baltimore
SAIS Review **(13243)** ....(Combined) 553

MASSACHUSETTS
Cambridge
International Organization **(14071)** ....‡3,000
International Security **(14072)** ....‡4,600
Journal of Cold War
Studies **(14075)** ....(Combined) 2,300

Malden
Middle East Policy **(14298)**

Medford
The Fletcher Forum of World
Affairs **(14321)** ....(Paid) 2,000

MICHIGAN
Ann Arbor
European Access **(14749)**

MINNESOTA
Minneapolis
Far Eastern Affairs **(16078)**

MISSOURI
Fort Leonard Wood
America's Insider **(17070)**
Cuba News **(17072)**

NEW HAMPSHIRE
Manchester
Le Canado-Americain **(18557)** ....(Paid) ‡36,000
(Controlled) ‡1,333

NEW JERSEY
Princeton
World Politics **(19478)** ....(Paid) ‡3940
(Non-paid) ‡107

NEW YORK
Amityville
A Current Bibliography on African Affairs **(20037)**

Armonk
Annual Survey of Eastern Europe and the Former
Soviet Union **(20064)**
China Briefing **(20067)**
India Briefing **(20078)**
International Journal of Political
Economy **(20081)** ....(Paid) 279
Korea Briefing **(20088)**

Binghamton
Journal on African Immigration (JAI) **(20161)**

Brooklyn
Kurdish Life **(20328)**

Jamaica
International Chinese Application Psychology
Journal **(20833)**
International Chinese Nursing Journal **(20834)**
International Chinese Sexology Journal **(20835)**

Nanuet
Wazobia News **(21105)**

New York
American Foreign Policy Interests **(21187)**
Asia Pacific Journal of Environmental Law **(21262)**
Asia-Pacific Journal on Human Rights and the
Law **(21263)**
Asia Pacific Law Review **(21264)**
Cepal Review **(21390)**
Continental Philosophy Review **(21495)**
East European Politics & Societies **(21578)**
Ethics and International Affairs **(21633)**
European Foreign Affairs Review **(21638)**
European Journal of Crime, Criminal Law and
Criminal Justice **(21640)**
European Journal of Criminal Policy and
Research **(21641)**
European Journal for Education Law and
Policy **(21642)**
European Journal of Epidemiology **(21643)**
European Journal of Health Law **(21644)**
European Journal of Law Reform **(21646)**
European Migration and Law **(21655)**
European Public Law **(21656)**
European Review of Private Law **(21657)**
Foreign Affairs **(21725)** ....(Paid) 124,000
German Politics and Society **(21759)**
International Environmental Agreements **(21896)**
International Insurance Law Journal **(21898)**
International Journal for the Advancement of
Counseling **(21899)**

International Journal on Minority and Group
Rights **(21911)**
International Negotiation **(21928)**
International Peacekeeping **(21929)**
International Politics **(21930)**
Japanese Journal of Political
Science **(21957)** 400
Journal of International Affairs **(22102)**
Journal of Latin American Studies **(22110)** 1,900
Journal of the Royal Asiatic
Society **(22181)** ....(Paid) ‡544
(Non-paid) ‡839
Leiden Journal of International Law **(22246)**
Monthly Bibliography, Part II **(22361)**
NACLA Report on the
Americas **(22391)** ....(Paid) ‡6,000
New Leader **(22431)**
Permanent Missions to the United Nations **(22542)**
Review of Central and East European Law **(22657)**
Review of International Studies **(22661)** 1700
UN Chronicle **(22882)** ....(Paid) ‡9,000
(Controlled) ‡22,000
United Nations Treaty
Series **(22885)** ....(Combined) ‡1,500
World Policy Journal **(22944)** 5,000

Staten Island
International Migration Review **(23358)** ....‡2,000

NORTH CAROLINA
Chapel Hill
North Carolina Journal of International Law and
Commercial
Regulation **(23716)** ....(Combined) 395

Durham
Duke Journal of Comparative and International
Law **(23817)**

OHIO
Columbus
Current Digest of the Post-Soviet
Press **(25014)** ....(Paid) 1,000

PENNSYLVANIA
Carlisle
Parameters **(26760)** ....(Paid) ‡1,500
(Non-paid) ‡11,500

Hanover
Revista Panamericana de Salud
Publica **(26976)** ....‡12,000

Harrisburg
German Policy Studies **(26992)**

Philadelphia
Current History **(27433)** ....‡21,000
Energy Systems and
Policy **(27460)** ....(Controlled) ‡285
Peace and Freedom **(27613)**

Pittsburgh
Diplomatic List **(27781)**
Treaties and Other International Acts
Series **(27850)** 126

TEXAS
Austin
Texas International Law
Journal **(29826)** ....(Paid) 600

College Station
Journal of Politics **(30046)** 4,000

Dallas
Clements' International Report **(30137)**

Houston
Houston Journal of International Law **(30486)**
Sarmatian Review **(30526)**

VIRGINIA
Fairfax
Comparative Strategy **(32014)** ....(Paid) 700

Norfolk
International Journal of Educational
Telecommunications **(32284)**

WISCONSIN
Milwaukee
Digest of Middle East Studies
(DOMES) **(34065)** ....(Paid) 1,000

WYOMING
Laramie
Energy Sources **(34548)** ....(Controlled) ‡345

Circ.   Circ.   Circ.

INTERNATIONAL AFFAIRS (continued)

ALBERTA, CANADA
Edmonton
Global Governance **(34714)** ....(Paid) 1,600

BRITISH COLUMBIA, CANADA
Vancouver
Pacific Affairs **(35157)** ....‡2,500

NEWFOUNDLAND AND LABRADOR, CANADA
St. John's
Labour/Le Travail **(35488)** 900

ONTARIO, CANADA
Ottawa
Canadian Review of American
  Studies **(36227)** ....(Paid) 475

Toronto
Behind the Headlines **(36473)** ....(Paid) 1,200
Bulletin on Current Research in Soviet and East
  European Law **(36480)** ....(Paid) 130
                                                   150
Canada & Arab World **(36487)** ....(Paid) ‡7,900
                    (Non-paid) ‡5,300
International Journal **(36623)** ....‡1,300
Southern Africa Report **(36744)** ....(Paid) 900
                       (Non-paid) 100

Willowdale
International Journal of Comparative
  Sociology **(36879)**

INTERNATIONAL BUSINESS AND ECONOMICS

ALABAMA
Birmingham
International Review of Financial Analysis **(74)**

ARIZONA
Flagstaff
Journal of the Flagstaff
  Institute **(697)** ....(Combined) 150

CALIFORNIA
Palm Springs
Futures **(2759)**

San Francisco
World Trade **(3464)**

Thousand Oaks
Economic Development
  Quarterly **(3862)** ....(Paid) ‡1,300
                     (Non-paid) ‡164

DISTRICT OF COLUMBIA
Washington
Alam Attijarat (The World of
  Business) **(5320)** ....(Non-paid) ‡20,954
Asian Affairs **(5366)** 364
The Brookings Review **(5385)** ....(Paid) ‡6,000
                   (Controlled) ‡10,000
The China Business Review **(5411)** ....(Paid) ‡5,600
                   (Non-paid) ‡100
East Asian Executive Reports **(5467)** ....(Paid) ‡400
                   (Non-paid) 500
Economia **(5471)**
Export America **(5487)**
Export Today's Global Business
  Magazine **(5488)** ....‡86,000
Finance &
  Development **(5495)** ....(Controlled) 95,000
Financial Market Trends **(5496)**
Foreign Service
  Journal **(5500)** ....(Combined) ‡15,000
Franchising World **(5503)** ....(Paid) ‡233
                   (Controlled) ‡10,200
Journal of International Business
  Studies **(5599)** ....(Paid) 4,200
Law and Policy in International Business **(5633)**
Main Economic Indicators **(5641)**
Middle East Executive
  Reports **(5649)** ....(Paid) ‡500
                   (Non-paid) ‡400
The Middle East Journal **(5650)** ....‡3,500
Monthly Statistics of International Trade **(5661)**
OECD Economic Studies **(5699)**
OECD Observer **(5703)**
Quarterly National Accounts **(5756)**
The World Bank Economic
  Review **(5868)** ....(Paid) 1,800
                 (Non-paid) 10,000
World Economic Outlook **(5869)**

World Watch **(5871)** ....(Paid) ‡15,000
                   (Non-paid) ‡1,200

FLORIDA
Coral Gables
Artes Graficas **(6004)** 24,112

Odessa
WWS/World Wide Shipping **(6480)** 9,500

Ormond Beach
Foreign Tax Law Bi-Weekly Bulletin **(6533)**

GEORGIA
Atlanta
Textile World Latina **(7055)** ....(Combined) 12,500

ILLINOIS
Carol Stream
Global Cosmetic Industry **(8144)**

Champaign
Comparative Labor Law & Policy
  Journal **(8184)** ....(Combined) 800

Chicago
Chamber Way
  Germany/Midwest **(8303)** ....(Controlled) 6,000

Riverwoods
Doing Business in Europe **(9502)** ....‡1,000
Doing Business in Europe **(9503)** ....(Paid) ‡125
Tax Treaties **(9509)**

KANSAS
Overland Park
International Construction **(11715)** ....△25,000
World Broadcast
  News **(11738)** ....(Non-paid) ‡12,665

LOUISIANA
Thibodaux
Global Business and Finance
  Review **(12859)** ....(Paid) 400
                   (Non-paid) 150

MASSACHUSETTS
Belmont
IDB America **(13840)**

Boston
China Telecom **(13873)**
Journal of Transnational Management
  Development **(13919)** ....(Paid) 107
The WorldPaper **(13973)** ....(Paid) 1,800,000

Cambridge
International Organization **(14071)** ....‡3,000

Newton
EDN Europe **(14390)**
Electronic Business Asia **(14395)**
Global Design News **(14397)**

Quincy
American Journal of Transportation **(14488)**

MICHIGAN
Ann Arbor
European Access **(14749)**

Kalamazoo
Journal of International Accounting, Auditing and
  Taxation **(15239)**

Southfield
Ward's Automotive International **(15551)**

MINNESOTA
Minneapolis
Far Eastern Affairs **(16078)**

MISSOURI
Fort Leonard Wood
America's Insider **(17070)**

St. Louis
International Advances in Economic
  Research **(17446)**

NEBRASKA
Lincoln
Journal of World Business **(18088)** ....‡2,000

NEW JERSEY
East Rutherford
Latin Finance **(18784)**

Fort Lee
Quick Frozen Foods
  International **(18834)** ....(Paid) ‡6,011
                   (Controlled) ‡5,528

Hoboken
Public Administration and
  Development **(19092)** ....(Paid) 7,000

Newark
Journal of Commerce Import
  Bulletin **(19356)** ....‡1,608

NEW MEXICO
Albuquerque
SourceMex Economic News and Analysis on
  Mexico **(19788)**

NEW YORK
Armonk
Eastern European
  Economics **(20074)** ....(Paid) ⊕422
Emerging Markets Finance and
  Trade **(20076)** ....(Paid) ⊕196
International Journal of Political
  Economy **(20081)** ....(Paid) 279
The Japanese Economy **(20083)** ....(Paid) ⊕225

Binghamton
Journal of African Business **(20160)**

Great Neck
Petroleo Internacional **(20694)** ....(Non-paid) 9,313
World Industrial Reporter (Reportero
  Industrial) **(20695)** ....(Non-paid) ‡71,101

Nanuet
Wazobia News **(21105)**

New York
Asia-Pacific Financial Markets **(21261)**
Business Europe **(21356)**
Business Latin America **(21358)**
Commodity Trade Statistics **(21457)**
Cong Thuong **(21482)** ....‡5,000
Development Business **(21547)**
European Finance Review **(21636)**
European Financial Law Review **(21637)**
European Journal of Law and Economics **(21645)**
Experimental Economics **(21666)**
The Exporter **(21669)** ....(Paid) ‡2,500
                   (Controlled) ‡2,500
Foreign Affairs **(21725)** ....(Paid) 124,000
Fortune International **(21728)**
International Journal of Comparative Labour Law and
  Industrial Relations **(21902)**
International Journal of Franchising and Distribution
  Law **(21907)**
International Tax and Public Finance **(21939)**
Intertax **(21943)**
Journal of Management and Governance **(22120)**
MSI Europe **(22376)**
The Nikkei Weekly **(22463)**
Rundt's World Business Intelligence **(22680)**
Television Europe **(22820)**
Transnational Corporations **(22854)**
UK & USA **(22880)** ....(Paid) 14,000
World Mining Equipment **(22942)**

OREGON
Portland
Pacific Marketer **(26498)**

PENNSYLVANIA
Indiana
Advances in Competitiveness Research **(27071)**
Competitiveness Review **(27072)** .....(Combined) 700
Global Competitiveness **(27074)**
International Journal of Commerce and
  Management **(27075)**

Middletown
Journal of East-West Business **(27254)** 250
Journal of Euromarketing **(27255)** ....(Paid) 300
                   (Non-paid) 50
Journal of Global Marketing **(27256)** 432
Journal of International Consumer
  Marketing **(27257)** ....(Paid) 371
Journal of Teaching in International
  Business **(27259)** 245

PUERTO RICO
San Juan
Caribbean Business **(28290)** ....(Paid) 39,500
                   (Free) 4,500

SOUTH CAROLINA
Charleston
Port News **(28516)** ....(Combined) 9,000

Columbia
Essays in International Business **(28548)**

TENNESSEE
Johnson City
Journal of Asia-Pacific Business **(29252)**

TEXAS
Austin
Journal of Organizational Computing and Electronic
   Commerce **(29789)**

El Paso
Twin Plant News **(30283)** ....(Controlled) 9,600

Houston
Oil & Gas Journal Latinoamerica **(30517)**

Irving
The Journal of African Human Resources and
   Business Issues **(30605)**

Laredo
The International Trade
   Journal **(30669)** ....(Paid) ‡649

VIRGINIA
Arlington
Tax Notes International **(31836)** ....(Paid) 1,365

Ashburn
Business Today Egypt **(31850)**
Egypt Today **(31851)**

WASHINGTON
Seattle
Asia Pacific Economic
   Review **(32942)** ....(Combined) 30,500

Woodinville
China Markets for Melamine **(33208)**
China Paints and Coatings: Market and
   Opportunities **(33209)**
China Synthetic Rubber Markets **(33210)**
China Wood Preservatives **(33211)**
Chinese Markets for Dimethylacetamide **(33212)**

BRITISH COLUMBIA, CANADA
Burnaby
B. C. Business **(34890)**

Vancouver
Pacific Affairs **(35157)** ....‡2,500

West Vancouver
Harbour & Shipping **(35238)** 2,000

NEW BRUNSWICK, CANADA
Fredericton
Journal of Comparative International
   Management **(35396)**

ONTARIO, CANADA
Toronto
Canada & Arab World **(36487)** ....(Paid) ‡7,900
                     (Non-paid) ‡5,300
Canada Journal **(36488)** ....(Combined) 24,000

JEWELRY, WATCHES, AND CLOCKS

CALIFORNIA
Carlsbad
Gems & Gemology **(1665)** 10,000

COLORADO
Denver
Watch & Clock Review **(4365)** ....(Paid) ‡3,000
                  (Non-paid) ‡12,500

CONNECTICUT
Norwalk
Accessories **(5048)** ....(Paid) 11,000
                  (Non-paid) 11,000

NEW JERSEY
Mahwah
Fashion Accessories **(19190)** ....(Paid) 1,650
                  (Non-paid) 7,651

NEW YORK
Melville
Modern Jeweler **(21049)**

New York
Accent Magazine **(21134)** ....(Paid) 4,429
                (Non-paid) 10,179
American Time **(21208)** ....(Non-paid) 8,000
Couture International Jeweler **(21508)** 20,000
Diamond Intelligence Briefs **(21550)**
Jewelers' Circular-Keystone **(21960)** ....(Paid) 24,792
National Jeweler **(22397)** ....(Paid) 9,000
                (Controlled) 21,300

New York Diamonds **(22441)**

PENNSYLVANIA
Columbia
Bulletin of the National Association of Watch and
   Clock Collectors **(26798)** ....‡31,000

Devon
Colored Stone **(26823)** ....(Paid) ‡10,230
Lapidary Journal **(26824)** ....‡53,000

King of Prussia
JCK's High-Volume Jeweler **(27124)**

ONTARIO, CANADA
Ottawa
Canadian Gemmologist **(36197)** ....(Paid) 650

Toronto
Canadian Jeweller **(36508)** ....(Combined) 5,500

JOURNALISM AND PUBLISHING
See also Book Trade and Author News; Communications

ALABAMA
Tuscaloosa
American Journalism **(484)** ....(Paid) 800

ARKANSAS
State University
Southwestern Mass Communication
   Journal **(1350)** ....(Paid) 500

CALIFORNIA
Fresno
The Collegian **(1949)** ....(Free) 5,000

Los Angeles
Amass **(2206)** ....(Paid) 6,000

Sacramento
California Publisher **(2987)** ....‡1,300

Thousand Oaks
Journal of Communication Inquiry **(3884)**

COLORADO
Denver
Colorado Editor **(4313)** ....‡1,100
The New Review **(4342)** ....‡73,000
Newspapers &
   Technology **(4343)** ....(Non-paid) ‡17,822

CONNECTICUT
Middletown
Journal of Scholarly Publishing **(4945)** 1,800

Stamford
Circulation
   Management **(5142)** ....(Controlled) ‡10,009
Folio **(5151)** ....(Paid) 8,063
                 (Non-paid) 661

DISTRICT OF COLUMBIA
Washington
APF Reporter **(5357)** ....(Controlled) 4,000

FLORIDA
Miami
Hora de Cierre **(6361)** ....(Controlled) 10,000

Sarasota
Writer's Guidelines Magazine **(6669)** .....(Paid) ‡750
                (Non-paid) ‡250

INDIANA
Indianapolis
Quill **(10165)** ....‡11,000

IOWA
Iowa City
Quill & Scroll **(10986)** ....(Paid) ‡11,500
                (Non-paid) ‡152

KENTUCKY
Frankfort
The Kentucky Press **(12074)** ....‡750

MAINE
Bangor
The Write Markets Report **(12905)** ......(Paid) 1,000

MARYLAND
Adelphi
NABJ Journal **(13088)** ....(Paid) 3,000

College Park
American Journalism Review **(13410)** ....(Paid) 8,447
                (Controlled) 18,033

MASSACHUSETTS
Cambridge
The Harvard International Journal of
   Press/Politics **(14059)**
Nieman Reports **(14086)** ....(Combined) 5,822

MICHIGAN
Traverse City
Independent Publisher Online **(15597)** 30,000
Publishing Entrepreneur **(15601)**

MISSOURI
Columbia
Missouri Press News **(17001)** ....‡900

St. Louis
The St. Louis Journalism Review **(17502)** 3,000

MONTANA
Missoula
Montana Journalism
   Review **(17871)** ....(Non-paid) 1,000

NEW YORK
Melville
Printing News **(21060)**

New York
American Writer **(21209)** ....(Controlled) 6,400
                (Non-paid) 3,500
Bookseller **(21335)** 11,050
Columbia Journalism
   Review **(21447)** ....(Paid) ‡22,253
Editor & Publisher **(21585)** ....(Paid) 14,278
                (Non-paid) 3,905
EXTRA! **(21670)** ....(Paid) ‡17,000
                (Non-paid) ‡700
                6,000
Forbes MediaCritic **(21721)**
Publishers Weekly **(22610)** ....(Paid) 32,863
Publishing Research
   Quarterly **(22611)** ....(Paid) ‡800

OHIO
Lebanon
The Lebanon Light **(25294)** ....(Controlled) 1,500

OKLAHOMA
Edmond
ByLine **(25813)** 3,500

Oklahoma City
Oklahoma Publisher **(25986)** ....‡1,200

OREGON
Portland
Oregon Publisher **(26493)** ....(Controlled) ‡650

SOUTH CAROLINA
Columbia
Journalism and Mass Communication
   Quarterly **(28555)** ....‡5,096

SOUTH DAKOTA
Brookings
Grassroots Editor **(28814)** ....‡1,000

TENNESSEE
Knoxville
Journalism and Mass Communication
   Educator **(29279)** ....‡3,718

Memphis
Newspaper Research Journal **(29377)** ....‡1,175

Trade, Technical, and Professional Publications

Circ.   Circ.   Circ.

JOURNALISM AND PUBLISHING
(continued)

Nashville
Media Studies Journal (29471) .....(Combined) 5,000
(Non-paid) 20,000

TEXAS
Austin
Texas Press Messenger (29841) ....‡760

UTAH
Provo
Journal of Media and Religion (31404)

VIRGINIA
Arlington
The News Media & the
Law (31814) ....(Paid) ‡1,000
(Non-paid) ‡1,000

Falls Church
Print Media (32052)
PrintMedia Magazine (32054) ....(Controlled) ‡24,000

Vienna
Foundation Update (32577)
Presstime (32579) ....(Paid) 15,994
(Non-paid) 1,545

WASHINGTON
Auburn
The Current (32655) ....(Controlled) ‡1,500

Seattle
The Washington Newspaper (33039) ....‡970

WISCONSIN
Clam Lake
Brilliant Ideas for
Publishers (33634) ....(Controlled) ‡17,000

ONTARIO, CANADA
Cornwall
Writer's Lifeline (35756) ....(Paid) ‡1,200
(Non-paid) ‡300

Mississauga
Masthead (36077) ....(Controlled) 4,445

Toronto
Journal of Scholarly Publishing (36639) 1,500
Press Review (36715) ....‡14,000
Victorian Periodicals
Review (36786) ....(Combined) 800

LABOR

See also Employment and Human Resources

CALIFORNIA
Berkeley
California Public Employee Relations (1505)

Los Angeles
Overture (2355) ....(Paid) ‡10,000
(Free) ‡450

Mountain View
The People (2608) 10,900

Oakland
East Bay Labor
Journal (2679) ....(Controlled) 25,000
Journal of Employee Ownership Law and
Finance (2684) ....(Combined) 550

San Francisco
The Dispatcher (3350) ....(Non-paid) ‡44,000
Musical News (3393) ....(Free) ‡3,200
Pipelines (3414) ....(Non-paid) 2,500

San Jose
Construction Labor News (3514) ......(Paid) ‡25,000
(Free) ‡300

DISTRICT OF COLUMBIA
Washington
America Work (5322) ....‡168,000
The American Postal Worker (5339) 300,000
American Teacher (5346) ....(Paid) 850,000
The Carpenter (5396) 473,104
Catering Industry Employee (5397) ....‡215,000
Graphic Communicator (5519) ....‡140,000
IBEW Journal (5539) ....(Paid) 800,000
In Transit (5541) ....(Non-paid) 175,000

Journal of the International Union of Bricklayers &
Allied Craftworkers (5601) ....(Paid) ‡2,000
(Controlled) ‡110,000
The Laborer (5627)
Postal Record (5724) 310,000
The Teamster (5816) ....‡1,760,000
U.A. Journal (5834) ....(Controlled) 330,000
Working America (5865) ......(Controlled) ‡1,000,000

GEORGIA
Cochran
The Robins Review (7180) ....(Free) ‡13,800

ILLINOIS
Champaign
Comparative Labor Law & Policy
Journal (8184) ....(Combined) 800

Peoria
The Labor Paper (9420) ....‡10,500

Riverwoods
Labor Law Journal (9506) ....‡2,059

Rock Island
Tri-City Labor Review (9521) ....‡4,700

INDIANA
Indianapolis
ISTA Advocate (10137) ....(Controlled) ‡50,000

KANSAS
Kansas City
Boilermaker Reporter (11525) ......(Non-paid) 85,000

KENTUCKY
Lexington
Labor Studies Journal (12171) ....(Paid) ‡800

MARYLAND
Camp Springs
Seafarers LOG (13402) ....(Non-paid) ‡43,000

Rockville
Interchange
(Rockville) (13683) ....(Controlled) 95,000
The Winning Edge (13700)

MASSACHUSETTS
Boston
Tomorrow Magazine (13968)

MICHIGAN
Detroit
Detroit Labor News (14926) ....(Paid) ⊕4,770
(Non-paid) ⊕100
Solidarity (14947) ....(Non-paid) 1,355,000

Lansing
Michigan AFL-CIO News (15279) ....‡30,000

Southfield
BMWE Journal (15542) ....‡60,000

MINNESOTA
Duluth
Labor World (15838) ....(Paid) ‡14,800

Minneapolis
Minneapolis Labor Review (16099) ....‡60,000

St. Paul
Union Advocate (16411) ....‡37,153

MISSOURI
St. Louis
St. Louis/Southern Illinois Labor
Tribune (17508) ....‡78,000

NEW JERSEY
Montvale
JobWatch (19259)

NEW YORK
Albany
Employment Review (19984) ....(Non-paid) ‡600

Amityville
Journal of Individual Employment Rights (20046)

Armonk
Working USA (20101) ....(Paid) 1,271

Brooklyn
Darbininkas (The Worker) (20311) ....‡14,000

Ithaca
Industrial and Labor Relations
Review (20804) ....(Paid) ‡2,400
(Non-paid) ‡165

New York
American Writer (21209) ....(Controlled) 6,400
(Non-paid) 3,500
Arbitration Times (21241) ....(Non-paid) 60,000
Employee Responsibilities and Rights
Journal (21603)
Frontpage (21737) ....‡4,500
Human Resource Planning (21833)
International Journal of Comparative Labour Law and
Industrial Relations (21902)
International Labor and Working-Class
History (21926) 900
International Musician (21927) 150,000
Labor Arbitration in
Government (22230) ....(Paid) ‡5,000
(Non-paid) ‡2,000
The Militant (22336) ....(Paid) ‡8,000
(Free) ‡217
New York Generator (22444)
New York Metro Area Postal Union, Union
Mail (22447) ....(Paid) 13,000
(Controlled) 500
P S C Clarion (22516)
People's Weekly World (22541) ....(Paid) ‡40,000
(Non-paid) ‡1,500
The Punch List (22614)
RWDSU Record (22698) ....‡250,000
Summary of Labor Arbitration
Awards (22806) ....(Paid) ‡750
(Non-paid) ‡4,000
TWU Express (22879)
Unite! Magazine (22884) ....‡500,000
Workers World (22938) ....(Paid) 3000 Approx.
Yiddisher Kemfer (Jewish Fighter) (22949)

OHIO
Cleveland
Locomotive Engineers Journal (24921) ....‡54,000
UTU News (24960) ....(Controlled) 130,000
Worker's Compensation Journal of Ohio (24966)

Toledo
Toledo Union Journal (25572) ....‡12,000

OREGON
Portland
Northwest Labor Press (26487) ....‡53,500
Oregon Teamster (26494) ....(Non-paid) 35,000
The Union Register (26513) ....‡25,000

PENNSYLVANIA
Pittsburgh
Employment and Earnings (27784)
Monthly Labor Review (27818)
Steelabor (27847) ....‡840,000
U.E. News (27851)

TENNESSEE
Nashville
The PACEsetter (29478) ....(Free) ‡320,000

TEXAS
Austin
Texas Public Employee (29844) 14,000

Dallas
Occupational Health &
Safety (30174) ....(Combined) △81,000

VIRGINIA
Arlington
ABC Today (31767) ....(Paid) ‡20,000
(Non-paid) ‡2,000

Fairfax
Journal of Labor Research (32022) ....‡1,200
United Mine Workers Journal (32033)

WASHINGTON
Federal Way
WEA Action (32765) ....(Paid) 74,000

WISCONSIN
Kenosha
The Labor Paper (33873) 15,000

Milwaukee
Milwaukee Labor Press,
AFL-CIO (34085) ....(Paid) ‡60,000
(Free) ‡642

Racine
The Racine Labor (34275) ....‡4,500

NEWFOUNDLAND AND LABRADOR, CANADA
St. John's
Labour/Le Travail (35488) 900

NOVA SCOTIA, CANADA
Halifax
Labor Legislation in Nova Scotia (35569)

ONTARIO, CANADA
Aurora
Workplace News (35652) ....(Paid) 760

Kingston
Worklife Report (35949) ....‡1,500

North York
Our Ontario (36131) ....(Controlled) 80,000

Ottawa
The Canadian Postmaster (Le Maitre de Poste
Canadien) (36226) ....‡9,500

Windsor
The Guardian (36886) ....‡26,000

QUEBEC, CANADA
Montreal
La Flute (37149) ....(Controlled) 8,500
Nouvelles CEQ (37197) ....(Non-paid) 95,498

Quebec
Revue Relations Industrielles/Industrial
Relations (37296) ....(Paid) 1,500
(Non-paid) 150

LABORATORY RESEARCH (SCIENTIFIC AND MEDICAL)

ARIZONA
Tempe
Multivariate Behavioral Research (911)

CALIFORNIA
Irvine
Biomedical Optics (2076)

San Diego
Experimental and Molecular Pathology (3149)
Journal of Magnetic Resonance (3201)
Journal of Surgical Research (3214)
Methods (3229)
Methods in Immunology and
Immunochemistry (3231)
Molecular and Cellular Neurosciences (3234)
Molecular Phylogenetics and Evolution (3236)
NeuroImage (3241)
Protein Expression and Purification (3250)
Virology (3288)

CONNECTICUT
Farmington
Acta Haematologica (4794) 1,300
American Journal of Nephrology (4795) 2,900
Cells Tissues Organs (4804) 1,200

New Haven
Journal of Marine Research (4995) ....(Paid) 800
Laboratory Investigation (4997) ....(Paid) ‡3,200

Shelton
American Biotechnology
Laboratory (5117) ....(Non-paid) ‡70,792
International Biotechnology
Laboratory (5124) ....(Controlled) ‡26,432
International Laboratory (5125) ....(Paid) 86
(Non-paid) 37,967

Wilton
Labmedica (5229) ....(Non-paid) ‡26,000

DISTRICT OF COLUMBIA
Washington
Clinical and Diagnostic Laboratory
Immunology (5419) ....(Paid) 938
Clinical Laboratory
News (5420) ....(Controlled) 25,000

ILLINOIS
Chicago
Archives of Pathology & Laboratory
Medicine (8271) ....(Paid) ‡3,070
(Controlled) ‡13,274
Laboratory Medicine (8454) ....(Paid) 150,205
(Non-paid) 15,583

Northfield
CAP Today (9325) ....(Paid) 8,500
(Non-paid) 42,200

MARYLAND
Baltimore
Addictive Disorders & Their Treatment (13107)
Alzheimer Disease and Associated
Disorders (13112) 692
American Journal of Clinical
Oncology (13114) 1,450
The American Journal of
Dermatopathology (13115) 2348
The American Journal of Forensic Medicine and
Pathology (13117) 1,691
The Clinical Journal of Pain (13146) 2,128
Clinical Journal of Sport Medicine (13147) 3,230
Clinical Neuropharmacology (13148) 558
Convulsive Therapy (13151) 1017
Cornea (13152) 1,343
Diagnostic Molecular Pathology (13156) 1,073
International Journal of Gynecological
Pathology (13173) 1,134
Journal of Cardiovascular
Pharmacology (13181) 1451
Journal of Clinical Gastroenterology (13183) ...1,235
Journal of Electromyography and
Kinesiology (13189) 1,000
Journal of Glaucoma (13190) 1,566
Journal of Immunotherapy (13193) ....(Paid) 696
Journal of Neurosurgical
Anesthesiology (13196) 914
Journal of Orthopaedic Trauma (13197) 3173
Journal of Pediatric
Hematology/Oncology (13199) ....(Paid) 1,674
Journal of Rehabilitation Research and
Development (13201) ....(Non-paid) 6,000
Journal of Spinal Disorders &
Techniques (13202) 1,696
Molecular Medicine (13221) ....(Combined) 500
Neuropsychiatry, Neuropsychology, and Behavioral
Neurology (13224) 1181
Neurosurgery Quarterly (13225) 764
Ophthalmic Plastic and Reconstructive
Surgery (13228) 1,168
Pancreas (13232) 540
Surgical Laparoscopy Endoscopy & Percutaneous
Techniques (13250) 1,330
Ultrasound Quarterly (13256) 1468

Bethesda
The American Journal of
Pathology (13302) ....‡4,500
Entomology Abstracts (13334)
The Journal of Molecular
Diagnostics (13352) ....(Paid) 3,000

Gaithersburg
Experimental Aging Research (13539) 1,000
Inside Laboratory Management (13543)

Kensington
Undersea & Hyperbaric
Medicine (13592) ....(Controlled) 2,200

Lanham
Journal for Vascular
Ultrasound (13606) ....(Combined) 3,900

MASSACHUSETTS
Boston
Obesity Research (13942) ....(Paid) 1,200

Cambridge
Journal of Biopharmaceutical
Statistics (14074) 550
Neural Computation (14084) ....‡1,500
‡1,500

Malden
Journal of Neurochemistry (14295) 2333

Norwood
Clinical Laboratory MarketPlace (14446) 61,555

Westborough
BioTechniques (14635) 62,000

MICHIGAN
Ann Arbor
Journal of Neuro-Ophthalmology (14757) 1574

MINNESOTA
Minneapolis
Journal of Andrology (16086) ....‡1,200

MISSISSIPPI
Jackson
Journal of Pharmacoepidemiology (16698) 175

MISSOURI
St. Louis
The Journal of Laboratory and Clinical
Medicine (17456) ....(Paid) 2,617
(Non-paid) 289

NEW JERSEY
Edison
Applied Clinical
Trials (18786) ....(Combined) △14,972

Hoboken
Chirality (18912) ....(Paid) 4200
Fire and Materials (18948)
Genes, Chromosomes and Cancer (18950) 5950
Human Brain Mapping (18965) 4200
Journal of Clinical Laboratory
Analysis (19013) 3850
Luminescence (19054)
Movement Disorders (19067) 2,301
NMR in Biomedicine (19074)
Phytotherapy Research (19084) 4,200
Statistics in Medicine (19106) ....(Paid) 12,600

Montvale
Clinical Laboratory Reference
(CLR) (19246) ....(Free) 53,000
Medical Laboratory Observer
(MLO) (19266) ....(Free) ‡53,000

Morris Plains
Laboratory
Equipment (19295) ....(Non-paid) ‡120,018

Piscataway
Rutgers Center of Alcohol
Studies (19431) ....(Combined) ⊕2,100

Springfield
Progress in Research (19596) .....(Non-paid) 25,000

Thorofare
Occupational Therapy Journal of
Research (19630) ....(Paid) 900

NEW YORK
Binghamton
Journal of Forensic Neuropsychology (20174)
Journal of Forensic Psychology Practice (20175)

Cold Spring Harbor
Learning & Memory (20484)

Garrison
IRB (20648) ....(Paid) 1,100

Larchmont
Journal of Aerosol Medicine (20904)
Journal of Anti-Aging Medicine (20907)
Vector-Borne and Zoonotic Diseases (20929)

New York
AIDS and Behavior (21167)
Aquatic Ecology (21237)
Domestic Animal Endocrinology (21566)
Heart Failure Reviews (21797)
Investigational New Drugs (21945)
Journal of Computer-Aided Molecular Design (22036)
Lab Animal (22229) ....(Paid) 156
(Non-paid) 10,200
Learning Environments Research (22243)
Medicine, Health Care and Philosophy (22312)
Nature (22409) ....(Non-paid) 681
Nutrient Cycling in Agroecosystems (22475)
Pulmonary Pharmacology (22612)
Vaccine (22894)

NORTH CAROLINA
Chapel Hill
The Cleft Palate-Craniofacial Journal (23704)

OHIO
Cleveland
Molecular Endocrinology (24927)

OREGON
Astoria
Journal of Aquatic Food Product
Technology (26225) 170

Portland
Tinnitus Today (26510) ....(Paid) 200,000

PENNSYLVANIA
King of Prussia
ADVANCE for Administrators of the
Laboratory (27107)
ADVANCE for Medical Laboratory
Professionals (27114) ....(Controlled) ‡65,300

Circulation: ★ = ABC; △ = BPA; ♦ = CAC; • = CCAB; ❏ = VAC; ⊕ = PO Statement; ‡ = Publisher's Report; Boldface figures = sworn; Light figures = estimated.

3169

Circ.   Circ.   Circ.

LABORATORY RESEARCH (SCIENTIFIC AND MEDICAL) (continued)

Philadelphia
Annals of Diagnostic Pathology (27377)
Cancer Research (27392) ....(Paid) ‡9,621
Cell Stress and Chaperones (27396)
Chinese Medical Sciences Journal (27402)
Clinics in Laboratory Medicine (27416)
Medical Informatics & The Internet in Medicine (27566)
Molecular Cancer Research (27572) .....(Paid) 2,400

TENNESSEE
Memphis
Comparative Medicine (29363) ....‡3,000
Journal of Biomolecular Techniques (29371)

TEXAS
Austin
Infancy (29783)

Houston
Clinical Cancer Research (30463) ....(Combined) ⊕4,552
Visual Neuroscience (30541) 600

VERMONT
Burlington
Methods in Cell Science (31515) ....‡700

ONTARIO, CANADA
Hamilton
Canadian Journal of Medical Laboratory Science (CJLMS) (35877) ....(Paid) 14,326
(Controlled) 451

Oakville
Canadian Journal of Clinical Pharmacology (36138) ....(Controlled) 7,000

Ottawa
Canadian Association of Radiologists Journal (36189) 1,600

Toronto
Laboratory Product News (36647) ....(Combined) •20,359

QUEBEC, CANADA
Montreal
Sante Mentale au Quebec (37221) ....(Paid) 750

LANDSCAPE ARCHITECTURE

See also Botany; Florists and Floriculture; Seed and Nursery Trade

CALIFORNIA
Berkeley
Design Book Review (1513) ....‡7,000

Tustin
Landscape Architect and Specifier News (3962) ....(Controlled) ‡27,487

DISTRICT OF COLUMBIA
Washington
Landscape Architecture (5629)

FLORIDA
Clearwater
Interiorscape (5986)

ILLINOIS
Chicago
American Nurseryman (8261) ....(Paid) 14,961
Arbor Age (8266) ....(Paid) 120
18,469
Landscape Design (8456) ....‡38,000
Landscape & Irrigation (8457) ....(Paid) 63
(Controlled) 62,000
Outdoor Power Equipment (8521) ......(Paid) 1,089
(Controlled) 16,930
Recreation Resources (8553) .....(Controlled) 51,100

Oak Brook
The Landscape Contractor (9355) ......(Paid) ‡2,000
(Non-paid) ‡760

KANSAS
Overland Park
Grounds Maintenance (11713) ....(Non-paid) ‡65,050

MASSACHUSETTS
Cambridge
Harvard Design Magazine (14057) 12,000

Jamaica Plain
Arnoldia (14258) 4,450

NEW YORK
New York
Garden Design (21747) ....(Paid) 445,805
Landscape Ecology (22232)

OHIO
Cleveland
Landscape Management (24918) ....(Combined) ‡51,000
Lawn & Landscape Magazine (24919) ....(Combined) ‡63,000

Columbus
Ohio Florists Association Bulletin (25044) ....(Paid) 3,500

OREGON
Portland
Pacific Coast Nurseryman and Garden Supply Dealer (26496) ....(Paid) ‡6,840
(Non-paid) ‡3,624

Wilsonville
Digger (26614) ....(Controlled) ‡5,000

TEXAS
Fort Worth
Garden Center Merchandising & Management (30339) ....(Combined) ‡15,000

VIRGINIA
Herndon
CM News (32162) ....(Non-paid) ‡3,500

WISCONSIN
Fort Atkinson
Pro (33717) ....(Controlled) ‡49,000

Madison
Landscape Journal (33957) ....(Paid) 900

BRITISH COLUMBIA, CANADA
Surrey
Hort West (35108)

Vancouver
Landscaping & Groundskeeping Journal (35152) ....(Combined) 16,664

ONTARIO, CANADA
Milton
Landscape Trades (36049) ....(Combined) •8,240

QUEBEC, CANADA
Quebec
Espaces Verts (37283) ....‡2,250
Quebec Vert (37295) ....‡3,760

LAUNDRY AND DRY CLEANING

CALIFORNIA
Huntington Beach
New Era Magazine (2064) ....(Controlled) ‡18,211

Pasadena
Western Cleaner and Launderer (2828) ....(Non-paid) ⊕16,000

CONNECTICUT
Waterbury
Drycleaners News (5192) ....(Paid) 41
(Non-paid) 8,698

ILLINOIS
Chicago
American Coin-Op (8254) ......(Controlled) 18,800
American Drycleaner (8255) .....(Controlled) ‡23,600
American Laundry News (8258) ....‡15,050

Downers Grove
Journal of the Coin Laundry and Drycleaning Industry (8787) ....(Controlled) 26,000

MARYLAND
Silver Spring
Fabricare (13726) ....(Paid) 8,800

PENNSYLVANIA
Willow Grove
The National Clothesline (28193) ....(Controlled) ‡32,000

VIRGINIA
Alexandria
Textile Rental Magazine (31744) ....‡5,900

ONTARIO, CANADA
Oakville
Fabricare Canada (36144) ....(Controlled) 6,300

LAW

ALABAMA
Bessemer
The Western Star (52) ....⊕10,000

Maxwell AFB
Air Force Law Review (314)

ARIZONA
Phoenix
Arizona Business Gazette (775) ....(Paid) 10,208
(Free) 5,744
Business Law Today (797) ....(Paid) △50,664

Tempe
Jurimetrics (909) 7,400

Tucson
The Daily Territorial (944) ....(Paid) 892
(Free) 100
Legal Reference Services Quarterly (954) 1,101

ARKANSAS
Fayetteville
Arkansas Law Review (1117)

CALIFORNIA
Berkeley
American Journal of Comparative Law (1489) 2,000
Asian Law Journal (1491)
Asian Law Journal (1492) ....(Paid) 200
Berkeley Journal of Employment and Labor Law (1496) 582
Berkeley Journal of International Law (1497)
Berkeley Technology Law Journal (1498)
Berkeley Women's Law Journal (1500)
California Law Review (1502) ....‡1,500
Ecology Law Quarterly (1515)
Estate Planning and California Probate Reporter (1518)
Index to Foreign Legal Periodicals (1528) 600

Chatsworth
The National Notary (1689) ....‡200,000

Costa Mesa
Law Office Computing (1776)
Legal Assistant Today (1777) ....‡19,000

Long Beach
Reporter (2174) ....‡650

Los Angeles
Chicano-Latin Law Review (2237) 340
The Guild Practitioner (2282) ....(Paid) 2,300
Los Angeles Daily Journal (2321) ......(Paid) 12,433
(Free) 514
Los Angeles Lawyer (2324) ....(Paid) 22,536
(Non-paid) 2,723
NOMMO (2348) ....(Non-paid) 10,000
Southern California Law Review (2396) ....(Paid) ‡1,033
(Non-paid) ‡100
UCLA Journal of Environmental Law and Policy (2418)

Oakland
Alameda County Bar Association Bulletin (2664) ....(Controlled) 2,800
California Business Law Reporter (2672)
The Inter-City Express (2682) ....(Paid) ‡1,023
(Non-paid) ‡14
Real Property Law Reporter (2696)

Sacramento
The Daily Recorder (2995) ....‡1,122
McGeorge Law Review (3007)
Sacramento Lawyer (3015) ....(Controlled) 3500

San Diego
Legal Theory (3223) 600
Regulatory Toxicology and Pharmacology (3254)
San Diego Law Review (3264) 900

Thomas Jefferson Law
Review **(3279)** ....(Combined) 280

San Francisco
Cal Law **(3334)**
California Bar Journal **(3335)**
California Lawyer **(3337)** ....(Controlled) ‡130,000
California Official Reports **(3338)**
Golden Gate University Law
Review **(3366)** ....(Paid) 375
Hastings Communications and Entertainment Law
Journal (COMM/ENT) **(3370)** ....(Paid) 1,000
(Non-paid) 150
IP Magazine **(3375)**
New College of California Journal of Public Interest
Law **(3395)**
The Recorder **(3421)** ....‡6,600
San Francisco Attorney
Magazine **(3427)** ....(Paid) 10,000

San Jose
San Jose Post-Record **(3537)** 1,200

Santa Clara
Santa Clara Computer and High Technology Law
Journal **(3674)** ....(Paid) 463
Santa Clara Law Review **(3675)**

Stanford
Stanford Law Review **(3801)** ....(Combined) 2,167
Stanford Lawyer **(3802)** ....(Controlled) 15,000

Thousand Oaks
Criminal Justice Abstracts **(3859)** ....‡800
Family Court Review **(3870)** ....(Paid) 2,500

Torrance
Right of Way **(3941)** ....‡9,000

Walnut Creek
Contra Costa News Register **(4049)** ....‡500

COLORADO
Denver
The Colorado Lawyer **(4315)** ....(Paid) 14,000
Denver Journal of International Law and
Policy **(4323)**
Denver University Law Review **(4326)** ....‡600

Pueblo
The Colorado Tribune **(4598)** ....‡374

CONNECTICUT
Hartford
Connecticut Law
Review **(4888)** ....(Controlled) 1,450

New Britain
Connecticut Bar Journal **(4973)** ....(Paid) 11,500
Connecticut Lawyer **(4974)**

New Haven
Federal Sentencing Reporter **(4989)**
Yale Journal of Law and
Feminism **(5006)** ....(Paid) 1,100
The Yale Law Journal **(5007)** ....‡4,300

DELAWARE
Wilmington
Delaware Journal of Corporate
Law **(5291)** ....(Paid) 997

DISTRICT OF COLUMBIA
Washington
ACCA Docket **(5314)** ....(Paid) ⊕10,500
American Criminal Law Review **(5325)**
American Journal of International
Law **(5332)** ....‡6,800
The American University Law
Review **(5347)** ....(Paid) ‡570
(Non-paid) ‡700
ASAE Association Law and
Policy **(5363)** ....(Non-paid) 1,400
Bank & Corporate Governance Law Reporter **(5372)**
Catholic University Law Review **(5401)** ....‡1,400
Chemical Waste Litigation Reporter **(5405)**
Church & State **(5415)** ....(Paid) ‡33,000
(Controlled) ‡2,600
Class Action Reports **(5417)** ....(Controlled) 700
Computer Law Reporter **(5431)**
EPA Administrative Law Reporter **(5484)**
The Federal Lawyer **(5493)** ....‡15,000
George Washington Journal of International Law and
Economics **(5507)**
The George Washington Law
Review **(5508)** ....‡2,000
International Journal of Legal
Information **(5555)** ....(Paid) 600

The Journal of Arts Management, Law, and
Society **(5573)** ....(Paid) 491
Law Briefs **(5632)**
Law and Policy in International Business **(5633)**
Legal Times **(5635)** ....(Paid) ‡7,000
National Environmental Enforcement
Journal **(5670)** ....(Controlled) 750
National Tax Journal **(5681)**
NBA Magazine **(5691)**
OECD Journal of Competition Law & Policy **(5702)**
RICO Law Reporter **(5769)**
Section 504 Compliance Handbook **(5786)**
Securities Reform Act Litigation Reporter **(5787)**
Supreme Court Debates **(5808)**
The Tax Lawyer **(5812)** ....(Paid) 20,000
(Non-paid) 1,800
TRIAL **(5831)** ....(Paid) 45,611
(Non-paid) 7,713
The Washington Lawyer **(5847)** ....(Paid) 75,000
(Non-paid) 800

FLORIDA
Coral Gables
Entertainment & Sports Law Review **(6006)**

Fort Lauderdale
Broward Daily Business
Review **(6072)** ....(Paid) 2,736
(Non-paid) 154

Gainesville
Florida Journal of International
Law **(6137)** ....(Combined) 285
Journal of Law and Public
Policy **(6148)** ....(Paid) 225
Professional Ethics **(6153)** ....(Paid) 700

Longwood
New York Town Law **(6313)**

Miami
Daily Business Review **(6347)** ....(Paid) 10,184
(Controlled) 286
St. Thomas Law Review **(6378)** ....(Paid) ‡234
Tequesta **(6383)** ....(Paid) 3,600

Ormond Beach
Foreign Tax Law Bi-Weekly Bulletin **(6533)**

Tallahassee
The Florida Bar Journal **(6707)** ....‡63,762
The Journal of the Academy of Florida Trial
Lawyers **(6724)** ....(Paid) 4,000
Journal of Drug Issues **(6725)**

Tampa
Trial Advocate Quarterly **(6782)** ....(Combined) 2,000

GEORGIA
Athens
Georgia Law Review **(6939)**

Atlanta
Daily Report **(6997)** ....(Paid) ♦5,541
(Non-paid) ♦321
Daily Report **(6998)** ....(Combined) 6,701
Fulton County Daily Report **(7009)** ......(Paid) 5,270
(Non-paid) 552
Georgia Bar Journal **(7010)** 28,000

Macon
Mercer Lawyer **(7384)**

HAWAII
Honolulu
Hawaii Bar Journal **(7689)** ....(Paid) 5,400
(Non-paid) 500

IDAHO
Moscow
Idaho Law Review **(7916)**

ILLINOIS
Carbondale
Law Library Journal **(8119)** ....‡5,200

Champaign
Comparative Labor Law & Policy
Journal **(8184)** ....(Combined) 800
Northwestern University Law
Review **(8206)** ....‡1,500
University of Illinois Law Review **(8221)** 900

Chicago
ABA Journal **(8241)** ....(Paid) 320,100
(Non-paid) 106,251
The Brief **(8291)** ....(Paid) ‡32,000
(Non-paid) ‡1,741
Chicago Daily Law Bulletin **(8311)** ....‡6,633

Chicago Lawyer **(8314)** ....(Paid) 1,156
(Non-paid) 8,995
The Compleat Lawyer **(8339)** ....(Paid) ‡17,698
(Non-paid) ‡1,877
Criminal Justice Magazine **(8348)** ....(Paid) 8,603
(Non-paid) 1,252
Defense Counsel Journal **(8351)**
EDT **(8361)** ....(Paid) 28,557
Family Advocate **(8373)** ....(Paid) ‡11,517
(Non-paid) ‡1,387
ISBA Bar News **(8421)** ....(Controlled) ‡33,600
The Journal of Criminal Law and
Criminology **(8435)** 3,000
The Journal of Law and
Economics **(8441)** ....(Paid) ‡3,050
The Journal of Legal
Studies **(8442)** ....(Paid) ‡1,300
LAMPlighter **(8455)**
Law and History Review **(8458)**
Loyola University Chicago Law
Journal **(8472)** ....(Controlled) ‡650
National Security Law Report **(8500)**
Northwestern Journal of International Law &
Business **(8512)** ....(Combined) 598
Probate and Property **(8540)** ....(Paid) 30,000
(Controlled) 1,391
The Professional Lawyer **(8541)** ....(Paid) 1,000
(Non-paid) 250
Public Contract Law Journal **(8543)**
Student Lawyer **(8572)** ....(Paid) △38,000
Supreme Court Economic Review **(8576)**
Supreme Court Review **(8577)**
Tort & Insurance Law Journal **(8585)**
The University of Chicago Law
Review **(8592)** ....‡2,600
The Urban Lawyer **(8595)** ....(Paid) 6,200
(Non-paid) 300

Glen Ellyn
Law Enforcement Legal
Review **(8929)** ....(Paid) 1,000

O Fallon
The Legal Reporter **(9333)** ....(Paid) 1,000
(Free) 10

Riverwoods
Bankruptcy Law Reports **(9501)** ....‡500

Springfield
The Journal of Legal
Medicine **(9637)** ....(Paid) ‡1,622

Vernon Hills
ALA News **(9727)** ....(Controlled) 9,000
Legal Management **(9728)** ....(Controlled) ‡25,200

INDIANA
Bloomington
Federal Communications Law
Journal **(9826)** ....(Paid) ‡4,000
Indiana Law Journal **(9833)** ....(Combined) 750

Indianapolis
Court & Commercial
Record **(10105)** ....(Controlled) ⊕1,127
Indiana Law Review **(10128)** ....(Combined) 850
Res Gestaie **(10167)** ....(Non-paid) 10,500

Mishawaka
The Mishawaka
Enterprise **(10313)** ....(Controlled) 1,625

Notre Dame
Journal of College and University
Law **(10369)** ....(Paid) 248
Journal of Legislation **(10370)**
Notre Dame Journal of Law, Ethics & Public
Policy **(10371)** ....(Controlled) 490
Notre Dame Law Review **(10372)** ....‡1,500

Terre Haute
Issues in Law & Medicine **(10487)** ......(Paid) 1,000
(Controlled) 2,000

IOWA
Des Moines
Drake Law Review **(10782)**
The Iowa Lawyer **(10792)** ....(Controlled) 8,250

Iowa City
Iowa Law Review **(10976)** 1,500
Journal of Corporation Law **(10978)** ....(Paid) 800
(Non-paid) 200

KANSAS
Lawrence
University of Kansas Law Review **(11568)** 1,000

Circ.   Circ.   Circ.

LAW (continued)

Topeka
Family Law Quarterly **(11817)** 12,500

KENTUCKY
Frankfort
Kentucky Bench & Bar
  Magazine **(12068)** ....‡13,322

Lexington
Kentucky Law Journal **(12170)** ....(Paid) ‡880
(Controlled) ‡475

LOUISIANA
Baton Rouge
Louisiana Law Review **(12499)**

New Orleans
The Louisiana Bar Journal **(12737)** 18,319
Loyola Law Review **(12741)** ....(Paid) 800
Tulane Journal of Technology and Intellectual
  Property **(12759)**

Rayville
Richland Beacon News **(12803)** ....(Paid) ‡1,204
(Non-paid) ‡1,471

MARYLAND
Baltimore
ICSID Review **(13170)** ....‡707
Journal of Health Care Law and
  Policy **(13191)** ....(Paid) 250
The Law Forum **(13208)** ....(Controlled) 8,000
NAD KARU Case Reports **(13223)**

Silver Spring
Mental Health Report **(13738)**

South Easton
Case Digests, Human Resources Law Index **(13750)**

Waldorf
Accident Investigation
  Quarterly **(13769)** ....(Combined) 1,800
Accident Reconstruction
  Journal **(13770)** ....(Combined) 2800

MASSACHUSETTS
Amherst
Law & Society Review **(13800)** ....‡2,400

Andover
The Long Term View **(13813)** ....(Non-paid) 5,000

Boston
American Journal of Law &
  Medicine **(13849)** 3,700
Boston University Journal of Science & Technology
  Law **(13865)**
The Journal of Law, Medicine &
  Ethics **(13916)** ....‡5,000
Lawyer's Journal **(13921)** ....(Controlled) 19,000
Lawyers Weekly USA **(13922)**
Massachusetts Bar Association Lawyers
  Journal **(13925)** ....(Controlled) 18,000
Massachusetts Lawyers Weekly **(13928)** .....‡16,000
New England Law Review **(13936)**

Cambridge
Harvard Journal of Law and Public Policy **(14062)**
Harvard Journal of Legislation **(14063)** 800
Harvard Law Review **(14064)** ....‡5,275

Chestnut Hill
Massachusetts Civil Service Reporter **(14129)**
Massachusetts Discrimination Law Reporter **(14130)**

Newton
Alledger **(14383)** ....(Non-paid) 2,000
Boston College Environmental Affairs Law
  Review **(14384)** ....(Paid) 800

MICHIGAN
Ann Arbor
Michigan Journal of Gender &
  Law **(14764)** ....(Paid) 230
Michigan Law Review **(14765)** ....‡2,040

Crystal Falls
Indiana Law Reporter **(14894)** ....(Combined) 171

East Lansing
International Journal of Comparative and Applied
  Criminal Justice **(14985)** ....(Paid) 400

Jackson
Jackson County Legal News **(15222)** 1,900

Lansing
Michigan Bar Journal **(15281)** ....‡31,600

Novi
Michigan Lawyers Weekly **(15409)** .....(Paid) ‡4,700
(Controlled) ‡17,000

Shelby Township
Macomb County Legal News **(15536)** 1,279

Troy
Detroit Legal News **(15618)** ....⊕1,850

MINNESOTA
Edina
Specialty Law Digest **(15877)**

Minneapolis
Bench & Bar of
  Minnesota **(16060)** ....(Paid) ‡15,206
(Non-paid) ‡919
Constitutional Commentary **(16070)**
Minnesota Law &
  Politics **(16103)** ....(Controlled) 22,000
(Paid) 2,000
Minnesota Law Review **(16104)** 1,345

St. Paul
Journal of Law and Religion **(16382)** ....(Paid) 1,000

MISSISSIPPI
University
Mississippi Law Journal **(16867)** ....(Paid) 900

MISSOURI
Columbia
Journal of Dispute Resolution **(16995)** .....(Paid) 450
(Non-paid) 14
Missouri Law Review **(17000)** ....(Paid) ‡900
(Non-paid) ‡250

Jackson
The Cash-Book Journal **(17118)** 7,000
5,325
12,325

Jefferson City
Journal of the Missouri Bar **(17123)** ....‡26,500

Kansas City
Journal of Forensic Economics **(17174)**

St. Louis
St. Louis Lawyer **(17503)**
St. Louis Watchman
  Advocate **(17509)** ....(Combined) ‡40,000
The Washington University Global Studies Law
  Review **(17528)**
Washington University Journal of Law and
  Policy **(17529)**

Springfield
Forensic Examiner **(17600)**

Warrensburg
Probation and Parole Law Reports **(17669)**

MONTANA
Helena
Trial Trends **(17823)**

NEBRASKA
Lincoln
The Nebraska Lawyer **(18102)** .....(Combined) 8,700

NEVADA
Las Vegas
Nevada Lawyer **(18379)** ....(Controlled) 5,900

Reno
Juvenile and Family Court
  Journal **(18421)** ....(Combined) ⊕2,300

NEW HAMPSHIRE
Concord
New Hampshire Bar Journal **(18473)** 5,200

NEW JERSEY
Hoboken
Health Care Analysis **(18958)**
International Insolvency Review **(18974)**
Management Report for Nonunion
  Organizations **(19057)** 5,985
Remediation **(19097)** 5985

New Brunswick
New Jersey Lawyer **(19336)** 18,000

Newark
Corporate Counsel **(19352)**
New Jersey Law Journal **(19361)** .....(Mon.) ★8,175
Rutgers Computer and Technology Law
  Journal **(19364)**

Rutgers Law Review **(19365)**

Pitman
General Aviation Accident Report **(19434)**

NEW MEXICO
Albuquerque
New Mexico Law
  Review **(19781)** ....(Combined) 700

NEW YORK
Albany
Albany Law Review **(19980)**
Journal **(19991)** 65,000
New York State Register **(20000)** 2,400
State Bar News **(20004)**

Armonk
Chinese Law and
  Government **(20070)** ....(Paid) ⊕227
Russian Politics and Law **(20094)** ......(Paid) ⊕248
Statutes and Decisions: The Laws of the USSR and
  its Successor Stabey **(20100)** ....(Paid) ⊕145

Bronx
Index to Legal Periodicals & Books **(20272)**

Brooklyn
Daily Bulletin **(20309)** ....‡5,200

Buffalo
Buffalo Law Journal **(20366)** ....(Paid) 700
(Non-paid) 30
Buffalo Law Review **(20367)** ....(Paid) ⊕600
Chicago Journal of International Law **(20373)**
Immigration and Nationality Law
  Review **(20381)** 165
Journal of Legal Pluralism and Unofficial
  Law **(20382)** ....(Paid) 252

Flushing
Queens Bar Bulletin **(20610)** ....(Paid) 2,200

Huntington
The Suffolk Lawyer **(20776)** ......(Controlled) ‡3,500

Ithaca
Cornell International Law Journal **(20795)**
Cornell Journal of Law and Public
  Policy **(20796)** ....(Paid) 550
Cornell Law Review **(20797)** ....‡6,000

Jamaica
The Catholic Lawyer **(20832)** 1,000

Larchmont
Biotechnology Law Report **(20892)**
Election Law Journal **(20898)**
Gaming Law Review **(20900)**

New York
Air Space and Law **(21169)**
American Journal of Family Law **(21193)**
Art, Antiquity and Law **(21250)**
Asia Pacific Journal of Environmental Law **(21262)**
Asia-Pacific Journal on Human Rights and the
  Law **(21263)**
Asia Pacific Law Review **(21264)**
Asset Protection Journal **(21267)**
Banking Law Journal **(21289)** ....(Paid) 2,500
Benefits Law Journal **(21295)** 5,985
The Business Torts Reporter **(21360)**
The Cambridge Law Journal **(21367)** 1,600
City of New York Council Digest **(21426)**
Columbia Human Rights Law
  Review **(21444)** ....(Paid) 650
Columbia Journal of Asian
  Law **(21445)** ....(Paid) ‡270
Columbia Journal of Environmental
  Law **(21446)** ....(Paid) 1,200 Approx.
Columbia Law Review **(21448)** .....(Controlled) 2,175
(Non-paid) 20
The Computer & Internet Lawyer **(21475)**
Criminal Justice Ethics **(21517)**
Criminal Law Bulletin **(21518)** ....(Paid) 1,637
(Non-paid) 397
Dispute Resolution Times **(21559)**
Elder's Advisor **(21591)**
Environmental Claims Journal **(21614)**
European Environmental Law Review **(21635)**
European Financial Law Review **(21637)**
European Journal of Crime, Criminal Law and
  Criminal Justice **(21640)**
European Journal for Education Law and
  Policy **(21642)**
European Journal of Health Law **(21644)**
European Journal of Law and Economics **(21645)**
European Journal of Law Reform **(21646)**
European Journal of Social Security **(21652)**
European Migration and Law **(21655)**

European Public Law **(21656)**
European Review of Private Law **(21657)**
Expert Evidence **(21668)**
Feminist Legal Studies **(21683)**
Fordham Intellectual Property, Media & Entertainment
    Law Journal **(21722)** ....(Combined) 745
Fordham Law Review **(21723)** 2,800
Fordham Urban Law Journal **(21724)**
Insights **(21877)**
Intellectual Property and Technology Law
    Journal **(21887)**
International Children's Rights Monitor **(21893)**
International and Comparative Corporate Law
    Journal **(21894)**
International Corporate Law Bulletin **(21895)**
International Environmental Agreements **(21896)**
International Insurance Law Journal **(21898)**
The International Journal of Children's
    Rights **(21901)**
International Journal of Comparative Labour Law and
    Industrial Relations **(21902)**
International Journal of Franchising and Distribution
    Law **(21907)**
The International Journal of Marine and Coastal
    Law **(21910)**
International Journal on Minority and Group
    Rights **(21911)**
International Journal for the Semiotics of
    Law **(21917)**
IP Litigator **(21948)**
Journal of the History of International Law **(22090)**
Journal of Insurance Coverage **(22098)**
Journal of International Arbitration **(22103)**
Journal of International Wildlife Law and
    Policy **(22105)**
Journal of Internet Law **(22106)**
Journal of Network Industries **(22140)**
Journal of World Trade **(22215)**
Law and Critique **(22237)**
Law Enforcement News **(22238)** ....(Paid) ‡6,000
Law and Human Behavior **(22239)**
The Legal History Review **(22244)**
Legal Issues of Economic Integration **(22245)**
Leiden Journal of International Law **(22246)**
The Licensing Journal **(22253)**
NAFTA **(22392)**
The National Law Journal **(22398)** .....(Paid) 28,540
Negotiation Journal **(22414)**
The New York Law
    Journal **(22445)** ....(Mon.-Fri.) 13,745
New York University Law
    Review **(22456)** ....(Combined) 2,000
Numerical Algorithms **(22471)**
Of Counsel **(22485)**
Review of Central and East European Law **(22657)**
The Review of Securities & Commodities
    Regulation **(22662)**
Securities Regulation Law
    Journal **(22720)** ....(Paid) 1,074
                           (Non-paid) 107
South America–Basic Oil Laws & Concession
    Contracts **(22765)** ....‡5,000
Substance Use & Misuse **(22803)** 650
The Trial Lawyer **(22864)** 5,950
Trial Lawyers Quarterly **(22865)** ....(Controlled) 4,500

Staten Island
Migration World Magazine **(23360)** ....‡1,250

Syracuse
Syracuse Law Review **(23427)**

NORTH CAROLINA
Cary
Journal of Law, Economics, and
    Organization **(23692)**

Chapel Hill
North Carolina Journal of International Law and
    Commercial
    Regulation **(23716)** ....(Combined) 395
North Carolina Law Review **(23717)** ....(Paid) ‡1,100
                       (Controlled) ‡500
School Law Bulletin (Chapel
    Hill) **(23721)** ....(Combined) 1,000

Charlotte
The Mecklenburg Times **(23749)** ....(Paid) ‡857
                       (Non-paid) ‡81

Durham
Alaska Law Review **(23805)**
Duke Environmental Law and Policy Forum **(23816)**
Duke Journal of Comparative and International
    Law **(23817)**
Duke Law Journal **(23818)**
Law and Contemporary Problems **(23833)** ....‡1,985

Raleigh
North Carolina Lawyers
    Weekly **(24146)** ....(Paid) 3,300
                       (Non-paid) 120

NORTH DAKOTA
Grand Forks
North Dakota Law
    Review **(24455)** ....(Controlled) 2,300

OHIO
Ada
Ohio Northern University Law
    Review **(24571)** ....(Paid) 850

Akron
The Akron Legal News **(24573)** ....‡5,000

Cincinnati
University of Cincinnati Law
    Review **(24823)** ....(Combined) 600

Cleveland
Babbit's Ohio Municipal Service **(24858)**
Baldwin's Ohio Legislative Service,
    Annotated **(24860)**
Baldwin's Ohio Monthly Record **(24861)**
Cleveland Bar Journal **(24869)** .....(Controlled) 5,200
Daily Legal News **(24879)** ....‡1,300
Domestic Relations Journal of Ohio **(24882)**
Journal of Law and Health **(24915)**
Probate Law Journal of Ohio **(24944)**
SERB Official Reporter **(24953)**
Worker's Compensation Journal of Ohio **(24966)**

Columbus
The Daily Reporter **(25015)** ....(Paid) 5,300
                       (Free) 64
Ohio State Journal on Dispute
    Resolution **(25051)** ....(Paid) 800

Dayton
Ethics, Law and Aging
    Review **(25115)** ....(Combined) 1,000

Elyria
The Paper Book **(25179)** ....(Combined) 12,500

OKLAHOMA
Norman
American Indian Law
    Review **(25932)** ....(Combined) 630

Oklahoma City
The Oklahoma Bar
    Journal **(25974)** ....(Paid) ⊕**13,656**
                       (Non-paid) ⊕**164**

Tulsa
Tulsa Daily Commerce & Legal
    News **(26136)** ....‡450

OREGON
Eugene
Office Manager **(26327)** ....‡900

Lake Oswego
Oregon State Bar Bulletin **(26405)** ....(Paid) ‡13,988

Portland
Environmental Law
    (Portland) **(26476)** ....(Combined) 849

PENNSYLVANIA
Allentown
Lehigh Law Journal **(26628)** ....(Paid) 160
                       (Controlled) 575

Broomall
Gray Areas **(26737)** ....(Paid) ‡14,000

Carlisle
Dickinson Law Review **(26758)** ....‡2,000

Doylestown
Bucks County Law Reporter **(26830)** .....(Paid) ‡810
                       (Free) ‡50

Harrisburg
The PBA Quarterly **(27003)** 30,000
Pennsylvania Bar News **(27005)** ....(Paid) 30,000
                       (Controlled) 750
The Pennsylvania Lawyer **(27009)** 30,000

Horsham
Current Award Trends in Personal Injury **(27058)**
Early Childhood Law and Policy Reporter **(27059)**

Lancaster
Lancaster Law Review **(27142)** ....‡750

Norristown
Montgomery County Law Reporter **(27336)** ....‡2,100

Philadelphia
ALI-ABA Business Law Course Materials
    Journal **(27367)** ....(Paid) ‡2,802
                       (Non-paid) ‡61
ALI-ABA Estate Planning Course Materials
    Journal **(27368)**
The CLE Journal **(27407)**
The Practical Lawyer **(27641)** .....(Controlled) 15,100
The Practical Litigator **(27642)**
The Practical Real Estate Lawyer **(27643)**
The Practical Tax Lawyer **(27644)**
Temple Law Review **(27701)**
University of Pennsylvania Journal of International
    Economic Law **(27713)** ....(Paid) ‡650
University of Pennsylvania Law
    Review **(27714)** ....‡2,000

Pittsburgh
Journal of Law & Commerce **(27802)**
Juris **(27807)** ....(Controlled) 8,000
Military Law Review **(27813)**
The Pennsylvania Police Criminal Law
    Bulletin **(27826)** ....(Paid) 1,200
                       (Non-paid) 50

Reading
Berks County Law Journal **(27917)** ......(Paid) ‡796

Villanova
Villanova Law Review **(28098)** ....‡890

Washington
Washington County Reports **(28119)** ......(Paid) 287
                       (Non-paid) 25

Wayne
Asbestos Property Litigation Reporter **(28124)**
Automotive Litigation Reporter **(28125)**
Bank and Lender Liability Litigation Reporter **(28126)**
Civil RICO Litigation Reporter **(28128)**
Computer & Online Industry Litigation
    Reporter **(28130)**
Corporate Officers and Directors Liability Litigation
    Reporter **(28131)**
Hazardous Waste Litigation Reporter **(28132)**
Health Law Litigation Reporter **(28133)**
Securities Litigation & Regulation Reporter **(28135)**
Tobacco Industry Litigation Reporter **(28137)**

West Chester
Chester County Law Reporter **(28144)** 420

York
York Legal Record **(28209)** ....(Paid) ‡211
                       (Non-paid) ‡101

RHODE ISLAND
Providence
Medical Law's Regan Report **(28407)**
The Rhode Island Bar
    Journal **(28420)** ....(Combined) 5,200

SOUTH CAROLINA
Columbia
South Carolina Law Review **(28565)**
South Carolina
    Lawyer **(28566)** ....(Controlled) 10,500

TENNESSEE
Knoxville
Tennessee Law Review **(29283)** ....‡1,500

Nashville
The Business Lawyer **(29447)** ....(Paid) ‡56,011
                       (Non-paid) ‡5,064
Vanderbilt Journal of Transnational Law **(29499)**

TEXAS
Austin
The American Journal of Criminal
    Law **(29751)** ....(Combined) 600
Austin Lawyer **(29761)** ....(Controlled) ⊕**4,000**
The Review of Litigation **(29801)** 800
Texas Bar Journal **(29812)** ....(Paid) ‡78,000
                       (Non-paid) ‡1,500
Texas Environmental Law Journal **(29818)**
Texas Forum on Civil Liberties and Civil
    Rights **(29821)** ....(Combined) 400
Texas Hispanic Journal of Law and
    Policy **(29823)** ....(Combined) 300
Texas Intellectual Property Law
    Journal **(29825)** ....(Combined) 1,800
Texas International Law
    Journal **(29826)** ....(Paid) 600
Texas Journal of Business
    Law **(29827)** ....(Paid) 4,000

Circ.　　　　Circ.　　　　Circ.

LAW (continued)

Texas Journal of Women and the
Law **(29829)** ....(Combined) 450
Texas Law Review **(29830)** ....‡1,800
Texas Law Review Manual on Usage and
Style **(29831)** 10,000
Texas Law Review Texas Rules of
Form **(29832)** 10,000
The Texas Review of Entertainment and Sports
Law **(29846)**
Texas Review of Law and
Politics **(29847)** ....(Combined) 6,200

Dallas
Journal of Air Law and
Commerce **(30163)** ....‡2,000

Houston
Art Law & Accounting
Reporter **(30459)** ....(Paid) 1,500
Daily Court Review **(30469)** 2,120
Houston Journal of International Law **(30486)**

San Marcos
Journal of Police and Criminal
Psychology **(31084)** ....(Controlled) 350

Waco
Journal of Church and
State **(31249)** ....(Paid) ⊕1,700

UTAH
Salt Lake City
Journal of Land Resouces and Environmental
Law **(31434)**

VERMONT
Montpelier
The Vermont Bar Journal **(31564)**

South Royalton
The FORUM **(31602)** ....(Free) ‡1,100

VIRGINIA
Alexandria
The Prosecutor **(31730)**

Arlington
The Exempt Organization Tax
Review **(31792)** ....‡1,000
George Mason University School of Law **(31794)**
The National Jurist **(31811)** ....(Combined) 70,000
The News Media & the
Law **(31814)** ....(Paid) ‡1,000
(Non-paid) ‡1,000
SPLC Report **(31832)**
Victimology **(31839)** ....‡2,700

Blacksburg
Communication Law and Policy **(31868)**

Charlottesville
Army Lawyer **(31915)**
Virginia Journal of International
Law **(31945)** ....(Paid) 1,000
Virginia Law Review **(31946)** 2,200

Quantico
FBI Law Enforcement
Bulletin **(32340)** ....(Controlled) 45,000

Richmond
Virginia Lawyers Weekly **(32464)** ....‡3,250

Virginia Beach
Regent University Law
Review **(32588)** ....(Controlled) 450

Williamsburg
William & Mary Bill of Rights
Journal **(32621)** ....(Paid) ‡1,500
William and Mary Law Review **(32622)**

WASHINGTON
Seattle
Prison Legal News **(33006)** ....(Paid) 4,000
(Non-paid) 230
Seattle University Law Review **(33024)**
Violence and Victims **(33036)** ....(Paid) 2,500
(Non-paid) 100

WEST VIRGINIA
Charleston
The West Virginia
Lawyer **(33277)** ....(Combined) 6,500

WISCONSIN
Eau Claire
Journal of Nursing Law **(33671)** ....(Paid) 800

Madison
The Bar Examiner **(33923)** ....(Non-paid) ‡3,000
Wisconsin Law Review **(33984)** ....‡2,000
Wisconsin Lawyer **(33985)** ....‡21,500

Milwaukee
American Business Law Journal **(34058)**
Wisconsin Law Journal **(34110)** ....(Paid) 747

River Falls
Argumentation and
Advocacy **(34306)** ....(Paid) 1,000

WYOMING
Cheyenne
The Wyoming Lawyer **(34499)** ....(Paid) 2,500

Laramie
Wyoming Law Review **(34553)**

ALBERTA, CANADA
Edmonton
Health Law Journal **(34715)**
Health Law Review **(34716)**
LawNow **(34719)**

BRITISH COLUMBIA, CANADA
Vancouver
The Advocate **(35121)** ....(Paid) ‡9,500
(Non-paid) ‡500

MANITOBA, CANADA
Winnipeg
Manitoba Law Journal **(35339)** ....(Combined) 500

NEWFOUNDLAND AND LABRADOR, CANADA
Grand Bank
Provincial Judges Journal/Journal des Juges
Provinciaux **(35460)** ....(Controlled) 1,200

NOVA SCOTIA, CANADA
Halifax
Hearsay **(35567)** 5,000

ONTARIO, CANADA
Aurora
Canadian Business Law Journal **(35641)**
Canadian Lawyer **(35642)** ....(Controlled) 27,506
Criminal Law Quarterly **(35646)**
Estates, Trusts & Pensions Journal **(35648)**
Law Times **(35651)** ....(Paid) 10,000
(Non-paid) 3,800

London
Canadian Journal of Law &
Jurisprudence **(35979)** ....(Combined) 500

Markham
The Lawyers Weekly **(36026)** ....(Paid) 5,555
(Controlled) 14,357

Ottawa
The Canadian Bar Review (La Revue du Barreau
Canadien) **(36190)** ....(Paid) ‡38,128
(Non-paid) ‡2
NATIONAL **(36262)** ....(Paid) 33,131
(Non-paid) 835
Ottawa Law Review **(36267)**

Toronto
Banking and Finance Law Review **(36471)**
Bulletin on Current Research in Soviet and East
European Law **(36480)** ....(Paid) 130
150
Canadian Family Law Quarterly **(36497)**
Canadian Journal of Women and the Law/Revue
Femmes et Droit **(36513)** ....(Controlled) 15,000
Education & Law Journal **(36580)**
Intellectual Property Journal **(36622)**
Journal of Environmental Law and Practice **(36635)**
National Journal of Constitutional Law **(36672)**
Osgoode Hall Law Journal **(36691)** 465
900
University of Toronto Faculty of Law Review **(36779)**
University of Toronto Law Journal **(36780)** 1,000

QUEBEC, CANADA
Cowansville
Bulletin de Droit de L'Environnement **(36980)**
Bulletin de Droit de la Sante **(36981)**
Droit de cite **(36982)**
Gestion Plus Info-Employeur **(36983)**
Resumes de droit penal **(36984)**

Montreal
Annals of Air and Space Law/Annales de Droit
Aerien et Spatial **(37084)** ....(Controlled) 1,000
La Revue du Barreau **(37152)** ....‡9,662

McGill Law Journal/Revue de Droit de
McGill **(37183)** ....(Combined) 1,500
Revue Juridique Themis **(37219)**

LIBRARY AND INFORMATION SCIENCE

See also Book Trade and Author News

ARIZONA
Tucson
Legal Reference Services Quarterly **(954)** 1,101

CALIFORNIA
Culver City
Library Mosaics **(1794)** 5,000

Los Angeles
The Library Quarterly **(2316)** ....(Paid) 1,500

San Mateo
Slavic & East European Information
Resources **(3590)** 150

Santa Barbara
Journal of IS Financial
Management **(3645)** ....(Controlled) 925

COLORADO
Boulder
EDUCAUSE Quarterly **(4166)** ....(Paid) 7,600
(Free) ⊕170

Greeley
Technical Services Quarterly **(4500)** 768

CONNECTICUT
Middletown
Choice **(4943)** ....(Paid) ‡3,500
(Controlled) ‡141

Southport
The Small Press Book Review **(5138)**

Westport
MultiCultural Review **(5214)** ....(Paid) ‡5,000

Wilton
EMedia **(5226)** ....(Combined) △30,277

DISTRICT OF COLUMBIA
Washington
Information Outlook **(5544)** ....‡15,000
Science Books & Films **(5780)** ....(Paid) ‡4,500
(Non-paid) ‡600
SPEC Kit **(5800)** ....(Paid) 550
(Non-paid) 10
SpeciaList **(5801)** ....(Combined) 15,000
Update (Library of
Congress) **(5837)** ....(Non-paid) 7,600

FLORIDA
Gainesville
Art Reference Services Quarterly **(6130)** 321
Librarians at Liberty **(6150)**

Tallahassee
Orange Seed Technical
Bulletin **(6727)** ....(Non-paid) 2000

GEORGIA
Athens
College and Research Libraries **(6932)** ......‡12,000

IDAHO
Moscow
Focus on Security **(7914)** ....(Paid) 100

ILLINOIS
Carbondale
Law Library Journal **(8119)** ....‡5,200

Champaign
Library Trends **(8202)** 2,000

Chicago
The American Archivist **(8252)** 4,634
American Libraries **(8259)** ....(Combined) ‡59,300
Booklist **(8287)** ....(Paid) ‡26,119
(Non-paid) ‡2,385
College and Research Libraries
News **(8336)** ....‡12,200
Information Technology and
Libraries **(8413)** ....‡5,794
Journal of AHIMA **(8429)** ....(Paid) 45,000
(Non-paid) 450

Journal of the Medical Library
   Association **(8445)** ....(Non-paid) ‡5,000
                                        (Paid) ‡800
Library Administration &
   Management **(8462)** ....(Paid) ‡5,250
Library Resources & Technical
   Services **(8463)** ....‡6,756
Library Technology Reports **(8464)**
Public Libraries **(8545)** ....(Combined) ‡9,742
School Library Media
   Quarterly **(8561)** ....(Paid) ‡8,850
                                        (Non-paid) ‡311

DeKalb
Behavioral & Social Sciences
   Librarian **(8731)** 367
Music Reference Services Quarterly **(8738)** 213

Glen Ellyn
Church Libraries **(8925)** ....(Paid) ‡550
                                        (Controlled) ‡100

River Forest
World Libraries **(9493)** ....(Controlled) 298

INDIANA
Bloomington
Indiana Libraries **(9834)** ....(Controlled) 3,500

Indiana
The Information Society **(10076)** ....‡417

KENTUCKY
Bowling Green
Serials Review **(11948)**

Frankfort
Kentucky Libraries **(12072)** 1,800

LOUISIANA
Eunice
Louisiana Libraries **(12574)** ....(Paid) ‡1,500
                                        (Non-paid) ‡50

MARYLAND
Baltimore
Portal **(13237)** ....(Combined) 1,500
School Library Media Activities
   Monthly **(13244)** ....(Paid) ⊕11,500

MASSACHUSETTS
Boston
Congregational Library Bulletin **(13881)** ....(Paid) 925

Pittsfield
Catholic Library World **(14470)** ....‡1,200

MICHIGAN
Lansing
Media Spectrum **(15278)** 1,350

MISSISSIPPI
Jackson
Mississippi Libraries Association **(16705)** .....‡1,200

MISSOURI
Kansas City
Journal of Religious & Theological
   Information **(17176)** ....(Paid) 301

NEBRASKA
Lincoln
Science & Technology Libraries **(18119)** 1,035

NEW HAMPSHIRE
Hanover
Dartmouth College Library
   Bulletin **(18518)** ....(Non-paid) 1,200

NEW JERSEY
Fords
The Lit Page **(18827)** ....(Paid) ‡400
                                        (Non-paid) ‡200
On the Road **(18828)** ....(Paid) ‡700
                                        (Non-paid) ‡200

Hoboken
Journal of the American Society for Information
   Science **(19001)** 33,600

Medford
Computers in Libraries **(19223)** ....‡6,000
Information Science Abstracts **(19224)**
Marketing Library Services **(19230)**

New Providence
Microform Review **(19348)** 1,500

NEW YORK
Albany
The Acquisitions Librarian **(19979)** 512
The Reference Librarian **(20003)** ....(Paid) 964

Binghamton
Internet Reference Services Quarterly **(20158)**
Journal of Archival Organization **(20163)**
Journal of Hospital Librarianship **(20180)**
Journal of Internet Cataloging **(20185)**
Journal of Library & Information Services for Distance
   Learning **(20187)**
Medical Reference Services
   Quarterly **(20208)** 1,295
Public Library Quarterly **(20212)** 630
Public Services Quarterly **(20213)**
Resource Sharing & Information
   Networks **(20214)** ....(Paid) 424

Bronx
Library Literature & Information Science **(20275)**

Lancaster
Journal of Interlibrary Loan, Document Delivery, and
   Information Supply **(20882)** 691

New York
Archival Science **(21244)**
Archives and Museum Informatics **(21246)**
Data Mining and Knowledge Discovery **(21538)**
Kirkus Reviews **(22223)** ....(Paid) ‡4,000
Library Journal **(22251)** ....(Paid) 21,487
School Library Journal **(22710)** ....(Paid) 38,021

Syracuse
College & Undergraduate Libraries **(23396)** 300
Syracuse University Library Associates
   Courier **(23430)** ....(Paid) 600

OHIO
Cedarville
The Christian Librarian **(24745)** ....(Paid) 700
                                        (Non-paid) 100

Cincinnati
Content Networking Journal **(24790)**
The Journal of Academic Librarianship **(24805)**

Columbus
Journal of Business and Finance
   Librarianship **(25023)** 708

Worthington
The Book Report **(25678)** ....‡15,000
Library Talk **(25680)** 10,000

OKLAHOMA
Norman
Journal of Library Administration **(25935)** 600
Reference and User Services
   Quarterly **(25941)** ....‡7,645

PENNSYLVANIA
Pittsburgh
Answers **(27759)** ....‡5,000

Topton
Special Libraries Association, Geography & Map
   Division **(28052)** ....(Paid) ‡700
                                        (Controlled) ‡39

Wexford
Cataloging and Classification
   Quarterly **(28154)** 1,580

SOUTH CAROLINA
Charleston
Against the Grain **(28504)** ....(Paid) 2,000
                                        (Non-paid) 200

TEXAS
Austin
Community & Junior College
   Libraries **(29770)** ....(Paid) 587

VIRGINIA
Virginia Beach
Journal of Information Technology
   Management **(32587)**

WASHINGTON
Seabeck
Video Librarian **(32936)** ....(Paid) 2,000
                                        (Non-paid) 100

Seattle
Teacher Librarian **(33034)** ....(Combined) 9,700

WISCONSIN
Middleton
Notes **(34052)**

MANITOBA, CANADA
Winnipeg
Bibliotheca Medica Canadiana **(35315)**
CM **(35322)** ....(Paid) ‡1,700
                                        (Non-paid) ‡100

NOVA SCOTIA, CANADA
Halifax
APLA Bulletin **(35557)** ....(Paid) 350

ONTARIO, CANADA
Ottawa
Feliciter **(36242)** ....(Controlled) ‡5,000

Toronto
Canadian Journal of Information and Library
   Science **(36510)** ....(Paid) 500
Teaching Librarian **(36755)** ....(Paid) 1,374
Victorian Periodicals
   Review **(36786)** ....(Combined) 800

QUEBEC, CANADA
Montreal
Documentation et Bibliotheques **(37110)** 800,000
Education Libraries **(37112)** ....(Combined) 400
Infor **(37130)** 1,125

LIGHTING

See also Electrical Engineering

CALIFORNIA
Arcadia
Electrical News **(1428)** ....(Paid) ‡1,100
                                        (Free) ‡41,000

San Francisco
The Keeper's Log **(3387)** ....(Paid) ‡11,000
                                        (Non-paid) ‡200

COLORADO
Morrison
NETA World **(4587)** ....(Controlled) 6,000

FLORIDA
Tallahassee
Relay Magazine **(6730)** ....(Controlled) 7,500

ILLINOIS
Lincolnshire
Residential Lighting **(9087)** ....(Paid) 261
                                        (Non-paid) 11,057

NEW JERSEY
Clifton
Home Lighting &
   Accessories **(18755)** ....(Paid) 3,465
                                        (Non-paid) 6,529

NEW YORK
New York
Architectural Lighting **(21242)** ......(Non-paid) 25,000
LD+A **(22240)** ....‡10,000
Lighting Dimensions Magazine **(22256)** 14,052

ONTARIO, CANADA
Mississauga
Lighting Magazine **(36074)** ....(Controlled) 9,500

LITERATURE

ALABAMA
Auburn
Southern Humanities
   Review **(45)** ....(Combined) 700

Birmingham
Birmingham Poetry Review **(59)** ....(Paid) 700

Huntsville
Poem **(273)** 400

Tuscaloosa
Black Warrior Review **(485)** ....(Paid) 2,000

ALASKA
Juneau
UAS Explorations **(598)** 650

Circulation: ★ = ABC; △ = BPA; ♦ = CAC; ● = CCAB; ❑ = VAC; ⊕ = PO Statement; ‡ = Publisher's Report; Boldface figures = sworn; Light figures = estimated.

3175

Circ.

LITERATURE (continued)

ARIZONA
Tempe
Bilingual Review/Revista Bilingue **(900)**

Tucson
Arizona Quarterly **(933)** ....(Paid) ‡350
(Non-paid) ‡300

ARKANSAS
Eureka Springs
Aqua Terra, Meta-Ecology and Culture **(1113)**

CALIFORNIA
Berkeley
Classical Antiquity **(1508)**
Coracle **(1511)** ....(Paid) 50
Mystery Readers
Journal **(1544)** ....(Controlled) 2,000
Nineteenth-Century Literature **(1547)** ....‡1,980

Claremont
Women's Studies **(1726)** ....(Paid) 500

Cupertino
Red Wheelbarrow **(1799)** 500

Irvine
The Ear **(2078)**

Kensington
Blue Unicorn **(2100)** ....(Combined) 475

Long Beach
Pearl **(2173)** ....(Combined) 550

Los Angeles
Southern California Anthology **(2393)** ....(Paid) 1,200

Malibu
Pacific Coast Philology **(2493)**

Mountain View
La Red—The Net **(2607)** ....(Combined) 5,000

Oakland
Ruah **(2698)** ....(Combined) 300

Palm Springs
Shaw Annual **(2767)**

San Francisco
H2SO4 **(3372)** ....(Combined) ‡1000

San Leandro
Five Fingers Review **(3561)** ....(Paid) 1,000

Santa Cruz
Scintilla **(3689)**

Saratoga
Stanford French & Italian Studies **(3746)**

Ventura
Art/Life **(4000)**

COLORADO
Boulder
English Language Notes **(4167)** ....(Paid) ‡1,100
(Non-paid) ‡150
Many Mountains Moving **(4178)** ....(Paid) 1,800
(Non-paid) 200

Denver
Denver Quarterly **(4325)** ....(Paid) ‡700
(Non-paid) ‡200

Edgewater
Pleiades Magazine **(4410)** ....(Combined) 10,000

Fort Collins
Colorado Review **(4428)** ....(Paid) 1,300

Golden
Dayspring **(4466)** ....(Paid) 726
Fiction Forum **(4467)** ....(Paid) 608
(Non-paid) 12
Poet's Forum **(4473)** ....(Paid) 516

CONNECTICUT
Fairfield
George Herbert Journal **(4788)** ......(Combined) 500

Stratford
Small Pond Magazine of
Literature **(5172)** ....(Combined) 265

DISTRICT OF COLUMBIA
Washington
American Studies International **(5345)** ....‡800
ANQ **(5353)** 496

Critique **(5450)** ....(Paid) 916
The Explicator **(5486)** ....(Paid) 1,586
The Germanic Review **(5512)** ....(Paid) ‡700
Romance Quarterly **(5772)** ....(Paid) 422
Shakespeare Quarterly **(5790)** ....(Paid) ‡3,400
(Non-paid) ‡250
Symposium **(5809)** ....(Paid) ‡500
Washington Review **(5853)** ....(Controlled) 800

FLORIDA
Coral Gables
James Joyce Literary
Supplement **(6008)** ....(Combined) 475

Lakeland
Onionhead Literary
Quarterly **(6290)** ....(Combined) 320

Largo
Oasis **(6300)** ....(Combined) 290

Orlando
Faulkner Journal **(6489)**
Florida Review **(6493)** ....(Controlled) 1,000

Pensacola
Half Tones to Jubilee **(6566)**

Tampa
Tampa Review **(6779)** ....(Paid) 650

GEORGIA
Athens
The Georgia Review **(6942)** ......(Combined) ‡5,000

Atlanta
CLA Journal **(6985)** ....(Paid) ‡1,500
(Controlled) ‡10
Journal of Biblical Literature **(7020)**
South Atlantic Review **(7043)** ....(Paid) ‡2,000
(Non-paid) ‡200
Studies in the Literary
Imagination **(7047)** ....(Paid) 624

Carrollton
Christianity and Literature **(7156)** ....(Paid) 1,100

Forest Park
Parnassus Literary Journal **(7277)** ....(Paid) 150

Savannah
Southern Poetry Review **(7539)** ....(Controlled) 1,000

Valdosta
Snake Nation Review **(7614)** ....(Controlled) 700

HAWAII
Honolulu
Biography **(7681)** ....(Paid) ‡450
(Controlled) ‡50
China Review International **(7683)** ....(Paid) 600
(Controlled) 45
Chinese Language Teachers Association
Journal **(7684)** 650

IDAHO
Pocatello
Rendezvous **(7947)** ....(Paid) 100

ILLINOIS
Carbondale
American Journal of Semiotics **(8114)** ....‡600

Charleston
Karamu **(8235)** ....(Combined) 600

Chicago
Another Chicago Magazine **(8264)** 2,000
Insects are People Too **(8415)**
Keats-Shelley Journal **(8452)**
Lenox Avenue **(8460)**
Light **(8465)** ....(Combined) ‡923
Metmenys **(8484)** ....(Paid) 700
Other Voices **(8519)** 1,300-1,700

DeKalb
Bulletin de la Societe Americaine de Philosophie de
Langue Francaise **(8732)**

Edwardsville
Papers on Language &
Literature **(8814)** ....(Paid) 600
(Non-paid) 54

Evanston
Arsenal **(8849)**
Eighteenth-Century Studies **(8857)** ....‡4400
TriQuarterly **(8873)**

Gurnee
Children, Churches & Daddies **(8965)**

Highland Park
December **(8991)** ....(Paid) 1,000

Lincoln
Modern Haiku **(9083)** ....(Combined) 770

Loves Park
Rockford Review **(9120)** ....(Paid) 750

Normal
Review of Contemporary Fiction **(9304)**
Spoon River Poetry
Review **(9306)** ....(Combined) 1,000

Prospect Heights
Night Roses **(9471)** ....(Controlled) 300

Urbana
The Communication Review **(9702)**
Illinois Classical Studies **(9708)** ......(Controlled) 260
Journal of English and Germanic
Philology **(9712)** ....‡1,400

Wauconda
The Classical Bulletin **(9742)** ....(Paid) ‡520
(Non-paid) ‡480

INDIANA
Bloomington
Indiana Libraries **(9834)** ....(Controlled) 3,500
Indiana Review **(9836)** ....(Combined) 2,000
Journal of Modern Literature **(9843)** 1,200

Fort Wayne
CLIO **(9965)**

Greencastle
Science Fiction
Studies **(10035)** ....(Controlled) 1,150

Notre Dame
Religion and Literature **(10376)** ....(Paid) 450

Terre Haute
Poet's Roundtable **(10488)** ....(Controlled) 1,000

Valparaiso
The Cresset **(10508)** ....‡4,700

West Lafayette
Sycamore Review **(10554)**

IOWA
Cedar Rapids
Coe Review **(10670)** ....(Controlled) 1,500

Des Moines
Lyrical Iowa **(10803)**

Iowa City
The Iowa Review **(10977)** ....(Combined) 2,700
Midwest Modern Language Association
Journal **(10982)** ....(Paid) 2,000
Philological Quarterly **(10984)**
Syllecta Classica **(10989)** ....(Combined) 120
Walt Whitman Quarterly
Review **(10990)** ....(Paid) 500
(Non-paid) 250

KANSAS
Lawrence
First Intensity **(11551)** ....(Paid) ‡250

Saint John
Chiron Review **(11777)** ....(Combined) 2,000

KENTUCKY
Lexington
Journal of Caribbean Studies **(12167)** 1,000

Louisville
Henry James Review **(12217)** ....‡600

Nicholasville
French Forum **(12324)** ....(Controlled) 500

Pikeville
Pikeville Review **(12358)** ....(Paid) 500

LOUISIANA
Baton Rouge
New Delta Review **(12505)**
The Southern Review **(12506)** ....‡2,500

Lake Charles
McNeese Review **(12638)** ....(Combined) 200

Natchitoches
Louisiana English Journal **(12717)** ....(Paid) ‡399

New Orleans
New Laurel Review **(12743)**

Xavier Review **(12762)** ....(Combined) 300

MAINE
Orono
Puckerbrush Review **(13003)** ....(Paid) 300

Portland
The Cafe Review **(13006)** ....(Controlled) 500

Rangeley
Orgonomic Functionalism **(13043)**

Thomaston
Northwoods Journal **(13066)** ....(Paid) 125

MARYLAND
Baltimore
Arethusa **(13126)** ....‡759
Bookbird **(13138)** ·...................(Combined) 1,650
Diacritics **(13155)** ....‡1,256
English Literary History (ELH) **(13159)** ......‡1,908
Journal of Modern Greek Studies **(13194)** ......‡700
The Lion and the Unicorn **(13209)** ....‡89
Maryland Poetry Review **(13215)** ....(Paid) 500
Modernism/Modernity **(13220)** ....(Combined) 637
Philosophy and Literature **(13235)** ....‡1,320

Columbia
Abbey **(13450)** ....(Controlled) 200

Lanham
Voice of Youth
   Advocates **(13609)** ....(Combined) 6,000

Salisbury
Literature Film Quarterly **(13709)** ....‡800

Towson
Persuasions **(13762)**
Persuasions (Online Version) **(13763)**

Waldorf
Cochran's Corner **(13771)** ....(Combined) 7,000

MASSACHUSETTS
Amherst
English Literary
   Renaissance **(13793)** ....(Combined) 1,450
Peregrine **(13804)**

Arlington
the new renaissance **(13821)** ....(Combined) 910

Becket
Anais **(13834)** ....(Paid) 1,000

Boston
Gay and Lesbian Review Worldwide **(13895)**
The New England
   Quarterly **(13937)** ....(Paid) ‡2,000
                    (Non-paid) ‡400
Ploughshares **(13950)**
Studies in American Fiction **(13964)**
Studies in Romanticism **(13966)** ....‡1,800

Cambridge
The Boston Book
   Review **(14041)** ....(Combined) ‡10,000
Harvard Journal of Asiatic
   Studies **(14061)** ....(Paid) 1,100
Harvard Review **(14066)** ....(Controlled) 2,300
Speculum, A Journal of Medieval
   Studies **(14104)** ....‡6,000

Chestnut Hill
Method **(14131)** ....(Combined) 500

Malden
The Russian Review **(14299)** ....(Paid) ‡1,700
                     (Non-paid) ‡100

Medford
George Sand Studies **(14322)** ....(Paid) 300

Nantucket
The Hemingway
   Review **(14339)** ....(Combined) 1,200

Provincetown
Provincetown Arts **(14486)** ....(Combined) 10,000

Spencer
Nostoc Magazine **(14549)** ....(Non-paid) 500

MICHIGAN
Ann Arbor
Michigan Quarterly Review **(14768)** ....‡1,200

Detroit
Criticism **(14922)** ....‡1,200
Struggle **(14950)** ....(Combined) 600

East Lansing
Journal of South Asian
   Literature **(14987)** ....(Paid) 400
Red Cedar Review **(14992)**

Grand Rapids
Pedagogy **(15100)**

Kalamazoo
Comparative Drama **(15234)** ....(Paid) ‡850
                    (Controlled) ‡50

Lansing
way station magazine **(15296)** .....(Combined) 1,040

Mount Pleasant
Michigan Historical Review **(15376)**

MINNESOTA
Minneapolis
Spout **(16133)** ....(Combined) 250

Morris
Conradiana **(16197)**

Pine Island
Kumquat Meringue **(16271)** ....(Paid) 600

St. Joseph
Studio One/HCC **(16358)**

St. Paul
Ruminator Review **(16408)**

MISSISSIPPI
Hattiesburg
Mississippi Review **(16663)** ....,....(Combined) 1,500

Mississippi State
The Mississippi
   Quarterly **(16783)** ....(Combined) 900

MISSOURI
Columbia
Classical and Modern Literature **(16989)** 500
Minnesota Review **(16997)** ....(Combined) 1,100

Maryville
The Laurel Review
   (Maryville) **(17273)** ....(Controlled) 700

St. Louis
African American Review **(17406)** ....(Paid) 4,200
                    (Non-paid) 167
Manuscripta **(17470)** ....(Combined) 500
River Styx **(17489)** ....(Controlled) 1,700
Thalia **(17523)** 450

Springfield
Explorations in Renaissance
   Culture **(17598)** ....(Combined) 314

MONTANA
Missoula
CutBank **(17866)** ....(Controlled) 1000

NEBRASKA
Kearney
Platte Valley Review **(18060)** ......(Combined) 1,000

Lincoln
Legacy: A Journal of American Women
   Writers **(18089)**
Nineteenth Century French
   Studies **(18109)** ....(Combined) 800

Omaha
The Nebraska Review **(18204)**

NEVADA
Las Vegas
Art **(18360)** 100
Interim **(18364)** ....(Combined) 400

NEW HAMPSHIRE
Hanover
Revista de Critica Literaria Latinoamericana **(18519)**

Portsmouth
Red Owl **(18638)** ....(Paid) 50
                    (Non-paid) 50

Warner
Color Wheel **(18647)** ....(Paid) 300

NEW JERSEY
Cherry Hill
German Quarterly **(18735)** ....(Combined) 3,200

Cranbury
Shakespeare Studies **(18770)** ....(Paid) 1,000

Jersey City
Talisman **(19144)** ....(Paid) 1000

Madison
The Literary Review **(19182)** ....(Paid) ‡2,000
                    (Controlled) ‡200

New Brunswick
Italian Quarterly **(19332)** ....(Paid) 1,050

Ocean Grove
Sensations Magazine **(19391)** ....(Non-paid) 2,100

Paterson
The Paterson Literary
   Review **(19417)** ....(Controlled) 900

Princeton
Hesperia **(19461)** ....(Paid) ‡785
                    (Controlled) ‡217

Scotch Plains
The Armchair Detective **(19533)** ....(Paid) 6,500
                    (Non-paid) 100

Teaneck
Bravo **(19608)** ....(Non-paid) 500

NEW MEXICO
Albuquerque
American Literary Realism **(19765)**
Conceptions Helpless **(19770)** ....(Controlled) 700

Las Cruces
Whole Notes **(19878)** ....(Controlled) 300

Santa Fe
Countermeasures **(19933)** ....(Combined) 1,600

NEW YORK
Albany
Cervantes: Bulletin of the Cervantes Society of
   America **(19983)**
The Little Magazine **(19994)**
13th Moon **(20005)**
Twentieth Century
   Literature **(20007)** ....(Paid) ‡2,400
                    (Non-paid) ‡150

Amherst
1812 **(20033)**

Armonk
Russian Studies in
   Literature **(20097)** ....(Paid) ⊕157

Brooklyn
Semiotext **(20347)**

Flushing
Spring **(20613)** ....(Paid) 500

Garden City
Nassau Review **(20644)** ....(Non-paid) 1,200

Geneva
Seneca Review **(20655)** ....(Combined) 1000

Greenvale
Confrontation **(20698)** ....(Combined) 2,000

Jackson Heights
Editor's Choice **(20826)** ....(Paid) 3000
The Spirit That Moves Us **(20829)**

Kennedy
Arachne **(20858)**

Mohegan Lake
The Iconoclast (Mohegan
   Lake) **(21088)** ....(Combined) 1,000

New York
American Letters &
   Commentary **(21201)** ....(Controlled) 1,500
American Poet **(21205)** ....(Paid) 10,000
American Writer **(21209)** ....(Controlled) 6,400
                    (Non-paid) 3,500
Aristos **(21248)**
Book **(21334)**
Charioteer **(21397)** ....(Paid) 800
Comparative Criticism **(21463)**
Critical Survey **(21521)**
Free Focus **(21734)** 600
Independent Shavian **(21861)**
Journal of American Studies **(21986)** .....(Paid) ‡455
                    (Non-paid) ‡3,346
Modern Asian Studies **(22347)** 1150
National Review **(22400)** ....(Paid) 155,664
Neohelicon **(22415)**
Neophilologus **(22416)**
New York Quarterly **(22450)**

Circulation: ★ = ABC; △ = BPA; ♦ = CAC; • = CCAB; ❏ = VAC; ⊕ = PO Statement; ‡ = Publisher's Report; Boldface figures = sworn; Light figures = estimated.

3177

Circ.   Circ.   Circ.

LITERATURE (continued)

Novyj Zhurnal (The New Review) (22470) 500
NYC Poetry Calendar (22479) ....(Combined) 30,000
Outerbridge (22512) ....(Non-paid) 500
Parnassus (22531) ....(Paid) 1,500
Renaissance Quarterly (22646) ....‡3,500
Romanic Review (22676) ....(Paid) 900
Rural History (22681) 500
Sartre Studies International (22705)
The Serpentine Muse (22733)
Yugntruf (22954) ....(Paid) 1000

Port Washington
Hypotheses (23128) ....(Combined) 220

Potsdam
Blueline (Potsdam) (23137) ....(Combined) 600
Wallace Stevens Journal (23141) ....(Paid) 600
(Non-paid) 100

Rochester
Blake/An Illustrated Quarterly (23211) ....(Paid) ‡500
Fifteenth Century Studies (23226) 400

Staten Island
Waterways: Poetry in the
    Mainstream (23365) ....(Paid) ‡50
(Non-paid) ‡100

Stony Brook
North Atlantic Review (23374) ....(Non-paid) 900

Syracuse
Salt Hill (23420) ....(Combined) 2,000
Syracuse University Library Associates
    Courier (23430) ....(Paid) 600

Water Mill
Literary Rocket (23513) 2,000

NORTH CAROLINA
Chapel Hill
a/b (23696) ....(Paid) 400
Annali D'Italianistica (23698) 600
The Carolina Quarterly (23701) ......(Combined) 900
Early American Literature (23707) ......(Paid) 850
Journal of African
    Travel-Writing (23709) ....(Combined) 525
Southern Literary Journal (23725) ....(Paid) 800
Studies in Philology (23726) ....(Combined) 1,250

Durham
American Literature (23806) ....‡5,500
Boundary 2 (23810) ....(Paid) 850
Poetics Today (23840) ....(Paid) 900
SAQ (23843) ....‡1,300

Greensboro
English Literature in Transition (23922) ....‡900
The Greensboro Review (23923) ...(Combined) 800
Parting Gifts (23933)

Greenville
NCLR (23966) ....(Paid) 750
Tar River Poetry (23970) ....(Paid) 600

Mount Olive
Mount Olive Review (24085)

Pembroke
Pembroke Magazine (24115) ....(Combined) 750

OHIO
Athens
Milton Quarterly (24630) ....‡950

Berea
Grasslands Review (24677) ....(Paid) 200

Bowling Green
Clues: A Journal of Detection (24690)
Mid-American Review (24696) .....(Controlled) 1,600
Modern Austrian Literature (24697) ....‡700

Cincinnati
America Drama (24769)

Cleveland
The Emily Dickinson
    Journal (24890) ....(Combined) 500
Whiskey Island
    Magazine (24965) ....(Controlled) 1,500

Columbus
Lost and Found Times (25029) ......(Combined) 300
Narrative (25033)
Pudding Magazine (25057)
Research in African
    Literatures (25058) ....(Paid) 800
(Controlled) 200

Oberlin
Field: Contemporary Poetry and
    Poetics (25445) ....(Paid) 1,500
(Non-paid) 200

OKLAHOMA
Edmond
ByLine (25813) 3,500

Norman
World Literature Today (25944) ....(Paid) ‡1,980
(Non-paid) ‡200

Stillwater
Cimarron Review (26076) ....(Paid) ‡450
(Non-paid) ‡150

Tulsa
James Joyce Quarterly (26118) ....(Paid) ‡1,450
(Non-paid) ‡20

OREGON
Corvallis
CALYX (26285) ....(Paid) 4,500
(Non-paid) 500

Eugene
Northwest Review (26326) ....(Controlled) 1,250

Portland
Hubbub (26481) ....(Combined) 350

PENNSYLVANIA
Ambridge
Taproot Literary
    Review (26656) ....(Controlled) 1,000

Grantville
Fat Tuesday (26948) ....(Paid) 200

Hellertown
The Baker Street Journal (27037) ....‡1,800

Indiana
Studies in the Humanities (27077) ....(Paid) 300
Works and Days (27078) 350

Mc Keesport
Latin America Indian Literatures
    Journal (27229) ....(Combined) 260

Philadelphia
The Classical World (27406) ....‡3,000
CrossConnect (27432)
L I T: Literature Interpretation Theory (27557)

Pittsburgh
Creative Nonfiction (27772) ....(Paid) 4,500
Critica Hispanica (27773)
Latin American Literary
    Review (27809) ....(Combined) 1,250
Milton Studies (27814)

University Park
Book History (28071)
The Chaucer Review (28072) ....‡1,350
Comparative Literature Studies (28073) 1,000
Resources for Literary
    Study (28084) ....(Combined) 700
Studies in American Jewish
    Literature (28085) ....(Combined) 450

Washington
Topic (Washington) (28117) ....(Combined) 500

West Chester
College Literature (28145) ....(Combined) 700

RHODE ISLAND
Cranston
Inti (28335) ....(Controlled) 1,000

Kingston
ATQ (28358) ....(Paid) ‡404
(Controlled) ‡42

Providence
Brasil - Brazil (28389)
Gavea-Brown (28398)
Literature and Psychology (28403) 1,000

SOUTH CAROLINA
Charleston
Mark Twain Circular (28515) ....(Paid) 450

Clemson
South Carolina Review (28533)

Newberry
Studies in Short Fiction (28717) ....‡1,900

TENNESSEE
Bristol
American Journal of Italian Studies (29065) 300

Gallatin
Firefly Magazine (29202) ....(Controlled) 1,200

Memphis
River City (29378) ....(Controlled) 1,500

Murfreesboro
Tennessee Folklore Society
    Bulletin (29434) ....(Paid) ‡380
(Non-paid) ‡47

Nashville
Bulletin Baudelairien (29446) 250

TEXAS
Austin
Borderlands: Texas Poetry Review (29766)
Nerve Cowboy (29793) ....(Combined) 275
Sulphur River Literary
    Review (29810) ....(Combined) 350

Brownsville
Extrapolation (29960) ....‡1,000

College Station
Helios (Lubbock) (30042)
Seventeenth-Century News (30049) 1,200
South Central Review (30050) ....(Paid) 1,300

Dallas
Arthuriana (30124) ....(Paid) ‡750

Fort Worth
Linden Lane Magazine (30345) ....(Paid) 2000

Houston
Studies in English Literature, 1500-1900
    (SEL) (30531) ....(Paid) ‡1,742
(Non-paid) ‡100

Huntsville
The Texas Review (30597)

Leakey
Fine Print (30679) 2000

Lubbock
Intertexts (30712)

Nacogdoches
RE:AL (30852)

Victoria
Symploke (31235)

Waxahachie
Integra (31270) ....(Paid) 1,430

UTAH
Logan
Western American
    Literature (31354) ....(Paid) ‡1,200
(Non-paid) ‡50

Ogden
Weber Studies (31379) ....(Combined) 1,000

Provo
Children's Book and Play Review (31401)
Rhetoric Society Quarterly (31407) ....(Paid) 900

VERMONT
Middlebury
New England Review (31558) ....‡2,000,000

VIRGINIA
Abingdon
Sow's Ear Poetry
    Review (31626) ....(Combined) 650

Arlington
Bogg (31782) ....(Controlled) 850

Blacksburg
Stephen Crane Studies (31878) .....(Combined) 127

Fairfax
The Comparatist (32013) ....(Paid) 450
Phoebe (32026) ....(Combined) 1,000

Hollins College
The Hollins Critic (32169) ....‡500

Richmond
The Poe Messenger (32445) ....(Paid) 450

Williamsburg
Chasqui (32615) ....(Combined) 385

William and Mary
   Review **(32624)** ....(Combined) 3,500

WASHINGTON
Bellingham
Bellingham Review **(32676)** ....(Controlled) 2,100

Nordland
Pangolin Papers **(32853)** ....(Paid) 500

Pullman
Poe Studies/Dark
   Romanticism **(32906)** ....(Combined) 500
Rocky Mountain Review of Language and
   Literature **(32907)** ....(Controlled) 1,000

Sammamish
Tundra **(32935)** ....(Combined) 700

Seattle
Jack Mackerel Magazine **(32974)** .....(Non-paid) 500
Modern Language
   Quarterly **(32988)** ....(Paid) ‡1,350
                                          (Non-paid) ‡75
PoetsWest Online **(33003)** ....(Free) 300
Raven Chronicles **(33011)** ....(Paid) 2,000

WEST VIRGINIA
Bluefield
Commonwealth Novel in
   English **(33254)** ....(Paid) 450

Morgantown
Victorian Poetry **(33397)** ....(Paid) 692
                                          (Non-paid) 86

WISCONSIN
Madison
L'Anello Che Non Tiene **(33919)**
Contemporary Literature **(33928)** ....(Paid) 2,000
Madison Review **(33960)**
Monatshefte **(33963)** ....‡1,000
Prime **(33971)**
Substance **(33975)** ....(Paid) 500

Milwaukee
Renascence **(34096)** ....(Paid) ‡650
                                          (Non-paid) ‡25

Oshkosh
Wisconsin Review **(34228)** ....(Combined) ‡2,000

WYOMING
Laramie
Owen Wister Review **(34550)**

ALBERTA, CANADA
Calgary
ARIEL **(34628)** ....(Combined) 950
Opuntia **(34653)**
The Prairie Journal of Canadian
   Literature **(34654)** ....(Paid) 600

Lethbridge
Victorian Review **(34798)** ....(Paid) 350

BRITISH COLUMBIA, CANADA
Burnaby
West Coast Line **(34909)** ....(Paid) 550

New Westminster
Event **(35028)** ....(Combined) 1,300

North Vancouver
The Capilano Review **(35034)** ....(Combined) 900

Sardis
Teak Roundup **(35087)** ....(Controlled) 100

Vancouver
Raddle Moon **(35161)** ....(Paid) 700

MANITOBA, CANADA
Winnipeg
Mosaic **(35345)** ....(Paid) ‡750
                                          (Non-paid) ‡150

NEW BRUNSWICK, CANADA
Fredericton
ellipse **(35393)** ....(Combined) 560
International Fiction Review **(35395)**

ONTARIO, CANADA
Guelph
CCL Canadian Children's Literature (Litterature
   Canadienne pour la Jeunesse) **(35860)** .....‡1,000
Essays in Theatre/Etudes
   Theatrales **(35862)** ....(Combined) 350

Kingston
Revue Frontenac/Frontenac Review **(35947)**

Ottawa
Canadian Review of American
   Studies **(36227)** ....(Paid) 475
English Studies in Canada
   (ESC) **(36241)** ....(Controlled) 1,150
Journal of Canadian
   Poetry **(36254)** ....(Combined) 500

Toronto
Brick **(36477)** ....(Paid) 3,000
Canadian Review of Comparative
   Literature **(36529)** ....(Combined) 300
Exile **(36586)** 1,100
Lang Van **(36648)** ....(Controlled) 1,800
Parchment **(36697)** ....(Combined) 525
Renaissance and Reformation/Renaissance et
   Reforme **(36726)** ....(Combined) 700
University of Toronto Quarterly **(36782)** 945

Windsor
Windsor Review **(36892)** ....(Paid) 250

QUEBEC, CANADA
L'Annonciation
Emploi Plus **(36939)** ....(Combined) 500

Chicoutimi
Protee **(36967)**

Montreal
Journal of Canadian Fiction **(37138)** 1,500
KOLA **(37148)** ....(Combined) 325
Scrivener **(37222)** ....(Combined) 500

Quebec
Nuit Blanche **(37293)** ....(Controlled) 3,400

SASKATCHEWAN, CANADA
Regina
Green's Magazine **(37530)** ....(Controlled) 250
Wascana Review of Contemporary Poetry and Short
   Fiction **(37535)** ....(Controlled) 278

Saskatoon
Lumen **(37552)** ....(Paid) 300
Semeia **(37556)** 1,500

LOCAL, STATE, AND REGIONAL PUBLICATIONS

See also History and Genealogy; Chambers of Commerce and Boards of Trade

ALABAMA
Birmingham
Business Alabama Monthly **(63)** ....(Paid) 10,000
                                          (Controlled) 8,000

Montgomery
Alabama Municipal Journal **(359)** ....(Paid) ‡200
                                          (Controlled) ‡4,500
Developing Alabama **(364)** ....(Non-paid) 7,000

ALASKA
Anchorage
Alaska History **(522)** ....(Paid) 500

ARIZONA
Bisbee
Pay Dirt Magazine **(660)** ....‡3,500

Phoenix
Arizona Business Gazette **(775)** ....(Paid) 10,208
                                          (Free) 5,744
Business Journal - Serving Phoenix and the Valley of
   the Sun **(796)**
Southwest Contractor **(811)** ....(Combined) 6,000

Tucson
Arizona's Economy **(935)**

ARKANSAS
Fort Smith
Fort Smith Historical Society
   Journal **(1142)** ....(Paid) 450

Little Rock
Arkansas Business **(1213)** ....(Paid) 6,500
                                          (Controlled) 2,000

Rogers
Backtracker **(1326)** ....(Combined) 240

CALIFORNIA
Arroyo Grande
Times Press Recorder **(1434)**

Bakersfield
Historic Kern **(1452)** ....(Controlled) 450

Berkeley
California Public Employee Relations **(1505)**

Irvine
Orange County Business
   Journal **(2086)** ....(Paid) 13,456
                                          (Non-paid) 599

Los Angeles
The Los Angeles Business
   Journal **(2320)** ....(Paid) ★20,956
Southern California Quarterly **(2397)** .....(Paid) 1,200

Sacramento
The Business Journal **(2978)** ....(Paid) 12,727
California State Association of Counties California
   County **(2988)** ....(Non-paid) 7,000

San Diego
Journal of San Diego
   History **(3212)** ....(Combined) 3,500
San Diego Business Journal **(3258)** ....‡22,500
San Diego Daily
   Transcript **(3262)** ....(Mon.-Fri.) 15,000

San Francisco
New California Media (NCM) **(3394)**
San Francisco Attorney
   Magazine **(3427)** ....(Paid) 10,000
San Francisco Business
   Times **(3431)** ....(Paid) 19,929

San Jose
San Jose Business Journal **(3535)** .....(Paid) 16,000

COLORADO
Boulder
The Boulder County Business
   Report **(4157)** ....(Paid) 10,000

Centennial
ColoradoBiz **(4223)**

Denver
The Mining Record **(4339)** ....‡5,260

CONNECTICUT
Bridgeport
Business Woman **(4712)** ....(Combined) 15,000

Hartford
Connecticut Housing Production and Permit
   Authorized Construction **(4887)**

New Haven
Business Times **(4984)** ....(Non-paid) ‡22,400
Fairfield County Business Times **(4988)** ....‡7,400

Tolland
Connecticut Maple Leaf **(5175)** 700

DELAWARE
Wilmington
Archaeological Society of Delaware
   Bulletin **(5288)** ....(Paid) 100

DISTRICT OF COLUMBIA
Washington
Washington Business
   Journal **(5843)** ....(Paid) 20,208
Washington History **(5845)** ....(Paid) 3,000

FLORIDA
Fort Lauderdale
Business in Broward **(6073)** ....(Paid) ‡14,200
                                          (Controlled) ‡5,800

Miami
Daily Business Review **(6347)** ....(Paid) 10,184
                                          (Controlled) 286
Miami Today **(6373)** ....(Controlled) △32,146
                                          (Paid) △601

Orlando
Orlando Business Journal **(6502)** ....(Paid) 11,536

Pensacola
Pensacola History
   Illustrated **(6567)** ....(Controlled) 700

Sarasota
Sarasota Magazine **(6664)** ....(Combined) ‡13,000

Circulation: ★ = ABC; △ = BPA; ♦ = CAC; ● = CCAB; ❑ = VAC; ⊕ = PO Statement; ‡ = Publisher's Report; Boldface figures = sworn; Light figures = estimated.

3179

Circ.   Circ.   Circ.

LOCAL, STATE, AND REGIONAL PUBLICATIONS (continued)

Tallahassee
Florida Engineering Society
Journal **(6710)** ....(Paid) ‡4,500

West Palm Beach
Palm Beach and The Naples
Times **(6849)** ....(Combined) 150,000

GEORGIA
Athens
Georgia Business and Economic
Conditions **(6938)** ....(Free) ‡2,000

Atlanta
Atlanta History Center **(6969)** ....(Paid) 5,500
TechLINKS **(7051)** ....‡23,000

Thomasville
South Georgia Business
Journal **(7586)** ....(Paid) ⊕1,000
(Controlled) ⊕7,000

HAWAII
Honolulu
Hawaii Business **(7691)** ....(Paid) ‡3,057
(Non-paid) ‡10,197
Hawaiian Journal of
History **(7699)** ....(Combined) ⊕1,800

IDAHO
Boise
The Idaho Business Review **(7809)** .....(Paid) 3,100
(Free) 450

Rexburg
Snake River Echoes **(7964)** ....(Controlled) 250

ILLINOIS
Chicago
Chicago Tribune Magazine **(8328)**
Today's Chicago
Woman **(8583)** ....(Non-paid) 70,000
Windy City Sports
Magazine **(8607)** ....(Controlled) ‡100,000

Clinton
Dewitt County Genealogical Society
Quarterly **(8683)** ....(Controlled) 200

Springfield
Broker News **(9620)** ....(Controlled) 500,000
Illinois Banker **(9621)** ....‡2,200

Urbana
Champaign County Genealogical Society
Quarterly **(9699)** ....(Controlled) 250

INDIANA
Bloomington
Indiana Business
Review **(9831)** ....(Controlled) 2,000

Indianapolis
Indiana Business
Magazine **(10124)** ....(Controlled) 3,175
(Non-paid) 26,622
2,619

Rochester
Fulton County Images **(10430)** ....(Controlled) 700

IOWA
Des Moines
Des Moines Business
Record **(10780)** ....(Paid) ‡3,932

KANSAS
Shawnee Mission
Texas Banking **(11805)** ....(Paid) ‡5,000
(Controlled) ‡300

Topeka
Topeka Genealogical Society
Quarterly **(11839)** ....(Controlled) 1,095

Wichita
Wichita Business Journal **(11890)** ....(Paid) 5,088

KENTUCKY
Campbellsville
Central Kentucky
Researcher **(12007)** ....(Controlled) 315

LOUISIANA
Baton Rouge
Greater Baton Rouge Business
Report **(12489)** ....(Paid) ‡2,657
(Non-paid) ‡6,001

Shreveport
North Louisiana History **(12817)** ....(Paid) 500

MARYLAND
Annapolis
Municipal Maryland **(13094)** ....(Paid) ‡1,750
(Non-paid) ‡190

Baltimore
Baltimore Business Journal **(13129)** .....(Paid) 9,089

Elkton
Cecil Historical Journal **(13494)**

Frostburg
Journal of the Alleghenies **(13527)** ....(Paid) 200

Ocean City
Oceana Magazine **(13639)** ....(Non-paid) ‡27,000

MASSACHUSETTS
Boston
Boston Airport Journal **(13855)** ....(Non-paid) 21,000
Boston Seaport Journal **(13862)** ....(Non-paid) 6,000
Massachusetts Lawyers Weekly **(13928)** .....‡16,000
New England Economic
Review **(13933)** ....(Non-paid) ‡15,000

Cambridge
Foodservice East **(14054)** ....‡23,000

East Boston
Travel New England **(14166)** ....(Non-paid) 8,000

Westfield
Historical Journal of
Massachusetts **(14640)** ....(Paid) 1000

MICHIGAN
Boyne City
Outstate Business **(14833)** ....(Non-paid) ‡10,000

Detroit
Crain's Detroit Business **(14920)** ......(Paid) ★34,685
Detroiter **(14929)** ....(Paid) 18,535
(Controlled) 2,000

Kalamazoo
Business Outlook for West
Michigan **(15233)** ....(Paid) 100
(Controlled) 25

Lansing
Journal of Small
Business **(15276)** ....(Non-paid) 9,000

MINNESOTA
Duluth
The Duluthian **(15837)** ....‡1,800

Minneapolis
Architecture Minnesota **(16058)** ....(Paid) ‡3,000
(Controlled) ‡4,000
CityBusiness **(16066)** ....(Paid) 11,278
Minnesota Law &
Politics **(16103)** ....(Controlled) 22,000
(Paid) 2,000

MISSISSIPPI
Jackson
Mississippi Business
Journal **(16700)** ....(Paid) ‡8,620
(Non-paid) ‡2,460
Mississippi Magazine **(16706)** ....(Paid) ‡34,000
(Non-paid) ‡500

Louisville
Winston County Journal **(16750)** ....(Paid) ‡4,900
(Non-paid) ‡4,400

Lucedale
George County Times **(16753)**

Tupelo
Northeast Mississippi Historical and Genealogical
Society Quarterly **(16850)** ....(Combined) 475

MISSOURI
Cape Girardeau
Big Muddy **(16943)**

Columbia
Missouri State Genealogical Association
Journal **(17005)** ....(Paid) 705

Kansas City
Kansas City Business
Journal **(17178)** ....(Paid) 10,941

Rolla
Phelps County Genealogical Society
Quarterly **(17379)** ....(Paid) 190

St. Louis
St. Louis Business Journal **(17496)** ....(Paid) 18,400
St. Louis Countian **(17499)** 1,300

MONTANA
Missoula
The Montana Business
Quarterly **(17870)** ....(Paid) ‡1,300
(Non-paid) ‡200

NEBRASKA
Omaha
The Lincoln Business Journal **(18202)**
The Omaha Business Journal **(18205)**

NEVADA
Las Vegas
Nevada Business Journal **(18378)** ......(Paid) ‡6,000
(Controlled) ‡9,000

NEW HAMPSHIRE
Manchester
Business NH Magazine **(18556)** ....(Paid) ‡600
(Controlled) ‡13,850
New Hampshire Business Review **(18558)** 15,000
Northeast Export
Magazine **(18561)** ....(Controlled) 11,750

NEW JERSEY
Fairfield
New Jersey Business **(18814)** ....‡20,000

Morristown
New Jersey Monthly **(19313)** ....(Paid) 94,000

Princeton
Princeton History **(19470)** 1,500

NEW YORK
Buffalo
Business First of Buffalo **(20371)** ....(Paid) 9,696

Latham
Capital District Business
Review **(20931)** ....(Paid) 9,273

New York
Crain's New York
Business **(21511)** ....(Paid) ★42,420
(Non-paid) ★21,574

Ronkonkoma
Long Island Business News **(23271)** ....(Paid) 8,500
(Non-paid) 3,500

Syracuse
The Business
Record **(23391)** ....(Controlled) ‡17,500
Central N.Y. Business
Journal **(23393)** ....(Paid) ‡1,300
(Controlled) ‡6,700

NORTH CAROLINA
Charlotte
The Business Journal of
Charlotte **(23736)** ....(Paid) 13,922
Business Journal - Serving Metropolitan Kansas
City **(23737)**

Greenville
North Carolina Genealogical Society
Journal **(23967)** ....(Controlled) 2,000

Horse Shoe
A Lot of Bunkum **(24010)** ....(Controlled) 750

Raleigh
North Carolina **(24143)** ....‡16,000
North Carolina Insight **(24145)** ....(Paid) ‡1,300

Research Triangle Park
Southern Growth Magazine **(24187)**

OHIO
Cincinnati
Cincinnati Business Courier **(24783)** ....(Paid) 12,701

Cleveland
Babbit's Ohio Municipal Service **(24858)**
Baldwin's Ohio Legislative Service,
Annotated **(24860)**
Baldwin's Ohio Monthly Record **(24861)**

Crain's Cleveland
Business **(24877)** ....(Paid) ★21,109
Probate Law Journal of Ohio **(24944)**
Worker's Compensation Journal of Ohio **(24966)**

Columbus
Business First-Columbus **(25003)** ......(Paid) ‡10,612

Mansfield
Ohio Records & Pioneer
Families **(25333)** ....(Controlled) 1,605

OKLAHOMA
Durant
Red River Valley Historical Journal **(25807)**

Lawton
Tree Tracers **(25889)** ....(Combined) 400

Norman
Oklahoma Business Bulletin **(25938)** ....‡500

OREGON
Portland
Daily Journal of Commerce **(26475)** ......(Paid) 3,341
(Controlled) 809

Roseburg
Umpqua Trapper **(26556)** ....(Paid) 340

PENNSYLVANIA
Enola
Pennsylvania Township
News **(26886)** ....(Paid) ‡9,215
(Non-paid) ‡1,063

Philadelphia
Advertising/Communications Times **(27364)**
Philadelphia Business
Journal **(27624)** ....(Paid) 11,506

Pittsburgh
Pittsburgh Business Times **(27830)** ....(Paid) 16,731

Warren
Stepping Stones **(28104)**

RHODE ISLAND
Providence
Providence Business News **(28414)** ......(Paid) 5,785

SOUTH CAROLINA
Columbia
Business & Economic Review **(28546)** ....‡6,100

Conway
Independent Republic
Quarterly **(28590)** ....(Combined) 400

SOUTH DAKOTA
Yankton
South Dakota Magazine **(29039)** ....(Paid) 32,800

TENNESSEE
Memphis
Ansearchin' News **(29357)**

Murfreesboro
Border States **(29429)**

Nashville
Nashville Business Journal **(29472)** ......(Paid) 6,200

Sevierville
Smoky Mountain Historical Society
Journal **(29590)** ....(Combined) 725

TEXAS
Austin
Austin Business Journal **(29756)** ......(Paid) ★7,027
Austin Genealogical Society Quarterly **(29758)**
Texas Petroleum and C-Store
Journal **(29839)** ....‡1,200

Dallas
Daily Commercial Record **(30142)**

McAllen
The South Texas Business
Journal **(30787)** ....(Paid) ‡3,500
(Controlled) ‡3,000

San Antonio
The San Antonio Business
Journal **(31045)** ....(Paid) 11,932

VERMONT
Williston
Business People
Vermont **(31618)** ....(Controlled) ⊕6,000

VIRGINIA
Arlington
State Tax Notes **(31833)**

Richmond
Virginia Business **(32460)** ....(Controlled) 32,500

Staunton
Augusta Historical
Bulletin **(32553)** ....(Controlled) 500

WASHINGTON
Bellevue
Washington CEO **(32669)** ....(Controlled) 37,000

Olympia
Olympia Genealogical Society
Quarterly **(32859)** ....(Controlled) 200

Pullman
Rocky Mountain Review of Language and
Literature **(32907)** ....(Controlled) 1,000

Seattle
Puget Sound Business
Journal **(33007)** ....(Paid) 20,000

Wenatchee
Wenatchee Business
Journal **(33195)** ....(Paid) ‡1,900
(Non-paid) ‡2,300

WISCONSIN
Black Earth
Corporate Report Wisconsin **(33588)** ....(Paid) 71
(Controlled) 30,000

Madison
Wisconsin Beverage Business **(33979)** ....‡6,000
The Wisconsin Taxpayer **(33991)** ....‡9,000
(Non-paid) ‡700

Milwaukee
The Business Journal Serving Greater
Milwaukee **(34060)** ....(Paid) 10,100

Oshkosh
Michigan Botanist **(34223)** ....(Combined) ⊕800

ALBERTA, CANADA
Edmonton
Commerce News **(34706)** ....(Non-paid) 36,000
Edmonton and Homersham Commerce &
Industry **(34709)** ....(Non-paid) ‡5,000

BRITISH COLUMBIA, CANADA
Cranbrook
Kootenay Business Magazine **(34936)** ......(Paid) 24
(Controlled) ‡9,100

Richmond
British Columbia Genealogist **(35074)** ....(Paid) 1,000

Vancouver
Business in Vancouver Media
Group **(35128)** ....(Paid) 10,000

Victoria
British Columbia Division of Vital Statistics Quarterly
Digest **(35209)**

MANITOBA, CANADA
Winnipeg
Exports of Canadian Grain and Wheat
Flour **(35328)** ....(Paid) 150
Generations **(35329)** ....(Controlled) 800
Manitoba History **(35338)**

NEWFOUNDLAND AND LABRADOR, CANADA
St. John's
Newfoundland Studies **(35492)** ....(Controlled) 300

ONTARIO, CANADA
Hamilton
B12-Hamilton/Halton Business
Report **(35875)** ....(Controlled) ‡23,375

Mississauga
Mississauga Business
Times **(36080)** ....(Controlled) ‡19,500

Scarborough
Northern Ontario
Business **(36379)** ....(Controlled) ‡10,500

Toronto
Canada Journal **(36488)** ....(Combined) 24,000
Vitality Magazine **(36789)** ....(Paid) 50,000
York Pioneer **(36795)** ....(Controlled) 400

QUEBEC, CANADA
Cookshire
Journal Regional le Haut-Saint-Francois **(36977)**

Ste.-Foy
Quebec Info **(37339)** 2,000

Stanstead
Stanstead Historical Society Journal **(37407)**

SASKATCHEWAN, CANADA
Saskatoon
Saskatoon History
Review **(37555)** ....(Combined) 400

LUMBER

NEW YORK
Manhasset
Wood Technology **(21019)** ....(Paid) 472
(Controlled) 22,500

MANITOBA, CANADA
Winnipeg
WRLA Yardstick **(35365)** ....(Controlled) 1,650

MACHINERY AND EQUIPMENT

See also Commerce and Industry; Metal,
Metallurgy, and Metal Trade; Vending
Machines

ALABAMA
Montgomery
Power Equipment Trade **(375)** ....(Controlled) 21,559

CALIFORNIA
Los Angeles
Respiratory Therapy
Products **(2379)** ....(Controlled) 30,000

San Clemente
Industrial West **(3101)** ....(Controlled) ‡24,700

Tarzana
RePlay Magazine **(3839)** ....(Combined) 4,000

COLORADO
Englewood
www.industry.net **(4417)** ....(Non-paid) 500,000

CONNECTICUT
Prospect
Job Shop Technology
(JST) **(5092)** ....(Controlled) ‡32,000

ILLINOIS
Bensenville
Process Heating **(8070)** ....(Controlled) 23,000

Chicago
Utillaje **(8596)** ....(Paid) 500
(Controlled) 30,250

Rockford
TPJ—The Tube & Pipe
Journal **(9534)** ....(Controlled) ‡30,000

Skokie
Computer Listing Service's Machinery & Equipment
Guide **(9603)** ....(Non-paid) ‡4,000
Industrial Market
Place **(9606)** ....(Controlled) ‡100,000

IOWA
Fort Dodge
Contractors Hot Line **(10896)** ....(Paid) ‡3,658
(Non-paid) ‡36,342
Contractors Hot Line Monthly Equipment
Guide **(10897)** ....(Paid) 10,000
Farm Equipment Guide **(10898)** ....(Paid) ‡11,500
(Non-paid) ‡7,500
Farmers Hot Line **(10900)** ....(Non-paid) ‡47,540
(Paid) ‡1,660
Industrial Machine
Trader **(10901)** ....(Combined) ‡12,000
Plastics Hot Line **(10907)** ....(Controlled) ‡6,000

MAINE
Pownal
Fine Tool Journal **(13033)** ....(Paid) 2,500

Yarmouth
HME News **(13079)** ....(Paid) △17,100

Circulation: ★ = ABC; △ = BPA; ◆ = CAC; • = CCAB; ❑ = VAC; ⊕ = PO Statement; ‡ = Publisher's Report; Boldface figures = sworn; Light figures = estimated.

3181

Trade, Technical, and Professional Publications

Circ.

Circ.

Circ.

MACHINERY AND EQUIPMENT (continued)

MASSACHUSETTS
Norwell
DDIN International **(14439)** ....(Combined) 6,000

MICHIGAN
Dearborn
Forming &
  Fabricating **(14902)** ....(Controlled) 65,496

MINNESOTA
Plymouth
Precision Manufacturing **(16279)** ....(Non-paid) 6,535

MISSOURI
Independence
Lift Equipment **(17115)** ....(Combined) 16,500

NEBRASKA
Lincoln
Machinery Trader (Central Edition) **(18092)**
Machinery Trader (Eastern Edition) **(18093)**
Machinery Trader (Western Edition) **(18094)**

NEW JERSEY
Princeton Junction
Card Manufacturing **(19483)** ....(Paid) 3,000

Washington
Compressed Air **(19706)** ....(Controlled) 130,000

NEW YORK
Larchmont
Metalworking Insiders' Report **(20920)**

Montclair
The Tube Council
  News **(21092)** ....(Non-paid) 2,300

New York
Foodservice Equipment and Supplies **(21715)**
Plastics Technology **(22564)** ....(Paid) ⊕46,530
                                 (Non-paid) ⊕3,728

OHIO
Cleveland
Hydraulics &
  Pneumatics **(24910)** ....(Controlled) ‡49,878
Machine Design **(24923)** ....(Non-paid) ‡180,619
New Equipment
  Digest **(24932)** ....(Controlled) 206,000

Columbus
Finer Points Magazine **(25017)** ....(Controlled) 4,500

Solon
Medical Equipment
  Designer **(25526)** ....(Non-paid) ‡12,000

TENNESSEE
Crossville
Rock and Dirt **(29159)** ....(Paid) 36,000
                                 (Free) 137,000

WISCONSIN
Fort Atkinson
Professional Tool & Equipment
  News **(33718)** ....(Non-paid) ‡110,143
Today's Distributor **(33721)** ....(Controlled) 41,050

Waukesha
Compressor Tech
  Two **(34400)** ....(Controlled) 11,529
Diesel & Gas Turbine
  Worldwide **(34401)** ....(Paid) ‡675
                                 (Controlled) ‡20,050
Diesel Progress International
  Edition **(34402)** ....(Paid) ‡91
                                 (Controlled) ‡13,247
Diesel Progress North American
  Edition **(34403)** ....(Paid) 255
                                 (Controlled) 27,462

BRITISH COLUMBIA, CANADA
Vancouver
Heavy Equipment
  Guide **(35147)** ....(Combined) 30,978

ONTARIO, CANADA
Mississauga
Equipment Journal **(36067)**
Manufacturing
  Automation **(36075)** ....(Combined) 21,295

Toronto
Canadian Machinery and
  Metalworking **(36515)** ....(Paid) •306
                                 (Non-paid) •19,120
IT Magazine **(36626)** 20,000
Machinery & Equipment
  MRO **(36653)** ....(Combined) 18,828

MANAGEMENT AND ADMINISTRATION

ARKANSAS
Little Rock
The Case Manager **(1226)** ....(Combined) 20,000

CALIFORNIA
Berkeley
California Management Review
  (CMR) **(1503)** ....‡5,500
Journal of High Technology Management
  Research **(1533)**

Irvine
Organization Science **(2087)** ....‡1,700

Los Angeles
Association News **(2215)** ....(Controlled) ‡40,000
Fitness Management Magazine **(2271)** ....(Paid) 243
                                 (Controlled) 26,000

Malibu
Special Events **(2496)** ....(Controlled) 24,408
                                 (Paid) 1,557

San Diego
Journal of Environmental Economics and
  Management **(3190)**

San Francisco
Nonprofit Management and
  Leadership **(3406)** ....(Paid) 1,500
Public Productivity & Management Review **(3418)**

Thousand Oaks
Management Communication
  Quarterly **(3902)** ....(Paid) ‡600
Public Works Management &
  Policy **(3910)** ....(Paid) 4,000

COLORADO
Englewood
MGMA Connexion **(4414)** ....(Controlled) 19,000

CONNECTICUT
Hartford
CBIA News **(4886)** ....‡11,000
The Journal of Private Enterprise **(4896)**

Norwalk
Accessories **(5048)** ....(Paid) 11,000
                                 (Non-paid) 11,000

Southport
Private Power Executive **(5137)**

DELAWARE
Newark
International Journal of Conflict
  Management **(5274)** ....(Paid) 500

DISTRICT OF COLUMBIA
Washington
Air Transport World **(5318)** ......(Controlled) ‡43,300
Association Management **(5370)** ....(Paid) 29,055
Healthplan **(5524)** ....(Paid) ‡6,700
Lodging Magazine **(5640)** ....(Paid) 4,885
                                 (Non-paid) 52,000
Research-Technology
  Management **(5763)** ....(Paid) ‡4,200
                                 (Non-paid) ‡800

FLORIDA
Fort Lauderdale
Journal of Psychotherapy in Independent
  Practice **(6079)** 399

Fort Myers
AFSM International Professional
  Journal **(6093)** 20,000

Miami
Journal of Security
  Administration **(6366)** ....(Paid) 2,500

Naples
Emergence **(6438)**

North Miami
FIU Hospitality Review **(6465)** .....(Controlled) 7,000

St. Petersburg
Florida Marine Research Institute Technical
  Reports **(6626)** ....(Non-paid) 600

GEORGIA
Atlanta
Corporate Cashflow **(6993)** ....(Controlled) 40,000

Marietta
OR/MS Today **(7415)** ....(Combined) 14,268

Tucker
Performance Management Ezine **(7611)** 3,000

HAWAII
Honolulu
Hawaii Business **(7691)** ....(Paid) ‡3,057
                                 (Non-paid) ‡10,197

ILLINOIS
Arlington Heights
FacilityCare **(8023)** ....(Paid) 37,000

Chicago
Journal of AHIMA **(8429)** ....(Paid) 45,000
                                 (Non-paid) 450
The Journal of Medical Practice
  Management **(8446)** ....(Paid) ‡2,430
                                 (Non-paid) ‡110
Materials Management in Health
  Care **(8481)** ....(Non-paid) 30,000

Deerfield
Harmony **(8724)** ....(Combined) 8,000

Evanston
Journal of Economics and Management
  Strategy **(8864)** 1,000

Itasca
Today's Supervisor **(9020)** ....‡80,000

Lincolnshire
Salon Today Magazine **(9088)** ....‡30,000

Normal
Journal of Management
  Education **(9300)** ....(Paid) 1,000

Vernon Hills
Legal Management **(9728)** ....(Controlled) ‡25,200

IOWA
Burlington
Supervision **(10640)** ....‡2,600

Davenport
Operations Research/Management Science **(10737)**

KANSAS
Pittsburg
Journal of Managerial
  Issues **(11752)** ....(Controlled) 1,000

KENTUCKY
Bowling Green
International Journal of Organizational
  Analysis **(11946)** ....(Paid) 450

Frankfort
Workforce Professional **(12077)** ....(Paid) ‡16,000

MARYLAND
Bethesda
Association Trends **(13318)** ....(Paid) ‡4,154
                                 (Free) ‡2,997
North American Journal of Fisheries
  Management **(13366)** ....‡3,200
U.S.A.E. **(13386)** 2,000

Gaithersburg
Quality Management in Health
  Care **(13547)** ....(Paid) 1,400

Linthicum
Management Science **(13622)** ....(Paid) 4,300
M&SOM (Manufacturing & Service Operations
  Management) **(13623)**
OR/MS Today **(13624)**

Silver Spring
Manager's Source Guide **(13737)** 10,000

MASSACHUSETTS
Boston
CFO **(13872)** ....(Controlled) ‡350,000
Harvard Business Review **(13898)** ....(Paid) 249,100

Journal of Transnational Management
   Development **(13919)** ....(Paid) 107

Burlington
European Journal of Purchasing and Supply
   Management **(14027)**

Cambridge
Sloan Management Review **(14101)** ....‡25,000

Concord
Perspective **(14148)** ....‡6,700

Framingham
CIO Magazine **(14192)** ....(Paid) ‡5,052
                  (Controlled) ‡125,000

Newton
Supply Chain Management Review **(14411)**

Norwood
Meeting Planners MarketPlace **(14449)** 78,817

Wellesley Hills
Contingency Planning and Recovery Journal
   (CPR-J) **(14621)**

MICHIGAN
Chelsea
Personnel Management Abstracts **(14877)** ......‡645

Detroit
Journal of Organizational
   Behavior-Management **(14934)**.(Controlled)‡583

Flint
Journal of Leadership and Organizational
   Studies **(15036)**

Okemos
The Corporate Board **(15415)** ....‡4,000

MINNESOTA
Minneapolis
MIS Quarterly **(16110)** ....(Paid) 3,000
                  (Non-paid) 100

NEBRASKA
Lincoln
Journal of Database
   Management **(18087)** ....(Controlled) 300

NEW HAMPSHIRE
Salem
Journal of Innovative
   Management **(18644)** ....(Paid) 2,500
                 (Non-paid) 1,000

NEW JERSEY
Florham Park
Financial Executive **(18825)** 18,000

Hoboken
Human Factors in Ergonomics and
   Manufacturing **(18966)** ....(Combined) 3,325
International Journal of Intelligent Systems in
   Accounting, Finance, and Management **(18987)**
International Journal of Satellite Communications
   Networking **(18997)**
Journal of Multi-Criteria Decision
   Analysis **(19034)** ....(Paid) 3,500
Management Report for Nonunion
   Organizations **(19057)** 5,985
Public Administration and
   Development **(19092)** ....(Paid) 7,000
Strategic Management
   Journal **(19108)** ....(Paid) 28,000
Thunderbird International Business
   Review **(19119)** 5950

Montvale
Chief Executive **(19244)** ....(Controlled) 42,000

NEW MEXICO
Santa Fe
OR Manager **(19939)** ....(Combined) 3,500

NEW YORK
Binghamton
Journal of Convention & Exhibition
   Management **(20168)**
Journal of Promotion Management **(20193)** 305

Ithaca
Administrative Science
   Quarterly **(20787)** ....(Paid) ‡4,600
Coaching
   Management **(20790)** ....(Controlled) ‡109,567

New York
Across the Board **(21144)** ....(Paid) ‡31,600
                 (Non-paid) ‡600
Business Horizons **(21357)** ...:..................3,300
Credit Card Management **(21513)** ....(Paid) 3,252
                (Non-paid) 8,524
Employee Benefit
   News **(21600)** ....(Combined) ‡61,000
Employee Relations Law Journal **(21602)** 5985
Group Decision and Negotiation **(21781)**
Health Care Management Science **(21793)**
The Health Care Manager **(21794)** ......(Paid) 1,899
                  (Free) 66
Journal of Ambulatory Care
   Management **(21981)** ....(Paid) 2,598
                 (Non-paid) 123
Journal of Market-Focused Management **(22122)**
Leaders Magazine **(22242)** ....(Non-paid) ‡35,120
Organizational Dynamics **(22502)** ....(Paid) 3,947
The TV Executive **(22874)** ....(Paid) 100
                 (Non-paid) 8,000

Rensselaerville
Innovating Magazine **(23182)** ....(Paid) ‡800
                 (Non-paid) ‡27

Syracuse
American Journal of Mathematical and Management
   Sciences **(23386)** ....‡1,000

OHIO
Chesterland
Organization Development
   Journal **(24760)** ....(Combined) 720

Cincinnati
Automotive Design and
   Production **(24777)** ....(Non-paid) ‡55,000
The Journal for Quality and
   Participation **(24808)** ....‡5,000

Cleveland
Behavioral Health Management **(24863)** 21,802
Convenience Store Decisions **(24876)** ....‡41,800
IndustryWeek **(24911)** ....(Paid) 7,229
                (Controlled) 233,000
Journal of Systems
   Management **(24917)** ....(Paid) ‡8,000
Nursing Homes **(24934)**

Columbus
Rinksider **(25059)** ....(Paid) ‡750
                 (Non-paid) ‡1,750

Dayton
Manage **(25122)** ....(Controlled) ‡40,000

PENNSYLVANIA
Ardmore
Podiatry Management
   Magazine **(26663)** ....(Paid) ‡541
                 (Non-paid) 15,000

Hershey
Annals of Cases on Information Technology
   (ACIT) **(27039)** ....(Paid) 200

King of Prussia
ADVANCE for Administrators of the
   Laboratory **(27107)**

Narberth
Physicians News Digest **(27310)** ....(Paid) ‡20
               (Controlled) ‡28,809

Newtown Square
PM Network **(27330)** ....(Paid) ‡103,270
               (Non-paid) ‡1,437
Project Management
   Journal **(27332)** ....(Paid) ‡85,000
               (Non-paid) ‡1,437

Philadelphia
Directors & Boards **(27452)** ....(Paid) ‡1,500
               (Non-paid) ‡3,500
Maritime Policy & Management **(27561)**
Work & Stress **(27722)**

Pittsburgh
Mathematics of Operations
   Research **(27812)** ....‡2,800

University Park
Interfaces **(28077)** ....‡6,900

Wayne
Corporate Officers and Directors Liability Litigation
   Reporter **(28131)**

Yardley
Managed Care **(28201)** ....(Controlled) 60,000

SOUTH CAROLINA
Columbia
Journal of Management **(28553)**

TENNESSEE
Knoxville
Information Management Journal **(29272)** 11,000

Nashville
Journal of Service Research **(29464)**

TEXAS
Corpus Christi
SAM Advanced Management
   Journal **(30078)** ....‡5,000

Denton
The Journal of Personal Selling and Sales
   Management **(30240)** ....(Paid) ‡700

Hurst
Self-Employed America **(30602)** ......(Paid) ‡250,000

Lubbock
The Leadership Quarterly **(30714)**

Waco
Entrepreneurship Theory and
   Practice **(31246)** ....‡1,600

VIRGINIA
Alexandria
Airport Magazine **(31632)** 7,000
Balance **(31646)** ....(Combined) 6,900
PaperTronix, Document Management Merging Paper
   & Electronics **(31720)** ....(Paid) 1,874
                (Non-paid) 800

Arlington
Management Quarterly **(31806)**

Chesapeake
Journal of Management Systems **(31965)** 1,200

Reston
Journal of Management in Engineering **(32386)**
Journal of Professional Issues in Engineering
   Education and Practice **(32391)**

Virginia Beach
Journal of Information Technology
   Management **(32587)**

WEST VIRGINIA
Morgantown
Journal of Small Business
   Management **(33395)** ....‡4,500

WISCONSIN
Milwaukee
Quality Management
   Journal **(34095)** ....(Paid) 14,000

NEW BRUNSWICK, CANADA
Fredericton
Journal of Comparative International
   Management **(35396)**

ONTARIO, CANADA
Mississauga
Charitable Business
   Magazine **(36061)** ....(Controlled) 12,000
Church Business **(36062)** ....(Controlled) ‡12,487

Ottawa
Healthcare Management
   Forum **(36247)** ....(Controlled) 3,270

Toronto
Association **(36464)** ....(Combined) 15,000
The Canadian Manager **(36516)** ....(Paid) ‡5,000
               (Controlled) ‡10,000
Investment Executive **(36624)** .....(Controlled) 45,600
Ivey Business Quarterly **(36629)** ....(Paid) ‡8,500
               (Non-paid) ‡6,500
Physician's Management
   Manuals **(36707)** ....(Combined) 41,101

QUEBEC, CANADA
Montreal
Geston **(37120)** ....(Paid) 5,500

Circulation: ★ = ABC; △ = BPA; ♦ = CAC; ● = CCAB; ❑ = VAC; ⊕ = PO Statement; ‡ = Publisher's Report; Boldface figures = sworn; Light figures = estimated.

3183

Circ.   Circ.   Circ.

MARRIAGE AND FAMILY

CALIFORNIA
San Diego
San Diego Family
  Magazine **(3263)** ....(Free) ‡119,862
                            (Paid) ‡143

Thousand Oaks
Journal of Family Issues **(3889)** ....(Paid) ‡800

COLORADO
Colorado Springs
Focus on the Family
  Magazine **(4247)** ....(Free) 2,200,000

Fort Collins
Journal of Feminist Family Therapy **(4435)**

DISTRICT OF COLUMBIA
Washington
Journal of Family Psychology **(5591)** ....‡4,700

HAWAII
Honolulu
Population Reports **(7718)**

ILLINOIS
Downers Grove
Matrimony **(8790)**

Normal
Personal Relationships **(9303)** ....(Paid) ‡567
                           (Non-paid) ‡74

INDIANA
Hammond
Journal of Family Psychotherapy **(10052)** 479

Indianapolis
Marriage and Family Review **(10150)** .....(Paid) 589

MINNESOTA
Minneapolis
Family Relations **(16077)** ....‡5,000
Journal of Marriage and Family **(16088)** ......‡7,500

St. Paul
Marriage Magazine **(16387)** 11,000

NEW YORK
Binghamton
Journal of Family Social Work **(20173)** 654

New York
Guttmacher Report on Public Policy **(21784)**

OHIO
Cleveland
Domestic Relations Journal of Ohio **(24882)**

TENNESSEE
Franklin
Above Rubies **(29193)** ....(Non-paid) ‡130,000

VIRGINIA
Norfolk
Journal of Family Communication **(32286)**

WISCONSIN
Milwaukee
Life Without Limits **(34073)** ....(Non-paid) ⊕35,000

ALBERTA, CANADA
Calgary
Journal of Comparative Family Studies **(34651)**

NEWFOUNDLAND AND LABRADOR, CANADA
Pouch Cove
Resource Links **(35481)**

MATERIALS HANDLING

CONNECTICUT
Stamford
Operations and Fulfillment **(5157)** .....(Paid) ‡13,000

ILLINOIS
East Peoria
Material Handling Network **(8806)** ....(Paid) 155
                         (Non-paid) 13,475

Northbrook
Journal of Nuclear Materials
  Management **(9318)** ....(Paid) ‡8,000

MASSACHUSETTS
Newton
Modern Materials
  Handling **(14406)** ....(Non-paid) ‡105,841

NEW JERSEY
Morris Plains
Material Handling Product
  News **(19297)** ....(Controlled) 90,000

NEW YORK
Stony Brook
Journal of Thermal Spray
  Technology **(23371)** ....(Paid) ⊕481
                        (Non-paid) 199

OHIO
Cleveland
Material Handling
  Management **(24925)** ....(Non-paid) 95,000
                        (Paid) 95,497

VIRGINIA
Ashland
Pallet Enterprise **(31857)** ....(Paid) ‡150
                        (Controlled) ‡14,000

Reston
Journal of Materials in Civil Engineering **(32387)**

ONTARIO, CANADA
Toronto
Materials Management &
  Distribution **(36658)** ....(Combined) 19,226

QUEBEC, CANADA
Ste.-Therese
Logistics Magazine **(37369)** ....(Combined) 21,919

MATHEMATICS

See also Statistics

ALABAMA
Birmingham
Russian Journal of Mathematical
  Physics **(89)** 5985

CALIFORNIA
Berkeley
Probability in the Engineering and Informational
  Sciences **(1552)** 350

El Monte
Journal of Fuzzy Mathematics **(1866)**

Emeryville
Mathematics in Education and Research **(1878)**

La Jolla
Mathematical Research
  Letters **(2117)** ....(Combined) 250

Los Angeles
Pacific Journal of Mathematics **(2356)**

Palo Alto
Journal of Oughtred Society **(2797)** ....(Paid) 400

San Diego
Advances in Applied Mathematics **(3107)**
Applied and Computational Harmonic Analysis **(3115)**
Finite Fields and Their Applications **(3154)**
Historia Mathematica **(3167)**
Journal of Algebra **(3176)**
Journal of Algorithms **(3177)**
Journal of Approximation Theory **(3180)**
Journal of Colloid and Interface Science **(3181)**
Journal of Combinatorial Theory, Series A **(3182)**
Journal of Combinatorial Theory, Series B **(3183)**
Journal of Complexity **(3184)**
Journal of Computational Physics **(3185)**
Journal of Computer and System Sciences **(3186)**
Journal of Differential Equations **(3187)**
Journal of Functional Analysis **(3197)**
Journal of Mathematical Psychology **(3204)**
Journal of Multivariate Analysis **(3207)**
Journal of Number Theory **(3209)**

Santa Monica
Journal of Applied Mathematics and Decision
  Sciences **(3712)**

Stanford
Communications in Partial Differential
  Equations **(3795)** 625

Thousand Oaks
Simulation & Gaming **(3916)** ....(Paid) ‡600

CONNECTICUT
Danbury
Scholastic DynaMath **(4754)** ....‡235,000
Scholastic MATH Magazine **(4755)** ....‡200,000

Storrs Mansfield
The IMS Bulletin **(5171)** ....(Paid) 4,200

DISTRICT OF COLUMBIA
Washington
American Mathematical Monthly **(5335)** ......‡20,000
College Mathematics Journal **(5424)**
Journal of Online Mathematics and Its
  Applications **(5607)**
Mathematics Magazine **(5645)**

FLORIDA
Miami
International Journal of Mathematical and Statistical
  Sciences **(6363)**

Orlando
Numerical Functional Analysis and
  Optimization **(6501)** 400

Palm Harbor
Algebras, Groups &
  Geometries **(6550)** ....(Paid) 200

Ponte Vedra Beach
The International Journal of Logistics
  Management **(6595)** 2,000

Tampa
Journal of Theoretical
  Probability **(6772)** ....(Paid) 350

ILLINOIS
Chicago
Mathematical Finance **(8482)** ....‡800

Urbana
Illinois Journal of
  Mathematics **(9709)** ....(Paid) ‡1,200

INDIANA
Bloomington
Indiana University Mathematics
  Journal **(9837)** ....(Paid) 630
                        (Non-paid) 165

IOWA
Webster City
Modern Logic: International Journal for the History of
  Mathematical Logic, Set Theory, and Foundation of
  Mathematics **(11314)** ....(Paid) 125
                        (Non-paid) 20

KANSAS
Emporia
The Pentagon **(11431)** ....(Paid) 3,000

MARYLAND
Baltimore
American Journal of Mathematics **(13118)** 1,200

College Park
CHAOS **(13414)**

Silver Spring
Science Weekly **(13745)**

MASSACHUSETTS
Boston
The Bulletin of Symbolic Logic **(13868)** ....‡2,500

Cambridge
Econometrica **(14050)** ....‡7,000
Information and Computation **(14070)**

Massachusetts
Advances in Mathematics **(14312)**

Natick
Experimental Mathematics **(14346)** ....(Paid) 500

Somerville
Advances in Theoretical and Mathematics
  Physics **(14530)**
Asian Journal of
  Mathematics **(14531)** ....(Combined) 1,100

Journal of Differential
Geometry **(14535)** ....(Combined) 1,250
Methods and Applications of
Analysis **(14536)** ....(Combined) 100

Worcester
Pi Mu Epsilon Journal **(14686)** .....(Controlled) 3,600

MICHIGAN
Ann Arbor
Michigan Mathematical
Journal **(14766)** ....(Paid) 900

MISSOURI
Chesterfield
Journal of Parametrics **(16975)** 650

NEW JERSEY
Hoboken
Applied Stochastic Models in Business and
Industry **(18894)**
Communications in Numerical Methods in
Engineering **(18918)**
Communications on Pure and Applied
Mathematics **(18919)** 10,150
Complexity **(18920)** 14,000
Environmetrics **(18942)**
International Journal of Adaptive Control and Signal
Processing **(18975)**
International Journal of Circuit Theory and
Applications **(18978)**
International Journal for Numerical and Analytical
Methods in Geomechanics **(18989)**
International Journal for Numerical Methods in
Engineering **(18990)**
International Journal for Numerical Methods in
Fluids **(18991)**
Journal of Chemometrics **(19011)** ....(Paid) 4,200
Journal of Combinatorial Designs **(19015)** 2800
Journal of Graph Theory **(19025)** 6230
Mathematical Methods in the Applied
Sciences **(19059)**
Naval Research Logistics **(19070)** 7000
Numerical Linear Algebra with Applications **(19075)**
Numerical Methods for Partial Differential
Equations **(19076)** 4200
Random Structures & Algorithms **(19095)** 3850
Systems and Computers in Japan **(19115)** .....‡300

Mahwah
Mathematical Thinking and Learning **(19201)**

New Brunswick
Studies in Nonlinear Dynamics and
Econometrics **(19341)**

Princeton
Annals of Mathematics **(19453)** ....‡2,000

River Edge
Journal of Computational Geometry and
Applications **(19515)**
Journal of Knot Theory and Its Ramifications
(JKTR) **(19516)**

NEW MEXICO
Rehoboth
Smarandache Notions
Journal **(19912)** ....(Combined) 1,000

NEW YORK
Albany
New York Journal of Mathematics **(19995)**

Amityville
Journal of Recreational Mathematics **(20047)**

Geneseo
SUNY Geneseo Journal of Science and
Mathematics **(20650)**

New York
Acta Numerica **(21145)** ....(Paid) ‡148
(Non-paid) ‡5
Adsorption **(21151)**
Advances in Computational Mathematics **(21154)**
Algebra and Logic **(21171)**
Algebras and Representation Theory **(21172)**
Algorithmica **(21173)** ....(Combined) 700
Applications of Mathematics **(21227)**
Applied Mathematics and Mechanics **(21230)**
Applied Mathematics and
Optimization **(21231)** ....(Combined) 650
Approximation Theory and Its Applications **(21234)**
Bulletin of the London Mathematical Society **(21351)**
Collected Algorithms (CALGO) Supplements **(21437)**
Communications in Statistics: Simulation &
Computation **(21460)** 725

Communications in Statistics: Theory &
Methods **(21461)** 800
Computational Geosciences **(21469)**
Computational & Mathematical Organization
Theory **(21470)**
Computational Mathematics and Modeling **(21471)**
Constructive
Approximation **(21489)** ....(Combined) 450
Czechoslovak Mathematical Journal **(21530)**
Differential Equations **(21551)**
Discrete and Computational
Geometry **(21557)** ....(Combined) 600
Ergodic Theory and Dynamical
Systems **(21626)** 600
European Journal of Applied
Mathematics **(21639)** 350
Functional Analysis and Its Applications **(21741)**
Georgian Mathematical Journal **(21756)**
International Journal of Computers for Mathematical
Learning **(21904)**
Journal of Algebraic Combinatorics **(21980)**
Journal of Combinatorial Optimization **(22030)**
Journal of Computational Analysis and
Applications **(22034)**
Journal of Cryptology **(22042)** ......(Combined) 1,800
Journal of Dynamic and Control Systems **(22050)**
Journal of Dynamics and Differential
Equations **(22052)**
Journal of Engineering Mathematics **(22063)**
Journal of Experimental Algorithmics (JEA) **(22067)**
Journal of Fluid Mechanics **(22070)** 1700
Journal of the London Mathematical
Society **(22116)** ....(Paid) ‡894
(Non-paid) ‡432
Journal of Mathematical Chemistry **(22126)**
Journal of Mathematical Imaging and Vision **(22127)**
Journal of Mathematical Science **(22128)**
Journal of Mathematics Teacher Education **(22129)**
K-Theory **(22217)**
Letters in Mathematical Physics **(22247)**
Lithuanian Mathematical Journal **(22262)**
LMS Journal of Computation and
Mathematics **(22264)**
The Mathematical Intelligencer **(22294)** 4,500
Mathematical Notes of the Academy of Sciences of
the USSR **(22295)**
Mathematical Physics, Analysis and
Geometry **(22296)**
Mathematical Proceedings of the Cambridge
Philosophical Society **(22297)**
Mathematical Structures in Computer
Science **(22298)** 350
Open Systems & Information Dynamics **(22495)**
Order **(22501)**
Positivity **(22585)**
Potential Analysis **(22586)**
Quantitative Microbiology **(22616)**
Reliable Computing **(22644)**
Semigroup Forum **(22723)** ....(Combined) 500
Sequential Analysis **(22731)** ....(Paid) 325
Siberian Mathematical Journal **(22739)**
Stochastic Models **(22792)** ....(Paid) 600
Theoretical and Mathematical Physics **(22828)**
Theory of Computing
Systems **(22830)** ....(Combined) 650
Ukrainian Mathematical Journal **(22881)**

Poughkeepsie
The Journal of Symbolic Logic **(23147)** ....‡2,500

Syracuse
American Journal of Mathematical and Management
Sciences **(23386)** ....‡1,000

NORTH CAROLINA
Durham
Duke Mathematical Journal **(23819)** ....‡915
IMRN **(23827)** ....(Paid) 237

Greensboro
Integers **(23924)**

OHIO
Beachwood
The Annals of Applied Probability **(24648)** 2,200
The Annals of Probability **(24649)** ....‡2,700

Columbus
School Science and Mathematics **(25061)** .....‡3500

PENNSYLVANIA
Philadelphia
Cybernetics and
Systems **(27447)** ....(Combined) ‡341
International Journal of Mathematical Education in
Science and Technology **(27501)**
SIAM Journal on Applied
Mathematics **(27678)** ....‡2,573

SIAM Journal on Computing **(27679)** ....‡2,076
SIAM Journal on Control and
Optimization **(27680)** ....‡1,993
SIAM Journal on Discrete
Mathematics **(27681)** ....‡1,758
SIAM Journal on Mathematical
Analysis **(27682)** ....‡1,754
SIAM Journal on Matrix Analysis and
Applications **(27683)** ....‡1,623
SIAM Journal on Numerical
Analysis **(27684)** ....‡2,482
SIAM Journal on Optimization **(27685)** ....‡1,736
SIAM Journal on Scientific
Computing **(27686)** ....‡2,152
SIAM News **(27687)** ....(Paid) ‡9,161
(Non-paid) ‡512
SIAM Review **(27688)** ....‡11,669
Theory of Probability and Its
Applications **(27704)** ....‡1,609

Pittsburgh
Mathematics of Operations
Research **(27812)** ....‡2,800

RHODE ISLAND
Providence
Abstracts of Papers Presented to the American
Mathematical Society **(28384)** ....(Paid) ‡2,640
Bulletin (New Series) of the American Mathematical
Society **(28392)** ....(Paid) 25,937
Current Mathematical
Publications **(28394)** ....(Paid) ‡1,180
Employment Information in the Mathematical
Sciences **(28396)** ....(Paid) ‡580
Journal of Algebraic Geometry **(28401)**
Journal of the American Mathematical
Society **(28402)** 987
Mathematical Reviews **(28404)** ....(Paid) ‡1,500
Mathematics of
Computation **(28405)** ....(Paid) ‡1,567
Memoirs of the American Mathematical
Society **(28409)** ....(Paid) ‡645
Notices of the American Mathematical
Society **(28410)** ....(Paid) ‡33,008
Proceedings of the American Mathematical
Society **(28413)** ....(Paid) ‡1,300
St. Petersburg Mathematical
Journal **(28423)** ....(Paid) ‡115
Sugaku Expositions **(28424)** ....(Paid) ‡200
Theory of Probability & Mathematical
Statistics **(28425)** ....(Paid) ‡225
Transactions of the American Mathematical
Society **(28426)** ....(Paid) ‡1,200
Transactions of the Moscow Mathematical
Society **(28427)** ....(Paid) ‡340

SOUTH CAROLINA
Clemson
The Electronic Journal of Combinatorics **(28532)**

SOUTH DAKOTA
Aurora
The Fibonacci Quarterly **(28806)** .....(Combined) 830

TEXAS
Arlington
Libertas Mathematica **(29734)** 200

Houston
Houston Journal of Mathematics **(30487)** ....‡460
Journal of Optimization Theory and
Applications **(30497)**

VIRGINIA
Alexandria
Journal of Computational and Graphical
Statistics **(31690)**

Arlington
Quantum **(31822)**

Reston
Journal for Research in Mathematics
Education **(32393)** ....‡11,844
The Mathematics Teacher **(32403)** .....(Paid) 49,000
Mathematics-Teaching in the Middle
School **(32404)** ....(Paid) 36,000
Teaching Children Mathematics **(32417)** 48,000

WISCONSIN
Madison
Substance **(33975)** ....(Paid) 500

Milwaukee
Communications in Algebra **(34063)** 725

Circulation: ★ = ABC; △ = BPA; ♦ = CAC; ● = CCAB; ❏ = VAC; ⊕ = PO Statement; ‡ = Publisher's Report; Boldface figures = sworn; Light figures = estimated.

3185

Trade, Technical, and Professional Publications

Circ.   Circ.   Circ.

MATHEMATICS (continued)

BRITISH COLUMBIA, CANADA
Vancouver
Canadian Journal of Mathematics **(35132)** 1,226

Victoria
YES Mag **(35231)** ....(Paid) 18,000

MANITOBA, CANADA
Winnipeg
Ars Combinatoria **(35310)**

ONTARIO, CANADA
London
Ontario Mathematics
  Gazette **(35991)** ....(Paid) 1,200

Ottawa
Crux Mathematicorum with Mathematical
  Mayhem **(36240)** 800
Physics Essays **(36272)** ....‡171

Toronto
Canadian Mathematical
  Bulletin **(36517)** ....(Paid) 775

MEDICINE AND SURGERY

See also Chiropractic; Drugs and
Pharmaceuticals; Health and Healthcare;
Hospitals and Healthcare Institutions;
Laboratory Research (Scientific and
Medical); Osteopathy; Physiology and
Anatomy; Podiatry; Psychology and
Psychiatry; Substance Abuse and
Treatment; Toxicology

ALABAMA
Birmingham
Southern Medical Journal **(97)** ....‡21,500

ARIZONA
Phoenix
AZ Med **(793)** ....(Controlled) 5,000

ARKANSAS
Little Rock
Arkansas Pharmacist **(1219)**
Drug Metabolism Reviews **(1228)** 800
The Journal of the Arkansas Medical
  Society **(1231)** ....(Paid) ‡3,000
                     (Non-paid) ‡1,200

CALIFORNIA
Berkeley
Journal of Lipid Research **(1535)** ....(Paid) ‡2,029

Davis
American Journal of Clinical
  Nutrition **(1810)** ....‡7,934
Clinical Reviews in Allergy & Immunology **(1813)**

Encinitas
Alternative Therapies in Health and
  Medicine **(1882)** ....(Paid) 14,000

Irvine
Biomedical Optics **(2076)**
Ostomy Quarterly **(2088)** ....‡30,000

La Jolla
Annals of Behavioral Medicine **(2112)** ....‡3,000

Long Beach
Journal of Electrocardiology **(2170)** .....(Paid) 1,000

Los Angeles
Endocrinology **(2264)** ....(Paid) ‡4,540
                     (Non-paid) ‡453
LACMA Physician **(2314)** ....(Paid) ‡10,154
                     (Non-paid) ‡651
Ophthalmology Journal **(2352)** 25,498
Plastic Surgery
  Products **(2369)** ....(Controlled) 12,000

Menlo Park
The Pharos **(2525)** ....(Controlled) 70,000

Mission Viejo
Medical Industry Information
  Report **(2555)** ....(Controlled) 16,500

Oakland
Alameda-Contra Medical
  Association **(2663)** ....(Non-paid) 3,000

Palo Alto
Annual Review of Medicine **(2791)**

Playa del Rey
Cancer Victors Journal **(2851)** ....(Paid) ‡20,000

Riverside
Women's Imaging **(2949)**

Sacramento
California Journal of Health-System Pharmacy **(2984)**
Sierra Sacramento Valley
  Medicine **(3019)** ....(Controlled) 2,000

San Diego
Blood Cells, Molecules, & Diseases **(3122)**
Brain, Behavior, and Immunity **(3124)**
Brain and Cognition **(3125)**
Cryobiology **(3137)**
Epilepsy & Behavior **(3146)**
Fire-Rescue Magazine **(3155)** ....(Paid) 9,709
                    (Non-paid) 35,991
Gynecologic Oncology **(3166)**
JEMS **(3175)** ....(Paid) 28,000
                   (Controlled) 12,000
Journal of Invertebrate Pathology **(3199)**
Journal of Surgical Research **(3214)**
Molecular Genetics and Metabolism **(3235)**
Molecular Therapy **(3237)**
Neurobiology of Disease **(3239)**
Real-Time Imaging **(3253)**
San Diego County Physician **(3261)** .....(Paid) 3,000
Virology **(3288)**

San Francisco
Anesthesia & Analgesia **(3326)** ....‡22,084
California Family Physician **(3336)** ....‡7,000
Journal of Cardiac Failure **(3378)**
Pain Management Nursing **(3411)**
San Francisco Medicine **(3436)**

Santa Monica
Neonatal Intensive Care **(3713)**

Santa Rosa
Sonoma Medicine **(3735)** ....(Combined) 1,000

Stockton
IAL News **(3805)** ....(Non-paid) 8,000

Thousand Oaks
AWHONN Lifelines **(3851)** ....(Paid) 21,500
Journal of the American Medical Directors Association
  (JAMDA) **(3878)** ....(Paid) 7,200
Journal of the Association of Nurses in AIDS
  Care **(3880)** ....(Paid) ‡3,000
The Journal of Diagnostic Medical Sonography
  (JDMS) **(3887)** ....(Paid) 14,000
Journal of Neuroimaging **(3895)** ....(Paid) 1,100
Neurohabilitation and Neural
  Repair **(3904)** ....(Paid) 1,100
                    (Non-paid) 50

Torrance
Contemporary
  Orthopaedics **(3930)** ....(Non-paid) 30,000
Contemporary Surgery **(3931)** .....(Combined) 48,876
                  (Combined) 50,077
Emergency **(3933)** 29,000

Van Nuys
Dialysis &
  Transplantation **(3987)** ....(Non-paid) △22,701
Emergency Medical Services **(3988)** 48,125

COLORADO
Boulder
Nutrition Science News **(4182)** ....(Combined) 21,000

Dencer
Journal of Asthma **(4303)** ....(Paid) 8,500

Denver
American Journal of Bariatric
  Medicine **(4304)** ....(Controlled) 1,800
Colorado Medicine **(4317)** 5,500
Primary Care Case Reviews **(4349)**
Seminars in Hearing **(4356)** ....(Paid) 2,155
                    (Non-paid) 78
SSM **(4358)** ....(Combined) 14,000

Dillon
Binocular Vision & Strabismus
  Quarterly **(4399)** ....(Combined) 800

Englewood
MGMA Connexion **(4414)** ....(Controlled) 19,000

Littleton
The Journal of Pediatric Pharmacology and
  Therapeutics **(4549)**

Silverthorne
Seminars in Vascular Surgery **(4625)** ....‡2,006

CONNECTICUT
Darien
American Journal of Geriatric
  Cardiology **(4769)** ....(Controlled) 20,000
Cardiovascular Reviews &
  Reports **(4770)** ....(Controlled) ‡81,107
Congestive Heart
  Failure **(4771)** ....(Controlled) ‡20,000

Farmington
Acta Haematologica **(4794)** 1,300
American Journal of Nephrology **(4795)** 2,900
Analytic Psychology **(4796)** 1,700
Annals of Nutrition and Metabolism **(4797)** 1,250
Audiology and Neuro-Otology **(4798)** 1,650
Biology of the Neonate **(4799)** 1,150
Blood Purification **(4800)** 950
Brain, Behavior and Evolution **(4801)** 1,000
Cardiology **(4802)** 1,300
Cells Tissues Organs **(4804)** 1,200
Cellular Physiology and
  Biochemistry **(4805)** ....‡1,450
Cerebrovascular Diseases **(4806)** ....‡1,050
Chemotherapy **(4807)** 1,300
Chirurgische
  Gastroenterologie **(4808)** ....(Combined) 4,000
Community Genetics **(4809)** ....(Combined) 1,000
Cytogenetics and Cell Genetics **(4810)** 1,800
Dementia and Geriatric Cognitive
  Disorders **(4811)** ....‡1,050
Dermatologica Helvetica **(4812)** ....(Combined) 500
Dermatology **(4813)** ....‡2,350
Dermatology Psychosomatics **(4814)**
Developmental Neuroscience **(4815)** 800
Digestion **(4816)** ....‡800
Digestive Diseases **(4817)** 1,500
Digestive Surgery **(4818)** 3,500
European Addiction
  Research **(4819)** ....(Combined) 1,000
European Neurology **(4820)** 1,050
European Surgical Research **(4821)** 800
Fetal Diagnosis and Therapy **(4823)** 1,100
Folia Phoniatrica et Logopaedica **(4824)** 1,100
Forschende Komplementarmedizin und Klassische
  Naturheilkunde **(4826)** ....(Combined) 4,000
Gynaekologisch-geburtshilfliche
  Rundschau **(4828)** 1,750
Gynecologic and Obstetric
  Investigation **(4829)** 950
HeartDrug **(4830)**
Hormone Research **(4831)** 1,250
Human Development **(4832)** 1,950
Human Heredity **(4833)** 1,000
International Archives of Allergy and
  Immunology **(4834)** 1,400
Intervirology **(4835)** 800
Journal of Biomedical Science **(4836)**
Journal of Vascular Research **(4838)** 1,800
Kidney and Blood Pressure
  Research **(4839)** 1,950
Medical Principles and Practice **(4840)** 1,950
Nephron **(4841)** 3,050
Neuroendocrinology **(4842)** 1,650
Neuroepidemiology **(4843)** 800
Neuroimmunomodulation **(4844)**
Neuropsychobiology **(4845)** 1,000
Neurosignals **(4846)** 800
Oncology **(4847)** 1,250
Onkologie **(4848)** 800
ORL **(4851)** 850
Oto-Rhino-Laryngologia Nova **(4852)** ....‡1,000
Pathobiology **(4853)** 1,050
Pediatric Neurosurgery **(4854)** 1,150
Phonetica **(4856)** 1,150
Psychopathology **(4857)** 800
Psychotherapy and Psychosomatics **(4858)** 1,000
Respiration **(4859)** 1,200
Skin Pharmacology and Applied Skin
  Physiology **(4860)** 1,000
Stereotactic and Functional
  Neurosurgery **(4861)** 1,050
Tumor Biology **(4862)** 1,000
Urologia Internationalis **(4863)** 2,000
Verhaltenstherapie **(4864)** ....‡4,000

Madison
Journal of Developmental and Learning
  Disorders **(4932)**

New Haven
Connecticut Medicine **(4986)** 7,200
The Yale Journal of Biology &
  Medicine **(5005)** ....‡600

Numbers cited after listings are entry numbers rather than page numbers.

Shelton
American Clinical
 Laboratory **(5118)** ....(Non-paid) ‡43,567

Wilton
Critical Care
 International **(5224)** ....(Controlled) ‡26,000

DELAWARE
Newark
Delaware Medical Journal **(5271)** ....(Paid) 1,800
(Free) 24

DISTRICT OF COLUMBIA
Washington
Academic Medicine **(5313)** ....‡5,900
Antimicrobial Agents and
 Chemotherapy **(5355)** ....(Paid) ‡5,810
(Non-paid) ‡30
Behavioral Medicine **(5374)** 552
Clinical and Diagnostic Laboratory
 Immunology **(5419)** ....(Paid) 938
Good Medicine Magazine **(5516)**
Infection and Immunity **(5543)** ....(Combined) ‡4,240
Journal of Motor Behavior **(5602)** ....(Paid) 986
Journal of the National Medical
 Association **(5603)** ....(Paid) 6,000
(Controlled) 31,000
The Journal of
 Neuroscience **(5606)** ....(Paid) ‡3,341
(Non-paid) ‡303
Journals of Gerontology **(5620)**
Minority Health Today **(5652)**
Modern Drug Discovery **(5656)**
Seminars in Hematology **(5788)** ....‡6,377
State Health Monitor **(5804)**
Today's Internist **(5825)** ....(Paid) ‡20,979
(Non-paid) ‡15,013
U.S. Medicine **(5835)** ....(Paid) 70
(Free) 40,192

FLORIDA
Boca Raton
Medical Marketing &
 Media **(5936)** ....(Controlled) ‡10,000

Fort Myers
Children's Health Care **(6094)**

Miami
Seminars in Arthritis and
 Rheumatism **(6379)** ....‡4,072

Naples
Operative Techniques in Thoracic and Cardiovascular
 Surgery **(6448)**
Seminars in Thoracic and Cardiovascular
 Surgery **(6449)**

Orlando
Flying Physician **(6495)**
The Journal of Human Performance in Extreme
 Environments **(6499)** ....(Paid) 200

Tallahassee
Florida Medical Association **(6715)**

Tampa
Cancer Control Journal **(6759)**
The Journal of Craniofacial
 Surgery **(6770)** ....(Paid) 2,000
Journal of Mental Health and
 Aging **(6771)** ....(Combined) 300

GEORGIA
Atlanta
Blood Weekly **(6980)**
The Complete European Trade Digest Medical
 Edition **(6991)**
Emerging Infectious Diseases **(7003)**
Journal of the Medical Association of
 Georgia **(7022)** 8,000
Stem Cell Week **(7046)**

Augusta
Journal of PeriAnesthesia Nursing **(7100)**
Seminars in Laparoscopic Surgery **(7102)** .....‡1,172

Milledgeville
The Pre- & Perinatal Psychology Journal **(7435)**

HAWAII
Honolulu
Hawaii Medical Journal **(7697)** ....‡1800

IDAHO
Dover
Alternative Medicine Review **(7852)** ....(Paid) ⊕7,500

ILLINOIS
Arlington Heights
Journal of Occupational and Environmental
 Medicine **(8025)** ....(Paid) 9,200
(Non-paid) 170

Champaign
Athletic Therapy Today **(8181)** 3,000
Motor Control **(8204)** ....(Paid) ‡307

Chicago
AMA Alliance Today **(8251)** .....(Controlled) ‡40,000
American Medical News **(8260)** ......(Paid) 332,331
(Non-paid) 7,685
Archives of
 Dermatology **(8267)** ....(Combined) ‡14,515
Archives of Internal
 Medicine **(8268)** ....(Combined) ‡103,271
Archives of Otolaryngology–Head & Neck
 Surgery **(8270)** ....(Combined) ‡12,086
Archives of Pathology & Laboratory
 Medicine **(8271)** ....(Paid) ‡3,070
(Controlled) ‡13,274
Archives of Pediatrics & Adolescent
 Medicine **(8272)** ....(Combined) ‡30,334
Archives of Physical Medicine and
 Rehabilitation **(8273)** 11,500
Archives of Surgery **(8274)**
Chicago Medicine **(8318)** ....(Paid) 10,915
The Diabetes Educator **(8353)** ....(Paid) ‡12,300
(Non-paid) ‡200
Headache Quarterly **(8391)** ....(Paid) ‡3,500
Health Data Management **(8392)**
Hospitals & Health Networks **(8401)**
JAMA **(8424)** ....‡348,746
The Journal of Medical Practice
 Management **(8446)** ....(Paid) ‡2,430
(Non-paid) ‡110
Modern Physician **(8492)**
Ultrastructural Pathology **(8590)** 779

Chicago Heights
Journal of Irreproducible Results **(8667)** ....‡5,000

Des Plaines
Critical Care Medicine **(8757)** ....(Paid) 14,089
(Non-paid) ‡351

Elgin
International Journal of Dermatology **(8824)**

Lyons
Human Gene Therapy **(9124)**

Northbrook
AWHP's Worksite
 Health **(9312)** ....(Controlled) 2,900

Oak Brook
RadioGraphics **(9363)** 28,000

Oak Park
Doody's Health Sciences Book Review
 Journal **(9374)** ....(Paid) 750
(Non-paid) 100

Park Ridge
AANA Journal **(9403)** ....(Paid) ‡627
(Non-paid) ‡30,120
AMT Events **(9404)** ....(Controlled) 26,000

Schaumburg
MEEN Diagnostic and Invasive
 Technology **(9586)** ....(Combined) 29,104
MEEN Imaging Technology News **(9587)** 36,961

Springfield
The Journal of Legal
 Medicine **(9637)** ....(Paid) ‡1,622
The Post-Abortion
 Review **(9641)** ....(Controlled) 1050
Teaching and Learning in Medicine **(9643)**

INDIANA
Indianapolis
American Journal of Physical Medicine and
 Rehabilitation **(10078)** ....(Paid) ‡4,091
(Non-paid) ‡216
The Journal of Cognitive
 Rehabilitation **(10139)** 1,000
Journal of Pediatric Surgery **(10141)** ....‡2,900
Journal of Stroke and Cerebrovascular
 Diseases **(10142)**
Medical Care **(10152)** ....(Paid) 2,293
Medicine and Science in Sports and
 Exercise **(10153)** ....(Paid) ‡14,000
(Non-paid) ‡128
Seminars in Pediatric Surgery **(10170)**
Seminars in Respiratory Infections **(10171)**

Terre Haute
Issues in Law & Medicine **(10487)** ......(Paid) 1,000
(Controlled) 2,000

IOWA
Iowa City
Arteriosclerosis, Thrombosis, and Vascular
 Biology **(10969)** ....‡3,242

Lamoni
Annals of Plastic Surgery **(11027)** 2,020

West Des Moines
Iowa Medicine **(11320)** ....(Paid) 4,297
(Non-paid) 150

KANSAS
Lawrence
Ambulatory Pediatrics **(11546)**
American Journal of Cosmetic
 Surgery **(11547)** ....‡3,000

Leawood
American Family
 Physician **(11583)** ....(Controlled) 179,315
Family Practice Management **(11584)** ....‡97,348

Overland Park
Home Care Magazine **(11714)**

KENTUCKY
Lexington
Aphasiology **(12159)**
Journal of Oral and Maxillofacial
 Surgery **(12168)** ....‡10,037

Louisville
Journal of Cardiothoracic and Vascular
 Anesthesia **(12220)**
Journal of the Kentucky Medical
 Association **(12221)** ....(Controlled) ⊕6,234
Unique Opportunities **(12242)** .....(Controlled) 80,000

LOUISIANA
New Orleans
Health Sciences at
 Tulane **(12732)** ....(Non-paid) 21,000
Journal for Minority Medical
 Students **(12735)** ....(Non-paid) 10,000
The Ochsner Journal **(12749)** ......(Combined) 9,496

MAINE
Yarmouth
HME News **(13079)** ....(Paid) △17,100

MARYLAND
Baltimore
Advances in Anatomic Pathology **(13108)** 1,550
Advances in Gastroenterology, Hepatology and
 Clinical Nutrition **(13109)**
Alzheimer Disease and Associated
 Disorders **(13112)** 692
American Journal of Epidemiology **(13116)** ....‡6,100
The American Journal of Surgical Pathology
 (AJSP) **(13119)** 6,865
Applied Immunohistochemistry & Molecular
 Morphology **(13125)** 1,064
Bulletin of the History of Medicine **(13140)** ....‡2,394
CA: A Cancer Journal for
 Clinicians **(13141)** ....‡150,000
Cardiovascular and Thoracic Anesthesia
 Journal **(13142)**
Caring for the Ages **(13143)** ....(Paid) 47,946
Clinical and Applied
 Thrombosis/Hemostasis **(13145)** 878
Clinical Orthopaedics and Related
 Research **(13149)** ....(Paid) 10,150
Diagnostic Molecular Pathology **(13156)** 1,073
Emergency Medicine News **(13158)** ....(Paid) 25,060
Inflammatory Bowel Diseases **(13171)** 3,829
Johns Hopkins
 Magazine **(13174)** ....(Controlled) ‡121,000
Journal of Bronchology **(13180)** 1,549
Journal of Cerebral Blood Flow and
 Metabolism **(13182)** 1,151
Journal of Clinical Neuromuscular
 Disease **(13184)** 800
Journal of Clinical Neurophysiology **(13185)** 1,637
Journal of Nervous and Mental
 Disease **(13195)** ....(Combined) ‡1,698
Journal of Neurosurgical
 Anesthesiology **(13196)** 914
Journal of Pediatric Gastroenterology &
 Nutrition **(13198)** ....(Paid) 2,076
Journal of Pediatric Orthopaedics **(13200)** 2,560
Journal of Urology **(13204)** ....(Paid) ‡18,356
(Non-paid) ‡423
Literature and Medicine **(13210)** 606

Circulation: ★ = ABC; △ = BPA; ◆ = CAC; ● = CCAB; ❏ = VAC; ⊕ = PO Statement; ‡ = Publisher's Report; Boldface figures = sworn; Light figures = estimated.

3187

Circ.

MEDICINE AND SURGERY (continued)

Maryland Medical Journal (13212) ....‡7,500
Medicine (13216) ....(Paid) ‡3,381
                                        (Non-paid) ‡135
Menopause (13217) 2,639
Molecular Medicine (13221) ....(Combined) 500
Obstetric Anesthesia Digest (13226) 1,010
Oncology Times (13227) 45,000
The Otolaryngology Journal (13229) 1,025
Otology & Neurotology (13230) ....(Paid) 1,464
The Pain Medicine Journal (13231) 1,000
Pathology Case Reviews (13233) ....(Paid) 1,327
Pediatric Critical Care Medicine (13234) 1,700
Sports Medicine and Arthroscopy
  Review (13249) 1,404
                                                934
Techniques in Neurosurgery (13251) 909
Techniques in Orthopaedics (13252) 2955
Topics in Magnetic Resonance Imaging
  (TMRI) (13255) 3,031
World Federation for Mental Health Annual
  Report (13263) ....(Paid) 2500

Bethesda
The American Journal of Occupational
  Therapy (13301) 40,000
The American Journal of
  Pathology (13302) ....‡4,500
Immunology Abstracts (13344)
The Journal of Molecular
  Diagnostics (13352) ....(Paid) 3,000
Journal of Nutrition (13354) ....(Paid) ‡4,420
                                        (Non-paid) ‡204
Medical and Pharmaceutical Biotechnology
  Abstracts (13359)
Military Medicine (13361) ....(Paid) ‡12,500
OT Practice (13370)

Bowie
The Journal of
  Histotechnology (13392) ....(Paid) ‡4,950
                                        (Controlled) ‡250

College Park
Medical Dosimetry (13434)

Ellicott City
International Journal of Emergency Mental
  Health (13498)

Gaithersburg
Topics in Emergency
  Medicine (13550) ....(Paid) 2,000

Hagerstown
Ambulatory Medicine Letter (13561)

Kensington
Undersea & Hyperbaric
  Medicine (13592) ....(Controlled) 2,200

Lanham
Journal for Vascular
  Ultrasound (13606) ....(Combined) 3,900

Linthicum
Emergency Medicine (13619) ....(Paid) 3,110
                                        (Non-paid) 48,258

Potomac
Immunopharmacology and
  Immunotoxicology (13652) ....(Paid) 325

Rockville
Family Practice News (13678) ....(Controlled) 80,432
Journal of Speech, Language, and Hearing
  Research (13685)
Ob Gyn News (13690) ....(Controlled) 32,131
Skin & Allergy News (13697) .....(Controlled) 18,782

Silver Spring
Journal of Ethnomedicine and Drug
  Development (13730)
JPEN: Journal of Parenteral and Enteral
  Nutrition (13734) ....(Paid) ‡9,129
                                        (Non-paid) ‡620
NCP: Nutrition in Clinical
  Practice (13742) ....(Paid) ‡7,609
                                        (Non-paid) ‡520

Towson
The IN-REPORT (13759) ....‡2,200
JNMS: Journal of the Neuromusculoskeletal
  System (13760) ....(Paid) 7,000
Research in Healthcare Financial
  Management (13765)

Circ.

MASSACHUSETTS
Andover
Journal of Toxicology, Cutaneous and Ocular
  Toxicology (13812) ....(Paid) 425

Belmont
Archives of General
  Psychiatry (13838) ....(Combined) ‡30,771

Boston
American Journal of Law &
  Medicine (13849) 3,700
International Anesthesiology
  Clinics (13906) ....(Paid) ‡1,700
The Journal of Law, Medicine &
  Ethics (13916) ....‡5,000
Journal of Ultrasound in
  Medicine (13920) ....(Paid) 10,000
The New England Journal of
  Medicine (13935) ....(Paid) ‡230,000
                                        (Non-paid) ‡10,132
Obesity Research (13942) ....(Paid) 1,200
Seminars in Thoracic & Cardiovascular
  Surgery (13959)

Brookline
Medicine & Global Survival (14022)
Plastic and Reconstructive
  Surgery (14023) ....(Paid) ‡13,240
                                        (Non-paid) ‡315

Burlington
The Knee (14031) ....‡2,250
Seminars in Colon and Rectal
  Surgery (14032) ....‡947
Supramolecular Science (14033)
Ultrasonics Sonochemistry (14035)

Cambridge
AJOB (14036)
Neural Computation (14084) ....‡1,500
                                                ‡1,500

Malden
Epilepsia (14291) 5471
Journal of Experimental Therapeutics and
  Oncology (14294)

Needham
The Journal of Bone and Joint
  Surgery (14357) ....(Paid) ‡35,842
                                        (Non-paid) 398

Newton
Innovations in End-of-Life Care (14399)

Norwood
Journal of Infusion Nursing (14448) .....(Paid) 7,000

Shrewsbury
Journal of Intensive Care
  Medicine (14524) ....‡2,200

Sudbury
The Cancer Journal (14578)

Weston
American Journal of Alzheimers
  Disease (14648) ....(Paid) ‡2,200
Healing Ministry (14650) 1,100
Journal of Healthcare Safety, Compliance & Infection
  Control (14651) ....(Paid) ‡2,200

MICHIGAN
Detroit
Clinical Journal of Women's Health (14919)
Neurological Research (14941)

East Lansing
Michigan Medicine (14989) ....‡14,000

Kalamazoo
Journal of Investigative
  Surgery (15240) ....(Paid) ‡571

Midland
Phi Rho Sigma
  Journal (15356) ....(Non-paid) 12,500

Okemos
Triad (15417) ....(Paid) ⊕4,200

Southfield
Health Care Weekly Review (15543)

MINNESOTA
Edina
Specialty Law Digest (15877)

Mendota Heights
Journal of Forensic
  Identification (16052) ....(Combined) 5,500

Circ.

Minneapolis
American Journal of Kidney Diseases (16056)
Genetics in Medicine (16083) ....(Paid) ‡1,405
Journal of Toxicology Toxin
  Reviews (16090) ....(Paid) 225
Minnesota Medicine (16105) ....‡9,500
Postgraduate
  Medicine (16121) ....(Controlled) 140,000
Transfusion (16136) ....(Paid) ‡13,790
                                        (Non-paid) ‡158

Rochester
Annals of Allergy, Asthma, &
  Immunology (16306) ....(Paid) ‡6,000
                                        (Non-paid) ‡200
Diseases of the Colon and
  Rectum (16307) ....(Paid) 4,809
                                        (Non-paid) 730
Fertility and Sterility (16308) ....‡14,000
Mayo Clinic
  Proceedings (16309) ....(Non-paid) ‡127,000
Operative Techniques in General Surgery (16310)

MISSISSIPPI
Ridgeland
Journal of the Mississippi State Medical
  Association (16834) ....(Paid) ‡3,300
                                        (Non-paid) ‡100

MISSOURI
Columbia
Seminars in Oncology (17009) ....‡9,614

Jefferson City
Missouri Medicine (17126) ....‡6,600

Kansas City
Medical Directory of Greater Kansas
  City (17183) ....‡2,880

Rolla
Original Internist (17378) 7,500

St. Louis
ACTA Cytologica (17403) ....(Paid) 5,836
                                        (Controlled) 22
American Journal of Obstetrics and
  Gynecology (17410) ....(Combined) ‡12,245
Annals of Emergency
  Medicine (17414) ....(Paid) 26,410
                                        (Non-paid) 813
Annals of Otology, Rhinology and
  Laryngology (17415) ....‡5,613
Breast Diseases (17418)
Catholic Health World (17420) ....(Paid) ‡300
                                        (Non-paid) ‡10,500
Computer Aided Surgery (17426) ....(Paid) 12,500
Current Problems in Cardiology (17427)
Current Problems in Dermatology (17428)
Current Problems in Obstetrics, Gynecology and
  Fertility (17429)
Disease-A-Month (17435)
Gastrointestinal
  Endoscopy (17440) ....(Combined) ‡10,250
The Journal of Allergy and Clinical
  Immunology (17451) ....(Paid) ‡8,800
Journal of the American Academy of
  Dermatology (17452) ....(Paid) ‡19,149
Journal of Hand Surgery (17455)
The Journal of Laboratory and Clinical
  Medicine (17456) ....(Paid) 2,617
                                        (Non-paid) 289
The Journal of Reproductive
  Medicine (17461) ....(Controlled) ‡33,659
                                        (Paid) ‡1,514
Journal of Shoulder and Elbow
  Surgery (17462) ....(Paid) 2,866
                                        (Free) 231
Patient Drug Facts (17482)
St. Louis Metropolitan
  Medicine (17505) ....(Paid) 2,066
                                        (Non-paid) 190
Somatosensory and Motor
  Research (17513) ....(Paid) 250
Topics in Stroke
  Rehabilitation (17525) ....(Paid) 1,000

MONTANA
Missoula
St. Patrick Hospital Health
  Update (17876) ....(Controlled) 30,000

NEBRASKA
Lincoln
Comments on Toxicology (18081)

Omaha
Journal of Child Neurology **(18201)** ......(Paid) 3,000
(Non-paid) 60

NEVADA
Reno
Journal of Renal Nutrition **(18420)**

NEW HAMPSHIRE
Lebanon
Dartmouth Medicine **(18542)** ....(Non-paid) 25,000

Nashua
Healthcare Review **(18590)** .....(Combined) ❑52,503

NEW JERSEY
Belle Mead
Physician Assistant **(18669)** .....(Controlled) ‡31,259

Chatham
The American Journal of
Anesthesiology **(18725)** ....‡45,185
The American Journal of
Orthopedics **(18726)** ....(Controlled) ‡28,313
CUTIS **(18728)**
The Female Patient **(18729)** .....(Controlled) 104,234

Clifton
Clinician Reviews **(18753)**

Hoboken
American Journal of Hematology **(18884)** 9800
American Journal of Industrial
Medicine **(18886)** 7700
Annals of Neurology **(18891)** ....(Paid) 7,384
Bioelectromagnetics **(18903)** 5950
Catheterization and Cardiovascular
Diagnosis **(18908)** 23,800
Chirality **(18912)** ....(Paid) 4200
Circulatory Shock **(18913)** 375
Clinical Anatomy **(18914)** 7000
Clinical Neuroscience **(18915)** 4550
Concepts in Magnetic Resonance **(18922)**
Diabetes/Metabolism Review **(18930)** 500
Diagnostic Cytopathology **(18931)** 11,200
Dyslexia **(18933)**
Genes, Chromosomes and Cancer **(18950)** 5950
Genetic Epidemiology **(18951)** 6300
Head & Neck **(18956)**
Head & Neck Surgery **(18957)** 2,650
Health Care Analysis **(18958)**
Health Economics **(18959)**
Hematological Oncology **(18961)**
Hippocampus **(18963)** 4550
Human Brain Mapping **(18965)** 4200
Human Psychopharmacology **(18968)**
In Session **(18972)**
International Journal of Cancer **(18976)** 10,150
Journal of Biomedical Materials
Research **(19007)** 17,500
Journal of Clinical Apheresis **(19012)** 8750
Journal of Clinical Ultrasound **(19014)** 21,700
The Journal of Comparative
Neurology **(19018)** 7000
Journal of Labelled Compounds and
Radiopharmaceuticals **(19028)** ....(Paid) 4,900
Journal of Medical Virology **(19030)** 7000
Journal of Molecular
Recognition **(19032)** ....(Paid) 4,200
Journal of Neurobiology **(19035)** 5250
Journal of Neuroscience Research **(19036)** 5950
Journal of Pathology **(19039)** ....(Paid) 18,900
Journal of Surgical Oncology **(19040)** 7000
The Journal of Trace Elements in Experimental
Medicine **(19051)** 2800
Lasers in Surgery and Medicine **(19053)** 25,200
Medical and Pediatric Oncology **(19060)** 11,200
Medicinal Research Reviews **(19061)** 3850
Microsurgery **(19063)** 6650
Molecular Carcinogenesis **(19065)** 4550
Molecular Reproduction and
Development **(19066)** 5600
Muscle & Nerve **(19068)** 36,400
Neurology and Urodynamics **(19072)**
NMR in Biomedicine **(19074)**
Pharmacoepidemiology and Drug
Safety **(19082)** 2,800
Phytotherapy Research **(19084)** 4,200
The Prostate **(19088)** 6300
Radiation Oncology Investigations **(19094)** 3500
Seminars in Surgical Oncology **(19103)** 3850
Synapse **(19113)** ....(Paid) 290
Teratogenesis, Carcinogenesis and
Mutagenesis **(19117)** ....(Paid) 3,850
Teratology **(19118)** 11,550

Jamesburg
Cardiology Review **(19127)** ....(Controlled) △65,009

Family Practice
Recertification **(19129)** ....(Controlled) ‡94,957
Resident & Staff Physician **(19132)**
Surgical Rounds **(19133)** ....(Controlled) △51,556

Lawrenceville
New Jersey Medicine **(19163)** 9,200

Mahwah
Clinical Cardiology **(19189)** ....(Paid) 894
(Non-paid) 34,404
International Journal of Behavioral Medicine **(19192)**

Maplewood
Clinical Trials Monitor **(19215)**

Montvale
Clinical Cardiology Alert **(19245)**
Clinical Laboratory Reference
(CLR) **(19246)** ....(Free) 53,000
Contemporary
OB/GYN **(19248)** ....(Non-paid) 36,901
(Non-paid) 36,901
Contemporary
Pediatrics **(19249)** ....(Controlled) 48,289
Contemporary Urology **(19250)** ....(Paid) 42742
Contraceptive Technology Update **(19251)**
Infectious Disease Alert **(19256)**
Internal Medicine Alert **(19257)**
Journal of the American Academy of Physician
Assistants (JAAPA) **(19260)** ....(Controlled) 40,500
Medical Economics **(19262)** ....(Paid) 94,000
(Controlled) 64,000
Medical Economics—Orthopedic Surgery
Edition **(19264)**
Medical Economics for
Surgeons **(19265)** ....(Paid) 1,202
(Controlled) 48,300
OB/GYN Clinical Alert **(19268)**
Patient Care **(19270)** ....(Controlled) 145,000
(Controlled) 145,000
Podiatry Today **(19272)** ....(Free) ‡15,218
Strategic Medicine **(19276)**
Trauma Reports **(19277)**

Morris Plains
Biomedical Products **(19288)** ....(Controlled) ‡71,000
Medical Design
Technology **(19298)** ....(Non-paid) 35,450
Patient Management **(19299)** .....(Controlled) 60,100
Surgical Products **(19307)** ....(Controlled) ‡71,023

Newark
Journal of ECT **(19357)** ....(Paid) 820

Old Tappan
The American Academy of Orthopaedic Surgeons
Bulletin **(19393)** ....(Combined) 27,000
Journal of the American Academy of Orthopaedic
Surgeons **(19394)** ....(Paid) 29,000

Piscataway
Journal of Studies on
Alcohol **(19429)** ....(Paid) ‡2,400

Pitman
Dermatology Nursing **(19433)** ....(Paid) ‡5,000
MedSurg Nursing **(19435)**

Plainsboro
Home Healthcare
Consultant **(19441)** ....(Paid) 65,000
The Journal of Gender-Specific Medicine **(19442)**

Princeton
International Journal of Occupational Medicine,
Immunology and Toxicology **(19462)**

Somerset
Integrative Physiological and Behavioral
Science **(19562)** ....(Paid) ‡500

Thorofare
Hem/Onc Today **(19616)** ....(Controlled) ⊕33,000
Infection Control and Hospital
Epidemiology **(19617)** 5,810
Infectious Disease
News **(19618)** ....(Controlled) ‡6,200
Infectious Diseases in
Children **(19619)** ....(Controlled) ‡42,000
The Journal of Knee
Surgery **(19622)** ....(Paid) ‡750
Journal of Refractive Surgery **(19626)** 2,582
Journal of Spirochetal and Tick-borne
Diseases **(19627)**
O&P Business News **(19628)**
O&P World **(19629)**
Ocular Surgery
News **(19631)** ....(Controlled) ‡17,000
Ocular Surgery News Europe/Asia-Pacific
Edition **(19632)** ....(Controlled) ‡33,346

Ocular Surgery News Latin America Edition **(19633)**
Orthopaedics Today
International **(19635)** ....(Combined) 24,461
Orthopedics **(19636)** ....(Controlled) ‡25,100
Orthopedics Today **(19637)** ....(Free) ‡23,435
Today in Cardiology **(19641)**

NEW MEXICO
Santa Fe
OR Manager **(19939)** ....(Combined) 3,500

NEW YORK
Amityville
The International Journal of Psychiatry in
Medicine **(20040)**

Armonk
Journal of Cardiac Surgery **(20084)** ....‡2,417
Journal of Cardiovascular
Electrophysiology **(20085)** ....‡3,164
Journal of Interventional Cardiology **(20086)** ...2,333
Noninvasive Electrocardiology **(20089)**
PACE: Pacing and Clinical
Electrophysiology **(20090)** ....(Paid) ‡6,616

Binghamton
Journal of Cannabis Therapeutics **(20165)**
Journal of Forensic Neuropsychology **(20174)**
Journal of Forensic Psychology Practice **(20175)**
Journal of Herbal Pharmacotherapy **(20177)**
Journal of HIV/AIDS & Social Services **(20179)**
Journal of Hospital Librarianship **(20180)**
Journal of Infectious Disease
Pharmacotherapy **(20184)** ....(Paid) 16
Journal of Managed Pharmaceutical
Care **(20188)** ....(Paid) 2,200
Journal of Neurotherapy **(20189)**
Journal of Whiplash & Related Disorders **(20207)**
Medical Reference Services
Quarterly **(20208)** 1,295

Bronx
Progress in Cardiovascular
Diseases **(20281)** ....‡3,914

Brooklyn
Doctor's Shopper **(20314)** .....(Controlled) ‡155,000

Buffalo
Endocrine Research **(20379)** 350
Techniques in Regional Anesthesia and Pain
Management **(20389)**

Garden City
American Journal of Chinese Medicine **(20634)**

Garrison
Hastings Center Report **(20647)** ....(Paid) 7,500
(Controlled) 1,000
IRB **(20648)** ....(Paid) 1,100

Glen Head
Angiology **(20661)** ....(Paid) ‡5,722
(Non-paid) ‡349
Clinical Pediatrics **(20662)** ....(Paid) ‡4,910
International Journal of Surgical
Pathology **(20663)** ....(Combined) 2,865
Trends in Amplification **(20664)** ....(Combined) 1,865
Vascular and Endovscular
Surgery **(20665)** ....‡4,440

Hawthorne
Cortland Forum **(20725)** ....(Non-paid) ⊕141,500

Lake Success
The News of New
York **(20881)** ....(Controlled) 26,000

Larchmont
Alternative & Complementary Therapies **(20888)**
Antioxidants and Redox Signaling **(20889)**
Antisense and Nucleic Acid Drug
Development **(20890)**
Cancer Biotherapy and
Radiopharmaceuticals **(20893)**
Cloning and Stem Cells **(20894)**
Disease Management **(20896)**
Genetic Testing **(20902)**
Hybridoma and Hybridomics **(20903)**
Journal of Aerosol Medicine **(20904)**
Journal of Aerosol Medicine **(20905)**
The Journal of Alternative & Complementary
Medicine **(20906)**
Journal of Anti-Aging Medicine **(20907)**
Journal of Child and Adolescent
Psychopharmacology **(20908)**
Journal of Clinical Laser Medicine &
Surgery **(20909)**
Journal of Computational Biology **(20910)**
Journal of Endourology **(20911)**

Circ.   Circ.   Circ.

MEDICINE AND SURGERY (continued)

Journal of Gynecologic Surgery **(20912)**
Journal of Hematotherapy & Stem Cell
  Research **(20913)**
Journal of Interferon & Cytokine Research **(20914)**
Journal of Laparoendoscopic and Advanced Surgical
  Techniques **(20915)**
Journal of Men's Health **(20916)**
Journal of Neurotrauma **(20917)**
Journal of Women's Health **(20919)**
Microbial Drug Resistance **(20921)**
Natural Pharmacy **(20922)**
Omics: A Journal of Integrative Biology **(20923)**
Pediatric Endosurgery & Innovative
  Techniques **(20925)**
Telemedicine Journal and E-Health **(20926)**
Thyroid **(20927)** 900
Tissue Engineering **(20928)**
Vector-Borne and Zoonotic Diseases **(20929)**

Melville
Oncology **(21052)** ....(Controlled) △**30,016**
                  (Paid) △**1,875**
Primary Care &
  Cancer **(21059)** ....(Controlled) 70,451

Mineola
Journal of Toxicology: Clinical Toxicology **(21085)**

New York
Academic Physician & Scientist **(21132)**
ACC Current Journal Review **(21133)**
Advanced in Renal Replacement Therapy **(21153)**
Aesthetic Plastic
  Surgery **(21160)** ....(Combined) **3,000**
Aesthetic Surgery
  Journal **(21161)** ....(Combined) ‡**5,389**
AIDS and Behavior **(21167)**
Alzheimer's Care Quarterly **(21175)**
The American Journal of
  Cardiology **(21190)** ....‡**20,897**
The American Journal of
  Gastroenterology **(21194)** ....(Paid) 8,185
              (Non-paid) ‡197
American Journal of Medicine **(21195)** ....‡**53,751**
American Journal of Preventive
  Medicine **(21198)** ....(Paid) ‡**2,500**
              (Non-paid) ‡18
American Journal of Surgery **(21200)** 14,241
American Review of Respiratory
  Disease **(21206)** ....‡**16,637**
Anesthesiology
  News **(21213)** ....(Combined) ‡**34,922**
Angiogenesis **(21215)**
Annals of Vascular
  Surgery **(21220)** ....(Combined) **2,300**
Apoptosis **(21225)**
Applied Psychophysiology and Biofeedback **(21233)**
Artificial Cells, Blood Substitutes and Immobilization
  Biotechnology **(21256)** 325
Biomedical Engineering **(21320)**
Biomedical Microdevices **(21321)**
Biomedical Safety and Standards **(21322)**
BioMetals **(21323)**
Brain and Mind **(21336)**
Bulletin of Experimental Biology and
  Medicine **(21350)**
Bulletin of the New York Academy of
  Medicine **(21352)** ....‡**3,900**
Calcified Tissue
  International **(21365)** ....(Combined) **1,650**
Cancer Causes and Control **(21370)**
Cancer Investigation **(21371)** ....(Controlled) ‡**17,420**
Cardiac Electrophysiology Review **(21374)**
Cardiology Special
  Edition **(21375)** ....(Non-paid) 22,343
Cell and Tissue Banking **(21386)**
Clinics in Developmental Medicine **(21430)**
Complementary Health Practice
  Review **(21468)** ....(Controlled) 350
Contemporary Dialysis &
  Nephrology **(21491)** ....(Combined) 18,395
Critical Care Nursing Quarterly **(21519)** ....‡**3,000**
Critical Reviews in Therapeutic Drug Carrier
  Systems **(21520)** ....(Paid) 500
Data Centrum **(21537)** ....(Non-paid) 127,500
Developmental Medicine and Child
  Neurology **(21548)** 4,000
Diabetes
  Self-Management **(21549)** ....(Paid) 374,156
              (Non-paid) 30,075
Dysphagia **(21573)** ....(Combined) 2,200
Epidemiology and Infection **(21624)** 1000
European Journal of Epidemiology **(21643)**
Facial Plastic Surgery **(21672)** ....(Paid) 2,093
Familial Cancer **(21676)**
Federal Practitioner **(21681)** ....(Controlled) ‡**25,853**

Fetal and Maternal Medicine
  Review **(21687)** ....(Paid) ‡240
              (Non-paid) ‡58
Gastroenterology and Endoscopy
  News **(21748)** ....(Non-paid) ‡**8,261**
General Surgery & Laparoscopy
  News **(21749)** ....(Controlled) ‡**38,303**
Glycoconjugate **(21773)**
Health Care Management Science **(21793)**
Heart Failure Reviews **(21797)**
Hemoglobin **(21799)** 325
Hospital for Joint Diseases
  Bulletin **(21818)** ....(Paid) 1,200
Immunological Investigations **(21852)** 375
Inflammation **(21868)**
Inside MS **(21876)** 680,000
International Family Planning
  Perspectives **(21897)** ....(Paid) ‡**30,000**
              (Non-paid) ‡**1,000**
International Journal of Cardiovascular
  Imaging **(21900)**
International Journal of Obstetric Anesthesia **(21912)**
International Journal of Rehabilitation and
  Health **(21916)**
International Journal of Technology Assessment in
  Health Care **(21921)** 1500
International
  Psychogeriatrics **(21932)** ....(Combined) 1,400
International Urology and Nephrology **(21940)**
Internet Health Care **(21941)**
Investigational New Drugs **(21945)**
JMPT: Journal of Manipulative and Physiological
  Therapeutics **(21968)** ....(Paid) ‡**13,823**
Journal of AAPOS (American Association for Pediatric
  Ophthalmology and
  Strabismus) **(21971)** ....(Combined) ‡**1,283**
Journal of the American College of
  Surgeons **(21982)** ....(Paid) ‡**13,176**
             (Controlled) ‡**6,832**
Journal of the American Medical Women's
  Association **(21983)** ....‡**10,000**
Journal of Assisted Reproduction and
  Genetics **(22000)**
The Journal of Biomedical Informatics **(22012)**
Journal of Clinical Immunology **(22026)**
Journal of Clinical Monitoring and
  Computing **(22027)** ....(Paid) 1,300
Journal of Controversial Medical Claims **(22039)**
Journal of Cutaneous
  Medicine **(22045)** ....(Combined) 2,500
The Journal of Experimental
  Medicine **(22068)** ....‡**2,730**
Journal of Genetic Couseling **(22079)**
Journal of Head Trauma
  Rehabilitation **(22083)** ....(Paid) 2,500
              (Free) 66
Journal of Health Care Compliance **(22084)**
Journal of Inherited Metabolic Disease **(22095)**
Journal of Interventional Cardiac
  Electrophysiology **(22107)**
Journal of Liposome
  Research **(22113)** ....(Paid) 400
Journal of Mammary Gland Biology and
  Neoplasia **(22119)**
Journal of Medical Humanities **(22130)**
Journal of Medical Systems **(22131)**
Journal of Muscle Research and Cell
  Motility **(22137)**
Journal of Nonverbal Behavior **(22146)**
Journal of Psychosocial
  Oncology **(22171)** ....(Paid) 1,002
Journal of Radiosurgery **(22176)**
Journal of Reconstructive
  Microsurgery **(22177)** 1,935
The Journal of Thoracic and Cardiovascular
  Surgery **(22205)** ....(Combined) ‡**8,341**
Journal of Vascular
  Surgery **(22212)** ....(Combined) ‡**7,634**
Kidney **(22219)** ....(Combined) 700
Lung **(22270)** ....(Combined) 725
Materials and Processing Report **(22290)**
Maternal and Child Health Journal **(22292)**
Medical Physics **(22310)** ....‡**4,182**
Medicine and Health **(22311)**
Medicine, Health Care and Philosophy **(22312)**
Metabolic Brain Disease **(22318)**
Modern Medicine **(22349)** ......(Controlled) ‡**125,000**
Molecular and Cellular Biochemistry **(22356)**
The Mount Sinai Journal of
  Medicine **(22373)** ....‡**2,000**
Neurochemical Research **(22423)**
Neurophysiology **(22424)**
Neuropsychology Review **(22425)**
NUTRITION **(22476)**
NYSSA Sphere **(22480)** ....(Combined) 3,500
Orthopedic Special
  Edition **(22506)** ....(Controlled) 20,411

Osteoporosis International **(22507)**
Otolaryngology–Head and Neck
  Surgery **(22508)** ....(Paid) ‡**11,300**
Pain Digest **(22518)** ....(Combined) 1,000
Perspectives on Sexual and Reproductive
  Health **(22545)** ....(Paid) 5,000
              (Non-paid) 2,000
Pituitary **(22554)**
Practical Diabetology **(22590)** ....(Controlled) ‡**52,086**
Quality of Life Research **(22615)**
Reviews in Endocrine & Metabolic Disorders **(22663)**
Seminars in Neurology **(22724)** ....(Paid) 3,000
Seminars in Respiratory and Critical Care
  Medicine **(22725)** ....(Paid) 2,785
Seminars in Thrombosis and
  Hemostasis **(22727)** ....(Paid) 2,582
Sepsis **(22730)**
Skull Base **(22742)** ....(Paid) ‡**1,517**
Substance Use & Misuse **(22803)** 650
Surgery **(22810)** ....(Combined) ‡**5,635**
Surgical Endoscopy **(22811)** ....(Paid) 5,090
Thrombosis Research **(22833)** ....‡**1,580**
Topics in Clinical Chiropractic **(22844)** 1,037
Topics in Geriatric
  Rehabilitation **(22845)** ....(Paid) 1,768
              (Non-paid) 70
Transplantation **(22855)** ....(Paid) ‡**2,449**
              (Non-paid) ‡401
Urology **(22891)** ....(Paid) ‡**7,228**
Vaccine **(22894)**
World Journal of
  Surgery **(22941)** ....(Combined) 5,000

Port Washington
International Journal of Fertility and Women's
  Medicine **(23129)**

Rhinebeck
FOCUS: Journal for Respiratory Care Managers and
  Educators **(23183)**

Rochester
Families, Systems &
  Health **(23225)** ....(Controlled) ⊕**1,250**
INQUIRY **(23228)** ....‡**2,000**

Valhalla
Survey of Anesthesiology **(23483)** ......(Paid) ‡**1,067**
              (Non-paid) ‡142
Toxicology Pathology **(23484)** ......(Combined) 1,000

NORTH CAROLINA
Cary
Cerebral Cortex **(23687)** ....(Paid) 700
Journal of the History of Medicine and Allied
  Sciences **(23691)** 1,100

Chapel Hill
The Cleft Palate-Craniofacial Journal **(23704)**
Journal of Autism and Developmental
  Disorders **(23710)** ....‡**2,000**
Renal Failure **(23720)** 425
Seminars in Radiation Oncology **(23722)**

Durham
Arthritis and Rheumatism **(23808)** ....‡**9,000**
Lasers in the Life Sciences **(23832)**
North Carolina Medical Journal **(23838)** ......‡**10,000**

Raleigh
Inhalation Toxicology **(24138)** ....‡287

Research Triangle Park
Experimental Lung Research **(24184)** ....‡390

Wilmington
Health Care for Women
  International **(24295)** ....‡696

Winston-Salem
Arthroscopy **(24318)**

OHIO
Cleveland
Applied Nursing Research **(24856)**
Cleveland Clinic Journal of
  Medicine **(24870)** ....(Paid) ‡509
             (Controlled) ‡**91,879**
Cleveland Physician **(24873)** ....(Paid) 1,300
Dermatology Times **(24880)** ...(Controlled) 9,839
Ear, Nose & Throat
  Journal **(24884)** ....(Combined) △**13,784**
Molecular Endocrinology **(24927)**
Urology Times **(24959)** ....(Controlled) 9,500

Columbus
Columbus Physician **(25010)** ....(Non-paid) 2,000

Dayton
Dayton Medicine **(25114)** ....(Non-paid) ‡**2,700**

Kettering
Journal of Nutrition, Health & Aging **(25283)**

Solon
Medical Equipment Designer **(25526)** ....(Non-paid) ‡12,000

Toledo
Toledo Medicine **(25571)** ....(Paid) ‡1,568
(Controlled) ‡208

OKLAHOMA

Oklahoma City
Journal **(25967)** ....(Paid) ‡3,900
(Non-paid) ‡440

Tulsa
Tulsa Medicine **(26137)** ....(Paid) ‡1,050
(Non-paid) ‡50

OREGON

Portland
The Scribe **(26508)** ....‡3,000
Seminars in Reproductive Endocrinology **(26509)** ....(Paid) 1,811
(Non-paid) 97

PENNSYLVANIA

Gladwyne
RETINA **(26944)** 2,476

Harrisburg
Journal of the Pennsylvania Osteopathic Medical Association **(26996)** ....(Combined) ⊕**4,035**
Pennsylvania Medicine **(27010)** ....(Paid) 20,000
(Non-paid) 350

King of Prussia
ADVANCE for Administrators in Radiation & Radiation Oncology **(27108)** ....(Controlled) ‡21,987
ADVANCE for Directors in Rehabilitation **(27109)**
ADVANCE for Health Information Executives **(27110)**
ADVANCE for Health Information Professionals **(27111)**
ADVANCE for Imaging and Radiation Therapy Professionals **(27112)** ....(Controlled) ‡69,000
ADVANCE for Managers of Respiratory Care **(27113)** ....(Controlled) ‡21,000
ADVANCE for Medical Laboratory Professionals **(27114)** ....(Controlled) ‡65,300
ADVANCE for Nurses **(27116)** ....(Combined) 510,000
ADVANCE for Physician Assistants **(27119)** ....(Non-paid) ‡31,900
ADVANCE for Providers of Post-Acute Care **(27120)**
ADVANCE for Respiratory Care Practitioners **(27121)** ....(Controlled) 44,800
ADVANCE for Speech-Language Pathologists & Audiologists **(27122)** ....(Controlled) ‡61,000

Malvern
The Journal of Invasive Cardiology **(27212)** ....(Paid) ‡5,450
(Non-paid) ‡5,000

Narberth
Physicians News Digest **(27310)** ....(Paid) ‡20
(Controlled) ‡28,809

Philadelphia
Academic Emergency Medicine **(27361)** ....(Paid) 5,600
ACP Observer **(27362)** ....(Paid) 76,074
(Non-paid) 1,551
Advances in Skin & Wound Care **(27363)** ....(Controlled) 20,389
American Heart Journal **(27370)** ....(Combined) ‡5,948
The American Journal of Emergency Medicine **(27371)** ....‡2,561
American Journal of the Medical Sciences **(27372)** 1,430
American Journal of Otolaryngology **(27373)** ....‡1,565
Anesthesiology **(27375)** ....(Paid) 38,643
Anesthesiology Clinics of North America **(27376)**
Annals of Diagnostic Pathology **(27377)**
Annals of Internal Medicine **(27379)** ....(Paid) 91,224
Archives of Family Medicine **(27383)**
ASA Refresher Courses in Anesthesiology **(27384)**
ASAIO Journal **(27385)** 1,609
AUA News **(27386)** ....(Combined) 12,405
Biomedical Instrumentation & Technology **(27388)** ....(Paid) ‡7,000
Blood **(27389)** ....‡14,043
Cancer Epidemiology, Biomarkers & Prevention **(27391)** ....(Controlled) 1,421
Cancer Research **(27392)** ....(Paid) ‡9,621
Cardiology Clinics **(27393)**
Cardiology Clinics: Annual of Drug Therapy **(27394)**
Cell Stress and Chaperones **(27396)**
Chest Surgery Clinics **(27399)**
Child and Adolescent Psychiatric Clinics **(27401)**
Circulation **(27403)** ....(Paid) ‡25,000
Circulation Research **(27404)** ....(Paid) ‡3,100
Clinical Oncology **(27408)** ....(Paid) ‡16,275
Clinical Pediatric Emergency Medicine **(27409)**
Clinical Perspectives in Gastroenterology **(27410)**
Clinics in Chest Medicine **(27413)**
Clinics in Family Practice **(27414)**
Clinics in Liver Disease **(27417)**
Clinics in Perinatology **(27418)**
Clinics in Plastic Surgery **(27419)**
Clinics in Podiatric Medicine and Surgery **(27420)**
Clinics in Sports Medicine **(27421)**
Complementary Medicine for the Physician **(27425)**
Coronary Artery Disease **(27428)** ....(Paid) 534
Critical Care Clinics **(27429)**
CRNA **(27431)**
Current Opinion in Anesthesiology **(27434)** ....(Paid) ‡3,250
Current Opinion in Cardiology **(27435)** ....(Paid) ‡1,550
Current Opinion in Gastroenterology **(27436)** ....(Paid) ‡1,540
Current Opinion in Lipidology **(27437)** ....(Paid) ‡5,500
Current Opinion in Neurology **(27438)** ....(Paid) ‡2,809
Current Opinion in Obstetrics & Gynecology **(27439)** ....(Paid) ‡2,000
Current Opinion in Oncology **(27440)** ....(Paid) ‡1,800
Current Opinion in Ophthalmology **(27441)** ....(Paid) ‡1,011
Current Opinion in Orthopaedics **(27442)** ....(Paid) ‡2,000
Current Opinion in Pediatrics **(27443)** ....(Paid) ‡3,005
Current Opinion in Psychiatry **(27444)** ....(Paid) ‡4,750
Current Opinion in Rheumatology **(27445)** ....(Paid) ‡5,500
Current Surgery **(27446)** ....(Combined) 1,542
Dermatologic Clinics **(27450)**
Ear and Hearing **(27455)** ....(Paid) ‡3,121
(Non-paid) ‡77
Emergency Medicine Clinics of North America **(27457)** ....‡5,300
The Endocrinologist **(27458)** ....(Paid) ‡2,872
(Non-paid) ‡85
Endocrinology and Metabolism Clinics **(27459)**
Epidemiology **(27462)** ....(Combined) **1,747**
European Journal of Gastroenterology & Hepatology **(27465)**
Facial Plastic Surgery Clinics **(27466)**
Foot & Ankle **(27470)** ....(Paid) ‡3,941
(Non-paid) ‡48
Foot and Ankle Clinics **(27471)**
Gastroenterology **(27473)** 15,851
Gastroenterology Clinics **(27474)**
Gastrointestinal Endoscopy Clinics **(27475)**
Growth Hormone and IGF Research **(27477)**
Hand Clinics **(27478)** ....(Paid) 2,986
Hematology/Oncology Clinics **(27480)**
Home Care Manager **(27485)**
Human Pathology **(27487)** ....‡7,549
Hypertension **(27488)** ....‡4,050
Immunology and Allergy Clinics **(27489)**
Infectious Disease Clinics **(27491)**
Infertility and Reproductive Medicine Clinics **(27492)**
Journal of the American Society of Echocardiography **(27513)** ....‡8,347
Journal of the American Society of Nephrology **(27514)** ....(Paid) 6,720
(Non-paid) 274
Journal of the American Society for Surgery **(27515)**
The Journal of Arthroplasty **(27516)** ....‡7,800
Journal of Cardiopulmonary Rehabilitation **(27518)** ....(Paid) 3,694
Journal of Cardiovascular Pharmacology and Therapeutics **(27519)**
Journal of Child and Family Nursing **(27521)**
Journal of Gynecologic Techniques **(27529)**
Journal of Hand Therapy **(27530)** ....‡4,500
Journal of Hypertension **(27531)** ....(Paid) 1,843
Journal of Intravenous Nursing **(27532)** ....(Paid) 9,185
Journal of Investigative Medicine **(27533)** ....‡14,000
Journal of Nuclear Cardiology **(27539)** ....(Combined) ‡6,499
Journal of Pain **(27542)**
Journal of Pediatric Orthopaedics, Part B. **(27544)** ....(Paid) 1,000
Journal of Pelvic Medicine & Surgery **(27545)** 486
Journal of Surgical Outcomes **(27552)**
Journal of Vascular and Interventional Radiology (JVIR) **(27555)**
The Lancet (North American Edition) **(27559)** ....‡19,614
The Medical Clinics **(27564)**
Medical Decision Making **(27565)** ....‡1,600
Medical Problems of Performing Artists **(27567)** ....(Paid) ‡1,500
Molecular Cancer Research **(27572)** .....(Paid) 2,400
Molecular Diagnosis **(27573)**
Neurologic Clinics **(27576)**
Neurology **(27577)** ....(Paid) 20,339
Neurology Network Commentary **(27578)**
Neurosurgery **(27579)** ....(Paid) ‡8,950
(Non-paid) ‡365
Neurosurgery Clinics **(27580)**
Nursing Case Management **(27589)** .....(Paid) 2,017
Obstetrics and Gynecology Clinics **(27594)**
Operative Techniques in Cataract and Refractive Surgery **(27600)**
Operative Techniques in Gynecologic Surgery **(27601)**
Operative Techniques in Neurosurgery **(27602)**
Operative Techniques in Oculoplastic, Orbital and Reconstructive Surgery **(27603)**
Operative Techniques in Orthopaedics **(27604)**
Operative Techniques in Otolaryngology **(27605)** ....(Paid) ‡2,419
Operative Techniques in Plastic and Reconstructive Surgery **(27606)**
Operative Techniques in Sports Medicine **(27607)**
Oral and Maxillofacial Surgery Clinics **(27608)**
The Orthopedic Clinics **(27609)**
The Otolaryngologic Clinics **(27611)**
Pediatric Hematology and Oncology **(27616)** ....(Paid) ‡357
Pediatric Physical Therapy **(27618)** .....(Paid) ‡5,696
(Non-paid) ‡72
Philadelphia Medicine **(27628)** .....(Non-paid) ‡4,500
Physical Medicine and Rehabilitation Clinics **(27638)**
Physical Therapy Case Reports **(27639)**
Primary Care **(27645)**
Problems in Anesthesia **(27647)** 2,354
Psychosomatic Medicine **(27651)** ....(Paid) ‡2,035
(Non-paid) ‡117
Seizure **(27657)**
Seminars in Anesthesia, Perioperative Medicine and Pain **(27658)** ....‡2,628
Seminars in Arthroplasty **(27659)**
Seminars in Breast Disease **(27661)**
Seminars in Cardiothoracic and Vascular Anesthesia **(27662)**
Seminars in Cutaneous Medicine and Surgery **(27663)**
Seminars in Cutaneous Medicine and Surgery **(27664)** 1,019
Seminars in Diagnostic Pathology **(27665)**
Seminars in Gastrointestinal Disease **(27666)**
Seminars in Neonatology **(27667)**
Seminars in Oncology Nursing **(27668)**
Seminars in Pediatric Neurology **(27669)**
Seminars in Perinatology **(27670)** 2,171
Seminars in Perioperative Nursing **(27671)**
Seminars in Spine Surgery **(27674)** ....(Paid) ‡2,010
Seminars in Urologic Oncology **(27676)**
Sexually Transmitted Diseases **(27677)** 1,402
Spine **(27693)** 7,464
Sports Chiropractic & Rehabilitation **(27695)** ....(Paid) 2121
Stroke **(27696)** ....(Paid) ‡6,500
The Surgical Clinics of North America **(27697)**
Techniques in Gastrointestinal Endoscopy **(27698)**
Techniques in Hand and Upper Extremity Surgery **(27699)** 1,160
Techniques in Vascular and Interventional Radiology **(27700)**
Transactions and Studies of the College of Physicians of Philadelphia **(27709)** ....(Combined) 1,900
Transplantation Reviews **(27710)**
The Urologic Clinics **(27715)**

Pittsburgh
Abridged Index Medicus **(27753)**
Bulletin of Allegheny County Medical Society **(27763)** ....(Paid) ‡3,687
(Controlled) ‡219
Clinical Journal of Oncology Nursing **(27765)** ....(Combined) ‡30,000
Digestive Diseases and Sciences **(27780)**
Index Medicus **(27798)**
Navy Medicine **(27820)**
Pittsburgh Hospital News **(27833)** 30,000

Spring City
For the Record **(28008)** ....(Controlled) 58,000

Circulation: ★ = ABC; △ = BPA; ♦ = CAC; • = CCAB; ❑ = VAC; ⊕ = PO Statement; ‡ = Publisher's Report; Boldface figures = sworn; Light figures = estimated.

3191

Circ.   Circ.   Circ.

MEDICINE AND SURGERY (continued)
Wayne
Health Law Litigation Reporter **(28133)**

Wynnewood
Clinical Nuclear Medicine **(28197)** ....(Paid) 1,678

Yardley
Managed Care **(28201)** ....(Controlled) 60,000

RHODE ISLAND
Providence
Allergy and Asthma
    Proceedings **(28385)** ....(Combined) 3,000
American Journal of Rhinology **(28386)** 3,000
Healthcare Technology
    Management **(28399)** ....(Controlled) 21,748
Medical Imaging **(28406)** ....(Controlled) 21,195
Medical Law's Regan Report **(28407)**
Medicine and Health Rhode
    Island **(28408)** ....(Paid) ‡1,900
                                       (Non-paid) ‡175
24x7 **(28429)** ....(Controlled) 15,766

SOUTH CAROLINA
Columbia
Journal of the South Carolina Medical
    Association **(28554)** ....‡5,870

Fort Mill
Aquatic Therapy Journal **(28611)**

Kiawah Island
Archives of Andrology, an International
    Journal **(28673)** 453

SOUTH DAKOTA
Sioux Falls
South Dakota Journal of
    Medicine **(28967)** ....(Controlled) 1,940

TENNESSEE
Bristol
Today's Christian Doctor **(29066)** .....(Paid) ⊕20,000

Chattanooga
CRANIO **(29088)** ....(Paid) ‡1,638
                                       (Non-paid) ‡308

Nashville
California Medicine **(29448)**
Healthcare Business
    Month **(29457)** ....(Combined) 38,109
Obstetrical & Gynecological
    Survey **(29477)** ....(Combined) ‡8,055
X-Ray News **(29504)**

TEXAS
Arlington
Gastroenterology Nursing **(29732)** ....(Paid) 6,719

Austin
Texas Medicine **(29835)** ....(Paid) ‡26,090

Dallas
AARC Times **(30120)** ....(Paid) ‡32,500
                                       (Non-paid) ‡150
American Journal of Contact
    Dermatitis **(30122)** ....‡765
Archives of Neurology **(30123)** ....(Paid) ‡6,095
                                       (Controlled) ‡8,874
Federation Bulletin **(30155)** ....(Paid) 4,000
Federation Exchange **(30156)**
Model for the Preparation of a Guidebook on Medical
    Discipline **(30168)**

Galveston
Endocrine Reviews **(30379)** ....(Paid) ‡4,333
                                       (Non-paid) ‡378
Medical Humanities Review **(30382)**

Houston
Annals of Biomedical Engineering **(30457)**
Applied Neuropsychology **(30458)**
Clinical Cancer
    Research **(30463)** ....`.(Combined) ⊕4,552
Clinical and Experimental
    Hypertension **(30464)** 425
Research Initiative/Treatment
    Action! **(30524)** 1,200

Lubbock
Seminars in Nephrology **(30717)** ....‡2,198

San Antonio
Family Medicine **(31030)** ....(Paid) ‡5,000
                                       (Controlled) ‡513
Journal of Trauma **(31036)** ....(Paid) ‡6,436
                                       (Non-paid) ‡278

Medical Gazette **(31038)** ....(Free) ‡12,000
Medical Gazette **(31039)**
Pharmacology Biochemistry and Behavior **(31041)**
Physiology & Behavior **(31042)**

Sugar Land
Internet Journal of Academic Physician
    Assistants **(31138)**
Internet Journal of Advanced Nursing
    Practice **(31139)**
The Internet Journal of Anesthesiology **(31140)**
Internet Journal of Asthma, Allergy and
    Immunology **(31141)**
Internet Journal of Emergency and Intensive Care
    Medicine **(31142)**
Internet Journal of Family Practice **(31143)**
Internet Journal of Gastroenterology **(31144)**
Internet Journal of Gynecology and
    Obstetrics **(31145)**
Internet Journal of Health **(31146)**
Internet Journal of Healthcare Administration **(31147)**
Internet Journal of Infectious Disease **(31148)**
Internet Journal of Internal Medicine **(31149)**
Internet Journal of Law, Healthcare and
    Ethics **(31150)**
Internet Journal of Neuromonitoring **(31151)**
Internet Journal of Neurosurgery **(31152)**
Internet Journal of Ophthalmology and Visual
    Science **(31153)**
Internet Journal of Orthopedic Surgery **(31154)**
Internet Journal of Pain, Symptom Control and
    Palliative Care **(31155)**
Internet Journal of Pathology **(31156)**
Internet Journal of Pediatrics and
    Neonatology **(31157)**
Internet Journal of Perfusionists **(31158)**
Internet Journal of Pulmonary Medicine **(31159)**
Internet Journal of Radiology **(31160)**
Internet Journal of Rescue and Disaster
    Medicine **(31161)**
Internet Journal of Surgery **(31162)**
Internet Journal of Thoracic and Cardiovascular
    Surgery **(31163)**

UTAH
Salt Lake City
Clinical Obstetrics Gynecology **(31424)** ....‡11,170

VERMONT
Sharon
Journal of Cognitive Neuroscience **(31598)**

VIRGINIA
Alexandria
Annals of Surgical Oncology **(31641)** 2,424
Aviation, Space, and Environmental
    Medicine **(31645)** ....‡4,000
Diabetes Care **(31665)**
Diabetes Forecast **(31666)** ....(Paid) 434,780
Group Practice Journal **(31677)** ....(Paid) △60,000
The Journal of Orthopaedic and Sports Physical
    Therapy (JOSPT) **(31700)** ....(Paid) ‡16,971
                                       (Non-paid) ‡272
Liver Transplantation **(31707)**
Physical Therapy **(31722)** ....(Paid) ‡78,000

Arlington
Psychosomatics **(31820)** ....(Paid) 1,747
                                       (Non-paid) 781

Charlottesville
The American Journal of Sports
    Medicine **(31914)** ....(Paid) ‡10,000
                                       (Non-paid) ‡125
AUA Today **(31916)** ....‡18,723
Clinical Chemistry **(31924)** ....(Combined) 12,000
Journal of Neurosurgery **(31934)** ....‡11,000
Neurosurgical Focus **(31935)**

Fairfax
Journal of Cataract and Refractive
    Surgery **(32019)** ....‡14,000

Mc Lean
Science Illustrated **(32255)** .....(Controlled) ‡110,000

Reston
Journal of Nuclear Medicine
    Technology **(32388)** ....‡7,000

Richmond
Infection Control & Sterilization
    Technology **(32438)** ....(Paid) △25,000
The Journal of Perinatal
    Education **(32442)** ....(Paid) ‡5,224
                                       (Non-paid) ‡408
Virginia Medical Quarterly **(32466)** ....‡7,000

Springfield
Journal of Environmental Science and Health, Part C:
    Environmental Carcinogenesis and Ectoxicology
    Reviews **(32545)** 250

WASHINGTON
Issaquah
Journal of Heart-Centered Therapies **(32785)**

Port Townsend
Townsend Letter for Doctors &
    Patients **(32896)** ....(Controlled) 6,000

Seattle
Bulletin of the King County Medical
    Society **(32952)** ....‡5,000
Outlook **(32999)** ....(Non-paid) 20,000
Regional Anesthesia and Pain Medicine **(33014)**

WEST VIRGINIA
Charleston
West Virginia Medical
    Journal **(33278)** ....(Paid) ‡2,500
                                       (Controlled) ‡100

WISCONSIN
Hudson
Neurology & Clinical Neurophysiology **(33796)**

Madison
American Orthoptic Journal **(33917)** .....(Paid) 1,600
Annals of Surgery **(33920)** ....‡7,806
Prehospital and Disaster
    Medicine **(33970)** ....(Controlled) 1,569
Wisconsin Medical Journal **(33987)** ....‡9,000

ALBERTA, CANADA
Calgary
Canadian Journal of Neurological
    Sciences **(34637)** 1,600

Edmonton
The Alberta Doctors'
    Digest **(34698)** ....(Non-paid) 6,000
Health Law Review **(34716)**

BRITISH COLUMBIA, CANADA
Nanaimo
Canadian Bulletin of Medical History/Bulletin Canadien
    D'historie de la Medecine **(35018)** ......(Paid) 300

Vancouver
BCMJ (The British Columbia Medical
    Journal) **(35126)** ....(Controlled) ‡8,700
Healthcare Product
    News **(35146)** ....(Combined) 15,388

White Rock
Occupational Therapy
    NOW **(35242)** ....(Combined) 6,500

ONTARIO, CANADA
Arnprior
Long Term Care **(35637)** ....(Controlled) 5,600

Hamilton
International Journal of Infectious
    Diseases **(35882)** ....(Paid) 2,769
Journal of the American Academy of
    Audiology **(35883)** ....(Paid) 9,065
Journal of Continuing Education in the Health
    Professions **(35884)** ....(Paid) 2,790
Journal of Travel Medicine **(35886)** ....(Paid) ‡2,486
Seminars in Headache Management **(35889)**
Transfusion Medicine Reviews **(35892)**

Milton
The Renal Family **(36051)** ....(Non-paid) ‡9,000

Mississauga
Canadian Family
    Physician **(36058)** ....(Combined) 33,908

Oakville
The Canadian Journal of Cardiology (Journal
    Canadien de
    Cardiologie) **(36137)** ....(Combined) 15,500
The Canadian Journal of
    Gastroenterology **(36139)** ....(Paid) ‡200
                                       (Controlled) ‡15,500
The Canadian Journal of Plastic Surgery **(36140)**
Canadian Respiratory
    Journal **(36141)** ....(Controlled) 15,500

Ottawa
Canadian Association of Radiologists
    Journal **(36189)** 1,600

Numbers cited after listings are entry numbers rather than page numbers.

Canadian Journal of Medical Radiation
  Technology (36207) ....(Paid) ‡9,798
                              (Non-paid) ‡89
The Canadian Journal of Occupational Therapy
  (Revue Canadienne
  d'Ergotherapie) (36209) ....(Paid) ‡7,000
                              (Non-paid) ‡76
Canadian Journal of Rural
  Medicine (36218) 6,300
Canadian Journal of
  Surgery (36220) ....(Combined) 2,700
CMA News (36235) ....‡45,600
CMAJ/JAMC (Canadian Medical Association Journal)/
  (Journal de l'Association Medicale
  Canadienne) (36236) ....(Combined) •62,008
Compendium of Pharmaceuticals and
  Specialties (36238)
Provincial Drug Benefit Programs (36273)

Port Burwell
The Canadian Journal of
  Herbalism (36331) 1,000

Toronto
Canadian Oncology Nursing Journal (36522)
Diabetes Dialogue (36573) ......(Controlled) ‡60,928
Journal of Critical Care (36634)
Journal of Orthomolecular Medicine (36636)
The Journal of
  Rheumatology (36637) ....(Paid) ‡3,500
                              (Non-paid) ‡60
The Medical Post (36659) ....(Combined) 43,241
Obesity Surgery (36679)
Ontario Medical
  Review (36684) ....(Combined) •24,029
Ontario Medicine (36685) ....(Combined) 17,087
Patient Care (36698) ....(Combined) 25,932
Physician's Management
  Manuals (36707) ....(Combined) 41,101
Physiotherapy Canada (36708)

QUEBEC, CANADA
Montreal
L'Actualite Medicale (37081) ....(Combined) 17,157
Canadian Journal of Anesthesia (Journal canadien
  d'anesthesie) (37095) 5,100
Doctor's Review (37109) ....(Combined) 38,500
Journal of Palliative Care (37144) ......(Paid) ‡1,200
                              (Non-paid) ‡79
L'Actualite Medicale (37154) ....(Non-paid) 16,511
                              (Paid) 730
Le Medecin du
  Quebec (37170) ....(Combined) 18,200
Parkhurst Exchange (37205) ......(Combined) 38,500

Pointe-Claire
The Canadian Journal of CME (Continuing Medical
  Education) (37272) ....(Controlled) 35,886
The Canadian Journal of
  Diagnosis (37273) ....(Combined) 35,733
Le Clinicien (37274) ....(Controlled) 12,416
Perspectives in
  Cardiology (37276) ....(Controlled) 15,269

METAL, METALLURGY, AND METAL TRADE

**See also Machinery and Equipment;
Engineering (Various branches); Plumbing
and Heating; Air Conditioning and
Refrigeration; Mining and Minerals; Welding**

CALIFORNIA
Georgetown
The Anvil's Ring (2002) ....(Paid) 4,574

Los Angeles
Journal of Materials Engineering and
  Performance (2303) ....(Paid) ⊕541
                              (Non-paid) ⊕141

Pico Rivera
Armenian Numismatic Journal (2839) ......(Paid) 200

Rancho Santa Fe
Silver Magazine (2882) ....‡6,000

San Clemente
Industrial West (3101) ....(Controlled) ‡24,700

South San Francisco
Light Metal Age (3789) ....(Paid) 5,380

COLORADO
Littleton
Mining Engineering (4553) ....(Paid) 17,057

CONNECTICUT
Guilford
Wire Journal
  International (4879) ....(Controlled) ‡14,100

DISTRICT OF COLUMBIA
Washington
The Ironworker (5561)
Scrap (5784) ....(Paid) 7322
Valve Magazine (5839)

FLORIDA
Nokomis
Modern Applications News
  (MAN) (6464) ....(Controlled) ‡85,001
                              (Free) ‡118
                              (Paid) ‡17

Orlando
Plating & Surface Finishing (6507) ....(Paid) ‡508

GEORGIA
Forest Park
Ornamental Miscellaneous Metal
  Fabricator (7276) ....(Combined) ‡8,000

ILLINOIS
Bensenville
Process Heating (8070) ....(Controlled) 23,000

Chicago
Modern Metals (8491) ....(Controlled) ‡40,000

Des Plaines
Modern Casting Magazine (8764) ....(Paid) 1,684
                              (Controlled) 24,806

Glenview
Finishers' Management (8934) ....(Paid) 422
                              (Non-paid) 10,466

Oak Brook
Metal Center News (9360) ....(Non-paid) ‡13,542
Springs (9366) ....(Non-paid) 9,754

Rockford
The FABRICATOR (9527) ....(Controlled) 55,000
Stamping Journal (9533) ....(Controlled) 35,000
TPJ—The Tube & Pipe
  Journal (9534) ....(Controlled) ‡30,000

Rosemont
Die Casting Engineer (9555) ....(Paid) ‡3,400
                              (Non-paid) ‡350

Wonder Lake
Die Casting Management (9770) ....(Paid) ‡55
                              (Non-paid) ‡4,369

KANSAS
Kansas City
Boilermaker Reporter (11525) ....(Non-paid) 85,000

MARYLAND
Bethesda
World Calendar (13389)

MICHIGAN
Dearborn
Forming &
  Fabricating (14902) ....(Controlled) 65,496

Novi
American Tool, Die & Stamping
  News (15407) ....(Controlled) 34,000

Traverse City
Machinist's Workshop (15599) ....(Paid) ‡19,911
                              (Non-paid) ‡91

MISSOURI
St. Louis
Synthesis and Reactivity in Inorganic and Metal-
  Organic Chemistry (17519) 300

NEW JERSEY
Clark
Wire Rope News & Sling
  Technology (18749) ....(Controlled) ‡4,000
                              (Paid) ‡470

Hoboken
Magnetic Resonance in Chemistry (19056)

Morris Plains
Production Technology
  News (19304) ....(Controlled) ‡81,000

Princeton
International Journal of Powder
  Metallurgy (19463) ....‡3,400

NEW YORK
Larchmont
Metalworking Insiders' Report (20920)

New York
Foodservice Equipment and Supplies (21715)
Industrial Laboratory (21866)
Journal of Light Metals (22111)
Metal Finishing (22321) ....(Paid) 2,042
                              (Non-paid) 17,745

Metals Week (22324)
Protection of Metals (22601)
Soviet Journal of Non-Ferrous Metals (22767)
Soviet Metal Technology (22768)
Soviet Powder Metallurgy and Metal
  Ceramics (22769)

Webster
Automatic Machining (23526) 13,000

NORTH CAROLINA
Charlotte
Direct From Midrex (23743) ....(Controlled) 3,100

OHIO
Beachwood
Alloys Index (24647)
Metalforming Technology Digest (24652)
Metals Abstracts (24653)
Nonferrous Alert (24654)
Polymers/Ceramics/Composites Alert (24655)
Steels Alert (24657)

Cincinnati
Automotive Design and
  Production (24777) ....(Non-paid) ‡55,000
Modern Machine Shop (24810) ....(Free) 117,000
Products Finishing (24813) ....(Controlled) ‡45,677

Cleveland
American Machinist (24855) ....(Non-paid) ‡80,000
Forging (24897) ....(Combined) 5,000
Foundry Management &
  Technology (24899) ....(Non-paid) ‡18,500
33 Metal Producing (24956) .....(Controlled) ‡18,760
Welding Design &
  Fabrication (24961) ....(Controlled) ‡40,000

Independence
Metalforming (25251) ....(Non-paid) 60,000

Materials Park
Advanced Materials &
  Processes (25363) ....(Paid) 30,000
Alloy Digest (25364) 250
International Materials
  Reviews (25366) ....(Paid) 200
                              (Non-paid) 30
Journal of Phase Equilibria (25367) .....(Paid) ‡201
                              (Non-paid) ‡104

Powell
American Fastener Journal (25489) ....(Paid) 844
                              (Controlled) 10,042

Solon
Tooling &
  Production (25529) ....(Controlled) ‡80,845

Stow
Fastener Technology
  International (25545) ....(Controlled) ‡13,050
Wire & Cable Technology
  International (25548) ....(Controlled) ‡10,500

PENNSYLVANIA
Pittsburgh
AISE Steel Technology (27754) ....(Paid) ‡12,034
                              (Non-paid) ‡589
Industrial Heating (27799) ....(Paid) 265
                              (Non-paid) 24,000
Steelabor (27847) ....‡840,000

Warrendale
Iron & Steel Maker
  Magazine (28112) ....(Paid) 8,572
                              (Non-paid) 1,000

TENNESSEE
Collierville
Cutting Tool Business (29134)

TEXAS
Houston
Corrosion (30466) ....‡3,500

Circulation: ★ = ABC; △ = BPA; ♦ = CAC; • = CCAB; ❑ = VAC; ⊕ = PO Statement; ‡ = Publisher's Report; Boldface figures = sworn; Light figures = estimated.

3193

Trade, Technical, and Professional Publications

Circ.   Circ.   Circ.

METAL, METALLURGY, AND METAL TRADE
(continued)
Materials Performance (30506) ....(Paid) ‡15,835

WISCONSIN
Iola
Metal Roofing Magazine (33835)

Milwaukee
Metalsmith (34080) ....(Paid) ‡5,994
(Controlled) ‡50
(Controlled) ‡6,200

ONTARIO, CANADA
Burlington
Canadian Industrial
Machinery (35715) ....(Combined) 17,464

Markham
Metalworking Production and
Purchasing (36028) ....(Combined) •20,234

Toronto
Canadian Machinery and
Metalworking (36515) ....(Paid) •306
(Non-paid) •19,120

Communique (36555)

QUEBEC, CANADA
Jonquiere
Le Lingot (37012) ....‡16,000

Montreal
CIM Bulletin (Canadian Mining & Metallurgical
Bulletin) (37103) ....‡10,140

METEOROLOGY

DISTRICT OF COLUMBIA
Washington
Weatherwise (5858)

MASSACHUSETTS
Boston
Journal of Applied Meteorology (13912) ....‡2,721

NEW JERSEY
Hoboken
International Journal of Climatology (18979)

NEW YORK
New York
Journal of Seismology (22185)
Meteorological Applications (22325) 600

MILITARY AND NAVY
See also Veterans

ALABAMA
Marion
Marion Military Institute Alumni
Bulletin (311) ....(Controlled) ‡10,000

Maxwell AFB
Air Force Journal of Logistics (313) 14,000
Air Force Law Review (314)
Air and Space Power Journal (315) ....(Paid) ‡1,200
(Controlled) ‡20,000

ALASKA
Anchorage
Sourdough Sentinel (532) ....(Free) 7,500

ARIZONA
Fort Huachuca
Commander (708) ....(Paid) ‡2,300
(Controlled) ‡5,000
Military Intelligence Professional Bulletin (709)

Glendale
Thunderbolt (716) ....(Free) ‡11,500

Tucson
Vietnam War Generation Journal (971)

CALIFORNIA
Bakersfield
Strategy & Tactics (1453) ....(Paid) ⊕5,200

Barstow
Barstow Log (1480) ....(Non-paid) 3,500

Camp Pendleton
Flight Jacket (1651) ....(Free) ‡13,000

The Scout (1652)

Edwards AFB
Desert Wings (1841) ....(Non-paid) 10,000

El Segundo
Astro News (1867) ....(Non-paid) 5,500

Fort Irwin
Tiefort Telegraph (1925) ....(Non-paid) 6,500

Lancaster
Aerotech News &
Review (2146) ....(Non-paid) 15,000

Lompoc
Space and Missile Times (2163) ....(Free) ‡8,500

Los Angeles
The Lighthouse (2317) ....(Non-paid) ‡11,000
Soldiers Today (2391)

March Air Force Base
The Beacon (2503) ....(Free) 9,100

Newport Beach
Ex-CBI Roundup (2626) ....‡5,247

Palm Springs
GEO Europe (2760)

Redlands
Globetrotter (2904) ....(Free) 10,000

Sacramento
Military (3008) ....‡26,000

San Diego
San Diego Navy
Dispatch (3266) ....(Non-paid) 40,000

San Luis Obispo
Command Magazine (3564) ....‡24,000
(Non-paid) ‡100

Woodland Hills
Airpower (4100)

COLORADO
Colorado Springs
Space Observer (4257) ....(Free) ‡7,500

USAF Academy
Academy Spirit (4651) ....(Free) ‡7,500

CONNECTICUT
Monroe
Army Aviation Magazine (4962) ....‡14,500

Torrington
The Dolphin (5177)

DELAWARE
Dover
The Airlifter (5242) ....(Free) 7,000

DISTRICT OF COLUMBIA
Ft. McNair
Military Psychology (5306)

Washington
Interservice (5559) ....(Paid) ‡10,000
Joint Force Quarterly (5565)
Marines Magazine (5644) 62,000
National Guard Magazine (5676) ....‡42,000
Navy Civil Engineer (5690) ....(Paid) ‡200
(Non-paid) ‡16,000
The Officer (5705) 80,000

FLORIDA
Gulf Breeze
Russia & Eurasia Military Review Annual (6181)

Mayport
The Mirror (6333) ....(Free) ‡9,700

GEORGIA
Fort Benning
Infantry (7281) ....(Paid) ‡3,700
(Controlled) ‡10,360

Fort Gordon
Army Communicator (7282) ....(Controlled) ‡5,000
The Signal (7283) ....‡16,000

Robins AFB
Citizen Airman (7499) ....(Controlled) 75,000

Warner Robins
Robins Rev-Up (7637) ....(Free) ‡20,000

HAWAII
Camp H M Smith
Asia-Pacific Defense
Forum (7660) ....(Non-paid) 27,000

Kaneohe
Hawaii Army Weekly (7769) ....(Free) 13,489
Hawaii Marine (7771) ....(Free) 9,000
Hawaii Navy News (7772) ....(Free) 15,873
Hawaiian Falcon (7773) ....(Free) 7,315
Military Sun Press (7775) ....(Free) ‡7,374

IDAHO
Boise
Gunfighter (7808) ....(Free) ‡5,400

ILLINOIS
Chicago
JMNR (8426) ....(Paid) 900
(Non-paid) 1,500

Edwardsville
Command Post (8811) ....‡14,100

Springfield
Patriots of the
Heartland (9640) ....(Controlled) ‡15,000

KANSAS
Fort Leavenworth
Military Review (11440) ....(Paid) ‡5,000
(Controlled) ‡20,000

Fort Riley
Fort Riley Post (11442) ....(Paid) ‡250
(Free) ‡7,391

KENTUCKY
Fort Campbell
Ft. Campbell Courier (12060) ....(Free) 23,000

Fort Knox
Armor (12061) ....(Paid) 7,000
(Non-paid) 7,000
Inside the Turret (12062) ....(Free) ‡20,000

LOUISIANA
Deridder
Guardian (12565) ....(Free) ‡15,000

New Orleans
Naval Reservist
News (12742) ....(Controlled) ‡100,000

MARYLAND
Annapolis
Naval History (13095) 32,000
Proceedings (13096) ....‡125,000
Shipmate (13097) ....‡42,500

Bethesda
Military Grocer (13360) ....(Controlled) 8,000
Military Medicine (13361) ....(Paid) ‡12,500

Fort Meade
Soundoff (13504) ....(Non-paid) 11,841
(Paid) 8

Pasadena
Minerva (13644) ....(Paid) ‡500
(Non-paid) ‡20

Temple Hills
Sergeants (13754) ....(Non-paid) ‡131,000

MASSACHUSETTS
Ayer
Fort Devens Dispatch (13828) ....(Free) 5,200

Cambridge
International Security (14072) ....‡4,600
Journal of Cold War
Studies (14075) ....(Combined) 2,300

Norwood
Journal of Electronic
Defense (14447) ....(Paid) ‡15,084

MINNESOTA
Minneapolis
Military Thought (16098) 200

MISSISSIPPI
Columbus
Silver Wings (16605) ....(Free) 3,000

Vicksburg
Dredging Research (16870) ....(Non-paid) 2200

Numbers cited after listings are entry numbers rather than page numbers.

MISSOURI
Fort Leonard Wood
CML Army Chemical Review **(17071)**
Engineer: The Professional Bulletin for Army
   Engineers **(17073)**

Independence
Army Motors **(17105)** ....(Controlled) 10,000

NEBRASKA
Offutt A F B
The Air Pulse **(18187)** ....(Free) ‡13,000

NEW HAMPSHIRE
Nashua
Military & Aerospace
   Electronics **(18597)** ....(Paid) 200
                              (Controlled) 48,000

NEW JERSEY
Somerset
Armed Forces & Society **(19561)** ....(Paid) ‡1,700

Willingboro
Airtides **(19752)** ....(Non-paid) ♦9,291
The Post **(19754)** ....(Non-paid) ♦9,196

NEW MEXICO
Albuquerque
Focus KAFB Newspaper **(19771)** .....(Free) ‡15,000

NEW YORK
Floral Park
Salute **(20606)** ....(Controlled) ‡200,000

Westbury
Exchange & Commissary
   News **(23554)** ....(Paid) ⊕642
                              8,300
Government Food
   Service **(23555)** ....(Controlled) 10,500
Military Club & Hospitality **(23557)** ....(Paid) ‡61
                              ‡9,079
R & R Shopper's
   News **(23559)** ....(Controlled) ‡100,000

NORTH CAROLINA
Fort Bragg
Special Warfare **(23897)** ....(Combined) 10,200

Raeford
Fort Bragg Paraglide **(24120)** ....(Free) 25,000

OHIO
Toledo
Warship International **(25573)** ....(Paid) 3,000
                              (Non-paid) 62

Wright Patterson AFB
Skywrighter **(25684)** ....(Free) ‡35,000

OKLAHOMA
Altus
Patriot **(25731)** ....(Free) 5,000

Fort Sill
The Cannoneer **(25837)** ....(Free) ‡14,500
Field Artillery **(25838)** ....(Paid) ‡7,000
                              (Non-paid) ‡7,000

PENNSYLVANIA
Carlisle
Parameters **(26760)** ....(Paid) ‡1,500
                              (Non-paid) ‡11,500

Harrisburg
MHQ **(26998)** ....(Paid) ‡29,000

Pittsburgh
All Hands **(27756)**
Military Law Review **(27813)**
The Mobility Forum **(27815)**
Naval Aviation News **(27819)**
Navy Medicine **(27820)**
United States Army Aviation Digest **(27852)**

RHODE ISLAND
Newport
Naval War College
   Review **(28367)** ....(Controlled) ‡10,000
The Newport Navalog **(28371)** ....(Free) ‡6,000

TEXAS
Denton
Military History of the
   West **(30242)** ....(Combined) 550

San Angelo
Goodfellow Monitor **(31004)** ....(Controlled) 5,000

San Antonio
Airman **(31024)** ....(Controlled) 750,000

UTAH
Ogden
Hilltop Times **(31377)** ....(Free) ‡20,000

Tooele
Shopper's Guide (UT) **(31479)** ....(Free) ‡3,500

VERMONT
Tunbridge
The Civil War News **(31608)** ....(Paid) 9,000
                              (Free) 400

VIRGINIA
Alexandria
Armed Forces Comptroller **(31643)** ....‡20,000
Defense Transportation Journal **(31664)** ......‡10,000
The Military Engineer **(31709)** ....(Paid) 20,066
Naval Affairs **(31715)** ....(Controlled) ‡145,000
Officer Review **(31718)** ....(Paid) ‡11,000
                              (Non-paid) ‡100
The Retired Officer
   Magazine **(31733)** ....(Paid) 385,088
The Sojourner **(31738)** ....(Paid) ‡9,500
                              (Non-paid) ‡200
Translog: Journal of Military Transportation
   Management **(31746)**
Wings of Gold **(31753)** ....(Paid) ‡9,200
                              (Non-paid) ‡905

Arlington
Air Force Magazine **(31768)** ....(Paid) 182,330
                              (Non-paid) 6,165
ARMY Magazine **(31780)** ....(Paid) 79,091
National Defense **(31810)** ....(Paid) 24,000
                              (Non-paid) 1,720
Pentagram **(31816)** ....(Free) 26,000
Sea Power **(31830)** ....(Paid) 75,000
                              (Controlled) 5,919

Charlottesville
Army Lawyer **(31915)**

Fairfax
SIGNAL **(32029)** ....(Paid) △26,483
                              (Non-paid) △2,046

Fort Belvoir
Acquisition Review
   Quarterly **(32078)** ....(Free) 14,397

Hampton
The Flyer **(32127)** ....(Controlled) ‡13,500

Harrisonburg
Journal of Mine Action **(32140)**

Langley AFB
Combat Edge **(32176)**

Leesburg
Vietnam **(32187)**

Lexington
The Journal of Military
   History **(32189)** ....(Paid) ‡2,900
                              (Non-paid) ‡30

Norfolk
Profile (Norfolk) **(32292)** ....(Non-paid) 30,000

Quantico
Leatherneck **(32341)** 97,600
Marine Corps Gazette **(32342)** ....(Paid) ‡28,718
                              (Controlled) ‡894

Springfield
Air Force Times **(32537)** ....(Paid) 61,846
Armed Forces Journal
   International **(32539)** ....(Paid) 4,000
                              (Non-paid) 34,000
Army Times **(32540)** ....(Paid) 94,099
Defense News **(32542)** ....(Paid) 11,309
                              (Controlled) 27,177
Navy Times **(32549)** ....(Paid) 51,170

Woodbridge
Belvoir Eagle **(32636)** ....(Free) 19,000
Quantico Sentry **(32638)** ....(Free) ‡11,000

WASHINGTON
Mill Creek
Defense Communities **(32831)**

Silverdale
N.W. Navigator **(33084)** ....(Combined) ♦6,696

Tacoma
The Ranger **(33149)** ....(Free) ‡24,700

WISCONSIN
Iola
Military Trader **(33837)** ....(Combined) 9,778

ALBERTA, CANADA
Coldlake
Canadian Forces Base Cold Lake
   Courier **(34688)** ....(Free) ‡3,000

Edmonton
Sealandair **(34728)** ....(Paid) 21
                              (Free) 3,200

Medicine Hat
Demining Technology Information Forum
   Journal **(34809)**

BRITISH COLUMBIA, CANADA
Lazo
CFB Comox Totem
   Times **(35008)** ....(Combined) 2,150
Totem Times **(35009)** ....(Free) 2,100

Victoria
The Lookout **(35220)** ....‡5,000

MANITOBA, CANADA
Winnipeg
Voxair **(35357)** ....(Free) 4,850

NEW BRUNSWICK, CANADA
Moncton
The Moncton Provider **(35412)** ....‡700

Oromocto
The Oromocto
   Post-Gazette **(35424)** ....(Paid) ‡3,240
                              (Free) ‡540

NOVA SCOTIA, CANADA
Greenwood
Aurora **(35556)** ....(Free) ‡5,800

Halifax
TRIDENT **(35571)** ....(Free) ‡10,000
                              (Paid) ‡200

ONTARIO, CANADA
Borden
Borden Citizen **(35691)** ....(Paid) ‡300
                              (Free) ‡3,700

Hornel Heights
The Shield **(35915)** ....(Free) ‡1,000

Ottawa
Airforce **(36184)** ....(Paid) 15,738
                              (Non-paid) 3,752
Radio Aids to Marine Navigation **(36274)**

Toronto
Canadian Defence Quarterly (Revue Canadienne de
   Defense) **(36496)** ....(Combined) ‡5,850

Trenton
CONTACT **(36824)** ....(Free) ‡3,500

QUEBEC, CANADA
Alouette
Phare/Beacon **(36931)** ....(Controlled) 2,500

Montreal
ADSUM **(37083)** ....(Free) ‡5,000

Richelain
Servir **(37306)** 3,300

MILK AND DAIRY PRODUCTS
**See also Confectionaries and Frozen Dairy
Products**

ILLINOIS
Bensenville
Dairy Foods **(8066)** ....(Paid) 656
                              (Controlled) 20,230

Rolling Meadows
The National Dipper **(9549)** ....(Non-paid) 17,000

IOWA
Des Moines
Journal of Food Protection **(10800)** ....‡3,100

Circulation: ★ = ABC; △ = BPA; ♦ = CAC; • = CCAB; ❑ = VAC; ⊕ = PO Statement; ‡ = Publisher's Report; Boldface figures = sworn; Light figures = estimated.

Circ.   Circ.   Circ.

MILK AND DAIRY PRODUCTS (continued)

WISCONSIN
Appleton
Milk & Liquid Food
Transporter **(33538)** ....(Controlled) 4,812

Middleton
Cheese Market News **(34050)** ....(Paid) ‡2,325

QUEBEC, CANADA
Longueuil
Le Producteur de Lait
Quebecois **(37055)** ....(Combined) •10,278

MINING AND MINERALS

See also Stone and Rock Products;
Petroleum, Oil, and Gas; Metal, Metallurgy,
and Metal Trade

ALASKA
Anchorage
Petroleum News Alaska **(530)** ....(Paid) ‡1,600
(Non-paid) ‡800

ARIZONA
Bisbee
Pay Dirt Magazine **(660)** ....‡3,500

Phoenix
Southwest Contractor **(811)** ....(Combined) 6,000

CALIFORNIA
Aptos
International California Mining
Journal **(1426)** ....‡10,000

Carlsbad
Gems & Gemology **(1665)** 10,000

Irvine
World Dredging, Mining &
Construction **(2093)** ....‡3,400

Ventura
Rock & Gem **(4009)** ....‡65,000

COLORADO
Denver
The Mining Record **(4339)** ....‡5,260

Golden
Colorado School of Mines Quarterly **(4465)** .....‡300
Mines Magazine **(4470)** ....‡20,000

Littleton
Economic Geology **(4547)** 5,000
Minerals and Metallurgical
Processing **(4552)** ....‡587
Mining Engineering **(4553)** ....(Paid) 17,057

DISTRICT OF COLUMBIA
Washington
Federal Mine Safety and Health Review **(5494)**
Rocks & Minerals **(5770)** ....(Paid) ‡3,100
(Controlled) 1,000

IDAHO
Boise
Miner's News **(7814)** ....(Paid) ‡2,520
(Non-paid) ‡3,879

INDIANA
Indianapolis
Mine & Quarry Trader **(10154)** ....(Non-paid) 35,309

KANSAS
Overland Park
Coal Age **(11705)** ....(Controlled) ‡19,609

MINNESOTA
Duluth
Skillings Mining Review **(15842)** ....(Paid) 2,370
(Controlled) 60

Minneapolis
Engineering and Mining
Journal **(16074)** ....(Non-paid) 14,082

NEW YORK
New York
American Museum Novitates **(21202)**
Geotechnical and Geological Engineering **(21758)**
Journal of Mining Science **(22134)**
Lithology and Mineral Resources **(22261)**
Natural Resources Research **(22408)**

World Mining Equipment **(22942)**

OHIO
Bowling Green
Equipment Echoes **(24691)** ....(Paid) 4,300

Cleveland
Journal of Explosives
Engineering **(24914)** ....(Combined) 36,000
Pit & Quarry **(24942)** ....(Non-paid) 23,564
(Paid) 2,437

PENNSYLVANIA
Pittsburgh
Monthly Energy Review **(27817)**

University Park
Earth and Mineral
Sciences **(28075)** ....(Controlled) ‡18,500

VIRGINIA
Fairfax
United Mine Workers Journal **(32033)**

WEST VIRGINIA
Charleston
Coal People Magazine **(33269)** ....(Paid) ‡3,000
(Non-paid) ‡8,500
West Virginia Coal Facts **(33274)**

BRITISH COLUMBIA, CANADA
Victoria
BC Mine Rescue Manual **(35207)**

ONTARIO, CANADA
Toronto
Canadian Mining
Journal **(36519)** ....(Combined) •10,158
Nickel **(36674)** ....(Non-paid) 37,000
The Northern Miner **(36677)**

QUEBEC, CANADA
Montreal
CIM Bulletin (Canadian Mining & Metallurgical
Bulletin) **(37103)** ....‡10,140
CIM Reporter **(37104)** ....(Controlled) 8,106

MOTION PICTURES

See also Photography

ARIZONA
Tempe
Java Magazine **(906)** ....(Controlled) 27,000

CALIFORNIA
Berkeley
Film Quarterly **(1521)** ....‡5,626
Jump Cut **(1539)** ....(Paid) 3,000

Culver City
Film Score Monthly **(1793)** ....(Combined) 11,000

Los Angeles
The Agencies **(2203)** ....(Paid) 487
(Combined) 3,390
International Documentary **(2297)** 12,000
Journal of Film and Video **(2301)** 1,400
Variety **(2427)** ....(Mon.) 34,293
Variety's on Production **(2428)** ....(Paid) ‡200
(Controlled) ‡28,000

Pasadena
BOXOFFICE Magazine **(2812)** ....(Paid) 5,940

Riverside
Cinefex **(2935)** ....(Paid) 36,000
(Non-paid) 1,000

San Francisco
Cinematograph **(3343)** ....(Controlled) 3,000
Film/Tape World **(3361)** ....(Controlled) 4,000
Release Print **(3423)** ....(Combined) 9,000

Van Nuys
Entertainment Employment Journal **(3989)**
Update Magazine **(3996)** 24,000

West Hollywood
ICG Magazine **(4063)** ....(Combined) ⊕12,000

CONNECTICUT
Fairfield
Hitchcock Annual **(4789)** ....(Combined) 1,000

DISTRICT OF COLUMBIA
Washington
Journal of Popular Film and
Television **(5613)** ....(Paid) ‡780

FLORIDA
Palatka
Cinevue Worldwide Talent Directory and Festival
Program Book **(6536)** ....(Paid) ‡2,000
(Controlled) ‡2,000

GEORGIA
Savannah
Animation Journal **(7530)** ....(Paid) 200

ILLINOIS
Chicago
Screen Magazine **(8562)** ....‡15,000

KANSAS
Overland Park
Millimeter Magazine **(11721)** ....(Paid) 207
(Paid) 30,201

MARYLAND
Baltimore
Wide Angle **(13262)** ....‡828

Salisbury
Literature Film Quarterly **(13709)** ....‡800

NEW YORK
Albany
Film Literature Index **(19986)** ....‡525

New York
Film Comment **(21693)** ....‡47,000
Film Journal International **(21694)** 10,200
Scene at the
Movies **(22709)** ....(Non-paid) ‡652,720

Wantagh
Films in Review **(23500)** 38,500

White Plains
SMPTE Journal **(23573)** ....(Paid) ‡9,200

OKLAHOMA
Cleveland
Film & History **(25789)** ....(Paid) 1,000

PENNSYLVANIA
Indiana
Studies in the Humanities **(27077)** ....(Paid) 300

Meadville
Film Criticism **(27234)** ....(Combined) 650

TENNESSEE
Memphis
Cinema Revue **(29361)** ....(Paid) 1,000

TEXAS
Dallas
Cinema Journal **(30136)** ....(Combined) ⊕2,858

ONTARIO, CANADA
Toronto
CineAction! **(36550)** ....(Paid) 400
(Non-paid) 2,000
Playback **(36711)** ....(Controlled) ‡8,500

Waterloo
Kinema **(36854)**

MOTORCYCLES

CALIFORNIA
Agoura
V-Twin News **(1384)**

Costa Mesa
Cycle News **(1773)** ....(Paid) 35,496
(Free) 1,247

NEVADA
Gardnerville
Motorcycle Industry
Magazine **(18348)** ....(Non-paid) 20,202

BRITISH COLUMBIA, CANADA
Langley
MPH **(35004)** 2,000

MUSEUMS

CALIFORNIA
Walnut Creek
Curator (4051)

Woodland Hills
Exhibit Builder (4103) 15,000

CONNECTICUT
Mystic
Log of Mystic Seaport (4968) ....(Paid) 22,000
(Controlled) 300

DISTRICT OF COLUMBIA
Washington
Museum News (5664) ....‡17,000
Smithsonian Magazine (5794) ....(Paid) 2,055,887

IDAHO
Moscow
Focus on Security (7914) ....(Paid) 100

ILLINOIS
Springfield
The Living Museum (9639) ....(Non-paid) ‡18,000

INDIANA
Indianapolis
Previews (10162) ....(Controlled) ‡12,000

MASSACHUSETTS
Deerfield
Historic Deerfield (14157)

Salem
The American Neptune (14512) ....‡1,550

Sturbridge
Old Sturbridge Visitor (14577) ....(Combined) 12,000

MICHIGAN
Detroit
Bulletin of the Detroit Institute of
Arts (14917) ....(Combined) 5,500

MISSOURI
Columbia
Muse (17007) ....(Controlled) 660
(Paid) 1,200

NEW YORK
Bronx
Art Index (20253)

New York
Archives and Museum Informatics (21246)
MoMA Magazine (22359) ....(Combined) 60,000

PENNSYLVANIA
Philadelphia
Philadelphia Museum of Art
Bulletin (27629) ....(Paid) ‡4,000
(Non-paid) ‡4,000

TENNESSEE
Nashville
History News (29458) ....(Paid) ‡5,100
(Non-paid) ‡828

MANITOBA, CANADA
Winnipeg
The Manitoba Museum Annual
Report (35340) ....(Non-paid) 2,700

ONTARIO, CANADA
Toronto
Rotunda (36732) 25,000

MUSIC AND MUSICAL INSTRUMENTS

See also Performing Arts

ARIZONA
Tempe
General Music Today (904)
Journal of Historical Research in Music
Education (907) ....(Combined) 227

CALIFORNIA
Berkeley
Music Perception (1543) ....‡1,450

19th-Century Music (1548) 1,382

Burbank
Entertainment Today (1617) ....‡215,000

Concord
CMEA News (1751) ....(Paid) ‡3,250

Culver City
Film Score Monthly (1793) ....(Combined) 11,000

Emeryville
Electronic Musician (1877) ....(Paid) △49,775
(Non-paid) △17,697
Mix (1879) ....(Paid) 2,044
(Controlled) 53,597
Mix—Edicion en
Espanol (1880) ....(Combined) 20,000

Fresno
Pollstar (1956)

Los Angeles
The Beat (Los Angeles) (2217) ....(Non-paid) 25,000
Overture (2355) ....(Paid) ‡10,000
(Free) ‡450
Polish Music Journal (2372)

Lynwood
World of Pageantry (2488) ....(Paid) ⊕12,000

Malibu
Windplayer (2497)

Orange
The Jazzologist (2723) ....‡3,600

San Anselmo
Acoustic Guitar Magazine (3081) ....(Paid) 50,000
STRINGS (3084) ....‡15,000

San Diego
American Federation of Musicians (3110) .....‡1,200

San Francisco
Musical News (3393) ....(Free) ‡3,200

Studio City
Music Connection Magazine (3822) ....⊕75,000

COLORADO
Boulder
American Music Research Center
Journal (4155) ....(Combined) 400
American Suzuki Journal (4156) ....‡9,000
Recording (4186) ....(Paid) ‡24,679
(Non-paid) ‡2,857

DISTRICT OF COLUMBIA
Washington
The World & I (5870) ....(Paid) 20,056
(Non-paid) 2,781

FLORIDA
Tallahassee
Florida Music Director (6716) ....(Paid) ‡4,500
Psychomusicology (6728)

GEORGIA
Athens
Georgia Music News (6941) 3,200
Southeastern Journal of Music
Education (6951) ....(Paid) 300

ILLINOIS
Champaign
American Music (8179) ....‡1,600
Ethnomusicology (8186)

Chicago
Black Music Research Journal (8285)
Lenox Avenue (8460)

Deerfield
Harmony (8724) ....(Combined) 8,000

DeKalb
Music Reference Services Quarterly (8738) 213

Des Plaines
The DIAPASON (8760) ....‡5,100

Elmhurst
Music Inc. (8836) ....(Controlled) ‡8,900

Northfield
Clavier (9326) ....‡16,700
The Instrumentalist (9330) ....‡18,200

Springfield
Illinois Music Educator (9627) ....(Controlled) 3,500

Urbana
Bulletin of the Council for Research in Music
Education (9698) ....(Paid) ‡1,000
(Non-paid) ‡100

INDIANA
Bloomington
Philosophy of Music Education
Review (9849) ....(Paid) 500

Muncie
Indiana Musicator (10327) ....(Paid) 2,000

Notre Dame
American Musicology Society
Journal (10367) ....(Combined) 4,800

West Lafayette
The Woman Conductor (10555)

IOWA
Iowa City
Syllecta Classica (10989) ....(Combined) 120

KANSAS
Lawrence
International Journal of Research in Choral
Singing (11553)

Manhattan
Jazz Education Journal (11621) ....(Paid) 7,500
(Non-paid) 300

Wichita
Kansas Music Review (11886) 2,500

KENTUCKY
Russellville
Bluegrass Music News (12388) ....‡2,100

LOUISIANA
Baton Rouge
Journal for Research in Music
Education (12491) ....(Paid) ‡3,500
(Controlled) ‡19
Update (12507)

MARYLAND
Baltimore
Modernism/Modernity (13220) ....(Combined) 637

Silver Spring
JazzTimes (13728) ....(Paid) ‡80,898
(Non-paid) ‡9,000

Journal of Music Therapy (13731)
Uno Mas Magazine (13747)

Thurmont
Maryland Music
Educator (13755) ....(Combined) 1,400

MASSACHUSETTS
Babson Park
Journal of Popular Music Studies (13831)

Boston
Berklee Today (13854) ....(Non-paid) ‡41,000

Cambridge
Computer Music Journal (14046) 2,193
Leonardo Music Journal (14080)

Medfield
Jazz Player (14316)
Saxophone Journal (14318)

Needham
Musical Merchandise
Review (14363) ....(Paid) 1,338
(Non-paid) △9,913

Newton Highlands
Plainsong and Medieval
Music (14415) ....(Paid) ‡414
(Non-paid) ‡47

West Stockbridge
Lingo Magazine (14627) 3,500,000

MICHIGAN
Royal Oak
Alarm Clock (15476) ....(Non-paid) 200

Warren
The Music Index (15660) ....‡750

MINNESOTA
Bloomington
The Hymn (15758) ....(Paid) ⊕2,847

Circulation: ★ = ABC; △ = BPA; ♦ = CAC; ● = CCAB; ❑ = VAC; ⊕ = PO Statement; ‡ = Publisher's Report; Boldface figures = sworn; Light figures = estimated.

3197

Trade, Technical, and Professional Publications

Circ.   Circ.   Circ.

MUSIC AND MUSICAL INSTRUMENTS
(continued)

Minnetonka
REQUEST **(16175)** ....(Paid) 1,000,000

MISSOURI
Kansas City
Live Sound! International **(17181)** ....(Paid) 2,800
(Non-paid) 7,950
Piano Technicians Journal **(17192)** 4,000

Springfield
Explorations in Renaissance
Culture **(17598)** ....(Combined) 314

NEBRASKA
Lincoln
Nebraska Music Educator **(18104)** ....(Paid) 1,650
Women and Music **(18128)**

NEW JERSEY
Cedar Grove
Drum Business **(18720)** ....(Controlled) 6,600

Englewood
Music Trades **(18796)** ....(Paid) 5,668

NEW YORK
Manhasset
Gavin **(21001)**

New Rochelle
New on the Charts **(21119)** ....‡2,500

New York
The American Organist **(21203)** ....‡24,000
British Journal of Music Education **(21341)** 750
Cambridge Opera Journal **(21368)** 750
Chamber Music **(21395)** ....(Paid) $10,000
(Non-paid) $2,000
CMJ New Music Report **(21433)**
Country Airplay Monitor **(21505)** 2,803
CVC Report **(21527)** ....(Paid) 800
Early Music History **(21574)** 550
Historic Brass Society **(21805)** ....(Paid) 800
Impact! **(21853)**
International Musician **(21927)** 150,000
Journal of Jewish Music and Liturgy **(22109)**
Music Alive! **(22384)**
Music and Media **(22386)** 1,600
Popular Music **(22580)** 800
Pro Sound News **(22595)** ....(Controlled) ‡24,653
Renaissance Quarterly **(22646)** ....‡3,500
RILM Abstracts of Music
Literature **(22668)** ....‡1,200
Rock Airplay Monitor **(22674)** 2,803
SYMPHONY **(22813)** ....‡18,500
Top 40 Airplay Monitor **(22843)** 2,803

Port Washington
DJ Times **(23125)** 20,000
The Music & Sound
Retailer **(23131)** ....(Controlled) 11,300

Rochester
Integral **(23230)**
Music Theory Spectrum **(23233)**
The Opera Quarterly **(23234)** ....(Combined) 3800

NORTH CAROLINA
Chapel Hill
Beethoven Forum **(23699)**

OHIO
Bowling Green
Popular Music and Society **(24700)**

Cincinnati
American Music Teacher **(24771)** .....(Paid) ‡24,000
(Free) ‡300

Columbus
Journal of Music Teacher Education **(25026)**

Youngstown
Contributions to Music
Education **(25696)** ....(Paid) 400

OKLAHOMA
Lawton
Choral Journal **(25885)** ....‡18,500

Norman
Journal of Music Theory
Pedagogy **(25936)** ....(Paid) 500

PENNSYLVANIA
Bethlehem
Sing Out! **(26705)** ....(Paid) ‡13,000
(Non-paid) ‡500

Broomall
Contemporary Record Society News
Magazine **(26735)** ....(Combined) 90,000
Gray Areas **(26737)** ....(Paid) ‡14,000

Philadelphia
Journal of Musicological Research **(27537)**

TENNESSEE
Jackson
The Matthay News **(29230)** ....(Paid) 142

Nashville
American Songwriter **(29440)** ....(Paid) 1,728
Close Up Magazine **(29451)**
International Fan Club Organization **(29460)**
Pedalpoint **(29480)** ....(Paid) 48,000
Worship **(29503)** ....(Paid) 5,000

TEXAS
Austin
Piano Guild Notes **(29797)** ....(Paid) ‡12,168
(Non-paid) ‡525
The Southwestern Musician **(29808)** ....‡10,500

Dallas
Bass World **(30128)** ....(Paid) 3,200

Denton
The Clarinet **(30233)** ....(Paid) ‡4,000
(Non-paid) ‡50

Houston
Angbase **(30456)**
Journal of American
Organbuilding **(30495)** ....(Paid) 650

UTAH
South Jordan
Classical Singer
Magazine **(31472)** ....(Combined) 4000

VIRGINIA
Falls Church
The American Harp Journal **(32041)**

Front Royal
Sacred Music **(32095)** ....‡1,000

Reston
Journal of Research in Music Education **(32394)**
Music Educators Journal **(32405)** .....(Paid) ‡80,000
Teaching Music **(32418)** ....(Paid) 80,000
Update: Applications of Research in Music
Education **(32422)**

Richmond
The Tracker **(32457)** ....‡3,800

Winchester
Dulcimer Players News **(32627)** ....(Paid) 4,500

WASHINGTON
Eastsound
NAPRA Review **(32742)** ....(Non-paid) 10,000

Edmonds
Voice of Washington Music
Educators **(32747)** ....(Controlled) 1,500

Tacoma
American Lutherie **(33143)**

WEST VIRGINIA
Salem
Blues Revue **(33463)** ....(Paid) 18,000

WISCONSIN
Middleton
Notes **(34052)**

BRITISH COLUMBIA, CANADA
Victoria
Fermata **(35216)** ....(Combined) 100

NOVA SCOTIA, CANADA
Dartmouth
Kodaly Society of Canada, Alla
Breve **(35548)** ....(Paid) 400

ONTARIO, CANADA
London
Studies in Music **(35993)** ....(Non-paid) 310

Maple
Incursion Music Review **(36010)**

St. Catharines
Canadian Music
Trade **(36352)** ....(Controlled) ‡3,500
Canadian Musician **(36353)** ....‡29,500

Toronto
Musicworks Magazine **(36671)**

QUEBEC, CANADA
Montreal
Circuit **(37105)** ....(Combined) 1,500

NATURAL HISTORY AND NATURE STUDY

See also Ecology and Conservation;
Entomology; Ornithology and Oology

ARIZONA
Tucson
Paleoclimates **(958)**

CALIFORNIA
Berkeley
The Four Seasons **(1522)** ....(Combined) 431

Manhattan Beach
Lepidopterists Society Journal **(2501)** ....(Paid) 1,500

Santa Barbara
The Veliger **(3661)** ....(Paid) ‡640
(Non-paid) ‡10

Walnut Creek
Curator **(4051)**

DISTRICT OF COLUMBIA
Washington
DEFENDERS Magazine **(5460)** ....‡275,000
ZooGoer **(5875)** ....(Paid) 31,000

ILLINOIS
Chicago
Mushroom the Journal **(8497)** ....‡2,000

Edwardsville
Illinois Wildlife **(8813)** ....‡12,684

Springfield
Illinois Parks & Recreation
Magazine **(9628)** 6,000

INDIANA
Notre Dame
American Midland
Naturalist **(10366)** ....(Paid) ‡1,137
(Controlled) ‡54

KENTUCKY
Louisville
American Conchologist **(12210)** ....(Combined) 1,700

LOUISIANA
Hammond
Journal of Herpetology **(12591)** ....(Combined) 2,550

MAINE
Augusta
Maine Fish and Wildlife **(12893)** ....(Paid) 12,500
(Non-paid) 400

Steuben
The Northeastern Naturalist **(13060)**
The Southeastern Naturalist **(13061)**

MARYLAND
Lanham
Environmental Entomology **(13601)**

MICHIGAN
Ann Arbor
Journal of Great Lakes Research **(14756)**
Wetlands **(14772)**

Charlevoix
The North Woods Call **(14865)** ....‡8,000

MINNESOTA
Minneapolis
The Loon **(16093)** ....(Combined) 1,400

MISSISSIPPI
University
Estuaries (16864)

MISSOURI
North Kansas City
AFA Watchbird (17318) ....(Paid) 10,000
(Non-paid) 100

NEBRASKA
Lincoln
Great Plains Research (18086) ......(Combined) 500

NEW HAMPSHIRE
Nashua
CleanRooms (18584) ....(Controlled) △35,156

NEW JERSEY
Bernardsville
Records of New Jersey
Birds (18680) ....(Controlled) 4,200

NEW YORK
New York
Journal of Aquatic Ecosystem Stress and
Recovery (21996)
Journal of Insect Conservation (22097)
Micropaleontology (22332) ....(Combined) 780
Natural History Magazine (22405) .....(Paid) 300,000

Troy
Northeastern Geology and Environmental
Sciences (23454) ....(Paid) 400

NORTH CAROLINA
Raleigh
Wildlife in North Carolina (24159) .....(Paid) ‡66,319
(Non-paid) ‡3,626

OHIO
Cleveland
Explorer (24894) ....‡11,000

Columbus
Ohio Biological Survey Miscellaneous
Contributions (25040) ....(Paid) 80

Marietta
Bird Watcher's Digest (25343) ....‡90,000

OKLAHOMA
Tulsa
Bulletin of the Oklahoma Ornithological
Society (26107) ....(Paid) ‡425
(Non-paid) ‡10

OREGON
Cave Junction
Mountains & Rivers (26265)

PENNSYLVANIA
Dingmans Ferry
Nature Study (26828) ....(Non-paid) ‡800

Pittsburgh
Carnegie Magazine (27764) ....(Paid) 28,679

TEXAS
College Station
American Association of Stratigraphic Palynologists
Contributions Series (30036) ....(Combined) 952

UTAH
Provo
Western North American
Naturalist (31409) ....(Paid) 225

VIRGINIA
Arlington
Endangered Species Bulletin (31788)

WYOMING
Cheyenne
Wyoming Wildlife (34501) ....(Paid) ‡35,000
(Controlled) ‡1,100

ONTARIO, CANADA
Ottawa
Canadian
Field-Naturalist (36194) ....(Controlled) ‡2,180
Nature Canada (36263) **31,400**
Trail and Landscape (36277)

Toronto
Rotunda (36732) 25,000

NATURAL RESOURCES

COLORADO
Fort Collins
Human Dimensions of Wildlife (4432)
RMRScience (4437) ....(Controlled) 2,000

MINNESOTA
St. Paul
Minnesota Conservation
Volunteer (16390) 125,000

MISSISSIPPI
University
Estuaries (16864)

NEW JERSEY
Hoboken
Environmetrics (18942)
Natural Gas (19069) 5,985
Permafrost and Periglacial
Processes (19080) 3,500

OKLAHOMA
Tulsa
Utility Automation International (26142)

OREGON
Bend
Natural Areas Journal (26243) .....(Combined) 2,250

Portland
Environmental Law
(Portland) (26476) ....(Combined) 849

PENNSYLVANIA
Philadelphia
Progress in Natural Science (27649)

TEXAS
Dallas
Gas Utility and Pipeline
Industries (30160) ....(Non-paid) 10,878

Houston
Hart's E&P (30475) ....(Paid) ‡1,145
(Non-paid) ‡44,281
Oil & Gas Journal Latinoamerica (30517)

VIRGINIA
Richmond
Virginia Forests (32462) ....(Paid) 3,250

ALBERTA, CANADA
Calgary
Alberta Drilling Progress Weekly Report (34626)

NUCLEAR ENGINEERING

See also Power and Power Plants; Physics

CALIFORNIA
Berkeley
Experimental Heat Transfer (1520) ....(Paid) ‡267

San Diego
Nuclear Data Sheets (3243)

CONNECTICUT
Hebron
Radiation Protection
Management (4916) ....(Paid) 750
RSO Magazine (4917) ....(Paid) 950

GEORGIA
Norcross
Engineering Economist (7459)
NAC Focus (7468)

ILLINOIS
Glen Ellyn
Nuclear Plant Journal (8931) .....(Non-paid) △20,012

La Grange Park
Nuclear News (9052) ....(Paid) 10,500
(Controlled) 1,500
Nuclear Science and Engineering (9053) 1,200
Nuclear Technology (9054) 1,300

Northbrook
Journal of Nuclear Materials
Management (9318) ....(Paid) ‡8,000

Urbana
Fusion Technology (9705) 600

NEW JERSEY
Hoboken
Progress in Photovoltaics (19087) ......(Paid) 17,500

NEW YORK
New York
Atomic Energy (21269)
Hyperfine Interactions (21840)
Journal of Computer-Aided Materials Design (22035)
Journal of Radioanalytical and Nuclear
Chemistry (22175)
Journal of Reducing Space Mission Cost (22178)

PENNSYLVANIA
Philadelphia
Energy Systems and
Policy (27460) ....(Controlled) ‡285

TENNESSEE
Oak Ridge
Nuclear Safety (29549) ....(Paid) ‡2,000
(Controlled) ‡1,475

VIRGINIA
Reston
International Aerospace Abstracts (32366)

WYOMING
Laramie
Energy Sources (34548) ....(Controlled) ‡345

NURSING

**See also Hospitals and Healthcare
Institutions; Medicine and Surgery**

ARKANSAS
Little Rock
Geriatric Nursing (1230) ....(Paid) ‡6,050
Nursing Outlook (1234) ....(Paid) ‡4,881

CALIFORNIA
Aliso Viejo
American Journal of Critical
Care (1389) ....(Combined) 66,500
Critical Care Nurse (1391) ....‡96,000

Glendale
Cumulative Index to Nursing & Allied Health
Literature (Print Index) (2008) ....‡1,800

Los Angeles
Journal of Intravenous Therapy (2302) ....‡1,000
Journal of Pediatric Nursing (2304) ......(Paid) 2,752

Oakland
California Nurse (2674) ....(Paid) ‡47,000
(Controlled) ‡500

RevolutioN Magazine (2697)

San Francisco
Pain Management Nursing (3411)

Santa Rosa
Neonatal Network (3730) ....(Controlled) 11,000

Sunnyvale
Nurseweek (3830) ....(Controlled) ‡225,000

Thousand Oaks
AWHONN Lifelines (3851) ....(Paid) 21,500
Clinical Nursing Research (3854) ....(Paid) ‡700
Home Health Care Management and
Practice (3872) 1,000
Journal of the Association of Nurses in AIDS
Care (3880) ....(Paid) ‡3,000
Journal of Family Nursing (3890) ......(Paid) 500
Journal of Obstetric, Gynecologic and Neonatal
Nursing (JOGNN) (3896) ....(Paid) 23,000

COLORADO
Denver
AORN Journal (4305) ....(Paid) 44,000

Lakewood
Nurse Author and Editor (4534) ....(Paid) ‡500

CONNECTICUT
New Haven
Archives of Psychiatric Nursing (4983)

DISTRICT OF COLUMBIA
Washington
The American Nurse (5337) ....‡210,000

Circulation: ★ = ABC; △ = BPA; ◆ = CAC; ● = CCAB; ❏ = VAC; ⊕ = PO Statement; ‡ = Publisher's Report; Boldface figures = sworn; Light figures = estimated.

3199

Circ.   Circ.   Circ.

NURSING (continued)

FLORIDA
Fort Lauderdale
Nursing Spectrum—Florida Edition **(6082)**

Gainesville
Cancer Nursing **(6133)** ....(Paid) 3,250

Tallahassee
Thanatos **(6739)** ....(Paid) ‡7,000
(Non-paid) ‡200

GEORGIA
Atlanta
Journal of Nursing
Measurement **(7023)** ....(Combined) 400

Augusta
Journal of PeriAnesthesia Nursing **(7100)**

ILLINOIS
Aurora
Nursing Management **(8041)** ....(Paid) 109,492
(Controlled) 19,337

Chicago
JMNR **(8426)** ....(Paid) 900
(Non-paid) 1,500

Chicago Heights
Journal of Irreproducible Results **(8667)** ....‡5,000

Glenview
Rehabilitation Nursing **(8941)** ....‡10,300

Hoffman Estates
Nursing Spectrum—Greater Chicago/Tri-State
Edition **(9001)**

Lisle
ABNF Journal **(9109)** ....(Combined) 562

Northfield
McKnight's Long-Term Care
News **(9331)** ....(Paid) ‡850
(Controlled) ‡50,025

Park Ridge
AANA Journal **(9403)** ....(Paid) ‡627
(Non-paid) ‡30,120

INDIANA
Indianapolis
Journal of Nursing Scholarship **(10140)** 115,000

IOWA
Iowa City
Insight **(10973)** ....(Paid) 1,306
(Free) 210

KANSAS
Overland Park
Home Care Magazine **(11714)**

Topeka
Kansas Nurse **(11830)** ....(Paid) ‡1,700
(Non-paid) ‡100

KENTUCKY
Louisville
Home Healthcare Nurse **(12218)** ....(Paid) 8,192

MAINE
Portland
Computers in Nursing **(13009)** ....(Paid) 3,100

MARYLAND
Baltimore
A.J.N. International Nursing Index **(13110)**
Caring for the Ages **(13143)** ....(Paid) 47,946

Hagerstown
Nurse Educator **(13569)**

Silver Spring
Journal of Practical
Nursing **(13733)** ....(Paid) ‡6,000

MASSACHUSETTS
Lexington
Nursing Spectrum—New England Edition **(14273)**

Natick
Clinical Excellence for Nurse Practitioners **(14345)**

Norwood
Journal of Infusion Nursing **(14448)** .....(Paid) 7,000

MICHIGAN
Detroit
Outcomes Management **(14942)** ....(Paid) ‡1,100

MISSOURI
Jefferson City
The Missouri Nurse **(17128)**

St. Louis
International Journal of Trauma
Nursing **(17447)** ....(Paid) 1,019
(Non-paid) 257
Journal of the American Psychiatric Nurses
Association **(17453)** ....(Paid) ‡5,733
Journal of Vascular Nursing **(17463)** ....(Paid) 1,220
(Free) 326

NEW JERSEY
Hoboken
Catheterization and Cardiovascular
Diagnosis **(18908)** 23,800
Research in Nursing & Health **(19098)** 13,300

Montvale
ED Nursing **(19253)**
Nursing Opportunities **(19267)**
Office Nurse **(19269)**
Patient Care for the Nurse Practitioner **(19271)**
RN **(19274)** ....(Paid) 199,243
(Non-paid) 25,557

Pitman
Dermatology Nursing **(19433)** ....(Paid) ‡5,000
MedSurg Nursing **(19435)**
Nephrology Nursing Journal **(19436)** ....‡15,500
Nursing Economics **(19437)** ....‡6,752
Orthopaedic Nursing **(19438)** ....(Paid) ‡12,000
Pediatric Nursing **(19439)** ....‡14,011
Plastic Surgery Nursing **(19440)**

Rocky Hill
Issues in Comprehensive Pediatric
Nursing **(19524)** ....(Combined) 740

Thorofare
AAOHN Journal **(19615)** ....‡14,800
The Journal of Continuing Education in
Nursing **(19620)** ....‡4,439
Journal of Gerontological
Nursing **(19621)** ....(Paid) ‡10,000
Journal of Nursing
Education **(19623)** ....(Paid) 4,000
Journal of Psychosocial Nursing and Mental Health
Services **(19625)** ....‡6,000

Wood Ridge
Journal of Community Health Nursing **(19755)**

NEW YORK
Binghamton
Journal of Social Work in Long-Term Care **(20199)**

Chautauqua
Journal of Multicultural Nursing and Health
(JMCNH) **(20454)**

Huntington Bay
MCN, The American Journal of Maternal/Child
Nursing **(20777)** ....(Paid) 10,397

Jackson Heights
SCI Nursing **(20828)** 2,500

Jamaica
International Chinese Nursing Journal **(20834)**

New York
AACN's Clinical Issues in Critical Care
Nursing **(21129)** 2,478
Advances in Nursing Science **(21156)** 2,343,169
Critical Care Nursing Quarterly **(21519)** ....‡3,000
Holistic Nursing Practice **(21807)**
Imprint **(21856)** 40,000
Journal of Cardiovascular
Nursing **(22018)** ....(Paid) 2,271
(Non-paid) 4
Journal of Nursing Care
Quality **(22147)** ....(Paid) 5,362
(Non-paid) 108
Journal of Perinatal and Neonatal
Nursing **(22154)** ....(Paid) 2,501
(Non-paid) 92
Nursing Administration
Quarterly **(22472)** ....(Paid) 4,239
(Non-paid) 47
Nursing Leadership Forum **(22474)** ....(Paid) 240
(Free) 50
Research and Theory for Nursing
Practice **(22649)** ....(Free) 600

Westbury
Nursing Spectrum—New York & New Jersey
Edition **(23558)**

OHIO
Cleveland
Applied Nursing Research **(24856)**

Columbus
Ohio Nurses Review **(25047)** .....(Controlled) 10,000

PENNSYLVANIA
Harrisburg
Clinical Nurse Specialist **(26987)** ....(Paid) 3,319
(Non-paid) 110

King of Prussia
ADVANCE for Nurse
Practitioners **(27115)** ....(Controlled) ‡41,000
ADVANCE for
Nurses **(27116)** ....(Combined) 510,000
ADVANCE for Physician
Assistants **(27119)** ....(Non-paid) ‡31,900
Nursing Spectrum—Philadelphia/Tri-State
Edition **(27126)**

Philadelphia
Critical Care Nursing Clinics **(27430)**
CRNA **(27431)**
Home Care Manager **(27485)**
Home Healthcare Nurse Manager **(27486)**
Journal of Ambulatory Monitoring **(27511)**
Journal of Child and Adolescent Psychiatric
Nursing **(27520)** ....(Paid) ‡2500
Journal of Child and Family Nursing **(27521)**
Journal of Emergency
Nursing **(27527)** ....(Combined) ‡27,120
Journal of Intravenous
Nursing **(27532)** ....(Paid) 9,185
Journal for Nurses in Staff Development
(JNSD) **(27540)** ....(Paid) 3,400
Journal of Nursing Administration
(JONA) **(27541)** ....(Paid) 6,000
Journal of Professional Nursing **(27548)**
Journal of the Society of Pediatric
Nurses **(27550)** ....‡3,000
Journal of Trauma Nursing **(27554)**
Nurse Educator **(27587)** ....(Paid) 2,950
Nurse Practitioner Forum **(27588)** ....‡1,785
Nursing Case Management **(27589)** .....(Paid) 2,017
The Nursing Clinics of North America **(27590)**
Nursing Forum **(27591)** ....(Paid) 2,200
Nursing History Review **(27592)**
Nursing 96 **(27593)** ....(Paid) 350,000
Online Journal of Knowledge Synthesis for
Nursing **(27598)**
ONS Nursing Scan in Oncology **(27599)**
Seminars in Oncology Nursing **(27668)**
Seminars in Perioperative Nursing **(27671)**

Pittsburgh
Clinical Journal of Oncology
Nursing **(27765)** ....(Combined) ‡30,000
Oncology Nursing Forum **(27824)** ....‡31,225

Springhouse
American Journal of
Nursing **(28013)** ....(Paid) 317,111
(Non-paid) 20,191
The Nurse Practitioner **(28014)** ....(Paid) △27,393

TENNESSEE
Knoxville
Issues in Mental Health Nursing **(29273)**

TEXAS
Austin
Infancy **(29783)**
Journal of Holistic Nursing **(29788)**

Houston
The Journal of Pediatric Oncology
Nursing **(30498)** ....‡2,982

Sugar Land
Internet Journal of Advanced Nursing
Practice **(31139)**

VIRGINIA
Falls Church
Nursing Spectrum—Washington D.C. & Baltimore
Edition **(32050)**

WASHINGTON
Seattle
The Washington Nurse **(33040)** ....(Controlled) 7,600

WEST VIRGINIA
Charleston
West Virginia Nurse **(33279)** ....(Paid) ⊕32,000

WISCONSIN
Eau Claire
Journal of Nursing Law **(33671)** ....(Paid) 800

Madison
Journal of Christian
   Nursing **(33950)** ....(Paid) ‡10,000
   (Controlled) ‡150

ALBERTA, CANADA
Calgary
Dynamics **(34642)**

Edmonton
Western Journal of Nursing
   Research **(34735)** ....(Paid) ‡1,950
   (Non-paid) ‡110

BRITISH COLUMBIA, CANADA
Vancouver
Nursing BC **(35153)** ....(Combined) 34,454

White Rock
Canadian Operating Room Nursing
   Journal **(35241)** ....‡3,500

ONTARIO, CANADA
North York
Body Cast **(36121)**

Ottawa
Canadian Nurse (L'Infirmiere
   Canadienne) **(36223)** ....(Combined) 111,563

Toronto
Canadian Oncology Nursing Journal **(36522)**
The Registered Nurse
   Journal **(36725)** ....(Controlled) ‡19,000

QUEBEC, CANADA
Laval
C'est Pour Quand? **(37035)** ....(Non-paid) 44,000

Montreal
L'infirmiere du
   Quebec **(37126)** ....(Combined) 65,853

OCEANOGRAPHY AND MARINE STUDIES

ALABAMA
Dauphin Island
Gulf of Mexico Science **(169)**

CALIFORNIA
San Diego
ICES Journal of Marine Science **(3170)**

San Francisco
The Keeper's Log **(3387)** ....(Paid) ‡11,000
   (Non-paid) ‡200

San Pedro
Whalewatcher **(3597)**

CONNECTICUT
New Haven
Journal of Marine Research **(4995)** ....(Paid) 800

FLORIDA
Miami
The Bulletin of Marine Science **(6343)**

St. Petersburg
Florida Marine Research Institute Technical
   Reports **(6626)** ....(Non-paid) 600
Florida Marine Research
   Publications **(6627)** ....(Non-paid) 600
Memoirs of the Hourglass
   Cruises **(6631)** ....(Non-paid) 600

HAWAII
Honolulu
Indo-Pacific Fishes **(7704)**
Marine Geodesy **(7710)** ....(Paid) ‡200
Marine Georesources and Geotechnology **(7711)**

ILLINOIS
Moline
Aquatic Mammals **(9202)** 350

MARYLAND
Bethesda
ASFA 2: Ocean Technology, Policy & Non-Living
   Resources **(13313)**
ASFA 3: Aquatic Pollution and Environmental
   Quality **(13314)**
ASFA Marine Biotechnology Abstracts **(13317)**
Oceanic Abstracts **(13369)**
Transactions of the American Fisheries
   Society **(13385)** ....‡3,700

MASSACHUSETTS
Boston
Journal of Atmospheric and Oceanic
   Technology **(13913)** ....‡1,588
Journal of Physical Oceanography **(13917)** ...‡2,067

Woods Hole
The Biological Bulletin **(14672)** .....(Controlled) 1,690
Oceanus Magazine **(14673)** ....(Controlled) 5,000

MINNESOTA
St. Paul
Hydrological Science and
   Technology **(16380)** ....(Controlled) 500

NEW JERSEY
Highlands
Underwater Naturalist **(18874)** ....‡9,500

Newark
Marine and Freshwater Behavior and
   Physiology **(19359)**

NEW YORK
New York
Aquaculture International **(21235)**
Aquarium Sciences and Conservation **(21236)**
Aquatic Ecology **(21237)**
Aquatic Geochemistry **(21238)**
Biological Invasions **(21317)**
The International Journal of Marine and Coastal
   Law **(21910)**
JMBA: Journal of the Marine Biological
   Association **(21967)** 1600
Journal of the Marine Biological Association of the
   United Kingdom **(22121)** 1,600
Journal of Oceanography **(22149)**
Marine Geophysical Researches **(22282)**
Natural Hazards **(22404)**
Reviews in Fish Biology and Fisheries **(22664)**

Southampton
Journal of Shellfish
   Research **(23344)** ....(Controlled) 1,000

OREGON
Astoria
Journal of Aquatic Food Product
   Technology **(26225)** 170

PENNSYLVANIA
Philadelphia
Ocean Development and International Law **(27595)**

RHODE ISLAND
Kingston
Marine Resource Economics **(28360)** ....‡300

SOUTH CAROLINA
Mount Pleasant
The Water Log Maritime
   Journal **(28697)** ....(Combined) 10,000

TEXAS
Houston
UnderWater Magazine **(30539)** .....(Non-paid) 16,300

VIRGINIA
Arlington
Sea Technology **(31831)** ....(Paid) 250
   (Controlled) 20,500

Chesapeake
Calypso Log **(31964)** ....‡100,000

WASHINGTON
Seattle
Coastal Management **(32955)**

OILS AND FATS (ANIMAL & VEGETABLE)

ILLINOIS
Champaign
INFORM (International News on Fats, Oils and
   Related Materials) **(8190)** 6,000

TEXAS
Houston
Oil Mill Gazetteer **(30518)** ....‡1,750

VIRGINIA
Falls Church
Lube Report **(32049)** ....(Controlled) 10,000

OPHTHALMOLOGY, OPTOMETRY, AND OPTICS

CALIFORNIA
Carlsbad
Fiber and Integrated Optics **(1664)** ....‡443

San Diego
Experimental Eye Research **(3148)**
Graphical Models **(3163)**

San Francisco
EyeNet **(3359)**

COLORADO
Dillon
Binocular Vision & Strabismus
   Quarterly **(4399)** ....(Combined) 800

CONNECTICUT
Farmington
Ophthalmic Research **(4849)** 850
Ophthalmologica **(4850)** 1,250

Madison
Annals of Ophthalmology **(4926)** 8,844

DISTRICT OF COLUMBIA
Washington
Applied Optics **(5359)** 3,200
Journal of the Optical Society of America A: Optics,
   Image Science,and Vision **(5608)** ...(Paid) 2,200
Journal of the Optical Society of America B: Optical
   Physics **(5609)**
Optics Letters **(5709)** ....(Paid) 2400
Optics & Photonics News **(5710)** ......(Paid) ‡15,000

FLORIDA
Tallahassee
Focal Point **(6721)** 1,200

ILLINOIS
Chicago
Archives of
   Ophthalmology **(8269)** ....(Combined) ‡18,373
The Microscope **(8487)** ....(Paid) ‡900
   (Controlled) ‡50

Niles
Journal of the Illinois Optometric
   Association **(9289)** 1,200

MARYLAND
Baltimore
Cornea **(13152)** 1,343
Eye and Contact Lens: Science and Clinical
   Practice **(13160)** ....‡3,100

College Park
Journal of Optical Technology **(13429)** ....‡470

Rockville
Optometric Education **(13691)** ....‡2,800

MASSACHUSETTS
Andover
Journal of Toxicology, Cutaneous and Ocular
   Toxicology **(13812)** ....(Paid) 425

MICHIGAN
Lansing
The Michigan Optometrist **(15288)** ....(Paid) ‡856
   (Controlled) ‡99

MISSOURI
Kansas City
Journal of Low Vision and Neuro-Optometric
   Rehabilitation **(17175)** ....(Paid) 500

Circulation: ★ = ABC; △ = BPA; ♦ = CAC; • = CCAB; ❑ = VAC; ⊕ = PO Statement; ‡ = Publisher's Report; Boldface figures = sworn; Light figures = estimated.

Circ.   Circ.   Circ.

OPHTHALMOLOGY, OPTOMETRY, AND OPTICS (continued)

St. Louis
AOA News (17416) ....(Paid) ‡22,189
                                  (Free) ‡7,823

Journal of Optometric Vision
    Development (17457) ....(Paid) 1,600
Optometry (17479) ....(Paid) ‡20,535
                            (Non-paid) ‡6,700

NEW HAMPSHIRE
Nashua
Vision Systems Design (18602)

NEW JERSEY
Thorofare
Journal of Pediatric Ophthalmology &
    Strabismus (19624) ....‡2,179
Journal of Refractive Surgery (19626) 2,582
Ocular Surgery
    News (19631) ....(Controlled) ‡17,000
Ocular Surgery News Latin America Edition (19633)
Ophthalmic Surgery Lasers and
    Imaging (19634) ....‡4,358
Primary Care Optometry News (19639)

NEW YORK
Larchmont
Journal of Ocular Pharmacology and
    Therapeutics (20918)

New York
American Journal of
    Ophthalmology (21196) ....(Paid) 11,169
Journal of AAPOS (American Association for Pediatric
    Ophthalmology and
    Strabismus) (21971) ....(Combined) ‡1,283
Metabolic Pediatric and Systems
    Ophthalmology (22319) ....‡1,000
Survey of Ophthalmology (22812) ......(Paid) ‡9,271
                            (Non-paid) ‡971

OHIO
Cleveland
Ophthalmology
    Times (24938) ....(Controlled) △18,769

PENNSYLVANIA
Fort Washington
Contact Lens
    Spectrum (26926) ....(Non-paid) ‡32,000
Eyecare Business (26930) ....(Non-paid) 52,200
Optometric
    Management (26932) ....(Non-paid) 33,500

Newtown Square
Review of Optometry (27333) ....(Paid) 7,273
                            (Controlled) 27,419

Philadelphia
Current Opinion in
    Ophthalmology (27441) ....(Paid) ‡1,011
Journal of Modern Optics (27536)
Operative Techniques in Cataract and Refractive
    Surgery (27600)
Operative Techniques in Oculoplastic, Orbital and
    Reconstructive Surgery (27603)

Pittsburgh
Seminars in Ophthalmology (27841) ....‡831

WASHINGTON
Bellingham
Optical Engineering (32678) ....(Paid) 10,000

ONTARIO, CANADA
Ottawa
Canadian Journal of Ophthalmology (Journal
    Canadien
    d'Ophtalmologie) (36210) ....(Paid) ‡1,300

Toronto
Optical Prism (36689) ....(Controlled) 11,500

QUEBEC, CANADA
Montreal
L'Optometriste (37198) ....(Controlled) ‡4,400

Saint-Laurent
Practical Optometry (37366) 3,065

ORNITHOLOGY AND OOLOGY
See also Natural History and Nature Study

ARIZONA
Tempe
The Condor (901) ....‡3,300

CALIFORNIA
Mission Viejo
WildBird Magazine (2558) ....(Paid) 127,775

Pacifica
Western Birds (2741) ....(Paid) 1,100

FLORIDA
Tallahassee
Florida Field Naturalist (6711) ....‡575

HAWAII
Honolulu
Elepaio (7688) ....‡2,000
Waterbirds (7728) ....‡800

INDIANA
Indianapolis
Indiana Audubon
    Quarterly (10122) ....(Combined) 556

KANSAS
Lawrence
Wilson Bulletin (11572) ....(Paid) 3,200

MINNESOTA
Minneapolis
The Loon (16093) ....(Combined) 1,400

St. Cloud
Interpretive Birding Bulletin (16342)

NEW YORK
New York
Field Notes (21690) ....‡6,000

South Hempstead
Kingbird (23343) ....(Paid) 650

NORTH CAROLINA
Raleigh
The Chat (24132) ....‡1,000

OHIO
Marietta
Bird Watcher's Digest (25343) ....‡90,000

OKLAHOMA
Tulsa
Bulletin of the Oklahoma Ornithological
    Society (26107) ....(Paid) ‡425
                            (Non-paid) ‡10

SOUTH DAKOTA
Aberdeen
South Dakota Bird
    Notes (28791) ....(Controlled) 800

WISCONSIN
Granton
APWS Magazine (33736) ....(Paid) 1,800

BRITISH COLUMBIA, CANADA
Chemainus
Avicultural Journal (34923) ....(Paid) 300

OSTEOPATHY

ILLINOIS
Chicago
The DO (8355) ....(Non-paid) ‡47,000
Journal of the American Osteopathic
    Association (8432) ....(Controlled) ‡36,615

PENNSYLVANIA
Harrisburg
Journal of the Pennsylvania Osteopathic Medical
    Association (26996) ....(Combined) ⊕4,035

Philadelphia
Digest (27451) ....(Controlled) ‡10,600

PACKAGING
See also Paper

GEORGIA
Atlanta
TAPPI JOURNAL (7049) ....(Paid) 29,707
                            (Non-paid) 10,313

ILLINOIS
Chicago
Boxboard Containers (8289) ....(Paid) 2,356
                            (Non-paid) 12,392
Packaging World (8524) ....(Controlled) 92,000
Paper, Film & Foil
    Converter (8526) ....(Non-paid) ‡42,548

St. Charles
Food & Drug
    Packaging (9568) ....(Combined) 65,000

IOWA
Fort Dodge
Packaging and Converting
    Hotline (10906) ....(Combined) 10,000

MICHIGAN
Troy
Packaging Strategies (15631)

NEW JERSEY
Avon by the Sea
Board Converting News (18662) 5,914

NEW YORK
Farmingdale
Distribution Sales and
    Management (20594) ....(Controlled) 17,000

New York
Converting Magazine (21499) ....(Controlled) ‡44,414
Packaging Digest (22517) ....(Paid) 4,700
                            (Controlled) 111,600

OHIO
Cleveland
Paperboard Packaging
    Worldwide (24939) ....(Paid) 1,577
                            (Controlled) 12,478

WASHINGTON
Yakima
Carrot Country (33218) ....(Controlled) ‡2,650

ONTARIO, CANADA
Toronto
Canadian Packaging (36523) .....(Combined) 13,188

PAINT AND WALLCOVERINGS
See also Interior Design/Decorating

COLORADO
Colorado Springs
American Painting Contractor (4235) ....‡30,736

Loveland
American Paint and Coatings
    Journal (4565) ....(Paid) 2,006
                            (Non-paid) 2,798

CONNECTICUT
Norwalk
Journal of Water Borne
    Coatings (5067) ....(Paid) 250
                            (Non-paid) 750

GEORGIA
Atlanta
Modern Paint and Coatings (7027) ....(Paid) 397
                            (Non-paid) 17,636

MARYLAND
Millersville
Cleaning & Restoration (13630) ....‡2,600

MASSACHUSETTS
Newton
Interior Design (14401) ....(Paid) 54,584

MICHIGAN
Troy
Paint & Coatings
    Industry (15632) ....(Non-paid) ‡20,889

MINNESOTA
Hopkins
Mirror News Magazine **(15964)** ....(Paid) ‡42,230
(Non-paid) ‡5,660

St. Paul
Wall Fashions
   Magazine **(16415)** ....(Controlled) 31,905

MISSOURI
Fenton
Paint & Decorating
   Retailer **(17063)** ....(Combined) ‡26,201

St. Louis
Painting & Wallcovering
   Contractor **(17481)** ....(Paid) 1,926
(Non-paid) 26,202

NEBRASKA
Omaha
Heartland Retailer **(18197)** ....(Free) ‡15,250

NEW JERSEY
Red Bank
Today's Facility
   Manager **(19501)** ....(Controlled) ❏50,000

NEW YORK
New York
House Beautiful **(21821)** ....(Paid) 853,748
INTERIORS **(21891)** ....(Paid) 11,009
(Non-paid) 15,351

PENNSYLVANIA
Blue Bell
Journal of Coatings Technology **(26725)** .....‡10,500

Pittsburgh
Journal of Protective Coatings &
   Linings **(27803)** ....(Paid) ‡9,854
(Non-paid) ‡5,146

ONTARIO, CANADA
Toronto
Coatings Magazine **(36553)** ....(Non-paid) •6,148
(Paid) •114

QUEBEC, CANADA
Outremont
Les Idees de Ma Maison **(37267)** ......(Paid) 53,529

PAPER

See also Packaging

ALABAMA
Montgomery
Paper Industry **(374)** ....(Controlled) 18,880

CALIFORNIA
San Francisco
Pulp and Paper **(3419)** ....(Paid) 2,000
(Controlled) 40,000

CONNECTICUT
Danbury
Party & Paper Retailer **(4749)** ....‡15,000

DISTRICT OF COLUMBIA
Washington
Paper, Paperboard, and Wood Pulp Monthly
   Statistical Summary **(5714)**

GEORGIA
Atlanta
TAPPI JOURNAL **(7049)** ....(Paid) 29,707
(Non-paid) 10,313

MICHIGAN
Troy
Packaging Strategies **(15631)**

NEW JERSEY
Glen Rock
Paper Age **(18847)** ......:............(Paid) 207
(Controlled) 30,555

Hoboken
Abstract Bulletin of the Institute of Paper Science
   and Technology **(18880)** ....(Paid) ‡660
(Controlled) ‡90

NEW YORK
Farmingdale
Distribution Sales and
   Management **(20594)** ....(Controlled) 17,000

Manhasset
Pulp & Paper
   International **(21012)** ....(Controlled) 15,134

TENNESSEE
Nashville
The PACEsetter **(29478)** ....(Free) ‡320,000

QUEBEC, CANADA
Montreal
Journal of Pulp & Paper
   Science **(37145)** ....(Combined) 13,150

Pointe-Claire
Les Papetieres du
   Quebec **(37275)** ....(Combined) ‡4,348
Pulp & Paper
   Canada **(37277)** ....(Combined) •10,131

Sainte-Foy
Papetier **(37375)** 11,500

PARKS

ALABAMA
Montgomery
Outdoor Alabama **(372)** ....‡12,000

DISTRICT OF COLUMBIA
Washington
National Parks **(5679)** ....(Paid) 348,951

IDAHO
Idaho Falls
Today's Playground **(7872)**

ILLINOIS
Chicago
At the Park **(8278)** ....(Controlled) 9,000

Springfield
Illinois Parks & Recreation
   Magazine **(9628)** 6,000

INDIANA
Syracuse
WOODALL's Campground
   Management **(10479)** ....(Paid) 100
(Non-paid) 11,700

PENNSYLVANIA
Ardmore
Tourist Attractions & Parks
   Magazine **(26665)** ....(Combined) ‡31,424

TEXAS
Sugar Land
Splash Magazine **(31164)**

VIRGINIA
Ashburn
Parks & Recreation Magazine **(31854)** ....‡24,000

ONTARIO, CANADA
Delhi
Turf & Recreation **(35771)** ....(Combined) 15,000

PATENTS, TRADEMARKS, AND COPYRIGHTS

CALIFORNIA
Santa Barbara
The Lightbulb/Invent!
   Journal **(3649)** ....(Combined) 6,000

FLORIDA
St. Petersburg
Copyright Law Reports **(6622)** ....‡950

LOUISIANA
New Orleans
Tulane Journal of Technology and Intellectual
   Property **(12759)**

MASSACHUSETTS
Boston
Inventors' Digest **(13908)** ....‡20,000

PENNSYLVANIA
Pittsburgh
Patents-Official Gazette **(27825)**

TEXAS
Austin
Texas Intellectual Property Law
   Journal **(29825)** ....(Combined) 1,800

VIRGINIA
Alexandria
les Nouvelles **(31705)**
Trademarks **(31745)**

PEACE

ARIZONA
Flagstaff
International Journal of Humanities and
   Peace **(696)** ....(Paid) 2000

CALIFORNIA
Santa Barbara
The Sunflower **(3659)** ....(Non-paid) 8,000

Thousand Oaks
Peace Research Abstracts
   Journal **(3906)** ....(Paid) 200

CONNECTICUT
New Haven
Journal of Conflict
   Resolution **(4993)** ....(Paid) ‡2,363
(Non-paid) ‡114

DISTRICT OF COLUMBIA
Washington
Arms Control Today **(5361)** ....‡3,000
Foreign Policy **(5499)** ....(Paid) 34,000
(Non-paid) 40,000
(Combined) **70,000**

ILLINOIS
Champaign
Peace, Prosperity & Democracy **(8209)**

Chicago
Bulletin of the Atomic Scientists **(8295)** ......‡10,000

IOWA
Denison
U.S. Farm News **(10767)** ....‡1,500

MAINE
Lewiston
Peace and Conflict **(12977)**

MASSACHUSETTS
Cambridge
International Security **(14072)** ....‡4,600

NEW YORK
New York
International Peacekeeping **(21929)**

PENNSYLVANIA
Erie
The Catholic Peace Voice **(26895)** .....(Paid) 15,000
(Non-paid) 10,000

Philadelphia
Peace and Freedom **(27613)**

Villanova
Journal of Peace & Justice Studies **(28097)**

ONTARIO, CANADA
Toronto
Peace Magazine **(36699)** 6,000

Waterloo
Ploughshares Monitor **(36857)** ....(Paid) 7,000

PEDIATRICS

CALIFORNIA
Thousand Oaks
Journal of Early Adolescence **(3888)** ......(Paid) 700

COLORADO
Littleton
The Journal of Pediatric Pharmacology and
   Therapeutics **(4549)**

Circ.   Circ.   Circ.

PEDIATRICS (continued)

CONNECTICUT
Farmington
Pediatric Neurosurgery **(4854)** 1,150

ILLINOIS
Chicago
Archives of Pediatrics & Adolescent
  Medicine **(8272)** ....(Combined) ‡30,334
Journal of Dentistry for
  Children **(8437)** ....(Paid) ‡4,265
                  (Controlled) ‡29

Elk Grove Village
Pediatrics **(8833)** ....(Paid) 4,000
                 (Non-paid) 57,000

INDIANA
Indianapolis
Journal of Pediatric Surgery **(10141)** ....‡2,900

KANSAS
Lawrence
Ambulatory Pediatrics **(11546)**

MARYLAND
Baltimore
Pediatric Critical Care Medicine **(13234)** 1,700

Rockville
Pediatric News **(13692)** ....(Controlled) 41,690

MISSOURI
St. Louis
Current Problems in Pediatric and Adolescent Health
  Care **(17430)**
The Journal of Pediatrics **(17458)** ......(Paid) 13,040
                    (Free) 514

NEW JERSEY
Hoboken
Medical and Pediatric Oncology **(19060)** 11,200
Pediatric Pulmonology **(19079)** 9800

Montvale
Contemporary
  Pediatrics **(19249)** ....(Controlled) 48,289

Pitman
Pediatric Nursing **(19439)** ....‡14,011

Rocky Hill
Issues in Comprehensive Pediatric
  Nursing **(19524)** ....(Combined) 740

Thorofare
Journal of Pediatric Ophthalmology &
  Strabismus **(19624)** ....‡2,179
Pediatric Annals **(19638)** ....(Controlled) ‡45,000

NEW YORK
Binghamton
Physical and Occupational Therapy in
  Pediatrics **(20210)** ....(Controlled) ‡1,178

Glen Head
Clinical Pediatrics **(20662)** ....(Paid) ‡4,910

Larchmont
Pediatric Asthma, Allergy & Immunology **(20924)**

New York
Journal of AAPOS (American Association for Pediatric
  Ophthalmology and
  Strabismus) **(21971)** ....(Combined) ‡1,283
Journal of Pediatric Psychology **(22151)**
Journal of Perinatal and Neonatal
  Nursing **(22154)** ....(Paid) 2,501
                (Non-paid) 92
Metabolic Pediatric and Systems
  Ophthalmology **(22319)** ....‡1,000
Pediatric Cardiology **(22536)** ....(Combined) 1,300

Rochester
Development and Psychopathology **(23223)** 1300

PENNSYLVANIA
Philadelphia
Clinical Pediatric Emergency Medicine **(27409)**
Current Opinion in
  Pediatrics **(27443)** ....(Paid) ‡3,005
Journal of Developmental & Behavioral
  Pediatrics **(27524)** ....(Paid) ‡1,321
                (Non-paid) ‡140
Journal of Pediatric Health
  Care **(27543)** ....(Combined) ‡7,645
Pediatric Clinics **(27614)**

Pediatric Emergency Care **(27615)** .....(Paid) ‡1,576
                (Non-paid) ‡215
Pediatric Pathology & Molecular
  Medicine **(27617)** ....‡834
Pediatric Research **(27619)** ....(Paid) ‡3,888
                (Non-paid) ‡23

TEXAS
Austin
Infancy **(29783)**

Dallas
The Pediatric Infectious Disease
  Journal **(30177)** ....(Paid) ‡13,432
                (Non-paid) ‡302

Houston
The Journal of Pediatric Oncology
  Nursing **(30498)** ....‡2,982
Seminars in Pediatric Infectious
  Diseases **(30529)** ....‡1,007

Sugar Land
Internet Journal of Pediatrics and
  Neonatology **(31157)**

ONTARIO, CANADA
Toronto
Mere Nouvelle **(36662)** ....(Non-paid) 45,025
Today's Parent
  Newborn **(36763)** ....(Non-paid) 154,755

PERFORMING ARTS

See also Drama and Theatre; Music and Musical Instruments

ALABAMA
Auburn University
Bulletin of the Comediantes **(49)** ....(Paid) 500

ARIZONA
Tempe
Stage of the Art **(915)**
Youth Theatre Journal **(918)**

CALIFORNIA
Los Angeles
The Agencies **(2203)** ....(Paid) 487
                (Combined) 3,390

COLORADO
Boulder
On-Stage Studies **(4183)**

Steamboat Springs
Vail International Dance
  Festival **(4635)** ....(Non-paid) ‡10,000

CONNECTICUT
New Haven
Theater **(5003)** ....(Combined) 2,400

DISTRICT OF COLUMBIA
Washington
INTERMISSION **(5549)** ....(Paid) ‡1,000
                (Non-paid) ‡9,000
The Journal of Arts Management, Law, and
  Society **(5573)** ....(Paid) 491
The World & I **(5870)** ....(Paid) 20,056
                (Non-paid) 2,781

FLORIDA
Apopka
Bow & Swing **(5909)** ....(Paid) 1,250
                (Non-paid) 200

Palatka
Cinevue Worldwide Talent Directory and Festival
  Program Book **(6536)** ....(Paid) ‡2,000
                (Controlled) ‡2,000

GEORGIA
Atlanta
Art Papers Magazine **(6965)** ....(Paid) 135,000

ILLINOIS
Carbondale
Sacred Dance Guild Journal **(8120)**

Chicago
At the Park **(8278)** ....(Controlled) 9,000
Lenox Avenue **(8460)**

Elmhurst
Marquee **(8835)** ....(Controlled) ‡1,000

IOWA
Pella
Theatre History Studies **(11152)** ....(Paid) 1,000

KANSAS
Lawrence
Journal of Dramatic Theory and Criticism **(11555)**

NEVADA
Las Vegas
Juggle **(18368)** 3,000
Magic **(18377)** ....(Controlled) 10,500

NEW YORK
Brooklyn
Asian Theater Journal **(20297)** ....(Paid) 550
                (Controlled) 40

Chautauqua
Chautauquan Daily **(20453)** ....‡2,500

East Hampton
2wice **(20547)** ....(Paid) ‡2,500

New York
Art Bulletin **(21251)**
Art Journal **(21253)**
Back Stage West **(21284)** 95,011
Ballet Review **(21285)** ....(Paid) 2,000
Dance Chronicle **(21534)** ....(Paid) 450
Dance Magazine **(21535)** ....(Paid) ‡55,000
                (Non-paid) ‡1,082
The Dramatist **(21568)** ....(Paid) 8,000
Journal of Cultural Economics **(22043)**
Music and Media **(22386)** 1,600
New Theatre Quarterly **(22436)** 1,250
Opera News **(22497)** ....(Paid) 100,000
PAJ: A Journal of Performing **(22519)** ....‡2,640
PIX **(22555)**
Ross Reports Television and
  Film **(22677)** ....(Combined) 15,103
Show Biz News & Model News **(22738)** 350,000

TEXAS
Austin
Folk Dance Problem
  Solver **(29776)** ....(Combined) 650

VIRGINIA
Falls Church
The American Harp Journal **(32041)**

WASHINGTON
Seattle
ENCORE **(32963)** ....(Combined) ‡1,126,000

BRITISH COLUMBIA, CANADA
Vancouver
Dance International **(35138)** ....(Paid) 3,500

MANITOBA, CANADA
Winnipeg
Ballet-Hoo **(35312)** ....(Paid) ‡100
                (Non-paid) ‡14,000

ONTARIO, CANADA
Guelph
Essays in Theatre/Etudes
  Theatrales **(35862)** ....(Combined) 350

Toronto
C Magazine **(36482)**
Performing Arts in Canada **(36701)** ....‡20,000
Performing Arts and Entertainment in
  Canada **(36702)** ....(Paid) 44,630
Theatre Research in Canada/Recherches Theatrales
  Au Canada **(36758)**

PETROLEUM, OIL, AND GAS

ALASKA
Anchorage
Petroleum News Alaska **(530)** ....(Paid) ‡1,600
                (Non-paid) ‡800

CALIFORNIA
Anaheim
O & A Marketing News **(1411)** ....(Paid) ‡4,522
                (Free) ‡2,732

DISTRICT OF COLUMBIA
Washington
American Gas **(5330)** ....(Paid) 3,800
                (Non-paid) 6,000
Annual Energy Review 2000 **(5352)**

Energy Prices and Taxes **(5478)**
Natural Gas Monthly **(5688)**
Oil, Gas, Coal and Electricity Quarterly
    Statistics **(5706)**
Petroleum Supply Monthly **(5718)**

GEORGIA
Norcross
Engineering Economist **(7459)**

ILLINOIS
Champaign
Oil and Gas **(8208)** ....(Paid) ‡200
                        (Controlled) ‡120

Chicago
NPN International **(8513)** ....(Controlled) ‡7,500

Des Plaines
gasLine **(8762)**

INDIANA
Indianapolis
Fueling Indiana **(10113)** ....(Controlled) 1,000

KANSAS
Derby
The American Oil and Gas
    Reporter **(11406)** ....‡13,540

LOUISIANA
Baton Rouge
LOMA Line **(12493)** ....(Non-paid) 600

MARYLAND
Potomac
Diesel Fuel News **(13651)**
Oil and Gas Interests **(13656)**
Petroleum Finance Week **(13657)**

MASSACHUSETTS
Beverly
Oil and Energy **(13841)** ....(Controlled) ‡6,605
                        (Paid) ‡2,045

MICHIGAN
Mount Pleasant
Michigan Oil and Gas News **(15377)** ....‡700
                        (Non-paid) ‡40

Troy
National Driller **(15630)**

MISSOURI
Jefferson City
MLPGA News **(17131)** ....(Paid) ‡345
                        (Non-paid) ‡337

Kansas City
NLGI Spokesman **(17189)** ....(Paid) ‡2,200
                        (Non-paid) ‡50

NEBRASKA
Lincoln
Marketer **(18095)** ....(Combined) ‡1,400

NEW JERSEY
Hoboken
Journal of Mass Spectrometry **(19029)**
Natural Gas **(19069)** 5,985

NEW YORK
Great Neck
Petroleo Internacional **(20694)** ....(Non-paid) 9,313

New York
Asia & Australasia–Basic Oil Laws & Concession
    Contracts **(21260)** ....‡5,000
Central American & Caribbean–Basic Oil Laws &
    Concession Contracts **(21389)** ....‡5,000
Chemical and Petroleum Engineering **(21403)**
Chemistry and Technology of Fuels and
    Oils **(21407)**
Europe–Basic Oil Laws & Concession
    Contracts **(21634)** 5,000
Lubricants World **(22268)**
Middle East–Basic Oil Laws & Concession
    Contracts **(22333)** ....‡5,000
Natural Gas Week **(22403)**
North Africa–Basic Oil Laws & Concession
    Contracts **(22469)** ....‡5,000
South America–Basic Oil Laws & Concession
    Contracts **(22765)** ....‡5,000
South & Central Africa–Basic Oil Laws & Concession
    Contracts **(22766)** ....‡5,000

NORTH CAROLINA
Raleigh
NGA News **(24142)** 850

OHIO
Cleveland
LP-Gas **(24922)** ....(Paid) 4,178
                        (Non-paid) 10,756
                                    15,600

OKLAHOMA
Oklahoma City
The Marketer **(25971)**
Propaneorist **(25994)** ....(Controlled) 1,540

Tulsa
AAPG Bulletin **(26104)** ....‡30,000
AAPG Explorer **(26105)** ....(Paid) ‡30,000
                        (Controlled) ‡300
Oil, Gas & Petrochem
    Equipment **(26121)** ....(Combined) ‡32,000
Petroleum Abstracts **(26125)**

PENNSYLVANIA
Philadelphia
Energy Systems and
    Policy **(27460)** ....(Controlled) ‡285

Pittsburgh
Monthly Energy Review **(27817)**

TENNESSEE
Crossville
International
    Tradequip **(29158)** ....(Combined) 51,000

TEXAS
Austin
Texas Petroleum and C-Store
    Journal **(29839)** ....‡1,200
Texas Propane **(29843)** ....(Controlled) ‡1,050

Dallas
Gas Industries **(30159)** ....(Combined) 10,338

Houston
Drilling Contractor **(30470)** ....(Paid) 130
                        (Non-paid) 29,000
Gulf of Mexico Drilling Report **(30473)** ....(Paid) 450
Gulf of Mexico Field Development
    Report **(30474)** ....(Paid) 275
Hart's Fuel Technology &
    Management **(30476)** ....(Paid) 1,400
                        (Non-paid) 9,078
Hart's Lubricants
    World **(30477)** ....(Controlled) 10,240
Hydrocarbon Processing **(30490)** ....(Paid) 11,099
                        (Non-paid) 24,885
Offshore **(30513)** ....(Paid) 841
                        (Controlled) ‡37,289
Offshore Engineer **(30514)** ......(Combined) △31,269
Oil & Gas Journal **(30516)** ....(Paid) 31,354
Pipeline News **(30520)**
Power & Gas
    Marketing **(30521)** ....(Combined) **20,000**
Rehabilitation
    Technology **(30523)** ....(Combined) 32,000
World Oil **(30542)** 35,947

Richardson
Journal of Petroleum
    Technology **(30976)** ....(Paid) 51,000
                        (Non-paid) 4,000
SPE Drilling and Completion **(30979)** ....‡5,800
SPE Production and Facilities **(30980)** ....‡5,000
SPE Reservoir Evaluation &
    Engineering **(30981)** ....‡5,000

VIRGINIA
Falls Church
Lube Report **(32049)** ....(Controlled) 10,000

Vienna
Public Utilities Fortnightly **(32580)**

WASHINGTON
Kirkland
Pacific Builder & Engineer **(32799)** ....(Paid) 251
                        (Controlled) 12,274

WYOMING
Laramie
Energy Sources **(34548)** ....(Controlled) ‡345
Petroleum Science & Technology **(34551)**

ALBERTA, CANADA
Calgary
Alberta Drilling Progress Weekly Report **(34626)**
Energy
    Processing/Canada **(34643)** ......(Combined) 9,800
Propane/Canada **(34655)** ....(Combined) ‡5,200

BRITISH COLUMBIA, CANADA
Vancouver
Oil & Gas Product
    News **(35154)** ....(Combined) 17,511

Victoria
PIMS (Petroleum Information Management
    System) **(35224)**

MANITOBA, CANADA
Winnipeg
The Oil Can **(35347)** ....(Controlled) ‡1,000

PETS

See also Veterinary Medicine

CALIFORNIA
La Honda
Schnauzer Shorts **(2109)** ....(Combined) ⊕1,000
Terrier Type **(2110)** ....(Combined) ‡1,900

Mission Viejo
Pet Product News **(2556)** ....(Controlled) ‡23,000

Norco
Animals Exotic and Small **(2640)** 3,500

Sacramento
Animal Issues **(2976)** ....(Paid) ‡30,000
                        (Non-paid) ‡1,000

CONNECTICUT
Darien
Friends of Animals Actionline **(4772)** 150,000

DISTRICT OF COLUMBIA
Washington
Animal Sheltering Magazine **(5350)** ......(Paid) 7,000

ILLINOIS
Mount Morris
Petfood Industry **(9243)** ....(Controlled) ‡9,291

INDIANA
Butler
The National Stock Dog **(9877)**

MISSOURI
St. Louis
Schutzhund USA **(17510)** ....(Paid) 7,500
                        (Non-paid) 500

NEW YORK
Melville
The Pet Dealer **(21053)** ....(Paid) 564
                        (Non-paid) 16,597

TENNESSEE
Jackson
Sheltie Pacesetter **(29231)** ....(Combined) ⊕2,600

PHILANTHROPY AND HUMANITARIANISM

CALIFORNIA
San Francisco
Harmony **(3369)** ....(Paid) ‡1,000
                        (Non-paid) ‡100

DISTRICT OF COLUMBIA
Washington
The Chronicle of
    Philanthropy **(5414)** ....(Paid) 45,063
Foundation News & Commentary **(5501)** .....‡13,000
The Humanitarian **(5537)**

ILLINOIS
Chicago
Advancing Philanthropy **(8243)**

MARYLAND
Baltimore
Human Rights Quarterly **(13169)** ....‡1,770

Circulation: ★ = ABC; △ = BPA; ♦ = CAC; ● = CCAB; ❑ = VAC; ⊕ = PO Statement; ‡ = Publisher's Report; Boldface figures = sworn; Light figures = estimated.

3205

Circ.   Circ.   Circ.

PHILANTHROPY AND HUMANITARIANISM (continued)

MICHIGAN
Detroit
Crain's Nonprofit News **(14921)**

NEW JERSEY
Parsippany
Non-profit Times **(19412)**
The Nonprofit Times **(19413)** ....(Paid) 2,000
(Non-paid) 34,000

NEW YORK
Brookville
Journal of Counseling &
Development **(20360)** ....‡60,500

New York
Amnesty Action **(21210)** ....‡300,000
Hoosharar Mioutune **(21817)** ....‡7,500
JCC Circle **(21958)** ....‡35,000
Journal of Social Distress and the
Homeless **(22186)**

PENNSYLVANIA
Philadelphia
The Soroptimist of the Americas
Magazine **(27690)** ....(Paid) 50,000

VIRGINIA
Alexandria
Catholic Charities USA **(31652)** ....‡3,000
The War Cry **(31750)** 25,000

WASHINGTON
Seattle
Nonprofit and Voluntary Sector
Quarterly **(32990)** 1,700

PHILOLOGY, LANGUAGE, AND LINGUISTICS

ARIZONA
Tucson
Language in Society **(953)** 1900

CALIFORNIA
Berkeley
Journal of Chinese Linguistics **(1532)**
Linguistics of the Tibeto-Burma Area **(1540)**

Concord
ETC: A Review of General
Semantics **(1753)** 1,500

La Jolla
Linguistic Notes from La Jolla **(2116)**

Los Angeles
Issues in Applied Linguistics
(IAL) **(2299)** ....(Paid) 250
(Non-paid) 50
Scientific Studies of Reading **(2385)**

Malibu
Pacific Coast Philology **(2493)**

Monterey
Applied Language
Learning **(2581)** ....(Non-paid) 4,500

San Diego
Computer Speech & Language **(3130)**

Santa Barbara
Journal of French Language Studies **(3644)** 600
Research on Language and Social Interaction **(3652)**

Santa Cruz
Metaphor and Symbol **(3686)**

Santa Rosa
Maledicta **(3729)** ....(Paid) 2,000

COLORADO
Fort Collins
Statement (Fort Collins) **(4439)** ....(Paid) 850

DISTRICT OF COLUMBIA
Washington
The Germanic Review **(5512)** ....(Paid) ‡700
The Journal of Indo-European
Studies **(5598)** ....(Paid) ‡856
(Non-paid) ‡56
The Mankind Quarterly **(5643)** ....(Paid) ‡1,075
(Non-paid) ‡60

GEORGIA
Atlanta
CLA Journal **(6985)** ....(Paid) ‡1,500
(Controlled) ‡10
South Atlantic Review **(7043)** ....(Paid) ‡2,000
(Non-paid) ‡200

HAWAII
Honolulu
Oceanic Linguistics **(7712)** ....(Paid) 400
(Controlled) 30

ILLINOIS
Carbondale
American Journal of Semiotics **(8114)** ....‡600

Chicago
Visible Language **(8599)** ....‡1,300

DeKalb
Names **(8739)** ....(Paid) 850

Edwardsville
Papers on Language &
Literature **(8814)** ....(Paid) 600
(Non-paid) 54

Urbana
Journal of English and Germanic
Philology **(9712)** ....‡1,400

Wauconda
The Classical Bulletin **(9742)** ....(Paid) ‡520
(Non-paid) ‡480

INDIANA
Bloomington
Journal of Japanese Linguistics **(9842)**
Studies in Second Language
Acquisition **(9852)** 1750

IOWA
Iowa City
Philological Quarterly **(10984)**

KENTUCKY
Wilmore
Buddhist-Christian Studies **(12450)** ....(Paid) 700
(Controlled) 60

LOUISIANA
Baton Rouge
Journal of Mayan Linguistics **(12490)** ......(Paid) 100

MARYLAND
Bethesda
Linguistics and Language Behavior
Abstracts **(13357)** ....‡900

Rockville
Journal of Speech, Language, and Hearing
Research **(13685)**

MASSACHUSETTS
Cambridge
Linguistic Inquiry **(14081)** 2,800

MICHIGAN
Hillsdale
IMPRIMIS **(15164)**

MINNESOTA
Bemidji
Germanic Notes and Reviews **(15737)**
Oshkaabewis Native Journal **(15738)**

MISSOURI
St. Louis
Manuscripta **(17470)** ....(Combined) 500

NEW JERSEY
Cherry Hill
Die Unterrichtspraxis/Teaching
German **(18734)** ....(Combined) 4,100

Mahwah
Language Acquisition **(19200)**
Mind, Culture, and Activity **(19202)**

Morristown
WORD WAYS **(19314)** ....‡500

NEW YORK
Clinton
American Journal of Philology **(20469)** ....‡1,517

New York
Applied Psycholinguistics **(21232)** 1,000
English Digest **(21605)** ....(Controlled) 50,000
English Today **(21606)** 1750
Journal of Child Language **(22024)** 1,650
Journal of Comparative Germanic Linguistics **(22031)**
Journal of Germanic Languages **(22080)** 350
Journal of Linguistics **(22112)** 2,100
Journal of Logic, Language and Information **(22115)**
Language Teaching **(22233)** ....(Paid) 2,300
(Non-paid) 1700
Language Variation and Change **(22234)** 850
Linguistics and Philosophy **(22258)**
Machine Translation **(22273)**
Natural Language & Linguistic Theory **(22406)**
Natural Language Semantics **(22407)**
Neophilologus **(22416)**
Phonology **(22550)** ....(Paid) ‡698
(Non-paid) 68
PMLA **(22567)** ....‡32,350
Reading and Writing **(22628)**
Romanic Review **(22676)** ....(Paid) 900
Russian Linguistics **(22695)**

Stony Brook
Language **(23372)** ....(Paid) ‡6,079
(Non-paid) ‡89

Yonkers
Foreign Language Annals **(23599)** ....‡8,000

Yorktown Heights
Natural Language
Engineering **(23608)** ....(Paid) ‡245
(Non-paid) ‡59

NORTH CAROLINA
Chapel Hill
Studies in Philology **(23726)** ....(Combined) 1,250

Durham
American Speech **(23807)** 2,000

OHIO
Columbus
Italica **(25022)** ....‡1,600

OKLAHOMA
Ada
Communication Studies **(25724)**

PENNSYLVANIA
Philadelphia
History and Philosophy of the Life Sciences **(27483)**

TENNESSEE
Memphis
Discourse Processes **(29369)**

TEXAS
Austin
Communication Disorders
Quarterly **(29769)** ....(Paid) 2,300

Dallas
Journal of Translation and Textlinguistics **(30164)**
Notes on Linguistics **(30171)**
Notes on Literacy **(30172)** ....‡500

UTAH
Provo
Scandinavian Studies **(31408)** ....‡1,000

VIRGINIA
Alexandria
TESOL Journal **(31742)** ....(Combined) 15,000
TESOL Quarterly **(31743)** ....‡10,000

Charlottesville
Classical Journal **(31923)** ....‡3,000

Fairfax
Women and Language **(32034)** ......(Combined) 400

WASHINGTON
Pullman
Rocky Mountain Review of Language and
Literature **(32907)** ....(Controlled) 1,000

Seattle
Modern Language
Quarterly **(32988)** ....(Paid) ‡1,350
(Non-paid) ‡75

Vashon Island
Linguistics Analysis **(33185)** ....(Controlled) 1,900

WEST VIRGINIA
Morgantown
West Virginia University Philological
Papers **(33399)** 400

WISCONSIN
Madison
The Modern Language
Journal **(33962)** ....(Paid) ‡5,000
(Controlled) ‡74

ONTARIO, CANADA
Kingston
Revue Frontenac/Frontenac Review **(35947)**

Toronto
The Canadian Journal of Linguistics/Revue
canadienne de
linguistique **(36511)** ....(Combined) 800
The Canadian Modern Language Review/La Revue
canadienne des langues
vivantes **(36520)** ....(Combined) 1,200
Journal of Cognition and Development **(36633)**
Onomastica Canadiana **(36681)** ....(Paid) 250

Waterloo
Germano-Slavica **(36851)** ....(Paid) ‡200

QUEBEC, CANADA
Montreal
Journal CAJLE **(37137)**
Meta **(37186)** ....‡1,800

PHILOSOPHY

ARKANSAS
Fayetteville
Philosophical Topics **(1123)**

CALIFORNIA
Berkeley
Classical Antiquity **(1508)**
Rhetorica **(1556)** 875

La Mirada
Journal of Psychology and
Theology **(2126)** ....‡1,350

Los Angeles
Ancient Wisdom for Modern
Living **(2210)** ....(Free) 20,000
Theosophy **(2412)** ....(Paid) 800

Pasadena
Sunrise **(2827)**

San Jose
Rosicrucian Digest **(3534)** ......(Combined) ‡20,000

San Pedro
Sudden Enlightenment Digest **(3596)**

Santa Clara
Hume Studies **(3672)**

Thousand Oaks
Philosophy of the Social
Sciences **(3907)** ....(Paid) ‡1,350
(Non-paid) ‡114
Science, Technology & Human
Values **(3915)** ....(Paid) 1,600

COLORADO
Colorado Springs
Journal of Regional Criticism **(4250)**

Golden
Dayspring **(4466)** ....(Paid) 726

DISTRICT OF COLUMBIA
Washington
The Humanist **(5536)** ....(Paid) ‡9,485
(Non-paid) ‡5,664
Kennedy Institute of Ethics Journal **(5623)** 2,000
Perspectives on Political
Science **(5717)** ....(Paid) 467
Review of Metaphysics **(5766)** ....‡2,500
ReVision **(5768)** ....(Paid) ‡900
The Thomist **(5822)** ....(Paid) 1000
(Controlled) 50
The World & I **(5870)** ....(Paid) 20,056
(Non-paid) 2,781

FLORIDA
Ft. Pierce
International Journal of Applied Philosophy **(6118)**

Gainesville
Business & Professional Ethics
Journal **(6131)** 700
Professional Ethics **(6153)** ....(Paid) 700

Panama City
The Journal of Ideas **(6555)** ....‡200

Tallahassee
Social Theory and
Practice **(6735)** ....(Combined) 800

GEORGIA
Atlanta
New Vico Studies **(7032)** ....(Combined) 300

HAWAII
Honolulu
Philosophy East & West **(7717)** ....(Paid) ‡1,400
(Controlled) ‡50

ILLINOIS
Carbondale
American Journal of Semiotics **(8114)** ....‡600

Chicago
The Owl of Minerva **(8523)**
Philosophy Today **(8529)** ....(Paid) ‡1124
(Non-paid) ‡60

DeKalb
Bulletin de la Societe Americaine de Philosophie de
Langue Francaise **(8732)**

Normal
Southwest Philosophy Review **(9305)** ......(Paid) 250

Peru
The Monist **(9449)** ....(Paid) ‡1,500
(Non-paid) ‡200

INDIANA
Bloomington
Hypatia **(9829)** 1,600
Philosophy of Music Education
Review **(9849)** ....(Paid) 500

Fort Wayne
CLIO **(9965)**

Notre Dame
Review of Politics **(10378)** 1,700

KENTUCKY
Wilmore
Faith and Philosophy **(12451)** ....(Paid) 1,800

LOUISIANA
Shreveport
Q.J.I. **(12818)** ....(Paid) 100

MAINE
Orono
The Journal of Mind and
Behavior **(13000)** ....(Paid) ‡1,191

MARYLAND
Baltimore
Journal of the History of
Philosophy **(13192)** 1,600
Philosophy and Literature **(13235)** ....‡1,320
Philosophy, Psychiatry &
Psychology **(13236)** ....(Paid) 592

MASSACHUSETTS
Boston
The Bulletin of Symbolic Logic **(13868)** ....‡2,500
Radical Philosophy Review **(13955)**
Studies in Practical Philosophy **(13965)**

Chestnut Hill
Method **(14131)** ....(Combined) 500
Philosophy & Social Criticism **(14132)**

Malden
The Journal of Aesthetics and Art
Criticism **(14292)** ....‡2,500

Norwell
Journal of Agricultural and Environmental
Ethics **(14441)** ....(Paid) 211
(Non-paid) 27

Worcester
Idealistic Studies **(14683)**

MINNESOTA
Minneapolis
NST (Nature, Society and Thought) **(16118)** 500

MISSOURI
Centerview
International Journal of Philosophical Practice
(IJPP) **(16968)**

Kansas City
Philosophy of Science **(17191)** ....(Paid) 2,280
(Non-paid) 20

St. Joseph
Creation Research Society
Quarterly **(17391)** 2,000

St. Louis
The Modern Schoolman **(17474)** ....(Paid) ‡600
(Non-paid) ‡50

NEW JERSEY
New Brunswick
Journal of the History of
Ideas **(19333)** ....(Paid) ‡3,300
(Controlled) ‡140

Princeton
Philosophy & Public Affairs **(19467)** ....(Paid) ‡2,127
(Non-paid) ‡59

Rutherford
The Fountain **(19526)**

Upper Montclair
Thinking **(19694)** ....(Paid) ‡250
(Non-paid) ‡100

NEW YORK
Amherst
Free Inquiry **(20030)** ....(Paid) ‡30,000
(Non-paid) ‡7,000

Armonk
Contemporary Chinese
Thought **(20073)** ....(Paid) ⊕154
Russian Studies in
Philosophy **(20098)** ....(Paid) ⊕158

Binghamton
African Philosophy **(20151)**

Farmingdale
Aitia/Humanities
Magazine **(20593)** ....(Controlled) 5,000

Ithaca
Cornell Political Forum **(20798)** .....(Non-paid) 8,000
Philosophical Review **(20813)** ....‡3,200

New York
Arabic Sciences and Philosophy **(21239)** 450
Biological Reviews of the Cambridge Philosophical
Society **(21318)**
Continental Philosophy Review **(21495)**
Criminal Justice Ethics **(21517)**
Economics and Philosophy **(21581)** 1,100
Ethical Theory and Moral Practice **(21631)**
Ethics and Information Technology **(21632)**
Ethics and International Affairs **(21633)**
Human Studies **(21835)**
Husserl Studies **(21837)**
Journal of Ethics **(22065)**
Journal for General Philosophy of Science **(22078)**
Journal of Indian Philosophy **(22093)**
Journal of Logic, Language and Information **(22115)**
Journal of Philosophical Logic **(22157)**
The Journal of Philosophy **(22158)** ....‡4,611
The Journal of Value Inquiry **(22211)**
Lapis **(22235)** ....(Combined) 18,000
Minds and Machines **(22337)**
Philosophical Studies **(22549)**
Sartre Studies International **(22705)**
Science & Society **(22713)** 1,923

Port Washington
Hypotheses **(23128)** ....(Combined) 220

OHIO
Bowling Green
The Philosopher's Index **(24699)** ....(Paid) ‡1,322
(Non-paid) ‡175
Social Philosophy and Policy **(24702)** 1,000

Oxford
Teaching Philosophy **(25461)** ....(Paid) ‡1,110
(Non-paid) ‡47

OKLAHOMA
Oklahoma City
The Personalist Forum **(25992)** ......(Combined) 230

Circ.   Circ.   Circ.

PHILOSOPHY (continued)

PENNSYLVANIA
Bryn Athyn
The New Philosophy **(26740)** ....(Paid) ‡340
(Non-paid) ‡87

Harrisburg
Global Virtue Ethics Review **(26993)**
Journal of Power and Ethics **(26997)**

Philadelphia
History and Philosophy of Logic **(27484)**
Journal of Ecumenical Studies **(27525)**
World Futures **(27723)**

Pittsburgh
Ancient Philosophy **(27758)** ....(Combined) 750
Public Affairs Quarterly **(27839)**

University Park
American Philosophical Quarterly **(28069)**
The Journal of Speculative
Philosophy **(28079)** ....‡300
Philosophy and Rhetoric **(28082)** ....‡1,000

Villanova
Epoche **(28096)**

RHODE ISLAND
Providence
Philosophy and Phenomenological Research **(28412)**

TENNESSEE
Memphis
The Southern Journal of
Philosophy **(29382)** ....(Paid) ‡1,200
(Non-paid) ‡60

TEXAS
Arlington
Utopian Studies **(29739)** ....(Paid) 375

College Station
Journal of Philosophical
Research **(30045)** ....(Paid) 300

Denton
Environmental Ethics **(30237)** ....(Paid) 2,000

Irving
American Catholic Philosophical
Quarterly **(30603)** ....‡1,800

VIRGINIA
Charlottesville
Augustinian Studies **(31917)**
HYLE **(31929)**
International Philosophical
Quarterly **(31931)** ....(Paid) ‡1,500
(Controlled) ‡50
Philosophy Now **(31937)**
Questions **(31939)**

WASHINGTON
Bainbridge Island
Gurukulam **(32658)** ....(Paid) ‡100
(Non-paid) ‡300

Seattle
Review of Existential Psychology and
Psychiatry **(33015)** ....(Paid) 250

WISCONSIN
Madison
Substance **(33975)** ....(Paid) 500

Milwaukee
Philosophy & Theology **(34093)** ....(Paid) 500

ALBERTA, CANADA
Athabasca
The Trumpeter **(34610)** ....(Paid) ‡600
(Non-paid) ‡200

Edmonton
Philosophy in Review/Comptes rendus
Philosophiques **(34725)** ....(Combined) 260

Lethbridge
Canadian Journal of Philosophy **(34794)** 950

BRITISH COLUMBIA, CANADA
Vancouver
History of Philosophy Quarterly **(35148)**

MANITOBA, CANADA
Winnipeg
Ultimate Reality and Meaning **(35355)** 370

NEW BRUNSWICK, CANADA
Fredericton
Sociology of Religion **(35397)**

ONTARIO, CANADA
Burks Falls
Canadian Theosophist **(35713)**

Hamilton
Russell: The Journal of Bertrand Russell
Studies **(35888)** ....(Paid) 360

London
Canadian Journal of Law &
Jurisprudence **(35979)** ....(Combined) 500

Toronto
University of Toronto Quarterly **(36782)** 945

Windsor
Informal Logic **(36887)** ....(Controlled) 400

QUEBEC, CANADA
Quebec
Laval Theologique et Philosophique **(37286)**

SASKATCHEWAN, CANADA
Saskatoon
Lumen **(37552)** ....(Paid) 300

PHOTOGRAPHY
See also Motion Pictures

CALIFORNIA
Berkeley
Jump Cut **(1539)** ....(Paid) 3,000

Cedarville
Floating Island **(1681)**

Los Angeles
Outdoor Photographer **(2354)** ....(Paid) 215,189
Petersen's Photographic
Magazine **(2365)** ....(Paid) 204,537

Ojai
Imaging News Online **(2713)**

Santa Monica
Focus on Imaging **(3709)** ....(Controlled) ‡20,873
The RangeFinder **(3716)** ....(Paid) 8,412
(Controlled) 40,959

Ventura
Art/Life **(4000)**

CONNECTICUT
Stamford
Kids Creative Resources **(5152)**

FLORIDA
Titusville
PhotoPro **(6818)** ....(Paid) 26,919
(Non-paid) 11,977
Shutterbug **(6819)** ....(Paid) 87,000

GEORGIA
Atlanta
Art Papers Magazine **(6965)** ....(Paid) 135,000
PEI Magazine **(7036)** ....(Paid) 11,000
(Non-paid) 28,000
Professional Photographer
Storytellers **(7039)** ....(Paid) 25,332

MICHIGAN
Jackson
Photo Marketing **(15223)** ....(Controlled) 15,500

NEW YORK
East Hampton
2wice **(20547)** ....(Paid) ‡2,500

Melville
The Commerical
Image **(21041)** ....(Non-paid) ‡22,607
Modern Reprographics **(21050)** 18,000
Photo Trade News **(21054)**
Photographic Video Trade
News **(21055)** ....(Paid) 3,755
(Non-paid) 9,204
PTN (Photographic Trade
News) **(21062)** ....(Paid) 280
(Non-paid) 12,770

Rochester
AFTERIMAGE **(23208)** ....(Non-paid) ‡5,000
(Paid) ‡5,000

Woodstock
Photography Quarterly **(23595)** ....(Paid) 10,000

NORTH CAROLINA
Durham
News Photographer **(23836)** ....(Paid) ‡9,500

Greensboro
Photo Imaging
Entrepreneur **(23934)** ....(Non-paid) ‡22,651

OKLAHOMA
Oklahoma City
PSA Journal **(25995)** 6,000

PENNSYLVANIA
Langhorne
The Photo Review **(27158)** ....(Paid) ‡2,000
(Non-paid) ‡250

VIRGINIA
Fairfax
So to Speak **(32031)**

Springfield
Journal of Imaging Science and Technology **(32546)**

MANITOBA, CANADA
Winnipeg
Professional Photographers of
Canada **(35350)** ....‡1,700

ONTARIO, CANADA
North York
Applied Arts
Magazine **(36120)** ....(Combined) 13,000

Wellington
Canadian Camera **(36869)** ....‡4,000

QUEBEC, CANADA
Montreal
Scrivener **(37222)** ....(Combined) 500

Quebec
Master Guide **(37292)** ....(Combined) 5,250

PHYSICAL EDUCATION AND ATHLETICS

ALABAMA
Mobile
Journal of Sport Behavior **(322)**

CALIFORNIA
Rancho Cordova
Journal of Applied Sport Psychology **(2875)**

San Diego
IDEA Health & Fitness
Source **(3171)** ....(Paid) 23,000
IDEA Personal Trainer **(3172)** ....(Combined) 10,000

COLORADO
Colorado Springs
Strength and Conditioning
Journal **(4258)** ....(Paid) 26,000

CONNECTICUT
Danbury
Coach and Athletic Director **(4737)** 2,50,000
Scholastic Coach & Athletic
Director **(4753)** ....(Paid) 35,360
(Non-paid) 14,935

GEORGIA
Atlanta
Club Industry **(6987)** ....(Combined) 30,107

ILLINOIS
Champaign
Canadian Journal of Applied
Physiology **(8183)** ....(Paid) ‡879
(Non-paid) ‡37
International Journal of Sport Nutrition & Exercise
Metabolism **(8191)** ....(Paid) ‡1,372
Journal of Applied
Biomechanics **(8195)** ....(Paid) ‡1,164
(Non-paid) ‡40
Journal of Sport & Exercise
Psychology **(8198)** ....(Paid) ‡1,891
Journal of Sport Rehabilitation **(8200)** ....(Paid) ‡880
Journal of Teaching in Physical
Education **(8201)** ....(Paid) ‡1,300

Pediatric Exercise Science **(8210)** ....(Paid) ‡650
(Non-paid) ‡32
Quest **(8215)** ....(Paid) 1,562
(Non-paid) 44
The Sport Psychologist **(8218)** ....(Paid) ‡1,202
‡45

Evanston
Wrestling Digest **(8874)**

Macomb
PALAESTRA **(9131)** ....(Combined) ‡5000

INDIANA
Indianapolis
Physical Educator **(10160)**

MASSACHUSETTS
Springfield
Measurement in Physical Education and Exercise
Science **(14551)**

NEBRASKA
Lincoln
Nine **(18108)**

NEVADA
Las Vegas
ACSM's Health & Fitness
Journal **(18359)** ....‡10,700
Women in Sport and Physical Activity
Journal **(18387)** ....(Paid) 250

NEW YORK
Ithaca
Coaching
Management **(20790)** ....(Controlled) ‡109,567

OHIO
Cleveland
Athletics Administration **(24857)** ....‡7,100

PENNSYLVANIA
Philadelphia
Journal of Spiritual
Bodywork **(27551)** ....(Combined) 150

SOUTH CAROLINA
Hilton Head Island
TennisPro **(28662)** ....(Combined) 15,000

TEXAS
Houston
ADDvantage **(30454)**

VIRGINIA
Reston
AAHPERD Update **(32354)** ....(Paid) 24,165
American Journal of Health Education **(32360)**
Journal of Physical Education, Recreation & Dance
(JOPERD) **(32390)** ....(Paid) 20,000
Strategies **(32415)** ....‡10,000
Strategies **(32416)** ....(Paid) 7,460

WISCONSIN
Racine
Referee Magazine **(34276)** ....(Paid) ‡35,000
(Non-paid) ‡200

ONTARIO, CANADA
Ottawa
Avante **(36185)**
Physical & Health Education Journal **(36270)**

Sudbury
Physical Education Digest **(36418)** ....(Paid) 2,000

Waterloo
Leisure/Loisir **(36855)** ....(Paid) ‡350
(Non-paid) ‡50

PRINCE EDWARD ISLAND, CANADA
Charlottetown
Island Sport Scene **(36916)** ....(Non-paid) 350

QUEBEC, CANADA
Montreal
Ascent Magazine **(37088)** ....(Controlled) 10,000

PHYSICS
See also Nuclear Engineering; Science
(General)

ALABAMA
Birmingham
Russian Journal of Mathematical
Physics **(89)** 5985

ARIZONA
Tucson
Oxidation of Metals **(957)**

CALIFORNIA
Berkeley
Probability in the Engineering and Informational
Sciences **(1552)** 350

San Diego
Annals of Physics **(3114)**
Archives of Biochemistry and Biophysics **(3116)**
Atomic Data and Nuclear Data Tables **(3118)**
Biochemical and Biophysical Research
Communications **(3120)**
Icarus **(3169)**
Journal of Colloid and Interface Science **(3181)**
Journal of Computational Physics **(3185)**
Journal of Magnetic Resonance **(3203)**
Journal of Molecular Spectroscopy **(3206)**

Santa Barbara
Physics of Fluids **(3651)**

Thousand Oaks
The Journal of Diagnostic Medical Sonography
(JDMS) **(3887)** ....(Paid) 14,000

DISTRICT OF COLUMBIA
Washington
Applied Optics **(5359)** 3,200
Journal of the Optical Society of America B: Optical
Physics **(5609)**

FLORIDA
Naples
Journal of Thermal Stresses **(6442)** ....‡308

Palm Harbor
Hadronic Journal **(6551)** ....(Paid) 150
Hadronic Journal Supplement **(6552)** ......(Paid) 100

GEORGIA
Athens
Molecular Physics **(6947)**

HAWAII
Honolulu
Pacific Science **(7715)** ....(Paid) ‡680
(Controlled) ‡30

ILLINOIS
Chicago
Numerical Heat Transfer, Part A:
Applications **(8515)** ....‡586

Urbana
Journal of Macromolecular Science, Part B,
Physics **(9713)** 600

INDIANA
West Lafayette
International Reviews in Physical Chemistry **(10547)**

MARYLAND
Bethesda
Solid State and Superconductivity Abstracts **(13380)**

College Park
Announcer **(13411)** ....(Paid) ‡11,000
Applied Physics Letters **(13412)** 4,600
Bulletin of the American Physical
Society **(13413)** ....‡39,757
CHAOS **(13414)**
Current Physics Index **(13415)** ....‡279
The Industrial
Physicist **(13421)** ....(Controlled) 60,000
JETP Letters **(13422)** ....‡845
Journal of Applied Physics **(13423)**
The Journal of Chemical Physics **(13425)** ....‡N/A
Journal of Experimental and Theoretical Physics
(JETP) **(13427)** ....‡1,080
Journal of Mathematical Physics **(13428)**
Journal of Physical and Chemical Reference
Data **(13430)**
Low Temperature Physics **(13433)** ....‡150

Physics of Particles and Nuclei **(13435)**
Physics Today **(13436)** ....‡127,000
Semiconductors **(13440)** ....‡570
Technical Physics **(13441)** ....‡300
Technical Physics Letters **(13442)** ....‡180
Virtual Journal of Biological Physics
Research **(13444)**
Virtual Journal of Quantum Information **(13446)**

Laurel
Johns Hopkins APL Technical
Digest **(13613)** ....(Controlled) ⊕4,330

MASSACHUSETTS
Amherst
American Journal of Physics **(13789)** 8,100

Arlington
Galilean
Electrodynamics **(13819)** ....(Combined) ‡320

Burlington
Supramolecular Science **(14033)**

Chestnut Hill
Advances in Physics **(14126)**

Lexington
CryoGas International **(14271)**

Somerville
Advances in Theoretical and Mathematics
Physics **(14530)**
Journal of Differential
Geometry **(14535)** ....(Combined) 1,250

NEW JERSEY
Hoboken
Complexity **(18920)** 14,000
International Journal for Numerical and Analytical
Methods in Geomechanics **(18989)**
International Journal for Numerical Methods in
Fluids **(18991)**
Journal of Polymer Science **(19042)** 12,950
Journal of Raman Spectroscopy **(19044)**
Numerical Linear Algebra with Applications **(19075)**
Random Structures & Algorithms **(19095)** 3850
X-Ray Spectrometry **(19120)**

Princeton
Physics of Plasmas **(19468)** ....‡2,611

River Edge
International Journal of Nonlinear Optical Physics
(IJNOP) **(19511)**
International Journal of PIXE **(19512)**
Journal of Modern Physics A **(19517)**

NEW MEXICO
Rehoboth
Smarandache Notions
Journal **(19912)** ....(Combined) 1,000

NEW YORK
Hauppauge
Nova Journal of Theoretical Physics **(20720)**

Melville
Physical Review Abstracts **(21056)** 3,000
Physiological Chemistry and Physics and Medical
NMR **(21057)** ....(Combined) 353

New York
Adsorption **(21151)**
Astrophysics **(21268)**
Atomization and Sprays **(21270)** ....(Paid) 500
Cellulose **(21388)**
Comments on Nuclear and Particles Physics **(21455)**
Communications in Theoretical Physics **(21462)**
Computational Geosciences **(21469)**
Czechoslovak Journal of Physics **(21529)**
Foundations of Physics **(21731)**
Foundations of Physics Letters **(21732)**
Fullerene Science &
Technology **(21740)** ....(Paid) 250
High Temperature **(21802)**
Hyperfine Interactions **(21840)**
Interface Science **(21890)**
International Journal of Infrared and Millimeter
Waves **(21909)**
International Journal of Theoretical Physics **(21923)**
International Journal of Thermophysics **(21924)**
Journal of Applied Mechanics and Technical
Physics **(21992)**
Journal of Applied Spectroscopy **(21995)**
Journal of Biological Physics **(22010)**
Journal of Biomolecular NMR **(22013)**
Journal of Computer-Aided Materials Design **(22035)**

Circulation: ★ = ABC; △ = BPA; ♦ = CAC; • = CCAB; ❑ = VAC; ⊕ = PO Statement; ‡ = Publisher's Report; Boldface figures = sworn; Light figures = estimated.

3209

Circ.

PHYSICS (continued)

Journal of Engineering Physics and
   Thermophysics **(22064)**
Journal of Fusion Energy **(22074)**
Journal of Low Temperature Physics **(22117)**
Journal of Nondestructive Evaluation **(22144)**
Journal of Plasma Physics **(22161)** 400
Journal of Rheology **(22179)**
Journal of Statistical Physics **(22193)**
Journal of Superconductivity **(22198)**
Laser and Particle Beams **(22236)** 400
Letters in Mathematical Physics **(22247)**
Mathematical Physics, Analysis and
   Geometry **(22296)**
Mathematical Proceedings of the Cambridge
   Philosophical Society **(22297)**
Neutron News **(22427)** ....(Combined) 4,100
Open Systems & Information Dynamics **(22495)**
Russian Physics Journal **(22697)**

Ridge
Physical Review A **(23190)** 2,200
Physical Review B **(23191)** 2,550
Physical Review C **(23192)** 1,500
Physical Review D **(23193)** 1,900
Physical Review E **(23194)** 1,900
Physical Review Letters **(23195)** 5,900
Physical Review Special Topics **(23196)**

NORTH CAROLINA
Boone
The Physics Teacher **(23655)** 10,000

OKLAHOMA
Tulsa
Geophysics **(26116)** ....‡16,530

OREGON
Klamath Falls
Radio Science **(26385)**

PENNSYLVANIA
Philadelphia
Contemporary Physics **(27427)**
Philosophical Magazine **(27636)**
Philosophical Magazine Letters **(27637)**

Pittsburgh
Journal of Research of the National Institute of
   Standards and Technology **(27804)**

VIRGINIA
Charlottesville
Transport Theory and Statistical
   Physics **(31942)** 300

Reston
Journal of Propulsion and Power **(32392)** .....‡2,000
Journal of Thermophysics and Heat
   Transfer **(32398)** ....‡1,600

WASHINGTON
Seattle
Reviews of Modern Physics **(33016)** ....(Paid) 4,300

ONTARIO, CANADA
Ottawa
Physics in Canada **(36271)** ....‡2,050
Physics Essays **(36272)** ....‡171

PHYSIOLOGY AND ANATOMY

See also Biology; Zoology

CALIFORNIA
San Diego
Methods **(3230)**

Thousand Oaks
Neurohabilitation and Neural
   Repair **(3904)** ....(Paid) 1,100
                             (Non-paid) 50

ILLINOIS
Champaign
Motor Control **(8204)** ....(Paid) ‡307

MARYLAND
Baltimore
Journal of Orthopaedic Trauma **(13197)** 3173

Bethesda
Advances in Physiology
   Education **(13294)** ....(Combined) ‡9,739
American Journal of Physiology: Cell
   Physiology **(13303)** ....(Combined) ‡3,310

American Journal of Physiology
   (Consolidated) **(13304)** ....(Combined) ‡2,639
American Journal of Physiology: Endocrinology and
   Metabolism **(13305)** ....(Combined) ‡3,231
American Journal of Physiology: Gastrointestinal and
   Liver Physiology **(13306)** ......(Combined) ‡3,241
American Journal of Physiology: Heart and Circulatory
   Physiology **(13307)** ....(Combined) ‡3,231
American Journal of Physiology: Lung Cellular and
   Molecular
   Physiology **(13308)** ....(Combined) ‡3,388
American Journal of Physiology: Regulatory,
   Integrative and Comparative
   Physiology **(13309)** ....(Combined) ‡3,126
American Journal of Physiology: Renal
   Physiology **(13310)** ....(Combined) ‡3,421
Journal of Applied
   Physiology **(13348)** ....(Combined) ‡3,092
Journal of Neurophysiology **(13353)** ....(Paid) ‡1,931
News in Physiological Sciences
   (NIPS) **(13364)** ....(Paid) ‡10,505
Physiological Reviews **(13374)** ....(Paid) ‡3,187

MASSACHUSETTS
Cambridge
Immunity **(14069)** 3,000

MINNESOTA
Minneapolis
Journal of Andrology **(16086)** ....‡1,200

MISSOURI
St. Louis
Analytical and Quantitative Cytology and
   Histology **(17413)** ....(Paid) ‡3,090

NEW JERSEY
Hoboken
Developmental Dynamics **(18927)** 8750
GLIA **(18954)** 4200
Journal of Cellular Physiology **(19009)** 9800
Microscopy Research and
   Technique **(19062)** 5600
Movement Disorders **(19067)** 2,301
Reviews in Medical Virology **(19099)** ....(Paid) 3,500
Yeast **(19121)**

Somerset
Integrative Physiological and Behavioral
   Science **(19562)** ....(Paid) ‡500

Thorofare
Occupational Therapy Journal of
   Research **(19630)** ....(Paid) 900

NEW YORK
New York
European Journal of Phycology **(21647)**
Experimental Physiology **(21667)** 650
Human Physiology **(21831)**
Journal of Anatomy **(21988)**
Journal of Evolutionary Biochemistry and
   Physiology **(22066)**
Journal of Physiology **(22159)** 2200
Medical Physics **(22310)** ....‡4,182
Neuroscience and Behavioral Physiology **(22426)**
Psychophysiology **(22606)**
Pulmonary Pharmacology **(22612)**

OHIO
Toledo
Clinical Kinesiology **(25565)**

PENNSYLVANIA
King of Prussia
ADVANCE for Occupational Therapy
   Practitioners **(27117)** ....(Non-paid) ‡60,000

Philadelphia
Annals of Human Biology **(27378)**
Annals of Internal Medicine **(27379)** ....(Paid) 91,224
Disability and Rehabilitation **(27453)**
Ergonomics **(27463)**
Medical Informatics & The Internet in
   Medicine **(27566)**
Modern Pathology **(27571)** ....(Paid) ‡5,514
                           (Non-paid) ‡87
Seizure **(27657)**
Sexually Transmitted Diseases **(27677)** 1,402

SOUTH CAROLINA
Kiawah Island
Archives of Andrology, an International
   Journal **(28673)** 453

Circ.

TEXAS
Dallas
Journal of the Academy of Rehabilitative
   Audiology **(30162)** ....(Paid) ‡600

Houston
Visual Neuroscience **(30541)** 600

San Antonio
Physiology & Behavior **(31042)**

VIRGINIA
Alexandria
JPO: Journal of Prosthetics &
   Orthotics **(31704)** ....(Paid) ‡4,600
O & P Almanac **(31717)** ....‡8,700

Hampton
Metabolism - Clinical and
   Experimental **(32130)** ....‡3,506

ONTARIO, CANADA
Ottawa
Canadian Journal of Physiology and Pharmacology
   (Revue Canadienne de Physiologie et
   Pharmacologie) **(36211)** ....‡1,000

PLASTIC AND COMPOSITION MATERIALS

See also Chemistry, Chemicals, and Chemical Engineering

COLORADO
Denver
Injection Molding
   Magazine **(4330)** ....(Combined) ‡37,500
Plastics Auxiliaries &
   Machinery **(4348)** ....(Controlled) 30,000

Wheat Ridge
Composites
   Technology **(4673)** ....(Controlled) ‡25,000
High-Performance
   Composites **(4676)** ....(Controlled) ‡20,000

CONNECTICUT
Bethel
Experimental Mechanics **(4697)** 4,500

Brookfield
Journal of Vinyl and Additive
   Technology **(4726)** ....‡535
Plastics Engineering **(4727)** 32,035
Polymer Engineering and Science **(4728)** 1,400

FLORIDA
Coral Gables
Tecnologia del Plastico **(6013)** ....(Controlled) 15,109

ILLINOIS
Riverside
The Plastics Distributor & Fabricator
   Magazine **(9498)** ....(Non-paid) ‡28,142

KANSAS
Leawood
The IAPD Magazine **(11585)** ....(Paid) 10,000
                          (Non-paid) 10,000

MINNESOTA
St. Paul
Powder and Bulk
   Engineering **(16407)** ....(Free) ‡35,005

NEW YORK
Melville
Plastics World **(21058)** ....(Controlled) ‡57,311

New York
Modern Plastics **(22350)** ....(Paid) 14,750
                       (Non-paid) 20,197
Plastics Technology **(22564)** ....(Paid) ⊕46,530
                       (Non-paid) ⊕**3,728**

OHIO
Akron
Plastics News **(24585)** ....(Paid) 21,350
                       (Non-paid) 39,920
Rubber & Plastics News **(24587)** ......(Paid) △**6,322**
                       (Non-paid) △**9,995**

Beachwood
Polymers/Ceramics/Composites Alert **(24655)**

Cincinnati
Automotive Finishing **(24778)**
Products Finishing **(24813)** ......(Controlled) ‡45,677

Materials Park
Advanced Materials &
  Processes **(25363)** ....(Paid) 30,000
Alloy Digest **(25364)** 250
Engineered Materials Abstracts **(25365)**

VIRGINIA
Richmond
Polymer-Plastics Technology and
  Engineering **(32446)** 325

ONTARIO, CANADA
Toronto
Canadian Plastics **(36525)** ....(Combined) 10,244
Plastics in Canada **(36710)** ....(Combined) 10,550

PLUMBING AND HEATING
See also Air Conditioning and Refrigeration

ALABAMA
Birmingham
Associated Plumbing Heating &
  Cooling **(55)** ....(Non-paid) ‡2,000

CALIFORNIA
Laguna Hills
Reeves Journal **(2135)** ....(Controlled) ‡13,500

Ontario
Official Magazine **(2717)** ....(Paid) ‡5,000

San Francisco
Pipelines **(3414)** ....(Non-paid) 2,500

CONNECTICUT
Waterbury
Alternative Energy
  Retailer **(5190)** ....(Controlled) ⊕9,837
                                      (Paid) ⊕332

FLORIDA
Altamonte Springs
Ohio Perspective **(5901)** ....(Controlled) ‡8,000
Wisconsin Perspective **(5903)** .....(Controlled) ‡7,200

Boca Raton
HVAC/R Distribution Today **(5932)** ....(Paid) 500
                                      (Non-paid) 250

Tallahassee
Florida Contractor **(6708)**

GEORGIA
Atlanta
ASHRAE Journal **(6966)** ....(Paid) 49,200
                                      (Non-paid) 11,157
International Journal of Heating, Ventilating, Air-
  Conditioning and Refrigeration Research (HVAC &
  R Research) **(7018)**

ILLINOIS
Des Plaines
Contractor Magazine **(8755)** ......(Controlled) 48,504
                                      (Controlled) 48,504

Springfield
Illinois Master Plumber **(9626)** ....‡2,000

INDIANA
Indianapolis
Indiana Contractor **(10125)** ....(Controlled) ‡5,579

KENTUCKY
Louisville
Kentucky Plumbing-Heating-Cooling
  Index **(12225)** ....‡4,500

MARYLAND
Ellicott City
Maryland PHCC News &
  Views **(13499)** ....(Non-paid) 2,500

MASSACHUSETTS
Westborough
District Energy **(14637)** ....‡3,520

MICHIGAN
Lansing
Michigan Master Plumber and Mechanical
  Contractor **(15287)** ....(Controlled) ‡3,100

Troy
Air Conditioning, Heating and Refrigeration
  News **(15616)** ....(Paid) 25,938
                                      (Non-paid) 4,706

NEW YORK
New York
Consulting-Specifying
  Engineer **(21490)** ....(Controlled) ‡47,508

NORTH CAROLINA
Garner
North Carolina Plumbing-Heating-Cooling
  Forum **(23905)** ....(Non-paid) ‡1,000

Greensboro
Southern PHC
  Magazine **(23939)** ....(Non-paid) ‡12,274

OHIO
Cleveland
Heating/Piping/Air Conditioning Engineering
  (HPAC) **(24906)** ....(Paid) 1,250
                                      (Non-paid) 56,000

OREGON
Klamath Falls
SNEWS **(26387)** ....(Paid) 625

SOUTH CAROLINA
Columbia
Palmetto Piper **(28559)** ....‡2,700

ONTARIO, CANADA
Etobicoke
Plumbing & HVAC Product
  News **(35819)** ....(Combined) •18,031

Toronto
Heating, Plumbing, Air Conditioning Buyers'
  Guide **(36613)** ....(Controlled) 15,528
HPAC (Heating-Plumbing-Air Conditioning
  Magazine) **(36620)** ....(Combined) 16,528

QUEBEC, CANADA
Montreal
Inter-Mecanique du
  Batiment **(37134)** ....(Combined) •6,350

PODIATRY

CALIFORNIA
Los Angeles
Hospital Podiatrist **(2294)** ....(Non-paid) 1,000
Podiatric Products **(2371)** ....(Controlled) 13,000

ILLINOIS
Park Ridge
Journal of Foot and Ankle
  Surgery **(9405)** ....(Paid) ‡6,400
                                      (Non-paid) ‡200

MARYLAND
Bethesda
APMA News **(13312)** ....(Paid) ‡12,375
                                      (Non-paid) ‡125
Journal of the American Podiatric Medical
  Association **(13347)** ....(Paid) ‡13,397
                                      (Non-paid) ‡1,693

NEW JERSEY
Montvale
Podiatry Today **(19272)** ....(Free) ‡15,218

PENNSYLVANIA
Philadelphia
Clinics in Podiatric Medicine and Surgery **(27420)**

POLICE, PENOLOGY, AND PENAL INSTITUTIONS
See also Safety

CALIFORNIA
Orange
Law Enforcement
  Journal **(2724)** ....(Controlled) 1,600

San Rafael
Correctional News **(3600)** ....(Combined) 13,218

Thousand Oaks
Crime & Delinquency **(3858)** ....(Paid) 1,500

Criminal Justice and
  Behavior **(3860)** ....(Paid) ‡1,100
Journal of Research in Crime and
  Delinquency **(3899)** ....(Paid) ‡1,100
Violence Against Women **(3920)**

Torrance
Police **(3940)** ....‡52,000

COLORADO
Denver
Law Enforcement Product
  News **(4338)** ....(Non-paid) 26,417
Public Safety Product
  News **(4350)** ....(Non-paid) 14,292

CONNECTICUT
Hartford
Campus Law Enforcement
  Journal **(4885)** ....(Paid) 1,700

DISTRICT OF COLUMBIA
Washington
American Criminal Law Review **(5325)**

FLORIDA
Miami
The Chief of Police **(6345)**

ILLINOIS
Deerfield
Law and Order **(8726)** ....(Paid) 11,890
                                      (Controlled) 19,888

Menard
The Menard Time **(9172)** ....(Non-paid) ‡3,400

KENTUCKY
Louisville
National Police Review **(12232)** ....(Paid) ‡4,000
                                      (Non-paid) ‡1,000

LOUISIANA
Angola
Angolite **(12472)** ....(Paid) ⊕3,100

MARYLAND
Hagerstown
American Jails **(13562)** ....(Paid) 5,100
                                      (Non-paid) 2,500

Lanham
CORRECTIONS TODAY **(13599)** ....‡20,000
Journal of Correctional Best Practices **(13603)**

MASSACHUSETTS
Cambridge
American Police Beat **(14037)** ....(Paid) ★11,500
                                      (Non-paid) ★45,500

MICHIGAN
East Lansing
International Journal of Comparative and Applied
  Criminal Justice **(14985)** ....(Paid) 400

MINNESOTA
Mendota Heights
Journal of Forensic
  Identification **(16052)** ....(Combined) 5,500

MISSOURI
Springfield
Forensic Examiner **(17600)**

Warrensburg
Probation and Parole Law Reports **(17669)**

NEW JERSEY
Hasbrouck Heights
National Missing Persons
  Report **(18866)** ....(Controlled) ‡45,000

Somerset
Trends in Organized Crime **(19568)** ......(Paid) ‡300

NEW YORK
Albany
The Journal of Criminal Justice & Popular
  Culture **(19992)** ....(Free) 2,343

Binghamton
Journal of Threat Assessment **(20204)**

New York
Criminal Justice Ethics **(21517)**
European Journal of Crime, Criminal Law and
  Criminal Justice **(21640)**

Circulation: ★ = ABC; △ = BPA; ♦ = CAC; • = CCAB; ❑ = VAC; ⊕ = PO Statement; ‡ = Publisher's Report; Boldface figures = sworn; Light figures = estimated.

3211

Circ.   Circ.   Circ.

POLICE, PENOLOGY, AND PENAL INSTITUTIONS (continued)

European Journal of Criminal Policy and
   Research **(21641)**
Journal of Quantitative Criminology **(22174)**
Law Enforcement News **(22238)** ....(Paid) ‡6,000

PENNSYLVANIA
Doylestown
Journal of Offender Rehabilitation **(26833)** 540

Philadelphia
The Prison Journal **(27646)**

Pittsburgh
The Pennsylvania Police Criminal Law
   Bulletin **(27826)** ....(Paid) 1,200
                     (Non-paid) 50

Quakertown
Police & Security News **(27915)** ....(Paid) ‡449
                   (Non-paid) ‡22,160

Shippensburg
Women & Criminal
   Justice **(27993)** ....(Controlled) ‡382

TENNESSEE
Chattanooga
Polygraph **(29091)**

TEXAS
Fort Worth
Journal of Police Crisis Negotiations **(30343)**

San Marcos
Journal of Police and Criminal
   Psychology **(31084)** ....(Controlled) 350

VIRGINIA
Alexandria
The Police Chief **(31723)** ....‡20,000
Sheriff **(31737)** ....‡19,000

Arlington
International Counterterrorism & Security **(31799)**
Victimology **(31839)** ....‡2,700

Quantico
FBI Law Enforcement
   Bulletin **(32340)** ....(Controlled) 45,000

WISCONSIN
Fort Atkinson
Law Enforcement
   Technology **(33713)** ....(Non-paid) ‡30,000

ONTARIO, CANADA
Markham
Blue Line Magazine **(36014)** ....(Combined) ⊕12,000

Ottawa
Canadian Journal of Criminology/Revue Canadienne
   de Criminologie **(36204)** ....(Controlled) 1,100
Forum on Corrections Research **(36244)**
RCMP Veterans' Association Quarterly/Association
   des anciens de la GRC
   Trimestrialle **(36275)** 13,000

QUEBEC, CANADA
Cowansville
Resumes de droit penal **(36984)**

Montreal
La Flute **(37149)** ....(Controlled) 8,500

POLITICAL SCIENCE

CALIFORNIA
Fullerton
Structural Equation Modeling **(1990)**

Los Angeles
Studies in American Political
   Development **(2407)** 400

COLORADO
Boulder
Latin American Politics and
   Society **(4176)** ....(Paid) 1,300
                    (Controlled) 202

Denver
Denver Journal of International Law and
   Policy **(4323)**

CONNECTICUT
New Haven
Journal of Conflict
   Resolution **(4993)** ....(Paid) ‡2,363
                   (Non-paid) ‡114

Storrs
Public Perspective **(5167)** ....(Combined) 3,000

DISTRICT OF COLUMBIA
Washington
Civil Rights Journal **(5416)**
Journal of Democracy **(5580)** 4,500
Policy and Practice of Public Human
   Services **(5720)**
Presidential Studies Quarterly **(5728)**
The Responsive Community **(5764)** ......(Paid) 2,000

GEORGIA
Athens
State and Local Government
   Review **(6952)** ....(Controlled) 1,000

Statesboro
Politics and Policy **(7561)** ....(Paid) 485

ILLINOIS
Champaign
State Politics & Policy Quarterly **(8219)**

DeKalb
Crossroads **(8733)** ....(Paid) 300

Springfield
Journal of the Abraham Lincoln Association **(9635)**

INDIANA
West Lafayette
Journal of the Early
   Republic **(10549)** ....(Combined) 1,450

MARYLAND
Baltimore
Theory & Event **(13253)**

College Park
Politics and the Life Sciences **(13437)**

MASSACHUSETTS
Burlington
Transport Policy **(14034)**

Cambridge
Asian American Policy
   Review **(14039)** ....(Combined) 700
The Harvard International Journal of
   Press/Politics **(14059)**
Harvard Journal of Legislation **(14063)** 800

Malden
Middle East Policy **(14298)**

MICHIGAN
Ann Arbor
Comparative Studies in Society &
   History **(14745)** ....(Paid) ‡2028

MINNESOTA
St. Cloud
Journal of Information Ethics **(16344)** .....(Paid) 200
                   (Controlled) 50

NEW JERSEY
Somerset
Armed Forces & Society **(19561)** ....(Paid) ‡1,700

NEW MEXICO
Silver City
Foreign Policy in Focus **(19952)** ....(Paid) 800
                   (Non-paid) 250

NEW YORK
Albany
Legislative Gazette **(19993)** ....(Paid) 385
                   (Non-paid) 18,200

Brooklyn
New Politics **(20332)** ....(Paid) 3000

Hauppauge
White House Studies **(20723)**

Ithaca
Cornell Journal of Law and Public
   Policy **(20796)** ....(Paid) 550
Cornell Political Forum **(20798)** .....(Non-paid) 8,000

Larchmont
Election Law Journal **(20898)**

New York
British Journal of Political
   Science **(21342)** ....(Paid) ‡1231
                   (Non-paid) ‡88
Dispute Resolution Times **(21559)**
European Journal of Political Research **(21649)**
Integrated Assessment **(21885)**
Japanese Journal of Political
   Science **(21957)** 400
Journal of Comparative Policy Analysis **(22032)**
Journal of International Affairs **(22102)**
The Journal of Socio-Economics **(22188)**
Political Affairs **(22573)**
Risk, Decision and Policy **(22670)**
Social Research **(22756)** ....‡3,000
Theoria **(22829)**

Rhinebeck
The Trends Journal **(23186)**

NORTH CAROLINA
Durham
Socialist Review **(23844)**

Raleigh
Social Science Computer Review **(24153)** 1,000

PENNSYLVANIA
Carlisle
Parameters **(26760)** ....(Paid) ‡1,500
                  (Non-paid) ‡11,500

Harrisburg
Journal of Power and Ethics **(26997)**

Pittsburgh
Public Affairs Quarterly **(27839)**

TEXAS
Dallas
Clements' International Report **(30137)**
World of Politics **(30190)**

Waco
Journal of Church and
   State **(31249)** ....(Paid) ⊕1,700

VIRGINIA
Arlington
Political and Legal Anthropological Review **(31818)**

Vienna
Government Union Review **(32578)**

WASHINGTON
Ferndale
The North American Technocrat **(32768)** 1,500

BRITISH COLUMBIA, CANADA
Burnaby
International History
   Review **(34903)** ....(Controlled) 900

ONTARIO, CANADA
Ottawa
Canadian Review of American
   Studies **(36227)** ....(Paid) 475

POLITICS

**See also Congressional and Federal
Government Affairs**

ARIZONA
Phoenix
Arizona Capitol Times **(776)** ....(Combined) 5,000

ARKANSAS
Little Rock
Arkansas Register **(1220)** ....(Combined) 206

CALIFORNIA
Berkeley
Bad Subjects **(1493)**
Studies in Comparative International
   Development **(1563)** ....(Paid) ‡600
Tikkun Magazine **(1565)** ....(Combined) 20,000

Beverly Hills
TVI Report **(1579)** ....(Paid) ‡1,000
                   (Non-paid) ‡100

Culver City
Turning the Tide **(1795)** ....(Paid) ‡750
(Non-paid) ‡9,250

Los Angeles
Amass **(2206)** ....(Paid) 6,000
New Perspectives Quarterly **(2345)** .....(Paid) 11,002
(Non-paid) 559
REASON **(2378)** ....(Paid) 55,000

Mountain View
The People **(2608)** 10,900

Nevada City
Wild Duck Review **(2616)** ....(Paid) ‡3,500

Oakland
Asian Survey **(2667)** ....‡3,300

Palo Alto
Meanderings **(2798)**

Sacramento
California Journal **(2983)** ....(Paid) 9,500
(Non-paid) 225
California State Association of Counties California
County **(2988)** ....(Non-paid) 7,000

Santa Cruz
Capitalism, Nature,
Socialism **(3681)** ....(Combined) ‡1,983

Thousand Oaks
American Politics Research **(3849)** ....(Paid) 700
The Annals of the American Academy of Political and
Social Science **(3850)** ....(Paid) ‡4,000
Comparative Political Studies **(3857)** .....(Paid) ‡900
Politics & Society **(3908)** ....(Paid) 800

COLORADO
Denver
NEXUS Magazine **(4344)** ....(Paid) 25,000
(Non-paid) 200
State Legislatures **(4361)** ....(Paid) ‡18,385

CONNECTICUT
New Haven
Journal of Health Politics, Policy and
Law **(4994)** ....‡2500

Storrs
Public Perspective **(5167)** ....(Combined) 3,000

DELAWARE
Wilmington
Parliamentary Journal **(5294)** 1,800

DISTRICT OF COLUMBIA
Washington
The American Enterprise **(5328)** ....(Paid) 25,000
American Political Science
Review **(5338)** ....‡16,000
The American Spectator **(5344)** ....(Paid) 60,000
Church & State **(5415)** ....‡33,000
(Controlled) ‡2,600
CovertAction Quarterly **(5446)** ....‡12,000
The CQ Researcher **(5447)** ....(Paid) ‡5,000
Current **(5453)** ....‡2,174
The Hill **(5526)** 22,500
Human Events **(5535)** ....‡72,000
Insight on the News **(5547)**
The Journal of International Security Affairs **(5600)**
Journal of Palestine Studies **(5610)** .....(Paid) 3,500
Journal of Social, Political & Economic
Studies **(5615)** ....(Paid) ‡1,150
(Non-paid) ‡55
Legal Briefs **(5634)** 3,600
National Journal **(5678)** ....(Paid) 9,600
The National Voter **(5683)** ....(Paid) ‡89,500
Perspectives on Political
Science **(5717)** ....(Paid) 467
Political Money Monitor **(5721)** 3,600
PS **(5736)** ....‡16,000
The Public Interest **(5750)** 8,000
The Republican
Woman **(5762)** ....(Controlled) 100,000
Scoop **(5782)** ....(Non-paid) 3,600
TransCaucasus, A Chronology **(5828)** 2,000
The Washington Monthly **(5848)** ....(Paid) 18,000
(Non-paid) 2,000
Women & Politics Journal **(5863)** 635
Women's Political Times **(5864)**
The World & I **(5870)** ....(Paid) 20,056
(Non-paid) 2,781

FLORIDA
Gainesville
Republican Liberty **(6157)** ....(Paid) 600
(Non-paid) 100

GEORGIA
Athens
State and Local Government
Review **(6952)** ....(Controlled) 1,000

Marietta
The Truth at Last **(7421)** ....(Paid) ‡30,000
(Free) ‡12,000

ILLINOIS
Champaign
Peace, Prosperity & Democracy **(8209)**
Policy Studies Journal **(8212)** ....(Paid) ‡2,350
(Non-paid) ‡50
Policy Studies Review **(8213)** ....(Paid) ‡2,350
(Non-paid) ‡50

Chicago
In These Times **(8410)** ....‡20,000
People's Tribune **(8528)**
The Revolutionary Worker **(8556)**

Gurnee
Children, Churches & Daddies **(8965)**

Mount Morris
The American
Prospect **(9236)** ....(Combined) 51,000

Rockford
Chronicles **(9526)** ....‡8,000

Springfield
Legislative Synopsis and Digest **(9638)**

INDIANA
Notre Dame
Notre Dame Journal of Law, Ethics & Public
Policy **(10371)** ....(Controlled) 490
Rethinking Marxism **(10377)** ....(Paid) ‡900
(Non-paid) ‡105
Review of Politics **(10378)** 1,700

IOWA
Iowa City
Legislative Studies
Quarterly **(10980)** ....(Paid) ‡1100
(Non-paid) ‡40

KENTUCKY
Lexington
Journal of Caribbean Studies **(12167)** 1,000

LOUISIANA
Baton Rouge
Louisiana Municipal Review **(12501)**

MAINE
Orono
Canadian-American Public Policy **(12999)**

MASSACHUSETTS
Amherst
POLITY: The Journal of the Northeastern Political
Science Association **(13805)** ....(Paid) ‡1,000
(Non-paid) ‡100

Burlington
Transport Policy **(14034)**

Cambridge
Asian American Policy
Review **(14039)** ....(Combined) 700
Dollars & Sense **(14049)** ....‡8,400
Harvard International Review **(14060)**
International Security **(14072)** ....‡4,600
The Washington Quarterly **(14111)** .....(Paid) ‡3,300
(Non-paid) ‡250

Chestnut Hill
Massachusetts Civil Service Reporter **(14129)**

Malden
Middle East Policy **(14298)**

MICHIGAN
Detroit
Against the Current **(14914)** ....(Paid) ‡1,600

Sandusky
Official Michigan **(15520)** ....(Paid) 800
(Free) 100

MINNESOTA
Minneapolis
Minnesota Law &
Politics **(16103)** ....(Controlled) 22,000
(Paid) 2,000
New Rules Journal **(16114)** ....(Paid) 4,000

Xcp: Cross Cultural
Poetics **(16142)** ....(Combined) 850
St. Paul
New Unionist **(16401)** ....(Non-paid) 8,600
(Paid) 400

MISSISSIPPI
Jackson
Mississippi Municipalities **(16707)**

MISSOURI
Fort Leonard Wood
Cuba News **(17072)**

St. Louis
Synthesis/Regeneration **(17520)**

NEW JERSEY
Hoboken
Journal of International
Development **(19027)** ....(Paid) 2,800

Montclair
Shelterforce **(19241)** ....(Combined) ⊕5,000

Princeton
Philosophy & Public Affairs **(19467)** ....(Paid) ‡2,127
(Non-paid) ‡59
World Politics **(19478)** ....(Paid) ‡3940
(Non-paid) ‡107

NEW YORK
Albany
Legislative Gazette **(19993)** ....(Paid) 385
(Non-paid) 18,200

Armonk
Problems of Post-Communism **(20092)**

Brooklyn
Kurdish Life **(20328)**
New Politics **(20332)** ....(Paid) 3000
Semiotext **(20347)**

New York
Amnesty Action **(21210)** ....‡300,000
Comparative Politics **(21464)** ....‡2,000
East European Politics & Societies **(21578)**
European Foreign Affairs Review **(21638)**
Human Rights Case Digest **(21834)**
India Abroad **(21862)** ....(Fri.) 53,851
Integrated Assessment **(21885)**
International Politics **(21930)**
Journal of American Studies **(21986)** .....(Paid) ‡455
(Non-paid) ‡3,346
Journal of Modern African Studies **(22135)** 1600
Journal of World Trade **(22215)**
MOCT-MOST **(22343)**
Monthly Review **(22364)** ....(Paid) ‡5,321
(Non-paid)· ‡97
National Review **(22400)** ....(Paid) 155,664
Nations and Nationalism **(22401)**
The Nonviolent Activist **(22467)** ....(Paid) 8,000
(Non-paid) 1,500
People's Weekly World **(22541)** ....(Paid) ‡40,000
(Non-paid) ‡1,500
Perspectiva Mundial **(22544)** ....‡4,300
Political Affairs **(22573)**
Political Affairs **(22574)** ....‡5,000
Political Behavior **(22575)**
Political Psychology **(22576)**
Political Science Quarterly **(22577)** ....‡8,000
Socialist Forum **(22758)** ....(Combined) 5,000
Telos **(22821)** 2,500
Workers Vanguard **(22937)** ....‡17,895

NORTH CAROLINA
Chapel Hill
Daily Bulletin **(23705)** ....(Combined) 1,100
Popular Government **(23719)** ....(Combined) 8,000

Durham
Political Communication **(23841)** 450
Socialist Review **(23844)**

OHIO
Cincinnati
Criminal Politics Magazine **(24791)**

Wright Patterson AFB
DISAM Journal **(25683)**

OREGON
Eugene
Dendron News **(26315)** ....(Paid) 20,000

Circulation: ★ = ABC; △ = BPA; ♦ = CAC; • = CCAB; ❑ = VAC; ⊕ = PO Statement; ‡ = Publisher's Report; Boldface figures = sworn; Light figures = estimated.

3213

Circ. Circ. Circ.

POLITICS (continued)

Salem
Oregon Secretary of State Administration Rule
Compilation **(26571)**

PENNSYLVANIA
Easton
Publius: The Journal of
Federalism **(26851)** ....‡1,200
(Non-paid) ‡100

Middletown
International Journal of Public
Administration **(27252)** ....‡450

Philadelphia
Middle East Quarterly **(27569)** ....(Paid) ‡2,100

Pittsburgh
Background Notes on the Countries of the
World **(27762)**
Weekly Compilation of Presidential
Documents **(27855)**

TENNESSEE
Nashville
Tennessee Town & City **(29494)** ....(Paid) ‡5,600
(Non-paid) ‡300

TEXAS
Austin
Texas Review of Law and
Politics **(29847)** ....(Combined) 6,200

College Station
Journal of Politics **(30046)** 4,000

Dallas
Clements' International Report **(30137)**
World of Politics **(30190)**

Tyler
Both Sides Now **(31196)** ....‡200
Texas Tribune **(31199)** ....(Paid) ‡300

VIRGINIA
Arlington
Studies in Conflict and Terrorism **(31834)** 850
Women's Quarterly **(31842)**

Charlottesville
Political Theory **(31938)** ....(Paid) ‡2,350
(Non-paid) ‡95

Ivy
World Climate Report **(32174)** .....(Combined) 3,000

Vienna
Government Union Review **(32578)**

WASHINGTON
Seattle
Freedom Socialist **(32967)** 10,000
Prison Legal News **(33006)** ....(Paid) 4,000
(Non-paid) 230

WISCONSIN
Cornucopia
The Dandelion **(33645)** ....‡400

Madison
The Progressive **(33972)** ....(Paid) ‡32,000
(Non-paid) ‡1,000

Milwaukee
Life Without Limits **(34073)** ....(Non-paid) ⊕35,000

ALBERTA, CANADA
Edmonton
Global Governance **(34714)** ....(Paid) 1,600

BRITISH COLUMBIA, CANADA
Burnaby
The Democrat **(34896)** 25,684

Vancouver
Outlook **(35156)** 2,000

ONTARIO, CANADA
New Hamburg
Inroads **(36102)** ....(Paid) 120
(Non-paid) 100

Ottawa
Canadian Journal of Political Science (Revue
canadienne de science politique) **(36213)** 3,000
Canadian Parliamentary Review **(36224)** 2,000
500

Toronto
Behind the Headlines **(36473)** ....(Paid) 1,200
Kick It Over **(36642)** ....(Paid) ‡1,500
(Non-paid) ‡500
Public Sector Management/Management et Secteur
Public **(36720)** ....(Paid) 3,500
Socialist Worker **(36742)** ....‡2,000
Technology in
Government **(36756)** ....(Combined) 18,318
The Tocqueville Review/La Revue
Tocqueville **(36761)** ....(Combined) 500

Waterloo
Ploughshares Monitor **(36857)** ....(Paid) 7,000

Woodville
Canadian Speeches **(36910)** ....(Paid) 1,000

QUEBEC, CANADA
Montreal
L'Action Nationale **(37079)** ....(Paid) ‡3,000

SASKATCHEWAN, CANADA
Regina
Briarpatch **(37525)** ....(Paid) ‡2,500
(Controlled) ‡1,400
The Commonwealth **(37529)** 14,000

POSTAL AND SHIPPING SUPPLIES

DISTRICT OF COLUMBIA
Washington
The American Postal Worker **(5339)** 300,000
Postal Record **(5724)** 310,000

MINNESOTA
St. Paul
Dakota Collector **(16373)** ....(Combined) 70

NEW YORK
New York
New York Metro Area Postal Union, Union
Mail **(22447)** ....(Paid) 13,000
(Controlled) 500

PENNSYLVANIA
Pittsburgh
Postal Bulletin **(27838)**

RHODE ISLAND
North Providence
Rhode Island Postal History Journal **(28377)** 80

VIRGINIA
Alexandria
The National Rural Letter
Carrier **(31714)** ....(Controlled) ‡100,000

Fairfax
Postmasters Gazette **(32027)** ....‡42,000

ONTARIO, CANADA
Ottawa
The Canadian Postmaster (Le Maitre de Poste
Canadien) **(36226)** ....‡9,500

POULTRY PRODUCTS AND SUPPLIES

ALABAMA
Cullman
WATT Poultry USA **(162)** ....(Combined) 20,126

GEORGIA
Gainesville
Poultry and Egg
Marketing **(7293)** ....(Controlled) ‡11,600
Poultry Times **(7294)** ....(Paid) 10,661

ILLINOIS
Mount Morris
Poultry International **(9245)** ......(Combined) 23,620

POWER AND POWER PLANTS

See also Electrical Engineering; Nuclear Engineering

ARKANSAS
Little Rock
Rural Arkansas **(1236)** ....(Paid) 312,186

CALIFORNIA
Palo Alto
EPRI Journal **(2795)**

COLORADO
Boulder
Journal of Energy and
Development **(4175)** ....(Combined) 1,000
Solar Today **(4191)** ....(Paid) 9,500

CONNECTICUT
Norwalk
Turbomachinery International **(5078)** .....(Paid) 1,597
(Non-paid) 9,479

Southport
Gas Turbine World **(5136)** ....(Paid) 910
(Controlled) 9,666

DISTRICT OF COLUMBIA
Washington
Electric Perspectives **(5476)** ....(Paid) 308
(Controlled) 18,200
Public Power **(5752)** ....(Controlled) 14,700
(Paid) 138

FLORIDA
Boca Raton
Powerline **(5938)**

Tallahassee
Relay Magazine **(6730)** ....(Controlled) 7,500

GEORGIA
Lilburn
Strategic Planning for Energy and the
Environment **(7374)** ....(Paid) 8,600

Norcross
Engineering Economist **(7459)**
NAC Focus **(7468)**

ILLINOIS
Glen Ellyn
Nuclear Plant Journal **(8931)** .....(Non-paid) △20,012

KANSAS
Overland Park
Energy Manager **(11710)**
Power Quality
Assurance **(11726)** ....(Non-paid) 30,011
Transmission and Distribution
World **(11732)** ....(Controlled) ‡34,750
Utility Business **(11733)** ....(Combined) 50,000

MASSACHUSETTS
Chicopee
National Engineer **(14136)** ....(Paid) ‡5,422
(Controlled) ‡56

MICHIGAN
Troy
Energy User News **(15622)** ....(Paid) 894
(Non-paid) 50,027

National Driller **(15630)**

NEW YORK
New York
The Electricity Journal **(21592)** ....‡1,800
Energy in the News **(21604)** ......(Controlled) 30,000
International Private Power Quarterly **(21931)**
Journal of Engineering for Gas Turbines and
Power **(22061)** 2,224
Power **(22587)** ....(Paid) 5,977
(Non-paid) 60,463

OHIO
Cleveland
Energy Journal **(24893)** ....(Controlled) 4,000
The Motion Systems
Distributor **(24931)** ....(Controlled) ‡12,879

OKLAHOMA
Tulsa
Electric Light &
Power **(26115)** ....(Controlled) ‡30,000

Numbers cited after listings are entry numbers rather than page numbers.

Potencia **(26126)**
Power Engineering **(26127)** ....(Controlled) 58,000
Power Engineering International **(26128)**
Utility Automation **(26141)** ......(Controlled) ‡25,000
Utility Automation International **(26142)**

PENNSYLVANIA
Philadelphia
Electric Machines Components and
  Systems **(27456)** ....(Combined) ‡376
Energy Systems and
  Policy **(27460)** ....(Controlled) ‡285

Pittsburgh
Monthly Energy Review **(27817)**

TENNESSEE
Chattanooga
TVPPA News **(29093)** ....(Controlled) ‡2,855

Oak Ridge
Concentrating Solar Power **(29547)**
Geothermal Energy Technology **(29548)**
Oak Ridge National Laboratory
  Review **(29550)** ....(Non-paid) ‡6,100

TEXAS
Dallas
Gas Utility and Pipeline
  Industries **(30160)** ....(Non-paid) 10,878

Houston
Oil & Gas Journal Latinoamerica **(30517)**
Power & Gas
  Marketing **(30521)** ....(Combined) **20,000**

VIRGINIA
Alexandria
Utility Fleet Management **(31748)** ....‡22,014

Arlington
R.E. Magazine **(31823)** ....(Paid) 32,000

Vienna
Public Utilities Fortnightly **(32580)**
Public Utilities Fortnightly **(32581)** 7,000

WASHINGTON
Vancouver
Northwest Public Power Association
  Bulletin **(33177)** ....(Paid) ‡6,300

WYOMING
Laramie
Energy Sources **(34548)** ....(Controlled) ‡345

ALBERTA, CANADA
Calgary
International Journal of Power and Energy
  Systems **(34648)**

ONTARIO, CANADA
Mississauga
Energy Manager **(36065)** ....(Controlled) 10,161

PRINTING AND TYPOGRAPHY

CALIFORNIA
Berkeley
Design Book Review **(1513)** ....‡7,000

Glendale
Print-Equip News **(2012)** ....(Controlled) 23,258

Ojai
Imaging News Online **(2713)**

COLORADO
Broomfield
Printwear **(4206)** ....(Combined) △**20,046**
Sign Business **(4208)** ....(Paid) △**7,732**
                        (Non-paid) △**10,319**

CONNECTICUT
Stamford
Folio **(5151)** ....(Paid) 8,063
                 (Non-paid) 661

FLORIDA
Fort Myers
SignCraft **(6098)** ....(Paid) ★**12,947**

Margate
Dealer Communicator **(6324)** ....(Controlled) ‡13,633

Ponte Vedra Beach
Digital Output **(6594)** 30,000

ILLINOIS
Chicago
Serif **(8563)**

Libertyville
High Volume Printing **(9077)** ....(Controlled) ‡39,047
In-Plant Printer & Electronic
  Publisher **(9078)** ....(Controlled) ‡25,502
Instant and Small Commercial
  Printer **(9079)** ....(Controlled) ‡49,289

Peoria
Step-By-Step Graphics **(9427)** ....‡42,000

South Holland
IPA Bulletin **(9615)** ....‡1,600

KANSAS
Overland Park
American Printer **(11695)** ....(Controlled) ‡89,755

MICHIGAN
Brighton
The Engravers Journal **(14836)**

NEW HAMPSHIRE
Nashua
Computer Graphics World **(18588)** ....(Paid) 9,706
                      (Non-paid) 54,961

NEW JERSEY
Paramus
Printing Manager **(19406)**

NEW YORK
Melville
Modern Reprographics **(21050)** 18,000
Printing News **(21060)**
Printing News/East **(21061)** ....(Paid) ‡7,000
                          (Free) ‡500
Quick Printing **(21063)** ....(Paid) 3,917
                      (Non-paid) 56,133

New York
Editor & Publisher **(21585)** ....(Paid) 14,278
                      (Non-paid) 3,905
Graphic Arts Monthly **(21779)** .....(Combined) 86,895
Graphis **(21780)** ....(Paid) 20,000

Ronkonkoma
FLEXO **(23268)** ....(Paid) 1,963
                   (Controlled) 19,000
FLEXO ESPANOL **(23269)** ....(Paid) ‡2,500
                    (Non-paid) ‡5,500

OHIO
Cincinnati
The Big Picture **(24779)** ....(Paid) 762
                    (Non-paid) 47,420
HOW **(24804)** ....(Paid) 37,008
Screen Printing **(24815)** ....(Paid) 4,360
                    (Non-paid) 13,101
Signs of the Times & Screen Printing en
  Espanol **(24818)** ....(Paid) 540
                    (Non-paid) 15,950

PENNSYLVANIA
Harrisburg
Press **(27012)** 3,000

TEXAS
Austin
Texas Press Messenger **(29841)** ....‡760

Houston
COPI Press **(30465)**

Leakey
Fine Print **(30679)** 2000

VIRGINIA
Alexandria
PaperTronix, Document Management Merging Paper
  & Electronics **(31720)** ....(Paid) 1,874
                    (Non-paid) 800

Falls Church
Package Printing **(32051)** ....(Non-paid) ‡26,000
Printing Impressions **(32053)** ....(Non-paid) 88,210
PrintMedia Magazine **(32054)** ....(Controlled) ‡24,000

ONTARIO, CANADA
Mississauga
The Graphic Monthly **(36069)** .....(Controlled) 10,413

North York
Applied Arts
  Magazine **(36120)** ....(Combined) 13,000

Toronto
Canadian Printer
  Magazine **(36526)** ....(Non-paid) 11,302
                       (Paid) 143
PrintAction **(36716)** ....(Combined) 10,287

PSYCHOLOGY AND PSYCHIATRY

ALABAMA
Livingston
Alabama Counseling Association
  Journal **(305)** ....(Non-paid) 2000

Mobile
Journal of Instructional Psychology **(321)** ....‡450
Journal of Sport Behavior **(322)**

Tuscaloosa
Media Psychology **(488)**

ALASKA
Anchorage
Journal of Personality Assessment **(528)**

ARIZONA
Tucson
Environment and Behavior **(946)** ....(Paid) ‡1,600
                      (Non-paid) ‡152

CALIFORNIA
Azusa
Journal of Psychology and
  Christianity **(1446)** ....(Paid) ‡2,300
                    (Non-paid) ‡200

Berkeley
Issues in Education **(1530)**
Measurement **(1541)**

Fullerton
Structural Equation Modeling **(1990)**

Irvine
The Psychiatric
  Times **(2089)** ....(Controlled) ‡42,583

La Jolla
Annals of Behavioral Medicine **(2112)** ....‡3,000
JINS **(2114)** 3,500

La Mirada
Journal of Psychology and
  Theology **(2126)** ....‡1,350

Los Altos
The Psychoanalytic Quarterly **(2195)** ....‡3,200

Los Angeles
Ancient Wisdom for Modern
  Living **(2210)** ....(Free) 20,000
Psychological Perspectives **(2374)** ....(Paid) 2,000
                    (Non-paid) 2,000

Newport Beach
American Journal of Forensic
  Psychiatry **(2621)** ....‡1,000
American Journal of Forensic
  Psychology **(2622)** ....‡800

Novato
Journal of Social Behavior and
  Personality **(2650)** ....(Paid) ‡600

Oakland
Transactional Analysis
  Journal **(2701)** ....(Paid) 1,800

Palo Alto
Annual Review of Psychology **(2793)**

Rancho Cordova
Journal of Applied Sport Psychology **(2875)**
Journal of Loss & Trauma **(2876)**

San Diego
Adolescence **(3106)** ....(Paid) ‡2,300
                    (Non-paid) ‡55

Brain and Cognition **(3125)**
Cognitive Psychology **(3129)**
Consciousness and Cognition **(3134)**
Contemporary Educational Psychology **(3135)**
Developmental Review **(3141)**
Family Therapy **(3153)** ....(Paid) ‡1,100
                    (Non-paid) ‡50

Hormones and Behavior **(3168)**
Journal of Environmental Psychology **(3192)**

Circulation: ★ = ABC; △ = BPA; ♦ = CAC; ● = CCAB; ❑ = VAC; ⊕ = PO Statement; ‡ = Publisher's Report; Boldface figures = sworn; Light figures = estimated.

3215

Circ.   Circ.   Circ.

PSYCHOLOGY AND PSYCHIATRY (continued)

Journal of Experimental Child Psychology (3193)
Journal of Experimental Social Psychology (3194)
Journal of Mathematical Psychology (3204)
Journal of Memory and Language (3205)
Journal of Research in Personality (3211)
Journal of Vocational Behavior (3217)
Learning and Motivation (3222)
Neurobiology of Learning and Memory (3240)
Organizational Behavior and Human Decision Processes (3245)

San Francisco
(a) (3323)
Conflict Resolution Quarterly (3344) ....(Paid) ‡2,108
                                      (Non-paid) ‡98
Journal of Homosexuality (3382) 1,298
New Directions for Child and Adolescent
  Development (3397) ....(Paid) 400
                                      (Non-paid) 50
New Directions for Evaluation (3399) ....(Paid) 2,900
                                      (Non-paid) 82
New Directions for Mental Health
  Services (3402) ....(Paid) 1,303
                                      (Non-paid) 70

Santa Barbara
The International Journal for the Psychology of
  Religion (3642)

Stanford
Social Psychology Quarterly (3797) ....‡3,250

Thousand Oaks
American Behavioral Scientist (3848)
Behavior Modification (3852) ....(Paid) 700
Criminal Justice and
  Behavior (3860) ....(Paid) ‡1,100
Educational and Psychological
  Measurement (3865) ....(Paid) ‡1,250
Evaluation Review (3868) ....(Paid) ‡1,600
                                      (Non-paid) ‡208
Hispanic Journal of Behavioral
  Sciences (3871) ....(Paid) 500
Journal of Adolescent
  Research (3876) ....(Paid) ‡600
Journal of Black Psychology (3881) .....(Paid) 1,200
Journal of Cross-Cultural
  Psychology (3886) ....(Paid) 1,500
Journal of Early Adolescence (3888) ...(Paid) 700
Journal of Humanistic
  Psychology (3892) ....(Paid) ‡1,500
Journal of Interpersonal
  Violence (3893) ....(Paid) ‡6,250
                                      (Non-paid) ‡157
Journal of Language and Social
  Psychology (3894) ....(Paid) 300
Journal of Research in Crime and
  Delinquency (3899) ....(Paid) ‡1,100
The Journal for Specialists in Group
  Work (3900) ....‡2,300

COLORADO
Fort Collins
Journal of Feminist Family Therapy (4435)

CONNECTICUT
Bloomfield
Journal of the American Academy of
  Psychoanalysis (4702) 10,000

Farmington
Analytic Psychology (4796) 1,700
Brain, Behavior and Evolution (4801) 1,000
Journal of Personality (4837) ....‡2,000
Psychopathology (4857) 800
Psychotherapy and Psychosomatics (4858) ...1,000

Hartford
Digest of Neurology and Psychiatry (4889)
Ecological Psychology (4890)
Human Development (4894) ....(Paid) ‡10,000
                                      (Non-paid) ‡300

Madison
Depression and Stress (4928)
Gender and Psychoanalysis (4929)
Integrative Psychiatry (4930)
Journal of Clinical Psychoanalysis (4931)
Journal of Geriatric Psychiatry (4933)
Journal of Imago Relationship Therapy (4934)
Psychoanalysis and Contemporary
  Thought (4935) 1,000

New Haven
Archives of Psychiatric Nursing (4983)
Imagination, Cognition and Personality (4990)

DISTRICT OF COLUMBIA
Ft. McNair
Military Psychology (5306)

Washington
American Psychologist (5340) ....‡105,500
APA Monitor (5356) ....‡102,350
Behavioral Medicine (5374) 552
Behavioral Neuroscience (5375) ....‡1,850
Consulting Psychology Journal: Practice and
  Research (5437) ....(Paid) ‡1,050
Contemporary Psychology (5440) ....‡3,400
Developmental Psychology (5463) ....‡5,400
Family Therapy News (5491) 22,000
Genetic, Social, and General Psychology
  Monographs (5506) ....(Paid) ‡450
The International Journal of Action
  Methods (5552) ....(Combined) 351
Journal of Abnormal Psychology (5566) ....‡7,900
Journal of Applied Psychology (5572) ....‡5,500
The Journal of Consulting and Clinical
  Psychology (5579) ....‡9,650
Journal of Educational Psychology (5584) .....‡5,100
Journal of Experimental Psychology: Animal Behavior
  Processes (5588) ....‡1,900
Journal of Experimental Psychology: Human
  Perception and Performance (5589) ....‡2,500
Journal of Experimental Psychology: Learning,
  Memory and Cognition (5590) ....‡3,300
Journal of Family Psychology (5591) ....‡4,700
The Journal of General
  Psychology (5592) ....(Paid) ‡1,100
The Journal of Genetic
  Psychology (5593) ....(Paid) 795
Journal of Health Communication (5595)
Journal of Personality and Social
  Psychology (5611) ....‡5,600
The Journal of Psychology (5614) ......(Paid) ‡1,400
The Journal of Social
  Psychology (5616) ....(Paid) ‡1,700
Journals of Gerontology (5620)
Monitor on Psychology (5660) ....(Paid) 155,000
Neuropsychology Abstracts (5693) ....‡1,500
Professional Psychology: Research and
  Practice (5732) ....‡7,800
Psychiatry (5737) 2,017
Psychological Abstracts (5738) ....‡1,000
Psychological Assessment (5739) ...(Paid) ‡5,700
Psychological Bulletin (5740) ....‡6,800
Psychological Review (5741) ....‡5,900
Psychology of Addictive
  Behaviors (5742) ....(Paid) ‡725
Psychology and Aging (5743) ....‡3,200
PsycSCAN: Applied Psychology (5744) ......‡1,400
PsycSCAN: Clinical Psychology (5746) ......‡3,600
PsycSCAN: LD/MR (5747) ....‡900

FLORIDA
Deerfield Beach
Counselor (6048) ....(Paid) 30,000

Fort Lauderdale
Journal of Psychotherapy in Independent
  Practice (6079) 399

Fort Myers
Children's Health Care (6094)

Gainesville
Relationships Today (6156) 160,000

Miami
Journal of Personality Disorders (6365) 1,313

Naples
Emergence (6438)

Orlando
The Journal of Human Performance in Extreme
  Environments (6499) ....(Paid) 200

Tallahassee
Florida Psychologist (6718) ....(Controlled) 1,800
Journal of Drug Issues (6725)
Thanatos (6739) ....(Paid) ‡7,000
                                      (Non-paid) ‡200

Tampa
Journal of Behavioral Health Services &
  Research (6769) ....(Paid) 3,500
                                      (Non-paid) 100
Journal of Mental Health and
  Aging (6771) ....(Combined) 300

GEORGIA
Athens
Journal of Learning Disabilities (6945) ....‡8,500

Kennesaw
Teaching of Psychology (7355)

Milledgeville
The Pre- & Perinatal Psychology Journal (7435)

HAWAII
Hilo
Creativity Research Journal (7670)

ILLINOIS
Champaign
American Journal of Psychology (8178) ....‡2,108
Journal of Sport & Exercise
  Psychology (8198) ....(Paid) ‡1,891
The Sport Psychologist (8218) ....(Paid) ‡1,202
                                      ‡45

Chicago
Journal of Graphoanalysis (8438)
Residential Treatment for Children and
  Youth (8555) ....(Paid) 799
Suicide and Life-Threatening
  Behavior (8575) 1,739

DeKalb
Names (8739) ....(Paid) 850

Normal
Personal Relationships (9303) ....(Paid) ‡567
                                      (Non-paid) ‡74

INDIANA
Hammond
Journal of Clinical Activities, Assignments & Handouts
  in Psychotherapy (10051)
Journal of Family Psychotherapy (10052) 479

West Lafayette
Social Cognition (10553) 756

IOWA
Iowa City
Journal of Loss & Trauma (10979)

KANSAS
Topeka
Bulletin of the Menninger
  Clinic (11815) ....(Combined) ‡1,220

Wichita
Multivariate Experimental Clinical Research (11887)

KENTUCKY
Louisville
Developmental Neuropsychology (12214)

LOUISIANA
Lafayette
Deviant Behavior: An Interdisciplinary
  Journal (12616) 600

New Orleans
Infant Mental Health
  Journal (12734) ....(Paid) ‡1,010
                                      (Controlled) ‡47

MAINE
Lewiston
Peace and Conflict (12977)

Orono
The Journal of Mind and
  Behavior (13000) ....(Paid) ‡1,191

MARYLAND
Baltimore
American Imago (13113) 728
Clinical Neuropharmacology (13148) 558
Journal of Clinical Neurophysiology (13185) 1,637
Journal of Nervous and Mental
  Disease (13195) ....(Combined) ‡1,698
Philosophy, Psychiatry &
  Psychology (13236) ....(Paid) 592

Bethesda
Communique (13325)
School Psychology Review (13378)

College Park
Journal of Counseling Psychology (13426) ....‡8,500

Ellicott City
International Journal of Emergency Mental
  Health (13498)

Hyattsville
Personality and Social Psychology Review (13588)

Rockville
Clinical Psychiatry
  News (13677) ....(Controlled) 32,946

Numbers cited after listings are entry numbers rather than page numbers.

Silver Spring
Journal of Music Therapy **(13731)**

Wheaton
Psychiatric Services **(13781)** ....(Paid) ‡10,000
(Non-paid) ‡13,500

MASSACHUSETTS
Belmont
Archives of General
Psychiatry **(13838)** ....(Combined) ‡30,771

Boston
Journal of Clinical
Psychopharmacology **(13915)** ....(Paid) ‡8,614
(Non-paid) ‡163
Psychiatric Rehabilitation
Journal **(13953)** ....(Paid) 4,000

MICHIGAN
Detroit
Merrill-Palmer Quarterly **(14935)** ....(Paid) ‡1,200
(Non-paid) ‡100

Flint
Journal of Leadership and Organizational
Studies **(15036)**

Michigan
Brain and Language **(15353)**

MINNESOTA
Minneapolis
Journal of Psychology and Human
Sexuality **(16089)** 226

MISSOURI
Columbia
The Counseling
Psychologist **(16992)** ....(Paid) ‡5,400
(Non-paid) ‡128

St. Louis
Journal of the American Psychiatric Nurses
Association **(17453)** ....(Paid) ‡5,733

Springfield
Annals of the American Psychotherapy
Association **(17592)**

MONTANA
Missoula
Perceptual and Motor Skills **(17874)** ....‡2,000
Psychological Reports **(17875)** ....‡2,000

NEBRASKA
Lincoln
School Psychology Quarterly **(18118)** ....(Paid) 3,000

NEW JERSEY
Hillsdale
Gestalt Review **(18876)** 707
Psychoanalytic Dialogues **(18877)** ....(Paid) 2,500
Psychoanalytic Inquiry **(18878)** 1,500

Hoboken
Aggressive Behavior **(18882)** 3,850
Applied Cognitive Psychology **(18892)**
Behavioral Interventions **(18901)**
Behavioral Sciences and the Law **(18902)** 700
Child Abuse Review **(18911)**
Clinical Psychology & Psychotherapy **(18916)**
Depression and Anxiety **(18926)** 3150
Dyslexia **(18933)**
European Eating Disorders Review **(18943)**
European Journal of Personality **(18944)**
European Review of Social Psychology **(18945)**
Human Psychopharmacology **(18968)**
In Session **(18972)**
Infant and Child Development **(18973)**
International Journal of Eating
Disorders **(18981)** 8400
International Journal of Geriatric Psychiatry **(18983)**
International Journal of Short-Term
Psychotherapy **(18998)** 700
International Review of Industrial and Organizational
Psychology **(19000)**
Journal of Community & Applied Social
Psychology **(19017)** ....(Paid) 2,800
Journal of Organizational
Behavior **(19037)** ....(Paid) 6,300
Psycho-Oncology **(19090)**
Psychology and Marketing **(19091)** 5600
Stress and Health **(19109)** ....(Paid) 3,500
Systems Research and Behavioral Science **(19116)**

Mahwah
The American Psychoanalyst **(19184)**

Applied Developmental Science **(19185)**
Basic and Applied Social Psychology **(19187)**
Children's Services **(19188)**
International Journal of Behavioral Medicine **(19192)**
International Journal of Cognitive
Ergonomics **(19193)**
The Journal of Behavioral Finance **(19195)**
Journal of Clinical Child Psychology **(19196)**
Journal of Consumer Psychology **(19197)**
Mind, Culture, and Activity **(19202)**
Neural Computing Surveys **(19203)**
Understanding Statistics **(19207)**

Newark
Journal of ECT **(19357)** ....(Paid) 820

Piscataway
Current Psychology **(19422)** ....(Paid) ‡500
Journal of Applied School
Psychology **(19428)** 800

Thorofare
Journal of Psychosocial Nursing and Mental Health
Services **(19625)** ....‡6,000
Psychiatric Annals **(19640)** ......(Controlled) ‡33,000

NEW YORK
Albany
Group & Organization
Management **(19989)** ....(Paid) ‡1,550
(Non-paid) ‡146
NYSPA Notebook/Psychologist **(20002)** ....‡3,500

Amityville
The International Journal of Psychiatry in
Medicine **(20040)**
OMEGA-Journal of Death and Dying **(20053)**

Armonk
International Journal of Mental
Health **(20080)** ....(Paid) ⊕213
Journal of Russian and East European
Psychology **(20087)** ....(Paid) ⊕217

Binghamton
Journal of Aggression, Maltreatment &
Trauma **(20162)**
Journal of Clinical Activities, Assignments & Handouts
in Psychotherapy Practice **(20166)**
Journal of Forensic Neuropsychology **(20174)**
Journal of Forensic Psychology Practice **(20175)**
Journal of Lesbian Studies **(20186)**
Journal of Prevention & Intervention in the
Community **(20192)** 237
Journal of Religion & Abuse **(20195)**
Journal of Threat Assessment **(20204)**
Journal of Trauma & Dissociation **(20205)**
Journal of Trauma Practice **(20206)**
Occupational Therapy in Mental
Health **(20209)** 906
Social Work with Groups **(20217)** 1,063
Women & Therapy **(20221)** ....(Paid) 823

Bronx
Journal of Maintenance in the
Addictions **(20274)** ....(Paid) 450

Buffalo
Child Study Journal **(20374)**
The Clinical Supervisor **(20376)** ....(Paid) 488
Psychology in the Schools **(20385)** .....(Paid) ‡1,684
(Non-paid) ‡78

Flushing
Journal of Educational and Psychological
Consultation **(20609)**

Jamaica
International Chinese Application Psychology
Journal **(20833)**
International Chinese Sexology Journal **(20835)**

Larchmont
CyberPsychology and Behavior **(20895)**

New Rochelle
Journal of Pastoral Counseling **(21118)**

New York
American Journal of Community Psychology **(21191)**
The American Journal of Drug and Alcohol
Abuse **(21192)** 825
American Journal of
Orthopsychiatry **(21197)** ....‡10,000
The American Journal of Psychoanalysis **(21199)**
Applied Psycholinguistics **(21232)** 1,000
Applied Psychophysiology and Biofeedback **(21233)**
Archives of Sexual Behavior **(21247)**
Behavioral and Brain Sciences **(21294)** 2,100
Biofeedback and Self-Regulation **(21314)**

Clinical Child and Family Psychology
Review **(21429)**
Cognitive Science **(21435)**
Cognitive Therapy & Research **(21436)**
Contemporary Family Therapy **(21493)**
Current Directions in Psychological Science **(21524)**
Dreaming **(21569)**
Educational Psychology Review **(21589)**
Expert Evidence **(21668)**
Human Relations **(21832)**
Intelligence **(21888)**
International Journal of Sexuality and Gender
Studies **(21918)**
International Journal of Stress Management **(21920)**
International
Psychogeriatrics **(21932)** ....(Combined) 1,400
Journal of Abnormal Child Psychology **(21972)**
Journal of the American Psychoanalytic
Association **(21984)** 5,500
Journal of the American Society for Psychical
Research **(21985)** 1,600
Journal of Applied Psychoanalytic Studies **(21994)**
Journal of Behavioral Education **(22006)**
Journal of Behavioral Medicine **(22007)**
Journal of Brief Therapy **(22014)**
Journal of Child and Adolescent Group
Therapy **(22022)**
Journal of Child and Family Studies **(22023)**
Journal of Clinical Geropsychology **(22025)**
Journal of Clinical Psychology in Medical
Settings **(22028)**
Journal of Cognitive
Psychotherapy **(22029)** ....(Paid) 700
(Controlled) 80
Journal of Family Violence **(22069)**
Journal of Gambling Studies **(22075)**
Journal of Gender, Culture, and Health **(22077)**
Journal of Genetic Cooneling **(22079)**
Journal of Happiness Studies **(22082)**
Journal of Nonverbal Behavior **(22146)**
Journal of Pediatric Psychology **(22151)**
The Journal of Psychohistory **(22168)** ....‡7,000
Journal of Psycholinguistic Research **(22169)**
Journal of Psychopathology & Behavioral
Assessment **(22170)**
Journal of Psychosocial
Oncology **(22171)** ....(Paid) 1,002
Journal of Psychotherapy Integration **(22172)**
The Journal of Socio-Economics **(22188)**
Journal of Traumatic Stress **(22207)**
Journal of Youth and Adolescence **(22216)**
Law and Human Behavior **(22239)**
Loss, Grief and Care **(22267)**
Motivation and Emotion **(22370)**
Neuropsychology Review **(22425)**
Nonlinear Dynamics, Psychology, and Life
Sciences **(22466)**
Political Psychology **(22576)**
Pre- and Peri-Natal Psychology Journal **(22592)**
Psychoanalytic Books **(22602)** ....(Paid) 1,000
The Psychoanalytic Review **(22603)** 1,250
Psychological Medicine **(22604)** 1,450
Psychology Today **(22605)** ....(Paid) 323,003
Psychophysiology **(22606)**
The Psychotherapy Patient **(22607)** 199
Readings **(22629)** 8,000
Social Work in Health Care **(22757)** 1,608

Rochester
Development and Psychopathology **(23223)** 1300

NORTH CAROLINA
Cary
The Journal of Deaf Studies and Deaf
Education **(23690)** ....(Paid) 396

Greensboro
Psychology of Women
Quarterly **(23936)** ....(Paid) 4437
(Non-paid) 75

Raleigh
Social Science Computer Review **(24153)** 1,000

Wilmington
Health Care for Women
International **(24295)** ....‡696

OHIO
Bowling Green
Personnel Psychology **(24698)** ....(Paid) 2,300

Cleveland
Behavioral Health Management **(24863)** 21,802
Journal of Applied Social Studies **(24913)**
Journal of Sex & Marital Therapy **(24916)** ....‡1,500
Psychological Inquiry **(24946)**

Circulation: ★ = ABC; △ = BPA; ♦ = CAC; • = CCAB; ⚇ = VAC; ⊕ = PO Statement; ‡ = Publisher's Report; Boldface figures = sworn; Light figures = estimated.

Trade, Technical, and Professional Publications

3217

Circ.   Circ.   Circ.

PSYCHOLOGY AND PSYCHIATRY (continued)

Columbus
Journal for the Psychoanalysis of Culture and
Society (25028)
The National
Psychologist (25034) ....(Combined) 30,000

Gambier
The Psychological Record (25213) .....(Paid) ‡1,450
(Non-paid) ‡242

Johnstown
The International Journal of Aviation
Psychology (25270)

Oxford
Psychotherapy
Research (25459) ....(Combined) ‡1,350

OKLAHOMA
Grove
American Journal of Pastoral
Counseling (25846) 1,000

Oklahoma City
Journal of Clinical
Psychology (25968) ....(Paid) ‡3,001
(Controlled) ‡45

PENNSYLVANIA
Doylestown
Journal of Offender Rehabilitation (26833) 540

Hazleton
Journal of Emotional Abuse (27033) ......(Paid) ‡25
(Non-paid) ‡4

Philadelphia
Child and Adolescent Psychiatric Clinics (27401)
Comprehensive Psychiatry (27426)
Current Opinion in
Psychiatry (27444) ....(Paid) ‡4,750
Ergonomics Abstracts (27464)
International Journal of Personal Construct
Psychology (27503) ....(Paid) ‡356
Journal of the American Academy of Child and
Adolescent Psychiatry (27512) ......(Paid) ‡10,508
(Non-paid) ‡486
Journal of Child and Adolescent Psychiatric
Nursing (27520) ....(Paid) ‡2500
Journal of Community
Psychology (27522) ....(Paid) ‡678
(Non-paid) ‡49
Journal of Developmental & Behavioral
Pediatrics (27524) ....(Paid) ‡1,321
(Non-paid) ‡140
Psychiatric Clinics (27650)
Psychosomatic Medicine (27651) ....(Paid) ‡2,035
(Non-paid) ‡117

Wallingford
Journal of College Student
Psychotherapy (28101) 565

RHODE ISLAND
Providence
Literature and Psychology (28403) 1,000
Psychopharmacology Update (28418)

SOUTH CAROLINA
Orangeburg
Psychology and Education (28732)

SOUTH DAKOTA
Lennox
Reclaiming Children and Youth (28885)

TENNESSEE
Chattanooga
Polygraph (29091)

Knoxville
Issues in Mental Health Nursing (29273)

Memphis
Death Studies (29368)
Journal of Clinical
Psychiatry (29372) ....(Paid) ‡7,100
(Controlled) ‡28,400
Journal of Constructivist Psychology (29373)

TEXAS
Arlington
Journal of Technology in Human
Services (29733) ....(Controlled) ‡513

Austin
Animal Learning and Behavior (29754) ....‡1,200
Behavior Research Methods, Instruments, &
Computers (29763) ....‡1,150
Cognitive, Affective, & Behavioral
Neuroscience (29768) ....‡1,100
Individual Psychology (29782) 1,900
Infancy (29783)
Journal of the History of Sexuality (29787) 1,000
Journal of Positive Behavior Interventions (29790)
Memory & Cognition (29792) ....‡2,400
Perception & Psychophysics (29796) ....‡1,800
Psychonomic Bulletin & Review (29800) ......‡3,000

College Station
Reading Psychology (30048)

Houston
Applied Neuropsychology (30458)
Menninger Perspective (30507)

Lubbock
Journal of Marital & Family
Therapy (30713) ....(Paid) 20,000
(Non-paid) 200

VIRGINIA
Alexandria
Adultspan Journal (31630)
Counseling Today (31661) ....(Paid) ‡56,000
(Free) ‡59
Counselor Education and
Supervision (31663) ....(Paid) 3,500
Government Relations Update (31676)
Journal of Addictions and Offender
Counseling (31685)
Journal of Counseling and
Development (31692) ....(Paid) 59,000
Journal of Humanistic Counseling &
Development (31698) ....(Paid) ‡1,700
Journal of Multicultural Counseling and
Development (31699) ....(Paid) ‡3,000
Measurement and Evaluation in Counseling and
Development (31708) ....(Paid) 1,900
Professional School Counseling (31729) .....‡15,500

Arlington
American Journal of
Addictions (31772) ....(Paid) 1,400
(Non-paid) 25
American Journal of
Psychiatry (31773) ....(Paid) ‡45,633
(Non-paid) ‡700
EAP Association Exchange (31785)
Ethos (31789) ....(Paid) ‡1,200
Journal of Neuropsychiatry and Clinical
Neurosciences (31803) ....(Paid) 1,700
Journal of Psychiatric
Research (31804) ....(Paid) 1,600
(Non-paid) 25
Psychiatric News (31819) ....(Paid) ‡37,436
(Non-paid) ‡1,219
Psychosomatics (31820) ....(Paid) 1,747
(Non-paid) 781

Fairfax
Journal of Social and Clinical
Psychology (32023) 1,000

Norfolk
Journal of Family Communication (32286)

Williamsburg
Journal of Psychoeducational
Assessment (32618) ....(Paid) ‡865
(Controlled) ‡74

WASHINGTON
Seattle
Review of Existential Psychology and
Psychiatry (33015) ....(Paid) 250
Seminars in Clinical Neuropsychiatry (33029)
Violence and Victims (33036) ....(Paid) 2,500
(Non-paid) 100

WEST VIRGINIA
Morgantown
Journal of the Experimental Analysis of
Behavior (33394) ....(Paid) 2,000
(Non-paid) 90

BRITISH COLUMBIA, CANADA
Vancouver
International Journal of Testing (35150)

ONTARIO, CANADA
London
Identity (35984)

Journal of Systemic
Therapies (35985) ....(Paid) ‡2,500

Ottawa
The Canadian Journal of
Psychiatry (36214) 7,500
Journal of Psychiatry and
Neuroscience (36255) ....(Paid) 5,000

Toronto
Canadian Journal of Human Sexuality (36509)
CrossCurrents (36564) ....(Paid) ‡1,100
(Controlled) ‡1,500
Journal of Cognition and Development (36633)

QUEBEC, CANADA
Montreal
Revue Canadienne de Psycho-Education (37216)
Sante Mentale au Quebec (37221) ....(Paid) 750

PUBLIC RELATIONS

See also Advertising and Marketing; Communications

DISTRICT OF COLUMBIA
Washington
Currents (5455) ....‡15,000

FLORIDA
Gainesville
Journal of Public Relations Research (6149)

ILLINOIS
Chicago
Journal of Public Policy &
Marketing (8449) ....(Paid) ‡472

MARYLAND
Coltons Point
Public Relations Review (13449) ....(Paid) ‡1,500
(Non-paid) ‡55

MINNESOTA
Maple Grove
Format Magazine (16038) ....(Non-paid) 3,000

NEW YORK
New York
O'Dwyer's PR Services
Report (22484) ....(Paid) ‡2,000
(Non-paid) ‡2,000
Public Relations Strategist (22608) .....(Paid) ‡8,000
(Controlled) ‡25,000
Public Relations Tactics (22609)

Rhinebeck
Public Relations Quarterly (23185) ....‡5,000

WISCONSIN
Madison
PR Watch (33969) ....(Combined) 2,000

PUBLIC SAFETY AND EMERGENCY RESPONSE

CALIFORNIA
Tustin
9-1-1 Magazine (3963) ....(Paid) 13,000

MASSACHUSETTS
Quincy
Fire Technology (14489) ....‡4,000

TEXAS
Dallas
Occupational Health &
Safety (30174) ....(Combined) △81,000

WISCONSIN
Madison
Prehospital and Disaster
Medicine (33970) ....(Controlled) 1,569

PUBLIC SPEAKING AND LECTURING

ARIZONA
Tempe
Professional Speaker (913) ....(Controlled) ⊕4,200

CALIFORNIA
Glendora
Sharing Ideas News
    Magazine (2026) ....(Paid) ‡3,000
                             (Controlled) ‡1,000

Rancho Santa Margarita
The Toastmaster (2883) 170,000

LOUISIANA
Dodson
Quote (12568) ....‡5,000

PUBLIC TRANSPORTATION

ARIZONA
Phoenix
Bus Ride (794) ....(Paid) ‡7,200
                            (Non-paid) ‡6,500

CALIFORNIA
Torrance
Metro Magazine (3937) ....(Controlled) 20,500
School Bus Fleet (3942) ....(Controlled) 24,000
                                    (Paid) 231

DISTRICT OF COLUMBIA
Washington
Destinations (5462) ....(Paid) ‡3,379
                            (Controlled) ‡2,621

ILLINOIS
Polo
National Bus Trader (9461) ....(Paid) ‡5,800

IOWA
Cedar Rapids
Russell's Official National Motor Coach
    Guide (10677) ....‡14,100

VIRGINIA
Reston
Journal of Bridge
    Engineering (32371) ....(Paid) 2,300

WISCONSIN
Fort Atkinson
Mass Transit (33714) ....(Controlled) ‡20,506
                                    (Paid) ‡0

ONTARIO, CANADA
Toronto
Taxi News (36753) ....(Free) 10,100

PURCHASING

ARIZONA
Tempe
Inside Supply Management (905) .....(Paid) ‡45,000
                             (Non-paid) ‡300
The Journal of Supply Chain
    Management (908) ....‡1,800

KANSAS
Topeka
Mid-America Commerce and
    Industry (11833) ....(Controlled) ‡8,500

MASSACHUSETTS
Burlington
European Journal of Purchasing and Supply
    Management (14027)
Journal of Retailing and Consumer Services (14029)

Newton
Electronic Business (14394) .....(Combined) ‡52,000
Purchasing
    Magazine (14408) ....(Non-paid) ‡100,203

NEW YORK
Great Neck
American Industry (20685) ....(Controlled) ‡25,000
Industrial Purchasing
    Agent (20689) ....(Controlled) ‡25,000

Manhasset
EBN (20998) ....(Non-paid) ‡57,100

Mount Kisco
ABD (21098) ....(Combined) ‡20,000

PENNSYLVANIA
Spring House
Office Systems 96 (28009) ......(Controlled) 100,225

VIRGINIA
Alexandria
Utility Fleet Management (31748) ....‡22,014

McLean
Contract Management (32264) ....(Controlled) 22,000
National Contract Management
    Journal (32266) ....(Controlled) 4,800

ONTARIO, CANADA
Mississauga
Government
    Business (36068) ....(Controlled) ‡20,661

Toronto
Government Purchasing
    Guide (36608) ....(Combined) •16,401
Materials Management &
    Distribution (36658) ....(Combined) 19,226
Modern Purchasing (36666) ....(Combined) 18,313

RADIO, TELEVISION, CABLE, AND VIDEO

See also Electrical Engineering; Electronics Engineering; Music and Musical Instruments

ARIZONA
Dewey
World Scanner Report (684) ....(Paid) 800
                            (Non-paid) 50

CALIFORNIA
Berkeley
Jump Cut (1539) ....(Paid) 3,000

Chatsworth
Adult Video News (1685)

Chico
Smart TV & Sound
    Magazine (1696) ....(Combined) 50,000

Culver City
Film Score Monthly (1793) ....(Combined) 11,000

Emeryville
Mix (1879) ....(Paid) 2,044
                            (Controlled) 53,597

Mix—Edicion en
    Espanol (1880) ....(Combined) 20,000

Fresno
One to One (1954) ....(Paid) 1,000
One to One II (1955) ....(Paid) 300

Los Angeles
The Agencies (2203) ....(Paid) 487
                            (Combined) 3,390
Journal of Film and Video (2301) 1,400
Radio & Records (2375) ....(Paid) 8000
                            (Non-paid) 500
Spectator (Los Angeles) (2404)
Variety (2427) ....(Mon.) 34,293
Variety's on Production (2428) ....(Paid) ‡200
                            (Controlled) ‡28,000

Riverside
Sufism (2948)

San Francisco
DV Media Group (3351) ....‡60,000
Film/Tape World (3361) ....(Controlled) 4,000
Game Developer (3364)
Release Print (3423) ....(Combined) 9,000

Santa Ana
Response TV (3631) ....(Paid) 700
                            (Non-paid) 21,000
Video Store (3635) ....(Non-paid) 43,885
                                    (Paid) 422

Santa Monica
Entertainment Law Reporter; Movies Music
    Broadcasting Theater Publishing Multimedia
    Sports (3706) ....(Paid) 730

Torrance
Cable Yellow Pages (3929) ....(Non-paid) ‡33,000

Van Nuys
Entertainment Employment Journal (3989)

West Hollywood
ICG Magazine (4063) ....(Combined) ⊕12,000

COLORADO
Denver
The New Review (4342) ....‡73,000
RCR Wireless News (4351) ....(Paid) 9,173
                            (Free) 33,603

Englewood
Cable World (4412) ....(Paid) 5,000
                            (Non-paid) 15,000

RadioResource
    International (4415) ....(Non-paid) 12,000

Greenwood Village
Cable Avails (4504)

Littleton
Wireless Week (4556) ....(Controlled) ‡28,809

CONNECTICUT
Wilton
IE Magazine (5228) ....(Controlled) ‡36,000

DISTRICT OF COLUMBIA
Washington
Communicator (5426) ....‡3,500
Journal of Broadcasting & Electronic
    Media (5576) ....(Paid) ‡2,230
                            (Non-paid) ‡120
Journal of Popular Film and
    Television (5613) ....(Paid) ‡780
Television & Cable Factbook (5819)

FLORIDA
Orange City
Markee (6486) ....(Non-paid) ⊕21,367

Palatka
Cinevue Worldwide Talent Directory and Festival
    Program Book (6536) ....(Paid) ‡2,000
                            (Controlled) ‡2,000

GEORGIA
Savannah
Animation Journal (7530) ....(Paid) 200

HAWAII
Honolulu
Pacific Telecommunications
    Review (7716) ....(Controlled) 2,500

ILLINOIS
Chicago
Eleven (8365) ....‡160,000
Screen Magazine (8562) ....‡15,000

Des Plaines
Financial Manager for the Media
    Professional (8761) ....(Controlled) 1,600

IOWA
Burlington
Radio Campaigns (10639)

KANSAS
Overland Park
Broadcast
    Engineering (11699) ....(Controlled) ‡32,000
Millimeter Magazine (11721) ....(Paid) 207
                                    (Paid) 30,201
Mobile Radio Technology (11722) ....‡25,002
Radio Magazine (11727) ....(Controlled) △15,000
Sound & Video
    Contractor (11731) ....(Controlled) ‡20,536
Video Systems (11734) ....(Controlled) ‡52,000
World Broadcast
    Engineering (11737) ....(Combined) 14,017
World Broadcast
    News (11738) ....(Non-paid) ‡12,665

Shawnee
Government Video (11800) ....(Non-paid) 15,000

MARYLAND
Potomac
Communications (13649) ....(Controlled) ‡25,000

MASSACHUSETTS
Wayland
Electronic House (14614) ....‡80,000

MICHIGAN
Detroit
Electronic Media (14931) ....(Paid) ‡10,708
                            (Non-paid) ‡16,124

Circulation: ★ = ABC; △ = BPA; ♦ = CAC; • = CCAB; ❑ = VAC; ⊕ = PO Statement; ‡ = Publisher's Report; Boldface figures = sworn; Light figures = estimated.

3219

Circ.   Circ.   Circ.

RADIO, TELEVISION, CABLE, AND VIDEO
(continued)

MISSOURI
St. Louis
The St. Louis Journalism Review **(17502)** 3,000

NEW HAMPSHIRE
Littleton
Media Market Guide **(18549)** ....(Paid) ‡1,000
(Controlled) ‡100

Peterborough
audioXpress **(18617)** ....(Paid) 15,000
Video Event **(18632)** ....(Paid) ‡1,098,659

NEW JERSEY
Lakewood
SHOOT **(19158)** 15,100

Westfield
Palmer Video Magazine **(19744)**
Palmer Video News **(19745)**

NEW YORK
Albany
Film Literature Index **(19986)** ....‡525

Commack
db, The Sound Engineering
Magazine **(20488)** ....(Controlled) ‡15,000
(Paid) ‡5,000

Farmingdale
TV Blueprint **(20597)** ....(Paid) ‡2,200,000

Hauppauge
Electronics Now **(20717)** ....(Paid) 76,889
Poptronics **(20722)** ....(Paid) 71,253

Manhasset
Gavin **(21001)**

New Windsor
The Journal of College Radio **(21127)** ....‡3,000

New York
Broadcasting & Cable **(21343)** ....(Paid) 24,765
(Non-paid) 10,405
Country Airplay Monitor **(21505)** 2,803
CVC Report **(21527)** ....(Paid) 800
DigitalTV **(21553)** ....(Non-paid) ‡30,072
Impact! **(21853)**
Journal of the Audio Engineering
Society **(22003)** ....‡13,561
Mediaweek Magazine **(22309)** ....(Paid) 6,989
(Non-paid) 15,038
Pro Sound News **(22595)** ....(Controlled) ‡24,653
Producers Masterguide **(22598)** ....(Paid) ‡1,000
(Non-paid) ‡13,000
R&B Airplay Monitor **(22625)** 2,803
Rock Airplay Monitor **(22674)** 2,803
Studies in Gender and
Sexuality **(22801)** ....(Combined) 700
Television Europe **(22820)**
Top 40 Airplay Monitor **(22843)** 2,803
The TV Executive **(22874)** ....(Paid) 100
(Non-paid) 8,000
TV Executive Daily **(22875)** ....(Non-paid) ‡8,000
TWICE **(22878)** ....(Non-paid) ‡33,000
Video Age Daily **(22897)** ....(Non-paid) ‡8,000
Video Age International **(22898)** ....(Paid) 800
(Non-paid) 11,200
Videography **(22899)** ....(Controlled) ‡40,978

Port Washington
Popular Communications **(23132)** .....(Paid) ⊕59,340
(Non-paid) ⊕876
Post **(23134)** 30,550
Sound & Communications
Magazine **(23136)** ....(Paid) 458
(Non-paid) 16,640

Salamanca
Electronic Retailer **(23291)** ....(Controlled) ‡18,000

White Plains
AV Video & Multimedia
Producer **(23568)** ....(Paid) ‡471
(Controlled) ‡101,420
SMPTE Journal **(23573)** ....(Paid) ‡9,200

OKLAHOMA
Cleveland
Film & History **(25789)** ....(Paid) 1,000

Oklahoma City
CATJ **(25958)** ....(Controlled) 2,000

OREGON
Eugene
QCWA News **(26332)** 10,000

PENNSYLVANIA
East Stroudsburg
Feedback **(26847)** ....(Paid) ‡1,600
(Non-paid) ‡100

Lansdowne
Radio-TV Interview
Report **(27162)** ....(Non-paid) 4,000

Levittown
North American Shortwave Association (NASWA)—
The Journal **(27188)** ....(Paid) 1,200

Radnor
TV Host Monthly **(27916)** ....(Paid) 1,024,472
(Non-paid) 209,485

TENNESSEE
Nashville
Television News Index and
Abstracts **(29487)** ....‡200

TEXAS
Dallas
Cinema Journal **(30136)** ....(Combined) ⊕2,858

VIRGINIA
Arlington
The News Media & the
Law **(31814)** ....(Paid) ‡1,000
(Non-paid) ‡1,000

Falls Church
Radio World **(32056)** ....(Controlled) ‡14,000
TV Technology **(32059)** ....(Controlled) ‡35,000

Manassas
NRB **(32224)** ....(Controlled) ‡8,500

WASHINGTON
Seattle
Media Inc. **(32986)**

WISCONSIN
Madison
Telemedium **(33976)** ....(Combined) 600

ALBERTA, CANADA
Calgary
Broadcast Technology+Media
Production **(34629)** ....(Controlled) ‡7,100

ONTARIO, CANADA
North York
Marketnews **(36130)** ....(Combined) •10,538

Ottawa
Radio Aids to Marine Navigation **(36274)**

Toronto
Broadcaster **(36478)** ....(Controlled) 7,697
Cablecaster **(36484)** ....(Controlled) 6,075
Listening In **(36651)** ....(Paid) 700
(Non-paid) 200
Playback **(36711)** ....(Controlled) ‡8,500

QUEBEC, CANADA
Montreal
Info Presse Communications **(37127)** ....(Paid) 5,500
(Controlled) 2,500

RADIOLOGY, ULTRASOUND, AND NUCLEAR MEDICINE

CALIFORNIA
Glendale
Administrative Radiology
Journal **(2006)** ....(Paid) 11,380

Oakland
The Radiologist **(2695)** 910

San Diego
Journal of Structural Biology **(3213)**

FLORIDA
Gainesville
Journal of Digital Imaging **(6147)** ....‡1,527

ILLINOIS
Oak Brook
RadioGraphics **(9363)** 28,000

MARYLAND
Baltimore
Journal of Computer-Assisted
Tomography **(13186)** ....‡2,051
Journal of Thoracic Imaging **(13203)** 1,007

Hagerstown
Lippincott's Reviews: Radiology **(13565)**

MASSACHUSETTS
Burlington
Ultrasonics Sonochemistry **(14035)**

NEW HAMPSHIRE
Nashua
Vision Systems Design **(18602)**

NEW JERSEY
Ocean
Applied Radiology **(19387)** ....(Paid) 14
(Controlled) 32,000

NEW MEXICO
Albuquerque
Radiologic Technology **(19785)** ....(Paid) ‡65,000

NEW YORK
Armonk
Echocardiography **(20075)** ....‡2,449

Bronx
Seminars in Nuclear Medicine **(20286)** ....‡4,897

Manhasset
Diagnostic Imaging **(20996)** ....(Paid) 31,240
(Non-paid) 30,283

New York
Abdominal Imaging **(21131)** ....(Combined) 1,350
CardioVascular and Interventional
Radiology **(21376)** ....(Combined) 2,400
Dysphagia **(21573)** ....(Combined) 2,200
Journal of Radiosurgery **(22176)**

NORTH CAROLINA
Chapel Hill
Seminars in Radiation Oncology **(23722)**

Durham
Lasers in the Life Sciences **(23832)**

PENNSYLVANIA
King of Prussia
ADVANCE for Administrators in Radiation & Radiation
Oncology **(27108)** ....(Controlled) ‡21,987
ADVANCE for Imaging and Radiation Therapy
Professionals **(27112)** ....(Controlled) ‡69,000

Philadelphia
AJNR: American Journal of
Neuroradiology **(27366)** ....(Paid) ‡5,934
(Non-paid) ‡130
Journal of Vascular and Interventional Radiology
(JVIR) **(27555)**
Radiologic Clinics of North America **(27652)**
Seminars in Breast Disease **(27661)**
Seminars in Radiologic Technology **(27672)**
Seminars in Roentgenology **(27673)** ....‡5,518
Seminars in Ultrasound, CT and
MRI **(27675)** ....‡4,880
Techniques in Vascular and Interventional
Radiology **(27700)**

Wynnewood
Clinical Nuclear Medicine **(28197)** ....(Paid) 1,678

TEXAS
Sugar Land
Internet Journal of Radiology **(31160)**

Temple
Investigative Radiology **(31178)** ....(Paid) 614

VIRGINIA
Leesburg
American Journal of
Roentgenology **(32182)** ....(Paid) ‡23,131
(Non-paid) ‡351

Reston
Journal of Nuclear Medicine
Technology **(32388)** ....‡7,000

ONTARIO, CANADA
Ottawa
Canadian Journal of Medical Radiation
Technology **(36207)** ....(Paid) ‡9,798
(Non-paid) ‡89

RAILROAD

See also Public Transportation

ILLINOIS
Chicago
Railway Track & Structures **(8546)** ......(Paid) 5,452
(Controlled) 3,048

Mount Prospect
Signalman's Journal **(9250)** ....‡15,000

Peoria
The Short Line **(9424)** ....(Paid) 1,100
(Non-paid) 20

Urbana
Railroad History **(9716)** ....(Paid) 3,500

MASSACHUSETTS
Somerville
B&M Bulletin **(14532)** ....‡2,200

MICHIGAN
Southfield
BMWE Journal **(15542)** ....‡60,000

NEW YORK
New York
International Railway
Journal **(21933)** ....(Combined) 10,314
Railway Age **(22624)** ....(Paid) 998
(Non-paid) 23,730

OHIO
Cleveland
Locomotive Engineers Journal **(24921)** ....‡54,000

PENNSYLVANIA
Berwyn
The Mutual Magazine **(26697)** ....‡8,500

WISCONSIN
Milwaukee
Progressive
Railroading **(34094)** ....(Controlled) △25,052

Waukesha
Model Railroader **(34407)** ....(Paid) ★175,051
Trains **(34413)** ....(Paid) ★109,329

QUEBEC, CANADA
Montreal
Canadian Rail/Rail
Canadien **(37099)** ....(Combined) 1,050
Movin' **(37194)** ....(Non-paid) ‡30,000

REAL ESTATE

CALIFORNIA
Costa Mesa
New Homes
Magazine **(1778)** ....(Non-paid) ‡100,000

Los Angeles
Apartment Age Magazine **(2211)** ......(Paid) ‡11,000
(Controlled) ‡29,000
California Real Estate
Journal **(2231)** ....(Paid) ‡2,842
(Non-paid) ‡194
Daily Commerce **(2251)** ....(Free) 279
(Paid) 2,829

Oakland
The Inter-City Express **(2682)** ....(Paid) ‡1,023
(Non-paid) ‡14
Real Property Law Reporter **(2696)**

Riverside
First Tuesday **(2936)** ....(Paid) 5,087
(Non-paid) 90,000

Sacramento
The Daily Recorder **(2995)** ....‡1,122

San Diego
Business Opportunities Journal **(3126)** ......‡132,000
Mortgage Originator
Magazine **(3238)** ....(Combined) 16,522
San Diego Commerce **(3259)** ....(Paid) 670
(Free) 209

Santa Monica
Unique Homes **(3719)** ....(Paid) 56,410

Sherman Oaks
California Real Estate
Magazine **(3761)** ....(Paid) 95,000
(Non-paid) 350

Torrance
Right of Way **(3941)** ....‡9,000

Walnut Creek
The Institutional Real Estate
Letter **(4054)** ....(Paid) 500
(Non-paid) 1,000
REITStreet Magazine **(4055)** ....(Non-paid) 4,000

COLORADO
Castle Rock
The CF Apartment Reporter **(4220)**
Clayton-Fillmore Report **(4221)**

Denver
The Daily Journal **(4320)** ....(Paid) ‡1,206
(Controlled) ‡3,859

DISTRICT OF COLUMBIA
Washington
The Corridor Real Estate
Journal **(5443)** ....(Paid) ‡5,000
(Controlled) ‡3,000
Developments **(5464)** 2,800
Housing Policy Debate **(5530)** ......(Non-paid) 7,000
Journal of Housing
Research **(5597)** ....(Non-paid) 6,200
Mobility **(5655)** ....(Paid) ‡11,970
(Non-paid) ‡498
Professional Report **(5733)** ....(Paid) 3,500
Real Estate Journal/Tri-State
(REJ) **(5759)** ....(Paid) ⊕6,211
Urban Land Magazine **(5838)** ....(Paid) 15,000

FLORIDA
Gainesville
Journal of College and University Student
Housing **(6146)**

Miami
Daily Business Review **(6347)** ....(Paid) 10,184
(Controlled) 286

Naples
Naples Guide **(6446)** ....(Controlled) ‡270,000

Orlando
Florida Realtor **(6492)** ....(Paid) △78,025
(Non-paid) △2,495

St. Petersburg
The duPont Registry: A Buyer's Gallery of Fine
Homes **(6625)** ....(Paid) 22,000
(Controlled) 28,000
Maddux Report **(6630)** ....(Paid) 1,040
(Controlled) 13,180

Vero Beach
Florida Real Estate **(6835)** ....(Non-paid) ‡77,622

GEORGIA
Atlanta
Atlanta Homes and Lifestyles **(6970)** ....‡33,828
Corporate Real Estate
Executive **(6994)** ....(Paid) 3,800
Corporate Real Estate
Leader **(6995)** ....(Controlled) 8,000
National Real Estate
Investor **(7030)** ....(Paid) ‡3,971
(Controlled) ‡29,075
Shopping Center World **(7042)** ....(Paid) 830
(Controlled) 35,000

Norcross
Site Selection
Magazine **(7469)** ....(Combined) 45,000

ILLINOIS
Chicago
Commercial Investment Real
Estate **(8337)** ....(Paid) ‡600
(Controlled) ‡11,000
Journal of Property Management **(8448)** .....‡23,000
Manufactured Home
Merchandiser **(8476)** ....(Controlled) ‡18,452
Metro Chicago Real
Estate **(8485)** ....(Controlled) ‡8,582
Probate and Property **(8540)** ....(Paid) 30,000
(Controlled) 1,391
Real Estate Issues **(8548)**
Real Estate Today **(8549)** ....(Paid) 784,469
(Controlled) 1,182
REALTOR Magazine **(8550)** ....(Paid) 763,219
(Free) 1,077

REALTORS Land Institute **(8551)** ......(Paid) ‡1,600
(Non-paid) ‡500
Realty and Building **(8552)** ....(Paid) ‡13,280
(Controlled) ‡1,130
The Residential Specialist **(8554)** ....‡43,000
Today's Realtor **(8584)** ....(Paid) 725,000
(Free) 1,323

INDIANA
Bloomington
Real Estate Economics **(9850)**

Indianapolis
The Voice **(10181)** ....(Paid) 5,000

MARYLAND
Bethesda
New Homes Register **(13363)** ......(Non-paid) 17,000

MASSACHUSETTS
Boston
The Commercial Record **(13879)** 3,200
(Free) 408

Norwell
New England Real Estate
Journal **(14442)** ....(Paid) ‡8,000
(Free) ‡1,200
New York Real Estate
Journal **(14443)** ....(Paid) 3,700

Wilmington
Property Digest and Economic Development
Magazine **(14663)** ....(Controlled) ‡6,000

Winchester
Real Estate Finance **(14667)** 2,600

MICHIGAN
Southfield
The Michigan Real Estate Journal **(15546)**

MISSISSIPPI
Olive Branch
Home Market Magazine **(16805)** ......(Free) ‡16,000

MISSOURI
Columbia
The Missouri Realtor **(17002)** ....‡18,000

MONTANA
Billings
Montana Land
Magazine **(17732)** ....(Controlled) ‡100,000

NEW HAMPSHIRE
Manchester
The Registry Review **(18563)**

NEW JERSEY
Edison
New Jersey Realtors
Magazine **(18788)** ....(Non-paid) 41,000

Red Bank
Business Facilities **(19500)** ....(Free) 43,500

NEW YORK
Buffalo
Buffalo Law Journal **(20366)** ....(Paid) 700
(Non-paid) 30

Freeport
Realty **(20626)** ....‡6,000

New York
The Real Estate Finance Journal **(22631)** 2,500
Real Estate Forum **(22632)** ......(Controlled) 33,251
Real Estate New York **(22633)** ....(Paid) ‡551
(Controlled) ‡16,661
Real Estate Review **(22634)** 8,200
Real Estate Weekly **(22635)** ....(Paid) 8,453
(Free) 512

Setauket
North Shore Homes **(23327)** ......(Non-paid) ‡42,000

NORTH CAROLINA
Charlotte
The Mecklenburg Times **(23749)** ....(Paid) ‡857
(Non-paid) ‡81

Greensboro
Plants Sites & Parks **(23935)** ....(Paid) 81
(Controlled) 44,500

Greenville
Homes Magazine **(23964)** ....(Non-paid) ‡7,500

Circulation: ★ = ABC; △ = BPA; ♦ = CAC; ● = CCAB; ❑ = VAC; ⊕ = PO Statement; ‡ = Publisher's Report; Boldface figures = sworn; Light figures = estimated.

3221

Circ.   Circ.   Circ.

REAL ESTATE (continued)

PENNSYLVANIA
West Chester
The Homes Magazine **(28147)**

RHODE ISLAND
Providence
Real Estate Software
   Guide **(28419)** ....(Paid) 63,000

SOUTH CAROLINA
Charleston
Commerce Magazine **(28512)**

TEXAS
Austin
Texas Realtor **(29845)** ....(Paid) ‡45,920
                 (Non-paid) ‡630

College Station
Tierra Grande **(30055)** ....‡118,000

Dallas
Dallas/Fort Worth New Homes
   Guide **(30144)** ....(Controlled) ‡80,000

Fort Worth
Commercial Recorder **(30335)** ....‡600

Houston
Daily Court Review **(30469)** 2,120

VIRGINIA
Alexandria
Common Ground **(31656)** ....(Paid) ‡30,000

WASHINGTON
Bellevue
Timber Bulletin **(32668)** ....(Paid) 10,000

Bothell
Vacation Ownership World **(32691)** ....‡3,000

Edmonds
Real Estate
   Northwest **(32745)** ....(Controlled) 25,000

MANITOBA, CANADA
Winnipeg
The Canadian Appraiser **(35319)** 6,000

ONTARIO, CANADA
Ottawa
CMHC Housing Outlook, National Edition **(36237)**

Thunder Bay
Thunder Bay Real Estate
   News **(36444)** ....(Paid) **30,000**

Toronto
Real Estate News **(36722)** ......(Controlled) ‡98,720

Unionville
Active Adult **(36827)**
Condo Life **(36828)**
Homes Magazine **(36829)** 100,000
Moving to Alberta **(36830)**
Moving to Montreal **(36831)**
Moving to Ottawa/Outaouais **(36832)**
Moving to Saskatchewan **(36833)**
Moving to Southwestern Ontario **(36834)**
Moving to Toronto **(36835)**
Moving to Vancouver & British Columbia **(36836)**
Moving to Winnipeg & Manitoba **(36837)**

RENTAL EQUIPMENT

See also Machinery and Equipment

CALIFORNIA
Malibu
Rental Equipment
   Register **(2494)** ....(Non-paid) ‡18,532

Newport Beach
Truck Sales & Leasing **(2636)** ....(Non-paid) ‡20,074

FLORIDA
Tallahassee
Florida Rental Association News **(6719)** 1600

ILLINOIS
Moline
Rental Management **(9207)** ....(Paid) 5,491
               (Non-paid) 12,933

TEXAS
Austin
Progressive Rentals **(29799)** ....‡5,000

WISCONSIN
Fort Atkinson
Rental Product News **(33720)** ....(Controlled) 20,500

ONTARIO, CANADA
Exeter
Canadian Rental
   Service **(35824)** ....(Controlled) ‡3,762

RETAIL

See also General Merchandise

ARIZONA
Phoenix
Asian Sources Gifts & Home Products **(788)**

CALIFORNIA
Palm Springs
JQ **(2762)**
Tobacco Retailer **(2768)**

Rocklin
Web Commerce Today **(2957)**

COLORADO
Colorado Springs
CBA Marketplace **(4239)** ....(Paid) ‡8,514
               (Non-paid) ‡567

DISTRICT OF COLUMBIA
Washington
Stores **(5805)** ....(Paid) 15,776
               (Non-paid) 19,966

FLORIDA
Lake Mary
Inspirational Giftware **(6277)**

GEORGIA
Atlanta
Retail Ink **(7041)**

Roswell
Point Of Purchase **(7516)** ....(Controlled) 19,500
Retail Operations &
   Construction **(7518)** ....(Controlled) 25,500

ILLINOIS
Chicago
M **(8475)** ....(Non-paid) 17,000
NPN International **(8513)** ....(Controlled) ‡7,500

St. Charles
Country Business **(9563)** ....(Combined) 30,000

Skokie
P-O-P Design **(9608)** ....(Non-paid) △**18,005**
P-O-P Times **(9609)** ....(Non-paid) △**19,379**

IOWA
Des Moines
Embroidery Professional & Sewing Professional/Round
   Bobbin **(10784)** ....(Non-paid) ‡10,000

MAINE
Waldoboro
Today Magazine **(13070)** 6,500

Yarmouth
Kitchenware News **(13081)** ......(Combined) ‡12,122

MASSACHUSETTS
Burlington
Journal of Retailing and Consumer Services **(14029)**

MISSOURI
Fenton
Paint & Decorating
   Retailer **(17063)** ....(Combined) ‡26,201

St. Louis
DECOR **(17432)** ....(Paid) 24,245
               (Non-paid) 785

NEW JERSEY
Morris Plains
Vertical Application Reseller **(19308)**

Randolph
Retail Info Systems
   News **(19497)** ....(Controlled) ‡18,500

Retail Systems
   Reseller **(19498)** ....(Controlled) 15,000

NEW YORK
Centerport
Retailers Forum
   Magazine **(20446)** ....(Non-paid) 70,000
Swap Meet Magazine **(20447)** .....(Non-paid) 72,000

New York
Action Sports Retailer **(21147)**
American Time **(21208)** ....(Non-paid) 8,000
Bicycle Retailer and Industry
   News **(21308)** 12,337
Chain Store Age **(21393)** ....(Paid) 2,253
               (Non-paid) 33,398
Couture International Jeweler **(21508)** 20,000
Credit Card Management **(21513)** ....(Paid) 3,252
               (Non-paid) 8,524
Discount Store News **(21554)** ....(Paid) 7,904
               (Non-paid) 24,957
Fly Fishing Retailer **(21709)**
Home Furnishings News (HFN) **(21808)**
MMR **(22340)** ....(Paid) 6,498
               (Non-paid) 28,123
Retail Merchandiser **(22653)** .....(Controlled) ‡35,000
Retail Tech **(22654)**
Target The Family **(22815)**
Variety and General Merchandise
   TradeNews **(22896)**

Salamanca
Electronic Retailer **(23291)** ....(Controlled) ‡18,000

NORTH CAROLINA
High Point
High Points **(23999)**

OHIO
Sandusky
Retail News **(25509)** 8,845

OREGON
Corvallis
Tipsico Bulletin **(26291)**

PENNSYLVANIA
Pittsburgh
Baby Shop **(27761)**

RHODE ISLAND
Providence
Bedroom **(28388)** ....(Controlled) 21,700

VIRGINIA
Falls Church
Catalog Success
   Magazine **(32042)** ....(Combined) 15,245
Dealerscope: The Business of CE Retailing **(32043)**

WASHINGTON
Bellingham
New Age Retailer **(32677)** ....(Non-paid) 10,000

Seattle
Pike Place Market Merchants Association & Market
   News **(33002)**

WISCONSIN
Fort Atkinson
Yard and Garden **(33723)** 17,500

Iola
Blade Trade **(33806)** ....(Combined) 2,410

MANITOBA, CANADA
Winnipeg
C Store Canada **(35318)**

ROADS AND STREETS

See also Construction, Contracting, Building, and Excavating

ARIZONA
Phoenix
Southwest Contractor **(811)** ....(Combined) 6,000

DISTRICT OF COLUMBIA
Washington
ITE Journal **(5562)** ....‡14,000

Numbers cited after listings are entry numbers rather than page numbers.

ILLINOIS
Des Plaines
Roads & Bridges
  Magazine **(8770)** ....(Controlled) ‡65,000

MICHIGAN
Lansing
Michigan Roads and
  Construction **(15291)** ....(Paid) **1,043**
                                        (Non-paid) **436**

MISSOURI
Independence
The Asphalt Contractor **(17106)** 11,152

NEW HAMPSHIRE
Concord
New Hampshire Highways **(18474)** ....‡1,600

NEW YORK
New York
Construction Products **(21488)** ....(Non-paid) 101,000
                                        (Non-paid) 101,000

OHIO
Columbus
Ohio Contractor **(25041)** ....(Paid) ‡850
                                        (Non-paid) ‡5,500

PENNSYLVANIA
Harrisburg
HIGHWAY BUILDER **(26995)** ....‡3,000

TEXAS
Dallas
Better Roads **(30131)** ....(Non-paid) 39,424

ROOFING

See also Building Materials, Concrete, Brick, and Tile; Metal, Metallurgy, and Metal Trade; Construction, Contracting, Building, and Excavating

DISTRICT OF COLUMBIA
Washington
Journeyman Roofer and
  Waterproofer **(5622)** 23,000

FLORIDA
Winter Park
Florida Forum **(6879)** ....(Controlled) ‡4,500

ILLINOIS
Bensenville
Contractors Guide **(8065)** ....(Paid) 148
                                        (Non-paid) 23,434

Rosemont
Professional Roofing **(9556)** ....(Paid) 5,898
                                        (Controlled) 13,609

MICHIGAN
Troy
Roofing Contractor **(15638)**

NEVADA
Reno
Western
  Roofing/Insulation/Siding **(18426)** .....(Paid) ‡3,017
                                        (Controlled) ‡20,345

PENNSYLVANIA
Philadelphia
The Trade News **(27707)** ....(Non-paid) 850

WISCONSIN
Iola
Metal Roofing Magazine **(33835)**

RUBBER TRADE

See also Automotive (Trade)

OHIO
Akron
European Rubber
  Journal **(24580)** ....(Combined) △8,186
Rubber Chemistry and
  Technology **(24586)** ....‡3,000
Rubber & Plastics News **(24587)** ......(Paid) △6,322
                                        (Non-paid) △9,995

Rubber World **(24588)** ....(Paid) 2,413
                                        (Non-paid) 7,937
Urethanes
  Technology **(24592)** ....(Combined) △7,118

WASHINGTON
Woodinville
China Synthetic Rubber Markets **(33210)**

SAFETY

ALABAMA
Mobile
Elevator World **(319)** ....(Paid) ‡6,200
                                        (Non-paid) ‡162

CALIFORNIA
Auburn
FPC/Fire Protection
  Contractor **(1438)** ....(Controlled) 2,300

Moffett Field
ASRS Directline **(2573)**
Callback **(2574)** ....(Combined) 85,000

San Diego
Fire-Rescue Magazine **(3155)** ....(Paid) 9,709
                                        (Non-paid) 35,991
JEMS **(3175)** ....(Paid) 28,000
                                        (Controlled) 12,000
Molecular Therapy **(3237)**

Torrance
Security Sales **(3943)** 25,140

COLORADO
Denver
Law Enforcement Product
  News **(4338)** ....(Non-paid) 26,417
Public Safety Product
  News **(4350)** ....(Non-paid) 14,292

CONNECTICUT
Hartford
Campus Law Enforcement
  Journal **(4885)** ....(Paid) 1,700

DISTRICT OF COLUMBIA
Washington
Federal Mine Safety and Health Review **(5494)**
Modern Drug Discovery **(5656)**
Youth Today **(5874)** ....(Combined) 58,000

FLORIDA
Daytona Beach
Public Safety
  Communications **(6039)** ....(Paid) ‡14,000
                                        (Controlled) ‡135

North Palm Beach
National PAL CopsnKids
  Chronicles **(6470)** ....(Controlled) 22,000

GEORGIA
Atlanta
The Complete European Trade Digest Electrical
  Edition **(6989)**
The Complete European Trade Digest Machinery
  Edition **(6990)**
The Complete European Trade Digest Medical
  Edition **(6991)**

IDAHO
Moscow
Focus on Security **(7914)** ....(Paid) 100

ILLINOIS
Bensenville
SECURITY **(8071)** ....(Controlled) 40,541

Des Plaines
Professional Safety **(8769)** ....‡30,000

Glen Ellyn
Law Enforcement Legal
  Review **(8929)** ....(Paid) 1,000

Itasca
Family Safety & Health **(9013)** ....‡500,000
Safe Driver **(9017)** ....(Paid) 80,000
Safety+Health **(9018)** ....(Controlled) 51,000
Safeworker **(9019)** ....(Paid) 40,000
Today's Supervisor **(9020)** ....‡80,000
Traffic Safety **(9021)** ....(Paid) ‡25,000
                                        (Non-paid) ‡66

Streamwood
National Locksmith **(9667)** ....(Paid) 12,705

INDIANA
Franklin
Access **(10004)** ....(Controlled) 3,000

KANSAS
Overland Park
Seguridad Latina **(11730)** ....(Combined) 16,000

MAINE
Augusta
Fatal Occupational Injuries in
  Maine **(12891)** ....(Non-paid) 1,000

MARYLAND
Bethesda
Health and Safety Science Abstracts **(13342)**
Lead Detection and Abatement
  Contractor **(13356)** ....(Paid) 10,000

Rockville
Inspection Monitor **(13682)**

MASSACHUSETTS
Weston
Journal of Healthcare Safety, Compliance & Infection
  Control **(14651)** ....(Paid) ‡2,200

MICHIGAN
East Lansing
International Journal of Comparative and Applied
  Criminal Justice **(14985)** ....(Paid) 400

Troy
Security Distributing & Marketing
  (SDM) **(15639)** ....(Combined) ‡28,003

NEVADA
Carson City
MOTION **(18327)** ....(Non-paid) 33,000

NEW HAMPSHIRE
Nashua
CleanRooms International **(18585)**

NEW JERSEY
Cranford
Safety Briefs **(18772)** ....(Non-paid) ‡8,000

NEW YORK
Binghamton
Journal of Threat Assessment **(20204)**

New York
Biomedical Safety and Standards **(21322)**
Home Systems **(21813)**
Mundo Mercantil **(22381)** ....(Combined) 10,000
SDM Dealer/Installer
  Marketplace **(22716)** ....(Combined) 28,000

Salamanca
Security Professional **(23294)** ......(Non-paid) 20,000

OHIO
Cleveland
Occupational
  Hazards **(24936)** ....(Controlled) ‡65,000

OREGON
Creswell
SAFE Journal **(26298)** ....(Combined) 950
SAFE Symposium Proceedings **(26299)**

PENNSYLVANIA
Norristown
Industrial Safety and Hygiene
  News **(27335)** ....(Controlled) ‡62,057

Philadelphia
Toxicology & Ecotoxicology
  News/Reviews **(27706)** 600

Pittsburgh
Industrial Hygiene
  News **(27800)** ....(Controlled) 62,000

Quakertown
Police & Security News **(27915)** ....(Paid) ‡449
                                        (Non-paid) ‡22,160

TEXAS
College Station
Food Additives and Contaminants **(30041)** 650
Industrial Fire World **(30043)** ....(Paid) 18,000

Circulation: ★ = ABC; △ = BPA; ♦ = CAC; • = CCAB; ❑ = VAC; ⊕ = PO Statement; ‡ = Publisher's Report; Boldface figures = sworn; Light figures = estimated.

3223

Circ.   Circ.   Circ.

SAFETY (continued)

Dallas
Keynotes **(30166)** ....(Controlled) ‡10,000
Occupational Health &
Safety **(30174)** ....(Combined) △81,000

Fort Worth
Journal of Police Crisis Negotiations **(30343)**

VIRGINIA
Alexandria
Aviation Mechanics Bulletin **(31644)** 2,700
Flight Safety Digest **(31673)**

Arlington
Quantum **(31822)**

Fairfax
Synergist **(32032)**

Richmond
Compliance
Magazine **(32435)** ....(Non-paid) △60,014

WISCONSIN
Spooner
Underground Focus **(34338)** ......(Combined) 18,200

BRITISH COLUMBIA, CANADA
Victoria
BC Mine Rescue Manual **(35207)**

ONTARIO, CANADA
Aurora
CANADIAN SECURITY **(35643)** ....‡14,832

Burlington
Canadian Occupational
Safety **(35716)** ....(Combined) 12,528

Ottawa
Living Safety Magazine **(36260)** ....‡100,000

Toronto
Accident Prevention **(36460)** ......(Combined) 11,173
The Canadian Locksmith Magazine **(36514)** 500
Canadian Occupational Health and Safety News
(COHSN) **(36521)** ....‡1,100
OH&S Canada **(36680)** ....(Paid) 8,271
(Non-paid) 2,405

SAVINGS AND LOAN

INDIANA
Franklin
Access **(10004)** ....(Controlled) 3,000

TEXAS
Austin
The S & L Quarterly **(29803)**

SCIENCE (GENERAL)

See also Anthropology and Ethnology;
Archaeology; Astronautics; Biology;
Botany; Chemistry, Chemicals, and
Chemical Engineering; Engineering (Various
branches); Entomology; Forestry; Genetics;
Geology; Laboratory Research (Scientific
and Medical), etc.

ALABAMA
Auburn
Journal of the Alabama Academy of
Science **(42)** ....‡1,200

ARIZONA
Tempe
Copeia **(902)**

CALIFORNIA
Berkeley
Historical Studies in the Physical and Biological
Sciences **(1525)**
Measurement **(1541)**
PaleoBios **(1549)**

Eureka
The Journal of Borderland
Research **(1893)** ....(Paid) ‡1,100
(Non-paid) ‡100

Los Angeles
Innovation and Ideas **(2296)** ....(Paid) ‡120,000

The World & Science **(2441)**

Palo Alto
Annual Review of Earth and Planetary
Sciences **(2789)**
Annual Review of Genetics **(2790)**
Annual Review of Microbiology **(2792)**

Pasadena
Engineering & Science **(2815)** ....(Paid) 200
(Non-paid) 15,500

San Diego
Cell Biology International **(3128)**
Cytokine **(3138)**
Finite Fields and Their Applications **(3154)**
Frontiers in Neuroendocrinology **(3157)**
Fungal Genetics and Biology **(3158)**
Journal of Magnetic Resonance **(3202)**
Journal of Multivariate Analysis **(3207)**
Metabolic Engineering **(3228)**
Methods **(3229)**
Neurobiology of Disease **(3239)**
Nuclear Data Sheets **(3243)**
Quality Assurance **(3251)**
Real-Time Imaging **(3253)**
Seminars in Cell & Developmental Biology **(3273)**

San Pedro
Whalewatcher **(3597)**

Santa Cruz
Invertebrate Biology **(3684)**

Santa Monica
Human Factors **(3711)** ....(Combined) 6,300
Journal of Applied Mathematics and Decision
Sciences **(3712)**
RAND Review **(3715)** ....(Controlled) 15,000

Stevenson Ranch
Journal of Nanoscience and
Nanotechnology **(3804)** ....(Paid) 120

Thousand Oaks
Science, Technology & Human
Values **(3915)** ....(Paid) 1,600

Woodland Hills
Airpower **(4100)**

COLORADO
Greeley
Journal of the Colorado-Wyoming Academy of
Science **(4498)**

Whitewater
Journal of Pyrotechnics **(4685)** ....(Combined) 500

CONNECTICUT
Danbury
Science World **(4763)** ....(Paid) 395,228

Farmington
Folia Primatologica **(4825)** 850

New Haven
Yale Scientific Magazine **(5010)** ....(Paid) ‡1,900
(Non-paid) ‡3,000

Shelton
American Laboratory
News **(5119)** ....(Non-paid) 92,847

Stamford
Current Science **(5146)** ....‡357,583

DISTRICT OF COLUMBIA
Washington
American Mineralogist **(5336)** ....(Paid) 3,200
Current Antarctic
Literature **(5454)** ....(Controlled) ‡1,100
Main Science & Technology Indicators **(5642)**
Nature International Weekly Journal of
Science **(5689)** ....(Paid) 53,861
(Non-paid) 686
Optics Letters **(5709)** ....(Paid) 2400
Paleobiology **(5713)**
Proceedings of the National Academy of Sciences of
the United States of
America **(5731)** ....(Paid) 7,200
(Non-paid) 2,300
Research-Technology
Management **(5763)** ....(Paid) ‡4,200
(Non-paid) ‡800
Reviews of Geophysics **(5767)**
ReVision **(5768)** ....(Paid) ‡900
Science **(5778)** ....(Paid) 155,911
Science Activities **(5779)** 1,042
Science Books & Films **(5780)** ....(Paid) ‡4,500
(Non-paid) ‡600

Science News **(5781)** ....(Paid) 168,621
21st Century Science &
Technology **(5833)** ....(Paid) 19,500

FLORIDA
Boca Raton
International Journal of Geomechanics **(5934)**

Boynton Beach
Instrumentation Science & Technology **(5950)** 325

Seminole
Journal of Crustacean Biology **(6684)** ....(Paid) ‡952

GEORGIA
Atlanta
BioWorld Magazine **(6978)** ....(Controlled) ‡10,000

Lawrenceville
Georgia Journal of Science **(7367)**

IDAHO
Pocatello
Journal of the Idaho Academy of
Science **(7946)** ....(Paid) 500

ILLINOIS
Argonne
Solvent Extraction and Ion
Exchange **(8020)** ....(Paid) 325

Carbondale
Knowledge, Technology &
Policy **(8118)** ....(Paid) ‡500

Champaign
Motor Control **(8204)** ....(Paid) ‡307

Chicago
Insights **(8418)**
Numerical Heat Transfer **(8514)**
Osiris **(8517)**
Scanning Microscopy **(8560)** ....‡1,000

Lisle
Journal of Theory Construction
Testing **(9111)** ....(Combined) 570

Macomb
Journal of Elementary Science Education **(9129)**

Oak Brook
Semiconductor International **(9365)** ......(Paid) 1,015
(Non-paid) 45,541

Urbana
Fusion Technology **(9705)** 600

Wheaton
Journal of Outcome Measurement **(9756)**

INDIANA
Lafayette
Protein Science **(10254)**

IOWA
Ames
Aeon **(10588)** ....(Paid) 500
(Non-paid) 100

KANSAS
Lawrence
International Journal of Research in Choral
Singing **(11553)**
Journal of Scientific
Exploration **(11558)** ....(Paid) 3,000
Transactions of the Kansas Academy of
Science **(11566)**
Weed Science **(11570)**

LOUISIANA
Lake Charles
Applied Spectroscopy Reviews **(12635)** ....(Paid) 400

MAINE
Salsbury Cove
MDIBL Bulletin **(13048)**

Steuben
The Northeastern Naturalist **(13060)**
The Southeastern Naturalist **(13061)**

MARYLAND
Baltimore
American Journal of Epidemiology **(13116)** ....‡6,100
Molecular Medicine **(13221)** ....(Combined) 500

Bethesda
Conference Papers Index **(13327)**

Numbers cited after listings are entry numbers rather than page numbers.

The Journal of Molecular
Diagnostics (13352) ....(Paid) 3,000
Risk Abstracts (13377)
Solid State and Superconductivity Abstracts (13380)

College Park
CHAOS (13414)
Transportation Science (13443)
Virtual Journal of Nanoscale Science &
Technology (13445)
Virtual Journal of Quantum Information (13446)

Frederick
Professional
Surveyor (13520) ....(Controlled) ‡52,000

Gaithersburg
Inside Laboratory Management (13543)

Silver Spring
Science Weekly (13745)

MASSACHUSETTS
Amherst
Main Group Chemistry News (13801)

Boston
Boston University Journal of Science & Technology
Law (13865)

Cambridge
Catalyst (14044) ....(Paid) 50,000
Journal of Machine Learning Research (14078)

Medford
Applied Biochemistry and Biotechnology (14319)

Pittsfield
Photonics Spectra (14471) ....(Controlled) ‡86,500

Worcester
Science & Engineering Network News (14688)

MICHIGAN
Ann Arbor
Michigan Academician (14759) ....(Paid) ⊕850
Wetlands (14772)

MINNESOTA
St. Paul
Hydrological Science and
Technology (16380) ....(Controlled) 500

MISSISSIPPI
Jackson
Mississippi Geology (16703) ....(Non-paid) 1,100

MISSOURI
Kansas City
Philosophy of Science (17191) ....(Paid) 2,280
(Non-paid) 20

St. Joseph
Creation Research Society
Quarterly (17391) 2,000

Springfield
Forensic Examiner (17600)

NEBRASKA
Lincoln
Transactions of the Nebraska Academy of
Sciences (18123)

NEW JERSEY
Edison
Spectroscopy (18789) ....(Controlled) ‡28,612

Hoboken
Color Research and Application (18917) 1,700
Cytometry (18925) 24,500
Earth Surface Processes and Landforms (18934)
Environmental and Molecular
Mutagenesis (18940) 10,850
Heat Transfer - Japanese Research (18960) 400
Hematological Oncology (18961)
International Journal for Numerical Methods in
Engineering (18990)
International Journal of Quantum
Chemistry (18995) 5950
Journal of Applied Polymer
Science (19003) 10,500
Journal of Applied Toxicology (19004)
Journal of Quaternary
Science (19043) ....(Paid) 4,200
Journal of Research in Science
Teaching (19045) 19,950
Journal of Thermal Analysis and Calorimetry (19050)

Microscopy Research and
Technique (19062) 5600
Microwave and Optical Technology
Letters (19064) 4900
Packaging Technology and
Science (19078) 2,800
Pharmacoepidemiology and Drug
Safety (19082) 2,800
Phytochemical Analysis (19083) 3,500
Phytotherapy Research (19084) 4,200
Polymer International (19085)
Polymers for Advanced Technologies (19086)
Proteins: Structure, Function, and
Genetics (19089) 8400
Reviews in Medical Virology (19099) ....(Paid) 3,500
Science Education (19101) 14,350

Mahwah
Neural Computing Surveys (19203)
Transportation Human Factors (19206)

Morris Plains
R & D Magazine (19305) ....(Controlled) 90,230

Newark
Polymer Preprints (19363) ....(Controlled) 9,000

River Edge
International Journal on Artificial Intelligence
Tools (19508)
International Journal of Intelligent and Cooperative
Information Systems (19510)
Journal of Knot Theory and Its Ramifications
(JKTR) (19516)
Journal of Modern Physics B (19518)

Totowa
Molecular Biotechnology (19652) ....(Paid) 350

NEW MEXICO
Albuquerque
New Mexico Journal of Science (19780)
The Skeptical Inquirer (19786) ....(Paid) ‡34,091
(Non-paid) ‡1,598

Las Cruces
Tamara (19877)

Socorro
New Mexico Geology (19959) ....(Combined) 650

NEW YORK
Bronx
Applied Science & Technology Index (20252)
General Science Index (20270)

Forest Hills
The Velikovskian (20617) 235

Geneseo
SUNY Geneseo Journal of Science and
Mathematics (20650)

Hauppauge
International Journal of Space Research (20718)

Ithaca
Cornell Science & Technology
Magazine (20799) ....‡3,000
ISIS (20805) ....‡3,836

Larchmont
Antioxidants and Redox Signaling (20889)
Astrobiology (20891)
Cloning and Stem Cells (20894)
Journal of Aerosol Medicine (20904)
Journal of Anti-Aging Medicine (20907)

Melville
Physiological Chemistry and Physics and Medical
NMR (21057) ....(Combined) 353

New York
Acta Numerica (21145) ....(Paid) ‡148
(Non-paid) ‡5
Adsorption (21151)
Advances in Health Sciences Education (21155)
American Journal of Preventive
Medicine (21198) ....(Paid) ‡2,500
(Non-paid) ‡18
Applied Composite Materials (21229)
Aquaculture International (21235)
Arabic Sciences and Philosophy (21239) 450
Archival Science (21244)
Behavioral and Brain Sciences (21294) 2,100
BioComplexity (21311)
BioControl (21312)
Biomedical Safety and Standards (21322)
Brain and Mind (21336)
The British Journal for the History of
Science (21340) 1,600

Catalysis Surveys from Japan (21380)
Cellular and Molecular Neurobiology (21387)
Cellulose (21388)
Chromosome Research (21414)
Combustion, Explosion, and Shock Waves (21452)
Communications in Theoretical Physics (21462)
Computational Geosciences (21469)
Computational & Mathematical Organization
Theory (21470)
Cybernetics (21528)
Dangerous Properties of Industrial Materials
Report (21536)
Discover (21555) ....(Paid) 1,005,981
Environmental Fluid Mechanics (21617)
Environmental Modeling & Assessment (21620)
Environmental Monitoring and Assessment (21621)
The Environmentalist (21623)
Evolution and Human Behavior (21659)
Evolutionary Ecology (21660)
Extremes (21671)
Flow, Turbulence and Combustion (21707)
Genetic Resources and Crop Evolution (21751)
GeoJournal (21754)
Geotechnical and Geological Engineering (21758)
Global Change & Human Health (21769)
Glycoconjugate (21773)
High-Purity Substances (21801)
Higher-Order and Symbolic Computation (21803)
The Histochemical Journal (21804)
Hyperfine Interactions (21840)
IEEE Spectrum (21849) ....(Paid) 3,39,000
(Non-paid) 30,699
Inorganic Materials (21875)
Instructional Science (21882)
Instruments and Experimental Techniques (21883)
Integrated Pest Management (21886)
Interface Science (21890)
International Journal of Food Properties (21905)
International Journal of Fracture (21906)
International Journal of Speech Technology (21919)
Investigational New Drugs (21945)
Journal of Algebraic Combinatorics (21980)
Journal of the American Society for Psychical
Research (21985) 1,600
Journal of Applied Electrochemistry (21990)
Journal of Applied Phycology (21993)
Journal of Atmospheric Chemistry (22002)
Journal of Biological Physics (22010)
Journal of Biomolecular NMR (22013)
Journal of Computer-Aided Materials Design (22035)
Journal of Computer-Aided Molecular Design (22036)
Journal of Computer-Assisted Microscopy (22037)
Journal of Cryptology (22042) ....(Combined) 1,800
Journal of Cultural Heritage (22044)
Journal of Dispersion Science &
Technology (22049) 400
Journal of Elasticity (22057)
Journal of Electroceramics (22058)
Journal of Fluorescence (22072)
Journal for General Philosophy of Science (22078)
Journal of Inclusion Phenomena and Macrocyclic
Chemistry (22092)
Journal of Intelligent and Robotic Systems (22101)
Journal of Mammalian Evolution (22118)
Journal of Materials Science (22123)
Journal of Materials Science Letters (22124)
Journal of Mathematical Chemistry (22126)
Journal of Nanoparticle Research (22138)
Journal of Neurocytology (22142)
Journal of Nonlinear
Science (22145) ....(Combined) 425
Journal of Paleolimnology (22150)
Journal of Plant Growth
Regulation (22160) ....(Combined) 825
Journal of Porous Materials (22163)
Journal of Science Education and
Technology (22182)
Journal of Science Teacher Education (22183)
Journal of Scientific Computing (22184)
Journal of Sol-Gel Science and Technology (22189)
Journal of Soviet Laser Research (22191)
Journal of Structural Chemistry (22195)
Kinetics and Catalysis (22222)
Letters in Mathematical Physics (22247)
Letters in Peptide Science (22248)
Lifetime Data Analysis (22255)
Machine Learning (22272)
Magnetohydrodynamics (22275)
Materials Science (22291)
Measurement Techniques (22304)
Mechanics of Composite Materials (22307)
Melts (22314)
Metal Science and Heat Treatment (22322)
Metallurgist (22323)
Micropaleontology (22332) ....(Combined) 780
Minds and Machines (22337)
Molecular Biology Reports (22354)

Circ.   Circ.   Circ.

SCIENCE (GENERAL) (continued)

Molecular Breeding (22355)
Molecular Engineering (22358)
Multibody System Dynamics (22378)
Mycopathologia (22389)
NASA Tech Briefs (22393) .....(Controlled) ‡200,000
Neural Processing Letters (22422)
Neutron News (22427) ....(Combined) 4,100
Nonlinear Dynamics (22465)
Nonlinear Dynamics, Psychology, and Life
   Sciences (22466)
Nutrient Cycling in Agroecosystems (22475)
Optical Networks Magazine (22499)
Optimization and Engineering (22500)
Origins of Life and Evolution of the
   Biosphere (22504)
Pharmacy World & Science (22548)
Photosynthesis Research (22553)
Pituitary (22554)
Plant Cell, Tissue and Organ Culture (22557)
Plant Foods for Human Nutrition (22560)
Plant and Soil (22561)
Popular Science (22582) ....(Paid) 1,566,817
Prevention Science (22593)
Quantitative Microbiology (22616)
Reaction Kinetics and Catalysis Letters (22627)
ReCall (22638) 650
Refractories (22641)
Risk Analysis (22669)
RNA (22672)
Science in Context (22711) 450
Science & Education (22712)
Scientific American (22714) ....(Paid) 687,437
Subsurface Sensing Technologies and
   Applications (22804)

Paul Smiths
Adirondack Journal of Environmental
   Studies (23083) ....(Combined) 350

Troy
Separation Science and
   Technology (23458) ....(Paid) 600

Woodbury
Genome Research (23590)

Yorktown Heights
IBM Journal of Research and
   Development (23606) ....(Combined) ‡14,000

NORTH CAROLINA
Cary
Cerebral Cortex (23687) ....(Paid) 700

Chapel Hill
The Cleft Palate-Craniofacial Journal (23704)

Durham
Journal of Parapsychology (23831) ....(Paid) ‡872
                                       (Non-paid) ‡117

Research Triangle Park
American Scientist (24183) ....(Paid) 92,407
Experimental Lung Research (24184) ....‡390
Journal of Vacuum Science and Technology A &
   B (24186) ....‡6,900

Winston-Salem
The Journal of Parasitology (24320)

OHIO
Cleveland
Molecular Endocrinology (24927)

Columbus
Batelle Solutions
   Update (25000) ....(Non-paid) 40,000
School Science and Mathematics (25061) .....‡3500

Kent
The Ohio Journal of
   Science (25277) ....(Paid) ‡2,000

OKLAHOMA
Tulsa
The Leading Edge (26120) ....⊕16,990

OREGON
Eugene
LCGC (26321) ....(Controlled) ‡51,482

PENNSYLVANIA
Emmaus
Compost Science & Utilization (26876) ....(Paid) 800

Exton
Maro Polymer Links/Alerts (26918) ....(Paid) ‡100
                                       (Controlled) ‡5

Media
Age (27241)

Philadelphia
Annals of Science (27380)
History and Philosophy of the Life Sciences (27483)
International Journal of Geographical Information
   Science (27498)
International Journal of Hyperthermia (27499)
International Journal of Pest Management (27504)
International Journal of Remote Sensing (27507)
International Journal of Science Education (27508)
Mechanics of Advanced Materials and
   Structures (27562)
Proceedings of the American Philosophical
   Society (27648) ....(Paid) ‡650
                                       (Non-paid) ‡1,200
Progress in Natural Science (27649)
The Scientist (27656) ....(Paid) 1,240
                                       50,041
                                       4,419

Pittsburgh
Ancient Philosophy (27758) ....(Combined) 750
Carnegie Magazine (27764) ....(Paid) 28,679
Journal of Research of the National Institute of
   Standards and Technology (27804)

Warrendale
Journal of Materials Research (28113) ....‡2,300

RHODE ISLAND
Providence
Employment Information in the Mathematical
   Sciences (28396) ....(Paid) ‡580

SOUTH CAROLINA
Columbia
Journal of Cluster Science (28551)

TENNESSEE
Hixson
Tennessee Academy of Science
   Journal (29222) ....‡1,100

Memphis
Journal of Biomolecular Techniques (29371)

Oak Ridge
Oak Ridge National Laboratory
   Review (29550) ....(Non-paid) ‡6,100

TEXAS
College Station
Palynology (30047) ....(Controlled) 952

Richardson
Issues in Science and
   Technology (30975) ....‡18,000

VIRGINIA
Arlington
NSTA Reports! (31815) ....(Paid) 53,000
Science Scope (31828) ....(Paid) ‡15,000
                                       (Non-paid) ‡26,000
The Science Teacher (31829) ....‡27,000

Blacksburg
Wood & Fiber Science (31880) ....‡800

Fairfax
Journal of Environmental Science and Health, Part B:
   Pesticides, Food Contaminants, and Agricultural
   Wastes (32021) ....(Paid) 325

Harrisonburg
Journal of Mine Action (32140)

Ivy
World Climate Report (32174) .....(Combined) 3,000

Mc Lean
Science Illustrated (32255) .....(Controlled) ‡110,000

Middleburg
Journal of the American Water Resources
   Association (32272) 3,000

Norfolk
Journal of Interactive Learning Research (32288)

Reston
Journal of Cold Regions Engineering (32372)

Richmond
Brain Injury (32430)

Springfield
Environmental Carcinogenesis & Ecotoxicology
   Reviews (32543) ....(Paid) ‡250

Journal of Environmental Science and Health, Part C:
   Environmental Carcinogenesis and Ectoxicology
   Reviews (32545) 250
Journal of Imaging Science and Technology (32546)

WASHINGTON
Ferndale
The North American Technocrat (32768) 1,500

Pullman
Northwest Science (32905) ....(Paid) ‡687
                                       (Non-paid) ‡70

Seattle
Bamboo Science & Culture (32946)

WISCONSIN
Madison
Crop Science (33931) ....‡4,500
Ground Water (33944)
The Journal of Sex Research (33955)
Soil Science Society of America
   Journal (33973) ....‡4,500

Waukesha
Astronomy (34394) ....(Paid) ★152,821

ALBERTA, CANADA
Calgary
Arctic (34627)

Medicine Hat
Demining Technology Information Forum
   Journal (34809)

BRITISH COLUMBIA, CANADA
Victoria
Archaea (35206) ....(Paid) 500
                                       (Non-paid) 500
naturalSCIENCE (35223) 16,000
YES Mag (35231) ....(Paid) 18,000

NOVA SCOTIA, CANADA
Dartmouth
Journal of Northwest Atlantic Fishery
   Science (35547)
NAFO Scientific Council Studies (35549)

ONTARIO, CANADA
Ottawa
Physics Essays (36272) ....‡171

Port Burwell
The Canadian Journal of
   Herbalism (36331) 1,000

QUEBEC, CANADA
L'Annonciation
Emploi Plus (36939) ....(Combined) 500

Montreal
Canadian Journal of Regional Science (37098)
Les Debrouillards (37176) ....(Controlled) 37,500
Quebec Science (37213) ....(Paid) 22,601

Westmount
The Dawson Research Journal of Experimental
   Science (DRJES) (37442)

SEED AND NURSERY TRADE

**See also Florists and Floriculture;
Landscape Architecture; Turf and Turf
Maintenance**

FLORIDA
Clearwater
Nursery Business Retailer (5989) ....(Paid) ‡1,806
                                       (Non-paid) ‡5,932

Winter Park
Ornamental Outlook (6884) 13,175

ILLINOIS
Batavia
Grower Talks (8054) ....(Paid) 9,230

Chicago
American Nurseryman (8261) ....(Paid) 14,961
Arbor Age (8266) ....(Paid) 120
                                       18,469
Nursery News (8516) ....(Paid) ‡2,246
                                       (Non-paid) ‡19,446

Des Plaines
Seed World (8771) ....(Paid) 1,493
                                       (Non-paid) 3,649

IOWA
Cedar Falls
Seed & Crops Digest　**(10662)** ....(Paid) 2,000
(Controlled) 3,000

KANSAS
Lecompton
Christmas Trees　**(11588)** ....(Paid) ‡4,391
(Controlled) ‡41

MISSOURI
St. Louis
American Christmas Tree Journal　**(17409)** ....‡1,600

OHIO
Columbus
Ohio Florists Association
Bulletin　**(25044)** ....(Paid) 3,500

OREGON
Portland
Pacific Coast Nurseryman and Garden Supply
Dealer　**(26496)** ....(Paid) ‡6,840
(Non-paid) ‡3,624

Wilsonville
Digger　**(26614)** ....(Controlled) ‡5,000

TEXAS
Fort Worth
Garden Center Products &
Supplies　**(30340)** 15,000

ONTARIO, CANADA
Milton
Landscape Trades　**(36049)** ....(Combined) •8,240

QUEBEC, CANADA
Quebec
Espaces Verts　**(37283)** ....‡2,250
Option Serre　**(37294)** ....‡1,580
Quebec Vert　**(37295)** ....‡3,760

SEISMOLOGY

CALIFORNIA
El Cerrito
Bulletin　**(1859)** ....(Paid) ‡2,737
Seismological Research Letters　**(1862)**

DISTRICT OF COLUMBIA
Washington
Computational Seismology　**(5430)**

SELLING AND SALESMANSHIP

See also Advertising and Marketing;
General Merchandise

CALIFORNIA
Lake Forest
Agency Sales Magazine　**(2141)** ....‡18,000

DISTRICT OF COLUMBIA
Washington
ASMC Sales & Marketing
Magazine　**(5369)** ....‡4,000
Sales & Marketing Ideas　**(5776)** 14,000

FLORIDA
Lake Mary
Christian Retailing　**(6276)** ....(Controlled) ‡10,500

Palm Beach Gardens
Selling　**(6545)**

ILLINOIS
Chicago
Velocity　**(8597)** ....(Controlled) 2,500
4,000

Mount Prospect
NSGA Retail Focus　**(9248)** ....(Paid) ‡3,000

Tinley Park
Money Maker's Monthly　**(9686)** ......(Paid) ‡125,000
(Non-paid) ‡125,000

IOWA
Burlington
American Salesman　**(10637)** ....‡1,500

KANSAS
Overland Park
The Auctioneer　**(11697)** ....‡5,800
Retail Store Image　**(11728)** ....(Controlled) 25,000

NEW YORK
Binghamton
Journal of Convention & Exhibition
Management　**(20168)**
Journal of Promotion Management　**(20193)** 305

Great Neck
Journal of Business Forecasting
Methods　**(20691)** ....(Paid) 3,500

Manhasset
CRN　**(20994)** ....(Free) 117,500

New York
Sales & Marketing Management　**(22701)** .....‡70,000

OHIO
Akron
Counterman　**(24578)** ....(Controlled) 50,062

Fairborn
Contractor Marketing　**(25186)** ......(Controlled) 4,500

Powell
Electronic Distribution Today　**(25491)** 5,000

TEXAS
Arlington
Used Car Dealer　**(29738)** ....(Paid) ‡15,537
(Non-paid) ‡358

Dallas
Home Health Products　**(30161)**
Retailer and Marketing
News　**(30180)** ....(Controlled) ‡7,500

Denton
The Journal of Personal Selling and Sales
Management　**(30240)** ....(Paid) ‡700

VIRGINIA
Fredericksburg
Selling Power　**(32087)** ....(Paid) 100,000
(Controlled) 90,000

WISCONSIN
Iola
Comics & Games
Retailer　**(33814)** ....(Non-paid) ‡4,434

Milwaukee
Spare Time　**(34103)** ....‡200,000

SERVICE INDUSTRIES

CALIFORNIA
Agoura
Tattoo Industry　**(1382)**

Richmond
American Window Cleaner
Magazine　**(2920)** ....(Paid) 1,100
(Controlled) 7,900

Sacramento
Fair Dealer　**(2999)** ....(Controlled) 2,200

CONNECTICUT
Stamford
Customer Support
Management　**(5147)** ....(Combined) 42,000

DISTRICT OF COLUMBIA
Washington
Quotarian　**(5757)** ....(Controlled) ⊕8,322

FLORIDA
Fort Myers
Sbusiness　**(6097)** ....(Controlled) 22,000

MAINE
Waldoboro
Today Magazine　**(13070)** 6,500

MISSOURI
Springfield
Fairs and Expos　**(17599)**

WISCONSIN
Milwaukee
Contracting Profits　**(34064)** ....(Paid) 50
(Controlled) 35,000

SHIPS AND SHIPPING

See also Boats and Marine

CALIFORNIA
Irvine
World Dredging, Mining &
Construction　**(2093)** ....‡3,400

Long Beach
Pacific Shipper　**(2172)** ....(Paid) 5,083

FLORIDA
Odessa
WWS/World Wide Shipping　**(6480)** 9,500

MAINE
Portland
Professional Mariner　**(13018)** ....(Paid) ‡31,000

MARYLAND
Camp Springs
Seafarers LOG　**(13402)** ....(Non-paid) ‡43,000

Towson
Port of Baltimore　**(13764)** ....(Controlled) ‡11,500

MASSACHUSETTS
Indian Orchard
Titanic Commutator　**(14256)**

Quincy
American Journal of Transportation　**(14488)**

Salem
The American Neptune　**(14512)** ....‡1,550

MICHIGAN
Boyne City
Seaway Review　**(14834)** ....(Paid) ‡10,200
(Non-paid) ‡400

MISSOURI
St. Louis
The Waterways Journal　**(17530)** ....‡5,728

NEW YORK
Garden City
CNS Focus　**(20636)** ....(Non-paid) 7,000

New York
Journal of Navigation　**(22139)** ....(Paid) 455
(Non-paid) 3,346
Marine Log　**(22283)** ....(Paid) 500
(Non-paid) 25,000
Maritime Reporter and Engineering
News　**(22284)** ....(Non-paid) ‡30,822

SOUTH CAROLINA
Charleston
Port News　**(28516)** ....(Combined) 9,000

WASHINGTON
Seattle
MARINE DIGEST　**(32984)** ....(Controlled) ‡7,200

BRITISH COLUMBIA, CANADA
West Vancouver
Harbour & Shipping　**(35238)** 2,000

SHOES, LEATHER, AND LUGGAGE

CONNECTICUT
Norwalk
Accessories　**(5048)** ....(Paid) 11,000
(Non-paid) 11,000
Travelware　**(5077)** ....(Paid) 661
(Non-paid) 11,778

MASSACHUSETTS
Arlington
American Shoemaking　**(13816)** ....(Paid) 1,836
(Non-paid) 719
The Leather Manufacturer　**(13820)** ....‡2,000

NEW JERSEY
Princeton
Travel Goods Showcase　**(19476)** ....(Paid) ‡9,897
(Non-paid) ‡981

Circulation: ★ = ABC; △ = BPA; ♦ = CAC; • = CCAB; ☐ = VAC; ⊕ = PO Statement; ‡ = Publisher's Report; Boldface figures = sworn; Light figures = estimated.

3227

Trade, Technical, and Professional Publications

Circ.   Circ.   Circ.

SHOES, LEATHER, AND LUGGAGE (continued)

NEW YORK
New York
Footwear News (FN) (21716) ....(Paid) 11,725
(Non-paid) 3,311
Outerwear Magazine (22513) ....‡17,000

ONTARIO, CANADA
Markham
Luggage, Leathergoods &
Accessories (36027) ....(Non-paid) 4,500

SOCIAL PROGRAMS

See also Philanthropy and Humanitarianism

CALIFORNIA
Santa Monica
RAND Review (3715) ....(Controlled) 15,000

Thousand Oaks
AFFILIA: Journal of Women and Social
Work (3847) ....(Paid) ‡700

DISTRICT OF COLUMBIA
Washington
Children's Voice (5410) 15,000
Housing Policy Debate (5530) ......(Non-paid) 7,000
The Humanitarian (5537)

ILLINOIS
Skokie
School Social Work Journal (9610)

MICHIGAN
Detroit
Psychoanalytic Social Work (14945) ....(Paid) 569

MINNESOTA
Minneapolis
New Rules Journal (16114) ....(Paid) 4,000

St. Paul
Child and Youth Services (16370) ....(Paid) 417

NEW JERSEY
New Brunswick
Journal of Religion, Disability &
Health (19334) ....(Paid) 335

NEW YORK
Binghamton
Journal of Ethnic & Cultural Diversity in Social
Work (20171) 732
Journal of Family Social Work (20173) 654
Journal of Health Care
Chaplaincy (20176) ....(Controlled) 417
Journal of HIV/AIDS & Social Services (20179)
Journal of Human Behavior in the Social
Environment (20181)
Journal of Immigrant & Refugee Services (20183)
Journal of Religion & Spirituality in Social Work:
Social Thought (20196) ....‡1,000
Journal of Social Service Research (20198) 535
Social Policy Journal (20216)
Social Work with Groups (20217) 1,063
Social Work in Mental Health (20218)

New York
European Journal of Social Security (21652)
Journal of Cognitive
Psychotherapy (22029) ....(Paid) 700
(Controlled) 80

VIRGINIA
Alexandria
Catholic Charities USA (31652) ....‡3,000
Journal of Addictions and Offender
Counseling (31685)

SOCIAL SCIENCES

ARIZONA
Tucson
Perspectives in Mexican American
Studies (959) ....(Paid) 500
Studies in Latin American Popular Culture (965)

CALIFORNIA
Berkeley
Contexts (1510) ....(Paid) ❏1,040
Journal of Social and Evolutionary Systems (1537)

Measurement (1541)

Hayward
Journal of Gay and Lesbian Social
Services (2043) ....(Paid) 422

Long Beach
Sexuality & Culture (2175) 1,000

Los Altos
The Future of Children (2192)

Los Angeles
Administration in Social
Work (2199) ....(Controlled) ‡1,577

Palm Springs
Futures (2759)

Palo Alto
Annual Review of Sociology (2794)

Pasadena
Journal of Interdisciplinary
Studies (2819) ....(Non-paid) 1,000

San Diego
Legal Theory (3223) 600

San Francisco
(a) (3323)

Thousand Oaks
Cross-Cultural Research (3861) ....(Paid) ‡500
Politics & Society (3908) ....(Paid) 800

CONNECTICUT
New Britain
Multicultural Perspectives (4976)

DISTRICT OF COLUMBIA
Washington
American Review of Canadian Studies (5342)
Health & Social Work (5523) 6,500
Mediterranean Quarterly (5646) ....(Paid) 650
Youth Today (5874) ....(Combined) 58,000

FLORIDA
Bonita Springs
Cultic Studies Review (5947)

Orlando
The Journal of Human Performance in Extreme
Environments (6499) ....(Paid) 200

ILLINOIS
Chicago
The Journal of Comparative Asian
Development (8434)
Public Culture (8544) ....(Combined) 1000
Signs (8564) ....‡3,149

Wheaton
Journal of Outcome Measurement (9756)

INDIANA
Bloomington
Mongolian Studies (9845)

IOWA
Cedar Falls
Journal of Social Studies Research (10658)

KANSAS
Topeka
The Social Science Journal (11836) ....‡1,400

Winfield
International Social Science
Review (11909) ....(Paid) ‡7,000
(Non-paid) ‡150

MAINE
Orono
Northeast Folklore (13002)

MARYLAND
Baltimore
Theory & Event (13253)

Cheverly
Romani Studies (13407) ....(Paid) 272

College Park
Science Communication (13439) ....(Paid) ‡418
(Non-paid) ‡12

Silver Spring
Demography (13724) ....(Paid) 3,000
Social Education (13746) ....(Paid) ‡29,000

MASSACHUSETTS
Boston
Health and Human Rights (13899) ....(Paid) ‡970
Journal of Progressive Human
Services (13918) ....(Controlled) ‡1,099

Cambridge
DAEDALUS (14048) ....‡20,000
The Harvard International Journal of
Press/Politics (14059)

Chestnut Hill
Philosophy & Social Criticism (14132)

Malden
Sociological Methodology (14300)
Sociological Theory (14301)

Williamstown
Gastronomica (14659)

MINNESOTA
Minneapolis
Cultural Critique (16071)
NST (Nature, Society and Thought) (16118) 500

NEBRASKA
Lincoln
Great Plains Quarterly (18085) ......(Controlled) 600
Great Plains Research (18086) ......(Combined) 500

NEW JERSEY
Hoboken
Behavioral Interventions (18901)
International Journal of Population
Geography (18994)
System Dynamics Review (19114) ....(Paid) 7000

Mahwah
Mind, Culture, and Activity (19202)
Understanding Statistics (19207)

New Brunswick
Social Text (19339) ....(Combined) 650

Princeton
Child and Family Behavior
Therapy (19457) ....(Controlled) ‡598

Rutherford
The Fountain (19526)

Somerset
Journal of Income
Distribution (19563) ....(Combined) 200

NEW MEXICO
Albuquerque
Human Nature (19773)

NEW YORK
Armonk
Russian Social Science
Review (20095) ....(Paid) ⊕487

Binghamton
Adoption Quarterly (20150)
African Philosophy (20151)
Ijele (20155)
Jenda (20159)
Journal on African Immigration (JAI) (20161)
Journal of Human Behavior in the Social
Environment (20181)
Journal of Lesbian Studies (20186)
Journal of Religion & Abuse (20195)
Journal of Religion & Spirituality in Social Work:
Social Thought (20196) ....‡1,000
Journal of Social Work in Long-Term Care (20199)
Journal of Social Work Practice in the
Addictions (20200)
Journal of Teaching in the Addictions (20201)
Social Policy Journal (20216)
Social Work in Mental Health (20218)
Theory and Research in Social
Education (20219) 896
West Africa Review (20220)

Bronx
Social Sciences Index (20287)

Buffalo
Child Study Journal (20374)

Ithaca
Human Ecology Forum (20802) ....(Paid) ‡600
(Non-paid) ‡2,500

Larchmont
CyberPsychology and Behavior (20895)

Numbers cited after listings are entry numbers rather than page numbers.

New York
European Journal of Population **(21650)**
European Journal of Social Quality **(21651)**
European Judaism **(21654)**
GeoJournal **(21754)**
German Politics and Society **(21759)**
Guttmacher Report on Public Policy **(21784)**
Human Life Review **(21830)** ....(Paid) 6,000
Human Studies **(21835)**
Indo-Iranian Journal **(21864)**
International Journal of Sexuality and Gender
　Studies **(21918)**
Journal of Aging and Identity **(21978)**
Journal of Comparative Policy Analysis **(22032)**
Journal of Cultural Heritage **(22044)**
Journal of Gender, Culture, and Health **(22077)**
Journal of Happiness Studies **(22082)**
Journal of Heuristics **(22088)**
Journal of Social Policy **(22187)** 2,000
Nomadic Peoples **(22464)**
Prospects **(22600)** 600
Social Research **(22756)** ....‡3,000
Studies in Gender and
　Sexuality **(22801)** ....(Combined) 700

Staten Island
Migration World Magazine **(23360)** ....‡1,250

NORTH CAROLINA
Chapel Hill
Southern Cultures **(23724)** ....(Paid) 2,400

Durham
Comparative Studies of South Asia, Africa, and the
　Middle East **(23815)** ....(Paid) 450
GLQ **(23822)** ....(Combined) 1400
Nepantla **(23835)**

OHIO
Bowling Green
Popular Music and Society **(24700)**

Columbus
Journal of Poverty **(25027)**
Journal for the Psychoanalysis of Culture and
　Society **(25028)**

Oxford
Journal of African American
　Men **(25455)** ....(Paid) ‡1,100

PENNSYLVANIA
Glenolden
Journal of Scotch-Irish Studies **(26946)**

Harrisburg
Global Virtue Ethics Review **(26993)**
The New Social Worker **(27000)** ....(Paid) 2,000
　　　　　　　　　　　　　　　　(Non-paid) 1,000

Hazleton
Journal of Emotional Abuse **(27033)** ......(Paid) ‡25
　　　　　　　　　　　　　　　(Non-paid) ‡4

Johnstown
The Pennsylvania
　Geographer **(27088)** ....(Combined) 450

Media
Voices **(27244)** ....(Controlled) 500

Pittsburgh
Public Affairs Quarterly **(27839)**

TEXAS
Austin
Social Studies and the Young
　Learner **(29805)** ....(Paid) 6,000

Lubbock
The Leadership Quarterly **(30714)**

San Marcos
Journal of Police and Criminal
　Psychology **(31084)** ....(Controlled) 350

VIRGINIA
Ashburn
Journal of Leisure Research **(31852)**

Fairfax
Journal of Social
　History **(32024)** ....(Combined) 1,500

Herndon
American Journal of Islamic Social
　Sciences **(32160)** 1,700

Richmond
The Journal of the Jamestown Rediscovery
　Center **(32441)**

WASHINGTON
Ferndale
The North American Technocrat **(32768)** 1,500

WISCONSIN
Madison
The Journal of Sex Research **(33955)**
Substance **(33975)** ....(Paid) 500

ALBERTA, CANADA
Calgary
Journal of Comparative Family Studies **(34651)**

MANITOBA, CANADA
Winnipeg
Canadian Journal of Urban Research **(35320)**

ONTARIO, CANADA
London
Identity **(35984)**

Ottawa
Canadian Social Trends **(36228)** ....(Paid) 4,500

Sudbury
Canadian Journal of Program Evaluation/Revue
　Canadienne D'evaluation de
　Programme **(36415)** 1,525

Toronto
Canadian Journal of Sociology/Cahiers canadiens de
　sociologie **(36512)** ....(Combined) 1000
C.D. Howe Institute Commentary **(36543)**
The Tocqueville Review/La Revue
　Tocqueville **(36761)** ....(Combined) 500
Urban History Review **(36783)** ....(Paid) 400

PRINCE EDWARD ISLAND, CANADA
Charlottetown
Canadian Review of Studies in
　Nationalism **(36913)** ....(Controlled) 600

QUEBEC, CANADA
Montreal
Canadian Journal of Regional Science **(37098)**
Canadian Review of Sociology and
　Anthropology **(37100)**

Ste.-Foy
Anthropologie et Societes **(37335)**

SOCIETY FOR THE PREVENTION OF CRUELTY TO ANIMALS AND ANTI-VIVISECTION

CALIFORNIA
San Francisco
Our Animals **(3410)** ....(Non-paid) ‡52,000

DISTRICT OF COLUMBIA
Washington
HSUS News **(5534)** ....(Free) 300,000

MASSACHUSETTS
Boston
Animals Magazine **(13850)** ....(Paid) 70,000

PENNSYLVANIA
Jenkintown
The AV Magazine **(27083)** ......(Combined) ‡10,000

SOCIOLOGY

See also Philanthropy and Humanitarianism

ARIZONA
Tucson
Language in Society **(953)** 1900

CALIFORNIA
Berkeley
Contexts **(1510)** ....(Paid) ❏1,040
Social Problems **(1561)** 3,757
Sociological Perspectives **(1562)** ....‡1,200

Fullerton
Structural Equation Modeling **(1990)**

Los Angeles
REASON **(2378)** ....(Paid) 55,000

Novato
Journal of Social Behavior and
　Personality **(2650)** ....(Paid) ‡600

Palo Alto
Annual Review of Sociology **(2794)**

San Diego
Social Science Research **(3276)**

San Francisco
Harmony **(3369)** ....(Paid) ‡1,000
　　　　　　　　　　　　　　　(Non-paid) ‡100
Social Justice **(3443)** ....(Paid) ‡3,000
　　　　　　　　　　　　　　　(Non-paid) ‡50

Stanford
Social Psychology Quarterly **(3797)** ....‡3,250

Thousand Oaks
Administration & Society **(3846)** ....(Paid) ‡700
AFFILIA: Journal of Women and Social
　Work **(3847)** ....(Paid) ‡700
American Behavioral Scientist **(3848)**
The Annals of the American Academy of Political and
　Social Science **(3850)** ....(Paid) ‡4,000
Criminal Justice Abstracts **(3859)** ....‡800
Evaluation Review **(3868)** ....(Paid) ‡1,600
　　　　　　　　　　　　　　(Non-paid) ‡208
Indian Economic and Social History Review **(3874)**
Journal of Applied Behavioral
　Science **(3879)** ....(Paid) 1,500
Journal of Black Studies **(3882)** ....(Paid) ‡1,000
Journal of Family Issues **(3889)** ....(Paid) ‡800
Journal of Language and Social
　Psychology **(3894)** ....(Paid) 300
Journal of Sport & Social
　Issues **(3901)** ....(Paid) 600
Philosophy of the Social
　Sciences **(3907)** ....(Paid) ‡1,350
　　　　　　　　　　　　　　(Non-paid) ‡114
Politics & Society **(3908)** ....(Paid) 800
Research on Social Work
　Practice **(3911)** ....(Paid) ‡1,700
Sage Family Studies
　Abstracts **(3912)** ....(Paid) ‡300
Sage Urban Studies Abstracts **(3914)** ....(Paid) ‡300
SMR/Sociological Methods and
　Research **(3917)** ....(Paid) ‡700
Urban Affairs Review **(3918)** ....(Paid) ‡1,110
Work and Occupations **(3921)** ....(Paid) ‡700
Youth & Society **(3923)** ....(Paid) ‡700

CONNECTICUT
New Haven
Journal of Conflict
　Resolution **(4993)** ....(Paid) ‡2,363
　　　　　　　　　　　　　　(Non-paid) ‡114

DISTRICT OF COLUMBIA
Washington
Child Welfare **(5408)** ....‡6,000
Children & Schools **(5409)** 2,400
The CQ Researcher **(5447)** ....(Paid) ‡5,000
Current **(5453)** ....‡2,174
Gender Issues **(5505)** ....(Paid) ‡700
Health & Social Work **(5523)** 6,500
Journal of Social, Political & Economic
　Studies **(5615)** ....(Paid) ‡1,150
　　　　　　　　　　　　　　(Non-paid) ‡55
The Mankind Quarterly **(5643)** ....(Paid) ‡1,075
　　　　　　　　　　　　　　(Non-paid) ‡60
National Right to Life News **(5680)**
Policy and Practice of Public Human
　Services **(5720)**
Population Bulletin **(5722)** ....‡5,000
The Public Interest **(5750)** 8,000
The Responsive Community **(5764)** ......(Paid) 2,000
The Social Studies **(5795)** ....(Paid) 1,727
Social Work **(5796)** 152,000
Social Work Research **(5797)** ....(Paid) 2,200
Sociology of Education **(5798)** ....‡3,000
Teaching Sociology **(5815)** ....‡2,400

FLORIDA
Orlando
The Journal of Human Performance in Extreme
　Environments **(6499)** ....(Paid) 200

HAWAII
Honolulu
Population Reports **(7718)**

ILLINOIS
Champaign
Policy Studies Journal **(8212)** ....(Paid) ‡2,350
　　　　　　　　　　　　　　(Non-paid) ‡50

Circulation: ★ = ABC; △ = BPA; ♦ = CAC; ● = CCAB; ❏ = VAC; ⊕ = PO Statement; ‡ = Publisher's Report; Boldface figures = sworn; Light figures = estimated.

3229

Circ.

SOCIOLOGY (continued)

Policy Studies Review **(8213)** ....(Paid) ‡2,350
                                      (Non-paid) ‡50
Sociology of Sport Journal **(8216)** ......(Paid) ‡1,119

Chicago
City & Community **(8333)**
Signs **(8564)** ....‡3,149

Normal
Personal Relationships **(9303)** ....(Paid) ‡567
                                      (Non-paid) ‡74

INDIANA
West Lafayette
Contemporary Sociology **(10545)** ....‡7,200

IOWA
Iowa City
The Sociological Quarterly **(10987)** ....‡2,800

KENTUCKY
Lexington
Journal of Caribbean Studies **(12167)** 1,000

LOUISIANA
Lafayette
Deviant Behavior: An Interdisciplinary
   Journal **(12616)** 600
Sociological Spectrum **(12619)**

MARYLAND
Baltimore
American Quarterly **(13120)** ....‡6,240

Bethesda
Futures Research Quarterly **(13338)** ....‡1,500
The Futurist **(13339)** ....‡31,000
Sociological Abstracts **(13379)** ....‡1,900

Silver Spring
Social Education **(13746)** ....(Paid) ‡29,000

MASSACHUSETTS
Boston
Central European History **(13871)**
Ethics & Behavior **(13890)**
Health and Human Rights **(13899)** ....(Paid) ‡970
The WorldPaper **(13973)** ....(Paid) 1,800,000

Malden
Sociological Methodology **(14300)**
Sociological Theory **(14301)**

Waltham
Proof Texts **(14603)** ....‡960

Wellesley
Society **(14617)** ....(Paid) ‡4,500

MICHIGAN
Ann Arbor
Comparative Studies in Society &
   History **(14745)** ....(Paid) ‡2028

Detroit
Against the Current **(14914)** ....(Paid) ‡1,600

Kalamazoo
Journal of Sociology and Social
   Welfare **(15241)** ....‡650

MINNESOTA
Minneapolis
Family Relations **(16077)** ....‡5,000

MISSOURI
St. Louis
Social Justice Review **(17512)** ....(Paid) 4,600
                                      (Non-paid) 500

NEW JERSEY
Hoboken
Applied Cognitive Psychology **(18892)**
Behavioral Interventions **(18901)**
Child Abuse Review **(18911)**
European Journal of Personality **(18944)**
Infant and Child Development **(18973)**
International Journal of Population
   Geography **(18994)**
Journal of International
   Development **(19027)** ....(Paid) 2,800
Psycho-Oncology **(19090)**
Stress and Health **(19109)** ....(Paid) 3,500

Kendall Park
Journal of Jewish Communal
   Service **(19152)** ....‡4,000

Circ.

Somerset
The American Sociologist **(19560)** ....(Paid) ‡800
Armed Forces & Society **(19561)** ....(Paid) ‡1,700

NEW MEXICO
Albuquerque
Business & Society **(19768)**

NEW YORK
Albany
Gender & Society **(19988)** ....(Paid) ‡2,650
                                      (Non-paid) ‡153

Armonk
Chinese Sociology and
   Anthropology **(20071)** ....(Paid) ⊕199
International Journal of Electronic
   Commerce **(20079)** ....(Paid) 254
International Journal of
   Sociology **(20082)** ....(Paid) ⊕302
Sociological Research **(20099)** ....(Paid) ⊕272

Binghamton
Journal of Bisexuality **(20164)**
Journal of Elder Abuse and
   Neglect **(20169)** 1,193
Journal of Ethnic & Cultural Diversity in Social
   Work **(20171)** 732
Journal of Ethnicity in Substance Abuse **(20172)**
Journal of Social Service Research **(20198)** 535
Social Work with Groups **(20217)** 1,063

New York
Continuity and Change **(21496)** 650
European Journal of Sociology **(21653)** 950
Evolution and Human Behavior **(21659)**
Human Ecology **(21828)**
International Journal of Politics, Culture, and
   Society **(21914)**
Journal of Gerontological Social
   Work **(22081)** 998
Journal of Social Distress and the
   Homeless **(22186)**
The Journal of Socio-Economics **(22188)**
Modern Asian Studies **(22347)** 1150
Nations and Nationalism **(22401)**
Population and Development
   Review **(22583)** ....(Paid) ‡2,400
                                  (Controlled) ‡2,600
Population Research and Policy Review **(22584)**
Race & Society **(22620)**
Science & Society **(22713)** 1,923
Social Justice Research **(22754)**
Social Work in Health Care **(22757)** 1,608
Sociological Forum **(22759)**
Studies in Family
   Planning **(22800)** ....(Non-paid) ‡4,400
                                      (Paid) ‡1,200
Studies in Gender and
   Sexuality **(22801)** ....(Combined) 700
Substance Use & Misuse **(22803)** 650
The Urban League Review **(22890)** 500

Rensselaerville
Innovating Magazine **(23182)** ....(Paid) ‡800
                                      (Non-paid) ‡27

Rhinebeck
The Trends Journal **(23186)**

Saratoga Springs
Salmagundi **(23302)** ....(Paid) ‡5,100
                                  (Controlled) ‡200

Staten Island
International Migration Review **(23358)** ....‡2,000
Migration World Magazine **(23360)** ....‡1,250

NORTH CAROLINA
Chapel Hill
Leisure Sciences **(23714)** ....‡311
Social Forces **(23723)** ....(Paid) ‡3,192
                                  (Controlled) ‡110

Raleigh
Social Science Computer Review **(24153)** 1,000

OHIO
Bowling Green
Journal of American Culture **(24693)** ....‡1,300

Cleveland
Journal of Applied Social Studies **(24913)**

OKLAHOMA
Oklahoma City
Human Organization **(25966)** ....‡3,999

Circ.

PENNSYLVANIA
Broomall
Gray Areas **(26737)** ....(Paid) ‡14,000

Pittsburgh
Current Population Reports **(27777)**

University Park
Human Performance **(28076)**

TEXAS
Austin
Journal of the History of Sexuality **(29787)** 1,000

College Station
Contemporary Economic
   Policy **(30039)** ....(Paid) ‡3,200
                                      (Non-paid) ‡75
South Central Review **(30050)** ....(Paid) 1,300

UTAH
Salt Lake City
Journal of Land Resouces and Environmental
   Law **(31434)**

VIRGINIA
Alexandria
Journal of Addictions and Offender
   Counseling **(31685)**
Journal of Social Work Education **(31702)**

Arlington
Studies in Conflict and Terrorism **(31834)** 850

Ashburn
Journal of Leisure Research **(31852)**

Blacksburg
Journal of Health & Social
   Behavior **(31875)** ....‡3,500

WASHINGTON
Seattle
Nonprofit and Voluntary Sector
   Quarterly **(32990)** 1,700
Violence and Victims **(33036)** ....(Paid) 2,500
                                      (Non-paid) 100

WISCONSIN
Madison
American Sociological Review **(33918)** ....‡12,500
The Journal of Sex Research **(33955)**

Milwaukee
Families in Society **(34067)** ....‡4,000

NEW BRUNSWICK, CANADA
Fredericton
Sociology of Religion **(35397)**

ONTARIO, CANADA
London
Identity **(35984)**

Ottawa
Human Rights Tribune/Tribune Des Droits
   Humains **(36249)** ....(Controlled) 1,500

Willowdale
International Journal of Comparative
   Sociology **(36879)**

QUEBEC, CANADA
Montreal
Canadian Review of Sociology and
   Anthropology **(37100)**

SOVIET INTERESTS

MARYLAND
Baltimore
Vestnik **(13260)** ....(Combined) 10,000

MASSACHUSETTS
Malden
The Russian Review **(14299)** ....(Paid) ‡1,700
                                      (Non-paid) ‡100

NEW YORK
Armonk
Anthropology & Archeology of
   Eurasia **(20065)** ....(Paid) ⊕322
Emerging Markets Finance and
   Trade **(20076)** ....(Paid) ⊕196
Journal of Russian and East European
   Psychology **(20087)** ....(Paid) ⊕217

Numbers cited after listings are entry numbers rather than page numbers.

Problems of Economic
  Transition (20091) ....(Paid) ⊕360
Russian Education and
  Society (20093) ....(Paid) ⊕211
Russian Politics and Law (20094) ....(Paid) ⊕248
Russian Social Science
  Review (20095) ....(Paid) ⊕487
Russian Studies in History (20096) ......(Paid) ⊕256
Russian Studies in
  Literature (20097) ....(Paid) ⊕157
Russian Studies in
  Philosophy (20098) ....(Paid) ⊕158
Sociological Research (20099) ....(Paid) ⊕272
Statutes and Decisions: The Laws of the USSR and
  its Successor Stabey (20100) ....(Paid) ⊕145

SPORTING GOODS/RETAIL SPORTS

ALABAMA
Montgomery
Fishing Tackle Retailer (365) ....(Controlled) ‡22,884

CALIFORNIA
Los Angeles
Aquatics International (2213) .....(Non-paid) ★26,500
Pool & Spa News (2373) ....(Paid) 7,800
                                    (Non-paid) 8,000

COLORADO
Boulder
Skiing Trade News (4190) ....(Free) ‡16,875

CONNECTICUT
Woodbury
Ski Area Management (5236) ....(Paid) ‡4,056

FLORIDA
Tallahassee
Bluewater Scuba Electronic & Fax
  Update (6701) 700
Scuba Retailer (6734) 3,000

GEORGIA
Atlanta
Swimming Pool/Spa
  Age (7048) ....(Controlled) 17,064
                                 (Controlled) 17,064

Roswell
Sporting Goods
  Dealer (7519) ....(Controlled) ‡18,000

ILLINOIS
Mount Prospect
NSGA Retail Focus (9248) ....(Paid) ‡3,000

Peoria
Shotgun News (9425) ....(Controlled) 115,000

MINNESOTA
Maple Grove
Archery Business (16036) ....(Controlled) 11,000
Powersports
  Business (16039) ....(Controlled) ‡16,000

Minnetonka
Tack'n Togs
  Merchandising (16176) ....(Controlled) ‡14,264

NEW YORK
Manhasset
Action Sports (20990) ....(Paid) ‡6,500
                                    (Controlled) ‡1,500

New York
Action Sports Retailer (21147)
Fly Fishing Retailer (21709)
Sporting Goods
  Business (22774) ....(Controlled) ‡28,700

WISCONSIN
Iola
Card Trade (33807) ....(Combined) 5,776

ONTARIO, CANADA
Markham
Pool & Spa Marketing (36030) ....(Paid) ‡2,000
                                    (Non-paid) ‡7,000

Woodbridge
Sports Business (36906) ....(Combined) 6,519

QUEBEC, CANADA
Montreal
Bike, Boat & R.V. Trader/Moto, Bateau & Vehicules
  Recreatif Hebdo (37091)

STATE, MUNICIPAL, AND COUNTY ADMINISTRATION
See also Chambers of Commerce and Boards of Trade

ALABAMA
Montgomery
Alabama Municipal Journal (359) ....(Paid) ‡200
                                     (Controlled) ‡4,500

ARIZONA
Phoenix
Southwest Contractor (811) ....(Combined) 6,000

ARKANSAS
North Little Rock
City & Town (1299) ....‡7,400

CALIFORNIA
Berkeley
California Public Employee Relations (1505)
Representations (1555) ....‡1273

Sacramento
The Daily Recorder (2995) ....‡1,122
Western City (3022) ....(Paid) ‡10,500

Thousand Oaks
Journal of Planning Literature (3898) .....(Paid) ‡500
Sage Public Administration
  Abstracts (3913) ....(Paid) ‡300

COLORADO
Denver
Colorado Municipalities (4318) ....(Paid) 4,950
                                     (Controlled) 350
State Legislatures (4361) ....(Paid) ‡18,385

DISTRICT OF COLUMBIA
Washington
County News (5445) ....(Paid) 25,000
                                        (Free) 2,500
Governing Magazine (5517) ....(Controlled) 86,000
Government Executive (5518) ....(Paid) 900
                                     (Controlled) 60,450
National Civic Review (5669) ....‡2,250
Nation's Cities Weekly (5686) ....‡32,500
PA Times (5712) 13,500
Public Administration Review (5748) ......‡16,000
The Public Employee
  Magazine (5749) ....‡1,400,000
Public Management
  (PM) (5751) ....(Controlled) ‡14,000

FLORIDA
Tallahassee
Florida Administrative
  Weekly (6705) ....(Paid) ‡2,600
                                     (Non-paid) ‡190
Quality Cities (6729) ....(Paid) ‡3,324
                                     (Non-paid) ‡1,368

GEORGIA
Atlanta
American City and County (6962) ....(Paid) 420
                                     (Controlled) 74,100

ILLINOIS
Chicago
City & Community (8333)
Government Finance Review (8388) 14,000
Planning (8532) ....(Paid) ⊕32,136

Country Club Hills
International Code Council (8689) ....‡14,000

Springfield
Illinois Issues (9625) ....(Paid) ‡6,000
                                     (Non-paid) ‡500
Township Perspective (9644) ....(Paid) ‡12,000
                                     (Non-paid) ‡200

INDIANA
Indianapolis
Construction Digest (10104) ....(Paid) 496
                                     (Non-paid) 12,576

KANSAS
Topeka
Kansas Government Journal (11828) ....‡6,000

KENTUCKY
Lexington
Spectrum: Journal of State
  Government (12176) 4,000
State Government News (12177) ....(Paid) 669
                                     (Non-paid) 18,000

Louisville
Journal of Urban Affairs (12222)

MARYLAND
Annapolis
Municipal Maryland (13094) ....(Paid) ‡1,750
                                     (Non-paid) ‡190

College Park
Journal of Policy Analysis and
  Management (13431) 22,400

MASSACHUSETTS
Boston
The Mass Municipal
  Directory (13924) ....(Combined) 5,884

Burlington
Transport Policy (14034)

MICHIGAN
Ann Arbor
Michigan Municipal Review (14767) ....‡11,300

Lansing
Michigan Roads and
  Construction (15291) ....(Paid) 1,043
                                     (Non-paid) 436

MISSOURI
Columbia
American Review of Public
  Administration (16987) ....(Paid) ‡1,100

Jefferson City
Missouri Municipal Review (17127) ....‡6,200

St. Louis
Journal of Policy History (17459) ....(Paid) 700

NEBRASKA
Lincoln
Nebraska Municipal Review (18103) ....‡3,200

NEW JERSEY
Ridgewood
Public Works (19503) ....(Paid) 458
                                     (Controlled) 67,083

Trenton
New Jersey Municipalities (19661) .....(Paid) ‡8,000
                                     (Non-paid) ‡300
New Jersey Reporter (19663) ....(Paid) ‡1,200
                                     (Controlled) ‡500

NEW YORK
Albany
New York State Register (20000) 2,400

Mount Vernon
Empire State Report (21102) ....(Paid) 1,600
                                     (Non-paid) 14,000

New York
The Chief Civil Service
  Leader (21408) ....(Fri.) ★52,087
The Housing Authority
  Journal (21824) ....(Non-paid) ‡230,000
Journal of Public Policy (22173) 800

NORTH CAROLINA
Raleigh
Southern City (24154) ....(Paid) ‡5,700
                                     (Controlled) ‡500

OHIO
Cleveland
Government Product
  News (24905) ....(Controlled) ‡85,054

PENNSYLVANIA
Enola
Pennsylvania Township
  News (26886) ....(Paid) ‡9,215
                                     (Non-paid) ‡1,063

Circulation: ★ = ABC; △ = BPA; ♦ = CAC; • = CCAB; ▢ = VAC; ⊕ = PO Statement; ‡ = Publisher's Report; Boldface figures = sworn; Light figures = estimated.

3231

Circ.   Circ.   Circ.

STATE, MUNICIPAL, AND COUNTY ADMINISTRATION (continued)

Harrisburg
The Borough News Magazine **(26983)**
Community Affairs **(26988)** ....(Free) 24,000

TENNESSEE
Nashville
Tennessee Town & City **(29494)** ....(Paid) ‡5,600
(Non-paid) ‡300

TEXAS
Abilene
County Progress **(29653)** ....‡5,000

Austin
COUNTY Magazine **(29772)** ....(Paid) 5,200
(Free) 500
Texas Town & City **(29849)** ....(Paid) ‡10,500
(Non-paid) ‡750

VERMONT
Burlington
Planning Commissioners
Journal **(31517)** ....(Paid) 7,700
(Non-paid) 70

VIRGINIA
Alexandria
Public Personnel Management **(31732)** ....‡7,000

Falls Church
Federal Computer Week **(32044)** .....(Free) ‡86,000
Government E-Business **(32047)**

Richmond
Virginia Town & City **(32467)** ....(Paid) ‡4,505
(Non-paid) ‡575

Springfield
Federal Times **(32544)** ....(Paid) 32,589

WISCONSIN
Madison
The Municipality **(33964)** ....‡9,446
Wisconsin Counties **(33980)** ....(Paid) ‡3,500
(Non-paid) ‡3,500

ALBERTA, CANADA
Calgary
Canadian Public Policy–Analyse de
Politiques **(34638)** ....(Paid) ‡1,100
(Non-paid) ‡32

MANITOBA, CANADA
Portage La Prairie
Municipal Leader **(35283)** ....(Paid) 1,450

ONTARIO, CANADA
St. Thomas
Municipal World **(36362)** ....(Combined) 7,500

Toronto
Canadian Public Administration (Administration
publique du Canada) **(36528)** 3,400
Civic Public Works **(36551)** ....(Combined) 13,085
Government Purchasing
Guide **(36608)** ....(Combined) •16,401

STATIONERY, OFFICE EQUIPMENT, AND COLLEGE STORE SUPPLIES

CONNECTICUT
Danbury
Party & Paper Retailer **(4749)** ....‡15,000

ILLINOIS
Chicago
Giftware News **(8387)** ....(Paid) 15,239
(Non-paid) 21,766

MISSOURI
Kansas City
BTA Solutions **(17158)** ....‡5,000

NEW YORK
Geneva
Educational Dealer **(20652)** ......(Controlled) ‡10,500

Westbury
College Store Executive **(23553)** ....(Paid) 185
(Controlled) 9,167

OHIO
Oberlin
The College Store **(25444)** ....‡8,500

PENNSYLVANIA
Philadelphia
Office Dealer **(27596)** ....(Controlled) ‡18,500

VIRGINIA
Alexandria
Print Solutions **(31726)** ....(Paid) ‡13,800
(Non-paid) ‡625

ONTARIO, CANADA
Scarborough
Comda Key **(36375)** ....(Non-paid) ‡1,600

Toronto
Gifts & Tablewares **(36604)** ....(Paid) 1,796
(Non-paid) 14,065

STATISTICS

See also Mathematics

ALABAMA
Birmingham
Russian Journal of Mathematical
Physics **(89)** 5985

CALIFORNIA
San Francisco
Disability Statistics Report **(3349)**

COLORADO
Denver
Technometrics **(4362)** ....(Combined) ⊕6,377

CONNECTICUT
Storrs Mansfield
The IMS Bulletin **(5171)** ....(Paid) 4,200

DISTRICT OF COLUMBIA
Washington
Biometrics **(5377)** ....‡8,500
Journal of Agricultural, Biological, and Environmental
Statistics **(5567)**
Journal of Educational and Behavioral
Statistics **(5583)**
Paper, Paperboard, and Wood Pulp Monthly
Statistical Summary **(5714)**
Population Bulletin **(5722)** ....‡5,000
Quarterly Labour Force Statistics **(5755)**

FLORIDA
Miami
International Journal of Mathematical and Statistical
Sciences **(6363)**

ILLINOIS
Chicago
Mathematical Finance **(8482)** ....‡800

IOWA
Davenport
Quality Control and Applied Statistics **(10739)**

MARYLAND
Hyattsville
Advance Data **(13585)** ....(Non-paid) 15,000
National Vital Statistics
Report **(13587)** ....(Non-paid) ‡9,000

MASSACHUSETTS
Cambridge
Econometrica **(14050)** ....‡7,000

NEW JERSEY
Hoboken
Applied Stochastic Models in Business and
Industry **(18894)**
Journal of Applied Econometrics **(19002)**
Journal of Chemometrics **(19011)** ....(Paid) 4,200
Journal of Forecasting **(19023)** ....(Paid) 9,800
Managerial and Decision Economics **(19058)**
Mathematical Methods in the Applied
Sciences **(19059)**
Statistics in Medicine **(19106)** ....(Paid) 12,600

Mahwah
Understanding Statistics **(19207)**

New Brunswick
Studies in Nonlinear Dynamics and
Econometrics **(19341)**

River Edge
International Journal of Uncertainty, Fuzziness, and
Knowledge-Based Systems **(19514)**

NEW YORK
New York
Chance **(21396)** ....(Combined) **5,000**
Constructive
Approximation **(21489)** ....(Combined) **450**
Environmental and Ecological Statistics **(21615)**
Extremes **(21671)**
Health Services and Outcomes Research
Methodology **(21795)**
Journal of Dynamic and Control Systems **(22050)**
Lifetime Data Analysis **(22255)**
Mathematical Proceedings of the Cambridge
Philosophical Society **(22297)**
Methodology and Computing in Applied
Probability **(22326)**
Monthly Bulletin of Statistics **(22362)**
Quantitative Microbiology **(22616)**
Sequential Analysis **(22731)** ....(Paid) **325**
Stochastic Models **(22792)** ....(Paid) **600**

Rhinebeck
The Trends Journal **(23186)**

OHIO
Beachwood
The Annals of Statistics **(24650)** ....‡4,300
Statistical Science **(24656)** ....(Paid) 4,700

Marion
American Demographics **(25350)** ....(Paid) 26,310

OREGON
Portland
Export Report **(26477)** 275
Injury and Illness Incidence **(26482)** 275
Monthly F.O.B. Price Summary, Past Sales (Coast
Mills) **(26485)** 280
Monthly F.O.B. Price Summary, Past Sales (Inland
Mills) **(26486)** 300
Western Lumber Facts **(26514)** 380

PENNSYLVANIA
Pittsburgh
Monthly Labor Review **(27818)**
Official Summary of Security Transactions and
Holdings **(27823)**

VIRGINIA
Alexandria
The American Statistician **(31638)** .....(Paid) ‡15,500
(Controlled) ‡13
Amstat News **(31640)** ....(Controlled) 17,000
Journal of the American Statistical
Association **(31688)** ....(Paid) ‡14,500
(Controlled) ‡195
Journal of Business & Economic Statistics **(31689)**
Journal of Computational and Graphical
Statistics **(31690)**
Journal of Statistics
Education **(31703)** ....(Non-paid) 2,230

Fairfax
ITEA Journal of Test and
Evaluation **(32018)** ....(Combined) 2,575

WASHINGTON
Blaine
Grey Book **(32688)**

Seattle
Journal of Financial and Quantitative
Analysis **(32977)** ....‡3,200

BRITISH COLUMBIA, CANADA
Victoria
British Columbia Business Indicators **(35208)**
British Columbia Division of Vital Statistics Quarterly
Digest **(35209)**
British Columbia Origin Exports **(35211)**
British Columbia Regional Index **(35212)**
Economic Accounts **(35215)**
Labour Force Survey **(35218)**

ONTARIO, CANADA
London
Canadian Plant Disease
Survey **(35980)** ....(Controlled) 500

Ottawa
Canadian Social Trends **(36228)** ....(Paid) 4,500

STONE AND ROCK PRODUCTS

See also Building Materials, Concrete, Brick, and Tile; Cemeteries and Monuments; Mining and Minerals

ILLINOIS
Chicago
Rock Products (8558) ....(Non-paid) △22,172

NEW YORK
New York
Stone Magazine (22794) ....(Paid) 1,700
(Non-paid) 20,000
Tile & Decorative Surfaces (22836) .....(Paid) 1,137
(Non-paid) 20,441

VIRGINIA
Alexandria
Stone, Sand & Gravel
Review (31739) ....(Paid) ‡2,558
(Non-paid) ‡1,412

QUEBEC, CANADA
Westmount
Aggregates & Roadbuilding
Magazine (37441) ....(Combined) •12,175

STORAGE AND WAREHOUSING

ARIZONA
Phoenix
The Mini-Storage Messenger (807) ......(Paid) 6,000
(Non-paid) 500

NEW HAMPSHIRE
Nashua
InfoStor (18592) ....△30,189

NEW JERSEY
Morris Plains
Material Handling Product
News (19297) ....(Controlled) 90,000

NEW YORK
New York
Logistics Management and Distribution
Report (22266) ....(Controlled) ‡83,250

VIRGINIA
Alexandria
Direction (31667) ....(Combined) ‡5,000

SUBSTANCE ABUSE AND TREATMENT

CALIFORNIA
Van Nuys
The N.A. Way
Magazine (3993) ....(Non-paid) 28,000

DISTRICT OF COLUMBIA
Washington
Youth Today (5874) ....(Combined) 58,000

FLORIDA
Fort Lauderdale
Journal of Child and Adolescent Substance
Abuse (6077) ....(Paid) 325

INDIANA
Indianapolis
Alcoholism: Clinical and Experimental
Research (10077) ....(Paid) ‡1,333
(Non-paid) ‡408

KANSAS
Hutchinson
Union Signal (11502) ....‡2,000

MARYLAND
Baltimore
Addictive Disorders & Their Treatment (13107)

Bethesda
Alcohol Research & Health (13298)

Hagerstown
Listen (13566) ....‡35,000
Winner (13571) ....(Paid) 15,000

Rockville
Prevention Pipeline (13696)

MICHIGAN
Lansing
Monday Morning Report (15294) ......(Paid) ‡1,000
(Non-paid) ‡100

MINNESOTA
St. Paul
Journal of Ministry in Addiction and
Recovery (16383) ....(Paid) 274

NEBRASKA
Omaha
Journal of Alcohol and Drug
Education (18200) ....(Paid) 1,000

NEW JERSEY
Piscataway
Journal of Studies on
Alcohol (19429) ....(Paid) ‡2,400

NEW YORK
Amityville
Journal of Drug Education (20043)

New York
The American Journal of Drug and Alcohol
Abuse (21192) 825
Journal of Addictive
Diseases (21974) ....(Paid) 3,676
Journal of Substance Abuse Treatment (22196)
Substance Use & Misuse (22803) 650

PENNSYLVANIA
Pittsburgh
Alcohol, Health and Research World (27755)

TEXAS
Lubbock
Alcoholism Treatment Quarterly (30708)

VIRGINIA
Arlington
American Journal of
Addictions (31772) ....(Paid) 1,400
(Non-paid) 25

Richmond
Brain Injury (32430)

ONTARIO, CANADA
Toronto
CrossCurrents (36564) ....(Paid) ‡1,100
(Controlled) ‡1,500

SUGAR AND SUGAR BEETS

GEORGIA
Atlanta
Textile World Latina (7055) ....(Combined) 12,500

IDAHO
Idaho Falls
The Sugar Producer (7871) .....(Controlled) ‡16,000

LOUISIANA
New Orleans
Sugar Journal (12754) ....(Paid) 654
(Non-paid) 3,319

NEW JERSEY
Cresskill
Sugar y Azucar (18773) ....(Paid) 506
(Controlled) 4,707

NORTH DAKOTA
Fargo
The Sugarbeet
Grower (24414) ....(Non-paid) ‡12,000

TAXATION AND TARIFF

CALIFORNIA
Los Angeles
PBC Federal Tax Guide (2359)

DISTRICT OF COLUMBIA
Washington
National Tax Journal (5681)
The Tax Executive (5811) ....(Combined) 5,556
The Tax Management International Forum (5813)

Tax Practice Adviser (5814) ....(Paid) 1,000
(Non-paid) 279

ILLINOIS
Riverwoods
Tax Treaties (9509)
Taxes–The Tax Magazine (9510) .....(Paid) ‡10,745
(Non-paid) ‡500

MARYLAND
Gaithersburg
EA Journal (13537) 10,000

MASSACHUSETTS
Boston
Massachusetts CPA Review Online (13927)

MICHIGAN
Kalamazoo
Journal of International Accounting, Auditing and
Taxation (15239)

NEW JERSEY
Jersey City
Tax Adviser (19145)

NEW YORK
New York
Business Entities (21355)
Corporate Business Taxation Monthly (21500)
Corporate Taxation (21501)
The International Tax Journal (21938)
International Tax and Public Finance (21939)
Intertax (21943)
The Journal of California Taxation (22017)
Journal of International
Taxation (22104) ....(Paid) 2,500
The Journal of New York Taxation (22143)
Journal of Property Tax Management (22166)
Journal of State Taxation (22192)
The Journal of Taxation (22201) ....(Paid) 12,935
Practical Tax Strategies (22591) ....(Paid) ‡8831
(Non-paid) ‡115

PENNSYLVANIA
Berwyn
Vertex National SalesTax
Manuals (26698) ....‡1,010

Pittsburgh
Internal Revenue Bulletin (27801)
United States Tax Court Reports (27853)

VIRGINIA
Arlington
The Exempt Organization Tax
Review (31792) ....‡1,000
Highlights and Documents (31795)
The Insurance Tax Review (31797)
State Tax Notes (31833)
Tax Notes (31835)
Tax Notes International (31836) ....(Paid) 1,365

WISCONSIN
Appleton
TAXPRO Quarterly Journal (33545) ....(Paid) 16,000
(Non-paid) 1,000

Madison
The Wisconsin Taxpayer (33991) ....‡9,000
(Non-paid) ‡700

ONTARIO, CANADA
Toronto
Canadian Tax Journal (Revue fiscale
canadienne) (36531) ....‡8,300

TELECOMMUNICATIONS

ARIZONA
Phoenix
Asian Sources Telecom Sources (790)

CALIFORNIA
Brisbane
The Net (1607)

Chatsworth
The Industry Standard (1687)

Chico
Smart TV & Sound
Magazine (1696) ....(Combined) 50,000

Circulation: ★ = ABC; △ = BPA; ♦ = CAC; • = CCAB; ▢ = VAC; ⊕ = PO Statement; ‡ = Publisher's Report; Boldface figures = sworn; Light figures = estimated.

3233

Circ.   Circ.   Circ.

TELECOMMUNICATIONS (continued)

Elk Grove
Web Publisher **(1874)**

La Jolla
IEEE Antennas &
  Propogation **(2113)** ....(Controlled) 10,400

Los Alamitos
IEEE Internet Computing **(2186)** ....(Paid) 14,455

Mountain View
Global Technology Business **(2606)**

Palo Alto
Java Pro **(2796)**
Microsoft Interactive Developer **(2799)**

San Diego
Lotus Advisor
  Magazine **(3227)** ....(Combined) 15,000

San Francisco
The Red Herring **(3422)** ....(Paid) 162,666
                    (Non-paid) 5,611

Santa Ana
America's Network **(3619)** ....(Paid) 1,914
                   (Non-paid) 51,374
Comunicaciones **(3623)** ....(Controlled) 10,000
InfoText **(3628)** ....(Controlled) ‡18,000
Telecom Asia **(3633)** ....(Controlled) 20,000

COLORADO
Broomfield
Digital Graphics **(4204)** ....(Paid) △72
                (Non-paid) △18,513

Denver
The Telephone Pioneer **(4363)** ....‡756,350

Englewood
RadioResource
  International **(4415)** ....(Non-paid) 12,000

Golden
CLEC Magazine **(4464)**

Littleton
Wireless Week **(4556)** ....(Controlled) ‡28,809

CONNECTICUT
Norwalk
CTI **(5053)**
Customer Interaction Solutions **(5055)**
Telemarketing & Call Center
  Solutions **(5076)** ....(Paid) 2,170
                (Non-paid) 28,331

Tolland
International Journal of Instructional Media
  (IJIM) **(5176)** 2000

DISTRICT OF COLUMBIA
Washington
Mobile Communications Report **(5654)**
OPASTCO Roundtable **(5708)** ....(Paid) ‡2,900
                (Non-paid) ‡600
Optics & Photonics News **(5710)** ......(Paid) ‡15,000
Satellite Week **(5777)**
TeleTimes **(5818)** 5,000

FLORIDA
Brandon
NewMedia **(5961)** ....(Combined) 250,000

Nokomis
Communications News **(6462)** ....‡100,000

GEORGIA
Norcross
Applied Microwave & Wireless **(7455)** .....(Paid) 100
                (Non-paid) 43,000

HAWAII
Honolulu
Pacific Telecommunications
  Review **(7716)** ....(Controlled) 2,500

ILLINOIS
Cary
Outside Plant Magazine **(8169)** ....(Paid) 995
               (Controlled) 18,211
Utility & Telephone Fleets **(8171)** ......(Paid) ‡259
               (Controlled) ‡18,804

Chicago
Telephony **(8581)** ....(Paid) 2,685
               (Non-paid) 70,065

Upstart **(8594)** ....(Combined) 65,000

Northbrook
Semiconductor
  Magazine **(9322)** ....(Non-paid) 43,000

KANSAS
Overland Park
Cellular & Mobile
  International **(11704)** ....(Combined) 10,000
Mobile Radio Technology **(11722)** ....‡25,002
Wireless Review **(11736)** ....(Paid) 1,797
               (Controlled) 30,028

MARYLAND
Potomac
Mobile Products Europe **(13655)**
Telecommunications Regulatory Monitor **(13661)**
Via Satellite **(13662)** 22,000
Wireless Business & Technology **(13663)**
Wireless Data News **(13664)** ....(Controlled) ‡28,000
Wireless Networks **(13665)**

Rockville
411 **(13680)**

MASSACHUSETTS
Boston
China Telecom **(13873)**

Brookline
Server/Workstation
  Expert **(14024)** ....(Controlled) 85,000

Cambridge
Presence **(14090)** ....(Paid) 1000

Norwood
Telecommunications
  Magazine **(14451)** ....(Paid) 1,600
              (Controlled) 85,068

Southborough
IntraNet Magazine **(14545)**

Wayland
Popular Home Automation **(14615)** ....(Paid) ‡19,889

NEW HAMPSHIRE
Nashua
Cabling Installation &
  Maintenance **(18583)** ....(Non-paid) 23,600
Integrated Communications
  Design **(18593)** ....‡23,406
Portable Design **(18599)**
Wireless Integration **(18605)**

NEW JERSEY
Lakewood
SHOOT **(19158)** 15,100

Medford
Information Today **(19225)** ....(Paid) ‡5,000
              (Non-paid) ‡5,000

Montvale
Java Developer's Journal **(19258)**

Morris Plains
Fiberoptic Product
  News **(19290)** ....(Non-paid) ‡35,000
Wireless Design and
  Development **(19309)** 42,000

Paramus
Wireless Systems Design **(19408)** ....△37,200

NEW YORK
Manhasset
Call Center Magazine **(20991)** ....(Paid) 60,795
              (Non-paid) 37,179
Communication Systems Design **(20992)** 37,000
Digital Video Magazine **(20997)**
Internet Week **(21005)** ....(Non-paid) 200,000
Teleconnect Magazine **(21015)** ....(Non-paid) 46
               (Paid) 27,000

New York
IEEE Communications
  Magazine **(21844)** ....(Paid) 50,000
              (Non-paid) 1,000
International Journal of Wireless Information
  Networks **(21925)**
Journal of Network and Systems
  Management **(22141)**
Mobile Networks and Applications **(22342)**
netWorker **(22419)**
Online Learning **(22492)**
R&B Airplay Monitor **(22625)** 2,803
Satellite Broadband **(22706)** 21,531

TWICE **(22878)** ....(Non-paid) ‡33,000
Wireless & Mobility **(22922)**
Year/2000 Journal **(22948)**

Port Washington
Popular Communications **(23132)** .....(Paid) ⊕59,340
             (Non-paid) ⊕876

Sound & Communications
  Magazine **(23136)** ....(Paid) 458
             (Non-paid) 16,640

White Plains
Tape/Disc Business **(23575)** ....(Paid) 400
             (Non-paid) 11,600

NORTH CAROLINA
Cary
Journal of Communication **(23689)** .....(Paid) ‡5,000

OKLAHOMA
Tulsa
Utility Automation **(26141)** ....(Controlled) ‡25,000

PENNSYLVANIA
Spring House
Office Systems 96 **(28009)** ......(Controlled) 100,225

TENNESSEE
Memphis
Roaming Guide **(29379)**

TEXAS
Houston
Telecom Business **(30532)** ....(Combined) 35,000

VIRGINIA
Alexandria
Utility Fleet Management **(31748)** ....‡22,014

Annandale
Communication Booknotes Quarterly **(31763)**

Arlington
Intercom **(31798)** 20,000
Rural Telecommunications **(31825)** .....(Paid) ‡4,090
             (Non-paid) ‡250

Fairfax
SIGNAL **(32029)** ....(Paid) △26,483
             (Non-paid) △2,046

Norfolk
International Journal of Educational
  Telecommunications **(32284)**

Vienna
Public Utilities Fortnightly **(32580)**
Public Utilities Fortnightly **(32581)** 7,000

WASHINGTON
Seattle
Linux Gazette **(32981)**
Linux Journal **(32982)** ....(Combined) 30,000

ONTARIO, CANADA
Mississauga
Structured Cabling **(36088)** ....(Combined) 9,089

Toronto
Cabling Systems **(36485)** ....(Combined) 11,000

TEXTILES

ARIZONA
Phoenix
Embroidery Business News **(802)**

COLORADO
Broomfield
Printwear **(4206)** ....(Combined) △20,046

Greenwood Village
Stitches Magazine **(4505)** ....(Combined) 18,302
THE PRESS
  Magazine **(4506)** ....(Controlled) ‡22,979

DISTRICT OF COLUMBIA
Washington
Cotton **(5444)**
The Textile Museum Journal **(5821)** 5,000
                    1,000
                    400

GEORGIA
Atlanta
Textile Industries **(7053)** ....(Paid) △**152**
(Controlled) △**32,074**
Textile World **(7054)** ....(Paid) 617
(Controlled) 31,803

MINNESOTA
Roseville
Geotechnical Fabrics Report **(16332)** ....(Paid) 2,061
(Controlled) 13,939
Industrial Fabric Products
Review **(16333)** ....(Paid) 3,437
(Non-paid) 4,652
(Controlled) 1,911

St. Paul
Marine Textiles **(16386)** ....(Paid) ‡3,000
(Non-paid) ‡5,000

MISSISSIPPI
Greenwood
Staplreview **(16645)** ....‡4,500

NEW JERSEY
Englewood
Surface Design
Journal **(18798)** ....(Combined) 5,700

Princeton
Textile Research Journal **(19473)** ....‡2,000

Ramsey
Nonwovens Industry **(19492)** ....(Paid) 544
(Controlled) 11,055

NEW YORK
New York
Daily News Record **(21531)** ....(Paid) 17,069
Embroidery Monogram Business **(21598)** 26,192
Home Textiles
Today **(21814)** ....(Controlled) ‡11,000
LDB Interior Textiles **(22241)** ....(Paid) ‡146
(Free) ‡12,253

NORTH CAROLINA
Charlotte
Hosiery News **(23745)** ....(Controlled) ‡2,500
Southern Textile News **(23754)** ....‡6,000

Research Triangle Park
AATCC Review **(24182)** ....:..(Paid) 5,800
(Non-paid) 1,000

PENNSYLVANIA
Fleetwood
The Apparel Strategist **(26920)**

SOUTH CAROLINA
Columbia
Bobbin Magazine **(28545)** ....△**20,883**
La Bobina **(28556)** ....(Controlled) ‡13,600

Greenville
Textiles
Panamericanos **(28627)** ....(Controlled) 13,000

TEXAS
Houston
Cotton Digest International **(30467)** .....(Paid) ‡6000
(Controlled) ‡3300

Mesquite
Cotton Gin & Oil Mill
Press **(30807)** ....(Paid) ‡1,700
(Non-paid) ‡200

VIRGINIA
Charlottesville
Textile Technology Digest **(31941)**

Dillwyn
EGA Needle Arts
Magazine **(31996)** ....(Paid) 30,000

QUEBEC, CANADA
Saint-Hyacinthe
Canadian Textile Journal (La Revue Canadienne du
Textile) **(37348)** ....(Controlled) 2,500

THEOLOGY

CALIFORNIA
Pasadena
Sunrise **(2827)**

Quartz Hill
Quartz Hill Journal of Theology **(2868)** 200

San Diego
Journal of Druze Studies **(3188)**

San Pedro
Sudden Enlightenment Digest **(3596)**

ILLINOIS
Chicago
Insights **(8418)**

INDIANA
Indianapolis
Religion and American Culture **(10166)**

Notre Dame
Religion and Literature **(10376)** ....(Paid) 450

MARYLAND
Baltimore
Journal of Early Christian
Studies **(13187)** ....(Combined) 1,444

MICHIGAN
Riverview
Journal of Biblical Studies **(15465)**

MINNESOTA
St. Paul
Journal of Law and Religion **(16382)** ....(Paid) 1,000

MISSOURI
St. Louis
Social Justice Review **(17512)** ....(Paid) 4,600
(Non-paid) 500

NEW JERSEY
Cherry Hill
Journal of Religion and Psychical
Research **(18737)** ....(Controlled) 347

NEW YORK
Binghamton
Journal of Religion & Abuse **(20195)**

Brooklyn
The Watchtower **(20355)** ....‡23,042,000

New York
European Judaism **(21654)**
Journal of Jewish Music and Liturgy **(22109)**

OKLAHOMA
Oklahoma City
The Personalist Forum **(25992)** ......(Combined) 230

OREGON
Milwaukie
New Moon Rising **(26438)** 4,000

Williams
Shaman's Drum **(26612)** ....(Combined) 12,000

PENNSYLVANIA
Harrisburg
Journal of Power and Ethics **(26997)**

Philadelphia
Journal of Ecumenical Studies **(27525)**
Journal of Spiritual
Bodywork **(27551)** ....(Combined) 150

TENNESSEE
Nashville
Pedalpoint **(29480)** ....(Paid) 48,000
Worship **(29503)** ....(Paid) 5,000

TEXAS
Arlington
Utopian Studies **(29739)** ....(Paid) 375

UTAH
Provo
Journal of Media and Religion **(31404)**

WISCONSIN
Milwaukee
Philosophy & Theology **(34093)** ....(Paid) 500

NEW BRUNSWICK, CANADA
Fredericton
Sociology of Religion **(35397)**

ONTARIO, CANADA
Ottawa
Logos **(36261)**

Toronto
Catholic Insight **(36539)** ....(Paid) 3,300
(Non-paid) 400
Historical Studies **(36615)**

QUEBEC, CANADA
Montreal
Ascent Magazine **(37088)** ....(Controlled) 10,000

Quebec
Laval Theologique et Philosophique **(37286)**

TOBACCO

CALIFORNIA
Marina del Rey
Lott's 3—in—1 Buyer's Guide **(2509)** ....(Paid) ‡300
(Controlled) ‡1,700

Palm Springs
Tobacco Retailer **(2768)**

NEW YORK
New York
Tobacco International **(22842)** ......(Combined) 4,176

NORTH CAROLINA
Raleigh
The Burley Tobacco
Farmer **(24128)** ....(Controlled) 17,318
The Flue Cured Tobacco
Farmer **(24136)** ....(Paid) 85
(Controlled) 14,461

PENNSYLVANIA
Wayne
Tobacco Industry Litigation Reporter **(28137)**

ONTARIO, CANADA
Delhi
The Canadian Tobacco
Grower **(35766)** ....(Paid) ‡2,000

TOXICOLOGY

**See also Drugs and Pharmaceuticals;
Ecology and Conservation**

ARKANSAS
Little Rock
Drug Metabolism Reviews **(1228)** 800

CALIFORNIA
San Diego
Regulatory Toxicology and Pharmacology **(3254)**
Toxicological Sciences **(3281)**
Toxicology and Applied Pharmacology **(3282)**

DELAWARE
Newark
Drug and Chemical Toxicology **(5272)** 350

ILLINOIS
Niles
Journal of Analytical
Toxicology **(9287)** ....(Paid) ‡1,250
(Non-paid) ‡64

KANSAS
Manhattan
Veterinary and Human
Toxicology **(11630)** ....(Paid) ‡1,000
(Controlled) ‡25

MARYLAND
Baltimore
Therapeutic Drug Monitoring **(13254)** 813

Bethesda
Toxicology Abstracts **(13384)**

NEW JERSEY
Hoboken
Journal of Biochemical and Molecular
Toxicology **(19006)**
Journal of Mass Spectrometry **(19029)**
The Journal of Trace Elements in Experimental
Medicine **(19051)** 2800
Packaging Technology and
Science **(19078)** 2,800

Circulation: ★ = ABC; △ = BPA; ♦ = CAC; • = CCAB; ❏ = VAC; ⊕ = PO Statement; ‡ = Publisher's Report; Boldface figures = sworn; Light figures = estimated.

3235

Trade, Technical, and Professional Publications

Circ.   Circ.   Circ.

TOXICOLOGY (continued)

Pharmacoepidemiology and Drug
   Safety (19082) 2,800
Phytotherapy Research (19084) 4,200
Teratology (19118) 11,550

NEW MEXICO
New Mexico
Ecotoxicology and Environmental Safety (19903)

NEW YORK
New York
Archives of Environmental Contamination and
   Toxicology (21245) ....(Combined) 800
Bulletin of Environmental Contamination and
   Toxicology (21349) ....(Combined) 1,100
Human & Experimental
   Toxicology (21829) ....(Paid) 500

NORTH CAROLINA
Raleigh
Inhalation Toxicology (24138) ....‡287

PENNSYLVANIA
Philadelphia
Journal of Toxicology and Environmental
   Health (27553) 855
Toxicology & Ecotoxicology
   News/Reviews (27706) 600
Xenobiotica (27724)

TEXAS
Houston
Environmental Toxicology and
   Chemistry (30471) 5,500

TRAILERS AND ACCESSORIES
**See also Transportation, Traffic, and
Shipping**

CALIFORNIA
Ventura
RV Business (4010) ....(Combined) 21,000
WOODALL'S Southern RV (4023) ......(Paid) 30,000

COLORADO
Broomfield
Restyling Magazine (4207)

GEORGIA
Roswell
Truck Accessory
   News (7520) ....(Controlled) ‡10,000

ILLINOIS
Deerfield
Successful Dealer (8729) ....(Controlled) ‡21,049

IOWA
Cedar Falls
Trucking Times & Sport Utility
   News (10663) ....(Combined) 13,500

MISSOURI
Cassville
Trendsetter (16966)

TEXAS
Houston
Trailer/Body Builders (30535) ....(Controlled) ‡14,110

ONTARIO, CANADA
Mississauga
Camping Canada Dealer
   News (36055) ....(Non-paid) ‡6,000

TRANSPORTATION, TRAFFIC, AND SHIPPING
See also Trucks and Trucking

ARKANSAS
Little Rock
Arkansas Trucking Report (1222) 9,000

CALIFORNIA
Redondo Beach
School Transportation News (2911) ....(Paid) ‡1,756
   (Non-paid) ‡21,403

Santa Monica
RAND Review (3715) ....(Controlled) 15,000

Santa Rosa
Northwesterner (3732) ....(Non-paid) 700

Torrance
Automotive Fleet (3927) ....(Paid) 252
   (Non-paid) 21,706

CONNECTICUT
Norwalk
Advanced Transportation Technology News (5049)

DISTRICT OF COLUMBIA
Washington
In Transit (5541) ....(Non-paid) 175,000
Traffic World (5827) ....(Paid) 8,562
Transportation
   Quarterly (5829) ....(Controlled) ‡1,500

FLORIDA
Jacksonville
American Shipper (6209) ....(Paid) 2,005
   (Controlled) ‡11,770

GEORGIA
Atlanta
Transportation Journal (7056) ......(Controlled) 1,913

ILLINOIS
Cary
Transport Technology
   Today (8170) ....(Non-paid) 40,000
Utility & Telephone Fleets (8171) ....(Paid) ‡259
   (Controlled) ‡18,804

Downers Grove
OAG Air Cargo Guide (8792) ....‡6,029

Itasca
Safe Driver (9017) ....(Paid) 80,000
Traffic Safety (9021) ....(Paid) ‡25,000
   (Non-paid) ‡66

MAINE
Augusta
Maine Trails (12895) ....(Controlled) ‡1,300

MARYLAND
Annapolis
The Best from American Canals (13089)

College Park
Transportation Science (13443)

Kensington
Transportation Leader (13591) ....‡5,500

Rockville
Interchange
   (Rockville) (13683) ....(Controlled) 95,000
The Winning Edge (13700)

MASSACHUSETTS
Newton
Logistics Management and Distribution
   Report (14405) ....(Non-paid) ‡83,285

MICHIGAN
Farmington Hills
NTEA Technical Report (15019) ....(Paid) 2,000

NEW HAMPSHIRE
Manchester
Bus Industry Magazine (18555) ......(Combined) 500

NEW JERSEY
Mahwah
Transportation Human Factors (19206)

NEW YORK
Jamaica
Airport Press (20830) ....(Free) 18,000

New York
Auto Interiors (21274) 13,642
Logistics Management and Distribution
   Report (22266) ....(Controlled) ‡83,250
TWU Express (22879)

OHIO
Cincinnati
Automotive Design and Production (24776)
Automotive Finishing (24778)

OREGON
Eugene
GPS World (26317) 38,000

PENNSYLVANIA
Harrisburg
HIGHWAY BUILDER (26995) ....‡3,000

King of Prussia
Commercial Carrier Journal (CCJ) (27123)

Philadelphia
Transport Reviews (27711)

SOUTH CAROLINA
Columbia
SCTA Hi-Lights (28564) ....‡2,500

TEXAS
Dallas
Better Roads (30131) ....(Non-paid) 39,424

Houston
Modern Bulk
   Transporter (30508) ....(Controlled) ‡14,772
Refrigerated
   Transporter (30522) ....(Controlled) 12,022

VIRGINIA
Alexandria
Defense Transportation Journal (31664) ......‡10,000
Direction (31667) ....(Combined) ‡5,000
Direction (31668) ....‡3,500
The Moving World (31711) ....‡3,000
Translog: Journal of Military Transportation
   Management (31746)

Fredericksburg
The Parking Professional (32086)

Norfolk
Towing and Recovery
   Footnotes (32295) ....(Controlled) 40,000

WASHINGTON
Chehalis
Log Trucker (32710) ....(Combined) ‡12,000

WISCONSIN
Appleton
Milk & Liquid Food
   Transporter (33538) ....(Controlled) 4,812

Madison
MAST (Mailing Systems Technology) (33961)

ALBERTA, CANADA
Calgary
Journal of Advanced
   Transportation (34650) ....(Combined) 355

MANITOBA, CANADA
Winnipeg
Western Canada Highway
   News (35358) ....(Non-paid) ‡4,000

ONTARIO, CANADA
Toronto
Canadian Transportation &
   Logistics (36532) ....(Combined) ‡18,382
Materials Management &
   Distribution (36658) ....(Combined) 19,226

QUEBEC, CANADA
Laval
Gestion Logistique (37038) 10,104
Guide du Transport par Camion (37039) 3,000

TRAVEL AND TOURISM

CALIFORNIA
Carmel
Community Spirit Magazine
   (Carmel) (1671) ....(Combined) 125,000

San Francisco
Palate and Spirit (3412)
TravelAge West (3453) ....(Controlled) ‡34,001

San Rafael
ASU Travel Guide (3598) ....‡60,000

Valencia
Traveling Times (3982) ....‡1,650,000

CONNECTICUT
South Norwalk
Travel World News
  Magazine **(5132)** ....(Non-paid) ‡30,000

Stamford
Motorcycle Tour &
  Cruiser **(5155)** ....(Combined) 45,000

DISTRICT OF COLUMBIA
Washington
Destinations **(5462)** ....(Paid) ‡3,379
                      (Controlled) ‡2,621
Developments **(5464)** 2,800
The World & I **(5870)** ....(Paid) 20,056
                     (Non-paid) 2,781

FLORIDA
Boca Raton
Corporate & Incentive
  Travel **(5929)** ....(Non-paid) 40,123

Miami
Vacation Industry
  Review **(6387)** ....(Controlled) 23,000

Miami Lakes
Recommend **(6419)** ....(Non-paid) △55,094

North Miami
FIU Hospitality Review **(6465)** .....(Controlled) 7,000

GEORGIA
Blakely
Southern Festivals **(7131)** ....(Paid) 3,000
                     (Non-paid) 20,000

ILLINOIS
Downers Grove
OAG Pocket Flight Guide - Pacific Asia
  Edition **(8793)** ....(Paid) ‡5,303
                     (Non-paid) ‡996
TRAVELtips **(8796)** ....(Controlled) 13,000

Polo
National Bus Trader **(9462)** ....(Paid) 4,500

INDIANA
Carmel
Timeshare Business **(9880)** ....(Controlled) 9,000

MASSACHUSETTS
Stow
Corporate Meetings &
  Incentives **(14572)** ....(Controlled) ‡36,776

MICHIGAN
East Lansing
Journal of Hospitality and Leisure
  Marketing **(14986)** 396

Holland
Group Tour Magazine Great Lakes
  Region **(15168)** ....(Controlled) 15,000
Group Tour Magazine Mid-Atlantic
  Region **(15169)** ....(Controlled) 15,000
Group Tour Magazine New England
  Region **(15170)** ....(Controlled) 15,000
Group Tour Magazine Southeastern
  Region **(15171)** ....(Controlled) 15,000
Group Tour Magazine Western
  Region **(15172)** ....(Controlled) 15,000

MINNESOTA
Duluth
Lake Superior Magazine **(15839)** ...(Paid) ‡22,500

NEVADA
Incline Village
Adventure Travel
  Business **(18356)** ....(Non-paid) 15,000

NEW JERSEY
Chatham
Physicians' Travel & Meeting
  Guide **(18732)** ....(Paid) 6,929
                    (Non-paid) 135,367

Englewood Cliffs
Hi Class Living **(18801)** ....(Controlled) ‡16,000

Florham Park
AAA Traveler **(18823)** ....(Free) 220,000

Hoboken
International Journal of Tourism Research **(18999)**

Morristown
Cruise and Vacation
  Views **(19311)** ....(Controlled) 30,000

Pleasantville
Whoot Newspaper **(19445)** ....(Paid) 527
                     (Free) 38,000

Secaucus
Business Travel Planner - European Edition **(19535)**
Business Travel Planner - North American
  Edition **(19536)**
Business Travel Planner - Pacific/Asia
  Edition **(19537)**
Hotel & Travel Index–International
  Edition **(19539)** ....(Paid) 57,000
Travel Weekly **(19542)** ....(Paid) 50,020

West Atlantic City
New Jersey Casino
  Journal **(19716)** ....(Paid) 15,000
                    (Controlled) 10,000

NEW YORK
Binghamton
International Journal of Hospitality & Tourism
  Administration **(20157)**
Journal of Convention & Exhibition
  Management **(20168)**
Journal of Human Resources in Hospitality &
  Tourism **(20182)**
Journal of Quality Assurance in Hospitality &
  Tourism **(20194)**
Journal of Teaching in Travel & Tourism **(20202)**

New York
Business Travel
  News **(21361)** ....(Non-paid) ‡54,795
Diversion **(21560)** ....(Controlled) 177,000
Open World for Disability and Mature
  Travel **(22496)** ....(Paid) 1,500
                    (Non-paid) 8,500
Successful Meetings **(22805)** ....(Controlled) ‡75,000
Travel Agent **(22856)** ....(Controlled) 51,500
                    (Paid) 122
Travel Trade **(22859)** ....(Paid) 38,727
                    (Non-paid) 5,974

NORTH CAROLINA
Candler
Belize First Magazine **(23682)** ....(Paid) 5,050
                    (Non-paid) 150,000

PENNSYLVANIA
Harrisburg
British Heritage **(26984)** ....(Paid) 80,166

TENNESSEE
Nashville
Key Magazine Nashville **(29466)** 25,000

TEXAS
Fort Worth
Chile Pepper Magazine **(30332)** ....(Paid) 70,000
                    (Controlled) 30,000
Southwest Airlines Spirit **(30352)** 371,020

Sugar Land
Asia Pacific Journal of Tourism
  Research **(31136)** ....(Paid) 400

VIRGINIA
Richmond
Journal of Hospitality & Tourism Research **(32440)**

WASHINGTON
Seattle
Horizon Air Magazine **(32971)** ....‡300,000

BRITISH COLUMBIA, CANADA
New Westminster
B.C. Sport Fishing
  Magazine **(35027)** ....(Paid) ‡19,481
                    (Non-paid) ‡982

Vancouver
Canadian Traveller **(35134)** ......(Combined) ‡14,954

ONTARIO, CANADA
Toronto
Canadian Travel
  Press **(36533)** ....(Controlled) 13,551
Meetings & Incentive
  Travel **(36660)** ....(Combined) •10,422
Rendez-Vous Canada **(36727)**
Travel Courier **(36772)** ....(Controlled) 10,034
Travelweek **(36773)** ....(Combined) 13,563

QUEBEC, CANADA
Montreal
Spa Destinations **(37225)** ......(Non-paid) 20,500
Tourisme Plus **(37229)** ....(Combined) 9,341

Ste.-Foy
Agenda **(37334)** 2,000

Ville D'Anjou
Le Magazine L'agent de
  voyages **(37436)** ....(Combined) 8,456

TRUCKS AND TRUCKING

See also Transportation, Traffic, and Shipping

ALABAMA
Anniston
Through the Gears Trucking
  Magazine **(16)** 130,000

Tuscaloosa
NATSO Truckers
  News **(489)** ....(Non-paid) ‡206,000
Overdrive **(490)** ....(Paid) 6,138
                   (Controlled) 141,969
Trucking Co. **(491)** ....(Controlled) ‡40,000

CALIFORNIA
Anaheim
MiniTruckin' **(1409)** ....‡325,000

Irvine
Truck Sales & Leasing
  Magazine **(2091)** ....(Controlled) ‡20,000

Los Angeles
Petersen's 4 Wheel & Off
  Road **(2363)** ....(Paid) 451,260
Sport Truck **(2405)** ....(Paid) 202,635

Newport Beach
Heavy Duty
  Trucking **(2627)** ....(Controlled) ‡101,976
Truck Sales & Leasing **(2636)** ....(Non-paid) ‡20,074

Palm Springs
Truck Fleet Management **(2769)** ....(Paid) 383
                    (Non-paid) 25,058

CONNECTICUT
Hartford
Motor Transport Association Bullitin **(4898)**

Norwalk
Advanced Transportation Technology News **(5049)**

Stamford
Fleet Owner **(5150)** ....(Non-paid) ‡101,240

FLORIDA
Longwood
Tow Times **(6314)** ....(Paid) 10,749
                    (Controlled) 21,062

Tallahassee
Florida Truck News **(6720)** ....(Paid) ‡1,600
                    (Controlled) ‡800

GEORGIA
Norcross
Trucker's Connection **(7471)** ....△201,000

Roswell
Over the Road **(7515)** ....(Paid) 131
                    (Non-paid) 74,293
Pro Trucker **(7517)** ....(Paid) 14
                    (Non-paid) 125,000
Truck Accessory
  News **(7520)** ....(Controlled) ‡10,000

ILLINOIS
Deerfield
Successful Dealer **(8729)** ....(Controlled) ‡21,049
Truck Parts &
  Service **(8730)** ....(Controlled) ‡26,566

Itasca
Safe Driver **(9017)** ....(Paid) 80,000

River Grove
Illinois Truck News **(9496)** ....(Controlled) ‡7,500

INDIANA
Indianapolis
American Trucker—Badger
  Edition **(10081)** ....(Combined) 33,990

Circ.   Circ.   Circ.

TRUCKS AND TRUCKING (continued)

American Trucker—Buckeye
  Edition (10082) ....(Combined) 44,008
American Trucker—California
  Edition (10083) ....(Combined) 55,429
American Trucker—Cascade
  Edition (10084) ....(Combined) 44,195
American Trucker—Central States
  Edition (10085) ....(Combined) 61,924
American Trucker—Illinois
  Edition (10087) ....(Combined) 48,387
American Trucker—Indiana
  Edition (10088) ....(Combined) 38,045
American Trucker—Metro East
  Edition (10090) ....(Combined) 48,419
American Trucker—Michigan
  Edition (10091) ....(Combined) 51,151
American Trucker—Mid-Atlantic
  Edition (10092) ....(Combined) 85,124
American Trucker—Minn/Dakota Truck
  Edition (10093) ....(Paid) 44,773
American Trucker—Mountain America
  Edition (10094) ....(Combined) 46,023
American Trucker—New England
  Edition (10095) ....(Combined) 62,335
American Trucker—New York/Pennsylvania
  Edition (10096) ....(Combined) 41,007
American Trucker—South Central
  Edition (10097) ....(Combined) 79,058

IOWA
Des Moines
The Iowa Trucking Lifeliner (10797) 3,000

Fort Dodge
Mid-America Weekly
  Trucking (10904) ....(Non-paid) 100,000

KANSAS
Topeka
Mid-America Transporter (11834) ....(Paid) 3,758
      (Non-paid) 352

KENTUCKY
Buckner
Fastline—Bluegrass Truck
  Edition (11968) ....(Combined) 22,000
Fastline—Dixie Truck
  Edition (11970) ....(Combined) 22,000
      (Combined) 22,000
Fastline—Florida Truck
  Edition (11972) ....(Combined) 22,000
Fastline—Georgia Truck
  Edition (11973) ....(Combined) 22,000
Fastline—Mid-West Truck
  Edition (11981) ....(Combined) 22,000
Fastline—Northland Truck
  Edition (11986) ....(Combined) 22,000
Fastline—South Central Truck
  Edition (11992) ....(Combined) 22,000
Fastline—Tennessee Truck
  Edition (11995) ....(Combined) 22,000
Fastline—Tri-State Truck
  Edition (11997) ....(Combined) 22,000

MAINE
Augusta
Maine Motor Transport
  News (12894) ....(Paid) 2,452
      (Non-paid) 1,500

MICHIGAN
Farmington Hills
NTEA Technical Report (15019) ....(Paid) 2,000

MISSOURI
Grain Valley
Land Line (17084) ....(Controlled) ‡140,000

Kansas City
Wheels of Time (17203) 22,500

NEBRASKA
Lincoln
Nebraska Trucker (18105) ....‡2,200
Truck Paper (18124) ....(Controlled) ‡445,186
      (Paid) ‡28,577

NEW JERSEY
East Brunswick
Bulletin of the New Jersey Motor Truck
  Association (18780) ....‡1500

NEW YORK
New York
Commercial Carrier
  Journal (21456) ....(Non-paid) ‡85,000
Owner Operator (22515) ....(Paid) 15,856
      (Non-paid) 77,152

NORTH DAKOTA
Bismarck
Rolling Along (24359) 3,000

OKLAHOMA
Oklahoma City
Oklahoma Motor Carrier (25982) ....‡3,000

PENNSYLVANIA
Camp Hill
Penntrux (26754) ....(Controlled) ‡2,500

King of Prussia
Commercial Carrier Journal (CCJ) (27123)

Slippery Rock
Movin' Out (27996) ....(Paid) ‡1,000
      (Non-paid) ‡54,000

SOUTH CAROLINA
Columbia
SCTA Hi-Lights (28564) ....‡2,500

SOUTH DAKOTA
Sioux Falls
South Dakota Trucking News (28968) ....‡750

TENNESSEE
Nashville
Road King (29483) ....(Non-paid) 250,000
Tennessee Trucking News (29496) 853

VIRGINIA
Alexandria
Light & Medium Truck (31706) ....‡50,086
Transport Topics (31747) ....(Paid) 30,592
Utility Fleet Management (31748) ....‡22,014

Norfolk
Towing and Recovery
  Footnotes (32295) ....(Controlled) 40,000

WISCONSIN
Fort Atkinson
Fleet Maintenance
  Supervisor (33710) ....(Controlled) △44,018

WYOMING
Casper
Wyoming Trucker (34486) ....(Non-paid) ‡3,700

MANITOBA, CANADA
Winnipeg
Western Canada Highway
  News (35358) ....(Non-paid) ‡4,000

ONTARIO, CANADA
Etobicoke
Today's Trucking (35821) ....(Combined) •29,945
Transport Routier (35822) ....(Combined) •12,022

Toronto
Atlantic Trucking (36466) ....(Paid) ‡1,400
      (Non-paid) ‡100
Motor Truck (36669) ....(Combined) •21,194
Truck News (36774) ....(Combined) 50,952
Truck West (36775) ....(Combined) 21,417

QUEBEC, CANADA
Laval
L'Echo du Transport (37036) ....(Controlled) 18,625

Montreal
Truck Trader/Camion Hebdo (37230)

TURF AND TURF MAINTENANCE

ILLINOIS
Chicago
sportsTURF (8571) ....(Combined) 18,431

IOWA
Cedar Falls
Western Turf & Landscape Press (10664)

MASSACHUSETTS
Amherst
Journal of Turf Grass
  Management (13799) ....(Paid) 127

VERMONT
St. Johnsbury
TURF (31594) ....(Controlled) ‡68,600

WISCONSIN
Fort Atkinson
Pro (33717) ....(Controlled) ‡49,000

VENDING MACHINES

LOUISIANA
New Orleans
Play Meter Magazine (12751) ....‡6,000

NEW JERSEY
Medford
STAR TECH Journal (19233) ....‡2,500

WISCONSIN
Fort Atkinson
Automatic
  Merchandiser (33705) ....(Controlled) 15,000

ONTARIO, CANADA
Delhi
Canadian Vending Magazine (35767) ....(Paid) ‡600
      (Non-paid) ‡2,600

VETERANS

ARIZONA
Tucson
Vietnam War Generation Journal (971)

CALIFORNIA
Canoga Park
Warbirds International (1661)

Clovis
California Legionnaire (1732) ....(Paid) 153,800
      (Free) 1,000

Sacramento
The California Veteran (2989) 120,000
Military (3008) ....‡26,000

GEORGIA
Atlanta
Veterans' Bulletin (7058) ....(Controlled) ‡2,500

INDIANA
Indianapolis
American Legion Auxiliary's National
  News (10079) ....(Paid) 780,000
American Legion
  Magazine (10080) ....(Paid) 2,602,005
The Hoosier Legionnaire (10117) ....(Free) ‡133,000

IOWA
Des Moines
Iowa Legionnaire (10793) ....‡78,000

KENTUCKY
Cold Spring
DAV Magazine (12017) ....‡1,100,000

MARYLAND
Lanham
The National AMVET (13607) ....(Paid) ‡175,000
      (Controlled) ‡4,000

Pasadena
Minerva (13644) ....(Paid) ‡500
      (Non-paid) ‡20

MINNESOTA
St. Paul
Minnesota Legionnaire (16394) ....‡116,000

MISSISSIPPI
Jackson
Mississippi Legionnaire (16704) 26,000

MISSOURI
Kansas City
VFW Auxiliary (17200) ....‡700,000
VFW Magazine (17201) ....(Paid) 18,000,000

NEW YORK
Albany
New York State Assembly Standing Committee on
Veterans' Affairs Annual Report **(19996)**

New York
Federal Practitioner **(21681)** .....(Controlled) ‡25,853
Weteran/Veteran **(22916)**

OHIO
Perrysburg
The American Legion Press **(25474)** ....‡5,000

SOUTH DAKOTA
Watertown
South Dakota Legion News **(29018)** ....‡27,815

TEXAS
Austin
TEXAS LEGION TIMES **(29833)** ....‡110,000

Richardson
Mexican War Journal **(30977)** ....(Combined) 135

VIRGINIA
Alexandria
The Catholic War Veteran **(31653)** ....(Paid) ‡24,000
(Free) ‡1,000

WASHINGTON
Langley
Alarming Cry News **(32805)** ....(Combined) 1,500

ONTARIO, CANADA
Ottawa
Legion Magazine **(36258)** ....(Paid) 362,274

VETERINARY MEDICINE

CALIFORNIA
Davis
Veterinary Surgery **(1818)** ....‡2,195

Pico Rivera
Pulse **(2841)** ....(Paid) ‡1,060
(Non-paid) ‡78

Sacramento
California Veterinarian **(2990)** ....(Paid) ‡4,300
(Non-paid) ‡3,000

COLORADO
Denver
Journal of the American Animal Hospital
Association **(4333)** 13,500
TRENDS Magazine **(4364)** 16,000

ILLINOIS
Schaumburg
American Journal of Veterinary
Research **(9583)** ....(Paid) 6,700
(Non-paid) 211
Journal of the American Veterinary Medical
Association **(9584)** ....(Paid) 48,504
(Non-paid) 3,198

KANSAS
Lawrence
Journal of Avian Medicine and Surgery **(11554)**

Lenexa
Swine Practitioner **(11597)** ....△3,340
Veterinary Economics **(11598)** 54,236

Manhattan
Veterinary and Human
Toxicology **(11630)** ....(Paid) ‡1,000
(Controlled) ‡25

KENTUCKY
Lexington
The Horse **(12165)** ....(Paid) 40,000

MARYLAND
Bethesda
Animal Behavior Abstracts **(13311)**
Journal of Aquatic Animal
Health **(13349)** ....(Paid) 1,500

NEBRASKA
Crawford
Rare Breeds Journal **(17990)** ....(Paid) 4,000

NEW JERSEY
Montvale
FirstLine **(19254)**
Veterinary Medicine **(19278)** ....△43,648

NEW YORK
New York
Domestic Animal Endocrinology **(21566)**
Experimental and Applied Acarology **(21664)**
Vaccine **(22894)**

Valhalla
Toxicology Pathology **(23484)** ......(Combined) 1,000

NORTH CAROLINA
Raleigh
Veterinary Radiology &
Ultrasound **(24158)** ....(Controlled) 1,200

OHIO
Cleveland
DVM Newsmagazine **(24883)** ....(Paid) 3,000
(Non-paid) 54,000

PENNSYLVANIA
Media
Journal of Zoo and Wildlife
Medicine **(27242)** 1,500

Philadelphia
Clinical Techniques in Small Animal Practice **(27411)**
Clinical Techniques in Small Animal
Practice **(27412)** ....‡1,144
Journal of Natural History **(27538)** ....(Paid) 333,180
Seminars in Avian and Exotic Pet Medicine **(27660)**
Veterinary Clinics **(27717)**

Yardley
Compendium on Continuing Education for the
Practicing Veterinarian **(28199)** ......(Paid) ‡20,035
(Non-paid) ‡11,446

TEXAS
Austin
Texas Veterinarian **(29850)** ....(Paid) ‡3,000
(Controlled) ‡500

VIRGINIA
Blacksburg
Journal of Veterinary Medical Education **(31877)**

ONTARIO, CANADA
Ottawa
Canadian Journal of Veterinary
Research **(36221)** ....‡2,000
Canadian Veterinary Journal **(36229)** ....‡6,600
5,500

QUEBEC, CANADA
Montreal
Nos Animaux **(37195)** ....(Paid) 14,000
(Non-paid) 11,000

Saint-Hyacinthe
Le Medecin Veterinaire du
Quebec **(37351)** ....(Non-paid) ‡2,700

VOCATIONAL EDUCATION

DISTRICT OF COLUMBIA
Washington
Youth Today **(5874)** ....(Combined) 58,000

MASSACHUSETTS
Burlington
Journal of Vocational Rehabilitation **(14030)**

MICHIGAN
Ann Arbor
Tech Directions **(14770)** ....(Paid) 500
(Controlled) 40,000

NEW YORK
New York
International Journal for the Advancement of
Counseling **(21899)**

PENNSYLVANIA
Pittsburgh
Journal for Vocational Special Needs
Education **(27805)**

VIRGINIA
Alexandria
Techniques **(31741)** ....(Paid) ‡42,000

ONTARIO, CANADA
Ottawa
Canadian Vocational Journal **(36230)** ....‡1,000

WASTE MANAGEMENT AND RECYCLING

**See also Water Supply and Sewage
Disposal; Ecology and Conservation**

DISTRICT OF COLUMBIA
Washington
Scrap **(5784)** ....(Paid) 7322

FLORIDA
Winter Park
Florida Specifier **(6881)** ....(Paid) ‡1,000
(Controlled) ‡11,000

GEORGIA
Atlanta
Waste Age **(7059)** ....(Paid) 1,000
(Non-paid) 43,000

Waste Age Product
News **(7060)** ....(Combined) 30,000

IOWA
Ankeny
Conservation Voices **(10605)** .....(Combined) 12,032

MICHIGAN
Detroit
Waste News **(14952)** ....(Paid) 16,231
(Non-paid) 24,147

Troy
Pollution Engineering **(15635)** ....(Controlled) ‡58,000

MINNESOTA
St. Louis Park
El Digest **(16360)**

NEVADA
Las Vegas
Recharger Magazine **(18384)** ....(Paid) ‡5,000
(Non-paid) ‡750

NEW HAMPSHIRE
Nashua
CleanRooms International **(18585)**
Water & Wastewater International **(18603)**

NEW JERSEY
Hoboken
Environmental Quality Management **(18941)**

NEW YORK
Amityville
Journal of Environmental
Systems **(20045)** ....(Paid) 1,200

Larchmont
Environmental Engineering Science **(20899)**

New York
Dangerous Properties of Industrial Materials
Report **(21536)**
Ecotoxicology **(21583)**

OHIO
Cleveland
Recycling Today **(24948)** 16,869

OKLAHOMA
Tulsa
Prevencion de la Contaminacion **(26129)**
Worldwide Waste Management **(26144)**

OREGON
Portland
Resource Recycling **(26505)** ....(Paid) 2,697
(Controlled) 14,350

PENNSYLVANIA
Emmaus
BioCycle **(26875)** 12,500
Compost Science & Utilization **(26876)** ....(Paid) 800

Pittsburgh
EM **(27783)** ....‡10,000
Pollution Equipment
News **(27836)** ....(Controlled) 90,600

Wayne
Hazardous Waste Litigation Reporter **(28132)**

Circulation: ★ = ABC; △ = BPA; ♦ = CAC; ● = CCAB; ▫ = VAC; ⊕ = PO Statement; ‡ = Publisher's Report; Boldface figures = sworn; Light figures = estimated.

3239

Trade, Technical, and Professional Publications

Circ.

WASTE MANAGEMENT AND RECYCLING
(continued)

VIRGINIA
Alexandria
Water Environment & Technology (31752)

Reston
Practice Periodical of Hazardous, Toxic, and
Radioactive Waste Management (32410)

WISCONSIN
Appleton
Progress in Paper
Recycling (33543) ....(Combined) 700

BRITISH COLUMBIA, CANADA
Vancouver
Canadian Environmental
Protection (35131) ....(Combined) 21,304

ONTARIO, CANADA
Aurora
Environmental Science &
Engineering (35647) ....(Combined) 19,095

Burlington
Water Quality Research Journal of
Canada (35719) ....(Paid) 300

Toronto
Solid Waste &
Recycling (36743) ....(Combined) •9,600

WATER SUPPLY AND SEWAGE DISPOSAL

See also Ecology and Conservation; Waste Management and Recycling

ALABAMA
Birmingham
U.S. Piper (98) ....(Non-paid) 8,500

ARIZONA
Tucson
Water Conditioning &
Purification (972) ....(Paid) 1,071
(Controlled) 19,824

CALIFORNIA
Davis
California Water Resources Center
Contribution (1812) ....(Non-paid) 450

Sacramento
Management of the California State Water
Project (3006)

COLORADO
Denver
Journal of the American Water Works
Association (4334) ....(Paid) ‡39,040
(Controlled) ‡3,993

Fort Collins
International Dredging Review (4433) ....(Paid) 1,500
(Controlled) 1,450

DISTRICT OF COLUMBIA
Washington
Water Resources Research (5857)

FLORIDA
Winter Park
Florida Specifier (6881) ....(Paid) ‡1,000
(Controlled) ‡11,000

GEORGIA
Atlanta
Waste Age (7059) ....(Paid) 1,000
(Non-paid) 43,000

ILLINOIS
Chicago
Irrigation Journal (8420) ....(Controlled) ‡16,500
Landscape & Irrigation (8457) ....(Paid) 63
(Controlled) 62,000

Des Plaines
Water Engineering &
Management (8773) ....(Paid) 3,648
(Non-paid) 37,442
Water & Wastes
Digest (8774) ....(Non-paid) ‡100,332

Circ.

IOWA
Ankeny
Journal of Soil and Water
Conservation (10606) 9,358

Fort Dodge
Land & Water (10902) ....(Paid) 4,000
(Non-paid) 16,000

KANSAS
Halstead
U.S. Water News (11477) ....(Paid) ‡1,700
(Controlled) ‡18,300

MAINE
Waldoboro
Journal of Maine Water Utilities
Association (13068) 400

MASSACHUSETTS
Holliston
Journal of the New England Water Works
Association (14239) ....(Paid) ‡2,800
(Non-paid) ‡243

MICHIGAN
Kalamazoo
Ground Water Monitoring and
Remediation (15237) ....‡15,500

MISSISSIPPI
Vicksburg
Dredging Research (16870) ....(Non-paid) 2200

NEW HAMPSHIRE
Nashua
Water & Wastewater International (18603)

NEW JERSEY
Hoboken
River Research and Applications (19100)

NEW YORK
Amityville
Journal of Environmental
Systems (20045) ....(Paid) 1,200

Latham
Water Technology (20934) ....(Paid) 67
(Controlled) 20,219

New York
Ecotoxicology (21583)
Geotechnical and Geological Engineering (21758)
Water Resources (22910)

Syracuse
Clearwaters (23395) ....(Paid) ‡2,400
(Non-paid) ‡300

OHIO
Columbus
Critical Reviews in Environmental Science and
Technology (25013) ....(Controlled) 700

Westerville
Water Well Journal (25645) ......(Non-paid) ‡25,000
(Paid) ‡1,500

OKLAHOMA
Tulsa
Prevencion de la Contaminacion (26129)
WaterWorld (26143) ....(Non-paid) 65,000
Worldwide Waste Management (26144)

PENNSYLVANIA
Emmaus
BioCycle (26875) 12,500

Pittsburgh
Pollution Equipment
News (27836) ....(Controlled) 90,600

TEXAS
Austin
Texas Water Utilities
Journal (29851) ....(Controlled) ⊕9,010

VERMONT
Danville
The American Dowser (31538)

VIRGINIA
Alexandria
Operations Forum (31719) ....(Paid) ‡14,451
Utility Fleet Management (31748) ....‡22,014

Circ.

Water Environment Research (31751) ....‡8,500
Water Environment & Technology (31752)

Middleburg
Journal of the American Water Resources
Association (32272) 3,000

Reston
Journal of Irrigation and Drainage
Engineering (32385)
Journal of Water Resources Planning and
Management (32401) ....(Paid) ⊕1,500

WISCONSIN
Madison
Ground Water (33944)

BRITISH COLUMBIA, CANADA
Vancouver
Canadian Environmental
Protection (35131) ....(Combined) 21,304

ONTARIO, CANADA
Aurora
Environmental Science &
Engineering (35647) ....(Combined) 19,095

Burlington
Water Quality Research Journal of
Canada (35719) ....(Paid) 300

Exeter
Ground Water
Canada (35827) ....(Controlled) ‡3,920

QUEBEC, CANADA
Montreal
Vecteur Environnement (37233) ....(Combined) 4,000

WEIGHTS AND MEASURES

TENNESSEE
Hendersonville
Weighing & Measurement (29221) ....‡15,000

WELDING

See also Metal, Metallurgy, and Metal Trade

FLORIDA
Miami
Welding Journal (6391) ....(Paid) 47,719

ILLINOIS
Rockford
Practical Welding
Today (9530) ....(Controlled) 40,000

OHIO
Cleveland
Gases & Welding Distributor (24901) ......(Paid) 668
(Non-paid) 5,000

Welding Design &
Fabrication (24961) ....(Controlled) ‡40,000
Welding Innovation (24962) ......(Controlled) ‡78,000

WILDLIFE AND EXOTIC ANIMALS

CALIFORNIA
Berkeley
Journal of Wildlife
Rehabilitation (1538) ....(Paid) 2,000

Los Angeles
Zoo View (2444) ....(Paid) 57,000
(Non-paid) 1,000

Oakland
California Coast &
Ocean (2673) ....(Combined) 10,000

Sacramento
Animal Issues (2976) ....(Paid) ‡30,000
(Non-paid) ‡1,000

COLORADO
Fort Collins
Human Dimensions of Wildlife (4432)

ILLINOIS
Ava
Illinois Audubon (8045) ....(Combined) 3,000

Chicago
Physiological and Biochemical Zoology (8530)

MARYLAND
Takoma Park
Endangered Species & Wetlands Report (13751)

Washington Grove
Journal of Applied Animal Welfare Science (13774)

MASSACHUSETTS
Northampton
Mammalian Species (14429)

MISSOURI
Jefferson City
Missouri
   Conservationist (17124) ....(Combined) 440,000

NEW YORK
Bronx
Wildlife Conservation (20290) ....(Paid) 150,000

New York
Journal of International Wildlife Law and
   Policy (22105)

OHIO
Marietta
Bird Watcher's Digest (25343) ....‡90,000

PENNSYLVANIA
Media
Journal of Zoo and Wildlife
   Medicine (27242) 1,500

TEXAS
Bowie
Exotic Market Review (29940)

VIRGINIA
Arlington
Endangered Species Bulletin (31788)

ONTARIO, CANADA
Thunder Bay
Alices (36436)

WOOD AND WOODWORKING

See also Forestry

ALABAMA
Gulf Shores
Crossties (251) ....(Controlled) ‡3,500

Montgomery
Panel World (373) ....(Controlled) ‡12,192

CALIFORNIA
Los Angeles
Woodworkers West (2439) ....(Combined) 10,000

Newport Beach
Building Products
   Digest (2623) ....(Controlled) ‡12,750
The Merchant Magazine (2630) ....(Paid) ‡3,798
                                   (Controlled) 269

Novato
Woodwork (2654) ....‡50,000

CONNECTICUT
Essex
Woodshop News (4785) ....(Paid) ⊕72,176
                                   (Free) ⊕21,500

Newtown
Fine Woodworking (5043) ....(Paid) 265,029

ILLINOIS
Des Plaines
CabinetMaker (8751) ....(Controlled) 40,000

Lincolnshire
CWB: Custom Woodworking
   Business (9085) ....(Controlled) ‡60,000
Wood & Wood
   Products (9089) ....(Non-paid) ‡51,573

Springfield
ILMDA Advantage (9633) ....(Combined) ‡918

IOWA
Des Moines
ShopNotes (10808)

WOOD (10815) ....(Paid) 551,121
Woodsmith (10816) ....(Paid) 375,000

MAINE
Pownal
Fine Tool Journal (13033) ....(Paid) 2,500

MICHIGAN
Troy
Modern Woodworking (15629) 57,000

MINNESOTA
Eagan
American Woodworker (15861) ....(Paid) 332,911

Medina
Woodworker's Journal (16049) ....(Paid) ‡223,758
                                   (Non-paid) ‡2,256

Shoreview
American Woodturner (16446) ....(Paid) 9,700

NEW YORK
Manhasset
Wood Technology (21019) ....(Paid) 472
                                   (Controlled) 22,500

New York
Building Supply Home
   Centers (21347) ....(Non-paid) ‡51,305

Syracuse
Journal of Wood Chemistry and
   Technology (23406) 300

OHIO
Cincinnati
Chip Chats (24781) ....‡35,000

TENNESSEE
Cordova
Shelter (29152) ....(Non-paid) ‡26,723

VERMONT
Newbury
Timber Framing (31571) ....(Paid) 1,800

VIRGINIA
Ashland
Pallet Enterprise (31857) ....(Paid) ‡150
                                   (Controlled) ‡14,000

Blacksburg
Wood & Fiber Science (31880) ....‡800

WASHINGTON
Woodinville
China Wood Preservatives (33211)

WISCONSIN
Fort Atkinson
Wood Digest (33722) ....(Controlled) ‡51,010

Madison
Forest Products Journal (33941) 3,800
Hardwood Floors (33945) ....(Controlled) 24,300

BRITISH COLUMBIA, CANADA
Vancouver
Specialty Wood
   Journal (35168) ....(Combined) 9,942

ONTARIO, CANADA
Markham
Woodworking (36033) ....(Combined) •11,171

Mississauga
The LBMAO Reporter (36073) .....(Non-paid) ‡1,500

Ottawa
Wood Design & Building (36281) ....(Paid) 8,000
                                   (Non-paid) 25,000
Wood Lebois (36282) ....(Combined) 67,000

Toronto
Centre (36544) ....,..........(Controlled) 15,749

QUEBEC, CANADA
Baie D'urfe'
Canadian Wood
   Products (36945) ....(Combined) 7,358

Victoriaville
2x4 (All About Wood) (37433) ....(Controlled) ‡7,569

ZOOLOGY

ALABAMA
Montgomery
Outdoor Alabama (372) ....‡12,000

ARIZONA
Phoenix
Arizoo (783) ....(Paid) ‡34,000
                                   (Non-paid) ‡2,000

Tucson
Cryptozoology (943) ....(Paid) 900

CALIFORNIA
San Diego
ZOONOOZ (3290) ....‡200,000

CONNECTICUT
Farmington
Folia Primatologica (4825) 850

DELAWARE
Newark
Journal of Foraminiferal Research (5276)

DISTRICT OF COLUMBIA
Washington
ZooGoer (5875) ....(Paid) 31,000

FLORIDA
Gainesville
Contributions on Entomology International (6134)
Holarctic Lepidoptera (6143) ....(Combined) 425
Oriental Insects (6152)
Tropical Lepidoptera (6159) ....(Combined) 805

HAWAII
Honolulu
Elepaio (7688) ....‡2,000

ILLINOIS
Chicago
Physiological and Biochemical Zoology (8530)

KANSAS
Topeka
Animal Keepers'
   Forum (11814) ....(Controlled) 2,850

LOUISIANA
Baton Rouge
The Coleopterists Bulletin (12487) ....‡850

MARYLAND
College Park
Journal of Arachnology (13424) 650

Washington Grove
Journal of Applied Animal Welfare Science (13774)

Westminster
Miniature Donkey Talk (13777) ....(Combined) 7,300

MASSACHUSETTS
Northampton
Mammalian Species (14429)

MICHIGAN
West Bloomfield
International Journal of Acarology (15675)

NEW JERSEY
Hoboken
American Journal of Primatology (18889) 4,900
The Journal of Experimental
   Zoology (19022) 1,200
Zoo Biology (19122) 3850

Newark
Marine and Freshwater Behavior and
   Physiology (19359)

NEW YORK
Larchmont
Vector-Borne and Zoonotic Diseases (20929)

New York
American Museum Novitates (21202)
Fish Physiology and Biochemistry (21702)
International Journal of Primatology (21915)

NORTH CAROLINA
Greensboro
Journal of Mammalogy (23925)

Circulation: ★ = ABC; △ = BPA; ♦ = CAC; • = CCAB; ⧠ = VAC; ⊕ = PO Statement; ‡ = Publisher's Report; Boldface figures = sworn; Light figures = estimated.

3241

Trade, Technical, and Professional Publications

Circ.

ZOOLOGY (continued)

PENNSYLVANIA
Media
Journal of Zoo and Wildlife
  Medicine **(27242)** 1,500

Philadelphia
Journal of Natural History **(27538)** ....(Paid) 333,180

VIRGINIA
Blacksburg
Herpetologica **(31872)** ....‡1,700

ONTARIO, CANADA
Kitchener
Megadrilogica **(35963)** ....(Paid) 1,000

North York
Canadian Journal of Zoology (Revue Canadienne de
  Zoologie) **(36125)** ....‡1,300

Newspaper Feature Editors

This section provides the names and telephone numbers of editors contributing to daily newspapers with circulations of 50,000 or more. This index lists newspapers geographically (by state or province, and by city). Listings within each city appear alphabetically by publication title.

The following is an alphabetical list of newspapers that are represented in the Newspaper Feature Editors index:

Abilene Reporter-News (Abilene, TX)
The Advocate (Baton Rouge, LA)
Albuquerque Journal (Albuquerque, NM)
Amarillo Globe-News (Amarillo, TX)
The Ann Arbor News (Ann Arbor, MI)
Argus Leader (Mc Lean, VA)
The Arizona Daily Star (Tucson, AZ)
The Arizona Republic (Phoenix, AZ)
Arkansas Democrat-Gazette (Little Rock, AR)
Asbury Park Press (East Brunswick, NJ)
Asheville Citizen-Times (Asheville, NC)
The Atlanta Journal and Constitution (Atlanta, GA)
The Atlanta Voice (Atlanta, GA)
The Bakersfield Californian (Bakersfield, CA)
The Baltimore Sun (Baltimore, MD)
Baptist Messenger (Oklahoma City, OK)
Battle Creek Shopper News (Battle Creek, MI)
The Bay City Times (Bay City, MI)
The Beacon-News (Aurora, IL)
Beaumont Enterprise (Beaumont, TX)
Belleville News-Democrat (Belleville, IL)
The Billings Gazette (Billings, MT)
The Birmingham News (Birmingham, AL)
Birmingham Post-Herald (Birmingham, AL)
The Blade (Toledo, OH)
The Boston Globe (Boston, MA)
Boston Herald (Boston, MA)
Bucks County Courier Times (Levittown, PA)
The Buffalo News (Buffalo, NY)
The Burlington Free Press (Burlington, VT)
Calgary Herald (Calgary, AB)
The Calgary Sun (Calgary, AB)
Cape Cod Times (Hyannis, MA)
Charleston Daily Mail (Charleston, WV)
The Chronicle Herald (Halifax, NS)
The Cincinnati Enquirer (Cincinnati, OH)
The Cincinnati Post (Cincinnati, OH)
The Clarion Ledger (Jackson, MS)
The Collingwood Connection (Midland, ON)
Columbus Alive (Columbus, OH)
The Columbus Dispatch (Columbus, OH)
Contra Costa Times (Walnut Creek, CA)
The Courier-Journal (Louisville, KY)
The Courier-News (Bridgewater, NJ)
Courier-Post (Cherry Hill, NJ)
Crain's Chicago Business (Chicago, IL)
Daily Commercial (Leesburg, FL)
Daily Herald (Arlington Heights, IL)
Daily Local News (West Chester, PA)
Daily Press (Newport News, VA)

Daily Record (Parsippany, NJ)
The Daily Times (Primos, PA)
The Daily-Mail (Hagerstown, MD)
The Dallas Morning News (Dallas, TX)
Democrat and Chronicle (Rochester, NY)
The Denver Post (Denver, CO)
Des Moines News (Burien, WA)
The Des Moines Register (Des Moines, IA)
Deseret News (Salt Lake City, UT)
Detroit Free Press (Detroit, MI)
The Detroit News (Detroit, MI)
Diario las Americas (Miami, FL)
The Eagle-Tribune (Lawrence, MA)
The Edmonton Journal (Edmonton, AB)
The Edmonton Sun (Edmonton, AB)
Education Update (New York, NY)
El Paso Times (El Paso, TX)
El Vocero de Puerto Rico (San Juan, PR)
The Enterprise (Brockton, MA)
Erie Times-News (Erie, PA)
Express-News (San Antonio, TX)
The Flint Journal (Flint, MI)
The Florida Times-Union (Jacksonville, FL)
Florida Today (Melbourne, FL)
The Fort Saskatchewan Record (Fort Saskatchewan, AB)
The Forum (Fargo, ND)
The Free Lance-Star (Fredericksburg, VA)
The Fresno Bee (Fresno, CA)
The Gazette (Montreal, QC)
The Grand Rapids Press (Grand Rapids, MI)
Green Bay Press-Gazette (Green Bay, WI)
The Greenville News (Greenville, SC)
The Halifax Herald (Halifax, NS)
The Herald (Everett, WA)
Herald & Review (Decatur, IL)
The Herald-Sun (Durham, NC)
The Honolulu Advertiser (Honolulu, HI)
Honolulu Star-Bulletin (Honolulu, HI)
Houston Press (Houston, TX)
The Huntsville Times (Huntsville, AL)
The Hutchinson News (Hutchinson, KS)
The Idaho Statesman (Boise, ID)
The Indianapolis Star (Indianapolis, IN)
Irish Voice Newspaper (New York, NY)
Isthmus (Madison, WI)
Journal Star (Peoria, IL)
Kalamazoo Gazette (Kalamazoo, MI)
The Kansas City Star (Kansas City, MO)
The Knoxville News-Sentinel (Knoxville, TN)

La Presse (Montreal, QC)
Lansing State Journal (Lansing, MI)
Las Vegas Review-Journal (Las Vegas, NV)
Las Vegas Weekly (Las Vegas, NV)
Le Journal de Montreal (Montreal, QC)
Le Journal de Quebec (Quebec, QC)
Le Soleil (Quebec, QC)
Leader-Post (Regina, SK)
Leader-Telegram (Eau Claire, WI)
The Liberal (Richmond Hill, ON)
Lincoln Journal (Lincoln, NE)
The London Free Press (London, ON)
Lowell Sun (Lowell, MA)
The Macomb Daily (Mount Clemens, MI)
Milwaukee Journal Sentinel (Milwaukee, WI)
The Mobile Register (Mobile, AL)
The Modesto Bee (Modesto, CA)
The Morning Call (Allentown, PA)
National Post (Don Mills, ON)
News & Record (Greensboro, NC)
News Journal (Mansfield, OH)
The News-Gazette (Champaign, IL)
The News-Journal (Daytona Beach, FL)
The News-Leader (Staunton, VA)
News-Register (Wheeling, WV)
Newsday (Melville, NY)
North Jersey Prospector (Clifton, NJ)
Now (Toronto, ON)
Oakland Press (Pontiac, MI)
The Oakland Tribune (Oakland, CA)
Oklahoman (Oklahoma City, OK)
Omaha World-Herald (Omaha, NE)
The Oregonian (Portland, OR)
The Ottawa Citizen (Ottawa, ON)
The Palm Beach Post (West Palm Beach, FL)
The Patriot Ledger (Quincy, MA)
Pennysaver (Hanover, MD)
Pensacola News Journal (Pensacola, FL)
Philadelphia Daily News (Philadelphia, PA)
Philadelphia Inquirer (Philadelphia, PA)
Pittsburgh City Paper (Pittsburgh, PA)
Plain Dealer (Cleveland, OH)
The Post-Crescent (Appleton, WI)
Post-Gazette (Pittsburgh, PA)
The Post-Standard (Syracuse, NY)
Poughkeepsie Journal (Poughkeepsie, NY)
Press & Sun-Bulletin (Binghamton, NY)
The Press of Atlantic City (Pleasantville, NJ)
Quad-City Times (Davenport, IA)
Reading Eagle (Reading, PA)

The Record (Hackensack, NJ)
The Record (Stockton, CA)
The Register-Guard (Eugene, OR)
The Repository (Canton, OH)
Republican-American (Waterbury, CT)
Results Media Shopper's Guide (Hicksville, NY)
Richmond Times-Dispatch (Richmond, VA)
The Roanoke Times (Roanoke, VA)
Sacramento News & Review (Sacramento, CA)
The Saginaw News (Saginaw, MI)
The Salt Lake Tribune (Salt Lake City, UT)
The San Bernardino County Sun (San Bernardino, CA)
San Francisco Chronicle (San Francisco, CA)
San Gabriel Valley Tribune (West Covina, CA)
San Jose Mercury News (San Jose, CA)
Santa Barbara News-Press (Santa Barbara, CA)
Sarasota Herald-Tribune (Sarasota, FL)
Seattle Post-Intelligencer (Seattle, WA)
Sioux City Journal (Sioux City, IA)
South Bend Tribune (South Bend, IN)
The Spokesman-Review (Spokane, WA)
St. Louis Post-Dispatch (St. Louis, MO)
St. Paul Pioneer Press (St. Paul, MN)

St. Petersburg Times (St. Petersburg, FL)
Standard-Examiner (Ogden, UT)
The Standard-Times (New Bedford, MA)
Star Tribune (Minneapolis, MN)
Star-Gazette (Elmira, NY)
Star-Ledger (Newark, NJ)
State Journal-Register (Springfield, IL)
Staten Island Advance (Staten Island, NY)
Statesman Journal (Salem, OR)
Stockbridge Town Crier (Stockbridge, MI)
Suburban News (Hackettstown, NJ)
Sunday Dispatch (Pittston, PA)
Telegram & Gazette (Worcester, MA)
The Times (Shreveport, LA)
The Times (Munster, IN)
Times Herald-Record (Middletown, NY)
The Times Leader (Wilkes Barre, PA)
The Times-Picayune (New Orleans, LA)
TimesDaily (Florence, FL)
The Topeka Capital-Journal (Topeka, KS)
The Toronto Star (Toronto, ON)
The Trentonian (Trenton, NJ)
The Tribune (Mesa, AZ)

Tribune-Democrat (Johnstown, PA)
Tribune-Review (Greensburg, PA)
Tulsa World (Tulsa, OK)
The Union Leader (Manchester, NH)
Union-News & Sunday Republican (Springfield, MA)
USA Today (Mc Lean, VA)
Valley Times (Pleasanton, CA)
The Vancouver Courier (Vancouver, BC)
The Vancouver Sun (Vancouver, BC)
Ventura County Star (Ventura, CA)
The Vindicator (Youngstown, OH)
The Virginian-Pilot (Norfolk, VA)
Wapakoneta Daily News (Wapakoneta, OH)
The Washington Post (Washington, DC)
Waterloo-Cedar Falls Courier (Waterloo, IA)
Waupaca County News (Iola, WI)
Wichita Eagle (Wichita, KS)
Willamette Week (Portland, OR)
The Winnipeg Sun (Winnipeg, MB)
Winston-Salem Journal (Winston-Salem, NC)
Wisconsin State Journal (Madison, WI)
York Daily Record (York, PA)
York Sunday News (York, PA)

ALABAMA-Anniston

(15) THE ANNISTON STAR
PO Box 189
Anniston, AL 36202
Lifestyle..............Cathi Downing.......................(256)235-9235

ALABAMA-Birmingham

(58) THE BIRMINGHAM NEWS
PO Box 2553
Birmingham, AL 35202
City.....................Randy Henderson...................(205)325-2444
Financial/Business.....Jerry Underwood....................(205)325-3250
Lifestyle................Betsy Butgereit......................(205)325-2282
Lifestyle................Alec Harvey.........................(205)325-2100
Metro...................Wayne Hester.......................(205)325-2478
Sports..................Tom Arenberg......................(205)325-2433
State...................Glenn Stephens.....................(205)325-2482
Sunday.................Kenneth Carter.....................(205)325-3419
Weekend..............Pamela Dugan......................(205)325-3449

(60) BIRMINGHAM POST-HERALD
2200 4th Ave. N.
Birmingham, AL 35203
Editorials..............Karl Seitz...........................(205)325-2411
Metro...................John Staed.........................(205)325-2344
Sports..................Tim Stephens.......................(205)325-2127

ALABAMA-Huntsville

(270) THE HUNTSVILLE TIMES
PO Box 1487, West Sta.
Huntsville, AL 35807-0487
Aviation.................Martin Burkey.......................(205)532-4418
Book....................Ann Marie Martin..................(205)532-4407
City.....................Lee Roop...........................(205)532-4423
Drama..................Ann Marie Martin..................(205)532-4412
Editorials..............John Ehinger........................(205)532-4218
Entertainment..........Mike Kaylor........................(205)532-4406
Environmental.........Martin Burkey.......................(205)532-4418
Family..................Melinda Joiner......................(205)532-4404
Financial/Business.....Ray Garner.........................(205)532-4424
Food...................Mickey Ellis.........................(205)532-4403
Garden/Home.........Don Cox...........................(205)532-4443
News...................Joe Duncan.........................(205)532-4402
Political.................John Anderson......................(205)532-4293
Religion................Yvonne White......................(205)532-4419
Sports..................John Pruett..........................(205)532-4430
State...................Guy Hollis..........................(205)532-4000

ALABAMA-Mobile

(325) THE MOBILE REGISTER
304 Government St.
PO Box 2488
Mobile, AL 36602
Art.....................Thomas Harrison...................(334)694-6714
Book....................John Sledge........................(334)433-1551
City.....................David Helms........................(334)434-8614
Drama..................Thomas Harrison...................(334)694-6714
Editorials..............Frances Coleman...................(334)434-8607
Education.............Casandra Andrews..................(334)439-7158
Family..................Eleanor Ransburg..................(334)439-7106
Fashion................Debra Braggs......................(334)434-8539
Features...............Eleanor Ransburg..................(334)439-7106
Financial/Business.....Jerald Hyche........................(334)434-8644
Food...................David Holloway.....................(334)434-8682
Garden/Home.........Bill Finch...........................(334)434-8535
Lifestyle................David Helms........................(334)434-8614
Medical................Jean Helms.........................(334)434-8537
Metro...................Jim Van Anglen....................(334)434-8608
Movie..................Mike Brantley.......................(334)434-8642
Music..................Carol Cain.........................(334)434-8606
Photo..................Robie Ray..........................(334)434-7194
Political.................Gene Owens........................(334)434-8587
Radio..................Mike Brantley.......................(334)434-8642
Real Estate...........Kathy Jumper......................(334)434-8538
Religion................Kristen Campbell....................(334)434-8579
Rural Development...Charles Croft.......................(334)433-1551
Saturday..............Robert Buchanan...................(334)433-1551
Society................Susie Cloos........................(334)434-8691
Sports..................Kim Shugart........................(334)433-1551
TV.....................Mike Brantley.......................(334)434-8642
Travel..................Eleanor Ransburg..................(334)439-7106
Women's..............Debra Braggs......................(334)434-8539

ARIZONA-Mesa

(746) THE TRIBUNE
120 W. 1st Ave.
Mesa, AZ 85210
Editorials..............Bob Schuster.......................(602)898-6507

Features..............Liz Merritt........................(602)898-6572

ARIZONA-Phoenix

(782) THE ARIZONA REPUBLIC
200 E. Van Buren St.
Phoenix, AZ 85004-2238
Entertainment..........Vinton Supplee.....................(602)444-4823
Financial/Business.....David Fritze........................(602)444-8640
Garden/Home.........Zada Blayton......................(602)444-8977
Lifestyle................Stacy Sullivan......................(602)444-8749
Metro...................Kristin Gilger.......................(602)444-8306
Photo..................Dave Seibert.......................(602)444-8954
Sports..................Dave Lumia........................(602)444-8166
Travel..................Mike Stephens.....................(602)444-8745

ARIZONA-Tucson

(929) THE ARIZONA DAILY STAR
4850 S. Park Ave.
Tucson, AZ 85726-6807
City.....................Debbie Kornmiller..................(602)573-4127
Editorials..............Jim Kiser...........................(602)573-4235
Financial/Business.....John Bolton........................(602)573-4177
Food...................Tom Turner........................(602)573-4124
Medical................Jane Erikson.......................(602)573-4118
Music..................James Reel.........................(602)573-4128
News...................Joe McDermott....................(602)573-4173
News...................Ann-Eve Petersen..................(602)573-4101
Photo..................Linda Salazar.......................(602)573-4155
Sports..................B. J. Bartlett.......................(602)573-4150
Travel..................Tom Turner........................(602)573-4124

ARKANSAS-Little Rock

(1216) ARKANSAS DEMOCRAT-GAZETTE
Capitol Ave. & Scott St.
PO Box 2221
Little Rock, AR 72203
City.....................Todd Stone........................(501)378-3867
Editorials..............Paul Greenberg....................(501)378-3482
Family..................Rhonda Owen......................(501)378-3495
Features...............Jack Schnedler.....................(501)399-3677
Food...................Irene Wassell.......................(501)378-3497
Photo..................Barry Arthur........................(501)378-3484
Political.................Bill Simmons........................(501)399-3657
Religion................Laurie Pierce........................(501)378-3471
Travel..................Libby Smith.........................(501)378-3888

CALIFORNIA-Bakersfield

(1447) THE BAKERSFIELD CALIFORNIAN
PO Box BIN 440
Bakersfield, CA 93302
Features...............Andy Kehe.........................(661)395-7434
Metro...................Bob Christie........................(661)395-7413
Photo..................Alex Horvath.......................(661)395-7490
Sports..................Tony Lacava........................(661)395-7737

CALIFORNIA-Fresno

(1950) THE FRESNO BEE
1626 E St.
Fresno, CA 93786
Entertainment..........Tom Becker.......................(209)441-6281
Features...............Alison Lucian.......................(209)441-6368
Financial/Business.....Ron Trujillo........................(209)441-6329
Food...................Lanny Larson......................(209)441-6297
Garden/Home.........Guy Keeler........................(209)441-6383
Metro...................John Rich..........................(209)441-6436
Movie..................Rick Bentley........................(209)441-6352
News...................Kris Eldred.........................(209)441-6486
Photo..................William (Bill) Haines................(209)441-6376
Political.................Jim Boren..........................(209)441-6307
Real Estate...........Sanford Nax.......................(209)441-6495
Religion................Ron Orozco........................(559)441-6304
Sports..................Robert Zizzo.......................(559)441-6340
TV & Radio...........Lanny Larson......................(209)441-6297
Travel..................Alison Lucian.......................(209)441-6368

CALIFORNIA-Modesto

(2561) THE MODESTO BEE
1325 H St.
Modesto, CA 95354
Editorials..............Dick LeGrand......................(209)578-2317
Financial/Business.....Dave Hill...........................(209)578-2336
Lifestyle................Mike Dunbar.......................(209)578-2012
Photo..................Ted Benson........................(209)578-2322
Sports..................Ted Brock..........................(209)578-2301

CALIFORNIA-Oakland

(2692) THE OAKLAND TRIBUNE
Tribune Tower
401 13th St.
Oakland, CA 94612
Financial/Business	Dave Tong	
Photo	Ron Reisterer	
Sports	Steve Herendeen	

CALIFORNIA-Pleasanton

(2856) VALLEY TIMES
127 Spring St.
PO Box 607
Pleasanton, CA 94566
City	Kelly Gust	(510)847-2111
City	Mark Mazzaferro	(510)847-2111
Features	Linda Davis	(510)847-2111
Photo	Jim Ketsdever	(510)847-2111
Religion	Dave Goll	(510)847-2111

CALIFORNIA-Sacramento

(3017) SACRAMENTO NEWS & REVIEW
1015 20th St.
Sacramento, CA 95814
Editorials	Tom Walsh	(916)498-1234

CALIFORNIA-San Bernardino

(3092) THE SAN BERNARDINO COUNTY SUN
399 N. D St.
San Bernardino, CA 92401-1518
Editorials	Richard Kimball	(909)889-9666
Entertainment	Ian Cahir	(909)889-9666
Features	John Weeks	(909)889-9666
Financial/Business	Jim Steinberg	(909)889-9666
Metro	Bill Diepenbrock	(909)889-9666
Movie	Owen Sheeran	(909)889-9666
Music	Owen Sheeran	(909)889-9666
News	Jill Jess	(909)889-9666
Photo	Gary Miller	(909)889-9666
Real Estate	Mike Murphy	(909)889-9666
Religion	Carla Wheeler	(909)889-9666
Sports	Paul Oberjuerge	(909)889-9666
Travel	Owen Sheeran	(909)889-9666

CALIFORNIA-San Francisco

(3432) SAN FRANCISCO CHRONICLE
901 Mission St.
San Francisco, CA 94103
Financial/Business	Kathleen Pender	(415)777-8440
Food	Michael Bauer	(415)777-7044
Photo	Scott Sommerdorf	(415)777-7077
TV	John Carman	(415)777-1111

CALIFORNIA-San Jose

(3536) SAN JOSE MERCURY NEWS
750 Ridder Park Dr.
San Jose, CA 95190-0001
Drama	Karen D'Souza	(408)271-3772
Education	Mark Brown	(408)920-5221
Entertainment	Katherine Fong	(408)278-3448
Fashion	Crystal Chow	(408)920-5954
Features	Katherine Fong	(408)278-3448
Financial/Business	David Satterfield	(408)920-5352
Food	Carolyn Jung	(408)920-5451
Garden/Home	Holly Hayes	(408)920-5374
Movie	Glenn Lovell	(408)920-5639
Music	Brad Kava	(408)920-5040
Photo	Geri Migielicz	(408)920-5090
Religion	Richard Scheinin	(408)920-5974
Sports	Mike Guersch	(408)920-5648
TV	Steve Marinucci	(408)920-5963

CALIFORNIA-Santa Barbara

(3655) SANTA BARBARA NEWS-PRESS
715 Anacapa St.
Santa Barbara, CA 93102-1359
Financial/Business	Mark Van de Kamp	(805)564-5212
Metro	Jane Hulse	(805)564-5131
News	Don Murphy	(805)564-5272

CALIFORNIA-Stockton

(3807) THE RECORD
530 E. Market St.
PO Box 900
Stockton, CA 95201-0900
Editorials	Kevin Parrish	(209)546-8264
Features	Robert Wagner	(209)546-8260
Financial/Business	Eric Grunder	(209)546-8260
Photo	David Finch	(209)546-8268
Sports	Sam Smith	(209)546-8282

CALIFORNIA-Ventura

(4014) VENTURA COUNTY STAR
5250 Ralston St.
Ventura, CA 93003
Editorials	Marianne Ratchiff	(805)655-7108
Entertainment	Mark Wyckoff	(805)655-1754
Lifestyle	Rich Welch	(805)645-1032
Sports	Mike Blackwell	(805)655-5821
TV	Dave Mason	(805)655-5831

CALIFORNIA-Walnut Creek

(4050) CONTRA COSTA TIMES
2640 Shadelands Dr.
Walnut Creek, CA 94598-2513
News	Jim Day	(925)935-2525
Photo	Jon Manlove	(925)935-2525
Political	Daniel Borenstein	(925)935-2525

CALIFORNIA-West Covina

(4060) SAN GABRIEL VALLEY TRIBUNE
1210 N. Azusa Canyon Rd.
West Covina, CA 91790
Automotive	Vernor Rodgers	
Editorials	Steve Scauzillo	
Entertainment	Liz Smilor	
Fashion	Carla Sanders	
Features	Catherine Gaugh	
Financial/Business	Jason Schaff	
Food	Linda Alquist	
Photo	Tim Berger	
Sports	Steve Hunt	
Travel	Rich Irwin	

COLORADO-Denver

(4324) THE DENVER POST
1560 Broadway
Denver, CO 80202-1577
Sports	Jin Armstrong	(303)820-1010

CONNECTICUT-Waterbury

(5193) REPUBLICAN-AMERICAN
389 Meadow St.
Waterbury, CT 06722
City	Suzan Bibisi	(203)574-3636
Entertainment	Ed Goodman	(203)574-3636
Fashion	James V. Ruocco	(203)574-3636
Financial/Business	Howard Fielding	(203)574-3636
Food	Claire LaFleur	(203)574-3636
Food	Jean Reid	(203)574-3636
Metro	Robert Fredericks	(203)574-3636
News	Robert Veillette	(203)574-3636
Photo	Thomas Kabelka	(203)574-3636
Political	Bill Leulchardt	(203)574-3636
Real Estate	Colleen Kelly	(203)574-3636
Religion	Colleen Kelly	(203)574-3636
Society	Ed Goodman	(203)574-3636
Sports	Lee Lewis	(203)574-3636
Suburban	John Crowell	(203)574-3636
Suburban	Thomas Hennick	(203)574-3636
TV & Radio	Russell Shaddox	(203)574-3636
Travel	Ed Goodman	(203)574-3636
Women's	Claire LaFleur	(203)574-3636

DISTRICT OF COLUMBIA-Washington

(5850) THE WASHINGTON POST
1150 15th St. NW
Washington, DC 20071-2400
Family	Margaret Mason	(202)334-6565
Fashion	Nina Hyde	(202)334-7548
Features	Mary Hadar	(202)334-6030
Financial/Business	Peter Behr	(202)334-7320
Food	Phyllis Richman	(202)334-7590
Garden/Home	Henry Mitchell	(202)334-7570

Living................Judy Weintraub.....................(202)334-6291
Medical................Abigail Trafford....................(202)334-5011
Metro................Milton Coleman.....................(202)334-6224
Movie................Rita Kempley.......................(202)334-7565
Music................Joseph McLellan....................(202)334-7565
News................Robert Kaiser......................(202)334-7549
Photo................Joe Elbert.........................(202)334-7383
Political................David Broder......................(202)334-7444
Real Estate............Ken Bredemeier....................(202)334-7124
Religion................Majorie Hyer......................(202)334-7334
Rural Development......Ward Sinclair.....................(202)334-7440
Society................Donnie Radcliffe...................(202)334-7556
Sports................George Solomon....................(202)334-7367
Sunday................Bob Thompson......................(202)334-6468
TV & Radio............John Carmody......................(202)334-7568
Travel................Linda Halsey.......................(202)334-7591

FLORIDA-Daytona Beach

(6037) THE NEWS-JOURNAL
901 6th St.
Daytona Beach, FL 32117-8099
Financial/Business......Tom Brown.........................(386)252-1511

FLORIDA-Florence

(6071) TIMESDAILY
PO Box 797
Florence, FL
Features................Vicky Pounders....................(256)740-5757
Sports................Josh Bean.........................(256)740-5757

FLORIDA-Jacksonville

(6212) THE FLORIDA TIMES-UNION
1 Riverside Ave.
Jacksonville, FL 32202-4904
Editorials................Lloyd Brown.......................(904)359-4307
News................Mike Marino.......................(904)359-4513
Photo................Dennis Hamilton...................(904)359-4215
Photo................M. Jack Luedke....................(904)359-4287
Suburban................David Bauer.......................(904)359-4182

FLORIDA-Leesburg

(6301) DAILY COMMERCIAL
PO Box 490007
Leesburg, FL 34749-0007
News................Scott Callahan....................(352)365-8200
Photo................Jack Hardman......................(352)365-8200
Sports................Brian Campbell....................(352)365-8200

FLORIDA-Melbourne

(6334) FLORIDA TODAY
Gannett Plaza
PO Box 419000
Melbourne, FL 32941-9000
Entertainment............Colleen Moore.....................(407)242-3717
Family................Hanna Krause......................(407)242-3779
Fashion................Amy Clark.........................(407)242-3784
Features................Suzy Fleming......................(321)242-3614

FLORIDA-Miami

(6348) DIARIO LAS AMERICAS
2900 NW 39th St.
Miami, FL 33142
City................Yolanda Gonzales Alfaro...........(305)633-3341
Entertainment............Vivian Crucet.....................(305)633-3341
Fashion................Magda Gonzalez....................(305)633-3341
Financial/Business......Enrique Llaca.....................(305)633-3341
Food................Carmencita San Miguel.............(305)633-3341
Garden/Home............Oscar Grau........................(305)633-3341
Lifestyle................Magda Gonzalez....................(305)633-3341
Living................Magda Gonzalez....................(305)633-3341
Metro................Yolanda Gonzales Alfaro...........(305)633-3341
Movie................Buddy Clarke......................(305)633-3341
Music................Luis Felipe Marsans...............(305)633-3341
News................Luis Mario........................(305)633-3341
Photo................Alex Gort.........................(305)633-3341
Political................Ariel Remos.......................(305)633-3341
Real Estate............Oscar Grau........................(305)633-3341
Society................Chichi Aloy.......................(305)633-3341
Sports................Luis B. De Lima...................(305)633-3341
Travel................Miguel A. Suarez..................(305)633-3341
Women's................Magda Gonzalez....................(305)633-3341

FLORIDA-Pensacola

(6568) PENSACOLA NEWS JOURNAL
1 News-Journal Plaza
Pensacola, FL 32501-5670
Fashion................Alice Crann.......................(904)435-8632
Features................Susan Catron......................(904)435-8621
Financial/Business......Mike Mika.........................(904)435-8517
Food................Sandra Burnett....................(904)435-8655
Lifestyle................Susan Catron......................(904)435-8621
Medical................Susan Catron......................(904)435-8621
Travel................Susan Catron......................(904)435-8621

FLORIDA-St. Petersburg

(6633) ST. PETERSBURG TIMES
490 1st Ave. S.
PO Box 1121
St. Petersburg, FL 33701
Editorials................Phil Gailey.......................(727)893-8268
Features................Jeanne Grinstead..................(727)893-8769
Financial/Business......Alecia Swasy......................(727)893-8113
Metro................Tim Nickens.......................(727)893-8532
Photo................Sue Morrow........................(727)893-8231
Sports................Jack Sheppard.....................(727)893-8495

FLORIDA-Sarasota

(6663) SARASOTA HERALD-TRIBUNE
801 S. Tamiami Trail
Sarasota, FL 34236
Entertainment............Joel Welin........................(941)957-5175
Fashion................Janet Uffinger....................(941)957-5417
Features................Susan Rite........................(941)957-5271
Sports................Scott Peterson....................(941)957-5172

FLORIDA-West Palm Beach

(6848) THE PALM BEACH POST
2751 S Dixie Hwy.
West Palm Beach, FL 33405
Art................Gary Schwan.......................(561)820-4574
Financial/Business......Joe Chudicek......................(561)820-4401
Food................Jan Norris........................(561)820-4737
Garden/Home............Pat Morgan........................(561)820-4733
Lifestyle................Nicole Piscopo....................(561)820-4704
Metro................Bill Rose.........................(561)820-4402
Photo................Pete Cross........................(561)820-4466
Political................Brian Crowley.....................(561)820-4723
Radio................Carl Hardy........................(561)820-4483
Religion................Elizabeth Clarke..................(561)820-4485
Society................Thom Smith........................(561)820-4430
Sports................Tim Burke.........................(561)820-4480
State................Price Patton......................(561)820-4583
TV................Kevin Thompson....................(561)820-4436
Travel................Cheryl Blackerby..................(561)820-4727

GEORGIA-Atlanta

(6972) THE ATLANTA JOURNAL AND CONSTITUTION
72 Marietta St. NW
PO Box 4689
Atlanta, GA 30303
Entertainment............Kathy Janich......................(404)526-5971
Features................Bob Longino.......................(404)526-5430
Features................Frank Rizzo.......................(404)526-5494
Financial/Business......Jennifer Hill.....................(404)526-5869
Food................Susan Puckett.....................(404)526-5443
Garden/Home............Sheila Reed.......................(404)526-5485
Medical................Nick Tate.........................(404)526-5671
Movie................Eleanor Ringel....................(404)526-5468
Religion................Ron Feinberg......................(404)526-5491
Science................Nick Tate.........................(404)526-5671
Travel................Howard Pousner....................(404)526-5479

(6974) THE ATLANTA VOICE
633 Pryor St. SW
Box 92405
Atlanta, GA 30314-0405
Lifestyle................Gloria McKinley...................(404)524-6426

HAWAII-Honolulu

(7700) THE HONOLULU ADVERTISER
News Bldg.
605 Kapiolani Blvd.
PO Box 3110
Honolulu, HI 96802
Drama................Wayne Harada......................(808)525-8067

(7702) HONOLULU STAR-BULLETIN
500 Ala Moana Blvd., 7-210
Honolulu, HI 96813

City	Ed Lynch	(808)529-4758
Editorials	Mary Poole	(808)529-4787
Features	Nadine Kam	(808)529-4775
News	Steven Petranik	(808)529-4764

IDAHO-Boise

(7811) THE IDAHO STATESMAN
1200 N. Curtis Rd.
PO Box 40
Boise, ID 83707

Columnist	Dan Popkey	(208)377-6200
Editorials	Chuck Malloy	(208)377-6200
Entertainment	Michael Deeds	(208)377-6200
Family	Vickie Ashwell	(208)377-6200
Financial/Business	Mike Maharry	(208)377-6200
Metro	Roya Camp	(208)377-6200
News	Holly Anderson	(208)377-6200
Sports	Jennifer Swindell	(208)377-6200

ILLINOIS-Arlington Heights

(8022) DAILY HERALD
PO Box 280
Arlington Heights, IL 60006

Editorials	David Beery	(847)427-4541
Financial/Business	James Kane	(847)427-4565
Metro	Colleen Thomas	(847)427-4763
Movie	Dann Gire	(847)427-4530
News	Theresa Schmedding	(847)427-4574
News	Colleen Thomas	(847)427-4763
Sports	Scot Gregor	(847)427-4449
Sports	Mike Imrem	(847)427-4456
Sports	Bob Logan	(847)427-4431
Sports	Tom Quinlan	(847)427-4455
Sports	Tim Sassone	(847)427-4452
TV & Radio	Ted Cox	(847)427-4528

ILLINOIS-Aurora

(8040) THE BEACON-NEWS
101 S River St.
Aurora, IL 60506

Features	Penny Falcon	(630)844-5963

ILLINOIS-Belleville

(8060) BELLEVILLE NEWS-DEMOCRAT
120 S. Illinois St.
PO Box 427
Belleville, IL 62222-0427

Editorials	Lori Browning	(618)239-2472
Sports	Joe Ostermeier	(618)239-2516
Sunday	Maureen Houston	(618)239-2641

ILLINOIS-Champaign

(8205) THE NEWS-GAZETTE
15 Main St.
PO Box 677
Champaign, IL 61820

Aviation	Don Dodson	(217)351-5223
Book	Tom Kacich	(217)351-5221
Consumer Affairs	Tom Kacich	(217)351-5221
Drama	Julie Kistler	(217)351-5368
Entertainment	Tom Kacich	(217)351-5221
Family	Tom Kacich	(217)351-5221
Farm	Anne Cook	(217)351-5217
Fashion	Tom Kacich	(217)351-5221
Features	Tom Kacich	(217)351-5221
Financial/Business	Don Dodson	(217)351-5223
Food	Tom Kacich	(217)351-5221
Garden/Home	Tom Kacich	(217)351-5221
Lifestyle	Tom Kacich	(217)351-5221
Living	Tom Kacich	(217)351-5221
Medical	Paul Wood	(217)351-5222
Metro	Mary Sharp	(217)351-5211
Movie	Tom Kacich	(217)351-5221
Music	Tom Kacich	(217)351-5221
News	John Beck	(217)351-5212
Photo	Darrell Hoemann	(217)351-5214
Political	Mary Sharp	(217)351-5211
Radio	Mike Howie	(217)351-5368
Real Estate	Don Dodson	(217)351-5223
Religion	Dan Corkery	(217)351-5213
Rural Development	Mary Sharp	(217)351-5211
Saturday	Dan Corkery	(217)351-5213
Science	Paul Wood	(217)351-5222
Society	Tom Kacich	(217)351-5221

Sports	Jean McDonald	(217)351-5231
Suburban	Mary Sharp	(217)351-5211
TV	Tom Kacich	(217)351-5221
Travel	Tom Kacich	(217)351-5221
Women's	Tom Kacich	(217)351-5221

ILLINOIS-Chicago

(8346) CRAIN'S CHICAGO BUSINESS
360 N Michigan Ave.
Chicago, IL 60601

Advertising News	Albert Gallun	(312)649-7844
Consumer Affairs	Albert Gallun	(312)649-7844
Education	Greg Hinz	(312)649-7844
Entertainment	Brian McCormick	(312)649-7844
Financial/Business	Steve Strahler	(312)649-7844
Food	Albert Gallun	(312)649-7844
Medical	Sarah Klein	(312)649-7844
Political	Greg Hinz	(312)649-7844
Real Estate	Steve Daniels	(312)649-7844
Regional	Patricia Richardson	(312)649-7844
Travel	Brian McCormick	(312)649-7844

ILLINOIS-Decatur

(8711) HERALD & REVIEW
601 E. William St.
Decatur, IL 62525

Automotive	Ron Ingram	(217)429-5151
Consumer Affairs	Steve Cahalan	(217)429-5151
Education	Burton Cole	(217)429-5151
Entertainment	Bob Fallstrom	(217)429-5151
Environmental	Amy Ragsdale	(217)429-5151
Family	Bob Fallstrom	(217)429-5151
Farm	Steve Cahalan	(217)429-5151
Fashion	Bob Fallstrom	(217)429-5151
Features	Bob Fallstrom	(217)429-5151
Financial/Business	Mike Carr	(217)429-5151
Financial/Business	Ron Ingram	(217)429-5151
Food	Bob Fallstrom	(217)429-5151
Garden/Home	Bob Fallstrom	(217)429-5151
Lifestyle	Bob Fallstrom	(217)429-5151
Living	Bob Fallstrom	(217)429-5151
Medical	Amy Ragsdale	(217)429-5151
Metro	Carol Alexander	(217)429-5151
Movie	Bob Fallstrom	(217)429-5151
Music	Bob Fallstrom	(217)429-5151
News	Carol Alexander	(217)429-5151
Photo	Damon Cain	(217)429-5151
Political	Dawn Morville	(217)429-5151
Radio	Bob Fallstrom	(217)429-5151
Real Estate	Steve Cahalan	(217)429-5151
Real Estate	Mike Carr	(217)429-5151
Religion	Theresa Churchill	(217)429-5151
Rural Development	Mike Carr	(217)429-5151
Rural Development	Ron Ingram	(217)429-5151
Saturday	Bob Fallstrom	(217)429-5151
Science	Carol Alexander	(217)429-5151
Society	Bob Fallstrom	(217)429-5151
Sports	Steve Cameron	(217)429-5151
Suburban	Carol Alexander	(217)429-5151
TV	Bob Fallstrom	(217)429-5151
Travel	Bob Fallstrom	(217)429-5151
Women's	Bob Fallstrom	(217)429-5151

ILLINOIS-Peoria

(9419) JOURNAL STAR
1 News Plaza
Peoria, IL 61643

Art	Gary Panetta	(309)686-3132
Lifestyle	Dennis Dimond	(309)686-3243
Metro	Jerry McDowell	(309)686-3117
Movie	Gary Panetta	(309)686-3132
Music	Gary Panetta	(309)686-3132
News	Jerry McDowell	(309)686-3256
Photo	Eric Behrens	(309)686-3137
Religion	Mike Miller	(309)686-3106
Rural Development	Ken Kirchoefer	(309)686-3041
Sports	Kirk Wessler	(309)686-3216
TV & Radio	Mike Miller	(309)686-3106

ILLINOIS-Springfield

(9642) STATE JOURNAL-REGISTER
1 Copley Plz.
PO Box 219
Springfield, IL 62701-1927

Education	Sean Noble	(217)788-1300
Entertainment	Tom Alesia	(217)788-1300
Fashion	Charlyn Fargo	(217)788-1300
Features	Paul Povse	(217)788-1300
Financial/Business	Chris Dettro	(217)788-1300
Food	Charlyn Fargo	(217)788-1300
Lifestyle	Paul Povse	(217)788-1300

Movie	Paul Povse	(217)788-1300
Music	Paul Povse	(217)788-1300
News	Ted Wolf	(217)788-1300
Sports	Jim Ruppert	(217)788-1300
Sunday	Ted Wolf	(217)788-1300
TV	Tom Alesia	(217)788-1300
Travel	Jim Betzold	(217)788-1300

INDIANA-Indianapolis

(10133) THE INDIANAPOLIS STAR
307 N. Pennsylvania St.
Indianapolis, IN 46204

Art	Zach Dunkin	(317)444-6079
Aviation	Chris O'Malley	(317)444-6081
Drama	Peter Szatmary	(317)444-6078
Editorials	Lisa Coffey	(317)444-6206
Entertainment	Zach Dunkin	(317)444-6079
Family	Courtenay Edelhart	(317)444-6481
Financial/Business	Chris O'Malley	(317)444-6081
Food	Patti Denton	(317)444-6132
Medical	Diana Penner	(317)444-6249
Movie	Bonnie Britton	(317)444-6258
Music	David Lindquist	(317)444-6404
Music	Whitney Smith	(317)444-6226
Photo	Greg Fisher	(317)444-6198
Political	Mary Beth Schneider	(317)444-6827
Science	Diana Penner	(317)444-6249
Sports	Jim Lefko	(317)444-6352
Suburban	Kevin Morgan	(317)444-6292
Travel	David Mannweiler	(317)444-6084

INDIANA-Munster

(10053) THE TIMES
601 W 45th Ave.
Munster, IN 46321

Fashion	Lane Brown	(219)933-3246
Financial/Business	Phil Britt	(219)933-3399
Food	Lane Brown	(219)933-3246
Garden/Home	Lane Brown	(219)933-3246
Lifestyle	Lane Brown	(219)933-3246
Real Estate	Nancy Pieters	(219)933-3216
Sports	Ron Brow	(219)933-3232
TV & Radio	Lane Brown	(219)933-3246
Travel	Lane Brown	(219)933-3246

INDIANA-South Bend

(10458) SOUTH BEND TRIBUNE
225 W. Colfax Ave.
South Bend, IN 46626

Art	Joe Vince	(574)235-6479
Editorials	Gayle Dantzler	(574)235-6349
Editorials	Paul Lamirand	(574)235-6324
Entertainment	Joe Vince	(574)235-6479
Features	Chris Benninghoff	(574)235-6345
Financial/Business	Ed Semmler	(574)235-6466
Lifestyle	Deanna Francis	(574)235-6248
Metro	Virginia Black	(574)235-6321
Regional	Rick Martinez	(616)687-7006
Society	Kathy Sechowski	(574)235-6360
Sports	Bill Bilinski	(574)235-6331

IOWA-Davenport

(10738) QUAD-CITY TIMES
500 E. 3rd St.
PO Box 3828
Davenport, IA 52801

Editorials	Deborah Brasier	(319)383-2452
Photo	Craig Chandler	(319)383-2361

IOWA-Des Moines

(10781) THE DES MOINES REGISTER
PO Box 957
Des Moines, IA 50304

Metro	Rick Tapscott	(515)284-8461
Sports	Jeanne Abbott	(515)284-8000

IOWA-Sioux City

(11213) SIOUX CITY JOURNAL
515 Pavonia St.
Sioux City, IA 51102

Book	Marcia Poole	(712)279-5070
TV & Radio	Bruce Miller	(712)279-5075
Travel	Larry Myhre	(712)279-5070
Women's	Marcia Poole	(712)279-5083

IOWA-Waterloo

(11289) WATERLOO-CEDAR FALLS COURIER
501 Commercial St.
Waterloo, IA 50701

Aviation	Pat Kinney	(319)291-1481
Book	Phyllis Singer	(319)291-1461
City	Nancy Raffensperger	(319)291-1481
Consumer Affairs	Nancy Raffensperger	(319)291-1481
Drama	Melody Parker	(319)291-1462
Editorials	George Saucer	(319)291-1458
Education	Anne Phillips	(319)291-1481
Entertainment	Melody Parker	(319)291-1462
Environmental	William Slakey	(319)291-1481
Family	Phyllis Singer	(319)291-1461
Farm	William Slakey	(319)291-1481
Fashion	Carolyn Cole	(319)291-1467
Features	Carolyn Cole	(319)291-1467
Financial/Business	Pat Kinney	(319)291-1481
Food	Carolyn Cole	(319)291-1467
Garden/Home	Melody Parker	(319)291-1462
Lifestyle	Carolyn Cole	(319)291-1467
Living	Carolyn Cole	(319)291-1467
Medical	Jackie Young	(319)291-1481
Metro	Nancy Raffensperger	(319)291-1481
Movie	Melody Parker	(319)291-1462
Music	Melody Parker	(319)291-1462
News	Nancy Raffersperger	(319)291-1481
Photo	Dan Nierling	(319)291-1476
Political	Eric Woolson	(319)291-1481
Radio	Phyllis Singer	(319)291-1461
Real Estate	Pat Kinney	(319)291-1481
Religion	Amy Gades	(319)291-1454
Rural Development	Amy Gades	(319)291-1454
Society	Phyllis Singer	(319)291-1461
Sports	Kevin Evans	(319)291-1469
Suburban	Nancy Raffensperger	(319)291-1481
TV	Curt Glenn	(319)291-1481
Travel	Carolyn Cole	(319)291-1463
Women's	Phyllis Singer	(319)291-1461

KANSAS-Hutchinson

(11501) THE HUTCHINSON NEWS
PO Box 190
300 W. 2nd St
Hutchinson, KS 67504-0190

City	Mary Rintoul	(620)694-5769
Lifestyle	Joyce Hall	(620)694-5740
News	Greg Nucifora	(620)694-5740

KANSAS-Topeka

(11838) THE TOPEKA CAPITAL-JOURNAL
616 SE Jefferson St.
Topeka, KS 66607

Features	Karen Sipes	(785)295-1283

KANSAS-Wichita

(11891) WICHITA EAGLE
PO Box 820
Wichita, KS 67201

Features	Lori Linenberger	(316)268-6298
Lifestyle	Lori Linenberger	(316)268-6298
News	Tom Shine	(316)268-6268
Photo	Bo Rader	(316)268-6231
Travel	Arlice Davenport	(316)268-6256
Weekend	Macia Werts	(316)268-6267

KENTUCKY-Louisville

(12213) THE COURIER-JOURNAL
525 W. Broadway St.
Louisville, KY 40202-7431

Aviation	Ric Manning	(502)582-4240
Book	Keith Runyon	(502)582-4594
City	Jean Porter	(502)582-4691
Consumer Affairs	Arlene Jacobson	(502)582-4651
Family	Greg Johnson	(502)582-7077
Farm	Judy Egerton	(502)582-7088
Features	Greg Johnson	(502)582-7077
Food	Sarah Fritschner	(502)582-4203
Music	Jeffrey Puckett	(502)582-4160
Political	Al Cross	(502)875-5136
Radio	Tom Dorsey	(502)582-4474
Sports	Harry Bryan	(502)582-4060
Suburban	Linda Raymond	(502)582-4120
Travel	Ed Bennett	(502)582-4615

LOUISIANA-Baton Rouge

(12484) THE ADVOCATE
525 Lafayette St.
Baton Rouge, LA 70802-5410

Editorials	Bill Bankston	(504)383-1111
Education	Curt Eysink	(504)383-1111
Entertainment	John Wirt	(504)383-1111
Environmental	Bob Anderson	(504)383-1111
Fashion	Karen Martin	(504)383-1111
Features	Freda Yarbrough	(504)383-1111
Financial/Business	Kathryn Flournoy	(504)383-1111
Food	Tommy Simmons	(504)383-1111
Lifestyle	Pat Tessier	(504)383-1111
Metro	Dan Hatfield	(504)383-1111
Movie	John Wirt	(504)383-1111
News	Dan Hatfield	(504)383-1111
Photo	Mark Keedy	(504)383-1111
Religion	Greg Toney	(504)383-1111
Sports	Butch Muir	(504)383-1111
Sunday	Art Adams	(504)383-1111
Travel	Cynthia Campbell	(504)383-1111

LOUISIANA-New Orleans

(12758) THE TIMES-PICAYUNE
3800 Howard Ave.
New Orleans, LA 70125-1429

Aviation	Robert Rhoden	(504)586-3365
City	Peter Kovacs	(504)586-3560
Drama	Dominic Papatola	(504)586-3687
Editorials	Malcolm Forsyth	(504)586-3605
Family	Bettye Anding	(504)586-3575
Fashion	Chris Bynum	(504)586-3655
Features	Cindy Hardy	(504)826-3729
Financial/Business	Robert Scott	(504)586-3418
Food	Dale Curry	(504)586-3575
Movie	Renee Peck	(504)586-3467
Music	Frank Gagnard	(504)586-3687
News	Jim Amoss	(504)586-3560
Photo	Doug Parker	(504)586-3686
Real Estate	Greg Thomas	(504)586-3678
Religion	Valerie Faciane	(504)586-3560
Religion	Bruce Nolan	(504)586-3344
Society	Nell Nolan	(504)586-3655
Sports	Steve Rocca	(504)586-3405
Sunday	Bettye Anding	(504)586-3575
TV & Radio	Mark Lorando	(504)586-3665
Travel	Millie Ball	(504)586-3668
Women's	MaryLou Atkinson	(504)586-3655

LOUISIANA-Shreveport

(12820) THE TIMES
222 Lake St.
Shreveport, LA 71101

TV & Radio	Bill Cooksey	(318)459-3200
Travel	Sheri Conover	(318)459-3200
Women's	Martha Fitzgerald	(318)459-3200

MARYLAND-Baltimore

(13135) THE BALTIMORE SUN
501 N. Calvert St.
Baltimore, MD 21278-0001

Columnist	John McIntyre	(410)332-6133
Features	Kim Marcum	(410)332-6106
Financial/Business	Gerald Merrell	(410)332-6000
Sports	Molly Dunham	(410)332-6717
Travel	Jeff Price	(410)332-6748

MARYLAND-Hagerstown

(13563) THE DAILY-MAIL
PO Box 439
Hagerstown, MD 21741

Features	Jake Womer	(301)733-5131

MARYLAND-Hanover

(13580) PENNYSAVER
1342 Charwood Rd.
Hanover, MD 21076

News	Patti Trujillo	(410)684-2600

MASSACHUSETTS-Boston

(13857) THE BOSTON GLOBE
135 Morrissey Blvd.
PO Box 2378
Boston, MA 02107-3310

Art	Scott Powers	(617)929-2536
Art	Christine Temin	(617)929-2781
City	Joe Williams	(617)929-3000
Drama	Ed Siegel	(617)929-2832
Editorials	H.D.S. Greenway	(617)929-3222
Education	Doug Bailey	(617)929-3077
Education	Marilyn Garateix	(617)929-3100
Education	Don MacGillis	(617)929-3059
Entertainment	Matthew Gilbert	(617)929-2808
Fashion	Suzanne Ryan	(617)929-2957
Financial/Business	Peter Mancusi	(617)929-3058
Food	Louise Kennedy	(617)929-2924
Living	Fiona Luis	(617)929-3278
Medical	Doug Bailey	(617)929-3077
Medical	Don MacGillis	(617)929-3059
Metro	Peter Canellos	(617)929-3100
Political	Carolyn Ryan	(617)929-3100
Religion	Marilyn Garateix	(617)929-3100
Science	Don MacGillis	(617)929-3059
TV	Matthew Gilbert	(617)929-2808

(13858) BOSTON HERALD
One Herald Sq.
PO Box 2096
Boston, MA 02106-2096

Book	Mark Chapman	(617)426-3000
City	Dan Rosenfeld	(617)426-3000
City	Janet Walsh	(617)426-3000
Editorials	Rachelle Cohen	(617)426-3000
Entertainment	Bill Weber	(617)426-3000
Food	Jane Dornbusch	(617)426-3000
Movie	James Verniere	(617)426-3000
Music	Larry Katz	(617)426-3000
News	Howie Carr	(617)426-3000
News	Margery Eagan	(617)426-3000
News	Joe Fitzgerald	(617)426-3000
News	Peter Gelzinis	(617)426-3000
News	Leonard Greene	(617)426-3000
Photo	Kevin Cole	(617)426-3000
Political	Walter Roche	(617)426-3000
Society	Dana Bisbee	(617)426-3000
Sunday	Eric Norment	(617)426-3000
TV	Monica Collins	(617)426-3000
Travel	Mark Chapman	(617)426-3000

MASSACHUSETTS-Brockton

(14012) THE ENTERPRISE
60 Main St.
PO Box 1450
Brockton, MA 02303

City	Steve Damish	(508)427-4022

MASSACHUSETTS-Hyannis

(14250) CAPE COD TIMES
319 Main St.
Hyannis, MA 02601

Entertainment	Tim Miller	(508)862-1140
Lifestyle	Bill O'Neill	(508)862-1168
Sports	William Higgins	(508)775-1200

MASSACHUSETTS-Lawrence

(14266) THE EAGLE-TRIBUNE
PO Box 100
Lawrence, MA 01842

Art	Gretchen Putnam	(978)946-2000
City	John Macone	(978)946-2000
Editorials	Ken Johnson	(978)946-2000
Features	Gretchen Putnam	(978)946-2000
Medical	Marjory Sherman	(978)946-2000
News	Alan White	(978)946-2000
Sports	Bill Burt	(978)946-2000

MASSACHUSETTS-Lowell

(14278) LOWELL SUN
15 Kearney Sq.
Lowell, MA 01853

City	Charles St. Armand	(508)970-4645
Financial/Business	Gail Ross	(508)970-4660
Lifestyle	Carol McQuaid	(508)970-4631
Photo	David Gregory	(508)970-4663
Sports	Dennis Whitton	(508)970-4628
Suburban	Thomas Zuppa	(508)970-4644
Sunday	John Greenwald	(508)970-4637

Women's..............Carol McQuaid.....................(508)458-7100

MASSACHUSETTS-New Bedford

(14377) THE STANDARD-TIMES
25 Elm St.
New Bedford, MA 02740

City.....................Richard Lodge....................(508)997-7411
Consumer Affairs.......Rachel Thomas....................(508)997-7411
Drama...................Brad Hathaway....................(508)997-7411
Editorials..............Steve Urbon.....................(508)997-7411
Education...............Susan Pawlack-Seaman............(508)997-7411
Entertainment..........Brad Hathaway....................(508)997-7411
Environmental..........Natalie White...................(508)997-7411
Fashion.................Brad Hathaway....................(508)997-7411
Features................Brad Hathaway....................(508)997-7411
Financial/Business......Steve DeCosta...................(508)997-7411
Food....................Brad Hathaway....................(508)997-7411
Lifestyle...............Brad Hathaway....................(508)997-7411
Living..................Brad Hathaway....................(508)997-7411
Medical.................Brad Hathaway....................(508)997-7411
Metro...................Richard Lodge...................(508)997-7411
Movie...................Brad Hathaway....................(508)997-7411
Music...................Brad Hathaway....................(508)997-7411
News....................Mike Conery.....................(508)997-7411
Photo...................George Patisteas................(508)997-7411
Political...............Mike Conery.....................(508)997-7411
Religion................Robert Barcellos................(508)997-7411
Rural Development.....Michael Bailey....................(508)997-7411
Saturday................Michael Bailey..................(508)997-7411
Science.................Brad Hathaway....................(508)997-7411
Society.................Brad Hathaway....................(508)997-7411
Sports..................Bob Stern.......................(508)997-7411
Suburban................Michael Bailey..................(508)997-7411
TV......................Steve Varnum....................(508)997-7411
Travel..................Anne Eisenmenger................(508)997-7411

MASSACHUSETTS-Quincy

(14491) THE PATRIOT LEDGER
PO Box 699159
Quincy, MA 02269-9159

Entertainment..........Jon Lehman.......................(617)786-7066
Fashion.................Jon Lehman......................(617)786-7066
Food....................Lisa McManus....................(617)786-7082
Lifestyle...............Lisa McManus....................(617)786-7082
Religion................Ann Doyle.......................(617)786-7098
Science.................Lisa McManus....................(617)786-7082
Sports..................Earl LaChance...................(617)786-7057

MASSACHUSETTS-Springfield

(14552) UNION-NEWS & SUNDAY REPUBLICAN
1860 Main St.
Springfield, MA 01101

Book....................Arnold Friedman..................(413)788-1212
City....................Larry Rivais....................(413)788-1304
Consumer Affairs.......Kevin McGurk....................(413)788-1335
Drama...................Dorris Schmidt..................(413)788-1279
Editorials..............Joseph Hopkins..................(413)788-1255
Education...............Phyllis Andreoni................(413)788-1269
Education...............William Freebairn...............(413)788-1269
Entertainment..........Doris Schmidt....................(413)788-1331
Environmental..........Stan Freeman....................(413)788-1264
Family..................Mimi Rigali.....................(413)788-1291
Fashion.................Jean O'Connell..................(413)788-1298
Features................Mimi Rigali.....................(413)788-1291
Financial/Business......Carolyn Robbins.................(413)788-1298
Food....................Jean O'Connell..................(413)788-1208
Garden/Home.............Mimi Rigali.....................(413)788-1291
Lifestyle...............Mimi Rigali.....................(413)788-1291
Medical.................Laurie Bobskill.................(413)788-1338
Metro...................Jame Gillen.....................(413)788-1303
Movie...................Doris Schmidt...................(413)788-1331
Music...................Doris Schmidt...................(413)788-1331
News....................Lawrence Sullivan...............(413)788-1342
Photo...................Norman Roy......................(413)788-1045
Political...............John Appleton...................(413)788-1288
Real Estate.............Mimi Rigali.....................(413)788-1291
Rural Development.....Larry Rivais......................(413)788-1304
Science.................Stan Freeman....................(413)788-1264
Society.................Mimi Rigali.....................(413)788-1291
Sports..................Richard Osgood..................(413)788-1210
State...................Robert Chipkin..................(413)788-1201
Suburban................James Gillen....................(413)788-1303
TV......................Ruth O'Brien....................(413)788-1293
Travel..................Mimi Rigali.....................(413)788-1291
Women's.................Mimi Rigali.....................(413)788-1291

MASSACHUSETTS-Worcester

(14690) TELEGRAM & GAZETTE
20 Franklin St.
PO Box 15012
Worcester, MA 01615

Art.....................Frank Magiera...................(508)793-9292
Environmental..........John J. Monahan..................(508)793-9172
Features................David Mawson....................(508)793-9227
Food....................Barbara Houle...................(508)793-9145
Music...................David Mawson....................(508)793-9227
Photo...................Leonard J. Lazure...............(508)767-9549
Religion................Kathleen Shaw...................(508)793-9242
Sports..................David Nathan....................(508)793-9350
Travel..................Diana Scott.....................(508)793-9434

MICHIGAN-Ann Arbor

(14742) THE ANN ARBOR NEWS
340 E. Huron St., PO Box 1147
Ann Arbor, MI 48104-1147

Automotive..............Mike Kersmarki..................(313)994-6872
Editorials..............Kay Semion......................(313)994-6863
Education...............Jud Branam......................(734)994-6989
Education...............Steve Cain......................(313)994-6820
Entertainment..........Bruce Martin.....................(313)994-6838
Environmental..........Karl Bates......................(313)994-6825
Fashion.................Steve Cagle.....................(313)994-6701
Financial/Business......Mike Kersmarki..................(313)994-6825
Food....................Steve Cagle.....................(313)994-6880
Lifestyle...............Julie Wiernik...................(313)994-6872
Living..................Julie Wiernik...................(313)994-6841
Medical.................Julie Wiernik...................(313)994-6827
Metro...................Rick Fitzgerald.................(313)994-6862
Movie...................Bruce Martin....................(313)994-6835
News....................Andy Chapelle...................(313)994-6858
Photo...................Judy Nies Tell..................(313)994-6823
Political...............Andy Chapelle...................(313)994-6817
Real Estate.............Mike Kersmarki..................(313)994-6857
Religion................Don Faber.......................(313)994-6873
Science.................Julie Wiernik...................(734)994-6989
Sports..................Geoff Larcom....................(734)994-6989
Travel..................Steve Cagle.....................(734)994-6989
Women's.................Julie Wiernik...................(734)994-6989

MICHIGAN-Battle Creek

(14792) BATTLE CREEK SHOPPER NEWS
1361 E. Columbia Ave.
Battle Creek, MI 49014

Sports..................Carl Olson.......................(616)965-3955

MICHIGAN-Bay City

(14802) THE BAY CITY TIMES
311 5th St.
Bay City, MI 48708

Entertainment..........Jalene Jameson...................(989)894-9675
Food....................Jalene Jameson..................(989)894-9675
Religion................Jalene Jameson..................(989)894-9675

MICHIGAN-Detroit

(14924) DETROIT FREE PRESS
600 W. Fort St.
Detroit, MI 48226

City....................Jeff Taylor.....................(313)222-6600
Features................Tina Croley.....................(313)222-8774
Metro...................Bob Campbell....................(313)223-4549
Metro...................James Hill......................(734)432-6505
Science.................David Bloomquist................(313)223-4288

(14927) THE DETROIT NEWS
615 W. Lafayette Blvd.
Detroit, MI 48226-3197

Art.....................Rhonda Rudd.....................(313)222-2300
Editorials..............Tom Bray........................(313)222-2300
Garden/Home.............Marge Colburn...................(313)222-2300
Movie...................Susan Stark.....................(313)222-2300
Religion................Rhonda Rudd.....................(313)222-2300
Sports..................Phil Laciura....................(313)222-2300

MICHIGAN-Flint

(15033) THE FLINT JOURNAL
200 E. 1st St.
Flint, MI 48502-1925

City....................John Foren......................(810)766-6382
Food....................Ron Krueger.....................(810)766-6117
Medical.................Shantell Kirkendoll.............(810)766-6366
Sports..................Dave Poniers....................(810)766-6125
Suburban................Jim Larkin......................(810)766-6305

MICHIGAN-Grand Rapids

(15096) THE GRAND RAPIDS PRESS
155 Michigan St. NW
Grand Rapids, MI 49503-2302

Book	Ann Byle	(616)459-1612
City	Andy Angelo	(616)459-1456
Drama	David Nicolette	(616)459-1594
Editorials	Joe Crawford	(616)459-1483
Education	Tracy Supert	(616)459-1492
Entertainment	Sue Wallace	(616)459-1604
Environmental	John Sinkevics	(616)459-1471
Family	Sue Schroder	(616)459-1627
Fashion	Cathy Bissell	(616)459-1501
Features	Susan Schroder	(616)459-1627
Financial/Business	Jim Harger	(616)459-1592
Food	Ann Wells	(616)459-1503
Garden/Home	Sue Schroder	(616)459-1626
Lifestyle	Susan Schroder	(616)459-1627
Medical	Chris Meehan	(616)459-1461
Movie	John Douglas	(616)459-1631
Music	Sue Wallace	(616)459-1604
News	Andy Angelo	(616)459-1456
Photo	Jim Starkey	(616)459-1619
Political	Ted Roelofs	(616)459-1497
Real Estate	Jim Harger	(616)459-1592
Religion	Ed Golder	(616)459-1613
Society	Susan Schroder	(616)459-1627
Sports	Bob Becker	(616)459-1674
Sunday	Bob Keveney	(616)459-1489
TV & Radio	Ruth Butler	(616)459-1586
Travel	Hank Bornheimer	(616)459-1490
Women's	Susan Schroder	(616)459-1627

MICHIGAN-Kalamazoo

(15242) KALAMAZOO GAZETTE
401 S. Burdick St.
Kalamazoo, MI 49007

Book	Kathy Doud	(269)345-3511
Drama	Kathy Doud	(269)345-3511
Editorials	Tom Thinnes	(269)345-3511
Education	Becky Payne	(269)345-3511
Entertainment	Mary Wade	(269)345-3511
Environmental	Jeff Alexander	(269)345-3511
Family	Mary Wade	(269)345-3511
Fashion	Peggy Guthaus	(269)345-3511
Features	Mary Wade	(269)345-3511
Financial/Business	Paul Keep	(269)345-3511
Food	Peggy Guthaus	(269)345-3511
Garden/Home	Norman Sparks	(269)345-3511
Lifestyle	Mary Wade	(269)345-3511
Medical	Bill Krasean	(269)345-3511
Metro	Mary Kramer	(269)345-3511
Movie	Doug Pullen	(269)345-3511
Music	Kathy Doud	(269)345-3511
Photo	Robert Maxwell	(269)345-3511
Real Estate	Paul Keep	(269)345-3511
Religion	Craig Thomas	(269)345-3511
Sports	Jack Moss	(269)345-3511
Sunday	Harold Smith	(269)345-3511
TV & Radio	Tom Haroldson	(269)345-3511
Travel	Larry Pratt	(269)345-3511

MICHIGAN-Lansing

(15277) LANSING STATE JOURNAL
120 E. Lenawee
Lansing, MI 48919

City	Rich Jackson	(517)377-1206
Editorials	Mark Nixon	(517)377-1038
Entertainment	Mike Hughes	(517)377-1156
Features	Tim Makinen	(517)377-1053
Financial/Business	Jim McMiller	(517)377-1056
Political	Chris Andrews	(517)377-1054
Sports	Vince Ellis	(517)377-1071

MICHIGAN-Mount Clemens

(15372) THE MACOMB DAILY
100 Macomb Daily Dr.
PO Box 707
Mount Clemens, MI 48046

Editorials	Mitch Kehetian	(810)783-0327
Education	Frank DeFrank	(810)783-0309
Entertainment	Debbie Komar	(810)783-0251
Financial/Business	Bill Fleming	(810)783-0253
Food	Debbie Komar	(810)783-0251
Medical	Debbie Komar	(810)783-0251
Political	Chad Selweski	(810)783-0218
Real Estate	Niky Hachigian	(810)783-0323
Religion	Bob Selna	(810)783-0229
Sports	George Pohly	(810)783-0270

MICHIGAN-Pontiac

(15450) OAKLAND PRESS
48 W. Huron St., No. 436009
PO Box 9
Pontiac, MI 48342-2101

City	Susan Belniak	(248)332-8181
Drama	Kenn Jones	(248)332-8181
Editorials	Neil Munro	(248)332-8181
Entertainment	Kenn Jones	(248)332-8181
Fashion	Sybil Little	(248)332-8181
Features	Holly Shreve	(248)332-8181
Financial/Business	Daniel Grantham	(248)332-8181
Food	Sybil Little	(248)332-8181
Garden/Home	Jody Headlee	(248)332-8181
Movie	Kenn Jones	(248)332-8181
Music	Kenn Jones	(248)332-8181
News	Susan Hood	(248)332-8181
Photo	Ed Noble	(248)332-8181
Political	Steve Spalding	(248)332-8181
Religion	Sandra Birdiett	(248)332-8181
Society	Sybil Little	(248)332-8181
Sports	Keith Langlois	(248)332-8181

MICHIGAN-Saginaw

(15491) THE SAGINAW NEWS
203 S. Washington Ave.
Saginaw, MI 48607

Book	Janet Martineau	(517)776-9707
Drama	Janet Martineau	(517)776-9707
Editorials	Terence Smith	(517)776-9684
Education	Paul Rau	(517)776-9777
Entertainment	Janet Martineau	(517)776-9707
Family	Ken Tabacsko	(517)776-9705
Fashion	Ken Tabacsko	(517)776-9705
Features	Ken Tabacsko	(517)776-9705
Financial/Business	Jean Spenner	(517)776-9683
Food	Mary Foreman	(517)776-9676
Garden/Home	Bill Cornish	(517)776-9780
Metro	Rob Handeyside	(517)776-9678
Movie	Janet Martineau	(517)776-9707
Music	Janet Martineau	(517)776-9707
News	Brian Hlavaty	(517)776-9778
Political	Mike Thompson	(517)776-9691
Society	Ken Tabacsko	(517)776-9705
Sports	Paul Neumeyer	(517)776-9770
TV & Radio	Sue White	(517)776-9705
Travel	John Walker	(517)776-9713
Women's	Ken Tabacsko	(517)776-9705

MICHIGAN-Stockbridge

(15579) STOCKBRIDGE TOWN CRIER
PO Box 548
Stockbridge, MI 49285-0548

News	Sandra Kay	(517)851-7833

MINNESOTA-Minneapolis

(16134) STAR TRIBUNE
425 Portland Ave.
Minneapolis, MN 55488

Book	Chris Waddington	(612)673-4000
Education	Mary Jane Smetanka	(612)673-7380
Fashion	Kristin Tillotson	(612)673-7844
Features	John Habich	(612)673-1736
Food	Lee Dean	(612)673-4000
Garden/Home	Connie Nelson	(612)673-4000
Movie	Jeff Strickler	(612)673-7392
Music	Michael Anthony	(612)673-4445
Music	Jon Bream	(612)673-1719
News	Roger Buoen	(612)673-1729
Photo	Darlene Pfister	(612)673-4280
Real Estate	Neal Gendler	(612)673-7242
Religion	Martha Sawyer Allen	(612)673-4139
Rural Development	Sharon Schmickle	(612)673-4361
Sunday	John Habich	(612)673-1736
Travel	Catherine Watson	(612)673-4282
Women's	Rosalind Bentley	(612)673-7844

MINNESOTA-St. Paul

(16409) ST. PAUL PIONEER PRESS
345 Cedar St.
St. Paul, MN 55101

Family	Sue Campbell	(651)228-5326
Food	Sue Campbell	(651)228-5326
Travel	Sue Campbell	(651)228-5326

MISSISSIPPI-Jackson

(16695) THE CLARION LEDGER
201 S. Congress
PO Box 40
Jackson, MS 39205

Aviation	David Hampton	(601)961-7000
Book	Orley Hood	(601)961-7000
Medical	Katharine Dougan	(601)961-7000
Photo	Chris Todd	(601)961-7000
Political	Shawn McIntosh	(601)961-7000
Sports	Rick Cleveland	(601)961-7000

MISSOURI-Kansas City

(17180) THE KANSAS CITY STAR
1729 Grand Blvd.
Kansas City, MO 64108-1413

City	Randall Smith	(816)234-4884
Drama	Robert Butler	(816)234-4392
Editorials	James Scott	(816)234-4478
Education	Lynn Horsley	(816)234-4300
Entertainment	Robert Butler	(816)234-4392
Family	Clayton Keller	(816)234-4396
Fashion	Jackie White	(816)234-4462
Features	Jeanne Meyer	(816)234-4461
Financial/Business	Doug Weaver	(816)234-4370
Food	John Martellaro	(816)234-4395
Garden/Home	Clayton Keller	(816)234-4396
Lifestyle	Clayton Keller	(816)234-4396
Movie	Robert Butler	(816)234-4392
Music	Scott Cantrell	(816)234-4380
Music	Brian McTavish	(816)234-4380
News	Diane Stafford	(816)234-4300
Photo	Tim Janicke	(816)234-4342
Political	Rich Hood	(816)234-4300
Real Estate	Chris Lester	(816)234-4370
Society	Laura Rollins Hockaday	(816)234-4391
Sports	Dale Bye	(816)234-4355
Sunday	Jeanne Meyer	(816)234-4461
TV & Radio	Barry Garron	(816)234-4394
Travel	Mary Lou Nolan	(816)234-4397
Women's	Clayton Keller	(816)234-4390

MISSOURI-St. Louis

(17506) ST. LOUIS POST-DISPATCH
1 Metropolitain Sq., Ste. 1300
St. Louis, MO 63102

Art	Jeff Daniel	(314)340-8399
Art	Susan Hegger	(314)340-8348
Book	Jane Henderson	(314)340-8107
Drama	Judith Newmark	(314)340-8243
Entertainment	Susan Hegger	(314)340-8348
Food	Judy Evans	(314)340-8235
Garden/Home	Barbara Hertenstein	(314)340-8236
Garden/Home	Becky Homan	(314)340-8238
Lifestyle	Nancy Miller	(314)340-8340
Living	Mary Leonard	(314)340-8260
Movie	Joe Williams	(314)340-8344
Music	Kevin Johnson	(314)340-8237
Music	Sarah Bryan Miller	(314)340-8249
TV	Gail Pennington	(314)340-8136
Travel	Ron Cobb	(314)340-8231

MONTANA-Billings

(17729) THE BILLINGS GAZETTE
401 N Broadway
PO Box 36300
Billings, MT 59107

Features	Christine Rubich	(406)657-1301
Metro	Mike Gast	(406)657-1200
Movie	Christene Meyers	(406)657-1200
Music	Christene Meyers	(406)657-1200
News	Mike Gast	(406)657-1200
Photo	Larry Mayer	(406)657-1200
Political	Jim Gransbery	(406)657-1200
Religion	Mike Gast	(406)657-1200
Society	Chris Rubich	(406)657-1200
Sports	Warren Rogers	(406)657-1200
TV & Radio	Christene Meyers	(406)657-1200
Travel	Christene Meyers	(406)657-1200

NEBRASKA-Lincoln

(18090) LINCOLN JOURNAL
PO Box 81609
Lincoln, NE 68508-1609

Book	Herb Hyde	(402)473-7287
City	Bob Moyer	(402)473-7249
Consumer Affairs	John Barrette	(402)473-7285
Drama	Tom Ineck	(402)473-7256
Editorials	Richard Herman	(402)473-7225
Education	Jack Kennedy	(402)473-7254
Entertainment	L. Kent Wolgamott	(402)473-7244
Environmental	Al Laukaitis	(402)473-7257
Family	Susan Kreifel	(402)473-7213
Farm	Arthur J. Hovey	(402)473-7321
Fashion	Kathryn Cates Moore	(402)473-7212
Features	Susan Kreifel	(402)473-7213
Financial/Business	John Barrette	(402)473-7285
Food	Susan Kreifel	(402)473-7213
Garden/Home	Susan Kreifel	(402)473-7213
Lifestyle	Susan Kreifel	(402)473-7213
Living	Susan Kreifel	(402)473-7213
Medical	Martha Stoddard	(402)473-7248
Metro	Bob Moyer	(402)473-7249
Movie	Kent Wolgamott	(402)473-7244
Music	Tom Ineck	(402)473-7256
Music	L. Kent Wolgamott	(402)473-7244
News	Robert T. Moyer	(402)473-7222
Photo	Randy Hampton	(402)473-7481
Political	Kathleen Rutledge	(402)473-7250
Radio	Donna Peate	(402)473-7231
Real Estate	Gene Kelly	(402)473-7240
Religion	Susan Willey	(402)473-7214
Rural Development	Arthur J. Hovey	(402)473-7321
Society	Susan Kreifel	(402)473-7213
Sports	Brian Hill	(402)473-7434
State	Fred Knapp	(402)473-7242
Suburban	Fred Knapp	(402)473-7242
Sunday	Catharine L. Huddle	(402)473-7245
TV	Donna Peate	(402)473-7231
Travel	Margaret Ehlers	(402)473-7219
Women's	Susan Kreifel	(402)473-7213

NEBRASKA-Omaha

(18206) OMAHA WORLD-HERALD
1334 Dodge St.
Omaha, NE 68102-1122

Art	Kay MacMillan	(402)444-1000
Editorials	Frank Partsch	(402)444-1000
Education	Deb Shanahan	(402)444-1000
Entertainment	Jim Minge	(402)444-1000
Fashion	Kathleen Brown	(402)444-1000
Financial/Business	Steve Jordan	(402)444-1000
Financial/Business	Chris Olson	(402)444-1000
Food	Jane Palmer	(402)444-1000
Medical	Mary McGrath	(402)444-1000
Movie	Jim Delmont	(402)444-1000
News	Kent Savery	(402)444-1000
Political	C. David Kotok	(402)444-1000
Religion	Julia McCord	(402)444-1000
Sports	Steve Sinclair	(402)444-1000

NEVADA-Las Vegas

(18374) LAS VEGAS REVIEW-JOURNAL
1111 W. Bonanza Rd.
PO Box 70
Las Vegas, NV 89125

City	Mary Hines	(702)383-0286
Features	Frank Fertado	(702)383-0274
Financial/Business	Michael Hiesigner	(702)383-0258
News	Mary Greeley	(703)383-0424
Sports	Jim Fossum	(702)383-4618

(18376) LAS VEGAS WEEKLY
PO Box 230657
Las Vegas, NV 89123-0011

Features	Richard Abowitz	(702)990-2411
News	Rob Bhatt	(702)990-2411

NEW HAMPSHIRE-Manchester

(18565) THE UNION LEADER
100 William Loeb Dr.
PO Box 9555
Manchester, NH 03109-5309

Book	Barry Palmer	(603)668-4321
City	Tami Plyler	(603)668-4321
Family	Ellie Ferriter	(603)668-4321
Financial/Business	Bill Regan	(603)668-4321
Religion	Norm Welsh	(603)668-4321
Sports	Maureen Milliken	(603)668-4321
Sunday	Pat Sheeran	(603)668-4321

NEW JERSEY-Bridgewater

(19572) THE COURIER-NEWS
1201 Rte. 22 W
PO Box 6600
Bridgewater, NJ 08807

Entertainment	Bob Makin	(908)707-3113
Features	Damian Fanelli	(908)707-3255
Lifestyle	Paul Grzella	(908)707-3113

NEW JERSEY-Bridgewater (continued)

Real Estate	Pam Mackenzie	(908)707-3113
Sports	Dave Siminoff	(908)707-3157

NEW JERSEY-Cherry Hill

(18733) COURIER-POST
301 Cuthbert Blvd.
Cherry Hill, NJ 08002

Editorials	Robert E. Ingle	(609)486-2411
Features	Alan Jaffe	(609)486-2411
Sports	Chuck Bausman	(609)486-2411

NEW JERSEY-Clifton

(18757) NORTH JERSEY PROSPECTOR
85 Crooks Ave.
Clifton, NJ 07011

Lifestyle	N. Razumov	(973)773-8300

NEW JERSEY-East Brunswick

(18779) ASBURY PARK PRESS
35 Kennedy Blvd.
East Brunswick, NJ 08816

Editorials	Andrew Sharp	(732)922-6000
Financial/Business	Robert Hordt	(732)922-6000

NEW JERSEY-Hackensack

(18854) THE RECORD
150 River St.
Hackensack, NJ 07601-7172

Food	Pat Mack	(201)646-4000

NEW JERSEY-Hackettstown

(18858) SUBURBAN NEWS
106 E Moore St.
Hackettstown, NJ 07840

Entertainment	Ellen Dooley	(732)396-4203

NEW JERSEY-Newark

(19366) STAR-LEDGER
1 Star-Ledger Plaza
Newark, NJ 07102-1200

Editorials	Richard Aregood	(973)877-4120
Education	Joanne Sills	(973)877-1803
Financial/Business	David Allen	(973)877-4229
Photo	Pim Van Hemmen	(973)877-1782

NEW JERSEY-Parsippany

(19411) DAILY RECORD
800 Jefferson Rd.
PO Box 217
Parsippany, NJ 07054

Editorials	Lorraine Ash	(973)428-6200
Financial/Business	Ron Stepneski	(973)428-6200
Photo	Karen Fucito	(973)428-6200
Sports	Mike Buffaglino	(973)428-6200

NEW JERSEY-Pleasantville

(18658) THE PRESS OF ATLANTIC CITY
11 Devins Ln.
Pleasantville, NJ 08232-3806

City	Charles Wray	(609)272-1234
Editorials	Carla Linz	(609)272-1234
Financial/Business	Kevin Post	(609)272-1234
News	Peter Brophy	(609)272-1234
Photo	Gary Shivers	(609)272-1234
Sports	Michael Sheperd	(609)272-1234

NEW JERSEY-Trenton

(19670) THE TRENTONIAN
Southand at Perry St.
Trenton, NJ 08602

Book	Bill Dwyer	(609)989-7800
City	Wilson Barto	(609)989-7800
Drama	Diane Dixon	(609)989-7800
Editorials	Ed Hawkins	(609)989-7800
Education	Daniel Riben	(609)989-7800
Entertainment	Jim Dixon	(609)989-7800
Family	Diane Dixon	(609)989-7800
Fashion	Diane Dixon	(609)989-7800
Features	Diane Dixon	(609)989-7800
Financial/Business	Jim Fitzsimmons	(609)989-7800
Food	Jim Dixon	(609)989-7800
Garden/Home	Diane Dixon	(609)989-7800
Lifestyle	Diane Dixon	(609)989-7800
Movie	Jim Dixon	(609)989-7800
Music	Claude Lewis	(609)989-7800
News	Pete Sherwood	(609)989-7800
Photo	Steve Mervish	(609)989-7800
Political	Tony Wilson	(609)989-7800
Real Estate	Stan Lavis	(609)989-7800
Religion	Ford Bothwell	(609)989-7800
Rural Development	Jim Fitzsimmons	(609)989-7800
Saturday	Ken Vegotsky	(609)989-7800
Society	Diane Dixon	(609)989-7800
Sports	Joe Logue	(609)989-7800
Sunday	Ken Vegotsky	(609)989-7800
TV	Bob Zera	(609)989-7800
Travel	Jim Dixon	(609)989-7800
Women's	Diane Dixon	(609)989-7800

NEW MEXICO-Albuquerque

(19763) ALBUQUERQUE JOURNAL
7777 Jefferson NE
Albuquerque, NM 87109

Book	Tom Mayer	(505)823-3939
City	Tom Harmon	(505)823-3840
Drama	Dave Steinberg	(505)823-3925
Editorials	Bill Hume	(505)823-3860
Education	Chris Miller	(505)823-3951
Entertainment	Dave Steinberg	(505)823-3925
Environmental	Rene Kimball	(505)823-3958
Family	Steve Hallock	(505)823-3936
Fashion	Susan Stiger	(505)823-3926
Features	Steve Hallock	(505)823-3936
Financial/Business	A.C. Etheridge	(505)823-3830
Food	Susan Stiger	(505)823-3926
Garden/Home	Susan Stiger	(505)823-3926
Lifestyle	Steve Hallock	(505)823-3936
Living	Steve Hallock	(505)823-3936
Medical	Byron Spice	(505)823-3950
Metro	Dan Ritchey	(505)823-3844
Movie	Dave Steinberg	(505)823-3925
Music	David Noble	(505)823-3921
Photo	Ray Cary	(505)823-3991
Political	John Robertson	(505)823-3929
Real Estate	Robert Hagan	(505)823-3836
Religion	Demetria Martinez	(505)823-3800
Society	Steve Hallock	(505)823-3936
Sports	Dennis Latta	(505)823-3903
TV	Rick Nathanson	(505)823-3929
Travel	Roger Ruvolo	(505)823-3927

NEW YORK-Binghamton

(20211) PRESS & SUN-BULLETIN
Binghamton Press Co.
Vestal Pkwy. E.
PO Box 1270
Binghamton, NY 13902

Editorials	Frank Roessner	(607)798-1124
Education	George Basler	(607)798-1172
Entertainment	Barb Van Atta	(607)798-1171
Environmental	Tom Wilber	(607)798-1177
Financial/Business	Jeff Platsky	(607)798-1178
Movie	Sarah Miller	(607)798-1176
News	Chris Kocher	(607)798-1184
Religion	Michelle Terry	(607)798-1317
Society	Mary Ann Rogan	(607)798-1189
Sports	Charlie Jaworski	(607)798-1191
TV	Laurie Miner	(607)798-1115

NEW YORK-Buffalo

(20368) THE BUFFALO NEWS
1 News Plz.
Buffalo, NY 14203-2994

Drama	Mark Sommer	(716)849-5484
Fashion	Susan Martin	(716)849-4450
Food	Janice Okun	(716)849-4468
Movie	Jeff Simon	(716)849-4438
Music	Mary Kunz	(716)849-4001
Political	Robert McCarthy	(716)849-5593
Religion	Jay Tokasz	(716)849-4408
Sports	Howard Smith	(716)849-4465
TV	Alan Pergament	(716)849-4566

NEW YORK-Elmira

(20573) STAR-GAZETTE
PO Box 285
Elmira, NY 14902

Lifestyle	Annie-Laurie Blair	(607)734-5151

NEW YORK-Hicksville

(20744) RESULTS MEDIA SHOPPER'S GUIDE
250 Miller Pl.
Hicksville, NY 11801
　　Consumer Affairs........ Juliana McCabe....................(516)812-3757

NEW YORK-Melville

(21051) NEWSDAY
235 Pinelawn Rd.
Melville, NY 11747-4250
　　Editorials.............. James Klurfeld.....................(516)843-2700

NEW YORK-Middletown

(21081) TIMES HERALD-RECORD
40 Mulberry St.
Middletown, NY 10940
　　City....................Robert Quinn.......................(914)343-2181
　　Drama...................Dennis Sprick......................(914)343-2181
　　Editorials..............Robert J. Gaydos...................(914)343-2181
　　Education...............Traci Williams.....................(914)343-2181
　　Entertainment..........Emily Morrison......................(914)343-2181
　　Environmental..........Wayne Hall..........................(914)343-2181
　　Family.................Brenda Gilhooly.....................(914)343-2181
　　Fashion................Brenda Gilhooly.....................(914)343-2181
　　Features...............Brenda Gilhooly.....................(914)343-2181
　　Financial/Business..... Adam Bryant........................(914)343-2181
　　Food...................Brenda Gilhooly.....................(914)343-2181
　　Garden/Home............Brenda Gilhooly.....................(914)343-2181
　　Lifestyle..............Brenda Gilhooly.....................(914)343-2181
　　Living.................Brenda Gilhooly.....................(914)343-2181
　　Medical................Beth Mullally.......................(914)343-2181
　　Movie..................Dennis Sprick.......................(914)343-2181
　　Music..................Steve Israel........................(914)343-2181
　　News...................Alan Gaul...........................(914)343-2181
　　Photo..................Michael Carey.......................(914)343-2181
　　Political..............Robert Quinn........................(914)343-2181
　　Radio..................Dennis Sprick.......................(914)343-2181
　　Real Estate............Adam Bryant.........................(914)343-2181
　　Religion...............Wayne Hall..........................(914)343-2181
　　Rural Development..... Adam Bryant.........................(914)343-2181
　　Society................Barbara Bedell......................(914)343-2181
　　Sports.................Chuck Bausman.......................(914)343-2181
　　Sunday.................Emily Morrison......................(914)343-2181
　　TV.....................Dennis Sprick.......................(914)343-2181
　　Travel.................Moe Mitterling......................(914)343-2181
　　Women's................Brenda Gilhooly.....................(914)343-2181

NEW YORK-New York

(21588) EDUCATION UPDATE
276 5th Ave., Ste. 1005
New York, NY 10001
　　Education...............Jacob Appel........................(212)481-5519

(21951) IRISH VOICE NEWSPAPER
432 Park Ave. S Ste. 1503
New York, NY 10016
　　News....................Jack Flynn.........................(212)684-3366

NEW YORK-Poughkeepsie

(23149) POUGHKEEPSIE JOURNAL
85 Civic Center Plaza
Poughkeepsie, NY 12601-2410
　　City....................Gerry McNulty......................(914)454-2000
　　Consumer Affairs....... Craig Wolf.........................(914)454-2000
　　Drama...................Florence Pennella..................(914)454-2000
　　Editorials..............Meg Downey.........................(914)454-2000
　　Education...............Linda Montanari....................(914)454-2000
　　Entertainment..........Carol Trapani.......................(914)454-2000
　　Environmental..........Dennis Kipp.........................(914)454-2000
　　Family.................Carol Trapani.......................(914)454-2000
　　Farm...................Kent Gibbons........................(914)454-2000
　　Fashion................Carol Trapani.......................(914)454-2000
　　Features...............Carol Trapani.......................(914)454-2000
　　Financial/Business..... Craig Wolf.........................(914)454-2000
　　Food...................Carol Trapani.......................(914)454-2000
　　Garden/Home............Carol Trapani.......................(914)454-2000
　　Lifestyle..............Carol Trapani.......................(914)454-2000
　　Living.................Carol Trapani.......................(914)454-2000
　　Medical................Dennis Kipp.........................(914)454-2000
　　Metro..................Gerry McNulty.......................(914)454-2000
　　Music..................Carol Trapani.......................(914)454-2000
　　News...................Gerry McNulty.......................(914)454-2000
　　Photo..................Jack Kurtz..........................(914)454-2000
　　Political..............David L'Heureux.....................(914)454-2000
　　Real Estate............Harvey Auster.......................(914)454-2000
　　Religion...............Diane McKeon........................(914)454-2000
　　Rural Development..... Harvey Auster.......................(914)454-2000
　　Saturday...............Tom Tobin...........................(914)454-2000
　　Science................Dennis Kipp.........................(914)454-2000
　　Society................Carol Trapani.......................(914)454-2000
　　Sports.................Dan Cohen...........................(914)454-2000
　　Sports.................Paul Hurley.........................(914)454-2000
　　State..................David L'Heureux.....................(914)454-2000
　　Travel.................Carol Trapani.......................(914)454-2000
　　Women's................Carol Trapani.......................(914)454-2000

NEW YORK-Rochester

(23222) DEMOCRAT AND CHRONICLE
55 Exchange Blvd.
Rochester, NY 14614-2001
　　Editorials..............James Lawrence.....................(716)232-7100
　　Features...............Mike Johansson......................(716)232-7100
　　Financial/Business...... Brahm Resnik......................(716)232-7100
　　Metro..................Robert Finnery......................(716)232-7100
　　News...................Mike Johansson......................(716)232-7100
　　News...................Stan Wischnowski....................(716)232-7100
　　Photo..................Alan English........................(716)232-7100
　　Sports.................Tom Batzold.........................(716)232-7100

NEW YORK-Staten Island

(23361) STATEN ISLAND ADVANCE
950 Fingerboard Rd.
Staten Island, NY 10305
　　Art....................Michael Fressola....................(718)981-1234
　　City...................Tom Checchi.........................(718)981-1234
　　Fashion................Elaine Boies........................(718)981-1234
　　Food...................Jane Milza..........................(718)981-1234
　　Lifestyle..............Dan Breen...........................(718)981-1234
　　Metro..................Tom Checchi.........................(718)981-1234
　　Movie..................John Hurley.........................(718)981-1234
　　News...................Ed Donnelly.........................(718)981-1234
　　Photo..................Steve Zaffarano.....................(718)981-1234
　　Political..............Judy Randall........................(718)981-1234
　　Real Estate............Stevie Lacy.........................(718)981-1234
　　Religion...............Julia Martin........................(718)981-1234
　　Society................Dan Breen...........................(718)981-1234
　　Sports.................Lou Bergonzi........................(718)981-1234
　　Sunday.................Chuck Schmdit.......................(718)981-1234
　　TV.....................Dan Breen...........................(718)981-1234
　　Travel.................Cassondra Phares....................(718)981-1234
　　Women's................Dan Breen...........................(718)981-1234

NEW YORK-Syracuse

(23419) THE POST-STANDARD
PO Box 4915
Syracuse, NY 13221
　　City...................Janis Barth.........................(315)470-0011
　　Editorials..............Fred Fiske.........................(315)470-0011
　　Photo..................Harry DiOrio........................(315)470-0011
　　Sports.................Steve Carlic........................(315)470-0011

NORTH CAROLINA-Asheville

(23627) ASHEVILLE CITIZEN-TIMES
14 O. Henry Ave.
Asheville, NC 28801
　　City...................Robyn Tomlin........................(828)232-5883
　　Editorials..............Joy Franklin.......................(828)232-5895
　　Features...............Lydia Carrington....................(828)232-5848
　　News...................Scott Bowers........................(828)232-5852
　　Regional...............Geoff Cantrell......................(828)232-5922

NORTH CAROLINA-Durham

(23824) THE HERALD-SUN
2828 Picket Rd.
Durham, NC 27705
　　Consumer Affairs....... Tom Beavers........................(919)419-6627
　　Drama...................Jim Wise...........................(919)419-6680
　　Editorials..............Bob Wilson.........................(919)419-6662
　　Entertainment..........Jim Wise............................(919)419-6680
　　Environmental..........Bill Stagg..........................(919)419-6630
　　Family.................Jim Wise............................(919)419-6680
　　Fashion................Jim Wise............................(919)419-6680
　　Features...............Jim Wise............................(919)419-6680
　　Financial/Business...... Tom Beavers.......................(919)419-6627
　　Food...................Jim Wise............................(919)419-6680
　　Garden/Home............Jim Wise............................(919)419-6680
　　Lifestyle..............Jim Wise............................(919)419-6680
　　Living.................Jim Wise............................(919)419-6680
　　Medical................Jeff Zimmer.........................(919)419-6633
　　Metro..................Bill Stagg..........................(919)419-6630
　　Movie..................Jim Wise............................(919)419-6680
　　Music..................Jim Wise............................(919)419-6680
　　Radio..................Jim Wise............................(919)419-6680
　　Real Estate............Tom Beavers.........................(919)419-6627
　　Religion...............Flo Johnston........................(919)419-6638
　　Science................Mark Donovan........................(919)419-6633

NORTH CAROLINA-Durham (continued)

Society	Jim Wise	(919)419-6680
Sports	Jimmy Dupree	(919)419-6667
State	Bill Stagg	(919)419-6630
Suburban	Bill Stagg	(919)419-6630
TV	Rachael Barden	(919)419-6615
Travel	Jim Wise	(919)419-6680
Women's	Jim Wise	(919)419-6664

NORTH CAROLINA-Greensboro

(23930) NEWS & RECORD
200 E. Market St.
PO Box 20848
Greensboro, NC 27401-2910

Aviation	Jack Scism	(919)373-7004
Book	Ann Alexander	(919)373-7040
City	Mike Massoglia	(919)373-7033
Drama	Abe Jones	(919)373-7090
Editorials	Dave Dubuisson	(919)373-7038
Education	Mike Massoglia	(919)373-7033
Environmental	Bill Hancock	(919)373-7070
Family	Carla Bagley	(919)373-7344
Fashion	Doris Paysour	(919)373-7059
Features	Carla Bagley	(919)373-7054
Financial/Business	Pete Fields	(919)373-7085
Food	Carla Bagley	(919)373-7057
Garden/Home	Carla Bagley	(919)373-7054
Lifestyle	Carla Bagley	(919)373-7054
Living	Carla Bagley	(919)373-7054
Medical	Ann Morris	(919)373-7083
Movie	Leigh Pressley	(919)373-7058
Music	Abe Jones	(919)373-7090
News	Mike Massoglia	(919)373-7070
Photo	Al Spicer	(919)373-7087
Political	Jim Schlosser	(919)373-7081
Radio	Leigh Pressley	(919)373-7058
Real Estate	Mark Sutter	(919)373-7023
Religion	Ann Morris	(919)373-7098
Saturday	Tom Corrigan	(919)373-7023
Society	Martha Long	(919)373-7097
Sports	Larry Keech	(919)373-7080
Sunday	Tom Corrigan	(919)373-7023
TV	Leigh Pressley	(919)373-7058
Travel	Carla Bagley	(919)373-7054
Women's	Doris Paysour	(919)373-7059

NORTH CAROLINA-Winston-Salem

(24324) WINSTON-SALEM JOURNAL
PO Box 3159
Winston-Salem, NC 27102-3159

Features	Lynn Felder	(336)727-7339

NORTH DAKOTA-Fargo

(24411) THE FORUM
Box 2020
101 5th St. N.
Fargo, ND 58102-4826

Editorials	Jack Zaleski	(701)235-7311

OHIO-Canton

(24731) THE REPOSITORY
500 Market Ave. S
Canton, OH 44702-2112

Aviation	Ed Semmler	(216)454-5611
Book	Michael Hanke	(216)454-5611
City	Jim Hillibish	(216)454-5611
Drama	Dan Kane	(216)454-5611
Editorials	William Hopper	(216)454-5611
Education	Susan Glaser	(216)454-5611
Entertainment	Dan Kane	(216)454-5611
Environmental	Jim Weber	(216)454-5611
Family	Mark Price	(216)454-5611
Fashion	Diana Rossetti	(216)454-5611
Features	Jim Hillibish	(216)454-5611
Financial/Business	Ed Semmler	(216)454-5611
Food	Kathie Smith	(216)454-5611
Garden/Home	Jim Hillibish	(216)454-5611
Lifestyle	Mark Price	(216)454-5611
Metro	Jim Hillibish	(216)454-5611
Movie	Dan Kane	(216)454-5611
Music	Dan Kane	(216)454-5611
News	Jim Weber	(216)454-5611
Photo	Stan Myers	(216)454-5611
Political	Rick Senften	(216)454-5611
Real Estate	William McIntire	(216)454-5611
Religion	Becky Clover	(216)454-5611
Rural Development	Jim Hillibish	(216)454-5611
Society	Mark Price	(216)454-5611
Sports	Bob Stewart	(216)454-5611
Sunday	David Kaminski	(216)454-5611
TV	Dan Kane	(216)454-5611

Travel	Diana Rossetti	(216)454-5611
Women's	Mark Price	(216)454-5611

OHIO-Cincinnati

(24785) THE CINCINNATI ENQUIRER
312 Elm St.
Cincinnati, OH 45202

City	Ron Liebau	(513)369-1951
Drama	Sara Pearce	(513)369-1984
Editorials	Thom Gephart	(513)369-1854
Education	Krista Ramsey	(513)369-1933
Entertainment	Sara Pearce	(513)369-1984
Environmental	Betsy News	(513)369-1951
Family	Sue Bedinghaus	(513)369-1984
Fashion	Mary Beth Crocker	(513)369-1967
Features	Sara Pearce	(513)369-1984
Food	Toni Cashnelli	(513)369-1985
Garden/Home	Peggy Lane	(513)369-1981
Lifestyle	Sara Pearce	(513)369-1984
Living	Sara Pearce	(513)369-1984
Medical	Sue MacDonald	(513)369-1991
Metro	Ron Liebau	(513)369-1951
Movie	Joe DeChick	(513)369-1863
Music	Ray Cooklis	(513)369-1982
Music	Cliff Radel	(513)369-1973
News	Jim Smith	(513)369-1951
Photo	Liz Dufour	(513)369-1952
Political	Howard Wilkinson	(513)369-1034
Real Estate	Mike Boyer	(513)369-1009
Religion	Chris Wolff	(513)369-1988
Society	Jackie Barrett-Sant	(513)369-1046
Sports	Greg Noble	(513)369-1029
Sunday	Jim Dean	(513)369-1812
TV	John Kiesewetter	(513)369-1970
Travel	Sara Pearce	(513)369-1984

(24788) THE CINCINNATI POST
125 E. Court St.
Cincinnati, OH 45202

Book	Bob Hahn	(513)352-2785
City	Mike Philipps	(513)352-2706
Consumer Affairs	Nancy Berlier	(513)352-2752
Drama	Jerry Stein	(513)352-2794
Editorials	Byron While	(513)352-2773
Education	Laurie Petrie	(513)352-2714
Entertainment	David Lyman	(513)352-2790
Fashion	Gayle Harden	(513)352-2754
Features	Mark Gavert	(513)352-2752
Financial/Business	Dan Adriacco	(513)352-2761
Food	Joyce Rosencrans	(513)352-2753
Garden/Home	Lee Cain	(513)352-2750
Lifestyle	Nancy Berlier	(513)352-2752
Living	Nancy Berlier	(513)352-2752
Medical	Lisa Rose	(513)352-2738
Metro	Mike Philipps	(513)352-2706
Movie	David Lyman	(513)352-2790
Music	Larry Nager	(513)352-2793
News	Mike Philipps	(513)352-2706
Photo	Winston Townsend	(513)352-2711
Political	Randy Ludlow	(513)352-2730
Radio	Greg Paeth	(513)352-2792
Real Estate	Dan Andriacco	(513)352-2761
Religion	Terry Boschert	(513)352-2710
Rural Development	Nadine Louthan	(513)352-2744
Saturday	Amy Culbertson	(513)352-2754
Society	Mary Linn White	(513)352-2754
Sports	Mark Tomasik	(513)352-2705
State	Doug Henry	(513)352-2712
Suburban	Doug Henry	(513)352-2712
TV	Greg Paeth	(513)352-2775
Travel	Mark Gavert	(513)352-2752

OHIO-Cleveland

(24943) PLAIN DEALER
1801 Superior Ave.
Cleveland, OH 44114

Book	Janice Harayda	(216)344-4410
City	John Griffith	(216)344-4803
Drama	Marianne Evett	(216)344-4545
Editorials	Mary Anne Sharkey	(216)344-4252
Education	Ron Rutti	(216)344-4819
Entertainment	Cheryl Kushner	(216)344-4109
Fashion	Janet McCue	(216)344-4542
Features	Christine Jindra	(216)344-4839
Financial/Business	Tom Coscarelli	(216)344-4405
Food	Iris Bailin	(216)344-4401
Garden/Home	Suzanne Hively	(216)344-4554
Medical	Doug Lefton	(216)344-4871
Metro	Ted Diadiun	(216)344-4833
Music	Robert Finn	(216)344-4269
News	Van Richmond	(216)344-4395
Photo	Bob Dorksen	(216)344-4356
Political	Jim Linderwood	(216)344-4820
Political	Steve Luttner	(216)344-4820

Radio	David Sowd	(216)344-4559
Real Estate	Bill Lubinger	(216)344-4112
Religion	Darrell Holland	(216)344-4812
Saturday	Kim Taylor	(216)344-4296
Society	Mary Strassmeyer	(216)344-4848
Sports	Gene Williams	(216)344-4106
Sunday	Bob McAuley	(216)344-4878
TV	Tom Feran	(216)344-4905
Travel	David Molyneaux	(216)344-4560

OHIO-Columbus

(25007) COLUMBUS ALIVE
1079 N High St.
Columbus, OH 43201-2439

Art	Melissa Storker	(614)221-2449

(25008) THE COLUMBUS DISPATCH
34 S. 3rd St.
Columbus, OH 43215

City	Mark Ellis	(614)461-5097
Columnist	Richard Fenlon	(614)461-8528
Columnist	Mike Harden	(614)461-5027
Columnist	John McNeely	(614)461-5215
Columnist	John Switzer	(614)461-5203
Columnist	Barbara Zuck	(614)461-5078
Editorials	Richard Carson	(614)461-5072
Entertainment	Michele Toney	(614)461-5075
Features	T.R. Fitchko	(614)461-8890
Financial/Business	Gerald Tebben	(614)461-5231
Food	Sue Dawson	(614)461-5529
News	Dennis Mahoney	(614)461-5157
Sports	George Strode	(614)461-8522
State	Frank Hinchey	(614)461-5569
Travel	Lisa Reuter	(614)461-8531

OHIO-Mansfield

(25332) NEWS JOURNAL
70 W. 4th St.
PO Box 25
Mansfield, OH 44903

City	Cynthia Jakubick	(419)522-3311
Consumer Affairs	Chriss Harris	(419)522-3311
Drama	Miriam Smith	(419)522-3311
Editorials	Terry Mapes	(419)522-3311
Entertainment	Miriam Smith	(419)522-3311
Environmental	Jeannie Gorgas	(419)522-3311
Family	Jim Krummel	(419)522-3311
Farm	Ron Simon	(419)522-3311
Fashion	Anne Miller	(419)522-3311
Features	Cynthia Jakubick	(419)522-3311
Financial/Business	Chriss Harris	(419)522-3311
Food	Ray Dyson	(419)522-3311
Garden/Home	Jeanne Bishop	(419)522-3311
Lifestyle	Jim Krummel	(419)522-3311
Living	Jim Krummel	(419)522-3311
Medical	Carol Zito	(419)522-3311
Metro	Jeannie Gorgas	(419)522-3311
Movie	Miriam Smith	(419)522-3311
Music	Miriam Smith	(419)522-3311
News	Dan Kopp	(419)522-3311
Photo	Alan King	(419)522-3311
Political	Roger Nielsen	(419)522-3311
Radio	Miriam Smith	(419)522-3311
Real Estate	Margaret Mershon	(419)522-3311
Religion	Karen Palmer	(419)522-3311
Rural Development	Ron Simon	(419)522-3311
Saturday	Carl Hunnell	(419)522-3311
Science	Carol Zito	(419)522-3311
Society	Anne Miller	(419)522-3311
Sports	Mark Naegele	(419)522-3311
State	Jeannie Gorgas	(419)522-3311
Suburban	Jeannie Gorgas	(419)522-3311
TV	Melinda McKenna	(419)522-3311
Travel	John Domer	(419)522-3311
Women's	Jeanne Bishop	(419)522-3311

OHIO-Toledo

(25564) THE BLADE
541 N. Superior St.
Toledo, OH 43660-1000

Features	Richard Paton	(419)724-6000

OHIO-Wapakoneta

(25615) WAPAKONETA DAILY NEWS
8 Willipie St.
PO Box 389
Wapakoneta, OH 45895

Sports	Joe Menden	(419)738-2120

OHIO-Youngstown

(25699) THE VINDICATOR
Vindicator Sq. No. 107
PO Box 780
Youngstown, OH 44501

Editorials	Dennis Mangan	(330)747-1471
News	Richard Logan	(330)747-1471
Photo	Robert Yosay	(330)747-1471
Political	David Skolnick	(330)747-1471
Regional	Anthony Paglia	(330)747-1471
Society	Barbara Shaffer	(330)747-1471
Sports	Robert Todor	(330)747-1471

OKLAHOMA-Oklahoma City

(25954) BAPTIST MESSENGER
PO Box 12130
Oklahoma City, OK 73157-2130

State	Dana Williamson	

(25989) OKLAHOMAN
9000 N. Broadway
PO Box 25125
Oklahoma City, OK 73114

Food	Sharon Dowell	(405)475-3304
Sports	Bob Colon	(405)475-3313
TV	Penny Hanley	(405)475-3108

OKLAHOMA-Tulsa

(26139) TULSA WORLD
315 S. Boulder Ave.
PO Box 1770
Tulsa, OK 74103

City	Debbie Jackson	(918)581-8325
Drama	John Wooley	(918)581-8335
Editorials	Alex Adwan	(918)581-8330
Education	Laureen Gilroy	(918)581-8350
Education	Ray Johnson	(918)581-8350
Family	Rusty Lang	(918)581-8340
Fashion	Laurie Winslow	(918)581-8300
Features	Pat Atkinson	(918)581-8300
Financial/Business	Dwayne Hartnett	(918)581-8315
Food	Suzanne Holloway	(918)581-8340
Movie	Dennis King	(918)581-8335
Music	John Wooley	(918)581-8335
Photo	Johnny Walker	(918)581-8350
Real Estate	Cynthia Dees	(918)581-8315
Religion	Carolyn Jenkins	(918)581-8300
Rural Development	Mark Lee	(918)581-8300
Society	Danna Sue Walker	(918)581-8340
Sports	Bill Connors	(918)581-8355
Sunday	Joe Worley	(918)581-8345
TV	Rita Sherrow	(918)581-8360
Women's	Danna Sue Walker	(918)581-8340

OREGON-Eugene

(26334) THE REGISTER-GUARD
3500 Chad Dr., 97408
PO Box 10188
Eugene, OR 97440-2188

City	Grant Podelco	(503)485-1234
Consumer Affairs	Christian Wihtol	(503)485-1234
Political	David Steves	(541)363-3451
Sports	John Conrad	(541)485-1234
TV	Steve Irvin	(541)485-1234

OREGON-Portland

(26495) THE OREGONIAN
1320 SW Broadway
Portland, OR 97201-3469

Book	Jeff Baker	(503)221-8165
Entertainment	Karen Brooks	(503)221-8230
Fashion	Vivian McInerny	(503)294-4076
Financial/Business	Mark Hester	(503)221-8548
Food	Chris Christensen	(503)294-5191
Medical	Vicki Martin	(503)221-8313
Music	Marty Hughley	(503)221-8383
News	John Harvey	(503)221-8149
Political	Jeff Mapes	(503)221-8213
Sports	Dennis Peck	(503)221-8164
TV	Pete Carlin	(503)221-8232
Travel	Sue Hobart	(503)221-8191

(26515) WILLAMETTE WEEK
822 SW 10th
Portland, OR 97205

Art	Caryn Brooks	(503)243-2122

OREGON-Salem

(26573) STATESMAN JOURNAL
280, Church St. NE
PO Box 13009
Salem, OR 97301

Financial/Business	Don Currie	(503)399-6677
Lifestyle	Michelle Maxwell	(503)399-6930
Metro	Matt Misterek	(503)399-6862
Sports	Kathy Sheldon	(503)399-6801

PENNSYLVANIA-Allentown

(26629) THE MORNING CALL
101 N. 6th St., No. 1260
Allentown, PA 18101-1403

Book	Paul Willistein	(215)820-6546
City	Al Roberts	(215)820-6566
Drama	Paul Willistein	(215)820-6546
Editorials	Van Cavett	(215)820-6728
Family	Jame Kelly	(215)820-6117
Fashion	Polly Rayner	(215)820-6515
Features	Paul Willistein	(215)820-6546
Financial/Business	Charles Jaffe	(215)820-6694
Food	Diane Stoneback	(215)820-6526
Garden/Home	Diane Stoneback	(215)820-6526
Lifestyle	James Kelly	(215)820-6741
Medical	Ann Wtazelek	(215)820-6745
Movie	Paul Willistein	(215)820-6546
Music	Paul Willistein	(215)820-6546
News	Al Roberts	(215)820-6566
Photo	Joel Bieler	(215)820-6537
Political	Al Roberts	(215)820-6566
Real Estate	Al Roberts	(215)820-6566
Religion	David Venditta	(215)820-6566
Rural Development	Al Roberts	(215)820-6566
Science	Rosa Salter	(215)820-6750
Society	Polly Rayner	(215)820-6783
Sports	Paul F. Reinhard	(215)820-6515
Sunday	Linda Luther	(215)820-6656
TV	Sylvia Lawler	(215)820-6733
Travel	Randy Kraft	(215)820-6557
Women's	Polly Rayner	(215)820-6515

PENNSYLVANIA-Erie

(26897) ERIE TIMES-NEWS
205 W. 12th St.
Erie, PA 16534-0001

Features	Kevin Cuneo	(814)870-1701

PENNSYLVANIA-Greensburg

(26956) TRIBUNE-REVIEW
622 Cabin Hill Dr.
Greensburg, PA 15601

Book	Robin Jennings	(412)834-1151
Drama	Cathy Lubenski	(412)834-1151
Editorials	Paul Koloski	(412)834-1151
Entertainment	Cathy Lubenski	(412)834-1151
Family	Phyllis Pack	(412)834-1151
Fashion	Phyllis Pack	(412)834-1151
Financial/Business	Jack Markowitz	(412)834-1151
Food	Lynn Kuhn	(412)834-1151
Garden/Home	Paul Teske	(412)834-1151
Lifestyle	Phyllis Pack	(412)834-1151
News	Frank Myers	(412)834-1151
Political	Paul Koloski	(412)834-1151
Radio	Bill Dymond	(412)834-1151
Real Estate	Ron DaParma	(412)834-1151
Religion	David Lester	(412)834-1151
Society	Phyllis Pack	(412)834-1151
Sports	Dave Ailes	(412)834-1151
Sunday	Bill Dymond	(412)834-1151
TV	Christy Slewinski	(412)834-1151
Travel	Sue McFarland	(412)834-1151
Women's	Phyllis Pack	(412)834-1151

PENNSYLVANIA-Johnstown

(27089) TRIBUNE-DEMOCRAT
425 Locust St.
Johnstown, PA 15907

Aviation	Terry Altemus	(814)536-0711
Book	Marcia Lewis	(814)536-0711

PENNSYLVANIA-Levittown

(27186) BUCKS COUNTY COURIER TIMES
8400 Rte. 13
Levittown, PA 19057

Editorials	Guy Petroziello	(215)949-4000
Entertainment	Denise Yourse	(215)949-4000

Features	Tom Haines	(215)949-4000
Food	Betty Cichy	(215)949-4000
Lifestyle	Tom Haines	(215)949-4000
Sports	Gary Silvers	(215)949-4000

PENNSYLVANIA-Philadelphia

(27625) PHILADELPHIA DAILY NEWS
400 N. Broad St.
Philadelphia, PA 19130-4015

City	Kurt Heine	(213)854-5941
Editorials	Frank Burgos	(213)854-5149
Movie	Gary Thompson	(215)854-5855
Music	Jon Takiff	(215)854-5960
Political	Gar Joseph	(215)854-5895
Society	Stu Bykofsky	(215)854-5977
Sports	Pat Mcloone	(215)854-5700

(27627) PHILADELPHIA INQUIRER
400 N. Broad St.
Philadelphia, PA 19130

Book	Mike Leary	(215)854-5616
City	William Marimow	(215)854-2772
Drama	Cliff Ridley	(215)854-5610
Editorials	David Boldt	(215)854-4530
Education	Dale Mezzacappa	(215)854-2790
Family	Lucia Herndon	(215)854-5724
Fashion	Roy Campbell	(215)854-2799
Features	Ron Patel	(215)854-4519
Financial/Business	Craig Stock	(215)854-2455
Food	Ken Bookman	(215)854-5743
Movie	Carrie Rickey	(215)854-5627
Movie	Desmond Ryan	(215)854-5614
Music	Daniel Webster	(215)854-5598
Real Estate	Gene Austin	(215)854-2578
Religion	Mike Schaffer	(215)854-2781
Society	David Iams	(215)854-5726
Sports	David Tucker	(215)854-4550
Sunday	Paul Moore	(215)854-5140
TV	Jonathan Storm	(215)854-5618
Travel	Mike Shoup	(215)854-5727

PENNSYLVANIA-Pittsburgh

(27832) PITTSBURGH CITY PAPER
650 Smithfield St., Ste. 2200
Pittsburgh, PA 15222

Art	Mary Binder	(412)316-3342
Entertainment	Mary Binder	(412)316-3342

(27837) POST-GAZETTE
34 Blvd. of the Allies
Pittsburgh, PA 15222

Editorials	Michael McGough	(412)263-1343
News	Ced Kurtz	(412)263-1764
Photo	John Beale	(412)263-1688
Sports	Fritz Huysman	(412)263-1653

PENNSYLVANIA-Pittston

(27885) SUNDAY DISPATCH
109 New St.
Pittston, PA 18640

News	Tom Bubul	(717)655-1418

PENNSYLVANIA-Primos

(27907) THE DAILY TIMES
500 Mildred Ave.
Primos, PA 19018

Editorials	Linda DeMeglio	(610)622-8817
Education	Matthew Zager	(610)622-8803
Entertainment	Lynn Keyser	(610)622-8813
Family	Trish Cofiell	(610)622-8819
Fashion	Lynn Keyser	(610)622-8813
Features	Trish Cofiell	(610)622-8819
Financial/Business	Joseph Monchecourt	(610)622-8886
Food	Lynn Keyser	(610)622-8813
Garden/Home	Trish Cofiell	(610)622-8819
Metro	Joseph Hart	(610)622-8894
Religion	Harry Maitland	(610)622-8816
Sports	Tom McNichol	(610)622-8884

PENNSYLVANIA-Reading

(27919) READING EAGLE
PO Box 582
Reading, PA 19603-0582

City	Dennis V. Deysher	(610)371-5011
News	Jim Deegan	(610)371-5009

PENNSYLVANIA-West Chester

(28146) DAILY LOCAL NEWS
250 N Bradford Ave.
West Chester, PA 19382-2800
```
City.....................Michael Rellahan...................(610)430-1195
Features.................Natalie Smith......................(610)430-1125
Financial/Business.......Brian McCullogh....................(610)430-1126
Photo....................Larry McDevitt.....................(610)430-1132
Sports...................Kevin Scott........................(610)430-1179
```

PENNSYLVANIA-Wilkes Barre

(28167) THE TIMES LEADER
15 N. Main St.
Wilkes Barre, PA 18711
```
Art......................Sandra Snyder......................(570)829-5537
```

PENNSYLVANIA-York

(28207) YORK DAILY RECORD
122 S George St.
PO Box 15122
York, PA 17405-7122
```
Features.................Buffy Andrews......................(717)771-2052
```

(28210) YORK SUNDAY NEWS
1891 Loucks
PO Box 14401
York, PA 17404
```
City.....................J. P. Kurish.......................(717)767-6397
```

PUERTO RICO-San Juan

(28294) EL VOCERO DE PUERTO RICO
PO Box 9023831
San Juan, PR 00902-3831
```
Book.....................Elia Gonzalez-Ramos................(809)721-2300
City.....................German Martin-Negroni..............(809)721-2300
Drama....................Elia Gonzalez-Ramos................(809)721-2300
Editorials...............German Martin-Negroni..............(809)721-2300
Education................Luis Collado.......................(809)721-2300
Environmental............Luis Collado.......................(809)721-2300
Family...................Elia Gonzalez-Ramos................(809)721-2300
Fashion..................Elia Gonzalez-Ramos................(809)721-2300
Features.................Jose Purcell.......................(809)721-2300
Financial/Business.......Miguel Rivera......................(809)721-2300
Food.....................Elia Gonzalez-Ramos................(809)721-2300
Garden/Home..............Elia Gonzalez-Ramos................(809)721-2300
Movie....................Elia Gonzalez-Ramos................(809)721-2300
Music....................Elia Gonzalez-Ramos................(809)721-2300
News.....................Jose Purcell.......................(809)721-2300
Photo....................Rafael A. Rivera...................(809)721-2300
Political................Miguel Rivera......................(809)721-2300
Real Estate..............Miguel Rivera......................(809)721-2300
Religion.................Luis Collado.......................(809)721-2300
Society..................Elia Gonzalez-Ramos................(809)721-2300
Sports...................Luis Colon.........................(809)721-2300
TV.......................Elia Gonzalez-Ramos................(809)721-2300
Travel...................Elia Gonzalez-Ramos................(809)721-2300
Women's..................Elia Gonzalez-Ramos................(809)721-2300
```

SOUTH CAROLINA-Greenville

(28623) THE GREENVILLE NEWS
PO Box 1688
Greenville, SC 29602
```
Drama....................Jan Phillips.......................(803)298-4100
Editorials...............Tom Inman..........................(803)298-4100
Education................Lucy May...........................(803)298-4100
Entertainment............Jan Phillips.......................(803)298-4100
Environmental............Jim Hammond........................(803)298-4100
Family...................Jan Phillips.......................(803)298-4100
Fashion..................Jan Phillips.......................(803)298-4100
Features.................Jan Phillips.......................(803)298-4100
Financial/Business.......Robert Scott.......................(803)298-4100
Food.....................Jan Phillips.......................(803)298-4100
Garden/Home..............Jan Phillips.......................(803)298-4100
Lifestyle................Jan Phillips.......................(803)298-4100
Metro....................Marion Elliott.....................(803)298-4100
Movie....................Jan Phillips.......................(803)298-4100
Music....................Jan Phillips.......................(803)298-4100
News.....................Mark Murphy........................(803)298-4100
Photo....................Fred Rollins.......................(803)298-4100
Political................Wayne Rope.........................(803)298-4100
Real Estate..............Robert Scott.......................(803)298-4100
Religion.................Frances Evans......................(803)298-4100
Rural Development........Marion Elliott.....................(803)298-4100
Society..................Jan Phillips.......................(803)298-4100
Sports...................Ed McGranahan......................(803)298-4100
Sunday...................Mark Murphy........................(803)298-4100
TV.......................Jan Phillips.......................(803)298-4100
Travel...................Jan Phillips.......................(803)298-4100
```
```
Women's..................Jan Phillips.......................(803)298-4100
```

TENNESSEE-Knoxville

(29280) THE KNOXVILLE NEWS-SENTINEL
2332 News Sentinel Dr.
Knoxville, TN 37921
```
Drama....................Doug Mason.........................(865)342-6441
Editorials...............Hoyt Canady........................(865)342-6250
Entertainment............Chuck Campbell.....................(865)342-6443
Family...................Amy McRary.........................(423)342-6437
Fashion..................Kevin Cowan........................(865)342-6426
Features.................Sherri Gardner-Howell..............(865)342-6430
Financial/Business.......David Keim.........................(865)342-6311
Food.....................Louise Durman......................(865)342-6432
Movie....................Betsy Pickle.......................(865)342-6442
Travel...................Linda Lange........................(865)342-6433
```

TEXAS-Abilene

(29652) ABILENE REPORTER-NEWS
101 Cypress St.
PO Box 30
Abilene, TX 79604
```
Book.....................Larry Lawrence.....................(915)673-4271
City.....................Richard Horn.......................(915)673-4271
Entertainment............Bob Lapham.........................(915)673-4271
Farm.....................J.T. Smith.........................(915)673-4271
Food.....................Pam Percival.......................(915)673-4271
Political................Richard Horn.......................(915)673-4271
Sports...................Al Pickett.........................(915)673-4271
```

TEXAS-Amarillo

(29694) AMARILLO GLOBE-NEWS
PO Box 2091
Amarillo, TX 79166
```
City.....................Vivian Salazar.....................(806)345-3353
```

TEXAS-Beaumont

(29897) BEAUMONT ENTERPRISE
380 Main St.
PO Box 3071
Beaumont, TX 77704-3071
```
City.....................Dan Anderson.......................(409)838-2859
Editorials...............Thomas Taschinger..................(409)838-2887
Features.................Beth Gallaspy......................(409)838-2872
Features.................Jane McBride.......................(409)838-2809
Financial/Business.......Chris Clausen......................(408)838-2876
Photo....................Ron Jaap...........................(409)838-2807
Sports...................Gerry Dickert......................(409)838-2806
```

TEXAS-Dallas

(30147) THE DALLAS MORNING NEWS
508 Young St.
PO Box 655237
Dallas, TX 75265
```
Features.................Sue Smith..........................(214)977-8222
Science..................Tom Siegfried......................(214)977-8443
```

TEXAS-El Paso

(30280) EL PASO TIMES
Times Plaza
El Paso, TX 79901-1470
```
Book.....................Josie Cantu-Weber..................(915)546-6154
City.....................Bob Locke..........................(915)546-6124
Drama....................Josie Cantu-Weber..................(915)546-6154
Editorials...............Barbara Funkhouser.................(915)546-6118
Education................Ramon Renteria.....................(915)546-6124
Entertainment............Josie Cantu-Weber..................(915)546-6154
Environmental............Bob Locke..........................(915)546-6124
Family...................Josie Cantu-Weber..................(915)546-6154
Fashion..................Josie Cantu-Weber..................(915)546-6154
Features.................Josie Cantu-Weber..................(915)546-6154
Financial/Business.......John Barrett.......................(915)546-6145
Food.....................Josie Cantu-Weber..................(915)546-6154
Garden/Home..............Roxanne Schroeder..................(915)546-6157
Lifestyle................Josie Cantu-Weber..................(915)546-6154
Medical..................Bob Locke..........................(915)546-6124
Movie....................Josie Cantu-Weber..................(915)546-6154
Music....................Josie Cantu-Weber..................(915)546-6154
News.....................Bob Locke..........................(915)546-6124
Photo....................Jay Bryant.........................(915)546-6172
Political................Gary Scharrer......................(915)546-6130
Real Estate..............John Barrett.......................(915)546-6145
Religion.................Karen Peterson.....................(915)546-6154
Rural Development........Bob Locke..........................(915)546-6124
Society..................Mary Margaret Davis................(915)546-6157
Sports...................Ray Hagar..........................(915)546-6170
```

TEXAS-El Paso (continued)

Sunday	Nan Keck	(915)546-6174
TV	Josie Cantu-Weber	(915)546-6154
Travel	Josie Cantu-Weber	(915)546-6154
Women's	Josie Cantu-Weber	(915)546-6154

TEXAS-Houston

(30488) 'HOUSTON PRESS
1621 Milam, Ste. 100
Houston, TX 77002

Political	Tim Fleck	(713)280-2400

TEXAS-San Antonio

(31029) EXPRESS-NEWS
PO Box 2171
San Antonio, TX 78297-2171

Book	Steve Bennett	(210)250-3413
Entertainment	Jim Kiest	(210)250-3415
Entertainment	Kristina Paledes	(210)250-3442
Garden/Home	Tracy Lehmann	(210)250-3000
Photo	Doug Sehres	(210)250-3411
Sunday	Elaine Ayala	(210)250-3405
TV	Jeanne Jakle	(512)250-3461

UTAH-Ogden

(31378) STANDARD-EXAMINER
332 Standard Way
PO Box 12790
Ogden, UT 84412-2790

City	Mark Saal	(801)625-4272
Lifestyle	Vanessa Zimmer	(801)625-4270
Photo	Colin Braley	(801)625-4280
Sports	Chris Miller	(801)625-4261

UTAH-Salt Lake City

(31426) DESERET NEWS
30 East 100 South
Salt Lake City, UT 84111

Art	David Gagon	(801)237-2149
Book	Jerry Johnston	(801)237-2150
City	Angie Hutchinson	(801)237-2132
Drama	Ivan Lincoln	(801)237-2146
Environmental	Joseph Bauman	(801)237-2100
Financial/Business	Max Knudson	(801)237-2118
Food	Jean Williams	(801)236-6099
Movie	Jeff Vice	(801)236-6019
Photo	Tom Smart	(801)237-2127
Political	Bob Bernick, Jr.	(801)237-2111
Radio	Lynn Arave	(801)237-2150
Real Estate	Max Knudson	(801)237-2118
Religion	Carrie Moore	(801)237-2100
Rural Development	Jerry Spangler	(801)237-2100
Sports	Marilyn Karras	(801)236-6079
TV	Scott Pierce	(801)237-2146
Travel	Kathryn Clayton	(801)237-2170

(31440) THE SALT LAKE TRIBUNE
143 S. Main St.
Salt Lake City, UT 84111

Art	Ann Wilson	(801)257-8741
Editorials	Vern Anderson	(801)257-8743
Education	Tom Harvey	(801)257-8767
Entertainment	Ann Wilson	(801)257-8741
Environmental	Greg Burton	(801)257-8797
Financial/Business	Lisa Carricaburu	(801)257-8716
Garden/Home	Anna Cekola	(801)257-8769
Lifestyle	Anna Cekola	(801)257-8769
Photo	Lori Post	(801)257-8940
Political	Tom Harvey	(801)257-8767
Regional	Peg McEntee	(801)257-8726
Sports	Mike Gottschamer	(801)257-8931
Sports	Jim Halley	(801)257-8961
Travel	Greg Burton	(801)257-8797

VERMONT-Burlington

(31514) THE BURLINGTON FREE PRESS
191 College St.
Burlington, VT 05402-0010

Book	Sally Pollak	(802)660-1859
City	Ed Shamy	(802)660-1862
Editorials	Stephen Kiernan	(802)660-1841
Entertainment	Elizabeth Munding	(802)660-1863
Features	Elizabeth Munding	(802)660-1863
Financial/Business	Aki Soga	(802)660-1866
Food	Debbie Salomon	(802)863-3441
Garden/Home	Becky Holt	(802)660-1808
Living	Elizabeth Munding	(802)660-1863
News	Dennis Redmond	(802)660-1850

Photo	Karen Pike	(802)660-1879
Political	Tom Zolper	(802)229-9141
Sports	Ted Ryan	(802)660-1855

VIRGINIA-Fredericksburg

(32085) THE FREE LANCE-STAR
616 Amelia St.
Fredericksburg, VA 22401

Art	Neva Trenis	(540)374-5412
Entertainment	Neva Trenis	(540)374-5412
Family	Laura Hutchinson	(540)374-5485
Food	Laura Hutchinson	(540)374-5485
Living	Laura Hutchinson	(540)374-5485

VIRGINIA-Mc Lean

(32240) ARGUS LEADER
7950 Jones Branch Dr.
Mc Lean, VA 22107

Book	Ann Grauvogl	(605)331-2300
City	Maricarrol Kueter	(605)331-2300
Consumer Affairs	Brenda Wade Schmidt	(605)331-2300
Drama	Ann Grauvogl	(605)331-2300
Editorials	Rob Swenson	(605)331-2300
Education	Anne Marie Otey	(605)331-2300
Entertainment	Ann Grauvogl	(605)331-2300
Environmental	Maricarrol Kueter	(605)331-2300
Family	Joyce Terveen	(605)331-2300
Farm	Brenda Wade Schmidt	(605)331-2300
Fashion	Jean Shea	(605)331-2300
Features	Jean Shea	(605)331-2300
Financial/Business	Brenda Wade Schmidt	(605)331-2300
Food	Joyce Terveen	(605)331-2300
Garden/Home	Brenda Schmidt	(605)331-2300
Lifestyle	Joyce Terveen	(605)331-2300
Living	Joyce Terveen	(605)331-2300
Medical	Joyce Terveen	(605)331-2300
Metro	Maricarrol Kueter	(605)331-2300
Movie	Ann Grauvogl	(605)331-2300
Music	Ann Grauvogl	(605)331-2300
News	Maricarrol Kueder	(605)331-2300
Photo	Lloyd Cunningham	(605)331-2300
Political	David Kranz	(605)331-2300
Radio	Ann Grauvogl	(605)331-2300
Real Estate	Brenda Schmidt	(605)331-2300
Religion	Joyce Terveen	(605)331-2300
Rural Development	Brenda Schmidt	(605)331-2300
Saturday	Rosemary McCoy	(605)331-2300
Science	Joyce Terveen	(605)331-2300
Society	Sheryl Steele	(605)331-2300
Sports	Greg Hansen	(605)331-2300
Suburban	Maricarrol Kueter	(605)331-2300
TV	Sheryl Steele	(605)331-2300
TV & Radio	Ann Grauvogl	(605)331-2300
Women's	Jean Shea	(605)331-2300

(32257) USA TODAY
7950 Jones Branch Dr.
Mc Lean, VA 22107

Book	Robert Wilson	(703)276-5486
Drama	David Patrick Stearurs	(202)715-5405
Editorials	John Seigenthaler	(703)276-3400
Education	Pat OrDovensky	(703)276-3467
Entertainment	Jack Curry	(703)276-3475
Environmental	Rae Tyson	(703)276-3424
Family	Linda Kauss	(703)276-6532
Fashion	Liz Sporkin	(202)715-5414
Features	Linda Kauss	(703)276-6532
Financial/Business	Hal Ritter	(703)276-3400
Food	Linda Kauss	(703)276-6532
Garden/Home	David Landis	(703)276-3470
Lifestyle	Susan Weiss	(703)276-3475
Medical	Tim Friend	(703)276-5455
Movie	Mike Clark	(703)276-6537
Music	Edna Gunderson	(703)276-3793
News	David Colton	(703)276-3422
Photo	Paul White	(703)276-5527
Political	Richard Benedetto	(703)276-3621
Radio	Haya El Nasser	(703)276-3470
Real Estate	David Landis	(703)276-3470
Rural Development	David Landis	(703)276-3470
Society	Jeannie Williams	(703)276-3773
Sports	Henry Freeman	(703)276-3735
TV & Radio	Matt Roush	(703)276-3783
Travel	Ron Schoolmeester	(703)276-3785
Women's	Shawn Sell	(703)276-5433

VIRGINIA-Newport News

(32279) DAILY PRESS
7505 Warwick Blvd,
Newport News, VA 23607

Entertainment	Lucretia McDine	(757)247-4733
Family	Rhonda Swan	(757)247-7892

Financial/Business...... Holly Roberson..................(757)247-4766
Metro..................Mark DiVincenzo...................(757)247-4737
News...................Bob Evans........................(757)247-4758
Photo..................Dennis Tennant...................(757)247-4764
Regional...............Jesse Todd.......................(757)928-6448
Sports.................Mario Orlikoff...................(757)247-4764
Sports.................Doug Roberson....................(757)247-4639
Suburban...............Vic Monaco.......................(757)229-3715

VIRGINIA-Norfolk

(32296) THE VIRGINIAN-PILOT
150 W. Brambleton Ave.
Norfolk, VA 23510-2018
Book.................Peggy Earle......................(757)446-2254
Editorials...........Alan Sorensen....................(757)446-2304
Education............Lorraine Eaton...................(757)222-5112
Features.............Latane Jones.....................(757)446-2977
Financial/Business...Carl Fincke......................(757)446-2359
Food.................Melinda Forbes...................(757)446-2360
Garden/Home..........Melinda Forbes...................(757)446-2360
Music................David Simpson....................(757)446-2546
Real Estate..........Ann-Marie Sradomski..............(757)446-2262
Sports...............Tom White........................(757)446-2368
Weekend..............Donald Luzzatto..................(757)446-2424

VIRGINIA-Richmond

(32452) RICHMOND TIMES-DISPATCH
300 E. Franklin St.
PO Box 85333
Richmond, VA 23293
Education............Ruth Intress.....................(804)649-6438
Entertainment........Margaret Graves..................(804)649-6819
Environmental........Rex Springston...................(804)649-6815
Family...............Robert Walsh.....................(804)649-6405
Features.............Robert Walsh.....................(804)649-6405
Financial/Business...Pam Feibish......................(804)649-6331
Food.................Jann Malone......................(804)649-6820
Garden/Home..........Cindy Creasy.....................(804)649-6363
Lifestyle............Robert Walsh.....................(804)649-6405
Medical..............Jammi Smith......................(804)649-6355
Movie................Dan Neman........................(804)649-6408
Music................Clarke Bustard...................(804)649-6362
News.................Bob Diehl........................(804)649-6356
News.................Harry Meem.......................(804)649-6356
Photo................Perk Gormus......................(804)649-6541
Political............Michael Hardy....................(804)649-6810
Real Estate..........Donna Rogers.....................(804)649-6990
Religion.............Alberta Lindsey..................(804)649-6754
Society..............Robert Walsh.....................(804)649-6405
Sports...............Jack Berninger...................(804)649-6558
Sunday...............John Clarke......................(804)649-6819
TV...................Ms. Douglas Durden...............(804)649-6359
Travel...............Katherine Calos..................(804)649-6433
Women's..............Robert Walsh.....................(804)649-6355

VIRGINIA-Roanoke

(32491) THE ROANOKE TIMES
PO Box 2491
Roanoke, VA 24010-2491
Food.................Nancy Gleiner....................(703)981-3253
Garden/Home..........Marty Horne......................(703)981-3207
News.................Rich Martin......................(703)981-3210
Real Estate..........Sandra Kelly.....................(703)981-3393
Religion.............Cody Lowe........................(703)981-3425
Saturday.............Rich Martin......................(703)981-3210
Sports...............Bill Bern........................(703)981-3128
Sunday...............Rich Martin......................(703)981-3210
Travel...............Carolyn Daugherty................(703)981-3244
Travel...............Liz Hock.........................(703)981-3326

VIRGINIA-Staunton

(32556) THE NEWS-LEADER
11 N. Central Ave.
PO Box 59
Staunton, VA 24402
City.................Louise Whall.....................(417)836-1258
Drama................Bil Tatum........................(417)836-1185
Editorials...........George Freeman...................(417)836-1113
Education............Tami Wicker......................(417)836-1198
Entertainment........Ron Sylvester....................(417)836-1172
Environmental........Deborah Barnes...................(417)836-1276
Family...............Patti Dutcher....................(417)836-1272
Farm.................Willard Woods....................(417)836-1241
Fashion..............Ron Davis........................(417)836-1256
Features.............Ron Davis........................(417)836-1256
Financial/Business...Connie Farrow....................(417)836-1283
Food.................Ron Davis........................(417)836-1256
Garden/Home..........Ron Davis........................(417)836-1256
Lifestyle............Ron Davis........................(417)836-1256
Living...............Ron Davis........................(417)836-1256
Medical..............Kathleen O'Dell..................(417)836-1276

Metro................Louise Whall.....................(417)836-1258
Movie................Ron Davis........................(417)836-1256
Music................Ron Davis........................(417)836-1256
News.................Louise Whall.....................(417)836-1258
Photo................Bob Linder.......................(417)836-1182
Political............Bob Edwards......................(417)836-1195
Real Estate..........Connie Farrow....................(417)836-1283
Religion.............Ron Davis........................(417)836-1256
Rural Development....Chick Howland....................(417)836-1258
Rural Development....Willard Woods....................(417)836-1241
Society..............Ron Davis........................(417)836-1256
Sports...............Kelley Bass......................(417)836-1373
State................Louise Whall.....................(417)836-1258
TV...................Marty Eddleman...................(417)836-1120
Travel...............Ron Davis........................(417)836-1256

WASHINGTON-Burien

(32699) DES MOINES NEWS
133 SW 153rd St. SW
Burien, WA 98166
Features.............Ralph Nichols....................(206)444-4873

WASHINGTON-Everett

(32761) THE HERALD
1213 Grand & California Sts.
PO Box 930
Everett, WA 98206
City.................Robert Frank.....................(425)339-3426
Columnist............Julie Muhlstein..................(425)339-3460
Editorials...........Bob Bolerjack....................(425)339-3466
Financial/Business...Mike Benbow......................(425)339-3459
Sports...............Kevin Brown......................(425)339-3474

WASHINGTON-Seattle

(33021) SEATTLE POST-INTELLIGENCER
101 Elliott Ave. W.
Seattle, WA 98119
Art..................Duston Harvey....................(206)448-8343
Book.................John Marshall....................(206)448-8170
Drama................Joe Adcock.......................(206)448-8369
Editorials...........Joann Byrd.......................(206)448-8387
Entertainment........Duston Harvey....................(206)448-8343
Environmental........Rob McClure......................(206)448-8092
Fashion..............Susan Phinney....................(206)448-8397
Financial/Business...Don Smith........................(206)448-8098
Food.................Steph Simons.....................(206)448-8157
Lifestyle............John Engstrom....................(206)448-8351
Medical..............Tom Paulson......................(206)443-8318
Movie................William Arnold...................(206)448-8185
Music................R.M. Campbell....................(206)448-8396
Music................Gene Stout.......................(206)448-6383
Sports...............Pete Wovurski....................(206)448-8224
Travel...............John Engstrom....................(206)448-8351

WASHINGTON-Spokane

(33101) THE SPOKESMAN-REVIEW
999 W Riverside Ave.
PO Box 2160
Spokane, WA 99210
Editorials...........Doug Floyd.......................(509)459-5466
Entertainment........Jim Kershner.....................(509)459-5493
Fashion..............Jamie Neely......................(509)459-5443
Garden/Home..........Jamie Neely......................(509)459-5443
Lifestyle............Jamie Neely......................(509)459-5443
Medical..............Carla Johnson....................(509)459-5148
Movie................Dan Webster......................(509)459-5483
Music................Isamu Jordan.....................(509)459-5299
Political............Jim Camden.......................(509)459-5461
Saturday.............Richard Wagoner..................(509)459-5403
Sports...............Joe Palmquist....................(509)459-5503
Travel...............Chris Willie.....................(509)459-5481

WEST VIRGINIA-Charleston

(33267) CHARLESTON DAILY MAIL
1001 Virginia St. E.
Charleston, WV 25331
Aviation.............Becky Fleming....................(304)348-1244
Book.................Becky Fleming....................(304)348-1244
City.................Frank Hutchins...................(304)348-4834
Drama................Julianne Kemp....................(304)348-4806
Editorials...........David Greenfield.................(304)348-4870
Education............Karen Klein......................(304)348-4810
Entertainment........Julianne Kemp....................(304)348-4806
Environmental........Pat Sanders......................(304)348-4836
Family...............Therese Cox......................(304)348-4874
Fashion..............Therese Cox......................(304)348-4872
Features.............Julianne Kemp....................(304)348-4806
Financial/Business...Phil Nussel......................(304)348-4804

WEST VIRGINIA-Charleston (continued)

Food	Julianne Kemp	(304)348-4806
Garden/Home	Julianne Kemp	(304)348-4806
Lifestyle	Julianne Kemp	(304)348-4806
Medical	Becky Fleming	(304)348-1244
Movie	Greg Wood	(304)348-4849
Music	Kay Michael	(304)348-4819
News	Nanya Friend	(304)348-4849
Photo	Chip Ellis	(304)348-4825
Political	Richard Grimes	(304)348-4841
Real Estate	Becky Fleming	(304)348-1244
Religion	Therese Cox	(304)348-4874
Saturday	Monica Orosz	(304)348-4830
Society	Julianne Kemp	(304)348-4806
Sports	Don Hager	(304)348-4807
TV & Radio	Ron Hutchison	(304)348-4884
Travel	Julianne Kemp	(304)348-4806
Women's	Julianne Kemp	(304)348-4806

WEST VIRGINIA-Wheeling

(33503) NEWS-REGISTER
1500 Main St.
Wheeling, WV 26003

Aviation	Margaret Beltz	(304)233-0100
Book	Don Fise	(304)233-0100
City	Margaret Beltz	(304)233-0100
Consumer Affairs	Margaret Beltz	(304)233-0100
Drama	Don Fise	(304)233-0100
Editorials	Mike Myer	(304)233-0100
Education	Margaret Beltz	(304)233-0100
Entertainment	Don Fise	(304)233-0100
Environmental	Margaret Beltz	(304)233-0100
Family	Gladys Van Horne	(304)233-0100
Farm	Margaret Beltz	(304)233-0100
Fashion	Gladys Van Horne	(304)233-0100
Features	Margaret Beltz	(304)233-0100
Financial/Business	Margaret Beltz	(304)233-0100
Food	Judi Tarowsky	(304)233-0100
Garden/Home	Gladys Van Horne	(304)233-0100
Lifestyle	Gladys Van Horne	(304)233-0100
Living	Gladys Van Horne	(304)233-0100
Medical	Margaret Beltz	(304)233-0100
Metro	Margaret Beltz	(304)233-0100
Movie	Don Fise	(304)233-0100
Music	Don Fise	(304)233-0100
News	Margaret Beltz	(304)233-0100
Photo	Art Limann	(304)233-0100
Political	Linda Comins	(304)233-0100
Radio	Don Fise	(304)233-0100
Real Estate	Margaret Beltz	(304)233-0100
Religion	Linda Comins	(304)233-0100
Science	Margaret Beltz	(304)233-0100
Society	Gladys Van Horne	(304)233-0100
Sports	Bill Van Horne	(304)233-0100
Suburban	Margaret Beltz	(304)233-0100
TV	Don Fise	(304)233-0100
Travel	Don Fise	(304)233-0100
Women's	Gladys Van Horne	(304)233-0100

WISCONSIN-Appleton

(33542) THE POST-CRESCENT
PO Box 59
Appleton, WI 54912

Aviation	Don Dastonia	(414)733-4411
Book	Ed Berthiaume	(414)733-4411
City	Bernie Peterson	(414)733-4411
Drama	Dan Roherty	(414)733-4411
Editorials	Michael C. Walter	(414)733-4411
Education	Kathy Walsh Nufer	(414)733-4411
Entertainment	Dan Roherty	(414)733-4411
Environmental	Ed Berthiaume	(414)733-4411
Family	Judy Williams	(414)733-4411
Fashion	Ed Berthiaume	(414)733-4411
Features	Peter Geniesse	(414)733-4411
Financial/Business	Arlen Boardman	(414)733-4411
Food	Pat Stenson	(414)733-4411
Garden/Home	Donald Mendyke	(414)733-4411
Lifestyle	Ed Berthiaume	(414)733-4411
Medical	Maija Penikis	(414)733-4411
Metro	Bernie Peterson	(414)733-4411
Movie	Dan Roherty	(414)733-4411
Music	Dan Roherty	(414)733-4411
News	Dan Flannery	(414)733-4411
Photo	Dwight Nale	(414)733-4411
Political	James Meyer	(414)733-4411
Real Estate	Arlen Boardman	(414)733-4411
Religion	Maija Penikis	(414)733-4411
Rural Development	Roger Pitt	(414)733-4411
Saturday	Peter Geniesse	(414)733-4411
Society	Ed Berthiaume	(414)733-4411
Sports	Larry Gallup	(414)733-4411
Sunday	Peter Geniesse	(414)733-4411
TV	Tom Richards	(414)733-4411
Travel	Myrna Collins	(414)733-4411
Women's	Ed Berthiaume	(414)733-4411

WISCONSIN-Eau Claire

(33672) LEADER-TELEGRAM
PO Box 570
Eau Claire, WI 54702

Food	Blythe Wachter	(715)830-5828
Lifestyle	Susan Barber	(715)833-9213
Medical	Jennifer Schmidt	(715)833-9206
Religion	Blythe Wachter	(715)830-5828
Sports	Julian Emerson	(715)830-5911
Sports	Todd Golden	(715)833-9200

WISCONSIN-Green Bay

(33741) GREEN BAY PRESS-GAZETTE
PO Box 23430
Green Bay, WI 54305-3430

Drama	Warren Gerds	(920)431-8352
Editorials	Mike Blecha	(920)431-8248
Entertainment	Kendra Meinert	(920)431-8347
Environmental	Peter Rebhahn	(920)431-8212
Features	Kim McAuliffe	(920)431-8385
Financial/Business	Steve Bruss	(920)431-8221
Food	Kim McAuliffe	(920)431-8221
Garden/Home	Kim McAuliffe	(920)431-8221
Lifestyle	Kim McAuliffe	(920)431-8221
Metro	Roger Schneider	(920)431-8221
Movie	Warren Gerds	(920)431-8221
Music	Warren Gerds	(920)431-8221
Photo	Steve Levin	(920)431-8329
Political	Joanne Zipperer	(920)431-8327
Real Estate	Steve Bruss	(920)431-8327
Religion	Jean Peerenboom	(920)431-8219
Rural Development	Joanne Zipperer	(920)431-4411
Society	Kim McAuliffe	(920)431-4411
Sports	Bob Berghaus	(920)431-8413
TV	Warren Gerds	(920)431-8389
Travel	Steve Kirchman	(920)431-8389
Women's	Kim McAuliffe	(920)431-8389

WISCONSIN-Iola

(33854) WAUPACA COUNTY NEWS
PO Box 235
Iola, WI 54945

News	Jane Myhra	(715)445-6397

WISCONSIN-Madison

(33949) ISTHMUS
101 King St.
Madison, WI 53703

Features	Tenaya Darlington	(608)251-5627

(33990) WISCONSIN STATE JOURNAL
1901 Fish Hatchery Rd.
PO Box 8058
Madison, WI 53713

Book	William Wineke	(608)252-6146
City	Phil Glende	(608)252-6117
Consumer Affairs	Jennifer Sereno	(608)252-6155
Drama	Chris Juzwik	(608)252-6180
Editorials	Tom Still	(608)252-6110
Education	Doug Erickson	(608)252-6149
Entertainment	Chris Juzwik	(608)252-6180
Environmental	Ron Seely	(608)252-6131
Family	Chris Juzwik	(608)252-6180
Farm	Jennifer Sereno	(608)252-6155
Fashion	Sandy Kallio	(608)252-6181
Features	Chris Juzwik	(608)252-6180
Financial/Business	Jennifer Sereno	(608)252-6155
Food	Chris Martell	(608)252-6179
Garden/Home	Chris Juzwik	(608)252-6180
Lifestyle	Chris Juzwik	(608)252-6180
Living	Chris Juzwik	(608)252-6180
Medical	Pat Simms	(608)252-6126
Metro	Phil Glende	(608)252-6117
Movie	Chris Juzwik	(608)252-6180
Music	Natasha Kassulke	(608)252-6187
Photo	Meg Theno	(608)252-6151
Political	Scott Milfred	(608)252-6129
Radio	Chris Juzwik	(608)252-6180
Real Estate	Jennifer Sereno	(608)252-6155
Religion	William Wineke	(608)252-6146
Science	Ron Seely	(608)252-6131
Society	Chris Juzwik	(608)252-6180
Sports	Greg Sprout	(608)252-6170
TV	Chris Juzwik	(608)252-6180
Travel	Chris Juzwik	(608)252-6180
Women's	Chris Juzwik	(608)252-6180

WISCONSIN-Milwaukee

(34084) MILWAUKEE JOURNAL SENTINEL
PO Box 661
Milwaukee, WI 53201
- Entertainment........... Diane Bacha.....................(414)224-2333
- Features................ Diane Bacha.....................(414)224-2333
- Photo................... Jill Williams...................(414)224-2349

CANADA

ALBERTA-Calgary

(34631) CALGARY HERALD
215-16 St. SE
Calgary AB, Canada T2P 0W8
- City.................... Don Campbell....................(403)235-7486
- Editorials.............. Peter Menzies...................(403)235-7594
- Entertainment.......... Eric Dawson.....................(403)235-7580
- Fashion................ Monica Zurowski.................(403)235-7291
- Financial/Business..... Ron Nowell......................(403)235-7485
- Garden/Home............ Monica Zurowski.................(403)235-7291
- Living................. Monica Zurowski.................(403)235-7291
- News................... Roman Cooney....................(403)235-7517
- Photo.................. Peter Brosseau..................(403)235-7597
- Religion............... Gordon Legge....................(403)235-7560
- Sports................. Mark Tremblay...................(403)235-7578
- Travel................. Debra Cummings..................(403)235-2317

(34633) THE CALGARY SUN
2615 12th St. NE
Calgary AB, Canada T2E 7W9
- Entertainment.......... Anika VanWyke...................(403)250-4308
- Features............... Kit Poole.......................(403)250-4118
- Garden/Home........... Myke Thomas.....................(403)250-4324
- Lifestyle.............. Kevin Franchuk..................(403)250-4148
- Sports................ Martin Hudson...................(403)250-4351

ALBERTA-Edmonton

(34711) THE EDMONTON JOURNAL
PO Box 2421
Edmonton AB, Canada T5J 0S1
- Automotive............. Dave Halliday...................(780)498-5685
- Book................... Gordon Morash...................(780)429-5368
- City.................. Heather Boyd....................(780)429-5386
- Editorials............. Susan Ruttan....................(780)429-5206
- Entertainment......... Richard Helm....................(780)429-5346
- Features.............. Barb Wilkinson..................(780)429-5374
- Financial/Business.... Kathy Kerr......................(780)429-5325
- Sports................ John McKinnon...................(780)429-5303

(34712) THE EDMONTON SUN
4990 92nd Ave., Ste. 250
Edmonton AB, Canada T6B 3A1
- Financial/Business..... Dan Healing.....................(780)468-0283
- Photo................. Gary Bartlett...................(780)468-0297
- Sports................ Phil Rivers.....................(780)468-0262
- Travel................ Erik Floren.....................(780)768-0271

ALBERTA-Fort Saskatchewan

(34771) THE FORT SASKATCHEWAN RECORD
10420 98th Ave., No. 155
Fort Saskatchewan AB, Canada T8L 2N6
- Sports................ Corey Osmak.....................(403)998-7070

BRITISH COLUMBIA-Vancouver

(35173) THE VANCOUVER COURIER
1574 W. 6th Ave.
Vancouver BC, Canada V6J 1R2
- Entertainment.......... Fiona Hughes....................(604)630-3505

(35175) THE VANCOUVER SUN
1-200 Granville St.
Vancouver BC, Canada V6C 3N3
- City.................. John Drabble....................(604)605-2111
- Editorials............. Don Cayo........................(604)605-2111
- Features.............. Lucy Hyslop.....................(604)605-2111
- Financial/Business..... Harvey Enchin...................(604)605-2111
- News.................. Valerie Casselton...............(604)605-2111

MANITOBA-Winnipeg

(35364) THE WINNIPEG SUN
1700 Church Ave.
Winnipeg MB, Canada R2X 3A2
- Automotive............. John K. White...................(204)632-2708
- Book................... Pat St. Germain.................(204)632-2710
- City.................. Rachel Morgan...................(204)632-2780
- City.................. John K. White...................(204)632-2708
- Entertainment......... John Kendle.....................(204)632-2783
- Photo................. James O'Connor..................(204)632-2640
- Sports................ Mark Hamm.......................(204)632-2794
- Sunday................ John Kendle.....................(204)632-2783

NOVA SCOTIA-Halifax

(35561) THE CHRONICLE HERALD
1650 Argyle St.
Halifax NS, Canada B3J 2T2
- Book................... Deborah Wiles...................(902)426-1146
- City.................. Brian Ward......................(902)426-3088
- Editorials............. Bob Howse.......................(902)426-3098
- Features.............. Margaret MacKay.................(902)426-1143
- Financial/Business.... Roger Taylor....................(902)426-2815
- Food.................. Marie Nightingale...............(902)426-1187
- Lifestyle............. Margaret MacKay.................(902)426-1143
- Medical............... Susan LeBlanc...................(902)426-3304
- Music................. Stephen Cooke...................(902)426-3083
- Political............. Amy Smith.......................(902)426-3301
- Religion.............. Ellenor Gray....................(902)426-1106
- Sports................ Mike Flemming...................(902)426-3068
- TV.................... Pat Lee.........................(902)426-0207
- Travel................ Ellenor Gray....................(902)426-1106

(35566) THE HALIFAX HERALD
1650 Argyle St.
Halifax NS, Canada B3J 2T2
- Entertainment.......... Greg Guy........................(902)426-3039
- Financial/Business..... Roger Taylor....................(902)426-2815
- Living................ Margaret MacKay.................(902)426-1143
- Sports................ Mike Flemming...................(902)426-3069

ONTARIO-Don Mills

(35776) NATIONAL POST
1450 Don Mills Rd.
Don Mills ON, Canada M3B 2X7
- Features............... Sarah Murdoch...................(416)383-2349

ONTARIO-London

(35987) THE LONDON FREE PRESS
369 York St.
London ON, Canada N6A 4G1
- Automotive............. Clare Dear......................(519)667-4576
- City.................. Julie Carl......................(519)667-4596
- Financial/Business.... Greg Van Moorsel................(519)667-4550
- News.................. Chris Nixon.....................(519)667-4609
- Photo................. Susan Bradnam...................(519)667-4509
- Real Estate........... Clare Dear......................(519)667-4576
- Sports................ David Langford..................(519)667-4506

ONTARIO-Midland

(36040) THE COLLINGWOOD CONNECTION
206-9170 County Rd. 93
Box 77
Mountainview Mall
RR 2
Midland ON, Canada L4R 4K4
- News.................. Lee Ballantyne..................(705)527-5500

ONTARIO-Ottawa

(36265) THE OTTAWA CITIZEN
1101 Baxter Rd.
PO Box 5020
Ottawa ON, Canada K2C 3M4
- Financial/Business..... Drew Gragg......................(613)596-3799
- Food.................. Ron Eade........................(613)596-3793
- Garden/Home........... Sheila Brady....................(613)596-3709
- Sports................ Hugh Adami......................(613)596-3510

ONTARIO-Richmond Hill

(36343) THE LIBERAL
9350 Yonge St.
PO Box 390
Richmond Hill ON, Canada L4C 4Y6
- Automotive............. John Frechette..................(905)881-3373

ONTARIO-Toronto

(36678) NOW
189 Church St.
Toronto ON, Canada M5B 1Y7
- News.................. Glenn Wheeler...................(416)364-1300

ONTARIO-Toronto (continued)

(36770) THE TORONTO STAR
1 Yonge St., 5th Fl.
Toronto ON, Canada M5E 1E6

Drama	Geoff Chapman	(416)869-4475
Editorials	John Honderich	(416)869-4940
Entertainment	Vian Ewart	(416)869-4480
Fashion	Carola Vyhnak	(416)869-4843
Features	Jim Atkins	(416)869-4870
Financial/Business	Adam Mayers	(416)869-4810
Food	Marion Kane	(416)869-4853
Garden/Home	Dale Anne Freed	(416)869-4851
Garden/Home	Fred Dale	(416)869-4851
Lifestyle	Linwood Barclay	(416)869-4924
Medical	Marilyn Dunlop	(416)869-4450
Metro	Dave Ellis	(416)869-4420
Movie	Craig MacInnis	(416)869-4477
Music	William Littler	(416)869-4480
News	Mary Deanne Shears	(416)869-4404
Photo	Brad Henderson	(416)869-4925
Political	Gord Barthos	(416)869-4910
Radio	Henry Mietkiewicz	(416)869-4476
Real Estate	Pat Brennan	(416)869-4820
Religion	Michael McAteer	(416)869-4879
Saturday	Dennis Morgan	(416)869-4882
Sports	Phil Bingley	(416)869-4361
Sunday	Ellie Tesher	(416)869-4860
TV	Jim Bawden	(416)869-4474
Travel	Mitch Smyth	(416)869-4877

QUEBEC-Montreal

(37118) THE GAZETTE
250 St-Antoine St. W.
Montreal QC, Canada H2Y 3R7

Automotive	Doug Sweet	(514)987-2596
Book	Bryan Demchinsky	(514)987-2486
Columnist	Jack Todd	(514)987-2621
Drama	Pat Donnelly	(514)987-2576
Entertainment	Lucinda Chodan	(514)987-2460
Fashion	Eva Friede	(514)987-2434
Financial/Business	Peter Hadekel	(514)987-2531
Financial/Business	David Yates	(514)987-2459
Food	Julian Armstrong	(514)987-2550
Garden/Home	Annabelle King	(514)987-2551
Movie	John Griffin	(514)987-2571
Music	Arthur Kaptainis	(514)987-2570
Photo	Barry Gray	(514)987-2588
Radio	Peggy Curran	(514)987-2529
Religion	Harvey Shepherd	(514)987-2651
Sports	Mark Tremblay	(514)987-2474
TV	Peggy Curran	(514)987-2529
Travel	Paul Waters	(514)987-2468
Women's	Donna Nebenzahl	(514)987-2501

(37150) LA PRESSE
7, rue St-Jacques
Montreal QC, Canada H2Y 1K9

Drama	Jean Beaunoyer	(514)285-7070
Editorials	Alain Dubuc	(514)285-7070
Education	Michele Ouimet	(514)285-7070
Fashion	Jacques Gagnon	(514)285-7070
Fashion	Vivianne Roy	(514)285-7070
Financial/Business	Rudy LeCours	(514)285-7070
Garden/Home	Florian Bernard	(514)285-7070
Movie	Serge Dussault	(514)285-7070
News	Pierre Vincent	(514)285-7070
Photo	Roland Forget	(514)285-7070
Political	Mario Fontaine	(514)285-7070
Religion	Jules Beliveau	(514)285-7070
Sports	Michel Blanchard	(514)285-7070
TV	Louise Cousineau	(514)285-7070
Travel	Francois Trepanier	(514)285-7070
Women's	Martha Gagnon	(514)285-7070

(37163) LE JOURNAL DE MONTREAL
4545, rue Frontenac
Montreal QC, Canada H2H 2R7

City	Jean-Maurice Duddin	(514)521-4545
Drama	Carmen Montessuit	(514)521-4545
Entertainment	Jean-Paul Sylvain	(514)521-4545
Fashion	Monelle Saindon	(514)521-4545
Features	Yves Rochon	(514)521-4545
Financial/Business	Michel Van De Walle	(514)521-4545
Food	Monique Girard-Solomita	(514)521-4545
Garden/Home	Pascale Perrault	(514)521-4545
Lifestyle	Clair Harting	(514)521-4545
Medical	Michele Coude-Lord	(514)521-4545
Movie	Franco Nuovo	(514)521-4545
Movie	Daniel Rioux	(514)521-4545
Music	Manon Guilbert	(514)521-4545
Sports	Guy Perras	(514)521-4545
Travel	Paul Simier	(514)521-4545

QUEBEC-Quebec

(37288) LE JOURNAL DE QUEBEC
450, rue Bechard, Vanier
Quebec QC, Canada G1M 2E9

Aviation	Michel Poirier	(418)683-1573
Book	Jocelyn Bourque	(418)683-1573
City	M.F. Bernier	(418)683-1573
Drama	Denise Martel	(418)683-1573
Editorials	Serge Cote	(418)683-1573
Editorials	Serge Gosselin	(418)683-1573
Education	Regys Caron	(418)683-1573
Entertainment	Serge Drouin	(418)683-1573
Environmental	Michel Poirier	(418)683-1573
Family	Jocelyn Bourque	(418)683-1573
Fashion	Jocelyn Bourque	(418)683-1573
Features	Serge Gosselin	(418)683-1573
Financial/Business	Michel Poirier	(418)683-1573
Food	Louise Larouche	(418)683-1573
Garden/Home	Guy St. Laurent	(418)683-1573
Lifestyle	Jocelyn Bourque	(418)683-1573
Medical	Johanne Roy	(418)683-1573
Metro	Michel Poirier	(418)683-1573
Movie	Denise Martel	(418)683-1573
Music	Pierre O. Nadeau	(418)683-1573
News	Serge Gosselin	(418)683-1573
Photo	Serge St. Hilaire	(418)683-1573
Political	Serge Gosselin	(418)683-1573
Real Estate	Guy St. Laurent	(418)683-1573
Religion	Michel Poirier	(418)683-1573
Rural Development	M.F. Bernier	(418)683-1573
Saturday	Jocelyn Bourque	(418)683-1573
Society	Michel Poirier	(418)683-1573
Sports	Claude Bedard	(418)683-1573
Sunday	Michel Poirier	(418)683-1573
TV	Pierre Nadeau	(418)683-1573
Travel	Michel Poirier	(418)683-1573
Women's	Michel Poirier	(418)683-1573

(37290) LE SOLEIL
925 Chemin St. Louis
PO Box 1547
Quebec QC, Canada G1K 7J6

Drama	Jean Hilaire	(418)686-3394
Education	Michele LaFerriere	(418)686-3394
Family	Suzanne Colpron	(418)686-3369
Food	Gilles Ouellet	(418)686-3420
Real Estate	Giles Angers	(418)686-3394
Rural Development	Rejean Lacombe	(418)686-3394
Sports	Maurice Dumas	(418)686-3405
TV	Richard Therrien	(514)235-0722
Travel	Gilles Ouellet	(418)686-3420

SASKATCHEWAN-Regina

(37532) LEADER-POST
1964 Park St.
Regina SK, Canada S4P 3G4

City	Andy Cooper	(306)565-8211

Master Index

The Master Index is a comprehensive listing of all entries, both print and broadcast, included in this *Directory*. Citations in this index are interfiled alphabetically throughout regardless of media type. Publications are cited according to title and important keywords within titles; broadcast citations are by station call letters or cable company names. Indexed here also are: notices of recent cessations; former call letters or titles; foreign language and other alternate publication titles; other types of citations. Indexing is word-by-word rather than letter-by-letter, so that "New York" files before "News". Listings in the Master Index include geographic locations and entry numbers. An asterisk (*) after a number indicates that the title is mentioned within the text of the cited entry.

A

A+ **37167***
A+ (Chatsworth, CA) *Unable to locate*
(a) (San Francisco, CA) **3323**
A & A (Plano, TX) **37796**
A & A (Fort Worth, TX) *Unable to locate*
a/b (Chapel Hill, NC) **23696**
A/C FLYER (Rye Brook, NY) **23282**
A/E/C Magazine; Construction Market Data, (Norcross, GA) **7457**
A/E/C Systems: The Magazine of Computer Solutions (Cleveland, OH) *Ceased*
A+, Le Magazine Affaires **37167***
A-1 Cablesystems Inc. (Golden, BC, Can.) **34967**
A-R Cable Inc. **23611***
A-R Cable Investments, Inc. (Hudson, MA) **14245**
A-R Cable Service, Inc. **12906***
A-R Cable Services Inc. **14245***
A-R Cable Services, Inc. **9535***
A & E Magazine (Broomfield, CO) *Unable to locate*
A & T Register (Greensboro, NC) **23915**
AAA—Chicago Motor Club Home & Away (Aurora, IL) **8037**
AAA Delware Motorist **27354***
AAA Going Places (Tampa, FL) **6757**
AAA Keystone Motorist **27355***
AAA Maryland Motorist **27356***
AAA Motorist **26624***
AAA Reading-Berks (Reading, PA) *Unable to locate*
AAA Shore Motorist **27358***
AAA Southern Traveler (St. Louis, MO) **17402**
AAA Today **26624***
AAA Today **24802***
AAA Today (Bluefield, WV) **33252**
AAA Today Magazine (Columbus, OH) *Unable to locate*
AAA Traveler **28205***
AAA Traveler (Florham Park, NJ) **18823**
AAA Traveler (Allentown, PA) **26624***
AAA Valley Motorist **27359***
AAA Virginia Motorist **27360***
AAA World **28205***
AAA World **33947***
AAA World (Philadelphia, PA) **27353**
AAA World—Delaware (Philadelphia, PA) **27354**
AAA World—Keystone (Philadelphia, PA) **27355**
AAA World—Maryland (Philadelphia, PA) **27356**
AAA World—Potomac (Philadelphia, PA) **27357**
AAA World—Shore (Philadelphia, PA) **27358**
AAA World—Valley (Philadelphia, PA) **27359**
AAA World—Virginia (Philadelphia, PA) **27360**
AAC (Lincoln, NE) **18077**
AACN's Clinical Issues in Critical Care Nursing (New York, NY) **21129**
AAFCS Action (Alexandria, VA) **31629**
AAHPERD Update (Reston, VA) **32354**
AAII Journal (Chicago, IL) **8240**
AAIW Show Daily; Aftermarket Business (Cleveland, OH) **24854**
aakpRENALIFE (Tampa, FL) **6758**
AANA Journal (Park Ridge, IL) **9403**
A&E (Arts and Entertainment Network) (New York, NY) **37723**
AANNT Journal **19436***
AAOHN Journal (Thorofare, NJ) **19615**
AAPG Bulletin (Tulsa, OK) **26104**
AAPG Explorer (Tulsa, OK) **26105**
AARC Times (Dallas, TX) **30120**

AARP Bulletin (Washington, DC) **5307**
AARP News Bulletins **5307***
AARTimes **30120***
AASHTO Quarterly (Washington, DC) *Ceased*
AATCC Review (Research Triangle Park, NC) **24182**
AAUP; Academe: Bulletin of the (Washington, DC) **5312**
AAUW in Action (Washington, DC) **5308**
AAUW Outlook (Washington, DC) **5309**
AB Bookman's Weekly (Clifton, NJ) *Ceased*
ABA Bank Marketing Magazine (Washington, DC) **5310**
ABA Banking Journal (New York, NY) **21130**
ABA Consumer Credit Delinquency Bulletin (Washington, DC) **5311**
ABA Journal (Chicago, IL) **8241**
The ABA Journal Annual Buyers Guide (Chicago, IL) *Ceased*
ABA Retail Banking Digest (Washington, DC) *Ceased*
Abaka (Saint-Laurent, QC, Can.) **37361**
Abbeville Cablevision **28465***
The Abbeville Herald (Abbeville, AL) **1**
Abbeville Meridional (Abbeville, LA) **12455**
Abbey (Columbia, MD) **13450**
Abbey's Own **36149***
Abbotsford Clearbrook Times **34876***
Abbotsford News (Hope, BC, Can.) *Unable to locate*
Abbotsford Times (Abbotsford, BC, Can.) **34876**
Abbotsford Times (Abbotsford, BC, Can.) **34877**
Abby Oaks News **36149***
ABC (New York, NY) **37681**
ABC Radio Networks (New York, NY) **37609**
ABC Today (Arlington, VA) **31767**
ABD (Mount Kisco, NY) **21098**
Abdominal Imaging (New York, NY) **21131**
Aberdeen American News (San Jose, CA) **3508**
Aberdeen Examiner (Aberdeen, MS) **16543**
The Aberdeen Times (Aberdeen, ID) **7797**
Aberdeen's Concrete Construction **8000***
Aberdeen's Magazine of Masonry Construction **8002***
Abernathy Weekly Review (Abernathy, TX) **29651**
Aberrations (San Francisco, CA) *Unable to locate*
Abilene Reflector Chronicle (Abilene, KS) **11332**
Abilene Reporter-News (Abilene, TX) **29652**
Ability Magazine (Costa Mesa, CA) **1771**
Ability Magazine (Miami, FL) *Unable to locate*
Abingdon Argus (Macomb, IL) **9128**
Abingdon Virginian (Abingdon, VA) **31625**
Abington Journal (Clarks Summit, PA) **26785**
Abington/Rockland Mariner (Abington, MA) **13785**
Abington Standard (Rockland, MA) **14506**
Abitibi Quest; L'Echo d' (La Sarre, QC, Can.) **37022**
Abitibiens; Les Echos **36928***
Able Cable **35579***
Able Cablevision Ltd. (Liverpool, NS, Can.) **35591**
Able Newspaper (Old Bethpage, NY) **23036**
ABN Radio Network (Columbus, OH) **37610**
ABN TV (Columbus, OH) **37682**
ABNF Journal (Lisle, IL) **9109**
Abnormal Psychology; Journal of (Washington, DC) **5566**
Aboard, Dominicana (Coral Gables, FL) *Ceased*
Aboard, Ecuatoriana (Coral Gables, FL) *Ceased*
Aboard, Lan-Chile (Coral Gables, FL) *Ceased*
Aboard, Lineas Aereas Paraguayas (Coral Gables, FL) *Ceased*
Aboard, Lloyd Aero Boliviano (Coral Gables, FL) *Ceased*
Aboard Magazine (Coral Gables, FL) *Unable to locate*
Aboard, TACA (Coral Gables, FL) *Ceased*

Aboard, Tan Sahsa (Coral Gables, FL) *Ceased*
Aboard, Viasa (Coral Gables, FL) *Ceased*
Aboriginal Science Fiction (Woburn, MA) *Unable to locate*
Abortion Review; The Post- (Springfield, IL) **9641**
About Action Unlimited (Concord, MA) **14142**
About Alfords *Ceased*
About Children (Tuscaloosa, AL) *Unable to locate*
About.Time (Rochester, NY) **23207**
Above & Beyond (Yellowknife, NT, Can.) *Unable to locate*
Above Rubies (Franklin, TN) **29193**
ABP Flower Marketing **11591***
ABP Writers Syndicate **38011***
Abraham Lincoln Association; Journal of the (Springfield, IL) **9635**
Abrahamian Feature Syndicate (Williamsville, NY) **37797**
Abrasive Engineering Society Magazine **26742***
Abrasive Users News Fax (Butler, PA) **26742**
Abrasives Magazine (Grand Rapids, MI) *Unable to locate*
Abraxas (Madison, WI) **33915**
Abridged Index Medicus (Pittsburgh, PA) **27753**
Abridged Readers' Guide to Periodical Literature (Bronx, NY) **20250**
ABS Magazine (Wichita, KS) **11879**
Absolute Magnitude (Radford, VA) **32344**
Absolute Reference (Plainfield, IN) *Unable to locate*
The Absolute Sound (Sea Cliff, NY) *Unable to locate*
The Abstract **1232***
Abstract Bulletin of the Institute of Paper Chemistry **18880***
Abstract Bulletin of the Institute of Paper Science and Technology (Hoboken, NJ) **18880**
Abstracts in Anthropology (Amityville, NY) **20034**
Abstracts of Entomology (Philadelphia, PA) *Unable to locate*
Abstracts on Health Effects of Environmental Pollutants (Philadelphia, PA) *Ceased*
Abstracts in Human-Computer Interaction (Lawrence, KS) *Ceased*
Abstracts of Mycology (Philadelphia, PA) *Unable to locate*
Abstracts of Papers Presented to the American Mathematical Society (Providence, RI) **28384**
Abstracts with Programs (Boulder, CO) **4154**
Abstracts in Social Gerontology (Thousand Oaks, CA) **3845**
Abstracts of Working Papers in Economics (AWPE) (La Jolla, CA) **2111**
Abuse; Journal of Emotional (Hazleton, PA) **27033**
Abuse; Journal of Religion & (Binghamton, NY) **20195**
Abuse Review; Child (Hoboken, NJ) **18911**
Abya Yala News (Oakland, CA) *Unable to locate*
AC Current (Amarillo, TX) **29692**
ACA Bulletin **5574***
Academe: Bulletin of the AAUP (Washington, DC) **5312**
Academic Computing (McKinney, TX) *Ceased*
Academic Emergency Medicine (Philadelphia, PA) **27361**
Academic Exchange Quarterly (Stuyvesant Falls, NY) **23379**
Academic Library Book Review (Lynbrook, NY) *Ceased*
Academic Life; Akademiska Dzive/ (Minneapolis, MN) **16055**
Academic Medicine (Washington, DC) **5313**

The Advertiser (Greenfield, IN) **10039**
The Advertiser (Muncie, IN) **10325**
The Advertiser (Ames, IA) **10587**
The Advertiser (Iowa Falls, IA) **10999**
Advertiser (Concordia, KS) **11397**
Advertiser (Maysville, KY) **12288**
The Advertiser (Springhill, LA) **12846**
Advertiser (Danvers, MA) **14152**
Advertiser (Iron Mountain, MI) *Unable to locate*
The Advertiser (McMurray, PA) *Unable to locate*
Advertiser (Edgefield, SC) **28599**
The Advertiser (Jefferson City, TN) *Ceased*
The Advertiser (Athens, TX) **29745**
Advertiser (Edgerton, WI) **33685**
The ADvertiser (Riverton, WY) **34575**
The Advertiser (Beaverlodge, AB, Can.) **34617**
Advertiser (St. John's, NL, Can.) **35484**
Advertiser-Courier (Hermann, MO) **17096**
Advertiser-Democrat (Norway, ME) **12993**
The Advertiser, Expanded Edition (Muncie, IN) *Ceased*
The Advertiser-Gleam (Guntersville, AL) **254**
Advertiser; Marion (Marion, WI) **34023**
Advertiser-News **36309***
The Advertiser-News (Ithaca, MI) *Unable to locate*
The Advertiser News (Hattiesburg, MS) *Unable to locate*
Advertiser - North and South Edition (Jefferson, WI) **33867**
Advertiser Post **37509***
Advertiser-Register (Rockford, IA) **11182**
The Advertiser/The Security Advertiser **4452***
Advertiser-Tribune (Tiffin, OH) **25559**
The Advertisers News *Unable to locate*
Advertising Age (Chicago, IL) **8245**
Advertising Age/Europe (New York, NY) *Ceased*
Advertising Age's Creativity (New York, NY) *Unable to locate*
Advertising/Communications Times (Philadelphia, PA) **27364**
Advertising; Journal of (Ames, IA) **10590**
Advertising Law Anthology *Ceased*
Advertising & Marketing Review (Golden, CO) **4462**
Advertising and Marketing; What's New in (Richmond, VA) **32470**
Advertising; Medical (West Trenton, NJ) **19743**
Advertising Rates & Data; Canadian (Toronto, ON, Can.) **36490**
Advertising Research; Journal of (New York, NY) **21976**
Advertising Review; Healthcare (Centennial, CO) **4224**
Advertising Techniques (New York, NY) *Unable to locate*
Advertising Workshop (Anchorage, AK) **37802**
The Advertizer **28479***
Advertizer-Herald (Bamberg, SC) **28479**
Advice Goddess (Santa Monica, CA) **37803**
Adviser; Central Alberta (Red Deer, AB, Can.) **34828**
Advisor **606***
The Advisor (North Haven, CT) **5047**
The Advisor (Eastpointe, MI) **14998**
The Advisor (Mount Clemens, MI) **15370**
Advisor (Bensalem, PA) *Ceased*
Advisor (Mitchell, SD) **28899**
The Advisor Group (Grosse Pointe Farms, MI) **37804**
Advisor Journal (Neptune, NJ) *Unable to locate*
Advisor Magazine (Tampa, FL) *Unable to locate*
Advisor Today (Falls Church, VA) **32039**
Advisor; Twin Valley News & (West Alexandria, OH) **25631**
The Advisor - Youngwood (Mount Pleasant, PA) **27300**
The Advocate **24851***
The Advocate **20417***
The Advocate **19351***
The Advocate **32666***
Advocate **34867***
The Advocate **34830***
Advocate **15934***
Advocate **7945***
The Advocate (Los Angeles, CA) **2200**
The Advocate (San Pablo, CA) **3594**
The Advocate (Stamford, CT) **5139**
Advocate (Clifton, IL) **8681**
The Advocate (Kansas City, KS) **11524**
The Advocate (Baton Rouge, LA) **12484**
The Advocate (Fairhaven, MA) **14177**
The Advocate (North Adams, MA) **14417**
The Advocate (North Adams, MA) **14416**
The Advocate (Newark, OH) **25424**
Advocate (Allen, OK) **25729**
The Advocate (Houston, TX) *Unable to locate*
Advocate (Spooner, WI) *Unable to locate*
The Advocate (Athabasca, AB, Can.) **34609**
The Advocate (Vancouver, BC, Can.) **35121**
Advocate-Leader (Kennebec, SD) *Ceased*
Advocate-Messenger (Danville, KY) **12036**
Advocate; The Mitchell (Mitchell, ON, Can.) **36094**

Advocate Penny Saver (Sweetwater, TN) **29623**
The Advocate-Tribune (Granite Falls, MN) **15934**
AdvocateMEN **2328***
Adweek (New York, NY) **21157**
Adweek/Midwest (Chicago, IL) **8246**
Adweek/New England (Boston, MA) **13846**
Adweek/Southeast (Lakewood, NJ) *Unable to locate*
Adweek/Southwest (Dallas, TX) *Unable to locate*
Adweek Western Edition (New York, NY) **21158**
Adweek's AD DAY (New York, NY) *Ceased*
AEDS Bulletin **11622***
AEDS Monitor **11622***
Aegis (Bel Air, MD) **13289**
Aeon (Ames, IA) **10588**
Aeqlitas **22226***
Aerial Applicator (Santa Fe Springs, CA) *Unable to locate*
Aerial Applicator Farm, Forest & Fire (Santa Fe Springs, CA) *Unable to locate*
Aero Digest **22665***
Aero Magazine (Mission Viejo, CA) *Ceased*
AERO Sun-Times (Helena, MT) **17817**
Aerobics and Fitness **3759***
Aeronautica & Air Label Collectors Club (Elgin, IL) **8822**
Aeronomy; International Journal of Geomagnetism and (Washington, DC) **5553**
Aerosol Medicine; Journal of (Larchmont, NY) **20904**
Aerospace Abstracts; International (Reston, VA) **32366**
Aerospace America (Reston, VA) **32356**
Aerospace America (Reston, VA) **32355**
Aerospace Composites and Materials (Colonia, NJ) *Unable to locate*
Aerospace & Defence Technology (Toronto, ON, Can.) *Ceased*
Aerospace and Defense International Product News (New York, NY) *Ceased*
Aerospace & Defense Science (Indialantic, FL) *Ceased*
Aerospace and Electronic Systems Magazine; IEEE (New York, NY) **21843**
Aerospace Electronics; Military & (Nashua, NH) **18597**
Aerospace Engineering (Warrendale, PA) **28110**
Aerospace Engineering; Journal of (Reston, VA) **32368**
Aerospace Power Journal **315***
Aerospace Products News (Morris Plains, NJ) *Unable to locate*
Aerospace Research Bulletins *Ceased*
Aerostation (San Diego, CA) *Unable to locate*
Aerotech News & Review (Lancaster, CA) **2146**
AES Daily (New York, NY) **21159**
Aescelepian Chronicle (Chapel Hill, NC) *Unable to locate*
Aesthetic Plastic Surgery (New York, NY) **21160**
Aesthetic Surgery Journal (New York, NY) **21161**
Aesthetic Surgery Quarterly **21161***
Aesthetics and Art Criticism; The Journal of (Malden, MA) **14292**
AETN **1032***
AFA Watchbird (North Kansas City, MO) **17318**
AFAS Quarterly **15269***
AFB News (New York, NY) *Unable to locate*
AFE Facilities Engineering Journal (Cincinnati, OH) **24767**
Affaire de Coeur (Oakland, CA) **2662**
AFFAIRES; LES (Montreal, QC, Can.) **37175**
Affaires Plus; Le Magazine (Montreal, QC, Can.) **37167**
(Affaires Universitaires); University Affairs (Ottawa, ON, Can.) **36278**
AFFILIA: Journal of Women and Social Work (Thousand Oaks, CA) **3847**
Affirmative Action Register (St. Louis, MO) **17405**
Affordable Aircraft (Canoga Park, CA) *Unable to locate*
AFL-CIO; Milwaukee Labor Press, (Milwaukee, WI) **34085**
AFL-CIO News; Michigan (Lansing, MI) **15279**
Afn Shvel (New York, NY) **21162**
AFP Exchange (Bethesda, MD) **13295**
Africa Information Afrique (New York, NY) *Ceased*
Africa, and the Middle East; Comparative Studies of South Asia, (Durham, NC) **23815**
Africa Now **36385***
Africa Report (New York, NY) *Ceased*
Africa Report; Southern (Toronto, ON, Can.) **36744**
Africa Review; West (Binghamton, NY) **20220**
Africa Today (bloomington, IN) **9822**
African Affairs; A Current Bibliography on (Amityville, NY) **20037**
African American Men; Journal of (Oxford, OH) **25455**
African-American News & Issues (Houston, TX) **30455**
African American Review (St. Louis, MO) **17406**
African Archaeological Review (New York, NY) **21163**

African Arts (Los Angeles, CA) **2201**
African Business; Journal of (Binghamton, NY) **20160**
African Herald (Dallas, TX) **30121**
African History; The Journal of (New York, NY) **21977**
African Human Resources and Business Issues; The Journal of (Irving, TX) **30605**
African Immigration (JAI); Journal on (Binghamton, NY) **20161**
African Literatures; Research in (Columbus, OH) **25058**
African Methodist Episcopal Church; Journal of Christian Education of the (Nashville, TN) **29461**
African Philosophy (Binghamton, NY) **20151**
African Studies; Journal of Asian and (Willowdale, ON, Can.) **36880**
African Studies; Journal of Modern (New York, NY) **22135**
African Studies; Northeast (East Lansing, MI) **14991**
African Studies Quarterly (Gainesville, FL) **6129**
African Studies Review (New Brunswick, NJ) **19324**
African Time Broadcasting, Inc. (New York, NY) *Unable to locate*
African Travel-Writing; Journal of (Chapel Hill, NC) **23709**
Afro-American (East Orange, NJ) *Unable to locate*
Afro-American; Baltimore (Baltimore, MD) **13128**
Afro-American Historical and Genealogical Society Journal (Washington, DC) **5315**
Afro-American Times (Brooklyn, NY) **20295**
Afro-Americans in New York Life and History (Buffalo, NY) **20362**
The Afro News (Aldergrove, BC, Can.) **34879**
Afroasiatic Linguistics (Lancaster, CA) *Ceased*
Afronet Magazine (Los Angeles, CA) **2202**
AFSM International Professional Journal (Fort Myers, FL) **6093**
After Five Magazine (Redding, CA) **2886**
AFTERIMAGE (Rochester, NY) **23208**
Aftermarket Business (Cleveland, OH) **24853**
Aftermarket Business AAIW Show Daily (Cleveland, OH) **24854**
Aftermarket Insider (Bethesda, MD) **13296**
Aftermarket Journal; Eastern (Boynton Beach, FL) **5949**
Aftermarket Today **13296***
The Afton-Fairland American (Fairland, OK) **25832**
Afton Star-Enterprise (Afton, IA) **10573**
Ag Alert (Sacramento, CA) **2974**
Ag Consultant (Willoughby, OH) **25655**
Ag Equipment Power (Spokane, WA) **33092**
Ag Journal (La Junta, CO) **4526**
AG-PILOT International (Mount Vernon, WA) *Unable to locate*
Ag Retailer Magazine (New Prague, MN) **16208**
AGA Monthly **5330***
AGAIN Magazine (Ben Lomond, CA) **1486**
Against the Current (Detroit, MI) **14914**
Against the Grain (Charleston, SC) **28504**
Agape **16387***
Agassiz-Harrison Advance (Agassiz, BC, Can.) *Unable to locate*
Agave (Phoenix, AZ) **771**
AGB Reports **5832***
AGD Impact (Chicago, IL) **8247**
AGE **27241***
Age (Media, PA) **27241**
The Age Dispatch (Strathroy, ON, Can.) **36412**
Age d'Or - Vie Nouvelle (Montreal, QC, Can.) *Unable to locate*
Ageing International (Victoria, BC, Can.) **35205**
Ageing and Society (New York, NY) **21164**
Agence France-Presse (Washington, DC) **37805**
Agencia Efe/Efe News Service (Washington, DC) **37806**
The Agencies (Los Angeles, CA) **2203**
The Agency (Kings Park, NY) **37807**
Agency (New York, NY) *Ceased*
Agency Sales Magazine (Lake Forest, CA) **2141**
Agenda (Ste.-Foy, QC, Can.) **37334**
Agenda New York (New York, NY) *Unable to locate*
Agent Canada Travel Magazine (Vancouver, BC, Can.) *Unable to locate*
Agent & Manager **21674***
Agent; Professional (Alexandria, VA) **31727**
AgeVenture Syndicated News Service (Boca Raton, FL) **37808**
AgExporter (Pittsburgh, PA) *Unable to locate*
Aggie; The California (Davis, CA) **1811**
Aggies Illustrated (Tulsa, OK) **26106**
Aggregates & Roadbuilding Magazine (Westmount, QC, Can.) **37441**
Aggression, Maltreatment & Trauma; Journal of (Binghamton, NY) **20162**
Aggressive Behavior (Hoboken, NJ) **18882**
AGI Cablevision, Inc. **35655***
AGI Cablevision, Inc. (Simcoe, ON, Can.) *Unable to locate*
Agile Enterprise (Hoboken, NJ) *Ceased*

All Hit Country **35060***
All-Man (New York, NY) *Unable to locate*
All Number-Finds (Ambler, PA) **26645**
All Points Cable TV (Fall City, WA) **32763**
The All State (Clarksville, TN) **29114**
All-Stater Sports (Watertown, MA) *Ceased*
Allamakee Journal (Black Earth, WI) **33587**
Allan Kaye's Sports Cards News & Price Guides (St. Louis, MO) **17408**
Alledger (Newton, MA) **14383**
Allegan County Cablevision, Inc. **14726***
The Allegan County News (Allegan, MI) **14719**
Allegan County News & Gazette **14719***
Allegan Flashes (Allegan, MI) **14720**
The Allegany County Pennysaver (Wellsville, NY) **23532**
Alleghany Highlander (Covington, VA) **31981**
The Alleghany News (Sparta, NC) **24240**
Alleghenies; Journal of the (Frostburg, MD) **13527**
Allegheny Business News (Pittsburgh, PA) *Unable to locate*
Allegheny Literary Review **27232***
The Allegheny Review (Meadville, PA) **27232**
The Allen American (Allen, TX) **29681**
(Allen County Edition); Senior Life (Milford, IN) **10310**
Allen County News (Scottsville, KY) *Ceased*
Allen Memorial Art Museum Bulletin (Oberlin, OH) **25443**
Allen's TV Cable Service Inc. (Morgan City, LA) **12709**
Aller Simple (Los Angeles, CA) *Unable to locate*
Allergies and Asthma; Coping with (Franklin, TN) **29196**
Allergy, Asthma, & Immunology; Annals of (Rochester, MN) **16306**
Allergy and Asthma Proceedings (Providence, RI) **28385**
Allergy & Clinical Immunology; Canadian Journal of (Saint-Laurent, QC, Can.) **37362**
Allergy and Clinical Immunology; The Journal of (St. Louis, MO) **17451**
Allergy Clinics; Immunology and (Philadelphia, PA) **27489**
Allergy & Immunology; Clinical Reviews in (Davis, CA) **1813**
Allergy/Immunology Guide (Belle Mead, NJ) *Unable to locate*
Allergy and Immunology; International Archives of (Farmington, CT) **4834**
Allergy and Immunology; Internet Journal of Asthma, (Sugar Land, TX) **31141**
Allergy & Immunology; Pediatric Asthma, (Larchmont, NY) **20924**
Allergy News; Skin & (Rockville, MD) **13697**
Allergy Proceedings **28385***
Alliance (Beaufort, SC) **28486**
Alliance (Ottawa, ON, Can.) *Ceased*
Alliance Communications Cooperative, Inc. (Garretson, SD) **28859**
Alliance Magazine (Mississauga, ON, Can.) **36053**
The Alliance Newspaper (Bradford, MA) *Unable to locate*
The Alliance Review **24605***
Alliance Times-Herald (Alliance, NE) **17927**
(Alliancer); Zwiazkowiec (Toronto, ON, Can.) **36798**
Allied Feature Syndicate/Electronic Manufacturing News (Webb City, MO) *Unable to locate*
Allied News (Grove City, PA) **26963**
Alloy Digest (Materials Park, OH) **25364**
Alloys Index (Beachwood, OH) **24647**
Allsport Photography USA (Santa Monica, CA) **37812**
Allston Brighton Citizen Journal (Boston, MA) *Ceased*
Allure (New York, NY) **21174**
Alma Reminder (Alma, MI) **14728**
Alma Times (Alma, GA) **6914**
Alma Times-Statesman **6914***
The Almaguin News (Burks Falls, ON, Can.) **35712**
The Almanac (Menlo Park, CA) **2522**
Almanac (Oakland, CA) **2665**
The Almanac (McMurray, PA) **27231**
Almanac; Wapsipinicon (Anamosa, IA) **10602**
Almanecer in English (New York, NY) *Ceased*
Almena Plaindealer (Almena, KS) *Ceased*
Almond Facts (Sacramento, CA) **2975**
Almonte Gazette **35631***
Aloha Breeze (Hillsboro, OR) *Ceased*
Aloha, The Magazine of Hawaii & the Pacific (Honolulu, HI) *Unable to locate*
Alpena Journal (Wessington Springs, SD) *Unable to locate*
Alpena News (Alpena, MI) **14735**
Alpena Star (Gaylord, MI) **15066**
Alpena Star Advertiser **15066***
Alpha Epsilon Pi; The Lion of (Indianapolis, IN) **10149**
Alpharetta Neighbor (Alpharetta, GA) **6916**
Alpine Avalanche (Alpine, TX) **29682**
Alpine Sun (Alpine, CA) **1392**
Alsea River Cable TV (Waldport, OR) **26607**

Alsip Express (Midlothian, IL) *Unable to locate*
Alta Advertiser (Alta, IA) **10585**
Alta Vista Journal **11878***
Altamont Enterprise and Albany County Post (Altamont, NY) **20027**
The Altamont Journal (Altamont, KS) *Unable to locate*
The Altamont News (Altamont, IL) **8008**
The Altavista Journal (Altavista, VA) **31756**
Alternate View Network (Shreveport, LA) *Unable to locate*
Alternative Cinema (Montclair, NJ) **19240**
Alternative & Complementary Therapies (Larchmont, NY) **20888**
Alternative Energy Retailer (Waterbury, CT) **5190**
Alternative Medicine Review (Dover, ID) **7852**
The Alternative Orange **23417***
Alternative Press (Cleveland, OH) *Unable to locate*
Alternative Press Index (Baltimore, MD) **13111**
Alternative Therapies in Health and Medicine (Encinitas, CA) **1882**
Alternatives (Atlanta, GA) *Unable to locate*
Alternatives Journal (Waterloo, ON, Can.) **36845**
Alternatives: Perspectives on Society, Technology & Environment **36845***
The Alto Herald **30999***
Alton Citizen Journal (Warrenton, MO) *Unable to locate*
Alton Telegraph **8009***
Altoona Herald-Mitchellville Index (Altoona, IA) **10586**
Altoona Mirror (Altoona, PA) **26635**
Altus Times (Altus, OK) **25730**
AlumiNews (Pierrefonds, QC, Can.) *Ceased*
Alumnae Magazine; Douglass (New Brunswick, NJ) **19330**
Alumnae Quarterly; Smith (Northampton, MA) **14430**
Alumnews (Moorhead, MN) **16187**
The Alumni Bulletin **25673***
Alumni Gazette (Williamsburg, VA) **32613**
Alumni Journal (Winnipeg, MB, Can.) **35309**
Alumni; Kansas (Lawrence, KS) **11561**
Alumni Magazine; Alabama (Tuscaloosa, AL) **481**
Alumni Magazine; Brown (Providence, RI) **28390**
Alumni Magazine; Dartmouth (Hanover, NH) **18517**
Alumni Magazine; Georgia Tech (Atlanta, GA) **7013**
Alumni Magazine; MSU (East Lansing, MI) **14990**
Alumni Magazine; Ohio State (Columbus, OH) **25050**
Alumni Report **8600***
Alumni Review; Carolina (Chapel Hill, NC) **23700**
Alumni Review; Hamilton (Clinton, NY) **20472**
Alumni Review; Ole Miss (University, MS) **16868**
Alumni Review; University of North Dakota (Grand Forks, ND) **24458**
Alumni Review; University of Southern California **2426***
Alumni Review; Williams (Williamstown, MA) **14660**
The Alumnus **33967***
Alumnus (Carbondale, IL) **8113**
Alumnus; City College (New York, NY) **21421**
Alumnus; Tennessee (Knoxville, TN) **29282**
Alura (Novinger, MO) *Ceased*
Alva Review-Courier (Alva, OK) **25737**
Alverno Today (Milwaukee, WI) **34057**
The Alvin Advertiser (Alvin, TX) **29689**
Alvin and the Chipmunks (Santa Monica, CA) *Unable to locate*
The Alvin Sun (Alvin, TX) **29690**
The Alvord-Sunset Gazette (Alvord, TX) *Unable to locate*
Always Jukin' Magazine (Seattle, WA) **32938**
Alzheimer Disease and Associated Disorders (Baltimore, MD) **13112**
Alzheimer's Care Quarterly (New York, NY) **21175**
Alzheimers Disease; American Journal of (Weston, MA) **14648**
Am-Pol Eagle (Cheektowaga, NY) **20455**
AMA Alliance Today (Chicago, IL) **8251**
Amador Ledger-Dispatch (El Cajon, CA) **1842**
aMagazine (New York, NY) **21176**
Amalgam (Dayton, OH) *Unable to locate*
Amanda y Rocinante (West Haven, CT) *Unable to locate*
Amarillo Daily News **29694***
Amarillo Daily News (Augusta, GA) *Ceased*
Amarillo Globe-News (Amarillo, TX) **29694**
Amarillo Globe-Times **29694***
Amarillo Globe-Times (Augusta, GA) *Ceased*
Amarillo Sunday News-Globe **29694***
Amarillo; TV Cable of **29720***
Amass (Los Angeles, CA) **2206**
The Amateur Telescope Making Journal (Seattle, WA) **32939**
Amateur Writer's Journal (Bellaire, OH) *Ceased*
Amazing Heroes (Seattle, WA) *Ceased*
The Amazing Maze Magazine (Manchester by the Sea, MA) *Ceased*
Amazing Stories (Renton, WA) *Ceased*
Amazon Times (Owings Mills, MD) *Unable to locate*
Amber Waves (Washington, DC) **5321**
Ambiance (Portage, MI) *Ceased*

Ambler Gazette (Fort Washington, PA) **26924**
The Amboy News (Amboy, IL) **8012**
Ambulatory Care Management; Journal of (New York, NY) **21981**
Ambulatory Medicine Letter (Hagerstown, MD) **13561**
Ambulatory Pediatrics (Lawrence, KS) **11546**
Ambush Magazine (New Orleans, LA) **12726**
AMC Outdoors (Boston, MA) **13848**
AMCA Trucking Report **1222***
Amelia (Bakersfield, CA) *Ceased*
Amelia Bulletin Monitor (Amelia Court House, VA) **31759**
Amerasia Journal (Los Angeles, CA) **2207**
America (Philadelphia, PA) **27369**
America; Alba de (Westminster, CA) **4073**
America Drama (Cincinnati, OH) **24769**
America Entertains (New York, NY) *Ceased*
America; Travel (Evanston, IL) **8871**
America West Airlines Magazine (Phoenix, AZ) **773**
America Work (Washington, DC) **5322**
The American **25832***
American **30872***
American (Washington, DC) *Ceased*
American (Brookville, IN) **9873**
The American (Blackduck, MN) **15753**
The American (Provo, UT) *Unable to locate*
The American (West Jordan, UT) *Ceased*
American Academy of Dermatology; Journal of the (St. Louis, MO) **17452**
The American Academy of Orthopaedic Surgeons Bulletin (Old Tappan, NJ) **19393**
American Academy of Political and Social Science; The Annals of the (Thousand Oaks, CA) **3850**
American Academy of Psychoanalysis; Journal of the (Bloomfield, CT) **4702**
American Academy of Religion; Journal of the (Whittier, CA) **4077**
American Advertising (Washington, DC) *Ceased*
American Ag Network (Pierre, SD) **37613**
American Agent & Broker (St. Louis, MO) *Unable to locate*
American Agriculturist (Carol Stream, IL) *Unable to locate*
American; The Allen (Allen, TX) **29681**
American Amateur Journalist (Fountain Hills, AZ) **710**
American Angler (Bennington, VT) **31496**
American Angler & Fly Tyer **31496***
American Annals of the Deaf (Washington, DC) **5323**
American Anthropologist (Arlington, VA) **31770**
American Antiquity (Washington, DC) **5324**
American; Antlers (Antlers, OK) **25743**
American-Arab Message (Detroit, MI) *Unable to locate*
The American Archivist (Chicago, IL) **8252**
American Art (Washington, DC) *Unable to locate*
American Art Journal (New York, NY) **21177**
American Artist (New York, NY) **21178**
American; Askov (Askov, MN) **15722**
American Association for the Education of the Severely & Profoundly Handicapped Review **13179***
(American Association for Pediatric Ophthalmology and Strabismus); Journal of AAPOS (New York, NY) **21971**
American Association of Stratigraphic Palynologists Contributions Series (College Station, TX) **30036**
American Association of Variable Star Observers; Journal of the (Cambridge, MA) **14073**
American Astrology (Ambler, PA) **26646**
American Astronomical Society; Bulletin of the (Washington, DC) **5388**
American Atheist (Parsippany, NJ) **19410**
American Baby (New York, NY) **21179**
American Banker (New York, NY) **21180**
American Bankers Association Banking Literature Index **12241***
The American Baptist **28090***
American Baptist Quarterly (Valley Forge, PA) **28089**
American Baptists in Mission (Valley Forge, PA) **28090**
American Bee Journal (Hamilton, IL) **8968**
American Beef Cattleman (Allen, KS) **11336**
American Behavioral Scientist (Thousand Oaks, CA) **3848**
The American Benedictine Review (Richardton, ND) **24533**
American Bible Society Record (New York, NY) **21181**
American Bicyclist (New York, NY) *Unable to locate*
The American Biology Teacher (Reston, VA) **32359**
American Biotechnology Laboratory (Shelton, CT) **5117**
American Birds **21690***
The American Blade **33805***
American Board of Family Practice; Journal of the (Seattle, WA) **32976**
American Bonanza Society Magazine **11879***

American Book Collector (Ossining, NY) *Unable to locate*
The American Book Review (Normal, IL) **9295**
American Bookseller (Tarrytown, NY) *Ceased*
American Bowhunter (Pillager, MN) *Unable to locate*
American; Breckenridge (Breckenridge, TX) **29946**
American Brewer **31635***
American Brewer (Alexandria, VA) **31635**
American Breweriana (Pueblo, CO) **4597**
American Breweriana Journal **4597***
American Bungalow (Sierra Madre, CA) **3764**
American Business (New York, NY) **21182**
American Business Law Journal (Milwaukee, WI) **34058**
American Buyer's Review **2506***
American Cable **5265***
American Cable **30649***
American Cable Co. **12936***
American Cable Entertainment (Wilton, CT) **5233**
American Cable Entertainment (Madison, IN) *Unable to locate*
American Cable Entertainment (Marksville, LA) **12675**
American Cable TV (Millsboro, DE) **5265**
American Cable TV of Lower Delaware (Dagsboro, DE) **5241**
American Cablevision **7317***
American Cablevision **16044***
American Cablevision (Leavenworth, KS) **11581**
American Cablevision (Jackson, MS) *Ceased*
American Cablevision (Kansas City, MO) *Unable to locate*
American Cablevision of Queens **22959***
American Cablevision of Queens (Flushing, NY) *Ceased*
American Cablevision Services Inc. (Kissimmee, FL) **6265**
American Cablevision of South Pasadena (South Pasadena, CA) **3787**
American Cake Decorating (St. Paul, MN) **16363**
The American Cartographer **13532***
American Catholic Philosophical Quarterly (Irving, TX) **30603**
American Cemetery (New York, NY) *Unable to locate*
American Ceramic Society Bulletin (Westerville, OH) **25636**
American Ceramic Society; Journal of the (Westerville, OH) **25641**
American Ceramics (New York, NY) **21183**
American Cheerleader (New York, NY) **21184**
American Chianina Journal (Platte City, MO) **17348**
American Chinese Herald (New York, NY) *Unable to locate*
The American Chiropractor (Fort Wayne, IN) *Unable to locate*
American Christmas Tree Journal (St. Louis, MO) **17409**
American Cinematographer (Los Angeles, CA) *Ceased*
American Cinemediator (Encino, CA) *Ceased*
American City and County (Atlanta, GA) **6962**
American Classic Screen (Shawnee Mission, KS) *Unable to locate*
American Clean Car (Chicago, IL) **8253**
American Clinical Laboratory (Shelton, CT) **5118**
American Cocker Magazine (Midway City, CA) *Ceased*
American Coin-Op (Chicago, IL) **8254**
American Collector's Journal (Kewanee, IL) *Unable to locate*
American College of Dentists; Journal of the (San Diego, CA) **3178**
American College of Physicians Observer **27362***
American Community Cablevision **20817***
American Conchologist (Louisville, KY) **12210**
American Cooner (Sesser, IL) **9597**
American Counselor (Alexandria, VA) *Ceased*
American Country Collectibles (New York, NY) **21185**
American Cowboy (Sheridan, WY) **34587**
American Craft (New York, NY) **21186**
American Criminal Law Review (Washington, DC) **5325**
American Croat (Americki Hrvat) (Arcadia, CA) *Unable to locate*
American Crossword Federation (Massapequa Park, NY) **37813**
American Cueist Magazine (McKinney, TX) **30801**
American Culture; Journal of (Bowling Green, OH) **24693**
American Culture; Religion and (Indianapolis, IN) **10166**
American; The Daily (Monmouth, IL) **9214**
American; Daily (Somerset, PA) **28002**
American Dane (Omaha, NE) *Unable to locate*
American Demographics (Marion, OH) **25350**
American Dental Association; Journal of the (Chicago, IL) **8430**
American; Downey Herald (Downey, CA) **1834**
The American Dowser (Danville, VT) **31538**
American Druggist (New York, NY) *Unable to locate*

American Drycleaner (Chicago, IL) **8255**
American Economic Review (Princeton, NJ) **19452**
American Economist (Tuscaloosa, AL) *Unable to locate*
American Educational History Journal (Dayton, OH) **25106**
American Educational Research Journal (Washington, DC) **5326**
American Educator (Washington, DC) **5327**
American Ensemble **21395***
The American Enterprise (Washington, DC) **5328**
American Entomologist (Lanham, MD) **13597**
American Environmental Laboratory (Shelton, CT) *Ceased*
American Equine Magazine (Plymouth, PA) *Unable to locate*
American Ethnic History; Journal of (Atlanta, GA) **7019**
American Ethnologist (Arlington, VA) **31771**
American Family Physician (Leawood, KS) **11583**
American Farriers Journal (Brookfield, WI) **33602**
American Fastener Journal (Powell, OH) **25489**
American Federation of Musicians (San Diego, CA) **3110**
American Fern Journal (Little Rock, AR) **1211**
American Field (Chicago, IL) **8256**
American Film (Hollywood, CA) *Ceased*
American Fire Journal (Bellflower, CA) **1484**
American Firearms Industry (Fort Lauderdale, FL) *Unable to locate*
American Fitness (Sherman Oaks, CA) **3759**
American Fly Tyer **31496***
American Food and Ag. Exporter (Bloomfield, MI) *Ceased*
American Foreign Policy Interests (New York, NY) **21187**
American Forests (Washington, DC) **5329**
American Forum Radio (Colorado Springs, CO) *Unable to locate*
American Fruit Grower (Willoughby, OH) **25656**
American Funeral Director (New York, NY) *Unable to locate*
The American Gardener (Alexandria, VA) **31636**
American Gas (Washington, DC) **5330**
The American Genealogist (Demorest, GA) **7239**
American Girl (Middleton, WI) **34049**
American Glass Review (Clifton, NJ) *Ceased*
American Gold News (Las Vegas, NV) *Unable to locate*
American; Griswold (Griswold, IA) **10934**
The American Grocer (Bay Harbor Islands, FL) *Ceased*
American Guardian **32006***
American Guernsey Cattle Club **25494***
American Guidance for Seniors (Falls Church, VA) **32040**
American Handgunner (San Diego, CA) **3111**
The American Harp Journal (Falls Church, VA) **32041**
American Health Care Association Journal **5735***
American Health for Women (New York, NY) *Unable to locate*
American Heart Journal (Philadelphia, PA) **27370**
American Hereford Journal **17171***
American Heritage (New York, NY) **21188**
American Heritage Cablevision **10729***
The American Historical Review (Bloomington, IN) **9823**
American History (Harrisburg, PA) **26982**
American History Illustrated **26982***
American History; Reviews in (Baltimore, MD) **13242**
American Hockey Magazine (Colorado Springs, CO) **4234**
American Homestyle **21189***
American Homestyle and Gardening (New York, NY) **21189**
American Horticulturist **31636***
American How-To **16171***
American Hunter (Fairfax, VA) **32003**
American Imago (Baltimore, MD) **13113**
American Immigration Report (Jericho, NY) *Unable to locate*
American Indian Art Magazine (Scottsdale, AZ) *Ceased*
American Indian Basketry Magazine (Portland, OR) **26467**
American Indian Culture and Research Journal (Los Angeles, CA) **2208**
American Indian Higher Education (TCJ); Tribal College Journal of (Mancos, CO) **4572**
American Indian Law Review (Norman, OK) **25932**
American Indian Quarterly (Flagstaff, AZ) **693**
American Industrial Hygiene Association Journal (Fairfax, VA) **32004**
American Industry (Great Neck, NY) **20685**
American Ink Maker (Melville, NY) *Unable to locate*
American Institute of Baking Technical Bulletin (Manhattan, KS) **11619**
American Institute for Conservation of Historic and Artistic Works Journal (Washington, DC) **5331**

American International College Journal of Business (Chicago, IL) **8257**
American International Syndicate (St. Joseph, MO) *Unable to locate*
American Iron Magazine (Stamford, CT) *Unable to locate*
American Jails (Hagerstown, MD) **13562**
American Jewelry Manufacturer (Providence, RI) *Unable to locate*
American Jewish Archives (Cincinnati, OH) **24770**
American Jewish History (Newton Centre, MA) **14414**
American Jewish World (St. Louis Park, MN) **16359**
American Jones Building & Maintenance (Seattle, WA) **32940**
American Journal (Westbrook, ME) **13074**
American Journal of Addictions (Arlington, VA) **31772**
American Journal of Agricultural Economics (Malden, MA) **14289**
American Journal of Alzheimer's Care and Related Disorders and Research **14648***
American Journal of Alzheimers Disease (Weston, MA) **14648**
American Journal of Anatomy **18927***
American Journal of Ancient History (New Brunswick, NJ) **19325**
The American Journal of Anesthesiology (Chatham, NJ) **18725**
American Journal of Art Therapy (Montpelier, VT) *Ceased*
The American Journal of Asthma & Allergy for Pediatricians (Thorofare, NJ) *Ceased*
American Journal of Bariatric Medicine (Denver, CO) **4304**
American Journal of Botany (Ithaca, NY) **20789**
American Journal of Cardiac Imaging (Philadelphia, PA) *Ceased*
The American Journal of Cardiology (New York, NY) **21190**
American Journal of Chinese Medicine (Garden City, NY) **20634**
American Journal of Clinical Nutrition (Davis, CA) **1810**
American Journal of Clinical Oncology (Baltimore, MD) **13114**
American Journal of Clinical Pathology (Philadelphia, PA) *Unable to locate*
American Journal of Community Psychology (New York, NY) **21191**
American Journal of Comparative Law (Berkeley, CA) **1489**
American Journal of Contact Dermatitis (Dallas, TX) **30122**
American Journal of Cosmetic Surgery (Lawrence, KS) **11547**
The American Journal of Criminal Law (Austin, TX) **29751**
American Journal of Critical Care (Aliso Viejo, CA) **1389**
American Journal of Dance Therapy (Columbia, MD) **13451**
The American Journal of Dermatopathology (Baltimore, MD) **13115**
The American Journal of Drug and Alcohol Abuse (New York, NY) **21192**
American Journal of Economics and Sociology (New York, NY) *Unable to locate*
American Journal of Education (Seattle, WA) *Unable to locate*
American Journal of EEG Technology **33329***
American Journal of Electroneurodiagnostic Technology (Green Bank, WV) **33329**
The American Journal of Emergency Medicine (Philadelphia, PA) **27371**
American Journal of Epidemiology (Baltimore, MD) **13116**
American Journal of Family Law (New York, NY) **21193**
The American Journal of Family Therapy (Philadelphia, PA) *Unable to locate*
The American Journal of Forensic Medicine and Pathology (Baltimore, MD) **13117**
American Journal of Forensic Psychiatry (Newport Beach, CA) **2621**
American Journal of Forensic Psychology (Newport Beach, CA) **2622**
The American Journal of Gastroenterology (New York, NY) **21194**
American Journal of Geriatric Cardiology (Darien, CT) **4769**
American Journal of Health Education (Reston, VA) **32360**
American Journal of Health Promotion (St. Louis, MO) *Ceased*
American Journal of Health-System Pharmacy (Bethesda, MD) **13300**
American Journal of Hematology (Hoboken, NJ) **18884**
The American Journal of Hospice Care **14649***

American Journal of Hospice and Palliative Care (Weston, MA) **14649**
American Journal of Hospital Pharmacy **13300***
American Journal of Human Biology (Hoboken, NJ) **18885**
The American Journal of Human Genetics (Seattle, WA) *Unable to locate*
American Journal of Industrial Medicine (Hoboken, NJ) **18886**
(American Journal of Infection Control); AJIC (Little Rock, AR) **1210**
American Journal of International Law (Washington, DC) **5332**
American Journal of Islamic Social Sciences (Herndon, VA) **32160**
American Journal of Islamic Studies **32160***
American Journal of Italian Studies (Bristol, TN) **29065**
American Journal of Kidney Diseases (Minneapolis, MN) **16056**
The American Journal of Knee Surgery **19622***
American Journal of Law & Medicine (Boston, MA) **13849**
American Journal of Maternal/Child Nursing; MCN, The (Huntington Bay, NY) **20777**
American Journal of Mathematical and Management Sciences (Syracuse, NY) **23386**
American Journal of Mathematics (Baltimore, MD) **13118**
American Journal of Medical Genetics (Hoboken, NJ) **18887**
American Journal of the Medical Sciences (Philadelphia, PA) **27372**
American Journal of Medicine (New York, NY) **21195**
American Journal on Mental Retardation (Washington, DC) **5333**
American Journal of Nephrology (Farmington, CT) **4795**
American Journal of Noninvasive Cardiology (Farmington, CT) *Ceased*
American Journal of Nursing (Springhouse, PA) **28013**
American Journal of Obstetrics and Gynecology (St. Louis, MO) **17410**
The American Journal of Occupational Therapy (Bethesda, MD) **13301**
American Journal of Ophthalmology (New York, NY) **21196**
American Journal of Orthodontics and Dentofacial Orthopedics (St. Louis, MO) **17411**
The American Journal of Orthopedics (Chatham, NJ) **18726**
American Journal of Orthopsychiatry (New York, NY) **21197**
American Journal of Otolaryngology (Philadelphia, PA) **27373**
The American Journal of Otology **13230***
American Journal of Pastoral Counseling (Grove, OK) **25846**
The American Journal of Pathology (Bethesda, MD) **13302**
American Journal of Pharmaceutical Education (Augusta, GA) **7095**
American Journal of Philology (Clinton, NY) **20469**
American Journal of Physical Anthropology (Hoboken, NJ) **18888**
American Journal of Physical Medicine and Rehabilitation (Indianapolis, IN) **10078**
American Journal of Physics (Amherst, MA) **13789**
American Journal of Physiology: Cell Physiology (Bethesda, MD) **13303**
American Journal of Physiology (Consolidated) (Bethesda, MD) **13304**
American Journal of Physiology: Endocrinology and Metabolism (Bethesda, MD) **13305**
American Journal of Physiology: Gastrointestinal and Liver Physiology (Bethesda, MD) **13306**
American Journal of Physiology: Heart and Circulatory Physiology (Bethesda, MD) **13307**
American Journal of Physiology: Lung Cellular and Molecular Physiology (Bethesda, MD) **13308**
American Journal of Physiology: Regulatory, Integrative and Comparative Physiology (Bethesda, MD) **13309**
American Journal of Physiology: Renal, Fluid and Electrolyte Physiology **13310***
American Journal of Physiology: Renal Physiology (Bethesda, MD) **13310**
American Journal of Political Science (Madison, WI) *Unable to locate*
American Journal of Potato Research (Orono, ME) **12998**
American Journal of Preventive Medicine (New York, NY) **21198**
American Journal of Primatology (Hoboken, NJ) **18889**
American Journal of Psychiatry (Arlington, VA) **31773**
The American Journal of Psychoanalysis (New York, NY) **21199**

American Journal of Psychology (Champaign, IL) **8178**
American Journal of Public Health (Washington, DC) **5334**
American Journal of Respiratory Cell and Molecular Biology (New York, NY) *Ceased*
American Journal of Rhinology (Providence, RI) **28386**
American Journal of Roentgenology (Leesburg, VA) **32182**
American Journal of Science (New Haven, CT) **4982**
American Journal of Semiotics (Carbondale, IL) **8114**
American Journal of Small Business **31246***
American Journal of Sociology (Seattle, WA) *Unable to locate*
The American Journal of Sports Medicine (Charlottesville, VA) **31914**
American Journal of Surgery (New York, NY) **21200**
The American Journal of Surgical Pathology (AJSP) (Baltimore, MD) **13119**
American Journal of Tax Policy (Tuscaloosa, AL) *Ceased*
American Journal of Transportation (Quincy, MA) **14488**
American Journal of Tropical Medicine and Hygiene (Lawrence, KS) *Unable to locate*
American Journal of Veterinary Research (Schaumburg, IL) **9583**
American Journalism (Tuscaloosa, AL) **484**
American Journalism Review (College Park, MD) **13410**
American Kennel Club Awards (New York, NY) *Unable to locate*
American Kennel Club Gazette (New York, NY) *Unable to locate*
American Laboratory News (Shelton, CT) **5119**
American; Lakota (Lakota, ND) **24488**
American Laundry Digest (Chicago, IL) *Ceased*
American Laundry News (Chicago, IL) **8258**
American Lawn Applicator **24919***
The American Lawyer (New York, NY) *Unable to locate*
American Legion Auxiliary's National News (Indianapolis, IN) **10079**
American Legion Magazine (Indianapolis, IN) **10080**
The American Legion Press (Perrysburg, OH) **25474**
American Letters & Commentary (New York, NY) **21201**
American Libraries (Chicago, IL) **8259**
American Literary Realism (Albuquerque, NM) **19765**
American Literary Scholarship (Durham, NC) *Unable to locate*
American Literature (Durham, NC) **23806**
American Literature; Western (Logan, UT) **31354**
American Lutherie (Tacoma, WA) **33143**
American Machinist (Cleveland, OH) **24855**
American Mathematical Monthly (Washington, DC) **5335**
American Mathematical Society; Abstracts of Papers Presented to the (Providence, RI) **28384**
American Mathematical Society; Bulletin (New Series) of the (Providence, RI) **28392**
American Mathematical Society; Journal of the (Providence, RI) **28402**
American Mathematical Society; Memoirs of the (Providence, RI) **28409**
American Mathematical Society; Notices of the (Providence, RI) **28410**
American Mathematical Society; Proceedings of the (Providence, RI) **28413**
American Mathematical Society; Transactions of the (Providence, RI) **28426**
American Medical Directors Association (JAMDA); Journal of the (Thousand Oaks, CA) **3878**
American Medical News (Chicago, IL) **8260**
American Metal Market (New York, NY) *Unable to locate*
American Metric Journal (Camarillo, CA) *Unable to locate*
American Midland Naturalist (Notre Dame, IN) **10366**
American Mineralogist (Washington, DC) **5336**
American Mining Congress Journal (Washington, DC) *Ceased*
American Modeler (Whitsett, NC) **24288**
American Mosquito Control Association Journal (New Brunswick, NJ) *Unable to locate*
American Mother **5243***
The American Mother (Dover, DE) **5243**
American Motorcyclist (Pickerington, OH) **25477**
American Mover **31668***
American Mover **31667***
American Movie Classics (Boston, MA) *Ceased*
American Movie Classics (Bethpage, NY) **37725**
American; Murphysboro (Monmouth, IL) **9217**
American Museum Novitates (New York, NY) **21202**
American Music (Champaign, IL) **8179**
American Music Research Center Journal (Boulder, CO) **4155**
American Music Teacher (Cincinnati, OH) **24771**

American Musicology Society Journal (Notre Dame, IN) **10367**
The American Muslim (St. Louis, MO) **17412**
The American Naturalist (Seattle, WA) *Unable to locate*
The American Neptune (Salem, MA) **14512**
American News (Montevideo, MN) **16180**
American News; The San Bernardino (San Bernardino, CA) **3090**
The American News Service (Brattleboro, VT) *Unable to locate*
American; Norwalk Herald (Norwalk, CA) **2648**
The American Nurse (Washington, DC) **5337**
American Nurseryman (Chicago, IL) **8261**
American Office Dealer (New York, NY) *Ceased*
American Oil Chemists' Society; Journal of the (Champaign, IL) **8194**
The American Oil and Gas Reporter (Derby, KS) **11406**
The American Organist (New York, NY) **21203**
American Oriental Society; Journal of the (Boulder, CO) **4173**
American Orthoptic Journal (Madison, WI) **33917**
American Ostrich (Fort Worth, TX) *Unable to locate*
American Pacific Co. (Desert Center, CA) **1825**
American Paint and Coatings Journal (Loveland, CO) **4565**
American Painting Contractor (Colorado Springs, CO) **4235**
American Paper Convention Daily (Rosemont, IL) *Unable to locate*
American Papermaker (Atlanta, GA) *Unable to locate*
American; Paramount/Bellflower Herald (Paramount, CA) **2809**
American Patchwork and Quilting (Des Moines, IA) **10770**
The American Patriot (Scottsdale, AZ) *Ceased*
The American Patriot (New York, NY) *Unable to locate*
American Penstemon Society Bulletin (Lakewood, CO) **4530**
American Pharmacy **5570***
The American Philatelist (State College, PA) **28016**
American Philosophical Quarterly (University Park, PA) **28069**
American Philosophical Society; Proceedings of the (Philadelphia, PA) **27648**
American Photo (New York, NY) **21204**
American Physical Society; Bulletin of the (College Park, MD) **13413**
The American Physics Teacher **13789***
American Pigeon Journal (Warrenton, MO) *Unable to locate*
American Planning Association (JAPA); Journal of the (Portland, OR) **26483**
American Podiatric Medical Association; Journal of the (Bethesda, MD) **13347**
American Poet (New York, NY) **21205**
American Poetry Anthology (Seattle, WA) *Unable to locate*
The American Poetry Review (Philadelphia, PA) **27374**
American Police Beat (Cambridge, MA) **14037**
American Political Development; Studies in (Los Angeles, CA) **2407**
American Political Science Review (Washington, DC) **5338**
American Politics (Washington, DC) *Unable to locate*
American Politics Quarterly **3849***
American Politics Quarterly **3849***
American Politics Research (Thousand Oaks, CA) **3849**
The American Postal Worker (Washington, DC) **5339**
American Potato Journal **12998***
American Premiere **1575***
American Presbyterians: Journal of Presbyterian History **27547***
American Press Service and Features Syndicate (Van Nuys, CA) **37814**
American Printer (Overland Park, KS) **11695**
The American Prospect (Mount Morris, IL) **9236**
American Psychiatric Nurses Association; Journal of the (St. Louis, MO) **17453**
The American Psychoanalyst (Mahwah, NJ) **19184**
American Psychoanalytic Association; Journal of the (New York, NY) **21984**
American Psychologist (Washington, DC) **5340**
American Psychotherapy Association; Annals of the (Springfield, MO) **17592**
American Public Radio **37657***
The American Quarter Horse Journal (Amarillo, TX) **29695**
American Quarterly (Baltimore, MD) **13120**
American Quilter (Paducah, KY) **12337**
American Racing Pigeon News **24665***
American Radio **20404***
American Radio System **20414***
American Radio Systems **29858***

American Railway Engineering Association Bulletin (Landover, MD) *Ceased*
The American Rationalist (St. Louis, MO) *Unable to locate*
American; Real (Leakey, TX) **30680**
American Record Guide (Cincinnati, OH) **24772**
American Recorder (Littleton, CO) *Unable to locate*
American Red Angus (Denton, TX) **30232**
American Red Brangus Journal (Dripping Springs, TX) **30250**
American Rehabilitation (Washington, DC) **5341**
American Rennaissance (Oakton, VA) **32315**
American Republic; Daily (Poplar Bluff, MO) **17357**
The American Revenuer (Rockford, IA) **11183**
American Review of Canadian Studies (Washington, DC) **5342**
American Review of Management and Inventiveness Report (Albuquerque, NM) *Unable to locate*
American Review of Public Administration (Columbia, MO) **16987**
American Review of Respiratory Disease (New York, NY) **21206**
American Revolution Magazine; Daughters of the (Washington, DC) **5459**
American Rider (Camarillo, CA) *Unable to locate*
American Rifleman (Fairfax, VA) **32005**
American Rodder (Agoura, CA) **1376**
American Romanian Review (Cleveland, OH) *Ceased*
American Rose (Shreveport, LA) **12816**
The American Rose Magazine **12816***
American Rowing **10180***
American Sailings (New York, NY) *Ceased*
American Sailor (Portsmouth, RI) *Unable to locate*
American; St. Louis (St. Louis, MO) **17493**
American Salers (Parker, CO) **4596**
American Salesman (Burlington, IA) **10637**
American Salon (Milford, CT) **4952**
The American-Scandinavian Review **22708***
The American Scholar (Washington, DC) **5343**
The American School Board Journal (Alexandria, VA) **31637**
American School & University (Overland Park, KS) **11696**
American Scientific Affiliation; Journal of the **14257***
American Scientist (Research Triangle Park, NC) **24183**
American Seaports **6480***
American Self Protection Review (Marina del Rey, CA) *Ceased*
The American Senior (Los Angeles, CA) **2209**
American Shipper (Jacksonville, FL) **6209**
American Shoemaking (Arlington, MA) **13816**
American Short Fiction (Austin, TX) *Ceased*
American Skating World (Pittsburgh, PA) *Unable to locate*
American Skier (Englewood, CO) *Ceased*
American SMALL FARM (Westerville, OH) *Unable to locate*
American Snowmobiler (St. Paul, MN) *Unable to locate*
American Soccer Magazine *Ceased*
American Society of Echocardiography; Journal of the (Philadelphia, PA) **27513**
American Society for Horticultural Science; Journal of the (Alexandria, VA) **31687**
American Society for Information Science; Journal of the (Hoboken, NJ) **19001**
American Society of Nephrology; Journal of the (Philadelphia, PA) **27514**
American Society for Psychical Research; Journal of the (New York, NY) **21985**
American Society for Surgery; Journal of the (Philadelphia, PA) **27515**
American Sociological Review (Madison, WI) **33918**
The American Sociologist (Somerset, NJ) **19560**
American Songwriter (Nashville, TN) **29440**
American Spacemodeling **19894***
The American Spectator (Washington, DC) **5344**
American Speech (Durham, NC) **23807**
American Spirit Newspaper (Berkeley, CA) **1490**
American Sports (Rosemead, CA) **2967**
American Sportswear & Knitting Times (Summit, NJ) *Unable to locate*
American Squaredance (Salinas, CA) **3066**
American Srbobran (Pittsburgh, PA) **27757**
American; Stamford (Stamford, TX) **31128**
American-Statesman; Austin (Austin, TX) **29755**
American Statistical Association; Journal of the (Alexandria, VA) **31688**
The American Statistician (Alexandria, VA) **31638**
American Stock Exchange Radio AMEX (New York, NY) **37614**
American Stock Exchange Reports **22784***
American; Stroud (Stroud, OK) **26089**
American Studies; Canadian Review of (Ottawa, ON, Can.) **36227**
American Studies International (Washington, DC) **5345**
American Studies; Journal of (New York, NY) **21986**

The American Sunbeam **29558***
The American Surgeon (New York, NY) *Ceased*
American Suzuki Journal (Boulder, CO) **4156**
American; Talihina (Talihina, OK) **26098**
American Taxation Association Journal (Austin, TX) **29752**
American Teacher (Washington, DC) **5346**
American Technical Education Association Journal (Wahpeton, ND) **24547**
American Telecommunications Group Assn. (Des Plaines, IL) **37683**
American Televenture of Utah, Inc. (Monticello, UT) *Unable to locate*
American Theatre (New York, NY) **21207**
American Time (New York, NY) **21208**
American Tool, Die & Stamping News (Novi, MI) **15407**
American Trapper (Riverton, WY) **34576**
American Trucker—Badger Edition (Indianapolis, IN) **10081**
American Trucker—Buckeye Edition (Indianapolis, IN) **10082**
American Trucker—California Edition (Indianapolis, IN) **10083**
American Trucker—Cascade Edition (Indianapolis, IN) **10084**
American Trucker—Central States Edition (Indianapolis, IN) **10085**
American Trucker—Florida Edition (Indianapolis, IN) **10086**
American Trucker—Illinois Edition (Indianapolis, IN) **10087**
American Trucker—Indiana Edition (Indianapolis, IN) **10088**
American Trucker—Kentucky/Tennessee Edition (Indianapolis, IN) **10089**
American Trucker Magazine (Indianapolis, IN) *Ceased*
American Trucker—Metro East Edition (Indianapolis, IN) **10090**
American Trucker—Michigan Edition (Indianapolis, IN) **10091**
American Trucker—Mid-Atlantic Edition (Indianapolis, IN) **10092**
American Trucker—Minn/Dakota Truck Edition (Indianapolis, IN) **10093**
American Trucker—Mountain America Edition (Indianapolis, IN) **10094**
American Trucker—New England Edition (Indianapolis, IN) **10095**
American Trucker—New York/Pennsylvania Edition (Indianapolis, IN) **10096**
American Trucker—South Central Edition (Indianapolis, IN) **10097**
American Trucker—Southern Edition (Indianapolis, IN) **10098**
The American University Law Review (Washington, DC) **5347**
American Urban Radio Networks (New York, NY) **37615**
American Vedantist (Elmhurst, NY) **20571**
American Vegetable Grower (Willoughby, OH) **25657**
The American Veteran **13607***
American Visions (Washington, DC) **5348**
The American Voice (Louisville, KY) *Ceased*
American Voice (New York, NY) *Unable to locate*
The American Wanderer (Universal City, TX) **31224**
American Water Resources Association; Journal of the (Middleburg, VA) **32272**
American Water Works Association; Journal of the (Denver, CO) **4334**
American Way (Fort Worth, TX) **30329**
The American Way Features (Blowing Rock, NC) *Unable to locate*
American; Weiser Signal (Weiser, ID) **7998**
The American West (Tucson, AZ) *Ceased*
American; Whitney Point Reporter, and Oxford Review Times; Chenango (Greene, NY) **20697**
American Window Cleaner Magazine (Richmond, CA) **2920**
American Wine Society Journal (Rochester, NY) **23209**
American Woman Motorscene (Troy, MI) *Unable to locate*
American Women Writers; Legacy: A Journal of (Lincoln, NE) **18089**
American Woodturner (Shoreview, MN) **16446**
American Woodworker (Eagan, MN) **15861**
The American Worker (Millersville, MD) *Unable to locate*
American Writer (New York, NY) **21209**
The American Zionist (New York, NY) *Ceased*
American Zoologist (Chicago, IL) *Unable to locate*
Americana Magazine (New York, NY) *Ceased*
Americans for Legal Reform (Washington, DC) *Ceased*
(Americanski Slovenec); Glasilo KSKJ (Joliet, IL) **9033**
AmericanStyle Magazine (Baltimore, MD) **13121**
The Americas (Washington, DC) **5349**

America's Barrel Racer (Terrell, TX) **31182**
America's Christian Newspaper (Madisonville, KY) **12270**
America's Cup Challenge (New York, NY) *Unable to locate*
America's Family Support Magazine (Chicago, IL) **8262**
America's Insider (Fort Leonard Wood, MO) **17070**
America's Network (Santa Ana, CA) **3619**
America's 1st Freedom (Fairfax, VA) **32006**
America's Pharmacist (Alexandria, VA) **31639**
The Americas Review (Houston, TX) *Ceased*
America's Talking (Fort Lee, NJ) *Unable to locate*
Americus Times-Recorder (Americus, GA) **6920**
(Amerikai Magyar SZO); Hungarian Word (New York, NY) **21836**
Amerikan Uutiset (Lantana, FL) **6298**
Amery Free Press (Amery, WI) **33527**
Amesbury News (Needham, MA) *Unable to locate*
Amethyst Review (Truro, NS, Can.) *Ceased*
Amherst (Amherst, MA) **13790**
Amherst Bee **20540***
Amherst Bulletin (Amherst, MA) **13791**
Amherst Daily News (Amherst, NS, Can.) **35532**
Amherst News-Times (Amherst, OH) *Unable to locate*
Amherst Press (Littlefield, TX) **30696**
Amherst Student (Amherst, MA) **13792**
Amherst Tomorrow River Times (Iola, WI) **33799**
The Amherstburg Echo (Amherstburg, ON; Can.) **35632**
The Amicus Journal **22488***
AMIGA Plus (San Francisco, CA) *Unable to locate*
Amiga World (Chatsworth, CA) *Unable to locate*
Amino Acids: Peptides & Proteins: CSA Biochemistry Abstracts, Part 3 (Bethesda, MD) *Ceased*
Amite Tangi-Digest (Amite, LA) **12470**
The Amity Observer (Shelton, CT) **5120**
Amityville/Copiague Pennysaver (Farmingdale, NY) *Ceased*
Amityville Record (Amityville, NY) **20035**
Amityville Suffolk Life (Amityville, NY) **20036**
AMM Magazine (New York, NY) *Ceased*
Amnesty Action (New York, NY) **21210**
The Amory Advertiser (Amory, MS) **16545**
Ampersand Communications (Miami, FL) **37815**
Amphibious Warfare Review (Alexandria, VA) *Unable to locate*
Amplitude *Ceased*
AMPRA Review **5753***
Amrac Cable **18462***
Amrac Clearview (Belchertown, MA) **13837**
AMS; Bulletin of the (Boston, MA) **13867**
Amstat News (Alexandria, VA) **31640**
Amsterdam News (New York, NY) **21211**
AMT Events (Park Ridge, IL) **9404**
Amtelecom Communications (Aylmer, ON, Can.) **35655**
Amtrak Express (Huntington, NY) *Unable to locate*
Amusement Business (Nashville, TN) **29441**
AMVET; The National (Lanham, MD) **13607**
AMW Cablevision (Metcalfe, MS) *Unable to locate*
Amzak Cable (New Ulm, MN) **16215**
The Anaconda Leader (Anaconda, MT) **17721**
Anacortes American (Mount Vernon, WA) *Unable to locate*
Anadarko Cable TV (Anadarko, OK) *Unable to locate*
Anadarko Daily News (Anadarko, OK) *Unable to locate*
Anaerobe (San Diego, CA) **3112**
Anagram (Baltimore, MD) **13122**
Anaheim Bulletin (Santa Ana, CA) *Unable to locate*
Anaheim Hills Highlander **1398***
Anaheim Hills News (Anaheim, CA) **1398**
Anahuac Progress (Anahuac, TX) **29721**
Anais (Becket, MA) **13834**
Analgesia; Anesthesia & (San Francisco, CA) **3326**
Analog Computing *Ceased*
Analog Science Fiction & Fact (New York, NY) *Unable to locate*
Analyse de Politiques; Canadian Public Policy— (Calgary, AB, Can.) **34638**
Analysis; Methods and Applications of (Somerville, MA) **14536**
Analysis Solutions Magazine (Santa Fe, NM) *Unable to locate*
Analytic Psychology (Farmington, CT) **4796**
Analytical Biochemistry (San Diego, CA) **3113**
Analytical Chemistry (Washington, DC) *Unable to locate*
Analytical Letters (New York, NY) **21212**
Analytical Methods and Instrumentation (Hoboken, NJ) *Ceased*
Analytical and Quantitative Cytology and Histology (St. Louis, MO) **17413**
Anamosa Journal-Eureka (Anamosa, IA) **10601**
Anarchy (Columbia, MO) **16988**
Anatomic Pathology; Advances in (Baltimore, MD) **13108**
The Anatomical Record (Hoboken, NJ) **18890**

Anthropology; SACC Notes—Teaching (Arlington, VA) 31826
Anthropology; Social (New York, NY) 22753
Anthropology; Transforming (Arlington, VA) 31837
Anthrozoos (West Lafayette, IN) 10544
Anti-Aging Medicine; Journal of (Larchmont, NY) 20907
Antic, The Atari Resource (San Francisco, CA) Ceased
Antic's Amiga Plus (San Francisco, CA) Ceased
Antietam Cable TV (Hagerstown, MD) 13572
Antigo Area Shoppers Guide (Antigo, WI) 33530
Antigo Daily Journal (Antigo, WI) 33531
Antigonish Cablevision 35601*
The Antigonish Review (Antigonish, NS, Can.) 35536
Antimicrobial Agents and Chemotherapy (Washington, DC) 5355
Antioch News (Antioch, IL) 8016
Antioch News Reporter 8016*
Antioch Publication (Kansas City, MO) Unable to locate
The Antioch Review (Yellow Springs, OH) 25690
Antioxidants and Redox Signaling (Larchmont, NY) 20889
Antique Automobile (Hershey, PA) 27040
Antique Bottle and Glass Collector (East Greenville, PA) 26845
Antique & Collectables (El Cajon, CA) 1843
Antique Detective Syndicate (Ft. Lauderdale, FL) Unable to locate
Antique Digest; Maine (Waldoboro, ME) 13069
Antique Gazette (Iola, WI) Ceased
Antique Gazette; Cotton & Quail (Iola, WI) 33815
ANTIQUE GUIDE; Renninger's (Lafayette Hill, PA) 27132
Antique Journal for California & Nevada (El Cajon, CA) 1844
Antique Journal for the Northwest (El Cajon, CA) 1845
The Antique Label Collectors Magazine (Rapid City, SD) Unable to locate
Antique Monthly (Tuscaloosa, AL) Ceased
Antique Motor News (Long Beach, CA) Ceased
Antique Radio Classified (Carlisle, MA) 14120
Antique Review (Groveport, OH) 25234
Antique Showcase (St. Catharines, ON, Can.) 36349
The Antique Trader Price Guide to Antiques and Collectors' Items 33811*
Antique Trader Weekly (Iola, WI) 33800
The Antiquer (New York, NY) 21223
The Antiquer (New York, NY) 21222
Antiquer; The Hudson Valley 21223*
Antiques! (Toronto, ON, Can.) Ceased
Antiques; Art & (Atlanta, GA) 6963
Antiques and the Arts Weekly (Newtown, CT) 5039
Antiques & Classics Boat 34201*
Antiques & Collectibles Magazine (Westbury, NY) 23551
Antiques and Collecting Hobbies 8265*
Antiques & Collecting Magazine (Chicago, IL) 8265
Antiques Journal; The New England (Ware, MA) 14609
Antiques; The Magazine (New York, NY) 22274
Antiques; Mass Bay (Needham, MA) 14360
The Antiques News 21223*
AntiqueWeek (Eastern Edition) (Knightstown, IN) 10233
AntiqueWeek (Mid-Central Edition) (Knightstown, IN) 10234
Antiquities; Technology & Conservation of Art, Architecture & (Somerville, MA) 14539
Antiquity; American (Washington, DC) 5324
Antiquity; Classical (Berkeley, CA) 1508
Antiquity and Law; Art, (New York, NY) 21250
Antisense and Nucleic Acid Drug Development (Larchmont, NY) 20890
Antisense Research and Development 20890*
The AntiShyster News Magazine (Dallas, TX) Unable to locate
The Antitrust Bulletin (New York, NY) Unable to locate
Antitrust Law and Economics Review (Vero Beach, FL) 6834
Antlers American (Antlers, OK) 25743
Antrim County News (Bellaire, MI) 14805
Antwerp Bee-Argus (Antwerp, OH) 24612
Anvil Herald; Hondo (Hondo, TX) 30451
The Anvil's Ring (Georgetown, CA) 2002
Anxiety 18926*
Anxiety; Depression and (Hoboken, NJ) 18926
Anxiety Research: An International Journal (New York, NY) Unable to locate
AOA News (St. Louis, MO) 17416
AOAC International; Journal of (Gaithersburg, MD) 13544
AOI Business Viewpoint (Salem, OR) Unable to locate
AONE's Leadership Prospectives (Philadelphia, PA) Ceased

AOPA Almanac 31717*
AOPA Pilot (Frederick, MD) 13505
AORN Journal (Denver, CO) 4305
AP Business Plus; AP-TMS Information Service (Washington, DC) 37684
AP-TMS Information Service AP Business Plus (Washington, DC) 37684
apa magazine (New York, NY) Ceased
APA Monitor (Washington, DC) 5356
The Apache 685*
The Apache County Reporter (Eagar, AZ) 691
Apache Junction Independent (Apache Junction, AZ) 656
Apache News (Apache, OK) 25744
Apalachee Quarterly (Tallahassee, FL) Unable to locate
Apartment Age Magazine (Los Angeles, CA) 2211
The Apartment Book (Raleigh, NC) Unable to locate
Apartment Management; Building Business & (Farmington Hills, MI) 15016
Apartment Management Magazine (Huntington Beach, CA) 2059
Apartment News (Garden Grove, CA) 1997
Apartment Owner/Builder 2059*
Apartment Reporter; The CF (Castle Rock, CO) 4220
Apartments for Rent Magazine (Bothell, WA) 32690
APCO BULLETIN 6039*
Aperture (New York, NY) 21224
APF Reporter (Washington, DC) 5357
APG News (Bel Air, MD) Unable to locate
Aphasiology (Lexington, KY) 12159
Apheresis; Journal of Clinical (Hoboken, NJ) 19012
Aphrodite Gone Berserk (Staten Island, NY) Ceased
APICS-The Performance Advantage (Marietta, GA) 7409
The Apis 804*
APLA Bulletin (Halifax, NS, Can.) 35557
Aplikace Matematiky 21227*
APMA News (Bethesda, MD) 13312
Apogee Photo Magazine (Conifer, CO) Unable to locate
Apollo Cablevision Inc. 1684*
Apollo News-Record (Leechburg, PA) 27180
The Apopka Chief (Apopka, FL) 5908
Apoptosis (New York, NY) 21225
The Apostle (Birmingham, AL) 54
Apostolat 37085*
Apostolat International (Montreal, QC, Can.) 37085
Apostolate of the Little Flower (San Antonio, TX) Unable to locate
Apostolic Times 12270*
Appalachian Bulletin 13848*
Appalachian Heritage (Berea, KY) 11936
Appalachian Journal (Boone, NC) 23652
The Appalachian Log 33272*
Appalachian News Express (Pikeville, KY) 12357
Appalachian Notes (Santa Monica, CA) Ceased
Appalachian Trailway News (Harpers Ferry, WV) 33333
Appaloosa Journal (Moscow, ID) 7911
Appaloosa News 7911*
Apparel Industry International (Roswell, GA) 7512
Apparel Industry Magazine (Atlanta, GA) Unable to locate
APPAREL Merchandising (New York, NY) 21226
Apparel News; California (Los Angeles, CA) 2230
Apparel News; Chicago (Chicago, IL) 8306
Apparel News; Dallas (Dallas, TX) 30143
Apparel News; New York (Los Angeles, CA) 2346
Apparel News South (Los Angeles, CA) 2212
The Apparel Strategist (Fleetwood, PA) 26920
Appeal Democrat (Marysville, CA) 2515
Appeal Tribune/Mt. Angel News (Silverton, OR) 26584
L'Appel (Quebec, QC, Can.) Unable to locate
Appellate Courts Edition (Minneapolis, MN) Unable to locate
Appendx (Cambridge, MA) 14038
Applause (Philadelphia, PA) 27381
Apple (Tarrytown, NY) Unable to locate
Apple Cable TV 23589*
The Apple II GS Buyer's Guide (Vero Beach, FL) Ceased
Apple Valley News (Apple Valley, CA) Unable to locate
Apple Valley/Rosemount Sun Current (Apple Valley, MN) 15718
Appleseeds (Peterborough, NH) 18616
Appleton City Journal (Appleton City, MO) Unable to locate
Appleton Press (Appleton, MN) 15719
Appliance (Oak Brook, IL) 9337
Appliance China Edition (Oak Brook, IL) 9338
Appliance European Edition (Oak Brook, IL) 9339
Appliance Latin America Edition (Oak Brook, IL) 9340
Appliance Manufacturer (Solon, OH) 25524
Appliance New Product Digest (Oak Brook, IL) Ceased
Appliance Retailing (Derby, CT) Ceased
Appliance Service News (St. Charles, IL) 9562

Appliance Service News (St. Charles, IL) 9561
Application Development Advisor (Chatsworth, CA) Unable to locate
Application Development Trends (Framingham, MA) 14191
Applications of Mathematics (New York, NY) 21227
Applications News (MAN); Modern (Nokomis, FL) 6464
Applicator (Chicago, IL) Unable to locate
Applied Artificial Intelligence (Philadelphia, PA) 27382
Applied Arts Magazine (North York, ON, Can.) 36120
Applied Behavioral Science; Journal of (Thousand Oaks, CA) 3879
Applied Behavioral Science Review (Berkeley, CA) Unable to locate
Applied Biochemistry and Biotechnology (Medford, MA) 14319
Applied Biochemistry and Microbiology (New York, NY) 21228
Applied Clinical Trials (Edison, NJ) 18786
Applied Cognitive Psychology (Hoboken, NJ) 18892
Applied Composite Materials (New York, NY) 21229
Applied and Computational Harmonic Analysis (San Diego, CA) 3115
Applied Computing Technologies (St. Clair Shores, MI) Unable to locate
Applied Developmental Science (Mahwah, NJ) 19185
Applied Engineering in Agriculture (St. Joseph, MI) 15511
Applied and Environmental Microbiology (Washington, DC) 5358
Applied Geographic Studies (Hoboken, NJ) Ceased
Applied Immunohistochemistry & Molecular Morphology (Baltimore, MD) 13125
Applied Industrial Hygiene 24774*
Applied Language Learning (Monterey, CA) 2581
Applied Mathematics and Decision Sciences; Journal of (Santa Monica, CA) 3712
Applied Mathematics and Mechanics (New York, NY) 21230
Applied Mathematics and Optimization (New York, NY) 21231
Applied Measurement in Education (Mahwah, NJ) 19186
Applied Mechanics Reviews (Fairfield, NJ) 18811
Applied Microwave Magazine 7455*
Applied Microwave & Wireless (Norcross, GA) 7455
Applied Neuropsychology (Houston, TX) 30458
Applied Nursing Research (Cleveland, OH) 24856
Applied Occupational & Environmental Hygiene (Cincinnati, OH) 24774
Applied Optics (Washington, DC) 5359
Applied Organometallic Chemistry (Hoboken, NJ) 18893
Applied Pathology (Farmington, CT) Ceased
Applied Physics Communications (New York, NY) Ceased
Applied Physics Letters (College Park, MD) 13412
Applied and Preventive Psychology (New York, NY) Unable to locate
Applied Psycholinguistics (New York, NY) 21232
Applied Psychophysiology and Biofeedback (New York, NY) 21233
Applied Radiology (Ocean, NJ) 19387
Applied Science & Technology Index (Bronx, NY) 20252
Applied Sciences; Mathematical Methods in the (Hoboken, NJ) 19059
Applied Skin Physiology; Skin Pharmacology and (Farmington, CT) 4860
Applied Spectroscopy (Frederick, MD) Unable to locate
Applied Spectroscopy Reviews (Lake Charles, LA) 12635
Applied Stochastic Models in Business and Industry (Hoboken, NJ) 18894
Applied Stochastic Models and Data Analysis 18894*
Appraisal Institute Magazine (AIM) 35319*
The Appraisal Journal (Chicago, IL) Unable to locate
Appraisal Review (St. Louis, MO) Ceased
Appraiser; The Canadian (Winnipeg, MB, Can.) 35319
The Appraisers Standard (Ludlow, VT) 31548
APPRISE 26985*
Approach, The Naval Aviation Safety Review (Pittsburgh, PA) Unable to locate
Approximation Theory and Its Applications (New York, NY) 21234
Approximation Theory; Journal of (San Diego, CA) 3180
APWA Reporter (Chicago, IL) Unable to locate
APWS Magazine (Granton, WI) 33736
Aqua Dulce News; Acton/ (Rosamond, CA) 2966
Aqua-Field Turkey Hunting Guide (Shrewsbury, NJ) 19546
AQUA Magazine (Madison, WI) 33921
Aqua Terra, Meta-Ecology and Culture (Eureka Springs, AR) 1113
Aquaculture International (New York, NY) 21235
Aquaculture; Journal of Applied (Frankfort, KY) 12064

Arizona Silver Belt (Globe, AZ) **717**
Arizona Texas Cotton; California- (Fresno, CA) **1945**
Arizona Trend (St. Petersburg, FL) *Ceased*
Arizona Trends (Scottsdale, AZ) **867**
Arizona and the West **951***
Arizona West (Parker, AZ) **762**
Arizona's Economy (Tucson, AZ) **935**
Arizoo (Phoenix, AZ) **783**
The Ark (Tiburon, CA) **3926**
Ark; Bellowing (Seattle, WA) **32949**
Ark Valley News (Valley Center, KS) **11857**
Arka Tech (Russellville, AR) **1331**
Arkansas; Aging (Little Rock, AR) **1208**
Arkansas Banker (Little Rock, AR) **1212**
Arkansas Business (Little Rock, AR) **1213**
Arkansas Business & Economic Review (Fayetteville, AR) **1115**
Arkansas Catholic (Little Rock, AR) **1214**
Arkansas Cattle Business (Little Rock, AR) **1215**
Arkansas Democrat **1216***
Arkansas Democrat-Gazette (Little Rock, AR) **1216**
Arkansas Educator (Little Rock, AR) **1217**
The Arkansas Episcopalian (Little Rock, AR) *Unable to locate*
Arkansas Family Historian (Hot Springs, AR) **1183**
Arkansas Farm Research (Fayetteville, AR) *Ceased*
Arkansas Farmer (Carol Stream, IL) *Unable to locate*
Arkansas Game and Fish Magazine **1223***
Arkansas Grocer (Pine Bluff, AR) *Unable to locate*
Arkansas Grocers & Retail Merchants News (Little Rock, AR) *Unable to locate*
Arkansas Historical Quarterly (Fayetteville, AR) **1116**
Arkansas Homes **1218***
Arkansas Law Review (Fayetteville, AR) **1117**
Arkansas Living (Little Rock, AR) **1218**
Arkansas Medical Society; The Journal of the (Little Rock, AR) **1231**
Arkansas; The Morning News of Northwest (Rogers, AR) **1327**
The Arkansas Motor Carrier **1222***
Arkansas News Leader; East (Wynne, AR) **1371**
Arkansas Pharmacist (Little Rock, AR) **1219**
Arkansas Propane Gas News (Little Rock, AR) *Unable to locate*
Arkansas Radio Network (Little Rock, AR) *Unable to locate*
Arkansas Register (Little Rock, AR) **1220**
Arkansas Review (State University, AR) **1348**
Arkansas; Rural (Little Rock, AR) **1236**
Arkansas State Press (Little Rock, AR) *Ceased*
Arkansas State University; The Herald of (State University, AR) **1349**
Arkansas Times (Little Rock, AR) **1221**
Arkansas Times; Northwest (Fayetteville, AR) **1122**
Arkansas Times; Northwest (Fayetteville, AR) **1121**
The Arkansas Traveler (Fayetteville, AR) **1118**
Arkansas Trucking Report (Little Rock, AR) **1222**
Arkansas Wildlife (Little Rock, AR) **1223**
Arlington Advocate (Arlington, MA) **13817**
Arlington Catholic Herald (Arlington, VA) **31777**
Arlington Citizen (Arlington, NE) **17935**
The Arlington Citizen-Journal (Arlington, TX) *Ceased*
Arlington Courier **32423***
Arlington Enterprise (Arlington, MN) **15721**
Arlington Heights Post (Arlington Heights, IL) **8021**
Arlington Historical Magazine (Arlington, VA) **31778**
The Arlington Journal (Arlington, VA) **31779**
Arlington News (Arlington, TX) *Ceased*
Arlington Sun (Arlington, SD) **28803**
Arlington Sun Gazette (Alexandria, VA) **31642**
Arlington TeleCable Inc. **29743***
Arlington Times (Arlington, WA) **32654**
Armada Times (Armada, MI) **14782**
The Armchair Detective (Scotch Plains, NJ) **19533**
Armed Forces Comptroller (Alexandria, VA) **31643**
Armed Forces Journal International (Springfield, VA) **32539**
Armed Forces & Society (Somerset, NJ) **19561**
The Armenian Mirror-Spectator (Watertown, MA) **14610**
Armenian Numismatic Journal (Pico Rivera, CA) **2839**
The Armenian Reporter International (Fresh Meadows, NY) *Unable to locate*
The Armenian Weekly (Watertown, MA) **14611**
Armor **12061***
Armor (Fort Knox, KY) **12061**
Armour Cable TV (Mitchell, SD) *Unable to locate*
Armour Chronicle (Armour, SD) **28804**
Arms Control Today (Washington, DC) **5361**
Arms; Man at (Lincoln, RI) **28362**
Arms & the World **37887***
Armstrong Advertiser (Armstrong, BC, Can.) **34882**
Armstrong Cable Services (North Lima, OH) **25437**
Armstrong Communications Ltd. **36114***
The Armstrong Journal (Armstrong, IA) **10607**
Armstrong Utilities Inc. (Butler, PA) **26744**
Armstrong Utilities Inc. (Zelienople, PA) **28220**
Army Aviation Digest; United States (Pittsburgh, PA) **27852**

Army Aviation Magazine (Monroe, CT) **4962**
Army Chemical Review; CML (Fort Leonard Wood, MO) **17071**
Army Communicator (Fort Gordon, GA) **7282**
Army Engineers; Engineer: The Professional Bulletin for (Fort Leonard Wood, MO) **17073**
Army Flier (Enterprise, AL) *Ceased*
Army Lawyer (Charlottesville, VA) **31915**
Army Logistician (Pittsburgh, PA) *Unable to locate*
ARMY Magazine (Arlington, VA) **31780**
Army Man (Boulder, CO) *Unable to locate*
Army Motors (Independence, MO) **17105**
Army-Navy Store and Outdoor Merchandiser (Melville, NY) **21040**
Army Reserve Magazine (Washington, DC) *Unable to locate*
Army Times (Springfield, VA) **32540**
Army Transportation Journal **31664***
Army Weekly; Hawaii (Kaneohe, HI) **7769**
Arnazella (Bellevue, WA) **32662**
Arnold Sentinel (Stapleton, NE) **18285**
Arnoldia (Jamaica Plain, MA) **14258**
Aroostook Republican & News (Caribou, ME) **12946**
Around the Town (Lexington, KY) **12160**
Around Town Publication (Pompano Beach, FL) *Unable to locate*
ARQ **32078***
ARQ/Architecture-Quebec **37370***
ARQ, La revue d'architecture (Sainte-Adele, QC, Can.) **37370**
Arrig Communication Systems (Perham, MN) **16266**
Arrigoni Travel Syndication (Fairfax, CA) **37818**
Arrival (Berkeley, CA) *Unable to locate*
Arrive (Bethesda, MD) *Ceased*
Arrived (St. Paul, MN) *Ceased*
The Arrow **27767***
The Arrow (Rochester, NY) **23210**
The Arrow (Staten Island, NY) **23357**
Arrow Lakes News (Nakusp, BC, Can.) **35017**
Arrow Shopper (Ettrick, WI) **33691**
Arrowsmith Star **35043***
Ars Combinatoria (Winnipeg, MB, Can.) **35310**
Ars-; Scholastic (Danbury, CT) **4752**
Arsenal (Evanston, IL) **8849**
Art (Las Vegas, NV) **18360**
Art Access (Seattle, WA) **32941**
Art in America (New York, NY) **21249**
Art & Antiques (Atlanta, GA) **6963**
Art, Antiquity and Law (New York, NY) **21250**
Art and Archaeology Bulletin; University of Michigan Museums of (Ann Arbor, MI) **14771**
Art, Architecture & Antiquities; Technology & Conservation of (Somerville, MA) **14539**
Art Bulletin (New York, NY) **21251**
Art Bulletin; Philadelphia Museum of (Philadelphia, PA) **27629**
Art Business News (New York, NY) **21252**
Art Calendar (Salisbury, MD) **13706**
Art of California (Napa, CA) *Unable to locate*
Art; Canadian (Toronto, ON, Can.) **36492**
Art Conference Review; Southeastern College (Pueblo, CO) **4601**
Art & Crafts Catalyst **12534***
Art Criticism; The Journal of Aesthetics and (Malden, MA) **14292**
Art Culinaire (Morristown, NJ) **19310**
Art and Design News (Indianapolis, IN) *Unable to locate*
Art Direction (New York, NY) *Unable to locate*
The Art of Eating (Peacham, VT) **31578**
Art Education (University Park, PA) **28070**
Art Education; Studies in (Tallahassee, FL) **6736**
Art Examiner; New (Chicago, IL) **8504**
Art; Friends of French (Rancho Palos Verdes, CA) **2880**
Art Impressions (Richmond Hill, ON, Can.) *Unable to locate*
Art Index (Bronx, NY) **20253**
Art Institute of Chicago Museum Studies (Chicago, IL) **8275**
Art Institute Magazine; San Francisco (San Francisco, CA) **3426**
Art Issues (West Hollywood, CA) **4061**
Art Journal (New York, NY) **21253**
Art Journal; American (New York, NY) **21177**
Art Journal; Woman's (Laverock, PA) **27168**
Art Law & Accounting Reporter (Houston, TX) **30459**
Art/Life (Ventura, CA) **4000**
Art & Man (Danbury, CT) **4735**
Art Material Trade News (Atlanta, GA) **6964**
Art Museum Bulletin; Allen Memorial (Oberlin, OH) **25443**
Art Museum Bulletin; Saint Louis (St. Louis, MO) **17495**
Art Now Gallery Guide—Boston/New England Edition (Clinton, NJ) **18759**
Art Now Gallery Guide—Chicago/Midwest Edition (Clinton, NJ) **18760**

Art Now Gallery Guide—Europe Edition (Clinton, NJ) *Ceased*
Art Now Gallery Guide—International Edition (Clinton, NJ) **18761**
Art Now Gallery Guide—New York Edition (Clinton, NJ) **18762**
Art Now Gallery Guide—Philadelphia Edition (Clinton, NJ) **18763**
Art Now Gallery Guide—Southeast Edition (Clinton, NJ) **18764**
Art Now Gallery Guide—Southwest Edition (Clinton, NJ) **18765**
Art Now Gallery Guide—West Coast Edition (Clinton, NJ) **18766**
Art Papers **6965***
Art Papers Magazine (Atlanta, GA) **6965**
Art Quarterly; Inuit (Ottawa, ON, Can.) **36252**
Art Reference Services Quarterly (Gainesville, FL) **6130**
Art Society Journal; Glass (Seattle, WA) **32968**
Art; Southwest (Houston, TX) **30530**
Art and Style International (Champlain, NY) *Unable to locate*
Art Therapy (Mundelein, IL) **9256**
ART TIMES (Mount Marion, NY) **21100**
Art Today (Iola, WI) *Ceased*
ART; U.S. (Minneapolis, MN) **16137**
Art; West (Auburn, CA) **1441**
Art of the West (Minnetonka, MN) **16167**
Art&Artists (New York, NY) *Unable to locate*
ArtByte (New York, NY) **21254**
Artere (Montreal, QC, Can.) **37086**
Arteriosclerosis and Thrombosis: A Journal of Vascular Biology **10969***
Arteriosclerosis, Thrombosis, and Vascular Biology (Iowa City, IA) **10969**
Artery (Fulton, MI) *Unable to locate*
Artes Graficas (Coral Gables, FL) **6004**
Artesia Daily Press (Artesia, NM) **19817**
Artesian Commonwealth (Woonsocket, SD) *Ceased*
ARTFOCUS (Toronto, ON, Can.) **36463**
Artforum International Magazine (New York, NY) *Unable to locate*
Arthritis Care and Research (Hoboken, NJ) **18898**
Arthritis and Rheumatism (Durham, NC) **23808**
Arthritis and Rheumatism; Seminars in (Miami, FL) **6379**
Arthritis/Rheumatology Guide (Lawrenceville, NJ) *Ceased*
Arthritis Today (Atlanta, GA) *Unable to locate*
Arthroplasty; The Journal of (Philadelphia, PA) **27516**
Arthroplasty; Seminars in (Philadelphia, PA) **27659**
Arthroscopy (Baltimore, MD) *Ceased*
Arthroscopy (Winston-Salem, NC) **24318**
Arthroscopy Review; Sports Medicine and (Baltimore, MD) **13249**
Arthur (Peterborough, ON, Can.) **36313**
Arthur Enterprise (Arthur, NE) **17936**
Arthur Frommer's Budget Travel (New York, NY) **21255**
Arthur Graphic Clarion (Arthur, IL) **8027**
Arthuriana (Dallas, TX) **30124**
Arthur's International (Las Vegas, NV) **37819**
Artichoke (Vancouver, BC, Can.) **35122**
Artificial Cells, Blood Substitutes and Immobilization Biotechnology (New York, NY) **21256**
Artificial Intelligence; Applied (Philadelphia, PA) **27382**
Artillery; Field (Fort Sill, OK) **25838**
The Artilleryman (Tunbridge, VT) **31607**
Artique (Quakertown, PA) **27913**
L'Artisan (Montreal, QC, Can.) **37087**
Artist; American (New York, NY) **21178**
Artist; Sunshine (Orlando, FL) **6508**
Artistic Works Journal; American Institute for Conservation of Historic and (Washington, DC) **5331**
ArtistMarket.com (Farmington Hills, MI) **37820**
The Artist's Magazine (Cincinnati, OH) **24775**
Artists; Medical Problems of Performing (Philadelphia, PA) **27567**
Artist's Workbook **24792***
Artist's Workbook; Decorative (Cincinnati, OH) **24792**
Artists and Writers Syndicate (Washington, DC) **37821**
ArtistWriter (Pleasanton, CA) *Ceased*
ArtLinc Magazine (Fort Collins, CO) *Ceased*
ARTnews Magazine (New York, NY) **21257**
Arton Paper (New York, NY) **21258**
ArtPaper (Minneapolis, MN) *Unable to locate*
ARTPOST **36463***
ARTS (Coconut Grove, FL) *Unable to locate*
Arts & Activities (San Diego, CA) **3117**
Arts; African (Los Angeles, CA) **2201**
Arts; Alabama (Montgomery, AL) **355**
ARTS ALIVE! Magazine (Allentown, PA) **26626**
Arts Alive Magazine (North Vancouver, BC, Can.) *Unable to locate*
Arts and Antiques Network (Washington, DC) *Unable to locate*

Astronomical Society; Bulletin of the American (Washington, DC) 5388
Astronomical Society of Canada (R.A.S.C.); Journal of the Royal (Toronto, ON, Can.) 36638
Astronomical Society of the Pacific; Publication of the (Tempe, AZ) 914
Astronomy (Waukesha, WI) 34394
Astronomy and Astrophysics; Annual Review of (Palo Alto, CA) 2788
Astronomy; Experimental (New York, NY) 21665
Astronomy Letters (College Park, MD) Unable to locate
Astrophysical Journal (Chicago, IL) Unable to locate
Astrophysical Journal Supplement Series (Tucson, AZ) 936
Astrophysics (New York, NY) 21268
Astrophysics; Annual Review of Astronomy and (Palo Alto, CA) 2788
ASU Travel Guide (San Rafael, CA) 3598
ASUCLA Together 2268*
At Bowling Green 24689*
At the Crossroads (St. Paul, AR) Ceased
At the Park (Chicago, IL) 8278
At the Shore (Pleasantville, NJ) 19443
AT & T Broadband (Mishawaka, IN) 10314
AT & T Broadband (Pittsburgh, PA) 27857
AT & T Cable Services (Kankakee, IL) 9040
AT & T Media Services (Richmond, VA) 32471
At Your Leisure (Camas, WA) 32700
The ATA Magazine (Edmonton, AB, Can.) 34701
AT&T Broad Band (Garland, TX) 30386
AT&T Broadband 18427*
AT&T Broadband 17637*
AT&T Broadband 15101*
AT&T Broadband (Cypress, CA) 1801
AT&T Broadband (Fresno, CA) 1961
AT&T Broadband (Denver, CO) Unable to locate
AT&T Broadband (Branford, CT) 4709
AT&T Broadband (Miami, FL) 6393
AT&T Broadband (Twin Falls, ID) 7989
AT&T Broadband (Ames, IA) 10595
AT&T Broadband (Valparaiso, IN) 10511
AT&T Broadband (Revere, MA) 14504
AT&T Broadband (Muskegon, MI) 15391
AT&T Broadband (St. Paul, MN) 16419
AT&T Broadband (Missoula, MT) 17877
AT&T Broadband (Logan, UT) 31356
AT&T Broadband (Olympia, WA) 32865
AT&T Broadband & Internet Service (Peoria, IL) 9429
AT&T Broadband New England Region CT Properties (Kensington, CT) 4919
AT&T Cable (Burlingame, CA) 1633
AT&T Cable (Merrillville, IN) 10300
AT&T Cable Services (Overland, MO) 17326
AT&T Cable Services (Billings, MT) 17735
AT&T Comcast 27904*
AT&T Media Services (Jacksonville, FL) 6218
AT&T Media Services (Coeur d'Alene, ID) 7847
AT&T Media Services (Portland, OR) 26517
AT&T Technical Journal (Murray Hill, NJ) Ceased
Atari Explorer (Duluth, MN) Unable to locate
Atarian (Sunnyvale, CA) Ceased
Atascadero News (Atascadero, CA) 1435
ATC Cablevision Program Guide (Boston, MA) Ceased
The Atchison County Mail (Rock Port, MO) 17377
Atchison Daily Globe (Atchison, KS) 11345
Atelier (Boston, MA) Ceased
Atheist; American (Parsippany, NJ) 19410
Athenaeum; The Daily (Morgantown, WV) 33392
Athens Banner Herald (Athens, GA) 6928
Athens Daily News (Athens, GA) Unable to locate
Athens Daily Review (Athens, TX) 29746
Athens Magazine (Athens, GA) 6929
The Athens Messenger (Athens, OH) 24628
The Athens News (Athens, OH) 24629
Athens News Courier (Athens, AL) 27
Athens Observer (Athens, GA) Unable to locate
Athens Star (Athens, GA) 6930
The Athlete 9602*
Athlete; Chicago's Amateur (Skokie, IL) 9602
Athletes in Action (Xenia, OH) 25685
Athletic Administration 24857*
Athletic Business (Madison, WI) Unable to locate
Athletic Management (Ithaca, NY) Unable to locate
Athletic Therapy Today (Champaign, IL) 8181
Athletic Training; Journal of (Charlottesville, VA) 31933
Athletics Administration (Cleveland, OH) 24857
Athletics Magazine (Toronto, ON, Can.) 36465
Athol Daily News (Athol, MA) 13824
The Athol/Orange Town Crier (Greenfield, MA) 14219
ATI—America's Textile Industries 7053*
ATI—America's Textiles International 7053*
The Atikokan Progress (Atikokan, ON, Can.) 35639
ATIN: AIDS Targeted Information (Philadelphia, PA) Ceased
Atkinson-Annawan News (Kewanee, IL) 9044
Atkinson County Citizen (Pearson, GA) 7482

The Atkinson Graphic (Atkinson, NE) 17938
Atlanta Baby (Atlanta, GA) Unable to locate
Atlanta Bulletin (Atlanta, GA) Unable to locate
Atlanta; Business (Atlanta, GA) 6982
Atlanta Business Chronicle (Atlanta, GA) 6967
The Atlanta Constitution 6972*
Atlanta Daily World (Atlanta, GA) 6968
Atlanta Historical Journal 6969*
Atlanta History Center (Atlanta, GA) 6969
Atlanta Homes and Lifestyles (Atlanta, GA) 6970
The Atlanta Inquirer (Atlanta, GA) 6971
The Atlanta Jewish Times (Atlanta, GA) Unable to locate
The Atlanta Journal 6972*
The Atlanta Journal and Constitution (Atlanta, GA) 6972
Atlanta; Key Magazine (Sugar Hill, GA) 7573
Atlanta Magazine (Indianapolis, IN) Unable to locate
Atlanta Main Events Guide (Norcross, GA) Unable to locate
The Atlanta Metro (Union City, GA) 7613
Atlanta Parent (Atlanta, GA) 6973
Atlanta Small Business Monthly (Norcross, GA) Unable to locate
Atlanta Sports & Fitness Magazine (Atlanta, GA) Unable to locate
The Atlanta Times (Atlanta, TX) Ceased
Atlanta Tribune: The Magazine (Roswell, GA) 7513
Atlanta University Magazine; Clark (Atlanta, GA) 6986
The Atlanta Voice (Atlanta, GA) 6974
Atlanta; WHERE (Atlanta, GA) 7061
The Atlantic 13851*
Atlantic Advocate (Fredericton, NB, Can.) Ceased
Atlantic Baptist (Wolfville, NS, Can.) Unable to locate
Atlantic Beef Quarterly (Liverpool, NS, Can.) 35587
Atlantic Books Today (Halifax, NS, Can.) Unable to locate
Atlantic Business (Halifax, NS, Can.) Unable to locate
Atlantic Business Magazine (St. John's, NL, Can.) 35485
Atlantic Business Report (Moncton, NB, Can.) Unable to locate
Atlantic City Magazine 19444*
Atlantic City; The Press of (Atlantic City, NJ) 18658
The Atlantic Co-operator (Moncton, NB, Can.) 35411
Atlantic Communicator (Southampton, PA) Ceased
Atlantic Control States Beverage Journal (Wheeling, WV) 33500
The Atlantic Council News (Washington, DC) Ceased
Atlantic County Record (Hammonton, NJ) 18862
Atlantic Economic Journal (St. Louis, MO) 17417
Atlantic Feature Syndicate (Melrose, MA) 37827
Atlantic Fisherman (Halifax, NS, Can.) Unable to locate
Atlantic Fishery Science; Journal of Northwest (Dartmouth, NS, Can.) 35547
Atlantic Forestry Review (Liverpool, NS, Can.) 35588
Atlantic Geology (Wolfville, NS, Can.) 35623
Atlantic Horse & Pony (Liverpool, NS, Can.) 35589
Atlantic Insight (Halifax, NS, Can.) Unable to locate
Atlantic LifeStyle Business 35485*
The Atlantic Monthly (Boston, MA) 13851
Atlantic News-Telegraph (Atlantic, IA) 10610
Atlantic Progress Magazine (Halifax, NS, Can.) 35559
Atlantic Review; South (Atlanta, GA) 7043
Atlantic Salmon Journal (St. Andrews, NB, Can.) 35429
Atlantic Snowmobiler (Fredericton, NB, Can.) 35390
Atlantic Tech 28092*
Atlantic Trucking (Toronto, ON, Can.) 36466
ATLAS 22945*
Atlas; The Delta (Delta, OH) 25164
Atloona Video Corp. 26636*
Atmore Advance (Atmore, AL) 33
Atmosphere (Washington, DC) 5371
Atmosphere (Etobicoke, ON, Can.) Unable to locate
Atmospheric Chemistry; Journal of (New York, NY) 22002
Atmospheric and Oceanic Technology; Journal of (Boston, MA) 13913
The ATO Palm (Champaign, IL) Unable to locate
Atom Mind (Albuquerque, NM) 19767
Atom Tabloid (Rahway, NJ) Unable to locate
Atomic Data and Nuclear Data Tables (San Diego, CA) 3118
Atomic Energy (New York, NY) 21269
Atomic Scientists; Bulletin of the (Chicago, IL) 8295
Atomization and Sprays (New York, NY) 21270
ATQ (Kingston, RI) 28358
Attacheair Magazine (Greensboro, NC) 23916
L'Attention 37151*
Attica Hub (Attica, OH) 24638
Attica Independent (Attica, KS) 11347
Attica Pennysaver (Attica, NY) 20104
Attorney Magazine; San Francisco (San Francisco, CA) 3427
ATV (Atlantic Television System) (Halifax, NS, Can.) 37685
ATV Sports (Costa Mesa, CA) Ceased

ATW China (Cleveland, OH) Ceased
Atwater Herald 16454*
Atwater's New Times (Winton, CA) 4095
Atwood Cable Systems Inc. (Atwood, KS) 11349
Atwood Herald (Atwood, IL) 8031
Au Courant (Ottawa, ON, Can.) Ceased
Au Fil Du Bois (Quebec, QC, Can.) Ceased
Au Fil des Evenements (Quebec, QC, Can.) 37281
AUA News (Philadelphia, PA) 27386
AUA Today (Charlottesville, VA) 31916
The Auburn Alumnews 39*
The Auburn Bulletin (Auburn, AL) 38
Auburn Cablevision 17941*
Auburn Cablevision Inc. (Auburn, NY) 20107
Auburn Citizen (Auburn, IL) 8032
Auburn Journal (Auburn, CA) 1436
Auburn Magazine (Auburn, AL) 39
Auburn News (Auburn, MA) Unable to locate
Auburn News; Opelika- (Opelika, AL) 409
Auburn Pennysaver (Syracuse, NY) 23387
The Auburn Plainsman (Auburn, AL) 40
Auburn Press-Tribune (Auburn, NE) 17939
Auburndale Star 6869*
AUC Digest (Atlanta, GA) 6975
Auction & Surplus (Glendale, CA) Ceased
Auction Times for the West (Iola, WI) Ceased
The Auctioneer (Overland Park, KS) 11697
Auctions and Sales; National (Los Angeles, CA) 2342
Audio (New York, NY) Ceased
The Audio Amateur 18617*
Audio Electronics 18617*
Audio and Electronics; Car (Anaheim, CA) 1402
Audio Engineering Society; Journal of the (New York, NY) 22003
Audio Times (New York, NY) Ceased
Audio/Video Interiors (Anaheim, CA) 1399
AudioFile (Portland, ME) 13005
Audiology; Journal of the Academy of Rehabilitative (Dallas, TX) 30162
Audiology and Neuro-Otology (Farmington, CT) 4798
AudioVideo International (New York, NY) 21271
audioXpress (Peterborough, NH) 18617
Audit Guides; Federal (Riverwoods, IL) 9504
Auditing (Atlanta, GA) 6976
Auditing; International Journal of Government (Washington, DC) 5554
Auditing and Taxation; Journal of International Accounting, (Kalamazoo, MI) 15239
Auditions U.S.A.; Music Gigs & (New York, NY) 22385
Auditor; Internal (Altamonte Springs, FL) 5900
Audubon (New York, NY) 21272
Audubon County Advocate Journal (Audubon, IA) 10614
Audubon County Journal (Audubon, IA) Ceased
Audubon News Advocate 10614*
Audubon Quarterly; Indiana (Indianapolis, IN) 10122
AUFBAU - The Transatlantic Jewish Paper (New York, NY) 21273
Augusta Advocate 1271*
Augusta Area Times (Augusta, WI) 33559
The Augusta Chronicle (Augusta, GA) 7096
Augusta Daily Gazette (Augusta, KS) 11350
Augusta Focus (Augusta, GA) 7097
Augusta Historical Bulletin (Staunton, VA) 32553
Augustana College Magazine (Rock Island, IL) 9516
Augustana Mirror (Sioux Falls, SD) 28961
Augustana Observer (Rock Island, IL) 9517
Augustinian Studies (Charlottesville, VA) 31917
Aujourd'hui Credo (Longueuil, QC, Can.) 37051
The Auk (Washington, DC) Unable to locate
Aum Namo Narayanay Journal 3596*
The Aumnibus (Montgomery, AL) Unable to locate
Aumsville/Sublimity Cablevision 26590*
Aura Literary/Arts Review (Birmingham, AL) 56
The Aurelia Sentinel (Aurelia, IA) Unable to locate
The Aurora (Labrador City, NL, Can.) 35469
Aurora (Greenwood, NS, Can.) 35556
The Aurora Advertiser (Aurora, MO) 16894*
Aurora Advocate (Aurora, OH) 24639
The Aurora Beacon-News 8040*
Aurora Borealis (Aurora, IL) 8039
Aurora Cable TV, Ltd. (Aurora, ON, Can.) 35653
Aurora County Standard (Stickney, SD) Unable to locate
Aurora-Hoyt Lakes Range Facts (Aurora, MN) Unable to locate
Aurora Rising (Decatur, GA) 7234
Aurora Sentinel (Minneapolis, MN) Unable to locate
Austell Neighbor (Austell, GA) 7115
Austin American-Statesman (Austin, TX) 29755
Austin Broadcasting Corp. 29616*
Austin Broadcasting Corp. 29615*
Austin Business Journal (Austin, TX) 29756
Austin Cable Vision 29885*
Austin Chronicle (Pekin, IN) 10392
Austin Chronicle (Austin, TX) 29757
Austin Daily Herald (Austin, MN) 15723

B

Babson Bulletin **13830***
Baby; American (New York, NY) **21179**
Baby & Child; Northwest (Renton, WA) **32925**
The Baby Connection News Journal (San Antonio, TX) *Unable to locate*
Baby Huey (Los Angeles, CA) *Unable to locate*
Baby Journal; South Shore (Kingston, MA) **14265**
Baby Magazine (New York, NY) *Unable to locate*
Baby Shop (Pittsburgh, PA) **27761**
Baby Talk (New York, NY) **21283**
Baby Times (Miami, FL) *Unable to locate*
Babybug (Peru, IL) **9446**
Babyfish...Lost Its Momma (Detroit, MI) *Unable to locate*
Babylon Advertiser (Farmingdale, NY) *Ceased*
Babylon Beacon **20111***
Babylon South Bay's Shopper (Lindenhurst, NY) **20946**
babysue (Decatur, GA) **7235**
babysue review **7235***
Bachelor Book Magazine (Coral Springs, FL) *Unable to locate*
Bachelor No. 1 (New York, NY) *Unable to locate*
Bachelorette Book Magazine (Coral Springs, FL) *Unable to locate*
Bachow and Elkin Communications Inc. (Bala Cynwyd, PA) **26669**
Back Country Trader **3259***
The Back Forty (Wahpeton, ND) *Unable to locate*
Back to Godhead (San Diego, CA) *Unable to locate*
Back to Health Magazine (Deerfield Beach, FL) *Ceased*
Back Home (Hendersonville, NC) **23983**
Back Home in Kentucky (Franklin, TN) **29194**
Back Stage (New York, NY) *Unable to locate*
Back Stage/SHOOT **19158***
Back Stage West (New York, NY) **21284**
Back of the Yards Journal (Chicago, IL) **8279**
Background Notes on the Countries of the World (Pittsburgh, PA) **27762**
BackOffice Magazine (Nashua, NH) **18582**
Backpacker Magazine (Emmaus, PA) **26873**
Backspin (Winnipeg, MB, Can.) **35311**
Backstreets (Seattle, WA) *Ceased*
The Backstretch (Southfield, MI) *Unable to locate*
Backtracker (Rogers, AR) **1326**
Backwoods Home Magazine (Gold Beach, OR) **26359**
Bacteriology; Journal of (Washington, DC) **5575**
Bacteriology; Microbiology Abstracts, Section B (Bethesda, MD) **13319**
Bad Attitude (Cambridge, MA) **14040**
Bad Subjects (Berkeley, CA) **1493**
Badger Builder (Frankfort, KY) *Ceased*
The Badger Common'Tater (Antigo, WI) **33532**
Badger Farm Bureau News **33937***
The Badger Herald (Madison, WI) *Unable to locate*
Badger Legionnaire & American Legion Auxiliary Wisconsin (Milwaukee, WI) *Unable to locate*
The Badger Sportsman (Chilton, WI) **33623**
The Baffler Magazine (Chicago, IL) **8280**
Bagley Public Utilities (Bagley, MN) **15728**
Bagot; La Pensee de (Acton Vale, QC, Can.) **36929**
The Bagpipe (Denver, CO) **4306**
Baha'i News (Wilmette, IL) *Ceased*
The Baha'is (New York, NY) *Ceased*
Bahamas Magazine (Miami, FL) *Unable to locate*
Baikar Armenian Weekly (Watertown, MA) *Ceased*
Bailey County Journal (Muleshoe, TX) **30845**
Bailey News; Spring Hope Enterprise/ (Spring Hope, NC) **24244**
Bainbridge Cable (Bainbridge, NY) *Unable to locate*
The Bainbridge Island Review (Bainbridge Island, WA) **32657**
Baja Explorer (La Jolla, CA) *Unable to locate*
Bajo El Sol (Yuma, AZ) **1016**
Baker Cable TV **7985***
Baker City Herald (Baker City, OR) **26232**
The Baker County Press (Macclenny, FL) **6316**
Baker Observer (Baker, LA) **12478**
The Baker Street Journal (Hellertown, PA) **27037**
Bakers Journal (Delhi, ON, Can.) **35763**
The Bakersfield Californian (Bakersfield, CA) **1447**
Bakersfield News Observer (Bakersfield, CA) **1448**
Bakersfield's Shopper (Bakersfield, CA) **1449**
Bakery Production and Marketing (Chicago, IL) *Unable to locate*
Bakery; Snack Food and Wholesale (Deerfield, IL) **8728**
Baking (Itasca, IL) *Ceased*
Baking Buyer (Kansas City, MO) **17155**
Baking; Christmas Helps & Holiday (New York, NY) **21413**
Baking Management (Cleveland, OH) **24859**
Baking; Modern (Des Plaines, IL) **8763**
Baking News; Milling & (Kansas City, MO) **17185**
Baking & Snack (Kansas City, MO) **17156**
Baking Technical Bulletin; American Institute of (Manhattan, KS) **11619**
Baking; Woman's Day Holiday (New York, NY) **22928**

Balance (Birmingham, MI) **14823**
Balance (Alexandria, VA) **31646**
The Balance Sheet **7693***
Balaton-Press-Tribune (Balaton, MN) **15729**
Balaton-Russell-Press-Tribune-Record **15729***
Balcony Square **36386***
Bald Knob Banner (Bald Knob, AR) **1038**
Baldur Gazette **35251***
The Baldwin Citizen (Lynbrook, NY) *Unable to locate*
The Baldwin City Signal (Baldwin City, KS) **11351**
Baldwin Herald (Baldwin, NY) **20113**
Baldwin Leader; The Freeport- (Merrick, NY) **21071**
The Baldwin Ledger (Lawrence, KS) **11548**
Baldwin Park Highlander (City of Industry, CA) *Ceased*
Baldwin Shopper's Guide (Ontario, ON, Can.) **36157**
Baldwin Times (Bay Minette, AL) **51**
Baldwin's Ohio Legislative Service, Annotated (Cleveland, OH) **24860**
Baldwin's Ohio Monthly Record (Cleveland, OH) **24861**
Baldwinsville Messenger (Syracuse, NY) **23388**
Baldwinsville Pennysaver (Syracuse, NY) **23389**
The Baldwyn News (Baldwyn, MS) **16549**
Ball State Daily News (Muncie, IN) **10326**
Ball State University Forum (Muncie, IN) *Ceased*
Ballard News Tribune (Seattle, WA) **32944**
Ballard Strikes Softball Magazine (Oklahoma City, OK) **25953**
Ballet-Hoo (Winnipeg, MB, Can.) **35312**
Ballet Review (New York, NY) **21285**
The Ballinger Ledger (Ballinger, TX) **29887**
Balloon History and Museology; Annals of (Mayer, MN) **16048**
Balloon Life (Seattle, WA) **32945**
Balloons & Parties **18851***
Balloons & Parties Magazine (Hackensack, NJ) **18851**
Balloons & Parties Today **18851***
Ballston Journal (Ballston Spa, NY) **20119**
Ballston-Malta Pennysaver (Ballston, NY) **20118**
Baltimore Afro-American (Baltimore, MD) **13128**
Baltimore Business Journal (Baltimore, MD) **13129**
The Baltimore Chronicle (Baltimore, MD) **13130**
Baltimore City Paper (Baltimore, MD) **13131**
Baltimore Edition; Nursing Spectrum—Washington D.C. & (Falls Church, VA) **32050**
Baltimore Engineer **13240***
The Baltimore Enterprise and Inner Harbor News (Baltimore, MD) *Unable to locate*
Baltimore Gay Paper (Baltimore, MD) **13132**
The Baltimore Guide (Baltimore, MD) **13133**
Baltimore Guide; The (Baltimore, MD) **13133**
Baltimore Magazine (Baltimore, MD) **13134**
The Baltimore Messenger (Columbia, MD) **13453**
Baltimore; Port of (Towson, MD) **13764**
The Baltimore Sun (Baltimore, MD) **13135**
Baltimore Times (Baltimore, MD) **13136**
Baltimore; WHERE (Baltimore, MD) **13261**
Baltimore's Child (Baltimore, MD) **13137**
BAM Magazine (Concord, CA) **1750**
The Bamberg Herald **28479***
Bamboo Ridge (Honolulu, HI) **7680**
Bamboo Science & Culture (Seattle, WA) **32946**
The Bancroft Register (Bancroft, IA) **10616**
B&M Bulletin (Somerville, MA) **14532**
Bandwagon (Mulvane, KS) **11663**
Bandwagon (Columbus, OH) **24999**
Banff Crag & Canyon (Banff, AB, Can.) **34613**
Banff Crag and Canyon (Banff, AB, Can.) **34612**
Bangor Daily News (Bangor, ME) **12903**
Bank Accounting & Finance (Concord, MA) **14143**
Bank Automation Newsletter (New York, NY) *Ceased*
Bank of Boston Regional Review; Federal Reserve (Boston, MA) **13893**
Bank Compliance Alert (New York, NY) *Unable to locate*
Bank & Corporate Governance Law Reporter (Washington, DC) **5372**
Bank Director (Brentwood, TN) **29060**
Bank Director's Report (New York, NY) *Ceased*
Bank Facts (Toronto, ON, Can.) **36470**
Bank Financial Management International (Atlanta, GA) *Unable to locate*
Bank Financial Quarterly (Hartland, WI) **33776**
Bank Financial Quarterly; S & L—Savings (Hartland, WI) **33783**
Bank Investment Marketing (New York, NY) **21286**
Bank and Lender Liability Litigation Reporter (Wayne, PA) **28126**
The Bank Loan Officers Journal (New York, NY) *Ceased*
Bank Management **8281***
Bank Management (New York, NY) *Unable to locate*
Bank Marketing **5310***
Bank Marketing (Washington, DC) **5373**
Bank New Product News **21287***
Bank News (Shawnee Mission, KS) **11803**
Bank Note Reporter (Iola, WI) **33802**
The Bank Quarterly (Austin, TX) **29762**

Bank of Richmond Economic Quarterly; Federal Reserve (Richmond, VA) **32437**
Bank Systems & Technology (New York, NY) *Unable to locate*
Bank Tax Report (New York, NY) *Ceased*
Bank Technology News (New York, NY) **21287**
Banker; American (New York, NY) **21180**
Banker; Arkansas (Little Rock, AR) **1212**
Banker; Canadian (Toronto, ON, Can.) **36493**
Banker; Carolina (Raleigh, NC) **24129**
Banker; Future (New York, NY) **21743**
Banker; Hoosier (Indianapolis, IN) **10115**
Banker; Illinois (Springfield, IL) **9621**
Banker; Independent (Washington, DC) **5542**
Banker; The Kansas (Topeka, KS) **11826**
Banker; Kentucky (Louisville, KY) **12223**
Banker Magazine; Michigan (Lansing, MI) **15280**
Banker; The Mississippi (Jackson, MS) **16699**
Banker; The Ohio **25048***
Banker; Oklahoma (Oklahoma City, OK) **25973**
Banker; The Tennessee (Nashville, TN) **29488**
Banker & Tradesman (Boston, MA) *Unable to locate*
Bankers Digest (Dallas, TX) **30126**
The Bankers Magazine (New York, NY) *Ceased*
Bankers Monthly (New York, NY) *Ceased*
Banking Abstracts; World (New York, NY) **22940**
Banking and Finance Law Review (Toronto, ON, Can.) **36471**
Banking & Financial Services Policy Report (New York, NY) **21288**
Banking; Florida (Tallahassee, FL) **6706**
Banking Issues and Innovations in Products Marketing & Technology (Chicago, IL) *Ceased*
Banking Journal; ABA (New York, NY) **21130**
Banking; Journal of Money, Credit, and (Columbus, OH) **25025**
Banking Law Anthology *Ceased*
Banking Law Journal (New York, NY) **21289**
Banking Law Review (New York, NY) *Ceased*
Banking Magazine; Mortgage (Washington, DC) **5662**
Banking Software Review (Indianapolis, IN) *Ceased*
Banking Strategies (Chicago, IL) **8281**
Banking; Texas (Shawnee Mission, KS) **11805**
Banking Today **6706***
Bankruptcy Law Reports (Riverwoods, IL) **9501**
Bankruptcy Law Review (New York, NY) *Ceased*
Banks County News (Jefferson, GA) **7345**
Banks in Insurance Report (Hoboken, NJ) **18899**
The Banner (Riverside, CA) **2930**
Banner (San Francisco, CA) *Unable to locate*
Banner (St. Elmo, IL) **9576**
The Banner (Grand Rapids, MI) **15089**
Banner (Creighton, MO) *Ceased*
Banner (Deer Lodge, MT) **17780**
Banner (Russell, MB, Can.) **35288**
Banner-Democrat (Lake Providence, LA) **12652**
Banner Extra **36172***
The Banner-Gazette (Pekin, IN) **10393**
Banner-Graphic (Greencastle, IN) **10033**
Banner Independent (Booneville, MS) **16571**
Banner Journal (Black River Falls, WI) **33591**
Banner-News (Magnolia, AR) **1258**
Banner Post (Manning, AB, Can.) **34806**
The Banner-Press (Marble Hill, MO) **17262**
The Banner Press (Brenham, TX) **29448**
The Banner Press Newspaper (Columbus, TX) **30064**
Banner Sheep Magazine (Cuba, IL) **8699**
Bapist True Union **13454***
Baptist; The California Southern (Fresno, CA) **1946**
Baptist; The Canadian (Etobicoke, ON, Can.) **35813**
The Baptist Challenge (Little Rock, AR) **1224**
The Baptist Courier (Greenville, SC) **28621**
Baptist Herald (Oakbrook Terrace, IL) *Ceased*
Baptist Informer (Raleigh, NC) **24125**
Baptist Leader (Valley Forge, PA) *Ceased*
Baptist Message (LBM); Louisiana (Alexandria, LA) **12459**
Baptist Messenger (Oklahoma City, OK) **25954**
Baptist Messenger; Ohio (Columbus, OH) **25039**
The Baptist Program **29484***
Baptist Progress (Waxahachie, TX) **31269**
Baptist Quarterly; American (Valley Forge, PA) **28089**
The Baptist Record (Jackson, MS) **16694**
Baptist and Reflector (Brentwood, TN) **29061**
Baptist; Rocky Mountain (Centennial, CO) **4227**
The Baptist Standard (Dallas, TX) **30127**
Baptist Trumpet (Little Rock, AR) **1225**
The Baptist Visitor **35817***
Baptist Witness; Florida (Jacksonville, FL) **6210**
BaptistLIFE (Columbia, MD) **13454**
Bar Association Lawyers Journal; Massachusetts (Boston, MA) **13925**
Bar & Beverage Business Magazine (Winnipeg, MB, Can.) **35313**
Bar Bulletin; Queens (Flushing, NY) **20610**
Bar Code News **18630***
The Bar Examiner (Madison, WI) **33923**
The Bar Harbor Times (Bar Harbor, ME) **12917**
Bar Journal; California (San Francisco, CA) **3335**

Beach Bay News (Florala, AL) *Unable to locate*
Beach & Bay Press (San Diego, CA) **3119**
Beach Haven Times (Setauket, NY) *Unable to locate*
The Beach Journal (Aberdeen, WA) *Ceased*
The Beach Reporter (Manhattan Beach, CA) **2500**
The Beach Weekly (Sarasota, FL) **6654**
The Beachcomber (Surf City, NJ) *Unable to locate*
The Beacher (Michigan City, IN) **10303**
Beaches Leader/Ponte Vedra Leader (Jacksonville Beach, FL) **6247**
The Beacon **19210***
The Beacon (March Air Force Base, CA) **2503**
The Beacon (Spirit Lake, IA) **11236**
The Beacon (Concord, MA) **14144**
Beacon (Cannon Falls, MN) **15788**
Beacon (Melrose, MN) **16051**
The Beacon (Clifton, NJ) **18751**
Beacon (Princeton, NJ) *Unable to locate*
Beacon (Grants, NM) **19862**
The Beacon (Port Clinton, OH) **25480**
The Beacon (Portland, OR) **26468**
Beacon (Wilkes Barre, PA) **28163**
Beacon; The (Gander, NL, Can.) **35455**
The Beacon (Gander, NL, Can.) **35455**
The Beacon (Kipling, SK, Can.) *Ceased*
Beacon Express (Niceville, FL) **6461**
Beacon Free Press (Wappingers Falls, NY) **23501**
The Beacon Herald (Stratford, ON, Can.) **36409**
The Beacon Hill News (Seattle, WA) **32948**
The Beacon Hill Times (Boston, MA) **13853**
Beacon and Leader **17100***
Beacon Light (Beacon, NY) **20139**
Beacon Mailbag (Manahawkin, NJ) **19209**
The Beacon-News (Aurora, IL) **8040**
Beacon-News (Paris, IL) **9399**
The Beacon Newspaper (New Baltimore, MI) *Unable to locate*
The Beacon-Observer (Overton, NE) **18242**
Beacon Preview **14792***
Bead and Button (Waukesha, WI) **34395**
Beads (Ottawa, ON, Can.) **36186**
Beans & Bears! (Iola, WI) **33803**
The Bear Deluxe Magazine (Portland, OR) **26469**
The Bear Essential Magazine **26469***
Bear Essential News for Kids (Tempe, AZ) *Unable to locate*
The Bear Laker (Montpelier, ID) **7908**
Bear News (Hornepayne, ON, Can.) **35916**
Bear Report (Mundelein, IL) **9257**
Bears!; Beans & (Iola, WI) **33803**
Beasley Broadc **1238***
The Beat **10063***
Beat; The Hart (Hart, TX) **30432**
The Beat (Los Angeles) (Los Angeles, CA) **2217**
Beatles Fan Magazine (Orange, CT) **5090**
Beatrice Daily Sun (Beatrice, NE) **17947**
Beattyville Enterprise (Jackson, KY) **12143**
Beau (White Plains, NY) **23570**
Beauce Media-La Vallee de la Chaudiere (Ste.-Marie, QC, Can.) *Unable to locate*
The Beaufort Gazette (Beaufort, SC) **28487**
Beaumont Enterprise (Beaumont, TX) **29897**
Beaumont; Metropolitan (Beaumont, TX) **29899**
Beaumont Nouvelle **34692***
Beaumont Nouvelle (Devon, AB, Can.) **34692**
Beauport Express (Beauport, QC, Can.) **36948**
Beauregard Daily News (Deridder, LA) **12564**
Beautiful British Columbia **35210***
Beauty (New York, NY) *Unable to locate*
Beauty Age (New York, NY) *Ceased*
Beauty Education (Clifton Park, NY) *Unable to locate*
Beauty Fashion (New York, NY) *Unable to locate*
Beauty Inc. (Scottsdale, AZ) *Ceased*
The Beaver **2994***
The Beaver (Winnipeg, MB, Can.) **35314**
Beaver County Legal Journal (Beaver, PA) *Unable to locate*
Beaver County News (St George, UT) *Unable to locate*
Beaver County Times (Beaver, PA) **26684**
Beaver Creek Features (Cleveland, OH) **37832**
Beaver; Napanee (Napanee, ON, Can.) **36098**
Beaver; Oakville (Oakville, ON, Can.) **36147**
The Beaver Press (Beaver, UT) **31320**
Beaver Valley Times **26684***
Beavercreek News (Kettering, OH) *Unable to locate*
Beaverton Clarion; Gladwin County Record and (Gladwin, MI) **15080**
Beaverton Valley Times (Portland, OR) **26470**
Bebidas (Overland Park, KS) *Unable to locate*
Bec- Producer; The Western (Elk Grove, CA) **1875**
Bece Cable Inc. **509***
Becker County Record (Detroit Lakes, MN) **15828**
Beckett Baseball Card Monthly (Dallas, TX) *Unable to locate*
Beckett Basketball Card Monthly (Dallas, TX) *Unable to locate*
Beckett Focus on Future Stars (Dallas, TX) *Ceased*

Beckett Football Card Monthly (Dallas, TX) *Unable to locate*
Beckett Hockey Monthly (Dallas, TX) *Unable to locate*
Beckett Sports Collectibles and Autographs (Dallas, TX) **30130**
Becks Cable Systems (Ramsey, IL) **9485**
Bedding Magazine **31647***
Bedford/Blair Shoppers' Guide **26914***
Bedford Bullet (Bedford, VA) **31860**
The Bedford Bulletin (Bedford, NH) *Unable to locate*
Bedford Bulletin (Bedford, VA) **31861**
Bedford Cablevision (Bedford, VA) **31862**
Bedford Cablevision Ltd. (Temperance, MI) *Unable to locate*
Bedford Daily Gazette (Bedford, PA) **26688**
Bedford Historical Quarterly (Normandy, TN) **29546**
Bedford Journal (Milford, NH) **18576**
Bedford Minuteman (Bedford, MA) **13835**
The Bedford Sackville Daily News **35545***
Bedford Sun Banner (Bedford, OH) **24660**
Bedford Times-Register (Bedford, OH) **24661**
Bedminster Press; Hills- (Bedminster, NJ) **18668**
Bedroom (Providence, RI) **28388**
Bedroom Magazine (Torrance, CA) *Ceased*
BEDTimes (Alexandria, VA) **31647**
The Bee **31991***
The Bee (Jefferson, IA) **11005**
The Bee (Hutchinson, KS) *Unable to locate*
The Bee (Portland, OR) *Unable to locate*
The Bee (Daingerfield, TX) **30118**
The Bee (Phillips, WI) **34237**
Bee County Enterprise (Beeville, TX) *Ceased*
Bee Culture (Medina, OH) **24772**
Bee-Journal (Canastota, NY) *Unable to locate*
Bee; Phillips (Phillips, WI) **34239**
Beebe News (Beebe, AR) **1045**
Beecher City Journal (Beecher City, IL) **8058**
Beecher Herald (Beecher, IL) **8057**
BEEF (Minneapolis, MN) **16059**
Beef Cattleman; American (Allen, KS) **11336**
Beef Cattleman; Missouri (Kansas City, MO) **17186**
Beef Extra **11403***
Beef; Illinois (Springfield, IL) **9622**
Beef; Indiana (Indianapolis, IN) **10123**
Beef Magazine; Alberta (Calgary, AB, Can.) **34625**
The Beef Producer (Decatur, IL) **8709**
Beef Producer; Oregon (Salem, OR) **26569**
Beef Quarterly; Atlantic (Liverpool, NS, Can.) **35587**
Beef Today (Council Grove, KS) **11403**
The Beefmaster Cowman (San Antonio, TX) **31025**
Beefweek (Macon, GA) *Unable to locate*
Beer (Hayward, CA) *Ceased*
Beer Magazine (Ottawa, ON, Can.) *Unable to locate*
Beethoven Forum (Chapel Hill, NC) **23699**
The Beethoven Journal (San Jose, CA) **3511**
The Beethoven Newsletter **3511***
Beetle Bailey (Santa Monica, CA) *Unable to locate*
The Beeton Record Sentinel (Beeton, ON, Can.) **35673**
Beeville Bee—Picayune (Picayune, TX) **30934**
Before & After (Roseville, CA) **2970**
Behavior Abstracts; Linguistics and Language (Bethesda, MD) **13357**
Behavior; AIDS and (New York, NY) **21167**
Behavior Analysis & Therapy; PsycSCAN: (Washington, DC) **5745**
Behavior; Animal Learning and (Austin, TX) **29754**
Behavior; CyberPsychology and (Larchmont, NY) **20895**
Behavior; Environment and (Tucson, AZ) **946**
Behavior; Ethics & (Boston, MA) **13890**
Behavior and Evolution; Brain, (Farmington, CT) **4801**
Behavior Genetics (New York, NY) **21293**
Behavior, and Immunity; Brain, (San Diego, CA) **3124**
Behavior & Information Technology (Philadelphia, PA) **27387**
Behavior; Journal of Health & Social (Blacksburg, VA) **31875**
Behavior; The Journal of Mind and (Orono, ME) **13000**
Behavior; Journal of Nonverbal (New York, NY) **22146**
Behavior; Journal of Organizational (Hoboken, NJ) **19037**
Behavior Modification (Thousand Oaks, CA) **3852**
Behavior and Personality; Journal of Social (Novato, CA) **2650**
Behavior; Pharmacology Biochemistry and (San Antonio, TX) **31041**
Behavior; Physiology & (San Antonio, TX) **31042**
Behavior Research Methods, Instruments, & Computers (Austin, TX) **29763**
Behavioral Assessment; Journal of Psychopathology & (New York, NY) **22170**
Behavioral and Brain Sciences (New York, NY) **21294**
Behavioral Decision Making; Journal of (Hoboken, NJ) **19005**
Behavioral Disorders (Arlington, VA) *Unable to locate*

Behavioral Education; Journal of (New York, NY) **22006**
Behavioral Finance; The Journal of (Mahwah, NJ) **19195**
Behavioral Health Management (Cleveland, OH) **24863**
Behavioral Health Services & Research; Journal of (Tampa, FL) **6769**
Behavioral Interventions (Hoboken, NJ) **18901**
Behavioral Medicine (Washington, DC) **5374**
Behavioral Medicine Abstracts **2112***
Behavioral Medicine; Annals of (La Jolla, CA) **2112**
Behavioral Medicine; International Journal of (Mahwah, NJ) **19192**
Behavioral Medicine; Journal of (New York, NY) **22007**
Behavioral Medicine Update **2112***
Behavioral Neurology; Neuropsychiatry, Neuropsychology, and (Baltimore, MD) **13224**
Behavioral Neuroscience (Washington, DC) **5375**
Behavioral Research in Accounting (East Lansing, MI) **14982**
Behavioral Research; Multivariate (Tempe, AZ) **911**
Behavioral Residential Treatment (Hoboken, NJ) *Ceased*
Behavioral Science (Fallbrook, CA) *Unable to locate*
Behavioral Science; Integrative Physiological and (Somerset, NJ) **19562**
Behavioral Science; Journal of Applied (Thousand Oaks, CA) **3879**
Behavioral Sciences; Hispanic Journal of (Thousand Oaks, CA) **3871**
Behavioral Sciences and the Law (Hoboken, NJ) **18902**
Behavioral Scientist; American (Thousand Oaks, CA) **3848**
Behavioral & Social Sciences Librarian (DeKalb, IL) **8731**
Behavioral Statistics; Journal of Educational and (Washington, DC) **5583**
Behaviors; Psychology of Addictive (Washington, DC) **5742**
Behavorial Assessment *Ceased*
Behind the Headlines (Toronto, ON, Can.) **36473**
Beirut Times (Los Angeles, CA) **2218**
The Bel Air Post (Los Angeles, CA) *Ceased*
Belarusan; Bielarus/The (Jamaica, NY) **20831**
Belgrade Observer (Belgrade, MN) **15735**
Belhaven Cable TV (Belhaven, NC) **23641**
Belize First Magazine (Candler, NC) **23682**
Bell-Enterprise; Remsen (Remsen, IA) **11175**
Bell Gardens Review (Bell Gardens, CA) **1483**
Bell Journal of Economics **3714***
Bell/Maywood/Cudahy Industrial Post (Bell, CA) **1482**
Bellaire Monthly (Houston, TX) *Unable to locate*
The Belle Banner (Belle, MO) **16899**
Belle Mead/Hillsborough Beacon and Manville House (Princeton, NJ) *Unable to locate*
Belle Plaine Herald (Belle Plaine, MN) **15736**
The Belle Plaine News (Belle Plaine, KS) **11354**
The Belle Plaine Union (Marengo, IA) **11059**
Belle River North Essex News **35675***
The Bellefontaine Examiner (Bellefontaine, OH) **24666**
Bellerose North Pennysaver; Floral Park (Floral Park, ON, Can.) **35833**
Bellerose South Pennysaver; Floral Park (Floral Park, ON, Can.) **35834**
Belles Lettres (Charlottesville, VA) **31918**
The Belletrist Review (Plainville, CT) *Ceased*
Belleville Cable TV (Belleville, KS) **11359**
The Belleville Enterprise (Belleville, WI) **14806**
Belleville Journal (Belleville, IL) **8059**
Belleville News-Democrat (Belleville, IL) **8060**
Belleville Post (Bloomfield, NJ) **18685**
Belleville Recorder (Belleville, WI) **33572**
Belleville Telescope (Belleville, KS) **11356**
Belleville Times (West Paterson, NJ) **19726**
The Bellevue Gazette (Bellevue, OH) **24669**
Bellevue-Geddes Pennysaver (Syracuse, NY) **23390**
Bellevue Leader (Bellevue, NE) **17951**
Bellevue RFD News (Bellevue, OH) **24670**
Bellflower Herald American; Paramount/ (Paramount, CA) **2809**
The Bellingham Business Journal (Bellingham, WA) **32675**
The Bellingham Herald (Mc Lean, VA) **32242**
Bellingham Review (Bellingham, WA) **32676**
Bellmore Life (Merrick, NY) **21070**
Bellmore/Merrick North Shopper's Guide (Ontario, ON, Can.) **36159**
Bellmore/Merrick Observer (Bellmore, NY) **20146**
Bellmore South This Week/Pennysaver (Bellmore, HI) **7659**
Bellowing Ark (Seattle, WA) **32949**
The Bellows Falls Town Crier (Bellows Falls, VT) **31494**
Bellport/East Patchogue Suffolk Life (Bellport, NY) **20148**
The Bells (Belton, TX) **29915**

Numbers cited in bold after listings are entry numbers rather than page numbers.

The Bi-County Messenger (Monett, MO) *Unable to locate*
Bi-State Reporter (Grayslake, IL) *Ceased*
Bible Advocate (Denver, CO) **4307**
The Bible Friend (Minneapolis, MN) **16061**
Bible Reader; Weekly (Cincinnati, OH) **24828**
Bible Review (Washington, DC) *Unable to locate*
Bible Society Record; American (New York, NY) **21181**
Bible and Spade (Landisville, PA) **27157**
Bible Standard and Herald of Christ's Kingdom (Chester Springs, PA) **26777**
The Bible Today (Collegeville, MN) **15805**
Biblical Archaeologist (Champaign, IL) *Unable to locate*
Biblical Archaeology Review (Washington, DC) *Unable to locate*
The Biblical Evangelist (Ingleside, TX) *Ceased*
Biblical History (Leesburg, VA) *Ceased*
Biblical Literature; Journal of (Atlanta, GA) **7020**
Biblical Quarterly; The Catholic (Washington, DC) **5399**
Biblical Recorder (Raleigh, NC) **24126**
Biblical Studies; Journal of (Riverview, MI) **15465**
Biblical Theology Bulletin (South Orange, NJ) **19583**
Biblio (Eugene, OR) *Ceased*
Bibliographical Society of America; Papers of the (Columbia, SC) **28561**
Bibliography; Bulletin of (Raleigh, NC) **24127**
Bibliography; Inter-American Review of (Washington, DC) **5548**
Biblion (Westport, CT) *Ceased*
Bibliotheca Medica Canadiana (Winnipeg, MB, Can.) **35315**
Bibliotheca Sacra (Dallas, TX) **30132**
Bichon Frise News *Ceased*
Bicycle Business Journal (Fort Worth, TX) *Ceased*
Bicycle Dealer Strategies (Beaverton, OR) *Unable to locate*
Bicycle Guide (Lehigh Valley, PA) *Unable to locate*
The Bicycle Paper (Seattle, WA) **32951**
Bicycle Retailer and Industry News (New York, NY) **21308**
BICYCLE USA (Baltimore, MD) *Unable to locate*
Bicycling (Emmaus, PA) **26874**
Bid & Ask (Blaine, WA) *Unable to locate*
Bielarus/The Belarusan (Jamaica, NY) **20831**
Bielarus/The Byelorussian **20831***
Bielaruskaya Dumka (South River, NJ) **19592**
Bielaruski Holas (Byelorussian Voice) (Toronto, ON, Can.) *Unable to locate*
Bienvenidos a Miami (Miami, FL) **6341**
Bienville Democrat/Ringgold Record (Arcadia, LA) **12476**
BiereMag (Ottawa, ON, Can.) **36187**
Big Apple Parents (New York, NY) *Unable to locate*
Big Bear Life & the Grizzly (Big Bear Lake, CA) **1580**
The Big Bend Sentinel (Marfa, TX) **30764**
Big Bend Studies; Journal of (Alpine, TX) **29683**
Big Bend/Vernon Bulletin **34159***
Big Buck (Saskatoon, SK, Can.) **37548**
Big Canoe Cable TV System (Big Canoe, GA) **7127**
Big City Blues Magazine (Royal Oak, MI) **15477**
Big Country Farm & Ranch News (Anson, TX) *Unable to locate*
Big Horn County News (Hardin, MT) **17811**
Big Island; This Week (Honolulu, HI) **7724**
The Big Lake Wildcat (Big Lake, TX) **29919**
Big Muddy (Cape Girardeau, MO) **16943**
Big Pasture News (Grandfield, OK) **25845**
The Big Picture (Cincinnati, OH) **24779**
Big Pine Key Free Press; Marathon/ (Marathon, FL) **6322**
Big Red Hen Productions (New York, NY) **37836**
Big Red News **22437***
The Big Reel (Iola, WI) **33804**
Big River Cablevision **34387***
The Big Sandy & Hawkins Journal and Tri Area News (Big Sandy, TX) **29920**
Big Sandy Mountaineer (Big Sandy, MT) **17726**
The Big Sandy News (Louisa, KY) **12208**
Big Sandy TV Cable, Inc. (West Van Lear, KY) **12436**
Big Saver (Middletown, NY) **21079**
Big Shout Magazine (Wilmington, DE) *Unable to locate*
Big South Fork Cablevision **29555***
Big Spring Herald (Big Spring, TX) **29924**
The Big Takeover (New York, NY) **21309**
The Big Timber Pioneer (Big Timber, MT) **17727**
Big Truck Trader (Park Hills, KY) *Unable to locate*
Big White Mountaineer (Big White, BC, Can.) **34885**
Big World (Lancaster, PA) **27139**
Bigfoot Prints **33098***
Bigfork Eagle (Bigfork, MT) **17728**
The Biggs News/Butte County Reporter (Biggs, CA) *Unable to locate*
Bijo Cablevision Inc. **7570***

Bijou (Montreal, QC, Can.) *Ceased*
Bike Action; Mountain (Valencia, CA) **3981**
Bike, Boat & R.V. Trader/Moto, Bateau & Vehicules Recreatif Hebdo (Montreal, QC, Can.) **37091**
Bike; Hot (Anaheim, CA) **1406**
Bike Magazine; Dirt (Valencia, CA) **3977**
Bike Racing Nation **4259***
Bike Tech (Emmaus, PA) *Ceased*
Biker (Agoura, CA) **1377**
Biker Lifestyle **1377***
Biking; Mountain (Canoga Park, CA) **1658**
Bildgebung/Imagaing (Farmington, CT) *Ceased*
Bildor **15016***
Bilingual Review/Revista Bilingue (Tempe, AZ) **900**
Bill Austin **29614***
Bill of Fare *Ceased*
Bill of Rights Journal; William & Mary (Williamsburg, VA) **32621**
Billboard (New York, NY) *Unable to locate*
Billerica Minuteman (Needham, MA) **14349**
The Billerica News (Somerville, MA) *Unable to locate*
Billiards Digest (Chicago, IL) **8283**
Billings Business Journal (Billings, MT) *Ceased*
Billings County Pioneer (Beach, ND) **24343**
The Billings Gazette (Billings, MT) **17729**
Billings News; Garber- (Garber, OK) **25842**
The Billings Outpost (Billings, MT) **17730**
Billings Tele-Communications Inc. **17735***
The Billings Times (Billings, MT) **17731**
The Biloxi-D'Iberville Press (Biloxi, MS) *Unable to locate*
BIN Merchandiser **2852***
Bingo Bugle (Plantation, FL) *Unable to locate*
Bingo Bugle (Vancouver, BC, Can.) *Unable to locate*
Bingo and Gaming News (Vacaville, CA) **3973**
Bingo Today (Bellevue, WA) *Unable to locate*
Binnewater Tides (Rosendale, NY) **23277**
Binocular Vision & Eye Muscle Surgery **4399***
Binocular Vision & Strabismus Quarterly (Dillon, CO) **4399**
Bio File (Teaneck, NJ) **37837**
Bio/Technology **22410***
Biocatalysis (New York, NY) *Unable to locate*
Biochemical and Biophysical Research Communications (San Diego, CA) **3120**
Biochemical Genetics (Austin, TX) **29764**
Biochemical and Molecular Medicine **3235***
Biochemical and Molecular Toxicology; Journal of (Hoboken, NJ) **19006**
Biochemistry (Washington, DC) *Unable to locate*
Biochemistry; Analytical (San Diego, CA) **3113**
Biochemistry and Behavior; Pharmacology (San Antonio, TX) **31041**
Biochemistry and Biophysics; Archives of (San Diego, CA) **3116**
Biochemistry and Biotechnology; Applied (Medford, MA) **14319**
Biochemistry & Biotechnology; Preparative (Boynton Beach, FL) **5952**
Biochemistry and Cell Biology (Biochimie et Biologie Cellulaire) (Winnipeg, MB, Can.) **35316**
Biochemistry; Cellular Physiology and (Farmington, CT) **4805**
Biochemistry; Fish Physiology and (New York, NY) **21702**
Biochemistry and Function; Cell (Hoboken, NJ) **18909**
Biochemistry; Journal of Cellular (Hoboken, NJ) **19008**
Biochemistry and Microbiology; Applied (New York, NY) **21228**
Biochemistry; Molecular and Cellular (New York, NY) **22356**
Biochemistry (Moscow) (New York, NY) **21310**
Biochemistry and Physiology; Archives of Insect (Hoboken, NJ) **18897**
Biochemistry and Physiology; Journal of Evolutionary (New York, NY) **22066**
Biochemistry and Physiology; Pesticide (Davis, CA) **1817**
(Biochimie et Biologie Cellulaire); Biochemistry and Cell Biology (Winnipeg, MB, Can.) **35316**
BioChromatography (Westborough, MA) *Ceased*
BioComplexity (New York, NY) **21311**
Bioconjugate Chemistry (Washington, DC) *Unable to locate*
BioControl (New York, NY) **21312**
BioCycle (Emmaus, PA) **26875**
Biodiversity and Conservation (New York, NY) **21313**
Biodynamics (San Francisco, CA) **3331**
Bioeconomics; Journal of (New York, NY) **22008**
Bioelectromagnetics (Hoboken, NJ) **18903**
Bioenergetics and Biomembranes; Journal of (New York, NY) **22009**
BioEngineering Abstracts (Bethesda, MD) **13320**
Bioengineering; Biotechnology & (Hoboken, NJ) **18907**
Biofeedback; Applied Psychophysiology and (New York, NY) **21233**
Biofeedback and Self-Regulation (New York, NY) **21314**

Biofouling (New York, NY) *Unable to locate*
Biogerontology (New York, NY) **21315**
Biographical Record; The New York Genealogical and (New York, NY) **22443**
Biography (Honolulu, HI) **7681**
Biography (New York, NY) **21316**
Biography; Current (Bronx, NY) **20265**
Biography Index (Bronx, NY) **20254**
Biography; Pennsylvania Magazine of History and (Philadelphia, PA) **27623**
Biography; Virginia Magazine of History and (Richmond, VA) **32465**
Biological Abstracts (Philadelphia, PA) *Unable to locate*
Biological Abstracts/RRM (Reports, Reviews, Meetings) (Philadelphia, PA) *Unable to locate*
Biological & Agricultural Index (Bronx, NY) **20255**
Biological Association of the United Kingdom; Journal of the Marine (New York, NY) **22121**
The Biological Bulletin (Woods Hole, MA) **14672**
Biological Chemistry; The Journal of (Bethesda, MD) **13350**
Biological Control (San Diego, CA) **3121**
Biological, and Environmental Statistics; Journal of Agricultural, (Washington, DC) **5567**
Biological Farming News (Albuquerque, NM) *Unable to locate*
Biological Invasions (New York, NY) **21317**
Biological Mass Spectrometry **19029***
Biological Membranes: CSA Biochemistry Abstracts, Part 1 (Bethesda, MD) *Ceased*
Biological Oceanography (Philadelphia, PA) *Ceased*
Biological Physics; Journal of (New York, NY) **22010**
Biological Physics Research; Virtual Journal of (College Park, MD) **13444**
Biological Reviews of the Cambridge Philosophical Society (New York, NY) **21318**
Biological Rhythms; Journal of (Evanston, IL) **8863**
Biological Sciences; Doklady (New York, NY) **21563**
Biological Sciences; Historical Studies in the Physical and (Berkeley, CA) **1525**
Biological Sciences & Living Resources; ASFA/ Aquatic Sciences & Fisheries Abstracts Part 1: (Bethesda, MD) **13316**
Biological Signals and Receptors **4846***
Biological Survey Miscellaneous Contributions; Ohio (Columbus, OH) **25040**
Biological Therapies in Dentistry (Hamilton, ON, Can.) **35874**
Biologie Cellulaire); Biochemistry and Cell Biology (Biochimie et (Winnipeg, MB, Can.) **35316**
Biology; American Journal of Human (Hoboken, NJ) **18885**
Biology; Annals of Human (Philadelphia, PA) **27378**
Biology; Arteriosclerosis, Thrombosis, and Vascular (Iowa City, IA) **10969**
Biology (Biochimie et Biologie Cellulaire); Biochemistry and Cell (Winnipeg, MB, Can.) **35316**
Biology Bulletin (New York, NY) **21319**
Biology Bulletin Monthly (Northbrook, IL) *Ceased*
Biology; Developmental (San Diego, CA) **3140**
Biology Digest (Medford, NJ) **19221**
Biology; DNA and Cell (Larchmont, NY) **20897**
Biology and Fisheries; Reviews in Fish (New York, NY) **22664**
Biology of Fishes; Environmental (New York, NY) **21613**
Biology; Fungal Genetics and (San Diego, CA) **3158**
Biology; Human (Lawrence, KS) **11552**
Biology; Invertebrate (Santa Cruz, CA) **3684**
Biology; The Journal of Cell (New York, NY) **22019**
Biology; Journal of Computational (Larchmont, NY) **20910**
Biology; Journal of Crustacean (Seminole, FL) **6684**
Biology; Journal of the History of (New York, NY) **22089**
Biology; Journal of Membrane (New York, NY) **22132**
Biology; Journal of Structural (San Diego, CA) **3213**
Biology Magazine; IEEE Engineering in Medicine and (Piscataway, NJ) **19424**
Biology and Medicine; Bulletin of Experimental (New York, NY) **21350**
Biology & Medicine; The Yale Journal of (New Haven, CT) **5005**
Biology; Molecular (New York, NY) **22353**
Biology; Molecular and Cellular (Washington, DC) **5658**
Biology of the Neonate (Farmington, CT) **4799**
Biology and Neoplasia; Journal of Mammary Gland (New York, NY) **22119**
Biology; The Quarterly Review of (Stony Brook, NY) **23375**
Biology Reporter; Plant Molecular (Athens, GA) **6948**
Biology of Reproduction (Madison, WI) **33924**
Biology Reviews; Microbiology and Molecular (Washington, DC) **5648**
Biology; Russian Journal of Developmental (New York, NY) **22686**

3286

Numbers cited in bold after listings are entry numbers rather than page numbers.

Blake/An Illustrated Quarterly (Rochester, NY) 23211
Blakely Cable Television, Inc. (Blakely, GA) Unable to locate
Blanco County News (Blanco, TX) 29927
Bland Courier (Belle, MO) 16900
The Bland Messenger Unable to locate
Blandinsville Star Gazette (Macomb, IL) Ceased
Blasdell Lackawanna Pennysaver (Blasdell, NY) 20234
Blast! Magazine (Nashville, TN) Unable to locate
The Blazer (Joliet, IL) 9030
Blazer News (Jackson, MI) 15220
The Bledsonian Banner (Pikeville, TN) 29567
Blenheim News-Tribune (Blenheim, ON, Can.) 35686
Blessing, Inc. 28430*
The Blessings of Liberty (Pinehurst, NC) Ceased
Bley Cable Inc. (Beardstown, IL) Unable to locate
Blind; Matilda Ziegler Magazine for the (New York, NY) 22299
Blissfield Advance 14827*
Blitz (Los Angeles, CA) 2222
The Blitz (Oakland, CA) 2669
BLK (Los Angeles, CA) 2223
Block Island Cable TV Inc. (Block Island, RI) 28325
Blockbuster (Fort Lauderdale, FL) Unable to locate
Blockstone Cable TV (Coeur d'Alene, ID) Unable to locate
Blood (Philadelphia, PA) 27389
Blood Alley (Vancouver, BC, Can.) Unable to locate
Blood Cells, Molecules, & Diseases (San Diego, CA) 3122
Blood Flow and Metabolism; Journal of Cerebral (Baltimore, MD) 13182
The Blood-Horse (Lexington, KY) 12161
Blood Pressure Research; Kidney and (Farmington, CT) 4839
Blood Purification (Farmington, CT) 4800
Blood Substitutes and Immobilization Biotechnology; Artificial Cells, (New York, NY) 21256
Blood Weekly (Atlanta, GA) 6980
Bloodlines (Kalamazoo, MI) 15232
Bloodlines; Coonhound (Kalamazoo, MI) 15235
Bloomberg Business News (New York, NY) 37839
Bloomberg Magazine 19454*
Bloomberg Markets Magazine (Princeton, NJ) 19454
Bloomer Advance (Bloomer, WI) 33596
The Bloomfield Democrat (Bloomfield, IA) 10622
Bloomfield Journal (Bloomfield, CT) 4700
Bloomfield Life (West Paterson, NJ) 19727
Bloomfield Monitor (Bloomfield, NE) 17961
The Bloomfield News (Bloomfield, IN) 9820
The Bloomfield Vindicator 16907*
Blooming Prairie News 15757*
Blooming Prairie Times (Blooming Prairie, MN) 15757
Bloomingdale/Glendale Heights Press (Oak Brook, IL) 9342
Bloomingdale Voice (Schaumburg, IL) Ceased
Bloomington Cable Inc. (Bloomington, TX) 29928
The Bloomington Independent (Bloomington, IN) 9824
Bloomington/Normal, Inc.; TCI of (Normal, IL) 9307
Bloomington Sun Current (Eden Prairie, MN) 15866
The Bloomington Voice 9824*
The Bloomsbury Review (Denver, CO) 4309
Bloomville Gazette (Bloomville, OH) 24681
Blossom Times (Blossom, TX) 29929
Blountstown County Record 5925*
The Blount Countian (Oneonta, AL) 404
The Blount County Shopping Guide (Oneonta, AL) 405
The Blowing Rocket (Blowing Rock, NC) 23650
Blue Book of Fur Farming (Eden Prairie, MN) Unable to locate
Blue Chart Report Ceased
Blue & Gold Illustrated—Notre Dame Football (Notre Dame, IN) 10368
Blue and Gray (Harrogate, TN) Ceased
The Blue and Grey 13514*
Blue Hill Leader (Blue Hill, NE) 17962
Blue Island Sun-Standard (Chicago, IL) Unable to locate
blue jean magazine (Victor, NY) Unable to locate
Blue Line Magazine (Markham, ON, Can.) 36014
Blue List of Current Municipal and Corporate Offerings (New York, NY) Unable to locate
Blue Mound Leader (Blue Mound, IL) 8088
Blue Mountain Buyer's Guide (Collingwood, ON, Can.) Ceased
Blue Mountain Eagle (John Day, OR) 26378
Blue Mountain TV Cable Co. (Mount Vernon, OR) 26441
The Blue Penny Quarterly (Charlottesville, VA) 31919
Blue Rapids Times (Westmoreland, KS) Ceased
Blue Ridge Business Journal (Greenville, SC) Unable to locate
Blue Ridge Cable (Palmerton, PA) 27349
Blue Ridge Cable Television Inc. (Milford, PA) 27264
Blue Ridge CATV (York Haven, PA) Ceased
Blue Ridge CATV Inc. (Ephrata, PA) 26890
Blue Ridge Country (Roanoke, VA) 32489

The Blue Ridge Digest 23628*
Blue Ridge Leader (Purcellville, VA) 32339
The Blue Ridge Sun 32172*
Blue Springs Examiner (Daily Edition) (Blue Springs, MO) 16908
Blue Springs Examiner (Wednesday Edition) (Blue Springs, MO) 16909
Blue Springs & Independence Examiner Extra (Daily Edition) (Independence, MO) 17108
Blue Springs & Independence Examiner Suburban Life (Wednesday Edition) (Independence, MO) 17109
Blue Stocking (Portland, OR) Unable to locate
Blue Unicorn (Kensington, CA) 2100
Blue Valley Edition; Leawood Sun, (Lake Quivera, KS) 11543
Blue Valley Gazette (Shawnee Mission, KS) Ceased
Blue Water Legal and Business News (Port Huron, MI) Unable to locate
Blue and White 27324*
Blueboy (New York, NY) Unable to locate
Bluefield Motorist 33252*
Bluefieldian (Bluefield, WV) 33253
Bluegrass Music News (Russellville, KY) 12388
Bluegrass Truck Edition; Fastline— (Buckner, KY) 11968
Bluegrass Unlimited (Warrenton, VA) 32599
Bluejacket (Memphis, TN) Unable to locate
Blueline (Potsdam) (Potsdam, NY) 23137
Blueridge Cable Co. (Mansfield, PA) 27220
Blues Access (Boulder, CO) Ceased
Blues; Living (University, MS) 16866
Blues Magazine; Big City (Royal Oak, MI) 15477
Blues Magazine; Cadence Jazz and (Redwood, NY) 23179
Blues Revue (Salem, WV) 33463
Blues Revue Quarterly 33463*
Bluewater Scuba Electronic & Fax Update (Tallahassee, FL) 6701
Bluewater TV Cable Ltd. (Clinton, ON, Can.) 35738
Bluffs Monitor Birch Cliff News (Scarborough, ON, Can.) Ceased
Bluffs Times (Bluffs, IL) 8089
Bluffton News (Bluffton, OH) 24682
Bluffton News-Banner (Bluffton, IN) 9863
Blushing Bride (Jamaica, NY) Unable to locate
The Blythe Advertiser 1588*
Blythe Spirit (Blytheville, AR) Ceased
Blytheville Courier News (Blytheville, AR) 1057
Blytheville TV Cable Co. 1060*
BME (New York, NY) Unable to locate
BMWE Journal (Southfield, MI) 15542
BMX Plus! (Valencia, CA) 3976
BNA Online (Washington, DC) Ceased
BNA Topics (Deep River, ON, Can.) 35761
BNAC Communicator (Silver Spring, MD) Unable to locate
B'nai B'rith (Washington, DC) 5379
BNA's International Letter (Washington, DC) Ceased
BNH The Business of New Hampshire 18556*
Board Converting News (Avon by the Sea, NJ) 18662
The Boardman 12495*
Boardman Leader (Warren, OH) Ceased
Boardman News (Boardman, OH) 24684
The Boardmember 12495*
Boardwatch Magazine (Golden, CO) 4463
Boat Journal 6981*
Boat Magazine; Pontoon & Deck (Idaho Falls, ID) 7867
Boat Modeler; Radio Control (Ridgefield, CT) 5100
Boat and Motor Dealer (Niles, IL) 9286
Boat Owner; DIY (Dallas, TX) 30151
Boat & RV Trader (Park Hills, KY) Unable to locate
Boat & R.V. Trader/Moto, Bateau & Vehicules Recreatif Hebdo; Bike, (Montreal, QC, Can.) 37091
BOAT/U.S. Reports 31648*
BoatBuilder; Professional (Brooklin, ME) 12932
Boating Business (Oakville, ON, Can.) Unable to locate
Boating; Classic (Oconomowoc, WI) 34201
Boating Digest (Yarmouth, ME) Ceased
Boating Life (Winter Park, FL) 6877
Boating Magazine (New York, NY) 21329
Boating; Mid-America (Cleveland Heights, OH) 24994
Boating News (Vancouver, BC, Can.) Unable to locate
Boating Product News (New York, NY) Unable to locate
Boating; Rhode Island (East Greenwich, RI) 28342
Boating & Sailing; Motor (New York, NY) 22371
Boating World (Atlanta, GA) 6981
Boatings Caribbean Sports & Travel Magazine; Pleasure (Miami, FL) 6376
Boatracing Magazine (Monroe, WA) Ceased
Boats; The duPont Registry: A Buyer's Gallery of Fine (St. Petersburg, FL) 6624
Boats Magazine; Trailer (Carson, CA) 1677
BoatU.S. Magazine (Alexandria, VA) 31648

Bob Watkins Sports 24 Magazine (Glendale, KY) Ceased
Bobbin Magazine (Columbia, SC) 28545
Bobina; La (Columbia, SC) 28556
Bob's Feints (Escondido, CA) Unable to locate
Boca Community News; West (Chicago, IL) 8603
Boca Isles (Delray Beach, FL) Ceased
Boca Raton Community News (Boca Raton, IL) 8092
Boca Raton/Delray Beach Monday Paper (Chicago, IL) Ceased
Boca Raton Magazine (Boca Raton, FL) 5928
The Boca Raton News (Boca Raton, FL) Unable to locate
Boca's Best (Hollywood, FL) Unable to locate
The Bodega Bay Navigator (Bodega Bay, CA) 1590
Body (New York, NY) Unable to locate
Body Cast (North York, ON, Can.) 36121
Body Copy (Los Angeles, CA) Unable to locate
Body Fashions and Intimate Apparel (BFIA) (New York, NY) Unable to locate
Body Mind Spirit Magazine (Providence, RI) Ceased
Body Positive (New York, NY) 21330
Body & Soul Magazine (Watertown, MA) 14612
BodyBoarding Magazine (San Clemente, CA) 3100
Bodybuilding Lifestyles (Stamford, CT) Unable to locate
Bodyshop (Toronto, ON, Can.) 36476
BodyShop Business (Akron, OH) 24575
Bodyshop Expo (Laguna Hills, CA) Ceased
Bodywise Magazine (St. Paul, MN) Unable to locate
Boer Trader & Meat Goat News 31006*
The Bogalusa Daily News (Bogalusa, LA) 12533
Bogata News (Bogata, TX) 29932
Bogg (Arlington, VA) 31782
Bohemia Suffolk Life; Holbrook/ (Medford, NY) 21033
Bohemio News; El (San Francisco, CA) 3357
Boilermaker Reporter (Kansas City, KS) 11525
Boiling Point (Chapel Hill, NC) Unable to locate
The Boise City News (Boise City, OK) 25766
Boise Family Magazine (Boise, ID) 7803
Boise Weekly (Boise, ID) 7804
Boissevain Recorder (Boissevain, MB, Can.) 35252
Bolingbrook/Romeoville Reporter (Downers Grove, IL) 8780
The Bolingbrook Sun (Naperville, IL) 9261
Bolivar Commercial (Cleveland, MS) 16590
Bolivar Herald-Free Press (Bolivar, MO) 16911
The Bolton Enterprise 35690*
Boma (Washington, DC) 5380
Bomb (New York, NY) 21331
Bon Appetit (Los Angeles, CA) 2224
Bon Homme Richard (Petersburg, VA) 32329
Bon Vivant 18767*
Bon Vivant (Macon, GA) Unable to locate
The Bona Venture (St. Bonaventure, NY) 23286
BONAT's Diversified (Palm Springs, CA) 37840
The Bond Buyer (New York, NY) 21332
Bond Guide (New York, NY) 21333
Bone (New York, NY) Unable to locate
Bone and Joint Surgery; The Journal of (Needham, MA) 14357
Bone and Mineral Research; Journal of (Durham, NC) 23829
The Bonham Daily Favorite (Durant, OK) 25803
Bonita Banner (Bonita Springs, FL) 5946
Bonjour Chez-Nous (Rockland, ON, Can.) Unable to locate
Bonjour Chez-Nous (Montreal, QC, Can.) Ceased
Bonjour Dimanche (Montreal, QC, Can.) Ceased
Bonkers? (Palm Beach, FL) 6541
The Bonner County Daily Bee (Sandpoint, ID) 7977
Bonners Ferry Herald (Bonners Ferry, ID) 7836
Bonneville International Corp. 33065*
Bonni Buy'rr (Mid Valley Edition) (Plainfield, IL) Ceased
Bonni Buy'rr (South Valley Edition) (Plainfield, IL) Ceased
Bonnyville Nouvelle (Bonnyville, AB, Can.) 34621
Bonsai Journal (Huson, MT) 17835
Bonsai Today (Watertown, MA) 14613
Bonsall Messenger (Valley Center, CA) Ceased
The Bonus Paper (Oconto Falls, WI) 34207
Book (New York, NY) 21334
Book Alert (Bridgewater, NJ) Ceased
Book Dealers World (Cottage Grove, OR) 26294
Book Exchange and Collector's Newspaper 31608*
Book Finder; Provident (Scottdale, PA) 27955
Book Forum (Niantic, CT) Ceased
Book History (University Park, PA) 28071
Book Links: Connecting Books, Libraries and Classrooms (Chicago, IL) 8286
Book & Magazine Production 9077*
Book News & Book Business Mart (Fort Worth, TX) 30330
Book and Play Review; Children's (Provo, UT) 31401
The Book Report (Worthington, OH) 25678
Book Review; The American (Normal, IL) 9295
Book Review; Braille (Washington, DC) 5381
Book Review; Design (Berkeley, CA) 1513

Brant News (Brantford, ON, Can.) *Unable to locate*
The Brantford Expositor (Brantford, ON, Can.) **35703**
Brantford Pennysaver (Brantford, ON, Can.) **35704**
Brantley Enterprise (Nahunta, GA) **7451**
Brasil - Brazil (Providence, RI) **28389**
The Brasilians (New York, NY) *Unable to locate*
Brass Society; Historic (New York, NY) **21805**
BRAT-FM - 107.3 (Sleepy Eye, MN) **16452**
Bratrsky Vestnik **10673***
Bratstvo (Brotherhood) (Independence, OH) *Unable to locate*
Bratstvo (Fraternity) (North York, ON, Can.) **36122**
Brattleboro Reformer (Brattleboro, VT) **31508**
The Brattleboro Town Crier (Brattleboro, VT) **31509**
Bravo (Teaneck, NJ) **19608**
Bravo (Bethpage, NY) **37730**
Bravo! Newsmagazine (San Diego, CA) *Unable to locate*
Braxton Citizens' News (Sutton, WV) **33475**
Braxton Democrat-Central (Sutton, WV) **33476**
Braymer Bee (Braymer, MO) **16926**
Brazil Project Advisor *Ceased*
The Brazil Times (Brazil, IN) **9869**
The Brazoria County News (West Columbia, TX) **31283**
The Brazorian News (Lake Jackson, TX) *Unable to locate*
Brazosport Facts (Clute, TX) **30033**
Brazzil (Los Angeles, CA) **2227**
Brea Progress (Santa Ana, CA) *Unable to locate*
The Bread of Life (Gloucester, ON, Can.) **35849**
Breakaway Magazine (Colorado Springs, CO) **4237**
BREAKTHROUGHS in Health and Science (New York, NY) *Ceased*
Breast Disease; Seminars in (Philadelphia, PA) **27661**
Breast Diseases (St. Louis, MO) **17418**
Breast Implant Litigation Reporter (Wayne, PA) **28127**
Breastcare (Riverside, CA) **2932**
Breckenridge American (Breckenridge, TX) **29946**
Breckenridge Journal (Breckenridge, CO) *Unable to locate*
Breckinridge County Herald-News (Hardinsburg, KY) **12103**
Breda News (Breda, IA) **10630**
Breeders' Journal; Guernsey (Reynoldsburg, OH) **25494**
Breese Journal (Breese, IL) **8097**
The Breeze (Mathiston, MS) **16760**
The Breeze (Harrisonburg, VA) **32137**
Breeze-Courier (Taylorville, IL) **9678**
The Breeze Herald (Andover, OH) *Unable to locate*
Bremen Enquirer (Bremen, IN) **9872**
Bremen Messenger; Midlothian- (Midlothian, IL) **9189**
Bremer Butler Super Shopper (Waverly, IA) *Ceased*
Bremer County Independent (Waverly, IA) **11306**
Bremerton Patriot (Bremerton, WA) **32692**
Bremond Press (Bremond, TX) **29947**
Brenafeatures (Needham, MA) **37843**
Brentwood Cable Co. Ltd. **34673***
Brentwood Journal (Franklin, TN) **29195**
Brentwood News (Walnut Creek, CA) *Unable to locate*
Brentwood Post (Pacific Palisades, CA) *Ceased*
Brentwood Suffolk Life (Brentwood, NY) **20240**
Bresnan Communications **16530***
Bresnan Communications (Glencoe, MN) **15919**
Bresnan Communications (Marshall, MN) **16044**
Bresnan Communications (Madison, WI) **33992**
Bresnan Communications (Richland Center, WI) **34299**
Bresnan Communications Co. (Hinesville, GA) **7333**
Bresnan Communications Co. (Hinesville, GA) **7332**
Bresnan Communications Co. (Duluth, MN) **15844**
Bresnan Communications Co. (White Plains, NY) **23576**
The Brethren Journal (Brenham, TX) **29950**
Brethren Missionary Herald (Winona Lake, IN) *Ceased*
Brevard Shopping News (Central Edition) (Melbourne, FL) *Unable to locate*
Brevard Shopping News (North Edition) (Melbourne, FL) *Unable to locate*
Brevard Shopping News (South Edition) (Melbourne, FL) *Unable to locate*
Brewer; American (Alexandria, VA) **31635**
Breweriana; American (Pueblo, CO) **4597**
The Brewers Bulletin (Thiensville, WI) **34365**
Brewers Digest (Thiensville, WI) **34366**
Brewery Age; Modern (Norwalk, CT) **5068**
Brewery Age Tabloid Edition; Modern (Norwalk, CT) **5069**
Brewery Gulch Gazette (Bisbee, AZ) *Unable to locate*
Brewing Chemists; Journal of the American Society of (St. Paul, MN) **16381**
The Brewing Industry News (Riverdale, IL) *Ceased*
BrewingTechniques (Eugene, OR) *Unable to locate*
Brewster Oracle (Brewster, MA) **14005**
Brewster Quad-City Herald (Brewster, WA) **32696**
Brewster Times (Brewster, NY) **20242**

The Brewton Standard & The Plus (Brewton, AL) **136**
Briarpatch (Regina, SK, Can.) **37525**
Brick (Toronto, ON, Can.) **36477**
Bricklayer (Red Deer, AB, Can.) **34827**
Bricklayers & Allied Craftworkers; Journal of the International Union of (Washington, DC) **5601**
Bridal Crafts (Des Plaines, IL) **8750**
Bridal Guide (New York, NY) **21338**
Bridal Trends (Ogden, UT) *Unable to locate*
Bride by Demetrios; For the (New York, NY) **21717**
Bride; Elegant (Greensboro, NC) **23921**
Bride Magazine; Contemporary (South Plainfield, NJ) **19588**
Bride Magazine; Today's (Etobicoke, ON, Can.) **35820**
Bride; Modern (New York, NY) **22348**
Bride; New England (Peabody, MA) **14463**
Bride's **21339***
Bride's Magazine (New York, NY) **21339**
Brides; Southern California (Riverside, CA) **2945**
Bride's and Your New Home **21339***
Bridesburg Guide (Philadelphia, PA) *Unable to locate*
The Bridge (Washington, DC) **5383**
Bridge (Farmington Hills, MI) *Unable to locate*
The Bridge (Port Clinton, OH) *Ceased*
The Bridge (Portland, OR) **26471**
Bridge Engineering; Journal of (Reston, VA) **32371**
Bridge of Eta Kappa Nu (Rolla, MO) *Unable to locate*
Bridge River-Lillooet News (Lillooet, BC, Can.) **35010**
Bridge U.S.A. (Torrance, CA) **3928**
Bridgeport/Back of the Yards EXTRA (Chicago, IL) *Unable to locate*
Bridgeport-Birch Run Weekly News (Chesaning, MI) *Ceased*
Bridgeport Leader-Times (Bridgeport, IL) *Unable to locate*
Bridgeport News (Bridgeport, CT) **4711**
Bridgeport News (Chicago, IL) **8290**
Bridgeport News-Blade (Bridgeport, NE) **17964**
Bridgeport Pennysaver; East Syracuse/Minoa/Kirkville/ (Syracuse, NY) **23401**
The Bridgeport Post **4713***
Bridger Record (Red Lodge, MT) *Ceased*
The Bridger Valley General Store (Rochelle, IL) *Ceased*
Bridger Valley Pioneer (Lyman, WY) **34563**
Bridges Magazine; Roads & (Des Plaines, IL) **8770**
Bridgeton Evening News (Bridgeton, NJ) **18690**
Bridgetown Monitor (New Minas, NS, Can.) *Unable to locate*
Bridgeview Independent (Midlothian, IL) **9184**
Bridgeville Area News (Monroeville, PA) *Unable to locate*
Bridgewater Independent (Bridgewater, MA) **14006**
Bridgewater Townsman **14006***
Bridgewater Townsman (Bridgewater, MA) **14007**
The Bridgton News (Bridgton, ME) **12930**
The Brief (Chicago, IL) **8291**
The Brief Case **3427***
Brigham Young Magazine **31399***
Bright Lights (San Francisco, CA) *Unable to locate*
Bright Side (Kennesaw, GA) **7353**
Brighton Argus (Howell, MI) **15190**
Brighton Independent (Brighton, ON, Can.) **35707**
Brighton Park-McKinley Park Life (Chicago, IL) **8292**
Brighton Pittsford Post (Canandaigua, NY) **20419**
Brighton Standard (Brighton, CO) *Unable to locate*
Brilliant Ideas for Publishers (Clam Lake, WI) **33634**
The Brillion News (Brillion, WI) **33599**
Brimleyana (Raleigh, NC) *Ceased*
Brio Magazine (Colorado Springs, CO) *Unable to locate*
Bristol Bay News (Anchorage, AK) *Ceased*
The Bristol BayTimes (Dillingham, AK) **562**
Bristol Express (Burlington, NJ) **18705**
Bristol Phoenix (Bristol, RI) **28326**
The Bristol Press (Bristol, CT) **4721**
The Bristow News (Bristow, OK) **25767**
Britannia (Yorklyn, DE) **5305**
Britannia (Ottawa, ON, Can.) **36188**
British-American Communications (Sunland, CA) **3826**
British Car (Los Altos, CA) *Ceased*
British Columbia Business Indicators (Victoria, BC, Can.) **35208**
British Columbia Division of Vital Statistics Quarterly Digest (Victoria, BC, Can.) **35209**
British Columbia Genealogist (Richmond, BC, Can.) **35074**
British Columbia Magazine; (Victoria, BC, Can.) **35210**
British Columbia Magazine (Victoria, BC, Can.) **35210**
British Columbia Medical Journal); BCMJ (The (Vancouver, BC, Can.) **35126**
British Columbia; Moving to Vancouver & (Unionville, ON, Can.) **36836**
British Columbia Origin Exports (Victoria, BC, Can.) **35211**

British Columbia Regional Index (Victoria, BC, Can.) **35212**
British Columbia; Westworld (Burnaby, BC, Can.) **34912**
British Heritage (Harrisburg, PA) **26984**
British History Illustrated **26984***
The British Journal for the History of Science (New York, NY) **21340**
British Journal of Management (Hoboken, NJ) *Ceased*
British Journal of Music Education (New York, NY) **21341**
British Journal of Political Science (New York, NY) **21342**
British-Telecom, Inc **3826***
Britt (Los Angeles, CA) *Ceased*
The Britt News-Tribune (Britt, IA) **10631**
Brittany World (Wheat Ridge, CO) *Ceased*
Brittonia (Bronx, NY) *Unable to locate*
Broad Top Bulletin (Saxton, PA) **27944**
Broadband; Satellite (New York, NY) **22706**
Broadband Systems & Design (Morris Plains, NJ) *Ceased*
The Broadcast (Vicksburg, MI) **15653**
Broadcast Cable Financial Journal **8761***
Broadcast Engineering (Overland Park, KS) **11699**
Broadcast Engineering; World (Overland Park, KS) **11737**
Broadcast News Ltd. (Toronto, ON, Can.) **37844**
Broadcast News; World (Overland Park, KS) **11738**
Broadcast Technology+Media Production (Calgary, AB, Can.) **34629**
The Broadcaster (Rockville, CT) **5105**
Broadcaster (Toronto, ON, Can.) **36478**
Broadcaster; 1590 (Nashua, NH) **18598**
Broadcaster/Progress; Deer Park (Deer Park, TX) **30223**
Broadcasting **21343***
Broadcasting, **991***
Broadcasting & Cable (New York, NY) **21343**
Broadcasting & Electronic Media; Journal of (Washington, DC) **5576**
Broadcast+Technology **34629***
Broadn Ripple-Glendale Northside Topics **10356***
The Broadside (Bend, OR) **26240**
Broadside (Fairfax, VA) **32010**
Broadside (Toronto, ON, Can.) *Ceased*
Broadview/Berkeley/Westchester Suburban Life; Hillside/ (Oak Brook, IL) **9352**
Broadview Express (Broadview, SK, Can.) **37453**
Brock Citizen (Beaverton, ON, Can.) **35672**
The Brock Press (St. Catharines, ON, Can.) **36350**
Brockport Post (Brockport, NY) **20244**
Brockton News Tribune (Brockton, MA) **14011**
Brockville Cable TV (Brockville, ON, Can.) **35709**
The Brockville Recorder and Times (Brockville, ON, Can.) **35708**
Brockway Record **27908***
Broiler Industry **162***
Broken Arrow Scout **25771***
Broken Bow Cable TV (Broken Bow, OK) **25775**
Broken Bow News (Broken Bow, OK) **25774**
Broken Pencil (Toronto, ON, Can.) **36479**
Broken Streets (Bristol, CT) *Unable to locate*
The Broker (San Francisco, CA) *Ceased*
Broker; California (Burbank, CA) **1616**
Broker; Kansas Insurance Agent and (Topeka, KS) **11829**
Broker Magazine (New York, NY) **21344**
Broker News (Springfield, IL) **9620**
Broker World (Overland Park, KS) **11700**
Bromeliad Society Journal (Auburn, CA) **1437**
Bronchology; Journal of (Baltimore, MD) **13180**
The Bronson Journal (Bronson, MI) **14837**
Bronte Enterprise **30984***
Bronx Press Blue (Bronx, NY) **20258**
Bronx Press Gold (Bronx, NY) **20259**
Bronx Press Red (Bronx, NY) **20260**
Bronx Press-Review (Bronx, NY) **20261**
Bronxville Review Press-Reporter (Mc Lean, VA) *Unable to locate*
Brook Reporter (Brook, IN) *Unable to locate*
The Brooke County Review (Wellsburg, WV) **33494**
Brooke News **33494***
Brookfield Journal (Brookfield, CT) **4725**
Brookfield News (New Berlin, WI) **34167**
Brookhaven Review (Smithtown, NY) **23336**
Brookings Papers on Economic Activity (Washington, DC) **5384**
The Brookings Register (Brookings, SD) **28812**
The Brookings Review (Washington, DC) **5385**
Brookline Citizen **17677***
Brookline Journal; Hollis (Milford, NH) **18578**
Brookline TAB (Brookline, MA) **14017**
Brooklyn Center Sun-Post (Brooklyn Center, MN) **15774**
Brooklyn Chronicle (Brooklyn, IA) **10633**
Brooklyn Heights Press (Brooklyn, NY) **20301**
Brooklyn Marketeer (Brooklyn, NY) *Unable to locate*
Brooklyn New York Recorder (Brooklyn, NY) **20302**

The Brooklyn Paper/Brooklyn's Weekly Newspaper (Brooklyn, NY) **20303**
Brooklyn Park Sun-Post (Eden Prairie, MN) **15867**
Brooklyn Public Library Bulletin *Ceased*
Brooklyn/Queens Cable **23189**
Brooklyn Queens Cable TV **20615***
Brooklyn Record (Brooklyn, NY) **20304**
Brooklyn Sun Journal (Brooklyn, OH) **24711**
Brooks Bulletin (Brooks, AB, Can.) **34623**
The Brookville American **26733***
Broom Brush and Mop (Arcola, IL) **8019**
Broome Pennysaver (Owego, NY) **23065**
Broomfield Enterprise Sentinel (Minneapolis, MN) *Unable to locate*
Broomstick (San Francisco, CA) *Ceased*
Brossard-Eclair (Brossard, QC, Can.) **36951**
Brotherhood of Maintenance of Way Employees Railway Journal (Southfield, MI) *Ceased*
Broward; Business in (Fort Lauderdale, FL) **6073**
Broward Daily Business Review (Fort Lauderdale, FL) **6072**
The Broward Informer (Sunrise, FL) **6699**
Broward Jewish Journal (Chicago, IL) **8293**
Broward Neighbors **6076***
Broward-Palm Beach; New Times (Fort Lauderdale, FL) **6081**
Broward Review **6072***
Broward Sunrise Informer **6699***
Browbeat Magazine (Oakland, CA) **2670**
Brown Alumni Magazine (Providence, RI) **28390**
Brown Alumni Monthly **28390***
The Brown City Banner (Brown City, MI) **14839**
Brown County Chronicle **33738***
Brown County Democrat (Nashville, IN) **10337**
Brown County Independent (Groton, SD) **28862**
Brown County KIDS **33965***
Brown County News & Hecla Independent **28862***
Brown County Press (Mount Orab, OH) **25396**
Brown Daily Herald (Providence, RI) **28391**
Brown Deer Herald (New Berlin, WI) **34168**
Brown Gold Magazine (Sanford, FL) **6646**
Brown Swiss Bulletin (Beloit, WI) *Unable to locate*
Brown and White (Bethlehem, PA) **26699**
Brownfield Network (Jefferson City, MO) **37618**
Brownfield News (Brownfield, TX) **29953**
Brownsboro Statesman; Chandler & (Brownsboro, TX) **29955**
Brownsville Herald (Brownsville, TX) **29959**
Brownsville States-Graphic (Brownsville, TN) **29070**
Brownton Bulletin **15776***
Brownwood Bulletin (Brownwood, TX) **29965**
Brownwood TV Cable Service, Inc. (Brownwood, TX) *Unable to locate*
BRQ - Blues Revue **33463***
Bruce Jenner's Better Health & Living (New York, NY) *Unable to locate*
Bruin; Daily (Los Angeles, CA) **2250**
Brule-Buffalo County News (Kimball, SD) **28879**
Brule County News **28879***
Brunswick Beacon (Shallotte, NC) **24223**
The Brunswick Business Journal (Moncton, NB, Can.) *Unable to locate*
The Brunswick Citizen (Brunswick, MD) **13395**
Brunswick County News & Shopper (Shallotte, NC) *Unable to locate*
The Brunswick News (Brunswick, GA) **7139**
Brunswick Sun Times (Brunswick, OH) **24713**
Brunswick Times-Gazette (Lawrenceville, VA) **32178**
Brunswick Times Record (Brunswick, ME) **12935**
The Brunswickan (Fredericton, NB, Can.) **35391**
The Brunswicker (Brunswick, MO) **16928**
Brush and Mop; Broom (Arcola, IL) **8019**
Brush News-Tribune (Brush, CO) **4209**
Brushware (Huddleston, VA) **32171**
Bryan-College Station Eagle (Bryan, TX) **29973**
The Bryan Press **29975***
The Bryan Times (Bryan, OH) **24714**
Bryant & Stratton News **28442***
Bryn Mawr-Haverford College News **27028***
The Bryn Mawr & Haverford News (Haverford, PA) **27028**
The Bryologist (Carbondale, IL) **8115**
BSDA News Magazine (Surrey, BC, Can.) **35106**
BT Technology Journal (New York, NY) **21345**
BTA Solutions (Kansas City, MO) **17158**
BtoB Magazine (Chicago, IL) **8294**
B12-Hamilton/Halton Business Report (Hamilton, ON, Can.) **35875**
Buc In Print (Charleston, SC) **28506**
Buc 'N Print **28506***
The Buccaneer (Tampa, FL) *Unable to locate*
Buchanan County News (Faucett, MO) *Unable to locate*
The Buchtelite (Akron, OH) **24576**
Buckeye; Archbold (Archbold, OH) **24613**
Buckeye Cablevision (Toledo, OH) **25574**
Buckeye Farm News (Columbus, OH) **25002**
The Buckeye Lake Advertiser (New Lexington, OH) **25411**

The Buckeye Review (Youngstown, OH) **25694**
Buckeye Valley News (Buckeye, AZ) **662**
Bucklin Banner (Cimarron, KS) **11381**
Buckmasters Whitetail Magazine (Montgomery, AL) **362**
Bucknell World (Lewisburg, PA) **27191**
Bucks County; The Advance of (Newtown, PA) **27327**
Bucks County Courier Times (Levittown, PA) **27186**
Bucks County Law Reporter (Doylestown, PA) **26830**
Bucks County Midweek (Trevose, PA) **28055**
Bucks County Telegraph (Doylestown, PA) **26831**
Bucks County Tribune (Feasterville, PA) **26919**
Bucks Mont Courier **26981***
Bucksport Free Press (Belfast, ME) *Ceased*
Bucktail Broadcasting Corp. (Emporium, PA) **26883**
Bucyrus RFD News (Bellevue, OH) **24671**
The Bucyrus Telegraph-Forum (Bucyrus, OH) **24718**
Buddhist-Christian Studies (Wilmore, KY) **12450**
Buddhist Contemplatives; The Journal of the Order of (Mount Shasta, CA) **2604**
The Buddhist Monthly (Talmage, CA) *Unable to locate*
Buddhist Text Information (Carmel, NY) *Ceased*
Buddy (Dallas, TX) *Unable to locate*
Buddy Basch Feature Syndicate (New York, NY) **37845**
Budget; Meredosia (Bluffs, IL) **8090**
Budget Travel; Arthur Frommer's (New York, NY) **21255**
Budget Watch (Washington, DC) *Ceased*
Budgeteer News; Duluth (Duluth, MN) **15836**
Budgeteer Press **15836***
Budgeting and Finance; Public (Coral Gables, FL) **6011**
Budgeting; OECD Journal on (Washington, DC) **5701**
Bud's Cable Service **26789***
Budstikken (Minneapolis, MN) *Unable to locate*
Buena Park/La Palma/Cypress News *Unable to locate*
Buena Salud **28289***
Buena Vida (San Juan, PR) **28289**
Buena Vista County Journal (Newell, IA) **11114**
Buena Vista Today (Storm Lake, IA) **11243**
Buenavision Cable TV (Los Angeles, CA) **2445**
Buenhogar (Miami, FL) **6342**
Buffalo Bulletin (Buffalo, WY) **34478**
The Buffalo Business Journal (Buffalo, NY) *Ceased*
Buffalo County Journal (Cochrane, WI) **33640**
Buffalo Criterion (Buffalo, NY) **20364**
Buffalo Fine Print News (Buffalo, NY) *Unable to locate*
Buffalo Grove Countryside (Buffalo Grove, IL) **8100**
Buffalo Jewish Review (Buffalo, NY) **20365**
Buffalo Law Journal (Buffalo, NY) **20366**
Buffalo Law Review (Buffalo, NY) **20367**
The Buffalo News (Buffalo, NY) **20368**
Buffalo Press (Buffalo, TX) **29986**
Buffalo Reflex (Buffalo, MO) **16929**
Buffalo Ridge Gazette (Ruthton, MN) **16339**
The Buffalo Rocket (Buffalo, NY) **20369**
Buffalo Spree (Williamsville, NY) **23582**
Buffalo Tri City Register (Riverton, IL) **9499**
BuffaloBeat (Buffalo, NY) **20370**
Buford Television Inc. (Tyler, TX) **31204**
The Bugle **9291***
Bugle (Missoula, MT) **17865**
The Bugle (Woodstock, NB, Can.) **35440**
Bugle; Journal of Elk Country **17865***
Buhl Herald (Buhl, ID) **7838**
Build and Green (Vancouver, BC, Can.) *Ceased*
Buildcore Product Source (Toronto, ON, Can.) *Ceased*
Builder (Washington, DC) **5386**
Builder Architect (Phoenix, AZ) *Unable to locate*
Builder; Ask the (Cincinnati, OH) **37824**
Builder; Automated (Ventura, CA) **4001**
Builder; Central Oklahoma Home (Oklahoma City, OK) **25959**
Builder & Contractor **31767***
Builder/Dealer (Erie, PA) **26893**
Builder & Engineer; California (Riverside, CA) **2933**
Builder & Engineer; Pacific (Kirkland, WA) **32799**
Builder Insider (Dallas, TX) **30134**
Builder Magazine; Indiana (Spencer, IN) **10470**
Builder Magazine, Uniform Series Edition (Evanston, IL) **8854**
Builder News Extra (Westlake, LA) **12878**
Builder Report; The Rhode Island (East Providence, RI) **28345**
Builder Review (Durham, NC) *Ceased*
Builder; Western (Brookfield, WI) **33606**
Builders Association News (Fort Worth, TX) *Unable to locate*
Builder's Best Home Plans (Washington, DC) *Ceased*
Building (Toronto, ON, Can.) *Unable to locate*
Building Business & Apartment Management (Farmington Hills, MI) **15016**
Building Design & Construction (New York, NY) **21346**
Building Energy Technology (Oak Ridge, TN) *Ceased*

Building Homes & Renovations (Toronto, ON, Can.) *Ceased*
Building Ideas; Better Homes and Gardens (New York, NY) **21296**
Building Magazine (Toronto, ON, Can.) *Ceased*
Building Magazine; Utah (Salt Lake City, UT) **31441**
Building Management & Design (Toronto, ON, Can.) *Unable to locate*
Building Management Hawaii (Honolulu, HI) **7682**
Building Material Dealer (Minneapolis, MN) **16062**
Building Material Retailer **16062***
Building News; Frame (Iola, WI) **33827**
Building News; Nation's (Washington, DC) **5684**
Building Oklahoma (Oklahoma City, OK) *Ceased*
Building Operating Management (Milwaukee, WI) **34059**
Building Products (Washington, DC) **5387**
Building Products Digest (Newport Beach, CA) **2623**
Building Products Report (Atlanta, GA) *Ceased*
Building; Realty and (Chicago, IL) **8552**
Building Services Contractor (Melville, NY) *Ceased*
Building; Southern (Birmingham, AL) **92**
Building Supply Home Centers (New York, NY) **21347**
Building; Traditional (Brooklyn, NY) **20349**
Buildings (Cedar Rapids, IA) **10669**
Buildings; The Structural Design of Tall (Hoboken, NJ) **19110**
The Buletin **24662***
Bulk Solids; Powder/ (Morris Plains, NJ) **19302**
Bull & Bear Financial Report (Longwood, FL) **6312**
The Bull Mountain Bugle (Stuart, VA) *Ceased*
The Bull Terrier Quarterly (Wheat Ridge, CO) *Ceased*
Bulldog Weekly (Redlands, CA) **2901**
The Bullet (Fredericksburg, VA) **32084**
The Bulletin **32272***
The Bulletin **25010***
The Bulletin **25571***
BULLETIN **28052***
Bulletin (El Cerrito, CA) **1859**
The Bulletin (Walnut Creek, CA) *Unable to locate*
The Bulletin (Milford, CT) **4953**
The Bulletin (Washington, DC) *Unable to locate*
The Bulletin (Sarasota, FL) **6655**
Bulletin (Denison, IA) **10765**
The Bulletin (Brownton, MN) **15776**
The Bulletin (New York, NY) **21348**
The Bulletin (Rochester, NY) **23212**
Bulletin (Litchville, ND) **24496**
The Bulletin (Bend, OR) **26241**
The Bulletin (Angleton, TX) **29726**
The Bulletin (Austin, TX) *Ceased*
Bulletin (Bandera, TX) **29888**
The Bulletin (Santa Fe, TX) *Unable to locate*
The Bulletin (Crozet, VA) *Unable to locate*
Bulletin (Baldwin, WI) **33560**
The Bulletin (Summerland, BC, Can.) **35102**
Bulletin of the Academy of Sciences of the USSR, Division of Chemical Sciences **22682***
Bulletin des Agriculteurs; Le (Montreal, QC, Can.) **37156**
Bulletin of Allegheny County Medical Society (Pittsburgh, PA) **27763**
Bulletin of Alloy Phase Diagrams **25367***
Bulletin of the American Astronomical Society (Washington, DC) **5388**
Bulletin of American Mideast Business (Tuckerton, NJ) *Ceased*
Bulletin of the American Physical Society (College Park, MD) **13413**
Bulletin of the American Schools of Oriental Research (Champaign, IL) *Unable to locate*
Bulletin of the American Society of Papyrologists (Upper Montclair, NJ) **19692**
Bulletin of the AMS (Boston, MA) **13867**
Bulletin of the Args **4352***
The Bulletin of the Association for Business Communication **21353***
Bulletin of the Atomic Scientists (Chicago, IL) **8295**
Bulletin Baudelairien (Nashville, TN) **29446**
Bulletin of Bibliography (Raleigh, NC) **24127**
Bulletin Canadien D'historie de la Medecine; Canadian Bulletin of Medical History/ (Nanaimo, BC, Can.) **35018**
The Bulletin of the Center for Children's Books (Champaign, IL) **8182**
Bulletin of the Cincinnati Historical Society **12233***
The Bulletin of the Cleveland Museum of Art (Cleveland, OH) *Ceased*
Bulletin of the Comediantes (Auburn University, AL) **49**
Bulletin: Committee on South Asian Women (College Station, TX) **30038**
Bulletin of Concerned Asian Scholars (Cedar, MI) **14863**
Bulletin of the Council for Research in Music Education (Urbana, IL) **9698**
Bulletin on Current Research in Soviet and East European Law (Toronto, ON, Can.) **36480**

Bulletin in Defense of Marxism (New York, NY) *Unable to locate*

Bulletin of the Detroit Institute of Arts (Detroit, MI) **14917**

Bulletin de Droit Immobilier (Cowansville, QC, Can.) *Ceased*

Bulletin de Droit de L'Environnement (Cowansville, QC, Can.) **36980**

Bulletin de Droit Municipal (Cowansville, QC, Can.) *Ceased*

Bulletin de Droit de la Sante (Cowansville, QC, Can.) **36981**

Bulletin of the Entomological Society of America **13597***

Bulletin of Environmental Contamination and Toxicology (New York, NY) **21349**

Bulletin of Experimental Biology and Medicine (New York, NY) **21350**

The Bulletin of Historical Research in Music Education **907***

Bulletin of the History of Dentistry **8024***

Bulletin of the History of Medicine (Baltimore, MD) **13140**

Bulletin of the International Bureau of Education (Paris Cedex 15,) *Ceased*

Bulletin of the King County Medical Society (Seattle, WA) **32952**

Bulletin; Le (Buckingham, QC, Can.) **36952**

Bulletin of the London Mathematical Society (New York, NY) **21351**

The Bulletin of Marine Science (Miami, FL) **6343**

Bulletin of the Medical Library Association **8445***

Bulletin of the Menninger Clinic (Topeka, KS) **11815**

Bulletin of the Midwest Modern Language Association **10982***

Bulletin on Narcotics (New York, NY) *Ceased*

Bulletin of the National Association of Watch and Clock Collectors (Columbia, PA) **26798**

Bulletin of the New Jersey Motor Truck Association (East Brunswick, NJ) **18780**

Bulletin (New Series) of the American Mathematical Society (Providence, RI) **28392**

Bulletin of the New York Academy of Medicine (New York, NY) **21352**

Bulletin of the Oklahoma Ornithological Society (Tulsa, OK) **26107**

Bulletin of the Orleans Parish Medical Society (New Orleans, LA) *Ceased*

Bulletin of the Orton Society **13123***

Bulletin/Progress Enterprise (Bridgewater, NS, Can.) **35542**

Bulletin of Prosthetics Research **13201***

Bulletin of the Psychonomic Society **29800***

Bulletin of the Railway and Locomotive Historical Society **9716***

Bulletin of the Science Fiction Writers of America (Enfield, CT) *Unable to locate*

Bulletin de la Societe Americaine de Philosophie de Langue Francaise (DeKalb, IL) **8732**

The Bulletin of Symbolic Logic (Boston, MA) **13868**

Bulletin—The Magazine for Utility Management **33177***

Bulletin Times (Bolivar, TN) **29057**

Bulletin of the Torrey Botanical Club **11559***

Bulletin Voyages (Montreal, QC, Can.) *Unable to locate*

Bullish on Crafts (Durango, CO) *Unable to locate*

Bullpen (Trenton, NJ) **19654**

Bullseye (Poughkeepsie, NY) *Unable to locate*

Bulverde Community News (San Antonio, TX) **31027**

The Bunker Hill Gazette-News (Bunker Hill, IL) **8101**

The Bunkie Record (Bunkie, LA) **12542**

Buoyant Flight (Akron, OH) **24577**

Burbank Daily Review **1614***

Burbank Leader (Burbank, CA) **1614**

Burbank Stickney Independent (Midlothian, IL) **9185**

The Burden Times **11368***

Bureau of Alcohol, Tobacco, and Firearms Bulletin (Pittsburgh, PA) *Unable to locate*

Bureau County Republican (Princeton, IL) **9467**

Bureau News (Atlanta, GA) *Unable to locate*

Bureau of Wholesale Sales Representatives News (Atlanta, GA) *Unable to locate*

The Bureaucrat **13659***

Burke County Tribune (Bowbells, ND) **24379**

The Burke/Fairfax Station Connection (Burke, VA) **31908**

Burke Gazette (Burke, SD) **28827**

Burks Falls Powassan Almaguin News **35712***

Burleson County Citizen-Tribune (Caldwell, TX) **29994**

Burleson Star (Burleson, TX) **29988**

The Burley Tobacco Farmer (Raleigh, NC) **24128**

Burlingame Enterprise-Chronicle **11369***

Burlington County Times (Willingboro, NJ) **19753**

The Burlington Daily Times News **23672***

The Burlington Free Press (Burlington, VT) **31514**

Burlington Mail (Burlington, NJ) **18706**

Burlington Post (Burlington, ON, Can.) **35714**

Burlington Record **4210***

Burlington Record & Plains Dealer (Burlington, CO) **4210**

Burlington Standard Press (Burlington, WI) **33608**

Burlington Times-Union (Concord, MA) *Unable to locate*

Burlington Union (Needham, MA) **14351**

The Burnaby-New Westminster News Leader (Burnaby, BC, Can.) **34893**

Burnaby Now (Burnaby, BC, Can.) **34894**

Burnet Bulletin (Burnet, TX) **29991**

Burnet Bulletin-Marble Falls Messenger **29991***

Burnett County Sentinel (Grantsburg, WI) **33737**

Burnham/Calumet City Star (Calumet City, IL) **8107**

Burns Times-Herald (Burns, OR) **26259**

Burnsville/Savage Sun Current (Burnsville, MN) **15781**

Burping Lula (Richmond, VA) **32431**

Burr Ridge/Pleasantdale Suburban Life; Countryside/Indian Head Park/Willow Springs/ (Oak Brook, IL) **9346**

Burroughs Bulletin (Louisville, KY) **12211**

Burroughs World **31255***

Burt County Plaindealer (Tekamah, NE) **18296**

Burton Antenna Co. Inc. (Melvin, KY) *Unable to locate*

Burtonsville Gazette (Frederick, MD) **13507**

Burwell Tribune (Sargent, NE) **18259**

Bus Conversions (Westminster, CA) **4074**

Bus Fleet; School (Torrance, CA) **3942**

Bus Industry Magazine (Manchester, NH) **18555**

Bus Ride (Phoenix, AZ) **794**

Bus Trader; National (Polo, IL) **9462**

Bus World (Long Beach, CA) *Unable to locate*

The Bush Blade (Anchor Point, AK) **519**

Bushong Bulletin (North Jackson, OH) **25436**

Business (Atlanta, GA) **6982**

Business AAIW Show Daily; Aftermarket (Cleveland, OH) **24854**

Business Access/Access aux Affaires (Ottawa, ON, Can.) *Unable to locate*

Business; Adventure Travel (Incline Village, NV) **18356**

The Business Advocate (Washington, DC) **5389**

Business; Aftermarket (Cleveland, OH) **24853**

Business Age (Milwaukee, WI) *Ceased*

Business Air Today (Fort Dodge, IA) **10895**

Business Alabama **63***

Business Alabama Monthly (Birmingham, AL) **63**

Business Almanac; The Finger Lakes (Auburn, NY) **20106**

Business; American (New York, NY) **21182**

Business; Arkansas (Little Rock, AR) **1213**

Business Atlanta (Atlanta, GA) **6982**

The Business Blanket (Bad Axe, MI) *Unable to locate*

Business in Broward (Fort Lauderdale, FL) **6073**

Business Bulletin; Oklahoma (Norman, OK) **25938**

Business to Business (Seattle, WA) *Unable to locate*

Business to Business (Bracebridge, ON, Can.) *Ceased*

Business in Calgary (Calgary, AB, Can.) **34630**

Business; Caribbean (San Juan, PR) **28290**

Business; Carolina (New Bern, NC) **24095**

Business Change and Re-engineering (Hoboken, NJ) *Ceased*

Business; Chicago (Chicago, IL) **8307**

Business Chronicle; Atlanta (Atlanta, GA) **6967**

Business; CIO Web (Framingham, MA) **14193**

Business & Commercial Aviation (Rye Brook, NY) *Unable to locate*

Business Communication; The Journal of (Flint, MI) **15035**

Business Communication Quarterly (New York, NY) **21353**

Business Communications Review (Westmont, IL) **9753**

Business Computer News (Toronto, ON, Can.) *Ceased*

Business Computer Systems (Boston, MA) *Ceased*

Business Concepts (Los Angeles, CA) **2228**

Business Conditions Digest (Pittsburgh, PA) *Ceased*

Business Consumer Guide (Watertown, MA) *Unable to locate*

Business; Contracting (Cleveland, OH) **24875**

Business; Country (St. Charles, IL) **9563**

Business Courier; Cincinnati (Cincinnati, OH) **24783**

Business; Crain's Chicago (Chicago, IL) **8346**

Business; Crain's Detroit (Detroit, MI) **14920**

Business; Crain's New York (New York, NY) **21511**

Business Credit (Columbia, MD) **13455**

The Business Daily (Des Moines, IA) **10772**

Business; Development (New York, NY) **21547**

Business Digest (New Milford, CT) **5028**

Business Digest of Central Massachusetts (Worcester, MA) *Unable to locate*

Business Digest of Greater Burlington **31618***

Business Digest of Greater Waterbury (Middlebury, CT) **4941**

Business Digest; Lafayette (Lafayette, IN) **10252**

Business Digest of Lehigh Valley (Philadelphia, PA) *Ceased*

Business Digest of Lower Fairfield County (Norwalk, CT) *Unable to locate*

Business Documents (Overland Park, KS) *Unable to locate*

Business Eastern Europe (New York, NY) **21354**

Business and Economic Conditions; Georgia (Athens, GA) **6938**

Business and Economic History (Williamsburg, VA) **32614**

Business & Economic Journal; Southern (Montgomery, AL) **377**

Business and Economic Perspectives; Journal of (Martin, TN) **29342**

Business and Economic Report **11885***

Business & Economic Review (Columbia, SC) **28546**

Business & Economic Review; Arkansas (Fayetteville, AR) **1115**

Business & Economic Statistics; Journal of (Alexandria, VA) **31689**

Business and Economic Studies; Journal of (Oakdale, NY) **23029**

Business Economics (Washington, DC) **5390**

Business & Economics; Quarterly Journal of (Lincoln, NE) **18116**

Business Education Forum (Reston, VA) **32362**

Business Entities (New York, NY) **21355**

Business Entrepreneur; Minority (Torrance, CA) **3938**

Business; Essays in International (Columbia, SC) **28548**

Business Ethics (Minneapolis, MN) **16063**

Business Ethics Quarterly (Washington, DC) **5391**

Business Ethics: The Magazine of Socially Responsible Business **16063***

Business Europe (New York, NY) **21356**

The Business Examiner (Tacoma, WA) **33144**

Business Executive (Oakville, ON, Can.) **36136**

Business Facilities (Red Bank, NJ) **19500**

Business & Facility Concepts (Salamanca, NY) *Unable to locate*

Business Farmer (Scottsbluff, NE) **18262**

Business Farmer-Stockman (Scottsbluff, NE) **18263**

Business Features Syndicate (North Stratford, NH) **37846**

Business Finance (Calabasas, CA) *Unable to locate*

Business and Finance Librarianship; Journal of (Columbus, OH) **25023**

Business and Finance Review; Global (Thibodaux, LA) **12859**

Business; Financial Studies of the Small (Winter Haven, FL) **6866**

Business First (Charlotte, NC) **23735**

Business First of Buffalo (Buffalo, NY) **20371**

Business First-Columbus (Columbus, OH) **25003**

Business Forecasting Methods; Journal of (Great Neck, NY) **20691**

Business Formations and Failures *Ceased*

Business Forms, Labels, & Systems (Minneapolis, MN) *Ceased*

Business Forum (Los Angeles, CA) **2229**

Business Forum Digest **25107***

Business Forum Software Digest (Dayton, OH) **25107**

Business Gazette (Frederick, MD) **13508**

Business Gazette; Arizona (Phoenix, AZ) **775**

Business Geographics (Norwalk, CT) **5051**

Business; Global Technology (Mountain View, CA) **2606**

Business; Government (Mississauga, ON, Can.) **36068**

Business; Greenhouse (Rolling Meadows, IL) **9547**

Business; GSA (Greenville, SC) **28624**

Business; Hawaii (Honolulu, HI) **7691**

Business & Health (Montvale, NJ) **19243**

Business; Health Products (Melville, NY) **21045**

The Business of Herbs (Jemez Springs, NM) *Ceased*

Business; Hispanic (Santa Barbara, CA) **3641**

Business History Review (Boston, MA) **13869**

Business; Home (Huntington Beach, CA) **2062**

Business Horizons (New York, NY) **21357**

Business & Incentive Strategies (New York, NY) *Unable to locate*

Business Indicators; British Columbia (Victoria, BC, Can.) **35208**

Business & Industry (Carlisle, IA) **10648**

Business and Industry; Applied Stochastic Models in (Hoboken, NJ) **18894**

Business Insight (Kalamazoo, MI) *Unable to locate*

Business Insurance (Chicago, IL) **8296**

Business Intelligence; Rundt's World (New York, NY) **22680**

Business Interiors **19501***

Business Issues; The Journal of African Human Resources and (Irving, TX) **30605**

The Business Journal **29472***

The Business Journal (Fresno, CA) **1943**

The Business Journal (Sacramento, CA) **2978**

The Business Journal (Mason City, IA) **11070**

Business; Journal of African (Binghamton, NY) **20160**

Business; Journal of Asia-Pacific (Johnson City, TN) **29252**

3296

Numbers cited in bold after listings are entry numbers rather than page numbers.

Canadian Auto Review (Toronto, ON, Can.) *Ceased*

Canadian Auto World (Mississauga, ON, Can.) **36057**

Canadian Aviation and Aircraft for Sale (Hamilton, ON, Can.) *Unable to locate*

Canadian Aviation News (Calgary, AB, Can.) *Unable to locate*

Canadian Ayrshire Review (Ottawa, ON, Can.) *Unable to locate*

Canadian Banker (Toronto, ON, Can.) **36493**

The Canadian Baptist (Etobicoke, ON, Can.) **35813**

The Canadian Bar Review (La Revue du Barreau Canadien) (Ottawa, ON, Can.) **36190**

Canadian Beverage Review (Ajax, ON, Can.) *Ceased*

Canadian Biker (Victoria, BC, Can.) **35213**

Canadian Biosystems Engineering (Saskatoon, SK, Can.) **37549**

Canadian Boating (Mississauga, ON, Can.) *Unable to locate*

Canadian Bowhunting (Vancouver, BC, Can.) *Ceased*

Canadian Broadcasting Corporation CBC/Societe Radio Canada SRC (Ottawa, ON, Can.) **37620**

Canadian Broadcasting Corporation (CBC)/Societe Radio Canada (SRC) (Ottawa, ON, Can.) **37688**

Canadian Bulletin of Medical History/Bulletin Canadien D'historie de la Medecine (Nanaimo, BC, Can.) **35018**

Canadian Business (Toronto, ON, Can.) **36494**

Canadian Business Law Journal (Aurora, ON, Can.) **35641**

Canadian Business Life (Toronto, ON, Can.) *Unable to locate*

Canadian Business Review (Ottawa, ON, Can.) *Ceased*

Canadian Camera (Wellington, ON, Can.) **36869**

The Canadian Camp (Mississauga, ON, Can.) *Unable to locate*

Canadian Camper (Rexdale, ON, Can.) **36341**

The Canadian Catholic Review (Saskatoon, SK, Can.) *Ceased*

Canadian Ceramics Quarterly (Willowdale, ON, Can.) **36876**

The Canadian Champion (Richmond Hill, ON, Can.) *Unable to locate*

Canadian Charolais Banner **37527***

Canadian Chemical News (L'Actualite Chimique Canadienne) (Ottawa, ON, Can.) **36191**

Canadian Children's Literature (Litterature Canadienne pour la Jeunesse); CCL (Guelph, ON, Can.) **35860**

Canadian Churchman Anglican Journal Episcopal **36462***

Canadian Cleaner and Launderer **36144***

Canadian Clinical Laboratory *Ceased*

Canadian Coin Box Magazine **35767***

Canadian Coin News (St. Catharines, ON, Can.) **36351**

Canadian Computer Wholesaler (Vancouver, BC, Can.) **35130**

Canadian Construction Record (Toronto, ON, Can.) *Unable to locate*

Canadian Consulting Engineer (Toronto, ON, Can.) **36495**

Canadian Cooperative Wool Growers Magazine (Cookstown, ON, Can.) **35752**

Canadian Courier; Corriere Canadese/ (Toronto, ON, Can.) **36560**

Canadian Courier/Nowy Kurier; Polish (Toronto, ON, Can.) **36713**

Canadian Critical Care Nursing Journal (White Rock, BC, Can.) *Ceased*

Canadian Curling News (Don Mills, ON, Can.) *Unable to locate*

Canadian Dairy (Toronto, ON, Can.) *Unable to locate*

Canadian Datasystems (Toronto, ON, Can.) *Ceased*

Canadian Defence Quarterly (Revue Canadienne de Defense) (Toronto, ON, Can.) **36496**

Canadian Dental Management (Lachine, QC, Can.) *Ceased*

Canadian Dimension (CD) (Winnipeg, MB, Can.) *Unable to locate*

Canadian Direct Marketing News (Scarborough, ON, Can.) *Unable to locate*

Canadian Doctor (Markham, ON, Can.) *Unable to locate*

Canadian Economic Observer (Ottawa, ON, Can.) **36192**

Canadian Electronics (Markham, ON, Can.) **36016**

Canadian Electronics Engineering **36016***

Canadian Emergency News (Calgary, AB, Can.) *Unable to locate*

The Canadian Entomologist (Ottawa, ON, Can.) **36193**

Canadian Environmental Protection (Vancouver, BC, Can.) **35131**

Canadian Ethnic Studies Journal (Calgary, AB, Can.) **34634**

Canadian Family Law Quarterly (Toronto, ON, Can.) **36497**

Canadian Family Physician (Mississauga, ON, Can.) **36058**

Canadian Fiction Magazine (Toronto, ON, Can.) *Unable to locate*

Canadian Field-Naturalist (Ottawa, ON, Can.) **36194**

The Canadian Firefighter (Toronto, ON, Can.) **36498**

Canadian Flight (Ottawa, ON, Can.) **36195**

Canadian Flight Annual (Ottawa, ON, Can.) **36196**

Canadian Florist Greenhouse & Nursery (Mississauga, ON, Can.) *Unable to locate*

The Canadian Fly Fisher (Belleville, ON, Can.) **35677**

Canadian Food & Drug Packaging News (Toronto, ON, Can.) *Ceased*

Canadian Footwear Journal (Ste.-Anne-de-Bellevue, QC, Can.) *Unable to locate*

Canadian Forces Base Cold Lake Courier (Coldlake, AB, Can.) **34688**

Canadian Forest Industries (Baie D'urfe', QC, Can.) **36944**

The Canadian Forum (Halifax, NS, Can.) *Ceased*

Canadian Free Press (Toronto, ON, Can.) **36499**

(Canadian-French Edition); Selection du Reader's Digest (Montreal, QC, Can.) **37223**

Canadian Fruitgrower **35769***

Canadian Funeral Director (Ajax, ON, Can.) *Unable to locate*

Canadian Funeral News (Calgary, AB, Can.) *Unable to locate*

Canadian Gardening (Markham, ON, Can.) **36017**

Canadian Gemmologist (Ottawa, ON, Can.) **36197**

The Canadian Geographer (Montreal, QC, Can.) **37093**

Canadian Geographic (Ottawa, ON, Can.) **36198**

Canadian Geotechnical Journal (Revue Canadienne de Geotechnique) (Mississauga, ON, Can.) **36059**

Canadian German Trade (Toronto, ON, Can.) *Ceased*

Canadian Gladiolus Annual (Surrey, BC, Can.) *Unable to locate*

Canadian Governments Buyer **36068***

Canadian Grain and Wheat Flour; Exports of (Winnipeg, MB, Can.) **35328**

Canadian Grey Panthers; Panthers' Plus, (Toronto, ON, Can.) **36695**

Canadian Grocer (Toronto, ON, Can.) **36500**

Canadian Guernsey Journal (Guelph, ON, Can.) *Unable to locate*

Canadian Guider (Toronto, ON, Can.) **36501**

Canadian Hairdresser (Mississauga, ON, Can.) *Unable to locate*

Canadian Heavy Equipment Guide (Vancouver, BC, Can.) *Unable to locate*

Canadian Hereford Digest (Calgary, AB, Can.) **34635**

Canadian Heritage (Toronto, ON, Can.) *Ceased*

Canadian Historical Review (Toronto, ON, Can.) **36502**

Canadian Home and Country (Markham, ON, Can.) **36018**

Canadian Home Economics Journal (Revue Canadienne d'Economie Familiale) (Ottawa, ON, Can.) **36199**

Canadian Home Workshop (Markham, ON, Can.) **36020**

Canadian Home Workshop (Markham, ON, Can.) **36019**

Canadian Horse **35644***

Canadian Horseman Magazine **35649***

Canadian Hotel & Restaurant (Toronto, ON, Can.) *Ceased*

Canadian House & Home Magazine (Toronto, ON, Can.) **36503**

Canadian HR Reporter (Toronto, ON, Can.) **36504**

Canadian Human Rights Advocate (Maniwaki, QC, Can.) *Ceased*

Canadian Hunting and Shooting (Vancouver, BC, Can.) *Ceased*

Canadian Independent Adjuster (Toronto, ON, Can.) **36505**

Canadian Industrial Equipment News (Toronto, ON, Can.) **36506**

Canadian Industrial Machinery (Burlington, ON, Can.) **35715**

Canadian Inflight (Toronto, ON, Can.) *Unable to locate*

Canadian Information Processing (Toronto, ON, Can.) *Ceased*

Canadian Insurance X Canadian Insurance Magazine (Toronto, ON, Can.) **36507**

Canadian Interiors (Toronto, ON, Can.) *Ceased*

Canadian Jersey Breeder (Guelph, ON, Can.) *Unable to locate*

Canadian Jeweller (Toronto, ON, Can.) **36508**

The Canadian Jewish News (North York, ON, Can.) **36124**

Canadian Jewish Outlook **35156***

Canadian Jewish Studies/Etudes Juives Canadiennes (Montreal, QC, Can.) **37094**

Canadian Journal on Aging (La Revue Canadienne du vieillissement) (Hamilton, ON, Can.) **35876**

Canadian Journal of Agricultural Economics (Ottawa, ON, Can.) **36200**

Canadian Journal of Allergy & Clinical Immunology (Saint-Laurent, QC, Can.) **37362**

Canadian Journal of Analytical Sciences and Spectroscopy (Laval, QC, Can.) *Ceased*

Canadian Journal of Anesthesia (Journal canadien d'anesthesie) (Montreal, QC, Can.) **37095**

Canadian Journal of Animal Science (Ottawa, ON, Can.) **36201**

Canadian Journal of Applied Physiology (Champaign, IL) **8183**

Canadian Journal of Botany (Revue Canadienne de Botanique) (Ottawa, ON, Can.) *Unable to locate*

The Canadian Journal of Cardiology (Journal Canadien de Cardiologie) (Oakville, ON, Can.) **36137**

Canadian Journal of Chemical Engineering (Montreal, QC, Can.) **37096**

Canadian Journal of Chemistry (Revue Canadienne de Chimie) (Ottawa, ON, Can.) **36202**

Canadian Journal of Civil Engineering (Revue Canadienne de Genie Civil) (Ottawa, ON, Can.) **36203**

Canadian Journal of Clinical Pharmacology (Oakville, ON, Can.) **36138**

The Canadian Journal of CME (Continuing Medical Education) (Pointe-Claire, QC, Can.) **37272**

Canadian Journal of Communication (Calgary, AB, Can.) **34636**

Canadian Journal of Comparative Medicine/Veterinary Science **36221***

Canadian Journal of Criminology/Revue Canadienne de Criminologie (Ottawa, ON, Can.) **36204**

The Canadian Journal of Dermatology (Baie-D'Urfe, QC, Can.) *Unable to locate*

The Canadian Journal of Diagnosis (Pointe-Claire, QC, Can.) **37273**

Canadian Journal of Dietetic Practice and Research (Markham, ON, Can.) **36021**

Canadian Journal of Earth Sciences (Revue Canadienne des Sciences de la Terre) (Edmonton, AB, Can.) **34703**

Canadian Journal of Economics (Revue Canadienne d'Economique) (Montreal, QC, Can.) **37097**

Canadian Journal of Fisheries & Aquatic Science (Ottawa, ON, Can.) **36205**

Canadian Journal of Forest Research (Revue Canadienne de Recherches Forestiere) (Ottawa, ON, Can.) *Unable to locate*

The Canadian Journal of Gastroenterology (Oakville, ON, Can.) **36139**

Canadian Journal of Genetics and Cytology **36128***

The Canadian Journal of Geriatrics (Pointe-Claire, QC, Can.) *Ceased*

The Canadian Journal of Herbalism (Port Burwell, ON, Can.) **36331**

Canadian Journal of History/Annales canadiennes d'histoire (Saskatoon, SK, Can.) **37550**

Canadian Journal of Hospital Pharmacy (Ottawa, ON, Can.) **36206**

Canadian Journal of Human Sexuality (Toronto, ON, Can.) **36509**

The Canadian Journal of Infectious Diseases (Oakville, ON, Can.) *Unable to locate*

Canadian Journal of Information and Library Science (Toronto, ON, Can.) **36510**

Canadian Journal of Information Science **36510***

Canadian Journal of Italian Studies **29065***

Canadian Journal of Latin American and Caribbean Studies (London, ON, Can.) **35978**

Canadian Journal of Law & Jurisprudence (London, ON, Can.) **35979**

The Canadian Journal of Linguistics/Revue canadienne de linguistique (Toronto, ON, Can.) **36511**

Canadian Journal of Mathematics (Vancouver, BC, Can.) **35132**

Canadian Journal of Medical Laboratory Science (CJLMS) (Hamilton, ON, Can.) **35877**

Canadian Journal of Medical Radiation Technology (Ottawa, ON, Can.) **36207**

Canadian Journal of Medical Technology (CJMT) **35877***

Canadian Journal of Microbiology (Revue Canadienne de Microbiologie) (Ottawa, ON, Can.) **36208**

Canadian Journal of Neurological Sciences (Calgary, AB, Can.) **34637**

Canadian Journal of Nursing Administration (White Rock, BC, Can.) *Ceased*

The Canadian Journal of Ob/Gyn (Baie-D'Urfe, QC, Can.) *Unable to locate*

The Canadian Journal of Occupational Therapy (Revue Canadienne d'Ergotherapie) (Ottawa, ON, Can.) **36209**

Canadian Journal of Ophthalmology (Journal Canadien d'Ophtalmologie) (Ottawa, ON, Can.) **36210**

Canadian Journal of Optometry (La Revue Canadienne d'Optometrie) (Ottawa, ON, Can.) *Unable to locate*

Canadian Journal of Philosophy (Lethbridge, AB, Can.) **34794**

Canadian Journal of Physiology and Pharmacology (Revue Canadienne de Physiologie et Pharmacologie) (Ottawa, ON, Can.) **36211**

Canadian Journal of Plant Science (Ottawa, ON, Can.) **36212**

The Canadian Journal of Plastic Surgery (Oakville, ON, Can.) **36140**

Canadian Journal of Political Science (Revue canadienne de science politique) (Ottawa, ON, Can.) **36213**

Canadian Journal of Program Evaluation/Revue Canadienne D'evaluation de Programme (Sudbury, ON, Can.) **36415**

Canadian Journal of Psychiatric Nursing (Winnipeg, MB, Can.) *Ceased*

The Canadian Journal of Psychiatry (Ottawa, ON, Can.) **36214**

Canadian Journal of Public Health (Ottawa, ON, Can.) **36215**

Canadian Journal of Radiography, Radiation Therapy & Nuclear Medicine **36207***

Canadian Journal of Regional Science (Montreal, QC, Can.) **37098**

Canadian Journal of Rehabilitation (Edmonton, AB, Can.) *Ceased*

Canadian Journal of Remote Sensing (Ottawa, ON, Can.) **36216**

Canadian Journal of Respiratory Therapy (Ottawa, ON, Can.) **36217**

Canadian Journal of Rural Medicine (Ottawa, ON, Can.) **36218**

Canadian Journal of Sociology/Cahiers canadiens de sociologie (Toronto, ON, Can.) **36512**

Canadian Journal of Soil Science (Ottawa, ON, Can.) **36219**

Canadian Journal of Surgery (Ottawa, ON, Can.) **36220**

Canadian Journal of Urban Research (Winnipeg, MB, Can.) **35320**

Canadian Journal of Veterinary Research (Ottawa, ON, Can.) **36221**

Canadian Journal of Women and the Law/Revue Femmes et Droit (Toronto, ON, Can.) **36513**

Canadian Journal of Zoology (Revue Canadienne de Zoologie) (North York, ON, Can.) **36125**

Canadian Laboratory (Willowdale, ON, Can.) *Ceased*

Canadian Labour and Employment Law Journal (Toronto, ON, Can.) *Ceased*

Canadian Labour (Le Monde Syndical) (Ottawa, ON, Can.) *Ceased*

Canadian Lawyer (Aurora, ON, Can.) **35642**

The Canadian Leader (Ottawa, ON, Can.) **36222**

The Canadian League (Winnipeg, MB, Can.) *Ceased*

Canadian Literature (Vancouver, BC, Can.) **35133**

Canadian Literature; The Prairie Journal of (Calgary, AB, Can.) **34654**

Canadian Living (Markham, ON, Can.) *Unable to locate*

The Canadian Locksmith Magazine (Toronto, ON, Can.) **36514**

Canadian Machinery and Metalworking (Toronto, ON, Can.) **36515**

The Canadian Manager (Toronto, ON, Can.) **36516**

Canadian Mathematical Bulletin (Toronto, ON, Can.) **36517**

(Canadian Medical Association Journal)/(Journal de l'Association Medicale Canadienne); CMAJ/JAMC (Ottawa, ON, Can.) **36236**

Canadian Mennonite (Waterloo, ON, Can.) **36847**

Canadian Messenger (Toronto, ON, Can.) **36518**

Canadian Mill Product News (Burnaby, BC, Can.) *Unable to locate*

Canadian Mining Journal (Toronto, ON, Can.) **36519**

(Canadian Mining & Metallurgical Bulletin); CIM Bulletin (Montreal, QC, Can.) **37103**

The Canadian Missionary Link **35817***

The Canadian Modern Language Review/La Revue canadienne des langues vivantes (Toronto, ON, Can.) **36520**

Canadian MoneySaver (Bath, ON, Can.) **35667**

Canadian Music Trade (St. Catharines, ON, Can.) **36352**

Canadian Musician (St. Catharines, ON, Can.) **36353**

Canadian Nature **36263***

Canadian Nurse (L'Infirmiere Canadienne) (Ottawa, ON, Can.) **36223**

Canadian Nursing Home Journal (White Rock, BC, Can.) **35240**

Canadian Occupational Health and Safety News (COHSN) (Toronto, ON, Can.) **36521**

Canadian Occupational Safety (Burlington, ON, Can.) **35716**

Canadian Office Products and Stationery (Willowdale, ON, Can.) *Ceased*

Canadian Oncology Nursing Journal (Toronto, ON, Can.) **36522**

Canadian Operating Room Nursing Journal (White Rock, BC, Can.) **35241**

Canadian Packaging (Toronto, ON, Can.) **36523**

(Canadian Pages); Kanadske Listy (Mississauga, ON, Can.) **36072**

Canadian Parliamentary Review (Ottawa, ON, Can.) **36224**

Canadian Pharmaceutical Journal (Ottawa, ON, Can.) **36225**

Canadian Philatelist (Toronto, ON, Can.) **36524**

Canadian Philosophical Reviews **34725***

Canadian Pizza Magazine (Delhi, ON, Can.) **35765**

Canadian Plant Disease Survey (London, ON, Can.) **35980**

Canadian Plastics (Toronto, ON, Can.) **36525**

Canadian Plastics Technology Showcase (Toronto, ON, Can.) *Ceased*

Canadian Poetry; Journal of (Ottawa, ON, Can.) **36254**

Canadian Pool & Spa Marketing **36030***

The Canadian Postmaster (Le Maitre de Poste Canadien) (Ottawa, ON, Can.) **36226**

Canadian Power Illustrated (Mississauga, ON, Can.) *Unable to locate*

The Canadian Press & Broadcast News (Toronto, ON, Can.) **37851**

Canadian Printer Magazine (Toronto, ON, Can.) **36526**

Canadian Printer and Publisher **36526***

Canadian Process Equipment & Control News (Toronto, ON, Can.) **36527**

Canadian Public Administration (Administration publique du Canada) (Toronto, ON, Can.) **36528**

Canadian Public Policy—Analyse de Politiques (Calgary, AB, Can.) **34638**

Canadian Rail/Rail Canadien (Montreal, QC, Can.) **37099**

Canadian Railway Modeller (Winnipeg, MB, Can.) *Unable to locate*

The Canadian Record (Canadian, TX) **29997**

Canadian Rental Service (Exeter, ON, Can.) **35824**

Canadian Resources (Regina, SK, Can.) *Unable to locate*

Canadian Respiratory Journal (Oakville, ON, Can.) **36141**

Canadian Retailer (Winnipeg, MB, Can.) *Ceased*

Canadian Review of American Studies (Ottawa, ON, Can.) **36227**

Canadian Review of Comparative Literature (Toronto, ON, Can.) **36529**

Canadian Review of Sociology and Anthropology (Montreal, QC, Can.) **37100**

Canadian Review of Studies in Nationalism (Charlottetown, PE, Can.) **36913**

Canadian Rockies; WHERE (Calgary, AB, Can.) **34660**

Canadian Rodeo News (Calgary, AB, Can.) **34639**

Canadian RV Dealer **36055***

Canadian Sailings (Montreal, QC, Can.) *Unable to locate*

Canadian Secretary (Toronto, ON, Can.) *Ceased*

CANADIAN SECURITY (Aurora, ON, Can.) **35643**

Canadian Select Homes **36752***

Canadian Seniority Magazine (Pickering, ON, Can.) *Unable to locate*

Canadian Serbian (Hamilton, ON, Can.) **35878**

Canadian Shareowner (Toronto, ON, Can.) **36530**

Canadian Shipping and Marine Engineering (Mississauga, ON, Can.) *Ceased*

Canadian Slavonic Papers/Revue Canadienne des Slavistes (Edmonton, AB, Can.) **34704**

Canadian Social Trends (Ottawa, ON, Can.) **36228**

Canadian Specialty Foods Retailer (Port Credit, ON, Can.) *Ceased*

Canadian Speeches (Woodville, ON, Can.) **36910**

Canadian Sportfishing (Waterdown, ON, Can.) **36844**

The Canadian Sportsman (Straffordville, ON, Can.) **36408**

The Canadian Stamp News (St. Catharines, ON, Can.) **36354**

Canadian Statesman (Bowmanville, ON, Can.) *Unable to locate*

Canadian Statistical Review **36192***

Canadian Studies; American Review of (Washington, DC) **5342**

Canadian Studies (Revue d'Etudes Canadiennes); Journal of (Peterborough, ON, Can.) **36316**

The Canadian Surveyor **36246***

Canadian Swine (Ottawa, ON, Can.) *Unable to locate*

Canadian Tax Journal (Revue fiscale canadienne) (Toronto, ON, Can.) **36531**

Canadian Telecom (Toronto, ON, Can.) *Unable to locate*

Canadian Textile Journal (La Revue Canadienne du Textile) (Saint-Hyacinthe, QC, Can.) **37348**

Canadian Theatre Review (Guelph, ON, Can.) **35859**

Canadian Theosophist (Burks Falls, ON, Can.) **35713**

Canadian Thoroughbred (Aurora, ON, Can.) **35644**

The Canadian Tobacco Grower (Delhi, ON, Can.) **35766**

Canadian Transport (Ottawa, ON, Can.) *Unable to locate*

Canadian Transportation **36532***

Canadian Transportation and Distribution Management **36532***

Canadian Transportation Logistics **36532***

Canadian Transportation & Logistics (Toronto, ON, Can.) **36532**

Canadian Transportation Logistics/Including Canadian Warehousing Logistics **36532***

The Canadian Trapper (North Battleford, SK, Can.) *Ceased*

Canadian Travel Courier **36772***

Canadian Travel Press (Toronto, ON, Can.) **36533**

Canadian Travel Press Weekly **36533***

The Canadian Traveller **36750***

Canadian Traveller (Vancouver, BC, Can.) **35134**

Canadian Treasurer (Toronto, ON, Can.) **36534**

Canadian Treasurey Management Review *Ceased*

Canadian Underwriter (Don Mills, ON, Can.) **35772**

Canadian Vending Magazine (Delhi, ON, Can.) **35767**

Canadian Vet Supplies (Montreal, QC, Can.) *Unable to locate*

Canadian Veterinary Journal (Ottawa, ON, Can.) **36229**

Canadian Vocational Journal (Ottawa, ON, Can.) **36230**

Canadian Water Well **35827***

Canadian West (Langley, BC, Can.) *Ceased*

Canadian Wings **36092***

Canadian Woman Golfer **36737***

Canadian Woman Studies (Les Cahiers de la Femme) (Toronto, ON, Can.) **36535**

Canadian Wood Products (Baie D'urfe', QC, Can.) **36945**

Canadian Workshop **36020***

Canadian Workshop **36019***

Canadian Yachting Magazine (Mississauga, ON, Can.) **36060**

canadienne); Canadian Tax Journal (Revue fiscale (Toronto, ON, Can.) **36531**

Canadienne Grecque; La Tribune (Montreal, QC, Can.) **37153**

Canado-Americain; Le (Manchester, NH) **18557**

Canals; The Best from American (Annapolis, MD) **13089**

Canarsie Courier (Brooklyn, NY) **20305**

Canarsie Digest (Brooklyn, NY) **20306**

Canastota Bee-Journal (Canastota, NY) **20425**

The Canby Herald (Wilsonville, OR) **26613**

Cancer (New York, NY) *Ceased*

Cancer Biochemistry Biophysics (New York, NY) *Unable to locate*

Cancer Biotherapy and Antibody, Immunoconjuates, and Radiopharmaceuticals **20893***

Cancer Biotherapy and Radiopharmaceuticals (Larchmont, NY) **20893**

The Cancer Bulletin for University of Texas M.D. Anderson Cancer Center (Houston, TX) *Ceased*

Cancer Case Presentations (Philadelphia, PA) *Ceased*

Cancer Causes and Control (New York, NY) **21370**

Cancer Control Journal (Tampa, FL) **6759**

Cancer Epidemiology, Biomarkers & Prevention (Philadelphia, PA) **27391**

Cancer; Familial (New York, NY) **21676**

Cancer; Genes, Chromosomes and (Hoboken, NJ) **18950**

Cancer; International Journal of (Hoboken, NJ) **18976**

Cancer Investigation (New York, NY) **21371**

The Cancer Journal (Sudbury, MA) **14578**

Cancer Journal for Clinicians; CA: A (Baltimore, MD) **13141**

Cancer Magazine (Philadelphia, PA) *Ceased*

Cancer News Journal **2851***

Cancer Nursing (Gainesville, FL) **6133**

Cancer; Nutrition and (Mahwah, NJ) **19204**

Cancer Practice (Philadelphia, PA) *Unable to locate*

Cancer Prevention (Philadelphia, PA) *Ceased*

Cancer; Primary Care & (Melville, NY) **21059**

Cancer Research (Philadelphia, PA) **27392**

Cancer Research; Clinical (Houston, TX) **30463**

Cancer Research; Molecular (Philadelphia, PA) **27572**

Cancer Victors Journal (Playa del Rey, CA) **2851**

CANDIS **36699***

Candy Business (Palm Springs, CA) **2755**

Candy Buyer; Professional (Palm Springs, CA) **2765**

Candy Industry (Deerfield, IL) **8722**

Candy Marketer (Cleveland, OH) *Ceased*

Candy Wholesaler **5465***

Candy World Illustrated (Marina del Rey, CA) **2505**

Caney Chronicle **11374***

Canfield Family Association (Wichita, KS) *Ceased*

Canine Practice (Los Angeles, CA) *Ceased*

Canisteo Penn-E-Saver; Hornell- (Canisteo, NY) **20428**

Canmore Leader (Canmore, AB, Can.) **34678**

3300

Numbers cited in bold after listings are entry numbers rather than page numbers.

CED (Communications Engineering & Design) (Highlands Ranch, CO) 4516
Cedar County News (Hartington, NE) 18034
Cedar County Republican (Stockton, MO) 17639
Cedar Creek Pilot (Cedar Creek, TX) 30009
Cedar Grove Times; Verona- (Cedar Grove, NJ) 18722
Cedar Hill Chronicle (Cedar Hill, TX) Unable to locate
Cedar Hill Sentinel (Cedar Hill, TX) 30010
Cedar Hill Today (Cedar Hill, TX) 30011
Cedar Key Beacon (Cedar Key, FL) 5979
Cedar Lake Journal (Lowell, IN) 10279
Cedar Lake-Lowell Star (Crown Point, IN) 9914
The Cedar Post (Cedar Park, TX) Unable to locate
Cedar Rapids Gazette (Cedar Rapids, IA) Unable to locate
Cedar Rapids Press (Cedar Rapids, NE) 17971
Cedar Springs Advance; Rockford/ (Rockford, MI) 15469
Cedar Valley Cable Co. (Austin, TX) 29857
Cedar Valley Times (Vinton, IA) 11282
Cedarhurst/Lawrence Shopper's Guide (Ontario, ON, Can.) 36160
Cedarhurst Pennysaver (Cedarhurst, HI) 7661
The Cedartown Standard (Cedartown, GA) 7165
CEE News (Overland Park, KS) 11703
Ceilings; Walls & (Troy, MI) 15644
Celebrate Life! (Indian Rocks Beach, FL) Ceased
Celebrating Voices (Binghamton, NY) 20152
Celebration (Kansas City, MO) 17160
Celebrity Plus (New York, NY) Ceased
Celina Record (Plano, TX) Unable to locate
Cell (Cambridge, MA) 14045
Cell Biochemistry and Function (Hoboken, NJ) 18909
Cell Biology (Biochimie et Biologie Cellulaire); Biochemistry and (Winnipeg, MB, Can.) 35316
Cell Biology; DNA and (Larchmont, NY) 20897
Cell Biology International (San Diego, CA) 3128
Cell Genetics; Cytogenetics and (Farmington, CT) 4810
Cell Growth & Differentiation 27572*
Cell Motility and the Cytoskeleton (Hoboken, NJ) 18910
Cell Motility; Journal of Muscle Research and (New York, NY) 22137
Cell Physiology; American Journal of Physiology: (Bethesda, MD) 13303
Cell Research; Experimental (San Diego, CA) 3147
Cell Science; Methods in (Burlington, VT) 31515
Cell Stress and Chaperones (Philadelphia, PA) 27396
Cell and Tissue Banking (New York, NY) 21386
Cells Tissues Organs (Farmington, CT) 4804
Cellulaire); Biochemistry and Cell Biology (Biochimie et Biologie (Winnipeg, MB, Can.) 35316
Cellular Biology; Molecular and (Washington, DC) 5658
Cellular Business & Wireless World 11736*
Cellular Immunology (Bethesda, MD) 13323
Cellular Marketing (Greenwood Village, CO) Ceased
Cellular & Mobile International (Overland Park, KS) 11704
Cellular and Molecular Neurobiology (New York, NY) 21387
Cellular News Today (Everett, WA) Unable to locate
Cellular One Roaming Guide 29379*
Cellular Physiology and Biochemistry (Farmington, CT) 4805
Cellulose (New York, NY) 21388
Celtic Heritage (Halifax, NS, Can.) 35560
Cemetery; Catholic (Des Plaines, IL) 8752
Cemetery Management 32367*
Cencom 9150*
Cencom of Abbeville 28465*
Cencom Cable of Alabama, L.P. (Fultondale, AL) Unable to locate
Cencom Cable Associates 9150*
Cencom Cable Associates Inc. 30620*
Cencom Cable Associates Inc. (Dallas, TX) Unable to locate
Cencom Cable Television 30649*
Cencom Cable Television 1477*
Cencom Cable Television (Grovetown, GA) 7317
Cencom of Kingsville (Kingsville, TX) 30649
Cent Saver Buyer's Guide (Portage, WI) 34252
Cent Saver Extra (Portage, WI) 34253
Cent Saver Reminder (Portage, WI) 34254
Centel Cable (Germantown, OH) Unable to locate
Center Grove Gazette (Fishers, IN) 9956
Center Magazine 2345*
Center Magazine (Louisville, KY) Ceased
Center Management Ceased
Center Municipal Cable System (Center, CO) 4230
Center Post-Dispatch (Center, CO) 4229
Center Quarterly 23595*
Center Republican (Washburn, ND) 24553
Centereach/Lake Grove Suffolk Life (Centereach, NY) 20445
Centereach/Selden Suffolk Life 20445*
Centereach Weekender (Farmingdale, NY) Ceased

The Centerville-Bellbrook Times (Centerville, OH) 24753
Centerville News (Centerville, TX) 30015
Centerville Times (Herndon, VA) 32161
Central Alberta Adviser (Red Deer, AB, Can.) 34828
Central Alberta Life (Red Deer, AB, Can.) 34829
Central America Newspak (Austin, TX) Ceased
Central American & Caribbean—Basic Oil Laws & Concession Contracts (New York, NY) 21389
Central Asia Monitor (Benson, VT) 31504
Central Boca Times (Chicago, IL) Ceased
Central Cable TV 35601*
The Central California Catholic Life (Fresno, CA) 1947
Central California Jewish Heritage (Winnetka, CA) Unable to locate
Central City Times-Argus (Central City, KY) 12014
Central Coast Sun Bulletin (Redding, CA) Ceased
Central Coast This Week (Santa Maria, CA) 3695
Central Coast Times (Paso Robles, CA) 2830
Central County (Eau Claire, MI) 15001
Central County Trade Lines Shopper's Guide (Eau Claire, MI) 15002
Central European History (Riverside, CA) 2934
Central European History (Boston, MA) 13871
Central Florida Family Magazine (Orlando, FL) 6488
The Central Florida Future (Orlando, FL) Unable to locate
Central Florida Magazine (Winter Park, FL) Unable to locate
Central Florida Newcomer (Raleigh, NC) Ceased
Central Huntington Pennysaver (Huntington, NY) Unable to locate
Central Independent Television USA, Inc. (New York, NY) 37690
Central Islip/Hauppauge Suffolk Life (Central Islip, NY) 20448
Central Islip Suffolk Life 20448*
Central Kentucky News-Journal (Campbellsville, KY) 12006
Central Kentucky Researcher (Campbellsville, KY) 12007
Central Kitsap Reporter (Silverdale, WA) 33083
Central Kitsap Style 33083*
Central Maine Morning Sentinel (Waterville, ME) Unable to locate
Central Marketplace (Abilene, KS) 11333
Central Michigan Life (Mount Pleasant, MI) 15375
Central Military Sun Press 7775*
Central Minnesota Shopping News (St. Cloud, MN) Ceased
Central Missouri News (Sedalia, MO) 17569
Central Nervous System Trauma 20917*
Central News Agency (New York, NY) Unable to locate
Central Newspapers Inc. (Washington, DC) Unable to locate
Central N.Y. Business Journal (Syracuse, NY) 23393
Central Oklahoma Home Builder (Oklahoma City, OK) 25959
Central Oregon Rancher (Powell Butte, OR) Unable to locate
Central Oregonian (Prineville, OR) 26548
Central PA (Harrisburg, PA) 26985
The Central Peace Signal (Rycroft, AB, Can.) 34840
Central Penn Business Journal (Harrisburg, PA) Unable to locate
Central Pennsylvania's APPRISE 26985*
Central Post (Dayton, NJ) 18776
Central Post Tempo (North Brunswick, NJ) 19380
Central Press Features of London (New York, NY) Ceased
Central Railway Chronicle (Buffalo, NY) Unable to locate
Central Record (Lancaster, KY) 12152
The Central Record (Medford, NJ) 19222
Central St. Croix News (Hammond, WI) 33773
Central Shopper (Des Moines, IA) 10774
Central Shopper (Lisbon, OH) 25307
Central Square Citizen Outlet (Central Square, NY) 20451
Central Star/Journal Wave (Los Angeles, CA) 2234
Central States 34323*
Central States Archaeological Journal (Chesterfield, MO) 16974
Central Sun-Press (Kaneohe, HI) 7768
Central Valley Cable (Gualala, CA) 2035
The Central Virginian (Louisa, VA) 32200
Central Washington Catholic (Yakima, WA) 33219
Central Weekend (Eden Prairie, MN) Ceased
Central West End Journal (Warrenton, MO) 17675
Centralia Sentinel (Centralia, IL) 8174
Centre (Toronto, ON, Can.) 36544
Centre County Heritage (State College, PA) 28017
Centre County Legal Journal (State College, PA) Unable to locate
Centre Daily News (San Francisco, CA) Unable to locate

Centre Daily News (Long Island City, NY) Unable to locate
Centre Daily Times (State College, PA) 28018
Centre D'Etudes de L'Asie de L'Est/Cahiers (Montreal, QC, Can.) 37101
Centrepiece (Danville, KY) 12037
Centretown News (Ottawa, ON, Can.) 36233
CentreView (Centreville, VA) 31910
Centreville Press (Centreville, AL) 151
Centroamerica (Minneapolis, MN) Unable to locate
Centrum Guide (Worcester, MA) Ceased
Century (Hastings-on-Hudson, NY) Unable to locate
Century Cable 10351*
Century Cable (Owensboro, KY) 12328
Century Cable (Hartsville, SC) 28658
Century Cable (Coeburn, VA) Ceased
Century Cable (Dellslow, WV) Ceased
Century Cable Television 34444*
Century Cable TV 16646*
Century Cable TV (Fort Payne, AL) Ceased
Century Cable TV (Vanceburg, KY) 12424
Century Cable TV (Dellslow, WV) 33301
Century Comm. 32773*
Century Communication (Brunswick, GA) 7141
Century Communications 4120*
Century Communications 7847*
Century Communications 34523*
Century Communications (Brea, CA) Unable to locate
Century Communications (Santa Monica, CA) 3721
Century Communications (Owensboro, KY) 12329
Century Communications (Greenwood, MS) 16646
Century Communications (Lovington, NM) 19898
Century Communications Corp. (Newburgh, IN) 10351
Century Cullman Corp. (Cullman, AL) 163
Century Home 36018*
Century Huntington Co. (Huntington, WV) 33338
Century ML Cable Venture (Toa Baja, PR) 28317
Century New Mexico Cable TV 19898*
Century News Service (Falls Church, VA) 37859
Century Ohio Cable TV Corp. (Struthers, OH) Unable to locate
Century Shenango Cable TV, Inc. (Hermitage, PA) Unable to locate
Century Southwest Cable 3721*
CenturyTel TeleVideo (Casco, WI) 33617
CenturyTel TeleVideo (Platteville, WI) 34244
Centurytel Televideo (Thorp, WI) 34368
CenturyTel Telview (Randolph, WI) 34279
CEO/International Strategies (New York, NY) Unable to locate
CEO; Washington (Bellevue, WA) 32669
Cepal Review (New York, NY) 21390
Ceramic Abstracts (Bethesda, MD) Ceased
Ceramic Arts & Crafts 33826*
Ceramic Engineering and Science Proceedings (Westerville, OH) 25637
Ceramic Industry (Solon, OH) Unable to locate
Ceramic Society Bulletin; American (Westerville, OH) 25636
Ceramic Society; Journal of the American (Westerville, OH) 25641
Ceramic Source (Westerville, OH) 25638
Ceramics; American (New York, NY) 21183
Ceramics/Composites Alert; Polymers/ (Beachwood, OH) 24655
Ceramics; Glass and (New York, NY) 21765
Ceramics Magazine (Muskegon, MI) Ceased
Ceramics Monthly (Westerville, OH) 25639
Ceramics Quarterly; Canadian (Willowdale, ON, Can.) 36876
Cereal Chemistry (St. Paul, MN) 16368
Cereal Foods World (St. Paul, MN) 16369
Cerebral Blood Flow and Metabolism; Journal of (Baltimore, MD) 13182
Cerebral Cortex (Cary, NC) 23687
Cerebrovascular and Brain Metabolism Reviews (Baltimore, MD) Unable to locate
Cerebrovascular Diseases (Farmington, CT) 4806
Cerebrovascular Diseases; Journal of Stroke and (Indianapolis, IN) 10142
Cerebus (Kitchener, ON, Can.) 35959
The Ceres Courier (Ceres, CA) 1682
Cerritos/Artesia Community Advocate (Los Angeles, CA) Ceased
Certified Engineering Technician (Flowery Branch, GA) 7273
Cervantes: Bulletin of the Cervantes Society of America (Albany, NY) 19983
C'est Pour Quand? (Laval, QC, Can.) 37035
The CF Apartment Reporter (Castle Rock, CO) 4220
GF Cable TV Inc. (Montreal, QC, Can.) 37242
CFA Digest (Charlottesville, VA) 31922
CFAB-AM - 1450 (Windsor, NS, Can.) 35620
CFAC-AM (Calgary, AB, Can.) Unable to locate
CFAI-FM - 101.1 (Edmundston, NB, Can.) 35386
CFAM-AM - 950 (Altona, MB, Can.) 35248
CFAN-FM - 99.3 (Miramichi, NB, Can.) 35410
CFAP-TV (Quebec, QC, Can.) Unable to locate
CFAR-AM - 590 (Flin Flon, MB, Can.) 35267

CFAX-AM - 1070 (Victoria, BC, Can.) **35232**
CFB Comox Totem Times (Lazo, BC, Can.) **35008**
CFBC-AM (St. John, NB, Can.) *Unable to locate*
CFBG-FM - 99.5 (Bracebridge, ON, Can.) **35697**
CFBR-AM **36423***
CFBR-FM - 100.3 (Edmonton, AB, Can.) **34744**
CFBV-AM - 870 (Smithers, BC, Can.) **35091**
CFCA-FM **36860***
CFCA-FM - 105.3 (Waterloo, ON, Can.) **36860**
CFCB-AM - 570 (Corner Brook, NL, Can.) **35451**
CFCH-AM (North Bay, ON, Can.) *Ceased*
CFCL-AM **36457***
CFCN-AM **34671***
CFCN-TV - Channel 4 (Calgary, AB, Can.) **34665**
CFCO-AM - 630 (Chatham, ON, Can.) **35731**
CFCP-FM - 98.9 (Courtenay, BC, Can.) **34933**
CFCR **34979***
CFCR-FM - 90.5 (Saskatoon, SK, Can.) **37561**
CFCV-FM - 97.7 (Port-aux-Basques, NL, Can.) **35478**
CFCW-AM - 790 (Edmonton, AB, Can.) **34745**
CFCY-AM - 630 (Charlottetown, PE, Can.) **36918**
CFDA-FM - 101.9 FM (Victoriaville, QC, Can.) **37434**
(CFDJ); ColdFusion Developer's Journal (Montvale, NJ) **19247**
CFDL-FM - 97.9 (Deer Lake, NL, Can.) **35454**
CFDR-AM (Dartmouth, NS, Can.) *Unable to locate*
CFED-AM (Chibougamau, QC, Can.) *Unable to locate*
CFEI-FM - 106.5 (Saint-Hyacinthe, QC, Can.) **37352**
CFEK-AM - 1240 (Fernie, BC, Can.) **34954**
CFEL-FM - 102.1 (Montmagny, QC, Can.) **37078**
CFFB-AM **35520***
CFFB-AM - 1230 (Iqaluit, NT, Can.) **35520**
CFFC-AM **34823***
CFFF-FM - 92.7 (Peterborough, ON, Can.) **36320**
CFFM-FM **34981***
CFFM-FM - 97.5 (Williams Lake, BC, Can.) **35245**
CFFR-AM - 660 (Calgary, AB, Can.) **34666**
CFFX-AM - 960 (Kingston, ON, Can.) **35950**
CFGB-AM (Happy Valley, NL, Can.) *Ceased*
CFGB-FM - 89.5 (Happy Valley, NL, Can.) **35467**
CFGL-FM - 105.7 (Laval, QC, Can.) **37045**
CFGN-AM - 1230 (Port-aux-Basques, NL, Can.) **35479**
CFGO **36288***
CFGO-AM - 1200 (Ottawa, ON, Can.) **36288**
CFGP-AM **34776***
CFGP-FM - 97.7 (Grande Prairie, AB, Can.) **34776**
CFGS-TV - Channel 49 (Hull, QC, Can.) **37005**
CFGT-AM (Quebec, QC, Can.) *Unable to locate*
CFGX-FM - 99.9 (Sarnia, ON, Can.) **36367**
CFHK-FM - 103.1 (London, ON, Can.) **35995**
CFHK-FM (London/St. Thomas, ON, Can.) *Ceased*
CFIM-FM - 92.7 (Cap-aux-Meules, QC, Can.) **36955**
CFIQ-AM (Saint John's, NL, Can.) *Ceased*
CFIX-FM - 96.9 (Chicoutimi, QC, Can.) **36972**
CFJB-FM - 95.7 (Barrie, ON, Can.) **35660**
CFJC-TV - Channel 4 (Kamloops, BC, Can.) **34979**
CFJO-FM - 97.3 (Thetford Mines, QC, Can.) **37411**
CFJR-FM - 104.9 FM (Brockville, ON, Can.) **35710**
CFKC-AM - 1340 (Creston, BC, Can.) **34940**
CFKS-TV - Channel 30 (Sherbrooke, QC, Can.) **37396**
CFLC-FM - 97.9 (Churchill Falls, NL, Can.) **35444**
CFLG-FM - 104.5 mhz (Cornwall, ON, Can.) **35757**
CFLM-AM - 1240 (La Tuque, QC, Can.) **37024**
CFLN-AM - 1230 (Goose Bay, NL, Can.) **35459**
CFLO-FM - 104.7 (L'Annonciation, QC, Can.) **36940**
CFLS-AM **37050***
CFLS-FM **37050***
CFLV-AM **37427***
CFLW-AM - 1340 (Wabush, NL, Can.) **35512**
CFLY-FM - 98.3 (Kingston, ON, Can.) **35951**
C.F.M.A. Building Profits (Princeton, NJ) **19456**
CFMB-AM - 1280 (Westmount, QC, Can.) **37447**
CFMC-FM - 95.1 (Saskatoon, SK, Can.) **37562**
CFMF-FM - 103.1 (Fermont, QC, Can.) **36995**
CFMG-FM (St. Albert, AB, Can.) *Unable to locate*
CFMI-FM (Vancouver, BC, Can.) *Unable to locate*
CFMK-FM - 96.3 (Kingston, ON, Can.) **35952**
CFMM-FM - 99.1 (Prince Albert, SK, Can.) **37519**
CFMO-FM **36297***
CFMQ-FM **37540***
CFMS-FM (Victoria, BC, Can.) *Ceased*
CFMT-TV - Channel 47/60/69 (Toronto, ON, Can.) **36802**
CFMU-FM - 93.3 (Hamilton, ON, Can.) **35893**
CFMX-FM - 96.3 (Toronto, ON, Can.) **36803**
CFNB-AM **35404***
CFNI-AM - 1240 (Port Hardy, BC, Can.) **35053**
CFNJ-FM - 99.1 (Saint-Gabriel, QC, Can.) **37340**
CFNL-AM - 590 (Fort Nelson, BC, Can.) **34957**
CFNN-FM - 97.9 (St. Anthony, NL, Can.) **35483**
CFNO-FM - 93.1 (Marathon, ON, Can.) **36012**
CFNW-AM - 790 (Port au Choix, NL, Can.) **35480**
CFNY-FM - 102.1 (Toronto, ON, Can.) **36804**
CFO (Boston, MA) **13872**
CFOB-AM - 640 (Fort Francis, ON, Can.) **35842**
CFOK-AM - 1370 (Westlock, AB, Can.) **34872**
CFOM-FM - 102.9 (Levis, QC, Can.) **37050**

CFOR-AM **36177***
CFOS-AM - 560 (Owen Sound, ON, Can.) **36300**
CFOX-FM (Vancouver, BC, Can.) *Unable to locate*
CFOZ-FM, CJOZ-FM, CKCV-FM, CKOZ-FM, CIOZ-FM, CHOS-FM, CKSS-FM, CIOS-FM **35499***
CFPL-AM - 980 (London, ON, Can.) **35996**
CFPL-FM - 95.9 (London, ON, Can.) **35997**
CFPL-TV **35998***
CFPL-TV (The New PL) - Channel 10 (London, ON, Can.) **35998**
CFPS-AM - 1490 (Owen Sound, ON, Can.) **36301**
CFQC-AM (Saskatoon, SK, Can.) *Unable to locate*
CFQC-TV - Channel 8 (Saskatoon, SK, Can.) **37563**
CFQM-FM - 103.9 (Moncton, NB, Can.) **35418**
CFQR-FM (Montreal, QC, Can.) *Unable to locate*
CFQX-FM (Winnipeg, MB, Can.) *Unable to locate*
CFRA-AM - 580 (Ottawa, ON, Can.) **36289**
CFRB-AM - 1010 (Toronto, ON, Can.) **36805**
CFRC-AM **35953***
CFRC-FM - 101.9 (Kingston, ON, Can.) **35953**
CFRE-TV - Channel 11 (Regina, SK, Can.) **37539**
CFRG-AM (Regina, SK, Can.) *Unable to locate*
CFRH-FM - 88.1 (Penetanguishene, ON, Can.) **36311**
CFRM-FM **37250***
CFRN-AM - 1260 (Edmonton, AB, Can.) **34746**
CFRN-TV - Channel 3; Cable 2 (Edmonton, AB, Can.) **34747**
CFRO-FM - 102.7 (Vancouver, BC, Can.) **35185**
CFRP-AM (Baie-Comeau, QC, Can.) *Unable to locate*
CFRQ-FM (Dartmouth, NS, Can.) *Unable to locate*
CFRS-AM **36392***
CFRS-TV - Channel 4 (Jonquiere, QC, Can.) **37014**
CFRU-FM - 93.3 (Guelph, ON, Can.) **35868**
CFRV-FM - 107.7 (Lethbridge, AB, Can.) **34799**
CFRW-AM **35369***
CFRW-AM - 1290 (Winnipeg, MB, Can.) **35369**
CFRW-FM **35370***
CFRY-AM - 920 (Portage La Prairie, MB, Can.) **35284**
CFS Mont Apica Cable TV System (Bagotville, QC, Can.) *Unable to locate*
CFSK-TV - Channel 4 (Saskatoon, SK, Can.) **37564**
CFSL-AM - 1190 (Weyburn, SK, Can.) **37593**
CFST-AM **35369***
CFSX-AM - 870 (Stephenville, NL, Can.) **35509**
CFTI-FM **36458***
CFTK-AM - 590 (Terrace, BC, Can.) **35112**
CFTK-TV - Channel 3 (Terrace, BC, Can.) **35113**
CFTO-TV - Channel 9 (Scarborough, ON, Can.) **36387**
CFTR-AM - 680 (Toronto, ON, Can.) **36806**
CFTU-TV **37243***
CFTU-TV - Channel 29 (Montreal, QC, Can.) **37243**
CFUN **35410***
CFUN-AM (Vancouver, BC, Can.) *Unable to locate*
CFUV-FM - 101.9 (Victoria, BC, Can.) **35233**
CFVD-FM - 95.5 (Degelis, QC, Can.) **36985**
CFVM-AM - 99.9 (Amqui, QC, Can.) **36936**
CFWB-AM - 1490 (Campbell River, BC, Can.) **34920**
CFWE-FM (Lac La Biche, AB, Can.) *Unable to locate*
CFWF-FM (Regina, SK, Can.) *Unable to locate*
CFWM-FM (Winnipeg, MB, Can.) *Unable to locate*
CFXL-AM (Calgary, AB, Can.) *Unable to locate*
CFXU-AM - 690 (Antigonish, NS, Can.) **35539**
CFXYFM - 105.3 (Fredericton, NB, Can.) **35402**
CFYK-AM - 1340 (Yellowknife, NT, Can.) **35529**
CFYK-TV (Yellowknife, NT, Can.) *Unable to locate*
CFYM-AM - 1210 (Kindersley, SK, Can.) **37484**
CFYN-AM (Sault Sainte Marie, ON, Can.) *Ceased*
CFYQ-AM **35458***
CFYR-AM - 1400 (Edson, AB, Can.) **34759**
CFZZ-AM (St. Jean, QC, Can.) *Unable to locate*
CG Professional (San Francisco, CA) *Unable to locate*
CGA Magazine (Vancouver, BC, Can.) **35135**
CGA World (Olyphant, PA) **27347**
CH & R Product News & Menu Planner (Don Mills, ON, Can.) *Ceased*
CHAB-AM - 800 (Moose Jaw, SK, Can.) **37503**
CHAD-AM - 1340 (Amos, QC, Can.) **36933**
Chadron Record (Chadron, NE) **17973**
Chaffee County Times (Salida, CO) **4618**
Chagrin Herald Sun (Chagrin Falls, OH) **24755**
The Chagrin Valley Times (Chagrin Falls, OH) **24756**
The Chagrin Valley Times (Geauga Edition) (Chagrin Falls, OH) *Ceased*
CHAI-FM - 101.9 (Chateauguay, QC, Can.) **36963**
Chai Today (Miami Beach, FL) *Unable to locate*
Chain Drug Review (New York, NY) **21391**
Chain Leader (New York, NY) **21392**
Chain Merchandiser Magazine (Baker City, OR) *Ceased*
Chain Saw Age **375***
Chain Saw Age/Power Equipment Trade **375***
Chain Store Age (New York, NY) **21393**
Chain Store Age Executive (New York, NY) *Ceased*
CHAK-AM - 860 (Inuvik, NT, Can.) **35518**
CHAL-AM (La Pocatiere, QC, Can.) *Ceased*
Chalcedon Report (Vallecito, CA) **3983**

Chalk Circle (Hoboken, NJ) *Unable to locate*
Challenge (Fort Lauderdale, FL) *Unable to locate*
Challenge (Armonk, NY) **20066**
Challenge Magazine (Rockville, MD) **13676**
Challenge Magazine (Rochester, NY) *Unable to locate*
Challenge New York (New York, NY) **21394**
The Challenger (Buffalo, NY) **20372**
Challenger; The Greenwood and Southside (Greenwood, IN) **10046**
Challenger; The Weekly (St. Petersburg, FL) **6635**
Challenges (Stamford, CT) *Ceased*
The Challis Messenger (Challis, ID) **7842**
CHAM-AM - 820 (Hamilton, ON, Can.) **35894**
Chamber of Commerce of Chicago Bulletin; Italian American (Chicago, IL) **8422**
Chamber Music (New York, NY) **21395**
Chamber Way Germany/Midwest (Chicago, IL) **8303**
Chamberlain-Oacoma Register (Chamberlain, SD) **28831**
Chambers Cable of Edmonds (Edmonds, WA) *Unable to locate*
Chamblee De Kalb Neighbor (Chamblee, GA) **7167**
Chambly Inc.; Le Journal de (Chambly, QC, Can.) **36959**
Champaign County Genealogical Society Quarterly (Urbana, IL) **9699**
The Champion (Washington, DC) *Unable to locate*
The Champion (Kissimmee, FL) **6260**
Champion Bugle **37358***
Champion; Chino (Chino, CA) **1708**
Championship Racing Magazine (Waukesha, WI) **34397**
The Champlain Edge (Saint-Lambert, QC, Can.) **37358**
Champlin Dayton Press (Champlin, MN) **15791**
Champs-Elysees (Nashville, TN) **29449**
Chance (New York, NY) **21396**
Chancellor Broadcasting Network (Las Vegas, NV) **37624**
Chancellor LMA **6851***
Chancellor Media Corporation **30563***
Chandler Arizonan Tribune (Mesa, AZ) *Unable to locate*
Chandler & Brownsboro Statesman (Brownsboro, TX) **29955**
Chandler Independent (Chandler, AZ) **674**
Chandler News-Publicist **25780***
Chandler Post **10349***
Chandler Register; Newburgh (Newburgh, IN) **10349**
Change (Washington, DC) **5403**
Change; Continuity and (New York, NY) **21496**
Change Review; Confrontation/ (Dayton, OH) **25112**
Changes (Hoboken, NJ) *Ceased*
Changes Magazine (Deerfield Beach, FL) *Ceased*
Changes Socialist Monthly **14914***
Changing Men (Madison, WI) *Unable to locate*
Changing Times **5625***
Changing Times-The Kiplinger Washington Editors Inc. (Washington, DC) **37860**
Chanhassen Excelsior (Eden Prairie, MN) *Unable to locate*
Chanhassen Sun-Sailor; Excelsior/Shorewood/ (Excelsior, MN) **15887**
The Chanhassen Villager (Chanhassen, MN) **15792**
Channel **9322***
Channel (San Jose, CA) *Unable to locate*
Channel Business (Toronto, ON, Can.) **36545**
Channel Communication (Green Bay, WI) **33743**
Channel Town Press (La Conner, WA) **32801**
Channels - The Business of Communications (New York, NY) *Ceased*
Channelvision Cable TV, Inc. (Texarkana, AR) *Unable to locate*
Channelvision Inc. **33743***
The Chanticleer (Conway, SC) **28588**
Chantilly/Centreville Times (Reston, VA) *Unable to locate*
The Chanute Tribune (Chanute, KS) **11377**
CHAOS (College Park, MD) **13414**
Chaparral Guide (Truth or Consequences, NM) **19967**
Chapel Hill News (Chapel Hill, NC) **23702**
(Chapel Hill); School Law Bulletin (Chapel Hill, NC) **23721**
Chapel News (Chapel Hill, NC) **23703**
Chaplaincy; Journal of Health Care (Binghamton, NY) **20176**
The Chapleau Sentinel (Chapleau, ON, Can.) *Ceased*
The Chapman Advertiser & Enterprise Journal (Salina, KS) **11781**
The Chappell Register (Chappell, NE) **17977**
Chapter & Verse TV (Providence, RI) **28430**
Char-Jay (Shelton, WA) **33078**
Char-Koosta News (Pablo, MT) **17889**
Charhdi Kala (Surrey, BC, Can.) **35107**
The Chariho Times (Wyoming, RI) **28463**
Charioteer (New York, NY) **21397**
Charisma (Lake Mary, FL) **6274**

Chemistry of Natural Compounds (New York, NY) 21406

Chemistry News; Main Group (Amherst, MA) 13801

Chemistry and Physics and Medical NMR; Physiological (Melville, NY) 21057

Chemistry (Revue Canadienne de Chimie); Canadian Journal of (Ottawa, ON, Can.) 36202

Chemistry; Russian Journal of Applied (New York, NY) 22683

Chemistry; Russian Journal of Biorganic (New York, NY) 22684

Chemistry; Russian Journal of Coordination (New York, NY) 22685

Chemistry; Russian Journal of General (New York, NY) 22689

Chemistry; Russian Journal of Organic (New York, NY) 22693

Chemistry; Structural (Durham, NH) 18502

Chemistry; Synthesis and Reactivity in Inorganic and Metal-Organic (St. Louis, MO) 17519

Chemistry and Technology of Fuels and Oils (New York, NY) 21407

Chemistry and Technology; Journal of Wood (Syracuse, NY) 23406

Chemistry and Technology; Rubber (Akron, OH) 24586

Chemistry; Theoretical and Experimental (New York, NY) 22826

Chemists; Journal of the American Society of Brewing (St. Paul, MN) 16381

Chemists' Society; Journal of the American Oil (Champaign, IL) 8194

ChemMatters (Washington, DC) 5406

Chemometrics; Journal of (Hoboken, NJ) 19011

Chemoreception Abstracts (Bethesda, MD) 13324

Chemotherapy (Farmington, CT) 4807

Chemotherapy; Antimicrobial Agents and (Washington, DC) 5355

CHEMTECH (Washington, DC) Unable to locate

Chemung Historical Journal (Elmira, NY) 20572

Chemung Valley Reporter (Horseheads, NY) Unable to locate

Chenango American, Whitney Point Reporter, and Oxford Review Times (Greene, NY) 20697

Cheney Free Press (Cheney, WA) 32714

The Cheney Sentinel (Belle Plaine, KS) Ceased

CHEQ-FM 36298*

CHEQ-FM - 101.3 (Sainte-Marie, QC, Can.) 37382

CHER-AM - 950 (Sydney, NS, Can.) 35611

The Cheraw Chronicle (Cheraw, SC) 28527

Cherokee Advocate (Washington, DC) 5407

Cherokee County Banner (Jacksonville, TX) Ceased

Cherokee County Herald (Centre, AL) 148

Cherokee Daily Times (Cherokee, IA) 10699

Cherokee Messenger & Republican (Cherokee, OK) 25783

The Cherokee One Feather (Cherokee, NC) 23783

Cherokee Plus (Cherokee, GA) 7169

Cherokee Scout (Murphy, NC) 24088

Cherokee Tribune (Tulsa, OK) Ceased

Cherokeean/Herald (Rusk, TX) 30999

The Cherotic (r)Evolutionary (Berkeley, CA) Ceased

Cherry Diamond (St. Louis, MO) 17421

Cherryville Eagle (Cherryville, NC) 23784

The Chesapeake Banner (Cambridge, MD) Ceased

Chesapeake Bay Magazine (Annapolis, MD) 13091

Chesapeake Children 13092*

Chesapeake Family (Annapolis, MD) 13092

The Chesapeake Post (Chesapeake, VA) Unable to locate

The Cheshire Herald (Cheshire, CT) 4733

The Chesley Enterprise (Chesley, ON, Can.) 35734

Chesnee Tribune (Chesnee, SC) 28530

Chess Life (New Windsor, NY) 21126

Chess Life and Review 21126*

Chesstours (Reno, NV) 37862

Chest (Northbrook, IL) Unable to locate

Chest Medicine; Clinics in (Philadelphia, PA) 27413

Chest Surgery Clinics (Philadelphia, PA) 27399

Chester County Guide (Exton, PA) Ceased

The Chester County Homes 28147*

Chester County Law Reporter (West Chester, PA) 28144

Chester County Press (Oxford, PA) 27348

Chester Herald (Lincoln, NE) 18078

Chester News and Reporter (Chester, SC) 28531

Chester Progressive (Chester, CA) 1691

The Chesterfield Advertiser (Chesterfield, SC) Unable to locate

Chesterfield Cablevision 32472*

Chesterfield County Shopper (Cheraw, SC) 28528

Chesterfield Gazette (Glen Allen, VA) Ceased

Chesterfield Journal (Warrenton, MO) 17676

The Chesterton Review (South Orange, NJ) 19584

Chesterton Tribune (Chesterton, IN) 9886

Chesterville Record (Chesterville, ON, Can.) 35735

Chestnut Hill Local (Philadelphia, PA) 27400

The Chetek Alert (Chetek, WI) 33622

The Chetopa Advance (Chetopa, KS) 11380

Chetwynd Echo (Chetwynd, BC, Can.) 34924

Chevrolet High Performance (Los Angeles, CA) 2235

Chevrolet Preview (Troy, MI) Ceased

Chevy; All (Anaheim, CA) 1397

Chevy Camper 15657*

Chevy Chase Gazette (Frederick, MD) Unable to locate

Chevy Outdoors (Warren, MI) 15657

Chevy; Super (Anaheim, CA) 1416

Chevy Truck (Los Angeles, CA) 2236

CHEX-AM 36324*

CHEX-TV - Channel 12 (Peterborough, ON, Can.) 36321

CHEY-FM - 94.7 (Trois-Rivieres, QC, Can.) 37417

CHEZ-FM (Ottawa, ON, Can.) Unable to locate

CHFA-AM - 680 (Edmonton, AB, Can.) 34748

CHFC-AM - 1230 (Churchill, MB, Can.) 35262

CHFD-TV - Channel 6 (Thunder Bay, ON, Can.) 36446

CHFI-FM - 98.1 (Toronto, ON, Can.) 36807

CHFM-FM (Calgary, AB, Can.) Unable to locate

CHFX-FM - 101.9 (Halifax, NS, Can.) 35573

Chg-; Parent & (Danbury, CT) 4748

CHGA-FM - 97.3 (Maniwaki, QC, Can.) 37066

CHGG-FM (Winnipeg, MB, Can.) Unable to locate

Chianina Journal; American (Platte City, MO) 17348

Chic Magazine (Beverly Hills, CA) 1570

Chicago Advertising & Media (CAM) (Chicago, IL) Unable to locate

Chicago Apparel News (Chicago, IL) 8306

The Chicago Bowler (Lombard, IL) Unable to locate

Chicago Bulletin; Italian American Chamber of Commerce of (Chicago, IL) 8422

Chicago Business (Chicago, IL) 8307

Chicago Business; Crain's (Chicago, IL) 8346

Chicago Cable TV (Chicago, IL) Unable to locate

The Chicago Catechumenate 8300*

The Chicago Catholic 8301*

Chicago Catholic (Chicago, IL) Ceased

Chicago Chronicle (Chicago, IL) 8308

Chicago Cigar Smoker Magazine (Glen Ellyn, IL) 8924

Chicago Citizen (Chicago, IL) Unable to locate

The Chicago Computer Guide (Chicago, IL) 8309

Chicago Computers & Users (Chicago, IL) Unable to locate

Chicago County Press (Lindstrom, MN) 16002

Chicago Crusader (Chicago, IL) 8310

Chicago Daily Law Bulletin (Chicago, IL) 8311

Chicago Dental Society News (Chicago, IL) 8312

Chicago District Golfer (Lake Forest, IL) Ceased

Chicago Food Market News (Chicago, IL) Ceased

Chicago Heights Star (Tinley Park, IL) 9684

Chicago History (Chicago, IL) 8313

Chicago Home and Garden (Lake Forest, IL) 9061

(Chicago); Insight (Chicago, IL) 8417

Chicago Journal of International Law (Buffalo, NY) 20373

Chicago Law Journal; Loyola University (Chicago, IL) 8472

Chicago Lawyer (Chicago, IL) 8314

Chicago Life (Chicago, IL) 8315

Chicago Magazine (Chicago, IL) 8316

Chicago Magazine; Another (Chicago, IL) 8264

Chicago Magazine; Gay (Chicago, IL) 8384

The Chicago Maroon (Chicago, IL) 8317

Chicago Medicine (Chicago, IL) 8318

Chicago Metro News (Chicago, IL) Unable to locate

(Chicago); Mid-America (Chicago, IL) 8488

Chicago/Midwest Edition; Art Now Gallery Guide— (Clinton, NJ) 18760

Chicago Motor Club Home & Away; AAA— (Aurora, IL) 8037

Chicago Museum Studies; Art Institute of (Chicago, IL) 8275

Chicago Parent Magazine (Oak Park, IL) 9373

Chicago Press; West (St. Charles, IL) 9573

Chicago Purchasor Magazine (Chicago, IL) Unable to locate

Chicago Reader (Chicago, IL) 8319

Chicago Real Estate; Metro (Chicago, IL) 8485

The Chicago Reporter (Chicago, IL) 8320

Chicago Review (Chicago, IL) 8321

Chicago Ridge Citizen (Midlothian, IL) 9186

Chicago Runner Magazine (Skokie, IL) Ceased

Chicago Sentinel News 8323*

Chicago Shimpo (Chicago, IL) 8322

The New #Chicago Shoreland News (Chicago, IL) 8323

Chicago South Shore Scene (Chicago, IL) 8324

Chicago Standard News (Chicago Heights, IL) 8666

Chicago Studies (Chicago, IL) 8325

Chicago Sun-Times (Chicago, IL) 8326

Chicago-Sun Times Features Inc. (Chicago, IL) 37863

Chicago Times Magazine (Chicago, IL) Ceased

Chicago/Tri-State Edition; Nursing Spectrum—Greater (Hoffman Estates, IL) 9001

Chicago Tribune (Chicago, IL) 8327

Chicago Tribune Magazine (Chicago, IL) 8328

Chicago Weekend (Chicago, IL) 8329

Chicago; WHERE (Chicago, IL) 8605

Chicago Woman; Today's (Chicago, IL) 8583

Chicagoland Golf (Woodridge, IL) 9771

Chicagoland Quarterly Business Review (Tinley Park, IL) Ceased

ChicagoLand TV (CLTV) (Oak Brook, IL) 37735

Chicago's Amateur Athlete (Skokie, IL) 9602

Chicago's Northwest Side Press (Chicago, IL) 8330

Chicano; El (San Bernardino, CA) 3086

Chicano-Latin Law Review (Los Angeles, CA) 2237

Chickadee (Toronto, ON, Can.) 36548

Chickasha Daily Express 25785*

The Chickasha Star (Chickasha, OK) Unable to locate

Chico Enterprise-Record (Chico, CA) 1692

Chico Examiner (Chico, CA) Unable to locate

Chico New Voice Newspaper (Chico, CA) Unable to locate

Chico News & Review (Chico, CA) 1693

Chico Texan (Chico, TX) 30016

Chicopee Herald Weekly (Westfield, MA) Unable to locate

Chicot County Spectator (Lake Village, AR) 1205

The Chief Civil Service Leader (New York, NY) 21408

Chief (Division of American-Chief Co.); The Pawnee (Pawnee, OK) 26031

Chief Engineer (Orland Park, IL) Unable to locate

Chief Executive (Montvale, NJ) 19244

Chief Fire Executive (Melville, NY) Ceased

Chief Information Officer Journal (New York, NY) Ceased

Chief; The Mukwonago (Mukwonago, WI) 34158

The Chief of Police (Miami, FL) 6345

Chief-Union (Upper Sandusky, OH) 25604

Chiefland Citizen (Chiefland, FL) 5981

Chiefland Shopper (Perry, IA) 11155

Chiefland's Central Iowa Farm Magazine (Perry, IA) Ceased

The Chieftain (Moline, IL) 9203

Chieftain (Bonner Springs, KS) 11363

Chieftain (Fulton, MS) 16627

Chieftain (Tecumseh, NE) 18295

The Chieftain (Iroquois, ON, Can.) 35923

Chieftain; Jicarilla (Dulce, NM) 19843

Chieftain; Lamar Daily News and Holly (Lamar, CO) 4537

Chieftain; Poway News (Poway, CA) 2867

Chieftain; The Pueblo (Pueblo, CO) 4599

Chieftain Shopper (Bonner Springs, KS) 11364

Chieftain; Wallowa County (Enterprise, OR) 26310

Chihuahua News Ceased

CHIK-FM - 98.9 (Quebec, QC, Can.) 37298

Child (New York, NY) 21409

Child Abuse Review (Hoboken, NJ) 18911

Child and Adolescent Group Therapy; Journal of (New York, NY) 22022

Child and Adolescent Psychiatric Clinics (Philadelphia, PA) 27401

Child and Adolescent Psychiatric Nursing; Journal of (Philadelphia, PA) 27520

Child and Adolescent Psychiatry; Journal of the American Academy of (Philadelphia, PA) 27512

Child and Adolescent Psychopharmacology; Journal of (Larchmont, NY) 20908

Child and Adolescent Social Work Journal (New York, NY) Unable to locate

Child Birth Planner 22529*

Child-Care Administration; Journal of (Holbrook, NY) 20749

Child Care Center (Libertyville, IL) Ceased

Child of Colors Magazine (Burbank, CA) Ceased

Child; Dallas (Addison, TX) 29671

Child Development (Seattle, WA) Unable to locate

Child Development; Infant and (Hoboken, NJ) 18973

Child Education Resources; Exceptional (Arlington, VA) 31790

Child and Family Behavior Therapy (Princeton, NJ) 19457

Child and Family Nursing; Journal of (Philadelphia, PA) 27521

Child and Family Psychology Review; Clinical (New York, NY) 21429

Child and Family Studies; Journal of (New York, NY) 22023

Child First-Year Planner (New York, NY) Ceased

Child; FortWorth (Addison, TX) 29672

Child Health Journal; Maternal and (New York, NY) 22292

Child Language; Journal of (New York, NY) 22024

Child Life (Indianapolis, IN) 10100

Child Nephrology and Urology (Farmington, CT) Ceased

Child Neurology; Developmental Medicine and (New York, NY) 21548

Child Neurology; Journal of (Omaha, NE) 18201

Child; Northwest Baby & (Renton, WA) 32925

Child Nursing; MCN, The American Journal of Maternal/ (Huntington Bay, NY) **20777**

Child; Parent & (Bethesda, MD) **13371**

Child Pregnancy Planner (New York, NY) *Ceased*

Child Psychiatry and Human Development (New York, NY) *Unable to locate*

Child Psychology; Journal of Abnormal (New York, NY) **21972**

Child Psychology; Journal of Clinical (Mahwah, NJ) **19196**

Child Psychology; Journal of Experimental (San Diego, CA) **3193**

Child; Seattle's (Seattle, WA) **33027**

Child Study Journal (Buffalo, NY) **20374**

Child Today Magazine; Gifted (Waco, TX) **31247**

Child Welfare (Washington, DC) **5408**

Child and Youth Care Forum (New York, NY) *Unable to locate*

Child and Youth Services (St. Paul, MN) **16370**

Childhood Education (Olney, MD) *Unable to locate*

Childhood Education Annual; Information Technology in (Norfolk, VA) **32283**

Childhood Education; Journal of Research in (Olney, MD) **13643**

Children (Emmaus, PA) *Unable to locate*

Children, Churches & Daddies (Gurnee, IL) **8965**

Children; Exceptional (Arlington, VA) **31791**

Children and Families (Alexandria, VA) **31654**

Children; The Future of (Los Altos, CA) **2192**

Children; Good News for (Dayton, OH) **25118**

Children; Highlights for (Honesdale, PA) **27048**

Children; Infants and Young (Gaithersburg, MD) **13542**

Children; Infectious Diseases in (Thorofare, NJ) **19619**

Children; Journal of Dentistry for (Chicago, IL) **8437**

Children Magazine; LA **1884***

Children; Potomac (Chevy Chase, MD) **13408**

Children & Schools (Washington, DC) **5409**

Children; Teaching Exceptional (Chestnut Hill, MA) **14134**

Children; Technology and (Reston, VA) **32419**

Children Today (Pittsburgh, PA) *Unable to locate*

Children; Young (Washington, DC) **5873**

Children and Youth; Reclaiming (Lennox, SD) **28885**

Children and Youth; Residential Treatment for (Chicago, IL) **8555**

Children's Album (Concord, CA) *Ceased*

Children's Book and Play Review (Provo, UT) **31401**

Children's Book Review **31401***

Children's Books; The Bulletin of the Center for (Champaign, IL) **8182**

Children's Broadcasting **30576***

Children's Business (New York, NY) **21410**

Children's Digest (Indianapolis, IN) **10101**

Children's Express (Washington, DC) *Unable to locate*

The Children's Friend (Lincoln, NE) **18079**

Children's Health Care (Fort Myers, FL) **6094**

Children's House/Children's World (Caldwell, NJ) **18711**

Children's Literature Association Quarterly (Battle Creek, MI) **14793**

Children's Literature in Education (New York, NY) **21411**

Children's Literature (Litterature Canadienne pour la Jeunesse); CCL Canadian (Guelph, ON, Can.) **35860**

Children's Magic Window Magazine (Minneapolis, MN) *Ceased*

Children's Ministry Magazine (Loveland, CO) **4566**

Children's Playmate Magazine (Indianapolis, IN) **10102**

Children's Rights; The International Journal of (New York, NY) **21901**

Children's Rights Monitor; International (New York, NY) **21893**

Children's Services (Mahwah, NJ) **19188**

Children's Software Revue (CSR) (Flemington, NJ) **18818**

Children's Surprises **16135***

Children's Syndicated Radio Network (Eaton Rapids, MI) *Unable to locate*

Children's Voice (Washington, DC) **5410**

The Childress Index (Childress, TX) **30017**

Childsplay **14168***

Chile Pepper Magazine (Fort Worth, TX) **30332**

Chilkat Valley News (Haines, AK) **584**

Chillicothe Bulletin (Peoria, IL) *Unable to locate*

Chillicothe Gazette (Chillicothe, OH) **24761**

Chillicothe Times-Bulletin (Chillicothe, IL) **8670**

Chilliwack Market Place (Sardis, BC, Can.) *Unable to locate*

The Chilliwack Progress (Chilliwack, BC, Can.) **34926**

Chilliwack Progress Advertiser Edition **34927***

Chilliwack Progress Weekender Edition (Chilliwack, BC, Can.) **34927**

Chilliwack Times (Chilliwack, BC, Can.) **34928**

Chilton County News (Clanton, AL) **154**

Chilton Spirit **33882***

Chilton's Motor Age (Chicago, IL) **8331**

CHIM-FM **34993***

The Chimes (La Mirada, CA) **2125**

Chimes (Grand Rapids, MI) **15090**

The Chimes (Columbus, OH) **25006**

Chimie); Canadian Journal of Chemistry (Revue Canadienne de (Ottawa, ON, Can.) **36202**

Chimique Canadienne); Canadian Chemical News (L'Actualite (Ottawa, ON, Can.) **36191**

CHIN-AM - 1540 (Toronto, ON, Can.) **36808**

CHIN-FM - 100.7 (Toronto, ON, Can.) **36809**

China Briefing (Armonk, NY) **20067**

The China Business Review (Washington, DC) **5411**

China Clipper (Norman, OK) **25933**

China Daily Newspaper (San Francisco, CA) *Unable to locate*

China; Early (Berkeley, CA) **1514**

China Economic Review (Berkeley, CA) **1507**

China Edition; Appliance (Oak Brook, IL) **9338**

China Glass & Tableware (Clifton, NJ) *Ceased*

China; Late Imperial (Baltimore, MD) **13207**

China Law Reporter (Washington, DC) *Ceased*

China Markets for Melamine (Woodinville, WA) **33208**

China; Modern (Thousand Oaks, CA) **3903**

China Network World (San Mateo, CA) *Unable to locate*

China News Digest—Canada (Gaithersburg, MD) **13533**

China News Digest—Global (Gaithersburg, MD) **13534**

China News Digest—US (Gaithersburg, MD) **13535**

China News—Europe/Pacific (Gaithersburg, MD) **13536**

The China Painter (Oklahoma City, OK) **25960**

China Paints and Coatings: Market and Opportunities (Woodinville, WA) **33209**

China Press (New York, NY) *Unable to locate*

China Report (Thousand Oaks, CA) **3853**

China Review International (Honolulu, HI) **7683**

China Synthetic Rubber Markets (Woodinville, WA) **33210**

China Telecom (Boston, MA) **13873**

China Transport (Princeton, NJ) *Ceased*

China; Ward's Automotive International Focus on (Southfield, MI) **15552**

China Wood Preservatives (Woodinville, WA) **33211**

The Chincoteague Beachcomber (Chincoteague, VA) **31971**

Chinese America (San Francisco, CA) **3340**

Chinese American Daily News (Monterey Park, CA) **2592**

Chinese American Forum (St. Charles, MO) **17383**

Chinese Application Psychology Journal; International (Jamaica, NY) **20833**

Chinese Business Journal (Seattle, WA) *Ceased*

Chinese Daily News,Inc (Monterey Park, CA) **2593**

Chinese Economic Studies **20068***

The Chinese Economy (Armonk, NY) **20068**

Chinese Education & Society (Armonk, NY) **20069**

Chinese Educational **20069***

Chinese Environment and Development (Armonk, NY) *Ceased*

Chinese Free Daily News **1865***

Chinese L.A. Daily News (El Monte, CA) **1865**

Chinese Language Teachers Association Journal (Honolulu, HI) **7684**

Chinese Law and Government (Armonk, NY) **20070**

Chinese Linguistics; Journal of (Berkeley, CA) **1532**

Chinese Markets for Dimethylacetamide (Woodinville, WA) **33212**

Chinese Medical Sciences Journal (Philadelphia, PA) **27402**

Chinese Medicine; American Journal of (Garden City, NY) **20634**

Chinese News (Seattle, WA) *Ceased*

Chinese News (Toronto, ON, Can.) *Unable to locate*

Chinese Nursing Journal; International (Jamaica, NY) **20834**

Chinese Physics (College Park, MD) *Unable to locate*

Chinese Science Section B: Chemistry; Current Topics in (New York, NY) **21526**

Chinese Sexology Journal; International (Jamaica, NY) **20835**

Chinese Snuff Bottle Society of America Newsletter **13172***

Chinese Snuff Bottle Society Journal; International (Baltimore, MD) **13172**

Chinese Sociology and Anthropology (Armonk, NY) **20071**

Chinese Studies in History (Armonk, NY) **20072**

Chinese Studies In Philosophy **20073***

Chinese Times (San Francisco, CA) **3341**

Chinese Times (Vancouver, BC, Can.) *Unable to locate*

The Chinese Voice (Vancouver, BC, Can.) *Unable to locate*

ChinMusic Magazine (San Francisco, CA) **3342**

Chino Champion (Chino, CA) **1708**

Chino Hills Champion (Chino, CA) **1709**

Chino Hills News **1709***

Chino Valley Cable Television Co. Century **1710***

Chino Valley Champion **1709***

Chino Valley News **1708***

Chino Valley Review (Prescott, AZ) **846**

Chinook (Casper, WY) **34483**

Chinook Observer (Long Beach, WA) **32810**

The Chinook Opinion (Chinook, MT) **17770**

Chinook Progressive Club TV (Chinook, WA) **32717**

Chip Chats (Cincinnati, OH) **24781**

CHIP-FM - 101.7 (Fort Coulonge, QC, Can.) **36996**

Chippewa Herald (Chippewa Falls, WI) **33626**

Chippewa Herald-Telegram **33626***

Chippewa Herald Telegram (Chippewa Falls, WI) **33627**

Chip's Closet Cleaner (Chicago, IL) *Ceased*

Chips from Many Trees and Growing Roots (Milton, NH) **18580**

Chips-O-Wood (Mathiston, MS) **16761**

CHIQ-FM - 94.3 (Winnipeg, MB, Can.) **35370**

Chirality (Hoboken, NJ) **18912**

Chiron Review (Saint John, KS) **11777**

Chiropractic (Fort Wayne, IN) *Ceased*

Chiropractic Association; Journal of the Canadian (Toronto, ON, Can.) **36632**

Chiropractic; Dynamic (Huntington Beach, CA) **2060**

Chiropractic History (Richlands, VA) **32425**

Chiropractic Products (Los Angeles, CA) **2238**

Chiropractic & Rehabilitation; Sports (Philadelphia, PA) **27695**

Chiropractic Sports Medicine (Baltimore, MD) *Unable to locate*

Chiropractic; Texas Journal of (Austin, TX) **29828**

Chiropractic; Topics in Clinical (New York, NY) **22844**

Chirp (Toronto, ON, Can.) **36549**

Chirurgische Gastroenterologie (Farmington, CT) **4808**

The Chisholm Tribune-Press (Chisholm, MN) **15796**

Chittenango-Bridgeport Times (Canastota, NY) **20426**

CHJM-FM - 99.7 (Saint-Georges-de-Beauce, QC, Can.) **37342**

CHKG-FM - 96.1 (Vancouver, BC, Can.) **35186**

CHKG-FM 96.1 **35186***

CHKS-FM - 106.3 (Sarnia, ON, Can.) **36368**

CHLB-FM - 95.5 (Lethbridge, AB, Can.) **34800**

CHLC-FM (Baie-Comeau, QC, Can.) *Unable to locate*

CHLM-FM **37260***

CHLN-AM - 550 (Trois-Rivieres, QC, Can.) **37418**

CHLQ-FM - 93.1 (Charlottetown, PE, Can.) **36919**

CHLT-AM - 630 (Sherbrooke, QC, Can.) **37397**

CHLW-AM - 1310 (St. Paul, AB, Can.) **34845**

CHMA-AM **35428***

CHMA-FM - 106.9 (Sackville, NB, Can.) **35428**

CHMB-AM (Vancouver, BC, Can.) *Ceased*

CHML-AM - 900 (Hamilton, ON, Can.) **35895**

CHMM-FM **35371***

CHMN-AM - 106.5 (Canmore, AB, Can.) **34679**

CHMO-AM - 1450 (Moosonee, ON, Can.) **36095**

CHMR-AM **35498***

CHMR-FM - 93.5 (St. John's, NL, Can.) **35498**

CHMS-FM - 97.7 (Bancroft, ON, Can.) **35657**

CHMX-FM - 92.1 (Regina, SK, Can.) **37540**

CHNB-TV - Channel 4 (North Bay, ON, Can.) **36117**

CHNC-AM - 610 (New Carlisle, QC, Can.) **37257**

CHNC-AM - 1150 (New Carlisle, QC, Can.) **37256**

CHNL-AM - 610 (Kamloops, BC, Can.) **34980**

CHNO-FM - 103.9 (Sudbury, ON, Can.) **36422**

CHNR-AM **36392***

CHNS-AM - 960 (Halifax, NS, Can.) **35574**

CHNV-FM - 103.5 (Castlegar, BC, Can.) **34921**

CHOA-AM **34856***

CHOA-FM - 103.5/96.5/103.9 (Noranda, QC, Can.) **37260**

CHOC-FM - 92.5 (Jonquiere, QC, Can.) **37015**

Chocolate News (New York, NY) *Unable to locate*

Chocolate and Nut World **2509***

Chocolate Singles (Jamaica, NY) *Unable to locate*

Chocolatier (New York, NY) **21412**

Choctaw Advocate (Butler, AL) **140**

Choctaw County Times (Hugo, OK) **25871**

Choctaw/Nicoma Park Free Press (Midwest City, OK) *Unable to locate*

Choctaw Plaindealer (Ackerman, MS) **16544**

CHOG-AM (North York, ON, Can.) *Unable to locate*

CHOH-AM (Timmins, ON, Can.) *Unable to locate*

CHOI **37402***

CHOI-FM - 98.1 (Sillery, QC, Can.) **37402**

Choice (Middletown, CT) **4943**

Choices (Danbury, CT) **4736**

Choices (Malden, MA) **14290**

Choices for Entrepreneurial Women (Los Angeles, CA) *Ceased*

CHOK-AM (Sarnia, ON, Can.) *Unable to locate*

Chokio Review (Chokio, MN) **15797**

CHOM-FM - 97.7 (Westmount, QC, Can.) **37448**

The Chomedey News (Chomedey, QC, Can.) *Unable to locate*

CHON-FM - 98.1 (Whitehorse, YT, Can.) **37607**

CHOO-AM **35628***

Cicindela (Prairie Village, KS) *Unable to locate*
CICS Update (Westminster, CO) **4660**
CICT-TV - Channel 2 (Calgary, AB, Can.) **34668**
CICU-FM - 94.1 (Eskasoni First Nation, NS, Can.) **35553**
CICX-FM - 105.9 (Orillia, ON, Can.) **36177**
CIDC-FM (Orangeville, ON, Can.) *Unable to locate*
CIDR-FM - 93.9 (Bingham Farms, MI) **14822**
Cie Cable Vision de Hawkesbury Ltd **35910***
CIEG-FM - 107.5 (Squamish, BC, Can.) **35095**
CIEL-FM (Longueuil, QC, Can.) *Unable to locate*
CIEL-FM - 103.7 (Riviere-du-Loup, QC, Can.) **37315**
CIEU-FM **36958***
CIEU-FM - 94.9 (Carleton, QC, Can.) **36958**
CIFA-FM - 104.1 (Yarmouth, NS, Can.) **35625**
CIFJ-AM - 1480 (Fort St. James, BC, Can.) **34959**
CIFL-AM - 1450 (Fraser Lake, BC, Can.) **34961**
CIFM-FM - 98.3 (Kamloops, BC, Can.) **34981**
CIFX-AM **35369***
Cigar Aficionâdo (New York, NY) **21418**
Cigar Smoker Magazine; Chicago (Glen Ellyn, IL) **8924**
Cigar / Tobacco World (Marina del Rey, CA) **2506**
CIGB-FM (Trois-Rivieres, QC, Can.) *Unable to locate*
CIGL-FM - 97.1 (Belleville, ON, Can.) **35680**
CIGM-AM - 790 (Sudbury, ON, Can.) **36424**
CIGM-FM **36426***
CIGO-FM (Port Hawkesbury, NS, Can.) *Unable to locate*
CIGV-FM - 100.7 (Princeton, BC, Can.) **35067**
CIHO-FM - 96.3 (Saint-Hilarion, QC, Can.) **37344**
CIII-TV - Channel 2 (Don Mills, ON, Can.) **35780**
CIKI-FM - 98.7 (Rimouski, QC, Can.) **37309**
CILA-FM **34799***
CILK-FM - 101.5 (Kelowna, BC, Can.) **34992**
CILQ-FM - 107.1 (Toronto, ON, Can.) **36813**
CILT-FM - 96.7 (Altona, MB, Can.) **35250**
CILW-AM **34870***
CIM Bulletin (Canadian Mining & Metallurgical Bulletin) (Montreal, QC, Can.) **37103**
CIM Construction Journal (Norwood, MA) **14445**
CIM Reporter (Montreal, QC, Can.) **37104**
Cimarron Review (Stillwater, OK) **26076**
CIME-FM (Longueuil, QC, Can.) *Unable to locate*
CIMF-FM - 94.9 (Hull, QC, Can.) **37007**
CIMG-FM - 94.1 (Swift Current, SK, Can.) **37576**
CIMJ-FM - 106.1 (Guelph, ON, Can.) **35869**
CIMO-FM - 106.1 (Sherbrooke, QC, Can.) **37398**
CIMT-TV - Channel 9 (Riviere-du-Loup, QC, Can.) **37316**
CIMX-FM - 88.7 (Windsor, ON, Can.) **36898**
Cincinnati Business Courier (Cincinnati, OH) **24783**
Cincinnati CityBeat (Cincinnati, OH) **24784**
The Cincinnati Enquirer (Cincinnati, OH) **24785**
The Cincinnati Herald (Cincinnati, OH) **24786**
Cincinnati Journal of Magic (Logan, OH) **25310**
Cincinnati; Key Magazine (Maineville, OH) **25327**
Cincinnati Law Review; University of (Cincinnati, OH) **24823**
Cincinnati Magazine (Cincinnati, OH) **24787**
Cincinnati Mèdicine (Cincinnati, OH) *Ceased*
Cincinnati News Record; University of (Cincinnati, OH) **24824**
The Cincinnati Post (Cincinnati, OH) **24788**
Cincinnati Purchasor (Cincinnati, OH) *Unable to locate*
Cincinnati Wedding (Cincinnati, OH) **24789**
CineAction! (Toronto, ON, Can.) **36550**
Cineaste (New York, NY) **21419**
Cinefantastique (Los Angeles, CA) **2239**
Cinefex (Riverside, CA) **2935**
Cinema; Alternative (Montclair, NJ) **19240**
Cinema Canada (Montreal, QC, Can.) *Unable to locate*
Cinema Journal (Dallas, TX) **30136**
Cinema Revue (Memphis, TN) **29361**
Cinema, Video & Cable Movie Digest (Ambler, PA) *Ceased*
Cinemagic *Ceased*
Cineman Syndicate, LLC (Rye, NY) **37865**
Cinematograph (San Francisco, CA) **3343**
Cinemax (New York, NY) **37736**
Cinevue (New York, NY) *Unable to locate*
Cinevue Worldwide Talent Directory and Festival Program Book (Palatka, FL) **6536**
CING-FM (Burlington, ON, Can.) *Unable to locate*
CINN-FM - 91.1 (Hearst, ON, Can.) **35912**
CINQ-FM - 102.3 (Montreal, QC, Can.) **37245**
CINR-FM **35687***
CIO Canada (Scarborough, ON, Can.) **36374**
CIO Magazine (Framingham, MA) **14192**
CIO Web Business (Framingham, MA) **14193**
CIOC-FM - 98.5 (Victoria, BC, Can.) **35235**
CIOI-FM - 101.3 (Prince George, BC, Can.) **35058**
CIOK-FM - 100.5 (St. John, NB, Can.) **35434**
CION-FM (Riviere-du-Loup, QC, Can.) *Ceased*
CIOO-FM - 100.1 (Halifax, NS, Can.) **35575**
CIOR-AM (Princeton, BC, Can.) *Unable to locate*
CIOS-FM - 98.5 (Stephenville, NL, Can.) **35510**
CIOX-FM - 101.1 (Ottawa Falls, ON, Can.) **36298**
CIOZ-FM - 94.7 (Marystown, NL, Can.) **35474**
CIPA-TV - Channel 9 (Prince Albert, SK, Can.) **37521**
CIPC-AM **37278***
CIPC-FM - 99.1 (Port-Cartier, QC, Can.) **37278**
CIPN-FM - 104.7 (Squamish, BC, Can.) **35096**
CIQB-FM - 101.1 (Barrie, ON, Can.) **35662**
CIQC-AM (Montreal, QC, Can.) *Unable to locate*
CIQM-FM (London, ON, Can.) *Unable to locate*
CIRB-AM (Lac Etchemin, QC, Can.) *Ceased*
Circle **21958***
The Circle (Minneapolis, MN) **16064**
The Circle (Poughkeepsie, NY) **23145**
Circle Bar Cable Television, Inc. (Ozona, TX) **30892**
Circle C Cable Partners, Ltd. (Austin, TX) *Unable to locate*
Circle Track; Petersen's (Los Angeles, CA) **2362**
Circleville Herald (Circleville, OH) **24850**
Circuit (Montreal, QC, Can.) **37105**
Circuit Cellar INK (Hanover, NH) **18515**
Circuit Design & Manufacture; Printed (Manhasset, NY) **21010**
Circuit Design; Printed **21010***
Circuit Network; Printed (Sparta, NJ) **19593**
Circuit News Digest (Alba, MO) *Unable to locate*
Circuit Rider (Nashville, TN) **29450**
Circuit Theory and Applications; International Journal of (Hoboken, NJ) **18978**
CircuiTree (Troy, MI) **15617**
Circuits Assembly (Atlanta, GA) **6984**
Circulating Pines (Circle Pines, MN) *Ceased*
Circulation (Philadelphia, PA) **27403**
Circulation Management (Stamford, CT) **5142**
Circulation Research (Philadelphia, PA) **27404**
Circulatory Shock (Hoboken, NJ) **18913**
Circus Magazine (New York, NY) **21420**
CIRK-FM (Edmonton, AB, Can.) *Unable to locate*
CIRO-FM **37342***
CIRV-FM - 88.7 (Toronto, ON, Can.) **36814**
CIRX-FM - 94.3 (Prince George, BC, Can.) **35059**
CISA-TV (Lethbridge, AB, Can.) *Unable to locate*
CISC-FM - 107.5 (Squamish, BC, Can.) **35097**
The Cisco Press (Cisco, TX) **30020**
Cisco World (Austin, TX) **29767**
CISE-FM - 104.7 (Squamish, BC, Can.) **35098**
CISL-AM - 650 (Vancouver, BC, Can.) **35188**
CISM Journal ACSGC **36246***
CISN-FM - 103.9 (Edmonton, AB, Can.) **34750**
CISP-FM - 104.5 (Squamish, BC, Can.) **35099**
CISQ-FM - 107.1 (Squamish, BC, Can.) **35100**
Cissna Park News (Cissna Park, IL) **8678**
CISV **35308***
CISW-FM - 102.1 (Whistler, BC, Can.) **35239**
The Citadel (Middletown, NY) **21080**
CITE-FM - 107.3 (Montreal, QC, Can.) **37246**
Cites Nouvelles (Ste.-Genevieve, QC, Can.) *Unable to locate*
CITF-FM - 107.5 (Quebec, QC, Can.) **37301**
CITI-FM (Winnipeg, MB, Can.) *Unable to locate*
Cities (Armdale, NS, Can.) *Unable to locate*
Cities and Roads (Greensboro, NC) *Ceased*
Cities & Villages (Columbus, OH) *Unable to locate*
The Citizen **35057***
The Citizen **15161***
The Citizen **2108***
The Citizen (Boyne City, MI) **14832**
The Citizen (Detroit, MI) **14918**
Citizen (Laconia, NH) **18536**
The Citizen (Hillside, NJ) *Unable to locate*
The Citizen (Rahway, NJ) **19485**
The Citizen (Auburn, NY) **20105**
Citizen (American Fork, UT) **31316**
The Citizen (Duncan, BC, Can.) **34949**
The Citizen (Thompson, MB, Can.) **35300**
The Citizen (St. John, NB, Can.) *Unable to locate*
The Citizen (Blyth, ON, Can.) *Ceased*
The Citizen (Kipling, SK, Can.) **37485**
Citizen Advance **29054***
Citizen-Advertiser (Paris, KY) **12354**
Citizen Airman (Robins AFB, GA) **7499**
Citizen Gazette (Burnet, TX) **29992**
Citizen Herald (Jesup, IA) **11007**
Citizen-Journal (Osceola, AR) *Unable to locate*
Citizen Journal (Warrenton, MO) **17677**
The Citizen of Morris County (Denville, NJ) **18777**
The Citizen (Mount Forest Citizen) (Durham, ON, Can.) **35797**
Citizen; The New Age (Dearborn Heights, MI) **14909**
The Citizen-News (Edgefield, SC) **28600**
Citizen; Orangeville (Orangeville, ON, Can.) **36173**
The Citizen-Patriot (Atwood, KS) *Ceased*
The Citizen Record (Oakland, MD) *Unable to locate*
The Citizen Shopper **10999***
Citizen-Standard (Valley View, PA) **28093**
Citizen-Statesman (Celina, TN) **29084**
Citizen Telegram (Rifle, CO) *Unable to locate*
The Citizen-Times (Scottsville, KY) **12394**
Citizen Tribune (Steubenville, OH) *Ceased*
Citizen Tribune (Morristown, TN) **29418**
Citizen Voice & Times (Irvine, KY) **12141**
Citizens Centre Report (Edmonton, AB, Can.) **34705**
Citizens Journal (Atlanta, TX) **29748**
Citizens News & Record (Aberdeen, NC) *Unable to locate*
Citizens' Voice (Wilkes Barre, PA) **28164**
CITL-TV - Channel 4 (Lloydminster, AB, Can.) **34804**
CITR-FM - 101.9 (Vancouver, BC, Can.) **35189**
Citroen Club Magazine (San Diego, CA) *Unable to locate*
Citrograph (Fresno, CA) **1948**
Citrus County Chronicle (Crystal River, FL) **6030**
The Citrus Industry (Bartow, FL) **5917**
Citrus and Vegetable Magazine (Tampa, FL) **6760**
Cittadino Canadese; Il (Montreal, QC, Can.) **37124**
CITV-TV - Channel 13 (Edmonton, AB, Can.) **34751**
City (Indianapolis, IN) *Ceased*
City of Baxter Springs (Baxter Springs, KS) **11353**
City of Cascade Locks (Cascade Locks, OR) **26263**
City of Cawker Cable TV (Cawker City, KS) **11376**
City College Alumnus (New York, NY) **21421**
The City Collegian (Seattle, WA) **32954**
City & Community (Chicago, IL) **8333**
City & Country Club Life (Miami Springs, FL) **6422**
City & Country Home (Toronto, ON, Can.) *Ceased*
City-County Magazine (Burlington, NC) **23671**
City of Covington CATV (Covington, GA) **7212**
City Detroit Magazine (Farmington Hills, MI) *Ceased*
City Edition Pennysaver (Syracuse, NY) **23394**
City Family (New York, NY) **21422**
City of Fosston Cable TV (Fosston, MN) **15909**
City Guide Magazine (New York, NY) **21423**
City on a Hill (Santa Cruz, CA) **3682**
The City Journal (New York, NY) **21424**
City Limits (New York, NY) **21425**
City Line News (Bala Cynwyd, PA) *Unable to locate*
City Link (Fort Lauderdale, FL) **6074**
City of New York Council Digest (New York, NY) **21426**
City News (New Rochelle, NY) *Unable to locate*
City News Bureau of Chicago (Chicago, IL) *Ceased*
City News Service Inc. (Los Angeles, CA) **37866**
City Newspaper (Rochester, NY) **23216**
City of Norway CATV (Norway, MI) **15406**
City Pages (Minneapolis, MN) **16065**
City Paper (Washington, DC) *Unable to locate*
City Paper (Philadelphia, PA) **27405**
City Paper; Baltimore (Baltimore, MD) **13131**
City Parent (Oakville, ON, Can.) **36143**
City Rant (Austin, TX) *Ceased*
City Reports (Cleveland, OH) *Unable to locate*
The City Scene (Santa Monica, CA) *Unable to locate*
City Scene (Windsor, ON, Can.) *Unable to locate*
City & Society (Arlington, VA) *Ceased*
City Sports (Solana Beach, CA) **3767**
City & State (Chicago, IL) *Unable to locate*
The City Sun (Brooklyn, NY) *Unable to locate*
City of Taconite Cable TV (Taconite, MN) **16465**
City Terrace Comet (Los Angeles, CA) **2240**
City & Town (North Little Rock, AR) **1299**
City Trees (Peabody, MA) **14461**
CITY-TV - Channel 57 (Toronto, ON, Can.) **36815**
City of Unionville CATV (Unionville, MO) **17659**
City of Williamstown Cable (Williamstown, KY) **12449**
CityBusiness (Minneapolis, MN) **16066**
Cityview (Des Moines, IA) **10776**
CIUT-FM - 89.5 (Toronto, ON, Can.) **36816**
CIVA-TV - Channel 8 (Val d'Or, QC, Can.) **37421**
CIVH-AM - 1340 (Vanderhoof, BC, Can.) **35199**
Civic Center News, Inc. **2322***
Civic Center NewSource (Los Angeles, CA) **2241**
Civic League Record; The Christian (Augusta, ME) **12890**
Civic Public Works (Toronto, ON, Can.) **36551**
Civic Review; National (Washington, DC) **5669**
Civil Air Patrol News (Montgomery, AL) **363**
Civil Engineer; Navy (Washington, DC) **5690**
Civil Engineering-ASCE (Reston, VA) **32363**
Civil Engineering; Journal of Computing in (Reston, VA) **32374**
Civil Engineering; Journal of Materials in (Reston, VA) **32387**
Civil Engineering News **6918***
Civil Engineering Practice (Boston, MA) **13878**
Civil Liberties and Civil Rights; Texas Forum on (Austin, TX) **29821**
Civil RICO Litigation Reporter (Wayne, PA) **28128**
Civil Rights Journal (Washington, DC) **5416**
Civil Rights; Texas Forum on Civil Liberties and (Austin, TX) **29821**
Civil Service Reporter; Massachusetts (Chestnut Hill, MA) **14129**
Civil War Chronicles (New York, NY) *Ceased*
Civil War History (Kent, OH) **25272**
The Civil War Lady (Clarinda, IA) **10701**
The Civil War News (Tunbridge, VT) **31608**
Civil War Times Illustrated (Harrisburg, PA) **26986**
Civilization (Washington, DC) *Unable to locate*

Numbers cited in bold after listings are entry numbers rather than page numbers.

Civitan Magazine (Birmingham, AL) 64
CIWW-AM (Ottawa, ON, Can.) Unable to locate
CIXK-FM - 106.5 (Owen Sound, ON, Can.) 36302
CIXX-FM - 106.9 (London, ON, Can.) 36000
CIYR-AM - 1230 (Edson, AB, Can.) 34760
CIZL-FM - 98.9 (Regina, SK, Can.) 37541
CIZN-FM (Cambridge, ON, Can.) Unable to locate
CIZZ-FM - 98.9 (Red Deer, AB, Can.) 34834
CJAB-FM - 94.5 (Chicoutimi, QC, Can.) 36973
CJAD-AM - 800 (Montreal, QC, Can.) 37247
CJAN-FM - 99.3 (Asbestos, QC, Can.) 36942
CJAR-AM - 1240 (The Pas, MB, Can.) 35279
CJAT-AM 35116*
CJAT-FM - 95.7 (Trail, BC, Can.) 35116
CJAV-AM - 1240 (Port Alberni, BC, Can.) 35050
CJAY-FM - 92.1 (Calgary, AB, Can.) 34669
CJAZ 35193*
CJBC-AM - 860 (Toronto, ON, Can.) 36817
CJBC-FM - 90.3 (London, ON, Can.) 36001
CJBK-AM - 1290 (London, ON, Can.) 36002
CJBN-TV - Channel 13 (Keewatin, ON, Can.) 35927
CJBQ-AM - 800 (Belleville, ON, Can.) 35681
CJBQ-FM 35680*
CJBR-FM - 101.5 (Rimouski, QC, Can.) 37310
CJBX-FM - 92.7 (London, ON, Can.) 36003
CJBZ-AM 36288*
CJCA-AM - 930 (Edmonton, AB, Can.) 34752
CJCB-AM - 1270 (Sydney, NS, Can.) 35612
CJCB-TV - Channel 4 (Sydney, NS, Can.) 35613
CJCD-AM (Yellowknife, NT, Can.) Ceased
CJCD-FM - 100.1 (Hay River, NT, Can.) 35516
CJCD 1240 35516*
CJCH-AM - 920 (Halifax, NS, Can.) 35576
CJCH-TV - Channel 5 (Halifax, NS, Can.) 35577
CJCI-AM - 620 (Prince George, BC, Can.) 35060
CJCJ-FM - 104.1 (Woodstock, NB, Can.) 35441
CJCL-AM - 590 (Toronto, ON, Can.) 36818
CJCR-AM 35458*
CJCS-AM - 1240 (Stratford, ON, Can.) 36411
CJCW-AM - 590 (Sussex, NB, Can.) 35439
CJCY-AM - 1390 (Medicine Hat, AB, Can.) 34814
CJDC-AM - 890 (Dawson Creek, BC, Can.) 34942
CJDC-FM - 92.7 (Dawson Creek, BC, Can.) 34943
CJDM-FM - 92.1 (Drummondville, QC, Can.) 36993
CJDV-AM 34697*
CJEM-FM - 92.7 (Edmundston, NB, Can.) 35387
CJEN-FM (Winnipeg, MB, Can.) Unable to locate
CJER-AM (Saint-Jerome, QC, Can.) Unable to locate
CJET-AM - 630 (Smiths Falls, ON, Can.) 36396
CJET-FM 36298*
CJEV-AM - 1340 (Blairmore, AB, Can.) 34620
CJEZ-FM - 97.3 (Toronto, ON, Can.) 36819
CJFB-TV - Channel 5 (Swift Current, SK, Can.) 37577
CJFI-FM 36367*
CJFM-FM - 95.9 (Montreal, QC, Can.) 37248
CJFP-FM 37315*
CJFT-AM (Fort Erie, ON, Can.) Unable to locate
CJFW-FM - 103.1 (Terrace, BC, Can.) 35114
CJFX-AM - 98.9 (Antigonish, NS, Can.) 35540
CJGC-AM 35996*
CJGL-FM 37576*
CJGR-FM - 100 (Gold River, BC, Can.) 34965
CJGX-AM - 940 (Yorkton, SK, Can.) 37602
CJIB-AM - 940 (Vernon, BC, Can.) 35204
CJIV-AM 34914*
CJJD-AM 35894*
CJJR-FM - 93.7 (Vancouver, BC, Can.) 35190
CJKK-FM (St. John's, NL, Can.) Unable to locate
CJKL-FM - 101.5 FM (Kirkland Lake, ON, Can.) 35958
CJKR-FM - 97.5 (Winnipeg, MB, Can.) 35371
CJKX-FM - 95.9 (Ajax, ON, Can.) 35628
CJLA-FM - 104.9 (Lachute, QC, Can.) 37031
CJLB-AM (Thunder Bay, ON, Can.) Unable to locate
CJLF-FM - 100.3 (Barrie, ON, Can.) 35663
CJLM-AM (Joliette, QC, Can.) Unable to locate
CJLP-FM - 107.1 (Thetford Mines, QC, Can.) 37412
CJLR-FM 37487*
CJLS-FM - 96.3 (Shelburne, NS, Can.) 35605
CJLS-FM - 95.5 (Yarmouth, NS, Can.) 35626
CJLX-FM - 92.3 (Belleville, ON, Can.) 35682
CJMC-AM 37373*
CJMC-AM - 1490 (Sainte-Anne-des-Monts, QC, Can.) 37373
CJMD-AM (Chibougamau, QC, Can.) Unable to locate
CJME-AM - 980 (Regina, SK, Can.) 37542
CJMF-FM - 93.3 (Quebec, QC, Can.) 37302
CJMG-FM - 97.1 (Penticton, BC, Can.) 35046
CJMH-AM (Medicine Hat, AB, Can.) Ceased
CJMM-FM - 99.1 (Rouyn-Noranda, QC, Can.) 37323
CJMO-FM - 103.1 (Moncton, NB, Can.) 35420
CJMR-AM - 1320 (Oakville, ON, Can.) 36153
CJMS-AM (Montreal, QC, Can.) Ceased
CJMT-AM (Chicoutimi, QC, Can.) Unable to locate
CJMV-FM - 102.7 (Val d'Or, QC, Can.) 37422
CJMX-FM - 105.3 (Sudbury, ON, Can.) 36425
CJNB-AM - 1050 (North Battleford, SK, Can.) 37513
CJNH-AM 35657*
CJNR-FM 35687*
CJNS-AM - 1240 (Meadow Lake, SK, Can.) 37496
CJOA-FM - 95.1 (Thunder Bay, ON, Can.) 36447
CJOB-AM - 680 (Winnipeg, MB, Can.) 35372
CJOC-AM (Lethbridge, AB, Can.) Ceased
CJOH-TV - Channel 13 (Ottawa, ON, Can.) 36292
CJOI-AM 34874*
CJOI-FM - 109.8 (Rimouski, QC, Can.) 37311
CJOJ-FM - 95.5 (Belleville, ON, Can.) 35683
CJOK-FM - 93.3 (Fort McMurray, AB, Can.) 34768
CJOM-FM 36898*
CJON-AM 35501*
CJON-TV (NTV) - Channel 5 (St. John's, NL, Can.) 35500
CJOR-AM 35192*
CJOV-FM 34993*
CJOY-AM - 1460 (Guelph, ON, Can.) 35870
CJOZ-FM - 92.1 (Bonavista Bay, NL, Can.) 35442
CJPM-TV (Chicoutimi, QC, Can.) 36974
CJPR-AM - 1490 (Crowsnest Pass, AB, Can.) 34691
CJPT-FM - 103.7 (Brockville, ON, Can.) 35711
CJQM-FM - 104.3 (Sault Sainte Marie, ON, Can.) 36372
CJQQ-FM - 92.1 (Timmins, ON, Can.) 36458
CJRB-AM - 1220 (Boissevain, MB, Can.) 35253
CJRC-AM (Gatineau, QC, Can.) Unable to locate
CJRE-FM (Gaspe, QC, Can.) Ceased
CJRG-FM (Gaspe, QC, Can.) Ceased
CJRL-AM - 1220 (Kenora, ON, Can.) 35930
CJRM-AM 37543*
CJRN-AM - 710 (Niagara Falls, ON, Can.) 36112
CJRP-AM (Sillery, QC, Can.) Unable to locate
CJRQ-FM - 92.7 (Sudbury, ON, Can.) 36426
CJRS-AM (Sherbrooke, QC, Can.) Unable to locate
CJRT-FM - 91.1 (Toronto, ON, Can.) 36820
CJRV-FM (Gaspe, QC, Can.) Ceased
CJRW-AM - 102.1 (Summerside, PE, Can.) 36926
CJRX-FM - 106.7 (Lethbridge, AB, Can.) 34801
CJRY-FM 36810*
CJSA-AM (Saint-Jerome, QC, Can.) Unable to locate
CJSB-AM 36295*
CJSD-FM (Thunder Bay, ON, Can.) Ceased
CJSF-FM - 90.1 FM (Burnaby, BC, Can.) 34914
CJSL-AM (Estevan, SK, Can.) Unable to locate
CJSN-AM - 1490 (Shaunavon, SK, Can.) 37570
CJSO-FM - 101.7 (Sorel-Tracy, QC, Can.) 37406
CJSR-FM - 88.5 (Edmonton, AB, Can.) 34753
CJSS-AM - 1220 (Cornwall, ON, Can.) 35758
CJSW-FM - 90.9 (Calgary, AB, Can.) 34670
CJTK-FM - 95.5 (Sudbury, ON, Can.) 36427
CJTR-AM (Trois-Rivieres, QC, Can.) Ceased
CJTT-FM - 104.5 FM (New Liskeard, ON, Can.) 36106
CJUL-AM - 1220 (Cornwall, ON, Can.) 35759
CJVA-AM (Caraquet, NB, Can.) Unable to locate
CJVB-AM - 1470 (Vancouver, BC, Can.) 35191
CJVR-AM - 750 (Melfort, SK, Can.) 37499
CJWA-AM - 1240 (Wawa, ON, Can.) 36866
CJWW-AM - 600 (Saskatoon, SK, Can.) 37565
CJXX-FM - 93.1 (Grande Prairie, AB, Can.) 34777
CJXY-FM - 107.9 (Hamilton, ON, Can.) 35896
CJYC-FM (St. John, NB, Can.) Unable to locate
CJYE-AM - 1250 (Oakville, ON, Can.) 36154
CJYM-AM - 1330 (Rosetown, SK, Can.) 37546
CJYQ-AM - 930 (St. John's, NL, Can.) 35501
CJYR-AM - 970 (Edson, AB, Can.) 34761
The CK of A Journal (St. Louis, MO) 17422
CKAD-AM - 1350 (Middleton, NS, Can.) 35595
CKAL-AM (Vernon, BC, Can.) Ceased
CKAL-FM 35203*
CKAL-FM (Vernon, BC, Can.) Ceased
CKAM-AM - 990 (Westmount, QC, Can.) 37449
CKAP-AM (Kapuskasing, ON, Can.) Unable to locate
CKAR-AM 36182*
CKAT-AM - 600 (North Bay, ON, Can.) 36119
CKAY-AM (Duncan, BC, Can.) Unable to locate
CKBA-AM - 850 (Athabasca, AB, Can.) 34611
CKBB-AM 35662*
CKBC-AM - 1360 (Bathurst, NB, Can.) 35381
CKBD-AM - 600 (Vancouver, BC, Can.) 35192
CKBI-AM - 900 (Prince Albert, SK, Can.) 37522
CKBL-FM (Kelowna, BC, Can.) Unable to locate
CKBS-AM 37352*
CKB2-FM - 100.1 MHZ (Kamloops, BC, Can.) 34982
CKBW-AM - 1000 (Bridgewater, NS, Can.) 35544
CKBW-FM - 98.1 (Liverpool, NS, Can.) 35592
CKBX-AM - 840 (100 Mile House, BC, Can.) 35041
CKBY-FM (Ottawa, ON, Can.) Unable to locate
CKCB-AM 35749*
CKCB-FM - 95.1 (Collingwood, ON, Can.) 35749
CKCH-AM (Hull, QC, Can.) Ceased
CKCH-FM 37007*
CKCK-AM (Regina, SK, Can.) Unable to locate
CKCK-TV 37544*
CKCL-AM - 600 (Truro, NS, Can.) 35617
CKCM-AM 35463*
CKCM-AM - 620 (Grand Falls, NL, Can.) 35463
CKCN-AM 37388*
CKCN-FM - 94.1 (Sept-Iles, QC, Can.) 37388
CKCO-TV - Channel 42/13/2/ (Kitchener, ON, Can.) 35965
CKCQ-AM - 920 (Quesnel, BC, Can.) 35070
CKCR-AM - 1340 (Revelstoke, BC, Can.) 35072
CKCU-FM - 93.1 (Ottawa, ON, Can.) 36293
CKCV-AM (Quebec, QC, Can.) Ceased
CKCW-FM - 94.5 (Moncton, NB, Can.) 35421
CKCW-TV - Channel 2 (Moncton, NB, Can.) 35422
CKDA-AM (Victoria, BC, Can.) Unable to locate
CKDH-AM - 900 (Amherst, NS, Can.) 35533
CKDK-FM - 103.9 (Woodstock, ON, Can.) 36909
CKDM-AM - 730 (Dauphin, MB, Can.) 35264
CKDO-AM - 1350 (Oshawa, ON, Can.) 36182
CKDO-FM (Baie-Comeau, QC, Can.) Unable to locate
CKDQ-AM - 910 (Drumheller, AB, Can.) 34697
CKDR-AM - 800 (Dryden, ON, Can.) 35791
CKDS-FM 35896*
CKDU-FM - 97.5 (Halifax, NS, Can.) 35578
CKDX-AM (Newmarket, ON, Can.) Unable to locate
CKDY-AM - 1420 (Kentville, NS, Can.) 35583
CKEC-AM - 1320 (New Glasgow, NS, Can.) 35597
CKEG-AM - 1570 (Nanaimo, BC, Can.) 35022
CKEK-AM 34937*
CKEN-AM - 97.7 (Kentville, NS, Can.) 35584
CKER-AM 34754*
CKER-FM - 101.9 (Edmonton, AB, Can.) 34754
CKEY-FM - 101.1 (Niagara Falls, ON, Can.) 36113
CKFH-AM 36818*
CKFL-AM (Lac Megantic, QC, Can.) Unable to locate
CKFM-FM - 99.9 (Toronto, ON, Can.) 36821
CKFR-AM (Kelowna, BC, Can.) Unable to locate
CKGA-AM - 650 (Gander, NL, Can.) 35457
CKGB-FM 36458*
CKGB-FM - 750 (Timmins, ON, Can.) 36459
CKGE-FM - 94.9 (Oshawa, ON, Can.) 36183
CKGF-AM - 1340 (Grand Forks, BC, Can.) 34972
CKGL-AM - 570 (Kitchener, ON, Can.) 35966
CKGO-AM (Hope, BC, Can.) Unable to locate
CKGR-AM - 1400 (Golden, BC, Can.) 34968
CKGY-FM - 95.5 (Red Deer, AB, Can.) 34835
CKHJ-FM - 105.3 (Fredericton, NB, Can.) 35405
CKHL-AM 34823*
CKHR-FM - 107.3 (Hay River, NT, Can.) 35517
CKIA-FM - 96.1 (Quebec, QC, Can.) 37303
CKIK-FM (Calgary, AB, Can.) Unable to locate
CKIM-AM - 1240 (Grand Falls, NL, Can.) 35464
CKIQ-AM (Kelowna, BC, Can.) Unable to locate
CKIR-AM - 870 (Golden, BC, Can.) 34969
CKIS-AM 37449*
CKIS-FM 35371*
CKIX-FM - 99.1 (St. John's, NL, Can.) 35502
CKJD-AM 36368*
CKJR-AM - 1440 (Wetaskiwin, AB, Can.) 34874
CKJS-AM - 810 (Winnipeg, MB, Can.) 35373
CKKC-AM - 880 (Nelson, BC, Can.) 35026
CKKC-FM - 101.9 (Crawford Bay, BC, Can.) 34938
CKKL-FM - 93.9 (Ottawa, ON, Can.) 36294
CKKN-FM - 101.3 (Prince George, BC, Can.) 35061
CKKQ-FM (Victoria, BC, Can.) Unable to locate
CKKR-AM 37546*
CKKS-FM - 96.9 (Vancouver, BC, Can.) 35193
CKKW-AM - 1090 (Waterloo, ON, Can.) 36861
CKKX-TV 34668*
CKKY-AM - 830 (Wainwright, AB, Can.) 34870
CKLA-AM 34823*
CKLA-FM 35869*
CKLB-FM - 101.9 (Yellowknife, NT, Can.) 35530
CKLC-AM - 1380 (Kingston, ON, Can.) 35954
CKLD-FM - 105.5 (Thetford Mines, QC, Can.) 37413
CKLE-FM (Caraquet, NB, Can.) Unable to locate
CKLG-AM (Vancouver, BC, Can.) Ceased
CKLH-FM - 102.9 (Hamilton, ON, Can.) 35897
CKLM-AM (Laval, QC, Can.) Unable to locate
CKLN-FM - 88.1 (Toronto, ON, Can.) 36822
CKLP-FM (Parry Sound, ON, Can.) Unable to locate
CKLQ-AM - 880 (Brandon, MB, Can.) 35256
CKLR-AM (L'Annonciation, QC, Can.) Ceased
CKLS-AM - 1240 (La Sarre, QC, Can.) 37023
CKLW-AM - 800 (Windsor, ON, Can.) 36899
CKLW-FM, The River 14822*
CKLW-TV 36897*
CKLY-AM - 910 (Lindsay, ON, Can.) 35974
CKLZ-FM - 104.7 (Kelowna, BC, Can.) 34993
CKMA-AM (Abbotsford, BC, Can.) Unable to locate
CKMF-FM - 94.3 (Montreal, QC, Can.) 37249
CKMG-FM (Maniwaki, QC, Can.) Unable to locate
CKMI Global TV - Channel UHF 20 (Sainte-Foy, QC, Can.) 37380
CKMI-TV 37380*
CKML-FM 36940*
CKMM-FM (Winnipeg, MB, Can.) Unable to locate
CKMO-AM 35898*
CKMO-FM - 103.1 (Victoria, BC, Can.) 35236
CKMP-FM 36045*
CKMR 35410*
CKMS-FM - 100.3 (Waterloo, ON, Can.) 36862
CKMV-AM - 1490 (Grand Falls, NB, Can.) 35407
CKMW-AM - 1570 (Winkler, MB, Can.) 35308
CKMX-AM - 1060 (Calgary, AB, Can.) 34671

CKNB-AM - 950 (Campbellton, NB, Can.) **35384**
CKND-TV - Channel 9 (Winnipeg, MB, Can.) **35374**
CKNG-FM - 92.5 (Edmonton, AB, Can.) **34755**
CKNL-AM - 560 (Fort St. John, BC, Can.) **34960**
CKNR-AM - 1340 (Elliot Lake, ON, Can.) **35804**
CKNR-FM - 94.1 (Blind River, ON, Can.) **35687**
CKNS-FM **35687***
CKNS-FM **35687***
CKNW-AM - 980 (Vancouver, BC, Can.) **35194**
CKNX-AM - 920 (Wingham, ON, Can.) **36903**
CKNX-FM - 101.7 (Wingham, ON, Can.) **36904**
CKNX-TV - Channel 8 (Wingham, ON, Can.) **36905**
CKO-AM (Montreal, QC, Can.) *Ceased*
CKO-FM (Calgary, AB, Can.) *Ceased*
CKOC-AM - 1150 (Hamilton, ON, Can.) **35898**
CKOD-AM **37427***
CKOD-FM - 103.1 (Valleyfield, QC, Can.) **37427**
CKOI-FM - 96.9 (Verdun, QC, Can.) **37429**
CKOK-AM **35047***
CKOM-AM - 650 (Saskatoon, SK, Can.) **37566**
CKON-FM - 97.3 (Rooseveltown, NY) **23276**
CKOO-AM (Osoyoos, BC, Can.) *Ceased*
CKOR-AM - 800 (Penticton, BC, Can.) **35047**
CKOS-TV - Channel 5 (Yorkton, SK, Can.) **37603**
CKOT-AM - 1510 (Tillsonburg, ON, Can.) **36451**
CKOT-FM - 101.3 (Tillsonburg, ON, Can.) **36452**
CKOV-AM - 630 (Kelowna, BC, Can.) **34994**
CKOX-FM **36909***
CKOY-AM **36457***
CKPC-AM - 1380 (Brantford, ON, Can.) **35705**
CKPC-FM - 92.1 (Brantford, ON, Can.) **35706**
CKPE-FM - 94.9 (Sydney, NS, Can.) **35614**
CKPG-AM - 550 (Prince George, BC, Can.) **35062**
CKPG-TV - Channel 2 (Prince George, BC, Can.) **35063**
CKPR-AM (Thunder Bay, ON, Can.) *Ceased*
CKPR-TV - Channel 2 (Thunder Bay, ON, Can.) **36448**
CKPT-AM - 1420 (Peterborough, ON, Can.) **36322**
CKQB-FM - 106.9 (Ottawa, ON, Can.) **36295**
CKQM-FM - 105.1 (Peterborough, ON, Can.) **36323**
CKQN-FM - 99.3 (Baker Lake, NT, Can.) **35513**
CKQR-AM - 99.3 (Castlegar, BC, Can.) **34922**
CKQT-FM **36183***
CKRB-FM - 103.3 (Saint-Georges-de-Beauce, QC, Can.) **37343**
CKRC-AM (Winnipeg, MB, Can.) *Unable to locate*
CKRD-AM **34833***
CKRD-TV - Channel 6 (Red Deer, AB, Can.) **34836**
CKRK-FM - 103.7 (Kahnawake, QC, Can.) **37019**
CKRL-FM - 89.1 (Quebec, QC, Can.) **37304**
CKRM-AM - 620 (Regina, SK, Can.) **37543**
CKRN-AM - 1400 (Noranda, QC, Can.) **37261**
CKRN-TV - Channel 4 (Noranda, QC, Can.) **37262**
CKRO-MF **35425***
CKRS-AM (Jonquiere, QC, Can.) *Unable to locate*
CKRS-TV - Channel 12 (Jonquiere, QC, Can.) **37016**
CKRU-AM - 980 (Peterborough, ON, Can.) **36324**
CKRV-FM - 97.5 (Kamloops, BC, Can.) **34983**
CKRW-AM - 610 (Whitehorse, YT, Can.) **37608**
CKRX-AM (Lethbridge, AB, Can.) *Ceased*
CKRX-FM **34800***
CKRY-FM - 105.1 (Calgary, AB, Can.) **34672**
CKRZ-FM - 100.3 (Ohsweken, ON, Can.) **36156**
CKSA-AM - 1080 (Lloydminster, AB, Can.) **34805**
CKSB-AM - 1050 (Winnipeg, MB, Can.) **35375**
CKSF-AM **35758***
CKSJ-AM (Saint-Jerome, QC, Can.) *Unable to locate*
CKSL-AM (London, ON, Can.) *Unable to locate*
CKSM-AM (Shawinigan, QC, Can.) *Unable to locate*
CKSO-AM **36424***
CKSO-TV **36428***
CKSP-AM **35104***
CKSQ-AM - 1400 (Stettler, AB, Can.) **34856**
CKSR-AM **34850***
CKSR-FM (Chilliwack, BC, Can.) *Unable to locate*
CKST-AM - 1040 (Vancouver, BC, Can.) **35195**
CKSW-AM - 570 (Swift Current, SK, Can.) **37578**
CKSY-FM - 94.3 (Chatham, ON, Can.) **35732**
CKTA-AM (Taber, AB, Can.) *Unable to locate*
CKTB-AM - 610 (St. Catharines, ON, Can.) **36359**
CKTB-FM **36358***
CKTF-FM - 104.1 (Ottawa, ON, Can.) **36296**
CKTK-AM - 1230 (Kitimat, BC, Can.) **35000**
CKTO-FM - 100.9 (Truro, NS, Can.) **35618**
CKTS-AM (Sherbrooke, QC, Can.) *Ceased*
CKTY-AM **36368***
CKUA-AM - 580 (Edmonton, AB, Can.) **34756**
CKUE-FM **36298***
CKUE-FM - 95.1 (Chatham, ON, Can.) **35733**
CKUT-AM - 1600 (Wollaston Lake, SK, Can.) **37596**
CKUT-FM - 90.3 (Montreal, QC, Can.) **37250**
CKUW-FM - 95.9 FM (Winnipeg, MB, Can.) **35376**
CKVD-AM - 900 (Val d'Or, QC, Can.) **37423**
CKVH-AM - 1020 (High Prairie, AB, Can.) **34782**
CKVL-AM - 850 (Verdun, QC, Can.) **37430**
CKVM-AM - 710 (Ville-Marie, QC, Can.) **37438**
CKVO-AM - 710 (Clarenville, NL, Can.) **35445**
CKVR-TV - Channel 3 (Barrie, ON, Can.) **35664**
CKVT-AM **37438***
CKVU-TV **35196***
CKVU-TV - Channel 10 (Vancouver, BC, Can.) **35196**
CKWA-AM - 1210 (Slave Lake, AB, Can.) **34850**
CKWF-FM - 101.5 (Peterborough, ON, Can.) **36325**
CKWK-AM **35453***
CKWL-AM - 570 (Williams Lake, BC, Can.) **35246**
CKWM-FM - 97.7 (Kentville, NS, Can.) **35585**
CKWR-FM - 98.5 (Waterloo, ON, Can.) **36863**
CKWS-AM **35950***
CKWS-FM **35952***
CKWS-TV - Channel 11 (Kingston, ON, Can.) **35955**
CKWW-AM - 580 (Windsor, ON, Can.) **36900**
CKWX-AM - 1130 (Vancouver, BC, Can.) **35197**
CKX-AM - 1150 (Brandon, MB, Can.) **35257**
CKX-FM - 96.1 (Brandon, MB, Can.) **35258**
CKXB-AM - 670 (Musgravetown, NL, Can.) **35476**
CKXD-AM - 1010 (Gander, NL, Can.) **35458**
CKXG-AM (Grand Falls, NL, Can.) *Unable to locate*
CKXJ-AM (Grand Bank, NL, Can.) *Ceased*
CKXM-AM - 1200 (Victoria, BC, Can.) **35237**
CKXM-FM **34744***
CKXR-AM - 580 (Salmon Arm, BC, Can.) **35083**
CKXR-FM - 102.1 (Salmon Arm, BC, Can.) **35084**
CKXX-AM **35453***
CKXX-FM - 103.9 (Corner Brook, NL, Can.) **35453**
CKY-AM (Winnipeg, MB, Can.) *Unable to locate*
CKYC-AM (Toronto, ON, Can.) *Unable to locate*
CKYC-FM - 93.7 (Owen Sound, ON, Can.) **36303**
CKYL-AM **34823***
CKYL-AM - 610 (Peace River, AB, Can.) **34823**
CKYQ-FM - 95.7 (Plessisville, QC, Can.) **37271**
CKYQ-FM - 95.7 (Plessisville, QC, Can.) **37270**
CKYR-AM **34762***
CKYX-FM - 97.9 (Fort McMurray, AB, Can.) **34769**
CKZZ-FM - 95.3 (Richmond, BC, Can.) **35078**
CLA Journal (Atlanta, GA) **6985**
Clackamas County News (Estacada, OR) **26313**
The Clackamas County Review (Clackamas, OR) *Unable to locate*
Claiborne Progress (Tazewell, TN) **29625**
CLAIMS (Brier, WA) **32698**
Claims Journal; Environmental (New York, NY) **21614**
Clairon Regional de St. Hyacinthe; Le (Saint-Hyacinthe, QC, Can.) **37350**
The Clansman **35560***
The Clanton Advertiser (Clanton, AL) **155**
The CLAO Journal **13160***
Clap; Magazine Le (Sainte-Foy, QC, Can.) **37374**
Clara City Herald (Clara City, MN) **15798**
Clare County Buyers Guide (Alma, MI) **14730**
Clare County Cleaver (Harrison, MI) *Unable to locate*
Clare County Review (Clare, MI) **14878**
The Clare Sentinel (Clare, MI) **14879**
Claremont Collegian **1724***
Claremont Courier (Claremont, CA) *Unable to locate*
The Claremont Review (Victoria, BC, Can.) **35214**
Claremore Daily Progress (Claremore, OK) **25788**
Clarence Bee (Clarence, NY) **20461**
The Clarence Courier (Clarence, MO) **16980**
Clarence-Lowden Sun News (Tipton, IA) **11268**
The Clarendon Enterprise (Clarendon, TX) **30021**
Clarendon Hills Progress (Downers Grove, IL) **8781**
Clarendon Press **30021***
Claresholm Local Press (Claresholm, AB, Can.) **34683**
The Clarinet (Denton, TX) **30233**
Clarington / Courtice (Bowmanville, ON, Can.) **35692**
Clarington-Port Perry This Week; Oshawa-Whitby-(Oshawa, ON, Can.) **36181**
The Clarion (Denver, CO) **4310**
The Clarion (Corydon, IN) **9904**
Clarion (Rochester Hills, MI) *Unable to locate*
The Clarion (St. Paul, MN) **16371**
Clarion (Dayton, OH) **25110**
The Clarion (Palestine, TX) **30896**
Clarion (Madison, WI) **33927**
The Clarion (Nepean, ON, Can.) *Unable to locate*
The Clarion Call (Clarion, PA) **26779**
Clarion Herald (New Orleans, LA) **12727**
The Clarion Ledger (Jackson, MS) **16695**
Clarion News (Clarion, PA) **26780**
Clarissa Independent **15799***
Clark Atlanta University Magazine (Atlanta, GA) **6986**
Clark Cablevision (Laughlin, NV) **18411**
Clark County Clipper (Ashland, KS) **11344**
Clark County Courier (Clark, SD) **28832**
Clark County Journal (Jeffersonville, IN) **10224**
The Clark County Press (Neillsville, WI) **34163**
The Clark/Cranford Eagle (Clark, NJ) **18747**
Clark Now (Worcester, MA) *Ceased*
Clark Patriot (Rahway, NJ) *Unable to locate*
Clarke County Democrat (Grove Hill, AL) **247**
Clarke County Tribune (Quitman, MS) *Unable to locate*
Clarke Courier (Dubuque, IA) **10841**
Clarke Times-Courier (Berryville, VA) **31864**
The Clarkfield Advocate **15934***
Clarksburg Exponent (Clarksburg, WV) **33293**
Clarksburg Telegram (Clarksburg, WV) **33294**
The Clarksdale Press Register (Clarksdale, MS) **16588**
Clarkston Eccentric (Clarkston, MI) **14880**
The Clarkston News (Clarkston, MI) **14881**
Clarksville Star (Clarksville, IA) **10705**
The Clarksville Times **31959***
The Clarksville Times (Clarksville, TX) **30022**
Clasificado; El (Los Angeles, CA) **2262**
Class Action Reports (Washington, DC) **5417**
Class Magazine (New York, NY) *Unable to locate*
Classic American Homes (New York, NY) **21427**
Classic Auto Restorer (Mission Viejo, CA) *Unable to locate*
Classic Boating (Oconomowoc, WI) **34201**
Classic Cable **31206***
Classic Cable (Breckenridge, CO) *Unable to locate*
Classic Cable (Lampasas, TX) **30666**
Classic Cable (Tyler, TX) **31205**
Classic Cable Co. (Spearman, TX) *Unable to locate*
Classic Cable, Inc. (Tyler, TX) **31206**
Classic Communications Ltd. (Richmond Hill, ON, Can.) **36348**
Classic Cookbooks (Minneapolis, MN) **16067**
Classic Images (Muscatine, IA) **11102**
Classic Toy Trains Magazine (Waukesha, WI) **34398**
Classic Trains (Waukesha, WI) **34399**
Classic Truck **25691***
Classic Trucks (Anaheim, CA) **1403**
Classical Antiquity (Berkeley, CA) **1508**
The Classical Bulletin (Wauconda, IL) **9742**
Classical Calliope **18619***
Classical Journal (Charlottesville, VA) **31923**
Classical and Modern Literature (Columbia, MO) **16989**
The Classical Network **19679***
Classical Philology (Seattle, WA) *Unable to locate*
Classical Singer Magazine (South Jordan, UT) **31472**
Classical Tradition; International Journal of the (Boston, MA) **13907**
The Classical World (Philadelphia, PA) **27406**
The Classified Flea Market (Oakland, CA) **2676**
Classified Gazette (San Rafael, CA) **3599**
The Classified Gazette (Sonoma County Edition) (Sonoma, CA) **3773**
The Classified News (Mississauga, ON, Can.) **36063**
Classroom; Cable in the (Boston, MA) **13870**
Classy 99.9 **33135***
Clatskanie Chief (Clatskanie, OR) **26268**
Claude Brisebois Engineering (Montreal, QC, Can.) *Unable to locate*
Clause (Azusa, CA) **1445**
Clavier (Northfield, IL) **9326**
Claws; Paws & (Indianapolis, IN) **10159**
Clawson Mirror (Royal Oak, MI) **15478**
Clay Cablevision (Orange Park, FL) *Unable to locate*
The Clay City Times (Clay City, KY) *Unable to locate*
Clay County Advocate-Press; Daily (Flora, IL) **8890**
Clay County Courier (Corning, AR) **1090**
Clay County Crescent (Green Cove Springs, FL) *Unable to locate*
Clay County Democrat (Rector, AR) **1324**
Clay County Free Press (Clay, WV) **33297**
Clay County Leader (Henrietta, TX) **30442**
Clay County News (Sutton, NE) **18292**
The Clay County Progress **23980***
The Clay County Progress (Hayesville, NC) **23980**
The Clay County Progress—Mountain News **23980***
Clay County Republican; Louisville (Louisville, IL) **9119**
Clay Dispatch-Tribune **17162***
Clay & Platte Dispatch-Tribune (Kansas City, MO) **17162**
Clay Times (Waterford, VA) **32609**
The Clay Times Journal (Lineville, AL) **304**
Clay Today (Orange Park, FL) **6487**
Clay West Shopper News **17082***
The Clayton County Register (Elkader, IA) **10873**
Clayton-Fillmore Report (Castle Rock, CO) **4221**
The Clayton Neighbor (Forest Park, GA) **7275**
The Clayton News **23644***
Clayton News/Daily (Jonesboro, GA) **7351**
The Clayton News-Star (Benson, NC) **23644**
The Clayton Record (Clayton, AL) **158**
Clayton Sun (College Park, GA) *Unable to locate*
Clayton Sun; Smyrna **5287***
Clayton Sun-Times; Smyrna/ (Smyrna, DE) **5287**
The Clayton Tribune (Clayton, GA) *Unable to locate*
Clayton Word; West End- (St. Louis, MO) **17531**
CLC Observer **22482***
The CLE Journal (Philadelphia, PA) **27407**
The CLE Journal and Register **27407***
Clean Scene Magazine (Alexandria, VA) *Ceased*
Cleaner and Launderer; Western (Pasadena, CA) **2828**
Cleaning Business (Seattle, WA) *Unable to locate*
Cleaning-Finishing-Coating Digest (Materials Park, OH) *Ceased*

Numbers cited in bold after listings are entry numbers rather than page numbers.

Club Specials Magazine (Sandy Hook, CT) **5111**
Club TV de Matagami/Matagami TV Club (Matagami, QC, Can.) **37067**
Clubdate Magazine (Cleveland, OH) *Unable to locate*
The Clubhouse (Nashua, NH) **18586**
Clubhouse Jr. (Colorado Springs, CO) **4241**
Clubwoman Magazine; GFWC (Washington, DC) **5514**
Clues: A Journal of Detection (Bowling Green, OH) **24690**
The Cluster (Macon, GA) **7380**
Cluster Computing (New York, NY) **21431**
Cluster; The Mercer (Macon, GA) **7383**
The Clyde Enterprise (Clyde, OH) **24996**
Clyde Republican (Clyde, KS) **11385**
Clydesdale News (Pecatonica, IL) **9413**
CM (Winnipeg, MB, Can.) **35322**
CM News **32243***
CM News (Herndon, VA) **32162**
CMA Management (Mississauga, ON, Can.) *Unable to locate*
CMA News (Ottawa, ON, Can.) **36235**
CMAJ/JAMC (Canadian Medical Association Journal)/ (Journal de l'Association Medicale Canadienne) (Ottawa, ON, Can.) **36236**
CME (Continuing Medical Education); The Canadian Journal of (Pointe-Claire, QC, Can.) **37272**
CMEA News (Concord, CA) **1751**
CMHC Housing Outlook, National Edition (Ottawa, ON, Can.) **36237**
CMJ New Music Monthly (New York, NY) **21432**
CMJ New Music Report (New York, NY) **21433**
CML Army Chemical Review (Fort Leonard Wood, MO) **17071**
CMP Bulletin (Riverside, CA) *Ceased*
(CMR); California Management Review (Berkeley, CA) **1503**
CN Club News (New York, NY) *Ceased*
CNA (Iola, WI) **33808**
CNBC (Consumer News & Business Channel) (Fort Lee, NJ) **37737**
CNEWA World (New York, NY) **21434**
CNN (Cable News Network)/Headline News (Atlanta, GA) **37738**
CNN Radio Network (Atlanta, GA) **37625**
CNS Drugs (Langhorne, PA) *Unable to locate*
CNS Focus (Garden City, NY) **20636**
Co-Ette Magazine (Detroit, MI) *Unable to locate*
Co-Laborer (Antioch, TN) **29049**
Co-op America Quarterly *Unable to locate*
Co-Op City News (Bronx, NY) **20263**
The Co-Pilot (Walker, MN) **16493**
Coach and Athletic Director (Danbury, CT) **4737**
Coach; Texas (Austin, TX) **29814**
Coachella Valley Sun (Palm Springs, CA) **2756**
Coaching Management (Ithaca, NY) **20790**
Coaching Volleyball (Colorado Springs, CO) **4242**
Coaching Women's Basketball (Lilburn, GA) **7371**
Coal **11705***
Coal Age (Overland Park, KS) **11705**
The Coal City Courant (Wilmington, IL) **9765**
Coal and Electricity Quarterly Statistics; Oil, Gas, (Washington, DC) **5706**
Coal Facts; West Virginia (Charleston, WV) **33274**
The Coal Journal (Lexington, KY) *Unable to locate*
Coal People Magazine (Charleston, WV) **33269**
Coal and Synfuels Technology (Arlington, VA) *Unable to locate*
Coal Valley News (Madison, WV) **33374**
Coal Voice (Washington, DC) *Unable to locate*
The Coalfield Progress (Norton, VA) **32310**
Coalgate Record-Register (Coalgate, OK) **25793**
Coalinga CATV (Coalinga, CA) **1736**
Coalinga Courier **1735***
Coalinga Record (Coalinga, CA) **1735**
COAS: New Mexico Archaeology and History (Las Cruces, NM) *Ceased*
Coast (Bay Head, NJ) *Ceased*
The Coast (Halifax, NS, Can.) **35562**
Coast Cable (Dana Point, CA) **1808**
Coast Cable (San Jose, CA) *Unable to locate*
Coast Cable Communications Ltd. (Sechelt, BC, Can.) **35088**
Coast Cable TV **2035***
Coast Cable Vision Ltd. **35088***
Coast & Country (Marblehead, MA) *Ceased*
The Coast Guard (Shelburne, NS, Can.) **35604**
Coast Magazine (Newport Beach, CA) **2624**
Coast Magazine—Alaska Edition. (Vancouver, BC, Can.) *Unable to locate*
Coast Magazine—Alberta Edition (Vancouver, BC, Can.) *Unable to locate*
Coast Magazine—British Columbia Edition (Vancouver, BC, Can.) *Unable to locate*
Coast Magazine—Ontario Edition (Toronto, ON, Can.) **36552**
(Coast Mills); Monthly F.O.B. Price Summary, Past Sales (Portland, OR) **26485**
Coast Mountain Courier **34974***
Coast Mountain News (Hagensborg, BC, Can.) **34974**

Coast News (Dade City, FL) *Ceased*
Coast Papers **12941***
Coast Press; Delaware (Rehoboth Beach, DE) **5284**
The Coast Star (Manasquan, NJ) **19213**
Coast TV Cable Inc. **16654***
Coast Weekly (Seaside, CA) **3750**
The Coastal Bend Herald (Rockport, TX) *Unable to locate*
The Coastal Carolinian (Wilmington, NC) *Unable to locate*
The Coastal Courier (Hinesville, GA) **7330**
The Coastal Courier (Glace Bay, NS, Can.) *Unable to locate*
Coastal Guide (Myrtle Beach, SC) *Unable to locate*
Coastal Journal (Bath, ME) **12918**
Coastal Law; The International Journal of Marine and (New York, NY) **21910**
Coastal Living (Birmingham, AL) **65**
Coastal Management (Seattle, WA) **32955**
Coastal Observer (Pawleys Island, SC) **28742**
Coastal Post (Bolinas, CA) **1591**
The Coastal Times (Charleston, SC) *Unable to locate*
Coastal View (Carpinteria, CA) **1676**
The Coaster (Harbour Breton, NL, Can.) **35468**
Coastland Times (Manteo, NC) **24053**
Coastside Cable TV Inc. (El Granada, CA) **1864**
Coastside Chronicle (San Mateo, CA) **3584**
Coatings; Journal of Water Borne (Norwalk, CT) **5067**
Coatings & Linings; Journal of Protective (Pittsburgh, PA) **27803**
Coatings Magazine (Toronto, ON, Can.) **36553**
Coatings; Modern Paint and (Atlanta, GA) **7027**
Coatings Technology; Journal of (Blue Bell, PA) **26725**
Coaxial Cable Corp. (Edinboro, PA) **26863**
Coaxial Communications of Central Ohio (Columbus, OH) **25070**
Coaxial Communications of Southern Ohio (Amelia, OH) **24609**
Cobblestone (Peterborough, NH) **18621**
The Cobden Sun (Cobden, ON, Can.) **35740**
Cobourg Daily Star (Cobourg, ON, Can.) **35741**
Cobourg-Port Hope Shoppers Market (Cobourg, ON, Can.) *Unable to locate*
The Cochran Journal (Cochran, GA) **7178**
Cochrane This Week **34685***
Cochrane Times (Cochrane, AB, Can.) **34685**
Cochran's Corner (Waldorf, MD) **13771**
Cockatiel & Parakeet World **2585***
Cocktails Magazine (Las Vegas, NV) **18361**
Coconut Creek Forum; Margate/ (Margate, FL) **6325**
Coda Magazine (Toronto, ON, Can.) **36554**
Coda: Poets & Writers Newsletter **22568***
Codata Bulletin (New York, NY) *Ceased*
C.O.D.E. (Minnetonka, MN) *Unable to locate*
Code of Federal Regulations (Pittsburgh, PA) **27766**
Code One (Fort Worth, TX) **30334**
CodeWorks (Tacoma, WA) *Ceased*
Cody Enterprise (Cody, WY) **34513**
Coe Review (Cedar Rapids, IA) **10670**
Coeur d'Alene Press (Coeur d'Alene, ID) **7844**
CoEvolution Quarterly **3603***
Coffee County News (Douglas, GA) **7243**
Coffee & Cuisine (Seattle, WA) *Unable to locate*
Coffee Journal (Minneapolis, MN) *Ceased*
Coffee Trade Journal; Tea and (New York, NY) **22816**
Coffey County Republican (Burlington, KS) **11370**
Coffey County Today **11370***
Coffeyville Journal (Coffeyville, KS) **11386**
Cogeco (Sept-Iles, QC, Can.) **37389**
Cogeco Cable (Baie-Comeau, QC, Can.) **36943**
Cogeco Cable (Saint-Hyacinthe, QC, Can.) **37353**
Cogeco Cable Inc. (Hawkesbury, ON, Can.) **35910**
Cogeco Cable Inc. (Windsor, ON, Can.) **36901**
COGECO Cable, Inc. (Trois-Rivieres, QC, Can.) **37419**
Cogeco Cable Solutions (Belleville, ON, Can.) **35684**
Cogeco Cable Systems (Niagara Falls, ON, Can.) **36114**
Cogeneration (Southport, CT) *Ceased*
Cogeneration and Competitive Power Journal (Lilburn, GA) **7372**
Cognition; Brain and (San Diego, CA) **3125**
Cognition and Development; Journal of (Toronto, ON, Can.) **36633**
Cognition and Instruction (Nashville, TN) **29452**
Cognition; Memory & (Austin, TX) **29792**
Cognitive, Affective, & Behavioral Neuroscience (Austin, TX) **29768**
Cognitive Psychology (San Diego, CA) **3129**
Cognitive Psychology; Applied (Hoboken, NJ) **18892**
Cognitive Psychotherapy; Journal of (New York, NY) **22029**
Cognitive Science (New York, NY) **21435**
Cognitive Therapy & Research (New York, NY) **21436**
Cohasset Mariner (Cohasset, MA) **14141**
Cohasset Shoppinguide (Pembroke, MA) *Ceased*

Coin Launderer & Cleaner (Northbrook, IL) *Ceased*
Coin Laundry and Drycleaning Industry; Journal of the (Downers Grove, IL) **8787**
Coin Magazine; Error Trends (Oceanside, NY) **23030**
Coin News; Canadian (St. Catharines, ON, Can.) **36351**
Coin News; World (Iola, WI) **33857**
Coin-Op; American (Chicago, IL) **8254**
Coin Prices (Iola, WI) **33809**
Coin Review; Rare (Wolfeboro, NH) **18655**
The Coin Slot (Wheat Ridge, CO) *Ceased*
Coin World (Sidney, OH) **25516**
COINage (Ventura, CA) **4002**
Coins Magazine (Iola, WI) **33810**
Coins Magazine; Fell's U.S. (Hollywood, FL) **6194**
Cokato Enterprise **15824***
Cokefish (New Hope, PA) *Unable to locate*
Colbert County Reporter (Tuscumbia, AL) *Unable to locate*
Colborne Chronicle (Colborne, ON, Can.) **35746**
Colby (Waterville, ME) **13071**
Colby Echo (Waterville, ME) **13072**
Colby Free Press (Colby, KS) **11388**
The Colchester Chronicle (Macomb, IL) *Ceased*
Colchester Sunday (Truro, NS, Can.) **35615**
Cold Lake Courier; Canadian Forces Base (Coldlake, AB, Can.) **34688**
Cold Lake Sun (Cold Lake, AB, Can.) **34687**
Cold Spring Record (Cold Spring, MN) **15803**
Cold War International History Project (Washington, DC) **5423**
Cold War Studies; Journal of (Cambridge, MA) **14075**
ColdFusion Developer's Journal (CFDJ) (Montvale, NJ) **19247**
Coldwater Daily Reporter **14887***
Coldwater Daily Reporter (Coldwater, MI) **14887**
Cole Camp Courier (Windsor, MO) **17720**
The Coleopterists Bulletin (Baton Rouge, LA) **12487**
Coleraine Cable Communications System (Coleraine, MN) **15804**
Coleridge Blade (Coleridge, NE) **17979**
The Colfax County Press (Clarkson, NE) **17978**
Colfax Gazette **32720***
Colfax Highline Cable (Colfax, WA) **32721**
Colfax Record (Colfax, CA) **1739**
Colfax Tribune **10717***
The Colgate Maroon **20706***
The Colgate Maroon-News (Hamilton, NY) **20706**
The Colgate News **20706***
Colgate Scene (Hamilton, NY) **20707**
Collaboration (Mount Tremper, NY) *Unable to locate*
Collage (Claremont, CA) **1724**
Collage (Ottawa, ON, Can.) *Ceased*
Collectables; Antique & (El Cajon, CA) **1843**
Collected Algorithms (CALGO) Supplements (New York, NY) **21487**
Collectible Automobile (Lincolnwood, IL) **9091**
Collectibles; American Country (New York, NY) **21185**
Collectibles Canada (St. Catharines, ON, Can.) **36356**
Collectibles; Car Toy (Canoga Park, CA) **1655**
Collectibles, Flea Market Finds (New York, NY) **21438**
Collectibles Magazine; Antiques & (Westbury, NY) **23551**
Collectif; Le (Sherbrooke, QC, Can.) **37394**
Collecting Magazine; Antiques & (Chicago, IL) **8265**
Collecting; Pop Culture (Corona, CA) **1767**
Collecting Toys Magazine (Waukesha, WI) *Ceased*
Collection Management (Binghamton, NY) *Unable to locate*
Collections (Columbia) *Ceased*
Collections & Credit Risk (Chicago, IL) **8335**
The Collective (Alexandria, VA) **31655**
Collector (Minneapolis, MN) **16068**
Collector Editions (New York, NY) *Unable to locate*
Collector; Jukebox (Pleasant Hill, IA) **11160**
Collector Magazine & Price Guide (Iola, WI) **33811**
Collector Magazine; Professional (Boston, MA) **13952**
Collector; The New York-Pennsylvania (Canandaigua, NY) **20422**
The Collectors Club Philatelist (Riva, MD) **13672**
Collector's Mart (Iola, WI) **33812**
Collectors Motor News (Long Beach, CA) *Ceased*
Collectors News (Grundy Center, IA) **10935**
Collectors News & the Antique Reporter **10935***
Collectors' Showcase (Tulsa, OK) **26109**
The College (Annapolis, MD) **13093**
College Athletic Management **20790***
College of the Bible Quarterly **12174***
College Boulevard News (Overland Park, KS) **11706**
College Broadcaster (Providence, RI) *Unable to locate*
College & Career Guide News for College Students (Tucson, AZ) **940**
College & Career Guide News for High School Teens **940***
College Composition and Communication (Urbana, IL) **9700**
College English (Urbana, IL) **9701**

College Health; Journal of American (Washington, DC) **5569**
College Heights Herald (Bowling Green, KY) **11941**
College Hoops Illustrated (New York, NY) **21439**
College Journal; The Connecticut (New London, CT) **5017**
College Literature (West Chester, PA) **28145**
College Mathematics Journal (Washington, DC) **5424**
College Musician (Burbank, CA) *Unable to locate*
College News (Chicago, IL) *Unable to locate*
College Outlook (Kansas City, MO) **17163**
College Outlook and Career Opportunities **17163***
College Park Gazette (Frederick, MD) **13509**
College of Physicians of Philadelphia; Transactions and Studies of the (Philadelphia, PA) **27709**
College Planning and Management (Dayton, OH) **25111**
College Point-Malba Pennysaver (Ontario, ON, Can.) *Unable to locate*
College Radio; The Journal of (New Windsor, NY) **21127**
College Reading and Learning; Journal of (Prince George, BC, Can.) **35056**
The College Reporter (Lancaster, PA) **27140**
College and Research Libraries (Athens, GA) **6932**
College and Research Libraries News (Chicago, IL) **8336**
College Review (Wahpeton, ND) **24548**
College Services (Charlottesville, VA) **31925**
College Services Administration **31925***
College Sports (South Plainfield, NJ) *Unable to locate*
The College Store (Oberlin, OH) **25444**
College Store Executive (Westbury, NY) **23553**
The College Store Journal **25444***
College Student Affairs Journal (Natchitoches, LA) **12715**
College Student Journal (Mobile, AL) **318**
College Student Psychotherapy; Journal of (Wallingford, PA) **28101**
College Teaching (Washington, DC) **5425**
College Teaching; Journal on Excellence in (Oxford, OH) **25456**
College & Undergraduate Libraries (Syracuse, NY) **23396**
College Union **23555***
College and University Foodservice; Journal of (Blacksburg, VA) **31873**
College and University Student Housing; Journal of (Gainesville, FL) **6146**
The College Voice (New London, CT) **5016**
The College Voice (Staten Island, NY) *Unable to locate*
College Week; Community (Fairfax, VA) **32012**
College Woman (Burbank, CA) *Unable to locate*
Colleges; Careers & (Keyport, NJ) **19155**
Colleges Journal; Community (Washington, DC) **5429**
Colleges; New Directions for Community (San Francisco, CA) **3398**
The Collegian (Fresno, CA) **1949**
Collegian (Fayette, IA) **10888**
The Collegian (Coffeyville, KS) **11387**
Collegian (Glendive, MT) *Ceased*
The Collegian (Hastings, NE) **18035**
The Collegian (Jamestown, ND) **24475**
Collegian (Ashland, OH) **24618**
The Collegian (Toledo, OH) **25566**
Collegian (Lawton, OK) **25886**
The Collegian (Grove City, PA) **26964**
The Collegian (Philadelphia, PA) **27422**
The Collegian (Richmond, VA) **32433**
Collegian Chief **11212***
Collegian; The City (Seattle, WA) **32954**
Collegian; The Daily (University Park, PA) **28074**
Collegian; Hutchinson (Hutchinson, KS) **11500**
Collegian; Kansas State (Manhattan, KS) **11626**
Collegian Newspaper (Tulsa, OK) **26110**
Collegian Reporter (Sioux City, IA) **11212**
Collegian; The Rocky Mountain (Fort Collins, CO) **4438**
Collegian; St. Mary's (Moraga, CA) **2597**
Collegian; The SDSU (Brookings, SD) **28816**
Collegian; Tech (Montgomery, WV) **33387**
The Collegiate (Grand Rapids, MI) **15092**
The Collegiate (Wilson, NC) **24311**
Collegiate Baseball Newspaper (Tucson, AZ) **941**
Collegiate Insider **9607***
Collegiate Microcomputer (Terre Haute, IN) *Ceased*
Collegiate Times (Blacksburg, VA) **31867**
Collegio (Pittsburg, KS) **11751**
Colleton Shopper (Walterboro, SC) **28780**
Colleyville News and Times (Southlake, TX) **31122**
Collie Variety (Wheat Ridge, CO) *Ceased*
The Collierville Herald (Collierville, TN) **29133**
The Collingwood Connection (Midland, ON, Can.) **36040**
Collinsville Herald-Journal (Warrenton, MO) **17678**
Collision Magazine (Franklin, MA) **14204**
Collision Quarterly (Burnaby, BC, Can.) **34895**

Colloid and Interface Science; Journal of (San Diego, CA) **3181**
Colloid Journal (New York, NY) **21440**
Colloid Journal of the USSR **21440***
Colon and Rectal Surgery; Seminars in (Burlington, MA) **14032**
Colon and Rectum; Diseases of the (Rochester, MN) **16307**
The Colonial (Trenton, NJ) **19655**
Colonial Free Press (Allenhurst, NJ) *Unable to locate*
Colonial History; Journal of Colonialism & (Towson, MD) **13761**
Colonial Homes (New York, NY) **21441**
Colonial Latin America Historical Review (Albuquerque, NM) **19769**
Colonial Waterbirds **7728***
Colonialism & Colonial History; Journal of (Towson, MD) **13761**
Colonie Spotlight (Colonie, NY) **20485**
Colony Cablevision **14378***
Colony Communications, Inc. (Tujunga, CA) **3951**
Colony Communications Inc. (Providence, RI) *Unable to locate*
The Colony Courier-Leader (The Colony, TX) **30062**
Colony Leader **30062***
The Colony Leader (Lewisville, TX) **30685**
Color Country Shopper (Kanab, UT) **31341**
Color Research and Application (Hoboken, NJ) **18917**
Color Wheel (Warner, NH) **18647**
Coloradan; South (Alamosa, CO) **4131**
Colorado Alumnus (Boulder, CO) *Ceased*
Colorado Beverage Analyst (Denver, CO) **4311**
Colorado Business Magazine (Englewood, CO) *Unable to locate*
Colorado Business Report; The Northern (Fort Collins, CO) **4436**
Colorado; The Business Times of Western (Grand Junction, CO) **4477**
Colorado City Record (Colorado City, TX) **30063**
Colorado Country Life (Denver, CO) **4312**
Colorado County Citizen (Columbus, TX) **30065**
Colorado Daily (Boulder, CO) **4161**
Colorado Editor (Denver, CO) **4313**
Colorado Engineer (Boulder, CO) **4162**
Colorado Episcopalian (Denver, CO) **4314**
Colorado Expression (Denver, CO) *Unable to locate*
Colorado Farmer-Stockman (Vancouver, WA) **33174**
Colorado Homes & Lifestyles (Englewood, CO) *Unable to locate*
Colorado; Key Magazine (Littleton, CO) **4550**
The Colorado Lawyer (Denver, CO) **4315**
The Colorado Leader (Denver, CO) **4316**
Colorado Legionnaire (Denver, CO) *Unable to locate*
Colorado Medicine (Denver, CO) **4317**
Colorado Municipalities (Denver, CO) **4318**
Colorado; Out Front (Denver, CO) **4346**
Colorado Outdoors (Denver, CO) **4319**
The Colorado Pharmacist (Denver, CO) *Unable to locate*
Colorado Review (Fort Collins, CO) **4428**
Colorado River Life (Lake Havasu City, AZ) *Ceased*
Colorado River Weekender (Bullhead City, AZ) **664**
Colorado School of Mines Quarterly (Golden, CO) **4465**
Colorado Ski Industry (Boulder, CO) *Ceased*
Colorado Springs Cablevision **4262***
Colorado Springs Independent (Colorado Springs, CO) **4243**
Colorado State Review **4428***
Colorado; TCI Cablevision of (Pueblo, CO) **4612**
Colorado; TCI Cablevision of Central (Aspen, CO) **4144**
Colorado Transcript **4468***
The Colorado Tribune (Pueblo, CO) **4598**
Colorado Woman News (Denver, CO) *Unable to locate*
Colorado-Wyoming Academy of Science; Journal of the (Greeley, CO) **4498**
ColoradoBiz (Centennial, CO) **4223**
Colorado's Front Range Quarterly **4653***
Colored Stone (Devon, PA) **26823**
ColorsNW Magazine (Seattle, WA) **32956**
Colposcopy & Gynecologic Laser Surgery **20912***
Colton Cable TV (Colton, OR) **26269**
Colton City News (Colton, CA) **1740**
Colton Courier (Colton, CA) **1741**
Coltsfoot (Shipman, VA) *Ceased*
Columban Mission (St. Columbans, NE) **18256**
Columbia (New Haven, CT) **4985**
The Columbia (Rhinebeck, NY) *Ceased*
Columbia Basin Cable (Umatilla, OR) **26600**
Columbia Basin Cable (Goldendale, WA) *Unable to locate*
Columbia Basin Herald (Moses Lake, WA) **32838**
Columbia Cable **32795***
Columbia Cable of Nevada **18351***
Columbia Cable of Oregon **26239***
Columbia Cable of Virginia (Woodbridge, VA) **32639**

Columbia Cable of Washington (Vancouver, WA) **33181**
Columbia Chronicle **32734***
Columbia College Today (New York, NY) **21442**
Columbia County News Times (Martinez, GA) **7426**
Columbia Daily Spectator (New York, NY) **21443**
Columbia Daily Tribune (Columbia, MO) **16990**
Columbia Flier (Columbia, MD) **13457**
Columbia Human Rights Law Review (New York, NY) **21444**
Columbia International Inc. (Greenwich, CT) **4876**
Columbia Journal of Asian Law (New York, NY) **21445**
Columbia Journal of Environmental Law (New York, NY) **21446**
Columbia Journalism Review (New York, NY) **21447**
Columbia Law Review (New York, NY) **21448**
Columbia Law School News (New York, NY) **21449**
Columbia Magazine (Columbia, MD) **13458**
Columbia Missourian (Columbia, MO) **16991**
The Columbia News (Shrewsbury, PA) *Ceased*
Columbia News/Martinez-Evans Times **7426***
The Columbia Press (Warrenton, OR) **26610**
Columbia Request (Philmont, NY) *Ceased*
The Columbia Star (Columbia, SC) **28547**
The Columbia Star *Ceased*
Columbia Union Visitor (Columbia, MD) **13459**
Columbia University Record (New York, NY) **21450**
The Columbian (Indianapolis, IN) **10103**
The Columbian (Vancouver, WA) **33175**
Columbian-Progress/Marion County Advertiser (Columbia, MS) **16599**
Columbus Alive (Columbus, OH) **25007**
Columbus Area Choice (Columbus, NE) **17980**
Columbus Business Journal (Gahanna, OH) *Unable to locate*
Columbus County News **23695***
Columbus Daily Advocate (Columbus, KS) **11395**
The Columbus Dispatch (Columbus, OH) **25008**
Columbus Free Press (Columbus, OH) *Unable to locate*
The Columbus Gazette (Columbus Junction, IA) **10718**
Columbus, Inc.; TeleCable of (Columbus, GA) **7185**
Columbus Journal-Republican (Columbus, WI) **33642**
Columbus Ledger-Enquirer (San Jose, CA) **3513**
Columbus Monthly (Columbus, OH) **25009**
Columbus Physician (Columbus, OH) **25010**
Columbus Telegram (Columbus, NE) **17981**
The Columbus Times (Columbus, GA) **7183**
Columbus TV Cable Corp. (Columbus, MS) **16606**
The Columns (Fairmont, WV) **33312**
Colusa Sun-Herald (Willows, CA) **4085**
Com-Link Inc. (Union Springs, AL) **511**
Comanche Cable **4368***
Comb Magazine *Ceased*
Combat (Circleville, WV) **33292**
Combat Crew (Pittsburgh, PA) *Ceased*
Combat Edge (Langley AFB, VA) **32176**
Combinatorial Optimization; Journal of (New York, NY) **22030**
Combinatorial Theory, Series A; Journal of (San Diego, CA) **3182**
Combinatorial Theory, Series B; Journal of (San Diego, CA) **3183**
Combinatorics; The Electronic Journal of (Clemson, SC) **28532**
Combinatorics, Probability and Computing (New York, NY) **21451**
Comboni Missions (Cincinnati, OH) *Ceased*
Combustion, Explosion, and Shock Waves (New York, NY) **21452**
Combustion; Flow, Turbulence and (New York, NY) **21707**
Comcast (Leesburg, FL) **6302**
Comcast (Ann Arbor, MI) **14773**
Comcast (Grand Rapids, MI) **15101**
Comcast (Jersey City, NJ) **19148**
Comcast (Pottsville, PA) **27904**
Comcast Aftervision (Richmond, VA) **32472**
Comcast Cable (Sarasota, FL) **6671**
Comcast Cable (Elizabethtown, KY) **12045**
Comcast Cable (Carlisle, PA) **26762**
Comcast Cable Communications (Las Cruces, NM) **19879**
Comcast Cable Communications (Alexandria, VA) **31754**
Comcast Cable Communications Inc. (Philadelphia, PA) **27725**
Comcast Cable Co. (Lancaster, PA) **27147**
Comcast Cable TV (Taylor, MI) **15588**
Comcast Cablevision (Huntsville, AL) **276**
Comcast Cablevision (Little Rock, AR) **1237**
Comcast Cablevision (Santa Ana, CA) **3636**
Comcast Cablevision (New Haven, CT) *Unable to locate*
Comcast Cablevision (Fort Wayne, IN) **9975**
Comcast Cablevision (Detroit, MI) **14955**

Comcast Cablevision (Eatontown, NJ) *Unable to locate*
Comcast Cablevision (Willow Grove, PA) **28194**
Comcast Cablevision of Baltimore County (Timonium, MD) *Unable to locate*
Comcast Cablevision of California, Inc. (Ontario, CA) **2719**
Comcast Cablevision of Flint (Flint, MI) **15038**
Comcast Cablevision of Harford County (Aberdeen, MD) **13086**
Comcast Cablevision of Hillsdale (Hillsdale, MI) **15165**
Comcast Cablevision of Indiana (Indianapolis, IN) **10185**
Comcast Cablevision of Mercer County (Trenton, NJ) **19673**
Comcast Cablevision of Meridian (Meridian, MS) **16771**
Comcast Cablevision of Middletown (Middletown, CT) *Unable to locate*
Comcast Cablevision of Newport Beach (Newport Beach, CA) **2638**
Comcast Cablevision of Paducah (Paducah, KY) **12341**
Comcast Cablevision of Philadelphia (Philadelphia, PA) **27726**
Comcast Cablevision of Southeast Michigan (Sterling Heights, MI) **15577**
Comcast Cablevision of Tuscaloosa (Tuscaloosa, AL) **493**
Comcast Communications (Longmont, CO) **4562**
Comcast Communications, Inc. (Fort Lauderdale, FL) **6089**
Comda Key (Scarborough, ON, Can.) **36375**
Come Home *Ceased*
Comedy Central (New York, NY) **37739**
The Comedy Channel **37739***
The Comedy Magazine (Seattle, WA) **32957**
The Comenian (Bethlehem, PA) **26700**
The Comer News (Comer, GA) **7197**
The Comet **34680***
ComeUnity (St. Petersburg, FL) *Ceased*
Comfrey Cable TV (Redwood Falls, MN) **16296**
The Comfrey Times (Comfrey, MN) **15811**
Comic Artist Magazine; Cartoonist and (Santa Ana, CA) **3622**
Comic News **26325***
Comic News (New York, NY) *Ceased*
Comic News; Northwest (Eugene, OR) **26325**
The Comic Reader (Menomonee Falls, WI) *Ceased*
Comic Relief (Arcata, CA) *Unable to locate*
Comic Shop News (Marietta, GA) **7410**
Comic Syndicate; Creative (Sioux Falls, SD) **37876**
Comics Buyer's Guide (Iola, WI) **33813**
Comics & Games Retailer (Iola, WI) **33814**
Comics Heritage **37357***
The Comics Journal (Seattle, WA) **32958**
Comics Retailer **33814***
Comics Review **29428***
Comics Revue (Mountain Home, TN) **29428**
Comics Scene (New York, NY) *Ceased*
Comics Scene 2000 (New York, NY) **21453**
Coming Attractions (Jersey City, NJ) *Unable to locate*
Coming Up (Jersey City, NJ) **19134**
Comitatus (Los Angeles, CA) **2244**
(COMM/ENT); Hastings Communications and Entertainment Law Journal (San Francisco, CA) **3370**
Commack/Kings Park Suffolk Life (Commack, NY) **20486**
Commack News (Commack, NY) **20487**
Commack Pennysaver (Huntington, NY) *Unable to locate*
Commack Weekender (Farmingdale, NY) *Ceased*
Command Cable of Eastern Illinois (Effingham, IL) **8817**
Command Magazine (San Luis Obispo, CA) **3564**
Command Post (Edwardsville, IL) **8811**
Commander (Fort Huachuca, AZ) **708**
Commentary (New York, NY) **21454**
The Commentator (Los Angeles, CA) **2245**
Commentator; The Catholic (Baton Rouge, LA) **12486**
Commentator; The 40-Mile County (Bow Island, AB, Can.) **34622**
Comments on Agricultural and Food Chemistry (New York, NY) *Unable to locate*
Comments on Atomic and Molecular Physics (New York, NY) *Unable to locate*
Comments from the Friends (Assonet, MA) **13823**
Comments on Molecular and Cellular Biophysics (New York, NY) *Unable to locate*
Comments on Nuclear and Particles Physics (New York, NY) **21455**
Comments of Plasma Physics and Controlled Fusion (New York, NY) *Unable to locate*
Comments on Theoretical Biology (New York, NY) *Unable to locate*
Comments on Toxicology (Lincoln, NE) **18081**
Commerce (Chicago, IL) *Ceased*

Commerce Business Daily (Pittsburgh, PA) *Unable to locate*
Commerce City Sentinel (Denver, CO) *Ceased*
Commerce; Daily (Los Angeles, CA) **2251**
Commerce; Daily Journal of (Portland, OR) **26475**
Commerce; Finance and (Minneapolis, MN) **16081**
Commerce and Industry; Mid-America (Topeka, KS) **11833**
Commerce; International Journal of Electronic (Armonk, NY) **20079**
Commerce Journal (Commerce, TX) **30067**
Commerce; Journal of (Burnaby, BC, Can.) **34904**
Commerce; Journal of Internet (Monroe, LA) **12691**
Commerce; Journal of Law & (Pittsburgh, PA) **27802**
Commerce; Kansas City (Millstadt, IL) **9197**
Commerce & Legal News; Tulsa Daily (Tulsa, OK) **26136**
Commerce Magazine (Charleston, SC) **28512**
The Commerce News (Commerce, GA) **7198**
Commerce News (Edmonton, AB, Can.) **34706**
Commerce; Revue (Montreal, QC, Can.) **37217**
Commerce; San Diego (San Diego, CA) **3259**
Commerce; Seattle Daily Journal of (Seattle, WA) **33019**
Commerce Spinal Column Newsweekly (Commerce, MI) **14890**
Commerce; Trade and (Winnipeg, MB, Can.) **35353**
Commercial **16603***
The Commercial Appeal (Memphis, TN) **29362**
Commercial Carrier Journal (New York, NY) **21456**
Commercial Carrier Journal (CCJ) (King of Prussia, PA) **27123**
The Commercial Dispatch (Columbus, MS) **16603**
Commercial-Express (Vicksburg, MI) **15654**
The Commercial and Financial Chronicle (Daytona Beach, FL) *Unable to locate*
Commercial Fisheries News (Stonington, ME) **13062**
Commercial Floor Care (Woodland Hills, CA) **4101**
Commercial Investment Real Estate (Chicago, IL) **8337**
Commercial Lenders Alert (New York, NY) *Ceased*
Commercial Lending Review (Concord, MA) **14146**
Commercial-News (Danville, IL) **8701**
Commercial Property News (New York, NY) *Ceased*
The Commercial Record (Boston, MA) **13879**
The Commercial Record (Saugatuck, MI) **15525**
Commercial Recorder (Fort Worth, TX) **30335**
Commercial Renovation (Chicago, IL) *Unable to locate*
The Commercial Review (Portland, IN) **10403**
Commercial Review (Portland, OR) *Unable to locate*
Commercial West **16117***
The Commerical Image (Melville, NY) **21041**
Commodities; Technical Analysis of Stocks & (Seattle, WA) **33035**
Commodity Markets and the Developing Countries (Philadelphia, PA) *Ceased*
Commodity News Services Inc. (Leawood, KS) *Unable to locate*
Commodity Price Charts (Palm Springs, CA) **2757**
Commodity Quotations Inc. (Harrison, NY) **37867**
Commodity Trade Statistics (New York, NY) **21457**
Commodore Magazine (West Chester, PA) *Ceased*
Common Boundary Magazine (Bethesda, MD) *Unable to locate*
Common Cause Magazine (Washington, DC) *Ceased*
Common Ground (San Anselmo, CA) **3082**
Common Ground (Alexandria, VA) **31656**
Common Knowledge (Cary, NC) *Unable to locate*
Common Lives/Lesbian Lives (Iowa City, IA) **10970**
Common Market Reporter Doing Business in Europe **9502***
Common Sense **29384***
Common'Tater; The Badger (Antigo, WI) **33532**
Commonweal (New York, NY) **21458**
Commonwealth (Ash Grove, MO) **16892**
The Commonwealth (Norfolk, VA) *Unable to locate*
The Commonwealth (Regina, SK, Can.) **37529**
Commonwealth Express; The Ripon (Ripon, WI) **34302**
Commonwealth; Greenwood (Greenwood, MS) **16644**
Commonwealth-Journal (Somerset, KY) **12403**
Commonwealth Novel in English (Bluefield, WV) **33254**
Commonwealth Progress (Ahoskie, NC) **23613**
Commonwealth Times (Richmond, VA) **32434**
Communi Comm Services (Eatonton, GA) **7266**
Communicade (Rochester, NY) **23217**
Communicare (Wichita, KS) *Ceased*
Communicating Together (Thornhill, ON, Can.) *Unable to locate*
CommuniCAtion **35127***
Communication Abstracts (Thousand Oaks, CA) **3855**
Communication Administration (JACA); Journal of the Association for (Washington, DC) **5574**
Communication Arts (Menlo Park, CA) **2523**
Communication Booknotes Quarterly (Annandale, VA) **31763**

Communication; Canadian Journal of (Calgary, AB, Can.) **34636**
Communication; College Composition and (Urbana, IL) **9700**
Communication; Critical Studies in Media (Athens, GA) **6935**
Communication Disorders Quarterly (Austin, TX) **29769**
Communication Education (Athens, GA) **6933**
Communication Inquiry; Journal of (Thousand Oaks, CA) **3884**
Communication; Journal of (Cary, NC) **23689**
Communication; The Journal of Business (Flint, MI) **15035**
Communication; Journal of Family (Norfolk, VA) **32286**
Communication; Journal of Health (Washington, DC) **5595**
Communication Journal; Southern (Detroit, MI) **14949**
Communication Journal; Southwestern Mass (State University, AR) **1350**
Communication Law and Policy (Blacksburg, VA) **31868**
Communication Monographs (Philadelphia, PA) **27423**
Communication Outlook (East Lansing, MI) **14983**
Communication Quarterly (Newark, DE) **5270**
Communication Quarterly; Management (Thousand Oaks, CA) **3902**
Communication Quarterly; Technical (St. Paul, MN) **16410**
Communication Research (Thousand Oaks, CA) **3856**
Communication Research; Journal of Applied (Washington, DC) **5571**
The Communication Review (Urbana, IL) **9702**
Communication in Statistics, Stochastic Models **22792***
Communication Studies (Ada, OK) **25724**
Communication Systems Design (Manhasset, NY) **20992**
Communication Systems, Inc. (Columbia, SC) *Unable to locate*
Communication Systems; International Journal of (Hoboken, NJ) **18890**
Communication; Western Journal of (Fresno, CA) **1960**
Communication; Women's Studies in (Athens, GA) **6953**
Communication World; IABC (San Francisco, CA) **3374**
Communication; Written (Thousand Oaks, CA) **3922**
Communications (Englewood, CO) *Ceased*
Communications (Potomac, MD) **13649**
Communications Abstracts Journal; Electronics & (Bethesda, MD) **13333**
Communications of the ACM (New York, NY) **21459**
Communications in Algebra (Milwaukee, WI) **34063**
Communications on Applied Nonlinear Analysis (Orlando, FL) *Unable to locate*
Communications Consultant (New York, NY) *Ceased*
Communications Cuivor, Inc. **37323***
Communications Design; Integrated (Nashua, NH) **18593**
(Communications Engineering & Design); CED (Highlands Ranch, CO) **4516**
Communications; The Howard Journal of (Washington, DC) **5532**
Communications International/National News (Los Angeles, CA) **37868**
Communications in Japan; Electronics and (Hoboken, NJ) **18937**
Communications and the Law (Westport, CT) *Ceased*
Communications Law Journal; Federal (Bloomington, IN) **9826**
Communications Magazine; IEEE (New York, NY) **21844**
Communications Magazine; Personal (New York, NY) **22543**
Communications Magazine; Sound & (Port Washington, NY) **23136**
Communications in Mass Spectrometry; Rapid (Hoboken, NJ) **19096**
Communications Networking; International Journal of Satellite (Hoboken, NJ) **18997**
Communications News (Nokomis, FL) **6462**
Communications in Numerical Methods in Engineering (Hoboken, NJ) **18918**
Communications in Partial Differential Equations (Stanford, CA) **3795**
Communications; Popular (Port Washington, NY) **23132**
Communications on Pure and Applied Mathematics (Hoboken, NJ) **18919**
Communications Report; Mobile (Washington, DC) **5654**
Communications Services Inc. **30378***
Communications in Soil Science and Plant Analysis (Athens, GA) **6934**
Communications Standards Review (Palo Alto, CA) *Ceased*

Computational Mathematics and Modeling (New York, NY) **21471**

Computational Seismology (Washington, DC) **5430**

COMPUTE (Greensboro, NC) *Unable to locate*

Compute (Los Alamitos, CA) *Unable to locate*

Computer Access Newspaper (Minneapolis, MN) *Unable to locate*

Computer-Aided Engineering (Cleveland, OH) *Unable to locate*

Computer-Aided Materials Design; Journal of (New York, NY) **22035**

Computer-Aided Molecular Design; Journal of (New York, NY) **22036**

Computer Aided Surgery (St. Louis, MO) **17426**

Computer Animation; Journal of Visualization and (Hoboken, NJ) **19052**

Computer Applications in Engineering Education (Hoboken, NJ) **18921**

Computer Applications; Journal of Network and (San Diego, CA) **3208**

Computer-Assisted Microscopy; Journal of (New York, NY) **22037**

Computer-Assisted Tomography; Journal of (Baltimore, MD) **13186**

Computer Bits (Clackamas, OR) **26266**

Computer Book Review (Honolulu, HI) *Ceased*

Computer Bulletin (New York, NY) **21472**

Computer Buyer's Guide & Handbook (New York, NY) **21473**

Computer Careers; Graduating Engineer & (Evanston, IL) **8860**

Computer and Communications Decisions (Hasbrouck Heights, NJ) *Unable to locate*

The Computer Consultant (Syracuse, NY) *Ceased*

Computer Craft **23130***

Computer Currents (El Cerrito, CA) **1860**

Computer Curriculum Resource (Bradenton Beach, FL) *Ceased*

Computer Dealer News (Toronto, ON, Can.) **36556**

Computer Design (Nashua, NH) **18587**

Computer Digest (Rockville, MD) *Unable to locate*

Computer-Disability News (Chicago, IL) *Unable to locate*

Computer/Electronic Service News **13080***

Computer Fair Show Program (Morgan Hill, CA) **2601**

Computer Game Review (Lombard, IL) *Unable to locate*

Computer Gaming World (Anaheim Hills, CA) *Unable to locate*

Computer Graphics and Applications; IEEE (Los Alamitos, CA) **2183**

Computer Graphics Review (Overland Park, KS) *Ceased*

Computer Graphics Today (Midland Park, NJ) *Unable to locate*

Computer Graphics World (Nashua, NH) **18588**

Computer Guide; The Chicago (Chicago, IL) **8309**

Computer and High Technology Law Journal; Santa Clara (Santa Clara, CA) **3674**

Computer-Human Interaction (TOCHI) (New York, NY) **21474**

Computer Information Review (Commack, NY) *Ceased*

Computer and Information Systems Abstracts Journal (Bethesda, MD) **13326**

Computer Interaction; Human- (Mahwah, NJ) **19191**

Computer Interaction; International Journal of Human (Mahwah, NJ) **19194**

The Computer & Internet Lawyer (New York, NY) **21475**

The Computer Journal (Citrus Heights, CA) *Unable to locate*

The Computer Journal (New York, NY) *Ceased*

The Computer Journal (Tulsa, OK) *Unable to locate*

Computer/Law Journal (Manhattan Beach, CA) *Unable to locate*

Computer Law Reporter (Washington, DC) **5431**

Computer Life (New York, NY) **21476**

Computer Link Magazine (Rochester, NY) **23218**

Computer Listing Service's Machinery & Equipment Guide (Skokie, IL) **9603**

Computer Literature Index (Phoenix, AZ) **800**

Computer Living/New York (Bronx, NY) **20264**

Computer Magazine (Los Alamitos, CA) **2181**

Computer Marketplace Show Program **2601***

Computer Monthly; Southwest (Glendale, AZ) **715**

Computer Music Journal (Cambridge, MA) **14046**

Computer & Office Product Evaluations (COPE) (Berkeley, CA) *Ceased*

Computer & Online Industry Litigation Reporter (Wayne, PA) **28130**

The Computer Paper (Toronto, ON, Can.) *Unable to locate*

The Computer Post (Winnipeg, MB, Can.) *Ceased*

Computer Products; Asian Sources (Phoenix, AZ) **784**

Computer Publishing Magazine (Santa Monica, CA) *Ceased*

Computer-R-Digital (Metuchen, NJ) *Unable to locate*

Computer Retail News **20994***

Computer Retail Week (Manhasset, NY) **20993**

Computer Review; Social Science (Raleigh, NC) **24153**

Computer Science Education (Eau Claire, WI) **33667**

Computer Science & Engineering Journals (Bethesda, MD) *Ceased*

Computer Science; Mathematical Structures in (New York, NY) **22298**

Computer Security Products Report (Madison, WI) *Ceased*

Computer Shopper (New York, NY) **21477**

Computer Simulation; International Journal of (Eau Claire, WI) **33670**

Computer Simulation International; Transactions of the Society for (San Diego, CA) **3283**

Computer Simulation (TOMACS); Modeling and (New York, NY) **22344**

Computer & Software News (New York, NY) *Ceased*

Computer Software; Programming and (New York, NY) **22599**

Computer Speech & Language (San Diego, CA) **3130**

Computer Support; Journal of End User (Binghamton, NY) **20170**

Computer Survival Guide (New York, NY) **21478**

Computer Survival Journal (New York, NY) **21479**

Computer and System Sciences; Journal of (San Diego, CA) **3186**

Computer Systems; ACM Transactions on (New York, NY) **21137**

Computer Technology Review (Beverly Hills, CA) **1571**

Computer Telephony (New York, NY) *Unable to locate*

Computer Times (Bardstown, KY) **11925**

Computer User (Minneapolis, MN) **16069**

Computer User; KC (Overland Park, KS) **11718**

Computer User; Puget Sound (Seattle, WA) **33008**

Computer User's Survival Guide **21478***

Computer Vision and Image Understanding (San Diego, CA) **3131**

Computer Vision; International Journal of (New York, NY) **21903**

Computer Wave (Seattle, WA) *Unable to locate*

Computer Week; Federal (Falls Church, VA) **32044**

Computer Wholesaler; Canadian (Vancouver, BC, Can.) **35130**

Computerized Investing (Chicago, IL) **8341**

Computerized Manufacturing (Roanoke, VA) *Ceased*

Computers in Accounting **21135***

Computers and Applications; International Journal of (Calgary, AB, Can.) **34646**

Computers in Banking (New York, NY) *Ceased*

Computers; Behavior Research Methods, Instruments, & (Austin, TX) **29763**

Computers and Biomedical Research **22012***

Computers & Communications Library (Pennsauken, NJ) *Ceased*

Computers for Design & Construction (New York, NY) *Unable to locate*

Computers in Education (Toronto, ON, Can.) *Ceased*

Computers in HR Management (New York, NY) *Ceased*

Computers in Human Services **20203***

Computers in Human Services **29733***

Computers; IEEE Design and Test of (Los Alamitos, CA) **2184**

Computers in Japan; Systems and (Hoboken, NJ) **19115**

Computers in Libraries (Medford, NJ) **19223**

Computers for Mathematical Learning; International Journal of (New York, NY) **21904**

Computers and Medicine (Chicago, IL) *Unable to locate*

Computers in Nursing (Portland, ME) **13009**

Computers and People (Newtonville, MA) *Unable to locate*

Computers in Physics (College Park, MD) *Unable to locate*

Computers in the Schools (Reno, NV) **18419**

ComputerTalk for the Pharmacist (Blue Bell, PA) **26723**

ComputerUser (Minneapolis, MN) **37870**

Computerworld (Framingham, MA) **14194**

ComputerWorld Campus Edition (Framingham, MA) *Unable to locate*

Computerworld Canada (Scarborough, ON, Can.) **36376**

Compute!'s Amiga Resource *Ceased*

Compute!'s Gazette *Ceased*

Compute!'s PC Magazine *Ceased*

Computin-; Family (Danbury, CT) **4740**

Computing Abstracts; Internet & Personal (Medford, NJ) **19226**

-Computing & -Automation; Scientific (Morris Plains, NJ) **19306**

Computing Canada (Toronto, ON, Can.) **36557**

Computing; Client/Server (Westborough, MA) **14636**

Computing; Cluster (New York, NY) **21431**

Computing; Combinatorics, Probability and (New York, NY) **21451**

Computing in Education; Journal of Research on (Manhattan, KS) **11622**

Computing and Electronic Commerce; Journal of Organizational (Austin, TX) **29789**

Computing; Genealogical (Provo, UT) **31403**

Computing in Higher Education; Journal of (Amherst, MA) **13797**

Computing; Home-Office (Danbury, CT) **4741**

Computing; INFORMS Journal on (Linthicum, MD) **13621**

Computing; Journal of Clinical Monitoring and (New York, NY) **22027**

Computing; Journal of End User (Hershey, PA) **27043**

Computing; Journal of Parallel and Distributed (San Diego, CA) **3210**

Computing; Journal of Scientific (New York, NY) **22184**

Computing Machinery; Journal of the Association for (New York, NY) **22001**

Computing; Network (Manhasset, NY) **21007**

Computing News (Eugene, OR) *Unable to locate*

Computing News & Reviews (Aliso Viejo, CA) **1390**

Computing Now! (Toronto, ON, Can.) *Ceased*

Computing; On Target (Spanaway, WA) **33091**

Computing; PC (New York, NY) **22533**

Computing; Reliable (New York, NY) **22644**

Computing Research; Journal of Educational (Amityville, NY) **20044**

Computing Resources for the Professional (Seattle, WA) *Ceased*

Computing Reviews (New York, NY) **21480**

Computing in Science & Engineering (Los Alamitos, CA) **2182**

Computing; SIAM Journal on (Philadelphia, PA) **27679**

Computing; SIAM Journal on Scientific (Philadelphia, PA) **27686**

Computing; Smart (Lincoln, NE) **18120**

Computing Software Review (Danbury, CT) **4738**

Computing Surveys; ACM (New York, NY) **21136**

Computing Systems (Cambridge, MA) *Ceased*

The Computing Teacher **26322***

Computing & Technology; MultiLingual (Sandpoint, ID) **7979**

ComputorEdge (San Diego, CA) **3133**

ComputorEdge (San Diego, CA) **3132**

Comstock's Business Magazine (Sacramento, CA) **2993**

Comtemporary Oncology (Montvale, NJ) *Ceased*

Comunicaciones (Santa Ana, CA) **3623**

Comunita Viva (Toronto, ON, Can.) *Unable to locate*

Conceive (Danville, CA) *Ceased*

Concentrating Solar Power (Oak Ridge, TN) **29547**

Concept Cablevision **10186***

Conceptions Helpless (Albuquerque, NM) **19770**

Concepts in Magnetic Resonance (Hoboken, NJ) **18922**

Concern **12219***

Concert Music Network (New York, NY) **37626**

The Concho Herald (Miles, TX) **30828**

Conchologist; American (Louisville, KY) **12210**

Conchologists of America Bulletin **12210***

Concord Cable TV (Concord, CA) *Unable to locate*

The Concord Item (Dover, NH) *Ceased*

Concord Journal (Needham, MA) *Unable to locate*

Concord Monitor (Concord, NH) **18471**

Concord North **18559***

The Concord Tribune **24016***

Concorde; La (Saint-Eustache, QC, Can.) **37332**

The Concordia Sentinel (Ferriday, LA) **12579**

Concordia Theological Quarterly (Fort Wayne, IN) **9966**

The Concordian (Moorhead, MN) **16188**

The Concordian (Concordia, MO) **17026**

Concrete Abstracts (Farmington Hills, MI) **15017**

Concrete Cunstruction (Addison, IL) **8000**

The Concrete Foundation Contractor **31406***

Concrete Herald (Concrete, WA) *Ceased*

Concrete Industry Bulletin (Escondido, CA) *Unable to locate*

Concrete International (Farmington Hills, MI) **15018**

Concrete International; Design & Construction **15018***

Concrete Masonry News **32162***

Concrete Producer News (Cleveland, OH) *Ceased*

Concrete Products (Overland Park, KS) **11707**

Concrete Repair Bulletin (Des Plaines, IL) **8753**

The Concrete Trader (Dublin, OH) *Unable to locate*

Concurrency **18923***

Concurrency and Computation: Practice and Experience (Hoboken, NJ) **18923**

Conde Nast Traveler (New York, NY) **21481**

Conde News (Doland, SD) **28844**

Conditioning Journal; Strength and (Colorado Springs, CO) **4258**

Conditioning; Training and (Ithaca, NY) **20815**

Condo Informer **6699***

Contemporary Family Therapy (New York, NY) **21493**
Contemporary Gastroenterology (Montvale, NJ) *Ceased*
Contemporary Gerontology (New York, NY) **21494**
Contemporary Impressions (Peachtree City, GA) **7479**
Contemporary Internal Medicine (Stamford, CT) *Unable to locate*
Contemporary Jewry (Melrose Park, PA) **27245**
Contemporary Literature (Madison, WI) **33928**
Contemporary Long Term Care (Los Angeles, CA) **2246**
Contemporary Management in Critical Care *Ceased*
Contemporary Management in Internal Medicine *Ceased*
Contemporary Management in Obstetrics and Gynecology *Ceased*
Contemporary Management in Otolaryngology *Ceased*
The Contemporary Management Series *Ceased*
Contemporary OB/GYN (Montvale, NJ) **19248**
Contemporary Optometry (New York, NY) *Ceased*
Contemporary Orthopaedics (Torrance, CA) **3930**
The Contemporary Pacific (Honolulu, HI) **7685**
Contemporary Pediatrics (Montvale, NJ) **19249**
Contemporary Physics (Philadelphia, PA) **27427**
Contemporary Podiatric Physician (Los Angeles, CA) *Ceased*
Contemporary Policy Issues **30039***
Contemporary Psychiatry (New York, NY) *Ceased*
Contemporary Psychology (Washington, DC) **5440**
Contemporary Record Society News Magazine (Broomall, PA) **26735**
Contemporary Sociology (West Lafayette, IN) **10545**
Contemporary South Asia (Dunnellon, FL) *Unable to locate*
Contemporary Stone and Tile Design (Paramus, NJ) **19401**
Contemporary Surgery (Torrance, CA) **3931**
Contemporary Times (Alexandria, VA) *Unable to locate*
Contemporary Urology (Montvale, NJ) **19250**
Contemporary Verse Two (Winnipeg, MB, Can.) *Unable to locate*
Content (Mountain, ON, Can.) *Unable to locate*
Content Networking Journal (Cincinnati, OH) **24790**
Contents (Savannah, GA) *Unable to locate*
Contexts (Berkeley, CA) **1510**
Continental Cablevision **1961***
Continental Cablevision **6218***
Continental Cablevision **7989***
Continental Cablevision **8840***
Continental Cablevision **15449***
Continental Cablevision **32749***
Continental Cablevision **18567***
Continental Cablevision **16424***
Continental Cablevision (Downey, CA) *Unable to locate*
Continental Cablevision (Los Angeles, CA) *Unable to locate*
Continental Cablevision (Stockton, CA) **3810**
Continental Cablevision (Naples, FL) **6450**
Continental Cablevision (Folkston, GA) *Unable to locate*
Continental Cablevision (Belleville, IL) **8061**
Continental Cablevision (Elmhurst, IL) **8839**
Continental Cablevision (Morton Grove, IL) *Unable to locate*
Continental Cablevision (Brockton, MA) **14013**
Continental Cablevision (Cambridge, MA) **14113**
Continental Cablevision (Lawrence, MA) **14268**
Continental Cablevision (Quincy, MA) *Unable to locate*
Continental Cablevision (Westfield, MA) **14644**
Continental Cablevision (Lansing, MI) *Unable to locate*
Continental Cablevision (Madison Heights, MI) *Unable to locate*
Continental Cablevision (Southfield, MI) **15556**
Continental Cablevision (Dayton, OH) **25131**
Continental Cablevision (Lancaster, OH) *Unable to locate*
Continental Cablevision, Inc. (Boston, MA) *Unable to locate*
Continental Cablevision, Inc. of Springfield (Springfield, MA) **14554**
Continental Cablevision of Massachusetts, Inc. (Needham, MA) **14374**
Continental Cablevision, Mediaone **32471***
Continental Cablevision of New England, Inc. (Manchester, NH) **18566**
Continental Cablevision of New Hampshire, Inc. (Portsmouth, NH) *Unable to locate*
Continental Cablevision System (Richmond, VA) *Unable to locate*
Continental Features/Continental News Service (San Diego, CA) **37873**
Continental Magazine (Boston, MA) **13884**
Continental News Service; Continental Features/ (San Diego, CA) **37873**
Continental Newstime (San Diego, CA) **3136**

Continental Philosophy Review (New York, NY) **21495**
Continental Profiles *Unable to locate*
Continental Reporter (Seattle, WA) *Unable to locate*
Contingencies (Washington, DC) **5441**
Contingency Journal (Dallas, TX) *Ceased*
Contingency Planning and Recovery Journal (CPR-J) (Wellesley Hills, MA) **14621**
Continuing Care Magazine (Dallas, TX) *Unable to locate*
Continuing Education; New Directions for Adult and (San Francisco, CA) **3396**
Continuite (Quebec, QC, Can.) **37282**
Continuity and Change (New York, NY) **21496**
Continuo (Hammondsport, NY) *Unable to locate*
Continuum (Alexandria, VA) *Ceased*
Contours (Greenwich, CT) *Unable to locate*
Contra Costa Lawyer (Concord, CA) *Unable to locate*
Contra Costa News Register (Walnut Creek, CA) **4049**
Contra Costa Sun (Lafayette, CA) **2131**
Contra Costa Times (Walnut Creek, CA) **4050**
Contraband (Lake Charles, LA) **12636**
Contraceptive Technology Update (Montvale, NJ) **19251**
Contract (New York, NY) **21498**
Contract (New York, NY) **21497**
Contract Design **21497***
Contract Management (McLean, VA) **32264**
Contracting Business (Cleveland, OH) **24875**
Contracting Profits (Milwaukee, WI) **34064**
Contractor; American Painting (Colorado Springs, CO) **4235**
Contractor; The Asphalt (Independence, MO) **17106**
Contractor Engineer **811***
Contractor; Florida (Tallahassee, FL) **6708**
Contractor; Indiana (Indianapolis, IN) **10125**
Contractor; Louisiana (Baton Rouge, LA) **12496**
Contractor Magazine (Des Plaines, IL) **8755**
Contractor Marketing (Fairborn, OH) **25186**
Contractor; Michigan Master Plumber and Mechanical (Lansing, MI) **15287**
Contractor, Midwest (Kansas City, MO) **17184**
Contractor; The National Utility (Arlington, VA) **31812**
Contractor; Southwest (Phoenix, AZ) **811**
Contractors Equipment Guide (Needham Heights, MA) **14376**
Contractors Guide (Bensenville, IL) **8065**
Contractors Hot Line (Fort Dodge, IA) **10896**
Contractors Hot Line Monthly Equipment Guide (Fort Dodge, IA) **10897**
Contracts; Middle East—Basic Oil Laws & Concession (New York, NY) **22333**
Contributions on Entomology International (Gainesville, FL) **6134**
Contributions to Music Education (Youngstown, OH) **25696**
Control (Itasca, IL) **9010**
Control Ad-Lits (Itasca, IL) **9011**
Control Ambiental Magazine (Glen Ellyn, IL) *Unable to locate*
Control and Computers **34641***
Control Engineering (Bensenville, IL) *Unable to locate*
Control and Intelligent Systems (Calgary, AB, Can.) **34641**
Control Isa Show Reporter (Itasca, IL) **9012**
Control News; Canadian Process Equipment & (Toronto, ON, Can.) **36527**
Control and Optimization; SIAM Journal on (Philadelphia, PA) **27680**
Control Solutions (Tulsa, OK) **26111**
Control Systems; Journal of Dynamic and (New York, NY) **22050**
Controller (Lincoln, NE) **18082**
Controls; International Instrumentation and (Great Neck, NY) **20690**
Controls and Systems *Ceased*
Convene (Chicago, IL) **8343**
Convenience Store Decisions (Cleveland, OH) **24876**
Convenience Store Merchandiser (New York, NY) *Ceased*
Convenience Store News (New York, NY) *Unable to locate*
Convention & Exhibition Management; Journal of (Binghamton, NY) **20168**
Conventions; Meetings & (Secaucus, NJ) **19540**
ConventionSouth (Gulf Shores, AL) **250**
Converge (Folsom, CA) **1917**
Conversion and Empaque Magazine (Melville, NY) *Ceased*
Converting Hotline; Packaging and (Fort Dodge, IA) **10906**
Converting Magazine (New York, NY) **21499**
Convulsive Therapy (Baltimore, MD) **13151**
Convulsive Therapy Dedicated to the Science of Electroconvulsive Therapy and Related Treatments **19357***
Conway Broadcasting **7954***
Conway Broadcasting **7951***

Conway Corp. (Conway, AR) **1084**
Conway County/Petit Jean Country Headlight (Morrilton, AR) *Unable to locate*
The Conway Daily Sun (North Conway, NH) **18614**
Conway Springs Star and the Argonia Argosy (Conway Springs, KS) **11400**
Cook County News-Herald (Grand Marais, MN) **15926**
Cook News-Herald (Cook, MN) **15813**
Cookbook Digest (New York, NY) *Unable to locate*
Cookbook Revue; ICR: The International (New York, NY) **21841**
Cookbooks; Pillsbury Classic (Minneapolis, MN) **16119**
Cooke Cablevision **16634***
Cooke Cablevision **19838***
Cooke Cablevision **26407***
Cooke Cablevision **28663***
Cooke Cablevision **33191***
Cooke Cablevision **7218***
Cooke Cablevision Inc. **9040***
Cooke County's Best Values (Muenster, TX) *Ceased*
Cooking; Healthy (Riverside, CA) **2937**
Cooking; Home (Berne, IN) **9812**
COOKING LIGHT (Birmingham, AL) **66**
Cooking Magazine; Fine (Newtown, CT) **5040**
Cooking Magazine; Specialty (Hollywood, FL) **6198**
Cooking Pleasures (Minnetonka, MN) **16168**
Cooking for Profit (Fond du Lac, WI) **33696**
COOK'S (Palm Coast, FL) *Ceased*
Cook's Illustrated (Brookline, MA) **14018**
Coolidge Examiner (Coolidge, AZ) **677**
Cooling Forum; North Carolina Plumbing-Heating- (Garner, NC) **23905**
Cooling Magazine; Southern Plumbing, Heating, **23939***
The Coon-Hound Corner (Stockport, OH) *Ceased*
Coon Rapids Enterprise (Coon Rapids, IA) **10720**
Coon Rapids Herald (Coon Rapids, MN) **15816**
Coon Rapids Municipal Cable (Coon Rapids, IA) **10721**
Cooney Cable Associates **20755***
Coonhound Bloodlines (Kalamazoo, MI) **15235**
Cooper County Record (Boonville, MO) *Ceased*
Cooperateur Agricole; Le (Montreal, QC, Can.) **37157**
The Cooperative Accountant (Springfield, VA) **32541**
Cooperative Business Journal (Washington, DC) **5442**
Cooperative de Cablodistribution de l'Arriere-Pays (Charlesbourg, QC, Can.) **36961**
The CoopersTown Crier (Cooperstown, NY) **20497**
Coos County Democrat (Lancaster, NH) **18541**
Coos Magazine **18469***
Cope *Ceased*
Copeia (Tempe, AZ) **902**
COPI Press (Houston, TX) **30465**
Copiah County Courier (Hazlehurst, MS) **16678**
Coping **29197***
Coping with Allergies and Asthma (Franklin, TN) **29196**
Coping with Cancer (Franklin, TN) **29197**
Copley/Colony Cablevision **1801***
Copley/Colony Harbor Cablevision (Wilmington, CA) **4091**
Copley News Service (San Diego, CA) **37874**
Coppell Gazette (Coppell, TX) **30072**
Copper Basin News (Kearny, AZ) **727**
Copper Country News (Globe, AZ) **718**
The Copper Era (Sierra Vista, AZ) **886**
Copper Mountain Metropolitan District (Copper Mountain, CO) **4288**
Copper News; Ajo (Ajo, AZ) **655**
Copperas Cove Leader-Press (Copperas Cove, TX) **30074**
Copperopolis Herald (Copperopolis, CA) **1763**
Copy Imaging and Reproduction (Melville, NY) *Ceased*
Copy Magazine (Melville, NY) *Ceased*
Copyright Law Reports (St. Petersburg, FL) **6622**
Coqeco Cable Solutions (Belleville, ON, Can.) **35685**
Coquille Valley Sentinel (Coquille, OR) **26281**
Coquitlam Now (Coquitlam, BC, Can.) **34930**
Coracle (Berkeley, CA) **1511**
Coral Gables News (Coral Gables, FL) **6005**
Coral Springs Forum/Margate Forum **6018***
Coral Springs Monthly (Coral Springs, FL) *Unable to locate*
Coral Springs News (Hollywood, FL) *Unable to locate*
Coral Springs/Parkland Forum (Coral Springs, FL) **6017**
Coram/Middle Island Suffolk Life (Coram, NY) **20501**
Coram/Ridge Suffolk Life **20501***
Coraopolis Record Star (Monroeville, PA) **27276**
Corbin Times Tribune **12020***
The Corcoran Journal (Corcoran, CA) **1765**
The Cord (St. Bonaventure, NY) **23287**
The Cord (Waterloo, ON, Can.) **36849**
The Cord Weekly **36849***
Cordele Dispatch (Cordele, GA) **7203**
Cordiality (New York, NY) *Unable to locate*
The Cordova Times (Cordova, AK) **558**

Country Living (Wappingers Falls, NY) *Ceased*
Country Living Gardener (New York, NY) 21507
Country Living (Ohio) (Columbus, OH) 25012
The Country Mailbox (Marshfield, MO) 17270
Country Mile Media, Inc. (Creswell, OR) 26297
Country Music (Westport, CT) 5213
Country Music; Journal of (Nashville, TN) 29462
Country Music News (Ottawa, ON, Can.) 36239
Country Music Television (Nashville, TN) 37740
Country News 2831*
Country News (Paso Robles, CA) *Unable to locate*
Country News-Press 2831*
Country Peddler (Bowling Green, KY) 11942
Country Road Chronicles (Dingmans Ferry, PA) 26827
Country Roads (Salina, KS) 11782
Country Roads Magazine 18664*
Country Roads Quarterly (Oakland, MD) *Unable to locate*
Country Sampler (St. Charles, IL) 9564
Country Sampler Decorating Ideas (St. Charles, IL) 9565
Country Sampler's West (St. Charles, IL) *Ceased*
The Country Shopper (Goodhue, MN) 15925
Country Song Roundup (Paramus, NJ) *Unable to locate*
Country Style Homes Plans and Designs (St. Paul, MN) 16372
Country Sun (Peterborough, ON, Can.) *Ceased*
Country Times; Gunnison (Gunnison, CO) 4509
The Country Today (Eau Claire, WI) 33668
Country Wagon Journal 18872*
Country Weekly (Boca Raton, FL) 5930
Country Woman (Greendale, WI) 33760
The Countryman (Romeo, MI) 15472
Countrypolitan Home Plans 16400*
Countryside Cablevision (Bowling Green, OH) *Unable to locate*
Countryside/Indian Head Park/Willow Springs/Burr Ridge/Pleasantdale Suburban Life (Oak Brook, IL) 9346
Countryside & Small Stock Journal (Withee, WI) *Unable to locate*
Countryside Sun (Naperville, IL) *Ceased*
The County Courier 7101*
County Courier (Buffalo, MO) 16930
County Courier (Enosburg, VT) 31541
The County Democrat Publishing Co. (Shawnee, OK) 26061
The County Journal (Percy, IL) 9445
County Journal (Warrenton, MO) 17679
The County Journal (Washburn, WI) 34388
County Ledger-Press (Balsam Lake, WI) 33561
The County Line (Madison Heights, MI) *Unable to locate*
County Line Advertiser (Chillicothe, OH) 24762
County Line Observer (Illiopolis, IL) 9007
The County Line Reminder (Lapeer, MI) *Unable to locate*
County Lines (Westtown, PA) 28153
COUNTY Magazine (Austin, TX) 29772
County Neighbors (Punxsutawney, PA) 27908
County News (Washington, DC) 5445
County News (Cambridge, MN) 15785
County News (Statesville, NC) 24246
County News-Enterprise (Forest City, NC) 23893
County Pennysaver (Massena, NY) 21026
County Press (Lapeer, MI) 15308
County Press (Newtown Square, PA) 27328
County Progress (Abilene, TX) 29653
The County Record (Blountstown, FL) 5925
County Reporter (Cinnaminson, NJ) *Unable to locate*
County Review (Raymond, AB, Can.) *Unable to locate*
County Shopper—Catskill Park Edition (Delhi, NY) 20523
County Shopper—Delaware Edition (Delhi, NY) 20524
County Star (Tolono, IL) 9692
County Star (Warrenton, MO) *Unable to locate*
County Star Journal West (Warrenton, MO) 17680
County Transcript (Susquehanna, PA) 28041
County Wide News (Westminster, MD) *Ceased*
County Wide Newspaper (Machias, ME) 12985
The Countyline (Bryan, OH) 24715
The Countywide (Karnes City, TX) 30632
Countywide News (Tecumseh, OK) 26099
Coup d'Oeil (Napierville, QC, Can.) 37254
Coup de Peigne (Montreal, QC, Can.) *Ceased*
Coup de Pouce (Montreal, QC, Can.) 37106
Cour Supreme en Bref (Cowansville, QC, Can.) *Ceased*
Courant (Bottineau, ND) 24376
The Courier 24725*
Courier 26801*
Courier 30070*
The Courier (Dardanelle, AR) 1097
The Courier (Pasadena, CA) 2814
The Courier (Plant City, FL) 6585
Courier (Glen Ellyn, IL) 8926

Courier (Lincoln, IL) 9082
The Courier (Monmouth, IL) 9213
Courier (South Holland, IL) 9614
Courier (Washington, IL) 9735
Courier (Reinbeck, IA) 11174
Courier (Sutherland, IA) 11259
The Courier (Houma, LA) 12601
The Courier (Winona, MN) 16526
The Courier (Littleton, NH) 18548
The Courier (Middletown, NJ) 19234
The Courier (Cobleskill, NY) 20477
The Courier (New York, NY) *Unable to locate*
The Courier (Valley Stream, NY) 23486
The Courier (Findlay, OH) 25194
The Courier (Reedsport, OR) 26553
Courier (Freeman, SD) 28857
Courier (Sisseton, SD) 28991
Courier (Savannah, TN) 29584
The Courier (Farmers Branch, TX) 30314
The Courier (Mequon, WI) *Ceased*
The Courier (Waterloo, WI) 34391
Courier Chronicle 29224*
The Courier and Citizens Journal 28785*
The Courier (Conneaut) (Jefferson, OH) 25261
Courier-Crescent (Orrville, OH) *Unable to locate*
Courier-Democrat (Russellville, AR) *Unable to locate*
The Courier Express (Glasgow, MT) 17792
Courier Express (Du Bois, PA) 26837
Courier 4 26566*
Courier and Freeman 21027*
Courier-Gazette (Newark, NY) 22994
The Courier Herald (Dublin, GA) 7251
Courier-Herald (Thornbury, ON, Can.) 36434
Courier-Index (Marianna, AR) 1267
Courier-Islander; Campbell River (Campbell River, BC, Can.) 34917
Courier-Journal 23215*
Courier Journal (Crescent City, FL) 6022
The Courier-Journal (Louisville, KY) 12213
Courier-Journal (Marine City, MI) *Unable to locate*
Courier Journal (Festus, MO) 17065
Courier Journal (Rochester, NY) 23219
Courier Laval du Jeudi (Montreal, QC, Can.) 37107
The Courier-Leader (Paw Paw, MI) 15433
Courier Magazine (Manassas, VA) *Unable to locate*
Courier News (Blytheville, AR) 1058
The Courier News (Elgin, IL) 8823
The Courier-News (Somerville, NJ) 19572
The Courier-News (Clinton, TN) 29129
Courier News Weekly (Harleysville, PA) 26981
Courier Plus 16678*
Courier-Post (Cherry Hill, NJ) 18733
Courier-Post/This Week (Cherry Hill, NJ) *Unable to locate*
Courier-Press (Prairie du Chien, WI) 34267
Courier-Press (Prairie du Chien, WI) 34266
The Courier Press (Wallaceburg, ON, Can.) 36843
The Courier-Publications (Rockland, ME) 13044
Courier-Record (Blackstone, VA) 31892
The Courier-Sentinel (Kiester, MN) 15985
Courier-Standard-Enterprise (Fort Plain, NY) 20618
Courier-Times (New Castle, IN) 10342
Courier-Times (Sutherland, NE) 18291
Courier-Times (Roxboro, NC) 24209
Courier Tribune (Seneca, KS) 11798
The Courier-Tribune (Asheboro, NC) 23621
The Courier-Wedge (Durand, WI) 33661
Courier Weekend (St. Stephen, NB, Can.) 35436
Courrier-Ahuntsic (Montreal, QC, Can.) *Unable to locate*
Courrier-Bordeaux/Cartierville (Montreal, QC, Can.) *Unable to locate*
Courrier Deux-Montagnes (Montreal, QC, Can.) *Unable to locate*
Courrier d'Oshawa; Le (Toronto, ON, Can.) 36650
Courrier Laval du Dimanche; Le (Montreal, QC, Can.) 37158
Courrier; Le (Trois-Pistoles, QC, Can.) 37414
Courrier Mag Expansion (Saint-Hubert, QC, Can.) *Ceased*
Courrier de Malartic; Le (Malartic, QC, Can.) 37063
Courrier des Moulins (Montreal, QC, Can.) *Ceased*
Courrier des Moulins; Le (Laval, QC, Can.) 37041
Courrier de Portneuf; Le (Donnacona, QC, Can.) 36987
Courrier Saint-Hubert 37345*
Courrier-Sud; Le (Nicolet, QC, Can.) 37259
Court-Butternut Pennysaver (Syracuse, NY) 23398
Court & Commercial Record (Indianapolis, IN) 10105
Court Journal; Juvenile and Family (Reno, NV) 18421
Court Review; Daily (Houston, TX) 30469
Court TV (New York, NY) 37741
Courtenay Comox Valley Record 34931*
Courtland Cable TV (New Ulm, MN) *Unable to locate*
Courtland Journal-Empire (Courtland, KS) 11405
Courtroom Television Network (New York, NY) 37742
Courts, Health Science and the Law (Philadelphia, PA) *Ceased*
The Coushatta Citizen (Coushatta, LA) 12551

The Coushatta Citizen Shopper (Coushatta, LA) 12552
Couture International Jeweler (New York, NY) 21508
The Covenant Companion (Chicago, IL) 8345
The Coventry Courier (Wakefield, RI) 28444
Cover Story (Foothill, CA) 1920
Cover Story (Ontario, CA) *Unable to locate*
Cover Story (Palmdale, CA) 2783
Cover Story (Cordele, GA) 7204
Coverings (Picton, ON, Can.) 36328
CoverStory (Marysville, CA) 2516
CoverSTORY (Wallaceburg, ON, Can.) *Ceased*
Covert Action Information Bulletin 5446*
CovertAction Quarterly (Washington, DC) 5446
Covina Highlander Press Courier (West Covina, CA) *Unable to locate*
The Covington Leader (Covington, TN) 29153
Covington News (Covington, GA) 7210
Covington Record (Covington, OK) 25795
Covington Virginian 31982*
Cow Country (Cheyenne, WY) 34495
Cow Country News (Lexington, KY) 12163
Cow Neck Peninsula Historical Society Journal (Port Washington, NY) 23123
Cowboy; American (Sheridan, WY) 34587
Cowboys & Indians (Dallas, TX) 30139
Cowichan News Leader (Duncan, BC, Can.) 34950
The Cowl (Providence, RI) 28393
The Cowley County Reporter (Burden, KS) 11368
Cowlitz County Advocate (Castle Rock, WA) *Unable to locate*
Cowlitz-Wahkiakum Senior News (Longview, WA) 32811
COWMAN; Oklahoma (Oklahoma City, OK) 25977
Cowpens/Pacolet Tribune (Cowpens, SC) 28594
Cox Cable 30244*
Cox Cable (Macon, GA) *Unable to locate*
Cox Cable Bakersfield (Bakersfield, CA) 1455
Cox Cable Cedar Rapids Inc. 10684*
Cox Cable Cleveland Area, Inc. (Parma, OH) 25468
Cox Cable Greater Hartford, Inc. 4939*
Cox Cable of Hampton Roads (Hampton Roads, VA) 32136
Cox Cable Jefferson Parish (Harahan, LA) 12597
Cox Cable Lubbock (Lubbock, TX) 30721
Cox Cable of New Orleans 12763*
Cox Cable Ocala 6473*
Cox Cable Oklahoma City 25998*
Cox Cable Quad Cities (Moline, IL) 9208
Cox Cable Rhode Island, Inc. (Cranston, RI) *Unable to locate*
Cox Cable Saginaw (Saginaw, MI) 15493
Cox Cable San Diego (San Diego, CA) 3293
Cox Cable Santa Barbara (Goleta, CA) 2028
Cox Cable South Carolina 28706*
Cox Cable Spokane 33138*
Cox Cable TV (Destrehan, LA) *Unable to locate*
Cox Cable TV of Pensacola (Pensacola, FL) 6571
Cox Cable-University City (Gainesville, FL) *Unable to locate*
Cox Communication (West Warwick, RI) 28456
Cox Communications 28184*
Cox Communications 25426*
Cox Communications 25352*
Cox Communications 14655*
Cox Communications (Phoenix, AZ) 814
Cox Communications (Tucson, AZ) 975
Cox Communications (Fort Smith, AR) 1144
Cox Communications (Irvine, CA) 2094
Cox Communications (Rancho Santa Margarita, CA) 2884
Cox Communications (Vista, CA) *Unable to locate*
Cox Communications (Ocala, FL) 6473
Cox Communications (Springfield, IL) 9645
Cox Communications (McPherson, KS) 11643
Cox Communications (Ashland, KY) 11918
Cox Communications (Violet, LA) 12870
Cox Communications (Enid, OK) 25824
Cox Communications (Stillwater, OK) 26083
Cox Communications (Midland, TX) 30816
Cox Communications (Texarkana, TX) 31185
Cox Communications, Inc. (Medicine Lodge, KS) 11650
Cox Communications, Inc. (Wichita, KS) 11893
Cox Communications Louisiana (New Orleans, LA) 12763
Cox Communications New England (Manchester, CT) 4939
Cox Communications Oklahoma City (Oklahoma City, OK) 25998
Cox Communications, Omaha, LLC (Omaha, NE) 18210
Cox Communications Roanoke (Roanoke, VA) 32494
Cox Communications & Times Mirror Cable TV of Sprinfield 9645*
Cox Enterprises (Atlanta, GA) 7063
Cox Newspapers Inc. (Washington, DC) 37875
CP Air Express (Toronto, ON, Can.) *Ceased*
CPA; California (Redwood City, CA) 2913

Numbers cited in bold after listings are entry numbers rather than page numbers.

The Daily Journal (Vineland, NJ) 19698
Daily Journal of Commerce 33019*
Daily Journal of Commerce (New Orleans, LA) 12728
Daily Journal of Commerce (Portland, OR) 26475
Daily Journal Messenger (Seneca, SC) 28754
Daily Kent Stater (Kent, OH) 25273
Daily Lass-O 30241*
Daily Leader (Pontiac, IL) 9464
Daily Leader (Brookhaven, MS) 16578
Daily Ledger 1425*
The Daily Ledger (Canton, IL) 8110
The Daily Ledger (Fishers, IN) 9957
Daily Legal News (Cleveland, OH) 24879
Daily Local News (West Chester, PA) 28146
The Daily-Mail (Hagerstown, MD) 13563
Daily Mail (Catskill, NY) 20438
The Daily Mercury 35864*
Daily Mercury (Medford, MA) 14320
The Daily Messenger (Canandaigua, NY) 20420
Daily Midway Driller (Taft, CA) Unable to locate
Daily Miner & News (Kenora, ON, Can.) 35929
The Daily Mining Gazette (Houghton, MI) 15183
The Daily Mississippian (University, MS) 16863
Daily Nebraskan (Lincoln, NE) 18083
Daily News 30309*
The Daily News 32888*
Daily News 33142*
The Daily News 13707*
Daily News 4080*
The Daily News (Mountain Home, AR) Ceased
Daily News (Red Bluff, CA) 2885
Daily News (Woodland Hills, CA) 4102
Daily News (Moscow, ID) 7912
Daily News (Bowling Green, KY) 11943
Daily News (Middlesboro, KY) 12293
The Daily News (Greenville, MI) 15135
The Daily News (Iron Mountain, MI) 15208
The Daily News (Richmond, MO) 17375
Daily News (Jacksonville, NC) 24011
Daily News (Wahpeton, ND) 24549
The Daily News (Bangor, PA) Unable to locate
The Daily News (Huntingdon, PA) 27068
The Daily News (Mc Keesport, PA) 27228
The Daily News (Memphis, TN) 29367
The Daily News (Longview, WA) 32812
Daily News (Pullman, WA) Unable to locate
The Daily News (West Bend, WI) 34445
The Daily News (Prince Rupert, BC, Can.) 35064
The Daily News (Dartmouth, NS, Can.) 35545
The Daily News-Bulletin (Brookfield, MO) 16927
Daily News Democrat-Courier Journal 17689*
Daily News Express (Bowling Green, KY) 11944
Daily News-Journal (Murfreesboro, TN) 29430
The Daily News Leader (Staunton, VA) 32555
Daily News Mercury 14296*
Daily News Press 4222*
Daily News Record (New York, NY) 21531
Daily News-Record (Harrisonburg, VA) 32138
Daily News Shopping Guide 11944*
Daily News Shopping Guide (Bowling Green, KY) 11945
Daily News-Sun (Sun City, AZ) 895
The Daily News Worldwide (Halifax, NS, Can.) 35563
The Daily Nonpareil (Council Bluffs, IA) 10726
The Daily Northwestern (Evanston, IL) 8856
The Daily O'Collegian (Stillwater, OK) 26077
The Daily Oklahoman 25989*
The Daily Orange (Syracuse, NY) 23399
The Daily Other (Jacksonville, IL) 9022
Daily Pacific Builder (San Francisco, CA) Unable to locate
Daily Packet and Times (Orillia, ON, Can.) 36174
The Daily Pasadena Citizen 30914*
The Daily Pennsylvanian (Philadelphia, PA) 27448
Daily Pilot (Costa Mesa, CA) 1774
Daily Post-Athenian (Athens, TN) 29052
Daily Prayer Guide 2817*
Daily Press 2831*
The Daily Press 23466*
The Daily Press (Victorville, CA) 4031
The Daily Press (Escanaba, MI) 15007
The Daily Press (St. Marys, PA) 27942
Daily Press (Newport News, VA) 32279
The Daily Press (Ashland, WI) 33554
The Daily Press (Timmins, ON, Can.) 36453
The Daily Press, E.M.C. (Timmins, ON, Can.) 36454
Daily Press Leader 17054*
Daily Press Preview (Victorville, CA) 4032
The Daily Progress (Charlottesville, VA) 31926
Daily Racing Form (New York, NY) 21532
Daily Racing Form (Toronto, ON, Can.) Unable to locate
Daily Racing Form (West Coast Edition) (Gardena, CA) Unable to locate
The Daily Record 28146*
The Daily Record 9421*
Daily Record (Canon City, CO) 4213
Daily Record (Lawrenceville, IL) 9068
The Daily Record (Baltimore, MD) 13154

The Daily Record (Kansas City, MO) Unable to locate
The Daily Record (Omaha, NE) Unable to locate
Daily Record (Parsippany, NJ) 19411
The Daily Record (Rochester, NY) 23220
The Daily Record (Dunn, NC) 23803
The Daily Record (Wooster, OH) 25672
Daily Record (Ellensburg, WA) 32748
The Daily Recorder (Sacramento, CA) 2995
The Daily Reflector (Greenville, NC) 23962
The Daily Register (Harrisburg, IL) 8972
Daily Register (Portage, WI) 34255
Daily Register; Gainesville (Gainesville, TX) 30376
Daily Report (Atlanta, GA) 6998
Daily Report (Atlanta, GA) 6997
Daily Reporter (Greenfield, IN) 10040
Daily Reporter (Sioux City, IA) Unable to locate
The Daily Reporter (Spencer, IA) 11230
The Daily Reporter (Derby, KS) 11407
The Daily Reporter (Columbus, OH) 25015
The Daily Reporter Advertiser 10039*
Daily Republic (Fairfield, CA) 1909
The Daily Republic (Mitchell, SD) 28900
Daily Republican Register (Mount Carmel, IL) 9231
Daily Review 31982*
The Daily Review (Hayward, CA) 2041
The Daily Review (Morgan City, LA) 12707
The Daily Review (Towanda, PA) 28053
Daily Review Atlas (Monmouth, IL) 9216
Daily Rocket-Miner (Rock Springs, WY) 34581
The Daily Sentinel (Scottsboro, AL) 445
The Daily Sentinel (Grand Junction, CO) 4478
Daily Sentinel (Le Mars, IA) 11034
The Daily Sentinel (Le Mars, IA) 11033
Daily Sentinel (Rome, NY) 23264
The Daily Sentinel (Gallipolis, OH) 25208
The Daily Sentinel (Nacogdoches, TX) 30849
The Daily Sentinel-Review (Woodstock, ON, Can.) 36907
The Daily Sentry-News 12843*
Daily Shipping News (Portland, OR) Unable to locate
Daily Siftings Herald (Arkadelphia, AR) 1030
The Daily Sitka Sentinel (Sitka, AK) 638
Daily South Town/News Marketer (Lansing, IL) Unable to locate
The Daily Southerner (Tarboro, NC) 24254
Daily Southtown (Tinley Park, IL) 9685
Daily Sparks Tribune (Sparks, NV) 18445
The Daily Spectrum 31417*
The Daily Standard 27270*
The Daily Standard (Excelsior Springs, MO) 17050
The Daily Standard (Celina, OH) 24749
The Daily Star (Oneonta, NY) 23049
The Daily Star-Journal (Warrensburg, MO) 17666
The Daily Statesman (Dexter, MO) 17032
The Daily Sun (Warner Robins, GA) Unable to locate
Daily Sun News (Sunnyside, WA) 33142
Daily Sun Post 3103*
Daily & Sunday Freeman (Kingston, NY) 20860
The Daily Sundial (Northridge, CA) 2646
The Daily Tar Heel (Chapel Hill, NC) 23706
The Daily Targum (New Brunswick, NJ) 19329
Daily TaxFax (Arlington, VA) Ceased
The Daily Telegram (Adrian, MI) 14708
The Daily Telegram (Superior, WI) 34359
Daily Telegraph (Bluefield, WV) 33255
The Daily Territorial (Tucson, AZ) 944
The Daily Texan (Austin, TX) 29773
The Daily Times 35698*
The Daily Times (Ottawa, IL) 9390
Daily Times (Sullivan, IN) 10474
The Daily Times (Salisbury, MD) 13707
The Daily Times (Farmington, NM) 19846
The Daily Times (Primos, PA) 27907
The Daily Times (Maryville, TN) 29347
The Daily Times (Weirton, WV) 33489
Daily Times (Rawlins, WY) 34572
Daily Times-Call (Longmont, CO) 4558
Daily Times Chronicle (Woburn, MA) 14669
Daily Times Leader (West Point, MS) 16875
Daily Titan (Fullerton, CA) 1989
Daily Transcript (Dedham, MA) 14154
The Daily Tribune 10594*
Daily Tribune (Cheboygan, MI) 14872
Daily Tribune (Royal Oak, MI) 15480
The Daily Tribune (Bay City, TX) 29891
The Daily Tribune (Wisconsin Rapids, WI) 34463
The Daily Tribune News (Cartersville, GA) Ceased
Daily Trojan (Los Angeles, CA) 2252
Daily Union (Junction City, KS) 11519
Daily Union Extra (Junction City, KS) 11520
The Daily Universe (Provo, UT) 31402
The Daily University Star 31086*
The Daily of the University of Washington 32959*
Daily Utah Chronicle (Salt Lake City, UT) 31425
Daily Variety (New York, NY) 21533
Daily Vidette (Normal, IL) 9296
The Daily Whale 5246*
Daily Word (Unity Village, MO) 17660

Daily Worker 22541*
The Daily World (Helena, AR) 1174
Daily World (Opelousas, LA) 12791
The Daily World (Aberdeen, WA) 32647
Dairy; California (Clovis, CA) 1731
Dairy Extra 16184*
Dairy; Farm and Salem, OH) 25505
Dairy Farmer; Ontario (London, ON, Can.) 35988
Dairy Field (Troy, MI) Unable to locate
Dairy and Field Crops Digest (Owego, NY) 23066
Dairy, Food and Environmental Sanitation (Des Moines, IA) Unable to locate
Dairy Foods (Bensenville, IL) 8066
Dairy Goat Journal (Withee, WI) 34468
Dairy Guide 35326*
Dairy Herd Management Ceased
Dairy Magazine (St. Paul, MN) Ceased
Dairy Research; Journal of (New York, NY) 22046
Dairy Science; Journal of (Blacksburg, VA) 31874
Dairy Today (Monticello, MN) 16184
Dairy Update-Demographic Section of Country Guide Magazine (Winnipeg, MB, Can.) 35326
Dairy World (Millbury, MA) 14334
The Dairyman 1768*
Dairyman; Hoard's (Fort Atkinson, WI) 33711
Dairyman; The Western (Corona, CA) 1768
Dairymen's Digest (North Central Region Edition) (Arlington, TX) Unable to locate
Dairymen's Digest (Southern Region Edition) (Arlington, TX) Unable to locate
Dairynews (Syracuse, NY) Ceased
Dakota Catholic Action (Bismarck, ND) 24350
Dakota Central Telecommunications Cooperative Assn. (Carrington, ND) 24384
Dakota Collector (St. Paul, MN) 16373
Dakota Country (Bismarck, ND) 24351
Dakota County Tribune (Burnsville, MN) 15782
Dakota Farm Edition; Fastline— (Buckner, KY) 11969
Dakota Farmer (Glyndon, MN) 15922
Dakota Giant Network (Bismarck, ND) 37692
Dakota Outdoors (Pierre, SD) 28916
Dakota Scientist 24548*
Dakota Student (Grand Forks, ND) 24454
Dakotan; The Isabel (Isabel, SD) 28876
Dakotan; Yankton Daily Press & (Yankton, SD) 29040
The Dale News 9917*
Daleville Sun Courier (Enterprise, AL) 200
Dalhart Daily Texan (Dalhart, TX) 30119
Dalhousie Alumni Magazine (Halifax, NS, Can.) 35564
The Dalhousie Gazette (Halifax, NS, Can.) 35565
Dalhousie News (Dalhousie, NB, Can.) Ceased
Dalhousie Review (Halifax, NS, Can.) Ceased
Dallas Apparel News (Dallas, TX) 30143
Dallas City Enterprise (Dallas City, IL) Unable to locate
Dallas County News (Adel, IA) Unable to locate
Dallas County Round-up 10572*
Dallas Examiner (Dallas, TX) Unable to locate
Dallas & Fort Worth Home Living (Addison, TX) Ceased
Dallas/Fort Worth New Homes Guide (Dallas, TX) 30144
Dallas Greensheet (Dallas, TX) 30145
Dallas, Inc.; TCI Cablevision of (Dallas, TX) 30218
Dallas Journal (Dallas, TX) 30146
Dallas; Key Magazine (Dallas, TX) 30165
Dallas Magazine (Dallas, TX) Ceased
The Dallas Morning News (Dallas, TX) 30147
Dallas New Era (Dallas, GA) 7221
Dallas/Oak Cliff Tribune 30173*
Dallas Observer (Dallas, TX) 30148
The Dallas Post (Dallas, PA) 26816
Dallas Post Tribune (Dallas, TX) 30149
The Dallas Quarterly 30146*
Dallas Times Herald 30147*
The Dallas Weekly Newspaper (Dallas, TX) 30150
Dallas; WHERE (Dallas, TX) 30188
Dallas Woman (Dallas, TX) Unable to locate
DallasChild (Addison, TX) 29671
The Dalles Chronicle (The Dalles, OR) Ceased
The Dalmatian Quarterly (Wheat Ridge, CO) 4674
The Dalton Carpet Journal (Dalton, GA) Ceased
The Dalton Gazette & Kidron News (Dalton, OH) 25105
Daly City Record (Daly City, CA) 1802
Damascus Courier-Gazette (Damascus, MD) 13481
Damascus/Mt. Airy Express (Alexandria, VA) Unable to locate
Dan Chung News (Irvine, CA) 2077
Dana Point/Laguna Niguel News 2136*
Dana Point/Laguna Niguel News 1805*
Dana Point News (Dana Point, CA) 1805
Danbury Reporter (Walnut Cove, NC) 24267
Danbury Review (Holstein, IA) Ceased
Dance in Canada (Danse au Canada) (Toronto, ON, Can.) Unable to locate
Dance Chronicle (New York, NY) 21534

Deposit Television Inc. (Deposit, NY) **20530**
Depression (Hoboken, NJ) *Ceased*
Depression and Anxiety (Hoboken, NJ) **18926**
Depression and Stress (Madison, CT) **4928**
The DeQuincy News (DeQuincy, LA) **12563**
Der Kanadier (Belleville, ON, Can.) *Unable to locate*
Der Yid (Brooklyn, NY) **20313**
Derivatives; The Journal of (New York, NY) **22048**
Derivatives Quarterly (New York, NY) **21544**
Dermatitis; American Journal of Contact (Dallas, TX) **30122**
Dermatologic Clinics (Philadelphia, PA) **27450**
Dermatologica Helvetica (Farmington, CT) **4812**
Dermatology (Farmington, CT) **4813**
Dermatology; Archives of (Chicago, IL) **8267**
Dermatology Clinical Digest Series (New York, NY) *Ceased*
Dermatology; Current Problems in (St. Louis, MO) **17428**
Dermatology; International Journal of (Elgin, IL) **8824**
Dermatology; Journal of the American Academy of (St. Louis, MO) **17452**
Dermatology Nursing (Pitman, NJ) **19433**
Dermatology Psychosomatics (Farmington, CT) **4814**
Dermatology; Seminars in **27664***
Dermatology Times (Cleveland, OH) **24880**
Dermatology Times of Canada (Mississauga, ON, Can.) *Unable to locate*
Dermatopathology; The American Journal of (Baltimore, MD) **13115**
The Derrick (Oil City, PA) **27346**
Derry News (Derry, NH) **18488**
DES Litigation Reporter (Wayne, PA) *Ceased*
Des Moines Business Record (Des Moines, IA) **10780**
Des Moines County News (West Burlington, IA) **11319**
Des Moines News (Burien, WA) **32699**
The Des Moines Register (Des Moines, IA) **10781**
Des Plaines Times (Des Plaines, IL) **8759**
Des Plaines Valley News (Summit, IL) **9674**
DESANEWS (Ocoee, FL) *Unable to locate*
Desarrollo Nacional **4957***
Descant (Toronto, ON, Can.) **36570**
Deseret News (Salt Lake City, UT) **31426**
Desert Advertiser (Indio, CA) *Unable to locate*
Desert Airman (Tucson, AZ) *Unable to locate*
Desert Call (Crestone, CO) **4300**
Desert Dispatch (Barstow, CA) **1481**
Desert Hot Springs Cablevision (Desert Hot Springs, CA) **1826**
Desert Magazine (Palm Desert, CA) *Ceased*
Desert Mailer News (Palmdale, CA) **2784**
Desert Plants (Tucson, AZ) **945**
Desert Post WEEKLY (Cathedral City, CA) **1679**
Desert Rancher (Indio, CA) *Unable to locate*
Desert Sentinel **1679***
Desert Sentinel (Desert Hot Springs, CA) *Unable to locate*
The Desert Sun (Palm Springs, CA) **2758**
The Desert Trail (Twentynine Palms, CA) **3964**
The Desert Weekly (Palm Springs, CA) *Unable to locate*
Desert Wings (Edwards AFB, CA) **1841**
Deshler Flag (Liberty Center, OH) *Unable to locate*
The Deshler Rustler (Deshler, NE) **17998**
DesigeNet **29771***
Design Automation of Electronic Systems (TODAES) (New York, NY) **21545**
Design Automation for Embedded Systems (New York, NY) **21546**
Design Book Review (Berkeley, CA) **1513**
Design; Computer (Nashua, NH) **18587**
Design Computing (Hoboken, NJ) *Ceased*
Design Cost Data (Tampa, FL) **6761**
Design and Development; Product (Morris Plains, NJ) **19303**
Design Education; International Journal of Technology and (New York, NY) **21922**
Design; Electronic (Paramus, NJ) **19402**
Design Engineering (Toronto, ON, Can.) **36571**
Design; Entertainment (Overland Park, KS) **11711**
Design; Ergonomics in (Santa Monica, CA) **3707**
Design & Fabrication; Welding (Cleveland, OH) **24961**
Design with Flowers (Costa Mesa, CA) *Unable to locate*
Design; Hospitality (New York, NY) **21819**
Design House Review (Long Beach, CA) *Unable to locate*
Design; Interior (Newton, MA) **14401**
Design; Machine (Cleveland, OH) **24923**
Design Magazine; Harvard (Cambridge, MA) **14057**
Design Management (Atlanta, GA) *Ceased*
Design Management Journal (Boston, MA) **13885**
Design & Manufacture; Printed Circuit (Manhasset, NY) **21010**
Design & Manufacturing; IIE Transactions on (Norcross, GA) **7463**
Design Methods (San Luis Obispo, CA) **3565**

Design News (Newton, MA) **14387**
Design; Printed Circuit **21010***
Design Product News (Markham, ON, Can.) **36023**
Design; PT (Cleveland, OH) **24947**
Design Quarterly (Cambridge, MA) *Ceased*
Design Solutions (Centreville, VA) *Ceased*
Design South (Miami Beach, FL) *Ceased*
Design of Tall Buildings; The Structural (Hoboken, NJ) **19110**
Design and Test of Computers; IEEE (Los Alamitos, CA) **2184**
Design Times (Boston, MA) *Unable to locate*
Design; Visual Merchandising and Store (Cincinnati, OH) **24827**
Designer/Builder (Santa Fe, NM) **19934**
Designer Specifier (Falls Church, VA) *Ceased*
Designers' Collection Home Plans (Minneapolis, MN) *Unable to locate*
Designers West (Los Angeles, CA) *Unable to locate*
Designfax (Solon, OH) **25525**
DesignMart (Cleveland, OH) **24881**
Designs; Journal of Combinatorial (Hoboken, NJ) **19015**
Desktop Communications (New York, NY) *Unable to locate*
Desktop Press (Los Angeles, CA) *Unable to locate*
Desktop Publisher (Maple Glen, PA) *Unable to locate*
DeSoto County Tribune (Olive Branch, MS) **16804**
DeSoto Times Today (Hernando, MS) **16679**
DeSoto Today (DeSoto, TX) **30246**
Desserts! (Berne, IN) *Ceased*
The Destin Log (Destin, FL) **6059**
Destination **36442***
Destinations (Englewood, CO) *Unable to locate*
Destinations (Washington, DC) **5462**
Destinations (Toronto, ON, Can.) *Ceased*
Details (New York, NY) *Unable to locate*
Detective; The Armchair (Scotch Plains, NJ) **19533**
Detective Cases (Montreal, QC, Can.) *Ceased*
Detective Dragnet (Montreal, QC, Can.) *Ceased*
Detective Files (Montreal, QC, Can.) *Ceased*
Detroit Business; Crain's (Detroit, MI) **14920**
Detroit Free Press (Detroit, MI) **14924**
Detroit; HOUR (Royal Oak, MI) **15481**
Detroit Institute of Arts; Bulletin of the (Detroit, MI) **14917**
The Detroit Jewish News (Detroit, MI) **14925**
The Detroit Journal **15413***
The Detroit Journal (Detroit, MI) *Unable to locate*
Detroit Labor News (Detroit, MI) **14926**
Detroit Lakes Tribune (Detroit Lakes, MN) **15829**
Detroit Legal News (Troy, MI) **15618**
Detroit Lutheran (Troy, MI) **15619**
Detroit Metropolitan Woman (Southfield, MI) *Unable to locate*
Detroit Monitor **14939***
Detroit Monthly (Detroit, MI) *Ceased*
The Detroit News (Detroit, MI) **14927**
Detroit Press & Guide; Warrendale-West (Dearborn, MI) **14907**
Detroit Society for Genealogical Research Magazine (Detroit, MI) **14928**
Detroit; Sport (Royal Oak, MI) **15486**
Detroit Weekly; Real (Ferndale, MI) **15030**
Detroiter (Detroit, MI) **14929**
Deutsche Presse (German Press) (Toronto, ON, Can.) **36572**
Deux Rives; Les (Sorel, QC, Can.) **37405**
Devachan *Ceased*
The DeValls Bluff Times (Hazen, AR) **1171**
Developing Alabama (Montgomery, AL) **364**
Development (Herndon, VA) *Unable to locate*
Development Business (New York, NY) **21547**
Development; Finance & (Washington, DC) **5495**
Development; IBM Journal of Research and (Yorktown Heights, NY) **23606**
Development; Infant and Child (Hoboken, NJ) **18973**
Development; Journal of International (Hoboken, NJ) **19027**
Development Magazine; Area (Westbury, NY) **23552**
Development Pharmacology and Therapeutics (Farmington, CT) *Ceased*
Development and Psychopathology (Rochester, NY) **23223**
Development; Public Administration and (Hoboken, NJ) **19092**
Development Review; Population and (New York, NY) **22583**
Developmental & Behavioral Pediatrics; Journal of (Philadelphia, PA) **27524**
Developmental Biology (San Diego, CA) **3140**
Developmental Brain Dysfunction (Farmington, CT) *Ceased*
Developmental Dynamics (Hoboken, NJ) **18927**
Developmental Genetics (Hoboken, NJ) **18928**
Developmental and Learning Disorders; Journal of (Madison, CT) **4932**
Developmental Medicine and Child Neurology (New York, NY) **21548**

Developmental Medicine; Clinics in (New York, NY) **21430**
Developmental Neuropsychology (Louisville, KY) **12214**
Developmental Neuroscience (Farmington, CT) **4815**
Developmental Psychobiology (Hoboken, NJ) **18929**
Developmental Psychology (Washington, DC) **5463**
Developmental Review (San Diego, CA) **3141**
Developmental Science; Applied (Mahwah, NJ) **19185**
Developments (Washington, DC) **5464**
Deviant Behavior: An Interdisciplinary Journal (Lafayette, LA) **12616**
Devilirium (Durham, NC) *Ceased*
Devil's Millhopper (Aiken, SC) *Ceased*
Devil's River News (Sonora, TX) **31119**
The Devine News (Devine, TX) **30247**
Devoir; Le (Montreal, QC, Can.) **37159**
Devon Dispatch (Devon, AB, Can.) **34693**
DeWitt Bath Review (Charlotte, MI) **14868**
Dewitt County Genealogical Society Quarterly (Clinton, IL) **8683**
DeWitt County View **31313***
Dewitt/Fayetteville/Manlius Pennysaver; Jamesville/ (Manlius, NY) **21020**
DeWitt Suburban Life **20531***
DeWitt Times (DeWitt, NY) **20531**
The Dexter Leader (Dexter, MI) **14976**
DFW People (Euless, TX) **30310**
DG Review (Austin, TX) *Ceased*
Dharma Journal (Madison, WI) *Unable to locate*
Dia por Dia **24793***
Dia a Dia (Cincinnati, OH) **24793**
Dia Newspaper; El (Cicero, IL) **8673**
Diabetes (St. Louis, MO) **17433**
Diabetes Care (Alexandria, VA) **31665**
Diabetes Countdown (New York, NY) *Unable to locate*
Diabetes Dialogue (Toronto, ON, Can.) **36573**
The Diabetes Educator (Chicago, IL) **8353**
Diabetes Forecast (Alexandria, VA) **31666**
Diabetes Management Guide (Belle Mead, NJ) *Unable to locate*
Diabetes/Metabolism Review (Hoboken, NJ) **18930**
Diabetes in the News (Chicago, IL) *Unable to locate*
Diabetes Prevention and Therapy (Hoboken, NJ) *Ceased*
Diabetes Professional **22590***
Diabetes Self-Management (New York, NY) **21549**
Diabetes Spectrum (Alexandria, VA) *Unable to locate*
Diabetic; Voice of the (Columbia, MO) **17012**
Diabetology; Practical (New York, NY) **22590**
Diablo (Walnut Creek, CA) **4052**
Diablo Arts (Walnut Creek, CA) **4053**
Diablo Business (Walnut Creek, CA) *Ceased*
Diaconate Magazine *Ceased*
Diacritics (Baltimore, MD) **13155**
Diagnosis **37273***
Diagnosis; The Canadian Journal of (Pointe-Claire, QC, Can.) **37273**
Diagnostic Cytopathology (Hoboken, NJ) **18931**
Diagnostic Imaging (Manhasset, NY) **20996**
Diagnostic and Invasive Technology; MEEN (Schaumburg, IL) **9586**
Diagnostic Laboratory Immunology; Clinical and (Washington, DC) **5419**
Diagnostic Medical Sonography (JDMS); The Journal of (Thousand Oaks, CA) **3887**
Diagnostic Molecular Pathology (Baltimore, MD) **13156**
Diagnostic Oncology (Farmington, CT) *Ceased*
Diagnostic Pathology; Seminars in (Philadelphia, PA) **27665**
Diagnostics & Clinical Testing (New York, NY) *Ceased*
Diagnostique **28505***
The Diagonal Progress (Diagonal, IA) **10839**
Dial; The Boscobel (Boscobel, WI) **33598**
Dial Weta **31841***
The Dialog (Wilmington, DE) **5293**
Dialogue (Deerfield, IL) *Ceased*
Dialogue (Salem, OR) **26567**
DIALOGUE (Salt Lake City, UT) *Unable to locate*
Dialogue (Toronto, ON, Can.) *Unable to locate*
Dialysis & Nephrology; Contemporary (New York, NY) **21491**
Dialysis & Transplantation (Van Nuys, CA) **3987**
Diamond (Sioux Center, IA) **11205**
Diamond Bar/Phillips Ranch Highlander (West Covina, CA) *Unable to locate*
The Diamond Drill (Crystal Falls, MI) *Unable to locate*
Diamond Head Radio Inc. **7744***
Diamond Intelligence Briefs (New York, NY) **21550**
Diamond; Murfreesboro (Murfreesboro, AR) **1293**
Diamond Trail News (Sully, IA) **11257**
Diamondback (College Park, MD) **13416**
Diamonds; New York (New York, NY) **22441**
The DIAPASON (Des Plaines, IL) **8760**
Diario las Americas (Miami, FL) **6348**

Diario/La Prensa; El (New York, NY) 21590
Diarist's Journal (Covington, KY) 12026
Diaspora (Toronto, ON, Can.) 36574
Diaspora; Journal of the Hellenic (New York, NY) 22087
Dick Tracy Adventures (Prescott, AZ) *Unable to locate*
The Dickey County Leader (Ellendale, ND) 24407
Dickey Rural Services Inc. (Ellendale, ND) 24408
Dickey Rural Telephone 24408*
Dickinson Journal; The Emily (Cleveland, OH) 24890
Dickinson Law Review (Carlisle, PA) 26758
The Dickinson Press (Dickinson, ND) 24394
The Dickinsonian (Carlisle, PA) 26759
The Dickson Herald (Dickson, TN) 29165
DICP, The Annals of Pharmacotherapy 24773*
Didato Associates (Ossining, NY) 37885
The Didsbury Booster 34694*
The Didsbury Booster and County of Mountain View News 34694*
Didsbury Chronicle (Airdrie, AB, Can.) *Ceased*
The Didsbury Pioneer 34694*
The Didsbury Review (Didsbury, AB, Can.) 34694
Die Casting Engineer (Rosemont, IL) 9555
Die Casting Management (Wonder Lake, IL) 9770
Die Hausfrau 6936*
Die Mennonitische Post (Steinbach, MB, Can.) 35295
Die Unterrichtspraxis/Teaching German (Cherry Hill, NJ) 18734
Dieciocho (Charlottesville, VA) 31928
Diehard Game Fan (Agoura, CA) *Unable to locate*
Diemaking, Stamping and EDMing 15407*
Diesel Equipment Superintendent 2769*
Diesel Fuel News (Potomac, MD) 13651
Diesel & Gas Turbine Worldwide (Waukesha, WI) 34401
Diesel Magazine (Kitchener, ON, Can.) *Unable to locate*
Diesel Progress Engines & Drives 34403*
Diesel Progress International Edition (Waukesha, WI) 34402
Diesel Progress North American Edition (Waukesha, WI) 34403
Diet and Exercise Guide; Fitness (New York, NY) 21704
Diet & Fitness (Hollywood, FL) 6192
Dietary Manager Magazine (St. Charles, IL) 9567
Dieterich Special Gazette; Teutopolis Press and (Teutopolis, IL) 9682
Dietetic Association; Journal of the American (Chicago, IL) 8431
Dietetique en Action (Montreal, QC, Can.) 37108
Differences (Providence, RI) 28395
Differential Equations (New York, NY) 21551
Differential Equations; Communications in Partial (Stanford, CA) 3795
Differential Equations; Journal of (San Diego, CA) 3187
Differential Geometry; Journal of (Somerville, MA) 14535
The Digby Courier (Digby, NS, Can.) 35552
The Digest (Hallandale, FL) 6184
The Digest (Asheville, NC) 23628
Digest (Philadelphia, PA) 27451
Digest, BC Edition; Community (Vancouver, BC, Can.) 35136
The Digest of Chiropractic Economics (Livonia, MI) *Unable to locate*
Digest for Home Furnishers (Eden Prairie, MN) *Unable to locate*
Digest; Lubbock Southwest (Lubbock, TX) 30716
Digest of Middle East Studies (DOMES) (Milwaukee, WI) 34065
Digest of Neurology and Psychiatry (Hartford, CT) 4889
The Digest of Non-Profit Management (Louisville, KY) *Unable to locate*
Digest of Philadelphia College of Osteopathic Medicine 27451*
Digestion (Farmington, CT) 4816
Digestive Diseases (Farmington, CT) 4817
Digestive Diseases and Sciences (Pittsburgh, PA) 27780
Digestive Surgery (Farmington, CT) 4818
Digests of Environmental Impact Statements; EIS: (Bethesda, MD) 13331
The Digger 2728*
The Digger 26614*
Digger (Wilsonville, OR) 26614
The Digger Shopper & News (Oroville, CA) 2728
The Dighton Herald (Dighton, KS) 11412
Digital Age (Fort Washington, PA) *Ceased*
Digital Audio Review 18620*
Digital Coast Reporter (New York, NY) 21552
Digital Creativity *Ceased*
Digital Desktop *Ceased*
Digital Graphics (Broomfield, CO) 4204
Digital Imaging; Journal of (Gainesville, FL) 6147
Digital Journal.com (Toronto, ON, Can.) 36575

Digital News (Framingham, MA) *Ceased*
Digital News & Review (Newton, MA) 14388
Digital Output (Ponte Vedra Beach, FL) 6594
Digital Review 14388*
Digital Signal Processing (San Diego, CA) 3142
Digital Systems Report (Carlsbad, CA) *Ceased*
Digital Unix News *Ceased*
Digital Video Magazine (Manhasset, NY) 20997
Digital's Rdb World (Austin, TX) *Ceased*
digitalsouth Dispatch (Fort Lauderdale, FL) *Unable to locate*
DigitalTV (New York, NY) 21553
The Dillon Herald (Dillon, SC) 28597
Dillon Tribune (Dillon, MT) 17782
Dillon Tribune-Examiner 17782*
Dillsburg Banner (Dillsburg, PA) 26826
Dimanche; Le Richelieu (Saint-Jean, QC, Can.) 37355
Dime Novel Roundup (Dundas, MN) 15860
Dimension (Birmingham, AL) 68
Dimension Cable 2884*
Dimension Cable 11918*
Dimension Cable 25426*
Dimension Cable 28456*
Dimension Cable 28184*
Dimension Cable 30230*
Dimension Cable Services 30816*
Dimension Cable Services 31185*
Dimension Cable Services 10256*
Dimension Cable Services 14655*
Dimension Cable Services 814*
Dimension Cable Services (Midland, TX) 30817
Dimension PSX Magazine 1934*
Dimensions of Critical Care Nursing (Lakewood, CO) *Ceased*
Dimensions of Critical Care Nursing (Philadelphia, PA) *Ceased*
Dimethylacetamide; Chinese Markets for (Woodinville, WA) 33212
Dining Guide; Buying & (New York, NY) 21364
Dinuba Sentinel (Dinuba, CA) 1828
Dinwiddie Monitor (Dinwiddie, VA) 31997
Dinwiddig Cable Partners L.P. 32332*
Diocesan News (Charlottetown, PE, Can.) *Ceased*
The Diocesan Review (Corner Brook, NL, Can.) *Ceased*
Diocese of Orange Bulletin (Orange, CA) 2722
Dionysos (Seattle, WA) *Unable to locate*
Diplomatic List (Pittsburgh, PA) 27781
Direct (Stamford, CT) 5148
Direct From Midrex (Charlotte, NC) 23743
Direct and Interactive Marketing; Journal of (Hoboken, NJ) 19021
Direct Marketing Magazine (Garden City, NY) 20637
DirectGuide (Seattle, WA) 32960
Direction (Alexandria, VA) 31668
Direction (Alexandria, VA) 31667
Direction Informatique (Toronto, ON, Can.) 36576
Directions (Bridgewater, NJ) *Newsweek*
DirecTIons (Dallas, TX) *Unable to locate*
The Director (Brookfield, WI) 33604
Directors & Boards (Philadelphia, PA) 27452
Directory World (East Windsor, NJ) *Ceased*
Dirt Bike Magazine (Valencia, CA) 3977
Dirt Late Model (Enfield, CT) 4780
Dirt Rider (Los Angeles, CA) 2253
Dirt Wheels (Valencia, CA) 3978
Dirty Linen (Baltimore, MD) 13157
Dirva (The Field) (Cleveland, OH) *Unable to locate*
Disabilities—Education & Related Services; Physical (Arlington, VA) 31817
Disabilities; Focus on Autism and Other Developmental (Kansas City, KS) 11526
Disabilities; Information Technology and (New York, NY) 21872
Disabilities; Journal of Developmental and Physical (Fort Lauderdale, FL) 6078
Disabilities; Journal of Learning (Athens, GA) 6945
Disabilities Research and Practice; Learning (Ann Arbor, MI) 14758
Disability & Health; Journal of Religion, (New Brunswick, NJ) 19334
Disability and Mature Travel; Open World for (New York, NY) 22496
Disability Network (Washington, DC) *Ceased*
Disability Policy Studies; Journal of (Austin, TX) 29786
Disability Quarterly; Learning (Overland Park, KS) 11719
The Disability Rag 12215*
Disability Rag & Resource 12215*
The Disability Rag's Ragged Edge Magazine (Louisville, KY) 12215
Disability and Rehabilitation (Philadelphia, PA) 27453
Disability Statistics Report (San Francisco, CA) 3349
Disability Studies Quarterly (Chicago, IL) 8354
Disability; Technology and (Buffalo, NY) 20390
Disabled Outdoors Magazine (Chicago, IL) *Unable to locate*

DISAM Journal (Wright Patterson AFB, OH) 25683
Disarmament: A Periodic Review by the United Nations (Bellevue, WA) *Ceased*
Disaster Medicine; Internet Journal of Rescue and (Sugar Land, TX) 31161
Disaster Medicine; Prehospital and (Madison, WI) 33970
Disaster Recovery Journal (St. Louis, MO) 17434
Disc Golf Journal (Champaign, IL) *Unable to locate*
Disc Golf World News (Overland Park, KS) *Unable to locate*
Disc Sports (Fair Haven, VT) *Ceased*
Discipleship Journal (Colorado Springs, CO) 4245
Discipliana (Nashville, TN) 29454
Disclosure Record (Floral Park, NY) *Unable to locate*
Discography; The Jazz Review and Collectors (Long Beach, CA) 2169
Discount Merchandiser (New York, NY) *Unable to locate*
Discount Store News (New York, NY) 21554
Discourse Processes (Memphis, TN) 29369
Discover (New York, NY) 21555
Discover Aventura 5912*
Discover Mid-America (Kansas City, MO) 17164
DISCOVER/Naples Marco Bonita (Naples, FL) *Ceased*
Discover: Peninsula & Silicon Valley (Redwood City, CA) *Unable to locate*
Discoveries (Iola, WI) 33818
Discoveries; Mercer University (Macon, GA) 7385
Discovering and Exploring New Jersey's Fishing Streams and the Delaware River (Somerdale, NJ) 19557
Discovering and Exploring New Jersey's Streams 19557*
Discovery (Warren, MI) *Ceased*
DISCOVERY (Colborne, ON, Can.) *Ceased*
The Discovery Channel (Bethesda, MD) 37744
Discovery Magazine (New York, NY) 21556
Discrete and Computational Geometry (New York, NY) 21557
Discrimination Law Reporter; Massachusetts (Chestnut Hill, MA) 14130
Disease-A-Month (St. Louis, MO) 17435
Disease Alert; Infectious (Montvale, NJ) 19256
Disease Clinics; Infectious (Philadelphia, PA) 27491
Disease; Coronary Artery (Philadelphia, PA) 27428
Disease Management (Larchmont, NY) 20896
Disease; Neurobiology of (San Diego, CA) 3239
Disease News; Infectious (Thorofare, NJ) 19618
Disease Pharmacotherapy; Journal of Infectious (Binghamton, NY) 20184
Diseased Pariah News (Oakland, CA) 2677
Diseases; Blood Cells, Molecules, & (San Diego, CA) 3122
Diseases; Cerebrovascular (Farmington, CT) 4806
Diseases in Children; Infectious (Thorofare, NJ) 19619
Diseases of the Colon and Rectum (Rochester, MN) 16307
Diseases; Digestive (Farmington, CT) 4817
Diseases; International Journal of Infectious (Hamilton, ON, Can.) 35882
Diseases; Journal of Addictive (New York, NY) 21974
Diseases; Journal of Spirochetal and Tick-borne (Thorofare, NJ) 19627
Diseases and Sciences; Digestive (Pittsburgh, PA) 27780
Diseases; Seminars in Pediatric Infectious (Houston, TX) 30529
Diseases; Sexually Transmitted (Philadelphia, PA) 27677
Disgusting Comics (New York, NY) *Unable to locate*
The Disney Channel (Burbank, CA) 37745
The Disney Channel Magazine (Burbank, CA) *Ceased*
Disney's Colossal Comics Collection (Burbank, CA) *Ceased*
Disorders; Journal of Developmental and Learning (Madison, CT) 4932
The Dispatch 19139*
The Dispatch 16603*
Dispatch (Kenai, AK) 606
The Dispatch (Gilroy, CA) 2003
The Dispatch (Maunaloa, HI) 7788
Dispatch (Clay Center, KS) *Unable to locate*
Dispatch (Brainerd, MN) 15766
The Dispatch (Hatch, NM) *Unable to locate*
The Dispatch (Lexington, NC) 24040
Dispatch (Blairsville, PA) 26714
The Dispatch (Midland, TX) *Unable to locate*
Dispatch: City Edition 32950*
Dispatch Features (Hollister, CA) *Unable to locate*
The Dispatch News (Dracut, MA) 14161
Dispatch-News (Spartanburg, SC) 28758
Dispatch/Plaines News 32744*
The Dispatch and the Rock Island Argus (Moline, IL) 9204
The Dispatcher (San Francisco, CA) 3350

Dispersion Science & Technology; Journal of (New York, NY) **22049**
DISPLAY & DESIGN IDEAS (Atlanta, GA) *Unable to locate*
Dispute Resolution; Journal of (Columbia, MO) **16995**
Dispute Resolution Journal (New York, NY) **21558**
Dispute Resolution; Ohio State Journal on (Columbus, OH) **25051**
Dispute Resolution Times (New York, NY) **21559**
Dissent (New York, NY) *Unable to locate*
Dissociation; Journal of Trauma & (Binghamton, NY) **20205**
Distinguished Home Plans (Minneapolis, MN) *Unable to locate*
Distinguished Home Plans (St. Paul, MN) **16374**
Distressed Real Estate Law Alert *Ceased*
Distributed Computing (Mountain Lakes, NJ) *Ceased*
Distributed Systems and Networks; International Journal of Parallel and (Calgary, AB, Can.) **34647**
Distribution Channels (Washington, DC) **5465**
Distribution Report; Logistics Management and (Newton, MA) **14405**
Distribution Sales (Cleveland, OH) *Unable to locate*
Distribution Sales and Management (Farmingdale, NY) **20594**
Distribution; Transportation & (Cleveland, OH) **24958**
Distribution World; Transmission and (Overland Park, KS) **11732**
Distributor (Chicago, IL) *Unable to locate*
Distributor; Food (Falls Church, VA) **32045**
Distributor; Today's (Fort Atkinson, WI) **33721**
District Cablevision, Inc. (Washington, DC) **5876**
District Energy (Westborough, MA) **14637**
District Heating & Cooling **14637***
District Lawyer **5847***
The District News (Red Lake, ON, Can.) *Unable to locate*
Dive Boat Calendar & Travel Guide (La Verne, CA) *Unable to locate*
Dive Notes **6701***
Dive Training (Parkville, MO) **17335**
The Diver (Portland, CT) *Unable to locate*
Diver Magazine (Delta, BC, Can.) **34946**
Diver; Skin (Los Angeles, CA) **2390**
Diversion (New York, NY) **21560**
Diversity Magazine (Winchester, CA) **4092**
Diversity; Workforce (Melville, NY) **21066**
Divine Reflections **31606***
Divine Word Missionaries (Techny, IL) **9681**
Diving World (Van Nuys, CA) *Ceased*
Dix Hills/Melville Suffolk Life (Melville, NY) **21042**
Dixie Cable TV (Alma, GA) **6915**
Dixie Contractor (Norcross, GA) *Unable to locate*
Dixie County Advocate (Cross City, FL) **6029**
Dixie News (Florence, KY) **12059**
Dixie Truck Edition; Fastline— (Buckner, KY) **11970**
The Dixon Tribune (Dixon, CA) **1831**
Dixon's Independent Voice (Dixon, CA) **1832**
DIY Boat Owner (Dallas, TX) **30151**
DJ Times (Port Washington, NY) **23125**
DM News (New York, NY) **21561**
DM Review (Washington, DC) *Unable to locate*
DMI Academic Review (Boston, MA) **13886**
DNA **8278***
DNA **10326***
DNA: A Journal of Molecular Biology **20897***
DNA and Cell Biology (Larchmont, NY) **20897**
The DO (Chicago, IL) **8355**
Do-It-Yourself Retailing (Indianapolis, IN) *Unable to locate*
Doane Owl (Crete, NE) **17994**
Doberman World (Wheat Ridge, CO) *Ceased*
Dock Age; Marina/ (Niles, IL) **9290**
Docket **3015***
Dr. Dobb's Journal (San Mateo, CA) **3585**
Doctor Strange, Sorcerer Supreme (New York, NY) **21562**
Doctor; Today's Christian (Bristol, TN) **29066**
Doctors' Digest; The Alberta (Edmonton, AB, Can.) **34698**
Doctors Office Products (Amherst, NH) *Ceased*
Doctors' Orders (New York, NY) *Unable to locate*
Doctors & Patients; Townsend Letter for (Port Townsend, WA) **32896**
Doctor's Review (Montreal, QC, Can.) **37109**
Doctor's Shopper (Brooklyn, NY) **20314**
Document Delivery World (Westport, CT) *Ceased*
Document Management (Scottsdale, AZ) **868**
Document Management and Windows Imaging **868***
Documentation et Bibliotheques (Montreal, QC, Can.) **37110**
(Documentation sur la Recherche Feministe); Resources for Feminist Research (Toronto, ON, Can.) **36728**
Dodge Center Star-Record (Dodge Center, MN) **15833**
Dodge City Daily Globe (Dodge City, KS) **11414**

Dodge Construction News Green Sheet (Southern California Edition) (Monterey Park, CA) *Unable to locate*
Dodge Construction News (Illinois, Indiana, Wisconsin Edition) (Chicago, IL) **8356**
Dodge County Cablevision (Verona, WI) **34381**
Dodge County Independent (Kasson, MN) **15982**
Dodge County Independent News (Juneau, WI) **33869**
Dodge Criterion (Dodge, NE) **17999**
Dodge Magazine (Troy, MI) **15620**
The Dodgeville Chronicle (Dodgeville, WI) **33658**
Dog Fancy Magazine (Mission Viejo, CA) **2550**
Dog; Gun (Los Angeles, CA) **2283**
Dog; The National Stock (Butler, IN) **9877**
Dog World (Mission Viejo, CA) **2551**
Dog; You & Your (Des Moines, IA) **10819**
Dogs in Canada (Etobicoke, ON, Can.) **35814**
Dogs USA (Mission Viejo, CA) **2552**
Dogtown Territorial Quarterly **2805***
Dogwood Tales Magazine (Memphis, TN) *Unable to locate*
Doing Business in Europe (Riverwoods, IL) **9503**
Doing Business in Europe (Riverwoods, IL) **9502**
The Doings (Hinsdale, IL) **8997**
Doklady Biological Sciences (New York, NY) **21563**
Doklady Chemistry (New York, NY) **21564**
Doklady Earth Sciences (Birmingham, AL) **69**
Doklady Physical Chemistry (New York, NY) **21565**
Doland Times Record (Doland, SD) **28845**
Dolbeau TV Service Inc. **37333***
The Doll Artisan (Iola, WI) **33819**
Doll Artistry (Grantsville, MD) *Ceased*
Doll Castle News (Washington, NJ) **19707**
Doll Costuming (Iola, WI) **33820**
Doll Crafter (Iola, WI) **33821**
Doll Designs (Berne, IN) *Ceased*
Doll Life (Newton, NJ) *Ceased*
Doll Reader (Cumberland, MD) *Unable to locate*
Doll World (Berne, IN) **9808**
Doll World Collector's Price Guide (Berne, IN) *Ceased*
Dollar Saver (Thomson, GA) **7591**
Dollar Saver (Somerville, MA) **14533**
Dollar Saver (Livonia, MI) **15314**
Dollars & Sense (Cambridge, MA) **14049**
Dollars & Sense (Brantford, ON, Can.) *Ceased*
Dollars & Sense Magazine (Chicago, IL) *Unable to locate*
Dollarsaver (Hemet, CA) **2047**
Dollhouse Miniatures Magazine (Waukesha, WI) **34404**
Dollmaking (Iola, WI) **33822**
DOLLS (Iola, WI) **33823**
Dolls & Animals; Soft (Muskegon, MI) **15389**
Dolores Star (Durango, CO) **4401**
The Dolphin (Torrington, CT) **5177**
The Dolphin (Syracuse, NY) **23400**
Dolphin Digest (Miami, FL) **6349**
Dolphin Log (Chesapeake, VA) *Unable to locate*
Domain (Austin, TX) *Ceased*
The Dome (Chester, PA) **26774**
(DOMES); Digest of Middle East Studies (Milwaukee, WI) **34065**
Domestic Animal Endocrinology (New York, NY) **21566**
Domestic Relations Journal of Ohio (Cleveland, OH) **24882**
DOMESTIQUE (Kokomo, IN) *Ceased*
Dominion Post (Morgantown, WV) **33393**
Domino (Toronto, ON, Can.) *Ceased*
Domino Update (Westminster, CO) *Ceased*
DominoPro (Calabasas, CA) *Unable to locate*
Don Danske Pioneer **8999***
(Don Mills); Dental Guide (Toronto, ON, Can.) **36568**
Dona Z. Meilach Features (Carlsbad, CA) **37886**
Donaldsonville Chief (Donaldsonville, LA) **12569**
Donalsonville News (Donalsonville, GA) **7240**
The Dong-A Daily News (Elkins Park, PA) **26870**
Dong A Il Bo (San Francisco, CA) *Ceased*
Dongola Tri-County Record (Dongola, IL) **8778**
The Doniphan Herald (Doniphan, NE) **18000**
Donkey Talk; Miniature (Westminster, MD) **13777**
Donna Events News (Donna, TX) *Unable to locate*
Donnellson Star (West Point, IA) **11324**
Donrey Cablevision (Rogers, AR) *Unable to locate*
Donrey Washington News Bureau (Washington, DC) *Unable to locate*
Don't Laugh, You're Next (Washington, DC) **37887**
Doody's Health Sciences Book Review Journal (Oak Park, IL) **9374**
Doon Press (Doon, IA) **10840**
Door County Advocate (Sturgeon Bay, WI) **34350**
The Door Opener (Vernon, CT) **5187**
Door Reminder (Sister Bay, WI) **34329**
Door & Window Business (Hackettstown, NJ) *Unable to locate*
The Doors Collectors Magazine (Orem, UT) **31384**
Doors and Hardware (Chantilly, VA) **31911**

Dorado Gazette/Georgetown Gazette and Town Crier; El (El Dorado, CA) **1863**
Doraville De Kalb Neighbor (Doraville, GA) **7241**
Dorchester Argus-Citizen (Dorchester, MA) **14159**
Dorchester Eagle-Record **28750***
The Dorchester Star (Cambridge, MD) **13399**
Dorothy Ahle Caricatures (Malden, MA) **37888**
Dorsey Communications (Los Angeles, CA) *Unable to locate*
Dos Mundos Bilingual Newspaper (Kansas City, MO) **17165**
Dos Mundos Newspaper **17165***
Dos Palos Star (Merced, CA) *Unable to locate*
DOS Resource Guide (Chatsworth, CA) *Unable to locate*
Dosimetry; Medical (College Park, MD) **13434**
The Dothan Eagle (Dothan, AL) **185**
The Dothan Progress (Dothan, AL) **186**
Double Take (Somerville, MA) **14534**
Douglas Broadcasting **33074***
Douglas Budget (Douglas, WY) **34519**
Douglas Cable Communications (Logan, IA) *Unable to locate*
Douglas Cable Communications (Topeka, KS) *Unable to locate*
Douglas Communications Mid-South **1068***
Douglas County Cablevision (Omaha, NE) *Unable to locate*
Douglas County Gazette **18002***
Douglas County Herald (Ava, MO) **16896**
Douglas County News Press/Highlands Ranch Herald (Castle Rock, CO) **4222**
Douglas County Post-Gazette (Elkhorn, NE) **18002**
Douglas County Sentinel (Douglasville, GA) **7249**
The Douglas Enterprise **7244***
The Douglas Enterprise & Bonus (Douglas, GA) **7244**
The Douglas Neighbor (Marietta, GA) **7411**
Douglas News **7243***
The Douglas Shopper (Douglas, GA) **7245**
Douglass Alumnae Bulletin **19330***
Douglass Alumnae Magazine (New Brunswick, NJ) **19330**
Douglaston/Little Neck Pennysaver (Farmingdale, NY) *Ceased*
Douglaston/Little Neck Shopper's Guide (Ontario, ON, Can.) **36161**
Dove Creek Press (Dove Creek, CO) **4400**
Dover Post (Dover, DE) **5247**
The Dover/Sherborn Gazette **14160***
Dover-Sherborn Suburban Press (Sherborn, MA) **14523**
Dover-Sherborn TAB (Dover, MA) **14160**
The Dover TAB **14160***
The Dover Times (Rochester, NH) *Unable to locate*
Dow Jones Financial News Service (New York, NY) **37889**
Dow Jones Radio Network (New York, NY) **37629**
Dow Theory Forecasts (Hammond, IN) **10050**
Dowagiac Daily News (Dowagiac, MI) **14977**
Dowline (Princeton, NJ) **19459**
Down Beat (Elmhurst, IL) **8834**
Down East Magazine (Camden, ME) **12942**
Downers Grove Progress (Downers Grove, IL) **8783**
Downers Grove Reporter (Downers Grove, IL) **8784**
Downers Grove Sun (Naperville, IL) **9262**
Downey Herald American (Downey, CA) **1834**
Downieville TV (Downieville, CA) **1838**
Downs News and Times (Downs, KS) **11420**
Downtown (Grand Gorge, NY) **37890**
Downtown (New York, NY) *Unable to locate*
Downtown Express (New York, NY) **21567**
Downtown Gazette (Long Beach, CA) **2166**
Downtown News (Brooklyn, NY) **20315**
Downtown Planet (Honolulu, HI) **7686**
Downtown Source (Seattle, WA) *Ceased*
The Downtowner **23357***
Downtowner Newspaper (Cincinnati, OH) **24794**
Dowry; Agnieszka's (Chicago, IL) **8248**
Dows Advocate (Dows, IA) *Ceased*
Dowser; The American (Danville, VT) **31538**
DPH Journal **31817***
The Draft Horse Journal (Waverly, IA) **11307**
Drag Racing Monthly (Santa Monica, CA) *Unable to locate*
Drag Racing Today (Waco, TX) *Ceased*
Dragon Ball Z Collector (Dallas, TX) **30152**
The Dragon Chronicle (Cortland, NY) **20513**
Dragon Magazine (Renton, WA) **32923**
Dragonfly (Arlington, VA) *Ceased*
Dragonfly (Olympia, WA) *Ceased*
The Dragon's Blood (Sussex, NJ) **19607**
Dragster; National (Glendora, CA) **2024**
The Drain Enterprise (Drain, OR) **26306**
Drainage Systems; Irrigation and (New York, NY) **21953**
Drake Law Review (Des Moines, IA) **10782**
Drake Update (Des Moines, IA) **10783**
Drama; America (Cincinnati, OH) **24769**
Drama; Comparative (Kalamazoo, MI) **15234**

Drama-Logue (Hollywood, CA) *Unable to locate*
Drama; Modern (Toronto, ON, Can.) **36665**
Drama Service; National (Nashville, TN) **29474**
Dramatic Theory and Criticism; Journal of (Lawrence, KS) **11555**
Dramatics Magazine (Cincinnati, OH) **24795**
The Dramatist (New York, NY) **21568**
Dramatists Guild Quarterly **21568***
Draperies and Window Coverings (West Palm Beach, FL) **6846**
Draugas **8381***
Drawing (New York, NY) *Unable to locate*
Drawings; Master (New York, NY) **22289**
Drayton Valley Western Review (Drayton Valley, AB, Can.) **34695**
Dread of Night (Prescott, AZ) *Unable to locate*
Dream Home Magazine (Cincinnati, OH) *Unable to locate*
Dream Magazine (Nevada City, CA) **2615**
Dreamin' (Granbury, TX) *Ceased*
Dreaming (New York, NY) **21569**
Dreams and Nightmares (Tuscaloosa, AL) **486**
Dreams and Visions (Orillia, ON, Can.) **36175**
Dreamworks (New York, NY) *Ceased*
Dredging, Mining & Construction; World (Irvine, CA) **2093**
Dredging Research (Vicksburg, MS) **16870**
Dredging Review; International (Fort Collins, CO) **4433**
Dresden Enterprise (Dresden, TN) **29170**
Dresden Transcript (Dresden, OH) **25167**
Dresden Village News **25167***
Dress (Earleville, MD) **13485**
Dress for Excellence; Just for Men/Male Call/ (Mamaroneck, NY) **37972**
DRESSAGE & CT (Unionville, PA) *Ceased*
Drew County Shopper's Guide (Monticello, AR) **1279**
Drew Magazine (Madison, NJ) **19180**
Drexel Hill Press **27334***
Drexel Polymer Notes **26918***
Drexel Star (Drexel, MO) **17039**
Drilling (Dallas, TX) *Ceased*
Drilling and Completion; SPE (Richardson, TX) **30979**
Drilling Contractor (Houston, TX) **30470**
Drilling; Foundation (Dallas, TX) **30158**
Drilling Progress Weekly Report; Alberta (Calgary, AB, Can.) **34626**
Drilling Report; Gulf of Mexico (Houston, TX) **30473**
Drillsite (Calgary, AB, Can.) *Ceased*
DRIVE! (Concord, CA) **1752**
Driver; Car and (New York, NY) **21372**
Driving **18823***
(DRJES); The Dawson Research Journal of Experimental Science (Westmount, QC, Can.) **37442**
DRMS Communications, Inc. **10333***
Droit de cite (Cowansville, QC, Can.) **36982**
Droit de Cite **36982***
Droit; Le (Ottawa, ON, Can.) **36257**
Drop Shipping News (New York, NY) **21570**
Drovers (Lenexa, KS) **11590**
Drovers Journal **11590***
Drug Abuse Update (Atlanta, GA) *Ceased*
Drug and Alcohol Abuse; The American Journal of (New York, NY) **21192**
Drug Benefit Programs; Provincial (Ottawa, ON, Can.) **36273**
Drug Carrier Systems; Critical Reviews in Therapeutic (New York, NY) **21520**
Drug and Chemical Toxicology (Newark, DE) **5272**
Drug & Cosmetic Industry (New York, NY) *Unable to locate*
Drug and Crime Prevention Funding News *Ceased*
Drug Delivery (San Diego, CA) **3143**
Drug Design and Discovery (New York, NY) *Unable to locate*
Drug Development and Industrial Pharmacy (Austin, TX) **29775**
Drug Development; Journal of Ethnomedicine and (Silver Spring, MD) **13730**
Drug Development Research (Hoboken, NJ) **18932**
Drug Discovery; Modern (Washington, DC) **5656**
Drug Disposition; Biopharmaceutics and (Hoboken, NJ) **18905**
Drug Education; Journal of (Amityville, NY) **20043**
Drug Education; Journal of Alcohol and (Omaha, NE) **18200**
Drug Facts; Patient (St. Louis, MO) **17482**
Drug Intelligence & Clinical Pharmacy **24773***
Drug Issues; Journal of (Tallahassee, FL) **6725**
Drug Merchandising (Toronto, ON, Can.) *Ceased*
Drug Metabolism and Disposition (Philadelphia, PA) **27454**
Drug Metabolism Reviews (Little Rock, AR) **1228**
Drug Protocol (Toronto, ON, Can.) *Ceased*
Drug Resistance; Microbial (Larchmont, NY) **20921**
Drug Safety; Pharmacoepidemiology and (Hoboken, NJ) **19082**
Drug Store News (New York, NY) **21571**

Drug Therapy (Belle Mead, NJ) *Ceased*
Drug Therapy; Cardiology Clinics: Annual of (Philadelphia, PA) **27394**
Drug Topics (Montvale, NJ) **19252**
Drugs; Investigational New (New York, NY) **21945**
Drugs; Journal of Psychoactive (San Francisco, CA) **3384**
Drugs Magazine; Wholesale **4532***
Drum Business (Cedar Grove, NJ) **18720**
Drum Corps World (Madison, WI) **33934**
The Drumheller Mail (Drumheller, AB, Can.) **34696**
The Drummer **26808***
The Drummer (Buffalo, NY) **15777**
Drummer Magazine; Modern (Cedar Grove, NJ) **18721**
Drummer News; Vandalia (Vandalia, OH) **25611**
The Drummer Pennysaver (Batavia, NY) **20120**
Drumright News Journal (Cushing, OK) *Ceased*
Drums and Drumming (Cupertino, CA) *Ceased*
Drums; Tundra (Bethel, AK) **554**
The Drury Mirror (Springfield, MO) **17595**
Druze Studies; Journal of (San Diego, CA) **3188**
Drych (The Mirror); Y (Utica, NY) **23469**
Drycleaner; American (Chicago, IL) **8255**
Drycleaners News (Waterbury, CT) **5192**
Drycleaning Industry; Journal of the Coin Laundry and (Downers Grove, IL) **8787**
The Dryden Observer (Dryden, ON, Can.) **35790**
Drying Technology (New York, NY) **21572**
DSNA Mini Journal **33040***
DSP Engineering (St. Clair Shores, MI) *Unable to locate*
Du Page County Voice (Chicago, IL) *Ceased*
Du Page Progress; Darien (Downers Grove, IL) **8782**
Duarte Cable Communications (Duarte, CA) *Ceased*
Dublin News (Dublin, OH) **25168**
Dublin Progress (Dublin, TX) *Unable to locate*
Dublin Villager (Columbus, OH) *Unable to locate*
The Dubois Frontier (Dubois, WY) **34520**
The Dubuque Advertiser (Dubuque, IA) **10842**
The Dubuque Area Magazine (Dubuque, IA) **10843**
Duchess County Cablevision **23589***
The Duckburg Times (Los Angeles, CA) **2254**
Ducks Unlimited (Memphis, TN) **29370**
DuckTales *Ceased*
Duclos Cable Vision **37009***
Duclos Cable Vision Ltee. (Iles de la Madeleine, QC, Can.) **37009**
Ducom Communications Inc. (Du Bois, PA) **26838**
Duke; The Duquesne (Pittsburgh, PA) **27782**
Duke Environmental Law and Policy Forum (Durham, NC) **23816**
Duke Journal of Comparative and International Law (Durham, NC) **23817**
Duke Law Journal (Durham, NC) **23818**
Duke Mathematical Journal (Durham, NC) **23819**
Dulcimer Players News (Winchester, VA) **32627**
Duluth Budgeteer News (Duluth, MN) **15836**
Duluth Manney Shopper (Two Harbors, MN) *Unable to locate*
Duluth News Tribune (San Jose, CA) **3515**
The Duluthian (Duluth, MN) **15837**
Dumas Clarion (Dumas, AR) **1105**
Dumont Cablevision (Dumont, IA) **10856**
The Duncan Banner (Duncan, OK) **25800**
Duncan Cable TV (Wilmington, VT) **31620**
Duncannon Record (Duncannon, PA) **26842**
Duncanville Suburban **30254***
Duncanville Today (Duncanville, TX) **30254**
Dundalk Eagle (Dundalk, MD) **13484**
Dundalk Herald (Dundalk, ON, Can.) **35793**
The Dundee Observer (Dundee, NY) **20534**
Dundee Reporter (Toledo, OH) *Unable to locate*
Dune Buggies & Hot VWs (Costa Mesa, CA) **1775**
Dunedin/Countryside Herald (Tarpon Springs, FL) *Unable to locate*
The Dunedin Times/The Palm Harbor Sounder (Dunedin, FL) **6061**
Dungeonmaster; Checkmate Incorporating (Wyoming, PA) **28198**
Dunkel Sports Research Service, News-Journal Com. (Daytona Beach, FL) **37891**
Dunkirk/Fredonia Quality Guide **23564***
Dunkirk-Fredonia-Westfield Pennysaver (Fredonia, NY) **20621**
Dunkirk News & Sun (Portland, IN) **10404**
Dunklin County Press (Senath, MO) **17575**
Dunklin Democrat; The Daily (Kennett, MO) **17217**
The Dunlap Reporter (Dunlap, IA) **10857**
The Dunlap Tribune (Dunlap, TN) **29171**
Dunn County Herald (Killdeer, ND) **24485**
Dunn County News, Shopper, and Reminder (Menomonie, WI) **34038**
Dunn County Reminder (Menomonie, WI) **34039**
The Dunnville Chronicle (Dunnville, ON, Can.) **35795**
Dunnville Shoppers Guide (Dunnville, ON, Can.) **35796**
Dunsmuir News (Dunsmuir, CA) *Unable to locate*
Dunwoody De Kalb Neighbor (Dunwoody, GA) **7259**

DuPage Business Ledger **9343***
DuPage County Voice (Morton Grove, IL) *Ceased*
DuPage Press; North (Glen Ellyn, IL) **8930**
DuPage Press; West (St. Charles, IL) **9574**
DuPage Progress; Southeast (Downers Grove, IL) **8795**
DuPage Suburban LIFE/Reporter; SE (Downers Grove, IL) **8794**
The Duplex Planet (Saratoga Springs, NY) **23301**
Duplin Times Progress (Kenansville, NC) **24019**
Dupo Journal; Cahokia- (Warrenton, MO) **17674**
The duPont Registry: A Buyer's Gallery of Fine Automobiles (St. Petersburg, FL) **6623**
The duPont Registry: A Buyer's Gallery of Fine Boats (St. Petersburg, FL) **6624**
The duPont Registry: A Buyer's Gallery of Fine Homes (St. Petersburg, FL) **6625**
The Duquesne Duke (Pittsburgh, PA) **27782**
Durand Cable Co. (Durand, WI) *Ceased*
The Durand Express (Owosso, MI) **15429**
Durango Herald (Durango, CO) **4402**
Durant Daily Democrat (Durant, OK) **25804**
Durham Cablevision (Durham, NC) *Unable to locate*
The Durham Chronicle (Durham, ON, Can.) **35798**
Durham Morning Herald **23824***
The Durham Sun **23824***
Duroc News **10552***
Duroc News (West Lafayette, IL) *Ceased*
The Duster (Lubbock, TX) **30709**
The Dutch Harbor Fisherman (Dutch Harbor, AK) **564**
Dutton Advance (Dutton, ON, Can.) **35799**
Duxbury Clipper (Duxbury, MA) **14162**
Duxbury Reporter (Duxbury, MA) **14163**
Duxbury Shoppinguide (Pembroke, MA) *Ceased*
DV Media Group (San Francisco, CA) **3351**
DVM Newsmagazine (Cleveland, OH) **24883**
DVS Guide (Boston, MA) **13887**
Dwight Star & Herald (Dwight, IL) **8801**
DX Ontario **36651***
Dyepot; Shuttle Spindle & (Duluth, GA) **7257**
Dyer County Tennessean (Dyersburg, TN) *Ceased*
Dyersburg News (Dyersburg, TN) **29174**
Dyersville Commercial (Dyersville, IA) **10859**
Dying; OMEGA-Journal of Death and (Amityville, NY) **20053**
Dykes, Disability, & Stuff (Madison, WI) *Unable to locate*
DynaMath; Scholastic (Danbury, CT) **4754**
Dynamic Business (Pittsburgh, PA) *Unable to locate*
Dynamic Chiropractic (Huntington Beach, CA) **2060**
Dynamic and Control Systems; Journal of (New York, NY) **22050**
Dynamic Systems, Measurement, and Control; Journal of (New York, NY) **22051**
Dynamic Years (Long Beach, CA) *Ceased*
Dynamical Systems; Ergodic Theory and (New York, NY) **21626**
Dynamics (Calgary, AB, Can.) **34642**
Dynamics and Differential Equations; Journal of (New York, NY) **22052**
Dynamics and Econometrics; Studies in Nonlinear (New Brunswick, NJ) **19341**
Dynamics Review; System (Hoboken, NJ) **19114**
The Dynamo (Alliance, OH) **24604**
The Dysart Reporter (Dysart, IA) **10862**
Dyslexia (Hoboken, NJ) **18933**
Dyslexia; The Annals of (Baltimore, MD) **13123**
Dysphagia (New York, NY) **21573**
Dziennik Chicagowski (Chicago, IL) *Unable to locate*
Dziennik Zwiazkowy **8536***

E

E! (Los Angeles, CA) **37746**
E (Norwalk, CT) **5057**
E (Norwalk, CT) **5056**
e-Business Advisor (San Diego, CA) **3144**
E-COMM Magazine **3744***
E-Health; Telemedicine Journal and (Larchmont, NY) **20926**
A & E Monthly **21316***
E-Now Report (New York, NY) *Ceased*
E-Z Read Crosswords (New York, NY) *Ceased*
E-Z Shopper (Merced, CA) *Unable to locate*
EA Journal (Gaithersburg, MD) **13537**
EAA Experimenter (Oshkosh, WI) **34221**
EAA Sport Aviation (Oshkosh, WI) **34222**
Eagan Sun Current (Eagan, MN) **15862**
The Eagle **16364***
Eagle **31323***
Eagle (Ekalaka, MT) **17786**
The Eagle (Chadron, NE) **17974**
The Eagle (Cambridge, NY) **20416**
The Eagle (Price, UT) **31392**
The Eagle Bulletin **21021***

Numbers cited in bold after listings are entry numbers rather than page numbers.

Economics and Management; Journal of Environmental (San Diego, CA) **3190**

Economics and Management Strategy; Journal of (Evanston, IL) **8864**

Economics; Managerial and Decision (Hoboken, NJ) **19058**

Economics; Marine Resource (Kingston, RI) **28360**

Economics; Medical (Montvale, NJ) **19262**

Economics; Networks and Spatial (New York, NY) **22421**

Economics; Nursing (Pitman, NJ) **19437**

Economics and Nutrition Review; Family (Alexandria, VA) **31672**

Economics—Obstetrics/Gynecology Edition; Medical (Montvale, NJ) **19263**

Economics, and Organization; Journal of Law, (Cary, NC) **23692**

Economics—Orthopedic Surgery Edition; Medical (Montvale, NJ) **19264**

Economics and Philosophy (New York, NY) **21581**

Economics; The Quarterly Journal of (Cambridge, MA) **14094**

Economics; Quarterly Journal of Austrian (New York, NY) **22618**

Economics; Quarterly Journal of Business & (Lincoln, NE) **18116**

Economics; RAND Journal of (Santa Monica, CA) **3714**

Economics; Real Estate (Bloomington, IN) **9850**

Economics Report; Agricultural (East Lansing, MI) **14981**

Economics; Research in (San Diego, CA) **3255**

Economics Review; Antitrust Law and (Vero Beach, FL) **6834**

Economics; The Review of Austrian (New York, NY) **22656**

Economics (Revue Canadienne d'Economique); Canadian Journal of (Montreal, QC, Can.) **37097**

Economics and Statistics; Review of (Cambridge, MA) **14098**

Economics for Surgeons; Medical (Montvale, NJ) **19265**

Economie Familiale); Canadian Home Economics Journal (Revue Canadienne d' (Ottawa, ON, Can.) **36199**

Economique); Canadian Journal of Economics (Revue Canadienne d' (Montreal, QC, Can.) **37097**

The Economist (New York, NY) **21582**

Economist; Free Press & (Shelburne, ON, Can.) **36389**

Economist; Louisiana Rural (Baton Rouge, LA) **12503**

Economist & Sun (Markham, ON, Can.) **36024**

L'Economiste Medicale (Montreal, QC, Can.) *Ceased*

Economy; Arizona's (Tucson, AZ) **935**

Economy; The International (Washington, DC) **5550**

Economy; International Journal of Political (Armonk, NY) **20081**

Economy; The Review of Black Political (Somerset, NJ) **19564**

Economy Shopper (West Salem, WI) **34449**

EconSouth (Atlanta, GA) **7001**

EContent (Wilton, CT) **5225**

Ecorse Telegram (Ecorse, MI) *Unable to locate*

Ecoscience (Ste.-Foy, QC, Can.) **37336**

EcoSource (Guelph, ON, Can.) *Ceased*

Ecotoxicology (New York, NY) **21583**

Ecotoxicology and Environmental Safety (New Mexico, NM) **19903**

Ecotoxicology News/Reviews; Toxicology & (Philadelphia, PA) **27706**

Ecotoxicology Reviews; Environmental Carcinogenesis & (Springfield, VA) **32543**

Ectoxicology Reviews; Journal of Environmental Science and Health, Part C: Environmental Carcinogenesis and (Springfield, VA) **32545**

Ecumenical Studies; Journal of (Philadelphia, PA) **27525**

Ecumenical Trends (Ludlow, KY) *Unable to locate*

The Ecumenist (Mahwah, NJ) *Ceased*

Ed. (Cambridge, MA) **14051**

ED News **18110***

ED Nursing (Montvale, NJ) **19253**

ED-Tech Review **32282***

Ed, The Official Publication of USDLA (United States Distance Learning Association) (San Ramon, CA) *Unable to locate*

Eddyville Tribune (Eddyville, IA) **10865**

Eden Daily News (Eden, NC) **23855**

The Eden Echo (Eden, TX) **30269**

Eden Prairie News (Eden Prairie, MN) **15868**

Eden Prairie Sun Current (Eden Prairie, MN) **15869**

EDGE (Indianapolis, IN) *Ceased*

EDGE (Toronto, ON, Can.) **36577**

Edgebrook Reporter (Chicago, IL) **8359**

Edgebrook-Sauganash Passage (Highland Park, IL) *Unable to locate*

Edgebrook Times Review (Edgebrook, IL) **8809**

The Edgeley Mail (Edgeley, ND) **24404**

Edgemont Herald-Tribune (Edgemont, SD) **28849**

The Edgerton Earth (Edgerton, OH) **25176**

The Edgerton Enterprise (Edgerton, MN) **15873**

The Edgerton Reporter (Edgerton, WI) **33687**

Edgewater/Uptown News-Star; Rogers Park/ (Lincolnwood, IL) **9103**

Edgewood Enterprise (Edgewood, TX) **30270**

Edgewood Reminder (Edgewood, IA) **10867**

EDI Forum (Oak Park, IL) *Unable to locate*

The EDI Law Review (Norwell, MA) **14440**

Edicion Bilingue Independent (Los Angeles, CA) **2260**

Edina Sun Current (Edina, MN) **15874**

Edinburgh Journal of Botany (New York, NY) **21584**

Edison-Norwood Times Review (Chicago, IL) **8360**

Edison Review; Metuchen (Edison, NJ) **18787**

Editor; Colorado (Denver, CO) **4313**

Editor; Grassroots (Brookings, SD) **28814**

Editor; Nurse Author and (Lakewood, CO) **4534**

Editor & Publisher (New York, NY) **21585**

Editorial Consultant Service (West Hempstead, NY) **37892**

Editorial Pace (Westmont, IL) **9754**

Editorial Research Reports **5447***

Editorials On File (New York, NY) **21586**

Editor's Choice (Jackson Heights, NY) **20826**

Editor's Copy Syndicate (Sarasota, FL) **37893**

Editors Press Service Inc. (Sarasota, FL) *Unable to locate*

EDM Digest **15407***

Edmonson News (Brownsville, KY) *Unable to locate*

The Edmonton Examiner (Edmonton, AB, Can.) **34708**

Edmonton Families (Vancouver, BC, Can.) *Ceased*

Edmonton and Homersham Commerce & Industry (Edmonton, AB, Can.) **34709**

Edmonton Jewish Life (Edmonton, AB, Can.) **34710**

The Edmonton Journal (Edmonton, AB, Can.) **34711**

Edmonton Magazine **34736***

The Edmonton Sun (Edmonton, AB, Can.) **34712**

Edmonton; WHERE (Edmonton, AB, Can.) **34737**

The Edmore Advertiser (Alma, MI) **14731**

Edmore Herald (Fordville, ND) **24440**

EDN China **14389***

EDN China (Newton, MA) **14389**

EDN Europe (Newton, MA) **14390**

EDN Magazine Edition (Newton, MA) **14391**

EDN News Edition **14392***

EDN Products and Careers (Newton, MA) **14392**

Edna Herald **30275***

The Edon Commercial (Edon, OH) **25177**

Edouard Benoit Telecable (Riviere-a-Pierre, QC, Can.) *Unable to locate*

EDP Auditing (New York, NY) *Unable to locate*

EDP Weekly's IT Monitor (Washington, DC) **5472**

Edson Leader (Edson, AB, Can.) **34758**

Edson Leader Report **34758***

EDT **14363***

EDT (Chicago, IL) **8361**

EDT (Summerside, PE, Can.) **36922**

Educacion Medica y Salud (Hanover, PA) *Ceased*

Education (Chula Vista, CA) **1714**

Education Administration Quarterly (Milwaukee, WI) **34066**

Education Administration and Supervision Journal; National Forum of (Lake Charles, LA) **12641**

Education; American Journal of Health (Reston, VA) **32360**

Education Annual; Information Technology in Childhood (Norfolk, VA) **32283**

Education; Applied Measurement in (Mahwah, NJ) **19186**

Education; Art (University Park, PA) **28070**

Education Association Journal; American Technical (Wahpeton, ND) **24547**

Education; British Journal of Music (New York, NY) **21341**

Education; Bulletin of the Council for Research in Music (Urbana, IL) **9698**

Education for Business; Journal of (Washington, DC) **5582**

Education California (EDCAL) (Sacramento, CA) **2996**

Education Canada (Toronto, ON, Can.) **36578**

Education Canada (EEC); Exceptionality (Charlottetown, PE, Can.) **36914**

Education); The Canadian Journal of CME (Continuing Medical (Pointe-Claire, QC, Can.) **37272**

Education; Children's Literature in (New York, NY) **21411**

Education; The Chronicle of Higher (Washington, DC) **5413**

Education; Communication (Athens, GA) **6933**

Education; Computer Applications in Engineering (Hoboken, NJ) **18921**

Education; Computer Science (Eau Claire, WI) **33667**

Education; Contributions to Music (Youngstown, OH) **25696**

Education; Current Index to Journals in (Phoenix, AZ) **801**

The Education Digest (Ann Arbor, MI) **14747**

Education; English (Urbana, IL) **9704**

Education; European (Armonk, NY) **20077**

Education Finance; Journal of (Champaign, IL) **8196**

Education Forum (Toronto, ON, Can.) **36579**

Education of the Gifted; Journal for the (Knoxville, TN) **29275**

Education Index (Bronx, NY) **20267**

Education and Information Technologies (New York, NY) **21587**

Education; Innovative Higher (New York, NY) **21874**

Education; International Journal of Lifelong (Philadelphia, PA) **27500**

Education; International Journal of Science (Philadelphia, PA) **27508**

Education; International Review of (New York, NY) **21935**

Education; Issues in (Berkeley, CA) **1530**

Education; The Journal of Adventist (Silver Spring, MD) **13729**

Education; The Journal of Aesthetic (Champaign, IL) **8192**

Education; Journal of Computing in Higher (Amherst, MA) **13797**

Education; Journal of Dental (San Antonio, TX) **31033**

Education; Journal of Developmental (Boone, NC) **23653**

Education; Journal of Distance (Edmonton, AB, Can.) **34718**

Education; Journal of Drug (Amityville, NY) **20043**

Education; The Journal of Environmental (Washington, DC) **5586**

Education; The Journal of Experimental (Washington, DC) **5587**

Education; Journal of General (University Park, PA) **28078**

Education; The Journal of Higher (Columbus, OH) **25024**

Education; Journal of Industrial Teacher (Knoxville, TN) **29276**

Education Journal; Jazz (Manhattan, KS) **11621**

Education; Journal of Language, Identity, and (San Antonio, TX) **31034**

Education; Journal of Latinos and (San Bernardino, CA) **3087**

Education Journal; Lutheran (River Forest, IL) **9492**

Education; Journal of Management (Normal, IL) **9300**

Education; Journal of Marketing for Higher (Cincinnati, OH) **24806**

Education; Journal of Mathematics Teacher (New York, NY) **22129**

Education Journal; National Forum of Teacher (Lake Charles, LA) **12643**

Education; The Journal of Negro (Washington, DC) **5605**

Education; The Journal of Perinatal (Richmond, VA) **32442**

Education; Journal of Personnel Evaluation in (New York, NY) **22155**

Education Journal; Physical & Health (Ottawa, ON, Can.) **36270**

Education; Journal of Research on Computing in (Manhattan, KS) **11622**

Education; Journal for Research in Mathematics (Reston, VA) **32393**

Education; Journal for Research in Music (Baton Rouge, LA) **12491**

Education; Journal of Science Teacher (New York, NY) **22183**

Education; Journal of Secondary Gifted (Evanston, IL) **8865**

Education; The Journal of Special (Nashville, TN) **29465**

Education; Journal of Statistics (Alexandria, VA) **31703**

Education; Journal of Teacher (Des Moines, IA) **10801**

Education; Journal of Teaching in Physical (Champaign, IL) **8201**

Education; Journal of Technology & Teacher (Norfolk, VA) **32289**

Education; Journal of Veterinary Medical (Blacksburg, VA) **31877**

Education; Journal for Vocational Special Needs (Pittsburgh, PA) **27805**

Education & Law Journal (Toronto, ON, Can.) **36580**

Education Law and Policy; European Journal for (New York, NY) **21642**

Education Leader; State (Denver, CO) **4360**

Education; Liberal (Washington, DC) **5636**

Education Libraries (Montreal, QC, Can.) **37112**

Education Magazine; Black Employment and (Atlanta, GA) **6979**

Education Magazine; Home (Tonasket, WA) **33165**

Education Management; Higher (Washington, DC) **5525**

Education; Multicultural (San Francisco, CA) **3392**

Education; New Directions for Adult and Continuing (San Francisco, CA) **3396**

El Sereno Star (Los Angeles, CA) **2263**
El Sol (Phoenix, AZ) *Unable to locate*
El Sol (Salinas, CA) *Unable to locate*
El Sol Del Valle (Sanger, CA) *Unable to locate*
El Sol de la Florida (Tampa, FL) *Unable to locate*
El Sol de Hialeah (Hialeah, FL) **6187**
El Tecolote (San Francisco, CA) *Unable to locate*
El Tiempo (Stockton, CA) *Unable to locate*
El Tiempo Latino (Arlington, VA) **31787**
El Tiempo Libre (Las Vegas, NV) **18362**
El Tiempo de New York (Jackson Heights, NY) **20827**
El Todo (Bayamon, PR) *Unable to locate*
El Vaquero (Glendale, CA) **2009**
El Visitante de Puerto Rico (San Juan, PR) **28293**
El Vistante **28293***
El Vocero de Puerto Rico (San Juan, PR) **28294**
E.L.A. Brooklyn-Belvedere Comet (Belvedere, CA) **1485**
Elan Image (Montreal, QC, Can.) *Unable to locate*
Elasticity; Journal of (New York, NY) **22057**
Elastomerics (Atlanta, GA) *Ceased*
The Elba Clipper (Elba, AL) **197**
Elbert County News (Woodland Park, CO) *Unable to locate*
The Elberton Star **7267***
The Elberton Star & Examiner (Elberton, GA) **7267**
Elbow Surgery; Journal of Shoulder and (St. Louis, MO) **17462**
The Elburn Herald (Elburn, IL) **8821**
Elder Abuse and Neglect; Journal of (Binghamton, NY) **20169**
Elder Update (Tallahassee, FL) **6703**
Elderly; Journal of Housing for the (Columbia, MO) **16996**
Elderly; Journal of Nutrition for the (Little Neck, NY) **20952**
Elder's Advisor (New York, NY) **21591**
The Eldon Advertiser (Eldon, MO) **17045**
Eldorado Courier (Eldorado, OK) **25818**
Election Law Journal (Larchmont, NY) **20898**
Electra Star-News (Electra, TX) **30306**
Electric Consumer (Indianapolis, IN) **10109**
Electric Cooperative Connections; South Dakota (Pierre, SD) **28920**
Electric Light & Power (Tulsa, OK) **26115**
Electric Machines Components and Systems (Philadelphia, PA) **27456**
Electric Machines and Power Systems **27456***
Electric Nebraskan; Rural (Lincoln, NE) **18117**
Electric News; Illinois Rural (Springfield, IL) **9630**
Electric Perspectives (Washington, DC) **5476**
Electric Power International (Columbus, OH) *Unable to locate*
Electrical Apparatus (Chicago, IL) **8363**
Electrical Business (Mississauga, ON, Can.) **36064**
Electrical Construction and Maintenance (EC&M) (Overland Park, KS) **11708**
Electrical Construction Technology **11703***
Electrical Contractor (Bethesda, MD) **13332**
Electrical Edition; The Complete European Trade Digest (Atlanta, GA) **6989**
Electrical Engineering in Japan (Hoboken, NJ) **18936**
Electrical Equipment News (Toronto, ON, Can.) *Ceased*
Electrical News (Arcadia, CA) **1428**
Electrical Standards and Product Guide (Rosslyn, VA) **32514**
Electrical Systems Design (Edgemont, PA) *Ceased*
Electrical Wholesaling (Overland Park, KS) **11709**
Electrical Workers Journal **5539***
Electrical World (Columbus, OH) *Unable to locate*
Electricien; Le Maitre **37113***
Electricite Quebec (Montreal, QC, Can.) **37113**
The Electricity Journal (New York, NY) **21592**
Electricity Quarterly Statistics; Oil, Gas, Coal and (Washington, DC) **5706**
Electricity Today (Ajax, ON, Can.) **35627**
Electrification Magazine; Rural (Arlington, VA) **31824**
Electrifying Times (Bend, OR) **26242**
Electro-Vision (La Tuque) Inc. (La Tuque, QC, Can.) **37025**
Electrocardiology; Journal of (Long Beach, CA) **2170**
Electrocardiology; Noninvasive (Armonk, NY) **20089**
Electroceramics; Journal of (New York, NY) **22058**
The Electrochemical Society Interface (Pennington, NJ) **19420**
Electrochemistry; Journal of Applied (New York, NY) **21990**
Electrochemistry; Russian Journal of (New York, NY) **22688**
Electrodynamics; Galilean (Arlington, MA) **13819**
ElectroIndustry (ei) (Rosslyn, VA) **32515**
Electromagnetics (Chicago, IL) **8364**
Electromyography and Kinesiology; Journal of (Baltimore, MD) **13189**
The Electron (Cleveland, OH) **24889**
Electronic Business (Newton, MA) **14394**

Electronic Business Asia (Newton, MA) **14395**
Electronic Business Buyer **14394***
Electronic Commerce; International Journal of (Armonk, NY) **20079**
Electronic Commerce; Journal of Organizational Computing and (Austin, TX) **29789**
Electronic Commerce World (Hollywood, FL) **6193**
(Electronic Component News); ECN (New York, NY) **21580**
Electronic Components; Asian Sources (Phoenix, AZ) **785**
Electronic Composition & Imaging (Willowdale, ON, Can.) *Unable to locate*
Electronic Defense; Journal of (Norwood, MA) **14447**
Electronic Design (Paramus, NJ) **19402**
Electronic Distribution Show Daily (Chagrin Falls, OH) *Unable to locate*
Electronic Distribution Today (Powell, OH) **25491**
Electronic Engineering Times (Manhasset, NY) **20999**
Electronic Gaming Monthly (Lombard, IL) *Unable to locate*
Electronic Green Journal (EGJ) (Moscow, ID) **7913**
Electronic House (Wayland, MA) **14614**
Electronic Imaging (College Station, TX) **30040**
The Electronic Journal of Combinatorics (Clemson, SC) **28532**
Electronic Learning (Danbury, CT) **4739**
The Electronic Library (Medford, NJ) *Ceased*
Electronic Manufacturing (Libertyville, IL) *Ceased*
Electronic Manufacturing News (New York, NY) *Ceased*
Electronic Media (Detroit, MI) **14931**
Electronic Media; Journal of Broadcasting & (Washington, DC) **5576**
Electronic Musician (Emeryville, CA) **1877**
Electronic News (Chatsworth, CA) *Unable to locate*
The Electronic and Optical Publishing Review (Medford, NJ) *Ceased*
Electronic Packaging & Production (New York, NY) **21593**
Electronic Payments International (Atlanta, GA) *Unable to locate*
Electronic Product News **36016***
Electronic Products (Garden City, NY) **20638**
(Electronic Products and Technology); EP&T (Mississauga, ON, Can.) **36066**
Electronic Publisher; In-Plant Printer & (Libertyville, IL) **9078**
Electronic Publishing (Nashua, NH) **18589**
Electronic Publishing (Hoboken, NJ) *Ceased*
Electronic Publishing Business (Los Altos, CA) *Unable to locate*
Electronic Purchasing **14394***
Electronic Retailer (Salamanca, NY) **23291**
Electronic Retailing (Los Angeles, CA) *Unable to locate*
Electronic Servicing & Technology (Port Washington, NY) **23126**
Electronic Systems Magazine; IEEE Aerospace and (New York, NY) **21843**
Electronic Systems; PCIM Power (Overland Park, KS) **11725**
Electronic Systems (TODAES); Design Automation of (New York, NY) **21545**
Electronic Testing; Journal of (New York, NY) **22059**
Electronic World News *Ceased*
Electronics (Cleveland, OH) *Ceased*
Electronics; Asian Sources (Phoenix, AZ) **786**
Electronics; Canadian (Markham, ON, Can.) **36016**
Electronics; Car Audio and (Anaheim, CA) **1402**
Electronics & Communications Abstracts Journal (Bethesda, MD) **13333**
Electronics and Communications in Japan (Hoboken, NJ) **18937**
Electronics Distribution Today (Stamford, CT) *Ceased*
Electronics; IEEE Transactions on Industrial (New York, NY) **21850**
Electronics; International Journal of High Speed (River Edge, NJ) **19509**
Electronics; Journal of Communications Technology and (Hoboken, NJ) **19016**
Electronics Magazine; Mobile (Torrance, CA) **3939**
Electronics; Military & Aerospace (Nashua, NH) **18597**
Electronics News for China (Evanston, IL) *Unable to locate*
Electronics Now **20722***
Electronics Now (Hauppauge, NY) **20717**
Electronics; Radiophysics and Quantum (New York, NY) **22623**
Electronics Specifier (Libertyville, IL) *Ceased*
Electronics and Technology Today (North York, ON, Can.) *Ceased*
Electronics Test (Manhasset, NY) *Ceased*
Electronics West (Tempe, AZ) *Ceased*
Electronique Industrielle et Commerciale (EIC) (Montreal, QC, Can.) **37114**
Electrophysiology; Journal of Cardiovascular (Armonk, NY) **20085**

Electrophysiology; PACE: Pacing and Clinical (Armonk, NY) **20090**
Electrophysiology Review; Cardiac (New York, NY) **21374**
Elegant Bride (Greensboro, NC) **23921**
Elegant Fashion (New York, NY) *Ceased*
Elegant Hair (New York, NY) *Ceased*
Elementary School Guidance & Counseling **31729***
The Elementary School Journal (Seattle, WA) *Unable to locate*
Elementary Science Education; Journal of (Macomb, IL) **9129**
Elementary Teacher's Ideas and Materials Workshop (Plainsboro, NJ) *Unable to locate*
Elepaio (Honolulu, HI) **7688**
The Elephant Ear **2078***
Elevator World (Mobile, AL) **319**
Eleven (Chicago, IL) **8365**
11 (New Wilmington, PA) **27322**
Eleventh Muse (Colorado Springs, CO) *Ceased*
ELF (Tonawanda, NY) *Ceased*
Elgin County Market (St. Thomas, ON, Can.) **36361**
The Elgin Echo (Elgin, IA) **10871**
Elgin Television Association (Elgin, OR) **26309**
(ELH); English Literary History (Baltimore, MD) **13159**
Eligible (Sherman Oaks, CA) **3762**
Eliot—George Henry Lewes Studies; George (DeKalb, IL) **8735**
Elite Cars (Lincolnwood, IL) *Ceased*
Elite; North Shore Today's (Syosset, NY) **23381**
Elizabeth City News (Clark, NJ) **18748**
Elizabeth-Hanover Gazette **8904***
Elizabeth Weekly News **8904***
Elizabethton Star (Elizabethton, TN) **29179**
Elizabethtown Chronicle (Elizabethtown, PA) **26865**
Elk City Daily News (Elk City, OK) *Unable to locate*
The Elk County Citizen-Advance News (Longton, KS) **11613**
Elk Grove Citizen (Galt, CA) **1993**
Elk Grove-Laguna Neighbors (Elk Grove, CA) **1872**
Elk Grove Neighbors **1872***
Elk Grove Times (Elk Grove Village, IL) **8831**
Elk Horn (Ridgway, PA) **27934**
Elk Horn-Kimballton Review **10872***
Elk Point Review (Elk Point, AB, Can.) **34763**
Elk River Star News (Elk River, MN) **15878**
Elk River Star Shopper (Elk River, MN) **15879**
Elk Valley Miner (Fernie, BC, Can.) *Ceased*
Elk Valley Times (Fayetteville, TN) **29188**
(Elkhart County Edition); The Paper (Goshen, IN) **10027**
Elkhart Tri-State News (Elkhart, KS) **11422**
Elkhart TV Cable Co. **11423***
Elkhorn Exchange **18002***
The Elkhorn Independent (Elkhorn, WI) **33688**
Elkhorn Valley-Post **18002***
Elkhorn Valley Shopper (West Point, NE) **18311**
Elkhound Annual (Wheat Ridge, CO) *Ceased*
The Elkhound Quarterly (Wheat Ridge, CO) *Ceased*
Elko Daily Free Press (Elko, NV) **18335**
Elko Independent (Elko, NV) *Unable to locate*
The Elks Magazine (Chicago, IL) **8366**
The Elkton Record (Elkton, SD) **28851**
Elle (New York, NY) **21594**
Elle Canada (New York, NY) **21595**
Elle Decor (New York, NY) **21596**
The Ellenville Press (Ellenville, NY) **20569**
Ellery Queen's Mystery Magazine (New York, NY) **21597**
The Ellinwood Leader (Ellinwood, KS) **11424**
The Elliott County News (West Liberty, KY) *Ceased*
ellipse (Fredericton, NB, Can.) **35393**
Ellis County Capital (Arnett, OK) **25750**
The Ellis County News **11480***
Ellis County News (Ennis, TX) **30308**
Ellis County News; Northwest Oklahoman and (Shattuck, OK) **26060**
Ellis County Star (Hays, KS) **11479**
The Ellis Review (Ellis, KS) **11425**
The Ellsworth American (Ellsworth, ME) **12955**
The Ellsworth Reporter (Ellsworth, KS) **11426**
Ellsworth Voice **15699***
Ellwood City Ledger (Ellwood City, PA) **26871**
Elm City Citizen Newspaper (Milford, CT) **4954**
Elm Grove Elm Leaves (New Berlin, WI) **34170**
Elm Leaves (Glenview, IL) *Unable to locate*
Elm Street (Toronto, ON, Can.) **36582**
Elma Reminder (Elma, IA) *Unable to locate*
Elma Review (Elma, NY) **20570**
Elmer Times (Elmer, NJ) **18793**
The Elmhurst College Magazine **8837***
Elmhurst College Magazine **8837***
Elmhurst Press (Oak Brook, IL) **9349**
Elmhurst Suburban LIFE (Oak Brook, IL) **9350**
The Elmira Independent (Elmira, ON, Can.) **35805**
Elmont Herald (Elmont, NY) **20572**
Elmont Pennysaver (Elmont, HI) **7663**
Elmont Shopper's Guide (Ontario, ON, Can.) **36163**
Elmvale Lance (Elmvale, ON, Can.) **35806**

3340

Numbers cited in bold after listings are entry numbers rather than page numbers.

Exhibit Builder (Woodland Hills, CA) **4103**
Exhibit Manager; TradeShow & (Santa Monica, CA) **3718**
Exhibit Marketing Magazine (Florham Park, NJ) **18824**
Exhibition Management; Journal of Convention & (Binghamton, NY) **20168**
Exhibitor Relations Co. (Encino, CA) **37898**
Exhibitor Times (Phoenix, AZ) **803**
Exile (Toronto, ON, Can.) **36586**
Exit (Rochester, NY) *Unable to locate*
Exit 13 Magazine (Fanwood, NJ) **18815**
Exito (Miami, FL) *Unable to locate*
Exito! (Chicago, IL) **8371**
Exodus Magazine (Toronto, ON, Can.) **36587**
Exotic Market Review (Bowie, TX) **29940**
Exotic Pet Medicine; Seminars in Avian and (Philadelphia, PA) **27660**
Expansion Management (Prairie Village, KS) **11761**
Expecting (Etobicoke, ON, Can.) **35815**
Expecting; Parents (New York, NY) **22527**
L'Expediteur **37038***
Expeditions; Great (Raleigh, NC) **24137**
Experience (Pittsburg, CA) **2846**
Experimental Aging Research (Gaithersburg, MD) **13539**
Experimental Agriculture (New York, NY) **21663**
Experimental Analysis of Behavior; Journal of the (Morgantown, WV) **33394**
Experimental and Applied Acarology (New York, NY) **21664**
Experimental Astronomy (New York, NY) **21665**
Experimental Cell Research (San Diego, CA) **3147**
Experimental and Clinical Immunogenetics (Farmington, CT) *Ceased*
Experimental Economics (New York, NY) **21666**
Experimental Eye Research (San Diego, CA) **3148**
Experimental Heat Transfer (Berkeley, CA) **1520**
Experimental Hematology (Charlottesville, VA) *Unable to locate*
Experimental Lung Research (Research Triangle Park, NC) **24184**
Experimental Mathematics (Natick, MA) **14346**
Experimental Mechanics (Bethel, CT) **4697**
Experimental Medicine; The Journal of (New York, NY) **22068**
Experimental Medicine; The Journal of Trace Elements in (Hoboken, NJ) **19051**
Experimental and Molecular Pathology (San Diego, CA) **3149**
Experimental Mycology **3159***
Experimental Neurology (San Diego, CA) **3150**
Experimental Parasitology (San Diego, CA) **3151**
Experimental Physiology (New York, NY) **21667**
Experimental Science (DRJES); The Dawson Research Journal of (Westmount, QC, Can.) **37442**
Experimental Techniques (Bethel, CT) **4698**
Experimental Zoology; The Journal of (Hoboken, NJ) **19022**
Expert Evidence (New York, NY) **21668**
Expert Systems (Medford, NJ) *Ceased*
Expert Systems (New York, NY) *Ceased*
Expert Systems; International Journal of (Urbana, IL) **9711**
Expert Systems Review **18987***
The Explicator (Washington, DC) **5486**
Explorations in Economic History (San Diego, CA) **3152**
Explorations in Renaissance Culture (Springfield, MO) **17598**
explore (Toronto, ON, Can.) **36588**
Explore Kansas City **17167***
Explore KC **17167***
Explorer (Los Angeles, CA) **2267**
Explorer (Cleveland, OH) **24894**
The Explorer (Sioux Lookout, ON, Can.) *Unable to locate*
Explorer; Catholic (Romeoville, IL) **9552**
Explorer; Nebraska & Iowa (Blair, NE) **17957**
Explorer; South American (Ithaca, NY) **20814**
Exploring (Irving, TX) *Ceased*
Expo (Overland Park, KS) **11712**
Expo/Extra **25623***
The Exponent (Huntsville, AL) **269**
The Exponent (Brooklyn, MI) **14838**
Exponent (East Grand Forks, MN) **15865**
The Exponent (Bozeman, MT) **17752**
The Exponent (Berea, OH) **24676**
Exponent (Platteville, WI) **34240**
Exponent II (Arlington, MA) **13818**
Export America (Washington, DC) **5487**
Export/Exportador (Elk Grove Village, IL) *Unable to locate*
Export Leads (Poulsbo, WA) **32897**
Export Magazine; Northeast (Manchester, NH) **18561**
Export Report (Portland, OR) **26477**
Export Today Magazine **5488***
Export Today's Global Business Magazine (Washington, DC) **5488**

The Exporter (New York, NY) **21669**
Exports; British Columbia Origin (Victoria, BC, Can.) **35211**
Exports of Canadian Grain and Wheat Flour (Winnipeg, MB, Can.) **35328**
The Expositor (Sparta, TN) **29613**
Expositor (Sparta, TN) **29612**
Express **29358***
The Express **26850***
The Express **19820***
Express (Berkeley, CA) *Unable to locate*
The Express (Colon, MI) *Ceased*
The Express (Marion, NC) **24055**
The Express (Fordville, ND) **24441**
The Express (Lock Haven, PA) **27204**
Express (Pleasanton, TX) **30952**
Express (Fort McMurray, AB, Can.) *Unable to locate*
The Express (St. John's, NL, Can.) **35487**
Express (St. John's, NL, Can.) **35486**
The Express (Meaford, ON, Can.) **36036**
L'Express (Orleans, ON, Can.) *Unable to locate*
L'Express (Toronto, ON, Can.) **36589**
L'Express (Drummondville, QC, Can.) **36989**
L'Express d'Outremont (Outremont, QC, Can.) **37264**
Express Line **19932***
The Express Line (El Cajon, CA) *Ceased*
L'Express de L'Ontario **36589***
Express-News (San Antonio, TX) **31029**
Express Shopper (Scottsbluff, NE) **18264**
Express Shopper (Memphis, TN) *Ceased*
Express-Star (Chickasha, OK) **25785**
Express du Sud-Est (Moncton, NB, Can.) *Unable to locate*
The Express-Times (Easton, PA) **26850**
Expression (Mesa, AZ) *Ceased*
Expressions (Montreal, QC, Can.) *Unable to locate*
The Expressline (Wilkes Barre, PA) **28166**
Exquisite Corpse (Baton Rouge, LA) *Ceased*
Extended Care Product News (Malvern, PA) **27211**
Extension (Chicago, IL) **8372**
Extension Connection (Hamden, NY) *Ceased*
Extension Network-Ontario, Wayne, Yates Counties (Canandaigua, NY) *Ceased*
Extension News **23171***
Extension Review (Pittsburgh, PA) *Unable to locate*
Exteriors (New York, NY) *Ceased*
EXTRA (Indianola, IA) **10964**
Extra (Great Bend, KS) *Ceased*
EXTRA! (New York, NY) **21670**
Extra (Hickory, NC) **23987**
Extra (Medford, OR) *Ceased*
The Extra *Ceased*
Extra; El (Dallas, TX) **30154**
Extra Equity for Homebuyers (Greens Farms, CT) **4871**
The Extra Express (Putnam, CT) *Unable to locate*
Extra Income (Santa Barbara, CA) *Unable to locate*
Extra; ISU (Pocatello, ID) **7945**
The Extra Mile (Coal Township, PA) **37899**
Extra Newspaper Features (Rochester, MN) **37900**
The Extra Shopper (Phillips, WI) **34238**
Extra Shopping Guide (Hoopeston, IL) **9004**
The Extra Touch Online (Livonia, MI) **15315**
Extrapolation (Brownsville, TX) **29960**
Extraprize **1912***
Extreme Environments; The Journal of Human Performance in (Orlando, FL) **6499**
ExtremeInk.com (Sherman Oaks, CA) **37901**
Extremes (New York, NY) **21671**
The Eye (Wilmington, DE) *Ceased*
Eye (New York, NY) *Unable to locate*
Eye (Greensboro, NC) *Ceased*
Eye (Toronto, ON, Can.) **36590**
Eye and Contact Lens: Science and Clinical Practice (Baltimore, MD) **13160**
Eye Research; Experimental (San Diego, CA) **3148**
Eye Weekly (Toronto, ON, Can.) **36591**
Eyecare Business (Fort Washington, PA) **26930**
EyeNet (San Francisco, CA) **3359**
Eyes Magazine (Los Angeles, CA) *Unable to locate*
Eyewitness (Wayne, MI) **15672**

F

F & B Marketplace (Lenexa, KS) *Ceased*
FAA Aviation News (Washington, DC) **5489**
Fabric Architecture (Roseville, MN) **16331**
Fabric Products Review; Industrial (Roseville, MN) **16333**
Fabricare (Silver Spring, MD) **13726**
Fabricare Canada (Oakville, ON, Can.) **36144**
Fabricating; Forming & (Dearborn, MI) **14902**
Fabrication; Welding Design & (Cleveland, OH) **24961**
The FABRICATOR (Rockford, IL) **9527**
Fabrics & Architecture **16331***

Fabrics Report; Geotechnical (Roseville, MN) **16332**
Face Magazine (Southwest Harbor, ME) **13058**
Faceoff (Winnipeg, MB, Can.) *Ceased*
Faces (Peterborough, NH) **18623**
Faces International (Los Angeles, CA) *Unable to locate*
Facets **8251***
Facial Plastic Surgery (New York, NY) **21672**
Facial Plastic Surgery Clinics (Philadelphia, PA) **27466**
Facilities Design & Management (New York, NY) **21673**
Facilities & Event Management (New York, NY) **21674**
Facilities Planning News **2727***
Facility Management Journal (Houston, TX) **30472**
Facility Manager (Coppell, TX) **30073**
Facility News **13642***
FacilityCare (Arlington Heights, IL) **8023**
The FACS CPA Chronicle (Hartford, CT) *Ceased*
Facts (Redlands, CA) **2903**
Facts; Brazosport (Clute, TX) **30033**
Facts about Coal (Washington, DC) *Ceased*
Facts and Comparisons (St. Louis, MO) **17437**
Facts Newspaper (Seattle, WA) **32964**
Facts Shoppers' Guide (Redlands, CA) *Ceased*
Factsheet Five (San Francisco, CA) *Unable to locate*
FAD Magazine (San Anselmo, CA) **3083**
The FADER (New York, NY) **21675**
Fag Rag (Boston, MA) **13891**
Fair Dealer (Sacramento, CA) **2999**
Fair Guide; The Crafts (Corte Madera, CA) **1770**
Fair Haven Register **23178***
Fair Lawn-Elmwood Park-Saddle Brook Shopper (Fair Lawn, NJ) **18806**
Fair Times (Arnold, MO) *Unable to locate*
Fair World; Horseman and (Lexington, KY) **12166**
Fairbanks Cablevision (Aurora, IN) **9791**
Fairbanks Daily News-Miner (Fairbanks, AK) **567**
Fairborn Daily Herald (Fairborn, OH) **25187**
Fairbury Cablevision **18008***
Fairbury Journal-News (Fairbury, NE) **18005**
Fairchild News Service (New York, NY) **37902**
Fairfax Chief (Fairfax, OK) **25831**
The Fairfax Connection (Fairfax, VA) **32015**
The Fairfax Forum (Fairfax, MO) **17053**
Fairfax Journal (Alexandria, VA) **31671**
The Fairfax News (Fairfax, VT) **31543**
Fairfax Standard (Fairfax, MN) **15888**
Fairfield Advertiser; Lancaster (Lancaster, OH) **25290**
Fairfield Citizen-News (Fairfield, CT) **4787**
Fairfield County Business Journal (Hawthorne, NY) *Unable to locate*
Fairfield County Business Times (New Haven, CT) **4988**
Fairfield County Catholic (Bridgeport, CT) **4714**
Fairfield County Weekly (Stamford, CT) **5149**
Fairfield County Woman (Stamford, CT) *Unable to locate*
Fairfield Echo (Fairfield, OH) **25188**
The Fairfield Independent **28787***
Fairfield Leader (Fairfield, OH) **25189**
The Fairfield Ledger (Fairfield, IA) **10882**
Fairfield Minuteman (New Milford, CT) **5029**
The Fairfield Recorder (Fairfield, TX) **30311**
Fairfield Sun Times (Fairfield, MT) **17789**
Fairfield Times **17789***
Fairfield Times-Wheat Center News **17789***
Fairhope Courier (Robertsdale, AL) **436**
Fairless Hills Express (Burlington, NJ) **18708**
Fairmont Photo Press (Fairmont, MN) **15889**
Fairplay Flume; Park County Republican and The (Bailey, CO) **4152**
Fairport/Penfield Community News (Fairport, NY) *Unable to locate*
Fairport Perinton Herald Mail (Pittsford, NY) *Ceased*
Fairport- Post; Perinton- (Fairport, NY) **20590**
Fairpress (Westport, CT) *Ceased*
Fairs and Expos (Springfield, MO) **17599**
Fairview Enterprise (Fairview, KS) **11439**
Fairview Heights/O'Fallon Journal (Swansea, IL) **9677**
Fairview Heights Tribune (Mascoutah, IL) **9151**
The Fairview Post (Fairview, AB, Can.) **34764**
Fairview Republican (Fairview, OK) **25833**
Fairway Sun (Overland Park, KS) *Ceased*
Fairways; California (Chicago, IL) **8297**
Faith and Fellowship (Fergus Falls, MN) **15896**
Faith and Philosophy (Wilmore, KY) **12451**
Faith & Reason (Front Royal, VA) **32094**
The Faithist Journal **730***
Falcon **1477***
Falcon (Ottawa, ON, Can.) *Unable to locate*
Falcon Cable **33191***
Falcon Cable **32749***
Falcon Cable (Gilroy, CA) **2005**
Falcon Cable (Klamath Falls, OR) **26388**
Falcon Cable (Wharton, TX) **31285**
Falcon Cable (Ellensburg, WA) **32749**

Falcon Cable Systems (Reedsport, OR) *Unable to locate*
Falcon Cable TV (Scottsboro, AL) **447**
Falcon Cable TV (Mojave, CA) **2575**
Falcon Cable TV (Perryville, MO) *Unable to locate*
Falcon Cable TV (Sedalia, MO) **17571**
Falcon Cable TV (Plattsburgh, NY) **23104**
Falcon Cable TV (Kill Devil Hills, NC) **24021**
Falcon Cable TV (Lakeview, OR) **26407**
Falcon Cable TV (Beaufort, SC) *Unable to locate*
Falcon Cable TV (Brownsville, TN) **29072**
Falcon Cable TV (Palacios, TX) **30895**
Falcon Cable TV (Portland, TX) **30960**
Falcon Cablevision **11775***
Falcon Cablevision (Malibu, CA) *Unable to locate*
Falcon Cablevision (CedarTown, GA) *Unable to locate*
Falcon Cablevision (Port Orchard, WA) **32892**
Falcon Cablevision of Corbin Inc. (Corbin, KY) **12021**
Falcon Capital Cable (Washington, MO) **17706**
Falcon/Capital Cable Partners L.P. (St. Louis, MO) *Unable to locate*
Falcon CATV Inc. (Onancock, VA) **32317**
Falcon Classic Cable (Morganton, NC) **24075**
Falcon; Fayette (Somerville, TN) **29608**
The Falcon Flyer **4651***
Falcon; Slovak Catholic (Passaic, NJ) **19416**
Falcon); Sokol Polski (Polish (Pittsburgh, PA) **27844**
Falcon Telecable (Denver, CO) **4368**
Falcon Telecable (Lincoln City, OR) *Unable to locate*
Falcon Video Communications (Weiser, ID) **7999**
Falconnews **4651***
Falcon's Eye (Misenheimer, NC) **24064**
Falfurrias Facts (Falfurrias, TX) **30313**
Fallon County Times (Baker, MT) **17722**
Fallon Eagle Standard; Lahontan Valley News/ (Fallon, NV) **18345**
The Falmouth Outlook (Pendleton, KY) **12355**
FAMA (Teaneck, NJ) *Unable to locate*
Famersville Herald **1907***
Familial Cancer (New York, NY) **21676**
Families (Toronto, ON, Can.) **36592**
Families; Adoptive (New York, NY) **21150**
Families; Children and (Alexandria, VA) **31654**
FAMILIES Magazine; North Florida (Jacksonville, FL) **6216**
FAMILIES Magazine; Washington (Herndon, VA) **32166**
Families in Michiana (La Porte, IN) *Unable to locate*
Families in Society (Milwaukee, WI) **34067**
Families, Systems & Health (Rochester, NY) **23225**
Families; Tidewater Virginia (Williamsburg, VA) **32619**
Families; WestCoast (Vancouver, BC, Can.) **35179**
The Family (Boston, MA) *Ceased*
Family (Kansas City, MO) *Ceased*
Family (Durham, NC) *Ceased*
Family Advocate (Chicago, IL) **8373**
Family Business (Philadelphia, PA) *Unable to locate*
Family Business Review (San Francisco, CA) *Unable to locate*
Family; Chesapeake (Annapolis, MD) **13092**
Family Chronicle (Toronto, ON, Can.) **36593**
Family Circle (New York, NY) **21677**
Family Communication; Journal of (Norfolk, VA) **32286**
Family & Community Health (New York, NY) **21678**
Family Computin- (Danbury, CT) **4740**
Family Computing **4741***
Family and Conciliation Courts Review **3870***
Family and Consumer Sciences Research Journal (Thousand Oaks, CA) **3869**
Family Court Review (Thousand Oaks, CA) **3870**
The Family Digest (Fort Wayne, IN) **9967**
Family Economics and Nutrition Review (Alexandria, VA) **31672**
Family Economics Review **31672***
Family; Essex County (Mountainside, NJ) **19316**
Family Features Editorial Syndicate Inc. (Shawnee Mission, KS) **37903**
The Family Friend (Milwaukee, WI) **34068**
Family Futures (Mahwah, NJ) *Ceased*
Family Genealogies *Ceased*
The Family Handyman (New York, NY) *Unable to locate*
Family; The History of the (Newark, DE) **5273**
Family History Magazine; Everton's (Logan, UT) **31348**
Family and Home-Office Computing **4741***
Family Issues; Journal of (Thousand Oaks, CA) **3889**
Family; Journal of Marriage and (Minneapolis, MN) **16088**
Family Law Quarterly (Topeka, KS) **11817**
Family Law Quarterly; Canadian (Toronto, ON, Can.) **36497**
Family Life (New York, NY) **21679**
Family & Life; Jewish (Newton, MA) **14402**
Family; Little Rock (Little Rock, AR) **1233**
Family Living (Anaheim, CA) *Unable to locate*

The Family Magazine (Kansas City, KS) *Unable to locate*
Family Magazine; Boise (Boise, ID) **7803**
Family Magazine; Los Angeles (Encino, CA) **1884**
Family Magazine; San Diego (San Diego, CA) **3263**
Family Magazine; South Bay (Encino, CA) **1885**
Family Magazine; Ventura (Encino, CA) **1886**
Family Medicine (San Antonio, TX) **31030**
Family Medicine; Archives of (Philadelphia, PA) **27383**
Family; Middlesex County (Mountainside, NJ) **19317**
Family; Morris County (Mountainside, NJ) **19318**
Family Motor Coaching (Cincinnati, OH) **24797**
Family; New York (Mamaroneck, NY) **20987**
Family Nursing; Journal of (Thousand Oaks, CA) **3890**
Family PC (New York, NY) **21680**
Family Pet (Tampa, FL) *Unable to locate*
Family Physician; Canadian (Mississauga, ON, Can.) **36058**
Family Planning Perspectives **22545***
Family Planning Perspectives; International (New York, NY) **21897**
Family Practice (Toronto, ON, Can.) *Unable to locate*
Family Practice; Clinics in (Philadelphia, PA) **27414**
Family Practice; Internet Journal of (Sugar Land, TX) **31143**
Family Practice; Journal of the American Board of (Seattle, WA) **32976**
Family Practice Management (Leawood, KS) **11584**
Family Practice News (Rockville, MD) **13678**
Family Practice Recertification (Jamesburg, NJ) **19129**
Family Process (Rochester, NY) *Unable to locate*
Family Psychology; Journal of (Washington, DC) **5591**
Family Psychology Review; Clinical Child and (New York, NY) **21429**
Family Psychotherapy; Journal of (Hammond, IN) **10052**
Family Records, TODAY (Kansas City, MO) **17168**
Family Relations (Minneapolis, MN) **16077**
Family Relations: Journal of Applied Family of Child Studies **16077***
Family Review; Marriage and (Indianapolis, IN) **10150**
Family Safety & Health (Itasca, IL) **9013**
Family Shopper (Waltham, MA) *Ceased*
Family Social Work; Journal of (Binghamton, NY) **20173**
Family Stations Inc. (Oakland, CA) **37632**
Family Studies Abstracts; Sage (Thousand Oaks, CA) **3912**
Family Studies; Journal of Child and (New York, NY) **22023**
Family Studies; Journal of Comparative (Calgary, AB, Can.) **34651**
Family Support Magazine; America's (Chicago, IL) **8262**
Family Systems (Washington, DC) **5490**
Family Systems Medicine **23225***
Family Therapy (San Diego, CA) **3153**
Family Therapy; Contemporary (New York, NY) **21493**
Family Therapy; Journal of Marital & (Lubbock, TX) **30713**
Family Therapy News (Washington, DC) **5491**
Family Times (Philadelphia, PA) **27467**
Family Vacations (New York, NY) *Unable to locate*
Family Violence; Journal of (New York, NY) **22069**
Family Weekly **32259***
Family; Westchester (Mamaroneck, NY) **20988**
Family Word Seek Puzzles (Norwalk, CT) **5059**
Family; Zellers (Toronto, ON, Can.) **36797**
Family.com (IFF); Interfaith (Newton, MA) **14400**
FamilyFun (Northampton, MA) **14428**
FamilyNet (Fort Worth, TX) **37750**
The Famuan (Tallahassee, FL) **6704**
The Fan (Norristown, PA) *Unable to locate*
Fancy Food **8374***
Fancy Food & Culinary Products (Chicago, IL) **8374**
Fanfare (Tenafly, NJ) **19613**
Fannin County Special (Bonham, TX) **29933**
Fannon Cable TV Co. (New Tazewell, TN) **29543**
Fantastic Films (Evanston, IL) *Ceased*
Fantasy & Science Fiction; The Magazine of (Hoboken, NJ) **19055**
Fantasy Sports (Iola, WI) **33825**
Fantasy Tapes (River Edge, NJ) *Unable to locate*
Fanwood Press; Scotch Plains- (Scotch Plains, NJ) **19534**
The Far East **18256***
Far East Business (Des Plaines, IL) *Ceased*
Far Eastern Affairs (Minneapolis, MN) **16078**
Far Gone (Lafayette, LA) *Unable to locate*
Far Northeast Citizen Sentinel (Horsham, PA) **27060**
Far Rockaway Pennysaver (Far Rockaway, HI) **7664**
Far West Farm Edition; Fastline— (Buckner, KY) **11971**
Farandula USA (Santa Ana, CA) **3625**
Faribault Area Shopper (Faribault, MN) *Ceased*
Faribault County Register (Blue Earth, MN) **15762**

Farina News (Farina, IL) **8884**
Farm Bureau News; Alabama **360***
Farm Bureau News; Arizona (Phoenix, AZ) **777**
Farm Bureau News; Georgia (Macon, GA) **7381**
Farm Bureau News; Mississippi (Jackson, MS) **16702**
Farm Bureau News; Nebraska (Lincoln, NE) **18100**
Farm Bureau News; San Joaquin (San Joaquin, CA) **3507**
Farm Bureau News; Show Me Missouri (Jefferson City, MO) **17133**
Farm Bureau News; Tennessee (Columbia, TN) **29138**
Farm Bureau News; Virginia (Richmond, VA) **32461**
Farm Bureau Press **1229***
Farm Bureau Spokesman; Montana (Bozeman, MT) **17753**
Farm Bureau's Rural Route (Madison, WI) **33937**
Farm Chemicals (Willoughby, OH) **25658**
Farm Chemicals International (Willoughby, OH) **25659**
Farm Chronicle (Palatine Bridge, NY) **23074**
Farm Collector (Topeka, KS) **11818**
Farm Computer News (Des Moines, IA) *Ceased*
Farm and Country **23074***
Farm & Country (Toronto, ON, Can.) *Unable to locate*
Farm and Dairy (Salem, OH) **25505**
Farm Edition; Fastline—Dakota (Buckner, KY) **11969**
Farm Edition; Fastline—Far West (Buckner, KY) **11971**
Farm Edition; Fastline—Illinois (Buckner, KY) **11974**
Farm Edition; Fastline—Indiana (Buckner, KY) **11975**
Farm Edition; Fastline—Iowa (Buckner, KY) **11976**
Farm Edition; Fastline—Kansas (Buckner, KY) **11977**
Farm Edition; Fastline—Kentucky (Buckner, KY) **11978**
Farm Edition; Fastline—Mid-Atlantic (Buckner, KY) **11979**
Farm Edition; Fastline—Mid-South (Buckner, KY) **11980**
Farm Edition; Fastline—Minnesota (Buckner, KY) **11982**
Farm Edition; Fastline—Missouri (Buckner, KY) **11983**
Farm Edition; Fastline—Nebraska (Buckner, KY) **11984**
Farm Edition; Fastline—Northeast (Buckner, KY) **11985**
Farm Edition; Fastline—Northwest (Buckner, KY) **11987**
Farm Edition; Fastline—Ohio (Buckner, KY) **11988**
Farm Edition; Fastline—Oklahoma (Buckner, KY) **11989**
Farm Edition; Fastline—Ontario (Buckner, KY) **11990**
Farm Edition; Fastline—Rocky Mountain (Buckner, KY) **11991**
Farm Edition; Fastline—Southeast (Buckner, KY) **11993**
Farm Edition; Fastline—Tennessee (Buckner, KY) **11994**
Farm Edition; Fastline—Texas (Buckner, KY) **11996**
Farm Edition; Fastline—Wisconsin (Buckner, KY) **11998**
Farm Equipment (Fort Atkinson, WI) **33708**
Farm Equipment Guide (Fort Dodge, IA) **10898**
Farm Equipment Quarterly (Exeter, ON, Can.) *Ceased*
Farm Focus (Halifax, NS, Can.) *Unable to locate*
Farm Futures (Onalaska, WI) *Unable to locate*
The Farm Gate and Regional Country News (Exeter, ON, Can.) **35825**
Farm & Home News **23306***
Farm and Home News (Nappanee, IN) **10335**
Farm and Home Pennysaver (Clinton, NY) **20471**
Farm & Home Research Quarterly (Brookings, SD) **28813**
Farm Impact (Mascoutah, IL) **9152**
Farm Industry News (Minneapolis, MN) **16079**
Farm Journal (Philadelphia, PA) **27468**
Farm Light & Power (Regina, SK, Can.) *Unable to locate*
The Farm Market **37590***
Farm News (Marion, IN) *Unable to locate*
Farm News; Buckeye (Columbus, OH) **25002**
Farm News of Erie and Wyoming Counties (East Aurora, NY) **20542**
Farm News; Michigan (Lansing, MI) **15282**
Farm News; U.S. (Denison, IA) **10767**
Farm News & Views (Oklahoma City, OK) **25963**
Farm & Power Equipment Dealer **17062***
Farm Press; California-Arizona (Overland Park, KS) **11701**
Farm Press; Delta (Minneapolis, MN) **16073**
Farm Press; Southeast (Minneapolis, MN) **16129**
Farm Press; Southwest (Minneapolis, MN) **16130**
Farm Press; Western (Minneapolis, MN) **16139**
Farm Pulp (Seattle, WA) **32965**
Farm/Ranch Exchange (Scottsbluff, NE) *Ceased*
Farm and Ranch Guide (Bismarck, ND) **24352**
Farm & Ranch Living (Greendale, WI) **33762**

Numbers cited in bold after listings are entry numbers rather than page numbers.

Government Purchasing Guide (Toronto, ON, Can.) 36608

Government Recreation and Fitness (Westbury, NY) 23556

Government Relations Update (Alexandria, VA) 31676

Government Review; State and Local (Athens, GA) 6952

Government Subsidized Programs 2280*

Government Technology (Sacramento, CA) Unable to locate

Government; Technology in (Toronto, ON, Can.) 36756

Government Union Review (Vienna, VA) 32578

Government Video (Shawnee, KS) 11800

Gowanda Pennysaver (Hamburg, NY) Unable to locate

The Gowrie News (Gowrie, IA) 10927

GPS Solutions (Hoboken, NJ) 18955

GPS World (Eugene, OR) 26317

GQ (Gentlemen's Quarterly) (New York, NY) 21777

Grace Citizen (Preston, ID) Ceased

Grace Tidings (Omaha, NE) 18196

Graceville Enterprise, Clinton Advocate 15800*

The Graceville News (Graceville, FL) 6173

Graduate Computerworld (Chatsworth, CA) Ceased

Graduate School of Public Affairs 32990*

The Graduate, University of Toronto Alumni Magazine 36781*

Graduate Women 5309*

Graduating Engineer 8860*

Graduating Engineer & Computer Careers (Evanston, IL) 8860

The Graettinger Times (Graettinger, IA) 10928

Graffiti; Le (Montreal, QC, Can.) 37161

Grafton Cable Communications Inc. (Grafton, OH) 25219

Grafton Sentinal 33325*

The Graham Leader (Graham, TX) 30402

Graham News Syndicate (Brooklyn, NY) 37928

Graham Star (Robbinsville, NC) 24200

Grail (Ottawa, ON, Can.) Ceased

Grain (Saskatoon, SK, Can.) Unable to locate

Grain Age (Eden Prairie, MN) Unable to locate

Grain; Feed & (Fort Atkinson, WI) 33709

Grain & Feed Marketing (Seattle, WA) 32969

Grain; Grass & (Manhattan, KS) 11620

Grain Journal (Decatur, IL) Unable to locate

Grain and Wheat Flour; Exports of Canadian (Winnipeg, MB, Can.) 35328

Grain; World (Kansas City, MO) 17205

Grainews (Winnipeg, MB, Can.) 35330

Grammar Gremlins (Knoxville, TN) Ceased

Grand Bend Sun (Dresden, ON, Can.) 35788

The Grand Blanc News (Grand Blanc, MI) 15083

Grand Blanc Press (Fenton, MI) Ceased

Grand Canyon News; Williams- (Williams, AZ) 1010

Grand Centre-Cold Lake Sun 34687*

The Grand Falls Advertiser 35484*

Grand Forks Herald (San Jose, CA) 3518

Grand Island Independent (Grand Island, NE) 18025

Grand Island PennySaver (Grand Island, NE) 20677

Grand Junction Globe Free Press (Grand Junction, IA) Unable to locate

Grand Lake! Magazine (Grove, OK) Unable to locate

Grand Lake Shopper's Guide (Grove, OK) Unable to locate

The Grand Ledge Independent (Charlotte, MI) 14870

Grand Marais Pilot & Pictured Rocks Review (Seney, MI) 15534

Grand Prairie Herald (Hazen, AR) 1172

Grand Prairie News (Arlington, TX) Ceased

Grand Rapids Advance (Grand Rapids, MI) 15094

Grand Rapids Business Journal (Grand Rapids, MI) Unable to locate

Grand Rapids Guest Book (Grand Rapids, MI) Unable to locate

Grand Rapids Magazine (Grand Rapids, MI) 15095

Grand Rapids Manney Shopper (Two Harbors, MN) Unable to locate

Grand Rapids Parent (Grand Rapids, MI) Unable to locate

The Grand Rapids Press (Grand Rapids, MI) 15096

The Grand Rapids Times (Grand Rapids, MI) 15097

The Grand River Sachem (Caledonia, ON, Can.) 35721

Grand Saline Sun (Austin, TX) Unable to locate

Grand Street (New York, NY) 21778

Grand Terrace City News (Colton, CA) 1742

Grand Times (El Cerrito, CA) 1861

The Grand Trunk Poplar Press (Evansburg, AB, Can.) Unable to locate

Grand Valley Business Times 4477*

Grand Valley East Advance (Caledonia, MI) 14851

Grand Valley West Advance (Jenison, MI) 15228

Grande Cache Mountaineer (Grande Cache, AB, Can.) 34773

Grande Prairie This Week (Grande Prairie, AB, Can.) Unable to locate

Grandmasters (San Francisco, CA) Unable to locate

Grandview Exponent (Grandview, MB, Can.) 35269

Grandview Herald (Grandview, WA) 32783

Grandview Tribune (Grandview, TX) 30408

The Grange News 32862*

Granger News (Cedar Park, TX) Unable to locate

Granger; Ohio (Columbus, OH) 25045

Granite City Journal (Warrenton, MO) 17684

Granite City Press Record (Collinsville, IL) Unable to locate

Granite City Press Record Journal (Warrenton, MO) Unable to locate

Granite Falls Tribune 15934*

Granite State News (Wolfeboro, NH) 18654

Granite State Vacationer (Dover, NH) Ceased

The Grant City Times-Tribune (Grant City, MO) 17087

Grant County Herald (Herman, MN) 15950

Grant County Herald Independent (Lancaster, WI) 33907

Grant County Journal (Ephrata, WA) 32756

Grant County Journal; Medford Patriot-Star and (Medford, OK) 25915

Grant County News (Williamstown, KY) 12448

Grant County News (Elgin, ND) 24406

Grant County Press (Petersburg, WV) 33429

Grant County Review (Milbank, SD) 28893

Grant, Iowa, Lafayette Shopping News (Platteville, WI) 34241

Grant Park Gazette (Grant Park, IL) 8950

Grant Tribune Sentinel (Grant, NE) 18032

Grants Magazine (New York, NY) Ceased

Grants Pass Daily Courier (Grants Pass, OR) 26362

Grantsville Gazette (Grantsville, UT) Unable to locate

Granville Booster 25220*

Granville Sentinel (Granville, OH) 25223

Grape Grower Magazine (Fresno, CA) 1951

Grape Times (Tallahassee, FL) 6723

Grape Vine 35608*

Grapeland Cablevison 31208*

The Grapeland Messenger (Grapeland, TX) 30410

Grapeline Northwest (Pacific, WA) Ceased

Grapevine; Homeless (Cleveland, OH) 24908

Grapevine Independent (Rancho Cordova, CA) 2874

The Grapevine Sun (Grapevine, TX) 30412

Grapevine Weekly (Pittsburgh, PA) 27793

Graph Theory; Journal of (Hoboken, NJ) 19025

Graphic (Lake Mills, IA) 11024

The Graphic (Petoskey, MI) 15435

The Graphic (Stapleton, NE) 18286

The Graphic (Mc Lean, VA) Ceased

Graphic Arts Literature Abstracts (Rochester, NY) Ceased

Graphic Arts Monthly (New York, NY) 21779

Graphic Arts Product News (Chicago, IL) Ceased

Graphic Communicator (Washington, DC) 5519

Graphic Design: USA (New York, NY) Unable to locate

The Graphic Monthly (Mississauga, ON, Can.) 36069

Graphic Syndicate (Toronto, ON, Can.) Unable to locate

The Graphic Weekly (Malibu, CA) 2489

Graphical Models (San Diego, CA) 3164

Graphical Models (San Diego, CA) 3163

Graphical Models and Image Processing 3164*

Graphical Models and Image Processing 3163*

GraphiCommunicator 5519*

Graphics; ACM Transactions on (New York, NY) 21139

Graphics and Applications; IEEE Computer (Los Alamitos, CA) 2183

Graphics; Digital (Broomfield, CO) 4204

Graphics Journal; Engineering Design (West Lafayette, IN) 10546

Graphics Tools; Journal of (Natick, MA) 14347

Graphics World; Computer (Nashua, NH) 18588

Graphis (New York, NY) 21780

Graphoanalysis; Journal of (Chicago, IL) 8438

Grass & Grain (Manhattan, KS) 11620

Grass Management; Journal of Turf (Amherst, MA) 13799

Grasslands Review (Berea, OH) 24677

Grassroots Cable Systems (Crossville, TN) Unable to locate

Grassroots Editor (Brookings, SD) 28814

Gratiot County Herald (Ithaca, MI) 15219

Grave Tales (Prescott, AZ) Unable to locate

Gravenhurst Banner (Gravenhurst, ON, Can.) 35856

Gravenhurst Cable System Ltd. 35857*

Gravenhurst News (Bracebridge, ON, Can.) Unable to locate

Gravette News Herald (Gravette, AR) Unable to locate

Gravois Watson Times 17514*

Gray Areas (Broomall, PA) 26737

The Gray News (Gray, ME) 12966

Grays Harbor Beacon (Ocean Shores, WA) Unable to locate

Gray's Sporting Journal (Augusta, GA) 7099

Grayslake Review (Grayslake, IL) 8955

Grayslake Times (Grayslake, IL) 8956

Grayson Cable TV Co. Inc. (Charleston, WV) Unable to locate

Grayson County News-Gazette (Leitchfield, KY) 12157

Grayson County Shopper (Durant, OK) 25805

Grayson Journal-Enquirer (Grayson, KY) 12093

Grayson Report (San Juan Capistrano, CA) Ceased

Great American Crafts (Iola, WI) 33829

Great Basin Naturalist 31409*

Great Bend Tribune (Great Bend, KS) 11468

Great Body (New York, NY) Ceased

Great Commission Handbook (Evanston, IL) Ceased

Great Crosswords (New York, NY) Unable to locate

Great Dane Reporter (Riverside, CA) Unable to locate

Great Dane Shopping News (Oregon, WI) 34216

Great Expectations 36764*

Great Expeditions (Raleigh, NC) 24137

Great Falls Cable TV (Lancaster, SC) Unable to locate

The Great Falls Connection (Great Falls, VA) 32118

Great Falls Current 32423*

Great Falls, Inc.; TCI Cablevision of (Great Falls, MT) 17806

Great Falls Tribune (Great Falls, MT) 17799

Great Foods Magazine (Fort Lee, NJ) Ceased

Great Lake Entomologist (Ann Arbor, MI) 14751

Great Lakes Boating (Kenosha, WI) Unable to locate

Great Lakes Fisherman (Port Stanley, ON, Can.) Ceased

The Great Lakes Fruit Growers News 15568*

Great Lakes Pilot News (Ann Arbor, MI) 14752

Great Lakes Region; Group Tour Magazine (Holland, MI) 15168

Great Lakes Research; Journal of (Ann Arbor, MI) 14756

Great Lakes Sailor (Cleveland, OH) Ceased

Great Lakes Skier (Ann Arbor, MI) Ceased

Great Lakes Travel and Living (Port Clinton, OH) Unable to locate

The Great Lakes Vegetable Grower News 15570*

The Great Neck News (Hicksville, NY) Unable to locate

Great Neck Pennysaver (Farmingdale, NY) Ceased

Great Neck Record (Great Neck, NY) 20688

Great Neck Shopper's Guide (Huntington, NY) Unable to locate

Great Plains Cable 11390*

Great Plains Cable TV Inc. (Blair, NE) 17959

Great Plains Quarterly (Lincoln, NE) 18085

Great Plains Research (Lincoln, NE) 18086

Great Windsor Newsmagazine (Windsor, ON, Can.) Unable to locate

Greater Baton Rouge Business Report (Baton Rouge, LA) 12489

Greater Beloit Shopping News 33577*

The Greater Cincinnati Business Record (Cincinnati, OH) Ceased

Greater Hartford Business Review (Cromwell, CT) Ceased

Greater Hartford Communications Corp. 4913*

Greater Lubbock (Lubbock, TX) Ceased

Greater Media Cable 14694*

Greater Philadelphia Cablevision, Inc. (Philadelphia, PA) 27727

Greater Phoenix Jewish News 805*

Greater Pine Island Treetop Gazette (St. James City, FL) Unable to locate

Greater Pittsburgh Newcomer (Raleigh, NC) Ceased

Greater Portland Cable Advertising 26517*

Greater Portland Magazine (Portland, ME) Unable to locate

Greater Pugent Sound Apartment Guide (Bellevue, WA) Unable to locate

Greater Reading Area Merchandiser (Reading, PA) 27918

Greater Rochester Advertiser 20554*

Greater Rochester Cablevision, Inc. (Rochester, NY) 23242

Greater San Juan; Cable TV of (San Juan, PR) 28296

Greater Seattle InfoGuide (Woodinville, WA) 33213

The Greater Waterbury Business Digest 4941*

Greater Worcester Cablevision 14694*

GreatLander Bush Mailer (Anchorage, AK) 526

Grecque; La Tribune Canadienne (Montreal, QC, Can.) 37153

Greece Pennysaver (Rochester, NY) 23227

The Greece Post (Greece, NY) 20696

Greek Orthodox Theological Review (Brookline, MA) 14019

Greek, Roman, and Byzantine Studies (Durham, NC) 23823

Greek Sunday News (Boston, MA) Ceased

Greeley County Republican (Tribune, KS) 11848

Green Acres (Troy, KS) 11849

Green Anarchy (Eugene, OR) 26318

Green Bay News 35507*

Green Bay News-Chronicle (Green Bay, WI) 33740

Green Bay Press-Gazette (Green Bay, WI) **33741**
The Green Bay Register **33739***
Green County Spectrum (Xenia, OH) **25686**
Green Forest Tribune **1054***
Green Grass Syndicated Features (Toledo, OH) **37929**
Green Industry (Appleton, WI) *Ceased*
Green Lake County Reporter (Berlin, WI) **33583**
Green Library Journal **7913***
Green Line **23632***
The Green Man (Point Arena, CA) *Ceased*
Green Owl **17075***
Green Profit Magazine (Batavia, IL) **8053**
Green River Cable TV Co. (Green River, WY) **34533**
Green River Star (Green River, WY) **34532**
Green Saver; Lake View Resort and (Lake View, IA) **11026**
Green Sheet **5965***
The Green Sheet **26057***
Green Sheet Newspapers **31323***
Green Sheet-Shopping News *Ceased*
Green Sheet-The San Jacinto Valley Advertiser (Palm Desert, CA) *Ceased*
Green Tab-Northern Valley (Moundsville, WV) **33407**
Green Teacher (Toronto, ON, Can.) **36609**
The Green Thumb (Naples, NY) **37930**
Green Valley News & Sun (Green Valley, AZ) **722**
The Green and White (Saskatoon, SK, Can.) **37551**
Green World (Randolph, VT) **31580**
Greenacres/Lantana/Lake Worth Forum (Wellington, FL) **6843**
Greenacres/Suburban Lake Worth Town-Crier (West Palm Beach, FL) *Unable to locate*
Greenacres Thursday Paper (Chicago, IL) *Ceased*
Greenbelt News Review (Greenbelt, MD) **13558**
(Greenbelt); Spectrum (Greenbelt, MD) **13560**
Greenbrier Historical Society Journal (Lewisburg, WV) **33363**
Greenbrier Valley Ranger (Lewisburg, WV) **33364**
Greenbrier Valley Trader (Lewisburg, WV) **33365**
Greenbrook-North Plainfield Edition); The Journal ((Somerville, NJ) **19573**
Greenbrook-North Plainfield Journal **19573***
The Greenburgh Inquirer **23313***
Greenbush Area News (East Greenbush, NY) *Unable to locate*
Greendale News **35507***
Greendale Village Life (New Berlin, WI) **34175**
Greene County Democrat (Eutaw, AL) **208**
Greene County Herald (Leakesville, MS) **16744**
Greene County News (West Coxsackie, NY) **23540**
Greene County Record (Stanardsville, VA) **32552**
Greene County Shopper (Carrollton, IL) **8160**
Greene Prairie Press (Carrollton, IL) **8161**
The Greene Recorder (Greene, IA) **10929**
The Greeneville Sun (Greeneville, TN) **29212**
Greenfield Daily Times (Greenfield, OH) *Ceased*
Greenfield/Greendale Enterprise **34412***
Greenfield/Greendale Enterprise (Greenfield, WI) **33765**
Greenfield News (Greenfield, CA) *Unable to locate*
Greenfield Observer (New Berlin, WI) **34176**
The Greenfield Town Crier (Greenfield, MA) **14220**
Greenfield Vedette (Greenfield, MO) **17088**
Greenhorn Valley-News (Colorado City, CO) **4233**
Greenhouse Business (Rolling Meadows, IL) **9547**
Greenhouse Canada (Delhi, ON, Can.) **35770**
Greenhouse Grower (Willoughby, OH) **25660**
Greenhouse; Hobby (Bedford, MA) **13836**
Greenhouse Management and Production (Fort Worth, TX) **30341**
The Greenly Tribune (Greeley, CO) **4497**
Greenmaster (Richmond Hill, ON, Can.) *Unable to locate*
Greenpeace Magazine (Washington, DC) **5520**
Greenpoint Gazette (Brooklyn, NY) **20318**
Greenprints (Fairview, NC) **23876**
Green's Magazine (Regina, SK, Can.) **37530**
Greensboro News & Record **23930***
The Greensboro Review (Greensboro, NC) **23923**
The Greensboro Watchman (Greensboro, AL) **243**
The Greensburg Daily News (Greensburg, IN) **10043**
Greensburg; TCI of (Greensburg, PA) **26957**
Greensburg Times (Greensburg, IN) **10044**
The Greenup News (Greenup, KY) **12098**
Greenup Press (Greenup, IL) **8960**
The Greenville Advocate (Greenville, IL) **8961**
Greenville Black Star **28544***
Greenville Black Star (Columbia, SC) *Ceased*
Greenville Community News (Dover, DE) **5248**
Greenville Herald Banner (Greenville, TX) **30413**
Greenville Local (Greenville, NY) **20700**
The Greenville News (Greenville, SC) **28623**
Greenville Piedmont (Greenville, SC) *Ceased*
The Greenville Shopper (Greenville, MS) *Unable to locate*
The Greenwich Journal **20701***
Greenwich News (Norwalk, CT) *Ceased*
Greenwich Time (Greenwich, CT) **4874**

Greenwich Village Villager (New York, NY) *Unable to locate*
Greenwood Commonwealth (Greenwood, MS) **16644**
Greenwood Democrat (Greenwood, AR) **1162**
The Greenwood Gazette (Greenwood, IN) *Unable to locate*
Greenwood Lake News **20702***
Greenwood Lake and West Milford News (Greenwood Lake, NY) **20702**
Greenwood News (Franklin, IN) *Ceased*
The Greenwood and Southside Challenger (Greenwood, IN) **10046**
The Greer Citizen (Greer, SC) **28652**
The Greeter (Plentywood, MT) **17894**
Greetings Magazine (New York, NY) *Ceased*
Gregory Times Advocate (Gregory, SD) **28861**
Grenada Lake Herald (Grenada, MS) **16653**
Grenfell Sun (Grenfell, SK, Can.) **37472**
Grenfell Times (Grenfell, SK, Can.) *Ceased*
Gresham Gazette (Gresham, NE) *Ceased*
The Gresham Outlook (Gresham, OR) **26365**
Gretna Breeze (Gretna, NE) *Unable to locate*
Gretna Guide & News (Gretna, NE) **18033**
Grey Book (Blaine, WA) **32688**
Grey Panthers; Panthers' Plus, Canadian (Toronto, ON, Can.) **36695**
Greybull Standard (Greybull, WY) **34534**
Greybull Standard Tribune **34534***
The Greyhound (Baltimore, MD) **13167**
The Greyhound Review (Abilene, KS) **11334**
The Gridley Herald (Gridley, CA) **2032**
The Griffin (Buffalo, NY) **20380**
Griffin Daily News (Griffin, GA) **7311**
Griffin-Larrabee News Bureau (Washington, DC) *Unable to locate*
The Griffin Report of Food Marketing (Chicago, IL) *Unable to locate*
Griffin's Modern Grocer **18852***
Griffin's Tri-State Food News (Pittsburgh, PA) **27794**
Griffith News (Merrillville, IN) *Unable to locate*
Griffith News Feature Service Worldwide (Albany, NY) **37931**
The Griffith Observer (Los Angeles, CA) **2281**
The Griffon News (St. Joseph, MO) **17392**
The Grifton Times **23977***
Griggs County Sentinel-Courier (Cooperstown, ND) **24388**
Grimsby Cable TV Ltd. (Grimsby, ON, Can.) *Unable to locate*
The Grimsby Independent (Beansville, ON, Can.) **35671**
Grinnell Herald-Register (Grinnell, IA) **10931**
Grinnell Town & Country (Oakley, KS) *Ceased*
Griswold American (Griswold, IA) **10934**
Grit (Topeka, KS) **11821**
Grit and Steel (Gaffney, SC) **28616**
The Grizzly (Collegeville, PA) **26796**
Grizzly; Big Bear Life & the (Big Bear Lake, CA) **1580**
Grocer; Canadian (Toronto, ON, Can.) **36500**
Grocer; Iowa (Des Moines, IA) **10791**
Grocer; Military (Bethesda, MD) **13360**
Grocer; Minnesota (St. Paul, MN) **16392**
Grocer; Missouri (Springfield, MO) **17606**
Grocer; Modern (Hackensack, NJ) **18852**
Grocer Today Magazine (Burnaby, BC, Can.) **34900**
Grocer; Today's (South Miami, FL) **6686**
Grocer; Western (Winnipeg, MB, Can.) **35359**
Grocergram; IGA (Chicago, IL) **8404**
Grocers Journal of California (Long Beach, CA) *Ceased*
Grocers Journal; Oklahoma (Oklahoma City, OK) **25980**
Grocers Report (San Rafael, CA) **3601**
Grocer's Spotlight **8389***
Grocery Communications (Clearwater, FL) *Ceased*
Grocery Distribution (Hinsdale, IL) *Unable to locate*
Grocery Equipment Product News *Ceased*
Grocery Headquarters (Chicago, IL) **8389**
Grocery Marketing **8389***
Groene & Groene (DeLand, FL) **37932**
Groleau TV Cable Engineering (Sainte-Thecle, QC, Can.) **37383**
Groom & Board (Chicago, IL) *Unable to locate*
Grosse Pointe News (Grosse Pointe Farms, MI) **15140**
Grosse Pointe Times (Warren, MI) *Unable to locate*
The Grosse Pointer (Bingham Farms, MI) *Unable to locate*
Groton Regional Independent (Groton, SD) **28863**
Ground Water (Madison, WI) **33944**
Ground Water Canada (Exeter, ON, Can.) **35827**
Ground Water Monitoring and Remediation (Kalamazoo, MI) **15237**
Ground Water Monitoring Review **15237***
Grounds Maintenance (Overland Park, KS) **11713**
Groundskeeping Journal; Landscaping & (Vancouver, BC, Can.) **35152**
GROUP (New York, NY) *Unable to locate*

Group Decision and Negotiation (New York, NY) **21781**
Group Magazine (Loveland, CO) **4567**
Group & Organization Management (Albany, NY) **19989**
Group and Organization Studies **19989***
Group Practice Journal (Alexandria, VA) **31677**
Group Research Report *Ceased*
Group Tour Magazine Great Lakes Region (Holland, MI) **15168**
Group Tour Magazine Mid-Atlantic Region (Holland, MI) **15169**
Group Tour Magazine New England Region (Holland, MI) **15170**
Group Tour Magazine Southeastern Region (Holland, MI) **15171**
Group Tour Magazine Western Region (Holland, MI) **15172**
Group Travel (Voyage en Groupe) (Laprairie, QC, Can.) **37033**
Group W **16419***
Group W Cable **19898***
Group W Cable **13036***
Grove City College Alumni Magazine (Grove City, PA) **26965**
Grove City News (Grove City, OH) **25232**
Grove City Record (Grove City, OH) **25233**
The Grove Examiner (Spruce Grove, AB, Can.) **34852**
Grove Sun (Grove, OK) **25847**
Groveton News (Groveton, TX) **30418**
The Grower (Lenexa, KS) **11593**
The Grower (Guelph, ON, Can.) **35863**
Grower; Hay & Forage (Minneapolis, MN) **16084**
Grower; Sun Diamond (Stockton, CA) **3809**
Grower Talks (Batavia, IL) **8054**
Growers News; The Fruit (Sparta, MI) **15568**
Growers News; The Vegetable (Sparta, MI) **15570**
Grower's Review Quarterly (Chicago, IL) *Ceased*
Growing Business (Hamilton, MO) *Ceased*
The Growing Edge (Corvallis, OR) **26288**
Growing Without Schooling (Cambridge, MA) *Ceased*
The Growl (Goodman, MS) **16630**
Growth Hormone and IGF Research (Philadelphia, PA) **27477**
The Growth & Income Letter *Ceased*
Grundy County Herald (Tracy City, TN) **29628**
The Grundy Register (Grundy Center, IA) **10936**
Grunion Gazette (Long Beach, CA) **2168**
Gruver Statesman **31124***
The Gruver Statesman (Gruver, TX) *Ceased*
The Grygla Eagle (Grygla, MN) **15936**
GS Communications **13503***
GS Communications, Inc. (Ranson, WV) **33444**
GSA Bulletin **4168***
GSA Business (Greenville, SC) **28624**
GSA Business Journal **28624***
GSB Chicago (Chicago, IL) *Ceased*
gsdReview **721***
GSM News Service **38004***
The GSU Innovator (University Park, IL) **9697**
Guadalupe Valley Communications Systems Inc. (Boerne, TX) **29931**
Guarantor (Chicago, IL) *Unable to locate*
Guard; Batesville (Batesville, AR) **1040**
The Guardian **1214***
Guardian (Deridder, LA) **12565**
The Guardian (Dayton, OH) **25119**
Guardian (Brampton, ON, Can.) **35700**
The Guardian (Windsor, ON, Can.) **36886**
The Guardian (Charlottetown, PE, Can.) **36915**
Guardian Communications, Inc. **24847***
The Guardian Express (Welland, ON, Can.) *Unable to locate*
The Guardian-Journal (Homer, LA) **12600**
Guardian Newsweekly (New York, NY) *Unable to locate*
The Guardsman (San Francisco, CA) **3368**
Guayama; Periodico El Regional de (Humacao, PR) **28250**
Guelph Magazine (Guelph, ON, Can.) *Ceased*
Guelph Mercury (Guelph, ON, Can.) **35864**
Guelph Pennysaver (Guelph, ON, Can.) **35865**
The Guelph Tribune (Waterloo, ON, Can.) *Unable to locate*
Guernsey Breeders' Journal (Reynoldsburg, OH) **25494**
Guernsey Gazette (Lingle, WY) **34559**
The Guernsey-Noble Advertiser (Cambridge, OH) **24725**
Guest Life Monterey Bay (Carmel, CA) **1672**
Guidance, Control, and Dynamics; Journal of (Reston, VA) **32380**
The Guide **35635***
The Guide (Boston, MA) **13897**
The Guide (Rapid City, SD) *Unable to locate*
Guide (Killarney, MB, Can.) **35270**
Guide Magazine (St. Petersburg, FL) *Unable to locate*

H

Hang Gliding (Colorado Springs, CO) *Unable to locate*
Hanging Loose (Brooklyn, NY) **20319**
Hankinson News **24467***
Hanna City Trivoli Index (Glasford, IL) *Ceased*
The Hanna Herald (Hanna, AB, Can.) **34779**
Hannibal Courier-Post (Hannibal, MO) **17090**
Hanover Area Journal **27305***
Hanover Area Merchandiser (Hanover, PA) **26975**
Hanover Branch (Hanover, MA) **14227**
Hanover Cable TV Inc. (Hanover, PA) **26978**
Hanover Eagle & Weekly Regional News (Madison, NJ) **19181**
Hanover Mariner (Hanover, MA) **14228**
Hanover News (Worcester, MA) **14681**
Hanover Park Examiner (Hanover Park, IL) **8970**
Hanover Park North Voice (Lincolnwood, IL) *Unable to locate*
Hanover Park/Steamwood Press; Itasca/Roselle Press: Serving Bartlett/ (Oak Brook, IL) **9354**
The Hanover Post (Hanover, ON, Can.) **35900**
Hanover Remnder **8904***
Hanover Shoppinguide (Pembroke, MA) *Ceased*
The Hansford County Reporter-Statesman (Spearman, TX) **31124**
Hansford Plainsman **31124***
Hanska Cable TV (Redwood Falls, MN) **16298**
The Hanska Herald (Hanska, MN) **15939**
Hanson Mariner **14229***
Hanson Mariner; Whitman/ (Whitman, MA) **14657**
Hanson Reporter (Plymouth, MA) *Ceased*
Hanson Town Crier (Hanson, MA) **14229**
The Hants Journal (Windsor, NS, Can.) **35619**
Happenings Magazine **26786***
Happenings Magazine (Clarks Summit, PA) **26786**
Happi Household & Personal Products Industry (Ramsey, NJ) **19488**
Happiness Studies; Journal of (New York, NY) **22082**
Happy Times (St. Louis, MO) **17442**
The Haralson Gateway Beacon (Bremen, GA) **7137**
Harbinger (Palatine, IL) **9394**
Harbor City Star (Nanaimo, BC, Can.) **35019**
Harbor Independent News; Random Lengths/ (San Pedro, CA) **3595**
Harbor Light; Harbor Springs (Harbor Springs, MI) **15144**
Harbor Sound (Brunswick, GA) **7140**
Harbor Springs Harbor Light (Harbor Springs, MI) **15144**
Harbour & Shipping (West Vancouver, BC, Can.) **35238**
Hard Hat News (Palatine Bridge, NY) **23075**
Hardboiled (Brooklyn, NY) *Unable to locate*
Hardin County Independent (Elizabethtown, IL) **8830**
Hardin County Index (Eldora, IA) **10868**
Hardin County Times **11001***
Hardin Tribune **17811***
Hardin Tribune Herald **17811***
Hardware Age **21789***
Hardware Age's Home Improvement Market (New York, NY) **21789**
Hardware; Doors and (Chantilly, VA) **31911**
Hardware and Farm Equipment **17197***
Hardware and Home Centre Magazine (Toronto, ON, Can.) **36610**
Hardware Merchandising (Toronto, ON, Can.) **36611**
Hardware Trade (Hull, IA) **10955**
Hardwares; Asian Sources (Phoenix, AZ) **789**
The Hardwick Gazette (Hardwick, VT) **31544**
Hardwood Floors (Madison, WI) **33945**
Hare Krishna World (Alachua, FL) **5898**
Harford Business Ledger, Inc. (Aberdeen, MD) **13085**
Harford Post (Bel Air, MD) *Unable to locate*
Harlan Community Television Inc. (Harlan, KY) **12105**
Harlan County Journal (Alma, NE) **17933**
The Harlan Daily Enterprise (Harlan, KY) **12104**
Andy #Harle **26463***
Harlem-Foster Times (Lincolnwood, IL) **9094**
Harlem-Irving Leader **8511***
Harlem-Irving Times (Chicago, IL) **8390**
Harlem News (Cedar Rapids, IA) *Unable to locate*
Harlem U.S.A.; The New York Voice/ (Jamaica, NY) **20839**
Harlem Valley Times (Amenia, NY) **20029**
Harley Women/ Asphault Angels Magzine (Anamosa, IA) *Ceased*
Harmon Cable Communications **16477***
Harmon Cable Communications (Tracy, MN) **16477**
Harmon Football Forecast (Long Beach, NY) **37934**
The Harmonizer (Kenosha, WI) **33870**
Harmony (San Francisco, CA) **3369**
Harmony (Deerfield, IL) **8724**
Harmony (Skokie, IL) **9605**
Harmony Cable Inc. (Harmony, MN) **15940**
Harmony Magazine (Brooklyn, NY) *Unable to locate*
Harmony News **16017***
Harness Horse (Harrisburg, PA) *Ceased*
The Harness Shop News **24110***
Harnett County News (Lillington, NC) **24044**

Harp Journal; The American (Falls Church, VA) **32041**
Harper Advocate (Harper, KS) **11478**
Harper County Journal (Buffalo, OK) **25777**
Harper Herald (Harper, TX) *Unable to locate*
Harper Woods Herald; Northeast Detroiter (Birmingham, MI) **14826**
Harper's Bazaar (New York, NY) **21790**
Harper's Bazaar en Espanol (Miami, FL) **6357**
Harper's Magazine (New York, NY) **21791**
Harrah Herald (Midwest City, OK) *Unable to locate*
The Harrah News (Oklahoma City, OK) **25965**
Harriman Record (Shelbyville, KY) *Unable to locate*
Harrington Gay Men's Fiction Quarterly (Hampton, VA) **32129**
Harrington Journal (Harrington, DE) **5257**
Harrington Lesbian Fiction Quarterly (Binghamton, NY) **20154**
Harris County Herald (Pine Mountain, GA) **7485**
Harris County Journal (Manchester, GA) **7407**
The Harrison City Post (Jeannette, PA) *Ceased*
Harrison Daily Times (Marion, IL) **9142**
The Harrison Independent (Harrison, NY) **20712**
Harrison News Herald (Cadiz, OH) **24722**
Harrison Post (Lawrence, IN) *Ceased*
Harrison Press (Harrison, OH) **25238**
Harrison Sun; The Crawford Clipper/ (Crawford, NE) **17989**
The Harriston Review (Harriston, ON, Can.) **35902**
The Harrodsburg Herald (Harrodsburg, KY) **12111**
Harron Cable of New York (Utica, NY) **23470**
Harron Cable TV (Bad Axe, MI) **14787**
Harron Cablevision (Londonderry, NH) *Unable to locate*
Harrow & Colchester South This Week (Harrow, ON, Can.) **35903**
The Harrow News (Harrow, ON, Can.) **35904**
Harrowsmith **37251***
Harrowsmith Country Life (Montreal-Nord, QC, Can.) **37251**
Harrowsmith Magazine (Toronto, ON, Can.) *Ceased*
The Hart Beat (Hart, TX) **30432**
Hart County News-Herald (Horse Cave, KY) **12137**
Harte Hanks Cable **6483***
Harte-Hanks Newspapers (Washington, DC) *Unable to locate*
Hartford Advocate (Hartford, CT) **4891**
The Hartford Automobiler **5204***
Hartford City News Times (Hartford City, IN) **10060**
The Hartford Courant (Hartford, CT) **4892**
Hartford Democrat **13291***
Hartford Inquirer (Hartford, CT) **4893**
Hartford News-Herald (Geneva, AL) **240**
Hartford Times-Press (Hartford, WI) *Unable to locate*
Hartland Observer (Hartland, NB, Can.) *Unable to locate*
Hartland Shopper (Hartland, MI) **15149**
Hartley Municipal Cable TV (Hartley, IA) **10949**
Hartley Sentinel (Hartley, IA) **10948**
Hart's E&P (Houston, TX) **30475**
Hart's Fuel Technology & Management (Houston, TX) **30476**
Hart's Lubricants World (Houston, TX) **30477**
Hart's Oil and Gas World **30475***
Hartselle Enquirer (Hartselle, AL) **264**
Hartselle Shopping Guide (Hartselle, AL) **265**
Hartshorne Sun (Hartshorne, OK) **25858**
The Hartsville Vidette (Hartsville, TN) **29218**
The Hartville News (Hartville, OH) **25239**
The Hartwell Sun (Hartwell, GA) **7321**
Harvard Advocate (Cambridge, MA) **14055**
Harvard Business Review (Boston, MA) **13898**
Harvard Crimson (Cambridge, MA) **14056**
Harvard Design Magazine (Cambridge, MA) **14057**
Harvard Education Buletin **14051***
Harvard Educational Review (Cambridge, MA) **14058**
The Harvard Independent (Cambridge, MA) *Unable to locate*
The Harvard International Journal of Press/Politics (Cambridge, MA) **14059**
Harvard International Review (Cambridge, MA) **14060**
Harvard Journal of Asiatic Studies (Cambridge, MA) **14061**
Harvard Journal of Law and Public Policy (Cambridge, MA) **14062**
Harvard Journal of Legislation (Cambridge, MA) **14063**
Harvard Law Review (Cambridge, MA) **14064**
Harvard Magazine (Cambridge, MA) **14065**
Harvard Review (Cambridge, MA) **14066**
Harvard Review of Psychiatry (St. Louis, MO) *Ceased*
The Harvard Salient (Palmer, MA) **14455**
Harvard Theological Review (Cambridge, MA) **14067**
Harvard University Gazette (Cambridge, MA) **14068**
Harvest (Trenton, NJ) *Unable to locate*
Harvest (Montreal, QC, Can.) *Unable to locate*
Harvest Magazine (Salem, OR) *Ceased*

Harvest States AgriVisions (St. Paul, MN) *Unable to locate*
Harvest Weekly; Random (Spencer, NY) **23349**
Harvesting; Timber (Montgomery, AL) **379**
Harvey for Loving People (New York, NY) *Ceased*
Harvey/Markham Star (Harvey, IL) **8976**
Harwich Oracle (Harwich, MA) **14230**
Harwood Heights News; Norridge- (Harwood Heights, IL) **8978**
Harwood Heights-Norridge Harlem & Irving Passage (Highland Park, IL) *Unable to locate*
Hasbrouck Heights-Woodridge-Maywood-Rochelle Park Shopper; Lodi- (Lodi, NJ) **19179**
Haskell County Monitor-Chief (Cimarron, KS) **11382**
The Haskell Free Press (Haskell, TX) **30433**
Haskell News (Haskell, OK) **25859**
Hastad Cable **15698***
Hastad Engineering Co. (Halstad, MN) *Ceased*
The Hastings Banner (Hastings, MI) **15152**
Hasting's Cable Vision Ltd. (Madoc, ON, Can.) **36006**
Hastings Center Report (Garrison, NY) **20647**
Hastings Communications and Entertainment Law Journal (COMM/ENT) (San Francisco, CA) **3370**
The Hastings Enterprise **20716***
Hastings Reminder (Hastings, MI) **15153**
Hastings Star (Hastings, ON, Can.) **35905**
Hastings Star Gazette (Hastings, MN) **15941**
Hastings Today (Hastings, NE) **18036**
The Hastings Tribune (Hastings, NE) **18037**
Hatboro Progress (Hatboro, PA) **27027**
Hatchet; The GW (Washington, DC) **5521**
Hattiesburg American (Hattiesburg, MS) **16661**
Hattiesburg; Impact of (Laurel, MS) **16739**
Hatton Free Press (Fordville, ND) **24442**
Haunts (Cranston, RI) **28334**
Hauppauge-Nesconset Pennysaver (Huntington, NY) *Unable to locate*
Hauppauge/Nesconset Suffolk Life **23290***
Hauppauge Suffolk Life; Central Islip/ (Central Islip, NY) **20448**
Hauser Communications Inc. (New York, NY) *Ceased*
Haut Decor (Oakland Park, FL) *Unable to locate*
Haut St-Francois; Le (Cookshire, QC, Can.) **36978**
Haut-Ville Express (Quebec, QC, Can.) *Ceased*
Havana Herald (Havana, FL) **6185**
Havana Mason County Democrat (Havana, IL) **8979**
Have Fun at the Movies (Dallas, TX) **37935**
Havelock Citizen (Havelock, ON, Can.) **35906**
Haven Journal (Haven, KS) *Unable to locate*
Haverford News; The Bryn Mawr & (Haverford, PA) **27028**
Haverford Press (Newtown Square, PA) **27329**
The Haverhill Gazette (Haverhill, MA) **14232**
Havre Daily News (Havre, MT) **17813**
Havre; Le (Chandler, QC, Can.) **36960**
Hawaii (Mission Viejo, CA) **2553**
Hawaii (Boulder, CO) **4170**
Hawaii Army Weekly (Kaneohe, HI) **7769**
Hawaii Bar Journal (Honolulu, HI) **7689**
Hawaii Bar News **7689***
Hawaii Beverage Guide (Honolulu, HI) **7690**
Hawaii; Building Management (Honolulu, HI) **7682**
Hawaii Business (Honolulu, HI) **7691**
Hawaii Catholic Herald (Honolulu, HI) **7692**
Hawaii CPA News (Honolulu, HI) **7693**
Hawaii Crop Weather (Honolulu, HI) **7694**
Hawaii Dental Journal (Honolulu, HI) **7695**
Hawaii Hochi (Honolulu, HI) **7696**
Hawaii Hospitality (Honolulu, HI) *Unable to locate*
Hawaii Kai/East Oahu Sun Press (Kaneohe, HI) **7770**
Hawaii Marine (Kaneohe, HI) **7771**
Hawaii Medical Journal (Honolulu, HI) **7697**
Hawaii Navy News (Kaneohe, HI) **7772**
Hawaii Orchid Journal (Waianae, HI) **7794**
Hawaii Pacific Review (Honolulu, HI) **7698**
Hawaii Realtor Journal (Wahiawa, HI) *Unable to locate*
Hawaii Today; West (Kailua Kona, HI) **7766**
Hawaii Tribune-Herald (Birmingham, AL) *Unable to locate*
Hawaiian Cable Vision Co. (Lahaina, HI) **7778**
Hawaiian Cablevision (Hilo, HI) **7671**
Hawaiian Falcon (Kaneohe, HI) **7773**
Hawaiian Journal of History (Honolulu, HI) **7699**
Hawgs Illustrated (Fayetteville, AR) **1120**
Hawk Eye (Burlington, IA) **10638**
Hawk Reporter (Big Spring, TX) *Ceased*
Hawkesbury Express (Le Moniteur & The Echo) **35908***
HAWKEYE (Tampa, FL) **6767**
Hawkeye Booster (Elgin, IA) *Ceased*
Hawkeye Heritage (Des Moines, IA) **10787**
Hawkinsville Dispatch and News (Hawkinsville, GA) **7323**
Hawley Herald (Hawley, MN) **15943**
Hawthorne Community News/Lawndale Tribune (Culver City, CA) *Unable to locate*
Hawthorne-Glen Rock-Haledon-North Haledon-Prospect Park Shopper (Hawthorne, NJ) **18870**

3358

Numbers cited in bold after listings are entry numbers rather than page numbers.

Healthcare Forum Journal 8395*
Healthcare Informatics (Evergreen, CO) Unable to
  locate
Healthcare; Managed (Cleveland, OH) 24924
Healthcare Management Forum (Ottawa, ON, Can.)
  36247
Healthcare Marketing Report (Atlanta, GA) 7015
Healthcare; Modern (Chicago, IL) 8490
Healthcare New Orleans Ceased
Healthcare Nurse; Home (Louisville, KY) 12218
Healthcare Nurse Manager; Home (Philadelphia, PA)
  27486
Healthcare Product News (Vancouver, BC, Can.)
  35146
Healthcare Products Today (Richmond, VA) Ceased
Healthcare Purchasing News (Highland Park, IL) 8992
Healthcare Review (Nashua, NH) 18590
Healthcare Risk Management; Journal of (Chicago,
  IL) 8440
Healthcare Safety, Compliance & Infection Control;
  Journal of (Weston, MA) 14651
Healthcare Technology Management (Providence, RI)
  28399
Healthcare Technology Management International
  28399*
The Healthkeepers Journal (Chula Vista, CA) Unable
  to locate
Healthplan (Washington, DC) 5524
Healthplan Magazine 5524*
HealthQuest (Chalfont, PA) 26767
Healthsharing (Toronto, ON, Can.) Ceased
Healthstate (Newark, NJ) 19353
HealthTexas (Austin, TX) Ceased
HealthWeek Ceased
Healthy Cooking (Riverside, CA) 2937
Healthy Heart (Montvale, NJ) Ceased
Healthy Magazine; Living (Boston, MA) 13923
Healthy Pregnancy (New York, NY) 21796
Healthy Weight Journal (Hamilton, ON, Can.) 35880
Healy's Highlights 3827*
Hearing; Ear and (Philadelphia, PA) 27455
Hearing Health (Washington, DC) Unable to locate
Hearing Instruments (Cleveland, OH) Ceased
The Hearing Journal (Philadelphia, PA) Unable to
  locate
Hearing Loss (Bethesda, MD) 13343
The Hearing Professional (Livonia, MI) 15316
Hearing Research; Journal of Speech and (Geneseo,
  NY) 20649
Hearing; Seminars in (Denver, CO) 4356
Hearing Services in Schools; Language, Speech, and
  (Rockville, MD) 13686
Hearne Cablevision 29984*
The Hearne Democrat (Hearne, TX) 30435
Hearsay (Halifax, NS, Can.) 35567
Hearst 2481*
Hearst News Service (Washington, DC) 37939
Heart Beat (New York, NY) Unable to locate
Heart-Centered Therapies; Journal of (Issaquah, WA)
  32785
Heart and Circulatory Physiology; American Journal of
  Physiology: (Bethesda, MD) 13307
Heart of the City (Wichita, KS) Unable to locate
Heart Failure (Greenwich, CT) Ceased
Heart Failure; Congestive (Darien, CT) 4771
Heart Failure Reviews (New York, NY) 21797
Heart Journal; American (Philadelphia, PA) 27370
Heart and Lung (Philadelphia, PA) 27479
Heart & Soul (New York, NY) Unable to locate
HeartCare (Westlake Village, CA) Unable to locate
HeartDrug (Farmington, CT) 4830
Hearth & Home Magazine (Laconia, NH) 18537
The Hearthstone Collection of Folklore, Nostalgia &
  History (Ironton, OH) Ceased
The Hearthstone Press 27926*
The Hearthstone Town and Country (Red Hill, PA)
  27926
Heartland (Indianapolis, IN) Unable to locate
Heartland (Edinboro, PA) 26861
Heartland Boating (Martin, TN) Unable to locate
Heartland Retailer (Omaha, NE) 18197
Heartland Shopper (Neepawa, MB, Can.) 35277
The Heartland Shopping News (Fergus Falls, MN)
  15898
Heartland Trader (Wauseon, OH) 25623
Hearts Aflame (Washington, NJ) 19708
Heat Exchanger Design Update (New York, NY)
  21798
Heat Processing Digest (Materials Park, OH) Ceased
Heat Transfer Engineering: An International Quarterly
  (Stillwater, OK) 26078
Heat Transfer; Experimental (Berkeley, CA) 1520
Heat Transfer - Japanese Research (Hoboken, NJ)
  18960
Heat Transfer; Journal of (New York, NY) 22086
Heat Transfer-Recent Contents (Fairfield, NJ) 18813
Heat Transfer - Soviet Research (Hoboken, NJ)
  Ceased
Heat Treating (New York, NY) Unable to locate

Heat Treatment; Metal Science and (New York, NY)
  22322
Heating, Air Conditioning & Plumbing Products
  (Morris Plains, NJ) Ceased
Heating-Cooling Forum; North Carolina Plumbing-
  (Garner, NC) 23905
Heating, Cooling Magazine; Southern Plumbing,
  23939*
Heating; Industrial (Pittsburgh, PA) 27799
Heating/Piping/Air Conditioning Engineering (HPAC)
  (Cleveland, OH) 24906
Heating, Plumbing, Air Conditioning Buyers' Guide
  (Toronto, ON, Can.) 36613
Heating; Process (Bensenville, IL) 8070
Heaven Bone (Chester, NY) 20460
The Heavener Ledger (Heavener, OK) 25861
Heaven's Metal 30931*
Heavy Construction News (Toronto, ON, Can.) 36614
Heavy Duty Distribution 8730*
Heavy Duty Trucking (Newport Beach, CA) 2627
Heavy Equipment Guide (Vancouver, BC, Can.)
  35147
Heavy Metal (Rockville Centre, NY) 23261
Heavy Metal Thunder (New York, NY) Ceased
The Heavyweight Champions: Ring Special (Rockville
  Centre, NY) Unable to locate
L'Hebdo-Journal (Cap-de-la-Madeleine, QC, Can.)
  36956
L'Hebdo de Laval (Laval, QC, Can.) Unable to locate
Hebdo de Le Droit (Ottawa, ON, Can.) Ceased
L'Hebdo Mekinac/des Chenaux (Shawinigan, QC,
  Can.) 37390
L'Hebdo le Plus (Caraquet, NB, Can.) Ceased
Hebdo de la Pointe (Montreal, QC, Can.) Unable to
  locate
L'Hebdo Rive-Nord (Montreal, QC, Can.) 37122
L'Hebdo du St. Maurice (Shawinigan, QC, Can.)
  37391
L'Hebdo St-Tite/Normandie 37390*.
Heber Springs Arkansas Sun 1173*
Hebron Herald (Hebron, ND) 24471
Hebron Journal Register (Hebron, NE) 18045
Hechizos (Elizabeth, NJ) Unable to locate
Heckler (Sacramento, CA) 3001
Heck's TV & Cable (Armstrong, IA) 10609
The Hegewisch News (Portage, IN) Unable to locate
The Heights (Chestnut Hill, MA) 14128
Heights Herald (Fishers, IN) Ceased
Heights Independent 14910*
The Helena-West Helena Daily World 1174*
Helicon Cable Communications (Bourg, LA) 12539
Helicon Cable Communications (Boone, NC) 23658
Helicon CableVision 12539*
Helicopter Society; Journal of the American
  (Alexandria, VA) 31686
Helicopters Magazine (Mississauga, ON, Can.) 36070
Heliograph, Arrow, Messenger 685*
Helios (Lubbock) (College Station, TX) 30042
The Hellenic Calendar (Santa Ana, CA) 3626
Hellenic Chronicle (Natick, MA) Ceased
Hellenic Diaspora; Journal of the (New York, NY)
  22087
Hellenic Hamilton News (Hamilton, ON, Can.) 35881
The Hellenic News (London, ON, Can.) 35982
Hellenism; Journal of Modern (Brookline, MA) 14021
Hello Orting! News 32874*
Helmut Newton's Illustrated (New York, NY) Unable
  to locate
Hem/Onc Annals (Thorofare, NJ) Ceased
Hem/Onc Today (Thorofare, NJ) 19616
Hematological Oncology (Hoboken, NJ) 18961
Hematology; American Journal of (Hoboken, NJ)
  18884
Hematology/Oncology Clinics (Philadelphia, PA) 27480
Hematology/Oncology; Journal of Pediatric (Baltimore,
  MD) 13199
Hematology and Oncology; Pediatric (Philadelphia,
  PA) 27616
Hematology; Seminars in (Washington, DC) 5788
Hematopathology and Molecular Hematology (New
  York, NY) Ceased
Hematotherapy & Stem Cell Research; Journal of
  (Larchmont, NY) 20913
The Hemet News (Birmingham, AL) Ceased
Hemingway Notes 14339*
The Hemingway Review (Nantucket, MA) 14339
Hemlo News 36442*
Hemlock Shoppers Guide (Alma, MI) 14732
Hemmings Motor News (Bennington, VT) 31499
Hemoglobin (New York, NY) 21799
Hemostasis; Clinical and Applied Thrombosis/
  (Baltimore, MD) 13145
Hemostasis; Seminars in Thrombosis and (New York,
  NY) 22727
Hemotherapy; Journal of 20913*
Hempstead Beacon (Hempstead, NY) 20728

Hempstead Shopper's Guide (Ontario, ON, Can.)
  36164
The Henderson County Quill (Stronghurst, IL) 9672
Henderson Daily Dispatch (Henderson, NC) 23981
Henderson Daily News (Henderson, TX) 30440
Henderson Home News (Henderson, NV) 18353
Henderson Independent (Henderson, MN) 15947
The Henderson News (Henderson, NE) 18047
Hendrick County Flyer/Weekend Edition (Avon, IN)
  9793
The Hendricks County Flyer (Avon, IN) 9794
Hendricks County Newsleader (Brownsburg, IN)
  Ceased
Hendricks Pioneer (Hendricks, MN) 15948
The Henning Advocate (Henning, MN) 15949
Henrico Gazette (Mechanicsville, VA) Ceased
Henrietta Post (Henrietta, NY) 20731
Henry County Advertizer Shopper (Geneseo, IL) 8915
Henry County Local (New Castle, KY) 12321
Henry County Local & Shopper (New Castle, KY)
  12322
Henry County News Republican (New Castle, IN)
  Unable to locate
The Henry Herald 7429*
Henry James Review (Louisville, KY) 12217
The Henry Neighbor (Henry, GA) 7328
Henry News-Republican (Henry, IL) 8981
Henryetta Daily Free-Lance (Henryetta, OK) 25863
Hepatology and Clinical Nutrition; Advances in
  Gastroenterology, (Baltimore, MD) 13109
Hepatology; European Journal of Gastroenterology &
  (Philadelphia, PA) 27465
Heppner TV Inc. (Heppner, OR) 26368
Hera (Binghamton, NY) Ceased
Herald 31477*
The Herald 34025*
Herald 25423*
Herald 11164*
Herald, 7496*
The Herald 2582*
Herald (Nogales, AZ) 754
Herald (El Centro, CA) Unable to locate
The Herald (New Britain, CT) 4975
The Herald (Cahokia, IL) 8104
Herald (Cairo, IL) 8105
Herald (Chicago, IL) Ceased
Herald (Metamora, IL) 9177
The Herald (Rockton, IL) 9546
The Herald (Columbus, IN) Ceased
The Herald (Jasper, IN) 10219
The Herald (Oakland, IA) 11120
Herald (New York Mills, MN) 16220
Herald (Sauk Centre, MN) 16436
Herald (Spring Grove, MN) 16455
Herald (Independence, MO) 17112
Herald (Independence, MO) 17111
Herald (Three Forks, MT) 17915
The Herald (Farmingdale, NJ) Unable to locate
The Herald (Truth or Consequences, NM) 19968
The Herald (Geneva, NY) 20654
The Herald (New Paltz, NY) 21112
The Herald (New England, ND) 24522
The Herald (Andover, OH) Unable to locate
The Herald (Aspinwall, PA) 26666
The Herald (Pittsburgh, PA) 27796
The Herald (Sharon, PA) 27986
The Herald (Rock Hill, SC) 28744
Herald (San Antonio, TX) 31032
The Herald (Everett, WA) 32761
The Herald (Winnipeg, MB, Can.) 35331
The Herald (Alliston, ON, Can.) 35630
The Herald (London, ON, Can.) 35983
The Herald (Herbert, SK, Can.) 37474
Herald Advertiser (Sanger, CA) 3616
The Herald Advertiser (Holly, MI) Unable to locate
The Herald-Advocate (Wauchula, FL) 6841
The Herald of Arkansas State University (State
  University, AR) 1349
The Herald Breeze (DeFuniak Springs, FL) 6053
The Herald of Christian Science (Boston, MA) 13900
Herald-Chronicle (Winchester, TN) 29647
Herald Citizen 8105*
Herald-Citizen Plus (Cookeville, TN) 29143
The Herald Citizen Tri-County Shopper (Crystal Lake,
  IL) Ceased
The Herald Coaster (Rosenberg, TX) 30992
Herald Coaster Extra (Rosenberg, TX) 30993
The Herald/Country Market (Bourbonnais, IL) 8094
Herald-Courier/Virginia-Tennessean (Bristol, VA) 31897
The Herald-Democrat 1050*
The Herald Democrat (Salida, CO) 4619
The Herald-Democrat (Beaver, OK) 25757
Herald Democrat (Sherman, TX) 31103
Herald Dispatch (Los Angeles, CA) 3288
The Herald-Dispatch (Mc Lean, VA) 32245
Herald-Enterprise (Golconda, IL) 8945
The Herald-Gazette (Barnesville, GA) 7121
The Herald-Gazette (Trenton, TN) 29629

The Human Resources Professional (New York, NY) *Ceased*
Human Rights Case Digest (New York, NY) **21834**
Human Rights; Health and (Boston, MA) **13899**
Human Rights and the Law; Asia-Pacific Journal on (New York, NY) **21263**
Human Rights Law Review; Columbia (New York, NY) **21444**
Human Rights Quarterly (Baltimore, MD) **13169**
Human Rights Review (New Orleans, LA) **12733**
Human Rights Tribune/Tribune Des Droits Humains (Ottawa, ON, Can.) **36249**
Human Services; Journal of Progressive (Boston, MA) **13918**
Human Services; Journal of Technology in (Binghamton, NY) **20203**
Human Services; Journal of Technology in (Arlington, TX) **29733**
Human Sexuality; Canadian Journal of (Toronto, ON, Can.) **36509**
Human Sexuality; Journal of Psychology and (Minneapolis, MN) **16089**
Human Studies (New York, NY) **21835**
Human Toxicology; Veterinary and (Manhattan, KS) **11630**
Humane Medicine (Ottawa, ON, Can.) *Ceased*
Humanism; Anthropology and (Arlington, VA) **31776**
The Humanist (Washington, DC) **5536**
Humanist in Canada (Ottawa, ON, Can.) **36250**
Humanistic Counseling & Development; Journal of (Alexandria, VA) **31698**
Humanistic Psychology; Journal of (Thousand Oaks, CA) **3892**
The Humanitarian (Washington, DC) **5537**
Humanitas (Washington, DC) **5538**
Humanities Collections (Binghamton, NY) *Ceased*
Humanities Index (Bronx, NY) **20271**
Humanities; Journal of Medical (New York, NY) **22130**
Humanities and Peace; International Journal of (Flagstaff, AZ) **696**
Humanities Review; Medical (Galveston, TX) **30382**
Humanities Review; Southern (Auburn, AL) **45**
Humanities Review; Western (Salt Lake City, UT) **31443**
Humanities; Studies in the (Indiana, PA) **27077**
Humansville Star-Leader (Osceola, MO) **17323**
Humber Log (Corner Brook, NL, Can.) **35446**
Humble Sun (Pasadena, TX) *Unable to locate*
HumbleSun **30651***
Humboldt Beacon & Advance (Fortuna, CA) **1928**
Humboldt Independent (Humboldt, IA) **10957**
Humboldt Reminder (Humboldt, IA) **10958**
Humboldt Republican (Humboldt, IA) *Ceased*
The Humboldt Standard (Humboldt, NE) **18053**
The Humboldt Sun (Winnemucca, NV) **18450**
Hume Studies (Santa Clara, CA) **3672**
The Humeston New Era (Humeston, IA) **10960**
Humor Books Syndicate (Stafford, VA) *Unable to locate*
Humornet (New York, NY) *Unable to locate*
Humpty Dumpty's Magazine (Indianapolis, IN) **10119**
Hungarian Word (Amerikai Magyar SZO) (New York, NY) **21836**
Hungarians; California (Reseda, CA) **2917**
Hungry Horse News (Columbia Falls, MT) **17773**
Hungry Mind Review **16408***
Hungry Mind Review: Children's Book Section **16408***
Hunt County Shopper (Greenville, TX) **30414**
The Hunted News (Warwick, RI) **28450**
Hunter; American (Fairfax, VA) **32003**
Hunter & Angler; Arizona (Mesa, AZ) **743**
Hunter Ed (Seattle, WA) *Ceased*
Hunter; Musky (St. Germain, WI) **34312**
Hunter; North American (Minnetonka, MN) **16173**
Hunter & Sport Horse (Fort Wayne, IN) **9970**
Hunterdon County Democrat (Flemington, NJ) **18820**
Hunterdon Profile **18821***
Hunterdon Review (Stirling, NJ) **19602**
Hunterdon; Strictly (Bridgewater, NJ) **18701**
Hunter's Frontier Times (Cave Creek, AZ) *Ceased*
The Hunter's Horn (Sesser, IL) **9598**
Huntia (Pittsburgh, PA) **27797**
Hunting; Bow and Arrow (Orange, CA) **2721**
Hunting; Deer & Deer (Iola, WI) **33817**
Hunting & Fishing News; Mid-South (Brownsville, TN) **29071**
Hunting; Hounds and (Bradford, PA) **26728**
Hunting Magazine; Turkey and Turkey (Iola, WI) **33853**
Hunting News; Fishing and (Seattle, WA) **32966**
Hunting; Petersen's (Los Angeles, CA) **2364**
Hunting Retriever (Kalamazoo, MI) **15238**
Huntington Beach/Fountain Valley Independent (Fountain Valley, CA) **1935**
Huntington Beach Independent **1935***
Huntington Beach News (Huntington Beach, CA) *Unable to locate*
Huntington Beach Weekly **1935***

The Huntington Harbour Journal **2065***
Huntington Herald (Shelton, CT) **5123**
Huntington Library Quarterly (San Marino, CA) **3580**
Huntington Park Bulletin (Huntington Park, CA) **2068**
Huntington Pennysaver (Huntington, NY) *Unable to locate*
Huntington Station Suffolk Life (Huntington Station, NY) **20778**
Huntington Station Weekender (Farmingdale, NY) *Ceased*
Huntington Suffolk Life (Huntington, NY) **20772**
Huntington Weekender (Farmingdale, NY) *Ceased*
Huntington Woods/Berkley Mirror (Royal Oak, MI) **15482**
Huntley, Marengo; The Farmside: (Huntley, IL) **9006**
Huntsville Forester (Huntsville, ON, Can.) **35917**
Huntsville Herald News (Huntsville, ON, Can.) *Unable to locate*
The Huntsville Item (Huntsville, TX) **30595**
Huntsville News (Huntsville, AL) *Ceased*
Huntsville; Old (Huntsville, AL) **271**
The Huntsville Times (Huntsville, AL) **270**
Huntsville TV Cable Inc. (Huntsville, AR) **1193**
Huron CATV (Coalinga, CA) **1737**
Huron County Press & Newsweekly (Sebewaing, MI) **15533**
Huron Daily Plainsman (Huron, SD) *Unable to locate*
Huron Daily Tribune (Bad Axe, MI) **14785**
Huron Expositor (Seaforth, ON, Can.) **36388**
Huronia Business Times (Barrie, ON, Can.) *Unable to locate*
Huronia Sunday Saver (Midland, ON, Can.) *Ceased*
Huronia Weekend (Midland, ON, Can.) *Ceased*
Hurricane Alice (Providence, RI) **28400**
The Hurricane Breeze (Hurricane, WV) **33348**
Huskers Illustrated (Brentwood, TN) **29062**
Husserl Studies (New York, NY) **21837**
Hustler Busty Beauties (Beverly Hills, CA) **1573**
Hustler Letters Magazine *Ceased*
Hustler Magazine (Beverly Hills, CA) **1574**
Hustler; South Pittsburg (South Pittsburg, TN) **29610**
Hustler; Vanderbilt (Nashville, TN) **29498**
Hutchinson Collegian (Hutchinson, KS) **11500**
Hutchinson Herald (Menno, SD) **28892**
Hutchinson Leader (Hutchinson, MN) **15967**
The Hutchinson News (Hutchinson, KS) **11501**
HVAC (Chicago, IL) *Unable to locate*
HVAC/R Distribution Today (Boca Raton, FL) **5932**
(HVAC & R Research); International Journal of Heating, Ventilating, Air-Conditioning and Refrigeration Research (Atlanta, GA) **7018**
HVAC/Refrigeration **35819***
HVAC/Refrigeration (Etobicoke, ON, Can.) *Ceased*
HVS Partners **6743***
HVS Partners **6750***
HW (West Hartford, CT) *Ceased*
HX Magazine (New York, NY) **21838**
Hybrid Circuit Technology (Libertyville, IL) *Ceased*
Hybridoma **20903***
Hybridoma and Hybridomics (Larchmont, NY) **20903**
Hybridomics; Hybridoma and (Larchmont, NY) **20903**
Hyde Park Citizen (Chicago, IL) **8402**
Hyde Park Herald (Chicago, IL) **8403**
Hyde Park Mattapan Tribune (Hyde Park, MA) **14255**
Hyde Park Townsman (Hyde Park, NY) **20779**
Hydraulic Engineering; Journal of (Reston, VA) **32382**
Hydraulics & Pneumatics (Cleveland, OH) **24910**
Hydro Review (Atlanta, GA) *Ceased*
The Hydro Review-North Caddo News (Hydro, OK) *Unable to locate*
Hydrobiological Journal (Hoboken, NJ) **18970**
Hydrocarbon Processing (Houston, TX) **30490**
Hydrologic Engineering; Journal of (Reston, VA) **32383**
Hydrological Processes (Hoboken, NJ) **18971**
Hydrological Science and Technology (St. Paul, MN) **16380**
Hydrology; Journal of Environmental (Sacramento, CA) **3004**
Hydrotechnical Construction (New York, NY) **21839**
Hygiene Association Journal; American Industrial (Fairfax, VA) **32004**
Hygiene; The Journal of Practical (Mahwah, NJ) **19198**
Hygiene News; Industrial (Pittsburgh, PA) **27800**
Hygiene News; Industrial Safety and (Norristown, PA) **27335**
HYLE (Charlottesville, VA) **31929**
The Hymn (Bloomington, MN) **15758**
Hymn Society of America **15758***
Hypatia (Bloomington, IN) **9829**
Hype Magazine, Inc. (Seattle, WA) *Ceased*
Hyperbaric Medicine; Undersea & (Kensington, MD) **13592**
Hyperfine Interactions (New York, NY) **21840**
Hypertension (Philadelphia, PA) **27488**
Hypertension; Clinical and Experimental (Houston, TX) **30464**
Hypertension; Journal of (Philadelphia, PA) **27531**

Hyphen Magazine (Somonauk, IL) *Unable to locate*
Hypotheses (Port Washington, NY) **23128**
Hysteria (Bridgeport, CT) *Ceased*

I

I Am Nation News (Pioneer, TN) **29569**
I-97 Rocks Cutting Edge 2000-2002 **9309***
IABC Communication World (San Francisco, CA) **3374**
IAEI News (Richardson, TX) **30974**
IAL News (Stockton, CA) **3805**
iAm Magazine! (Edina, MN) **15875**
The IAPD Magazine (Leawood, KS) **11585**
IAPES News **12077***
IB (Independent Business) (Thousand Oaks, CA) *Unable to locate*
Iberian; Daily (New Iberia, LA) **12722**
IBEW Journal (Washington, DC) **5539**
IBIS Review (Chicago, IL) *Ceased*
IBM Journal of Research and Development (Yorktown Heights, NY) **23606**
IBM Systems Journal (Yorktown Heights, NY) **23607**
IC Card Systems & Design (Atlanta, GA) *Unable to locate*
ICA Review (Arlington, VA) **31796**
ICAO Bulletin **37123***
The ICAO Journal (Montreal, QC, Can.) **37123**
Icarus (San Diego, CA) **3169**
ICCN/Outpatient Care **9590***
Ice Skating; Recreational (Dallas, TX) **30179**
ICEP, Inc. - Channel 44 (El Paso, TX) **30284**
ICES Journal of Marine Science (San Diego, CA) **3170**
ICG Magazine (West Hollywood, CA) **4063**
ICN (Los Angeles, CA) *Unable to locate*
Icon (Westfield, IN) **10559**
The Iconoclast (Mohegan Lake) (Mohegan Lake, NY) **21088**
ICP Manufacturing Software (Indianapolis, IN) *Ceased*
ICR: The International Cookbook Revue (New York, NY) **21841**
ICS Cleaning Specialist (Woodland Hills, CA) **4107**
ICSID Review (Baltimore, MD) **13170**
ICUC: I See You See (Quincy, IL) **9473**
ID (New York, NY) *Unable to locate*
ID Magazine (Guelph, ON, Can.) *Unable to locate*
ID Systems **18630***
ID: The Information Source for Managers and DSRs (New York, NY) **21842**
Ida County Courier-Reminder (Ida Grove, IA) **10961**
Ida County Pioneer-Record (Ida Grove, IA) *Unable to locate*
Idaho Academy of Science; Journal of the (Pocatello, ID) **7946**
Idaho Argonaut (Moscow, ID) **7915**
Idaho Beverage Analyst (Denver, CO) *Ceased*
The Idaho Business Review (Boise, ID) **7809**
Idaho Catholic Register (Boise, ID) **7810**
Idaho City Cable TV (Idaho City, ID) **7861**
Idaho County Free Press (Grangeville, ID) **7857**
Idaho Enterprise; Malad City (Malad City, ID) **7904**
Idaho FarmekraHJJmpw- (Urbandale, IA) **11275**
Idaho Golf (Idaho Falls, ID) **7865**
Idaho Law Review (Moscow, ID) **7916**
Idaho Moneysaver (Moscow, ID) **7917**
Idaho Mountain Express (Ketchum, ID) **7887**
Idaho Outdoor Digest (Rupert, ID) *Ceased*
Idaho Press Tribune (Nampa, ID) **7930**
Idaho Register **7810***
Idaho State Journal (Pocatello, ID) *Unable to locate*
The Idaho Statesman (Boise, ID) **7811**
Idaho Wildlife (Boise, ID) *Ceased*
The Idaho World (Garden Valley, ID) **7856**
The IDB (Washington, DC) **5540**
IDB America (Belmont, MA) **13840**
IDB Communications Group Inc. (Culver City, CA) **37696**
IDB Communications Group Inc. (Culver City, CA) **37638**
IDEA Health & Fitness Source (San Diego, CA) **3171**
IDEA Personal Trainer (San Diego, CA) **3172**
Idea Source Guide (Devon, PA) *Unable to locate*
IDEA Today **3171***
The Ideal Traveler (Los Angeles, CA) *Unable to locate*
Idealistic Studies (Worcester, MA) **14683**
IDEALS (Nashville, TN) *Ceased*
Ideas for Better Living (Columbus, OH) *Ceased*
Ideas; The Journal of (Panama City, FL) **6555**
Ideas; Journal of the History of (New Brunswick, NJ) **19333**
Ideas para Su Hogar (Ideas for Your Home) (Miami, FL) **6362**

International Instrumentation and Controls (Great Neck, NY) **20690**

International Insurance Law Journal (New York, NY) **21898**

International Insurance Monitor (Mount Vernon, NY) *Ceased*

International Journal (Toronto, ON, Can.) **36623**

International Journal of Acarology (West Bloomfield, MI) **15675**

The International Journal of Accounting (Berkeley, CA) **1529**

The International Journal of Action Methods (Washington, DC) **5552**

International Journal of Adaptive Control and Signal Processing (Hoboken, NJ) **18975**

The International Journal of Addictions **22803***

The International Journal of Adult Orthodontics and Orthognathic Surgery (Carol Stream, IL) *Unable to locate*

International Journal for the Advancement of Counseling (New York, NY) **21899**

International Journal of Aging and Human Development (Amityville, NY) **20038**

The International Journal of Air Pollution Control and Hazardous Waste Management **27783***

International Journal of Algebra and Computation (River Edge, NJ) *Ceased*

International Journal of American Linguistics (Seattle, WA) *Unable to locate*

International Journal of Applied Economics and Econometrics (Somerset, NJ) *Ceased*

International Journal of Applied Philosophy (Ft. Pierce, FL) **6118**

International Journal on Artificial Intelligence Tools (River Edge, NJ) **19508**

The International Journal of Aviation Psychology (Johnstown, OH) **25270**

International Journal of Behavioral Medicine (Mahwah, NJ) **19192**

International Journal of Cancer (Hoboken, NJ) **18976**

International Journal of Cardiovascular Imaging (New York, NY) **21900**

International Journal of Chemical Kinetics (Hoboken, NJ) **18977**

The International Journal of Children's Rights (New York, NY) **21901**

International Journal of Circuit Theory and Applications (Hoboken, NJ) **18978**

International Journal of the Classical Tradition (Boston, MA) **13907**

International Journal of Climatology (Hoboken, NJ) **18979**

International Journal of Clinical Monitoring and Computing **22027***

International Journal of Clinical Neuropsychology (Madison, WI) *Unable to locate*

International Journal of Cognitive Ergonomics (Mahwah, NJ) **19193**

International Journal of Commerce and Management (Indiana, PA) **27075**

International Journal of Communication Systems (Hoboken, NJ) **18980**

International Journal of Comparative and Applied Criminal Justice (East Lansing, MI) **14985**

International Journal of Comparative Labour Law and Industrial Relations (New York, NY) **21902**

International Journal of Comparative Psychology (New York, NY) *Ceased*

International Journal of Comparative Sociology (Willowdale, ON, Can.) **36879**

International Journal of Computer Aided VLSI Design (Eau Claire, WI) *Ceased*

International Journal of Computer Integrated Manufacturing (Philadelphia, PA) **27495**

International Journal of Computer Simulation (Eau Claire, WI) **33670**

International Journal of Computer Vision (New York, NY) **21903**

International Journal of Computers and Applications (Calgary, AB, Can.) **34646**

International Journal of Computers for Mathematical Learning (New York, NY) **21904**

International Journal of Conflict Management (Newark, DE) **5274**

International Journal of Control (Philadelphia, PA) **27496**

International Journal of Cross-Cultural Consumer Behavior **27257***

International Journal of Dermatology (Elgin, IL) **8824**

International Journal of Developmental Neuroscience (Galveston, TX) **30381**

International Journal of Digital and Analog Communication Systems **18980***

International Journal of Eating Disorders (Hoboken, NJ) **18981**

International Journal of Educational Reform (Lanham, MD) **13602**

International Journal of Educational Telecommunications (Norfolk, VA) **32284**

International Journal of Electronic Commerce (Armonk, NY) **20079**

International Journal of Electronics (Philadelphia, PA) **27497**

International Journal of Emergency Mental Health (Ellicott City, MD) **13498**

International Journal of Energy Research (Hoboken, NJ) **18982**

International Journal of Engineering Fluid Mechanics (Houston, TX) *Ceased*

International Journal of Environmental Studies: Sections A & B (Kings Point, NY) **20859**

International Journal of Expert Systems (Urbana, IL) **9711**

International Journal of Family Psychiatry (Chicago, IL) *Ceased*

International Journal of Fertility and Menopausal Studies **23129***

International Journal of Fertility and Women's Medicine (Port Washington, NY) **23129**

International Journal of Food Properties (New York, NY) **21905**

International Journal of Fracture (New York, NY) **21906**

International Journal of Franchising and Distribution Law (New York, NY) **21907**

International Journal of Genome Research (River Edge, NJ) *Ceased*

International Journal of Geographical Information Science (Philadelphia, PA) **27498**

International Journal of Geomagnetism and Aeronomy (Washington, DC) **5553**

International Journal of Geomechanics (Boca Raton, FL) **5934**

International Journal of Geriatric Psychiatry (Hoboken, NJ) **18983**

International Journal of Government Auditing (Washington, DC) **5554**

International Journal of Group Psychotherapy (Chicago, IL) *Unable to locate*

International Journal of Group Tensions (New York, NY) *Ceased*

International Journal of Gynecological Pathology (Baltimore, MD) **13173**

International Journal of Health Care Finance and Economics (New York, NY) **21908**

International Journal of Health Planning and Management (Hoboken, NJ) **18984**

International Journal of Health Services (Amityville, NY) **20039**

International Journal of Heating, Ventilating, Air-Conditioning and Refrigeration Research (HVAC & R Research) (Atlanta, GA) **7018**

International Journal of High Speed Electronics (River Edge, NJ) **19509**

International Journal of Historical Archaeology (Normal, IL) **9299**

International Journal of Hospitality & Tourism Administration (Binghamton, NY) **20157**

International Journal for Housing Science and Its Applications (Coral Gables, FL) **6007**

International Journal of Human Computer Interaction (Mahwah, NJ) **19194**

International Journal of Human Factors in Manufacturing (Hoboken, NJ) *Ceased*

International Journal of Human Resource Management (Greenwich, CT) *Ceased*

International Journal of Humanities and Peace (Flagstaff, AZ) **696**

International Journal of Hyperthermia (Philadelphia, PA) **27499**

International Journal of Imaging Systems and Technology (Hoboken, NJ) **18985**

International Journal of Infectious Diseases (Hamilton, ON, Can.) **35882**

International Journal of Infrared and Millimeter Waves (New York, NY) **21909**

International Journal of Instructional Media (IJIM) (Tolland, CT) **5176**

International Journal of Intelligent and Cooperative Information Systems (River Edge, NJ) **19510**

International Journal of Intelligent Systems (Hoboken, NJ) **18986**

International Journal of Intelligent Systems in Accounting, Finance, and Management (Hoboken, NJ) **18987**

International Journal of Kurdish Studies (Brooklyn, NY) **20321**

International Journal of Law Libraries **5555***

International Journal of Legal Information (Washington, DC) **5555**

International Journal of Lifelong Education (Philadelphia, PA) **27500**

The International Journal of Logistics Management (Ponte Vedra Beach, FL) **6595**

The International Journal of Marine and Coastal Law (New York, NY) **21910**

International Journal of Mathematical Education in Science and Technology (Philadelphia, PA) **27501**

International Journal of Mathematical and Statistical Sciences (Miami, FL) **6363**

International Journal of Mental Health (Armonk, NY) **20080**

International Journal of Methods in Psychiatric Research (Hoboken, NJ) *Ceased*

International Journal of Microwave and Millimeter-Wave Computer-Aided Engineering (Hoboken, NJ) *Ceased*

International Journal of Middle East Studies (Ann Arbor, MI) **14753**

International Journal of Mini and Microcomputers **34646***

International Journal on Minority and Group Rights (New York, NY) **21911**

International Journal of Modelling & Simulation (Calgary, AB, Can.) **34071**

International Journal of Network Management (Hoboken, NJ) **18988**

The International Journal of Neural Networks Expert Systems (Medford, NJ) *Ceased*

International Journal of Neuroradiology (Philadelphia, PA) *Ceased*

International Journal of Neuroscience (New York, NY) *Unable to locate*

International Journal of Nonlinear Optical Physics (IJNOP) (River Edge, NJ) **19511**

International Journal for Numerical and Analytical Methods in Geomechanics (Hoboken, NJ) **18989**

International Journal for Numerical Methods in Engineering (Hoboken, NJ) **18990**

International Journal for Numerical Methods in Fluids (Hoboken, NJ) **18991**

International Journal of Numerical Modelling (Hoboken, NJ) **18992**

International Journal of Obstetric Anesthesia (New York, NY) **21912**

International Journal of Occupational Medicine, Immunology and Toxicology (Princeton, NJ) **19462**

International Journal of Offshore and Polar Engineering (Cupertino, CA) **1797**

International Journal of Optoelectronics (Philadelphia, PA) **27502**

The International Journal of Oral & Maxillofacial Implants (Carol Stream, IL) *Unable to locate*

International Journal of Organizational Analysis (Bowling Green, KY) **11946**

International Journal of Orthodontics (Milwaukee, WI) **34071**

International Journal of Osteoarchaeology (Hoboken, NJ) **18993**

International Journal of Parallel and Distributed Systems and Networks (Calgary, AB, Can.) **34647**

International Journal of Parallel Programming (New York, NY) **21913**

International Journal of Partial Hospitalization (New York, NY) *Ceased*

The International Journal of Periodontics & Restorative Dentistry (Carol Stream, IL) *Unable to locate*

International Journal of Personal Construct Psychology (Philadelphia, PA) **27503**

International Journal of Pest Management (Philadelphia, PA) **27504**

International Journal of Pharmaceutical Advances (Thousand Oaks, CA) *Ceased*

International Journal of Philosophical Practice (IJPP) (Centerview, MO) **16968**

International Journal of PIXE (River Edge, NJ) **19512**

International Journal of Plant Sciences (Seattle, WA) *Unable to locate*

The International Journal of Police Negotiations and Crisis Management **30343***

International Journal of Political Economy (Armonk, NY) **20081**

International Journal of Politics, Culture, and Society (New York, NY) **21914**

International Journal of Population Geography (Hoboken, NJ) **18994**

International Journal of Powder Metallurgy (Princeton, NJ) **19463**

International Journal of Power and Energy Systems (Calgary, AB, Can.) **34648**

International Journal of Primatology (New York, NY) **21915**

International Journal of Production Research (Philadelphia, PA) **27505**

The International Journal of Prosthodontics (Carol Stream, IL) *Unable to locate*

The International Journal of Psychiatry in Medicine (Amityville, NY) **20040**

The International Journal for the Psychology of Religion (Santa Barbara, CA) **3642**

International Journal of Public Administration (Middletown, PA) **27252**

International Journal of Purchasing & Materials Management **908***

International Journal of Qualitative Studies in Education (Austin, TX) **29785**

Interpersonal Violence; Journal of (Thousand Oaks, CA) **3893**
Interpress of London and New York (New York, NY) **37958**
Interpress Service (Washington, DC) **37959**
Interpretation (Richmond, VA) **32439**
Interpretive Birding Bulletin (St. Cloud, MN) **16342**
Interrace Magazine (Burbank, CA) *Ceased*
Interracial Books for Children Bulletin (New York, NY) *Unable to locate*
Interservice (Washington, DC) **5559**
Interstate News Service (St. Louis, MO) **37960**
The Interstate Progress (Mansfield, LA) **12667**
Interstate Radio Network, Inc. (Nashville, TN) *Unable to locate*
The InterStudy Competitive Edge (Bloomington, MN) *Unable to locate*
Intertax (New York, NY) **21943**
Intertexts (Lubbock, TX) **30712**
InterTown Record (North Sutton, NH) **18615**
Intertrade and Investment (Atlanta, GA) *Unable to locate*
Intervention; Journal of Early (Chapel Hill, NC) **23711**
Intervention in School and Clinic (Fairfax, VA) **32017**
Interview (New York, NY) **21944**
Intervirology (Farmington, CT) **4835**
Inti (Cranston, RI) **28335**
Intimacies (New York, NY) *Unable to locate*
Intimate Fashion News (New York, NY) *Unable to locate*
Intimate Story (New York, NY) *Ceased*
The InTowner Newspaper (Washington, DC) **5560**
Intranet Journal (Scarborough, ON, Can.) *Ceased*
IntraNet Magazine (Southborough, MA) **14545**
Intravenous Therapy; Journal of (Los Angeles, CA) **2302**
Intravenous Therapy News **22547***
Intrepid (Denver, CO) *Ceased*
Intrigue (Woodbridge, NJ) *Unable to locate*
Intro (Des Moines, IA) **10788**
Intro Magazine (Los Angeles, CA) *Ceased*
Intuition (San Francisco, CA) *Unable to locate*
INTV-TV (River Forest, IL) **9494**
Inuit Art Quarterly (Ottawa, ON, Can.) **36252**
Inuit Broadcasting Corporation (Ottawa, ON, Can.) **37697**
Inuvik Drum (Yellowknife, NT, Can.) **35524**
Invasion and Metastasis (Farmington, CT) *Ceased*
Invasive Technology; MEEN Diagnostic and (Schaumburg, IL) **9586**
Invention Convention (Hollywood, CA) *Unable to locate*
Inventors' Digest (Boston, MA) **13908**
Inver Grove Heights Sun Current; South St. Paul/ (South St. Paul, MN) **16453**
The Inverness Oran (Inverness, NS, Can.) **35581**
Invertebrate Biology (Santa Cruz, CA) **3684**
Invertebrate Pathology; Journal of (San Diego, CA) **3199**
Invest Canada (Toronto, ON, Can.) *Unable to locate*
Investext Advisor *Ceased*
Investigational New Drugs (New York, NY) **21945**
Investigative Ophthalmology & Visual Science (Philadelphia, PA) *Unable to locate*
Investigative Radiology (Temple, TX) **31178**
Investing; Better (Madison Heights, MI) **15326**
Investing; The Journal of (Plano, TX) **30947**
Investing Licensing & Trading Conditions Abroad (New York, NY) *Unable to locate*
Investment Advisor Magazine (Shrewsbury, NJ) **19556**
Investment Compliance; The Journal of (New York, NY) **22108**
Investment Dealers' Digest (New York, NY) **21946**
Investment Executive (Toronto, ON, Can.) **36624**
Investment Magazine; Global (New York, NY) **21772**
Investment Management Weekly (New York, NY) **21947**
Investment News (Chicago, IL) **8419**
Investment Profiles (Boston, MA) *Unable to locate*
Investment Real Estate; Commercial (Chicago, IL) **8337**
Investment Report; EBRI Quarterly Pension (Washington, DC) **5470**
The Investment Reporter (Newport Beach, CA) **2628**
Investment Vision **22946***
Investments; The Journal of Alternative (Amherst, MA) **13796**
Investments/Opportunities Around The World (Hollywood, FL) *Unable to locate*
Investments; Pensions & (New York, NY) **22537**
Investor Direct (Palm Springs, CA) **2761**
Investor; Institutional (New York, NY) **21880**
Investor (International Edition); Institutional (New York, NY) **21881**
Investor Relations; Strategic (Washington, DC) **5806**
Investor's Business Daily (Los Angeles, CA) **2298**
Investor's Daily **2298***
Investor's Digest of Canada (Toronto, ON, Can.) **36625**

InVitro Cellular & Developmental Biology - PLANT (Largo, MD) **13612**
Inyo Register (Bishop, CA) **1583**
IOL and Ocular Surgery News **19631***
Iola Herald (Iola, WI) **33832**
The Iola Register (Iola, KS) **11513**
Ion Exchange; Solvent Extraction and (Argonne, IL) **8020**
The Ionian (New Rochelle, NY) **21117**
Iosco County News Herald (East Tawas, MI) **14997**
Iowa; Annals of (Iowa City, IA) **10968**
The Iowa Appetizer **10785***
Iowa Bird Life (Ames, IA) *Unable to locate*
Iowa Broadcasting **16321***
Iowa Broadcasting **16315***
Iowa Business & Technology Resource Guide (Des Moines, IA) **10789**
Iowa Cattleman (Ames, IA) *Unable to locate*
Iowa City Magazine (Iowa City, IA) *Unable to locate*
Iowa City Press Citizen (Iowa City, IA) **10974**
Iowa Conservationist (Des Moines, IA) **10790**
Iowa County Farmer (Marengo, IA) **11061**
Iowa Explorer; Nebraska & (Blair, NE) **17957**
Iowa Falls Citizen **11001***
Iowa Farm Edition; Fastline— (Buckner, KY) **11976**
Iowa Farmer Today (Cedar Rapids, IA) **10674**
Iowa Food Dealer **10791***
Iowa Grocer (Des Moines, IA) **10791**
Iowa Heritage Illustrated (Iowa City, IA) **10975**
Iowa Image (Nixa, MO) *Ceased*
Iowa Law Review (Iowa City, IA) **10976**
The Iowa Lawyer (Des Moines, IA) **10792**
Iowa Legionnaire (Des Moines, IA) **10793**
Iowa; Lyrical (Des Moines, IA) **10803**
Iowa Medicine (West Des Moines, IA) **11320**
The Iowa News (Sulphur, LA) **12851**
Iowa Oil Spout (West Des Moines, IA) *Ceased*
Iowa Parent **10794***
Iowa Parent & Family (Des Moines, IA) **10794**
Iowa Pork Producer (Clive, IA) **10716**
Iowa Pork Today (Cedar Rapids, IA) **10675**
Iowa Public Television (Johnston, IA) **37698**
Iowa REC News (Urbandale, IA) **11276**
The Iowa Review (Iowa City, IA) **10977**
The Iowa School Board Dialogue (Des Moines, IA) **10795**
Iowa Shopping News; Eastern (Dyersville, IA) **10860**
Iowa Small Business Resource Guide **10789***
Iowa Smoke-Eater (Des Moines, IA) **10796**
Iowa State Daily (Ames, IA) **10589**
The Iowa Stater (Ames, IA) *Ceased*
Iowa; TCI of (Dubuque, IA) **10853**
The Iowa Trucking Lifeliner (Des Moines, IA) **10797**
Iowa Union Farmer **10767***
Iowa Woman (Iowa City, IA) *Unable to locate*
The Iowan (Des Moines, IA) **10798**
Iowan; The Daily (Iowa City, IA) **10972**
Iowan; Northern (Cedar Falls, IA) **10661**
Iowegian (Centerville, IA) **10688**
IP Litigator (New York, NY) **21948**
IP Magazine (San Francisco, CA) **3375**
IPA Bulletin (South Holland, IL) **9615**
The IP.com Journal (West Henrietta, NY) **23543**
IPS Industrial Products and Services **35718***
Ipswich Chronicle (Needham, MA) **14356**
The Ipswich Tribune (Ipswich, SD) **28873**
IRA Investor (Youngstown, OH) *Unable to locate*
Iranian Community Newspaper (Scarborough, ON, Can.) **36377**
Iranian Journal; Indo- (New York, NY) **21864**
IRB (Garrison, NY) **20648**
IRB: A Review of Human Subjects Researh **20648***
Iredell County News **24246***
Ireland; Eire- (Morristown, NJ) **19312**
Ireland of the Welcomes (Westport, CT) *Unable to locate*
Ireton Examiner (Ireton, IA) **11004**
IRIS (Charlottesville, VA) **31932**
Irish Advocate (New York, NY) *Ceased*
Irish America Magazine (New York, NY) **21949**
Irish American News (Oak Park, IL) **9376**
Irish Echo (New York, NY) **21950**
Irish Families; Journal of (Kansas City, MO) **17173**
Irish Focus News (San Francisco, CA) **3376**
The Irish Herald **3376***
Irish Hills Cablevision LP (Brooklyn, MI) *Unable to locate*
Irish Studies; Journal of Scotch- (Glenolden, PA) **26946**
Irish Voice Newspaper (New York, NY) **21951**
The Irish Wolfhound Quarterly (Wheat Ridge, CO) **4677**
Iron County Miner (Hurley, WI) **33797**
Iron Feather Journal (Boulder, CO) **4172**
Iron Man (New York, NY) **21952**
Iron River Pioneer (Washburn, WI) *Unable to locate*
Iron River Reporter (Iron River, MI) **15211**
Iron & Steel Engineer **27754***

Iron & Steel Maker Magazine (Warrendale, PA) **28112**
Iron Trader News **367***
Irondequoit-Penfield News & Shopper **23231***
Irondequoit Post (Irondequoit, NY) **20783**
Irondequoit Press **20783***
Irondequoit Shopper (Rochester, NY) **23231**
Ironman (Oxnard, CA) **2730**
Ironwood Daily Globe (Ironwood, MI) **15213**
Ironwood Publications (Charleston, IL) *Unable to locate*
The Ironworker (Washington, DC) **5561**
IronWorks (Montgomery, AL) **367**
Iroquois County's Times-Republic (Watseka, IL) **9739**
The Irregular and Mt. Washington Valley News (North Conway, NH) *Ceased*
Irreproducible Results; Journal of (Chicago Heights, IL) **8667**
Irricana Rocky View/Five Village Weekly; Crossfield/ (Irricana, AB, Can.) **34788**
Irrigation and Drainage Engineering; Journal of (Reston, VA) **32385**
Irrigation and Drainage Systems (New York, NY) **21953**
Irrigation Journal (Chicago, IL) **8420**
Irrigation; Landscape & (Chicago, IL) **8457**
IRS Practice and Policy **5814***
Irvine World News (Irvine, CA) *Unable to locate*
Irving News (Arlington, TX) *Ceased*
Irving Park Booster; North Center- (Lincolnwood, IL) **9101**
Irvington Herald (Irvington, NJ) **19125**
ISA Journal **24185***
The Isabel Dakotan (Isabel, SD) **28876**
Isanti County News **15785***
ISBA Bar News (Chicago, IL) **8421**
ISBA Journal (Indianapolis, IN) **9837**
ISI Atlas of Science: Animal and Plant Sciences *Ceased*
ISI Atlas of Science: Biochemistry *Ceased*
ISI Atlas of Science: Immunology *Ceased*
ISI Atlas of Science: Pharmacology *Ceased*
ISIS (Ithaca, NY) **20805**
ISKCON World Review (San Diego, CA) *Unable to locate*
Iskon World Review **5898***
Islamic Social Sciences; American Journal of (Herndon, VA) **32160**
The Island (San Francisco, CA) *Unable to locate*
Island Ad-Vantages (Stonington, ME) **13064**
Island Business (Honolulu, HI) *Ceased*
Island Cablevision **35579***
Island Dispatch (Grand Island, NY) **20678**
The Island-Ear (Garden City, NY) **20643**
Island; The Garden (Lihue, HI) **7779**
Island Gazette (Carolina Beach, NC) **23684**
Island Home (Honolulu, HI) *Unable to locate*
Island Life Magazine (Sanibel, FL) **6649**
Island Navigator **6208***
Island News (Thorne Bay, AK) **643**
The Island Packet (Hilton Head Island, SC) **28661**
Island Park Herald; Oceanside- (Oceanside, NY) **23031**
Island Reporter (Sanibel, FL) **6650**
Island Sport Scene (Charlottetown, PE, Can.) **36916**
Island Visitor (Victoria, BC, Can.) **35217**
Islander (Gulf Shores, AL) **252**
The Islander (Sanibel, FL) **6651**
The Islander (St. Simons Island, GA) **7525**
Islander (Hilton Head Island, SC) *Unable to locate*
Islander (South Hero, VT) **31601**
Islander; The Catalina (Avalon, CA) **1443**
The Islander News (Key Biscayne, FL) **6251**
Islands Magazine (Santa Barbara, CA) **3643**
The Islands' Sounder (Eastsound, WA) **32741**
Island's Sounder Hot Sheet (Bainbridge Island, WA) *Ceased*
Isleton Journal; River News Herald & (Rio Vista, CA) **2927**
Islip Advertiser (Farmingdale, NY) *Ceased*
Islip News (Islip, NY) **20786**
Isolation and Purification (New York, NY) *Unable to locate*
ISP Business News (Potomac, MD) **13654**
(ISR); Information Systems Research (Linthicum, MD) **13620**
Israel Horizons (New York, NY) *Unable to locate*
Israel Journal of Psychiatry and Related Sciences (Chicago, IL) *Ceased*
Israel Scene (New York, NY) *Ceased*
Israel Studies (Bloomington, IN) **9838**
Israel Viewpoint; Young (New York, NY) **22952**
Israelite; Las Vegas (Las Vegas, NV) **18373**
The Issaquah Press (Issaquah, WA) **32784**
Issaquah Valley Shopper **32784***
Issue Watch (Seattle, WA) *Ceased*
Issues (St. Louis, MO) **17448**
Issues in Accounting Education (Sarasota, FL) **6657**

Jefferson County Journal (Warrenton, MO) **17685**
Jefferson County Journal (Adams, NY) **19976**
Jefferson County Leader; Port Townsend/ (Port Townsend, WA) **32894**
Jefferson County Pennysaver (Watertown, NY) *Unable to locate*
Jefferson County Sunday Journal **17685***
The Jefferson County Transcript (Golden, CO) **4469**
Jefferson County Weekender (Jefferson, WI) *Unable to locate*
The Jefferson Herald (Jefferson, IA) **11006**
Jefferson Jimplecute (Jefferson, TX) **30624**
Jefferson Law Review; Thomas (San Diego, CA) **3279**
Jefferson Parish; Cox Cable (Harahan, LA) **12597**
Jefferson Park Leader **8573***
Jefferson Park Passage (Highland Park, IL) *Unable to locate*
Jefferson Park/Portage Park Times (Lincolnwood, IL) **9095**
The Jefferson Post (West Jefferson, NC) **24283**
Jefferson Recorder-Times (San Antonio, TX) *Ceased*
Jefferson Reporter (Thomson, GA) *Ceased*
Jefferson Reporter; News & Former & Wadley Herald/The (Louisville, GA) **7376**
Jefferson Republic (De Soto, MO) *Ceased*
Jefferson Star (Rigby, ID) **7967**
The Jefferson Times **24283***
The Jefferson Times Too (West Jefferson, NC) *Ceased*
Jeffersonian (Columbia, MD) **13463**
Jeffersonian (Croswell, MI) **14892**
Jeffersonian; The Daily (Cambridge, OH) **24724**
Jeffersonian Democrat (Brookville, PA) **26732**
Jeffersonville Cable (Stowe, VT) *Unable to locate*
Jellico Advance-Sentinel (Jellico, TN) *Unable to locate*
JEMS (San Diego, CA) **3175**
The Jena Times (Jena, LA) *Unable to locate*
Jenda (Binghamton, NY) **20159**
Jennings Daily News (Jennings, LA) **12606**
Jericho News Journal (Jericho, NY) **20849**
Jericho Pennysaver; Plainview/ (Plainview, NY) **23099**
Jericho Tribune; Syosset/ (Jericho, NY) **20850**
Jerry D. Mead Enterprises (Carson City, NV) *Unable to locate*
Jersey Beat (Weehawken, NJ) **19711**
The Jersey City Reporter (Jersey City, NJ) **19140**
Jersey City; This Week in (Jersey City, NJ) **19147**
Jersey County Shopper (Carrollton, IL) **8162**
Jersey Journal (Jersey City, NJ) **19141**
Jersey Journal (Reynoldsburg, OH) **25495**
Jersey Journeys (Newark, NJ) **19355**
Jersey Parents Express; South (Fort Washington, PA) **26934**
Jersey Shore Art & Antiques (Bay Head, NJ) *Ceased*
The Jerusalem Journal of International Relations (Baltimore, MD) *Ceased*
The Jerusalem Post Foreign Service (New York, NY) **37967**
The Jerusalem Post, International Edition (New York, NY) **21959**
The Jerusalem Quarterly (New York, NY) *Ceased*
The Jessamine Journal (Nicholasville, KY) **12325**
Jesuit Bulletin (St. Louis, MO) **17449**
Jesuits; Studies in the Spirituality of (St. Louis, MO) **17518**
Jet (Chicago, IL) **8425**
Jet Cargo News (Houston, TX) *Ceased*
Jet Gazette (Austin, TX) *Unable to locate*
Jet Lag Magazine (St. Louis, MO) *Unable to locate*
Jet Skier Magazine **1921***
Jet Sports (Foothill Ranch, CA) **1921**
The Jetmore Republican (Jetmore, KS) **11516**
(JETP); Journal of Experimental and Theoretical Physics (College Park, MD) **13427**
JETP Letters (College Park, MD) **13422**
Jets Journal (Red Bank, NJ) *Ceased*
Jewel (New York, NY) *Ceased*
Jeweler; Couture International (New York, NY) **21508**
Jeweler; JCK's High-Volume (King of Prussia, PA) **27124**
Jeweler; Modern (Melville, NY) **21049**
Jeweler; National (New York, NY) **22397**
Jewelers' Circular-Keystone (New York, NY) **21960**
Jewelers Inc. (Albert Lea, MN) *Unable to locate*
Jewelers, Inc. (Rochford, SD) *Unable to locate*
Jewell County News (Mankato, KS) **11637**
Jewell County Post **11638***
Jewell County Record (Mankato, KS) **11638**
Jeweller; Canadian (Toronto, ON, Can.) **36508**
Jewellery World (Toronto, ON, Can.) *Ceased*
The Jewett Messenger (Jewett, TX) **30625**
Jewish Action (New York, NY) *Unable to locate*
The Jewish Advocate (Boston, MA) **13910**
Jewish Archives; American (Cincinnati, OH) **24770**
Jewish Braille Review (New York, NY) **21961**
Jewish Bulletin of Northern California (San Francisco, CA) *Unable to locate*
Jewish Bulletin; Ottawa (Ottawa, ON, Can.) **36266**

Jewish Chronicle (Worcester, MA) **14685**
Jewish Chronicle; Kansas City (Overland Park, KS) **11717**
Jewish Chronicle; The Wisconsin (Milwaukee, WI) **34109**
Jewish Communal Service; Journal of (Kendall Park, NJ) **19152**
The Jewish Community Voice (Cherry Hill, NJ) **18736**
Jewish Currents (New York, NY) **21962**
Jewish Exponent Inside (Philadelphia, PA) **27509**
Jewish Family & Life (Newton, MA) **14402**
(Jewish Fighter); Yiddisher Kemfer (New York, NY) **22949**
Jewish Floridian of Palm Beach County (Miami, FL) *Ceased*
Jewish Floridian of South Broward (Miami, FL) *Ceased*
Jewish Floridian of South County (Miami, FL) *Ceased*
Jewish Forward (New York, NY) **21963**
The Jewish Herald (Brooklyn, NY) **20322**
Jewish Herald-Voice (Houston, TX) **30494**
Jewish History; American (Newton Centre, MA) **14414**
Jewish History; Western States (Woodland Hills, CA) **4117**
Jewish Horizon **19749***
The Jewish Journal (Youngstown, OH) *Unable to locate*
Jewish Journal; Broward (Chicago, IL) **8293**
Jewish Journal Dade (Deerfield Beach, FL) **6050**
The Jewish Journal/North of Boston (Salem, MA) **14513**
Jewish Journal North; Palm Beach (Chicago, IL) **8525**
Jewish Journal South; Palm Beach (West Palm Beach, FL) **9750**
Jewish Leader (New London, CT) *Unable to locate*
Jewish Ledger (Rochester, NY) **23232**
Jewish Ledger; Connecticut (West Hartford, CT) **5202**
Jewish Light; St. Louis (St. Louis, MO) **17501**
Jewish Link; New Mexico (Albuquerque, NM) **19779**
Jewish Literature; Studies in American (University Park, PA) **28085**
Jewish Music and Liturgy; Journal of (New York, NY) **22109**
Jewish News; Akron (Akron, OH) **24572**
Jewish News; The Canadian (North York, ON, Can.) **36124**
Jewish News—Central Edition; New Jersey (Whippany, NJ) **19749**
Jewish News; Cleveland (Beachwood, OH) **24651**
Jewish News; The Detroit (Detroit, MI) **14925**
Jewish News of Greater Phoenix (Phoenix, AZ) **805**
Jewish News; Intermountain (Denver, CO) **4332**
Jewish News; Savannah (Savannah, GA) **7535**
Jewish News; Stark (Canton, OH) **24732**
Jewish News; Toledo (Sylvania, OH) **25556**
Jewish Observer (DeWitt, NY) **20532**
The Jewish Observer (New York, NY) **21964**
Jewish Post of New York (New York, NY) **21965**
The Jewish Post & News (Winnipeg, MB, Can.) **35334**
Jewish Post and Opinion; The Indiana (Indianapolis, IN) **10127**
Jewish Press (Omaha, NE) **18199**
Jewish Press (Brooklyn, NY) **20323**
Jewish Press of Pinellas County (Clearwater, FL) **5987**
Jewish Press of Tampa (Clearwater, FL) **5988**
Jewish Press; Toronto (Downsview, ON, Can.) **35785**
The Jewish Quarterly Review (Philadelphia, PA) **27510**
The Jewish Reporter (Las Vegas, NV) **18365**
Jewish Reporter; Wyoming Valley (Vestal, NY) **23489**
Jewish Review; Buffalo (Buffalo, NY) **20365**
Jewish Singles News **23010***
Jewish Singles News/Single News & Views/Singles Style (North Bellmore, NY) **23010**
Jewish Social Studies (Bloomington, IN) **9839**
The Jewish Standard (Toronto, ON, Can.) **36630**
The Jewish Star (Birmingham, AL) **75**
Jewish Star (San Francisco, CA) *Unable to locate*
The Jewish Star (Calgary Edition) (Calgary, AB, Can.) *Ceased*
The Jewish Star (Edmonton Edition) (Calgary, AB, Can.) *Ceased*
Jewish Studies/Etudes Juives Canadiennes; Canadian (Montreal, QC, Can.) **37094**
Jewish Studies; Latin American (Swarthmore, PA) **28042**
Jewish Telegraphic Agency Inc. (New York, NY) **37968**
Jewish Television Network (Beverly Hills, CA) **37765**
Jewish Times (Huntingdon Valley, PA) *Unable to locate*
Jewish Times; The Boston (Boston, MA) **13859**
Jewish Times; San Diego (La Mesa, CA) **2123**
The Jewish Transcript (Seattle, WA) **32975**
The Jewish Veteran (Washington, DC) **5563**
The Jewish Voice (Wilmington, DE) *Unable to locate*
Jewish Voice; Deep South (Birmingham, AL) **67**

The Jewish Week (New York, NY) **21966**
Jewish Week; Washington (Rockville, MD) **13699**
Jewish Weekly News (Springfield, MA) *Unable to locate*
The Jewish Western Bulletin (Vancouver, BC, Can.) **35151**
Jewish Woman (Washington, DC) **5564**
The Jewish World (Albany, NY) **19990**
Jewish World; American (St. Louis Park, MN) **16359**
JewishSports.com (Newton, MA) **14403**
Jewry; Contemporary (Melrose Park, PA) **27245**
(JHEOE); Journal of Higher Education Outreach and Engagement (Athens, GA) **6944**
JIAPAC (Journal of the International Association of Physicians in AIDS Care) (Chicago, IL) *Unable to locate*
The Jibsheet (Bellevue, WA) **32666**
Jicarilla Chieftain (Dulce, NM) **19843**
Jiji Press America Ltd. (New York, NY) **37969**
Jim Hogg County Enterprises (Hebbronville, TX) *Unable to locate*
Jimplecute; Jefferson (Jefferson, TX) **30624**
The Jimplicate **16971***
The Jimplicute (Chaffee, MO) *Ceased*
JINN Magazine (San Francisco, CA) **3377**
JINS (La Jolla, CA) **2114**
JIT (Joplin, MO) *Ceased*
JMBA: Journal of the Marine Biological Association (New York, NY) **21967**
J.M.C.I. Cable (Big Clifty, KY) *Unable to locate*
JMCI - The Journal of Molecular and Cellular Immunology (New York, NY) *Ceased*
(JMCNH); Journal of Multicultural Nursing and Health (Chautauqua, NY) **20454**
JMNR (Chicago, IL) **8426**
JMPT: Journal of Manipulative and Physiological Therapeutics (New York, NY) **21968**
(JNCHC); Journal of the National Collegiate Honors Council (Birmingham, AL) **76**
JNMS: Journal of the Neuromusculoskeletal System (Towson, MD) **13760**
(JNSD); Journal for Nurses in Staff Development (Philadelphia, PA) **27540**
Job Corps in Action (Ogden, UT) *Ceased*
Job Ready; St. Petersburg, FL) *Unable to locate*
Job Scan **18464***
Job Shop Technology (JST) (Prospect, CT) **5092**
Jobber Executive *Ceased*
Jobber News (Toronto, ON, Can.) **36631**
Jobber Topics Reports (Barrington, IL) *Unable to locate*
Jobs Digest; Air (Washington, DC) **5317**
Jobs Today (Detroit, MI) *Ceased*
JobWatch (Montvale, NJ) **19259**
Jock Erotic Novels (Los Angeles, CA) *Unable to locate*
Jock Stars Collection Stryker (Los Angeles, CA) *Unable to locate*
Joe Magazine (New York, NY) **21969**
Johannes Schwalm Historical Association Journal (State Line, PA) **28032**
John Milton Magazine (New York, NY) **21970**
John Rice & Charles Strauser **17643***
Johns Hopkins APL Technical Digest (Laurel, MD) **13613**
Johns Hopkins Magazine (Baltimore, MD) **13174**
The Johns Hopkins News-Letter (Baltimore, MD) **13175**
Johns Hopkins University Gazette **13163***
Johnson City Press (Johnson City, TN) **29251**
Johnson City Press-Chronicle **29251***
Johnson City Record Courier (Johnson City, TX) **30626**
Johnson County Graphic (Clarksville, AR) **1080**
Johnson County Marketplace (Shawnee Mission, KS) *Unable to locate*
Johnson County Sun (Overland Park, KS) **11716**
The Johnson Pioneer (Johnson, KS) **11518**
Johnsonburg Community TV Co. Inc. (Johnsonburg, PA) **27086**
The Johnsonburg Press (Johnsonburg, PA) **27085**
Johnston County Capital Democrat (Tishomingo, OK) **26100**
Johnston Sunrise (Greenville, RI) **28354**
Johnstown Breeze (Johnstown, CO) **4522**
Johnstown Independent (Johnstown, OH) **25271**
The Joint Commission Journal on Quality Improvement (Oakbrook Terrace, IL) **9380**
Joint Diseases Bulletin; Hospital for (New York, NY) **21818**
Joint Force Quarterly (Washington, DC) **5565**
Jolicoeur's Business NH **18556***
The Joliet Herald News (Joliet, IL) **9035**
Jolly Shopper (Lockport, IL) *Unable to locate*
JOM (Mount Prospect, IL) *Unable to locate*
(JONA); Journal of Nursing Administration (Philadelphia, PA) **27541**
Jonathan (Los Angeles, CA) **2300**
Billy R. #Jones **7570***

Journal of the American Leather Chemists Association (Lubbock, TX) *Unable to locate*

Journal of the American Mathematical Society (Providence, RI) **28402**

Journal of the American Medical Directors Association (JAMDA) (Thousand Oaks, CA) **3878**

Journal of the American Medical Women's Association (New York, NY) **21983**

The Journal of American Military History (Fort Collins, CO) *Ceased*

Journal of the American Oil Chemists' Society (Champaign, IL) **8194**

Journal of American Organbuilding (Houston, TX) **30495**

Journal of the American Oriental Society (Boulder, CO) **4173**

Journal of the American Osteopathic Association (Chicago, IL) **8432**

Journal of the American Pharmaceutical Association (Washington, DC) **5570**

Journal of the American Planning Association (Chicago, IL) *Unable to locate*

Journal of the American Planning Association (JAPA) (Portland, OR) **26483**

Journal of the American Podiatric Medical Association (Bethesda, MD) **13347**

Journal of the American Psychiatric Nurses Association (St. Louis, MO) **17453**

Journal of the American Psychoanalytic Association (New York, NY) **21984**

Journal of the American Rhododendron Society (Fortuna, CA) **1929**

Journal of the American Scientific Affiliation **14257***

Journal of the American Society of Brewing Chemists (St. Paul, MN) **16381**

Journal of the American Society of CLU & ChFC **26741***

Journal of the American Society of Echocardiography (Philadelphia, PA) **27513**

Journal of the American Society for Horticultural Science (Alexandria, VA) **31687**

Journal of the American Society for Information Science (Hoboken, NJ) **19001**

Journal of the American Society of Nephrology (Philadelphia, PA) **27514**

Journal of the American Society for Psychical Research (New York, NY) **21985**

Journal of the American Society for Surgery (Philadelphia, PA) **27515**

Journal of the American Statistical Association (Alexandria, VA) **31688**

Journal of American Studies (New York, NY) **21986**

Journal of the American Veterinary Medical Association (Schaumburg, IL) **9584**

Journal of the American Water Resources Association (Middleburg, VA) **32272**

Journal of the American Water Works Association (Denver, CO) **4334**

Journal of AMRA **8429***

Journal of Analytic Social Work **14945***

Journal of Analytical Chemistry (New York, NY) **21987**

Journal of Analytical Toxicology (Niles, IL) **9287**

Journal of Anatomy (New York, NY) **21988**

Journal of Andrology (Minneapolis, MN) **16086**

Journal of Anthropological Archaeology (San Diego, CA) **3179**

Journal of Anthropological Research (Albuquerque, NM) **19774**

Journal of Anthroposophical Medicine (Ann Arbor, MI) *Ceased*

Journal of Anti-Aging Medicine (Larchmont, NY) **20907**

Journal of AOAC International (Gaithersburg, MD) **13544**

Journal of Applied Animal Welfare Science (Washington Grove, MD) **13774**

Journal of Applied Aquaculture (Frankfort, KY) **12064**

Journal of Applied Asphalt Binder Technology (Blooming Glen, PA) **26716**

Journal of Applied Behavior Analysis (Lawrence, KS) *Unable to locate*

Journal of Applied Behavioral Science (Thousand Oaks, CA) **3879**

Journal of Applied Biomechanics (Champaign, IL) **8195**

Journal of Applied Chemistry of the USSR **22683***

Journal of Applied Communication Research (Washington, DC) **5571**

Journal of Applied Corporate Finance (New York, NY) **21989**

Journal of Applied Econometrics (Hoboken, NJ) **19002**

Journal of Applied Electrochemistry (New York, NY) **21990**

Journal of Applied Fire Science (Amityville, NY) **20041**

Journal of Applied Gerontology (Thousand Oaks, CA) *Ceased*

Journal of Applied Mathematics and Decision Sciences (Santa Monica, CA) **3712**

Journal of Applied Mechanics (New York, NY) **21991**

Journal of Applied Mechanics and Technical Physics (New York, NY) **21992**

Journal of Applied Meteorology (Boston, MA) **13912**

Journal of Applied Phycology (New York, NY) **21993**

Journal of Applied Physics (College Park, MD) **13423**

Journal of Applied Physiology (Bethesda, MD) **13348**

Journal of Applied Polymer Science (Hoboken, NJ) **19003**

Journal of Applied Psychoanalytic Studies (New York, NY) **21994**

Journal of Applied Psychology (Washington, DC) **5572**

Journal of Applied Recreation Research **36855***

Journal of Applied Rehabilitation Counseling (Manassas, VA) **32222**

Journal of Applied School Psychology (Piscataway, NJ) **19428**

Journal of Applied Social Studies (Cleveland, OH) **24913**

Journal of Applied Spectroscopy (New York, NY) **21995**

Journal of Applied Sport Psychology (Rancho Cordova, CA) **2875**

Journal of Applied Toxicology (Hoboken, NJ) **19004**

Journal of Approximation Theory (San Diego, CA) **3180**

Journal of Aquatic Animal Health (Bethesda, MD) **13349**

Journal of Aquatic Ecosystem Stress and Recovery (New York, NY) **21996**

Journal of Aquatic Food Product Technology (Astoria, OR) **26225**

Journal of Arachnology (College Park, MD) **13424**

Journal of Arboriculture (Champaign, IL) *Unable to locate*

Journal of Archaeological Method and Theory (New York, NY) **21997**

Journal of Archaeological Research (New York, NY) **21998**

Journal of Architectural Education (JAE) (Cambridge, MA) *Unable to locate*

Journal of Architectural Engineering (Reston, VA) **32370**

Journal of Architectural and Planning Research (Chicago, IL) **8433**

Journal of Architectural Research **8433***

Journal of Archival Organization (Binghamton, NY) **20163**

Journal-Argus (St. Mary's, ON, Can.) **36360**

Journal of Arizona History (Tucson, AZ) **950**

The Journal of the Arkansas Medical Society (Little Rock, AR) **1231**

Journal of the Arnold Arboretum (Cambridge, MA) *Ceased*

The Journal of Art (New York, NY) *Ceased*

The Journal of Arthroplasty (Philadelphia, PA) **27516**

Journal of Artificial Intelligence in Education (Norfolk, VA) *Unable to locate*

Journal of Artificial Intelligence Research (Marina del Rey, CA) *Unable to locate*

The Journal of Arts Management, Law, and Society (Washington, DC) **5573**

Journal of the ASFMRA (Denver, CO) **4335**

Journal of Asia-Pacific Business (Johnson City, TN) **29252**

Journal of Asian and African Studies (Willowdale, ON, Can.) **36880**

Journal of Asian American Studies (Baltimore, MD) **13178**

Journal of Asian Economics (New York, NY) **21999**

The Journal of Asian Martial Arts (Erie, PA) **26900**

The Journal of Asian Studies (Salt Lake City, UT) **31433**

Journal of Assisted Reproduction and Genetics (New York, NY) **22000**

Journal of the Association for Communication Administration (JACA) (Washington, DC) **5574**

Journal of the Association for Computing Machinery (New York, NY) **22001**

Journal of the Association of Nurses in AIDS Care (Thousand Oaks, CA) **3880**

Journal of the Association of Official Analytical Chemists **13544***

The Journal of the Association for Persons with Severe Handicaps (Baltimore, MD) **13179**

Journal of Asthma (Dencer, CO) **4303**

The Journal of the Astronautical Sciences (West Lafayette, IN) **10548**

Journal of Athletic Training (Charlottesville, VA) **31933**

Journal of Atmospheric Chemistry (New York, NY) **22002**

Journal of Atmospheric and Oceanic Technology (Boston, MA) **13913**

Journal of the Audio Engineering Society (New York, NY) **22003**

Journal of Autism and Developmental Disorders (Chapel Hill, NC) **23710**

Journal of Automated Reasoning (New York, NY) **22004**

Journal of Automatic Chemistry (Philadelphia, PA) **27517**

Journal of Automation and Information Sciences (New York, NY) **22005**

Journal of Avian Medicine and Surgery (Lawrence, KS) **11554**

Journal of the AVMA (Schaumburg, IL) *Unable to locate*

Journal of Bacteriology (Washington, DC) **5575**

The Journal of Bank Accounting and Auditing (New York, NY) *Ceased*

The Journal of Bank Taxation (New York, NY) *Ceased*

Journal of Behavioral Decision Making (Hoboken, NJ) **19005**

Journal of Behavioral Education (New York, NY) **22006**

The Journal of Behavioral Finance (Mahwah, NJ) **19195**

Journal of Behavioral Health Services & Research (Tampa, FL) **6769**

Journal of Behavioral Medicine (New York, NY) **22007**

Journal of Biblical Literature (Atlanta, GA) **7020**

Journal of Biblical Studies (Riverview, MI) **15465**

Journal of Big Bend Studies (Alpine, TX) **29683**

Journal of Biochemical and Molecular Toxicology (Hoboken, NJ) **19006**

Journal of Biochemical Toxicology **19006***

Journal of Biochemistry, Molecular Biology and Biophysics (Langhorne, PA) *Ceased*

Journal of Bioeconomics (New York, NY) **22008**

Journal of Bioenergetics and Biomembranes (New York, NY) **22009**

The Journal of Biological Chemistry (Bethesda, MD) **13350**

Journal of Biological Physics (New York, NY) **22010**

Journal of Biological Rhythms (Evanston, IL) **8863**

Journal of Biomechanical Engineering (New York, NY) **22011**

The Journal of Biomedical Informatics (New York, NY) **22012**

Journal of Biomedical Materials Research (Hoboken, NJ) **19007**

Journal of Biomedical Science (Farmington, CT) **4836**

Journal of Biomolecular NMR (New York, NY) **22013**

Journal of Biomolecular Screening (Larchmont, NY) *Ceased*

Journal of Biomolecular Techniques (Memphis, TN) **29371**

Journal of Biopharmaceutical Statistics (Cambridge, MA) **14074**

Journal of Bisexuality (Binghamton, NY) **20164**

Journal of Black Psychology (Thousand Oaks, CA) **3881**

Journal of Black Studies (Thousand Oaks, CA) **3882**

The Journal of Bone and Joint Surgery (Needham, MA) **14357**

Journal of Bone and Mineral Research (Durham, NC) **23829**

Journal of Border Health (El Paso, TX) *Unable to locate*

The Journal of Borderland Research (Eureka, CA) **1893**

Journal of the Boston Society of Civil Engineers **13878***

Journal of Bridge Engineering (Reston, VA) **32371**

Journal of Brief Therapy (New York, NY) **22014**

Journal of British Studies (Seattle, WA) *Unable to locate*

Journal of Broadcasting **5576***

Journal of Broadcasting & Electronic Media (Washington, DC) **5576**

Journal of Bronchology (Baltimore, MD) **13180**

Journal of Burn Care & Rehabilitation (New York, NY) *Unable to locate*

Journal of Business **19585***

The Journal of Business (Seattle, WA) *Unable to locate*

Journal of Business (Spokane, WA) *Unable to locate*

The Journal of Business Communication (Flint, MI) **15035**

Journal of Business and Economic Perspectives (Martin, TN) **29342**

Journal of Business & Economic Statistics (Alexandria, VA) **31689**

Journal of Business and Economic Studies (Oakdale, NY) **23029**

Journal of Business and Finance Librarianship (Columbus, OH) **25023**

Journal of Business Forecasting Methods (Great Neck, NY) **20691**

Journal of Business and Psychology (New York, NY) *Unable to locate*

Journal of Business and Public Affairs (Murray, KY) **12315**
Journal of Business Strategies (Huntsville, TX) **30596**
Journal of Business Strategy (New York, NY) **22015**
Journal of Business and Technical Communications (Thousand Oaks, CA) **3883**
Journal of Business-to-Business Marketing (New York, NY) **22016**
The Journal of C Language Translation (Trumansburg, NY) *Ceased*
Journal CAJLE (Montreal, QC, Can.) **37137**
Journal of the California Dental Association (Sacramento, CA) **3003**
The Journal of California Taxation (New York, NY) **22017**
Journal of the Canadian Ceramic Society **36876***
Journal of the Canadian Chiropractic Association (Toronto, ON, Can.) **36632**
Journal of the Canadian Dental Association (Journal de l'Association Dentaire Canadienne) (Ottawa, ON, Can.) **36253**
Journal of Canadian Fiction (Montreal, QC, Can.) **37138**
Journal of the Canadian Jewish Historical Society **37094***
Journal of Canadian Petroleum Technology (Montreal, QC, Can.) *Unable to locate*
Journal of Canadian Poetry (Ottawa, ON, Can.) **36254**
Journal of Canadian Studies (Revue d'Etudes Canadiennes) (Peterborough, ON, Can.) **36316**
(Journal Canadien de Cardiologie); The Canadian Journal of Cardiology (Oakville, ON, Can.) **36137**
Journal Canadien De Pharmacologie Clinique **36138***
(Journal Canadien d'Ophtalmologie); Canadian Journal of Ophthalmology (Ottawa, ON, Can.) **36210**
Journal Canadien de Gastroenterologie **36139***
Journal of Cannabis Therapeutics (Binghamton, NY) **20165**
The Journal of CAPEA **3356***
Journal of Carbohydrate Chemistry (Missoula, MT) **17867**
Journal of Cardiac Failure (San Francisco, CA) **3378**
Journal of Cardiac Surgery (Armonk, NY) **20084**
Journal of Cardiopulmonary Rehabilitation (Philadelphia, PA) **27518**
Journal of Cardiothoracic and Vascular Anesthesia (Louisville, KY) **12220**
Journal of Cardiovascular Diagnosis & Procedures (Larchmont, NY) *Ceased*
Journal of Cardiovascular Electrophysiology (Armonk, NY) **20085**
Journal of Cardiovascular Nursing (New York, NY) **22018**
Journal of Cardiovascular Pharmacology (Baltimore, MD) **13181**
Journal of Cardiovascular Pharmacology and Therapeutics (Philadelphia, PA) **27519**
Journal of Career Development (New York, NY) *Unable to locate*
Journal of Career Planning & Employment (Bethlehem, PA) **26701**
Journal of Caribbean Studies (Lexington, KY) **12167**
Journal of Case Management **21377***
The Journal of Case Management (New York, NY) *Ceased*
Journal of Cash Management **13295***
Journal of Catalysis (Berkeley, CA) **1531**
Journal of Cataract and Refractive Surgery (Fairfax, VA) **32019**
The Journal of Cell Biology (New York, NY) **22019**
Journal of Cellular Biochemistry (Hoboken, NJ) **19008**
Journal of Cellular Physiology (Hoboken, NJ) **19009**
Journal of Cerebral Blood Flow and Metabolism (Baltimore, MD) **13182**
Journal de Chambly **36959***
Journal of Chemical Crystallography (New York, NY) **22020**
Journal of Chemical Dependency Treatment (Binghamton, NY) *Unable to locate*
Journal of Chemical Ecology (New York, NY) **22021**
Journal of Chemical Education (Westport, CT) *Unable to locate*
Journal of Chemical and Engineering Data (Washington, DC) *Unable to locate*
Journal of Chemical Information and Computer Sciences (Washington, DC) *Unable to locate*
Journal of Chemical Neuroanatomy (Hoboken, NJ) *Ceased*
The Journal of Chemical Physics (College Park, MD) **13425**
Journal of Chemical Technology and Biotechnology (Hoboken, NJ) **19010**
Journal of Chemical Vapor Deposition (Thousand Oaks, CA) *Ceased*
Journal of Chemometrics (Hoboken, NJ) **19011**
Journal of Child and Adolescent Group Therapy (New York, NY) **22022**

Journal of Child & Adolescent Psychiatric and Mental Health Nursing **27520***
Journal of Child and Adolescent Psychiatric and Mental Health Nursing (Philadelphia, PA) *Ceased*
Journal of Child and Adolescent Psychiatric Nursing (Philadelphia, PA) **27520**
Journal of Child and Adolescent Psychopharmacology (Larchmont, NY) **20908**
Journal of Child and Adolescent Substance Abuse (Fort Lauderdale, FL) **6077**
Journal of Child-Care Administration (Holbrook, NY) **20749**
Journal of Child and Family Nursing (Philadelphia, PA) **27521**
Journal of Child and Family Studies (New York, NY) **22023**
Journal of Child Language (New York, NY) **22024**
Journal of Child Neurology (Omaha, NE) **18201**
Journal of Child Sexual Abuse (Binghamton, NY) *Unable to locate*
Journal of Children's Communication Development **29769***
Journal of Chinese Law **21445***
Journal of Chinese Linguistics (Berkeley, CA) **1532**
Journal of Chiropractic **17469***
Journal of Christian Camping **4240***
Journal of Christian Education of the African Methodist Episcopal Church (Nashville, TN) **29461**
Journal of Christian Nursing (Madison, WI) **33950**
Journal of Chromatographic Science (Niles, IL) **9288**
Journal of Chronic Fatigue Syndrome (Binghamton, NY) *Unable to locate*
Journal of Church and State (Waco, TX) **31249**
Journal of Climate (Boston, MA) **13914**
Journal of Climate and Applied Meteorology **13914***
Journal of Clinical Activities, Assignments & Handouts in Psychotherapy (Hammond, IN) **10051**
Journal of Clinical Activities, Assignments & Handouts in Psychotherapy Practice (Binghamton, NY) **20166**
Journal of Clinical Anesthesia (Burlington, MA) *Ceased*
Journal of Clinical Apheresis (Hoboken, NJ) **19012**
Journal of Clinical Child Psychology (Mahwah, NJ) **19196**
Journal of Clinical Endocrinology & Metabolism (Bethesda, MD) *Unable to locate*
Journal of Clinical Engineering (New York, NY) *Unable to locate*
Journal of Clinical and Experimental Gerontology (New York, NY) *Ceased*
Journal of Clinical Gastroenterology (Baltimore, MD) **13183**
Journal of Clinical Geropsychology (New York, NY) **22025**
Journal of Clinical Hypnotherapy and Hypnoanalysis (Madison, CT) *Ceased*
Journal of Clinical Immunoassay (Wayne, MI) *Unable to locate*
Journal of Clinical Immunology (New York, NY) **22026**
Journal of Clinical Investigation (New York, NY) *Unable to locate*
Journal of Clinical Laboratory Analysis (Hoboken, NJ) **19013**
Journal of Clinical Laser Medicine & Surgery (Larchmont, NY) **20909**
Journal of Clinical Microbiology (Washington, DC) **5577**
Journal of Clinical Monitoring **22027***
Journal of Clinical Monitoring and Computing (New York, NY) **22027**
Journal of Clinical Neurology (Jamesburg, NJ) *Ceased*
Journal of Clinical Neuromuscular Disease (Baltimore, MD) **13184**
Journal of Clinical Neurophysiology (Baltimore, MD) **13185**
Journal of Clinical Orthodontics (Boulder, CO) **4174**
Journal of the Clinical Orthopaedic Society (Hoboken, NJ) *Ceased*
The Journal of Clinical Pharmacology (Philadelphia, PA) *Unable to locate*
Journal of Clinical Psychiatry (Memphis, TN) **29372**
Journal of Clinical Psychoanalysis (Madison, CT) **4931**
Journal of Clinical Psychology (Oklahoma City, OK) **25968**
Journal of Clinical Psychology in Medical Settings (New York, NY) **22028**
Journal of Clinical Psychopharmacology (Boston, MA) **13915**
Journal of Clinical Ultrasound (Hoboken, NJ) **19014**
Journal of Cluster Science (Columbia, SC) **28551**
The Journal of Coal Quality (Bowling Green, KY) *Ceased*
Journal of Coatings Technology (Blue Bell, PA) **26725**
Journal of Cognition and Development (Toronto, ON, Can.) **36633**

Journal of Cognitive Neuroscience (Sharon, VT) **31598**
Journal of Cognitive Psychotherapy (New York, NY) **22029**
The Journal of Cognitive Rehabilitation (Indianapolis, IN) **10139**
Journal of the Coin Laundry and Drycleaning Industry (Downers Grove, IL) **8787**
Journal of Cold Regions Engineering (Reston, VA) **32372**
Journal of Cold War Studies (Cambridge, MA) **14075**
Journal of Collective Negotiations in the Public Sector (Amityville, NY) **20042**
Journal of College Counseling (Baltimore, MD) *Unable to locate*
Journal of College Placement **26701***
The Journal of College Radio (New Windsor, NY) **21127**
Journal of College Reading and Learning (Prince George, BC, Can.) **35056**
Journal of College Science Teaching (Arlington, VA) **31801**
Journal of College Student Development (Alexandria, VA) *Ceased*
Journal of College Student Psychotherapy (Wallingford, PA) **28101**
Journal of College and University Foodservice (Blacksburg, VA) **31873**
Journal of College and University Law (Notre Dame, IN) **10369**
Journal of College and University Student Housing (Gainesville, FL) **6146**
Journal of Colloid and Interface Science (San Diego, CA) **3181**
Journal of Colonialism & Colonial History (Towson, MD) **13761**
Journal of the Colorado-Wyoming Academy of Science (Greeley, CO) **4498**
Journal of Combinatorial Chemistry (Washington, DC) **5578**
Journal of Combinatorial Designs (Hoboken, NJ) **19015**
Journal of Combinatorial Optimization (New York, NY) **22030**
Journal of Combinatorial Theory, Series A (San Diego, CA) **3182**
Journal of Combinatorial Theory, Series B (San Diego, CA) **3183**
The Journal of Commerce (Newark, NJ) *Unable to locate*
Journal of Commerce (Burnaby, BC, Can.) **34904**
Journal of Commerce Import Bulletin (Newark, NJ) **19356**
The Journal of Commercial Bank Lending **27654***
The Journal of Commercial Lending **27654***
Journal of Communication (Cary, NC) **23689**
Journal of Communication Inquiry (Thousand Oaks, CA) **3884**
Journal of Communications Technology and Electronics (Hoboken, NJ) **19016**
Journal of Community & Applied Social Psychology (Hoboken, NJ) **19017**
Journal of Community Health (New York, NY) *Unable to locate*
Journal of Community Health Nursing (Wood Ridge, NJ) **19755**
Journal of Community Practice (Binghamton, NY) *Unable to locate*
Journal of Community Psychology (Philadelphia, PA) **27522**
The Journal of Comparative Asian Development (Chicago, IL) **8434**
Journal of Comparative Economics (Middletown, CT) **4944**
Journal of Comparative Family Studies (Calgary, AB, Can.) **34651**
Journal of Comparative Germanic Linguistics (New York, NY) **22031**
Journal of Comparative International Management (Fredericton, NB, Can.) **35396**
The Journal of Comparative Neurology (Hoboken, NJ) **19018**
Journal of Comparative Policy Analysis (New York, NY) **22032**
Journal of Comparative Psychology (Washington, DC) *Unable to locate*
Journal of Compensation and Benefits (New York, NY) **22033**
Journal of Complexity (San Diego, CA) **3184**
Journal of Composites for Construction (Reston, VA) **32373**
Journal of Composites Technology and Research (West Conshohocken, PA) *Unable to locate*
Journal of Computational Analysis and Applications (New York, NY) **22034**
Journal of Computational Biology (Larchmont, NY) **20910**
Journal of Computational Chemistry (Hoboken, NJ) **19019**

Journal of Computational Geometry and Applications (River Edge, NJ) **19515**

Journal of Computational and Graphical Statistics (Alexandria, VA) **31690**

Journal of Computational Intelligence in Finance (Haymarket, VA) *Ceased*

Journal of Computational Physics (San Diego, CA) **3185**

Journal of Computer-Aided Materials Design (New York, NY) **22035**

Journal of Computer-Aided Molecular Design (New York, NY) **22036**

Journal of Computer-Assisted Microscopy (New York, NY) **22037**

Journal of Computer-Assisted Tomography (Baltimore, MD) **13186**

Journal of Computer and System Sciences (San Diego, CA) **3186**

Journal of Computer and Systems Sciences International (Hoboken, NJ) *Ceased*

Journal of Computers in Math and Science Teaching (Norfolk, VA) *Unable to locate*

Journal of Computing in Childhood Education (Norfolk, VA) *Unable to locate*

Journal of Computing in Civil Engineering (Reston, VA) **32374**

Journal of Computing in Higher Education (Amherst, MA) **13797**

Journal of Computing and Society (Eau Claire, WI) *Ceased*

Journal of Conflict Resolution (New Haven, CT) **4993**

Journal of Construction Accounting and Taxation (New York, NY) **22038**

Journal of Construction Engineering and Management (Reston, VA) **32375**

Journal of Constructivist Psychology (Memphis, TN) **29373**

Journal Constructo (Saint-Laurent, QC, Can.) **37363**

The Journal of Consulting and Clinical Psychology (Washington, DC) **5579**

Journal of Consumer Affairs (Ames, IA) **10591**

Journal of Consumer Health on the Internet (Binghamton, NY) **20167**

The Journal of Consumer Lending (New York, NY) *Ceased*

Journal of Consumer Psychology (Mahwah, NJ) **19197**

Journal of Consumer Research (Seattle, WA) *Unable to locate*

Journal of Contemporary Ethnography (Thousand Oaks, CA) **3885**

Journal of Contemporary Law **31434***

Journal of Contemporary Neurology **33796***

Journal of Contemporary Psychotherapy (New York, NY) *Unable to locate*

Journal of Continuing Education in the Health Professions (Hamilton, ON, Can.) **35884**

The Journal of Continuing Education in Nursing (Thorofare, NJ) **19620**

Journal of Controversial Medical Claims (New York, NY) **22039**

Journal of Convention & Exhibition Management (Binghamton, NY) **20168**

Journal of the Copyright Society of the U.S.A. (New York, NY) *Unable to locate*

Journal de Cornwall; Le (Cornwall, ON, Can.) **35753**

The Journal of Corporate Accounting and Finance (Hoboken, NJ) **19020**

Journal of Corporate Computing (Santa Monica, CA) *Unable to locate*

Journal of Corporate Taxation (New York, NY) *Unable to locate*

Journal of Corporation Law (Iowa City, IA) **10978**

Journal of Correctional Best Practices (Lanham, MD) **13603**

Journal of Correctional Health Care (Chicago, IL) *Unable to locate*

Journal of Cost Analysis and Management (Alexandria, VA) **31691**

Journal of Cost Management (New York, NY) **22040**

Journal Cote-des-Neiges (Montreal, QC, Can.) *Ceased*

Journal of Counseling & Development (Brookville, NY) **20360**

Journal of Counseling and Development (Alexandria, VA) **31692**

Journal of Counseling Psychology (College Park, MD) **13426**

Journal of Country Music (Nashville, TN) **29462**

Journal of Couple & Relationship Therapy (Binghamton, NY) *Unable to locate*

Journal and Courier (Lafayette, IN) **10251**

Journal of Court Reporting (Vienna, VA) *Unable to locate*

Journal of Craniofacial Surgery **6770***

The Journal of Craniofacial Surgery (Tampa, FL) **6770**

The Journal of Criminal Justice & Popular Culture (Albany, NY) **19992**

The Journal of Criminal Law and Criminology (Chicago, IL) **8435**

Journal of Criminal Law, Criminology, & Political Science **8435***

Journal of Crisis Negotiations **30343***

Journal of Critical Care (Toronto, ON, Can.) **36634**

The Journal of Critical Illness (Greenwich, CT) *Unable to locate*

Journal of Critical Inquiry into Curriculum and Instruction (San Francisco, CA) **3379**

Journal of Cross-Cultural Gerontology (New York, NY) **22041**

Journal of Cross-Cultural Psychology (Thousand Oaks, CA) **3886**

Journal of Crustacean Biology (Seminole, FL) **6684**

Journal of Cryptology (New York, NY) **22042**

Journal of Culinary Practice (Binghamton, NY) *Ceased*

Journal of Cultural Diversity (Lisle, IL) **9110**

Journal of Cultural Economics (New York, NY) **22043**

Journal of Cultural Geography (Bowling Green, OH) **24694**

Journal of Cultural Heritage (New York, NY) **22044**

Journal of Cuneiform Studies (Ann Arbor, MI) **14755**

Journal of Current Laser Abstracts (Tulsa, OK) *Ceased*

Journal of Curriculum Studies (Philadelphia, PA) **27523**

Journal of Curriculum Theorizing (San Francisco, CA) **3380**

Journal of Customer Service in Marketing & Management **1536***

Journal of Cutaneous Aging & Cosmetic Dermatology (Larchmont, NY) *Ceased*

Journal of Cutaneous Medicine (New York, NY) **22045**

Journal of Dairy Research (New York, NY) **22046**

Journal of Dairy Science (Blacksburg, VA) **31874**

(Journal canadien d'anesthesie); Canadian Journal of Anesthesia (Montreal, QC, Can.) **37095**

Journal of Database Administration **18087***

Journal of Database Management (Lincoln, NE) **18087**

The Journal of Deaf Studies and Deaf Education (Cary, NC) **23690**

The Journal of Decorative and Propaganda Arts (Miami, FL) *Ceased*

Journal of Defense & Diplomacy (Mc Lean, VA) *Ceased*

Journal of Deferred Compensation (New York, NY) **22047**

Journal of Democracy (Washington, DC) **5580**

Journal Dentaire du Quebec (JDQ) (Montreal, QC, Can.) **37139**

Journal of Dental Education (San Antonio, TX) **31033**

Journal of Dental Hygiene (Chicago, IL) **8436**

Journal of Dental Research (Alexandria, VA) **31693**

Journal of Dentistry for Children (Chicago, IL) **8437**

The Journal of Derivatives (New York, NY) **22048**

The Journal of Developing Areas (Macomb, IL) *Ceased*

Journal of Developmental & Behavioral Pediatrics (Philadelphia, PA) **27524**

Journal of Developmental Education (Boone, NC) **23653**

Journal of Developmental and Learning Disorders (Madison, CT) **4932**

Journal of Developmental and Physical Disabilities (Fort Lauderdale, FL) **6078**

The Journal of Diagnostic Medical Sonography (JDMS) (Thousand Oaks, CA) **3887**

Journal of Differential Equations (San Diego, CA) **3187**

Journal of Differential Geometry (Somerville, MA) **14535**

Journal of Digital Imaging (Gainesville, FL) **6147**

Journal of Direct and Interactive Marketing (Hoboken, NJ) **19021**

Journal of Direct Marketing **19026***

Journal of Disability Policy Studies (Austin, TX) **29786**

Journal of Dispersion Science & Technology (New York, NY) **22049**

Journal of Dispute Resolution (Columbia, MO) **16995**

Journal of Distance Education (Edmonton, AB, Can.) **34718**

Journal of the Division for Early Childhood **23711***

Journal of Divorce and Remarriage (Binghamton, NY) *Unable to locate*

Journal of Documentation (Medford, NJ) *Ceased*

Journal of Dramatic Theory and Criticism (Lawrence, KS) **11555**

Journal of Drug Education (Amityville, NY) **20043**

Journal of Drug Issues (Tallahassee, FL) **6725**

Journal of Druze Studies (San Diego, CA) **3188**

Journal of Dynamic and Control Systems (New York, NY) **22050**

Journal of Dynamic Systems, Measurement, and Control (New York, NY) **22051**

Journal of Dynamics and Differential Equations (New York, NY) **22052**

Journal of Early Adolescence (Thousand Oaks, CA) **3888**

Journal of Early Christian Studies (Baltimore, MD) **13187**

Journal of Early Intervention (Chapel Hill, NC) **23711**

Journal of the Early Republic (West Lafayette, IN) **10549**

Journal of Early Southern Decorative Arts (Winston-Salem, NC) **24319**

Journal of East-West Business (Middletown, PA) **27254**

The Journal of Ecclesiastical History (New York, NY) **22053**

The Journal of Economic Education (Washington, DC) **5581**

Journal of Economic Entomology (Lanham, MD) **13604**

Journal of Economic Growth (New York, NY) **22054**

The Journal of Economic History (New York, NY) **22055**

Journal of Economic Literature (Stanford, CA) **3796**

Journal of Economic Perspectives (Minneapolis, MN) **16087**

Journal of Economic Theory (San Diego, CA) **3189**

The Journal of Economics and Economic Education Research (Candler, NC) *Unable to locate*

Journal of Economics and Management Strategy (Evanston, IL) **8864**

Journal of ECT (Newark, NJ) **19357**

Journal of Ecumenical Studies (Philadelphia, PA) **27525**

Journal of Education for Business (Washington, DC) **5582**

Journal of Education Finance (Champaign, IL) **8196**

Journal for the Education of the Gifted (Knoxville, TN) **29275**

Journal of Education for Library and Information Science (State College, PA) *Ceased*

Journal of Education Policy (Philadelphia, PA) **27526**

Journal of Education for Students Placed at Risk (Baltimore, MD) **13188**

Journal of Educational and Behavioral Statistics (Washington, DC) **5583**

Journal of Educational Change (New York, NY) **22056**

Journal of Educational Communication **26752***

Journal of Educational Computing Research (Amityville, NY) **20044**

Journal of Educational Multimedia and Hypermedia (Norfolk, VA) **32285**

Journal of Educational and Psychological Consultation (Flushing, NY) **20609**

Journal of Educational Psychology (Washington, DC) **5584**

Journal of Educational Public Relations **26752***

Journal of Educational Relations (Camp Hill, PA) **26752**

The Journal of Educational Research (Washington, DC) **5585**

Journal of Educational Technology Systems (Stony Brook, NY) **23370**

Journal of Elasticity (New York, NY) **22057**

Journal of Elder Abuse and Neglect (Binghamton, NY) **20169**

Journal of Electrocardiology (Long Beach, CA) **2170**

Journal of Electroceramics (New York, NY) **22058**

Journal of Electromyography and Kinesiology (Baltimore, MD) **13189**

Journal of Electron Microscopy Technique (Hoboken, NJ) *Ceased*

Journal of Electronic Defense (Norwood, MA) **14447**

Journal of Electronic Materials (Mount Prospect, IL) *Unable to locate*

Journal of Electronic Testing (New York, NY) **22059**

Journal of Electrophysiology **20085***

Journal of Elementary Science Education (Macomb, IL) **9129**

Journal of Emergency Nursing (Philadelphia, PA) **27527**

Journal do Emigrante (Montreal, QC, Can.) **37140**

Journal of Emotional Abuse (Hazleton, PA) **27033**

Journal of Emotional and Behavioral Disorders (DeKalb, IL) **8736**

Journal of Employee Ownership Law and Finance (Oakland, CA) **2684**

Journal of Employment Counseling (Alexandria, VA) **31694**

Journal of End User Computer Support (Binghamton, NY) **20170**

Journal of End User Computing (Hershey, PA) **27043**

Journal of Endodontics (Hagerstown, MD) **13564**

Journal of Endourology (Larchmont, NY) **20911**

Journal of Endovascular Surgery (Armonk, NY) *Ceased*

Journal of Energetics & Fluids Engineering (Hoboken, NJ) *Ceased*

3380

Numbers cited in bold after listings are entry numbers rather than page numbers.

Journal of Energy and Development (Boulder, CO) **4175**
Journal of Energy Engineering (Reston, VA) **32376**
Journal of Energy, Finance and Development (Anchorage, AK) **527**
Journal of Energy Resources Technology (New York, NY) **22060**
Journal of Engineering for Gas Turbines and Power (New York, NY) **22061**
Journal of Engineering for Industry (New York, NY) **22062**
Journal of Engineering Mathematics (New York, NY) **22063**
Journal of Engineering Mechanics (Reston, VA) **32377**
Journal of Engineering and Physics **22064***
Journal of Engineering Physics and Thermophysics (New York, NY) **22064**
Journal of English and Germanic Philology (Urbana, IL) **9712**
The Journal-Enterprise (Providence, KY) **12378**
Journal of Entrepreneurial and Small Firm Finance (Waco, TX) **31250**
Journal of Environmental Economics and Management (San Diego, CA) **3190**
The Journal of Environmental Education (Washington, DC) **5586**
Journal of Environmental Engineering (Reston, VA) **32378**
Journal of Environmental Health (Denver, CO) **4336**
Journal of Environmental Hydrology (Sacramento, CA) **3004**
Journal of Environmental Law and Practice (Toronto, ON, Can.) **36635**
Journal of Environmental Management (San Diego, CA) **3191**
Journal of Environmental Pathology, Toxicology & Oncology (Boca Raton, FL) *Ceased*
Journal of Environmental Permitting (Hoboken, NJ) *Ceased*
Journal of Environmental Polymer Degradation **22162***
Journal of Environmental Psychology (San Diego, CA) **3192**
Journal of Environmental Quality (Madison, WI) **33951**
Journal of Environmental Regulation (Hoboken, NJ) *Ceased*
Journal of Environmental Science and Health, Part A: Toxic/Hazardous Substances & Environmental Engineering (Fairfax, VA) **32020**
Journal of Environmental Science and Health, Part B: Pesticides, Food Contaminants, and Agricultural Wastes (Fairfax, VA) **32021**
Journal of Environmental Science and Health, Part C: Environmental Carcinogenesis and Ectoxicology Reviews (Springfield, VA) **32545**
Journal of Environmental Sciences **9548***
Journal of Environmental Systems (Amityville, NY) **20045**
Journal of Enzyme Inhibition (New York, NY) *Unable to locate*
The Journal Era (Berrien Springs, MI) **14812**
Journal of Esthetic Dentistry **35885***
Journal of Esthetic and Restorative Dentistry (Hamilton, ON, Can.) **35885**
Journal of ET Nursing **17464***
Journal of Ethical Studies (Chicago, IL) *Unable to locate*
Journal of Ethics (New York, NY) **22065**
Journal of Ethics, Law, and Aging **25115***
Journal of Ethnic & Cultural Diversity in Social Work (Binghamton, NY) **20171**
Journal of Ethnic and Multicultural Marketing (Binghamton, NY) *Ceased*
Journal of Ethnic Studies (Bellingham, WA) *Ceased*
Journal of Ethnicity in Substance Abuse (Binghamton, NY) **20172**
Journal of Ethnomedicine and Drug Development (Silver Spring, MD) **13730**
Journal of Euromarketing (Middletown, PA) **27255**
The Journal of European Business (New York, NY) *Ceased*
Journal of the Evangelical Homiletics Society (South Hamilton, MA) **14544**
Journal of the Evangelical Theological Society (Wake Forest, NC) **24261**
The Journal of Evidence-Based Dental Practice (St. Louis, MO) **17454**
Journal of Evidence Photography (Honesdale, PA) **27050**
Journal of Evolutionary Biochemistry and Physiology (New York, NY) **22066**
Journal on Excellence in College Teaching (Oxford, OH) **25456**
Journal of Experimental Algorithmics (JEA) (New York, NY) **22067**
Journal of the Experimental Analysis of Behavior (Morgantown, WV) **33394**

Journal of Experimental Child Psychology (San Diego, CA) **3193**
The Journal of Experimental Education (Washington, DC) **5587**
The Journal of Experimental Medicine (New York, NY) **22068**
Journal of Experimental Pathology *Ceased*
Journal of Experimental Psychology: Animal Behavior Processes (Washington, DC) **5588**
Journal of Experimental Psychology: General (Washington, DC) *Unable to locate*
Journal of Experimental Psychology: Human Perception and Performance (Washington, DC) **5589**
Journal of Experimental Psychology: Learning, Memory and Cognition (Washington, DC) **5590**
Journal of Experimental Social Psychology (San Diego, CA) **3194**
Journal of Experimental and Theoretical Physics (JETP) (College Park, MD) **13427**
Journal of Experimental Therapeutics and Oncology (Malden, MA) **14294**
The Journal of Experimental Zoology (Hoboken, NJ) **19022**
Journal of Explosives Engineering (Cleveland, OH) **24914**
Journal-Express (Knoxville, IA) **11019**
The Journal Express (Antigo, WI) **33533**
Journal of Family Communication (Norfolk, VA) **32286**
Journal of Family and Consumer Sciences: From Research to Practice (Alexandria, VA) **31695**
Journal of Family and Economic Issues (New York, NY) *Unable to locate*
Journal of Family History (Berkeley, CA) *Ceased*
Journal of Family Issues **5591***
Journal of Family Issues (Thousand Oaks, CA) **3889**
Journal of Family Nursing (Thousand Oaks, CA) **3890**
The Journal of Family Practice (Blacklick, OH) *Unable to locate*
Journal of Family Psychology (Washington, DC) **5591**
Journal of Family Psychotherapy (Hammond, IN) **10052**
Journal of Family Social Work (Binghamton, NY) **20173**
Journal of Family Violence (New York, NY) **22069**
Journal of Farm Economics **14289***
Journal for Farming Systems Research-Extension (AFSRE) (East Lansing, MI) *Ceased*
Journal of Federalism; Publius: The (Easton, PA) **26851**
Journal of Feminist Family Therapy (Fort Collins, CO) **4435**
Journal of Film and Video (Los Angeles, CA) **2301**
Journal of Finance (Columbus, OH) *Unable to locate*
Journal of Financial Intermediation (San Diego, CA) **3195**
Journal of Financial Planning (Denver, CO) **4337**
Journal of Financial and Quantitative Analysis (Seattle, WA) **32977**
Journal of Financial Research (Columbia, SC) **28552**
Journal of Financial Service Professionals (Bryn Mawr, PA) **26741**
Journal of Financial Software (Santa Monica, CA) *Ceased*
Journal of the Fisheries Research Board of Canada **36205***
The Journal of Fixed Income (Chapel Hill, NC) **23712**
Journal of the Flagstaff Institute (Flagstaff, AZ) **697**
The Journal of the Florida Medical Association (Tallahassee, FL) *Ceased*
Journal of Fluid Mechanics (New York, NY) **22070**
Journal of Fluids Engineering (New York, NY) **22071**
Journal of Fluorescence (New York, NY) **22072**
Journal of Folklore Research (Bloomington, IN) **9841**
Journal of Food Composition and Analysis (San Diego, CA) **3196**
Journal of Food and Milk Technology **10800***
Journal of Food Products Marketing (Philadelphia, PA) **27528**
Journal of Food Protection (Des Moines, IA) **10800**
Journal of Food Science (Chicago, IL) *Unable to locate*
Journal of Foot and Ankle Surgery (Park Ridge, IL) **9405**
Journal of Foot Surgery **9405***
Journal of Foraminiferal Research (Newark, DE) **5276**
Journal of Forecasting (Hoboken, NJ) **19023**
Journal of Forensic Economics (Kansas City, MO) **17174**
Journal of Forensic Identification (Mendota Heights, MN) **16052**
Journal of Forensic Neuropsychology (Binghamton, NY) **20174**
Journal of Forensic Psychology Practice (Binghamton, NY) **20175**
Journal of Forestry (Bethesda, MD) **13351**
Journal Francais (San Francisco, CA) **3381**
Journal of French Language Studies (Santa Barbara, CA) **3644**

The Journal Friday Home Report (Alexandria, VA) **31696**
Journal of Functional Analysis (San Diego, CA) **3197**
Journal of Functional Programming (New York, NY) **22073**
Journal of Fusion Energy (New York, NY) **22074**
The Journal of Futures Markets (Hoboken, NJ) **19024**
Journal of Fuzzy Mathematics (El Monte, CA) **1866**
Journal of Gambling Studies (New York, NY) **22075**
Journal of Gay, Lesbian, and Bisexual Indentity **21918***
Journal of Gay and Lesbian Information Resources (Binghamton, NY) *Ceased*
Journal of the Gay and Lesbian Medical Association (New York, NY) **22076**
Journal of Gay & Lesbian Politics (Binghamton, NY) *Ceased*
Journal of Gay and Lesbian Psychotherapy (Binghamton, NY) *Unable to locate*
Journal of Gay and Lesbian Social Services (Hayward, CA) **2043**
Journal-Gazette (Mattoon, IL) **9159**
The Journal Gazette (Fort Wayne, IN) **9971**
The Journal Gazette (Indianapolis, IN) *Unable to locate*
Journal of Gender, Culture, and Health (New York, NY) **22077**
The Journal of Gender-Specific Medicine (Plainsboro, NJ) **19442**
Journal of General Chemistry of the USSR **22689***
Journal of General Education (University Park, PA) **28078**
Journal of General Internal Medicine (Philadelphia, PA) *Ceased*
Journal of General Orthodontics **34071***
Journal for General Philosophy of Science (New York, NY) **22078**
The Journal of General Physiology (New York, NY) *Unable to locate*
The Journal of General Psychology (Washington, DC) **5592**
Journal of Genetic Couseling (New York, NY) **22079**
The Journal of Genetic Psychology (Washington, DC) **5593**
Journal of Geography (St. Cloud, MN) **16343**
The Journal of Geology (Seattle, WA) *Unable to locate*
Journal of Geophysical Research (Washington, DC) **5594**
Journal of Geotechnical and Geoenvironmental Engineering (Reston, VA) **32379**
Journal of Geriatric Drug Therapy (Binghamton, NY) *Ceased*
Journal of Geriatric Psychiatry (Madison, CT) **4933**
Journal of Germanic Languages (New York, NY) **22080**
Journal of Gerontological Nursing (Thorofare, NJ) **19621**
Journal of Gerontological Social Work (New York, NY) **22081**
The Journal of Gerontology **5621***
Journal of Glaucoma (Baltimore, MD) **13190**
Journal of Global Business (Harrisonburg, VA) **32139**
Journal of Global Information Management (Hershey, PA) **27044**
Journal of Global Marketing (Middletown, PA) **27256**
Journal of Government Financial Management (Alexandria, VA) **31697**
Journal of Graph Theory (Hoboken, NJ) **19025**
Journal of Graphics Tools (Natick, MA) **14347**
Journal of Graphoanalysis (Chicago, IL) **8438**
Journal of Great Lakes Research (Ann Arbor, MI) **14756**
The Journal of the Greater Houston Dental Society (Houston, TX) **30496**
The Journal (Greenbrook-North Plainfield Edition) (Somerville, NJ) **19573**
Journal of Guidance, Control, and Dynamics (Reston, VA) **32380**
Journal & Guide (Norfolk, VA) *Unable to locate*
Journal of Gynecologic Surgery (Larchmont, NY) **20912**
Journal of Gynecologic Techniques (Philadelphia, PA) **27529**
Journal of the Gypsy Lore Society **13407***
Journal of Hand Surgery (St. Louis, MO) **17455**
Journal of Hand Therapy (Philadelphia, PA) **27530**
Journal of Happiness Studies (New York, NY) **22082**
Journal of Head Trauma Rehabilitation (New York, NY) **22083**
Journal of Health Care Chaplaincy (Binghamton, NY) **20176**
Journal of Health Care Compliance (New York, NY) **22084**
Journal of Health Care Finance (New York, NY) **22085**
Journal of Health Care Law and Policy (Baltimore, MD) **13191**
Journal of Health Care Marketing **8477***

Journal of Health Care Material Management 32438*
Journal of Health Care for the Poor and Underserved (Thousand Oaks, CA) 3891
Journal of Health Communication (Washington, DC) 5595
Journal of Health Education (Reston, VA) 32381
Journal of Health and Human Behavior 31875*
Journal of Health Politics, Policy and Law (New Haven, CT) 4994
Journal of Health & Social Behavior (Blacksburg, VA) 31875
Journal of Health and Social Policy (Norfolk, VA) 32287
Journal of Healthcare Management (Chicago, IL) 8439
Journal for Healthcare Quality (Glenview, IL) 8938
Journal of Healthcare Resource Management (Richmond, VA) Unable to locate
Journal of Healthcare Risk Management (Chicago, IL) 8440
Journal of Healthcare Safety, Compliance & Infection Control (Weston, MA) 14651
Journal of Heart-Centered Therapies (Issaquah, WA) 32785
The Journal of Heart and Lung Transplantation (St. Louis, MO) Ceased
Journal of Heat Transfer (New York, NY) 22086
Journal of the Hellenic Diaspora (New York, NY) 22087
Journal of Hematotherapy & Stem Cell Research (Larchmont, NY) 20913
Journal of Hemotherapy 20913*
Journal Herald 25113*
Journal Herald (Pomeroy, IA) 11164
The Journal Herald (White Haven, PA) 28155
Journal of Herbal Pharmacotherapy (Binghamton, NY) 20177
Journal of Herbs, Spices & Medicinal Plants (Binghamton, NY) 20178
Journal of Herpetology (Hammond, LA) 12591
Journal of Heuristics (New York, NY) 22088
Journal of High Technology Management Research (Berkeley, CA) 1533
The Journal of Higher Education (Columbus, OH) 25024
Journal of Higher Education Outreach and Engagement (JHEOE) (Athens, GA) 6944
Journal of Historic Madison, Inc. 33946*
Journal of Historical Research in Music Education (Tempe, AZ) 907
The Journal of Historical Review (Newport Beach, CA) 2629
Journal of History of the Behavioral Sciences (Brandon, VT) Unable to locate
Journal of the History of Biology (New York, NY) 22089
Journal of the History of Dentistry (Arlington Heights, IL) 8024
Journal of the History of Economic Thought (Durham, NH) 18500
Journal of the History of Ideas (New Brunswick, NJ) 19333
Journal of the History of International Law (New York, NY) 22090
Journal of the History of Medicine and Allied Sciences (Cary, NC) 23691
Journal of the History of Philosophy (Baltimore, MD) 13192
Journal of the History of Sexuality (Austin, TX) 29787
The Journal of Histotechnology (Bowie, MD) 13392
Journal of HIV/AIDS Education and Prevention for Children and Adolescents 5203*
Journal of HIV/AIDS Prevention and Education for Adolescents & Children (West Hartford, CT) 5203
Journal of HIV/AIDS & Social Services (Binghamton, NY) 20179
Journal of Holistic Nursing (Austin, TX) 29788
Journal of Home and Consumer Horticulture (Binghamton, NY) Ceased
Journal of Home Economics 31695*
Journal of Home Health Care Practice 3872*
Journal of Home Health Care Products (New York, NY) Unable to locate
Journal of Homosexuality (San Francisco, CA) 3382
Journal of the Hong Kong College of Radiologists (Philadelphia, PA) Ceased
Journal of Hospital Librarianship (Binghamton, NY) 20180
Journal of Hospital Marketing (Berkeley, CA) 1534
Journal of Hospitality and Leisure Marketing (East Lansing, MI) 14986
Journal of Hospitality & Tourism Research (Richmond, VA) 32440
Journal of Housing 5596*
Journal of Housing and Community Development (Washington, DC) 5596
Journal of Housing Economics (San Diego, CA) 3198
Journal of Housing for the Elderly (Columbia, MO) 16996

Journal of Housing Research (Washington, DC) 5597
Journal of Human Behavior in the Social Environment (Binghamton, NY) 20181
The Journal of Human Performance in Extreme Environments (Orlando, FL) 6499
Journal of Human Resources (Madison, WI) 33952
Journal of Human Resources in Hospitality & Tourism (Binghamton, NY) 20182
Journal of Human Virology (Philadelphia, PA) Ceased
Journal of Humanistic Counseling & Development (Alexandria, VA) 31698
Journal of Humanistic Education & Development 31698*
Journal of Humanistic Psychology (Thousand Oaks, CA) 3892
Journal of Hydraulic Engineering (Reston, VA) 32382
Journal of Hydrologic Engineering (Reston, VA) 32383
Journal of Hypertension (Philadelphia, PA) 27531
Journal of Ichthyology (Hoboken, NJ) Ceased
Journal of the Idaho Academy of Science (Pocatello, ID) 7946
The Journal of Ideas (Panama City, FL) 6555
Journal of the IES 9548*
Journal of Illinois History (Springfield, IL) 9636
Journal of the Illinois Optometric Association (Niles, IL) 9289
Journal of Image Guided Surgery 17426*
Journal of Imaging Science 32546*
Journal of Imaging Science and Technology (Springfield, VA) 32546
Journal of Imaging Technology 32546*
Journal of Imago Relationship Therapy (Madison, CT) 4934
Journal of Immigrant Health (New York, NY) 22091
Journal of Immigrant & Refugee Services (Binghamton, NY) 20183
Journal of Immunoassay and Immunochemistry (Boynton Beach, FL) 5951
Journal of Immunology (Baltimore, MD) Ceased
Journal of Immunotherapy (Baltimore, MD) 13193
Journal of In Vitro Fertilization and Embryo Transfer 22000*
Journal of Inclusion Phenomena and Macrocyclic Chemistry (New York, NY) 22092
Journal of Income Distribution (Berkeley, CA) Unable to locate
Journal of Income Distribution (Somerset, NJ) 19563
The Journal Independent (Piedmont, AL) 427
Journal of Independent Social Work (Binghamton, NY) Ceased
Journal of Indian Philosophy (New York, NY) 22093
Journal of Indigenous Studies (Saskatoon, SK, Can.) Ceased
Journal of Individual Employment Rights (Amityville, NY) 20046
The Journal of Indo-European Studies (Washington, DC) 5598
Journal of Industrial Ecology (Cambridge, MA) 14076
Journal of Industrial Teacher Education (Knoxville, TN) 29276
Journal Industriel du Quebec (Montreal, QC, Can.) 37141
Journal of Industry, Competition and Trade (New York, NY) 22094
Journal of Inequalities and Applications (New York, NY) Unable to locate
Journal of Infectious Disease Pharmacotherapy (Binghamton, NY) 20184
The Journal of Infectious Diseases (Seattle, WA) Unable to locate
Journal of Inflammation (Hoboken, NJ) Ceased
Journal of Information Ethics (St. Cloud, MN) 16344
Journal of Information Systems (Sarasota, FL) 6658
Journal of Information Technology Management (Virginia Beach, VA) 32587
Journal of Infrastructure Systems (Reston, VA) 32384
Journal of Infusion Nursing (Norwood, MA) 14448
Journal of Inherited Metabolic Disease (New York, NY) 22095
Journal of Innovative Management (Salem, NH) 18644
Journal of Inorganic and Organometallic Polymers (Staten Island, NY) 23359
Journal Inquirer (Manchester, CT) Unable to locate
Journal of Insect Behavior (New York, NY) 22096
Journal of Insect Conservation (New York, NY) 22097
Journal of Instructional Psychology (Mobile, AL) 321
Journal of Insurance Coverage (New York, NY) 22098
Journal of Insurance Regulation (Madison, WI) 33953
Journal of Intelligent Information Systems (New York, NY) 22099
Journal of Intelligent Manufacturing (New York, NY) 22100
Journal of Intelligent and Robotic Systems (New York, NY) 22101
Journal of Intensive Care Medicine (Shrewsbury, MA) 14524

Journal of Interactive Learning Research (Norfolk, VA) 32288
Journal of Interactive Marketing 19021*
Journal of Interactive Marketing (Hoboken, NJ) 19026
The Journal of Interdisciplinary History (Cambridge, MA) 14077
Journal of Interdisciplinary Studies (Pasadena, CA) 2819
Journal of Interferon & Cytokine Research (Larchmont, NY) 20914
Journal of Intergroup Relations (Nashville, TN) 29463
Journal of Interlibrary Loan, Document Delivery, and Information Supply (Lancaster, NY) 20882
Journal of the International Academy for Case Studies (Candler, NC) Unable to locate
Journal of International Accounting, Auditing and Taxation (Kalamazoo, MI) 15239
Journal of International Affairs (New York, NY) 22102
Journal of International Arbitration (New York, NY) 22103
Journal of the International Association of Jazz Record Collectors (Dundas, ON, Can.) 35794
Journal of the International Association for Mathematical Geology 22293*
Journal of International Business Law 27713*
Journal of International Business Studies (Washington, DC) 5599
Journal of International Consumer Marketing (Middletown, PA) 27257
Journal of International Development (Hoboken, NJ) 19027
Journal of International Financial Markets, Institutions and Money (Binghamton, NY) Ceased
Journal of International Food and Agribusiness Marketing (Middletown, PA) 27258
Journal of International Management (Hoboken, NJ) Ceased
The Journal of International Security Affairs (Washington, DC) 5600
Journal of International Taxation (New York, NY) 22104
Journal of the International Union of Bricklayers & Allied Craftworkers (Washington, DC) 5601
Journal of International Wildlife Law and Policy (New York, NY) 22105
Journal of Internet Cataloging (Binghamton, NY) 20185
Journal of Internet Commerce (Monroe, LA) 12691
Journal of Internet Law (New York, NY) 22106
Journal of Interpersonal Violence (Thousand Oaks, CA) 3893
Journal of Interventional Cardiac Electrophysiology (New York, NY) 22107
Journal of Interventional Cardiology (Armonk, NY) 20086
Journal of Intravenous Nursing (Philadelphia, PA) 27532
Journal of Intravenous Therapy (Los Angeles, CA) 2302
The Journal of Invasive Cardiology (Malvern, PA) 27212
Journal of Invertebrate Pathology (San Diego, CA) 3199
Journal of Investigative Medicine (Philadelphia, PA) 27533
Journal of Investigative Surgery (Kalamazoo, MI) 15240
The Journal of Investing (Plano, TX) 30947
The Journal of Investment Compliance (New York, NY) 22108
Journal of Irreproducible Results (Chicago Heights, IL) 8667
Journal of Irrigation and Drainage Engineering (Reston, VA) 32385
Journal of IS Financial Management 3646*
Journal of IS Financial Management (Santa Barbara, CA) 3645
Journal of IT Financial Management (Santa Barbara, CA) 3646
Journal L'Itineraire (Montreal, QC, Can.) 37142
The Journal of the Jamestown Rediscovery Center (Richmond, VA) 32441
Journal of the Japanese and International Economics (San Diego, CA) 3200
Journal of Japanese Linguistics (Bloomington, IN) 9842
Journal of Japanese Studies (Seattle, WA) 32978
Journal of Jewish Communal Service (Kendall Park, NJ) 19152
Journal of Jewish Music and Liturgy (New York, NY) 22109
Journal of the Johannes Schwalm Historical Association (State Line, PA) 28033
Journal des Juges Provinciaux; Provincial Judges Journal/ (Grand Bank, NL, Can.) 35460
The Journal of the Kafka Society of America (New York, NY) Unable to locate
Journal of the Kansas Entomological Society (Lawrence, KS) Unable to locate

3382

Numbers cited in bold after listings are entry numbers rather than page numbers.

Journal of Kansas Pharmacy (Topeka, KS) **11823**

Journal of the Kentucky Medical Association (Louisville, KY) **12221**

The Journal of Knee Surgery (Thorofare, NJ) **19622**

Journal of Knot Theory and Its Ramifications (JKTR) (River Edge, NJ) **19516**

Journal 'L' Actif College Shawinigan (Shawinigan, QC, Can.) *Ceased*

Journal La Petite-Nation (Saint-Andre-Avellin, QC, Can.) **37325**

Journal La Voix (Sorel, QC, Can.) **37403**

Journal of Labelled Compounds and Radiopharmaceuticals (Hoboken, NJ) **19028**

Journal of Labor Economics (Seattle, WA) *Unable to locate*

Journal of Labor Research (Fairfax, VA) **32022**

The Journal of Laboratory and Clinical Medicine (St. Louis, MO) **17456**

Journal of Land Resouces and Environmental Law (Salt Lake City, UT) **31434**

Journal of Language, Identity, and Education (San Antonio, TX) **31034**

Journal of Language and Social Psychology (Thousand Oaks, CA) **3894**

Journal of Laparoendoscopic and Advanced Surgical Techniques (Larchmont, NY) **20915**

Journal of Laparoendoscopic Surgery **20915***

Journal de l'Association Canadienne des Radiologistes (Ottawa, ON, Can.) *Unable to locate*

Journal de l'Assurance (Montreal, QC, Can.) **37143**

Journal of Latin American Affairs (Washington, DC) *Unable to locate*

Journal of Latin American Anthropology (Arlington, VA) **31802**

Journal of Latin American Studies (New York, NY) **22110**

Journal of Latinos and Education (San Bernardino, CA) **3087**

Journal L'Avenir **36994***

Journal of Law & Commerce (Pittsburgh, PA) **27802**

The Journal of Law and Economics (Chicago, IL) **8441**

Journal of Law, Economics, and Organization (Cary, NC) **23692**

Journal of Law and Health (Cleveland, OH) **24915**

The Journal of Law, Medicine & Ethics (Boston, MA) **13916**

Journal of Law and Public Policy (Gainesville, FL) **6148**

Journal of Law and Religion (St. Paul, MN) **16382**

Journal Le Crieur (Montreal, QC, Can.) *Unable to locate*

Journal Le Madawaska Ltee (Edmundston, NB, Can.) **35385**

Journal Le Nord (Saint-Jerome, QC, Can.) **37356**

Journal Le Voyageur (Sudbury, ON, Can.) **36416**

Journal of Leadership and Organizational Studies (Flint, MI) **15036**

Journal of Learning Disabilities (Athens, GA) **6945**

The Journal of the Learning Sciences (Atlanta, GA) **7021**

Journal L'Eau Vive (Regina, SK, Can.) **37531**

Journal of Legal Economics (Florence, AL) **219**

The Journal of Legal Medicine (Springfield, IL) **9637**

Journal of Legal Pluralism and Unofficial Law (Buffalo, NY) **20382**

The Journal of Legal Studies (Chicago, IL) **8442**

Journal of Legislation (Notre Dame, IN) **10370**

Journal of Leisure Research (Ashburn, VA) **31852**

The Journal of Lending & Credit Risk Management **27654***

Journal of Lesbian Studies (Binghamton, NY) **20186**

Journal of Leukocyte Biology (Hoboken, NJ) *Ceased*

Journal L'Hebdo le Point (Montreal, QC, Can.) *Ceased*

Journal Liaison St-Louis (Montreal, QC, Can.) *Unable to locate*

Journal of Library Administration (Norman, OK) **25935**

Journal of Library Automation **8413***

Journal of Library & Information Services for Distance Learning (Binghamton, NY) **20187**

The Journal of Light Construction (Richmond, VT) *Unable to locate*

Journal of Light Metals (New York, NY) **22111**

Journal of Lightwave Technology (New York, NY) *Ceased*

Journal of the Lincoln Assassination (Lorton, VA) **32198**

Journal L'Information Regionale **36962***

Journal of Linguistic Anthropology (Santa Barbara, CA) **3647**

Journal of Linguistics (New York, NY) **22112**

Journal of Lipid Research (Berkeley, CA) **1535**

Journal of Liposome Research (New York, NY) **22113**

Journal of Liquid Chromatography & Related Technologies (New York, NY) **22114**

Journal of Logic, Language and Information (New York, NY) **22115**

Journal of the London Mathematical Society (New York, NY) **22116**

Journal of Long-Term Care Administration **31646***

The Journal of Long Term Home Health Care **21377***

Journal of the Los Angeles International Fern Society (Pasadena, CA) **2820**

Journal of Loss & Trauma (Rancho Cordova, CA) **2876**

Journal of Loss & Trauma (Iowa City, IA) **10979**

Journal of the Louisiana State Medical Society (Metairie, LA) *Unable to locate*

Journal of Low Temperature Physics (New York, NY) **22117**

Journal of Low Vision and Neuro-Optometric Rehabilitation (Kansas City, MO) **17175**

The Journal—Lynnwood Edition (Lynnwood, WA) **32823**

Journal of Machine Learning Research (Cambridge, MA) **14078**

Journal of Macromolecular Science, Part B, Physics (Urbana, IL) **9713**

Journal of Magnetic Resonance (San Diego, CA) **3203**

Journal of Magnetic Resonance (San Diego, CA) **3202**

Journal of Magnetic Resonance (San Diego, CA) **3201**

Journal of Magnetic Resonance - Series B **3201***

Journal of Maine Water Utilities Association (Waldoboro, ME) **13068**

Journal of Maintenance in the Addictions (Bronx, NY) **20274**

Journal of Mammalian Evolution (New York, NY) **22118**

Journal of Mammalogy (Greensboro, NC) **23925**

Journal of Mammary Gland Biology and Neoplasia (New York, NY) **22119**

Journal of Managed Pharmaceutical Care (Binghamton, NY) **20188**

Journal of Management (Columbia, SC) **28553**

Journal of Management Accounting Research (Waterloo, ON, Can.) **36853**

Journal of Management Education (Normal, IL) **9300**

Journal of Management in Engineering (Reston, VA) **32386**

Journal of Management and Governance (New York, NY) **22120**

Journal of Management Information Systems (Armonk, NY) *Unable to locate*

Journal of Management Inquiry (Thousand Oaks, CA) *Unable to locate*

Journal of Management Systems (Chesapeake, VA) **31965**

Journal of Managerial Issues (Pittsburg, KS) **11752**

Journal of Manipulative and Physiological Therapeutics; JMPT: (New York, NY) **21968**

Journal of Manufacturing Systems (Dearborn, MI) **14903**

Journal of the Marine Biological Association; JMBA: (New York, NY) **21967**

Journal of the Marine Biological Association of the United Kingdom (New York, NY) **22121**

Journal of Marine Biotechnology (New York, NY) *Ceased*

Journal of Marine Research (New Haven, CT) **4995**

Journal of Marine Science **169***

Journal of Marital & Family Therapy (Lubbock, TX) **30713**

Journal of Market-Focused Management (New York, NY) **22122**

Journal of Marketing (Chicago, IL) **8443**

Journal of Marketing Channels (Denton, TX) **30238**

Journal of Marketing for Higher Education (Cincinnati, OH) **24806**

Journal of Marketing for Mental Health **368***

Journal of Marketing Research (Chicago, IL) **8444**

Journal of Marriage and Family (Minneapolis, MN) **16088**

Journal of Mass Media Ethics (St. Petersburg, FL) **6629**

Journal of Mass Spectrometry (Hoboken, NJ) **19029**

Journal of Materials in Civil Engineering (Reston, VA) **32387**

Journal of Materials Engineering and Performance (Los Angeles, CA) **2303**

Journal of Materials Research (Warrendale, PA) **28113**

Journal of Materials Science (New York, NY) **22123**

Journal of Materials Science Letters (New York, NY) **22124**

Journal of Materials Shaping Technology (New York, NY) *Ceased*

Journal of Materials Synthesis and Processing (New York, NY) **22125**

Journal of Materials Technology and Performance **2303***

Journal of Mathematical Analysis and Applications (San Diego, CA) *Ceased*

Journal of Mathematical Chemistry (New York, NY) **22126**

Journal of Mathematical Imaging and Vision (New York, NY) **22127**

Journal of Mathematical Physics (College Park, MD) **13428**

Journal of Mathematical Psychology (San Diego, CA) **3204**

Journal of Mathematical Science (New York, NY) **22128**

Journal of Mathematics Teacher Education (New York, NY) **22129**

Journal of Mayan Linguistics (Baton Rouge, LA) **12490**

Journal of the Mechanics and Physics of Solids (New York, NY) *Ceased*

The Journal of Media Economics (Denton, TX) **30239**

Journal of Media and Religion (Provo, UT) **31404**

Journal of Mediated Communication *Ceased*

Journal of the Medical Association of Georgia (Atlanta, GA) **7022**

Journal of Medical Engineering & Technology (Philadelphia, PA) **27534**

Journal of Medical Entomology (Lanham, MD) **13605**

Journal of Medical Humanities (New York, NY) **22130**

Journal of the Medical Library Association (Chicago, IL) **8445**

The Journal of Medical Practice Management (Chicago, IL) **8446**

Journal Medical Society of New Jersey **19163***

Journal of Medical Systems (New York, NY) **22131**

Journal of Medical Virology (Hoboken, NJ) **19030**

Journal of Medicinal Chemistry (Washington, DC) *Unable to locate*

Journal of Medieval and Early Modern Studies (Durham, NC) **23830**

Journal of Membrane Biology (New York, NY) **22132**

Journal of Memory and Language (San Diego, CA) **3205**

Journal of Men's Health (Larchmont, NY) **20916**

Journal of Men's Studies (Harriman, TN) **29216**

Journal of Mental Health Administration **6769***

Journal of Mental Health and Aging (Tampa, FL) **6771**

Journal of Mental Health Counseling (Thousand Oaks, CA) *Ceased*

Journal of Mercury (Warren, MI) *Unable to locate*

Journal Messenger **32223***

Journal-Messenger (Marissa, IL) **9149**

Journal of the Michigan Dental Association (Lansing, MI) **15275**

Journal Michigan Pharmacist **15290***

Journal of Microcolumn Separations (Hoboken, NJ) **19031**

Journal of Microelectronic Systems Integration (New York, NY) **22133**

Journal of Microencapsulation (Philadelphia, PA) **27535**

Journal of the Midwest History of Education Society **25106***

The Journal of Military History (Lexington, VA) **32189**

Journal of Milk Technology **10800***

The Journal of Mind and Behavior (Orono, ME) **13000**

Journal of Mine Action (Harrisonburg, VA) **32140**

Journal of Mining Science (New York, NY) **22134**

Journal of Ministry in Addiction and Recovery (St. Paul, MN) **16383**

Journal of Ministry Marketing & Management (Binghamton, NY) *Ceased*

Journal for Minority Medical Students (New Orleans, LA) **12735**

Journal of the Mississippi Academy of Sciences (Jackson, MS) *Unable to locate*

The Journal of Mississippi History (Jackson, MS) **16697**

Journal of the Mississippi State Medical Association (Ridgeland, MS) **16834**

Journal of the Missouri Bar (Jefferson City, MO) **17123**

Journal of Modern African Studies (New York, NY) **22135**

Journal of Modern Greek Studies (Baltimore, MD) **13194**

Journal of Modern Hellenism (Brookline, MA) **14021**

The Journal of Modern History (Seattle, WA) *Unable to locate*

Journal of Modern Literature (Bloomington, IN) **9843**

Journal of Modern Optics (Philadelphia, PA) **27536**

Journal of Modern Physics A (River Edge, NJ) **19517**

Journal of Modern Physics B (River Edge, NJ) **19518**

The Journal of Molecular Diagnostics (Bethesda, MD) **13352**

Journal of Molecular Evolution (New York, NY) **22136**

Journal of Molecular Recognition (Hoboken, NJ) **19032**

Journal of Molecular Spectroscopy (San Diego, CA) **3206**

Journal of Money, Credit, and Banking (Columbus, OH) 25025

Journal and Monitor-Herald (Tomah, WI) 34369

Journal de Montreal; Le (Montreal, QC, Can.) 37163

Journal of Morphology (Hoboken, NJ) 19033

Journal of the Moscow Aviation Institute (Philadelphia, PA) Ceased

Journal of Motor Behavior (Washington, DC) 5602

The Journal of the Mount Sinai Hospital 22373*

Journal of Multi-Criteria Decision Analysis (Hoboken, NJ) 19034

Journal of Multicultural Counseling and Development (Alexandria, VA) 31699

Journal of Multicultural Nursing and Health 20454*

Journal of Multicultural Nursing and Health (JMCNH) (Chautauqua, NY) 20454

Journal of Multicultural Social Work 20171*

Journal of the Multihandicapped Person 6078*

Journal of Multinational Financial Management (Binghamton, NY) Ceased

Journal of Multivariate Analysis (San Diego, CA) 3207

Journal of Muscle Research and Cell Motility (New York, NY) 22137

Journal of Muscle Shoals History (Florence, AL) 220

The Journal of Musculoskeletal Medicine (Greenwich, CT) Unable to locate

Journal of Musculosketal Pain (San Antonio, TX) 31035

Journal of Music Teacher Education (Columbus, OH) 25026

Journal of Music Theory Pedagogy (Norman, OK) 25936

Journal of Music Therapy (Silver Spring, MD) 13731

Journal of Musicological Research (Philadelphia, PA) 27537

Journal of Musicology (Berkeley, CA) Unable to locate

The Journal of Myocardial Ischemia Ceased

Journal of Nanoparticle Research (New York, NY) 22138

Journal of Nanoscience and Nanotechnology (Stevenson Ranch, CA) 3804

Journal of the National Cancer Institute (Pittsburgh, PA) Ceased

Journal of the National Collegiate Honors Council (JNCHC) (Birmingham, AL) 76

Journal of the National Medical Association (Washington, DC) 5603

Journal of the National Technical Association (New Orleans, LA) Ceased

Journal of Natural History (Philadelphia, PA) 27538

Journal of Natural Products (Washington, DC) 5604

Journal of Navigation (New York, NY) 22139

Journal of Near Death Studies (New York, NY) Ceased

Journal of Near Eastern Studies (Seattle, WA) Unable to locate

The Journal of Negro Education (Washington, DC) 5605

Journal of Negro History (Silver Spring, MD) 13732

Journal Neighbors (Alton, IL) Unable to locate

The Journal Neighbors (Alton, IL) Ceased

Journal of Nematology (Knoxville, TN) 29277

Journal of Nephrology Nursing (Ashland City, TN) Unable to locate

Journal of Nervous and Mental Disease (Baltimore, MD) 13195

Journal of Network and Computer Applications (San Diego, CA) 3208

Journal of Network Industries (New York, NY) 22140

Journal of Network and Systems Management (New York, NY) 22141

Journal of Neuro-AIDS (San Francisco, CA) 3383

Journal of Neuro-Ophthalmology (Ann Arbor, MI) 14757

Journal of Neurobiology (Hoboken, NJ) 19035

Journal of Neurochemistry (Malden, MA) 14295

Journal of Neurocytology (New York, NY) 22142

Journal of Neurogenetics (Waltham, MA) 14600

Journal of Neuroimaging (Thousand Oaks, CA) 3895

Journal of Neurologic Rehabilitation 3904*

Journal of Neurological and Orthopaedic Medicine and Surgery (New York, NY) Ceased

Journal of Neuropathology & Experimental Neurology (Lawrence, KS) 11556

Journal of Neurophysiology (Bethesda, MD) 13353

Journal of Neuropsychiatry and Clinical Neurosciences (Arlington, VA) 31803

The Journal of Neuroscience (Washington, DC) 5606

Journal of Neuroscience Nursing (Chicago, IL) Unable to locate

Journal of Neuroscience Research (Hoboken, NJ) 19036

Journal of Neurosurgery (Charlottesville, VA) 31934

Journal of Neurosurgical Anesthesiology (Baltimore, MD) 13196

Journal of Neurotherapy (Binghamton, NY) 20189

Journal of Neurotrauma (Larchmont, NY) 20917

Journal of Neurovascular Disease (Weston, MA) Ceased

Journal of the New England Water Works Association (Holliston, MA) 14239

Journal of the New Jersey Dental Association (North Brunswick, NJ) 19381

Journal of New Jersey Poets (Randolph, NJ) 19495

Journal of New Seeds (Binghamton, NY) 20190

Journal of the New York State Nurses Association (Guilderland, NY) Unable to locate

The Journal of New York Taxation (New York, NY) 22143

Journal-News (Hamilton, OH) 25235

The Journal-News (Spencerville, OH) 25530

The Journal of NIH Research (Washington, DC) Unable to locate

Journal & Noble County Leader (Caldwell, OH) 24723

Journal of Nondestructive Evaluation (New York, NY) 22144

Journal of Nonlinear Science (New York, NY) 22145

Journal of Nonprofit & Public Sector Marketing (Montgomery, AL) 368

Journal of Nonverbal Behavior (New York, NY) 22146

Journal of Nonverbal Behavior (New York, NY) Unable to locate

The Journal—North Seattle Edition (North Seattle, WA) 32854

Journal of Northeast Asian Studies 19331*

Journal of the Northeastern Political Science Association; POLITY: The (Amherst, MA) 13805

The Journal—Northgate Edition (Northgate, WA) 32855

Journal of Northwest Atlantic Fishery Science (Dartmouth, NS, Can.) 35547

Journal of Nuclear Cardiology (Philadelphia, PA) 27539

Journal of Nuclear Materials Management (Northbrook, IL) 9318

The Journal of Nuclear Medicine (Reston, VA) Unable to locate

Journal of Nuclear Medicine Technology (Reston, VA) 32388

Journal of Number Theory (San Diego, CA) 3209

Journal of Nurse Assistants (Chagrin Falls, OH) Unable to locate

Journal for Nurses in Staff Development (JNSD) (Philadelphia, PA) 27540

Journal of Nursing Administration (JONA) (Philadelphia, PA) 27541

Journal of Nursing Care Quality (New York, NY) 22147

Journal of Nursing Education (Thorofare, NJ) 19623

Journal of Nursing Jocularity (Mesa, AZ) Unable to locate

Journal of Nursing Law (Eau Claire, WI) 33671

Journal of Nursing Measurement (Atlanta, GA) 7023

Journal of Nursing Quality Assurance 22147*

Journal of Nursing Scholarship (Indianapolis, IN) 10140

Journal of Nutraceuticals, Functional & Medical Foods (Hazleton, PA) 27034

Journal of Nutrition (Bethesda, MD) 13354

Journal of Nutrition Education (Dallas, TX) Ceased

Journal of Nutrition for the Elderly (Little Neck, NY) 20952

Journal of Nutrition, Health & Aging (Kettering, OH) 25283

Journal of Nutrition in Recipe and Menu Development (Blacksburg, VA) 31876

Journal of Object-Oriented Programming (New York, NY) Unable to locate

Journal of Obstetric, Gynecologic and Neonatal Nursing (JOGNN) (Thousand Oaks, CA) 3896

Journal of Occupational Behavior 19037*

Journal of Occupational and Environmental Medicine (Arlington Heights, IL) 8025

Journal of Occupational Medicine 8025*

Journal of Occupational Rehabilitation (New York, NY) 22148

Journal of Oceanography (New York, NY) 22149

Journal of Ocular Pharmacology 20918*

Journal of Ocular Pharmacology and Therapeutics (Larchmont, NY) 20918

Journal Of Negro History 13732*

Journal of Offender Counseling, Services, and Rehabilitation 26833*

Journal of Offender Rehabilitation (Doylestown, PA) 26833

Journal of Online Mathematics and Its Applications (Washington, DC) 5607

Journal of the Ontario Herbalists Association 36331*

Journal of Open Source Medical Computing (JOSMC) (Houston, TX) Unable to locate

Journal of Operations Management (Falls Church, VA) Ceased

Journal of Ophthalmic Nursing & Technology (Thorofare, NJ) Ceased

Journal Opinion (Bradford, VT) 31506

Journal of the Optical Society of America A: Optics, Image Science,and Vision (Washington, DC) 5608

Journal of the Optical Society of America B: Optical Physics (Washington, DC) 5609

Journal of Optical Technology (College Park, MD) 13429

Journal of Optimization Theory and Applications (Houston, TX) 30497

Journal of Optometric Education 13691*

Journal of Optometric Vision Development (St. Louis, MO) 17457

Journal of Oral Implantology (Alexandria, VA) Unable to locate

Journal of Oral and Maxillofacial Surgery (Lexington, KY) 12168

The Journal of the Order of Buddhist Contemplatives (Mount Shasta, CA) 2604

The Journal of Organic Chemistry (Washington, DC) Unable to locate

Journal of Organic Chemistry of the USSR 22693*

Journal of Organizational Behavior (Hoboken, NJ) 19037

Journal of Organizational Behavior-Management (Detroit, MI) 14934

Journal of Organizational Computing and Electronic Commerce (Austin, TX) 29789

Journal of Organizational Excellence (Hoboken, NJ) 19038

Journal of Orofacial Pain (Carol Stream, IL) 8146

Journal of Orthomolecular Medicine (Toronto, ON, Can.) Unable to locate

Journal of Orthomolecular Medicine (Toronto, ON, Can.) 36636

Journal of Orthopaedic Research (Baltimore, MD) Ceased

The Journal of Orthopaedic and Sports Physical Therapy (JOSPT) (Alexandria, VA) 31700

Journal of Orthopaedic Trauma (Baltimore, MD) 13197

The Journal of Osteopathic Medicine (New York, NY) Unable to locate

The Journal of Otolaryngology (Le Journal d'Oto-Rhino-Laryngologie) (Toronto, ON, Can.) Unable to locate

Journal of Oughtred Society (Palo Alto, CA) 2797

Journal of Outcome Measurement (Wheaton, IL) 9756

Journal of Packaging Technology (Danbury, CT) Unable to locate

Journal of Pain (Philadelphia, PA) 27542

Journal of Pain and Palliative Care Pharmacotherapy (Salt Lake City, UT) 31435

Journal of Paleolimnology (New York, NY) 22150

Journal of Paleontology (Lawrence, KS) 11557

Journal of Palestine Studies (Washington, DC) 5610

Journal of Palliative Care (Montreal, QC, Can.) 37144

Journal of Pan African Studies (Fresno, CA) Unable to locate

Journal of Parallel and Distributed Computing (San Diego, CA) 3210

Journal of Parametrics (Chesterfield, MO) 16975

Journal of Parapsychology (Durham, NC) 23831

The Journal of Parasitology (Winston-Salem, NC) 24320

Journal of Parenteral and Enteral Nutrition; JPEN: (Silver Spring, MD) 13734

Journal of Parenteral Science and Technology 10983*

Journal of Pascal, ADA and Modula-2 (Hoboken, NJ) Ceased

The Journal of Pastoral Care 23681*

The Journal of Pastoral Care and Counseling (Calabash, NC) 23681

Journal of Pastoral Counseling (New Rochelle, NY) 21118

Journal of Pastoral Psychotherapy 25846*

Journal des Pates et Papiers (Montreal, QC, Can.) Ceased

Journal of Pathology (Hoboken, NJ) 19039

The Journal of Patient Account Management (Fort Lauderdale, FL) Unable to locate

Journal-Patriot (North Wilkesboro, NC) 24108

Journal of Peace & Justice Studies (Villanova, PA) 28097

Journal of Pediatric Gastroenterology & Nutrition (Baltimore, MD) 13198

Journal of Pediatric Health Care (Philadelphia, PA) 27543

Journal of Pediatric Hematology/Oncology (Baltimore, MD) 13199

Journal of Pediatric Nursing (Los Angeles, CA) 2304

The Journal of Pediatric Oncology Nursing (Houston, TX) 30498

Journal of Pediatric Ophthalmology & Strabismus (Thorofare, NJ) 19624

Journal of Pediatric Orthopaedics (Baltimore, MD) 13200

Journal of Pediatric Orthopaedics, Part B. (Philadelphia, PA) 27544

Journal of Technology in Human Services (Binghamton, NY) 20203

Journal of Technology in Human Services (Arlington, TX) 29733

Journal of Technology & Teacher Education (Norfolk, VA) 32289

Journal of Technology Transfer (New York, NY) 22203

Journal of the Tennessee Medical Association (Nashville, TN) Unable to locate

Journal of Testing and Evaluation (West Conshohocken, PA) Unable to locate

Journal of Texture Studies (Trumbull, CT) 5185

Journal of The Canadian Dietetic Association 36021*

Journal of The Institute of Environmental Sciences and Technology (Rolling Meadows, IL) 9548

Journal of Theoretical Probability (Tampa, FL) 6772

Journal of Theory Construction Testing (Lisle, IL) 9111

Journal of Therapeutic Horticulture (Gaithersburg, MD) Unable to locate

Journal of Thermal Analysis 22204*

Journal of Thermal Analysis 19050*

Journal of Thermal Analysis and Calorimetry (Hoboken, NJ) 19050

Journal of Thermal Analysis and Calorimetry (New York, NY) 22204

Journal of Thermal Spray Technology (Stony Brook, NY) 23371

Journal of Thermal Stresses (Naples, FL) 6442

Journal of Thermophysics and Heat Transfer (Reston, VA) 32398

Journal of Third World Studies (Americus, GA) 6922

The Journal of Thoracic and Cardiovascular Surgery (New York, NY) 22205

Journal of Thoracic Imaging (Baltimore, MD) 13203

Journal of Thought (San Francisco, CA) 3385

Journal of Threat Assessment (Binghamton, NY) 20204

The Journal Times (Racine, WI) 34273

Journal of Tissue Culture Methods 31515*

Journal of the Torrey Botanical Society (Lawrence, KS) 11559

Journal of Toxicology: Clinical Toxicology (Mineola, NY) 21085

Journal of Toxicology, Cutaneous and Ocular Toxicology (Andover, MA) 13812

Journal of Toxicology and Environmental Health (Philadelphia, PA) 27553

Journal of Toxicology Toxin Reviews (Minneapolis, MN) 16690

The Journal of Trace Elements in Experimental Medicine (Hoboken, NJ) 19051

Journal of Trace and Microprobe Techniques (New York, NY) 22206

Journal Transcript (Danielson, CT) Ceased

The Journal Transcript (Franklin, NH) Unable to locate

Journal of Translation and Textlinguistics (Dallas, TX) 30164

Journal of Transnational Management Development (Boston, MA) 13919

Journal of Transplant Coordination (Aliso Viejo, CA) Unable to locate

Journal of Transportation Engineering (Reston, VA) 32399

Journal of Trauma (San Antonio, TX) 31036

Journal of Trauma & Dissociation (Binghamton, NY) 20205

Journal of Trauma Nursing (Philadelphia, PA) 27554

Journal of Trauma Nursing; International (St. Louis, MO) 17447

Journal of Trauma Practice (Binghamton, NY) 20206

Journal of Traumatic Stress (New York, NY) 22207

Journal of Travel Medicine (Hamilton, ON, Can.) 35886

Journal of Tree Fruit Production (Amherst, MA) 13798

Journal of Tribology (New York, NY) 22208

Journal-Tribune 28754*

Journal-Tribune (Marengo, IA) 11062

Journal Tribune (Biddeford, ME) 12922

Journal of Tropical Ecology (New York, NY) 22209

Journal of Turbomachinery (New York, NY) 22210

Journal of Turf Grass Management (Amherst, MA) 13799

Journal of Turkish Studies/Turkluk Bilgisi Arastirmalari (Duxbury, MA) 14164

The Journal of Typographic Research 8599*

Journal of Ultrasound in Medicine (Boston, MA) 13920

Journal of Unconventional History (Cardiff by the Sea, CA) Ceased

Journal of the University Film & Video Association 2301*

Journal of Urban Affairs (Louisville, KY) 12222

Journal of Urban and Contemporary Law 17529*

Journal of Urban Economics (San Diego, CA) 3215

Journal of Urban History (Charlotte, NC) 23746

Journal of Urban Planning and Development (Reston, VA) 32400

Journal of Urology (Baltimore, MD) 13204

Journal of Vacuum Science and Technology A & B (Research Triangle Park, NC) 24186

Journal Valley News (White Haven, PA) 28157

The Journal of Value Inquiry (New York, NY) 22211

Journal of Vascular and Interventional Radiology (JVIR) (Philadelphia, PA) 27555

Journal of Vascular Nursing (St. Louis, MO) 17463

Journal of Vascular Research (Farmington, CT) 4838

Journal of Vascular Surgery (New York, NY) 22212

Journal of Vascular Technology 13606*

Journal for Vascular Ultrasound (Lanham, MD) 13606

Journal of Vegetable Crop Production (Lane, OK) 25881

Journal of Veterinary & Comparative Oncology (Larchmont, NY) Ceased

Journal of Veterinary Internal Medicine (New York, NY) Ceased

Journal of Veterinary Medical Education (Blacksburg, VA) 31877

Journal of Vietnamese Music (Kent, OH) Ceased

Journal of Vinyl and Additive Technology (Brookfield, CT) 4726

Journal of Vinyl Technology 4726*

Journal of Virology (Washington, DC) 5618

Journal of Vision Rehabilitation 17175*

Journal of Visual Communication and Image Representation (San Diego, CA) 3216

Journal of Visual Impairment & Blindness (New York, NY) Unable to locate

Journal of Visualization and Computer Animation (Hoboken, NJ) 19052

Journal of VLSI Signal Processing-Systems for Signal, Image, and Video Technology (New York, NY) 22213

Journal of Vocational Behavior (San Diego, CA) 3217

Journal of Vocational Rehabilitation (Burlington, MA) 14030

Journal for Vocational Special Needs Education (Pittsburgh, PA) 27805

Journal of Voice (Baltimore, MD) 13205

Journal of Voluntary Action Research 32990*

Journal of Water Borne Coatings (Norwalk, CT) 5067

Journal Water Pollution Control Ferderation 31751*

Journal of Water Resources Planning and Management (Reston, VA) 32401

Journal of Waterway, Port, Coastal, and Ocean Engineering (Reston, VA) 32402

Journal of Wave-Material Interaction (University Park, PA) 28080

The Journal of Wealth Management (New York, NY) Unable to locate

Journal of Weight Engineering 8779*

Journal of the West (Manhattan, KS) 11623

Journal of Whiplash & Related Disorders (Binghamton, NY) 20207

Journal of Wildlife Rehabilitation (Berkeley, CA) 1538

Journal of Winston Churchill (Washington, DC) 5619

Journal of the Wisconsin Optometric Association (Middleton, WI) Ceased

Journal of WOCN (Wound, Ostomy, and Continence Nursing) (St. Louis, MO) 17464

Journal of Women and Aging (Sarasota, FL) 6659

Journal of Women's Health 20919*

Journal of Women's Health (Larchmont, NY) 20919

The Journal of Women's History (Bloomington, IN) 9844

Journal of Women's Imaging (Baltimore, MD) Unable to locate

Journal of Wood Chemistry and Technology (Syracuse, NY) 23406

Journal-World (Lawrence, KS) 11560

Journal of World Business (Lincoln, NE) 18088

Journal of World History (Honolulu, HI) 7705

Journal of World Prehistory (New York, NY) 22214

Journal of World Trade (New York, NY) 22215

Journal of X-Ray Science and Technology (San Diego, CA) Ceased

Journal of Youth and Adolescence (New York, NY) 22216

Journal of Youth Services in Libraries (Chicago, IL) Ceased

Journal of Zoo and Wildlife Medicine (Media, PA) 27242

Journalism; American (Tuscaloosa, AL) 484

Journalism Educator 29279*

Journalism and Mass Communication Educator (Knoxville, TN) 29279

Journalism and Mass Communication Quarterly (Columbia, SC) 28555

Journalism Quarterly 28555*

Journalism Review; American (College Park, MD) 13410

Journalism Review; Columbia (New York, NY) 21447

Journalism Review; Montana (Missoula, MT) 17871

Journalism Review; The St. Louis (St. Louis, MO) 17502

Journalist; American Amateur (Fountain Hills, AZ) 710

Journals of Gerontology (Washington, DC) 5620

The Journals of Gerontology; Psychological Sciences & Social Sciences (Washington, DC) 5621

Journey Magazine (Lynchburg, VA) Ceased

Journey Press (Seattle, WA) Unable to locate

Journeyman Roofer 5622*

Journeyman Roofer and Waterproofer (Washington, DC) 5622

Journeys (West Hartford, CT) 5204

Journeywoman Online Magazine (Toronto, ON, Can.) 36640

Joy of Travel (Bethesda, MD) Ceased

Joyce Literary Supplement; James (Coral Gables, FL) 6008

Joyce Quarterly; James (Tulsa, OK) 26118

The Joyful Woman (Greenville, SC) Unable to locate

JP (Los Angeles, CA) 2305

JPEN: Journal of Parenteral and Enteral Nutrition (Silver Spring, MD) 13734

JPO: Journal of Prosthetics & Orthotics (Alexandria, VA) 31704

JQ (Palm Springs, CA) 2762

JRMMRA 34552*

(JSAH); Journal of the Society of Architectural Historians (Chicago, IL) 8450

Jubilee (Duvall, WA) 32740

Juco Review (Colorado Springs, CO) 4251

Judaean; Young (New York, NY) 22953

Judaism (Santa Cruz, CA) 3685

Judaism; Conservative (New York, NY) 21485

Judaism; European (New York, NY) 21654

Judges Journal/Journal des Juges Provinciaux; Provincial (Grand Bank, NL, Can.) 35460

Judicature (Des Moines, IA) Unable to locate

Judicial Conduct Reporter (Des Moines, IA) Unable to locate

Judith Basin Press (Stanford, MT) 17912

Judson Cameo (Marion, AL) Ceased

JUF News (Chicago, IL) 8451

Juggle (Las Vegas, NV) 18368

Jukebox Collector (Pleasant Hill, IA) 11160

Julesburg Advocate (Julesburg, CO) 4523

Julian Cablevision 1594*

Julian News (Julian, CA) 2098

Jumble Word Puzzles (Norwalk, CT) Ceased

Jump Cut (Berkeley, CA) 1539

The Junction Eagle (Junction, TX) 30630

Juneau County Reminder/Wisconsin Reminder (Mauston, WI) Ceased

Juneau Empire (Juneau, AK) 596

Juniata News (Philadelphia, PA) 27556

Juniata Sentinel (Mifflintown, PA) 27263

Junior Baseball Magazine (Canoga Park, CA) 1656

Junior Chronicle (Sylvania, OH) Ceased

Jr. High Ministry Magazine (Loveland, CO) Ceased

Junior League Baseball 1656*

Junior Magazine (Pittsburgh, PA) 27806

Junior Scholastic (Danbury, CT) 4743

Junior Statement (San Mateo, CA) 3588

Jupiter Ceased

The Jupiter Courier (Jupiter, FL) 6249

Jupiter/Tequesta Thursday (Chicago, IL) Ceased

Jurimetrics (Tempe, AZ) 909

Jurimetrics Journal 909*

Juris (Pittsburgh, PA) 27807

Jurist; The National (Arlington, VA) 31811

Just Crochet (New York, NY) Unable to locate

Just Hockey (Oklahoma City, OK) 25970

Just Horsin' Around (Franklin, TN) Unable to locate

Just for Men/Male Call/Dress for Excellence (Mamaroneck, NY) 37972

Justice 22884*

The Justice (Waltham, MA) 14601

Justice Abstracts; Criminal (Thousand Oaks, CA) 3859

Justice; Social (San Francisco, CA) 3443

Juvenile and Family Court Journal (Reno, NV) 18421

Juvenile Merchandising (New York, NY) Unable to locate

Juxtapoz (San Francisco, CA) 3386

JVibe.com (Newton, MA) 14404

JW Plus (Toronto, ON, Can.) Unable to locate

JWB Circle 21958*

JWV Publishing 17720*

K

K-SIX-TV 30098*

K-State Radio Network (Manhattan, KS) 37640

K-Stater (Manhattan, KS) Unable to locate

K-Theory (New York, NY) 22217

K & V Cable TV Co. (Haysi, VA) 32157

K-Vision Services Ltd. 35598*

KAAA-AM 16294*

KAAA-AM - 1230 (Kingman, AZ) **732**
KAAB-AM (Batesville, AR) *Unable to locate*
KAAK-FM - 98.9 (Spokane, WA) **33104**
KAAL-TV - Channel 6 (Austin, MN) **15724**
KAAM-AM - 1310 (Dallas, TX) **30192**
KAAM-AM - 770 (Irving, TX) **30610**
KAAN-AM - 870 (Bethany, MO) **16904**
KAAN-FM - 95.5 (Bethany, MO) **16905**
KAAP-FM - 99.5 (Wenatchee, WA) **33197**
KAAQ-FM - 105.9 (Alliance, NE) **17928**
KAAR-FM - 95.3 (Spokane, WA) **33105**
KAAR-TV **3305***
KAAS-TV - Channel 18 (Salina, KS) **11785**
KAAT-FM - 103.1 & translators 104.3 (Oakhurst, CA) **2660**
Kaatskill Life (Delhi, NY) **20526**
KAAY-AM - 1090 (Little Rock, AR) **1238**
KABB-TV - Channel 29 (San Antonio, TX) **31050**
KABC-AM - 790 (Los Angeles, CA) **2446**
KABC-FM **2459***
KABC-TV - Channel 7 (Glendale, CA) **2014**
KABF-FM (Little Rock, AR) *Unable to locate*
KABG-FM **15787***
KABI-AM - 1560 (Abilene, KS) **11335**
KABL-AM - 960 (San Francisco, CA) **3468**
KABL-FM (San Francisco, CA) *Unable to locate*
KABN-AM - 840 (Anchorage, AK) **533**
KABQ-AM (Albuquerque, NM) *Unable to locate*
KABR-AM **28795***
KABR-AM - 1500 (Magdalena, NM) **19901**
KABX-FM - 97.5 (Merced, CA) **2529**
KABY-TV - Channel 9 (Aberdeen, SD) **28792**
KACC-AM - 89.7 (Alvin, TX) **29691**
KACD-FM - 103.1 (Whittier, CA) **4081**
KACE-FM - 103.9 & 98.3 (Los Angeles, CA) **2447**
KACH-AM - 1340 (Preston, ID) **7961**
KACI-AM - 1300 (The Dalles, OR) **26301**
KACI-FM - 97.7 (The Dalles, OR) **26302**
KACJ-AM **1153***
KACO-AM (Houston, TX) *Unable to locate*
KACQ-AM **1185***
KACS Christian Radio - 90.5 (Chehalis, WA) **32712**
KACS-FM **32712***
KACT-FM - 105.5 (Andrews, TX) **29724**
KACU-FM - 89.7 (Abilene, TX) **29657**
KACV-FM - 89.9 (Amarillo, TX) **29700**
KACV-TV - Channel 2 (Amarillo, TX) **29701**
KACW-FM **30909***
KACW-FM - 107.3 (Coos Bay, OR) **26275**
KACY-AM **12624***
KACY-FM **4028***
KADA-AM - 1230 (Ada, OK) **25725**
KADA-FM - 99.3 (Ada, OK) **25726**
KADI-AM **17550***
KADI-FM (Springfield, MO) *Unable to locate*
KADN-TV - Channel 15 (Lafayette, LA) **12622**
KADO-AM **31190***
Kadoka Press (Kadoka, SD) **28877**
KADQ-FM - 94.3 (Rexburg, ID) **7965**
KADR-AM - 1400 (Elkader, IA) **10874**
KADS-AM (Tulsa, OK) *Unable to locate*
KADU-FM - 90.1 (Yucaipa, CA) **4126**
KADV-FM - 90.5 (Ceres, CA) **1683**
KADX-FM **4421***
KADX-FM - 94.7 (Anchorage, AK) **534**
KADY-FM (Kealakekua, HI) *Unable to locate*
KADY-TV - Channel 63 (Camarillo, CA) **1643**
KAEH-FM - 100.9 (Sun City, CA) **3825**
KAEP-FM - 105.7 (Spokane, WA) **33106**
KAET Magazine (Tempe, AZ) **910**
KAET-TV - Channel 8 (Tempe, AZ) **919**
KAEZ-FM - 105.7 (Amarillo, TX) **29702**
KAFA-FM - 104.5 (USAF Academy, CO) **4652**
KAFE-AM **19950***
KAFE-FM - 104.3 (Bellingham, WA) **32680**
KAFF-AM (Flagstaff, AZ) *Unable to locate*
KAFF-FM **3970***
KAFF-FM (Flagstaff, AZ) *Unable to locate*
KAFR-FM **32886***
KAFR-FM **19965***
KAFT-TV - Channel 13 (Fayetteville, AR) **1125**
KAFX-FM - 95.5 (Lufkin, TX) **30742**
KAFY-AM (Bakersfield, CA) *Unable to locate*
KAGC-AM - 1510 (Bryan, TX) **29976**
KAGE-AM - 1380 (Winona, MN) **16532**
KAGE-FM - 95.3 (Winona, MN) **16533**
KAGG-FM - 96.1 (Bryan, TX) **29977**
KAGH-AM - 800 (Crossett, AR) **1093**
KAGH-FM - 104.9 (Crossett, AR) **1094**
KAGI-AM - 930 (Ashland, OR) **26219**
KAGL-TV (Glendale, CA) *Unable to locate*
KAGM-FM **26390***
KAGO-AM - 1150 (Klamath Falls, OR) **26389**
KAGO-FM - 99.5 (Klamath Falls, OR) **26390**
KAGR-TV (Ventura, CA) *Unable to locate*
KAGT-AM **32653***
KAGU-FM - 88.7 (Spokane, WA) **33107**
KAGY-AM - 1510 (Buras, LA) **12543**
KAHI-AM - 950 (Auburn, CA) **1442**

KAHK-FM **29878***
Kahoka Communications Cable (Kahoka, MO) **17152**
KAHR-FM (Poplar Bluff, MO) *Unable to locate*
KAHU **7672***
KAHU-AM - 1060 (Hilo, HI) **7672**
KAHY-FM **26562***
KAHZ-AM (Hurst, TX) *Unable to locate*
KAID-TV - Channel 4 (Boise, ID) **7816**
KAIL-TV - Channel 53 (Clovis, CA) **1734**
KAIM-AM - 870 (Honolulu, HI) **7729**
KAIM-FM - 95.5 (Honolulu, HI) **7730**
Kaimin; Montana (Missoula, MT) **17872**
KAIN-AM (Natchez, MS) *Ceased*
Kainai News (Standoff, AB, Can.) **34854**
KAIR-FM - 93.7 (Atchison, KS) **11346**
KAIT-TV - Channel 8 (Jonesboro, AR) **1199**
KAJ-TV - Channel 18 (Kalispell, MT) **17838**
KAJA-FM - 97.3 (San Antonio, TX) **31051**
KAJJ-FM **1159***
KAJK-AM (Fortuna, CA) *Unable to locate*
KAJN-FM - 102.9 (Crowley, LA) **12560**
KAJO-AM - 1270 (Grants Pass, OR) **26363**
KAJX-FM (Aspen, CO) *Unable to locate*
KAJZ-FM **4081***
KAJZ-FM **4081***
KAKC-AM (Tulsa, OK) *Unable to locate*
KAKE-TV - Channel 10 (Wichita, KS) **11894**
KAKI-FM - 107.1 (Benton, AR) **1048**
KAKN-FM - 100.9-FM (Naknek, AK) **624**
KAKS-AM (Canyon, TX) *Unable to locate*
KAKT-FM - 105.1 (Medford, OR) **26419**
KALA-FM - 88.5 (Davenport, IA) **10740**
Kalamazoo Flashes (Allegan, MI) **14721**
Kalamazoo Gazette (Kalamazoo, MI) **15242**
KALB-AM (Alexandria, LA) *Ceased*
KALB-TV - Channel 5 (Alexandria, LA) **12460**
KALC-FM - 105.9 (Denver, CO) **4369**
KALE-AM - 960 (Kennewick, WA) **32789**
Kaleidoscope (Birmingham, AL) **77**
Kaleidoscope (Brockport, NY) **20245**
Kaleidoscope (Akron, OH) **24582**
Kaleidoscope: International Magazine of Literature,
Fine Arts, and Disability **24582***
Kaleidoscope Music (Chicago, IL) *Unable to locate*
Kaleidoscope Television (San Antonio, TX) *Unable to locate*
KALF-FM (Chico, CA) *Unable to locate*
KALI-AM (Hollywood, CA) *Unable to locate*
KALI-FM (Orange, CA) *Unable to locate*
Kalispell News (Kalispell, MT) *Unable to locate*
Kalkaskian; The Leader and the (Kalkaska, MI) **15261**
KALL-AM - 910 (West Valley City, UT) **31487**
Kalliope (Jacksonville, FL) **6215**
KALM-AM - 1290 (Thayer, MO) **17649**
KALN-AM - 1370 (Iola, KS) **11514**
KALO-AM (Port Arthur, TX) *Unable to locate*
The Kalona News (Kalona, IA) **11010**
KALP-FM - 92.7 (Alpine, TX) **29686**
KALQ-FM - 93.5 (Alamosa, CO) **4133**
KALS-FM - 97.1 (Kalispell, MT) **17839**
KALT-AM - 900 (Houston, TX) **30544**
KALU-FM - 89.3 (Langston, OK) **25882**
KALV-AM - 1430 (Alva, OK) **25739**
KALW-FM - 91.7 (San Francisco, CA) **3469**
KALX-FM - 90.7 (Berkeley, CA) **1567**
KALZ-FM - 102.7 (Fresno, CA) **1962**
KAMA-AM (El Paso, TX) *Unable to locate*
KaMai Forum (Glendale, CA) **2010**
KAMB-FM - 101.5 (Merced, CA) **2530**
KAMC-TV - Channel 28 (Lubbock, TX) **30722**
KAMD-AM (Camden, AR) *Ceased*
KAMD-FM - 97.1 (Camden, AR) **1071**
KAME-TV - Channel 21 (Reno, NV) **18428**
Kamehameha Cablevision **7668***
KAMG-AM - 1340 (Victoria, TX) **31237**
KAMI-AM - 1580 (Cozad, NE) **17987**
KAMI-FM - 104.5 (Cozad, NE) **17988**
KAMJ-AM **823***
KAMJ-FM **845***
KAML-AM - 990 (Kenedy, TX) **30636**
KAML-FM - 96.9 (Gillette, WY) **34528**
The Kamloops News (Kamloops, BC, Can.) **34977**
Kamloops This Week (Kamloops, BC, Can.) **34978**
KAMO-AM **1130***
KAMO-FM - 94.3 (Fayetteville, AR) **1126**
Kampana—Campana (Long Island City, NY) **20964**
KAMQ-AM - 1240 (Carlsbad, NM) **19823**
KAMR-TV (Amarillo, TX) *Unable to locate*
KAMS-FM - 95.1 (Thayer, MO) **17650**
Kamsack Times (Kamsack, SK, Can.) **37478**
KAMU-FM - 90.9 (College Station, TX) **30056**
KAMU-TV - Channel 15 (College Station, TX) **30057**
KAMX-FM (Albuquerque, NM) *Ceased*
KAMX-FM - 94.7 (Austin, TX) **29858**
KAMZ-FM (El Paso, TX) *Unable to locate*
KANA-AM (Anaconda, MT) *Ceased*
Kanabec County Times (Mora, MN) **16195**
KANADA KURIER (Winnipeg, MB, Can.) **35335**

Kanadske Listy (Canadian Pages) (Mississauga, ON, Can.) **36072**
Kanadsky Slovak (Toronto, ON, Can.) *Unable to locate*
Kanata Kourier **35925***
Kanata Kourier-Standard (Kanata, ON, Can.) **35925**
Kanata Standard **35925***
The Kanawha Reporter (Kanawha, IA) **11011**
KAND-AM - 1340 (Corsicana, TX) **30103**
KAND-FM **30104***
Kandiyohi County Times (Spicer, MN) **16454**
KANE-AM - 1240 (New Iberia, LA) **12723**
Kane County Chronicle (Geneva, IL) **8918**
Kane County Herald (Chicago, IL) *Unable to locate*
Kane Republican (Kane, PA) **27103**
KANG-FM **1424***
Kanhistique (Ellsworth, KS) **11427**
KANI **31286***
KANI-AM - 1500 (Wharton, TX) **31286**
KANJ-FM - 91.5 (Houston, TX) **30545**
Kankakee Valley Post News (Rensselaer, IN) **10412**
KANM-FM - 99.9 (College Station, TX) **30058**
KANS-AM **11471***
KANS-FM - 92.9 (Emporia, KS) **11432**
Kansan; Kansas City (Kansas City, KS) **11527**
Kansan; Newton (Newton, KS) **11669**
Kansan; The University Daily (Lawrence, KS) **11567**
Kansas! (Topeka, KS) **11824**
Kansas Academy of Science; Transactions of the (Lawrence, KS) **11566**
Kansas Agriculture Network/Kansas Information Network (Topeka, KS) **37641**
Kansas Alumni (Lawrence, KS) **11561**
The Kansas Anthropologist (Topeka, KS) **11825**
The Kansas Banker (Topeka, KS) **11826**
Kansas Beverage News (Wichita, KS) **11884**
Kansas Biology Teacher (Emporia, KS) **11430**
Kansas Business News (Augusta, KS) *Unable to locate*
Kansas Chief (Troy, KS) **11851**
Kansas City Business Journal (Kansas City, MO) **17178**
Kansas City Commerce (Millstadt, IL) **9197**
Kansas City Genealogist (Kansas City, MO) **17179**
Kansas City Globe (Kansas City, MO) *Unable to locate*
Kansas City Hispanic News (Kansas City, MO) *Unable to locate*
Kansas City Homes & Gardens (Prairie Village, KS) **11762**
Kansas City Jewish Chronicle (Overland Park, KS) **11717**
Kansas City Kansan (Kansas City, KS) **11527**
Kansas City Live! (Kansas City, MO) *Unable to locate*
Kansas City Magazine *Unable to locate*
Kansas City Medical Guide (Kansas City, MO) *Unable to locate*
Kansas City North News **17190***
Kansas City Small Business Monthly (Kansas City, MO) *Unable to locate*
The Kansas City Star (Kansas City, MO) **17180**
The Kansas City Times **17180***
The Kansas City Times (Kansas City, MO) *Ceased*
The Kansas City Voice (Kansas City, KS) *Unable to locate*
Kansas City Wyandotte Echo (Kansas City, KS) **11528**
Kansas Country Living (Topeka, KS) **11827**
Kansas Economic Report (Wichita, KS) **11885**
Kansas Farm Edition; Fastline— (Buckner, KY) **11977**
Kansas Farmer (Jewell, KS) **11517**
Kansas Food Dealers Bulletin (Shawnee Mission, KS) **11804**
Kansas 4-H Journal (Manhattan, KS) **11624**
Kansas Government Journal (Topeka, KS) **11828**
Kansas History: A Journal of the Central Plains (Topeka, KS) *Unable to locate*
Kansas, Inc.; TCI of (Salina, KS) **11792**
Kansas Insurance **11829**
Kansas Insurance Agent and Broker (Topeka, KS) **11829**
Kansas Living (Manhattan, KS) **11625**
Kansas Music Review (Wichita, KS) **11886**
Kansas Nurse (Topeka, KS) **11830**
Kansas Pharmacy; Journal of (Topeka, KS) **11823**
Kansas Professional Engineer (Topeka, KS) *Unable to locate*
Kansas Quarterly **1348***
Kansas Quarterly/Arkansas Review **1348***
Kansas Register; Northwestern (Salina, KS) **11783**
Kansas State Collegian (Manhattan, KS) **11626**
Kansas State Engineer (Manhattan, KS) **11627**
Kansas Stockman (Topeka, KS) **11831**
Kansas Transporter **11834***
Kansas Works (Ellsworth, KS) *Ceased*
KANU-FM - 91.5 (Lawrence, KS) **11573**
KANW-FM - 89.1 (Albuquerque, NM) **19791**
KANZ-FM - 91.1 (Garden City, KS) **11450**

Numbers cited in bold after listings are entry numbers rather than page numbers.

KBHE-TV - Channel 9 (Vermillion, SD) **29009**
KBHK-TV - Channel 44 (San Francisco, CA) **3470**
KBHL-FM - 103.9 (Osakis, MN) **16246**
KBHP-FM - 101.1 (Bemidji, MN) **15741**
KBHS-AM (Hot Springs, AR) *Unable to locate*
KBHT-FM - 93.5 (Grapeland, TX) **30411**
KBHU-FM - 89.1 (Spearfish, SD) **28995**
KBIA-FM - 91.3 (Columbia, MO) **17013**
KBIB-AM (Marion, TX) *Unable to locate*
KBIC-FM (Alice, TX) *Unable to locate*
KBID-FM **27133***
KBIF-AM (Fresno, CA) *Unable to locate*
KBIG-FM (Los Angeles, CA) *Unable to locate*
KBIL-AM **17250***
KBIL-AM (San Angelo, TX) *Unable to locate*
KBIM-AM - 910 (Roswell, NM) **19915**
KBIM-FM - 94.9 (Roswell, NM) **19916**
KBIM-TV - Channel 10 (Roswell, NM) **19917**
KBIQ-FM **33049***
KBIS-AM (Little Rock, AR) *Ceased*
KBIX-AM (Tulsa, OK) *Unable to locate*
KBIZ-AM - 1240 (Ottumwa, IA) **11141**
KBJJ-FM **16045***
KBJM-AM - 1400 (Lemmon, SD) **28883**
KBJR-TV (Duluth, MN) *Unable to locate*
KBJS-FM - 90.3 (Jacksonville, TX) **30616**
KBJT-AM - 1570 (Fordyce, AR) **1136**
KBKB-AM (Fort Madison, IA) *Unable to locate*
KBKB-FM (Fort Madison, IA) *Unable to locate*
KBKH-AM **32912***
KBKN-FM **26228***
KBKN-FM **26451***
KBKR-AM - 1490 (Baker City, OR) **26234**
KBKR-FM **26235***
KBKS-FM (Seattle, WA) *Unable to locate*
KBKW-AM **32648***
KBKW-AM - 1450 (Aberdeen, WA) **32648**
KBLA-AM (Los Angeles, CA) *Unable to locate*
KBLE-AM (Mercer Island, WA) *Ceased*
KBLF-AM (Red Bluff, CA) *Unable to locate*
KBLG-AM - 910 (Billings, MT) **17737**
KBLI-AM **7801***
KBLJ-FM **4528***
KBLL-AM - 1240 (Helena, MT) **17825**
KBLL-FM - 99.5 (Helena, MT) **17826**
KBLP-FM - 105.1 (Lindsay, OK) **25901**
KBLQ-AM **31359***
KBLQ-FM - 92.9 (Logan, UT) **31357**
KBLR-AM **16913***
KBLR-AM **11467***
KBLR-TV - Channel 39 (Las Vegas, NV) **18391**
KBLS-FM - 102.5 (Manhattan, KS) **11631**
KBLU-AM - 560 (Yuma, AZ) **1024**
KBLV-AM **33074***
KBLX AM **3504***
KBLX AM **3504***
KBLX-AM **3502***
KBLX-FM - 102.9 (San Francisco, CA) **3472**
KBLX-FM - 102.9 (San Francisco, CA) **3471**
KBLZ-FM (Omaha, NE) *Unable to locate*
KBMA-FM - 99.5 (College Station, TX) **30059**
KBMA-TV **17214***
KBMB-TV **24372***
KBMC-FM **26342***
KBME-TV - Channel 3 (Bismarck, ND) **24362**
KBMG-AM **17881***
KBMG-FM - 95.9 (Hamilton, MT) **17809**
KBMN-AM (Bozeman, MT) *Unable to locate*
KBMO-AM - 1290 (Benson, MN) **15748**
KBMR-AM - 1130 (Bismarck, ND) **24363**
KBMS-AM (Portland, OR) *Unable to locate*
KBMT-TV - Channel 12 (Beaumont, TX) **29902**
KBMV-AM (Birch Tree, MO) *Unable to locate*
KBMV-FM (Birch Tree, MO) *Unable to locate*
KBMW-AM - 1450 (Wahpeton, ND) **24551**
KBMW-FM - 107.1 (Wahpeton, ND) **24550**
KBMX-FM - 101.9 (Bowling Green, MO) **16917**
KBMY-TV - Channel 17 (Bismarck, ND) **24364**
KBNA-AM - 920 (El Paso, TX) **30285**
KBNA-FM - 97.5 (El Paso, TX) **30286**
KBND-AM - 1110 (Bend, OR) **26244**
KBNJ-FM - 91.7 (Corpus Christi, TX) **30080**
KBNL-FM - 89.9 (Laredo, TX) **30671**
KBNN-AM - 750 (Lebanon, MO) **17239**
KBNO-AM - 1280 (Denver, CO) **4372**
KBNP-AM (Portland, OR) *Unable to locate*
KBNR-FM - 88.3 (Brownsville, TX) **29961**
KBNT-TV - Channel 19 (San Diego, CA) **3294**
KBOB-FM (La Puente, CA) *Ceased*
KBOB-FM - 99.7 (Davenport, IA) **10741**
KBOC-FM - 98.3 (Bridgeport, TX) **29952**
KBOE-AM - 740 (Oskaloosa, IA) **11136**
KBOE-FM - 104.9 (Oskaloosa, IA) **11137**
KBOG-FM **26187***
KBOI **4199***
KBOI-AM - 670 (Boise, ID) **7817**
KBOI-FM **7828***
KBOK-AM - 1310 (Malvern, AR) **1264**
KBOL-AM (Boulder, CO) *Unable to locate*

KBOM-AM **24369***
KBOM-FM - 106.7 (Santa Fe, NM) **19947**
KBOO-FM - 90.7 (Portland, OR) **26519**
KBOP-AM (Pleasanton, TX) *Ceased*
KBOQ-FM - 95.5 (Monterey, CA) **2586**
KBOR-AM - 1700 (Brownsville, TX) **29962**
KBOR-FM **29963***
KBOS-FM (Fresno, CA) *Unable to locate*
KBOT-FM - 104.1 (Detroit Lakes, MN) **15831**
KBOV-AM - 1230 (Bishop, CA) **1585**
KBOX-FM - 104.1 (Santa Maria, CA) **3697**
KBOY-FM - 95.7 (Medford, OR) **26420**
KBOZ-AM - 1090 (Bozeman, MT) **17754**
KBOZ-FM - 97.5 (Bozeman, MT) **17755**
KBPA-AM (San Francisco, CA) *Unable to locate*
KBPI-FM **4369***
KBPI-FM (Denver, CO) *Unable to locate*
KBPK-FM - 90.1 (Fullerton, CA) **1991**
KBPR-FM - 90.7 (Brainerd, MN) **15768**
KBPS-AM - 1450 (Portland, OR) **26520**
KBPS-FM - 89.9 (Portland, OR) **26521**
KBQI-FM - 107.9 (Albuquerque, NM) **19795**
KBQQ-FM **24512***
KBQQ-FM (Minot, ND) *Ceased*
KBRA-FM - 95.9 (Freer, TX) **30368**
KBRB-AM - 1400 (Ainsworth, NE) **17924**
KBRB-FM - 92.7 (Ainsworth, NE) **17925**
KBRC-AM - 1430 (Mount Vernon, WA) **32848**
KBRD-AM - 680 (Olympia, WA) **32868**
KBRD-FM **33062***
KBRE-AM - 940 (Cedar City, UT) **31325**
KBRE-FM - 92.5 (Merced, CA) **2531**
KBRE-FM - 94.9 (Cedar City, UT) **31326**
KBRF-AM - 1250 (Fergus Falls, MN) **15900**
KBRF-FM **15903***
KBRG-FM (San Jose, CA) *Unable to locate*
KBRI-AM - 1570 (Brinkley, AR) **1064**
KBRI-FM **1065***
KBRJ-FM - 104.1 (Anchorage, AK) **537**
KBRK-AM - 1430 (Brookings, SD) **28818**
KBRK-FM - 93.7 (Brookings, SD) **28819**
KBRL-AM - 1300 (McCook, NE) **18154**
KBRN-AM - 1500 (McAllen, TX) **30791**
KBRO-AM (Tacoma, WA) *Unable to locate*
KBRR-TV - Channel 10 (Thief River Falls, MN) **16469**
KBRS-AM (Fayetteville, AR) *Unable to locate*
KBRT-AM - 740 (Costa Mesa, CA) **1784**
KBRU-FM - 101.7 (Fort Morgan, CO) **4447**
KBRV-AM - 790 (Pocatello, ID) **7949**
KBRV-AM - 790 (Soda Springs, ID) **7983**
KBRW-AM - 680 (Barrow, AK) **552**
KBRW-FM - 91.9 (Barrow, AK) **553**
KBRX-AM - 1350 (Oneill, NE) **18233**
KBRX-FM - 102.9 (Oneill, NE) **18234**
KBRZ-AM - 1460 (Freeport, TX) **30366**
KBS Inc. (Wichita, KS) **37699**
KBSB-FM - 89.7 (Bemidji, MN) **15742**
KBSD-TV - Channel 6 (Dodge City, KS) **11416**
KBSF-AM - 1460 (Springhill, LA) **12848**
KBSG-AM - 1210 (Seattle, WA) **33046**
KBSG-FM - 97.3 (Seattle, WA) **33047**
KBSH-TV - Channel 7 (Hays, KS) **11484**
KBSI-TV - Channel 23 (Cape Girardeau, MO) **16948**
KBSL-TV - Channel 10 (Goodland, KS) **11465**
KBSM-FM - 91.7 (McCall, ID) **7906**
KBSN-AM - 1470 (Moses Lake, WA) **32841**
KBSP-TV (Salem, OR) *Unable to locate*
KBSR-AM - 1490 (Laurel, MT) **17847**
KBSR-FM **17741***
KBST-AM - 1490 (Big Spring, TX) **29925**
KBSU-FM - 90.3 (Boise, ID) **7818**
KBSW-FM - 91.7 (Twin Falls, ID) **7991**
KBSY-FM (Fort Smith, AR) *Unable to locate*
KBSY-FM - 88.5 (Boise, ID) **7819**
KBSZ-AM - 1250 (Wickenburg, AZ) **1006**
KBSZ-FM **1007***
KBTA-AM - 1340 (Batesville, AR) **1043**
KBTB-FM (Seattle, WA) *Unable to locate*
KBTC-AM - 1250 (Houston, MO) **17103**
KBTC-FM - 91.7 (Tacoma, WA) **33155**
KBTC-TV - Channel 28 (Tacoma, WA) **33156**
KBTN-AM - 1420 (Neosho, MO) **17305**
KBTN-FM - 99.7 (Neosho, MO) **17306**
KBTO-FM - 101.9 (Bottineau, ND) **24377**
KBTR-FM (Tucson, AZ) *Unable to locate*
KBTV-TV **30219***
KBTV-TV **4391***
KBTV-TV - Channel 4 (Beaumont, TX) **29903**
KBTX-TV - Channel 3 (Bryan, TX) **29978**
KBUB-FM - 90.3 (Brownwood, TX) **29967**
KBUC-AM (San Antonio, TX) *Unable to locate*
KBUC-FM (San Antonio, TX) *Unable to locate*
KBUF-AM - 1030 (Garden City, KS) **11451**
KBUG-AM **17629***
KBUG-FM (Warsaw, MO) *Unable to locate*
KBUK-AM **29896***
KBUK-FM - 104.9 (La Grange, TX) **30657**
KBUL-AM - 970 (Billings, MT) **17738**

KBUL-FM (Reno, NV) *Unable to locate*
KBUM-AM **24373***
KBUN-AM - 1450 (Bemidji, MN) **15743**
KBUR-AM - 1490 (Burlington, IA) **10641**
KBUR-FM **10644***
KBUS-AM - 101.9 (Paris, TX) **30906**
KBUT-FM - 90.3 (Crested Butte, CO) **4299**
KBUX-FM - 94.3 (Quartzsite, AZ) **859**
KBUY-AM - 1360 (Ruidoso, NM) **19929**
KBUY-FM - 94.1 (Amarillo, TX) **29704**
KBVC-FM **11249***
KBVI **4199***
KBVM-FM - 88.3 (Portland, OR) **26522**
KBVO-TV **29862***
KBVR-FM - 88.7 (Corvallis, OR) **26292**
KBVU-FM - 97.5 (Storm Lake, IA) **11249**
KBWB-TV - Channel 20 (San Francisco, CA) **3473**
KBWC-FM - 91.1 (Marshall, TX) **30767**
KBWD-AM - 1380 (Brownwood, TX) **29968**
KBWH-FM (Blair, NE) *Unable to locate*
KBWL-FM **31461***
KBX-TV **30723***
KBXG-AM (Denver, CO) *Unable to locate*
KBXL-FM - 94.1 (Boise, ID) **7820**
KBXR-FM - 102.3 (Columbia, MO) **17014**
KBXS-FM **18342***
KBYB-FM (El Dorado, AR) *Unable to locate*
KBYG-AM - 1400 (Big Spring, TX) **29926**
KBYI-FM - 100.5 (Rexburg, ID) **7966**
KBYO-FM - 104.9 (Tallulah, LA) **12856**
KBYR-AM - 700 (Anchorage, AK) **538**
KBYU-FM - 89.1, 89.5 (Provo, UT) **31410**
KBYU-TV - Channel 11 (Provo, UT) **31411**
KBYZ-FM - 96.5 (Bismarck, ND) **24365**
KBZB-AM (Sierra Vista, AZ) *Unable to locate*
KBZC-AM - 1300 (Colorado Springs, CO) **4263**
KBZD-FM - 99.7 (Amarillo, TX) **29705**
KBZE-FM - 105.9 (Morgan City, LA) **12710**
KBZG-FM (Payson, AZ) *Unable to locate*
KBZK-TV - Channel 7 (Bozeman, MT) **17756**
KBZN-FM - 97.9 (Ogden, UT) **31380**
KBZO-AM (Lubbock, TX) *Unable to locate*
KBZO-TV - Channel 51 (Lubbock, TX) **30723**
KBZQ-FM - 99.5 (Lawton, OK) **25890**
KBZR-FM **30571***
KBZS-AM - 620 (Grand Junction, CO) **4481**
KBZS-FM **3295***
KBZS-FM **3295***
KBZT-FM **3295***
KBZT-FM **2752***
KBZT-FM **2748***
KBZT-FM - 94.9 (San Diego, CA) **3295**
KBZX-FM (Paso Robles, CA) *Unable to locate*
KBZY-AM **15932***
KBZY-AM - 1490 (Salem, OR) **26575**
KC Computer User (Overland Park, KS) **11718**
KCAC-FM - 89.5 (Camden, AR) **1072**
KCAD-AM **29669***
KCAD-FM - 99.1 (Dickinson, ND) **24397**
KCAD-FM - 99.1 (Dickinson, ND) **24396**
KCAJ-FM - 102.1 (Roseau, MN) **16329**
KCAK-FM **1744***
KCAL-AM (Highland, CA) *Unable to locate*
KCAL-FM (Redlands, CA) *Unable to locate*
KCAL-TV - Channel 9 (Los Angeles, CA) **2448**
KCAM-AM - 790 (Glennallen, AK) **583**
KCAP-AM - 1340 (Helena, MT) **17827**
KCAP-FM **17832***
KCAQ-FM - 104.7 (Ventura, CA) **4028**
KCAR-AM - 1350 (Clarksville, TX) **30023**
KCAS-FM - 91.5 (Mission, TX) **30834**
KCAT-AM - 1340 (Pine Bluff, AR) **1315**
KCAW-FM - 104.7 (Sitka, AK) **639**
KCAZ-AM (Kansas City, KS) *Ceased*
KCBA-TV - Channel 35 (Salinas, CA) **3068**
KCBC-AM - 770 (Oakdale, CA) **2657**
KCBD-TV - Channel 11 (Lubbock, TX) **30724**
KCBF-AM - 820 (Fairbanks, AK) **571**
KCBI-FM - 90.9 (Dallas, TX) **30194**
KCBJ-TV **17018***
KCBL-FM **4503***
KCBQ-AM (San Diego, CA) *Unable to locate*
KCBQ-FM **3303***
KCBQ-FM (San Diego, CA) *Unable to locate*
KCBR-AM (Monument, CO) *Unable to locate*
KCBS-AM - 740 (San Francisco, CA) **3474**
KCBS-FM - 93.1 (Los Angeles, CA) **2449**
KCBS-TV - Channel 2 (Los Angeles, CA) **2450**
KCBW-FM **17573***
KCBX-FM (San Luis Obispo, CA) *Ceased*
KCBY-TV - Channel 11 (Coos Bay, OR) **26277**
KCBZ-FM **30024***
KCBZ-FM - 96.5 (Astoria, OR) **26229**
KCCA-FM - 107.1 (Colorado City, AZ) **676**
KCCB-AM - 1260 (Corning, AR) **1091**
KCCC-AM - 930 (Carlsbad, NM) **19825**
KCCD-FM - 90.3 (Moorhead, MN) **16190**
KCCI-TV - Channel 8 (Des Moines, IA) **10820**
KCCK-FM - 88.3 (Cedar Rapids, IA) **10678**

Numbers cited in bold after listings are entry numbers rather than page numbers.

KCCL-FM **1039***
KCCL-FM (Paris, AR) *Unable to locate*
KCCM-FM - 91.1 (Moorhead, MN) **16191**
KCCN-FM (Honolulu, HI) *Unable to locate*
KCCN-TV **3072***
KCCO-TV - Channel 7 (Alexandria, MN) **15714**
KCCQ-FM - 105.1 (Ames, IA) **10597**
KCCR-AM - 1240 (Pierre, SD) **28924**
KCCS-FM **17015***
KCCT-AM - 1150 (Corpus Christi, TX) **30081**
KCCU-FM - 89.3 (Lawton, OK) **25891**
KCCV-AM - 760 (Overland Park, KS) **11739**
KCCV-FM - 92.3 (Overland Park, KS) **11740**
KCCY-FM - 96.9 (Colorado Springs, CO) **4264**
KCD-FM **1819***
KCDA-FM (Spokane, WA) *Unable to locate*
KCDC-FM - 90.7 (Longmont, CO) **4563**
KCDI-FM - 93.3 (Bryant, AR) **1066**
KCDL-FM - 99.3 (Weatherford, OK) **26187**
KCDR-AM **10683***
KCDR-FM **31329***
KCDS-FM **1424***
KCDU-FM (Dallas, TX) *Unable to locate*
KCDY-FM - 104.1 (Carlsbad, NM) **19826**
KCDZ-FM - 107.7 (Joshua Tree, CA) **2097**
KCEC-TV - Channel 50 (Denver, CO) **4373**
KCED-FM - 91.3 (Centralia, WA) **32705**
KCEL-FM **26450***
KCEL-FM - 106.9 (California City, CA) **1640**
KCEN-TV - Channel 6 (Temple, TX) **31180**
KCEO-AM - 1000 (Carlsbad, CA) **1668**
KCEP-FM - 88.1 (Las Vegas, NV) **18392**
KCET Magazine (Los Angeles, CA) *Ceased*
KCET-TV - Channel 28 (Los Angeles, CA) **2451**
KCEV-FM **11411***
KCEZ-FM **1073***
KCFA-AM **33120***
KCFA-AM (Eagle River, AK) *Ceased*
KCFA-FM **33121***
KCFB-FM - 91.5 (St. Cloud, MN) **16349**
KCFI-AM **10665***
KCFM **26166***
KCFO-AM - 970 (Tulsa, OK) **26145**
KCFO-FM **26169***
KCFS-FM - 94.5 (Sioux Falls, SD) **28970**
KCFV-FM - 89.5 (St. Louis, MO) **17534**
KCFW-TV - Channel 9 (Kalispell, MT) **17840**
KCFX-FM (Overland Park, KS) *Unable to locate*
KCFY-FM - 88.1 (Yuma, AZ) **1025**
KCGL-FM **31454***
KCGL-FM - 104.1 (Cody, WY) **34514**
KCGM-FM - 95.7 (Scobey, MT) **17904**
KCGN-AM **28835***
KCGN-FM - 101.5 (Osakis, MN) **16247**
KCGQ-FM - 99.3 (Cape Girardeau, MO) **16949**
KCGR-FM - 100.5 (Cottage Grove, OR) **26295**
KCGS-AM - 960 (Marshall, AR) **1270**
KCGY-FM - 95.1 (Laramie, WY) **34554**
KCHA-AM - 1580 (Charles City, IA) **10696**
KCHA-FM - 95.9 (Charles City, IA) **10697**
KCHE-AM - 1440 (Cherokee, IA) **10700**
KCHF-TV - Channel 11 (Santa Fe, NM) **19948**
KCHG-AM (San Antonio, TX) *Unable to locate*
KCHH-FM **1700***
KCHI-AM - 1010 (Chillicothe, MO) **16978**
KCHI-FM - 98.5 (Chillicothe, MO) **16979**
KCHJ-AM - 1010 (Bakersfield, CA) **1458**
KCHK-AM - 1350 (New Prague, MN) **16210**
KCHK-FM - 95.5 (New Prague, MN) **16211**
KCHL-AM (San Antonio, TX) *Unable to locate*
KCHR-AM - 1350 (Charleston, MO) **16973**
KCHS-AM - 1400 (Truth or Consequences, NM) **19970**
KCHU-AM - 770 (Valdez, AK) **646**
KCHU-FM - 88.1 (Valdez, AK) **647**
KCHV-FM **2772***
KCHX-FM - 106.7 (Odessa, TX) **30873**
KCHZ-FM (Overland Park, KS) *Unable to locate*
KCIB-FM **2891***
KCIC-FM - 88.5 (Grand Junction, CO) **4482**
KCID-AM (Caldwell, ID) *Unable to locate*
KCID-FM (Boise, ID) *Unable to locate*
KCIF-FM (Hilo, HI) *Unable to locate*
KCII-AM - 106.1 (Washington, IA) **11287**
KCII-FM - 106.1 (Washington, IA) **11288**
KCIJ-AM **12826***
KCIK-TV **30290***
KCIL-FM - 107.5 (Houma, LA) **12602**
KCIM-AM - 1380 (Carroll, IA) **10653**
KCIR-FM **30104***
KCIR-FM - 90.7 (Twin Falls, ID) **7992**
KCIS-AM - 630 (Seattle, WA) **33048**
KCIT-TV - Channel 14 (Amarillo, TX) **29706**
KCIV-FM **26303***
KCIV-FM - 99.9 (Mount Bullion, CA) **2603**
KCIW-AM **1006***
KCIW-FM **836***
KCIX-FM - 105.9 (Boise, ID) **7821**
KCIY-FM - 106.5 (Westwood, KS) **11871**

KCJB-AM - 910 (Minot, ND) **24507**
KCJB-TV **24515***
KCJC-FM (Russellville, AR) *Unable to locate*
KCJH-FM **3820***
KCJH-FM - 89.1 (Stockton, CA) **3811**
KCJJ-AM - 1630 (Iowa City, IA) **10991**
KCJZ-FM - 106.7 (San Antonio, TX) **31052**
KCKC-AM (San Bernardino, CA) *Ceased*
KCKK-AM - 1600 (Denver, CO) **4374**
KCKL-FM - 95.9 (Malakoff, TX) **30756**
KCKN-AM **19914***
KCKR-FM **30411***
KCKR-FM (Waco, TX) *Unable to locate*
KCKS-FM - 94.9 (Concordia, KS) **11398**
KCKX-AM (Stayton, OR) *Unable to locate*
KCKY-AM (Coolidge, AZ) *Unable to locate*
KCLA-AM (Pine Bluff, AR) *Unable to locate*
KCLB-AM - 970 (Palm Springs, CA) **2771**
KCLB-FM **3041***
KCLB-FM - 93.7 (Palm Springs, CA) **2772**
KCLC-FM - 89.1 (St. Charles, MO) **17385**
KCLD-FM - 104.7 (St. Cloud, MN) **16350**
KCLE-AM - 1140 (Cleburne, TX) **30026**
KCLI-AM - 1320 (Clinton, OK) **25792**
KCLI-FM **26189***
KCLI-FM (Clinton, OK) *Ceased*
KCLK-AM - 1430 (Lewiston, ID) **7894**
KCLK-FM - 94.1 (Lewiston, ID) **7895**
KCLL-AM **3704***
KCLN-AM - 1390 (Clinton, IA) **10712**
KCLN-FM **10714***
KCLO-AM **11582***
KCLO-TV - Channel 15 (Rapid City, SD) **28937**
KCLQ-AM **2039***
KCLQ-FM **1975***
KCLQ-FM - 107.9 (Lebanon, MO) **17240**
KCLR-AM (Lubbock, TX) *Unable to locate*
KCLS-FM - 101.7 (Ely, NV) **18341**
KCLT-FM - 104.9 (West Helena, AR) **1368**
KCLU-AM - 88.3 Ventura County, 102.3 FM Santa Barbara County (Thousand Oaks, CA) **3924**
KCLV-AM - 1240 (Clovis, NM) **19831**
KCLV-FM - 99.1 (Clovis, NM) **19832**
KCLW-AM - 900 (Hamilton, TX) **30421**
KCLX-AM - 1450 (Colfax, WA) **32722**
KCLX-FM **32724***
KCLX-FM **3306***
KCLY-FM - 100.9 (Clay Center, KS) **11384**
KCMA-FM **3503***
KCMA-FM (Tulsa, OK) *Unable to locate*
KCMB-FM (Baker, OR) *Unable to locate*
KCMC-AM (Texarkana, TX) *Unable to locate*
KCME-FM (Colorado Springs, CO) *Unable to locate*
KCMG-AM **17301***
KCMG-FM **17302***
KCMH-FM - 91.5 (Mountain Home, AR) **1286**
KCMI-FM - 96.9 (Scottsbluff, NE) **18267**
KCMJ-AM - 1140 (Palm Springs, CA) **2773**
KCMJ-FM - 92.7 (Palm Springs, CA) **2774**
KCML-FM **1975***
KCMN-AM - 1530 (Colorado Springs, CO) **4265**
KCMO-AM (Westwood, KS) *Unable to locate*
KCMO-TV **17207***
KCMR-FM - 97.9 (Mason City, IA) **11074**
KCMS Bulletin (Brooklyn, NY) *Unable to locate*
KCMS-FM - 105.3 (Seattle, WA) **33049**
KCMT-FM **15715***
KCMT-FM (Folsom, CA) *Unable to locate*
KCMT-TV **15714***
KCMU-FM - 90.3 (Seattle, WA) **33050**
KCMV **33050***
KCMX-AM - 580 (Ashland, OR) **26220**
KCMY-TV **2849***
KCMZ-AM (Dallas, TX) *Unable to locate*
KCNC-TV - Channel 4 (Denver, CO) **4375**
KCND-FM - 90.5 (Bismarck, ND) **24366**
KCNE-FM - 91.9 (Lincoln, NE) **18131**
KCNI-AM - 1280 (Broken Bow, NE) **17967**
KCNL-AM **590***
KCNO-AM **1396***
KCNO-FM - 94.5 (Alturas, CA) **1395**
KCNQ-FM - 102.5 (Kernville, CA) **2103**
KCNR-AM - 860 (Salt Lake City, UT) **31445**
KCNS-TV - Channel 38 (San Francisco, CA) **3475**
KCNT-FM - 88.1 (Hastings, NE) **18038**
KCNW-AM - 1380 (Kansas City, KS) **11537**
KCNY-AM (Moab, UT) *Unable to locate*
KCNZ-AM - 1250 (Cedar Falls, IA) **10665**
KCOB-AM - 1280 (Newton, IA) **11116**
KCOB-FM - 95.9 (Newton, IA) **11117**
KCOE-FM - 105.5 (Johnson, NE) **18057**
KCOG-AM - 1400 (Centerville, IA) **10689**
KCOH-AM - 1430 AM (Houston, TX) **30546**
KCOK-AM **3955***
KCOL-AM - 600 (Fort Collins, CO) **4440**
KCOL-FM - 92.5 (Beaumont, TX) **29904**
KCOM-AM - 1550 (Comanche, TX) **30066**
KCON-AM - 1230 (Conway, AR) **1085**
KCOP-TV - Channel 13 (Los Angeles, CA) **2452**

KCOR-AM - 1350 (San Antonio, TX) **31053**
KCOR-TV **31078***
KCOS-TV - Channel 13 (El Paso, TX) **30287**
KCOT-FM **30824***
KCOU-FM - 88.1 (Columbia, MO) **17015**
KCOW-AM **32752***
KCOW-AM - 1400 (Alliance, NE) **17929**
KCOY-TV - Channel 12 (Santa Maria, CA) **3698**
KCOZ-FM - 91.7 (Point Lookout, MO) **17355**
KCPB-FM - 91.1 (Thousand Oaks, CA) **3925**
KCPI-FM **15709***
KCPI-FM - 94.9 (Albert Lea, MN) **15709**
KCPL-AM (Olympia, WA) *Unable to locate*
KCPM-TV - Channel 24 (Chico, CA) **1698**
KCPP-AM **31447***
KCPQ-TV - Channel 13 (Seattle, WA) **33051**
KCPR-FM - 91.3 (San Luis Obispo, CA) **3570**
KCPS-AM - 1150 (Burlington, IA) **10642**
KCPS-FM 1955-1971 **33160***
KCPT-TV - Channel 19/Digital 18 (Kansas City, MO) **17206**
KCR-AM - 1620 (San Diego, CA) **3296**
KCR-FM - 98.9 (San Diego, CA) **3297**
KCRA-AM **3025***
KCRA-TV - Channel 3 (Sacramento, CA) **3024**
KCRB-FM - 88.5 (Bemidji, MN) **15744**
KCRC-AM - 1390 (Enid, OK) **25825**
KCRF-FM - 96.7 (Newport, OR) **26447**
KCRG-AM - 1600 (Cedar Rapids, IA) **10679**
KCRG-TV - Channel 9 (Cedar Rapids, IA) **10680**
KCRH-FM - 89.9 (Hayward, CA) **2045**
KCRI-FM **1177***
KCRK-FM - 92.1 (Colville, WA) **32728**
KCRL-TV **18440***
KCRM-FM (Austin, TX) *Unable to locate*
KCRN-AM - 1340 (San Angelo, TX) **31012**
KCRN-FM - 93.9 (San Angelo, TX) **31013**
KCRO-AM - 660 (Omaha, NE) **18213**
KCRR-FM - 97.7 (Waterloo, IA) **11291**
KCRS-AM **10666***
KCRS-FM - 103.3 (Odessa, TX) **30874**
KCRT-AM - 1240 (Trinidad, CO) **4649**
KCRT-FM - 92.5 (Trinidad, CO) **4650**
KCRU-FM **89.1 3722***
KCRV-AM - 1370 (Kennett, MO) **17219**
KCRV-FM **17220***
KCRV-FM - 105.1 (Kennett, MO) **17220**
KCRW-FM - 89.9 (Santa Monica, CA) **3722**
KCRX-AM - 1430 (Roswell, NM) **19918**
KCRY-FM **89.3 3722***
KCSB-FM - 91.9 (Santa Barbara, CA) **3662**
KCSC-FM - 90.1 (Edmond, OK) **25815**
KCSD-FM - 90.9 (Sioux Falls, SD) **28971**
KCSD-TV **17206***
KCSF-FM - 90.9 (San Francisco, CA) **3476**
KCSI-FM - 95.3 (Red Oak, IA) **11171**
KCSJ-AM - 590 (Pueblo, CO) **4603**
KCSJ-FM **4287***
KCSM-FM - 91.1 (San Mateo, CA) **3592**
KCSM-TV - Channel 60 (San Mateo, CA) **3593**
KCSN-FM - 88.5 (Northridge, CA) **2647**
KCSO-TV **3053***
KCSP-FM - 90.3 (Casper, WY) **34487**
KCSR-AM - 610 (Chadron, NE) **17975**
KCSS-FM - 91.9 (Turlock, CA) **3960**
KCST-AM - 1250 (Florence, OR) **26354**
KCSU-FM - 90.5 (Fort Collins, CO) **4441**
KCSY-AM (Soldotna, AK) *Unable to locate*
KCTA-AM (Corpus Christi, TX) *Unable to locate*
KCTC-AM - 1320 (Sacramento, CA) **3025**
KCTE-AM - 1510 (Independence, MO) **17116**
KCTI-AM (Gonzales, TX) *Unable to locate*
KCTM-FM (Rio Grande City, TX) *Unable to locate*
KCTN-FM - 100.1 (Elkader, IA) **10875**
KCTO-AM - 1540 (Columbia, LA) **12550**
KCTO-FM (Columbia, LA) *Unable to locate*
KCTQ-AM (Thousand Oaks, CA) *Unable to locate*
KCTR-AM **17738***
KCTR-FM - 102.9 (Billings, MT) **17739**
KCTS Magazine (Seattle, WA) **32980**
KCTS-TV - Channel 9 (Seattle, WA) **33052**
KCTT-FM - 101.7 (Yellville, AR) **1375**
KCTV-TV **17756***
KCTV-TV - Channel 5 (Kansas City, MO) **17207**
KCTX-AM - 1510 (Childress, TX) **30018**
KCTY-AM **3069***
KCTY-FM - 106.9 (Omaha, NE) **18214**
KCUB-AM - 1290 (Tucson, AZ) **976**
KCUE-AM - 1250 (Red Wing, MN) **16294**
KCUI-FM - 89.1 (Pella, IA) **11153**
KCUL-AM - 1410 (Marshall, TX) **30768**
KCUL-FM - 92.3 (Marshall, TX) **30769**
KCUR-FM - 89.3 (Kansas City, MO) **17208**
KCUV-AM (Denver, CO) *Unable to locate*
KCUZ-AM - 1490 (Safford, AZ) **862**
KCVL-AM - 1240 (Colville, WA) **32729**
KCVO-FM (Camdenton, MO) *Unable to locate*
KCVR-AM (Stockton, CA) *Unable to locate*
KCVS-FM - 91.7 (Milwaukee, WI) **34111**

KCVW-FM - 94.3 (Hutchinson, KS) **11503**
KCWA **16891***
KCWC-FM - 88.1 (Riverton, WY) **34578**
KCWC-TV - Channel 4 (Riverton, WY) **34579**
KCWD-FM - 96.7 (Harrison, AR) **1167**
KCWE-TV (Kansas City, MO) *Unable to locate*
KCWM-AM **31237***
KCWM-AM - 1460 (Hondo, TX) **30452**
KCWR-AM **1473***
KCWR-FM - 107.1 (Bakersfield, CA) **1459**
KCWT-TV (Seattle, WA) *Unable to locate*
KCWU-FM - 88.1 (Ellensburg, WA) **32750**
KCWW-AM - 1580 (Dallas, TX) **30195**
KCWY-TV **34503***
KCXL-AM - 1140 (Liberty, MO) **17250**
KCXX-FM - 103.9 (San Bernardino, CA) **3094**
KCXY-FM - 95.3 (Camden, AR) **1073**
KCYI-FM **26006***
KCYL-AM - 1450 (Lampasas, TX) **30667**
KCYN-FM **1319***
KCYX-AM **26417***
KCYY-FM - 100.3 (San Antonio, TX) **31054**
KCZE-FM - 95.1 (Charles City, IA) **10698**
KCZO-FM - 92.1 (McAllen, TX) **30792**
KCZQ-FM - 102.3 (Cresco, IA) **10731**
KCZY-FM **11132***
KDAB-FM (Prairie Grove, AR) *Unable to locate*
KDAC-AM - 1230 (Ukiah, CA) **3968**
KDAE-AM (Corpus Christi, TX) *Ceased*
KDAF-TV - Channel 33 (Dallas, TX) **30196**
KDAK-AM - 1600 (Carrington, ND) **24385**
KDAL-AM - 610 (Duluth, MN) **15845**
KDAL-FM - 95.7 (Duluth, MN) **15846**
KDAL-TV **15848***
KDAM-FM (Monroe City, MO) *Unable to locate*
KDAO-AM - 1190 (Marshalltown, IA) **11067**
KDAP-AM - 1450 (Douglas, AZ) **689**
KDAP-FM (Douglas, AZ) *Unable to locate*
KDAQ-FM - 89.9 (Shreveport, LA) **12823**
KDAR-FM - 98.3 (Oxnard, CA) **2732**
KDAS-AM **1264***
KDAZ-AM - 730 (Albuquerque, NM) **19796**
KDB-FM **3663***
KDB-FM - 93.7 (Santa Barbara, CA) **3663**
KDB-TV - Channel 59 (Albuquerque, NM) **19797**
KDBB-FM - 104.3 (Flat River, MO) **17067**
KDBC-TV - Channel 4 (El Paso, TX) **30288**
KDBH-FM (Natchitoches, LA) *Unable to locate*
KDBK-FM (San Francisco, CA) *Unable to locate*
KDBM-AM - 1490 (Dillon, MT) **17785**
KDBM-FM (Dillon, MT) *Unable to locate*
KDBQ-FM (San Francisco, CA) *Unable to locate*
KDBS-AM - 1410 (Alexandria, LA) **12462**
KDBS-FM **12467***
KDBV-AM - 980 (Salinas, CA) **3069**
KDCE-AM - 950 (Espanola, NM) **19845**
KDCI **1667***
KDCK-FM **11418***
KDCO-FM - 93.5 (Coos Bay, OR) **26278**
KDCQ **30875***
KDCR-FM - 88.5 (Sioux Center, IA) **11209**
KDCV-FM - 91.1 (Blair, NE) **17960**
KDDA-AM (Dumas, AR) *Unable to locate*
KDDB-FM - 102.7 (Honolulu, HI) **7732**
KDDD-AM - 800 (Dumas, TX) **30252**
KDDD-FM - 95.3 (Dumas, TX) **30253**
KDDK-FM **1250***
KDDK-FM (Little Rock, AR) *Unable to locate*
KDDQ-FM (Duncan, OK) *Unable to locate*
KDDR-AM - 1220 (Oakes, ND) **24528**
KDDR-FM (Oakes, ND) *Ceased*
KDDS-AM - 1490 (Duluth, MN) **15847**
KDDX-FM - 101.1 103.5 (Spearfish, SD) **28996**
KDEA-FM **12725***
KDEB-TV - Channel 27 (Springfield, MO) **17619**
KDEC-AM - 1240 (Decorah, IA) **10759**
KDEC-FM - 100.5 (Decorah, IA) **10760**
KDEF-AM (Albuquerque, NM) *Unable to locate*
KDEL-FM - 100.9 (Arkadelphia, AR) **1031**
KDEM-FM - 94.3 (Deming, NM) **19841**
KDEN-AM (Aurora, CO) *Unable to locate*
KDES-AM **2775***
KDES-AM - 920 (Palm Springs, CA) **2775**
KDES-FM - 104.7 (Palm Springs, CA) **2776**
KDEW-AM (North Little Rock, AR) *Ceased*
KDEW-FM (De Witt, AR) *Unable to locate*
KDEX-AM - 1590 (Dexter, MO) **17033**
KDEX-FM - 102.3 (Dexter, MO) **17034**
KDEY-FM **30747***
KDEZ-FM (Jonesboro, AR) *Unable to locate*
KDFC-AM (San Francisco, CA) *Ceased*
KDFC-FM - 102.1 (San Francisco, CA) **3477**
KDFI-TV - Channel 27 (Dallas, TX) **30197**
KDFL-AM (Tacoma, WA) *Unable to locate*
KDFM-FM **1760***
KDFN-AM - 1500 (Doniphan, MO) **17037**
KDFR-FM - 91.3 (Des Moines, IA) **10821**
KDFT-AM - 540 (Dallas, TX) **30198**
KDFW-TV - Channel 4 (Dallas, TX) **30199**

KDFX-FM **30612***
KDFX-FM **10850***
KDGB-FM - 93.1 (Pratt, KS) **11765**
KDGE-FM (Irving, TX) *Unable to locate*
KDGO-AM (Durango, CO) *Unable to locate*
KDHI-AM **3965***
KDHI-FM - 92.1 (Twentynine Palms, CA) **3965**
KDHL-AM - 920 (Faribault, MN) **15895**
KDHN-AM (Dimmitt, TX) *Unable to locate*
KDHX-FM - 88.1 (St. Louis, MO) **17535**
KDIA-AM **3492***
KDIC-FM - 88.5 (Grinnell, IA) **10932**
KDIF-AM - 1440 (Riverside, CA) **2950**
KDIL **31052***
KDIN-TV - Channel 11 (Des Moines, IA) **10822**
KDIO-AM - 1350 (Milbank, SD) **28894**
KDIS-AM - 1110 (Los Angeles, CA) **2453**
KDIX-AM - 1230 (Dickinson, ND) **24398**
KDIX-TV **24401***
KDIZ-AM - 1440 (Minneapolis, MN) **16146**
KDJI-AM - 1270 (Holbrook, AZ) **725**
KDJK-FM (Oakdale, CA) *Unable to locate*
KDJR-FM (Columbia, MO) *Unable to locate*
KDJS-AM - 1590 (Willmar, MN) **16520**
KDJS-FM - 95.3 (Willmar, MN) **16521**
KDJW-AM - 1360 (Amarillo, TX) **29707**
KDKA-AM - 1020 (Pittsburgh, PA) **27858**
KDKA-TV - Channel 2 (Pittsburgh, PA) **27859**
KDKB-FM - 93.3 (Mesa, AZ) **750**
KDKD-AM - 1280 (Clinton, MO) **16985**
KDKD-FM - 95.3 (Clinton, MO) **16986**
KDKF-TV - Channel 31 (Klamath Falls, OR) **26391**
KDKK-FM - 97.5 (Park Rapids, MN) **16257**
KDKO-AM - 1510 (Evergreen, AL) **210**
KDKR-FM - 91.3 (Tulsa, OK) **26146**
KDLA-AM (De Ridder, LA) *Ceased*
KDLG-AM - 670 (Dillingham, AK) **563**
KDLH-TV - Channel 3 (Duluth, MN) **15848**
KDLK-AM **30228***
KDLK-FM - 94.1 (Del Rio, TX) **30226**
KDLL-FM - 91.9 (Kenai, AK) **608**
KDLM-AM - 1340 (Detroit Lakes, MN) **15832**
KDLO-FM - 96.9 (Watertown, SD) **29020**
KDLO-TV - Channel 3 (Florence, SD) **28856**
KDLP-AM (Morgan City, LA) *Ceased*
KDLR-AM - 1240 (Devils Lake, ND) **24391**
KDLS-AM - 1310 (Perry, IA) **11157**
KDLS-FM - 105.5 (Perry, IA) **11158**
KDLT-TV - Channel 46 (Sioux Falls, SD) **28972**
KDLV-TV - Channel 5 (Sioux Falls, SD) **28973**
KDLX-FM - 106.7 (Maryville, MO) **17278**
KDLY-FM - 97.5 (Lander, WY) **34544**
KDMA-AM - 1460 (Montevideo, MN) **16181**
KDMC-FM **10861***
KDMD-TV - Channel 33 (Anchorage, AK) **539**
KDMG-FM **11154***
KDMG-FM - 103.1 (Burlington, IA) **10643**
KDMI-AM **10834***
KDMM-AM (Dallas, TX) *Ceased*
KDMM-FM - 105.7 (Herington, KS) **11489**
KDMO-AM - 1490 (Carthage, MO) **16960**
KDMX-FM - 102.9 (Dallas, TX) **30200**
KDNA-FM - 91.9 (Yakima, WA) **33227**
KDND-FM - 107.9 (Sacramento, CA) **3026**
KDNK-FM - 90.5 (Carbondale, CO) **4219**
KDNL-TV - Channel 30 (St. Louis, MO) **17536**
KDNS-FM **3478***
KDNW-FM - 97.3 (Duluth, MN) **15849**
KDNZ-FM - 88.7 (San Francisco, CA) **3478**
KDOB-TV, KUZZ-TV **1472***
KDOC-TV (Anaheim, CA) *Unable to locate*
KDOG-FM - 96.7 (Mankato, MN) **16031**
KDOK-AM **31220***
KDOK-AM **31212***
KDOK-FM - 92.1 (Tyler, TX) **31209**
KDOL-AM **18393***
KDON-FM - 102.5 (Salinas, CA) **3070**
KDOR-TV - Channel 17 (Broken Arrow, OK) **25772**
KDOS-AM - 1490 (Laredo, TX) **30672**
KDOT-FM - 104.5 (Reno, NV) **18429**
KDOV-AM (Phoenix, OR) *Unable to locate*
KDOX-AM - 1280 (Las Vegas, NV) **18393**
KDPR-FM - 89.9 (Bismarck, ND) **24367**
KDPS-FM - 88.1 (Des Moines, IA) **10823**
KDQN-AM - 1390 (De Queen, AR) **1101**
KDQN-FM - 92.1 (De Queen, AR) **1102**
KDR-TV (Phoenix, AZ) *Unable to locate*
KDRG-AM (Anaconda, MT) *Unable to locate*
KDRK-FM - 93.7 (Spokane, WA) **33110**
KDRM-FM - 99.3 (Moses Lake, WA) **32842**
KDRO-AM - 1490 (Sedalia, MO) **17572**
KDRQ-AM (Wishek, ND) *Ceased*
KDRS-AM - 1490 (Paragould, AR) **1309**
KDRS-FM - 107.1 (Paragould, AR) **1310**
KDRV-TV - Channel 12 (Medford, OR) **26421**
KDRY-AM - 1100 (San Antonio, TX) **31055**
KDSD-AM - 90.9 (Pierpont, SD) **28915**
KDSD-TV - Channel 16 (Aberdeen, SD) **28794**
KDSE-TV - Channel 9 (Dickinson, ND) **24399**

KDSI-AM **29679***
KDSJ-AM - 980 (Deadwood, SD) **28842**
KDSM-TV - Channel 17 (Des Moines, IA) **10824**
KDSN-AM - 1530 (Denison, IA) **10768**
KDSN-FM - 107.1 (Denison, IA) **10769**
KDSQ-FM (Denison, TX) *Unable to locate*
KDSR-FM - 101.1 (Williston, ND) **24561**
KDSS-FM - 92.7 (Ely, NV) **18342**
KDST-FM - 99.3 (Dyersville, IA) **10861**
KDSU-FM - 91.9 (Fargo, ND) **24417**
KDSX-AM (Denison, TX) *Unable to locate*
KDTH-AM - 1370 (Dubuque, IA) **10848**
KDTL-FM **16633***
KDTN-TV - Channel 2 (Dallas, TX) **30201**
KDTU-TV **994***
KDTV-TV - Channel 14 (San Francisco, CA) **3479**
KDTX-TV - Channel 58 (Irving, TX) **30611**
KDUB-TV **10849***
KDUC-FM (Barstow, CA) *Unable to locate*
KDUH-TV - Channel 4 (Scottsbluff, NE) **18268**
KDUK-FM (Eugene, OR) *Ceased*
KDUK-FM - 104.7 (Eugene, OR) **26336**
KDUN-AM **26554***
KDUN-AM - 1030 (Reedsport, OR) **26554**
KDUN-AM (Reedsport, OR) *Unable to locate*
KDUP-AM - 830 (Portland, OR) **26523**
KDUQ-FM (Barstow, CA) *Unable to locate*
KDUV-FM **29675***
KDUX-FM - 104.7 (Aberdeen, WA) **32649**
KDUZ-AM (Hutchinson, MN) *Unable to locate*
KDVE-AM **29908***
KDVL-FM - 102.5 (Devils Lake, ND) **24392**
KDVR-TV - Channel 31 (Denver, CO) **4376**
KDVS-FM - 90.3 (Davis, CA) **1819**
KDVV-FM (Topeka, KS) *Unable to locate*
KDWA-AM - 1460 (Hastings, MN) **15942**
KDWB-FM - 101.3 (Minneapolis, MN) **16147**
KDWD-FM **10645***
KDWD-FM - 100.1 (Spencer, IA) **11232**
KDWG-AM **17738***
KDWN-AM - 720 (Las Vegas, NV) **18394**
KDXE-FM **31167***
KDXI-FM - 1360 (Center, TX) **30014**
KDXL-FM - 106.5 (St. Louis Park, MN) **16362**
KDXY-FM (Paragould, AR) *Unable to locate*
KDYL-TV **31462***
KDYN-AM - 1540 (Ozark, AR) **1306**
KDYS-AM - 1520 (Lafayette, LA) **12624**
KDZA-AM (Lakewood, CO) *Ceased*
KDZA-FM **4264***
KEA News (Frankfort, KY) **12065**
KEAG-FM (Anchorage, AK) *Unable to locate*
KEAL-FM - 95.3 (Douglas, AZ) **690**
KEAN-AM - 1280 (Abilene, TX) **29659**
KEAN-FM - 105.1 (Abilene, TX) **29660**
KEAP-AM **1644***
KEAR-FM - 106.9 (Oakland, CA) **2704**
The Kearney Courier (Kearney, MO) **17216**
Kearney Daily Hub **18059***
Kearney Hub (Kearney, NE) **18059**
Kearsarge Cable Communications Inc. (New London, NH) **18609**
KEAS-AM - 1590 (Eastland, TX) **30267**
Keats-Shelley Journal (Chicago, IL) **8452**
KEAZ-FM (De Ridder, LA) *Unable to locate*
KEBC-AM - 1340 (Oklahoma City, OK) **26001**
KEBC-FM (Oklahoma City, OK) *Unable to locate*
KEBE-AM - 1400 (Jacksonville, TX) **30617**
KEBR-AM - 88.1 (Sacramento, CA) **3027**
KEBR-FM - 88.1 (Sacramento, CA) **3028**
KEBS-TV **3309***
KECG-FM (El Cerrito, CA) *Unable to locate*
KECH-FM (Sun Valley, ID) *Unable to locate*
KECI-TV - Channel 13 (Missoula, MT) **17879**
KECN-AM - 690 (Blackfoot, ID) **7801**
KECO-FM - 96.5 (Elk City, OK) **25820**
KECR-AM (El Cajon, CA) *Unable to locate*
KECR-FM (El Cajon, CA) *Unable to locate*
KECY-TV - Channel 9 (El Centro, CA) **1853**
KEDA-AM - 1540 (San Antonio, TX) **31056**
KEDG-AM **3050***
KEDG-FM **2020***
KEDJ-FM (Phoenix, AZ) *Unable to locate*
KEDM-FM - 90.3 (Monroe, LA) **12694**
KEDO-AM - 1400 (Longview, WA) **32816**
KEDP-FM - 91.1 (Las Vegas, NM) **19890**
KEDT-FM - 90.3 (Corpus Christi, TX) **30082**
KEDT-TV (Corpus Christi, TX) *Unable to locate*
KEED-AM **26340***
KEED-AM (Eugene, OR) *Ceased*
KEEE-AM (Nacogdoches, TX) *Unable to locate*
KEEL-AM - 710 (Shreveport, LA) **12824**
KEEN-FM **3547***
The Keene Sentinel (Keene, NH) **18530**
The Keene Town Crier (Brattleboro, VT) *Unable to locate*
Keene Valley Sun (Keenesburg, CO) *Unable to locate*
Keene Valley Video Inc. (Keene Valley, NY) **20857**

KEEP-FM **30769***
The Keeper's Log (San Francisco, CA) **3387**
Keeping Posted with NCSY (New York, NY) *Unable to locate*
The Keepsake (New Orleans, LA) **12736**
KEES-AM - 1430 (Tyler, TX) **31210**
KEET-TV - Channel 13 (Eureka, CA) **1898**
KEEY-FM - 102.1 (Minneapolis, MN) **16148**
KEEZ-FM - 99.1 (Mankato, MN) **16032**
KEFM-FM - 96.1 (Omaha, NE) **18215**
KEFR-FM - 89.9 (Le Grand, CA) **2151**
KEGE-FM **16157***
KEGG-AM **30387***
KEGL-FM - 97.1 (Dallas, TX) **30202**
KEGX-FM - 106.5 (Kennewick, WA) **32790**
KEHG-AM **15910***
KEIN-AM - 1310 (Black Eagle, MT) **17748**
KEIN-FM **17749***
Keister-Williams Newspaper Services, Inc. (Charlottesville, VA) **37974**
Keith County News (Ogallala, NE) **18188**
Keizertimes (Keizer, OR) **26380**
KEJO-AM (Corvallis, OR) *Unable to locate*
KEJO-FM **26208***
KEKA-FM - 101.5 (Eureka, CA) **1899**
KEKB-FM - 99.9 (Grand Junction, CO) **4483**
KEKR-TV **11538***
KELA-AM - 1470 (Centralia, WA) **32706**
KELB-FM **2772***
KELD-AM - 1400 (El Dorado, AR) **1108**
KELD-FM **1109***
KELE-AM - 1360 (Mountain Grove, MO) **17301**
KELE-FM - 92.5 (Mountain Grove, MO) **17302**
KELG-AM - 1440 (Austin, TX) **29861**
KELI-FM - 98.7 (San Angelo, TX) **31014**
KELK-AM - 1240 (Elko, NV) **18336**
The Keller Citizen (Keller, TX) **30635**
Kelly Observer (San Antonio, TX) *Unable to locate*
KELN-FM - 97.1 (North Platte, NE) **18178**
KELQ-AM - 1320 (Sioux Falls, SD) **28974**
KELO-FM - 92.5 (Sioux Falls, SD) **28975**
KELO-LAND TV (Sioux Falls, SD) **37700**
KELO-TV - Channel 11 (Sioux Falls, SD) **28976**
Kelowna Capital News (Kelowna, BC, Can.) **34989**
Kelowna and District Real Estate This Week (Kelowna, BC, Can.) *Unable to locate*
KELP-AM - 1590 (El Paso, TX) **30289**
KELP-TV **30304***
KELR-FM - 105.3 (Chariton, IA) **10694**
KELT-FM **30795***
Keltria Journal (Minneapolis, MN) *Ceased*
Kelvington Radio (Wadena, SK, Can.) **37582**
KELY-AM - 1230 (Ely, NV) **18343**
KELY-FM **18341***
KEMB-FM **11232***
KEMM-FM (Gatesville, TX) *Ceased*
Kemmerer Gazette (Kemmerer, WY) **34541**
KEMO-TV **3479***
KEMP-FM (St. George, UT) *Ceased*
Kemper County Messenger (De Kalb, MS) **16621**
KEMV-TV - Channel 6 (Mountain View, AR) **1292**
Ken-Ton Bee (Buffalo, NY) **20383**
KENA-AM - 1450 (Mena, AR) **1276**
KENA-FM - 102.1 (Mena, AR) **1277**
KENB-FM **34605***
Kenbridge-Victoria Dispatch (Victoria, VA) **32576**
KEND-AM **30730***
KEND-FM - 106.5 (Roswell, NM) **19919**
Kendall County Record (Yorkville, IL) **9776**
Kendall News (Kendall, FL) **6250**
KENE-AM **33169***
Kenedy City Cable Co. (Kenedy, TX) *Unable to locate*
KENI-AM - 650 (Anchorage, AK) **540**
Kenilworth Leader **19154***
Kenly News (Kenly, NC) **24020**
KENM-AM **19907***
Kenmare News (Kenmare, ND) **24484**
KENN-AM - 1390 (Farmington, NM) **19847**
Kennebec CATV Inc. (Kennebec, SD) **28878**
Kennebec Journal (Augusta, ME) **12892**
Kennedale News (Everman, TX) *Ceased*
Kennedy Advance-Times **30632***
Kennedy Cablevision, Inc. (Reidsville, GA) **7489**
Kennedy Institute of Ethics Journal (Washington, DC) **5623**
Kennel Review (Studio City, CA) *Unable to locate*
Kenner City News (Kenner, LA) *Ceased*
Kennesaw Neighbor (Kennesaw, GA) **7354**
Kennett Cablevision (Kennett, MO) **17221**
The Kennett Paper (Kennett Square, PA) **27106**
KENO-AM - 1460 (Las Vegas, NV) **18395**
Kenosha Bulletin (Kenosha, WI) **33871**
Kenosha Evening News **33872***
The Kenosha Labor **33873***
Kenosha News (Kenosha, WI) **33872**
Kenosha 34 **33874***
KENR-FM **705***
KENS-TV - Channel 5 (San Antonio, TX) **31057**

Kensington Gazette (Frederick, MD) **13515**
Kensington/Richmond Guide (Philadelphia, PA) *Unable to locate*
Kent **25275***
Kent Alumni (Kent, OH) **25275**
Kent City Advance; Sparta/ (Jenison, MI) **15230**
The Kent County Daily Times (West Warwick, RI) **28455**
Kent County News (Chestertown, MD) **13405**
Kent Good Times Dispatch (Kent, CT) **4920**
Kenton County Recorder (Florence, KY) *Unable to locate*
KentonTimes (Kenton, OH) **25281**
The Kentuckiana Purchasor (Indianapolis, IN) *Unable to locate*
Kentucky Afield (Frankfort, KY) **12066**
Kentucky Afield, The Magazine **12066***
Kentucky; All Around (Louisville, KY) **12209**
Kentucky Ancestors (Frankfort, KY) **12067**
Kentucky; Back Home in (Franklin, TN) **29194**
Kentucky Banker (Louisville, KY) **12223**
Kentucky Bench & Bar Magazine (Frankfort, KY) **12068**
Kentucky Beverage Journal (Frankfort, KY) *Unable to locate*
Kentucky Builder (Louisville, KY) *Unable to locate*
Kentucky Business Ledger (Louisville, KY) *Ceased*
The Kentucky City (Lexington, KY) *Unable to locate*
Kentucky Constructor (Frankfort, KY) *Ceased*
Kentucky Educational TV - Channel 15 (Lexington, KY) **12180**
Kentucky Engineer (Frankfort, KY) **12069**
Kentucky English Bulletin (Bowling Green, KY) **11947**
The Kentucky Explorer (Jackson, KY) **12145**
Kentucky Farm Bureau News **12209***
Kentucky Farm & Dairy Family Living (Columbia, KY) *Ceased*
Kentucky Farm Edition; Fastline— (Buckner, KY) **11978**
Kentucky Farmer (Carol Stream, IL) *Unable to locate*
Kentucky Farmer (Frankfort, KY) **12070**
Kentucky Grocer's Banner (Louisville, KY) *Unable to locate*
The Kentucky Journal (Frankfort, KY) **12071**
Kentucky Journal of Commerce and Industry (Louisville, KY) *Unable to locate*
Kentucky Journal; Western (Newburgh, IN) **10350**
Kentucky Kernel (Lexington, KY) **12169**
Kentucky Law Journal (Lexington, KY) **12170**
Kentucky Libraries (Frankfort, KY) **12072**
Kentucky Living (Louisville, KY) **12224**
Kentucky Marquee (Louisville, KY) *Ceased*
Kentucky Medical Association; Journal of the (Louisville, KY) **12221**
Kentucky New Era (Hopkinsville, KY) **12132**
Kentucky News-Journal; Central (Campbellsville, KY) **12006**
The Kentucky Pharmacist (Frankfort, KY) **12073**
Kentucky Plumbing-Heating-Cooling Index (Louisville, KY) **12225**
The Kentucky Post (Covington, KY) **12027**
Kentucky Prairie Farmer **12070***
The Kentucky Press (Frankfort, KY) **12074**
Kentucky Researcher; Central (Campbellsville, KY) **12007**
Kentucky Review (Lexington, KY) *Ceased*
Kentucky Standard (Bardstown, KY) **11926**
Kentucky/Tennessee Edition; American Trucker— (Indianapolis, IN) **10089**
Kentucky Travel Guide (Louisville, KY) **12226**
Kentucky Trucker (Louisville, KY) *Unable to locate*
The Kentville Advertiser (New Minas, NS, Can.) **35599**
Kentwood Advance (Kentwood, MI) **15263**
Kentwood News **12613***
The Kentwood News-Ledger (Kentwood, LA) **12612**
KENU-AM (Tacoma, WA) *Unable to locate*
KENV-TV - Channel 10 (Elko, NV) **18337**
KENW-FM - 89.5 (Portales, NM) **19905**
KENW-TV - Channel 3 (Portales, NM) **19906**
KENY-FM **591***
The Kenyon Leader (Kenyon, MN) **15983**
The Kenyon Review (Gambier, OH) **25212**
KENZ-FM (Salt Lake City, UT) *Unable to locate*
KEOK-FM - 101.7 (Tahlequah, OK) **26096**
KEOL-FM - 91.7 (La Grande, OR) **26400**
KEOM-FM - 88.5 (Mesquite, TX) **30809**
KEOR-AM - 1110 (Atoka, OK) **25752**
KEOS-FM - 89.1 (Bryan, TX) **29979**
KEOT-FM **31420***
The Keota Eagle (Keota, IA) **11017**
KEOV-TV **30430***
Keowee Courier (Walhalla, SC) **28778**
KEPC-FM - 89.7 (Colorado Springs, CO) **4266**
KEPI-FM - 88.7 (McAllen, TX) **30793**
KEPO-AM **30291***
KEPO-FM - 92.9 (Eagle Point, OR) **26308**
KEPR-AM **32883***
KEPR-TV - Channel 19 (Pasco, WA) **32878**

KEPX-FM - 89.5 (McAllen, TX) **30794**
KERA-FM - 90.1 (Dallas, TX) **30203**
KERA-TV - Channel 13 (Dallas, TX) **30204**
Kerala Express (Toronto, ON, Can.) **36641**
KERB-AM (Kermit, TX) *Unable to locate*
KERB-FM (Kermit, TX) *Unable to locate*
Kerby News for Seniors *Unable to locate*
KERC **30267***
KERC-FM **30266***
Keremeos Review (Keremeos, BC, Can.) **34996**
Kerens Tribune (Kerens, TX) **30637**
The Kerf (Crescent City, CA) **1787**
KERI-AM - 1180 (Bakersfield, CA) **1460**
The Kerkhoven Banner (Kerkhoven, MN) **15984**
KERM-FM - 98.3 (Torrington, WY) **34598**
The Kerman News (Kerman, CA) **2101**
KERN-AM - 1410 (Bakersfield, CA) **1461**
Kern Shopper (Bakersfield, CA) *Ceased*
Kern Valley Sun (Lake Isabella, CA) *Unable to locate*
Kernel (Cochran, GA) **7179**
Kernel; Kentucky (Lexington, KY) **12169**
KERO-TV - Channel 23 (Bakersfield, CA) **1462**
KERP-FM (Winterville, GA) *Unable to locate*
KERR-AM - 750 (Polson, MT) **17900**
Kerrobert Citizen-Dispatch (Kerrobert, SK, Can.) **37480**
Kerrville Daily Times (Kerrville, TX) **30639**
Kerrville Mountain Sun (Kerrville, TX) **30640**
KERX-FM - 95.3 (Barling, AR) **1039**
KESD-FM/South Dakota Public Broadcasting - 88.3 (Brookings, SD) **28820**
KESD-TV - Channel 8 (Brookings, SD) **28821**
KESE-AM - 1190 (Bentonville, AR) **1052**
KESM-AM - 1580 (El Dorado Springs, MO) **17043**
KESM-FM - 105.5 (El Dorado Springs, MO) **17044**
KESP-AM (Santa Barbara, CA) *Ceased*
KESQ-AM - 1400 (Palm Desert, CA) **2748**
KESQ-TV - Channel 42 (Palm Desert, CA) **2749**
KESS-AM - 1270 (Dallas, TX) **30205**
KEST-AM - 1450 (San Francisco, CA) **3480**
KESY-AM **18212***
KESY-FM **18227***
KESZ-FM - 99.9 (Phoenix, AZ) **817**
KETA-TV - Channel 13 (Oklahoma City, OK) **26002**
KETC Guide (St. Louis, MO) **17465**
KETC-TV - Channel 9 (St. Louis, MO) **17537**
The Ketch Pen (Ellensburg, WA) *Unable to locate*
Ketchikan Daily News (Ketchikan, AK) **611**
The Ketchum Co./Bisbee Observer **659***
KETG - Channel 9 (Arkadelphia, AR) **1032**
KETK-TV - Channel 56 (Tyler, TX) **31211**
Ketmarket Communications Radio Division of River City Broadcasting **27890***
KETR-FM - 88.9 (Commerce, TX) **30069**
KETS-TV - Channel 2 (Conway, AR) **1086**
Kettering-Oakwood Times (Kettering, OH) **25284**
Kettle Moraine Advertiser **34157***
KETV-TV - Channel 7 (Omaha, NE) **18216**
KETX-AM - 1440 (Livingston, TX) **30701**
KETX-FM (Livingston, TX) *Unable to locate*
KETX-TV (Livingston, TX) *Unable to locate*
KEUG-FM - 105.5 (Portland, OR) **26524**
KEUN-AM - 1490 (Eunice, LA) **12576**
KEVA-AM - 1240 (Evanston, WY) **34524**
KEVN-TV - Channel 7 (Rapid City, SD) **28938**
Kew Gardens Hills Pennysaver (Rockville Centre, NY) *Ceased*
Kewaskum Statesman (Kewaskum, WI) **33879**
The Kewaunee County Star (Algoma, WI) **33521**
Kewaunee County Sunday Chronicle (Algoma, WI) **33522**
Kewaunee Enterprise (Kewaunee, WI) **33880**
The Kewaunee Star **33521***
KEWB-FM (Redding, CA) *Unable to locate*
KEWC-FM **32715***
KEWE-FM **3060***
KEWL-AM - 1400 (Texarkana, TX) **31186**
KEWL-FM - 95.1 (Texarkana, TX) **31187**
KEWQ-AM **1702***
KEWS-AM **30116***
KEWU-FM - 89.5 (Cheney, WA) **32715**
KEX-AM - 1190 (Portland, OR) **26525**
KEXL-FM - 106.7 (Norfolk, NE) **18171**
KEXO-AM - 1230 (Grand Junction, CO) **4484**
KEXS-AM - 1090 (Excelsior Springs, MO) **17052**
KEXT-FM - 104.7 (Albuquerque, NM) **19798**
Key to Christian Education (Cincinnati, OH) *Ceased*
Key to the Door...Illustrated (Sturgeon Bay, WI) **34351**
Key; Frontier Country (Shawnee, OK) **26063**
Key Horizons (Indianapolis, IN) *Ceased*
Key to Kingston (Kingston, ON, Can.) **35937**
KEY Magazine (Culver City, CA) *Unable to locate*
Key Magazine Atlanta (Sugar Hill, GA) **7573**
KEY Magazine, Carmel and Monterey Peninsula (Carmel, CA) **1673**
Key Magazine Cincinnati (Maineville, OH) **25327**
Key Magazine Colorado (Littleton, CO) **4550**

Numbers cited in bold after listings are entry numbers rather than page numbers.

KFTL-TV - Channel 64 (San Leandro, CA) **3563**
KFTM-AM - 1400 (Fort Morgan, CO) **4448**
KFTR-TV (Waterloo, IN) *Unable to locate*
KFTS-TV - Channel 518 (Medford, OR) **26422**
KFTV-TV - Channel 21 (Fresno, CA) **1968**
KFTW-AM **17056***
KFTX-FM **10913***
KFTX-FM - 97.5 (Corpus Christi, TX) **30085**
KFTY-TV - Channel 50 (Santa Rosa, CA) **3739**
KFTZ-FM - 103.3 (Idaho Falls, ID) **7873**
KFUN-AM - 1230 (Las Vegas, NM) **19891**
KFUO-AM - 850 (Clayton, MO) **16982**
KFUO-FM - 99.1 (St. Louis, MO) **17540**
KFVE-TV (Honolulu, HI) *Unable to locate*
KFVS-TV - Channel 12 (Cape Girardeau, MO) **16951**
KFWB-AM - 980 (Los Angeles, CA) **2456**
KFWJ-AM - 980 (Lake Havasu City, AZ) **739**
KFXB-TV - Channel 40 (Dubuque, IA) **10849**
KFXD-AM - 580 (Boise, ID) **7822**
KFXI-FM - 92.1 (Marlow, OK) **25906**
KFXK-TV - Channel 51 (Longview, TX) **30705**
KFXS-FM - 100.3 (Rapid City, SD) **28939**
KFXT-FM - 100.9 (Marlow, OK) **25907**
KFXX-AM - 910 (Portland, OR) **26526**
KFXX-FM - 106.7 (Ulysses, KS) **11855**
KFXY-FM - 96.7 (Morgan City, LA) **12711**
KFXZ-FM - 106.3 (Lafayette, LA) **12625**
KFYE-FM **1983***
KFYE-FM - 106.3 (Sacramento, CA) **3030**
KFYI-AM - 910 (Phoenix, AZ) **820**
KFYN-AM - 1420 (Bonham, TX) **29934**
KFYO-AM - 790 (Lubbock, TX) **30725**
KFYR-TV - Channel 5 (Bismarck, ND) **24368**
KFYX-FM - 107.1 (Texarkana, TX) **31188**
KFYZ-FM - 98.3 (Bonham, TX) **29935**
KFZX-FM - 102.1 (Odessa, TX) **30875**
KGA-AM - 1510 (Spokane, WA) **33114**
KGAA-AM **32800***
KGAC-FM (St. Peter, MN) *Unable to locate*
KGAF-AM - 1580 (Gainesville, TX) **30377**
KGAL-AM **26410***
KGAL-AM - 1580 (Lebanon, OR) **26409**
KGAM-AM **1463***
KGAM-FM **11907***
KGAN-TV - Channel 2 (Cedar Rapids, IA) **10681**
KGAP-FM - 98.5 (Clarksville, TX) **30024**
KGAS-AM - 1590 (Carthage, TX) **30006**
KGAS-FM - 104.3 (Carthage, TX) **30007**
KGB-FM - 101.5 (San Diego, CA) **3301**
KGBA-FM - 100.1 (El Centro, CA) **1854**
KGBC-AM - 1540 (Galveston, TX) **30383**
KGBI-FM - 100.7 (Omaha, NE) **18218**
KGBM-FM (Palmdale, CA) *Unable to locate*
KGBR-FM - 92.7 (Gold Beach, OR) **26361**
KGBS-AM (Dallas, TX) *Unable to locate*
KGBS-TV **31450***
KGBT-AM (Harlingen, TX) *Unable to locate*
KGBT-TV - Channel 4 (Harlingen, TX) **30426**
KGBX-FM - 105.9 (Springfield, MO) **17620**
KGBY-FM - 92.5 (Sacramento, CA) **3031**
KGCA-AM **24536***
KGCB-FM - 90.9 (Prescott, AZ) **851**
KGCR-FM - 107.7 (Brewster, KS) **11366**
KGCT-TV **26165***
KGCU-AM **24369***
KGCX-AM (Sidney, MT) *Unable to locate*
KGDD-AM (Paris, TX) *Unable to locate*
KGDE-AM **15900***
KGDE-AM **15900***
KGDN-AM **33048***
KGDN-FM - 101.3 (Spokane, WA) **33115**
KGDP-AM (Santa Maria, CA) *Unable to locate*
KGEE-AM **1463***
KGEE-FM **1464***
KGEE-FM (Odessa, TX) *Unable to locate*
KGEK **4642***
KGEM-AM (Boise, ID) *Unable to locate*
KGEN-AM - 1370-AM (Tulare, CA) **3953**
KGEN-FM **3954***
KGEN-FM - 94.5 (Tulare, CA) **3954**
KGEO-AM - 1230 (Bakersfield, CA) **1463**
KGEO-TV **26009***
KGER-AM **2018***
KGER-FM - 95.9 (Spokane, WA) **33116**
KGET-TV (Bakersfield, CA) *Unable to locate*
KGEZ-AM - 600 (Kalispell, MT) **17841**
KGFE-TV - Channel 2 (Grand Forks, ND) **24460**
KGFF-AM - 1450 (Shawnee, OK) **26066**
KGFL **19918***
KGFM-FM - 101.5 (Bakersfield, CA) **1464**
KGFT-FM - 100.7 (Colorado Springs, CO) **4267**
KGFW-AM - 1340 (Kearney, NE) **18061**
KGFX-AM - 1060 (Pierre, SD) **28925**
KGFX-FM - 92.7 (Pierre, SD) **28926**
KGFY-FM (Stillwater, OK) *Unable to locate*
KGGG-FM **28939***
KGGG-FM - 94.7 (Hutchinson, KS) **11504**
KGGI-FM - 99.1 (Riverside, CA) **2951**
KGGK-FM **1421***

KGGL-FM - 93.3 (Missoula, MT) **17880**
KGGO-FM (Urbandale, IA) *Unable to locate*
KGGR-AM (Dallas, TX) *Unable to locate*
KGGY-FM - 102.3 (Dubuque, IA) **10850**
KGHF-AM - 1350 (Pueblo, CO) **4605**
KGHI-FM **1288***
KGHL-AM - 790 (Billings, MT) **17740**
KGHL-FM **17741***
KGHL-TV **17745***
KGHO-FM (Olympia, WA) *Unable to locate*
KGHP-FM - 89.9 (Gig Harbor, WA) **32775**
KGHR-AM **16315***
KGHR-FM - 91.5 (Tuba City, AZ) **926**
KGHS-AM - 1230 (International Falls, MN) **15969**
KGHT-AM (North Little Rock, AR) *Unable to locate*
KGIL-AM (Mission Hills, CA) *Ceased*
KGIL-FM **26599***
KGIM-AM - 1420 (Aberdeen, SD) **28795**
KGIN-TV - Channel 11 (Grand Island, NE) **18028**
KGIR-AM - 1220 (Cape Girardeau, MO) **16952**
KGIW-AM - 1450 (Alamosa, CO) **4135**
KGIW-FM **4133***
KGJF-AM **1240***
KGKB-AM **31220***
KGKG-FM **28819***
KGKL-AM - 960 (San Angelo, TX) **31015**
KGKL-FM - 97.5 (San Angelo, TX) **31016**
KGKO-AM (Benton, AR) *Unable to locate*
KGLA-AM - 1540 (New Orleans, LA) **12764**
KGLC-AM **25918***
KGLC-FM - 100.9 (Miami, OK) **25917**
KGLD-AM - 1330 (Tyler, TX) **31212**
KGLD-FM **31209***
KGLD-TV **11454***
KGLE-AM - 590 (Glendive, MT) **17796**
KGLF-AM (Robstown, TX) *Unable to locate*
KGLI-FM - 95.5 (Sioux City, IA) **11215**
KGLL-FM (Fort Collins, CO) *Unable to locate*
KGLN-AM - 980 (Glenwood Springs, CO) **4460**
KGLO-AM - 1300 (Mason City, IA) **11075**
KGLO-TV **11077***
KGLP-FM **19860***
KGLS-FM **11765***
KGLS-FM **4461***
KGLT-FM - 91.9 (Bozeman, MT) **17757**
KGLW-AM (Arroyo Grande, CA) *Unable to locate*
KGLX-FM - 99.1 (Gallup, NM) **19859**
KGLY-FM - 91.3 (Tyler, TX) **31213**
KGMB-AM **7751***
KGMB-TV **7733***
KGMC-TV **26007***
KGMC-TV - Channel 43 (Fresno, CA) **1969**
KGMD-TV - Channel 9 (Honolulu, HI) **7733**
KGME-AM - 1360 (Phoenix, AZ) **821**
KGMG-FM **3303***
KGMI-AM - 790 (Bellingham, WA) **32682**
KGMN-FM - 99.9 (Kingman, AZ) **733**
KGMO-AM **16947***
KGMS-FM **980***
KGMT-AM - 1310 (Fairbury, NE) **18006**
KGMX-FM - 106.3 (Palmdale, CA) **2785**
KGMY-AM - 1400 (Springfield, MO) **17621**
KGMY-FM - 100.5 (Springfield, MO) **17622**
KGNA-FM - 89.9 (Arnold, MO) **16891**
KGNB-AM - 1420 (New Braunfels, TX) **30862**
KGNC-AM - 710 (Amarillo, TX) **29709**
KGNC-FM - 97.9 (Amarillo, TX) **29710**
KGND-AM - 1470 (Grove, OK) **25850**
KGND-FM - 107.5 (Grove, OK) **25851**
KGNG-AM (San Angelo, TX) *Unable to locate*
KGNM-AM - 1270 (St. Joseph, MO) **17396**
KGNN-AM **17031***
KGNN-FM - 90.3 (Cuba, MO) **17031**
KGNO-AM - 1370 (Dodge City, KS) **11417**
KGNO-FM **11418***
KGNS-AM **30675***
KGNS-TV - Channel 8 (Laredo, TX) **30673**
KGNT-FM - 103.9 (Logan, UT) **31358**
KGNU-FM - 88.5 (Boulder, CO) **4197**
KGNV-FM - 89.9 (Washington, MO) **17707**
KGNW-AM - 820 (Seattle, WA) **33053**
KGNZ-FM - 88.1 (Abilene, TX) **29662**
KGO-AM - 810 (San Francisco, CA) **3484**
KGO-TV - Channel 7 (San Francisco, CA) **3485**
KGOE-AM - 1480 (Eureka, CA) **1901**
KGOK-FM - 97.7 (Sulphur, OK) **26091**
KGOL-AM (Humble, TX) *Unable to locate*
KGOL-FM **30575***
KGON-FM - 92.3 (Portland, OR) **26527**
KGOR-FM - 99.9 (Omaha, NE) **18219**
KGOS-AM - 1490 (Torrington, WY) **34599**
KGOT-FM (Anchorage, AK) *Unable to locate*
KGOU-FM - 106.3 (Norman, OK) **25945**
KGOZ-FM - 101.7 (Trenton, MO) **17653**
KGPC-AM **24452***
KGPC-FM **24451***
KGPE-TV - Channel 47 (Fresno, CA) **1970**
KGPL-AM (Monticello, AR) *Ceased*
KGPO-FM (Monticello, AR) *Unable to locate*

KGRA-FM - 98.9 (Stuart, IA) **11256**
KGRB-AM (La Puente, CA) *Unable to locate*
KGRC-FM - 92.9 (Quincy, IL) **9475**
KGRD-FM (Marquette, NE) *Unable to locate*
KGRE-AM - 1450 (Greeley, CO) **4501**
KGRG-FM - 89.9 (Auburn, WA) **32656**
KGRI-FM (Henderson, TX) *Ceased*
KGRK-AM - 970 (Cedar Falls, IA) **10666**
KGRM-FM - 91.5 (Grambling, LA) **12588**
KGRN-AM - 1410 (Grinnell, IA) **10933**
KGRO-AM - 1230 (Pampa, TX) **30901**
KGRS-FM - 107.3 (Burlington, IA) **10644**
KGRT-AM - 103.9 (Las Cruces, NM) **19880**
KGRV-AM - 700 (Winston, OR) **26618**
KGRW-FM (Austin, TX) *Unable to locate*
KGRZ-AM - 1450 (Missoula, MT) **17881**
KGSC-TV **3548***
KGSG-FM - 93.7 (Pasco, WA) **32881**
KGSR-FM - 107.1 (Austin, TX) **29863**
KGST-AM (Fresno, CA) *Unable to locate*
KGSU-FM **31329***
KGSW-TV **19792***
KGTL-AM - 620 (Homer, AK) **590**
KGTM-AM **27136***
KGTM-FM (Rexburg, ID) *Unable to locate*
KGTN-AM (Gonzales, TX) *Unable to locate*
KGTO-AM - 1050 (Tulsa, OK) **26147**
KGTR-FM - 96.7 (Great Bend, KS) **11469**
KGTS-FM - 91.3 (College Place, WA) **32725**
KGTV-TV - Channel 10 (San Diego, CA) **3302**
KGTW-FM - 106.7 (Ketchikan, AK) **612**
KGU-AM - 760 (Honolulu, HI) **7734**
KGUC-AM-FM **4511***
KGUC-FM **4512***
KGUL-AM - 1560 (Port Lavaca, TX) **30959**
KGUN-TV - Channel 9 (Tucson, AZ) **979**
KGVE-FM - 99.3 (Grove, OK) **25852**
KGVL-AM - 1400 (Greenville, TX) **30415**
KGVM-FM - 99.3 (Gardnerville, NV) **18350**
KGVN-FM - 93.7 (Reno, NV) **18430**
KGVO-TV **17879***
KGVW-AM - 640 (Belgrade, MT) **17725**
KGVW-FM (Belgrade, MT) *Unable to locate*
KGVY-AM - 1080 (Green Valley, AZ) **723**
KGW-AM (Portland, OR) *Ceased*
KGW-TV - Channel 8 (Portland, OR) **26528**
KGWA-AM - 960 (Enid, OK) **25826**
KGWC-TV - Channel 14 (Cheyenne, WY) **34503**
KGWL-TV - Channel 5 (Lander, WY) **34545**
KGWN-TV - Channel 5 (Cheyenne, WY) **34504**
KGWR-TV - Channel 13 (Rock Springs, WY) **34582**
KGWY-FM - 100.7 (Gillette, WY) **34529**
KGY-FM - 96.9 (Olympia, WA) **32869**
KGYN-AM - 1210 (Guymon, OK) **25856**
KGZO-FM - 90.9 (Camarillo, CA) **1645**
KHAC-AM - 880 (Window Rock, AZ) **1012**
KHAD-AM (De Soto, MO) *Unable to locate*
KHAI-TV **7740***
KHAK-AM - 98.1 (Cedar Rapids, IA) **10682**
Khang Chien Magazine (San Jose, CA) **3520**
KHAP-FM (Paradise, CA) *Unable to locate*
KHAR-AM - 590 (Anchorage, AK) **542**
KHAS-AM - 1230 (Hastings, NE) **18039**
KHAS-TV - Channel 5 (Hastings, NE) **18040**
KHAY-FM (Ventura, CA) *Unable to locate*
KHAZ-FM - 99.5 (Hays, KS) **11485**
KHBM-AM - 1430 (Monticello, AR) **1280**
KHBM-FM - 93.5 (Monticello, AR) **1281**
KHBN-FM **19960***
KHBR-AM - 1560 (Hillsboro, TX) **30450**
KHBS-TV - Channel 40 (Fort Smith, AR) **1150**
KHBT-FM - 97.7 (Humboldt, IA) **10959**
KHBV-TV **18355***
KHCA-FM - 95.3 (Manhattan, KS) **11632**
KHCB-AM - 1400 (Houston, TX) **30547**
KHCB-FM - 105.7 (Houston, TX) **30548**
KHCC-FM - 90.1 (Hutchinson, KS) **11505**
KHCD-FM - 89.5 (Salina, KS) **11786**
KHCE-TV - Channel 23 (San Antonio, TX) **31058**
KHCH-AM - 1400 (Houston, TX) **30549**
KHCL-FM - 92.5 (Houston, TX) **30550**
KHCP-FM - 89.3 (Houston, TX) **30551**
KHDC-FM - 90.9 (Salinas, CA) **3071**
KHDL-AM (Spokane, WA) *Unable to locate*
KHDX-FM - 93.1 (Conway, AR) **1088**
KHET-TV - Channel 11 (Honolulu, HI) **7735**
KHEX-FM **4125***
KHEY-AM - 1380 (El Paso, TX) **30291**
KHEY-FM - 96.3 (El Paso, TX) **30292**
KHEZ-FM (Boise, ID) *Unable to locate*
KHFI-FM - 96.7 (Austin, TX) **29864**
KHFI-TV **29883***
KHFM-FM - 96.3 (Albuquerque, NM) **19799**
KHGG-AM - 1580 (Fort Smith, AR) **1151**
KHGI-TV - Channel 13/6 (Kearney, NE) **18062**
KHHC-FM **1053***
KHHH-AM **30901***
KHHH-FM (Honolulu, HI) *Unable to locate*
KHHK-FM (Yakima, WA) *Unable to locate*

KHHL-FM - 98.9 (Austin, TX) **29865**
KHHT-FM **24516***
KHID-FM - 88.1 (Harlingen, TX) **30427**
KHIH-FM - 95.7 (Denver, CO) **4378**
KHII-FM **4281***
KHIN-TV - Channel 36 (Red Oak, IA) **11172**
KHIS-AM - 800 (Bakersfield, CA) **1465**
KHIS-FM (Bakersfield, CA) *Unable to locate*
KHIT-AM **30667***
KHIT-AM - 1450 (Reno, NV) **18431**
KHIT-FM **18429***
KHIT-FM **32886***
KHIZ-TV - Channel 64 (Victorville, CA) **4035**
KHJ-AM - 930 (Burbank, CA) **1624**
KHJJ-AM **2787***
KHJM-FM - 100.3 (Taft, OK) **26093**
KHKC-FM - 103.1 (Atoka, TX) **29749**
KHKE-FM - 89.5 (Cedar Falls, IA) **10667**
KHKK-FM - 104.1 (Modesto, CA) **2566**
KHKR-AM (Helena, MT) **17828**
KHKR-FM - 104.1 (Helena, MT) **17829**
KHKS-FM - 106.1 (Dallas, TX) **30206**
KHLA-FM - 99.5 (Lake Charles, LA) **12645**
KHLB-AM - 1340 (Marble Falls, TX) **30763**
KHLC-FM (Bandera, TX) *Unable to locate*
KHLO-AM - 850 (Hilo, HI) **7673**
KHLS-FM - 96.3 (Blytheville, AR) **1061**
KHLT-AM - 1520 (Hallettsville, TX) **30419**
KHLT-FM **1245***
KHME-FM (Winona, MN) *Unable to locate*
KHMO-AM - 1070 (Hannibal, MO) **17091**
KHMX-FM (Houston, TX) *Unable to locate*
KHND-AM - 1470 (Harvey, ND) **24469**
KHNE-FM - 89.1 (Hastings, NE) **18041**
KHNE-TV - Channel 29 (Hastings, NE) **18042**
KHNS-FM - 102.3 (Haines, AK) **586**
KHOB-AM - 1390 (Hobbs, NM) **19866**
KHOE-FM - 90.5 (Fairfield, IA) **10884**
KHOG-TV - Channel 29 (Fayetteville, AR) **1128**
KHOK-FM - 100.7 (Great Bend, KS) **11470**
KHOL-AM - 1410 (Beulah, ND) **24348**
KHOL-TV **18062***
KHOM-FM (New Orleans, LA) *Unable to locate*
KHON-TV - Channel 2 (Honolulu, HI) **7736**
KHOP-FM - 95.1 (Modesto, CA) **2567**
KHOS-AM **987***
KHOS-AM (Sonora, TX) *Unable to locate*
KHOS-FM (Sonora, TX) *Unable to locate*
KHOT-AM - 1250 (Fresno, CA) **1971**
KHOU-TV (Houston, TX) *Unable to locate*
KHOW-AM - 630 (Denver, CO) **4379**
KHOW-FM **4378***
KHOX-FM **1201***
KHOY-FM - 88.1 (Laredo, TX) **30674**
KHOZ-AM - 900 (Harrison, AR) **1168**
KHOZ-FM - 102.9 (Harrison, AR) **1169**
KHPA-FM - 104.9 (Hope, AR) **1179**
KHPE-FM - 107.9 (Albany, OR) **26209**
KHPR-FM - 88.1 (Honolulu, HI) **7737**
KHPX-FM - 98.3 (El Paso, TX) **30293**
KHQ-AM **33108***
KHQ-FM **33118***
KHQ-TV - Channel 6 (Spokane, WA) **33117**
KHQA-TV - Channel 7 (Quincy, IL) **9476**
KHQN-AM - 1480 (Spanish Fork, UT) **31475**
KHQT-FM - 103.1 (Las Cruces, NM) **19881**
KHR-TV **981***
KHRN-FM **29983***
KHRR-FM - 101.7 (Tucson, AZ) **980**
KHRR-TV - Channel 40 (Tucson, AZ) **981**
KHRT-FM - 106.9 (Minot, ND) **24508**
KHSC-FM **1431***
KHSC-TV - Channel 46 (Ontario, CA) **2720**
KHSH-TV - Channel 67 (Houston, TX) **30552**
KHSL-FM - 103.5 (Chico, CA) **1700**
KHSL-TV - Channel 12 (Chico, CA) **1701**
KHSN-AM - 1230 (Coos Bay, OR) **26279**
KHSP-AM **31186***
KHSS-FM - 100.7 (Milton-Freewater, OR) **26436**
KHSU-FM - 90.5 (Arcata, CA) **1431**
KHSX-TV (Irving, TX) *Unable to locate*
KHTA-TV - 92.5 (Houston, TX) **30553**
KHTE-AM **2892***
KHTH-AM (Breckenridge, CO) *Ceased*
KHTK-AM - 1140 (Sacramento, CA) **3032**
KHTN-FM (Merced, CA) *Unable to locate*
KHTR-FM - 104.3 (Pullman, WA) **32911**
KHTT-FM **3738***
KHTT-FM - 106.9 (Tulsa, OK) **26148**
KHTV-TV - Channel 39 (Houston, TX) **30554**
KHTX-AM (Salinas, CA) *Ceased*
KHTY-FM (Santa Barbara, CA) *Unable to locate*
KHTZ-AM (Reno, NV) *Ceased*
KHTZ-FM **18433***
KHTZ-FM **2460***
KHUB-AM - 1340 (Fremont, NE) **18014**
KHUI-FM **7762***
KHUM-FM **4392***
KHUQ-FM **11855***

KHUT-FM - 102.9 (Hutchinson, KS) **11506**
KHUZ-AM **29938***
KHVH-AM (Honolulu, HI) *Unable to locate*
KHVH-TV **7743***
KHVL-AM - 1490 (Huntsville, TX) **30598**
KHVN-AM - 970 (Dallas, TX) **30207**
KHVO-TV (Reno, NV) *Unable to locate*
KHWB-TV - Channel 59 (Eugene, OR) **26338**
KHWI-FM - 101.5 (Hilo, HI) **7674**
KHWK-FM - 92.7 (Tonopah, NV) **18448**
KHYE-FM (Hemet, CA) *Unable to locate*
KHYI-FM - 95.3 (Plano, TX) **30949**
KHYL-FM (Sacramento, CA) *Unable to locate*
KHYM-AM (Longview, TX) *Unable to locate*
KHYM-FM - 103.9 (Meade, KS) **11647**
KHYS-FM (Houston, TX) *Unable to locate*
KHYT-FM **33233***
KHYT-FM - 107.5 (Tucson, AZ) **982**
KIA-FM - 93.9 (Mason City, IA) **11076**
KIAB-FM **11279***
KIAB-FM **11279***
KIAH-FM **3970***
KIAK-AM - 970 (Fairbanks, AK) **573**
KIAK-FM - 102.5 (Fairbanks, AK) **574**
KIAL-AM - 1450 (Unalaska, AK) **645**
KIAM-AM - 630 (Nenana, AK) **625**
KIAM-FM **33199***
KIAQ-FM - 96.9 (Fort Dodge, IA) **10908**
KIBC-FM **18189***
KIBC-FM - 90.5 (Burney, CA) **1636**
KIBG-FM - 106.3 (Merced, CA) **2532**
KIBS-AM **1585***
KIBS-FM - 100.7 (Bishop, CA) **1586**
KICA-AM - 980 (Clovis, NM) **19833**
KICA-FM - 98.3 (Clovis, NM) **19834**
KICB-FM - 88.1 (Fort Dodge, IA) **10909**
KICC-FM (International Falls, MN) *Unable to locate*
KICD-AM - 1240 (Spencer, IA) **11233**
KICD-FM - 107.7 (Spencer, IA) **11234**
KICE-AM (Bend, OR) *Unable to locate*
KICE-FM **26246***
KICI-AM *Ceased*
KICI-FM - 107.9 (Corsicana, TX) **30104**
Kick It Over (Toronto, ON, Can.) **36642**
Kicks (New York, NY) **22218**
KICM-FM - 93.7 (Ardmore, OK) **25747**
KICO-AM - 1490 (Calexico, CA) **1637**
KICR-FM **12464***
KICR-FM **26280***
KICT-FM - 95.1 (Wichita, KS) **11898**
KICU-TV - Channel 36 (San Jose, CA) **3548**
KICX-FM - 96.1 (McCook, NE) **18155**
KICX-FM - 104.1 (Midland, ON, Can.) **36045**
KICY-AM - 850 (Nome, AK) **626**
KICY-FM - 100.3 (Nome, AK) **627**
KID-AM - 590 (Idaho Falls, ID) **7874**
Kid City (New York, NY) *Ceased*
KID-FM - 96.1 (Idaho Falls, ID) **7875**
KIDA-FM **11250***
KIDA-FM **24431***
KIDD-AM (Monterey, CA) *Unable to locate*
KIDD-FM **2589***
KIDE-FM - 91.3 (Hoopa, CA) **2057**
KIDI-TV **19797***
KIDK-TV - Channel 3 (Idaho Falls, ID) **7876**
KIDN-AM **4605***
KIDN-FM (Steamboat Springs, CO) *Unable to locate*
Kidney (New York, NY) **22219**
Kidney and Blood Pressure Research (Farmington, CT) **4839**
Kidney Diseases; American Journal of (Minneapolis, MN) **16056**
KIDO-AM - 580 (Boise, ID) **7823**
KIDO-TV **7831***
Kidpreneurs News (New York, NY) **22220**
KIDR-AM - 740 (Phoenix, AZ) **822**
Kidron News; The Dalton Gazette & (Dalton, OH) **25105**
KIDS! (Chicago, IL) *Ceased*
KIDS-AM (Springfield, MO) *Ceased*
Kids; Connecticut's County (Westport, CT) **5212**
Kids Courier (Hamburg, NY) **20704**
KIDS CREATIONS (Montreal, QC, Can.) **37147**
Kids; Creative (Waco, TX) **31245**
Kids Creative Resources (Stamford, CT) **5152**
KIDS; Dane County (Madison, WI) **33933**
Kids Discover (New York, NY) **22221**
KIDS; Fox Valley (Madison, WI) **33942**
Kids; Guideposts for (Chesterton, IN) **9887**
Kids Magazine (Park Ridge, NJ) **19409**
Kids; Michigan History for (Lansing, MI) **15286**
Kids' News (Atlanta, GA) *Unable to locate*
Kids Parade **37147***
Kids; Sports Illustrated for (New York, NY) **22777**
Kids; Time for (New York, NY) **22840**
Kids Toronto **36143***
Kids Tribute (Don Mills, ON, Can.) *Unable to locate*
KidSmart (White House Station, NJ) *Unable to locate*
KidSports (Arlington, VA) *Ceased*

Kidstuff (Lake Park, FL) **6284**
Kidsworld (Toronto, ON, Can.) **36643**
KIDX-FM - 98.5 (Billings, MT) **17741**
KIDY-TV - Channel 6 (San Angelo, TX) **31017**
Kidz Magazine (Omaha, NE) *Unable to locate*
KIDZ-TV - Channel 54 (Abilene, TX) **29663**
KIEA-FM (Ethete, WY) *Unable to locate*
Kiel Record **33882***
Kiel Tri-County Record (Kiel, WI) *Ceased*
KIEM-TV - Channel 3 (Eureka, CA) **1902**
KIEV-AM **2019***
KIEZ-AM (Salinas, CA) *Unable to locate*
KIEZ-FM **12510***
KIFG **11002***
KIFG-FM - 95.3 (Iowa Falls, IA) **11002**
KIFG-FM - 95.3 (Iowa Falls, IA) **11003**
KIFH-AM **7746***
KIFI-TV - Channel 8 (Idaho Falls, ID) **7877**
KIFM-FM (San Diego, CA) *Unable to locate*
KIFO-AM (Honolulu, HI) *Ceased*
KIFS-FM - 107.5 (Medford, OR) **26423**
KIFW-AM (Sitka, AK) *Unable to locate*
KIFW-TV **576***
KIGC-FM - 88.7 (Oskaloosa, IA) **11138**
KIGS-AM - 620 (Hanford, CA) **2039**
Kihei Times (Makawao, HI) **7787**
KIHN-AM - 1340 (Hugo, OK) **25873**
KIHR-AM - 1340 (Hood River, OR) **26377**
KIHS-TV **2720***
KIHX **857***
KII-FM - 98.9 (Punta Gorda, FL) **6608**
KIII-TV - Channel 3 (Corpus Christi, TX) **30086**
KIIK-FM - 95.9 (Fairfield, IA) **10885**
KIIM-FM - 99.5 (Tucson, AZ) **983**
KIIN-TV - Channel 12 (Des Moines, IA) **10825**
KIIQ-FM **18429***
KIIS-AM - 102.7 (Burbank, CA) **1625**
KIIS-FM - 102.7 (Burbank, CA) **1626**
KIIX-AM - 1410 AM (Fort Collins, CO) **4442**
KIIX-FM **4390***
KIIZ-AM - 1050 (Harker Heights, TX) **30423**
KIJK-FM **26252***
KIJN-AM - 1060 (Farwell, TX) **30316**
KIJN-FM - 92.3 (Farwell, TX) **30317**
KIJV-AM (Huron, SD) *Unable to locate*
KIKF-FM - 94.3 (Anaheim, CA) **1421**
KIKI-AM - 990 (Honolulu, HI) **7738**
KIKI-FM - 93.9 (Honolulu, HI) **7739**
KIKK-AM - 650 (Houston, TX) **30555**
KIKK-FM - 95.7 (Houston, TX) **30556**
KIKN-AM **30431***
KIKN-FM **4606***
KIKO-AM - 1340 (Miami, AZ) **752**
KIKO-FM - 106.1 (Claypool, AZ) **675**
KIKS-AM **11514***
KIKS-FM - 99.3 (Iola, KS) **11515**
KIKT-FM - 93.5 (Greenville, TX) **30416**
KIKU-TV - Channel 20 (Honolulu, HI) **7740**
KIKV-FM - 100.7 (Alexandria, MN) **15715**
KIKX-FM (Colorado Springs, CO) *Unable to locate*
KIKZ-AM - 1250 (Seminole, TX) **31099**
KILA-FM (Las Vegas, NV) *Unable to locate*
KILE-AM (Galveston, TX) *Unable to locate*
Kilgore Cable TV Co. (Kilgore, TX) **30642**
Kilgore News Herald (Birmingham, AL) **78**
KILJ-AM - 1130 (Mount Pleasant, IA) **11095**
Killeen Daily Herald (Killeen, TX) **30644**
KILO-AM **32800***
KILO-FM - 94.3 (Colorado Springs, CO) **4268**
KILR-AM - 1070 (Estherville, IA) **10879**
KILR-FM - 95.9 (Estherville, IA) **10880**
KILS-AM **11607***
KILT-AM - 610 (Houston, TX) **30557**
KILT-FM - 100.3 (Houston, TX) **30558**
KIMA-AM **33232***
KIMA-TV - Channel 29 (Yakima, WA) **33229**
Kimberling City Southwest Missourian (Branson, MO) *Ceased*
KIML-AM - 1270 (Gillette, WY) **34530**
KIMM-AM - 1150 (Rapid City, SD) **28940**
KIMN-FM **4443***
KIMO-TV - Channel 13 (Anchorage, AK) **543**
KIMP-AM - 960 (Mount Pleasant, TX) **30841**
KIMP-FM **30842***
KIMT-TV - Channel 3 (Mason City, IA) **11077**
KIMX-FM - 105.5 (Laramie, WY) **34555**
KIMY-FM - 93.9 (Watonga, OK) **26181**
Kin Mag (Cambridge, ON, Can.) **35726**
KIN Magazine **35726***
KINA-AM (Salina, KS) *Unable to locate*
Kincardine Cable TV Ltd. (Kincardine, ON, Can.) **35935**
Kincardine News (Kincardine, ON, Can.) **35934**
KIND-AM - 1010 (Independence, KS) **11511**
KIND-FM - 102.9 (Independence, KS) **11512**
KIND News (East Haddam, CT) **4777**
Kinder Courier-News (Kinder, LA) **12614**
Kindersley Clarion (Kindersley, SK, Can.) **37481**
The Kindred Spirit **11777***

Kindred Spirit (Kensington, PE, Can.) 36920
KINE-FM (Honolulu, HI) *Unable to locate*
Kinema (Waterloo, ON, Can.) 36854
Kinesiology; Clinical (Toledo, OH) 25565
Kinesiology; Journal of Electromyography and (Baltimore, MD) 13189
Kinesis (Whitefish, MT) *Unable to locate*
Kinesis (Vancouver, BC, Can.) *Unable to locate*
Kinetics and Catalysis (New York, NY) 22222
Kinetics and Catalysis Letters; Reaction (New York, NY) 22627
KINF-AM - 1020 (Roswell, NM) 19920
KINF-FM 11419*
KING-AM (Seattle, WA) *Ceased*
King City Rustler (Soledad, CA) 3769
King County Dental Society; The Journal of the Seattle- (Seattle, WA) 32979
King County Medical Society; Bulletin of the (Seattle, WA) 32952
King Features Syndicate Inc. (New York, NY) 37976
KING-FM - 98.1 (Seattle, WA) 33054
King & Kango (Vallejo, CA) 37977
King of Prussia Courier (King of Prussia, PA) 27125
KING-TV - Channel 5 (Seattle, WA) 33055
King Videocable 7989*
King Videocable Co. 2618*
King Videocable Co. 1827*
King Videocable Company 32749*
King Videocable Co. (Mount Shasta, CA) *Unable to locate*
King Videocable Co. (Brooklyn Park, MN) 15775
King Weekly (King City, ON, Can.) *Unable to locate*
Kingbird (South Hempstead, NY) 23343
The Kingdom Daily Sun-Gazette 17076*
Kingfisher Times and Free Press (Kingfisher, OK) 25879
Kingfisher Times; Kingfisher Free Press 25879*
Kingman Daily Miner (Kingman, AZ) 729
Kingman Journal (Kingman, KS) 11539
Kingman Leader-Courier (Kingman, KS) 11540
Kings Bay Communications, Inc. (Kingsland, GA) 7356
Kings County News 2038*
Kings County Record (Sussex, NB, Can.) 35438
Kings Courier (Brooklyn, NY) 20325
Kings Kable Ltd. 35582*
Kings Mountain Herald (Kings Mountain, NC) 24025
Kings Park Suffolk Life; Commack/ (Commack, NY) 20486
Kings Park Weekender (Farmingdale, NY) *Ceased*
Kingsman (Brooklyn, NY) 20326
Kingsport Times News (Kingsport, TN) 29260
Kingston Independent Voice (Kingston, MA) 14263
Kingston; Profile (Kingston, ON, Can.) 35942
Kingston Reporter (Kingston, MA) 14264
Kingston This Week (Kingston, ON, Can.) 35938
The Kingston Whig-Standard (Kingston, ON, Can.) 35939
Kingstree News 28674*
Kingsville Record (Kingsville, TX) 30647
The Kingsville Reporter (Kingsville, ON, Can.) 35956
Kingwood Cablevision, Inc. (Kingwood, TX) 30652
Kingwood Echo (Pasadena, TX) *Unable to locate*
Kingwood Observer (Kingwood, TX) 30650
KINI-FM - 96.1 (Crookston, NE) 17996
Kinistino—Birch Hills Post—Gazette (Melfort, SK, Can.) 37497
Kinistino Post 37497*
Kinky Fetishes (Port Chester, NY) *Unable to locate*
KINL-FM - 92.7 (Eagle Pass, TX) 30259
Kinmundy Express (Kinmundy, IL) 9049
KINN-AM - 1270 (Alamogordo, NM) 19759
Kinneloa Television Systems (Alhambra, CA) *Unable to locate*
The Kinney Cavalryman (Brackettville, TX) *Ceased*
KINO-AM - 1230 (Winslow, AZ) 1015
KINQ-FM 1760*
KINS-AM - 980 (Eureka, CA) 1903
Kinsley Graphic (Larned, KS) *Ceased*
The Kinsley Mercury 11601*
KINT-FM 30286*
KINT-FM - 93.9 (El Paso, TX) 30294
KINT-TV - Channel 26 (El Paso, TX) 30295
KINY-AM - 800 (Juneau, AK) 599
KIOA-AM 10835*
KIOA-FM - 93.3 (Des Moines, IA) 10826
KIOC-FM (Vidor, TX) *Unable to locate*
KIOD-FM - 105.3 (McCook, NE) 18156
KIOI-FM (San Francisco, CA) *Unable to locate*
KIOK-FM - 94.9 (Kennewick, WA) 32791
KIOL-K-LITE 30824*
KION-TV - Channel 5 (Salinas, CA) 3072
KIOO-FM (Porterville, CA) *Unable to locate*
KIOQ-FM 1586*
KIOS-FM - 91.5 (Omaha, NE) 18220
KIOT-FM (Santa Fe, NM) *Unable to locate*
KIOU-AM - 1480 (Shreveport, LA) 12826
KIOU-FM 30088*
KIOV-AM - 1450 (Payette, ID) 7944

KIOV-FM 28977*
KIOW-FM - 107.3 (Forest City, IA) 10892
Kiowa County Democrat (Snyder, OK) 26073
Kiowa County Press (Eads, CO) 4407
Kiowa County Signal (Greensburg, KS) 11475
Kiowa County Star-Review 25865*
KIOX-AM - 1270 (Bay City, TX) 29892
KIOZ-FM - 105.3 (San Diego, CA) 3303
KIPA-AM - 620 (Hilo, HI) 7675
KIPA-FM 7674*
The Kiplinger Texas Letter *Ceased*
Kiplinger's Personal Finance Magazine (Washington, DC) 5625
KIPO-FM - 89.3 (Honolulu, HI) 7741
KIPR-FM 30742*
KIPR-FM - 92.3 (Little Rock, AR) 1243
KIQI-AM - 1010 (San Francisco, CA) 3486
KIQK-FM - 104.1 (Rapid City, SD) 28941
KIQO-FM (Atascadero, CA) *Unable to locate*
KIQQ-AM (Hesperia, CA) *Unable to locate*
KIQS-AM - 1560 (Willows, CA) 4089
KIQS-FM (Willows, CA) *Unable to locate*
KIQX-FM - 101.3 (Durango, CO) 4403
KIQY-FM 26214*
KIQZ-FM - 92.7 (Rawlins, WY) 34573
KIRC-FM - 105.9 (Shawnee, OK) 26067
KIRK-AM 16904*
KIRK-FM 16905*
KIRK-FM 26067*
Kirkland Courier (Kirkland, WA) 32798
Kirkland Courier Review 32798*
Kirkland Lake Gazette (New Liskeard, ON, Can.) *Unable to locate*
Kirksville Daily Express and News (Kirksville, MO) 17227
Kirkus Reviews (New York, NY) 22223
Kirkville/Bridgeport Pennysaver; East Syracuse/Minoa/ (Syracuse, NY) 23401
KIRL-AM - 1460 (St. Charles, MO) 17386
KIRN-AM - 670 (Los Angeles, CA) 2457
KIRO-AM - 710 (Seattle, WA) 33056
KIRO-TV - Channel 7 (Seattle, WA) 33057
KIRQ-FM (Lawton, OK) *Unable to locate*
KIRT-AM - 1580 (McAllen, TX) 30796
Kirtland Enterprise (Willoughby, OH) *Ceased*
KIRV-AM - 1510 (Fresno, CA) 1972
KIRX-AM - 1450 (Kirksville, MO) 17230
KISA-AM - 1540 (Honolulu, HI) 7742
KISC-FM - 98.1 (Spokane, WA) 33118
KISD-FM - 98.7 (Pipestone, MN) 16276
KISF-FM 17212*
KISF-FM (Las Vegas, NV) *Unable to locate*
KISI-FM - 101.5 (Malvern, AR) 1265
Kiski News (Vandergrift, PA) *Ceased*
KISM-FM - 92.9 (Bellingham, WA) 32683
KISN-AM - 570 (Salt Lake City, UT) 31448
KISN-FM - 97.1 (Salt Lake City, UT) 31449
KISO-AM 30301*
KISO-AM - 1230 (Phoenix, AZ) 823
KISP-AM 823*
KISQ-FM - 98.1 (San Francisco, CA) 3487
KISS-AM 31062*
KISS-FM 4291*
KISS-FM - 99.5 (San Antonio, TX) 31059
KIST-AM - 1340 (Santa Barbara, CA) 3666
KIST-FM 26018*
KISU-TV - Channel 10 (Pocatello, ID) 7950
KISW-FM (Seattle, WA) *Unable to locate*
KISX-FM (Bryan, TX) *Unable to locate*
KISZ-AM 4294*
KISZ-FM - 97.9 (Cortez, CO) 4291
KIT-AM - 1280 (Yakima, WA) 33230
Kit Builders Magazine (Placentia, CA) 2847
Kit Car (Los Angeles, CA) 2306
Kit Car Illustrated (Anaheim, CA) 1407
KIT-FM 33225*
KITA-AM - 1440 (Little Rock, AR) 1244
Kitbuilders and Glue Sniffers Magazine 2847*
Kitchen and Bath Business (New York, NY) 22224
Kitchen & Bath Concepts (Chicago, IL) *Ceased*
Kitchen & Bath Design Guide 5626*
Kitchen and Bath Design Ideas (Melville, NY) 21046
Kitchen and Bath Design News (Melville, NY) 21047
Kitchen & Bath Showroom (Washington, DC) 5626
Kitchen Gardener (Newtown, CT) 5044
Kitchen Plans; Better Homes and Gardens (New York, NY) 21300
Kitchener-Waterloo Pennysaver (Kitchener, ON, Can.) 35960
Kitchener-Waterloo Record (Kitchener, ON, Can.) 35961
Kitchens and Baths; Woman's Day (New York, NY) 22931
Kitchenware News (Yarmouth, ME) 13081
Kite Lines (Cockeysville, MD) *Ceased*
KITH-AM 4038*
The Kithara (Portland, OR) 26484
KITI-AM - 1420 (Centralia, WA) 32707
KITI-FM - 95.1 (Centralia, WA) 32708

KITN-TV 16161*
KITO - 96.1 (Vinita, OK) 26177
KITPLANES (San Diego, CA) 3218
KITR-FM - 101.3 (Creston, IA) 10733
KITS-FM - 105.3 (San Francisco, CA) 3488
Kitsap Neighbors; North (Bremerton, WA) 32693
Kitsap Neighbors; South (Bremerton, WA) 32694
Kitsap Reporter; Central (Silverdale, WA) 33083
KITT-FM 12842*
Kittitas County Tribune; Northern (Cle Elum, WA) 32718
Kittson County Enterprise (Hallock, MN) 15937
KITV-TV - Channel 4 (Honolulu, HI) 7743
KITX-FM - 95.5 (Hugo, OK) 25874
KITZ-AM (Silverdale, WA) *Unable to locate*
KIUL-AM - 1240 (Garden City, KS) 11452
KIUN-AM - 1400 (Pecos, TX) 30925
KIUP-AM - 930 (Durango, CO) 4404
KIUP-FM 4406*
KIUS-FM (Hutchinson, KS) *Unable to locate*
The Kiva 952*
Kiva (Tucson, AZ) 952
KIVA-AM (Albuquerque, NM) *Unable to locate*
KIVI-TV - Channel 6 (Nampa, ID) 7932
KIVV-TV - Channel 5 (Rapid City, SD) 28942
KIVY-AM - 1290 (Crockett, TX) 30107
KIVY-FM - 92.7 (Crockett, TX) 30108
KIWA-AM - 1550 (Sheldon, IA) 11196
KIWA-FM - 105.3 (Sheldon, IA) 11197
Kiwanis Magazine (Indianapolis, IN) 10145
KIWD FM - 101.9 (Las Vegas, NV) 18396
KIWI-FM - 92.1 (Bakersfield, CA) 1466
KIWR-FM - 89.7 (Council Bluffs, IA) 10727
KIWW-FM (Harlingen, TX) *Unable to locate*
KIXB-FM - 103.3 (El Dorado, AR) 1109
KIXC-AM 30965*
KIXC-FM - 100.9 (Quanah, TX) 30964
KIXI-AM (Bellevue, WA) *Unable to locate*
KIXL-AM - 970 (Austin, TX) 29866
KIXQ-FM - 102.5 (Joplin, MO) 17144
KIXR-FM - 104.7 (Ponca City, OK) 26039
KIXS-FM 30424*
KIXS-FM - 107.9 (Victoria, TX) 31239
KIXT-AM 1188*
KIXT-AM 3571*
KIXT-AM - 930 (Bellingham, WA) 32684
KIXV-FM 29945*
KIXW-AM - 960 (Victorville, CA) 4036
KIXX-FM - 96.1 (Watertown, SD) 29021
KIXY-FM - 94.7 (San Angelo, TX) 31018
KIXZ-AM (Amarillo, TX) *Unable to locate*
KIYS-FM (Jonesboro, AR) *Unable to locate*
KIYU-AM - 910 (Galena, AK) 582
KIZN-FM 7835*
KIZN-FM - 92.3 (Boise, ID) 7824
KIZS-FM (Reno, NV) *Unable to locate*
KIZZ-FM (Minot, ND) *Unable to locate*
KJAA-AM 819*
KJAA-AM - 1240 (Globe, AZ) 720
KJAA-TV 30737*
KJAB-FM - 88.3 (Mexico, MO) 17286
KJAC-TV 29903*
KJAE-FM - 93.5 (Leesville, LA) 12659
KJAK-FM - 92.7 (Lubbock, TX) 30726
KJAM-AM - 1390 (Madison, SD) 28887
KJAM-FM - 103.1 (Madison, SD) 28888
KJAN-AM - 1220 (Atlantic, IA) 10611
KJAQ-FM 16949*
KJAS-FM - 107.3 (Jasper, TX) 30621
KJAV-FM - 104.9 (Alamo, TX) 29674
KJAX-AM 2571*
KJAY-AM - 1430 (West Sacramento, CA) 4067
KJAZ-AM (Oroville, CA) *Unable to locate*
KJAZ-FM (Alameda, CA) *Unable to locate*
KJBC-AM - 1150 (Midland, TX) 30818
KJBE-AM (Ogden, UT) *Unable to locate*
KJBX-AM (Lubbock, TX) *Unable to locate*
KJBZ-FM (Laredo, TX) *Unable to locate*
KJCB-AM - 770 (Lafayette, LA) 12626
KJCD-FM - 104.3 (Denver, CO) 4380
KJCE-AM - 1370 (Austin, TX) 29867
KJCF-AM 17066*
KJCK-AM - 1420 (Junction City, KS) 11521
KJCK-FM - 94.5 (Junction City, KS) 11522
KJCO-FM (Yuma, CO) *Unable to locate*
KJCR-FM - 88.3 (Keene, TX) 30634
KJCS-FM (Nacogdoches, TX) *Unable to locate*
KJCT-TV - Channel 8 (Grand Junction, CO) 4485
KJCY-FM 7927*
KJDJ-AM (Santa Maria, CA) *Unable to locate*
KJDM-FM 32867*
KJDX-FM - 93.3 (Susanville, CA) 3833
KJEF-AM (Jennings, LA) *Unable to locate*
KJEF-FM - 92.9 (Jennings, LA) 12607
KJEL-AM 17239*
KJEM-FM - 93.3 (Bentonville, AR) 1053
KJEO-TV 1970*
KJET-AM (Hoquiam, WA) *Unable to locate*
KJET-FM 3030*

KJET-FM - 105.7 (Aberdeen, WA) **32650**
KJEZ-FM - 95.5 (Poplar Bluff, MO) **17358**
KJFF-AM - 1400 (Festus, MO) **17066**
KJFJ-AM **11315***
KJFK-FM **29865***
KJFK-FM **29865***
KJFK-FM **29865***
KJFM-FM - 102.1 (Louisiana, MO) **17257**
KJFP-FM (Yakutat, AK) *Unable to locate*
KJFX-FM - 95.7 (Fresno, CA) **1973**
KJHK-FM - 90.7 (Lawrence, KS) **11574**
KJHY-FM - 101.9 (Nampa, ID) **7933**
KJIA-AM **28835***
KJIC-FM (Pasadena, TX) *Unable to locate*
KJIL-FM - 99.1 (Meade, KS) **11648**
KJIN-AM - 1490 (Houma, LA) **12603**
KJJB-FM - 105.5 (Eunice, LA) **12577**
KJJC-FM (Indianola, IA) *Unable to locate*
KJJG-FM/KIGL **11235***
KJJJ-AM **820***
KJJJ-FM (Tucson, AZ) *Unable to locate*
KJJK-AM - 1020 (Fergus Falls, MN) **15901**
KJJK-FM - 96.5 (Fergus Falls, MN) **15902**
KJJL-AM - 1370 (Cheyenne, WY) **34505**
KJJO-AM **16153***
KJJO-FM **16164***
KJJQ-AM - 910 (Brookings, SD) **28822**
KJJT-AM **30877***
KJJY-FM (Des Moines, IA) *Unable to locate*
KJJZ-FM **619***
KJKJ-FM (Grand Forks, ND) *Unable to locate*
KJKT-FM **17144***
KJLA-AM **17116***
KJLH-FM - 102.3 (Inglewood, CA) **2074**
KJLO-FM - 104.1 (Monroe, LA) **12695**
KJLS-FM - 103.3 (Hays, KS) **11486**
KJLT-AM - 970 (North Platte, NE) **18179**
KJLT-FM - 94.9 (North Platte, NE) **18180**
KJLU-FM - 88.9 (Jefferson City, MO) **17136**
KJLY-FM - 104.5 (Blue Earth, MN) **15765**
KJMB-FM - 100.3 (Blythe, CA) **1589**
KJME-AM - 1390 (Denver, CO) **4381**
KJMH-TV (Burlington, IA) *Unable to locate*
KJMO-FM - 100.1 (Jefferson City, MO) **17137**
KJMQ-FM **2531***
KJMS-FM (Memphis, TN) *Unable to locate*
KJMZ-FM **30212***
KJNA-AM (Jena, LA) *Ceased*
KJNA-FM (Jena, LA) *Unable to locate*
KJNB-FM - 99.9 (Collegeville, MN) **15807**
KJNE-FM (Waco, TX) *Unable to locate*
KJNO-AM - 630 (Juneau, AK) **600**
KJNP-AM (North Pole, AK) *Unable to locate*
KJNP-FM (North Pole, AK) *Unable to locate*
KJNP-TV - Channel 4 (North Pole, AK) **630**
KJOC-AM - 1170 (Davenport, IA) **10742**
KJOE-AM **12826***
KJOE-FM - 106.1 (Slayton, MN) **16450**
KJOI-FM **1630***
KJOI-FM **1984***
KJOJ-AM (Conroe, TX) *Unable to locate*
KJOJ-FM - 103.3 (Houston, TX) **30559**
KJOK-AM - 1400 (Yuma, AZ) **1026**
KJOK-FM **1027***
KJOL-FM - 90.3 (Grand Junction, CO) **4486**
KJOP-AM - 1240 (Lemoore, CA) **2153**
KJOT-FM (Boise, ID) *Unable to locate*
KJOX-AM - 980 (Yakima, WA) **33231**
KJOY-FM (Stockton, CA) *Unable to locate*
KJPN-AM (Waipahu, HI) *Unable to locate*
KJPW-AM - 1390 (Waynesville, MO) **17710**
KJPW-FM - 102.3 (Waynesville, MO) **17711**
KJQI-AM **1785***
KJQN-FM (Ogden, UT) *Unable to locate*
KJQY-FM **3310***
KJR-AM (Seattle, WA) *Unable to locate*
KJRB-AM (Spokane, WA) *Unable to locate*
KJRC-AM (Kings Beach, CA) *Unable to locate*
KJRE-TV - Channel 19 (Ellendale, ND) **24409**
KJRG-AM - 950 (Newton, KS) **11672**
KJRH-TV - Channel 2 (Tulsa, OK) **26149**
KJRR-TV - Channel 7 (Jamestown, ND) **24479**
KJSA-AM - 1140 (Weatherford, TX) **31274**
KJSN-FM - 102.3 (Modesto, CA) **2568**
KJSR-FM - 103.3 (Tulsa, OK) **26150**
KJTL-TV - Channel 18 (Wichita Falls, TX) **31297**
KJTM-TV **1241***
KJTT-AM (Oak Harbor, WA) *Unable to locate*
KJTV-AM - 950 (Lubbock, TX) **30727**
KJTV-TV **29706***
KJTV-TV - Channel 34 (Lubbock, TX) **30728**
KJTX-FM - 104.5 (Longview, TX) **30706**
KJTY-FM - 88.1 (Topeka, KS) **11840**
KJUD-TV - Channel 8 (Juneau, AK) **601**
KJUG-AM - 1270 (Tulare, CA) **3955**
KJUG-FM - 106.7 (Tulare, CA) **3956**
KJUL-FM - 104.3 (Las Vegas, NV) **18397**
KJVC-FM - 92.7 (Logansport, LA) **12662**
KJVH-FM - 89.5 (Longview, WA) **32817**

KJVI-TV **34537***
KJWH-AM (Camden, AR) *Unable to locate*
KJWY-TV - Channel 2 (Jackson, WY) **34537**
KJYE-FM - 92.3 (Grand Junction, CO) **4487**
KJYK-AM **977***
KJYO-FM - 102.7 (Oklahoma City, OK) **26004**
KJYR-AM (Tucson, AZ) *Ceased*
KJZZ-FM - 91.5 (Tempe, AZ) **921**
KJZZ-TV - Channel 14 (Salt Lake City, UT) **31450**
KKAA-AM - 1560 (Aberdeen, SD) **28796**
KKAJ-AM **25749***
KKAJ-FM - 95.7 (Ardmore, OK) **25748**
KKAN-AM - 1490 (Phillipsburg, KS) **11749**
KKAP-AM **30323***
KKAP-AM **30324***
KKAQ-AM - 1460 (Thief River Falls, MN) **16470**
KKAR-AM - 1290 (Omaha, NE) **18221**
KKAS-AM 1959-1999 **31108***
KKAT-AM - 101.9 (Salt Lake City, UT) **31451**
KKAY-AM - 1590 (Donaldsonville, LA) **12570**
KKAY-FM (Donaldsonville, LA) *Ceased*
KKAZ-FM (Cheyenne, WY) *Unable to locate*
KKBB-FM (Shafter, CA) *Unable to locate*
KKBC-FM - 95.3 (Baker City, OR) **26235**
KKBE-FM - 105.5 (Ventura, CA) **4029**
KKBG-FM - 97.9 (Hilo, HI) **7676**
KKBH-FM **3306***
KKBI-FM - 106.1 (Broken Bow, OK) **25776**
KKBJ-AM - 1360 (Bemidji, MN) **15745**
KKBJ-FM (Bemidji, MN) *Unable to locate*
KKBL-FM - 95.9 (Monett, MO) **17294**
KKBN-FM - 93.5 (Sonora, CA) **3781**
KKBQ-AM (Houston, TX) *Unable to locate*
KKBQ-FM (Houston, TX) *Unable to locate*
KKBR-FM (White Rock, NM) *Unable to locate*
KKBS-FM - 92.7 (Guymon, OK) **25857**
KKBT-FM (Hollywood, CA) *Unable to locate*
KKBY-FM (Tacoma, WA) *Unable to locate*
KKBZ-FM - 99.3 (Clarinda, IA) **10703**
KKCA-FM - 100.5 (Jefferson City, MO) **17138**
KKCB-AM **3571***
KKCC-AM **25792***
KKCD-FM - 92.3 KEZO, 105.9 KKLD, 104.5 KRSZ, 97.7 KQLH, 94.1 KMXM,KBBX (Omaha, NE) **18222**
KKCI-FM - 102.5 (Goodland, KS) **11466**
KKCK-FM - 99.7 (Marshall, MN) **16046**
KKCL-FM (Lubbock, TX) *Unable to locate*
KKCM-AM **15795***
KKCO-TV - Channel 11 (Grand Junction, CO) **4488**
KKCQ-AM - 1480 (Fosston, MN) **15910**
KKCQ-FM **15912***
KKCQ-FM - 96.7 (Fosston, MN) **15911**
KKCR-AM **27136***
KKCR-FM - 90.9 (Hanalei, HI) **7667**
KKCS-AM - 1460 (Colorado Springs, CO) **4269**
KKCS-FM - 101.9 (Colorado Springs, CO) **4270**
KKCW-FM (Portland, OR) *Unable to locate*
KKDA-AM - 730 (Grand Prairie, TX) **30406**
KKDA-FM - 104.5 (Grand Prairie, TX) **30407**
KKDD-AM (Las Vegas, NV) *Unable to locate*
KKDD-FM **4502***
KKDJ-FM (Kingsburg, CA) *Unable to locate*
KKDQ-FM (Thief River Falls, MN) *Unable to locate*
KKDS-AM - 1060 (Salt Lake City, UT) **31452**
KKDY-FM - 102.5 (West Plains, MO) **17717**
KKDZ-AM (Seattle, WA) *Unable to locate*
KKEA-AM - 1420 (Honolulu, HI) **7744**
KKED-FM **30082***
KKEE-FM (Astoria, OR) *Unable to locate*
KKEG-FM - 92.1 (Fayetteville, AR) **1129**
KKEL-AM (Hobbs, NM) *Ceased*
KKEQ-FM - 107.1 (Fosston, MN) **15912**
KKER-FM (Casa Grande, AZ) *Unable to locate*
KKEZ-FM - 94.5 (Fort Dodge, IA) **10910**
KKFG-FM (Farmington, NM) *Unable to locate*
KKFI-FM - 90.1 (Kansas City, MO) **17209**
KKFJ-AM - 570 (Alturas, CA) **1396**
KKFM-FM - 98.1 (Colorado Springs, CO) **4271**
KKFN-AM - 950 (Denver, CO) **4382**
KKFO-AM (Coalinga, CA) *Unable to locate*
KKFR-FM - 92.3 (Phoenix, AZ) **824**
KKFX-AM (Seattle, WA) *Unable to locate*
KKGB-FM (Sulphur, LA) *Unable to locate*
KKGD-AM - 810 (Silt, CO) **4624**
KKGL-FM - 96.9 (Boise, ID) **7825**
KKGM-AM **4481***
KKGO-AM (Los Angeles, CA) *Ceased*
KKGR-AM (Timonium, MD) *Ceased*
KKGT-AM - 1150 (Clackamas, OR) **26267**
KKGZ-AM **4450***
KKHI-AM (San Francisco, CA) *Unable to locate*
KKHI-FM - 100.7 (San Rafael, CA) **3605**
KKHJ-AM **1624***
KKHJ-FM **28944***
KKHK-FM - 99.5 (Denver, CO) **4383**
KKHN-FM **7732***
KKHQ-FM (Corpus Christi, TX) *Unable to locate*
KKHR-FM **2449***
KKIA-FM - 92.9 (Storm Lake, IA) **11250**

KKIC-AM - 950 (Boise, ID) **7826**
KKID-AM (Sallisaw, OK) *Ceased*
KKIK-FM **30738***
KKIM-AM (Albuquerque, NM) *Unable to locate*
KKIM-FM - 94.3 (Aitkin, MN) **15702**
KKIN-AM - 930 (Aitkin, MN) **15703**
KKIQ-FM - 101.7 (Pleasanton, CA) **2857**
KKIS-FM **1760***
KKIT-AM - 1340 (Taos, NM) **19964**
KKIT-FM - 99.9 (Taos, NM) **19965**
KKIX-FM (Fayetteville, AR) *Unable to locate*
KKJG-FM (San Luis Obispo, CA) *Unable to locate*
KKJJ **26423***
KKJL-AM - 1400 (San Luis Obispo, CA) **3571**
KKJM-FM - 92.9 (Sauk Rapids, MN) **16438**
KKJO-AM **17399***
KKJO-FM - 105.5 (St. Joseph, MO) **17397**
KKJQ-FM - 97.3 (Garden City, KS) **11453**
KKJR-FM (Hutchinson, MN) *Unable to locate*
KKJX-AM - 960 (Klamath Falls, OR) **26393**
KKJY-FM (Albuquerque, NM) *Unable to locate*
KKJZ-FM - 106.7 (Portland, OR) **26529**
KKKK-FM **2959***
KKKK-FM - 101.3 (Odessa, TX) **30876**
KKLA-AM - 1240 (Glendale, CA) **2015**
KKLA-FM - 99.5 (Glendale, CA) **2016**
KKLB-AM **7949***
KKLB-FM **7843***
KKLB-FM - 92.5 (Austin, TX) **29868**
KKLD-FM **986***
KKLE-AM - 1550 (Winfield, KS) **11911**
KKLF-FM (Salinas, CA) *Unable to locate*
KKLH-FM - 104.7 (Springfield, MO) **17623**
KKLI-FM - 106.3 (Colorado Springs, CO) **4272**
KKLL-AM (Joplin, MO) *Unable to locate*
KKLL-FM (Webb City, MO) *Unable to locate*
KKLO-AM - 1410 (Leavenworth, KS) **11582**
KKLQ-AM **3307***
KKLQ-AM (Oceanside, CA) *Unable to locate*
KKLQ-FM (San Diego, CA) *Ceased*
KKLS-AM - 920 (Rapid City, SD) **28943**
KKLS-FM **28944***
KKLS-FM - 104.7 (Sioux Falls, SD) **28977**
KKLT-FM - 98.7 (Phoenix, AZ) **825**
KKLV-FM **537***
KKLV-FM - 94.7 (West Memphis, AR) **1369**
KKLX-FM - 96.1 (Worland, WY) **34605**
KKLY-FM **4489***
KKLZ-FM (Las Vegas, NV) *Unable to locate*
KKMA-FM - 99.5 (Sioux City, IA) **11216**
KKMC-AM (Salinas, CA) *Unable to locate*
KKMG-FM - 98.9 (Colorado Springs, CO) **4273**
KKMG-FM - 93.3 (Oklahoma City, OK) **26005**
KKMI-FM - 93.5 (Burlington, IA) **10645**
KKMJ-AM **30301***
KKMJ-FM - 95.5 (Austin, TX) **29869**
KKMK-FM - 93.9 (Rapid City, SD) **28944**
KKMV-FM - 92.5 (Jerome, ID) **7883**
KKMY-FM (Beaumont, TX) *Unable to locate*
KKND-AM **977***
KKND-FM - 106.7 (New Orleans, LA) **12765**
KKNN-FM - 95.1 (Grand Junction, CO) **4489**
KKNO-AM (Gretna, LA) *Unable to locate*
KKNU-FM - 93.1 (Eugene, OR) **26339**
KKOA-AM **24513***
KKOB-AM - 770 (Albuquerque, NM) **19800**
KKOB-FM (Albuquerque, NM) *Unable to locate*
KKOH-AM (Reno, NV) *Unable to locate*
KKOJ-AM - 1190 (Jackson, MN) **15977**
KKON-AM (Kealakekua, HI) *Unable to locate*
KKOR-FM - 94.5 (Gallup, NM) **19860**
KKOS-FM **3304***
KKOT-FM - 93.5 (Columbus, NE) **17982**
KKOW-AM - 860 (Pittsburg, KS) **11755**
KKOW-FM - 96.9 (Pittsburg, KS) **11756**
KKOY-AM - 1460 (Chanute, KS) **11378**
KKOY-FM - 105.5 (Chanute, KS) **11379**
KKOZ-AM - 1430 (Ava, MO) **16897**
KKOZ-FM - 92.1 (Ava, MO) **16898**
KKPL-FM (Spokane, WA) *Unable to locate*
KKPN-FM (Houston, TX) *Unable to locate*
KKPR-AM - 1460 (Kearney, NE) **18063**
KKPR-FM - 98.9 (Kearney, NE) **18064**
KKPS-FM - 99.5 (McAllen, TX) **30797**
KKPT-FM - 94.1 (Little Rock, AR) **1245**
KKQQ-FM **19832***
KKQQ-FM - 102.3 (Brookings, SD) **28823**
KKQV-FM **27135***
KKQX-FM **4272***
KKRB-FM - 106.9 (Klamath Falls, OR) **26394**
KKRC-AM **28981***
KKRD-FM (Wichita, KS) *Unable to locate*
KKRE-AM (Florence, KY) *Unable to locate*
KKRK-FM **690***
KKRL-FM - 93.7 (Carroll, IA) **10654**
KKRN-FM - 102.5 (Little Rock, AR) **1246**
KKRO-FM (Anchorage, AK) *Unable to locate*
KKRQ-FM - 100.7 (Iowa City, IA) **10992**
KKRT-AM - 900 (Wenatchee, WA) **33198**

Numbers cited in bold after listings are entry numbers rather than page numbers.

KKRV-AM - 104.7 (Wenatchee, WA) 33199
KKRV-FM 2103*
KKRW-FM - 93.7 (Houston, TX) 30560
KKRX-AM 25895*
KKRY-FM - 92.5 (Miles City, MT) 17863
KKRZ-FM - 100.3 (Portland, OR) 26530
KKSA-AM (Sacramento, CA) *Unable to locate*
KKSA-AM - 1260 (San Angelo, TX) 31019
KKSC-AM 1597*
KKSD-AM (Anchorage, AK) *Unable to locate*
KKSD-FM 34112*
KK7J-AM 1396*
KKSF-FM - 103.7 (San Francisco, CA) 3489
KKSI-FM - 101.5 (Eddyville, IA) 10866
KKSJ-AM (San Jose, CA) *Ceased*
KKSL-AM - 1290 (Portland, OR) 26531
KKSM-AM - 1320 (San Marcos, CA) 3579
KKSN-AM (Portland, OR) *Unable to locate*
KKSN-FM (Portland, OR) *Unable to locate*
KKSO-AM 11278*
KKSR-FM (St. Cloud, MN) *Unable to locate*
KKSS-FM - 97.3 (Albuquerque, NM) 19801
KKST-FM - 98.7 (Alexandria, LA) 12464
KKSU-AM 37640*
KKSY-FM - 107.1 (Searcy, AR) 1342
KKTK-AM 4481*
KKTK-AM 30027*
KKTR-AM (Fresno, CA) *Unable to locate*
KKTU-FM 3970*
KKTV-TV - Channel 11 (Colorado Springs, CO) 4274
KKTX-AM - 1360 (Corpus Christi, TX) 30087
KKTX-AM - 1240 (Tyler, TX) 31214
KKTX-FM (Longview, TX) *Unable to locate*
KKTY-AM (Douglas, WY) *Ceased*
KKTY-FM 18050*
KKTY-FM (Douglas, WY) *Ceased*
KKTZ-FM - 93.5 (Mountain Home, AR) 1287
KKUA-AM - 90.7 (Honolulu, HI) 7745
KKUB-AM - 1300 (Brownfield, TX) 29954
KKUL-AM (Billings, MT) *Ceased*
KKUP-FM - 91.5 (Cupertino, CA) 1800
KKUR-FM (Ventura, CA) *Unable to locate*
KKUZ-FM (Barling, AR) *Ceased*
KKVO-FM - 90.9 (Altus, OK) 25734
KKVS-FM - 98.7 (Las Cruces, NM) 19882
KKVV-AM - 1060 AM (Las Vegas, NV) 18398
KKWD-FM - 97.9 (Oklahoma City, OK) 26006
KKWK-FM 25924*
KKWM-AM (Dallas, TX) *Ceased*
KKWQ-FM - 92.5 (Warroad, MN) 16498
KKWS-FM - 105.9 (Wadena, MN) 16491
KKWY-AM - 1630 (Cheyenne, WY) 34506
KKWY-FM 31380*
KKWZ-FM (Richfield, UT) *Unable to locate*
KKXK-FM - 94.1 (Montrose, CO) 4581
KKXL-AM - 1440 (Grand Forks, ND) 24461
KKXL-FM (Grand Forks, ND) *Unable to locate*
KKXO-AM - 1450 (Eugene, OR) 26340
KKXX-AM - 930 (Chico, CA) 1702
KKXX-FM 1474*
KKXX-FM - 105.3 (Bakersfield, CA) 1467
KKYA-FM - 93.1 (Yankton, SD) 29041
KKYC-FM - 102.3 (Clovis, NM) 19835
KKYK-FM (Little Rock, AR) *Unable to locate*
KKYN-AM - 1090 (Plainview, TX) 30941
KKYN-FM - 106.9 (Plainview, TX) 30942
KKYR-AM - 790 (Texarkana, AR) 1355
KKYR-FM - 102.5 (Texarkana, AR) 1356
KKYS-FM - 104.7 (Bryan, TX) 29980
KKYT-FM 18156*
KKYX-AM - 680 (San Antonio, TX) 31060
KKYY-FM 4512*
KKZR-FM (Houston, TX) *Unable to locate*
KKZX-AM 10742*
KKZX-FM - 98.9 (Spokane, WA) 33119
KKZZ-AM - 1400 (Santa Paula, CA) 3723
KLAA-FM (Alexandria, LA) *Unable to locate*
KLAA-TV 12875*
KLAC-AM - 570 (Glendale, CA) 2017
KLAD-FM - 92.5 (Klamath Falls, OR) 26395
KLAL-FM (Chariton, IA) *Ceased*
KLAM-AM - 1450 (Cordova, AK) 559
KLAN-FM 24567*
KLAQ-FM - 95.5 (El Paso, TX) 30296
KLAR-AM - 1300 (Laredo, TX) 30675
KLAS-TV - Channel 8 (Las Vegas, NV) 18399
KLAT-AM - 1010 (Houston, TX) 30561
KLAU-AM (Salinas, CA) *Unable to locate*
KLAV-AM (Las Vegas, NV) *Unable to locate*
KLAW Broadcasting, Inc. 25892*
KLAW-FM - 101.3 (Lawton, OK) 25892
KLAX-FM (Los Angeles, CA) *Unable to locate*
KLAX-TV - Channel 31 (Alexandria, LA) 12465
KLAY-AM - 1180 (Tacoma, WA) 33157
KLAZ-FM - 105.9 (Hot Springs, AR) 1185
KLBA-AM - 1370 (Albia, IA) 10577
KLBA-FM - 96.7 (Albia, IA) 10578
KLBB-AM - 1400 (Minneapolis, MN) 16150
KLBC-FM - 106.3 (Durant, OK) 25810

KLBJ-AM - 590 (Austin, TX) 29870
KLBJ-FM - 93.7 (Austin, TX) 29871
KLBK-TV (Lubbock, TX) *Unable to locate*
KLBM-AM - 1450 (La Grande, OR) 26401
KLBM-FM 26402*
KLBO-AM - 1330 (Monahans, TX) 30836
KLBQ-FM - 99.3 (El Dorado, AR) 1110
KLBS-AM - 1330 (Los Banos, CA) 2476
KLBY-TV - Channel 4 (Colby, KS) 11391
KLCB-AM - 1230 (Libby, MT) 17853
KLCC-FM - 89.7 (Eugene, OR) 26341
KLCD-FM - 89.5 (Rochester, MN) 16313
KLCE-FM (Idaho Falls, ID) *Unable to locate*
KLCJ-AM - 1360 (Amarillo, TX) 29711
KLCJ-FM 19955*
KLCK-AM - 1400 (Goldendale, WA) 32777
KLCL-AM - 1470 (Lake Charles, LA) 12646
KLCM-FM - 95.9 (Lewistown, MT) 17849
KLCN-AM - 910 (Blytheville, AR) 1062
KLCO-AM 26047*
KLCQ-FM 3738*
KLCR-FM - 96.9 (Dubuque, IA) 10851
KLCS-TV - Channel 58 (Los Angeles, CA) 2458
KLCU-FM 7313*
KLCU-FM - 90.3 (Lawton, OK) 25893
KLCV-FM - 88.5 (Lincoln, NE) 18135
KLCX-FM 26336*
KLCY-AM - 930 (Missoula, MT) 17882
KLCY-FM - 105.9 (Vernal, UT) 31484
KLDE-FM - 107.5 (Houston, TX) 30562
KLDI-AM (Laramie, WY) *Unable to locate*
KLDN-FM 17153*
KLDO-TV - Channel 27 (Laredo, TX) 30676
KLDY-AM 17250*
KLDY-AM 32868*
KLDY-AM - 1280 (Olympia, WA) 32870
KLDZ-FM (Lincoln, NE) *Unable to locate*
KLEA-AM - 630 (Lovington, NM) 19899
KLEA-FM - 101.7 (Lovington, NM) 19900
KLEB-AM - 1600 (Larose, LA) 12657
KLEE-AM - 1480 (Ottumwa, IA) 11142
KLEE-FM 11143*
KLEF-AM - 98.1 (Anchorage, AK) 544
KLEH-AM (Anamosa, IA) *Unable to locate*
KLEI-AM - 1130 (Kailua, HI) 7765
KLEL-FM - 89.3 (San Jose, CA) 3549
KLEM-AM - 1410 (Le Mars, IA) 11035
KLEN-FM - 106.3 (Cheyenne, WY) 34507
KLER-AM - 1300 (Orofino, ID) 7939
KLER-FM - 95.3 (Orofino, ID) 7940
KLEU-AM 11298*
KLEV-AM (Cleveland, TX) *Unable to locate*
KLEW-TV - Channel 3 (Lewiston, ID) 7896
KLEX-AM (Lexington, MO) *Unable to locate*
KLEY-AM - 1130 (Wellington, KS) 11867
KLFA-FM (Salinas, CA) *Unable to locate*
KLFB-AM - 1420 (Lubbock, TX) 30729
KLFC-FM - 88.1 (Branson, MO) 16921
KLFD-AM - 1410 (Litchfield, MN) 16005
KLFE-AM 2015*
KLFF-AM 821*
KLFF-FM - 89.3 (San Luis Obispo, CA) 3572
KLFJ-AM (Springfield, MO) *Unable to locate*
KLFM-FM 10827*
KLFM-FM - 92.9 (Great Falls, MT) 17801
KLFT-AM 12657*
KLFX-FM - 107.3 (Harker Heights, TX) 30424
KLFY-TV - Channel 10 (Lafayette, LA) 12627
KLGA-AM - 1600 (Algona, IA) 10582
KLGA-FM - 92.7 (Algona, IA) 10583
KLGD-FM (Abilene, TX) *Ceased*
KLGG-FM (St. George, UT) *Unable to locate*
KLGM-FM 34480*
KLGN-AM - 1390 (Logan, UT) 31359
KLGR-AM - 1490 (Redwood Falls, MN) 16299
KLGR-FM - 97.7 (Redwood Falls, MN) 16300
KLGS-FM 17664*
KLGT 16420*
KLGT-FM - 92.9 (Buffalo, WY) 34480
KLGV-AM (Longview, TX) *Unable to locate*
KLHI-FM (Lahaina, HI) *Unable to locate*
KLHS-FM - 88.9 (Lewiston, ID) 7897
KLHT-AM - 1040 (Honolulu, HI) 7746
KLIB-AM 11607*
KLIC-AM - 1230 (Monroe, LA) 12696
KLID-AM - 1340 (Poplar Bluff, MO) 17359
KLIF-AM - 570 (Dallas, TX) 30208
KLIK-AM - 1240 (Jefferson City, MO) 17139
KLIL-FM 3971*
KLIL-FM - 92.1 (Moreauville, LA) 12706
KLIM-AM (Limon, CO) *Ceased*
KLIN-AM - 1400 (Lincoln, NE) 18136
KLIN-FM 18130*
Kline's TV and Two Way (Kinsley, KS) *Ceased*
KLIO-FM 10744*
KLIS-FM (Palestine, TX) *Unable to locate*
KLIT-FM 3667*
KLIT-FM 2020*

KLIT-FM 2020*
KLIV-AM - 1590 (San Jose, CA) 3550
KLIX-AM - 1310 (Twin Falls, ID) 7995
KLIX-FM - 96.5 (Twin Falls, ID) 7996
KLIZ-AM - 1380 (Brainerd, MN) 15769
KLJB-TV - Channel 18 (Davenport, IA) 10743
KLJC-FM - 88.5 (Kansas City, MO) 17210
KLJZ-FM - 93.1 (Yuma, AZ) 1027
KLKC-AM - 1540 (Parsons, KS) 11745
KLKC-FM - 93.5 (Parsons, KS) 11746
KLKE-TV - Channel 24 (Lincoln, NE) 18137
KLKI-AM - 1340 (Anacortes, WA) 32653
KLKK-FM (Clear Lake, IA) *Unable to locate*
KLKL-FM (Shreveport, LA) *Unable to locate*
KLKN-TV - Channel 8 (Lincoln, NE) 18138
KLKO-FM - 93.7 (Elko, NV) 18338
KLKS-FM - 104.3 (Breezy Point, MN) 15772
KLKT-FM (Incline Village, NV) *Ceased*
KLLA-AM - 1570 (Leesville, LA) 12660
KLLC-FM - 97.3 (San Francisco, CA) 3490
KLLF-AM 27134*
KLLI-FM - 95.9 (Texarkana, AR) 1357
KLLK-AM (Willits, CA) *Unable to locate*
KLLL-AM - 1590 (Lubbock, TX) 30730
KLLL-FM - 96.3 (Lubbock, TX) 30731
KLLM-FM - 103.9 (Forks, WA) 32770
KLLP-FM (Idaho Falls, ID) *Unable to locate*
KLLR-AM 15770*
KLLR-FM 29705*
KLLT-FM - 104.9 (Spencer, IA) 11235
KLLU-FM 2953*
KLLV-AM - 550 (Breen, CO) 4200
KLLY-FM - 95.3 (Bakersfield, CA) 1468
KLLZ-AM - 1600 (Brainerd, MN) 15770
KLMA-FM - 96.5 (Hobbs, NM) 19867
KLMG-TV 30705*
KLMJ-FM - 104.9 (Hampton, IA) 10941
KLMN-FM - 89.1 (Amarillo, TX) 29712
KLMN-TV 1154*
KLMO-AM - 1060 (Longmont, CO) 4564
KLMP-FM - 97.9 (Rapid City, SD) 28945
KLMR-AM - 920 (Lamar, CO) 4539
KLMT-FM 31259*
KLMX-AM - 1450 (Clayton, NM) 19829
KLND-FM - 89.5 (Mc Laughlin, SD) 28891
KLNE-FM - 88.7 (Lexington, NE) 18073
KLNE-TV - Channel 3 (Lexington, NE) 18074
KLNG-AM - 1560 (Council Bluffs, IA) 10728
KLNR-FM (Las Vegas, NV) *Unable to locate*
KLNT-AM 10712*
KLNT-FM 10714*
KLO-AM - 1430 (Ogden, UT) 31381
KLOA-AM - 1240 (Ridgecrest, CA) 2924
KLOA-FM - 104.9 (Ridgecrest, CA) 2925
KLOC-AM - 920 (Stockton, CA) 3812
KLOE-AM - 730 (Goodland, KS) 11467
KLOE-TV 11465*
KLOG-AM - 1490 (Kelso, WA) 32787
KLOH-AM - 1050 (Pipestone, MN) 16277
KLOI-Laramie 34510*
KLOK-AM (San Jose, CA) *Unable to locate*
KLOK-FM 3489*
KLOL-FM - 101.1 (Houston, TX) 30563
KLOM-AM (Lompoc, CA) *Unable to locate*
KLON-FM - 88.1 (Long Beach, CA) 2179
KLOO-AM - 1340 (Albany, OR) 26210
KLOQ-AM 2535*
KLOQ-FM - 98.7 (Merced, CA) 2533
KLOR-FM 10851*
KLOR-FM - 99.3 (Ponca City, OK) 26040
KLOS-FM - 95.5 (Los Angeles, CA) 2459
KLOU-FM (St. Louis, MO) *Unable to locate*
KLOV-AM (Loveland, CO) *Unable to locate*
KLOV-FM - 89.3 (Sacramento, CA) 3033
KLOZ-FM 30298*
KLOZ-FM - 92.7 (Kaiser, MO) 17153
KLPA-TV - Channel 25 (Alexandria, LA) 12466
KLPB-TV - Channel 24 (Lafayette, LA) 12628
KLPC-FM 3697*
KLPI-FM - 89.1 (Ruston, LA) 12808
KLPL-AM - 1050 (Lake Providence, LA) 12653
KLPL-FM - 92.7 (Lake Providence, LA) 12654
KLPQ-FM 1245*
KLPR-FM - 91.3 (Kearney, NE) 18065
KLPW-AM - 1220 (Washington, MO) 17708
KLPX-FM - 96.1 (Tucson, AZ) 984
KLPZ-AM - 1380 (Parker, AZ) 765
KLQL-FM - 101.1 (Luverne, MN) 16015
KLQP-FM - 92.1 (Madison, MN) 16021
KLQZ-FM 1310*
KLRA-AM (North Little Rock, AR) *Unable to locate*
KLRA-FM (North Little Rock, AR) *Unable to locate*
KLRC-FM - 101.1 (Siloam Springs, AR) 1344
KLRD-FM - 90.1 (Yucaipa, CA) 4127
KLRE-FM - 90.5 (Little Rock, AR) 1247
KLRG-AM - 1150 (North Little Rock, AR) 1301
KLRK 26238*
KLRN-TV 29872*
KLRN-TV - Channel 9 (San Antonio, TX) 31061

KLRR-FM - 01.75 (Bend, OR) 26245
KLRS-AM 17301*
KLRS-FM 17302*
KLRT-TV - Channel 16 (Little Rock, AR) 1248
KLRU-TV - Channel 18 (Austin, TX) 29872
KLRX-FM 30193*
KLSA-FM - 90.7 (Shreveport, LA) 12827
KLSB-TV - Channel 19 (Nacogdoches, TX) 30853
KLSC-AM 4421*
KLSC-FM 30732*
KLSE-FM - 91.7 (Decorah, IA) 10761
KLSK-FM - 98.1 (Albuquerque, NM) 19802
KLSN-AM 33108*
KLSN-FM 29972*
KLSN-FM 11256*
KLSP-FM - 91.7 (Angola, LA) 12473
KLSQ-AM - 870 (Las Vegas, NV) 18400
KLSR-AM (Memphis, TX) Ceased
KLSR-FM - 105.3 (Memphis, TX) 30803
KLSS-AM 11078*
KLST-TV - Channel 8 (San Angelo, TX) 31020
KLSU-FM - 91.1 (Baton Rouge, LA) 12508
KLSX-FM - 97.1 (Los Angeles, CA) 2460
KLSY-FM - 92.5 (Bellevue, WA) 32673
KLSZ-FM - 102.7 (Van Buren, AR) 1360
KLTA-FM - 105.1 (Fargo, ND) 24424
KLTB-AM 16913*
KLTB-FM - 104.3 (Boise, ID) 7827
KLTC-AM (Dickinson, ND) Unable to locate
KLTD-FM 29865*
KLTE-FM 26018*
KLTF-AM - 960 (Little Falls, MN) 16008
KLTG-FM - 96.5 (Corpus Christi, TX) 30088
KLTI-AM (Macon, MO) Unable to locate
KLTI-FM - 104.1 (Des Moines, IA) 10827
KLTJ-TV - Channel 22 (Houston, TX) 30564
KLTK-AM (Grove, OK) Unable to locate
KLTL-TV - Channel 18 (Lake Charles, LA) 12647
KLTM-TV - Channel 13 (Monroe, LA) 12697
KLTN-AM (Albuquerque, NM) Unable to locate
KLTO-FM (El Paso, TX) Unable to locate
KLTR-FM 30560*
KLTS-TV - Channel 24 (Shreveport, LA) 12828
KLTT-AM - 670 (Brighton, CO) 4203
KLTV-TV - Channel 7 (Tyler, TX) 31215
KLTW-AM 890*
KLTX-AM - 1390 (Glendale, CA) 2018
KLTY-FM (Irving, TX) Unable to locate
KLTZ-AM - 1240 (Glasgow, MT) 17794
KLUB-AM 31448*
Klublife (Toronto, ON, Can.) 36644
KLUH-FM - 90.3 (Poplar Bluff, MO) 17360
KLUJ-TV - Channel 44 (Harlingen, TX) 30428
KLUM-FM 17136*
KLUP-AM - 930 (San Antonio, TX) 31062
KLUR-FM (Wichita Falls, TX) Unable to locate
KLUV-FM - 98.7 (Dallas, TX) 30209
KLUX-FM - 89.5 (Corpus Christi, TX) 30089
KLUZ-TV - Channel 41 (Albuquerque, NM) 19803
KLVA-FM - 105.5 (Sacramento, CA) 3034
KLVB-AM - 730 (Sacramento, CA) 3035
KLVC-FM - 88.3 (Sacramento, CA) 3036
KLVE-FM (Hollywood, CA) Unable to locate
KLVF-FM - 100.7 (Las Vegas, NM) 19892
KLVG-FM - 103.7 (Sacramento, CA) 3037
KLVI-AM - 560 (Beaumont, TX) 29906
KLVJ-AM (Mountain Home, ID) Unable to locate
KLVJ-FM - 100.1 (Sacramento, CA) 3038
KLVK-FM 3030*
KLVL-AM (Houston, TX) Unable to locate
KLVN-FM 11117*
KLVN-FM - 100.1 (Sacramento, CA) 3039
KLVO-FM (Albuquerque, NM) Unable to locate
KLVP-AM - 1040 (Portland, OR) 26532
KLVP-FM - 88.7 (Sacramento, CA) 3040
KLVQ-AM - 1410 (Athens, TX) 29747
KLVR-FM - 91.9 (Sacramento, CA) 3041
KLVS-AM 26531*
KLVS-FM 3030*
KLVS-FM - 99.3 (Sacramento, CA) 3042
KLVT-AM - 1230 (Levelland, TX) 30683
KLVT-FM - 105.3 (Levelland, TX) 30684
KLVU-AM (Joliet, IL) Unable to locate
KLVU-FM 30209*
KLVU-FM - 107.1 (Sacramento, CA) 3043
KLVV-FM 31467*
KLVV-FM - 88.7 (Ponca City, OK) 26041
KLVW-FM - 99.1 (Rocklin, CA) 2959
KLVX-TV - Channel 10 (Las Vegas, NV) 18401
KLVY-AM - 1260 (Powell, WY) 34570
KLVY-FM - 91.1 (Sacramento, CA) 3044
KLWD-FM 34591*
KLWN-AM - 1320 (Lawrence, KS) 11575
KLWN-FM 11576*
KLWT-AM - 1230 (Lebanon, MO) 17241
KLWT-FM 17240*
KLWW-AM 10683*
KLXQ-FM 1189*
KLXR-AM (Redding, CA) Unable to locate

KLXS-FM (Pierre, SD) Unable to locate
KLXV-TV (San Jose, CA) Unable to locate
KLXX-AM - 1270 (Bismarck, ND) 24369
KLYC-AM - 1260 (McMinnville, OR) 26417
KLYD-AM (Bakersfield, CA) Ceased
KLYF-AM 10829*
KLYF-FM - 106.3 (Des Moines, IA) 10828
KLYK-FM - 105.5 (Longview, WA) 32818
KLYN-FM 32822*
KLYQ-AM - 1240 (Hamilton, MT) 17810
KLYQ-FM 17809*
KLYR-AM - 1360 (Clarksville, AR) 1081
KLYT-FM - 88.3 (Albuquerque, NM) 19804
KLYV-FM - 105.3 (Dubuque, IA) 10852
KLZ-AM - 560 (Denver, CO) 4384
KLZE-FM (Owensville, MO) Unable to locate
KLZR-FM - 105.9 (Lawrence, KS) 11576
KLZX-FM 31463*
KLZZ-AM 3307*
KMA-AM - 960 (Shenandoah, IA) 11200
KMA Chief II (Mukwonago, WI) 34157
KMA-FM 10703*
KMAC-AM 31072*
KMAC-FM 16428*
KMAD-AM - 1550 (Madill, OK) 25903
KMAG-FM - 99.1 (Fort Smith, AR) 1152
KMAI-FM 7739*
KMAJ-AM - 1440 (Topeka, KS) 11841
KMAJ-FM - 107.7 (Topeka, KS) 11842
KMAL-FM - 92.9 (Sikeston, MO) 17585
KMAM-AM - 1530 (Butler, MO) 16932
KMAN-AM - 1350 (Manhattan, KS) 11633
KMAP-AM 1475*
KMAQ-AM - 1320 (Maquoketa, IA) 11056
KMAQ-FM - 95.1 (Maquoketa, IA) 11057
KMAR-AM (Winnsboro, LA) Ceased
KMAS-AM - 1030 (Shelton, WA) 33081
KMAT-FM - 105.1 (Houston, TX) 30565
KMAU-TV (Reno, NV) Unable to locate
KMAV-AM - 1520 (Mayville, ND) 24500
KMAV-FM 26103*
KMAV-FM - 105.5 (Mayville, ND) 24501
KMAX-FM - 107.1 (Los Angeles, CA) 2461
KMAX-TV - Channel 31 (Sacramento, CA) 3045
KMAY-AM 2952*
KMAZ-FM 18145*
KMBA-AM (Albuquerque, NM) Unable to locate
KMBC-AM 11872*
KMBC-TV - Channel 9 (Kansas City, MO) 17211
KMBD-AM - 1590 (Tillamook, OR) 26598
KMBH-FM - 88.9 (Harlingen, TX) 30429
KMBH-TV - Channel 60 (Harlingen, TX) 30430
KMBI-AM - 1330 (Spokane, WA) 33120
KMBI-FM - 107.9 (Spokane, WA) 33121
KMBL-AM - 1450 (Junction, TX) 30631
KMBQ-FM 12842*
KMBQ-FM - 99.7 (Wasilla, AK) 651
KMBR-FM - 95.5 (Butte, MT) 17763
KMBS-AM (West Monroe, LA) Unable to locate
KMBS-TV 1150*
KMBY-FM (Salinas, CA) Unable to locate
KMBZ-AM - 980 (Westwood, KS) 11872
KMCA-AM - 1450 (Redding, CA) 2889
KMCA-FM 15697*
KMCD-AM - 1570 (Fairfield, IA) 10886
KMCG-FM - 95.7 (San Diego, CA) 3304
KMCH-FM - 94.7 (Manchester, IA) 11046
KMCI-TV (Lawrence, KS) Unable to locate
KMCK-TV (Fayetteville, AR) Unable to locate
KMCL-FM - 101.1 (McCall, ID) 7907
KMCM-AM 26417*
KMCM-FM - 96.9 (Midland, TX) 30819
KMCO-FM - 101.3 (McAlester, OK) 25910
KMCQ-FM - 104.5 (The Dalles, OR) 26303
KMCR-FM 921*
KMCR-FM - 103.9 (Montgomery City, MO) 17297
KMCT-TV - Channel 39 (West Monroe, LA) 12876
KMCX-FM - 106.5 (Ogallala, NE) 18189
KMDL-FM (Lafayette, LA) Unable to locate
KMDO-AM - 1600 (Fort Scott, KS) 11444
KMDX-FM (Parker, AZ) Unable to locate
KMED-AM - 1440 (Medford, OR) 26424
KMED-TV 26431*
KMEG-TV - Channel 14 (Sioux City, IA) 11217
KMEL-FM - 106.1 (San Francisco, CA) 3491
KMEM-FM - 100.5 (Memphis, MO) 17282
KMEN-FM (San Bernardino, CA) Unable to locate
KMEO-AM 822*
KMEO-FM 826*
KMEO-FM 1007*
KMER-AM - 950 (Kemmerer, WY) 34542
KMET-AM (Riverside, CA) Ceased
KMET-FM 1796*
KMEX-TV - Channel 34 (Los Angeles, CA) 2462
KMEZ-FM 30212*
KMEZ-FM - 102.9 (Belle Chasse, LA) 12530
KMFA-FM - 89.5 (Austin, TX) 29873
KMFB-FM - 92.7 (Mendocino, CA) 2520
KMFC-FM - 92.1 (Centralia, MO) 16970

KMFG-FM - 102.9 (Hibbing, MN) 15955
KMFX-AM - 1190 (Rochester, MN) 16314
KMFY-FM - 96.9 (Grand Rapids, MN) 15931
KMGA-FM (Albuquerque, NM) Unable to locate
KMGC-FM 30200*
KMGE-FM - 94.5 (Eugene, OR) 26342
KMGG-FM 1628*
KMGG-FM (Santa Rosa, CA) Unable to locate
KMGH-TV (Denver, CO) Unable to locate
KMGI-FM 33063*
KMGI-FM - 102.5 (Pocatello, ID) 7951
KMGJ-FM - 93.1 (Grand Junction, CO) 4490
KMGK-FM 10826*
KMGL-FM (Oklahoma City, OK) Unable to locate
KMGM-FM - 105.5 (Montevideo, MN) 16182
KMGN-FM (Flagstaff, AZ) Unable to locate
KMGO-FM - 98.7 (Centerville, IA) 10690
KMGP-FM 30875*
KMGQ-FM (Santa Barbara, CA) Unable to locate
KMGR-AM (Salt Lake City, UT) Ceased
KMGR-FM - 95.7 (Fillmore, UT) 31334
KMGW-FM - 94.5 (Casper, WY) 34489
KMGX-AM 987*
KMGX-FM (Mission Hills, CA) Ceased
KMGX-FM - 100.7 (Bend, OR) 26246
KMGZ-FM - 95.3 (Lawton, OK) 25894
KMHA-FM - 91.3 (Four Bears, ND) 24447
KMHC Inc. (Kingston Mines, IL) 9048
KMHD-FM - 89.1 (Gresham, OR) 26366
kMHI-AM - 1240 (Mountain Home, ID) 7927
KMHK-AM 28903*
KMHL-AM - 1400 (Marshall, MN) 16047
KMHM-FM - 104.1 (Marble Hill, MO) 17263
KMHT-AM - 1450 (Huntsville, TX) 30599
KMHT-FM - 103.9 (Huntsville, TX) 30600
KMIA-AM 29742*
KMIA-FM (Rosenberg, TX) Unable to locate
KMIC-AM - 1590 (Houston, TX) 30566
KMID-TV - Channel 2 (Midland, TX) 30820
KMIH-FM - 104.5 (Mercer Island, WA) 32830
KMIL-AM - 1330 (Cameron, TX) 29996
KMIN-AM (Grants, NM) Unable to locate
KMIR-TV - Channel 36 (Palm Desert, CA) 2751
KMIS-AM - 1050 (Kennett, MO) 17222
KMIT-FM - 105.9 (Mitchell, SD) 28902
KMIX-AM - 1390 (Stockton, CA) 3813
KMIX-FM - 100.9 (Stockton, CA) 3814
KMIZ-TV - Channel 17 (Columbia, MO) 17018
KMJ-AM - 580 (Fresno, CA) 1974
KMJ-TV 1982*
KMJC-AM (San Diego, CA) Ceased
KMJC-FM 10744*
KMJI-FM 4369*
KMJK-FM 17212*
KMJK-FM 26529*
KMJK-FM - 107.3 (Kansas City, MO) 17212
KMJM-FM - 104.9 (St. Louis, MO) 17541
KMJQ-FM - 102.1 (Houston, TX) 30567
KMJX-FM (Little Rock, AR) Unable to locate
KMJY-AM - 700 (Oldtown, ID) 7936
KMJY-FM - 104.5 (Oldtown, ID) 7937
KMJZ-FM - 95.1 (Bend, OR) 26247
KMKF-FM - 101.5 (Manhattan, KS) 11634
KMKS-FM - 102.5 (Bay City, TX) 29893
KMKX-FM 3310*
KMKX-FM (Rock Springs, WY) Unable to locate
KMKY-AM - 1310 (San Francisco, CA) 3492
KMLA-AM 31186*
KMLA-FM (Ashdown, AR) Unable to locate
KMLA-FM - 103.7 (Oxnard, CA) 2733
KMLB-AM - 1440 (Monroe, LA) 12698
KMLE-FM (Dallas, TX) Unable to locate
KMLM-TV - Channel 42 (Midland, TX) 30821
KMLT-FM 29710*
KMLW-FM - 88.3 (Spokane, WA) 33122
KMMJ-AM (Grand Island, NE) Unable to locate
KMMK-FM 30782*
KMML-FM - 96.9 (Amarillo, TX) 29713
KMMO-AM - 102.9 (Marshall, MO) 17266
KMMO-FM - 102.9 (Marshall, MO) 17267
KMMR-FM - 100.1 (Malta, MT) 17859
KMMT-FM - 106.5 (Mammoth Lakes, CA) 2499
KMMX-FM - 100.3 (Lubbock, TX) 30732
KMMX-FM (San Antonio, TX) Unable to locate
KMMY-FM - 97.1 (Muskogee, OK) 25924
KMMZ-AM 34517*
KMND-AM - 1510 (Midland, TX) 30822
KMNE-FM - 90.3 (Lincoln, NE) 18139
KMNE-TV - Channel 7 (Bassett, NE) 17944
KMNR-FM - 89.7 (Rolla, MO) 17381
KMNS-AM (Sioux City, IA) Unable to locate
KMNT-FM - 102.9 (Centralia, WA) 32709
KMNY-AM (Anaheim, CA) Unable to locate
KMOA-AM (Searcy, AR) Ceased
KMOC-FM - 89.5 (Wichita Falls, TX) 31298
KMOD-FM - 97.5 (Tulsa, OK) 26151
KMOE-FM - 92.1 (Butler, MO) 16933
KMOG-AM - 1420 (Payson, AZ) 768
KMOH-TV (Bullhead City, AZ) Unable to locate

KMOJ-FM - 89.9 (Minneapolis, MN) 16151
KMOK-FM - 106.9 (Lewiston, ID) 7898
KMOL-TV - Channel 4 (San Antonio, TX) 31063
KMOM-AM (Monticello, MN) Unable to locate
KMON-AM - 560 (Great Falls, MT) 17802
KMON-FM - 94.5 (Great Falls, MT) 17803
KMOO-AM (Mineola, TX) Ceased
KMOO-FM - 99.9 (Mineola, TX) 30831
KMOQ-FM (Joplin, MO) Unable to locate
KMOR-FM - 92.9 (Scottsbluff, NE) 18269
KMOS-TV - Channel 6 (Warrensburg, MO) 17671
KMOT-TV - Channel 10 (Minot, ND) 24509
KMOU-FM - 104.7 (Roswell, NM) 19921
KMOV-TV - Channel 4 (St. Louis, MO) 17542
KMOX-AM - 1120 (St. Louis, MO) 17543
KMOX-TV 17542*
KMOZ-AM (Rolla, MO) Unable to locate
KMPC-AM 2453*
KMPG-AM (Hollister, CA) Unable to locate
KMPH-FM - 107.5 (Fresno, CA) 1975
KMPH-TV - Channel 26 (Fresno, CA) 1976
KMPL-AM 17586*
KMPO-FM (Fresno, CA) Unable to locate
KMPQ-AM (Houston, TX) Unable to locate
KMPR-FM - 88.9 (Minot, ND) 24510
KMPS 575*
KMPS-AM - 1090 (Seattle, WA) 33059
KMPS-FM 546*
KMPS-FM - 94.1 FM (Seattle, WA) 33060
KMRC-AM - 1430 (Morgan City, LA) 12712
KMRF-AM (Marshfield, MO) Unable to locate
KMRI-AM - 1550 (Salt Lake City, UT) 31453
KMRJ-FM - 99.5 (San Juan Capistrano, CA) 3560
KMRN-AM - 1360 (Cameron, MO) 16940
KMRO-FM - 90.3 (Camarillo, CA) 1647
KMRO-FM (Camarillo, CA) 1646
KMRR-AM (Tucson, AZ) Unable to locate
KMRS-AM - 1230 (Morris, MN) 16199
KMRY-AM - 1450 (Cedar Rapids, IA) 10683
KMSA-FM - 91.3 (Grand Junction, CO) 4491
KMSB-TV - Channel 11 (Tucson, AZ) 985
KMSC-FM - 88.3 (Sioux City, IA) 11218
KMSD-AM - 1510 (Milbank, SD) 28895
KMSD-FM 29022*
KMSG-TV - Channel 59 (Fresno, CA) 1977
KMSI-FM - 88.1 (Tulsa, OK) 26152
KMSL-AM 33124*
KMSM-FM 17381*
KMSO-FM - 102.5 (Missoula, MT) 17883
KMSO-TV 17879*
KMSP-TV - Channel 9 (Eden Prairie, MN) 15870
KMSS-TV - Channel 33 (Shreveport, LA) 12829
KMST-TV 3072*
KMSU - 19 (Minot, ND) 24511
KMSU-FM - 89.7 (Mankato, MN) 16034
KMT (Sebastopol, CA) 3751
KMTA-AM - 1050 (Miles City, MT) 17864
KMTA-FM 17863*
KMTB-FM - 99.5 (Nashville, AR) 1296
KMTC-FM - 91.1 (Russellville, AR) 1333
KMTC-TV 17619*
KMTF-TV 1986*
KMTH-FM - 98.7 (Maljamar, NM) 19902
KMTI-AM - 650 (Manti, UT) 31367
KMTL-AM - 760 (North Little Rock, AR) 1302
KMTN-FM - 1290 (Jackson, WY) 34538
KMTP-TV (San Francisco, CA) Unable to locate
KMTR-TV - Channel 16 (Springfield, OR) 26587
KMTS-FM - 99.1 (Glenwood Springs, CO) 4461
KMTT-FM - 103.7 (Seattle, WA) 33062
KMTT-FM - 103.7 (Seattle, WA) 33061
KMTV-TV - Channel 3 (Omaha, NE) 18223
KMTX-FM - 105.3 (Helena, MT) 17830
KMTY-FM 19832*
KMTY-FM 26199*
KMTY-FM - 97.7 (Holdrege, NE) 18050
KMUD-FM - 91.1 (Redway, CA) 2912
KMUL-AM - 1380 (Muleshoe, TX) 30847
KMUN-FM - 91.9 (Astoria, OR) 26230
KMUS (Muskogee, OK) Ceased
KMUT-FM - 105.7 (Salt Lake City, UT) 31454
KMUV-TV 3045*
KMUW-FM - 89.1 (Wichita, KS) 11899
KMUZ-AM - 1230 (Washougal, WA) 33192
KMVC-FM - 91.7 (Marshall, MO) 17268
KMVI-AM - 550 (Kahului, HI) 7760
KMVI-FM - 98.3 (Pukalani, HI) 7791
KMVL-AM - 1220 (Madisonville, TX) 30753
KMVL-FM - 100.5 (Madisonville, TX) 30754
KMVR-FM - 104.9 (Las Cruces, NM) 19883
KMVT-TV - Channel 11 (Twin Falls, ID) 7997
KMVX-FM - 102.9 (Jerome, ID) 7884
KMWB-TV - Channel 23 (St. Paul, MN) 16420
KMWorld (Medford, NJ) 19227
KMWX-AM - 1460 (Yakima, WA) 33232
KMWX-FM 33228*
KMXA-FM - 99.9 (Minot, ND) 24512
KMXC-FM - 97.3 (Sioux Falls, SD) 28978
KMXD-FM - 100.3 (Des Moines, IA) 10829

KMXE-FM (Red Lodge, MT) Unable to locate
KMXG-FM - 96.1 (Davenport, IA) 10744
KMXI-FM 26529*
KMXI-FM - 95.1 (Chico, CA) 1703
KMXJ-FM - 94.1 (Amarillo, TX) 29714
KMXL-FM 31362*
KMXL-FM - 95.1 (Carthage, MO) 16961
KMXO-AM (Abilene, TX) Unable to locate
KMXP-FM - 96.9 (Phoenix, AZ) 827
KMXP-FM - 96.9 (Phoenix, AZ) 826
KMXQ-FM 19798*
KMXQ-FM - 92.9 (Socorro, NM) 19960
KMXR-FM (Corpus Christi, TX) Unable to locate
KMXS-FM - 103.1 (Anchorage, AK) 545
KMXT-FM - 100.1 (Kodiak, AK) 617
KMXU-FM - 105.1 (Manti, UT) 31368
KMXV-FM (Kansas City, MO) Unable to locate
KMXX-FM 845*
KMXX-FM 4641*
KMXX-FM - 99.3 (Brawley, CA) 1596
KMXZ-FM - 94.9 (Tucson, AZ) 986
KMYC-AM - 1410 (Marysville, CA) 2517
KMYL-AM - 1190 (Phoenix, AZ) 828
KMYO-FM 1251*
KMYT-FM 2529*
KMYX-AM (Bakersfield, CA) Unable to locate
KMYX-FM (Bakersfield, CA) Unable to locate
KMYZ-AM - 1570 (Tulsa, OK) 26153
KMYZ-FM - 104.5 (Tulsa, OK) 26154
KMZE-FM - 92.1 (Woodward, OK) 26199
KMZQ-FM (Las Vegas, NV) Unable to locate
KMZT-FM - 105.1 (Los Angeles, CA) 2463
KMZU-FM - 100.7 (Carrollton, MO) 16957
KMZX-FM - 106.3 (North Little Rock, AR) 1303
KMZZ-FM (San Bernardino, CA) Unable to locate
KNAB-AM - 1140 (Burlington, CO) 4211
KNAB-FM (Orange, CA) Unable to locate
KNAB-FM - 104.1 (Burlington, CO) 4212
KNAC-FM (Los Angeles, CA) Unable to locate
KNAF-AM - 910 (Johnson City, TX) 30628
KNAK-AM (Delta, UT) Unable to locate
KNAL-AM (Victoria, TX) Ceased
KNAN-FM (West Monroe, LA) Unable to locate
KNAQ-FM 7883*
KNAS-FM - 105.5 (Nashville, AR) 1297
KNAT-TV - Channel 23 (Albuquerque, NM) 19805
KNAU-FM - 88.7 (Flagstaff, AZ) 700
KNAX-FM (Fresno, CA) Unable to locate
KNAZ-TV - Channel 2 (Flagstaff, AZ) 701
KNBC-TV - Channel 4 (Burbank, CA) 1627
KNBO-AM - 1530 (New Boston, TX) 30861
KNBQ-FM 33047*
KNBR-AM - 680 (San Francisco, CA) 3493
KNBT-FM - 92.1 (New Braunfels, TX) 30863
KNBU-FM - 89.7 (Baldwin City, KS) 11352
KNBZ-FM 651*
KNCB-AM - 1320 (Vivian, LA) 12872
KNCI-FM (Sacramento, CA) Unable to locate
KNCK-AM - 1390 (Concordia, KS) 11399
KNCM-AM 17291*
KNCN-FM - 101.3 (Corpus Christi, TX) 30090
KNCO-AM - 830 (Grass Valley, CA) 2030
KNCO-FM - 94.1 (Grass Valley, CA) 2031
KNCQ-FM - 97.3 (Redding, CA) 2890
KNCT-FM - 91.3 (Killeen, TX) 30645
KNCT-TV - Channel 46 (Killeen, TX) 30646
KNCW-AM 32781*
KNCW-FM 32782*
KNDA-AM - 1000 (Odessa, TX) 30877
KNDC-AM - 1490 (Hettinger, ND) 24473
KNDD-FM - 107.7 (Seattle, WA) 33063
KNDE-FM 983*
KNDI-AM - 1270 (Honolulu, HI) 7747
KNDK-AM - 1080 (Langdon, ND) 24490
KNDK-FM - 95.7 (Langdon, ND) 24491
KNDL-FM - 89.9 (Angwin, CA) 1424
KNDN-AM - 960 (Farmington, NM) 19848
KNDR-FM - 104.7 (Mandan, ND) 24499
KNDU-TV - Channel 25 (Richland, WA) 32930
KNDY-AM - 1570 (Marysville, KS) 11640
KNDY-FM - 95.5 (Marysville, KS) 11641
KNEA-AM (Jonesboro, AR) Unable to locate
KNEB-AM - 960 (Scottsbluff, NE) 18270
KNEB-FM - 94.1 (Scottsbluff, NE) 18271
KNED-AM - 1150 (McAlester, OK) 25911
The Knee (Burlington, MA) 14031
Knee Surgery; The Journal of (Thorofare, NJ) 19622
KNEI-AM - 1140 (Waukon, IA) 11304
KNEI-FM - 103.5 (Waukon, IA) 11305
KNEK-AM - 1190 (Lafayette, LA) 12629
KNEK-FM (Washington, LA) Unable to locate
KNEL-AM - 1490 (Brady, TX) 29944
KNEL-FM - 95.3 (Brady, TX) 29945
KNEM-AM - 1240 (Nevada, MO) 17309
KNEO-FM - 91.7 (Neosho, MO) 17307
KNES-FM - 99.1 (Fairfield, TX) 30312
KNET-AM - 1450 (Palestine, TX) 30898
KNEU-AM - 1250 (Roosevelt, UT) 31416

KNEV-FM (Reno, NV) Unable to locate
KNEW-AM (San Francisco, CA) Unable to locate
KNEX-AM 11645*
KNEX-FM 11644*
KNEZ-AM 3704*
KNFL-AM (Logan, UT) Ceased
KNFL-FM - 104.9 (Logan, UT) 31360
KNFP-FM 2953*
KNFR-FM (San Diego, CA) Unable to locate
KNFT-AM - 950 (Silver City, NM) 19954
KNFT-FM - 102.9 (Silver City, NM) 19955
KNFX-AM - 970 (Rochester, MN) 16315
KNGL-AM - 1540 (McPherson, KS) 11645
KNGM-FM - 91.9 (Emporia, KS) 11433
KNGN-AM - 1360 (McCook, NE) 18157
KNGS-AM 2039*
KNGS-FM (Coalinga, CA) Unable to locate
KNGT-FM - 94.3 (Jackson, CA) 2096
KNGV-FM (Kingsville, TX) Unable to locate
KNHC-FM - 89.5 (Seattle, WA) 33064
KNHK-FM - 92.9 (Reno, NV) 18432
KNIA-AM - 1320 (Knoxville, IA) 11021
KNIC-FM 4541*
KNID-FM - 99.7 (Enid, OK) 25827
Knife Magazine; National (Chattanooga, TN) 29090
Knife Show Calendar; Gun & (Iola, WI) 33830
Knight Examiner 19138*
Knight; The Gannon (Erie, PA) 26899
Knight-Ridder Financial News (Leawood, KS) Unable
   to locate
Knight-Ridder/Tribune Information Services
   (Washington, DC) 37978
Knightstown Banner (Knightstown, IN) 10236
KNIK-FM (Anchorage, AK) Unable to locate
KNIN-FM - 92.9 (Lafayette Hill, PA) 27133
KNIQ-FM 11076*
KNIR-AM - 1360 (New Iberia, LA) 12724
KNIS-FM - 91.3 (Carson City, NV) 18332
KNIT-AM 29659*
KnitNet (Toronto, ON, Can.) 36645
Knitter's (Sioux Falls, SD) 28964
Knitting Digest (Berne, IN) 9813
Knitting World 9813*
Knives Illustrated (Anaheim, CA) 1408
KNIX-FM (Tempe, AZ) Unable to locate
KNJO-FM (Thousand Oaks, CA) Unable to locate
KNKN-FM - 107.1 (Pueblo, CO) 4606
KNKT-FM (Albuquerque, NM) Unable to locate
KNLA-FM (Los Alamos, NM) Unable to locate
KNLB-FM - 91.1 (Lake Havasu City, AZ) 740
KNLC-TV - Channel 24 (St. Louis, MO) 17544
KNLF-FM - 95.9 (Quincy, CA) 2871
KNLG-FM - 90.3 (New Bloomfield, MO) 17311
KNLJ-TV - Channel 25 (New Bloomfield, MO) 17312
KNLR-FM - 97.5 (Bend, OR) 26248
KNLT-FM (Walla Walla, WA) Unable to locate
KNLU 12703*
KNLV-AM - 1060 (Ord, NE) 18237
KNLV-FM - 103.9 (Ord, NE) 18238
KNMC-FM (Havre, MT) Unable to locate
KNME-TV - Channel 5 (Albuquerque, NM) 19806
KNMI-FM - 88.9 (Farmington, NM) 19849
KNMO-FM - 97.5 (Nevada, MO) 17310
KNMQ-FM 702*
KNMX-AM (Las Vegas, NM) Unable to locate
KNNB-FM - 88.1 (Whiteriver, AZ) 1004
KNNC-FM 29878*
KNNC-FM (Austin, TX) Unable to locate
KNND-AM - 1400 (Cottage Grove, OR) 26296
KNNG-FM - 104.7 (Sterling, CO) 4640
KNNK-FM - 100.5 (Hereford, TX) 30445
KNNN-FM - 99.3 (Redding, CA) 2891
KNNS-AM 821*
KNNS-AM - 1510 (Great Bend, KS) 11471
KNNS-FM 15931*
KNNT-AM (Kennett, MO) Unable to locate
Knob Noster Item (Knob Noster, MO) 17233
KNOC-AM - 1450 (Natchitoches, LA) 12719
KNOD-FM - 105.3 (Harlan, IA) 10947
KNOE-AM - 101.9 (Monroe, LA) 12699
KNOE-FM - 101.9 (Monroe, LA) 12700
KNOE-TV - Channel 8 (Monroe, LA) 12701
KNOF-FM - 95.3 (St. Paul, MN) 16421
KNOI-AM 32912*
KNOK-FM 12530*
KNOM-AM - 780 (Nome, AK) 628
KNOM-FM - 96.1 (Nome, AK) 629
KNON-FM - 89.3 (Dallas, TX) 30210
KNOP-TV - Channel 2 (North Platte, NE) 18181
KNOR-AM - 1400 (Norman, OK) 25946
KNOS-FM 17268*
KNOT-AM - 1450 (Prescott, AZ) 852
KNOT-FM - 99.1 (Prescott, AZ) 853
Knot Theory and Its Ramifications (JKTR); Journal of
   (River Edge, NJ) 19516
Knotes (New York, NY) 22225
KNOW Atlanta Magazine (Atlanta, GA) 7024
KNOW-FM (St. Paul, MN) Unable to locate
Know Your World Extra (Stamford, CT) 5153

Knowledge, Creation, Diffusion, Utilization 13439*
Knowledge Engineeg; International Journal of Software Engineering and (River Edge, NJ) 19513
The Knowledge Engineering Review (Brooklyn, NY) 20327
Knowledge Magazine (Fort Worth, TX) *Unable to locate*
Knowledge Management (Irvine, CA) 2082
Knowledge, Technology & Policy (Carbondale, IL) 8118
KNOX-AM - 1310 (Grand Forks, ND) 24462
The Knox County Citizen (Fredericktown, OH) 25201
Knox County Daily News (Bicknell, IN) *Unable to locate*
Knox County News (Knox City, TX) 30653
KNOX-FM (Grand Forks, ND) *Unable to locate*
Knox Student (Galesburg, IL) 8905
The Knoxville Journal (Galesburg, IL) *Unable to locate*
The Knoxville Journal (Maryville, TN) *Ceased*
The Knoxville News-Sentinel (Knoxville, TN) 29280
KNPR-FM (Las Vegas, NV) *Unable to locate*
KNPT-AM - 1310 (Newport, OR) 26448
KNPT-FM 26451*
KNRO-AM - 1670 (Redding, CA) 2892
KNRR-TV - Channel 12 (Pembina, ND) 24532
KNRY-AM - 1240 (Sand City, CA) 3614
KNSD-TV - Channel 39 (San Diego, CA) 3305
KNSE-AM (Glendora, CA) *Unable to locate*
KNSG-FM - 94.7 (New Ulm, MN) 16216
KNSI-AM - 1450 (St. Cloud, MN) 16351
KNSN-AM (Chico, CA) *Unable to locate*
KNSN-FM 32886*
KNSP-AM (Staples, MN) *Unable to locate*
KNSR-FM - 88.9 (Collegeville, MN) 15808
KNSS-AM - 1240 (Wichita, KS) 11900
KNST-AM - 790 (Tucson, AZ) 987
KNSU-FM 12720*
KNSU-FM - 91.5 (Thibodaux, LA) 12861
KNTA-AM 3472*
KNTB-FM (Rifle, CO) *Unable to locate*
KNTI-FM (Lakeport, CA) *Unable to locate*
KNTL-FM (Oklahoma City, OK) *Unable to locate*
KNTN-FM - 102.7 (Moorhead, MN) 16192
KNTO-FM (Livingston, CA) *Unable to locate*
KNTR-AM (Ferndale, WA) *Unable to locate*
KNTS-AM (Abilene, TX) *Unable to locate*
KNTU-FM - 88.1 (Denton, TX) 30243
KNTV-TV - Channel 11 (San Jose, CA) 3551
KNTX-AM - 1410 (Bowie, TX) 29942
KNUC-FM 31358*
KNUE-FM - 101.5 (Tyler, TX) 31216
KNUI-AM - 900 (Kahului, HI) 7761
KNUI-FM - 99.9 (Kahului, HI) 7762
KNUJ-AM - 860 (New Ulm, MN) 16217
KNUJ-FM - 107.3 (New Ulm, MN) 16218
KNUS-AM (Lakewood, CO) *Unable to locate*
KNUU-AM - 970 (Las Vegas, NV) 18402
KNUZ-AM (Houston, TX) *Ceased*
KNVR-FM 1706*
KNWC-AM - 1270 (Sioux Falls, SD) 28979
KNWC-FM - 96.5 (Sioux Falls, SD) 28980
KNWD-FM - 91.7 (Natchitoches, LA) 12720
KNWR-FM 32680*
KNWS-AM - 101.9 (Waterloo, IA) 11293
KNWS-FM - 101.9 (Waterloo, IA) 11294
KNWX-AM - 1210 (Seattle, WA) 33065
KNWX-FM 33065*
KNWX-FM 33065*
KNWZ-AM (Palm Desert, CA) *Unable to locate*
KNX-AM - 1070 (Los Angeles, CA) 2464
KNX-FM 2449*
KNXN-AM (Tucson, AZ) *Unable to locate*
KNXR-FM (Rochester, MN) *Unable to locate*
KNXT 2450*
KNXT-TV - Channel 49 (Fresno, CA) 1978
KNXV-TV (Phoenix, AZ) *Unable to locate*
KNYD-FM - 90.5 (Tulsa, OK) 26155
KNYO-AM (Independence, CA) *Ceased*
KNZ-AM 26525*
KNZA-FM - 103.9 (Hiawatha, KS) 11493
KNZR-AM - 1560 (Bakersfield, CA) 1469
KNZZ-AM (Grand Junction, CO) *Unable to locate*
KO Magazine Superfight Color Special No. 1 (Ambler, PA) 26651
KOA-AM - 850 (Denver, CO) 4385
KOA-FM 4388*
KOAA-TV - Channel 5 & 30 (Pueblo, CO) 4607
KOAB-TV (Portland, OR) *Ceased*
KOAC-AM 31214*
KOAC-AM - 550 (Corvallis, OR) 26293
KOAC-TV (Portland, OR) *Ceased*
KOAI-FM 30206*
KOAI-TV 701*
KOAK-AM - 1080 (Red Oak, IA) 11173
KOAK-FM 11171*
KOAL-AM - 750 (Price, UT) 31395
KOAM-AM 11755*
KOAM-TV - Channel 7 (Pittsburg, KS) 11757

KOAP-TV 26534*
KOAQ-AM - 690 (Scottsbluff, NE) 18272
KOAQ-FM 4388*
KOAT-TV - Channel 7 (Albuquerque, NM) 19807
KOAZ-FM 843*
KOAZ-FM - 97.5 (Tucson, AZ) 988
KOB-TV - Channel 4 (Albuquerque, NM) 19808
KOBC-FM - 90.7 (Joplin, MO) 17145
KOBE-AM - 1450 (Las Cruces, NM) 19884
KOBF-TV - Channel 12 (Farmington, NM) 19850
KOBH-AM 28946*
KOBI-TV - Channel 5 (Medford, OR) 26425
KOBN-TV (Kailua, HI) *Unable to locate*
KOBO-AM (Yuba City, CA) *Unable to locate*
KOBR-TV - Channel 8 (Roswell, NM) 19922
KOCB-TV - Channel 34 (Oklahoma City, OK) 26007
KOCC-FM 2960*
KOCC-FM - 88.9 (Oklahoma City, OK) 26008
KOCE-TV - Channel 50 (Huntington Beach, CA) 2067
KOCE Viewers Guide (Huntington Beach, CA) 2063
KOCL-FM - 94.1 (San Diego, CA) 3306
KOCN-FM - 105.1 (Salinas, CA) 3073
KOCO-TV - Channel 5 (Oklahoma City, OK) 26009
KOCR-AM - 1310 (Joplin, MO) 17146
KOCR-TV (Cedar Rapids, IA) *Unable to locate*
KOCV-TV - Channel 36 (Odessa, TX) 30878
KOCY-FM - 105.3 (Jonesboro, AR) 1201
KODA-FM - 99.1 (Houston, TX) 30568
Kodaly Society of Canada, Alla Breve (Dartmouth, NS, Can.) 35548
KODE-TV - Channel 12 (Joplin, MO) 17147
KODI-AM - 1400 (Cody, WY) 34515
Kodiak Cablevision (Kodiak, AK) 618
Kodiak Daily Mirror (Kodiak, AK) 616
KODJ-FM 2449*
KODL-AM (The Dalles, OR) *Unable to locate*
KODM-FM - 97.9 (Midland, TX) 30823
KODS-FM - 103.7 (Reno, NV) 18433
KODY-AM - 1240 (North Platte, NE) 18182
KODZ-FM - 99.1 (Eugene, OR) 26343
KOEA-FM (Lafayette, LA) *Ceased*
KOEA-FM - 97.5 (Doniphan, MO) 17038
KOED-TV - Channel 11 (Tulsa, OK) 26156
KOEL-AM - 950 (Oelwein, IA) 11124
KOEL-FM - 92.3 (Waterloo, IA) 11295
KOET-TV - Channel 3 (Oklahoma City, OK) 26010
KOEZ-FM - 92.3 (Newton, KS) 11673
KOEZ 105.1 FM - 91.7, 105.1 (St. George, UT) 31419
KOFC-AM (Fayetteville, AR) *Unable to locate*
KOFE-AM 32912*
KOFE-AM - 1240 (St. Maries, ID) 7973
KOFI-AM - 1180 (Kalispell, MT) 17842
KOFI-FM - 103.9 (Kalispell, MT) 17843
KOFK-AM (Grants, NM) *Unable to locate*
KOFM-FM - 103.1 (Enid, OK) 25828
KOFO-AM - 1220 (Ottawa, KS) 11692
KOFX-FM - 92.3 (El Paso, TX) 30297
KOFY-AM (San Francisco, CA) *Ceased*
KOFY-TV 3473*
KOGA-AM - 930 (Ogallala, NE) 18190
KOGA-FM - 99.7 (Ogallala, NE) 18191
KOGM-FM - 107.1 (Opelousas, LA) 12792
KOGO-AM - 600 (San Diego, CA) 3307
KOGT-AM - 1600 (Orange, TX) 30889
KOHI-AM - 1600 (St. Helens, OR) 26564
KOHL-FM - 89.3 (Fremont, CA) 1940
KOHM-FM - 89.1 (Lubbock, TX) 30733
KOHO-AM (Honolulu, HI) *Unable to locate*
KOHS-FM - 91.7 (Orem, UT) 31386
KOHT-FM - 98.3 (Tucson, AZ) 989
KOHU-AM - 1360 (Hermiston, OR) 26370
KOHU-FM 26371*
Koi USA (San Diego, CA) *Unable to locate*
KOIA-TV 11146*
KOIL-AM - 1180 (Omaha, NE) 18224
KOIN-TV - Channel 6 (Portland, OR) 26533
KOIR-FM - 88.5 (Edinburg, TX) 30272
KOIT-AM - 1260 (San Francisco, CA) 3494
KOIT-FM - 96.5 (San Francisco, CA) 3495
KOJC-FM (Cedar Rapids, IA) *Unable to locate*
KOJJ-FM - 100.5 (Reseda, CA) 2918
KOJM-AM - 610 (Havre, MT) 17814
KOJY-FM 1984*
KOJY-FM - 106.9 (Bloomfield, IA) 10623
KOKA-AM (Shreveport, LA) *Unable to locate*
KOKB-AM - 1580 (Ponca City, OK) 26042
KOKC-AM (Tulsa, OK) *Unable to locate*
KOKE-AM - 1370 (Austin, TX) 29874
KOKE-FM 29869*
KOKE-FM (Austin, TX) *Unable to locate*
KOKF-FM - 90.9 (Oklahoma City, OK) 26011
KOKH-TV - Channel 25 (Oklahoma City, OK) 26012
KOKI-TV - Channel 23 (Tulsa, OK) 26157
KOKK-AM - 1210 (Huron, SD) 28872
KOKL-AM - 1240 (Okmulgee, OK) 26025
KOKO-AM - 1450 (Warrensburg, MO) 17672
Kokomo Perspective (Kokomo, IN) 10240
Kokomo Tribune (Kokomo, IN) 10241

KOKS-FM - 89.5 (Poplar Bluff, MO) 17361
KOKX-AM - 1310 (Keokuk, IA) 11014
KOKX-FM - 95.3 (Keokuk, IA) 11015
KOKY-AM 1244*
KOKY-AM 1244*
KOKY-FM - 102.1 (Little Rock, AR) 1249
KOKZ-FM - 105.7 (Waterloo, IA) 11296
KOLA (Montreal, QC, Can.) 37148
KOLA-FM (Riverside, CA) *Unable .to locate*
KOLD-TV - Channel 13 (Tucson, AZ) 990
KOLE-AM - 1340 (Beaumont, TX) 29907
KOLJ-AM 30965*
KOLL-FM 34528*
KOLL-FM (Little Rock, AR) *Unable to locate*
KOLM-AM - 1520 (Rochester, MN) 16316
KOLN-TV - Channel 10 (Lincoln, NE) 18140
KOLO-TV - Channel 8 (Reno, NV) 18434
KOLR-TV - Channel 10 (Springfield, MO) 17624
KOLS-FM - 95.5 (Dodge City, KS) 11418
KOLT-AM - 1320 (Scottsbluff, NE) 18273
KOLT-FM - 105.7 (Flagstaff, AZ) 702
KOLU-FM - 90.1 (Pasco, WA) 32882
KOLX-FM (Barling, AR) *Unable to locate*
KOLY-AM - 1300 (Mobridge, SD) 28907
KOLY-FM - 99.5 (Mobridge, SD) 28908
KOLZ-FM (Fayetteville, AR) *Unable to locate*
KOMA-AM (Oklahoma City, OK) *Unable to locate*
KOMA-FM (Moore, OK) *Unable to locate*
KOMB-FM - 103.9 (Fort Scott, KS) 11445
KOMC-AM - 1220 (Branson, MO) 16922
KOMC-FM 17297*
KOMC-FM - 100.1 (Branson, MO) 16923
KOMC-TV 11682*
KOME-FM (San Jose, CA) *Unable to locate*
KOMO-AM - 1000 (Seattle, WA) 33066
KOMO-TV - Channel 4 (Seattle, WA) 33067
KOMP-FM - 92.3 (Las Vegas, NV) 18403
KOMS-FM 26214*
KOMU-TV - Channel 8 (Columbia, MO) 17019
KOMW-AM (Omak, WA) *Unable to locate*
KOMW-FM (Omak, WA) *Unable to locate*
KOMX-FM - 100.3 (Pampa, TX) 30902
KOMY-AM (Watsonville, CA) *Unable to locate*
KONA-AM - 610 (Pasco, WA) 32883
KONA-FM - 105.3 (Pasco, WA) 32884
KONA-TV 7736*
Konawa Leader (Konawa, OK) 25880
KONE-AM 18437*
KONE-FM - 101.1 (Lubbock, TX) 30734
KONG-AM 7782*
KONG-FM 7783*
KONG-FM 1966*
KONO-AM - 860 (San Antonio, TX) 31064
KONO-FM - 101.1 (San Antonio, TX) 31065
KONO-TV 31070*
KONP-AM - 1450 (Port Angeles, WA) 32889
KONQ-FM - 91.9 (Dodge City, KS) 11419
KONY-AM (St. George, UT) *Unable to locate*
KONY-FM - 99.9 (St. George, UT) 31420
KOOC-FM 17988*
KOOD-TV - Channel 9 (Bunker Hill, KS) 11367
KOOG-TV (Ogden, UT) *Unable to locate*
KOOI-FM - 106.5 (Jacksonville, TX) 30618
KOOJ-FM (Baton Rouge, LA) *Unable to locate*
KOOK-FM 17739*
KOOK-TV 17744*
KOOL-AM 26160*
KOOL-AM 835*
KOOL-FM 26161*
KOOL-FM 26018*
KOOL-FM - 94.5 (Phoenix, AZ) 829
KOOL-FM - 93.9 (Ottawa, ON, Can.) 36297
KOOL-TV 837*
KOOO-AM 18212*
KOOQ-AM - 1410 (North Platte, NE) 18183
Kootenai Cable Inc. 7847*
Kootenai Cable Inc. (Libby, MT) 17854
Kootenai Valley Eagle (Libby, MT) *Ceased*
The Kootenay Advertiser (Cranbrook, BC, Can.) 34935
Kootenay Business Magazine (Cranbrook, BC, Can.) 34936
Kootenay Cable Ltd. (Fernie, BC, Can.) 34955
KOPA-AM (Scottsdale, AZ) *Unable to locate*
KOPB-TV - Channel 10 (Portland, OR) 26534
KOPN-FM - 89.5 (Columbia, MO) 17020
KOPO-AM 978*
KOPO-FM 989*
KOPR-FM - 94.1 (Butte, MT) 17764
KOPY-AM - 1070 (Alice, TX) 29679
KOPY-FM - 92.1 (Alice, TX) 29680
KOQL-FM - 106.1 (Columbia, MO) 17021
KOQO-AM - 790 (Fresno, CA) 1979
KOQO-FM - 101.9 (Fresno, CA) 1980
KORA-FM - 98.3 (Bryan, TX) 29981
KORC-AM 31274*
KORC-AM - 820 (Waldport, OR) 26608
KORD-AM 32880*
KORD-FM - 102.7 (Pasco, WA) 32885

KQAD-AM - 800 (Luverne, MN) 16016
KQAI-FM 30019*
KQAK-FM - 105.7 (Bend, OR) 26249
KQAL-FM - 89.5 (Winona, MN) 16534
KQAQ-AM 16315*
KQAR-AM - 100.3 (Little Rock, AR) 1250
KQAY-FM - 92.7 (Tucumcari, NM) 19972
KQAZ-FM - 101.7 (Show Low, AZ) 882
KQBE-FM - 103.1 (Ellensburg, WA) 32751
KQBR-FM (Davis, CA) Unable to locate
KQCA-TV (Rancho Cordova, CA) Unable to locate
KQCD-TV - Channel 7 (Dickinson, ND) 24400
KQCR-FM (Cedar Rapids, IA) Unable to locate
KQCS-FM (Davenport, IA) Ceased
KQCV-AM - 800 (Oklahoma City, OK) 26013
KQCV-FM - 95.1 (Shawnee, OK) 26068
KQDF-FM 11469*
KQDI-AM - 1450 (Spokane, WA) 33124
KQDJ-AM - 1400 (Jamestown, ND) 24480
KQDJ-FM 24483*
KQDJ-FM - 101.1 (Valley City, ND) 24546
KQDS-AM 15847*
KQDS-AM 24546*
KQDS-FM - 94.9 (Duluth, MN) 15850
KQDY-FM - 94.5 (Bismarck, ND) 24370
KQED-FM - 88.5 (San Francisco, CA) 3498
KQED-TV (San Francisco, CA) Unable to locate
KQEG-TV - Channel 23 (La Crosse, WI) 33887
KQEN-AM - 1240 (Roseburg, OR) 26558
KQEO-AM (Albuquerque, NM) Unable to locate
KQEQ-AM - 1210 (Fresno, CA) 1981
KQEW-FM - 102.3 (Fordyce, AR) 1137
KQEX-FM - 100.3 (Fortuna, CA) 1931
KQEZ-FM (Scottsdale, AZ) Unable to locate
KQFC-FM - 97.9 (Boise, ID) 7829
KQFC-FM - 97.9 (Boise, ID) 7828
KQFM-FM - 100.5 (Hermiston, OR) 26371
KQFX-FM (Austin, TX) Ceased
KQFX-TV - Channel 11 (Columbia, MO) 17023
KQHC-FM - 92.7 (Burns, OR) 26260
KQHN-AM - 1510 (Beaumont, TX) 29908
KQHT-FM (Grand Forks, ND) Unable to locate
KQIK-AM (Lakeview, OR) Unable to locate
KQIK-FM (Lakeview, OR) Unable to locate
KQIL-AM 4496*
KQIN-AM 33053*
KQIP-FM 30819*
KQIT-FM 1261*
KQIX 31188*
KQIX-FM 4490*
KQIZ-FM (Amarillo, TX) Unable to locate
KQKD-AM - 1380 (Redfield, SD) 28954
KQKI-FM - 95.3 (Morgan City, LA) 12713
KQKQ-FM - 98.5 (Omaha, NE) 18226
KQKS-FM - 107.5 (Denver, CO) 4387
KQKY-FM - 105.9 (Kearney, NE) 18066
KQLA-FM - 103.5 (Junction City, KS) 11523
KQLD-FM (New Orleans, LA) Unable to locate
KQLI-FM 25897*
KQLL-AM - 1430 (Tulsa, OK) 26160
KQLL-FM - 106.1 (Tulsa, OK) 26161
KQLM-FM - 107.9 (Odessa, TX) 30882
KQLO-AM (Reno, NV) Unable to locate
KQLT-FM (Casper, WY) Unable to locate
KQLV-FM (Little Rock, AR) Unable to locate
KQLX-AM - 890 (Lisbon, ND) 24494
KQLX-FM - 106.1 (Lisbon, ND) 24495
KQLZ-FM (Culver City, CA) Unable to locate
KQMA-FM - 92.5 (Phillipsburg, KS) 11750
KQMC-FM - 102.3 (Brinkley, AR) 1065
KQMD-AM 1971*
KQMG-AM - 1220 (Independence, IA) 10962
KQMG-FM - 95.3 (Independence, IA) 10963
KQMJ-FM 26164*
KQMN-FM - 91.1 (Moorhead, MN) 16193
KQMO-FM 17636*
KQMQ-FM (Honolulu, HI) Unable to locate
KQMS-AM - 1400 (Redding, CA) 2893
KQMT-FM 4151*
KQMX-FM (Rolla, MO) Unable to locate
KQNA-AM - 1130 (Prescott Valley, AZ) 858
KQNG-AM - 570 (Lihue, HI) 7782
KQNG-FM - 93.5 (Lihue, HI) 7783
KQNK-AM - 106.7 (Norton, KS) 11679
KQNM-FM 19861*
KQNN-FM 29680*
KQNS-FM - 95.5 (Salina, KS) 11787
KQNV-FM (Reno, NV) Ceased
KQOD-FM - 100.1 (Stockton, CA) 3815
KQOK-FM 610*
KQPT-FM (Rancho Cordova, CA) Unable to locate
KQPW-FM 1980*
KQQK-FM (Houston, TX) Unable to locate
KQQL-FM - 107.9 (Minneapolis, MN) 16152
KQQQ-AM - 1150 (Pullman, WA) 32912
KQQQ-FM 32911*
KQRC-FM - 98.9 (Westwood, KS) 11873
KQRN-FM - 107.3 (Mitchell, SD) 28904
KQRO-AM 30116*

KQRO-FM 30117*
KQRS-AM 16146*
KQRS-FM (Minneapolis, MN) Ceased
KQRZ-FM 574*
KQSA-AM 31019*
KQSB-AM (Santa Barbara, CA) Unable to locate
KQSK-FM - 97.5 (Chadron, NE) 17976
KQSN-FM - 92.9 (Yakima, WA) 33233
KQSP-FM 33119*
KQSR-FM - 94.7 (Oklahoma City, OK) 26014
KQSS-FM - 98.3 (Miami, AZ) 753
KQST-FM (Sedona, AZ) Unable to locate
KQSW-FM - 96.5 (Rock Springs, WY) 34583
KQTL-AM (Tucson, AZ) Unable to locate
KQTV-TV - Channel 2 (St. Joseph, MO) 17398
KQTY-AM - 1490 (Borger, TX) 29938
KQTZ-FM - 105.9 (Hobart, OK) 25867
KQUA-FM 17263*
KQUS-FM - 97.5 (Hot Springs, AR) 1186
KQUY-FM 17763*
KQV-AM - 1410 (Pittsburgh, PA) 27860
KQVO-FM - 97.7 (Calexico, CA) 1638
KQWB-AM - 1660 (Fargo, ND) 24425
KQWB-FM - 98.7 (Fargo, ND) 24426
KQWC-AM - 1570 (Webster City, IA) 11315
KQWC-FM - 95.7 (Webster City, IA) 11316
KQXI-AM (Englewood, CO) Unable to locate
KQXK-AM (Springdale, AR) Unable to locate
KQXL-FM - 106.5 (Baton Rouge, LA) 12509
KQXT-FM - 101.9 (San Antonio, TX) 31067
KQXX-FM - 98.5 (McAllen, TX) 30798
KQXY-FM (Nederland, TX) Unable to locate
KQYB-FM - 98.3 (Spring Grove, MN) 16456
KQYN-AM - 1250 (Twentynine Palms, CA) 3966
KQYX-AM - 1450 (Joplin, MO) 17148
KRAC-AM 19759*
KRAD-AM 24464*
KRAE-AM - 1480 (Cheyenne, WY) 34509
KRAF-AM 26554*
KRAF-AM (Holdenville, OK) Unable to locate
KRAI-AM - 550 (Craig, CO) 4296
KRAI-FM - 93.7 (Craig, CO) 4297
KRAK-AM - 1470 (Hesperia, CA) 2049
KRAK-FM - 98.5 (Sacramento, CA) 3046
KRAL-AM - 1240 (Rawlins, WY) 34574
KRAN-AM (Altus, AR) Unable to locate
KRAO-FM - 102.5 (Colfax, WA) 32723
KRAV-FM - 96.5 (Tulsa, OK) 26162
KRAW-FM 12649*
KRAY-AM 29711*
KRAY-FM - 103.5 (Salinas, CA) 3074
KRAZ-FM (Farmington, NM) Unable to locate
KRBA-AM - 1340 (Lufkin, TX) 30743
KRBB-FM (Wichita, KS) Unable to locate
KRBB-TV 12877*
KRBC-TV - Channel 9 (Abilene, TX) 29665
KRBD-FM - 105.9 (Ketchikan, AK) 613
KRBE-FM - 104 (Houston, TX) 30572
KRBI-AM - 1310 (St. Peter, MN) 16432
KRBI-FM - 105.5 (St. Peter, MN) 16433
KRBK-TV 3045*
KRBL-FM (Albuquerque, NM) Unable to locate
KRBM-FM (Pendleton, OR) Unable to locate
KRBR-FM - 102.5 (Duluth, MN) 15851
KRBT-AM - 1340 (Eveleth, MN) 15885
KRBV-FM - 100.3 (Dallas, TX) 30212
KRBW-FM - 90.5 (Ottawa, KS) 11693
KRBZ-FM - 96.5 (Westwood, KS) 11874
KRCB-TV - Channel 22 (Rohnert Park, CA) 2962
KRCC-FM - 91.5 (Colorado Springs, CO) 4275
KRCD-AM 7949*
KRCD-FM - 1490 (Chubbuck, ID) 7843
KRCG-TV - Channel 13 (Jefferson City, MO) 17140
KRCH-FM - 101.7 (Rochester, MN) 16317
KRCK-AM (Los Angeles, CA) Unable to locate
KRCL-FM (Salt Lake City, UT) Unable to locate
KRCO-AM - 690 (Prineville, OR) 26551
KRCR-TV - Channel 7 (Redding, CA) 2894
KRCS-FM - 93.1 (Rapid City, SD) 28948
KRCU-FM - 90.9 (Cape Girardeau, MO) 16953
KRCV-AM 18431*
KRCV-AM (Orlando, FL) Ceased
KRCX-AM (Sacramento, CA) Unable to locate
KRCY-FM (Lake Havasu City, AZ) Unable to locate
KRDD-AM - 1320 (Roswell, NM) 19925
KRDG-AM (Sacramento, CA) Ceased
KRDG-FM - 105.3 (Redding, CA) 2895
KRDI-FM 10760*
KRDM-FM (Ardmore, OK) Unable to locate
KRDO-AM - 1240 (Colorado Springs, CO) 4276
KRDO-FM - 95.1 (Colorado Springs, CO) 4277
KRDO-TV - Channel 13 (Colorado Springs, CO) 4278
KRDS-FM - 1190 (Phoenix, AZ) 836
KRDU-AM - 1130 (Dinuba, CA) 1830
KRDZ-AM - 1440 (Wray, CO) 4693
KRDZ-FM 4695*
KRE-AM 3504*
KRE-FM 3471*
KREB-AM - 1190 (Fayetteville, AR) 1130

Krebs Cycle Productions (Eugene, OR) 37979
KREC-FM (Cedar City, UT) Unable to locate
KRED-AM 1901*
KRED-FM - 92.3 (Eureka, CA) 1904
KREE-AM 19929*
KREG-TV (Carbondale, CO) Unable to locate
KREI-AM - 800 (Farmington, MO) 17055
KREK-FM - 104.9 (Bristow, OK) 25770
KREL-AM 18393*
KREL-AM - 1420 (California, MO) 16936
KREM-TV - Channel 2 (Spokane, WA) 33125
KREN-TV - Channel 27 (Reno, NV) 18438
KREO-FM 3738*
KREP-FM - 92.1 (Belleville, KS) 11360
Kress Chronicle (Kress, TX) 30654
KREW-AM 33238*
KREW-FM 33237*
KREX-TV - Channel 5 (Grand Junction, CO) 4493
KREZ-TV - Channel 6 (Durango, CO) 4405
KRFA-FM - 91.7 (Pullman, WA) 32913
KRFD-AM 2517*
KRFD-FM 2518*
KRFD-FM 31334*
KRFH-AM - 610 (Arcata, CA) 1432
KRFI-AM 17301*
KRFI-FM 17302*
KRFM-FM (Show Low, AZ) Unable to locate
KRFS-AM - 1600 (Superior, NE) 18290
KRFS-FM (Superior, NE) Unable to locate
KRFX-FM - 103.5 (Denver, CO) 4388
KRGE-AM - 1290 (Weslaco, TX) 31279
KRGI-AM - 1430 (Grand Island, NE) 18029
KRGI-FM - 96.5 (Grand Island, NE) 18030
KRGK-FM 16961*
KRGN-FM - 103.1 (Amarillo, TX) 29716
KRGO-AM 1981*
KRGO-AM (Fresno, CA) Ceased
KRGO-FM - 107.9 (Magna, UT) 31365
KRGS-AM - 690 (Grand Junction, CO) 4494
KRGT-FM (Austin, TX) Ceased
KRGV-AM 31279*
KRGV-TV - Channel 5 (Weslaco, TX) 31280
KRHD-AM - 1350 (Duncan, OK) 25801
KRHD-FM - 102.3 (Duncan, OK) 25802
KRHS-FM - 90.1 (Overland, MO) 17327
KRHW-AM - 1520 (Sikeston, MO) 17586
KRIA-AM 31062*
KRIC-FM 7966*
KRIG-AM 30883*
KRIJ-FM 1700*
KRIL-AM - 1410 (Odessa, TX) 30883
KRIN-TV - Channel 32 (Johnston, IA) 11009
KRIO-AM - 910 (Edinburg, TX) 30273
KRIS-TV - Channel 6 (Corpus Christi, TX) 30093
KRIT-FM 10908*
KRIV-TV (Houston, TX) Unable to locate
KRIX-FM 30797*
KRIZ-AM - 1420 (Seattle, WA) 33069
KRJB-FM - 106.3 (Ada, MN) 15697
KRJC-FM - 95.3 (Elko, NV) 18339
KRJF-AM 17862*
KRJM-FM - 101.5 (Mahnomen, MN) 16024
KRJT-AM 29942*
KRJT-AM Feb. 2000 29942*
KRJY-FM - 96.3 (St. Louis, MO) 17547
KRKC-AM - 1490 (King City, CA) 2104
KRKC-FM - 102.1 (King City, CA) 2105
KRKD-FM 2455*
KRKI-AM (Estes Park, CO) Unable to locate
KRKK-AM - 1360 (Rock Springs, WY) 34584
KRKM-FM (Granby, CO) Unable to locate
KRKN-FM - 104.3 (Ottumwa, IA) 11144
KRKO-AM - 1380 (Everett, WA) 32762
KRKQ-FM - 98.3 (Urbandale, IA) 11279
KRKS-AM (Englewood, CO) Unable to locate
KRKT-AM - 990 (Albany, OR) 26211
KRKT-FM - 99.9 (Albany, OR) 26212
KRKU-FM - 98.5 (McCook, NE) 18158
KRKX-FM - 94.1 (Billings, MT) 17742
KRKY-AM (Granby, CO) Unable to locate
KRKZ-FM - 93.5 (Altus, OK) 25735
KRLA-AM - 870 (Glendale, CA) 2019
KRLA-AM - 1110 (Los Angeles, CA) 2466
KRLB-FM (Lubbock, TX) Unable to locate
KRLC-AM - 1350 (Lewiston, ID) 7901
KRLD-AM - 1080 (Arlington, TX) 29740
KRLD-TV 30199*
KRLF-FM - 88.5 (Pullman, WA) 32914
KRLI-FM - 97.5 (Carrollton, MO) 16958
KRLL-AM (Albuquerque, NM) Unable to locate
KRLN-AM - 1400 (Canon City, CO) 4214
KRLN-FM 4215*
KRLS-FM (Pella, IA) Unable to locate
KRLT-FM (South Lake Tahoe, CA) Unable to locate
KRLV-AM (Las Vegas, NV) Unable to locate
KRLW-AM - 1320 (Pocahontas, AR) 1320
KRLW-FM - 106.3 (Pocahontas, AR) 1321
KRMA-TV - Channel 6 (Denver, CO) 4389
KRMD-AM - 1340 (Shreveport, LA) 12830

Numbers cited in bold after listings are entry numbers rather than page numbers.

KRMD-FM - 101.1 (Shreveport, LA) **12831**
KRME-AM **30452***
KRMG-AM - 740 (Tulsa, OK) **26163**
KRMH-AM - 1230 (Colorado Springs, CO) **4279**
KRMH-FM - 93.5 (Colorado Springs, CO) **4280**
KRMK-FM **26187***
KRML-AM - 1410 (Carmel, CA) **1674**
KRMO-AM - 990 (Monett, MO) **17295**
KRMP-AM - 103.5 (Anadarko, OK) **25741**
KRMS-AM - 1150 (Osage Beach, MO) **17322**
KRMT-FM - 103.7 (Anadarko, OK) *
KRMT-TV - Channel 41 (Arvada, CO) **4139**
KRMW-AM (Santa Ana, CA) *Unable to locate*
KRMX-AM - 107.1 (Pueblo, CO) **4608**
KRNA-FM (Iowa City, IA) *Unable to locate*
KRNE-FM - 91.5 (Lincoln, NE) **18142**
KRNE-TV - Channel 12 (Merriman, NE) **18161**
KRNI-AM - 1010 (Mason City, IA) **11078**
KRNL-FM - 89.7 (Mount Vernon, IA) **11100**
KRNN-AM **31062***
KRNO-FM (Reno, NV) *Unable to locate*
KRNQ-FM/Q-102 **10832***
KRNR-AM - 1490 (Roseburg, OR) **26559**
KRNS-AM **26261***
KRNT-AM - 1350 (Des Moines, IA) **10831**
KRNT-TV **10820***
KRNU-FM - 90.3 (Lincoln, NE) **18143**
KRNV-FM - 102.1 (Reno, NV) **18439**
KRNV-TV - Channel 4 (Reno, NV) **18440**
KROA-FM - 95.7 (Doniphan, NE) **18001**
KROB-AM - 1510 (Robstown, TX) **30986**
KROB-FM **30095***
KROC-AM - 1340 (Rochester, MN) **16318**
KROC-FM - 106.9 (Rochester, MN) **16319**
KROC-TV **16320***
KROD-AM - 600 (El Paso, TX) **30299**
KROD-TV **30288***
KROD-TV **30359***
KROE-AM - 930 (Sheridan, WY) **34589**
KROE-FM **34592***
KROF-AM (Abbeville, LA) *Unable to locate*
KROF-FM (Abbeville, LA) *Unable to locate*
KROG-AM (Redding, CA) *Unable to locate*
KROG-FM - 96.9 (Grants Pass, OR) **26364**
KROK-FM **12832***
KROK-FM - 92.1 (Deridder, LA) **12566**
KRON-TV - Channel 4 (San Francisco, CA) **3499**
KROO-FM (Breckenridge, TX) *Ceased*
KROP-AM - 1300 (Brawley, CA) **1597**
KROQ-FM - 106.7 (Burbank, CA) **1629**
KROR-FM (Yucca Valley, CA) *Unable to locate*
KROS-AM - 1340 (Clinton, IA) **10713**
KROU-FM - 105.7 (Norman, OK) **25947**
KROW-AM **3468***
KROX-AM - 1260 (Crookston, MN) **15821**
KROX-FM - 101.5 (Austin, TX) **29876**
KROY-AM - 1590 (Victorville, CA) **4037**
KROZ-FM **31209***
KRPL-AM - 1400 (Moscow, ID) **7923**
KRPM-AM **33059***
KRPQ-FM - 104.9 (Rohnert Park, CA) **2963**
KRPV-TV - Channel 27 (Roswell, NM) **19926**
KRPX-AM - 1080 (Price, UT) **31397**
KRQE-FM (Albuquerque, NM) *Unable to locate*
KRQK-FM (Santa Maria, CA) *Unable to locate*
KRQQ-FM - 93.7 (Tucson, AZ) **992**
KRQR-FM **3490***
KRQS-FM **4592***
KRQT-FM **30575***
KRQU-FM (Laramie, WY) *Unable to locate*
KRQZ-FM **25925***
KRRB-FM **24402***
KRRC-FM - 104.1 (Portland, OR) **26539**
KRRG-FM - 98.1 (Laredo, TX) **30677**
KRRI-FM (Boulder City, NV) *Unable to locate*
KRRO-FM - 103.7 (Sioux Falls, SD) **28981**
KRRP-AM - 950 (Coushatta, LA) **12553**
KRRQ-FM - 95.5 (Lafayette, LA) **12631**
KRRR-AM **19929***
KRRR-FM - 104.9 (Cheyenne, WY) **34510**
KRRS-AM - 1460 (Santa Rosa, CA) **3740**
KRRT-TV (San Antonio, TX) *Unable to locate*
KRRU-AM (Manitou Springs, CO) *Unable to locate*
KRRV-AM **12462***
KRRV-FM - 100.3 (Alexandria, LA) **12467**
KRRW-FM **30193***
KRRX-FM - 106.1 (Redding, CA) **2896**
KRRZ-AM - 1390 (Minot, ND) **24513**
KRSA-AM - 580 (Petersburg, AK) **633**
KRSB-FM - 103.1 (Roseburg, OR) **26560**
KRSC-AM (Othello, WA) *Unable to locate*
KRSD-AM **28951***
KRSD-FM - 88.1 (Sioux Falls, SD) **28982**
KRSE-FM - 105.7 (Yakima, WA) **33234**
KRSH-FM **17327***
KRSJ-FM - 100.5 (Durango, CO) **4406**
KRSL-AM - 990 (Russell, KS) **11774**
KRSN-AM - 1490 (Los Alamos, NM) **19895**

KRSO-AM (Redlands, CA) *Unable to locate*
KRSP-AM **31452***
KRSP-FM - 103.5 (Salt Lake City, UT) **31455**
KRSR-FM **30217***
KRST-AM - 92.3 (Albuquerque, NM) **19810**
KRSV-AM - 1210 (Afton, WY) **34475**
KRSV-FM - 98.7 (Afton, WY) **34476**
KRSY-AM - 1230 (Alamogordo, NM) **19760**
KRSY-FM - 92.7 (Alamogordo, NM) **19761**
KRTA-AM - 610 (Medford, OR) **26426**
KRTH-AM **1624***
KRTH-FM - 101.1 (Los Angeles, CA) **2467**
KRTN-AM - 1490 (Raton, NM) **19911**
KRTR-FM - 96.3 (Honolulu, HI) **7750**
KRTS-FM - 92.1 (Houston, TX) **30573**
KRTV-TV - Channel 3 (Great Falls, MT) **17804**
KRTY-FM - 95.3 (San Jose, CA) **3552**
KRTZ-FM - 98.7 (Cortez, CO) **4292**
KRUA-AM - 88.1 (Anchorage, AK) **546**
KRUB-FM (Boise, ID) *Unable to locate*
KRUE-FM - 92.1 (Owatonna, MN) **16255**
KRUF-FM - 94.5 (Shreveport, LA) **12832**
KRUI-AM - 1490 (Ruidoso Downs, NM) **19931**
KRUI-FM - 89.7 (Iowa City, IA) **10993**
KRUN-AM (Ballinger, TX) *Unable to locate*
KRUS-AM - 1490 (Ruston, LA) **12810**
KRUS-FM **12811***
KRUU-FM **11279***
KRUZ-FM (Santa Barbara, CA) *Unable to locate*
KRVA-AM **30215***
KRVA-FM **30782***
KRVC-AM **3035***
KRVE-FM **3552***
KRVE-FM - 96.1 (Baton Rouge, LA) **12510**
KRVI-FM - 95.1 (Fargo, ND) **24428**
KRVI-FM - 95.1 (Fargo, ND) **24427**
KRVM-FM - 91.9 (Eugene, OR) **26345**
KRVN-AM - 880 (Lexington, NE) **18075**
KRVN-FM - 93.1 (Lexington, NE) **18076**
KRVQ-FM - 102.1 (Shreveport, LA) **12833**
KRVR-FM - 105.5 (Modesto, CA) **2570**
KRVV-FM - 100.1 (Monroe, LA) **12702**
KRVZ-AM - 1400 (Springerville, AZ) **894**
KRWA-FM (Waldron, AR) *Unable to locate*
KRWB-AM (Roseau, MN) *Unable to locate*
KRWC-AM - 1360 (Buffalo, MN) **15779**
KRWG-FM - 90.7 (Las Cruces, NM) **19885**
KRWG-TV - Channel 22 (Las Cruces, NM) **19886**
KRWM-FM (Bellevue, WA) *Unable to locate*
KRWN-FM - 93 (Farmington, NM) **19852**
KRWQ-FM - 100.3 (Medford, OR) **26427**
KRWR-FM (Vienna, VA) *Unable to locate*
KRWV-FM - 99.5 (Emporia, KS) **11434**
KRX-AM - 1050 (Lawton, OK) **25895**
KRXK-AM (Rexburg, ID) *Unable to locate*
KRXL-FM - 94.5 (Kirksville, MO) **17231**
KRXO-FM (Oklahoma City, OK) *Unable to locate*
KRXQ-FM - 93.7 (Sacramento, CA) **3047**
KRXV-FM (Los Angeles, CA) *Ceased*
KRXX-AM **16157***
KRXX-FM **31259***
KRXX-FM - 101.1 (Kodiak, AK) **619**
KRXY-FM (Denver, CO) *Unable to locate*
KRYD-FM - 105 (Grand Junction, CO) **4495**
KRYK-FM (Chinook, MT) *Unable to locate*
KRYS-AM **30087***
KRYS-FM - 99.1 (Corpus Christi, TX) **30094**
KRYT-FM (Pueblo, CO) *Unable to locate*
KRZA-FM - 88.7 (Alamosa, CO) **4136**
KRZE-AM (Farmington, NM) *Unable to locate*
KRZE-FM (Ontario, CA) *Unable to locate*
KRZI-AM - 1580 (Waco, TX) **31260**
KRZK-FM - 106.3 (Branson, MO) **16924**
KRZN-AM (Denver, CO) *Ceased*
KRZQ-FM (Reno, NV) *Unable to locate*
KRZR-FM (Fresno, CA) *Unable to locate*
KRZY-AM (Albuquerque, NM) *Unable to locate*
KRZY-FM - 105.9 (Albuquerque, NM) **19811**
KRZZ-FM - 96.3 (Wichita, KS) **11902**
KSAB-FM - 99.9 (Corpus Christi, TX) **30095**
KSAC-AM **37640***
KSAC-AM (Reno, NV) *Unable to locate*
KSAH-AM - 720 (San Antonio, TX) **31068**
KSAJ-FM - 98.5 (Salina, KS) **11788**
KSAL-AM - 1150 (Salina, KS) **11789**
KSAM-AM **30598***
KSAN-AM (San Francisco, CA) *Unable to locate*
KSAQ-FM - 96.1 (San Antonio, TX) **31069**
KSAR-FM - 92.3 (Salem, AR) **1336**
KSAS-TV - Channel 24 (Wichita, KS) **11903**
KSAT-TV - Channel 12 (San Antonio, TX) **31070**
KSAU-FM - 90.1 (Nacogdoches, TX) **30854**
KSAX-TV - Channel 42 (Alexandria, MN) **15716**
KSAY-FM **10744***
KSAY-FM - 98.5 (Fort Bragg, CA) **1924**
KSAZ-TV - Channel 10 (Phoenix, AZ) **837**
KSBC-FM - 90.1 (Hot Springs, AR) **1187**
KSBH-FM - 94.9 (Natchitoches, LA) **12721**
KSBI-TV (Billings, MT) *Ceased*

KSBI-TV - Channel 52 (Oklahoma City, OK) **26015**
KSBJ-FM - 89.3 (Humble, TX) **30592**
KSBL-FM - 101.7 (Santa Barbara, CA) **3667**
KSBN-AM (Spokane, WA) *Unable to locate*
KSBQ-AM (Santa Maria, CA) *Unable to locate*
KSBR-FM - 88.5 (Mission Viejo, CA) **2560**
KSBT-FM **4637***
KSBW-TV - Channel 8 (Salinas, CA) **3075**
KSBY-TV - Channel 6 (San Luis Obispo, CA) **3573**
KSBZ-FM - 103.1 (Sitka, AK) **640**
KSCA-FM - 101.9 (Glendale, CA) **2020**
KSCB-AM (Liberal, KS) *Unable to locate*
KSCB-FM (Liberal, KS) *Unable to locate*
KSCC-FM **1056***
KSCE-TV - Channel 38 (El Paso, TX) **30300**
KSCH-FM - 95.9 (Sulphur Springs, TX) **31167**
KSCI-TV - Channel 18 (Los Angeles, CA) **2468**
KSCJ-AM - 1360 (Sioux City, IA) **11219**
KSCL-FM - 91.3 (Shreveport, LA) **12834**
KSCM-FM **17104***
KSCN-FM - 96.9 (Mount Pleasant, TX) **30842**
KSCO-AM - 1080 (Santa Cruz, CA) **3691**
KSCQ-FM - 92.9 (Silver City, NM) **19957**
KSCR-AM **15748***
KSCR-FM - 93.5 (Benson, MN) **15749**
KSCS-FM - 96.3 (Arlington, TX) **29741**
KSCU-FM - 103.3 (Santa Clara, CA) **3677**
KSCV-FM **18065***
KSD-FM (St. Louis, MO) *Unable to locate*
KSD-TV **17548***
KSDA-FM **2953***
KSDB-FM - 91.9 (Manhattan, KS) **11635**
KSDJ-FM - 90.7 (Brookings, SD) **28824**
KSDK-TV - Channel 5 (St. Louis, MO) **17548**
KSDL-FM - 92.1 (Sedalia, MO) **17573**
KSDM-FM - 104.1 (International Falls, MN) **15970**
KSDN-AM - 930 (Aberdeen, SD) **28798**
KSDN-FM - 94.1 (Aberdeen, SD) **28799**
KSDO-AM - 1130 (San Diego, CA) **3313**
KSDO-FM **3306***
KSDP-AM - 830 (Sand Point, AK) **635**
KSDR-AM - 1480 (Watertown, SD) **29023**
KSDR-FM - 92.9 (Watertown, SD) **29024**
KSDS-FM - 88.3 (San Diego, CA) **3314**
KSDT-AM (Hemet, CA) *Unable to locate*
KSDT-FM - 95.5 (La Jolla, CA) **2122**
KSDZ-FM - 95.5 (Gordon, NE) **18023**
KSED-FM - 107.5 (Flagstaff, AZ) **703**
KSEE-TV - Channel 24 (Fresno, CA) **1982**
KSEG-FM (Sacramento, CA) *Unable to locate*
KSEI-AM - 930 (Pocatello, ID) **7954**
KSEI-FM **7951***
KSEK-AM - 1340 (Pittsburg, KS) **11758**
KSEL-AM - 1450 (Portales, NM) **19907**
KSEL-FM **30738***
KSEL-FM - 95.3 (Portales, NM) **19908**
KSEL-TV **30722***
KSEM-AM **32841***
KSEM-FM **32842***
KSEM-FM - 106.3 (Seminole, TX) **31100**
KSEN-AM - 1150 (Shelby, MT) **17907**
KSEO-AM - 750 (Durant, OK) **25811**
KSEQ-FM - 97.1 (Visalia, CA) **4043**
KSER-FM - 90.7 (Lynnwood, WA) **32826**
KSES-AM (Yucca Valley, CA) *Unable to locate*
KSET-AM - 1300 (Silsbee, TX) **31108**
KSEV-AM - 700 (Houston, TX) **30574**
KSEZ-FM (Sioux City, IA) *Unable to locate*
KSFA-AM - 860 (Lufkin, TX) **30744**
KSFC-FM - 91.9 (Spokane, WA) **33126**
KSFI-FM - 100.3 (Salt Lake City, UT) **31456**
KSFM-FM - 102.5 (Sacramento, CA) **3048**
KSFO-AM - 560 (San Francisco, CA) **3500**
KSFQ-FM - 101.1 (Santa Fe, NM) **19949**
KSFS-AM - 1520 (Crooks, SD) **28835**
KSFT-AM - 1550 (St. Joseph, MO) **17399**
KSFT-FM **17397***
KSFT-FM - 107.1 (Sioux City, IA) **11220**
KSFX-FM - 100.5 (Roswell, NM) **19927**
KSFY-TV - Channel 13 (Sioux Falls, SD) **28983**
KSGB-AM **29742***
KSGI-AM (St. George, UT) *Ceased*
KSGL-AM - 900 (Wichita, KS) **11904**
KSGN-FM - 89.7 (Riverside, CA) **2953**
KSGO-AM **26526***
KSGO-FM (Stockton, CA) *Unable to locate*
KSGR-AM **4689***
KSGS-AM - 950 (Minneapolis, MN) **16153**
KSGT-AM - 1340 (Jackson, WY) **34539**
KSHA-FM - 104.3 (Redding, CA) **2897**
KSHB-TV - Channel 41 (Kansas City, MO) **17214**
KSHE-FM - 94.7 (St. Louis, MO) **17549**
KSHN-FM - 99.9 (Liberty, TX) **30692**
KSHO-AM - 920 (Lebanon, OR) **26410**
KSHO-TV **18405***
KSHP-AM - 1400 (Las Vegas, NV) **18404**
KSHR-FM - 97.3 (Coquille, OR) **26283**
KSHU-FM - 90.5 (Huntsville, TX) **30601**

KSHY-AM **34505***
KSIB-AM - 1520 (Creston, IA) **10734**
KSID-AM - 1340 (Sidney, NE) **18279**
KSIG-AM - 1450 (Crowley, LA) **12561**
KSIL-AM (Silver City, NM) *Unable to locate*
KSIM-AM - 1400 (Sikeston, MO) **17587**
KSIN-TV - Channel 27 (Sioux City, IA) **11221**
KSIQ-FM - 96.1 (Brawley, CA) **1598**
KSIR-AM - 1010 (Fort Morgan, CO) **4450**
KSIR-FM - 107.1 (Greeley, CO) **4502**
KSIS-AM - 1050 (Sedalia, MO) **17574**
KSIV-AM - 1320 (St. Louis, MO) **17550**
KSIW-AM (Woodward, OK) *Unable to locate*
KSIX-AM - 1230 (Corpus Christi, TX) **30096**
KSJB-AM - 600 (Jamestown, ND) **24481**
KSJC-FM - 89.5 (Stockton, CA) **3816**
KSJD-FM - 91.5 (Cortez, CO) **4293**
KSJJ-FM - 102.9 (Bend, OR) **26250**
KSJL-AM - 760 (San Antonio, TX) **31071**
KSJM-FM **24482***
KSJM-FM (Tucson, AZ) *Unable to locate*
KSJN-FM - 99.5 (St. Paul, MN) **16422**
KSJO-FM - 92.7 (San Jose, CA) **3553**
KSJR-FM - 90.1 (Collegeville, MN) **15809**
KSJS-FM - 90.5 (San Jose, CA) **3554**
KSJT-FM **31016***
KSJT-FM - 107.5 (San Angelo, TX) **31021**
KSJU-FM **15807***
KSJV-FM (Fresno, CA) *Unable to locate*
KSJX-AM - 1500 (San Jose, CA) **3555**
KSJY-FM (Lafayette, LA) *Unable to locate*
KSJZ-FM - 93.3 (Jamestown, ND) **24482**
KSKA-FM - 91.1 (Anchorage, AK) **547**
KSKB-FM - 99.1 (Brooklyn, IA) **10634**
KSKD-FM **3043***
KSKD-FM **3039***
KSKE-AM (Vail, CO) *Unable to locate*
KSKE-FM (Vail, CO) *Unable to locate*
KSKF-FM - 90.9 (Ashland, OR) **26221**
KSKG-FM - 99.9 (Salina, KS) **11790**
KSKI-AM (Hailey, ID) *Ceased*
KSKI-FM - 103.7 (Ketchum, ID) **7889**
KSKN-TV - Channel 22 (Spokane, WA) **33127**
KSKO-AM - 870 (McGrath, AK) **623**
KSKR-FM **1277***
KSKS-FM - 93.7 (Fresno, CA) **1983**
KSKT-FM **11632***
KSKU-FM **11508***
KSKX-FM - 105.5 (Colorado Springs, CO) **4281**
KSKY-AM (Irving, TX) *Unable to locate*
KSKZ-FM (Garden City, KS) *Unable to locate*
KSL-AM - 1160 (Salt Lake City, UT) **31457**
KSL-TV - Channel 5 (Salt Lake City, UT) **31458**
KSLA-TV - Channel 12 (Shreveport, LA) **12835**
KSLC-FM (McMinnville, OR) *Unable to locate*
KSLD-TV (Los Angeles, CA) *Unable to locate*
KSLE-FM **26067***
KSLH-FM (St. Louis, MO) *Ceased*
KSLI-FM - 104.1 (Lincoln, NE) **18144**
KSLM-AM (Salem, OR) *Unable to locate*
KSLO-AM - 1230 (Opelousas, LA) **12793**
KSLO-FM **12792***
KSLQ-FM **17555***
KSLR-AM - 630 (San Antonio, TX) **31072**
KSLS-FM - 101.5 (Liberal, KS) **11606**
KSLT-FM **31218***
KSLT-FM - 107.3 (Rapid City, SD) **28949**
KSLU-FM - 90.9 (Hammond, LA) **12595**
KSLV-AM - 1240 (Monte Vista, CO) **4578**
KSLV-FM - 95.3 (Monte Vista, CO) **4579**
KSLX-FM (Scottsdale, AZ) *Unable to locate*
KSLY-FM - 96.1 (San Luis Obispo, CA) **3574**
KSMA-AM - 1240 (Santa Maria, CA) **3699**
KSMA-FM (Amarillo, TX) *Unable to locate*
KSMB-FM - 94.5 (Lafayette, LA) **12632**
KSMB/KDYS Radio Broadcasting Co. **12632***
KSMC-FM - 89.5 (Moraga, CA) **2598**
KSMF-FM - 89.1 (Ashland, OR) **26222**
KSMG-FM (Des Moines, IA) *Unable to locate*
KSMG-FM - 105.3 (San Antonio, TX) **31073**
KSMI-AM **26069***
KSMI-AM **12570***
KSMJ-AM - 1380 (Sacramento, CA) **3049**
KSML-AM **720***
KSML-AM **31099***
KSMM-AM - 1530 (Chaska, MN) **15795**
KSMO-AM - 1340 (Salem, MO) **17564**
KSMO-TV - Channel 62 (Kansas City, KS) **11538**
KSMQ-TV - Channel 15 (Austin, MN) **15725**
KSMR-FM - 92.5 (Winona, MN) **16535**
KSMS-FM **17627***
KSMS-TV - Channel 67 (Monterey, CA) **2587**
KSMT-FM (Breckenridge, CO) *Unable to locate*
KSMU-FM - 91.1 (Springfield, MO) **17627**
KSMW-FM **16535***
KSMX-AM (Walla Walla, WA) *Unable to locate*
KSMX-FM **10913***
KSN Television Group (Wichita, KS) **37701**
KSNB-TV - Channel 4 (Kearney, NE) **18067**

KSNC-TV - Channel 2 (Great Bend, KS) **11472**
KSND-FM **26339***
KSNE-FM (Las Vegas, NV) *Unable to locate*
KSNF-TV - Channel 16 (Joplin, MO) **17149**
KSNG-TV - Channel 11 (Garden City, KS) **11454**
KSNI-FM - 102.5 (Santa Maria, CA) **3700**
KSNK-TV - Channel 8 (Oberlin, KS) **11682**
KSNM-AM - 570 (Las Cruces, NM) **19887**
KSNM-FM (from 1984 through 2000) **19882***
KSNN-FM (Dallas, TX) *Ceased*
KSNN-FM - 93.5 (St. George, UT) **31421**
KSNO-AM (Aspen, CO) *Ceased*
KSNO-FM **4143***
KSNP-FM - 95.3 (Burlington, KS) **11371**
KSNR-FM - 100.3 (Thief River Falls, MN) **16471**
KSNS-FM **12651***
KSNT-TV - Channel 27 (Topeka, KS) **11843**
KSNW-TV - Channel 3 (Wichita, KS) **11905**
KSNY-AM - 1450 (Snyder, TX) **31116**
KSNY-FM - 101.5 (Snyder, TX) **31117**
KSNZ **4540***
KSNZ-FM - 93.3 (Lamar, CO) **4540**
KSOA-AM **16898***
KSOF-FM - 92.9 (Fresno, CA) **1984**
KSOL-FM **3505***
KSOL-FM - 98.9 (San Francisco, CA) **3501**
KSON-FM - 97.3 (San Diego, CA) **3315**
KSOO-AM - 1140 (Sioux Falls, SD) **28984**
KSOO-TV **28983***
KSOP-AM (East Providence, RI) *Unable to locate*
KSOP-FM - 104.3 (Salt Lake City, UT) **31459**
KSOR-FM - 90.1 (Ashland, OR) **26223**
KSOS-AM (Ogden, UT) *Unable to locate*
KSOS-FM (Ogden, UT) *Unable to locate*
KSOU-AM - 1090 (Sioux Center, IA) **11210**
KSOU-FM - 93.9 (Sioux Center, IA) **11211**
KSOX-AM - 1240 (Raymondville, TX) **30971**
KSOX-FM - 107.1 (Raymondville, TX) **30972**
KSOZ-FM **17355***
KSPA-AM **1669***
KSPB-FM - 91.9 (Pebble Beach, CA) **2834**
KSPC-FM - 88.7 (Claremont, CA) **1727**
KSPD-AM - 790 (Boise, ID) **7830**
KSPE-AM (Santa Barbara, CA) *Unable to locate*
KSPE-FM (Santa Barbara, CA) *Unable to locate*
KSPI-AM - 780 (Stillwater, OK) **26085**
KSPI-FM - 93.7 (Stillwater, OK) **26086**
KSPK-FM - 102.3, 103.5 (Walsenburg, CO) **4657**
KSPL-AM (San Marcos, TX) *Unable to locate*
KSPL-FM **30742***
KSPL-FM - 102.9 (Bakersfield, CA) **1470**
KSPN-FM - 103.1, 97.3, and 98.3 (Aspen, CO) **4143**
KSPN-FM (Aspen, CO) *Unable to locate*
KSPO-AM **33111***
KSPO-FM - 106.5 (Dishman, WA) **32738**
KSPR-TV - Channel 33 (Springfield, MO) **17628**
KSPS-TV - Channel 7 (Spokane, WA) **33128**
KSPT-AM (Sandpoint, ID) *Unable to locate*
KSPX-TV - Channel 29 (Placerville, CA) **2849**
KSPZ-FM - 92.9 (Colorado Springs, CO) **4282**
KSQY-FM (Deadwood, SD) *Unable to locate*
KSRA-AM - 92.7 (Salmon, ID) **7975**
KSRA-FM (Salmon, ID) *Unable to locate*
KSRC-AM (Socorro, NM) *Unable to locate*
KSRE-TV - Channel 6 (Minot, ND) **24514**
KSRF-FM **4081***
KSRH-FM - 88.1 (San Rafael, CA) **3606**
KSRM-AM - 920 (Kenai, AK) **609**
KSRO-AM - 1350 (Santa Rosa, CA) **3741**
KSRQ-FM - 90.1 (Thief River Falls, MN) **16472**
KSRR-AM (Orem, UT) *Unable to locate*
KSRV-AM - 1380 (Ontario, OR) **26456**
KSRW-FM - 96.1 (Childress, TX) **30019**
KSRX-AM (El Dorado, KS) *Unable to locate*
KSRZ-FM - 104.5 (Omaha, NE) **18227**
KSSA-AM **30215***
KSSA-FM **30782***
KSSD-FM - 92.5 (Cedar City, UT) **31327**
KSSI-FM - 102.7 (Ridgecrest, CA) **2926**
KSSK-AM - 590 (Honolulu, HI) **7751**
KSSK-FM - 92.3 (Honolulu, HI) **7752**
KSSM-FM **25917***
KSSM-FM (Copperas Cove, TX) *Unable to locate*
KSSN-FM - 95.7 (Little Rock, AR) **1251**
KSSR-AM (Santa Rosa, NM) *Unable to locate*
KSSR-FM **29863***
KSSS-AM **4284***
KSSS-FM - 101.5 (Bismarck, ND) **24371**
KSST-AM - 1230 (Sulphur Springs, TX) **31168**
KSSU-AM - 1580 (Sacramento, CA) **3050**
KSSU-FM - 91.9 (Durant, OK) **25812**
KSSX-FM (Redding, CA) *Unable to locate*
KSSY-FM **33199***
KSTB-AM (Breckenridge, TX) *Ceased*
KSTC-AM - 1230 (Sterling, CO) **4642**
KSTC-FM **4640***
KSTE-AM - 650 (Sacramento, CA) **3051**
KSTE-FM - 105.9 (Portland, OR) **26540**
KSTF-TV - Channel 10 (Gering, NE) **18019**

KSTH-FM **12580***
KSTK-FM - 101.7 (Wrangell, AK) **654**
KSTL-AM (St. Louis, MO) *Unable to locate*
KSTM-FM - 99.5 (Tulsa, OK) **26164**
KSTN-AM - 1420 (Stockton, CA) **3817**
KSTN-FM - 107.3 (Stockton, CA) **3818**
KSTP-AM (St. Paul, MN) *Unable to locate*
KSTP-FM - 94.5 (Minneapolis, MN) **16154**
KSTP-TV - Channel 5 (St. Paul, MN) **16423**
KSTQ-FM - 99.3 (Glenwood, MN) **15921**
KSTR **4481***
KSTR-FM - 96.1 (Montrose, CO) **4582**
KSTS-TV - Channel 48 (San Jose, CA) **3556**
KSTT-AM **10742***
KSTU-TV - Channel 13 (Salt Lake City, UT) **31460**
KSTV-AM - 1510 (Stephenville, TX) **31132**
KSTV-FM - 93.1 (Stephenville, TX) **31133**
KSTW-TV - Channel 11 (Renton, WA) **32928**
KSTX-FM **4215***
KSTY-FM - 104.5 (Canon City, CO) **4215**
KSTZ-FM - 102.5 (Des Moines, IA) **10832**
KSTZ-FM (Clayton, CO) *Ceased*
KSUA-FM - 91.5 (Fairbanks, AK) **575**
KSUB-AM - 590 (Cedar City, UT) **31328**
KSUB-FM **31327***
KSUC-FM **30634***
KSUD-AM - 730 (West Memphis, AR) **1370**
KSUD-FM **1369***
KSUE-AM - 1240 (Susanville, CA) **3834**
KSUE-FM **3833***
KSUI-FM - 91.7 (Iowa City, IA) **10994**
KSUM-AM - 1370 (Fairmont, MN) **15892**
KSUN-AM - 1400 (Phoenix, AZ) **838**
KSUN-FM - 95 (Rohnert Park, CA) **2964**
KSUP-FM - 106.3 (Juneau, AK) **602**
KSUT-FM - 91.3 (Ignacio, CO) **4520**
KSUU-FM - 91.1 (Cedar City, UT) **31329**
KSUV-FM **1470***
KSUX-FM - 105.7 (Sioux City, IA) **11222**
KSUZ-FM (Los Angeles, CA) *Ceased*
KSVC-AM (Richfield, UT) *Unable to locate*
KSVE-AM - 1150 (El Paso, TX) **30301**
KSVI-TV - Channel 6 (Billings, MT) **17743**
KSVN-AM - 730 (Hooper, UT) **31339**
KSVP-AM - 990 (Artesia, NM) **19818**
KSVR-FM - 90.1 (Mount Vernon, WA) **32849**
KSVY-AM (Spokane, WA) *Unable to locate*
KSWB-AM - 840 (Seaside, OR) **26581**
KSWB-TV (Chula Vista, CA) *Unable to locate*
KSWC-FM - 100.3 (Winfield, KS) **11912**
KSWD-AM (Seward, AK) *Unable to locate*
KSWG-FM - 96.3 (Wickenburg, AZ) **1007**
KSWH-FM - 91.9 (Arkadelphia, AR) **1033**
KSWK-TV - Channel 3 (Lakin, KS) **11545**
KSWN-FM - 93.9 (McCook, NE) **18159**
KSWO-AM (Lawton, OK) *Unable to locate*
KSWO-TV - Channel 7 (Lawton, OK) **25896**
KSWS-AM **19923***
KSWT-TV - Channel 13 (Yuma, AZ) **1028**
KSWV-AM - 810 (Santa Fe, NM) **19950**
KSWV-FM **3306***
KSWW **32651***
KSWW-FM - 102.1 (Aberdeen, WA) **32651**
KSXM **26462***
KSXT-FM **32886***
KSXX-AM **31473***
KSXX-FM - 99.9 (Marysville, CA) **2518**
KSXY-FM **18439***
KSXY-FM (Fresno, CA) *Unable to locate*
KSYC-AM - 1490 (Yreka, CA) **4122**
KSYC-FM - 103.9 (Yreka, CA) **4123**
KSYE-FM (Frederick, OK) *Unable to locate*
KSYL-AM - 970 (Alexandria, LA) **12468**
KSYM-FM - 90.1 (San Antonio, TX) **31074**
KSYN-FM - 92.5 (Joplin, MO) **17150**
KSYR-FM - 95.7 (Shreveport, LA) **12836**
KSYS-TV - Channel 8 (Medford, OR) **26428**
KSYU-FM - 95.1 (Albuquerque, NM) **19812**
KSYV-FM - 96.7 (Solvang, CA) **3772**
KSYY-FM (Denver, CO) *Ceased*
KSYZ-FM - 107.7 (Grand Island, NE) **18031**
KSZL-AM (Barstow, CA) *Unable to locate*
KTA-TV - Channel 7 (Santa Maria, CA) **3701**
KTAB-TV - Channel 32 (Abilene, TX) **29666**
KTAC-AM **33061***
KTAC-FM - 93.9 (Spokane, WA) **33129**
KTAE-AM - 1260 (Austin, TX) **29877**
KTAG-FM - 97.9 (Cody, WY) **34516**
KTAJ-TV - Channel 16 (St. Joseph, MO) **17400**
KTAK-FM (Riverton, WY) *Unable to locate*
KTAL-FM - 98.1 (Shreveport, LA) **12837**
KTAL-TV - Channel 6 (Shreveport, LA) **12838**
KTAM-AM - 1240 (Bryan, TX) **29982**
KTAN-AM - 1420 (Sierra Vista, AZ) **890**
KTAO-FM - 101.9 (Taos, NM) **19966**
KTAP-AM - 1600 (Santa Maria, CA) **3702**
KTAR-AM - 620 (Phoenix, AZ) **839**
KTAS-TV - Channel 33 (Santa Maria, CA) **3703**
KTAT-AM (Breckenridge, TX) *Unable to locate*

KTAW-FM **30060***
KTAZ-FM **893***
KTBA-AM - 1050 (Tuba City, AZ) **927**
KTBB-AM - 600 (Tyler, TX) **31217**
KTBC-FM **30745***
KTBC-TV (Austin, TX) *Unable to locate*
KTBG-FM - 90.9 (Warrensburg, MO) **17673**
KTBI-AM (Spokane, WA) *Unable to locate*
KTBI-FM (Spokane, WA) *Unable to locate*
KTBL-FM (Albuquerque, NM) *Unable to locate*
KTBN-TV - Channel 40 (Santa Ana, CA) **3637**
KTBO-TV - Channel 14 (Oklahoma City, OK) **26016**
KTBQ-FM - 107.7 (Lufkin, TX) **30745**
KTBR-AM - 950 (Roseburg, OR) **26561**
KTBR-FM - 94.1 (Roseburg, OR) **26562**
KTBS-TV - Channel 3 (Shreveport, LA) **12839**
KTBT-AM **30574***
KTBW-TV - Channel 20 (Federal Way, WA) **32767**
KTBY-TV (Anchorage, AK) *Unable to locate*
KTBZ-FM - 94.5 (Houston, TX) **30575**
KTCA-TV **16426***
KTCB-AM - 1470 (Sikeston, MO) **17588**
KTCC-FM - 91.9 (Colby, KS) **11392**
KTCE-FM - 92.3 (Salt Lake City, UT) **31461**
KTCF-FM **10668***
KTCH-AM - 1590 (Wayne, NE) **18308**
KTCH-FM - 104.9 (Wayne, NE) **18309**
KTCI-TV **16425***
KTCJ-AM (Minneapolis, MN) *Unable to locate*
KTCL-FM - 93.3 (Denver, CO) **4390**
KTCN-FM (Deer, AR) *Ceased*
KTCR-AM - 1340 (Kennewick, WA) **32792**
KTCS-AM - 1410 (Fort Smith, AR) **1155**
KTCS-FM - 99.9 (Fort Smith, AR) **1156**
KTCS/Nine Magazine **32980***
KTCU-FM - 88.7 (Fort Worth, TX) **30358**
KTCV-FM - 88.1 (Kennewick, WA) **32793**
KTCW-FM **32879***
KTCY-FM - 104.9 (Mc Kinney, TX) **30782**
KTCZ-FM - 97.1 (Minneapolis, MN) **16155**
KTDB-FM - 89.7 (Pinehill, NM) **19904**
KTDL-AM (Farmerville, LA) *Ceased*
KTDO-AM **26449***
KTDR-FM - 96.3 (Del Rio, TX) **30227**
KTEC-FM - 89.5 (Klamath Falls, OR) **26397**
KTED-FM **1963***
KTEE-AM (Blackfoot, ID) *Unable to locate*
KTEG-FM - 104.7 (Albuquerque, NM) **19813**
KTEH-TV - Channel 54 (San Jose, CA) **3557**
KTEJ-TV - Channel 19 (Jonesboro, AR) **1203**
KTEK-AM - 1110 (Houston, TX) **30576**
KTEK-FM - 88.7 (Socorro, NM) **19961**
KTEL-AM - 1490 (Milton-Freewater, OR) **26437**
KTEL-FM (Milton-Freewater, OR) *Unable to locate*
KTEM-AM - 1400 (Temple, TX) **31181**
KTEN-FM **25727***
KTEN-TV (Denison, TX) *Unable to locate*
KTEO-AM **31012***
KTEQ-FM - 91.3 (Rapid City, SD) **28950**
KTER-AM 1947-1992 **31183***
KTEW-TV **26149***
KTEX-FM - 100.3 (Alamo, TX) **29675**
KTEZ-AM (Lubbock, TX) *Unable to locate*
KTEZ-FM **30734***
KTFC-FM - 103.3 (Sioux City, IA) **11223**
KTFH-TV - Channel 49 & 33 (Houston, TX) **30577**
KTFI-AM (Twin Falls, ID) *Unable to locate*
KTFM-AM **2535***
KTFM-FM - 102.7 (San Antonio, TX) **31075**
KTFO **31099***
KTFO-TV - Channel 41 (Tulsa, OK) **26165**
KTFS-AM **31186***
KTFS-AM - 940 (Texarkana, TX) **31190**
KTFS-FM (Ashdown, AR) *Ceased*
KTFW-AM - 1460 (Cleburne, TX) **30027**
KTFX-AM - 1340 (Sand Springs, OK) **26055**
KTFX-FM **26150***
KTFX-FM - 102.1 (Muskogee, OK) **25925**
KTFY-FM **29954***
KTGE-AM (Salinas, CA) *Unable to locate*
KTGF-TV - Channel 16 (Great Falls, MT) **17805**
KTGG-AM - 1540 (Spring Arbor, MI) **15572**
KTGL-FM - 92.9 (Lincoln, NE) **18145**
KTGO-AM - 1090 (Tioga, ND) **24540**
KTGR-AM (Columbia, MO) *Unable to locate*
KTHC-FM - 95.1 (Sidney, MT) **17911**
KTHE-AM - 1240 (Thermopolis, WY) **34596**
KTHI-TV **24429***
K39BJ **12714***
KTHN-FM - 92.1 (La Junta, CO) **4528**
KTHO-AM (South Lake Tahoe, CA) *Unable to locate*
KTHS-AM - 1480 (Berryville, AR) **1055**
KTHS-FM - 107.1 (Berryville, AR) **1056**
KTHT-FM (Fresno, CA) *Unable to locate*
KTHV-TV - Channel 11 (Little Rock, AR) **1252**
KTHX-FM **18439***
KTI Cablevision (Fulton, MO) **17079**
KTIB-AM - 640 (Thibodaux, LA) **12862**
KTIC-AM - 840 (West Point, NE) **18313**

KTID-AM (San Rafael, CA) *Unable to locate*
KTID-FM **3605***
KTID-FM **3605***
KTIE-FM **1459***
KTIE-TV **1643***
KTIG-FM - 102.7 (Pequot Lakes, MN) **16263**
KTIK-AM (Boise, ID) *Unable to locate*
KTIL-AM **26598***
KTIL-FM - 94.1 (Tillamook, OR) **26599**
KTIM-AM **1006***
KTIM-FM **3605***
KTIN-TV - Channel 21 (Fort Dodge, IA) **10911**
KTIP-AM - 1450 (Porterville, CA) **2863**
KTIS-AM - 900 (Roseville, MN) **16335**
KTIS-FM - 98.5 (Roseville, MN) **16336**
KTIV-TV - Channel 4 (Sioux City, IA) **11224**
KTIX-AM (Pendleton, OR) *Unable to locate*
KTJC-FM - 92.3 (Rayville, LA) **12805**
KTJK-AM - 1230 (Del Rio, TX) **30228**
KTJN-FM - 106 (Brownsville, TX) **29963**
KTJO-FM - 88.9 (Ottawa, KS) **11694**
KTJS-AM - 1420 (Hobart, OK) **25868**
KTKA-TV (Topeka, KS) *Unable to locate*
KTKC-FM - 92.7 (Springhill, LA) **12849**
KTKK-AM - 630 (South Jordan, UT) **31473**
KTKN-AM - 930 (Ketchikan, AK) **614**
KTKP-AM (Phoenix, AZ) *Unable to locate*
KTKR-AM (Las Vegas, NV) *Unable to locate*
KTKS-AM - 95.1 (Versailles, MO) **17664**
KTKT-AM - 990 (Tucson, AZ) **993**
KTKU-FM - 105.1 (Juneau, AK) **603**
KTLA/KTVT (Tulsa, OK) *Unable to locate*
KTLA-TV - Channel 5 (Hollywood, CA) **2053**
KTLB-FM (Rockwell City, IA) *Unable to locate*
KTLC-TV **26000***
KTLE-AM (Tooele, UT) *Unable to locate*
KTLE-FM (Tooele, UT) *Unable to locate*
KTLF-FM - 90.5 (Colorado Springs, CO) **4283**
KTLM-FM (Taft, CA) *Unable to locate*
KTLN-FM - 90.5 (New Orleans, LA) **12766**
KTLO-AM - 1240 (Mountain Home, AR) **1289**
KTLO-FM - 97.9 (Mountain Home, AR) **1290**
KTLQ-AM - 1350 (Tahlequah, OK) **26097**
KTLQ-FM **26096***
KTLS-FM - 106.5 (Ada, OK) **25727**
KTLT-FM (Wichita Falls, TX) *Unable to locate*
KTLU-AM - 1580 (Rusk, TX) **31000**
KTLV-AM - 1220 (Midwest City, OK) **25919**
KTLW-FM - 88.9 (Van Nuys, CA) **3998**
KTLX-FM - 91.9 (Columbus, NE) **17983**
KTMA-AM **1901***
KTMA-TV **16420***
KTMC-AM - 1400 (McAlester, OK) **25912**
KTMD-TV - Channel 48 (Houston, TX) **30578**
KTME-AM (Santa Maria, CA) *Unable to locate*
KTMF-AM **16210***
KTMF-TV - Channel 23 (Missoula, MT) **17885**
KTMG-AM (Deer Trail, CO) *Unable to locate*
KTMM-AM - 1340 (Grand Junction, CO) **4496**
KTMP-AM - 1340 (Heber City, UT) **31338**
KTMS-AM (Santa Barbara, CA) *Unable to locate*
KTMT-AM - 580 (Medford, OR) **26429**
KTMT-FM - 93.7 (Medford, OR) **26430**
KTMX-FM **1705***
KTMX-FM - 104.9 (York, NE) **18323**
KTNA-FM - 88.5 (Talkeetna, AK) **642**
KTNC-AM - 1230 (Falls City, NE) **18010**
KTNC-TV - Channel 42 (Concord, CA) **1761**
KTND-FM **4029***
KTND-FM - 107.7 (Austin, TX) **29878**
KTNE-FM - 91.1 (Alliance, NE) **17931**
KTNE-TV - Channel 13 (Alliance, NE) **17932**
KTNL-TV - Channel 13 (Fairbanks, AK) **576**
KTNM-AM - 1400 (Tucumcari, NM) **19973**
KTNN-AM - 660 (Window Rock, AZ) **1013**
KTNO-AM - 1540 (Arlington, TX) **29742**
KTNQ-AM - 1020 (Glendale, CA) **2021**
KTNS-AM **30215***
KTNS-AM - 1060 (Oakhurst, CA) **2661**
KTNT-FM **19930***
KTNT-FM - 102.5 (Eufaula, OK) **25830**
KTNV-TV - Channel 13 (Las Vegas, NV) **18405**
KTNW-TV - Channel 31 (Richland, WA) **32931**
KTNY-FM - 101.7 (Libby, MT) **17855**
KTNZ-AM - 1010 (Amarillo, TX) **29717**
KTOB-AM (Mill Valley, CA) *Unable to locate*
KTOC-FM (Jonesboro, LA) *Unable to locate*
KTOD-FM - 92.7 (Conway, AR) **1089**
KTOE-AM - 1420 (Mankato, MN) **16035**
KTOF-FM **11299***
KTOK-AM - 1000 (Oklahoma City, OK) **26054**
KTOL-AM **32870***
KTOM-AM - 1380 (Salinas, CA) **3076**
KTOM-FM - 100.7 (Salinas, CA) **3077**
KTON-AM - 940 (Belton, TX) **29917**
KTOO-FM - 104.3 (Juneau, AK) **604**
KTOO-TV - Channel 3 (Juneau, AK) **605**
KTOQ-AM - 1340 (Rapid City, SD) **28951**
KTOU-FM **31470***

KTOW-AM **26055***
KTOX-AM (Needles, CA) *Unable to locate*
KTOY-FM **33155***
KTOZ-AM - 1060 (Springfield, MO) **17629**
KTOZ-FM (Springfield, MO) *Unable to locate*
KTPA-AM - 1370 (Hope, AR) **1180**
KTPB-FM - 88.7 (Kilgore, TX) **30643**
KTPH-FM - 91.7 (Tonopah, NV) **18449**
KTPI-FM (Palmdale, CA) *Unable to locate*
KTPK-FM - 106.9 (Topeka, KS) **11844**
KTPR-FM - 91.1 (Fort Dodge, IA) **10912**
KTPS-TV **33156***
KTPX-TV **30825***
KTQM-FM - 99.9 (Clovis, NM) **19836**
KTQN-FM (Belton, TX) *Unable to locate*
KTQX-FM - 90.1 (Bakersfield, CA) **1471**
KTRA-FM (Farmington, NM) *Unable to locate*
KTRB-AM - 860 (Fresno, CA) **1985**
KTRC-AM (Santa Fe, NM) *Unable to locate*
KTRE-TV - Channel 9 (Lufkin, TX) **30746**
KTRF-AM - 1230 (Thief River Falls, MN) **16473**
KTRH-AM - 740 (Houston, TX) **30579**
KTRK-TV - Channel 13 (Houston, TX) **30580**
KTRN-AM **27134***
KTRO-AM (Oxnard, CA) *Unable to locate*
KTRR-FM (Fort Collins, CO) *Unable to locate*
KTRS-AM - 550 (St. Louis, MO) **17551**
KTRS-FM - 104.7 (Casper, WY) **34490**
KTRT-AM (Tulsa, OK) *Unable to locate*
KTRU-FM - 91.7 (Houston, TX) **30581**
KTRV-TV - Channel 12 (Nampa, ID) **7934**
KTRW-AM (Spokane, WA) *Ceased*
KTRX-FM - 93.5 (Tarkio, MO) **17647**
KTRY-AM (Bastrop, LA) *Unable to locate*
KTRZ-FM - 93.1 (Riverton, WY) **34580**
KTSA-AM - 550 (San Antonio, TX) **31076**
KTSB-FM **29881***
KTSB-TV **11843***
KTSC-FM - 89.5 (Pueblo, CO) **4609**
KTSC-TV - Channel 8 (Pueblo, CO) **4610**
KTSD-FM - 91.1 (Reliance, SD) **28956**
KTSD-TV - Channel 10 (Reliance, SD) **28957**
KTSF-TV - Channel 26 (Brisbane, CA) **1612**
KTSJ-AM (Claremont, CA) *Unable to locate*
KTSL-FM - 101.9 (Spokane, WA) **33130**
KTSM-AM (El Paso, TX) *Unable to locate*
KTSM-FM (El Paso, TX) *Unable to locate*
KTSM-TV - Channel 9 (El Paso, TX) **30302**
KTSO-FM - 94.1 (Tulsa, OK) **26166**
KTSP-AM **31422***
KTSP-FM **837***
KTSR-FM - 92.1 (College Station, TX) **30060**
KTST-FM - 101.9 (Oklahoma City, OK) **26018**
KTSU-FM - 90.9 (Houston, TX) **30582**
KTSW-FM - 89.9 MAZ (San Marcos, TX) **31087**
KTTC-TV - Channel 10 (Rochester, MN) **16320**
KTTI-FM (Yuma, AZ) *Unable to locate*
KTTK-FM - 90.7 (Lebanon, MO) **17242**
KTTN-AM - 1600 (Trenton, MO) **17654**
KTTN-FM - 92.3 (Trenton, MO) **17655**
KTTS-FM - 94.7 (Springfield, MO) **17630**
KTTS-TV **17624***
KTTT-AM - 1510 (Columbus, NE) **17984**
KTTT-FM **17982***
KTTU-TV - Channel 18 (Tucson, AZ) **994**
KTTV-TV - Channel 11 (Los Angeles, CA) **2469**
KTTW-TV - Channel 17 (Sioux Falls, SD) **28985**
KTTX-AM **29951***
KTTX-FM (Bryan, TX) *Unable to locate*
KTUC-AM (Tucson, AZ) *Unable to locate*
KTUE-AM (Tulia, TX) *Unable to locate*
KTUF-AM **30195***
KTUH-FM - 90.3 (Honolulu, HI) **7753**
KTUI-AM - 1560 (Sullivan, MO) **17642**
KTUI-FM - 100.9 (Sullivan, MO) **17643**
KTUL-TV - Channel 8 (Tulsa, OK) **26167**
KTUN-FM - 101.5 (Avon, CO) **4151**
KTUO-FM (Sonora, CA) *Ceased*
KTUS-AM **4143***
KTUU-TV (Anchorage, AK) *Unable to locate*
KTUX-FM (Shreveport, LA) *Unable to locate*
KTV (Korean American Network News) (Flushing, NY) *Unable to locate*
KTVA-TV - Channel 11 (Anchorage, AK) **548**
KTVB-TV - Channel 7 (Boise, ID) **7831**
KTVC-TV **11416***
KTVD-TV - Channel 20 (Englewood, CO) **4418**
KTVE-TV - Channel 10 (West Monroe, LA) **12877**
KTVF-TV - Channel 11 (Fairbanks, AK) **577**
KTVG-TV (Grand Island, NE) *Unable to locate*
KTVH-TV **11906***
KTVH-TV - Channel 12 (Helena, MT) **17831**
KTVI-TV - Channel 2 (St. Louis, MO) **17552**
KTVK-TV - Channel 3 (Phoenix, AZ) **840**
KTVL-TV - Channel 10 (Medford, OR) **26431**
KTVM-TV - Channel 6 (Butte, MT) **17765**
KTVN-TV - Channel 2 (Reno, NV) **18441**
KTVO-AM - 1400 (San Francisco, CA) **3502**
KTVO-TV - Channel 3 (Kirksville, MO) **17232**

KTVP-TV **1128***
KTVQ-TV - Channel 2 (Billings, MT) **17744**
KTVS-TV (Sterling, CO) *Unable to locate*
KTVT-TV - Channel 11 (Fort Worth, TX) **30359**
KTVU-TV - Channel 2 (Oakland, CA) **2705**
KTVW-TV - Channel 33 (Phoenix, AZ) **841**
KTVX-TV - Channel 4 (Salt Lake City, UT) **31462**
KTVZ-TV - Channel 21 (Bend, OR) **26251**
KTWA-FM - 92.7 (Ottumwa, IA) **11145**
KTWB-FM - 101.9 (Sioux Falls, SD) **28986**
KTWB-TV - Channel 22 (Seattle, WA) **33070**
KTWC-FM **817***
KTWI-FM **26253***
KTWK-AM - 1300 (Colorado Springs, CO) **4284**
KTWN **31188***
KTWN-AM **31190***
KTWO-AM - 1030 (Casper, WY) **34491**
KTWO-TV - Channel 2 (Casper, WY) **34492**
KTWS-TV **30197***
KTWU-TV - Channel 11 (Topeka, KS) **11845**
KTWV-FM - 94.7 (Culver City, CA) **1796**
KTXA-TV - Channel 21 (Dallas, TX) **30213**
KTXC-AM - 1600 (Cuero, TX) **30116**
KTXC-FM - 104.7 (Midland, TX) **30824**
KTXH-TV (Houston, TX) *Unable to locate*
KTXJ-AM - 1350 (Jasper, TX) **30622**
KTXL-TV **31020***
KTXL-TV - Channel 40 (Sacramento, CA) **3052**
KTXQ-FM (Dallas, TX) *Unable to locate*
KTXR-FM - 101.3 (Springfield, MO) **17631**
KTXS-TV - Channel 12 (Abilene, TX) **29667**
KTXT-FM - 88.1 (Lubbock, TX) **30735**
KTXT-TV - Channel 5 (Lubbock, TX) **30736**
KTXU-FM **30909***
KTXZ-AM (Austin, TX) *Unable to locate*
KTYD-FM - 99.9 (Santa Barbara, CA) **3668**
KTYE-FM **29658***
KTYL-AM **31212***
KTYL-FM - 93.1 (Tyler, TX) **31218**
KTYL-TV **834***
KTYM-AM - 1460 (Inglewood, CA) **2075**
KTYN-AM (Minot, ND) *Unable to locate*
KTYX-FM **25747***
KTZA-FM - 92.9 (Artesia, NM) **19819**
KTZN-AM **2453***
KTZN-FM (Cincinnati, OH) *Unable to locate*
KTZO-FM - 103.3 (Albuquerque, NM) **19814**
KTZR-AM (Tucson, AZ) *Unable to locate*
KTZZ-FM - 93.7 (Black Eagle, MT) **17749**
KTZZ-TV **33070***
KUAC-FM - 89.9 (Fairbanks, AK) **578**
KUAC-TV - Channel 9 (Fairbanks, AK) **579**
KUAD-FM - 99.1 (Windsor, CO) **4688**
KUAF-FM - 91.3 (Fayetteville, AR) **1131**
KUAI-AM - 720 (Eleele, HI) **7662**
KUAM-FM **25821***
Kuang Hua Hua Pao; Sinorama/ (Los Angeles, CA)
  2388
KUAR-FM - 89.1 (Little Rock, AR) **1253**
KUAS-TV - Channel 27 (Tucson, AZ) **995**
KUAT-AM **997***
KUAT-FM (Tucson, AZ) *Unable to locate*
KUAT-TV - Channel 6 (Tucson, AZ) **996**
KUAZ-AM - 1550 (Tucson, AZ) **997**
KUAZ-FM - 89.1 (Tucson, AZ) **998**
KUBA-AM - 1600 (Yuba City, CA) **4124**
KUBB-FM - 96.3 (Merced, CA) **2534**
KUBC-AM - 580 (Montrose, CO) **4583**
KUBE-FM - 93.3 (Seattle, WA) **33071**
KUBL-FM - 93.3 (Salt Lake City, UT) **31463**
KUBO **3071***
KUBO-FM - 88.7 (El Centro, CA) **1855**
KUBQ-FM - 98.7 (La Grande, OR) **26402**
KUBS-FM - 91.5 (Newport, WA) **32852**
KUCB-FM (Des Moines, IA) *Unable to locate*
KUCD-FM - 101.9 (Honolulu, HI) **7754**
KUCI-FM (Irvine, CA) *Ceased*
KUCL-AM (Boise, ID) *Unable to locate*
KUCR-FM - 88.3 (Riverside, CA) **2954**
KUCU-AM **19866***
KUCV-FM - 91.1 FM (Lincoln, NE) **18146**
KUDA-FM (Las Vegas, NV) *Unable to locate*
KUDL-FM (Westwood, KS) *Unable to locate*
KUDY-FM (Spokane, WA) *Ceased*
KUED-TV - Channel 7 (Salt Lake City, UT) **31464**
KUEL-FM - 92.1 (Fort Dodge, IA) **10913**
KUEN-AM **33198***
KUER-FM - 90.1 (Salt Lake City, UT) **31465**
KUET-AM (Glendale, AZ) *Ceased*
KUEZ-FM **17883***
KUEZ-FM - 100.1 (Lufkin, TX) **30747**
KUFO-FM - 101.1 (Portland, OR) **26541**
KUFX-FM - 98.5 (San Jose, CA) **3558**
KUGM-FM **32683***
KUGN-AM - 590 (Eugene, OR) **26346**
KUGN-FM - 97.9 (Eugene, OR) **26347**
KUGR-AM (Green River, WY) *Unable to locate*
KUGS-FM - 89.3 (Bellingham, WA) **32685**
KUGT-AM (Cape Girardeau, MO) *Unable to locate*

KUHB-FM - 91.9 (St. Paul Island, AK) **634**
KUHD-AM (North Port Arthur, TX) *Unable to locate*
KUHF-FM - 88.7 (Houston, TX) **30583**
KUHL-AM (Santa Maria, CA) *Unable to locate*
KUHL-AM - 1410 (Santa Maria, CA) **3704**
KUHT-TV - Channel 8 (Houston, TX) **30584**
KUIC-FM - 95.3 (Vacaville, CA) **3975**
KUID-AM **32913***
KUIK-AM - 1360 (Hillsboro, OR) **26375**
KUIN-AM **26219***
KUIN-FM **31484***
KUJ-AM (Walla Walla, WA) *Unable to locate*
KUKI-AM - 1400 (Ukiah, CA) **3969**
KUKI-FM - 103.3 (Ukiah, CA) **3970**
KUKN-FM - 105.5 (Kelso, WA) **32788**
KUKQ-AM - 1060 (Tempe, AZ) **922**
KULA-AM (Kailua, HI) *Unable to locate*
KULA-FM **7752***
KULC-TV - Channel 9 (Salt Lake City, UT) **31466**
KULE-AM - 730 (Ephrata, WA) **32757**
KULE-FM - 92.3 (Ephrata, WA) **32758**
KULM-FM - 98.3 (Broken Arrow, OK) **25773**
The Kulm Messenger (Kulm, ND) **24486**
KULP-AM - 1390 (El Campo, TX) **30277**
KULP-FM - 96.9 (El Campo, TX) **30278**
KULR-TV - Channel 8 (Billings, MT) **17745**
Kultur Und Leben (New York, NY) *Ceased*
KULV-AM **2129***
KULV-AM - 550 (La Verne, CA) **2129**
KULV-FM - 107.9 (La Verne, CA) **2130**
KULY-AM - 1420 (Ulysses, KS) **11856**
KUMA-AM - 1290 (Pendleton, OR) **26461**
KUMA-FM - 107.7 (Pendleton, OR) **26462**
KUMD-FM - 103.3 (Duluth, MN) **15852**
KUMM-FM - 89.7 (Morris, MN) **16200**
Kumquat Meringue (Pine Island, MN) **16271**
KUMR-FM - 88.5 (Rolla, MO) **17382**
KUMU-FM - 94.7 (Honolulu, HI) **7755**
KUMV-TV - Channel 8 (Williston, ND) **24564**
KUNA-AM **2748***
KUNA-FM - 96.7 (Palm Desert, CA) **2752**
KUNC-FM - 91.5 (Greeley, CO) **4503**
KUND-AM - 1370 (Grand Forks, ND) **24463**
Kung-Fu; Inside (Burbank, CA) **1619**
Kung Fu/Qigong (Fremont, CA) **1939**
KUNI-FM - 90.9 (Cedar Falls, IA) **10668**
KUNM-FM - 89.9 (Albuquerque, NM) **19815**
KUNO-AM (Corpus Christi, TX) *Unable to locate*
KUNQ-FM - 99.3 (Houston, MO) **17104**
KUNR-FM - 88.7 (Reno, NV) **18442**
KUNV-FM - 91.5 (Las Vegas, NV) **18406**
KUNY-FM - 91.5 (Mason City, IA) **11079**
KUOA-AM - TER0 (Siloam Springs, AR) **1345**
KUOI-FM (Moscow, ID) *Unable to locate*
KUOL-FM **1277***
KUOM-AM - 770 (Minneapolis, MN) **16156**
KUON-TV - Channel 12 (Lincoln, NE) **18147**
KUOO-FM - 103.9 (Spirit Lake, IA) **11239**
KUOP-FM - 91.3 (Stockton, CA) **3819**
KUOR-FM (Redlands, CA) *Ceased*
KUOW-FM - 94.9 (Seattle, WA) **33072**
KUPD-FM - 97.9 (Tempe, AZ) **923**
KUPI-AM - 980 (Idaho Falls, ID) **7878**
KUPI-FM - 99.1 (Idaho Falls, ID) **7879**
KUPL-AM - 970 (Portland, OR) **26542**
KUPL-FM - 98.7 (Portland, OR) **26543**
KUPR-FM **3304***
KUPS-FM - 90.1 (Tacoma, WA) **33159**
KUPT-TV - Channel 22 (Lubbock, TX) **30737**
KURA-FM (Ridgway, CO) *Unable to locate*
KURB-FM (Little Rock, AR) *Unable to locate*
Kurdish Life (Brooklyn, NY) **20328**
Kurdish Studies; International Journal of (Brooklyn,
  NY) **20321**
Kurdish Times **20321***
Kurenai: Japanese Embroidery Journal (Roswell, GA)
  Ceased
KURIER; KANADA (Winnipeg, MB, Can.) **35335**
KURL-AM - 730 (Billings, MT) **17746**
KURM-AM - 790 (Rogers, AR) **1329**
KURV-AM - 710 (Edinburg, TX) **30274**
KURY-AM - 910 (Brookings, OR) **26256**
KURY-FM - 95.3 (Brookings, OR) **26257**
Kuryer Zjednoczenia (Cleveland, OH) *Unable to
  locate*
KUSA-TV - Channel 9 (Denver, CO) **4391**
KUSC-FM - 91.5 (Los Angeles, CA) **2470**
KUSD-AM (Vermillion, SD) *Ceased*
KUSD-FM - 89.7 (Vermillion, SD) **29010**
KUSD-TV - Channel 2 (Vermillion, SD) **29011**
KUSF-AM **3478***
KUSF-FM - 90.3 (San Francisco, CA) **3503**
KUSH-AM - 1600 (Cushing, OK) **25796**
KUSI-TV - Channel 51 (San Diego, CA) **3316**
KUSK-TV - Channel 7 (Prescott, AZ) **854**
KUSM-TV - Channel 9 (Bozeman, MT) **17758**
KUSO-FM **26169***
KUSP-FM - 88.9 (Santa Cruz, CA) **3692**

KUSU-FM - 89.5, 91.5 (Logan, UT) **31361**
KUT-FM - 90.5 (Austin, TX) **29879**
KUTA-AM - 790 (Blanding, UT) **31321**
KUTF-TV (Salem, OR) *Unable to locate*
KUTI-AM **33231***
KUTO-AM - 1400 (San Francisco, CA) **3504**
KUTP-TV - Channel 45 (Phoenix, AZ) **842**
KUTQ-FM - 99.5 (Salt Lake City, UT) **31467**
KUTR-AM **31445***
KUTT-FM - 99.5 (Fairbury, NE) **18007**
KUTV-TV - Channel 2 (Salt Lake City, UT) **31468**
KUTX-FM - 90.1 (San Angelo, TX) **31022**
KUTY-AM - 1380 (Palmdale, CA) **2786**
KUTZ-FM **29865***
KUUL-FM **19859***
KUUL-FM - 103.7 (Davenport, IA) **10745**
Kuumba (Los Angeles, CA) **2310**
KUUY-AM (Cheyenne, WY) *Unable to locate*
KUUZ-FM - 95.9 (Greenville, MS) **16632**
KUVI-TV - Channel 45 (Bakersfield, CA) **1472**
KUVN-TV - Channel 23 (Dallas, TX) **30214**
KUVO-FM - 89.3 (Denver, CO) **4392**
KUVR-AM - 1380 (Holdrege, NE) **18051**
KUVR-FM **18050***
KUVS-TV - Channel 19 (Sacramento, CA) **3053**
KUWL-FM (Fairbanks, AK) *Unable to locate*
KUWR-FM - 91.9 (Laramie, WY) **34557**
KUWS-FM - 91.3 (Superior, WI) **34362**
KUYL-AM - 1280 (Modesto, CA) **2571**
KUYO-AM - 830 (Casper, WY) **34493**
KUZZ-AM - 550 (Bakersfield, CA) **1473**
KUZZ-FM - 107.9 (Bakersfield, CA) **1474**
KVAB-FM - 102.9 (Lewiston, ID) **7902**
KVAC-AM - 1490 (Forks, WA) **32771**
KVAK-AM - 1230 (Valdez, AK) **648**
KVAL-TV - Channel 13 (Eugene, OR) **26348**
KVAN-AM (Vancouver, WA) *Unable to locate*
KVAR-FM - 1160 (Riverside, CA) **2955**
KVAS-AM - 1230 (Astoria, OR) **26231**
KVAY-FM - 105.7 (Lamar, CO) **4541**
KVBC-TV - Channel 3 (Las Vegas, NV) **18407**
KVBR-AM (Brainerd, MN) *Unable to locate*
KVCA-AM **2457***
KVCA-FM - 670 (Los Angeles, CA) **2471**
KVCE-FM (Winnemucca, NV) *Ceased*
KVCI-AM - 1510 (Canton, TX) **29999**
KVCL-AM - 1270 (Winnfield, LA) **12881**
KVCL-FM - 92.1 (Winnfield, LA) **12882**
KVCM-FM **17297***
KVCQ-FM - 97.7 (Cuero, TX) **30117**
KVCR-FM - 91.9 (San Bernardino, CA) **3095**
KVCR-TV - Channel 24 (San Bernardino, CA) **3096**
KVCS-AM - 1020 (Perry, OK) **26033**
KVCS-FM (Perry, OK) *Unable to locate*
KVCT-TV (Victoria, TX) *Ceased*
KVCU-AM - 1190 (Boulder, CO) **4198**
KVCX-FM - 101.5 (Milwaukee, WI) **34112**
KVCY-FM (Fort Scott, KS) *Unable to locate*
KVDA-TV - Channel 60 (San Antonio, TX) **31077**
KVDB-AM **11210***
KVDB-FM **11211***
KVDL-AM - 1150 (Quanah, TX) **30965**
KVDP-FM - 89.1 (Dry Prong, LA) **12572**
KVEA-TV (Glendale, CA) *Unable to locate*
KVEC-AM (San Luis Obispo, CA) *Unable to locate*
KVEE-FM - 107.5 (Lake Charles, LA) **12649**
KVEG-AM **18409***
KVEL-AM - 920 (Vernal, UT) **31485**
KVEN-AM (Ventura, CA) *Unable to locate*
KVEO-TV - Channel 23 (Brownsville, TX) **29964**
KVER-FM - 91.1 FM (El Paso, TX) **30303**
KVET-AM - 1300 (Austin, TX) **29880**
KVEW-TV - Channel 42 (Kennewick, WA) **32794**
KVEZ-FM **31358***
KVFC-AM - 740 (Cortez, CO) **4294**
KVFD-AM - 1400 (Fort Dodge, IA) **10914**
KVFG-FM **12861***
KVFG-FM - 103.1 (Colton, CA) **1745**
KVFM-FM **31362***
KVFW-AM **11911***
KVFX-FM - 94.5 (Logan, UT) **31362**
KVGB-AM - 1590 (Great Bend, KS) **11473**
KVGB-FM - 104.3 (Great Bend, KS) **11474**
KVHP-TV - Channel 29 (Lake Charles, LA) **12650**
KVHS-FM - 90.5 (Concord, CA) **1762**
KVHT-FM - 106.3 (Yankton, SD) **29042**
KVI-AM - 570 (Seattle, WA) **33073**
KVIA-TV - Channel 7 (El Paso, TX) **30304**
KVIC-FM - 95.1 (Victoria, TX) **31240**
KVIE-TV - Channel 6 (Sacramento, CA) **3054**
KVIH-TV - Channel 12 (Clovis, NM) **30032**
KVII-TV - Channel 7 (Amarillo, TX) **29718**
KVIJ-TV (Amarillo, TX) *Ceased*
KVIL-FM (Dallas, TX) *Unable to locate*
KVIM-AM **2771***
KVIN-AM **25850***
KVIO-AM **683***
KVIP-AM - 540 (Redding, CA) **2898**
KVIP-FM - 98.1 (Redding, CA) **2899**

KVIP-TV **2894***
KVIQ-TV - Channel 6 (Eureka, CA) **1905**
KVIS-AM - 910 (Miami, OK) **25918**
KVIV-AM (El Paso, TX) *Unable to locate*
KVJM-FM - 103.1 (Bryan, TX) **29983**
KVJY-AM - 840 (Harlingen, TX) **30431**
KVKI-AM (Shreveport, LA) *Ceased*
KVKI-FM - 96.5 (Shreveport, LA) **12840**
KVKM-AM **30836***
KVLA-AM - 1400 (Vidalia, LA) **12864**
KVLE-FM - 102.3 (Bala Cynwyd, PA) **26670**
KVLG-FM **30657***
KVLH-AM - 1470 (Sulphur, OK) **26092**
KVLI-FM (Lake Isabella, CA) *Unable to locate*
KVLL-AM (Woodville, TX) *Unable to locate*
KVLO-FM - 102.9 (Little Rock, AR) **1254**
KVLT-FM **26161***
KVLT-FM - 92.3 (Victoria, TX) **31241**
KVLU-FM - 91.3 (Beaumont, TX) **29909**
KVLV-AM - 980 (Fallon, NV) **18346**
KVLV-FM - 99.3 (Fallon, NV) **18347**
KVLY-FM - 107.9 (McAllen, TX) **30799**
KVLY-TV - Channel 11 (Fargo, ND) **24429**
KVMA-AM - 630 (Magnolia, AR) **1259**
KVMA-FM - 107.9 (Magnolia, AR) **1260**
KVML-AM - 1450 (Sonora, CA) **3782**
KVMR-FM (Nevada City, CA) *Unable to locate*
KVMX-FM - 96.7 (Duncanville, TX) **30255**
KVNA-AM - 600 (Flagstaff, AZ) **704**
KVNA-FM - 97.5 (Flagstaff, AZ) **705**
KVNE-FM - 89.5 (Tyler, TX) **31219**
KVNF-FM - 90.9 (Paonia, CO) **4595**
KVNI-AM - 1080 (Coeur d'Alene, ID) **7848**
KVNO-FM - 90.7 (Omaha, NE) **18228**
KVNU-AM - 610 (Logan, UT) **31363**
KVOA-TV - Channel 4 (Tucson, AZ) **999**
KVOB-AM **12702***
KVOC-AM (Casper, WY) *Unable to locate*
KVOD-FM - 90.1 FM (Denver, CO) **4394**
KVOD-FM - 92.5 (Denver, CO) **4393**
KVOE-AM (Emporia, KS) *Unable to locate*
KVOE-FM - 101.7 (Emporia, KS) **11435**
KVOI-AM - 690 (Oro Valley, AZ) **757**
KVOK-AM - 560 (Kodiak, AK) **620**
KVOL-AM - 1330 (Lafayette, LA) **12633**
KVOL-FM - 105.9 (Lafayette, LA) **12634**
KVON-AM - 1440 (Napa, CA) **2612**
KVOO-AM - 1170 (Tulsa, OK) **26168**
KVOO-FM - 98.5 (Tulsa, OK) **26169**
KVOO-TV **26149***
KVOP-AM - 1090 (Plainview, TX) **30944**
KVOP-FM - 106.9 (Plainview, TX) **30945**
KVOR-AM - 740 (Colorado Springs, CO) **4285**
KVOS-AM **32682***
KVOS-TV - Channel 12 (Bellingham, WA) **32686**
KVOU-AM - 1400 (Uvalde, TX) **31226**
KVOW-AM **30698***
KVOW-AM (Riverton, WY) *Unable to locate*
KVOX-AM - 1280 (Fargo, ND) **24430**
KVOX-FM - 99.9 (Fargo, ND) **24431**
KVOY-AM **2148***
KVOY-AM **1026***
KVOZ-AM **30672***
KVOZ-AM (Laredo, TX) *Unable to locate*
KVPA-FM - 101.1 (South Padre Island, TX) **31120**
KVPI-AM - 1050 (Ville Platte, LA) **12866**
KVPI-FM - 92.5 (Ville Platte, LA) **12867**
KVPT-TV - Channel 18 (Fresno, CA) **1986**
KVRA-AM **29043***
KVRC-AM - 1240 (Arkadelphia, AR) **1034**
KVRD-AM **683***
KVRD-FM - 105.7 (Cottonwood, AZ) **682**
KVRE-FM **3742***
KVRF-FM **29042***
KVRH-FM - 92.3 (Salida, CO) **4622**
KVRH-FM - 92.3 (Salida, CO) **4621**
KVRI-FM **31444***
KVRO-FM - 98.1 (Stillwater, OK) **26087**
KVRP-AM (Haskell, TX) *Unable to locate*
KVRP-FM - 95.5 (Haskell, TX) **30434**
KVRQ-FM **2531***
KVRR-TV - Channel 15 (Fargo, ND) **24432**
KVRX-FM - 91.7 (Austin, TX) **29881**
KVSA-AM - 1220 (McGehee, AR) **1273**
KVSC-FM **31361***
KVSC-FM - 88.1 (St. Cloud, MN) **16352**
KVSD-AM **1668***
KVSF-AM (Santa Fe, NM) *Unable to locate*
KVSH-AM - 940 (Valentine, NE) **18300**
KVSI-AM - 1450 (Montpelier, ID) **7910**
KVSL-AM (Show Low, AZ) *Unable to locate*
KVSN-AM - 1340 (Tumwater, WA) **33170**
KVSO-AM - 1240 (Ardmore, OK) **25749**
KVSP-AM - 1140 (Oklahoma City, OK) **26019**
KVSR-FM **28945***
KVST-FM - 103.7 (Conroe, TX) **30071**
KVTI-FM - 90.9 (Tacoma, WA) **33160**
KVTK-AM - 1570 (Yankton, SD) **29043**
KVTN-TV - Channel 25 (Little Rock, AR) **1255**

KVTO-AM (San Francisco, CA) *Unable to locate*
KVTV-TV - Channel 13 (Laredo, TX) **30678**
KVTY-FM - 105.1 (Lewiston, ID) **7903**
KVTY-FM (McAllen, TX) *Unable to locate*
KVUE-TV - Channel 24 (Austin, TX) **29882**
KVUU-FM - 99.9 (Pueblo, CO) **4611**
KVVA-AM (Phoenix, AZ) *Unable to locate*
KVVA-FM (Phoenix, AZ) *Unable to locate*
KVVP-FM - 105.7 (Leesville, LA) **12661**
KVVQ-AM (Hesperia, CA) *Unable to locate*
KVVQ-FM (Hesperia, CA) *Unable to locate*
KVVS-AM - 1170 (Windsor, CO) **4689**
KVVT-TV **4035***
KVVU-TV - Channel 5 (Henderson, NV) **18355**
KVVV-FM **3738***
KVVY-AM - 1580 (Merced, CA) **2535**
KVWC-AM - 1490 (Vernon, TX) **31232**
KVWC-FM - 103.1 (Vernon, TX) **31233**
KVWG-AM - 1280 (Pearsall, TX) **30921**
KVWG-FM - 95.3 (Pearsall, TX) **30922**
KVWJ-FM **31362***
KVWM-AM - 970 (Show Low, AZ) **883**
KVWM-FM - 93.5 (Show Low, AZ) **884**
KVYN-FM - 99.3 (Napa, CA) **2613**
KW Real Estate News (Kitchener, ON, Can.) **35962**
KW Television **20403***
KWAB-AM - 1490 (Boulder, CO) **4199**
KWAC-AM - 1490 (Bakersfield, CA) **1475**
KWAD-AM - 920 (Wadena, MN) **16492**
KWAI-AM - 1080 (Honolulu, HI) **7756**
KWAK-AM - 1240 (Stuttgart, AR) **1353**
KWAK-FM - 105.5 (Stuttgart, AR) **1354**
KWAL-AM - 620 (Osburn, ID) **7941**
KWAM-AM (Memphis, TN) *Unable to locate*
KWAR-FM - 89.1 (Waverly, IA) **11310**
KWAT-AM - 950 (Watertown, SD) **29025**
KWAT-FM **29021***
KWAV-FM - 96.9 (Monterey, CA) **2588**
KWAY-AM - 1470 (Waverly, IA) **11311**
KWAY-FM - 99.3 (Waverly, IA) **11312**
KWBB-TV **3475***
KWBE-AM - 1450 (Beatrice, NE) **17949**
KWBG-AM **11507***
KWBG-AM - 1590 (Boone, IA) **10629**
KWBG-FM **11279***
KWBI-FM (Morrison, CO) *Unable to locate*
KWBI-TV **4139***
KWBJ-TV - Channel 39 (Morgan City, LA) **12714**
KWBM-AM **24562***
KWBR-AM **3492***
KWBR-FM **3575***
KWBU-FM - 103.3 (Waco, TX) **31261**
KWBW-AM - 1450 (Hutchinson, KS) **11507**
KWBY-AM - 940 (Woodburn, OR) **26620**
KWCB-FM - 89.7 (Floresville, TX) **30320**
KWCC-FM - 93.1 (Muscatine, IA) **11105**
KWCD-FM - 92.3 (Sierra Vista, AZ) **891**
KWCD-FM (Santa Barbara, CA) *Unable to locate*
KWCH-TV - Channel 12 (Wichita, KS) **11906**
KWCL-AM (Oak Grove, LA) *Ceased*
KWCL-FM - 96.7 (Oak Grove, LA) **12789**
KWCM-TV **15720***
KWCO-AM - 105.5 (Chickasha, OK) **25786**
KWCO-FM - 105.5 (Chickasha, OK) **25787**
KWCR-AM **10683***
KWCR-FM - 88.1 (Ogden, UT) **31382**
KWCS-FM **29952***
KWCW-FM - 90.5 (Walla Walla, WA) **33190**
KWCX-FM (Page, AZ) *Unable to locate*
KWCY-FM - 103.5 (Phoenix, AZ) **843**
KWDF-AM - 840 (Ball, LA) **12481**
KWDG-FM **25877***
KWDM-FM - 88.7 (West Des Moines, IA) **11321**
KWDS-AM (Prescott Valley, AZ) *Unable to locate*
KWDX-FM - 101.7 (Silsbee, TX) **31109**
KWEB-AM - 1270 (Rochester, MN) **16321**
KWED-AM - 1580 (Seguin, TX) **31097**
KWEG-FM **26253***
KWEI-AM - 1260 (Boise, ID) **7832**
KWEI-FM - 99.5 (Boise, ID) **7833**
KWEN-FM - 95.5 (Tulsa, OK) **26170**
KWEO-FM **3037***
KWES-FM **30875***
KWES-FM - 93.5 (Ruidoso, NM) **19930**
KWES-TV - Channel 9 (Midland, TX) **30825**
KWEX-TV - Channel 41 (San Antonio, TX) **31078**
KWEY-AM - 1590 (Weatherford, OK) **26188**
KWEY-FM - 97.3 (Weatherford, OK) **26189**
KWEZ-AM **12698***
KWEZ-FM **12695***
KWFC-FM - 89.1 (Springfield, MO) **17632**
KWFH-FM - 90.1 (Parker, AZ) **766**
KWFM-FM - 92.9 (Tucson, AZ) **1000**
KWFN-AM **3740***
KWFR-FM - 101.9 (San Angelo, TX) **31023**
KWFS-AM - 1290 (Lafayette Hill, PA) **27134**
KWFS-FM - 103.3 (Lafayette Hill, PA) **27135**
KWFT-AM - 990 (Lafayette Hill, PA) **27136**
KWFX-FM (Woodward, OK) *Unable to locate*

KWGB-AM **11467***
KWGG-AM **10941***
KWGN-TV - Channel 2 (Englewood, CO) **4419**
KWHB-TV - Channel 47 (Tulsa, OK) **26171**
KWHE-TV - Channel 14 (Honolulu, HI) **7757**
KWHI-AM - 1280 (Brenham, TX) **29951**
KWHK-AM (Hutchinson, KS) *Unable to locate*
KWHK-FM - 103.9 (Spokane, WA) **33131**
KWHL-FM - 106.5 (Anchorage, AK) **549**
KWHN-AM - 1650 (Fort Smith, AR) **1157**
KWHN-FM - 105.5 (Haynesville, LA) **12599**
KWHP-AM **25796***
KWHQ-FM - 100.1 (Kenai, AK) **610**
KWHT-FM - 103.5 (Pendleton, OR) **26463**
KWHW-AM - 1450 (Altus, OK) **25736**
KWHW-FM **25735***
KWHY-TV - Channel 22 (Glendale, CA) **2022**
KWIC-AM (Beaumont, TX) *Unable to locate*
KWIC-FM (Beaumont, TX) *Unable to locate*
KWIK-AM - 1240 (Pocatello, ID) **7955**
KWIL-AM - 790 (Albany, OR) **26213**
KWIN-FM (Stockton, CA) *Unable to locate*
KWIQ-AM - 100.3 (Moses Lake, WA) **32843**
KWIQ-FM - 100.3 (Moses Lake, WA) **32844**
KWIT-FM - 90.3 (Sioux City, IA) **11225**
KWIX-AM - 1230 (Moberly, MO) **17291**
KWIZ-AM (Santa Ana, CA) *Unable to locate*
KWIZ-FM - 96.7 (Santa Ana, CA) **3638**
KWJC-FM - 91.9 (Liberty, MO) **17251**
KWJJ-AM - 1080 (Portland, OR) **26544**
KWJJ-FM - 99.5 (Portland, OR) **26545**
KWJL-AM - 1470 (Palmdale, CA) **2787**
KWJM-FM (Farmerville, LA) *Ceased*
KWJZ-FM (Seattle, WA) *Unable to locate*
KWKA-AM - 680 (Clovis, NM) **19837**
KWKC-AM - 1340 (Abilene, TX) **29668**
KWKH-AM - 1130 (Shreveport, LA) **12841**
KWKH-FM **12832***
KWKT-TV - Channel 44 (Waco, TX) **31262**
KWKW-AM - 1330 (Hollywood, CA) **2054**
KWKY-AM - 1150 (Des Moines, IA) **10833**
KWLA-AM - 1400 (Many, LA) **12671**
KWLC-AM - 1240 (Decorah, IA) **10762**
KWLD-FM - 91.5 (Plainview, TX) **30946**
KWLF-FM - 98.1 (Fairbanks, AK) **580**
KWLI-FM **4151***
KWLK-AM **32816***
KWLM-AM - 1340 (Willmar, MN) **16522**
KWLO-AM - 1330 (Waterloo, IA) **11297**
KWLS-AM - 1290-AM (Pratt, KS) **11766**
KWLT-FM **3295***
KWLT-FM - 102.7 (Crossett, AR) **1095**
KWLV-FM - 107.1 (Many, LA) **12672**
KWLZ-FM - 96.5 (Bend, OR) **26252**
KWMB-AM **16314***
KWMC-AM - 1490 (Del Rio, TX) **30229**
KWME-FM - 93.5 (Wellington, KS) **11868**
KWMG-FM **17982***
KWMM-FM - 98.7 (Osage, IA) **11132**
KWMT-AM - 540 (Fort Dodge, IA) **10915**
KWMT-FM **30874***
KWMU-FM - 90.7 (St. Louis, MO) **17553**
KWMX-FM - 96.7 (Flagstaff, AZ) **706**
KWNA-FM - 92.7 (Winnemucca, NV) **18452**
KWNB-TV - Channel 6 (Hayes Center, NE) **18044**
KWNC-AM - 1370 (Quincy, WA) **32920**
KWNE-FM - 94.5 (Ukiah, CA) **3971**
KWNM-TV **19956***
KWNN-FM (Stockton, CA) *Unable to locate*
KWNO-AM (Winona, MN) *Unable to locate*
KWNO-FM - 99.3 (Winona, MN) **16536**
KWNQ-FM **1169***
KWNR-FM - 95.5 (Las Vegas, NV) **18408**
KWNS-FM **11766***
KWNS-FM - 104.7 (Winnsboro, TX) **31306**
KWNW-AM **33203***
KWNZ-FM - 97.3 (Reno, NV) **18443**
KWOA-AM - 730 (Worthington, MN) **16541**
KWOD-FM - 106.5 (Sacramento, CA) **3055**
KWOF-AM - 850 & 89.1 FM (Waterloo, IA) **11298**
KWOF-FM - 88.1 (Waterloo, IA) **11299**
KWON-AM - 1400 (Bartlesville, OK) **25755**
KWOR-AM - 1340 (Worland, WY) **34606**
KWOX-FM - 101.1 (Woodward, OK) **26200**
KWPB-FM **17251***
KWPC-AM - 860 (Muscatine, IA) **11106**
KWPK-FM - 104.1 (Bend, OR) **26253**
KWPN-AM **18313***
KWPN-FM - 107.9 (West Point, NE) **18314**
KWPZ-FM - 106.5 (Lynden, WA) **32822**
KWQC-TV - Channel 6 (Davenport, IA) **10746**
KWRB-FM - 90.9 (Sierra Vista, AZ) **892**
KWRC-AM **26620***
KWRD-AM - 1470 (Henderson, TX) **30441**
KWRD-FM - 100.7 (Irving, TX) **30612**
KWRE-AM - 730 (Warrenton, MO) **17702**
KWRF-AM - 860 (Warren, AR) **1366**
KWRF-FM - 105.5 (Warren, AR) **1367**
KWRL-FM - 99.9 (La Grande, OR) **26403**

KWRM-AM - 1370 (Corona, CA) **1769**
KWRN-AM - 1550 (Victorville, CA) **4038**
KWRO-AM - 630 (Coquille, OR) **26284**
KWRO-FM **26283***
KWRS-FM - 90.3 (Spokane, WA) **33132**
KWRU-AM - 940 (Fresno, CA) **1987**
KWRW-FM - 97.7 (Rusk, TX) **31001**
KWSA-AM (Garden Grove, CA) *Unable to locate*
KWSB-FM - 91.1 (Gunnison, CO) **4513**
KWSC-FM - 91.9 (Wayne, NE) **18310**
KWSE-TV - Channel 4 (Williston, ND) **24565**
KWSH-AM - 1260 (Shawnee, OK) **26069**
KWSH-FM - 104.7 (Shawnee, OK) **26070**
KWSL-AM **11226***
KWSL-AM - 1470 (Sioux City, IA) **11226**
KWSM-FM **3956***
KWSN-AM - 1230 (Sioux Falls, SD) **28987**
KWSO-AM **1460***
KWSO-FM - 91.9 (Warm Springs, OR) **26609**
KWSP-FM (Agoura Hills, CA) *Unable to locate*
KWSS-FM **3558***
KWST-AM - 1430 (El Centro, CA) **1856**
KWST-FM **2589***
KWSU-AM - 1250 (Pullman, WA) **32915**
KWSU-TV - Channel 10 (Pullman, WA) **32916**
KWTD-FM **1303***
KWTO-AM - 560 (Springfield, MO) **17633**
KWTO-FM - 98.7 (Springfield, MO) **17634**
KWTR-AM **2144***
KWTS-FM - 91.1 (Canyon, TX) **30001**
KWTV-TV - Channel 9 (Oklahoma City, OK) **26020**
KWTX-AM - 1230 (Waco, TX) **31263**
KWTX-FM - 97.5 (Waco, TX) **31264**
KWTX-TV - Channel 10 (Waco, TX) **31265**
KWTY-FM - 102.9 (Big Pine, CA) **1582**
KWUF-AM - 1400 (Pagosa Springs, CO) **4591**
KWUF-FM - 106.3 (Pagosa Springs, CO) **4592**
KWUN-AM (Concord, CA) *Ceased*
KWUR-FM - 90.3 (St. Louis, MO) **17554**
KWVA-AM - 88.1 (Eugene, OR) **26349**
KWVE-FM - 107.9 (Santa Ana, CA) **3639**
KWVR-AM - 1340 (Enterprise, OR) **26311**
KWVR-FM - 92.1 (Enterprise, OR) **26312**
KWVS-FM **26451***
KWVS-FM **30085***
KWVV-FM - 105 (Homer, AK) **592**
KWWC-FM - 90.5 (Columbia, MO) **17024**
KWWF-FM **7888***
KWWJ-AM - 1360 (Baytown, TX) **29896**
KWWK-FM - 96.5 (Rochester, MN) **16322**
KWWL-AM **11297***
KWWL-FM **11292***
KWWL-TV - Channel 7 (Waterloo, IA) **11300**
KWWM-FM **31133***
KWWN-FM (Cameron Park, CA) *Unable to locate*
KWWR-FM - 95.7 (Mexico, MO) **17287**
KWWW-AM **33203***
KWWW-FM (Quincy, WA) *Unable to locate*
KWWX-AM - 1340 (Wenatchee, WA) **33204**
KWWX-AM - 1340 (Wenatchee, WA) **33203**
KWXE-FM - 104.5 (Glenwood, AR) **1160**
KWXI-AM - 670 (Glenwood, AR) **1161**
KWXI-FM **30202***
KWXX-FM - 94.7 (Hilo, HI) **7678**
KWXY-AM - 1340 (Palm Springs, CA) **2781**
KWXY-FM - 98.5 (Cathedral City, CA) **1680**
KWYD-AM - 1580 (Fountain, CO) **4453**
KWYD-FM **4281***
KWYK-AM **19848***
KWYK-FM - 94.9 (Farmington, NM) **19853**
KWYN-AM - 1400 (Wynne, AR) **1373**
KWYN-FM - 92.5 (Wynne, AR) **1374**
KWYO-AM - 1410 (Sheridan, WY) **34590**
KWYO-FM **34591***
KWYR-AM - 1260 (Winner, SD) **29033**
KWYR-FM **29034***
KWYR-FM - 93.7 (Winner, SD) **29034**
KWYS-AM - 920 (Ketchum, ID) **7890**
KWYX-FM - 102.7 (Jasper, TX) **30623**
KWYZ-AM (Everett, WA) *Unable to locate*
KWYZ-FM **30623***
KWZD-FM (Abilene, TX) *Unable to locate*
KXAA-FM - 99.5 (Spokane, WA) **33133**
KXAL-FM (Pittsburg, TX) *Unable to locate*
KXAM-AM - 1310 (Mesa, AZ) **751**
KXAN-TV - Channel 36 (Austin, TX) **29883**
KXAR-AM - 1490 (Hope, AR) **1181**
KXAR-FM - 101.7 (Hope, AR) **1182**
KXAS-TV - Channel 5 (Fort Worth, TX) **30360**
KXAZ-FM - 93.3 (Page, AZ) **760**
KXBS-FM (Ventura, CA) *Unable to locate*
KXBT-AM (Vallejo, CA) *Unable to locate*
KXBX-AM - 1270 (Lakeport, CA) **2144**
KXBX-FM (Lakeport, CA) *Unable to locate*
KXCI-FM - 91.3 (Tucson, AZ) **1001**
KXCL-FM **30104***
KXCL-FM - 103.9 (Yuba City, CA) **4125**
KXCV-FM - 90.5 (Maryville, MO) **17279**
KXDA-FM **19881***

KXDC-FM - 101.7 (Monterey, CA) **2589**
KXDD-FM (Yakima, WA) *Unable to locate*
KXDL-FM - 99.7 (Long Prairie, MN) **16011**
KXDX-FM **1354***
KXDZ-FM (Anchorage, AK) *Unable to locate*
KXEB-AM - 910 (Dallas, TX) **30215**
KXED-AM (Los Angeles, CA) *Unable to locate*
KXEG-AM (Phoenix, AZ) *Unable to locate*
KXEI-FM - 95.1 (Havre, MT) **17815**
KXEL-AM - 1540 (Waterloo, IA) **11301**
KXEM-FM **1470***
KXEN-AM (Mitchell, IL) *Unable to locate*
KXEO-AM - 1340 (Mexico, MO) **17288**
KXEQ-AM - 1340 (Reno, NV) **18444**
KXEW-AM - 1600 (Tucson, AZ) **1002**
KXEX-AM - 1550 (Fresno, CA) **1988**
KXEZ-FM **4125***
KXFE-FM (Dumas, AR) *Unable to locate*
KXFM-FM - 99.1 (Santa Maria, CA) **3705**
KXFX-FM - 101.7 (Santa Rosa, CA) **3742**
KXGN-TV - Channel 5 (Glendive, MT) **17797**
KXGO-FM - 93.1 (Eureka, CA) **1906**
KXGT-FM - 95.5 (Jamestown, ND) **24483**
KXIA-FM - 101.1 (Marshalltown, IA) **11069**
KXIC-AM - 800 (Iowa City, IA) **10995**
KXII-TV - Channel 12 (Sherman, TX) **31104**
KXIV **31450***
KXIX-FM - 94.1 (Bend, OR) **26254**
KXJB-TV - Channel 4 (Fargo, ND) **24433**
KXJX-FM **11154***
KXKC-FM - 99.1 (New Iberia, LA) **12725**
KXKK-FM (Dover, NM) *Unable to locate*
KXKL-AM **4395***
KXKL-FM - 105.1 (Denver, CO) **4395**
KXKQ-FM - 94.1 (Safford, AZ) **864**
KXKS-FM - 93.7 (Shreveport, LA) **12842**
KXKT-FM - 103.7 (Atlantic, IA) **10612**
KXKU-FM - 97.1 (Hutchinson, KS) **11508**
KXKW-AM **12624***
KXKX-FM **10850***
KXKZ-FM - 107.5 (Ruston, LA) **12811**
KXL-AM (Portland, OR) *Unable to locate*
KXL-FM (Portland, OR) *Unable to locate*
KXLA-AM (Rayville, LA) *Unable to locate*
KXLC-FM - 91.1 (Rochester, MN) **16323**
KXLE-AM - 1240 (Ellensburg, WA) **32752**
KXLE-FM - 95.3 (Ellensburg, WA) **32753**
KXLF-TV - Channel 4 (Butte, MT) **17766**
KXLI-TV **16324***
KXLJ-AM **17825***
KXLK-FM (Wichita, KS) *Unable to locate*
KXLN-TV - Channel 45 (Houston, TX) **30585**
KXLO-AM - 1230 (Lewistown, MT) **17850**
KXLP-FM - 93.1 (North Mankato, MN) **16222**
KXLQ-AM (Chariton, IA) *Ceased*
KXLR-FM (Fairbanks, AK) *Unable to locate*
KXLS-FM (Enid, OK) *Unable to locate*
KXLT-FM **4369***
KXLT-FM - 107.9 (Boise, ID) **7834**
KXLT-TV - Channel 47 (Rochester, MN) **16324**
KXLU-FM - 88.9 (Los Angeles, CA) **2472**
KXLV-FM **15787***
KXLY-AM - 920 (Spokane, WA) **33134**
KXLY-FM - 99.9 (Spokane, WA) **33135**
KXLY-TV - Channel 4 (Spokane, WA) **33136**
KXMA-TV - Channel 2 (Dickinson, ND) **24401**
KXMB-TV - Channel 12 (Bismarck, ND) **24372**
KXMC-TV - Channel 13 (Minot, ND) **24515**
KXMD-TV - Channel 11 (Williston, ND) **24566**
KXMG-FM **989***
KXMS-FM (Joplin, MO) *Ceased*
KXNE-FM - 89.3 (Norfolk, NE) **18172**
KXNE-TV - Channel 19 (Norfolk, NE) **18173**
KXNO-AM - 1460 (Des Moines, IA) **10834**
KXNP-FM - 103.5 (North Platte, NE) **18185**
KXNT-AM - 840 (Las Vegas, NV) **18409**
KXO-AM - 1230 (El Centro, CA) **1857**
KXO-FM - 107.5 (El Centro, CA) **1858**
KXOC-FM **2589***
KXOF-FM **10623***
KXOJ-FM - 100.9 (Tulsa, OK) **26172**
KXOK-FM (St. Louis, MO) *Unable to locate*
KXOL-AM **25792***
KXOL-FM - 96.3 (Los Angeles, CA) **2473**
KXON-TV **28972***
KXOO-AM - 94.3 (Elk City, OK) **25821**
KXOR-FM - 106.3 (Houma, LA) **12604**
KXOW-AM - 1420 (Hot Springs, AR) **1188**
KXOX-AM - 1240 (Sweetwater, TX) **31171**
KXOX-FM - 96.7 (Sweetwater, TX) **31172**
KXPC-FM - 103.7 (Albany, OR) **26214**
KXPH-AM - 1540 (Seattle, WA) **33074**
KXPK-FM - 92.1 (Englewood, CO) **4420**
KXPO-AM - 1340 (Grafton, ND) **24452**
KXPO-FM **24451***
KXPR-FM - 90.9 (Sacramento, CA) **3056**
KXPT-FM - 97.1 (Las Vegas, NV) **18410**
KXPZ-FM **3061***
KXRB-AM - 1000 (Sioux Falls, SD) **28988**

KXRI-FM - 91.9 (Amarillo, TX) **29719**
KXRJ-FM - 91.9 (Russellville, AR) **1334**
KXRK-FM - 96.3 (Salt Lake City, UT) **31469**
KXRM-TV - Channel 21 (Colorado Springs, CO) **4286**
KXRO-AM - 1320 (Aberdeen, WA) **32652**
KXRS-FM **32886***
KXRX-FM - 97.1 (Pasco, WA) **32886**
KXSA-FM - 103.1 (Monticello, AR) **1282**
KXTD-AM (Broken Arrow, OK) *Unable to locate*
KXTF-TV (Pocatello, ID) *Unable to locate*
KXTL-AM - 1370 (Butte, MT) **17767**
KXTP-AM (Duluth, MN) *Unable to locate*
KXTQ-FM - 93.7 (Lubbock, TX) **30738**
KXTR-AM - 1660 (Westwood, KS) **11875**
KXTR-FM - 96.5 (Mission, KS) **11657**
KXTV-TV - Channel 10 (Sacramento, CA) **3057**
KXTX-AM - 940 (Des Moines, IA) **10835**
KXTX-TV - Channel 39 (Dallas, TX) **30216**
KXTZ-FM - 95.3 (San Luis Obispo, CA) **3575**
KXTZ-FM (Las Vegas, NV) *Unable to locate*
KXUL-FM - 91.1 (Monroe, LA) **12703**
KXUM-AM - 670 (Bismarck, ND) **24373**
KXVI-AM - 91.1 (Garland, TX) **30387**
KXVO-TV - Channel 15 (Omaha, NE) **18229**
KXVQ-AM (Pawhuska, OK) *Unable to locate*
KXWY-TV **34488***
KXXI-FM **1360***
KXXI-FM - 93.7 (Gallup, NM) **19861**
KXXK-FM **25787***
KXXL-FM **30876***
KXXO-FM - 96.1 (Olympia, WA) **32871**
KXXR-FM **17212***
KXXR-FM - 93.7 (Minneapolis, MN) **16157**
KXXS-FM **33233***
KXXV-TV (Waco, TX) *Unable to locate*
KXXX-AM - 790 (Colby, KS) **11393**
KXXX-FM **3483***
KXXY-FM **26001***
KXXY-FM - 96.1 (Oklahoma City, OK) **26021**
KXYL-AM - 1240 (Brownwood, TX) **29971**
KXYL-FM - 96.9 (Brownwood, TX) **29972**
KXYQ-FM (Portland, OR) *Unable to locate*
KXYZ-AM - 1320 (Houston, TX) **30586**
KXZZ-AM (Lake Charles, LA) *Unable to locate*
KYAC-AM **32800***
KYAK-AM (Anchorage, AK) *Unable to locate*
KYAL-AM - 1550 (Tulsa, OK) **26173**
KYAP-AM **19929***
KYAX-FM **1395***
KYBA-FM - 105.3 (Rochester, MN) **16325**
KYBC-AM - 1600 (Cottonwood, AZ) **683**
KYBE-FM - 95.9 (Frederick, OK) **25841**
KYBG-AM - 1090 (Englewood, CO) **4421**
KYBS-FM **17755***
KYCA-AM - 1490 (Prescott, AZ) **855**
KYCC-FM **3811***
KYCC-FM - 90.1 (Stockton, CA) **3820**
KYCN-AM - 1340 (Wheatland, WY) **34602**
KYCN-FM **34603***
KYCR-AM (Minneapolis, MN) *Unable to locate*
KYCS-AM **30791***
KYCS-FM (Green River, WY) *Unable to locate*
KYCW-FM (Seattle, WA) *Unable to locate*
KYCX-FM - 104.9 (Mexia, TX) **30812**
KYCY-FM (San Francisco, CA) *Unable to locate*
KYDL-FM - 96.7 (Hot Springs, AR) **1189**
KYDS-FM - 91.5 (Sacramento, CA) **3058**
KYDZ-FM (Cody, WY) *Unable to locate*
KYEA-FM - 98.3 (Monroe, LA) **12704**
KYED-AM **10642***
KYES-AM **26561***
KYES-TV - Channel 5 (Anchorage, AK) **550**
KYEZ-FM - 93.7 (Salina, KS) **11791**
KYFA-FM **29719***
KYFC-TV (Shawnee Mission, KS) *Unable to locate*
KYFM-FM - 100.1 (Bartlesville, OK) **25756**
KYFO-AM - 1490 (Ogden, UT) **31383**
KYFR-AM - 920 (Shenandoah, IA) **11201**
KYFW-FM - 88.3 (Derby, KS) **11411**
KYFX-FM (Little Rock, AR) *Unable to locate*
KYGO-AM **4374***
KYGO-FM - 98.5 (Denver, CO) **4396**
KYHT-FM (Lancaster, CA) *Unable to locate*
KYIN-TV - Channel 24 (Mason City, IA) **11080**
KYIS-FM - 98.9 (Oklahoma City, OK) **26022**
KYJC-AM **26426***
KYJC-FM **26364***
KYKC-AM **28987***
KYKD-FM - 100.1 (Bethel, AK) **555**
KYKN-AM - 1430 (Salem, OR) **26576**
KYKR-FM - 95.1 (Beaumont, TX) **29910**
KYKS-FM - 105.1 (Lufkin, TX) **30748**
KYKX-FM - 105.7 (Longview, TX) **30707**
KYKY-FM - 98.1 (St. Louis, MO) **17555**
KYKZ-FM - 96.1 (Lake Charles, LA) **12651**
KYLD-FM - 94.9 (San Francisco, CA) **3505**
KYLR-AM (Huntsville, TX) *Unable to locate*
KYLS-AM - 1450 (Farmington, MO) **17056**
KYLS-FM - 95.9 (Farmington, MO) **17057**

KYLT-AM - 1340 (Missoula, MT) **17886**
KYLV-FM - 88.9 (Rocklin, CA) **2960**
KYMA-TV - Channel 11 (Yuma, AZ) **1029**
KYMC-FM - 89.7 (Chesterfield, MO) **16976**
KYMG-FM (Anchorage, AK) *Unable to locate*
KYMN-AM - 1080 (Northfield, MN) **16239**
KYMX-FM - 96.1 (Sacramento, CA) **3059**
KYND-AM - 1520 (Houston, TX) **30587**
KYND-FM **24516***
KYNE-TV - Channel 26 (Omaha, NE) **18230**
KYNG-AM (Coos Bay, OR) *Ceased*
KYNG-FM (Portland, OR) *Ceased*
KYNG-FM - 105.3 (Dallas, TX) **30217**
KYNN-FM (Omaha, NE) *Unable to locate*
KYNO-AM (Fresno, CA) *Unable to locate*
KYNO-FM **1973***
KYNR-AM **33169***
KYNT-AM - 1450 (Yankton, SD) **29044**
KYNU-FM **24483***
KYOC-FM (Yoakum, TX) *Unable to locate*
Kyodo News Serivce (New York, NY) **37980**
KYOO-AM - 1200 (Bolivar, MO) **16913**
KYOO-FM (Bolivar, MO) *Ceased*
KYOS-AM - 1480 (Merced, CA) **2536**
KYOT-FM - 95.5 (Phoenix, AZ) **844**
KYOT-FM **1972 4640***
KYOU-TV - Channel 15 (Ottumwa, IA) **11146**
KYPA-AM (West Hollywood, CA) *Unable to locate*
KYQQ-FM (Wichita, KS) *Unable to locate*
KYQT-FM **26451***
KYRK-FM **18410***
KYRO-AM - 1280 (Potosi, MO) **17365**
KYRS-FM **10694***
KYSC-FM - 88.5 (Yakima, WA) **33235**
KYSL-FM - 93.9 (Frisco, CO) **4457**
KYSM-AM - 1230 (North Mankato, MN) **16223**
KYSM-FM - 103.5 (North Mankato, MN) **16224**
KYSN-FM - 97.7 (Wenatchee, WA) **33205**
KYSR-FM **30286***
KYSR-FM - 98.7 (Burbank, CA) **1630**
KYSS-FM - 94.9 (Missoula, MT) **17887**
KYTC-AM **10666***
KYTC-FM - 102.7 (Albert Lea, MN) **15710**
KYTE-AM **26542***
KYTE-FM - 102.7 (Newport, OR) **26451**
KYTI-FM - 93.7 (Sheridan, WY) **34591**
KYTT-FM - 98.7 (Coos Bay, OR) **26280**
KYTV-TV - Channel 3 (Springfield, MO) **17635**
KYUF-FM - 104.9 (Uvalde, TX) **31227**
KYUK-AM - 640 (Bethel, AK) **556**
KYUK-TV - Channel 4 (Bethel, AK) **557**
KYUM-AM **1024***
KYUU-AM - 1470 (Liberal, KS) **11607**
KYVE-TV - Channel 47 (Yakima, WA) **33236**
KYW-AM - 1060 (Philadelphia, PA) **27728**
KYW-TV - Channel 3 (Philadelphia, PA) **27729**
KYXE-AM (Yakima, WA) *Unable to locate*
KYXI-FM (Yuma, AZ) *Unable to locate*
KYXK-FM (Gurdon, AR) *Unable to locate*
KYXS-AM **31274***
KYXS-FM - 95.9 (Weatherford, TX) **31275**
KYXX-FM (Sonora, TX) *Unable to locate*
KYXY-FM - 96.5 (San Diego, CA) **3317**
KYYA-FM - 93.3 (Billings, MT) **17747**
KYYD-AM **29668***
KYYK-FM - 98.3 (Palestine, TX) **30899**
KYYS-FM - 99.7 (Westwood, KS) **11876**
KYYT-FM - 102.3 (The Dalles, OR) **26304**
KYYX-FM - 97.1 (Minot, ND) **24516**
KYYY-FM - 92.9 (Bismarck, ND) **24374**
KYYZ-FM - 96.1 (Williston, ND) **24567**
KYZS-AM - 1490 (Tyler, TX) **31220**
KYZX-FM - 103.9 (Colorado Springs, CO) **4287**
KZAK-AM **31212***
KZAK-FM **31218***
KZAK-FM (Reno, NV) *Unable to locate*
KZAM-FM - 104.7 (Victoria, TX) **31242**
KZAN-FM **31380***
KZAP-FM **3046***
KZAP-FM - 96.7 (Chico, CA) **1706**
KZAT-FM - 95.5 (Tama, IA) **11264**
KZAZ-TV **985***
KZBA-FM **11279***
KZBB-FM - 97.9 (Fort Smith, AR) **1158**
KZBL-FM - 100.7 (Many, LA) **12673**
KZBQ-AM - 1290 (Pocatello, ID) **7956**
KZBQ-FM - 93.7 (Pocatello, ID) **7957**
KZBS-FM **26022***
KZCD-FM - 94.1 (Lawton, OK) **25897**
KZCO-FM - 97.7 (Sacramento, CA) **3060**
KZCR-FM - 103.3 (Fergus Falls, MN) **15903**
KZDX-FM - 99.9 (Rupert, ID) **7970**
KZED-FM **11868***
KZEE-AM (Weatherford, TX) *Ceased*
KZEG-FM - 94.7 (Clinton, IA) **10714**
KZEL-FM (Eugene, OR) *Unable to locate*
KZEN-FM - 100.3 (Columbus, NE) **17985**
KZEW-FM **30193***
KZEW-FM - 101.7 (Wheatland, WY) **34603**

KZEY-AM - 690 (Tyler, TX) **31221**
KZEZ-FM **31421***
KZEZ-FM - 95.7 (Fillmore, UT) **31335**
KZFF-FM (South Lake Tahoe, CA) *Unable to locate*
KZFM-FM - 95.5 (Corpus Christi, TX) **30097**
KZFN-FM - 106.1 (Moscow, ID) **7924**
KZFR-FM - 90.1 (Chico, CA) **1707**
KZFX-FM **30575***
KZGL-FM (Cottonwood, AZ) *Unable to locate*
KZHE-FM - 100.5 (Magnolia, AR) **1261**
KZHI-AM **7756***
KZHR-FM **33233***
KZHT-FM - 94.9 (Salt Lake City, UT) **31470**
KZIA-AM - 1610 (Portales, NM) **19909**
KZIG-FM - 89.9 (Cave City, AR) **1075**
KZII-FM (Lubbock, TX) *Unable to locate*
KZIM-AM - 960 (Cape Girardeau, MO) **16954**
KZIN-FM - 96.3 (Shelby, MT) **17908**
KZIO **15851***
KZIQ-AM (Ridgecrest, CA) *Unable to locate*
KZIX-AM **4442***
KZIZ-AM - 1420 (Tacoma, WA) **33161**
KZJH-FM - 95.3 (Jackson, WY) **34540**
KZKC-TV **11538***
KZKL-FM (Albuquerque, NM) *Unable to locate*
KZKS-FM (Grand Junction, CO) *Unable to locate*
KZKX-FM (Lincoln, NE) *Unable to locate*
KZKZ-AM **1153***
KZKZ-FM - 106.3 (Fort Smith, AR) **1159**
KZLA-FM - 93.9 (Los Angeles, CA) **2474**
KZLE-FM - 93.1 (Batesville, AR) **1044**
KZLN-FM - 97.5 (Othello, WA) **32876**
KZLS-FM (Great Bend, KS) *Unable to locate*
KZLT-FM - 104.3 (Grand Forks, ND) **24464**
KZLV-FM - 91.3 (Sacramento, CA) **3061**
KZMC-FM **18156***
KZMG-FM - 93.1 (Boise, ID) **7835**
KZMK-FM **891***
KZMK-FM - 100.9 (Sierra Vista, AZ) **893**
KZMO-AM **16936***
KZMQ-AM - 1140 (Cody, WY) **34517**
KZMQ-FM - 100.3 (Cody, WY) **34518**
KZMT-FM - 101.1 (Helena, MT) **17832**
KZMX-AM - 580 (Hot Springs, SD) **28868**
KZMX-FM - 96.7 (Hot Springs, SD) **28869**
KZMZ-FM - 96.9 (Alexandria, LA) **12469**
KZNC-FM (Huron, SD) *Unable to locate*
KZNG-AM - 1340 (Hot Springs, AR) **1190**
KZNS-AM - 1280 (Salt Lake City, UT) **31471**
KZNU-AM - 1450 (St. George, UT) **31422**
KZOC-FM (Osage City, KS) *Unable to locate*
KZOE-FM - 90.3 (Longview, WA) **32819**
KZOK-AM (Seattle, WA) *Unable to locate*
KZOK-FM (Seattle, WA) *Unable to locate*
KZOL-AM **30316***
KZOL-FM **30317***
KZOL-FM (Provo, UT) *Unable to locate*
KZON-FM - 101.5 (Phoenix, AZ) **845**
KZOO-AM - 1210 (Honolulu, HI) **7758**
KZOQ-FM - 100.1 (Missoula, MT) **17888**
KZOR-FM - 94.1 (Hobbs, NM) **19870**
KZOW-FM - 91.9 (Forest City, IA) **10893**
KZOZ-FM - 93.3 (San Luis Obispo, CA) **3576**
KZPH-FM - 106.7 (Spokane, WA) **33137**
KZPR-FM - 105.3 (Minot, ND) **24517**
KZPS-FM (Dallas, TX) *Unable to locate*
KZPT-FM - 104.1 (Tucson, AZ) **1003**
KZQQ-AM **31453***
KZQQ-AM - 1560 (Abilene, TX) **29669**
KZRA-AM - 1590 (Fayetteville, AR) **1132**
KZRK-AM **1306***
KZRK-FM (Amarillo, TX) *Unable to locate*
KZRK-FM (Dallas, TX) *Unable to locate*
KZRQ-FM - 104.1 (Springfield, MO) **17636**
KZRR-FM (Albuquerque, NM) *Unable to locate*
KZRX-AM (Prosser, WA) *Unable to locate*
KZRX-FM - 92.1 (Dickinson, ND) **24402**
KZRZ-FM **4420***
KZSC-FM - 88.1 (Santa Cruz, CA) **3693**
KZSD-TV - Channel 8 (Martin, SD) **28890**
KZSE-FM - 90.7 (Rochester, MN) **16326**
KZSN-AM (Wichita, KS) *Unable to locate*
KZSN-FM (Wichita, KS) *Unable to locate*
KZSP-FM - 95.3 (South Padre Island, TX) **31121**
KZSS-AM (Albuquerque, NM) *Unable to locate*
KZST-FM - 100.1 (Santa Rosa, CA) **3743**
KZSU-FM - 90.1 (Palo Alto, CA) **2803**
KZTA-AM (Yakima, WA) *Unable to locate*
KZTA-FM (Yakima, WA) *Unable to locate*
KZTB-FM - 96.7 (Yakima, WA) **33237**
KZTO-FM (Lawrence, KS) *Unable to locate*
KZTS-AM - 1210 (Yakima, WA) **33238**
KZTV-TV **18434***
KZTV-TV - Channel 10 (Corpus Christi, TX) **30098**
KZUA-AM - 92.1 (Holbrook, AZ) **726**
KZUE-AM - 1460 (El Reno, OK) **25817**
KZUL-AM **765***
KZUL-FM - 104.5 (Lake Havasu City, AZ) **741**
KZUM-FM - 89.3 (Lincoln, NE) **18148**

KZUU-FM - 90.7 (Pullman, WA) **32917**
KZWA-FM (Lake Charles, LA) *Unable to locate*
KZWC-FM **1760***
KZWY-FM - 94.9 (Sheridan, WY) **34592**
KZXR-FM (Prosser, WA) *Unable to locate*
KZXX-AM (Kenai, AK) *Ceased*
KZXY-AM **4036***
KZXY-FM - 102.3 (Victorville, CA) **4039**
KZYQ-FM - 103.5 (Greenville, MS) **16633**
KZYR-FM (Avon, CO) *Unable to locate*
KZYX-FM - 90.7 (Philo, CA) **2838**
KZZB-AM (St. Joseph, MO) *Unable to locate*
KZZB-AM - 990 (Beaumont, TX) **29911**
KZZD-FM - 90.7 (Wichita, KS) **11907**
KZZE-AM **29971***
KZZE-FM - 106.3 (Medford, OR) **26432**
KZZF-FM (Carson City, NV) *Ceased*
KZZJ-AM - 1450 (Rugby, ND) **24536**
KZZK-AM (Eugene, OR) *Unable to locate*
KZZK-FM (Eugene, OR) *Unable to locate*
KZZL-FM - 99.5 (Colfax, WA) **32724**
KZZN-AM - 1490 (Littlefield, TX) **30698**
KZZO-FM (Clovis, NM) *Unable to locate*
KZZOKY-FM - 100.5 (Sacramento, CA) **3062**
KZZP-FM (Mesa, AZ) *Unable to locate*
KZZP-FM (Chico, CA) *Unable to locate*
KZZQ-FM **29703***
KZZR-AM - 1230 (Burns, OR) **26261**
KZZT-FM - 105.5 (Moberly, MO) **17292**
KZZU-FM (Spokane, WA) *Unable to locate*
KZZX-FM (Alamogordo, NM) *Unable to locate*
KZZY-FM - 103.5 (Devils Lake, ND) **24393**
KZZZ-FM **667***

L

The L (New York, NY) **22226**
L I T: Literature Interpretation Theory (Philadelphia, PA) **27557**
L.A. Asian Journal (Los Angeles, CA) *Unable to locate*
La Barrique (Montreal, QC, Can.) *Ceased*
The La Belle Star (La Belle, MO) **17234**
La Belle Vision, Inc. **37419***
La Bobina (Columbia, SC) **28556**
La Boite a Nouvelles (Iroquois Falls, ON, Can.) *Unable to locate*
La Breche (Montreal, QC, Can.) *Unable to locate*
La Canada Valley Sun (La Canada, CA) **2107**
La Carta (Long Island City, NY) *Unable to locate*
LA Children Magazine **1884***
La Compagnie de Television de Sept-Iloe Ltee. **37807***
La Concorde (Saint-Eustache, QC, Can.) **37332**
La Crosse County Countryman **34449***
La Crosse Tribune (La Crosse, WI) **33885**
La Estrella De Puerto Rico (Hato Rey, PR) **28248**
La Familia de la Ciudad (New York, NY) **22227**
La Familia de Hoy (Knoxville, TN) *Unable to locate*
La Feria News (La Feria, TX) **30655**
La Florida Magazine (Boca Raton, FL) *Unable to locate*
La Flute (Montreal, QC, Can.) **37149**
La Follette Press (La Follette, TN) **29308**
La Fournee (Montreal, QC, Can.) *Unable to locate*
La Frontiere (Rouyn-Noranda, QC, Can.) **37321**
La Gaceta (Tampa, FL) **6773**
La Gatineau (Maniwaki, QC, Can.) **37065**
La Gazette de Maniwaki (Maniwaki, QC, Can.) *Unable to locate*
La Gazette Populaire (Trois-Rivieres, QC, Can.) **37415**
La Gente (Los Angeles, CA) **2311**
La Gente de Aztlan **2311***
La Grange Countian (LaGrange, IN) **10264**
La Grange Independent (La Grange, NY) **20866**
La Grange Journal (La Grange, TX) *Ceased*
La Grange/La Grange Park Sun (Naperville, IL) *Ceased*
The La Grange Ledger **23109***
La Grange News (LaGrange, IN) **10265**
La Grange Standard (LaGrange, IN) **10266**
La Guia Familiar (Van Nuys, CA) **3991**
La Habra Star (Anaheim, CA) *Unable to locate*
La Hacienda (North Miami, FL) *Unable to locate*
La Informacion (Houston, TX) **30501**
L.A. Jewish Times (Los Angeles, CA) *Unable to locate*
La Jolla Light (La Jolla, CA) **2115**
La Jolla; Linguistic Notes from (La Jolla, CA) **2116**
La Jolla Village News (San Diego, CA) **3219**
La Junta Tribune-Democrat (La Junta, CO) **4527**
La Latina Presencia (Gardner, KS) **11456**
La Liberte (St. Boniface, MB, Can.) **35289**

3412

Numbers cited in bold after listings are entry numbers rather than page numbers.

Lake Forester (Lake Forest, IL) 9062
Lake Front News (Port Clinton, OH) 25481
Lake Geneva Regional News (Lake Geneva, WI) 33903
Lake George Mirror (Warrensburg, NY) Ceased
Lake George News; The Warrensburg- (Warrensburg, NY) 23505
Lake Grove Suffolk Life; Centereach/ (Centereach, NY) 20445
The Lake Houston Sun (Pasadena, TX) 30911
Lake Hughes Television Cable Service (Ventura, CA) 4030
Lake to Lake Shopper (Brillion, WI) 33600
Lake Life Magazine (Atlanta, GA) Unable to locate
Lake Livingston Progress (Livingston, TX) 30699
Lake Michigan Journal (Benton Harbor, MI) 14808
Lake Mills Cablevision 11025*
The Lake Mills Leader (Lake Mills, WI) 33906
Lake News (Mount Dora, FL) Unable to locate
The Lake News (Lake Cowichan, BC, Can.) 35002
Lake Oconee Breeze (Madison, GA) Unable to locate
Lake Orion Eccentric (Lake Orion, MI) 15270
Lake Orion Review (Lake Orion, MI) 15271
Lake Oswego Review (Lake Oswego, OR) 26404
Lake of the Ozarks Senior Living (Springfield, MO) 17603
The Lake Placid News (Lake Placid, NY) 20875
Lake Powell Chronicle (Page, AZ) Unable to locate
Lake Region Echo/Press 15712*
Lake Region Life (Waterville, MN) 16504
Lake Region Monitor (Starke, FL) 6690
Lake Region Times (Madison Lake, MN) 16022
Lake River Times (Flippin, AR) Ceased
Lake Shore Cablevision 10511*
Lake Shore Shopper (Courtland, ON, Can.) Unable to locate
Lake Shore Visitor (Erie, PA) Unable to locate
Lake Station Herald (Merrillville, IN) Unable to locate
The Lake Sun Leader (Camdenton, MO) 16937
Lake Superior Magazine (Duluth, MN) 15839
Lake Tahoe Action Magazine (South Lake Tahoe, CA) 3783
Lake Union Herald (Berrien Springs, MI) 14813
The Lake Union Review 33022*
The Lake Union Review (Seattle, WA) Ceased
Lake View Resort and Green Saver (Lake View, IA) 11026
Lake Villa/Lindenhurst; The Review of (Lindenhurst, IL) 9108
Lake Villa Record (Lake Villa, IL) 9064
Lake Wales Highlander (Winter Haven, FL) 6868
The Lake Wales News (Lake Wales, FL) 6286
Lake Wallowa TV Cable 26550*
Lake Windermere Valley Echo 34976*
Lake Worth Forum; Greenacres/Lantana/ (Wellington, FL) 6843
Lake Worth Herald (Lake Worth, FL) 6288
Lake Worth News (Fort Worth, TX) Ceased
Lake Worth Town-Crier (West Palm Beach, FL) Ceased
Lake Zurich Courier (Lake Zurich, IL) 9065
Lake Zurich Enterprise (Grayslake, IL) Ceased
Lakefield Standard (Lakefield, MN) 15993
Lakeland Boating (Evanston, IL) Unable to locate
Lakeland Cablevision 16266*
Lakeland Review 34763*
Lakeland Shopper; North (Winter Haven, FL) 6870
Lakeland Shopper; South (Winter Haven, FL) 6872
Lakeland Shopping Guide (Alexandria, MN) 15713
Lakeland Times (Minocqua, WI) 34146
Lakeland Today (West Paterson, NJ) 19731
The Laker (Tampa, FL) 6774
The Laker (Mound, MN) 16201
Laker Shopper 15965*
Lakes Area Advertiser (Antioch, IL) 8017
The Lakes Area Shopper (Howell, MI) 15195
Lakes Cablevision 9167*
Lakes District News (Burns Lake, BC, Can.) 34915
Lakes Region Courier (Rochester, NH) Ceased
Lakes Region Radio-Current 31540*
Lakes Research; Journal of Great (Ann Arbor, MI) 14756
The Lakeshore Advance (Grand Bend, ON, Can.) 35854
Lakeshore Chronicle (Manitowoc, WI) Unable to locate
Lakeshore Community Television Ltd. 36431*
Lakeshore Flashes Shopping Guide (Allegan, MI) 14722
Lakeshore Life and Products News (St. Paul, MN) Ceased
Lakeshore News (Belle River, ON, Can.) 35675
Lakeshore Pennysaver (Fredonia, NY) 20622
Lakeshore Times (Lowell, MI) Ceased
Lakeshore Times; The Rowlett (Rowlett, TX) 30998
Lakeshore Weekly News (Wayzata, MN) Unable to locate
Lakeside Auburn Pennysaver 23387*
Lakeside Cortland Sunday/Democrat 23397*

Lakeside Leader (Slave Lake, AB, Can.) 34848
Lakeside Review (Layton, UT) 31343
Lakeside Town & Country Pennysaver 23431*
The Lakesider Magazine (Green Bay, WI) Ceased
Lakeview Cable TV 26407*
Lakeview Enterprise (Lakeview, MI) 15272
Lakeville Independent (Boston, MA) Unable to locate
Lakeville Journal (Lakeville, CT) 4921
Lakeville Life & Times 15996*
Lakewood Jefferson Sentinel (Minneapolis, MN) Unable to locate
Lakewood Journal (Vashon, WA) 33182
Lakewood News (Lake Odessa, MI) 15268
Lakewood Sun Post (Lakewood, OH) 25287
Lakota American (Lakota, ND) 24488
Lamar County Echo (Paris, TX) Ceased
Lamar County News (Hattiesburg, MS) 16662
Lamar Daily News and Holly Chieftain (Lamar, CO) 4537
The Lamar Democrat (Vernon, AL) 512
Lamar Democrat (Lamar, MO) 17235
Lamar Leader (Sulligent, AL) 460
Lamaze Para Padres (Darien, CT) 4774
Lamaze Parents' Magazine (Darien, CT) 4775
LamazeBaby (Darien, CT) Ceased
Lamb County Leader-News (Littlefield, TX) 30697
Lambda (Sudbury, ON, Can.) 36417
Lambda Book Report (Washington, DC) 5628
Lambda Rising Book Report 5628*
Lamberton News (Lamberton, MN) 15997
Lamborghini Club Magazine (Orinda, CA) Unable to locate
The Lambton Gazette 36364*
Lambton Shopping News (Sarnia, ON, Can.) 36364
Lamesa Press-Reporter (Lamesa, TX) 30663
Laminating Design and Technology (Fort Atkinson, WI) 33712
Lamishpaha (New York, NY) Unable to locate
Lamont Reporter (Lamont, CA) 2145
Lamp Journal 18755*
Lamp (New York) (Irving, TX) 30606
Lampasas Dispatch Record (Lampasas, TX) 30665
LAMPlighter (Chicago, IL) 8455
LAN Ceased
LAN Technology (San Mateo, CA) Unable to locate
LAN Times (San Francisco, CA) Unable to locate
Lancaster Bee/Depew Bee (Lancaster, NY) 20883
Lancaster Cable (Lancaster, SC) Unable to locate
Lancaster Excelsior 17236*
Lancaster Fairfield Advertiser (Lancaster, OH) 25290
Lancaster Farming (Ephrata, PA) 26888
Lancaster Independent Press (Lancaster, PA) Unable to locate
Lancaster Law Review (Lancaster, PA) 27142
Lancaster New Era (Lancaster, PA) 27143
The Lancaster News (Lancaster, SC) 28680
Lancaster News (Lancaster, TX) Unable to locate
Lancaster Sunday News (Lancaster, PA) 27144
Lancaster Today (Lancaster, TX) 30668
The Lance (Redding, CA) 2887
The Lance (Springfield, MO) 17604
The Lance (Winnipeg, MB, Can.) 35336
Lance; Elmvale (Elmvale, ON, Can.) 35806
Lance; The Free (Hollister, CA) 2050
The Lancet (North American Edition) (Philadelphia, PA) 27559
The Land (Mankato, MN) 16028
Land Degradation & Rehabilitation (Hoboken, NJ) Ceased
Land Economics (Madison, WI) 33956
Land Information Science; Surveying and (Gaithersburg, MD) 13548
Land Line (Grain Valley, MO) 17084
Land O' Lakes Mirror (St. Paul, MN) Ceased
Land 'O Lakes Recipe Collection (St. Paul, MN) Unable to locate
Land Research and Management; Arid (Logan, UT) 31346
Land Surveyor; The Ontario (Toronto, ON, Can.) 36683
Land & Water (Fort Dodge, IA) 10902
Land and Water Law Review 34553*
The Lander Wyoming State Journal (Lander, WY) 34543
Lander's Herald (Clayton, NJ) Ceased
Landforms; Earth Surface Processes and (Hoboken, NJ) 18934
The Landmark (Holden, MA) 14237
The Landmark (Platte City, MO) 17349
Landmark (Regina, SK, Can.) Unable to locate
Landmark Designs Inc. (Cottage Grove, OR) 37981
Landmark; Statesville Record and (Statesville, NC) 24247
Landmarks (Toronto, ON, Can.) Ceased
Landowner; Forest (Atlanta, GA) 7008
Landscape Architect and Specifier News (Tustin, CA) 3962
Landscape Architectural Review/Revue Ceased
Landscape Architecture (Washington, DC) 5629

Landscape Construction & Maintenance 3962*
The Landscape Contractor (Oak Brook, IL) 9355
Landscape Design (Chicago, IL) 8456
Landscape Ecology (New York, NY) 22232
Landscape & Irrigation (Chicago, IL) 8457
Landscape Journal (Madison, WI) 33957
Landscape Management (Cleveland, OH) 24918
Landscape and Nursery Digest (Hollywood, FL) Ceased
Landscape Trades (Milton, ON, Can.) 36049
Landscaping & Groundskeeping Journal (Vancouver, BC, Can.) 35152
Landsculptor (Bingham Farms, MI) Unable to locate
The Lane Report (Lexington, KY) 12172
Lang Van (Toronto, ON, Can.) 36648
Langford Bugle (Britton, SD) 28811
The Langley Advance (Langley, BC, Can.) Unable to locate
The Langley Times (Langley, BC, Can.) 35003
Langmuir (Washington, DC) Unable to locate
Language (Stony Brook, NY) 23372
Language Acquisition (Mahwah, NJ) 19200
Language Acquisition; Studies in Second (Bloomington, IN) 9852
Language Arts (Urbana, IL) 9714
Language Association Journal; Midwest Modern (Iowa City, IA) 10982
Language; Brain and (Michigan, MI) 15353
Language Bridges Quarterly (Richardson, TX) Unable to locate
Language Disorders; Topics in (New York, NY) 22847
Language Engineering; Natural (Yorktown Heights, NY) 23608
Language, Identity, and Education; Journal of (San Antonio, TX) 31034
Language and Information; Journal of Logic, (New York, NY) 22115
Language; Journal of Child (New York, NY) 22024
Language Journal; The Modern (Madison, WI) 33962
Language Learning; Applied (Monterey, CA) 2581
Language Learning and Technology (Honolulu, HI) 7708
Language & Linguistic Theory; Natural (New York, NY) 22406
Language & Literature; Papers on (Edwardsville, IL) 8814
Language and Literature; Rocky Mountain Review of (Pullman, WA) 32907
Language Notes; English (Boulder, CO) 4167
Language Quarterly; Modern (Seattle, WA) 32988
Language Review/La Revue canadienne des langues vivantes; The Canadian Modern (Toronto, ON, Can.) 36520
Language Semantics; Natural (New York, NY) 22407
Language; Seminars in Speech and (New York, NY) 22726
Language and Social Interaction; Research on (Santa Barbara, CA) 3652
Language and Social Psychology; Journal of (Thousand Oaks, CA) 3894
Language in Society (Tucson, AZ) 953
Language, Speech, and Hearing Services in Schools (Rockville, MD) 13686
Language Studies; Journal of French (Santa Barbara, CA) 3644
Language Studies; Sign (Burtonsville, MD) 13398
Language Teachers Association Journal; Chinese (Honolulu, HI) 7684
Language Teaching (New York, NY) 22233
Language Variation and Change (New York, NY) 22234
Language; Visible (Chicago, IL) 8599
Language; Women and (Fairfax, VA) 32034
Lanier County News (Lakeland, GA) 7366
Lanigan Advisor (Lanigan, SK, Can.) 37490
Lanigan Advisor (Lanigan, SK, Can.) 37489
Lannon-Lisbon News; Sussex- (New Berlin, WI) 34187
Lansing/Lynwood Star (Lansing, IL) 9067
Lansing State Journal (Lansing, MI) 15277
Lansing Sun Journal (Lansing, IL) Ceased
Lantana/Lake Worth Forum; Greenacres/ (Wellington, FL) 6843
The Lantern (Baytown, TX) 29895
Lantern; Campus (Willimantic, CT) 5219
Laparoendoscopic and Advanced Surgical Techniques; Journal of (Larchmont, NY) 20915
Laparoscopy News; General Surgery & (New York, NY) 21749
Lapeer Buyer's Guide (Lapeer, MI) 15309
Lapeer County Press 15308*
Lapidary Journal (Devon, PA) 26824
Lapis (New York, NY) 22235
The LaPorte County Magazine (La Porte, IN) Unable to locate
LaPorte Herald-Argus (La Porte, IN) 10247
LAP's Dimension 6003*

3414

Numbers cited in bold after listings are entry numbers rather than page numbers.

3418

Numbers cited in bold after listings are entry numbers rather than page numbers.

Literatures Journal; Latin America Indian (Mc Keesport, PA) **27229**
Literatures; Research in African (Columbus, OH) **25058**
Lithology and Mineral Resources (New York, NY) **22261**
Lithosphere Broadcasting Lp **1467***
Lithuanian Days (Los Angeles, CA) *Ceased*
Lithuanian Mathematical Journal (New York, NY) **22262**
Lithuanian Museum Review (Chicago, IL) **8467**
Litigation & Regulation Reporter; Securities (Wayne, PA) **28135**
Litigation Reporter; Asbestos Property (Wayne, PA) **28124**
Litigation Reporter; Automotive (Wayne, PA) **28125**
Litigation Reporter; Bank and Lender Liability (Wayne, PA) **28126**
Litigation Reporter; Chemical Waste (Washington, DC) **5405**
Litigation Reporter; Civil RICO (Wayne, PA) **28128**
Litigation Reporter; Computer & Online Industry (Wayne, PA) **28130**
Litigation Reporter; Hazardous Waste (Wayne, PA) **28132**
Litigation Reporter; Health Law (Wayne, PA) **28133**
Litigation Reporter; Securities Reform Act (Washington, DC) **5787**
Litigation Reporter; Tobacco Industry (Wayne, PA) **28137**
Litigation; The Review of (Austin, TX) **29801**
Litigator; IP (New York, NY) **21948**
Litigator; The Practical (Philadelphia, PA) **27642**
Lititz Record-Express (Lititz, PA) **27203**
Little Acres (Easton, MD) *Ceased*
Little Audrey (Los Angeles, CA) *Unable to locate*
Little Bell; Varpelis (The (Brooklyn, NY) **20352**
The Little Elm Journal (Little Elm, TX) **30695**
Little India (New York, NY) **22263**
Little Lotta (Los Angeles, CA) *Unable to locate*
The Little Magazine (Albany, NY) **19994**
The Little Neck-Glen Oaks Ledger **20939***
The Little Neck Ledger (Little Neck, NY) **20953**
Little Nickel Classifieds (Lynnwood, WA) **32824**
Little Nickel Want Ads **32822***
Little River News (Ashdown, AR) **1036**
Little River Rice County Monitor Journal (Ellsworth, KS) *Ceased*
Little Rock Family (Little Rock, AR) **1233**
Littlefork Times (St. Paul, MN) *Ceased*
Littleton Independent (Littleton, CO) **4551**
Littleton Independent (Littleton, MA) **14276**
The Littleton Observer (Littleton, NC) **24048**
Lituanus (Chicago, IL) **8468**
Liturgy (Washington, DC) **5638**
Liturgy 80 **8557***
Liturgy 90 **8557***
Liturgy 70 **8557***
Live Oak Cable TV, Inc. (Live Oak, CA) *Ceased*
Live Oak Independent Press (Live Oak, FL) *Ceased*
Live Oak Suwannee Democrat (Live Oak, FL) **6306**
Live Sound! International (Kansas City, MO) **17181**
Live Steam (Traverse City, MI) **15598**
Live Steam Newsletter **15598***
Live Wire (Manchester, CT) **4937**
Live Wire (New York, NY) *Unable to locate*
Lively Arts & Fine Arts (Pebble Beach, CA) *Unable to locate*
Liver Disease; Clinics in (Philadelphia, PA) **27417**
Liver Transplantation (Alexandria, VA) **31707**
Livermore Falls Advertiser (Livermore Falls, ME) **12984**
The Livermore Herald **2155***
Livermore Telephone and Communications (Livermore, IA) *Unable to locate*
Liverpool-Phoenix Pennysaver (Syracuse, NY) **23408**
Liverpool Review (Liverpool, NY) **20954**
Livestock Journal; Florida Cattleman and (Kissimmee, FL) **6261**
Livestock Journal; Western (Denver, CO) **4366**
Livestock Market Digest (Albuquerque, NM) **19775**
Livestock News; Tri-State (Sturgis, SD) **29001**
Livestock Report; Monthly Crop and (Guelph, ON, Can.) **35866**
Livestock Reporter; Weekly (Fort Worth, TX) **30355**
Livestock Reporter; Western (Billings, MT) **17734**
Livestock Weekly (San Angelo, TX) **31005**
Livewire (Jackson, MN) **15975**
Living (Harrisonburg, VA) **32141**
Living Among Nature Daringly (Silverton, OR) *Unable to locate*
Living Blues (University, MS) **16866**
Living with Cancer **29197***
Living with Christ (Ottawa, ON, Can.) **36259**
Living Church (Milwaukee, WI) **34074**
Living City (Bronx, NY) **20276**
Living Faith (Fenton, MO) **17061**
Living Fit (Woodland Hills, CA) *Ceased*
Living Healthy Magazine (Boston, MA) **13923**

The Living Light (Washington, DC) **5639**
Living Message (Toronto, ON, Can.) *Ceased*
The Living Museum (Springfield, IL) **9639**
Living Prayer (Barre, VT) *Ceased*
Living Safety Magazine (Ottawa, ON, Can.) **36260**
Living in South Carolina (Cayce, SC) **28503**
Living The Word (Schiller Park, IL) **9595**
Living The Word: Not Only on Sunday **9595***
Living Trends *Ceased*
Living Words **17061***
Livingston County Agricultural News (Mount Morris, NY) **21101**
Livingston County Leader/Livingston Republican (Geneseo, NY) *Unable to locate*
Livingston County Press and Argus (Howell, MI) **15196**
Livingston Enterprise (Livingston, MT) **17856**
The Livingston Ledger (Smithland, KY) **12402**
Livonia Gazelle (Geneseo, NY) *Unable to locate*
The Livonia Gazette (Livonia, NY) *Ceased*
Livonia Observer (Livonia, MI) **15317**
LLA Bulletin **12574***
Llamas Magazine (Jackson, CA) *Unable to locate*
Llano News (Llano, TX) **30702**
Llewellyn New Times **16384***
Llewellyn's New Worlds of Mind and Spirit (St. Paul, MN) **16384**
Lloydminster Daily Times (Lloydminster, AB, Can.) **34802**
Lloydminster Weekly Times **34802***
LMS Journal of Computation and Mathematics (New York, NY) **22264**
LMT (Monroe, CT) **4963**
Loadstar (Shreveport, LA) *Ceased*
Loadstar Quarterly (Shreveport, LA) *Ceased*
Loafer's Choice (Plantation, FL) **6587**
Loafing; Creative (Atlanta, GA) **6996**
Loan Officer's Legal Alert (Hoboken, NJ) *Ceased*
Lobo; New Mexico Daily (Albuquerque, NM) **19777**
The Local Exchange (Fort Qu'appelle, SK, Can.) *Ceased*
The Local Ledger (Quarryville, PA) *Unable to locate*
Location Update **3996***
Lockhart Post-Register (Lockhart, TX) **30703**
Lockney Beacon **30322***
Lockport/Lemont Sun; Homer/ (Naperville, IL) **9266**
The Locksmith Gazette (Columbus, OH) *Unable to locate*
Locksmith Ledger International (Notre Dame, IN) *Unable to locate*
Locksmith Magazine; The Canadian (Toronto, ON, Can.) **36514**
Locksmith; National (Streamwood, IL) **9667**
Locomotive (Lawrence, NE) **18070**
Locomotive Engineers Journal (Cleveland, OH) **24921**
Locomotive and Railway Preservation (Pasadena, CA) *Ceased*
Locus (Oakland, CA) **2687**
Loda Times (Paxton, IL) **9410**
Lode Star (Newberg, OR) **37643**
Lodge Journal and Guide **32291***
Lodging Magazine (Washington, DC) **5640**
The Lodi Enterprise (Lodi, WI) **33911**
Lodi-Hasbrouck Heights-Woodridge-Maywood-Rochelle Park Shopper (Lodi, NJ) **19179**
Lodi News-Merchandiser (Lodi, CA) **2157**
Lodi News-Sentinel (Lodi, CA) **2158**
The Log (Lantzville, BC, Can.) **35007**
Log Cabin Democrat (Conway, AR) **1083**
Log; The Destin (Destin, FL) **6059**
Log Home and Alternative Housing Builder **26893***
Log Home Living (Chantilly, VA) *Unable to locate*
Log Homes Illustrated (New York, NY) **22265**
Log; Lighthouse (Bridgewater, NS, Can.) **35543**
The Log (Los Angeles/Ventura County Edition) (San Diego, CA) **3224**
Log of Mystic Seaport (Mystic, CT) **4968**
The Log (Orange County Edition) (San Diego, CA) **3225**
Log; The Salem State (Salem, MA) **14515**
Log Trucker (Chehalis, WA) **32710**
The Logan Banner (Logan, WV) **33370**
Logan Daily News (Logan, OH) **25312**
Logan Herald-Observer (Logan, IA) **11040**
Logan Leader (Leitchfield, KY) *Ceased*
The Logan Republican (Logan, KS) **11612**
Logan Square Extra (Chicago, IL) **8469**
Logan Square Times (Harwood Heights, IL) *Ceased*
Logger and Lumberman (Wadley, GA) **7635**
Logger and Timber Processor; Northern (Old Forge, NY) **23037**
Loggers World (Chehalis, WA) **32711**
Loggin' Times; Southern (Montgomery, AL) **378**
Logging & Sawmilling Journal (North Vancouver, BC, Can.) **35035**
Logic; Algebra and (New York, NY) **21171**
Logic; The Bulletin of Symbolic (Boston, MA) **13868**
Logic; The Journal of Symbolic (Poughkeepsie, NY) **23147**

Logic, Language and Information; Journal of (New York, NY) **22115**
Logistics; Air Force Journal of (Maxwell AFB, AL) **313**
Logistics; Canadian Transportation & (Toronto, ON, Can.) **36532**
Logistics; IIE Transactions on Scheduling & (Norcross, GA) **7465**
Logistics Magazine (Ste.-Therese, QC, Can.) **37369**
Logistics Management **14405***
Logistics Management and Distribution Report (Newton, MA) **14405**
Logistics Management and Distribution Report (New York, NY) **22266**
Logistics Management; The International Journal of (Ponte Vedra Beach, FL) **6595**
Logistics Spectrum (Hyattsville, MD) *Unable to locate*
Logos (Mason City, IA) **11072**
Logos (San Antonio, TX) **31037**
Logos (Ottawa, ON, Can.) **36261**
Loisir **36855***
Loma Linda City News (Colton, CA) **1743**
LOMA Line (Baton Rouge, LA) **12493**
LOMA Resource (Atlanta, GA) **7026**
Lombard Spectator (Oak Brook, IL) **9358**
Lombard Suburban LIFE (Oak Brook, IL) **9359**
Lombardian (Lombard, IL) **9116**
LoMo Magazine (Birmingham, AL) **79**
Lompoc Record (Lompoc, CA) **2162**
Lona O'Connor (Boca Raton, FL) **37987**
London Bridge Cablevision **737***
London Business Monthly Magazine (London, ON, Can.) **35986**
The London Free Press (London, ON, Can.) **35987**
London Guidebook (London, ON, Can.) *Unable to locate*
London Magazine (London, ON, Can.) *Unable to locate*
London Mathematical Society; Bulletin of the (New York, NY) **21351**
London Mathematical Society; Journal of the (New York, NY) **22116**
London Pennysaver (London, ON, Can.) *Unable to locate*
Lone Peak Edition; New Utah! (American Fork, UT) **31318***
Lone Pine Television (Lone Pine, CA) **2164**
Lone Star Cablevision **29678***
Lone Star Horse Report (Fort Worth, TX) **30346**
Lone Star Softball (College Station, TX) *Ceased*
Lone Tree Reporter (Lone Tree, IA) **11041**
Long Beach Community News (Long Beach, CA) *Unable to locate*
Long Beach Express (Long Beach, CA) **2171**
Long Beach Herald (Long Beach, NY) **20960**
Long Beach Independent Voice (Lynbrook, NY) **20974**
Long Beach Pennysaver (Long Beach, HI) **7784**
Long Beach Shopper's Guide (Ontario, ON, Can.) **36166**
Long Beach Weekly (Long Beach, CA) *Unable to locate*
Long Island (Commack, NY) **20489**
Long Island Advance (Patchogue, NY) **23076**
Long Island Business News (Ronkonkoma, NY) **23271**
The Long Island Catholic (Roosevelt, NY) **23274**
Long Island Edition; The Fisherman- (Shirley, NY) **23331**
Long Island Examiner (Hempstead, NY) *Ceased*
Long Island Family (Huntington Station, NY) *Unable to locate*
Long Island Forum (Woodbury, NY) **23591**
Long Island Graphic (Freeport, NY) **20625**
Long Island Heritage (Mineola, NY) *Ceased*
The Long Island Journal (Long Beach, NY) *Unable to locate*
Long Island Local News (Malverne, NY) *Unable to locate*
Long Island Parenting News (Island Park, NY) *Unable to locate*
The Long Island Times (Syosset, NY) *Unable to locate*
The Long Island Traveler/Watchman **23347***
The Long Island Voice (Mineola, NY) *Unable to locate*
The Long Islander (Huntington, NY) **20774**
Long Lake Sun-Sailor; Wayzata/Orono/ (Plymouth, MN) **16280**
Long Prairie Leader (Long Prairie, MN) **16009**
The Long Story (Lawrence, MA) **14267**
Long Term Care (Arnprior, ON, Can.) **35637**
Long-Term Care; Journal of Social Work in (Binghamton, NY) **20199**
Long Term Care Monitor *Ceased*
Long-Term Care News; McKnight's (Northfield, IL) **9331**
The Long Term View (Andover, MA) **13813**
The Longboat Observer (Longboat Key, FL) **6311**
Longevity (New York, NY) *Unable to locate*

Longhorn Radio Network (Austin, TX) **37644**
The Longhorn Scene (Fort Worth, TX) *Unable to locate*
Longlac Times-Star; Geraldton- (Geraldton, ON, Can.) **35846**
The Longmeadow News (Westfield, MA) **14641**
Longueuil Extra (Longueuil, QC, Can.) **37056**
The Longview Current (Lees Summit, MO) **17245**
Longview Morning Journal (Longview, TX) *Ceased*
Longview News-Journal (Longview, TX) **30704**
Lonoke Democrat (Lonoke, AR) **1257**
Loogootee Tribune (Loogootee, IN) **10278**
The Looking Glass (Murfreesboro, AR) *Unable to locate*
Looking Up (Montreal, QC, Can.) *Ceased*
The Lookout (Cincinnati, OH) **24809**
The Lookout (Victoria, BC, Can.) **35220**
Lookout Foods (Naples, NY) *Ceased*
Lookout Non-Foods (Naples, NY) *Ceased*
Loomis News (Loomis, CA) **2180**
The Loon (Minneapolis, MN) **16093**
Loose Change (Las Vegas, NV) *Ceased*
Lorain Cable Television **25316***
Lorain County Times (Bay Village, OH) **24645**
Lordsburg Liberal (Lordsburg, NM) *Unable to locate*
Loretel Cablevision (Ada, MN) **15698**
The Loris Scene (Conway, SC) **28591**
The Loris Sentinel **28591***
Loris Times (Loris, SC) **28686**
Los Alamos Monitor (Los Alamos, NM) **19893**
Los Altos Town Crier (Los Altos, CA) **2193**
(Los Angeles); The Beat (Los Angeles, CA) **2217**
Los Angeles Bulletin (Los Angeles, CA) **2319**
The Los Angeles Business Journal (Los Angeles, CA) **2320**
(Los Angeles County Edition); Southern California Senior Life (Los Angeles, CA) **2399**
Los Angeles Daily Journal (Los Angeles, CA) **2321**
Los Angeles Downtown News (Los Angeles, CA) **2322**
Los Angeles Family Magazine (Encino, CA) **1884**
Los Angeles Features Syndicate (Winnetka, IL) **37988**
Los Angeles Herald-Examiner (Los Angeles, CA) *Ceased*
Los Angeles Independent (Los Angeles, CA) **2323**
Los Angeles International Fern Society; Journal of the (Pasadena, CA) **2820**
Los Angeles Lawyer (Los Angeles, CA) **2324**
Los Angeles Loyolan (Los Angeles, CA) **2325**
Los Angeles Magazine (Los Angeles, CA) *Unable to locate*
Los Angeles Philippine News (Los Angeles, CA) *Unable to locate*
Los Angeles Sentinel (Los Angeles, CA) *Unable to locate*
Los Angeles Times (Los Angeles, CA) **2326**
Los Angeles Times Magazine (Los Angeles, CA) **2327**
Los Angeles Times Syndicate (Los Angeles, CA) **37989**
Los Angeles Times Syndicate International (New York, NY) **37990**
Los Angeles Times—Ventura County Edition (Ventura, CA) **4005**
Los Angeles Times/Washington Post News Service (Washington, DC) **37991**
Los Angeles; WHERE (Los Angeles, CA) **2435**
Los Banos Enterprise (El Cajon, CA) **1846**
Los Cabos Magazine (San Diego, CA) **3226**
Los Gatos Times Observer **2478***
Los Gatos Weekly **2478***
Los Gatos Weekly Times (Los Gatos, CA) **2478**
Loss, Grief and Care (New York, NY) **22267**
Lost and Found Times (Columbus, OH) **25029**
Lost River Star (Merrill, OR) **26434**
Lost Treasure (Grove, OK) **25848**
A Lot of Bunkum (Horse Shoe, NC) **24010**
Lotbiniere; Le Peuple de (Quebec, QC, Can.) **37289**
Lottery Player's Magazine (Marlton, NJ) **19216**
Lott's 3—in—1 Buyer's Guide (Marina del Rey, CA) **2509**
Lotus Advisor Magazine (San Diego, CA) **3227**
Lotus Remarque (College Park, MD) **13432**
Loud (Phoenix, AZ) **806**
The Loudonville Times and The Loudonville Mohican Area Shopper (Loudonville, OH) **25317**
The Loudoun Connection (Mc Lean, VA) **32248**
Loudoun Easterner (Ashburn, VA) **31853**
Loudoun Times-Mirror (Loudoun, VA) **32199**
Louisburg Herald (Louisburg, KS) **11614**
Louisiana Agri-News Network/Louisiana Network (Baton Rouge, LA) **37645**
Louisiana Agriculture Magazine (Baton Rouge, LA) **12494**
Louisiana Baptist Builder (Denham Springs, LA) *Unable to locate*
Louisiana Baptist Message (LBM) (Alexandria, LA) **12459**
The Louisiana Bar Journal (New Orleans, LA) **12737**

The Louisiana Boardmember (Baton Rouge, LA) **12495**
The Louisiana Cattleman (Port Allen, LA) **12798**
The Louisiana Cattleman/The Louisiana Dairyman **12798***
Louisiana Contractor (Baton Rouge, LA) **12496**
Louisiana Cookin' (New Orleans, LA) **12738**
Louisiana Country (Baton Rouge, LA) **12497**
The Louisiana Engineer **12498***
Louisiana Engineer & Surveyor Journal (Baton Rouge, LA) **12498**
Louisiana English Journal (Natchitoches, LA) **12717**
Louisiana Farmer (New Orleans, LA) **12739**
Louisiana Good News; North (Minden, LA) **12688**
Louisiana Grocer (Metairie, LA) *Unable to locate*
Louisiana History (Lafayette, LA) **12618**
Louisiana History; North (Shreveport, LA) **12817**
Louisiana Journal (Baton Rouge, LA) *Unable to locate*
Louisiana Law Review (Baton Rouge, LA) **12499**
Louisiana Libraries (Eunice, LA) **12574**
Louisiana Life Magazine (Metairie, LA) **12677**
Louisiana Life—Magazine of the Bayou State **12677***
Louisiana Market Bulletin (Baton Rouge, LA) **12500**
Louisiana Municipal Review (Baton Rouge, LA) **12501**
Louisiana News (Kentwood, LA) **12613**
The Louisiana Pharmacist (Baton Rouge, LA) **12502**
The Louisiana Press-Journal (Louisiana, MO) **17256**
Louisiana Roots (Marksville, LA) **12674**
Louisiana Rural Economist (Baton Rouge, LA) **12503**
Louisiana Weekly (New Orleans, LA) **12740**
Louisville (Louisville, KY) **12227**
Louisville Business First (Charlotte, NC) *Unable to locate*
The Louisville Cardinal (Louisville, KY) **12228**
Louisville Clay County Republican (Louisville, IL) **9119**
Louisville Defender (Louisville, KY) **12229**
Louisville Eccentric Observer (LEO) (Louisville, KY) **12230**
Louisville Free Public Library **12251***
The Louisville Herald (Louisville, OH) **25319**
Louisville Magazine, Inc. (Louisville, KY) *Unable to locate*
Louisville Times (Louisville, CO) *Unable to locate*
LOVE 103.7 **24225***
Loveland Daily Reporter-Herald (Loveland, CO) **4568**
Loveland Herald (Loveland, OH) *Unable to locate*
The Lovell Chronicle (Lovell, WY) **34561**
Lovelock Review-Miner (Lovelock, NV) **18412**
Lovelock Review-Miner and Lovelock Tribune **18412***
lovematters.com (Redondo Beach, CA) **2910**
The Loves Park Post - Machesney Park Journal **9529***
The Loves Park Post-Machesney Park Pilot-Buyer's Guide **9529***
Lovetrance World Journal **3596***
Loving More (Boulder, CO) **4177**
The Lovington Daily Leader (Lovington, NM) **19897**
Low Calorie/Low Fat Recipes; Better Homes and Gardens Special Interest Publications (New York, NY) **21301**
Low Country Parent (Savannah, GA) *Ceased*
The Low Down to Hull & Back News (Wakefield, QC, Can.) **37439**
Low Fat Recipes; Better Homes and Gardens Special Interest Publications Low Calorie/ (New York, NY) **21301**
Low Rider Magazine (Walnut, CA) *Unable to locate*
Low Temperature Physics (College Park, MD) **13433**
Low Temperature Physics; Journal of (New York, NY) **22117**
Lowell Cable TV (Lowell, MI) **15321**
Lowell Cable TV Co., Inc. (Lowell, MA) **14280**
Lowell Ledger (Lowell, MI) **15320**
The Lowell Review (Florissant, MO) **17069**
Lowell Sun (Lowell, MA) **14278**
Lowell Tribune (Lowell, IN) **10280**
Lower Cape Shoppers Guide (Orleans, MA) *Ceased*
Lower Township Lantern (Rio Grande, NJ) *Unable to locate*
Lowndes Signal (Fort Deposit, AL) *Unable to locate*
Lowry Airman (Minneapolis, MN) *Unable to locate*
Loyalist Gazette (Toronto, ON, Can.) **36652**
Loyola Law Review (New Orleans, LA) **12741**
Loyola Magazine (Chicago, IL) **8470**
Loyola Phoenix (Chicago, IL) **8471**
Loyola University of Chicago Law Journal **8472***
Loyola University Chicago Law Journal (Chicago, IL) **8472**
Loyolan; Los Angeles (Los Angeles, CA) **2325**
LP-Gas (Cleveland, OH) **24922**
LPTV Reporter *Ceased*
LQ (Ladies Quarterly) (New York, NY) *Unable to locate*
LRC News (Seattle, WA) *Unable to locate*
LSU Alumni News **12504***
LSU Magazine (Baton Rouge, LA) **12504**
LUAC Forum **36123***

Lubbock Avalanche-Journal (Lubbock, TX) **30715**
Lubbock; Cox Cable (Lubbock, TX) **30721**
(Lubbock); Helios (College Station, TX) **30042**
Lubbock Southwest Digest (Lubbock, TX) **30716**
Lube Report (Falls Church, VA) **32049**
Lubricants World **30477***
Lubricants World (New York, NY) **22268**
Lubricants World; Hart's (Houston, TX) **30477**
Lubrication Engineering (Park Ridge, IL) **9406**
Lucas-Sylvan News (Lucas, KS) **11615**
The Lucasfilm Fan Club **4150***
Lucerne Valley Leader **2485***
Lucha/Struggle (New York, NY) *Ceased*
The Lucid Stone (Scottsdale, AZ) *Ceased*
Lucidity (Houston, TX) **30504**
The Lucknow Sentinel (Lucknow, ON, Can.) **36004**
Lucky (New York, NY) **22269**
Ludington Daily News (Ludington, MI) **15322**
The Ludowici News (Hinesville, GA) *Unable to locate*
The Lufkin Daily News (Lufkin, TX) **30739**
Luggage, Leathergoods & Accessories (Markham, ON, Can.) **36027**
Luggage & Leathergoods News **36027***
Luling Cablevision (Luling, TX) **30750**
The Luling Newsboy & Signal (Luling, TX) **30749**
The Lumber Co-Operator (Rensselaer, NY) **23181**
Lumber Facts; Western (Portland, OR) **26514**
The Lumberjack Newspaper (Arcata, CA) **1429**
Lumberman; Southern (Franklin, TN) **29199**
Lumen (Saskatoon, SK, Can.) **37552**
The Luminary (Muncy, PA) **27306**
Luminescence (Hoboken, NJ) **19054**
Lumpen (Chicago, IL) *Unable to locate*
Luna Negra (Kent, OH) **25276**
Lundi; Le (Outremont, QC, Can.) **37266**
Lung (New York, NY) **22270**
Lung Cellular and Molecular Physiology; American Journal of Physiology: (Bethesda, MD) **13308**
Lung; Heart and (Philadelphia, PA) **27479**
Lung Research; Experimental (Research Triangle Park, NC) **24184**
Lupus Today (Torrance, CA) *Unable to locate*
Lurzer's International Archive (New York, NY) **22271**
Lurzer's International Archive Magazine (New York, NY) *Unable to locate*
The Lusk Herald (Lusk, WY) **34562**
The Luso-Americano (Newark, NJ) **19358**
Luther Alumni Magazine (Decorah, IA) **10757**
Luther Alumni Quarterly **10757***
The Lutheran (Chicago, IL) **8473**
Lutheran Education Journal (River Forest, IL) **9492**
Lutheran Journal (Minneapolis, MN) **16094**
The Lutheran Layman (St. Louis, MO) **17467**
Lutheran Partners (Chicago, IL) **8474**
Lutheran Witness (St. Louis, MO) **17468**
Lutheran Woman Today (Minneapolis, MN) **16095**
Lutheran Women **16095***
Lutherie; American (Tacoma, WA) **33143**
The Lutz Community News (Lutz, FL) **6315**
Lutz Partyline **6315***
Luverne Announcer (Luverne, MN) **16013**
The Luverne Journal (Luverne, AL) *Unable to locate*
Luverne TV Cable Service (Luverne, AL) **308**
Luxemburg News (Luxemburg, WI) **33914**
Lyman County Herald (Presho, SD) **28930**
Lynbrook/East Rockaway/Malverne Shopper's Guide (Ontario, ON, Can.) **36167**
Lynbrook Herald **20978***
Lynbrook News Herald **20978***
Lynbrook Observer; East Rockaway/ (Lynbrook, NY) **20973**
Lynbrook Pennysaver (Lynbrook, HI) **7785**
Lynbrook USA (Lynbrook, NY) **20975**
Lynch News Service (Bethesda, MD) **37992**
Lynch TV Inc. (Lynch, KY) **12269**
The Lynchburg Ledger (Rustburg, VA) **32519**
Lynchburg News (Greenfield, OH) *Ceased*
Lyncourt Pennysaver (Syracuse, NY) **23409**
Lynden Tribune (Lynden, WA) **32821**
Lynden Tribune (Lynden, WA) **32820**
The Lyndon Independent (Medford, NJ) *Unable to locate*
Lyndon News Herald **11369***
Lynn Canal Cablevision **585***
Lynn County News (Tahoka, TX) **31174**
Lynn Enterprises; Richard (Lagro, IN) **38050**
Lynn—Linn Lineage Quarterly (McHenry, IL) **9165**
Lynnfield Edition; Peabody- (Peabody, MA) **14464**
Lynnfield-Peabody Edition (Peabody, MA) **14462**
Lynnfield/Peabody Observer (Somerville, MA) *Ceased*
The Lynnfield Villager (Lynnfield, MA) **14288**
Lynnwood Edition; The Journal— (Lynnwood, WA) **32823**
Lynwood Journal (Lynwood, CA) **2486**
Lynwood Press (Lynwood, CA) **2487**
Lynx (Toutle, WA) *Unable to locate*
Lynx Eye (Los Osos, CA) **2482**
Lyon County News (George, IA) **10920**
Lyon County Reporter (Rock Rapids, IA) **11179**

Lyons CATV Inc. (Lyons, KS) **11617**
Lyons Daily News (Lyons, KS) **11616**
Lyons Mirror Sun (Lyons, NE) **18151**
Lyons Recorder; The Old (Lyons, CO) **4570**
Lyons Republican **20979***
Lyons Shopping Guide (Newark, NY) **22995**
Lyra (Guttenberg, NJ) *Unable to locate*
The Lyric (Jericho, VT) **31545**
Lyrical Iowa (Des Moines, IA) **10803**

M

M (Chicago, IL) **8475**
M (New York, NY) *Ceased*
M & M Journal (Hillsboro, IL) **8995**
M & S Times (Alexandria, VA) *Ceased*
M-Tek Systems Inc. (New Ulm, MN) **16219**
The 'M' Voice Newspaper (Greenville, NC) **23965**
MA Training (Santa Clarita, CA) *Ceased*
Mabel Record **16017***
Mableton Neighbor (Marietta, GA) **7414**
The MAC Bulletin (Bellevue, OH) *Ceased*
Mac Design Magazine (Oldsmar, FL) **6484**
Mac Today **6484***
The Mac Weekly (St. Paul, MN) **16385**
MacAddict (Brisbane, CA) **1605**
The Macdonald Journal (Ste.-Anne-de-Bellevue, QC, Can.) *Ceased*
The Mace and Crown (Norfolk, VA) **32290**
Macedonia (West Hill, ON, Can.) **36870**
Macedonian Tribune (Fort Wayne, IN) **9972**
The MacEwan Journalist (Edmonton, AB, Can.) **34721**
MacGuide Report (Denver, CO) *Unable to locate*
Machias Valley News Observer (Machias, ME) **12986**
Machine Design (Cleveland, OH) **24923**
Machine Learning (New York, NY) **22272**
Machine Learning Research; Journal of (Cambridge, MA) **14078**
Machine-Mediated Learning (Hoboken, NJ) *Ceased*
Machine Shop; Modern (Cincinnati, OH) **24810**
Machine and Tool Blue Book (Bensenville, IL) *Ceased*
Machine Translation (New York, NY) **22273**
Machinerie Lourde (La Salle, QC, Can.) *Ceased*
Machinery; Canadian Industrial (Burlington, ON, Can.) **35715**
Machinery Edition; The Complete European Trade Digest (Atlanta, GA) **6990**
Machinery & Equipment Guide; Computer Listing Service's (Skokie, IL) **9603**
Machinery & Equipment MRO (Toronto, ON, Can.) **36653**
Machinery and Metalworking; Canadian (Toronto, ON, Can.) **36515**
Machinery; Plastics Auxiliaries & (Denver, CO) **4348**
Machinery Trader (Central Edition) (Lincoln, NE) **18092**
Machinery Trader (Eastern Edition) (Lincoln, NE) **18093**
Machinery Trader (Western Edition) (Lincoln, NE) **18094**
Machining Science and Technology (Gaithersburg, MD) **13545**
The Machinist (Washington, DC) *Unable to locate*
Machinist; American (Cleveland, OH) **24855**
Machinist's Workshop (Traverse City, MI) **15599**
MacII Review (Fairfield, CT) **4791**
Macintosh-Aided Design (New York, NY) *Ceased*
Macintosh News **20994***
Mackenzie Media Ltd. **35531***
The Mackinac Island Town Crier (Mackinac Island, MI) **15325**
Macklin Mirror (Macklin, SK, Can.) **37492**
Macksville Gazette (Terre Haute, IN) *Unable to locate*
MACLAS Latin American Essays (Newark, DE) **5278**
Maclean Hunter Cable TV **15588***
Maclean Hunter Cable TV (Ajax, ON, Can.) *Unable to locate*
Maclean Hunter Cable TV (Etobicoke, ON, Can.) **35823**
Maclean Hunter Cable TV Niagara **36114***
Maclean Hunter 4-Rogers 4 **35910***
Maclean's (Toronto, ON, Can.) **36654**
The Macleod Gazette (Fort Macleod, AB, Can.) **34766**
MacLine (Philadelphia, PA) *Unable to locate*
Macomb County Legal News (Shelby Township, MI) **15536**
The Macomb Daily (Mount Clemens, MI) **15372**
Macomb Journal (Macomb, IL) **9130**
Macomb-North Clinton Advisor **14998***
Macomb Plus (Shelby Township, MI) *Ceased*
Macomb Plus-St. Clair Shores (Shelby Township, MI) *Ceased*

Macon Beacon (Macon, MS) **16754**
Macon Chronicle-Herald (Macon, MO) **17259**
Macon County Times (Lafayette, TN) **29312**
Macon Magazine (Macon, GA) **7382**
The Macon Telegraph (San Jose, CA) **3523**
Macoupin County Enquirer **8126***
Macoupin County Shopper (Hillsboro, IL) *Unable to locate*
Macrobiotics Today (Oroville, CA) *Unable to locate*
Macromolecular Science, Part B, Physics; Journal of (Urbana, IL) **9713**
Macromolecules (Washington, DC) *Unable to locate*
MacTech Magazine (Westlake Village, CA) **4071**
MacTech Quarterly (Kent, WA) *Ceased*
MacTutor **4071***
MacUser (Foster City, CA) *Unable to locate*
MacWeek (San Francisco, CA) *Ceased*
Macworld (San Francisco, CA) **3388**
Mad Rhythms (Chesapeake, VA) *Unable to locate*
(Madame au Foyer); Homemaker's Magazine (Toronto, ON, Can.) **36617**
MadAminA! (Englewood, NJ) *Ceased*
Madawaska Ltee; Journal Le (Edmundston, NB, Can.) **35385**
Maddux Report (St. Petersburg, FL) **6630**
Made to Measure (Highland Park, IL) **8993**
Made in Mexico Magazine (Denver, CO) *Ceased*
Mademoiselle (New York, NY) *Ceased*
Madera Tribune (El Cajon, CA) **1847**
The Madill Record (Madill, OK) **25902**
Madison county journals (Collinsville, IL) **8687**
Madison Avenue (New York, NY) *Unable to locate*
Madison County Carrier (Madison, FL) **6317**
Madison County Chronicle (Worden, IL) **9773**
Madison County Eagle (Madison, VA) **32220**
Madison County Herald (Canton, MS) **16583**
Madison County Record (Madison, AL) **310**
Madison County Record (Huntsville, AR) **1192**
The Madison Courier (Madison, IN) **10283**
Madison Daily Leader (Madison, SD) **28886**
The Madison Eagle (Stirling, NJ) **19603**
Madison Enterprise-Recorder (Madison, FL) **6318**
Madison; Historic (Madison, WI) **33946**
The Madison Journal (Tallulah, LA) **12855**
Madison Livestock Belt **11618***
Madison Magazine (Madison, WI) **33959**
Madison Messenger (Madison, OH) **25325**
The Madison News (Madison, KS) **11618**
Madison-Park News (Warren, MI) *Unable to locate*
Madison Park Times (Seattle, WA) **32983**
Madison Press (Madison, OH) **25326**
Madison Review (Madison, WI) **33960**
Madison Review (Tailahassee) *Ceased*
Madison Spirit **11618***
Madison Square Garden Network (New York, NY) **37767**
Madison Tribune **25451***
The Madisonian **11618***
The Madisonian (Ennis, MT) **17787**
The Madisonville Meteor and Times (Madisonville, TX) **30752**
Madoc Review (Madoc, ON, Can.) **36005**
The Madras Pioneer (Madras, OR) **26412**
Madrid Register-News (Madrid, IA) **11043**
Madrono (Berkeley, CA) *Unable to locate*
Maes National Magazine (Houston, TX) **30505**
MAFES Research Highlights (Mississippi State, MS) **16782**
The Magazine Antiques (New York, NY) **22274**
Magazine and Bookseller (Falls Church, VA) *Unable to locate*
The Magazine for Christian Youth! (Nashville, TN) *Ceased*
Magazine Circuit Industriel (Quebec, QC, Can.) **37291**
The Magazine of Fantasy & Science Fiction (Hoboken, NJ) **19055**
Magazine Finance (Montreal, QC, Can.) **37180**
Magazine Jeunesse; Le (Montreal, QC, Can.) **37168**
Magazine Le Clap (Sainte-Foy, QC, Can.) **37374**
Magazine; Marquee (Mississauga, ON, Can.) **36076**
The Magazine of Positive Thinking **23086***
The Magazine of Sigma Chi (Evanston, IL) **8866**
Magazine of Speculative Poetry (Beloit, WI) **33575**
Magazine Temps Libre **37228***
Magazine of Virginia Genealogy (Richmond, VA) **32444**
Magazine VIVRE *Ceased*
MagazineWeek (New York, NY) *Ceased*
The Magee Courier (Magee, MS) **16755**
Maggots (Prescott, AZ) *Unable to locate*
Magic (Las Vegas, NV) **18377**
Magic; Cincinnati Journal of (Logan, OH) **25310**
Magic Realism (Sylmar, CA) **3836**
Magic Realism; North American **3836***
Magical Blend Magazine (Chico, CA) **1694**
Magna (Rockville, MD) *Unable to locate*
Magna Times & West Valley News (Magna, UT) **31364**

Magnesium and Trace Elements (Farmington, CT) *Ceased*
MAGNET (Philadelphia, PA) **27560**
Magnetic Resonance in Chemistry (Hoboken, NJ) **19056**
Magnetic Resonance; Concepts in (Hoboken, NJ) **18922**
Magnetic Resonance Imaging (TMRI); Topics in (Baltimore, MD) **13255**
Magnetic Resonance; Journal of (San Diego, CA) **3203**
Magnetic Resonance; Journal of (San Diego, CA) **3202**
Magnetic Resonance; Journal of (San Diego, CA) **3201**
Magnetic Resonance in Medicine (San Diego, CA) *Ceased*
Magnetic Resonance Quarterly (Baltimore, MD) *Ceased*
Magnetic Resonance - Series B; Journal of **3201***
Magnetohydrodynamics (New York, NY) **22275**
Magnetohydrodynamics: An International Journal (Philadelphia, PA) *Ceased*
Magnificat (Mount-Tremblant, QC, Can.) **37253**
Magnolia Gazette (Magnolia, MS) **16758**
Magnolia News; Queen Anne/ (Seattle, WA) **33010**
Magyar Elet (Hungarian Life) (North York, ON, Can.) *Unable to locate*
Magyar Naplo (Toronto, ON, Can.) **36655**
Magyarsag; Californiai **2917***
Mahomet Citizen (Mahomet, IL) **9138**
Mahopac Press (Mahopac, NY) **20980**
Maiden Evening News **14296***
Maiden Times (Newton, NC) *Ceased*
Maiden Voyages (San Francisco, CA) *Unable to locate*
Mail; The Atchison County (Rock Port, MO) **17377**
Mail Call (Blytheville, AR) *Ceased*
Mail; Charleston Daily (Charleston, WV) **33267**
Mail; Daily (Catskill, NY) **20349**
Mail; The Drumheller (Drumheller, AB, Can.) **34696**
Mail; The Edgeley (Edgeley, ND) **24404**
The Mail-Journal (Milford, IN) **10309**
Mail; The Merkel (Merkel, TX) **30806**
Mail; Mt. Horeb (Mount Horeb, WI) **34156**
Mail; The Mountain (Salida, CO) **4620**
The Mail-Star (Halifax, NS, Can.) *Unable to locate*
Mail-Sun; Sheldon (Sheldon, IA) **11195**
Mail and Terril Record; Milford (Spirit Lake, IA) **11237**
The Mail Tribune (Medford, OR) **26418**
Mail; Wayne County (Webster, NY) **23527**
Mail; The Winslow (Winslow, AZ) **1014**
Mailbox News Packet (Searcy, AR) **1338**
Mailbox Values Shopper (El Paso, TX) *Unable to locate*
The MAIleader (Lynbrook, NY) **20976**
Mailers Review (Portland, OR) *Unable to locate*
Mailing & Shipping Technology **33961***
Mailing Systems Technology); MAST ((Madison, WI) **33961**
MAIN magazine **29569***
Main Economic Indicators (Washington, DC) **5641**
The Main Event (Fair Lawn, NJ) *Ceased*
Main Group Chemistry (Langhorne, PA) *Unable to locate*
Main Group Chemistry News (Amherst, MA) **13801**
Main Line Life (Trenton, NJ) **19657**
Main Line Life (Ardmore, PA) **26661**
Main Line Magazine (Devon, PA) *Unable to locate*
Main Line Times (Ardmore, PA) **26662**
Main Science & Technology Indicators (Washington, DC) **5642**
Main Sheet (St. Clair Shores, MI) *Ceased*
Main Street (Charlottetown, PE, Can.) *Unable to locate*
Main Street Press (Patchogue, NY) *Unable to locate*
Maine Antique Digest (Waldoboro, ME) **13069**
Maine Beverage Journal (Boston, MA) *Ceased*
Maine Boats & Harbors (Camden, ME) **12944**
Maine Enterprise (Portland, ME) *Ceased*
Maine; Fatal Occupational Injuries in (Augusta, ME) **12891**
Maine Fish and Wildlife (Augusta, ME) **12893**
Maine Genealogist (Farmington, ME) **12961**
Maine History (Portland, ME) **13011**
Maine Magazine (Machias, ME) **12987**
Maine Motor Transport News (Augusta, ME) **12894**
Maine Organic Farmer and Gardener (Lincolnville, ME) **12982**
Maine Potato News (Presque Isle, ME) **13034**
Maine Real Estate Guide (Andover, MA) *Ceased*
The Maine Seine **12961***
The Maine Sportsman (Yarmouth, ME) **13082**
Maine Sunday Telegram (Portland, ME) **13012**
Maine Times (Bangor, ME) **12904**
Maine Times; Gulf of (Annapolis Royal, NS, Can.) **35534**
Maine Trails (Augusta, ME) **12895**

Medical History/Bulletin Canadien D'historie de la Medecine; Canadian Bulletin of (Nanaimo, BC, Can.) **35018**

Medical Humanities; Journal of (New York, NY) **22130**

Medical Humanities Review (Galveston, TX) **30382**

Medical Imaging (Providence, RI) **28406**

Medical Industry Information Report (Mission Viejo, CA) **2555**

Medical Informatics & The Internet in Medicine (Philadelphia, PA) **27566**

Medical Insights (Chicago, IL) *Unable to locate*

Medical Insurance Claims Inc. (Kinnelon, NJ) **38001**

Medical Journal; Air (Little Rock, AR) **1209**

Medical Journal); BCMJ (The British Columbia (Vancouver, BC, Can.) **35126**

Medical Journal; Delaware (Newark, DE) **5271**

Medical Journal; Hawaii (Honolulu, HI) **7697**

Medical Journal; Maryland (Baltimore, MD) **13212**

Medical Journal; North Carolina (Durham, NC) **23838**

Medical Journal; Southern (Birmingham, AL) **97**

Medical Journal; West Virginia (Charleston, WV) **33278**

Medical Journal; Wisconsin (Madison, WI) **33987**

Medical Laboratory Observer (MLO) (Montvale, NJ) **19266**

Medical Laboratory Professionals; ADVANCE for (King of Prussia, PA) **27114**

Medical Law's Regan Report (Providence, RI) **28407**

Medical Library Association; Journal of the (Chicago, IL) **8445**

Medical Marketing & Media (Boca Raton, FL) **5936**

Medical Meetings (Stow, MA) **14574**

Medical News; American (Chicago, IL) **8260**

Medical NMR; Physiological Chemistry and Physics and (Melville, NY) **21057**

Medical Patriot (San Antonio, TX) *Unable to locate*

Medical and Pediatric Oncology (Hoboken, NJ) **19060**

Medical and Pharmaceutical Biotechnology Abstracts (Bethesda, MD) **13359**

Medical Physics (New York, NY) **22310**

The Medical Post (Toronto, ON, Can.) **36659**

Medical Practice Management; The Journal of (Chicago, IL) **8446**

Medical Principles and Practice (Farmington, CT) **4840**

Medical Problems of Performing Artists (Philadelphia, PA) **27567**

Medical Product Manufacturing News (Los Angeles, CA) *Unable to locate*

Medical Quarterly; Virginia (Richmond, VA) **32466**

Medical Radiation Technology; Canadian Journal of (Ottawa, ON, Can.) **36207**

Medical Reference Services Quarterly (Binghamton, NY) **20208**

The Medical Rehabilitation Report (Reston, VA) *Unable to locate*

Medical Review; Ontario (Toronto, ON, Can.) **36684**

Medical Sciences; American Journal of the (Philadelphia, PA) **27372**

Medical Self Care (Providence, RI) *Ceased*

Medical Services; Emergency (Van Nuys, CA) **3988**

Medical Society; Bulletin of Allegheny County (Pittsburgh, PA) **27763**

Medical Society; Bulletin of the King County (Seattle, WA) **32952**

Medical Society; The Journal of the Arkansas (Little Rock, AR) **1231**

Medical Sonography (Santa Monica, CA) *Ceased*

Medical Sonography (JDMS); The Journal of Diagnostic (Thousand Oaks, CA) **3887**

Medical Students; Journal for Minority (New Orleans, LA) **12735**

Medical & Surgical Dermatology **22045***

Medical Systems; Journal of (New York, NY) **22131**

Medical Times (Jamesburg, NJ) *Ceased*

Medical Tribune (New York, NY) *Unable to locate*

Medical Virology; Journal of (Hoboken, NJ) **19030**

Medical Virology; Reviews in (Hoboken, NJ) **19099**

Medical Women's Association; Journal of the American (New York, NY) **21983**

Medical World News (New York, NY) *Unable to locate*

Medical World News *Ceased*

Medicale; L'Actualite (Montreal, QC, Can.) **37081**

Medicale Canadienne; CMAJ/JAMC (Canadian Medical Association Journal)/(Journal de l'Association (Ottawa, ON, Can.) **36236**

MediCenter Management (Florham Park, NJ) *Unable to locate*

Medicina Experimentis **4855***

Medicina Y Cultura (Ridgefield, CT) **5098**

Medicinal Plants; Journal of Herbs, Spices & (Binghamton, NY) **20178**

Medicinal Research Reviews (Hoboken, NJ) **19061**

Medicine (Baltimore, MD) **13216**

Medicine; Academic Emergency (Philadelphia, PA) **27361**

Medicine Alert; Internal (Montvale, NJ) **19257**

Medicine and Allied Sciences; Journal of the History of (Cary, NC) **23691**

Medicine; Alternative Therapies in Health and (Encinitas, CA) **1882**

Medicine; American Journal of (New York, NY) **21195**

Medicine; American Journal of Chinese (Garden City, NY) **20634**

Medicine; The American Journal of Emergency (Philadelphia, PA) **27371**

Medicine; American Journal of Industrial (Hoboken, NJ) **18886**

Medicine; American Journal of Preventive (New York, NY) **21198**

Medicine; Annals of Behavioral (La Jolla, CA) **2112**

Medicine; Annals of Emergency (St. Louis, MO) **17414**

Medicine; Annals of Internal (Philadelphia, PA) **27379**

Medicine; Archives of Internal (Chicago, IL) **8268**

Medicine; Archives of Pathology & Laboratory (Chicago, IL) **8271**

Medicine and Arthroscopy Review; Sports (Baltimore, MD) **13249**

Medicine; Aviation, Space, and Environmental (Alexandria, VA) **31645**

Medicine; Behavioral (Washington, DC) **5374**

Medicine and Biology Magazine; IEEE Engineering in (Piscataway, NJ) **19424**

The Medicine Bow Post (Medicine Bow, WY) *Unable to locate*

Medicine; Bulletin of Experimental Biology and (New York, NY) **21350**

Medicine; Bulletin of the History of (Baltimore, MD) **13140**

Medicine; Bulletin of the New York Academy of (New York, NY) **21352**

Medicine; California (Nashville, TN) **29448**

Medicine; Canadian Journal of Rural (Ottawa, ON, Can.) **36218**

Medicine and Child Neurology; Developmental (New York, NY) **21548**

Medicine; Cleveland Clinic Journal of (Cleveland, OH) **24870**

Medicine; Clinical Journal of Sport (Baltimore, MD) **13147**

Medicine; Clinical Nuclear (Wynnewood, PA) **28197**

Medicine; Clinics in Chest (Philadelphia, PA) **27413**

Medicine; Clinics in Developmental (New York, NY) **21430**

Medicine; Clinics in Geriatric (Philadelphia, PA) **27415**

Medicine Clinics; Infertility and Reproductive (Philadelphia, PA) **27492**

Medicine; Clinics in Laboratory (Philadelphia, PA) **27416**

Medicine Clinics of North America; Emergency (Philadelphia, PA) **27457**

Medicine; Clinics in Sports (Philadelphia, PA) **27421**

Medicine; Colorado (Denver, CO) **4317**

Medicine & Computer (White Plains, NY) *Ceased*

Medicine; Connecticut (New Haven, CT) **4986**

Medicine; Critical Care (Des Plaines, IL) **8757**

Medicine; Dartmouth (Lebanon, NH) **18542**

Medicine; Dayton (Dayton, OH) **25114**

Medicine; Emergency (Linthicum, MD) **13619**

Medicine & Ethics; The Journal of Law, (Boston, MA) **13916**

Medicine; Family (San Antonio, TX) **31030**

Medicine; Genetics in (Minneapolis, MN) **16083**

Medicine & Global Survival (Brookline, MA) **14022**

The Medicine Hat News (Medicine Hat, AB, Can.) **34810**

The Medicine Hat Shopper (Medicine Hat, AB, Can.) **34811**

Medicine and Health (New York, NY) **22311**

Medicine, Health Care and Philosophy (New York, NY) **22312**

Medicine/Health Information Review (Commack, NY) *Ceased*

Medicine and Health Rhode Island (Providence, RI) **28408**

Medicine, Immunology and Toxicology; International Journal of Occupational (Princeton, NJ) **19462**

Medicine; International Journal of Behavioral (Mahwah, NJ) **19192**

Medicine; The International Journal of Psychiatry in (Amityville, NY) **20040**

Medicine; Internet Journal of Emergency and Intensive Care (Sugar Land, TX) **31142**

Medicine; Internet Journal of Internal (Sugar Land, TX) **31149**

Medicine; Internet Journal of Pulmonary (Sugar Land, TX) **31159**

Medicine; Internet Journal of Rescue and Disaster (Sugar Land, TX) **31161**

Medicine; Iowa (West Des Moines, IA) **11320**

Medicine; Issues in Law & (Terre Haute, IN) **10487**

Medicine; Journal of Aerosol (Larchmont, NY) **20905**

Medicine; Journal of Aerosol (Larchmont, NY) **20904**

Medicine; The Journal of Alternative & Complementary (Larchmont, NY) **20906**

Medicine; Journal of Anti-Aging (Larchmont, NY) **20907**

Medicine; Journal of Behavioral (New York, NY) **22007**

Medicine; Journal of Cutaneous (New York, NY) **22045**

Medicine; The Journal of Experimental (New York, NY) **22068**

Medicine; The Journal of Gender-Specific (Plainsboro, NJ) **19442**

Medicine; Journal of Intensive Care (Shrewsbury, MA) **14524**

Medicine; Journal of Investigative (Philadelphia, PA) **27533**

Medicine; The Journal of Laboratory and Clinical (St. Louis, MO) **17456**

Medicine; The Journal of Legal (Springfield, IL) **9637**

Medicine; Journal of Occupational and Environmental (Arlington Heights, IL) **8025**

Medicine; Journal of Orthomolecular (Toronto, ON, Can.) **36636**

Medicine Journal; The Pain (Baltimore, MD) **13231**

Medicine; The Journal of Reproductive (St. Louis, MO) **17461**

Medicine; The Journal of Trace Elements in Experimental (Hoboken, NJ) **19051**

Medicine; Journal of Travel (Hamilton, ON, Can.) **35886**

Medicine; Journal of Ultrasound in (Boston, MA) **13920**

Medicine; Journal of Zoo and Wildlife (Media, PA) **27242**

Medicine; Laboratory (Chicago, IL) **8454**

Medicine; Lasers in Surgery and (Hoboken, NJ) **19053**

Medicine; Literature and (Baltimore, MD) **13210**

Medicine Lodge CATV **11650***

Medicine Magazine; Good (Washington, DC) **5516**

Medicine; Michigan (East Lansing, MI) **14989**

Medicine; Minnesota (Minneapolis, MN) **16105**

Medicine; Missouri (Jefferson City, MO) **17126**

Medicine; Modern (New York, NY) **22349**

Medicine; Molecular (Baltimore, MD) **13221**

Medicine; The Mount Sinai Journal of (New York, NY) **22373**

Medicine; Navy (Pittsburgh, PA) **27820**

Medicine; The New England Journal of (Boston, MA) **13935**

Medicine; New Jersey (Lawrenceville, NJ) **19163**

Medicine News; Internal (Rockville, MD) **13684**

Medicine North America (Montreal, QC, Can.) *Ceased*

Medicine; Operative Techniques in Sports (Philadelphia, PA) **27607**

Medicine and Pain; Seminars in Anesthesia, Perioperative (Philadelphia, PA) **27658**

Medicine; Pediatric Critical Care (Baltimore, MD) **13234**

Medicine; Pediatric Pathology & Molecular (Philadelphia, PA) **27617**

Medicine; Pennsylvania (Harrisburg, PA) **27010**

Medicine for the Physician; Complementary (Philadelphia, PA) **27425**

Medicine; Postgraduate (Minneapolis, MN) **16121**

Medicine; Preventive (San Diego, CA) **3248**

Medicine; Psychological (New York, NY) **22604**

Medicine; Psychosomatic (Philadelphia, PA) **27651**

Medicine Quarterly; Geriatric (Toronto, ON, Can.) **36601**

Medicine and Rehabilitation; American Journal of Physical (Indianapolis, IN) **10078**

Medicine Review; Alternative (Dover, ID) **7852**

Medicine Review; Fetal and Maternal (New York, NY) **21687**

Medicine Reviews; Transfusion (Hamilton, ON, Can.) **35892**

Medicine; St. Louis Metropolitan (St. Louis, MO) **17505**

Medicine; San Francisco (San Francisco, CA) **3436**

Medicine and Science in Sports and Exercise (Indianapolis, IN) **10153**

Medicine; Seminars in Nuclear (Bronx, NY) **20286**

Medicine; Seminars in Respiratory and Critical Care (New York, NY) **22725**

Medicine; Sonoma (Santa Rosa, CA) **3735**

Medicine; South Dakota Journal of (Sioux Falls, SD) **28967**

Medicine; Statistics in (Hoboken, NJ) **19106**

Medicine; Strategic (Montvale, NJ) **19276**

Medicine and Surgery; Clinics in Podiatric (Philadelphia, PA) **27420**

Medicine and Surgery; Journal of Avian (Lawrence, KS) **11554**

Medicine; Teaching and Learning in (Springfield, IL) **9643**

Medicine Technology; Journal of Nuclear (Reston, VA) **32388**

Medicine; Texas (Austin, TX) **29835**

Medicine; Toledo (Toledo, OH) **25571**

The Miami Chief (Miami, TX) 30813
Miami County Advocate 25592*
Miami County Advocate (Troy, OH) 25592
Miami County Republic (Paola, KS) 11741
Miami Daily Business Review (New York, NY) Ceased
The Miami Herald (San Jose, CA) 3526
The Miami Hurricane (Coral Gables, FL) 6010
Miami Magazine (Miami, FL) Unable to locate
Miami Mensual (Miami, FL) Unable to locate
Miami Metro Magazine (Miami, FL) Unable to locate
Miami New Times (Miami, FL) 6370
Miami Review 6347*
Miami Shores News (Miami, FL) 6371
Miami Springs News (Miami, FL) Unable to locate
The Miami Student (Oxford, OH) 25457
Miami Tele-Communications, Inc. (Miami, FL) 6394
The Miami Times (Miami, FL) 6372
Miami Today (Miami, FL) 6373
Miami Valley Business News 25108*
Miami Valley Fifty Plus (Troy, OH) 25593
Miami Valley Home Finder (Troy, OH) 25594
Miami Valley Parents (Troy, OH) 25595
Miami Valley Sunday News (Troy, OH) 25596
Miami Valley Wednesday 25592*
Miami Valley's New Business 25108*
Miami; WHERE (Miami, FL) 6392
Miami-Whitewater Press (Cincinnati, OH) Ceased
Miamisburg News 25375*
Miamisburg Sun (Sidney, OH) 25519
Miamisburg/West Carrollton News (Miamisburg, OH) 25375
Miata Magazine (Vista, CA) 4046
The Michael Connection (Orinda, CA) Unable to locate
Michael's Create! (Iola, WI) 33836
Michaels News (Black River Falls, WI) 38005
Michigan Academician (Ann Arbor, MI) 14759
Michigan AFL-CIO News (Lansing, MI) 15279
Michigan Alumnus (Ann Arbor, MI) 14760
Michigan Antiques Trading Post (Williamston, MI) Unable to locate
Michigan Banker Magazine (Lansing, MI) 15280
Michigan Banking and Business News 15280*
Michigan Bar Journal (Lansing, MI) 15281
Michigan Beverage News (Pontiac, MI) Unable to locate
Michigan Botanist (Oshkosh, WI) 34223
Michigan; Business Outlook for West (Kalamazoo, MI) 15233
The Michigan Catholic (Detroit, MI) 14937
Michigan Christian Advocate (Adrian, MI) 14709
Michigan Christmas Tree Journal (Howell, MI) 15197
Michigan Chronicle (Detroit, MI) 14938
Michigan Citizen (Highland Park, MI) 15161
Michigan Columbian (Dearborn Heights, MI) Unable to locate
Michigan ComputerUser Magazine (Linden, MI) Unable to locate
Michigan Contractor and Builder (Detroit, MI) Unable to locate
Michigan Country Lines (Okemos, MI) 15416
The Michigan Daily (Ann Arbor, MI) 14761
Michigan Dry Bean Digest (Saginaw, MI) Ceased
The Michigan Entomologist 14751*
Michigan Farm News (Lansing, MI) 15282
Michigan Farm Radio Network (Milan, MI) Unable to locate
Michigan Farmer (Carol Stream, IL) Unable to locate
Michigan Feminist Studies (Ann Arbor, MI) 14762
Michigan Florist (Haslett, MI) 15150
Michigan Food News (Lansing, MI) 15283
Michigan Golfer (Ann Arbor, MI) 14763
Michigan Health and Hospitals (Lansing, MI) 15284
Michigan Historical Review (Mount Pleasant, MI) 15376
Michigan History (Lansing, MI) 15285
Michigan History for Kids (Lansing, MI) 15286
Michigan History Magazine 15285*
Michigan Hunting and Fishing (Harrisburg, PA) Unable to locate
Michigan Industry (Detroit, MI) Unable to locate
The Michigan Journal (Marshall, MI) Ceased
Michigan Journal of Gender & Law (Ann Arbor, MI) 14764
Michigan Law Review (Ann Arbor, MI) 14765
Michigan Lawyers Weekly (Novi, MI) 15409
Michigan Life; Central (Mount Pleasant, MI) 15375
Michigan Living (Dearborn, MI) 14905
The Michigan Lutheran (Ann Arbor, MI) Ceased
Michigan Master Plumber and Mechanical Contractor (Lansing, MI) 15287
Michigan Mathematical Journal (Ann Arbor, MI) 14766
Michigan Medicine (East Lansing, MI) 14989
Michigan Municipal Review (Ann Arbor, MI) 14767
Michigan Natural Resources Magazine (West Bloomfield, MI) 15676
Michigan News (Haslett, MI) 15151
Michigan; Official (Sandusky, MI) 15520

Michigan Oil and Gas News (Mount Pleasant, MI) 15377
The Michigan Optometrist (Lansing, MI) 15288
Michigan Out-of-Doors (Lansing, MI) 15289
Michigan Overseas Veteran (Lansing, MI) Unable to locate
Michigan Patron 15151*
Michigan Pharmacist (Lansing, MI) 15290
The Michigan Post (Oak Park, MI) 15413
Michigan Prairie Farmer (Indianapolis, IN) Ceased
Michigan Quarterly Review (Ann Arbor, MI) 14768
The Michigan Real Estate Journal (Southfield, MI) 15546
Michigan Restaurateur (Lansing, MI) Unable to locate
Michigan Roads and Construction (Lansing, MI) 15291
Michigan Runner & Fitness Sports (Ann Arbor, MI) 14769
Michigan Senior Times; West (Allegan, MI) 14724
The Michigan Sentinel (Lathrup Village, MI) Unable to locate
Michigan Snowmobiler (East Jordan, MI) 14980
Michigan Sportsman (Lansing, MI) 15292
Michigan Tech Lode (Houghton, MI) 15184
Michigan Technic (Ann Arbor, MI) Ceased
Michigan Traveler (Lansing, MI) 15293
Michigan Woman Magazine (Birmingham, MI) Ceased
Michigan Women's Times (Kalamazoo, MI) Ceased
Mickey Mouse Magazine's Guide for Grown-Ups (New York, NY) Unable to locate
Micmac News (Sydney, NS, Can.) Unable to locate
Micro (Los Angeles, CA) Unable to locate
Micro Computer Abstracts 19226*
Micro Computer Journal (Port Washington, NY) 23130
Micro Cornucopia (Bend, OR) Ceased
Micro-Gazette (Montreal, QC, Can.) Unable to locate
Micro; IEEE (Los Alamitos, CA) 2187
Micro Marketworld (New York, NY) Ceased
Micro Publishing News (Laguna Hills, CA) Unable to locate
MicroAge Quarterly (Tempe, AZ) Ceased
Microbe Interactions (MPMI); Molecular Plant- (St. Paul, MN) 16397
Microbial & Comparative Genomics 20923*
Microbial Drug Resistance (Larchmont, NY) 20921
Microbial Ecology (New York, NY) 22330
Microbiological Reviews 5648*
Microbiologie; Canadian Journal of Microbiology (Revue Canadienne de (Ottawa, ON, Can.) 36208
Microbiology (New York, NY) 22331
Microbiology Abstracts, Section B; Bacteriology: (Bethesda, MD) 13319
Microbiology Abstracts, Section C; Algology, Mycology & Protozoology: (Bethesda, MD) 13299
Microbiology; Annual Review of (Palo Alto, CA) 2792
Microbiology; Applied Biochemistry and (New York, NY) 21228
Microbiology; Applied and Environmental (Washington, DC) 5358
Microbiology; Current (New York, NY) 21525
Microbiology; Journal of Clinical (Washington, DC) 5577
Microbiology; Microbiology Abstracts, Section A; Industrial and Applied (Bethesda, MD) 13345
Microbiology and Molecular Biology Reviews (Washington, DC) 5648
Microbiology; Quantitative (New York, NY) 22616
Microbiology Reviews; Clinical (Washington, DC) 5421
Microbiology (Revue Canadienne de Microbiologie); Canadian Journal of (Ottawa, ON, Can.) 36208
Microchemical Journal (Lake Charles, LA) 12639
Microcolumn Separations; Journal of (Hoboken, NJ) 19031
Microcomputers for Libraries (Wayne, PA) Ceased
Microcosm - Lyrical Ways Ceased
Microdevices; Biomedical (New York, NY) 21321
Microelectronic Manufacturing and Technology (Libertyville, IL) Ceased
Microelectronic Systems Integration; Journal of (New York, NY) 22133
Microelectronics; Russian (New York, NY) 22696
Microform Review (New Providence, NJ) 19348
Microlithography World (Nashua, NH) 18596
Micropaleontology (New York, NY) 22332
Micropendium (Round Rock, TX) Unable to locate
Microprobe Techniques; Journal of Trace and (New York, NY) 22206
The Microscope (Chicago, IL) 8487
Microscopy; Journal of Computer-Assisted (New York, NY) 22037
Microscopy Research and Technique (Hoboken, NJ) 19062
Microscopy; Scanning (Chicago, IL) 8560
Microsoft Certified Professional Magazine (Chatsworth, CA) Unable to locate
Microsoft Interactive Developer (Palo Alto, CA) 2799
Microsoft Networking Journal (Rochester, NY) Ceased
MicroStation World 26917*
Microsurgery (Hoboken, NJ) 19063

Microsurgery; Journal of Reconstructive (New York, NY) 22177
Microthought (Santa Monica, CA) Ceased
MicroTimes (Norcross, GA) 7467
Microvascular Research (San Diego, CA) 3232
Microwave Journal (Norwood, MA) 14450
Microwave and Optical Technology Letters (Hoboken, NJ) 19064
Microwave Product Digest (Hastings on Hudson, NY) Unable to locate
Microwave Systems News 6999*
Microwave & Wireless; Applied (Norcross, GA) 7455
MicroWaves 19405*
Microwaves & RF Magazine (Paramus, NJ) 19405
Mid-America Ag Network (Wichita, KS) 37646
Mid-America Boating (Cleveland Heights, OH) 24994
Mid-America (Chicago) (Chicago, IL) 8488
Mid-America Commerce and Industry (Topeka, KS) 11833
Mid-America Folklore (Batesville, AR) 1041
Mid-America Insurance (Overland Park, KS) Ceased
Mid-America Transporter (Topeka, KS) 11834
Mid-America Weekly Trucking (Fort Dodge, IA) 10904
Mid-American Journal of Business (Muncie, IN) Unable to locate
Mid-American Review (Bowling Green, OH) 24696
Mid-Atlantic Builder (Baltimore, MD) 13218
Mid-Atlantic Cable (Ladysmith, FL) Unable to locate
Mid-Atlantic Country (Greenbelt, MD) Unable to locate
Mid-Atlantic Farm Edition; Fastline— (Buckner, KY) 11979
Mid-Atlantic Food Service News (Columbia, MD) Ceased
Mid-Atlantic Journal of Business (South Orange, NJ) 19585
Mid-Atlantic Region; Group Tour Magazine (Holland, MI) 15169
Mid-Atlantic Tech 28092*
Mid-Atlantic Thoroughbred (Timonium, MD) 13758
Mid Cities News (Arlington, TX) Ceased
Mid-Coast Cable TV (El Campo, TX) 30279
Mid-Communications Cablevision Inc 16030*
Mid Continent Bottler (Lake Lotawana, MO) Ceased
Mid County Chronicle (Nederland, TX) 30857
Mid County Journal (Warrenton, MO) 17687
Mid-Hampton Suffolk Life (Riverhead, NY) 23200
Mid-Hudson CableVision (Catskill, NY) 20440
Mid Iowa Enterprise (State Center, IA) 11242
Mid Island Herald (Hempstead, NY) Ceased
Mid Island News (Smithtown, NY) 23337
Mid-Island Times (Hicksville, NY) 20741
Mid-Kansas Cable Services, Inc. (Moundridge, KS) 11660
Mid-Missouri Business (Columbia, MO) Unable to locate
Mid-Missourian (Columbia, MO) Unable to locate
Mid-North Monitor (Espanola, ON, Can.) 35808
Mid-South Business Journal 29359*
Mid-South Cable 16816*
Mid-South Farm Edition; Fastline— (Buckner, KY) 11980
Mid-South Farmer (Carol Stream, IL) Unable to locate
Mid-South Folklore 1041*
Mid-South Gospel News 1198*
Mid-South Horse Review (Columbus, MS) 16604
Mid-South Hunting & Fishing News (Brownsville, TN) 29071
Mid South Management 24283*
Mid-State Community TV (Aurora, NE) 17942
Mid-Town Mt. Pleasant Review 35139*
Mid-Valley Cablevision 35601*
The Mid-Valley Neighbor 26207*
Mid-Valley Town Crier (Weslaco, TX) 31278
Mid-Week (Trenton, NJ) Ceased
Mid-Week Messenger (Waynesville, NC) 24279
Mid-Week Messenger (Shippensburg, PA) Ceased
Mid-West Truck Edition; Fastline— (Buckner, KY) 11981
Mid-West Truckman (Topeka, KS) Ceased
Mid-York Weekly (Hamilton, NY) 20708
MidAmerica Farmer Grower (Perryville, MO) 17337
MidAmerica Guide (Chicago, IL) Unable to locate
Midcontinent Cable Co. (Aberdeen, SD) 28800
Midcontinent Communications (Bismarck, ND) 24375
Midcontinent Communications (Aberdeen, SD) Unable to locate
Midcontinent Communications (Sioux Falls, SD) 28989
MidContinent Oil World (New York, NY) Ceased
Midcontinental (Winnipeg, MB, Can.) Ceased
Midcontinental Journal of Archeology (Iowa City, IA) 10981
The Midday Record 10772*
Middle East Affairs; Washington Report on (Washington, DC) 5852
Middle East—Basic Oil Laws & Concession Contracts (New York, NY) 22333
Middle East; Comparative Studies of South Asia, Africa, and the (Durham, NC) 23815

Master Index Gale Directory of Publications & Broadcast Media/138th Ed.

Middle East Executive Reports (Washington, DC) **5649**
Middle East Insight (Washington, DC) *Unable to locate*
The Middle East Journal (Washington, DC) **5650**
Middle East Labor Bulletin (San Francisco, CA) *Ceased*
Middle East Policy (Malden, MA) **14298**
Middle East Quarterly (Philadelphia, PA) **27569**
Middle East Research & Information Project (Washington, DC) **5651**
Middle East Review (New York, NY) *Unable to locate*
Middle East Studies (DOMES); Digest of (Milwaukee, WI) **34065**
Middle East Studies; International Journal of (Ann Arbor, MI) **14753**
Middle Eastern Dancer (Casselberry, FL) *Ceased*
Middle Island Suffolk Life; Coram/ (Coram, NY) **20501**
Middle Park Times (Kremmling, CO) **4525**
Middle School Journal (Westerville, OH) **25642**
Middle Tennessee Shopper (Columbia, TN) **29137**
Middleboro Gazette (Middleboro, MA) **14331**
Middlebourne TV Cable (Jerusalem, OH) **25269**
The Middlebury Campus **31557***
Middlebury College Magazine (Middlebury, VT) **31557**
Middlebury College Newsletter **31557***
Middlebury Independent (Middlebury, IN) **10307**
Middlesex Buyer's Guide (New Brunswick, NJ) **19335**
Middlesex Chronicle (Somerville, NJ) **19574**
Middlesex County Family (Mountainside, NJ) **19317**
Middlesex County Shopper **19335***
Middlesex East Update (Woburn, MA) **14670**
Middlesex Magazine & Business Review (Cromwell, CT) *Ceased*
The Middlesex News (Needham, MA) *Unable to locate*
Middleton Times-Tribune (Middleton, WI) **34051**
Middletown Independent (Middletown, NJ) **19235**
Middletown Journal (Middletown, OH) **25378**
Middletown News (Middletown, IN) **10308**
The Middletown Press (Lawrence, MA) *Unable to locate*
Middletown Times Star (Middletown, CA) **2538**
Middletown Transcript (Middletown, DE) **5261**
The Middletown Valley Citizen (Middletown, MD) **13628**
Midi Dealer (Trumbull, CT) *Ceased*
The Midland (Fremont, NE) **18012**
Midland Buyer's Guide (Mount Pleasant, MI) **15378**
Midland, Continental Journal of Applied Corporate Finance **21989***
Midland Daily News (Midland, MI) **15355**
The Midland Mirror (Midland, ON, Can.) **36043**
Midland Reporter-Telegram (Midland, TX) **30814**
Midland Stars Times (Midland, ON, Can.) *Ceased*
Midland Times (Wyoming, IA) **11331**
The Midlands Business Journal (Omaha, NE) **18203**
Midlothian-Bremen Messenger (Midlothian, IL) **9189**
The Midlothian Mirror (Midlothian, TX) **30826**
Midlothian Reporter **30827***
Midlothian Today (Midlothian, TX) **30827**
Midrange (Glen Ellyn, IL) *Ceased*
Midrange Computing (Double Oak, TX) *Unable to locate*
Midrange Enterprise (Hampton, NH) **18514**
Midrange ERP **18514***
MIDRANGE Systems (Horsham, PA) *Unable to locate*
Midsouthwest Restaurant (Oklahoma City, OK) **25972**
Midstream (New York, NY) **22334**
Midway Magazine (Beaverton, OR) *Ceased*
The MidWeek (DeKalb, IL) **8737**
The Midweek (Fergus Falls, MN) **15899**
The Midweek (West Fargo, ND) **24556**
Midweek Bulletin **33871***
Midweek Extra **35615***
Midweek Extra **28745***
Midweek Magazine (Kaneohe, HI) **7774**
The Midweek Review **18924***
Midwest Airlines Magazine (Seattle, WA) **32987**
Midwest Art **16137***
Midwest Automotive & Autobody News (Chicago, IL) *Unable to locate*
The Midwest BEAT Magazine (Highland, IN) **10063**
Midwest Cable Communications Inc. (Bemidji, MN) **15746**
Midwest Cablevision (Eureka, IL) *Unable to locate*
Midwest Cablevision (Watseka, IL) *Unable to locate*
Midwest CableVision (Preston, MN) *Ceased*
Midwest Cablevision (Prairie du Chien, WI) **34269**
Midwest Cablevision (Waseca, WI) **34387**
Midwest City Sun (Midwest City, OK) *Unable to locate*
Midwest Contractor (Kansas City, MO) **17184**
Midwest Edition; Art Now Gallery Guide—Chicago/ (Clinton, NJ) **18760**
Midwest Engineer (Chicago, IL) **8489**
Midwest Equine Market (Elgin, IL) *Unable to locate*
Midwest Express Magazine **32987***
The Midwest Extra **25686***
Midwest; Farmer Stockman of the (Belleville, KS) **11357**
Midwest Features (Madison, WI) *Ceased*
Midwest Flyer Magazine (Oregon, WI) **34217**
Midwest Foodservice News (Columbus, OH) **25031**
Midwest Home & Garden (Minneapolis, MN) **16097**
Midwest Hospitality (Kansas City, MO) *Ceased*
Midwest Living Magazine (New York, NY) **22335**
Midwest Men (Magazine for Women) (St. Charles, IL) *Unable to locate*
Midwest Messenger (Tekamah, NE) **18297**
Midwest Modern Language Association Journal (Iowa City, IA) **10982**
The Midwest Motorist **17471***
The Midwest Music Review **17488***
Midwest Musicians Hotline **10905***
MidWest Outdoors (Elgin, IL) *Unable to locate*
Midwest Players (St. Paul, MN) **16389**
Midwest Poetry Review (Atlanta, GA) *Ceased*
The Midwest Quarterly (Pittsburg, KS) **11753**
Midwest Racing News (Milwaukee, WI) **34081**
Midwest Real Estate News (Atlanta, GA) *Unable to locate*
Midwest Retailer (Bloomington, MN) **15759**
Midwest Review of Public Administration **16987***
Midwest Traveler (St. Louis, MO) **17471**
Midwest Truck Trader **10904***
Midwest Video **19838***
Midwest Video Electronics (Rhinelander, WI) **34287**
Midwestern **4368***
Midwestern History; Traces of Indiana and (Indianapolis, IN) **10175**
Midwestern States Salvage Guide (Moore, OK) **25920**
Midwifery Today (Eugene, OR) **26323**
Midwifery Today and Childbirth Education with International Midwife **26323***
Miesiecznik Franciszkanski (Pulaski, WI) *Ceased*
Mifflinburg Telegraph (Mifflinburg, PA) **27262**
Mighty Mouse Adventure Magazine (Waterbury, CT) *Unable to locate*
Mighty Nickel (Grand Island, NE) **18026**
Migration and Law; European (New York, NY) **21655**
Migration Review; International (Staten Island, NY) **23358**
Migration Today **23360***
Migration World Magazine (Staten Island, NY) **23360**
Mikero Entertainments (Blanco, TX) *Ceased*
Mike's TV Inc. (Morton, WA) **32837**
Milan Leader **15517***
Milan Mirror-Exchange (Milan, TN) **29414**
Milan News **15517***
Milan News-Leader (Saline, MI) **15517**
Milan River Cities Reader (Milan, IL) *Ceased*
The Milan Standard (Milan, MO) **17289**
Milan Standard-Watson Journal (Milan, MN) **16054**
Milbank Herald Advance (Milbank, SD) *Ceased*
The Milbank Quarterly (New York, NY) *Ceased*
Mildmay Town & Country Crier (Mildmay, ON, Can.) **36046**
Mile Hi Cablevision Associates Ltd. (Denver, CO) *Ceased*
Mile Zero News (Grimshaw, AB, Can.) **34778**
Miles City Star (Miles City, MT) **17861**
Milestone Communications (Monument, CO) **4585**
Milford Advertiser-Press (Milford, OH) **25384**
The Milford Cabinet & Wilton Journal **18577***
Milford Daily News (Needham, MA) **14362**
Milford Herald-News (Milford, IL) **9196**
Milford Mail and Terril Record (Spirit Lake, IA) **11237**
The Milford Mirror (Shelton, CT) **5126**
Milford Reporter (Milford, CT) **4956**
Milford Spinal Column Newsweekly (Milford, MI) **15358**
Milford Times (Milford, MI) **15359**
The Milford Times (Milford, NE) **18162**
The Militant (New York, NY) **22336**
Military (Sacramento, CA) **3008**
The Military Advisor (San Jose, CA) *Unable to locate*
Military & Aerospace Electronics (Nashua, NH) **18597**
Military Affairs **32189***
Military Business Review (Virginia Beach, VA) *Ceased*
The Military Chaplain (Arlington, VA) *Unable to locate*
Military Club & Hospitality (Westbury, NY) **23557**
Military Clubs and Recreation (Alexandria, VA) *Unable to locate*
Military Collectors News Press (Tulsa, OK) *Ceased*
The Military Engineer (Alexandria, VA) **31709**
Military Forum (Ridgefield, CT) *Unable to locate*
Military Forum (Washington, DC) *Ceased*
Military Grocer (Bethesda, MD) **13360**
Military History (Leesburg, VA) *Unable to locate*
Military History Presents: Great Battles (Leesburg, VA) *Unable to locate*
Military History Review **3008***
Military History of the Southwest **30242***
Military History of the West (Denton, TX) **30242**
Military Institute Alumni Bulletin; Marion (Marion, AL) **311**
Military Intelligence Professional Bulletin **708***
Military Intelligence Professional Bulletin (Fort Huachuca, AZ) **709**
Military Law Review (Pittsburgh, PA) **27813**
Military Lifestyle (Bethesda, MD) *Ceased*
Military Living Magazine (Falls Church, VA) *Ceased*
Military Market Magazine (Springfield, VA) *Ceased*
Military Media Inc. (Poughkeepsie, NY) *Unable to locate*
Military Medicine (Bethesda, MD) **13361**
Military Police (Fort Mc Clellan, AL) *Unable to locate*
Military Psychology (Ft. McNair, DC) **5306**
Military Recorder-Times (San Antonio, TX) *Ceased*
Military Review (Fort Leavenworth, KS) **11440**
Military/Space Electronic Design (New York, NY) *Ceased*
Military Sun Press (Kaneohe, HI) **7775**
Military Thought (Minneapolis, MN) **16098**
Military Trader (Iola, WI) **33837**
Military Transportation Management; Translog: Journal of (Alexandria, VA) **31746**
Military Update (Centreville, VA) **38006**
Military Vehicles (Iola, WI) **33838**
Milk & Liquid Food Transporter (Appleton, WI) **33538**
Milk Producer; Ontario (Mississauga, ON, Can.) **36082**
The Mill City Enterprise (Mill City, OR) *Unable to locate*
Mill Creek Cable TV, Inc. (Salem, OR) **26577**
Mill Creek Community News (Dover, DE) **5250**
Mill Creek Enterprise (Lynnwood, WA) *Unable to locate*
Mill Trade Journal Recycling Markets (Avon by the Sea, NJ) *Unable to locate*
Millard County Chronicle Progress (Delta, UT) **31331**
Millard County Gazette (Delta, UT) **31332**
Millard Courier **18002***
Millbrae Sun (Millbrae, CA) **2543**
Millbrook Highlighter **36047***
Millbrook Round Table (Millbrook, NY) **21083**
Millbrook Times (Millbrook, ON, Can.) **36047**
Millburn- and Sho- Hills; The Item of (West Paterson, NJ) **19730**
Millcreek Sun (Erie, PA) *Ceased*
Millcreek Valley News-Press (Cincinnati, OH) *Ceased*
Mille Iles; La Voix des (Ste.-Therese, QC, Can.) **37368**
Mille Lacs County Times (Milaca, MN) **16053**
Mille Lacs Messenger (Isle, MN) **15972**
Millen News (Millen, GA) **7441**
Miller County Autogram-Sentinel (Eldon, MO) **17046**
Miller County Liberal (Colquitt, GA) **7182**
Miller Features Syndicate Inc. (Toronto, ON, Can.) *Unable to locate*
The Miller Press (Miller, MO) **17290**
The Miller Press (Miller, SD) **28896**
Millersburg TV Co. (Millersburg, PA) **27266**
Millheim TV Transmission Co. (Millheim, PA) **27269**
Milligan Syndicate (Barrington, IL) **38007**
Millimeter Magazine (Overland Park, KS) **11721**
Millimeter Waves; International Journal of Infrared and (New York, NY) **21909**
Milling & Baking News (Kansas City, MO) **17185**
Milling Journal (Decatur, IL) **8713**
Millington Herald and Lake Ville Aerial (Millington, MI) *Unable to locate*
The Millington Star (Millington, TN) **29416**
Millionaire (West Palm Beach, FL) *Unable to locate*
Millstadt Enterprise (Columbia, IL) *Unable to locate*
The Millville Daily **19698***
Milpitas Post (Milpitas, CA) **2545**
The Milton Courier (Milton, WI) **34054**
The Milton Daily Standard/The Lewisburg Daily Journal (Milton, PA) **27270**
Milton-Freewater Valley Times (Milton-Freewater, OR) **26435**
Milton Independent (Milton, VT) **31563**
Milton Magazine; John (New York, NY) **21970**
Milton Quarterly (Athens, OH) **24630**
Milton Record Transcript (Milton, MA) **14336**
Milton Shopping News (Oakville, ON, Can.) **36146**
Milton Studies (Pittsburgh, PA) **27814**
Milton Townsman (Milton, MA) **14337**
Milverton Sun (Milverton, ON, Can.) *Ceased*
Milwaukee; The Business Journal Serving Greater (Milwaukee, WI) **34060**
Milwaukee Community Journal (Milwaukee, WI) **34082**
Milwaukee Courier (Milwaukee, WI) **34083**
Milwaukee Journal **34084***
Milwaukee Journal Sentinel (Milwaukee, WI) **34084**
Milwaukee Labor Press, AFL-CIO (Milwaukee, WI) **34085**
Milwaukee Magazine (Milwaukee, WI) **34086**
Milwaukee Magazine; Key (Milwaukee, WI) **34072**
Milwaukee Sentinel **34084***
Milwaukee Star (Milwaukee, WI) **34087**
Milwaukee Times (Milwaukee, WI) **34088**

Numbers cited in bold after listings are entry numbers rather than page numbers.

Milwaukee Voice Graphic; South (New Berlin, WI) 34186

The Minco Minstrel (Chickasha, OK) *Unable to locate*

MIND 4180*

Mind and Behavior; The Journal of (Orono, ME) 13000

Mind, Culture, and Activity (Mahwah, NJ) 19202

Mind Extension University (Englewood, CO) 37768

Minden Cable TV (Minden, LA) *Unable to locate*

Minden City Herald (Minden City, MI) 15361

The Minden Courier (Minden, NE) 18163

Minden Press-Herald (Minden, LA) 12687

Minds and Machines (New York, NY) 22337

Mine Action; Journal of (Harrisonburg, VA) 32140

Mine & Quarry Trader (Indianapolis, IN) 10154

Mine Rescue Manual; BC (Victoria, BC, Can.) 35207

Mine Safety and Health Review; Federal (Washington, DC) 5494

Mine Workers Journal; United (Fairfax, VA) 32033

Mineola American (Mineola, NY) 21086

Mineola Monitor (Mineola, TX) 30830

Mineola Pennysaver (Mineola, ON, Can.) 36052

Miner; Bradford Journal/ (Mount Jewett, PA) 27298

Miner County Pioneer (Howard, SD) 28871

Miner; Iron County (Hurley, WI) 33797

Miner; Kingman Daily (Kingman, AZ) 729

Miner & News; Daily (Kenora, ON, Can.) 35929

Mineral County Independent-News (Hawthorne, NV) 18352

Mineral County Miner (Monte Vista, CO) *Unable to locate*

Mineral Daily News-Tribune (Keyser, WV) 33352

Mineral and Electrolyte Metabolism (MEM) (Farmington, CT) *Ceased*

Mineral Independent (Superior, MT) *Unable to locate*

Mineral Research; Journal of Bone and (Durham, NC) 23829

Mineral Resources Engineering (Philadelphia, PA) *Ceased*

Mineral Resources; Lithology and (New York, NY) 22261

Mineral Sciences; Earth and (University Park, PA) 28075

Mineralogical Record (Tucson, AZ) *Unable to locate*

Mineralogist; American (Washington, DC) 5336

Minerals and Metallurgical Processing (Littleton, CO) 4552

Minerals; Rocks & (Washington, DC) 5770

Minerals Today (Washington, DC) *Ceased*

Miner's News (Boise, ID) 7814

Minerva (Pasadena, MD) 13644

The Minerva Leader 25392*

The Minerva Leader 25328*

Minerva's Bulletin Board (Pasadena, MD) *Ceased*

Mines Magazine (Golden, CO) 4470

Mines Oredigger (Golden, CO) 4471

Mines Quarterly; Colorado School of (Golden, CO) 4465

Ming Pao Daily News (New York, NY) *Unable to locate*

Mini Paper/Buyer's Guide 34512*

Mini-PEGG 34724*

The Mini-Storage Messenger (Phoenix, AZ) 807

Mini, The Magazine for IBM 34/36/38 Decision Makers (Gloucester, MA) *Ceased*

Miniature Collector (Muskegon, MI) *Unable to locate*

Miniature Donkey Talk (Westminster, MD) 13777

Miniature Quilts (Montrose, PA) 27290

Miniatures Dealer (Waukesha, WI) *Ceased*

Miniatures Showcase (Waukesha, WI) *Ceased*

Minilab Developments 23934*

Minimally Invasive Surgical Nursing (Larchmont, NY) *Ceased*

Mining & Construction; World Dredging, (Irvine, CA) 2093

Mining Engineering (Littleton, CO) 4553

Mining Equipment; World (New York, NY) 22942

Mining Gazette; The Daily (Houghton, MI) 15183

The Mining Journal (Marquette, MI) 15338

Mining Journal; Canadian (Toronto, ON, Can.) 36519

Mining Journal; Engineering and (Minneapolis, MN) 16074

Mining Journal; International California (Aptos, CA) 1426

Mining & Metallurgical Bulletin; CIM Bulletin (Canadian (Montreal, QC, Can.) 37103

Mining News 33695*

Mining News; The Florence (Florence, WI) 33695

Mining/Processing Equipment (Morris Plains, NJ) *Ceased*

The Mining Record (Denver, CO) 4339

Mining Review (North Vancouver, BC, Can.) *Unable to locate*

Mining Review; Rich Hill (Rich Hill, MO) 17372

Mining Review; Skillings (Duluth, MN) 15842

Mining Science; Journal of (New York, NY) 22134

Mining Voice (Washington, DC) *Ceased*

Miniondas (Santa Ana, CA) 3629

The Minister's Practical Idea Kit (Golden, CO) *Ceased*

Ministries Today (Lake Mary, FL) 6278

Ministries Today *Ceased*

Ministry (Silver Spring, MD) 13739

Ministry (New York, NY) *Ceased*

Ministry in Addiction and Recovery; Journal of (St. Paul, MN) 16383

Ministry & Liturgy (San Jose, CA) 3527

Ministry Quarterly; National Apostolate for Inclusion (Riverdale, MD) 13673

MiniTruckin' (Anaheim, CA) 1409

The Minjoong Shinmoon (Toronto, ON, Can.) *Unable to locate*

Minkus Stamp Journal (Charlotte, NC) *Unable to locate*

Minneapolis Labor Review (Minneapolis, MN) 16099

The Minneapolis Messenger (Minneapolis, KS) 11654

Minneapolis Quarterly Review; Federal Reserve Bank of (Minneapolis, MN) 16080

The Minneapolis Review of Baseball 16375*

Minneapolis/St. Paul City Business 16066*

Minneapolis-St. Paul CityBusiness (Charlotte, NC) 23750

Minneapolis Spokesman-Recorder 16107*

Minneapolis Spokesman & St. Paul Recorder 16107*

Minneapolis Star and Tribune 16134*

The Minnedosa Tribune (Minnedosa, MB, Can.) 35274

The Minneola Record (Minneola, KS) 11655

Minneota Mascot (Minneota, MN) 16165

Minnesota (Minneapolis, MN) 16100

Minnesota Cable Enterprises 16477*

Minnesota Christian Chronicle (Minneapolis, MN) 16101

Minnesota Cities (St. Paul, MN) *Unable to locate*

Minnesota Conservation Volunteer (St. Paul, MN) 16390

The Minnesota Daily (Minneapolis, MN) 16102

Minnesota/Dakota Truck Merchandiser (New Hope, MN) *Unable to locate*

Minnesota Direct Mailer (Princeton, MN) *Ceased*

(Minnesota Edition); Home & Away (Bettendorf, IA) 10621

Minnesota Educator (St. Paul, MN) 16391

Minnesota Farm Edition; Fastline— (Buckner, KY) 11982

Minnesota Flyer Magazine (Sandstone, MN) 16434

Minnesota Genealogical Journal (Roseville, MN) 16334

Minnesota Golfer (Edina, MN) 15876

Minnesota Grocer (St. Paul, MN) 16392

Minnesota History (St. Paul, MN) 16393

Minnesota Horticulturist 15893*

Minnesota Independent Network Inc. (St. Paul, MN) 37702

Minnesota Insurance (Chaska, MN) 15794

Minnesota Law & Politics (Minneapolis, MN) 16103

Minnesota Law Review (Minneapolis, MN) 16104

Minnesota Legionnaire (St. Paul, MN) 16394

Minnesota Medicine (Minneapolis, MN) 16105

Minnesota Monthly (Minneapolis, MN) 16106

Minnesota News; Rural (Chippewa Falls, WI) 33628

Minnesota Parent (Eagan, MN) 15863

Minnesota Pharmacist (Springfield, IL) *Unable to locate*

Minnesota PHC Contractor (Brooklyn Center, MN) *Unable to locate*

Minnesota Police Journal (Minneapolis, MN) *Ceased*

Minnesota Precision Manufacturing Association Journal 16279*

Minnesota Public Television Association (St. Paul, MN) 37703

Minnesota Review (Columbia, MO) 16997

Minnesota River Valley Shopper (Faribault, MN) *Ceased*

Minnesota Smoke-Eater (St. Paul, MN) 16395

Minnesota Spokesman (Minneapolis, MN) 16107

Minnesota Sports (Minneapolis, MN) 16108

Minnesota Technology (Minneapolis, MN) 16109

The Minnesota Volunteer 16390*

Minnesota Women's Press (St. Paul, MN) 16396

Minnesotan Uutiset 6298*

Minnesota's Journal of Law & Politics 16103*

Minnetonka/Deephaven Sun-Sailor; West (Minnetonka, MN) 16179

Minnetonka Sailor-Sun; Hopkins/East (Hopkins, MN) 15963

Minoa/Kirkville/Bridgeport Pennysaver; East Syracuse/ (Syracuse, NY) 23401

Minonk News Dispatch 9200*

Minorities and Women in Business (Burlington, NC) *Unable to locate*

Minority Business Entrepreneur (Torrance, CA) 3938

Minority Engineer (Melville, NY) *Unable to locate*

Minority Features Syndicate (Farrell, PA) 38008

Minority and Group Rights; International Journal on (New York, NY) 21911

Minority Health Today (Washington, DC) 5652

Minority Medical Students; Journal for (New Orleans, LA) 12735

The Minot Daily News (Minot, ND) 24505

(Minot); Going Places (Minot, ND) 24504

The Minuteman (Coraopolis, PA) *Ceased*

The Minuteman Chronicle (Concord, MA) *Ceased*

Minuteman; Lexington (Concord, MA) 14147

Mirabella (New York, NY) *Unable to locate*

The Miraculous Medal (Philadelphia, PA) 27570

The Mirage (Douglas, AZ) 687

Miramar (Hollywood, FL) *Ceased*

Miramichi Headwaters (Miramichi, NB, Can.) *Unable to locate*

Miramichi Leader (Miramichi, NB, Can.) 35408

Miramichi Weekend (Miramichi, NB, Can.) 35409

The Mirror 36881*

The Mirror 35594*

The Mirror (Greeley, CO) 4499

The Mirror (Mayport, FL) 6333

The Mirror (Somerset, KY) 12405

The Mirror (Springfield, MO) 17605

Mirror (Seattle, WA) *Ceased*

Mirror (Dawson Creek, BC, Can.) *Unable to locate*

Mirror (Maidstone, SK, Can.) 37493

Mirror; Altoona (Altoona, PA) 26635

Mirror; Augustana (Sioux Falls, SD) 28961

Mirror; Campbell River (Campbell River, BC, Can.) 34918

The Mirror-Examiner (Middleton, NS, Can.) 35594

Mirror; The Gilmer (Gilmer, TX) 30396

Mirror; The Inquirer and (Nantucket, MA) 14340

Mirror; Lake Chelan (Chelan, WA) 32713

The Mirror (Martin County Edition) (Stuart, FL) *Ceased*

Mirror; The Midlothian (Midlothian, TX) 30826

Mirror News Magazine (Hopkins, MN) 15964

Mirror; North York (Willowdale, ON, Can.) 36881

The Mirror-Northern Report (High Prairie, AB, Can.) *Unable to locate*

Mirror (Northside and Southside); The Calgary (Calgary, AB, Can.) 34632

Mirror-Recorder (Arkville, NY) *Ceased*

Mirror-Republican (Mansfield, MO) 17261

Mirror; The Scarborough (Willowdale, ON, Can.) 36883

Mirror; Sooke (Sooke, BC, Can.) 35093

Mirror; Tonganoxie (Tonganoxie, KS) 11813

Mirror; The Wolfe City (Wolfe City, TX) 31307

Mirror); Y Drych (The (Utica, NY) 23469

MIS Quarterly (Minneapolis, MN) 16110

MIS Week (New York, NY) *Ceased*

Misanthrope; Le (Montreal, QC, Can.) 37171

The Miscellany News (Poughkeepsie, NY) 23148

Mishawaka Enterprise (Mishawaka, IN) *Unable to locate*

The Mishawaka Enterprise (Mishawaka, IN) 10313

Miss-Lou Guide (Natchez, MS) 16792

The Missile 2317*

The Missile (Lancaster, CA) *Ceased*

Missile Times; Space and (Lompoc, CA) 2163

Missiology (Wilmore, KY) 12453

Mission (Bensalem, PA) 26695

Mission Cable (Woodward, OK) 26201

Mission Cable Co. 25836*

Mission Cable Co. 748*

Mission Cable Co. (Denver, CO) 4397

Mission Cable Co. (Friona, TX) *Unable to locate*

Mission Cable Co. (Idalou, TX) *Unable to locate*

Mission Cable Co. (Knox City, TX) *Unable to locate*

Mission Cable Co. (Muleshoe, TX) *Unable to locate*

Mission Cable Co. (Rockwall, TX) *Unable to locate*

Mission Cable L.P. 31205*

Mission Canada 36540*

The Mission City Record (Mission, BC, Can.) 35016

Mission Frontiers (Pasadena, CA) 2821

The Mission Helper (Baltimore, MD) 13219

Mission Hills Sun (Overland Park, KS) *Ceased*

Mission Magazine (New York, NY) 22338

Mission Sun (Mission, KS) 11656

Mission Today (Evanston, IL) *Ceased*

Mission Valley Review (Woodland Hills, CA) 4109

Missionary (Sacramento, CA) 3009

Missionary News; Spiritan (Toronto, ON, Can.) 36746

Missionary Research; International Bulletin of (New Haven, CT) 4992

Missionettes Memos 17594*

Missionhurst (Arlington, VA) 31808

Missions Etrangeres (Laval, QC, Can.) 37042

Missions des Franciscains (Montreal, QC, Can.) 37187

Missions & Missionaries (Portland, OR) *Ceased*

Missions Mosaic (Birmingham, AL) *Ceased*

Missions Quarterly (EMQ); Evangelical (Wheaton, IL) 9755

The Mississauga Booster (Mississauga, ON, Can.) 36079

Mississauga Business 36080*

Mississauga Business Times (Mississauga, ON, Can.) 36080

Montgomery County News (Clarksville, TN) 29115
Montgomery County Observer (Blue Bell, PA) *Unable to locate*
The Montgomery County Record 27063*
Montgomery County Sentinel (Rockville, MD) 13687
Montgomery Herald (Troy, NC) 24257
The Montgomery Herald (Montgomery, WV) 33386
Montgomery Independent (Montgomery, AL) 370
The Montgomery Journal (Rockville, MD) 13688
Montgomery Life (Trenton, NJ) 19660
Montgomery Messenger (Montgomery, MN) 16183
The Montgomery Monitor (Soperton, GA) 7558
Montgomery Standard (Montgomery City, MO) 17296
Montgomery-Tuskegee Times (Montgomery, AL) *Unable to locate*
Montgomery Village Gazette (Frederick, MD) 13516
Montgomeryville Spirit 26931*
Month Magazine (Seattle, WA) *Unable to locate*
The Monthly 1876*
Monthly Bibliography, Part II (New York, NY) 22361
Monthly Bulletin of Statistics (New York, NY) 22362
Monthly Catalog of U.S. Government Publications (Pittsburgh, PA) 27816
Monthly Checklist of State Publications (Pittsburgh, PA) *Ceased*
Monthly Crop and Livestock Report (Guelph, ON, Can.) 35866
Monthly Energy Review (Pittsburgh, PA) 27817
Monthly F.O.B. Price Summary, Past Sales (Coast Mills) (Portland, OR) 26485
Monthly F.O.B. Price Summary, Past Sales (Inland Mills) (Portland, OR) 26486
Monthly Labor Review (Pittsburgh, PA) 27818
The Monthly (Northwest Edition) (Seattle, WA) *Unable to locate*
Monthly Prescribing Reference (New York, NY) 22363
The Monthly Report to Booksellers 32677*
Monthly Review (New York, NY) 22364
Monthly and Seasonal Weather Outlook (Pittsburgh, PA) *Unable to locate*
Monthly Statement 2913*
Monthly Statistics of Foreign Trade 5661*
Monthly Statistics of International Trade (Washington, DC) 5661
Monthly Vital Statistics Report 13587*
Monthly Weather Review (Boston, MA) 13929
Monticello Big Lake Shopper 16185*
The Monticello Express (Monticello, IA) 11089
Monticello Herald Journal (Monticello, IN) 10320
Monticello Messenger (Monticello, WI) *Unable to locate*
Monticello News (Monticello, FL) 6435
The Monticello News (Monticello, GA) 7445
Monticello Shopper (Monticello, MN) 16185
Monticello Sun-Journal (Delphi, IN) *Ceased*
Montmorency County Tribune (Atlanta, MI) 14783
The Montpelier Herald (Montpelier, IN) 10321
Montreal Business (Montreal, QC, Can.) *Ceased*
Montreal Ce Mois Ci (Montreal, QC, Can.) *Unable to locate*
The Montreal Downtowner (Montreal, QC, Can.) *Unable to locate*
The Montreal Gazette (Montreal, QC, Can.) 37188
Montreal La Criee (Montreal, QC, Can.) *Unable to locate*
Montreal; Le Journal de (Montreal, QC, Can.) 37163
Montreal Magazine (Westmount, QC, Can.) *Ceased*
Montreal Mirror (Montreal, QC, Can.) 37189
Montreal; Moving to (Unionville, ON, Can.) 36831
Montreal Scope (Montreal, QC, Can.) 37190
Montreal Serai (Montreal, QC, Can.) 37191
Montrose Daily Press (Montrose, CO) 4580
Montrose Herald Journal; Howard Lake-Waverly (Howard Lake, MN) 15966
Montrose Independent 27292*
The Montrose Sun (Cleveland, OH) 24928
Moody Broadcasting Network (Chicago, IL) 37647
Moody County Enterprise (Henryville, PA) *Unable to locate*
Moody County Enterprise (Flandreau, SD) 28855
The Moody Courier (Moody, TX) 30837
Moody Magazine (Chicago, IL) 8494
Moody's Bond Survey (New York, NY) *Ceased*
Moon Miners' Manifesto (Milwaukee, WI) 34089
Moon; New (Duluth, MN) 15840
Moon Record Star (Monroeville, PA) 27278
Moondance (Columbia, MO) *Unable to locate*
Moonlight Chronicles (Minneapolis, MN) *Ceased*
Moorcroft Leader (Moorcroft, WY) *Unable to locate*
Moore American (Moore, OK) 25921
Moore County Citizen News-Record (Aberdeen, NC) *Unable to locate*
The Moore County News (Lynchburg, TN) 29337
Moore County News-Press (Dumas, TX) 30251
Moorefield CableVision (Moorefield, WV) 33390
The Moorefield Examiner (Moorefield, WV) 33389
Mooresville Tribune (Mooresville, NC) 24068
Moorhead State University Advocate (Moorhead, MN) 16189

The Mooring Mast (Tacoma, WA) 33146
Moorpark Star (Moorpark, CA) *Unable to locate*
Moorshead Magazines Ltd. 36346*
Moose Country 24420*
Moose Jaw This Week (Moose Jaw, SK, Can.) 37501
Moose Jaw This Weekend (Moose Jaw, SK, Can.) *Ceased*
The Moose Jaw Times-Herald (Moose Jaw, SK, Can.) 37502
Moose Magazine (Mooseheart, IL) 9224
Moosehead Enterprises (Greenville, ME) 12967
Moosonee Freighter (Timmins, ON, Can.) 36455
Mop; Broom Brush and (Arcola, IL) 8019
Mopar; High Performance (Saddle Brook, NJ) 19527
Mopar Muscle (Los Angeles, CA) 2333
Mor Music TV (St. Petersburg, FL) *Unable to locate*
Mora Advertiser 16196*
Mora Advertisers (Mora, MN) 16196
Moravia Pennysaver (Syracuse, NY) 23413
Moravia Union (Moravia, IA) 11090
Moravian (Bethlehem, PA) 26704
Morbidity and Mortality Weekly Report (Atlanta, GA) 7028
Morbius (New York, NY) 22365
more (New York, NY) 22366
MORE-FM - 105.5 (Huntsville, ON, Can.) 35918
The Morehead News (Morehead, KY) 12303
The Morenci Observer (Morenci, MI) 15369
Moreno Valley Butterfield Express 2600*
The Morgan County Advertiser (New Lexington, OH) 25412
Morgan County Herald (McConnelsville, OH) 25369
Morgan County News (Wartburg, TN) 29639
Morgan County News (Morgan, UT) 31371
Morgan County Press (Stover, MO) 17640
Morgan Directory Reviews (Blue Bell, PA) *Unable to locate*
Morgan Hill Times (El Cajon, CA) *Unable to locate*
The Morgan Horse (Shelburne, VT) 31599
The Morgan Messenger (Berkeley Springs, WV) 33247
The Moriches Bay Tide (Shirley, NY) *Unable to locate*
Moriches Suffolk Life (Moriches, NY) 21097
Morinville Gazette 34842*
Morinville Mirror (Morinville, AB, Can.) 34816
Mormon Historical Studies (Hyrum, UT) 31340
Morning Advocate 12484*
The Morning Call (Allentown, PA) 26629
The Morning Herald (Hagerstown, MD) 13568
Morning Journal (Lisbon, OH) 25308
The Morning Journal (Lorain, OH) 25315
The Morning News (Blackfoot, ID) 7800
Morning News (Erie, PA) 26901
Morning News, Eerie Daily Times, Sunday Times-News 26897*
The Morning News of Northwest Arkansas (Rogers, AR) 1327
The Morning News Tribune 33147*
Morning Sentinel (Centralia, IL) 8175
The Morning Star (Vernon, BC, Can.) 35201
Morning Star: The Shopping Guide (Albion, MI) 14716
Morning Sun (Pittsburg, KS) 11754
The Morning Sun (Mount Pleasant, MI) 15379
Morning Sun News-Herald (Morning Sun, IA) 11092
Morningstar Japan (Chicago, IL) *Unable to locate*
Moro Cooperative TV Club (Goldendale, WA) 32778
Morocco Courier (Rensselaer, IN) 10413
Morphology; Journal of (Hoboken, NJ) 19033
Morresville/Decatur Times (South Bend, IN) 10457
Morrill's Cable TV Ltd. (Schreiber, ON, Can.) *Unable to locate*
Morris County Family (Mountainside, NJ) 19318
Morris Daily Herald (Morris, IL) 9225
Morris News Bee (Stirling, NJ) 19604
Morris News Service (Atlanta, GA) 38009
Morrison County Record (Little Falls, MN) 16006
Morrisons Cove Herald (Martinsburg, PA) 27222
Morrisonville Times (Morrisonville, IL) 9228
Morrow County Independent (Cardington, OH) 24739
Morrow County Sentinel (Mount Gilead, OH) *Unable to locate*
Mortality Weekly Report; Morbidity and (Atlanta, GA) 7028
Mortgage Banking Magazine (Washington, DC) 5662
Mortgage News; National (New York, NY) 22399
Mortgage Originator Magazine (San Diego, CA) 3238
Mortgage Servicing News (New York, NY) 22367
Mortgage Technology (New York, NY) 22368
Morticians of the Southwest (Garland, TX) *Unable to locate*
Morton Grove Champion Review (Morton Grove, IL) 9230
Morton Grove-Niles Life (Lincolnwood, IL) 9098
The Morton Journal 32836*
Morton Times News (Morton, IL) 9229
Morton Tribune (Morton, TX) 30839

Mortuary Management (Monterey, CA) 2583
Mortuary Times (Clifton, NJ) 18756
The Mosaic (Cleveland, OH) 24929
Mosaic (Pittsburgh, PA) *Ceased*
Mosaic (Winnipeg, MB, Can.) 35345
Mosaik (Winnipeg, MB, Can.) *Unable to locate*
Moscow Moneysaver (Moscow, ID) 7919
The Mosinee Times (Mosinee, WI) 34155
Moss Bluff News; Westlake/ (Westlake, LA) 12879
Motel (River Edge, NJ) *Unable to locate*
Mother; The American (Dover, DE) 5243
Mother Baby Journal (Santa Rosa, CA) *Ceased*
Mother Earth International Journal (San Francisco, CA) *Unable to locate*
Mother Earth News (New York, NY) 22369
Mother Jones (San Francisco, CA) 3391
Mother Lode Monitor (Sutter Creek, CA) *Unable to locate*
Mother; New 36763*
Mothering Magazine (Santa Fe, NM) 19936
Mothers Today (Bronxville, NY) *Unable to locate*
MOTION (Carson City, NV) 18327
Motion Systems Consultant (Cleveland, OH) 24930
The Motion Systems Distributor (Cleveland, OH) 24931
Motivation and Emotion (New York, NY) 22370
Motivational Marketing (Toronto, ON, Can.) *Unable to locate*
Motley County Tribune (Matador, TX) 30772
Moto, Bateau & Vehicules Recreatif Hebdo; Bike, Boat & R.V. Trader/ (Montreal, QC, Can.) 37091
Moto Journal (Montreal, QC, Can.) 37192
Motocross Action (Valencia, CA) 3980
Motocycliste (Montreal, QC, Can.) 37193
Motor Age; Chilton's (Chicago, IL) 8331
Motor Behavior; Journal of (Washington, DC) 5602
Motor Boating & Sailing (New York, NY) 22371
Motor in Canada (Winnipeg, MB, Can.) *Ceased*
Motor Carrier; The Arkansas 1222*
Motor Carrier Manager (Etobicoke, ON, Can.) *Ceased*
Motor City News (Warren, MI) *Ceased*
Motor Club Home & Away; AAA—Chicago (Aurora, IL) 8037
Motor Club News (Newark, NJ) *Unable to locate*
Motor Coach Guide; Russell's Official National (Cedar Rapids, IA) 10677
Motor Control (Champaign, IL) 8204
Motor Magazine (Bloomington, MN) 15760
Motor Matters (Wilmington, DE) 38010
Motor News; Hemmings (Bennington, VT) 31499
Motor News Media Corp. (Urbandale, IA) 38011
Motor; Northwest (Seattle, WA) 32994
Motor Service (Chicago, IL) 8495
Motor Skills; Perceptual and (Missoula, MT) 17874
Motor Transport Association Bullitin (Hartford, CT) 4898
Motor Transport News; Maine (Augusta, ME) 12894
Motor Trend (Los Angeles, CA) 2334
Motor Truck (Toronto, ON, Can.) 36669
Motor World (Los Angeles, CA) 2335
MotoRacing (Pleasanton, CA) 2854
MotoRacing; Southern (Winston-Salem, NC) 24322
MotorBoat (New York, NY) *Unable to locate*
Motorboating (New York, NY) 22372
Motorbooty (Detroit, MI) 14940
Motorcycle Consumer News (Mission Viejo, CA) *Unable to locate*
Motorcycle Dealer & Trade 36670*
Motorcycle Dealernews 3624*
Motorcycle Events Magazine (Pierre, SD) 28917
Motorcycle Industry Magazine (Gardnerville, NV) 18348
Motorcycle Industry Shopper 18348*
Motorcycle Price Guide (Milwaukee, WI) *Ceased*
Motorcycle Product News (Van Nuys, CA) *Unable to locate*
Motorcycle Shopper (Deltona, FL) *Ceased*
Motorcycle Technology; Roadracing World & (Lake Elsinore, CA) 2140
Motorcycle Tour & Cruiser (Stamford, CT) 5155
Motorcycle Tour & Travel 5155*
Motorcycle Weekly (Irvine, CA) *Unable to locate*
Motorcyclist (Los Angeles, CA) 2336
The Motorcyclist's Post (Huntington, CT) 4918
MotorHome (Ventura, CA) 4006
Motoring Road (Franklin, MA) 38012
Motoring Road Magazine (Franklin, MA) 14206
The Motorist 33252*
The Motorist (Williamsville, NY) 23584
Motorist (Bellevue, WA) 32667
Motorist; National (Foster City, CA) 1933
Motorist; Ohio (Independence, OH) 25252
Motorist; Rocky Mountain (Denver, CO) 4353
Motorland 3459*
Motorland 3458*
Motorsport Dealer & Trade (Toronto, ON, Can.) 36670
Motorsports Illustrated; Christian (Mansfield, PA) 27217

Motoryacht; Power and (New York, NY) **22588**
Motour **24802***
Motrix (Des Plaines, IL) *Unable to locate*
Mott Pioneer Press (New England, ND) *Ceased*
The Moulton Advertiser (Moulton, AL) **396**
Moulton Tribune (Moravia, IA) **11091**
Moultrie News (Mount Pleasant, SC) **28694**
Moultrie Observer (Moultrie, GA) **7446**
Moultrie Telecommunications, Inc. (Lovington, IL) **9123**
Mound City News (Mound City, MO) **17298**
Moundsville Daily Echo (Moundsville, WV) **33408**
Mt. Airy Courier Gazette (Gaithersburg, MD) *Unable to locate*
Mt. Airy Express **27575***
Mt. Airy Express (Germantown, MD) *Ceased*
Mount Airy News (Mount Airy, NC) **24079**
Mt. Airy Times Express (Philadelphia, PA) **27575***
Mount Allison Record (Sackville, NB, Can.) **35426**
Mt. Angel News; Appeal Tribune/ (Silverton, OR) **26584**
Mt. Aukum Review (Mount Aukum, CA) *Ceased*
Mt. Ayr Record-News (Mount Ayr, IA) **11093**
Mount Clemens-South Clinton Advisor **15370***
Mt. Clemens, South Clinton, Harrison Advisor **15370***
Mt. Dora Topic (Mount Dora, FL) *Unable to locate*
Mt. Dutton Cable Corp. (King Cove, AK) **615**
Mt. Enterprise Progress (Mount Enterprise, TX) *Ceased*
(Mount Forest Citizen); The Citizen (Durham, ON, Can.) **35797**
The Mount Forest Confederate (Mount Forest, ON, Can.) **36097**
Mount Greenwood Express (Midlothian, IL) **9190**
Mount Holly Mail (Burlington, NJ) **18710**
Mt. Holly News (Belmont, NC) *Unable to locate*
The Mount Hope Clarion (Mount Hope, KS) **11661**
Mt. Horeb Mail (Mount Horeb, WI) **34156**
Mt. Juliet; The Chronicle of (Mount Juliet, TN) **29425**
Mt. Morris Enterprise (Geneseo, NY) *Unable to locate*
Mt. Morris Times (Mount Morris, IL) **9241**
Mount Olive Chronicle (Chester, NJ) **18741**
The Mt. Olive Herald (Mount Olive, IL) **9246**
Mount Olive Review (Mount Olive, NC) **24085**
Mount Olive Tribune (Mount Olive, NC) **24086**
Mount Pleasant Daily Tribune (Mount Pleasant, TX) **30840**
The Mount Pleasant Journal (Mount Pleasant, PA) **27301**
Mt. Pleasant News (Mount Pleasant, IA) **11094**
Mt. Pleasant Record (Columbia, TN) *Unable to locate*
Mount Prospect Times (Mount Prospect, IL) **9247**
Mt. Pulaski Weekly News (Mount Pulaski, IL) **9251**
Mount Shasta Herald, Weed Press, Dunsmuir News (Mount Shasta, CA) **2605**
The Mount Sinai Journal of Medicine (New York, NY) **22373**
Mt. Sterling Advocate (Mount Sterling, KY) **12311**
Mt. Sterling Advocate-Advertiser (Mount Sterling, KY) **12312**
Mt. Union Times (Huntingdon, PA) *Ceased*
Mount Vernon Cablevision Inc. (Mount Vernon, OH) **25400**
Mount Vernon Daily Argus (Mount Vernon, NY) **21103**
Mt. Vernon Democrate (Mount Vernon, IN) **10323**
Mt. Vernon Gazette (Alexandria, VA) **31710**
Mount Vernon Hawkeye **11098***
The Mt. Vernon Independent (Mount Vernon, NY) **21104**
Mt. Vernon News (Mount Vernon, OH) **25399**
Mt. Vernon Signal (Mount Vernon, KY) **12314**
Mt. Washington Press (Cincinnati, OH) *Unable to locate*
The Mount Washington Star (Mount Washington, KY) *Ceased*
Mount Washington Star-Review (Los Angeles, CA) **2337**
The Mount Washington Valley Mountain Ear (Conway, NH) **18483**
The Mountain (Welches, OR) *Unable to locate*
Mountain Area Shopper (Oakland, MD) *Unable to locate*
Mountain Bike Action (Valencia, CA) **3981**
Mountain Bike Magazine (Emmaus, PA) **26878**
Mountain Biking (Canoga Park, CA) **1658**
Mountain Brook Cablevision, Inc. (Mountain Brook, AL) *Unable to locate*
Mountain Cable TV (Pikeville, KY) **12359**
The Mountain Citizen (Inez, KY) **12140**
Mountain Democrat (Placerville, CA) **2848**
The Mountain Eagle (Whitesburg, KY) **12438**
The Mountain Eagle (Kingston, NY) **20861**
Mountain Eagle; Jasper (Jasper, AL) **296**
Mountain Ear; The Mount Washington Valley (Conway, NH) **18483**
Mountain Echo (Flippin, AR) **1134**
Mountain Echo (Fall River Mills, CA) **1911**
Mountain Echo (Ironton, MO) *Ceased*

Mountain Echo/X-Tra (Ironton, MO) **17117**
The Mountain Enterprise (Frazier Park, CA) **1936**
Mountain Express; Idaho (Ketchum, ID) **7887**
The Mountain Gardener (Idaho Falls, ID) **7866**
Mountain Geologist (Denver, CO) **4340**
Mountain Home News (Mountain Home, ID) **7926**
Mountain Lake/Butterfield Observer/Advocate (Mountain Lake, MN) **16202**
Mountain Lake PBS - Channel 57 (Plattsburgh, NY) **23105**
Mountain Life and Work (Pineville, KY) *Ceased*
Mountain Living (Centennial, CO) **4225**
The Mountain Mail (Salida, CO) **4620**
The Mountain Mail (Welches, OR) *Unable to locate*
Mountain Media (Las Vegas, NV) *Unable to locate*
The Mountain Messenger (Downieville, CA) **1837**
Mountain Messenger Newspaper (Lewisburg, WV) **33366**
Mountain Movers (Springfield, MO) **17607**
The Mountain News **23980***
Mountain News (Lake Arrowhead, CA) **2138**
Mountain Pennysaver (Catskill, NY) **20439**
Mountain Pilot (Anchorage, AK) *Ceased*
The Mountain/Plains Business Journal (Omaha, NE) *Ceased*
Mountain Press (Sevierville, TN) **29589**
Mountain Research and Development (Berkeley, CA) *Ceased*
Mountain Shopper (Lake Arrowhead, CA) **2139**
The Mountain Spirit (Hagerhill, KY) **12102**
Mountain Sports & Living (New York, NY) **22374**
Mountain Statesman (Grafton, WV) **33325**
Mountain Sun; Kerrville (Kerrville, TX) **30640**
The Mountain Times (Boone, NC) **23654**
The Mountain Times (Killington, VT) **31547**
The Mountain View News (Sierra Vista, AZ) **888**
Mountain View Weekly Almanac (Cupertino, CA) *Ceased*
Mountain Wave (Marshall, AR) **1269**
Mountain Xpress (Asheville, NC) **23632**
Mountain Zone TV Systems (Alpine, TX) **29687**
The Mountaineer (Walnut, CA) **4047**
Mountaineer (Colorado Springs, CO) **4252**
The Mountaineer (Waynesville, NC) **24280**
The Mountaineer (Rocky Mountain House, AB, Can.) **34839**
Mountaineer; Big Sandy (Big Sandy, MT) **17726**
Mountaineer; Big White (Big White, BC, Can.) **34885**
Mountaineer; Boundary Creek Times (Greenwood, BC, Can.) **34973**
Mountaineer; Grande Cache (Grande Cache, AB, Can.) **34773**
The Mountaineer-Herald (Ebensburg, PA) **26857**
Mountaineer; The Ozarks (Kirbyville, MO) **17224**
Mountaineer Progress (Phelan, CA) **2837**
Mountaineer; The Virginia (Grundy, VA) **32121**
Mountaineer; Walhalla (Walhalla, ND) **24552**
Mountainfreak (Telluride, CO) **4644**
Mountains Cablevision-Sapphire Valley (Fairfield Glade, TN) *Ceased*
Mountains & Rivers (Cave Junction, OR) **26265**
Mountainside Echo **19595***
Mountaintop Eagle (Mountain Top, PA) **27304**
Mountaintop Journal (Mountain Top, PA) **27305**
Mountrail County Promoter, Inc. (Stanley, ND) **24537**
Mountrail County Record (Parshall, ND) **24530**
Mouse River Farmers Press **24541***
Mouse River Journal (Towner, ND) **24541**
Mouseion (St. John's, NL, Can.) **35490**
Mouth (Chicago, IL) **8496**
MOUTH (Topeka, KS) **11835**
Mouth 2 Mouth (New York, NY) *Unable to locate*
Movement Disorders (Hoboken, NJ) **19067**
Movers Journal **31667***
Movers News (Albany, NY) *Unable to locate*
Moves (Bakersfield, CA) *Unable to locate*
The Movie Channel (TMC) (New York, NY) **37769**
Movie Club Magazine (Baltimore, MD) *Ceased*
Movie Collector's World (Roseville, MI) **15475**
Movie Marketplace (Evanston, IL) *Ceased*
Movie Memories (Metairie, LA) *Unable to locate*
Movie Mirror (New York, NY) *Unable to locate*
Movie/Video Age International **22898***
Movieline (Los Angeles, CA) **2338**
MovieMaker Magazine (Seattle, WA) *Unable to locate*
Movies USA (Roswell, GA) *Unable to locate*
Movies' Videoscope; The Phantom of the (Ocean Grove, NJ) **19390**
Movietime; E! (Entertainment Television) **37746***
Movietone News *Ceased*
Moville Record (Moville, IA) **11101**
Movin' (Montreal, QC, Can.) **37194**
Movin' Out (Slippery Rock, PA) **27996**
Moving to Alberta (Unionville, ON, Can.) **36830**
Moving Food *Ceased*
Moving to Montreal (Unionville, ON, Can.) **36831**
Moving to Ottawa/Outaouais (Unionville, ON, Can.) **36832**

Moving to Saskatchewan (Unionville, ON, Can.) **36833**
Moving to Southwestern Ontario (Unionville, ON, Can.) **36834**
Moving to Toronto (Unionville, ON, Can.) **36835**
Moving Up (Centreville, VA) *Unable to locate*
Moving to Vancouver & British Columbia (Unionville, ON, Can.) **36836**
Moving to Winnipeg & Manitoba (Unionville, ON, Can.) **36837**
The Moving World (Alexandria, VA) **31711**
Moxie (Woodland Hills, CA) *Ceased*
MPC Chronicle (Park Ridge, IL) *Unable to locate*
MPH (Langley, BC, Can.) **35004**
MPLS.ST.PAUL (Minneapolis, MN) **16112**
MQ Update (Westminster, CO) **4664**
Mr. Mazoo (Saline, MI) **15518**
Mr. Te Ve (Los Angeles, CA) *Ceased*
MRI Banker's Guide to Foreign Currency (Houston, TX) **30509**
MRN Motor Racing Network Radio (Daytona Beach, FL) **37648**
MS; Inside (New York, NY) **21876**
Ms. Magazine (New York, NY) *Unable to locate*
MSBA in Brief *Ceased*
MSDN Magazine (Boulder, CO) **4180**
MSI (New York, NY) **22375**
MSI Europe (New York, NY) **22376**
MSJ **4180***
MSO's Cable Marketing (Denver, CO) *Ceased*
MSOS Journal (Winnipeg, MB, Can.) **35346**
MSP Airport News (St. Paul, MN) **16399**
MSU Alumni Magazine (East Lansing, MI) **14990**
MSW Management (Santa Barbara, CA) *Unable to locate*
MTL (English Edition) *Ceased*
MTL (French Edition) (Montreal, QC, Can.) *Ceased*
MTV (Music Television) (New York, NY) **37770**
MUAE *Unable to locate*
Mudflap (San Francisco, CA) *Unable to locate*
Muenster Enterprise (Muenster, TX) **30844**
Muffler Digest **17617***
Muir's Original Log Home Guide for Builders & Buyers (Newport, TN) *Ceased*
Mukilteo Tribune (Snohomish, WA) **33087**
Mukluk News (Tok, AK) **644**
Mukwanago Pubications **34157***
The Mukwanago Chief (Mukwanago, WI) **34158**
Mules and More (Bland, MO) **16906**
Muleshoe and Baily County Journal (Muleshoe, TX) **30846**
Muleskinner (Warrensburg, MO) **17668**
Mullan Television Co. (Mullan, ID) **7968**
The Mullens Advocate (Mullens, WV) **33410**
Mullich Communications (Norristown, PA) *Unable to locate*
Mullins Enterprise; Marion Star and (Marion, SC) **28689**
Mullinville Development Association (Mullinville, KS) **11662**
Multi-Channel TV Cable Co. **32611***
Multi-Channel TV Cable, Inc. **25334***
Multi-County Star (Covington, GA) **7211**
Multi-Criteria Decision Analysis; Journal of (Hoboken, NJ) **19034**
Multi-Housing News (New York, NY) **22377**
Multi-Images Magazine (Tampa, FL) *Unable to locate*
Multi Media Inc. (Newton, KS) **11674**
Multi Racial Love (New York, NY) *Ceased*
The Multi-Sport Facility News (North Miami, FL) *Ceased*
Multibody System Dynamics (New York, NY) **22378**
Multichannel News (New York, NY) *Unable to locate*
Multicultural Education (San Francisco, CA) **3392**
Multicultural Nursing and Health (JMCNH); Journal of (Chautauqua, NY) **20454**
Multicultural Perspectives (New Britain, CT) **4976**
MultiCultural Review (Westport, CT) **5214**
Multidimensional Systems and Signal Processing (New York, NY) **22379**
Multilingual Communications & Computing **7979***
Multilingual Communications & Technology **7979***
Multilingual Computing **7979***
MultiLingual Computing & Technology (Sandpoint, ID) **7979**
Multimedia Cablevision **10511***
Multimedia Cablevision Co. (Oklahoma City, OK) **26023**
Multimedia Cablevision, Inc. **11893***
Multimedia Cablevision, Inc. (Arkansas City, KS) **11343**
Multimedia Cablevision, Inc. (Arkansas City, KS) **11342**
Multimedia Cablevision, Inc. (Manhattan, KS) **11636**
Multimedia Cablevision, Inc. (Newton, KS) **11675**
Multimedia Cablevision of McPherson **11643***
Multimedia Cablevision of Medicine Lodge **11650***
Multimedia and Hypermedia; Journal of Educational (Norfolk, VA) **32285**

N

National Petroleum News (Des Plaines, IL) *Unable to locate*
National Police Review (Louisville, KY) **12232**
National Pork Report (Des Moines, IA) **10804**
National Post (Don Mills, ON, Can.) **35776**
National Press Syndicate (New York, NY) **38016**
National Press Writers Group (Bethesda, MD) *Unable to locate*
National Productivity Review **19038***
The National Provisioner (Chicago, IL) *Unable to locate*
The National Psychologist (Columbus, OH) **25034**
National Public Accountant (Alexandria, VA) **31713**
National Public Radio NPR (Washington, DC) **37650**
National Racquetball (Clearwater, FL) *Unable to locate*
National Radio Guide (Vancouver, BC, Can.) *Unable to locate*
National Real Estate Investor (Atlanta, GA) **7030**
The National Record (Hollywood, CA) **2052**
National Register of Commercial Real Estate (Stamford, CT) *Unable to locate*
National Relocation & Real Estate Magazine (South Norwalk, CT) *Unable to locate*
The National Reporter (Washington, DC) *Ceased*
National Review (New York, NY) **22400**
National Right to Life News (Washington, DC) **5680**
National Road Traveler (Cambridge City, IN) *Unable to locate*
The National Rural Letter Carrier (Alexandria, VA) **31714**
National SalesTax Manuals; Vertex (Berwyn, PA) **26698**
National Scanning (Wagontown, PA) *Unable to locate*
National Scene Magazine (New York, NY) *Unable to locate*
National Sculpture Review **22715***
National Security Law Report (Chicago, IL) **8500**
The National Sheriff **31737***
National Shuffler *Ceased*
National Small Business Journal (Atlanta, GA) *Ceased*
National Softball Magazine (Ontario, CA) *Unable to locate*
National Speed Sport News (Harrisburg, NC) **23978**
National Spokesman (Landover, MD) *Unable to locate*
The National Stock Dog (Butler, IN) **9877**
The National Storytelling Journal **29259***
National Tax Journal (Washington, DC) **5681**
National Thrift and Mortgage News **22399***
The National Times (New York, NY) *Unable to locate*
The National Tombstone Epitaph (Tombstone, AZ) **925**
National Trial Lawyer Magazine (Millville, NJ) *Unable to locate*
National Truck Trader **10904***
National Trust Forum (Washington, DC) **5682**
National Underwriter Life and Health-Financial Services Edition (Erlanger, KY) **12053**
National Underwriter Property and Casualty/Risk and Benefits Management (Erlanger, KY) **12054**
The National Utility Contractor (Arlington, VA) **31812**
National Vanguard (Hillsboro, WV) **33336**
National Vital Statistics Report (Hyattsville, MD) **13587**
The National Voter (Washington, DC) **5683**
National Weather Digest (Washington, DC) *Unable to locate*
National Wildlife (Reston, VA) **32407**
Nationalism; Nations and (New York, NY) **22401**
Nationality Broadcasting Network (Lakewood, OH) **37771**
Nation's Building News (Washington, DC) **5684**
Nation's Business (Washington, DC) **5685**
Nation's Center News (Buffalo, SD) **28826**
Nation's Cities Weekly (Washington, DC) **5686**
The Nation's Health (Washington, DC) **5687**
Nations and Nationalism (New York, NY) **22401**
Nation's Restaurant News (New York, NY) **22402**
Nationwide **3301***
Nationwide Communications **25079***
Nationwide Communications Inc. (Columbus, OH) *Unable to locate*
Native Americas (Ithaca, NY) **20810**
Native California; News from (Berkeley, CA) **1546**
The Native Hawaiian Report (Honolulu, HI) *Ceased*
Native Journal; Oshkaabewis (Bemidji, MN) **15738**
Native Monthly Reader (Pauma Valley, CA) *Ceased*
The Native Nevadan (Sparks, NV) *Ceased*
Native Peoples Magazine (Phoenix, AZ) *Unable to locate*
Native Press **35526***
Natoma-Luray Independent (Natoma, KS) **11665**
Na.to.n Review (Lubbock, TX) *Unable to locate*
NATPE Programmer (Medford, NJ) *Ceased*
NATSO Truckers News (Tuscaloosa, AL) **489**
Natural Areas Journal (Bend, OR) **26243**
Natural Business (Broomfield, CO) **4205**
Natural Foods Merchandiser (Boulder, CO) **4181**

Natural Gas (Hoboken, NJ) **19069**
Natural Gas Monthly (Washington, DC) **5688**
Natural Gas Week (New York, NY) **22403**
Natural Hazards (New York, NY) **22404**
Natural Hazards Review (Reston, VA) **32408**
Natural Health (Boston, MA) *Unable to locate*
Natural Health World and the Naturopath (Vancouver, WA) *Unable to locate*
Natural History Magazine (New York, NY) **22405**
Natural Immunity (Farmington, CT) *Ceased*
Natural Language Engineering (Yorktown Heights, NY) **23608**
Natural Language & Linguistic Theory (New York, NY) **22406**
Natural Language Semantics (New York, NY) **22407**
Natural Life (Niagara Falls, NY) **23004**
Natural Pharmacy (Larchmont, NY) **20922**
Natural Products; Journal of (Washington, DC) **5604**
Natural Resources Journal (Albuquerque, NM) **19776**
Natural Resources Research (New York, NY) **22408**
Natural Resources; Society & (Logan, UT) **31351**
Natural Resources; Wisconsin (Madison, WI) **33988**
Natural Toxins (Hoboken, NJ) *Ceased*
Natural Way Magazine (White Plains, NY) *Unable to locate*
Naturalist; American Midland (Notre Dame, IN) **10366**
Naturalist; Canadian Field- (Ottawa, ON, Can.) **36194**
Naturalist; Florida Field (Tallahassee, FL) **6711**
Naturalist; Maryland (Baltimore, MD) **13213**
Naturalist; The Northeastern (Steuben, ME) **13060**
Naturalist; The Southeastern (Steuben, ME) **13061**
Naturalist; Underwater (Highlands, NJ) **18874**
naturalSCIENCE (Victoria, BC, Can.) **35223**
Nature (New York, NY) **22409**
Nature Biotechnology (New York, NY) **22410**
Nature Canada (Ottawa, ON, Can.) **36263**
Nature Conservancy (Arlington, VA) **31813**
The Nature Conservancy Magazine **31813***
The Nature Conservancy News **31813***
Nature; Democracy and (Littleton, CO) **4546**
Nature Genetics (New York, NY) **22411**
Nature International Weekly Journal of Science (Washington, DC) **5689**
Nature Photographer (Quincy, MA) *Unable to locate*
Nature, Society and Thought); NST ((Minneapolis, MN) **16118**
Nature Study (Dingmans Ferry, PA) **26828**
Naturist Life International (Troy, VT) **31606**
NATVOA Bulletin (Bensalem, PA) *Unable to locate*
Naugatuck Daily News **4972***
Naugatuck News (Naugatuck, CT) **4972**
Nautical Brass (Fort Myers, FL) *Unable to locate*
Nautical Quarterly (Essex, CT) *Ceased*
Nautical Research Journal (Newburyport, MA) **14380**
Nautical World (Harrisburg, PA) *Unable to locate*
The Nautilus (Sanibel, FL) *Unable to locate*
Nautilus Magazine (Independence, VA) *Ceased*
Nauvoo Grapevine **9279***
The Nauvoo Journal **31340***
Navajo-Hopi Observer (Flagstaff, AZ) **698**
The Navajo Times (Window Rock, AZ) **1011**
Navajo Times Today **1011***
Naval Affairs (Alexandria, VA) **31715**
Naval Aviation News (Pittsburgh, PA) **27819**
Naval Engineers Journal (Alexandria, VA) *Unable to locate*
Naval History (Annapolis, MD) **13095**
Naval Research Logistics (Hoboken, NJ) **19070**
Naval Reservist News (New Orleans, LA) **12742**
Naval Stores Review (New Orleans, LA) *Unable to locate*
Naval War College Review (Newport, RI) **28367**
Navalog; The Newport (Newport, RI) **28371**
Navarro County Sun Extra (Corsicana, TX) **30102**
Navarro County Sun Extra/Bi-Stone Star Extra **30102***
Navasota Examiner (Navasota, TX) **30856**
Navigation; Journal of (New York, NY) **22139**
Navigator; Ocean (Portland, ME) **13015**
Navioneer (Grand Junction, CO) **4479**
Navy **31830***
The Navy Channel **2317***
Navy Civil Engineer (Washington, DC) **5690**
Navy Dispatch; San Diego (San Diego, CA) **3266**
Navy Medicine (Pittsburgh, PA) **27820**
Navy News (Virginia Beach, VA) *Unable to locate*
Navy News; Hawaii (Kaneohe, HI) **7772**
Navy Seals (Canoga Park, CA) *Unable to locate*
Navy Times (Springfield, VA) **32549**
NAWGA Review **32045***
NBA Hoop (New York, NY) **22412**
NBA Inside Stuff (New York, NY) **22413**
NBA Magazine (Washington, DC) **5691**
NBC (National Broadcasting Company) (New York, NY) **37705**
NBC Radio Network (Arlington, VA) *Unable to locate*
NBER Reporter (Cambridge, MA) **14083**
NCGR Journal (Needham, MA) **14364**
NCJW Journal (Westport, CT) **5215**

N.C.K. Market Guide **11361***
NCLR (Greenville, NC) **23966**
(NCM); New California Media (San Francisco, CA) **3394**
The NCOA Journal (San Antonio, TX) *Unable to locate*
NCP: Nutrition in Clinical Practice (Silver Spring, MD) **13742**
NCSL Conference Report (Denver, CO) *Ceased*
NDA News **29806***
NDEJ: A Journal of Religion in Literature **10376***
N'DIGO (Chicago, IL) **8501**
NE AR Tribune (Paragould, AR) **1307**
NE Gwinnett Cablevision (Suwanee, GA) *Unable to locate*
N.E. Region Community Booster; Nipawin (Nipawin, SK, Can.) **37507**
NEA Action; CTA/ **1631***
NEA Today (Annapolis Junction, MD) **13104**
NEAA News **31548***
Near North Broadcasting **34022***
Near North Broadcasting **34021***
Near North News (Chicago, IL) **8502**
Near South Herald (Chicago, IL) *Ceased*
The Near West Gazette (Chicago, IL) *Unable to locate*
Nebo (Russellville, AR) **1332**
Nebraska (Lincoln, NE) **18097**
Nebraska Academy of Sciences; Transactions of the (Lincoln, NE) **18123**
Nebraska Agriculture **18100***
Nebraska Alumnus **18097***
Nebraska Beverage Analyst (Lincoln, NE) **18098**
The Nebraska Bird Review (Lincoln, NE) *Unable to locate*
Nebraska Cattleman (Lincoln, NE) **18099**
Nebraska City News-Press (Nebraska City, NE) **18166**
Nebraska Farm Bureau News (Lincoln, NE) **18100**
Nebraska Farm Edition; Fastline— (Buckner, KY) **11984**
Nebraska Farmer (Carol Stream, IL) **8150**
Nebraska History (Lincoln, NE) **18101**
Nebraska & Iowa Explorer (Blair, NE) **17957**
Nebraska-Iowa Retailer **18127***
Nebraska Journal of Economics & Business **18116***
Nebraska Journal-Leader (Ponca, NE) **18252**
The Nebraska Lawyer (Lincoln, NE) **18102**
Nebraska Medical Journal (Lincoln, NE) *Ceased*
Nebraska Mortar and Pestle (Lincoln, NE) *Unable to locate*
Nebraska Municipal Review (Lincoln, NE) **18103**
Nebraska Music Educator (Lincoln, NE) **18104**
Nebraska Newspaper (Lincoln, NE) *Unable to locate*
The Nebraska Observer (Omaha, NE) *Ceased*
Nebraska Oil Jobber **18095***
Nebraska Petroleum Marketer **18095***
Nebraska Pharmacist (Lincoln, NE) *Ceased*
Nebraska Register; Southern (Lincoln, NE) **18121**
The Nebraska Retailer **18127***
The Nebraska Review (Omaha, NE) **18204**
The Nebraska Signal (Geneva, NE) **18016**
Nebraska Smoke-Eater (Pierce, NE) **18247**
Nebraska Trucker (Lincoln, NE) **18105**
Nebraska Union Farmer (Lincoln, NE) **18106**
NEBRASKAland (Lincoln, NE) **18107**
Nebraskan; Daily (Lincoln, NE) **18083**
Neck; Head & (Hoboken, NJ) **18956**
NECN/New England Cable News (Newton, MA) **37772**
Nedelni Hlasatel (Woodridge, IL) *Unable to locate*
Nedge (Providence, RI) *Unable to locate*
Needham TAB (Needham, MA) **14365**
Needham Times (Needham, MA) **14366**
Needle Arts Magazine; EGA (Dillwyn, VA) **31996**
Needle & Craft (New York, NY) *Unable to locate*
Needlepoint Plus (Concord, CA) *Ceased*
Needles Desert Star (Needles, CA) *Unable to locate*
The Needle's Eye (Huntley, IL) *Ceased*
Needlework Retailer (Ames, IA) **10592**
Neenah/Menasha Buyers' Guide (Appleton, WI) **33539**
Negative Capability (Mobile, AL) **327**
Negotiation Journal (New York, NY) **22414**
Negotiations in the Public Sector; Journal of Collective (Amityville, NY) **20042**
Negro American Literature Forum **17406***
Negro Education; The Journal of (Washington, DC) **5605**
The Negro Educational Review (Jacksonville, FL) *Unable to locate*
Negro History Bulletin (Silver Spring, MD) *Unable to locate*
Negro History; Journal of (Silver Spring, MD) **13732**
The Neighbor **28969***
The Neighbor (Attica, IN) **9788**
Neighbor News (Rockaway, NJ) **19522**
Neighbor Shopper (Bentonville, AR) **1051**
Neighborhood Journal (St. Louis, MO) **17476**
Neighborhood News (Santa Ana, CA) *Ceased*

New York Times News Service (New York, NY) 38020

New York Times Syndication Sales Corporation (New York, NY) 38021

The New York Times Upfront (Danbury, CT) 4746

New York Town Law (Longwood, FL) 6313

New York Trend (Great Neck, NY) 20693

New York University Alumni News Magazine (New York, NY) Ceased

New York University Law Review (New York, NY) 22456

New York Update (Columbia, MO) Unable to locate

New York Vietnam Business News 21482*

The New York Voice/Harlem U.S.A. (Jamaica, NY) 20839

New York; WHERE (New York, NY) 22917

New York Woman (New York, NY) Ceased

New York Writer (New York, NY) Ceased

The New Yorker (New York, NY) 22457

New Yorker Staats Zeitung (Sarasota, FL) 6661

New Yorker Staats Zeitung & Herold 6661*

New Yorkin Uutiset (Brooklyn, NY) Unable to locate

New York's Food & Life Sciences Quarterly 20793*

New Youth Connections; NYC/ (New York, NY) 22478

Newark Churchman 19367*

The Newark-Licking Advertiser (Newark, OH) 25425

Newark Pennysaver (Newark, NY) 22996

The Newberg Graphic (Newberg, OR) 26444

Newberry News (Newberry, MI) 15400

Newborn; Today's Parent (Toronto, ON, Can.) 36763

Newburg Cable TV System (Newburg, MO) 17316

Newburgh Chandler Register (Newburgh, IN) 10349

Newburgh Register 10349*

Newbury Street and Back Bay Guide (Boston, MA) 13938

Newburyport Daily News (Newburyport, MA) 14381

Newcastle Independent 35692*

The Newcastle Pacer (Newcastle, OK) 25929

The Newcomerstown News (Newcomerstown, OH) 25431

NeWest Review (Saskatoon, SK, Can.) Unable to locate

The Newfoundland Herald (St. John's, NL, Can.) 35491

Newfoundland Studies (St. John's, NL, Can.) 35492

The NewHome Book (Raleigh, NC) Unable to locate

Newhouse News Service (Washington, DC) 38022

The Newington Town Crier (Newington, CT) 5036

Newkirk Herald-Journal (Newkirk, OK) 25930

Newman Independent (Newman, IL) 9283

NewMedia (Brandon, FL) 5961

The Newnan Times-Herald (Newnan, GA) 7453

NewPaper 28416*

Newport Beach; Comcast Cablevision of (Newport Beach, CA) 2638

Newport Beach/Costa Mesa Daily Pilot (Newport Beach, CA) 2631

Newport Beach 714 (Newport Beach, CA) 2632

Newport Cable TV Co. (Newport, VT) Unable to locate

Newport Cable TV Inc. (Waterford, CT) 5200

The Newport Daily Express (Newport, VT) 31572

Newport Daily Independent (Newport, AR) 1298

The Newport Daily News (Newport, RI) 28368

Newport Ensign (Newport Beach, CA) Ceased

Newport History (Newport, RI) 28369

Newport Mercury (Newport, RI) 28370

The Newport Miner & Gem State Miner (Newport, WA) 32851

The Newport Navalog (Newport, RI) 28371

Newport News Cablevision (Newport News, VA) 32281

Newport Plain Talk (Newport, TN) 29544

Newport This Week (Newport, RI) 28372

Newport Traveler (Newport, RI) Unable to locate

News 34893*

News 26901*

News 16475*

News 9514*

The News 14547*

The News 14643*

The News (Salem, AR) 1335

News (Benton, IL) 8072

News (Fairbury, IL) Ceased

The News (Clay City, IN) 9890

News (LaGrange, IN) Unable to locate

News (Paoli, IN) 10387

News (Spirit Lake, IA) 11238

News (Kiowa, KS) 11541

News (Denham Springs, LA) 12562

News (Grand Blanc, MI) Ceased

News (Faribault, MN) 15894

News (Merrimack, NH) Ceased

News (Belvidere, NJ) 18671

The News (Cherry Hill, NJ) Ceased

News (Batavia, NY) 20121

News (Newburgh, NY) Unable to locate

News (Sunbury, OH) 25552

News (Del City, OK) Unable to locate

News (Yale, OK) 26203

The News (Aliquippa, PA) Ceased

The News (Kingstree, SC) 28675

The News (Kingstree, SC) 28674

News (Nocona, TX) 30868

News (Williamson, WV) 33512

The News (New Richmond, WI) 34193

The News Advance (Lynchburg, VA) 32206

News-Advertiser 34873*

News Advertiser 36309*

News Advertiser (Lake City, FL) 6270

News & Advertiser (Winchester, IN) 10565

News-Advertiser (Harlan, IA) 10942

News & Advertiser (Boonville, MO) 16914

News Advertiser East 31323*

News Advertiser West 31323*

News Advertiser West (Salt Lake City, UT) Unable to locate

News-Advocate (Fordyce, AR) 1135

News-Argus 36403*

The News & Banner (Franklin, GA) 7292

The News Banner (Covington, LA) 12554

The News Beacon (Fair Lawn, NJ) 18808

The News Beacon (Nashville, IN) 29475

News and Bryan County Democrat (Durant, OK) Ceased

The News Bulletin (Peoria, IL) 9421

News Canada (Toronto, ON, Can.) Unable to locate

NEWS-CAPITAL & Democrat; The McAlester (McAlester, OK) 25909

News Chronicle 23085*

News Chronicle (Scott City, KS) 11794

The News-Chronicle (Shippensburg, PA) 27989

The News Chronicle (Belton, SC) 28492

News-Chronicle Sunday 33738*

News-Chronicle Weekend Edition 33738*

News Chronicles 4003*

News Circle (Glendale, CA) 2011

News Citizen 28095*

News and Citizen (Morrisville, VT) 31569

The News-Commercial (Collins, MS) 16598

The News & Daily Advance (Lynchburg, VA) 32207

News of Delaware County (Havertown, PA) 27030

News Democrat 17689*

The News-Democrat (Carrollton, KY) 12011

The News Democrat (Georgetown, OH) 25216

News-Democrat (Waverly, TN) 29642

News Democrat Journal (Warrenton, MO) 17689

News-Democrat & Leader (Russellville, KY) 12389

News Derrick and Journal (Cushing, OK) Unable to locate

News-Digest Tangi Talk 12470*

The News-Dispatch (Michigan City, IN) 10304

News and Eagle (Enid, OK) 25822

The News Eagle (Hawley, PA) 27032

News Editor 11140*

The News in Engineering (Columbus, OH) 25035

News-Enterprise 12044*

News-Enterprise (Los Alamitos, CA) 2191

The News Enterprise (Ludlow, KY) Ceased

News Era (Kershaw, SC) 28671

The News-Examiner (Montpelier, ID) 7909

News Examiner (Lutcher, LA) 12665

The News-Examiner (Gallatin, TN) 29203

News Extra (Crestview, FL) 6024

News and Farmer (Preston, MD) Unable to locate

News & Food Report (Manchester, NH) 18560

News & Former & Wadley Herald/The Jefferson Reporter (Louisville, GA) 7376

NEWS/400 (Calabasas, CA) Unable to locate

NEWS/400 (Loveland, CO) 4569

News From Brazil 2227*

The News-Gazette (Champaign, IL) 8205

News Gazette (Machesney Park, IL) 9126

The News Gazette (Winchester, IN) 10566

News Gazette (Bayard, IA) 10617

The News-Gazette (Lexington, VA) 32190

News Gleaner (Bustleton-Somerton Edition) (Philadelphia, PA) 27581

News Gleaner (Far Northeast Edition) (Philadelphia, PA) 27582

News Gleaner (Frankford Juniata Edition) (Philadelphia, PA) 27583

News Gleaner (Lawndale Edition) 27586*

News Gleaner (Mayfair-Northeast Edition) (Philadelphia, PA) 27584

News Gleaner (Northeast Breeze Edition) 27586*

News Gleaner (Six Editions) (Philadelphia, PA) 27585

News Graphic (Cedarburg, WI) 33619

News Graphic Pilot 33619*

The News Guard (Lincoln City, OR) 26411

News-Guide (Eagle Pass, TX) 30257

The News & Herald 28787*

The News-Herald 24624*

The News-Herald 23614*

News Herald (Panama City, FL) 6556

The News-Herald (Owenton, KY) 12334

The News-Herald (Southgate, MI) 15566

News-Herald (Ravena, NY) 23177

The News Herald (Morganton, NC) 24073

News Herald (Port Clinton, OH) 25482

The News-Herald (Willoughby, OH) 25662

News-Herald (Franklin, PA) Unable to locate

News-Herald (Souderton, PA) 28004

News-Herald (Lenoir City, TN) 29323

The News Herald (Nashville, TN) 29476

News-Herald and Journal (Los Angeles, CA) 2347

The News-Herald (Lincoln Park/Southgate/Ecorse/River Rouge Edition) (Southgate, MI) Ceased

The News-Herald (Riverview/Flat Rock/Gibraltar/Huron Township Edition) (Southgate, MI) Ceased

The News-Herald (Taylor/Melvindale/Allen Park/Romulus) (Southgate, MI) Ceased

The News-Herald (Woodhaven/Brownstown Edition) (Southgate, MI) Ceased

The News-Herald (Wyandotte/Trenton Edition) (Southgate, MI) Ceased

News of the Highlands (Highland Falls, NY) 20747

News-Independent 17298*

News/Independent (Cissna Park, IL) 8679

News India Times (New York, NY) 22458

News from Indian Country (Hayward, WI) 33785

News IS (Westminster, CO) 4666

News-Item (Shamokin, PA) 27984

News Journal 29430*

The News Journal (New Castle, DE) 5267

The News-Journal (Daytona Beach, FL) 6037

The News Journal (Rupert, ID) Unable to locate

The News Journal (North Manchester, IN) 10360

News Journal (Columbia, LA) 12549

News Journal (Mountain Grove, MO) 17300

News-Journal (Raeford, NC) 24121

News Journal (Mansfield, OH) 25332

The News Journal (Florence, SC) 28603

News for Kids (Corona Del Mar, CA) Unable to locate

The News-Leader 23977*

News-Leader (Fernandina Beach, FL) 6069

The News Leader (Royston, GA) 7521

News-Leader (Rochelle, IL) 9514

News-Leader (Netcong, NJ) 19323

The News Leader (Grifton, NC) Ceased

The News Leader (Malvern, OH) 25328

The News Leader (Minerva, OH) 25392

The News Leader (Landrum, SC) 28681

The News Leader (Maynardville, TN) 29351

The News-Leader (Staunton, VA) 32556

News-Ledger (West Sacramento, CA) 4065

News Letter Journal (Newcastle, WY) 34564

News & Letters (Chicago, IL) 8508

News Marketer (Lansing, IL) Unable to locate

News and McHenry County Guide (Crystal Lake, IL) Unable to locate

The News Media & the Law (Arlington, VA) 31814

News Messenger 32854*

News-Messenger 30651*

News Messenger 18525*

The News-Messenger (Fremont, OH) 25202

News and Messenger (Menard, TX) 30804

The News-Messenger (Christiansburg, VA) 31972

News Mirror (Buffalo Lake, MN) Ceased

News Mirror (Hector, MN) 15946

News-Mirror (Mansfield, TX) 30757

News from Native California (Berkeley, CA) 1546

The News of New York (Lake Success, NY) 20881

News/North (Yellowknife, NT, Can.) 35525

News & Observer 6458*

The News Observer (Blue Ridge, GA) 7133

The News Observer (Vienna, GA) 7633

The News and Observer (Raleigh, NC) 24141

News-Optimist (North Battleford, SK, Can.) 37508

News-Optimist; Sunday Edition (North Battleford, SK, Can.) 37511

News of Orange County (Chatham, VA) Unable to locate

The News Paper 888*

News Photographer (Durham, NC) 23836

News in Physiological Sciences (NIPS) (Bethesda, MD) 13364

News Plus 14332*

News Pointer (San Rafael, CA) 3602

News Press (Woodland Park, CO) Ceased

The News Press (Stillwater, OK) 26079

News and Press (Darlington, SC) 28596

News-Press (Mc Lean, VA) Unable to locate

News Progress (Sullivan, IL) 9673

News Progress (Hominy, OK) 25870

The News-Progress (Chase City, VA) 31959

The News Progress (Clarksville, VA) 31975

News Record 1268*

The News-Record (Cerro Gordo, IL) 8176

News-Record (Mabel, MN) 16017

The News Record (Wanamingo, MN) 16495

News-Record (Zumbrota, MN) 16542

The News Record (Oak Grove, MO) Ceased

News-Record (Union, NJ) 19685

News & Record (Greensboro, NC) 23930

The News Record (Marshall, NC) **24059**
News-Record (Ravia, OK) *Unable to locate*
The News Record (Gillette, WY) **34527**
News-Record of Maplewood and South Orange (Union, NJ) **19686**
News-Register (McMinnville, OR) **26416**
News-Register (McMinnville, OR) **26415**
News-Register (Wheeling, WV) **33503**
News Report (Blackwood, NJ) **18681**
News Reporter (Tampa, FL) *Ceased*
News-Reporter (Washington, GA) **7640**
The News Reporter (Whiteville, NC) **24285**
News and Reporter (Bensalem, PA) *Unable to locate*
News Republic Cent Saver (Baraboo, WI) **33563**
News & Review **3017***
News-Review (Ridgecrest, CA) **2923**
The News-Review (Mattituck, NY) **21031**
News-Review (Continental, OH) **25094**
The News-Review (Roseburg, OR) **26555**
The News-Review & Lakes Observer (Sumner, WA) *Ceased*
The News-Sentinel (San Jose, CA) **3528**
The News and Sentinel (Colebrook, NH) **18468**
News-Sentinel (Stigler, OK) **26075**
The News & Shopper **28603***
News Shopper (Woodstock, GA) **7656**
News & Shopper (Myrtle Beach, SC) *Unable to locate*
The News of Southern Berks (Boyertown, PA) *Unable to locate*
News-Standard (Coulee City, WA) **32731**
News-Star **6096***
The News-Star (Monroe, LA) **12692**
News-Star (Nixon, TX) *Ceased*
The News Star (Stockdale, TX) *Unable to locate*
The News-Star (Lambeth, ON, Can.) *Unable to locate*
News-Star-World **12692***
The News Sun (La Jolla, CA) *Unable to locate*
The News-Sun (Sebring, FL) **6679**
News-Sun (Fairmount, IN) **9954**
News-Sun (Kendallville, IN) **10228**
The News Sun (Berea, OH) **24678**
The News-Sun (Newport, PA) *Unable to locate*
News-Telegram (Sulphur Springs, TX) **31166**
News-Times (Danbury, CT) **4747**
News-Times (Chadbourn, NC) **23695**
News-Times (Forest Grove, OR) **26355**
News-Times (Newport, OR) **26445**
The News Transcript (Freehold, NJ) **18839**
News Tribune **18781***
News-Tribune **35686***
News Tribune (Costa Mesa, CA) *Unable to locate*
News-Tribune (La Salle, IL) **9056**
News-Tribune (Waltham, MA) **14602**
The News Tribune (East Brunswick, NJ) *Ceased*
The News Tribune (Hicksville, OH) **25241**
News-Tribune (Oberlin, OH) **25446**
The News Tribune (Tacoma, WA) **33147**
News & Views **35127***
The News-Virginian (Waynesboro, VA) **32610**
News-Wave (Whitehall, WI) **34452**
News Weekly **15533***
News for You (Syracuse, NY) **23414**
Newsbytes News Network (Stillwater, MN) **38023**
Newschief (Winter Haven, FL) **6869**
Newsday (Melville, NY) **21051**
NewsEAST (Columbus, OH) *Ceased*
NewsInc. (New York, NY) *Unable to locate*
Newslink (San Jose, CA) **3529**
Newsounds, Our Kids Magazine **5841***
The Newspaper of Cardiology **21375***
Newspaper Datatrak *Ceased*
Newspaper Enterprise Association (New York, NY) **38024**
Newspaper Features Council Inc. (Greenwich, CT) *Unable to locate*
Newspaper Features Inc. (Locust Valley, NY) **38025**
Newspaper Research Journal (Memphis, TN) **29377**
Newspapers & Technology (Denver, CO) **4343**
Newspeak **14689***
NewsPort (San Francisco, CA) **3403**
Newsportraits Syndicate (Hackensack, NJ) **38026**
Newsreal (Gilbert, AZ) *Ceased*
Newsreel (Columbus, OH) **25036**
NEWSREPORT (Washington, DC) *Unable to locate*
NewsUSA (Falls Church, VA) **38027**
NewsWatch (Washington, DC) *Ceased*
Newsweek (New York, NY) **22459**
Newsweek International (New York, NY) **22460**
Newsweek International - Latin America Edition (New York, NY) **22461**
Newsweekly (Somerville, MA) **14537**
Newsweekly (Riverton, NJ) **19521**
NewsWest (Natick, MA) *Unable to locate*
Newton Cable Communications Ltd. (Downsview, ON, Can.) *Unable to locate*
Newton Cable TV **11675***
Newton Cable TV **11674***
Newton County Enterprise (Kentland, IN) **10231**

Newton County News (Granby, MO) **17085**
Newton County News (Newton, TX) **30867**
Newton County Times (Jasper, AR) **1196**
The Newton Daily News (Newton, IA) **11115**
Newton Falls Herald (Newton Falls, OH) *Unable to locate*
Newton Graphic (Newton, MA) **14407**
Newton Kansan (Newton, KS) **11669**
Newton Press-Mentor (Newton, IL) **9284**
The Newton Record (Newton, MS) **16800**
Newton TAB (Needham, MA) **14367**
The Newtown Bee (Newtown, CT) **5045**
Nex-Tech, Inc. (Lenora, KS) **11599**
Next Generation (Brisbane, CA) **1608**
Next Level Delaware Magazine (Wilmington, DE) *Unable to locate*
The Next Step Magazine (Victor, NY) **23494**
NeXTWORLD (Chatsworth, CA) *Ceased*
Nexus (Hamilton, ON, Can.) **35887**
NEXUS Magazine (Denver, CO) **4344**
Nexxus (Farmington, ME) *Unable to locate*
The NFIB Foundation Quarterly Economic Report for Small Business **5695***
The NFIB Foundation Small Business Economic Trends (Washington, DC) **5695**
NFPA Journal (Quincy, MA) **14490**
NFPW Agenda (Arlington, VA) *Unable to locate*
NGA News (Raleigh, NC) **24142**
Ngay Nay (Houston, TX) *Unable to locate*
Nguoi Viet Daily News (Westminster, CA) *Unable to locate*
NHSA Journal **31654***
Niagara; Adelphia Cable Communications of (Niagara Falls, NY) **23008**
The Niagara Advance (Virgil, ON, Can.) **36841**
Niagara Community TV Co-op (Niagara, WI) **34197**
Niagara Falls Gazette **23006***
Niagara Farmers' Monthly (Smithville, ON, Can.) **36397**
Niagara Gazette (Niagara Falls, NY) **23006**
The Niagara Index (Niagara University, NY) **23009**
The Niagara Journal (Niagara, WI) **34196**
Niagara-North Towns **20680***
Niagara Pennysaver **20680***
Niagara Shopping News (Niagara Falls, ON, Can.) **36109**
Niagara-Wheatfield Tribune (Grand Island, NY) **20680**
Nibble Magazine (Lincoln, MA) *Ceased*
NIC Sentinel (Coeur d'Alene, ID) **7845**
Nicable TV (Dalhousie, NB, Can.) *Unable to locate*
Niceville Bayou Times (Crestview, FL) *Unable to locate*
NICHCY News Digest (Washington, DC) **5696**
Nichi Bei Times (San Francisco, CA) **3404**
The Nicholas Chronicle (Summersville, WV) **33473**
Nicholas County News Leader (Richwood, WV) **33447**
The Nicholls Worth (Thibodaux, LA) **12860**
Nickel (Toronto, ON, Can.) **36674**
Nickel Belt News; Thompson (Thompson, MB, Can.) **35301**
The Nickel-Chehalis (Chehalis, WA) *Unable to locate*
The Nickel-Kelso (Kelso, WA) **32786**
Nickel Saver (Moses Lake, WA) **32839**
Nickel; Thrifty (Falls Church, VA) **32058**
Nickel Trader (Aberdeen, WA) *Unable to locate*
The Nickel Want Ads (Grand Junction, CO) **4480**
Nickelodeon (New York, NY) *Unable to locate*
Nickelodeon/Nick at Nite (New York, NY) **37774**
Nickel's Worth (Coeur d'Alene, ID) **7846**
Nicklas Petervary **21836***
Nicollet Cable TV (Redwood Falls, MN) **16301**
Nicollet Ledger; Lafayette- (Lafayette, MN) **15989**
Nieman Reports (Cambridge, MA) **14086**
Niepodleglosc/Independence (New York, NY) **22462**
Nifty Nickel (Las Vegas, NV) **18382**
Nigerian Financial Review (Mount Vernon, NY) *Unable to locate*
Night Call (River Edge, NJ) *Unable to locate*
Night Call (Brooklyn, NY) **20334**
Night & Day (Seattle, WA) *Ceased*
Night Rock News **10063***
Night Roses (Prospect Heights, IL) **9471**
Nightclub & Bar Magazine (Oxford, MS) **16806**
Nightlife (River Edge, NJ) **19519**
Nightlife Magazine (Central Islip, NY) *Unable to locate*
Nightlines Weekly (Chicago, IL) **8509**
Nightmoves (Chicago, IL) *Unable to locate*
Nihon Keizai Shimbun (New York, NY) *Unable to locate*
NIJC Review **7845***
The Nikkei Weekly (New York, NY) **22463**
Nikkel Saaver **32839***
Nikon World of Big Game Hunting (Shrewsbury, NJ) *Ceased*
The Niles Bugle (Niles, IL) **9291**
Niles Daily Star (Niles, MI) **15404**
Niles Daily Times **25616***
Niles Herald-Spectator (Niles, IL) **9292**

The Niles Life (Lincolnwood, IL) **9099**
Niles Life; Morton Grove- (Lincolnwood, IL) **9098**
The Niles Times **25616***
Nine **17465***
Nine (Lincoln, NE) **18108**
940 **27176***
9-1-1 Magazine (Tustin, CA) **3963**
Nineteenth Century French Studies (Lincoln, NE) **18109**
Nineteenth-Century Literature (Berkeley, CA) **1547**
19th-Century Music (Berkeley, CA) **1548**
Nineteenth-Century Studies (Lancaster, PA) *Unable to locate*
The 99 News **11883***
99 North Magazine (Squamish, BC, Can.) **35094**
96 Lite until 8/01 **15846***
Ninnau (Basking Ridge, NJ) **18665**
Ninnescah Valley News (Pretty Prairie, KS) **11767**
Nipawin Journal (Nipawin, SK, Can.) **37506**
Nipawin N.E. Region Community Booster (Nipawin, SK, Can.) **37507**
Nipigon-Red Rock Gazette (Nipigon, ON, Can.) **36115**
(NIPS); News in Physiological Sciences (Bethesda, MD) **13364**
Nishna Valley Tribune (Audubon, IA) *Unable to locate*
Nisqually Valley News (Yelm, WA) **33239**
Nisqually Valley Shopper (Yelm, WA) **33240**
Nisswa Review (Pequot Lakes, MN) *Unable to locate*
NITA Journal **27532***
Nit&Wit (Geneva, IL) *Unable to locate*
Nite Owl Publications (Philadelphia, PA) *Unable to locate*
Nite-Writer's International Literary Arts Journal (Pittsburgh, PA) **27822**
Nite-Writer's Literary Arts Journal **27822***
Nitric Oxide (San Diego, CA) **3242**
Nixa Enterprise (Nixa, MO) *Unable to locate*
NJ Autoist **18823***
NJEA Review (Trenton, NJ) **19665**
NJW Magazine (New Jersey Woman) (Fort Lee, NJ) **18832**
NK Lawn & Garden (St. Paul, MN) *Unable to locate*
NLGI Spokesman (Kansas City, MO) **17189**
N.M.E.A. News (Tinton Falls, NJ) *Unable to locate*
NMR in Biomedicine (Hoboken, NJ) **19074**
NMR's Automobile Blue Book **11698***
No Sweat News (Olympia, WA) *Unable to locate*
Noah's Ark (Houston, TX) *Ceased*
Nob Hill Gazette (San Francisco, CA) **3405**
Noble Advertiser; The Guernsey- (Cambridge, OH) **24725**
The Noble County American (Albion, IN) *Ceased*
Nobles County Review (Adrian, MN) **15699**
Noblesville Daily Ledger (Noblesville, IN) *Unable to locate*
Noblesville Times (Noblesville, IN) **10355**
Nocturnal Lyric (Astoria, OR) **26226**
The Node (Larkspur, CA) *Ceased*
Nogales International (Nogales, AZ) **755**
Noh Quarter (San Francisco, CA) *Unable to locate*
The Noise (Boston, MA) **13939**
Noise (Toronto, ON, Can.) **36675**
Noise Control Engineer Journal (Auburn, AL) **43**
Noise Control Engineering Journal **43***
Nokomis Times **37574***
Nolan County Shopper (Sweetwater, TX) **31169**
Nomad (Kingston, ON, Can.) **35940**
Nomadic Peoples (New York, NY) **22464**
The Nome Nugget (Nome, AK) *Unable to locate*
NOMMO (Los Angeles, CA) **2348**
Nomos (Glen Ellyn, IL) *Ceased*
Non-Ferrous Metals; Soviet Journal of (New York, NY) **22144**
Non-Foods Merchandising (New York, NY) *Ceased*
Non-profit Times (Parsippany, NJ) **19412**
Nondestructive Evaluation; Journal of (New York, NY) **22144**
Nonferrous Alert (Beachwood, OH) **24654**
Nonfiction; Creative (Pittsburgh, PA) **27772**
Noninvasive Electrocardiology (Armonk, NY) **20089**
Nonlinear Control; International Journal of Robust and (Hoboken, NJ) **18996**
Nonlinear Dynamics (New York, NY) **22465**
Nonlinear Dynamics, Psychology, and Life Sciences (New York, NY) **22466**
Nonlinear Science; Journal of (New York, NY) **22145**
The Nonprofit Counsel (Hoboken, NJ) *Ceased*
Nonprofit Management and Leadership (San Francisco, CA) **3406**
Nonprofit News; Crain's (Detroit, MI) **14921**
Nonprofit & Public Sector Marketing; Journal of (Montgomery, AL) **368**
The Nonprofit Times (Parsippany, NJ) **19413**
Nonprofit and Voluntary Sector Quarterly (Seattle, WA) **32990**
Nonrenewable Resources **22408***
The Nonviolent Activist (New York, NY) **22467**
Nonwovens Industry (Ramsey, NJ) **19492**
The Nooner Magazine (San Ramon, CA) **3607**

NOPA Special Report 31650*
Nor-Del Cablevision Ltd. (Norwich, ON, Can.) 36135
Nora News Dispatch (Fishers, IN) Ceased
Norba News 4259*
Norborne Democrat-Leader (Norborne, MO) 17317
Norco Independent; Corona- (Norco, CA) 2641
Norcom Telecommunications Ltd. (Kenora, ON, Can.) Unable to locate
Nord-Est Plus; Le (Sept-Iles, QC, Can.) 37386
Nord Info; Le (Sainte-Therese, QC, Can.) 37384
Nord; Le (Hearst, ON, Can.) 35911
Norden News (New York, NY) Unable to locate
NordicReach (New Canaan, CT) 4980
Nordonia Hills Sun (Northfield, OH) 25440
Nordstjernan (Swedish News) (New York, NY) 22468
Nor'easter Leadership News (Syracuse, NY) Unable to locate
Norfolk Daily News (Norfolk, NE) 18170
Norfolk Journal and Guide 32291*
(Norfolk); Profile (Norfolk, VA) 32292
Normal (New York, NY) Ceased
Normal, Inc.; TCI of Bloomington/ (Normal, IL) 9307
Normal News 3139*
Normal Normalite (Normal, IL) 9301
Norman Cable TV (Norman, OK) 25948
Norman County Index (Ada, MN) 15696
The Norman Transcript (Norman, OK) 25937
The Normangee Star (Normangee, TX) 30869
Norquay North Star (Canora, SK, Can.) 37456
Norridge-Harwood Heights News (Harwood Heights, IL) 8978
Norridge Times (Lincolnwood, IL) 9100
Norris City Banner (Norris City, IL) 9311
Norseman (Saratoga, CA) 3745
Norseman Broadcasting Corp. 10833*
North Africa—Basic Oil Laws & Concession Contracts (New York, NY) 22469
North America (New York, NY) Unable to locate
North American Actuarial Journal (Schaumburg, IL) 9589
North American Archaeologist (Amityville, NY) 20052
The North American Deer Farmer (Appleton, WI) 33541
North American Edition; Business Travel Planner - (Secaucus, NJ) 19536
(North American Edition); Food Engineering (Bensenville, IL) 8067
North American Fisherman (Minnetonka, MN) 16172
North American Flora (Bronx, NY) 20278
North American Hunter (Minnetonka, MN) 16173
North American Journal of Aquaculture (Bethesda, MD) 13365
North American Journal of Economics and Finance (Claremont, CA) 1725
North American Journal of Fisheries Management (Bethesda, MD) 13366
North American Lily Society Quarterly (Owatonna, MN) 16252
North American Magic Realism 3836*
North American Mining (Reno, NV) Unable to locate
North American Moravian 26704*
North American Post (Seattle, WA) 32991
North American Pylon (Pleasanton, CA) 2855
The North American Review (Cedar Falls, IA) 10659
North American Review of Economics and Finance 1725*
North American Shortwave Association (NASWA)— The Journal (Levittown, PA) 27188
North American South Devon (Lynnville, IA) Unable to locate
The North American Technocrat (Ferndale, WA) 32768
North American Voice of Fatima (Youngstown, NY) Unable to locate
North Andover Citizen (Needham, MA) 14368
North Area Pennysaver (Syracuse, NY) 23415
North Atlantic Review (Stony Brook, NY) 23374
The North Baltimore News (North Baltimore, OH) 25432
North Bartow News (Adairsville, GA) 6898
North Bay Biz (Santa Rosa, CA) 3731
North Bay Near North Sun (Burks Falls, ON, Can.) Ceased
The North Bay Nugget (North Bay, ON, Can.) 36116
North Beach Now (San Francisco, CA) 3407
North Bellmore/Merrick Pennysaver (Farmingdale, NY) Ceased
North Bend Eagle (North Bend, NE) 18175
The North Bergen/North Hudson Reporter 18672*
The North Bergen/Reporter (Bergen, NJ) 18672
North Brentwood Advertiser (Farmingdale, NY) Ceased
North Brunswick Post/Franklin News Record/Central Post 19380*
North Carolina (Raleigh, NC) 24143
(North Carolina); Agricultural Review (Raleigh, NC) 24124
North Carolina Architect 23837*
North Carolina Architecture (Durham, NC) 23837

North Carolina Christian Advocate (Greensboro, NC) 23931
North Carolina Farm Bureau News (Raleigh, NC) Ceased
North Carolina Genealogical Society Journal (Greenville, NC) 23967
North Carolina Historical Review (Raleigh, NC) 24144
North Carolina Housing Network (Richmond, VA) Ceased
North Carolina Insight (Raleigh, NC) 24145
North Carolina Journal of International Law and Commercial Regulation (Chapel Hill, NC) 23716
North Carolina Law Review (Chapel Hill, NC) 23717
North Carolina Lawyers Weekly (Raleigh, NC) 24146
The North Carolina Mason (Washington, NC) 24272
North Carolina Medical Journal (Durham, NC) 23838
North Carolina News Network (Raleigh, NC) 37651
North Carolina Pharmacist (Chapel Hill, NC) 23718
North Carolina Plumbing-Heating-Cooling Forum (Garner, NC) 23905
North Carolina; This Week of Western (Asheville, NC) 23634
North Carolina; TWC of (Reidsville, NC) 24181
North Carolina; Vision Cable of 23760*
North Carolina; We the People of 24143*
North Carolina; Wildlife in (Raleigh, NC) 24159
The North Castle News (North Castle, NY) 23011
North Center-Irving Park Booster (Lincolnwood, IL) 9101
North Central Optometric Viewpoint (Altamonte Springs, FL) Ceased
North Central Outlook 32992*
North Central Television, Inc 25511*
The North Channel Sun (Pasadena, TX) 30912
North Coast Cable of Bratenahl Ltd. Partnership (Cleveland, OH) Unable to locate
The North Coast Farmer (Santa Rosa, CA) Unable to locate
North Coast Journal (Arcata, CA) 1430
North Coast Review (Duluth, MN) 15841
North Coast Tidings (Seaside, OR) 26579
North Country Angler (Ely, MN) 15881
North Country Cable TV 23104*
North Country Catholic (Ogdensburg, NY) Unable to locate
North Country Farm News (Plattsburgh, NY) Unable to locate
North Country Farmer 19975*
North Country Free Trader (Elizabethtown, NY) 20564
North Country Magazine 15069*
North Country Pennysaver (Boonville, NY) 20238
North Country Saver (Ely, MN) 15882
North Country Sun (Ironwood, MI) 15214
North Country This Week (Potsdam, NY) 23138
North Country Weekly (Littleton, NH) Unable to locate
The North Countryman (Plattsburgh, NY) 23102
North County (Escondido, CA) Unable to locate
The North County Blade-Citizen 2708*
North County Buyer's Guide 19932*
North County Guide (Carlsbad, CA) Ceased
North County Journal 2831*
North County Journal East (Warrenton, MO) 17690
North County News (Columbia, MD) 13466
North County News (Yorktown Heights, NY) 23609
North County Times (Escondido, CA) 1892
The North County Times (Oceanside, CA) 2708
The North County Times-Advocate 2708*
The North Creek News-Enterprise (North Creek, NY) 23012
North Crow River News (Osseo, MN) 16248
North Dakota Alumni Review; University of (Grand Forks, ND) 24458
North Dakota Education News (Bismarck, ND) 24353
North Dakota Historical Quarterly 24354*
North Dakota History (Bismarck, ND) 24354
North Dakota Horizons (Bismarck, ND) 24355
North Dakota, Inc.; TCI of (Grand Forks, ND) 24465
North Dakota Journal of Education (Bismarck, ND) Ceased
North Dakota Law Review (Grand Forks, ND) 24455
North Dakota Music Educator (Minot, ND) Unable to locate
North Dakota Outdoors (Bismarck, ND) 24356
North Dakota Quarterly (Grand Forks, ND) 24456
North Dakota REC Magazine (Mandan, ND) 24498
North Dakota Stockman (Bismarck, ND) 24357
North Dayton Advertiser (Dayton, OH) Ceased
North Delta Sentinel (Delta, BC, Can.) 34947
North DuPage Press (Glen Ellyn, IL) 8930
North East Breeze (North East, PA) 27340
North-East Independent (Wakefield, RI) 28446
North Eastern Cablevision Ltd. (Yorkton, SK, Can.) 37604
North End News 4711*
The North English Record (North English, IA) 11118
North Florida FAMILIES Magazine (Jacksonville, FL) 6216
North Flushing Pennysaver (Flushing, ON, Can.) 35837

North Force Magazine 14833*
North Fork Suffolk Life (Riverhead, NY) 23201
The North Freeway Leader (Houston, TX) 30510
North Georgia News (Blairsville, GA) 7129
The North Haven Post (Milford, CT) Unable to locate
The North Haven Wallingford Post (Milford, CT) Unable to locate
North Hills News Record (Mc Lean, VA) Unable to locate
North Iowa Times (Black Earth, WI) 33589
North Island Gazette (Port Hardy, BC, Can.) 35051
North Island News (Courtenay, BC, Can.) Unable to locate
North Island Televiewer (Port Hardy, BC, Can.) 35052
North Jackson Progress (Jackson, AL) 290
The North Jefferson News (Gardendale, AL) Unable to locate
The North Jersey Herald & News (Somerville, NJ) Unable to locate
North Jersey Prospector (Clifton, NJ) 18757
North Jersey Suburbanite (Closter, NJ) Unable to locate
North Jersey Times (Pompton Lakes, NJ) Unable to locate
The North Journal (Monroeville, PA) Unable to locate
The North Kawartha Times (Fenelon Falls, ON, Can.) Ceased
North Kent Leader (Kent, ON, Can.) 35931
North Kitsap Herald (Poulsbo, WA) 32899
North Kitsap Herald (Poulsbo, WA) 32898
North Kitsap Neighbors (Bremerton, WA) 32693
North Lake Tahoe Bonanza (Incline Village, NV) 18358
North Lakeland Shopper (Winter Haven, FL) 6870
North Light (Cincinnati, OH) 24811
The North Loop News (Chicago, IL) Unable to locate
North Louisiana Good News (Minden, LA) 12688
North Louisiana Historical Association Journal 12817*
North Louisiana History (Shreveport, LA) 12817
North Meridian Observer (Fishers, IN) Ceased
North Miami Beach News (North Miami Beach, FL) 6468
North Minneapolis & North Suburban Shopping Guide (Minneapolis, MN) Ceased
North Minneapolis Sun-Post (Eden Prairie, MN) Unable to locate
North Missourian (Gallatin, MO) 17081
North Myrtle Beach Times (North Myrtle Beach, SC) 28730
North Okaloosa Bulletin 6024*
North Okanogan County Gazette—Tribune 32873*
North Penn Life (Fort Washington, PA) 26931
North Plainfield Edition); The Journal (Greenbrook- (Somerville, NJ) 19573
North Plainfield Journal; Greenbrook- 19573*
North Platte Telegraph (North Platte, NE) 18176
North Pompano Shopper (Hollywood, FL) Unable to locate
North Port Sun Herald (North Port, FL) 6471
North Potomac Gazette (Frederick, MD) 13518
North Providence North Star (Greenville, RI) 28355
North Reading Transcript (North Reading, MA) 14426
North Renfrew Times (Deep River, ON, Can.) 35762
North Ridgeville Light 25508*
The North Ridgeville Press & Light (Sandusky, OH) 25508
North Riverside/Riverside/Riverside Lawn Suburban Life (Oak Brook, IL) 9361
North San Antonio Times (San Antonio, TX) Unable to locate
North San Bernardino Green Sheet (San Bernardino, CA) 3088
North Santiam Communications (Stayton, OR) 26590
North Scott County News 16971*
The North Scott Press (Eldridge, IA) 10870
North Scottsdale Independent (Scottsdale, AZ) 872
North Sea Monitor (Hoboken, NJ) Ceased
North Seattle Edition; The Journal— (North Seattle, WA) 32854
North Seattle Herald-Outlook (Seattle, WA) 32992
The North Seattle Press 33022*
North Shopping Bulletin (North St. Paul, MN) Ceased
North Shore Homes (Setauket, NY) 23327
North Shore Magazine (Glenview, IL) 8939
North Shore News (North Vancouver, BC, Can.) 35036
North Shore Radio 35687*
The North Shore Sentinel (Thessalon, ON, Can.) 36433
North Shore Sunday (Danvers, MA) 14153
North Shore Today (Syosset, NY) 23380
North Shore Today's Elite (Syosset, NY) 23381
North Side Journal (Warrenton, MO) 17691
North Side News (Jerome, ID) 7881
North Snohomish Weekly (Mount Vernon, WA) Unable to locate
North-South (Somerset, NJ) Ceased
North Star News (Karlstad, MN) 15981

Northwest Extra (Chicago, IL) **8510**
Northwest Farm Edition; Fastline— (Buckner, KY) **11987**
Northwest Farm Equipment Journal (Marshfield, WI) *Ceased*
Northwest Farm & Field Report (Lynden, WA) *Ceased*
Northwest Florida Daily News (Fort Walton Beach, FL) **6121**
Northwest Fun & Games (Des Moines, WA) **32737**
NorthWest Gay & Lesbian Reader (Seattle, WA) *Ceased*
Northwest Guardian (Bainbridge Island, WA) *Ceased*
Northwest Herald (Chicago, IL) **11194**
Northwest Herald (Crystal Lake, IL) **8695**
Northwest Herald (McHenry, IL) **9166**
Northwest Herald (Unity, SK, Can.) **37581**
Northwest Hospitality News **26568***
Northwest Houston Business News (Houston, TX) *Ceased*
Northwest Indiana Catholic (Merrillville, IN) **10298**
N'West Iowa Review (Sheldon, IA) **11194**
Northwest Iowa Shopper (Spencer, IA) **11231**
Northwest Kitchen and Bath Quarterly (Seattle, WA) *Ceased*
Northwest Labor Press (Portland, OR) **26487**
Northwest Leader (Chicago, IL) **8511**
Northwest Leader-Sun (Universal City, TX) *Ceased*
Northwest Lincoln Sun (Lincoln, NE) *Ceased*
Northwest Literary Forum *Ceased*
Northwest Magazine (Portland, OR) *Ceased*
Northwest Metro Times (Bethany, OK) **25759**
Northwest Michigan Vacationeer (Boyne City, MI) *Ceased*
Northwest Missourian (Maryville, MO) **17275**
Northwest Motor (Seattle, WA) **32994**
The Northwest Network (Kirkland, WA) *Ceased*
Northwest News Network **37643***
Northwest Nikkei (Seattle, WA) *Unable to locate*
Northwest Oklahoma and Ellis County News (Shattuck, OK) **26060**
Northwest Orient (New York, NY) *Unable to locate*
Northwest Palate Magazine (Portland, OR) **26488**
Northwest Parent Connection (Seattle, WA) *Ceased*
Northwest Pennysaver (Rochester, NY) *Ceased*
The Northwest Phoenix (Gary, IN) **10017**
Northwest PhotoNetwork (Seattle, WA) *Unable to locate*
Northwest Press (Cincinnati, OH) *Unable to locate*
Northwest Public Power Association Bulletin (Vancouver, WA) **33177**
Northwest Public Power Bulletin **33177***
Northwest Review (Eugene, OR) **26326**
Northwest Runner (Seattle, WA) **32995**
Northwest Sailor **32996***
Northwest Science (Pullman, WA) **32905**
Northwest Senior Life (Portland, OR) **26489**
Northwest Shopper (Des Moines, IA) **10807**
Northwest Side Press; Chicago's (Chicago, IL) **8330**
Northwest Side Sunday Press (Chicago, IL) *Ceased*
Northwest Signal (Napoleon, OH) **25402**
Northwest Star (Pikesville, MD) *Ceased*
The Northwest Technocrat **32768***
Northwest Trail Tracer (Vincennes, IN) **10521**
Northwest Travel (Florence, OR) **26351**
Northwest Washington Beverage Analyst (Denver, CO) *Ceased*
Northwest Writers Photographers and Design Artists (Seattle, WA) *Unable to locate*
Northwest Yachting (Seattle, WA) **32996**
Northwestel Cable Inc. (Yellowknife, NT, Can.) **35531**
Northwestern (Oshkosh, WI) **34224**
Northwestern Banker **16117***
Northwestern; The Daily (Evanston, IL) **8856**
Northwestern Financial Review (Minneapolis, MN) **16117**
Northwestern Illinois Dispatch (Savanna, IL) **9580**
Northwestern Illinois Farmer (Lena, IL) **9074**
Northwestern Journal of International Law & Business (Chicago, IL) **8512**
Northwestern Kansas Register (Salina, KS) **11783**
Northwestern Lutheran **34070***
Northwestern News (Virden, IL) *Unable to locate*
Northwestern News (Alva, OK) **25738**
Northwestern University Law Review (Champaign, IL) **8206**
Northwesterner (Santa Rosa, CA) **3732**
NorthwestLiving! Magazine (Edmonds, WA) *Ceased*
Northwoods Journal (Thomaston, ME) **13066**
Northwoods Press (Nevis, MN) **16204**
Norton Courier (Norton, MA) **14437**
Norton Daily Telegram (Norton, KS) **11678**
Norton Mirror (Needham, MA) *Unable to locate*
Norwalk Citizen-News (Norwalk, CT) **5072**
Norwalk Herald American (Norwalk, CA) **2648**
Norwalk Lifestyles (Norwalk, CT) **5073**
Norwalk News **5073***
Norwalk Reflector (Norwalk, OH) **25441**

The Norwalk Weekly Life & Times (Norwalk, CT) *Ceased*
Norway Cablevision Inc. (Kanawha, IA) **11012**
Norway Viking; The Sons of (Minneapolis, MN) **16128**
Norwegian American Commerce (New York, NY) *Ceased*
Norwegian-American Studies (Northfield, MN) **16238**
Norwell Mariner (Norwell, MA) **14444**
Norwell Shoppinguide (Pembroke, MA) *Ceased*
Nor'Wester (Springdale, NL, Can.) **35507**
Nor'westing (Seattle, WA) **32997**
Norwich Bulletin (Norwich, CT) **5084**
Norwich Gazette (Norwich, ON, Can.) **36134**
The Norwich Guidon (Northfield, VT) **31575**
Norwich Pennysaver (Norwich, NY) **23022**
Norwin Star Star (Monroeville, PA) **27280**
Norwood Enterprise-Press (Cincinnati, OH) *Ceased*
Norwood Park-Edison Passage (Highland Park, IL) *Unable to locate*
Norwood Times Review; Edison- (Chicago, IL) **8360**
Norwood-Young America Times (Norwood, MN) **16241**
Nos Animaux (Montreal, QC, Can.) **37195**
Nostalgia Television **37758***
Nostalgia - True Personal Experience & Party (Orangeburg, SC) *Ceased*
Nostalgiaworld (North Haven, CT) *Unable to locate*
Nostalgic Cars (Lakeland, FL) *Ceased*
Nostoc Magazine (Spencer, MA) **14549**
Not Born Yesterday (La Canada, CA) **2108**
Not for Kids Only (El Paso, TX) *Ceased*
Notary; The National (Chatsworth, CA) **1689**
The Notebook (Washington, DC) *Unable to locate*
Notes (Middleton, WI) **34052**
Notes and Abstracts in American and International Education (San Francisco, CA) **3408**
Notes on Linguistics (Dallas, TX) **30171**
Notes on Literacy (Dallas, TX) **30172**
Notes on Translation (Dallas, TX) *Ceased*
Nothern Hardware Trade **10955***
Notices of the American Mathematical Society (Providence, RI) **28410**
Noticia; La (Charlotte, NC) **23747**
Noticias del Mundo (Los Angeles, CA) *Ceased*
Noticias del Mundo (Long Island City, NY) **20965**
Noticias de la Semana (Washington, DC) *Ceased*
Notivest (Woodland Hills, CA) *Ceased*
Notre-Dame du Cap; Revue (Cap-de-la-Madeleine, QC, Can.) **36957**
Notre Dame Football; Blue & Gold Illustrated— (Notre Dame, IN) **10368**
Notre Dame Journal of Law, Ethics & Public Policy (Notre Dame, IN) **10371**
Notre Dame Law Review (Notre Dame, IN) **10372**
Notre Dame Magazine (Notre Dame, IN) **10373**
Notre Dame Technical Review (Notre Dame, IN) **10374**
Nous (Malden, MA) *Unable to locate*
Nouveau Journal de St.-Michel **37146***
The Nouveau Magazine (New Hope, PA) **27321**
Nouveau Quartier Libre (Montreal, QC, Can.) **37196**
Nouvelle; Bonnyville (Bonnyville, AB, Can.) **34621**
Nouvelle; La (Victoriaville, QC, Can.) **37431**
Nouvelles CEQ (Montreal, QC, Can.) **37197**
Nouvelles Saint-Laurent News (Saint-Laurent, QC, Can.) **37365**
Nouvelliste; Le (Trois-Rivieres, QC, Can.) **37416**
NOVA **30281***
Nova Cablevision Inc. (Galesburg, IL) **8908**
Nova Express (Austin, TX) **29795**
Nova Journal of Theoretical Physics (Hauppauge, NY) **20720**
NOVA Quarterly (El Paso, TX) **30281**
Nova Review (Big Rapids, MI) **14817**
Nova Scotia; Labor Legislation in (Halifax, NS, Can.) **35569**
The Nova Scotia Medical Journal (Dartmouth, NS, Can.) *Ceased*
Nova - Voice of Ministry (Lake Worth, FL) *Unable to locate*
Novato Advance (Novato, CA) **2652**
Novato Buyer's Guide (Sebastopol, CA) *Ceased*
Novedades (Los Angeles, CA) **2350**
Novedades De Industria Alimenticia *Ceased*
Novi News (Novi, MI) **15410**
Novi Spinal Column Newsweekly (Novi, MI) **15411**
Novitates; American Museum (New York, NY) **21202**
Novon (St. Louis, MO) **17477**
Novoye Russkoye Slovo **22434***
Novy Domov (New Homeland) (Scarborough, ON, Can.) **36380**
Novyj Zhurnal (The New Review) (New York, NY) **22470**
Now (Toronto, ON, Can.) **36678**
Now; Coquitlam (Coquitlam, BC, Can.) **34930**
Now Hear This (Bridgewater, NJ) **18697**
The Now Newspaper (Surrey, BC, Can.) **35109**
Now; North Beach (San Francisco, CA) **3407**
Now & Then (Johnson City, TN) **29253**

Nowata Daily Star **25949***
Nowata Star (Nowata, OK) **25949**
Nowi Dni (New Days) (Toronto, ON, Can.) *Unable to locate*
Nowy Dziennik **22571***
Nowy Kurier; Polish Canadian Courier/ (Toronto, ON, Can.) **36713**
The Nozzle **13608***
Nozzle & Wrench (Lanham, MD) **13608**
NPN International (Chicago, IL) **8513**
NRB (Manassas, VA) **32224**
NREL in Review *Ceased*
N.S. Conservation *Ceased*
NSBA Newsletter **18102***
NSBE Journal **31716***
NSBE Magazine (Alexandria, VA) **31716**
NSEA Voice (Lincoln, NE) **18110**
NSGA Retail Focus (Mount Prospect, IL) **9248**
NST (Nature, Society and Thought) (Minneapolis, MN) **16118**
NSTA Reports! (Arlington, VA) **31815**
NT Systems (San Mateo, CA) *Ceased*
NT Update (Westminster, CO) *Ceased*
NTEA Technical Report (Farmington Hills, MI) **15019**
NTID Focus (Rochester, NY) *Ceased*
NTSB Reporter (White Plains, NY) **23572**
NTV Network/KHGI-TV (Kearney, NE) **37706**
NTV (Newfoundland Television) (St. Johns, NL, Can.) **37707**
NTV-TV - Channel 5 (Dawson Creek, BC, Can.) **34944**
NuCity **19789***
Nuclear Cardiology; Journal of (Philadelphia, PA) **27539**
Nuclear Chemistry; Journal of Radioanalytical and (New York, NY) **22175**
Nuclear Data Sheets (San Diego, CA) **3243**
Nuclear Data Tables; Atomic Data and (San Diego, CA) **3118**
Nuclear Fuel Cycle (Oak Ridge, TN) *Ceased*
Nuclear Materials Management **9318***
Nuclear Materials Management; Journal of (Northbrook, IL) **9318**
Nuclear Medicine; Clinical (Wynnewood, PA) **28197**
Nuclear Medicine; Seminars in (Bronx, NY) **20286**
Nuclear Medicine Technology; Journal of (Reston, VA) **32388**
Nuclear News (La Grange Park, IL) **9052**
Nuclear Plant Journal (Glen Ellyn, IL) **8931**
Nuclear Reactor Safety (Oak Ridge, TN) *Ceased*
Nuclear Reactors and Technology (Oak Ridge, TN) *Ceased*
Nuclear Safety (Oak Ridge, TN) **29549**
Nuclear Science and Engineering (La Grange Park, IL) **9053**
Nuclear Technology (La Grange Park, IL) **9054**
Nuclear Times (Boston, MA) *Ceased*
Nuclei; Physics of Particles and (College Park, MD) **13435**
Nucleic Acid Drug Development; Antisense and (Larchmont, NY) **20890**
Nucleic Acids Abstracts (Bethesda, MD) **13368**
Nucleosides & Nucleotides & Nucleic Acids (Birmingham, AL) **82**
Nucleus **14044***
Nude & Natural (Oshkosh, WI) **34225**
Nueces County Record Star (Robstown, TX) **30985**
Nuestras Raices/Our Roots (Denver, CO) **4345**
Nuestro (New York, NY) *Unable to locate*
Nuestro Tiempo (Los Angeles, CA) *Ceased*
Nueva Luz (Bronx, NY) **20279**
Nueva Opinion (San Antonio, TX) *Unable to locate*
Nueva Vista (Midland, TX) **30815**
Nuevo Amanecer (Brooklyn, NY) *Ceased*
Nuevo Dia; El (San Juan, PR) **28292**
Nuevo Herald; El (Fort Lauderdale, FL) **6075**
Nuevo Hudson; El (Jersey City, NJ) **19136**
Nuevo Patria; El (Miami, FL) **6350**
Nuevo Tiempo Hispano (Miami, FL) *Unable to locate*
The Nugget **2689***
The Nugget and CGS News (Oakland, CA) **2689**
Nugget; The North Bay (North Bay, ON, Can.) **36116**
Nuit Blanche (Quebec, QC, Can.) **37293**
Number One **29202***
Number Theory; Journal of (San Diego, CA) **3209**
Numerical Algorithms (New York, NY) **22471**
Numerical Analysis; SIAM Journal on (Philadelphia, PA) **27684**
Numerical Functional Analysis and Optimization (Orlando, FL) **6501**
Numerical Heat Transfer (Chicago, IL) **8514**
Numerical Heat Transfer, Part A: Applications (Chicago, IL) **8515**
Numerical Linear Algebra with Applications (Hoboken, NJ) **19075**
Numerical Methods in Engineering; Communications in (Hoboken, NJ) **18918**
Numerical Methods for Partial Differential Equations (Hoboken, NJ) **19076**

OAG Pocket Flight Guide - Latin American/Caribbean Edition (Downers Grove, IL) *Unable to locate*

OAG Pocket Flight Guide - North American Edition (Downers Grove, IL) *Unable to locate*

OAG Pocket Flight Guide - Pacific Asia Edition (Downers Grove, IL) **8793**

OAG Travel Planner Hotel & Motel Redbook (North American Edition) **19536***

OAG Worldwide Cruise & Shipline Guide (Downers Grove, IL) *Ceased*

Oahu; Spotlight (Honolulu, HI) **7722**

Oahu; This Week (Honolulu, HI) **7726**

The Oak Bay Star (Victoria, BC, Can.) *Unable to locate*

Oak Cliff Tribune (Dallas, TX) **30173**

Oak Creek Pictorial (New Berlin, WI) **34182**

Oak Forest/Midlothian Star (Oak Forest, IL) **9371**

Oak Hill Times (Swayzee, IN) **10478**

Oak Lawn Independent (Midlothian, IL) **9191**

Oak Lawn Star (Oak Lawn, IL) **9372**

Oak Leaves (Glenview, IL) *Unable to locate*

Oak Park & River Forest; Wednesday Journal of (Oak Park, IL) **9378**

Oak Ridge National Laboratory Review (Oak Ridge, TN) **29550**

The Oak Ridger (Oak Ridge, TN) **29551**

Oakbrook Terrace Argus; Villa Park/ (Oak Brook, IL) **9368**

Oakdale Advertiser (Oakdale, CA) **2655**

Oakdale Journal (Oakdale, LA) **12790**

Oakdale-Lake Elmo Review (North St. Paul, MN) **16228**

Oakdale Leader (Oakdale, CA) **2656**

Oakdale Suffolk Life; Sayville/ (Sayville, NY) **23310**

Oakes Times (Bismarck, ND) **24358**

Oakland Bay Area Observer (Oakland, CA) **2690**

Oakland Business Monthly (Union Lake, MI) *Ceased*

Oakland City Journal (Oakland City, IN) **10381**

Oakland City Journal Dollar Saver (Oakland City, IN) **10382**

The Oakland County Legal News (Pontiac, MI) *Unable to locate*

Oakland Gardens Pennysaver; Bayside South/ (Bayside, ON, Can.) **35668**

The Oakland-Hindsboro Prairie Sun (Casey, IL) *Unable to locate*

Oakland Independent (Oakland, NE) **18186**

Oakland Life (Detroit, MI) *Unable to locate*

Oakland Post (Oakland, CA) **2691**

The Oakland Post (Rochester, MI) *Unable to locate*

Oakland Press (Pontiac, MI) **15450**

Oakland Tech News (Warren, MI) *Unable to locate*

The Oakland Tribune (Oakland, CA) **2692**

The Oakley Graphic (Oakley, KS) **11680**

Oakmont Advance Leader (Monroeville, PA) **27281**

Oakville Beaver (Oakville, ON, Can.) **36147**

Oakville Shopping News (Oakville, ON, Can.) **36148**

Oakville Today (Oakville, ON, Can.) **36149**

Oakwood Register (Dayton, OH) **25123**

O&P Business News (Thorofare, NJ) **19628**

O&P World (Thorofare, NJ) **19629**

The Oarsman **10180***

Oasis (Largo, FL) **6300**

OB/GYN Clinical Alert (Montvale, NJ) **19268**

OB/GYN; Contemporary (Montvale, NJ) **19248**

Ob Gyn News (Rockville, MD) **13690**

Oberlin Alumni Magazine (Oberlin, OH) **25447**

The Oberlin Herald (Oberlin, KS) **11681**

The Oberlin Review (Oberlin, OH) **25448**

Obesity & Health **35880***

Obesity Research (Boston, MA) **13942**

Obesity Surgery (Toronto, ON, Can.) **36679**

OBG Management (Montvale, NJ) *Unable to locate*

Object Magazine (New York, NY) *Unable to locate*

The Objector (San Francisco, CA) *Unable to locate*

The Oblate World and Voice of Hope (Tewksbury, MA) **14586**

Oblique Times **36878***

Oblong Gem (Oblong, IL) **9381**

Oblong Oracle **9381***

oboe (San Francisco, CA) *Ceased*

O'Brien County Bell (Primghar, IA) **11168**

Obscure Publications & Video (Milwaukee, WI) *Unable to locate*

Observador; El (San Jose, CA) **3516**

L'Observateur (LaPlace, LA) **12655**

Observer **9422***

The Observer **9517***

Observer **2161***

The Observer **7133***

Observer **34218***

Observer **27362***

The Observer (Monterey, CA) **2584**

The Observer (Southington, CT) **5134**

The Observer (Davie, FL) **6034**

The Observer (New Smyrna Beach, FL) **6458**

Observer (Chicago, IL) *Ceased*

The Observer (Rockford, IL) **9528**

The Observer (Kewanna, IN) **10232**

The Observer (Notre Dame, IN) **10375**

The Observer (De Witt, IA) **10755**

The Observer (Vail, IA) **11280**

Observer (Blackwood, NJ) *Ceased*

The Observer (Hasbrouck Heights, NJ) **18867**

The Observer (Kearny, NJ) **19151**

The Observer (Newark, NJ) **19362**

Observer (Dunkirk, NY) **20537**

The Observer (New York, NY) **22482**

Observer (Smithtown, NY) **23339**

The Observer (Cleveland, OH) **24935**

The Observer (La Grande, OR) **26399**

The Observer (Philadelphia, PA) *Unable to locate*

The Observer (Greenville, RI) **28356**

The Observer (Holly Hill, SC) *Unable to locate*

The Observer (Nashville, TN) *Unable to locate*

The Observer (Charlottesville, VA) **31936**

The Observer (Herndon, VA) **32164**

Observer (Seattle, WA) **32998**

Observer (Pembroke, ON, Can.) **36308**

Observer Community Newspaper (Deerfield Beach, FL) **6051**

Observer-Dispatch (Utica, NY) **23466**

Observer/Enterprise (Robert Lee, TX) **30984**

Observer/Freebee **34218***

Observer Herald News (Newberry, SC) *Unable to locate*

The Observer News (Ruskin, FL) **6615**

Observer-News (Clinton, TN) *Unable to locate*

Observer-News-Enterprise (Newton, NC) **24106**

Observer Newspapers (Kingwood, TX) **30651**

The Observer-Patriot (Putnam, CT) *Unable to locate*

Observer-Reporter (Washington, PA) **28115**

Observer-Reporter (Waynesburg, PA) *Unable to locate*

Observer and Sun **30651***

Observer & Sun Newspapers **30651***

Observer-Tribune (Chester, NJ) **18742**

Obstetric Anesthesia Digest (Baltimore, MD) **13226**

Obstetric Anesthesia; International Journal of (New York, NY) **21912**

Obstetric, Gynecologic and Neonatal Nursing (JOGNN); Journal of (Thousand Oaks, CA) **3896**

Obstetric Investigation; Gynecologic and (Farmington, CT) **4829**

Obstetrical & Gynecological Survey (Nashville, TN) **29477**

Obstetrics and Gynecology; American Journal of (St. Louis, MO) **17410**

Obstetrics Gynecology; Clinical (Salt Lake City, UT) **31424**

Obstetrics and Gynecology Clinics (Philadelphia, PA) **27594**

Obstetrics & Gynecology; Current Opinion in (Philadelphia, PA) **27439**

Obstetrics/Gynecology Edition; Medical Economics— (Montvale, NJ) **19263**

Obstetrics, Gynecology and Fertility; Current Problems in (St. Louis, MO) **17429**

Obstetrics; Internet Journal of Gynecology and (Sugar Land, TX) **31145**

The OBU Bison (Shawnee, OK) **26064**

OC Metro (Newport Beach, CA) **2633**

O.C. Weekly (Costa Mesa, CA) **1779**

Ocala Star-Banner (Ocala, FL) **6472**

Ocaw Reporter (Lakewood, CO) *Ceased*

OCAW Reporter (OCAW) **29478***

OCB Cablevision Inc. (Athens, GA) *Unable to locate*

OCB Tracker (Glendora, CA) **2025**

Occasional Bulletin of Missionary Research **4992***

Occasional Papers in Translation and Textlinguistics (OPTAT) **30164***

Occasional Papers in Women's Studies **14762***

The Occidental Weekly (Los Angeles, CA) **2351**

Occupational and Environmental Medicine; Journal of (Arlington Heights, IL) **8025**

Occupational Hazards (Cleveland, OH) **24936**

Occupational Health Nursing **19615***

Occupational Health & Safety (Dallas, TX) **30174**

Occupational Health and Safety News (COHSN); Canadian (Toronto, ON, Can.) **36521**

Occupational Injuries in Maine; Fatal (Augusta, ME) **12891**

Occupational Medicine, Immunology and Toxicology; International Journal of (Princeton, NJ) **19462**

Occupational Outlook Quarterly (Washington, DC) **5698**

Occupational Rehabilitation; Journal of (New York, NY) **22148**

Occupational Safety; Canadian (Burlington, ON, Can.) **35716**

Occupational Therapy Forum (Wayne, PA) **28134**

Occupational Therapy in Geriatrics; Physical & (Bronx, NY) **20280**

Occupational Therapy in Health Care (Greenville, NC) **23968**

Occupational Therapy Journal of Research (Thorofare, NJ) **19630**

Occupational Therapy in Mental Health (Binghamton, NY) **20209**

Occupational Therapy NOW (White Rock, BC, Can.) **35242**

Occupational Therapy Practitioners; ADVANCE for (King of Prussia, PA) **27117**

Occupational Therapy (Revue Canadienne d'Ergotherapie); The Canadian Journal of (Ottawa, ON, Can.) **36209**

Occupations; Work and (Thousand Oaks, CA) **3921**

OCCurrence (Des Plaines, IL) **8765**

Ocean City Sentinel (Ocean City, NJ) **19388**

Ocean City Times **13638***

Ocean County Business Today (Toms River, NJ) *Ceased*

Ocean County Journal (Waretown, NJ) **19705**

Ocean County Observer (Toms River, NJ) **19642**

Ocean County Reporter (Toms River, NJ) **19643**

Ocean County Review (Seaside Heights, NJ) *Unable to locate*

Ocean Development and International Law (Philadelphia, PA) **27595**

Ocean Engineering; Journal of Waterway, Port, Coastal, and (Reston, VA) **32402**

Ocean Grove & Neptune Times **19392***

Ocean Industry (Houston, TX) *Ceased*

Ocean Navigator (Portland, ME) **13015**

Ocean Reef Cable TV (Key Largo, FL) *Unable to locate*

Ocean Side Advertiser (Seabrook, NH) *Unable to locate*

Ocean Springs Record (Mc Lean, VA) *Unable to locate*

Ocean State Business (Providence, RI) *Unable to locate*

Ocean State Golf (Cranston, RI) **28336**

Ocean State Grapevine (Rumford, RI) *Unable to locate*

Oceana Magazine (Ocean City, MD) **13639**

Oceana's Herald-Journal (Hart, MI) **15147**

Oceanic Abstracts (Bethesda, MD) **13369**

Oceanic Cablevision, Inc. (Mililani, HI) **7789**

Oceanic Linguistics (Honolulu, HI) **7712**

Oceanic Technology; Journal of Atmospheric and (Boston, MA) **13913**

Oceanographic Monthly Summary (Washington, DC) *Ceased*

Oceanography; Journal of (New York, NY) **22149**

Oceanography; Journal of Physical (Boston, MA) **13917**

Oceans (Stamford, CT) *Ceased*

Oceanside Beacon (Mineola, NY) *Unable to locate*

Oceanside Blade-Citizen **1892***

Oceanside Breeze (Encinitas, CA) *Ceased*

Oceanside-Island Park Herald (Oceanside, NY) **23031**

Oceanside/Island Park Shopper's Guide (Hicksville, NY) **20743**

Oceanside Pennysaver (Oceanside, HI) **7790**

Oceanus Magazine (Woods Hole, MA) **14673**

OceanView (Ocean, NJ) *Unable to locate*

Ocheyedan Press and Melvin News (Ocheyedan, IA) **11121**

The Ochsner Journal (New Orleans, LA) **12749**

O'Collegian; The Daily (Stillwater, OK) **26077**

Oconee Enterprise (Watkinsville, GA) **7643**

Oconomowoc Buyers Guide (Hartland, WI) **33782**

Oconomowoc Enterprise (Oconomowoc, WI) **34203**

Oconto County Reporter (Oconto, WI) **34204**

Oconto County Times-Herald (Oconto Falls, WI) **34208**

Oconto Falls Cable TV (Oconto Falls, WI) **34209**

OCS News (New York, NY) **22483**

Octane (Edmonton, AB, Can.) *Unable to locate*

October (Cambridge, MA) *Unable to locate*

The Octopus (Champaign, IL) **8207**

Ocular Pharmacology and Therapeutics; Journal of (Larchmont, NY) **20918**

Ocular Surgery News (Thorofare, NJ) **19631**

Ocular Surgery News Europe/Asia-Pacific Edition (Thorofare, NJ) **19632**

Ocular Surgery News Latin America Edition (Thorofare, NJ) **19633**

Ocular Toxicology; Journal of Toxicology, Cutaneous and (Andover, MA) **13812**

Oculoplastic, Orbital and Reconstructive Surgery; Operative Techniques in (Philadelphia, PA) **27603**

Odd Fellow and Rebekah; California (Linden, CA) **2154**

Odebolt Chronicle **11122***

Odell Times (Dwight, IL) *Ceased*

The Odem-Edroy Times (Odem, TX) **30870**

Odessa American (Odessa, TX) **30872**

Odessa Poetry Review (Odessa, MO) *Unable to locate*

The Odessa Record (Odessa, WA) **32858**

The Odessan (Odessa, MO) **17319**

O'Donnell Index-Press (Odonnell, TX) **30884**

O'Dwyer's PR Services Report (New York, NY) **22484**

Odyssey (Peterborough, NH) **18626**
Odyssey (New York, NY) **37708**
OE Reports **18454***
OEA Communique **25011***
OEA Focus **25964***
OECD Economic Studies (Washington, DC) **5699**
OECD Economic Surveys (Washington, DC) **5700**
OECD Economic Surveys - CCEET (Washington, DC)
Ceased
OECD Journal on Budgeting (Washington, DC) **5701**
OECD Journal of Competition Law & Policy
(Washington, DC) **5702**
OECD Observer (Washington, DC) **5703**
L'Oeil Regional (Beloeil, QC, Can.) **36950**
OEM **33715***
OEM Magazine *Ceased*
OEM Off-Highway (Fort Atkinson, WI) **33715**
OEM Worldwide (Fort Atkinson, WI) *Ceased*
oemagazine (Amherst, NH) **18454**
Of Counsel (New York, NY) **22485**
Of a Like Mind (Madison, WI) *Ceased*
O'Fallon Journal; Fairview Heights/ (Swansea, IL)
9677
O'Fallon Progress (O Fallon, IL) **9334**
Oferta Review; La (San Jose, CA) **3521**
Off Campus (Northampton, MA) *Ceased*
Off Duty (Newport Beach, CA) *Unable to locate*
Off Duty. Europe (Newport Beach, CA) *Unable to
locate*
Off Duty Pacific (Newport Beach, CA) *Unable to
locate*
Off the Glass (King of Prussia, PA) *Unable to locate*
Off-Highway Engineering; SAE (Warrendale, PA)
28114
Off Lead (Canastota, NY) *Ceased*
Off Our Backs (Washington, DC) **5704**
Off Road (Anaheim, CA) **1412**
Off-Road (Los Angeles, CA) *Unable to locate*
Off-Road Advertiser (Arcata, CA) *Ceased*
OFF ROAD AMERICA (Sarasota, FL) *Ceased*
Off Road; Petersen's 4 Wheel & (Los Angeles, CA)
2363
OffBeat Magazine (New Orleans, LA) **12750**
The Office (Stamford, CT) *Unable to locate*
Office Automation (Toronto, ON, Can.) *Unable to
locate*
Office Dealer (Philadelphia, PA) **27596**
Office and Emergency Pediatrics (Larchmont, NY)
Ceased
Office Guide to Miami (Fort Lauderdale, FL) *Unable
to locate*
Office Guide to Orlando (Longwood, FL) *Unable to
locate*
Office Guide to Tampa Bay (St. Petersburg, FL)
Unable to locate
Office Leasing Guide (Columbus, OH) *Unable to
locate*
Office Manager (Eugene, OR) **26327**
Office Nurse (Montvale, NJ) **19269**
Office Product News (Toronto, ON, Can.) *Ceased*
Office Productivity (Toronto, ON, Can.) *Ceased*
Office Products Dealer *Ceased*
Office Supply & Equipment Dealer (Cary, IL) *Ceased*
Office Systems 96 (Spring House, PA) **28009**
Office World News (Lakewood, NJ) *Unable to locate*
OFFICE@Home (Bowen Island, BC, Can.) **34887**
OfficePRO (Springfield, VA) **32550**
The Officer (Washington, DC) **5705**
Officer Review (Alexandria, VA) **31718**
OfficeSolutions (Houston, TX) **30512**
Official Accommodations Guide (Orlando, FL) *Unable
to locate*
The Official Beverly Hills, 90210 Magazine (New
York, NY) *Unable to locate*
Official City Guide (New York, NY) *Unable to locate*
Official Detective (New York, NY) *Unable to locate*
The Official Guide to Howard County (Columbia, MD)
13470
Official Journal of the American Association for the
History of Nursing **27592***
Official Magazine (Ontario, CA) **2717**
Official Michigan (Sandusky, MI) **15520**
Official Railway Guide - North American Travel
Edition (East Windsor, NJ) *Ceased*
The Official Star Trek Fan Club Magazine (Toronto,
ON, Can.) *Ceased*
Official Star Wars Insider (Aurora, CO) *Unable to
locate*
Official Steamship Guide International (Knoxville, TN)
Unable to locate
Official Summary of Security Transactions and
Holdings (Pittsburgh, PA) **27823**
Official U.S. PlayStation Magazine (Lombard, IL)
Unable to locate
Official Visitors Guide (Orlando, FL) *Unable to locate*
Official's Cryptograms (Ambler, PA) **26652**
Offroad America (Sarasota, FL) *Ceased*
Offshore (Houston, TX) **30513**
Offshore Engineer (Houston, TX) **30514**

Offshore Field Development International (Houston,
TX) *Unable to locate*
Offshore Magazine (Needham, MA) *Unable to locate*
Offshore and Polar Engineering; International Journal
of (Cupertino, CA) **1797**
Offshore Resources (West Vancouver, BC, Can.)
Unable to locate
The Offshore Rig Locator (Houston, TX) *Unable to
locate*
Offshore Worldwide (Miami, FL) *Unable to locate*
offspring (New York, NY) **22486**
Ogden Leader (Ogden, IL) **9382**
Ogden Reporter (Ogden, IA) **11125**
Ogden Standard-Examiner **31378***
Ogemaw County Herald (West Branch, MI) **15680**
Ogle County Life (Oregon, IL) **9387**
Ogle Tempo; Northern (Machesney Park, IL) **9127**
Oglethorpe Echo (Oglethorpe, GA) **7477**
Oh! Zone (Marquette, MI) *Ceased*
OH&S Canada (Toronto, ON, Can.) **36680**
Ohio Antique Review **25234***
The Ohio Banker **25048***
Ohio Baptist Messenger (Columbus, OH) **25039**
Ohio Beverage Journal (Wheeling, WV) **33504**
Ohio Biological Survey Miscellaneous Contributions
(Columbus, OH) **25040**
Ohio Builder (Louisville, KY) *Unable to locate*
Ohio Cattleman (Marysville, OH) **25358**
Ohio; Coaxial Communications of Central (Columbus,
OH) **25070**
Ohio Contractor (Columbus, OH) **25041**
(Ohio); Country Living (Columbus, OH) **25012**
Ohio County Engineer (Columbus, OH) **25042**
Ohio County Messenger (Beaver Dam, KY) **11930**
Ohio County News (Rising Sun, IN) **10428**
Ohio County Times-News (Hartford, KY) **12112**
The Ohio CPA Journal (Dublin, OH) **25169**
Ohio; Domestic Relations Journal of (Cleveland, OH)
24882
(Ohio Edition); Home & Away (Worthington, OH)
25679
Ohio Educational Broadcasting Network Commission
37709*
Ohio Educational Telecommunications Network
Commission (Columbus, OH) **37709**
Ohio Engineer (Columbus, OH) **25043**
Ohio Engineer News **25043***
Ohio Farm Edition; Fastline— (Buckner, KY) **11988**
The Ohio Farmer (Lancaster, OH) **25291**
Ohio Florists Association Bulletin (Columbus, OH)
25044
Ohio Granger (Columbus, OH) **25045**
Ohio Graphic (Mc Lean, VA) *Ceased*
Ohio. History (Columbus, OH) **25046**
The Ohio Journal of Science (Kent, OH) **25277**
Ohio Law Newspaper (Cleveland, OH) *Unable to
locate*
Ohio Lawyer (Columbus, OH) *Unable to locate*
Ohio Legislative Service, Annotated; Baldwin's
(Cleveland, OH) **24860**
Ohio LIVE; Northern (Cleveland, OH) **24933**
Ohio Magazine (Cleveland, OH) **24937**
Ohio Magazine; Wild (Columbus, OH) **25069**
Ohio Media Spectrum (Columbus, OH) *Ceased*
Ohio Medicine Magazine (Columbus, OH) *Unable to
locate*
Ohio Monthly Record; Baldwin's (Cleveland, OH)
24861
Ohio Motorist (Independence, OH) **25252**
Ohio Municipal Service; Babbit's (Cleveland, OH)
24858
Ohio News (Wooster, OH) *Unable to locate*
Ohio Northern University Law Review (Ada, OH)
24571
Ohio Nurses Review (Columbus, OH) **25047**
Ohio Perspective (Altamonte Springs, FL) **5901**
Ohio Pharmacist (Dublin, OH) *Unable to locate*
Ohio PHC Contractor **5901***
Ohio; Probate Law Journal of (Cleveland, OH) **24944**
Ohio Public Accountant (Columbus, OH) *Unable to
locate*
Ohio Record (Columbus, OH) **25048**
Ohio Records & Pioneer Families (Mansfield, OH)
25333
Ohio Restaurant News **25031***
Ohio Runner (Westerville, OH) **25643**
Ohio Schools (Columbus, OH) **25049**
Ohio Shopper's Guide; South Central (Washington
Court House, OH) **25620**
Ohio Southland (Seaman, OH) *Unable to locate*
Ohio Speech Journal (Akron, OH) **24583**
Ohio Sportsman (Port Clinton, OH) **25483**
Ohio State Alumni Magazine (Columbus, OH) **25050**
Ohio State Bar Association Report (Columbus, OH)
Unable to locate
Ohio State Journal on Dispute Resolution (Columbus,
OH) **25051**
Ohio State Lantern (Columbus, OH) **25052**
Ohio Tavern News (Columbus, OH) **25053**

Ohio; TCI Cablevision of (Warren, OH) **25618**
Ohio Underwriter (Erlanger, KY) *Unable to locate*
Ohio Valley History (Louisville, KY) **12233**
Ohio Valley Retailer **25509***
Ohio Washington News Service (Washington, DC)
38028
Ohio Wesleyan Magazine (Delaware, OH) **25161**
Ohio Woodlands (Columbus, OH) *Unable to locate*
Ohio; Worker's Compensation Journal of (Cleveland,
OH) **24966**
Ohioana Quarterly (Columbus, OH) **25054**
Ohio's Country Journal (Columbus, OH) *Unable to
locate*
Ohio's Heritage (Columbus, OH) **25055**
Ohio's Outdoor Beacon **25483***
The Oil Can (Winnipeg, MB, Can.) **35347**
Oil!; Check the (Powell, OH) **25490**
Oil Chemists' Society; Journal of the American
(Champaign, IL) **8194**
The Oil Daily **30477***
Oil and Energy (Beverly, MA) **13841**
Oil and Gas (Champaign, IL) **8208**
Oil, Gas, Coal and Electricity Quarterly Statistics
(Washington, DC) **5706**
Oil and Gas Interests (Potomac, MD) **13656**
Oil and Gas Investor (Houston, TX) **30515**
Oil & Gas Journal (Houston, TX) **30516**
Oil & Gas Journal Latinoamerica (Houston, TX)
30517
Oil and Gas News; Michigan (Mount Pleasant, MI)
15377
Oil, Gas & Petrochem Equipment (Tulsa, OK) **26121**
Oil & Gas Product News (Vancouver, BC, Can.)
35154
Oil and Gas Report (West Vancouver, BC, Can.)
Ceased
Oil and Gas Reporter; The American (Derby, KS)
11406
Oil Heating Magazine (Fairfield, NJ) *Unable to locate*
Oil Laws & Concession Contracts; Asia &
Australasia—Basic (New York, NY) **21260**
Oil Laws & Concession Contracts; Central American
& Caribbean—Basic (New York, NY) **21389**
Oil Laws & Concession Contracts; Europe—Basic
(New York, NY) **21634**
Oil Laws & Concession Contracts; Middle East—
Basic (New York, NY) **22333**
Oil Laws & Concession Contracts; North Africa—
Basic (New York, NY) **22469**
Oil Laws & Concession Contracts; South America—
Basic (New York, NY) **22765**
Oil Laws & Concession Contracts; South & Central
Africa—Basic (New York, NY) **22766**
The Oil Marketer **25971***
Oil Mill Gazetteer (Houston, TX) **30518**
Oil Mill Press; Cotton Gin & (Mesquite, TX) **30807**
Oil Stocks; Institutional Holding of (Huntington, NY)
20773
The Oil Weekly **30542***
Oil; World (Houston, TX) **30542**
Oils; Chemistry and Technology of Fuels and (New
York, NY) **21407**
Oilweek (Calgary, AB, Can.) *Unable to locate*
Ojai Valley News (Ojai, CA) **2714**
Ojai Valley Shopper (Ojai, CA) **2715**
Okaloosa County Reporter (Fort Walton Beach, FL)
Unable to locate
Okaloosa News-Journal (Herndon, VA) *Ceased*
Okanagan Business Magazine (Kelowna, BC, Can.)
Unable to locate
Okanagan Falls Review (Okanagan Falls, BC, Can.)
35037
Okanagan Life Magazine (Kelowna, BC, Can.) *Unable
to locate*
Okanogan County Chronicle; The Omak- (Omak, WA)
32872
Okanogan Valley Gazette-Tribune (Oroville, WA)
32873
Okarche Chieftain (Okarche, OK) **25950**
OKC Action **25993***
Okeechobee News (Okeechobee, FL) **6481**
Okeechobee Shoppers Guide (Okeechobee, FL) **6482**
The Okeene Record (Okeene, OK) **25951**
Okemah News Leader (Okemah, OK) **25952**
Okinawa Today (Westbury, NY) *Ceased*
Oklahoma **25993***
Oklahoma Agrinet/Oklahoma News Network
(Oklahoma City, OK) **37652**
Oklahoma Banker (Oklahoma City, OK) **25973**
The Oklahoma Bar Journal (Oklahoma City, OK)
25974
Oklahoma Beverage News (Oklahoma City, OK)
25975
Oklahoma Business (Oklahoma City, OK) *Unable to
locate*
Oklahoma Business Bulletin (Norman, OK) **25938**
Oklahoma Cable Comm. (Fort Gibson, OK) **25836**
Oklahoma; The Chronicles of (Oklahoma City, OK)
25962

Oklahoma City; Cox Communications (Oklahoma City, OK) 25998
Oklahoma City Journal 25969*
Oklahoma City Living Magazine (Oklahoma City, OK) Unable to locate
Oklahoma City Trader (Oklahoma City, OK) Unable to locate
Oklahoma Country (Oklahoma City, OK) 25976
Oklahoma County News (Midwest City, OK) Unable to locate
Oklahoma COWMAN (Oklahoma City, OK) 25977
The Oklahoma Daily (Norman, OK) 25939
The Oklahoma Eagle (Tulsa, OK) 26122
Oklahoma Entertainment News (Oklahoma City, OK) 25978
Oklahoma Farm Bureau Farmer 25976*
Oklahoma Farm Bureau Journal 25976*
Oklahoma Farm Edition; Fastline— (Buckner, KY) 11989
Oklahoma Farmer-Stockman (Ponca City, OK) 26036
Oklahoma Gazette (Oklahoma City, OK) 25979
Oklahoma Geology Notes (Norman, OK) 25940
Oklahoma Grocers Journal (Oklahoma City, OK) 25980
Oklahoma Home & Lifestyle (Tulsa, OK) Ceased
The Oklahoma Hornet (Waukomis, OK) 26182
Oklahoma Living Magazine (Oklahoma City, OK) 25981
The Oklahoma Mason (Guthrie, OK) 25854
Oklahoma Motor Carrier (Oklahoma City, OK) 25982
The Oklahoma Observer (Oklahoma City, OK) 25983
The Oklahoma Odd Fellow (Stillwater, OK) Unable to locate
Oklahoma Ornithological Society; Bulletin of the (Tulsa, OK) 26107
Oklahoma; Outdoor (Oklahoma City, OK) 25990
Oklahoma Pharmacist (Oklahoma City, OK) 25984
Oklahoma Professional Engineer (Oklahoma City, OK) 25985
Oklahoma Publisher (Oklahoma City, OK) 25986
Oklahoma Retailer (Oklahoma City, OK) 25987
Oklahoma State University Magazine (Stillwater, OK) 26080
Oklahoma; TCI of (Muskogee, OK) 25926
Oklahoma; TCI Cablevision of (Alva, OK) 25740
Oklahoma Today Magazine (Oklahoma City, OK) 25988
Oklahoma Union Farmer 25963*
Oklahoman (Oklahoma City, OK) 25989
Oklahoman and Ellis County News; Northwest (Shattuck, OK) 26060
The Oklee Herald (Oklee, MN) 16242
Okmulgee Cable TV 26026*
Okmulgee Daily Times (Okmulgee, OK) Unable to locate
OKO (Lachine, QC, Can.) Unable to locate
Okolona Messenger (Okolona, MS) 16803
Okotoks Western Wheel (Okotoks, AB, Can.) 34818
Ola (Long Beach, CA) Unable to locate
The Olathe Daily News (Olathe, KS) 11683
Olathe Sun (Olathe, KS) 11684
The Old Berthoud Recorder (Berthoud, CO) 4153
Old Bike Journal (Stamford, CT) Unable to locate
Old Cars Price Guide (Iola, WI) 33840
Old Cars Weekly (Iola, WI) 33841
Old Colony Memorial (Plymouth, MA) 14479
The Old Farmer's Almanac Gardener's Companion (Dublin, NH) 18499
The Old Farmer's Almanac Good Cook's Companion (Dublin, NH) Ceased
The Old Fart (Toronto, ON, Can.) Unable to locate
Old Gold and Black (Winston-Salem, NC) 24321
Old-House Interiors (Gloucester, MA) 14210
Old-House Journal (Washington, DC) 5707
Old Huntsville (Huntsville, AL) 271
Old Lyme Pictorial (New Haven, CT) Ceased
The Old Lyons Recorder (Lyons, CO) 4570
Old Mill Marketing (Millers Falls, MA) 14335
Old Mill News (Kentwood, MI) 15264
Old News (Marietta, PA) 27221
Old Oregon 26329*
Old Sturbridge Visitor (Sturbridge, MA) 14577
Old-Time Crochet (Berne, IN) 9814
The Old-Time Herald (Durham, NC) 23839
Old Town Orono Times 12997*
Old West (Cave Creek, AZ) Ceased
The Older American (Boston, MA) 13943
The Oldham Era (La Grange, KY) 12151
Olds Gazette (Olds, AB, Can.) 34819
Oldsmar Herald (Tarpon Springs, FL) Unable to locate
Oldtimers' Hockey News 36315*
Ole Miss Alumni Review (University, MS) 16868
Olean Pennysaver 23292*
Olean Press; The Independent (Salamanca, NY) 23292
Olean Times-Herald (Olean, NY) 23040
Olentangy Valley News (Powell, OH) 25492
Olive Hill Times (Olive Hill, KY) 12326

Oliver Chronicle (Oliver, BC, Can.) 35038
Oliver Tele-Vue Ltd. 35039*
Olivia Times-Journal (Olivia, MN) 16243
Olney Daily Mail (Olney, IL) 9384
The Olney Enterprise (Olney, TX) 30885
Olney Express (Alexandria, VA) Unable to locate
Olney-Gazette (Gaithersburg, MD) Unable to locate
Olney Times (Philadelphia, PA) 27597
O'Lochlainn's Journal of Irish Families 17173*
O'Lochlainn's Personal Journal of Irish Families (Kansas City, MO) Ceased
OLOGOS (Orthodox Lore of the Gospel of Our Savior) (St. Louis, MO) Ceased
Olomeinu (Our World) (Brooklyn, NY) Unable to locate
Olshan's Sports Features (Los Angeles, CA) 38029
The Olton Enterprise (Olton, TX) 30886
Olympia Broadcasting Networks (St. Louis, MO) 37653
Olympia Genealogical Society Quarterly (Olympia, WA) 32859
Olympia News 52 (Olympia, WA) Ceased
Olympia Review (Minier, IL) 9199
The Olympian (Colorado Springs, CO) Ceased
The Olympian (Mc Lean, VA) 32251
Olympic Cablevision 32892*
Om Mani Padme Hum (Denton, TX) Unable to locate
The Omaha Business Journal (Omaha, NE) 18205
Omaha, LLC; Cox Communications, (Omaha, NE) 18210
Omaha World-Herald (Omaha, NE) 18206
The Omak-Okonogan County Chronicle (Omak, WA) 32872
Omega Cable 15594*
Omega Communications Inc. (Indianapolis, IN) 10187
OMEGA-Journal of Death and Dying (Amityville, NY) 20053
Omics: A Journal of Integrative Biology (Larchmont, NY) 20923
Omineca Express (Vanderhoof, BC, Can.) 35198
Omni (New York, NY) Unable to locate
Omnibus (Bolivar, MO) 16912
Omnibus (Piscataway, NJ) Unable to locate
L'Omnipraticien (Toronto, ON, Can.) Unable to locate
Omro Herald (Berlin, WI) 33584
On (New York, NY) 22487
On the Avenue (San Diego, CA) Ceased
On Cable (Norwalk, CT) Ceased
On Campus Hospitlaity 23555*
On Earth (New York, NY) 22488
On the Green (Bloomfield, NJ) 18688
On Indian Land (Seattle, WA) Ceased
On the Issues (Denville, NJ) Unable to locate
On the Issues (Flushing, NY) Unable to locate
On Line (New York, NY) Unable to locate
On the Line (Scottdale, PA) 27794
On Location: The Film & Videotape Production Magazine (Hollywood, CA) Unable to locate
On the Mark (Northbrook, IL) 9319
On and Off Off Broadway 22345*
On Our Backs (San Francisco, CA) Unable to locate
On Paper, The Print Collector's Newsletter 21258*
On Premise (Madison, WI) 33966
On Production 2428*
On the Road (Fords, NJ) 18828
On the Scene Magazine (Albuquerque, NM) Ceased
On Spec (Edmonton, AB, Can.) 34722
On-Stage Studies (Boulder, CO) 4183
On Target (Newark, OH) Ceased
On Target Computing (Spanaway, WA) 33091
On Target Weekly 36772*
On the Town (Jenison, MI) 15229
On Track (Tallahassee, FL) 6726
On Track (Las Vegas, NV) Unable to locate
On Trial (Seattle, WA) Unable to locate
On Wall Street (New York, NY) 22489
ON WISCONSIN (Madison, WI) 33967
Onaga Herald (Onaga, KS) 11685
Onalaska Community Life (Onalaska, WI) 34211
Onawa Democrat (Onawa, IA) 11126
The Onaway Outlook (Onaway, MI) 15420
OnCenter (Palo Alto, CA) Ceased
Oncogene Research (New York, NY) Ceased
Oncogenes & Growth Factors Abstracts (Bethesda, MD) Ceased
Oncology (Farmington, CT) 4847
Oncology (Melville, NY) 21052
Oncology; American Journal of Clinical (Baltimore, MD) 13114
Oncology; Annals of Surgical (Alexandria, VA) 31641
Oncology; Clinical (Philadelphia, PA) 27408
Oncology Clinics; Hematology/ (Philadelphia, PA) 27480
Oncology; Current Opinion in (Philadelphia, PA) 27440
Oncology; Gynecologic (San Diego, CA) 3166
Oncology; Hematological (Hoboken, NJ) 18961
Oncology Investigations; Radiation (Hoboken, NJ) 19094

Oncology; Journal of Experimental Therapeutics and (Malden, MA) 14294
Oncology; Journal of Pediatric Hematology/ (Baltimore, MD) 13199
Oncology; Journal of Psychosocial (New York, NY) 22171
Oncology; Journal of Surgical (Hoboken, NJ) 19049
Oncology; Medical and Pediatric (Hoboken, NJ) 19060
Oncology Nursing (St. Louis, MO) Ceased
Oncology Nursing; Clinical Journal of (Pittsburgh, PA) 27765
Oncology Nursing Forum (Pittsburgh, PA) 27824
Oncology Nursing Journal; Canadian (Toronto, ON, Can.) 36522
Oncology Nursing; The Journal of Pediatric (Houston, TX) 30498
Oncology Nursing; Seminars in (Philadelphia, PA) 27668
Oncology; ONS Nursing Scan in (Philadelphia, PA) 27599
Oncology; Pediatric Hematology and (Philadelphia, PA) 27616
Oncology; Seminars in (Columbia, MO) 17009
Oncology; Seminars in Radiation (Chapel Hill, NC) 23722
Oncology; Seminars in Surgical (Hoboken, NJ) 19103
Oncology; Seminars in Urologic (Philadelphia, PA) 27676
Oncology Times (Baltimore, MD) 13227
#1 Agents & Contacts (New York, NY) Ceased
One Church (Lehighton, PA) Ceased
14850 Magazine (Ithaca, NY) 20812
101 Fun Things to Do (Marble Falls, TX) 30760
128 News (Gloucester, MA) Unable to locate
One to One (Fresno, CA) 1954
One to One II (Fresno, CA) 1955
1812 (Amherst, NY) 20033
1590 Broadcaster (Nashua, NH) 18598
1907-1953: The Annual Report 36795*
The 1960 Sun (Houston, TX) 30519
1001 Home Ideas (New York, NY) Ceased
OnEarth (New York, NY) 22490
The Oneida Daily Dispatch (Oneida, NY) 23045
Oneida Edition); Pennysaver ((Clinton, NY) 20473
Oneonta Telephone Co. (Oneonta, AL) 406
Oneworld (New York, NY) 22491
Ongaku Otaku (San Francisco, CA) 3409
The Onida Watchman (Onida, SD) 28911
The Onion (Milwaukee, WI) 34091
Onion Creek Free Press 29985*
Onionhead Literary Quarterly (Lakeland, FL) 6290
Onkologie (Farmington, CT) 4848
Online (Anderson, SC) 28474
Online and CD-ROM Review (Medford, NJ) Ceased
Online Industry Litigation Reporter; Computer & (Wayne, PA) 28130
Online Journal of Knowledge Synthesis for Nursing (Philadelphia, PA) 27598
Online Learning (New York, NY) 22492
Online Mathematics and Its Applications; Journal of (Washington, DC) 5607
Online USA (Santa Monica, CA) 38030
+online user (Anderson, SC) 28475
The Onlooker (Foley, AL) Unable to locate
Only Music (On Stage Magazine) (Houston, TX) Unable to locate
Onomastica 36681*
Onomastica Canadiana (Toronto, ON, Can.) 36681
Onondaga Hill Pennysaver; Strathmore- (Syracuse, NY) 23424
Onondaga Valley News (Syracuse, NY) 23416
Onoway Community Voice (Onoway, AB, Can.) 34820
ONROADS (Rosemont, PA) Unable to locate
ONS Nursing Scan in Oncology (Philadelphia, PA) 27599
ONSAT (Shelby, NC) Unable to locate
Onsite Review (Calgary, AB, Can.) 34652
Ontario Amateur (Mississauga, ON, Can.) Unable to locate
Ontario Archaeology (Richmond Hill, ON, Can.) 36345
Ontario Beef (Guelph, ON, Can.) Unable to locate
Ontario Corn Producer (Delhi, ON, Can.) Ceased
Ontario Craft (Toronto, ON, Can.) Unable to locate
Ontario Dairy Farmer (London, ON, Can.) 35988
Ontario Dentist (Toronto, ON, Can.) 36682
Ontario; Earthkeeping (Guelph, ON, Can.) 35861
Ontario Edition; Coast Magazine— (Toronto, ON, Can.) 36552
Ontario Farm Edition; Fastline— (Buckner, KY) 11990
Ontario Farmer (London, ON, Can.) 35989
Ontario Farmer (Eastern Edition) (London, ON, Can.) Ceased
Ontario, Gazette; University of Western (London, ON, Can.) 35994
Ontario Green Sheet (Ontario, CA) 2718
Ontario History (Willowdale, ON, Can.) 36882
Ontario Hog Farmer (London, ON, Can.) 35990

Ontario Home Builder (Burlington, ON, Can.) *Unable to locate*

The Ontario Land Surveyor (Toronto, ON, Can.) **36683**

The Ontario Land Surveyor Quarterly **36683***

Ontario Lawyers Weekly **36026***

Ontario Living - London (London, ON, Can.) *Unable to locate*

Ontario Mathematics Gazette (London, ON, Can.) **35991**

Ontario Medical Review (Toronto, ON, Can.) **36684**

Ontario Medical Technologist (Toronto, ON, Can.) *Ceased*

Ontario Medicine (Toronto, ON, Can.) **36685**

Ontario Milk Producer (Mississauga, ON, Can.) **36082**

Ontario; Moving to Southwestern (Unionville, ON, Can.) **36834**

Ontario Out of Doors (Toronto, ON, Can.) **36686**

Ontario/Recherche Agro-alimentaire en Ontario; Agri-Food Research in (Guelph, ON, Can.) **35858**

Ontario Reports (Aurora, ON, Can.) *Ceased*

Ontario Restaurant News (Mississauga, ON, Can.) **36083**

Ontario Snowmobiler (Newmarket, ON, Can.) **36107**

The Ontario Technologist (Etobicoke, ON, Can.) **35818**

Ontario Tennis Association (Toronto, ON, Can.) **36687**

Ontario-TV (Toronto, ON, Can.) *Unable to locate*

Ontario's Common Ground Magazine (Toronto, ON, Can.) *Ceased*

The Ontonagon Herald (Ontonagon, MI) **15422**

Onward (Evanston, IL) *Ceased*

Oologah Lake Leader (Oologah, OK) **26027**

OP (Olympia, WA) *Ceased*

Opa Locka News; Carol City- **6359***

Opasquia Times (The Pas, MB, Can.) **35278**

OPASTCO Roundtable (Washington, DC) **5708**

Opelika-Auburn News (Opelika, AL) **409**

Open City (New York, NY) **22493**

Open Computing (San Francisco, CA) *Ceased*

Open Economies Review (New York, NY) **22494**

The Open Letter (Louisville, KY) *Ceased*

Open Road (Vancouver, BC, Can.) *Unable to locate*

Open Road USA (Chicago, IL) *Unable to locate*

Open Systems & Information Dynamics (New York, NY) **22495**

Open-to-Buy (Dallas, TX) *Ceased*

Open Wheel Magazine (New York, NY) *Unable to locate*

Open World for Accessible Travel **22496***

Open World for Disability and Mature Travel (New York, NY) **22496**

Openings (Atlanta, GA) **7034**

Opera Canada (Toronto, ON, Can.) **36688**

Opera Journal; Cambridge (New York, NY) **21368**

Opera Magazine; The Washington (Washington, DC) **5849**

Opera News (New York, NY) **22497**

The Opera Quarterly (Rochester, NY) **23234**

Operation Update (New York, NY) **22498**

Operations Engineering; IIE Transactions on (Norcross, GA) **7464**

Operations Forestieres et de Scierie (Baie D'urfe', QC, Can.) **36946**

Operations Forum (Alexandria, VA) **31719**

Operations and Fulfillment (Stamford, CT) **5157**

Operations Research (Cambridge, MA) **14087**

Operations Research; Annals of (New York, NY) **21218**

Operations Research/Management Science (Davenport, IA) **10737**

Operations Research; Mathematics of (Pittsburgh, PA) **27812**

Operative Dentistry (Indianapolis, IN) **10157**

Operative Techniques in Cataract and Refractive Surgery (Philadelphia, PA) **27600**

Operative Techniques in General Surgery (Rochester, MN) **16310**

Operative Techniques in Gynecologic Surgery (Philadelphia, PA) **27601**

Operative Techniques in Neurosurgery (Philadelphia, PA) **27602**

Operative Techniques in Oculoplastic, Orbital and Reconstructive Surgery (Philadelphia, PA) **27603**

Operative Techniques in Orthopaedics (Philadelphia, PA) **27604**

Operative Techniques in Otolaryngology (Philadelphia, PA) **27605**

Operative Techniques in Plastic and Reconstructive Surgery (Philadelphia, PA) **27606**

Operative Techniques in Sports Medicine (Philadelphia, PA) **27607**

Operative Techniques in Thoracic and Cardiovascular Surgery (Naples, FL) **6448**

Ophtalmologie); Canadian Journal of Ophthalmology (Journal Canadien d' (Ottawa, ON, Can.) **36210**

Ophthalmic Laser Therapy (Larchmont, NY) *Ceased*

Ophthalmic Plastic and Reconstructive Surgery (Baltimore, MD) **13228**

Ophthalmic Practice (Saint-Laurent, QC, Can.) *Unable to locate*

Ophthalmic Research (Farmington, CT) **4849**

Ophthalmic Surgery **19634***

Ophthalmic Surgery Lasers and Imaging (Thorofare, NJ) **19634**

Ophthalmologica (Farmington, CT) **4850**

Ophthalmology; American Journal of (New York, NY) **21196**

Ophthalmology; Annals of (Madison, CT) **4926**

Ophthalmology; Archives of (Chicago, IL) **8269**

Ophthalmology; Current Opinion in (Philadelphia, PA) **27441**

Ophthalmology Journal (Los Angeles, CA) **2352**

Ophthalmology (Journal Canadien d'Ophtalmologie); Canadian Journal of (Ottawa, ON, Can.) **36210**

Ophthalmology; Metabolic Pediatric and Systems (New York, NY) **22319**

Ophthalmology; Seminars in (Pittsburgh, PA) **27841**

Ophthalmology & Strabismus; Journal of Pediatric (Thorofare, NJ) **19624**

Ophthalmology; Survey of (New York, NY) **22812**

Ophthalmology Times (Cleveland, OH) **24938**

Ophthalmology and Visual Science; Internet Journal of (Sugar Land, TX) **31153**

Opinion; The Chinook (Chinook, MT) **17770**

Opinion Del Sur; Periodico La (Humacao, PR) **28251**

Opinion; La (Los Angeles, CA) **2312**

Opinion; Public (Decorah, IA) **10758**

Opp Cablevision (Opp, AL) **411**

The Opp News (Opp, AL) **410**

Opportunities (Evanston, IL) *Ceased*

Opportunity Magazine (New York, NY) *Unable to locate*

Opportunity Valley News (Orange, TX) **30887**

OPSEU News **36131***

Opthalmic Surgery & Lasers **19634***

Opthalmology Management **26932***

Optic-Herald (Mount Vernon, TX) **30843**

Optic-News; Wellsville (Wellsville, MO) **17715**

Optical Engineering (Bellingham, WA) **32678**

Optical Fiber Technology (San Diego, CA) **3244**

Optical Index (New York, NY) *Unable to locate*

Optical Networks Magazine (New York, NY) **22499**

Optical Physics (IJNOP); International Journal of Nonlinear (River Edge, NJ) **19511**

Optical Physics; Journal of the Optical Society of America B: (Washington, DC) **5609**

Optical Prism (Toronto, ON, Can.) **36689**

Optical Prism: Canada's Optical Goods and Service Magazine **36689***

Optical Society of America A: Optics, Image Science,and Vision; Journal of the (Washington, DC) **5608**

Optical Society of America B: Optical Physics; Journal of the (Washington, DC) **5609**

Optical Technology Letters; Microwave and (Hoboken, NJ) **19064**

Optics; Applied (Washington, DC) **5359**

Optics; Fiber and Integrated (Carlsbad, CA) **1664**

Optics, Image Science,and Vision; Journal of the Optical Society of America A: (Washington, DC) **5608**

Optics Letters (Washington, DC) **5709**

Optics News **5710***

Optics & Photonics News (Washington, DC) **5710**

Optimal Control Applications and Methods (Hoboken, NJ) **19077**

The Optimist **8207***

Optimist (Abilene, TX) **29654**

Optimist (Redvers, SK, Can.) **37524**

The Optimist Magazine (St. Louis, MO) **17478**

Optimization and Engineering (New York, NY) **22500**

Optimization; Journal of Combinatorial (New York, NY) **22030**

Optimization Theory and Applications; Journal of (Houston, TX) **30497**

Optimum (Ottawa, ON, Can.) *Unable to locate*

Option (Los Angeles, CA) **2353**

Option Serre (Quebec, QC, Can.) **37294**

Options Politiques; Policy (Montreal, QC, Can.) **37207**

Optoelectronics; International Journal of (Philadelphia, PA) **27502**

Optometric Association; Journal of the Illinois (Niles, IL) **9289**

Optometric Education (Rockville, MD) **13691**

Optometric Management (Fort Washington, PA) **26932**

Optometric Vision Development; Journal of (St. Louis, MO) **17457**

Optometrist; The Michigan (Lansing, MI) **15288**

L'Optometriste (Montreal, QC, Can.) **37198**

Optometry (St. Louis, MO) **17479**

Optometry News; Primary Care (Thorofare, NJ) **19639**

Optometry; Practical (Saint-Laurent, QC, Can.) **37366**

Optometry; Review of (Newtown Square, PA) **27333**

Optometry and Vision Science (Philadelphia, PA) *Ceased*

Optronics; Lasers & (Morris Plains, NJ) **19296**

Opuntia (Calgary, AB, Can.) **34653**

Oquawka Current (Oquawka, IL) **9386**

L'Or en Dossier (La Salle, QC, Can.) *Ceased*

OR Manager (Santa Fe, NM) **19939**

OR/MS Today (Marietta, GA) **7415**

OR/MS Today (Linthicum, MD) **13624**

The Oracle **9213***

Oracle (Tampa, FL) **6775**

The Oracle (St. Paul, MN) **16403**

The Oracle (New Paltz, NY) **21114**

The Oracle (Tulsa, OK) **26123**

The Oracle (Cookeville, TN) **29144**

Oracle Informant (Elk Grove, CA) *Ceased*

Oracle Magazine (Redwood City, CA) **2914**

Oracle Update (Westminster, CO) *Ceased*

Orah Magazine (Montreal, QC, Can.) **37199**

Oral Health (Toronto, ON, Can.) **36690**

Oral History Review (Huntsville, AL) **272**

Oral and Maxillofacial Surgery Clinics (Philadelphia, PA) **27608**

Oral and Maxillofacial Surgery; Journal of (Lexington, KY) **12168**

Oral Surgery, Oral Medicine, Oral Pathology **17480***

Oral Surgery, Oral Medicine, Oral Pathology, Oral Radiology, and Endodontics (St. Louis, MO) **17480**

Orange Bulletin **4953***

Orange City News (Anaheim, CA) *Unable to locate*

Orange Coast (Newport Beach, CA) **2634**

Orange Coast Daily Pilot **2631***

Orange Countian (Paoli, IN) **10388**

Orange County Auto World (Laguna Hills, CA) *Unable to locate*

Orange County Business First (Irvine, CA) *Unable to locate*

Orange County Business Journal (Irvine, CA) **2086**

Orange County Cablevision **21082***

(Orange County Edition); Southern California Senior Life (Los Angeles, CA) **2400**

Orange County Jewish Heritage (Los Angeles, CA) *Unable to locate*

Orange County Living (Anaheim, CA) *Unable to locate*

Orange County Magazine (Irvine, CA) *Unable to locate*

Orange County News (Garden Grove, CA) **1998**

Orange County Post (Washingtonville, NY) **23512**

Orange County Preview (San Clemente, CA) *Unable to locate*

Orange County Register (Santa Ana, CA) **3630**

Orange County Reporter (Los Angeles, CA) *Unable to locate*

Orange County Review (Orange, VA) **32321**

Orange County; WHERE (Costa Mesa, CA) **1782**

The Orange Leader (Orange, TX) **30888**

Orange Seed Technical Bulletin (Tallahassee, FL) **6727**

Orange Source (Syracuse, NY) **23417**

Orange Town Crier; The Athol/ (Greenfield, MA) **14219**

Orange Transcript (Orange, NJ) **19396**

Orangeburg Black Voice (Orangeburg, SC) **28731**

Orangevale News/Citrus Heights News (San Diego, CA) *Ceased*

Orangevale Shopper (Folsom, CA) *Unable to locate*

The Orangeville Banner (Orangeville, ON, Can.) **36172**

Orangeville Citizen (Orangeville, ON, Can.) **36173**

L'Oratoire (Montreal, QC, Can.) **37200**

The Oratory (Montreal, QC, Can.) **37201**

Orbis (Philadelphia, PA) *Unable to locate*

The Orbit (Wayland, MI) *Ceased*

Orbit Magazine (Royal Oak, MI) *Ceased*

Orbit Video (Fairfax, VA) *Ceased*

Orchard News (Orchard, NE) **18235**

Orchard Park Bee (Orchard Park, NY) **23057**

Orchard Park Pennysaver (Orchard Park, NY) **23058**

Orchid Advocate (Leucadia, CA) *Unable to locate*

Orchid Isle Television (Birmingham, AL) **84**

Orchid Journal; Hawaii (Waianae, HI) **7794**

The Ord Quiz (Ord, NE) **18236**

Order (New York, NY) **22501**

The Ordway New Era (Ordway, CO) **4589**

The Ore Bin **26491***

Oredigger; Mines (Golden, CO) **4471**

Oregon Beef Producer (Salem, OR) **26569**

Oregon Beverage Analyst (Denver, CO) *Ceased*

Oregon Broadcasting Inc.; California- (Medford, OR) **37687**

Oregon Business Magazine (Portland, OR) *Unable to locate*

Oregon Cattleman **26569***

Oregon City Enterprise-Courier (Oregon City, OR) *Ceased*

Oregon Coast (Florence, OR) **26352**

Oregon Computing Teacher **26322***

Oregon Daily Emerald (Eugene, OR) **26328**

The Oregon Episcopal Church News (Portland, OR) **26490**

Oregon Episcopal Churchman 26490*
Oregon FarmekraHJJmpw- (Concord, CA) 1754
Oregon Food Journal 26615*
Oregon Geology (Portland, OR) 26491
Oregon Grange Bulletin (Portland, OR) *Unable to locate*
Oregon Grocery Line (Wilsonville, OR) 26615
Oregon Historical Quarterly (Portland, OR) 26492
Oregon, Inc.; TCI Cablevision of (Burns, OR) 26262
Oregon Observer (Oregon, WI) 34218
Oregon Peaceworker (Salem, OR) 26570
Oregon Pharmacist (Wilsonville, OR) 26616
Oregon Publisher (Portland, OR) 26493
Oregon Purchasor Magazine (Portland, OR) *Ceased*
Oregon Quarterly (Eugene, OR) 26329
Oregon Secretary of State Administration Rule Compilation (Salem, OR) 26571
Oregon State Bar Bulletin (Lake Oswego, OR) 26405
Oregon Stater (Corvallis, OR) 26289
Oregon; TCI Cablevision of (Eugene, OR) 26350
Oregon; TCI Cablevision of (Medford, OR) 26433
Oregon; TCI Cablevision of (Portland, OR) 26547
Oregon Teamster (Portland, OR) 26494
Oregon/Washington Labor Press 26487*
Oregon Wheat (Pendleton, OR) 26459
The Oregonian (Portland, OR) 26495
Oregonian; Central (Prineville, OR) 26548
Oregonian; East (Pendleton, OR) 26458
Orem-Geneva Times (Orem, UT) 31385
Orfordville Journal and Footville News (Orfordville, WI) 34220
Organbuilding; Journal of American (Houston, TX) 30495
Organic Chemistry; Journal of Physical (Hoboken, NJ) 19041
Organic Chemistry; Russian Journal of (New York, NY) 22693
Organic Farmer (Montpelier, VT) *Ceased*
Organic Farmer and Gardener; Maine (Lincolnville, ME) 12982
Organic Gardening (Emmaus, PA) 26879
Organic Letters (Washington, DC) 5711
Organic Mass Spectrometry 19029*
Organic Preparations and Procedures International (Boston, MA) 13944
Organic Process Research & Development (Columbus, OH) 25056
Organist; The American (New York, NY) 21203
Organization Development Journal (Chesterland, OH) 24760
Organization; International Studies of Management & (New York, NY) 21937
Organization Management; Group & (Albany, NY) 19989
Organization Science (Irvine, CA) 2087
Organizational Behavior and Human Decision Processes (San Diego, CA) 3245
Organizational Behavior; Journal of (Hoboken, NJ) 19037
Organizational Behavior-Management; Journal of (Detroit, MI) 14934
Organizational Behavior Teaching Review 9300*
Organizational Dynamics (New York, NY) 22502
Organizational Excellence; Journal of (Hoboken, NJ) 19038
Organometallic Chemistry; Applied (Hoboken, NJ) 18893
Organometallics (Washington, DC) *Unable to locate*
Organs; Cells Tissues (Farmington, CT) 4804
Orgonomic Functionalism (Rangeley, ME) 13043
Orient (Montreal, QC, Can.) 37202
Oriental Insects (Gainesville, FL) 6152
Oriental; Periodico El (Humacao, PR) 28249
Oriental Rug Review (Meredith, NH) *Ceased*
Oriental Society; Journal of the American (Boulder, CO) 4173
The Original Entertainer 25978*
Original Internist (Rolla, MO) 17378
The "Original" Marshall County Shopper (Lewisburg, TN) *Unable to locate*
The Original Pennysaver (Brea, CA) 1599
Origination News (New York, NY) 22503
Origins (Washington, DC) *Unable to locate*
Origins of Life and Evolution of the Biosphere (New York, NY) 22504
Orillia Today (Midland, ON, Can.) 36044
The Orion (Chico, CA) 1695
Orion (Great Barrington, MA) 14216
Orion Gazette (Geneseo, IL) 8916
Orion Nature Quarterly, Orion: People and Nature 14216*
The Orion Times (Geneseo, IL) *Unable to locate*
ORL (Farmington, CT) 4851
Orland Park Star (Orland Park, IL) 9389
Orland Press-Register (Willows, CA) 4087
Orland Township Messenger (Midlothian, IL) 9192
Orlando Business Journal (Orlando, FL) 6502
Orlando Magazine (Winter Park, FL) *Unable to locate*
Orlando Reporter (Apopka, FL) *Ceased*

The Orlando Sentinel (Orlando, FL) 6503
The Orlando Times (Orlando, FL) 6504
Orlando Weekly (Orlando, FL) 6505
Orlando; WHERE (Orlando, FL) 6510
Orleans Magazine (Orleans, ON, Can.) *Unable to locate*
Orleans Oracle (Yarmouth Port, MA) 14703
Orleans Shopper (Medina, NY) 21038
The Orleans Star 36178*
Orleans Star (Montreal, QC, Can.) *Unable to locate*
Ornament Magazine (Vista, CA) *Unable to locate*
Ornamental Miscellaneous Metal Fabricator (Forest Park, GA) 7276
Ornamental Outlook (Winter Park, FL) 6884
Ornamentals Northwest (Corvallis, OR) 26290
Ornithological Society; Bulletin of the Oklahoma (Tulsa, OK) 26107
Oro Puro (Palm Desert, CA) *Ceased*
The Oro Valley Territorial *Ceased*
Oro Valley Voice (Tucson, AZ) *Ceased*
Orofacial Pain; Journal of (Carol Stream, IL) 8146
The Oromocto Post-Gazette (Oromocto, NB, Can.) 35424
Orono/Long Lake Sun-Sailor; Wayzata/ (Plymouth, MN) 16280
Orono Weekly Times (Orono, ON, Can.) 36179
Oroville Mercury-Register 1692*
Oroville Shopping News (Oroville, CA) 2729
Orthodontics and Dentofacial Orthopedics; American Journal of (St. Louis, MO) 17411
Orthodontics; Journal of Clinical (Boulder, CO) 4174
Orthodontist; The Functional (Winchester, VA) 32629
The Orthodox Catholic Voice (Akron, OH) 24584
Orthodox Christian Journal (Harrisburg, PA) 27001
Orthodox Life (Jordanville, NY) 20854
Orthodox Observer (New York, NY) 22505
The Orthodox Word (Platina, CA) 2850
Orthomolecular Medicine; Journal of (Toronto, ON, Can.) 36636
Orthopaedic Nursing (Pitman, NJ) 19438
Orthopaedic Review 18726*
Orthopaedic Surgeons Bulletin; The American Academy of (Old Tappan, NJ) 19393
Orthopaedic Surgeons; Journal of the American Academy of (Old Tappan, NJ) 19394
Orthopaedic Trauma; Journal of (Baltimore, MD) 13197
Orthopaedics; Contemporary (Torrance, CA) 3930
Orthopaedics; Current Opinion in (Philadelphia, PA) 27442
Orthopaedics; Journal of Pediatric (Baltimore, MD) 13200
Orthopaedics; Operative Techniques in (Philadelphia, PA) 27604
Orthopaedics, Part B.; Journal of Pediatric (Philadelphia, PA) 27544
Orthopaedics and Related Research; Clinical (Baltimore, MD) 13149
Orthopaedics; Techniques in (Baltimore, MD) 13252
Orthopaedics Today International (Thorofare, NJ) 19635
The Orthopedic Clinics (Philadelphia, PA) 27609
Orthopedic Product News (New York, NY) *Ceased*
Orthopedic Products (Los Angeles, CA) *Ceased*
Orthopedic Special Edition (New York, NY) 22506
Orthopedic Surgery Edition; Medical Economics— (Montvale, NJ) 19264
Orthopedic Surgery; Internet Journal of (Sugar Land, TX) 31154
Orthopedics (Thorofare, NJ) 19636
Orthopedics; American Journal of Orthodontics and Dentofacial (St. Louis, MO) 17411
Orthopedics Today (Thorofare, NJ) 19637
Orthopsychiatry; American Journal of (New York, NY) 21197
Orthoptic Journal; American (Madison, WI) 33917
Orthotics; JPO: Journal of Prosthetics & (Alexandria, VA) 31704
Orting Valley (Orting, WA) *Ceased*
The Ortonville Independent (Ortonville, MN) 16245
Orwell Cable TV Co. (Orwell, OH) *Unable to locate*
OS/2 Magazine 21018*
OS/2 and Windows Magazine 21018*
OSA Messenger (Pittsburgh, PA) *Unable to locate*
Osage City Journal Free-Press 11369*
Osage County Chronicle (Burlingame, KS) 11369
Osage County Journal (Osage City, KS) *Ceased*
The Osage County Review 26071*
Osawatomie Graphic (Paola, KS) 11742
Osborne Cable Television Inc. 11599*
Osborne County Farmer (Osborne, KS) 11686
Osceola County Gazette-Tribune (Sibley, IA) 11202
Osceola News-Gazette (Kissimmee, FL) 6262
Osceola Record 18239*
Osceola Sentinel-Tribune (Osceola, IA) *Unable to locate*
Osceola Sentinel-Tribune (Osceola, IA) 11133
Osceola Shopper (Kissimmee, FL) 6263
Osceola Times (Osceola, AR) 1304

Oscoda Press (Oscoda, MI) 15425
OSERS News in Print (Washington, DC) *Ceased*
Osgood Journal (Versailles, IN) 10516
Osgoode Hall Law Journal (Toronto, ON, Can.) 36691
The Oshawa Times (Oshawa, ON, Can.) *Unable to locate*
Oshawa-Whitby-Clarington-Port Perry This Week (Oshawa, ON, Can.) 36181
Oshawa-Whitby-Clarington This Week 36181*
Oshkaabewis Native Journal (Bemidji, MN) 15738
Oshkosh Advance-Titan (Oshkosh, WI) 34226
Oshkosh Advance-Titan and Normal Advance 34226*
Oshkosh Buyers' Guide (Oshkosh, WI) 34227
Osiris (Chicago, IL) 8517
The Oskaloosa Herald (Oskaloosa, IA) 11134
The Oskaloosa Independent (Oskaloosa, KS) 11687
Oskaloosa Shopper (Oskaloosa, IA) 11135
Osmond Republican (Osmond, NE) 18241
Osoyoos Times (Osoyoos, BC, Can.) 35042
OSP Engineering & Construction (Nashua, NH) *Ceased*
Osseo-Maple Grove Press (Osseo, MN) 16249
The Ossian Bee (Ossian, IA) 11139
The Ossian Journal (Ossian, IN) 10385
Ossining Citizen Register (Mc Lean, VA) 32252
OSSTF Forum 36579*
Ostentatious Mind (New York, NY) *Unable to locate*
Osteoarchaeology; International Journal of (Hoboken, NJ) 18993
Osteopathic Association; Journal of the American (Chicago, IL) 8432
Osteopathic Hospital Leadership Magazine (Washington, DC) *Unable to locate*
Osteopathic Medical Association; Journal of the Pennsylvania (Harrisburg, PA) 26996
Osteopathic Medical News (Newtown, PA) *Ceased*
Osteoporosis International (New York, NY) 22507
Ostomy, and Continence Nursing; Journal of WOCN (Wound, (St. Louis, MO) 17464
Ostomy Quarterly (Irvine, CA) 2088
Ostomy/Wound Management (Malvern, PA) 27215
Oswego Independent-Observer (Oswego, KS) 11688
Oswego/Montgomery Sun (Naperville, IL) *Ceased*
Oswego Valley News 20631*
The Oswegonian (Oswego, NY) 23061
OT Practice (Bethesda, MD) 13370
OT Week 13370*
OTC Chart Manual (New York, NY) *Ceased*
OTEC Communication Co. (Ottoville, OH) 25453
Otero County Shopper (Alamogordo, NM) *Unable to locate*
OTF (FEO) Interaction (Toronto, ON, Can.) 36692
The Othello Outlook (Othello, WA) 32875
Other; The Daily (Jacksonville, IL) 9022
Other Press (New Westminster, BC, Can.) 35030
The Other Side (Philadelphia, PA) 27610
The Other Side of the Lake (Chicago, IL) 8518
Other Voices (Chicago, IL) 8519
Oto-Rhino-Laryngologia Nova (Farmington, CT) 4852
The Otolaryngologic Clinics (Philadelphia, PA) 27611
Otolaryngology; American Journal of (Philadelphia, PA) 27373
Otolaryngology—Head and Neck Surgery (New York, NY) 22508
Otolaryngology—Head & Neck Surgery; Archives of (Chicago, IL) 8270
The Otolaryngology Journal (Baltimore, MD) 13229
Otolaryngology; Operative Techniques in (Philadelphia, PA) 27605
Otology; The American Journal of 13230*
Otology & Neurotology (Baltimore, MD) 13230
Otology, Rhinology and Laryngology; Annals of (St. Louis, MO) 17415
O'Toole; Tom & Joanne (Willoughby, OH) 38100
Ottawa Advance (Coopersville, MI) 14891
Ottawa Business Journal (Ottawa, ON, Can.) 36264
Ottawa Business Quarterly (Ottawa, ON, Can.) *Unable to locate*
The Ottawa Citizen (Ottawa, ON, Can.) 36265
Ottawa Computes! (Toronto, ON, Can.) *Unable to locate*
The Ottawa Construction News (Nepean, ON, Can.) 36101
The Ottawa County Exponent (Oak Harbor, OH) 25442
Ottawa Families (Vancouver, BC, Can.) *Ceased*
Ottawa Herald (Ottawa, KS) 11689
Ottawa Jewish Bulletin (Ottawa, ON, Can.) 36266
Ottawa Law Review (Ottawa, ON, Can.) 36267
Ottawa Magazine (Ottawa, ON, Can.) *Unable to locate*
Ottawa/Outaouais; Moving to (Unionville, ON, Can.) 36832
Ottawa Pennysaver (Nepean, ON, Can.) *Unable to locate*
Ottawa Spirit (Ottawa, KS) 11690
Ottawa Sun (Ottawa, ON, Can.) 36268
Ottawa Sunday Herald (Ottawa, ON, Can.) *Ceased*

P

Pacific Northwest Cable (Newport, WA) *Unable to locate*
Pacific Northwest Executive (Seattle, WA) *Ceased*
The Pacific Northwest Inlander (Spokane, WA) **33097**
Pacific Northwest Quarterly (Seattle, WA) **33001**
Pacific Oil **30475***
Pacific Oil World (New York, NY) *Ceased*
Pacific Purchasor (Burbank, CA) *Ceased*
(Pacific Review); Pazifische Rundschau (Richmond, BC, Can.) **35075**
Pacific Rim Business Digest (Santa Monica, CA) *Unable to locate*
Pacific Science (Honolulu, HI) **7715**
Pacific Shipper (Long Beach, CA) **2172**
Pacific Sun (Mill Valley, CA) **2541**
Pacific Tech **28092***
Pacific Telecommunications Review (Honolulu, HI) **7716**
Pacific, The Monterey Bay **1672***
Pacific Ties (Los Angeles, CA) **2357**
Pacific Traffic (Long Beach, CA) *Unable to locate*
Pacific Tribune (Vancouver, BC, Can.) *Unable to locate*
Pacific Union Recorder (Westlake Village, CA) **4072**
Pacific West Cable Television **3064***
Pacific Yachting (Vancouver, BC, Can.) **35158**
Pacifica Network News (Washington, DC) **37654**
Pacifica Tribune (Pacifica, CA) **2738**
The Pacifican (Stockton, CA) **3806**
Pacing and Clinical Electrophysiology; PACE: (Armonk, NY) **20090**
Pack-O-Fun (Des Plaines, IL) **8766**
Package Printing (Falls Church, VA) **32051**
Package Printing and Converting **32051***
Packaging; Advanced (Nashua, NH) **18581**
Packaging; Canadian (Toronto, ON, Can.) **36523**
Packaging and Converting Hotline (Fort Dodge, IA) **10906**
Packaging Digest (Bensenville, IL) *Unable to locate*
Packaging Digest (New York, NY) **22517**
Packaging; Food & Drug (St. Charles, IL) **9568**
Packaging Hotline **10906***
Packaging & Manufacturing Technology, Part A; IEEE Transactions on Components, (College Park, MD) **13420**
Packaging & Manufacturing Technology, Part B; IEEE Transactions on Components, (Piscataway, NJ) **19426**
Packaging & Manufacturing Technology, Part C; IEEE Transactions on Components, (Piscataway, NJ) **19427**
Packaging & Production; Electronic (New York, NY) **21593**
Packaging Strategies (Troy, MI) **15631**
Packaging Technology and Science (Hoboken, NJ) **19078**
Packaging World (Chicago, IL) **8524**
Packard Cormorant (Brentwood, CA) **1603**
The Packer (Lenexa, KS) **11594**
Packer Report (Sun Prairie, WI) *Unable to locate*
Packer/Shipper (Yakima, WA) *Ceased*
Packerland Trader (Appleton, WI) *Unable to locate*
Packet (St. John's, NL, Can.) **35493**
Packet/Ledger Extra (Princeton, NJ) *Ceased*
Packet and Times; Daily (Orillia, ON, Can.) **36174**
The Packet & Times This Week (Orillia, ON, Can.) **36176**
Pacolet Tribune; Cowpens/ (Cowpens, SC) **28594**
Paddle Sports (Santa Clara, CA) *Unable to locate*
Paddler (Toronto, ON, Can.) *Unable to locate*
Paducah; Comcast Cablevision of (Paducah, KY) **12341**
The Paducah Post (Paducah, TX) **30893**
The Paducah Sun (Paducah, KY) **12339**
Pagan Muse & World Report (San Jose, CA) *Ceased*
Page News and Courier (Luray, VA) **32203**
Pageantry (Altamonte Springs, FL) **5902**
Pageantry Press **2488***
Pageantry; World of (Lynwood, CA) **2488**
The Pageland Progressive-Journal (Pageland, SC) **28739**
PageMarker In-Depth (Concord, MA) *Unable to locate*
The Pagosa Springs Sun (Pagosa Springs, CO) **4590**
Pagosa Vision Inc. (Union Springs, AL) *Ceased*
Pahrump Valley Times (Pahrump, NV) **18414**
Pain Digest (New York, NY) **22518**
Pain; Journal of (Philadelphia, PA) **27542**
Pain; Journal of Musculosketal (San Antonio, TX) **31035**
Pain Management Nursing (San Francisco, CA) **3411**
Pain Management; Techniques in Regional Anesthesia and (Buffalo, NY) **20389**
The Pain Medicine Journal (Baltimore, MD) **13231**
Pain Medicine; Regional Anesthesia and (Seattle, WA) **33014**
Pain and Palliative Care Pharmacotherapy; Journal of (Salt Lake City, UT) **31435**
Pain; Seminars in Anesthesia, Perioperative Medicine and (Philadelphia, PA) **27658**

Pain, Symptom Control and Palliative Care; Internet Journal of (Sugar Land, TX) **31155**
Paint & Coatings Industry (Troy, MI) **15632**
Paint and Coatings Journal; American (Loveland, CO) **4565**
Paint and Coatings; Modern (Atlanta, GA) **7027**
Paint & Decorating Retailer (Fenton, MO) **17063**
Paint Horse Journal (Fort Worth, TX) **30350**
Paint and Powder; Industrial (Bensenville, IL) **8068**
Paint Works (Newton, NJ) **19373**
Paintball Magazine (Burbank, CA) **1622**
Painted Bride Quarterly (Philadelphia, PA) *Unable to locate*
Painter; The China (Oklahoma City, OK) **25960**
Painting (Des Plaines, IL) **8767**
Painting Contractor; American (Colorado Springs, CO) **4235**
Painting & Wallcovering Contractor (St. Louis, MO) **17481**
The Paintsville Herald (Paintsville, KY) **12349**
The Paisley Advocate (Paisley, ON, Can.) *Unable to locate*
PAJ: A Journal of Performing (New York, NY) **22519**
Pakeeza International (Oakville, ON, Can.) **36150**
Pakistan (Fontana, CA) **1919**
Palacios Beacon (Palacios, TX) **30894**
The Paladin (Greenville, SC) **28625**
PALAESTRA (Macomb, IL) **9131**
Palate and Spirit (San Francisco, CA) **3412**
Palatine Countryside (Palatine, IL) **9395**
Palatka Daily News (Palatka, FL) **6537**
Paleobiology (Washington, DC) **5713**
PaleoBios (Berkeley, CA) **1549**
Paleoclimates (Tucson, AZ) **958**
Paleolimnology; Journal of (New York, NY) **22150**
Paleontological Journal (Birmingham, AL) **85**
Paleontology; Journal of (Lawrence, KS) **11557**
Palestine Herald-Press (Palestine, TX) **30897**
Palestine Studies; Journal of (Washington, DC) **5610**
The Palimpsest, Palimpsest **10975***
The Palisade Tribune and Valley Report (Palisade, CO) **4593**
The Palisadian (Oradell, NJ) *Unable to locate*
Palisadian-Post (Pacific Palisades, CA) **2736**
Palladium-Item (Richmond, IN) **10420**
The Palladium-Times (Oswego, NY) **23062**
Pallet Digest (Wadley, GA) *Ceased*
Pallet Enterprise (Ashland, VA) **31857**
Palliative Care; American Journal of Hospice and (Weston, MA) **14649**
Palliative Care; Internet Journal of Pain, Symptom Control and (Sugar Land, TX) **31155**
Palliative Care; Journal of (Montreal, QC, Can.) **37144**
Palliative Medicine (New York, NY) *Ceased*
Palm Beach County Visions (West Palm Beach, FL) *Unable to locate*
Palm Beach Daily Business Review (West Palm Beach, FL) **6847**
Palm Beach Daily News (Palm Beach, FL) **6542**
Palm Beach Gardens/North Palm Beach Thursday Paper (Chicago, IL) *Ceased*
Palm Beach Illustrated (Palm Beach, FL) **6543**
Palm Beach Jewish Journal **9750***
Palm Beach Jewish Journal **8525***
Palm Beach Jewish Journal North (Chicago, IL) **8525**
Palm Beach Jewish Journal South (West Palm Beach, IL) **9750**
Palm Beach Life (Palm Beach, FL) *Ceased*
Palm Beach; New Times Broward- (Fort Lauderdale, FL) **6081**
The Palm Beach Post (West Palm Beach, FL) **6848**
Palm Beach Review **6847***
Palm Beach Society Magazine (Palm Beach, FL) **6544**
Palm Beach and The Naples Times (West Palm Beach, FL) **6849**
Palm Beach Times **6849***
Palm Cable Inc. **6549***
Palm Coast Cablevision Ltd. (Palm Coast, FL) **6549**
Palm Desert Post **1679***
Palm Harbor Sounder; The Dunedin Times/The (Dunedin, FL) **6061**
Palm Springs; Key Magazine (Scottsdale, AZ) **870**
Palm Springs Life (Palm Springs, CA) **2763**
Palm Springs Life's Desert Guide (Palm Springs, CA) **2764**
Palmer Video Magazine (Westfield, NJ) **19744**
Palmer Video News (Westfield, NJ) **19745**
Palmerston Observer (Palmerston, ON, Can.) **36305**
Palmetto Bay News (Homestead, FL) **6204**
Palmetto Cable TV (Fort Mill, SC) **28613**
Palmetto Pharmacist (Columbia, SC) **28558**
Palmetto Piper (Columbia, SC) **28559**
Palmetto Poultry Life (Columbia, SC) **28560**
Palmyra Enterprise (Palmyra, WI) **34232**
Palmyra Spectator (Palmyra, MO) **17331**
Palo Altan (Minneapolis, MN) *Unable to locate*
Palo Alto Daily News (Palo Alto, CA) **2800**

The Palo Alto Times *Ceased*
Palo Alto Weekly (Palo Alto, CA) **2801**
Palo Pinto Shopper (Weatherford, TX) *Ceased*
Palo Verde Valley Times (Blythe, CA) **1587**
Palomino Horses (Tulsa, OK) **26124**
Palos Area Star (Tinley Park, IL) **9687**
Palos Citizen (Midlothian, IL) **9193**
Palos Hills-Hickory Hills **9398***
Palos Regional **9397***
Palos Verdes Peninsula News (Palos Verdes Peninsula, CA) **2804**
Palynologists Contributions Series; American Association of Stratigraphic (College Station, TX) **30036**
Palynology (College Station, TX) **30047**
The Pampa News (Pampa, TX) **30900**
Pan Am Clipper *Unable to locate*
The Pan American (Edinburg, TX) **30271**
Pan-Japan (Normal, IL) **9302**
The Pan-Pacific Entomologist (San Jose, CA) **3530**
Pana News-Palladium (Pana, IL) *Unable to locate*
Panamericanos; Textiles (Greenville, SC) **28627**
Pancreas (Baltimore, MD) **13232**
Pandemonium **33151***
Pandora (Ferndale, MI) *Unable to locate*
Pandora Times **25091***
Pandora Times; Putnam County Vidette/ (Columbus Grove, OH) **25091**
Panel World (Montgomery, AL) **373**
Pangolin Papers (Nordland, WA) **32853**
Panhandle Herald (Panhandle, TX) **30903**
The Panhandle Press (Raymond, IL) **9489**
Panhandle Press (Lisbon, OH) *Unable to locate*
Panjandrum Poetry Journal (North Hollywood, CA) *Ceased*
PAN*NET **5468***
Panola Post-Watchman **30904***
Panola Watchman (Panola, TX) **30904**
The Panolian (Batesville, MS) **16550**
Panora Cooperative Cablevision Assoc. Inc. (Panora, IA) **11148**
Panorama (Boston, MA) **13946**
Panorama; Porsche (Atlanta, GA) **7038**
The Pantagraph (Bloomington, IL) **8079**
Pantera International News (Huntington Beach, CA) *Unable to locate*
Panther (Orange, CA) **2725**
The Panther Magazine **36917***
Panther Prints (Charlottetown, PE, Can.) **36917**
Panthers' Plus, Canadian Grey Panthers (Toronto, ON, Can.) **36695**
The Paper **6506***
The Paper (Orlando, FL) **6506**
The Paper (Barry, IL) **8049**
The Paper (Wabash, IN) **10528**
The Paper (Greenville, SC) *Ceased*
Paper Age (Glen Rock, NJ) **18847**
Paper Boat Press (Poulsbo, WA) *Ceased*
The Paper Book (Elyria, OH) **25179**
Paper Canada; Pulp & (Pointe-Claire, QC, Can.) **37277**
Paper; City (Philadelphia, PA) **27405**
Paper Clips (Bridgewater, NJ) **18698**
The Paper Cut (Montreal, QC, Can.) **37203**
The Paper (Elkhart County Edition) (Goshen, IN) **10027**
Paper, Film & Foil Converter (Chicago, IL) **8526**
The Paper (Goshen Edition) (Goshen, IN) **10028**
Paper Industry (Montgomery, AL) **374**
Paper Industry Equipment **374***
Paper International; Pulp & (Manhasset, NY) **21012**
The Paper (Kosciusko Edition) (Warsaw, IN) **10536**
Paper Lantern **3139***
Paper Magazine (New York, NY) **22520**
Paper Money (Dallas, TX) **30175**
Paper, Paperboard, and Wood Pulp Monthly Statistical Summary (Washington, DC) **5714**
Paper; Park Slope (Brooklyn, NY) **20335**
Paper; Pulp and (San Francisco, CA) **3419**
Paper Radio (Portland, OR) *Ceased*
Paper Recycling; Progress in (Appleton, WI) **33543**
Paper Retailer; Party & (Danbury, CT) **4749**
Paper Science; Journal of Pulp & (Montreal, QC, Can.) **37145**
Paper Science and Technology; Abstract Bulletin of the Institute of (Hoboken, NJ) **18880**
Paper & Twine Journal (Brooklyn, NY) *Unable to locate*
Paperboard Packaging Worldwide (Cleveland, OH) **24939**
Paperboard, and Wood Pulp Monthly Statistical Summary; Paper, (Washington, DC) **5714**
Paperplates (Toronto, ON, Can.) **36696**
Papers of the Bibliographical Society of America (Columbia, SC) **28561**
Papers on Language & Literature (Edwardsville, IL) **8814**
PaperTronix **31720***

Peninsula Business Journal (Sequim, WA) 33076
Peninsula Clarion (Kenai, AK) 607
Peninsula Daily News (Port Angeles, WA) 32888
Peninsula Gateway (Gig Harbor, WA) 32774
Peninsula Magazine (Redwood City, CA) Ceased
The Peninsula News Review (Sidney, BC, Can.)
    Unable to locate
Peninsula Times Tribune (Palo Alto, CA) Ceased
The Penn (Indiana, PA) 27076
Penn Dental Journal (Philadelphia, PA) 27620
Penn Franklin News (Murrysville, PA) 27307
Penn Hills Progress Star (Monroeville, PA) 27282
Penn Lines (Harrisburg, PA) 27004
Penn-Mar CATV 26978*
Penn State; Research/ (University Park, PA) 28083
The Penn Stater (University Park, PA) 28081
Penn Treaty Guide (Philadelphia, PA) Unable to
    locate
Penn Valley Times (Souderton, PA) Ceased
Penneysaver 34293*
Pennington County Courant (Wall, SD) 29016
Pennisula Reporter (Millbrae, CA) 2544
The Pennsboro News (Pennsboro, WV) 33428
Pennsylvania Bar News (Harrisburg, PA) 27005
Pennsylvania Business Journal; Northeast
    (Bloomsburg, PA) 26717
Pennsylvania Civil Appellate Reporter (Wayne, PA)
    Ceased
Pennsylvania Classic Cable Corp. (Philadelphia, PA)
    Unable to locate
Pennsylvania Classic Cable TV (East Berlin, PA)
    Unable to locate
Pennsylvania Collector; The New York- (Canandaigua,
    NY) 20422
Pennsylvania Contractor (Harrisburg, PA) Unable to
    locate
Pennsylvania CPA Journal (Philadelphia, PA) 27621
Pennsylvania Dental Journal (Harrisburg, PA) 27006
Pennsylvania Farm & Dairy (Ithaca, NY) Ceased
Pennsylvania Farmer (Carol Stream, IL) Unable to
    locate
Pennsylvania Forests (Mechanicsburg, PA) 27240
Pennsylvania Game News (Harrisburg, PA) 27007
Pennsylvania Gazette (Philadelphia, PA) 27622
The Pennsylvania Geographer (Johnstown, PA) 27088
Pennsylvania Heritage (Harrisburg, PA) 27008
Pennsylvania History (State College, PA) 28019
Pennsylvania Inc.; TCI of (Kane, PA) 27104
Pennsylvania Journal of International Economic Law;
    University of (Philadelphia, PA) 27713
Pennsylvania Law Weekly Ceased
The Pennsylvania Lawyer (Harrisburg, PA) 27009
Pennsylvania Magazine (Camp Hill, PA) 26753
Pennsylvania Magazine of History and Biography
    (Philadelphia, PA) 27623
Pennsylvania Medicine (Harrisburg, PA) 27010
Pennsylvania Mennonite Heritage (Lancaster, PA)
    27145
Pennsylvania Osteopathic Medical Association;
    Journal of the (Harrisburg, PA) 26996
Pennsylvania Pharmacist (Harrisburg, PA) 27011
The Pennsylvania Police Criminal Law Bulletin
    (Pittsburgh, PA) 27826
Pennsylvania Public Television Network (Hershey, PA)
    37711
Pennsylvania Township News (Enola, PA) 26886
Pennsylvania; Voices of Central (State College, PA)
    28022
Pennsylvanian (Harrisburg, PA) Ceased
Penntrux (Camp Hill, PA) 26754*
PennWell Publishing Co. 18594*
Penny Pincher (Grand Junction, CO) Ceased
Penny Pincher; Shopping News/ (Sonoma, CA) 3776
Penny Power 23604*
Penny Power (Coopersburg, PA) 26807
Penny Press 8 (Syracuse, NE) Ceased
Penny Press 5 (Beatrice, NE) 17948
Penny Press 4 (Hiawatha, KS) 11492
Penny Press 1 (Nebraska City, NE) 18167
Penny Press 7 18026*
Penny Press 6 18026*
Penny Press 6 (Syracuse, NE) Unable to locate
Penny Press 3 (Syracuse, NE) Ceased
Penny Press 2 (Maryville, MO) 17276
Penny Saver (Mascoutah, IL) Ceased
The Penny Saver (Tinley Park, IL) 9688
Penny Saver (South Bend, IN) Ceased
Penny Saver (Cedar Rapids, IA) 10676
Penny Saver (Three Rivers, MI) Unable to locate
The Penny Saver (Plymouth, NH) 18633
Penny Saver (Covington, OH) 25099
Penny-Saver (Mansfield, PA) 27219
Penny Wise/Exchange (Roselle, IL) Unable to locate
Pennypower Shopping News (Topeka, KS) Unable to
    locate
Pennypower Shopping News (Springfield, MO) 17609
Pennysaver 23532*
The Pennysaver 36364*
The Pennysaver 32642*

Pennysaver 7659*
PennySaver (Brea, CA) 1601
Pennysaver (Brea, CA) 1600
Pennysaver (Plantation, FL) 6588
Pennysaver (Monmouth, IL) 9218
PennySaver (Harlan, IA) 10943
Pennysaver (Marshalltown, IA) 11065
Pennysaver (Hanover, MD) 13580
Pennysaver (Reno, NV) 18422
Pennysaver (Mount Holly, NJ) Unable to locate
The Pennysaver (Elmsford, NY) 20583
Pennysaver (Farmingdale, NY) 20596
Pennysaver (Ebensburg, PA) 26859
Pennysaver (Warwick, RI) 28451
The Pennysaver (Greenville, SC) Unable to locate
Pennysaver (Racine, WI) 34274
The Pennysaver (Coquitlam, BC, Can.) Ceased
Pennysaver (Chittenango Edition) (Oneida, NY) 23046
Pennysaver/News (Corinth, NY) 20502
Pennysaver News of Brookhaven (Medford, NY)
    Unable to locate
Pennysaver (Oneida Edition) (Clinton, NY) 20473
PennySaver Press (Bennington, VT) 31500
PennySaver/San Diego South (Brea, CA) 1602
Pennysaver Town Crier 20596*
The Pennysaver/Westchester Life 20583*
The Pennysavers (Sandwich, MA) Unable to locate
Pennywise (Burlington, MA) Ceased
Pennywise/Villager (Syracuse, NY) 23418
Penobscot Times, Inc. (Old Town, ME) 12997
Penquin Dip (Malden, MA) Unable to locate
Pensacola; Cox Cable TV of (Pensacola, FL) 6571
Pensacola History Illustrated (Pensacola, FL) 6567
Pensacola News Journal (Pensacola, FL) 6568
Pensacola Voice (Pensacola, FL) 6569
Pensacola's Independent Newsweekly (Gulf Breeze,
    FL) Unable to locate
Pensee de Bagot; La (Acton Vale, QC, Can.) 36929
Pensez-Y Bien! (Vanier, QC, Can.) 37428
Pension Benefits; Journal of (New York, NY) 22152
Pension Fund News (New York, NY) Ceased
Pension Investment Report; EBRI Quarterly
    (Washington, DC) 5470
PENSION Management (Atlanta, GA) 7037
Pension Plan Guide (Riverwoods, IL) 9507
Pension Planning and Compliance; Journal of (New
    York, NY) 22153
PENSION WORLD 7037*
Pensions & Investments (New York, NY) 22537
Pensions & Investments Age 22537*
Pensions Monitor; Benefits and (Toronto, ON, Can.)
    36475
The Pentagon (Emporia, KS) 11431
Pentagram (Arlington, VA) 31816
Pentagram News 31816*
The Pentecostal Messenger (Joplin, MO) 17142
Pentecostal Testimony (Mississauga, ON, Can.)
    36085
Penthouse (New York, NY) 22538
Penthouse Letters (New York, NY) Unable to locate
Penthouse Variations (New York, NY) 22539
Penticton Herald (Penticton, BC, Can.) 35044
Penticton Western News (Penticton, BC, Can.) 35045
Penton Executive Network (Cleveland, OH) Ceased
The People (Mountain View, CA) 2608
People-Animals-Environment 32924*
People and Education (Thousand Oaks, CA) Unable
    to locate
People; Food (Acworth, GA) 6897
People of God (Albuquerque, NM) 19784
People In Action and Sports Parade (Ogden, UT)
    Unable to locate
People & Places (High Point Edition) (High Point,
    NC) Ceased
People-Sentinel (Barnwell, SC) 28482
People; Teen (New York, NY) 22818
People Weekly (New York, NY) 22540
PeopleNet (Levittown, NY) 20942
Peoples Broadband Communications System 34279*
People's Cable Inc. (Atlanta, GA) Unable to locate
Peoples CATV Inc. (Erin, TN) 29183
People's Daily World 22541*
People's Tribune (Chicago, IL) 8528
The People's Voice Unable to locate
People's Weekly World (New York, NY) 22541
Peoria Daily Record 9421*
Peoria Heights Herald (Peoria, IL) Unable to locate
Peoria Times (Peoria, AZ) 769
Peoria Times Observer (Peoria, IL) 9422
Peotone Vedette (Peotone, IL) 9444
Pep Talk - Group Marriage News 4177*
Peptide Research (Westborough, MA) 14638
Peptide Science; Journal of (Hoboken, NJ) 19040
Peptide Science; Letters in (New York, NY) 22248
Peptomist 34360*
Perception (Ottawa, ON, Can.) Unable to locate
Perception & Psychophysics (Austin, TX) 29796
Perceptions (Duluth, GA) Ceased
Perceptual and Motor Skills (Missoula, MT) 17874

Peregrine (Amherst, MA) 13804
The Perfect Vision (Glen Cove, NY) Unable to locate
Performance (Fort Worth, TX) Unable to locate
The Performance Advantage; APICS- (Marietta, GA)
    7409
Performance Computing (Manhasset, NY) 21009
Performance of Constructed Facilities; Journal of
    (Reston, VA) 32389
Performance in Extreme Environments; The Journal
    of Human (Orlando, FL) 6499
Performance Guide (Fort Worth, TX) Unable to locate
Performance Horseman (Unionville, PA) Ceased
Performance; Journal of Materials Engineering and
    (Los Angeles, CA) 2303
Performance Management Ezine (Tucker, GA) 7611
Performance Management Magazine 7611*
Performance Practice Review Ceased
The Performing Artist (Orlando, FL) Ceased
Performing Artists; Medical Problems of (Philadelphia,
    PA) 27567
Performing Arts (Los Angeles, CA) 2360
Performing Arts in Canada (Toronto, ON, Can.)
    36701
Performing Arts and Entertainment in Canada
    (Toronto, ON, Can.) 36702
Performing Arts Journa 22519*
Performing; PAJ: A Journal of (New York, NY) 22519
Perfumer and Flavorist (Carol Stream, IL) 8152
Perfusion (New York, NY) Ceased
Perfusionists; Internet Journal of (Sugar Land, TX)
    31158
Perham Enterprise Bulletin (Perham, MN) 16265
Peri-Natal Psychology Journal; Pre- and (New York,
    NY) 22592
PeriAnesthesia Nursing; Journal of (Augusta, GA)
    7100
Perido Pelican (Gulf Breeze, FL) 6179
Periglacial Processes; Permafrost and (Hoboken, NJ)
    19080
Perinatal Education; The Journal of (Richmond, VA)
    32442
Perinatal and Neonatal Nursing; Journal of (New
    York, NY) 22154
Perinatal Psychology Journal; The Pre- &
    (Milledgeville, GA) 7435
Perinatology; Clinics in (Philadelphia, PA) 27418
Perinatology/Neonatology (Los Angeles, CA) Unable
    to locate
Perinatology; Seminars in (Philadelphia, PA) 27670
Perinton-Fairport Post (Fairport, NY) 20590
Periodical Literature; Abridged Readers' Guide to
    (Bronx, NY) 20250
Periodical Literature; Readers' Guide to (Bronx, NY)
    20283
Periodicals Digest Dentistry (San Francisco, CA)
    Unable to locate
Periodico El Oriental (Humacao, PR) 28249
Periodico El Regional de Guayama (Humacao, PR)
    28250
Periodico Horizonte (Fajardo, PR) 28242
Periodico La Opinion Central (Humacao, PR) Ceased
Periodico La Opinion Del Sur (Humacao, PR) 28251
Periodico La Voz Latina (Corpus Christi, TX) Unable
    to locate
Periodico, U.S.A.; El (McAllen, TX) 30783
Periodontology; Journal of (Chicago, IL) 8447
Perioperative Medicine and Pain; Seminars in
    Anesthesia, (Philadelphia, PA) 27658
Perioperative Nursing; Seminars in (Philadelphia, PA)
    27671
Peritoneal Dialysis International (Milton, ON, Can.)
    36050
Perkasie News-Herald (Perkasie, PA) 27352
The Permaculture Activist (Black Mountain, NC)
    Unable to locate
Permaculture Review, Overview and Digest (Sparr,
    FL) 6688
Permafrost and Periglacial Processes (Hoboken, NJ)
    19080
Permanent Buildings & Foundations (Provo, UT)
    31406
Permanent Missions to the United Nations (New
    York, NY) 22542
Perquimans Weekly (Hertford, NC) 23986
The Perris Progress (Perris, CA) 2835
Perry Chief (Perry, IA) 11156
The Perry County Advertiser (New Lexington, OH)
    25413
The Perry County News (Tell City, IN) 10482
Perry County/Petit Jean Country Headlight (Pea
    Ridge, AR) Unable to locate
The Perry County Republic-Monitor (Perryville, MO)
    17339
Perry County Times (New Bloomfield, PA) 27313
Perry County Tribune (New Lexington, OH) 25414
The Perry Daily Journal (Perry, OK) 26032
Perry Herald (Perry, NY) 23094
Perry News-Herald (Perry, FL) 6581
Perry Shopper (Perry, NY) 23095

The Pickens Sentinel (Pickens, SC) **28743**
Pickering Post (Scarborough, ON, Can.) *Unable to locate*
The Pickerington Times-Sun (Columbus, OH) *Unable to locate*
Picket; The Shepherd College (Shepherdstown, WV) **33464**
Pickett County Press (Byrdstown, TN) **29076**
Pickney Express **15443***
Pickney Shopping Guide **15443***
Pickups & Mini-Trucks (Los Angeles, CA) *Ceased*
Pico-Rivera Community News (Santa Fe Springs, CA) *Ceased*
Pico Rivera/Santa Fe Springs News (Pico Rivera, CA) **2840**
Picton Gazette (Picton, ON, Can.) **36329**
The Pictorial (Duncan, BC, Can.) **34951**
Pictorial-Gazette (Old Saybrook, CT) **5088**
Pictorial; Oak Creek (New Berlin, WI) **34182**
Pictou Advocate (Pictou, NS, Can.) **35602**
Picture Framing Magazine (Morganville, NJ) **19287**
Pictured Rocks Review; Grand Marais Pilot & (Seney, MI) **15534**
Piedmont & Berkeley Observer (Piedmont, CA) **2842**
Piedmont Cable Corp. (Reidsville, GA) **7490**
The Piedmont Herald (Piedmont, WV) **33435**
Piedmont Literary Review (Lynchburg, VA) *Ceased*
Piedmont Pedlar (Winston-Salem, NC) *Unable to locate*
Piedmont Press (Piedmont, CA) **2843**
Piedmont-Surrey Gazette (Piedmont, OK) **26035**
Piedmont Triad Newcomer (Raleigh, NC) **24149**
Piedmont Triad Newcomer (Raleigh, NC) **24148**
The Piedmonter (Oakland, CA) *Unable to locate*
Pierce City Leader-Journal (Sarcoxie, MO) **17566**
Pierce County Herald **32918***
Pierce County Herald (Ellsworth, WI) **33689**
Pierce County Leader (Pierce, NE) **18248**
Pierce County Parent **33009***
Pierce County Tribune (Rugby, ND) **24535**
Piercy & Barclay Designers Inc. (Tigard, OR) *Unable to locate*
Pierre Capital Journal (Pierre, SD) **28918**
Pig International (Mount Morris, IL) **9244**
Pig Iron (Youngstown, OH) **25698**
Pigeon Bulletin; Racing (Bellbrook, OH) **24665**
Pigeon News *Ceased*
Pigeon Roost News (Holly Springs, MS) **16680**
The Piggott Times (Piggott, AR) **1313**
The Pike County Advertiser (Waverly, OH) **25624**
The Pike County Dispatch **10400***
Pike County Dispatch (Milford, PA) *Unable to locate*
Pike County Journal-Reporter (Zebulon, GA) **7658**
Pike Place Market Merchants Association & Market News (Seattle, WA) **33002**
Pike Press (Pittsfield, IL) **9455**
Pike Register **10357***
Pike Topics (Noblesville, IN) **10357**
Pikes Peak Journal (Colorado Springs, CO) *Unable to locate*
Pikeview Farmer, Raunchland News, amd Simla Sun **4627***
Pikeville Review (Pikeville, KY) **12358**
The Pillar (Salt Lake City, UT) **31437**
Pillsbury Classic Cookbooks (Minneapolis, MN) **16119**
Pillsbury Fast & Healthy Magazine (Minneapolis, MN) **16120**
The Pilot (Boston, MA) **13949**
Pilot (Dixon, MO) **17035**
The Pilot (Southern Pines, NC) **24235**
The Pilot (Lewisporte, NL, Can.) **35470**
Pilot; Air Line (Herndon, VA) **32159**
Pilot; Daily (Costa Mesa, CA) **1774**
Pilot Edition; Scholastic News (Danbury, CT) **4759**
The Pilot-Independent (Walker, MN) **16494**
The Pilot Log (Macon, GA) **7386**
Pilot Magazine; Northern (Anchorage, AK) **529**
Pilot; Newport Beach/Costa Mesa Daily (Newport Beach, CA) **2631**
Pilot News (Plymouth, IN) *Unable to locate*
Pilot News (Kansas City, MO) *Unable to locate*
Pilot News; Great Lakes (Ann Arbor, MI) **14752**
Pilot; Professional (Alexandria, VA) **31728**
Pilot; The Redding (Ridgefield, CT) **5102**
Pilot; The Rockport (Rockport, TX) **30988**
Pilot; Sportsman (Asheboro, NC) **23623**
Pilot; Steamboat (Steamboat Springs, CO) **4631**
The Pilot-Tribune (Storm Lake, IA) **11244**
Pilots Safety Exchange (Alexandria, VA) *Ceased*
Pilsen/Little Village/Cicero/Berwyn EXTRA (Chicago, IL) **8531**
PIMA's Papermaker Magazine (Glenview, IL) *Ceased*
PIME World (Detroit, MI) **14943**
Pimienta (Miami, FL) *Ceased*
PIMS (Petroleum Information Management System) (Victoria, BC, Can.) **35224**
The Pinal Pioneer (Casa Grande, AZ) *Unable to locate*
Pincher Creek Echo (Pincher Creek, AB, Can.) **34824**

The Pinckney Shopper (Pinckney, MI) **15443**
Pinconning Journal (Pinconning, MI) **15444**
Pine Bluff Commercial (Pine Bluff, AR) **1314**
Pine Bluff News (Pine Bluff, AR) *Unable to locate*
Pine Bluffs Community TV System (Pine Bluffs, WY) **34567**
Pine Bluffs Post (Pine Bluffs, WY) **34566**
Pine City Pioneer (Pine City, MN) **16268**
Pine Cone; Carmel (Carmel, CA) **1670**
Pine Cone Press **16012***
Pine Cone Press-Citizen (Longville, MN) **16012**
Pine County Courier (Sandstone, MN) **16435**
The Pine Island Eagle (Cape Coral, FL) **5974**
Pine Island Record **16495***
Pine Island Telephone Co. (Pine Island, MN) **16273**
The Pine Knot (Cloquet, MN) **15802**
The Pine Log (Nacogdoches, TX) **30851**
Pine Plains Register Herald (Millbrook, NY) **21084**
Pine River Journal (Pine River, MN) **16274**
Pine, The Plow and the Pioneer (Three Lakes, WI) *Unable to locate*
Pinebelt Cable (Hattiesburg, MS) **16666**
Pinecrest Tribune (Miami, FL) **6375**
Pinedale Roundup (Pinedale, WY) **34568**
Pinellas County Review (St. Petersburg, FL) *Unable to locate*
Pinellas News (St. Petersburg, FL) **6632**
Pinellas Park News **6632***
The Pineville Sun (Pineville, KY) **12367**
Pinewood Cable TV (Southern Pines, NC) **24236**
Pinewood Country Creations (Cochrane, ON, Can.) **35744**
The Piney Woods Journal (Dodson, LA) **12567**
Pinkerton World Status Map (Arlington, VA) *Unable to locate*
Pinnacle (Berea, KY) **11939**
Pioche Record Publishing Co., Inc. **18415***
Pioneer **16268***
The Pioneer (Brandenburg, KY) *Ceased*
Pioneer (Fitchburg, MA) **14183**
The Pioneer (Big Rapids, MI) **14818**
The Pioneer (Bemidji, MN) **15739**
Pioneer (Hendricks, MN) *Unable to locate*
Pioneer (Mahnomen, MN) **16023**
Pioneer (Greenvale, NY) **20699**
Pioneer (Rochester, NY) **23235**
The Pioneer (Pittsburgh, PA) **27827**
Pioneer (Cambridge, ON, Can.) *Ceased*
The Pioneer Advertiser *Ceased*
Pioneer Broadcasting **33199***
Pioneer Broadcasting **33198***
Pioneer Cablevision Ltd. (Agassiz, BC, Can.) *Unable to locate*
Pioneer Clubs Perspective (Wheaton, IL) *Ceased*
The Pioneer East (Big Rapids, MI) *Unable to locate*
The Pioneer Herald (Mount Vernon, IA) *Unable to locate*
Pioneer Journal (Wadena, MN) **16490**
The Pioneer Log (Portland, OR) **26499**
Pioneer News (Shepherdsville, KY) **12400**
Pioneer News (Chetwynd, BC, Can.) *Unable to locate*
Pioneer News Extra (Shepherdsville, KY) **12401**
Pioneer Press (Fort Jones, CA) **1926**
Pioneer Public Television - Channel 10 (Appleton, MN) **15720**
Pioneer Republican (Marengo, IA) **11063**
Pioneer Review (Philip, SD) **28914**
Pioneer-Tribune (Manistique, MI) **15333**
Pioneer Woman **22390***
Pipe Journal; TPJ—The Tube & (Rockford, IL) **9534**
Pipe Line & Gas Industry (Houston, TX) *Ceased*
Pipeline (Duluth, GA) *Unable to locate*
Pipeline (Mountain Home, ID) *Ceased*
Pipeline (Estevan, SK, Can.) *Ceased*
Pipeline Digest (Houston, TX) *Ceased*
Pipeline & Gas Journal (Houston, TX) *Unable to locate*
Pipeline Industries; Gas Utility and (Dallas, TX) **30160**
Pipeline News (Houston, TX) **30520**
Pipelines (San Francisco, CA) **3414**
Piper (Pequot Lakes, MN) *Unable to locate*
The Piper Press (Kansas City, KS) **11531**
Piper; U.S. (Birmingham, AL) **98**
Pipestone County Star (Pipestone, MN) **16275**
Piping/Air Conditioning Engineering (HPAC); Heating/ (Cleveland, OH) **24906**
Piqua Daily Call (Piqua, OH) *Unable to locate*
The Piscataquis Observer (Dover Foxcroft, ME) **12952**
Piscataway Review (Piscataway, NJ) **19430**
Pit & Quarry (Cleveland, OH) **24942**
The Pitch (Kansas City, MO) **17193**
PitchWeekly **17193***
Pitt Magazine (Pittsburgh, PA) **27828**
The Pitt News (Pittsburgh, PA) **27829**
The Pittsburg Gazette (Pittsburg, TX) **30936**
Pittsburg Hustler; South (South Pittsburg, TN) **29610**
Pittsburgh Business Times (Pittsburgh, PA) **27830**

Pittsburgh Catholic (Pittsburgh, PA) **27831**
Pittsburgh City Paper (Pittsburgh, PA) **27832**
Pittsburgh Homewood-Brushton News **27835***
Pittsburgh Hospital News (Pittsburgh, PA) **27833**
Pittsburgh; Key Magazine (Pittsburgh, PA) **27808**
Pittsburgh Legal Journal (Pittsburgh, PA) *Unable to locate*
Pittsburgh Magazine (Pittsburgh, PA) **27834**
Pittsburgh Newsweekly; In (Philadelphia, PA) **27490**
Pittsburgh Parent (Bakerstown, PA) **26668**
The Pittsburgh Press (Pittsburgh, PA) *Ceased*
Pittsburgh Renaissance News (Pittsburgh, PA) **27835**
Pittsburgh T.E.Q. (Pittsburgh, PA) *Unable to locate*
Pittsburgh's Child **26668***
Pittsfield Gazette (Pittsfield, MA) **14472**
Pittsfield Valley Times (Pittsfield, ME) *Ceased*
Pittsford Post; Brighton (Canandaigua, NY) **20419**
Pittsford This Week (Pittsford, NY) *Unable to locate*
Pittsville Record (Pittsville, WI) *Unable to locate*
Pituitary (New York, NY) **22554**
Pivot (New York, NY) *Unable to locate*
PIX (New York, NY) **22555**
Pixel Vision (New York, NY) **22556**
Pizza Magazine; Canadian (Delhi, ON, Can.) **35765**
Pizza & Pasta (Chicago, IL) *Ceased*
Pizza Today (Louisville, KY) **12234**
PJG Magazine (Miami, FL) *Ceased*
Place (Detroit, MI) **14944**
Placentia News-Times (Anaheim, CA) *Unable to locate*
Placer Herald (Rocklin, CA) **2956**
PLACES (Brooklyn, NY) **20337**
Placoteux; Le (Saint-Pascal, QC, Can.) **37367**
Plain City Advocate (Plain City, OH) **25479**
Plain Dealer (Wabash, IN) **10529**
Plain Dealer (Blackwood, NJ) **18682**
Plain Dealer (Cleveland, OH) **24943**
Plain Talk (Vermillion, SD) **29005**
The Plain Truth (Pasadena, CA) **2825**
Plaindealer (St. James, MN) **16355**
Plainedge/South Levittown Pennysaver (Farmingdale, NY) *Ceased*
Plainfield Sun (Naperville, IL) **9272**
Plains Cable TV (Plains, MT) *Unable to locate*
Plains Reporter (Williston, ND) **24559**
Plainsman-Clarion (Richland, IL) **11177**
Plainsman Edition **17893***
Plainsman Newspaper **37454***
Plainsong and Medieval Music (Newton Highlands, MA) **14415**
PLAINSWOMAN (Grand Forks, ND) *Ceased*
Plaintiffs' Advocate **22865***
Plainview Daily Herald (Plainview, TX) **30939**
Plainview Herald (Hempstead, NY) *Ceased*
Plainview Herald (Plainview, NY) **23098**
Plainview/Jericho Pennysaver (Plainview, NY) **23099**
Plainview News (Plainview, MN) **16278**
Plainview News (Plainview, NE) **18249**
Plainview/Old Bethpage Herald **23098***
Plainview Weekender (Farmingdale, NY) *Ceased*
Plainville Times (Plainville, KS) **11759**
Plaisirs de Vivre (Westmount, QC, Can.) **37444**
Plan (Montreal, QC, Can.) **37206**
Plan Sponsor (Greenwich, CT) **4875**
Plane & Pilot (Los Angeles, CA) *Unable to locate*
Planet Atlanta (Atlanta, GA) *Unable to locate*
Planetarian (Los Angeles, CA) **2368**
Planetary Sciences; Annual Review of Earth and (Palo Alto, CA) **2789**
Planned Parenthood Review (New York, NY) *Ceased*
Planner; Insurance Conference (Stow, MA) **14573**
Planning (Chicago, IL) **8532**
Planning Association (JAPA); Journal of the American (Portland, OR) **26483**
Planning Commissioners Journal (Burlington, VT) **31517**
Planning for Higher Education (Ann Arbor, MI) *Unable to locate*
Planning Literature; Journal of (Thousand Oaks, CA) **3898**
Planning and Recovery Journal (CPR-J); Contingency (Wellesley Hills, MA) **14621**
Plano Star Courier (Plano, TX) **30948**
Plant (Toronto, ON, Can.) **36709**
The Plant Cell (Rockville, MD) **13694**
Plant Cell, Tissue and Organ Culture (New York, NY) **22557**
Plant City Shopper (Plant City, FL) **6586**
Plant Digest; The Herb, Spice, and Medicinal (Amherst, MA) **13794**
Plant Disease (St. Paul, MN) **16406**
Plant Disease Survey; Canadian (London, ON, Can.) **35980**
Plant Ecology (New York, NY) **22558**
Plant Engineering (New York, NY) **22559**
Plant Engineering and Maintenance; PEM (Burlington, ON, Can.) **35718**
Plant Engineering Products (New York, NY) *Ceased*
Plant Food; Better Crops with (Norcross, GA) **7456**

Plant Foods for Human Nutrition (New York, NY) 22560

Plant Growth Regulation; Journal of (New York, NY) 22160

Plant Magazine; Outside (Cary, IL) 8169

Plant Management & Engineering 36709*

Plant-Microbe Interactions (MPMI); Molecular (St. Paul, MN) 16397

Plant Molecular Biology Reporter (Athens, GA) 6948

Plant Nutrition; Journal of (Athens, GA) 6946

Plant Pathology; European Journal of (New York, NY) 21648

Plant Physiology (Rockville, MD) 13695

Plant Physiology; Russian Journal of (New York, NY) 22694

Plant Protection News (Gainesville, FL) Ceased

Plant Science; Canadian Journal of (Ottawa, ON, Can.) 36212

Plant Services (Itasca, IL) 9015

Plant Shutdowns Monitor (Oakland, CA) Ceased

Plant and Soil (New York, NY) 22561

The Plantagenet Connection (Arvada, CO) 4138

Plantation CableVision Inc. 28663*

Plantation Star (Hollywood, FL) Unable to locate

The Planter 13836*

The Planter Newspaper (Apopka, FL) 5911

PlantFinder (Pembroke Pines, FL) Unable to locate

Plants; Desert (Tucson, AZ) 945

Plants & Gardens News (Brooklyn, NY) 20338

Plants Sites & Parks (Greensboro, NC) 23935

The Plantsman (Loudon, NH) 18554

Plaquemine Post-South (Plaquemine, LA) 12795

Plaquemines Cablevision (Belle Chasse, LA) 12531

The Plaquemines Gazette (Belle Chasse, LA) 12528

The Plaquemines Watchman (Belle Chasse, LA) 12529

Plasma Chemistry and Plasma Processing (New York, NY) 22562

Plasma Physics; Journal of (New York, NY) 22161

Plasmas and Polymers (New York, NY) 22563

Plasmid (San Diego, CA) 3246

Plastic Canvas Crafts (Berne, IN) 9815

Plastic Canvas Home & Holiday (Big Sandy, TX) 29922

Plastic Canvas! Magazine 29922*

Plastic Canvas and More 9815*

Plastic Canvas World (Berne, IN) Unable to locate

Plastic and Reconstructive Surgery (Brookline, MA) 14023

Plastic and Reconstructive Surgery; Operative Techniques in (Philadelphia, PA) 27606

Plastic Surgery; Aesthetic (New York, NY) 21160

Plastic Surgery; Annals of (Lamoni, IA) 11027

Plastic Surgery; The Canadian Journal of (Oakville, ON, Can.) 36140

Plastic Surgery; Clinics in (Philadelphia, PA) 27419

Plastic Surgery Clinics; Facial (Philadelphia, PA) 27466

Plastic Surgery; Facial (New York, NY) 21672

Plastic Surgery News (Philadelphia, PA) Unable to locate

Plastic Surgery Nursing (Pitman, NJ) 19440

Plastic Surgery Products (Los Angeles, CA) 2369

The Plastic Tower (Bowie, MD) 13393

Plastic Waste Strategies (Falls Church, VA) Ceased

Plastico; Tecnologia del (Coral Gables, FL) 6013

Plastics Auxiliaries 4348*

Plastics Auxiliaries & Machinery (Denver, CO) 4348

Plastics in Canada (Toronto, ON, Can.) 36710

Plastics; Canadian (Toronto, ON, Can.) 36525

Plastics Compounding (Edison, NJ) Ceased

Plastics Design Forum (Chatham, NJ) Unable to locate

The Plastics Distributor & Fabricator Magazine (Riverside, IL) 9498

Plastics Engineering (Brookfield, CT) 4727

Plastics Fabricating & Forming (Garrisonville, VA) 32104

Plastics Hot Line (Fort Dodge, IA) 10907

Plastics Machinery & Equipment (Edison, NJ) Unable to locate

Plastics Magazine (Santa Monica, CA) Unable to locate

Plastics; Modern (New York, NY) 22350

Plastics News (Akron, OH) 24585

Plastics News; Rubber & (Akron, OH) 24587

Plastics Technology (New York, NY) 22564

Plastics Today (Falls Church, VA) Ceased

Plastics World (Melville, NY) 21058

PlasticTrends (Malibu, CA) Ceased

Plate World (Niles, IL) Ceased

Plateau (Flagstaff, AZ) Ceased

Plating & Surface Finishing (Orlando, FL) 6507

Platte County Citizen (Platte City, MO) 17350

Platte County Record Times (Wheatland, WY) 34601

Platte County Sun Gazette (Liberty, MO) 17249

Platte Dispatch-Tribune 17162*

Platte Gazette (Liberty, MO) Unable to locate

Platte Valley Review (Kearney, NE) 18060

Platteville Cable TV Corp. 34244*

Platteville Herald (Platteville, CO) Unable to locate

Platteville Journal (Platteville, WI) 34242

Platteville Telephone Co. 34245*

Plattsburgh Cablevision, Inc. 23104*

Plattsburgh Free Trader (Elizabethtown, NY) 20565

Plattsburgh North County Living 20564*

Plattsmouth Journal (Plattsmouth, NE) 18250

Play & Culture (Champaign, IL) Unable to locate

Play Magazine (Boca Raton, FL) Ceased

Play Meter Magazine (New Orleans, LA) 12751

Play Review; Children's Book and (Provo, UT) 31401

Playback (Toronto, ON, Can.) 36711

Playbill (Philadelphia, PA) 27640

Playbill Magazine (New York, NY) Unable to locate

Playboard (Burnaby, BC, Can.) Unable to locate

Playboy (Chicago, IL) 8533

Players (Los Angeles, CA) 2370

Playgirl (New York, NY) 22565

Playguy Magazine (New York, NY) 22566

PLAYS (Waukesha, WI) 34410

Plays; Poems and (Murfreesboro, TN) 29431

(PlayStation Magazine); PSM (Brisbane, CA) 1611

Playthings (New York, NY) Unable to locate

Plaza Tsushin (New York, NY) Unable to locate

Pleasant Grove Review (Pleasant Grove, UT) 31390

Pleasant Hill Times (Pleasant Hill, MO) 17352

The Pleasant Press (Pleasant Plains, IL) 9460

Pleasant Ridge/Ferndale Mirror (Royal Oak, MI) 15483

Pleasant TV Co., Inc. (Saugerties, NY) Ceased

Pleasantdale Suburban Life; Countryside/Indian Head Park/Willow Springs/Burr Ridge/ (Oak Brook, IL) 9346

Pleasants County Leader (St. Marys, WV) 33460

Pleasure Boatings Caribbean Sports & Travel Magazine (Miami, FL) 6376

Pleasure Quest (Mesa, AZ) Unable to locate

Pleiades Magazine (Edgewater, CO) 4410

Plentywood Cable TV Co. (Plentywood, MT) 17897

The Plentywood Herald (Plentywood, MT) Unable to locate

Plexers Inc. (Cameron Park, CA) 38036

Plomberie-Chauffage et Climatisation (Pointe-Claire, QC, Can.) Ceased

Ploughshares (Boston, MA) 13950

Ploughshares Monitor (Waterloo, ON, Can.) 36857

Plover Profile (Iola, WI) Ceased

Plum Advance Leader Star (Monroeville, PA) 27283

Plum Cable TV (Pittsburgh, PA) Unable to locate

Plumber; Illinois Master (Springfield, IL) 9626

Plumber and Mechanical Contractor; Michigan Master (Lansing, MI) 15287

Plumbing, Air Conditioning Buyers' Guide; Heating, (Toronto, ON, Can.) 36613

Plumbing-Air Conditioning Magazine); HPAC (Heating- (Toronto, ON, Can.) 36620

Plumbing Business Ceased

Plumbing Engineer (Northbrook, IL) 9320

Plumbing Heating & Cooling; Associated (Birmingham, AL) 55

Plumbing-Heating-Cooling Forum; North Carolina (Garner, NC) 23905

Plumbing-Heating-Cooling Index; Kentucky (Louisville, KY) 12225

Plumbing, Heating, Cooling Magazine; Southern 23939*

Plumbing & HVAC Product News (Etobicoke, ON, Can.) 35819

Plumbing & Mechanical (Rosemont, IL) Unable to locate

Plumbing, Piping & Heating 35819*

Plumpers and Big Women (Hialeah, FL) Unable to locate

plumtrees (Milwaukee, WI) Unable to locate

Plus 23086*

Plus Magazine (San Luis Obispo, CA) 3568

PLUS/Market 34829*

Plus Pages (Riverton, WY) Ceased

Plus Sizes (New York, NY) Ceased

Plus Voice Magazine (Chicago, IL) Unable to locate

Plymouth County Business Review (Plymouth, MA) 14480

Plymouth Guide (Plymouth, MA) Unable to locate

Plymouth Observer (Plymouth, MI) 15448

Plymouth Post 16280*

Plympton Reporter; Halifax/ (Halifax, MA) 14224

Plywood & Panel World 373*

PM Engineer (Troy, MI) 15633

PM Network (Newtown Square, PA) 27330

PM Purchasing Management (Burlington, ON, Can.) Ceased

The PMA (Chicago, IL) 8534

PME; Le Magazine (Montreal, QC, Can.) 37169

PMLA (New York, NY) 22567

PMP Network (Stoughton, MA) 37656

Pneumatics; Hydraulics & (Cleveland, OH) 24910

PNPA Press 27012*

POA (Indianapolis, IN) 10161

P.O.B. (Point of Beginning) (Troy, MI) 15634

Pocahontas Cable Vision (Marlinton, WV) 33377

Pocahontas County Advertiser (Pocahontas, IA) 11161

Pocahontas Record Democrat (Pocahontas, IA) 11162

Pocahontas Star Herald (Pocahontas, AR) 1316

The Pocahontas Times (Marlinton, WV) 33376

Pocket Flight Guide - Pacific Asia Edition; OAG (Downers Grove, IL) 8793

Pocket PC (Fairfield, IA) 10883

Pocket Pro Golf Magazine 36489*

Pockets Magazine (Nashville, TN) 29481

Pocono Record (Stroudsburg, PA) 28035

Pocono World (Hope, NJ) Unable to locate

Podiatric Medical Association; Journal of the American (Bethesda, MD) 13347

Podiatric Medicine and Surgery; Clinics in (Philadelphia, PA) 27420

Podiatric Products (Los Angeles, CA) 2371

Podiatrist; Hospital (Los Angeles, CA) 2294

Podiatry Management Magazine (Ardmore, PA) 26663

Podiatry Today (Montvale, NJ) 19272

The Poe Messenger (Richmond, VA) 32445

Poe Newsletter 32906*

Poe Studies/Dark Romanticism (Pullman, WA) 32906

Poem (Huntsville, AL) 273

Poems and Plays (Murfreesboro, TN) 29431

POET (Campbell, CA) Unable to locate

Poet (Shreveport, LA) Unable to locate

Poet; American (New York, NY) 21205

Poet Lore (Bethesda, MD) 13375

Poetic Briefs (Albany, NY) Unable to locate

Poetic Space (Bemidji, MN) Ceased

Poetics Today (Durham, NC) 23840

Poetics; Xcp: Cross Cultural (Minneapolis, MN) 16142

Poetry (Chicago, IL) 8535

Poetry Calendar; NYC (New York, NY) 22479

Poetry Canada (Kingston, ON, Can.) 35941

Poetry Flash (Berkeley, CA) 1551

Poetry Journal; The Beloit (Farmington, ME) 12959

Poetry; Journal of Canadian (Ottawa, ON, Can.) 36254

Poetry; Magazine of Speculative (Beloit, WI) 33575

Poetry Northwest (Seattle, WA) Ceased

Poetry Pilot 21205*

Poetry and Poetics; Field: Contemporary (Oberlin, OH) 25445

Poetry Review; The American (Philadelphia, PA) 27374

Poetry Review; Birmingham (Birmingham, AL) 59

Poetry Review; Borderlands: Texas (Austin, TX) 29766

Poetry Review; Cumberland (Nashville, TN) 29453

Poetry Review; Hiram (Hiram, OH) 25247

Poetry Review; Maryland (Baltimore, MD) 13215

Poetry Review; Southern (Savannah, GA) 7539

Poetry Review; Sow's Ear (Abingdon, VA) 31626

Poetry Review; Spoon River (Normal, IL) 9306

Poetry; S.F. 3415*

Poetry and Short Fiction; Wascana Review of Contemporary (Regina, SK, Can.) 37535

Poetry; Tar River (Greenville, NC) 23970

Poetry Toronto (Willowdale, ON, Can.) Ceased

Poetry USA (San Francisco, CA) 3415

Poetry; Victorian (Morgantown, WV) 33397

Poet's Forum (Golden, CO) 4473

Poets; Journal of New Jersey (Randolph, NJ) 19495

Poets on the Line (Brooklyn, NY) 20339

Poet's Roundtable (Terre Haute, IN) 10488

Poets at Work (Lyndora, PA) 27208

Poets & Writers Magazine (New York, NY) 22568

PoetsWest Literary Journal 33003*

PoetsWest Online (Seattle, WA) 33003

Poiesis (Toronto, ON, Can.) 36712

Poinsett Register (Greenville, SC) Ceased

The Point (San Diego, CA) 3247

The Point! (Oklahoma City, OK) 25993

Point (Columbia, SC) 28562

Point of Beginning); P.O.B. ((Troy, MI) 15634

The Point Edward Gazette 36366*

Point; Le (Dolbeau-Mistassini, QC, Can.) 36986

Point Of Purchase (Roswell, GA) 7516

Point Pleasant Register (Point Pleasant, WV) 33439

Point Reyes Light (Point Reyes Station, CA) 2859

Point and Shoreland Journal (Perrysburg, OH) 25476

The Pointe Coupee Banner (New Roads, LA) 12787

Pointer (West Point, NY) 23546

The Pointer (Stevens Point, WI) 34343

Pointer; News (San Rafael, CA) 3602

Points West 31429*

Poise 'n Oak 2511*

The Poker Digest Magazine (West Atlantic City, NJ) 19717

Poland Leader (Warren, OH) Ceased

Polar Engineering; International Journal of Offshore and (Cupertino, CA) 1797

Polar and Glaciological Abstracts (New York, NY) 22569

Polar Record (New York, NY) 22570

Polar Star **568***
The Polaris **6034***
Police (Torrance, CA) **3940**
Police Beat; American (Cambridge, MA) **14037**
Police; The Chief of (Miami, FL) **6345**
The Police Chief (Alexandria, VA) **31723**
Police Criminal Law Bulletin; The Pennsylvania (Pittsburgh, PA) **27826**
Police and Criminal Psychology; Journal of (San Marcos, TX) **31084**
Police Crisis Negotiations; Journal of (Fort Worth, TX) **30343**
Police Product News **3940***
Police Review; National (Louisville, KY) **12232**
Police & Security News (Quakertown, PA) **27915**
Policy Analysis and Management; Journal of (College Park, MD) **13431**
Policy History; Journal of (St. Louis, MO) **17459**
Policy Issues; Contemporary **30039***
Policy; Journal of Health and Social (Norfolk, VA) **32287**
Policy; Journal of International Wildlife Law and (New York, NY) **22105**
Policy & Marketing; Journal of Public (Chicago, IL) **8449**
Policy Options Politiques (Montreal, QC, Can.) **37207**
Policy and Practice of Public Human Services (Washington, DC) **5720**
Policy Review (Stanford, CA) *Unable to locate*
Policy Studies Journal (Champaign, IL) **8212**
Policy Studies Review (Champaign, IL) **8213**
Policy; Transport (Burlington, MA) **14034**
Polio Living **897***
Polish-American Journal (Boston, NY) **20239**
Polish American Voice **20239***
Polish American World (Baldwin, NY) **20114**
Polish Canadian Courier/Nowy Kurier (Toronto, ON, Can.) **36713**
Polish Daily News (Chicago, IL) **8536**
Polish Daily News (New York, NY) **22571**
Polish Digest (Stevens Point, WI) *Unable to locate*
(Polish Falcon); Sokol Polski (Pittsburgh, PA) **27844**
Polish Heritage (Levittown, PA) **27189**
Polish Music Journal (Los Angeles, CA) **2372**
Polish Nation **8499***
The Polish Review (New York, NY) **22572**
The Polish Weekly (Hamtramck, MI) **15141**
Polish Woman; Polka— (Scranton, PA) **27961**
The Polish World **15141***
Political Affairs (New York, NY) **22574**
Political Affairs (New York, NY) **22573**
Political Behavior (New York, NY) **22575**
Political Communication (Durham, NC) **23841**
Political Development; Studies in American (Los Angeles, CA) **2407**
Political & Economic Studies; Journal of Social, (Washington, DC) **5615**
Political Economy; History of (Durham, NC) **23825**
Political Economy; International Journal of (Armonk, NY) **20081**
Political Economy; The Review of Black (Somerset, NJ) **19564**
Political and Legal Anthropological Review (Arlington, VA) **31818**
Political Money Monitor (Washington, DC) **5721**
Political Psychology (New York, NY) **22576**
Political Research; European Journal of (New York, NY) **21649**
Political Research Quarterly (Salt Lake City, UT) *Ceased*
Political Science Association; POLITY: The Journal of the Northeastern (Amherst, MA) **13805**
Political Science; British Journal of (New York, NY) **21342**
Political Science; Japanese Journal of (New York, NY) **21957**
Political Science; Perspectives on (Washington, DC) **5717**
Political Science Quarterly (New York, NY) **22577**
Political Science Review; American (Washington, DC) **5338**
Political Science (Revue canadienne de science politique); Canadian Journal of (Ottawa, ON, Can.) **36213**
Political and Social Science; The Annals of the American Academy of (Thousand Oaks, CA) **3850**
Political Studies; Comparative (Thousand Oaks, CA) **3857**
Political Theory (Charlottesville, VA) **31938**
Political Times; Women's (Washington, DC) **5864**
Politics; The Harvard International Journal of Press/ (Cambridge, MA) **14059**
Politics; International (New York, NY) **21930**
Politics; Journal of (College Station, TX) **30046**
Politics Journal; Women & (Washington, DC) **5863**
Politics and Law; Russian (Armonk, NY) **20094**
Politics and the Life Sciences (College Park, MD) **13437**
Politics Magazine; Criminal (Cincinnati, OH) **24791**

Politics; Minnesota Law & (Minneapolis, MN) **16103**
Politics; New (Brooklyn, NY) **20332**
Politics and Policy (Statesboro, GA) **7561**
Politics, Policy and Law; Journal of Health (New Haven, CT) **4994**
Politics & Policy Quarterly; State (Champaign, IL) **8219**
Politics and Probe: the intelligence journal of the workers left (New York, NY) *Ceased*
Politics Research; American (Thousand Oaks, CA) **3849**
Politics; Review of (Notre Dame, IN) **10378**
Politics & Societies; East European (New York, NY) **21578**
Politics & Society (Thousand Oaks, CA) **3908**
Politics and Society; Latin American (Boulder, CO) **4176**
Politics; Texas Review of Law and (Austin, TX) **29847**
Politics; World (Princeton, NJ) **19478**
Politics; World of (Dallas, TX) **30190**
Politiques; Canadian Public Policy—Analyse de (Calgary, AB, Can.) **34638**
Politiques; Policy Options (Montreal, QC, Can.) **37207**
POLITY: The Journal of the Northeastern Political Science Association (Amherst, MA) **13805**
Polk City Press (Mulberry, FL) *Unable to locate*
The Polk County Democrat (Bartow, FL) **5918**
Polk County Enterprise (Livingston, TX) **30700**
Polk County Itemizer Observer (Dallas, OR) **26300**
Polk County News **29054***
The Polk County News (Osceola, NE) **18239**
The Polk County News (Stromsburg, NE) **18288**
Polk County News-Citizen Advance (Benton, TN) **29054**
Polk County News Journal (Columbus, NC) **23792**
Polk Shopper **5916***
Polka—Polish Woman (Scranton, PA) **27961**
Polled Hereford World **17171***
Polled Hereford World (Kansas City, MO) *Unable to locate*
Pollstar (Fresno, CA) **1956**
Pollution Abstracts (Bethesda, MD) **13376**
Pollution Consultant; The Air (New York, NY) **21168**
Pollution Engineering (Troy, MI) **15635**
Pollution Equipment News (Pittsburgh, PA) **27836**
Pollution Prevention Review (Hoboken, NJ) *Ceased*
Polo **6844***
Polo Players Edition (Wellington, FL) **6844**
Polonia's Voice **20239***
Polskie Radio New York 910 am **23113***
The Poly Post (Pomona, CA) **2861**
Polygraph (Chattanooga, TN) **29091**
Polymer Connection; Cast (Mc Lean, VA) **32243**
Polymer Engineering and Science (Brookfield, CT) **4728**
Polymer International (Hoboken, NJ) **19085**
Polymer Links/Alerts; Maro (Exton, PA) **26918**
Polymer News (New York, NY) *Unable to locate*
Polymer-Plastics Technology and Engineering (Richmond, VA) **32446**
Polymer Preprints (Newark, NJ) **19363**
Polymer Reaction Engineering (New York, NY) **22578**
Polymer Science; Journal of (Hoboken, NJ) **19042**
Polymer Science; Journal of Applied (Hoboken, NJ) **19003**
Polymer Technology; Advances in (Newark, NJ) **19350**
Polymers for Advanced Technologies (Hoboken, NJ) **19086**
Polymers/Ceramics/Composites Alert (Beachwood, OH) **24655**
Polymers and the Environment; Journal of (New York, NY) **22162**
Polymers; Plasmas and (New York, NY) **22563**
The Polytechnic (Troy, NY) **23455**
Polytechnic Reporter **20340***
The Polytechnic Reporter (Brooklyn, NY) **20340**
Polytechnicable (Brooklyn, NY) *Ceased*
Pomeroy East Washingtonian **32887***
Pompano Beach Tribune (Chicago, IL) *Ceased*
The Pompano Ledger (Pompano Beach, FL) **6592**
Pompano Times (Chicago, IL) **8537**
The Ponca City News (Ponca City, OK) **26037**
The Ponchatoula Times (Ponchatoula, LA) **12797**
Pondscapes Magazine (Sarasota, FL) *Unable to locate*
Ponoka Herald (Red Deer, AB, Can.) *Ceased*
Ponoka News & Advertiser (Ponoka, AB, Can.) **34825**
Ponte Vedra Leader; Beaches Leader/ (Jacksonville Beach, FL) **6247**
Ponteix TV Club (Ponteix, SK, Can.) **37516**
Pontiac Driving Excitement **15636***
Pontiac Excitement (Troy, MI) **15636**
Pontiac; High Performance (Saddle Brook, NJ) **19528**
Pontoon & Deck Boat Magazine (Idaho Falls, ID) **7867**
The Pontotoc Progress (Pontotoc, MS) **16823**

Pony Express (Bethany, MO) **16903**
Pony Express Mail (Liberty, TX) **30691**
Poodle Review (Urbana, IL) **9715**
Pool Dust (Tempe, AZ) **912**
Pool & Spa Marketing (Markham, ON, Can.) **36030**
Pool & Spa News (Los Angeles, CA) **2373**
Poolesville Gazette (Frederick, MD) **13519**
Poor and Underserved; Journal of Health Care for the (Thousand Oaks, CA) **3891**
Pop Culture Collecting (Corona, CA) **1767**
Pop Rock (Montreal, QC, Can.) *Ceased*
Pop-tart (Vancouver, BC, Can.) *Unable to locate*
Pope County Tribune (Glenwood, MN) **15920**
The Pope Speaks (Huntington, IN) **10073**
Poplarville Democrat (Poplarville, MS) **16824**
POPsmear (Beverly Hills, CA) **1576**
Poptronics (Hauppauge, NY) **20722**
Poptronics (Hauppauge, NY) **20721**
Popular Cars (Anaheim, CA) *Ceased*
Popular Ceramics (Glendale, CA) *Unable to locate*
Popular Communications (Port Washington, NY) **23132**
Popular Culture; Journal of (Bowling Green, OH) **24695**
Popular Culture in Libraries (Binghamton, NY) *Ceased*
Popular Culture; Studies in Latin American (Tucson, AZ) **965**
Popular; El (Bakersfield, CA) **1451**
Popular; El (Toronto, ON, Can.) **36581**
Popular Electronics **20722***
Popular Government (Chapel Hill, NC) **23719**
Popular Home Automation (Wayland, MA) **14615**
Popular Hot Rodding (Los Angeles, CA) *Unable to locate*
Popular Mechanics (New York, NY) **22579**
Popular Music (New York, NY) **22580**
Popular Music and Society (Bowling Green, OH) **24700**
Popular Music Studies; Journal of (Babson Park, MA) **13831**
Popular Photography and Imaging (New York, NY) **22581**
Popular Science (New York, NY) **22582**
Popular Woodworking (Concord, CA) *Unable to locate*
Population Bulletin (Washington, DC) **5722**
Population Connection (Washington, DC) **5723**
Population and Development Review (New York, NY) **22583**
Population and Environment (New York, NY) *Unable to locate*
Population; European Journal of (New York, NY) **21650**
Population Geography; International Journal of (Hoboken, NJ) **18994**
Population Reports (Honolulu, HI) **7718**
Population Reports; Current (Pittsburgh, PA) **27777**
Population Research and Policy Review (New York, NY) **22584**
Populist; The Progressive (Austin, TX) **29798**
The Poquoson Post (Yorktown, VA) **32645**
Porc Quebec (Longueuil, QC, Can.) **37057**
Pork (Lenexa, KS) **11595**
Pork (Toronto, ON, Can.) *Unable to locate*
Pork Producer; Iowa (Clive, IA) **10716**
Porous Materials; Journal of (New York, NY) **22163**
Porsche Panorama (Atlanta, GA) **7038**
Port Allegany Reporter-Argus (Port Allegany, PA) **27897**
Port Angeles Telecable, Inc **32890***
Port Arthur News (Port Arthur, TX) **30953**
Port of Baltimore (Towson, MD) **13764**
Port Byron Shopping Guide (Port Byron, NY) **23114**
Port Chester Guide **23574***
Port Colborne News (Newmarket, ON, Can.) *Unable to locate*
Port Dover Maple Leaf (Port Dover, ON, Can.) **36332**
Port Folio (Glenwood, IA) *Unable to locate*
Port Folio Weekly (Virginia Beach, VA) *Unable to locate*
The Port Gibson Reveille (Port Gibson, MS) **16826**
The Port Hole (Le Hublot) (Scarborough, ON, Can.) **36383**
Port Hope Evening Guide (Port Hope, ON, Can.) **36334**
Port Hope-Guide (Cobourg, ON, Can.) *Ceased*
Port Isabel/South Padre Press (Port Isabel, TX) **30954**
Port Jefferson Suffolk Life (Port Jefferson, NY) **23116**
The Port Lavaca Wave **30956***
The Port Lavaca Wave & Calhoun County WAVE EXTRA (Port Lavaca, TX) **30956**
Port of New Orleans RECORD (Metairie, LA) *Unable to locate*
Port News (Charleston, SC) **28516**
Port Orchard Advantage **32891***
The Port Orchard Independent (Port Orchard, WA) **32891**
Port Orford News (Port Orford, OR) **26465**

Master Index Gale Directory of Publications & Broadcast Media/138th Ed.

Port Orford Today (Port Orford, OR) **26466**
Port Perry Star (Port Perry, ON, Can.) **36335**
Port Perry This Week; Oshawa-Whitby-Clarington- (Oshawa, ON, Can.) **36181**
Port Saint Lucie Mirror (Stuart, FL) *Ceased*
Port St. Lucie News (Port St. Lucie, FL) *Unable to locate*
Port Times Record (Port Jefferson Station, NY) **23118**
Port Townsend/Jefferson County Leader (Port Townsend, WA) **32894**
Port Townsend Leader **32894***
Port Townsend Leader **10372***
Port TV Cable Co. (Port Allegany, PA) *Unable to locate*
Port Washington News (Port Washington, NY) **23133**
Port Washington Shopper's Guide (Huntington, NY) *Unable to locate*
Portable Computing (Malibu, CA) *Ceased*
Portable Design (Nashua, NH) **18599**
Portage Daily Register (Portage, WI) **34259**
The Portage Dispatch (Portage, PA) **27898**
Portage Flashes (Allegan, MI) *Ceased*
Portage Journal-Press (Merrillville, IN) *Unable to locate*
Portage Lakes Herald *Ceased*
Portage Park Leader **8573***
Portage Park Passage (Highland Park, IL) *Unable to locate*
Portage Park Times; Jefferson Park/ (Lincolnwood, IL) **9095**
Portageville Review **17363***
Portal (Baltimore, MD) **13237**
Portales News-Tribune (Portales, NM) *Unable to locate*
Portals of Prayer (St. Louis, MO) **17484**
Porter County Herald (Hebron, IN) *Ceased*
Porterville Recorder (Porterville, CA) **2862**
Portfolio Management; The Journal of (New York, NY) **22164**
Porthole (Fort Lauderdale, FL) **6083**
Porticus (Rochester, NY) **23236**
Portland (Portland, ME) **13016**
Portland Alliance (Portland, OR) **26500**
Portland Business Journal (Portland, OR) **26501**
Portland Business Today **26475***
Portland Computer Bits **26266***
Portland Downtowner (Portland, OR) *Unable to locate*
(Portland); Environmental Law (Portland, OR) **26476**
The Portland Leader (Portland, TN) *Unable to locate*
Portland News (Sinton, TX) **31110**
Portland Observer (Portland, OR) *Unable to locate*
Portland Parent (Seattle, WA) **33004**
Portland Physician Scribe **26508***
Portland Press Herald (Portland, ME) **13017**
Portland Review & Observer (Charlotte, MI) *Unable to locate*
The Portland Skanner (Portland, OR) **26502**
Portneuf; Le Courrier de (Donnacona, QC, Can.) **36987**
Portola Reporter (Portola, CA) **2864**
Portsmouth Daily Times (Portsmouth, OH) **25484**
Portsmouth Herald (Portsmouth, NH) **18637**
Portsmouth Magazine (Portsmouth, NH) *Ceased*
The Portsmouth Press (Exeter, NH) *Ceased*
The Portsmouth Times (Chesapeake, VA) *Unable to locate*
Portugal; Voz de (Hayward, CA) **2044**
Portugal; A Voz de (Montreal, QC, Can.) **37237**
Portuguese Journal (El Sobrante, CA) **1869**
Posey County News (Poseyville, IN) **10407**
Poseyville News **10407***
positions (Seattle, WA) **33005**
A Positive Approach (Millville, NJ) *Ceased*
Positive Strokes (Lamont, AB, Can.) *Ceased*
Positive Thinking (Pawling, NY) **23086**
Positivity (New York, NY) **22585**
Poskinolt Press (New York, NY) *Unable to locate*
Possibilities (Washington, DC) *Unable to locate*
The Post **27249***
The Post **2861***
The Post (Muscatine, IA) **11104**
The Post (Willingboro, NJ) **19754**
Post (Port Washington, NY) **23134**
The Post (Athens, OH) **24631**
The Post (Big Stone Gap, VA) **31865**
The Post (Buckingham, QC, Can.) *Unable to locate*
The Post-Abortion Review (Springfield, IL) **9641**
Post-Acute Care; ADVANCE for Providers of (King of Prussia, PA) **27120**
Post-adoption Helper (Southampton, ON, Can.) **36400**
Post/Ambassador (Blue Earth, MN) *Unable to locate*
Post-Bulletin (Rochester, MN) **16311**
The Post Colonial (Trenton, NJ) *Unable to locate*
Post-Communism; Problems of (Armonk, NY) **20092**
The Post and Courier (Charleston, SC) **28517**
The Post-Crescent (Appleton, WI) **33542**
Post Dispatch **1425***
Post Dispatch (Dardanelle, AR) **1098**
The Post Dispatch (Post, TX) **30961**
Post/Dispatch Features (Hollister, CA) *Unable to locate*
Post Eagle (Clifton, NJ) **18758**
Post Falls Press (Post Falls, ID) **7958**
Post Falls Tribune (Post Falls, ID) **7959**
Post-Gazette (Boston, MA) **13951**
Post-Gazette (Pittsburgh, PA) **27837**
The Post-Gazette and Oromocto Post **35424***
Post Herald (Red Creek, NY) **23178**
The Post-Journal (Jamestown, NY) **20842**
The Post-Journal and Metro Rockford Journal (Rockford, IL) **9529**
The Post & Mail (Columbia City, IN) **9893**
Post-Newsweek Cable **719***
Post-Newsweek Cable **681***
Post Newsweek Cable **758***
Post-Newsweek Cable **25732***
Post-Newsweek Cable (Bisbee, AZ) **661**
Post-Newsweek Cable (Phoenix, AZ) *Unable to locate*
Post-Newsweek Cable (Modesto, CA) **2572**
Post-Newsweek Cable (Gulfport, MS) **16655**
Post-Newsweek Cable (Ada, OK) **25728**
Post Newsweek Cable of Lampasas **30666***
The Post-Register (Idaho Falls, ID) **7868**
The Post Review (Somerville, NJ) *Unable to locate*
Post Script (Hamilton, MT) **17807**
The Post Script (Columbia, SC) *Unable to locate*
The Post-Searchlight (Bainbridge, GA) **7118**
The Post-Searchlight Extra (Bainbridge, GA) **7119**
Post Shopper (Pacific Palisades, CA) **2737**
Post Signal (Pilot Point, TX) **30935**
The Post-Standard (Syracuse, NY) **23419**
The Post-Star (Glens Falls, NY) **20669**
Post-Telegraph (Princeton, MO) **17366**
Post-Transcript **25167***
Post Tribune **17260***
Post-Tribune (San Jose, CA) **3532**
Post-Tribune (Merrillville, IN) **10299**
Post-Tribune (Jefferson City, MO) *Unable to locate*
Postal Bulletin (Pittsburgh, PA) **27838**
Postal History Journal; Rhode Island (North Providence, RI) **28377**
Postal Life (Washington, DC) *Unable to locate*
Postal Record (Washington, DC) **5724**
The Postal Supervisor (Washington, DC) *Unable to locate*
Postal Worker; The American (Washington, DC) **5339**
Postcard Collector (Dubuque, IA) **10844**
Postgraduate Medicine (Minneapolis, MN) **16121**
Postgraduate Radiology (St. Louis, MO) *Ceased*
The Posthorn (Boulder, CO) **4184**
Postmasters Gazette (Fairfax, VA) **32027**
Postmodern Culture (Baltimore, MD) **13238**
The Postville Herald-Leader (Postville, IA) **11165**
Pot-Bellied Pigs (Pleasant Grove, CA) *Ceased*
Potashville-Miner Journal (Esterhazy, SK, Can.) **37464**
Potato Country (Yakima, WA) **33221**
Potato Eyes (Troy, ME) *Ceased*
Potato Grower (Idaho Falls, ID) **7869**
Potato Grower; Valley (Fargo, ND) **24415**
Potato News; Maine (Presque Isle, ME) **13034**
Potato Production and Postharvest Handling; Journal of (Parma, ID) **7942**
Potato Research; American Journal of (Orono, ME) **12998**
Poteau Daily News & Sun (Poteau, OK) **26045**
Poteau News & Sun **26045***
Potencia (Tulsa, OK) **26126**
Potential Analysis (New York, NY) **22586**
Potentials (Minneapolis, MN) **16122**
Potentials; IEEE (New York, NY) **21847**
Potentials in Marketing **16122***
Potomac; AAA World— (Philadelphia, PA) **27357**
Potomac/Bethesda Almanac (Potomac, MD) **13658**
Potomac Children (Chevy Chase, MD) **13408**
Potomac Express (Alexandria, VA) *Ceased*
Potomac Gazette (Frederick, MD) *Unable to locate*
Potomac Gazette; North (Frederick, MD) **13518**
Potomac News (Woodbridge, VA) **32637**
The Potpourri (Fremont, CA) *Unable to locate*
Potpourri (Santa Clara, CA) *Unable to locate*
Potpourri Newspaper (Magnolia, TX) *Unable to locate*
(Potsdam); Blueline (Potsdam, NY) **23137**
Potter County Leader **26811***
Potter County News (Gettysburg, SD) *Unable to locate*
Potter Enterprise **26811***
Potter Leader-Enterprise **26811***
The Potter Leader Enterprise (Coudersport, PA) **26811**
Potter Printing, Inc. **24386***
Pottersfield Portfolio (Sydney, NS, Can.) **35609**
Pottery Making Illustrated (Westerville, OH) **25644**
Pottery Southwest (Santa Fe, NM) **19941**
Pottsville Republican (Pottsville, PA) **27903**
Poughkeepsie Journal (Poughkeepsie, NY) **23149**
The Poultney News (East Poultney, VT) *Ceased*
Poultry Digest (Mount Morris, IL) *Ceased*
Poultry and Egg Marketing (Gainesville, GA) **7293**
Poultry International (Mount Morris, IL) **9245**
Poultry Life; Palmetto (Columbia, SC) **28560**
Poultry Magazine (Chicago, IL) **8538**
Poultry Magazine/La Revue Canadienne D'Aviculture; Canada (Delhi, ON, Can.) **35764**
Poultry Marketing & Technology **8538***
Poultry; Meat & (Kansas City, MO) **17182**
Poultry News (Rutland, VT) *Ceased*
Poultry Press (Connersville, IN) **9901**
Poultry Processing (Mount Morris, IL) *Ceased*
Poultry Science (Champaign, IL) *Unable to locate*
Poultry Times (Gainesville, GA) **7294**
Poultry USA; WATT (Cullman, AL) **162**
The Pound Ridge Review (Ridgefield, CT) *Unable to locate*
Pour Parler Profession; Professionally Speaking/ (Toronto, ON, Can.) **36717**
P.O.V. (New York, NY) *Unable to locate*
Poverty; Journal of (Columbus, OH) **25027**
The Pow Wow (Monroe, LA) **12693**
Poway News Chieftain (Poway, CA) **2867**
POWDER (Dana Point, CA) **1806**
Powder and Bulk Engineering (St. Paul, MN) **16407**
Powder/Bulk Solids (Morris Plains, NJ) **19302**
Powder Diffraction (Newtown Square, PA) **27331**
Powder River Cable TV (Douglas, WY) *Ceased*
Powder River Examiner (Broadus, MT) **17759**
Powder Springs Neighbor (Powder Springs, GA) **7486**
Powell County Shopper News (Clay City, KY) *Unable to locate*
The Powell River News (Powell River, BC, Can.) *Ceased*
The Powell River Peak (Powell River, BC, Can.) **35054**
The Powell Tribune (Powell, WY) **34569**
Powell Valley News (Pennington Gap, VA) **32326**
Power (New York, NY) **22587**
Power Association Bulletin; Northwest Public (Vancouver, WA) **33177**
The Power County Press (American Falls, ID) **7798**
Power Delivery (Tulsa, OK) *Ceased*
Power; Electric Light & (Tulsa, OK) **26115**
Power Energy Ecology (Philadelphia, PA) *Ceased*
Power and Energy Systems; International Journal of (Calgary, AB, Can.) **34648**
Power Engineering (Tulsa, OK) **26127**
Power Engineering International (Tulsa, OK) **26128**
Power Equipment; Outdoor (Chicago, IL) **8521**
Power Equipment Trade (Montgomery, AL) **375**
Power & Gas Marketing (Houston, TX) **30521**
Power and Motoryacht (New York, NY) **22588**
Power Quality Assurance (Overland Park, KS) **11726**
Power Quarterly; International Private (New York, NY) **21931**
Power; Texas Co-op (Austin, TX) **29813**
Powerboat Magazine (Ventura, CA) **4008**
PowerBuilder Developer's Journal (Montvale, NJ) **19273**
Powerlifting USA Magazine (Camarillo, CA) **1642**
Powerline (Boca Raton, FL) **5938**
Powersports Business (Maple Grove, MN) **16039**
Powersystems Journal *Unable to locate*
Powertechnics (Norco, CA) *Unable to locate*
PowerValue (Overland Park, KS) *Ceased*
Poynette Press (Poynette, WI) **34264**
The Poynor Group (New York, NY) **38037**
POZ (New York, NY) *Unable to locate*
PPI Detailed Report (Washington, DC) **5725**
PR Millenium Editions **19594***
PR Newswire (New York, NY) **38038**
PR Services Report; O'Dwyer's (New York, NY) **22484**
PR Watch (Madison, WI) **33969**
PR Week (New York, NY) *Unable to locate*
The Practical Accountant (New York, NY) **22589**
Practical Allergy & Immunology **37362***
Practical Anarchy (Madison, WI) *Unable to locate*
Practical Anthropology **12453***
Practical Cardiology (Montvale, NJ) *Ceased*
Practical Diabetology (New York, NY) **22590**
Practical Gastroenterology (Westhampton Beach, NY) *Unable to locate*
The Practical Homeowner (Redwood City, CA) *Ceased*
Practical Homeschooling (Fenton, MO) **17064**
Practical Horseman (Harrisburg, PA) *Unable to locate*
The Practical Lawyer (Philadelphia, PA) **27641**
The Practical Litigator (Philadelphia, PA) **27642**
Practical Nursing; Journal of (Silver Spring, MD) **13733**
Practical Optometry (Saint-Laurent, QC, Can.) **37366**
Practical Procedures & Aesthetic Dentistry (Mahwah, NJ) **19205**
The Practical Real Estate Lawyer (Philadelphia, PA) **27643**
Practical Survival (Boulder, CO) *Unable to locate*
The Practical Tax Lawyer (Philadelphia, PA) **27644**
Practical Tax Strategies (New York, NY) **22591**

Numbers cited in bold after listings are entry numbers rather than page numbers.

Princeton Times (Princeton, WV) **33441**
Princeton Times-Republic (Berlin, WI) **33585**
Princeton Union-Eagle (Princeton, MN) **16284**
Princeton Weekly Bulletin (Princeton, NJ) **19472**
Principal (Alexandria, VA) **31725**
Print (New York, NY) *Unable to locate*
Print-Equip News (Glendale, CA) **2012**
Print & Graphics (Timonium, MD) *Unable to locate*
Print Marketing Concepts (Houston, TX) **38043**
Print Media (Falls Church, VA) **32052**
Print Reporter South (Chicago, IL) *Unable to locate*
Print Solutions (Alexandria, VA) **31726**
PrintAction (Toronto, ON, Can.) **36716**
Printed Circuit Assembly (Manhasset, NY) *Unable to locate*
Printed Circuit Design **21010***
Printed Circuit Design & Manufacture (Manhasset, NY) **21010**
Printed Circuit Fabrication **7035***
Printed Circuit Fabrication (Manhasset, NY) **21011**
Printed Circuit Network (Sparta, NJ) **19593**
Printer; American (Overland Park, KS) **11695**
Printer & Electronic Publisher; In-Plant (Libertyville, IL) **9078**
Printer; Instant and Small Commercial (Libertyville, IL) **9079**
Printer Magazine; Canadian (Toronto, ON, Can.) **36526**
Printers Hot Line (Fort Dodge, IA) *Unable to locate*
Printer's News (Lufkin, TX) *Ceased*
Printing; High Volume (Libertyville, IL) **9077**
Printing Impressions (Falls Church, VA) **32053**
Printing Journal (Timonium, MD) *Unable to locate*
Printing Manager (Paramus, NJ) **19406**
Printing News (Melville, NY) **21060**
Printing News/East (Melville, NY) **21061**
Printing News Midwest (Chicago, IL) *Unable to locate*
Printing; Package (Falls Church, VA) **32051**
Printing Products International (Port St. Lucie, FL) *Ceased*
Printing; Quick (Melville, NY) **21063**
Printing; Screen (Cincinnati, OH) **24815**
Printing Views (Timonium, MD) *Unable to locate*
PrintMedia Magazine (Falls Church, VA) **32054**
Prints (Alton, IL) *Ceased*
Printwear (Broomfield, CO) **4206**
Prior Lake American (Prior Lake, MN) **16288**
Priorities (New York, NY) *Ceased*
PRIORITIES (Salt Lake City, UT) *Ceased*
Prism (San Francisco, CA) *Ceased*
Prism (Fort Lauderdale, FL) *Ceased*
PRISM (Bala Cynwyd, PA) *Unable to locate*
PRISM International (Vancouver, BC, Can.) **35159**
Prism Radio Partners, L.P. **11900***
The Prison Journal (Philadelphia, PA) **27646**
Prison Legal News (Seattle, WA) **33006**
Prison Life (Columbia, MO) *Unable to locate*
Prisoners' Legal News **33006***
Private Arts (Chicago, IL) *Unable to locate*
Private Banking (New York, NY) *Ceased*
Private Cable & Wireless Cable Magazine (Houston, TX) *Unable to locate*
Private Clubs (Dallas, TX) **30178**
Private Enterprise; The Journal of (Hartford, CT) **4896**
Private Equity; The Journal of (South Bend, IN) **10456**
Private Equity Week (New York, NY) **22594**
Private Eye **31438***
Private Eyes Magazine (Hollywood, CA) *Unable to locate*
Private Label (Fort Lee, NJ) **18833**
Private Label Executive Edition (Fort Lee, NJ) *Ceased*
Private Label International (Fort Lee, NJ) *Unable to locate*
Private Label News (Doylestown, PA) *Ceased*
Private Pilot Magazine (Mission Viejo, CA) *Unable to locate*
Private Power Executive (Southport, CT) **5137**
Private Practice (Oklahoma City, OK) *Unable to locate*
Private Varnish (Pasadena, CA) *Unable to locate*
Pro (Fort Atkinson, WI) **33717**
Pro-Am Sports Service/Mile Square Publisher (Indianapolis, IN) *Unable to locate*
Pro Athlete (San Jose, CA) *Ceased*
PRO BASS **25762***
PRO/E (Santa Fe, NM) **19942**
Pro-Farm (Regina, SK, Can.) *Unable to locate*
Pro Football Weekly (Riverwoods, IL) **9508**
Pro Kent (Richibucto, NB, Can.) *Unable to locate*
Pro-Life Action News (Chicago, IL) **8539**
PRO REGE (Sioux Center, IA) **11206**
Pro Serv Inc. (Raleigh, NC) *Unable to locate*
Pro Sound News (New York, NY) **22595**
Pro Tooner (Daly City, CA) **1804**
Pro Trucker (Roswell, GA) **7517**
Probability; The Annals of (Beachwood, OH) **24649**

Probability; The Annals of Applied (Beachwood, OH) **24648**
Probability and Computing; Combinatorics, (New York, NY) **21451**
Probability in the Engineering and Informational Sciences (Berkeley, CA) **1552**
Probability and Its Applications; Theory of (Philadelphia, PA) **27704**
Probability; Journal of Theoretical (Tampa, FL) **6772**
Probability & Mathematical Statistics; Theory of (Providence, RI) **28425**
Probability; Methodology and Computing in Applied (New York, NY) **22326**
Probate Law Journal of Ohio (Cleveland, OH) **24944**
Probate and Property (Chicago, IL) **8540**
Probate Reporter; Estate Planning and California (Berkeley, CA) **1518**
Probation and Parole Law Reports (Warrensburg, MO) **17669**
Probe (Chicago, IL) *Ceased*
Probe Post (Toronto, ON, Can.) *Ceased*
Problems in Anesthesia (Philadelphia, PA) **27647**
Problems in Critical Care (New York, NY) *Ceased*
Problems of Economic Transition (Armonk, NY) **20091**
Problems of Economics **20091***
Problems in General Surgery (New York, NY) *Unable to locate*
Problems of Information Transmission (New York, NY) **22596**
Problems in Optometry (New York, NY) *Ceased*
Problems in Plastic & Reconstructive Surgery (Hagerstown, MD) *Unable to locate*
Problems of Post-Communism (Armonk, NY) **20092**
Problems in Respiratory Care (Philadelphia, PA) *Ceased*
Problems in Urology (New York, NY) *Ceased*
Problems in Veterinary Medicine (New York, NY) *Ceased*
Proceedings (Annapolis, MD) **13096**
Proceedings of the American Mathematical Society (Providence, RI) **28413**
Proceedings of the American Philosophical Society (Philadelphia, PA) **27648**
Proceedings of the Entomological Society of Washington (Washington, DC) **5730**
Proceedings of the IEEE (New York, NY) **22597**
Proceedings of the National Academy of Sciences of the United States of America (Washington, DC) **5731**
The Proceedings of the Nutrition Society (New York, NY) *Ceased*
Proceedings of the Society for Experimental Biology and Medicine (Philadelphia, PA) *Ceased*
Process Cooling and Equipment (Troy, MI) **15637**
Process Equipment & Control News; Canadian (Toronto, ON, Can.) **36527**
Process Heating (Bensenville, IL) **8070**
Process Industries Canada (Exeter, ON, Can.) *Ceased*
Process Safety and Environmental Protection (Philadelphia, PA) *Ceased*
Processed World (San Francisco, CA) **3416**
Processing (Itasca, IL) **9016**
Processing; International Journal of Adaptive Control and Signal (Hoboken, NJ) **18975**
Processing Letters; IEEE Signal (New York, NY) **21848**
Processing Letters; Neural (New York, NY) **22422**
Processor (Lincoln, NE) **18115**
Procomm Enterprises Magazine (San Anselmo, CA) *Unable to locate*
Proctor Journal (Proctor, MN) **16289**
Produce Business (Boca Raton, FL) **5939**
Produce Merchandising (Lenexa, KS) **11596**
The Produce News (Englewood Cliffs, NJ) **18802**
Producer; The Seminole (Seminole, OK) **26058**
Producers Masterguide (New York, NY) **22598**
Product Design and Development (Morris Plains, NJ) **19303**
Product News **13065***
Product News; Mobile **13664***
Product News; New (Chicago, IL) **8506**
Product News; Rental (Fort Atkinson, WI) **33720**
Producteur de Lait Quebecois; Le (Longueuil, QC, Can.) **37055**
Production and Facilities; SPE (Richardson, TX) **30980**
Production and Inventory Management Journal (Alexandria, VA) *Unable to locate*
Production Technology News (Morris Plains, NJ) **19304**
Productores de Hortalizas (Willoughby, OH) **25663**
Products Finishing (Cincinnati, OH) **24813**
Produits Pour L'Industrie Quebecoise (Markham, ON, Can.) **36031**
Profane Existence (Minneapolis, MN) **16124**
Professional Agent (Alexandria, VA) **31727**

Professional American Society of Brewing Chemists **16381***
Professional BoatBuilder (Brooklin, ME) **12932**
Professional Builder (Des Plaines, IL) **8768**
Professional Candy Buyer (Palm Springs, CA) **2765**
Professional Carwashing & Detailing (Latham, NY) **20933**
Professional Check Casher (St. James, NY) **23289**
Professional Cleaning Journal (Dallas, TX) *Unable to locate*
Professional Collector Magazine (Boston, MA) **13952**
Professional Computing (New York, NY) *Ceased*
Professional Counselor **6048***
Professional Counselor (Deerfield Beach, FL) *Ceased*
Professional Educator (Auburn, AL) **44**
Professional Engineer **31670***
The Professional Engineer (Raleigh, NC) **24150**
Professional Engineer in Kentucky **12069***
Professional Ethics (Gainesville, FL) **6153**
The Professional Geographer (San Diego, CA) **3249**
Professional Insurance Agents (Glenmont, NY) **20668**
The Professional Lawyer (Chicago, IL) **8541**
Professional Mariner (Portland, ME) **13018**
Professional Medical Assistant **8534***
Professional Photographer **7039***
Professional Photographer Storytellers (Atlanta, GA) **7039**
Professional Photographers of Canada (Winnipeg, MB, Can.) **35350**
Professional Pilot (Alexandria, VA) **31728**
Professional Psychology: Research and Practice (Washington, DC) **5732**
Professional Purchasing **20719***
The Professional Quilter (Lewisberry, PA) *Unable to locate*
Professional Remodeler (Oak Brook, IL) **9362**
Professional Renovation Magazine **36838***
Professional Report (Washington, DC) **5733**
Professional Roofing (Rosemont, IL) **9556**
Professional Safety (Des Plaines, IL) **8769**
Professional School Counseling (Alexandria, VA) **31729**
Professional School Psychology **18118***
Professional Speaker (Tempe, AZ) **913**
Professional Stained Glass **27933***
Professional Stained Glass (Brewster, NY) *Unable to locate*
Professional Surveyor (Frederick, MD) **13520**
Professional Tool & Equipment News (Fort Atkinson, WI) **33718**
The Professional Upholsterer (High Point, NC) *Ceased*
Professionally Speaking/Pour Parler Profession (Toronto, ON, Can.) **36717**
Professor George's Lottery (Boca Raton, FL) *Ceased*
The Profile (Decatur, GA) **7237**
Profile Kingston (Kingston, ON, Can.) **35942**
Profile: Life in the Armed Forces **32292***
Profile (Norfolk) (Norfolk, VA) **32292**
Profiles (Toronto, ON, Can.) **36718**
Profit (Redwood City, CA) **2915**
Profit (Toronto, ON, Can.) **36719**
Profit: Business to E-Business **2915***
Profit Guide; Zacks (Chicago, IL) **8611**
Profit Home Business (Toronto, ON, Can.) *Ceased*
Profitable Craft Merchandising (New York, NY) *Ceased*
The Profitline **30602***
Profits; Contracting (Milwaukee, WI) **34064**
Program (Mount Prospect, IL) **9249**
Program (Medford, NJ) *Ceased*
Program TV **9249***
Programming and Computer Software (New York, NY) **22599**
Programming; Embedded Systems (Manhasset, NY) **21000**
Programming; Journal of Functional (New York, NY) **22073**
Programming Languages and Systems; ACM Transactions on (New York, NY) **21142**
Programming Magazine (Columbia, SC) **28563**
Programming Quarterly; Intergenerational (Binghamton, NY) **20156**
Programming; Scientific (Hoboken, NJ) **19102**
Progres de Coaticook; Le (Coaticook, QC, Can.) **36976**
Progres-Dimanche (Chicoutimi, QC, Can.) **36966**
Progres-Echo (Rimouski, QC, Can.) **37308**
Progres de St. Leonard (Montreal, QC, Can.) **37210**
Progres St. Leonard-Nouveau Rosemont (Montreal, QC, Can.) *Unable to locate*
Progreso (New York, NY) *Unable to locate*
The Progress **8672***
The Progress (Christopher, IL) **8672**
The Progress (Bernardsville, NJ) **18679**
The Progress (Havelock, NC) *Unable to locate*
The Progress (Clearfield, PA) **26788**
The Progress (Anahuac, TX) **29722**
The Progress (Three Rivers, TX) **31191**

Public Utilities Law Anthology *Ceased*
Public Welfare (Washington, DC) *Unable to locate*
Public Works (Ridgewood, NJ) **19503**
Public Works; Civic (Toronto, ON, Can.) **36551**
Public Works Management & Policy (Thousand Oaks, CA) **3910**
Publication of the Astronomical Society of the Pacific (Tempe, AZ) **914**
The Publick Enterprise (Annapolis, MD) *Ceased*
Publiquip/RouCam (La Salle, QC, Can.) *Unable to locate*
Publish (Chatsworth, CA) *Unable to locate*
The Publisher (Toronto, ON, Can.) *Unable to locate*
Publisher; California (Sacramento, CA) **2987**
Publisher; In-Plant Printer & Electronic (Libertyville, IL) **9078**
Publisher; Oklahoma (Oklahoma City, OK) **25986**
Publisher; Oregon (Portland, OR) **26493**
Publishers' Auxiliary (Washington, DC) *Unable to locate*
Publishers; Brilliant Ideas for (Clam Lake, WI) **33634**
Publishers Weekly (New York, NY) **22610**
Publishing; Electronic (Nashua, NH) **18589**
Publishing Entrepreneur (Traverse City, MI) **15601**
Publishing; Journal of Scholarly (Toronto, ON, Can.) **36639**
Publishing Market Place Reference Plus *Ceased*
Publishing News (East Windsor, NJ) *Unable to locate*
Publishing & Production Executive **32054***
Publishing Research Quarterly (New York, NY) **22611**
Publishing Technology **32054***
Publius: The Journal of Federalism (Easton, PA) **26851**
Puck (San Francisco, CA) *Unable to locate*
The Puck (Brookline, MA) *Unable to locate*
Puckerbrush Review (Orono, ME) **13003**
Pudding Magazine (Columbus, OH) **25057**
The Pueblo Chieftain (Pueblo, CO) **4599**
Puente; El (Goshen, IN) **10022**
Puerta del Sol (Nashville, TN) **29482**
Puerto Rico; El Visitante de (San Juan, PR) **28293**
Puerto Rico; El Vocero de (San Juan, PR) **28294**
Puerto Rico Journal of Agriculture; University of (Rio Piedras, PR) **28286**
Puerto Rico; La Estrella de (Hato Rey, PR) **28248**
Puerto Rico; TCI Cable of (Luquillo, PR) **28255**
Puerto Rico; WHERE (Guaynabo, PR) **28246**
Puget Sound Business Journal (Seattle, WA) **33007**
Puget Sound Computer User (Seattle, WA) **33008**
Puget Sound Navy News (Bainbridge Island, WA) *Unable to locate*
Puget Sound Parent (Seattle, WA) **33009**
Pulaski Cablevision (Pulaski, TN) *Unable to locate*
Pulaski Citizen (Pulaski, TN) **29572**
Pulaski County Journal (Winamac, IN) **10564**
Pulaski Democrat (Pulaski, NY) *Unable to locate*
Pulaski Democrat (Shopper) (Pulaski, NY) *Unable to locate*
The Pulaski Enterprise (Mounds, IL) *Ceased*
Pulaski Week **12406***
The Pullman Herald (San Mateo, CA) *Ceased*
Pullman TV Cable Co., Inc. (Moscow, ID) **7925**
Pulmonary Medicine; Internet Journal of (Sugar Land, TX) **31159**
Pulmonary Pharmacology (New York, NY) **22612**
Pulmonology; Pediatric (Hoboken, NJ) **19079**
Pulp and Paper (San Francisco, CA) **3419**
Pulp & Paper Canada (Pointe-Claire, QC, Can.) **37277**
Pulp & Paper Forecaster (Manhasset, NY) *Ceased*
Pulp & Paper International (Manhasset, NY) **21012**
Pulp & Paper Science; Journal of (Montreal, QC, Can.) **37145**
Pulpit Helps (Chattanooga, TN) **29092**
Pulse (Pico Rivera, CA) **2841**
Pulse! (West Sacramento, CA) **4066**
Pulse; The Air (Offutt A F B, NE) **18187**
Pulse Journal (Mason, OH) *Unable to locate*
Pulse of the Planet (Ashland, OR) **26216**
Punch Digest for Canadian Doctors **36108***
Punch In Travel & Entertainment News Syndicate (New York, NY) **38044**
Punch in International Travel and Entertainment Magazine (New York, NY) **22613**
The Punch List (New York, NY) **22614**
Puncture (Portland, OR) **26503**
Punjab Guardian **35105***
Puntos. (Dallas, TX) *Unable to locate*
Purcell Register (Purcell, OK) **26050**
Purchase; Point Of (Roswell, GA) **7516**
Purchaser; Southern (Greensboro, NC) **23940**
Purchasing Agent; Industrial (Great Neck, NY) **20689**
Purchasing; CPI (Newton, MA) **14385**
Purchasing; Electronic **14394***
Purchasing Guide; Government (Toronto, ON, Can.) **36608**
Purchasing Magazine (Newton, MA) **14408**
Purchasing Management (St. Cloud, MN) *Ceased*
Purchasing; Modern (Toronto, ON, Can.) **36666**

Purchasing News; Healthcare (Highland Park, IL) **8992**
Purchasing and Supply Management; European Journal of (Burlington, MA) **14027**
Purchasing Today **905***
PurchasingWorld (Cleveland, OH) *Ceased*
Purdue Alumnus (West Lafayette, IN) **10551**
Purdue Engineer (West Lafayette, IN) *Unable to locate*
Purdue University *Ceased*
Pure Heart Magazine (Birmingham, AL) **88**
The Purebred Picture (Prophetstown, IL) *Ceased*
Purple Cow (Atlanta, GA) *Unable to locate*
Purpose (Scottdale, PA) **27956**
PUSH! (New York, NY) *Unable to locate*
The Putnam - Cabell Post (Culloden, WV) **33298**
Putnam County Courier **5093***
The Putnam County Courier (New Milford, CT) **5034**
Putnam County Journal Courier **6022***
Putnam County Journal; Unionville Republican & (Unionville, MO) **17658**
Putnam County News & Recorder (Cold Spring, NY) **20483**
Putnam County Record (Granville, IL) **8951**
Putnam County Sentinel (Ottawa, OH) **25452**
Putnam County Vidette/Pandora Times (Columbus Grove, OH) **25091**
Putnam Courier Trader (Putnam, CT) **5093**
Putnam Democrat (Culloden, WV) **33299**
Putnam Pennysaver (Palatka, FL) **6538**
The Putnam Pit (Cookeville, TN) *Unable to locate*
The Putnam Post/The Cabell Bulletin **33298***
The Putnam Trader **5093***
Puxico Weekly Press (Puxico, MO) **17367**
Puyallup Herald (Puyallup, WA) **32918**
Puzzle Feature Syndicate (Sun City, CA) *Unable to locate*
Puzzles; Good Time Fill-in (Norwalk, CT) **5062**
Puzzles; Good Time Word Seek (Norwalk, CT) **5063**
Pygmy Goat Digest **2640***
Pymatuning Area News (Andover, OH) **24611**
The Pyramid (Detroit, MI) *Unable to locate*
The Pyramid (Mount Pleasant, UT) **31372**
The Pyramid Shopper (Mount Pleasant, UT) **31373**
Pyrotechnics; Journal of (Whitewater, CO) **4685**

Q

Q (Cambridge, MA) **14092**
Q Journal (Cambridge, MA) **14093**
Q-Notes (Charlotte, NC) **23751**
Q, The Magazine That Answers Questions About Relationships (Van Nuys, CA) *Ceased*
QCWA News (Eugene, OR) **26332**
QDT (Carol Stream, IL) **8153**
Q.J.I. (Shreveport, LA) **12818**
Q105 **5024***
QST (Newington, CT) **5037**
Quachita Communications, Inc. **1276***
The Quad (West Chester, PA) **28148**
Quad-City Herald; Brewster (Brewster, WA) **32696**
Quad-City News (Hollywood, FL) *Unable to locate*
Quad-City Times (Davenport, IA) **10738**
Quad Community Press (White Bear Lake, MN) **16510**
Quad River News (Sheridan, MO) **17580**
Quail Unlimited (Edgefield, SC) **28601**
Quaker Campus (Whittier, CA) **4079**
Quaker Life (Richmond, IN) **10421**
Quaker Queries (Spokane, WA) *Ceased*
The Quakertown Free Press **27914***
Qualicum Beach News; Parksville- (Parksville, BC, Can.) **35043**
Qualified Remodeler Magazine (Fort Atkinson, WI) **33719**
Qualitative Health Research (Edmonton, AB, Can.) **34726**
Qualitative Sociology (New York, NY) *Unable to locate*
Quality (Bensenville, IL) *Ceased*
Quality Assurance (San Diego, CA) **3251**
Quality Assurance in Hospitality & Tourism; Journal of (Binghamton, NY) **20194**
Quality Cable **10186***
Quality Cities (Tallahassee, FL) **6729**
Quality Control and Applied Statistics (Davenport, IA) **10739**
Quality Digest (Cottonwood, CA) *Unable to locate*
Quality Engineering (Lacey, WA) **32803**
Quality of Life Research (New York, NY) **22615**
Quality Management; Environmental (Hoboken, NJ) **18941**
Quality Management in Health Care (Gaithersburg, MD) **13547**
Quality Management Journal (Milwaukee, WI) **34095**

Quality in Manufacturing (Solon, OH) *Ceased*
Quality Matters (Washington, DC) **5753**
The Quality Observer (Fairfax, VA) *Unable to locate*
Quality and Participation; The Journal for (Cincinnati, OH) **24808**
Quality Progress (Milwaukee, WI) *Unable to locate*
Quality and Reliability Engineering International (Hoboken, NJ) **19093**
The Quality Review (New York, NY) *Ceased*
Quality Review Bulletin **9380***
Quality Shopper (Chattanooga, TN) *Unable to locate*
Quallity Advocate Matters **5753***
Quanah Tribune-Chief (Quanah, TX) **30963**
Quantico Sentry (Woodbridge, VA) **32638**
Quantitative Analysis; Journal of Financial and (Seattle, WA) **32977**
Quantitative Criminology; Journal of (New York, NY) **22174**
Quantitative Microbiology (New York, NY) **22616**
Quantum (Arlington, VA) **31822**
Quantum Chemistry; International Journal of (Hoboken, NJ) **18995**
Quantum Electronics (College Park, MD) *Unable to locate*
Quantum Information; Virtual Journal of (College Park, MD) **13446**
Quarante (Arlington, VA) *Unable to locate*
Quarry Magazine (Kingston, ON, Can.) **35943**
Quarry; Pit & (Cleveland, OH) **24942**
Quarry Trader; Mine & (Indianapolis, IN) **10154**
Quart de Rond (Longueuil, QC, Can.) **37058**
The Quarter Horse Journal **29695***
The Quarter Racing Journal (Amarillo, TX) **29697**
The Quarter Racing Record (Oklahoma City, OK) *Unable to locate*
The Quarterly (Canton, NY) **20430**
The Quarterly (New York, NY) **22617**
Quarterly Bulletin of the Archeological Society of Virginia (Courtland, VA) *Unable to locate*
The Quarterly Byte *Ceased*
Quarterly Financial Report for Manufacturing, Mining and Trade Corporations (Pittsburgh, PA) *Unable to locate*
Quarterly Journal of Austrian Economics (New York, NY) **22618**
Quarterly Journal of Business & Economics (Lincoln, NE) **18116**
The Quarterly Journal of Economics (Cambridge, MA) **14094**
Quarterly Journal For New Jersey Dentists **19381***
Quarterly Journal of Speech (Washington, DC) **5754**
Quarterly Labour Force Statistics (Washington, DC) **5755**
Quarterly Magazine **36175***
Quarterly National Accounts (Washington, DC) **5756**
Quarterly Oil Statistics and Energy Balances **5706***
The Quarterly Review *Ceased*
The Quarterly Review of Biology (Stony Brook, NY) **23375**
Quarterly Review of Biophysics (New Haven, CT) **5000**
Quarterly Review of Economics & Business **8214***
The Quarterly Review of Economics and Finance (Champaign, IL) **8214**
Quarterly Review of Film Studies (New York, NY) *Unable to locate*
Quarterly Review; Virginia (Charlottesville, VA) **31947**
The Quarterly Review of Wines (Winchester, MA) **14666**
The Quarterly-Royal Canadian Mounted Police **36275***
Quartermaster's Review **5559***
Quartier Libre; Nouveau (Montreal, QC, Can.) **37196**
Quartz Hill Journal of Theology (Quartz Hill, CA) **2868**
Quaternary Features (New York, NY) *Unable to locate*
Quaternary Research (San Diego, CA) **3252**
Quaternary Science; Journal of (Hoboken, NJ) **19043**
Quay County Sun (Tucumcari, NM) **19971**
The Quayle Quarterly (Bridgeport, CT) *Ceased*
Que Pasa (Hartford, CT) *Ceased*
Que Pasa (Teaneck, NJ) *Ceased*
Que Pasa San Antonio (San Antonio, TX) **31043**
Quebec; L'infirmiere du (Montreal, QC, Can.) **37126**
Quebec Chronicle Telegraph (Ste.-Foy, QC, Can.) **37338**
Quebec Construction (Saint-Laurent, QC, Can.) *Ceased*
Quebec Enterprise (Montreal, QC, Can.) *Unable to locate*
Quebec Etudiant (Montreal, QC, Can.) *Unable to locate*
Quebec Habitation (Anjou, QC, Can.) **36938**
Quebec Home & School News (Montreal, QC, Can.) **37211**
Quebec Info (Ste.-Foy, QC, Can.) **37339**
Quebec; Le Journal de (Quebec, QC, Can.) **37288**
Quebec; Mariage (Toronto, ON, Can.) **36656**

Quebec Micro! (Toronto, ON, Can.) *Unable to locate*
Quebec Pharmacie (Montreal, QC, Can.) 37212
Quebec; Sante Mentale au (Montreal, QC, Can.) 37221
Quebec Science (Montreal, QC, Can.) 37213
Quebec Vert (Quebec, QC, Can.) 37295
Quebec Yachting (Toronto, ON, Can.) *Unable to locate*
Quebecs Farmers Advocate (Ste.-Anne-de-Bellevue, QC, Can.) 37328
Queen of All Hearts (Bay Shore, NY) 20137
Queen Anne/Magnolia News (Seattle, WA) 33010
Queen Charlotte Islands Observer (Queen Charlotte, BC, Can.) 35068
Queen's Alumni Review (Kingston, ON, Can.) 35944
Queens Bar Bulletin (Flushing, NY) 20610
Queens Chronicle (Rego Park, NY) 23180
Queens; Forum of (Ozone Park, NY) 23072
Queens Gazette (Astoria, NY) 20102
Queens Inner Unity Cable Systems (Richmond Hill, NY) 23189
Queen's Journal (Kingston, ON, Can.) 35945
Queens Ledger (Queens, NY) 23169
Queen's Mystery Magazine; Ellery (New York, NY) 21597
Queen's Quarterly (Kingston, ON, Can.) 35946
Queens Tribune (Fresh Meadows, NY) 20629
Queens Village (Rockville Centre, NY) *Ceased*
Queens Village Shopper's Guide (Ontario, ON, Can.) 36168
The Queens Village Times (Queens Village, NY) 23170
Queens Voice 20839*
Quesnel Cariboo Observer (Quesnel, BC, Can.) 35069
Quest (Tucson, AZ) 960
Quest (Champaign, IL) 8215
The Quest (Wheaton, IL) 9758
Questions (Charlottesville, VA) 31939
Queueing Systems (New York, NY) 22619
Quick & Easy Crafts 9805*
Quick & Easy Plastic Canvas (Big Sandy, TX) 29923
Quick & Easy Quilting (Berne, IN) 9817
Quick Frozen Foods International (Fort Lee, NJ) 18834
Quick Frozen Foods Magazine 21738*
Quick Guide (Baltimore, MD) *Unable to locate*
Quick 'n Easy Country Cookin' (Davis, SD) *Unable to locate*
Quick Print Products (New York, NY) *Ceased*
Quick Printing (Melville, NY) 21063
Quicks Professional Journal (Baltimore, MD) 13240
Quidditas (Laramie, WY) 34552
Quill (Indianapolis, IN) 10165
The Quill (Troy, NY) 23456
The Quill (Brandon, MB, Can.) 35255
Quill & Quire (Toronto, ON, Can.) 36721
Quill & Scroll (Iowa City, IA) 10986
Quilt Craft (New York, NY) *Unable to locate*
Quilt World (Berne, IN) 9818
The Quilter (Newton, NJ) 19374
Quilter; American (Paducah, KY) 12337
Quilter's Newsletter Magazine (Wheat Ridge, CO) *Unable to locate*
Quilter's Treasury (Berne, IN) *Ceased*
Quilting; American Patchwork and (Des Moines, IA) 10770
Quilting; Quick & Easy (Berne, IN) 9817
Quilting Today 27291*
Quilting Today (Montrose, PA) *Ceased*
Quiltworks Today (Montrose, PA) 27291
Quin County Advertiser (Oak Ridge, TN) *Ceased*
Quincaillerie-Materiaux (Toronto, ON, Can.) *Unable to locate*
The Quincy Herald Whig (Quincy, IL) 9474
Quincy Valley Post-Register (Quincy, WA) 32919
Quinte Cablevision Ltd. (Picton, ON, Can.) 36330
Quinte Weekly News (Belleville, ON, Can.) *Unable to locate*
Quintessence International (Carol Stream, IL) 8154
Quinto Lingo (Alexandria, VA) *Unable to locate*
Quirk's Marketing Research Review (Minneapolis, MN) 16125
Quitaque Post 30967*
Quitman County Democrat (Marks, MS) 16759
Quitman Free Press (Adel, GA) 6900
Quiz Features (Washington, DC) 38045
Quiz; The Ord (Ord, NE) 18236
The Quoddy Tides (Eastport, ME) 12954
Quondanet Futurus; Arthurian Interpretations 30124*
Quota Connection 5757*
Quotarian (Washington, DC) 5757
Quote (Dodson, LA) 12568
Quotidien du Saguenay-Lac-Saint-Jean; Le (Chicoutimi, QC, Can.) 36965
QVC Network, Inc. (West Chester, PA) 37781
qvMagazine (North Hollywood, CA) *Unable to locate*

R

The R & B Music & Entertainment Monthly (Santa Monica, CA) *Unable to locate*
R/C Modeler (Sierra Madre, CA) 3766
R & D Magazine (Morris Plains, NJ) 19305
R Media (Thibodaux, LA) 12863
R & R Cable Co. (Roslyn, WA) 32934
R & R News 2713*
R & R Shopper's News (Westbury, NY) 23559
Rabbit Creek Journal (Clipper Mills, CA) 1729
Rabbit Gazette (Kansas City, KS) *Ceased*
Rabbits in Canada (Bewdley, ON, Can.) *Ceased*
Rabun Cablevision 7174*
RAC Journal (Rome, NY) 23265
RAC Newsletter 23265*
RAC Quarterly 23265*
Raccoon (Memphis, TN) *Unable to locate*
Race and Nation (Las Vegas, NV) *Ceased*
Race & Society (New York, NY) 22620
Racer; Late Model (Enfield, CT) 4781
RaceTime (Van Nuys, CA) *Unable to locate*
RACF Update (Westminster, CO) 4667
The Racine Labor (Racine, WI) 34275
Racine TeleCable Corp. (Racine, WI) *Unable to locate*
Racing Collectibles Price Guide (Orlando, FL) *Unable to locate*
Racing Digest (Dover, PA) *Ceased*
Racing Form; Daily (New York, NY) 21532
Racing Journal; The Quarter (Amarillo, TX) 29697
Racing Magazine; Championship (Waukesha, WI) 34397
The Racing News (Nashville, TN) *Unable to locate*
Racing News; Area Auto (Trenton, NJ) 19653
Racing News; Midwest (Milwaukee, WI) 34081
Racing Pictorial (Indianapolis, IN) *Ceased*
Racing Pigeon Bulletin (Bellbrook, OH) 24665
The Racing Report 25943*
Racing & Sports Car Magazine (Tustin, CA) *Ceased*
Racing WHEELS Newspaper (Vancouver, WA) 33178
Racketeering Litigation Reporter 28128*
The Racquet (La Crosse, WI) 33886
RACQUETBALL Magazine (Colorado Springs, CO) 4256
The Racquette (Potsdam, NY) 23140
Radar; Le (Cap-aux-Meules, QC, Can.) 36954
Radcliffe Quarterly (Cambridge, MA) 14095
Raddle Moon (Vancouver, BC, Can.) 35161
Radiance (Castro Valley, CA) 1678
Radiation Curing; Journal of (Norwalk, CT) 5066
Radiation Oncology Investigations (Hoboken, NJ) 19094
Radiation Oncology; Seminars in (Chapel Hill, NC) 23722
Radiation Protection Management (Hebron, CT) 4916
Radiation Research (San Diego, CA) *Ceased*
Radiation Technology; Canadian Journal of Medical (Ottawa, ON, Can.) 36207
Radical America (Somerville, MA) *Unable to locate*
Radical History Review (New York, NY) 22621
Radical Pedagogy (Pueblo, CO) 4600
Radical Philosophy Review (Boston, MA) 13955
Radical Philosophy Review of Books 13955*
Radical Teacher (Cambridge, MA) 14096
Radio AAHS Magazine (Tampa, FL) *Unable to locate*
Radio Aids to Marine Navigation (Ottawa, ON, Can.) 36274
Radio Campaigns (Burlington, IA) 10639
Radio Canon 1981*
Radio Chicago (Chicago, IL) *Unable to locate*
Radio Classified; Antique (Carlisle, MA) 14120
Radio Comm in Canada 36280*
Radio Comm Magazine 36280*
Radio Control Boat Modeler (Ridgefield, CT) 5100
Radio Control Car Action (Ridgefield, CT) 5101
Radio Control Model Cars (Capistrano Beach, CA) *Ceased*
Radio; CQ Amateur (Port Washington, NY) 23124
Radio-Electronics 20717*
Radio Futura L 37430*
Radio Ingstad now 11279*
Radio Ink (Boynton Beach, FL) *Unable to locate*
Radio Iowa (Des Moines, IA) 37658
Radio; The Journal of College (New Windsor, NY) 21127
Radio Magazine (Overland Park, KS) 11727
Radio Peninsule, Inc. - 97.1 (Pokemouche, NB, Can.) 35425
Radio Pennsylvania Inc. (Harrisburg, PA) 37659
Radio Program Director Report (Chicago, IL) *Unable to locate*
Radio Ranks (New York, NY) *Ceased*
Radio & Records (Los Angeles, CA) 2375
Radio San Jose 3474*
Radio Science (Klamath Falls, OR) 26385
Radio Technology; Mobile (Overland Park, KS) 11722

Radio Today; 73 Amateur (Peterborough, NH) 18628
Radio-TV Interview Report (Lansdowne, PA) 27162
RADIO VOID (Providence, RI) *Unable to locate*
Radio World (Falls Church, VA) 32056
Radioactive Waste Management (Oak Ridge, TN) *Ceased*
Radioactive Waste Management; Practice Periodical of Hazardous, Toxic, and (Reston, VA) 32410
Radioactivity & Radiochemistry (Atlanta, GA) *Ceased*
Radioanalytical and Nuclear Chemistry; Journal of (New York, NY) 22175
Radiochemistry (New York, NY) 22622
RadioGraphics (Oak Brook, IL) 9363
Radiologic Clinics of North America (Philadelphia, PA) 27652
Radiologic Technology (Albuquerque, NM) 19785
Radiologic Technology; Seminars in (Philadelphia, PA) 27672
The Radiologist (Oakland, CA) 2695
Radiologists Journal; Canadian Association of (Ottawa, ON, Can.) 36189
Radiology (Oak Brook, IL) *Unable to locate*
Radiology; Applied (Ocean, NJ) 19387
Radiology; CardioVascular and Interventional (New York, NY) 21376
Radiology; Internet Journal of (Sugar Land, TX) 31160
Radiology; Investigative (Temple, TX) 31178
Radiology Journal; Administrative (Glendale, CA) 2006
Radiology (JVIR); Journal of Vascular and Interventional (Philadelphia, PA) 27555
Radiology Management (Marietta, GA) *Unable to locate*
Radiology; Techniques in Vascular and Interventional (Philadelphia, PA) 27700
Radiology Today (Thorofare, NJ) *Ceased*
Radiology & Ultrasound; Veterinary (Raleigh, NC) 24158
Radiomutuel 37422*
Radiomutuel Inc. (Montreal, QC, Can.) 37660
Radiopharmaceuticals; Cancer Biotherapy and (Larchmont, NY) 20893
Radiopharmaceuticals; Journal of Labelled Compounds and (Hoboken, NJ) 19028
Radiophysics and Quantum Electronics (New York, NY) 22623
RadioResource International (Englewood, CO) 4415
Radiosurgery; Journal of (New York, NY) 22176
RadTech Report (Northbrook, IL) 9321
The Radville Star (Radville, SK, Can.) 37523
RAE Cable (Bottineau, ND) 24378
The Rafu Shimpo (Los Angeles, CA) 2376
RAG (Lake Worth, FL) *Unable to locate*
Rag Mag (Goodhue, MN) *Ceased*
Rahway News Record (Rahway, NJ) *Unable to locate*
Rahway Progress (Rahway, NJ) 19486
Rail/Rail Canadien; Canadian (Montreal, QC, Can.) 37099
Rail Whispers (Larchmont, NY) *Unable to locate*
RailFan & Railroad (Newton, NJ) 19375
RailNews (Waukesha, WI) *Unable to locate*
Railroad History (Urbana, IL) 9716
Railroad Information (Wolfeboro, NH) *Unable to locate*
Railroad Model Craftsman (Newton, NJ) 19376
Railroad Press (Higley, AZ) *Unable to locate*
Railroad; RailFan & (Newton, NJ) 19375
Railroader; Model (Waukesha, WI) 34407
Railroading; Model (Aurora, CO) 4147
Railroading; Progressive (Milwaukee, WI) 34094
Railroads of St. Louis Magazine (St. Louis, MO) 17485
Railway Age (New York, NY) 22624
Railway Clerk/Interchange 13683*
Railway Journal; International (New York, NY) 21933
Railway Track & Structures (Chicago, IL) 8546
Railways; Garden (Waukesha, WI) 34406
Rain Crow (Chicago, IL) 8547
Rain Magazine (Eugene, OR) 26333
Rain Magazine (Houston, TX) *Ceased*
The Rainbow (Prospect, KY) *Ceased*
Rainbow News 12 Co. (Woodbury, NY) 23593
Rainbow-Pcar Reviews On-Line (Prospect, KY) 12377
Rainbow Report (Chelmsford, ON, Can.) *Unable to locate*
Rainbow Vision Cable (Flanagan, IL) *Unable to locate*
Rains County Leader (Emory, TX) 30307
Rainy Lake Herald; Ft. Frances Times and (Fort Frances, ON, Can.) 35841
Rainy River Record (Rainy River, ON, Can.) 36338
Raise the Stakes (San Francisco, CA) *Ceased*
Raisin River Advocate (Blissfield, MI) *Ceased*
Raising Black and Biracial Children (Burbank, CA) *Unable to locate*
Raivaaja 14183*
Raleigh; Cablevision of 24160*
(Raleigh Edition); The AD-PAK (Raleigh, NC) 24123
Raleigh Extra (Wendell, NC) *Unable to locate*
Raleigh Magazine (Raleigh, NC) *Unable to locate*
The Raleigh Reporter (Raleigh, NC) *Unable to locate*

Register-Tribune (Union City, MI) **15646**
The Registered Nurse (Toronto, ON, Can.) *Ceased*
The Registered Nurse Journal (Toronto, ON, Can.) **36725**
Registered Rep. (New York, NY) **22642**
Registered Representative **22642**
Registry Management; Journal of (Little Rock, AR) **1232**
The Registry Review (Manchester, NH) **18563**
The Regular (Del Valle, TX) *Unable to locate*
Regulated Rivers **19100**
Regulation (Washington, DC) **5760**
Regulatory, Integrative and Comparative Physiology; American Journal of Physiology: (Bethesda, MD) **13309**
Regulatory Toxicology and Pharmacology (San Diego, CA) **3254**
Rehab Brief (Falls Church, VA) *Unable to locate*
Rehab Info (Iola, WI) *Ceased*
Rehab Management (Marina Del Rey, CA) *Unable to locate*
Rehabilitation; American (Washington, DC) **5341**
Rehabilitation; American Journal of Physical Medicine and (Indianapolis, IN) **10078**
Rehabilitation; Archives of Physical Medicine and (Chicago, IL) **8273**
Rehabilitation Clinics; Physical Medicine and (Philadelphia, PA) **27638**
Rehabilitation Counseling Bulletin (Alexandria, VA) *Ceased*
Rehabilitation Digest (Toronto, ON, Can.) *Ceased*
Rehabilitation Education (Fayetteville, AR) **1124**
Rehabilitation Gazette (St. Louis, MO) *Unable to locate*
Rehabilitation and Health; International Journal of (New York, NY) **21916**
Rehabilitation; Journal of (Alexandria, VA) **31701**
Rehabilitation; Journal of Cardiopulmonary (Philadelphia, PA) **27518**
Rehabilitation; The Journal of Cognitive (Indianapolis, IN) **10139**
Rehabilitation; Journal of Offender (Doylestown, PA) **26833**
Rehabilitation Journal; Psychiatric (Boston, MA) **13953**
Rehabilitation; Journal of Sport (Champaign, IL) **8200**
Rehabilitation; Journal of Vocational (Burlington, VA) **14030**
Rehabilitation; Journal of Wildlife (Berkeley, CA) **1538**
Rehabilitation Nursing (Glenview, IL) **8941**
Rehabilitation Psychology (New York, NY) *Ceased*
Rehabilitation Research and Development; Journal of (Baltimore, MD) **13201**
Rehabilitation Review; International (New York, NY) **21934**
Rehabilitation Technology (Houston, TX) **30523**
Rehabilitative Audiology; Journal of the Academy of (Dallas, TX) **30162**
The Reidsville Review (Reidsville, NC) **24180**
Reign of the Sacred Heart (Hales Corners, WI) **33769**
REITStreet Magazine (Walnut Creek, CA) **4055**
(REJ); Real Estate Journal/Tri-State (Washington, DC) **5759**
Rejoice! (Hillsboro, KS) *Ceased*
Rejoice! (University, MS) *Ceased*
Relational Database Journal (Dallas, TX) *Ceased*
Relations (Montreal, QC, Can.) **37215**
Relations Industrielles/Industrial Relations; Revue (Quebec, QC, Can.) **37296**
Relationship Marketing; Journal of (Berkeley, CA) **1536**
Relationships; Personal (Normal, IL) **9303**
Relationships Today (Gainesville, FL) **6156**
Relative Wind (Wahpeton, ND) *Unable to locate*
Relax (New York, NY) *Ceased*
Relay Magazine (Tallahassee, FL) **6730**
Release Print (San Francisco, CA) **3423**
Release 1.0 (New York, NY) **22643**
Reliable Computing (New York, NY) **22644**
Reliance Distributors of B.C. Ltd. (Squamish, BC, Can.) **35101**
Relief Report (Washington, DC) *Ceased*
Religion & Abuse; Journal of (Binghamton, NY) **20195**
Religion and American Culture (Indianapolis, IN) **10166**
Religion in Communist Dominated Areas **22626**
Religion, Disability & Health; Journal of (New Brunswick, NJ) **19334**
Religion; The International Journal for the Psychology of (Santa Barbara, CA) **3642**
Religion; Journal of the American Academy of (Whittier, CA) **4077**
Religion; Journal of Law and (St. Paul, MN) **16382**
Religion; Journal of Media and (Provo, UT) **31404**
Religion and Literature (Notre Dame, IN) **10376**
Religion News Service (Washington, DC) **38047**
Religion and Psychical Research; Journal of (Cherry Hill, NJ) **18737**

Religion)/(Sciences Religieuses); SR (Studies in (Edmonton, AB, Can.) **34731**
Religion; Sociology of (Fredericton, NB, Can.) **35397**
Religion & Spirituality in Social Work: Social Thought; Journal of (Binghamton, NY) **20196**
Religion Teacher's Journal (Mystic, CT) **4970**
Religious Broadcasting **32224**
Religious Conference Manager (Stow, MA) **14575**
Religious Drawings Inc. (Dallas, TX) *Unable to locate*
Religious Education (Champaign, IL) *Unable to locate*
Religious Gerontology; Journal of (Wheaton, IL) **9757**
The Religious Herald (Richmond, VA) **32449**
Religious & Intellectual Life **21522**
Religious News Service **38047**
The Religious Observer **20312**
Religious; Review for (St. Louis, MO) **17487**
Religious Studies (New York, NY) **22645**
Religious Studies; Perspectives in (Kansas City, KS) **11530**
Religious Studies Review (Valparaiso, IN) **10510**
Religious & Theological Information; Journal of (Kansas City, MO) **17176**
Relix Magazine (Brooklyn, NY) **20341**
Relocation Magazine (Dallas, TX) *Unable to locate*
Reluctant Hero (Toronto, ON, Can.) *Unable to locate*
REMark (Benton Harbor, MI) *Ceased*
Remarque; Lotus (College Park, MD) **13432**
Remedial and Special Education (RASE) (Lynchburg, VA) **32209**
Remediation (Hoboken, NJ) **19097**
Remedy (Westport, CT) **5216**
Reminder **11252**
Reminder (Stafford Springs, CT) *Ceased*
Reminder (Vernon, CT) *Unable to locate*
Reminder (Galena, IL) *Unable to locate*
The Reminder (Algona, IA) **10580**
The Reminder (Knoxville, IA) **11020**
The Reminder (East Longmeadow, MA) **14167**
The Reminder (Roanoke Rapids, NC) *Unable to locate*
The Reminder (Coventry, RI) **28330**
The Reminder (Flin Flon, MB, Can.) **35266**
Reminder Newspapers (Pontiac, MI) *Unable to locate*
The Reminder Plus (Pierre, SD) **28919**
Remington Press (Remington, IN) *Unable to locate*
Reminisce (Greendale, WI) **33763**
Remix (Emeryville, CA) **1881**
Remnant Christian Magazine (Crowley, LA) *Unable to locate*
Remodeler Magazine; Qualified (Fort Atkinson, WI) **33719**
Remodeler; Professional (Oak Brook, IL) **9362**
Remodeling (Washington, DC) **5761**
Remodeling; Woman's Day Home (New York, NY) **22930**
Remote Sensing; Canadian Journal of (Ottawa, ON, Can.) **36216**
Remsen Bell-Enterprise (Remsen, IA) **11175**
Renaissance (Salem, MA) *Unable to locate*
Renaissance Culture; Explorations in (Springfield, MO) **17598**
Renaissance Magazine (Nantucket, MA) **14342**
Renaissance Quarterly (New York, NY) **22646**
Renaissance and Reformation/Renaissance et Reforme (Toronto, ON, Can.) **36726**
Renaissance et Reforme; Renaissance and Reformation/ (Toronto, ON, Can.) **36726**
Renaissance Times—New Center News (Warren, MI) **15661**
Renal Failure (Chapel Hill, NC) **23720**
The Renal Family (Milton, ON, Can.) **36051**
Renal Nutrition; Journal of (Reno, NV) **18420**
Renal Physiology; American Journal of Physiology: (Bethesda, MD) **13310**
Renal Replacement Therapy; Advanced in (New York, NY) **21153**
Renalife **6758**
Renalife Bulletin **6758**
Renascence (Milwaukee, WI) **34096**
Rendez-Vous Canada (Toronto, ON, Can.) **36727**
Rendezvous (Pocatello, ID) **7947**
Renews (Deerfield, IL) *Ceased*
The Renfrew Weekend News (Renfrew, ON, Can.) **36340**
Renninger's ANTIQUE GUIDE (Lafayette Hill, PA) **27132**
Reno Evening Gazette; Nevada State Journal and **18423**
Reno Gazette-Journal (Reno, NV) **18423**
Renovation Bricolage (Outremont, QC, Can.) **37268**
Renovation & Decor (Unionville, ON, Can.) **36838**
Renovation Ideas *Ceased*
The Renovator's Supply **14335**
Rensselaer Republican (Rensselaer, IN) **10414**
Rent Smart! **487**
Rental Equipment Register (Malibu, CA) **2494**
Rental Guide (Tallahassee, FL) **6731**
Rental Management (Moline, IL) **9207**
Rental Product News (Fort Atkinson, WI) **33720**

Rental Service; Canadian (Exeter, ON, Can.) **35824**
Rentals; Progressive (Austin, TX) **29799**
Renville County Farmer (Mohall, ND) **24520**
Renville County Star Farmer News (Renville, MN) **16303**
Renville Star-Farmer **16303**
REP **17181**
R.E.P. (Overland Park, KS) *Ceased*
Repair News; Automotive Body (New York, NY) **21276**
Repair Shop Product News (Chicago, IL) *Unable to locate*
RePlay **3839**
RePlay Magazine (Tarzana, CA) **3839**
Replique; La (Victoriaville, QC, Can.) **37432**
Report (Ontario, CA) *Unable to locate*
The Report (Mansfield, OH) *Unable to locate*
The Report (Swan River, MB, Can.) *Ceased*
Report on the Americas **22391**
Report on Business Magazine **36731**
Report of Fatal Occupational Injuries in Maine **12891**
Report Newsmagazine **34705**
The Report Newsmagazine—Alberta Edition (Edmonton, AB, Can.) *Ceased*
The Report Newsmagazine—BC Edition (Edmonton, AB, Can.) *Ceased*
Report on Urologic Techniques *Ceased*
Reporter **33519**
The Reporter **20340**
Reporter **18021**
Reporter **23533**
The Reporter **9333**
The Reporter (Bald Knob, AR) *Ceased*
Reporter (Long Beach, CA) **2174**
The Reporter (Placerville, CA) *Unable to locate*
Reporter (Casey, IL) **8173**
The Reporter (Palos Heights, IL) **9398**
Reporter (Emmetsburg, IA) **10877**
Reporter (Mankato, MN) **16029**
The Reporter (Somerville, NJ) *Unable to locate*
The Reporter (New York, NY) **22647**
The Reporter (Lansdale, PA) **27159**
Reporter (Hillsboro, TX) **30449**
The Reporter (Spokane, WA) **33098**
The Reporter (Stony Plain, AB, Can.) **34857**
The Reporter (Port Hawkesbury, NS, Can.) *Unable to locate*
The Reporter (Gananoque, ON, Can.) **35844**
Reporter and Farmer (Webster, SD) **29027**
The Reporter (Fond du Lac) (Fond du Lac, WI) **33697**
Reporter Magazine (Rochester, NY) **23237**
Reporter-News **29652**
The Reporter Press (North Conway, NH) *Ceased*
The Reporter Shopper **3974**
Reporter-Times (Martinsville, IN) **10294**
(Reportero Industrial); World Industrial Reporter (Great Neck, NY) **20695**
The Repository (Canton, OH) **24731**
Representations (Berkeley, CA) **1555**
Representative; The Fox Lake (Berlin, WI) **33582**
Reprint Bulletin Book Reviews (Dobbs Ferry, NY) *Ceased*
Repro Report (Oak Brook, IL) *Ceased*
Reproduction; Biology of (Madison, WI) **33924**
Reproductive Endocrinology; Seminars in (Portland, OR) **26509**
Reproductive and Genetic Engineering (New York, NY) *Ceased*
Reproductive Medicine Clinics; Infertility and (Philadelphia, PA) **27492**
Reproductive Medicine; The Journal of (St. Louis, MO) **17461**
Reprographics; Modern (Melville, NY) **21050**
Reptile & Amphibian Magazine (Pottsville, PA) *Unable to locate*
Reptiles (Mission Viejo, CA) **2557**
The Republic **27248**
The Republic (Columbus, IN) **9895**
The Republic (Franklin, IN) **10008**
Republic Cable Partners **814**
The Republic/Extra **17341**
Republic Monitor (Republic, MO) **17371**
The Republic-Monitor Shopping Guide (Perryville, MO) **17341**
Republic Times (Waterloo, IL) **9736**
Republic Times Shopper **9737**
The Republican (Danville, IN) **9921**
Republican (Paoli, IN) **10389**
The Republican (Oakland, MD) **13635**
Republican (Preston, MN) *Unable to locate*
Republican (Washington, PA) *Ceased*
Republican-American (Waterbury, CT) **5193**
Republican-Eagle (Red Wing, MN) **16293**
Republican Express **20525**
The Republican Journal (Belfast, ME) **12920**
Republican Journal (Darlington, WI) **33649**
Republican Liberty (Gainesville, FL) **6157**

Republican Nonpareil (Central City, NE) 17972
Republican-Register (Moravia, NY) 21096
Republican-Reporter (Oregon, IL) 9388
Republican-Rustler (Basin, WY) 34477
Republican-Times (Trenton, MO) 17652
The Republican Valley Sun (Oxford, NE) Ceased
The Republican Woman (Washington, DC) 5762
Republique; La (Montreal, QC, Can.) 37151
REQUEST (Minnetonka, MN) 16175
The Request (Saugerties, NY) Ceased
Res: Anthropology and Aesthetics (New York, NY)
   Ceased
Res Gestaie (Indianapolis, IN) 10167
Res Ipsa Loquitur (Coral Gables, FL) 6012
Rescue and Disaster Medicine; Internet Journal of
   (Sugar Land, TX) 31161
Rescue-EMS Magazine (Nassau, DE) Unable to
   locate
Rescue Magazine 3155*
Research (San Francisco, CA) 3424
Research in African Literatures (Columbus, OH)
   25058
Research on Aging (Durham, NC) 23842
Research on Aging: A Quarterly of Social
   Gerontology and Adult Development 23842*
Research Bulletin on Southern Africa Ceased
Research in Crime and Delinquency; Journal of
   (Thousand Oaks, CA) 3899
Research & Development 19305*
Research and Development; IBM Journal of
   (Yorktown Heights, NY) 23606
Research in Economics (San Diego, CA) 3255
Research in Healthcare Financial Management
   (Towson, MD) 13765
Research in Higher Education (New York, NY) 22648
Research; Illinois (Urbana, IL) 9710
Research Initiative/Treatment Action! (Houston, TX)
   30524
Research Journal; Newspaper (Memphis, TN) 29377
Research Journal of the Water Pollution Control
   Federation 31751*
Research on Language and Social Interaction (Santa
   Barbara, CA) 3652
Research Management 5763*
Research in Music Education; Journal for (Baton
   Rouge, LA) 12491
Research News (Ann Arbor, MI) Ceased
Research News Reporter (Washington, DC) Unable to
   locate
Research in Nondestructive Evaluation (New York,
   NY) Unable to locate
Research in Nursing & Health (Hoboken, NJ) 19098
Research; Operations (Cambridge, MA) 14087
Research; Pediatric (Philadelphia, PA) 27619
Research/Penn State (University Park, PA) 28083
Research and Practice; Community/Junior College
   Journal of (Denton, TX) 30234
Research Quarterly for Exercise and Sport (Reston,
   VA) 32413
Research Report (Chicago, IL) Ceased
Research in Review (Tallahassee, FL) 6732
Research in Science Teaching; Journal of (Hoboken,
   NJ) 19045
Research on Social Work Practice (Thousand Oaks,
   CA) 3911
Research Studies (Cleveland, OH) 24949
Research in the Teaching of English (Urbana, IL)
   9717
Research-Technology Management (Washington, DC)
   5763
Research and Theory for Nursing Practice (New
   York, NY) 22649
Reseller Management (Washington, DC) Unable to
   locate
Reservoir Evaluation & Engineering; SPE
   (Richardson, TX) 30981
Residences (Westmount, QC, Can.) 37445
Resident Life 792*
Resident Rounds (Boston, MA) Ceased
Resident & Staff Physician (Jamesburg, NJ) 19132
Residential Lighting (Lincolnshire, IL) 9087
Residential Micro Systems (Charlotte, NC) Unable to
   locate
The Residential Specialist (Chicago, IL) 8554
Residential Treatment for Children and Youth
   (Chicago, IL) 8555
Resolution (Camden, ME) Unable to locate
Resonance in Chemistry; Magnetic (Hoboken, NJ)
   19056
Resort Broadcasting Co. 26251*
Resort Development & Operations 32691*
Resort and Green Saver; Lake View (Lake View, IA)
   11026
Resort Management & Operations (St. Louis, MO)
   17486
Resort TV Cable Co., Inc. (Hot Springs National
   Park, AR) 1191
Resorter (Lake Geneva, WI) 33905
Resorter; Hesperia (Hesperia, CA) 2048

Resorter; The Houghton Lake (Houghton Lake, MI)
   15188
Resorter; Straitsland (Indian River, MI) 15203
Resorts & Great Hotels (Santa Barbara, CA) 3653
Resource (Atlanta, GA) 7040
Resource (St. Joseph, MI) 15513
The Resource Center Bulletin (Albuquerque, NM)
   Ceased
Resource Library Magazine (Orange, CA) 2726
Resource Links (Pouch Cove, NL, Can.) 35481
Resource News 34719*
Resource Recycling (Portland, OR) 26505
Resource Sharing & Information Networks
   (Binghamton, NY) 20214
Resources in Education (Pittsburgh, PA) 27840
Resources for Feminist Research (Documentation sur
   la Recherche Feministe) (Toronto, ON, Can.)
   36728
Resources for Literary Study (University Park, PA)
   28084
Resources Research; Natural (New York, NY) 22408
Respiration (Farmington, CT) 4859
Respiratory Care (Dallas, TX) Unable to locate
Respiratory Care Managers and Educators; FOCUS:
   Journal for (Rhinebeck, NY) 23183
Respiratory and Critical Care Medicine; Seminars in
   (New York, NY) 22725
Respiratory Disease; American Review of (New York,
   NY) 21206
Respiratory Infections; Seminars in (Indianapolis, IN)
   10171
Respiratory Journal; Canadian (Oakville, ON, Can.)
   36141
Respiratory Management (Los Angeles, CA) Unable
   to locate
Respiratory Therapy; Canadian Journal of (Ottawa,
   ON, Can.) 36217
Respiratory Therapy Products (Los Angeles, CA)
   2379
Respiratory Times (Burlington, ON, Can.) Unable to
   locate
Response (New York, NY) Unable to locate
Response (New York, NY) 22650
Response TV (Santa Ana, CA) 3631
Response to the Victimization of Women and
   Children (Bethesda, MD) Ceased
The Responsive Community (Washington, DC) 5764
The Restatement (Cincinnati, OH) Ceased
Restaurant Administration Quarterly; The Cornell Hotel
   and (Ithaca, NY) 20794
Restaurant Business (New York, NY) 22651
Restaurant/Food Review (Brooklyn, NY) 20342
Restaurant and Foodservice Marketing; Journal of
   (Las Vegas, NV) 18366
Restaurant Hospitality (Cleveland, OH) 24950
Restaurant and Hotel Design 21819*
Restaurant Information Abstracts (Washington, DC)
   Ceased
Restaurant Management Insider Ceased
Restaurant; Midsouthwest (Oklahoma City, OK) 25972
Restaurant/Motel Design 21819*
Restaurant News; Nation's (New York, NY) 22402
Restaurant News; Ontario (Mississauga, ON, Can.)
   36083
Restaurant News; Western (Winnipeg, MB, Can.)
   35361
Restaurant Row Magazine (Long Beach, CA) Unable
   to locate
Restaurants & Institutions (New York, NY) 22652
Restaurants, Resorts & Hotels (Stratford, CT) Unable
   to locate
Restaurants USA (Washington, DC) Ceased
Restaurateur; Wisconsin (Madison, WI) 33989
The Reston Connection (Mc Lean, VA) 32253
Reston/Herndon Times-Mirror (Reston, VA) 32414
The Reston Recorder (Reston, MB, Can.) 35285
Reston Times 32414*
Restoration (Tucson, AZ) 961
Restoration (Wanaque, NJ) Ceased
Restoration (Combermere, ON, Can.) 35750
Restoration; Cleaning & (Millersville, MD) 13630
The Restoration Herald (Mason, OH) 25359
Restoration and Management Notes 33935*
Restyling Magazine (Broomfield, CO) 4207
Results Media Shopper's Guide (Hicksville, NY)
   20744
Resumen Newspaper (Flushing, NY) 20612
Resumes de droit penal (Cowansville, QC, Can.)
   36984
Resurrection Magazine (Oxon Hill, MD) Unable to
   locate
Retail Directions (Toronto, ON, Can.) Ceased
Retail Focus; NSGA (Mount Prospect, IL) 9248
Retail Info Systems News (Randolph, NJ) 19497
Retail Ink (Atlanta, GA) 7041
Retail Merchandiser (New York, NY) 22653
Retail Merchandising (Toronto, ON, Can.) Ceased
Retail News (Sandusky, OH) 25509
Retail News (Toronto, ON, Can.) Unable to locate

Retail News Bureau (New York, NY) 38048
Retail News; Value (Clearwater, FL) 5992
Retail Operations & Construction (Roswell, GA) 7518
Retail Pharmacy News (New York, NY) Unable to
   locate
Retail Roundup (Port Washington, NY) 23135
Retail Store Image (Overland Park, KS) 11728
Retail Systems Reseller (Randolph, NJ) 19498
Retail Tech (New York, NY) 22654
Retail Week; Computer (Manhasset, NY) 20993
Retailer (Shelby,. NC) Ceased
Retailer; Action Sports (New York, NY) 21147
Retailer; Heartland (Omaha, NE) 18197
Retailer and Marketing News (Dallas, TX) 30180
Retailer; Midwest (Bloomington, MN) 15759
Retailer; Model (Waukesha, WI) 34408
Retailer; New Age (Bellingham, WA) 32677
Retailer; Nursery Business (Clearwater, FL) 5989
Retailer; Oklahoma (Oklahoma City, OK) 25987
The Retailer Shopping News 20957*
Retailer; Southwestern (Kansas City, MO) 17197
Retailers Forum Magazine (Centerport, NY) 20446
Retailing; Christian (Lake Mary, FL) 6276
Retailing and Consumer Services; Journal of
   (Burlington, MA) 14029
Retailing; Farm Supply (Englewood, CO) 4413
Retailing; Journal of (Babson Park, MA) 13832
Retailing News (Victorville, CA) Unable to locate
Retardation; Mental (Washington, DC) 5647
Retel TV Cable Co. Inc. (Williamsport, PA) 28183
Rethinking Marxism (Notre Dame, IN) 10377
Rethinking Schools (Milwaukee, WI) 34097
RETINA (Gladwyne, PA) 26944
The Retired Officer Magazine (Alexandria, VA) 31733
Retirement Community Business (Memphis, TN)
   Unable to locate
Retirement Life (Washington, DC) Unable to locate
The Retort (Billings, MT) 17733
The Retrospect (Collingswood, NJ) 18768
Retroviruses; AIDS Research and Human (Larchmont,
   NY) 20887
Reunions Magazine (Milwaukee, WI) 34098
Reuters America Inc. (New York, NY) Unable to
   locate
Rev-Up; Robins (Warner Robins, GA) 7637
Reveil; Le (Jonquiere, QC, Can.) 37013
Reveille/Between the Lakes (Seneca Falls, NY)
   23324
Reveille; Cloverdale (Cloverdale, CA) 1730
Reveille-Enterprise; Vevay (Vevay, IN) 10520
Revelstoke Cable TV Ltd. (Revelstoke, BC, Can.)
   35073
Revelstoke Front Row Centre 35071*
Revelstoke Review 35071*
Revelstoke Times Review (Revelstoke, BC, Can.)
   35071
RevelstokeTimes 35071*
Revenue Bulletin; Internal (Pittsburgh, PA) 27801
Revenuer; The American (Rockford, IA) 11183
The Revere Independent (Revere, MA) Ceased
Revere Journal (Revere, MA) 14502
Review 15452*
The Review 8188*
Re:VIEW 5758*
The Review 5549*
Review 29606*
The Review 26071*
The Review (Newark, DE) 5281
The Review (Erie, IL) 8846
Review (Hinckley, IL) Ceased
Review (Morrison, IL) Ceased
Review (Tuscola, IL) 9695
Review (Denison, IA) 10766
Review (Garnett, KS) 11459
Review (Richmond, MI) Unable to locate
The Review (Somerville, NJ) Ceased
The Review (Somerville, NJ) 19577
Review (Interlaken, NY) Unable to locate
The Review (Liverpool, NY) 20955
The Review (Alliance, OH) 24605
The Review (East Liverpool, OH) 25171
The Review (Shidler, OK) 26071
Review (Yukon, OK) 26205
The Review (Philadelphia, PA) 27653
Review (Cross Plains, TX) 30110
The Review (Plymouth, WI) 34249
The Review (Niagara Falls, ON, Can.) 36110
The Review (Vankleek Hill, ON, Can.) 36840
Review Ceased
Review of Accounting Information Systems 4554*
Review of Accounting Studies (New York, NY) 22655
Review-Appeal (Franklin, TX) 30363
The Review of Austrian Economics (New York, NY)
   22656
The Review of Black Political Economy (Somerset,
   NJ) 19564
Review of Business (Jamaica, NY) 20840
Review of Business Information Systems (Littleton,
   CO) 4554

Ride Texas Magazine (Austin, TX) **29802**
Rider (Ventura, CA) *Unable to locate*
Rider (Ancaster, ON, Can.) **35634**
Rider; Horse & (Hicksville, NY) **20739**
The Rider News (Lawrenceville, NJ) **19164**
Rider University (Lawrenceville, NJ) **19165**
The Ridgefield Press (Ridgefield, CT) **5103**
The Ridgetown Dominion (Dresden, ON, Can.)
 Unable to locate
The Ridgewood News (West Paterson, NJ) **19737**
Ridgewood Times **23198***
The Ridgway Record (Ridgway, PA) **27935**
The Ridgway Sun (Ridgway, CO) **4615**
Riding; Trail Blazer Horseback Trail (Prescott Valley,
 AZ) **856**
Ridley Press (Folsom, PA) **26921**
The Riesel Rustler (Riesel, TX) **30982**
Rifkin & Assoc. **12371***
Rifle (Prescott, AZ) **850**
Rifleman; American (Fairfax, VA) **32005**
Rigel Communications Inc. (Sherman, CT) *Unable to
 locate*
Right On! (New York, NY) **22667**
Right On/Sisters In Style **22667***
Right of Way (Torrance, CA) **3941**
Riklis Broadcasting **1643***
The Riley Countian (Riley, KS) **11769**
Riley Video Services (Athens, OH) *Unable to locate*
RILM Abstracts of Music Literature (New York, NY)
 22668
Rimbey Record (Red Deer, AB, Can.) *Unable to
 locate*
Rimouskois; Le (Rimouski, QC, Can.) **37307**
The Ring (Ambler, PA) **26653**
The Ringgold Progress (Arcadia, LA) **12477**
Ringgold Record; Bienville Democrat/ (Arcadia, LA)
 12476
The Ringling Eagle (Ringling, OK) **26051**
The Ringsted Dispatch (Armstrong, IA) **10608**
Rinksider (Columbus, OH) **25059**
RINSE (Toronto, ON, Can.) **36730**
RIO (San Antonio, TX) **31044**
Rio Grande Sun (Espanola, NM) **19844**
Riondel Community Cable Video Society (Riondel,
 BC, Can.) **35079**
RIP (Beverly Hills, CA) *Ceased*
The Ripley Bee (Ripley, OH) **25498**
Ripley Video Cable Co. (Ripley, MS) **16837**
Ripon Buyers' Guide; Berlin/ (Berlin, WI) **33581**
The Ripon Commonwealth Express (Ripon, WI)
 34302
Ripon Forum (Washington, DC) *Unable to locate*
Ripon Magazine (Ripon, WI) **34303**
The Ripon Record (Ripon, CA) **2928**
Ripple; Yadkin (Yadkinville, NC) **24339**
RISC World (Austin, TX) *Ceased*
The Rising Star (Eastland, TX) **30265**
Rising Sun Recorder (Rising Sun, IN) **10429**
Risk Abstracts (Bethesda, MD) **13377**
Risk Analysis (New York, NY) **22669**
Risk and Benefits Management; National Underwriter
 Property and Casualty/ (Erlanger, KY) **12054**
Risk, Decision and Policy (New York, NY) **22670**
Risk Finance; The Journal of (New York, NY) **22180**
Risk & Insurance (Horsham, PA) **27064**
Risk and Insurance; The Journal of (Malvern, PA)
 27213
Risk Management (New York, NY) **22671**
Risk Management Magazine; Treasury and (New
 York, NY) **22860**
Ritchie Gazette and The Cairo Standard (Harrisville,
 WV) **33334**
RITE (Chicago, IL) **8557**
Rites (Toronto, ON, Can.) *Unable to locate*
Ritmo *Ceased*
The Ritzville Adams County Journal (Ritzville, WA)
 32932
Rive Sud Express (Levis, QC, Can.) *Unable to locate*
River Cities Reader (Davenport, IA) *Unable to locate*
River Cities Tribune (Marble Falls, TX) **30762**
River City (Memphis, TN) **29378**
River Communications **4368***
River Extra (Lake Havasu City, AZ) **734**
River Falls Journal (River Falls, WI) **34309**
River Forest; Wednesday Journal of Oak Park &
 (Oak Park, IL) **9378**
River Grove Messenger (Glenview, IL) *Unable to
 locate*
River Grove Post **8574***
River Grove Times; Elmwood Park/ (Lincolnwood, IL)
 9093
River Hills Herald; Fox Point-Bayside- (New Berlin,
 WI) **34171**
River News Herald & Isleton Journal (Rio Vista, CA)
 2927
River Oaks News (River Oaks, TX) **30983**
River Parishes Guide - 1993 **12540***
The River Press (Fort Benton, MT) **17791**
River Raisin Cable (Monroe, MI) **15366**

The River Reporter (Narrowsburg, NY) **21107**
River Research and Applications (Hoboken, NJ)
 19100
River Styx (St. Louis, MO) **17489**
River Valley News Shopper (Howard City, MI) **15189**
River Valley Shopper (Spring Valley, MN) **16457**
Riverain; Le (Sainte-Anne-des-Monts, QC, Can.)
 37372
The Riverbank News (Riverbank, CA) **2929**
The Riverbend Review (North Battleford, SK, Can.)
 37510
The Riverdale Press (Bronx, NY) **20284**
Riverdale Review (Bronx, NY) **20285**
Rivereast News Bulletin (Glastonbury, CT) **4870**
The Riverfront Times (St. Louis, MO) **17490**
Riverhead Suffolk Life (Riverhead, NY) **23202**
Rivers Banner (Rivers, MB, Can.) **35286**
Rivers; Mountains & (Cave Junction, OR) **26265**
Riverside Bulletin (Los Angeles, CA) **2380**
Riverside Cable TV **1237***
Riverside County Agriculture (Moreno Valley, CA)
 2599
Riverside Current (Riverside, IA) **11178**
Riverside Green Sheet (Riverside, CA) **2944**
Riverside Lawn Suburban Life; North Riverside/
 Riverside/ (Oak Brook, IL) **9361**
Riverside Quarterly (Lake Charles, LA) *Unable to
 locate*
Riverside Reporter (Cinnaminson, NJ) **18743**
Riverside Review (Buffalo, NY) **20387**
Riverside/Riverside Lawn Suburban Life; North
 Riverside/ (Oak Brook, IL) **9361**
The Riverton Ranger (Riverton, WY) **34577**
The Riverview Times (St. Paul, MN) *Unable to locate*
Riveting News (Cleveland, OH) *Unable to locate*
Riviera Utilities Cable TV (Foley, AL) **228**
R.L.E. Currents (Cambridge, MA) **14099**
The RMA Journal (Philadelphia, PA) **27654**
RMRScience (Fort Collins, CO) **4437**
RMS Syndication (Charlotte, NC) **38051**
RN (Montvale, NJ) **19274**
RNA (New York, NY) **22672**
RNABC News **35153***
RNAO News **36725***
RND (Revue Notre-Dame) (Sillery, QC, Can.) **37401**
RO Monthly (Houston, TX) *Unable to locate*
Road King (Nashville, TN) **29483**
Road & Track (Newport Beach, CA) **2635**
Roadbuilding Magazine; Aggregates & (Westmount,
 QC, Can.) **37441**
Roadracing World & Motorcycle Technology (Lake
 Elsinore, CA) **2140**
Roads to Adventure (Ventura, CA) *Ceased*
Roads; Better (Dallas, TX) **30131**
Roads & Bridges Magazine (Des Plaines, IL) **8770**
Roads and Construction; Michigan (Lansing, MI)
 15291
Roads; Two-Lane (Fort Lauderdale, FL) **6085**
Roadside (Watertown, MA) *Unable to locate*
Roaming Guide (Memphis, TN) **29379**
Roane County News (Kingston, TN) **29269**
The Roane County News/Record (Rockwood, TN)
 29578
Roane County Reporter (Spencer, WV) **33470**
Roanoke Beacon (Plymouth, NC) **24119**
Roanoke Chowen News-Herald (Ahoskie, NC) **23614**
Roanoke; Cox Communications (Roanoke, VA) **32494**
Roanoke Review **9511***
The Roanoke Times (Roanoke, VA) **32491**
Roanoke Times & World News **32491***
Roanoke Tribune (Roanoke, VA) **32492**
Roanoke Valley Cablevision **32494***
Roanoker Magazine (Roanoke, VA) **32493**
Roaring Fork Valley Journal (Carbondale, CO) *Unable
 to locate*
Rob Magazine (Toronto, ON, Can.) **36731**
Robb Report (Acton, MA) *Unable to locate*
Robbinsdale Sun Post; Crystal (Crystal, MN) **15823**
Robert Lee Observer **30984***
Robertson County Times (Springfield, TN) **29618**
The Robesonian (Lumberton, NC) **24051**
Robins Rev-Up (Warner Robins, GA) **7637**
The Robins Review (Cochran, GA) **7180**
Robinson Daily News (Robinson, IL) **9512**
Roblin Review (Roblin, MB, Can.) **35287**
Robotic Systems; Journal of (Hoboken, NJ) **19046**
Robotic Systems; Journal of Intelligent and (New
 York, NY) **22101**
Robotica (New York, NY) **22673**
Robotics Age (Peterborough, NH) *Ceased*
Robotics and Automation; International Journal of
 (Calgary, AB, Can.) **34649**
Robotics & Automation Magazine (Raleigh, NC)
 24152
Robotics World (Longmont, CO) **4560**
Robotics World (Atlanta, GA) *Ceased*
Robstown Record **30985***
Rochelle Park Shopper; Lodi-Hasbrouck Heights-
 Woodridge-Maywood- (Lodi, NJ) **19179**

Rochester Business Journal (Rochester, NY) **23238**
Rochester Cablevision, Inc.; Greater (Rochester, NY)
 23242
Rochester Courier (Conway, NH) *Ceased*
Rochester Eccentric (Rochester, MI) **15466**
Rochester Golf Week Newspaper (Rochester, NY)
 23239
Rochester History (Rochester, NY) **23240**
Rochester Observer **15466***
Rochester & Rule Twin Cities News (Rochester, TX)
 Unable to locate
The Rochester Sentinel (Rochester, IN) **10431**
The Rochester Times (Rochester, NH) *Unable to
 locate*
The Rock **4535***
Rock Airplay Monitor (New York, NY) **22674**
Rock Associates **32773***
Rock County Leader (Bassett, NE) **17943**
Rock County Star Herald (Luverne, MN) **16014**
The Rock Creek Current (Washington, DC) *Ceased*
Rock and Dirt (Crossville, TN) **29159**
Rock Garden Quarterly (Denver, CO) **4352**
Rock & Gem (Ventura, CA) **4009**
Rock Heroes (Derby, CT) *Ceased*
Rock Hill Black View **28544***
Rock & Ice (Carbondale, CO) **4217**
Rock Island Argus (Rock Island, IL) **9519**
Rock On (Lakewood, CO) **4535**
Rock Products (Chicago, IL) **8558**
Rock River Cablevision Co. **9515***
The Rock River Times (Rockford, IL) **9531**
Rock Talk (Danville, PA) *Ceased*
Rock on Tour (New York, NY) *Unable to locate*
The Rock Valley Bee (Rock Valley, IA) **11181**
Rock Valley Review (Rock Falls, IL) *Unable to locate*
Rockaway Journal (Far Rockaway, NY) **20591**
Rockbill (New York, NY) *Unable to locate*
The Rockbridge Weekly (Lexington, VA) *Ceased*
Rockdale Citizen (Conyers, GA) **7201**
Rockdale Neighbor (Rockdale, GA) **7500**
The Rockdale Reporter & Messenger (Rockdale, TX)
 30987
The Rocket (Fairbury, IL) **8879**
The Rocket (Slippery Rock, PA) **27997**
Rocket; The Buffalo (Buffalo, NY) **20369**
Rocket Common Supplement Shopper (Harlan, IA)
 10944
The Rocket-Courier (Wyalusing, PA) **28196**
Rocket Fuel Online (Philadelphia, PA) **27655**
Rocket-Miner; Daily (Rock Springs, WY) **34581**
Rocket Press **23513***
Rocketry; Sport (Los Alamos, NM) **19894**
Rockets; Journal of Spacecraft and (Reston, VA)
 32395
Rockford Area News Leader (Osseo, MN) **16250**
Rockford/Cedar Springs Advance (Rockford, MI)
 15469
Rockford Journal; The Post-Journal and Metro
 (Rockford, IL) **9529**
Rockford Magazine (Mc Lean, VA) *Ceased*
Rockford Register Star (Rockford, IL) **9532**
Rockford Review (Loves Park, IL) **9120**
Rockhead (Larkspur, CA) *Unable to locate*
The Rockhurst Hawk **17195***
The Rockhurst Sentinel (Kansas City, MO) **17195**
Rockin' 50s (Lubbock, TX) *Unable to locate*
Rockingham Gazette **18507***
The Rockingham News (Exeter, NH) **18507**
Rockingham People & Places (Greensboro, NC)
 Ceased
Rockingham Shopper (Greensboro, NC) *Ceased*
Rockland County Business Journal **23502***
Rockland County Times (Haverstraw, NY) *Unable to
 locate*
Rockland Journal-News (Mc Lean, VA) **32254**
Rockland Mariner; Abington/ (Abington, MA) **13785**
Rockland Review (New Rochelle, NY) *Unable to
 locate*
Rockland Shoppinguide (Pembroke, MA) *Ceased*
Rockland Standard (Rockland, MA) **14507**
Rockmart Journal (Rome, GA) *Unable to locate*
The Rockport Pilot (Rockport, TX) **30988**
Rocks & Minerals (Washington, DC) **5770**
Rocksprings-Canyon TV Co. Inc. (Camp Wood, TX)
 Unable to locate
Rockton-Roscoe Herald **9546***
Rockton-Roscoe Herald (Rockton, IL) *Unable to
 locate*
Rockville Centre Herald (Rockville, NY) **23260**
Rockville Centre News and Owl (Rockville Centre,
 NY) **23262**
Rockville Centre Pennysaver (Rockville Centre, HI)
 7792
Rockville Centre Shopper's Guide (Hicksville, NY)
 20745
The Rockville Express (Alexandria, VA) *Unable to
 locate*
The Rockville Gazette (Rockville, MD) *Unable to
 locate*

(Rockville); Interchange (Rockville, MD) **13683**
Rockwall Texas Success (Rockwall, TX) *Ceased*
Rockwood-Eramosa Review (Acton, ON, Can.) *Unable to locate*
Rockwood Times (Shelbyville, KY) *Unable to locate*
Rocky Ford Daily Gazette (Rocky Ford, CO) **4616**
Rocky Fork Enterprise (Worthington, OH) **25681**
Rocky Hill Post (Bristol, CT) **4722**
Rocky Mount Cablevision (Rocky Mount, VA) *Unable to locate*
Rocky Mount Telegram (Rocky Mount, NC) **24205**
Rocky Mountain Baptist (Centennial, CO) **4227**
Rocky Mountain Business Journal (Denver, CO) *Ceased*
The Rocky Mountain Collegian (Fort Collins, CO) **4438**
Rocky Mountain Construction (Norcross, GA) *Unable to locate*
Rocky Mountain Farm Edition; Fastline— (Buckner, KY) **11991**
Rocky Mountain Gardener (Eldorado Springs, CO) **4411**
Rocky Mountain Golf Magazine (Steamboat Springs, CO) **4630**
Rocky Mountain Magazine (Denver, CO) *Unable to locate*
Rocky Mountain Motorist (Denver, CO) **4353**
Rocky Mountain News (Denver, CO) **4354**
Rocky Mountain Oil Journal (Denver, CO) *Unable to locate*
Rocky Mountain Oyster & National Oyster Newspaper (Denver, CO) **4355**
Rocky Mountain PAY DIRT (Bisbee, AZ) *Ceased*
Rocky Mountain Review of Language and Literature (Pullman, WA) **32907**
Rocky Mountain Sports *Unable to locate*
Rocky Mountain Union Farmer (Aurora, CO) **4148**
Rocky Point Suffolk Life (Rocky Point, NY) **23263**
Rocky View/Five Village Weekly; Crossfield/Irricana (Irricana, AB, Can.) **34788**
Rocky View Times (Cochrane, AB, Can.) **34686**
Roctober (Chicago, IL) **8559**
Rod Action (Canoga Park, CA) *Unable to locate*
Rod & Custom Magazine (Los Angeles, CA) **2381**
Rod & Reel **12943***
Rod Serling's The Twilight Zone Magazine (New York, NY) *Ceased*
Rodale's Fitness Swimmer (Emmaus, PA) **26881**
Rodale's SCUBA Diving (Savannah, GA) **7533**
Rodder; American (Agoura, CA) **1376**
Rodeo News (Pauls Valley, OK) *Unable to locate*
Rodeo News; Canadian (Calgary, AB, Can.) **34639**
Roeland Park Sun (Roeland Park, KS) **11770**
Roentgenology; American Journal of (Leesburg, VA) **32182**
Roentgenology; Seminars in (Philadelphia, PA) **27673**
Roeper Review (Bloomfield Hills, MI) **14829**
Roger Cable Systems **26546***
Rogers Cable **35110***
Rogers Cable **1999***
Rogers Cable (Barrie, ON, Can.) **35665**
Rogers Cable (Don Mills, ON, Can.) **35781**
Rogers Cable (Kitchener, ON, Can.) *Unable to locate*
Rogers Cable-Calgary **34673***
Rogers Cable Systems (Burnaby, BC, Can.) *Unable to locate*
Rogers Cable Systems, Georgian Bay Ltd. (Midland, ON, Can.) *Unable to locate*
Rogers Cable TV Niagara Partnership **36114***
Rogers Cablesystem **1144***
Rogers Cablesystems (Guelph, ON, Can.) *Unable to locate*
Rogers Cablesystems of Alaska (Wasilla, AK) **652**
Rogers Communications Inc. (Toronto, ON, Can.) *Unable to locate*
Rogers Hometown News (Rogers, AR) **1328**
Rogers Ottawa Ltd. (Ottawa, ON, Can.) *Ceased*
Rogers Park/Edgewater/Uptown News-Star (Lincolnwood, IL) **9103**
Rogers Surrey **35110***
Rogersville Review (Rogersville, TN) **29580**
Rogue Digger (Phoenix, OR) **26464**
Rohm and Haas Reporter *Ceased*
Rohnert Park Buyer's Guide (Petaluma, CA) *Unable to locate*
Rohnert Park Community Voice (Sonoma, CA) **3775**
Rohnert Park-Cotati Clarion (Petaluma, CA) *Unable to locate*
Rohnert Park Cotati Times (San Rafael, CA) *Ceased*
Rola Boza (God's Field) (Scranton, PA) **27962**
Roll Call (Washington, DC) **5771**
Roll Call Report Syndicate (Washington, DC) **38052**
Rolla Daily News (Rolla, MO) **17380**
RollerCoaster! (Penfield, NY) **23090**
Rollerderby (Guerneville, CA) *Unable to locate*
Rollergames (Rockville Centre, NY) *Ceased*
Rolling Along (Bismarck, ND) **24359**
Rolling Hills Herald **2804***
Rolling Meadows Review (Rolling Meadows, IL) **9550**

The Rolling Pebble **27767***
Rolling Stone (New York, NY) **22675**
Roman Archaeology; Journal of (Portsmouth, RI) **28381**
Roman; Romulus (Romulus, MI) **15474**
Romance Philology (Berkeley, CA) *Ceased*
Romance Quarterly (Washington, DC) **5772**
Romance Quarterly (Lexington, KY) *Ceased*
Romances Presents True Life Stories; Modern (New York, NY) **22351**
Romani Studies (Cheverly, MD) **13407**
Romanic Review (New York, NY) **22676**
Romantic Homes (St. Charles, IL) *Ceased*
Romantic Times (Brooklyn, NY) **20343**
Romantica 1600 **28232***
Romanticism; Studies in (Boston, MA) **13966**
The Romantist (Nashville, TN) *Ceased*
Rome News-Tribune (Rome, GA) **7503**
Rome Pennysaver (Rome, NY) **23266**
The Romeo Observer (Romeo, MI) **15473**
Romeo-Washington Advisor **15537***
Romeo-Washington Source (Shelby Township, MI) **15537**
Romeoville Reporter; Bolingbrook/ (Downers Grove, IL) **8780**
The Romeoville Sun (Romeoville, IL) **9553**
Romulus Roman (Romulus, MI) **15474**
Ron Bernthal (Hurleyville, NY) **38053**
Ronan Pioneer/Mission Valley News **17899***
Ronceverte Television Corp. (Ronceverte, WV) **33454**
Ronkonkoma Review (Ronkonkoma, NY) **23272**
Ronkonkoma Suffolk Life (Ronkonkoma, NY) **23273**
Ronkonkoma Weekender (Farmingdale, NY) *Ceased*
ROOFER Magazine (Fort Myers, FL) *Unable to locate*
Roofer and Waterproofer; Journeyman (Washington, DC) **5622**
Roofing Contractor (Troy, MI) **15638**
Roofing/Insulation/Siding; Western (Reno, NV) **18426**
Roofing Magazine; Metal (Iola, WI) **33835**
Roofing; Professional (Rosemont, IL) **9556**
Roofing Spec **9556***
Rooks County Record (Stockton, KS) *Ceased*
Room (Windsor, ON, Can.) **36889**
Room of One's Own (Vancouver, BC, Can.) **35165**
Roosevelt Association Journal; Theodore (Oyster Bay, NY) **23071**
Roosevelt Shopper's Guide; Uniondale/ (Ontario, ON, Can.) **36169**
Rooster Valley Shopper **31413***
Roscoe-Hosmer Independent (Ipswich, SD) **28874**
Roscommon County Herald-News (Roscommon, MI) *Unable to locate*
Rose; American (Shreveport, LA) **12816**
The Rose Hill Reporter (Rose Hill, KS) **11771**
The Rose Sheet (Chevy Chase, MD) **13409**
The Rose Thorn (Terre Haute, IN) **10489**
Roseau Times-Region (Roseau, MN) **16328**
Rosebud (Cambridge, WI) **33615**
The Rosebud News (Rosebud, TX) **30991**
Rosedale Laurelton Pennysaver (Honolulu, HI) *Ceased*
Rosedale/Laurelton Shopper's Guide (Ontario, ON, Can.) *Unable to locate*
Roselle Press (Oak Brook, IL) **9364**
Roselle Press: Serving Bartlett/Hanover Park/Steamwood Press; Itasca/ (Oak Brook, IL) **9354**
Roselle Record (La Jolla, CA) *Ceased*
Roselle Spectator **19171***
Roselle Voice (Lincolnwood, IL) *Unable to locate*
Rosemead Independent (City of Industry, CA) *Ceased*
Rosemead/South San Gabriel Progress (Rosemead, CA) **2968**
Rosemont Times (Des Plaines, IL) *Ceased*
Rosemount Sun Current; Apple Valley/ (Apple Valley, MN) **15718**
Rosetown Eagle (Rosetown, SK, Can.) **37545**
Roseville Independent (Macomb, IL) **9132**
Roseville Review (North St. Paul, MN) **16230**
The Rosholt Review (Rosholt, SD) **28958**
Rosicrucian Digest (San Jose, CA) **3534**
The Roslyn News (Roslyn, NY) **23278**
Roslyn Shopper's Guide (Huntington, NY) *Unable to locate*
The Ross County Advertiser (Chillicothe, OH) **24764**
Ross Reports Television **22677***
Ross Reports Television and Film (New York, NY) **22677**
Ross Valley Reporter (Sausalito, CA) *Unable to locate*
Rossburn Review **35292***
The Rossburn Review (Shoal Lake, MB, Can.) *Ceased*
Rossford Record Journal (Rossford, OH) **25503**
Rosslyn Review **5549***
The Rossmoor Journal (Seal Beach, CA) *Ceased*
Rossmoor News (Walnut Creek, CA) **4056**
Roswell Daily Record (Roswell, NM) **19913**
Roswell Neighbor (Marietta, GA) **7416**

ROTA.GENE (Brookfield, CT) **4729**
The ROTARIAN (Evanston, IL) **8869**
Rotary Review (Los Angeles, CA) **2382**
Rotary Rocket (Palos Verdes Estates, CA) *Unable to locate*
Rothco Cartoons (Brooklyn, NY) *Unable to locate*
Rotonde; La (Ottawa, ON, Can.) **36256**
ROTOR (Alexandria, VA) **31734**
Rotor & Wing (Potomac, MD) **13660**
Rotorcraft (Clinton, LA) *Unable to locate*
Rotorgram (Alexandria, VA) *Ceased*
The Rottweiler Quarterly (Gilroy, CA) **2004**
The Rotunda (Farmville, VA) **32068**
Rotunda (Toronto, ON, Can.) **36732**
Rouanda Express (Montreal, QC, Can.) *Ceased*
Rough Notes (Carmel, IN) *Unable to locate*
Rough Notes; The Chatham Courier- (Chatham, NY) **20452**
The Roughneck (Calgary, AB, Can.) *Unable to locate*
Round Bobbin **10784***
Round Lake News (Round Lake, IL) **9557**
The Round Rock Leader (Round Rock, TX) **30995**
Round the Table (Park Ridge, IL) **9408**
Round Table (Beloit, WI) **33576**
The Round Top Register (Round Top, TX) **30996**
The Round-up (Adel, IA) **10572**
Round Up (Las Cruces, NM) **19875**
Round-Up (Sundre, AB, Can.) **34859**
Round Valley News (Covelo, CA) *Unable to locate*
The Round Valley Paper **691***
Roundel Magazine (Greenville, SC) **28626**
Roundup; Pinedale (Pinedale, WY) **34568**
Roundup Record-Tribune and Winnett Times (Roundup, MT) **17902**
Route 66 Magazine (Williams, AZ) **1009**
Route 202 Review (Norristown, PA) *Ceased*
Routes et Transports (Montreal, QC, Can.) *Unable to locate*
Rouyn-Noranda Press (Rouyn-Noranda, QC, Can.) *Ceased*
Roving Reporter **20340***
Row Awards (Petaluma, CA) *Unable to locate*
Rowan's TV Inc. **26550***
Rowena Press (Rowena, TX) **30997**
Rowing U.S.A. **10180***
Rowland Heights Highlander (West Covina, CA) *Unable to locate*
The Rowlett Lakeshore Times (Rowlett, TX) **30998**
Roxbury Register (Roxbury Township, NJ) **19525**
Royal Asiatic Society; Journal of the (New York, NY) **22181**
Royal Book News (Alexandria, VA) *Unable to locate*
Royal Center Record (Royal Center, IN) **10436**
Royal City Record (New Westminster, BC, Can.) *Unable to locate*
Royal City Record Now **35031***
Royal Features (Houston, TX) **38054**
Royal Historical Society Transactions (New York, NY) **22678**
The Royal Neighbor (Rock Island, IL) **9520**
Royal Oak Cablevision Ltd. (Victoria, BC, Can.) *Ceased*
Royal Oak Courier (Royal Oak, MI) **15484**
Royal Oak Mirror (Royal Oak, MI) **15485**
Royal Palm Beach/Loxahatchee Town-Crier (West Palm Beach, FL) *Unable to locate*
Royal People **34457***
Royal Purple (Whitewater, WI) **34457**
The Royal Spaniels (Midway City, CA) **2539**
Roze Maryi (Stockbridge, MA) **14568**
Rozek's (Seattle, WA) *Ceased*
RPM Weekly (Toronto, ON, Can.) *Ceased*
RQ **25941***
RRT **36217***
RS Wavelength (Albuquerque, NM) *Ceased*
RSC (Refrigeration Service and Contracting) **8826***
R.S.I. Magazine (Cleveland, OH) **24951**
RSO Magazine (Hebron, CT) **4917**
RT/The Journal for Respiratory Care Practitioners (Los Angeles, CA) *Unable to locate*
Ruah (Oakland, CA) **2698**
Rubber Chemistry and Technology (Akron, OH) **24586**
Rubber Journal; European (Akron, OH) **24580**
Rubber Markets; China Synthetic (Woodinville, WA) **33210**
Rubber & Plastics News (Akron, OH) **24587**
Rubber World (Akron, OH) **24588**
Ruby Valley Cable Co. (Sheridan, MT) **17909**
Rug Hooking Magazine (Lemoyne, PA) **27185**
Rug Industry; Carpet and (Ramsey, NJ) **19487**
Rug News (Arden, NC) **23620**
Rugby (New York, NY) **22679**
The Ruidoso News (Ruidoso, NM) **19928**
Ruminator Review (St. Paul, MN) **16408**
RUN (Peterborough, NH) *Ceased*
Rundt's Weekly Intelligence Briefs **22680***
Rundt's World Business Intelligence (New York, NY) **22680**

Rungh (Vancouver, BC, Can.) **35166**
Runner & Fitness Sports; Michigan (Ann Arbor, MI) **14769**
Runner Magazine; Youth (Lake Oswego, OR) **26406**
Runner; New York (New York, NY) **22452**
Runner; Northwest (Seattle, WA) **32995**
Runner; Ohio (Westerville, OH) **35643**
The Runner's Schedule (San Rafael, CA) *Ceased*
Runner's World (Emmaus, PA) **26882**
Running; Inside Texas (Houston, TX) **30493**
Running Journal (Greeneville, TN) *Unable to locate*
Running News; California Track and (Chilmark, MA) **14138**
Running Through Texas (Dallas, TX) *Ceased*
Running Times (Wilton, CT) **5230**
Running Wild (Shutesbury, MA) **14526**
Rural Arkansas (Little Rock, AR) **1236**
Rural Builder (Iola, WI) **33842**
Rural Construction (Acton, ON, Can.) *Unable to locate*
Rural Cooperatives (Washington, DC) **5773**
Rural Delivery (Liverpool, NS, Can.) **35590**
The Rural Educator Journal (Norman, OK) **25942**
Rural Electric Missourian **17132***
Rural Electric Nebraskan (Lincoln, NE) **18117**
Rural Electrification Magazine (Arlington, VA) **31824**
Rural Health FYI (Kansas City, MO) *Ceased*
Rural Heritage (Gainesboro, TN) **29201**
Rural History (New York, NY) **22681**
Rural Landscapes (Des Moines, IA) *Ceased*
Rural Letter Carrier; The National (Alexandria, VA) **31714**
Rural Living (Glen Allen, VA) **32112**
Rural Minnesota News (Chippewa Falls, WI) **33628**
Rural Missouri (Jefferson City, MO) **17132**
Rural Montana (RM) (Great Falls, MT) *Unable to locate*
Rural Pennysaver, Inc. (Conklin, NY) **20494**
Rural Rambler (Oxford, WI) **34231**
Rural Retreat Cable TV Inc. (Rural Retreat, VA) **32516**
Rural Roots (Prince Albert, SK, Can.) **37518**
Rural Route Video (Ignacio, CO) **4521**
Rural Sociology (Ithaca, NY) *Unable to locate*
Rural Special Education Quarterly (Morgantown, WV) **33396**
Rural Telecommunications (Arlington, VA) **31825**
Rural-Urban Record (Columbia Station, OH) **24998**
Rural and Urban Roads **8770***
Rural Virginia **32112***
Rural Virginian (Charlottesville, VA) **31940**
Rural Visitor **14577***
The Rural Voice (Blyth, ON, Can.) **35688**
Ruralist; Missouri (Columbia, MO) **17004**
Ruralite (Forest Grove, OR) **26357**
Ruralite; The Sylva Herald & (Sylva, NC) **24251**
The Rush County News (La Crosse, KS) **11542**
Rushville Republican (Rushville, IN) **10437**
The Rusk Cherokeean **30999***
Russell Cable TV Co. (Russell, KS) **11775**
Russell County News (Russell Springs, KY) *Unable to locate*
Russell Daily News (Russell, KS) **11772**
Russell Municipal Cable TV (Russell, MA) **14511**
The Russell Record (Russell, KS) **11773**
Russell Studies; Russell: The Journal of Bertrand (Hamilton, ON, Can.) **35888**
Russell: The Journal of the Bertrand Russell Archives **35888***
Russell: The Journal of Bertrand Russell Studies (Hamilton, ON, Can.) **35888**
Russell's Official National Motor Coach Guide (Cedar Rapids, IA) **10677**
Russia & Eurasia Documents Annual (Gulf Breeze, FL) **6180**
Russia & Eurasia Military Review Annual (Gulf Breeze, FL) **6181**
Russian Academy of the Sciences. Doklady, Mathematics (Providence, RI) *Ceased*
Russian Academy of Sciences. Izvestiya, Mathematics (Providence, RI) *Ceased*
Russian Academy of Sciences. Sbornik, Mathematics (Providence, RI) *Ceased*
Russian Chemical Bulletin (New York, NY) **22682**
Russian and East European Psychology; Journal of (Armonk, NY) **20087**
Russian & Eastern European Finance and Trade **20076***
Russian Education and Society (Armonk, NY) **20093**
Russian Journal of Applied Chemistry (New York, NY) **22683**
Russian Journal of Bioorganic Chemistry (New York, NY) **22684**
Russian Journal of Computational Mechanics (Hoboken, NJ) *Ceased*
Russian Journal of Coordination Chemistry (New York, NY) **22685**
Russian Journal of Developmental Biology (New York, NY) **22686**

Russian Journal of Ecology (New York, NY) **22687**
Russian Journal of Electrochemistry (New York, NY) **22688**
Russian Journal of Engineering Thermophysics (New York, NY) *Ceased*
Russian Journal of General Chemistry (New York, NY) **22689**
Russian Journal of Genetics (New York, NY) **22690**
Russian Journal of Marine Biology (New York, NY) **22691**
Russian Journal of Mathematical Physics (Birmingham, AL) **89**
Russian Journal of Nondestructive Testing (New York, NY) **22692**
Russian Journal of Organic Chemistry (New York, NY) **22693**
Russian Journal of Plant Physiology (New York, NY) **22694**
Russian Journal of Theoretical and Applied Mechanics (New York, NY) *Ceased*
Russian Linguistics (New York, NY) **22695**
Russian Microelectronics (New York, NY) **22696**
Russian Orthodox Journal **27001***
Russian Physics Journal (New York, NY) **22697**
Russian Politics and Law (Armonk, NY) **20094**
The Russian Review (Malden, MA) **14299**
Russian River News (Walnut Creek, CA) *Unable to locate*
Russian Social Science Review (Armonk, NY) **20095**
Russian Studies in History (Armonk, NY) **20096**
Russian Studies in Literature (Armonk, NY) **20097**
Russian Studies in Philosophy (Armonk, NY) **20098**
Russian Word; New (New York, NY) **22434**
Russkoye Slovo; Novoye **22434***
Rustic-Republican **17238***
Rustler; The Riesel (Riesel, TX) **30982**
Rustler Sentinel (Scribner, NE) **18274**
Ruston Cable TV (Ruston, LA) *Unable to locate*
Ruston Daily Leader (Ruston, LA) **12806**
Rutgers Center of Alcohol Studies (Piscataway, NJ) **19431**
Rutgers Computer and Technology Law Journal (Newark, NJ) **19364**
Rutgers Law Review (Newark, NJ) **19365**
Rutgers Magazine (New Brunswick, NJ) **19338**
Rutherford (Charlottesville, VA) *Ceased*
Rutherford County News-Enterprise **23893***
The Rutherford Courier (Smyrna, TN) **29605**
Rutland Cablevision (Rutland, VT) *Unable to locate*
Rutland Herald (Rutland, VT) **31585**
RV Business (Ventura, CA) **4010**
RV Life (Lynnwood, WA) **32825**
RV News (Tempe, AZ) *Unable to locate*
RV Trade Digest (Elkhart, IN) *Unable to locate*
RV Trader (Seattle, WA) *Unable to locate*
R.V. Trader/Moto, Bateau & Vehicules Recreatif Hebdo; Bike, Boat & (Montreal, QC, Can.) **37091**
RV Traveler; WOODALL's California (Ventura, CA) **4016**
RV Traveler; WOODALL's Carolina (Ventura, CA) **4019**
RV Traveler; WOODALL's Midwest (Ventura, CA) **4020**
RV West Magazine (Woodinville, WA) **33215**
RV; WOODALL's Texas (Ventura, CA) **4025**
RV'n **32825***
RWDSU Record (New York, NY) **22698**
RX Being Well - The Waiting Room Magazine (New York, NY) *Unable to locate*
RX Home Care (Akron, OH) *Ceased*
The Ryan Leader (Ryan, OK) **26052**
The Ryder (Bloomington, IN) **9851**
Rye Chronicle (Rye, NY) **23279**
Ryegate Cable TV (Harlowton, MT) *Ceased*
The Ryersoniam (Toronto, ON, Can.) **36733**

S

S A Y N *Ceased*
(S & C); Service and Contracting (Elgin, IL) **8826**
S Corporations (New Rochelle, NY) *Ceased*
S/F (Square Foot) (Woburn, MA) *Unable to locate*
S Gaugian (Forest Park, IL) **8893**
The S & L Quarterly (Austin, TX) **29803**
S & L—Savings Bank Financial Quarterly (Hartland, WI) **33783**
S & P's Insurance Digest/Life Insurance Edition (New York, NY) **22699**
S & P's Insurance Digest/Property-Casualty & Reinsurance Edition (New York, NY) **22700**
The SAA Archaeological Record (Washington, DC) **5774**
Saanich News (Victoria, BC, Can.) **35225**
The Sabbath Recorder (Janesville, WI) **33861**
The Sabbath Sentinel (Fairview, OK) **25834**

The Sabbath Watchman (Downey, CA) **1836**
The Sabetha Herald (Sabetha, KS) **11776**
Sabinal Sampler (Sabinal, TX) **31002**
Sabinal Times **31002***
Sabine County Reporter **30437***
Sabine County Reporter and the Rambler (Hemphill, TX) **30437**
Sabine Index (Many, LA) **12669**
Sac City Reminder (Sac City, IA) **11186**
SAC Newsmonthly (Bogalusa, LA) **12534**
Sac Sun (Sac City, IA) **11187**
SACC Notes—Teaching Anthropology (Arlington, VA) **31826**
Sachem; The Grand River (Caledonia, ON, Can.) **35721**
Sackville Cable TV **35601***
The Sackville Tribune-Post (Sackville, NB, Can.) **35427**
The Sacramento Bee (Sacramento, CA) **3011**
Sacramento Bulletin (Sacramento, CA) **3012**
Sacramento Business Journal (Charlotte, NC) **23752**
Sacramento Cable (Sacramento, CA) **3063**
Sacramento City College Express (Sacramento, CA) **3013**
The Sacramento Gazette (Sacramento, CA) **3014**
Sacramento Lawyer (Sacramento, CA) **3015**
Sacramento Magazine (Sacramento, CA) **3016**
Sacramento Medicine **3019***
Sacramento News & Review (Sacramento, CA) **3017**
Sacramento Observer (Sacramento, CA) **3018**
Sacramento Report **2985***
The Sacramento Union (Sacramento, CA) *Ceased*
Sacred Dance Guild Journal (Carbondale, IL) **8120**
Sacred Heart News **16303***
Sacred Heart News (Sacred Heart, MN) *Ceased*
Sacred Heart; Reign of the (Hales Corners, WI) **33769**
Sacred Music (Front Royal, VA) **32095**
Sacred River: Bay Area Women's Journal (Berkeley, CA) *Unable to locate*
Saddle & Bridle Magazine (St. Louis, MO) **17491**
Saddle Brook Shopper; Fair Lawn-Elmwood Park- (Fair Lawn, NJ) **18806**
Saddle Horse Report (Shelbyville, TN) **29599**
Saddle Up (Haysville, KS) *Unable to locate*
Saddleback Valley News (Santa Ana, CA) **3632**
The Sae Gae Times (Long Island City, NY) **20966**
SAE Off-Highway Engineering (Warrendale, PA) **28114**
Safari Magazine (Tucson, AZ) **962**
Safe Driver (Itasca, IL) **9017**
SAFE Journal (Creswell, OR) **26298**
SAFE Symposium Proceedings (Creswell, OR) **26299**
Safe and Vault Technology (Nicholasville, KY) *Unable to locate*
Safety Briefs (Cranford, NJ) **18772**
Safety Digest; Flight (Alexandria, VA) **31673**
Safety Harbor Herald (Tarpon Springs, FL) *Ceased*
Safety & Health; Family (Itasca, IL) **9013**
Safety and Health Review; Federal Mine (Washington, DC) **5494**
Safety and Hygiene News; Industrial (Norristown, PA) **27335**
The Safety Journal (Anderson, SC) *Ceased*
Safety Magazine; Living (Ottawa, ON, Can.) **36260**
Safety News (COHSN); Canadian Occupational Health and (Toronto, ON, Can.) **36521**
Safety; Nuclear (Oak Ridge, TN) **29549**
Safety; Occupational Health & (Dallas, TX) **30174**
Safety; Pharmacoepidemiology and Drug (Hoboken, NJ) **19082**
Safety Product News; Public (Denver, CO) **4350**
Safety; Professional (Des Plaines, IL) **8769**
Safety Science Abstracts; Health and (Bethesda, MD) **13342**
Safety+Health (Itasca, IL) **9018**
Safeworker (Itasca, IL) **9019**
The Sag Harbor Express (Sag Harbor, NY) **23283**
The Sagamore (Indianapolis, IN) **10168**
Sage: A Scholarly Journal on Black Women (Atlanta, GA) *Ceased*
Sage Family Studies Abstracts (Thousand Oaks, CA) **3912**
Sage Public Administration Abstracts (Thousand Oaks, CA) **3913**
Sage Urban Studies Abstracts (Thousand Oaks, CA) **3914**
Sagebrush (Reno, NV) **18424**
SageWoman Magazine (Point Arena, CA) **2858**
Saginaw; Cox Cable (Saginaw, MI) **15493**
The Saginaw News (Saginaw, MI) **15491**
The Saginaw Press (Saginaw, MI) **15492**
Saguache Crescent (Saguache, CO) **4617**
Saguenayensia (Chicoutimi, QC, Can.) **36968**
Saigon Times (Rosemead, CA) **2969**
SAIL (Boston, MA) **13956**
Sailaway (St. Petersburg, FL) *Ceased*
Sailboard News (Fair Haven, VT) *Unable to locate*
Sailing (Port Washington, WI) *Ceased*

Sailing Canada Magazine (Cort Hope, ON, Can.) *Unable to locate*
Sailing Magazine; Northern Breezes (Minneapolis, MN) **16116**
Sailing; Motor Boating & (New York, NY) **22371**
Sailing World (Newport, RI) **28373**
The Sailorman Star (Honolulu, HI) *Ceased*
Sailors' Gazette (Key West, FL) *Unable to locate*
The St. Albans Messenger (St. Albans, VT) **31590**
St. Albert Gazette **34842***
St. Albert Gazette (St. Albert, AB, Can.) **34842**
St. Albert & Sturgeon Gazette **34842***
The St. Anthony Bulletin (St. Anthony, MN) **16340**
St. Anthony Messenger (Cincinnati, OH) **24814**
The St. Augustine Record (St. Augustine, FL) **6617**
The Saint Bernard Quarterly (Wheat Ridge, CO) *Ceased*
Saint Bernard Voice (Arabi, LA) **12474**
Saint-Bruno; Le Journal de (Saint-Bruno, QC, Can.) **37329**
St. Charles Chronicle, Geneva Chronicle, Batavia Chronicle, and Elburn Chronicle **8918***
St. Charles Herald-Guide (Boutte, LA) **12540**
St. Charles Journal (Warrenton, MO) **17693**
St. Charles Republican (St. Charles, IL) **9571**
St. Charles Sun (Naperville, IL) **9273**
Saint Charles Watchman (St. Louis, MO) **17492**
St. Clair County Buyer's Guide (Osceola, MO) **17324**
St. Clair County Courier (Osceola, MO) **17325**
The St. Clair Examiner (Toronto, ON, Can.) *Unable to locate*
St. Clair Gazette **36366***
St. Clair News-Aegis (St. Clair, AL) **443**
St. Clair Shores Sentinel (Warren, MI) *Unable to locate*
St. Cloud Daily Times **16345***
St. Cloud Times (St. Cloud, MN) **16345**
St. Cloud Visitor (St. Cloud, MN) **16346**
St. Croix County Star (Somerset, WI) *Unable to locate*
Saint Croix Courier (St. Stephen, NB, Can.) **35437**
St. Croix News; Central (Hammond, WI) **33773**
The St. Croix Review (Stillwater, MN) *Unable to locate*
St. Croix Valley Peach (Forest Lake, MN) **15906**
St. Croix Valley Press (White Bear Lake, MN) **16511**
Saint-Donat Telecable (Saint-Donat, QC, Can.) *Unable to locate*
The St. Edward Advance (St. Edward, NE) **18257**
Saint Fancier (Kittrell, NC) **24032**
St. Francis Herald (St. Francis, KS) *Unable to locate*
St. Francisville Democrat (St. Francisville, LA) **12812**
Saint Francois; Le (Valleyfield, QC, Can.) **37425**
Ste. Genevieve Herald (Ste. Genevieve, MO) **17387**
St. Helena Echo (Greensburg, LA) **12589**
St. Helena Star (St. Helena, CA) **3065**
Saint-Hubert; Courrier **37345***
Saint-Hubert; Le Journal de (Saint-Hubert, QC, Can.) **37345**
The St. Ignace News (St. Ignace, MI) **15508**
St. James/Nesconset Suffolk Life (St. James, NY) **23290**
The Saint Jo Tribune (St. Jo, TX) **31003**
St. John News (St. John, KS) **11778**
Saint John Times Globe **35431***
Saint John Times Globe (St. John, NB, Can.) *Ceased*
St. John Valley Times (Madawaska, ME) **12989**
St. John's News (Quincy, MA) *Ceased*
St. John's Pennysaver (St. Augustine, FL) **6618**
St. Johns Reminder (St. Johns, MI) **15510**
St. John's Reporter **13093***
St. Johns Review (Portland, OR) *Unable to locate*
St. Joseph Cablevision (St. Joseph, MO) **17401**
St. Joseph Gazette **17394***
St. Joseph News-Press (St. Joseph, MO) **17394**
The St. Joseph Telegraph (St. Joseph, MO) **17395**
St. Joseph's Messenger & Advocate of the Blind (Jersey City, NJ) *Ceased*
St. Lambert Journal (Saint-Lambert, QC, Can.) **37360**
St. Laurent; Le Soleil du (Valleyfield, QC, Can.) **37426**
St. Laurent L'Echo (Riviere-du-Loup, QC, Can.) *Ceased*
Saint-Laurent News; Nouvelles (Saint-Laurent, QC, Can.) **37365**
Saint Laurent/Portage; Le (Riviere-du-Loup, QC, Can.) **37314**
St. Lawrence (Canton, NY) **20431**
St. Lawrence County Historical Association **20430***
St. Louis Advertising (St. Louis, MO) *Unable to locate*
St. Louis American (St. Louis, MO) **17493**
St. Louis Argus (St. Louis, MO) **17494**
Saint Louis Art Museum Bulletin (St. Louis, MO) **17495**
St. Louis Bar Journal (Millstadt, IL) *Ceased*
St. Louis Business Journal (St. Louis, MO) **17496**
St. Louis Commerce (St. Louis, MO) **17497**

St. Louis ComputerUser (St. Louis, MO) *Unable to locate*
St. Louis Construction News & Review (St. Louis, MO) **17498**
St. Louis Countian (St. Louis, MO) **17499**
St. Louis Crusader (St. Louis, MO) **17500**
St. Louis Jewish Light (St. Louis, MO) **17501**
St. Louis Journal; East (Warrenton, MO) **17681**
The St. Louis Journalism Review (St. Louis, MO) **17502**
St. Louis Lawyer (St. Louis, MO) **17503**
St. Louis Lawyer Magazine (Millstadt, IL) *Ceased*
St. Louis Magazine (St. Louis, MO) *Ceased*
St. Louis Medicine **17505***
The St. Louis Metro Evening Whirl (St. Louis, MO) **17504**
St. Louis Metropolitan Medicine (St. Louis, MO) **17505**
St. Louis Park Sun-Sailor (St. Louis Park, MN) **16361**
St. Louis Pharmacist (Maryland Heights, MO) *Unable to locate*
St. Louis Post-Dispatch (St. Louis, MO) **17506**
St. Louis Review (St. Louis, MO) **17507**
St. Louis Sentinel Newspaper (St. Louis, MO) *Unable to locate*
St. Louis/Southern Illinois Labor Tribune (St. Louis, MO) **17508**
St. Louis Sun (St. Louis, MO) *Unable to locate*
St. Louis Watchman Advocate (St. Louis, MO) **17509**
The St. Louis Weekly (St. Louis, MO) *Ceased*
St. Louis; WHERE (St. Louis, MO) **17532**
St. Marie's Gazette-Record (St. Maries, ID) **7972**
St. Mary Journal (Morgan City, LA) **12708**
Saint Mary's Beacon (Lexington Park, MD) *Ceased*
St. Mary's Collegian (Moraga, CA) **2597**
St. Mary's Enterprise (Lexington Park, MD) **13616**
The St. Marys Oracle (St. Marys, WV) **33461**
St. Marys Star (St. Marys, KS) **11779**
St. Michel; Journal de (Montreal, QC, Can.) **37146**
St. Patrick Hospital Health Update (Missoula, MT) **17876**
St. Patrick Hospital Messenger **17876***
St. Paul CityBusiness; Minneapolis- (Charlotte, NC) **23750**
St. Paul Journal (St. Paul, AB, Can.) **34844**
St. Paul Phonograph-Herald (St. Paul, NE) **18258**
St. Paul Pioneer Press (St. Paul, MN) **16409**
St. Paul Recorder (St. Paul, MN) *Unable to locate*
St. Paul's Family Magazine (Olathe, KS) *Unable to locate*
The St. Pauls Review (St. Pauls, NC) **24213**
St. Peter Herald (St. Peter, MN) *Unable to locate*
St. Peters Journal (Warrenton, MO) **17694**
St. Peters Star (St. Peters, MO) *Unable to locate*
St. Petersburg Mathematical Journal (Providence, RI) **28423**
St. Petersburg Times (St. Petersburg, FL) **6633**
Saint Raphael's Better Health (New Haven, CT) **5001**
Saint Tammany; Cablevision Industries of (Slidell, LA) **12844**
St. Tammany Farmer (Covington, LA) **12555**
St. Tammany News-Banner (Covington, LA) **12556**
St. Thomas Law Review (Miami, FL) **6378**
St. Thomas Times-Journal (St. Thomas, ON, Can.) **36363**
Saints Herald **17112***
SAIS Review (Baltimore, MD) **13243**
Sakonnet Times (Bristol, RI) **28327**
Salado Village Voice (Salado, TX) *Unable to locate*
Salary Survey (Washington, DC) **5775**
Sald **27207***
The Salem Democrat (Salem, IN) **10439**
Salem Evening News **14514***
Salem Evening News (Beverly, MA) **13842**
Salem Headlight **1335***
The Salem Leader (Salem, IN) **10440**
Salem News **13842***
Salem News **1335***
Salem News (Salem, MA) **14514**
The Salem News (Salem, MO) **17563**
Salem News (Salem, OH) **25506**
Salem Observer (Salem, NH) **18645**
Salem Press **20701***
The Salem State Log (Salem, MA) **14515**
Salem Times-Commoner (Salem, IL) **9577**
Salem Times-Register (Salem, VA) **32521**
The Salers Stockman (Wheat Ridge, CO) *Ceased*
The Sales Executive (New York, NY) *Ceased*
Sales Force (Scarborough, ON, Can.) *Ceased*
Sales Magazine; Agency (Lake Forest, CA) **2141**
Sales Management; The Journal of Personal Selling and (Denton, TX) **30240**
Sales & Marketing Ideas (Washington, DC) **5776**
Sales & Marketing Management (New York, NY) **22701**
Sales & Marketing Manager Canada (Winnepeg, MB, Can.) *Ceased*
Sales & Marketing Quarterly **5369***

Sales and Marketing Strategies & News (Rockford, IL) *Unable to locate*
Sales & Marketing Training (Westbury, NY) *Ceased*
SalesDoctors Magazine (Boca Raton, FL) *Unable to locate*
Salesian (New Rochelle, NY) **21122**
Salesian Bulletin (New Rochelle, NY) *Ceased*
Salesman; American (Burlington, IA) **10637**
SalesTax Manuals; Vertex National (Berwyn, PA) **26698**
The Salina Journal (Salina, KS) **11784**
The Salina Sun (Gunnison, UT) **31336**
The Salinas Californian **3067***
The Saline Reporter (Saline, MI) **15519**
Salisbury News & Advertiser (Dover, DE) *Ceased*
The Salisbury Post (Salisbury, NC) **24215**
Salisbury Press-Spectator (Salisbury, MO) **17565**
Salmagundi (Saratoga Springs, NY) **23302**
Salmo Cabled Programmes Ltd. (Salmo, BC, Can.) **35080**
Salmon Arm Observer (Salmon Arm, BC, Can.) **35081**
Salmon Journal; Atlantic (St. Andrews, NB, Can.) **35429**
Salmon Leader; The Trout & (Olympia, WA) **32861**
Salmon River News (Mexico, NY) **21077**
Salmon Syndication (Vallejo, CA) *Ceased*
Salmon Trout Steelheader (Portland, OR) **26506**
Salome (Chicago, IL) *Unable to locate*
Salon; American (Milford, CT) **4952**
Salon Biz (Los Angeles, CA) *Ceased*
Salon Magazine (Toronto, ON, Can.) **36734**
Salon; Modern (Lincolnshire, IL) **9086**
Salon News (New York, NY) **22702**
Salon Today Magazine (Lincolnshire, IL) **9088**
SalonNews (New York, NY) **22703**
Salt of the Earth (Chicago, IL) *Ceased*
Salt Hill (Syracuse, NY) **23420**
Salt Hill Journal **23420***
Salt Lake City Weekly (Salt Lake City, UT) **31438**
Salt Lake Magazine (Salt Lake City, UT) **31439**
Salt Lake Times (Salt Lake City, UT) *Unable to locate*
The Salt Lake Tribune (Salt Lake City, UT) **31440**
Salt Water Sportsman (Boston, MA) **13957**
Saltsburg Press (Saltsburg, PA) *Ceased*
Saltscapes (Dartmouth, NS, Can.) **35550**
Saltspring Cablevision (1981) Ltd. (Salt Spring, BC, Can.) **35085**
Saltville News-Messenger (Wytheville, VA) *Unable to locate*
Saltwater Fly Fishing (Bennington, VT) **31501**
Saluda Standard Sentinel (Saluda, SC) **28753**
Saludos Hispanos (Palm Desert, CA) **2743**
Salut Dimanche (Louiseville, QC, Can.) **37061**
Salute (Floral Park, NY) **20606**
Salvage Guide; Midwestern States (Moore, OK) **25920**
Salyersville Independent (Salyersville, KY) **12390**
SAM Advanced Management Journal (Corpus Christi, TX) **30078**
Sam Mantics Enterprises (Menlo Park, CA) *Ceased*
The Samford Crimson (Birmingham, AL) **90**
Sammons Cable **30244***
Sammons Cable Services (Fort Worth, TX) **30361**
Sammons Communications **5196***
Sammons Communications **9910***
Sammons Communications (Glendale, CA) **2023**
Sammons Communications (Seymour, IN) **10449**
Sammons Communications (Harrisburg, PA) **27015**
Sammons Communications of Illinois Inc. **9024***
Sammons Communications, Inc. (Absecon, NJ) **18657**
Sammons Communications Inc. (Black Mountain, NC) **23648**
Sammons Communications of Mississippi, Inc. (Pascagoula, MS) **16812**
Sammons Communications of New Jersey Inc. **19700***
Sammons Communications of New Jersey, Inc. (Dover, NJ) *Unable to locate*
Sammons Communications of Oklahoma Inc. **25819***
Sammons Communications of Pennsylvania Inc. (Emmaus, PA) *Unable to locate*
Sammons Communications of Pennsylvania Inc. (Fleetwood, PA) *Unable to locate*
The Samoyed Quarterly (Wheat Ridge, CO) **4682**
Sampan (Boston, MA) **13958**
SAMPE Journal (Covina, CA) **1786**
The Sample Case (Columbus, OH) **25060**
The Sampler (Monessen, PA) *Ceased*
The Sampler (Mc Lean, VA) *Unable to locate*
Sampler; Sabinal (Sabinal, TX) **31002**
Sampling Theory in Signal and Image Processing (Potsdam, NY) *Unable to locate*
The Sampson Independent (Clinton, NC) **23789**
Samson Ledger (Samson, AL) **444**
San Angelo Bridal Guide Magazine (San Angelo, TX) **31009**

San Angelo City Lites Magazine (San Angelo, TX) *Ceased*
San Angelo Standard-Times (San Angelo, TX) **31010**
The San Antonio Business Journal (San Antonio, TX) **31045**
San Antonio Current (San Antonio, TX) *Unable to locate*
San Antonio Homes & Gardens (San Antonio, TX) **31046**
San Antonio Light (San Antonio, TX) *Ceased*
San Antonio Monthly Magazine (San Antonio, TX) *Unable to locate*
San Antonio; Que Pasa (San Antonio, TX) **31043**
San Antonio Register (San Antonio, TX) **31047**
San Augustine Tribune (San Augustine, TX) **31080**
San Benito News (San Benito, TX) **31081**
San Benito & Port Elizabeth (San Benito, TX) *Unable to locate*
The San Bernardino American News (San Bernardino, CA) **3090**
San Bernardino Bulletin (San Bernardino, CA) **3091**
San Bernardino County Museum Association Quarterly (Redlands, CA) **2907**
The San Bernardino County Sun (San Bernardino, CA) **3092**
San Bernardino Green Sheet; North (San Bernardino, CA) **3088**
San Bernardino Green Sheet; West (San Bernardino, CA) **3093**
San Bruno Herald (San Bruno, CA) **3097**
San Bruno Municipal Cable TV (San Bruno, CA) **3098**
San Clemente News **3102***
San Clemente Sun-Post News (San Clemente, CA) **3102**
San Diego Bulletin (San Diego, CA) **3257**
San Diego Business Journal (San Diego, CA) **3258**
San Diego Commerce (San Diego, CA) **3259**
San Diego Computer Journal (San Diego, CA) **3260**
San Diego County Physician (San Diego, CA) **3261**
San Diego Daily Transcript (San Diego, CA) **3262**
San Diego Examiner (San Diego, CA) *Ceased*
San Diego Family Magazine (San Diego, CA) **3263**
San Diego Family Press **3263***
San Diego Gay Times (San Diego, CA) *Unable to locate*
San Diego History; Journal of (San Diego, CA) **3212**
San Diego Home/Garden (San Diego, CA) *Unable to locate*
San Diego Independent (San Diego, CA) *Ceased*
San Diego Jewish Press-Heritage (Los Angeles, CA) *Unable to locate*
San Diego Jewish Times (La Mesa, CA) **2123**
San Diego; La Prensa (San Diego, CA) **3220**
San Diego Law Review (San Diego, CA) **3264**
San Diego Lesbian Press (San Diego, CA) *Unable to locate*
San Diego Live (San Diego, CA) *Ceased*
San Diego Log (San Diego, CA) *Unable to locate*
San Diego Magazine (San Diego, CA) **3265**
San Diego Navy Dispatch (San Diego, CA) **3266**
San Diego Parent (San Diego, CA) **3267**
San Diego Reader (San Diego, CA) **3268**
San Diego South; PennySaver/ (Brea, CA) **1602**
San Diego This Week (San Diego, CA) **3269**
San Diego; Today in (San Diego, CA) **3280**
The San Diego Union-Tribune (San Diego, CA) **3270**
The San Diego Voice and Viewpoint (San Diego, CA) **3271**
San Diego Woman Magazine (La Jolla, CA) *Ceased*
San Dimas Highlander (West Covina, CA) *Unable to locate*
San Fernando Gazette Express (Pacoima, CA) **2742**
San Fernando Poetry Journal (Northridge, CA) *Ceased*
The San Fernando Sun Newspaper and Valley View (San Fernando, CA) **3322**
San Fernando Valley Business Journal (Los Angeles, CA) **2383**
San Francisco (San Francisco, CA) **3425**
San Francisco (San Antonio, CA) *Unable to locate*
San Francisco Art Institute Magazine (San Francisco, CA) **3426**
San Francisco Attorney Magazine (San Francisco, CA) **3427**
San Francisco Bar **3427***
The San Francisco and Bay Area Guide (San Francisco, CA) **3428**
The San Francisco Bay Guardian (San Francisco, CA) **3429**
San Francisco Bay Times (San Francisco, CA) *Unable to locate*
San Francisco Bay View (San Francisco, CA) **3430**
San Francisco Business Times (San Francisco, CA) **3431**
San Francisco Catholic (San Francisco, CA) *Ceased*
San Francisco Chronicle (San Francisco, CA) **3432**
San Francisco Daily Journal (Los Angeles, CA) *Unable to locate*

San Francisco Examiner (San Francisco, CA) **3433**
San Francisco Focus **3435***
San Francisco Independent (San Francisco, CA) **3434**
San Francisco Latino **3358***
San Francisco Magazine (San Francisco, CA) **3435**
San Francisco Magazine; University of (San Francisco, CA) **3455**
San Francisco Medicine (San Francisco, CA) **3436**
San Francisco Observer (San Francisco, CA) **3437**
San Francisco Peninsula Parent (Dallas, TX) *Unable to locate*
San Francisco Post (San Francisco, CA) **3438**
San Francisco Progress (San Francisco, CA) *Unable to locate*
San Francisco Review of Books (San Francisco, CA) *Unable to locate*
San Francisco Style International (San Francisco, CA) **38055**
San Francisco System; TCI, (San Francisco, CA) **3506**
San Francisco; WHERE (San Francisco, CA) **3462**
San Gabriel Progress (Los Angeles, CA) *Ceased*
San Gabriel Sun (City of Industry, CA) *Ceased*
San Gabriel Valley Business Journal (Covina, CA) *Unable to locate*
San Gabriel Valley Independent (San Gabriel, CA) *Unable to locate*
San Gabriel Valley Tribune (West Covina, CA) **4060**
San Jacinto News Times (San Jacinto, TX) **31082**
San Jacinto Valley Register (Birmingham, AL) *Ceased*
San Joaquin Farm Bureau News (San Joaquin, CA) **3507**
San Jose Business Journal (San Jose, CA) **3535**
San Jose Magazine *Unable to locate*
San Jose Mercury News (San Jose, CA) **3536**
San Jose Post-Record (San Jose, CA) **3537**
San Jose Studies *Ceased*
San Jose Sun-Evergreen (Cupertino, CA) *Ceased*
San Juan Cablevision **32773***
San Juan Islands; The Journal of the (Friday Harbor, WA) **32772**
San Juan Island's Sounder (Bainbridge Island, WA) *Unable to locate*
The San Juan Record (Monticello, UT) **31370**
The San Juan Star (San Juan, PR) *Unable to locate*
The San Juans Beckon (Eastsound, WA) **32743**
San Leandro Observer (Oakland, CA) **2699**
San Leandro and South County Observer **2699***
The San Luis Obispo County Telegram Tribune (San Luis Obispo, CA) **3569**
San Manuel Miner (San Manuel, AZ) **865**
San Marcos Courier (San Marcos, CA) *Unable to locate*
San Marcos Daily Record (San Marcos, TX) **31085**
San Marcos News (San Marcos, TX) *Ceased*
San Marcos News Reporter (San Marcos, CA) *Unable to locate*
San Marino Tribune (San Marino, CA) **3581**
San Mateo Times (San Mateo, CA) **3589**
San Miguel Basin Forum (Nucla, CO) **4588**
San Patricio County News (Sinton, TX) **31111**
San Pedro Valley News-Sun (Benson, AZ) **658**
San Ramon Valley Times (Danville, CA) **1809**
San Saba News and Star (San Saba, TX) **31089**
Sanborn Pioneer (Sanborn, IA) **11188**
The Sand Mountain Reporter (Albertville, AL) **3**
Sand Springs Leader (Sand Springs, OK) **26054**
Sand Studies; George (Medford, MA) **14322**
Sandara **8001***
Sanders County Ledger (Thompson Falls, MT) **17914**
The Sanderson Times (Sanderson, TX) **31092**
Sandersville Progress (Sandersville, GA) **7526**
Sandlapper (Lexington, SC) **28685**
Sandmutopia Guardian **22704***
The SandMUtopian Guardian (New York, NY) **22704**
The Sandpaper (Surf City, NJ) **19606**
The Sandspur (Winter Park, FL) **6885**
Sandusky Register (Sandusky, OH) **25510**
Sandwich Broadsider (Yarmouth Port, MA) *Unable to locate*
The Sandwich Generation (Wickatunk, NJ) *Ceased*
Sandy Post (Gresham, OR) *Unable to locate*
Sandy Springs Neighbor (Marietta, GA) **7417**
Sanford Herald (Sanford, FL) **6647**
The Sanford Herald (Sanford, NC) **24219**
The Sanford News (Sanford, ME) **13049**
Sanger Herald (Sanger, CA) **3617**
Sanger-Hilsen (Singer Greeting) (Decorah, IA) *Unable to locate*
Sangre de Cristo Chronicle (Angel Fire, NM) **19816**
Sanilac County Buyer's Guide (Sandusky, MI) **15521**
Sanilac County News (Sandusky, MI) **15522**
Sanitary Maintenance (Milwaukee, WI) **34099**
Sanmans Communications (Morristown, TN) **29419**
Santa Anna News (Santa Anna, TX) *Unable to locate*
Santa Barbara; Cox Cable (Goleta, CA) **2028**
Santa Barbara Independent (Santa Barbara, CA) **3654**

Santa Barbara Magazine (Santa Barbara, CA) *Unable to locate*
Santa Barbara News-Press (Santa Barbara, CA) **3655**
Santa Barbara Review (Bakersfield, CA) *Ceased*
The Santa Clara (Santa Clara, CA) **3673**
Santa Clara Computer and High Technology Law Journal (Santa Clara, CA) **3674**
Santa Clara County Business Magazine (San Jose, CA) *Unable to locate*
Santa Clara Law Review (Santa Clara, CA) **3675**
Santa Clara Sun (Cupertino, CA) *Ceased*
Santa Cruz County Business Journal (Santa Cruz, CA) *Ceased*
Santa Cruz County Sentinel (Santa Cruz, CA) **3688**
Santa Cruz; Metro (Santa Cruz, CA) **3687**
Santa Cruz Sentinel **3688***
The Santa Fe New Mexican (Santa Fe, NM) **19943**
Santa Fe Reporter (Santa Fe, NM) **19944**
Santa Fe Springs News **2840***
Santa Fe Springs News; Pico Rivera/ (Pico Rivera, CA) **2840**
The Santa Fe Times (Alma, MO) **16890**
The Santa Fean Magazine (Santa Fe, NM) **19945**
Santa Gertrudis Tribune (Valley Mills, TX) *Ceased*
Santa Maria Times (Santa Maria, CA) **3696**
Santa Monica College Corsair (Santa Monica, CA) **3717**
Santa Paula Times (Santa Paula, CA) *Unable to locate*
Santa Rosa Free Press (Milton, FL) **6424**
Santa Rosa News (Santa Rosa, NM) **19951**
Santa Rosa Press Gazette (Milton, FL) **6425**
Santa Ynez Valley News (Solvang, CA) **3771**
Santana (Huntington Beach, CA) *Unable to locate*
Sante Mentale au Quebec (Montreal, QC, Can.) **37221**
The Santee Striper (Bamberg, SC) **28481**
The Saponifier (Silvana, WA) **33082**
Sapulpa Daily Herald (Sapulpa, OK) **26056**
Sapulpa Herald Extra (Sapulpa, OK) **26057**
SAQ (Durham, NC) **23843**
The SAR Magazine (Milwaukee, WI) **34100**
Saraland News-Herald (Bayou la Batre, AL) *Unable to locate*
Sarasota Herald-Tribune (Sarasota, FL) **6663**
Sarasota Magazine (Sarasota, FL) **6664**
Sarasota Times (Sarasota, FL) *Unable to locate*
Sarasota Weekly (Bradenton, FL) *Unable to locate*
The Saratoga (Rhinebeck, NY) *Ceased*
Saratoga News (Los Gatos, CA) **2479**
Saratoga Sun (Saratoga, WY) **34586**
The Saratogian (Saratoga Springs, NY) **23303**
The Sarcoxie Record (Sarcoxie, MO) **17567**
Sargent Leader (Sargent, NE) **18260**
Sarmatian Review (Houston, TX) **30526**
The Sarnia Gazette **36366***
The Sarnia Observer (Sarnia, ON, Can.) **36365**
Sarnia This Week (Sarnia, ON, Can.) **36366**
Sarpy County Extra (Blair, NE) **17958**
Sartre Studies International (New York, NY) **22705**
Saskatchewan Archaeology (Saskatoon, SK, Can.) **37553**
Saskatchewan Business (Saskatoon, SK, Can.) *Unable to locate*
Saskatchewan Farm Life (Saskatoon, SK, Can.) *Unable to locate*
Saskatchewan Genealogical Society (Regina, SK, Can.) **37533**
Saskatchewan History (Saskatoon, SK, Can.) **37554**
Saskatchewan; Moving to (Unionville, ON, Can.) **36833**
Saskatchewan Record; The Fort (Fort Saskatchewan, AB, Can.) **34771**
Saskatchewan Trucking (Winnipeg, MB, Can.) *Ceased*
Saskatchewan Valley News (Rosthern, SK, Can.) **37547**
Saskatoon Free Press (Saskatoon, SK, Can.) *Unable to locate*
Saskatoon History **37555***
Saskatoon History Review (Saskatoon, SK, Can.) **37555**
Sassy (New York, NY) *Unable to locate*
SAT Guide: Cable's Satellite Magazine (Hailey, ID) *Ceased*
Satellite Broadband (New York, NY) **22706**
Satellite Cable Service, Inc. **28825***
Satellite Choice (Fortuna, CA) *Ceased*
Satellite College Network (Torrance, CA) *Unable to locate*
Satellite Communications (Overland Park, KS) *Unable to locate*
Satellite Entertainment Guide (Edmonton, AB, Can.) **34727**
Satellite 1-416 (Toronto, ON, Can.) **36735**
Satellite Orbit (Fairfax, VA) *Unable to locate*
Satellite TV Opportunities Magazine (Oxford, MS) *Ceased*
Satellite TV Pre Vue (Salamanca, NY) *Ceased*
Satellite TV Week (Fortuna, CA) **1930**

Numbers cited in bold after listings are entry numbers rather than page numbers.

Satellite; Via (Potomac, MD) 13662
Satellite Week (Washington, DC) 5777
Satellite World (Hailey, ID) *Ceased*
Satire (Hancock, MD) *Ceased*
The Saturday Evening Post (Indianapolis, IN) 10169
The Saturday Paper 14690*
Saturday Review (Washington, DC) *Ceased*
Satya (Brooklyn, NY) 20344
The Satyr (West Hempstead, NY) 23541
Saudi Aramco World (Houston, TX) 30527
Saugeen City Life (Durham, ON, Can.) *Ceased*
Saugeen Telecable Ltd. (Hanover, ON, Can.) 35901
Saugerties Post Star (Saugerties, NY) 23308
Saugus Advertiser (Medford, MA) 14324
Sauk County Publishing 34281*
Sauk-Prairie Star (Sauk City, WI) 34313
Sauk Rapids Herald (Sauk Centre, MN) 16437
Sault Ste. Marie Evening News (Sault Sainte Marie, MI) 15527
Sault Ste. Marie This Week (Sault Sainte Marie, ON, Can.) 36369
The Sault Star (Sault Sainte Marie, ON, Can.) 36370
Savage (Agoura, CA) 1379
Savage Pacer (Savage, MN) 16441
Savage Sun Current; Burnsville/ (Burnsville, MN) 15781
Savannah Business Journal (Savannah, GA) *Unable to locate*
The Savannah Business Report & Journal 7531*
The Savannah Herald (Savannah, GA) 7534
Savannah Jewish News (Savannah, GA) 7535
Savannah Morning News (Savannah, GA) 7536
Savannah Pennysaver (Savannah, GA) 7537
Savannah Reporter and Andrew County Democrat (Savannah, MO) 17568
The Savannah Tribune (Savannah, GA) 7538
Savannah TV Cable 7540*
Save Our World (Cleveland, TN) 29122
Savers Guide 33450*
Saveur (New York, NY) *Unable to locate*
Savings Banker (Boston, MA) *Ceased*
Savings & Community Banker (Chicago, IL) *Unable to locate*
Savoy (New York, NY) 22707
Savvy Woman (New York, NY) *Ceased*
Sawmilling Journal; Logging & (North Vancouver, BC, Can.) 35035
Sawyer County Gazette (Winter, WI) 34461
Sawyer County Record (Hayward, WI) 33786
Sawyer County Record and Hayward Republican 33786*
Saxophone Journal (Medfield, MA) 14318
The Saybrook Gazette (Farmer City, IL) *Ceased*
Sayre Journal (Sayre, OK) *Unable to locate*
Sayville/Oakdale Suffolk Life (Sayville, NY) 23310
Sayville Weekender (Farmingdale, NY) *Ceased*
SBC Life (Nashville, TN) 29484
SBC Media Ventures L.P. 31754*
SBM Communications (Kalamazoo, MI) *Unable to locate*
Sbornik/Documents (New York, NY) *Ceased*
SBS Network Inc. (New York, NY) 37662
Sbusiness (Fort Myers, FL) 6097
SC Magazine (Framingham, MA) 14200
Scaffold Industry Association Magazine (Woodland Hills, CA) 4113
Scale Auto Magazine (Waukesha, WI) 34411
Scale Cabinetmaker *Ceased*
Scale Ship Modeler (Canoga Park, CA) 1659
Scale Woodcraft (Georgetown, CT) *Ceased*
Scandia Journal (Belleville, KS) 11358
Scandinavian Forum *Ceased*
Scandinavian Press (Vancouver, BC, Can.) 35167
Scandinavian Review (New York, NY) 22708
Scandinavian Studies (Provo, UT) 31408
Scanning (Mahwah, NJ) *Unable to locate*
Scanning Electron Microscopy 8560*
Scanning Microscopy (Chicago, IL) 8560
Scarboro Missions (Scarborough, ON, Can.) 36384
The Scarborough Mirror (Willowdale, ON, Can.) 36883
Scarborough News (Scarborough, ON, Can.) *Unable to locate*
The Scarlet (Worcester, MA) 14687
Scarlet Street (Glen Rock, NJ) 18848
The Scarsdale Inquirer (Scarsdale, NY) 23313
An Scathan (Ashland, PA) *Unable to locate*
Scatologica (Tucson, AZ) *Unable to locate*
SCD's Price Guide Weekly (Iola, WI) 33843
Scene (Cleveland, OH) 24952
The Scene (Appleton, WI) 33544
Scene; Chicago South Shore (Chicago, IL) 8324
Scene at the Movies (New York, NY) 22709
Scepter (Brooklyn, NY) 20345
Schaller Herald (Schaller, IA) 11189
Schau ins Land (Nashville, TN) 29485
Schaumburg Review (Schaumburg, IL) 9591
Schaumburg Voice (Lincolnwood, IL) *Unable to locate*
SCHC (Santa Fe Springs, CA) *Unable to locate*

The Schenectady Gazette 23314*
Schererville News (Merrillville, IN) *Unable to locate*
Schiller Park (Lincolnwood, IL) 9104
Schiller Times 9104*
Schizophrenia Bulletin (Bethesda, MD) *Unable to locate*
Schlein News Bureau (Washington, DC) 38056
Schleswig Leader (Mapleton, IA) 11053
Schmidt Services Inc. (Attica, NY) 38057
Schnauzer Shorts (La Honda, CA) 2109
Scholar; The American (Washington, DC) 5343
Scholarly Inquiry for Nursing Practice 22649*
Scholastic Action (Danbury, CT) 4751
Scholastic Ars- (Danbury, CT) 4752
Scholastic Coach & Athletic Director (Danbury, CT) 4753
Scholastic DynaMath (Danbury, CT) 4754
Scholastic Magazine (Notre Dame, IN) 10379
Scholastic MATH Magazine (Danbury, CT) 4755
Scholastic News Citizen Edition (Danbury, CT) 4756
Scholastic News Explorer Edition (Danbury, CT) 4757
Scholastic News Newstime Edition (Danbury, CT) 4758
Scholastic News Pilot Edition (Danbury, CT) 4759
Scholastic News Ranger Edition (Danbury, CT) 4760
Scholastic News Trails Edition (Danbury, CT) 4761
Scholastic Scope (Danbury, CT) 4762
Scholastic Voice (Danbury, CT) *Ceased*
The School Administrator (Arlington, VA) 31827
School Arts Magazine (Kutztown, PA) 27131
School Board Dialogue; The Iowa (Des Moines, IA) 10795
School Board Journal; Illinois (Springfield, IL) 9631
School Boards Association School Leader; New Jersey (Trenton, NJ) 19664
School Bus Fleet (Torrance, CA) 3942
School Business Affairs (Reston, VA) *Unable to locate*
School Business Magazine (Mississauga, ON, Can.) 36086
School and Clinic; Intervention in (Fairfax, VA) 32017
School and College (Cleveland, OH) *Unable to locate*
School and Community (Columbia, MO) 17008
School Counseling; Professional (Alexandria, VA) 31729
The School Counselor 31729*
The School Counselor (Alexandria, VA) *Ceased*
School Failure; Preventing (Washington, DC) 5729
School Food Service Journal 31735*
School Foodservice & Nutrition (Alexandria, VA) 31735
School Health; Journal of (Kent, OH) 25274
School Improvement; Pathways to (Naperville, IL) 9271
School Intervention Report (Holmes Beach, FL) 6202
School Journal; Middle (Westerville, OH) 25642
School Law Bulletin (Chapel Hill) (Chapel Hill, NC) 23721
School Library Journal (New York, NY) 22710
School Library Media Activities Monthly (Baltimore, MD) 13244
School Library Media Quarterly (Chicago, IL) 8561
School of Mines Quarterly; Colorado (Golden, CO) 4465
School Music News (Hendersonville, NC) *Unable to locate*
School News; Quebec Home & (Montreal, QC, Can.) 37211
School Planning and Management (Dayton, OH) 25125
School Psychology; Journal of Applied (Piscataway, NJ) 19428
School Psychology Quarterly (Lincoln, NE) 18118
School Psychology Review (Bethesda, MD) 13378
School Science and Mathematics (Columbus, OH) 25061
School Selection Guide (Bridgewater, NJ) 18699
School Shop 14770*
School Shop/Tech Directions 14770*
School Social Work Journal (Skokie, IL) 9610
School Transportation News (Redondo Beach, CA) 2911
School Trustee (Regina, SK, Can.) 37534
SchoolMates (New Windsor, NY) 21128
Schools; Children & (Washington, DC) 5409
Schools; Computers in the (Reno, NV) 18419
Schools; Language, Speech, and Hearing Services in (Rockville, MD) 13686
Schools in the Middle (Reston, VA) *Ceased*
Schools; MultiMedia (Medford, MA) 19231
Schools; Ohio (Columbus, OH) 25049
Schools; Psychology in the (Buffalo, NY) 20385
Schools; Rethinking (Milwaukee, WI) 34097
The Schulenburg Sticker (Schulenburg, TX) 31093
Schutzhund USA (St. Louis, MO) 17510
Schwadron Cartoon & Illustration Service (Ann Arbor, MI) 38058
Schwalm Historical Association; Journal of the Johannes (State Line, PA) 28033

Schweizer Journal 3447*
SCI Cable Corp. (Marion, OH) *Ceased*
The Sci-Fi Channel (New York, NY) 37782
SCI Nursing (Jackson Heights, NY) 20828
Sci Tech Book News (Portland, OR) 26507
Science (Washington, DC) 5778
Science Activities (Washington, DC) 5779
Science; American Journal of (New Haven, CT) 4982
Science; Archival (New York, NY) 21244
Science Books & Films (Washington, DC) 5780
Science; The British Journal for the History of (New York, NY) 21340
Science and Children (Arlington, VA) *Unable to locate*
Science and Christian Faith; Perspectives on (Ipswich, MA) 14257
Science Communication (College Park, MD) 13439
Science Communications (Newark, CA) 38059
Science in Context (New York, NY) 22711
Science; Current (Stamford, CT) 5146
Science; Cycling (East Windsor, NJ) 18785
Science (DRJES); The Dawson Research Journal of Experimental (Westmount, QC, Can.) 37442
Science Education (Hoboken, NJ) 19101
Science & Education (New York, NY) 22712
Science Education; International Journal of (Philadelphia, PA) 27508
Science Education and Technology; Journal of (New York, NY) 22182
Science; Engineering & (Pasadena, CA) 2815
Science & Engineering; Computing in (Los Alamitos, CA) 2182
Science & Engineering; Environmental (Aurora, ON, Can.) 35647
Science & Engineering Network News (Worcester, MA) 14688
Science Features Service (North Hills, CA) *Unable to locate*
Science Fiction Chronicle (Radford, VA) 32346
Science Fiction Eye (Asheville, NC) 23633
Science Fiction; The Magazine of Fantasy & (Hoboken, NJ) 19055
Science Fiction Review (Allegany, OR) *Unable to locate*
Science Fiction Studies (Greencastle, IN) 10035
Science of Food and Agriculture; Journal of the (Hoboken, NJ) 19047
Science; Gulf of Mexico (Dauphin Island, AL) 169
Science and Health, Part C: Environmental Carcinogenesis and Ectoxicology Reviews; Journal of Environmental (Springfield, MA) 32545
Science Illustrated (Mc Lean, VA) 32255
Science Index; General (Bronx, NY) 20270
Science; Journal of Cluster (Columbia, SC) 28551
Science; Journal of Colloid and Interface (San Diego, CA) 3181
Science; Journal for General Philosophy of (New York, NY) 22078
Science; Journal of Nonlinear (New York, NY) 22145
Science; Journal of Quaternary (Hoboken, NJ) 19043
Science Journal; Tennessee Academy of (Hixson, TN) 29222
Science and Mathematics; SUNY Geneseo Journal of (Geneseo, NY) 20650
Science of Mind (Los Angeles, CA) 2384
Science; Monkeyshines on Health and (Greensboro, NC) 23929
Science; Nature International Weekly Journal of (Washington, DC) 5689
Science; New Mexico Journal of (Albuquerque, NM) 19780
Science News (Washington, DC) 5781
Science; Northwest (Pullman, WA) 32905
Science; The Ohio Journal of (Kent, OH) 25277
Science; Pacific (Honolulu, HI) 7715
Science, Part B, Physics; Journal of Macromolecular (Urbana, IL) 9713
Science; Pharmacy World & (New York, NY) 22548
Science; Philosophy of (Kansas City, MO) 17191
Science; Popular (New York, NY) 22582
Science PROBE! (Farmingdale, NY) *Ceased*
Science; Protein (Lafayette, IN) 10254
Science; Quebec (Montreal, QC, Can.) 37213
Science Scope (Arlington, VA) 31828
Science Section B: Chemistry; Current Topics in Chinese (New York, NY) 21526
Science Service (Washington, DC) 38060
Science & Society (New York, NY) 22713
Science; Supramolecular (Burlington, MA) 14033
The Science Teacher (Arlington, VA) 31829
Science Teacher Education; Journal of (New York, NY) 22183
Science Teaching; Journal of College (Arlington, VA) 31801
Science Teaching; Journal of Research in (Hoboken, NJ) 19045
Science & Techniques de l'Eau 37233*
Science and Technology (New York, NY) *Unable to locate*

Second Messengers and Phosphoproteins (New York, NY) *Ceased*
Second Ring Syndicate (Evanston, IL) *Unable to locate*
Second Source, Healthcare Technology Management. **28429***
Second Source Imaging **28406***
The Second Stone (New Orleans, LA) *Ceased*
Second Wind (Milford, CT) *Ceased*
Secondary Gifted Education; Journal of (Evanston, IL) **8865**
Secondary Marketing Executive (Waterbury, CT) **5194**
Secondary Mortgage Markets (Mc Lean, VA) *Ceased*
Seconds (New York, NY) **22717**
The Secret Place (Valley Forge, PA) **28091**
The Secretary **32550***
Secrets (New York, NY) *Ceased*
Section 504 Compliance Handbook (Washington, DC) **5786**
Secure Retirement, The Newsmagazine for Mature Americans (Washington, DC) *Unable to locate*
The Secured Lender (New York, NY) **22718**
Securities & Commodities Regulation; The Review of (New York, NY) **22662**
Securities Industry News (New York, NY) **22719**
Securities Litigation & Regulation Reporter (Wayne, PA) **28135**
Securities Reform Act Litigation Reporter (Washington, DC) **5787**
Securities Regulation Law Journal (New York, NY) **22720**
SECURITY (Bensenville, IL) **8071**
Security Administration; Journal of (Miami, FL) **6366**
Security Advisor (San Diego, CA) *Ceased*
Security Affairs; The Journal of International (Washington, DC) **5600**
Security; Auto Sound & (Anaheim, CA) **1400**
SECURITY; CANADIAN (Aurora, ON, Can.) **35643**
Security Dealer (Melville, NY) *Unable to locate*
Security Distributing & Marketing (SDM) (Troy, MI) **15639**
Security; Focus on (Moscow, ID) **7914**
Security; International (Cambridge, MA) **14072**
Security Management (Alexandria, VA) **31736**
Security News **23294***
Security News; Police & (Quakertown, PA) **27915**
Security Professional (Salamanca, NY) **23294**
Security Sales (Torrance, CA) **3943**
Security Systems Integration; Access Control & (Atlanta, GA) **6959**
Security Technology & Design (Notre Dame, IN) *Unable to locate*
Security Transactions and Holdings; Official Summary of (Pittsburgh, PA) **27823**
Security World **8071***
The Sedalia Democrat (Sedalia, MO) **17570**
Sedan (Sedan, KS) **11796**
Sedan Times-Star (Sedan, KS) **11797**
Sedona Cablevision (Sedona, AZ) **880**
Sedona Excentric (Sedona, AZ) **877**
Sedona Red Rock News (Sedona, AZ) **878**
See *Ceased*
SEE Beaches **6667***
SEE Emerald Coast (Sarasota, FL) **6665**
SEE Florida Keys (Sarasota, FL) **6666**
SEE Sarasota, Bradenton, Venice & Gulf Coast Islands Magazine (Sarasota, FL) **6667**
Seebreeze Cable **35579***
Seed & Crops Digest (Cedar Falls, IA) **10662**
Seed & Crops Industry **10662***
Seed Industry Journal **10662***
The Seed Pod (St. Petersburg, FL) **6634**
Seed Trade News (Edina, MN) *Unable to locate*
Seed World (Des Plaines, IL) **8771**
Seeds (Dayton, OH) **25126**
Seeds; Journal of New (Binghamton, NY) **20190**
Seeds of Unfolding (New York, NY) **22721**
Seedsman's Digest **10662***
Seedstock Edge (West Lafayette, IN) **10552**
Seek (Cincinnati, OH) **24816**
The Seeley Swan Pathfinder (Seeley Lake, MT) **17905**
The Sega Channel (New York, NY) *Unable to locate*
The Seguin Gazette-Enterprise (Seguin, TX) **31096**
Seguridad Latina (Overland Park, KS) **11730**
Seismological Research Letters (El Cerrito, CA) **1862**
Seismology; Computational (Washington, DC) **5430**
Seismology; Journal of (New York, NY) **22185**
Seizure (Philadelphia, PA) **27657**
Sel & Poivre *Ceased*
Selah Optimist (Selah, WA) *Unable to locate*
Selby Record (Selby, SD) **28960**
Selden/Farmingville Suffolk Life (Selden, NY) **23323**
Selden Weekender (Farmingdale, NY) *Ceased*
Selechon ARCHIE **37357***
Select Homes & Food (Toronto, ON, Can.) *Unable to locate*
Selection du Reader's Digest (Canadian-French Edition) (Montreal, QC, Can.) **37223**

Selective Cancer Therapeutics (Larchmont, NY) *Ceased*
Self-Employed America (Hurst, TX) **30602**
SELF Magazine (New York, NY) **22722**
Self-Realization (Los Angeles, CA) **2386**
Self Reliance Journal (Orange, CA) *Ceased*
Self Storage Journal (Northbrook, IL) *Ceased*
Selinsgrove Times **27249***
Selinsgrove Times-Tribune (Selinsgrove, PA) *Unable to locate*
Selkirk Communications Inc. **6089***
Selkirk Communications Ltd. (Toronto, ON, Can.) *Unable to locate*
Selkirk Enterprise **35297***
The Selkirk Journal (Stonewall, MB, Can.) **35297**
Selkirk Springfield Enterprise (Stonewall, MB, Can.) *Ceased*
Selling (Palm Beach Gardens, FL) **6545**
Selling AS/400 Solutions (Calabasas, CA) *Unable to locate*
Selling Christmas Decorations (Goshen, NJ) **18850**
Selling Direct (New York, NY) *Ceased*
Selling Magazine **6545***
Selling & Merchandising *Ceased*
Selling Power (Fredericksburg, VA) **32087**
Selling and Sales Management; The Journal of Personal (Denton, TX) **30240**
The Selma Enterprise (Selma, CA) **3755**
The Selma Times-Journal (Selma, AL) **452**
Semana (Houston, TX) **30528**
Semana; La (Orlando, FL) **6500**
Semanario Azteca **3620***
The Semaphore **7283***
Semaphore Signal (Aptos, CA) *Ceased*
Semeia (Saskatoon, SK, Can.) **37556**
Semi-Dwarf Review (Eureka, CA) *Ceased*
Semiconductor Equipment & Materials Edition; The Complete European Trade Digest (Atlanta, GA) **6992**
Semiconductor International (Oak Brook, IL) **9365**
Semiconductor Magazine (Northbrook, IL) **9322**
Semiconductors (College Park, MD) **13440**
Semigroup Forum (New York, NY) **22723**
Seminar (Edmonton, AB, Can.) **34729**
Seminars in Anesthesia, Perioperative Medicine and Pain (Philadelphia, PA) **27658**
Seminars in Arthritis and Rheumatism (Miami, FL) **6379**
Seminars in Arthroplasty (Philadelphia, PA) **27659**
Seminars in Avian and Exotic Pet Medicine (Philadelphia, PA) **27660**
Seminars in Breast Disease (Philadelphia, PA) **27661**
Seminars in Cardiothoracic and Vascular Anesthesia (Philadelphia, PA) **27662**
Seminars in Cell & Developmental Biology (San Diego, CA) **3273**
Seminars in Clinical Neuropsychiatry (Seattle, WA) **33029**
Seminars in Colon and Rectal Surgery (Burlington, MA) **14032**
Seminars in Cutaneous Medicine and Surgery (Philadelphia, PA) **27664**
Seminars in Cutaneous Medicine and Surgery (Philadelphia, PA) **27663**
Seminars in Dermatology **27664***
Seminars in Diagnostic Pathology (Philadelphia, PA) **27665**
Seminars in Dialysis (Philadelphia, PA) *Ceased*
Seminars in Gastrointestinal Disease (Philadelphia, PA) **27666**
Seminars in Headache Management (Hamilton, ON, Can.) **35889**
Seminars in Hearing (Denver, CO) **4356**
Seminars in Hematology (Washington, DC) **5788**
Seminars in Laparoscopic Surgery (Augusta, GA) **7102**
Seminars in Neonatology (Philadelphia, PA) **27667**
Seminars in Nephrology (Lubbock, TX) **30717**
Seminars in Neurology (New York, NY) **22724**
Seminars in Nuclear Medicine (Bronx, NY) **20286**
Seminars for Nurse Managers (Philadelphia, PA) *Ceased*
Seminars in Oncology (Columbia, MO) **17009**
Seminars in Oncology Nursing (Philadelphia, PA) **27668**
Seminars in Ophthalmology (Pittsburgh, PA) **27841**
Seminars in Orthopaedics (Philadelphia, PA) *Ceased*
Seminars in Pediatric Infectious Diseases (Houston, TX) **30529**
Seminars in Pediatric Neurology (Philadelphia, PA) **27669**
Seminars in Pediatric Surgery (Indianapolis, IN) **10170**
Seminars in Perinatology (Philadelphia, PA) **27670**
Seminars in Perioperative Nursing (Philadelphia, PA) **27671**
Seminars in Radiation Oncology (Chapel Hill, NC) **23722**

Seminars in Radiologic Technology (Philadelphia, PA) **27672**
Seminars in Reproductive Endocrinology (Portland, OR) **26509**
Seminars in Respiratory and Critical Care Medicine (New York, NY) **22725**
Seminars in Respiratory Infections (Indianapolis, IN) **10171**
Seminars in Respiratory Medicine **22725***
Seminars in Roentgenology (Philadelphia, PA) **27673**
Seminars in Speech and Language (New York, NY) **22726**
Seminars in Spine Surgery (Philadelphia, PA) **27674**
Seminars in Surgical Oncology (Hoboken, NJ) **19103**
Seminars in Thoracic and Cardiovascular Surgery (Naples, FL) **6449**
Seminars in Thoracic & Cardiovascular Surgery (Boston, MA) **13959**
Seminars in Thrombosis and Hemostasis (New York, NY) **22727**
Seminars in Ultrasound, CT and MRI (Philadelphia, PA) **27675**
Seminars in Urologic Oncology (Philadelphia, PA) **27676**
Seminars in Urology (Philadelphia, PA) *Ceased*
Seminars in Vascular Surgery (Silverthorne, CO) **4625**
Seminars in Veterinary Medicine & Surgery **27412***
Seminary and Graduate School Handbook (Evanston, IL) *Ceased*
Seminary Quarterly Review; Union (Richmond, VA) **32459**
Seminole Outlook (Biddeford, ME) *Unable to locate*
The Seminole Producer (Seminole, OK) **26058**
The Seminole Sentinel (Seminole, TX) **31098**
Seminole Tribune (Hollywood, FL) *Unable to locate*
Semiotext (Brooklyn, NY) **20347**
Semiotics; American Journal of (Carbondale, IL) **8114**
Semiotics of Law; International Journal for the (New York, NY) **21917**
SEMO News (Lilbourn, MO) *Ceased*
The Senator (Elkins, WV) **33305**
Seneca County Farm (Waterloo, NY) *Unable to locate*
Seneca Falls Pennysaver (Syracuse, NY) **23421**
Seneca News-Dispatch (Seneca, MO) **17576**
Seneca Review (Geneva, NY) **20655**
SENGA (New Orleans, LA) **12753**
The Senior Advocate News Service (Washington, DC) *Unable to locate*
Senior American Magazine (Dundee, IL) *Unable to locate*
Senior American News (Weston, MA) *Ceased*
Senior Beacon; Southwest Kansas (Syracuse, KS) **11811**
Senior Citizen News (Orlando, FL) *Unable to locate*
Senior Citizens Advocate (New York, NY) *Ceased*
Senior Citizens Today (Sacramento, CA) *Ceased*
The Senior Consumer **6703***
Senior Dynamics (Chehalis, WA) *Unable to locate*
The Senior Edition (Tuscaloosa, AL) *Ceased*
Senior Life (Allen County Edition) (Milford, IN) **10310**
Senior Life (El-Ko Edition) (Milford, IN) **10311**
Senior Life (Inland Empire Edition); Southern California (Los Angeles, CA) **2398**
Senior Life (Los Angeles County Edition); Southern California (Los Angeles, CA) **2399**
Senior Life Magazine (Colton, CA) *Ceased*
Senior Life; Northwest (Portland, OR) **26489**
Senior Life (Northwest Edition) (Milford, IN) **10312**
Senior Life (Orange County Edition); Southern California (Los Angeles, CA) **2400**
Senior Life; Southern California (El Cajon, CA) **1848**
Senior Life (Southern California Edition); Southern California (Los Angeles, CA) **2401**
Senior Life (Southland Edition); Southern California (Los Angeles, CA) **2402**
Senior Life Styles Vista; The New (Jefferson, OH) **25264**
Senior Living; East Tennessee (Springfield, MO) **17596**
Senior Living; 4-States (Springfield, MO) **17601**
Senior Living; Lake of the Ozarks (Springfield, MO) **17603**
Senior Living; Ozarks (Springfield, MO) **17608**
Senior Magazine **3568***
Senior Messenger (Vancouver, WA) **33179**
Senior News (Orlando, FL) *Ceased*
Senior News; Cowlitz-Wahkiakum (Longview, WA) **32811**
Senior News Monthly (Salem, OR) *Ceased*
Senior News; The Thurston-Mason (Olympia, WA) **32860**
Senior Patient *Ceased*
Senior Scene (Tacoma, WA) **33150**
Senior Scoop (Toms River, NJ) **19644**
Senior Spectrum Monthly, Alameda (Sacramento, CA) *Ceased*

Senior Spectrum Monthly, Bakersfield (Sacramento, CA) *Ceased*
Senior Spectrum Monthly, Marin (Sacramento, CA) *Ceased*
Senior Spectrum Monthly, North Santa Clara (Sacramento, CA) *Ceased*
Senior Spectrum Monthly, Salinas/Monterey (Sacramento, CA) *Ceased*
Senior Spectrum Monthly, San Mateo (Sacramento, CA) *Ceased*
Senior Spotlite (Arvada, CO) *Unable to locate*
Senior Times **18380***
Senior Times **14724***
Senior Times (San Jose, CA) *Unable to locate*
The Senior Times (Worcester, MA) *Unable to locate*
Senior Times (Allegan, MI) **14723**
Senior Times (Spokane, WA) **33099**
Senior Times Magazine (Winter Haven, FL) *Unable to locate*
Senior Times (Peninsula Edition) (Virginia Beach, VA) *Ceased*
Senior Times (Richmond Edition) (Virginia Beach, VA) *Ceased*
Senior Times; West Michigan (Allegan, MI) **14724**
Senior Travel Tips **8796***
The Senior Tribune (Alpharetta, GA) *Unable to locate*
Senior Voice (Anchorage, AK) **531**
Senior Wire News Service (Denver, CO) **38064**
Senior World; Arizona (Tucson, AZ) **934**
Senior World of the Central Coast *Ceased*
Senior World Newsmagazine (El Cajon, CA) *Ceased*
Senior World Newsmagazine Orange County Edition (Laguna Hills, CA) *Unable to locate*
Senior World of Santa Barbara/Ventura (Laguna Hills, CA) *Ceased*
Seniority; Boston (Boston, MA) **13863**
SeniorPlus Newspaper (Barrie, ON, Can.) *Unable to locate*
Seniors; American Guidance for (Falls Church, VA) **32040**
Seniors' Housing News (Washington, DC) **5789**
Seniors Lambton-Kent; Mainly for (Petrolia, ON, Can.) **36326**
Seniors Today (Winnipeg, MB, Can.) *Unable to locate*
Sensations Magazine (Ocean Grove, NJ) **19391**
Sensible Sound (Snyder, NY) **23342**
Sensing Technologies and Applications; Subsurface (New York, NY) **22804**
Sensory Systems (New York, NY) **22728**
Sentier Chasse-Peche (Montreal, QC, Can.) **37224**
Sentinal Blaze (1920s) **16274***
Sentinel (Auburn, CA) **1439**
The Sentinel (Chula Vista, CA) *Unable to locate*
Sentinel (Cortez, CO) **4290**
The Sentinel (Chicago, IL) *Unable to locate*
Sentinel (Onawa, IA) **11127**
Sentinel (Bonner Springs, KS) **11365**
The Sentinel (Radcliff, KY) **12379**
The Sentinel (Plymouth, MA) **14481**
Sentinel (Dawson, MN) **15825**
Sentinel (Fairmont, MN) **15890**
Sentinel (Edina, MO) **17041**
Sentinel (Freehold, NJ) **18840**
Sentinel (Granville, NY) **20682**
The Sentinel (New Windsor, NY) *Unable to locate*
The Sentinel (Jefferson, OH) **25265**
Sentinel (Woodsfield, OH) *Unable to locate*
Sentinel (Carlisle, PA) **26761**
The Sentinel (Lewistown, PA) *Unable to locate*
The Sentinel (Willowdale, ON, Can.) **36884**
The Sentinel-Advertiser (Dinuba, CA) **1829**
The Sentinel Courier (Pilot Mound, MB, Can.) **35280**
The Sentinel-Echo (London, KY) **12203**
Sentinel & Enterprise (Fitchburg, MA) **14184**
Sentinel Leader (Sentinel, OK) **26059**
Sentinel Ledger **19388***
Sentinel-Mist; Chronicle/ (St. Helens, OR) **26563**
Sentinel-News (Shelbyville, KY) **12399**
Sentinel Plus (Hanford, CA) **2038**
The Sentinel-Record (Hot Springs, AR) **1184**
Sentinel; The Rockhurst (Kansas City, MO) **17195**
Sentinel-Standard (Ionia, MI) **15206**
Sentinel-Tribune (Bowling Green, OH) **24701**
Sentinelle; La (Chibougamau, QC, Can.) **36964**
Sentry; Quantico (Woodbridge, VA) **32638**
Sentry; Stow (Stow, OH) **25547**
Separation Science and Technology (Troy, NY) **23458**
Sephardic Scholar (New York, NY) **22729**
Sepsis (New York, NY) **22730**
Sequatchie Valley Purchase (South Pittsburg, TN) **29609**
The Sequatchie Valley Shopper (Pikeville, TN) **29568**
Sequels (Toronto, ON, Can.) *Unable to locate*
Sequential Analysis (New York, NY) **22731**
The Sequim Gazette (Sequim, WA) **33077**
Sequim's Jimmy-Come-Lately Gazette **33077***
Sequoyah Communications, Inc. **29298***
Sequoyah County Times (Sallisaw, OK) **26053**
SER America (Irving, TX) *Unable to locate*

Ser Padres (New York, NY) **22732**
SERB Official Reporter (Cleveland, OH) **24953**
Serb World U.S.A. (Tucson, AZ) **963**
Serbian; Canadian (Hamilton, ON, Can.) **35878**
Serenity (Baltimore, MD) **13245**
Sergeants (Temple Hills, MD) **13754**
Serial World **16025***
The Serials Librarian (Binghamton, NY) *Unable to locate*
Serials Review (Bowling Green, KY) **11948**
Serif (Chicago, IL) **8563**
The Serpentine Muse (New York, NY) **22733**
The Serran (Chicago, IL) *Unable to locate*
The Server Foodservice News (Pittsburgh, PA) *Ceased*
Server/Workstation Expert (Brookline, MA) **14025**
Server/Workstation Expert (Brookline, MA) **14024**
Service and Contracting (S & C) (Elgin, IL) **8826**
Service Electric Cable TV (Bethlehem, PA) **26707**
Service Electric Cable TV Inc. **27209***
Service Electric Cablevision (Birdsboro, PA) **26713**
Service Electric Company (Mahanoy City, PA) **27209**
Service News **13080***
Service Quarterly (Lansing, MI) *Unable to locate*
Service Reporter (Chicago, IL) *Unable to locate*
Service Research; Journal of (Nashville, TN) **29464**
Service Station and Garage Management (Toronto, ON, Can.) **36738**
Service Station Management (Des Plaines, IL) *Unable to locate*
Service and Support Management (Austin, TX) *Ceased*
ServiceInsights (Arlington, TX) **29735**
Services (Fairfax, VA) **32028**
Services Marketing; The Journal of (Santa Barbara, CA) **3648**
Services Marketing Quarterly (Berkeley, CA) **1558**
Services Marketing Today (Chicago, IL) *Ceased*
The Servicing Dealer (Freeport, IL) *Ceased*
Servicing Management (Waterbury, CT) **5195**
Servir (Richelain, QC, Can.) **37306**
Setauket Suffolk Life; Stony Brook/ (Stony Brook, NY) **23377**
The Setonian (South Orange, NJ) **19586**
Setonian (Greensburg, PA) **26954**
7 DAYS (New York, NY) *Ceased*
Seven Days (Burlington, VT) **31518**
Seven Hills Extra (Lynchburg, VA) *Ceased*
Seventeen (New York, NY) **22734**
Seventeenth Century News **30049***
Seventeenth-Century News (College Station, TX) **30049**
73 Amateur Radio Today (Peterborough, NH) **18628**
73 Amateur Radio's Technical Journal **18628***
Severworld (Austin, TX) **29804**
Sew Beautiful (Brownsboro, AL) **139**
Sew Business (Dallas, TX) *Ceased*
Sew News (Golden, CO) **4474**
Sew On; And (Martinsville, VA) **37816**
Sew it Seams (Kirkland, WA) *Unable to locate*
Sewanee (Sewanee, TN) **29593**
Sewanee News **29593***
The Sewanee Purple (Sewanee, TN) **29594**
The Sewanee Review (Sewanee, TN) **29595**
Seward County Independent (Seward, NE) **18276**
The Seward Phoenix LOG (Seward, AK) **637**
Sewickley Herald Star (Monroeville, PA) **27285**
Sewickley Magazine (Sewickley, PA) *Unable to locate*
Sewing Decor (New York, NY) *Ceased*
Sewing Savvy (Berne, IN) **9819**
Sex & Marital Therapy; Journal of (Cleveland, OH) **24916**
Sex Research; The Journal of (Madison, WI) **33955**
Sex Roles (New York, NY) *Unable to locate*
Sexology Journal; International Chinese (Jamaica, NY) **20835**
Sextant (Washington, DC) *Ceased*
Sexual Behavior; Archives of (New York, NY) **21247**
Sexual Medicine Guide (Lawrenceville, NJ) *Ceased*
Sexuality; Canadian Journal of Human (Toronto, ON, Can.) **36509**
Sexuality & Culture (Long Beach, CA) **2175**
Sexuality and Disability (New York, NY) *Unable to locate*
Sexuality and Gender Studies; International Journal of (New York, NY) **21918**
Sexuality; Journal of the History of (Austin, TX) **29787**
Sexuality; Studies in Gender and (New York, NY) **22801**
Sexually Transmitted Diseases (Philadelphia, PA) **27677**
Seymour Buyers' Guide **34315***
Seymour Buyers' Guide and Times Press (Seymour, WI) **34315**
Seymour Daily Tribune (Seymour, IN) **10448**
The Seymour Herald (Seymour, IA) **11191**
Seymour Times Press **34315***
SF (San Francisco, CA) *Ceased*

SF Broadcasting **33751***
SF Weekly (San Francisco, CA) **3439**
SFX Broadcasting **32480***
SFX Broadcasting, Inc. **24173***
SGA Journal **29732***
Shades Valley Sun (Ponte Vedra, FL) *Unable to locate*
The Shadow (New York, NY) **22735**
Shafer Court Connections (Richmond, VA) **32453**
Shafter Press (Shafter, CA) **3757**
Shafter Shopper (Shafter, CA) **3758**
Shake, Rattle and Roll (Memphis, TN) *Unable to locate*
Shaker Spirit (Point Pleasant, NJ) *Ceased*
Shakespeare Quarterly (Washington, DC) **5790**
Shakespeare Studies (Cranbury, NJ) **18770**
Shakopee Valley News (Shakopee, MN) **16445**
Shalom (Birmingham, AL) *Ceased*
Shalom (Hollywood, FL) *Ceased*
Shaman's Drum (Williams, OR) **26612**
The Shamrock Texan (Shamrock, TX) *Unable to locate*
Shape (Woodland Hills, CA) **4114**
Share (Toronto, ON, Can.) **36739**
Share Guide (Santa Rosa, CA) **3734**
Share International (North Hollywood, CA) **2644**
Share the Word (Washington, DC) **5791**
Shareholder Value (Peterborough, NH) **18629**
Shareowner; Canadian (Toronto, ON, Can.) **36530**
Sharing Ideas **2026***
Sharing Ideas News Magazine (Glendora, CA) **2026**
Sharon Advocate (Needham, MA) **14370**
The Sharon Reporter (Sharon, WI) **34316**
Sharon Sentinel (Sharon, MA) **14519**
Joe #Sharpnack (Iowa City, IA) **38065**
Sharpsburg **26666***
Shattered Wig Review (Baltimore, MD) **13246**
Shaunavon Standard (Shaunavon, SK, Can.) **37569**
Shaw Annual (Palm Springs, CA) **2767**
Shaw Cable **35598***
Shaw Cable **35665***
Shaw Cable (Calgary, AB, Can.) **34673**
Shaw Cable (Fort McMurray, AB, Can.) **34770**
Shaw Cable (Red Deer, AB, Can.) **34837**
Shaw Cable (Cranbrook, BC, Can.) *Unable to locate*
Shaw Cable (Prince George, BC, Can.) *Unable to locate*
Shaw Cable (Listowel, ON, Can.) **35976**
Shaw Cable (Orangeville, ON, Can.) *Unable to locate*
Shaw Cable TV (Terrace Bay, ON, Can.) **36431**
Shaw Cable TV (Sault) Ltd. (Sault Sainte Marie, ON, Can.) **36373**
Shaw Cablesystems (Saskatoon, SK, Can.) **37568**
Shaw Cablesystems (B.C.) Ltd. (North Vancouver, BC, Can.) *Ceased*
Shaw Cablesystems C.P. (Surrey, BC, Can.) **35110**
Shaw Cablesystems Inc. (Kelowna, BC, Can.) **34995**
Shaw Cablesystems Ltd. (Edmonton, AB, Can.) **34757**
Shaw Cablevision, Ltd. (Nanaimo, BC, Can.) **35023**
Shaw Communications Inc. **36901***
Shaw Community 4 (Duncan, BC, Can.) **34952**
Shaw Historical Library Journal (Klamath Falls, OR) **26386**
Shawano Evening Leader **34317***
Shawano Leader (Shawano, WI) **34317**
The Shawano Shopper (Shawano, WI) **34318**
Shawnee Cridersville Press (Wapakoneta, OH) *Unable to locate*
Shawnee Journal Herald (Shawnee, KS) **11801**
Shawnee-Merriam Sun (Shawnee, KS) **11802**
The Shawnee News-Star (Shawnee, OK) **26065**
Shawnee Sun **11802***
Sheaf (Warren, MN) **16496**
The Sheaf (Saskatoon, SK, Can.) **37557**
Sheboygan Falls News (Plymouth, WI) **34250**
The Sheboygan Press (Sheboygan, WI) **34321**
Sheep Breeder and Sheepman (Columbia, MO) *Ceased*
Sheep Canada (Edmonton, AB, Can.) **34730**
Sheep! Magazine (Withee, WI) **34469**
Sheet Music Magazine (Bedford Hills, NY) **20144**
Sheffield Standard and Times (Sheffield, AL) *Unable to locate*
Shekel (North Miami, FL) **6466**
Shelbina Democrat (Shelbina, MO) **17578**
Shelburne Falls and West County News (Shelburne Falls, MA) **14521**
Shelby County Herald (Shelbyville, MO) **17579**
Shelby County News-Gazette (Windsor, IL) **9767**
Shelby County Reporter (Columbiana, AL) **159**
Shelby County Review (Wapakoneta, OH) *Unable to locate*
Shelby Daily Globe (Shelby, OH) **25514**
Shelby Daily Star **24227***
The Shelby Promoter (Shelby, MT) **17906**
Shelby Report of the Southeast (Gainesville, GA) **7295**

Shelby Report of the Southwest (Gainesville, GA) **7296**
The Shelby Star (Shelby, NC) **24227**
Shelby Sun (Shelby, NE) *Unable to locate*
Shelby Sun Times (Germantown, TN) **29206**
Shelby Utica News (Warren, MI) *Unable to locate*
The Shelbyville News (Shelbyville, IN) **10452**
Shelbyville Times-Gazette (Shelbyville, TN) **29600**
Sheldon Mail-Sun (Sheldon, IA) **11195**
Shellbrook Chronicle (Shellbrook, SK, Can.) **37571**
Shelley Journal; Keats- (Chicago, IL) **8452**
The Shelley Pioneer (Shelley, ID) **7980**
Shellfish Research; Journal of (Southampton, NY) **23344**
Shellsburg Cablevision Corp. (Shellsburg, IA) **11198**
Shelter (Cordova, MD) **29152**
Shelter (Garrisonville, VA) **32105**
Shelter Island Reporter (Southampton, NY) **23345**
Shelter Sense **5350***
Shelterforce (Montclair, NJ) **19241**
Sheltie Pacesetter (Jackson, TN) **29231**
The Shelton Clipper (Shelton, NE) **18277**
Shelton-Mason County Journal (Shelton, WA) **33079**
Shemp! (Kahului, HI) **7759**
Shemp!: The Low-life Culture Magazine **7759***
Shenandoah (Lexington, VA) **32191**
The Shenandoah Valley-Herald (Woodstock, VA) **32640**
The Shepherd (Cardington, OH) **24740**
Shepherd Argus (Shepherd, MI) **15538**
The Shepherd College Picket (Shepherdstown, WV) **33464**
Shepherd Express (Milwaukee, WI) **34101**
Sherborn Suburban Press; Dover- (Sherborn, MA) **14523**
Sherburne News (Sherburne, NY) **23329**
Sheridan Broadcasting Network **37615***
Sheridan Headlight (Sheridan, AR) **1343**
Sheridan News (Noblesville, IN) *Ceased*
The Sheridan Press (Sheridan, WY) **34588**
Sheriff (Alexandria, VA) **31737**
Sheriff and Police Reporter (Seattle, WA) *Unable to locate*
Sherman Cablevision (Houlton, ME) **12971**
Sherman County Herald *Ceased*
Sherman County Journal (Moro, OR) *Unable to locate*
Sherman County Star (Goodland, KS) *Ceased*
Sherman County Times (Loup City, NE) **18150**
Sherman Democrat **31103***
Sherwood Park News (Sherwood Park, AB, Can.) **34847**
Sherwood Voice (Cabot, AR) *Unable to locate*
Shetland Productions (Madison, WI) **38066**
SHHH Journal **13343***
The Shidler Review **26071***
The Shield (Hornel Heights, ON, Can.) **35915**
Shield & Diamond (Memphis, TN) **29380**
Shift (New York, NY) **22736**
Shift (Toronto, ON, Can.) *Unable to locate*
Shih Tzu News *Ceased*
The Shilling (Virginia Beach, VA) **32589**
Shilo Cablevision (Shilo, MB, Can.) **35291**
Shilo Stag (Brandon, MB, Can.) *Ceased*
The Shiner Gazette (Shiner, TX) **31105**
Shing Wah Daily News **36740***
Shing Wah News (Toronto, ON, Can.) **36740**
The Shinnston News/The Harrison County Journal (Shinnston, WV) **33466**
Ship & Catering ONBOARD SERVICES Magazine; Airline, (Miami Springs, FL) **6421**
Ship of Christ the King (Chicago, IL) *Ceased*
Ship Modeler; Scale (Canoga Park, CA) **1659**
Ship to Shore (Studio City, CA) **3823**
Shipherd's Record (Olivet, MI) **15418**
Shipmate (Annapolis, MD) **13097**
Shipper; American (Jacksonville, FL) **6209**
Shipper; Pacific (Long Beach, CA) **2172**
Shipping Digest (New York, NY) *Unable to locate*
Shipping; Harbour & (West Vancouver, BC, Can.) **35238**
Shipping News; Drop (New York, NY) **21570**
Shipping; WWS/World Wide (Odessa, FL) **6480**
The Ship's Log (Trenton, MO) *Ceased*
Ships in Scale **31478***
Ships in Scale; Seaways' (Taylorsville, UT) **31478**
Shipyard News (Dover, NH) *Ceased*
Shirley Suffolk Life; Mastic/ (Mastic, NY) **21030**
Shirts Illustrated (Dallas, TX) *Unable to locate*
Sh'ma (Newton, MA) **14409**
Shmate (Berkeley, CA) *Ceased*
Sho- Hills; The Item of Millburn- and (West Paterson, NJ) **19730**
Shoal Lake Star **35292***
Shoal Lake Star (Shoal Lake, MB, Can.) *Ceased*
The Shoals News (Shoals, IN) **9226**
Shoals News Leader (Florence, AL) *Unable to locate*
Shoe Service (Baltimore, MD) *Unable to locate*
Shoemaking; American (Arlington, MA) **13816**

Shofar (Washington, DC) **5792**
SHOOT (Lakewood, NJ) **19158**
Shooting Industry (San Diego, CA) **3274**
Shooting; Precision (Manchester, CT) **4938**
Shooting Review; Skeet (San Antonio, TX) **31048**
Shooting Sports Retailer (Cuba, NY) *Unable to locate*
SHOOTING SPORTS USA (Washington, DC) *Unable to locate*
Shooting Star Review (Pittsburgh, PA) *Unable to locate*
Shooting Times (Peoria, IL) **9423**
SHOP (Mississauga, ON, Can.) *Ceased*
Shop Owner (Cleveland, OH) *Ceased*
Shop-Right 1 (Ridgway, PA) **27936**
Shop-Right 1 & 2 (Ridgway, PA) **27937**
Shop-Right 2 **27937***
$hop and $ave *Ceased*
Shop Talk! (Oriental, NC) **24110**
Shop Television Network (Burbank, CA) **37783**
ShopNotes (Des Moines, IA) **10808**
The Shopper **8915***
The Shopper **30414***
The Shopper (Salinas, CA) *Unable to locate*
The Shopper (Hollywood, FL) *Unable to locate*
Shopper (Winter Haven, FL) **6871**
Shopper (Lockport, IL) *Unable to locate*
The Shopper (Naperville, IL) *Ceased*
The Shopper (Waterloo, IL) **9737**
The $hopper (Wabash, IN) **10530**
The Shopper (Horseheads, NY) **20760**
The Shopper (Wolcott, NY) *Unable to locate*
The Shopper (Seattle, WA) **33030**
Shopper (Beldenville, WI) **33571**
The Shopper (Black Earth, WI) *Unable to locate*
The Shopper (Red Deer, AB, Can.) *Ceased*
The Shopper (Saskatoon, SK, Can.) *Ceased*
Shopper; Bakersfield's (Bakersfield, CA) **1449**
Shopper; Canyon (Flagstaff, AZ) **695**
The Shopper Diversified (Halstad, MN) **15938**
The Shopper Express and Pinckney Post **15443***
Shopper Guide **34227***
Shopper News **1051***
The Shopper News (Wickenburg, AZ) *Unable to locate*
The Shopper News (Peru, IN) *Unable to locate*
The Shopper News (Fair Lawn, NJ) **18809**
Shopper-News Network (Des Moines, IA) **10809**
Shopper News Note (Lindsay, OK) **25900**
The Shopper Observer News **6615***
Shopper; Owatonna Area (Owatonna, MN) **16253**
Shopper Stopper (Portage, WI) **34260**
Shopper Xtra (Killdeer, ND) *Ceased*
The Shopper (Zone I) (Durant, OK) **25808**
The Shopper (Zone II) (Durant, OK) **25809**
Shoppers Advantage (Caro, MI) **14856**
Shopper's Edge (Enid, OK) **25823**
Shoppers Fair (Cheboygan, MI) **14873**
Shoppers Gazette *Ceased*
The Shopper's Guide **14866***
The Shopper's Guide (Atwater, CA) *Ceased*
Shopper's Guide (Caro, MI) **14857**
Shoppers Guide (Hartford, MI) *Unable to locate*
Shoppers Guide (Otsego, MI) **15426**
A Shopper's Guide (Newton, NJ) **19377**
The Shopper's Guide (Pennsauken, NJ) *Unable to locate*
Shoppers Guide (Hendersonville, NC) *Unable to locate*
The Shoppers Guide (Everett, PA) **26914**
The Shopper's Guide (Waverly, TN) **29643**
Shoppers Guide-East (Three Rivers, MI) *Ceased*
Shopper's Guide; Results Media (Hicksville, NY) **20744**
The Shoppers Guide of Three Rivers **15593***
Shopper's Guide (UT) (Tooele, UT) **31479**
Shoppers Guide Weekly (Warren, AR) **1364**
Shopper's Guide, Yankee Trader, Huntington Pennysaver, Pennysaver **20744***
The Shopper's Helper (Greenwich, OH) **25230**
Shopper's Market (Belleville, ON, Can.) **35679**
Shoppers News **36369***
Shoppers News **1371***
Shoppers News (Rensselaer, IN) **10415**
Shopper's Newsletter **34231***
The Shopper's Outlook (Pendleton, KY) **12356**
Shoppers Review (Marshall, MN) **16043**
Shoppers' Special **6447***
The Shopper's Weekly (Shelton, WA) **33080**
The Shopping Bag **20554***
Shopping Bag & Advertiser (East Rochester, NY) **20554**
Shopping Center world **7042***
Shopping Center World (Atlanta, GA) **7042**
Shopping Centers Today (New York, NY) *Unable to locate*
The Shopping Channel (Mississauga, ON, Can.) **37712**
The Shopping Guide (Griffin, GA) *Unable to locate*
Shopping Guide; Lyons (Newark, NY) **22995**

Shopping Guide News (Rochester, IN) **10432**
Shopping News **34241***
The Shopping News (Tempe, AZ) *Unable to locate*
Shopping News (Derby, CT) **4776**
The Shopping News (Wichita, KS) *Unable to locate*
The Shopping News (St. Cloud, MN) **16347**
Shopping News (Canandaigua, NY) **20424**
The Shopping News (Oberlin, OH) **25449**
Shopping News; Boone County (Boone, IA) **10624**
Shopping News; Freeport (Freeport, IL) **8899**
Shopping News; The Heartland (Fergus Falls, MN) **15898**
Shopping News of Lancaster County (Ephrata, PA) **26889**
Shopping News; Monroe Area (Monroe, WI) **34150**
Shopping News Northerner (Wittenberg, WI) **34470**
Shopping News/Penny Pincher (Sonoma, CA) **3776**
Shopping News South (Bristol, RI) **28328**
Shopping Reminder (Columbus, WI) **33643**
ShopTalk Trade Publication (Chicago, IL) *Unable to locate*
Shore; AAA World— (Philadelphia, PA) **27358**
Shore Cable of New Jersey Inc. (Longport, NJ) *Unable to locate*
Shore & Country Shopper **15591***
Shore Keystone Motorist **27358***
Shore Line Times (New Haven, CT) **5002**
Shore Times (Baltimore, MD) **13247**
Shoreeast Magazine (Pleasantville, NJ) **19444**
Shoreline Beacon Times (Port Elgin, ON, Can.) **36333**
Shoreline Chronicle (Sheboygan, WI) **34322**
Shoreline Leader (Racine, WI) *Unable to locate*
The Shoreline News (London, ON, Can.) **35992**
Shores News (Roaming Shores, OH) **25500**
ShoreView (Ocean, NJ) *Unable to locate*
Shoreview-Arden Hills Bulletin (Shoreview, MN) **16447**
Shoreview Bulletin **16447***
Shoreview Press (White Bear Lake, MN) **16512**
Shorewood/Chanhassen Sun-Sailor; Excelsior/ (Excelsior, MN) **15887**
Shorewood Herald (New Berlin, WI) **34185**
Short Fiction by Women (New York, NY) *Unable to locate*
Short Fuse (Santa Barbara, CA) **3656**
The Short Line (Peoria, IL) **9424**
Short Stories in Spanish (Miami, FL) *Unable to locate*
The Shorthorn (Arlington, TX) **29736**
Shorthorn Country (Omaha, NE) **18208**
Shortwave Association (NASWA)—The Journal; North American (Levittown, PA) **27188**
Shoshone County News-Press (Kellogg, ID) *Unable to locate*
Shoshoni Pioneer (Shoshoni, WY) **34593**
Shotgun News (Peoria, IL) **9425**
Shotgun Sports (Auburn, CA) **1440**
Shots (Minneapolis, MN) **16126**
Shoulder and Elbow Surgery; Journal of (St. Louis, MO) **17462**
Shout (New York, NY) *Unable to locate*
Show Biz News **22738***
Show Biz News (New York, NY) *Ceased*
Show Biz News & Model News (New York, NY) **22738**
Show Biz News & Model News (New York, NY) **22737**
Show Business (New York, NY) *Ceased*
Show Cablesystems Ltd. **37568***
Show Continental (Miami Beach, FL) *Unable to locate*
Show Me Missouri Farm Bureau News (Jefferson City, MO) **17133**
Show Music (East Haddam, CT) *Ceased*
Show Reporter (Newton Center, MA) *Unable to locate*
Show Ring Magazine (Albany, TX) *Unable to locate*
Show & Sell (New Albany, IN) *Ceased*
Show Technology Magazine (Austin, TX) *Ceased*
ShowBiz Weekly (Henderson, NV) **18354**
Showboat **31044***
Showcase International **19476***
Showcase Magazine (Philadelphia, PA) *Ceased*
Showcase Real Estate Magazine (Wilbraham, MA) *Ceased*
Showcase USA (Torrance, CA) *Ceased*
Showtime (New York, NY) **37784**
Showtime Magazine (Reno, NV) *Unable to locate*
Shreveport; Cablevision of (Shreveport, LA) **12821**
Shreveport Journal (Shreveport, LA) *Ceased*
Shreveport Magazine (Shreveport, LA) *Ceased*
The Shreveport Sun (Shreveport, LA) **12819**
Shrewsbury Electric Light Plant **14525***
The Shrewsbury Voice (Auburn, MA) *Ceased*
Shrewsbury's Community Cablevision (Shrewsbury, MA) **14525**
Shun Po (South San Francisco, CA) *Unable to locate*
Shuswap Market News (Salmon Arm, BC, Can.) **35082**
The Shuswap Sun (Salmon Arm, BC, Can.) *Unable to locate*

Shutterbug (Titusville, FL) 6819
Shutterbug's Outdoor & Nature Photography
   (Titusville, FL) 6820
The Shuttle Sheet (Greensboro, NC) 23937
Shuttle Spindle & Dyepot (Duluth, GA) 7257
SI Business (Toronto, ON, Can.) Ceased
Si Magazine (Los Angeles, CA) 2387
SIAM Journal on Algebraic & Discrete Methods
   27683*
SIAM Journal on Applied Mathematics (Philadelphia,
   PA) 27678
SIAM Journal on Computing (Philadelphia, PA) 27679
SIAM Journal on Control and Optimization
   (Philadelphia, PA) 27680
SIAM Journal on Discrete Mathematics (Philadelphia,
   PA) 27681
SIAM Journal on Mathematical Analysis (Philadelphia,
   PA) 27682
SIAM Journal on Matrix Analysis and Applications
   (Philadelphia, PA) 27683
SIAM Journal on Numerical Analysis (Philadelphia,
   PA) 27684
SIAM Journal on Optimization (Philadelphia, PA)
   27685
SIAM Journal on Scientific Computing (Philadelphia,
   PA) 27686
SIAM Journal on Scientific and Statistical Computing
   27686*
SIAM News (Philadelphia, PA) 27687
SIAM Review (Philadelphia, PA) 27688
Siberian Husky News Ceased
Siberian Mathematical Journal (New York, NY) 22739
The Siberian Quarterly (Wheat Ridge, CO) 4683
Sickle & Sheaf (Kansas City, MO) 17196
SIDA (AIDS) (Elizabeth, NJ) Ceased
Sidelines (Murfreesboro, TN) 29432
Sidell Journal 9601*
Sidell Reporter (Sidell, IL) 9601
Sidesaddle (Fort Worth, TX) Unable to locate
Sidewalks (Champlin, MN) Ceased
Siding; Western Roofing/Insulation/ (Reno, NV) 18426
The Sidney Argus-Herald (Sidney, IA) 11203
The Sidney Daily News (Sidney, OH) 25521
Sidney Daily Sun 18278*
Sidney Herald 17910*
The Sidney Herald-Leader (Sidney, MT) 17910
Sidney Pennysaver (Norwich, NY) 23023
Sidney Sun Telegraph (Sidney, NE) 18278
Sidney Telegraph 18278*
The Sidney Telegraph (Sidney, NE) Ceased
Siebring Cable (George, IA) 10921
SIECUS Report (New York, NY) 22740
Sierra (San Francisco, CA) 3440
Sierra Booster (Loyalton, CA) 2484
The Sierra Breeze (Shingle Springs, CA) Ceased
Sierra County Sentinel (Truth or Consequences, NM)
   19969
Sierra Home Advertiser (Oakhurst, CA) 2659
Sierra Madre News (Sierra Madre, CA) Unable to
   locate
Sierra Sacramento Valley Medicine (Sacramento, CA)
   3019
Sierra Star (El Cajon, CA) Unable to locate
The Sierra Sun (Truckee, CA) 3950
Sierra View (Woodland Hills, CA) Ceased
Sierra Vista Herald (Sierra Vista, AZ) 889
Siftings Herald; Daily (Arkadelphia, AR) 1030
Sightlines (Niles, IL) Unable to locate
Sigma Alpha Iota Quarterly: Pan Pipes (Sarasota, FL)
   Unable to locate
Sigma Chi; The Magazine of (Evanston, IL) 8866
Sigma Phi Epsilon Journal (Richmond, VA) 32454
Sign Builder Illustrated (Greenville, NC) 23969
Sign Business (Broomfield, CO) 4208
Sign Language Studies (Burtonsville, MD) 13398
The Signal 16971*
The Signal (Merced, CA) 2528
The Signal (Santa Clarita, CA) 3679
The Signal (Turlock, CA) 3957
The Signal (Fort Gordon, GA) 7283
Signal (Manly, IA) 11048
Signal (Detroit, MI) 14946
Signal (Springport, MI) 15574
Signal (Taylorsville, MS) Unable to locate
The Signal (Lisbon, OH) Ceased
SIGNAL (Fairfax, VA) 32029
Signal Cable (West Bend, IA) Ceased
The Signal-Enterprise (Alma, KS) 11337
Signal 56 14946*
Signal; Garner Leader and (Garner, IA) 10919
Signal Item Star (Monroeville, PA) 27286
Signal; Northwest (Napoleon, OH) 25402
Signal; Post (Pilot Point, TX) 30935
Signal Processing; International Journal of Adaptive
   Control and (Hoboken, NJ) 18975
Signal Processing; Multidimensional Systems and
   (New York, NY) 22379
Signal-Review; South Hardin (Hubbard, IA) 10953

Signal; Smoky Lake (Smoky Lake, AB, Can.) 34851
Signal-Star; The Goderich (Goderich, ON, Can.)
   35851
Signalman's Journal (Mount Prospect, IL) 9250
Signals (Chicago, IL) Unable to locate
Signals (Rio Grande, OH) 25497
Signature (Leawood, KS) Unable to locate
Signatures (Anderson, IN) 9784
SignCraft (Fort Myers, FL) 6098
Signet Cable 24181*
Signpost (Dorchester, ON, Can.) 35782
Signpost for NW Trails 33041*
Signs (Chicago, IL) 8564
Signs & Screen em Portugues (Cincinnati, OH)
   Ceased
Signs of the Times (Nampa, ID) 7931
Signs of the Times (Cincinnati, OH) 24817
Signs of the Times & Screen Printing en Espanol
   (Cincinnati, OH) 24818
Sigourney News-Review (Sigourney, IA) 11204
Silent Advocate (Cincinnati, OH) 24819
Silent but Deadly (Tampa, FL) Unable to locate
Silent News (Rochester, NY) Unable to locate
Silent Sports (Waupaca, WI) 34419
The Silhouette (Hmilton, ON, Can.) 35914
Silicon Alley Reporter (New York, NY) 22741
Silicon Graphics World (Austin, TX) Ceased
Silicon Valley Engineer (Los Altos, CA) Ceased
Silicon Valley North (Ottawa, ON, Can.) Unable to
   locate
Silicon Valley/San Jose Business Journal (Charlotte,
   NC) 23753
Silk & Satin (Dorval, QC, Can.) 36988
The Silsbee Bee (Silsbee, TX) 31106
Silver Bird Travel Features (Sausalito, CA) Unable to
   locate
Silver Circle (Irwindale, CA) Ceased
Silver City Daily Press (Silver City, NM) 19953
Silver Lake Leader (Silver Lake, MN) 16448
Silver Magazine (Rancho Santa Fe, CA) 2882
Silver Screen (Toronto, ON, Can.) Unable to locate
The Silver Spring Express (Alexandria, VA) Unable to
   locate
Silver Spring Gazette (Frederick, MD) 13521
Silver State Post (Deer Lodge, MT) 17781
Silver Wings 2833*
Silver Wings (Columbus, MS) 16605
Silver Wings Mayflower Pulpit (Pearblossom, CA)
   2833
Silver World (Lake City, CO) 4529
Silverthorn & District News (Toronto, ON, Can.)
   Unable to locate
The Silverton Standard and The Miner (Silverton,
   CO) 4626
Simcoe and Nanticoke Times (Simcoe, ON, Can.)
   36390
The Simcoe Reformer (Simcoe, ON, Can.) 36391
Simcoe Times 36390*
Similkameen Spotlight; Princeton- (Princeton, BC,
   Can.) 35066
Simmental Country (Calgary, AB, Can.) 34657
Simmental Shield (Lindsborg, KS) Unable to locate
Simmons Cable (Lebanon, MO) Unable to locate
Simmons Cable TV 2177*
Simmons Cable TV of Lower Delaware 5265*
Simmons Cable TV of Lower Delaware 5241*
Simmons Cablevision 12675*
Simmons Communications Inc. 5233*
Simmons Review (Boston, MA) 13960
SIMNOW (Scarborough, ON, Can.) 36385
Simple Pleasures (Mount Airy, NC) 24080
Simple; Real (New York, NY) 22636
Simply Cross Stitch (Big Sandy, TX) Ceased
Simply Seafood (Seattle, WA) 33031
Simpson County News (Magee, MS) 16756
The Simpson Shopper (Magee, MS) 16757
The Simpsonian (Indianola, IA) 10966
The Simpsons Illustrated (New York, NY) Unable to
   locate
Simsbury News (Simsbury, CT) 5130
Simulation (San Diego, CA) 3275
Simulation & Gaming (Thousand Oaks, CA) 3916
Sinclair Communications 29863*
Sing Out! (Bethlehem, PA) 26705
Sing Pao (South San Francisco, CA) Unable to
   locate
Sing Tao Daily (South San Francisco, CA) 3791
Sing Tao Daily (Vancouver, BC, Can.) Unable to
   locate
Sing Tao Jih Pao 3791*
Singer Magazine; Classical (South Jordan, UT) 31472
Singer Media Corp. 38136*
The Singing News Magazine (Boone, NC) 23656
Single Again Magazine (Roseville, CA) 2972
Single Dad's Magazine (Littleton, CO) Unable to
   locate
Single Free Press (Seminole, OK) Unable to locate
The Single Parent (Chicago, IL) Ceased
The Single Scene (Gahanna, OH) Ceased

Single Shot Rifle Journal (Delphos, OH) Unable to
   locate
SingleLife Magazine (Milwaukee, WI) Unable to locate
Singles Almanac (Jersey City, NJ) Unable to locate
Singles Free Press Shopper (Seminole, OK) Unable
   to locate
Singles News & Views (New York, NY) Unable to
   locate
Sinister Wisdom (Berkeley, CA) 1559
Sino-Japanese Studies (Santa Barbara, CA) 3657
Sinorama/Kuang Hua Hua Pao (Los Angeles, CA)
   2388
The Sioux Center News (Sioux Center, IA) 11207
Sioux Center Shopper (Sioux Center, IA) 11208
Sioux City Journal (Sioux City, IA) 11213
Sioux County Capital-Democrat (Orange City, IA)
   11130
Sioux County Index-Reporter (Hull, IA) 10956
Sioux Falls Cable TV (Sioux Falls, SD) 28990
Sioux Falls Shopping News (Sioux Falls, SD) 28965
Sioux Falls Shopping News Informer (Sioux Falls,
   SD) 28966
Sioux Rapids Bulletin-Press (Sioux Rapids, IA) 11227
Sioux Valley News (Correctionville, IA) 10723
Siouxland Press (Hospers, IA) 10952
SIPA News Service (New York, NY) 38067
Siren Magazine (Houston, TX) Unable to locate
Sirius Systems, Inc. 18461*
The Siskiyou (Ashland, OR) 26217
Siskiyou Cablevision Inc. (Fort Jones, CA) 1927
Siskiyou Daily News (Yreka, CA) 4121
Sister City News (Washington, DC) 5793
Sister Miriam Teresa League of Prayer Bulletin
   (Convent Station, NJ) 18769
Sister 2 Sister (Takoma Park, MD) 13752
SISTERS (Washington, DC) Ceased
Site Development News (Morris Plains, NJ) Unable to
   locate
Site Selection Magazine (Norcross, GA) 7469
Sitka Sentinel; The Daily (Sitka, AK) 638
Situations Digest (Los Angeles, CA) 2389
The Siuslaw News (Florence, OR) 26353
600 KIIX 4440*
Six Nations New Credit Reporter (Ohsweken, ON,
   Can.) Ceased
16 Magazine (New York, NY) Unable to locate
'68' Micro Journal (Hixson, TN) Ceased
60504 Sun; The Fox Valley Villages/ (Naperville, IL)
   9263
62 Years-Bowling News 1615*
SJ First (Voorhees, NJ) 19703
SJL Broadcast Management Corp. (Billings, MT)
   37713
Sjoberg's Inc. (Thief River Falls, MN) 16474
Skagit Argus (Mount Vernon, WA) Unable to locate
Skagit Today 32846*
Skagit Valley Herald (Mount Vernon, WA) 32845
Skagit Weekly (Mount Vernon, WA) 32846
Skagway Cable TV (Haines, AK) 587
Skagway Network TV 585*
The Skagway News (Skagway, AK) 641
Skamania County Pioneer (Stevenson, WA) 33141
Skaneateles-Marcellus Pennysaver (Syracuse, NY)
   23422
Skaneateles-Marcellus Shopper's Guide 23422*
Skaneateles Press (Syracuse, NY) Unable to locate
Skateboarding Magazine; TransWorld (Oceanside, CA)
   2711
Skating; International Figure (Worcester, MA) 14684
Skating; Recreational Ice (Dallas, TX) 30179
Skeena Cablevision (Terrace, BC, Can.) Unable to
   locate
Skeet Shooting Review (San Antonio, TX) 31048
Skeptic (Altadena, CA) 1393
The Skeptical Inquirer (Albuquerque, NM) 19786
Ski (Boulder, CO) 4187
Ski America (Lenox, MA) Unable to locate
Ski Area Management (Woodbury, CT) 5236
Ski Canada (Toronto, ON, Can.) 36741
Ski Presse (McMasterville, QC, Can.) 37072
Ski Quebec (Boisbriand, QC, Can.) Unable to locate
Ski Racing (Boulder, CO) 4188
Ski Tech (Boulder, CO) Ceased
Ski Week 18635*
Skiatook Journal (Skiatook, OK) 26072
Skidaway Cable TV 7541*
The Skidmore News (Saratoga Springs, NY) 23304
Skier; Cross Country (Cable, WI) 33612
Skier; The Water (Polk City, FL) 6589
Skies America Airline Network (Tualatin, OR) Ceased
Skiing (Boulder, CO) 4189
Skiing Trade Monthly News 4190*
Skiing Trade News (Boulder, CO) 4190
Skiing Utah (Salt Lake City, UT) Unable to locate
Skillings Mining Review (Duluth, MN) 15842
Skin & Allergy News (Rockville, MD) 13697
Skin Art (New York, NY) Unable to locate
Skin Diver (Los Angeles, CA) 2390
Skin Inc. (Carol Stream, IL) 8155

Social Psychology; Basic and Applied (Mahwah, NJ) 19187
Social Psychology; European Review of (Hoboken, NJ) 18945
Social Psychology; Journal of Community & Applied (Hoboken, NJ) 19017
Social Psychology; Journal of Experimental (San Diego, CA) 3194
Social Psychology; Journal of Language and (Thousand Oaks, CA) 3894
Social Psychology Quarterly (Stanford, CA) 3797
Social Psychology Review; Personality and (Hyattsville, MD) 13588
Social Quality; European Journal of (New York, NY) 21651
Social Register Observer (New York, NY) 22755
Social Research (New York, NY) 22756
Social Science; The Annals of the American Academy of Political and (Thousand Oaks, CA) 3850
Social Science Computer Review (Raleigh, NC) 24153
Social Science History (Pittsburgh, PA) 27843
The Social Science Journal (Topeka, KS) 11836
Social Science Quarterly (Madison, WI) Unable to locate
Social Science Research (San Diego, CA) 3276
Social Science Review; International (Winfield, KS) 11909
Social Science Review; Russian (Armonk, NY) 20095
Social Sciences 11909*
Social Sciences; American Journal of Islamic (Herndon, VA) 32160
Social Sciences Index (Bronx, NY) 20287
Social Sciences; Philosophy of the (Thousand Oaks, CA) 3907
Social Security and Acquiescence Rulings (Pittsburgh, PA) Unable to locate
Social Security Bulletin (Pittsburgh, PA) Unable to locate
Social Security; European Journal of (New York, NY) 21652
Social Service Research; Journal of (Binghamton, NY) 20198
Social Service Review (Seattle, WA) Unable to locate
Social Services; Journal of Gay and Lesbian (Hayward, CA) 2043
Social Services; Journal of HIV/AIDS & (Binghamton, NY) 20179
The Social Studies (Washington, DC) 5795
Social Studies; Jewish (Bloomington, IN) 9839
Social Studies; Journal of Applied (Cleveland, OH) 24913
Social Studies Research; Journal of (Cedar Falls, IA) 10658
Social Studies and the Young Learner (Austin, TX) 29805
Social Text (New Brunswick, NJ) 19339
Social Theory and Practice (Tallahassee, FL) 6735
Social Thought 20196*
Social Thought; Journal of Religion & Spirituality in Social Work; (Binghamton, NY) 20196
Social Trends; Canadian (Ottawa, ON, Can.) 36228
Social Welfare; Journal of Sociology and (Kalamazoo, MI) 15241
Social Work (Washington, DC) 5796
Social Work; Administration in (Los Angeles, CA) 2199
Social Work; AFFILIA: Journal of Women and (Thousand Oaks, CA) 3847
Social Work in Education 5409*
Social Work Education; Journal of (Alexandria, VA) 31702
Social Work with Groups (Binghamton, NY) 20217
Social Work; Health & (Washington, DC) 5523
Social Work in Health Care (New York, NY) 22757
Social Work; Journal of Ethnic & Cultural Diversity in (Binghamton, NY) 20171
Social Work; Journal of Family (Binghamton, NY) 20173
Social Work; Journal of Gerontological (New York, NY) 22081
Social Work Journal; School (Skokie, IL) 9610
Social Work; Journal of Teaching in (New York, NY) 22202
Social Work in Long-Term Care; Journal of (Binghamton, NY) 20199
Social Work in Mental Health (Binghamton, NY) 20218
Social Work Practice in the Addictions; Journal of (Binghamton, NY) 20200
Social Work; Psychoanalytic (Detroit, MI) 14945
Social Work Research (Washington, DC) 5797
Social Work Research & Abstracts 5797*
Social Work: Social Thought; Journal of Religion & Spirituality in (Binghamton, NY) 20196
SocialAction.com (Newton, MA) 14410
Socialism; Capitalism, Nature, (Santa Cruz, CA) 3681
Socialist Forum (New York, NY) 22758

Socialist; Freedom (Seattle, WA) 32967
Socialist Review (San Francisco, CA) Unable to locate
Socialist Review (Durham, NC) 23844
Socialist Worker (Toronto, ON, Can.) 36742
Society (Wellesley, MA) 14617
Society; Business & (Albuquerque, NM) 19768
Society for Commercial Archeology Journal (Atlanta, GA) Unable to locate
Society; Education and Urban (Thousand Oaks, CA) 3863
Society & History; Comparative Studies in (Ann Arbor, MI) 14745
Society; Latin American Politics and (Boulder, CO) 4176
Society Magazine; Palm Beach (Palm Beach, FL) 6544
Society & Natural Resources (Logan, UT) 31351
Society News 26735*
Society of Pediatric Nurses; Journal of the (Philadelphia, PA) 27550
Society of Photo-Technologists (Englewood, CO) Unable to locate
Society; Politics & (Thousand Oaks, CA) 3908
Society; Race & (New York, NY) 22620
Society Review; Law & (Amherst, MA) 13800
Society; Russian Education and (Armonk, NY) 20093
Society and Thought); NST (Nature, (Minneapolis, MN) 16118
Society; Youth & (Thousand Oaks, CA) 3923
Socio-Economics; The Journal of (New York, NY) 22188
Sociological Abstracts (Bethesda, MD) 13379
Sociological Forum (New York, NY) 22759
Sociological Inquiry (Madison, WI) Unable to locate
Sociological Methodology (Malden, MA) 14300
Sociological Methods and Research; SMR/ (Thousand Oaks, CA) 3917
Sociological Perspectives (Berkeley, CA) 1562
The Sociological Quarterly (Iowa City, IA) 10987
Sociological Research (Armonk, NY) 20099
Sociological Review; American (Madison, WI) 33918
Sociological Spectrum (Lafayette, LA) 12619
Sociological Theory (Malden, MA) 14301
Sociologist; The American (Somerset, NJ) 19560
Sociology; Annual Review of (Palo Alto, CA) 2794
Sociology and Anthropology; Canadian Review of (Montreal, QC, Can.) 37100
Sociology and Anthropology; Chinese (Armonk, NY) 20071
Sociology/Cahiers canadiens de sociologie; Canadian Journal of (Toronto, ON, Can.) 36512
Sociology; Contemporary (West Lafayette, IN) 10545
Sociology of Education (Washington, DC) 5798
Sociology; European Journal of (New York, NY) 21653
Sociology; International Journal of (Armonk, NY) 20082
Sociology; International Journal of Comparative (Willowdale, ON, Can.) 36879
Sociology of Religion (Fredericton, NB, Can.) 35397
Sociology and Social Research (Los Angeles, CA) Ceased
Sociology and Social Welfare; Journal of (Kalamazoo, MI) 15241
Sociology of Sport Journal (Champaign, IL) 8216
Sociology; Teaching (Washington, DC) 5815
Sociometry 3797*
Sodus Pennysaver (Newark, NY) 22997
Soft Dolls & Animals (Muskegon, MI) 15389
Softball; Let's Play (Minneapolis, MN) 16092
Software (Santa Monica, CA) Unable to locate
Software (Hoboken, NJ) 19104
Software; ACM Transactions on Mathematical (New York, NY) 21141
Software Developer & Publisher 4416*
Software Development (Manhasset, NY) 21013
Software Digest; Business Forum (Dayton, OH) 25107
Software Engineering (New York, NY) Ceased
Software Engineering; Annals of (New York, NY) 21219
Software Engineering; Empirical (New York, NY) 21599
Software Engineering and Knowledge Engineeg; International Journal of (River Edge, NJ) 19513
Software Engineering and Methodology; ACM Transactions on (New York, NY) 21143
Software Guide; Real Estate (Providence, RI) 28419
Software Magazine (Westborough, MA) Unable to locate
Software Magazine; IEEE (Los Alamitos, CA) 2189
Software Maintenance; Journal of (Hoboken, NJ) 19048
Software Management News (Staten Island, NY) Ceased
Software Process (Hoboken, NJ) 19105
Software Reviews On File (New York, NY) Unable to locate

Software Revue (CSR); Children's (Flemington, NJ) 18818
Software Testing, Verification and Reliability (Hoboken, NJ) Ceased
SOI Bulletin; Statistics of Income - (Langley AFB, VA) 32177
Soil Mechanics and Foundation Engineering (New York, NY) 22760
Soil; Plant and (New York, NY) 22561
Soil Science (New Brunswick, NJ) 19340
Soil Science; Canadian Journal of (Ottawa, ON, Can.) 36219
Soil Science; Eurasian (Birmingham, AL) 71
Soil Science Society of America Journal (Madison, WI) 33973
Soil and Water Conservation; Journal of (Ankeny, IA) 10606
Soil and Water Conservation News (Washington, DC) Ceased
Sojourner (Jamaica Plain, MA) 14262
The Sojourner (Alexandria, VA) 31738
Sojourners (Washington, DC) 5799
Sokol Polski (Polish Falcon) (Pittsburgh, PA) 27844
Sokol Times (East Orange, NJ) 18783
Sol de Hialeah; El (Hialeah, FL) 6187
Solaman Productions (San Bernardino, CA) 38072
Solar Detox Update Ceased
Solar Industry Journal (Washington, DC) Ceased
Solar Power; Concentrating (Oak Ridge, TN) 29547
Solar System Research (New York, NY) 22761
Solar Thermal Energy Technology 29547*
Solar Today (Boulder, CO) 4191
SOLARIS (Roberval, QC, Can.) Unable to locate
Soldier of Fortune (Boulder, CO) 4192
Soldier Support Journal (Fort Benjamin Harrison, IN) Ceased
SOLDIERS (Alexandria, VA) Unable to locate
Soldiers Today (Los Angeles, CA) 2391
Soledad Bee (Soledad, CA) 3770
Soleil de la Floride; Le (Hollywood, FL) 6195
Soleil; Le (Quebec, QC, Can.) 37290
Soleil du St. Laurent; Le (Valleyfield, QC, Can.) 37426
SOLID Solutions Magazine (Santa Fe, NM) 19946
Solid State and Supconductivity Abstracts (Bethesda, MD) 13380
Solid State Technology (Nashua, NH) 18600
Solid Waste & Recycling (Toronto, ON, Can.) 36743
Solid Waste Technologies (Atlanta, GA) Unable to locate
Solidarity (Detroit, MI) 14947
Solomon Valley Post 11361*
Solomon Valley Post (Beloit, KS) Ceased
Solomon Valley Shopper (Beloit, KS) Ceased
Solon Economist (Solon, IA) 11229
Solon Herald Sun (Solon, OH) 25527
The Solon Times (Solon, OH) 25528
Solution Chemistry; Journal of (New York, NY) 22190
Solutions 16208*
Solutions 17158*
Solutions 26724*
Solutions for Better Health (New York, NY) Ceased
Solvay-Camillus Pennysaver (Syracuse, NY) 23423
Solvent Extraction and Ion Exchange (Argonne, IL) 8020
SOMA: Engineering for the Human Body (Philadelphia, PA) Ceased
Somatic Cell and Molecular Genetics (New York, NY) 22762
Somatics (Novato, CA) 2653
Somatosensory and Motor Research (St. Louis, MO) 17513
Somatosensory Research 17513*
Somerfield Cable TV Co. (Addison, PA) 26622
Somerset County Buyer's Guide (Somerville, NJ) 19578
Somerset County Cable 28619*
Somerset County Shopper 28003*
Somerset County Shopper 19578*
Somerset/Crisfield Express (Princess Anne, MD) 13668
Somerset Herald (Princess Anne, MD) 13669
Somerset Messenger Gazette (Somerset, NJ) 19565
Somerset Pulaski News Journal (Somerset, KY) 12406
Somerset Spectator (Somerset, NJ) 19566
Somerville Chronicle; Charlestown Patriot & (Charlestown, MA) 14123
Somerville Journal (Needham, MA) Unable to locate
The Somerville News (Somerville, MA) 14538
Somerville Tribune 29994*
Something Better (Jefferson City, MO) 17134
The Something Better News (Grandville, MI) Unable to locate
Son Hi-Fi/Video Guide (Montreal, QC, Can.) Unable to locate
The Sondheim Review (Chicago, IL) 8565
Song Hits Heartbreakers (Derby, CT) Ceased
Song Hits' Superstars (Derby, CT) Unable to locate

Song Manh Magazine (San Jose, CA) **3538**
Songwriter; American (Nashville, TN) **29440**
Songwriter Magazine (Hollywood, CA) *Ceased*
Sonic Cable **31356***
Sonic Cable Television (Turlock, CA) **3961**
Sonic Cable Television of Northern California (West Sacramento, CA) **4069**
Sonic Cable TV of San Luis Obispo (San Luis Obispo, CA) **3577**
Sonic Cable TV of Santa Cruz (Salinas, CA) **3078**
Sonochemistry; Ultrasonics (Burlington, MA) **14035**
Sonography (JDMS); The Journal of Diagnostic Medical (Thousand Oaks, CA) **3887**
Sonoma Business Magazine **3731***
Sonoma County Daily Herald-Recorder (Los Angeles, CA) *Unable to locate*
(Sonoma County Edition); The Classified Gazette (Sonoma, CA) **3773**
The Sonoma County Independent (Santa Rosa, CA) *Unable to locate*
Sonoma County Physician **3735***
Sonoma County Women's Voices (Sebastopol, CA) **3752**
The Sonoma Index-Tribune (Sonoma, CA) **3777**
Sonoma Medicine (Santa Rosa, CA) **3735**
Sonoma Valley News (Sonoma, CA) **3778**
Sonoma West Exchange (Sebastopol, CA) **3753**
Sonoma West Times & News (Sebastopol, CA) **3754**
Sonoran News (Cave Creek, AZ) **672**
Sons of Italy News (Belmont, MA) *Unable to locate*
Sons of Italy Times (Philadelphia, PA) **27689**
The Sons of Norway Viking (Minneapolis, MN) **16128**
Sonus (Cambridge, MA) *Unable to locate*
Sony Style (New York, NY) **22763**
Sooke Mirror (Sooke, BC, Can.) **35093**
Sooland Cablecom Corp. **11214***
The Sooner Catholic (Oklahoma City, OK) **25996**
Sooner LPG Times **25994***
Sooners (Tulsa, OK) **26132**
The Soperton News (Soperton, GA) **7559**
Sophia (Roslindale, MA) *Unable to locate*
The Sophian (Northampton, MA) **14431**
Sophisticate's Black Hairstyles and Care Guide (Chicago, IL) *Unable to locate*
Sorel-O-Vision Inc. (Montreal, QC, Can.) *Unable to locate*
Sorento News (Hillsboro, IL) *Unable to locate*
The Soroptimist of the Americas Magazine (Philadelphia, PA) **27690**
Souderton Independent (Souderton, PA) **28005**
Soul Magazine (Washington, NJ) **19709**
The Sound (Madison, CT) **4936**
Sound Business *Ceased*
Sound Choice (Oceano, CA) *Unable to locate*
Sound & Communications Magazine (Port Washington, NY) **23136**
Sound Engineering Magazine; db, The (Commack, NY) **20488**
Sound; Harbor (Brunswick, GA) **7140**
Sound Management (New York, NY) *Ceased*
Sound Out (Olympia, WA) *Unable to locate*
Sound & Security; Auto (Anaheim, CA) **1400**
Sound; Sensible (Snyder, NY) **23342**
The Sound Shore Review (White Plains, NY) **23574**
Sound and Vibration (Bay Village, OH) **24646**
Sound & Video Contractor (Overland Park, KS) **11731**
The Sound View News (Yonkers, NY) **23601**
Sound & Vision (Toronto, ON, Can.) *Ceased*
Soundboard (Claremont, CA) *Unable to locate*
The Sounder (Random Lake, WI) **34280**
Sounding Line (Parry Sound, ON, Can.) *Unable to locate*
Soundings (Essex, CT) **4783**
Soundings (Knoxville, TN) **29281**
Soundings (Norfolk, VA) **32294**
Soundings Trade Only (Essex, CT) **4784**
Soundoff (Fort Meade, MD) **13504**
Soundtrack (Ringwood, NJ) *Unable to locate*
The Source (Costa Mesa, CA) *Unable to locate*
The Source (New York, NY) **22764**
The Source (Arlington, VA) *Unable to locate*
SourceBook (Albuquerque, NM) **19787**
SourceMex Economic News and Analysis on Mexico (Albuquerque, NM) **19788**
Sources (Austin, TX) **29806**
Sources from the Ancient Near East (Lancaster, CA) *Ceased*
Sourceview, Journal of Software Reviews, Evaluations, and Ratings (Martinez, CA) *Ceased*
Sourdough Sentinel (Anchorage, AK) **532**
The Souris Plaindealer (Souris, MB, Can.) **35293**
Souris River Telecommunications Cooperative (Minot, ND) **24518**
South Advance (Sparta, MI) **15569**
The South Advocate (Lee, MA) *Unable to locate*
The South Alabamian (Jackson, AL) **291**
The South Amboy Citizen **19485***

South America—Basic Oil Laws & Concession Contracts (New York, NY) **20765**
South American Explorer (Ithaca, NY) **20814**
South Antelope Valley Foothill News **2784***
South Arkansas Accent (Hampton, AR) **1165**
South Asia Journal (Thousand Oaks, CA) *Ceased*
South Asian Review (Jacksonville, FL) *Unable to locate*
The South Asian Voice (Oakville, ON, Can.) **36151**
South Atlantic Bulletin **7043***
The South Atlantic Quarterly **23843***
South Atlantic Review (Atlanta, GA) **7043**
South Bay Cablevision (Los Gatos, CA) **2481**
South Bay Extra (Torrance, CA) **3944**
South Bay Family Magazine (Encino, CA) **1885**
South Bay Sun Times/Bonita Valley News (Chula Vista, CA) *Unable to locate*
South Bay's Newspaper **20950***
South Bay's Shopping Newspaper (Lindenhurst, NY) **20950**
South Bellmore/Merrick Pennysaver (Farmingdale, NY) *Ceased*
South Bend Tribune (South Bend, IN) **10458**
South Benton Cablevision, Inc. (Keystone, IA) **11018**
South Benton Star-Press (Marengo, IA) **11064**
South - Bergenite (West Paterson, NJ) **19738**
South Boston Tribune (South Boston, MA) **14540**
South Brentwood Advertiser (Farmingdale, NY) *Ceased*
South Buffalo News (Lackawanna, NY) **20868**
South Carolina Builder (Columbia, SC) *Ceased*
South Carolina Business Journal (Columbia, SC) *Unable to locate*
South Carolina Engineer (Camden, SC) *Ceased*
South Carolina Farmer **8137***
South Carolina Food Journal (Columbia, SC) *Unable to locate*
South Carolina Historical Magazine (Charleston, SC) **28518**
South Carolina Law Quarterly **28565***
South Carolina Law Review (Columbia, SC) **28565**
South Carolina Lawyer (Columbia, SC) **28566**
South Carolina; Living in (Cayce, SC) **28503**
South Carolina Medical Association; Journal of the (Columbia, SC) **28554**
South Carolina News Network (Columbia, SC) **37663**
The South Carolina Policy Forum (Columbia, SC) *Ceased*
South Carolina Review (Clemson, SC) **28533**
South Carolina United Methodist Advocate (Columbia, SC) **28567**
South Carolina; Vision Cable of **28604***
South Carolina Wildlife (Columbia, SC) **28568**
South Carolina YR and FFA (Clemson, SC) **28534**
South Carolina's Young Farmer and Future Farmer **28534***
South Center Journal **32796***
South & Central Africa—Basic Oil Laws & Concession Contracts (New York, NY) **22766**
South Central Living (Lafayette, MN) *Unable to locate*
South Central Ohio Shopper's Guide (Washington Court House, OH) **25620**
South Central Review (College Station, TX) **30050**
South Central Truck Edition; Fastline— (Buckner, KY) **11992**
The South Charlotte News **24116***
South Cherokee Neighbor **7169***
South City Journal (Warrenton, MO) **17695**
South Coast Shopper (Coos Bay, OR) **26272**
South Coloradan (Alamosa, CO) **4131**
South County Chronicle (Leavenworth, KS) *Ceased*
South County Current (Easton, MD) *Ceased*
South County Gazette and Shopper (Three Oaks, MI) **15591**
South County Independent (Wakefield, RI) **28447**
South County Journal (Warrenton, MO) **17696**
South County Journal (Kent, WA) **32796**
South County News (Everman, TX) *Ceased*
South County News-Times **17514***
The South County Spotlight (Scappoose, OR) **26578**
South County Times (Prince Frederick, MD) *Ceased*
South County Times (St. Louis, MO) **17514**
South Crow River News (Osseo, MN) **16251**
South Dade News Leader (Homestead, FL) **6205**
South Dakota Bird Notes (Aberdeen, SD) **28791**
South Dakota Cable Inc. (Sturgis, SD) *Unable to locate*
South Dakota Electric Cooperative Connections (Pierre, SD) **28920**
South Dakota Farm & Home Research Quarterly **28813***
South Dakota Highliner **28920***
South Dakota History (Pierre, SD) **28921**
South Dakota Journal of Medicine (Sioux Falls, SD) **28967**
South Dakota Legion News (Watertown, SD) **29018**
South Dakota Magazine (Yankton, SD) **29039**
South Dakota Pharmacist (Pierre, SD) **28922**
South Dakota Review (Vermillion, SD) **29006**

South Dakota Stock Grower (Rapid City, SD) **28932**
South Dakota; TCI Cablevision of (Rapid City, SD) **28952**
South Dakota Trucking News (Sioux Falls, SD) **28968**
South Dayton Advertiser (Dayton, OH) *Ceased*
The South De Kalb Neighbor (Marietta, GA) **7418**
The South District Journal **32948***
South East Metro (Cottage Grove, MN) *Ceased*
South East Times (Cleveland, OH) *Unable to locate*
The South End (Detroit, MI) **14948**
South End Citizen (Chicago, IL) **8566**
The South End News (Boston, MA) **13961**
South End News (Cleveland, OH) *Unable to locate*
South Florida Business Journal (Charlotte, NC) *Unable to locate*
South Florida Commuter Times (Fort Lauderdale, FL) *Unable to locate*
South Florida Home Buyer's Guide (Deerfield Beach, FL) *Ceased*
South Florida Jewish Tribune Broward Edition (Miami, FL) *Unable to locate*
South Florida; Media One of (Hialeah, FL) **6188**
South Florida Medical Review (Miami, FL) *Ceased*
South Florida Office Guide (Fort Lauderdale, FL) *Unable to locate*
South Florida Parenting (Sunrise, FL) **6700**
South Florida Style (Miami, FL) *Ceased*
South Flushing/Kissena Park Pennysaver (Ontario, ON, Can.) *Ceased*
South Fork Times (South Fork, CO) **4628**
The South Fulton Neighbor (Marietta, GA) **7419**
South Gate Press (Los Angeles, CA) **2392**
South Georgia Business Journal (Thomasville, GA) **7586**
South Georgia Shopper (Cairo, GA) *Unable to locate*
The South Grand Laker (Grove, OK) **25849**
South Gibson Star-Times (Fort Branch, IN) **9963**
South Hamilton Record News (Jewell, IA) **11008**
South Hardin Signal-Review (Hubbard, IA) **10953**
South Haven Daily Tribune (South Haven, MI) *Unable to locate*
The South Haven New Era (Conway Springs, KS) **11401**
South Hicksville/North Levittown Pennysaver (Farmingdale, NY) *Ceased*
The South Hill Enterprise (South Hill, VA) **32534**
South Hills Record (Pittsburgh, PA) **27845**
South Holland/Dolton Star (South Holland, IL) **9617**
South Holt Cablevision Inc. (Oregon, MO) **17321**
South Huntington/Dix Hills Weekender (Farmingdale, NY) *Ceased*
South Huntington Pennysaver (Huntington, NY) *Unable to locate*
South Idaho Press (Burley, ID) **7839**
South Jersey Advisor (Cinnaminson, NJ) **18744**
South Jersey Parents Express (Fort Washington, PA) **26934**
South Jersey Shoppers Guide (Cherry Hill, NJ) **18738**
South Jewish Voice; Deep (Birmingham, AL) **67**
South Kitsap Neighbors (Bremerton, WA) **32694**
South Lake Advertiser (Lowell, IN) **10282**
South Lake Press (Clermont, FL) **5995**
South Lakeland Shopper (Winter Haven, FL) **6872**
The South Lance **35336***
South Lincoln County News (Waldport, OR) **26606**
South Look (Marshfield, MA) **14309**
The South Lyon Herald (South Lyon, MI) **15540**
South Maplewood Review; Woodbury- (North St. Paul, MN) **16232**
South Marion; Voice of (Belleview, FL) **5923**
South Mercer Extra *Ceased*
South Miami News (Miami, FL) **6381**
South Milwaukee Voice Graphic (New Berlin, WI) **34186**
South Minneapolis Shopping Guide (Minneapolis, MN) *Unable to locate*
South Missourian Democrat **17648***
The South Missourian News (Thayer, MO) **17648**
South Okanagan Review **35037***
South OKC Leader (Moore, OK) **25922**
South Ontario News (Chino, CA) *Ceased*
South Orange News (Kissimmee, FL) **6264**
South Orange; News-Record of Maplewood and (Union, NJ) **19686**
South Padre Press; Port Isabel/ (Port Isabel, TX) **30954**
South Pasadena Journal (Los Angeles, CA) *Ceased*
South Peace News (High Prairie, AB, Can.) **34781**
South Philadelphia American (Philadelphia, PA) **27691**
South Pierce County Dispatch (Eatonville, WA) **32744**
South Pittsburg Hustler (South Pittsburg, TN) **29610**
South Pittsburgh Reporter (Pittsburgh, PA) **27846**
South Plainfield Reporter (South Plainfield, NJ) **19590**
South Plains Catholic (Lubbock, TX) **30718**
The South Reporter (Holly Springs, MS) **16681**
South St. Louis County News **17514***
South St. Paul/Inver Grove Heights Sun Current (South St. Paul, MN) **16453**

Southwest Art (Houston, TX) **30530**
The Southwest Booster (Swift Current, SK, Can.) **37575**
Southwest Builder **811***
Southwest Cable (Decatur, TX) **30222**
Southwest Cablevision (Monroe, LA) **12705**
The Southwest Catholic (Lake Charles, LA) **12644**
Southwest City Journal (Warrenton, MO) **17698**
Southwest Computer & Business Equipment Review (Scottsdale, AZ) *Ceased*
Southwest Computer Monthly (Glendale, AZ) **715**
Southwest Contractor (Phoenix, AZ) **811**
Southwest County Journal (Warrenton, MO) **17699**
Southwest Courier **25996***
Southwest Daily News (Sulphur, LA) **12852**
Southwest Daily Times (Liberal, KS) **11605**
Southwest Edition; Art Now Gallery Guide— (Clinton, NJ) **18765**
Southwest Enterprise (Waukesha, WI) *Ceased*
Southwest EXTRA (Chicago, IL) **8568**
Southwest Farm Press (Minneapolis, MN) **16130**
Southwest Georgia News (Albany, GA) *Ceased*
Southwest Globe Times (Philadelphia, PA) **27692**
Southwest Jewish Chronicle (Kansas City, MO) *Ceased*
Southwest; Journal of the (Tucson, AZ) **951**
Southwest Journal (Minneapolis, MN) **16131**
Southwest Journal on Aging (Stillwater, OK) **26082**
Southwest Kansas Register (Dodge City, KS) *Unable to locate*
Southwest Kansas Senior Beacon (Syracuse, KS) **11811**
Southwest Lincoln Sun (Lincoln, NE) *Ceased*
Southwest Messenger (Columbus, OH) **25063**
Southwest Missouri Cable TV Inc. (Carthage, MO) **16962**
Southwest News (Miami, FL) *Ceased*
Southwest News-Herald (Chicago, IL) **8569**
Southwest News Wave (Los Angeles, CA) **2403**
The Southwest Newsweek (Louisville, KY) *Unable to locate*
Southwest Oil World (New York, NY) *Ceased*
Southwest Passage (North Hollywood, CA) *Unable to locate*
Southwest Philosophy Review (Normal, IL) **9305**
Southwest Profile (Taos, NM) *Ceased*
Southwest Quarter Horse Track Magazine (Morgan Mill, TX) **30838**
Southwest Real Estate News (Garland, TX) *Unable to locate*
Southwest Review (Dallas, TX) **30181**
Southwest; Shelby Report of the (Gainesville, GA) **7296**
Southwest Star; Fort Bend/ **30910***
Southwest Stockman (Wheat Ridge, CO) **4684**
Southwest Sun (Jackson, MS) *Ceased*
Southwest Sun (McComb, MS) **16763**
Southwest Sun; Fort Bend/ (Pasadena, TX) **30910**
Southwest & Texas Water Works Journal (Temple, TX) *Ceased*
Southwest Times Record (Fort Smith, AR) **1143**
Southwest Tulsa News **26135***
Southwest Virginia Enterprise (Wytheville, VA) **32643**
The Southwestern (Weatherford, OK) **26185**
Southwestern Cable TV **3318***
Southwestern Entomologist (College Station, TX) **30051**
Southwestern Historical Quarterly (Austin, TX) **29807**
The Southwestern Journal (Brighton, IL) **8098**
Southwestern Journal of Anthropology **19774***
Southwestern Lore (Denver, CO) **4357**
Southwestern Mass Communication Journal (State University, AR) **1350**
The Southwestern Musician (Austin, TX) **29808**
Southwestern Pay Dirt **660***
Southwestern Retailer (Kansas City, MO) **17197**
Southwestern Shoppers Guide (Brighton, IL) **8099**
The Southwestern Sportsman Magazine (Winkelman, AZ) *Ceased*
Southwestern Union Record (Burleson, TX) **29989**
Souvenir *Ceased*
Souvenir Card & Gift (Chicago, IL) *Unable to locate*
Souvenirs, Gifts, & Novelties Magazine (Ardmore, PA) **26664**
Souvenirs and Novelties Magazine **26664***
The Sou'Wester (Americus, GA) **6923**
Soviet Anthropology and Archeology **20065***
Soviet Applied Mechanics **21892***
Soviet Atomic Energy **21269***
Soviet Biographical Service (Minneapolis, MN) *Ceased*
Soviet and East European Law; Bulletin on Current Research in (Toronto, ON, Can.) **36480**
Soviet & Eastern European Foreign Trade **20076***
Soviet Education **20093***
Soviet Electrochemistry **22688***
Soviet Genetics **22690***
Soviet Journal of Automation and Information Sciences (Hoboken, NJ) *Ceased*

Soviet Journal of Biorganic Chemistry **22684***
Soviet Journal of Communications Technology & Electronics (Hoboken, NJ) *Ceased*
Soviet Journal of Coordination Chemistry **22685***
The Soviet Journal of Development Biology **22686***
The Soviet Journal of Ecology **22687***
The Soviet Journal of Glass Physics and Chemistry **21768***
The Soviet Journal of Marine Biology **22691***
Soviet Journal of Non-Ferrous Metals (New York, NY) **22767**
The Soviet Journal of Nondestructive Testing **22692***
Soviet Journal of Optical Technology **13429***
Soviet Laser Research; Journal of (New York, NY) **22191**
Soviet Law and Government **20094***
Soviet Materials Science **22291***
Soviet Materials Science Reviews *Ceased*
Soviet Metal Technology (New York, NY) **22768**
Soviet Microelectronics **22696***
Soviet Mining Science **22134***
Soviet Physics Journal **22697***
Soviet Plant Physiology **22694***
Soviet Powder Metallurgy and Metal Ceramics (New York, NY) **22769**
Soviet Press; Current Digest of the Post- (Columbus, OH) **25014**
Soviet Psychology **20087***
Soviet Radiochemistry **22622***
Soviet Review **20095***
Soviet Sociology **20099***
Soviet Statutes and Decisions **20100***
Soviet Studies in History **22096***
Soviet Studies In History **20080***
Soviet Studies in Literature **20097***
Soviet Studies in Philosophy **20098***
Soviet Union; Annual Survey of Eastern Europe and the Former (Armonk, NY) **20064**
The Sower (Stamford, CT) **5160**
Sow's Ear Poetry Review (Abingdon, VA) **31626**
Soybean Digest (Minneapolis, MN) **16132**
Spa (Santa Barbara, CA) **3658**
Spa Age; Swimming Pool/ (Atlanta, GA) **7048**
Spa Destinations (Montreal, QC, Can.) **37225**
Spa Management (Montreal, QC, Can.) **37226**
Spa Marketing; Pool & (Markham, ON, Can.) **36030**
Spa News; Pool & (Los Angeles, CA) **2373**
Spa and Sauna **33921***
Spa Vacations (Brookline, MA) *Unable to locate*
Space Abstracts **20718***
Space Age Bachelor Magazine (Columbia, SC) *Ceased*
Space for All People (San Francisco, CA) *Ceased*
Space, and Environmental Medicine; Aviation, (Alexandria, VA) **31645**
Space and Missile Times (Lompoc, CA) **2163**
Space Mission Cost; Journal of Reducing (New York, NY) **22177**
Space Observer (Colorado Springs, CO) **4257**
Space Power (Washington, DC) *Ceased*
Space R & D Alert (Alexandria, VA) *Unable to locate*
Space Research; International Journal of (Hauppauge, NY) **20718**
Space Technology; Aviation Week & (New York, NY) **21282**
Space and Time Magazine (New York, NY) **22770**
Spacecraft and Rockets; Journal of (Reston, VA) **32395**
Spalding Enterprise (Spalding, NE) **18281**
Spaniels in the Field (Orr, MN) **16244**
Spaniels; The Royal (Midway City, CA) **2539**
Spanish Broadcasting System (New York, NY) **37785**
Spanish Fork Press (Spanish Fork, UT) **31474**
Spare Change (Cambridge, MA) **14103**
Spare Time (Milwaukee, WI) **34103**
Spares & Strikes (Clarence, NY) *Unable to locate*
Spark! (Cincinnati, OH) *Ceased*
Sparta Cablevision (Sparta, TN) *Unable to locate*
The Sparta Herald (Sparta, WI) **34332**
Sparta/Kent City Advance (Jenison, MI) **15230**
Sparta News-Plaindealer (New York, NY) *Ceased*
Spartan Daily (San Jose, CA) **3539**
Spartanburg Tribune (Spartanburg, SC) *Unable to locate*
SPE Drilling and Completion (Richardson, TX) **30979**
SPE Drilling Engineering **30979***
SPE Formation Evaluation **30981***
SPE Production Engineering **30980***
SPE Production and Facilities (Richardson, TX) **30980**
SPE Reservoir Engineering **30981***
SPE Reservoir Evaluation & Engineering (Richardson, TX) **30981**
Speaker Builder **18617***
Speaker Builder (Peterborough, NH) *Ceased*
Speakin' Out News (Huntsville, AL) **274**
Speaking of Soaps Inc. (Totowa, NJ) **38075**

The Spear-Shaker Review (Watertown, MA) *Unable to locate*
Spearfish Queen City Mail **28993***
Spearman Reporter **31124***
The Spearville News (Spearville, KS) **11807**
The Spec-Com Journal (Dubuque, IA) *Unable to locate*
The SPEC-DATA Program (Alexandria, VA) *Ceased*
SPEC Kit (Washington, DC) **5800**
SpecFile (Mission Viejo, CA) *Unable to locate*
Special Advertising Sales, Inc. (SASI) **37974***
Special Care in Dentistry (Chicago, IL) **8570**
Special Education Journal; National Forum of (Lake Charles, LA) **12642**
Special Education (RASE); Remedial and (Lynchburg, VA) **32209**
Special Education Report (New York, NY) **22771**
Special Events (Malibu, CA) **2496**
Special and Individual Needs Technology Magazine **32562***
Special Interest Autos (Wimberley, TX) **31303**
Special Issues (Des Plaines, IL) *Ceased*
Special Libraries **5544***
Special Libraries Association, Geography & Map Division (Topton, PA) **28052**
Special Parent/Special Child (South Salem, NY) *Unable to locate*
Special Recreation Digest **10988***
Special Recreation Digest (Iowa City, IA) **10988**
Special Report (Knoxville, TN) *Ceased*
Special Services in the Schools **19428***
Special Warfare (Fort Bragg, NC) **23897**
SpeciaList (Washington, DC) **5801**
Specialists in Group Work; The Journal for (Thousand Oaks, CA) **3900**
Specialized Transportation Planning and Practice (Tallahassee, FL) *Ceased*
Specialty Advertising Business **30607***
Specialty Automotive Magazine (Van Nuys, CA) **3995**
Specialty Coffee Retailer (St. Paul, MN) *Ceased*
Specialty Cooking Magazine (Hollywood, FL) **6198**
Specialty Coverage Market Reports *Ceased*
Specialty & Custom Dealer (Akron, OH) *Ceased*
Specialty Features Syndicate (Detroit, MI) **38076**
Specialty Food Merchandising (Manhasset, NY) *Unable to locate*
Specialty Law Digest (Edina, MN) **15877**
Specialty & Performance Magazine (Toronto, ON, Can.) **36745**
Specialty Wood Journal (Vancouver, BC, Can.) **35168**
Spectator (Valdosta, GA) **7615**
The Spectator (Somerset, MA) **14527**
The Spectator (Jackson, MI) **15224**
The Spectator (Clinton, NY) **20474**
Spectator (Eau Claire, WI) **33673**
The Spectator (Hundred Mile House, BC, Can.) *Unable to locate*
The Spectator (Annapolis Royal, NS, Can.) **35535**
The Spectator (Hamilton, ON, Can.) **35890**
Spectator Gauntlet **19609***
Spectator Leader (Linden, NJ) **19171**
Spectator (Los Angeles) (Los Angeles, CA) **2404**
Spectator Magazine (Tampa, FL) **6778**
Spectrometry; Journal of Mass (Hoboken, NJ) **19029**
Spectrometry; Rapid Communications in Mass (Hoboken, NJ) **19096**
Spectrometry; X-Ray (Hoboken, NJ) **19120**
Spectroscopy (Edison, NJ) **18789**
Spectroscopy; Journal of Applied (New York, NY) **21995**
Spectroscopy; Journal of Raman (Hoboken, NJ) **19044**
Spectroscopy Letters (Storrs, CT) **5168**
The Spectrum (Buffalo, NY) **20388**
The Spectrum (Fargo, ND) **24413**
The Spectrum (St. George, UT) **31417**
Spectrum Features (Bloomsburg, PA) **38077**
Spectrum (Greenbelt) (Greenbelt, MD) **13560**
Spectrum; IEEE (New York, NY) **21849**
Spectrum: Journal of State Government (Lexington, KY) **12176**
Spectrum Newspaper Weekly (North Highlands, CA) *Unable to locate*
Spectrum Newspapers (North Highlands, CA) *Unable to locate*
Spectrum Newspapers Monthly, Denver (Rancho Cordova, CA) *Unable to locate*
Spectrum Newspapers Monthly, Greater Sacramento (Rancho Cordova, CA) *Unable to locate*
Spectrum Newspapers Monthly, Las Vegas (Rancho Cordova, CA) *Unable to locate*
Spectrum Newspapers Monthly, Modesto (Rancho Cordova, CA) *Unable to locate*
Spectrum Newspapers Monthly, Portland (North Highlands, CA) *Ceased*
Spectrum Newspapers Monthly, Reno (Rancho Cordova, CA) *Unable to locate*
Spectrum Newspapers Monthly, San Francisco/Marin/ San Mateo (Rancho Cordova, CA) *Ceased*

Spectrum Newspapers Monthly, Santa Clara/Monterey (North Highlands, CA) *Ceased*

Spectrum Newspapers Monthly, Seattle (North Highlands, CA) *Ceased*

Spectrum Newspapers Monthly, Sonoma (Rancho Cordova, CA) *Unable to locate*

Spectrum Newspapers Weekly, Sacramento (Rancho Cordova, CA) *Unable to locate*

Spectrum Newspapers Weekly, Stockton (Rancho Cordova, CA) *Unable to locate*

Speculations (Sunnyvale, CA) **3831**

Speculative Philosophy; The Journal of (University Park, PA) **28079**

The Speculator (Sarasota, FL) *Ceased*

Speculum Magazine (Yardley, PA) *Ceased*

Speculum, A Journal of Medieval Studies (Cambridge, MA) **14104**

Speech; American (Durham, NC) **23807**

Speech and Hearing Research; Journal of (Geneseo, NY) **20649**

Speech, and Hearing Services in Schools; Language, (Rockville, MD) **13686**

Speech Journal; Ohio (Akron, OH) **24583**

Speech, Language, and Hearing Research; Journal of (Rockville, MD) **13685**

Speech and Language; Seminars in (New York, NY) **22726**

Speech; Quarterly Journal of (Washington, DC) **5754**

Speech Technology; International Journal of (New York, NY) **21919**

Speech & Theatre Journal; Missouri (Warrensburg, MO) **17667**

Speech Therapy Forum (Wayne, PA) *Unable to locate*

The Speedhorse Magazine **25943***

Speedhorse Racing Report (Norman, OK) **25943**

Speedway-Northwest Press **10172***

Speedway Scene (North Easton, MA) **14422**

Speedway Town Press (Indianapolis, IN) **10172**

Speedway West Wayne Press **10172***

The Speedy Bee (Jesup, GA) **7348**

The Spencer Advocate (Spencer, NE) **18282**

The Spencer County Journal-Democrat (Rockport, IN) **10434**

Spencer County Leader (Dale, IN) **9917**

Spencer Owen Leader (Spencer, IN) **10471**

Sphere **34907***

Sphere Magazine (Burnaby, BC, Can.) **34907**

Spice Networks (New York, NY) *Unable to locate*

Spices & Medicinal Plants; Journal of Herbs, (Binghamton, NY) **20178**

Spider (Peru, IL) **9450**

The Spill Magazine (Mississauga, ON, Can.) **36087**

Spin **4260***

SPIN (New York, NY) **22772**

Spinal Column Newsweekly; Commerce (Commerce, MI) **14890**

Spinal Column Newsweekly; Highland (Highland, MI) **15160**

Spinal Column Newsweekly; Milford (Milford, MI) **15358**

Spinal Column Newsweekly; Novi (Novi, MI) **15411**

Spinal Column Newsweekly; Waterford (Waterford, MI) **15668**

Spinal Column Newsweekly; West Bloomfield (West Bloomfield, MI) **15678**

Spinal Column Newsweekly; White Lake (White Lake, MI) **15683**

Spinal Cord Injury Life (Woburn, MA) *Unable to locate*

Spinal Disorders & Techniques; Journal of (Baltimore, MD) **13202**

Spindle & Dyepot; Shuttle (Duluth, GA) **7257**

Spine (Philadelphia, PA) **27693**

Spine Surgery; Seminars in (Philadelphia, PA) **27674**

Spinning Jenny (New York, NY) **22773**

The Spirit **33739***

Spirit (Detroit, MI) *Unable to locate*

Spirit (Bridgewater, NJ) **18700**

The Spirit (Punxsutawney, PA) **27909**

Spirit *Unable to locate*

Spirit of Ability (Calgary, AB, Can.) *Ceased*

Spirit of Aloha (Honolulu, HI) **7719**

Spirit of Bucks County (Trenton, NJ) *Ceased*

Spirit; The Catholic (Wheeling, WV) **33501**

Spirit of Change Magazine (Grafton, MA) **14213**

The Spirit of Democracy (Woodsfield, OH) *Ceased*

The Spirit Extra (Punxsutawney, PA) **27910**

SPIRIT-FM - 90.9 (Blacksburg, VA) **31881**

Spirit of Jefferson-Advocate (Charles Town, WV) **33266**

Spirit Lake Cable TV (Spirit Lake, IA) **11240**

Spirit & Life (Tucson, AZ) **964**

The Spirit of Philadelphia (Philadelphia, PA) **27694**

Spirit +Plus (Toms River, NJ) **19645**

Spirit; The Public (Ayer, MA) **13829**

Spirit to Spirit (Blythe, CA) *Unable to locate*

The Spirit That Moves Us (Jackson Heights, NY) **20829**

The Spirit of Woman in the Moon (San Jose, CA) *Unable to locate*

Spiritan Missionary News (Toronto, ON, Can.) **36746**

SpiritLed Woman (Lake Mary, FL) **6280**

Spiritual Bodywork; Journal of (Philadelphia, PA) **27551**

Spiritual Life (Washington, DC) **5802**

Spiritual Women's Times **6374***

Spirituality of Jesuits; Studies in the (St. Louis, MO) **17518**

Spirituality in Social Work: Social Thought; Journal of Religion & (Binghamton, NY) **20196**

Spirituality Today (St. Louis, MO) *Ceased*

Spiritwood Herald (Shellbrook, SK, Can.) **37572**

Spiro Graphic (Spiro, OK) **26074**

Spirochetal and Tick-borne Diseases; Journal of (Thorofare, NJ) **19627**

Spitball (Cincinnati, OH) *Unable to locate*

Splash (Anaheim, CA) **1413**

SPLASH (New York, NY) *Unable to locate*

Splash Magazine (Sugar Land, TX) **31164**

SPLC Report (Arlington, VA) **31832**

Splitrock Telecom Cooperative, Inc. **28859***

Spokane Chronicle (Spokane, WA) *Ceased*

Spokane Valley News **33102***

Spokane, Washington, Official Gazette (Spokane, WA) **33100**

Spokane Woman (Spokane, WA) *Ceased*

Spokesman **17158***

The Spokesman (Herrin, IL) **8983**

Spokesman (Iowa Falls, IA) **11000**

The Spokesman-Review (Spokane, WA) **33101**

Spondylitis Plus (Sherman Oaks, CA) **3763**

Spoon River Poetry Review (Normal, IL) **9306**

Spoon River Quarterly **9306***

Spooner Advocate (Spooner, WI) **34337**

Sport Behavior; Journal of (Mobile, AL) **322**

Sport Detroit (Royal Oak, MI) **15486**

Sport Diver (Winter Park, FL) **6886**

Sport & Exercise Psychology; Journal of (Champaign, IL) **8198**

Sport Fishing (Winter Park, FL) **6887**

Sport History Review (Champaign, IL) **8217**

Sport Journal; Sociology of (Champaign, IL) **8216**

Sport Literate (Chicago, IL) *Unable to locate*

Sport Magazine (Los Angeles, CA) *Ceased*

Sport Medicine; Clinical Journal of (Baltimore, MD) **13147**

Sport News; National Speed (Harrisburg, NC) **23978**

Sport and Physical Activity Journal; Women in (Las Vegas, NV) **18387**

Sport Pilot & Ultralights (Canoga Park, CA) *Unable to locate*

The Sport Psychologist (Champaign, IL) **8218**

Sport Psychology; Journal of Applied (Rancho Cordova, CA) **2875**

Sport Rehabilitation; Journal of (Champaign, IL) **8200**

Sport; Research Quarterly for Exercise and (Reston, VA) **32413**

Sport Rocketry (Los Alamos, NM) **19894**

Sport Scene; Island (Charlottetown, PE, Can.) **36916**

Sport Shop News (Stratford, CT) *Unable to locate*

Sport & Social Issues; Journal of (Thousand Oaks, CA) **3901**

Sport Truck (Los Angeles, CA) **2405**

Sport Utility Buyer's Guide (Milwaukee, WI) *Ceased*

Sport Utility Magazine; 4-Wheel Drive & (Anaheim, CA) **1405**

Sport Utility News; Trucking Times & (Cedar Falls, IA) **10663**

SportCare & Fitness (Wilmington, DE) *Unable to locate*

Sportfishing; Canadian (Waterdown, ON, Can.) **36844**

Sporthirado (Toronto, ON, Can.) *Ceased*

SPORTING CLASSICS (Columbia, SC) **28569**

Sporting Goods Business (New York, NY) **22774**

Sporting Goods Dealer (Roswell, GA) **7519**

Sporting Guns (Ocala, FL) *Unable to locate*

Sporting Journal; Gray's (Augusta, GA) **7099**

The Sporting News (St. Louis, MO) **17515**

Sports; Action (Manhasset, NY) **20990**

Sports & Adventure (Seattle, WA) *Unable to locate*

Sports Adviser Features (St. Charles, IL) **38078**

Sports Afield (New York, NY) **22775**

Sports Biofile & Bio-Toons (West Milford, NJ) **38079**

Sports Business (Woodbridge, ON, Can.) **36906**

Sports Car International (Ross, CA) **2973**

Sports Card Review & Value Line (Sussex, WI) *Unable to locate*

Sports Cards Magazine & Price Guide (Iola, WI) *Ceased*

Sports Chiropractic & Rehabilitation (Philadelphia, PA) **27695**

Sports; City (Solana Beach, CA) **3767**

Sports Collectors Digest (Iola, WI) **33844**

Sports and Exercise; Medicine and Science in (Indianapolis, IN) **10153**

Sports; Fantasy (Iola, WI) **33825**

Sports Focus Magazine (Gaithersburg, MD) *Unable to locate*

Sports History (Leesburg, VA) *Ceased*

Sports Illustrated (New York, NY) **22776**

Sports Illustrated for Kids (New York, NY) **22777**

Sports Illustrated for Women (New York, NY) **22778**

Sports Inc. (New York, NY) *Ceased*

Sports; Jet (Foothill Ranch, CA) **1921**

The Sports Journal (Calgary, AB, Can.) *Unable to locate*

Sports Journal; ACC (Chapel Hill, NC) **23697**

Sports Law Review; Entertainment & (Coral Gables, FL) **6006**

Sports Law; The Texas Review of Entertainment and (Austin, TX) **29846**

Sports Magazine; Health & Fitness (Houston, TX) **30478**

Sports Magazine; Windy City (Chicago, IL) **8607**

Sports Medicine; The American Journal of (Charlottesville, VA) **31914**

Sports Medicine and Arthroscopy Review (Baltimore, MD) **13249**

Sports Medicine; Clinics in (Philadelphia, PA) **27421**

Sports Medicine Digest (Van Nuys, CA) *Unable to locate*

Sports Medicine; Operative Techniques in (Philadelphia, PA) **27607**

Sports; Michigan Runner & Fitness (Ann Arbor, MI) **14769**

Sports; Minnesota (Minneapolis, MN) **16108**

Sports 'n Spokes (Phoenix, AZ) *Ceased*

Sports News; Prorodeo (Colorado Springs, CO) **4255**

Sports Northwest (Seattle, WA) *Ceased*

Sports Physical Therapy (JOSPT); The Journal of Orthopaedic and (Alexandria, VA) **31700**

Sports Retailer; Action (New York, NY) **21147**

Sports Review; Bay (Berkeley, CA) **1495**

Sports Science Review (Champaign, IL) *Ceased*

Sports; Shotgun (Auburn, CA) **1440**

Sports; Silent (Waupaca, WI) **34419**

Sports Spectrum (Wayzata, MN) *Unable to locate*

Sports Tech (New York, NY) **22779**

Sports Trade **36906***

Sports Travel (Secaucus, NJ) *Ceased*

Sports Trend (Atlanta, GA) *Unable to locate*

Sports Truck Accessory Digest (Elkhart, IN) *Unable to locate*

Sports by Voort (Madison, NJ) **38080**

Sports Weekly; USA TODAY (Mc Lean, VA) **32258**

Sportsbuff Features (Hamilton, MA) **38081**

SportsCar (Foothill Ranch, CA) *Unable to locate*

Sportschannel America (Woodbury, NY) **37786**

Sports.com; Jewish (Newton, MA) **14403**

SportsFan Magazine (Bethesda, MD) **13382**

Sportsman; The Badger (Chilton, WI) **33623**

Sportsman; The Canadian (Straffordville, ON, Can.) **36408**

Sportsman; Florida (Stuart, FL) **6693**

Sportsman; Georgia (Marietta, GA) **7413**

Sportsman; The Maine (Yarmouth, ME) **13082**

Sportsman; Michigan (Lansing, MI) **15292**

Sportsman Pilot (Asheboro, NC) **23623**

Sportsman; Salt Water (Boston, MA) **13957**

Sportsman; Western (Vancouver, BC, Can.) **35180**

sportsTURF (Chicago, IL) **8571**

Sportstyle (New York, NY) *Unable to locate*

Sportswear International (New York, NY) *Unable to locate*

Sportwear International (New York, NY) **22780**

Spotlight **27353***

The Spotlight **27160***

The Spotlight (Washington, DC) **5803**

The Spotlight (Indianapolis, IN) **10173**

The Spotlight (Delmar, NY) **20528**

Spotlight (Grand Beach, MB, Can.) *Ceased*

Spotlight - Advertiser (Versailles, IN) **10517**

Spotlight Big Island (Honolulu, HI) **7720**

Spotlight Casting (Hollywood, CA) *Unable to locate*

Spotlight Kauai (Honolulu, HI) **7721**

Spotlight Magazine (Elmsford, NY) **20584**

Spotlight Oahu (Honolulu, HI) **7722**

Spotlight; Princeton-Similkameen (Princeton, BC, Can.) **35066**

Spotlight; Times Journal (Eastman, GA) **7261**

Spotlight on Travel **27353***

Spotlite (Napoleon, OH) **25403**

Spotlite; The Philadelphia (Philadelphia, PA) **27631**

Spotted News (Peoria, IL) **9426**

Spout (Minneapolis, MN) **16133**

The Sprague Advocate (Sprague, WA) **33139**

The Spray **17917***

Spray Technology MKH (Fairfield, NJ) *Unable to locate*

Spree; Buffalo (Williamsville, NY) **23582**

Spring (Flushing, NY) **20613**

Spring Arbor College Journal **15571***

Spring Arbor University Journal (Spring Arbor, MI) **15571**

Spring City Cable TV Inc. (Spring City, TN) **29617**

Spring Creek Sun (Brooklyn, NY) **20348**
The Spring-ford Reporter (Trenton, NJ) **19666**
The Spring Hill New Era (Gardner, KS) **11457**
Spring Hope Enterprise/Bailey News (Spring Hope, NC) **24244**
Spring Journal (Putnam, CT) **5094**
Spring Lake News (Fayetteville, NC) **23881**
Spring Mills TV Co. (Spring Mills, PA) **28011**
Spring Observer (Cleveland, TX) **30030**
Spring Valley Bulletin (Lemon Grove, CA) *Unable to locate*
Spring Valley Sun (Spring Valley, WI) **34340**
Spring Valley Tribune (Spring Valley, MN) **16458**
Spring Valley's Bureau County Republican (Princeton, IL) *Ceased*
Springdale News **35507***
Springer ExprESS (Orr, MN) *Ceased*
Springfield Advance-Press (Springfield, MN) **16459**
Springfield Business Journal (Springfield, MO) **17610**
Springfield Computing (Springfield, IL) *Unable to locate*
The Springfield Connection (Springfield, VA) **32551**
Springfield; Continental Cablevision, Inc. of (Springfield, MA) **14554**
Springfield Great Empire Broadcasting, Inc. **17630***
Springfield Leader **19595***
Springfield! Magazine (Springfield, MO) **17611**
Springfield Monitor (Gretna, NE) *Unable to locate*
The Springfield News (Springfield, OR) **26586**
Springfield News-Sun (Springfield, OH) **25532**
Springfield Parent, Inc. (Springfield, MO) **17612**
Springfield Press (Springfield, PA) **28012**
Springfield Reporter (Springfield, VT) **31603**
The Springfield Sun (Springfield, KY) **12415**
Springfield Sun (Trenton, NJ) **19667**
Springhill Cable TV **35601***
Springhill-Parrsboro Record (Springhill, NS, Can.) **35606**
Springhill Press & News Journal (Springhill, LA) **12847**
The Springhillian (Mobile, AL) **330**
Springs (Oak Brook, IL) **9366**
Springs Valley Herald (French Lick, IN) **10011**
Springtown Epigraph (Azle, TX) *Unable to locate*
Springview Herald (Springview, NE) **18283**
Springville Herald (Springville, UT) **31477**
Springville Journal (Springville, NY) **23354**
Springville PennySaver (Springville, NY) **23355**
Sprinkler Age (Dallas, TX) **30182**
SPSM&H (Bakersfield, CA) *Ceased*
Spudman Magazine (Monterey, CA) *Unable to locate*
SPUR MAGAZINE (Augusta, GA) **7103**
Spur; The Texas (Spur, TX) **31125**
Spy (New York, NY) *Unable to locate*
SQL Server (Calabasas, CA) *Unable to locate*
SQL Server Update (Westminster, CO) *Ceased*
Square Dancer Magazine; The Northeast (North Scituate, RI) **28378**
Squaredance; American (Salinas, CA) **3066**
The Squire (Rockford, MI) *Unable to locate*
The Squire (Kansas City, MO) *Unable to locate*
SR (Studies in Religion)/(Sciences Religieuses) (Edmonton, AB, Can.) **34731**
Srbobran; American (Pittsburgh, PA) **27757**
SRDS **21135***
SRDS Consumer Magazine and Agri-Media Rates and Data **8754***
The SRDS Recruitment Solution (Des Plaines, IL) *Ceased*
SRW Inc. (Hershey, PA) *Ceased*
SSM (Denver, CO) **4358**
SSM Online (Denver, CO) **4359**
St-Francois; Le Haut (Cookshire, QC, Can.) **36978**
St-Hubert Extra (Montreal, QC, Can.) *Ceased*
ST Log (Beverly Hills, CA) *Ceased*
Staats-Zeitung; California (Los Angeles, CA) **2232**
STACKS (New York, NY) **22781**
Stadium Circle Features (Brooklyn, NY) **38082**
The Stafford Courier (Stafford, KS) **11808**
Stafford Data *Ceased*
Stafford Press (Stafford Springs, CT) *Ceased*
Stage of the Art (Tempe, AZ) **915**
Stage Directions (New York, NY) **22782**
Stage & Studio (Port Washington, NY) *Ceased*
Stagebill Group (Chicago, IL) *Unable to locate*
Stages (Boston, MA) **13962**
Stages (New York, NY) **22783**
Stained Glass **17370***
Stained Glass Magazine (Raytown, MO) **17370**
Stainless Steels Digest (Materials Park, OH) *Ceased*
Stamford American (Stamford, TX) **31128**
Stamford Lifestyles **5065***
The Stamford Trader *Ceased*
Stamp Collector (Iola, WI) **33845**
Stamp Monthly; Scott (Sidney, OH) **25520**
Stamp News; The Canadian (St. Catharines, ON, Can.) **36354**
Stamp News; Linn's (Sidney, OH) **25518**
Stamp News; Mekeel's Weekly (Hollis, NH) **18527**

Stamp Wholesaler (Iola, WI) **33846**
Stampede Features (Saratoga, WY) *Unable to locate*
Stamping Arts & Crafts (Muskegon, MI) **15390**
Stamping Grounds (Long Beach, NY) *Unable to locate*
Stamping Journal (Rockford, IL) **9533**
Stamping News; American Tool, Die & (Novi, MI) **15407**
Stamping Quarterly **9533***
Stamps (Hornell, NY) **20752**
Stamps Auction News (Hornell, NY) **20753**
Stanberry Headlight **16889***
The Standard (Arlington Heights, IL) **8026**
The Standard (Boston, MA) **13963**
The Standard (Springfield, MO) **17613**
Standard (Westhope, ND) **24558**
The Standard (Elliot Lake, ON, Can.) **35802**
The Standard (St. Catharines, ON, Can.) **36357**
Standard Banner (Jefferson City, TN) **29247**
Standard Blade **4202***
Standard Blade (Brighton, CO) **4202**
Standard Broadcast News (Toronto, ON, Can.) **37666**
Standard Corporation Records (New York, NY) *Unable to locate*
The Standard Democrat (Sikeston, MO) **17581**
Standard-Examiner (Ogden, UT) **31378**
Standard-Freeholder (Cornwall, ON, Can.) **35755**
Standard-Herald (Warrensburg, MO) *Ceased*
Standard News (Mountain View, MO) **17303**
Standard-Observer (Greensburg, PA) **26955**
Standard & Poor's A.S.E. Stock Reports (New York, NY) **22784**
Standard & Poor's Corporation Records, Current News Edition (New York, NY) **22785**
Standard & Poor's Dividend Record (New York, NY) **22786**
Standard & Poor's Nasdaq and Regional Exchange Stock Reports (New York, NY) **22787**
Standard & Poor's N.Y.S.E. Stock Reports (New York, NY) **22788**
Standard & Poor's Over the Counter and Regional Stock Exchange Reports **22787***
Standard-Radio Post (Fredericksburg, TX) **30365**
The Standard-Register (Tekoa, WA) *Unable to locate*
The Standard Shopping News (Celina, OH) *Unable to locate*
Standard-Speaker (Hazleton, PA) **27035**
The Standard-Times (New Bedford, MA) **14377**
The Standard Times (North Kingstown, RI) **28376**
The Standardbred News (Acton, ON, Can.) *Ceased*
StandardView (New York, NY) **22789**
Stanford Business (Stanford, CA) **3798**
Stanford Business School Magazine **3798***
Stanford Chaparral (Palo Alto, CA) *Unable to locate*
The Stanford Daily (Stanford, CA) **3799**
Stanford French & Italian Studies (Saratoga, CA) **3746**
Stanford Journal of International Relations (Stanford, CA) **3800**
Stanford Law Alum. *Ceased*
Stanford Law Review (Stanford, CA) **3801**
Stanford Lawyer (Stanford, CA) **3802**
Stanford Magazine (Stanford, CA) **3803**
Stanford Observer (Stanford, CA) *Ceased*
The Stanley Republican (Stanley, WI) **34342**
Stanley Sun (Overland Park, KS) *Ceased*
Stanly News and Press (Albemarle, NC) **23618**
Stanstead Historical Society Journal (Stanstead, QC, Can.) **37407**
The Stanstead Journal (Stanstead, QC, Can.) **37408**
Stanton Cable TV Co. (Stanton, KY) *Unable to locate*
Stanwood/Camano News (Stanwood, WA) **33140**
Staples World (Staples, MN) **16460**
The Stapleton Enterprise (Stapleton, NE) **18287**
Staplreview (Greenwood, MS) **16645**
Star **29179***
Star **11113***
Star (Colorado Springs, CO) *Unable to locate*
Star (Golden, CO) *Unable to locate*
The Star (Lakewood, CO) **4536**
The Star (Port St. Joe, FL) **6601**
Star (Ocilla, GA) **7476**
Star (Gilman, IL) **8921**
The Star (New York, NY) **22790**
The Star (Peekskill, NY) **23088**
Star (Tarrytown, NY) *Unable to locate*
Star (West Winfield, NY) **23550**
Star (Brookville, OH) **24712**
Star (Geary, OK) **25843**
Star (Delta, PA) **26822**
The Star (North Augusta, SC) **28719**
The Star (Grand Coulee, WA) **32779**
The Star (Sun Prairie, WI) **34358**
The Star (Cardston, AB, Can.) **34680**
The Star (Orleans, ON, Can.) **36178**
The Star (Quebec, QC, Can.) *Ceased*
Star Advertiser (Gaylord, MI) **15073**
Star Advocate (Titusville, FL) **6821**
The Star-Beacon **24623***

The Star Beacon (Ashtabula, OH) **24624**
Star Buyer's Guide (Gaylord, MI) **15074**
Star Buyer's Guide (Grand Coulee, WA) **32780**
Star Cable (Wadesville, IN) *Unable to locate*
Star Cable Associates (West Columbia, SC) *Unable to locate*
Star Cable TV Co. (Ville Platte, LA) **12868**
Star Cable TV Co. (Dobson, NC) **23801**
Star Cablevision **16330***
Star Cablevision **34387***
Star Cablevision **34269***
Star Cablevision **33862***
Star Cablevision (Martinsville, IN) *Unable to locate*
Star City Cable TV (Minot, ND) **24519**
Star-Clipper (Traer, IA) **11273**
The Star Countyman **34358***
Star-Courier (Kewanee, IL) **9045**
Star Courier (Northern Cambria, PA) **27345**
The Star Courier (Northern Cambria, PA) **27344**
Star-Democrat & Sunday Star (Easton, MD) **13489**
Star-Exponent; Culpeper (Culpeper, VA) **31987**
Star-Gazette (Moose Lake, MN) **16194**
Star Gazette (Hackettstown, NJ) **18857**
Star-Gazette (Elmira, NY) **20573**
Star Gazette Extra (Beardstown, IL) **8056**
Star-Herald (Presque Isle, ME) **13035**
The Star-Herald (Kosciusko, MS) **16734**
The Star Herald (Belton, MO) **16901**
Star-Herald (Scottsbluff, NE) **18265**
Star Herald (Ripley, WV) **33450**
The Star Journal (Gulfport, MS) *Unable to locate*
Star-Journal (Ainsworth, NE) **17923**
Star Journal (Ledgewood, NJ) **19167**
Star Journal (Dundas, ON, Can.) *Unable to locate*
Star & Lamp (Charlotte, NC) **23755**
The Star & Lamp of Pi Kappa Phi **23755***
Star-Ledger (Newark, NJ) **19366**
Star Lite Shoppers Guide (Adrian, MO) **16888**
Star-Mail (Madison, NE) **18152**
Star-News **23014***
Star-News **2823***
Star-News (Chula Vista, CA) **1715**
The Star-News (McCall, ID) **7905**
The Star News (Syracuse, NY) *Ceased*
Star News (Hendersonville, TN) **29220**
The Star News (Medford, WI) **34034**
Star Observers; Journal of the American Association of Variable (Cambridge, MA) **14073**
The Star Press (Muncie, IN) **10328**
The Star Press (Springboro, OH) **25531**
The Star Reporter **28547***
Star Republican (Urbana, OH) **25606**
Star Review (Burleson, TX) **29990**
The Star Shopper **8056***
The Star-Shopper (Lebanon, TN) *Ceased*
Star Shoppers Aid **29417***
Star Shopping Guide (Hammond, LA) **12593**
STAR TECH Journal (Medford, NJ) **19233**
Star & Times (Swan River, MB, Can.) **35299**
Star Trek Communicator (Aurora, CO) **4149**
Star Tribune **9788***
Star Tribune (Berryville, AR) **1054**
Star Tribune (Rochester, MI) *Unable to locate*
Star Tribune (Minneapolis, MN) **16134**
Star-Tribune (Chatham, VA) **31962**
Star Valley Independent (Afton, WY) **34474**
Star and Vidette (Grand Valley, ON, Can.) **35855**
Star Wars Insider (Aurora, CO) **4150**
Star Watch (Rock Hill, SC) **28745**
Star and Wave (Cape May, NJ) **18719**
Star of Zion (Charlotte, NC) *Unable to locate*
Starbuck Times (Starbuck, MN) **16462**
StarDate (Austin, TX) **29809**
Stark Jewish News (Canton, OH) **24732**
The Starkville Daily News (Starkville, MS) **16845**
Starkville TV Cable Co. **16846***
Starlog (New York, NY) **22791**
Starquest S.F. Magazine (Temple City, CA) *Unable to locate*
The Stars and Stripes (Washington, DC) *Unable to locate*
Starstream Cable TV (Garberville, CA) **1996**
Starting Line (Yellow Springs, OH) *Unable to locate*
The Starting Line-Up *Ceased*
Startling Detective (Montreal, QC, Can.) *Ceased*
Starweek Magazine (Toronto, ON, Can.) **36747**
STAT (New Orleans, LA) *Ceased*
The STATE **23932***
State (Pittsburgh, PA) *Unable to locate*
The State (Columbia, SC) **28570**
State of the Art (Tulsa, OK) **26133**
State Bar News (Albany, NY) **20004**
State Cable TV Corp. (Augusta, ME) **12896**
State Court Journal *Ceased*
State Education Leader (Denver, CO) **4360**
State Gazette (Dyersburg, TN) **29175**
State Government News (Lexington, KY) **12177**
State Government; Spectrum: Journal of (Lexington, KY) **12176**

State Health Monitor (Washington, DC) 5804
The State Hornet (Sacramento, CA) 3020
State Journal (Frankfort, KY) 12076
State Journal; The Lander Wyoming (Lander, WY) 34543
State Journal-Register (Springfield, IL) 9642
State Journal; Wisconsin (Madison, WI) 33990
State Legislatures (Denver, CO) 4361
State Line Tribune (Farwell, TX) 30315
State and Local Government Review (Athens, GA) 6952
The State News (East Lansing, MI) 14993
State News; Delaware (Dover, DE) 5246
State Politics & Policy Quarterly (Champaign, IL) 8219
The State Port Pilot (Southport, NC) 24239
State Press (Tempe, AZ) 916
State Register; Leader & (Seaford, DE) 5285
State Reproductive Health Monitor (New York, NY) Ceased
State Tax Notes (Arlington, VA) 31833
State Taxation; Journal of (New York, NY) 22192
State Times (Oneonta, NY) 23052
State Watch (Minneapolis, MN) Unable to locate
Stateline Market Basket (Phillipsburg, KS) Ceased
Stateline Shopping News (Beloit, WI) 33577
Statement (Fort Collins) (Fort Collins, CO) 4439
Staten Island Advance (Staten Island, NY) 23361
Staten Island Cable 23366*
The Staten Island Magazine (Staten Island, NY) Unable to locate
Staten Island Pennysaver (Staten Island, NY) 23362
Staten Island Register (Staten Island, NY) 23363
Stater; Daily Kent (Kent, OH) 25273
States; Border (Murfreesboro, TN) 29429
States-Graphic; Brownsville (Brownsville, TN) 29070
States News Service (Washington, DC) 38083
Statesboro CATV Inc. 7565*
Statesboro Herald (Statesboro, GA) 7564
Statesman (Stony Brook, NY) 23376
Statesman-Examiner & The Sun (Colville, WA) 32726
Statesman Journal (Salem, OR) 26573
Statesville Record and Landmark (Statesville, NC) 24247
StateWays (Norwalk, CT) 5074
Statistical Association; Journal of the American (Alexandria, VA) 31688
Statistical Bulletin (Hanover, PA) Unable to locate
Statistical Physics; Journal of (New York, NY) 22193
Statistical Science (Beachwood, OH) 24656
Statistical Sciences; International Journal of Mathematical and (Miami, FL) 6363
Statistician; The American (Alexandria, VA) 31638
Statistics; The Annals of (Beachwood, OH) 24650
Statistics; Commodity Trade (New York, NY) 21457
Statistics Education; Journal of (Alexandria, VA) 31703
Statistics of Income - SOI Bulletin (Langley AFB, VA) 32177
Statistics; Journal of Agricultural, Biological, and Environmental (Washington, DC) 5567
Statistics; Journal of Biopharmaceutical (Cambridge, MA) 14074
Statistics; Journal of Business & Economic (Alexandria, VA) 31689
Statistics; Journal of Computational and Graphical (Alexandria, VA) 31690
Statistics; Journal of Educational and Behavioral (Washington, DC) 5583
Statistics in Medicine (Hoboken, NJ) 19106
Statistics; Monthly Bulletin of (New York, NY) 22362
Statistics; Quality Control and Applied (Davenport, IA) 10739
Statistics Quarterly Digest; British Columbia Division of Vital (Victoria, BC, Can.) 35209
Statistics; Review of Economics and (Cambridge, MA) 14098
Statistics: Simulation & Computation; Communications in (New York, NY) 21460
Statistics; Theory & Methods; Communications in (New York, NY) 21461
Statistics; Theory of Probability & Mathematical (Providence, RI) 28425
Statistics; Understanding (Mahwah, NJ) 19207
Statutes and Decisions: The Laws of the USSR and its Successor Stabey (Armonk, NY) 20100
Staunton Star-Times (Staunton, IL) 9661
Stayner Sun (Stayner, ON, Can.) 36401
Stayton Mail (Stayton, OR) 26589
Steam (San Francisco, CA) Unable to locate
The Steam Automobile 9396*
The Steam Automobile Bulletin (Palatine, IL) 9396
Steam; Live (Traverse City, MI) 15598
Steam Traction (Topeka, KS) 11837
Steamboat Bill (Providence, RI) Unable to locate
Steamboat Magazine (Vail, CO) 4653
Steamboat Pilot (Steamboat Springs, CO) 4631
Steamboat Today (Steamboat Springs, CO) 4632

Steamboat Vacation Guide (Steamboat Springs, CO) Ceased
The Steamboat Whistle (Steamboat Springs, CO) 4633
Steamshovel Press (St. Louis, MO) 17516
Steamwood Press; Itasca/Roselle Press: Serving Bartlett/Hanover Park/ (Oak Brook, IL) 9354
Stearns-Morrison Enterprise (Albany, MN) 15704
Steel Construction; Modern (Chicago, IL) 8493
Steel Technology; AISE (Pittsburgh, PA) 27754
Steel Valley Green Tab (Moundsville, WV) Ceased
Steelabor (Pittsburgh, PA) 27847
Steele County Press (Finley, ND) 24437
The Steele Enterprise (Steele, ND) 17638
Steeleville Ledger (Steeleville, IL) 9662
Steelheader; Salmon Trout (Portland, OR) 26506
Steels Alert (Beachwood, OH) 24657
Steels Supplement 24657*
Steelville Star/Crawford Mirror (Cuba, MO) 17030
Stem Cell Research; Journal of Hematotherapy & (Larchmont, NY) 20913
Stem Cell Week (Atlanta, GA) 7046
Step-By-Step Graphics (Peoria, IL) 9427
The Step Saver (Southington, CT) 5135
Stephen Crane Studies (Blacksburg, VA) 31878
The Stephens County Heritage (Duncan, OK) Unable to locate
Stephens Life (Columbia, MO) 17010
Stephens Star 1069*
Stephenville Empire-Tribune (Stephenville, TX) 31130
Steppin' Out Magazine (Westwood, NJ) 19748
Stepping Stones (Warren, PA) 28104
Stereo Review (New York, NY) Ceased
Stereo Video Guide (Toronto, ON, Can.) 36748
Stereophile (Santa Fe, NM) Unable to locate
Stereotactic and Functional Neurosurgery (Farmington, CT) 4861
Sterer Cable TV of Florida, Inc. 6671*
Sterility; Fertility and (Rochester, MN) 16308
Sterilization Technology; Infection Control & (Richmond, VA) 32438
Sterling Bulletin (Sterling, KS) 11809
Sterling City News-Record (Sterling City, TX) 31134
The Sterling Connection 32248*
Sterling Heights Source (Sterling Heights, MI) 15576
Sterling/Utica/Shelby Advisor 15576*
The Stettler Independent (Stettler, AB, Can.) 34855
Steuben Courier-Advocate (Bath, NY) 20125
The Steuben News (Ridgewood, NJ) 23197
The Steubenville Register (Steubenville, OH) 25540
Steve Brock Book Reviews on the Internet (Sausalito, CA) 38084
The Stevens Indicator (Hoboken, NJ) 19107
Stevens Journal; Wallace (Potsdam, NY) 23141
Stevens Point Buyers' Guide (Stevens Point, WI) 34344
Stevens Point Journal (Stevens Point, WI) Unable to locate
Steward Anthropological Society Journal (Urbana, IL) 9718
The Stewart-Houston Times (Erin, TN) 29182
Stewart Living; Martha (New York, NY) 22287
Stewart-Webster Journal (Stewart, GA) 7569
STI Review (Washington, DC) Ceased
The Stickney Argus (Stickney, SD) 28998
Stickney/Forest View LIFE; Berwyn/ (Berwyn, IL) 8075
Stickney Independent; Burbank (Midlothian, IL) 9185
Sticks & Mallets (Milford, MA) Unable to locate
Stillwater County News (Columbus, MT) 17775
Stillwater Gazette (Stillwater, MN) Unable to locate
The Stillwater Sun 17775*
Stillwater Valley Advertiser (Covington, OH) 25100
Stillwater Valley News 25100*
Stillwell Sun 11810*
The Sting (Marietta, GA) 7420
Stirling News-Argus (Stirling, ON, Can.) 36403
Stitches (Newmarket, ON, Can.) 36108
Stitches Magazine (Greenwood Village, CO) 4505
The Stittsville News (Stittsville, ON, Can.) 36404
STL 17465*
Stochastic Models (New York, NY) 22792
Stochastic Models in Business and Industry; Applied (Hoboken, NJ) 18894
Stock Car Racing (Lakeland, FL) 6292
Stock Chart Service; Mansfield (Jersey City, NJ) 19143
Stock Charts; Trendline Daily Action (New York, NY) 22862
The Stock Exchange (Edmond, OK) Unable to locate
Stock Guide (New York, NY) 22793
The Stock Market Magazine (Yonkers, NY) 23602
Stock Reports; Standard & Poor's A.S.E. (New York, NY) 22784
Stock Reports; Standard & Poor's N.Y.S.E. (New York, NY) 22788
Stock Service Digest (Hammond, IN) Ceased
Stockbridge Town Crier (Stockbridge, MI) 15579

Stockholders & Creditors News Service (Wayne, PA) Ceased
Stockman Farmer (Mid South) 16770*
The Stockman Grass Farmer (Meridian, MS) 16770
Stockman; Kansas (Topeka, KS) 11831
Stockman of the Midwest; Farmer (Belleville, KS) 11357
Stockman; New Mexico (Albuquerque, NM) 19782
Stockman; North Dakota (Bismarck, ND) 24357
Stockman; Record (Wheat Ridge, CO) 4680
Stockman; Western Farmer- (Carol Stream, IL) 8157
Stockon Herald News 8904*
Stocks & Commodities; Technical Analysis of (Seattle, WA) 33035
The Stockton Record 3807*
Stoddard County News (Dexter, MO) Ceased
Stokes Record 24267*
Stone in America (Mount Sterling, OH) 25397
Stone County Enterprise (Wiggins, MS) 16877
Stone County Leader (Mountain View, AR) 1291
Stone County Republican; The Crane Chronicle/ (Crane, MO) 17027
Stone Magazine (New York, NY) 22794
The Stone Mountain De Kalb Neighbor (Stone Mountain, GA) 7571
Stone Review 31739*
Stone, Sand & Gravel Review (Alexandria, VA) 31739
Stone Soup (Santa Cruz, CA) 3690
Stone Through the Ages (Farmington, MI) Ceased
Stone and Tile Design; Contemporary (Paramus, NJ) 19401
Stone World (Paramus, NJ) Unable to locate
The Stoneham Independent (Stoneham, MA) 14569
Stoneham News Weekender (Stoneham, MA) Ceased
Stonewall Argus & Teulon Times (Stonewall, MB, Can.) 35498
Stoney Creek News (Stoney Creek, ON, Can.) 36406
Stony Brook/Setauket Suffolk Life (Stony Brook, NY) 23377
Stony Brook Weekender (Farmingdale, NY) Ceased
Stoplight (Chippewa Falls, WI) 33629
Store Design; Visual Merchandising and (Cincinnati, OH) 24827
Store Equipment & Design (New York, NY) 22795
Store Image; Retail (Overland Park, KS) 11728
Storer Cable 13610*
Storer Cable 6395*
Storer Cable of Carolina, Inc. (North Charleston, SC) Unable to locate
Storer Cable Communications (North Little Rock, AR) Unable to locate
Storer Cable Communications of Southern Kentucky 11950*
Storer Cable TV of Houston (Houston, TX) 30589
Storer Cable TV of Texas, Inc. 30386*
Storer Communications 12029*
Stores (Washington, DC) 5805
Stork (Indianapolis, IN) Ceased
Storm Lake Times (Storm Lake, IA) 11245
Story (Cincinnati, OH) Ceased
Story Art (Tacoma, WA) Unable to locate
The Story City Herald (Story City, IA) 11251
The Story City Reminder (Story City, IA) 11252
Story Friends (Scottdale, PA) 27957
Storyette Magazine (Marina del Rey, CA) 2510
Storytelling Magazine (Jonesborough, TN) 29259
Storyworks (Danbury, CT) 4764
Stouffville Sun (Stouffville, ON, Can.) 36407
Stouffville Tribune (Stouffville, ON, Can.) Unable to locate
Stoughton Chronicle (Rockland, MA) 14508
Stoughton Courier Hub (Stoughton, WI) 34349
Stoughton Journal (Needham, MA) 14371
Stoughton News Sentinel 14508*
The Stoutonia (Menomonie, WI) 34040
Stow Sentry (Stow, OH) 25547
Stowe Cable (Stowe, VT) 31605
The Stowe Reporter (Stowe, VT) 31604
The Straight Dope, Chicago Reader (Chicago, IL) 38085
Straits Area Star (Gaylord, MI) 15075
Straitsland Resorter (Indian River, MI) 15203
Strand Magazine (Myrtle Beach, SC) 28703
Strange But True (Cleveland, OH) Unable to locate
Strange Days (Worcester, MA) Unable to locate
Strange Magazine (Rockville, MD) 13698
Strange Plasma Ceased
The Stranger (Seattle, WA) 33033
The Stranger Register: Investments and Strategies 19556*
Stranger's Investment Advisor 19556*
Strasburg Weekly News (Strasburg, PA) 28034
Strategic Finance (Montvale, NJ) 19275
Strategic Investor Relations (Washington, DC) 5806
Strategic Management Journal (Hoboken, NJ) 19108
Strategic Marketing; Journal of (New York, NY) 22194
Strategic Medicine (Montvale, NJ) 19276

Sumner Gazette (Sumner, IA) **11258**
The Sumner Press (Sumner, IL) **9676**
Sumter Black Post (Columbia, SC) *Unable to locate*
Sumter County Journal **306***
Sumter County Record **306***
Sumter County Record-Journal (Livingston, AL) **306**
Sumter County Times (Bushnell, FL) **5969**
The Sumter Daily Item **28768***
Sumter Shopper (Fruitland Park, FL) **6128**
Sumter; Vision Cable of (Sumter, SC) **28769**
Sun **30919***
Sun (La Puente, CA) *Unable to locate*
The Sun (San Diego, CA) *Unable to locate*
The Sun (Dover, DE) *Unable to locate*
Sun (Clearwater, FL) *Ceased*
The Sun (Sun City Center, FL) **6698**
Sun (Trenton, IL) **9694**
The Sun (Mount Vernon, IA) **11098**
Sun (Edna, KS) *Unable to locate*
Sun (Quincy, MA) **14492**
Sun (Las Vegas, NV) *Unable to locate*
The Sun (Ocean City, NJ) *Ceased*
The Sun (Chapel Hill, NC) **23727**
The Sun (Cleveland, OH) **24954**
The Sun (North Canton, OH) *Ceased*
The Sun (Sheridan, OR) **26582**
The Sun (Hummelstown, PA) **27066**
The Sun (Houston, TX) *Unable to locate*
Sun (Suffolk, VA) **32567**
The Sun (Bremerton, WA) **32695**
The Sun (Colville, WA) **32727**
The Sun (Swift Current, SK, Can.) *Ceased*
Sun Advertiser (Georgetown, TX) **30391**
Sun Advocate (Price, UT) **31393**
Sun Banner Pride (Wadsworth, OH) **25614**
Sun Belt Buildings Journal (Phoenix, AZ) *Ceased*
Sun Belt Floor Covering (Dallas, TX) *Unable to locate*
Sun Bulletin (Palisades Park, NJ) **19399**
Sun Cable TV (Manson, WA) **32827**
Sun Cablevision (Hawi, HI) **7668**
Sun Cablevision (Kailua Kona, HI) **7767**
The Sun Chronicle (Attleboro, MA) **13825**
Sun Cities Independent (Sun City, AZ) **896**
Sun Cities Life **770***
Sun City News (Sun City, CA) **3824**
Sun/Coast Architect/Builder (Glendale, CA) *Unable to locate*
The Sun Consumer Special (Clarksville, VA) *Ceased*
Sun Country Cable (Groveland, CA) **2033**
Sun Country Cable (Shady Cove, OR) *Unable to locate*
Sun Country Cable, Inc. **26600***
Sun Country Cable Inc. (Pleasanton, CA) *Unable to locate*
Sun Country Cable Inc. (Quincy, WA) **32921**
The Sun Courier (Brecksville, OH) **24706**
Sun Diamond Grower (Stockton, CA) **3809**
Sun & Erie County Independent (Hamburg, NY) **20705**
Sun Features Inc. (Cardiff, CA) **38087**
Sun Gazette **28182***
Sun Gazette (Merrifield, VA) **32270**
The Sun Herald (San Jose, CA) **3540**
The Sun Herald (North Olmsted, OH) **25438**
The Sun Journal (Huntington Beach, CA) **2065**
The Sun-Journal (Ithaca, NY) *Unable to locate*
Sun Journal (New Bern, NC) **24097**
The Sun Journal (North Canton, OH) *Ceased*
Sun-Journal Weekend (Brooksville, FL) *Ceased*
The Sun Ledger (Quarryville, PA) *Unable to locate*
Sun Life Magazine (Peoria, AZ) **770**
Sun Marketplace (Hanover, PA) **26977**
Sun Media Corporation (Toronto, ON, Can.) **38088**
The Sun Messenger (Beachwood, OH) **24658**
Sun/Midweek (Anniston, AL) *Unable to locate*
Sun News (De Land, FL) *Ceased*
Sun-News (Lowden, IA) **11042**
The Sun & News (Hastings, MI) **15155**
Sun-News (Las Cruces, NM) **19876**
Sun News Field and Herald (Conway, SC) *Unable to locate*
Sun Newspaper (Stillwell, KS) **11810**
Sun Observer **29804***
Sun Plus (Webster, TX) *Ceased*
Sun-Post (San Clemente, CA) *Unable to locate*
The Sun Post (Miami Beach, FL) **6417**
Sun Post News (San Clemente, CA) **3103**
Sun Prarie Sailor **15869***
The Sun Press (Beachwood, OH) **24659**
Sun Publications (Naperville, IL) **9274**
The Sun Reporter (Downey, CA) *Ceased*
Sun-Reporter (San Francisco, CA) **3445**
Sun Reporter/Sunrise Mirror **6417***
Sun Review (Vernon, BC, Can.) **35202**
Sun Scoop Journal (Euclid, OH) **25185**
Sun-Sentinel (Fort Lauderdale, FL) **6084**
Sun Server **29804***
Sun Star (Fairbanks, AK) **568**

The Sun Star (Strongsville, OH) **25550**
Sun Tech Journal (Peterborough, NH) *Unable to locate*
Sun Times **29804***
Sun Times **17789***
The Sun Times (Parker, AZ) *Unable to locate*
Sun Times (Heber Springs, AR) **1173**
Sun-Times (Jacksonville Beach, FL) **6248**
The Sun Times (Owen Sound, ON, Can.) **36299**
Sun-Tribune (Morris, MN) **16198**
The Sun-Tribune (Sutherlin, OR) **26591**
Sun Valley Magazine (Ketchum, ID) *Unable to locate*
Sun Valley Sun (Simms, MT) *Unable to locate*
The Sun Visitor (Yuma, AZ) **1019**
Sunbelt Foodservice (Gainesville, GA) **7297**
Sunbelt Publishing Co. **6698***
Sunbonnet Crafts (Berne, IN) *Ceased*
The Suncoast Beacon (Largo, FL) *Unable to locate*
The Suncoast Compass (Kenneth City, FL) *Unable to locate*
Suncoast News (New Port Richey, FL) **6455**
The Suncook Valley Item (Dover, NH) *Ceased*
The Sundance Times (Sundance, WY) **34594**
Sunday Advocate **12484***
Sunday Dispatch (Pittston, PA) **27885**
Sunday Edition News-Optimist (North Battleford, SK, Can.) **37511**
The Sunday Express **35486***
Sunday Extra **4032***
Sunday Gazette-Mail (Charleston, WV) **33273**
Sunday Home Journal (Granite City, IL) **8949**
Sunday Independent **2323***
Sunday Independent (Lehman, PA) *Unable to locate*
Sunday Mirror, The Columbian **16599***
The Sunday Missourian (Columbia, MO) *Unable to locate*
The Sunday News **29633***
Sunday News (Eagle Pass, TX) **30258**
The Sunday Newspapers **34831***
Sunday Post (Lynn, MA) *Unable to locate*
The Sunday Post (Milwaukee, WI) *Unable to locate*
The Sunday Post-Ozaukee County (Cedarburg, WI) **33620**
The Sunday Post (Washington County) (West Bend, WI) **34446**
The Sunday Reminder (Willmar, MN) **16517**
Sunday Rockingham **23930***
Sunday School Counselor **17593***
Sunday School Leadership (Nashville, TN) **29486**
The Sunday Shopper (Somerset, PA) **28003**
Sunday Square Shooter (Staples, MN) **16461**
Sunday Sun (Georgetown, TX) **30392**
The Sunday Telegram **14690***
Sunday Topic Korean News (Elkins Park, PA) *Unable to locate*
The Sunday Visitor **10250***
The Sundial (Lynchburg, VA) **32210**
SunExpert **14024***
The Sunfield Sentinel (Sunfield, MI) **15583**
The Sunflower (Santa Barbara, CA) **3659**
The Sunflower (Wichita, KS) **11888**
The Sunflower (Bismarck, ND) **24360**
The Sunflower Association **24360***
Sunflower Cablevision (Lawrence, KS) **11577**
The SUNlight (Mount Vernon, IA) **11099**
Sunman Cablevision Co. **10477***
Sunman Telecommunications Corp. (Sunman, IN) **10477**
Sunny Destinations; WOODALL'S (Ventura, CA) **4024**
Sunny South News (Coaldale, AB, Can.) **34684**
Sunnyside Sun **33142***
Sunnyvale Scribe (Cupertino, CA) *Ceased*
Sunrise (Pasadena, CA) **2827**
Sunrise News **6699***
The Sunriser News (Ossian, IN) **10386**
Sunset Magazine (Menlo Park, CA) **2527**
Sunshine **23110***
Sunshine (McAllen, TX) **30788**
Sunshine Advertising News (Madison, WI) *Unable to locate*
Sunshine Artist (Orlando, FL) **6508**
Sunshine Coast News (Gibsons, BC, Can.) *Unable to locate*
Sunshine Magazine (Litchfield, IL) *Ceased*
Sunshine Press Services (Washington, DC) **38089**
Sunstone (Salt Lake City, UT) *Unable to locate*
SUNY Geneseo Journal of Science and Mathematics (Geneseo, NY) **20650**
Super Chevy (Anaheim, CA) **1416**
Super Easy-To-Do (New York, NY) **22807**
Super Ecran (Montreal, QC, Can.) **37227**
Super Floral **11591***
Super Floral Floral Retailing **11591***
Super Ford (Los Angeles, CA) **2408**
Super Gaming (Lombard, IL) *Ceased*
Super Hebdo (Montreal, QC, Can.) *Ceased*
Super/Moto Cross (Los Angeles, CA) *Ceased*
Super Saver (Yorkton, SK, Can.) *Ceased*
Super Scrollsaw Patterns (Akron, PA) *Ceased*

Super Shopper (Yuma, AZ) **1020**
Super Shopper (Vista, CA) *Ceased*
Super Shopper (Burlington, KS) *Ceased*
Super Shopper (Petoskey, MI) **15437**
Super Shopper (Las Vegas, NV) *Ceased*
Super Shopper (Clarksville, VA) **31976**
Super Shopper (Surrey, BC, Can.) *Ceased*
Super Stars (New York, NY) *Unable to locate*
Super Sunday Shopper **35244***
Superadio Network (Southborough, MA) **37667**
SUPERAUDIO Cable Radio Service (Englewood, CO) *Ceased*
SuperAutomotive Service (Wauconda, IL) *Unable to locate*
Superb Crosswords (Ambler, PA) **26654**
Supercharger (Farmington Hills, MI) **15020**
Supercomputing; Journal of (New York, NY) **22197**
Supercomputing Review (San Diego, CA) *Unable to locate*
Superconductivity; Journal of (New York, NY) **22198**
Superconductor Industry (Los Angeles, CA) *Unable to locate*
Superconductor Industry (Ramsey, NJ) *Ceased*
SuperCycle (Beverly Hills, CA) *Ceased*
Superfight Color Special No. 1; KO Magazine (Ambler, PA) **26651**
Superfly (New York, NY) *Unable to locate*
SuperGroup Magazine (Salt Lake City, UT) *Unable to locate*
Superintendent's Profile & Pocket Equipment Directory (LaFayette, NY) *Unable to locate*
Superintendent's Profile Product-Service Directory (Alma, QC, Can.) **36930**
The Superior Express **11637***
The Superior Express (Superior, NE) **18289**
Superior Fill-Ins (Ambler, PA) **26655**
Superior Manney Shopper (Superior, WI) **34361**
Superior Sun (Superior, AZ) **898**
Supermarket Business (New York, NY) **22808**
Supermarket Floral **11591***
The Supermarket Gourmet (Fowler, IN) **9997**
Supermarket News (New York, NY) **22809**
SuperOnda (Santa Barbara, CA) **3660**
Supertrax International Magazine (Bloomington, MN) **15761**
Supervision (Burlington, IA) **10640**
Supervisor; The Clinical (Buffalo, NY) **20376**
Supervisor; Today's (Itasca, IL) **9020**
Supplied 96.1 for 103.3 on Aug 8, 2001 **31904***
Supply Chain Management Review (Newton, MA) **14411**
Supply Chain Systems Magazine (Peterborough, NH) **18630**
Supply Chain Technology News (Cleveland, OH) **24955**
Supply and Demand for Scientists and Engineers *Ceased*
Supply House Times (New York, NY) *Unable to locate*
Supply Management; Inside (Tempe, AZ) **905**
Supply Post (Langley, BC, Can.) **35005**
Support (Pasadena, CA) *Unable to locate*
Supra-Sonics! (Rolling Hills Estates, CA) *Unable to locate*
Supramolecular Science (Burlington, MA) **14033**
Supreme Cable (Kirkland Lake, ON, Can.) *Unable to locate*
Supreme Court Debates (Washington, DC) **5808**
Supreme Court Economic Review (Chicago, IL) **8576**
Supreme Court Review (Chicago, IL) **8577**
*Surface (San Francisco, CA) **3446**
Surface (Val David, QC, Can.) *Unable to locate*
Surface Design Journal (Englewood, NJ) **18798**
Surface and Interface Analysis (Hoboken, NJ) **19112**
Surface Mount Technology **8959***
Surface Processes and Landforms; Earth (Hoboken, NJ) **18934**
Surface Warfare Magazine (Pittsburgh, PA) *Unable to locate*
SURFER Magazine (Dana Point, CA) **1807**
Surfing Girl (Boulder, CO) **4193**
Surfing Magazine (Anaheim, CA) **1417**
Surgeons Bulletin; The American Academy of Orthopaedic (Old Tappan, NJ) **19393**
Surgeons; Journal of the American College of (New York, NY) **21982**
Surgeons; Medical Economics for (Montvale, NJ) **19265**
Surgery (New York, NY) **22810**
Surgery; Aesthetic Plastic (New York, NY) **21160**
Surgery; American Journal of (New York, NY) **21200**
Surgery; Annals of (Madison, WI) **33920**
Surgery; Annals of Plastic (Lamoni, IA) **11027**
Surgery; Annals of Vascular (New York, NY) **21220**
Surgery; Archives of (Chicago, IL) **8274**
Surgery; Archives of Otolaryngology—Head & Neck (Chicago, IL) **8270**
Surgery; Canadian Journal of (Ottawa, ON, Can.) **36220**

Surgery Clinics; Chest (Philadelphia, PA) **27399**
Surgery Clinics; Oral and Maxillofacial (Philadelphia, PA) **27608**
Surgery; Clinics in Plastic (Philadelphia, PA) **27419**
Surgery; Clinics in Podiatric Medicine and (Philadelphia, PA) **27420**
Surgery; Computer Aided (St. Louis, MO) **17426**
Surgery; Contemporary (Torrance, CA) **3931**
Surgery; Current (Philadelphia, PA) **27446**
Surgery; Digestive (Farmington, CT) **4818**
Surgery; Head & Neck (Hoboken, NJ) **18957**
Surgery; Internet Journal of (Sugar Land, TX) **31162**
Surgery; Internet Journal of Orthopedic (Sugar Land, TX) **31154**
Surgery Journal; Aesthetic (New York, NY) **21161**
Surgery; Journal of the American Society for (Philadelphia, PA) **27515**
Surgery; Journal of Avian Medicine and (Lawrence, KS) **11554**
Surgery; The Journal of Bone and Joint (Needham, MA) **14357**
Surgery; Journal of Cardiac (Armonk, NY) **20084**
Surgery; Journal of Cataract and Refractive (Fairfax, VA) **32019**
Surgery; Journal of Clinical Laser Medicine & (Larchmont, NY) **20909**
Surgery; Journal of Foot **9405***
Surgery; Journal of Foot and Ankle (Park Ridge, IL) **9405**
Surgery; Journal of Gynecologic (Larchmont, NY) **20912**
Surgery; Journal of Hand (St. Louis, MO) **17455**
Surgery; Journal of Investigative (Kalamazoo, MI) **15240**
Surgery; Journal of Oral and Maxillofacial (Lexington, KY) **12168**
Surgery; Journal of Pediatric (Indianapolis, IN) **10141**
Surgery; Journal of Shoulder and Elbow (St. Louis, MO) **17462**
Surgery; The Journal of Thoracic and Cardiovascular (New York, NY) **22205**
Surgery; Journal of Vascular (New York, NY) **22212**
Surgery & Laparoscopy News; General (New York, NY) **21749**
Surgery and Medicine; Lasers in (Hoboken, NJ) **19053**
Surgery News Latin America Edition; Ocular (Thorofare, NJ) **19633**
Surgery News; Ocular (Thorofare, NJ) **19631**
Surgery; Obesity (Toronto, ON, Can.) **36679**
Surgery; Operative Techniques in Cataract and Refractive (Philadelphia, PA) **27600**
Surgery; Operative Techniques in General (Rochester, MN) **16310**
Surgery; Operative Techniques in Gynecologic (Philadelphia, PA) **27601**
Surgery; Operative Techniques in Oculoplastic, Orbital and Reconstructive (Philadelphia, PA) **27603**
Surgery; Operative Techniques in Plastic and Reconstructive (Philadelphia, PA) **27606**
Surgery; Operative Techniques in Thoracic and Cardiovascular (Naples, FL) **6448**
Surgery, Oral Medicine, Oral Pathology, Oral Radiology, and Endodontics; Oral (St. Louis, MO) **17480**
Surgery; Otolaryngology—Head and Neck (New York, NY) **22508**
Surgery; Plastic and Reconstructive (Brookline, MA) **14023**
Surgery; Seminars in Colon and Rectal (Burlington, MA) **14032**
Surgery; Seminars in Cutaneous Medicine and (Philadelphia, PA) **27663**
Surgery; Seminars in Laparoscopic (Augusta, GA) **7102**
Surgery; Seminars in Pediatric (Indianapolis, IN) **10170**
Surgery; Seminars in Spine (Philadelphia, PA) **27674**
Surgery; Seminars in Thoracic and Cardiovascular (Naples, FL) **6449**
Surgery; Seminars in Thoracic & Cardiovascular (Boston, MA) **13959**
Surgery; Seminars in Vascular (Silverthorne, CO) **4625**
Surgery; Techniques in Hand and Upper Extremity (Philadelphia, PA) **27699**
Surgery; Veterinary (Davis, CA) **1818**
Surgery; World Journal of (New York, NY) **22941**
The Surgical Clinics of North America (Philadelphia, PA) **27697**
Surgical Endoscopy (New York, NY) **22811**
Surgical Laparoscopy Endoscopy & Percutaneous Techniques (Baltimore, MD) **13250**
Surgical Oncology; Annals of (Alexandria, VA) **31641**
Surgical Oncology; Journal of (Hoboken, NJ) **19049**
Surgical Outcomes; Journal of (Philadelphia, PA) **27552**
Surgical Pathology (AJSP); The American Journal of (Baltimore, MD) **13119**

Surgical Pathology; International Journal of (Glen Head, NY) **20663**
Surgical Products (Morris Plains, NJ) **19307**
Surgical Research Communications (New York, NY) *Unable to locate*
Surgical Research; European (Farmington, CT) **4821**
Surgical Research; Journal of (San Diego, CA) **3214**
Surgical Rounds (Jamesburg, NJ) **19133**
Surgical Services Management **4358***
Surgical Techniques; Journal of Laparoendoscopic and Advanced (Larchmont, NY) **20915**
The Surgical Technologist (Englewood, CO) *Unable to locate*
Surplus Line Reporter & Insurance News (New Orleans, LA) **12755**
The Surplus Record (Chicago, IL) **8578**
Surprises (Minneapolis, MN) **16135**
Surrey Gazette; Piedmont- (Piedmont, OK) **26035**
The Surrey/North Delta Leader (Surrey, BC, Can.) *Unable to locate*
Surrey-North Delta Now (Surrey, BC, Can.) *Unable to locate*
Surrey Shopper (Surrey, BC, Can.) *Ceased*
Surry Scene (Mount Airy, NC) **24081**
Survey of Anesthesiology (Valhalla, NY) **23483**
Survey of Business (Knoxville, TN) *Ceased*
Survey of Current Business (Pittsburgh, PA) *Unable to locate*
Survey of Ophthalmology (New York, NY) **22812**
Surveying Engineering; Journal of (Reston, VA) **32397**
Surveying and Land Information Science (Gaithersburg, MD) **13548**
Surveying and Mapping **13548***
Surveyor; The California (Santa Rosa, CA) **3724**
Surveyor; The Ontario Land (Toronto, ON, Can.) **36683**
Surveyor; Professional (Frederick, MD) **13520**
Surveyor; The Texas (Austin, TX) **29848**
Surveys on Mathematics for Industry (New York, NY) *Ceased*
Survival; Medicine & Global (Brookline, MA) **14022**
Survival News (Mattapan, MA) **14313**
SusCom (Pearl, MS) **16816**
The Suspension Press (Covington, KY) **12028**
Susquehanna Alumnus **27975***
Susquehanna Cable Co. (York, PA) **28211**
Susquehanna Communications **16816***
Susquehanna Communications (Williamsport, PA) **28184**
Susquehanna County Independent (Montrose, PA) **27292**
Susquehanna County Press **27292***
Susquehanna Monthly Magazine (Marietta, PA) *Ceased*
Susquehanna Today (Selinsgrove, PA) **27975**
Susquehanna Transcript **28041***
Susquemanna Communications (York, PA) **28212**
Sussex Countian (Georgetown, DE) **5253**
The Sussex County Chronicle (Stanhope, NJ) **19599**
Sussex-Lannon-Lisbon News (New Berlin, WI) **34187**
The Sussex Post (Dover, DE) *Unable to locate*
Sussex Sun (Sussex, WI) **34364**
Sussex-Surry Dispatch (Wakefield, VA) **32598**
Sutton Capitol Associates (New York, NY) *Ceased*
Suwannee Democrat; Live Oak (Live Oak, FL) **6306**
Suwannee Valley News; Williston Sun- (Williston, FL) **6863**
Suzuki Journal; American (Boulder, CO) **4156**
SV Entertainment (Chicago, IL) *Ceased*
Svitlo (The Light) (Etobicoke, ON, Can.) *Unable to locate*
SVOBODA (Parsippany, NJ) **19414**
S.W. Pompano Shopper (Hollywood, FL) *Unable to locate*
Swampscott Reporter (Swampscott, MA) **14583**
Swan Hills Grizzly Gazette (Swan Hills, AB, Can.) **34860**
Swank (Paramus, NJ) **19407**
The Swanton Enterprise (Swanton, OH) **25553**
Swap Meet Magazine (Centerport, NY) **20447**
The Swap Shop (Picayune, MS) **16820**
Swap Shop News (Oakland Park, FL) *Ceased*
Swarthmore College Bulletin (Swarthmore, PA) **28044**
Swarthmore Phoenix (Swarthmore, PA) **28045**
The Swarthmorean (Swarthmore, PA) **28046**
The Swartz Creek News (Swartz Creek, MI) **15584**
S.W.A.T. Pro **13894***
S.W.A.T. (Special Weapons and Tactics) (Cornville, AZ) *Unable to locate*
SWE (Chicago, IL) **8579**
SWE Newsletter **8579***
Swea City Herald-Press (Swea City, IA) **11260**
SWEAT Magazine (Tempe, AZ) **917**
Sweden & America **4980***
Sweden; Fresh From (New York, NY) **21736**
Swedish American Genealogist (Longview, WA) **32814**

Swedish-American Historical Quarterly (St. Peter, MN) **16431**
Swedish Events **21736***
(Swedish News); Nordstjernan (New York, NY) **22468**
Swedish Pioneer Historical Quarterly **16431***
Swedish Press (Vancouver, BC, Can.) **35170**
Sweeping (Gaithersburg, MD) *Unable to locate*
Sweet Briar News (Sweet Briar, VA) *Unable to locate*
Sweet Potato (Oakland, CA) *Ceased*
Sweet Springs Herald (Sweet Springs, MO) **17644**
Sweetwater Cable Television Co. (Rock Springs, WY) **34585**
Sweetwater Reporter (Sweetwater, TX) **31170**
Swift County Monitor-News (Benson, MN) **15747**
Swim Fashion Quarterly (Phoenix, AZ) **812**
Swimmer; Rodale's Fitness (Emmaus, PA) **26881**
Swimming Pool/Spa Age (Atlanta, GA) **7048**
Swimming Pool and Spa Dealer News (Dallas, TX) *Ceased*
Swimming Technique (El Segundo, CA) *Unable to locate*
Swimming World and Junior Swimmer (El Segundo, CA) *Unable to locate*
Swimsuit Spectacular (Tarrytown, NY) *Ceased*
Swimwear Illustrated (Sunnyvale, CA) *Unable to locate*
Swine Practitioner (Lenexa, KS) **11597**
Swing Magazine (New York, NY) *Unable to locate*
Swiss-American Historical Society (Chicago, IL) **8580**
Swiss American Review (New York, NY) *Unable to locate*
Swiss Journal (San Francisco, CA) **3447**
Switch (San Jose, CA) **3541**
The Switzerland Democrat (Vevay, IN) **10519**
The Sword of the Lord (Murfreesboro, TN) **29433**
Sword of the Spirit (Baton Rouge, LA) *Ceased*
Sybase Magazine (Dublin, CA) **1839**
Sycamore Messenger (Cincinnati, OH) *Unable to locate*
Sycamore Review (West Lafayette, IN) **10554**
Sykesville Post-Dispatch **27908***
Syllabus Magazine (Chatsworth, CA) **1690**
Syllecta Classica (Iowa City, IA) **10989**
The Sylva Herald & Ruralite (Sylva, NC) **24251**
Sylvan Lake News (Sylvan Lake, AB, Can.) *Unable to locate*
Sylvan Valley CATV Co. (Brevard, NC) **23665**
Sylvania Herald (Sylvania, OH) **25554**
Sylvania Telephone (Sylvania, GA) **7581**
The Sylvester Local News (Sylvester, GA) **7582**
Sylvia Di Pietro (New York, NY) **38090**
Sylvia Syndicate (Chicago, IL) **38091**
Symbol (Atlanta, GA) *Unable to locate*
Symbolic Computation; Higher-Order and (New York, NY) **21803**
Symbolic Interaction (Berkeley, CA) *Unable to locate*
SYMPHONY (New York, NY) **22813**
Symphony Magazine **22813***
Symphony News **22813***
The Symphony User's Journal (Rochester, NY) *Ceased*
Symploke (Victoria, TX) **31235**
Symposium (Washington, DC) **5809**
Synapse (San Francisco, CA) **3448**
Synapse (Hoboken, NJ) **19113**
Syndicated Automotive News (Walnut Creek, CA) *Unable to locate*
Syndicated Columnists Weekly (Boston, MA) **13967**
Syndication Associates Inc. (Tulsa, OK) *Unable to locate*
Syndication Associates Inc. (St. Laurent, QC, Can.) *Unable to locate*
Synergist (Fairfax, VA) **32032**
Synthesis (Weston, VT) *Unable to locate*
Synthesis and Processing; Journal of Materials (New York, NY) **22125**
Synthesis and Reactivity in Inorganic and Metal-Organic Chemistry (St. Louis, MO) **17519**
Synthesis/Regeneration (St. Louis, MO) **17520**
Synthetic Communications (Pearl River, NY) **23087**
Syosset Advance (Syosset, NY) **23382**
Syosset Guardian; Oyster Bay- (Oyster Bay, NY) **23070**
Syosset/Jericho Tribune (Jericho, NY) **20850**
Syosset Tribune (Syosset, NY) **23383**
Syosset Weekender (Farmingdale, NY) *Ceased*
Syosset/Woodbury Pennysaver (Syosset, NY) **23384**
Syracuse Business **23391***
Syracuse East Pennysaver (Syracuse, NY) **23425**
Syracuse Herald-Journal (Syracuse, NY) **23426**
Syracuse Journal (Syracuse, KS) **11812**
Syracuse Journal-Democrat (Syracuse, NE) **18293**
Syracuse Law Review (Syracuse, NY) **23427**
Syracuse New Times (Syracuse, NY) **23428**
Syracuse NewChannels Corp. **23433***
The Syracuse Record (Syracuse, NY) **23429**
Syracuse University Library Associates Courier (Syracuse, NY) **23430**
Sys Admin (Lawrence, KS) **11565**

System Builder (Indianapolis, IN) *Ceased*
System Design; Formal Methods in (New York, NY) **21726**
System Dynamics Review (Hoboken, NJ) **19114**
System Gold (Harrington, DE) *Unable to locate*
Systemic Therapies; Journal of (London, ON, Can.) **35985**
Systems and Computers in Japan (Hoboken, NJ) **19115**
Systems Development Management (New York, NY) *Unable to locate*
Systems; Electric Machines Components and (Philadelphia, PA) **27456**
Systems Integration Business (Newton, MA) *Ceased*
Systems Integration; Journal of (New York, NY) **22200**
Systems Management; Journal of (Cleveland, OH) **24917**
Systems and Network Integration (Manhasset, NY) *Unable to locate*
Systems Practice (New York, NY) *Unable to locate*
Systems & Procedures Exchange Center (SPEC) Kit **5800***
Systems Research and Behavioral Science (Hoboken, NJ) **19116**
Systems 3X/400 **8276***
Systems User (Janesville, WI) *Ceased*

T

T & B **9607***
T H - ERS Express *Ceased*
T S I Journal of Particle Instrumentation (St. Paul, MN) *Ceased*
T-Shirt Retailer & Screen Printer **19589***
Ta Kung (South San Francisco, CA) *Unable to locate*
TAB **1222***
The Tab (Palo Alto, CA) *Ceased*
Tabaret (Ottawa, ON, Can.) **36276**
Taber Times (Taber, AB, Can.) *Unable to locate*
Tabernacle & Purgatory **964***
Table Rock Gazette (Kimberling City, MO) *Unable to locate*
Table Tennis Magazine; USA (Colorado Springs, CO) **4260**
Table Tennis Today **4260***
Table Tennis Topics **4260***
The Tablet (Brooklyn, NY) *Unable to locate*
Tabletalk (Orlando, FL) **6509**
The Tabloyd (Sudbury, ON, Can.) *Ceased*
Taboo (San Francisco, CA) **3449**
The Tabor City Tribune **24253***
Tabor-Loris Tribune (Tabor City, NC) **24253**
The Tack (Storm Lake, IA) **11246**
Tack'n Togs Merchandising (Minnetonka, MN) **16176**
Tacoma Reporter (Tacoma, WA) **33151**
Tacoma True Citizen (Tacoma, WA) **33152**
Tacoma Voice **33151***
Tactics; Strategy & (Bakersfield, CA) **1453**
TAD (Tool & Die) Magazine (Fairfield, NJ) *Unable to locate*
Taekwondo World (Yankton, SD) *Unable to locate*
The Taft Tribune (Taft, TX) **31173**
Tahlequah Daily Press (Westville, OK) **26191**
The Tahlequah Times Journal (Tahlequah, OK) **26095**
Tahoe Action **3783***
Tahoe Bonanza; North Lake (Incline Village, NV) **18358**
Tahoe Daily Tribune (South Lake Tahoe, CA) **3784**
Tahoe World (Reno, NV) **18425**
T'ai Chi (Los Angeles, CA) **2409**
Tailgate (Agoura, CA) **1380**
Tailor; The Custom (Washington, DC) **5457**
The Tailwind (Travis A F B, CA) *Unable to locate*
Taiwan Studies (Armonk, NY) *Ceased*
Take Off (San Jose, CA) *Unable to locate*
Take One (Peterborough, NH) **18631**
Takoma Park (Frederick, MD) **13522**
Talbott Tree *Ceased*
Talbotton New Era (Talbotton, GA) **7583**
Talco Times (Talco, TX) **31175**
Talebones (Auburn, WA) *Unable to locate*
Talihina American (Talihina, OK) **26098**
Talisman (Jersey City, NJ) **19144**
talk (New York, NY) **22814**
Talk; Bayou (Montebello, CA) **2579**
Talk of the Town (Moscow, ID) **7921**
Talk; Town (Media, PA) **27243**
Talk TV Network, Inc. (Phoenix, AZ) *Unable to locate*
Talk; Winnetka (Winnetka, IL) **9768**
Talking Book Topics (Washington, DC) **5810**
Talking Business (Hoboken, NJ) *Ceased*
Talking Drum (Topeka, KS) *Ceased*
Talking Medicine (Hoboken, NJ) *Ceased*
Talking Raven (Berkeley, CA) *Ceased*

Talknet (Arlington, VA) *Unable to locate*
Tall City 'N Cable **30816***
Tall City TV Cable **30817***
The Tallahassee Advertiser (Tallahassee, FL) **6737**
Tallahassee Democrat (San Jose, CA) **3542**
Tallahassee Magazine (Tallahassee, FL) **6738**
The Tallassee Tribune (Tallassee, AL) **467**
Tallmadge Express (Tallmadge, OH) **25557**
Tallulah Cablevision Corp. (Tallulah, LA) **12857**
Tallyho **716***
Talon (Colorado Springs, CO) *Ceased*
The Talon (Hattiesburg, MS) **16665**
Talon Marks (Norwalk, CA) **2649**
Tama County Shopper-Advisor (Tama, IA) **11262**
The Tama News-Herald (Tama, IA) **11263**
Tamara (Las Cruces, NM) **19877**
Tamarac/North Lauderdale Forum (Coral Springs, FL) **6018**
Taming the Workplace (Seattle, WA) **38092**
Tampa Bay Life (Tampa, FL) *Unable to locate*
Tampa Bay Magazine (Clearwater, FL) **5991**
Tampa Bay Newcomer (Raleigh, NC) *Ceased*
Tampa Business Journal (Charlotte, NC) *Unable to locate*
Tampa; Jewish Press of (Clearwater, FL) **5988**
Tampa Review (Tampa, FL) **6779**
The Tampa Tribune (Tampa, FL) **6780**
TAMS Journal (Bryantown, MD) **13397**
Tan (Jackson, MI) *Ceased*
Taney County Republican **17100***
Tangent TV Cable Co. (Corvallis, OR) *Unable to locate*
Tangerine (Utica, NY) **23467**
Tangi Talk (Amite, LA) *Ceased*
TANSTAAFL (Athens, GA) *Unable to locate*
Tantra: The Magazine (Albuquerque, NM) *Unable to locate*
Taos Magazine (Taos, NM) **19962**
The Taos News (Taos, NM) **19963**
Tap Talk (Pacific, WA) *Ceased*
Tape/Disc Business (White Plains, NY) **23575**
TAPPI JOURNAL (Atlanta, GA) **7049**
Taproot Literary Review (Ambridge, PA) **26656**
Taproot Literary Review Special Anniversary Edition **26656***
Taproot Mizmor Osage Orange Tree **26656***
Taproot Reviews (Lakewood, OH) **25288**
Taproot Willow Tree **26656***
Taproot's Sassafras Edition **26656***
Tar Heel; The Daily (Chapel Hill, NC) **23706**
Tar Heel Junior Historian (Raleigh, NC) **24155**
Tar River Poetry (Greenville, NC) **23970**
Tarentaise Recorder (Belfield, ND) *Ceased*
Target (Gibson City, IL) **8919**
Target Marketing (Falls Church, VA) **32057**
Target The Family (New York, NY) **22815**
Targum; The Daily (New Brunswick, NJ) **19329**
Tarheel Banker **24129***
Tarheel Banker (Raleigh, NC) *Ceased*
The Tarkio Avalanche (Tarkio, MO) **17646**
Tarpon Springs Herald (Tarpon Springs, FL) *Unable to locate*
Tarpon Springs Leader (New Port Richey, FL) *Ceased*
Tarrytown Daily News (Tarrytown, VA) **32569**
Tarrytown News **32569***
Tartan (Crystal Lake, IL) **8696**
The Tartan (Pittsburgh, PA) **27848**
The Tartan (Radford, VA) **32347**
TASB Journal **29834***
Tass News Agency **37961***
Taste of Home (Greendale, WI) **33764**
Taste of Latex (Seattle, WA) *Unable to locate*
T.A.T. Cablevision (Flora, MS) **16624**
Tate County Democrat **16841***
The Tattler-Reminder (Appleton, WI) *Ceased*
The Tattnall Journal (Reidsville, GA) **7488**
Tattoo (Agoura, CA) **1381**
Tattoo Industry (Agoura, CA) **1382**
Tau Beta Pi; The Bent of (Knoxville, TN) **29270**
Taunton Daily Gazette (Taunton, MA) **14584**
Tauy Talk **11690***
Tavern News; Ohio (Columbus, OH) **25053**
Tavern Sports International (Chicago, IL) *Ceased*
Tavistock Gazette (Tavistock, ON, Can.) **36430**
Tawakoni Area Advertiser (Quinlan, TX) *Ceased*
The Tawakoni News (Quinlan, TX) **30966**
Tax Adviser (Jersey City, NJ) **19145**
Tax Bulletin (Englewood Cliffs, NJ) *Unable to locate*
Tax Court Reports; United States (Pittsburgh, PA) **27853**
The Tax Executive (Washington, DC) **5811**
Tax Guide; PBC Federal (Los Angeles, CA) **2359**
Tax Journal; The International (New York, NY) **21938**
Tax Journal (Revue fiscale canadienne); Canadian (Toronto, ON, Can.) **36531**
Tax Law Bi-Weekly Bulletin; Foreign (Ormond Beach, FL) **6533**
Tax Law Review (New York, NY) *Ceased*

The Tax Lawyer (Washington, DC) **5812**
Tax Lawyer; The Practical (Philadelphia, PA) **27644**
The Tax Management International Forum (Washington, DC) **5813**
Tax Management; Journal of Property (New York, NY) **22166**
Tax News (New York, NY) *Ceased*
Tax Notes (Arlington, VA) **31835**
Tax Notes International (Arlington, VA) **31836**
Tax Practice (Arlington, VA) *Unable to locate*
Tax Practice Adviser (Washington, DC) **5814**
Tax Practitioners Journal **33545***
Tax and Public Finance; International (New York, NY) **21939**
Tax Review; The Exempt Organization (Arlington, VA) **31792**
Tax Review; The Insurance (Arlington, VA) **31797**
Tax Strategies; Practical (New York, NY) **22591**
Tax Treaties (Riverwoods, IL) **9509**
Taxada Community TV Assn. (Vananda, BC, Can.) **35119**
Taxation for Accountants **22591***
Taxation Association Journal; American (Austin, TX) **29752**
Taxation; The Journal of (New York, NY) **22201**
Taxation; The Journal of California (New York, NY) **22017**
Taxation; Journal of Construction Accounting and (New York, NY) **22038**
Taxation; Journal of International (New York, NY) **22104**
Taxation; Journal of International Accounting, Auditing and (Kalamazoo, MI) **15239**
Taxation; The Journal of New York (New York, NY) **22143**
Taxation; Journal of State (New York, NY) **22192**
Taxation for Lawyers **22591***
Taxation of Mergers and Acquisitions (New York, NY) *Ceased*
Taxation Monthly; Corporate Business (New York, NY) **21500**
Taxes; Energy Prices and (Washington, DC) **5478**
Taxes—The Tax Magazine (Riverwoods, IL) **9510**
TAXI (New York, NY) *Ceased*
Taxi and Livery Management **13591***
Taxi News (Toronto, ON, Can.) **36753**
Taxicab Management **13591***
Taxpayer; The Wisconsin (Madison, WI) **33991**
TAXPRO Quarterly Journal (Appleton, WI) **33545**
Taylor Clarion (Taylor, NE) **18294**
Taylor County News (Butler, GA) **7146**
Steve #Taylor **24099***
The Taylorsville Times (Taylorsville, NC) **24255**
Tazewell County Free Press (Richlands, VA) **32426**
TBS (Atlanta, GA) *Unable to locate*
TCA (Greenville, MS) **16634**
TCA Cable (Amarillo, TX) **29720**
TCA Cable TV **1144***
TCA Cable TV **1133***
TCA Cable TV (Bentonville, AR) *Unable to locate*
TCA Cable-TV (Fayetteville, AR) **1133**
TCA Cable TV (Jonesboro, AR) **1204**
TCA Cable TV (Clovis, NM) **19838**
TCA Cable TV (Abilene, TX) **29670**
TCA Cable TV (Bryan, TX) *Unable to locate*
TCA Cable TV (Snyder, TX) **31118**
TCA Cable TV of Arkadelphia (Arkadelphia, AR) **1035**
TCA Cable TV of Big Spring (Big Spring, TX) *Unable to locate*
TCA Cable TV Inc. (Tyler, TX) **31222**
TCA Cable TV of Jonesboro (Jonesboro, LA) **12609**
TCA Cablevision (Bryan, TX) **29984**
TCA Cable Business (Columbia, TN) *Unable to locate*
TCI **33162***
TCI **21608***
TCI **12029***
TCI **15101***
TCI **7989***
TCI **10595***
T.C.I. **10511***
TCI **975***
TCI (La Junta, CO) *Unable to locate*
TCI (Littleton, CO) **4557**
TCI (Decatur, IL) **8714**
TCI (Hammond, IN) **10054**
TCI (Des Moines, IA) **10836**
TCI (Waterloo, IA) **11302**
TCI (Baton Rouge, LA) **12511**
TCI (St. Louis, MO) *Unable to locate*
TCI (Papillion, NE) *Unable to locate*
TCI (Santa Fe, NM) *Unable to locate*
TCI (Mamaroneck, NY) **20989**
TCI (Tulsa, OK) **26174**
TCI (Tulsa, OK) *Unable to locate*
TCI (Milwaukie, OR) *Unable to locate*
TCI (Portsmouth, RI) **28382**
TCI (Watertown, SD) **29026**
TCI of Ark. **1144***
TCI of Arlington (Arlington, TX) **29743**

TCI of Bloomington/Normal, Inc. (Normal, IL) **9307**
TCI Cable (Tracy, CA) **3947**
TCI Cable (Blackfoot, ID) *Unable to locate*
TCI Cable (Idaho Falls, ID) **7880**
TCI Cable (Park City, UT) **31389**
TCI Cable of New Castle County **5268***
TCI Cable of New Mexico (Farmington, NM) **19854**
TCI Cable of Ohio (Marietta, OH) *Unable to locate*
TCI Cable of Puerto Rico (Luquillo, PR) **28255**
TCI Cable TV (Crystal City, TX) *Unable to locate*
TCI Cable TV (Eagle Pass, TX) **30260**
TCI Cable TV (Fredericksburg, TX) *Unable to locate*
TCI Cable TV (Hebbronville, TX) **30436**
TCI Cable TV (Sweetwater, TX) *Unable to locate*
TCI Cable TV (Zapata, TX) **31315**
TCI Cable TV Inc. (Salmon, ID) **7976**
TCI Cablevision **15391***
TCI Cablevision **1204***
TCI Cablevision **18427***
TCI Cablevision **32749***
TCI Cablevision (Miami, FL) *Ceased*
TCI Cablevision (Royal Oak, MI) **15488**
TCI Cablevision (Gardnerville, NV) **18351**
TCI Cablevision (Hillsboro, OH) **25244**
TCI Cablevision (Del Rio, TX) **30230**
TCI Cablevision (New Braunfels, TX) **30864**
TCI Cablevision (San Marcos, TX) **31088**
TCI Cablevision (Tacoma, WA) **33162**
TCI Cablevision (Walla Walla, WA) **33191**
TCI Cablevision (Worland, WY) **34607**
TCI Cablevision of Abilene **29670***
TCI Cablevision of Alabama (Piedmont, AL) **428**
TCI Cablevision of Alabama, Inc. (Hoover, AL) **267**
TCI Cablevision of California Inc. Arcadia (City of Industry, CA) **1720**
TCI Cablevision of Casper (Casper, WY) **34494**
TCI Cablevision of Central Colorado (Aspen, CO) **4144**
TCI Cablevision of Colorado (Boulder, CO) *Unable to locate*
TCI Cablevision of Colorado (Pueblo, CO) **4612**
TCI Cablevision of Dallas, Inc. (Dallas, TX) **30218**
TCI Cablevision of Davis (Davis, CA) **1820**
TCI Cablevision of East Oklahoma **26026***
TCI Cablevision of Eastern Shore (Ocean City, MD) **13640**
TCI Cablevision of Florida (Daytona Beach, FL) *Unable to locate*
TCI Cablevision of Georgia **6954***
TCI Cablevision of Georgia (Columbus, GA) **7184**
TCI Cablevision of Great Falls, Inc. (Great Falls, MT) **17806**
TCI Cablevision of Idaho **7948***
TCI Cablevision of Los Angeles County (City of Industry, CA) **1721**
TCI Cablevision Metroplex **30386***
TCI Cablevision of Missouri (Columbia, MO) **17025**
TCI Cablevision of Missouri (Hannibal, MO) **17092**
TCI Cablevision of Missouri (St. Peters, MO) **17562**
TCI Cablevision of Montana (Helena, MT) **17833**
TCI Cablevision of Nebraska (Sidney, NE) *Unable to locate*
TCI Cablevision of Nevada, Inc. (Carson City, NV) **18334**
TCI Cablevision of North Texas Inc. (Gainesville, TX) **30378**
TCI Cablevision of Ohio (Warren, OH) **25618**
TCI Cablevision of Ohio Inc. (East Liverpool, OH) *Unable to locate*
TCI Cablevision of Oklahoma **25824***
TCI Cablevision of Oklahoma (Alva, OK) **25740**
TCI Cablevision of Oregon **26388***
TCI Cablevision of Oregon (Eugene, OR) **26350**
TCI Cablevision of Oregon (Medford, OR) **26433**
TCI Cablevision of Oregon (Portland, OR) **26547**
TCI Cablevision of Oregon, Inc. (Burns, OR) **26262**
TCI Cablevision of South Dakota (Rapid City, SD) **28952**
TCI Cablevision of Southeast Washington (Kennewick, WA) **32795**
TCI Cablevision of Southwest Texas **31228***
TCI Cablevision of Stillwater **26083***
TCI Cablevision of Tacoma, Inc. (Tacoma, WA) *Unable to locate*
TCI Cablevision of Texas, Inc. (Beaumont, TX) **29912**
TCI Cablevision of Texas Inc. (The Colony, TX) *Unable to locate*
TCI Cablevision of Texas, Inc. (Corpus Christi, TX) **30099**
TCI Cablevision of Texas, Inc. (Galveston, TX) *Unable to locate*
TCI Cablevision of The Metroplex **30386***
TCI Cablevision of Tualatin Valley (Beaverton, OR) **26239**
TCI Cablevision of Utah, Inc. (Layton, UT) **31344**
TCI Cablevision of Utah, Inc. (Provo, UT) *Unable to locate*
TCI Cablevision of Utah, Inc. (Sandy, UT) *Unable to locate*

TCI Cablevision of Washington (Bellingham, WA) *Unable to locate*
TCI Cablevision of West Oakland County (Walled Lake, MI) **15656**
TCI Cablevision of Wisconsin **33992***
TCI Cablevision of Wisconsin **34299***
TCI Cablevision of Wyoming (Cheyenne, WY) **34511**
TCI Cablevision of Wyoming (Laramie, WY) **34558**
TCI of California (Englewood, CA) **1887**
TCI of Central Indiana (Anderson, IN) *Unable to locate*
TCI of Colorado (Englewood, CO) **4422**
TCI of Council Bluffs (Council Bluffs, IA) **10729**
TCI of Eastern Iowa **10997***
TCI of Eastern Iowa (Burlington, IA) **10646**
TCI of Eastern Iowa (Clinton, IA) **10715**
TCI of Eastern Iowa (Iowa City, IA) **10997**
TCI of Fort Collins (Fort Collins, CO) **4444**
TCI of Greensburg (Greensburg, PA) **26957**
TCI of Hamilton **19672***
TCI Hawaiian Islands (Kahului, HI) **7764**
TCI of Illinois (McHenry, IL) **9167**
TCI of Illinois, Inc. **9040***
TCI of Illinois, Inc. (Schaumburg, IL) **9593**
TCI of Indiana (New Castle, IN) **10343**
TCI of Indiana, Inc. (Bloomington, IN) **9855**
TCI of Iowa (Cedar Rapids, IA) **10684**
TCI of Iowa (Dubuque, IA) **10853**
TCI of Kansas Inc. **11674***
TCI of Kansas, Inc. **11636***
TCI of Kansas, Inc. (Salina, KS) **11792**
TCI of Kansas, Inc. (Topeka, KS) *Unable to locate*
T.C.I. of Lexington, Inc. **12179***
TCI of Louisiana **12870***
TCI of Louisiana (Baker, LA) **12479**
TCI of Louisiana (Lake Charles, LA) *Unable to locate*
TCI Media Services **16312***
TCI of Nantucket (Nantucket, MA) **14344**
TCI of New York (Buffalo, NY) **20394**
TCI of North Central Kentucky (Harrodsburg, KY) *Unable to locate*
TCI of North Dakota (Minot, ND) *Unable to locate*
TCI of North Dakota, Inc. (Grand Forks, ND) **24465**
TCI of Northern New Jersey (Oakland, NJ) **19386**
TCI of NY **20008***
TCI Oakland (Oakland, CA) **2706**
TCI of Ohio (Columbiana, OH) *Unable to locate*
TCI of Oklahoma (Muskogee, OK) **25926**
TCI of Oregon **26517***
TCI of Overland Park, Inc. (Overland Park, KS) *Unable to locate*
TCI of Pennsylvania, Inc. **27857***
TCI of Pennsylvania Inc. (Kane, PA) **27104**
TCI Radcliff Inc. (Radcliff, KY) **12380**
TCI, San Francisco System (San Francisco, CA) **3506**
TCI of Seattle, Inc. (Seattle, WA) *Unable to locate*
TCI of South Florida (Miami, FL) **6395**
TCI of Southern Minnesota **16530***
TCI Spokane (Spokane, WA) **33138**
TCI of Texas - Pasadena Office (Pasadena, TX) **30915**
TCI of Virginia, Inc. (Chesapeake, VA) *Unable to locate*
TCI of West Virginia (New Martinsville, WV) *Unable to locate*
TCI of West Virginia (Parkersburg, WV) **33422**
TCI of West Virginia (Webster Springs, WV) **33487**
TCI of West Virginia (Weston, WV) *Unable to locate*
TCI of West Virginia, Inc. (Bridgeport, OH) **24707**
(TCJ) Tribal College Journal of American Indian Higher Education (Mancos, CO) **4572**
TCL (Evansville, IN) **9937**
TCL (Biloxi, MS) **16563**
TCL Telecable (Beckley, WV) *Unable to locate*
TCP/SNA Update (Westminster, CO) **4668**
T+D Magazine (Alexandria, VA) **31740**
TD & T **12238***
TDR: The Drama Review (Cambridge, MA) **14105**
Tea and Coffee Trade Journal (New York, NY) **22816**
TEACH Magazine (Toronto, ON, Can.) **36754**
Teacher; American (Washington, DC) **5346**
Teacher; The American Biology (Reston, VA) **32359**
Teacher; American Music (Cincinnati, OH) **24771**
Teacher in the Church Today (Nashville, TN) *Ceased*
Teacher Education; Journal of (Des Moines, IA) **10801**
Teacher Education; Journal of Industrial (Knoxville, TN) **29276**
Teacher Education; Journal of Music (Columbus, OH) **25026**
Teacher Education Journal; National Forum of (Lake Charles, LA) **12643**
Teacher Education; Journal of Technology & (Norfolk, VA) **32289**
Teacher Education Quarterly (San Francisco, CA) **3450**

Teacher Education and Special Education (Cincinnati, OH) **24821**
The Teacher Educator (Muncie, IN) **10329**
Teacher; Feminist (Eau Claire, WI) **33669**
Teacher; Green (Toronto, ON, Can.) **36609**
Teacher Librarian (Seattle, WA) **33034**
Teacher Magazine (Bethesda, MD) **13383**
Teacher; The Mathematics (Reston, VA) **32403**
Teacher; The New York (Albany, NY) **20001**
Teacher; The Physics (Boone, NC) **23655**
Teacher; The Science (Arlington, VA) **31829**
Teacher; The Technology (Reston, VA) **32420**
Teachers Association Journal; Chinese Language (Honolulu, HI) **7684**
Teachers College Record (New York, NY) **22817**
Teachers in Focus Magazine (Colorado Springs, CO) *Ceased*
Teacher's Voice **14988***
Teaching in the Addictions; Journal of (Binghamton, NY) **20201**
Teaching Anthropology; SACC Notes— (Arlington, VA) **31826**
Teaching and Change (Thousand Oaks, CA) *Unable to locate*
Teaching Children Mathematics (Reston, VA) **32417**
Teaching Elementary Physical Education (Champaign, IL) **8220**
Teaching of English; Research in the (Urbana, IL) **9717**
Teaching English in the Two-Year College (Urbana, IL) **9720**
Teaching Exceptional Children (Chestnut Hill, MA) **14134**
Teaching History: A Journal of Methods (Point Lookout, MO) **17354**
Teaching in International Business; Journal of (Middletown, PA) **27259**
Teaching; Journal of College Science (Arlington, VA) **31801**
Teaching; Journal on Excellence in College (Oxford, OH) **25456**
Teaching; Journal of Research in Science (Hoboken, NJ) **19045**
Teaching/K-8 (Norwalk, CT) **5075**
Teaching; Language (New York, NY) **22233**
Teaching & Learning (Grand Forks, ND) **24457**
Teaching and Learning in Medicine (Springfield, IL) **9643**
Teaching Librarian (Toronto, ON, Can.) **36755**
Teaching in the Middle School; Mathematics- (Reston, VA) **32404**
Teaching Music (Reston, VA) **32418**
Teaching Philosophy (Oxford, OH) **25461**
Teaching of Psychology (Kennesaw, GA) **7355**
Teaching Secondary Physical Education (Champaign, IL) *Ceased*
Teaching in Social Work; Journal of (New York, NY) **22202**
Teaching Sociology (Washington, DC) **5815**
Teaching Theatre (Cincinnati, OH) **24822**
Teaching in Travel & Tourism; Journal of (Binghamton, NY) **20202**
The Teague Chronicle (Teague, TX) **31176**
Teak Roundup (Sardis, BC, Can.) **35087**
Team Licensing Business Magazine (Phoenix, AZ) *Ceased*
Team Sports Business (Phoenix, AZ) *Ceased*
TeamRehab Report (Malibu, CA) *Unable to locate*
The Teamster (Washington, DC) **5816**
Teamster; Oregon (Portland, OR) **26494**
Teaneck Suburbanite (Teaneck, NJ) **19610**
TEC Cosmetology Instruction (Falls Church, VA) *Ceased*
The Tech (Cambridge, MA) **14106**
The Tech (Rapid City, SD) **28933**
Tech Center News (Warren, MI) **15662**
Tech Collegian (Montgomery, WV) **33387**
Tech Directions (Ann Arbor, MI) **14770**
Tech Exec (Loveland, CO) *Ceased*
Tech Gazette (Frederick, MD) *Ceased*
Tech Market South (Atlanta, GA) *Unable to locate*
Tech Minnesota (St. Paul, MN) *Ceased*
Tech News (Worcester, MA) **14689**
Tech News (Southfield, MI) **15549**
Tech Notes (Atlanta, GA) *Unable to locate*
The Tech Talk (Ruston, LA) **12807**
Tech Topics (Atlanta, GA) **7050**
Teche News (St. Martinville, LA) **12814**
TechLINKS (Atlanta, GA) **7051**
Technical Analysis of Stocks & Commodities (Seattle, WA) **33035**
Technical Communication (Arlington, VA) *Unable to locate*
Technical Communication Quarterly (St. Paul, MN) **16410**
Technical Education Association Journal; American (Wahpeton, ND) **24547**
Technical Employment News (Austin, TX) *Ceased*
Technical Physics (College Park, MD) **13441**

Textile Maintenance Reporter (Austin, TX) *Ceased*
The Textile Museum Journal (Washington, DC) **5821**
Textile News; Southern (Charlotte, NC) **23754**
Textile Products & Processes (Atlanta, GA) *Ceased*
Textile Rental Magazine (Alexandria, VA) **31744**
Textile Research Journal (Princeton, NJ) **19473**
Textile Technology Digest (Charlottesville, VA) **31941**
Textile & Text (New York, NY) *Ceased*
Textile World (Atlanta, GA) **7054**
Textile World Latina (Atlanta, GA) **7055**
Textiles; LDB Interior (New York, NY) **22241**
Textiles; Marine (St. Paul, MN) **16386**
Textiles Panamericanos (Greenville, SC) **28627**
Textiles Today; Home (New York, NY) **21814**
Textlinguistics; Journal of Translation and (Dallas, TX) **30164**
Textures *Ceased*
TFR (San Diego, CA) *Ceased*
(TFTJ); Turn For The Judges (Houston, TX) **30537**
TG Magazine (Toronto, ON, Can.) **36757**
TG/Teen Generation **36757***
Thalia (St. Louis, MO) **17523**
Thamesana (New London, CT) *Ceased*
Thamesville Herald (Thamesville, ON, Can.) **36432**
Thanatos (Tallahassee, FL) **6739**
That's Country Magazine (Costa Mesa, CA) *Unable to locate*
Thayer News **17648***
The-A-Ki-Ki (Bourbonnais, IL) **8095**
the Chronicle (Barton, VT) **31493**
T.H.E. Journal (Tustin, CA) *Unable to locate*
(The Lights of Homeland); Teviskes Ziburiai (Mississauga, ON, Can.) **36089**
THE LINE (Victorville, CA) *Ceased*
the new renaissance (Arlington, MA) **13821**
THE PRESS Magazine (Greenwood Village, CO) **4506**
(The Smoke) Signal (Paducah, KY) **12340**
Theater (New Haven, CT) **5003**
A Theater of Blood (Sylmar, CA) **3838**
Theater; Home (Los Angeles, CA) **2293**
Theater Journal; Asian (Brooklyn, NY) **20297**
Theater Magazine; Preview (Burbank, CA) **1623**
Theatre; American (New York, NY) **21207**
Theatre Design & Technology (Louisville, KY) **12238**
Theatre/Etudes Theatrales; Essays in (Guelph, ON, Can.) **35862**
Theatre History in Canada **36758***
Theatre History Studies (Pella, IA) **11152**
Theatre Journal (Baltimore, MD) *Unable to locate*
Theatre Journal; Missouri Speech & (Warrensburg, MO) **17667**
Theatre Journal; Youth (Tempe, AZ) **918**
Theatre Quarterly; New (New York, NY) **22436**
Theatre Research in Canada/Recherches Theatrales Au Canada (Toronto, ON, Can.) **36758**
Theatre Review; Canadian (Guelph, ON, Can.) **35859**
Theatre Review; Latin American (Lawrence, KS) **11562**
Theatre Topics (Amherst, MA) **13806**
Theatrical Faces Magazine **26626***
THEATRUM (Toronto, ON, Can.) *Unable to locate*
theIndian (Westland, MI) **15681**
Their World (New York, NY) *Ceased*
Thema (Metairie, LA) **12679**
Theodore Roosevelt Association Journal (Oyster Bay, NY) **23071**
Theological Quarterly; Concordia (Fort Wayne, IN) **9966**
Theological Quarterly; Lexington (Lexington, KY) **12174**
Theological Review; Greek Orthodox (Brookline, MA) **14019**
Theological Review; Harvard (Cambridge, MA) **14067**
Theological Society; Journal of the Evangelical (Wake Forest, NC) **24261**
THEOLOGICAL STUDIES (Washington, DC) *Unable to locate*
Theologique et Philosophique; Laval (Quebec, QC, Can.) **37286**
Theology Digest (St. Louis, MO) **17524**
Theology; Journal of Psychology and (La Mirada, CA) **2126**
Theology; Philosophy & (Milwaukee, WI) **34093**
Theology; Quartz Hill Journal of (Quartz Hill, CA) **2868**
Theology Today (Princeton, NJ) **19474**
Theoretical and Experimental Chemistry (New York, NY) **22826**
Theoretical Foundations of Chemical Engineering (New York, NY) **22827**
Theoretical and Mathematical Physics (New York, NY) **22828**
Theoretical Physics; International Journal of (New York, NY) **21923**
Theoretical Population Biology (San Diego, CA) **3278**
Theoria (New York, NY) **22829**
Theory of Computing Systems (New York, NY) **22830**

Theory Construction Testing; Journal of (Lisle, IL) **9111**
Theory & Event (Baltimore, MD) **13253**
Theory into Practice (Columbus, OH) **25064**
Theory and Practice of Object Systems (Hoboken, NJ) *Ceased*
Theory of Probability and Its Applications (Philadelphia, PA) **27704**
Theory of Probability & Mathematical Statistics (Providence, RI) **28425**
Theory and Research in Social Education (Binghamton, NY) **20219**
Theosophical History (Yorba Linda, CA) **4119**
Theosophist; Canadian (Burks Falls, ON, Can.) **35713**
Theosophy (Los Angeles, CA) **2412**
Therapeutic Drug Carrier Systems; Critical Reviews in (New York, NY) **21520**
Therapeutic Drug Monitoring (Baltimore, MD) **13254**
Therapeutic Recreation Journal (Ashburn, VA) **31855**
Therapeutics; Clinical Pharmacology and (St. Louis, MO) **17423**
Therapeutics; Journal of Cannabis (Binghamton, NY) **20165**
Therapeutics; Journal of Ocular Pharmacology and (Larchmont, NY) **20918**
Therapeutics; Journal of Pharmacology & Experimental (Bethesda, MD) **13355**
Therapeutics and Oncology; Journal of Experimental (Malden, MA) **14294**
Therapies; Alternative & Complementary (Larchmont, NY) **20888**
Therapies; Journal of Heart-Centered (Issaquah, WA) **32785**
Therapy; The American Journal of Occupational (Bethesda, MD) **13301**
Therapy; Contemporary Family (New York, NY) **21493**
Therapy Forum; Occupational (Wayne, PA) **28134**
Therapy in Geriatrics; Physical & Occupational (Bronx, NY) **20280**
Therapy in Health Care; Occupational (Greenville, NC) **23968**
Therapy Journal; Aquatic (Fort Mill, SC) **28611**
Therapy; Journal of Brief (New York, NY) **22014**
Therapy; Journal of Child and Adolescent Group (New York, NY) **22022**
Therapy; Journal of Feminist Family (Fort Collins, CO) **4435**
Therapy; Journal of Hand (Philadelphia, PA) **27530**
Therapy; Journal of Imago Relationship (Madison, CT) **4934**
Therapy; Journal of Music (Silver Spring, MD) **13731**
Therapy in Mental Health; Occupational (Binghamton, NY) **20209**
Therapy News; Family (Washington, DC) **5491**
Therapy in Pediatrics; Physical and Occupational (Binghamton, NY) **20210**
Therapy; PsycSCAN: Behavior Analysis & (Washington, DC) **5745**
Therapy; PT, Magazine of Physical (Alexandria, VA) **31731**
Therapy Today; Athletic (Champaign, IL) **8181**
Therapy; Women & (Binghamton, NY) **20221**
Thermal Analysis and Calorimetry; Journal of (Hoboken, NJ) **19050**
Thermal Analysis and Calorimetry; Journal of (New York, NY) **22204**
Thermal Belt News Journal **23792***
Thermal Spray Technology; Journal of (Stony Brook, NY) **23371**
Thermal Stresses; Journal of (Naples, FL) **6442**
Thermophysics and Heat Transfer; Journal of (Reston, VA) **32398**
Thermophysics; International Journal of (New York, NY) **21924**
Thermophysics; Journal of Engineering Physics and (New York, NY) **22064**
TheRomantic.com (Cary, NC) **38095**
Thetford Video, Inc. (Thetford Mines, QC, Can.) *Unable to locate*
Thi Truong Tu Do (San Jose, CA) *Unable to locate*
Thief River Falls Times (Thief River Falls, MN) **16468**
Thielensiat (Greenville, PA) **26959**
Thiensville Courant; Mequon- (New Berlin, WI) **34178**
Things From Nowhere (Indianapolis, IN) *Unable to locate*
Thinking (Upper Montclair, NJ) **19694**
Third Coast (Kalamazoo, MI) **15245**
Third World News (Washington, DC) *Unable to locate*
Third World Studies; Journal of (Americus, GA) **6922**
The Thirteen Towns (Fosston, MN) **15908**
13th Moon (Albany, NY) **20005**
30 Days (San Francisco, CA) *Ceased*
39 Plus (Asheville, NC) *Unable to locate*
33 Metal Producing (Cleveland, OH) **24956**
33 Metal Producing—Nonferrous Edition (Cleveland, OH) *Ceased*
32 Pages (Chicago, IL) *Ceased*
This is Alaska (Anchorage, AK) *Ceased*

This Country Canada (Dunrobin, ON, Can.) *Unable to locate*
This is Indianapolis (Indianapolis, IN) **10174**
This is Laguna (Laguna Beach, CA) *Unable to locate*
This Magazine (Toronto, ON, Can.) *Unable to locate*
This Old House (New York, NY) **22831**
This Old Truck **25691***
This People (Provo, UT) *Unable to locate*
This Side of 60 (North Newton, KS) **38096**
This Week **36410***
This Week **11370***
This Week **7793***
This Week **1479***
This Week (Honolulu, HI) **7723**
This Week (Pittsford, NY) *Unable to locate*
This Week (Albany, OR) **26207**
This Week (Lansdale, PA) **27160**
This Week (London, ON, Can.) *Unable to locate*
This Week; Barry's Bay (Barry's Bay, ON, Can.) **35666**
This Week in Bayonne (Jersey City, NJ) **19146**
This Week Big Island (Honolulu, HI) **7724**
This Week in Business (Montreal, QC, Can.) *Ceased*
This Week Buyer's Guide (Northern Sonoma County Edition) (Walnut Creek, CA) *Ceased*
This Week in Chicago/Key Magazine (Chicago, IL) *Unable to locate*
This Week in Cleveland Magazine (Cleveland, OH) **24957**
This Week in East Metro **7200***
This Week in Fort Lauderdale (Miami Shores, FL) *Ceased*
This Week in Jersey City (Jersey City, NJ) **19147**
This Week Kauai (Honolulu, HI) **7725**
This Week Life & Times (Lakeville, MN) **15996**
This Week in the Madawaska Valley **35666***
This Week Magazine (Wilsonville, OR) *Ceased*
This Week in Marissa (Marissa, IL) *Ceased*
This Week Marketplace (Yorkton, SK, Can.) **37598**
This Week Maui (Honolulu, HI) *Unable to locate*
This Week; Moose Jaw (Moose Jaw, SK, Can.) **37501**
This Week New Orleans (New Orleans, LA) **12757**
This Week Oahu (Honolulu, HI) **7726**
This Week in Peachtree City (Norcross, GA) *Unable to locate*
This Week in the Piedmont Triad (Greensboro, NC) *Ceased*
This Week Publications (Waukesha, WI) **34412**
This Week; Sault Ste. Marie (Sault Sainte Marie, ON, Can.) **36369**
This Week in South Florida (Hollywood, FL) *Ceased*
This Week of Western North Carolina (Asheville, NC) **23634**
Thoi Bao (San Jose, CA) **3543**
Thoi Luan (Los Angeles, CA) *Unable to locate*
Thomas Jefferson Law Review (San Diego, CA) **3279**
The Thomas Tribune (New York, NY) **22832**
Thomaston Express (Thomaston, CT) **5174**
Thomaston Times (Thomaston, GA) **7585**
The Thomasville Times (Thomasville, AL) **470**
The Thomist (Washington, DC) **5823**
The Thompson Courier-Rake Register (Thompson, IA) **11266**
Thompson Nickel Belt News (Thompson, MB, Can.) **35301**
Thomson News Service (Washington, DC) *Ceased*
Thora-Zine Magazine (Austin, TX) *Ceased*
Thoracic Anesthesia Journal; Cardiovascular and (Baltimore, MD) **13142**
Thoracic and Cardiovascular Surgery; Internet Journal of (Sugar Land, TX) **31163**
Thoracic and Cardiovascular Surgery; The Journal of (New York, NY) **22205**
Thoracic and Cardiovascular Surgery; Operative Techniques in (Naples, FL) **6448**
Thoracic and Cardiovascular Surgery; Seminars in (Naples, FL) **6449**
Thoracic & Cardiovascular Surgery; Seminars in (Boston, MA) **13959**
Thoracic Imaging; Journal of (Baltimore, MD) **13203**
Thoreau Quarterly (Minneapolis, MN) *Ceased*
The Thornhill Liberal **36344***
Thornhill Post (Toronto, ON, Can.) **36759**
Thorny Locust (Kansas City, MO) **17198**
Thorold News (Thorold, ON, Can.) **36435**
The Thoroughbred of California **1427***
Thoroughbred; Mid-Atlantic (Timonium, MD) **13758**
Thoroughbred Record (Lexington, KY) *Ceased*
Thoroughbred Times (Lexington, KY) **12178**
Thorp Cablevision **34368***
Thorp Courier (Thorp, WI) **34367**
Thought (Bronx, NY) *Ceased*
Thought & Action (Washington, DC) **5823**
Thought; Journal of (San Francisco, CA) **3385**
Thoughts for All Seasons (Miami, FL) **6384**
Thousand Islands Sun (Alexandria Bay, NY) **20022**
Thousand Oaks Star **4003***
THRASHER (San Francisco, CA) **3452**

THRASHER Skateboard Magazine 3452*
Threads (Newtown, CT) 5046
Threat Assessment; Journal of (Binghamton, NY) 20204
3 & 4 Wheel Action 3979*
The Three Lakes News (Eagle River, WI) 33663
Three Rivers Chronicle (Parma, ID) *Unable to locate*
Three Rivers Commercial-News (Three Rivers, MI) 15592
Three Village Herald (East Setauket, NY) 20556
The Three Village Times (Elmont, NY) 20582
3Com Enterprise (Austin, TX) *Ceased*
3D Artist (Santa Fe, NM) *Ceased*
The Threepenny Review (Berkeley, CA) 1564
Thresholds in Education (DeKalb, IL) 8741
Thrif-T-Nickel Weekly News-Tab (Ottawa, IL) 9391
Thrifty Nickel (Falls Church, VA) 32058
Thrifty Nickel Want Ads (Evansville, IN) 9936
Thrifty Nickel Want Ads (Springfield, MO) *Unable to locate*
Thrifty Nickel Want Ads (Abilene, TX) 29655
Thrifty Nickel Want Ads (Lubbock, TX) 30719
Thrifty Nickel Want Ads (Texarkana, TX) *Unable to locate*
Thrifty Reporter (Windsor Locks-Suffield Edition) (Rockville, CT) *Unable to locate*
Thrifty Scot Shoppers Guide (Mapleton, MN) *Ceased*
Thrombosis/Hemostasis; Clinical and Applied (Baltimore, MD) 13145
Thrombosis and Hemostasis; Seminars in (New York, NY) 22727
Thrombosis Research (New York, NY) 22833
Thrombosis, and Vascular Biology; Arteriosclerosis, (Iowa City, IA) 10969
Through the Gears Trucking Magazine (Anniston, AL) 16
Thrut for Educational Leadership 3005*
The Thumb Blanket (Bad Axe, MI) 14786
Thunder Bay Business (Thunder Bay, ON, Can.) 36439
Thunder Bay Guest Magazine (Thunder Bay, ON, Can.) 36440
Thunder Bay Historical Museum Society, Papers and Records (Thunder Bay, ON, Can.) 36441
Thunder Bay Life (Thunder Bay, ON, Can.) 36442
Thunder Bay Post (Thunder Bay, ON, Can.) 36443
Thunder Bay Real Estate News (Thunder Bay, ON, Can.) 36444
Thunderbird International Business Review (Hoboken, NJ) 19119
Thunderbolt (Glendale, AZ) 716
Thundercurrent 20031*
Thurmont Gazette; Walkersville/ (Frederick, MD) 13525
Thursday Magazine 24109*
The Thursday Post (Lindsay, ON, Can.) *Ceased*
The Thurston County Senior News 32860*
The Thurston-Mason Senior News (Olympia, WA) 32860
Thyroid (Larchmont, NY) 20927
TI Computing News (Austin, TX) *Ceased*
Tichenor Media System (Dallas, TX) *Unable to locate*
Tick-borne Diseases; Journal of Spirochetal and (Thorofare, NJ) 19627
The Ticker (New York, NY) 22834
Ticonderoga; Times of (Elizabethtown, NY) 20566
Tideland News (Swansboro, NC) 24250
Tidewater Motorists (Norfolk, VA) *Unable to locate*
The Tidewater News (Franklin, VA) 32080
Tidewater Parent (Virginia Beach, VA) 32590
Tidewater Review (Easton, MD) *Ceased*
Tidewater Virginia Families (Williamsburg, VA) 32619
The Tidings (Los Angeles, CA) 2413
The Tidings (Ashland, OR) 26218
The Tie 12237*
TIE (The International Educator) (Cummaquid, MA) 14151
Tiefort Telegraph (Fort Irwin, CA) 1925
TIEMPO (Waco, TX) 31254
Tiempo Latino News 3457*
Tiempo Latino News 3456*
Tiempo de New York; El (Jackson Heights, NY) 20827
Tierra Grande (College Station, TX) 30055
TIES Magazine (Ewing, NJ) 18805
Tiftarea Shopper (Tifton, GA) 7598
The Tifton Gazette (Tifton, GA) 7599
Tifton Worth Turner Advertiser (Tifton, GA) *Unable to locate*
Tigard Times (Tigard, OR) 26596
Tigard/Tualatin Times 26596*
The Tiger (Clemson, SC) 28535
Tiger Beat Magazine (New York, NY) 22835
Tiger Tales (Santa Ana, CA) *Unable to locate*
Tight (Guerneville, CA) *Ceased*
The Tightwad Gazette *Ceased*
Tikkun Magazine (Berkeley, CA) 1565
The Tilbury Times (Tecumseh, ON, Can.) *Unable to locate*

Tilden Citizen (Tilden, NE) 18298
Tile & Decorative Surfaces (New York, NY) 22836
Tile Design; Contemporary Stone and (Paramus, NJ) 19401
Tile World (Paramus, NJ) *Unable to locate*
Till-Cable TV Ltd. (Saint Thomas, ON, Can.) *Unable to locate*
Tillamook County Shopping Guide (Tillamook, OR) *Unable to locate*
Tiller; Arvin (Shafter, CA) 3756
The Tillsonburg News (Tillsonburg, ON, Can.) 36450
TILT-UP (Provo, UT) *Ceased*
Timber Bulletin (Bellevue, WA) 32668
Timber Equipment Trader (Wadley, GA) *Ceased*
Timber Frame Homes (Chantilly, VA) *Unable to locate*
Timber Framing (Newbury, VT) 31571
Timber Harvesting (Montgomery, AL) 379
Timber Lake Topic (Timber Lake, SD) 29003
Timber Processing (Montgomery, AL) 380
Timber Processing Industry 380*
Timber Processor; Northern Logger and (Old Forge, NY) 23037
The Timber Producer (Rhinelander, WI) 34286
Timber/West 32746*
Timber West (Edmonds, WA) 32746
The Timberjay (Tower, MN) *Unable to locate*
Timbertimes (Hillsboro, OR) 26373
Time (New York, NY) 22837
Time; About. (Rochester, NY) 23207
Time (Asia) (New York, NY) 22838
Time (Atlantic) (New York, NY) *Unable to locate*
Time (Canada) (Toronto, ON, Can.) 36760
Time Data Syndicate (Manchester, NH) 38097
Time Digital (New York, NY) *Ceased*
Time; Greenwich (Greenwich, CT) 4874
Time International (New York, NY) 22839
Time for Kids (New York, NY) 22840
(Time); Laiks (Brooklyn, NY) 20329
Time (Latin America) (New York, NY) *Unable to locate*
Time Out New York (New York, NY) 22841
Time for Rhyme (Spiritwood, SK, Can.) *Unable to locate*
Time Table (Lenox, IA) 11036
Time Travel Magazine (Calgary, AB, Can.) *Ceased*
Time Warner 12863*
Time Warner (Dothan, AL) 188
Time Warner (Albany, NY) 20008
Time Warner (Charlotte, NC) 23760
Time Warner (Memphis, TN) 29385
Time Warner—Birmingham Division 100*
Time Warner Cable 17*
Time Warner Cable 880*
Time Warner Cable 6483*
Time Warner Cable 27904*
Time Warner Cable 26636*
Time Warner Cable (Bakersfield, CA) 1476
Time Warner Cable (Canyon Country, CA) 1662
Time Warner Cable (Englewood, CO) 4423
Time Warner Cable (Indianapolis, IN) 10188
Time Warner Cable (Marion, IN) 10288
Time Warner Cable (Terre Haute, IN) 10492
Time Warner Cable (Portland, ME) 13020
Time Warner Cable (Foxboro, MA) 14190
Time Warner Cable (Farmington Hills, MI) 15022
Time Warner Cable (Taylor, MI) 15589
Time Warner Cable (Jackson, MS) 16714
Time Warner Cable (Auburn, NE) 17941
Time Warner Cable (Fairbury, NE) 18008
Time Warner Cable (Palisades Park, NJ) 19400
Time Warner Cable (Hornell, NY) 20754
Time Warner Cable (Staten Island, NY) 23366
Time Warner Cable (Syracuse, NY) 23433
Time Warner Cable (Fayetteville, NC) 23883
Time Warner Cable (Greensboro, NC) 23944
Time Warner Cable (Havelock, NC) 23979
Time Warner Cable (Raleigh, NC) 24160
Time Warner Cable (Salisbury, NC) 24216
Time Warner Cable (Winston-Salem, NC) 24325
Time Warner Cable (Salem, OH) 25507
Time Warner Cable (Florence, SC) 28604
Time Warner Cable (Myrtle Beach, SC) 28706
Time Warner Cable (West Columbia, SC) *Unable to locate*
Time Warner Cable (Memphis, TN) 29386
Time Warner Cable (Austin, TX) 29885
Time Warner Cable (Waco, TX) 31266
Time Warner Cable (Altoona, WI) 33523
Time Warner Cable (Greenfield, WI) 33766
Time Warner Cable (Kenosha, WI) 33874
Time Warner Cable (Kimberly, WI) 33883
Time Warner Cable (Milwaukee, WI) 34113
Time Warner Cable (Wauwatosa, WI) 34444
Time Warner Cable of Florida (Orlando, FL) 6512
Time Warner Cable Ithaca (Ithaca, NY) 20817
Time Warner Cable of Maine (Presque Isle, ME) 13036

Time Warner Cable of Monroe/Union County (Monroe, NC) *Unable to locate*
Time Warner Cable of Nashua (Nashua, NH) 18606
Time Warner Cable of New York City (Flushing, NY) 20615
Time Warner Cable of New York City (New York, NY) 22959
Time Warner Cable - San Diego (San Diego, CA) 3318
Time Warner Cable - Western Ohio Division (Lima, OH) 25298
Time Warner Communications (Garden Grove, CA) 1999
Time Warner Communications (Stamford, CT) *Unable to locate*
Time Warner Communications (Columbus, OH) 25071
Time Warner Communications (El Paso, TX) 30305
Time Warner Communications (Kerrville, TX) 30641
Time Warner Communications (Uvalde, TX) 31228
Time Warner-Orange County Division (Middletown, NY) 21082
Timekeepers 26798*
Timeline (Columbus, OH) 25065
Timely Tips (Battle Creek, MI) *Unable to locate*
Timepieces; Asian Sources (Phoenix, AZ) 791
The Times 7962*
The Times 32526*
The Times 36390*
Times 23523*
Times 26896*
Times 30280*
The Times 30076*
The Times 28730*
Times 28667*
The Times 19746*
The Times 16468*.
Times 16462*
The Times (Cottonwood, AZ) *Ceased*
The Times (Melbourne, AR) 1274
The Times (North Little Rock, AR) 1300
Times (Blackshear, GA) 7128
The Times (Gainesville, GA) 7298
Times (Okawville, IL) 9383
Times (Rushville, IL) 9558
Times (Frankfort, IN) 9999
The Times (Hammond, IN) 10053
Times (Hebron, IN) *Ceased*
The Times (Mooresville, IN) 10322
Times (Poseyville, IN) *Ceased*
The Times (Maysville, KY) *Unable to locate*
The Times (Shreveport, LA) 12820
Times (Gloucester, MA) 14211
The Times (Webster, MA) *Unable to locate*
The Times (Harbor Beach, MI) 15143
The Times (Comfrey, MN) 15812
Times (Monticello, MN) 16186
Times (O Fallon, MO) *Ceased*
The Times (Hillside, NJ) *Unable to locate*
The Times (Trenton, NJ) 19668
The Times (Thomasville, NC) 24256
The Times (Columbus, OH) 25066
The Times (Warren, OH) 25616
Times (Okmulgee, OK) *Unable to locate*
Times (Pryor, OK) 26049
Times (Brownsville, OR) 26258
TIMES: in harness (Harrisburg, PA) 27013
The Times (Port Royal, PA) *Unable to locate*
The Times (Pawtucket, RI) 28379
Times (Lake Preston, SD) 28880
The Times (Pierre, SD) 28923
Times (Springfield, SD) 28997
Times (Bellville, TX) 29914
Times (Brownsville, TX) *Unable to locate*
Times (Wheeler, TX) 31287
The Times (Waitsburg, WA) 33186
The Times (Appleton, WI) *Ceased*
Times (Walworth, WI) 34386
The Times (Westby, WI) 34450
The Times (Mackenzie, BC, Can.) 35011
The Times (Treherne, MB, Can.) 35305
The Times (Winnipeg, MB, Can.) 35352
The Times (Haliburton, ON, Can.) 35873
The Times (Niagara Falls, ON, Can.) 36111
The Times of Acadiana (Lafayette, LA) 12620
Times Advantage (Brazil, IN) 9870
Times Advertiser (Dayton, OH) *Ceased*
The Times Advertiser (Fredericktown, OH) *Ceased*
Times Advocate (West Salem, IL) 9751
Times-Advocate (Exeter, ON, Can.) 35828
The Times of the Americas (Washington, DC) *Ceased*
The Times-Argus (Barre, VT) 31488
The Times At The Jersey Shore (Ocean Grove, NJ) 19392
Times Bonanza and Goldfield News (Tonopah, NV) 18447
The Times (Centerville Bellbrook Edition) 24753*
Times Chronicle (Trenton, NJ) 19669
Times Chronicle (Jenkintown, PA) *Unable to locate*

Toxicology and Pharmacology; Regulatory (San Diego, CA) **3254**
Toxicology Toxin Reviews; Journal of (Minneapolis, MN) **16090**
Toxicology; Veterinary and Human (Manhattan, KS) **11630**
The Toy Book (New York, NY) **22850**
Toy Cars & Models (Iola, WI) **33848**
Toy Collectibles; Car (Canoga Park, CA) **1655**
Toy Collector Magazine; U.S. (Helena, MT) **17824**
Toy and Hobby World (New York, NY) *Unable to locate*
Toy Magazine; Toyfare, The (Congers, NY) **20491**
Toy Shop (Iola, WI) **33849**
Toy Tips (Beverly Hills, CA) **1578**
Toy Trade News *Unable to locate*
Toyfare, The Guide to Collectible Toys **20491***
Toyfare, The Toy Magazine (Congers, NY) **20491**
Toys & Games (North York, ON, Can.) **36132**
Tozai Times (Los Angeles, CA) *Unable to locate*
TPA Messenger **29841***
TPC Cable TV **28272***
TPJ—The Tube & Pipe Journal (Rockford, IL) **9534**
TPQ—The Tube & Pipe Quarterly **9534***
TPT 17 - Channel 17 (St. Paul, MN) **16425**
TPT 2 - Channel 2 (St. Paul, MN) **16426**
TQ (Lincoln, NE) *Ceased*
TQS Television Network (Montreal, QC, Can.) **37715**
Trace: AIGA Journal of Design (New York, NY) **22851**
Trace Elements in Experimental Medicine; The Journal of (Hoboken, NJ) **19051**
Trace and Microprobe Techniques; Journal of (New York, NY) **22206**
Traces of Indiana and Midwestern History (Indianapolis, IN) **10175**
Tracings (Holyoke, MA) **14241**
Track & Field News (Mountain View, CA) **2609**
Track and Running News; California (Chilmark, MA) **14138**
The Tracker (Richmond, VA) **32457**
TRACKS MAGAZINE (Lansing, MI) **15295**
Trackside (Enfield, CT) **4782**
Tract Messenger (White Bear Lake, MN) **16513**
Tractor; Implement & (Cedar Falls, IA) **10657**
Tracy Press (Tracy, CA) **3946**
Trade Association News **27707***
Trade and Commerce (Winnipeg, MB, Can.) **35353**
Trade; Emerging Markets Finance and (Armonk, NY) **20076**
Trade Fax (Iola, WI) **33850**
Trade with Italy (New York, NY) *Unable to locate*
Trade; Italy Canada (Toronto, ON, Can.) **36627**
Trade; Journal of Industry, Competition and (New York, NY) **22094**
Trade Journal; The International (Laredo, TX) **30669**
Trade; Journal of World (New York, NY) **22215**
The Trade News (Philadelphia, PA) **27707**
Trade News Service (Canandaigua, NY) **38102**
Trade Service Corp. (San Diego, CA) *Unable to locate*
Trade & Transactions (York, NE) **18320**
Tradeline's Exclusive Reports Online (Orinda, CA) **2727**
The Trademark Reporter (New York, NY) *Unable to locate*
Trademarks (Alexandria, VA) **31745**
Trader Express (Estevan, SK, Can.) **37466**
Traders Guide (Ebensburg, PA) **26860**
Traders Magazine (New York, NY) *Unable to locate*
Trader's Shopper's Guide (Cheyenne, WY) **34496**
Traders World (Springfield, MO) **17615**
TradeShow & Exhibit Manager (Santa Monica, CA) **3718**
Tradeshow Week (Los Angeles, CA) **2414**
The Tradesman (Lexington, NC) *Unable to locate*
Tradeswomen (San Francisco, CA) *Ceased*
Tradewinds **17783***
Tradewinds (Los Angeles, CA) **2415**
Tradin' Times (Rocky River, OH) **25501**
Trading Cards (Beverly Hills, CA) *Ceased*
Trading Perspectives (San Francisco, CA) *Unable to locate*
The Trading Post (Minot, ND) **24506**
The Trading Post (Rittman, OH) **25499**
Tradition Magazine (Anita, IA) **10604**
Traditional Building (Brooklyn, NY) **20349**
Traditional Home (Chicago, IL) **8587**
Traditional Quilter **19374***
Traditional Quiltworks **27291***
Traditions **5169***
Traffic Control; Journal of Air (Arlington, VA) **31800**
Traffic Law Reports (Warrensburg, MO) *Ceased*
Traffic Management **14405***
Traffic Safety (Itasca, IL) **9021**
Traffic World (Washington, DC) **5827**
The Trail (Tacoma, WA) **33153**
Trail/Beaver Valley/Salmo Pennywise (Kaslo, BC, Can.) **34987**

The Trail Blazer (Morehead, KY) **12304**
Trail Blazer (Plainview, TX) **30940**
Trail Blazer Competition Horseback Riding **856***
Trail Blazer Horseback Trail Riding (Prescott Valley, AZ) **856**
Trail Daily Times (Trail, BC, Can.) **35115**
Trail-Gazette (Estes Park, CO) **4424**
Trail and Landscape (Ottawa, ON, Can.) **36277**
Trail Rider Magazine (Medford, NJ) *Unable to locate*
Trail Riding; Trail Blazer Horseback (Prescott Valley, AZ) **856**
Trail Times **35115***
Trailblazer (Frisco, TX) **30372**
Trailer Boats Magazine (Carson, CA) **1677**
Trailer/Body Builders (Houston, TX) **30535**
Trailer Life (Ventura, CA) **4011**
Traill County Tribune (Mayville, ND) *Unable to locate*
The Trailmarker **10148***
The Trailrider (Elliot Lake, ON, Can.) **35803**
Trails; Wisconsin (Black Earth, WI) **35390**
Training and Conditioning (Ithaca, NY) **20815**
Training & Development **31740***
Training & Development Journal **31740***
Training; Journal of Athletic (Charlottesville, VA) **31933**
Training Magazine (Minneapolis, MN) *Unable to locate*
Training Media Review (Cambridge, MA) **14108**
Trains (Waukesha, WI) **34413**
Trait d'Union; Le (Montreal, QC, Can.) **37173**
Tranputer Communications (Hoboken, NJ) *Ceased*
Trans (New York, NY) **22852**
Trans America Syndicate (Chicago, IL) *Unable to locate*
Trans-Video Inc. (Northfield, VT) **31576**
Trans Video; Warner Cable; Warner Amex Cable **27904***
Trans-Vision de Danville Inc. (Danville, QC, Can.) *Unable to locate*
Transactional Analysis Bulletin **2701***
Transactional Analysis Journal (Oakland, CA) **2701**
Transactions **9589***
Transactions (Montreal, QC, Can.) *Ceased*
Transactions of the American Entomological Society (Philadelphia, PA) **27708**
Transactions of the American Fisheries Society (Bethesda, MD) **13385**
Transactions of the American Mathematical Society (Providence, RI) **28426**
Transactions of the American Microscopical Society **3684***
Transactions of the ASAE (St. Joseph, MI) **15514**
Transactions on Automatic Control; IEEE (Brookline, MA) **14020**
Transactions of the Charles S. Peirce Society (Buffalo, NY) *Ceased*
Transactions (Doklady) of the Russian Academy of Sciences **69***
Transactions on Industrial Electronics; IEEE (New York, NY) **21850**
Transactions on Information Systems **21140***
Transactions of the Kansas Academy of Science (Lawrence, KS) **11566**
Transactions of the Moscow Mathematical Society (Providence, RI) **28427**
Transactions of the Nebraska Academy of Sciences (Lincoln, NE) **18123**
Transactions of the Society for Computer Simulation **3283***
Transactions of the Society for Computer Simulation International (San Diego, CA) **3283**
Transactions and Studies of the College of Physicians of Philadelphia (Philadelphia, PA) **27709**
Transactions of The Society of Rheology **22179***
Transactor (Richmond Hill, ON, Can.) *Unable to locate*
Transactor for the Amiga (Richmond Hill, ON, Can.) *Unable to locate*
Transafrica Forum (Somerset, NJ) *Unable to locate*
TransCaucasus, A Chronology (Washington, DC) **5828**
The Transcript **28566***
Transcript (North Adams, MA) **14418**
Transcript (New Rockford, ND) **24524**
The Transcript (Delaware, OH) **25162**
The Transcript (Morrisville, VT) **31570**
Transcript-Bulletin Review **31479***
Transcript & Free Press (Glencoe, ON, Can.) **35848**
Transcript-Pacific Maramec Valley (Pacific, MO) *Unable to locate*
Transcript-Telegram (Holyoke, MA) *Ceased*
Transform Magazine (New York, NY) **22853**
Transformations (Worcester, MA) **14691**
Transforming Anthropology (Arlington, VA) **31837**
Transfusion (Minneapolis, MN) **16136**
Transfusion Medicine Reviews (Hamilton, ON, Can.) **35892**
Transgender Tapestry (Waltham, MA) **14604**
Transition (Cambridge, MA) **14109**

Transitions Abroad (Bennington, VT) **31495**
Translation (New York, NY) *Ceased*
Translations Index (Materials Park, OH) *Ceased*
Translog: Journal of Military Transportation Management (Alexandria, VA) **31746**
Translog, The Journal of Military Transportation Management (Pittsburgh, PA) *Ceased*
Transmission Digest (Springfield, MO) **17616**
Transmission and Distribution **11732***
Transmission and Distribution International **11732***
Transmission and Distribution World (Overland Park, KS) **11732**
Transnational Corporations (New York, NY) **22854**
Transnational Law; Vanderbilt Journal of (Nashville, TN) **29499**
Transnational Management Development; Journal of (Boston, MA) **13919**
Transortation Intermediary *Ceased*
TRANSPACIFIC (Malibu, CA) *Unable to locate*
Transplantation (New York, NY) **22855**
Transplantation; Dialysis & (Van Nuys, CA) **3987**
Transplantation/Implantation Today *Ceased*
Transplantation Proceedings (Philadelphia, PA) *Ceased*
Transplantation Reviews (Philadelphia, PA) **27710**
The Transponder **23291***
Transport par Camion; Guide du (Laval, QC, Can.) **37039**
Transport Fleet News (South Holland, IL) *Unable to locate*
Transport Management; Journal of Air (Burlington, MA) **14028**
Transport News of Tennessee **29496***
Transport Policy (Burlington, MA) **14034**
Transport Reviews (Philadelphia, PA) **27711**
Transport Routier (Etobicoke, ON, Can.) **35822**
Transport Technology Today (Cary, IL) **8170**
Transport Theory and Statistical Physics (Charlottesville, VA) **31942**
Transport Topics (Alexandria, VA) **31747**
Transportation; American Journal of (Quincy, MA) **14488**
Transportation Business (Toronto, ON, Can.) *Ceased*
Transportation & Distribution (Cleveland, OH) **24958**
Transportation Energy Research (Oak Ridge, TN) *Ceased*
Transportation Engineering; Journal of (Reston, VA) **32399**
Transportation Executive Update (Alexandria, VA) *Unable to locate*
Transportation Human Factors (Mahwah, NJ) **19206**
Transportation Infrastructure Issues with Maine **12895***
Transportation Interiors; Automotive & (Roswell, GA) **7514**
Transportation International; Lifting & (Richmond, VA) **32443**
Transportation Journal (Atlanta, GA) **7056**
Transportation; Journal of Advanced (Calgary, AB, Can.) **34650**
Transportation Journal; Defense (Alexandria, VA) **31664**
Transportation Law Journal (Pittsburgh, PA) *Ceased*
Transportation Leader (Kensington, MD) **13591**
Transportation & Logistics; Canadian (Toronto, ON, Can.) **36532**
Transportation Management; Translog: Journal of Military (Alexandria, VA) **31746**
Transportation Quarterly (Washington, DC) **5829**
Transportation Science (College Park, MD) **13443**
Transportation Technology News; Advanced (Norwalk, CT) **5049**
Transporter; Mid-America (Topeka, KS) **11834**
Transporter; Milk & Liquid Food (Appleton, WI) **33538**
Transporter; Modern Bulk (Houston, TX) **30508**
Transporter; Refrigerated (Houston, TX) **30522**
Transvision Cookshire Inc. (Lennoxville, QC, Can.) **37048**
Transvision Pare Inc. (Fleurimont, QC, Can.) *Unable to locate*
Transvision Plus (Granby, QC, Can.) *Unable to locate*
Transvision Sawyerville Inc. (Sherbrooke, QC, Can.) **37399**
TransWorld Skateboarding Magazine (Oceanside, CA) **2711**
TransWorld Snowboarding Magazine (Oceanside, CA) **2712**
The Transylvania Times (Brevard, NC) **23664**
Trap & Field (Indianapolis, IN) **10176**
Trapper; American (Riverton, WY) **34576**
The Trapper & Predator Caller (Iola, WI) **33851**
Trauma and Abuse Today (Lancaster, PA) *Unable to locate*
Trauma & Dissociation; Journal of (Binghamton, NY) **20205**
Trauma; Journal of (San Antonio, TX) **31036**
Trauma; Journal of Aggression, Maltreatment & (Binghamton, NY) **20162**

The Triangle (Philadelphia, PA) **27712**
The Triangle (St. Michael, AB, Can.) **34843**
Triangle Business Journal (Charlotte, NC) *Unable to locate*
Triangle City Facts (Raleigh, NC) *Ceased*
The Triangle Comic Review (Carrboro, NC) *Ceased*
Triangle Communication System, Inc. (Havre, MT) *Ceased*
Triangle Newcomer (Raleigh, NC) **24157**
Triangle News (Coronach, SK, Can.) **37460**
Triangle Pointer (Chapel Hill, NC) **23728**
Triangle Shoppers Guide (Mount Dora, FL) *Unable to locate*
Triathlete (Cardiff, CA) **1663**
Triathlon; Inside (Boulder, CO) **4171**
Triax Cablevision (Chillicothe, IL) **8671**
Triax Cablevision (Carmel, IN) *Ceased*
Triax Cablevision (Grand Rapids, MN) **15933**
Triax Cablevision USA (Milton, WV) *Unable to locate*
Triax Cablevision - Waseca (Waseca, MN) **16502**
Triax Midwest and Associates (Robinson, IL) *Unable to locate*
Tribal College Journal of American Indian Higher Education (TCJ) (Mancos, CO) **4572**
Tribal: The Magazine of Tribal Art (San Francisco, CA) **3454**
Tribology; Journal of (New York, NY) **22208**
Triboro Banner (Scranton, PA) **27964**
Tribune **30263***
Tribune **31003***
The Tribune **24253***
The Tribune **25096***
Tribune **25209***
Tribune **27235***
The Tribune **35908***
The Tribune **32735***
The Tribune (Mesa, AZ) **746**
The Tribune (Monument, CO) **4584**
The Tribune (Fort Pierce, FL) *Unable to locate*
The Tribune (Mascoutah, IL) *Unable to locate*
The Tribune (Ames, IA) **10594**
Tribune (Buffalo Center, IA) **10635**
Tribune (Harlan, IA) **10945**
Tribune (New Hampton, IA) *Unable to locate*
Tribune (Grand Haven, MI) **15085**
Tribune (Union City, MI) **15647**
Tribune (Albert Lea, MN) **15706**
Tribune (Lake Crystal, MN) *Unable to locate*
Tribune (Minnesota Lake, MN) **16166**
Tribune (Deer Lodge, MT) *Ceased*
The Tribune (Liverpool, NY) *Unable to locate*
The Tribune (Elkin, NC) **23867**
Tribune (Ironton, OH) **25253**
The Tribune (Jefferson, OH) **25266**
The Tribune (Mount Sterling, OH) **25398**
Tribune (Toronto, OH) *Ceased*
The Tribune (Bethany, OK) **25761**
Tribune (Throckmorton, TX) **31192**
Tribune (Trenton, TX) **31193**
Tribune (Charlottesville, VA) **31943**
The Tribune (Williams Lake, BC, Can.) **35243**
The Tribune (Campbellton, NB, Can.) **35383**
Tribune (Sturgeon Falls, ON, Can.) **36414**
The Tribune (Welland, ON, Can.) **36867**
Tribune (Gravelbourg, SK, Can.) **37471**
The Tribune Advertiser **23868***
Tribune Advertiser (Dillon, MT) **17783**
Tribune Business Weekly (South Bend, IN) **10460**
Tribune Canadienne Grecque; La (Montreal, QC, Can.) **37153**
Tribune Chronicle (Warren, OH) **25617**
Tribune Courier (Benton, KY) **11933**
Tribune-Courier (Ontario, OH) **25451**
Tribune-Democrat (Johnstown, PA) **27089**
Tribune Des Droits Humains; Human Rights Tribune/ (Ottawa, ON, Can.) **36249**
The Tribune/Express (Hawkesbury, ON, Can.) **35908**
Tribune Express Progres Watchman (Lachute, QC, Can.) **37030**
Tribune & Georgian (St. Marys, GA) **7524**
The Tribune Hopper **12802***
Tribune Keystone **34257***
Tribune; La (Sherbrooke, QC, Can.) **37393**
Tribune Media Services Inc. (Chicago, IL) **38104**
Tribune News (South Whitley, IN) **10469**
Tribune-Phonograph (Abbotsford, WI) **33517**
Tribune Plus (Rayne, LA) **12802**
Tribune-Press **15796***
Tribune Press Reporter (Glenwood City, WI) **33734**
Tribune-Progress (Bartlett, TX) **29889**
Tribune Radio Networks (Chicago, IL) **37670**
Tribune-Record-Gleaner (Loyal, WI) **33913**
Tribune-Review **25761***
Tribune-Review (Greensburg, PA) **26956**
Tribune Shopping News (New Lexington, OH) **25415**
Tribune-Star (Terre Haute, IN) **10490**
Tribune-Times (Simpsonville, SC) **28756**
The Tribune Weekender (Williams Lake, BC, Can.) **35244**

Tribuno del Pueblo **8528***
Tribute (Don Mills, ON, Can.) *Unable to locate*
Tricycle (New York, NY) **22866**
The Trident **9495***
TRIDENT (Halifax, NS, Can.) **35571**
The Trident of Delta Delta Delta (Arlington, TX) **29737**
Trident Tides (Bainbridge Island, WA) *Ceased*
Trillium Cable Communications **35665***
Trillium Communications (Port Elgin, ON, Can.) *Unable to locate*
Trillum Cable Communications **35976***
The Trimble Banner (Bedford, KY) **11931**
The Trinitonian (San Antonio, TX) *Unable to locate*
Trinity Broadcasting Network (TBN) (Santa Ana, CA) **37790**
Trinity Journal (Weaverville, CA) **4059**
Trinity Missions (Silver Spring, MD) *Ceased*
The Trinity Standard (Trinity, TX) **31194**
The Trinity Tripod (Rocky Hill, CT) **5107**
Triopia Tribune (Bluffs, IL) **8091**
The Triplicate (Crescent City, CA) **1788**
Tripod; The Trinity (Rocky Hill, CT) **5107**
Tripoli Leader (Tripoli, IA) **11274**
The Tripp Star-Ledger (Parkston, SD) **28913**
Trips (Redwood City, CA) *Unable to locate*
Trips (Santa Cruz, CA) *Unable to locate*
TriQuarterly (Evanston, IL) **8873**
Tristar Cable, Inc. (Salina, KS) **11793**
Triton Times **2120***
Triumfo-FM **28316***
Trivia Quotient (Madison, WI) *Ceased*
Troika (Weston, CT) **5209**
Trojan Banner **26046***
Trojan; Daily (Los Angeles, CA) **2252**
Trojan Family **2426***
Trojan Family Magazine; USC (Los Angeles, CA) **2426**
Trona Argonaut (Trona, CA) **3948**
Trophy Striper (Boone, NC) *Unable to locate*
Tropical Ecology; Journal of (New York, NY) **22209**
Tropical Fish Hobbyist (Neptune, NJ) **19320**
Tropical Lepidoptera (Gainesville, FL) **6159**
Tropolitan (Troy, AL) **474**
Trot (Mississauga, ON, Can.) **36090**
The Trottingbred (Gouverneur, NY) **20675**
Troubled Company Prospector (Frederick, MD) **13523**
Troubled Company Reporter (Frederick, MD) **13524**
Troublesome Creek Times (Hindman, KY) **12128**
Trout (Arlington, VA) **31838**
The Trout & Salmon Leader (Olympia, WA) **32861**
Trout Steelheader; Salmon (Portland, OR) **26506**
Trout Wrapper (Belgrade, MT) **17724**
Troy Advocate (Tipp City, OH) **25562**
Troy Daily News (Troy, OH) **25597**
Troy Eccentric (Troy, MI) **15642**
Troy Free Press (Troy, MO) **17656**
Troy Gazette Register (Troy, PA) **28058**
Troy Observer **15642***
Troy Record **23457***
Troy-Somerset Gazette (Troy, MI) **15643**
Troy Source (Utica, MI) *Ceased*
Troy Television Cable Co. Inc. (Troy, ID) **7987**
Troy Times (Warren, MI) *Unable to locate*
TroyNewChannels **20008***
Truck Accessory News (Roswell, GA) **7520**
Truck Association; Bulletin of the New Jersey Motor (East Brunswick, NJ) **18780**
Truck; Chevy (Los Angeles, CA) **2236**
Truck & Commerce **25982***
Truck Edition; Fastline—Bluegrass (Buckner, KY) **11968**
Truck Edition; Fastline—Dixie (Buckner, KY) **11970**
Truck Edition; Fastline—Florida (Buckner, KY) **11972**
Truck Edition; Fastline—Georgia (Buckner, KY) **11973**
Truck Edition; Fastline—Mid-West (Buckner, KY) **11981**
Truck Edition; Fastline—Northland (Buckner, KY) **11986**
Truck Edition; Fastline—South Central (Buckner, KY) **11992**
Truck Edition; Fastline—Tennessee (Buckner, KY) **11995**
Truck Edition; Fastline—Tri-State (Buckner, KY) **11997**
Truck Fleet (Toronto, ON, Can.) *Ceased*
Truck Fleet Management (Palm Springs, CA) **2769**
The Truck Logger (Vancouver, BC, Can.) *Unable to locate*
Truck; Motor (Toronto, ON, Can.) **36669**
Truck News (Toronto, ON, Can.) **36774**
Truck News; Florida (Tallahassee, FL) **6720**
Truck News; Illinois (River Grove, IL) **9496**
Truck Paper (Lincoln, NE) **18124**
Truck Parts & Service (Deerfield, IL) **8730**
Truck Price Guide (Milwaukee, WI) *Ceased*
Truck Sales & Leasing (Newport Beach, CA) **2636**
Truck Sales & Leasing Magazine (Irvine, CA) **2091**
Truck; Sport (Los Angeles, CA) **2405**

Truck Trader (Park Hills, KY) *Unable to locate*
Truck Trader (Seattle, WA) *Unable to locate*
Truck Trader/Camion Hebdo (Montreal, QC, Can.) **37230**
Truck Trend (Los Angeles, CA) **2416**
Truck, Van, 4x4 Prices (Milwaukee, WI) *Ceased*
Truck West (Toronto, ON, Can.) **36775**
Truck World (North Vancouver, BC, Can.) *Unable to locate*
Truckee Week; North Tahoe/ (Truckee, CA) **3949**
Trucker—Badger Edition; American (Indianapolis, IN) **10081**
Trucker—Buckeye Edition; American (Indianapolis, IN) **10082**
Trucker—California Edition; American (Indianapolis, IN) **10083**
Trucker—Cascade Edition; American (Indianapolis, IN) **10084**
Trucker—Central States Edition; American (Indianapolis, IN) **10085**
Trucker—Florida Edition; American (Indianapolis, IN) **10086**
Trucker—Illinois Edition; American (Indianapolis, IN) **10087**
Trucker—Indiana Edition; American (Indianapolis, IN) **10088**
Trucker—Kentucky/Tennessee Edition; American (Indianapolis, IN) **10089**
Trucker; Log (Chehalis, WA) **32710**
Trucker—Metro East Edition; American (Indianapolis, IN) **10090**
Trucker—Michigan Edition; American (Indianapolis, IN) **10091**
Trucker—Mid-Atlantic Edition; American (Indianapolis, IN) **10092**
Trucker—Minn/Dakota Truck Edition; American (Indianapolis, IN) **10093**
Trucker—Mountain America Edition; American (Indianapolis, IN) **10094**
Trucker; Nebraska (Lincoln, NE) **18105**
Trucker—New England Edition; American (Indianapolis, IN) **10095**
Trucker—New York/Pennsylvania Edition; American (Indianapolis, IN) **10096**
Trucker; Pro (Roswell, GA) **7517**
Trucker—South Central Edition; American (Indianapolis, IN) **10097**
Trucker—Southern Edition; American (Indianapolis, IN) **10098**
Trucker; Wyoming (Casper, WY) **34486**
Trucker's Connection (Norcross, GA) **7471**
Truckers News; NATSO (Tuscaloosa, AL) **489**
Truckin' Magazine (Anaheim, CA) **1418**
Trucking; Atlantic (Toronto, ON, Can.) **36466**
Trucking Canada (Toronto, ON, Can.) *Ceased*
Trucking Co. (Tuscaloosa, AL) **491**
Trucking; Heavy Duty (Newport Beach, CA) **2627**
Trucking Lifeliner; The Iowa (Des Moines, IA) **10797**
Trucking Magazine; Through the Gears (Anniston, AL) **16**
Trucking News; South Dakota (Sioux Falls, SD) **28968**
Trucking Report; Arkansas (Little Rock, AR) **1222**
Trucking/South (Tuscaloosa, AL) *Ceased*
Trucking Technology (Palm Springs, CA) *Unable to locate*
Trucking Times & Sport Utility News (Cedar Falls, IA) **10663**
Trucking; Today's (Etobicoke, ON, Can.) **35821**
Trucks; Classic (Anaheim, CA) **1403**
Trucks; Custom Classic (Anaheim, CA) **1404**
TRUCKS Magazine (Southampton, PA) *Unable to locate*
Truckstop Travel Plaza (Newport Beach, CA) *Ceased*
The True Citizen (Waynesboro, GA) **7649**
True Citizen; Tacoma (Tacoma, WA) **33152**
True Confessions (New York, NY) **22867**
True Dakotan; Wessington Springs (Wessington Springs, SD) **29029**
True Detective (New York, NY) *Unable to locate*
True Experience (New York, NY) **22868**
True Love (New York, NY) **22869**
True Police Cases (Montreal, QC, Can.) *Ceased*
True Romance (New York, NY) **22870**
True Story (New York, NY) **22871**
True West (Cave Creek, AZ) **673**
Truly Portable *Ceased*
The Truman Tribune (Truman, MN) **16478**
Trumann Democrat (Trumann, AR) **1358**
Trumansburg Free Press (Trumansburg, NY) **23463**
Trumbull Monroe Reporter (Milford, CT) *Ceased*
Trumbull Times (Shelton, CT) **5128**
The Trumpet (West Liberty, WV) **33495**
The Trumpeter (Fritch, TX) **30374**
The Trumpeter (Athabasca, AB, Can.) **34610**
Truro Daily News (Truro, NS, Can.) **35616**
Trustee (Chicago, IL) **8588**
Trusteeship (Washington, DC) **5832**
Trusts and Estates (New York, NY) **22872**

The Truth (Elkhart, IN) 9924
The Truth (Mogadore, OH) *Unable to locate*
Truth on Fire! 35145*
The Truth at Last (Marietta, GA) 7421
Truth Radio Network - 5.4 and 5.8 (Nipomo, CA) 2639
Truth Seeker (San Diego, CA) 3284
Truth Semi-Weekly (San Francisco, CA) *Unable to locate*
The Tryon Daily Bulletin (Tryon, NC) 24259
TSO/ISPF Update (Westminster, CO) *Ceased*
TSTA Advocate (Austin, TX) 29852
The TSU Herald (Houston, TX) 30536
Tsvetnye Metally 22767*
Tu Internacional (Miami, FL) 6385
Tu Mundo 3992*
Tualatin Valley; TCI Cablevision of (Beaverton, OR) 26239
Tuba Frenzy (Chapel Hill, NC) 23729
The Tube Council News (Montclair, NY) 21092
Tube & Pipe Journal; TPJ—The (Rockford, IL) 9534
Tube Topics 21092*
Tucker De Kalb Neighbor (Marietta, GA) 7422
Tuckerman Record (Newport, AR) *Ceased*
Tuckerton Beacon (Tuckerton, NJ) 19681
Tucson Business Digest (Tucson, AZ) *Unable to locate*
Tucson Citizen (Tucson, AZ) 966
Tucson Comic News (Tucson, AZ) *Unable to locate*
(Tucson); Contact! (Tucson, AZ) 942
Tucson Gourmet (Tucson, AZ) 967
Tucson Guide Quarterly (Tucson, AZ) *Unable to locate*
Tucson Lifestyle Magazine (Tucson, AZ) 968
Tucson Shopper (Tucson, AZ) 969
Tucson Weekly (Tucson, AZ) 970
Tucumcari Literary Review (Los Angeles, CA) *Ceased*
Tuff Stuff (Iola, WI) 33852
Tuff Stuff jr. (Richmond, VA) *Ceased*
Tufty News Service (Washington, DC) *Unable to locate*
Tulane; Health Sciences at (New Orleans, LA) 12732
Tulane Journal of Technology and Intellectual Property (New Orleans, LA) 12759
Tulane Medicine 12732*
Tulanian (New Orleans, LA) 12760
Tulare County Life (Tulare, CA) *Ceased*
Tule River Times 3793*
The Tule Times (Springville, CA) 3793
The Tulia Herald (Tulia, TX) 31195
The Tullahoma News and Guardian (Tullahoma, TN) 29633
Tulsa Business Journal & Legal Record 26136*
Tulsa Cable Television 26174*
Tulsa County News 26135*
Tulsa County News (Tulsa, OK) 26135
Tulsa Daily Commerce & Legal News (Tulsa, OK) 26136
Tulsa Daily Legal News 26136*
Tulsa Magazine (Tulsa, OK) *Ceased*
Tulsa Medicine (Tulsa, OK) 26137
Tulsa Sentinel (Tulsa, OK) *Unable to locate*
Tulsa Studies in Women's Literature (Tulsa, OK) 26138
The Tulsa Tribune (Tulsa, OK) *Ceased*
Tulsa; Urban (Tulsa, OK) 26140
Tulsa World (Tulsa, OK) 26139
Tumbleweed Times (Moses Lake, WA) 32840
Tumor Biology (Farmington, CT) 4862
Tundra (Sammamish, WA) 32935
Tundra Drums (Bethel, AK) 554
Tundra Times (Anchorage, AK) *Unable to locate*
Tune; In (Lafayette, LA) 12617
The Tunica Times (Tunica, MS) 16848
The Tunica Times-Democrat 16848*
Tupelo Broadcasting Corporation 16857*
The Tupper Lake Free Press & Tupper Lake Herald (Tupper Lake, NY) *Unable to locate*
Turbine Worldwide; Diesel & Gas (Waukesha, WI) 34401
Turbo & Hi-Tech Performance (Anaheim, CA) 1419
Turbomachinery International (Norwalk, CT) 5078
TURF (St. Johnsbury, VT) 31594
Turf Grass Management; Journal of (Amherst, MA) 13799
Turf News (Rolling Meadows, IL) 9551
Turf & Recreation (Delhi, ON, Can.) 35771
Turf and Sport Digest (Baltimore, MD) *Ceased*
Turkey Letter; Weekly Insiders (Toms River, NJ) 19648
Turkey Show Previews; Deer and (Mequon, WI) 34043
Turkey & Turkey Hunter 33853*
Turkey and Turkey Hunting Magazine (Iola, WI) 33853
Turkey World 162*
Turkish Studies/Turkluk Bilgisi Arastirmalari; Journal of (Duxbury, MA) 14164

Turkluk Bilgisi Arastirmalari; Journal of Turkish Studies/ (Duxbury, MA) 14164
Turlock Journal (Turlock, CA) 3958
Turn For The Judges (TFTJ) (Houston, TX) 30537
Turner Classic Movies (Atlanta, GA) 37791
Turning the Tide (Culver City, CA) 1795
Turnpike Pennysaver (Richfield Springs, NY) 23187
Turtle 10177*
Turtle Lake Times (Turtle Lake, WI) 34376
Turtle Magazine for Preschool Kids (Indianapolis, IN) 10177
Turtle Mountain Star (Rolla, ND) 24534
Turtle Mountain Times (Belcourt, ND) 24345
Turtle Quarterly (Niagara Falls, NY) *Ceased*
The Tuscaloosa News (Tuscaloosa, AL) 492
Tuscarawas Bargain Hunter (Millersburg, OH) 25389
Tuscarawas Valley Life (Dover, OH) *Ceased*
Tuscola County Advertiser (Caro, MI) 14858
Tuskegee Cablevision 509*
The Tuskegee News (Tuskegee, AL) 508
Tustin News (Tustin, CA) *Unable to locate*
Tustin Outlook (Tustin, CA) *Unable to locate*
The Tuttle Times (Chickasha, OK) *Unable to locate*
TV Association of Coulee Dam (Coulee Dam, WA) 32732
TV Blueprint (Farmingdale, NY) 20597
TV Cable (Carmel, IN) *Ceased*
TV Cable of Amarillo 29720*
TV Cable of Berkeley County 33444*
TV Cable of Berkeley County (Inwood, WV) *Ceased*
TV Cable of Central Pennsylvania 28184*
TV Cable Co. of Andalusia Inc. (Andalusia, AL) 13
TV Cable of Elk City 25819*
TV Cable Inc. 16829*
TV Cable of Rensselaer Inc. (Rensselaer, IN) 10416
TV Cable of Winamac Inc. (Rensselaer, IN) 10417
TV Close-Up *Ceased*
TV Crosswords (New York, NY) 22873
TV Data (Glens Falls, NY) 38105
TV Enterprises Inc. (Brady, TX) *Unable to locate*
TV Entertainment (Horsham, PA) *Ceased*
The TV Executive (New York, NY) 22874
TV Executive Daily (New York, NY) 22875
TV Facts, Figures & Film (New York, NY) *Ceased*
TV & Film Extras (New York, NY) 22876
TV Guide (New York, NY) *Unable to locate*
TV Guide Canada (Toronto, ON, Can.) 36776
TV Hebdo (Montreal, QC, Can.) 37231
TV Horizons 34279*
TV Host Monthly (Radnor, PA) 27916
TV News (New York, NY) 22877
T.V. News (Oklahoma City, OK) *Unable to locate*
TV y Novelas (Miami, FL) 6386
TV Ontario (Toronto, ON, Can.) 37716
(TV Picture Life); Metal Edge (New York, NY) 22320
TV Plus (Shelby, NC) 24228
TV Plus (Montreal, QC, Can.) *Ceased*
TV Record (Watervliet, MI) *Ceased*
TV; Response (Santa Ana, CA) 3631
TV Service Inc. (Hindman, KY) 12129
T.V. Service Inc. & United Cable Systems Now T.V. Service Only. 12130*
TV & Sound Magazine; Smart (Chico, CA) 1696
TV Spot-Lite (Flushing, NY) *Unable to locate*
T.V. Star 31200*
TV Technology (Falls Church, VA) 32059
TV This Week (Yorkton, SK, Can.) 37599
TV Times (Baton Rouge, LA) *Ceased*
T.V. Week (Troy, OH) 25598
TV Week Magazine (Burnaby, BC, Can.) 34908
TV Week; Satellite (Fortuna, CA) 1930
TV West Inc. 37544*
TVA (Montreal, QC, Can.) 37717
TVI Report (Beverly Hills, CA) 1579
TVIQ Inc. (Eagle Grove, IA) *Ceased*
TVPPA News (Chattanooga, TN) 29093
TVRO Dealer (Fortuna, CA) *Ceased*
TW Fanch One Co. 26636*
TW/Fanch-Two Co. (Hornell, NY) 20755
TWA Ambassador (North Miami, FL) *Ceased*
Twain Circular; Mark (Charleston, SC) 28515
Twainian (Perry, MO) *Unable to locate*
TWC of North Carolina (Reidsville, NC) 24181
Tweed News (Tweed, ON, Can.) 36826
Twentieth Century Literature (Albany, NY) 20007
Twenty-four (Orlando, FL) *Ceased*
24 Hours (Santa Monica, CA) *Unable to locate*
24x7 (Providence, RI) 28429
20 de Mayo (Los Angeles, CA) 2417
21st Century Adventures (Hampton, GA) 7320
21st Century Science & Technology (Washington, DC) 5833
20/20 (Norwalk, CT) *Ceased*
Twentyone (Troy, MI) *Ceased*
TWICE (New York, NY) 22878
Twice Today Show Daily (New York, NY) *Unable to locate*
Twiggs County New Era (Cochran, GA) 7181
Twin-Boro News (Cresskill, NJ) 18774

Twin Cities (Minneapolis, MN) *Ceased*
Twin Cities Courier (Minneapolis, MN) *Unable to locate*
Twin Cities Reader (Minneapolis, MN) *Ceased*
Twin Cities Times (Sausalito, CA) *Unable to locate*
Twin Cities Visitor (Minneapolis, MN) *Ceased*
Twin Cities; WHERE (Minneapolis, MN) 16141
Twin City (Eau Claire, MI) 15003
The Twin City Community News (Bloomington, IL) 8081
Twin City Journal-Reporter (Gas City, IN) 10020
Twin City News (Chattahoochee, FL) 5980
Twin City News (Hollywood, FL) *Ceased*
The Twin-City News (Batesburg-Leesville, SC) 28485
Twin City Times-Riverdale Press (Lemoore, CA) *Unable to locate*
Twin City Trade Lines Shopper's Guide (Benton Harbor, MI) 14809
Twin County Cable 26706*
Twin County Cable TV, Inc. (Tuscaloosa, AL) 494
Twin County Cablevision (Quitman, MS) 16829
Twin County Trans Video Inc. (Bethlehem, PA) 26708
Twin Plant News (El Paso, TX) 30283
Twin Tiers Cable Comm. 20754*
Twin Valley CATV 15165*
Twin Valley Communications Inc. (Miltonvale, KS) 11653
Twin Valley News & Advisor (West Alexandria, OH) 25631
Twin Valley Times/Gary Graphic (Twin Valley, MN) 16479
TwinCity Shopper 18264*
Twins Magazine (Centennial, CO) 4228
Twinsburg Bulletin (Bedford, OH) 24662
The Twinsburg Sun (Twinsburg, OH) 25599
Twist Weekly (Seattle, WA) *Unable to locate*
Two Harbors Manney Shopper (Two Harbors, MN) 16481
Two Hills Times 34865*
256 Shades of Grey (Eau Claire, WI) *Unable to locate*
Two-Lane Roads (Fort Lauderdale, FL) 6085
2 Magazine (Los Angeles, CA) *Unable to locate*
2wice (East Hampton, NY) 20547
2x4 (All About Wood) (Victoriaville, QC, Can.) 37433
TWU Express (New York, NY) 22879
TY EDT (Vienna, VA) *Unable to locate*
Tygodnik Polski 15141*
Tyler Cableguide (Tyler, TX) 31200
Tyler County Journal & Sports Review (Sistersville, WV) *Ceased*
Tyler Courier-Times (Tyler, TX) *Ceased*
Tyler Courier-Times-Telegraph (Tyler, TX) 31201
Tyler Junior College News (Tyler, TX) 31202
Tyler Morning Telegraph (Tyler, TX) 31203
Tyler Review (Tyler, TX) *Unable to locate*
Tyler Star-News (Sistersville, WV) 33467
The Tyler Tribune (Tyler, MN) 16482
The Tylertown Times (Tylertown, MS) 16862
Tyndall Tribune & Register (Tyndall, SD) 29004
Type and Press (Hayward, CA) *Ceased*
Typesetters of Charleston (Charleston, SC) *Ceased*
The Typographer (Washington, DC) *Ceased*
Typographical Journal (Colorado Springs, CO) *Ceased*
Tyrone Daily Herald 28064*

U

U & lc (New York, NY) *Unable to locate*
U-Bild Newspaper Features (Van Nuys, CA) 38106
U. The National College Magazine (Los Angeles, CA) *Unable to locate*
UA Cablesystems of California 3947*
U.A. Journal (Washington, DC) 5834
UAE 7815*
UAE 15101*
UAE 15488*
UAE 12511*
UAE 10054*
UAE 9937*
UAE 8714*
UAE 32281*
UAE 29670*
UAE 20989*
UAE (Alameda, CA) *Unable to locate*
UAE (Van Nuys, CA) 3999
UAE (Bossier City, LA) 12538
UAE (Baltimore, MD) *Unable to locate*
UAE Cable, Mississippi Gulf Coast 16563*
UAH (The University of Alabama in Huntsville) Magazine (Huntsville, AL) 275
UAS Explorations (Juneau, AK) 598
UBC Alumni Chronicle 35171*
The Ubyssey (Vancouver, BC, Can.) 35172

UCLA Journal of Environmental Law and Policy (Los Angeles, CA) **2418**
UCLA Magazine (Los Angeles, CA) **2419**
The UCLA Monthly **2419***
UCLA Sports (Stamford, CT) *Ceased*
UConn Traditions (Storrs, CT) **5169**
UCSD Guardian (La Jolla, CA) **2120**
UDC Magazine (Richmond, VA) **32458**
udm/Upholstery Design and Management (Des Plaines, IL) **8772**
udm/Upholstery Design & Manufacturing **8772***
U.E. News (Pittsburgh, PA) **27851**
UEA Action (Murray, UT) **31374**
Ufahamu (Los Angeles, CA) **2420**
UHF Magazine (Longueuil, QC, Can.) **37059**
Uinta County Herald (Evanston, WY) **34521**
Uinta County Herald Shoppers Guide (Evanston, WY) **34522**
Uintah Basin Standard (Roosevelt, UT) **31415**
UJ (Raleigh, NC) *Unable to locate*
UK & USA (New York, NY) **22880**
Ukiah Daily Journal (Ukiah, CA) **3967**
Ukrainian Engineering News (New York, NY) *Unable to locate*
Ukrainian Mathematical Journal (New York, NY) **22881**
Ukrainian National Word (Chicago, IL) *Ceased*
Ukrainian News **34732***
Ukrainian News (Edmonton, AB, Can.) **34732**
Ukrainian Orthodox Word (South Bound Brook, NJ) **19582**
Ukrainian Philatelist (Chicago, IL) **8589**
Ukrainian Review; Forum—A (Scranton, PA) **27959**
Ukrainian Voice (Winnipeg, MB, Can.) **35354**
The Ukrainian Weekly (Parsippany, NJ) **19415**
The Ulen Union (Ulen, MN) **16483**
Ulster County Townsman (Woodstock, NY) **23596**
Ulster Request (Saugerties, NY) *Ceased*
Ultimate Reality and Meaning (Winnipeg, MB, Can.) **35355**
Ultra Magazine (Houston, TX) *Ceased*
Ultralight Aircraft Magazine (Encino, CA) *Ceased*
Ultralight Flying! (Chattanooga, TN) **29094**
Ultraproduct Focus *Ceased*
Ultrapure Water (Littleton, CO) *Ceased*
Ultrasonic Imaging (San Diego, CA) *Ceased*
Ultrasonics Sonochemistry (Burlington, MA) **14035**
Ultrasound, CT and MRI; Seminars in (Philadelphia, PA) **27675**
Ultrasound; Journal of Clinical (Hoboken, NJ) **19014**
Ultrasound; Journal for Vascular (Lanham, MD) **13606**
Ultrasound in Medicine; Journal of (Boston, MA) **13920**
Ultrasound Quarterly (Baltimore, MD) **13256**
Ultrasound; Veterinary Radiology & (Raleigh, NC) **24158**
Ultrastructural Pathology (Chicago, IL) **8590**
Ultreya Magazine (Dallas, TX) **30186**
The Ulysses News (Ulysses, KS) **11854**
UMASS Lowell Connector (Lowell, MA) **14279**
UMASS Magazine (Amherst, MA) **13807**
UMBC Review (Baltimore, MD) **13257**
UMD Statesman (Duluth, MN) **15843**
UMI's Banking Information Index (Louisville, KY) **12241**
Umpqua Free Press (Umpqua, OR) **26601**
The Umpqua Shopper (Sutherlin, OR) **26592**
Umpqua Trapper (Roseburg, OR) **26556**
UN Chronicle (New York, NY) **22882**
UN News (Huntsville, AL) *Ceased*
Unarius Light *Ceased*
UNC Media of Jacksonville **6245***
Uncertainty, Fuzziness, and Knowledge-Based Systems; International Journal of (River Edge, NJ) **19514**
Unclassified (Des Moines, IA) *Unable to locate*
Uncle; Farming (Bronx, NY) **20268**
Uncoverings (Lincoln, NE) **18125**
UNCW Magazine (Wilmington, NC) **24296**
UNCW Today **24296***
Under the Sun (Cookeville, TN) **29146**
Under Western Skies (Waynesville, NC) **24281**
Undercar Digest (Springfield, MO) **17617**
Undercurrent; The Bowen Island (Bowen Island, BC, Can.) **34886**
The Underground (Scarborough, ON, Can.) **36386**
Underground Construction (Houston, TX) **30538**
Underground Focus (Spooner, WI) **34338**
The Underground Wine Journal (Costa Mesa, CA) *Unable to locate*
Underground Zine Scene (Mason, MI) *Unable to locate*
Underhood Service (Akron, OH) **24591**
Undersea Biomedical Research **13592***
Undersea & Hyperbaric Medicine (Kensington, MD) **13592**
Undersea Technology **31831***
Understanding Statistics (Mahwah, NJ) **19207**
The Understory (Seattle, WA) *Unable to locate*

UnderWater Magazine (Houston, TX) **30539**
Underwater Naturalist (Highlands, NJ) **18874**
Underwater USA (Bloomsburg, PA) *Ceased*
Underwood News (Underwood, ND) **24543**
Underwriter; Canadian (Don Mills, ON, Can.) **35772**
Underwriter Property and Casualty/Risk and Benefits Management; National (Erlanger, KY) **12054**
Underwriters' Report (San Francisco, CA) *Unable to locate*
Undiscovered Countries Journal (Edmonds, WA) *Unable to locate*
UNDOC (New York, NY) **22883**
Unfinished Furniture Industry (Northfield, IL) *Ceased*
Unidos Magazine (Phoenix, AZ) *Unable to locate*
Uniforms and Accessories Review (New York, NY) *Ceased*
Uniforum's IT Solutions (Annapolis, MD) *Unable to locate*
Uninews *Ceased*
The Union **1928***
The Union (Arcata, CA) *Ceased*
The Union (Grass Valley, CA) **2029**
Union (Shelbyville, IL) **9599**
Union (Sullivan, IN) *Ceased*
L'Union (Woonsocket, RI) **28461**
Union (Arthabaska, QC, Can.) **36941**
Union Advocate (St. Paul, MN) **16411**
Union Banner (Carlyle, IL) **8129**
Union City Daily Messenger (Union City, TN) **29635**
The Union County Advocate (Morganfield, KY) **12307**
Union County Family (Mountainside, NJ) **19319**
Union County Leader (Clayton, NM) **19828**
Union County Review (Liberty, IN) *Unable to locate*
Union County Times (Starke, FL) **6691**
Union County Times (Middleburg, PA) **27250**
Union Daily Times (Union, SC) **28776**
Union-Democrat (Sonora, CA) **3780**
The Union Enterprise (Plainwell, MI) **15446**
Union Farmer (Saskatoon, SK, Can.) **37559**
Union Farmer; Nebraska (Lincoln, NE) **18106**
Union Hidpana (Santa Ana, CA) **3634**
Union Jack (La Mesa, CA) **2124**
(Union); Jednota (Middletown, PA) **27253**
The Union Leader (Manchester, NH) **18565**
Union Leader (Union, NJ) **19688**
L'Union Medicale du Canada (Montreal, QC, Can.) *Unable to locate*
Union News & Home **24060***
Union News Leader **29351***
Union-News & Sunday Republican (Springfield, MA) **14552**
Union Plus (Boston, MA) *Ceased*
Union Press-Courier **27345***
The Union-Recorder (Milledgeville, GA) **7436**
The Union Register (Portland, OR) **26513**
Union Republican (Albia, IA) **10576**
Union Seminary Quarterly Review (Richmond, VA) **32459**
Union Signal (Hutchinson, KS) **11502**
Union Springs Herald (Union Springs, AL) **510**
Union Springs News **21096***
Union Square Bulletin (San Francisco, CA) *Ceased*
The Union Star (Brookneal, VA) **31905**
Union-Sun and Journal (Lockport, NY) *Unable to locate*
Uniondale Beacon (Uniondale, NY) **23465**
Uniondale/Roosevelt Shopper's Guide (Ontario, ON, Can.) **36169**
Unionville Cable TV Authority **17659***
Unionville CATV; City of (Unionville, MO) **17659**
Unionville Republican & Putnam County Journal (Unionville, MO) **17658**
UNIPUB Impact of Science on Society (New York, NY) *Unable to locate*
Unique Homes (Santa Monica, CA) **3719**
Unique Opportunities (Louisville, KY) **12242**
Unirea (The Union) (Canton, OH) *Unable to locate*
UniReview (Austin, TX) *Unable to locate*
L'Uniscope (Hull, QC, Can.) **37003**
Unisphere Magazine (Chatham, NJ) *Unable to locate*
Unistar Radio Networks (New York, NY) *Unable to locate*
UNISYS/Network Computing News (Austin, TX) *Ceased*
UNISYS World (Waco, TX) **31255**
The Unit Circle (Seattle, WA) *Ceased*
Unite (Montreal, QC, Can.) *Ceased*
Unite! Magazine (New York, NY) **22884**
United Artist Cable **1721***
United Artist Cable **4422***
United Artists **13640***
United Artists Cable **3999***
United Artists Cable **4144***
United Artists Cable **19386***
United Artists Cable of Bossier City Inc. (Bossier City, LA) *Unable to locate*
United Artists Cable Corp. **4398***
United Artists Entertainment **9429***

United Artists Entertainment Co. (Santa Cruz, CA) *Unable to locate*
United Broadcasting Network (White Springs, FL) *Unable to locate*
United Cable **18567***
United Cable **13640***
United Cable of ESFV **3999***
United Cable Systems Inc. (Hindman, KY) **12130**
United Cable Television Services Corp. **4919***
United Cable TV **1721***
United Caprine News (Crowley, TX) **30113**
The United Church Observer (Toronto, ON, Can.) **36777**
United Communications Corp. **1701***
United Data-Vision (Sebeka, MN) **16444**
United Express (Beaverton, OR) *Ceased*
United Express (California) (Beaverton, OR) *Ceased*
United Feature Syndicate Inc. (New York, NY) **38107**
United Hemispheres (Greensboro, NC) **23942**
United Irish Press (Toronto, ON, Can.) *Unable to locate*
The United Journal (Forest Hills, NY) *Ceased*
United Kingdom; Journal of the Marine Biological Association of the (New York, NY) **22121**
United Media (New York, NY) **38108**
United Methodist Advocate; Mississippi (Jackson, MS) **16710**
United Methodist Advocate; Virginia (Glen Allen, VA) **32114**
United Methodist Connection (Baltimore, MD) *Ceased*
United Methodist; The Florida (Dallas, TX) **30157**
United Methodist Reporter (Dallas, TX) **30187**
United Mine Workers Journal (Fairfax, VA) **32033**
United Nations; Permanent Missions to the (New York, NY) **22542**
United Nations Treaty Series (New York, NY) **22885**
United Paramount Network (Los Angeles, CA) **37718**
United Press International (Washington, DC) **38109**
The United Rubber Worker (Akron, OH) *Ceased*
U.S. Agriculture (Minneapolis, MN) *Unable to locate*
United States Army Aviation Digest (Pittsburgh, PA) **27852**
U.S. ART (Minneapolis, MN) **16137**
U.S. Art, The Magazine of Realism in America **16137***
U.S. Auto Scene (Warren, MI) **15663**
U.S. Banker (New York, NY) **22886**
U.S. Bass (Mesa, AZ) *Unable to locate*
U.S. Black Engineer **13258***
U.S. Black Engineer & Information Technology **13258***
U.S. Cable (Johns Island, SC) **28668**
U.S. Cable Coastal Properties (Savannah, GA) **7541**
U.S. Cable of Lake County (Waukegan, IL) **9745**
U.S. Cable of Northern Indiana **10300***
U.S. Cable of Paterson (Paterson, NJ) *Unable to locate*
U.S. Cable of Southwest Texas (Alpine, TX) **29688**
U.S. Cable TV of Jekyll Island (San Luis Obispo, CA) **3578**
U.S. Catholic (Chicago, IL) **8591**
U.S. Catholic (Fort Washington, PA) *Ceased*
U.S. Catholic Historian (Huntington, IN) **10075**
U.S. Department of State Bulletin (Washington, DC) *Ceased*
U.S. Distribution Journal (New York, NY) *Ceased*
U.S. Farm News (Denison, IA) **10767**
U.S. Frontline News (New York, NY) **22887**
U.S. Geological Survey, Mineral Industry Surveys-Commodities: Barite (Reston, VA) *Ceased*
U.S. Gospel News (Jonesboro, AR) **1198**
U.S. Government Publications; Monthly Catalog of (Pittsburgh, PA) **27816**
U.S.A. Gymnastics (Indianapolis, IN) **10178**
United States Gypsum Co. (Empire, NV) **18344**
U.S. Immigration (Los Angeles, CA) **2421**
U.S. Japan Business News (Los Angeles, CA) **2422**
U.S. - Japan Women's Journal (Palo Alto, CA) **2802**
U.S. Kids (Indianapolis, IN) **10179**
U.S. Medicine (Washington, DC) **5835**
U.S. News & World Report (Washington, DC) **5836**
U.S. Newswire (Washington, DC) **38110**
U.S. 1 Newspaper (Princeton, NJ) **19477**
U.S. Pharmacist (Bloomfield, NJ) **18689**
U.S. Piper (Birmingham, AL) **98**
U.S. Professional Tennis Registry **28662***
U.S. Radio, Inc. **24168***
U.S. Roller Skating (Lincoln, NE) **18126**
U.S. Scots (Columbus, OH) *Unable to locate*
U.S. Sports (Chicago, IL) *Ceased*
United States Tax Court Reports (Pittsburgh, PA) **27853**
U.S. Tech (Valley Forge, PA) **28092**
U.S. Toy Collector Magazine (Helena, MT) **17824**
United States Trade Fair (Chicago, IL) *Unable to locate*
U.S. Water News (Halstead, KS) **11477**
United Video Cablevision **13046***
United Video Cablevision (Milo, ME) *Ceased*

Numbers cited in bold after listings are entry numbers rather than page numbers.

Numbers cited in bold after listings are entry numbers rather than page numbers.

Vaughan Liberal (Richmond Hill, ON, Can.) 36347
Vaughan Weekly (King City, ON, Can.) Unable to locate
The Vauxhall Advance (Vauxhall, AB, Can.) Unable to locate
VCA TeleCable, Inc. (Houston, TX) Unable to locate
VCC Voice 35176*
VCP 35535*
VEA Today 31566*
The Vealer (Madeira Beach, FL) Unable to locate
Vecinos del Valle (Woodland Hills, CA) 4116
Vecteur Environnement (Montreal, QC, Can.) 37233
Vector-Borne and Zoonotic Diseases (Larchmont, NY) 20929
Vedanta Free Press 20571*
Vedantist; American (Elmhurst, NY) 20571
Vedette; Greenfield (Greenfield, MO) 17088
Vedette; Guthrie County (Panora, IA) 11147
Veery (Chicago, IL) Unable to locate
The Vega Enterprise (Vega, TX) 31231
Vegetable (Fresno, CA) 1958
Vegetable Crop Production; Journal of (Lane, OK) 25881
Vegetable Grower; American (Willoughby, OH) 25657
The Vegetable Growers News (Sparta, MI) 15570
Vegetable Magazine; Citrus and (Tampa, FL) 6760
Vegetarian Gourmet (Montrose, PA) Ceased
Vegetarian Journal (Baltimore, MD) 13259
Vegetarian Times (Stamford, CT) 5162
Vegetarian Voice (Dolgeville, NY) 20533
Vegetatio 22558*
Veggie Life (Concord, CA) 1756
The Vegreville News Advertiser (Vegreville, AB, Can.) 34864
Vegreville Observer (Vegreville, AB, Can.) 34865
Vegreville Times Observer 34865*
Vehicle Leasing Today (Philadelphia, PA) 27716
Vehicle Technology Update; Ward's Engine and (Southfield, MI) 15555
The Veliger (Santa Barbara, CA) 3661
The Velikovskian (Forest Hills, NY) 20617
Velocity (Chicago, IL) 8597
VeloNews (Boulder, CO) 4194
Ven'd'Est (Bathurst, NB, Can.) 35379
Vending Magazine; Canadian (Delhi, ON, Can.) 35767
Vending Times (New York, NY) Unable to locate
The Venice Gondolier (Venice, FL) 6831
Venice Weekly (Sarasota, FL) 6668
Ventura Bulletin (Ventura, CA) 4012
Ventura County & Coast Reporter 4013*
Ventura County Edition; Los Angeles Times— (Ventura, CA) 4005
Ventura County Reporter (Ventura, CA) 4013
Ventura County Star (Ventura, CA) 4014
Ventura County Star (Camarillo Edition) (Ventura, CA) 4015
Ventura County Star Free Press 4014*
Ventura County Vida Newspaper (Oxnard, CA) 2731
Ventura Family Magazine (Encino, CA) 1886
Ventura Magazine (Westlake Village, CA) Unable to locate
Venture (Wheaton, IL) Ceased
Venture (New York, NY) Unable to locate
Venture (Dayton, OH) 25129
Venture Capital Journal (New York, NY) Unable to locate
Venue (Toronto, ON, Can.) Unable to locate
Veranda (Atlanta, GA) 7057
Verbatim, The Language Quarterly (Old Lyme, CT) Ceased
Verde Independent (Cottonwood, AZ) 680
Verdigre Eagle (Verdigre, NE) 18301
Verelk (Los Angeles, CA) 2429
Verhaltenstherapie (Farmington, CT) 4864
Veritas Catholic Youth Magazine (Agoura Hills, CA) Unable to locate
Verizon Americast (Cerritos, CA) 1684
The Vermilion (Lafayette, LA) 12621
Vermilion Free-Press (Amherst, OH) Ceased
Vermilion Photo Journal (Vermilion, OH) 25612
Vermilion Standard (Vermilion, AB, Can.) Unable to locate
The Vermont Bar Journal (Montpelier, VT) 31564
Vermont Beverage Journal (Avon, MA) Ceased
Vermont Business Magazine (Burlington, VT) 31519
Vermont; Business People (Williston, VT) 31618
The Vermont Catholic Tribune (Burlington, VT) 31520
Vermont Division of Geology and Mineral Ceased
Vermont ETV 31522*
Vermont ETV 31623*
Vermont ETV 31597*
Vermont ETV 31588*
Vermont Green Mountain Guide (North Springfield, VT) 31573
Vermont History (Barre, VT) 31489
Vermont Life (Montpelier, VT) 31565
Vermont Magazine (Middlebury, VT) 31559
Vermont-NEA Today (Montpelier, VT) 31566

Vermont News Guide (Manchester Center, VT) 31554
Vermont Outdoors 31516*
Vermont Real Estate Guide (Andover, MA) Ceased
The Vermont Standard (Woodstock, VT) 31624
Vermont Times (Shelburne, VT) Unable to locate
Vermont Woodlands Magazine 31537*
Vernal Express (Vernal, UT) 31483
The Verndale Sun (Verndale, MN) 16484
Vernon County Broadcaster (Viroqua, WI) 34383
The Vernon Daily News (Vernon, BC, Can.) Unable to locate
Vernon Hills News (Grayslake, IL) Ceased
Vernon Hills Review (Waukegan, IL) 9744
Vernon Township News/Voice (Highland Park, IL) Unable to locate
Vero Beach/Sebastian Advertiser (Melbourne, FL) Ceased
Verona-Cedar Grove Times (Cedar Grove, NJ) 18722
The Verona Press (Verona, WI) 34380
The Verona Press/Leader 34380*
The Versailles Policy (Versailles, OH) 25613
The Versailles Republican (Versailles, IN) 10518
Verse (Florence, MA) 14188
Vertex National SalesTax Manuals (Berwyn, PA) 26698
Vertica (New York, NY) Ceased
Vertical Application Reseller (Morris Plains, NJ) 19308
Vertical File Index (Bronx, NY) 20288
Vertiflite (Alexandria, VA) 31749
Verto Cable TV (Scranton, PA) Unable to locate
Verve (Simi Valley, CA) Unable to locate
The Vestal Town Crier (Conklin, NY) 20495
Vestkusten (Mill Valley, CA) 2542
Vestnik (Baltimore, MD) 13260
Veteran; The California (Sacramento, CA) 2989
Veteran; The Catholic War (Alexandria, VA) 31653
Veteran; The Jewish (Washington, DC) 5563
Veteran News; Texan (Fort Worth, TX) 30353
Veteran; Weteran/ (New York, NY) 22916
Veterans' Bulletin (Atlanta, GA) 7058
Veterinaire du Quebec; Le Medecin (Saint-Hyacinthe, QC, Can.) 37351
Veterinarian; California (Sacramento, CA) 2990
Veterinarian; Compendium on Continuing Education for the Practicing (Yardley, PA) 28199
Veterinarian; Texas (Austin, TX) 29850
Veterinary Clinical Nutrition (Los Angeles, CA) Ceased
Veterinary Clinics (Philadelphia, PA) 27717
Veterinary Economics (Lenexa, KS) Unable to locate
Veterinary Economics (Lenexa, KS) 11598
Veterinary and Human Toxicology (Manhattan, KS) 11630
Veterinary Journal; Canadian (Ottawa, ON, Can.) 36229
Veterinary Medical Association; Journal of the American (Schaumburg, IL) 9584
Veterinary Medical Education; Journal of (Blacksburg, VA) 31877
Veterinary Medicine (Lenexa, KS) Unable to locate
Veterinary Medicine (Montvale, NJ) 19278
Veterinary Practice Staff (Los Angeles, CA) Ceased
Veterinary Product News (Marietta, GA) Unable to locate
Veterinary Radiology 24158*
Veterinary Radiology & Ultrasound (Raleigh, NC) 24158
Veterinary Research; American Journal of (Schaumburg, IL) 9583
Veterinary Research; Canadian Journal of (Ottawa, ON, Can.) 36221
Veterinary Surgery (Davis, CA) 1818
Veterinary Toxicology 11630*
Vette (Saddle Brook, NJ) 19531
Vevay Reveille-Enterprise (Vevay, IN) 10520
VFW Auxiliary (Kansas City, MO) 17200
VFW Magazine (Kansas City, MO) 17201
VH-1 (Video Hits One) (New York, NY) 37794
Vi-Tel Inc. (Davenport, OK) 25798
VIA (San Francisco, CA) 3459
VIA (San Francisco, CA) 3458
Via Port of New York-New Jersey (New York, NY) Unable to locate
Via Satellite (Potomac, MD) 13662
Via Times Newsmagazine (Chicago, IL) 8598
Viacom Cable 33162*
Viacom Cable 26517*
Viacom Cable (Pleasanton, CA) Unable to locate
Viacom Cable (Nashville, TN) 29505
Viacom Cable of San Francisco 3506*
Viacom Cablevision 33766*
Viacom Cablevision (Livermore, CA) Unable to locate
Viacom Cablevision (Puget Sound, WA) 32901
Viacom Cablevision of Dayton (Dayton, OH) Unable to locate
Viacom Cablevision of Marion County (Livermore, CA) Unable to locate
Vibe Magazine (Boulder, CO) 4195
Vibrant Life (Hagerstown, MD) 13570

Vibration Engineering Ceased
Vic-Nic News Ceased
VICA Journal (Leesburg, VA) Ceased
Vice (Brooklyn, NY) 20353
Vici Beacon News (Vici, OK) Ceased
Vicksburg Evening Post (Vicksburg, MS) 16871
Victimology (Arlington, VA) 31839
Victims; Violence and (Seattle, WA) 33036
Victor This Week (Pittsford, NY) Unable to locate
The Victoria Advocate (Victoria, TX) 31236
Victoria County Record (Perth-Andover, NB, Can.) Unable to locate
Victoria Dispatch; Kenbridge- (Victoria, VA) 32576
Victoria Magazine (New York, NY) Ceased
The Victoria Pennysaver (Victoria, BC, Can.) Unable to locate
Victoria Today Ceased
Victoria; WHERE (Victoria, BC, Can.) 35230
Victorian Accents (New York, NY) Unable to locate
Victorian Homes (Brooklyn, NY) 20354
Victorian Periodicals Review (Toronto, ON, Can.) 36786
Victorian Poetry (Morgantown, WV) 33397
Victorian Review (Lethbridge, AB, Can.) 34798
Victorian Studies (Bloomington, IN) 9854
Victoria's Monday Magazine (Victoria, BC, Can.) Unable to locate
Victorville Green Sheet (Palm Desert, CA) 2744
Victory Music Review (Tacoma, WA) 33154
Vida Cristiana (Lake Mary, FL) 6281
Vida En El Valle (Fresno, CA) 1959
Vida Newspaper; Ventura County (Oxnard, CA) 2731
Vida Nueva (Los Angeles, CA) 2430
Vida Social (Miami, FL) 6389
Video Age Daily (New York, NY) 22897
Video Age International (New York, NY) 22898
Video Business (New York, NY) Unable to locate
Video Computing (Satellite Beach, FL) Unable to locate
Video Contractor; Sound & (Overland Park, KS) 11731
Video Derv Ltee (Baie St.-Paul, QC, Can.) 36947
Video Dery Ltee. (Ville de la Baie, QC, Can.) 37435
Video Digest (Fort Lauderdale, FL) Ceased
Video Event (Peterborough, NH) 18632
Video Extra (Philadelphia, PA) Unable to locate
Video Guide; Stereo (Toronto, ON, Can.) 36748
Video Insider (Wayne, PA) Unable to locate
Video Interiors; Audio/ (Anaheim, CA) 1399
Video; Journal of Film and (Los Angeles, CA) 2301
Video Librarian (Seabeck, WA) 32936
Video Life (Titusville, FL) Ceased
Video Magazine (New York, NY) Unable to locate
Video Magazine; Digital (Manhasset, NY) 20997
Video Magazine; Palmer (Westfield, NJ) 19744
Video Manager (Torrance, CA) Ceased
Video & Multimedia Producer; AV (White Plains, NY) 23568
Video News; Adult (Chatsworth, CA) 1685
Video News; Palmer (Westfield, NJ) 19745
Video PROphiles (Peterborough, NH) Unable to locate
Video Review (New Rochelle, NY) Unable to locate
Video Shopper (New York, NY) Ceased
Video Software Magazine (New York, NY) Ceased
Video Store (Santa Ana, CA) 3635
Video Systems (Overland Park, KS) 11734
Video Times (New York, NY) Unable to locate
Video Trade News; Photographic (Melville, NY) 21055
Video Tron (Saint-Felicien, QC, Can.) 37333
Video Vision Magazine (Miami, FL) Unable to locate
VIDEO WATCHDOG (Cincinnati, OH) 24826
Videogame Advisor 5228*
VideoGames & Computer Entertainment Magazine (Beverly Hills, CA) Ceased
Videography (New York, NY) 22899
Videomaker Magazine (Chico, CA) 1697
Videon Cable TV (Thompson, MB, Can.) 35304
Videon Cable TV (Atikokan, ON, Can.) 35640
Videoscope; The Phantom of the Movies' (Ocean Grove, NJ) 19390
Videotron Ltee. Division Telesag (Chicoutimi, QC, Can.) 36975
Vidette; Daily (Normal, IL) 9296
Vidette; The Highland (Troy, KS) 11850
Vidette/Pandora Times; Putnam County (Columbus Grove, OH) 25091
Vidette-Times (Valparaiso, IN) Ceased
Vidorian (Vidor, TX) 31243
Vidorian Shopper (Vidor, TX) 31244
Vie Des Arts (Montreal, QC, Can.) 37234
The Vienna News Observer 7633*
The Vienna/Oakton Connection (Vienna, VA) 32584
The Vienna Times (Vienna, IL) 9729
Vienna Times (Vienna, VA) 32585
Viet Bao Kinh Te (Westminster, CA) 4075
Viet Magazine (San Jose, CA) Unable to locate
Viet Nam Hai Ngoai (San Diego, CA) 3287
Vietnam (Leesburg, VA) 32187

Vogue Patterns Magazine (New York, NY) 22904
The Voice 23109*
VOICE 27014*
Voice 14988*
Voice 13630*
The Voice 6086*
The Voice 6352*
The Voice (Birmingham, AL) 99
The Voice (Kersey, CO) 4524
Voice (Daytona Beach, FL) 6040
The Voice (Indianapolis, IN) 10181
Voice (Grandville, MI) 15130
The Voice (Lincoln, NE) 18127
The Voice (Newark, NJ) 19367
The Voice (Bloomsburg, PA) 26719
The Voice (Vancouver, BC, Can.) 35176
The Voice of Agriculture (St. Paul, MN) 16414
Voice of Bensenville/Wood Dale (Schaumburg, IL) Ceased
Voice of Bloomingdale (Schaumburg, IL) Ceased
The Voice of Bowden (Bowden, AB, Can.) Unable to locate
The Voice Community Magazine (North Vancouver, BC, Can.) Unable to locate
Voice for the Defense (Dallas, TX) Unable to locate
Voice of the Diabetic (Columbia, MO) 17012
The VOICE for Education (Harrisburg, PA) 27014
Voice of the Elgin Farmer (Dresden, ON, Can.) Ceased
The Voice of Elk Grove Village (Schaumburg, IL) Ceased
Voice of the Essex Farmer (Essex, ON, Can.) 35810
Voice of the Farmer (Dresden, ON, Can.) 35789
Voice of Hanover Park North (Schaumburg, IL) Ceased
Voice of Hanover Park South (Schaumburg, IL) Ceased
The Voice of Hawai'i (Honolulu, HI) 7727
Voice of the Hawkeyes (Bloomington, IN) Unable to locate
Voice of Hoffman Estates (Schaumburg, IL) Ceased
Voice of the Huron Farmer 35789*
Voice of Itasca (Schaumburg, IL) Ceased
Voice; Journal of (Baltimore, MD) 13205
Voice of the Kent Farmer 35789*
Voice of the Lambton Farmer (Lambton, ON, Can.) 35967
Voice Ledger (Pleasant Valley, NY) 23109
Voice of the Middlesex Farmer (Middlesex, ON, Can.) 36037
Voice of Missions (New York, NY) Unable to locate
(Voice of the Nation); Hlas Naroda (Chicago, IL) 8398
The Voice News (New Baltimore, MI) 15398
The VOICE News (Hickman, NE) 18048
The Voice Newspaper (Fort Lauderdale, FL) 6086
The Voice Newspaper (Seattle, WA) 33037
Voice of Roselle/Medinah (Schaumburg, IL) Ceased
Voice of Schaumburg (Schaumburg, IL) Ceased
Voice of South Marion (Belleview, FL) 5923
The Voice of the Southwest (Gallup, NM) 19858
Voice of the Tennessee Walking Horse (Lewisburg, TN) 29326
The Voice & The Reporter (Huron, OH) Ceased
Voice of the Trapper 34576*
The Voice-Tribune (Louisville, KY) 12243
The Voice and the Vision (Dallas, TX) Ceased
Voice of Washington Music Educators (Edmonds, WA) 32747
Voice of Youth (Imperial, PA) 27070
Voice of Youth Advocates (Lanham, MD) 13609
Voices (Woodbury, CT) 5237
Voices (St. Louis, MO) 17527
Voices (Media, PA) 27244
Voices of Central Pennsylvania (State College, PA) 28022
Voices in Education (Cromwell, CT) Ceased
Voices of Experience (Seattle, WA) 33038
Voices International Ceased
Voices in Italian Americana (Lafayette, IN) 10255
Voices Magazine (Lisle, IL) 9112
VOICES Sunday-Weekly Star (Woodbury, CT) 5238
Voices: The Magazine of Ontario Public Sector Workers 36131*
VOILA QUEBEC (Quebec, QC, Can.) 37297
Voir (Montreal, QC, Can.) 37236
Voix du Dimanche; La (Matane, QC, Can.) 37068
Voix Gaspesienne; La (Matane, QC, Can.) 37069
Voix; Journal La (Sorel, QC, Can.) 37403
Voix de l'Est; La (Granby, QC, Can.) 37000
Voix des Mille Iles; La (Ste.-Therese, QC, Can.) 37368
Voix Sepharade (Montreal, QC, Can.) Unable to locate
Voix du Sud; La (Lac Etchemin, QC, Can.) 37027
Volando (Del Rio, TX) 30225
Volante (Vermillion, SD) 29007
Volcano Vision, Inc. (Pine Grove, CA) 2845
Volcano Vision, Inc. (Pine Grove, CA) 2844

Volga Tribune (Volga, SD) 29012
Volley (Custer, SD) Ceased
Volleyball (Anaheim, CA) Unable to locate
Volleyball; Coaching (Colorado Springs, CO) 4242
Volleyball Monthly (San Luis Obispo, CA) Ceased
Volt/Age 8363*
The Volta Review (Washington, DC) 5840
Volta Voices (Washington, DC) 5841
Voluntary Action Leadership (Washington, DC) Unable to locate
Voluntary Action Research; Journal of 32990*
Volunteer TV Cable Co. (Tellico Plains, TN) Ceased
VONA-AM 35475*
VONA-AM 35475*
VooDoo Magazine (Cambridge, MA) 14110
Voodoo Souls Quarterly (Lawrence, KS) 11569
Vortex (Mansfield, TX) Unable to locate
Voter; The National (Washington, DC) 5683
VOTRE SUCCES (Montreal, QC, Can.) Unable to locate
VOWR-AM - 800 (St. John's, NL, Can.) 35506
Vows (Longmont, CO) 4561
Voxair (Winnipeg, MB, Can.) 35357
(Voyage en Groupe); Group Travel (Laprairie, QC, Can.) 37033
Voyager (Pensacola, FL) 6570
Voyages Plus (Montreal, QC, Can.) Ceased
Voyageur (Green Bay, WI) 33742
Voyageur (Quebec, QC, Can.) Ceased
Voyageur; Journal Le (Sudbury, ON, Can.) 36416
Voz Catolica; La (Miami, FL) 6367
Voz Fronteriza (La Jolla, CA) 2121
Voz Hispana; La (New York, NY) 22228
Voz de Houston Newspaper; La (Houston, TX) 30503
Voz; La (Cupertino, CA) 1798
Voz; La (Pomona, CA) 2860
Voz; La (Elizabeth, NJ) 18790
Voz de Montreal (Montreal, QC, Can.) Unable to locate
Voz de Portugal (Hayward, CA) 2044
A Voz de Portugal (Montreal, QC, Can.) 37237
VR World (Darien, CT) Unable to locate
VSA Radio Network (Oklahoma City, OK) 37673
VSAM Update (Westminster, CO) Ceased
VSAWC Newsletter 34798*
VSE Update (Westminster, CO) Ceased
VU Magazine (Edmonton, AB, Can.) 34733
Vue (Miami, FL) Unable to locate
The Vulcan Advocate (Vulcan, AB, Can.) 34867
Vumore 31206*
Vumore Co. 25866*
The V.U.U. Informer (Richmond, VA) 32469
VW Trends (Anaheim, CA) 1420
VWs; Dune Buggies & Hot (Costa Mesa, CA) 1775
VXIJournal (St. Clair Shores, MI) Unable to locate
Vytis (The Knight) (Albany, NY) Unable to locate

W

W (New York, NY) 22905
W & J Magazine (Washington, PA) 28118
W & L (Lexington, VA) 32192
WAAA-AM - 980 (Winston-Salem, NC) 24326
WAAC 10495*
WAAC-FM - 92.9 (Valdosta, GA) 7618
WAAF-AM - 1440 (Boston, MA) 13974
WAAF-FM - 107.3 (Boston, MA) 13975
WAAG-FM - 94.9 (Galesburg, IL) 8909
WAAI-FM - 100.9 (Cambridge, MD) 13400
WAAJ-AM (Huntsville, AL) Ceased
WAAK-AM 23798*
WAAL-FM (Binghamton, NY) Unable to locate
WAAM-AM - 1600 (Ann Arbor, MI) 14774
WAAN-AM 29645*
WAAO-FM - 103.7 (Andalusia, AL) 14
WAAP-TV 23946*
WAAV-FM - 94.1 (Wilmington, NC) 24299
WAAW-FM 12318*
WAAX-AM (Gadsden, AL) Unable to locate
WAAY-TV - Channel 31 (Huntsville, AL) 277
WAAZ-FM - 104.9 (Crestview, FL) 6025
WAB-FM - 99.9 (Raleigh, NC) 24161
Wabamun Community Voice (Spruce Grove, AB, Can.) 34853
Wabash Cablevision 10523*
Wabash Valley Broadcasting Corp. 10504*
Wabash Valley Broadcasting, Inc. 5975*
Wabasha County Herald (Wabasha, MN) 16486
Wabasso Standard (Wabasso, MN) 16487
WABB-AM - 1480 (Mobile, AL) 332
WABB-FM - 97.5 (Mobile, AL) 333
WABC-AM - 770 (New York, NY) 22960
WABC-TV - Channel 7 (New York, NY) 22961
WABD-AM 29119*
WABD-FM 29118*

WABE-FM - 90.1 (Atlanta, GA) 7064
WABF-AM - 1220 (Fairhope, AL) 212
WABG-AM - 960 (Greenwood, MS) 16647
WABG-TV - Channel 6 (Greenville, MS) 16635
WABH-AM 31973*
WABH-AM - 1380 (Bath, NY) 20126
WABI-AM (Bangor, ME) Unable to locate
WABI-TV - Channel 5 (Bangor, ME) 12907
WABJ-AM - 1490 (Adrian, MI) 14711
WABK-FM - 104.3 (Augusta, ME) 12897
WABL-AM - 1570 (Amite, LA) 12471
WABM-TV - Channel 68 (Birmingham, AL) 102
WABN-AM 33889*
WABN-AM (Abingdon, VA) Unable to locate
WABN-FM - 92.7 (Abingdon, VA) 31628
WABQ-AM - 1540 (Cleveland, OH) 24967
WABR-FM 7603*
WABT-FM - 103.9 (Hammond, IN) 10055
WABU-TV 13977*
WABV-AM (Clemson, SC) Ceased
WABW-AM 13103*
WABX-AM (Mount Pleasant, MI) Ceased
WACA-AM 28501*
WACB-AM 27128*
WACD-AM (Alexander City, AL) Ceased
WACE-AM - 730 (Chicopee, MA) 14137
WACF-FM - 98.5 (Paris, IL) 9400
WACG-FM - 90.7 (Augusta, GA) 7104
WACH-TV - Channel 57 (Columbia, SC) 28571
Wachovia Moravian 26704*
WACI-FM 8900*
WACK-AM - 1420 (Newark, NY) 22998
WACL-AM - 570 (Waycross, GA) 7645
WACM-AM - 1490 (West Springfield, MA) 14626
WACO-AM 30027*
Waco Cablevision 31266*
Waco Citizen Newspaper (Waco, TX) 31256
WACO-FM - 99.9 (Waco, TX) 31267
The Waco Messenger (Waco, TX) Ceased
Waco Tribune-Herald (Waco, TX) 31257
Waconia Patriot (Waconia, MN) 16488
WACQ-AM - 1130 (Tallassee, AL) 468
WACQ-FM - 99.9 (Tallassee, AL) 469
WACR-AM - 1050 (Columbus, MS) 16607
WACR-FM - 103.9 (Columbus, MS) 16608
WACS-TV - Channel 25 (Dawson, GA) 7231
WACT-AM - 1420 (Tuscaloosa, AL) 495
WACT-FM 498*
WACV-AM (Montgomery, AL) Unable to locate
WACX-AM (Smyrna, GA) Unable to locate
WACX-TV - Channel 55 (Orlando, FL) 6513
WACY-TV - Channel 32 (Green Bay, WI) 33744
WACZ-AM 20521*
WADA-AM (Shelby, NC) Unable to locate
WADB-FM 19581*
WADC-AM 24602*
WADC-AM - 1050 (Parkersburg, WV) 33423
WADE-AM (Rockingham, NC) Unable to locate
Wade Cablevision (Philadelphia, PA) 27730
The Wadena News (Wadena, SK, Can.) 37583
WADI-FM - 95.3 (Corinth, MS) 16616
WADJ-AM 27102*
WADK-AM - 1540 (Newport, RI) 28374
WADL-TV - Channel 38 (Clinton Township, MI) 14884
Wadley Herald/The Jefferson Reporter; News & Former & (Louisville, GA) 7376
WADO-AM (New York, NY) Unable to locate
WADR-AM - 1480 (Utica, NY) 23471
WADS-AM (Ansonia, CT) Unable to locate
Wadsworth News (Warren, IL) 9733
WADU-AM (La Place, LA) Unable to locate
WADV-AM - 940 (Lebanon, PA) 27176
WADV-FM 20414*
WADX-AM 7609*
WADZ-FM 6924*
WAEB-AM - 790 (Whitehall, PA) 28159
WAEB-FM - 104.1 (Whitehall, PA) 28160
WAEC-AM - 860 (Atlanta, GA) 7065
WAEL-FM - 96.1 (Mayaguez, PR) 28259
WAEN-AM 27054*
WAEN-AM 27054*
WAER-FM - 88.3 (Syracuse, NY) 23434
WAES-AM 23769*
WAEV-FM - 97.3 (Savannah, GA) 7542
WAEW-AM - 1330 (Crossville, TN) 29160
WAEY-AM (Princeton, WV) Unable to locate
WAEY-FM (Princeton, WV) Unable to locate
WAEZ-FM - 99.3 (Bristol, VA) 31898
WAEZ-FM (Milton, WV) Unable to locate
WAFB-FM 12516*
WAFB-TV - Channel 9 (Baton Rouge, LA) 12512
WAFC-FM - 99.5 (Clewiston, FL) 5998
WAFC-FM (Clewiston, FL) Unable to locate
WAFD-FM - 100.3 (Webster Springs, WV) 33488
WAFF-TV - Channel 48 (Huntsville, AL) 278
WAFI-AM 12294*
WAFI-FM 7484*

WAFL-FM - 97.7 (Milford, DE) **5262**
WAFM-FM - 95.3 (Amory, MS) **16546**
WAFN-FM - 92.7 (Huntsville, AL) **279**
WAFS-AM - 920 (Atlanta, GA) **7066**
WAFT-FM - 101.1 (Valdosta, GA) **7619**
WAFX-FM (Chesapeake, VA) *Unable to locate*
WAFY-AM **33443***
WAFY-FM - 103.1 (Middletown, MD) **13629**
WAGA-TV - Channel 5 (Atlanta, GA) **7067**
WAGC-AM - 1560 (Centre, AL) **149**
WAGE-AM - 1200 (Leesburg, VA) **32188**
WAGG-AM (Birmingham, AL) *Unable to locate*
WAGI-FM (Gaffney, SC) *Unable to locate*
WAGL-AM (Lancaster, SC) *Unable to locate*
WAGM-TV - Channel 8 (Presque Isle, ME) **13037**
WAGN-AM - 1340 (Marinette, WI) **34019**
Wagner Announcer (Wagner, SD) **29013**
Wagner International Photos Inc. (New York, NY) **38113**
The Wagner Post Advertizer (Wagner, SD) *Ceased*
The Wagner Post and Announcer (Wagner, SD) **29014**
The Wagnerian (Staten Island, NY) **23364**
WAGO-AM **26891***
Wagoner Record-Democrat (Wagoner, OK) *Ceased*
Wagoner Tribune (Wagoner, OK) **26178**
WAGP-FM (Burton, SC) *Unable to locate*
WAGR-AM - 1340 (Durham, NC) **23847**
WAGS-AM - 1380 (Bishopville, SC) **28495**
WAGT-TV - Channel 26 (Augusta, GA) **7105**
WAGV-TV - Channel 44 (Vansant, VA) **32574**
WAGY-AM - 1320 (Forest City, NC) **23895**
WAH-TV (Boston, MA) *Unable to locate*
WAHC-FM **34161***
WAHD-FM - 90.5 (Raleigh, NC) **24162**
The Wahkiakum County Eagle (Cathlamet, WA) **32703**
Wahkiakum Senior News; Cowlitz- (Longview, WA) **32811**
Wahoo Newspaper (Wahoo, NE) **18302**
WAHR-FM - 99.1 (Huntsville, AL) **280**
WAHS-FM - 89.5 (Auburn Hills, MI) **14784**
WAHT-AM (Lebanon, PA) *Ceased*
WAHT-AM - 1560 (Clemson, SC) **28536**
WAIA-FM **6201***
WAIB-FM - 103.1 (Tallahassee, FL) **6741**
WAIC-FM - 91.9 (Springfield, MA) **14555**
WAID-FM - 106.5 (Clarksdale, MS) **16589**
WAIF-FM (Cincinnati, OH) *Unable to locate*
Waifs' Messenger (Chicago, IL) **8601**
WAIJ-FM - 90.3 (Grantsville, MD) **13557**
WAIK-AM (Galesburg, IL) *Unable to locate*
Waikiki Beach Press (Honolulu, HI) *Ceased*
WAIL-FM (Key West, FL) *Unable to locate*
WAIM-AM - 1230 (Anderson, SC) **28476**
WAIN-AM - 1270 (Columbia, KY) **12018**
WAIN-FM - 93.5 (Columbia, KY) **12019**
Wainwright Courier **34868***
Wainwright Edge (Wainwright, AB, Can.) **34868**
Wainwright Star Chronicle (Wainwright, AB, Can.) **34869**
WAIQ-TV - Channel 26 (Montgomery, AL) **382**
WAIR-FM - 92.5 (Traverse City, MI) **15605**
WAIS-AM - 770 (Nelsonville, OH) **25406**
WAIT-AM - 850 (Crystal Lake, IL) **8697**
WAIT-FM **8698***
WAIV-FM **9453***
WAIV-FM **6231***
WAJA-AM **23901***
WAJD-AM - 1390 (Gainesville, FL) **6161**
WAJF-AM - 1490 (Decatur, AL) **171**
WAJI-FM - 95.1 (Fort Wayne, IN) **9976**
WAJK-FM - 99.3 (La Salle, IL) **9057**
WAJL **6520***
WAJN-AM (Ashland City, TN) *Unable to locate*
WAJP-FM **8691***
WAJR-AM - 1440 (Morgantown, WV) **33400**
WAJV-FM (Columbus, MS) *Unable to locate*
WAJY-FM - 102.7 (Aiken, SC) **28470**
WAJZ **20935***
WAKA-TV - Channel 8 (Montgomery, AL) **383**
Wakarusa Tribune (Wakarusa, IN) **10533**
WAKB-FM - 96.9 (Augusta, GA) **7106**
WAKC-TV **24991***
WAKE-AM - 1500 (Valparaiso, IN) **10512**
Wake Boarding (Winter Park, FL) **6888**
WAKE-FM **10513***
WAKE-FM - 89.5 (Winston-Salem, NC) **24327**
Wake Weekly (Wake Forest, NC) **24262**
Wakeeney Cable TV Co. (Wa Keeney, KS) **11860**
The Wakefield Republican (Wakefield, NE) **18303**
WAKG-FM - 103.3 (Danville, VA) **31992**
WAKH-FM - 105.7 (McComb, MS) **16764**
WAKI-AM - 1230 (Mc Minnville, TN) **29354**
The Wakita Herald (Wakita, OK) **26179**
WAKK-AM (McComb, MS) *Unable to locate*
WAKM-AM (Franklin, TN) *Unable to locate*
WAKM-FM **26690***
WAKO-AM - 910 (Lawrenceville, IL) **9070**

WAKO-FM - 103.1 (Lawrenceville, IL) **9071**
Wakonda Times (Wakonda, SD) **29015**
Wakonda Times-Observer **29015***
WAKQ-FM - 105.5 (Paris, TN) **29560**
WAKR-AM - 1590 (Akron, OH) **24594**
WAKR-FM **24600***
WAKR-TV **24991***
WAKS **6798***
WAKS-FM (Fort Myers, FL) *Unable to locate*
The Wakulla News (Crawfordville, FL) **6021**
WAKW-FM - 93.3 (Cincinnati, OH) **24831**
WAKX-FM **15126***
WAKX-FM (Duluth, MN) *Unable to locate*
WAKY-AM (Greensburg, KY) *Unable to locate*
WAKY-TV **6893***
WAKZ-FM - 95.9 (Brookfield, OH) **24708**
WALA-TV - Channel 10 Digital Channel 9 (Mobile, AL) **334**
WALB-TV - Channel 10 (Albany, GA) **6905**
WALC-FM - 100.5 (Mt. Pleasant, SC) **28698**
WALCO Inc. (Bruce, MS) *Ceased*
WALD-AM - 1080 (Walterboro, SC) **28782**
Waldron News (Waldron, AR) **1361**
The Waldron News - Bulletin (Waldron, AR) **1362**
WALE-AM **14528***
WALE-AM - 990 (Providence, RI) **28431**
WALF-FM (Alfred, NY) *Unable to locate*
WALG-AM - 1590 (Albany, GA) **6906**
WALH-AM - 1340 (Mountain City, GA) **7450**
Walhalla Mountaineer (Walhalla, ND) **24552**
Walhill Citizen (Pender, NE) *Ceased*
WALI-AM **13478***
WALI-FM - 93.7 (Charleston, SC) **28519**
WALJ-FM - 107.1 (Macon, GA) **7388**
WALK-AM - 1370 (Patchogue, NY) **23078**
WALK-FM - 97.5 (Patchogue, NY) **23079**
Walker County Messenger (La Fayette, GA) **7360**
Walker/Westside Advance (Walker, MI) **15655**
Walker's Estimating & Construction Journal (Lisle, IL) *Ceased*
Walkersville/Thurmont Gazette (Frederick, MD) **13525**
Walking (New York, NY) *Unable to locate*
Walking Horse Report (Shelbyville, TN) **29601**
WALL-AM - 1340 (Poughkeepsie, NY) **23152**
Wall Fashions Magazine (St. Paul, MN) **16415**
Wall Lake Cable TV System (Wall Lake, IA) **11284**
The Wall Paper **16415***
Wall Street Journal (New York, NY) **22906**
The Wall Street Journal—Classroom Edition (New York, NY) **22907**
The Wall Street Journal (Midwest Edition) (Chicago, IL) **8602**
Wall Street Journal Radio Network (New York, NY) **37674**
Wall Street Journal Television Network (New York, NY) **37720**
Wall Street Journal Weekly Edition; The Asian (New York, NY) **21265**
Wall Street Journal (Western Edition) (San Francisco, CA) **3461**
Wall Street; On (New York, NY) **22489**
Wall Street Review of Books (New York, NY) *Unable to locate*
Wall Street and Technology (Manhasset, NY) **21017**
Wall Street Technology (New York, NY) *Unable to locate*
The Wall Street Transcript (New York, NY) *Unable to locate*
Wall Street Transcript Digest (New York, NY) *Unable to locate*
Wall & Window Trends (Melville, NY) **21065**
Walla Walla Union-Bulletin (Walla Walla, WA) **33188**
Wallace Enterprise (Wallace, NC) **24265**
The Wallace Miner (Kellogg, ID) *Unable to locate*
The Wallace Pennysaver (Westfield, MA) **14642**
Wallace Stevens Journal (Potsdam, NY) **23141**
The Wallaceburg News (Wallaceburg, ON, Can.) *Unable to locate*
Wallaces Farmer (Des Moines, IA) **10814**
Wallcovering Contractor; Painting & (St. Louis, MO) **17481**
Wallcoverings, Windows and Interior Fashions **21065***
The Waller County News-Citizen (Hempstead, TX) **30439**
Walleye In-Sider (Baxter, MN) **15732**
Walleye Magazine (Cleveland, OH) *Ceased*
Wallington-South Hackensack Shopper; Garfield- (Garfield, NJ) **18842**
Wallis News-Review (Wallis, TX) **31268**
Wallkill Valley Times (Walden, NY) **23496**
Wallowa County Chieftain (Enterprise, OR) **26310**
Walls & Ceilings (Troy, MI) **15644**
Wally's & Wimpy's Football Digest (Parkersburg, WV) *Unable to locate*
WALM-AM (Albion, MI) *Unable to locate*
The Walnut Leader (Walnut, IL) **9732**
Walnut Ridge Cablevision **1204***
WALO-AM (Humacao, PR) *Unable to locate*
The Walpole Times (Walpole, MA) **14594**

WALR-FM (Atlanta, GA) *Unable to locate*
WALS-FM - 102.1 (Peru, IL) **9451**
Walsh County Press (Park River, ND) **24529**
WALT-AM - 910 (Meridian, MS) **16772**
Walt Whitman Quarterly Review (Iowa City, IA) **10990**
Walters Herald (Walters, OK) **26180**
The Walton Log (Destin, FL) **6060**
The Walton Reporter (Walton, NY) **23497**
Walton Tribune/Advertiser (Monroe, GA) **7442**
Walworth County Shopper Advertiser & Shopper Sunday (Delavan, WI) **33654**
WALY-FM - 103.9 (Hollidaysburg, PA) **27047**
WALZ-FM - 95.3 (Machias, ME) **12988**
WAMA-AM - 1550 (Tampa, FL) **6784**
WAMB-AM - 1160 (Nashville, TN) **29506**
WAMB-FM - 98.7 (Donelson, TN) **29169**
WAMC-FM - 90.3 (Albany, NY) **20009**
WAMD-AM - 970 (Aberdeen, MD) **13087**
WAME-AM - 550 (Statesville, NC) **24248**
Wamego Smoke Signal **11861***
Wamego Times (Wamego, KS) **11862**
WAMF-AM - 1490 (Farmville, VA) **32069**
WAMF-FM **13808***
WAMF-FM - 90.5 (Tallahassee, FL) **6742**
WAMG-AM (Gallatin, TN) *Unable to locate*
WAMG-FM - 103.7 (Hales Corners, WI) **33770**
WAMH-FM - 89.3 (Amherst, MA) **13808**
WAMI-AM - 860 (Opp, AL) **412**
WAMI-FM - 102.3 (Opp, AL) **413**
WAMJ-AM **10462***
WAMK-FM - 90.9 (Kingston, NY) **20863**
WAML-AM - 1340 (Hattiesburg, MS) **16667**
WAMM-AM (Woodstock, VA) *Unable to locate*
WAMN-AM - 1050 (Blacksburg, VA) **31882**
WAMO-FM (Pittsburgh, PA) *Unable to locate*
WAMP-FM **25591***
Wampum Saver (Casa Grande, AZ) **670**
WAMQ-AM (Ebensburg, PA) *Unable to locate*
WAMR-AM - 1320 (Venice, FL) **6833**
WAMR-FM (Miami, FL) *Unable to locate*
WAMS-AM (Wilmington, DE) *Unable to locate*
WAMT-AM - 1060 (Titusville, FL) **6822**
WAMT-FM - 103.1 (Pittston, PA) **27886**
WAMU-FM - 88.5 (Washington, DC) **5877**
WAMV-AM - 1420 (Amherst, VA) **31762**
WAMW-AM - 1580 (Washington, IN) **10541**
WAMW-FM - 107.9 (Washington, IN) **10542**
WAMX-AM **33344***
WAMX-FM **33339***
WAMX-FM **14779***
WAMY-AM - 1580 (Amory, MS) **16547**
WAMZ-FM - 97.5 (Louisville, KY) **12245**
WANA-AM - 1490 (Anniston, AL) **18**
Wanamingo Progress **16495***
WANB-AM - 1580 (Waynesburg, PA) **28139**
WANB-FM - 103.1 (Waynesburg, PA) **28140**
WANC-AM **23612***
WANC-FM - 103.9 (Ticonderoga, NY) **23451**
WAND-TV - Channel 17 (Decatur, IL) **8715**
Wander Cable **2035***
Wander Telecommunications **26407***
The Wanderer (Mattapoisett, MA) **14314**
The Wanderer (St. Paul, MN) **16416**
WANE-TV - Channel 15 (Fort Wayne, IN) **9977**
Wang in the News (Austin, TX) *Ceased*
WANI-AM - 1400 (Auburn, AL) **46**
WANL-AM **26***
WANL-AM - 1250 (Albany, GA) **6907**
WANM-AM (Tallahassee, FL) *Unable to locate*
WANN-AM **13098***
WANO-AM (Pineville, KY) *Unable to locate*
WANR-AM (Warren, OH) *Unable to locate*
WANS-AM (Greenville, SC) *Unable to locate*
The WANT ADvertiser (Sudbury, MA) **14580**
WANT-AM (Richmond, VA) *Unable to locate*
Wantagh Observer; Seaford/ (Bellmore, NY) **20147**
Wantagh-Seaford Citizen (Merrick, NY) **21074**
Wantagh Seaford Pennysaver (Farmingdale, NY) *Ceased*
WANV-AM **32557***
WANX-TV **7073***
WANY-AM - 1390 (Albany, KY) **11915**
WANY-FM - 106.3 (Albany, KY) **11916**
WAOA-FM - 107.1 (Melbourne, FL) **6335**
WAOC-AM - 1420 (St. Augustine, FL) **6619**
WAOK-AM - 1380 (Atlanta, GA) **7068**
WAOR-FM - 95.3 (Mishawaka, IN) **10315**
WAOS-AM - 1460 (Austell, GA) **7116**
WAOV-AM - 1450 (Vincennes, IN) **10524**
WAOW-TV - Channel 9 (Wausau, WI) **34431**
WAOX-FM - 105.3 (Litchfield, IL) **9114**
WAOZ-AM **24836***
WAP-TV **29262***
WAPA-AM (Hato Rey, PR) *Unable to locate*
WAPA-TV (Guaynabo, PR) *Unable to locate*
Wapakoneta Daily News (Wapakoneta, OH) **25615**
Wapato Independent **33167***
WAPB-AM (Murfreesboro, TN) *Unable to locate*
WAPE-FM - 95.1 (Jacksonville, FL) **6219**

The Wapello Republican (Wapello, IA) **11285**
WAPF-AM - 980 (McComb, MS) **16765**
WAPG-AM **6895***
WAPI-AM - 1070 (Birmingham, AL) **103**
WAPI-FM **132***
WAPI-TV **131***
WAPK-TV - Channel 30 (Kingsport, TN) **29262**
WAPL-FM **33750***
WAPL-FM - 105.7 (Appleton, WI) **33546**
WAPN-FM - 91.5 (Daytona Beach, FL) **6041**
WAPP-FM **32634***
WAPR-AM (Sebring, FL) *Unable to locate*
WAPR-FM - 88.3 (Tuscaloosa, AL) **496**
WAPS-FM - 91.3 (Akron, OH) **24595**
Wapsipinicon Almanac (Anamosa, IA) **10602**
WAPT-TV - Channel 16 (Jackson, MS) **16715**
WAPW-FM **7078***
WAPX-FM - 91.7 (Clarksville, TN) **29117**
WAPZ-AM - 1250 (Wetumpka, AL) **516**
WAQE-AM - 1090 (Rice Lake, WI) **34295**
WAQE-FM - 97.7 (Rice Lake, WI) **34296**
WAQI-AM (Miami, FL) *Unable to locate*
WAQP-TV - Channel 49 (Saginaw, MI) **15494**
WAQQ-FM (Charlotte, NC) *Unable to locate*
WAQS-SM **23769***
WAQX-FM - 95.7 (Syracuse, NY) **23435**
WAQY-FM - 102.1 (East Longmeadow, MA) **14170**
WAQY-FM - 102.1 (East Longmeadow, MA) **14169**
The War Cry (Alexandria, VA) **31750**
War Generation Journal; Vietnam (Tucson, AZ) **971**
War Journal; Mexican (Richardson, TX) **30977**
War Studies; Journal of Cold (Cambridge, MA) **14075**
War Whoop (Abilene, TX) **29656**
WARA-AM (Attleboro, MA) *Unable to locate*
WARB-AM - 1580 (Oxford, AL) **416**
Warbirds International (Canoga Park, CA) **1661**
WARC-FM - 90.3 (Meadville, PA) **27236**
WARD-AM (Duryea, PA) *Ceased*
Ward's Auto Dealer (Southfield, MI) *Ceased*
Ward's Auto World (Southfield, MI) **15550**
Ward's Automotive International (Southfield, MI) **15551**
Ward's Automotive International Focus on China (Southfield, MI) **15552**
Ward's Automotive Reports (Southfield, MI) **15553**
Ward's Automotive Yearbook (Southfield, MI) **15554**
Ward's Dealer Business (Southfield, MI) *Unable to locate*
Ward's Engine and Vehicle Technology Update (Southfield, MI) **15555**
WARE-AM - 1250 (Palmer, MA) **14458**
Ware River News (Palmer, MA) **14457**
Wareham Courier (Plymouth, MA) **14482**
Warehousing Management (New York, NY) **22908**
WARF-AM - 95.3 (Jasper, AL) **297**
Warfare; Special (Fort Bragg, NC) **23897**
Warfield's Business Record **13154***
Warfield's Business Record (Baltimore, MD) *Ceased*
WARG-FM - 88.9 (Summit, IL) **9675**
WARK-AM - 1490 (Hagerstown, MD) **13573**
WARK-FM **13574***
The Warkworth Journal (Cobourg, ON, Can.) *Ceased*
WARM-AM (Avoca, PA) *Unable to locate*
WARM-AM - 590 (Wilkes Barre, PA) **28169**
WARM-FM - 103.3 (York, PA) **28213**
Warner Amex **24596***
Warner Amex **25435***
Warner Amex **26636***
Warner Amex Cable **18606***
Warner Brothers Studios (Burbank, CA) **37721**
Warner Cable **26636***
Warner Cable **1476***
Warner Cable (Flagstaff, AZ) *Unable to locate*
Warner Cable (Warsaw, IN) **10538**
Warner Cable (Akron, OH) **24596**
Warner Cable (Youngstown, OH) **25701**
Warner Cable of Canton (North Canton, OH) **25435**
Warner Cable of Columbus **25071***
Warner Cable Communications (Berlin, NH) **18456**
Warner Cable Communications (Cincinnati, OH) **24832**
Warner Cable Communications, Inc. **29261***
Warner Cable Communications, Inc. **1133***
Warner Cable Communications, Inc. (Lynn, MA) **14285**
Warner Cable Communications, Inc. (Medford, MA) *Unable to locate*
Warner Cable Communications, Inc. (Houston, TX) **30590**
Warner Cable of Danville (Danville, IL) **8704**
Warner Cable of De Kalb (De Kalb, IL) *Unable to locate*
Warner Cable of Greater Cincinnati **24832***
Warner Cable of Hampton (Hampton, VA) *Ceased*
Warner Cable of Nashua **18606***
The Warner Robins Buyers Guide (Warner Robins, GA) **7638**
Warner's New Paper (Warner, NH) **18648**
WARO-FM - 94.5 (Fort Myers, FL) **6099**

WARQ-FM - 93.5 (Columbia, SC) **28572**
WARR-AM - 1520 (Hampton, VA) **32131**
Warren Advisor (Warren, MI) **15665**
Warren County Guide (Warren, PA) *Unable to locate*
Warren County Magazine (Hackettstown, NJ) *Unable to locate*
Warren Eagle Democrat (Warren, AR) **1365**
Warren Newport Press **9733***
The Warren Record (Washington, DC) *Unable to locate*
Warren Sentinel (Front Royal, VA) **32096**
Warren Sentnel Leader **8904***
Warren Times-Gazette (Warren, RI) **28448**
Warren Times Observer (Warren, PA) **28105**
Warren Weekly (Warren, MI) **15666**
WarrenCable (Warren, IN) **10535**
Warrendale-West Detroit Press & Guide (Dearborn, MI) **14907**
Warrensburg Gazette (Warrensburg, MO) **17670**
Warrensburg/Lake George News **23504***
The Warrensburg-Lake George News (Warrensburg, NY) **23505**
Warrenton Banner (Warrenton, MO) *Ceased*
The Warrenton Clipper (Warrenton, GA) **7639**
Warrenton Journal (Warrenton, MO) **17700**
Warrenville Post (St. Charles, IL) **9572**
Warrick Enquirer (Boonville, IN) *Ceased*
The Warrior (Shearwater, NS, Can.) *Unable to locate*
The Warroad Pioneer (Warroad, MN) **16497**
Warsaw-Faison News (Warsaw, NC) **24271**
Warsaw Penny Saver (Warsaw, NY) **23506**
Warship International (Toledo, OH) **25573**
Wartburg Trumpet (Waverly, IA) **11308**
WARU-AM - 1600 (Peru, IN) **10398**
WARU-FM - 101.9 (Peru, IN) **10399**
WARV-AM - 1590 (Warwick, RI) **28454**
WARW-AM (Hoboken, NJ) *Unable to locate*
WARW-FM - 94.7 (Rockville, MD) **13701**
Warwhoop (Torrance, CA) *Ceased*
The Warwick Advertiser (Monroe, NY) **21091**
Warwick Beacon (Warwick, RI) **28453**
Warwick Valley Dispatch (Warwick, NY) **23508**
WARX-FM - 106.9 (Hagerstown, MD) **13574**
WARY-FM - 88.1 (Valhalla, NY) **23485**
WASA-AM (Havre de Grace, MD) *Unable to locate*
Wasatch Area Voices Express (Ogden, UT) *Unable to locate*
Wasatch Wave (Heber City, UT) **31337**
WASB-AM - 1590 (Brockport, NY) **20248**
WASC-AM - 1530 (Spartanburg, SC) **28760**
Wascana Review **37535***
Wascana Review of Contemporary Poetry and Short Fiction (Regina, SK, Can.) **37535**
Wasco Tribune (Bakersfield, CA) **1454**
WASE-FM - 103.5 (Elizabethtown, KY) **12046**
Waseca County Area Shopper (Faribault, MN) *Ceased*
Waseca County News (Waseca, MN) **16500**
Waseca Sun-Review **16500***
WASG-AM - 550 (Atmore, AL) **34**
WASH-FM - 97.1 (Washington, DC) **5878**
Washburn County Register (Shell Lake, WI) **34326**
Washburn Times **34388***
Washington (Kirkland, WA) *Ceased*
Washington Afro-American (Baltimore, MD) *Unable to locate*
Washington-Alaska Pharmacists **32927***
Washington Area Realtor (Laurel, MD) *Unable to locate*
The Washington Blade (Washington, DC) **5842**
Washington Business Journal (Washington, DC) **5843**
Washington Cable (Washington, DC) **5879**
The Washington Capital Spotlight Newspaper (Washington, DC) *Unable to locate*
Washington CEO (Bellevue, WA) **32669**
The Washington Citizens (Washington, DC) *Unable to locate*
Washington; Columbia Cable of (Vancouver, WA) **33181**
Washington County Bulletin **15817***
The Washington County Edition (Salem, IN) **10441**
Washington County News (Chatom, AL) **152**
Washington County News (Chipley, FL) **5984**
Washington County News (Washington, KS) **11863**
The Washington County News (St George, UT) *Unable to locate*
Washington County News (Abingdon, VA) **31627**
Washington County Observer (Prairie Grove, AR) *Ceased*
The Washington County Post **34446***
Washington County Post (Cambridge, NY) *Ceased*
Washington County Reports (Washington, PA) **28119**
Washington County Review **16228***
Washington County World **31490***
Washington Daily News (Washington, NC) **24273**
Washington D.C. & Baltimore Edition; Nursing Spectrum— (Falls Church, VA) **32050**
Washington DC Beverage Journal (Washington, DC) **5844**

The Washington Diplomat (Wheaton, MD) **13782**
Washington Dossier (Washington, DC) *Unable to locate*
The Washington Evening Journal (Washington, IA) **11286**
Washington FAMILIES Magazine (Herndon, VA) **32166**
Washington FarmekraHJJmpw- (Concord, CA) **1757**
Washington Flyer Magazine (Alexandria, VA) *Unable to locate*
Washington Food Dealer Magazine (Tacoma, WA) *Ceased*
Washington Foodservice News (Pacific, WA) *Ceased*
The Washington Free Press (Seattle, WA) *Ceased*
Washington G2 Reports (Washington, DC) **38114**
Washington History (Washington, DC) **5845**
The Washington Informer (Washington, DC) **5846**
Washington Jewish Week (Rockville, MD) **13699**
Washington Journal (Seattle, WA) *Unable to locate*
Washington Journal of International Law and Economics; George (Washington, DC) **5507**
Washington Journalism Review **13410***
The Washington Lawyer (Washington, DC) **5847**
Washington Libertarian (Seattle, WA) *Unable to locate*
The Washington Libertarian (Yakima, WA) *Unable to locate*
Washington Magazine (Bellevue, WA) **32670**
Washington Missourian (Washington, MO) **17705**
The Washington Monthly (Washington, DC) **5848**
The Washington Monthly Co. (Washington, DC) *Unable to locate*
Washington Music Educators; Voice of (Edmonds, WA) **32747**
The Washington New Observer (Washington, DC) *Unable to locate*
The Washington Newspaper (Seattle, WA) **33039**
The Washington Nurse (Seattle, WA) **33040**
Washington, Official Gazette; Spokane, (Spokane, WA) **33100**
The Washington Opera Magazine (Washington, DC) **5849**
Washington Pharmacist (Renton, WA) **32927**
The Washington Post (Washington, DC) **5850**
The Washington Post Magazine (Washington, DC) **5851**
The Washington Post Writers Group (Washington, DC) **38115**
Washington; Proceedings of the Entomological Society of (Washington, DC) **5730**
The Washington Quarterly (Cambridge, MA) **14111**
Washington Real Estate News **5443***
Washington Report on Middle East Affairs (Washington, DC) **5852**
Washington Reporter **9428***
Washington Review (Washington, DC) **5853**
Washington Review of Arts & Literature **5853***
Washington Small Business News Roundup (Kenner, LA) **38116**
Washington Source; Romeo- (Shelby Township, MI) **15537**
The Washington Square News (New York, NY) **22909**
Washington State Grange News (Olympia, WA) **32862**
Washington (State) Legislative Ethics Board *Ceased*
Washington State Migrant Education News (Toppenish, WA) *Unable to locate*
Washington State University Hilltopics (Pullman, WA) **32908**
Washington Technology (Washington, DC) **5854**
Washington Techway (Arlington, VA) **31840**
The Washington Times (Washington, DC) **5855**
Washington Times-Herald (Washington, IN) **10540**
Washington Times-Reporter (Peoria, IL) **9428**
(Washington); Topic (Washington, PA) **28117**
Washington Trails (Seattle, WA) **33041**
The Washington Trooper (Vancouver, WA) *Unable to locate*
The Washington University Global Studies Law Review (St. Louis, MO) **17528**
Washington University Journal of Law and Policy (St. Louis, MO) **17529**
Washington View (Washington, DC) *Unable to locate*
Washington; WHERE (Washington, DC) **5860**
Washington World **31490**
Washingtonian; East (Pomeroy, WA) **32887**
Washingtonian Magazine (Washington, DC) **5856**
Washita County Enterprise (Corn, OK) **25794**
Washougal Post-Record; Camas- (Camas, WA) **32701**
WASK-AM (Lafayette, IN) *Unable to locate*
WASK-FM **10261***
Waskom Review (Waskom, TX) *Unable to locate*
WASL-AM **13103***
WASL-FM - 100.1 (Dyersburg, TN) **29177**
WASN-AM (Youngstown, OH) *Unable to locate*
WASN-FM **20013***
WASO-AM (Covington, LA) *Unable to locate*
WASP-FM **26738***
WASR-AM - 1420 (Wolfeboro, NH) **18656**

WAYC-AM **26691***
WAYC-FM **26692***
WAYC-FM - 100.9 (Bedford, PA) **26690**
Waycross Cable Co. (Waycross, GA) **7646**
Waycross Journal Herald (Waycross, GA) **7644**
WAYE-AM (Birmingham, AL) *Unable to locate*
WAYF-FM **336***
WAYJ-FM - 88.7 (Fort Myers, FL) **6100**
Wayland Flashes Shopping Guide (Allegan, MI) *Unable to locate*
The Wayland Globe/Penasee Press **15670***
Wayland Pennysaver; Dansville- (Canisteo, NY) **20427**
The Wayland/Sudbury Gazette **14579***
The Wayland/Sudbury Gazette **14616***
Wayland Town Crier & TAB (Wayland, MA) **14616**
Wayland and Weston Town Crier **15671***
Wayland-Weston Town Crier (Wayland, MI) **15671**
WAYN-AM - 900 (Rockingham, NC) **24202**
Wayne Bargain Hunter **25390***
Wayne County Journal **25390***
Wayne County Journal-Banner (Piedmont, MO) **17343**
Wayne County Mail (Webster, NY) **23527**
Wayne County Mail (Sodus Edition) (Webster, NY) *Ceased*
The Wayne County News (Waynesboro, MS) **16872**
The Wayne County News (Waynesboro, TN) **29644**
Wayne County Outlook (Monticello, KY) **12298**
Wayne County Press (Fairfield, IL) **8880**
Wayne County Publication Inc (Wayne, WV) **33484**
Wayne County Star (Lyons, NY) **20979**
Wayne Eagle (Wayne, MI) **15673**
The Wayne Herald (Wayne, NE) **18306**
The Wayne Independent (Honesdale, PA) **27051**
The Wayne Journal (Millersburg, OH) **25390**
Wayne State Magazine (Detroit, MI) **14953**
Wayne Stater (Wayne, NE) **18307**
Wayne Today (West Paterson, NJ) **19741**
Waynedale News (Fort Wayne, IN) **9974**
WAYQ-TV (Palm Bay, FL) *Unable to locate*
WAYR-AM - 550 (Green Cove Springs, FL) **6174**
WAYS-FM - 99.1 (Macon, GA) **7389**
WAYT-FM **10531***
WAYX-AM (Nashville, TN) *Unable to locate*
WAYY **33678***
WAYY-AM - 790 (Altoona, WI) **33524**
WAYZ-AM (Waynesboro, PA) *Unable to locate*
WAYZ-FM - 104.7 (Greencastle, PA) **26950**
Wayzata/Orono/Long Lake Sun-Sailor (Plymouth, MN) **16280**
Wayzata Sun-Sailor (Minnetonka, MN) **16178**
WAZE-FM (Albany, GA) *Unable to locate*
WAZF-AM (Yazoo City, MS) *Unable to locate*
WAZK-FM (Decatur, AL) *Unable to locate*
WAZL-AM (Hazleton, PA) *Unable to locate*
Wazobia News (Nanuet, NY) **21105**
WAZR-FM - 93.7 (Woodstock, VA) **32641**
WAZS-AM - 980 (Summerville, SC) **28766**
WAZU-AM **24836***
WAZU-FM **25144***
WAZX-AM - 1550 (Smyrna, GA) **7556**
WAZY-AM - 1410 (Lafayette, IN) **10257**
WAZY-FM - 96.5 (Lafayette, IN) **10258**
WAZZ-AM - 1490 (Fayetteville, NC) **23884**
WAZZ-FM **23885***
WAZZ-FM **24099***
WBAA-AM - 920 (West Lafayette, IN) **10556**
WBAA-FM - 101.3 (West Lafayette, IN) **10557**
WBAB-FM - 102.3 (West Babylon, NY) **23537**
WBAC-AM (Cleveland, TN) *Unable to locate*
WBAD-FM - 94.3 (Greenville, MS) **16636**
WBAF-AM - 1090 (Barnesville, GA) **7122**
WBAG-AM - 1150 (Burlington, NC) **23674**
WBAI-FM (New York, NY) *Unable to locate*
WBAI Folio (New York, NY) *Unable to locate*
WBAK-TV - Channel 38 (Terre Haute, IN) **10494**
WBAL-AM - 1090 (Baltimore, MD) **13265**
WBAL-FM **13275***
WBAL-TV - Channel 11 (Baltimore, MD) **13266**
WBAM-AM **390***
WBAM-FM - 98.9 (Montgomery, AL) **384**
WBAP **30360***
WBAP-AM - 820 (Arlington, TX) **29744**
WBAQ-FM - 97.9 (Greenville, MS) **16637**
WBAR-AM - 1460 (Bartow, FL) **5919**
WBAR-FM - 94.7 (Cohoes, NY) **20480**
WBAT-AM - 1400 (Marion, IN) **10289**
WBAU-FM (Garden City, NY) *Unable to locate*
WBAV-AM - 1600 (Charlotte, NC) **23763**
WBAW-AM - 99.1 (Barnwell, SC) **28483**
WBAW-FM - 99.1 (Barnwell, SC) **28484**
WBAX-AM - 1240 (Scranton, PA) **27965**
WBAY-TV - Channel 2 (Green Bay, WI) **33745**
WBAZ-FM - 102.5 (Amagansett, NY) **20028**
WBBA-AM - 1580 (Pittsfield, IL) **9456**
WBBA-FM - 97.5 (Pittsfield, IL) **9457**
WBBB-AM **23677***
WBBC-FM - 93.5 (Blackstone, VA) **31893**
WBBD-AM **26765***

WBBD-AM - 1400 (Wheeling, WV) **33505**
WBBE-AM - 1580 (Lexington, KY) **12181**
WBBE-FM - 103.3 (Baton Rouge, LA) **12513**
WBBF-FM - 98.9 (Rochester, NY) **23243**
WBBG-FM - 93.3 (Youngstown, OH) **25702**
WBBH-TV - Channel 20 (Fort Myers, FL) **6101**
WBBI-FM - 107.5 (Cincinnati, OH) **24833**
WBBJ-TV - Channel 7 (Jackson, TN) **29233**
WBBK-AM (Blakely, GA) *Unable to locate*
WBBL-AM - 1340 (Grand Rapids, MI) **15102**
WBBM-AM - 780 (Chicago, IL) **8613**
WBBM-FM - 96.3 (Chicago, IL) **8614**
WBBM-TV - Channel 2 (Chicago, IL) **8615**
WBBN-FM - 95.9 (Laurel, MS) **16742**
WBBO-FM **28644***
WBBO-FM - 98.5 (Manahawkin, NJ) **19211**
WBBP-AM - 1480 (Memphis, TN) **29387**
WBBQ-AM (Augusta, GA) *Unable to locate*
WBBQ-FM (Augusta, GA) *Unable to locate*
WBBR-AM (Greenville, SC) *Unable to locate*
WBBS-FM (Great Barrington, MA) *Ceased*
WBBT-AM (Lyons, MS) *Unable to locate*
WBBV-FM (Vicksburg, MS) *Unable to locate*
WBBW-AM - 1240 (Youngstown, OH) **25703**
WBBY-FM (Westerville, OH) *Ceased*
WBBZ-AM - 1230 (Ponca City, OK) **26044**
WBCA-AM - 1110 (Atmore, AL) **35**
WBCB-AM - 1490 (Levittown, PA) **27190**
WBCC-TV - Channel 68 (Cocoa, FL) **6000**
WBCE-AM - 1200 (Wickliffe, KY) **12443**
WBCF-AM - 1240 (Florence, AL) **221**
WBCG-FM **24087***
WBCH-AM - 1220 (Hastings, MI) **15156**
WBCH-FM - 100.1 (Hastings, MI) **15157**
WBCI-FM - 105.9 (Topsham, ME) **13067**
WBCK-AM - 930 (Battle Creek, MI) **14794**
WBCL-FM - 90.3 (Fort Wayne, IN) **9978**
WBCM-AM (Bay City, MI) *Unable to locate*
WBCM-FM **15497***
WBCM-FM - 93.5 (Traverse City, MI) **15606**
WBCN-FM - 104.1 (Boston, MA) **13976**
WBCO-AM **53***
WBCO-AM - 1540 (Bucyrus, OH) **24719**
WBCP-AM - 1580 (Urbana, IL) **9721**
WBCR-AM (Scranton, PA) *Unable to locate*
WBCR-AM - 1470 (Alcoa, TN) **29048**
WBCR-FM - 90.3 (Beloit, WI) **33578**
WBCS-FM (Boston, MA) *Unable to locate*
WBCT-FM (Grand Rapids, MI) *Unable to locate*
WBCU-AM - 1460 (Union, SC) **28777**
WBCV-AM - 1550 (Bristol, TN) **29067**
WBCW-AM (Jeannette, PA) *Unable to locate*
WBCX-FM - 89.1 (Gainesville, GA) **7300**
WBCY-FM - 89.5 (Archbold, OH) **24615**
WBDC-FM - 100.9 (Jasper, IN) **10220**
WBDG-FM (Giant 90.0) - 90.9 (Indianapolis, IN) **10190**
WBDJ-FM **10500***
WBDK-FM - 96.7 (Sturgeon Bay, WI) **34353**
WBDN-AM **15009***
WBDR-FM - 102.7 (Watertown, NY) **23516**
WBDY-AM (Bluefield, WV) *Unable to locate*
WBDY-FM (Bluefield, WV) *Unable to locate*
WBEB-FM - 101.1 (Bala Cynwyd, PA) **26671**
WBEC-AM - 1420 (Pittsfield, MA) **14473**
WBEC-FM - 105.5 (Pittsfield, MA) **14474**
WBEE-AM - 1570 (Harvey, IL) **8977**
WBEE-FM - 92.5 (Rochester, NY) **23244**
WBEJ-AM - 1240 (Elizabethton, TN) **29180**
WBEL-AM (Beloit, WI) *Unable to locate*
WBEM-AM (Johnstown, PA) *Unable to locate*
WBEN-AM (Buffalo, NY) *Unable to locate*
WBEN-TV **20403***
WBER-AM **28523***
WBES-AM **28536***
WBES-FM (Charleston, WV) *Unable to locate*
WBET-AM - 1460 (Brockton, MA) **14014**
WBET-FM **14015***
WBEU-AM (Hilton Head Island, SC) *Unable to locate*
WBEV-AM - 1430 (Beaver Dam, WI) **33569**
WBEX-AM - 1490 (Chillicothe, OH) **24765**
WBEZ-FM (Chicago, IL) *Unable to locate*
WBFB-FM - 104.7 (Brewer, ME) **12926**
WBFC-AM (Stanton, KY) *Unable to locate*
WBFD **26693***
WBFD **26691***
WBFD-AM - 1310 (Bedford, PA) **26691**
WBFF-TV - Channel 45 (Baltimore, MD) **13267**
WBFG-FM (Effingham, IL) *Unable to locate*
WBFH-FM - 88.1 (Bloomfield Hills, MI) **14831**
WBFJ-AM **29650***
WBFJ-AM - 1550 (Winston-Salem, NC) **24328**
WBFJ-FM - 89.3 (Winston-Salem, NC) **24329**
WBFL-FM (Bellows Falls, VT) *Unable to locate*
WBFM-FM - 93.7 (Sheboygan, WI) **34323**
WBFN-AM - 1500 (Quitman, MS) **16830**
WBFO-FM - 88.7 (Buffalo, NY) **20395**
WBFR-FM - 89.5 (Birmingham, AL) **105**
WBFS-TV - Channel 33 (Miami, FL) **6397**

WBFX-FM - 101.3 (Grand Rapids, MI) **15103**
WBFX-TV **23959***
WBGC-AM - 1240 (Chipley, FL) **5985**
WBGF-FM - 93.5 (Belle Glade, FL) **5921**
WBGG-FM - 105.9 (Miramar, FL) **6428**
WBGL-FM - 91.7 (Champaign, IL) **8223**
WBGM-AM **6750***
WBGM-FM **6743***
WBGM-FM - 88.1 (Danville, PA) **26819**
WBGN-AM - 1340 (Bowling Green, KY) **11951**
WBGO-FM - 88.3 (Newark, NJ) **19368**
WBGQ-FM - 100.7 (Morristown, TN) **29420**
WBGR-AM (Baltimore, MD) *Unable to locate*
WBGS-AM - 1030 (Blacksburg, VA) **31883**
WBGT-AM **32558***
WBGT-FM **32559***
WBGU-FM - 88.1 (Bowling Green, OH) **24703**
WBGU-TV - Channel 27 (Bowling Green, OH) **24704**
WBGW-FM - 101.5 (Haubstadt, IN) **10061**
WBGZ-AM - 1570 (Alton, IL) **8011**
WBHB-AM - 1240 (Tifton, GA) **7600**
WBHD-FM - 94.3 (Wilkes Barre, PA) **28170**
WBHG-FM - 101.5 (Gilford, NH) **18511**
WBHK-FM - 98.7 (Birmingham, AL) **106**
WBHL-FM (Florence, AL) *Unable to locate*
WBHM-FM - 90.3 (Birmingham, AL) **107**
WBHN-AM - 1590 (Bryson City, NC) **23667**
WBHQ-FM (West Baden Springs, IN) *Ceased*
WBHR-AM - 660 (Sauk Rapids, MN) **16439**
WBHR-FM **15180***
WBHR-FM (Bellaire, OH) *Ceased*
WBHS-TV (St. Petersburg, FL) *Unable to locate*
WBHT-AM **29073***
WBHT-FM - 97.1 (Wilkes Barre, PA) **28171**
WBHV-FM - 103.1 (State College, PA) **28023**
WBHY-AM - 840 (Mobile, AL) **335**
WBHY-FM - 88.5 (Mobile, AL) **336**
WBIC-AM **20522***
WBIC-AM - 810 (Royston, GA) **7522**
WBIC-FM **7135***
WBIE-FM **7074***
WBIF-FM **9800***
WBIG-AM **23908***
WBIG-AM - 1280 (Aurora, IL) **8042**
WBIG-FM **23948***
WBIG-FM (Rockville, MD) *Unable to locate*
WBIL-AM (Tuskegee, AL) *Unable to locate*
WBIM-FM - 91.5 (Bridgewater, MA) **14009**
WBIP-AM - 1400 (Booneville, MS) **16572**
WBIP-FM - 99.3 (Booneville, MS) **16573**
WBIQ-TV - Channel 10 (Birmingham, AL) **108**
WBIR-AM **29289***
WBIR-FM **29290***
WBIR-TV - Channel 10 (Knoxville, TN) **29288**
WBIS-AM - 1190 (Annapolis, MD) **13098**
WBIU-AM **12524***
WBIW-AM - 1340 (Bedford, IN) **9799**
WBIZ-AM - 1400 (Eau Claire, WI) **33676**
WBIZ-FM - 100.7 (Eau Claire, WI) **33677**
WBJA-TV **20225***
WBJB-FM - 90.5 (Lincroft, NJ) **19170**
WBJC-FM - 91.5 (Baltimore, MD) **13268**
WBJH-FM **19676***
WBJW-FM **6525***
WBJZ-FM **23043***
WBJZ-FM - 104.7 (Ripon, WI) **34304**
WBKB-TV **8639***
WBKB-TV - Channel 11 (Alpena, MI) **14738**
WBKC-AM - 1460 (Painesville, OH) **25465**
WBKE-FM - 89.5 (North Manchester, IN) **10361**
WBKF-FM **6229***
WBKH-AM - 950 (Hattiesburg, MS) **16668**
WBKI-AM **7138***
WBKJ-FM - 105.1 (Kosciusko, MS) **16736**
WBKK-FM - 97.7 (Schenectady, NY) **23315**
WBKN-FM - 92.1 (Brookhaven, MS) **16579**
WBKO-TV - Channel 13 (Bowling Green, KY) **11952**
WBKV-AM - 1470 (West Bend, WI) **34447**
WBKV-FM **34448***
WBKX-FM **15349***
WBKX-FM - 96.5 (Fredonia, NY) **20623**
WBKY-FM **12197***
WBKZ-AM - 880 (Athens, GA) **6955**
WBLA-AM - 1440 (Elizabethtown, NC) **23865**
WBLB-AM - 1340 (Pulaski, VA) **32338**
WBLD-FM - 89.3 (West Bloomfield, MI) **15679**
WBLF-AM (Bellefonte, PA) *Unable to locate*
WBLG-FM **11962***
WBLG-TV **12196***
WBLI-FM - 106.1 (West Babylon, NY) **23538**
WBLJ-AM - 1230 (Dalton, GA) **7223**
WBLK-FM (Buffalo, NY) *Unable to locate*
WBLL-AM - 1390 (Bellefontaine, OH) **24667**
WBLM-FM - 102.9 (Portland, ME) **13021**
WBLN-FM **12318***
WBLO-AM **28735***
WBLR-AM (Grovetown, GA) *Unable to locate*
WBLS-FM - 107.5 (New York, NY) **22963**
WBLT-AM - 1350 (Bedford, VA) **31863**

WCPR-AM - 1450 (Coamo, PR) **28241**
WCPS-AM (Tarboro, NC) *Unable to locate*
WCPX-TV **6521***
WCPZ-FM - 102.7 (Sandusky, OH) **25512**
WCQA **20623***
WCQM-FM - 98.3 (Park Falls, WI) **34234**
WCQR-FM - 88.3 (Kingsport, TN) **29263**
WCQR-TV **5882***
WCQS-FM - 88.1 (Asheville, NC) **23635**
WCRA-AM - 1090 (Effingham, IL) **8819**
WCRA-FM **8820***
WCRB-FM - 102.5 (Waltham, MA) **14607**
WCRC-FM - 95.7 (Effingham, IL) **8820**
WCRD-AM - 540 (Muncie, IN) **10331**
WCRD-FM **9865***
WCRE-AM - 1420 (Cheraw, SC) **28529**
WCRF-FM - 103.3 (Cleveland, OH) **24971**
WCRH-FM - 90.5 (Williamsport, MD) **13783**
WCRI-AM **450***
WCRI Research Briefs (Cambridge, MA) *Unable to locate*
WCRJ-AM **6236***
WCRJ-FM (Jacksonville, FL) *Unable to locate*
WCRK-AM - 1150 (Morristown, TN) **29421**
WCRL-AM - 1570 (Oneonta, AL) **407**
WCRM-AM - 1350 (Fort Myers, FL) **6102**
WCRM-FM **10055***
WCRO-AM (Johnstown, PA) *Unable to locate*
WCRQ-FM **279***
WCRR-AM - 660 (Rural Retreat, VA) **32517**
WCRR-FM - 95.3 (Rural Retreat, VA) **32518**
WCRS-AM - 1450 (Greenwood, SC) **28647**
WCRS-FM **28650***
WCRT-AM (Birmingham, AL) *Unable to locate*
WCRV-AM - 640 (Memphis, TN) **29389**
WCRW 1926-1996/WEDC 1926-1997 **8651***
WCRX-FM - 88.1 (Chicago, IL) **8619**
WCRZ-FM - 107.9 (Flint, MI) **15039**
WCSB-FM - 89.3 (Cleveland, OH) **24972**
WCSC-TV (Charleston, SC) *Unable to locate*
WCSD-FM (Cookeville, TN) *Unable to locate*
WCSG-FM - 91.3 (Grand Rapids, MI) **15105**
WCSH-AM **13057***
WCSH-TV - Channel 6 (Portland, ME) **13023**
WCSI-AM - 1010 (Columbus, IN) **9896**
WCSJ-AM (Morris, IL) *Unable to locate*
WCSK-FM - 90.3 (Kingsport, TN) **29264**
WCSL-AM - 1590 (Cherryville, NC) **23785**
WCSM-AM - 1350 (Celina, OH) **24750**
WCSM-FM - 96.7 (Celina, OH) **24751**
WCSN-FM - 105.7 (Gulf Shores, AL) **253**
WCSO-FM **29096***
WCSP-AM (Crystal Springs, MS) *Unable to locate*
WCSR-AM - 1340 (Hillsdale, MI) **15166**
WCSR-FM - 92.1 (Hillsdale, MI) **15167**
WCSS-AM - 1490 (Amsterdam, NY) **20058**
WCST-AM - 1010 (Berkeley Springs, WV) **33248**
WCST-FM - 93.5 (Berkeley Springs, WV) **33249**
WCSU-AM **20514***
WCSU-FM **24972***
WCSU-FM - 88.9 (Wilberforce, OH) **25653**
WCSV-AM **29161***
WCSW-AM - 940 (Shell Lake, WI) **34327**
WCSX-FM - 94.7 (Southfield, MI) **15557**
WCSY-FM - 98.3 (South Haven, MI) **15539**
WCTA-AM - 810 (Alamo, TN) **29047**
WCTA-FM - 95.1 (Mayaguez, PR) **28260**
WCTC-AM - 1450 (New Brunswick, NJ) **19342**
WCTE-TV - Channel 22 (Cookeville, TN) **29148**
WCTF-AM (Vernon, CT) *Unable to locate*
WCTI-TV - Channel 12 (New Bern, NC) **24098**
WCTJ-FM **23161***
WCTK-FM (Warwick, RI) *Unable to locate*
WCTL-FM - 106.3 (Waterford, PA) **28123**
WCTM-AM - 1130 (Eaton, OH) **25175**
WCTN-AM - 950 (Potomac, MD) **13666**
WCTO-FM **20600***
WCTO-FM - 96.1 (Bethlehem, PA) **26709**
WCTQ-FM - 106.5 (Sarasota, FL) **6672**
WCTR-AM - 1530 (Chestertown, MD) **13406**
WCTS-AM - 1030 (Plymouth, MN) **16281**
WCTS-FM **16162***
WCTT-AM - 680 (Corbin, KY) **12022**
WCTT-FM - 107.3 (Corbin, KY) **12023**
WCTV-TV - Channel 6 (Tallahassee, FL) **6744**
WCTW-AM **10344***
WCTW-FM - 98.5 (Hudson, NY) **20769**
WCTX **27022***
WCTX-TV - Channel 59 (New Haven, CT) **5012**
WCTY-FM - 97.7 (Norwich, CT) **5085**
WCUB-AM - 980 (Manitowoc, WI) **34014**
WCUC-FM - 91.7 (Clarion, PA) **26783**
WCUE-AM - 1150 (Peninsula, OH) **25473**
WCUL-FM - 103.1 (Culpeper, VA) **31988**
WCUM-AM - 1450 (Bridgeport, CT) **4716**
WCUP-FM **6912***
WCUW-FM - 91.3 (Worcester, MA) **14696**
WCUZ-AM **15123***
WCUZ-FM **15103***

WCVA-AM - 1490 (Culpeper, VA) **31989**
WCVB-TV - Channel 5 (Needham, MA) **14375**
WCVC-AM - 1330 (Tallahassee, FL) **6745**
WCVC-FM **32635***
WCVE-FM - 88.9 (Richmond, VA) **32474**
WCVE-TV - Channel 23 (Richmond, VA) **32475**
WCVF-FM - 88.9 (Fredonia, NY) **20624**
WCVG-AM - 1320 (Latonia, KY) **12153**
WCVH-FM - 90.5 (Flemington, NJ) **18822**
WCVI-AM (Connellsville, PA) *Unable to locate*
WCVJ-FM - 90.9 (Jefferson, OH) **25268**
WCVK-FM - 90.7 (Bowling Green, KY) **11954**
WCVL-AM - 1550 (Crawfordsville, IN) **9911**
WCVM-FM **31561***
WCVN-TV - Channel 54 (Covington, KY) **12030**
WCVO-FM - 104.9 (Gahanna, OH) **25207**
WCVP-AM - 600 (Murphy, NC) **24090**
WCVP-FM - 95.9 (Murphy, NC) **24091**
WCVQ-FM - 107.9 (Clarksville, TN) **29118**
WCVR-FM - 102.1 (Randolph Center, VT) **31582**
WCVS-AM **9647***
WCVT-FM **13285***
WCVV-FM - 89.5 (Belpre, OH) **24674**
WCVW-TV - Channel 57 (Richmond, VA) **32476**
WCVX-TV (Valley Forge, PA) *Unable to locate*
WCVY-FM - 91.5 (Coventry, RI) **28331**
WCVZ-FM - 92.7 (Zanesville, OH) **25719**
WCW Magazine (Rockville Centre, NY) *Ceased*
WCWA-AM - 1230 (Toledo, OH) **25575**
WCWC-AM **34305***
WCWL-FM (Lenox, MA) *Unable to locate*
WCWM-FM - 90.7 (Williamsburg, VA) **32625**
WCWP-FM - 88.1 (Brookville, NY) **20361**
WCWS-FM - 90.9 (Wooster, OH) **25675**
WCWT-FM - 101.5 (Centerville, OH) **24754**
WCWV-FM - 92.9 (Summersville, WV) **33474**
WCXI-AM **15023***
WCXI-FM **15225***
WCXJ-AM (Pittsburgh, PA) *Unable to locate*
WCXL-FM **25135***
WCXN-AM - 1170 (Claremont, NC) **23786**
WCXR-FM **5887***
WCXR-FM (Lewisburg, PA) *Unable to locate*
WCXT-AM - 105.3 (Hart, MI) **15148**
WCXU-FM - 97.7 (Caribou, ME) **12947**
WCXX-FM - 102.3 (Caribou, ME) **12948**
WCYB-AM **31902***
WCYB-TV - Channel 5 (Bristol, VA) **31899**
WCYI-FM - 93.9 (Portland, ME) **13024**
WCYJ-FM - 88.7 (Waynesburg, PA) **28141**
WCYK-AM - 810 (Charlottesville, VA) **31950**
WCYK-FM - 99.7 (Charlottesville, VA) **31951**
WCYN-AM - 1400 (Cynthiana, KY) **12034**
WCYN-FM - 102.3 (Cynthiana, KY) **12035**
WCYO-FM - 100.7 (Richmond, KY) **12384**
WCYY-FM - 93.9 (Portland, ME) **13025**
WCZI-FM - 98.3 (Greenville, NC) **23971**
WCZN-AM **26667***
WCZQ-FM - 105.5 (Monticello, IL) **9223**
WCZR-AM (Charleston, WV) *Unable to locate*
WCZR-FM **6065***
WCZT-FM (Cape May, NJ) *Unable to locate*
WCZX-FM - 97.7 (Poughkeepsie, NY) **23155**
WCZY-FM **15414***
WCZY-FM - 104.3 (Mount Pleasant, MI) **15382**
WCZZ-AM - 1090 (Greenwood, SC) **28648**
W.D. Farmer Residence Designer Inc. (Tucker, GA) **38117**
WDAC-FM - 94.5 (Lancaster, PA) **27148**
WDAD-AM - 1450 (Indiana, PA) **27080**
WDAE-AM - 620 (Tampa, FL) **6786**
WDAF-AM - 610 (Westwood, KS) **11877**
WDAF-TV - Channel 4 (Kansas City, MO) **17215**
WDAK-AM - 540 (Columbus, GA) **7187**
WDAL-AM - 1430 (Dalton, GA) **7224**
WDAL-FM **16774***
WDAM-TV - Channel 7 (Hattiesburg, MS) **16669**
WDAN-AM - 1490 (Danville, IL) **8705**
WDAN-FM **8706***
WDAO-FM **25147***
WDAP-AM **8625***
WDAQ-FM - 98.3 (Danbury, CT) **4765**
WDAR-AM (Darlington, SC) *Ceased*
WDAR-FM (Darlington, SC) *Unable to locate*
WDAS-AM (Philadelphia, PA) *Unable to locate*
WDAS-FM - 105.3 (Bala Cynwyd, PA) **26672**
WDAT-AM **6534***
WDAU-TV **189***
WDAV-FM - 89.9 (Davidson, NC) **23800**
WDAX-AM **7428***
WDAY-AM - 970 (Fargo, ND) **24435**
WDAY-AM - 970 (Fargo, ND) **24434**
WDAY-TV - Channel 6 (Fargo, ND) **24436**
WDAZ-TV - Channel 8 (Grand Forks, ND) **24466**
WDBA-FM - 107.3 (Du Bois, PA) **26840**
WDBB-TV (Tuscaloosa, AL) *Unable to locate*
WDBC-AM - 680 (Escanaba, MI) **15010**
WDBD-TV - Channel 40 (Jackson, MS) **16716**
WDBF-AM - 1420 (Delray Beach, FL) **6058**

WDBJ-AM **32497***
WDBJ-TV - Channel 7 (Roanoke, VA) **32496**
WDBK-FM - 91.5 (Blackwood, NJ) **18684**
WDBL-AM - 1590 (Springfield, TN) **29619**
WDBL-FM - 94.3 (Springfield, TN) **29620**
WDBM-FM - 88.9 (East Lansing, MI) **14994**
WDBO-AM - 580 (Orlando, FL) **6515**
WDBO-FM **6530***
WDBO-TV **6521***
WDBQ-AM - 1490 (Dubuque, IA) **10854**
WDBQ-FM - 107.5 (Dubuque, IA) **10855**
WDBS-FM - 97.1 (Sutton, WV) **33477**
WDBT-FM - 95.5 (Jackson, MS) **16717**
WDBX-FM - 91.1 (Carbondale, IL) **8122**
WDCA-TV - Channel 20 (Washington, DC) **5880**
WDCB-FM - 90.9 (Glen Ellyn, IL) **8933**
WDCC-FM - 90.5 (Sanford, NC) **24220**
WDCF-AM - 1350 (Dade City, FL) **6033**
WDCG-FM (Durham, NC) *Unable to locate*
WDCL-FM - 89.7 (Bowling Green, KY) **11955**
WDCN-TV - Channel 8 (Nashville, TN) **29508**
WDCO-TV (Atlanta, GA) *Unable to locate*
WDCP-TV - Channel 35 (University Center, MI) **15648**
WDCQ-AM (Fort Myers, FL) *Unable to locate*
WDCQ-TV - Channel 19 (University Center, MI) **15649**
WDCR-AM - 1340 (Hanover, NH) **18520**
WDCT-AM (Fairfax, VA) *Unable to locate*
WDCU-FM - 90.1 (Washington, DC) **5881**
WDCV-FM - 88.3 (Carlisle, PA) **26763**
WDCX-FM - 99.5 (Buffalo, NY) **20397**
WDCY-AM - 1520 (Douglasville, GA) **7250**
WDDC-AM (Dallas, GA) *Unable to locate*
WDDC-FM - 100.1 (Portage, WI) **34262**
WDDD-AM - 810 (Marion, IL) **9145**
WDDD-FM - 107.3 (Marion, IL) **9146**
WDDD-TV **9148***
WDDH-FM - 97.5 (Ridgway, PA) **27939**
WDDJ-FM - 96.9 (Paducah, KY) **12342**
WDDK-FM (Greensboro, GA) *Unable to locate*
WDDO-AM - 1240 (Macon, GA) **7392**
WDDQ-FM - 92.1 (Valdosta, GA) **7620**
WDDW-AM **9145***
WDDY-AM **32116***
WDEA-AM - 1370 (Brewer, ME) **12927**
WDEA-FM **12929***
WDEB-AM - 1500 (Jamestown, TN) **29245**
WDEB-FM - 103.9 (Jamestown, TN) **29246**
WDEC-AM (Americus, GA) *Unable to locate*
WDEC-FM - 94.7 (Americus, GA) **6924**
WDEE-AM (Reed City, MI) *Unable to locate*
WDEF-AM - 1370 (Chattanooga, TN) **29097**
WDEF-FM - 92.3 (Chattanooga, TN) **29098**
WDEF-TV - Channel 12 (Chattanooga, TN) **29099**
WDEK-FM (De Kalb, IL) *Unable to locate*
WDEL-AM - 1150 (Wilmington, DE) **5297**
WDEN-AM - 1500 (Macon, GA) **7393**
WDEN-FM - 99.1 (Macon, GA) **7394**
WDEO-AM - 990 (Ann Arbor, MI) **14777**
WDEQ-FM - 103.3 (De Graff, OH) **25156**
WDER-AM - 1320 (Derry, NH) **18489**
WDET-FM - 101.9 (Detroit, MI) **14957**
WDEV-AM - 550 (Waterbury, VT) **31612**
WDEV-FM - 96.1 (Warren, VT) **31611**
WDEX-AM (Monroe, NC) *Unable to locate*
WDEY-AM **15310***
WDEY-FM **15312***
WDEZ-FM - 101.9 (Wausau, WI) **34432**
WDFB-AM - 1170 (Danville, KY) **12038**
WDFB-FM - 88.1 (Danville, KY) **12039**
WDFL-AM - 1240 (Trenton, FL) **6825**
WDFL-FM - 106.3 (Trenton, FL) **6826**
WDFM-FM **28026***
WDFM-FM - 98.1 (Defiance, OH) **25158**
WDFN-AM - 1130 (Farmington Hills, MI) **15023**
WDFX-TV - Channel 34 (Dothan, AL) **189**
WDGE-FM **23300***
WDGG-FM - 93.7 (Huntington, WV) **33339**
WDGL-AM **7250***
WDGL-FM - 98.1 (Baton Rouge, LA) **12516**
WDGO-FM **24969***
WDGR-AM (Dahlonega, GA) *Unable to locate*
WDGS-AM (Madison, IN) *Unable to locate*
WDGY-AM - 630 (St. Paul, MN) **16427**
WDHA-FM - 105.5 (Cedar Knolls, NJ) **18723**
WDHF-FM **8647***
WDHK-FM **25669***
WDHM-FM **10443***
WDHN-TV - Channel 18 (Dothan, AL) **190**
WDHO-TV **25582***
WDHR-FM - 93.1 (Pikeville, KY) **12361**
WDIA-AM - 1070 (Memphis, TN) **29390**
WDIC-AM - 1430 (Clintwood, VA) **31978**
WDIC-FM - 92.1 (Clintwood, VA) **31979**
WDIF-FM - 94.3 (Marion, OH) **25353**
WDIG-AM - 950 (Steubenville, OH) **25541**
WDIH-FM - 90.3 (Salisbury, MD) **13714**
WDIO-TV - Channel 10 (Duluth, MN) **15853**

WECS-FM - 90.1 (Willimantic, CT) **5221**
WECT-TV (Wilmington, NC) *Unable to locate*
WECU-FM **23976***
WECW-FM - 107.7 (Elmira, NY) **20574**
WECX-FM - 99.9 (St. Petersburg, FL) **6637**
WECZ-AM - 1540 (Punxsutawney, PA) **27911**
Wedding; Cincinnati (Cincinnati, OH) **24789**
WeddingBells Magazine (Toronto, ON, Can.) **36790**
WEDE-AM (Eden, NC) *Unable to locate*
WEDG-FM - 103.3 (Buffalo, NY) **20398**
WEDH-TV - Channel 24 (Hartford, CT) **4901**
WEDM-FM - 91.1 (Indianapolis, IN) **10193**
WEDN-TV - Channel 53 (Norwich, CT) **5086**
Wednesday Journal of Oak Park & River Forest (Oak
  Park, IL) **9378**
The Wednesday Magazine (Kansas City, MO) **17202**
Wednesday Morning American (Bartlesville, OK)
  Unable to locate
Wednesday-Sunday Missourian (Columbia, MO)
  Unable to locate
Wednesday Woman (Gretna, LA) *Ceased*
WEDO-AM - 810 (White Oak, PA) **28158**
WEDR-FM - 99.1 (Hollywood, FL) **6200**
WEDU-TV - Channel 3 (Tampa, FL) **6788**
WEDW-FM (Hartford, CT) *Unable to locate*
WEDW-TV - Channel 49 (Bridgeport, CT) **4718**
WEDY-TV - Channel 65 (New Haven, CT) **5013**
Wee Wisdom (Unity Village, MO) *Ceased*
WEEB-AM - 990 (Southern Pines, NC) **24237**
WEEC-FM - 100.7 (Springfield, OH) **25536**
WEED-AM - 1390 (Rocky Mount, NC) **24206**
Weed Science (Lawrence, KS) **11570**
Weed Technology (Lawrence, KS) **11571**
WEEE-FM **18740***
WEEE-FM (Delran, NJ) *Unable to locate*
WEEF-AM - 1430 (Highland Park, IL) **8994**
The Weehawken Reporter (Weehawken, NJ) **19712**
WEEI-AM - 850 (Boston, MA) **13982**
WEEI-FM **14010***
The Week (Delavan, WI) **33655**
The Week Ahead (Fair Lawn, NJ) **18810**
WEEK-TV - Channel 25 (Peoria, IL) **9432**
Weekend *Ceased*
Weekend Adventures Magazine (Cumberland, MD)
  13475
Weekend Advertiser (Kitimat, BC, Can.) **34999**
Weekend Balita (Glendale, CA) **2013**
The Weekend Deadline (Hackettstown, NJ) *Ceased*
Weekend Decorating Projects (New York, NY) **22913**
The Weekend Express (Algona, IA) **10581**
The Weekend Flyer **9793***
Weekend Gardener (Griffin, GA) *Ceased*
The Weekend Life (Morton Grove, IL) *Ceased*
Weekend News-Star (Lincolnwood, IL) *Ceased*
Weekend Plus (Winchester, KY) *Ceased*
Weekend Reporter (Toms River, NJ) **19647**
Weekend Woodcrafts (Concord, CA) **1758**
Weekend Woodworking Projects (Akron, PA) *Ceased*
The Weekender **18275***
Weekender (Cottonwood, AZ) *Ceased*
The Weekender (Bel Air, MD) **13291**
The Weekender (Somerville, MA) *Ceased*
The Weekender (Wilkes Barre, PA) **28168**
The Weekender (Lexington, VA) **32193**
The Weekender by the Bay (Bel Air, MD) *Unable to
  locate*
Weekender Cover Story (Lebanon, PA) *Ceased*
The Weekender Mountain Echo-News Tribune
  (Keyser, WV) **33355**
The Weekly **33026***
The Weekly (Bradenton, FL) *Unable to locate*
The Weekly (Norcross, GA) **7472**
The Weekly (Bangor, ME) *Unable to locate*
The Weekly (Rolla, MO) *Ceased*
The Weekly Advance **35928***
Weekly Alibi (Albuquerque, NM) **19789**
The Weekly American (Poplar Bluff, MO) *Ceased*
Weekly Bargain Bulletin (New Castle, PA) **27315**
Weekly Bargain Shopper (Maryville, MO) **17277**
Weekly Bible Lessons; Christian Science Quarterly-
  (Boston, MA) **13876**
Weekly Bible Reader (Cincinnati, OH) **24828**
Weekly Bulletin (New Orleans, LA) *Ceased*
The Weekly Calistogan (Calistoga, CA) **1641**
The Weekly Challenger (St. Petersburg, FL) **6635**
The Weekly Collegian (University Park, PA) **28086**
Weekly Commercial News (Inglewood, CA) *Unable to
  locate*
Weekly Compilation of Presidential Documents
  (Pittsburgh, PA) **27855**
The Weekly Courier **13045***
The Weekly Herald (Madison, IN) **10284**
The Weekly Herald (Williamston, NC) **24291**
The Weekly Home News (Spring Green, WI) **34339**
Weekly Insiders Turkey Letter (Toms River, NJ)
  19648
The Weekly Journal **5963***
The Weekly Leader **3974***
The Weekly Leader (Pearl, MS) **16815**

Weekly Livestock Reporter (Fort Worth, TX) **30355**
The Weekly Messenger (Prince Frederick, MD)
  Ceased
The Weekly News (Miami, FL) **6390**
The Weekly News (Hasbrouck Heights, NJ) **18868**
The Weekly News (Barton, VT) *Unable to locate*
Weekly Newspaper Service (Washington, DC) *Ceased*
The Weekly Observer (Tucson, AZ) **973**
The Weekly Observer (Hemingway, SC) **28659**
The Weekly Packet (Blue Hill, ME) **12924**
The Weekly Pennysaver (Syracuse, NY) *Ceased*
The Weekly Post (Rainsville, AL) **429**
Weekly Reader (Pre-K edition) (Stamford, CT) **5163**
The Weekly Record (New Madrid, MO) **17315**
Weekly Record (York, PA) **28206**
The Weekly Record (Red Deer, AB, Can.) *Unable to
  locate*
Weekly Record (Tumbler Ridge, BC, Can.) *Unable to
  locate*
The Weekly Record (Enfield, NS, Can.) *Unable to
  locate*
Weekly Recorder (Claysville, PA) **26787**
Weekly Register-Call (Central City, CO) **4231**
The Weekly Reminder (Paulding, OH) **25472**
The Weekly Review (Viking, AB, Can.) **34866**
Weekly Scene (Fort Lauderdale, FL) *Unable to locate*
The Weekly Shopper (Derby, KS) **11409**
The Weekly Standard (Washington, DC) **5859**
The Weekly Star **5238***
The Weekly Star (Vacaville, CA) **3974**
The Weekly Star (Pigeon Forge, TN) **29566**
The Weekly Terre Haute (Terre Haute, IN) *Ceased*
Weekly Territorial (Tucson, AZ) *Ceased*
Weekly Times (Rochester, NY) *Unable to locate*
The Weekly Transcript **4469***
The Weekly Tribune Plus (Royal Oak, MI) **15487**
Weekly Visalia Times-Daily (Visalia, CA) **4041**
The Weekly Vista (Bella Vista, AR) **1046**
Weekly Western Livestock Journal, Mountain Plain
  (Denver, CO) *Ceased*
Weekly World News (Boca Raton, FL) **5941**
WEEL-FM **33506***
WEEM-FM - 91.7 (Pendleton, IN) **10394**
WEEN-AM - 1460 (Lafayette, TN) **29313**
WEEO-AM (Waynesboro, PA) *Ceased*
WEEU-AM - 830 (Reading, PA) **27921**
WEEX-AM **26853***
WEEZ-AM **26667***
WEEZ-FM - 99.3 (Hattiesburg, MS) **16670**
WEFC **32502***
WEFG-AM **15063***
WEFG-FM - 97.5 (Fremont, MI) **15059**
WEFM-FM - 95.9 (Michigan City, IN) **10306**
WEFT-FM - 90.1 (Champaign, IL) **8226**
WEFX-FM (Norwalk, CT) *Unable to locate*
WEGA-AM - 1350 (Vega Baja, PR) **28320**
WEGE-FM - 102.5 (Crossville, TN) **29161**
WEGG-AM - 710 (Rose Hill, NC) **24208**
WEGK-FM **27216***
WEGL-FM - 91.1 (Auburn, AL) **48**
WEGN-FM **211***
WEGO-AM - 1410 (Concord, NC) **23793**
WEGP-AM (Presque Isle, ME) *Ceased*
WEGR-FM - 102.7 (Memphis, TN) **29391**
WEGW-FM (Wheeling, WV) *Ceased*
WEGX-FM (Dillon, SC) *Unable to locate*
WEGY-FM **29542***
WEGZ-FM - 105.9 (Washburn, WI) **34389**
WEHCO Video Inc. (Little Rock, AR) **1256**
WEHH-AM (Binghamton, NY) *Unable to locate*
WEHR-FM (Elberton, GA) *Unable to locate*
WEHS-TV (Chicago, IL) *Unable to locate*
WEHT-TV - Channel 25 (Evansville, IN) **9939**
WEHW-AM **5235***
WEIC-AM (Charleston, IL) *Unable to locate*
WEIC-FM (Charleston, IL) *Unable to locate*
Weighing & Measurement (Hendersonville, TN) **29221**
Weight Engineering (Dorsey, IL) **8779**
Weight Watchers Magazine (Birmingham, AL) *Ceased*
Weil Enterprises, Joyner Communications **23892***
WEIM-AM - 1280 (Fitchburg, MA) **14185**
Weimar Mercury (Weimar, TX) **31276**
WEIO-AM - 1050 (Eau Claire, WI) **33680**
WEIQ-TV - Channel 42 (Mobile, AL) **339**
WEIR-AM - 1430 (Weirton, WV) **33491**
Weird City *Ceased*
Weirton Daily Times **33489***
WEIS-AM - 990 (Centre, AL) **150**
Weiser Signal American (Weiser, ID) **7998**
WEIU-AM - 88.9 (Charleston, IL) **8237**
WEIU-TV - Channel 51 (Charleston, IL) **8238**
WEIZ-FM **7189***
WEIZ-FM **23056***
WEJC-TV **23959***
WEJE-FM - 96.3 (Fort Wayne, IN) **9982**
WEJL-AM - 630 (Scranton, PA) **27966**
WEJM-FM - 106.3 (Chicago, IL) **8620**
WEJY-FM - 97.5 (Monroe, MI) **15367**
WEJZ-FM - 96.1 (Jacksonville, FL) **6221**

WEKC-AM - 710 (Williamsburg, KY) **12446**
WEKG-AM - 810 (Jackson, KY) **12146**
WEKH-FM - 90.9 (Hazard, KY) **12117**
WEKL-FM - 102.3 (Augusta, GA) **7107**
WEKO-AM - 930 (Cabo Rojo, PR) **28234**
WEKR-AM (Fayetteville, TN) *Unable to locate*
WEKS-FM - 92.5 (Griffin, GA) **7313**
WEKT-AM - 1070 (Elkton, KY) **12052**
WEKU-FM - 88.9 (Richmond, KY) **12385**
WEKW-TV - Channel 52 (Keene, NH) **18532**
WEKY-AM - 1340 (Richmond, KY) **12386**
WEKZ-AM - 1260 (Monroe, WI) **34152**
WEKZ-FM - 93.7 (Monroe, WI) **34153**
WELA-FM - 104.3 (East Liverpool, OH) **25172**
WELB-AM - 1350 (Elba, AL) **198**
Welbac **12272***
WELC-AM - 1150 (Welch, WV) **33493**
The Welch Daily News (Welch, WV) **33492**
Welcomat, Center City Welcomat **27635***
Welcome to Greater Louisville (Louisville, KY) **12244**
Welcome Home Magazine of Denver (Littleton, CO)
  Unable to locate
Welcome Home Magazine of Las Vegas (Littleton,
  CO) *Unable to locate*
Welcome Homeowner Magazine (North Hollywood,
  CA) *Ceased*
Welcome to Miami and the Beaches (North Miami
  Beach, FL) **6469**
WELD-AM - 690 (Fisher, WV) **33317**
WELD-FM - 101.7 (Fisher, WV) **33318**
Welding Design & Fabrication (Cleveland, OH) **24961**
Welding & Fabricating Canada (Winnipeg, MB, Can.)
  Ceased
Welding Innovation (Cleveland, OH) **24962**
Welding Innovation Quarterly **24962***
Welding Journal (Miami, FL) **6391**
Welding Technology Digest (Materials Park, OH)
  Ceased
Welding Today; Practical (Rockford, IL) **9530**
Weldon Roanoke News (Weldon, NC) *Ceased*
WELE-AM - 1380 (Ormond Beach, FL) **6534**
The Weleetkan (Weleetka, OK) **26190**
Welfare Warriors (Milwaukee, WI) **34107**
WELI-AM - 960 (Hamden, CT) **4881**
WELK-FM - 94.7 (Elkins, WV) **33310**
WELL-AM **14800***
WELL-FM **14801***
WELL-FM - 88.7 (Dadeville, AL) **167**
Well Nations Magazine (Rapid City, SD) **28934**
Well Servicing (Houston, TX) *Unable to locate*
Wellesley Magazine (Wellesley, MA) *Ceased*
The Wellesley Townsman (Needham, MA) **14372**
Wellesley Townsman (Wellesley, MA) **14618**
Wellfleet Oracle (Wellfleet, MA) **14622**
Wellfleet Oracle; Eastham- (Eastham, MA) **14172**
The Wellington Advertiser (Fergus, ON, Can.) **35830**
Wellington Cable Communications Inc. (Wellington,
  OH) **25629**
Wellington Daily News (Wellington, KS) **11866**
Wellington Enterprise (Wellington, OH) **25628**
Wellington Leader (Wellington, TX) **31277**
Wellington Town-Crier (West Palm Beach, FL) *Unable
  to locate*
Wellman Advance (Wellman, IA) **11317**
Wellness MD (Richmond Hill, ON, Can.) *Unable to
  locate*
Wellness; Today's Health & (Minnetonka, MN) **16177**
Wells County Free Press (Harvey, ND) *Ceased*
The Wells Mirror (Wells, MN) **16505**
The Wells Progress (Gresham, OR) *Unable to locate*
Wellsboro Gazette (Lemont, PA) *Unable to locate*
The Wellston News (Wellston, OK) *Unable to locate*
The Wellston Sentry (Jackson, OH) *Unable to locate*
The Wellston Telegram **25630***
The Wellsville Daily Reporter (Wellsville, NY) **23533**
Wellsville Optic-News (Wellsville, MO) **17715**
WELM-AM - 1410 (Elmira, NY) **20575**
WELN-FM **23871***
WELO-AM - 580 (Tupelo, MS) **16851**
WELP-AM (Greenville, SC) *Unable to locate*
WELR-AM - 1360 (Roanoke, AL) **434**
WELR-FM - 102.3 (Roanoke, AL) **435**
WELS-AM - 1010 (Kinston, NC) **24029**
WELS-FM **24030***
WELS-FM - 102.9 (Kinston, NC) **24030**
Welsh Citizen (Welsh, LA) **12873**
WELV-AM - 1370 (Poughkeepsie, NY) **23156**
WELW-AM - 1330 (Willoughby, OH) **25665**
WELY-AM (Ely, MN) *Unable to locate*
WELY-FM (Ely, MN) *Unable to locate*
WELZ-AM - 1460 (Belzoni, MS) **16561**
WELZ-AM - 1460 (Belzoni, MS) **16560**
WEMB-AM - 1420 (Erwin, TN) **29185**
WEMC-FM - 91.7 (Harrisonburg, VA) **32143**
WEMD-AM **13490***
WEMG-AM (Chicago, IL) *Unable to locate*
WEMI-FM - 91.9 (Appleton, WI) **33548**
WEMJ-AM - 1490 (Gilford, NH) **18512**

WEMM-FM - 107.9 (Huntington, WV) **33340**
WEMO-FM **10750***
WEMP-AM - 1250 (Hales Corners, WI) **33771**
WEMR-AM - 1460 (Wilkes Barre, PA) **28175**
WEMR-FM - 107.7 (Wilkes Barre, PA) **28176**
WEMT-TV **12915***
WEMT-TV - Channel 39 (Johnson City, TN) **29254**
WEMU-FM - 89.1 (Ypsilanti, MI) **15692**
WEMX-FM - 94.1 (Baton Rouge, LA) **12517**
Wen Wei Po (South San Francisco, CA) *Unable to locate*
WENA-AM - 1330 (Gavco, PR) **28245**
Wenatchee Business Journal (Wenatchee, WA) **33195**
The Wenatchee World (Wenatchee, WA) **33196**
WENC-AM - 1220 (Whiteville, NC) **24286**
WEND-AM **6795***
WEND-FM - 106.5 (Charlotte, NC) **23768**
Wendell Clarion (Wendell, NC) **24282**
Wendy (Los Angeles, CA) *Unable to locate*
WENE-AM - 1430 (Vestal, NY) **23490**
WENG-AM - 1530 (Englewood, FL) **6063**
WENH-TV - Channel 11 (Durham, NH) **18503**
WENN-AM **53***
WENN-FM (Birmingham, AL) *Unable to locate*
WENO-AM - 760 (Nashville, TN) **29509**
Wenona Index (Henry, IL) **8982**
WENR-AM - 1090 (Englewood, TN) **29181**
WENS-FM (Indianapolis, IN) *Unable to locate*
WENT-AM - 1340 (Gloversville, NY) **20672**
WENU-AM **23172***
WENU-AM - 1410 (Queensbury, NY) **23172**
WENU-FM - 101.7 (Queensbury, NY) **23173**
WENY-AM - 1230 (Horseheads, NY) **20761**
WENY-FM - 92.7 (Horseheads, NY) **20762**
WENY-TV - Channel 36 (Horseheads, NY) **20763**
WENZ-FM (Cleveland, OH) *Unable to locate*
WEOK-AM - 1390 (Poughkeepsie, NY) **23157**
WEOL-AM - 930 (Elyria, OH) **25180**
WEOO-AM **32527***
WEOS-FM - 89.7 (Geneva, NY) **20657**
WEOW-FM - 92.7 (Key West, FL) **6254**
WEOZ-FM (Meadville, PA) *Unable to locate*
WEPA-AM (Eupora, MS) *Unable to locate*
WEPG-AM - 910 (South Pittsburg, TN) **29611**
WEPM-AM - 1340 (Martinsburg, WV) **33381**
WEPR-FM - 90.1 (Columbia, SC) **28575**
WEPS-FM - 88.9 (Elgin, IL) **8827**
WEQO-AM (Whitley City, KY) *Unable to locate*
WEQX-FM - 102.7 (Manchester, VT) **31552**
WERA-AM (Nutley, NJ) *Ceased*
WERC-AM - 960 (Birmingham, AL) **115**
WERD-AM **6245***
WERD-FM **19183***
WERE-AM (Cleveland, OH) *Unable to locate*
WERG-FM - 89.9 (Erie, PA) **26903**
WERH-AM - 970 (Hamilton, AL) **262**
WERI-AM (Westerly, RI) *Ceased*
WERK-AM (Muncie, IN) *Unable to locate*
WERK-FM (Muncie, IN) *Unable to locate*
WERL-AM - 950 (Eagle River, WI) **33666**
WERM-FM **25305***
WERO-FM - 93.3 (Washington, NC) **24275**
WERQ-AM - 1010 (Baltimore, MD) **13271**
WERQ-FM - 92.3 (Baltimore, MD) **13272**
WERR-FM - 104.1 (San Juan, PR) **28299**
WERS-FM - 88.9 (Boston, MA) **13983**
WERT-AM - 1220 (Van Wert, OH) **25610**
WERT-FM **9981***
WERU-AM **34004***
WERU-FM - 104.7 (Daytona Beach, FL) **6043**
WERX-FM - 102.5 (Edenton, NC) **23858**
WERZ-FM (Exeter, NH) *Unable to locate*
WESA-AM **26738***
WESA-AM - 940 (Pittsburgh, PA) **27866**
WESA-FM **27883***
WESB-AM - 1490 (Bradford, PA) **26730**
WESC-AM (Greenville, SC) *Unable to locate*
WESC-FM - 92.5 (Greenville, SC) **28629**
WESD-FM (Schofield, WI) *Unable to locate*
WESE-FM - 92.5 (Tupelo, MS) **16852**
WESH-TV - Channel 2 (Orlando, FL) **6516**
WESL-AM - 1490 (East St. Louis, IL) **8808**
Wesleyan (Middletown, CT) **4946**
The Wesleyan Advocate (Indianapolis, IN) **10182**
The Wesleyan Argus (Middletown, CT) **4947**
Wesleyan Christian Advocate (Stone Mountain, GA) **7572**
WESM-FM - 91.3 (Princess Anne, MD) **13670**
WESN-FM - 88.1 (Bloomington, IL) **8084**
WESO-AM (Southbridge, MA) *Unable to locate*
WESP-FM (Dothan, AL) *Unable to locate*
WESR-AM - 1330 (Onley, VA) **32319**
WESR-FM - 103.3 (Onley, VA) **32320**
WESS-FM - 90.3 (East Stroudsburg, PA) **26848**
Wessington Springs True Dakotan (Wessington Springs, SD) **29029**
Wessington Times Enterprise (Wessington, SD) **29028**
West (Toronto, ON, Can.) *Ceased*
West; Adventure (Incline Village, NV) **18357**

West Africa Review (Binghamton, NY) **20220**
West Akron Sun (Cleveland, OH) **24963**
West Alabama Cable TV **403***
West Alabama Gazette (Millport, AL) *Unable to locate*
West Alabama TV Cable Co. (Fayette, AL) **214**
West Allis Star (New Berlin, WI) **34189**
WEST-AM - 1400 (Easton, PA) **26852**
West Ark Cable TV (Rogers, AR) *Unable to locate*
West Art (Auburn, CA) **1441**
West Auglaize Merchandiser (Wapakoneta, OH) *Unable to locate*
West Babylon Advertiser *Ceased*
West Babylon Suffolk Life (Babylon, NY) **20112**
West Bank Guide (Metairie, LA) *Ceased*
West Bend Daily News **34445***
West Bend News **34445***
West Bloomfield Eccentric (West Bloomfield, MI) **15677**
West Bloomfield Observer & Eccentric **15677***
West Bloomfield Spinal Column Newsweekly (West Bloomfield, MI) **15678**
West Bloomington Sun-Current (Eden Prairie, MN) *Unable to locate*
West Boca Community News (Chicago, IL) **8603**
West Branch Times (West Branch, IA) **11318**
West Bridgewater Star **14624***
West Bridgewater Times (West Bridgewater, MA) **14624**
West Carleton Review (Arnprior, ON, Can.) **35638**
West Carroll Gazette (Oak Grove, LA) **12788**
West Carrollton News; Miamisburg/ (Miamisburg, OH) **25375**
West-Central Crossroads (Kindersley, SK, Can.) **37483**
West Central Tribune (Willmar, MN) **16518**
West Chester Week (Cincinnati, OH) *Unable to locate*
West Chicago Press (St. Charles, IL) **9573**
West Citizen Journal (Warrenton, MO) *Unable to locate*
West Coast Community Newspaper (El Cajon, CA) *Unable to locate*
West Coast Edition; Art Now Gallery Guide— (Clinton, NJ) **18766**
The West Coast Fisherman (Vancouver, BC, Can.) *Unable to locate*
West Coast Lifestyle Magazine (Sherman Oaks, CA) *Unable to locate*
West Coast Line (Burnaby, BC, Can.) **34909**
The West Coast Mariner (Vancouver, BC, Can.) *Unable to locate*
West Coast Online (San Jose, CA) *Ceased*
West Coast Review **34909***
West Coast Review of Books **2377***
West Coast Syndicate (Mill Valley, CA) **38119**
West County Journal (Warrenton, MO) **17701**
The West County Press (Brooklyn, NY) *Unable to locate*
West Des Moines Express (West Des Moines, IA) *Unable to locate*
West DuPage Press (St. Charles, IL) **9574**
West End-Clayton Word (St. Louis, MO) **17531**
West Ender (Vancouver, BC, Can.) *Unable to locate*
West Essex Tribune (Livingston, NJ) **19178**
West Fargo Pioneer (West Fargo, ND) **24557**
West Frankfort Daily American (West Frankfort, IL) **9749**
West Geauga Sun (Cleveland, OH) **24964**
West Hanover News (Ashland, VA) *Ceased*
West Hartford News (Bristol, CT) **4723**
West Haven News (West Haven, CT) **5207**
West Hawaii Today (Kailua Kona, HI) **7766**
West Hempstead Beacon (West Hempstead, NY) **23542**
West Hempstead Shopper's Guide (Ontario, ON, Can.) **36170**
West Hernando News (Brooksville, FL) *Unable to locate*
West Hill News (Scarborough, ON, Can.) *Unable to locate*
West Hollywood Independent (Los Angeles, CA) **2432**
West Islip Suffolk Life (West Islip, NY) **23544**
West Kentucky News (Paducah, KY) *Unable to locate*
West Kootenay Advertiser **35025***
West Kootenay Weekender (Nelson, BC, Can.) **35025**
West-Lane News (Veneta, OR) **26605**
The West Leader **8511***
West Liberty Index (West Liberty, IA) **11323**
West Life (Westlake, OH) **25649**
West Lincoln Review (Smithville, ON, Can.) **36398**
West Linn Tidings (West Linn, OR) **26611**
West Lorne Sun (West Lorne, ON, Can.) *Unable to locate*
West Lyon Herald (Inwood, IA) **10967**
West Michigan Family (Grand Rapids, MI) *Unable to locate*
West Michigan Senior Times (Allegan, MI) **14724**
West Mifflin Area Record (Monroeville, PA) *Ceased*

West Milford In-Depth (West Milford, NJ) *Unable to locate*
West Milford News; Greenwood Lake and (Greenwood Lake, NY) **20702**
West Milton Record (Tipp City, OH) **25563**
West Milwaukee Enterprise (Waukesha, WI) *Ceased*
West Minnetonka/Deephaven Sun-Sailor (Minnetonka, MN) **16179**
West Morris Star Journal (Ledgewood, NJ) **19168**
West Nebraska Register (Grand Island, NE) **18027**
The West News (West, TX) **31282**
West Orange Chronicle (Orange, NJ) **19397**
West Orange Times (Winter Garden, FL) **6865**
West Palm Beach Town-Crier (West Palm Beach, FL) *Ceased*
West Pasco Press (New Port Richey, FL) **6456**
West Plains Daily Quill (West Plains, MO) **17716**
West Point Bee (West Point, IA) **11325**
West Point News (West Point, NE) **18312**
West Prince Graphic (Alberton, PE, Can.) **36911**
West Proviso Herald (Proviso, IL) **9472**
West-Quebec Post (Aylmer, QC, Can.) *Unable to locate*
West River Catholic (Rapid City, SD) **28935**
West River Progress (Dupree, SD) **28846**
West Roxbury Transcript (Needham, MA) **14373**
West Saint Paul/Mendota Heights Sun Current (West St. Paul, MN) **16506**
West Salem Coulee News (Portage, WI) **34261**
West Salem Journal **26574***
West San Bernardino Green Sheet (San Bernardino, CA) **3093**
West Schuylkill Herald (Tower City, PA) **28054**
West Seattle Herald **33042***
West Seattle Herald/White Center News (Seattle, WA) **33042**
West Seneca Bee (West Seneca, NY) **23547**
West Seneca Pennysaver (West Seneca, NY) **23548**
West Sherburne Tribune (Big Lake, MN) **15751**
West Shore Shoppers Guide (Manistee, MI) **15330**
West Side **10042***
West Side (Salem, OR) **26574**
West Side Advance (Kerman, CA) **2102**
The West Side Index (Newman, CA) **2620**
West Side Journal (Port Allen, LA) **12799**
West Side Leader (Akron, OH) **24593**
West Side Messenger (Indianapolis, IN) **10183**
West Side Revue (Vancouver, BC, Can.) **35178**
West Side Story/Press Enterprise (Knoxville, TN) *Unable to locate*
West Side Sun News (North Olmsted, OH) **25439**
West Side Times (Buffalo, NY) **20391**
West Springfield Record (West Springfield, MA) **14625**
West Suburban Extra (Chicago, IL) **8604**
The West Tennessee Catholic (Memphis, TN) **29384**
West Texas Angelus (San Angelo, TX) **31011**
West Texas Catholic (Amarillo, TX) **29699**
West Texas County Courier (Horizon City, TX) **30453**
West Toledo Herald **25555***
West Town EXTRA; Wicker Park/ (Chicago, IL) **8606**
West Valley Cablevision (Chatsworth, CA) *Unable to locate*
West Valley Courier (Hillsboro, OR) **26374**
West Valley Eagle (West Valley City, UT) **31486**
West Valley View **31486***
West Valley View **31323***
West Valley View (Litchfield Park, AZ) **742**
West Virginia Beacon Digest (Charleston, WV) *Unable to locate*
West Virginia Coal Facts (Charleston, WV) **33274**
West Virginia Construction News (Charleston, WV) **33275**
West Virginia Daily News (Lewisburg, WV) **33367**
West Virginia Dental Journal (Charleston, WV) **33276**
West Virginia Educational Broadcasting Authority **33287***
West Virginia Educational Broadcasting Authority **33426***
West Virginia Forestry Notes *Ceased*
West Virginia Hillbilly (Minerva, OH) **25393**
West Virginia Hills and Streams (Renick, WV) *Ceased*
West Virginia, Inc.; TCI of (Bridgeport, OH) **24707**
The West Virginia Lawyer (Charleston, WV) **33277**
West Virginia Medical Journal (Charleston, WV) **33278**
West Virginia Metronews Radio Network (Morgantown, WV) **37676**
West Virginia News **33367***
West Virginia Nurse (Charleston, WV) **33279**
The West Virginia Pharmacist **33280***
West Virginia Pharmacists Association (Charleston, WV) **33280**
West Virginia University Alumni Magazine (Morgantown, WV) **33398**
West Virginia University Philological Papers (Morgantown, WV) **33399**
West Virginia; Wonderful (Charleston, WV) **33281**

West Volusia Blanket Shopper (De Land, FL) *Ceased*
West Volusia Pennysaver (De Land, FL) **6047**
West Whittier Independent **4070***
West; The Wyandotte (Kansas City, KS) **11536**
The Westborough News (Westborough, MA) **14639**
Westbrook Sentinel & Tribune (Westbrook, MN) **16507**
Westbury Pennysaver (Farmingdale, NY) *Ceased*
Westbury Shopper's Guide (Ontario, ON, Can.) **36171**
The Westbury Times (Westbury, NY) **23560**
Westchester Cable TV Inc. **23611***
WestChester Commerce (Elmsford, NY) *Unable to locate*
Westchester Country Club News (Rye, NY) **23281**
Westchester County Business Journal (Hawthorne, NY) *Unable to locate*
Westchester County Press (White Plains, NY) *Unable to locate*
Westchester County Weekly (Stamford, CT) **5164**
Westchester Family (Mamaroneck, NY) **20988**
Westchester Herald (Glenview, IL) *Unable to locate*
Westchester Historian (Elmsford, NY) **20585**
Westchester/Ladera Observer (La Jolla, CA) *Ceased*
Westchester Observer (Mount Vernon, NY) *Unable to locate*
Westchester Spotlight (Elmsford, NY) **20586**
Westchester Star (Los Angeles, CA) **2433**
Westchester Suburban Life; Hillside/Broadview/ Berkeley/ (Oak Brook, IL) **9352**
WestCoast Families (Vancouver, BC, Can.) **35179**
The Westerly News (Ucluelet, BC, Can.) **35117**
The Westerly Sun (Westerly, RI) **28458**
Western Agri-Radio Networks, Inc. DBA: California Agri-Radio Network; Southwest Agri-Radio Network. (Yuma, AZ) **37677**
Western American Literature (Logan, UT) **31354**
Western Association News **2215***
Western Banker (New York, NY) *Ceased*
The Western Bec- Producer (Elk Grove, CA) **1875**
Western Birds (Pacifica, CA) **2741**
The Western Boatman (Carson, CA) *Ceased*
Western Breeze (Cut Bank, MT) **17779**
Western Builder (Brookfield, WI) **33606**
Western Business (Billings, MT) *Ceased*
Western Cable TV (Bozeman, MT) *Unable to locate*
Western Cablesystems Ltd **35110***
Western Canada Highway News (Winnipeg, MB, Can.) **35358**
Western Canada Outdoors (North Battleford, SK, Can.) *Ceased*
The Western Canadian (Manitou, MB, Can.) **35272**
The Western Carolinian (Cullowhee, NC) **23795**
Western Catholic Reporter (Edmonton, AB, Can.) *Unable to locate*
Western CATV Inc. **1662***
Western Chronicle **30318***
Western City (Sacramento, CA) **3022**
Western Cleaner and Launderer (Pasadena, CA) **2828**
The Western Collegian **25162***
Western Commerce & Industry **35323***
Western Community TV Cable (San Angelo, TX) *Unable to locate*
Western Concept (Dickinson, ND) **24395**
Western Courier (Macomb, IL) **9133**
The Western Dairyman (Corona, CA) **1768**
Western Dakota Cable Inc. (Mott, ND) *Unable to locate*
Western Dakota Cable Inc. (New Leipzig, ND) **24523**
Western & Eastern Treasures (San Anselmo, CA) **3085**
Western Edition **3437***
Western Energy (Glendale, CA) *Unable to locate*
Western and English Fashions (Denver, CO) *Ceased*
Western European Education **20077***
Western Farm Press (Minneapolis, MN) **16139**
Western Farmer-Stockman (Carol Stream, IL) **8157**
Western Fire Journal **1484***
Western Floors **4112***
Western Flyfishing **26478***
The Western Front (Bellingham, WA) **32679**
Western Fruit Grower (Willoughby, OH) **25664**
Western Grocer (Winnipeg, MB, Can.) **35359**
Western Grower and Shipper (Newport Beach, CA) *Unable to locate*
Western Guard (Madison, MN) **16020**
Western Herald (Glenview, IL) *Ceased*
Western Herald (Kalamazoo, MI) **15246**
Western Hills Press (Cincinnati, OH) *Unable to locate*
Western Historical Quarterly (Logan, UT) **31355**
Western Hog Journal (Edmonton, AB, Can.) **34734**
Western Horseman (Colorado Springs, CO) **4261**
Western Hotelier (Winnipeg, MB, Can.) **35360**
Western Humanities Review (Salt Lake City, UT) **31443**
Western HVACR News (Los Angeles, CA) *Unable to locate*
Western Investor (Portland, OR) *Ceased*
Master Itasca Review (Deer River, MN) **15826**

Western Itasca Review & Deerpath Shopper (New York, NY) **22914**
Western Journal of Agricultural Economics **4434***
Western Journal of Applied Forestry (Bethesda, MD) **13388**
The Western Journal of Black Studies (Pullman, WA) **32909**
Western Journal of Communication (Fresno, CA) **1960**
Western Journal of Nursing Research (Edmonton, AB, Can.) **34735**
Western Journal of Speech Communications **1960***
Western Kansas World (Wa Keeney, KS) **11859**
Western Kentucky Catholic (Owensboro, KY) *Unable to locate*
Western Kentucky Journal (Newburgh, IN) **10350**
Western Links **5154***
Western Livestock Journal (Denver, CO) **4366**
Western Livestock Reporter (Billings, MT) **17734**
Western Living (Edmonton, AB, Can.) **34736**
Western Lumber Facts (Portland, OR) **26514**
Western Manitoba Profile on Business (Brandon, MB, Can.) *Ceased*
Western Maryland Genealogy (Gaithersburg, MD) **13551**
Western Massachusetts Commercial News (Feeding Hills, MA) *Ceased*
Western Micro Market (Pleasant Hill, CA) *Ceased*
Western Nebraska Observer (Kimball, NE) **18068**
Western New York Catholic (Buffalo, NY) **20392**
Western New York Catholic Visitor **20392***
Western New York Magazine (Buffalo, NY) *Ceased*
Western New Yorker (Geneseo, NY) *Unable to locate*
Western News (Libby, MT) **17852**
Western North American Naturalist (Provo, UT) **31409**
Western Observer (Anson, TX) *Unable to locate*
Western Oil World (New York, NY) *Ceased*
Western Ontario Business **35986***
Western Ontario Farmer **35989***
Western Ontario, Gazette; University of (London, ON, Can.) **35994**
Western Outdoors (Newport Beach, CA) **2637**
Western Outfitter, Retailers/Riding Apparel & Equipment (Houston, TX) *Ceased*
Western Photographer (Long Beach, CA) *Unable to locate*
The Western Planner (Soldotna, AK) *Unable to locate*
Western Polled Hereford Journal (Klamath Falls, OR) *Ceased*
Western Press **1021***
The Western Producer (Saskatoon, SK, Can.) **37560**
The Western Producer Newsfeature Service (Saskatoon, SK, Can.) **38120**
Western Real Estate News (South San Francisco, CA) *Unable to locate*
Western Recorder (Middletown, KY) **12297**
Western Region; Group Tour Magazine (Holland, MI) **15172**
Western Reserve Magazine (Cleveland, OH) *Unable to locate*
Western Restaurant News (Winnipeg, MB, Can.) **35361**
Western Review; Drayton Valley (Drayton Valley, AB, Can.) **34695**
Western Rider **35634***
Western Roofing/Insulation/Siding (Reno, NV) **18426**
Western RV Traveler **33215***
Western Shore Cable TV **13582***
Western Spirit *Ceased*
Western spirit/Miami Republican **11741***
Western Sportsman (Vancouver, BC, Can.) **35180**
Western Springs Suburban Life (Oak Brook, IL) **9370**
Western Springs Sun (Naperville, IL) *Ceased*
The Western Star **30985***
The Western Star (Bessemer, AL) **52**
The Western Star (Coldwater, KS) **11394**
Western Star (Lebanon, OH) **25295**
The Western Star (Corner Brook, NL, Can.) **35447**
Western States Jewish History (Woodland Hills, CA) **4117**
Western Styles (Lakewood, CO) *Ceased*
The Western Sun (Huntington Beach, CA) **2066**
The Western Texan (Snyder, TX) **31115**
Western Times (Sharon Springs, KS) **11799**
Western Trader (Custer, SD) **28838**
Western Trucking News (Port Coquitlam, BC, Can.) *Unable to locate*
Western Turf & Landscape Press (Cedar Falls, IA) **10664**
Western Turf Management **10664***
Western Underwriter (Property-Casualty-Life & Health) (San Rafael, CA) *Ceased*
Western United States; Hospitality News for the (Salem, OR) **26568**
Western Viking (Seattle, WA) **33043**
The Western Voice (Yuma, AZ) **1021**
Western Wheel; Okotoks (Okotoks, AB, Can.) **34818**
Western Wings **36092***

Western Wisconsin Communications Cooperative (Independence, WI) **33798**
Western World (Bandon, OR) **26236**
The Westerner **15247***
Westerns & Serial World; Favorite (Mankato, MN) **16025**
Westerville News **25646***
Westerville News & Public Opinion (Westerville, OH) **25646**
Westfield Community Antenna Association (Westfield, PA) **28152**
Westfield/Corry Quality Guide (Westfield, NY) **23563**
Westfield Enterprise (Fishers, IN) **9960**
The Westfield Evening News (Westfield, MA) **14643**
The Westfield Leader (Westfield, NJ) **19747**
Westfield Pennysaver; Dunkirk-Fredonia- (Fredonia, NY) **20621**
Westfield Quality Guide (Westfield, NY) **23564**
Westfield Republican (Westfield, NY) **23565**
The Westford Eagle (Westford, MA) **14646**
Westine Report (Burlington, WI) *Unable to locate*
Westinghouse/CBS, Inc. **2450***
Westlake/Moss Bluff News (Westlake, LA) **12879**
Westlake/Moss Bluff News Buyer's Guide **12878***
Westlake Picayune (Austin, TX) **29854**
The Westlaker **12879***
Westlaker Times (Rocky River, OH) **25502**
Westland Eagle (Wayne, MI) **15674**
Westland Observer (Westland, MI) **15682**
Westlock Hub (Westlock, AB, Can.) *Unable to locate*
Westlock News (Westlock, AB, Can.) **34871**
Westman Week (Brandon, MB, Can.) *Ceased*
WestMarc Cable **15391***
WestMarc Cable **10646***
WestMarc Cable TV **11302***
WestMare Cable **16312***
Westminister Herald (Westminster, CA) **4076**
Westminster Broadcasting Corp. **2773***
Westminster College Magazine (New Wilmington, PA) **27324**
The Westminster Forum **31427***
The Westminster News (Westminster, SC) **28784**
Westminster Window (Westminster, CO) **4669**
Westmont Progress (Downers Grove, IL) **8797**
WestMont Word **17820***
Westmore News (Port Chester, NY) **23115**
Westmoreland News (Montross, VA) **32275**
Westmoreland Recorder (Westmoreland, KS) **11870**
Westmoreland Star **27794***
The Westmount Examiner (Westmount, QC, Can.) **37446**
Weston Chronicle (Weston, MO) **17718**
Weston County Gazette (Upton, WY) **34600**
The Weston Democrat (Weston, WV) **33497**
The Weston Forum (Weston, CT) **5210**
Weston Town Crier & TAB (Weston, MA) **14652**
Weston Town Crier; Wayland and **15671***
Weston Voice (Black Rock, CT) **4699**
Westosha Report (Twin Lakes, WI) **34377**
Westport Minuteman (New Milford, CT) **5035**
Westport News (Norwalk, CT) **5080**
Westside Advance; Walker/ (Walker, MI) **15655**
Westside Enterprise (Greenfield, IN) **10042**
Westside Flashes (Allegan, MI) *Ceased*
Westside Flyer (Avon, IN) **9795**
Westside Gazette (Fort Lauderdale, FL) **6088**
Westside Messenger (Columbus, OH) **25068**
Westside Record-Journal (Ferndale, WA) **32769**
Westside Shopper (Woodbridge, CT) *Unable to locate*
Westside Shopping News (Taft, CA) *Unable to locate*
Westside Smart Shopper (Ferndale, WA) *Unable to locate*
Westside Sun (Pasadena, TX) *Unable to locate*
Westsider (Phoenix, AZ) *Unable to locate*
The Westsider (Los Angeles, CA) **2434**
Westsider (Deerfield Beach, FL) *Ceased*
The Westsider (New York, NY) **22915**
WestStar Cable TV (Rancho Cordova, CA) *Unable to locate*
WESTVIEW (Nashville, TN) **29502**
Westville Indicator (Westville, IN) **10561**
The Westville Reporter (Westville, OK) **26192**
Westways (Costa Mesa, CA) **1781**
Westwood One Radio Network (Culver City, CA) **37678**
Westwood Sun (Overland Park, KS) *Ceased*
Westword (Denver, CO) *Ceased*
Westworld (Burnaby, BC, Can.) **34910**
Westworld Alberta (Burnaby, BC, Can.) **34911**
Westworld British Columbia (Burnaby, BC, Can.) **34912**
Westworld Saskatchewan (Burnaby, BC, Can.) **34913**
WESU-FM - 88.1 (Middletown, CT) **4948**
WESX-AM - 1230 (Salem, MA) **14516**
WESY-AM - 1580 (Greenville, MS) **16639**
Wet Mountain Tribune (Westcliffe, CO) **4658**
WETA-FM - 90.9 (Arlington, VA) **31845**
WETA Magazine (Arlington, VA) **31841**
WETA-TV - Channel 26 (Arlington, VA) **31846**

Wetaskiwin Times **34873***
Wetaskiwin Times Advertiser (Wetaskiwin, AB, Can.) **34873**
WETB-AM - 790 (Johnson City, TN) **29255**
WETC-AM - 540 (Zebulon, NC) **24342**
WETD-FM - 90.9 (Alfred, NY) **20026**
Weteran/Veteran (New York, NY) **22916**
WETG-TV **26904***
WETH-FM - 89.1 (Arlington, VA) **31847**
Wethersfield Post (Bristol, CT) **4724**
WETK-TV - Channel 33 (Burlington, VT) **31522**
WETL-FM - 91.7 (South Bend, IN) **10461**
Wetlands (Ann Arbor, MI) **14772**
Wetlands Report; Endangered Species & (Takoma Park, MD) **13751**
WETM-TV - Channel 18 (Elmira, NY) **20576**
WETN-FM - 88.1 (Wheaton, IL) **9761**
WETO-TV **29254***
WETS-FM - 89.5 (Johnson City, TN) **29256**
WETT-AM (Ocean City, MD) Unable to locate
The Wetumpka Herald (Wetumpka, AL) **515**
WETV-TV **7079***
WETZ-AM - 1330 (New Martinsville, WV) **33415**
WETZ-FM - 103.9 (New Martinsville, WV) **33416**
Wetzel Chronicle (New Martinsville, WV) **33413**
Wetzel Green Tab (New Martinsville, WV) **33414**
WEUC-AM - 1420 (Ponce, PR) **28275**
WEUC-FM - 88.9 (Ponce, PR) **28276**
WEUL-FM - 98.1 (Kingsford, MI) **15266**
WEUP-AM - 1600 (Huntsville, AL) **282**
WEUS-AM **6813***
WEVA-AM - 860 (Emporia, VA) **32002**
WEVC-FM **9951***
WEVD-AM - 1050 (New York, NY) **22968**
WEVE-AM **15885***
WEVE-FM - 97.9 (Eveleth, MN) **15886**
WEVL-FM - 89.9 (Memphis, TN) **29392**
WEVO-FM - 89.1 (Concord, NH) **18476**
WEVR-AM - 1550 (River Falls, WI) **34310**
WEVR-FM - 106.3 (River Falls, WI) **34311**
WEVS-FM - 92.7 (Holland, MI) **15175**
WEVU-TV **6116***
WEVV-TV - Channel 44 (Evansville, IN) **9940**
WEVX-FM - 95.3 (Champaign, IL) **8227**
WEVZ-FM **14849***
WEW-AM (St. Louis, MO) Unable to locate
WEWO-AM (Laurinburg, NC) Unable to locate
Wewoka Daily Times (Wewoka, OK) **26194**
WEWS-TV - Channel 5 (Cleveland, OH) **24973**
WEXA Cable, Inc. (Conyers, GA) Unable to locate
WEXA-FM **16847***
WEXC-FM - 107.1 (Greenville, PA) **26960**
WEXI-AM **6241***
WEXI-FM - 102.9 (Fort Wayne, IN) **9983**
WEXL-AM - 1340 (Milford, MI) **15360**
WEXP **237***
WEXS-AM - 610 (Patillas, PR) **28274**
WEXT-AM **33767***
WEXT-FM - 104.7 (Kenosha, WI) **33875**
WEXY-AM - 1520 (Fort Lauderdale, FL) **6090**
Weyauwega Chronicle **34451***
Weyburn Review (Weyburn, SK, Can.) **37591**
Weyburn This Week (Weyburn, SK, Can.) **37592**
WEYE-AM **24222***
WEYE-FM - 104.3 (Rogersville, TN) **29581**
WEYI-TV - Channel 25 (Clio, MI) **14886**
Weymouth Dispatch (Weymouth, MA) **14653**
Weymouth News (Weymouth, MA) **14654**
WEYY-AM **416***
WEYY-FM - 92.7 (Talladega, AL) **466**
WEYZ-AM (North East, PA) Unable to locate
WEZB-FM (New Orleans, LA) Unable to locate
WEZC-AM - 1480 (Whitesburg, KY) **12439**
WEZC-FM (Charlotte, NC) Unable to locate
WEZE-AM - 590 (Boston, MA) **13984**
WEZF-FM - 92.9 (Burlington, VT) **31524**
WEZF-FM - 92.9 (Burlington, VT) **31523**
WEZG-FM (Syracuse, NY) Unable to locate
WEZI-AM **29406***
WEZI-FM - 94.3 (Memphis, TN) **29393**
WEZJ-FM - 104.3 (Williamsburg, KY) **12447**
WEZK-FM **29293***
WEZL-FM - 103.5 (Mount Pleasant, SC) **28699**
WEZN-FM - 99.9 (Milford, CT) **4959**
WEZO-AM - 950 (Rochester, NY) **23246**
WEZO-FM **23252***
WEZS-AM - 1350 (Laconia, NH) **18538**
WEZS-FM **32480***
WEZV-FM **10262***
WEZW-FM **33770***
WEZX-FM - 106.9 (Scranton, PA) **27967**
WEZY-FM **6338***
WEZY-FM - 92.1 (Racine, WI) **34277**
WEZZ-FM - 97.7 (Clanton, AL) **156**
WFAA **30208***
WFAA-TV - Channel 8 (Dallas, TX) **30219**
WFAD-AM - 1490 (Middlebury, VT) **31560**
WFAG-AM **23878***
WFAH-AM **24606***

WFAH-FM **24608***
WFAI-AM - 1510 (Wilmington, DE) **5298**
WFAI-AM (Fayetteville, NC) Unable to locate
WFAJ-FM (Terre Haute, IN) Ceased
WFAM-AM - 1050 (Augusta, GA) **7108**
WFAN-AM - 660 (Astoria, NY) **20103**
WFAR-FM (Danbury, CT) Unable to locate
WFAS-AM - 1230 (Hartsdale, NY) **20714**
WFAS-FM - 103.9 (Hartsdale, NY) **20715**
WFAT-FM - 96.5 (Kalamazoo, MI) **15248**
WFAU-AM - 1280 (Augusta, ME) **12899**
WFAW-AM - 940 (Fort Atkinson, WI) **33724**
WFAX-AM - 1220 (Falls Church, VA) **32062**
WFAY-TV - Channel 62 (Lumber Bridge, NC) **24050**
WFAZ-FM **24004***
WFBA-FM **28640***
WFBC-AM **28639***
WFBC-FM - 93.7 (Greenville, SC) **28630**
WFBE-FM - 95.1 (Flint, MI) **15041**
WFBG-AM (Altoona, PA) Unable to locate
WFBL-AM (East Longmeadow, MA) Unable to locate
WFBL-AM - 1050 (Baldwinsville, NY) **20116**
WFBM-TV **10208***
WFBN-TV **8622***
WFBS-AM - 1280 (Berwick, PA) **26696**
WFBZ **34147***
WFBZ-FM - 105.5 (La Crosse, WI) **33888**
WFCB-FM (Chillicothe, OH) Unable to locate
WFCB-TV **6564***
WFCC-FM - 107.5 (West Yarmouth, MA) **14630**
WFCD Communicator (Brandon, MB, Can.) Unable to locate
WFCE-FM **6600***
WFCF-AM **15042***
WFCG-AM - 1110 (Franklinton, LA) **12584**
WFCG-FM - 98.9 (Franklinton, LA) **12585**
WFCI-FM - 89.5 (Franklin, IN) **10009**
WFCJ-FM (Dayton, OH) Unable to locate
WFCL-AM - 1380 (Clintonville, WI) **33638**
WFCO-AM **13756***
WFCO-FM (Lancaster, OH) Unable to locate
WFCR-FM - 88.5 (Amherst, MA) **13809**
WFCS-FM - 107.7 (New Britain, CT) **4977**
WFCT-TV **24050***
WFCV-AM - 1090 (Fort Wayne, IN) **9984**
WFDD-FM - 88.5 (Winston-Salem, NC) **24330**
WFDF-AM - 910 (Flint, MI) **15042**
WFDL AM - 1170 (Waupun, WI) **34428**
WFDL-FM - 97.7 (Fond du Lac, WI) **33701**
WFDQ-FM - 91.9 (Teaneck, NJ) **19611**
WFDR-AM - 1370 (Manchester, GA) **7408**
WFDR-FM **7481***
WFDU-FM - 89.1 (Teaneck, NJ) **19612**
WFDV-AM **7507***
WFEA-AM - 1370 (Manchester, NH) **18568**
WFEB-AM - 1340 (Sylacauga, AL) **463**
WFEL-AM (Baltimore, MD) Unable to locate
WFEM-FM **27317***
WFEX-FM **12480***
WFFC-FM - 89.9 (Ferrum, VA) **32074**
WFFF-AM - 1360 (Columbia, MS) **16601**
WFFF-FM - 96.7 (Columbia, MS) **16602**
WFFG-AM (Marathon, FL) Unable to locate
WFFM-AM (Tifton, GA) Unable to locate
WFFN-FM - 95.3 (Jasper, AL) **298**
WFFT-TV - Channel 55 (Fort Wayne, IN) **9985**
WFFX-AM - 1450 (Meridian, MS) **16773**
WFGD-FM **7144***
WFGE-FM - 103.7 (Murray, KY) **12318**
WFGH-AM **31900***
WFGH-FM - 90.7 (Fort Gay, WV) **33319**
WFGL-AM (Santa Ana, CA) Unable to locate
WFGM-FM **33403***
WFGN-AM - 1180 (Gaffney, SC) **28617**
WFGW-AM (Black Mountain, NC) Unable to locate
WFGY-FM (Altoona, PA) Unable to locate
WFGZ-FM - 94.5 (Dickson, TN) **29167**
WFHC-FM - 91.5 (Henderson, TN) **29219**
WFHK-AM - 1430 (Pell City, AL) **423**
WFHL-TV - Channel 23 (Decatur, IL) **8718**
WFHM-AM **19701***
WFHN-FM - 107.1 (Fairhaven, MA) **14179**
WFHR-AM - 1320 (Wisconsin Rapids, WI) **34466**
WFIA-AM (Louisville, KY) Unable to locate
WFIC-AM - 1530 (Martinsville, VA) **32236**
WFIE-TV - Channel 14 (Evansville, IN) **9941**
WFIF-AM - 1500 (Milford, CT) **4960**
WFII-AM - 1230 (Columbus, IN) **25079**
WFIL-AM - 560 (Lafayette Hill, PA) **27137**
WFIN-AM - 1330 (Findlay, OH) **25196**
WFIN-FM **25197***
WFIQ-TV - Channel 36 (Florence, AL) **222**
WFIR-AM - 960 (Roanoke, VA) **32497**
WFIS-AM - 1600 (Fountain Inn, SC) **28614**
WFIT-AM - 530 (New York, NY) **22969**
WFIT-FM - 89.5 (Melbourne, FL) **6337**
WFIU-FM - 103.7 (Bloomington, IN) **9857**
WFIV-AM - 1080 (Kissimmee, FL) **6266**
WFIW-AM - 1390 (Fairfield, IL) **8881**

WFIW-FM - 104.9 (Fairfield, IL) **8882**
WFIX-AM **287***
WFIX-FM **227***
WFJA-FM - 105.5 (Sanford, NC) **24221**
WFJY-FM **6111***
WFKB-AM **29415***
WFKJ-AM - 890 (Cashtown, PA) **26766**
WFKN-AM - 1220 (Franklin, KY) **12083**
WFKO-FM **10244***
WFKS-FM **6535***
WFKX-FM - 95.7 (Jackson, TN) **29235**
WFKY-AM - 1490 (Frankfort, KY) **12080**
WFKZ-FM - 103.1 (Tavernier, FL) **6814**
WFLA-AM - 970 (Tampa, FL) **6789**
WFLA-TV - Channel 8 (Tampa, FL) **6790**
WFLB-AM **23884***
WFLB-FM - 96.5 (Fayetteville, NC) **23885**
WFLC-FM - 97.3 (Hollywood, FL) **6201**
WFLD-TV - Channel 32 (Chicago, IL) **8621**
WFLE-AM - 1060 (Flemingsburg, KY) **12058**
WFLE-FM - 95.1 (Lexington, KY) **12183**
WFLI-AM - 1070 (Chattanooga, TN) **29102**
WFLI-TV - Channel 53 (Chattanooga, TN) **29103**
WFLK-FM - 101.7 (Geneva, NY) **20658**
WFLM-FM **10058***
WFLO-AM - 870 (Farmville, VA) **32070**
WFLO-FM - 95.7 (Farmville, VA) **32071**
WFLP-AM (Erie, PA) Unable to locate
WFLQ-FM - 100.1 (French Lick, IN) **10012**
WFLR-AM - 1570 (Dundee, NY) **20535**
WFLR-FM - 95.9 (Dundee, NY) **20536**
WFLS-AM **32093***
WFLS-FM - 93.3 (Fredericksburg, VA) **32091**
WFLT-AM - 1420 (Flint, MI) **15043**
WFLW-AM - 1360 (Monticello, KY) **12300**
WFLW-FM **12301***
WFLX-TV - Channel 29 (West Palm Beach, FL) **6852**
WFLY-FM (Albany, NY) Unable to locate
WFLY-FM - 92.3 (Latham, NY) **20935**
WFLZ-FM - 93.3 (Tampa, FL) **6791**
WFMB-AM - 1450 (Springfield, IL) **9647**
WFMB-FM - 104.5 (Springfield, IL) **9648**
WFMC-AM - 730 (Goldsboro, NC) **23911**
WFMD-AM (Frederick, MD) Unable to locate
WFME-FM - 94.7 (West Orange, NJ) **19725**
WFMF-FM **12521***
WFMG-FM - 101.3 (Richmond, IN) **10423**
WFMH-AM - 1460 (Cullman, AL) **164**
WFMH-FM - 95.5 (Cullman, AL) **165**
WFMI-FM **384***
WFMJ-AM (Youngstown, OH) Ceased
WFMJ-TV - Channel 21 (Youngstown, OH) **25704**
WFMK-FM (Williamston, MI) Unable to locate
WFMN-AM **23003***
WFMO-AM - 860 (Fairmont, NC) **23873**
WFMP-AM **14702***
WFMR-FM - 106.9 (Milwaukee, WI) **34116**
WFMS-FM - 95.5 (Indianapolis, IN) **10194**
WFMT-FM (Chicago, IL) Unable to locate
WFMU-FM - 91.1 (Jersey City, NJ) **19149**
WFMV-FM **19378***
WFMW-AM - 730 (Madisonville, KY) **12273**
WFMY-TV - Channel 2 (Greensboro, NC) **23945**
WFMZ-FM - 100.7 (Allentown, PA) **26630**
WFMZ-TV - Channel 69 (Allentown, PA) **26631**
WFNC-AM - 640 (Fayetteville, NC) **23886**
WFNE-FM **7289***
WFNI-FM - 104.5 (Bala Cynwyd, PA) **26673**
WFNL-AM **7111***
WFNM-FM - 89.1 (Lancaster, PA) **27149**
WFNP-FM - 88.7 (New Paltz, NY) **21115**
WFNQ-FM **28644***
WFNR-AM - 710 (Radford, VA) **32348**
WFNS-AM (Tampa, FL) Unable to locate
WFNW-AM (Stamford, CT) Unable to locate
WFNX-FM - 101.7 (Lynn, MA) **14286**
WFNZ-AM - 610 (Charlotte, NC) **23769**
WFOB-AM - 1430 (Fostoria, OH) **25200**
WFOF-FM - 90.3 (Covington, IN) **9907**
WFOM-AM (Marietta, GA) Unable to locate
WFON-FM **33700***
WFOR-AM - 1400 (Hattiesburg, MS) **16671**
W46AR-TV - Channel 46 (Milwaukee, WI) **34117**
WFOX-FM - 97.1 (Atlanta, GA) **7072**
WFOY-AM - 1240 (St. Augustine, FL) **6620**
WFPA-AM **449***
WFPC-FM **10525***
WFPG-AM - 1450 (Northfield, NJ) **19382**
WFPG-FM - 96.9 (Northfield, NJ) **19383**
WFPK-FM - 91.9 (Louisville, KY) **12250**
WFPL-FM - 89.3 (Louisville, KY) **12251**
WFPM-AM **7291***
WFPR-AM (Hammond, LA) Unable to locate
WFPS-FM - 92.1 (Freeport, IL) **8900**
WFPT-TV - Channel 62 (Frederick, MD) **13526**
WFQR-AM **9859***
WFQS-FM - 91.3 (Asheville, NC) **23636**
WFQX-FM (Winchester, VA) Unable to locate
WFQX-TV - Channel 33/45 (Cadillac, MI) **14846**

WFRA-AM - 1450 (Franklin, PA) **26935**
WFRA-FM **26936***
WFRB-AM - 560 (Frostburg, MD) **13528**
WFRC-FM **14186***
WFRC-FM - 90.5 (Phenix City, AL) **426**
WFRD-FM - 99.3 (Hanover, NH) **18521**
WFRE-FM (Frederick, MD) *Unable to locate*
WFRG-FM - 104.3 (Whitesboro, NY) **23578**
WFRJ-FM - 88.9 FM (Windber, PA) **28195**
WFRK-AM (Red Bank, NJ) *Unable to locate*
WFRL-AM - 1570 (Freeport, IL) **8901**
WFRM-AM (Coudersport, PA) *Unable to locate*
WFRM-FM (Coudersport, PA) *Unable to locate*
WFRN-AM - 1270 (Elkhart, IN) **9925**
WFRN-FM - 104.7 (Elkhart, IN) **9926**
WFRO-AM - 900 (Fremont, OH) **25204**
WFRO-FM - 99.1 (Fremont, OH) **25205**
WFRQ-FM (Waynesboro, TN) *Ceased*
WFRS-FM - 88.9 (Islandia, NY) **20785**
WFRV-TV - Channel 5 (Green Bay, WI) **33747**
WFRW-FM - 88.1 (Newark, NY) **22999**
WFS **9219***
WFSB-FM **14202***
WFSB-TV - Channel 3 (Hartford, CT) **4902**
WFSC-AM - 1050 (Franklin, NC) **23899**
WFSC-FM **23900***
WFSE-FM (Edinboro, PA) *Unable to locate*
WFSF-AM (Ozark, AL) *Ceased*
WFSG-TV - Channel 56 (Panama City, FL) **6558**
WFSI-FM - 107.9 (Annapolis, MD) **13099**
WFSK-FM - 88.1 (Nashville, TN) **29510**
WFSL-TV **15305***
WFSP-AM - 1560 (Kingwood, WV) **33360**
WFSP-FM - 107.7 (Kingwood, WV) **33361**
WFSQ-FM - 91.5 (Tallahassee, FL) **6746**
WFSR-AM - 970 (Harlan, KY) **12106**
WFSS-FM - 91.9 (Fayetteville, NC) **23887**
WFSU-FM **6746***
WFSU-FM - 88.9 (Tallahassee, FL) **6747**
WFSU-TV - Channel 11 (Tallahassee, FL) **6748**
WFSY-FM - 98.5 (Panama City, FL) **6559**
WFTA-FM - 101.9 (Tupelo, MS) **16853**
WFTC-TV - Channel 29 (Minneapolis, MN) **16161**
WFTD-AM - 1080 (Marietta, GA) **7424**
WFTE-AM **10257***
WFTF-FM - 90.5 (Rutland, VT) **31586**
WFTG-AM - 1400 (London, KY) **12204**
WFTH-AM - 1590 (Richmond, VA) **32477**
WFTK-AM (Butner, NC) *Unable to locate*
WFTL-AM (Fort Lauderdale, FL) *Unable to locate*
WFTM-AM - 1240 (Maysville, KY) **12289**
WFTM-FM - 95.9 (Maysville, KY) **12290**
WFTN-AM - 1240 (Franklin, NH) **18509**
WFTN-FM - 94.1 (Franklin, NH) **18510**
WFTO-AM - 1330 (Tupelo, MS) **16854**
WFTR-AM - 1450 (Front Royal, VA) **32097**
WFTR-FM **32098***
WFTS-TV - Channel 28 (Tampa, FL) **6792**
WFTV-TV - Channel 9 (Orlando, FL) **6517**
WFTW-AM - 1260 (Fort Walton Beach, FL) **6123**
WFTW-FM **6124***
WFTX-TV - Channel 36/4 (Cape Coral, FL) **5975**
WFTY-TV - Channel 50 (Washington, DC) **5882**
WFTY-TV - Channel 67 (Central Islip, NY) **20450**
WFUB **14247***
WFUL-AM **12085***
WFUM-FM - 91.1 (Flint, MI) **15044**
WFUM-TV - Channel 28 (Flint, MI) **15045**
WFUN-AM - 970 (Ashtabula, OH) **24625**
WFUR-AM - 1570 (Grand Rapids, MI) **15106**
WFUR-FM (Grand Rapids, MI) *Unable to locate*
WFUV-FM - 90.7 (Bronx, NY) **20292**
WFVA-AM - 1230 (Fredericksburg, VA) **32092**
WFVA-FM **32090***
WFVR-AM (Gainesville, FL) *Unable to locate*
WFVX-TV - Channel 45 (Cadillac, MI) **14847**
WFWA-TV - Channel 39 (Fort Wayne, IN) **9986**
WFWC-AM **23356***
WFWL-AM - 1220 (Camden, TN) **29079**
WFWM-FM - 91.9 (Frostburg, MD) **13529**
WFWQ-FM **9976***
WFXA-FM - 103.1 (North Augusta, SC) **28720**
WFXB-FM **17561***
WFXB-TV - Channel 43 (Myrtle Beach, SC) **28707**
WFXC-FM (Morrisville, NC) *Unable to locate*
WFXD-FM - 103.3 (Marquette, MI) **15341**
WFXF-FM **10209***
WFXH-AM (Hilton Head Island, SC) *Unable to locate*
WFXH-FM (Hilton Head Island, SC) *Unable to locate*
WFXI-TV - Channel 8 (Morehead City, NC) **24071**
WFXK-FM (Raleigh, NC) *Unable to locate*
WFXL-TV - Channel 31 (Albany, GA) **6908**
WFXM-FM - 100.1 (Fort Valley, GA) **7289**
WFXO-FM - 104.9 (Iuka, MS) **16692**
WFXP-AM **4767***
WFXP-TV - Channel 66 (Erie, PA) **26904**
WFXQ-FM - 99.9 (Chase City, VA) **31960**
WFXR-TV - Channel 27 (Roanoke, VA) **32498**
WFXS-FM - 102.3 (Chattanooga, TN) **29104**

WFXT-TV - Channel 25 (Dedham, MA) **14156**
WFXV-TV **23267***
WFXW-AM (St. Charles, IL) *Ceased*
WFXX-AM (South Williamsport, PA) *Unable to locate*
WFXY-AM - 1490 (Middlesboro, KY) **12294**
WFYC-AM - 1280 (Alma, MI) **14733**
WFYF-TV **23522***
WFYI-FM - 90.1 (Indianapolis, IN) **10195**
WFYI-TV - Channel 20 (Indianapolis, IN) **10196**
WFYV-AM (Jacksonville, FL) *Ceased*
WFYV-FM - 104.5 (Jacksonville, FL) **6222**
WFYZ-AM **33446***
WFYZ-AM - 1360 (Ravenswood, WV) **33445**
WFYZ-FM **33445***
WFYZ-TV **29552***
WGA Update **33983***
WGAA-AM - 1340 (Cedartown, GA) **7166**
WGAB-AM - 1180 (Newburgh, IN) **10352**
WGAC-AM (Martinez, GA) *Unable to locate*
WGAD-AM - 1350 (Gadsden, AL) **235**
WGAI-AM - 560 (Elizabeth City, NC) **23862**
WGAJ-FM - 91.7 (Deerfield, MA) **14158**
WGAL-AM **27155***
WGAL-TV - Channel 8 (Lancaster, PA) **27150**
WGAM-AM - 1520 (Greenfield, MA) **14223**
WGAN-AM - 560 (South Portland, ME) **13054**
WGAN-TV **13026***
WGAO-FM - 88.3 (Franklin, MA) **14208**
WGAP-AM - 1400 (Maryville, TN) **29349**
WGAP-FM - 95.7 (Maryville, TN) **29350**
WGAQ-FM **10010***
WGAR-AM **24978***
WGAR-FM - 99.5 (Cleveland, OH) **24974**
WGAS-AM - 1420 (Charlotte, NC) **23770**
WGAT-AM - 1050 (Gate City, VA) **32109**
WGAU-AM - 1340 (Athens, GA) **6956**
WGAU-FM **6957***
WGAW-AM - 1340 (Hamilton, MA) **14226**
The WGAW Journal **2442***
WGAY-FM - 99.5 (Rockville, MD) **13702**
WGBA-TV - Channel 26 (Green Bay, WI) **33748**
WGBB-AM (West Babylon, NY) *Ceased*
WGBE-FM - 90.9 (Toledo, OH) **25576**
WGBF-AM - 1280 (Evansville, IN) **9942**
WGBF-FM - 103.1 (Evansville, IN) **9943**
WGBH-FM - 89.7 (Boston, MA) **13985**
WGBH-TV - Channel 2 (Boston, MA) **13986**
WGBI-AM - 910 (Pittston, PA) **27888**
WGBI-FM **27889***
WGBK-FM - 88.5 (Glenview, IL) **8943**
WGBM-FM **33756***
WGBM-AM **34385***
WGBO-TV - Channel 66 (Chicago, IL) **8622**
WGBR-AM (Goldsboro, NC) *Unable to locate*
WGBS-TV **27740***
WGBW-FM **33749***
WGBX-TV - Channel 44 (Boston, MA) **13987**
WGBY-TV - Channel 57 (Springfield, MA) **14557**
WGCA-FM - 88.5 (Quincy, IL) **9477**
WGCB-AM - 1440 (Red Lion, PA) **27928**
WGCB-FM - 96.1 (Red Lion, PA) **27929**
WGCB-TV - Channel 49 (Red Lion, PA) **27930**
WGCC-FM - 90.7 (Batavia, NY) **20123**
WGCD-AM (Chester, SC) *Unable to locate*
WGCH-AM - 1490 (Greenwich, CT) **4878**
WGCI-AM - 1390 (Chicago, IL) **8623**
WGCI-FM - 107.5 (Chicago, IL) **8624**
WGCL-AM - 1370 (Bloomington, IN) **9858**
WGCL-TV - Channel 46 (Atlanta, GA) **7073**
WGCM-FM - 102.3 (Gulfport, MS) **16656**
WGCO-FM **7145***
WGCO-FM - 98.3 (Savannah, GA) **7543**
WGCR-AM - 720 (Pisgah Forest, NC) **24117**
WGCS-FM - 91.1 (Goshen, IN) **10029**
WGCU-FM - 90.1 (Fort Myers, FL) **6104**
WGCU-TV - Channel 30 (Fort Myers, FL) **6105**
WGCV-AM - 620 (West Columbia, SC) **28783**
WGCX-FM (Mobile, AL) *Unable to locate*
WGDL-AM - 1200 (Lares, PR) **28254**
WGDN-AM - 1350 (Gladwin, MI) **15081**
WGDN-FM - 103.1 (Gladwin, MI) **15082**
WGDR-FM - 91.1 (Plainfield, VT) **31579**
WGEA-AM - 1150 (Geneva, AL) **242**
WGEE-AM **10206***
WGEL-FM - 101.7 (Greenville, IL) **8963**
WGEM-AM - 1440 (Quincy, IL) **9478**
WGEM-FM - 105.1 (Quincy, IL) **9479**
WGEM-TV - Channel 10 (Quincy, IL) **9480**
WGEN-AM - 1500 (Galva, IL) **8912**
WGEN-FM (Geneseo, IL) *Ceased*
WGER-FM (Saginaw, MI) *Unable to locate*
WGES-FM (Oswego, NY) *Unable to locate*
WGET-AM - 1320 (Gettysburg, PA) **26941**
WGEV-FM (Beaver Falls, PA) *Unable to locate*
WGEZ-AM - 1490 (Beloit, WI) **33579**
WGFA-AM - 1360 (Watseka, IL) **9740**
WGFA-FM - 94.1 (Watseka, IL) **9741**
WGFB-FM **31609***
WGFB-FM - 103.1 (Rockford, IL) **9536**

WGFC-AM - 1030 (Floyd, VA) **32077**
WGFP-AM - 940 (Worcester, MA) **14697**
WGFR-FM - 92.7 (Queensbury, NY) **23174**
WGFS-AM - 1430 (Covington, GA) **7213**
WGFT-FM - 101.1 (Youngstown, OH) **25705**
WGFX-FM - 104.5 (Nashville, TN) **29511**
WGGA-AM - 1240 (Gainesville, GA) **7302**
WGGB-TV - Channel 40 (Springfield, MA) **14558**
WGGC-FM - 95.1 (Bowling Green, KY) **11957**
WGGD-FM (Melbourne, FL) *Unable to locate*
WGGG-AM (Gainesville, FL) *Unable to locate*
WGGG-FM **6167***
WGGH-AM - 1150 (Marion, IL) **9147**
WGGL-FM - 91.1 (Houghton, MI) **15186**
WGGM-AM - 820 (Chesterfield, VA) **31970**
WGGN-AM - 820 (Chester, VA) **31968**
WGGN-FM - 97.7 (Castalia, OH) **24743**
WGGN-TV - Channel 52 (Castalia, OH) **24744**
WGGO-AM - 1590 (Salamanca, NY) **23295**
WGGS-TV - Channel 16 (Greenville, SC) **28631**
WGGT-TV **24335***
WGGY-FM - 101.3 (Pittston, PA) **27889**
WGGZ-FM **12516***
WGH-AM - 1310 (Virginia Beach, VA) **32593**
WGH-FM - 97.3 (Virginia Beach, VA) **32594**
WGHB-AM - 1250 (Farmville, NC) **23878**
WGHN-AM - 1370 (Grand Haven, MI) **15086**
WGHN-FM - 92.1 (Grand Haven, MI) **15087**
WGHP-TV - Channel 8 (High Point, NC) **24001**
WGHQ-AM - 920 (Poughkeepsie, NY) **23158**
WGHR-FM - 100.7 (Marietta, GA) **7425**
WGHT-AM - 1500 (Pompton Lakes, NJ) **19450**
WGHT-AM (Pompton Lakes, NJ) *Ceased*
WGHW-AM **27338***
WGIA-AM - 1350 (Waycross, GA) **7647**
WGIB-FM - 91.9 (Birmingham, AL) **116**
WGIC-AM **25689***
WGIC-FM - 98.5 (Cookeville, TN) **29149**
WGIL-AM - 1400 (Galesburg, IL) **8910**
WGIN-AM - 930 (Portsmouth, NH) **18639**
WGIP-AM - 1540 (Portsmouth, NH) **18640**
WGIQ-TV - Channel 43 (Louisville, AL) **307**
WGIR-AM - 610 (Manchester, NH) **18569**
WGIR-FM - 101.1 (Manchester, NH) **18570**
WGIV-AM **23763***
WGIX-FM - 95.3 (Gouverneur, NY) **20676**
WGKA-AM (Atlanta, GA) *Unable to locate*
WGKI-TV **14846***
WGKP-FM (Lake Katrine, NY) *Ceased*
WGKR-AM - 540 (Jersey City, NJ) **19150**
WGKS-FM - 96.9 (Lexington, KY) **12184**
WGKT-AM (Buffalo, NY) *Ceased*
WGKU-TV **14847***
WGKV-AM **33459***
WGKX-FM (Memphis, TN) *Unable to locate*
WGKY-FM - 95.9 (Wickliffe, KY) **12444**
WGL-AM (Fort Wayne, IN) *Unable to locate*
WGL-FM - 102 (Fort Wayne, IN) **9987**
WGLB-AM - 1560 (Milwaukee, WI) **34118**
WGLB-FM - 100.1 (Port Washington, WI) **34251**
WGLC-AM (Mendota, IL) *Ceased*
WGLC-FM - 100.1 (Mendota, IL) **9176**
WGLD-FM (Indianapolis, IN) *Unable to locate*
WGLE-FM - 90.7 (Lima, OH) **25300**
WGLF-FM - 104.1 (Tallahassee, FL) **6749**
WGLH-AM - 960 (La Follette, TN) **29309**
WGLI-AM (Babylon, NY) *Unable to locate*
WGLL-AM - 1570 (Auburn, IN) **9790**
WGLL-FM **26952***
WGLM-FM **10427***
WGLN-FM - 102.3 (Ashland, OH) **24619**
WGLQ-FM (Escanaba, MI) *Unable to locate*
WGLR-AM - 1280 (Lancaster, WI) **33908**
WGLR-FM - 97.7 (Lancaster, WI) **33909**
WGLS-FM - 89.7 (Glassboro, NJ) **18845**
WGLT-FM - 89.1 FM (Normal, IL) **9308**
WGLU-FM - 92.1 (Johnstown, PA) **27091**
WGLX-FM - 103.3 (Wisconsin Rapids, WI) **34467**
WGLY-FM - 93.5 (Essex, VT) **31542**
WGMA-AM - 1520 AM (Spindale, NC) **24242**
WGMB-AM - 640 (Bridgewater, VA) **31896**
WGMC-FM - 90.1, 105.1 (North Greece, NY) **23013**
WGMD-FM - 92.7 (Lewes, DE) **5260**
WGME-TV - Channel 13 (Portland, ME) **13026**
WGMF-AM (Horseheads, NY) *Unable to locate*
WGMI-AM - 1440 (Bremen, GA) **7138**
WGML-AM - 990 (Hinesville, GA) **7335**
WGMM-FM **15082***
WGMM-FM - 97.7 (Corning, NY) **20508**
WGMO-FM - 95.3 (Shell Lake, WI) **34328**
WGMR-FM - 101.1 (State College, PA) **28024**
WGMS-AM **13748***
WGMS-FM - 103.5 (Washington, DC) **5883**
WGMT-FM - 97.7 (Lyndonville, VT) **31550**
WGMX-FM (Marathon, FL) *Unable to locate*
WGMZ-FM **15039***
WGMZ-FM (Frankenmuth, MI) *Ceased*
WGN-AM - 720 (Chicago, IL) **8625**
WGN-TV - Channel 9 (Chicago, IL) **8626**

WGNA-AM - 1460 (Latham, NY) **20936**
WGNA-FM - 107.7 (Latham, NY) **20937**
WGNB-AM (Saint Petersburg, FL) *Ceased*
WGNB-FM - 89.3 (Zeeland, MI) **15695**
WGNC-AM - 1450 (Gastonia, NC) **23908**
WGNE-AM (Panama City, FL) *Unable to locate*
WGNE-FM **6559***
WGNE-FM - 99.9 (Ormond Beach, FL) **6535**
WGNI-FM - 102.7 (Wilmington, NC) **24300**
WGNM-TV - Channel 64 (Macon, GA) **7395**
WGNO-TV - Channel 26 (New Orleans, LA) **12770**
WGNR-AM **21125***
WGNR-FM **21124***
WGNR-FM (Zeeland, MI) *Unable to locate*
WGNS-AM - 1450 (Murfreesboro, TN) **29436**
WGNT-AM **33344***
WGNT-TV - Channel 27 (Portsmouth, VA) **32335**
WGNU-AM - 920 (St. Louis, MO) **17556**
WGNV-FM - 88.5 (Milladore, WI) **34053**
WGNX-TV **7073***
WGNY-AM - 1200 (Newburgh, NY) **23002**
WGNY-FM - 103.1 (Newburgh, NY) **23003**
WGNZ-AM - 1110 (Dayton, OH) **25138**
WGOC-AM - 640 (Gray, TN) **29208**
WGOG-FM - 96.3 (Walhalla, SC) **28779**
WGOH-AM - 1370 (Grayson, KY) **12094**
WGOJ-FM - 105.5 (Conneaut, OH) **25092**
WGOK-AM (Mobile, AL) *Unable to locate*
WGOL-FM **32219***
WGOL-FM (Lynchburg, VA) *Unable to locate*
WGOM-AM - 860 (Marion, IN) **10291**
WGOR-FM - 93.9 (Augusta, GA) **7109**
WGOS-AM - 1070 (High Point, NC) **24002**
WGOT-TV **18572***
WGOV-AM - 950 (Valdosta, GA) **7621**
WGOV-FM **7618***
WGOW-AM - 1150 (Chattanooga, TN) **29105**
WGPA-AM - 1100 (Bethlehem, PA) **26711**
WGPC-AM - 1450 (Albany, GA) **6909**
WGPC-FM - 104.5 (Albany, GA) **6910**
WGPH-FM - 91.5 (Vidalia, GA) **7630**
WGPR-FM - 107.5 (Detroit, MI) **14964**
WGPR-TV - Channel 62 (Detroit, MI) **14965**
WGPT-TV - Channel 36 (Oakland, MD) **13636**
WGPX-TV - Channel 16 (Greensboro, NC) **23946**
WGQR-FM - 105.7 (Elizabethtown, NC) **23866**
WGR-AM (Buffalo, NY) *Unable to locate*
WGRB-TV (Bardstown, KY) *Unable to locate*
WGRC-FM - 91.3 (Lewisburg, PA) **27194**
WGRD-AM (Grand Rapids, MI) *Ceased*
WGRD-FM - 97.9 (Grand Rapids, MI) **15107**
WGRE-FM - 91.5 (Greencastle, IN) **10037**
WGRF-FM - 96.9 (Buffalo, NY) **20399**
WGRG-FM **23492***
WGRM-AM - 1240 (Greenwood, MS) **16648**
WGRM-FM - 93.9 (Greenwood, MS) **16649**
WGRN-FM - 89.5 (Greenville, IL) **8964**
WGRO-AM - 960 (Lake City, FL) **6272**
WGRP-AM - 940 (Greenville, PA) **26961**
WGRP-FM **26960***
WGRQ-FM **20399***
WGRQ-FM (King George, VA) *Unable to locate*
WGRR-AM **344***
WGRR-FM (Cincinnati, OH) *Unable to locate*
WGRS-FM - 91.5 (Monroe, CT) **4964**
WGRT-AM **10210***
WGRT-FM **10211***
WGRT-FM - 102.3 (Port Huron, MI) **15454**
WGRV-AM - 1340 (Greeneville, TN) **29213**
WGRW-FM - 90.7 (Anniston, AL) **20**
WGRX-FM **13584***
WGRY-AM - 1230 (Grayling, MI) **15132**
WGRY-FM - 100.3 (Grayling, MI) **15133**
WGRZ-TV - Channel 2 (Buffalo, NY) **20400**
WGSE-TV **28707***
WGSE-TV (Myrtle Beach, SC) *Ceased*
WGSF-AM - 1210 (Memphis, TN) **29394**
WGSI-FM **28108***
WGSK-FM - 90.1 (Monroe, CT) **4965**
WGSL-AM **28632***
WGSL-FM - 91.1 (Loves Park, IL) **9121**
WGSN-AM (North Myrtle Beach, SC) *Unable to locate*
WGSO-AM - 990 (Metairie, LA) **12681**
WGSP-AM (Charlotte, NC) *Unable to locate*
WGSR-AM (Millen, GA) *Unable to locate*
WGSS-FM **23890***
WGST-AM (Atlanta, GA) *Unable to locate*
WGST-FM (Atlanta, GA) *Unable to locate*
WGSU-FM - 89.3 (Geneseo, NY) **20651**
WGSV-AM - 1270 (Guntersville, AL) **255**
WGSY-FM - 100.1 (Columbus, GA) **7189**
WGTA-AM - 950 (Summerville, GA) **7577**
WGTC-AM **9858***
WGTC-FM (La Porte, IN) *Unable to locate*
WGTD-FM - 91.1 (Kenosha, WI) **33876**
WGTE-FM - 91.3 (Toledo, OH) **25577**
WGTE-TV - Channel 30 (Toledo, OH) **25578**
WGTF-FM - 89.5 (Dothan, AL) **192**

WGTG-FM **29641***
WGTH-AM - 540 (Richlands, VA) **32427**
WGTH-FM - 105.5 (Richlands, VA) **32428**
WGTK-FM - 100.9 (Middlebury, VT) **31561**
WGTL-AM (Kannapolis, NC) *Unable to locate*
WGTM-AM - 590 (Wilson, NC) **24313**
WGTN-AM (Georgetown, SC) *Unable to locate*
WGTN-FM (Georgetown, SC) *Unable to locate*
WGTO-AM (Ocoee, FL) *Ceased*
WGTR-FM **6201***
WGTR-FM (Daytona Beach, FL) *Unable to locate*
WGTS-FM - 91.9 (Takoma Park, MD) **13753**
WGTT-AM - 1500 (Alabaster, AL) **2**
WGTU-TV - Channel 29 (Traverse City, MI) **15608**
WGTV-TV (Atlanta, GA) *Unable to locate*
WGTW-TV - Channel 48 (Philadelphia, PA) **27731**
WGTX-AM (De Funiak Springs, FL) *Ceased*
WGTY-FM - 107.7 (Gettysburg, PA) **26942**
WGTZ-FM - 92.9 (Dayton, OH) **25139**
WGUC-FM - 90.9 (Cincinnati, OH) **24839**
WGUD-AM - 1490 (Pascagoula, MS) **16813**
WGUL-AM **6485***
WGUL-AM - 860 (Palm Harbor, FL) **6553**
WGUL-FM - 106.3 (Palm Harbor, FL) **6554**
WGUN-AM - 1010 (Tucker, GA) **7612**
WGUR-FM - 88.9 (Milledgeville, GA) **7437**
WGUS-AM **28721***
WGUS-AM - 1380 (North Augusta, SC) **28721**
WGUS-FM **7107***
WGUY-FM - 102.1 (Newport, ME) **12992**
WGVA-AM - 1240 (Geneva, NY) **20659**
WGVC-FM **15110***
WGVE-FM - 88.7 (Gary, IN) **10019**
WGVK-TV - Channel 52 (Grand Rapids, MI) **15108**
WGVL-AM - 1440 (Greenville, MS) **28632**
WGVM-AM - 1260 (Greenville, MS) **16640**
WGVO-FM (Greenville, OH) *Unable to locate*
WGVP-TV **7625***
WGVU-AM - 1480 (Grand Rapids, MI) **15109**
WGVU-FM - 88.5 (Grand Rapids, MI) **15110**
WGVU-TV - Channel 35 (Grand Rapids, MI) **15111**
WGWD-FM - 93.3 (Gretna, FL) **6176**
WGWG-FM - 88.3 (Charlotte, NC) **23771**
WGWR-AM **23624***
WGWY-AM **14871***
WGXA-TV - Channel 24 (Macon, GA) **7396**
WGXM-AM - 98.1 (Dayton, OH) **25140**
WGY-AM - 810 (Albany, NY) **20011**
WGYE-FM - 102.7 (Fairmont, WV) **33314**
WGYI-FM - 98.5 (Meadville, PA) **27237**
WGYJ-AM **36***
WGYL-FM - 93.7 (Vero Beach, FL) **6837**
WGYM-AM **19176***
WGYV-AM - 1380 (Greenville, AL) **244**
WGYY-FM - 100.3 (Meadville, PA) **27238**
WGZO-FM (Hilton Head Island, SC) *Unable to locate*
WHA-TV - Channel 21 (Madison, WI) **33993**
WHAB-FM - 89.1 (Acton, MA) **13786**
WHAG-AM - 1410 (Hagerstown, MD) **13575**
WHAG-TV - Channel 25 (Hagerstown, MD) **13576**
WHAI-AM (Greenfield, MA) *Unable to locate*
WHAI-FM (Greenfield, MA) *Unable to locate*
WHAI-TV (Branford, CT) *Unable to locate*
WHAJ-FM - 104.5 (Bluefield, WV) **33256**
WHAK-AM (Alpena, MI) *Ceased*
WHAL-AM **29603***
Whalewatcher (San Pedro, CA) **3597**
Whaling City Cable TV **14378***
WHAM-AM - 1180 (Rochester, NY) **23247**
WHAM-TV **23253***
WHAN-AM - 1430 (Ashland, VA) **31858**
WHAP-AM (Hopewell, VA) *Unable to locate*
WHAR-AM **33296***
The Wharton Journal (Philadelphia, PA) **27719**
Wharton Journal-Spectator (Wharton, TX) **31284**
WHAS-AM - 840 (Louisville, KY) **12252**
WHAS-TV - Channel 11 (Louisville, KY) **12253**
What! A Magazine (Winnipeg, MB, Can.) **35362**
WHAT-AM - 1340 (Philadelphia, PA) **27732**
What Cheer Paper (What Cheer, IA) **11327**
What Is Enlightenment? (Lenox, MA) **14270**
What's Brewing (Meriden, CT) **38121**
What's Cooking Magazine (Don Mills, ON, Can.) **35779**
What's Happening **26316***
What's New in Advertising and Marketing (Richmond, VA) **32470**
What's New in Medicine (Kensington, CT) **38122**
What's On in Las Vegas Magazine **18385***
What's On Magazine **18385***
What's On, The Las Vegas Guide (Las Vegas, NV) **18385**
What's the Point? (Hollis, NH) *Unable to locate*
What's Up Information Services (Atlanta, GA) **38123**
What's Up Niagara Magazine (Niagara Falls, ON, Can.) *Unable to locate*
WHAV-AM - 1490 (Methuen, MA) **14330**
WHAW-AM - 980 (Weston, WV) **33499**
WHAZ-AM - 1330 (Cohoes, NY) **20481**

WHB-AM (Kansas City, MO) *Unable to locate*
WHBB-AM - 1490 (Selma, AL) **454**
WHBC-AM - 1480 (Canton, OH) **24734**
WHBC-FM - 94.1 (Canton, OH) **24735**
WHBF-AM **10748***
WHBF-TV - Channel 4 (Rock Island, IL) **9524**
WHBG-AM - 1360 (Harrisonburg, VA) **32144**
WHBI-FM **22978***
WHBL-AM - 1330 (Sheboygan, WI) **34324**
WHBN-AM - 1420 (Danville, KY) **12040**
WHBN-FM **12430***
WHBO-FM - 92.7 (Manheim, PA) **27216**
WHBP-AM **27092***
WHBQ-AM - 560 (Memphis, TN) **29395**
WHBQ-TV - Channel 13 (Memphis, TN) **29396**
WHBR-FM - 103.1 (Parkersburg, WV) **33424**
WHBR-TV - Channel 33 (Robertsdale, AL) **439**
WHBT-AM - 1410 (Tallahassee, FL) **6750**
WHBU-AM - 1240 (Daleville, IN) **9918**
WHBX-FM - 96.1 (Tallahassee, FL) **6751**
WHBY-AM - 1150 (Appleton, WI) **33549**
WHC-FM **20475***
WHCB-FM - 91.5 (Bluff City, TN) **29056**
WHCC-AM (Waynesville, NC) *Unable to locate*
WHCE-FM (Highland Springs, VA) *Unable to locate*
WHCF-FM - 88.5 (Bangor, ME) **12908**
WHCG-AM - 1360 (Metter, GA) **7433**
WHCG-FM **7432***
WHCH-AM **23896***
WHCH-FM **20730***
WHCH-FM - 98.3 (Marquette, MI) **15342**
WHCJ-FM - 90.3 (Savannah, GA) **7544**
WHCL-FM - 88.7 (Clinton, NY) **20475**
WHCM-AM **457***
WHCN-FM - 105.9 (Hartford, CT) **4903**
WHCO-AM - 1230 (Sparta, IL) **9618**
WHCR-FM - 90.3 (New York, NY) **22970**
WHCT-TV (Hartford, CT) *Ceased*
WHCU-AM - 870 (Ithaca, NY) **20818**
WHCU-FM **20825***
WHCY-FM - 106.3 (Newton, NJ) **19378**
WHDF-AM **15185***
WHDG-FM **13581***
WHDG-FM - 97.5 (Rhinelander, WI) **34288**
WHDH-TV - Channel 7 (Boston, MA) **13988**
WHDL-AM - 1450 (Olean, NY) **23041**
WHDM-AM - 1440 (Tavares, FL) **6812**
WHDQ-FM - 106.1 (Claremont, NH) **18466**
WHDZ-AM **26911***
Wheat Flour; Exports of Canadian Grain and (Winnipeg, MB, Can.) **35328**
The Wheat Grower (Washington, DC) *Ceased*
Wheat Life (Ritzville, WA) **32933**
Wheat; Oregon (Pendleton, OR) **26459**
Wheat Ridge Sentinel (Minneapolis, MN) *Unable to locate*
Wheat State Telecable Inc. (Udall, KS) **11853**
Wheatfield Tribune; Niagara- (Grand Island, NY) **20680**
Wheatley Journal (Wheatley, ON, Can.) **36872**
Wheaton Gazette (Wheaton, MN) **16508**
Wheaton Journal (Cassville, MO) **16967**
Wheaton Leader (Wheaton, IL) **9760**
Wheaton Sun (Naperville, IL) **9275**
Wheaton Wire (Norton, MA) **14438**
WHEB-AM (Portsmouth, NH) *Ceased*
WHEB-FM - 100.3 (Portsmouth, NH) **18641**
WHEC-TV - Channel 10 (Rochester, NY) **23248**
WHEE-AM - 1370 (Martinsville, VA) **32237**
The Wheel (Newport News, VA) **32280**
Wheel; The Emory (Atlanta, GA) **7005**
Wheel; Okotoks Western (Okotoks, AB, Can.) **34818**
The Wheeler County Eagle (Alamo, GA) **6901**
Wheeler County Independent (Sargent, NE) **18261**
Wheeler TV System (Wheeler, TX) **31288**
Wheelers (Yucca Valley, CA) **4129**
Wheeling Countryside (Wheeling, IL) **9762**
Wheelings -New England Mechanic (Franklin, MA) **14207**
Wheels, Etc. (Sudbury, MA) **14581**
Wheels and Keels **14581***
Wheels of Time (Kansas City, MO) **17203**
Wheels; World of (Mississauga, ON, Can.) **36093**
WHEI-FM - 88.9 (Tiffin, OH) **25560**
WHEN-AM - 620 (Syracuse, NY) **23438**
WHEN-FM **23448***
WHEN-TV **23447***
WHEO-AM - 1270 (Stuart, VA) **32565**
WHEP-AM - 1310 (Foley, AL) **229**
WHER-FM - 103.7 (Hattiesburg, MS) **16672**
WHERE Alaska & The Yukon (Vancouver, BC, Can.) **35181**
WHERE Atlanta (Atlanta, GA) **7061**
WHERE Baltimore (Baltimore, MD) **13261**
WHERE Boston (Boston, MA) **13971**
WHERE Calgary (Calgary, AB, Can.) **34659**
WHERE Canadian Rockies (Calgary, AB, Can.) **34660**
WHERE Chicago (Chicago, IL) **8605**

WHERE Dallas (Dallas, TX) **30188**
WHERE Denver (Denver, CO) **4367**
WHERE Edmonton (Edmonton, AB, Can.) **34737**
WHERE Ft. Worth (Fort Worth, TX) **30356**
WHERE Halifax (Halifax, NS, Can.) **35572**
Where Halifax/Dartmouth **35572***
WHERE Houston (Los Angeles, CA) *Unable to locate*
WHERE Indianapolis (Minneapolis, MN) **16140**
WHERE Las Vegas (Las Vegas, NV) **18386**
WHERE Los Angeles (Los Angeles, CA) **2435**
WHERE Miami (Miami, FL) **6392**
WHERE New Orleans (New Orleans, LA) **12761**
WHERE New York (New York, NY) **22917**
WHERE Orange County (Costa Mesa, CA) **1782**
WHERE Orlando (Orlando, FL) **6510**
WHERE Ottawa (Ottawa, ON, Can.) **36279**
WHERE Philadelphia (Philadelphia, PA) **27720**
WHERE Phoenix/Scottsdale (Scottsdale, AZ) **876**
WHERE Puerto Rico (Guaynabo, PR) **28246**
WHERE Rocky Mountains **34660***
WHERE St. Louis (St. Louis, MO) **17532**
WHERE San Francisco (San Francisco, CA) **3462**
WHERE Seattle (Seattle, WA) **33044**
WHERE Toronto (Toronto, ON, Can.) **36791**
WHERE Twin Cities (Minneapolis, MN) **16141**
WHERE Vancouver (Vancouver, BC, Can.) **35182**
WHERE Victoria (Victoria, BC, Can.) **35230**
WHERE Washington (Washington, DC) **5860**
Where & When Magazine **27299***
Where & When Pennsylvania's Travel Guide (Mount
  Joy, PA) **27299**
WHET-FM (Kaukauna, WI) *Unable to locate*
Whetstone (Sierra Vista) *Ceased*
WHEV-AM (Garner, NC) *Unable to locate*
WHEW-AM - 1380 (Franklin, TN) **29200**
WHEW-FM **6115***
WHEZ-AM **15248***
WHFB-AM (Benton Harbor, MI) *Unable to locate*
WHFB-FM - 99.9 (Benton Harbor, MI) **14811**
WHFC-FM - 91.1 (Bel Air, MD) **13292**
WHFD-FM **24616***
WHFH-FM - 88.5 (Flossmoor, IL) **8892**
WHFM-FM **23243***
WHFM-FM - 95.3 (Center Moriches, NY) **20444**
WHFR-FM - 89.3 (Dearborn, MI) **14908**
WHFS-FM (Hyattsville, MD) *Unable to locate*
WHFT-TV - Channel 45 (Pembroke Park, FL) **6564**
WHFX-FM **7144***
WHGG-FM - 90.1 (Bristol, TN) **29068**
WHGH-AM - 840 (Thomasville, GA) **7588**
WHGL-AM - 1310 (Troy, PA) **28060**
WHGL-FM - 100.3 (Troy, PA) **28061**
WHGM-FM **27047***
WHGR-AM (Houghton Lake, MI) *Unable to locate*
WHGS-FM **12972***
WHHB-FM - 99.9 (Holliston, MA) **14240**
WHHH-FM - 96.3 (Indianapolis, IN) **10197**
WHHM-FM - 107.7 (Jackson, MS) **19236**
WHHO-AM - 1320 (Hornell, NY) **20756**
WHHS-FM - 107.9 (Havertown, PA) **27031**
WHHS-FM (89.9) **27031***
WHHT-FM **12092***
WHHV-AM - 1400 (Hillsville, VA) **32168**
WHHY-AM (Montgomery, AL) *Unable to locate*
WHHY-FM (Montgomery, AL) *Unable to locate*
WHIA-AM (Dawson, GA) *Ceased*
WHIC-AM (Hardinsburg, KY) *Unable to locate*
WHIC-FM (Hardinsburg, KY) *Unable to locate*
WHID-FM - 88.1 (Green Bay, WI) **33749**
Whidbey News-Times (Oak Harbor, WA) **32857**
Whidbey News Times Hot Sheet (Oak Harbor, WA)
  Unable to locate
Whidbey Record; South (Langley, WA) **32806**
WHIE-AM - 1320 (Griffin, GA) **7314**
Whig; Cecil (Elkton, MD) **13495**
Whig-Standard (Kingston, ON, Can.) **35948**
WHII-AM **16555***
WHII-FM **16556***
WHIL-AM **24122***
WHIL-FM - 91.3 (Mobile, AL) **340**
WHIM-AM - 1520 (Altamonte Springs, FL) **5904**
WHIM-AM (Cumberland, RI) *Unable to locate*
WHIM-FM **28435***
WHIN-AM - 1010 (Gallatin, TN) **29204**
WHIO-AM - 1210 (Dayton, OH) **25141**
WHIO-FM **25142***
WHIP-AM - 1350 (Mooresville, NC) **24069**
Whiplash & Related Disorders; Journal of
  (Binghamton, NY) **20207**
WHIQ-TV - Channel 25 (Birmingham, AL) **117**
WHIR-AM - 1230 (Danville, KY) **12041**
The Whirlwind **20477***
WHIS-AM - 1440 (Bluefield, WV) **33257**
WHIS-TV **33261***
Whiskey Island Magazine (Cleveland, OH) **24965**
Whispering Wind (Folsom, LA) **12581**
Whistler Citizen (Whistler, BC, Can.) *Ceased*
The Whit (Glassboro, NJ) **18844**
WHIT-AM - 1550 (Madison, WI) **33994**

Whitby-Clarington-Port Perry This Week; Oshawa-
  (Oshawa, ON, Can.) **36181**
Whitby Free Press (Whitby, ON, Can.) *Ceased*
White Bear Press (White Bear Lake, MN) **16515**
White Castle Communications (Morris, CT) *Ceased*
The White Castle Times (Plaquemine, LA) *Ceased*
White Center News **33042***
White Center News; West Seattle Herald/ (Seattle,
  WA) **33042**
White City Reporter **11878***
White County Heritage (Searcy, AR) **1339**
White County News (Cleveland, GA) *Unable to locate*
White County Record (Bald Knob, AR) *Unable to
  locate*
White Deer News (White Deer, TX) **31289**
White Hall Journal (Pine Bluff, AR) *Unable to locate*
White House Studies (Hauppauge, NY) **20723**
White Lady (Maywood, NJ) *Unable to locate*
White Lake Beacon (Whitehall, MI) **15684**
White Lake Spinal Column Newsweekly (White Lake,
  MI) **15683**
White Leader **29030***
The White Light (Fremont, CA) *Ceased*
White Mountain Cablevision (Colebrook, NH) **18470**
White Mountain Independent (Show Low, AZ) **881**
White Plains Reporter Dispatch (Mc Lean, VA) **32262**
White River Cablevision (Martinsville, IN) **10296**
White River Gazette (Fishers, IN) **9961**
White River Journal (Des Arc, AR) *Unable to locate*
White River News (Bridgeport, IL) *Unable to locate*
White River Valley Herald **31581***
The White Rocker (Dallas, TX) **30189**
White Sands Cable Co. (Las Cruces, NM) **19888**
White Sands Missile Ranger (White Sands Missile
  Range, NM) **19974**
White Settlement Bomber News (White Settlement,
  TX) **31290**
The White Sheet (Columbus, OH) *Ceased*
White Sheet-The Blythe Advertiser (Blythe, CA) **1588**
White Sheet-The Imperial Valley Advertiser (Palm
  Desert, CA) *Ceased*
White Sheet-The Indio Advertiser (Palm Desert, CA)
  2745
White Sheet-The Lake Havasu City Advertiser (Lake
  Havasu City, AZ) **736**
White Sheet-The Morongo Basin Advertiser (Morongo
  Basin, CA) **2602**
White Sheet-The Palm Desert Advertiser (Palm
  Desert, CA) **2746**
White Sheet-The Palm Springs Advertiser (Palm
  Springs, CA) **2770**
White Sheet-The Palm Springs (North) Advertiser
  (Palm Desert, CA) *Ceased*
White Sheet-The Parker Advertiser (Parker, AZ) **764**
White Sheet-The Tri-State Advertiser (Palm Desert,
  CA) **2747**
The White Tops (Nashua, NH) **18604**
White Wing Messenger (Cleveland, TN) **29123**
Whitecourt Star (Whitecourt, AB, Can.) **34875**
Whitefish Bay Herald (New Berlin, WI) **34190**
Whitefish Pilot (Whitefish, MT) **17919**
Whitegate Features Syndicate (Providence, RI) **38124**
Whitehall Cable TV (Whitehall, MT) **17920**
Whitehall News (Whitehall, OH) **25652**
The Whitehall Times **34454***
Whitehall Times (Granville, NY) **20683**
Whitehall Times (Whitehall, WI) **34454**
The Whitehorse Star (Whitehorse, YT, Can.) **37605**
Whitesboro News-Record (Whitesboro, TX) **31291**
Whiteside News Sentinel (Morrison, IL) **9227**
Whiteside Shopper (Fulton, IL) **8903**
Whitestone Pennysaver (Whitestone, ON, Can.)
  36873
The Whitestone Times (Whitestone, NY) **23581**
Whitetail Business (Iola, WI) **33855**
Whitewater Register (Whitewater, WI) **34458**
Whitewater Valley Market Guide (Connersville, IN)
  9902
Whitewood Centennial **28881***
Whitewood Herald (Whitewood, SK, Can.) **37594**
The Whitewright Sun (Whitewright, TX) **31292**
The Whitley Republican **12445***
The Whitley Republican News Journal (Williamsburg,
  KY) **12445**
Whitman Academic Journal (Walla Walla, WA) **33189**
Whitman County Gazette (Colfax, WA) **32720**
Whitman/Hanson Mariner (Whitman, MA) **14657**
Whitman Mariner **14658***
Whitman Quarterly Review; Walt (Iowa City, IA)
  10990
Whitman Times (Whitman, MA) **14658**
Whitmark Magazine (Dallas, TX) *Ceased*
The Whitmire Courier **28785***
The Whitmire News (Whitmire, SC) **28785**
The Whitney Messenger (Whitney, TX) *Unable to
  locate*
Whitney Point Reporter, and Oxford Review Times;
  Chenango American, (Greene, NY) **20697**
Whittier Daily News (Whittier, CA) **4080**

Whittier Highlander (City of Industry, CA) *Ceased*
Whittier Independent (West Whittier, CA) **4070**
Whitworthian (Spokane, WA) **33103**
WHIY-AM - 1190 (Moulton, AL) **397**
WHIZ-AM - 1240 (Zanesville, OH) **25720**
WHIZ-FM - 102.5 (Zanesville, OH) **25721**
WHIZ-TV - Channel 18 (Zanesville, OH) **25722**
WHJB-AM **27343***
WHJB-AM - 1600 (Bedford, PA) **26693**
WHJC-AM - 1360 (Matewan, WV) **33384**
WHJE-FM - 91.3 (Carmel, IN) **9882**
WHJJ-AM - 920 (Providence, RI) **28434**
WHJT-FM - 96.3 (Clinton, MS) **16597**
WHJY-FM - 94.1 (Providence, RI) **28435**
WHK-AM (Cleveland, OH) *Unable to locate*
WHKC-FM **9943***
WHKO-FM - 99.1 (Dayton, OH) **25142**
WHKP-AM - 1450 (Hendersonville, NC) **23985**
WHKQ-FM **34277***
WHKQ-FM **34277***
WHKS-FM **27026***
WHKW-FM (Louisville, KY) *Unable to locate*
WHKY-AM - 1290 (Hickory, NC) **23991**
WHKY-TV - Channel 14 (Hickory, NC) **23992**
WHKZ-FM **28579***
WHLB-AM - 1400 (Hibbing, MN) **15956**
WHLD-AM - 1270 (Buffalo, NY) **20401**
WHLF-AM (South Boston, VA) *Ceased*
WHLF-FM - 95.3 (South Boston, VA) **32531**
WHLG-FM **6855***
WHLI-AM - 1100 (Farmingdale, NY) **20598**
WHLM-FM - 106.5 (Selinsgrove, PA) **27976**
WHLN-AM - 1410 (Harlan, KY) **12107**
WHLO-AM (Independence, OH) *Ceased*
WHLP-AM **29085***
WHLP-FM **29086***
WHLS-AM - 1450 (Port Huron, MI) **15455**
WHLT-TV (Hattiesburg, MS) *Unable to locate*
WHLV-AM (Ellisville, MS) *Unable to locate*
WHLX-AM - 1590 (Port Huron, MI) **15456**
WHLX-FM (Wheeling, WV) *Unable to locate*
WHLY-FM - 1620 (South Bend, IN) **10462**
WHLZ-FM (Manning, SC) *Ceased*
WHMA-AM - 1390 (Anniston, AL) **21**
WHMA-FM - 100.5 (Anniston, AL) **22**
WHMB-TV - Channel 40 (Noblesville, IN) **10359**
WHMC-FM **24058***
WHMC-FM (Columbia, SC) *Unable to locate*
WHMC-TV - Channel 23 (Conway, SC) **28593**
WHMD-FM - 107.1 (Hammond, LA) **12596**
WHME-FM - 103:1 (South Bend, IN) **10463**
WHMH-FM - 101.7 (Sauk Rapids, MN) **16440**
WHMI-AM (Howell, MI) *Ceased*
WHMI-FM - 93.5 (Howell, MI) **15199**
WHMM-TV **5885***
WHMP-AM - 1400 (Northampton, MA) **14432**
WHMP-FM - 99.3 (Northampton, MA) **14433**
WHMQ-FM **25433***
WHMS-FM - 97.5 (Champaign, IL) **8228**
WHMT-AM - 1190 (Humboldt, TN) **29225**
WHN-AM **20103***
WHNB-TV **5205***
WHNC-AM - 890 (Oxford, NC) **24113**
WHND-AM (Oak Park, MI) *Unable to locate*
WHNE-AM **7216***
WHNN-FM - 96.1 (Saginaw, MI) **15497**
WHNR-AM - 1360 (Winter Haven, FL) **6875**
WHNS-TV - Channel 21 (Greenville, SC) **28633**
WHNT-TV - Channel 19 (Huntsville, AL) **283**
WHNY-AM (McComb, MS) *Unable to locate*
WHNZ-AM - 1250 (Tampa, FL) **6793**
WHO-AM - 1040 (Des Moines, IA) **10837**
Who Cares (Washington, DC) *Unable to locate*
WHO-TV - Channel 13 (Des Moines, IA) **10838**
Who Writes What in Life and Health Insurance
  (Erlanger, KY) **12055**
WHOB-FM - 106.3 (Nashua, NH) **18607**
WHOC-AM - 1490 (Philadelphia, MS) **16817**
WHOD-AM - 1230 (Jackson, AL) **292**
WHOD-FM - 94.5 (Jackson, AL) **293**
WHOF-AM - 640 (Ocala, FL) **6474**
WHOI-TV - Channel 19 (Creve Coeur, IL) **8694**
WHOK-FM - 95.5 (Lancaster, OH) **25292**
WHOL-AM - 1600 (Allentown, PA) **26632**
Whole Earth (San Rafael, CA) **3603**
Whole Earth Review **3603***
Whole Foods (South Plainfield, NJ) **19591**
Whole Life (New York, NY) *Unable to locate*
Whole Notes (Las Cruces, NM) **19878**
The Whole Shebang! (Coos Bay, OR) **26273**
Wholesale Drugs Magazine **4532***
The Wholesaler (Chicago, IL) *Unable to locate*
WHOM-FM (Portland, ME) *Unable to locate*
WHON-AM - 930 (Richmond, IN) **10424**
WHOO-AM - 990 (Orlando, FL) **6518**
Whoot Newspaper (Pleasantville, NJ) **19445**
WHOP-AM - 1230 (Hopkinsville, KY) **12133**
WHOP-FM - 98.7 (Hopkinsville, KY) **12134**
WHOT-AM **25711***

WHOT-FM - 101.1 (Youngstown, OH) **25706**
WHOU-FM - 100.1 (Houlton, ME) **12972**
WHOU-FM (Presque Isle, ME) *Unable to locate*
WHOV **32133***
WHOV-FM - 88.1 (Hampton, VA) **32133**
WHOW-AM - 1520 (Clinton, IL) **8684**
WHOW-FM - 95.9 (Clinton, IL) **8685**
WHOY-AM - 1210 (Salinas, PR) **28288**
WHOZ-AM **338***
WHP-AM - 580 (Harrisburg, PA) **27016**
WHP-FM **27024***
WHP-TV - Channel 21 (Harrisburg, PA) **27017**
WHPA-AM **27054***
WHPA-FM (Altoona, PA) *Unable to locate*
WHPB-AM (Belton, SC) *Unable to locate*
WHPC-FM - 90.3 (Garden City, NY) **20645**
WHPE-AM **24002***
WHPE-FM - 95.5 (High Point, NC) **24003**
WHPK-FM - 88.5 (Chicago, IL) **8628**
WHPK-FM - 88.5 (Chicago, IL) **8627**
WHPO-FM - 100.9 (Hoopeston, IL) **9005**
WHPR-FM - 88.1 (Highland Park, MI) **15162**
WHPT-FM - 102.5 (St. Petersburg, FL) **6638**
WHPY-FM (Clayton, NC) *Unable to locate*
WHQR-FM - 91.3 (Wilmington, NC) **24301**
WHQT-FM (Miami, FL) *Ceased*
WHRB-FM - 95.3 (Cambridge, MA) **14114**
WHRD-AM (Huntington, WV) *Ceased*
WHRF-AM (Baltimore, MD) *Unable to locate*
WHRK-FM - 97.1 (Memphis, TN) **29397**
WHRL-FM - 103.1 (Albany, NY) **20012**
WHRM-TV - Channel 20 (Wausau, WI) **34433**
WHRO-FM - 90.3 (Norfolk, VA) **32299**
WHRO-TV - Channel 15 (Norfolk, VA) **32300**
WHRQ-AM **32212***
WHRS-AM (Winchester, KY) *Unable to locate*
WHRS-FM **5954***
WHRS-FM - 91.7 (Nashville, TN) **29512**
WHRS-TV **5955***
WHRV-AM **14774***
WHRV-FM - 89.5 (Norfolk, VA) **32301**
WHRW-FM - 90.5 (Binghamton, NY) **20223**
WHRZ-FM - 97.7 (Madisonville, KY) **12274**
WHSB-FM - 107.7 (Alpena, MI) **14741**
WHSC-AM - 1450 (Florence, SC) **28606**
WHSD-FM - 88.5 (Hinsdale, IL) **8998**
WHSE-TV (Newark, NJ) *Unable to locate*
WHSH **14247***
WHSI-TV **20450***
WHSL-FM - 100.3 (Greensboro, NC) **23947**
WHSM-AM - 910 (Hayward, WI) **33787**
WHSM-FM - 101.1 (Hayward, WI) **33788**
WHSN-FM - 89.3 (Bangor, ME) **12909**
WHSP-TV **19369***
WHSR-AM - 530 (Baltimore, MD) **13273**
WHSR-FM - 91.9 (Winchester, MA) **14668**
WHSS-FM - 89.5 (Hamilton, OH) **25236**
WHST-FM (Gaylord, MI) *Unable to locate*
WHSV-TV - Channel 3 (Harrisonburg, VA) **32145**
WHSW-TV - Channel 24 (Baltimore, MD) **13274**
WHSY-AM (Hattiesburg, MS) *Unable to locate*
WHSY-FM (Hattiesburg, MS) *Unable to locate*
WHTB-AM - 1400 (Somerset, MA) **14528**
WHTB-FM **466***
WHTC-AM - 1450 (Holland, MI) **15176**
WHTE-FM **13287***
WHTF-FM **27216***
WHTG-AM - 1410 (Neptune, NJ) **19321**
WHTG-FM - 106.3 (Neptune, NJ) **19322**
WHTH-AM - 790 (Newark, OH) **25429**
WHTI-FM - 96.7 (Daleville, IN) **9919**
WHTL-FM - 102.3 (Whitehall, WI) **34455**
WHTM-TV - Channel 27 (Harrisburg, PA) **27018**
WHTN-TV - Channel 39 (Old Hickory, TN) **29552**
WHTO **28185***
WHTO-FM - 93.3 (Williamsport, PA) **28185**
WHTQ-FM - 96.5 (Orlando, FL) **6519**
WHTR-FM (Queensbury, NY) *Ceased*
WHTS-FM - 98.9 (Davenport, IA) **10747**
WHTT-AM **20407***
WHTT-FM **10752***
WHTT-FM **14010***
WHTT-FM - 104.1 (Buffalo, NY) **20402**
WHTZ-FM (New York, NY) *Unable to locate*
WHUB **14247***
WHUB-AM (Cookeville, TN) *Unable to locate*
WHUC-AM - 1230 (Hudson, NY) **20770**
WHUC-FM **20771***
WHUD-FM - 100.7 (Beacon, NY) **20140**
WHUG-FM - 101.7 (Jamestown, NY) **20843**
WHUH-FM **15187***
WHUK-FM **31***
WHUN-AM - 1150 (Mount Union, PA) **27302**
WHUR-FM - 96.3 (Washington, DC) **5884**
WHUS-FM - 91.7 (Storrs, CT) **5170**
WHUT-AM - 1470 (Indianapolis, IN) **10198**
WHUT-TV - Channel 32 (Washington, DC) **5885**
WHVF-AM **34440***
WHVH-AM **23982***

WHVO-AM - 1480 (Hopkinsville, KY) **12135**
WHVR-AM - 1280 (Hanover, PA) **26979**
WHVT-FM **29527***
WHVT-FM (Clyde, OH) *Unable to locate*
WHVW-AM (Hyde Park, NY) *Unable to locate*
WHVW-FM, WJJB-FM **23155***
WHWB-AM (Rutland, VT) *Unable to locate*
WHWB-FM **31587***
WHWC-FM - 88.3 (Madison, WI) **33995**
WHWE-FM - 89.7 (Howe, IN) **10066**
WHWH-AM - 1350 (Princeton, NJ) **19480**
WHWK-FM - 98.1 (Binghamton, NY) **20224**
WHWL-FM - 95.7 (Marquette, MI) **15343**
WHXT-FM **26854***
WHXT-AM - 102.1 (Citronelle, AL) **153**
WHYB-FM - 103.7 (Marinette, WI) **34020**
WHYC-FM (Swanquarter, NC) *Unable to locate*
WHYI-FM (Fort Lauderdale, FL) *Unable to locate*
WHYL-AM (Carlisle, PA) *Unable to locate*
WHYL-FM (Carlisle, PA) *Unable to locate*
WHYM-AM **24248***
WHYN-FM - 93.1 (Tyler, TX) **31223**
WHYN-TV **14558***
WHYP-FM **27341***
WHYR-FM **13031***
WHYS-AM **6102***
WHYT-AM **15456***
WHYT-FM **14961***
WHYY-FM - 90.9 (Philadelphia, PA) **27733**
WHYY-TV - Channel 12 (Philadelphia, PA) **27734**
WHYZ-AM (Greenville, SC) *Unable to locate*
WHZI-AM **209***
WHZZ-FM - 101.7 (Lansing, MI) **15298**
WIAA-FM - 88.7 (Interlochen, MI) **15205**
WIAC-AM (San Juan, PR) *Unable to locate*
WIAC-FM (San Juan, PR) *Unable to locate*
WIAI-FM - 99.1 (Danville, IL) **8707**
WIAL-FM - 94.1 (Altoona, WI) **33526**
WIAM-AM - 900 (Williamston, NC) **24292**
WIAM-FM - 98.9 (Williamston, NC) **24293**
WIAN-AM - 1240 (Ishpeming, MI) **15218**
WIAN-FM **10195***
The Wiarton Echo (Wiarton, ON, Can.) **36874**
WIAV-FM **32305***
WIAZ-FM (San Juan, PR) *Unable to locate*
WIBA-AM - 1310 (Madison, WI) **33996**
WIBA-FM - 101.5 (Madison, WI) **33997**
The Wibaux Pioneer-Gazette (Wibaux, MT) **17921**
WIBB-AM (Macon, GA) *Unable to locate*
WIBC-AM (Indianapolis, IN) *Unable to locate*
WIBF-FM **26804***
WIBF-TV **27745***
WIBG-AM **27138***
WIBG-AM - 1020 (Ocean City, NJ) **19389**
WIBG-FM **27748***
WIBH-AM - 1440 (Metropolis, IL) **9179**
WIBI-FM - 91.1 (Carlinville, IL) **8128**
WIBL-FM - 101.7 (Louisville, KY) **12254**
WIBM-AM - 1450 (Jackson, MI) **15225**
WIBM-FM **15180***
WIBO-FM **25626***
WIBQ-FM **23580***
WIBR-AM (Baton Rouge, LA) *Unable to locate*
WIBU-AM - 900 (Poynette, WI) **34265**
WIBV-AM **17560***
WIBW-AM - 580 (Topeka, KS) **11846**
WIBW-FM - 97.3 (Topeka, KS) **11847**
WIBX-AM - 950 (Whitesboro, NY) **23579**
WIBZ-FM - 95.5 (Sumter, SC) **28771**
Wicazo Sa Review (Rapid City, MN) **16290**
Wicazo Sa Review/Red Pencil Review **16290***
WICB-AM - 91.7 (Ithaca, NY) **20819**
WICB.FM - 105.9 (Ithaca, NY) **20820**
WICC-AM - 600 (Bridgeport, CT) **4719**
WICD-TV - Channel 15 (Champaign, IL) **8229**
WICE-AM (Cumberland, RI) *Unable to locate*
Wichita Business Journal (Wichita, KS) **11890**
Wichita Eagle (Wichita, KS) **11891**
Wichita Eagle-Beacon **11891***
Wichita Falls Record News **31293***
Wichita Falls Times **31293***
Wichita Journal (Derby, KS) **11410**
Wichita Pennypower News (Wichita, KS) **11892**
Wichita WOMEN (Wichita, KS) *Unable to locate*
The Wichitan (Wichita Falls, TX) **31294**
WICK-AM - 1400 (Scranton, PA) **27968**
Wicked Mystic (New York, NY) *Unable to locate*
The Wickenburg Sun (Wickenburg, AZ) **1005**
Wicker Park/West Town EXTRA (Chicago, IL) **8606**
WICN-FM - 90.5 (Worcester, MA) **14698**
WICO-AM - 1320 (Salisbury, MD) **13715**
WICO-FM - 97.5 (Salisbury, MD) **13716**
WICR-FM - 88.7 (Indianapolis, IN) **10199**
WICS-TV - Channel 20 (Springfield, IL) **9649**
WICT-FM - 95.1 (Brookfield, OH) **24709**
WICU-TV - Channel 12 (Erie, PA) **26905**
WICY-AM - 1490 (Malone, NY) **20981**
WICZ-TV - Channel 40 (Vestal, NY) **23491**
WIDE-AM (Biddeford, ME) *Unable to locate*

Wide Angle (Baltimore, MD) **13262**
Widescreen Review (Temecula, CA) **3843**
WIDG-AM - 940 (Cheboygan, MI) **14875**
WIDI-FM (Quebradillas, PR) *Unable to locate*
WIDL-FM - 92.1 (Caro, MI) **14859**
WIDR-FM - 89.1 (Kalamazoo, MI) **15249**
WIDU-AM - 1600 (Fayetteville, NC) **23888**
Wieck Photo DataBase, Inc. (Addison, TX) **38125**
WIEL-AM - 1400 (Elizabethtown, KY) **12047**
WIEZ-AM **7647***
WIEZ-AM - 670 (Lewistown, PA) **27196**
WIFC-FM - 95.5 (Wausau, WI) **34434**
WIFE-FM - 100.3 (Connersville, IN) **9903**
WIFF-AM **9790***
WIFI-FM **26682***
WIFM-AM - 100.9 (Elkin, NC) **23869**
WIFM-FM - 100.9 (Elkin, NC) **23870**
WIFN-AM **15456***
WIFN-FM (Traverse City, MI) *Unable to locate*
WIFO-FM - 105.5 (Jesup, GA) **7349**
WIFR-TV - Channel 23 (Rockford, IL) **9537**
WIFX-FM - 94.3 (Whitesburg, KY) **12440**
WIGH-FM (Jackson, TN) *Unable to locate*
WIGL-AM **7108***
WIGL-FM **28585***
WIGL-FM - 102.9 (Orangeburg, SC) **28734**
WIGM-AM - 1490 (Medford, WI) **34035**
WIGM-FM **34036***
WIGO-AM (Atlanta, GA) *Unable to locate*
Wigwag (New York, NY) *Ceased*
WIGY-FM **13067***
WIHN-FM - 96.7 (Normal, IL) **9309**
WIHR-FM - 94.3 (Chambersburg, PA) **26771**
WIHT-TV **14775***
WIIC-TV **27873***
WIID-AM **15065***
WIII-FM (Cortland, NY) *Unable to locate*
WIII-TV **24846***
WIIL-FM - 95.1 (Kenosha, WI) **33877**
WIIL-TV **10494***
WIIN-AM **19382***
WIIN-AM (Jackson, MS) *Unable to locate*
WIIQ-TV - Channel 41 (Demopolis, AL) **179**
WIIS-FM - 107.1 (Key West, FL) **6255**
WIIT - 88.9 (Chicago, IL) **8629**
WIIT-FM **8629***
WIJK-AM (Evergreen, AL) *Unable to locate*
WIJY-FM - 95.9 (Franklin, IN) **10010**
WIKB-AM - 1230 (Iron River, MI) **15212**
WIKC-AM - 1490 (Bogalusa, LA) **12535**
WIKE-AM (Newport, VT) *Unable to locate*
WIKI-AM **31970***
WIKI-FM - 95.3 (North Vernon, IN) **10364**
WIKK-FM - 103.5 (Newton, IL) **9285**
WIKQ-FM - 103.1 (Greeneville, TN) **29214**
WIKS-FM - 101.9 (New Bern, NC) **24099**
WIKX-FM (Birmingham, AL) *Unable to locate*
WIKX-FM - 92.9 (Punta Gorda, FL) **6610**
WIKY-FM - 104.1 (Evansville, IN) **9944**
WIKZ-FM - 95.1 (Chambersburg, PA) **26772**
WIL-AM - 1430 (Creve Coeur, MO) **17028**
WIL-FM (St. Louis, MO) *Unable to locate*
WILA-AM - 1580 (Danville, VA) **31994**
The Wilber Republican (Wilber, NE) **18316**
The Wilbur Register (Wilbur, WA) **33207**
WILC-AM-VIVA900 - 900 (Laurel, MD) **13614**
Wilcox Progressive Era (Camden, AL) **143**
WILD-AM - 1090 (Roxbury, MA) **14510**
Wild Dog (Venice, FL) **6832**
Wild Duck Review (Nevada City, CA) **2616**
Wild Earth (Canton, NY) *Unable to locate*
Wild Ohio Magazine (Columbus, OH) **25069**
Wild Rivers Advertiser - North (Frederic, WI) **33730**
Wild Rivers Advertiser - South (Frederic, WI) **33731**
Wild West (Leesburg, VA) *Unable to locate*
Wild West News (Solomon, AZ) *Unable to locate*
The Wild Wood Reader (Miami, FL) *Unable to locate*
WildBird Magazine (Mission Viejo, CA) **2558**
Wildcat (Pineville, LA) **12794**
Wildcat; Arizona Daily (Tucson, AZ) **930**
Wildcat; The Big Lake (Big Lake, TX) **29919**
Wilde (San Francisco, CA) *Unable to locate*
Wilderness (Washington, DC) *Ceased*
Wilderness Trails (Petaluma, CA) *Unable to locate*
Wildfire (Fairfield) (Fairfield, WA) *Unable to locate*
Wildflower (Toronto, ON, Can.) *Unable to locate*
Wildfowl (Los Angeles, CA) **2436**
Wildfowl Carving and Collecting (Harrisburg, PA) *Unable to locate*
Wildlife; Arkansas (Little Rock, AR) **1223**
Wildlife Art (Eagan, MN) **15864**
Wildlife Art News **15864***
Wildlife Conservation (Bronx, NY) **20290**
Wildlife Crusader (Winnipeg, MB, Can.) *Unable to locate*
Wildlife Harvest (Goose Lake, IA) **10926**
Wildlife; Human Dimensions of (Fort Collins, CO) **4432**
Wildlife; Illinois (Edwardsville, IL) **8813**

Wildlife Journal **1538***
Wildlife Law and Policy; Journal of International (New York, NY) **22105**
Wildlife; Maine Fish and (Augusta, ME) **12893**
Wildlife Medicine; Journal of Zoo and (Media, PA) **27242**
Wildlife; Missouri (Jefferson City, MO) **17130**
Wildlife; National (Reston, VA) **32407**
Wildlife in North Carolina (Raleigh, NC) **24159**
Wildlife Rehabilitation; Journal of (Berkeley, CA) **1538**
Wildlife Review (Pittsburgh, PA) *Ceased*
Wildlife; South Carolina (Columbia, SC) **28568**
Wildlife; Texas Parks & (Austin, TX) **29838**
Wildlife; Virginia (Richmond, VA) **32468**
Wildlife; Wyoming (Cheyenne, WY) **34501**
WILE-AM - 1270 (Cambridge, OH) **24728**
WILE-FM **24727***
Wiley World *Ceased*
WILI-AM - 1400 (Willimantic, CT) **5222**
WILI-FM - 98.3 (Willimantic, CT) **5223**
WILK-AM - 980 (Pittston, PA) **27890**
Wilk-Amite Record (Meadville, MS) **16767**
The Wilkie Press (Wilkie, SK, Can.) **37595**
Wilkinson County News (Gordon, GA) **7307**
WILL-AM - 580 (Urbana, IL) **9723**
WILL-TV - Channel 12 (Urbana, IL) **9724**
Willacy County News; Raymondville Chronicle and (Raymondville, TX) **30970**
Willamette Week (Portland, OR) **26515**
The Willapa Harbor Herald (Raymond, WA) **32922**
The Willapa Harbor Marketplace (Raymond, WA) *Ceased*
Willard Times Junction (Willard, OH) **25654**
William A. Alan (Pittsburgh, PA) **38126**
William Carlos Williams Review (Austin, TX) **29855**
William & Mary Bill of Rights Journal (Williamsburg, VA) **32621**
William and Mary Law Review (Williamsburg, VA) **32622**
William and Mary Quarterly (Williamsburg, VA) **32623**
William and Mary Review (Williamsburg, VA) **32624**
Williams Alumni Review (Williamstown, MA) **14660**
Williams-Grand Canyon News (Williams, AZ) **1010**
Williams Northern Light **16516***
The Williams Record (Williamstown, MA) **14661**
The Williams Report **25754***
Williams-Sonoma TASTE (San Francisco, CA) *Ceased*
Williams Syndications Inc. (Chicago, IL) **38127**
Williamsfield Times (Williamsfield, IL) **9763**
Williamson County Cablevision Co., Inc. (Georgetown, TX) **30394**
Williamson County Sun (Georgetown, TX) **30393**
The Williamson Leader (Franklin, TN) *Ceased*
Williamson Sun and Sentinel (Williamson, WV) **33513**
Williamsport Sun-Gazette (Williamsport, PA) **28182**
Williamston Enterprise (East Lansing, MI) *Unable to locate*
Williamstown Cable; City of (Williamstown, KY) **12449**
Williamsville Sun (Riverton, IL) **9500**
Williston Daily Herald (Williston, ND) **24560**
Williston Sun-Suwannee Valley News (Williston, FL) **6863**
Williston Times (Williston Park, NY) **23585**
The Willits News (Willits, CA) **4083**
Willow Grove Guide (Trenton, NJ) **19671**
Willow Park Cable T.V. (Aledo, TX) **29678**
Willow Springs/Burr Ridge/Pleasantdale Suburban Life; Countryside/Indian Head Park/ (Oak Brook, IL) **9346**
Willow Springs News (Mountain View, MO) *Unable to locate*
Willowbrook Progress (Downers Grove, IL) **8798**
The Willows Journal (Willows, CA) **4088**
Wills Point Chronicle (Wills Point, TX) **31301**
WILM-AM - 1450 (Wilmington, DE) **5299**
The Wilmer Retina Update (Baltimore, MD) *Ceased*
Wilmette Life (Glenview, IL) **8942**
Wilmette News/Voice (Highland Park, IL) *Unable to locate*
The Wilmington Advocate (Wilmington, IL) *Unable to locate*
Wilmington Beacon (Wilmington, CA) **4090**
(Wilmington Edition); The AD-PAK (Wilmington, NC) **24294**
The Wilmington Journal (Wilmington, NC) **24297**
Wilmington Morning Star (Wilmington, NC) **24298**
Wilmington News-Journal (Wilmington, OH) **25667**
Wilmington-Tewksbury Town Crier (Tewksbury, MA) **14588**
The Wilmot Enterprise (Wilmot, SD) **29031**
WILN-FM - 105.9 (Panama City, FL) **6560**
WILO-AM - 1570 (Frankfort, IN) **10002**
WILP-AM **27892***
WILQ-FM (Williamsport, PA) *Unable to locate*
WILS-AM - 1320 (Lansing, MI) **15299**
WILS-FM **15298***
Wilshire Independent (Los Angeles, CA) **2437**
Wilson Bulletin (Lawrence, KS) **11572**

Wilson County Citizen (Fredonia, KS) **11447**
Wilson County News (Floresville, TX) **30319**
Wilson Daily Times (Wilson, NC) **24312**
Wilson Library Bulletin (Bronx, NY) *Ceased*
The Wilson Post-Democrat (Wilson, OK) **26197**
The Wilson Quarterly (Washington, DC) **5861**
Wilson World (Wilson, KS) **11908**
The Wilson World (Lebanon, TN) **29321**
Wilsonville Spokesman (Wilsonville, OR) **26617**
WILT-AM **27892***
WILT-AM (Mount Pocono, PA) *Unable to locate*
Wilton Bulletin (Wilton, CT) **5231**
Wilton-Durant Advocate News (Durant, IA) **10858**
Wilton Lifestyles (Norwalk, CT) **5081**
The Wilton Villager (Wilton, CT) **5232**
WILX-TV (Lansing, MI) *Unable to locate*
WILZ-FM - 104.5 (Saginaw, MI) **15498**
WIMA-AM - 1150 (Lima, OH) **25301**
The Wimberley View (Wimberley, TX) **31304**
WIMC-FM - 103.9 (Crawfordsville, IN) **9912**
WIMG-AM (Washington, PA) *Unable to locate*
WIMI-FM - 99.7 (Ironwood, MI) **15215**
WIMJ-FM **24845***
WIMM-FM **15060***
WIMO-AM (Winder, GA) *Unable to locate*
WIMS-AM - 1420 (Hammond, IN) **10056**
WIMX-AM (Camp Hill, PA) *Unable to locate*
WIMX-FM (Camp Hill, PA) *Unable to locate*
WIMZ-AM - 1240 (Knoxville, TN) **29289**
WIMZ-FM - 103.5 (Knoxville, TN) **29290**
Win Magazine **2071***
WIN News (Lexington, MA) **14274**
Win You, Ltd. **8990***
WINA-AM - 1070 (Charlottesville, VA) **31952**
WINC-AM - 1400 (Winchester, VA) **32631**
WINC-FM - 92.5 (Winchester, VA) **32632**
The Winchendon Courier (Winchendon, MA) **14664**
The Winchester Press (Winchester, ON, Can.) **36885**
Winchester Star (Lexington, MA) **14275**
The Winchester Star (Winchester, VA) **32630**
The Winchester Sun (Winchester, KY) **12454**
WIND-AM - 560 (Chicago, IL) **8630**
Wind Surf (Compton, CA) *Unable to locate*
WinDBreak Cable (Gering, NE) **18020**
Windcrest Area Recorder-Times (San Antonio, TX) *Ceased*
The Winder News **7652***
Windham Independent (Windham, NH) **18653**
The Windham Journal (Windham, NY) **23587**
Windham Phoenix *Ceased*
The Windhound (Wheat Ridge, CO) *Ceased*
The Windmill Herald (Langley, BC, Can.) **35006**
Windom Cable Communications (Windom, MN) **16524**
Window **18193***
Window Cleaner Magazine; American (Richmond, CA) **2920**
Window Coverings; Draperies and (West Palm Beach, FL) **6846**
Window Fashions (St. Paul, MN) **16418**
Window Fashions (St. Paul, MN) **16417**
Window Film (Garrisonville, VA) **32107**
Window Sources (New York, NY) **22918**
Windows Developer's Journal (San Mateo, CA) **3591**
Windows/DOS Developer's Journal **3591***
Windows Magazine (Manhasset, NY) **21018**
Windows NT Magazine (Calabasas, CA) *Unable to locate*
Windows and OS/2 **21018***
WindowsMagazine **21018***
Windplayer (Malibu, CA) **2497**
Windshield and Glass Repair **32102***
Windsor Beacon (Windsor, CO) **4687**
Windsor Cable TV (Windsor, NS, Can.) **35621**
The Windsor Chronicle (Windsor, VT) *Unable to locate*
Windsor Locks Journal (Windsor, CT) **5234**
Windsor Parent Magazine (Windsor, ON, Can.) **36891**
Windsor Pennysaver (London, ON, Can.) *Unable to locate*
Windsor Reminder (Vernon, CT) *Unable to locate*
Windsor Review (Windsor, ON, Can.) **36892**
The Windsor Standard (Conklin, NY) **20496**
The Windsor Star (Windsor, ON, Can.) **36893**
Windsor This Month (Windsor, ON, Can.) *Ceased*
Windspeaker (Edmonton, AB, Can.) **34738**
Windsport Magazine (Toronto, ON, Can.) **36792**
Windsurfing (Winter Park, FL) **6890**
Windward Sun-Press (Kaneohe, HI) **7776**
Windy City Sports Magazine (Chicago, IL) **8607**
Windy City Times (Chicago, IL) **8608**
WINE-AM - 940 (Brookfield, CT) **4730**
Wine; Best Buys In (Fort Worth, TX) **37833**
Wine Business Monthly (Sonoma, CA) *Unable to locate*
Wine Country International Magazine (Benicia, CA) *Ceased*
Wine East (Lancaster, PA) **27146**
Wine Enthusiast Magazine (Elmsford, NY) **20587**
Wine; Food & (New York, NY) **21713**

Wine and Food Magazine; Enoteca (Concord, ON, Can.) **35751**
Wine; The Friends of (Louisville, OH) **25318**
Wine Gazette; New England (Bernardsville, NJ) **18678**
Wine News; The (Coral Gables, FL) **6015**
The Wine News (Coral Gables, FL) **6015**
Wine Society Journal; American (Rochester, NY) **23209**
Wine Spectator (New York, NY) **22919**
Wine & Spirits Buying Guide **22920***
Wine & Spirits Magazine (New York, NY) **22920**
Wine Tidings (Montreal, QC, Can.) **37238**
The Wine Trader (Carson City, NV) *Unable to locate*
Wine; Travel, Food & (New York, NY) **22857**
Wine World (Canoga Park, CA) *Unable to locate*
Wine X Magazine (Santa Rosa, CA) **3736**
Wines; The Quarterly Review of (Winchester, MA) **14666**
Wines & Vines (San Rafael, CA) **3604**
WINF-AM (Winnsboro, SC) *Ceased*
WINF-AM - 970 (Staunton, VA) **32557**
Winfield Beacon & Wayland News (Winfield, IA) **11328**
Winfield Daily Courier (Winfield, KS) **11910**
Winfield Press (St. Charles, IL) **9575**
WING-AM - 1410 (Dayton, OH) **25143**
WING-FM - 102.9 (Dayton, OH) **25144**
Wing & Shot (Los Angeles, CA) **2438**
The Winged Foot (New York, NY) **22921**
The Wingham Advance-Times (Wingham, ON, Can.) **36902**
Wings (Portland, OR) **26516**
Wings of Alona *Ceased*
Wings Community Flyer (Bainbridge Island, WA) *Ceased*
Wings; Desert (Edwards AFB, CA) **1841**
Wings of Gold (Alexandria, VA) **31753**
Wings Magazine (Mississauga, ON, Can.) **36092**
Wings Newsmagazine **36092***
WINGS: Women's International News Gathering Service (Austin, TX) **38128**
Wingspan (Cheyenne, WY) **34497**
Wingspread (Universal City, TX) *Unable to locate*
WINH-AM **26843***
WINI-AM - 1420 (Murphysboro, IL) **9259**
WINK-AM - 1200 (Fort Myers, FL) **6106**
WINK-FM - 96.9 (Fort Myers, FL) **6107**
WINK-TV - Channel 11 (Fort Myers, FL) **6108**
The Winkler County News (Kermit, TX) **30638**
Winkler Pembina Times **35307***
The Winkler Times (Winkler, MB, Can.) **35307**
WINM-TV - Channel 63 (Butler, IN) **9878**
Winn Parish Enterprise (Winnfield, LA) **12880**
Winnebago Co-op Cablevision (Lake Mills, IA) **11025**
Winnebago News (Durand, IL) *Ceased*
The Winneconne News (Winneconne, WI) *Unable to locate*
The Winner **13571***
Winner (Hagerstown, MD) **13571**
Winner Advocate (Winner, SD) **29032**
Winners News Network (Boca Raton, FL) **37679**
Winnetka News/Voice (Highland Park, IL) *Unable to locate*
Winnetka Talk (Winnetka, IL) **9768**
Winnett Times; Roundup Record-Tribune and (Roundup, MT) **17902**
Winning Bicycling Illustrated (Lehigh Valley, PA) *Unable to locate*
The Winning Edge (Rockville, MD) **13700**
Winning Poker (Van Nuys, CA) *Ceased*
The Winnipeg Free Press (Winnipeg, MB, Can.) **35363**
Winnipeg & Manitoba; Moving to (Unionville, ON, Can.) **36837**
The Winnipeg Sun (Winnipeg, MB, Can.) **35364**
The Winnsboro News (Winnsboro, TX) **31305**
Winona Cablevision **16881***
Winona Daily News (Winona, MN) **16527**
Winona Post (Winona, MN) **16528**
Winona Post and Shopper **16528***
The Winona Times (Winona, MS) **16880**
Winonan (Winona, MN) **16529**
WINQ-FM - 97.7 (Winchendon, MA) **14665**
WINR-AM - 680 (Endwell, NY) **20588**
WINR-TV **23491***
WINS-AM - 1010 (New York, NY) **22971**
The Winslow Mail (Winslow, AZ) **1014**
Winsted-Lester Prairie Herald Journal (Winsted, MN) **16537**
Winsted Lester Prairie Journal (Winsted, MN) *Unable to locate*
Winston County Journal (Louisville, MS) **16750**
Winston Radio **27100***
Winston-Salem Chronicle (Winston-Salem, NC) **24323**
Winston-Salem Journal (Winston-Salem, NC) **24324**
Winston-Salem Magazine (Winston-Salem, NC) *Unable to locate*
WINT-FM **6295***

WINT-TV (Crossville, TN) *Unable to locate*
Winter Haven News Chief (Winter Haven, FL) **6873**
Winter Haven Shopper (Winter Haven, FL) **6874**
Winter Park/Maitland Observer (Winter Park, FL) **6891**
Winter Park Manifest (Granby, CO) **4476**
Winter Park Outlook (Orlando, FL) *Unable to locate*
Winter Texan (McAllen, TX) **30790**
Winter Visitor Independent (Phoenix, AZ) *Ceased*
Winters Express (Winters, CA) **4094**
Winterthur Portfolio (Winterthur, DE) **5304**
The Winthrop Independent (Revere, MA) *Ceased*
The Winthrop News (Winthrop, IA) **11329**
Winthrop Sun Transcript (Revere, MA) **14503**
Winton Times (Winton, CA) **4098**
WINV-AM (Inverness, FL) *Unable to locate*
WINW-AM - 1520 (Canton, OH) **24736**
WINX-FM - 94.3 (Warrenton, VA) **32603**
WINY-AM - 1350 (Putnam, CT) **5095**
WINZ-AM - 940 (Miramar, FL) **6429**
WIOA-FM (Santurce, PR) *Unable to locate*
WIOB-FM - 97.5 (Mayaguez, PR) **28261**
WIOC-FM - 105.1 (Ponce, PR) **28277**
WIOD-AM - 610 (Miramar, FL) **6430**
WIOG-FM - 102.5 (Saginaw, MI) **15499**
WIOJ-AM - 1010 (Jacksonville, FL) **6223**
WIOK-FM - 107.5 (Falmouth, KY) **12056**
WION-AM - 1430 (Ionia, MI) **15207**
WIOO-AM - 1000 (Carlisle, PA) **26764**
WIOQ-FM - 102.1 (Bala Cynwyd, PA) **26674**
WIOS-AM - 1480 (Tawas City, MI) **15586**
WIOT-FM - 104.7 (Toledo, OH) **25579**
WIOU-AM - 1350 (Kokomo, IN) **10242**
WIOV-AM - 1240 (Ephrata, PA) **26891**
WIOV-FM - 105.1 (Ephrata, PA) **26892**
WIOZ-AM - 550 (Southern Pines, NC) **24238**
WIOZ-FM (Southern Pines, NC) *Unable to locate*
WIP-AM - 610 (Philadelphia, PA) **26775**
WIPB-TV - Channel 49 (Muncie, IN) **10332**
WIPC-AM - 1280 (Lake Wales, FL) **6287**
WIPR-AM (San Juan, PR) *Unable to locate*
WIPR-FM - 91.3 (San Juan, PR) **28300**
WIPS-AM - 1250 (Crown Point, NY) **20516**
WIPS-FM (Ticonderoga, NY) *Ceased*
WIPU-FM **9979***
WIPX-TV - Channel 63 (Indianapolis, IN) **10200**
WIQB-FM - 102.9 (Ann Arbor, MI) **14778**
WIQH-FM - 88.3 (Concord, MA) **14150**
WIQO-FM - 100.9 (Covington, VA) **31983**
WIQQ-FM - 102.3 (Greenville, MS) **16641**
WIQT **20764***
WIRA-AM - 1400 (Port St. Lucie, FL) **6603**
WIRB-TV **6893***
WIRC-AM - 630 (Hickory, NC) **23993**
WIRD-AM - 920 (Lake Placid, NY) **20876**
WIRE-AM **10192***
Wire & Cable Technology International (Stow, OH) **25548**
WIRE-FM - 100.9 (Indianapolis, IN) **10201**
Wire Journal International (Guilford, CT) **4879**
Wire Rope News & Sling Technology (Clark, NJ) **18749**
Wire Technology International **25548***
Wire; Wheaton (Norton, MA) **14438**
Wired (San Francisco, CA) **3463**
The Wiregrass Farmer (Ashburn, GA) **6927**
Wireless Broadcasting Systems of Sacramento, Inc. (Sacramento, CA) **3064**
Wireless Business & Technology (Potomac, MD) **13663**
Wireless Business & Technology (Montvale, NJ) **19282**
Wireless Data News (Potomac, MD) **13664**
Wireless Design and Development (Morris Plains, NJ) **19309**
Wireless Flash News Service (San Diego, CA) **38129**
Wireless Integration (Nashua, NH) **18605**
Wireless & Mobility (New York, NY) **22922**
Wireless Networks (Potomac, MD) **13665**
Wireless Review (Overland Park, KS) **11736**
Wireless Systems Design (Paramus, NJ) **19408**
Wireless Telecom (Ottawa, ON, Can.) **36280**
Wireless Week (Littleton, CO) **4556**
WIRJ-AM - 740 (Humboldt, TN) **29226**
WIRK-FM (West Palm Beach, FL) *Unable to locate*
WIRO-AM (Ironton, OH) *Unable to locate*
WIRQ-FM - 94.3 (Rochester, NY) **23249**
WIRR-FM - 90.9 (Buhl, MN) **15780**
Wirt County Journal (Elizabeth, WV) **33304**
WIRT-TV - Channel 10 (Hibbing, MN) **15957**
WIRV-AM - 1550 (Irvine, KY) **12142**
WIRX-FM - 107.1 (St. Joseph, MI) **15515**
WIRY-AM - 1340 (Plattsburgh, NY) **23106**
WIS-AM **28586***
WIS-TV - Channel 10 (Columbia, SC) **28576**
WISA-AM - 1390 (Isabela, PR) **28252**
WISC-FM - 98.3 (High Point, NC) **24004**
WISC-TV - Channel 3 (Madison, WI) **33998**
Wisconsin Agriculturist (Urbandale, IA) **11277**

Wisconsin AIDS Update (Madison, WI) **33977**
Wisconsin Alumni **33967***
Wisconsin Archeologist (Milwaukee, WI) **34108**
Wisconsin Architect (Madison, WI) **33978**
Wisconsin Beverage Business (Madison, WI) **33979**
Wisconsin Beverage Journal **33979***
Wisconsin Counties (Madison, WI) **33980**
Wisconsin Dells Events (Wisconsin Dells, WI) **34462**
Wisconsin Edition; Dodge Construction News (Illinois, Indiana, (Chicago, IL) **8356**
Wisconsin Energy Cooperative News (Madison, WI) **33981**
Wisconsin Engineer (Madison, WI) **33982**
Wisconsin Farm Edition; Fastline— (Buckner, KY) **11998**
Wisconsin Fire Journal (Menomonee Falls, WI) *Unable to locate*
Wisconsin Grocer (Madison, WI) **33983**
Wisconsin Hi-Liter (Burlington, WI) **33610**
Wisconsin Home Gallery Magazine (Cedarburg, WI) **33621**
Wisconsin-Iowa Shopping News (Prairie du Chien, WI) **34268**
The Wisconsin Jewish Chronicle (Milwaukee, WI) **34109**
Wisconsin; Journal of the Pharmacy Society of (Madison, WI) **33954**
Wisconsin Law Journal (Milwaukee, WI) **34110**
Wisconsin Law Review (Madison, WI) **33984**
Wisconsin Lawyer (Madison, WI) **33985**
Wisconsin Light (Milwaukee, WI) *Unable to locate*
Wisconsin Magazine of History (Madison, WI) **33986**
Wisconsin Master Plumber **5903***
Wisconsin Medical Journal (Madison, WI) **33987**
Wisconsin in Motion (Mequon, WI) **34044**
Wisconsin Natural Resources (Madison, WI) **33988**
WISCONSIN; ON (Madison, WI) **33967**
Wisconsin Outdoor Journal (Iola, WI) **33856**
Wisconsin Perspective (Altamonte Springs, FL) **5903**
Wisconsin Pharmacist **33954***
Wisconsin PHC Contractor **5903***
Wisconsin Professional Engineer **34198***
Wisconsin Public Television Network (Madison, WI) **37722**
Wisconsin Rapids Buyers' Guide (Wisconsin Rapids, WI) **34464**
Wisconsin R.E.C. News **33981***
Wisconsin Restaurateur (Madison, WI) **33989**
Wisconsin Review (Oshkosh, WI) **34228**
Wisconsin Right to Life REPORTER **34073***
Wisconsin School Musician (Madison, WI) *Unable to locate*
Wisconsin Silent Sports **34419***
Wisconsin State Farmer (Waupaca, WI) **34422**
Wisconsin State Journal (Madison, WI) **33990**
The Wisconsin Taxpayer (Madison, WI) **33991**
Wisconsin Trails (Black Earth, WI) **33590**
Wisconsin West Magazine (Eau Claire, WI) **33674**
Wisconsin Woman (Menomonee Falls, WI) *Ceased*
Wise Buyer (Webb City, MO) **17713**
Wise County Messenger (Decatur, TX) **30221**
WISE-FM - 90.5 (Wise, VA) **32635**
The Wise Woman (Oakland, CA) **2703**
WISH-TV - Channel 8 (Indianapolis, IN) **10202**
The Wishek Star (Wishek, ND) **24568**
WISK-AM - 1390 (Americus, GA) **6925**
WISK-FM - 98.7 (Americus, GA) **6926**
WISL-AM - 1590 (Williamsport, PA) **28186**
WISL-FM - 95.3 (Williamsport, PA) **28187**
WISM-AM **33680***
WISM-FM - 98.1 (Eau Claire, WI) **33681**
WISN-AM - 1130 (Milwaukee, WI) **34119**
WISN-TV - Channel 12 (Milwaukee, WI) **34120**
Wisner News-Chronicle (Wisner, NE) **18317**
WISO-AM (Ponce, PR) *Unable to locate*
Wisonsin Bar Bulletin **33985***
WISP-AM (Kinston, NC) *Unable to locate*
WISR-AM - 680 (Butler, PA) **26746**
WISS-AM - 1090 (Berlin, WI) **33586**
WISS-FM **33586***
WISS-FM **34304***
WIST-AM **24248***
WIST-FM **29167***
WISU-FM - 89.7 (Terre Haute, IN) **10496**
WISV-AM **34384***
WISW-AM - 1320 (Columbia, SC) **28577**
WITA-AM - 1490 (Knoxville, TN) **29291**
WITB-FM (Salem, WV) *Unable to locate*
WITC-FM - 88.9 (Cazenovia, NY) **20443**
WITE-AM **10501***
WITF-TV - Channel 33 (Harrisburg, PA) **27019**
With (Newton, KS) **11671**
WITH-AM (Baltimore, MD) *Unable to locate*
WITI-TV - Channel 6 (Milwaukee, WI) **34121**
WITL-AM (Lansing, MI) *Unable to locate*
WITL-FM (Lansing, MI) *Unable to locate*
WITN-AM **24275***
WITN-TV - Channel 7 (Washington, NC) **24276**
The Witness (Dubuque, IA) **10846**

The Witness (Rockport, ME) **13047**
Witness (Farmington Hills, MI) **15021**
WITR-FM (Rochester, NY) *Unable to locate*
WITT-FM (Tuscola, IL) *Ceased*
Wittenberg Enterprise and Birnamwood News (Wittenberg, WI) **34471**
Wittenberg Torch (Springfield, OH) **25534**
WittyWorld International Cartoon Bulletin & WittyWorld Annual (North Wales, PA) *Ceased*
WITV-TV - Channel 7 (Charleston, SC) **28522**
WITW-FM **14849***
WITY-AM - 980 (Danville, IL) **8708**
WITZ-AM - 990 (Jasper, IN) **10221**
WITZ-FM - 104.7 (Jasper, IN) **10222**
WIUM-FM - 91.3 (Macomb, IL) **9134**
WIUM-TV **9137***
WIUP-FM - 90.1 (Indiana, PA) **27081**
WIUS-AM - 1570 (Bloomington, IN) **9859**
WIUS-FM - 88.3 (Macomb, IL) **9135**
WIUV-FM - 91.3 (Castleton, VT) **31529**
WIVA-FM (Caguas, PR) *Unable to locate*
WIVB-TV - Channel 4 (Buffalo, NY) **20403**
WIVE-FM **31859***
WIVK-AM **29304***
WIVK-AM **29296***
WIVK-FM - 107.7 (Knoxville, TN) **29292**
WIVQ-FM - 103.3 (Peru, IL) **9453**
WIVR **12286***
WIVR-AM **12285***
WIVT-TV - Channel 34 (Binghamton, NY) **20225**
WIVV-AM - 1370 (San Juan, PR) **28301**
WIVY-FM **6233***
WIWS-AM - 1070 (Beckley, WV) **33242**
WIXC-AM **29191***
WIXE-AM - 1190 (Monroe, NC) **24067**
WIXI-AM **123***
WIXI-FM (Naples, FL) *Unable to locate*
WIXK-AM - 1590 (New Richmond, WI) **34194**
WIXK-FM - 107.1 (New Richmond, WI) **34195**
WIXL-AM - 1190 (Orlando, FL) **6520**
WIXN-AM - 1460 (Dixon, IL) **8777**
WIXQ-FM - 91.7 (Millersville, PA) **27268**
WIXT-TV - Channel 9 (East Syracuse, NY) **20559**
WIXV-FM **32098***
WIXV-FM (Savannah, GA) *Unable to locate*
WIXX-FM (Green Bay, WI) *Unable to locate*
WIXY-AM **14169***
WIYD-AM - 1260 (Palatka, FL) **6539**
WIYE-TV **6513***
WIYN-AM **7509***
WIYN-FM **7510***
WIYN-FM (Deposit, NY) *Unable to locate*
WIYQ-FM **27097***
WIYY-FM - 97.9 (Baltimore, MD) **13275**
WIZA-AM (Savannah, GA) *Unable to locate*
Wizard (Congers, NY) **20492**
WIZB-FM (Dawson, GA) *Ceased*
WIZD-AM **36***
WIZD-FM - 99.9 (Wausau, WI) **34435**
WIZE-AM - 1340 (Dayton, OH) **25145**
WIZF-FM (Cincinnati, OH) *Unable to locate*
WIZK-AM - 1570 (Bay Springs, MS) **16555**
WIZK-FM - 94.3 (Bay Springs, MS) **16556**
WIZM-AM - 1410 (La Crosse, WI) **33889**
WIZM-FM - 93.3 (La Crosse, WI) **33890**
WIZO **29200***
WIZO-AM **29200***
WIZR-AM - 930 (Johnstown, NY) **20852**
WIZR-FM **20853***
WIZS-AM - 1450 (Henderson, NC) **23982**
WIZZ-AM **9670***
WJAB-FM - 90.9 (Normal, AL) **402**
WJAC-AM - 850 (Johnstown, PA) **27092**
WJAC-FM **27094***
WJAC-TV - Channel 6 (Johnstown, PA) **27093**
WJAD-AM **6911***
WJAG-AM - 780 (Norfolk, NE) **18174**
WJAK-AM **9929***
WJAL-AM **28701***
WJAL-TV - Channel 68 (Chambersburg, PA) **26773**
WJAM-AM **455***
WJAQ-FM - 100.9 (Marianna, FL) **6327**
WJAR-AM **28434***
WJAR-TV - Channel 10 (Cranston, RI) **28338**
WJAS-AM (Pittsburgh, PA) *Unable to locate*
WJAT-AM (Swainsboro, GA) *Unable to locate*
WJAT-FM (Swainsboro, GA) *Unable to locate*
WJAW-AM - 630 (Marietta, OH) **25348**
WJAW-FM - 100.9 (McConnelsville, OH) **25370**
WJAX-AM - 1220 (Jacksonville, FL) **6224**
WJAY-AM (Mullins, SC) *Unable to locate*
WJBB-AM - 1230 (Haleyville, AL) **259**
WJBB-FM - 92.7 (Haleyville, AL) **260**
WJBC-AM - 1230 (Bloomington, IL) **8085**
WJBD-AM - 1350 (Salem, IL) **9578**
WJBD-FM - 100.1 (Salem, IL) **9579**
WJBF-TV - Channel 6 (Augusta, GA) **7110**
WJBI-AM - 1290 (Batesville, MS) **16551**
WJBK-TV - Channel 2 (Detroit, MI) **14966**

WJXA-FM - 92.9 (Nashville, TN) **29513**
WJXB-FM - 97.5 (Knoxville, TN) **29293**
WJXL-AM (Jacksonville, AL) *Unable to locate*
WJXN-AM (Jackson, MS) *Unable to locate*
WJXR-FM - 92.1 (Jacksonville, FL) **6229**
WJXT-TV - Channel 4 (Jacksonville, FL) **6230**
WJXY-AM - 1050 (Murrells Inlet, SC) **28701**
WJXY-FM (Conway, SC) *Unable to locate*
WJYA-AM **7116***
WJYE-FM - 96.1 (Buffalo, NY) **20404**
WJYF-FM - 95.3 (Tifton, GA) **7601**
WJYI-AM - 1340 (Milwaukee, WI) **34122**
WJYJ-FM - 90.5 (Spotsylvania, VA) **32536**
WJYL-FM (Louisville, KY) *Ceased*
WJYM-AM (Perrysburg, OH) *Unable to locate*
WJYP-FM - 100.9 (South Charleston, WV) **33468**
WJYQ-FM (Charleston, SC) *Unable to locate*
WJYR-FM (Myrtle Beach, SC) *Unable to locate*
WJYW-FM - 88.9 (Union City, IN) **10507**
WJYY-FM - 105.5 (Concord, NH) **18477**
WJZ-TV - Channel 13 (Baltimore, MD) **13277**
WJZE-FM (Washington, DC) *Unable to locate*
WJZI-FM - 93.3 (Milwaukee, WI) **34123**
WJZQ-FM **33877***
WJZS-AM (Orangeburg, SC) *Unable to locate*
WJZW-FM - 105.9 (Washington, DC) **5887**
WJZY-TV - Channel 46 (Charlotte, NC) **23772**
WJZZ-FM - 105.9 (Detroit, MI) **14969**
WKAA-FM - 97.7 (Tifton, GA) **7602**
WKAB-TV **392***
WKAC-AM - 1080 (Athens, AL) **28**
WKAD-FM **28061***
WKAI-AM **9136***
WKAJ-AM (Saratoga Springs, NY) *Unable to locate*
WKAJ-FM **20013***
WKAK-FM (Albany, GA) *Unable to locate*
WKAL-AM - 1420 (Kalkaska, MI) **15262**
WKAL-AM (Traverse City, MI) *Ceased*
WKAL-FM **23578***
WKAM-AM - 1460 (Goshen, IN) **10030**
WKAN-AM - 1320 (Kankakee, IL) **9041**
WKAN-FM - 1320 (Kankakee, IL) **9042**
WKAP-AM **26634***
WKAP-AM - 1470 (Whitehall, PA) **28161**
WKAQ-AM - 580 (San Juan, PR) **28302**
WKAQ-FM - 104.7 (San Juan, PR) **28303**
WKAR-AM - 870 (East Lansing, MI) **14995**
WKAR-TV - Channel 23 (East Lansing, MI) **14996**
WKAS-TV - Channel 25 (Ashland, KY) **11920**
WKAT-AM - 1360 (Miami, FL) **6400**
WKAV-AM - 1400 (Charlottesville, VA) **31953**
WKAX-AM - 1500 (Russellville, AL) **442**
WKAY-AM - 1590 (Donaldsonville, LA) **12571**
WKAY-TV **23762***
WKAZ-AM **33459***
WKBA-AM - 1550 (Roanoke, VA) **32500**
WKBD-TV - Channel 50 (Southfield, MI) **15558**
WKBF-AM - 1270 (Davenport, IA) **10748**
WKBG-FM **28722***
WKBG-FM - 107.7 (North Augusta, SC) **28722**
WKBH-AM **33889***
WKBH-AM - 1570 (La Crosse, WI) **33891**
WKBH-FM **33888***
WKBI-AM - 1400 (St. Marys, PA) **27943**
WKBK-AM - 1290 (Winchester, NH) **18651**
WKBK-FM **18652***
WKBL-AM - 1250 (Covington, TN) **29154**
WKBL-FM **29155***
WKBN-AM - 570 (Boardman, OH) **24685**
WKBN-TV - Channel 27 (Youngstown, OH) **25707**
WKBO-AM - 1230 (Harrisburg, PA) **27020**
WKBQ-AM (St. Louis, MO) *Unable to locate*
WKBQ-FM - 104.1 (St. Louis, MO) **17557**
WKBQ-FM - 93.5 (Covington, TN) **29155**
WKBR-AM (Manchester, NH) *Unable to locate*
WKBS-TV - Channel 47 (Altoona, PA) **26639**
WKBT-TV - Channel 8 (La Crosse, WI) **33892**
WKBV-AM - 1490 (Richmond, IN) **10425**
WKBV-FM **10423***
WKBW-TV - Channel 7 (Buffalo, NY) **20405**
WKBX-FM - 106.3 (Kingsland, GA) **7358**
WKBY-AM - 1080 (Chatham, VA) **31963**
WKBZ-AM (Muskegon, MI) *Unable to locate*
WKBZ-FM (Muskegon, MI) *Unable to locate*
WKCA-FM - 107.7 (Owingsville, KY) **12336**
WKCC-FM - 96.7 (Grayson, KY) **12095**
WKCF-TV (Orlando, FL) *Unable to locate*
WKCG-FM - 101.3 (Augusta, ME) **12900**
WKCH-FM - 106.5 (Fort Atkinson, WI) **33725**
WKCH-TV **29302***
WKCI-FM - 101.3 (Hamden, CT) **4882**
WKCJ-FM (Lewisburg, WV) *Unable to locate*
WKCK-AM (Orocovis, PR) *Unable to locate*
WKCL-FM - 91.5 (Ladson, SC) **28678**
WKCQ-FM - 98.1 (Saginaw, MI) **15500**
WKCR-FM - 89.9 (New York, NY) **22972**
WKCS-FM - 91.1 (Knoxville, TN) **29294**
WKCT-AM - 930 (Bowling Green, KY) **11958**
WKCU-AM - 1350 (Corinth, MS) **16618**

WKCU-FM **16619***
WKCW-AM - 1420 (Warrenton, VA) **32604**
WKCX-FM - 97.7 (Rome, GA) **7504**
WKCY-AM - 1300 (Harrisonburg, VA) **32146**
WKCY-FM - 104.3 (Harrisonburg, VA) **32147**
WKDA-AM (Nashville, TN) *Ceased*
WKDA-AM - 1200 (Nashville, TN) **29514**
WKDA-FM **29515***
WKDC-AM **8074***
WKDD-FM - 98.1 (Akron, OH) **24598**
WKDE-AM - 1000 (Altavista, VA) **31757**
WKDE-FM - 105.5 (Altavista, VA) **31758**
WKDF-FM - 103.3 (Nashville, TN) **29515**
WKDI-AM - 840 (Denton, MD) **13483**
WKDK-AM - 1240 (Newberry, SC) **28718**
WKDL-FM **33888***
WKDM-AM - 1380 (New York, NY) **22973**
WKDN-FM - 106.9 (Camden, NJ) **18715**
WKDO-AM - 1560 (Liberty, KY) **12201**
WKDO-FM - 98.7 (Liberty, KY) **12202**
WKDP-AM - 1330 (Corbin, KY) **12024**
WKDP-FM - 99.5 (Corbin, KY) **12025**
WKDQ-FM - 99.5 (Evansville, IN) **9946**
WKDR-AM (South Burlington, VT) *Unable to locate*
WKDS-FM - 89.9 (Kalamazoo, MI) **15250**
WKDU-FM - 91.7 (Philadelphia, PA) **27737**
WKDW-AM - 900 (Staunton, VA) **32558**
WKDX-AM (Wadesboro, NC) *Unable to locate*
WKDZ-AM - 1110 (Cadiz, KY) **12004**
WKDZ-FM - 106.5 (Cadiz, KY) **12005**
WKEA-FM - 98.3 (Scottsboro, AL) **448**
WKEB-FM - 99.3 (Medford, WI) **34036**
WKED-AM - 1130 (Frankfort, KY) **12081**
WKED-FM - 103.7 (Frankfort, KY) **12082**
WKEE-FM - 100.5 (Huntington, WV) **33341**
WKEF-TV - Channel 22 (Dayton, OH) **25146**
WKEG-AM (Pittsburgh, PA) *Ceased*
WKEI-AM - 1450 (Kewanee, IL) **9047**
WKEQ-AM - 910 (Somerset, KY) **12407**
WKER-AM **19450***
WKES-FM **29107***
WKET-FM (Kettering, OH) *Unable to locate*
WKEU-AM - 1450 (Griffin, GA) **7315**
WKEU-FM **7316***
WKEW-AM (Greensboro, NC) *Unable to locate*
WKEX-AM - 1430 (Blacksburg, VA) **31887**
WKEY-AM - 1340 (Covington, VA) **31984**
WKEY-FM - 93.5 (Key West, FL) **6257**
WKFD-AM (Charlestown, RI) *Ceased*
WKFE-AM - 1550 (Yauco, PR) **28323**
WKFI-AM - 1090 (Wilmington, OH) **25668**
WKFL-AM (Bushnell, FL) *Unable to locate*
WKFM-FM **23578***
WKFM-FM **13025***
WKFM-FM (East Longmeadow, MA) *Unable to locate*
WKFM-FM - 96.1 (Milan, OH) **25381**
WKFN-FM **418***
WKFR-FM - 103.3 (Kalamazoo, MI) **15251**
WKFT-TV - Channel 40 (Fayetteville, NC) **23889**
WKFX-FM (Green Bay, WI) *Ceased*
WKGA-AM **33326***
WKGA-AM (Waukegan, IL) *Unable to locate*
WKGB-TV - Channel 53 (Bowling Green, KY) **11959**
WKGF-AM **6895***
WKGF-FM (Zolfo Springs, FL) *Ceased*
WKGL-FM **23163***
WKGL-FM - 97.7 (Muscle Shoals, AL) **398**
WKGM-AM - 940 (Smithfield, VA) **32527**
WKGN-AM (Sevierville, TN) *Unable to locate*
WKGO-FM - 106.1 (Cumberland, MD) **13477**
WKGQ-AM - 1060 (Milledgeville, GA) **7438**
WKGR-FM - 98.7 (West Palm Beach, FL) **6853**
WKGT-FM (Pensacola, FL) *Unable to locate*
WKGW **23578***
WKGW-FM (Oriskany, NY) *Unable to locate*
WKGX-AM - 1080 (Lenoir, NC) **24038**
WKHA-TV - Channel 35 (Hazard, KY) **12119**
WKHB-AM - 620 (North Versailles, PA) **27343**
WKHC-FM - 104.3 (Dahlonega, GA) **7220**
WKHF-AM **5914***
WKHI-FM **13721***
WKHI-FM (Onley, VA) *Unable to locate*
WKHJ-AM **28666***
WKHJ-FM - 104.5 (Mountain Lake Park, MD) **13633**
WKHK-FM (Richmond, VA) *Unable to locate*
WKHL-AM (Allentown, PA) *Unable to locate*
WKHL-FM (Stamford, CT) *Unable to locate*
WKHM-AM - 970 (Jackson, MI) **15226**
WKHQ-FM (Rochester, NY) *Unable to locate*
WKHR-FM - 88.3 (Chagrin Falls, OH) **24758**
WKHS-FM - 90.5 (Worton, MD) **13784**
WKHT-FM - 93.7 (Sumter, SC) **28772**
WKHV-FM **31758***
WKHX-AM **7071***
WKHX-FM - 101.5 (Atlanta, GA) **7074**
WKHY-FM - 93.5 (Lafayette, IN) **10260**
WKIC-AM - 1390 (Hazard, KY) **12120**
WKIE-FM - 92.7 (Chicago, IL) **8633**
WKIG-AM (Glennville, GA) *Unable to locate*

WKII-AM - 1070 (Punta Gorda, FL) **6611**
WKIJ-AM (Jasper, AL) *Unable to locate*
WKIK-AM (Leonardtown, MD) *Ceased*
WKIK-FM - 102.9 (La Plata, MD) **13594**
WKIN-AM (Kingsport, TN) *Unable to locate*
WKIO-FM - 92.5 (Champaign, IL) **8230**
WKIP-AM - 1450 (Poughkeepsie, NY) **23159**
WKIP-FM (Hyde Park, NY) *Unable to locate*
WKIQ-AM - 1240 (Tavares, FL) **6813**
WKIS-FM - 99.9 (Miami, FL) **6401**
WKIT-AM (Bangor, ME) *Unable to locate*
WKIX-AM **24171***
WKIX-FM - 96.1 (Burlington, NC) **23675**
WKJA-FM (Norfolk, VA) *Unable to locate*
WKJB-AM - 710 (Mayaguez, PR) **28262**
WKJB-FM - 99.1 (Mayaguez, PR) **28263**
WKJC-FM - 104.7 (Tawas City, MI) **15587**
WKJF-AM - 1370 (Cadillac, MI) **14848**
WKJG-AM **9993***
WKJG-FM **9990***
WKJG-TV - Channel 33 (Fort Wayne, IN) **9988**
WKJK-AM - 1080 (Louisville, KY) **12256**
WKJK-AM 1963-1985 **23914***
WKJM-AM **12285***
WKJM-AM - 1320 (Mayfield, KY) **12285**
WKJM-FM **10262***
WKJN-FM (Baton Rouge, LA) *Unable to locate*
WKJQ-AM - 1550 (Parsons, TN) **29564**
WKJQ-FM - 97.3 (Parsons, TN) **29565**
WKJR-FM (Mattoon, IL) *Unable to locate*
WKJV-AM - 1380 (Asheville, NC) **23637**
WKJX-FM (Elizabeth City, NC) *Unable to locate*
WKJY-FM - 98.3 (Farmingdale, NY) **20599**
WKKC-FM - 89.3 (Chicago, IL) **8634**
WKKD-AM - 1580 (Aurora, IL) **8043**
WKKD-FM - 95.9 (Aurora, IL) **8044**
WKKE-AM **16719***
WKKE-AM **23637***
WKKE-AM - 1080 (St. Pauls, NC) **24214**
WKKF-FM - 102.3 (Albany, NY) **20013**
WKKG-FM - 101.5 (Columbus, IN) **9897**
WKKI-FM - 94.3 (Celina, OH) **24752**
WKKJ-FM - 93.3 (Chillicothe, OH) **24766**
WKKL-FM - 90.7 (West Barnstable, MA) **14623**
WKKM-FM **15145***
WKKN-FM (Cordele, GA) *Unable to locate*
WKKO-FM - 99.9 (Toledo, OH) **25580**
WKKP-AM - 1410 (McDonough, GA) **7430**
WKKQ-AM **15960***
WKKQ-FM - 96.1 (Barbourville, KY) **11923**
WKKR-FM (Opelika, AL) *Unable to locate*
WKKS-AM - 1570 (Vanceburg, KY) **12425**
WKKS-FM - 104.9 (Vanceburg, KY) **12426**
WKKT-FM (Charlotte, NC) *Unable to locate*
WKKV-FM (West Allis, WI) *Unable to locate*
WKKW-FM - 97.9 (Morgantown, WV) **33403**
WKKX-FM - 106.5 (St. Louis, MO) **17558**
WKKY-FM (McComb, MS) *Ceased*
WKKY-FM - 104.7 (Geneva, OH) **25214**
WKKZ-FM - 92.7 (Dublin, GA) **7252**
WKLA-AM - 1450 (Ludington, MI) **15323**
WKLA-FM - 106.3 (Ludington, MI) **15324**
WKLB-AM - 1290 (Manchester, KY) **12279**
WKLB-FM **13996***
WKLB-FM (Boston, MA) *Ceased*
WKLC FM - 105.1 (St. Albans, WV) **33459**
WKLC-FM - 105.1 (St. Albans, WV) **33458**
WKLD-FM - 97.7 (Oneonta, AL) **408**
WKLE-TV - Channel 46 (Elizabethtown, KY) **12048**
WKLF-AM - 980 (Clanton, AL) **157**
WKLF-FM **156***
WKLG-FM (Key Largo, FL) *Unable to locate*
WKLH-FM (Milwaukee, WI) *Unable to locate*
WKLJ-AM - 1290 (Sparta, WI) **34335**
WKLJ-FM **16810***
WKLK-AM (Cloquet, MN) *Unable to locate*
WKLK-FM (Cloquet, MN) *Unable to locate*
WKLM-FM - 95.3 (Millersburg, OH) **25391**
WKLN-AM (Saint Augustine, FL) *Unable to locate*
WKLN-FM **166***
WKLP-AM - 1390 (Keyser, WV) **33357**
WKLP-FM **33358***
WKLQ-FM - 94.5 (Grand Rapids, MI) **15112**
WKLR-FM **10205***
WKLR-FM **25580***
WKLR-FM (Richmond, VA) *Unable to locate*
WKLS-FM - 96.1 (Atlanta, GA) **7075**
WKLT-FM (Traverse City, MI) *Unable to locate*
WKLU-AM (Midway, KY) *Ceased*
WKLV-AM (Bradenton, FL) *Unable to locate*
WKLV-AM - 1440 (Blackstone, VA) **31894**
WKLX-AM **23243***
WKLY-AM - 980 (Hartwell, GA) **7322**
WKLZ-FM (Petoskey, MI) *Unable to locate*
WKMA-TV - Channel 35 (Lexington, KY) **12185**
WKMB-AM - 1070 (Stirling, NJ) **19605**
WKMC-AM - 1370 (Roaring Spring, PA) **27940**
WKMG-AM (Newberry, SC) *Unable to locate*
WKMG-TV - Channel 6 (Orlando, FL) **6521**

WKMI-AM - 1360 (Kalamazoo, MI) **15252**
WKMJ-TV - Channel 68 (Louisville, KY) **12257**
WKMK-AM **5927***
WKML-FM - 95.7 (Fayetteville, NC) **23890**
WKMM-FM - 96.7 (Kingwood, WV) **33362**
WKMO-FM (Elizabethtown, KY) *Unable to locate*
WKMQ - Oldies **9544***
WKMR-TV - Channel 16 (Morehead, KY) **12305**
WKMS-FM - 91.3/92.1 Paducah, KY; 99.5 Paris, TN (Murray, KY) **12319**
WKMT-AM - 1220 (Kings Mountain, NC) **24026**
WKMU-TV - Channel 29 (Madisonville, KY) **12275**
WKMX-FM - 106.7 (Enterprise, AL) **203**
WKMY-FM **33442***
WKMZ-FM - 95.9 (Martinsburg, WV) **33382**
WKNA-FM - 88.9 (Senatobia, MS) **16843**
WKNB-FM - 104.3 (Warren, PA) **28106**
WKNB-TV **5205***
WKNC-FM - 88.1 (Raleigh, NC) **24164**
WKND-AM - 1480 (Windsor, CT) **5235**
WKNE-AM - 1290 (Keene, NH) **18533**
WKNE-FM - 103.7 (Keene, NH) **18534**
WKNG-AM - 1060 (Tallapoosa, GA) **7584**
WKNH-AM **15027***
WKNH-FM - 91.3 (Keene, NH) **18535**
WKNI-AM (Lexington, AL) *Unable to locate*
WKNK-FM (Glasgow, KY) *Unable to locate*
WKNN-AM **16814***
WKNN-FM - 99.1 (Biloxi, MS) **16564**
WKNO-FM - 91.1 (Memphis, TN) **29399**
WKNO-TV - Channel 10 (Memphis, TN) **29400**
WKNP-FM - 90.1 (Jackson, MS) **16721**
WKNQ-FM - 90.7 (Memphis, TN) **29401**
WKNR-AM - 850 (Cleveland, OH) **24978**
WKNS-FM (Kinston, NC) *Unable to locate*
WKNT-AM **24597***
WKNT-FM **24599***
WKNU-FM (Brewton, AL) *Unable to locate*
WKNV-AM - 890 (Fairlawn, VA) **32038**
WKNW-AM - 1400 (Sault Sainte Marie, MI) **15529**
WKNX-AM - 1250 (Saginaw, MI) **15501**
WKNX-TV **14886***
WKNY-AM - 1490 (Kingston, NY) **20864**
WKNZ-FM - 107.1 (Hattiesburg, MS) **16674**
WKOA-AM **12135***
WKOA-FM - 105.3 (Lafayette, IN) **10261**
WKOC-FM **8096***
WKOC-AM - 93.7 (Norfolk, VA) **32302**
WKOE-FM - 106.3 (Trenton, NJ) **19675**
WKOH-TV - Channel 31 (Henderson, KY) **12124**
WKOI-TV - Channel 43 (Richmond, IN) **10426**
WKOJ-FM **23163***
WKOJ-FM **23163***
WKOK-AM - 1070 (Sunbury, PA) **28039**
WKOL-AM (Amsterdam, NY) *Ceased*
WKOL-FM **23315***
WKOL-FM **23315***
WKOM-FM - 101.7 (Columbia, TN) **29139**
WKON-TV - Channel 52 (Owenton, KY) **12335**
WKOO-FM - 98.7 (Jacksonville, NC) **24013**
WKOP-AM - 1360 (Binghamton, NY) **20226**
WKOP-TV (Knoxville, TN) *Unable to locate*
WKOQ-FM **24042***
WKOR-AM - 980 (Columbus, MS) **16611**
WKOS-FM - 104.9 (Gray, TN) **29210**
WKOV-AM **25260***
WKOV-FM - 96.7 (Jackson, OH) **25259**
WKOW-TV - Channel 27 (Madison, WI) **33999**
WKOX-AM - 1200 (Framingham, MA) **14203**
WKOY-AM (Bluefield, WV) *Unable to locate*
WKOY-FM - 100.9 (Princeton, WV) **33442**
WKOZ-AM - 1340 (Kosciusko, MS) **16738**
WKPA-AM (New Kensington, PA) *Unable to locate*
WKPC-TV **12180***
WKPD-TV - Channel 29 (Lexington, KY) **12186**
WKPE-AM - 1170 (West Yarmouth, MA) **14631**
WKPE-FM - 104.7 (West Yarmouth, MA) **14632**
WKPI-TV - Channel 22 (Pikeville, KY) **12363**
WKPK-FM (Gaylord, MI) *Unable to locate*
WKPL-FM **34247***
WKPM-AM **16286***
WKPO-FM - 105.9 (Janesville, WI) **33866**
WKPQ-FM - 105.3 (Hornell, NY) **20757**
WKPR-AM - 1420 (Kalamazoo, MI) **15253**
WKPS-FM **27326***
WKPT-AM - 1400 (Kingsport, TN) **29265**
WKPT-FM **29268***
WKPT-TV - Channel 19 (Kingsport, TN) **29266**
WKPV-TV (San Juan, PR) *Unable to locate*
WKPW-FM - 90.7 (Knightstown, IN) **10237**
WKQA-FM **9442***
WKQD-FM **31***
WKQI-FM - 95.5 (Oak Park, MI) **15414**
WKQK-FM **207***
WKQL-FM - 96.9 (Jacksonville, FL) **6231**
WKQQ-FM - 98.1 (Lexington, KY) **12187**
WKQR-FM **153***
WKQS-FM **6401***
WKQS-FM **27095***

WKQS-FM - 101.9 (Marquette, MI) **15344**
WKQT-FM (Morehead City, NC) *Unable to locate*
WKQV-FM **19702***
WKQV-FM - 95.7 (Dunmore, PA) **26843**
WKQW-AM (Oil City, PA) *Unable to locate*
WKQX-FM - 101.1 (Chicago, IL) **8635**
WKQY-FM **33258***
WKQY-FM - 100.1 (Bluefield, WV) **33258**
WKQZ-FM - 93.3 (Saginaw, MI) **15502**
WKRA-AM - 1110 (Holly Springs, MS) **16682**
WKRA-FM - 92.7 (Holly Springs, MS) **16683**
WKRB-FM (Brooklyn, NY) *Unable to locate*
WKRC-AM - 550 (Cincinnati, OH) **24841**
WKRC-TV - Channel 12 (Cincinnati, OH) **24842**
WKRD-FM **346***
WKRD-FM - 93.7 (Schenectady, NY) **23316**
WKRG-AM **348***
WKRG-FM **346***
WKRG-TV - Channel 5 (Mobile, AL) **341**
WKRH-FM **13067***
WKRI-AM (West Warwick, RI) *Unable to locate*
WKRK-FM - 97.1 (Southfield, MI) **15559**
WKRL-FM **6811***
WKRM-AM - 1340 (Columbia, TN) **29140**
WKRN-TV - Channel 2 (Nashville, TN) **29516**
WKRO-AM - 1490 (Cairo, IL) **8106**
WKRP-TV - Channel 29 (Ridgefield, CT) **5104**
WKRR-FM - 92.3 (Greensboro, NC) **23949**
WKRS-AM - 1220 (Waukegan, IL) **9746**
WKRT-AM (Cortland, NY) *Unable to locate*
WKRU-AM - 1510 (Burnettown, SC) **28498**
WKRW-AM **7163***
WKRX-FM - 96.7 (Roxboro, NC) **24210**
WKRY **6257***
WKRZ-AM **26937***
WKRZ-FM - 98.5 (Pittston, PA) **27891**
WKSB-FM - 102.7 (Williamsport, PA) **28188**
WKSC-AM - 1300 (Kershaw, SC) **28672**
WKSC-FM **18535***
WKSE-FM - 98.5 (Buffalo, NY) **20406**
WKSF-FM - 99.9 (Asheville, NC) **23638**
WKSG-FM **14963***
WKSH-AM (Pewaukee, WI) *Unable to locate*
WKSI-FM **8974***
WKSI-FM - 98.7 (Greensboro, NC) **23950**
WKSJ-AM - 1270 (Mobile, AL) **342**
WKSJ-FM - 94.9 (Mobile, AL) **343**
WKSK-AM - 580 (West Jefferson, NC) **24284**
WKSL-FM **26771***
WKSL-FM (Greencastle, PA) *Ceased*
WKSM-FM - 99.5 (Fort Walton Beach, FL) **6124**
WKSN-AM - 1340 (Jamestown, NY) **20845**
WKSO-FM (Orangeburg, SC) *Unable to locate*
WKSO-TV - Channel 29 (Lexington, KY) **12188**
WKSQ-FM - 94.5 (Bangor, ME) **12911**
WKSR-AM - 1420 (Pulaski, TN) **29573**
WKSR-FM - 98.3 (Pulaski, TN) **29574**
WKSS-FM - 95.7 (Hartford, CT) **4904**
WKST-AM - 1200 (New Castle, PA) **27318**
WKSU-FM **11635***
WKSU-FM - 89.7 (Kent, OH) **25279**
WKSW-FM - 101.7 (Springfield, OH) **25537**
WKSX-FM - 92.7 (Johnston, SC) **28670**
WKSZ-FM **26805***
WKSZ-FM - 95.9 (Green Bay, WI) **33750**
WKTA-AM - 1330 (Evanston, IL) **8875**
WKTC-FM **23675***
WKTC-FM (Goldsboro, NC) *Unable to locate*
WKTE-AM - 1090 (King, NC) **24024**
WKTF-AM **32604***
WKTG-FM - 93.9 (Madisonville, KY) **12276**
WKTI-FM - 94.5 (Milwaukee, WI) **34124**
WKTJ-AM (West Farmington, ME) *Ceased*
WKTJ-FM - 99.3 (Farmington, ME) **12962**
WKTK-FM - 98.5 (Gainesville, FL) **6163**
WKTM-FM **28700***
WKTM-FM - 106.1 (Grovetown, GA) **7319**
WKTN-FM - 95.3 (Kenton, OH) **25282**
WKTP-AM **12994***
WKTQ-AM - 1450 (Norway, ME) **12994**
WKTR-AM - 840 (Quinque, VA) **32343**
WKTS-AM (Sheboygan, WI) *Unable to locate*
WKTV-TV - Channel 2 (Utica, NY) **23474**
WKTZ-FM - 90.9 (Jacksonville, FL) **6232**
WKUB-FM - 105.1 (Waycross, GA) **7648**
WKUL-FM - 92.1 (Cullman, AL) **166**
WKUN-AM - 1580 (Monroe, GA) **7444**
WKUS-AM **6648***
WKUZ-FM - 95.9 (Wabash, IN) **10532**
WKVA-AM - 920 (Lewistown, PA) **27197**
WKVE-FM **27939***
WKVG-AM - 1000 (Pound, VA) **32337**
WKVI-AM - 1520 (Knox, IN) **10239**
WKVM-AM - 810 (San Juan, PR) **28304**
WKVN-FM (Levittown, PR) *Unable to locate*
WKVR-FM - 92.3 (Huntingdon, PA) **27069**
WKVT-AM - 1490 (Brattleboro, VT) **31510**
WKVT-FM - 92.7 (Brattleboro, VT) **31511**
WKVV-AM **10192***

WKVX-AM - 960 (Wooster, OH) **25676**
WKWC-FM - 90.3 (Owensboro, KY) **12330**
WKWF-AM (Key West, FL) *Unable to locate*
WKWH-AM - 1520 (Shelbyville, IN) **10453**
WKWH-FM - 94.3 (Rushville, IN) **10438**
WKWI-FM - 101.7 (Kilmarnock, VA) **32175**
WKWK-AM **33505***
WKWK-FM - 97.3 (Wheeling, WV) **33506**
WKWL-AM - 1230 (Florala, AL) **217**
WKWL-FM - 100.9 (New London, CT) **5023**
WKWM-AM **15265***
WKWN-AM - 1420 (Trenton, GA) **7609**
WKWS-FM - 96.1 (Charleston, WV) **33283**
WKWT **29638***
WKWX-FM - 93.5 (Savannah, TN) **29586**
WKWZ-FM - 88.5 (Syosset, NY) **23385**
WKXA-FM - 100.5 (Findlay, OH) **25197**
WKXB-FM - 99.9 (Wilmington, NC) **24302**
WKXC-AM (Goldsboro, NC) *Unable to locate*
WKXC-FM (Atlanta, GA) *Ceased*
WKXD-FM (Monterey, TN) *Unable to locate*
WKXE-FM (White River Junction, VT) *Unable to locate*
WKXF-AM (Eminence, KY) *Unable to locate*
WKXF-FM **10340***
WKXG-AM - 1540 (Greenwood, MS) **16650**
WKXH-FM - 105.5 (St. Johnsbury, VT) **31595**
WKXI-FM - 107.5 (Ridgeland, MS) **16836**
WKXJ-AM **12009***
WKXK-FM **8665***
WKXK-FM **29542***
WKXK-FM - 97.9 (Fort Valley, GA) **7290**
WKXL-AM - 1450 (Concord, NH) **18478**
WKXL-FM **18478***
WKXN-FM - 95.9 (Greenville, AL) **245**
WKXO-AM (Richmond, VA) *Unable to locate*
WKXO-FM (Berea, KY) *Unable to locate*
WKXP-FM **3036***
WKXQ-FM - 92.5 (Rushville, IL) **9559**
WKXR-AM - 1260 (Asheboro, NC) **23624**
WKXT-TV **29306***
WKXU-FM - 101.1 (Burlington, NC) **23676**
WKXV-AM (Knoxville, TN) *Unable to locate*
WKXW-FM - 101.5 (Trenton, NJ) **19676**
WKXY-AM **6673***
WKXZ-FM - 93.9 (Norwich, NY) **23024**
WKY-AM (Oklahoma City, OK) *Unable to locate*
WKYA-FM - 105.5 (Greenville, KY) **12101**
WKYB-AM (Hemingway, SC) *Unable to locate*
WKYC-TV - Channel 3 (Cleveland, OH) **24979**
WKYD-AM (Andalusia, AL) *Ceased*
WKYE-FM - 95.5 (Johnstown, PA) **27094**
WKYG-AM (Parkersburg, WV) *Unable to locate*
WKYJ-FM **16613***
WKYK-AM - 940 (Burnsville, NC) **23679**
WKYM-FM - 101.7 (Monticello, KY) **12301**
WKYN-FM **27939***
WKYO-AM - 1360 (Caro, MI) **14860**
WKYQ-FM - 93.3 (Paducah, KY) **12345**
WKYR-AM - 1570 (Burkesville, KY) **12000**
WKYR-FM - 107.9 (Burkesville, KY) **12001**
WKYS-FM - 93.9 (Washington, DC) **5888**
WKYT-TV - Channel 27 (Lexington, KY) **12189**
WKYU-FM - 88.9 (Bowling Green, KY) **11960**
WKYU-TV - Channel 24 (Bowling Green, KY) **11961**
WKYW-FM (Frankfort, KY) *Unable to locate*
WKYX-AM - 570 (Paducah, KY) **12346**
WKYY-AM (Lancaster, KY) *Unable to locate*
WKYZ **29341***
WKYZ-FM (Corbin, KY) *Unable to locate*
WKZA-AM (Kane, PA) *Unable to locate*
WKZB-FM **16596***
WKZB-FM - 93.5 (Meridian, MS) **16775**
WKZC-FM (Ludington, MI) *Unable to locate*
WKZD-AM (Gainesville, GA) *Unable to locate*
WKZE-AM - 1020 (Sharon, CT) **5115**
WKZE-FM - 98.1 (Sharon, CT) **5116**
WKZG-FM **33356***
WKZI-AM - 800 (Dennison, IL) **8748**
WKZJ-AM **6287***
WKZK-AM - 1600 (Augusta, GA) **7111**
WKZL-FM - 107.5 (Greensboro, NC) **23951**
WKZM-FM (Sarasota, FL) *Unable to locate*
WKZO-AM - 590 (Kalamazoo, MI) **15254**
WKZO-TV **15260***
WKZQ-AM - 1450 (Myrtle Beach, SC) **28708**
WKZQ-FM - 101.7 (Myrtle Beach, SC) **28709**
WKZR-FM - 102.3 (Milledgeville, GA) **7439**
WKZS-FM **12888***
WKZS-FM - 103.1 (Covington, IN) **9908**
WKZT-AM - 1270 (Fulton, KY) **12085**
WKZW-AM **9436***
WKZW-FM **9438***
WKZW-FM **9438***
WLAB-FM - 88.3 (Fort Wayne, IN) **9989**
WLAC-AM - 1510 (Nashville, TN) **29518**
WLAC-FM - 105.9 (Nashville, TN) **29517**
WLAC-TV **29537***
WLAD-AM - 800 (Danbury, CT) **4766**

WLSI-AM - 900 (Pikeville, KY) **12364**
WLSK-FM - 100.9 (Lebanon, KY) **12156**
WLSM-AM - 1270 (Louisville, MS) **16751**
WLSM-FM - 107.1 (Louisville, MS) **16752**
WLSO-FM **10473***
WLSP-AM - 1530 (Lapeer, MI) **15310**
WLSQ-AM **7224***
WLSQ-FM - 94.3 (Humboldt, TN) **29227**
WLSR-FM **25306***
WLSR-FM (Galesburg, IL) *Unable to locate*
WLSS AM - 930 (Sarasota, FL) **6673**
WLSS-FM - 102.5 (Baton Rouge, LA) **12521**
WLST-AM **15009***
WLST-FM - 95.1 (Marinette, WI) **34021**
WLSU-FM - 88.9 (La Crosse, WI) **33894**
WLSV-AM - 790 (Wellsville, NY) **23535**
WLSW-FM - 103.9 (Connellsville, PA) **26802**
WLSY-FM - 94.7 (Louisville, KY) **12260**
WLSZ-FM - 105.3 (Humboldt, TN) **29228**
WLTA-AM **7170***
WLTA-AM - 1400 (Atlanta, GA) **7076**
WLTA-FM **10316***
WLTB-FM **23949***
WLTB-FM - 101.7 (Vestal, NY) **23492**
WLTC-AM (Gastonia, NC) *Unable to locate*
WLTD-AM **8877***
WLTD-FM (Jackson, MS) *Unable to locate*
WLTE-FM - 102.9 (Minneapolis, MN) **16163**
WLTF-FM **24982***
WLTG-AM (Panama City, FL) *Unable to locate*
WLTH-AM - 1370 (Merrillville, IN) **10301**
WLTI-FM **14959***
WLTI-FM **14282***
WLTI-FM - 105.9 (Syracuse, NY) **23439**
WLTJ-FM - 92.9 (Pittsburgh, PA) **27867**
WLTK-FM - 103.3 (Broadway, VA) **31904**
WLTM-AM **23901***
WLTN-AM - 1400 (Littleton, NH) **18551**
WLTN-FM - 96.7 (Littleton, NH) **18552**
WLTP-AM - 1450 (Vienna, WV) **33481**
WLTQ-FM - 97.3 (Milwaukee, WI) **34125**
WLTR-FM (Columbia, SC) *Unable to locate*
WLTS-FM - 105.3 (Metairie, LA) **12684**
WLTT-AM **13701***
WLTT-FM - 103.7 (Shallotte, NC) **24225**
WLTU-FM - 92.1 (Manitowoc, WI) **34015**
WLTV-TV **11952***
WLTV-TV - Channel 23 (Miami, FL) **6404**
WLTW (New York, NY) *Unable to locate*
WLTX-TV - Channel 19 (Columbia, SC) **28578**
WLTY-FM - 96.7 (Columbia, SC) **28579**
WLTZ-TV - Channel 38 (Columbus, GA) **7190**
WLUC-TV - Channel 6 (Negaunee, MI) **15397**
WLUJ-FM - 89.7 (Springfield, IL) **9651**
WLUK-TV - Channel 11 (Green Bay, WI) **33751**
WLUM-FM - 102.1 (Milwaukee, WI) **34126**
WLUN-FM - 95.3 (Wiggins, MS) **16878**
WLUP-FM - 97.9 (Chicago, IL) **8640**
WLUR-FM - 91.5 (Lexington, VA) **32194**
WLUS-AM - 980 (Gainesville, FL) **6164**
WLUV-AM (Rockford, IL) *Unable to locate*
WLUV-FM **31546***
WLUV-FM - 96.7 (Rockford, IL) **9538**
WLUW-FM - 88.7 (Chicago, IL) **8641**
WLUX-AM **12519***
WLUZ-AM - 1600 (Bayamon, PR) **28232**
WLVA-AM - 590 (Lynchburg, VA) **32214**
WLVA-TV **32216***
WLVE-FM **34006***
WLVE-FM - 93.9 (Miramar, FL) **6431**
WLVF-AM (Haines City, FL) *Unable to locate*
WLVF-FM (Haines City, FL) *Unable to locate*
WLVG-AM **14115***
WLVG-AM (Boston, MA) *Unable to locate*
WLVH-FM **4867***
WLVI-TV - Channel 56 (Boston, MA) **13989**
WLVJ-AM - 640 (West Palm Beach, FL) **6854**
WLVL-AM - 1340 (Lockport, NY) **20958**
WLVM-AM **14875***
WLVN-AM - 1080 (Luverne, AL) **309**
WLVO-FM - 106.1 (Live Oak, FL) **6307**
WLVQ-FM - 96.3 (Columbus, OH) **25080**
WLVR-FM (Bethlehem, PA) *Unable to locate*
WLVS-AM **6861***
WLVT-TV - Channel 39 (Bethlehem, PA) **26712**
WLVU-AM (Palm Harbor, FL) *Unable to locate*
WLVU-FM **26913***
WLVU-FM - 106.3 (Tampa, FL) **6794**
WLVV-FM **6560***
WLVX-AM (Bay Shore, NY) *Ceased*
WLVY-FM - 94.3 (Elmira, NY) **20577**
WLW-AM - 700 (Cincinnati, OH) **24843**
WLWC-TV **25077***
WLWD-TV **25137***
WLWI-AM **390***
WLWI-FM - 92.3 (Montgomery, AL) **387**
WLWI-TV **10213***
WLWL-AM - 770 (Rockingham, NC) **24203**
WLWT-TV (Cincinnati, OH) *Unable to locate*

WLXC-FM - 98.5 (Columbia, SC) **28580**
WLXG-AM - 1300 (Lexington, KY) **12192**
WLXI-TV - Channel 61 (Greensboro, NC) **23952**
WLXN-AM - 1440 (Lexington, NC) **24041**
WLXR-FM - 104.9 (Onalaska, WI) **34215**
WLXT-FM - 96.3 (Petoskey, MI) **15439**
WLXV-FM - 96.7 (Cadillac, MI) **14849**
WLXY-FM - 100.7 (Tuscaloosa, AL) **497**
WLYC-AM (Williamsport, PA) *Unable to locate*
WLYC-FM **28192***
WLYF-FM - 101.5 (Miami, FL) **6405**
WLYH-TV - Channel 15 (Harrisburg, PA) **27021**
WLYJ-TV (Clarksburg, WV) *Unable to locate*
WLYK-FM - 100.1 (Lynchburg, VA) **32215**
WLYN-AM - 101.7 (Marblehead, MA) **14305**
WLYT-FM **14233***
WLYT-FM - 102.9 (Charlotte, NC) **23774**
WLYU-FM (Lyons, GA) *Unable to locate*
WLYV-AM (Fort Wayne, IN) *Unable to locate*
WLYY-FM **15298***
WLZA-FM - 96.1 (Starkville, MS) **16847**
WLZK-FM - 94.1 (Paris, TN) **29561**
WLZR-AM **34122***
WLZR-FM **10262***
WLZR-FM - 102.9 (Milwaukee, WI) **34127**
WLZT-FM (Charleston, WV) *Unable to locate*
WLZW-FM - 98.7 (Whitesboro, NY) **23580**
WMAA-FM **16724***
WMAA-TV **16725***
WMAB-FM - 89.9 (Mississippi State, MS) **16786**
WMAB-TV - Channel 2 (Mississippi State, MS) **16787**
WMAC-AM **7433***
WMAC-AM - 940 (Macon, GA) **7397**
WMAD-AM **34004***
WMAD-FM (Sun Prairie, WI) *Unable to locate*
WMAE-FM - 91.3 (Booneville, MS) **16574**
WMAE-TV - Channel 12 (Jackson, MS) **16723**
WMAG-FM (High Point, NC) *Unable to locate*
WMAH-FM - 90.3 (Biloxi, MS) **16566**
WMAH-TV - Channel 19 (Biloxi, MS) **16567**
WMAJ-AM - 1450 (State College, PA) **28025**
WMAK-AM **29523***
WMAK-FM **29527***
WMAK-FM - 96.3 (Nashville, TN) **29519**
WMAL-AM - 630 (Washington, DC) **5889**
WMAL-FM **5894***
WMAL-FM **5886***
WMAM-AM - 570 (Marinette, WI) **34022**
WMAN-AM - 1400 (Mansfield, OH) **25335**
WMAO-FM - 90.9 (Greenwood, MS) **16651**
WMAO-TV - Channel 23 (Greenwood, MS) **16652**
WMAP-AM (Monroe, NC) *Unable to locate*
WMAP-FM **28740***
WMAQ-AM **8652***
WMAQ-AM - 670 (Chicago, IL) **8642**
WMAQ-TV - Channel 5 (Chicago, IL) **8643**
WMAR-TV - Channel 2 (Baltimore, MD) **13279**
WMAS-AM - 1450 (Springfield, MA) **14559**
WMAS-FM - 94.7 (Springfield, MA) **14560**
WMAU-FM - 88.9 (Meadville, MS) **16768**
WMAU-TV (Jackson, MS) *Unable to locate*
WMAV-FM - 90.3 (Oxford, MS) **16808**
WMAV-TV - Channel 18 (Oxford, MS) **16809**
WMAW-FM - 88.1 (Meridian, MS) **16776**
WMAW-TV - Channel 14 (Meridian, MS) **16777**
WMAX-AM **15109***
WMAX-AM (Grand Rapids, MI) *Ceased*
WMAX-FM **7363***
WMAY-AM - 970 (Spaulding, IL) **9619**
WMAZ-AM **7397***
WMAZ-AM (Macon, GA) *Unable to locate*
WMAZ-FM **7389***
WMAZ-TV - Channel 13 (Macon, GA) **7398**
WMBA-AM - 1460 (Beaver Falls, PA) **26687**
WMBB-TV - Channel 13 (Panama City, FL) **6561**
WMBC-AM **16610***
WMBC-FM - 103.1 (Columbus, MS) **16612**
WMBC-TV - Channel 63 (West Caldwell, NJ) **19720**
WMBD-AM - 1470 (Peoria, IL) **9433**
WMBD-TV - Channel 31 (Peoria, IL) **9434**
WMBE-AM (Chilton, WI) *Unable to locate*
WMBG-AM - 740 (Williamsburg, VA) **32626**
WMBH-FM **17144***
WMBI-AM - 1110 (Chicago, IL) **8644**
WMBI-FM - 90.1 (Chicago, IL) **8645**
WMBL-AM (Morehead City, NC) *Unable to locate*
WMBL-FM **24101***
WMBM-AM - 1490 (Miami Beach, FL) **6418**
WMBN-AM - 1340 (Petoskey, MI) **15440**
WMBO-AM (Auburn, NY) *Unable to locate*
WMBP-FM - 91.9 (Belpre, OH) **24675**
WMBR-FM - 88.1 (Cambridge, MA) **14116**
WMBR-TV **6230***
WMBS-AM - 590 (Uniontown, PA) **28068**
WMBT-AM - 1530 (Shenandoah, PA) **27987**
WMBV-FM - 91.9 (Dixons Mills, AL) **183**
WMBW-FM - 88.9 (Chattanooga, TN) **29107**
WMBX-FM - 102.3 (West Palm Beach, FL) **6855**
WMBY-FM **8631***

WMC-AM - 790 (Memphis, TN) **29403**
WMC-FM - 99.7 (Memphis, TN) **29404**
WMC-TV (Memphis, TN) *Unable to locate*
WMCA-AM - 570 (New York, NY) **22974**
WMCB-AM - 1540 (Martinsville, IN) **10297**
WMCB-FM **10306***
WMCD-FM - 100.1 (Statesboro, GA) **7566**
WMCF-TV - Channel 45 (Montgomery, AL) **388**
WMCG-FM - 104.9 (Dublin, GA) **7253**
WMCH-AM - 1260 (Church Hill, TN) **29113**
WMCJ-AM - 950 (Charleston, SC) **28523**
WMCL-AM - 1060 (McLeansboro, IL) **9168**
WMCL-FM **26747***
WMCM-FM (Rockland, ME) *Unable to locate*
WMCN-FM - 91.7 (St. Paul, Mn) **16428**
WMCO-FM - 90.7 (New Concord, OH) **25410**
WMCP-AM - 1280 (Columbia, TN) **29141**
WMCQ-FM (Richmond, KY) *Ceased*
WMCR-AM **9219***
WMCR-AM - 1600 (Oneida, NY) **23047**
WMCR-FM **15256***
WMCR-FM - 88.9 (Monmouth, IL) **9219**
WMCR-FM - 106.3 (Oneida, NY) **23048**
WMCRS **31562***
WMCS-AM - 1290 (Milwaukee, WI) **34128**
WMCT-AM - 1390 (Mountain City, TN) **29427**
WMCU-FM - 89.7 (Miami, FL) **6406**
WMCW-AM - 1600 (Harvard, IL) **8975**
WMCX-FM - 88.9 (West Long Branch, NJ) **19723**
WMDB-AM - 880 (Nashville, TN) **29520**
WMDC-FM - 98.7 (Mayville, WI) **34033**
WMDD-AM - 1480 (Fajardo, PR) **28244**
WMDH-AM - 1550 (New Castle, IN) **10344**
WMDH-FM - 102.5 (New Castle, IN) **10345**
WMDJ-FM - 101.1 (Martin, KY) **12283**
WMDK-FM **13030***
WMDM-AM - 1690 (Lexington Park, MD) **13617**
WMDM-FM - 97.7 (Lexington Park, MD) **13618**
WMDN-AM **16773***
WMDO-AM (Silver Spring, MD) *Ceased*
WMDT-TV - Channel 47 (Salisbury, MD) **13717**
WMEA-TV - Channel 26 (Lewiston, ME) **12979**
WMEB-FM (Orono, ME) *Unable to locate*
WMEB-TV - Channel 12 (Bangor, ME) **12913**
WMEC-TV - Channel 22 (Macomb, IL) **9137**
WMED-TV - Channel 13 (Calais, ME) **12939**
WMEE-FM - 97.3 (Fort Wayne, IN) **9990**
WMEG-FM - 106.9 (Guaynabo, PR) **28247**
WMEJ-FM - 91.9 (Huntington, WV) **33342**
WMEK-AM - 980 (Chase City, VA) **31961**
WMEM-TV - Channel 10 (Presque Isle, ME) **13039**
WMEN-AM **6745***
WMEQ-AM - 880 (Eau Claire, WI) **33682**
WMER-AM (Meridian, MS) *Unable to locate*
WMER-FM **24752***
WMET-AM - 1150 (Gaithersburg, MD) **13552**
WMET-FM **8647***
WMEV-AM - 1010 (Marion, VA) **32227**
WMEV-FM - 93.9 (Marion, VA) **32228**
WMEX-AM (Boston, MA) *Unable to locate*
WMEZ-FM - 94.1 (Gulf Breeze, FL) **6183**
WMFA-AM - 1400 (Raeford, NC) **24122**
WMFC-AM - 1360 (Monroeville, AL) **352**
WMFC-FM - 99.3 (Monroeville, AL) **353**
WMFD-AM - 630 (Wilmington, NC) **24303**
WMFE Program Guide (Orlando, FL) *Ceased*
WMFE-TV - Channel 24 (Orlando, FL) **6522**
WMFG-AM - 1240 (Hibbing, MN) **15958**
WMFG-FM - 106.3 (Hibbing, MN) **15959**
WMFJ-AM - 1450 (Port Orange, FL) **6598**
WMFL-AM (Monticello, FL) *Unable to locate*
WMFL-FM (West Palm Beach, FL) *Unable to locate*
WMFM-FM - 106.3 (Hattiesburg, MS) **16675**
WMFN-AM - 640 (Grand Rapids, MI) **15115**
WMFO-FM - 91.5 (Medford, MA) **14325**
WMFP-TV - Channel 62 (Boston, MA) **13990**
WMFQ-FM - 92.9 (Ocala, FL) **6475**
WMFR-AM - 1230 (High Point, NC) **24005**
WMFS-FM - 92.9 (Memphis, TN) **29405**
WMFT **10495***
WMFX-FM (Columbia, SC) *Unable to locate*
WMGA-AM (Moultrie, GA) *Unable to locate*
WMGB-FM **12195***
WMGB-FM - 93.7 (Macon, GA) **7399**
WMGC-TV **20225***
WMGE-AM **7406***
WMGE-FM (Danville, KY) *Unable to locate*
WMGF-FM (Orlando, FL) *Unable to locate*
WMGG-FM **25075***
WMGG-FM (Gallipolis, OH) *Unable to locate*
WMGH-FM - 105.5 (Lansford, PA) **27164**
WMGI-AM **6161***
WMGI-FM - 100.7 (Terre Haute, IN) **10498**
WMGK-FM - 102.9 (Bala Cynwyd, PA) **26675**
WMGL-FM (Charleston, SC) *Unable to locate*
WMGM-FM - 103.7 (Linwood, NJ) **19172**
WMGM-TV - Channel 40 (Linwood, NJ) **19173**
WMGN-FM (Madison, WI) *Unable to locate*
WMGO-AM - 1370 (Canton, MS) **16585**

3540

Numbers cited in bold after listings are entry numbers rather than page numbers.

WMXC-FM - 99.9 (Mobile, AL) 346
WMXD-FM - 92.3 (Detroit, MI) 14973
WMXE-FM 27342*
WMXF-FM 23885*
WMXH-FM - 105.7 (Harrisonburg, VA) 32151
WMXJ-FM - 102.7 (Miami, FL) 6408
WMXK-FM - 94.1 (Morristown, TN) 29424
WMXL-FM - 94.5 (Lexington, KY) 12193
WMXM-FM - 88.9 (Lake Forest, IL) 9063
WMXN-AM - 98.3 (Scottsboro, AL) 449
WMXO-FM - 101.5 (Olean, NY) 23043
WMXP-FM 9436*
WMXQ-FM 132*
WMXQ-FM 6856*
WMXQ-FM - 102.9 (Jacksonville, FL) 6233
WMXR-FM - 93.9 (Lebanon, NH) 18545
WMXS-FM - 103.3 (Montgomery, AL) 391
WMXT-FM - 102.1 (Pamplico, SC) 28741
WMXU-FM - 106.1 (Columbus, MS) 16613
WMXV-FM 22993*
WMXW-FM - 103.3 (Vestal, NY) 23493
WMXX-FM - 103.1 (Jackson, TN) 29237
WMXY-FM - 98.9 (Boardman, OH) 24686
WMXY-FM - 98.9 (Youngstown, OH) 25708
WMXZ-FM - 95.7 (Metairie, LA) 12685
WMYA-FM 32305*
WMYF-AM (Exeter, NH) Unable to locate
WMYI-FM - 102.5 (Greenville, SC) 28637
WMYK-FM 32302*
WMYK-FM - 92.1 (Norfolk, VA) 32303
WMYL-AM 20852*
WMYM 34147*
WMYN-AM - 1420 (Mayodan, NC) 24062
WMYQ-AM (Newton, MS) Unable to locate
WMYR-AM - 1410 (Fort Myers, FL) 6109
WMYT-AM (Wilmington, NC) Unable to locate
WMYU-FM - 102.1 (Knoxville, TN) 29295
WMYX-FM - 99.1 (Hales Corners, WI) 33772
WMYY-FM (Cohoes, NY) Unable to locate
WMZK-FM - 104.1 (Merrill, WI) 34047
WMZQ-FM - 98.7 (Rockville, MD) 13703
WNAA-FM - 90.1 (Greensboro, NC) 23954
WNAC-TV (Rehoboth, MA) Unable to locate
WNAE-AM - 1310 (Warren, PA) 28107
WNAH-AM - 1360 (Nashville, TN) 29521
WNAH-FM (Nashville, TN) Ceased
WNAI-AM - 680 (Louisville, KY) 12261
WNAK-AM - 730 (Nanticoke, PA) 27308
WNAL-TV 126*
WNAM-AM - 1280 (Neenah, WI) 34160
WNAN-FM 182*
WNAP-AM - 1110 (Norristown, PA) 27338
WNAP-FM 10205*
WNAQ-AM 4905*
WNAR-AM 27338*
WNAS-FM (New Albany, IN) Unable to locate
WNAT-AM - 1450 (Natchez, MS) 16795
WNAU-AM - 1470 (New Albany, MS) 16799
WNAV-AM - 1430 (Annapolis, MD) 13101
WNAW-AM - 1230 (North Adams, MA) 14421
WNAX-AM - 570 (Yankton, SD) 29045
WNAZ-FM - 89.1 (Nashville, TN) 29522
WNBC-AM 4907*
WNBC-FM 5205*
WNBC-TV (New York, NY) Unable to locate
WNBF-AM - 1290 (Binghamton, NY) 20227
WNBF-FM 20224*
WNBF-TV 20851*
WNBG-AM 29645*
WNBH-AM (New Bedford, MA) Unable to locate
WNBI-AM - 980 (Park Falls, WI) 34235
WNBI-FM 34234*
WNBK-FM 33551*
WNBN-AM - 1290 (Meridian, MS) 16778
WNBP-AM - 1450 (Newburyport, MA) 14382
WNBR-AM (Fuquay Varina, NC) Ceased
WNBR-FM - 94.1 (Statesville, NC) 24249
WNBS-AM - 1340 (Murray, KY) 12320
WNBT-AM - 1490 (Wellsboro, PA) 28143
WNBU-TV 13991*
WNBY-AM - 93.7 (Newberry, MI) 15401
WNBY-FM - 93.7 (Newberry, MI) 15402
WNBZ-AM - 1240 (Saranac Lake, NY) 23298
WNCA-AM - 1570 (Siler City, NC) 24231
WNCB-FM 23676*
WNCB-FM - 89.5 (Duluth, MN) 15856
WNCC-FM - 96.7 (Franklin, NC) 23900
WNCD-FM (Boardman, OH) Unable to locate
WNCE-FM 27156*
WNCE-FM - 92.1 (Harrisburg, PA) 27022
WNCF-TV - Channel 32 (Montgomery, AL) 392
WNCG-FM (Clyde, OH) Unable to locate
WNCI-FM (Columbus, OH) Unable to locate
WNCK-FM 28380*
WNCM-FM - 88.1 (Jacksonville, FL) 6234
WNCN-TV (Clayton, NC) Unable to locate
WNCO-AM - 1340 (Ashland, OH) 24620
WNCO-FM - 101.3 (Ashland, OH) 24621
WNCQ-FM 23517*

WNCR-AM (Fair Bluff, NC) Unable to locate
WNCS-FM - 104.7 (Montpelier, VT) 31567
WNCT-AM - 1070 (Greenville, NC) 23972
WNCT-FM - 107.9 (Greenville, NC) 23973
WNCT-TV - Channel 9 (Greenville, NC) 23974
WNCU-FM - 90.7 (Durham, NC) 23849
WNCW-FM - 88.7 (Spindale, NC) 24243
WNDA-FM (Huntsville, AL) Unable to locate
WNDB-AM - 1150 (Daytona Beach, FL) 6044
WNDC-AM - 910 (Baton Rouge, LA) 12522
WNDE-AM - 1260 (Indianapolis, IN) 10203
WNDH-FM - 103.1 (Napoleon, OH) 25404
WNDI-AM - 1550 (Sullivan, IN) 10475
WNDI-FM - 95.3 (Sullivan, IN) 10476
WNDJ-FM - 104.9 (Urbana, VA) 32573
WNDN-FM (Salisbury, NC) Ceased
WNDR-AM (Jamesville, NY) Unable to locate
WNDS-TV - Channel 50 (Derry, NH) 18490
WNDU-AM (South Bend, IN) Unable to locate
WNDU-FM (South Bend, IN) Unable to locate
WNDU-TV - Channel 16 (South Bend, IN) 10464
WNDY-FM (Crawfordsville, IN) Unable to locate
WNDY-TV - Channel 23 (Indianapolis, IN) 10204
WNDZ-AM (Portage, IN) Unable to locate
WNEA-AM (Newnan, GA) Unable to locate
WNEB-AM (Worcester, MA) Ceased
WNEC-FM - 91.7 (Henniker, NH) 18523
WNED-AM - 970 (Buffalo, NY) 20408
WNED-TV - Channel 17 (Buffalo, NY) 20409
WNEG-AM - 630 (Toccoa, GA) 7606
WNEG-TV (Toccoa, GA) Unable to locate
WNEH-TV - Channel 38 (Greenwood, SC) 28649
WNEK-FM - 105.1 (Springfield, MA) 14561
WNEL-AM - 1430 (Caguas, PR) 28235
WNEM-TV - Channel 5 (Saginaw, MI) 15503
WNEO-TV - Channel 45 (Kent, OH) 25280
WNEP-TV - Channel 16 (Moosic, PA) 27296
WNER-AM 6308*
WNES-AM - 1050 (Central City, KY) 12015
WNET-TV - Channel 13 (New York, NY) 22975
WNEV-TV 13988*
WNEW-AM (New York, NY) Unable to locate
WNEW-FM - 102.7 (New York, NY) 22976
WNEW-TV 22982*
WNEX-AM (Macon, GA) Ceased
WNEX-FM 7388*
WNEZ-AM 4865*
WNFA-FM - 88.3 (Port Huron, MI) 15457
WNFB-FM - 94.3 (Lake City, FL) 6273
WNFI-FM 6535*
WNFK-FM - 105.5 (Perry, FL) 6583
WNFL-AM - 1440 (Green Bay, WI) 33752
WNFM-FM - 104.9 (Reedsburg, WI) 34282
WNFT-TV 6242*
WNFZ-FM (Knoxville, TN) Unable to locate
WNGC-FM - 106.1 (Athens, GA) 6957
WNGE-TV 29516*
WNGM-TV (Marietta, GA) Unable to locate
WNGO-AM 12285*
WNGZ-FM (Horseheads, NY) Unable to locate
WNHC-AM (North Haven, CT) Unable to locate
WNHI-FM - 93.3 (Concord, NH) 18479
WNHQ-FM - 92.1 (Portland, ME) 13030
WNHU-FM - 88.7 (West Haven, CT) 5208
WNHV-AM (White River Junction, VT) Unable to
  locate
WNHW-FM - 92.3 (Wanchese, NC) 24268
WNIB-FM (Chicago, IL) Ceased
WNIC-FM - 100.3 (Farmington Hills, MI) 15025
WNIJ-FM - 90.5 (DeKalb, IL) 8744
WNIK-AM - 1230 (Arecibo, PR) 28228
WNIK-FM - 106.5 (Arecibo, PR) 28229
WNIL-AM - 1290 (Mishawaka, IN) 10317
WNIN-FM - 88.3 (Evansville, IN) 9947
WNIO-AM - 1540 (Boardman, OH) 24687
WNIR-AM 10206*
WNIR-FM - 100.1 (Akron, OH) 24599
WNIS-AM 32306*
WNIT-TV - Channel 34 (Elkhart, IN) 9927
WNIU-FM - 89.5 (DeKalb, IL) 8745
WNIV-AM - 970 (Atlanta, GA) 7077
WNIX-AM - 1330 (Greenville, MS) 16642
WNIZ-FM (Chicago, IL) Ceased
WNJA-AM - 89.7 (Buffalo, NY) 20410
WNJB-TV - Channel 58 (New Brunswick, NJ) 19344
WNJC-AM (Deptford, NJ) Unable to locate
WNJC-FM 16843*
WNJN-TV - Channel 50 (Montclair, NJ) 19242
WNJR-AM - 1430 (New York, NY) 22977
WNJR-FM - 91.7 (Washington, PA) 28122
WNJS-FM - 88.1 (Trenton, NJ) 19677
WNJS-TV - Channel 23 (Camden, NJ) 18716
WNJT-TV - Channel 52 (Trenton, NJ) 19678
WNJU-TV - Channel 47 (Teterboro, NJ) 19614
WNJX-TV - Channel 22 (Mayaguez, PR) 28264
WNJY-FM 6856*
WNJY-FM 10263*
WNKI-FM (Corning, NY) Unable to locate
WNKJ-FM - 89.3 (Hopkinsville, KY) 12136

WNKO-FM - 101.7 (Newark, OH) 25430
WNKR-FM (Dania, FL) Unable to locate
WNKS-FM (Boston, MA) Unable to locate
WNKT-FM - 107.5 (North Charleston, SC) 28725
WNKU-FM - 89.7 (Highland Heights, KY) 12127
WNKX-AM - 1570 (Centerville, TN) 29085
WNKX-FM - 96.7 (Centerville, TN) 29086
WNKY-AM (Whitesburg, KY) Ceased
WNLA-AM - 1380 (Indianola, MS) 16688
WNLA-FM - 105.5 (Indianola, MS) 16689
WNLC-AM (New London, CT) Ceased
WNLE-FM (Yulee, FL) Unable to locate
WNLF-AM 14871*
WNLK-AM (Norwalk, CT) Unable to locate
WNLR-AM - 1150 (Churchville, VA) 31973
WNLS-AM - 1270 (Tallahassee, FL) 6752
WNLT-FM 6803*
WNLT-FM - 104.3 (Fairfield, OH) 25191
WNMB-FM (North Myrtle Beach, SC) Unable to
  locate
WNMC-FM - 90.7 (Traverse City, MI) 15612
WNMH-FM - 91.5 (Northfield, MA) 14436
WNMP-AM 8877*
WNMR-FM 15346*
WNMT-AM - 1520 (Savannah, GA) 7547
WNMT-AM - 650 (Hibbing, MN) 15960
WNMU-FM - 90.1, 107.1, 91.9, 91.3, 91.1, 107.3
  (Marquette, MI) 15346
WNMU-TV - Channel 13 (Marquette, MI) 15347
WNMX-FM - 1240 (Charlotte, NC) 23775
WNNC-AM - 1230 (Newton, NC) 24107
WNND-FM - 100.3 (Chicago, IL) 8646
WNND-FM (Cary, NC) Unable to locate
WNNE-TV - Channel 31 (White River Junction, VT)
  31617
WNNH-FM - 99.1 (Bow, NH) 18459
WNNI-AM - 1260 (Radford, VA) 32349
WNNJ-AM (Newton, NJ) Unable to locate
WNNJ-FM (Newton, NJ) Unable to locate
WNNK-FM - 104.1 (Harrisburg, PA) 27023
WNNR-AM 4884*
WNNR-FM 23000*
WNNS-FM - 98.7 (Springfield, IL) 9653
WNNT-FM - 100.9 (Warsaw, VA) 32608
WNNT-FM - 100.9 (Warsaw, VA) 32607
WNNW-AM - 1110 (Salem, NH) 18646
WNNX-FM - 99.7 (Atlanta, GA) 7078
WNNY-AM 14871*
WNNZ-AM - 640 (Springfield, MA) 14562
WNOE-AM (New Orleans, LA) Unable to locate
WNOE-FM - 101.1 (New Orleans, LA) 12771
WNOG-AM - 1270 (Fort Myers, FL) 6110
WNOI-FM (Flora, IL) Unable to locate
WNOK-FM - 104.7 (Columbia, SC) 28581
WNOK-TV 28578*
WNOL-TV (New Orleans, LA) Unable to locate
WNON-FM 10201*
WNOO-AM (Chattanooga, TN) Unable to locate
WNOO-FM 29104*
WNOP-AM (Cincinnati, OH) Unable to locate
WNOR-AM (Chesapeake, VA) Unable to locate
WNOR-FM (Chesapeake, VA) Unable to locate
WNOU-FM 5223*
WNOU-FM - 93.1 (Indianapolis, IN) 10205
WNOV-AM - 860 (Milwaukee, WI) 34134
WNOW-AM 26867*
WNOW-AM - 1030 (Charlotte, NC) 23776
WNOW-FM 26868*
WNOX-AM - 990 (Knoxville, TN) 29296
WNOX-FM (Knoxville, TN) Unable to locate
WNOZ-AM (Aguadilla, PR) Unable to locate
WNPB-TV 15347*
WNPB-TV - Channel 24 (Morgantown, WV) 33404
WNPE-TV - Channel 16 (Watertown, NY) 23518
WNPI-TV - Channel 18 (Norwood, NY) 23025
WNPQ-FM - 95.9 (Uhrichsville, OH) 25601
WNPR-FM - 89.1 (Norwich, CT) 5087
WNPT-AM 505*
WNPT-FM (Northport, AL) Unable to locate
WNPV-AM - 1440 (Lansdale, PA) 27161
WNPX-AM - 750 (Metropolis, IL) 9181
WNQM-AM - 1300 (Nashville, TN) 29523
WNQV-FM 24729*
WNRB-AM 24687*
WNRB-AM 24687*
WNRG-AM - 940 (Grundy, VA) 32123
WNRI-AM - 1380 (Woonsocket, RI) 28462
WNRJ-AM 7303*
WNRJ-AM (Circleville, OH) Unable to locate
WNRK-AM - 1260 (Palm Desert, CA) 2753
WNRN-FM (Charlottesville, VA) Unable to locate
WNRQ-FM (Nashville, TN) Unable to locate
WNRR-FM - 92.1 (Bellevue, OH) 24672
WNRS-AM (Ann Arbor, MI) Ceased
WNRS-AM - 1420 (Ilion, NY) 20780
WNRT-FM 28316*
WNRT-FM - 96.9 (Santurce, PR) 28316
WNRW-FM 32596*
WNRZ-FM - 91.5 (Nashville, TN) 29524

Numbers cited in bold after listings are entry numbers rather than page numbers.

WNSC-TV - Channel 30 (Rock Hill, SC) **28747**
WNSH-AM - 1570 (Beverly, MA) **13844**
WNSI-AM **6648***
WNSN-FM - 101.5 (South Bend, IN) **10465**
WNSP-FM - 105.5 (Mobile, AL) **347**
WNSR-FM **22993***
WNSS-AM (Syracuse, NY) *Unable to locate*
WNST-AM (Milton, WV) *Unable to locate*
WNSV-FM - 104.7 (Nashville, IL) **9278**
WNSY-FM - 100.1 (Canton, GA) **7154**
WNTA-AM (Rockford, IL) *Ceased*
WNTH-FM - 88.1 (Winnetka, IL) **9769**
WNTI-FM - 91.9 (Hackettstown, NJ) **18859**
WNTJ-AM - 96.5 (Johnstown, PA) **27096**
WNTK-AM - 1020 (New London, NH) **18610**
WNTK-FM - 99.7 (New London, NH) **18611**
WNTL-AM (Waldorf, MD) *Unable to locate*
WNTM-AM - 710 (Mobile, AL) **348**
WNTN-AM - 1550 (Newton, MA) **14413**
WNTQ-FM - 93.1 (Syracuse, NY) **23442**
WNTR-AM - 1230 (Cumberland, MD) **13478**
WNTR-AM (Silver Spring, MD) *Ceased*
WNTS-AM - 1590 (Indianapolis, IN) **10206**
WNTT-AM - 1250 (Tazewell, TN) **29626**
WNTV-TV - Channel 29 (Greenville, SC) **28638**
WNTW-AM (Winchester, VA) *Unable to locate*
WNTX-FM (Marshfield, MA) *Ceased*
WNTY-AM - 990 (Plantsville, CT) **5091**
WNUA-FM - 95.5 (Chicago, IL) **8647**
WNUB-FM - 88.3 (Northfield, VT) **31577**
WNUE-AM (Hawkinsville, GA) *Unable to locate*
WNUF-FM **27884***
WNUR-FM - 89.3 (Evanston, IL) **8876**
WNUS-FM - 107.1 (Vienna, WV) **33482**
WNUV-TV - Channel 54 (Baltimore, MD) **13281**
WNUY-AM **6823***
WNUY-FM - 100.1 (Bluffton, IN) **9865**
WNVA-AM - 1350 (Norton, VA) **32312**
WNVA-FM - 106.3 (Norton, VA) **32313**
WNVC-TV - Channel 56 (Falls Church, VA) **32063**
WNVE-FM - 95.1 (Rochester, NY) **23250**
WNVI-AM - 1460 (North Vernon, IN) **10365**
WNVL-AM (Nicholasville, KY) *Unable to locate*
WNVR-AM - 1030 (Northbrook, IL) **9324**
WNVT-TV - Channel 53 (Falls Church, VA) **32064**
WNVU-AM **27289***
WNWC-AM - 1190 (Madison, WI) **34004**
WNWC-FM - 102.5 (Madison, WI) **34005**
WNWI-AM - 1080 (Valparaiso, IN) **10514**
WNWK-FM - 105.9 (New York, NY) **22978**
WNWN-FM - 98.5 (Battle Creek, MI) **14797**
WNWO-TV - Channel 24 (Toledo, OH) **25582**
WNWR-AM - 1540 (Bala Cynwyd, PA) **26676**
WNWS-AM **6407***
WNWS-AM - 1520 (Brownsville, TN) **29073**
WNWS-FM - 101.5 (Jackson, TN) **29238**
WNWV-FM - 107.3 (Elyria, OH) **25182**
WNWY-FM **12995***
WNWZ-AM - 1410 (Grand Rapids, MI) **15116**
WNWZ-AM - 1430 (Memphis, TN) **29406**
WNXT-AM - 1260 (Portsmouth, OH) **25485**
WNXT-FM - 99.3 (Portsmouth, OH) **25486**
WNYB-TV **20411***
WNYB-TV - Channel 26 (Orchard Park, NY) **23059**
WNYC-AM - 820 (New York, NY) **22979**
WNYC-FM - 93.9 (New York, NY) **22980**
WNYC Program Guide (New York, NY) **22923**
WNYE-FM - 91.5 (Brooklyn, NY) **20358**
WNYE-TV - Channel 25 (Brooklyn, NY) **20359**
WNYG-AM - 1440 (West Babylon, NY) **23539**
WNYK-FM - 88.7 (Nyack, NY) **23028**
WNYM-AM **19418***
WNYO-FM - 88.9 (Oswego, NY) **23063**
WNYO-TV - Channel 49 (Buffalo, NY) **20411**
WNYS-AM **20407***
WNYS-FM **20402***
WNYS-TV **20559***
WNYT-AM - 550 (Old Westbury, NY) **23038**
WNYT-TV - Channel 13 (Menands, NY) **21069**
WNYU-FM - 89.1 (New York, NY) **22981**
WNYV-FM - 94.1 (East Poultney, VT) **31540**
WNYW-TV - Channel 5 (New York, NY) **22982**
WNZE-FM - 94.3 (Plymouth, IN) **10401**
WNZK-AM (Southfield, MI) *Unable to locate*
WNZR-FM - 90.9 (Mount Vernon, OH) **25401**
WNZS-AM - 930 (Jacksonville, FL) **6235**
WNZT-AM (Washington Boro, PA) *Unable to locate*
WOAB-FM - 104.9 (Ozark, AL) **420**
WOAC-TV (Canton, OH) *Unable to locate*
WOAD-AM (Jackson, MS) *Unable to locate*
WOAI-AM - 1200 (San Antonio, TX) **31079**
WOAI-TV **31063***
WOAK-FM - 90.9 (LaGrange, GA) **7364**
WOAL-FM **12369***
WOAM-AM **12052***
WOAM-AM - 1350 (Peoria, IL) **9435**
WOAP-AM - 1090 (Owosso, MI) **15430**
WOAS-FM - 88.5 (Ontonagon, MI) **15423**
WOAY-AM - 860 (Oak Hill, WV) **33418**

WOAY-TV - Channel 4 (Oak Hill, WV) **33419**
WOAZ-FM **13996***
WOBB-FM - 100.3 (Albany, GA) **6912**
WOBC-FM (Oberlin, OH) *Unable to locate*
WOBE-FM - 101.5 (Iron Mountain, MI) **15210**
WOBL-AM - 1320 (Oberlin, OH) **25450**
WOBM-AM - 1160 (Bayville, NJ) **18667**
WOBM-FM - 92.7 (Toms River, NJ) **19651**
WOBN-FM - 101.5 (Westerville, OH) **25647**
WOBO-FM - 88.7 (Owensville, OH) **25454**
WOBR-FM - 95.3 (Wanchese, NC) **24269**
WOBS-AM - 1530 (Jacksonville, FL) **6236**
WOBT-AM - 1240 (Rhinelander, WI) **34290**
Woburn Advocate (Concord, MA) **14149**
WOC-AM - 1420 (Davenport, IA) **10751**
WOC-FM **10745***
WOC-TV **10746***
WOCA-AM - 1370 (Ocala, FL) **6477**
WOCC-AM - 1550 (Corydon, IN) **9906**
WOCD-TV **20018***
WOCG-FM - 90.1 (Huntsville, AL) **285**
WOCH-AM **10365***
WOCL-AM **20844***
WOCL-FM - 105.9 (Orlando, FL) **6524**
WOCM-FM - 98.1 (Selbyville, DE) **5286**
WOCN-AM - 1450 (Miami, FL) **6409**
WOCN-FM - 103.9 (Hyannis, MA) **14252**
WOCO-AM - 1260 (Oconto, WI) **34205**
WOCO-FM - 107.1 (Oconto, WI) **34206**
WOCQ-FM - 103.9 (Georgetown, DE) **5256**
WOCR-FM - 89.7 (Olivet, MI) **15419**
WOCT-FM - 104.3 (Baltimore, MD) **13282**
WOCV-AM - 1310 (Oneida, TN) **29557**
WOCW-FM (Beaufort, SC) *Unable to locate*
WOCX-FM - 106.5 (Apalachicola, FL) **5906**
Wod Cable TV **24705***
WODC-FM - 88.5 - 103.7 - 103.9 - 97.9 (Virginia Beach, VA) **32595**
WODE-AM - 1230 (Easton, PA) **26853**
WODE-FM - 99.9 (Easton, PA) **26854**
WODI-AM - 1230 (Brookneal, VA) **31906**
WODJ-FM - 107.3 (Grand Rapids, MI) **15117**
WODL-FM - 106.9 (Birmingham, AL) **125**
WODS-FM - 103.3 (Brighton, MA) **14010**
WODT-AM - 1280 (New Orleans, LA) **12772**
WODT-AM - 1280 (New Orleans, LA) **12773**
WODU-AM - 1630 (Norfolk, VA) **32304**
WODY-AM (Bassett, VA) *Unable to locate*
WODZ-AM - 680 (Memphis, TN) **29407**
WODZ-FM - 96.1 (Marcy, NY) **21022**
WOEI-FM **10507***
WOEL-FM - 89.9 (Elkton, MD) **13497**
WOES-FM - 91.3 (Elsie, MI) **15006**
WOET-TV **25149***
WOEZ-FM **27272***
WOFE-AM - 580 (Rockwood, TN) **29579**
WOFF-FM **6913***
WOFL-TV - Channel 35 (Lake Mary, FL) **6282**
WOFM-FM **23288***
WOFM-FM - 94.7 (Wausau, WI) **34436**
WOFN-FM - 88.7 (Tulsa, OK) **26175**
WOFX-FM - 92.5 (Cincinnati, OH) **24845**
WOGG-FM - 94.9 (Brownsville, PA) **26738**
WOGH-FM - 103.5 (Steubenville, OH) **25542**
WOGK-FM - 93.7 (Ocala, FL) **6478**
WOGL-AM **26678***
WOGL-FM (Philadelphia, PA) *Unable to locate*
WOGO-AM - 680 (Chippewa Falls, WI) **33632**
WOGR-AM - 1540 (Charlotte, NC) **23777**
WOGX-TV - Channel 51 (Lake Mary, FL) **6283**
WOGY-AM - 1300 (Pittston, PA) **27892**
WOGY-FM - 94.1 (Memphis, TN) **29408**
WOHC-FM - 90.1 (Cedarville, OH) **24747**
WOHI-AM - 1490 (East Liverpool, OH) **25173**
WOHO-AM **25581***
WOHP-AM **24667***
WOHP-FM - 88.3 (Cedarville, OH) **24748**
WOHS-AM - 730 (Shelby, NC) **24229**
WOHT-FM **16596***
WOHZ-AM - 1600 (Carnegie, PA) **26765**
WOI-AM - 640 (Ames, IA) **10599**
WOI-FM - 90.1 (Ames, IA) **10600**
WOI-TV - Channel 5 (West Des Moines, IA) **11322**
WOIC-AM **28577***
WOIC-AM (Columbia, SC) *Unable to locate*
WOIO-TV - Channel 19 (Cleveland, OH) **24983**
WOIR-AM - 1430 (Homestead, FL) **6206**
WOIV-FM **20561***
WOIZ-AM (Ponce, PR) *Unable to locate*
WOJB-FM - 88.9 (Hayward, WI) **33789**
WOJO-FM - 105.1 (Chicago, IL) **8648**
WOJY-AM (Chicago, IL) *Ceased*
WOJY-FM **23947***
WOKA-AM **23093***
WOKA-AM (Douglas, GA) *Unable to locate*
WOKA-FM (Douglas, GA) *Unable to locate*
WOKB-AM **6531***
WOKB-AM (Orlando, FL) *Unable to locate*
WOKC-AM (Okeechobee, FL) *Unable to locate*

WOKC-FM (Okeechobee, FL) *Unable to locate*
WOKE-AM (Charleston, SC) *Unable to locate*
WOKE-FM - 98.3 (Garrison, KY) **12086**
WOKF-FM - 92.5 (Kingsland, GA) **7359**
WOKH-FM - 96.7 (Bardstown, KY) **11928**
WOKI-FM - 100.3 (Knoxville, TN) **29297**
WOKJ-AM (Bolton, MS) *Unable to locate*
WOKK-FM - 97.1 (Meridian, MS) **16779**
WOKN-FM (Goldsboro, NC) *Unable to locate*
WOKO-FM - 98.9 (Burlington, VT) **31526**
WOKQ-FM - 97.5 (Dover, NH) **18493**
WOKR-TV - Channel 13 (Rochester, NY) **23251**
WOKT-AM - 1040 (Ashland, KY) **11921**
WOKU-AM - 1080 (Hurricane, WV) **33349**
WOKW-FM - 102.9 (Clearfield, PA) **26790**
WOKX-AM - 1590 (High Point, NC) **24006**
WOKY-AM - 920 (Greenfield, WI) **33767**
WOKZ-AM **8011***
WOKZ-FM - 105.9 (Fairfield, IL) **8883**
WOL-AM - 1450 (Lanham, MD) **13611**
WOLA-AM - 1380 (Barranquitas, PR) **28230**
WOLC-FM - 102.5 (Princess Anne, MD) **13671**
WOLD-AM - 1330 (Marion, VA) **32230**
WOLD-FM - 102.5 (Marion, VA) **32231**
WOLE-TV - Channel 12 (Aguadilla, PR) **28222**
WOLF-AM - 1490 (Syracuse, NY) **23443**
WOLF-FM **15187***
Wolf Tales (Wesson, MS) **16873**
WOLF-TV - Channel 56/53 (Wilkes Barre, PA) **28177**
The Wolfe City Mirror (Wolfe City, TX) **31307**
Wolfe County News (Campton, KY) **12010**
WOLL-FM - 105.5 (West Palm Beach, FL) **6856**
WOLN-FM **23044***
WOLO-TV - Channel 25 (Columbia, SC) **28582**
WOLR-FM (Lake City, FL) *Unable to locate*
WOLS-AM - 1230 (Florence, SC) **28610**
Wolseley News; Indian Head- (Indian Head, SK, Can.) **37477**
WOLV-FM - 97.7 (Houghton, MI) **15187**
WOLW-FM - 91.1 (Gaylord, MI) **15076**
WOLX-FM - 94.9 (Madison, WI) **34006**
WOLY-AM - 1500 (Battle Creek, MI) **14798**
WOLZ-FM - 95.3 (Fort Myers, FL) **6111**
Woman *Ceased*
The Woman Activist (Falls Church, VA) **32060**
Woman Bowler (Greendale, WI) *Ceased*
Woman; Business (Bridgeport, CT) **4712**
Woman; Carolina (Cary, NC) **23685**
Woman; Catholic (Washington, DC) **5402**
The Woman Conductor (West Lafayette, IN) **10555**
Woman; Country (Greendale, WI) **33760**
The Woman CPA (Cincinnati, OH) *Ceased*
Woman Engineer (Melville, NY) *Unable to locate*
Woman; Indianapolis (Indianapolis, IN) **10134**
Woman Magazine; Today's (Louisville, KY) **12240**
WOMAN; NA'AMAT (New York, NY) **22390**
Woman; Polka—Polish (Scranton, PA) **27961**
Woman of Power (Orleans, MA) *Ceased*
The Woman Rebel (Boston, MA) *Unable to locate*
Woman; SpiritLed (Lake Mary, FL) **6280**
Woman Studies (Les Cahiers de la Femme); Canadian (Toronto, ON, Can.) **36535**
Woman Today; Lutheran (Minneapolis, MN) **16095**
Woman; Today's Chicago (Chicago, IL) **8583**
Woman; Today's Christian (Wheaton, IL) **9759**
Woman; Today's Insurance (Tulsa, OK) **26134**
Woman; Working (New York, NY) **22939**
Womanews (New York, NY) *Unable to locate*
Woman's Art Journal (Laverock, PA) **27168**
Woman's Day (New York, NY) **22924**
Woman's Day Best Ideas for Christmas (New York, NY) **22925**
Woman's Day Crosswords (New York, NY) *Ceased*
Woman's Day Eating Light (New York, NY) **22926**
Woman's Day Gardening & Outdoor Living (New York, NY) **22927**
Woman's Day Holiday Baking (New York, NY) **22928**
Woman's Day Home Decorating Ideas (New York, NY) **22929**
Woman's Day Home Remodeling (New York, NY) **22930**
Woman's Day Kitchens and Baths (New York, NY) **22931**
Woman's Enterprise (Agoura, CA) *Ceased*
Woman's Life (Port Huron, MI) **15452**
Woman's Quarterly (Greenville, SC) *Unable to locate*
Woman's Touch (Springfield, MO) **17618**
Woman's Weal (Lynden, WA) *Ceased*
Woman's World (Englewood Cliffs, NJ) **18804**
WOMC-FM - 104.3 (Ferndale, MI) **15031**
Women and Aging; Journal of (Sarasota, FL) **6659**
Women Artists News Book Review (New York, NY) *Unable to locate*
Women in the Arts (Washington, DC) **5862**
Women in Business (Kansas City, MO) **17204**
Women in Business; Texas (The Woodlands, TX) **31308**
Women & Criminal Justice (Shippensburg, PA) **27993**
Women & Environments (Toronto, ON, Can.) **36793**

Women; First for (Englewood Cliffs, NJ) **18800**
Women in Forestry **7922***
Women and Guns (Buffalo, NY) **20393**
Women and Health (Binghamton, NY) *Ceased*
Women and Health (New York, NY) **22932**
Women International; Health Care for (Wilmington, NC) **24295**
Women and Language (Fairfax, VA) **32034**
Women and the Law/Revue Femmes et Droit; Canadian Journal of (Toronto, ON, Can.) **36513**
Women and the Law; Texas Journal of (Austin, TX) **29829**
Women Lawyers Journal (Chicago, IL) *Unable to locate*
Women and Music (Lincoln, NE) **18128**
Women in Natural Resources (Moscow, ID) **7922**
Women & Politics Journal (Washington, DC) **5863**
Women Quarterly; Psychology of (Greensboro, NC) **23936**
Women; Scoregolf for (Toronto, ON, Can.) **36737**
Women and Social Work; AFFILIA: Journal of (Thousand Oaks, CA) **3847**
Women in Sport and Physical Activity Journal (Las Vegas, NV) **18387**
Women; Sports Illustrated for (New York, NY) **22778**
Women Studies Abstracts (Somerset, NJ) **19570**
Women & Success (New York, NY) **22933**
Women & Therapy (Binghamton, NY) **20221**
Women Today (Washington, DC) *Ceased*
Women; Violence Against (Thousand Oaks, CA) **3920**
Women & Work (Washington, DC) *Ceased*
Women Writers; Legacy: A Journal of American (Lincoln, NE) **18089**
Women's Association; Journal of the American Medical (New York, NY) **21983**
Women's Basketball; Coaching (Lilburn, GA) **7371**
Women's Circle (Berne, IN) *Unable to locate*
Women's Education des femmes (Toronto, ON, Can.) *Ceased*
Women's Health; Clinical Journal of (Detroit, MI) **14919**
Women's Health; Journal of **20919***
Women's Health; Journal of (Larchmont, NY) **20919**
Women's Health Weekly (Atlanta, GA) **7062**
Women's History (Unionville, PA) *Unable to locate*
Women's Household (Berne, IN) *Ceased*
Women's Household Crochet (Berne, IN) *Ceased*
Women's Imaging (Riverside, CA) **2949**
The Women's Journal (Beaverton, OR) *Unable to locate*
Women's Journal; U.S. - Japan (Palo Alto, CA) **2802**
Women's Law Journal; Berkeley (Berkeley, CA) **1500**
Women's League Outlook (New York, NY) **22934**
Women's Literature; Tulsa Studies in (Tulsa, OK) **26138**
Women's Lives; Confronting Violence in (Toronto, ON, Can.) **36558**
Women's Medicine; International Journal of Fertility and (Port Washington, NY) **23129**
Women's News (Harrison, NY) **20713**
Women's News (Kirkland, WA) *Unable to locate*
Women's Outdoor World (WOW) (Califon, NJ) **18712**
Women's Policy Journal of Harvard **14093***
Women's Political Times (Washington, DC) **5864**
Women's Press; Minnesota (St. Paul, MN) **16396**
Women's Quarterly (Arlington, VA) **31842**
The Women's Record (Greenvale, NY) *Ceased*
The Women's Review of Books (Wellesley, MA) **14619**
Women's Sports & Fitness (Boulder, CO) *Unable to locate*
Women's Sports Traveler (New York, NY) *Ceased*
Women's Studies (Claremont, CA) **1726**
Women's Studies in Communication (Athens, GA) **6953**
Women's Studies Newsletter **22935***
Women's Studies Quarterly (New York, NY) **22935**
Women's Times (San Diego, CA) *Unable to locate*
Women's Wear Daily (New York, NY) **38130**
Women's Wear Daily (New York, NY) **22936**
Women's Work (Snohomish, WA) *Unable to locate*
Women's World **5564***
Womens's Music Plus (Chicago, IL) *Ceased*
WomenWise (Concord, NH) **18475**
Wometco **7473***
Wometco Cable (Douglasville, GA) *Unable to locate*
Wometco Cable (Jonesboro, GA) **7352**
Wometco Cable Corp. (Miami, FL) *Unable to locate*
Wometco Cable TV of Alabama **188***
Wometco Cable TV of Georgia Inc. (Marietta, GA) *Unable to locate*
Wometco of Gwinnett (Norcross, GA) **7475**
WOMG-AM **28577***
WOMG-FM - 103.1 (Columbia, SC) **28583**
WOMI-AM - 1490 (Owensboro, KY) **12331**
WOMP-AM - 1290 (Bellaire, OH) **24663**
WOMP-FM - 100.5 (Bellaire, OH) **24664**
WOMR-FM - 92.1 (Provincetown, MA) **14487**
WOMT-AM - 1240 (Manitowoc, WI) **34016**

WOMX-AM (Winter Park, FL) *Ceased*
WOMX-FM - 105.1 (Orlando, FL) **6525**
Womyn's Press (Eugene, OR) *Ceased*
WONC-FM - 89.1 (Naperville, IL) **9276**
WOND-AM - 1400 (Linwood, NJ) **19174**
Wonder Science (Kearneysville, WV) *Unable to locate*
Wonderful West Virginia (Charleston, WV) **33281**
WONE-AM - 980 (Dayton, OH) **25148**
WONE-FM **25153***
WONE-FM - 97.5 (Akron, OH) **24600**
Wonewoc Reporter (Wonewoc, WI) **34472**
WONN-AM - 1230 (Lakeland, FL) **6294**
WONO-FM **28519***
WONQ-AM **5978***
WONQ-AM - 1030 (Casselberry, FL) **5977**
WONT-FM **15424***
WONU-FM - 89.7 (Bourbonnais, IL) **8096**
WONW-AM - 1280 (Defiance, OH) **25159**
WONX-AM - 1590 (Evanston, IL) **8877**
WONY-FM - 90.9 (Oneonta, NY) **23053**
WONZ-AM **19176***
WONZ-AM (Hammonton, NJ) *Unable to locate*
WOOD (Des Moines, IA) **10815**
WOOD-AM - 1300 (Grand Rapids, MI) **15118**
Wood CableComm (Bowling Green, OH) **24705**
Wood County Democrat (Quitman, TX) **30968**
Wood Dale Press; Bensenville / (Oak Brook, IL) **9341**
Wood Design & Building (Ottawa, ON, Can.) **36281**
Wood Digest (Fort Atkinson, WI) **33722**
Wood & Fiber Science (Blacksburg, VA) **31880**
WOOD-FM - 105.7 (Grand Rapids, MI) **15120**
WOOD-FM - 105.7 (Grand Rapids, MI) **15119**
Wood Journal; Specialty (Vancouver, BC, Can.) **35168**
Wood Lake Cable TV (Redwood Falls, MN) **16302**
Wood Lebois (Ottawa, ON, Can.) **36282**
Wood 'n Energy **18537***
Wood Preservatives; China (Woodinville, WA) **33211**
Wood Pulp Monthly Statistical Summary; Paper, Paperboard, and (Washington, DC) **5714**
Wood-Ridge Independent (Wood-Ridge, NJ) *Ceased*
Wood River Journal (Hailey, ID) **7860**
The Wood River Sunbeam (Wood River, NE) **18318**
Wood Strokes & Woodcrafts (Concord, CA) **1759**
Wood Technology (Manhasset, NY) **21019**
WOOD-TV - Channel 8 (Grand Rapids, MI) **15121**
Wood); 2x4 (All About (Victoriaville, QC, Can.) **37433**
Wood & Wood Products (Lincolnshire, IL) **9089**
WOODALL's California RV Traveler (Ventura, CA) **4016**
WOODALL'S Camp-orama (Ventura, CA) **4017**
WOODALL'S Camperways (Ventura, CA) **4018**
WOODALL'S Campground Management (Syracuse, IN) **10479**
WOODALL's Carolina RV Traveler (Ventura, CA) **4019**
WOODALL's Discover RVing (Ventura, CA) *Ceased*
WOODALL's Midwest RV Traveler (Ventura, CA) **4020**
WOODALL's Northeast Outdoors (Ventura, CA) **4021**
WOODALL's Northeast Summers (Ventura, CA) **4022**
WOODALL'S Southern RV (Ventura, CA) **4023**
WOODALL'S Sunny Destinations (Ventura, CA) **4024**
WOODALL's Texas RV (Ventura, CA) **4025**
Woodbridge Advertiser (Beeton, ON, Can.) **35674**
Woodburn Independent (Woodburn, OR) **26619**
Woodbury Bulletin (Woodbury, MN) **16538**
Woodbury Pennysaver; Syosset/ (Syosset, NY) **23384**
Woodbury Photo News; Monroe (Woodbury, NY) **23592**
Woodbury-South Maplewood Review (North St. Paul, MN) **16232**
Woodcrafts; Weekend (Concord, CA) **1758**
The Wooden Horse (St. Petersburg, FL) **6636**
WoodenBoat (Brooklin, ME) **12933**
Woodford County Journal-Eureka Edition (Eureka, IL) **8847**
Woodford County Journal-Minonk Edition (Minonk, IL) **9200**
Woodford County Journal-Roanoke Edition (Roanoke, IL) **9511**
Woodford Star (Eureka, IL) **8848**
Woodford Sun (Versailles, KY) **12429**
Woodinville Citizen **32664***
Woodinville WEEKLY (Woodinville, WA) **33217**
Woodlake Echo (Exeter, CA) *Ceased*
Woodland Hills Progress (Monroeville, PA) **27288**
The Woodlands Sun (Pasadena, TX) *Unable to locate*
WOODMEN Magazine (Omaha, NE) **18209**
Woodmen Magazine; The Modern (Rock Island, IL) **9518**
Woodmen of the World Magazine **18209***
Woodmere Pennysaver; Hewlett/ (Hewlett, HI) **7669**
Woodmere Shopper's Guide; Hewlett/ (Ontario, ON, Can.) **36165**
Woodnotes, 1989-1997 **32935***
Woodridge-Maywood-Rochelle Park Shopper; Lodi-Hasbrouck Heights- (Lodi, NJ) **19179**

Woodridge Progress (Downers Grove, IL) **8799**
The Woodruff News (Woodruff, SC) **28788**
Woods County Enterprise (Waynoka, OK) **26184**
Woods County News **25737***
The Woods Lake News (Wood Lake, MN) *Unable to locate*
Woods and Waters; Eastern (Dartmouth, NS, Can.) **35546**
Woodshop News (Essex, CT) **4785**
Woodside Herald (Long Island City, NY) *Unable to locate*
Woodsman **31309***
Woodsmith (Des Moines, IA) **10816**
The Woodstock Independent (Woodstock, IL) **9772**
Woodstock Times (Kingston, NY) **20862**
Woodturner; American (Shoreview, MN) **16446**
Woodville Leader (Woodville, WI) **34473**
The Woodville Republican (Woodville, MS) **16882**
Woodward (Bloomfield Hills, MI) *Unable to locate*
Woodward News (Woodward, OK) **26198**
Woodwork (Novato, CA) **2654**
Woodworker; American (Eagan, MN) **15861**
Woodworker Projects & Techniques (Cincinnati, OH) *Ceased*
Woodworker's Journal (Medina, MN) **16049**
Woodworkers West (Los Angeles, CA) **2439**
Woodworking (Markham, ON, Can.) **36033**
Woodworking Business; CWB: Custom (Lincolnshire, IL) **9085**
Woodworking; Fine (Newtown, CT) **5043**
Woodworking; Modern (Troy, MI) **15629**
Woodworks and Crafts; Creative (Newton, NJ) **19370**
Woody Woodpecker (Santa Monica, CA) *Unable to locate*
WOOF-AM (Dothan, AL) *Unable to locate*
WOOF-FM (Dothan, AL) *Unable to locate*
Wool Growers Magazine; Canadian Cooperative (Cookstown, ON, Can.) **35752**
The Woonsocket Call **28460***
Woonsocket News (Woonsocket, SD) **29035**
WOOO-AM **10453***
WOOO-FM **10453***
Wooster (Wooster, OH) **25673**
WOOW-AM - 1340 (Greenville, NC) **23975**
WOOX-FM **26690***
WOOZ-AM **24287***
WOOZ-FM (Carbondale, IL) *Unable to locate*
WOPA-AM **9379***
WOPC-TV **27090***
WOPI-AM - 1490 (Bristol, TN) **29069**
WOPP-AM - 1290 (Opp, AL) **414**
WOPW-FM **7107***
WOPX-TV - Channel 56 (Winter Park, FL) **6893**
WOPY-AM **24012***
WOQI-FM - 93.3 (Ponce, PR) **28279**
WOR-AM - 710 (New York, NY) **22983**
WOR-TV **19543***
WORA-AM - 760 (Mayaguez, PR) **28265**
WORA-FM **32603***
WORA-TV - Channel 5 (Mayaguez, PR) **28266**
WORB-FM - 90.3 (Farmington Hills, MI) **15026**
WORC-AM (Worcester, MA) *Unable to locate*
WORC-FM - 98.9 (Worcester, MA) **14699**
Worcester Business Journal (Worcester, MA) **14692**
Worcester County Messenger (Pocomoke City, MD) **13645**
Worcester Magazine (Worcester, MA) **14693**
The Worcester Phoenix (Boston, MA) **13972**
Worcester Telegram **14690***
The Word (Chicago, IL) *Unable to locate*
The Word (Indianapolis, IN) **10184**
Word (Toronto, ON, Can.) **36794**
WORD-AM - 1330 (Greenville, SC) **28639**
The Word Among Us (Ijamsville, MD) **13589**
WORD-FM - 101.5 (Pittsburgh, PA) **27868**
Word & Image (Philadelphia, PA) **27721**
Word Up! (River Edge, NJ) *Unable to locate*
Word from Washington (Washington, DC) *Unable to locate*
Word and Way (Jefferson City, MO) **17135**
WORD WAYS (Morristown, NJ) **19314**
Word and Work (Louisville, KY) *Unable to locate*
Worddance (Wilmington, DE) **5295**
WordPerfect Suite Magazine (Orem, VT) *Unable to locate*
Words; Golden (Kingston, ON, Can.) **35936**
The Wordsworth Circle (Philadelphia, PA) *Unable to locate*
WORG-FM (Santee, SC) *Ceased*
Work (Andover, MA) **13814**
WORK-AM **28214***
WORK-FM - 107.1 (Barre, VT) **31491**
Work and Occupations (Thousand Oaks, CA) **3921**
Work; Perspectives on (Champaign, IL) **8211**
Work Related Abstracts (Warren, MI) *Ceased*
Work & Stress (Philadelphia, PA) **27722**
Workbasket (Haddonfield, NJ) *Ceased*
Workbench (Des Moines, IA) **10817**
WorkBoat (Mandeville, LA) *Unable to locate*

Worker Co-op Magazine (Toronto, ON, Can.) *Unable to locate*
Worker; Darbininkas (The (Brooklyn, NY) 20311
Worker; The Revolutionary (Chicago, IL) 8556
Worker's Compensation Journal of Ohio (Cleveland, OH) 24966
Workers Vanguard (New York, NY) 22937
Workers World (New York, NY) 22938
Workforce 12077*
Workforce (Costa Mesa, CA) 1783
Workforce Diversity (Melville, NY) 21066
Workforce Diversity for Engineering and IT Professionals (Melville, NY) 21067
Workforce Journal 12077*
Workforce Professional (Frankfort, KY) 12077
Working America (Washington, DC) 5865
Working-Class History; International Labor and (New York, NY) 21926
Working Moms & Dads Magazine (Tucson, AZ) 974
Working Money (Seattle, WA) 33045
Working Mother (New York, NY) *Unable to locate*
Working USA (Armonk, NY) 20101
Working Woman (New York, NY) 22939
Worklife Report (Kingston, ON, Can.) 35949
Workout (Beverly Hills, CA) *Ceased*
Workplace News (Aurora, ON, Can.) 35652
Works and Days (Indiana, PA) 27078
Works in Progress (Olympia, WA) 32863
Workstation News (New York, NY) *Unable to locate*
World (Spencer, IN) 10472
The World (Coos Bay, OR) 26274
World Affairs (Washington, DC) 5866
World Affairs; The Fletcher Forum of (Medford, MA) 14321
World Affairs Report (Stanford, CA) *Ceased*
World Airshow News (Oregon, WI) 34219
World Around You (Washington, DC) 5867
The World Bank Economic Review (Washington, DC) 5868
World Bank Research Observer (Philadelphia, PA) *Unable to locate*
World Banking Abstracts (New York, NY) 22940
World of Beef 34625*
World of Beef & Feedlot Management 34625*
World Book of IABC Communicators (San Francisco, CA) *Ceased*
World Broadcast Engineering (Overland Park, KS) 11737
World Broadcast News 11737*
World Broadcast News (Overland Park, KS) 11738
World of Business); Alam Attijarat (The (Washington, DC) 5320
World Business Review (Baltimore, MD) *Unable to locate*
World Calendar (Bethesda, MD) 13389
World Climate Report (Ivy, VA) 32174
World Coffee & Tea (Olney, MD) *Unable to locate*
World Coin News (Iola, WI) 33857
World Dredging, Mining & Construction (Irvine, CA) 2093
World Economic Outlook (Washington, DC) 5869
World Electronic Developments *Ceased*
World Encounter (Chicago, IL) *Ceased*
World of Fandom (Tampa, FL) 6783
World Features Syndicate (La Jolla, CA) 38131
World Federation for Mental Health Annual Report (Baltimore, MD) 13263
World Fence News (Austin, TX) *Unable to locate*
World Futures (Philadelphia, PA) 27723
World Grain (Kansas City, MO) 17205
World of Hibernia (New York, NY) *Unable to locate*
The World & I (Washington, DC) 5870
World Images News Service (Alexandria, VA) *Unable to locate*
World Industrial Reporter (Reportero Industrial) (Great Neck, NY) 20695
World Investment News (Blaine, WA) *Unable to locate*
World Journal 2593*
World Journal (Ackley, IA) 10570
World Journal of Surgery (New York, NY) 22941
The World at Large (Brooklyn, NY) 20357
World Libraries (River Forest, IL) 9493
World Literature Today (Norman, OK) 25944
World Magazine 13969*
World M&A Network (Bellevue, WA) *Unable to locate*
World of Martial Arts 1939*
World Mining Equipment (New York, NY) 22942
World Monitor (Boston, MA) *Unable to locate*
WORLD; National Geographic (Washington, DC) 5675
World News Digest (New York, NY) 22943
World News Syndicate Ltd. (Hollywood, CA) 38132
World Newsmap of the Week (Northbrook, IL) *Ceased*
World Observer (Rockford, IL) *Ceased*
World Oil (Houston, TX) 30542
World Order (Wilmette, IL) 9764
World of Pageantry (Lynwood, CA) 2488
World Policy Journal (New York, NY) 22944

World Politics (Princeton, NJ) 19478
World of Politics (Dallas, TX) 30190
World Ports — American Seaports 6480*
World Press (Dearborn, MI) 38133
World Press Review (New York, NY) 22945
World Progress (Chicago, IL) *Ceased*
World Reporter (Los Angeles, CA) 2440
World Scanner Report (Dewey, AZ) 684
The World & Science (Los Angeles, CA) 2441
The World of Senior Golf (Fort Lauderdale, FL) *Ceased*
World Spectator (Moosomin, SK, Can.) 37504
World Tennis (New York, NY) *Ceased*
World Trade (San Francisco, CA) 3464
World Traveling (Farmington Hills, MI) *Ceased*
The World of Tribal Arts 3454*
World Tribune (Santa Monica, CA) 3720
World Union Press (New York, NY) 38134
The World (Vermont) (Barre, VT) 31490
World Vision Today (Federal Way, WA) 32766
World War II (Leesburg, VA) *Unable to locate*
World Watch (Washington, DC) 5871
World Watch/Foreign Affairs Syndicate (Jamaica, NY) 38135
World Water & Environmental Engineer (Houston, TX) *Unable to locate*
World Waterskiing 6889*
World of Wheels (Mississauga, ON, Can.) 36093
World Wide Web Journal (Sebastopol, CA) *Ceased*
World Wood (Manhasset, NY) *Ceased*
World Wrestling Federation Battlemania (New York, NY) *Unable to locate*
The WorldPaper (Boston, MA) 13973
Worldprofit Online Magazine (Cambridge, MA) 14112
Worldradio (Sacramento, CA) 3023
World's Fair (Corte Madera, CA) *Ceased*
WorldViews (Cedar, MI) *Ceased*
Worldwatch Paper Series (Washington, DC) 5872
Worldwide Challenge (Orlando, FL) 6511
Worldwide Media (Laguna Niguel, CA) 38136
Worldwide Projects (Milford, CT) *Ceased*
Worldwide Travel Planner (Skokie, IL) *Ceased*
Worldwide Vacations for Families (Waltham, MA) *Unable to locate*
Worldwide Waste Management (Tulsa, OK) 26144
Worm Digest (Eugene, OR) 26335
The Wormwood Review (Stockton, CA) *Ceased*
WORO-FM - 92.5 (San Juan, PR) 28306
Worship (Collegeville, MN) 15806
Worship (Nashville, TN) 29503
WORT-FM - 89.9 (Madison, WI) 34007
Worth/Chicago Ridge Star (Tinley Park, IL) 9690
Worth Citizen (Midlothian, IL) 9195
Worth Magazine (New York, NY) 22946
Worth; The Nicholls (Thibodaux, LA) 12860
Worth-Palos Reporter 9398*
Worth-Ridge Reporter 9398*
Worthington Globe (Worthington, MN) 16540
Worthington News (Worthington, OH) 25682
Worthington Times (Worthington, IN) 10568
Wortington Suburbia News 25682*
WORV-AM - 1580 (Hattiesburg, MS) 16676
WORX-AM 10286*
WORX-FM - 96.7 (Madison, IN) 10285
WOSC-AM 20633*
WOSH-AM (Oshkosh, WI) *Unable to locate*
WOSM-FM - 103.1 (Ocean Springs, MS) 16802
WOSO-AM (San Juan, PR) *Unable to locate*
WOSQ-FM - 92.3 (Marshfield, WI) 34030
WOSS-FM - 91.1 (Ossining, NY) 23060
WOSU-AM - 820 (Columbus, OH) 25082
WOSU-FM - 89.7 (Columbus, OH) 25083
WOSU-TV - Channel 34 (Columbus, OH) 25084
WOSX-FM 34030*
Wotanin-Wowapi (Poplar, MT) 17901
WOTB-FM - 100.3 (Newport, RI) 28375
WOTL-FM - 90.3 (Toledo, OH) 25583
WOTR-AM 26810*
WOTR-FM - 96.3 (Lost Creek, WV) 33373
WOTS-AM (Kissimmee, FL) *Unable to locate*
WOTT-FM - 100.7 (Watertown, NY) 23519
WOTV-TV 15121*
WOTV-TV - Channel 41 (Battle Creek, MI) 14799
WOTW-FM 18607*
WOUB-AM - 1340 (Athens, OH) 24632
WOUB-FM - 91.3 (Athens, OH) 24633
WOUB-TV - Channel 20 (Athens, OH) 24634
WOUC-FM - 89.1 (Athens, OH) 24635
WOUC-TV - Channel 44 (Athens, OH) 24636
WOUL-FM - 89.1 (Ironton, OH) 25255
Wound Care; Advances in (Aurora, IL) 8038
(Wound, Ostomy, and Continence Nursing); Journal of WOCN (St. Louis, MO) 17464
Wound Repair and Regeneration (St. Louis, MO) *Ceased*
WOUR-FM - 96.9 (Utica, NY) 23475
WOUX-FM 15468*
WOVI-FM - 89.5 (Novi, MI) 15412
WOVK-FM - 98.7 (Wheeling, WV) 33507

WOVR-FM (Grosse Pointe, MI) *Unable to locate*
WOW-AM (Omaha, NE) *Unable to locate*
WOW-FM (Omaha, NE) *Unable to locate*
(WOW); Women's Outdoor World (Califon, NJ) 18712
WOWB-FM - 105.5 (Utica, NY) 23476
WOWF-FM (Royal Oak, MI) *Unable to locate*
WOWI-FM 10418*
WOWI-FM (Norfolk, VA) *Unable to locate*
WOWK-TV (Huntington, WV) *Unable to locate*
WOWL-AM 221*
WOWL-TV - Channel 15 (Florence, AL) 223
WOWN-FM - 99.3 (Shawano, WI) 34319
WOWO-AM - 1190 (Fort Wayne, IN) 9991
WOWO-FM (Fort Wayne, IN) *Unable to locate*
WOWQ-FM 26841*
WOWQ-FM - 102.1 (Du Bois, PA) 26841
WOWT-TV - Channel 6 (Omaha, NE) 18231
WOWW-FM 6580*
WOWZ-FM - 97.9 (Utica, NY) 23477
WOXF-AM 24112*
WOXF-FM 13992*
WOXO-FM - 92.7 (Norway, ME) 12995
WOXR-AM 416*
WOXX-FM - 99.3 (Franklin, PA) 26936
WOXY-FM - 97.7 (Oxford, OH) 25464
WOYE-FM - 94.1 (Mayaguez, PR) 28267
WOYK-AM - 1350 (York, PA) 28214
WOYL-AM - 1340 (Franklin, PA) 26937
WOYL-FM 27237*
WOYS-FM 5906*
WOZI-FM - 101.9 (Presque Isle, ME) 13040
WOZK-AM - 900 (Ozark, AL) 421
WOZN-AM 6244*
WOZN-FM - 98.7 (Key West, FL) 6258
WOZQ-FM - 91.9 (Northampton, MA) 14434
WOZZ-FM - 93.5 (Appleton, WI) 33551
WPAA-FM - 91.7 (Andover, MA) 13815
WPAB-AM - 550 (Ponce, PR) 28280
WPAB-FM 28279*
WPAC-FM - 92.7 (Ogdensburg, NY) 23034
WPAD-AM - 1560 (Paducah, KY) 12347
WPAG-AM 14780*
WPAJ-FM 28749*
WPAL-AM - 730 (North Charleston, SC) 28726
WPAM-AM - 1450 (Pottsville, PA) 27905
WPAN-TV (Fort Walton Beach, FL) *Unable to locate*
WPAP-FM (Panama City, FL) *Unable to locate*
WPAQ-AM - 740 (Mount Airy, NC) 24082
WPAR-AM 33481*
WPAR-FM 23994*
WPAR-FM - 91.3 (Salem, VA) 32522
WPAS-AM (Dade City, FL) *Unable to locate*
WPAT-AM (Clifton, NJ) *Unable to locate*
WPAT-FM - 93.1 (New York, NY) 22984
WPAX-AM - 1240 (Thomasville, GA) 7590
WPAY-AM - 1400 (Portsmouth, OH) 25487
WPAY-FM - 104.1 (Portsmouth, OH) 25488
WPAZ-AM - 1370 (Pottstown, PA) 27902
WPBA-TV - Channel 30 (Atlanta, GA) 7079
WPBC-FM - 99.5 (Bangor, ME) 12914
WPBF-TV - Channel 25 (Palm Beach Gardens, FL) 6547
WPBG-FM - 93.3 (Peoria, IL) 9436
WPBH-FM 4906*
WPBK-AM 15063*
WPBM-FM 28723*
WPBN-TV - Channel 7 (Traverse City, MI) 15613
WPBR-AM - 1340 (West Palm Beach, FL) 6857
WPBS-AM - 1040am (Conyers, GA) 7202
WPBS-FM 27746*
WPBT-TV - Channel 2 (Miami, FL) 6410
WPBX-FM - 88.3 (Southampton, NY) 23346
WPCB-TV - Channel 40 (Wall, PA) 28100
WPCC-AM - 1410 (Clinton, SC) 28541
WPCD-FM - 88.7 (Champaign, IL) 8232
WPCE-AM (Norfolk, VA) *Unable to locate*
WPCH-FM - 94.9 (Atlanta, GA) 7080
WPCJ-FM - 91.1 (Pittsford, MI) 15445
WPCK-FM - 104.9 (Oshkosh, WI) 34229
WPCM-AM - 920 (Burlington, NC) 23677
WPCM-FM 23676*
WPCN-FM - 88.1 (Point Pleasant, WV) 33440
WPCR-FM - 91.7 (Plymouth, NH) 18636
WPCT-AM 5095*
WPCT-FM 29167*
WPCV-FM - 97.5 (Lakeland, FL) 6295
WPCX-FM (Auburn, NY) *Unable to locate*
WPDC-AM - 1600 (Elizabethtown, PA) 26866
WPDC-FM 27045*
WPDE-TV - Channel 15 (Myrtle Beach, SC) 28710
WPDH-FM - 101.5 (Poughkeepsie, NY) 23160
WPDJ-AM (Huntington, IN) *Unable to locate*
WPDM-AM - 1470 (Potsdam, NY) 23142
WPDQ-AM (Boca Raton, FL) *Unable to locate*
WPDR-AM - 1350 (Portage, WI) 24263
WPDR-FM 34262*
WPDS-FM 6791*
WPDS-TV 10215*
WPDX-AM (Clarksburg, WV) *Unable to locate*

WPDX-FM (Clarksburg, WV) *Unable to locate*
WPEA-FM - 90.5 (Exeter, NH) **18508**
WPEC-TV - Channel 12 (West Palm Beach, FL) **6858**
WPED-AM **31950***
WPEG-AM **24328***
WPEG-FM (Concord, NC) *Unable to locate*
WPEH-AM - 1420 (Louisville, GA) **7377**
WPEH-FM - 92.1 (Louisville, GA) **7378**
WPEL-AM - 1250 (Montrose, PA) **27293**
WPEL-FM - 96.5 (Montrose, PA) **27294**
WPEN-AM - 950 (Bala Cynwyd, PA) **26677**
WPEO-AM - 1020 (Peoria, IL) **9437**
WPEP-AM - 1570 (Taunton, MA) **14585**
WPES-AM **31858***
WPET-AM - 950 (Greensboro, NC) **23955**
WPEX-AM (White Marsh, VA) *Unable to locate*
WPEZ-FM - 93.7 (Macon, GA) **7401**
WPFA-AM **6577***
WPFB-AM - 910 (Middletown, OH) **25379**
WPFB-FM - 105.9 (Middletown, OH) **25380**
WPFE-AM **7262***
WPFF-FM - 90.5 (Sturgeon Bay, WI) **34356**
WPFJ-AM - 1480 (Franklin, NC) **23901**
WPFM-FM (Panama City Beach, FL) *Unable to locate*
WPFP-AM **34235***
WPFP-FM **34234***
WPFR-FM **10497***
WPFR-FM - 93.9 (Dennison, IL) **8749**
WPFW-FM - 89.3 (Washington, DC) **5890**
WPFX-FM - 107.7 (North Baltimore, OH) **25433**
WPGA-AM - 980 (Macon, GA) **7402**
WPGA-FM (Perry, GA) *Unable to locate*
WPGC-AM - 1580 (Washington, DC) **5891**
WPGC-FM - 95.5 (Washington, DC) **5892**
WPGG-FM - 93.3 (Evergreen, AL) **211**
WPGH-AM **27872***
WPGH-TV - Channel 53 (Pittsburgh, PA) **27869**
WPGHY-AM - 1560 (Jasper, GA) **7343**
WPGI-FM - 100.9 (Elmira, NY) **20578**
WPGL-FM - 90.7 (Lake Katrine, NY) **20873**
WPGM-AM - 1570 (Danville, PA) **26820**
WPGM-FM - 96.7 (Danville, PA) **26821**
WPGO-FM **24224***
WPGS-AM - 840 (Titusville, FL) **6823**
WPGT-FM **29068***
WPGU-FM - 107.1 (Champaign, IL) **8233**
WPGW-AM - 1440 (Portland, IN) **10405**
WPGW-FM - 100.9 (Portland, IN) **10406**
WPGX-TV (Panama City, FL) *Unable to locate*
WPGX-TV - Channel 21 (Boston, MA) **13991**
WPHB-AM - 1260 (Philipsburg, PA) **27751**
WPHB-AM - 1260 (Philipsburg, PA) **27750**
WPHD-FM - 94.7, 95.3, 99.5 (Corning, NY) **20509**
WPHE-AM - 690 (Philadelphia, PA) **27738**
WPHG-AM - 1620 (Atmore, AL) **36**
WPHG-FM (Atmore, AL) *Unable to locate*
WPHI-FM - 103.9 (Conshohocken, PA) **26804**
WPHK-FM - 102.3 (Blountstown, FL) **5926**
WPHL-TV - Channel 17 (Philadelphia, PA) **27739**
WPHN-AM **12201***
WPHN-FM - 90.5 (Gaylord, MI) **15077**
WPHP-FM - 91.9 (Wheeling, WV) **33508**
WPHS-FM - 89.1 (Warren, MI) **15667**
WPHT-AM - 1210 (Bala Cynwyd, PA) **26678**
WPHY-AM **27137***
WPI Newspeak **14689***
WPIB-FM - 90.9 (Bluefield, WV) **33259**
WPIC-AM (Sharon, PA) *Unable to locate*
WPIE-AM - 1160 (Trumansburg, NY) **23464**
WPIG-FM - 95.7 (Olean, NY) **23044**
WPIM-FM - 90.5 (Martinsville, VA) **32239**
WPIN-AM - 810 (Blacksburg, VA) **31888**
WPIN-FM - 91.5 (Dublin, VA) **31999**
WPIQ-AM **7143***
WPIR-FM - 88.1 (Hickory, NC) **23994**
WPIT-AM - 730 (Pittsburgh, PA) **27870**
WPIT-FM **27868***
WPIX-TV - Channel 11 (New York, NY) **22985**
WPJB-FM - 102.7 (Narragansett, RI) **28364**
WPJK-AM - 1580 (Orangeburg, SC) **28735**
WPJL-AM - 1240 (Raleigh, NC) **24166**
WPJM-AM - 800 (Greer, SC) **28654**
WPJS-AM - 1330 (Naples, FL) **6453**
WPKE-AM - 1240 (Pikeville, KY) **12365**
WPKE-FM - 103.1 (Pikeville, KY) **12366**
WPKF-FM - 96.1 (Poughkeepsie, NY) **23161**
WPKH-FM (Portage, PA) *Unable to locate*
WPKK-FM **27939***
WPKM-FM **6802***
WPKM-FM (Scarborough, ME) *Unable to locate*
WPKN-FM - 89.5 (Bridgeport, CT) **4720**
WPKO-AM **25625***
WPKO-FM - 98.3 (Bellefontaine, OH) **24668**
WPKQ-FM - 103.7 (Dover, NH) **18494**
WPKR-FM - 99.5 (Oshkosh, WI) **34230**
WPKT-FM - 90.5 (Hartford, CT) **4906**
WPKY-AM - 1580 (Princeton, KY) **12376**

WPKZ-FM (Elkton, VA) *Unable to locate*
WPLA-FM - 93.3 (Jacksonville, FL) **6237**
WPLC-FM **6323***
WPLC-FM - 94.3 (Manassas, VA) **32225**
WPLG-FM **12508***
WPLG-TV - Channel 10 (Miami, FL) **6411**
WPLH-FM - 103.1 (Tifton, GA) **7603**
WPLJ-FM - 95.5 (New York, NY) **22986**
WPLK-AM **7501***
WPLK-AM - 800 (Palatka, FL) **6540**
WPLL-FM - 103.5 (Miramar, FL) **6432**
WPLM-AM - 1390 (Plymouth, MA) **14483**
WPLM-FM - 99.1 (Plymouth, MA) **14484**
WPLN-FM - 90.3 (Nashville, TN) **29525**
WPLO-AM **7071***
WPLO-AM - 610 (Lawrenceville, GA) **7369**
WPLP-AM **6793***
WPLR-FM - 99.1 (Milford, CT) **4961**
WPLS-FM - 96.7 (Greenville, SC) **28640**
WPLT-FM **14961***
WPLT-FM - 93.9 (Plattsburgh, NY) **23107**
WPLV-AM (Lanett, AL) *Unable to locate*
WPLW-AM (Pittsburgh, PA) *Ceased*
WPLX-AM - 1170 (Germantown, TN) **29207**
WPLY-AM (Muskegon, MI) *Ceased*
WPLY-FM - 100.3 (Conshohocken, PA) **26805**
WPLZ-AM **31969***
WPMB-AM - 1500 (Vandalia, IL) **9726**
WPMC-AM **26776***
WPME-AM **27911***
WPME-FM **27912***
WPMH-AM - 1010 (Chesapeake, VA) **31966**
WPMI-TV - Channel 15 (Mobile, AL) **349**
WPMO-AM **16814***
WPMP-FM **16564***
WPMR-FM (Mt. Pocono, PA) *Unable to locate*
WPMT-TV - Channel 43 (York, PA) **28215**
WPMW-FM (Mullens, WV) *Unable to locate*
WPNA-AM - 1490 (Oak Park, IL) **9379**
WPNC-FM (Plymouth, NC) *Ceased*
WPNE-TV - Channel 38 (Green Bay, WI) **33753**
WPNH-AM (Marlborough, NH) *Unable to locate*
WPNH-FM (Marlborough, NH) *Unable to locate*
WPNR-FM (Utica, NY) *Unable to locate*
WPNS-AM **14452***
WPNT-AM (Chicago, IL) *Ceased*
WPNT-FM **27867***
WPNT-FM **8646***
WPNT-FM (Milwaukee, WI) *Ceased*
WPNW AM - 1260 (Holland, MI) **15178**
WPNX-AM **7191***
WPNX-AM - 1460 (Columbus, GA) **7191**
WPOB-FM - 88.5 (Plainview, NY) **23101**
WPOC-FM - 93.1 (Baltimore, MD) **13283**
WPOE-AM **14223***
WPOK-AM (Pontiac, IL) *Ceased*
WPOK-FM **9466***
WPOL-AM - 1340 (Winston-Salem, NC) **24331**
WPOM-AM (West Palm Beach, FL) *Unable to locate*
WPON-AM - 1460 (Rochester, MI) **15467**
WPOP-AM - 1410 (Hartford, CT) **4907**
WPOR-AM (Portland, ME) *Unable to locate*
WPOR-AM (Portland, ME) *Unable to locate*
WPOS-FM - 102.3 (Holland, OH) **25248**
WPOW-FM - 96.5 (Miami, FL) **6412**
WPPA-AM - 1360 (Pottsville, PA) **27906**
WPPC-AM - 1570 (Ponce, PR) **28281**
WPPI-AM (Carrollton, GA) *Unable to locate*
WPPJ-AM - 670 (Pittsburgh, PA) **27871**
WPPK-FM **27939***
WPPL-FM - 103.9 (Blue Ridge, GA) **7134**
WPPT-FM **24845***
WPPX-TV - Channel 61 (Bala Cynwyd, PA) **26679**
WPQR-FM (Connellsville, PA) *Unable to locate*
WPRA-AM - 990 (Mayaguez, PR) **28268**
WPRB-FM - 103.3 (Princeton, NJ) **19481**
WPRD-AM (Orlando, FL) *Unable to locate*
WPRE-AM - 980 (Prairie du Chien, WI) **34270**
WPRE-FM **34271***
WPRH-FM **28583***
WPRI-TV - Channel 12 (East Providence, RI) **28346**
WPRJ-FM - 101.7 (Coleman, MI) **14889**
WPRK-FM - 91.5 (Winter Park, FL) **6894**
WPRL-FM - 91.7 (Lorman, MS) **16749**
WPRL-FM - 790 (East Providence, RI) **28347**
WPRM-FM (San Juan, PR) *Unable to locate*
WPRN-AM **141***
WPRN-FM - 107.7 (Butler, AL) **141**
WPRO-AM - 630 (East Providence, RI) **28348**
WPRO-FM - 92.3 (East Providence, RI) **28349**
WPRO-TV **28346***
WPRP-AM - 910 (Ponce, PR) **28282**
WPRQ-AM **29415***
WPRR-FM - 100.1 (Altoona, PA) **26640**
WPRS-AM - 1440 (Paris, IL) **9401**
WPRT-AM (Prestonburg, KY) *Unable to locate*
WPRU-FM **19481***
WPRV-TV (Rio Piedras, PR) *Unable to locate*
WPRW-AM (Manassas, VA) *Unable to locate*

WPRW-FM **6114***
WPRX-AM - 1120 (Hartford, CT) **4908**
WPRX-FM **11957***
WPRY-AM - 1400 (Perry, FL) **6584**
WPRZ-AM - 1250 (Warrenton, VA) **32605**
WPSA-FM - 98.3 (Paul Smiths, NY) **23084**
WPSC-FM - 88.7 (Wayne, NJ) **19710**
WPSD-TV - Channel 6 (Paducah, KY) **12348**
WPSE-AM - 1450 (Erie, PA) **26907**
WPSG-TV - Channel 57 (Philadelphia, PA) **27740**
WPSK-FM - 107.1 (Radford, VA) **32350**
WPSL-AM **27289***
WPSL-AM - 1590 (Port St. Lucie, FL) **6604**
WPSM-FM - 91.1 (Fort Walton Beach, FL) **6126**
WPSN-AM - 1590 (Honesdale, PA) **27054**
WPSO-AM - 1500 (Oldsmar, FL) **6485**
WPSR-FM - 90.7 (Evansville, IN) **9948**
WPST-FM - 97.5 (Princeton, NJ) **19482**
WPSU-FM - 91.5 (State College, PA) **28026**
WPSX-TV - Channel 3 (University Park, PA) **28087**
WPTA-TV - Channel 21 (Fort Wayne, IN) **9992**
WPTC-AM **7393***
WPTC-FM **20231***
WPTC-FM - 88.1 (Williamsport, PA) **28189**
WPTD-TV - Channel 16 (Dayton, OH) **25149**
WPTE-FM - 94.9 (Virginia Beach, VA) **32596**
WPTF-AM (Raleigh, NC) *Unable to locate*
WPTF-TV **24172***
WPTG-FM **27151***
WPTH-FM **9976***
WPTJ-TV (Johnstown, PA) *Unable to locate*
WPTL-AM - 920 (Canton, NC) **23683**
WPTM-FM - 102.3 (Roanoke Rapids, NC) **24196**
WPTN-AM - 780 (Cookeville, TN) **29150**
WPTO-TV - Channel 14 (Dayton, OH) **25150**
WPTQ-FM - 103.7 (Glasgow, KY) **12092**
WPTS-FM - 92.1 (Pittsburgh, PA) **27872**
WPTT-AM (Pittsburgh, PA) *Unable to locate*
WPTT-TV (Monroeville, PA) *Unable to locate*
WPTV-TV - Channel 5 (West Palm Beach, FL) **6859**
WPTW-AM - 1570 (Dayton, OH) **25151**
WPTW-FM **25141***
WPTW-FM **25134***
WPTX-AM **13617***
WPTY-TV (Memphis, TN) *Unable to locate*
WPTZ-TV - Channel 5 (Plattsburgh, NY) **23108**
WPUB-AM - 640 (New York, NY) **22987**
WPUB-FM - 94.3 (Camden, SC) **28502**
WPUL-AM **34246***
WPUL-AM **5920***
WPUL-AM - 1590 (South Daytona, FL) **6685**
WPUL-FM **34247***
WPUM-FM - 90.5 (Rensselaer, IN) **10418**
WPUP-AM **16553***
WPUP-FM - 103.7 (Bogart, GA) **7135**
WPUR-FM **6926***
WPUR-FM - 107.3 (Northfield, NJ) **19384**
WPUT-AM - 1510 (Patterson, NY) **23082**
WPUV-AM (Pulaski, VA) *Unable to locate*
WPVG-AM (Funkstown, MD) *Unable to locate*
WPVI-TV - Channel 6 (Philadelphia, PA) **27741**
WPVL-AM **25465***
WPVL-AM - 1590 (Platteville, WI) **34246**
WPVL-FM - 107.1 (Platteville, WI) **34247**
WPVO-AM - 1490 (Princeton, WV) **33443**
WPVR-FM - 94.9 (Roanoke, VA) **32501**
WPWA-AM - 1590 (Aston, PA) **26667**
WPWC-AM - 1480 (Triangle, VA) **32571**
WPWR-TV - Channel 50 (Chicago, IL) **8649**
WPWT-FM (Philadelphia, PA) *Ceased*
WPXA-TV (Marietta, GA) *Unable to locate*
WPXB-TV - Channel 60 (Manchester, NH) **18572**
WPXC-FM - 102.9 (Hyannis, MA) **14253**
WPXE-TV (Kenosha, WI) *Unable to locate*
WPXH-TV - Channel 44 (Birmingham, AL) **126**
WPXI-TV - Channel 11 (Pittsburgh, PA) **27873**
WPXN-FM - 104.9 (Paxton, IL) **9412**
WPXR-FM **10747***
WPXR-TV - Channel 38 (Roanoke, VA) **32502**
WPXT-TV - Channel 51 (Westbrook, ME) **13075**
WPXY-AM (Rochester, NY) *Unable to locate*
WPXY-FM (Rochester, NY) *Unable to locate*
WPXZ-FM - 104.1 (Punxsutawney, PA) **27912**
WPYK-AM - 1010 (Dora, AL) **184**
WPYX-FM - 106.5 (Albany, NY) **20014**
WPZA-AM **14780***
WQAA-FM **32205***
WQAB-FM - 91.3 (Philippi, WV) **33434**
WQAD-AM **9859***
WQAD-TV - Channel 8 (Moline, IL) **9209**
WQAI-AM (Fernandina Beach, FL) *Unable to locate*
WQAK-FM - 105.7 (Union City, TN) **29636**
WQAL-FM - 104.1 (Cleveland, OH) **24984**
WQAM-AM - 560 (Miami, FL) **6413**
WQAQ-FM - 98.1 (Hamden, CT) **4883**
WQAR-FM - 101.3 (Stillwater, NY) **23368**
WQAZ **16594***
WQAZ-FM (Cleveland, MS) *Ceased*
WQBA-AM (Miami, FL) *Unable to locate*

Numbers cited in bold after listings are entry numbers rather than page numbers.

WQBB-AM - 1040 (Knoxville, TN) **29298**
WQBE-AM - 97.5 (Charleston, WV) **33284**
WQBE-FM - 97.5 (Charleston, WV) **33285**
WQBH-AM - 1400 (Detroit, MI) **14974**
WQBK-AM (Albany, NY) *Unable to locate*
WQBK-FM (Albany, NY) *Unable to locate*
WQBN-AM - 1300 (Tampa, FL) **6799**
WQBR-AM (Jacksonville, FL) *Unable to locate*
WQBS-AM **28310***
WQBS-AM (Hato Rey, PR) *Unable to locate*
WQBX-AM **32348***
WQBX-FM (Alma, MI) *Unable to locate*
WQBZ-FM - 106.3 (Macon, GA) **7403**
WQCB-FM - 106.5 (Brewer, ME) **12928**
WQCC-AM **23777***
WQCC-FM - 106.3 (La Crosse, WI) **33895**
WQCD-FM - 101.9 (New York, NY) **22988**
WQCH-AM - 1590 (La Fayette, GA) **7361**
WQCK-AM **7408***
WQCK-FM **7481***
WQCK-FM - 92.7 (Baker, LA) **12480**
WQCM-FM - 96.7 (Halfway, PA) **26969**
WQCR-FM **31526***
WQCS-FM - 88.9 (Fort Pierce, FL) **6120**
WQCT-AM - 1520 (Bryan, OH) **24717**
WQCY-FM (Quincy, IL) *Unable to locate*
WQDE-AM **6907***
WQDK-FM - 99.3 (Ahoskie, NC) **23615**
WQDQ-AM - 1200 (Nashville, TN) **29526**
WQDR-FM - 94.7 (Raleigh, NC) **24167**
WQDW-FM (Kinston, NC) *Unable to locate*
WQDY-FM - 92.7 (Calais, ME) **12940**
WQEC-TV - Channel 27 (Quincy, IL) **9481**
WQED-FM - 89.3 (Pittsburgh, PA) **27874**
WQED-TV - Channel 13 (Pittsburgh, PA) **27875**
WQEL-FM - 92.7 (Bucyrus, OH) **24720**
WQEN-FM (Gadsden, AL) *Unable to locate*
WQEQ-FM **27886***
WQEX-TV - Channel 16 (Pittsburgh, PA) **27876**
WQEZ-FM - 94.3 (Peoria, IL) **9438**
WQFL-FM - 100.9 (Loves Park, IL) **9122**
WQFM-FM **34123***
WQFM-FM - 92.1 (Scranton, PA) **27969**
WQFN-FM **15124***
WQFN-FM (Muskegon, MI) *Ceased*
WQFN-FM - 100.1 (Scranton, PA) **27970**
WQFS-FM - 90.9 (Greensboro, NC) **23956**
WQFX-FM - 96.7 (Gulfport, MS) **16657**
WQGL-FM **16775***
WQGN-FM - 105.5 (New London, CT) **5024**
WQHH-FM - 96.5 (De Witt, MI) **14899**
WQHK-AM - 1380 (Fort Wayne, IN) **9993**
WQHL-AM - 1250 (Live Oak, FL) **6308**
WQHL-FM - 98.1 (Live Oak, FL) **6309**
WQHQ-FM - 104.7 (Salisbury, MD) **13718**
WQHR-FM - 96.1 (Presque Isle, ME) **13041**
WQHS-AM - 730 (Philadelphia, PA) **27742**
WQHS-TV - Channel 61 (Parma, OH) **25469**
WQHT-FM - 97.1 (New York, NY) **22989**
WQHY-FM - 95.5 (Prestonsburg, KY) **12373**
WQHZ-FM - 102.3 (Erie, PA) **26908**
WQIC-FM **16781***
WQIC-FM - 100.1 (Lebanon, PA) **27178**
WQID-FM **16568***
WQII-AM - 1140 (San Juan, PR) **28307**
WQIK-AM **6239***
WQIK-FM (Jacksonville, FL) *Unable to locate*
WQIN-AM - 1290 (Shenandoah, PA) **27988**
WQIS-AM - 890 (Laurel, MS) **16743**
WQIX-AM - 820 (Elmira, NY) **20579**
WQIX-FM **20578***
WQIZ-AM - 810 (St. George, SC) **28751**
WQJQ-FM - 105.1 (Jackson, MS) **16728**
WQJU-FM - 107.1 (State College, PA) **28027**
WQJZ-FM (Salisbury, MD) *Unable to locate*
WQKB-FM **27884***
WQKC-FM - 93.7 (Seymour, IN) **10450**
WQKI-AM (St. Matthews, SC) *Unable to locate*
WQKI-FM - 93.9 (Orangeburg, SC) **28736**
WQKK-FM **7432***
WQKK-FM - 99.1 (Johnstown, PA) **27097**
WQKL-FM - 107.1 (Ann Arbor, MI) **14779**
WQKR-AM - 1270 (Portland, TN) **29570**
WQKS-AM **12135***
WQKT-FM - 104.5 (Wooster, OH) **25677**
WQKX-FM - 94.1 (Sunbury, PA) **28040**
WQKY-FM - 99.3 (Emporium, PA) **26885**
WQKZ-FM **29059***
WQKZ-FM **20769***
WQKZ-FM - 98.5 (Jasper, IN) **10223**
WQLA-AM **29309***
WQLA-FM - 104.9 (La Follette, TN) **29311**
WQLH-FM - 98.5 (Green Bay, WI) **33754**
WQLJ-FM - 93.7 (Oxford, MS) **16810**
WQLK-FM - 96.1 (Richmond, IN) **10427**
WQLL-FM - 96.5 (Boston, MA) **13992**
WQLM-FM **6610***
WQLN-FM - 91.3 (Erie, PA) **26909**
WQLN-TV - Channel Q91.3 FM (Erie, PA) **26910**

WQLR-FM - 106.5 (Kalamazoo, MI) **15257**
WQLS-AM **25465***
WQLS-FM (Dothan, AL) *Unable to locate*
WQLT-FM - 107.3 (Florence, AL) **224**
WQLV-FM - 98.9 (Millersburg, PA) **27267**
WQLX-AM (Galion, OH) *Unable to locate*
WQLZ-FM - 92.7 (Springfield, IL) **9654**
WQME-FM - 98.7 FM (Anderson, IN) **9785**
WQMF-FM - 95.7 (Louisville, KY) **12262**
WQMG-AM (Greensboro, NC) *Unable to locate*
WQMG-FM - 97.1 (Greensboro, NC) **23957**
WQMR-AM **13053***
WQMR-FM **13627***
WQMR-FM **23588*** °
WQMR-FM **19343***
WQMS-AM **2***
WQMT-FM - 98.9 (Dalton, GA) **7225**
WQMU-FM - 103.1 (Indiana, PA) **27082**
WQMX-FM - 94.9 (Akron, OH) **24601**
WQMZ-FM - 95.1 (Charlottesville, VA) **31954**
WQNA-FM - 88.3 (Springfield, IL) **9655**
WQNI-FM **9479***
WQNS-FM (Waynesville, NC) *Unable to locate*
WQNX-AM - 1350 (Aberdeen, NC) **23612**
WQNY-FM - 103.7 (Ithaca, NY) **20821**
WQNZ-FM - 95.1 (Natchez, MS) **16796**
WQOD-FM **25702***
WQOK-FM - 97.5 (Raleigh, NC) **24168**
WQOL-FM - 103.7 (Port St. Lucie, FL) **6605**
WQON-FM (Grayling, MI) *Unable to locate*
WQOW-TV - Channel 18 (Eau Claire, WI) **33683**
WQOX-FM - 88.5 (Memphis, TN) **29409**
WQPC-FM - 94.3 (Prairie du Chien, WI) **34271**
WQPD-FM **6273***
WQPM-AM - 1300 (Princeton, MN) **16286**
WQPM-FM - 106.1 (Princeton, MN) **16287**
WQPO-FM - 100.7 (Harrisonburg, VA) **32152**
WQPR-FM - 88.7 (Muscle Shoals, AL) **400**
WQPT-TV - Channel 24 (Moline, IL) **9210**
WQPW-FM - 95.7 (Valdosta, GA) **7623**
WQQK-FM - 92.1 (Nashville, TN) **29527**
WQQQ-FM - 103.3 (Lakeville, CT) **4922**
WQQT-FM (Springfield, GA) *Unable to locate*
WQQW-AM (Waterbury, CT) *Unable to locate*
WQQY-FM **20013***
WQRC-FM - 99.9 (Hyannis, MA) **14254**
WQRF-TV - Channel 39 (Rockford, IL) **9539**
WQRI-FM - 88.3 (Bristol, RI) **28329**
WQRK-FM - 105.5 (Bedford, IN) **9800**
WQRL-FM - 106.3 (Benton, IL) **8073**
WQRP-FM (Dayton, OH) *Unable to locate*
WQRS-FM **15562***
WQRT-FM - 98.3 (Salamanca, NY) **23296**
WQRX-AM (Grovetown, GA) *Unable to locate*
WQRX-FM **8073***
WQSA-AM (Sarasota, FL) *Unable to locate*
WQSB-FM - 105.1 (Albertville, AL) **5**
WQSI-FM (Frederick, MD) *Unable to locate*
WQSM-FM - 98.1 (Fayetteville, NC) **23891**
WQSN-AM - 1660 (Kalamazoo, MI) **15258**
WQSR-FM (Towson, MD) *Unable to locate*
WQST-AM (Forest, MS) *Unable to locate*
WQST-FM (Forest, MS) *Unable to locate*
WQSU-FM - 88.9 (Selinsgrove, PA) **27979**
WQSY-FM - 103.9 (Hawkinsville, GA) **7324**
WQTC-AM **34378***
WQTC-FM - 102.3 (Manitowoc, WI) **34017**
WQTE-FM - 95.3 (Adrian, MI) **14713**
WQTL-FM (Ottawa, OH) *Unable to locate*
WQTQ-FM - 89.9 (Hartford, CT) **4909**
WQTR-FM (Amarillo, TX) *Unable to locate*
WQTU-FM - 102.3 (Rome, GA) **7506**
WQTW-AM - 1570 (Latrobe, PA) **27166**
WQUA-AM **10749***
WQUB-FM - 90.3 (Quincy, IL) **9482**
WQUE-FM - 93.3 (New Orleans, LA) **12774**
WQUL-FM - 97.7 (Griffin, GA) **7316**
WQUN-AM - 1220 (Hamden, CT) **4884**
WQUT-FM - 101.5 (Gray, TN) **29211**
WQVE-FM - 105.5 (Albany, GA) **6913**
WQVL-AM (Dover, DE) *Unable to locate*
WQVR-FM (Southbridge, MA) *Unable to locate*
WQWK-FM - 97.1 (State College, PA) **28028**
WQWM-AM (Kaukauna, WI) *Unable to locate*
WQWQ-AM (Muskegon, WI) *Unable to locate*
WQWV-FM - 103.7 (Petersburg, WV) **33430**
WQXA-AM - 1250 (Elizabethtown, PA) **26867**
WQXA-FM - 105.7 (Elizabethtown, PA) **26868**
WQXC-AM (Otsego, MI) *Ceased*
WQXC-FM - 100.9 (Otsego, MI) **15427**
WQXE-FM - 98.3 (Elizabethtown, KY) **12049**
WQXI-AM - 790 (Atlanta, GA) **7081**
WQXI-FM **7088***
WQXI-TV **7092***
WQXJ-FM **7175***
WQXK-FM - 105.1 (Youngstown, OH) **25709**
WQXL-AM - 1470 (Columbia, SC) **28584**
WQXM-FM **7388***
WQXO-AM - 1400 (Marquette, MI) **15348**

WQXO-FM **15342***
WQXQ-FM - 101.9 (Owensboro, KY) **12332**
WQXR-AM (New York, NY) *Ceased*
WQXR-FM - 96.3 (New York, NY) **22990**
WQXT-FM **23492***
WQXX **12435***
WQXX-FM **24078***
WQXX-FM - 106.1 (West Liberty, KY) **12435**
WQXY-AM (Hazard, KY) *Unable to locate*
WQXY-FM **12525***
WQYK-AM - 1010 (Tampa, FL) **6800**
WQYK-FM - 99.5 (Tampa, FL) **6801**
WQYT-FM **20224***
WQYX-FM - 93.1 (Clearfield, PA) **26791**
WQYZ-FM - 92.5 (Biloxi, MS) **16569**
WQZK-FM - 94.1 (Keyser, WV) **33358**
WQZQ-FM - 102.5 (Dickson, TN) **29168**
WQZX-FM - 94.3 (Greenville, AL) **246**
WQZY-FM - 95.9 (Dublin, GA) **7255**
WRAA-AM - 1330 (Luray, VA) **32204**
WRAB-AM - 1380 (Arab, AL) **24**
WRAC-FM - 103.1 (West Union, OH) **25634**
WRAD-AM (Radford, VA) *Unable to locate*
WRAF-FM **20223***
WRAF-FM - 90.9 & 88.5 (Toccoa Falls, GA) **7607**
WRAG-AM - 590 (Carrollton, AL) **147**
WRAI-AM (San Juan, PR) *Unable to locate*
WRAJ-AM **9179***
WRAJ-FM **9182***
WRAK-AM - 1400 (Williamsport, PA) **28190**
WRAL-AM **24166***
WRAL-FM - 101.5 (Raleigh, NC) **24169**
WRAL-TV - Channel 5 (Raleigh, NC) **24170**
WRAM-AM - 1330 (Monmouth, IL) **9221**
WRAN-FM - 98.3 (Shelbyville, IL) **9600**
Wrangell St. Elias News (Glennallen, AK) *Ceased*
Wrangell Sentinel (Wrangell, AK) **653**
The Wrap **34916***
WRAP (New York, NY) *Ceased*
WRAP-AM **32306***
WRAQ-AM **23637***
WRAS-FM - 88.5 (Atlanta, GA) **7082**
WRAT-FM - 95.9 (South Belmar, NJ) **19581**
WRAU-FM - 94.9 (Wheelersburg, OH) **25651**
WRAU-TV **8694***
WRAV-FM **6672***
WRAW-AM - 1340 (Reading, PA) **27922**
WRAX-FM **26690***
WRAX-FM - 107.7 (Birmingham, AL) **127**
WRAY-AM - 1250 (Princeton, IN) **10410**
WRAY-FM - 98.1 (Princeton, IN) **10411**
The Wray Gazette (Wray, CO) **4692**
WRBB-FM - 104.9 (Boston, MA) **13993**
WRBC-FM - 91.5 (Lewiston, ME) **12980**
WRBD-AM - 1470 (Stuart, FL) **6697**
WRBH-FM - 88.3 (New Orleans, LA) **12775**
WRBI-FM - 103.9 (Batesville, IN) **9797**
WRBL-TV - Channel 3 (Columbus, GA) **7192**
WRBN-FM - 104.1 (Clayton, GA) **7175**
WRBP-AM - 1440 (Youngstown, OH) **25710**
WRBQ-AM (Tampa, FL) *Ceased*
WRBQ-FM - 104.7 (Tampa, FL) **6802**
WRBR-FM - 103.9 (Mishawaka, IN) **10318**
WRBS-FM - 95.1 (Baltimore, MD) **13284**
WRBT-FM **9232***
WRBT-TV **12526***
WRBU-FM - 95.5 (Providence, RI) **28437**
WRBW-TV - Channel 65 (Orlando, FL) **6526**
WRBX-AM **23850***
WRBX-FM - 104.1 (Reidsville, GA) **7491**
WRBZ-AM - 850 (Raleigh, NC) **24171**
WRC-TV - Channel 4 (Washington, DC) **5893**
WRCA-AM - 1330 (Cambridge, MA) **14117**
WRCB-TV - Channel 13 (Chattanooga, TN) **29108**
WRCC-AM (Warner Robins, GA) *Ceased*
WRCC-AM - 1400 (Battle Creek, MI) **14800**
WRCC-FM **14801***
WRCC-FM (Warner Robins, GA) *Unable to locate*
WRCD-AM **7224***
WRCH-AM - 910 (Farmington, CT) **4865**
WRCH-FM - 100.5 (Farmington, CT) **4866**
WRCI-FM **15502***
WRCI-FM **18481***
WRCI-FM - 107.7 (Hillsboro, NH) **18526**
WRCI-Hillsboro **18478***
WRCK-FM **458***
WRCK-FM - 107.3 (Washington Mills, NY) **23510**
WRCL-FM (Richmond, VA) *Unable to locate*
WRCM-FM **24013***
WRCM-FM - 91.9 (Charlotte, NC) **23778**
WRCN-FM - 103.9 (Medford, NY) **21035**
WRCN-FM (Riverhead, NY) *Unable to locate*
WRCO-AM - 1450 (Richland Center, WI) **34300**
WRCO-FM - 100.9 (Richland Center, WI) **34301**
WRCP-AM (North Providence, RI) *Unable to locate*
WRCQ-FM **4865***
WRCQ-FM (Fayetteville, NC) *Unable to locate*
WRCR-AM - 1300 (Nanuet, NY) **21106**
WRCR-FM **16684***

Numbers cited in bold after listings are entry numbers rather than page numbers.

WRQT-FM - 95.7 (La Crosse, WI) **33896**
WRQX-FM - 107.3 (Washington, DC) **5894**
WRR-AM **30192***
WRR-FM - 101.1 (Dallas, TX) **30220**
WRRC-FM **32353***
WRRC-FM - 107.7 (Lawrenceville, NJ) **19166**
WRRD-AM - 540 (Brookfield, WI) **33607**
WRRE-AM (Juncos, PR) *Unable to locate*
WRRG-FM - 88.9 (River Grove, IL) **9497**
WRRH-FM - 88.7 (Franklin Lakes, NJ) **18836**
WRRK-FM - 96.9 (Pittsburgh, PA) **27878**
WRRL-AM - 1130 (Lewisburg, WV) **33369**
WRRL-FM **33368***
WRRM-FM (Cincinnati, OH) *Unable to locate*
WRRN-FM - 92.3 (Warren, PA) **28109**
WRRO **6575***
WRRO-AM **25710***
WRRR-AM (Rockford, IL) *Ceased*
WRRR-FM - 93.9 (St. Marys, WV) **33462**
WRRS-FM - 101.1 (Birmingham, AL) **128**
WRRV-FM - 92.7 (Poughkeepsie, NY) **23163**
WRRW-FM **29405***
WRRZ-AM - 880 (Clinton, NC) **23791**
WRSA-FM - 96.9 (Huntsville, AL) **286**
WRSC-AM - 1390 (State College, PA) **28029**
WRSC-FM **14434***
WRSD-FM - 94.9 (Folsom, PA) **26922**
WRSE-FM - 88.7 (Elmhurst, IL) **8841**
WRSF-FM - 105.7 (Nags Head, NC) **24093**
WRSH-FM (Rockingham, NC) *Unable to locate*
WRSI-FM - 93.9 (Northampton, MA) **14435**
WRSJ-AM - 1560 (San Juan, PR) **28308**
WRSK-FM - 88.1 (Slippery Rock, PA) **28000**
WRSL-AM - 1520 (Stanford, KY) **12417**
WRSL-FM - 95.9 (Stanford, KY) **12418**
WRSM-AM - 1540 (Sumiton, AL) **461**
WRSN-FM - 93.9 (Raleigh, NC) **24174**
WRSP-TV - Channel 55 (Springfield, IL) **9656**
WRSS-AM - 1410 (San Sebastian, PR) **28315**
WRSU-FM - 88.7 (New Brunswick, NJ) **19345**
WRSV-FM (Rocky Mount, NC) *Unable to locate*
WRSW-AM - 1480 (Warsaw, IN) **10539**
WRTA-AM - 1240 (Altoona, PA) **26641**
WRTB-FM **10543***
WRTC-FM - 89.3 (Hartford, CT) **4911**
WRTH-AM (St. Louis, MO) *Unable to locate*
WRTI-FM **6335***
WRTI-FM - 90.1 (Philadelphia, PA) **27744**
WRTK-AM **23258***
WRTK-AM - 1390 (Youngstown, OH) **25711**
WRTM-AM - 1490 (Jackson, MS) **16730**
WRTM-FM **5926***
WRTN-FM - 93.5 (New Rochelle, NY) **21124**
WRTO-FM (Miami, FL) *Unable to locate*
WRTP-AM - 1530 (Durham, NC) **23850**
WRTR-FM - 105.5 (Tuscaloosa, AL) **498**
WRTS-FM - 103.7 (North East, PA) **27342**
WRTU-FM - 89.7 (San Juan, PR) **28309**
WRTV-TV - Channel 6 (Indianapolis, IN) **10208**
WRUA-AM **27289***
WRUC-FM - 89.7 (Schenectady, NY) **23322**
WRUF-AM - 850 (Gainesville, FL) **6165**
WRUF-FM - 103.7 (Gainesville, FL) **6166**
WRUL-FM - 97.3 (Carmi, IL) **8133**
WRUN-AM (Oriskany, NY) *Unable to locate*
WRUP-FM **15341***
WRUR-FM - 88.5 (Rochester, NY) **23254**
WRUT-FM **31589***
WRUV-FM - 90.1 (Burlington, VT) **31527**
WRUW-FM - 91.1 (Cleveland, OH) **24985**
WRVA-AM (Richmond, VA) *Unable to locate*
WRVB-FM **34005***
WRVC-AM - 930 (Huntington, WV) **33344**
WRVC-FM **33339***
WRVC-FM - 92.7 (Huntington, WV) **33345**
WRVE-FM - 99.5 (Albany, NY) **20015**
WRVF-FM - 101.5 (Toledo, OH) **25584**
WRVG-FM - 89.9 (Georgetown, KY) **12089**
WRVH-FM **23081***
WRVI-FM - 105.9 (Louisville, KY) **12264**
WRVK-AM - 1460 (Renfro Valley, KY) **12381**
WRVM-FM - 102.7 (Suring, WI) **34363**
WRVO-FM - 89.9 (Oswego, NY) **23064**
WRVQ-FM - 94.5 (Richmond, VA) **32484**
WRVR-AM **29407***
WRVR-FM - 104.5 (Memphis, TN) **29412**
WRVS-FM - 89.9 (Elizabeth City, NC) **23863**
WRVT-FM - 88.7 (Colchester, VT) **31532**
WRVU-FM - 91.1 (Nashville, TN) **29530**
WRVV-FM - 97.3 (Harrisburg, PA) **27024**
WRVW-FM - 107.5 (Nashville, TN) **29531**
WRVX-FM **32219***
WRWA-FM - 88.7 (Troy, AL) **475**
WRWB-AM (Harrogate, TN) *Unable to locate*
WRWC-FM **9536***
WRWD-FM - 107.3 (Clintondale, NY) **20476**
WRWH-AM - 1350 (Cleveland, GA) **7176**
WRWR-TV (Bayamon, PR) *Unable to locate*
WRWX-FM (Fort Myers, FL) *Unable to locate*

WRXB-AM - 1590 (St. Petersburg, FL) **6639**
WRXC-FM - 90.1 (Monroe, CT) **4967**
WRXF-FM - 103.1 (Lapeer, MI) **15312**
WRXJ-AM **6235***
WRXK-FM - 96.1 (Estero, FL) **6067**
WRXL-FM - 102.1 (Richmond, VA) **32485**
WRXO-AM - 1430 (Roxboro, NC) **24211**
WRXO-FM **24211***
WRXO-FM **24210***
WRXR-AM (North Augusta, GA) *Ceased*
WRXR-FM **8647***
WRXR-FM - 96.3 (North Augusta, SC) **28723**
WRXY-TV (Venice, FL) *Unable to locate*
WRXZ-FM **8083***
WRYM-AM - 840 (Newington, CT) **5038**
WRYO-FM **6163***
WRYT-AM - 1080 (St. Louis, MO) **17559**
WRZA-FM - 99.9 (Chicago, IL) **8650**
WRZI-FM - 101.5 (Elizabethtown, KY) **12050**
WRZK-AM **29147***
WRZK-FM - 95.9 (Kingsport, TN) **29267**
WRZN-AM - 720 (Hernando, FL) **6186**
WRZQ-FM - 107.3 (Columbus, IN) **9898**
WRZX-FM - 103.3 (Indianapolis, IN) **10209**
WRZZ-FM - 106.1 (Vienna, WV) **33483**
WSAC-FM **12046***
WSAE-FM - 106.9 (Spring Arbor, MI) **15573**
WSAF-AM (Grovetown, GA) *Unable to locate*
WSAI-AM **24836***
WSAJ-AM - 1340 (Grove City, PA) **26966**
WSAJ-FM - 91.1 (Grove City, PA) **26967**
WSAK-FM - 102.1 (Dover, NH) **18495**
WSAL-AM - 1230 (Logansport, IN) **10277**
WSAL-FM **10276***
WSAM-AM - 1400 (Saginaw, MI) **15504**
WSAN-FM - 98.9 (Vieques, PR) **28321**
WSAO-AM - 1140 (Senatobia, MS) **16844**
WSAQ-FM - 107.1 (Port Huron, MI) **15458**
WSAR-AM - 1480 (Somerset, MA) **14529**
WSAU-AM - 550 (Wausau, WI) **34438**
WSAV-TV - Channel 3 (Savannah, GA) **7548**
WSAW-TV - Channel 7 (Wausau, WI) **34439**
WSAX-FM - 102.3 (Atlantic City, NJ) **18659**
WSAY-AM **23258***
WSAY-AM **32506***
WSAZ-TV - Channel 3 (Huntington, WV) **33346**
WSB-AM - 750 (Atlanta, GA) **7085**
WSB-FM - 98.5 (Atlanta, GA) **7086**
WSB-TV - Channel 2 (Atlanta, GA) **7087**
WSBA-AM - 910 (York, PA) **28216**
WSBA-TV **28215***
WSBB-AM - 1230 (New Smyrna Beach, FL) **6459**
WSBC-AM - 1240 (Chicago, IL) **8651**
WSBC-AM (Chicago, IL) *Unable to locate*
WSBE-TV (Providence, RI) *Unable to locate*
WSBF-FM - 88.1 (Clemson, SC) **28538**
WSBG-FM - 93.5 (Stroudsburg, PA) **28036**
WSBI-AM - 1210 (Byrdstown, TN) **29077**
WSBK-TV - Channel 38 (Boston, MA) **13995**
WSBK/WWOR (East Syracuse, NY) *Unable to locate*
WSBL-FM **5286***
WSBM-AM - 1340 (Florence, AL) **225**
WSBN-TV - Channel 47 (Norton, VA) **32314**
WSBR-AM - 740 (Boca Raton, FL) **5943**
WSBS-AM - 860 (Great Barrington, MA) **14218**
WSBT-AM - 960 (South Bend, IN) **10466**
WSBT-TV - Channel 22 (South Bend, IN) **10467**
WSBU-FM - 88.3 (St. Bonaventure, NY) **23288**
WSBV-AM - 1560 (South Boston, VA) **32533**
WSBY-FM (Salisbury, MD) *Unable to locate*
WSCB-AM **20396***
WSCB-FM - 89.9 (Springfield, MA) **14563**
WSCC-FM - 92.1 (Somerset, KY) **12408**
WSCD-FM - 92.9 (Duluth, MN) **15857**
WSCF-FM - 91.9 (Vero Beach, FL) **6838**
WSCG-FM (Corinth, NY) *Unable to locate*
WSCH-FM - 99.3 (Aurora, IN) **9792**
WSCI-FM (Mount Pleasant, SC) *Unable to locate*
WSCL-FM - 89.5 (Salisbury, MD) **13719**
WSCM-AM (Cobleskill, NY) *Unable to locate*
WSCO-TV - Channel 14 (Green Bay, WI) **33755**
WSCP-AM (Pulaski, NY) *Unable to locate*
WSCP-FM - 101.7 (Pulaski, NY) **23167**
WSCQ-FM (West Columbia, SC) *Unable to locate*
WSCR-AM **8663***
WSCR-AM - 670 (Chicago, IL) **8652**
WSCR-FM **23346***
WSCS-FM - 90.9 (New London, NH) **18612**
WSCT-FM **4768***
WSCV-TV - Channel 51 (Hialeah, FL) **6189**
WSCW-AM - 1410 (South Charleston, WV) **33469**
WSCZ-FM - 96.7 (Greenwood, SC) **28650**
WSDH-FM - 91.5 (East Sandwich, MA) **14171**
WSDL-AM **12845***
WSDL-FM - 90.7 (Salisbury, MD) **13720**
WSDM-AM **10501***
WSDM-FM **8640***
WSDM-FM - 97.7 (Terre Haute, IN) **10500**

WSDO-AM - 1400 (Sanford, FL) **6648**
WSDP-FM - 88.1 (Canton, MI) **14855**
WSDQ-AM - 1190 (Dunlap, TN) **29172**
WSDR-AM - 1240 (Sterling, IL) **9664**
WSDS-AM - 1480 (Ypsilanti, MI) **15693**
WSDT-AM (Rossville, GA) *Unable to locate*
WSDX-AM - 1130 (Terre Haute, IN) **10501**
WSDZ-AM - 1260 (St. Louis, MO) **17560**
WSEA-AM **5255***
WSEB-FM - 91.3 (Englewood, FL) **6064**
WSEC-TV - Channel 14/65 (Springfield, IL) **9657**
WSEE-TV - Channel 35 (Erie, PA) **26912**
WSEH-FM - 102.7 (Cumberland, KY) **12033**
WSEK-FM - 97.1 (Somerset, KY) **12409**
WSEL-AM (Pontotoc, MS) *Unable to locate*
WSEN-AM **20116***
WSEN-FM - 92.1 (Baldwinsville, NY) **20117**
WSEO-FM - 107.7 (Nelsonville, OH) **25407**
WSER-AM (Elkton, MD) *Unable to locate*
WSET-TV - Channel 13 (Lynchburg, VA) **32216**
WSEV-AM - 930 (Sevierville, TN) **29592**
WSEZ-AM - 1560 (Paoli, IN) **10390**
WSFA-TV - Channel 12 (Montgomery, AL) **393**
WSFB-AM - 1490 (Quitman, GA) **7487**
WSFC-AM - 1240 (Somerset, KY) **12410**
WSFJ-TV - Channel 51 (Thornville, OH) **25558**
WSFL-AM (New Bern, NC) *Unable to locate*
WSFL-FM (New Bern, NC) *Unable to locate*
WSFN-AM **15392***
WSFN-AM - 790 (Brunswick, GA) **7143**
WSFP-AM **6104***
WSFP-FM **6105***
WSFT-AM (Thomaston, GA) *Ceased*
WSFT-FM - 107.9 (Williamsport, PA) **28192**
WSFW-AM (Seneca Falls, NY) *Unable to locate*
WSFW-FM (Seneca Falls, NY) *Unable to locate*
WSFX-FM - 105.7 FM (Nanticoke, PA) **27309**
WSFX-TV - Channel 26 (Wilmington, NC) **24305**
WSGA-AM (Savannah, GA) *Unable to locate*
WSGA-FM - 104.7 (Hinesville, GA) **7336**
WSGB-AM - 1490 (Sutton, WV) **33478**
WSGC-FM **7268***
WSGD-FM (Moosic, PA) *Unable to locate*
WSGE-FM - 91.7 (Dallas, NC) **23797**
WSGH-AM (Winston-Salem, NC) *Unable to locate*
WSGI-AM - 1100 (Springfield, TN) **29621**
WSGL-FM - 103.1 (Naples, FL) **6454**
WSGM-FM **32559***
WSGN-FM - 91.5 (Gadsden, AL) **237**
WSGO-AM (Oswego, NY) *Unable to locate*
WSGR-FM - 91.3 (Port Huron, MI) **15459**
WSGS-FM - 101.1 (Hazard, KY) **12121**
WSGW-AM - 790 (Saginaw, MI) **15505**
WSGY-FM **6912***
WSGY-FM (Somerset, PA) *Unable to locate*
WSHA-FM - 88.9 (Raleigh, NC) **24175**
WSHC-FM - 89.7 (Shepherdstown, WV) **33465**
WSHE-FM **6432***
WSHE-FM - 100.3 (Maitland, FL) **6320**
WSHF-AM **457***
WSHG-FM **27887***
WSHG-FM **27887***
WSHH-FM (Pittsburgh, PA) *Unable to locate*
WSHJ-FM - 88.3 (Southfield, MI) **15560**
WSHK **398***
WSHL-FM - 91.3 (North Easton, MA) **14424**
WSHN-AM - 1550 (Fremont, MI) **15061**
WSHN-FM - 100.1 (Fremont, MI) **15062**
WSHO-AM - 800 (New Orleans, LA) **12776**
WSHP-AM (Shippensburg, PA) *Unable to locate*
WSHQ-FM (Cobleskill, NY) *Unable to locate*
WSHR-FM - 91.9 (Lake Ronkonkoma, NY) **20879**
WSHS-AM (Valdosta, GA) *Unable to locate*
WSHS-FM - 91.7 (Sheboygan, WI) **34325**
WSHU-FM - 91.1 (Fairfield, CT) **4792**
WSHW-FM - 99.7 (Frankfort, IN) **10003**
WSHY-AM (Decatur, IL) *Ceased*
WSHZ-FM - 107.9 (Muskegon, MI) **15396**
WSIA-FM - 88.9 (Staten Island, NY) **23367**
WSIB-AM **28491***
WSID-AM **13271***
WSIE-FM - 88.7 (Edwardsville, IL) **8815**
WSIF-AM - 90.9 (Wilkesboro, NC) **24289**
WSIG-FM - 96.9 (Mount Jackson, VA) **32277**
WSIL-TV - Channel 3 (Carterville, IL) **8164**
WSIP-AM - 1490 (Paintsville, KY) **12351**
WSIP-FM - 98.9 (Paintsville, KY) **12352**
WSIR-AM - 1490 (Winter Haven, FL) **6876**
WSIU-FM - 91.9 (Carbondale, IL) **8123**
WSIU-TV - Channel 8 (Carbondale, IL) **8124**
WSIV-AM - 1540 (East Syracuse, NY) **20560**
WSIX-FM - 97.9 (Nashville, TN) **29532**
WSJB-FM - 91.5 (Standish, ME) **13059**
WSJD-FM - 100.5 (Mount Carmel, IL) **9232**
WSJI-FM - 89.5 (Cherry Hill, NJ) **18740**
WSJK-TV - Channel 2 (Knoxville, TN) **29300**
WSJL-FM **18659***
WSJM-AM - 1400 (St. Joseph, MI) **15516**
WSJN-TV (Hato Rey, PR) *Unable to locate*

3550

Numbers cited in bold after listings are entry numbers rather than page numbers.

WTAE-AM 27865*
WTAE-TV - Channel 4 (Pittsburgh, PA) 27879
WTAG-AM - 580 (Paxton, MA) 14460
WTAI-AM - 1560 (Melbourne, FL) 6339
WTAI-FM 6335*
WTAJ-TV - Channel 10 (Altoona, PA) 26642
WTAK-AM 281*
WTAK-FM - 106.1 (Decatur, AL) 175
WTAL-AM (Tallahassee, FL) Unable to locate
WTAM-AM - 1100 (Cleveland, OH) 24986
WTAN-AM - 1340 (Clearwater, FL) 5994
WTAP-TV - Channel 15 (Parkersburg, WV) 33425
WTAQ-AM (Chicago, IL) Unable to locate
WTAR-AM - 850 (Norfolk, VA) 32306
WTAR-AM (Norfolk, VA) Unable to locate
WTAR-TV 32307*
WTAS-FM 15179*
WTAS-FM (Chicago, IL) Unable to locate
WTAT-TV - Channel 24 (Charleston, SC) 28525
WTAW-AM - 1620 (College Station, TX) 30061
WTAX-AM (Springfield, IL) Unable to locate
WTAZ-FM (Peoria, IL) Unable to locate
WTBB-FM - 97.7 (Panama City, FL) 6562
WTBC-AM - 1230 (Tuscaloosa, AL) 500
WTBC-AM - 1230 (Tuscaloosa, AL) 499
WTBF-AM - 970 (Troy, AL) 476
WTBF-FM - 94.7 (Troy, AL) 477
WTBG-FM - 95.3 (Brownsville, TN) 29074
WTBH-FM (Chiefland, FL) Unable to locate
WTBI-AM - 1540 (Greenville, SC) 28643
WTBJ-FM - 91 (Oxford, AL) 417
WTBK-FM - 105.7 (Manchester, KY) 12280
WTBL-AM (Central City, KY) Unable to locate
WTBO-AM - 1450 (Cumberland, MD) 13480
WTBO-TV 10212*
WTBP-AM 29564*
WTBQ-AM (Florida, NY) Unable to locate
WTBR-FM (Pittsfield, MA) Unable to locate
WTBS-FM 14116*
WTBS-TV (Atlanta, GA) Unable to locate
WTBU-FM - 89.3 (Boston, MA) 13997
WTBU-TV - Channel 69 (Indianapolis, IN) 10212
WTBY-TV - Channel 54 (Fishkill, NY) 20602
WTBZ-AM - 1260 (Grafton, WV) 33326
WTBZ-FM - 95.9 (Grafton, WV) 33327
WTCA-AM - 1050 (Plymouth, IN) 10402
WTCA-FM 10401*
WTCB-FM - 106.7 (Columbia, SC) 28585
WTCC-AM 4977*
WTCC-FM - 90.7 (Springfield, MA) 14564
WTCE-FM - 100.7 (Baton Rouge, LA) 12525
WTCH-AM - 960 (Shawano, WI) 34320
WTCI-TV - Channel 45 (Chattanooga, TN) 29110
WTCJ-AM - 1230 (Tell City, IN) 10483
WTCK-AM - 1320 (Greensboro, NC) 23958
WTCL-AM (Chattahoocheé, FL) Unable to locate
WTCM-AM - 580 (Traverse City, MI) 15614
WTCM-FM 15606*
WTCN-AM (Clearwater, MN) Ceased
WTCO-AM - 1450 (Campbellsville, KY) 12009
WTCO-FM 12008*
WTCQ-FM - 97.7 (Vidalia, GA) 7631
WTCR-AM - 1420 (Catlettsburg, KY) 12012
WTCR-FM - 103.3 (Catlettsburg, KY) 12013
WTCS-AM - 1490 (Fairmont, WV) 33316
WTCT-TV - Channel 27 (Marion, IL) 9148
WTCV-AM 12099*
WTCV-FM 29507*
WTCW-AM (Whitesburg, KY) Unable to locate
WTCX-FM - 96.1 (Fond du Lac, WI) 33702
WTCY-AM (Harrisburg, PA) Unable to locate
WTDY-AM (Madison, WI) Unable to locate
WTEB-FM - 89.3 (New Bern, NC) 24102
WTEL-AM - 860 (Bala Cynwyd, PA) 26680
WTEM-AM - 980 (Silver Spring, MD) 13748
WTEN-TV - Channel 10 (Albany, NY) 20016
WTEV-TV 28436*
WTEV-TV - Channel 47 (Jacksonville, FL) 6242
WTFM-FM - 98.5 (Kingsport, TN) 29268
WTFX-FM - 100.5 (Louisville, KY) 12266
WTGA-FM (Thomaston, GA) Unable to locate
WTGC-AM (Lewisburg, PA) Unable to locate
WTGE-FM 12525*
WTGI-TV 26679*
WTGL-TV - Channel 52 (Orlando, FL) 6528
WTGM-AM (Salisbury, MD) Unable to locate
WTGN-FM - 97.7 (Lima, OH) 25303
WTGP-FM - 88.1 (Greenville, PA) 26962
WTGR-AM 28708*
WTGR-FM - 97.5 (Greenville, OH) 25229
WTGS-TV - Channel 28 (Savannah, GA) 7550
WTGV-FM - 97.7 (Sandusky, MI) 15524
WTGY-FM (Charleston, MS) Unable to locate
WTHB-AM - 1550 (Augusta, GA) 7114
WTHD-AM 5264*
WTHD-FM - 105.5 (LaGrange, IN) 10267
WTHE-AM - 1520 (Mineola, NY) 21087
WTHI-AM - 1480 (Terre Haute, IN) 10502
WTHI-FM - 99.9 (Terre Haute, IN) 10503

WTHI-TV - Channel 10 (Terre Haute, IN) 10504
WTHK-FM 20771*
WTHL-FM 12413*
WTHO-FM - 101.7 (Thomson, GA) 7593
WTHP-FM 24004*
WTHQ 12254*
WTHR-TV - Channel 13 and HD Channel 46 (Indianapolis, IN) 10213
WTHS-FM 6402*
WTHS-FM - 89.9 (Holland, MI) 15179
WTHT-FM - 107.5 (Portland, ME) 13032
WTHU-AM - 1450 (Thurmont, MD) 13756
WTHZ-AM 6741*
WTHZ-FM - 94.1 (Lexington, NC) 24042
WTIB-FM 16692*
WTIC-AM (Hartford, CT) Unable to locate
WTIC-FM (Hartford, CT) Unable to locate
WTIC-TV - Channel 61 (Hartford, CT) 4912
WTIF-AM - 1340 (Tifton, GA) 7604
WTIG-AM - 990 (Massillon, OH) 25362
WTIJ-FM 31542*
WTIK-AM - 1310 (Durham, NC) 23852
WTIL-AM - 1300 (Mayaguez, PR) 28269
WTIM-AM 9680*
WTIM-FM - 97.3 (Taylorville, IL) 9680
WTIP-FM 33290*
WTIP-FM - 90.7 (Grand Marais, MN) 15927
WTIQ-AM - 1490 (Manistique, MI) 15334
WTIR-FM 13584*
WTIS-AM - 1110 (St. Petersburg, FL) 6641
WTIU-TV - Channel 30 (Bloomington, IN) 9860
WTIV-AM - 1230 (Titusville, PA) 28051
WTIX-AM (New Orleans, LA) Unable to locate
WTJA-TV (Syracuse, NY) Unable to locate
WTJB-FM - 91.7 (Troy, AL) 478
WTJC-TV (Springfield, OH) Unable to locate
WTJH-AM - 1260 (East Point, GA) 7260
WTJP-TV - Channel 60 (Gadsden, AL) 238
WTJR-TV (Quincy, IL) Unable to locate
WTJS-AM - 1390 (Jackson, TN) 29239
WTJT-FM - 90.1 (Crestview, FL) 6027
WTJU-FM - 91.1 (Charlottesville, VA) 31955
WTJY-FM 9654*
WTJY-FM - 89.5 (Blacksburg, VA) 31889
WTJZ-AM - 1270 (Hampton, VA) 32135
WTKA-AM - 1050 (Ann Arbor, MI) 14780
WTKB-FM - 93.7 (Trenton, TN) 29631
WTKF-FM - 107.3 (Newport, NC) 24105
WTKG-AM 15688*
WTKG-AM - 1230 (Grand Rapids, MI) 15123
WTKI-AM - 1450 (Huntsville, AL) 287
WTKK-AM (Pensacola, FL) Ceased
WTKL-AM (Baton Rouge, LA) Unable to locate
WTKM-AM - 1540 (Hartford, WI) 33774
WTKM-FM - 104.9 (Hartford, WI) 33775
WTKN-AM 6793*
WTKN-AM (Daleville, AL) Unable to locate
WTKO-AM - 1470 (Ithaca, NY) 20822
WTKR-TV - Channel 3 (Norfolk, VA) 32307
WTKT-FM - 103.3 (Lexington, KY) 12195
WTKU-FM - 98.3 (Linwood, NJ) 19175
WTKX-FM (Pensacola, FL) Unable to locate
WTKX-FM - 101.5 (Pensacola, FL) 6578
WTKY-FM (Tompkinsville, KY) Unable to locate
WTKZ-AM - 1320 (Allentown, PA) 26634
WTLA-AM (Bridgeport, NY) Unable to locate
WTLB-AM - 1310 (Washington Mills, NY) 23511
WTLC-AM (Indianapolis, IN) Unable to locate
WTLC-FM (Indianapolis, IN) Unable to locate
WTLH-TV - Channel 49 (Midway, FL) 6423
WTLJ-TV - Channel 54 (Allendale, MI) 14727
WTLN-AM - 950 (Altamonte Springs, FL) 5905
WTLO-AM - 1480 (Somerset, KY) 12412
WTLQ-AM - 1240 (Fort Myers, FL) 6113
WTLQ-FM 27887*
WTLR-FM - 89.9 (State College, PA) 28030
WTLS-AM (Tallassee, AL) Unable to locate
WTLT-FM - 93.5 (Fort Myers, FL) 6114
WTLT-FM (Columbus, OH) Unable to locate
WTLV-TV - Channel 12 (Jacksonville, FL) 6243
WTLW-TV - Channel 44 (Lima, OH) 25304
WTLZ-FM - 107.1 (Saginaw, MI) 15506
WTMA-AM - 1250 (North Charleston, SC) 28728
WTMB-AM - 1460 (Tomah, WI) 34371
WTMC-AM (Ocala, FL) Unable to locate
WTMD-FM - 89.7 (Baltimore, MD) 13285
WTME-AM - 780 (Norway, ME) 12996
WTMG-FM 6751*
WTMI-AM - 1290 (Hartford, CT) 4913
WTMI-FM (Coconut Grove, FL) Unable to locate
WTMJ-AM - 620 (Milwaukee, WI) 34135
WTMJ-TV - Channel 4 (Milwaukee, WI) 34136
WTMN-AM (Portsmouth, NH) Unable to locate
WTMP-AM - 1150 (Tampa, FL) 6804
WTMQ-AM (Chattanooga, TN) Unable to locate
WTMR-AM - 800 (Camden, NJ) 18718
WTMT-AM - 620 (Louisville, KY) 12267
WTMV-TV 6797*
WTMW-TV - Channel 14 (Silver Spring, MD) 13749

WTMX-FM (Skokie, IL) Unable to locate
WTMY-AM - 1280 (Sarasota, FL) 6676
WTMZ-AM - 910 (North Charleston, SC) 28729
WTN-FM - 99.7 (Nashville, TN) 29536
WTNC-AM (Thomasville, NC) Unable to locate
WTNC-FM 24004*
WTND-FM 23161*
WTNE-AM - 1500 (Brownsville, TN) 29075
WTNH-TV - Channel 8 (New Haven, CT) 5014
WTNJ-FM - 105.9 (Beckley, WV) 33245
WTNL-AM - 1390 (Reidsville, GA) 7492
WTNR-AM 29645*
WTNS-AM - 1560 (Coshocton, OH) 25097
WTNS-FM - 99.3 (Coshocton, OH) 25098
WTNT-FM - 94.9 (Tallahassee, FL) 6753
WTNV-FM - 104.1 (Jackson, TN) 29240
WTNW-AM 500*
WTNX-FM 24708*
WTNZ-TV - Channel 43 (Knoxville, TN) 29302
WTOA-FM 19482*
WTOB-AM - 1380 (Winston-Salem, NC) 24334
WTOC-TV - Channel 11 (Savannah, GA) 7551
WTOD-AM - 1560 (Toledo, OH) 25586
WTOE-AM - 1470 (Burnsville, NC) 23680
WTOG-TV - Channel 44 (St. Petersburg, FL) 6642
WTOJ-FM - 103.1 (Watertown, NY) 23520
WTOK-TV - Channel 11 (Meridian, MS) 16780
WTOL-TV - Channel 11 (Toledo, OH) 25587
WTOM-TV - Channel 4 (Traverse City, MI) 15615
WTON-AM - 1240 (Staunton, VA) 32560
WTON-FM - 94.3 (Staunton, VA) 32561
WTOO-AM 23637*
WTOO-FM 24668*
WTOP-AM - 1500 (Washington, DC) 5895
WTOP-FM - 94.3 (Rockville, MD) 13704
WTOP-TV 5897*
WTOQ-FM 34246*
WTOT-AM - 980 (Marianna, FL) 6329
WTOV-TV - Channel 9 (Steubenville, OH) 25544
WTOW-AM (Washington, NC) Unable to locate
WTOX-AM (Lincoln, ME) Unable to locate
WTOY-AM - 1480 (Roanoke, VA) 32506
WTPA-FM 27023*
WTPA-FM - 93.5 (Harrisburg, PA) 27025
WTPA-TV 27018*
WTPC-FM - 105.3 (Elsah, IL) 8845
WTPI-FM (Indianapolis, IN) Unable to locate
WTPL-FM - 107.7 (Concord, NH) 18481
WTPM-FM - 92.9 (Mayaguez, PR) 28270
WTPN-FM 13022*
WTPO-AM 7202*
WTPR-AM - 710 (Paris, TN) 29563
WTPT-FM - 93.3 (Greenville, SC) 28644
WTQR-FM (Winston-Salem, NC) Unable to locate
WTQX-AM (Selma, AL) Unable to locate
WTRA-TV (Mayaguez, PR) Unable to locate
WTRB-AM - 1570 (Ripley, TN) 29577
WTRC-AM - 1340 (Elkhart, IN) 9929
WTRE-AM - 1330 (Greensburg, IN) 10045
WTRE-FM 9898*
WTRF-TV - Channel 7 (Wheeling, WV) 33509
WTRG-FM - 100.7 (Raleigh, NC) 24176
WTRI-AM - 1520 (Brunswick, MD) 13396
WTRM-FM - 91.3 (Winchester, VA) 32633
WTRN-AM - 1340 (Tyrone, PA) 28065
WTRO-AM - 1450 (Dyersburg, TN) 29178
WTRP-AM - 620 (LaGrange, GA) 7365
WTRQ-AM (Warsaw, NC) Ceased
WTRR-AM 6648*
WTRS-AM (Ocala, FL) Ceased
WTRS-FM - 102.3 (Ocala, FL) 6479
WTRT-FM 25580*
WTRU-AM 15392*
WTRU-AM (Jupiter, FL) Unable to locate
WTRU-FM 15122*
WTRU-FM (Jupiter, FL) Unable to locate
WTRV-FM 33896*
WTRV-FM - 100.5 (Grand Rapids, MI) 15124
WTRW-AM - 1590 (Two Rivers, WI) 34378
WTRW-FM (Two Rivers, WI) Ceased
WTRX-AM (Flint, MI) Ceased
WTRY-AM - 980 (Latham, NY) 20938
WTRY-FM (Schenectady, NY) Unable to locate
WTRZ-FM 14561*
WTSA-AM - 1450 (Brattleboro, VT) 31512
WTSA-FM - 96.7 (Brattleboro, VT) 31513
WTSB-AM (Lumberton, NC) Unable to locate
WTSC-FM 9786*
WTSC-FM - 91.1 (Potsdam, NY) 23144
WTSF-TV - Channel 61 (Ashland, KY) 11922
WTSG-TV 6908*
WTSH-AM - 1360 (Rome, GA) 7509
WTSH-FM - 107.1 (Rome, GA) 7510
WTSJ-AM - 1050 (Cincinnati, OH) 24847
WTSK-AM - 790 (Tuscaloosa, AL) 501
WTSL-AM (Lebanon, NH) Unable to locate
WTSL-FM (Lebanon, NH) Unable to locate
WTSN-AM - 1270 (Dover, NH) 18496
WTSO-AM (Madison, WI) Unable to locate

WVEF-AM (Camden, SC) *Ceased*
WVEL-AM (East Peoria, IL) *Unable to locate*
WVEM-FM - 101.9 (Springfield, IL) **9659**
WVEN-FM **26936***
WVER-TV - Channel 28 (Rutland, VT) **31588**
WVEU-TV **7090***
WVEZ-FM (Louisville, KY) *Unable to locate*
WVFC-AM (McConnellsburg, PA) *Unable to locate*
WVFG-FM - 107.5 (Demopolis, AL) **180**
WVFI-AM - 640 (Notre Dame, IN) **10380**
WVFJ-FM - 93.3 (Peachtree City, GA) **7481**
WVFN-AM - 730 (Lansing, MI) **15306**
WVFS-FM - 89.7 (Tallahassee, FL) **6756**
WVFT-TV **32498***
WVGA-TV **7625***
WVGB-AM - 1490 (Beaufort, SC) **28491**
WVGR-FM - 104.1 (Grand Rapids, MI) **15125**
WVGS-FM - 91.9 (Statesboro, GA) **7567**
WVHC-FM **20730***
WVHC-FM - 91.5 (Herkimer, NY) **20734**
WVHI-AM - 1330 (Evansville, IN) **9952**
WVHI-FM **9953***
WVHN-FM (Dover, NH) *Unable to locate*
WVHQ-FM **14979***
WVHT-FM **33309***
WVHU-AM - 800 (Huntington, WV) **33347**
WVIA-FM - 89.9 (Pittston, PA) **27893**
WVIA-TV - Channel 44 (Pittston, PA) **27894**
WVIC-AM **15306***
WVIC-FM **15304***
WVIC-FM - 94.1 (Holt, MI) **15180**
WVIC-FM - 105.9 (Ithaca, NY) **20824**
WVID-FM - 90.3 (Trujillo Alto, PR) **28318**
WVII-TV - Channel 7 (Bangor, ME) **12915**
WVIJ-FM - 91.7 (Port Charlotte, FL) **6597**
WVIK-FM - 90.3 (Rock Island, IL) **9525**
WVIM-FM (Hernando, MS) *Unable to locate*
WVIN **20126***
WVIN-FM - 98.3 (Bath, NY) **20134**
WVIP-AM (Mount Kisco, NY) *Unable to locate*
WVIR-TV - Channel 29 (Charlottesville, VA) **31956**
WVIS-FM - 106.1 (San Juan, PR) **28312**
WVIT-TV - Channel 30 (West Hartford, CT) **5205**
WVIX-AM **16730***
WVIZ-TV - Channel 25 (Cleveland, OH) **24988**
WVJC-FM - 89.1 (Mount Carmel, IL) **9233**
WVJP **28236***
WVJP-AM - 1110 (Caguas, PR) **28236**
WVJP-FM - 103.3 (Caguas, PR) **28237**
WVJS-AM - 1420 (Owensboro, KY) **12333**
WVJV-TV **14247***
WVKC-FM (Galesburg, IL) *Unable to locate*
WVKM-FM - 106.7 (Matewan, WV) **33385**
WVKO-AM - 1580 (Columbus, OH) **25089**
WVKR-FM - 91.3 (Poughkeepsie, NY) **23164**
WVKS-FM (Toledo, OH) *Unable to locate*
WVKV-AM (Hurricane, WV) *Unable to locate*
WVKX-FM - 103.7 (Irwinton, GA) **7338**
WVKY-AM (Pikeville, KY) *Unable to locate*
WVKZ-AM (Clifton Park, NY) *Unable to locate*
WVLA-TV - Channel 33 (Baton Rouge, LA) **12526**
WVLC-AM - 1260 (Lake City, SC) **28679**
WVLD-AM (Valdosta, GA) *Unable to locate*
WVLE-FM - 99.3 (Scottsville, KY) **12396**
WVLJ-FM **9223***
WVLK-AM - 590 (Lexington, KY) **12198**
WVLK-FM - 92.9 (Lexington, KY) **12199**
WVLN-AM - 740 (Olney, IL) **9385**
WVLS-FM - 89.7 (Dunmore, WV) **33302**
WVLT-FM - 92.1 (Vineland, NJ) **19702**
WVLT-TV - Channel 8 (Knoxville, TN) **29306**
WVLY-FM - 100.9 (Milton, PA) **27272**
WVMC-AM - 1360 (Mount Carmel, IL) **9234**
WVMC-FM - 90.7 (Mansfield, OH) **25338**
WVMG-AM - 1440 (Macon, GA) **7404**
WVMG-FM - 96.7 (Macon, GA) **7405**
WVMH-FM - 90.5 (Mars Hill, NC) **24058**
WVMI-AM - 570 (Biloxi, MS) **16570**
WVMJ-FM - 104.5 (Conway, NH) **18487**
WVMJ-FM - 105.3 (Radford, VA) **32352**
WVMM-FM - 90.7 (Grantham, PA) **26947**
WVMN-AM - 90.1 (Cleveland, OH) **24989**
WVMR-FM - 89.7 (Dunmore, WV) **33303**
WVMS-FM **19695***
WVMS-FM - 89.5 (Cleveland, OH) **24990**
WVMT-AM - 620 (Colchester, VT) **31533**
WVMW-FM - 91.5 (Scranton, PA) **27972**
WVMX-FM - 101.9 (Cincinnati, OH) **24848**
WVMX-FM (Stowe, VT) *Ceased*
WVNC-FM - 96.7 (Canton, NY) **20434**
WVNE-AM - 760 (Springfield, MA) **14565**
WVNH-AM **18646***
WVNI-FM - 95.1 (Bloomington, IN) **9862**
WVNN-AM - 770 (Athens, AL) **30**
WVNO-FM - 106.1 (Mansfield, OH) **25339**
WVNP-FM - 89.9 (Charleston, WV) **33287**
WVNR-AM (Poultney, VT) *Unable to locate*
WVNS-FM **33283***
WVNU-FM - 97.5 (Greenfield, OH) **25226**

WVNV-FM - 96.5 (Malone, NY) **20982**
WVNY-TV - Channel 22 (Burlington, VT) **31528**
WVNZ-AM - 990 (Richmond, VA) **32487**
WVOA-FM - 103.9 (East Syracuse, NY) **20561**
WVOB-FM - 91.3 (Dothan, AL) **195**
WVOC-AM **14798***
WVOC-AM - 560 (Columbia, SC) **28586**
WVOD-FM - 99.1 (Manteo, NC) **24054**
WVOE-FM **10422***
WVOF-FM - 88.5 (Fairfield, CT) **4793**
WVOG-AM - 600 (Metairie, LA) **12686**
WVOH-AM - 920 (Hazlehurst, GA) **7326**
WVOH-FM - 93.5 (Hazlehurst, GA) **7327**
WVOJ-AM - 970 (Jacksonville, FL) **6244**
WVOK-AM **119***
WVOK-FM - 97.9 (Oxford, AL) **418**
WVOL-AM (Nashville, TN) *Unable to locate*
WVOM-AM - 1270 (Iuka, MS) **16693**
WVON-AM **8623***
WVON-AM - 1450 (Chicago, IL) **8658**
WVOP-AM - 970 (Vidalia, GA) **7632**
WVOR-FM - 100.5 (Rochester, NY) **23256**
WVOS-AM - 1240 (Liberty, NY) **20944**
WVOS-FM - 95.9 (Liberty, NY) **20945**
WVOT-AM - 1420 (Wilson, NC) **24315**
WVOV-AM **281***
WVOV-AM - 970 (Danville, VA) **31995**
WVOW-AM - 1290 (Logan, WV) **33371**
WVOW-FM - 101.9 (Logan, WV) **33372**
WVOX-AM - 1460 (New Rochelle, NY) **21125**
WVOZ-AM - 1180 (Knoxville, TN) **29307**
WVPB-FM - 91.7 (Charleston, WV) **33288**
WVPE-FM - 88.1 (Elkhart, IN) **9930**
WVPG-AM - 90.3 (Parkersburg, WV) **33426**
WVPH-FM - 90.3 (Piscataway, NJ) **19432**
WVPN-FM - 88.5 (Charleston, WV) **33289**
WVPO-AM - 840 (Stroudsburg, PA) **28037**
WVPR-FM - 89.5 (Windsor, VT) **31622**
WVPS-FM - 107.9 (Colchester, VT) **31534**
WVPT-TV - Channel 51 (Harrisonburg, VA) **32154**
WVPX-TV - Channel 23 (Cleveland, OH) **24991**
WVPY-TV - Channel 42 (Harrisonburg, VA) **32155**
WVRB-FM - 95.3 (Fairfield, OH) **25192**
WVRC-AM - 1400 (Spencer, WV) **33472**
WVRD-FM **16561***
WVRK-FM (Columbus, GA) *Unable to locate*
WVRQ-AM - 1360 (Viroqua, WI) **34384**
WVRQ-FM - 102.3 (Viroqua, WI) **34385**
WVRR-FM - 101.7 (Lebanon, NH) **18546**
WVRT-FM (Williamsport, PA) *Unable to locate*
WVRU-FM - 89.9 (Radford, VA) **32353**
WVRV-FM - 101.1 (St. Louis, MO) **17561**
WVSA-AM - 1380 (Vernon, AL) **514**
WVSB-FM - 104.1 (Romney, WV) **33453**
WVSB-TV **16855***
WVSC-AM - 990 (Johnstown, PA) **27100**
WVSD-FM - 91.7 (Itta Bena, MS) **16690**
WVSM-AM - 1500 (Rainsville, AL) **430**
WVSR-AM - 1240 (Charleston, WV) **33290**
WVSR-FM - 102.7 (Charleston, WV) **33291**
WVST-FM - 91.3 (Petersburg, VA) **32333**
WVSU-FM - 91.1 (Birmingham, AL) **130**
WVSV-FM (Stevenson, AL) *Unable to locate*
WVSX-TV - Channel 59 (Ghent, WV) **33321**
WVTA-TV - Channel 41 (Windsor, VT) **31623**
WVTB-TV - Channel 20 (St. Johnsbury, VT) **31597**
WVTC-FM - 90.7 (Randolph Center, VT) **31583**
WVTF-FM - 89.1 (Roanoke, VA) **32507**
WVTH-FM (Goodman, MS) *Unable to locate*
WVTI-FM - 96.1 (Grand Rapids, MI) **15126**
WVTM-TV - Channel 13 (Birmingham, AL) **131**
WVTR-FM - 91.9 (Roanoke, VA) **32508**
WVTT-TV (Manassas, VA) *Unable to locate*
WVTU-FM - 89.3 (Charlottesville, VA) **31957**
WVTV-TV - Channel 18 (Milwaukee, WI) **34143**
WVTY-FM (Pittsburgh, PA) *Unable to locate*
WVU-FM **29530***
WVUA-FM - 90.7 (Tuscaloosa, AL) **504**
WVUC-FM - 93.1 (Elkins, WV) **33311**
WVUD-FM - 91.3 (Newark, DE) **5282**
WVUE-TV - Channel 8 (New Orleans, LA) **12779**
WVUM-FM - 90.5 (Coral Gables, FL) **6016**
WVUR-FM - 95.1 (Valparaiso, IN) **10515**
WVUT-TV - Channel 22 (Vincennes, IN) **10526**
WVVA-TV - Channel 6 (Bluefield, WV) **33261**
WVVC-FM - 100.7 (New Hartford, NY) **21109**
WVVE-FM (Pawcatuck, CT) *Unable to locate*
WVVR-FM (Clarksville, TN) *Unable to locate*
WVVS-FM - 90.9 (Valdosta, GA) **7626**
WVVV-FM **32352***
WVVW-AM **33326***
WVVW-AM **25348***
WVVX-FM (Chicago, IL) *Unable to locate*
WVWR-FM **32507***
WVWV-FM **9908***
WVXA-FM - 96.7 (Rogers City, MI) **15471**
WVXH-FM - 92.1 (Harrison, MI) **15145**
WVXU-FM - 91.7 (Cincinnati, OH) **24849**

WVYC-FM - 99.7 (York, PA) **28218**
WVYH-FM **12886***
WVZN-AM - 1170 (Roanoke, VA) **32509**
WWAB-AM - 1330 (Lakeland, FL) **6297**
WWAC-TV - Channel 53 (Atlantic City, NJ) **18660**
WWAG-FM - 107.9 (Mc Kee, KY) **12292**
WWAK-AM (Hawthorne, FL) *Ceased*
WWAM-AM **14848***
WWAS-AM **28189***
WWAV-FM **12888***
WWAX-FM - 92.1 (Duluth, MN) **15858**
WWAY-TV - Channel 3 (Wilmington, NC) **24306**
WWAZ-AM **28347***
WWBA-FM **6644***
WWBB-AM **33300***
WWBB-FM - 101.5 (Providence, RI) **28439**
WWBC-AM - 1510 (Cocoa, FL) **6002**
WWBE-FM - 98.3 (Selinsgrove, PA) **27980**
WWBF-AM - 1130 (Bartow, FL) **5920**
WWBH-AM (New Smyrna Beach, FL) *Unable to locate*
WWBK-FM (Fredericktown, OH) *Unable to locate*
WWBL-FM - 106.5 (Washington, IN) **10543**
WWBN-FM - 101.5 (Burton, MI) **14841**
WWBT-TV - Channel 12 (Richmond, VA) **32488**
WWBZ-AM (Sewell, NJ) *Unable to locate*
WWCA-AM (Gary, IN) *Unable to locate*
WWCB-AM - 1370 (Corry, PA) **26810**
WWCC-AM **27054***
WWCH-AM - 1300 (Clarion, PA) **26784**
WWCK-AM - 105.5 (Flint, MI) **15048**
WWCL-FM **16874***
WWCM-AM **14777***
WWCM-AM **10501***
WWCM-AM (Ypsilanti, MI) *Unable to locate*
WWCM-FM **10500***
WWCO-AM - 1240 (Waterbury, CT) **5198**
WWCP-TV - Channel 8 (Johnstown, PA) **27101**
WWCS-AM (Canonsburg, PA) *Unable to locate*
WWCT-FM (Peoria, IL) *Unable to locate*
WWCU-FM - 90.5 (Cullowhee, NC) **23796**
WWCW-FM **26692***
WWDB-FM - 96.5 (Bala Cynwyd, PA) **26681**
WWDC-AM - 101.1 (Rockfield, MD) **13674**
WWDC-FM - 101.1 (Rockville, MD) **13705**
WWDE-FM (Virginia Beach, VA) *Unable to locate*
WWDE-FM - 101.3 (Virginia Beach, VA) **32597**
WWDF-AM (Shreveport, LA) *Unable to locate*
WWDJ-AM - 970 (Hasbrouck Heights, NJ) **18869**
WWDL-FM - 104.9 (Scranton, PA) **27973**
WWDM-FM - 103.1 (Columbia, SC) **28587**
WWDS **26915***
WWDX-FM (East Lansing, MI) *Unable to locate*
WWEB-FM - 89.9 (Wallingford, CT) **5189**
WWEC-FM **18523***
WWEC-FM - 88.3 (Elizabethtown, PA) **26869**
WWED-AM **14645***
WWEL-FM - 103.9 (London, KY) **12205**
WWET-FM **10262***
WWEV-FM - 91.5 (Cumming, GA) **7217**
WWEZ-FM **24845***
WWEZ-FM - 97.5 (Trenton, TN) **29632**
WWFG-FM - 99.9 (Salisbury, MD) **13721**
WWFH-FM **27886***
WWFM-FM **27149***
WWFM-The Classical Network - 89.1 (Trenton, NJ) **19679**
WWFN-FM (Florence, SC) *Unable to locate*
WWFX-FM **12926***
WWFX-FM - 100.1 (Worcester, MA) **14700**
WWGC-FM - 90.7 (Carrollton, GA) **7160**
WWGL **24042***
WWGM-AM (Gallatin, TN) *Unable to locate*
WWGR-AM **29309***
WWGR-FM - 101.9 (Fort Myers, FL) **6115**
WWGS-AM (Albany, GA) *Unable to locate*
WWGZ-AM **15310***
WWGZ-FM **15312***
WWHB-FM (Hampton Bays, NY) *Unable to locate*
WWHC-FM **9920***
WWHG-AM **20756***
WWHG-FM **20757***
WWHK-FM (Hartford, KY) *Unable to locate*
WWHL-AM (Cocoa, FL) *Unable to locate*
WWHN-AM (Joliet, IL) *Unable to locate*
WWHO-TV (Chillicothe, OH) *Unable to locate*
WWHP-FM - 98.3 (Farmer City, IL) **8887**
WWHP-FM - 98.3 (Farmer City, IL) **8886**
WWHR-AM **5944***
WWHS-FM - 92.1 (Hampden Sydney, VA) **32125**
WWHT-FM - 107.9 (Syracuse, NY) **23448**
WWHY-AM (Milan, TN) *Ceased*
WWIB-FM - 103.7 (Chippewa Falls, WI) **33633**
WWIC-AM - 1050 (Scottsboro, AL) **450**
WWIH-FM - 90.3 (High Point, NC) **24007**
WWII-AM - 720 (Shiremanstown, PA) **27995**
WWIL-AM - 1490 (Wilmington, NC) **24307**
WWIL-FM - 90.5 (Wilmington, NC) **24308**
WWIN-AM **9859***

WWIN-AM - 1400 (Baltimore, MD) **13286**
WWIN-FM - 95.9 (Baltimore, MD) **13287**
WWIS-AM - 1260 (Black River Falls, WI) **33592**
WWIS-FM - 99.7 (Black River Falls, WI) **33593**
WWIT-AM (Canton, NC) *Unable to locate*
WWIZ-FM - 103.9 (Hermitage, PA) **27038**
WWJ-AM - 950 (Southfield, MI) **15561**
WWJ-TV **14958***
WWJB-AM - 1450 (Brooksville, FL) **5966**
WWJC-AM - 850 (Duluth, MN) **15859**
WWJD-FM - 91.7 (Pippa Passes, KY) **12369**
WWJM-FM - 105.9 (New Lexington, OH) **25416**
WWJO-FM - 98.1 (St. Cloud, MN) **16354**
WWJR-FM **34323***
WWJY-FM - 103.9 (Hammond, IN) **10058**
WWKA-FM - 92.3 (Orlando, FL) **6530**
WWKB-AM (Buffalo, NY) *Unable to locate*
WWKC-FM - 104.9 (Cambridge, OH) **24729**
WWKE-AM **6477***
WWKI-FM - 100.5 (Kokomo, IN) **10244**
WWKJ-FM **14633***
WWKK-AM - 750 (Petoskey, MI) **15442**
WWKL-FM - 99.3 (Harrisburg, PA) **27026**
WWKM-AM (Harrison, MI) *Ceased*
WWKN-AM **14800***
WWKN-FM - 104.9 (Battle Creek, MI) **14801**
WWKO-AM **6614***
WWKS-FM **27882***
WWKX-FM - 106.3 (Pawtucket, RI) **28380**
WWKY-AM **12268***
WWKZ-FM - 105.3 (Tupelo, MS) **16859**
WWL-AM - 870 (New Orleans, LA) **12780**
WWL-TV - Channel 4 (New Orleans, LA) **12781**
WWLA-FM **33890***
WWLB-AM **6813***
WWLF-TV - Channel 56 (Wilkes Barre, PA) **28179**
WWLH-FM **32336***
WWLI-FM - 105 (East Providence, RI) **28351**
WWLL-FM - 105.7 (Sebring, FL) **6681**
WWLP-TV - Channel 22 (Springfield, MA) **14566**
WWLR-FM - 91.5 (Lyndonville, VT) **31551**
WWLS-AM (Norman, OK) *Unable to locate*
WWLS-FM - 104.9 (Oklahoma City, OK) **26024**
WWLT-FM - 103.1 (London, KY) **12206**
WWLV-FM **6514***
WWLV-FM **6514***
WWLV-FM - 93.9 (Miramar, FL) **6433**
WWLX-AM - 590 (Lawrenceburg, TN) **29320**
WWLZ-AM - 820 (Elmira, NY) **20580**
WWLZ-FM **14849***
WWMC-FM **27980***
WWMC-FM - 90.9 (Lynchburg, VA) **32217**
WWMG-FM - 96.1 (Charlotte, NC) **23782**
WWMH **34148***
WWMJ-FM - 95.7 (Brewer, ME) **12929**
WWMM-FM (Greenville, SC) *Unable to locate*
WWMO-AM (Eden, NC) *Unable to locate*
WWMO-FM **31889***
WWMS-FM - 97.5 (Tupelo, MS) **16860**
WWMT-TV - Channel 3 (Kalamazoo, MI) **15260**
WWMX-FM - 106.5 (Baltimore, MD) **13288**
WWMY-FM (Greensboro, NC) *Ceased*
WWNC-AM - 570 (Asheville, NC) **23640**
WWNH-AM - 1340 (Dover, NH) **18497**
WWNJ-FM - 91.1 (Trenton, NJ) **19680**
WWNK-FM (Cincinnati, OH) *Unable to locate*
WWNN-AM - 980 (Boca Raton, FL) **5944**
WWNO-FM - 89.9 (New Orleans, LA) **12782**
WWNR-AM - 620 (Beckley, WV) **33246**
WWNS-AM - 1240 (Statesboro, GA) **7568**
WWNT-AM (Dothan, AL) *Unable to locate*
WWNW-FM - 88.9 (New Wilmington, PA) **27326**
WWNY-TV - Channel 7 (Watertown, NY) **23521**
WWNZ-AM (Orlando, FL) *Unable to locate*
WWOD-AM (Lynchburg, VA) *Ceased*
WWOG-FM - 90.9 (Somerset, KY) **12413**
WWOJ-FM - 99.1 (Sebring, FL) **6682**
WWOK-AM **9942***
WWOK-FM **24093***
WWOL-AM - 780 (Forest City, NC) **23896**
WWOM-AM **12686***
WWOM-FM **23316***
WWOM-TV **12770***
WWON-AM (Woonsocket, RI) *Unable to locate*
WWON-AM - 930 (Waynesboro, TN) **29645**
WW1 Aero (Poughkeepsie, NY) **23151**
WWOO-FM **23796***
WWOO-FM **32634***
WWOR-TV - Channel 9 (Secaucus, NJ) **19543**
WWOW-AM - 1360 (Conneaut, OH) **25093**
WWOZ-FM - 90.7 (New Orleans, LA) **12783**
WWPA-AM (Williamsport, PA) *Unable to locate*
WWPB-TV - Channel 31 (Hagerstown, MD) **13578**
WWPD (Marion, SC) *Unable to locate*
WWPF-AM **6539***
WWPG-AM - 1280 (Tuscaloosa, AL) **505**
WWPH-FM - 107.9 (Princeton Junction, NJ) **19484**
WWPI-FM - 90.1 (Worcester, MA) **14701**
WWPJ-AM **505***

WWPR-AM **16851***
WWPR-FM - 105.1 (New York, NY) **22993**
WWPT-FM - 90.3 (Westport, CT) **5218**
WWPV-FM - 88.7 (Colchester, VT) **31535**
WWQC-FM **9482***
WWQI-TV **33893***
WWQM-FM - 106.3 (Madison, WI) **34010**
WWQQ-FM - 101.3 (Wilmington, NC) **24309**
WWRB-FM **29529***
WWRC-AM (Silver Spring, MD) *Unable to locate*
WWRC-FM **19166***
WWRE-FM - 105.5 (Winchester, VA) **32634**
WWRF-AM - 1380 (West Palm Beach, FL) **6861**
WWRK-FM - 92.1 (Elberton, GA) **7268**
WWRL-AM - 1600 (Woodside, NY) **23594**
WWRM-FM - 94.9 (St. Petersburg, FL) **6644**
WWRQ-FM - 107.7 (Valdosta, GA) **7627**
WWRV-AM - 1330 (Paterson, NJ) **19418**
WWRW-FM **34467***
WWRX-FM - 103.7 (Providence, RI) **28440**
WWS/World Ports **6480***
WWS/World Wide Shipping (Odessa, FL) **6480**
WWSB-TV (Sarasota, FL) **6677**
WWSC-AM - 1450 (Glens Falls, NY) **20670**
WWSE-FM - 93.3 (Jamestown, NY) **20846**
WWSH-FM **27887***
WWSH-FM (Hazleton, PA) *Unable to locate*
WWSJ-AM (St. Johns, MI) *Unable to locate*
WWSK-FM - 107.1 (Myrtle Beach, SC) **28712**
WWSL-FM - 102.3 (Philadelphia, MS) **16818**
WWSM-AM - 1510 (Lebanon, PA) **27179**
WWSN-FM **23773***
WWSN-FM - 103.3 (Brunswick, GA) **7144**
WWSP-FM - 89.9 (Stevens Point, WI) **34347**
WWSR-AM - 1420 (St. Albans, VT) **31592**
WWSS-AM - 1290 (Peoria, IL) **9441**
WWSS-FM (Laconia, NH) *Unable to locate*
WWST-AM **25676***
WWST-FM **25677***
WWSU-FM - 106.9 (Dayton, OH) **25154**
WWSW-AM - 970 (Pittsburgh, PA) **27880**
WWSW-FM - 94.5 (Pittsburgh, PA) **27881**
WWSY-FM **24708***
WWSY-FM - 95.9 (Brookfield, OH) **24710**
WWTC-AM (St. Louis Park, MN) *Unable to locate*
WWTI-TV - Channel 50 (Watertown, NY) **23522**
WWTK-AM - 730 (Sebring, FL) **6683**
WWTM-AM - 1400 (Decatur, AL) **176**
WWTN-FM - 99.7 (Nashville, TN) **29538**
WWTO-TV - Channel 35 (Ottawa, IL) **9393**
WWTR-FM **9652***
WWTR-FM (Ocean City, MD) *Unable to locate*
WWTV-TV - Channel 9 & 10 (Cadillac, MI) **14850**
WWUC-FM **29636***
WWUC-FM - 105.7 (Union City, TN) **29637**
WWUF-FM - 97.7 (Atlanta, GA) **7091**
WWUH-FM - 91.3 (West Hartford, CT) **5206**
WWUP-TV (Kinross, MI) *Unable to locate*
WWUS-FM - 104.1 (Big Pine Key, FL) **5924**
WWVA-AM - 1170 (Wheeling, WV) **33510**
WWVR-FM (West Terre Haute, IN) *Unable to locate*
WWVU-FM - 91.7 (Morgantown, WV) **33406**
WWVU-TV **33404***
WWVY-FM (New York, NY) *Unable to locate*
WWVZ-FM - 103.9 (Arlington, VA) **31848**
WWWA-FM **14595***
WWWB-AM **299***
WWWB-AM **23958***
WWWB-FM **23947***
WWWB-TV **6797***
WWWF-AM **215***
WWWG-AM - 1460 (Rochester, NY) **23257**
WWWI-AM - 1270 (Brainerd, MN) **15771**
www.industry.net (Englewood, CO) **4417**
WWWJ-AM - 1360 (Galax, VA) **32101**
WWWK-FM **32225***
WWWL-AM **31762***
WWWL-FM **6431***
WWWM-AM **25581***
WWWM-FM **24980***
WWWM-FM - 105.5 (Toledo, OH) **25590**
WWWO **9919***
WWWO-FM - 93.5 (Daleville, IN) **9920**
WWWQ-AM **6102***
WWWQ-FM (Glasgow, KY) *Unable to locate*
WWWR-AM - 910 (Roanoke, VA) **32510**
WWWS-AM (Buffalo, NY) *Unable to locate*
WWWS-FM **23976***
WWWS-FM **15506***
WWWT-AM - 1320 (Randolph Center, VT) **31584**
WWWV-FM - 97.5 (Charlottesville, VA) **31958**
WWWW-AM **15023***
WWWW-FM **14970***
WWWX-FM - 96.9 (Neenah, WI) **34161**
WWWY-FM - 104.9 (Columbus, IN) **9899**
WWWZ-FM (Charleston, SC) *Unable to locate*
WWXL-FM **12206***
WWXM-FM - 97.7 (Myrtle Beach, SC) **28713**
WWYD-FM **20715***

WWYN-FM - 106.9 (Jackson, TN) **29241**
WWYO-AM - 970 (Pineville, WV) **33438**
WWYZ-FM - 92.5 (Hartford, CT) **4915**
WWZB-AM - 93.9 (Somerset, KY) **12414**
WWZD-AM (Tupelo, MS) *Ceased*
WWZZ-FM - 104.1 (Arlington, VA) **31849**
WXAC-FM - 91.3 (Reading, PA) **27925**
WXAG-AM (Athens, GA) *Unable to locate*
WXAL-AM - 1400 (Demopolis, AL) **181**
WXAM-AM (Hodgenville, KY) *Unable to locate*
WXAN-FM - 103.9 (Ava, IL) **8046**
WXAR-FM - 95.7 (Wilkes Barre, PA) **28180**
WXAV-FM - 88.3 (Chicago, IL) **8659**
WXBA-FM - 88.1 (Brentwood, NY) **20241**
WXBB-FM - 105.3 (Dover, NH) **18498**
WXBC-AM - 540 (Annandale On Hudson, NY) **20061**
WXBE-FM - 97.9 (Wilkes Barre, PA) **28181**
WXBK-AM (Albertville, AL) *Ceased*
WXBM-FM (Pace, FL) *Unable to locate*
WXBQ-AM - 980 (Bristol, VA) **31900**
WXBQ-FM - 96.9 (Bristol, VA) **31901**
WXCC-FM - 96.5 (Williamson, WV) **33515**
WXCE-AM - 1260 (Amery, WI) **33528**
WXCF-FM - 103.9 (Clifton Forge, VA) **31977**
WXCI-FM - 91.7 (Danbury, CT) **4768**
WXCL-FM - 104.9 (Peoria, IL) **9442**
WXCO-AM - 1230 (Wausau, WI) **34440**
WXCR-FM **20013***
WXCR-FM **6645***
WXCT-AM **4884***
WXCT-FM **12525***
WXCV-FM - 95.3 (Homosassa, FL) **6207**
WXCY-FM - 103.7 (Havre de Grace, MD) **13581**
WXDG-FM - 105.1 (Southfield, MI) **15562**
WXDJ-FM (Miami, FL) *Unable to locate*
WXDR-FM **5282***
WXDT-FM **27737***
WXDU-FM - 88.7 (Durham, NC) **23854**
WXDX AM - 1310 (Farmington Hills, MI) **15027**
WXDX-FM - 105.9 (Pittsburgh, PA) **27882**
WXEE-AM (Welch, WV) *Ceased*
WXEG-FM - 103.9 (Dayton, OH) **25155**
WXEI-FM - 95.3 (Crestview, FL) **6028**
WXEL-FM - 90.7 (Boynton Beach, FL) **5954**
WXEL-TV - Channel 42 (Boynton Beach, FL) **5955**
WXEM-AM - 1460 (Austell, GA) **7117**
WXEW-AM - 840 (Yabucoa, PR) **28322**
WXEX-FM - 107.9 (Chicago, IL) **8660**
WXEX-TV **32481***
WXFG-FM **7107***
WXFL-FM - 96.1 (Florence, AL) **226**
WXFL-TV **6790***
WXFM-FM - 99.3 (Mount Zion, IL) **9255**
WXFN-AM - 1340 (Muncie, IN) **10334**
WXFX-FM (Prattville, AL) *Unable to locate*
WXGA-TV (Atlanta, GA) *Unable to locate*
WXGC-FM **7437***
WXGI-AM (Richmond, VA) *Unable to locate*
WXGL-AM **12996***
WXGL-FM **13025***
WXGM-AM - 1420 (Gloucester, VA) **32116**
WXGM-FM - 99.1 (Gloucester, VA) **32117**
WXGO-AM - 1270 (Madison, IN) **10286**
WXGT-FM **25078***
WXGZ-TV **33744***
WXHC-FM - 101.5 (Homer, NY) **20750**
WXHT-FM (Portsmouth, NH) *Unable to locate*
WXIA-TV - Channel 11 (Atlanta, GA) **7092**
WXIC-AM - 660 (Waverly, OH) **25625**
WXIE-FM - 92.3 (Oakland, MD) **13637**
WXII-AM - 830 (Winston-Salem, NC) **24336**
WXII-TV - Channel 12 (Winston-Salem, NC) **24337**
WXIK-FM **15180***
WXIL-FM (Parkersburg, WV) *Unable to locate*
WXIN-FM - 90.7 (Providence, RI) **28441**
WXIN-TV - Channel 59 (Indianapolis, IN) **10215**
WXIR-FM - 98.3 (Indianapolis, IN) **10216**
WXIS-FM - 103.9 (Erwin, TN) **29186**
WXIX-TV (Cincinnati, OH) *Unable to locate*
WXIY-AM **16555***
WXIY-FM **16556***
WXIZ-FM - 100.9 (Waverly, OH) **25626**
WXJM-FM - 88.7 (Harrisonburg, VA) **32156**
WXJN-FM (Salisbury, MD) *Unable to locate*
WXJX-FM **28122***
WXKC-FM - 99.9 (Erie, PA) **26913**
WXKE-FM - 103.9 (Fort Wayne, IN) **9994**
WXKL-AM - 1290 (Sanford, NC) **24222**
WXKO-AM - 1150 (Fort Valley, GA) **7291**
WXKO-FM **7290***
WXKO-FM, call letters changed to WZUS (FM) & city of license changed to Macon, IL 4/1/02. **29542***
WXKS-AM - 1430 (Medford, MA) **14326**
WXKS-FM - 107.9 (Medford, MA) **14327**
WXKT-FM - 100.1 (Washington, GA) **7642**
WXKU-AM **26867***
WXKW-AM **28161***
WXKX-AM - 1340 (Clarksburg, WV) **33296**
WXKX-FM (Parkersburg, WV) *Unable to locate*

Numbers cited in bold after listings are entry numbers rather than page numbers.

WXLA-AM - 1180 (Lansing, MI) **15307**
WXLC-FM - 102.3 (Waukegan, IL) **9747**
WXLE-FM **7189***
WXLF-AM **23761***
WXLI-AM - 1230 (Dublin, GA) **7256**
WXLI-FM **7252***
WXLK-FM **23949***
WXLK-FM - 92.3 (Roanoke, VA) **32511**
WXLL-AM (Decatur, GA) *Unable to locate*
WXLM-FM - 105.7 (New Albany, IN) **10340**
WXLN-AM - 1570 (New Albany, IN) **10341**
WXLN-FM **10340***
WXLN-FM **10340***
WXLO-FM - 104.5 (Worcester, MA) **14702**
WXLP-FM - 96.9 (Davenport, IA) **10752**
WXLQ-FM (Berlin, NH) *Unable to locate*
WXLR-FM **28023***
WXLR-FM - 104.9 (Harold, KY) **12110**
WXLS-FM **5223***
WXLT-TV **6677***
WXLV-FM - 90.3 (Schnecksville, PA) **27950**
WXLW-AM (Indianapolis, IN) *Unable to locate*
WXLX-AM **7438***
WXLX-FM - 103.7 (Bayamon, PR) **28233**
WXLY-FM - 102.5 (Mount Pleasant, SC) **28700**
WXLZ-AM - 1140 (Castlewood, VA) **31909**
WXLZ-FM - 107.3 (Lebanon, VA) **32181**
WXMC-AM (Parsippany, NJ) *Unable to locate*
WXMI-TV - Channel 17 (Grand Rapids, MI) **15127**
WXMJ-FM - 99.5 (Mount Union, PA) **27303**
WXMR-FM - 93.3 (Athens, AL) **31**
WXMT-TV - Channel 30 (Nashville, TN) **29539**
WXNE-TV **14156***
WXOD-FM - 98.7 (Winchester, NH) **18652**
WXOF-FM (Hernando, FL) *Unable to locate*
WXOK-AM (Baton Rouge, LA) *Unable to locate*
WXOL-AM **8658***
WXOL-AM (Oshkosh, WI) *Unable to locate*
WXON-TV **14962***
WXOQ-FM - 105.5 (Savannah, TN) **29587**
WXOR-FM **16569***
WXOU-FM - 88.3 (Rochester, MI) **15468**
WXOW-TV - Channel 19 (La Crescent, MN) **15988**
WXOX-AM (Bay City, MI) *Unable to locate*
WXOX-FM - 101.7 (Batavia, NY) **20124**
WXPL-FM - 91.3 (Fitchburg, MA) **14186**
WXPN-FM - 88.5 (Philadelphia, PA) **27747**
WXPQ-AM (Wauchula, FL) *Ceased*
WXPR-FM - 91.7 (Rhinelander, WI) **34292**
WXPS-FM **20726***
WXPT-FM - 104.1 (Minneapolis, MN) **16164**
WXPX-AM **27892***
WXPZ-FM - 101.3 (Milford, DE) **5263**
WXQK-AM - 970 (Cleveland, TN) **29128**
WXQR-FM (Jacksonville, NC) *Unable to locate*
WXQT-FM (Binghamton, NY) *Ceased*
WXRA-FM (Winston-Salem, NC) *Unable to locate*
WXRC-FM (Charlotte, NC) *Unable to locate*
WXRF-AM (Guayama, PR) *Unable to locate*
WXRF-FM **28247***
WXRI-FM - 91.3 (Blacksburg, VA) **31891**
WXRK-FM (New York, NY) *Unable to locate*
WXRL-AM - 1300 (Lancaster, NY) **20885**
WXRO-FM - 95.3 (Beaver Dam, WI) **33570**
WXRS-AM - 1590 (Swainsboro, GA) **7579**
WXRS-FM - 100.5 (Swainsboro, GA) **7580**
WXRT-FM - 93.1 (Chicago, IL) **8661**
WXRV-FM - 92.5 (Haverhill, MA) **14233**
WXRX-FM - 104.9 (Rockford, IL) **9543**
WXRY-FM **28572***
WXRZ-FM - 94.3 (Corinth, MS) **16619**
WXSR-FM (Tallahassee, FL) *Unable to locate*
WXSS-AM (Memphis, TN) *Unable to locate*
WXST-FM - 107.9 (Columbus, OH) **25090**
WXTA-FM - 97.9 (Edinboro, PA) **26864**
WXTB-FM - 97.8 (Tampa, FL) **6811**
WXTC-AM (Charleston, SC) *Unable to locate*
WXTC-FM (Charleston, SC) *Unable to locate*
WXTK-FM - 95.1 (West Yarmouth, MA) **14634**
WXTL-AM (Jacksonville, FL) *Unable to locate*
WXTN-AM - 1000 (Lexington, MS) **16747**
WXTO-AM - 1600 (Orlando, FL) **6531**
WXTQ-FM - 105.5 (Athens, OH) **24637**
WXTR-AM (Salt Lake City, UT) *Unable to locate*
WXTR-FM **31848***
WXTS-FM - 88.3 (Toledo, OH) **25591**
WXTU-FM - 92.5 (Bala Cynwyd, PA) **26682**
WXTV-TV (Secaucus, NJ) *Unable to locate*
WXTX-TV - Channel 54 (Columbus, GA) **7196**
WXTY-FM **23451***
WXTZ-AM **10192***
WXTZ-FM (Indianapolis, IN) *Unable to locate*
WXUR-FM - 92.7 (Ilion, NY) **20781**
WXUS-FM **10260***
WXVI-AM Montgomery, AL) *Unable to locate*
WXVL-FM - 99.3 (Crossville, TN) **29162**
WXVQ-AM - 1490 (Daytona Beach, FL) **6046**
WXVT-TV - Channel 15 (Greenville, MS) **16643**
WXVW-AM **10227***

WXVX-AM - 1510 (Monroeville, PA) **27289**
WXWX-FM (Greenville, SC) *Unable to locate*
WXWY-AM **438***
WXXA-AM - 790 (Louisville, KY) **12268**
WXXA-TV - Channel 23 (Albany, NY) **20017**
WXXB-FM - 102.9 (Lafayette, IN) **10263**
WXXI-AM - 1370 (Rochester, NY) **23258**
WXXI-TV - Channel 21 (Rochester, NY) **23259**
WXXK-FM **18546***
WXXK-FM - 100.5 (Lebanon, NH) **18547**
WXXL-FM (Altamonte Springs, FL) *Unable to locate*
WXXM-FM (Philadelphia, PA) *Unable to locate*
WXXO-FM (Clifton Park, NY) *Unable to locate*
WXXP-FM - 97.9 (Indianapolis, IN) **10217**
WXXQ-FM (Rockford, IL) *Unable to locate*
WXXR-AM (Cullman, AL) *Unable to locate*
WXXR-FM **165***
WXXU-AM (Cocoa, FL) *Unable to locate*
WXXV-TV - Channel 25 (Gulfport, MS) **16659**
WXXX-FM - 95.5 (Colchester, VT) **31536**
WXYB-FM **15695***
WXYC-FM - 89.3 (Chapel Hill, NC) **23733**
WXYM-FM - 96.1 (Tomah, WI) **34372**
WXYQ-AM **34345***
WXYT-AM - 1270 (Southfield, MI) **15563**
WXYU-AM **32212***
WXYV-FM (Baltimore, MD) *Unable to locate*
WXYZ-AM **15563***
WXYZ-TV - Channel 7 (Southfield, MI) **15564**
WXZQ-FM - 100.1 (Piketon, OH) **25478**
WYAB-FM - 93.1 (Yazoo City, MS) **16885**
WYAH-TV **32335***
WYAI-FM (Atlanta, GA) *Unable to locate*
WYAJ-FM - 97.7 (Sudbury, MA) **14582**
WYAK-AM - 1270 (Myrtle Beach, SC) **28714**
WYAK-FM - 103.1 (Myrtle Beach, SC) **28715**
WYAM-AM **53***
WYAM-AM - 890 (Decatur, AL) **177**
WYAM-FM (Hartselle, AL) *Unable to locate*
Wyandotte County Shopper (Kansas City, KS) **11535**
Wyandotte Echo; Kansas City (Kansas City, KS) **11528**
Wyandotte Municipal Services (Wyandotte, MI) **15686**
The Wyandotte West (Kansas City, KS) **11536**
WYAT-AM **12681***
WYAV-FM - 104.1 (Myrtle Beach, SC) **28716**
WYAY-FM - 106.7 (Atlanta, GA) **7093**
WYBB-FM - 98.1 (Charleston, SC) **28526**
WYBC-FM - 94.3 (New Haven, CT) **5015**
WYBE-TV (Philadelphia, PA) *Unable to locate*
WYBG-AM - 1050 (Massena, NY) **21029**
WYBN-FM - 93.1 (Grand Rapids, MI) **15128**
WYBR-FM **9543***
WYBT-AM - 1000 (Blountstown, FL) **5927**
WYCA-FM - 92.3 (Hammond, IN) **10059**
WYCB-AM (Washington, DC) *Unable to locate*
WYCC-TV - Channel 20 (Chicago, IL) **8662**
WYCE-FM (Wyoming, MI) *Unable to locate*
WYCK-AM - 1340 (Scranton, PA) **27974**
The Wyckoff Suburban News (Ridgewood, NJ) **19506**
WYCL-AM **31885***
WYCL-FM - 107.3 (Pensacola, FL) **6580**
WYCO-FM - 107.9 (Wausau, WI) **34441**
WYCP-FM **28218***
WYCQ-FM **29507***
WYCR-FM - 98.5 (Hanover, PA) **26980**
WYCS-FM - 91.5 (Smithfield, VA) **32528**
WYCV-AM - 900 (Granite Falls, NC) **23914**
WYCY-FM - 105.3 (Honesdale, PA) **27055**
WYDE-AM (Birmingham, AL) *Unable to locate*
WYDH-FM - 105.9 (Atmore, AL) **37**
WYDO-TV - Channel 14 (Morehead City, NC) **24072**
WYEA-AM - 1290 (Sylacauga, AL) **464**
WYEA-TV **7190***
WYER-AM **9234***
WYES-TV - Channel 12 (New Orleans, LA) **12784**
WYEZ-FM **10316***
WYFA-FM - 107.1 (Waynesboro, GA) **7650**
WYFB-FM - 90.5 (Keystone Heights, FL) **6259**
WYFD-FM - 91.7 (Huntsville, AL) **288**
WYFE-FM - 88.9 (Port Richey, FL) **6600**
WYFF-TV - Channel 4 (Greenville, SC) **28645**
WYFG-FM - 91.1 (Cowpens, SC) **28595**
WYFH-FM - 90.7 (Summerville, SC) **28767**
WYFI-FM - 99.7 (Chesapeake, VA) **31967**
WYFJ-FM - 100.1 (Ashland, VA) **31859**
WYFK-FM - 89.5 (Cataula, GA) **7164**
WYFM-FM - 102.9 (Youngstown, OH) **25713**
WYFN-AM - 980 (Madison, TN) **29339**
WYFQ-AM (Charlotte, NC) *Unable to locate*
WYFS-FM - 89.5 (Bloomingdale, GA) **7132**
WYFT-FM - 103.9 (Luray, VA) **32205**
WYFW-FM - 89.5 (Winder, GA) **7655**
WYFX-FM - 106.7 (Mount Vernon, IN) **10324**
WYFY-FM **29139***
WYGC-FM (Gainesville, FL) *Unable to locate*
WYGE-FM - 92.3 (London, KY) **12207**
WYGL-AM - 1240 (Selinsgrove, PA) **27981**
WYGL-FM - 100.5 (Selinsgrove, PA) **27982**

WYGO-AM **12024***
WYGO-FM **12025***
WYGR-AM - 1530 (Wyoming, MI) **15688**
WYGS **12309***
WYGS-AM **12308***
WYGY-FM (Cincinnati, OH) *Unable to locate*
WYHS-TV (Miramar, FL) *Unable to locate*
WYHT-FM - 105.3 (Mansfield, OH) **25340**
WYHY-FM - 95.3 (Rockford, IL) **9544**
WYIC-AM (Carmel, IN) *Unable to locate*
WYII-FM (Williamsport, MD) *Unable to locate*
WYIN-TV - Channel 56 (Merrillville, IN) **10302**
WYIS-AM - 1410 (Mc Rae, GA) **7428**
WYJB-FM (Albany, NY) *Unable to locate*
WYJD-FM (Brewton, AL) *Ceased*
WYKK-FM - 98.9 (Quitman, MS) **16831**
WYKM-AM - 1250 (Rupert, WV) **33457**
WYKR-FM - 101.3 (Wells River, VT) **31614**
WYKS-FM - 105.3 (Gainesville, FL) **6170**
WYKT-FM - 105.5 (Joliet, IL) **9038**
WYKX-FM - 104.7 (Escanaba, MI) **15012**
WYKZ-FM (Hilton Head Island, SC) *Unable to locate*
WYLD-AM - 940 (New Orleans, LA) **12785**
WYLD-FM - 98.5 (New Orleans, LA) **12786**
WYLE-TV (Tuscumbia, AL) *Unable to locate*
WYLF-AM - 850 (Penn Yan, NY) **23093**
WYLI-AM (Vienna, WV) *Unable to locate*
The Wylie News (Wylie, TX) **31310**
WYLL-AM - 1160 (Chicago, IL) **8663**
WYLO-AM **33607***
WYLR-FM (Glens Falls, NY) *Unable to locate*
WYLS-AM - 670 (York, AL) **518**
WYLX-FM (Lebanon, OH) *Unable to locate*
WYLZ-FM - 100.9 (Saginaw, MI) **15507**
WYMB-AM (Manning, SC) *Ceased*
WYMC-AM - 1430 (Mayfield, KY) **12287**
WYMC-FM **12444***
WYMG-FM - 100.5 (Springfield, IL) **9660**
WYMK-FM **28176***
Wymore Arbor State (Wymore, NE) **18319**
WYMR **6681***
WYMS-FM - 88.9 (Milwaukee, WI) **34144**
WYMT-TV - Channel 57 (Hazard, KY) **12122**
WYMX-FM (Greenwood, MS) *Unable to locate*
WYNA-FM (Tabor City, NC) *Unable to locate*
WYNC-AM (Yanceyville, NC) *Ceased*
WYND-AM - 1310 (DeLand, FL) **6057**
WYND-FM - 92.3 (Wanchese, NC) **24270**
WYNE-AM (Neenah, WI) *Ceased*
WYNF-FM - 105.9 (Sarasota, FL) **6678**
WYNG-FM - 105.3 (Evansville, IN) **9953**
WYNJ-FM **29243***
WYNK-AM - 1380 (Baton Rouge, LA) **12527**
WYNN-AM (Florence, SC) *Unable to locate*
WYNN-FM (Florence, SC) *Unable to locate*
Wynne Progress (Wynne, AR) **1372**
Wynnewood Gazette (Wynnewood, OK) **26202**
WYNO-AM (Nelsonville, OH) *Ceased*
WYNS-AM - 1160 (Lehighton, PA) **27184**
WYNT-FM - 95.9 (Upper Sandusky, OH) **25605**
WYNU-FM - 92.3 (Jackson, TN) **29243**
WYNU-FM - 92.3 (Jackson, TN) **29242**
WYNY-FM (New York, NY) *Unable to locate*
Wynyard Advance **37597***
Wynyard Advance/Gazette (Wynyard, SK, Can.) **37597**
WYNZ-AM **13057***
WYNZ-FM - 100.9 (South Portland, ME) **13056**
WYOC-FM (High Springs, FL) *Unable to locate*
WYOI-FM (Marietta, OH) *Unable to locate*
Wyoming Academy of Science; Journal of the Colorado- (Greeley, CO) **4498**
Wyoming Advance (Wyoming, MI) **15687**
Wyoming Archeologist (Casper, WY) **34485**
Wyoming Beverage Analyst (Denver, CO) *Ceased*
Wyoming Cable Television Inc. (Mullens, WV) **33411**
Wyoming Catholic Register (Cheyenne, WY) **34498**
Wyoming Counties; Farm News of Erie and (East Aurora, NY) **20542**
Wyoming County Farm News **20542***
Wyoming Daily News; Northern (Worland, WY) **34604**
Wyoming Eagle **34500***
Wyoming Law Journal **34553***
Wyoming Law Review (Laramie, WY) **34553**
The Wyoming Lawyer (Cheyenne, WY) **34499**
The Wyoming Plimpton Gazette **36366***
Wyoming Rural Electric News **34484***
Wyoming State Journal; The Lander (Lander, WY) **34543**
Wyoming State Tribune **34500***
Wyoming Stockman-Farmer (Cheyenne, WY) *Ceased*
Wyoming; TCI Cablevision of (Laramie, WY) **34558**
Wyoming Tribune-Eagle (Cheyenne, WY) **34500**
Wyoming Trucker (Casper, WY) **34486**
Wyoming Valley Jewish Reporter (Vestal, NY) **23489**
Wyoming Wildlife (Cheyenne, WY) **34501**
WYOO-FM **16147***
WYOS-FM (Wilkes Barre, PA) *Unable to locate*
WYOU-TV (Scranton, PA) *Unable to locate*

X

Y

Yachting; Pacific (Vancouver, BC, Can.) 35158
Yachtsman; Bay and Delta (Reno, NV) 18418
Yadkin Enterprises (Boonville, NC) *Unable to locate*
Yadkin Ripple (Yadkinville, NC) 24339
The Yadkin Valley Advertiser (Elkin, NC) 23868
Yahoo! Internet Life (New York, NY) 22947
Yakama Nation Radio - 1490 (Toppenish, WA) 33169
Yakima Herald-Republic (Yakima, WA) 33223
Yakima Nation Review (Toppenish, WA) *Unable to locate*
Yakuza (Wilmington, DE) 5296
Yale Daily News (New Haven, CT) 5004
Yale Expositor (Yale, MI) 15689
The Yale Herald (New Haven, CT) *Unable to locate*
The Yale Journal of Biology & Medicine (New Haven, CT) 5005
The Yale Journal of Criticism (Baltimore, MD) 13264
Yale Journal of Law and Feminism (New Haven, CT) 5006
The Yale Law Journal (New Haven, CT) 5007
The Yale Literary Magazine (New Haven, CT) 5008
Yale Record 26203*
The Yale Review (New Haven, CT) 5009
Yale Scientific Magazine (New Haven, CT) 5010
The Yancey Journal (Burnsville, NC) 5296
Yankee Food Service (Chicago, IL) *Unable to locate*
Yankee Homes (Dublin, NH) *Ceased*
Yankee Magazine (Dublin, NH) *Unable to locate*
Yankee Oilman Magazine 13841*
The Yankee Trader (Coram, NY) *Unable to locate*
Yankton Cable TV Ltd. (Yankton, SD) 29046
Yankton Daily Press & Dakotan (Yankton, SD) 29040
Yard and Garden (Fort Atkinson, WI) 33723
Yardley News (Yardley, PA) 28202
Yarmouth Register Sun (Yarmouth Port, MA) *Unable to locate*
Yarmouth Vanguard (Yarmouth, NS, Can.) 35624
The Yates Center News (Yates Center, KS) 11913
Yates City Banner (Yates City, IL) 9774
The Yazoo Herald (Yazoo City, MS) 16883
YB News (Youngstown, OH) 25700
Yeadon Times (Yeadon, PA) 28204
Year/2000 Journal (New York, NY) 22948
Yeast (Hoboken, NJ) 19121
Yell County Record (Danville, AR) 1096
Yellow Jacket (Springfield, MA) 14553
Yellow Jacket (Brownwood, TX) 29966
Yellow Springs News (Yellow Springs, OH) 25692
Yellowback Library (Des Moines, IA) 10818
Yellowknifer (Yellowknife, NT, Can.) 35528
Yellowstone County News, Inc. (Huntley, MT) 17834
Yes! A Journal of Positive Futures (Bainbridge Island, WA) 32659
YES Mag (Victoria, BC, Can.) 35231
YES Quarterly (Lansing, MI) 15297
Yesterday and Today in Lawrence County (Lawrenceburg, TN) 29317
Yesterday's Island (Nantucket, MA) 14343
Yesterday's Magazette (Sarasota, FL) 6670
Yesterdaze Toys (Clio, MI) *Ceased*
Yiddisher Kemfer (Jewish Fighter) (New York, NY) 22949
Yippi Yi Yea Western Lifestyles (Holly, MI) *Ceased*
YM (New York, NY) 22950
YO! (San Francisco, CA) 3466
Yoakum Herald-Times (Yoakum, TX) 31311
Yoga International (Honesdale, PA) 27052
Yoga Journal (Berkeley, CA) 1566
Yoga Magazine; Integral (Buckingham, VA) 31907
Yogi Bear (Santa Monica, CA) *Unable to locate*
YOLK (Los Angeles, CA) *Unable to locate*
Yomiuri America (New York, NY) 22951
Yonkers Herald Statesman (Mc Lean, VA) 32263
The Yonkers Home News & Times (Yonkers, NY) 23603
Yorba Linda Cable Television Co. 4120*
Yorba Linda Star (Santa Ana, CA) *Unable to locate*
YORK (Toronto, ON, Can.) *Ceased*
York Area Merchandiser; Northern Adams- (Lebanon, PA) 27175
York Cablevision Inc. (York, NE) 18324
York County Coast Star (Kennebunk, ME) 12973
York Daily Record (York, PA) 28207
The York Dispatch (York, PA) 28208
York Gazette (North York, ON, Can.) 36133
York Legal Record (York, PA) 28209

The York News (Newmarket, ON, Can.) *Unable to locate*
York News-Times (York, NE) 18321
York Pioneer (Toronto, ON, Can.) 36795
York Sunday News (York, PA) 28210
York Town Crier (Yorktown, VA) 32646
The York Weekly (York, ME) 13083
Yorkshire Journal 10552*
Yorkshire Journal (West Lafayette, IN) *Ceased*
Yorkton Broadcasting Co. Ltd. 37602*
Yorkton This Week & Enterprise (Yorkton, SK, Can.) 37600
Yorkton This Weekend (Yorkton, SK, Can.) *Ceased*
The Yorktown News (Yorktown, TX) 31312
Yorktown News-View (Yorktown, TX) 31313
Yorktown Pennysaver Corp. (Yorktown Heights, NY) 23610
Yorkville Enquirer (York, SC) 28790
Yossarian News Service (Millbrae, CA) 38137
YOU (Etobicoke, ON, Can.) *Ceased*
You! Magazine (Agoura Hills, CA) *Unable to locate*
You & Your Dog (Des Moines, IA) 10819
Young & Alive (Lincoln, NE) 18129
Young Bucks Outdoors (Montgomery, AL) 381
Young Children (Washington, DC) 5873
Young Country 30217*
Young Crusader (Hutchinson, KS) *Ceased*
Young Fashions Magazine (South Plainfield, NJ) *Ceased*
Young Horizons Indigo (Decatur, GA) 7238
Young Israel Viewpoint (New York, NY) 22952
Young Judaean (New York, NY) 22953
Young Learner; Social Studies and the (Austin, TX) 29805
Young Life (Yonkers, NY) *Ceased*
Young Miss 22950*
Young Rider (Mission Viejo, CA) 2559
Young Voices Magazine (Olympia, WA) 32864
Youngstown Jewish Times (Youngstown, OH) *Ceased*
Youngstown-Warren Call & Post (Cleveland, OH) *Ceased*
Youngsville TV Corp. (Youngsville, PA) 28219
Youngwood; The Advisor - (Mount Pleasant, PA) 27300
Your Big Backyard (Reston, VA) 32424
Your Black Books Guide (Hampton, VA) *Unable to locate*
Your Church (Carol Stream, IL) 8158
Your Community News (Three Rivers, MI) 15593
Your Family (New York, NY) *Ceased*
Your Family Shopper (Chippewa Falls, WI) 33630
Your Health (Boca Raton, FL) 5942
Your Health (Ogden, UT) *Unable to locate*
Your Health & Medical Bulletin 5942*
Your Home, Indoors & Out and Better Living (Ogden, UT) *Unable to locate*
Your Home Town News (Miami, FL) *Unable to locate*
Your Life Matters (Las Vegas, NV) 18388
Your Money (Skokie, IL) 9613
Your Neighbor (Davie, FL) *Unable to locate*
Your Neighbors (Bakersfield, CA) *Unable to locate*
Your World of Birds (Monterey, CA) 2585
Youth! (Nashville, TN) *Ceased*
Youth Action Forum (Toronto, ON, Can.) *Unable to locate*
Youth and Adolescence; Journal of (New York, NY) 22216
Youth Advocates; Voice of (Lanham, MD) 13609
Youth Connections; NYC/New (New York, NY) 22478
The Youth Leader (Springfield, MO) *Ceased*
Youth '96 (Pasadena, CA) *Unable to locate*
Youth Policy (Washington, DC) *Unable to locate*
Youth; Residential Treatment for Children and (Chicago, IL) 8555
Youth Runner Magazine (Lake Oswego, OR) 26406
Youth & Society (Thousand Oaks, CA) 3923
Youth Sports (Cocoa Beach, FL) *Unable to locate*
Youth Theatre Journal (Tempe, AZ) 918
Youth Today (Washington, DC) 5874
Youthworker (El Cajon, CA) 1850
Ypsilanti Press (Ypsilanti, MI) *Ceased*
YR Radio - 96.7 FM, 970 AM, 1230 AM, 1450 AM (Edson, AB, Can.) 34762
YSB (Washington, DC) *Unable to locate*
Yucaipa and Calimesa News-Mirror (Yucaipa, CA) *Ceased*

Yugntruf (New York, NY) 22954
Yukon News (Whitehorse, YT, Can.) 37606
Yukon; WHERE Alaska & The (Vancouver, BC, Can.) 35181
The Yuma Daily Sun (Yuma, AZ) 1022
Yuma Pioneer (Yuma, CO) 4694
Yunak (Toronto, ON, Can.) 36796

Z

Z Magazine *Unable to locate*
Z Paper (Boston, MA) *Unable to locate*
Zachary Plainsman-News (Zachary, LA) 12884
Zacks Analyst Watch (Chicago, IL) 8609
Zacks Earnings Forecaster (Chicago, IL) 8610
Zacks EPS Calendar (Chicago, IL) *Ceased*
Zacks Profit Guide (Chicago, IL) 8611
Zajednicar (Pittsburgh, PA) 27856
Zampelli Electronics (Lewistown, PA) 27199
Zanesville Muskingum Advertiser (Bristow, OK) 25769
ZAPAD (Waterloo, ON, Can.) *Unable to locate*
Zapata County News (Zapata, TX) 31314
Zavala County Sentinel (Crystal City, TX) 30114
ZD Internet Magazine (New York, NY) 22955
Zebulon Record 24341*
Zeeland Flashes Shopping Guide (Allegan, MI) 14725
Zeeland Record (Zeeland, MI) 15694
Zeit *Ceased*
Zeitung; Freie (Kenilworth, NJ) 19153
Zellers Family (Toronto, ON, Can.) 36797
Zenska Jednota; Fraternally, Yours, (Vandergrift, PA) 28094
Zeor; Companion in (Edgewood, MD) 13492
The Zephyr (Galesburg, IL) 8907
Zephyrhills News 5995*
Zephyrhills News (Washington, DC) *Ceased*
Zephyrhills Shopper (Clermont, FL) 5996
Zgoda (Cleveland, OH) *Unable to locate*
Ziegler Magazine for the Blind; Matilda (New York, NY) 22299
Ziff Davis Smart Business for the New Economy (New York, NY) 22956
Zillions (Yonkers, NY) 23604
Zine World 3420*
Zion Benton News (Zion, IL) 9780
Zionism Today (New York, NY) *Unable to locate*
Zion's Herald (Boston, MA) *Unable to locate*
Zion's Watch Tower Herald of Christ's Presence 20355*
Zionsville Eagle (Fishers, IN) *Ceased*
Zionsville Times Sentinel (Zionsville, IN) 10569
Zip Target Marketing 32057*
Zondervan Press Syndicate (Grand Rapids, MI) 38138
Zondervan Radio Network (Grand Rapids, MI) 37680
Zone Outaouais (Hull, QC, Can.) *Unable to locate*
The Zontian (Chicago, IL) 8612
Zoo Biology (Hoboken, NJ) 19122
Zoo View (Los Angeles, CA) 2444
Zoo and Wildlife Medicine; Journal of (Media, PA) 27242
ZooGoer (Washington, DC) 5875
ZooLife (Los Angeles, CA) *Ceased*
Zoology; The Journal of Experimental (Hoboken, NJ) 19022
Zoology (Revue Canadienne de Zoologie); Canadian Journal of (North York, ON, Can.) 36125
ZOOM Magazine (U.S. Edition) (New York, NY) *Ceased*
ZOONOOZ (San Diego, CA) 3290
Zoonotic Diseases; Vector-Borne and (Larchmont, NY) 20929
The ZPG Reporter 5723*
Zumbrota News 16495*
Zuzu's Petals Quarterly 20816*
Zuzu's Petals Quarterly Online (Ithaca, NY) 20816
Zwiazkowiec (Alliancer) (Toronto, ON, Can.) 36798
Zwita Productions (Stamford, CT) 38139
Zygon: Journal of Religion and Science (Chicago, IL) *Unable to locate*
Zygote (West Orange, NJ) 19724
ZYZZYVA (San Francisco, CA) 3467